ALABAMA · COLORADO · ARIZONA · MAINE · TEXAS · UTAH · ALASKA

IOWA · LOUISIANA · WISCONSIN · TENNESSEE · IDAHO

CALIFORNIA · MICHIGAN · MINNESOTA · MISSISSIPPI · MISSOURI · WEST VIRGINIA · NEW YORK · NEVADA

NORTH DAKOTA · PENNSYLVANIA · SOUTH CAROLINA · SOUTH DAKOTA · MARYLAND · ARKANSAS

GEORGIA · DELAWARE · ILLINOIS · KANSAS · NORTH CAROLINA · OREGON · NEBRASKA · KENTUCKY

NEW HAMPSHIRE · NEW JERSEY · NEW MEXICO · CONNECTICUT · FLORIDA · MASSACHUSETTS

1817  2001

The Official Catholic Directory

Anno Domini 2001

Published Annually by
P. J. Kenedy & Sons

INDIANA · OKLAHOMA · RHODE ISLAND · MONTANA

HAWAII · WASHINGTON · VIRGINIA · VERMONT · WYOMING · OHIO

The Official Catholic Directory
P.J. Kenedy & Sons, Publishers

Randy Mysel
Publisher

FOREWORD

P.J. Kenedy & Sons continues its proud tradition of excellence with the presentation of the 2001 edition of *The Official Catholic Directory*. Our efforts to produce a volume of uncompromising quality and accuracy is made possible by the numerous ecclesiastical authorities, diocesan officials, religious and laity who labor tirelessly with us to solicit, collect and organize the massive amounts of materials needed to complete this task. We would like to thank them for their cooperation and prayers which are essential to the success of our work.

Our directory expands each year with the inclusion of new parishes and institutions, and other elements. The growth reflects the relevance and vitality of the Catholic Church in the United States. However, nothing underscores the importance of the Church like the addition of a new diocese. This year we have the honor of presenting the diocese of Laredo in Volume One. The new see is a testimony to the diligence and commitment of those who minister in this area and all those who comprise the Catholic community. We share in their joy as they embark in their new journey of faith.

We also celebrate with the Church in the recent events which have given the United States three new cardinals whose gifts and insights are greatly needed. These men minister in areas where the value of Catholic education has been demonstrated by a dedication to preserve and strengthen our institutions as places of safety and academic integrity. In keeping with the mission of the Church, we have greatly expanded our listings of catechesis and religious programs. In addition, we provide extensive records on schools to assist those considering a Catholic education.

We are proud to be a part of the rich tradition of the Church which looks to the third millennium with eager anticipation. Our goal is to remain a valued resource to the Catholic community and to serve with intelligence and integrity.

Sincerely,

Randy Mysel

Randy Mysel
Publisher

121 Chanlon Road • New Providence, New Jersey 07974 • (908) 464-6800 • (800) 521-8110

Photo of His Holiness The Pope courtesy of Arturo Mari, L'Osservatore Romano.

His Holiness the Pope John Paul II

Is Your Fund Raising Headed in the *Right Direction?*

There are many paths and strategies to take in today's Catholic philanthropic world. Ruotolo Associates can provide the experience and vision necessary to navigate through all those challenges while successfully reaching your goals. For more than 21 years, we have proudly served hundreds of Catholic parishes, schools, dioceses and other institutions with quality, contemporary fund raising, development and public relations counsel.

Our Services Include:

- Increased Income/Stewardship Programs
- School Development Programs
- Public Relations
- Marketing/Recruitment
- Capital Campaigns
- Planning/Feasibility Studies
- Telephone/Communication Fund Raising
- Seminars/Workshops

When your needs call for counsel, join some of the clients we have guided in the *"Right Direction"*:

Academy of the Holy Angels, Demarest, NJ
Archdiocese of Boston
Archdiocese of New York
Archdiocese of Philadelphia
Carmelite Communion, Beacon, NY
Catholic Center at UVM, Burlington, VT
Catholic Chaplaincy at Harvard-Radcliffe, Cambridge, MA
Christian Brothers University, Memphis, TN
Diocese of Burlington
Holy Cross High School, Waterbury, CT
Holy Cross Parish, Stockton, IL
Holy Spirit Parish, St. Cloud, MN
Loyola Retreat House, Morristown, NJ
McAuley Regional High School, Joplin, MO
Mount St. Charles Academy, Woonsocket, RI
Our Lady of Good Counsel High School, Wheaton, MD
St. Ann Parish, Coppell, TX
St. Anthony's Parish, Cohasset, MA
St. Charles Borromeo Parish, Bloomington, IN
St. Francis of Assisi Parish, Manchester, NH
St. James Parish, Basking Ridge, NJ
St. Jane Frances de Chantal Parish, Easton, PA
St. Joseph's Parish, Springfield, MO
St. Luke's Parish, Barrington, RI
St. Ann's Parish, Nyack, NY
St. Mary's Monastery in Helfta, Germany
St. Mary's Parish, Colts Neck, NJ
St. Mary's Parish, Tiffin, OH
St. Patrick's Parish, Newcastle, ME
St. Patrick's Parish, Stoneham, MA
St. Vincent de Paul Parish, Rogers, AR
St. William's Church, Fort Lupton, CO
The Mary Louis Academy, Jamaica, NY
Ursuline Centre, Great Falls, MT

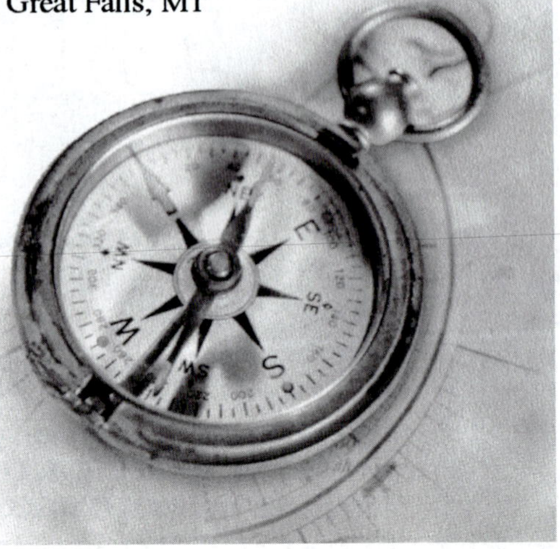

RUOTOLO ASSOCIATES INC.

Horizon Square • 29 Broadway • Suite 210 • Cresskill, N.J. 07626
Tel: 201-568-3898 • Fax: 201-568-8783 • RAssoc1@aol.com
www.ruotoloassoc.com

Divisions: • Mid-Atlantic • New England • Midwest • Balt./Washington, D.C.

Member:
AAFRC **American Association of Fundraising Counsel**
International Catholic Stewardship Council

THE I.T. VERDIN CO., CINCINNATI, OHIO

"Be to the
flock of Christ,
a Shepherd..."
Timeless style, noble materials
and old-time craftsmanship
are Almy hallmarks, creating
vestments and appointments
of heirloom quality.
Call or visit our website to
request a free catalog.
CM ALMY
Outfitters to the church
& clergy since 1892
THREE AMERICAN LANE
GREENWICH CT 06836–2644
CALL 800.225.2569
WEB www.almy.com
CM ALMY

Giving Glory to God through Art

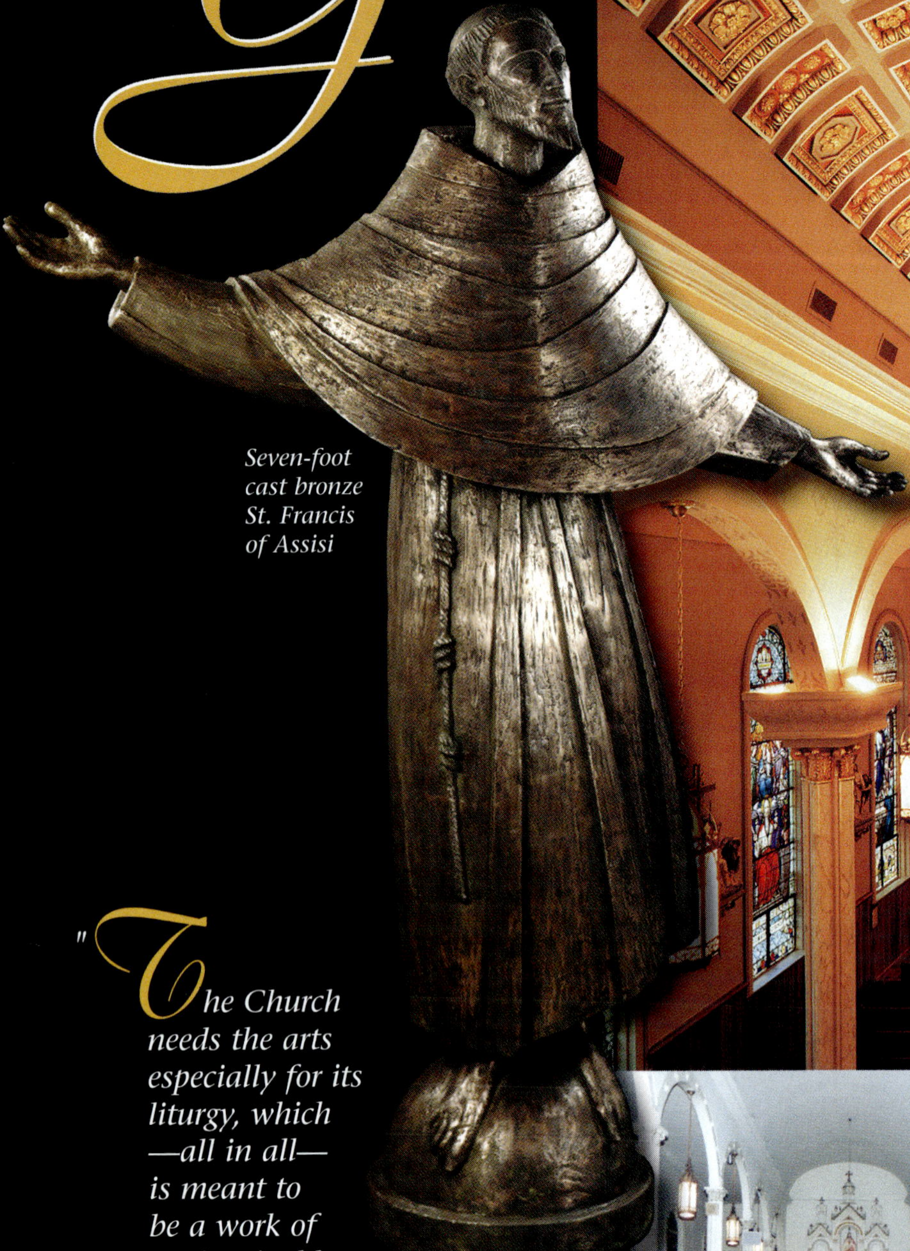

Seven-foot cast bronze St. Francis of Assisi

Before Restoration

After Restoration

St. Peter's Catholic Church, Montgomery, AL

"The Church needs the arts especially for its liturgy, which —all in all— is meant to be a work of art inspired by faith, drawing upon all the creative forces of architecture, sculpture and painting, music and poetry."

--Pope John Paul II

Since 1889, Conrad Schmitt Studios has been privileged to provide decoration, restoration and artwork to enhance worship spaces. Cathedrals, basilicas, churches, shrines and chapels throughout the country have called upon the Studio for guidance in creating environments that reach out to their communities and to God through art.

St. Hyacinth Catholic Church, Chicago IL

1885 window by John La Farge
After Conservation

INSTITUTIONAL STATUARY INC.
Distinctive Religious Works of Art
637 East 132nd Street
Bronx, New York 10454
1-800-847-3622
(718) 665-1125
(718) 665-1141
FAX # — (718) 665-0956
Designers Sculptors Manufacturers*
FULL COLOR CATALOG AVAILABLE UPON REQUEST.
IS&D
*Manufactured Exclusively in America

REFLECTIVE WORKS OF ART IN BRONZE AND FINE WOODS

A. J. Bellomo Studio's

The Black Forest Co.

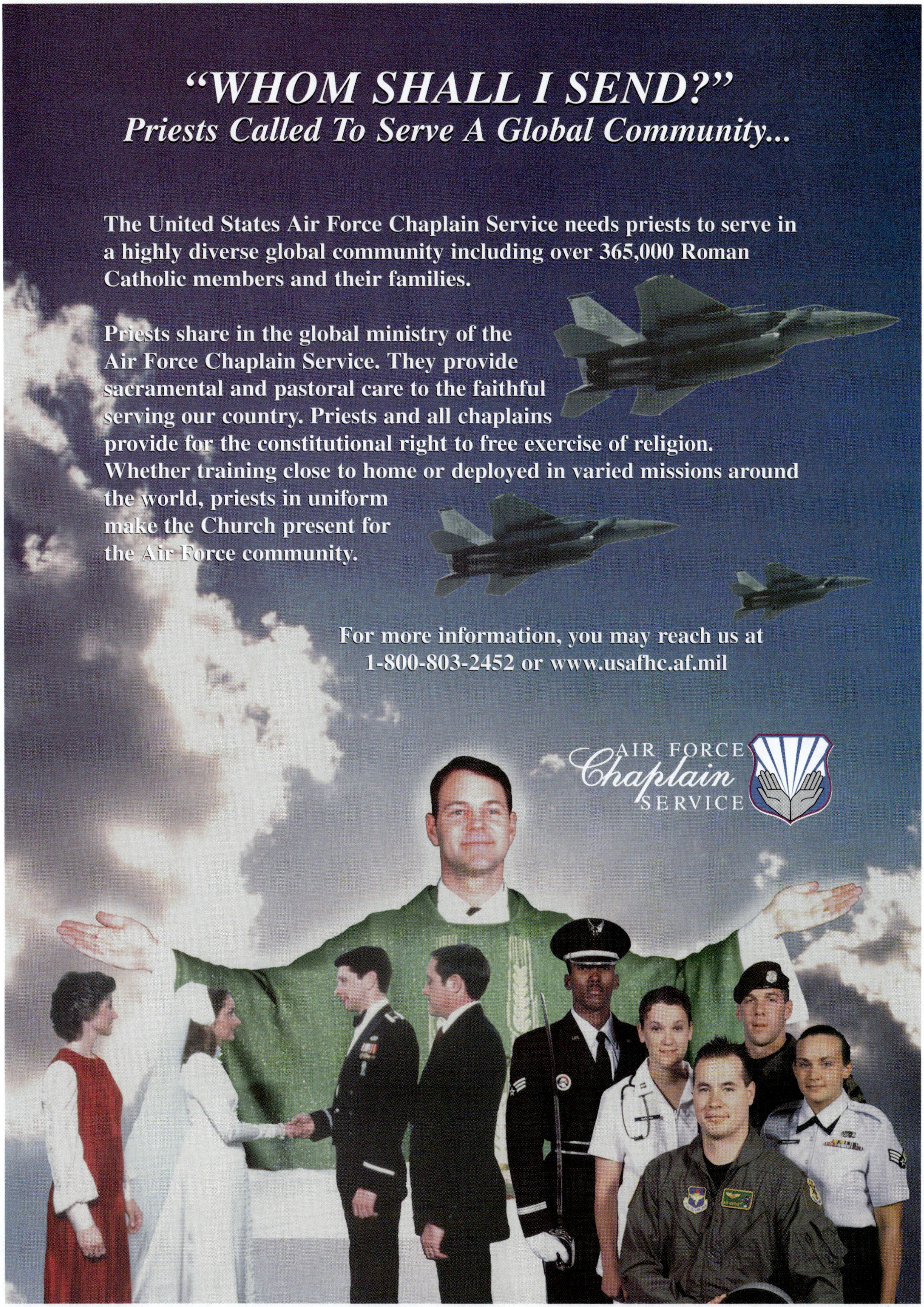
"WHOM SHALL I SEND?"
Priests Called To Serve A Global Community...
The United States Air Force Chaplain Service needs priests to serve in a highly diverse global community including over 365,000 Roman Catholic members and their families.
Priests share in the global ministry of the Air Force Chaplain Service. They provide sacramental and pastoral care to the faithful serving our country. Priests and all chaplains provide for the constitutional right to free exercise of religion. Whether training close to home or deployed in varied missions around the world, priests in uniform make the Church present for the Air Force community.
For more information, you may reach us at
1-800-803-2452 or www.usafhc.af.mil
AIR FORCE
Chaplain
SERVICE

Center Section of 30 foot high "Baptism of Christ" window - Blessed Trinity Church
Jacksonville, Florida - Rev. Denis O'Regan, Pastor: Photo by Vernon Nalley F.P.S.A.

The Original Metal Folding Kneeler

Special Offer on Replacement Kneeler Pad Orders

When you purchase Atwood Hamlin replacement kneeler pads you'll earn a 50% discount on our unbreakable replacement kneeler legs.

Call 1-800-545-8964 for complete details

Leg cross section view shows integrated rubber foot pad.

Hamlin

Silent, Comfortable, Durable Kneelers

After 50 years of continuous use in churches throughout North America, Hamlin Kneelers are still in service, thanks to flexible features like replaceable pads and legs. Over the years, these exclusive design features have been backed by Hamlin's highest quality craftsmanship and materials.

New, guaranteed unbreakable, kneeler leg design features integrated rubber foot pads that will never fall off.

Pew Form Cushions

Our cushions are designed for Catholic churches. Because they follow the countour of your existing pews, they stay firmly in place when getting on or off the pew seat.

Deluxe Pew Form Style

These cushions conform precisely to the contour of your pew seats. This design keeps the cushions in place without any fasteners.

Drop Front Style

Same as our deluxe pew form style. These cushions feature a drop front to completely cover worn front pew edges.

Upholstered Pew Comfort and Protection

A low-cost alternative to pew replacement, our exclusive pew form cushions give your pews a custom upholstered look. Best of all, no installation is required. Simply lay them in place. Optional upholstered backs and permanent installation are available.

Since 1949

Hamlin

ATWOOD-HAMLIN MANUFACTURING

P.O. Box 578
Richmond, IL 60071
Toll Free: 1-800-545-8964
Fax: 1-815-678-2130
www.atwood-hamlin.com
info@atwood-hamlin.com

expressing mystery and faith
across the centuries
Above right: William Willet, ca. 1898
Above left: St. Paul's Cathedral, Pittsburgh PA, ca. 1904
Right: St. Denis Catholic Church, Merwood, PA, ca. 1948
Below: Sacred Heart Catholic Church Southbury CT, ca. 1990
The Willet Stained Glass Studios
10 East Moreland Avenue - Philadelphia, PA 19118
Toll-free (877) 709-4106 - www.willetglass.com

EverGreene Painting Studios Inc

450 W. 31 Street New York, NY 10001
212-244-2800 Fax 212-244-6204
Chicago: 708-358-1642 Fax 708-358-1656
www.evergreene.com e-mail: info@evergreene.com

EverGreene is a full-service decorative arts studio committed to preserving the integrity of historic sacred spaces through conservation, restoration, and compatible new design. Services include investigation and analysis of original finishes, design of color schemes and architectural ornament, specifications, project management and implementation of work on site or in our studio.

St. Peter Church, San Francisco Photo: ©Ira Shrank

St. John's Seminary Chapel, Brighton, Mass. Photo:©Steve Rosenthal

Our Lady of Perpetual Help (Redemptorist Church), Kansas City

DECORATIVE PAINTING
MURALS & FINE ART
ORNAMENTAL PLASTER & SCAGLIOLA
SCULPTURE & STATUARY
ART GLASS & MOSAICS

St. Cecilia's Cathedral, Omaha Photo:©Scot Zimmerman

Fabric Art Tapestry
St. Stanislaus in Fall River, Massachusetts.

BEAUTIFUL ALL OCCASION PINS W/GIFT CARD

— *Select a Pin for Special Event* —

50% OFF SALE

Lent & Easter

D-101
Cross & Robe

D-102
Cross & Crown

St. Patrick's Day

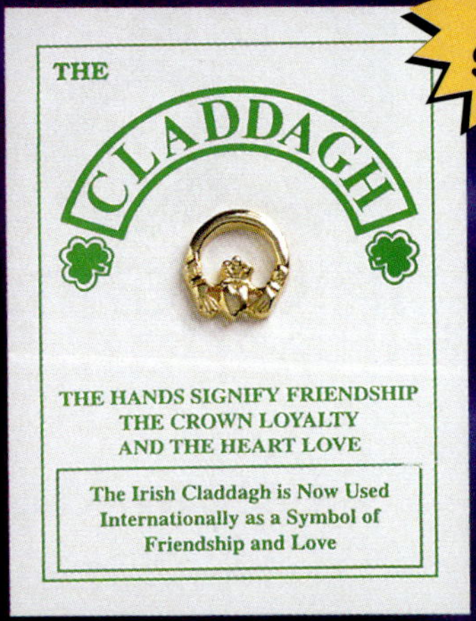

D-103
Claddagh

Mother's Day

D-104
Gold Cross

D-105
Angel w/Rose Crystal

Father's Day

D-106
Cross-Flag

Pins 80% Actual Size

D-107
Angel w/Pink Rose

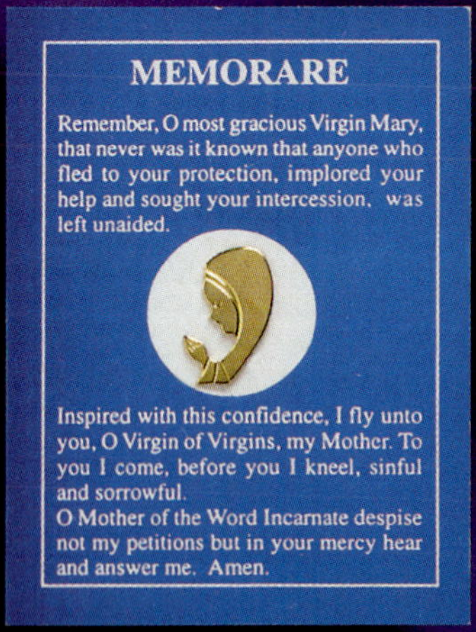

D-108
Praying Madonna

CONFIRMATION

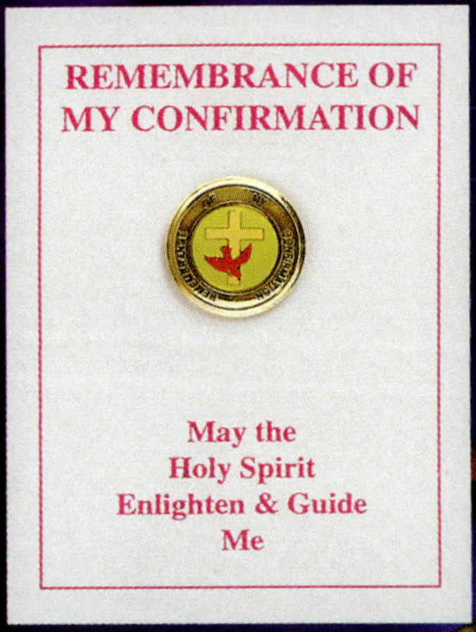

D-109
Confirmation

— PIN SALE PRICES —

	100	500	1000
Cross & Robe (D-101)	.69	.63	.59
Cross & Crown (D-102)	.69	.63	.59
Claddagh (D-103)	.69	.63	.59
Gold Cross (D-104)	.69	.63	.59

	100	500	1000
Angel w/Rose Crystal (D-105)	1.39	1.29	1.09
Cross-Flag (D-106)	1.00	.95	.85
Angel w/Pink Rose (D-107)	.95	.85	.75
Praying Madonna (D-108)	.69	.63	.59
Confirmation (D-109)	.69	.63	.59

James Doherty Inc. • 1-800-243-5305 • Fax: 570-346-2851

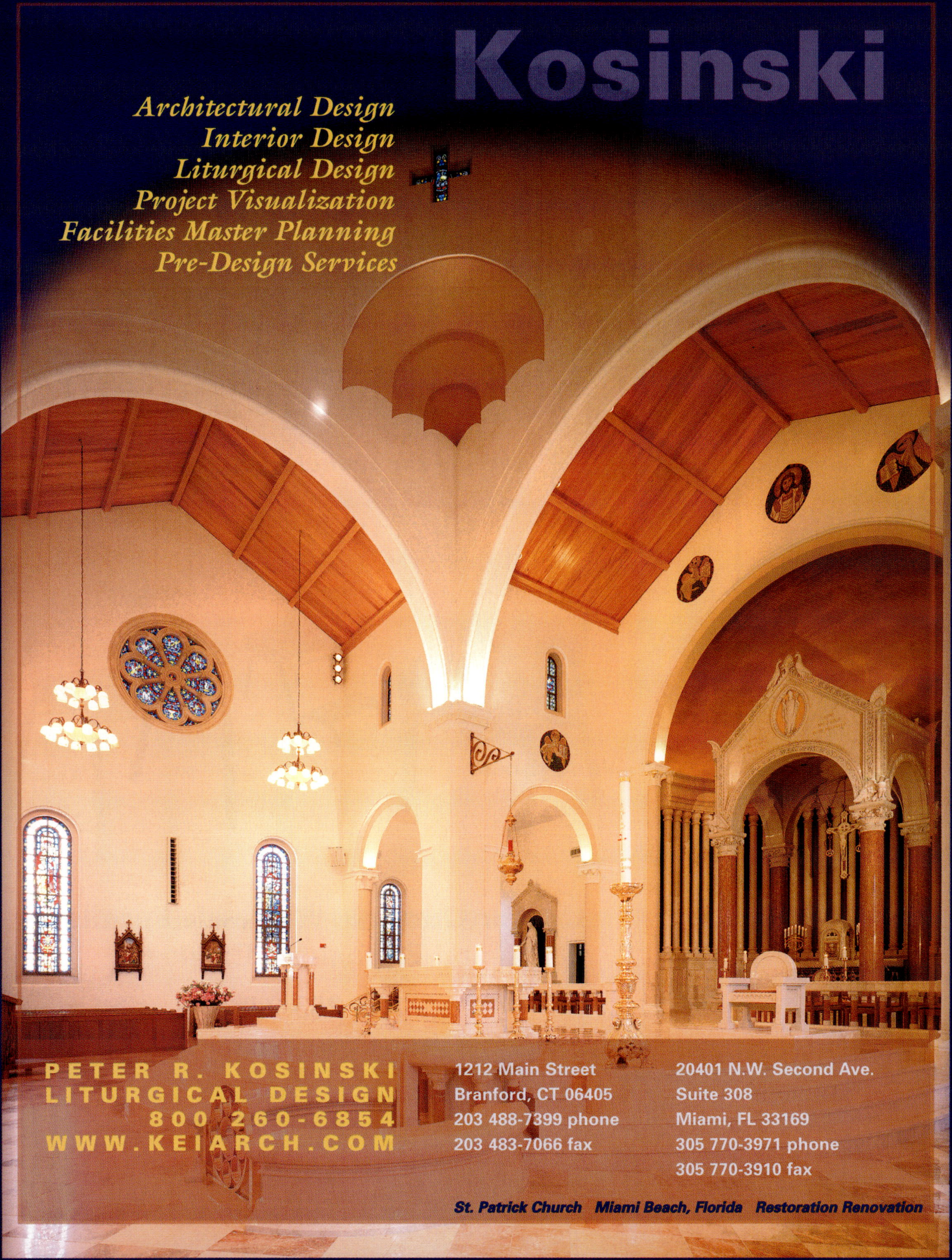
Kosinski
Architectural Design
Interior Design
Liturgical Design
Project Visualization
Facilities Master Planning
Pre-Design Services
PETER R. KOSINSKI
LITURGICAL DESIGN
800 260-6854
WWW.KEIARCH.COM
1212 Main Street
Branford, CT 06405
203 488-7399 phone
203 483-7066 fax
20401 N.W. Second Ave.
Suite 308
Miami, FL 33169
305 770-3971 phone
305 770-3910 fax
St. Patrick Church Miami Beach, Florida Restoration Renovation

Trust in a new beginning
As a child knows it can trust its parent, we want you to know you can trust us.
At Cokesbury, we want your trust and a lifelong partnership. We promise to serve you as you serve the church. We're committed to bringing you the finest resources to help you share the joyous message of God's love and help you grow and nurture your ministries—from books, Bibles, and teaching resources to vestments and church supplies. That has been our ministry for over 200 years. It lies at the heart of everything we do. Let us give you a hand. You can trust us. We guarantee it.
Call on us.
Click on us. Count on us.
Since 1789
Cokesbury
1-800-672-1789 • www.cokesbury.com
Altarware, Communionware, and Church Furnishings
Come Holy Spirit
Paraments, Apparel, & Vestments
I LIKE BEING CATHOLIC
Books for Church Leaders
Candles & Accessories, Offering Envelopes, Bulletins, and Supplies
Reference, Electronic, Music, and Teaching & Learning Resources
Look for Cokesbury's 2001 Liturgical Catalog, mailing February 28.
If you haven't received your catalog by the end of March, please call 1-800-672-1789 and request a free copy. Ask for catalog number CL1-508895.

DOMUSDEI

DOMUSDEI'S MANAGEMENT IS ABSOLUTELY AVAILABLE TO VISIT YOUR CHURCH IN ORDER TO VERIFY AND VALUATE ANY WORK TO BE DONE.

▲ **One of the three bronze doors made for Wichita's Cathedral - Kansas**
Sculptor: G. Savini

▲ **St. Francis - bronze - made for Card. Maida achbishop of Detroit**
Sculptor: G. Savini

▲ **Stained glass window made for Combonian fathers.**
Designed by artist: B. Ferabecoli

▲ **Rose window made for Mary, queen of the universe shrine in Orlando - Florida**
Artist: B. Ferabecoli

▲ **Byzantine mosaic**

▲ **Madonna - bronze - made for Card. Maida archbishop of Detroit**
Artist: G. Savini

▲ **Magnificent stained glass window in old style**
Artist: A. Positano

▲ **Wonderful stained glass window made for an important church in Rome - Italy.**
Artist: A. Positano

▲ **Precious mosaic made with enamels and gold.**

▲ **Absidal mosaic made with enamels.**
Artist: A. Positano

FACTORY: Via dei Tulipani 48 - 00040 CECCHINA DI ALBANO (ROMA) - ITALY
TEL: 011-39-06-9343369 - FAX: 011-39-06-9344971
SHOW ROOM: Via Scossacavalli 3/9 - 00193 ROMA - ITALY - Tel. 011-39-06-6868090
E-MAIL: info@domusdei.it - m.delmonte@domusdei.it
HTTP:/www.domusdei.it

IC XC
I AM
WHO AM

SANCTUS·SANCTUS·SANCTUS

TABLE OF CONTENTS

for
ver
ce to
install
ical

e myriad of
, the building
vorking within
nager, designer
aded windows,
ell as stone
ismal font,
candlesticks.
to Rambusch's
sitivity and
substance that
enterprise.

ch 1898-2001.
n a century of
nishing and lighting
of worship.

h generations dedicated to enhancing the atmosphere and the environment for
nstalling liturgical furnishings, interiors, decorative art and lighting systems for
with an understanding that is unique to Rambusch's century of experience,
Design Studios, Craft Workshops and Lighting division consistently produce.
Peace, Pheonix AZ; Holy Family College Chapel, Newtown, PA; St. Alberts, Huntingdon, PA; St. Vincent Ferrer, New York NY

SCH LIGHTING

ve., Jersey City NJ 07304 (201) 333-2525 Fax: (201) 433-3355
0 (212) 675-0400 Fax: (212) 620-4687 On-line: **www.rambuschlighting.com**

The Official Catholic Directory

for the Year of Our Lord

2001

GIVING STATUS OF THE CATHOLIC CHURCH AS OF JANUARY 1, 2001

Containing Ecclesiastical Statistics of

THE UNITED STATES, PUERTO RICO,
THE VIRGIN ISLANDS, AGANA, CAROLINE AND MARSHALL ISLANDS,
FOREIGN MISSIONARY ACTIVITIES, CANADA, AND MEXICO.

The information contained in this Directory is derived from reports submitted to the publishers by the ecclesiastical authorities of the countries concerned, and neither the publishers nor the ecclesiastical authorities assume responsibility for any errors or omissions.

P.J. KENEDY & SONS

Publishers of the Holy Apostolic See

For inquiries call: 908-665-3500, or write:
121 Chanlon Road, New Providence, NJ 07974
To place an order call: 1-800-521-8110

The 2001 edition of *The Official Catholic Directory* was prepared by National Register Publishing's Database Publishing Group.

Editorial Staff:
Managing Editor: Karen Chassie
Senior Editor: Kathleen F. Jurcsek
Associate Editor: Eileen Fanning
Assistant Editor: Sumitra B. Ramaprasad
Editorial Assistants: Aloy Achonwa, Linda Hummer, Jennifer Podolsky, Barry Vozar, Nancy Vozar, Lisa Woodley

Publisher's Staff:
Managing Editor: Jeanne Hanline

Editorial Systems:
Vice-President, Information Technology: John Roney
Manager, Reference & Biographic Systems: Helene Davis
Senior Programmer/Analyst: Benjamin Loh

Photo of His Holiness The Pope, courtesy of Arturo Mari, L'Osservatore Romano.

Published by P.J. Kenedy & Sons in association with National Register Publishing, a member of the LEXIS-NEXIS Group

President & Chief Executive Officer: John A. Lawler
Vice-President & Publisher: Randy H. Mysel
Vice-President, Database Production: Dean Hollister
Managing Director: Thomas M. Bachmann

Printed and bound in the United States of America
International Standard Book Number: 0-87217-402-6
International Standard Serial Number: 0078-3854
Library of Congress Catalog Card Number: 81-30961

CONTENTS

Part I

Part II

THE UNITED STATES

ARCHDIOCESES AND DIOCESES
(Archdioceses are in Boldface)

MISCELLANEOUS

EASTERN CHURCHES

TERRITORIAL SEES

Part III

CANADA AND MEXICO

Part IV

THE ARCHDIOCESES AND DIOCESES OF THE UNITED STATES—BY STATES

A—Indicates Archdiocese. The Archdiocese of Washington includes the District of Columbia and five counties of Maryland. Dioceses traverse state lines in the following instances only: Cheyenne includes all of Yellowstone National Park; South Norwich includes Fisher's Island; Wilmington includes the eastern shores of Maryland; and Gallup includes parts of Arizona and New Mexico.

Religious Order Initials for Men

A.A.	Assumptionists	[0130]
B.C.S.	Brothers of Christian Service	[]
B.G.S.	Little Brothers of the Good Shepherd	[0580]
B.S.O.	Basilian Salvatorian Fathers	[0190]
C.F.A.	Alexian Brothers	[0120]
C.F.C.	Congregation of Christian Brothers	[0310]
C. F.M.M.	Brothers of Our Lady, Mother of Mercy	[0980]
C.F.P.	Brothers of the Poor of St. Francis	[0460]
C.F.R.	Franciscan Friars of the Renewal	[0535]
C.F.X.	Brothers of St. Francis Xavier	[1350]
C.I.C.M.	Missionhurst Congregation of the Immaculate Heart of Mary	[0860]
C.J.	Josephite Fathers	[0710]
C.J.M.	Congregation of Jesus and Mary	[0450]
C.M.	Congregation of the Mission	[1330]
C.M.C.	Congregation of Mother Coredemptrix	[]
C.M.F.	Claretian Missionaries	[0360]
C.M.I.	Carmelites of Mary Immaculate	[0275]
C.M.L.M.	The Congregation of Maronite Lebanese Missionaries	[0785]
C.M.M.	Congregation of Mananhill Missionaries, Marianhill Fathers & Brothers	[0750]
C. M.Vd.	Mekhitarist Fathers	[]
C.O.	Oratorians	[0950]
C.P.	Congregation of the Passion	[1000]
C.P.M.	Congregation of the Fathers of Mercy	[0820]
C.PP.S.	Society of the Precious Blood	[1060]
C.R.	Congregation of the Resurrection	[1080]
C.R.	Theatine Fathers	[1300]
C.R.I.C.	Canons Regular of the Immaculate Conception	[]
C.R.L.	Canons Regular of the Lateran	[0250]
C.R.M.	Adorno Fathers	[0100]
C.R.S.	Somascan Fathers	[1250]
C.R.S.P.	Clerics Regular of St. Paul	[0160]
C.S.	Missionaries of St. Charles Scalabrinians	[1210]
C.S.B.	Basilian Fathers	[0170]
C.S.C.	Brothers of the Congregation of Holy Cross	[0600]
C.S.C.	Priests of the Congregation of Holy Cross	[0610]
C.S.J.	Congregation of St. Joseph	[1150]
C.S.J.B.	Congregation of St. John the Baptist	[]
C.S.P.	Paulist Fathers	[1030]
C.S.P.X.	Brothers of Saint Pius X	[1180]
C.S.S.	Stigmatine Fathers and Brothers.	[1280]
C.S.Sp.	Holy Ghost Fathers	[0650]
C.SS.R.	Redemptorist Fathers	[1070]
C.S.V.	Clerics of St. Viator	[1320]
D.L.P.	Diocesan Labor Priests	[]
Er.Cam.	Camaldolese Hermits of the Congregation of Monte Corona	[0230]
F.C.	Brothers of Charity	[0290]
F.D.P.	Sons of Divine Providence	[0410]
F.F.I.	Franciscan Friars of the Immaculate	[0533]
F.F.S C.	Franciscan Brothers of the Holy Cross	[0510]
F.I.C.	Brothers of Christian Instruction	[0320]
F.J.	Congregation of St. John	[]
F.M.M.	Brothers of Mercy	[0810]
F.M.M.	Missionary Fraternity of Mary	[]
F.M.S.	The Marist Brothers	[0770]
F.M.S.I.	Sons of Mary Missionary Society	[1270]
F.P.M.	Presentation Brothers	[]
F.S.C.	Brothers of the Christian Schools	[0330]
F.S.E.	Brothers of the Holy Eucharist	[0620]
F.S.P.	Brothers of St. Patrick	[1160]
F.S.R.	Brothers of the Congregation of Our Lady of the Holy Rosary	[0960]
F.S.S.P.	Priestly Fraternity of St. Peter	[1065]
G.H.M.	The Glenmary Home Missioners	[0570]
H.J.D.	Los Hermanos de Juan Diego	[]
H.M.C.	Hermits of Mount Carmel	[]
I.C.	Institute of Charity	[0300]
I.C.	Incarnational Consecration	[]
I.H.M.	Brothers of the Immaculate Heart of Mary	[0680]
I.M.C.	Consolata Missionaries	[0390]
I.S.S.S.	Schoenstatt Institute of Secular Priests	[]
L.B.S.F.	Little Brothers of Saint Francis	[1144]
L.C.	Legionaries of Christ	[0730]
M.Afr.	Missionaries of Africa	[0850]
M.C.B.S.	Missionary Congregation of the Blessed Sacrament	[]
M.C.C.J.	Comboni Missionaries of the Heart of Jesus (Verona)	[0380]
M.Des.	Mercedarios Descalzos	[]
M.E.P.	Paris Foreign Mission Society	[0897]
M.G.	Guadalupe Missioners	[]
M.H.M.	Mill Hill Missionaries	[0830]
M.I.C.	Congregation of Marians of the Immaculate Conception	[0740]
M.J.	Missionaries of St. Joseph (Mexico)	[]
M.M.	Maryknoll	[0800]
M.S.	The Missionaries of Our Lady of La Salette	[0720]
M.S.C.	Missionaries of the Sacred Heart	[1110]
M.S.F.	Congregation of the Missionaries of the Holy Family	[0630]
M.S.P.	Missionaries of St. Paul	[]
M.Sp.S.	Missionaries of the Holy Spirit	[0660]
M.Ss.A.	Missionaries of the Holy Apostles	[0590]
M.SS.CC.	Missionaries of the Sacred Hearts of Jesus and Mary	[1120]
O.A.R.	Order of the Augustinian Recollects	[0150]
O.Carm.	Carmelite Fathers and Brothers	[0270]
O.Cart.	Order of Carthusians	[0280]
O.C.D.	Discalced Carmelite Fathers	[0260]
O.Cist.	Cistercian Fathers	[0340]
O.C.S.O.	The Cistercian Order of the Strict Observance (Trappists)	[0350]
O.de.M.	Order of Our Lady of Mercy	[0970]
O.F.M.	Franciscan Friars	[0520]
O.F.M.Cap.	The Capuchin Friars	[0470]
O.F.M.Conv.	Conventual Franciscans	[0480]
O.H.	Hospitaller Brothers of St. John of God	[0670]
O.I.C.	Order of the Imitation of Christ	[]
O.L P.	Brothers of Our Lady of Providence	[]
O.M.	Minim Fathers	[0835]
O.Mar.	Congregation of Maronite Monks	[0790]
O.M.I.	Oblates of Mary Immaculate	[0910]
O.M.V.	Oblates of the Virgin Mary	[0940]
O.P.	Order of Preachers (Dominicans)	[0430]
O.Praem.	Canons Regular of Premontre	[0900]
O.R.C.	Operarios del Reina de Cristo	[]
O.S.A.	The Augustinians	[0140]
O.S.B.	Benedictine Monks	[0200]
O.S.B.Cam.	Camaldolese Hermits	[]
O S.B.M.	Order of St. Basil the Great	[0180]
O.S.C.	Canons Regular of the Order of the Holy Cross	[0400]
O.S.Cam.	Camillian Fathers and Brothers	[0240]
O.S.F.	Congregation of the Religious Brothers of the Third Order Regular of St Francis	[0490]
O.S.F.	Franciscan Brothers of Christ the King	[0500]
O.S.F.	Franciscan Brothers of the Third Order Regular	[0515]
O.S.F.	Franciscan Missionary Brothers of the Sacred Heart of Jesus	[0540]
O.S.F.S.	Oblates of St. Francis de Sales	[0920]
O.S.J.	Oblates of St. Joseph	[0930]
O.S.M.	Servites	[1240]
O.S.P.P.E.	Pauline Fathers	[1010]
O.Ss.S.	Brigittine Monks	[0895]
O.SS.T.	Order of the Holy Trinity	[1310]
P.I.M.E.	Pontifical Institute for Foreign Missions	[1050]
R.C.J.	Rogationist Fathers	[1090]
S.A.	Franciscan Friars of the Atonement	[0530]
S.A.C.	Society of the Catholic Apostolate	[0990]
S.C.	Brothers of the Sacred Heart	[1100]
S.C.	Servants of Charity	[1220]
S.Ch.	Society of Christ	[1260]
Sch.P.	Piarist Fathers.	[1040]
S.C.J.	Congregation of the Priests of the Sacred Heart	[1130]
S.D.B.	Salesians of Don Bosco	[1190]
S.D.S.	Society of the Divine Savior	[1200]
S.D.V.	Vocationist Fathers	[1340]
S.F.	Sons of the Holy Family	[0640]
S.F.M.	Scarboro Foreign Missions	[]
S.J.	Jesuit Fathers and Brothers	[0690]
S.M.	Society of Mary (Marianists)	[0760]
S.M.	Marist Fathers	[0780]
S.M.A.	Society of African Missions	[0110]
S.M.M.	Montfort Missionaries	[0870]
S.M.P.	Society of Our Mother of Peace	[]
S.O.Cist.	Cistercian Monks of the Strict Observance	[]
S.O.L.T.	Society of Our Lady of the Most Holy Trinity	[0975]
s.P.	Servants of the Paraclete	[1230]
S.P.S.	St. Patrick Missionary Society	[1170]
S.S.	Society of the Priests of Saint Sulpice	[1290]
S.S.C.	Society of St. Columban	[0370]
SS.CC.	Congregation of the Sacred Hearts of Jesus and Mary	[1140]
S.S.E.	Society of Saint Edmund	[0440]
S.S.J.	St. Joseph's Society of the Sacred Heart	[0700]
S.S.P.	Pauhne Fathers and Brothers	[1020]
S.S.S.	Congregation of the Blessed Sacrament	[0220]
S.S.T.	Missionary Society of St. Thomas the Apostle	[]
S.T.	Missionary Servants of the Most Holy Trinity	[0840]
S.X.	Xaverian Missionary Fathers	[1360]
S.V.D.	Society of the Divine Word	[0420]
T.O.R.	Third Order Regular of Saint Francis	[0560]
V.C.	Vincentian Congregation (India)	[]
V.D.C.	Verbum Dei Community	[]

Religious Order Initials for Women

Initials	Order	Code
A.B.S.	Auxiliaries of the Blessed Sacrament	[]
A.C.J.	Handmaids of the Sacred Heart of Jesus	[1870]
A.D.	Sisters of the Lamb of God	[2260]
A.I.M.	Association of Mary Immaculate	[]
A.N.G.	A New Genesis	[]
A.P.	Nuns of Perpetual Adoration of Blessed Sacrament	[3190]
A.P.B.	Adorers of the Precious Blood	[0110]
A.P.G.	Sisters of Perpetual Adoration	[3195]
A.R.	Handmaids of the Sacred Heart of Jesus for Reparation	[1880]
A.R.	Augustinian Recollects	[]
A.S.C.	Adorers of the Blood of Christ	[0100]
A.S.C.J.	Apostles of the Sacred Heart of Jesus	[0130]
B.C.	Notre Dame du Bon Conseil (Quebec)	[]
Bethl.	Bethlemita Daughters of the Sacred Heart of Jesus	[0910]
B.V.M.	Sisters of Charity of Blessed Virgin Mary	[0430]
B.V.M.C.	Blessed Virgin Missionaries of Carmel	[]
C.ach.	Carmeilte Sisters of Charity	[0340]
Carmel.D.C.J.	Carmelite Sisters of the Divine Heart of Jesus	[0360]
C.B.S.	Congregation of Bon Secours	[0270]
C.C.	Carmel Community	[0310]
C.C.V.I.	Sisters of Charity of Incarnate Word	[0460]
C.C.V.I.	Sisters of Charity of Incarnate Word (Houston, TX)	[0470]
C.C.W.	Carmelite Community of the Word	[0315]
C.D.P.	Sisters of Divine Providence	[0990]
C.D.P.	Sisters of Divine Providence of Kentucky	[1000]
C.D.P.	Sisters of Divine Providence of San Antonio, TX	[1010]
C.D.P.	Capuchin Sisters (Spain)	[]
C.D.S.	Congregation of Divine Spirit	[1040]
C.F.M.M.	Minim Daughters of Mary Immaculate	[2675]
C.F.P.	Feminine Congregation of the Passion	[]
C.F.P.	Mexican Passionist Sisters	[]
C.G.S.	Contemplatives of Good Shepherd	[1830]
C.H.F.	Sisters of Holy Faith	[1940]
C H.M.	Congregation of Humility of Mary	[2100]
C.H.S.	Community of the Holy Spirit	[2020]
C.I.C.	Sisters of Immaculate Conception	[2120]
C.I.J.	Congregation of Infant Jesus	[2230]
C.J.C.	Poor Sisters of Jesus Crucified and Sorrowful Mother	[3240]
C.K.	School Sisters of Christ the King	[]
C.L.H.C.	Congregation of Our Lady Help of the Clergy	[3090]
C.M.C.	Congregation of Mother of Carmel	[]
C.M.R.	Congregation of Mary Queen	[]
C.M.S.	Comboni Missionary Sisters	[0690]
C.M.S.	Cashel Mercy Sisters	[2515]
C.M.S.T.	Missionary Carmelites of St. Teresa	[0390]
C.N.D.	Congregation of Notre Dame	[2980]
C.O.C.	Companions of Christ	[]
C.P.	Religious of the Passion of Jesus Christ	[3170]
C.P.	Sisters of the Cross and Passion	[3180]
C.P.C.	Capuchin Poor Clares	[]
C.P.C.	St. Clare Capuchin Sisters	[]
C.P.P.S.	Sisters of the Precious Blood Dayton, Ohio	[3260]
C.P.P.S.	Sisters of the Most Precious Blood, (O'Fallon, MO)	[3270]
C.P.S.	Missionary Sisters of the Precious Blood	[2850]
C.R.	Sisters of the Resurrection	[3480]
C.S.	Company of the Savior	[0710]
C.S.	The Christian Sisters (Pious Union)	[]
C.S.A.	Sisters of Charity of St. Augustine	[0580]
C.S.A.	Sisters of St. Agnes	[3710]
C.S.A.	Albertine Sisters (Krakow, Poland)	[]
C.S.A.C.	Sisters of the Catholic Apostolate (Pallottine)	[3140]
C.S.B.	Congregation of St. Brigid	[3735]
C.S.C.	Congregation of Sisters of Holy Cross	[1920]
C.S.C.	Sisters of Holy Cross	[1930]
C.S.C.	Sisters of Holy Cross and Seven Dolors	[]
C.S.E.	Carmelite Sisters of the Eucharist	[]
C.S.F.N.	Sisters of Holy Family of Nazareth	[1970]
C.S.J.	Sisters of St. Joseph (Boston, Brighton)	[3830-01]
C.S.J.	Sisters of St. Joseph (Chicago, Lagrange Park)	[3830-02]
C.S.J.	Sisters of St. Joseph (Orange)	[3830-03]
C.S.J.	Sisters of St. Joseph (Rockville Centre, Brentwood)	[3830-05]
C.S.J.	Sisters of St. Joseph (Cleveland)	[3830-08]
C.S.J.	Sisters of St. Joseph (Lafayette, IN)	[3830-10]
C.S.J.	Sisters of St. Joseph (Pittsburgh, Baden)	[3830-13]
C.S.J.	Sisters of St. Joseph (Salina, Concordia)	[3830-15]
C.S.J.	Sisters of St. Joseph (Wichita)	[3830-18]
C.S.J.	Sisters of St. Joseph of Carondelet	[3840]
C.S.J.	Sisters of St. Joseph of Chambery	[3850]
C.S.J.	Sisters of St. Joseph (Lyons, France)	[3870]
C.S.J.	Sisters of St. Joseph of Medaille	[3880]
C.S.J.B.	Sisters of St. John the Baptist	[3820]
C.S.J.P.	Sisters of St. Joseph of Peace	[3890]
C.S.M.	Sisters of St. Martha of Antigonish N.S	[3937]
C.S.N.	Congregation of Sisters of Nazareth	[]
C.S.R.	Sisters of Holy Redeemer	[2000]
C.S.S.F.	Felician Sisters	[1170]
C.S.Sp.	Sisters of Holy Spirit	[2030]
C.S.S.T.	Carmelite Sisters of St. Teresa	[]
C.S.T.	Carmelite Sisters of St. Therese of Infant Jesus	[0380]
C.V.D.	Sisters of Bethany	[0250]
C.V.I.	Congregation of Incarnate Word and Blessed Sacrament	[2190]
C.V.I.	Religious of the Incarnate Word	[3449]
D.C.	Daughters of Charity of St. Vincent de Paul	[0760]
D.C.	Daughters of the Cross	[0770]
D.C.M.	Diocesan Carmelites of Maine	[]
D.C.P.B.	Daughters of Charity of Most Precious Blood	[0740]
D.H.M.	Daughters of Heart of Mary	[0810]
D.H.S.	Daughters of the Holy Spirit	[0820]
D.L.F.	Daughters of Our Lady of Fatima	[]
D.L.J.C.	Disciples of the Lord Jesus Christ	[0965]
D.M.	Daughters of Mary of the Immaculate Conception	[0860]
D.M.	Daughters of Our Lady of Mercy	[0890]
D.M.I.	Daughters of Mary Immaculate (Chaldean)	[]
D.M.J.	Daughters of Mary and Joseph	[0880]
D.O.M.	Daughters of Mercy (Croatian)	[]
D.S.F.	Daughters of St. Francis of Assisi	[0920]
D.S.M.P.	Daughters of St. Mary of Providence	[0940]
D.W.	Daughters of Wisdom	[0960]
E.F.M.S.	Eucharistic Franciscan Missionary Sisters	[1150]
E.M.S.	Eucharistic Missionary Society	[]
F.A.S.	Franciscan Apostolic Sisters	[]
F.C.	Daughters of the Cross of Liege	[0780]
F.C.J.	Society of Sisters Faithful Companions of Jesus	[4048]
F.C.S.C.J.	Daughters of Charity of the Sacred Heart of Jesus	[0750]
F.D.C.	Daughters of Divine Charity	[0790]
Fd.CC.	Canossian Daughters of Charity	[0730]
F.D.L.P.	Daughters of Providence	[]
F.D.N.S.C.	Daughters of Our Lady of the Sacred Heart	[0900]
F.D.P.	Daughters of Divine Providence	[0800]
F.D.Z.	Daughters of Divine Zeal	[0795]
F.H.I.C.	Franciscan Hospitaller Sisters of the Immaculate Conception	[1270]
F.H.M.	Franciscan Handmaids of the Most Pure Heart of Mary	[1260]
F.H.M.	Franciscan Sisters Daughters of Mercy	[1235]
F.I.	Daughters of Jesus	[0840]
F.J.	Congregation of the Daughters of Jesus	[0830]
F.L.G.	Franciscan Sisters of Our Lady of Grace	[]
F.M.A.	Daughters of Mary Help of Christians	[0850]
F.M.D.C.	Franciscan Missionaries of the Divine Child	[1340]
F.M.I.	Congregation of the Daughters of Mary Immaculate (Marianist Sisters)	[0870]
F.M.I.	Franciscan Sisters of Mary Immaculate of the Third Order of St. Francis of Assisi	[1500]
F.M.I.J.	Franciscan Missionaries of the Infant Jesus	[1365]
F.M.M.	The Franciscan Missionaries of Mary	[1370]
F.M.S.C.	Franciscan Missionary Sisters of the Sacred Heart	[1400]
F.M.S.J.	Mill Hill Sisters	[1410]
F.M.S.R.	Daughters of Our Lady of Holy Rosary	[]
F.N.S.S.C.	Franciscan Sisters of Our Lady of the Sacred Heart	[]
F.S.E.	The Institute of the Franciscan Sisters of the Eucharist	[1250]
F.S.J.	Religious Daughters of St. Joseph	[0930]
F.S.M.	Franciscan Sisters of Mary	[1415]
F.S.O.L.	Franciscan Sisters of Our Lady	[]
F.S.P.	Pious Society Daughters of St. Paul	[0950]
F.S.P.	Franciscan Sisters of Peace	[1425]
F.S.P.A.	Congregation of the Sisters of the Third Order of St. Francis of Perpetual Adoration	[1780]
F.S.R.	Franciscan Sisters of Ringwood	[1420]
F.S.S.C.	Franciscan Sisters of St. Clare (Pious Union)	[]
F.S.S.E.	Franciscan Sisters of St. Elizabeth	[1460]
F.S.S.J.	Franciscan Sisters of St. Joseph	[1470]
F.S.S.J.	Franciscan Sisters of St. Joseph	[1480]
F S.S.M.	Franciscan Sisters of the Sorrowful Mother	[]
F.S.Sp.J.	Franciscan Sisters of the Spirit of Jesus	[]
G.H.M.S.	Home Mission Sisters of America (Glenmary)	[2080]
G.N.S.H.	Grey Nuns of the Sacred Heart	[1840]
H.B.S.	Hermanas Contemplativas del Buen Pastor	[]
H.C.G.	Hermanas Catequistas Guadalupanas	[1900]
H.F.deS.J.	Franciscan Sisters of St. Joseph (Mexico City)	[]
H.G.S.	Congregation de Hermanas Guadalupanas de la Salle	[]

H.H.S.	Society of Helpers	[1890]
H.J.	Hermanas Josefinas	[1910]
H.J.D.	Las Hermanas de Juan Diego	[]
H.M.	Sisters of the Humility of Mary	[2110]
H.M.C.	Hermits of Mount Carmel	[]
H.M.S.S.	Mercedarian Sisters of the Blessed Sacrament	[2590]
H.M.S.S.	Religious Sisters of the Apostolate of the Blessed Sacrament	[3370]
H.O.Carm.	Hermits of Our Lady of Mt. Carmel	[]
H.P.B.	Congregation of the Handmaids of the Precious Blood	[1860]
H.R.F.	Sisters of the Holy Rosary of Fatima (Mexico)	[]
H.S.H.	Handmaids of the Sacred Heart of Pohang	[]
H.S.M.	Hermit Sisters of Mary	[]
H.Sp.S.	Daughters of the Holy Spirit Nazareth of the Good Shepherd	[]
H.S.S.	Hermanas del Servicio Social	[]
H.S.S.R.	Hermit Sisters of Romuald	[]
H.T.	Handmaids of the Most Holy Trinity	[]
H.V.M.	Sisters, Home Visitors of Mary	[2090]
I.B.V.M.	Institute of the Blessed Virgin Mary (Loretto Sisters)	[2370]
I.B.V.M.	Institute of the Blessed Virgin Mary (Loretto Sisters)	[2380]
I.C.	Vietnamese Sisters Incarnational Consecration	[]
I.C.M.	Missionary Sisters of the Immaculate Heart of Mary	[2750]
I.H.M.	Sisters of the Immaculate Heart of Mary at Mirinae	[2182]
I.H.M.	Sisters Servants of the Immaculate Heart of Mary	[2150]
I.H.M.	Sisters Servants of the Immaculate Heart of Mary	[2160]
I.H.M.	Sisters Servants of the Immaculate Heart of Mary	[2170]
I.H.M.	Sisters Servants of the Immaculate Heart of Mary	[2180]
I.H.M.	The California Institute of the Sisters of the Most Holy and Immaculate Heart of the Blessed Virgin Mary	[2930]
I.H.M.	Sisters of the Immaculate Heart of Mary of Wichita	[2185]
I.J.	Sisters of the Infant Jesus	[2240]
I.M.	Sisters of Charity of the Infant Mary	[]
I.S.S.M.	Secular Institute of Schoenstatt Sisters of Mary	[]
I.W.B.S.	Congregation of the Incarnate Word and Blessed Sacrament	[2200]
I.W.B.S.	Congregation of the Incarnate Word and Blessed Sacrament	[2205]
J.S.O.P.	Dominican Oblates of Jesus (Spain)	[]
L.B.	Ladies of Bethany	[]
L.C.M.	Sisters of the Little Company of Mary	[2270]
L.H.C.	Lovers of the Holy Cross Sisters	[2390]
L.M.S.C.	Little Missionary Sisters of Charity	[2290]
L.S.	Lasallian Sisters (Vietnam)	[]
L.S.A.	Little Sisters of the Assumption	[2310]
L.S.G.	Little Sisters of the Gospel (France)	[]
L.S.I.C.	Little Servant Sisters of the Immaculate Conception	[2300]
L.S.J.	Little Sisters of Jesus	[2330]
L.S.J.M.	Little Sisters of Jesus and Mary	[2331]
L.S.P.	Little Sisters of the Poor	[2340]
M.C.	Consolata Missionary Sisters	[0720]
M.C.	Missionaries of Charity	[2710]
M.C.	Poor Clare Missionary Sisters	[2840]
M.C.D.P.	Missionary Catechists of Divine Providence, San Antonio, TX	[2690]
M.C.M.	Cordi Marian Sisters	[]
M.C.P.	Missioneras Catequestas de los Pobres	[]
M.C.S.	Missionary Sisters of the Sacred Side	[]
M.C.S.J.M.	Congregation of Missionary Catechists of the Sacred Heart of Jesus and Mary	[]
M.D.	Mothers of the Helpless	[]
M.D.P.V.M.	Missionary Daughters of the Most Pure Virgin Mary	[]
M.E.	Missionary Ecumenical (Rome)	[]
M.C.SS.CC.J.M.	Missionary Catechists of the Sacred Hearts of Jesus and Mary	[2700]
M.E.S.S.T.	Eucharistic Missionaries of the Most Holy Trinity	[]
M.E.S.T.	Eucharistic Missionaries of St. Theresa (Mexico)	[]
M.F.P.	Franciscan Missionaries Our Lady of Peace	[]
M.G.Sp.S.	Guadalupan Missionaries of the Holy Spirit	[1845]
M.H.S.	Sisters of the Most Holy Sacrament	[2940]
M.H.S.H.	Mission Helpers of the Sacred Heart	[2720]
M.I.C.	Missionary Sisters of the Immaculate Conception (Canada)	[]
M.J.	Missionary Sisters of Jesus	[]
M.J.M.J.	Missionaries of Jesus, Mary and Joseph	[2770]
M.M.	Maryknoll Sisters of St. Dominic	[2470]
M.M.D.	Servite Missionary Sisters of the Sorrowful Mother	[]
M.M.M.	Medical Missionaries of Mary	[2480]
M.M.S.	Medical Mission Sisters	[2490]
M.O.M.	Missionary Sisters of Our Lady of Mercy	[2830]
M.P.F.	Religious Teachers Filippini	[3430]
M.P.H.	Missionary Sisters of Our Lady of Perpetual Help	[]
M.P.S.	Misioneras del Perpetual Socorro	[]
M.P.S.	Missionary Sisters of Our Lady of Perpetual Help	[]
M.P.V.	Religious Venerini Sisters	[4180]
M.R.	Marianist Sisters	[]
M.S.	Marian Sisters of the Diocese of Lincoln	[2400]
M.S.B.T.	Missionary Servants of the Most Blessed Trinity	[2790]
M.S.C.	Congregation of the Marianites of the Holy Cross	[2410]
M.S.C.	Missionary Sisters of the Most Sacred Heart of Jesus of Hiltrup	[2800]
M.S.C.	Missionary Sisters of the Sacred Heart	[2860]
M.S.C.Gpe.	Missionaries of the Sacred Heart of Jesus and of Our Lady of Guadalupe	[2865]
M.S.C.K.	Missionary Sisters of Christ the King	[2715]
M.S.F.	Missionary Sisters of the Holy Family	[]
M.S.H.F.	Missionary Sisters of the Holy Family (Poland)	[]
M.S.H.R.	Missionary Sisters of the Holy Rosary	[2730]
M.S.J.	Medical Sisters of St. Joseph	[2500]
M.S.K.C.P.	Missionary Sisters of Christ the King of Polonia	[]
M.S.M.G.	Missionary Sisters of Mother of God	[2810]
M.S.O.L.A.	Missionary Sisters of Our Lady of Africa	[2820]
M.S.S.A.	Missionary Servants of St. Anthony	[2890]
M.S.S.C.B.	Missionary Sisters of St. Charles Borromeo	[2900]
M.S.S.J.	Missionary Servants of St. Joseph (Spain)	[]
M.S.Sp.	Mission Sisters of the Holy Spirit	[2740]
M.SS.S.	Missionary Sisters of the Most Blessed Sacrament	[2780]
M.T.G.	Adorers of the Holy Cross	[4155]
M.X.Y.	The Yarumal Foreign Mission Institute (Colombia)	[]
N.A.U.-O.L.C.	North American Unions of Sisters of Our Lady of Charity	[3070]
N.D.	Notre Dame Sisters	[2960]
N.D.S.	Congregation of Notre Dame de Sion	[2950]
O.A.R.	Augustinian Recollect Sisters	[]
O.B.T.	Sisters Oblates to the Blessed Trinity	[3020]
O.C.A.	Carmelite Vietnamese of Our Lady of Mt. Carmel	[]
O.Carm.	Calced Carmelites	[0300]
O.Carm.	Carmelite Nuns of the Ancient Observance	[0320]
O.Carm.	Carmelite Sisters for Aged and Infirm	[0330]
O.Carm.	Carmelite Sisters (Corpus Christi)	[0350]
O.Carm.	Congregation of Our Lady of Mt. Carmel	[0400]
O.Carm.	Institute of the Sisters of Our Lady of Mt. Carmel	[0410]
O.C.D.	Carmelite Sisters of the Most Sacred Heart of Los Angeles	[0370]
O.C.D.	Discalced Carmelite Nuns	[0420]
O.C.D.	Carmelitas del Sagrado Corazon	[]
O.Cist.	Cistercian Nuns	[0680]
O.C.S.O.	Cistercian Nuns of the Strict Observance	[0670]
O.D.N.	Company of Mary	[0700]
O.L.C.	Sisters of Our Lady of Charity	[3071]
O.L.C.	Sisters of Our Lady of Charity	[3073]
O.L.G.	Sisters of Our Lady of the Garden	[]
O.L.L.	Sisters of Our Lady of Lourdes	[]
O.L.M.	Sisters of Charity of Our Lady of Mercy	[0510]
O.L.S.	Sisters of Our Lady of Sorrows	[3120]
O.L.V.M.	Our Lady of Victory Missionary Sisters	[3130]
O.M.M.I.	Oblate Missionaries of Mary Immaculate	[]
O.M.O.	Oblates of the Mother of Orphans	[3035]
O.P.	Dominican Contemplative Nuns (Cloistered)	[1050]
O.P.	Dominican Contemplative Sisters (Cloistered)	[1060]
O.P.	Dominican Sisters (St. Catharine, KY)	[1070-01]
O.P.	Dominican Sisters (Columbus, OH)	[1070-02]
O.P.	Dominican Sisters (Sinsinawa, WI)	[1070-03]
O.P.	Dominican Sisters (San Rafael, CA)	[1070-04]
O.P.	Dominican Sisters (Amityville, NY)	[1070-05]
O.P.	Dominican Sisters (Newburgh, NY)	[1070-06]
O.P.	Dominican Sisters (Nashville, TN)	[1070-07]
O.P.	Dominican Sisters (New Orleans, LA)	[1070-08]
O.P.	Dominican Sisters (Racine, WI)	[1070-09]
O.P.	Dominican Sisters (Springfield, IL)	[1070-10]
O.P.	Dominican Sisters (Sparkill, NY)	[1070-11]
O.P.	Dominican Sisters (San Jose, CA)	[1070-12]
O.P.	Dominican Sisters (Adrian, MI)	[1070-13]
O.P.	Dominican Sisters (Grand Rapids, MI)	[1070-14]
O.P.	Dominican Sisters (Blauvelt, NY)	[1070-15]
O.P.	Dominican Sisters (Ossining, NY)	[1070-16]
O.P.	Dominican Sisters (Media, PA)	[1070-17]
O.P.	Dominican Sisters (Caldwell, PA)	[1070-18]
O.P.	Dominican Sisters (Houston, TX)	[1070-19]
O.P.	Dominican Sisters (Tacoma, WA)	[1070-20]
O.P.	Dominican Sisters (Edmonds, WA)	[1070-21]
O.P.	Dominican Sisters (Fall River, MA)	[1070-22]
O.P.	Dominican Sisters (Hawthorne, NY)	[1070-23]
O.P.	Dominican Sisters (Great Bend, KS)	[1070-24]
O P.	Dominican Sisters (Kenosha, WI)	[1070-25]
O.P.	Dominican Sisters (Oxford, MI)	[1070-26]
O.P.	Dominican Sisters (Justice, IL)	[1070-27]
O.P.	Dominican Sisters (Akron, OH)	[1070-28]
O.P.	Dominican Sisters (Spokane, WA)	[1070-29]
O.P.	Dominican Sisters (Oxford, South Africa)	[1070-30]
O.P.	Marian Society of Dominican Catechists	[1090]
O.P.	Dominican Sisters of Charity of the Presentation of the Blessed Virgin	[1100]
O.P.	Dominican Sisters of Our Lady of the Rosary and of Saint Catherine of Siena, Cabra	[1110]
O.P.	Dominican Sisters of the Roman Congregation	[1120]

O.P.	Dominican Rural Missionaries	[1130]
O.P.	Eucharistic Missionaries of St. Dominic	[1140]
O.P.	Dominican Sisters of Carondelet	[]
O.P.	Religious Missionaries of St. Dominic (Spanish Prov.)	[]
O.P.	Dominican Sisters of Mt. Thabor	[]
O.P.	Dominican Sisters of Our Lady of the Most Holy Rosary	[]
O.P.	Dominican Sisters (Vietnam)	[]
O.P.	Dominican Contemplative Sisters	[]
O.P.	Dominican Sisters (Colombia)	[]
O.P.	Dominican Sisters (Ecuador)	[]
O.P.	Hermanas Dominicanas de la Doctrine Cristiana	[]
O.S.A.	Augustinian Nuns of Contemplative Life	[0160]
O.S.A.	Congregation of Augustinian Sisters Servants of Jesus and Mary	[2145]
O.S.A.	Sisters of St. Rita	[4010]
O.S.A.	Sisters of St. Augustine	[]
O.S.A.	Augustinian Sisters of Our Lady of Consolation	[]
O.S.B.	Benedictine Nuns of the Congregation of Solesmes	[0170]
O.S.B.	Benedictine Nuns of the Primitive Observance	[0180]
O.S.B.	Benedictine Sisters	[0190]
O.S.B.	Benedictine Sisters	[0200]
O.S.B.	Missionary Benedictine Sisters	[0210]
O.S.B.	Congregation of the Benedictine Sisters of Perpetual Adoration of Pontifical Jurisdiction	[0220]
O.S.B.	Benedictine Sisters of Pontifical Jurisdiction	[0230]
O.S.B.	Benedictine Nuns	[0233]
O.S.B.	Olivetan Benedictine Sisters	[0240]
O.S.B.	Congregation of Jesus Crucified	[2250]
O.S.B.	Benedictine Congregation of Our Lady of Monte	[]
O.S.B.	Benedictine Sisters of Sacred Heart	[]
O.S.B.	Contemplative Sisters of St. Benedict	[]
O.S.B.	Benedictine Sisters of Liberty	[]
O.S.B.	Congregation of the Benedictine Sisters of the Sacred Heart	[]
O.S.B.Cam.	Camaldolese Benedictine Sisters	[]
O.S.B.M.	Sisters of the Order of St. Basil the Great	[3730]
O.S.B.S.	Oblate Sisters of the Blessed Sacrament	[3010]
O.S.C.	Order of St. Clare	[3760]
O.S.C.	Sisters of St. Clare	[3770]
O.S.C.Cap.	Capuchin Poor Clares	[3765]
O.S.F.	Franciscan Sisters of Allegany New York	[1180]
O.S.F.	The Franciscan Sisters of Baltimore	[1200]
O.S.F.	Franciscan Sisters of Chicago	[1210]
O.S.F.	Franciscan Sisters of Christian Charity	[1230]
O.S.F.	Franciscan Sister, Daughters of the Sacred Hearts of Jesus and Mary	[1240]
O.S.F.	Franciscan Sisters of the Immaculate Conception	[1280]
O.S.F.	Franciscan Sisters of the Immaculate Conception and St. Joseph for the Dying	[1300]
O S.F.	Franciscan Sisters of Little Falls, Minnesota	[1310]
O.S.F.	Franciscan Missionary Sisters for Africa	[1320]
O.S.F.	Franciscan Missionary Sisters of the Immaculate Conception	[1350]
O.S.F.	Missionary Franciscan Sisters of the Immaculate Conception	[1360]
O.S.F.	Franciscan Missionaries of Our Lady	[1380]
O.S.F.	Franciscan Missionary Sisters of Our Lady of Sorrows	[1390]
O.S.F.	Franciscan Sisters of Our Lady of Perpetual Help	[1430]
O.S.F.	Franciscan Sisters of the Sacred Heart	[1450]
O.S.F.	Franciscan Sisters of St. Paul	[1485]
O.S.F.	Sisters of the Third Franciscan Order	[1490]
O.S.F.	St. Francis Mission Community	[1505]
O.S.F.	Sisters of St. Francis	[1510]
O.S.F.	Sisters of St. Francis of Christ the King	[1520]
O.S.F.	Sisters of St. Francis of the Congregation of Our Lady of Lourdes, Sylvania, Ohio	[1530]
O.S.F.	Sisters of Saint Francis, Clinton, Iowa	[1540]
O.S.F.	Sisters of St. Francis of the Holy Cross	[1550]
O.S.F.	Sisters of St. Francis of the Holy Eucharist	[1560]
O.S.F.	Sisters of St. Francis of the Holy Family	[1570]
O.S.F.	Sisters of St. Francis of the Immaculate Conception	[1580]
O.S.F.	Sisters of St. Francis of the Immaculate Heart of Mary (Hankinson, North Dakota)	[1590]
O.S.F.	Sisters of St. Francis of the Martyr St. George	[1600]
O.S.F.	Sisters of Saint Francis of Millvale, Pennsylvania	[1620]
O.S.F.	Sisters of St. Francis of Penance and Christian Charity	[1630]
O.S.F.	Sisters of St. Francis of Perpetual Adoration	[1640]
O.S.F.	The Sisters of St. Francis of Philadelphia	[1650]
O.S.F.	Sisters of Saint Francis of the Providence of God	[1660]
O.S.F.	Sisters of St. Francis of Savannah, MO	[1670]
O.S.F.	School Sisters of St. Francis	[1680]
O.S.F.	School Sisters of the Third Order of St. Francis (Pittsburgh, PA)	[1690]
O.S.F.	School Sisters of the Third Order of St. Francis (Panhandle, TX)	[1695]
O.S.F.	School Sisters of the Third Order of St. Francis (Bethlehem, PA)	[1700]
O S F.	The Sisters of St. Francis of Assisi	[1705]
O.S.F.	Congregation of the Third Order of St. Francis of Mary Immaculate (Joliet, IL)	[1710]
O.S.F.	Sisters of the Third Order Regular of St. Francis of the Congregation of Our Lady of Lourdes	[1720]
O.S.F.	Congregation of the Sisters of the Third Order of St. Francis (Oldenburg, IN)	[1730]
O.S.F.	Sisters of the Third Order of St. Francis of Penance and Charity	[1760]
O.S.F.	Sisters of the Third Order of St. Francis (Peoria, IL)	[1770]
O.S.F.	Sisters of St. Francis of the Third Order Regular (Williamsville, New York)	[1800]
O.S.F.	Bernardine Sisters of the Third Order of St. Francis	[1810]
O.S.F.	Hospital Sisters of the Third Order of St. Francis	[1820]
O.S.F.	Servants of the Holy Infancy of Jesus	[1980]
O.S.F.	Consolation Sisters (Highland, CA)	[]
O.S.F.	Franciscan Sisters of Christ the Divine Teacher	[]
O.S.F.	St. Francis Mission Community	[]
O.S.F.S.	Oblate Sisters of St. Francis de Sales	[3060]
O.S.H.J.	Oblate Sisters of the Sacred Heart of Jesus	[3050]
O.S.M.	Mantellate Sisters, Servants of Mary of Blue Island	[3570]
O.S.M.	Servants of Mary	[3580]
O.S.M.	Servants of Mary (Servite Sisters)	[3590]
O.S.M.	Oblates of St. Martha	[]
O.S.P.	Oblate Sisters of Providence	[3040]
O.S.S.	Sacramentine Nuns	[3490]
O.SS.R.	Order of the Most Holy Redeemer	[2010]
O.SS.R.	Oblates of the Most Holy Redeemer	[3030]
O.SS.S.	The Brigittine Sisters	[0280]
O.SS.T.	Sisters of the Most Holy Trinity	[0260]
O.S.U.	Ursuline Nuns (Roman Union)	[4110]
O.S.U.	Ursuline Nuns of the Congregation of Paris (St. Martin, OH)	[4120]
O.S.U.	Ursuline Nuns of the Congregation of Paris (Cincinnati, OH)	[4120-01]
O.S.U.	Ursuline Nuns of the Congregation of Paris (Kansas City, KS)	[4120-02]
O.S.U.	Ursuline Nuns of the Congregation of Paris (Louisville, KY)	[4120-03]
O.S.U.	Ursuline Nuns of the Congregation of Paris (Cleveland, OH)	[4120-04]
O.S.U.	Ursuline Nuns of the Congregation of Paris (Owensboro, KY)	[4120-05]
O.S.U.	Ursuline Nuns of the Congregation of Paris (Toledo, OH)	[4120-06]
O.S.U.	Ursuline Nuns of the Congregation of Paris (Youngstown, OH)	[4120-07]
O.S.U.	Ursuline Sisters of the Congregation of Tildonk, Belgium	[4130]
O.S.U.	Ursuline Sisters of Belleville	[4140]
O.S.U.	Irish Ursuline Union	[4150]
P.B.V.M.	Presentation of the Blessed Virgin Mary Sisters	[3280]
P.B.V.M.	Sisters of the Presentation of the B.V.M.	[3320]
P B.V.M.	Union of the Sisters of the Presentation of the Blessed Virgin Mary	[3330]
P.C.C.	Order of St. Clare	[3760]
P.C.I.	Pax Christi Institute	[]
P.C.J.	Sisters of the Poor Child Jesus	[3220]
P.C.P.A.	Poor Clares of Perpetual Adoration	[3210]
P.D.D.M.	Pious Disciples of the Divine Master	[0980]
P.F.M.	Franciscans of Mary	[2280]
P.H.J.C.	Poor Handmaids of Jesus Christ	[3230]
P.M.	Sisters of the Presentation of Mary	[3310]
P.O.S.C.	Little Workers of the Sacred Heart	[2345]
P.S.N.	Poor Sisters of Nazareth	[3242]
P.S.S.F.	The Little Sisters of the Holy Family	[2320]
P.S.S.J.	Poor Sisters of St. Joseph	[3250]
P.V.M.I.	The Parish Visitors of Mary Immaculate	[3160]
Q.M.H.C.	Quinhon Missionary Sisters of the Holy Cross	[]
R.A.	Religious of the Apostolate of the Sacred Heart	[3380]
R.A.	Religious of the Assumption	[3390]
R.A.	Antonine Sisters	[]
R.A.D.	Sisters of the Love of God	[]
R.C.	Congregation of Our Lady of Retreat in the Cenacle	[3110]
R.C.D.	Sisters of Our Lady of Christian Doctrine	[3080]
R.C.E.	Religious of Christian Education	[3410]
R.C.M.	Sisters of the Immaculate Conception	[2130]
R.C.S.C.J.	Sisters of the Cross of the Sacred Heart of Jesus (Mexico)	[]
R.D.C.	Sisters of the Divine Compassion	[0970]
R.E.	Religious of the Eucharist	[3420]
R.F.	Sisters of St. Philip Neri Missionary Teachers	[]
R.F.R.	Sisters of Our Lady of Refuge	[]
R.G.S.	The Sisters of the Good Shepherd	[1830]
R.H.S.J.	Religious Hospitallers of Saint Joseph	[3440]
R.J.M.	Religious of Jesus and Mary	[3450]
R.M.	Marianitas	[]
R.M.I.	Claretian Missionary Sisters	[0685]
R.M.I.	Religious of Mary Immaculate	[3460]
R.M.M.	Mercedarian Sisters	[]
R.O.D.A.	Sisters Oblates to Divine Love	[]
R.O.L.C.	Our Lady of Charity of Refuge	[3072]
R.S.C.	Religious Sisters of Charity	[3400]
R.S.C.J.	Society of the Sacred Heart	[4070]
R.S.H.M.	Religious of the Sacred Heart of Mary	[3465]
R.S.J.	Religious of St. Joseph of Australia	[]
R.S.M.	Religious Sisters of Mercy of Alma, Michigan	[2519]
R.S.M.	Sisters of Mercy	[2520]
R.S.M.	Sisters of Mercy of Ardagh & Clonmacnois	[2523]
R.S.M.	Sisters of Mercy (Galway)	[2535]
R.S.M.	Sisters of Mercy	[2540]
R.S.M.	Sisters of Mercy (Sligo)	[2549]
R.S.M.	Sisters of Mercy	[2550]
R.S.M.	Sisters of Mercy of the Americas	[2575]
R.S.M.	Sisters of Mercy (Ballyshannon, Ireland)	[]
R.S.M.	Sisters of Mercy (Mayo, Ireland)	[]
R.S.M.	Sisters of Mercy of Mississippi, Inc.	[]
R.S.M.	Sisters of Mercy of Portland	[2655]

R.S.M.	Diocesan Sisters of Mercy	[]
R.S.R.	Congregation of Our Lady of the Holy Rosary	[3100]
R.T.	Theatine Sisters of the Immaculate Conception	[]
R.V.M.	Religious of the Blessed Virgin Mary	[]
S.A.	Franciscan Sisters of the Atonement	[1190]
S.A.A.	Sisters Auxillaries of the Apostolate	[0140]
S.A.B.	Sisters of St. Anne Bangalone	[]
S.A.C.	Sisters of the Guardian Angel	[1850]
S.A.C.	Pallottine Missionary Sisters Queen of Apostles Prov	[3150]
S.A.S.V.	Sisters of the Assumption	[0150]
S.B.S.	The Sisters of the Blessed Sacrament for Indians and Colored People	[0260]
S.C.	Sisters of Charity of Cincinnati, Ohio	[0440]
S.C.	Sisters of Charity of Seton Hill, Greensburg, PA	[0570]
S.C.	Sisters of St. Elizabeth, Convent Station	[0590]
S.C.	Sisters of Charity of St. Vincent de Paul, Halifax	[0640]
S.C.	Sisters of Charity of St. Vincent de Paul, New York	[0650]
S.C.C.	Sisters of Christian Charity	[0660]
Sch.P.	Sisters of the Pious Schools	[3200]
S.C.I.C.	Sisters of Charity of the Immaculate Conception of Ivrea	[0450]
S.C.I.M.	Servants of the Immaculate Heart of Mary	[3550]
S.C.K.	Sisters of Christ the King	[]
S.C.L.	Sisters of Charity of Leavenworth, Kansas	[0480]
S.C.M.C.	Sisters of Charity of Our Lady, Mother of the Church	[0530]
S.C.M.M.	Sisters of Charity of Our Lady Mother of Mercy	[0520]
S.C.M.M.	Medical Mission Sisters	[2490]
S.C.N.	Sisters of Charity of Nazareth	[0500]
S.C.O.	Sisters of Charity of Ottawa (Grey Nuns of the Cross)	[0540]
S.C.O.	Sisters of Charity of Quebec (Grey Nuns)	[0560]
S.C.R.H.	Sisters of Charity of Rolling Meadows	[]
S.C.S.J.A.	Sisters of Charity of St. Joan Antida	[0600]
S.C.S.L.	Sisters of Charity of St. Louis	[0620]
S.C.S.H.	Sisters of Charity of St. Hyacinthe (Grey Nuns)	[0610]
S.deP.	Sister Servants of the Poor	[]
S.D.R.	Sisters of the Divine Redeemer	[1020]
S.D.S.	Sisters of the Divine Saviour	[1030]
S.D.S.H.	Sisters of the Society Devoted to the Sacred Heart	[4050]
S.D.V.	Vocationist Sisters	[4210]
S.E.	Sisters of Emanuel	[]
S.E.C.	Sisters of the Eucharistic Covenant	[]
S.F.C.C.	Sisters for Christian Community	[]
S.F.M.A.	Franciscan Missionary Sisters of Assisi	[1330]
S.F.p.	Franciscan Sisters of the Poor	[1440]
S.G.M.	Sisters of Charity of Montreal (Grey Nuns)	[0490]
S.G.S.	Hermanas del Buen Pastor	[]
S.H.C.J.	Society of the Holy Child Jesus	[4060]
S.H.F.	Sisters of the Holy Family	[1960]
S.H.J.M.	Sisters of the Sacred Hearts of Jesus and Mary	[3680]
S.H.S.	Sisters of the Holy Spirit	[2040]
S.H.Sp.	Sisters of the Holy Spirit and Mary Immaculate	[2050]
S.I.M.	Missionaries of the Kingship of Chnst	[]
S.I.W.	Sisters of the Incarnate Word and the Blessed Sacrament	[2210]
S.J.	Servants of Jesus	[3560]
S.J.A.	Sisters of Ste. Jeanne D'Arc	[3815]
S.J.B.	Sisters of St. John Bosco (Taylor, TX)	[]
S.J.C.	Sisters of St. Joseph of Cluny	[3860]
S.J.S.	Servants of the Blessed Sacrament	[3499]
S.J.S M.	Sisters of St. Joseph of St. Mark	[3910]
S.J.W.	Sisters of St. Joseph the Worker	[3920]
S.L.	Sisters of Loretto at the Foot of the Cross	[2360]
S.L.T.	Pious Society of Our Lady of the Most Holy Trinity	[]
S.L.W.	Sisters of the Living Word	[2350]
S.M.	Marist Sisters Congregation of Mary	[2430]
S.M.	Sisters of Mercy	[2516]
S.M.	Sisters of Mercy	[2518]
S.M.	Sisters of Mercy	[2570]
S.M.	Sisters of Mercy (Cork and Ross)	[2600]
S.M.	Misericordia Sisters	[2680]
S.M.	Sisters Servants of Mary	[3600]
S.M.	Sisters of Mercy (Loughrea, Ireland)	[]
S.M.	Sisters of Mercy of Tralee	[]
S.M.D.C.	Sisters of Mercy of Christian Charity of St. Vincent de Paul of Hungary	[2610]
S.M.G.	Poor Servants of the Mother of God	[3640]
S.M.I.	Sisters of Mary Immaculate	[2440]
S.M.I.C.	Missionary Sisters of the Immaculate Conception of the Mother of God	[2760]
S.M.M.G.	Sisters of Mary, Mother of God	[]
S.M.M.I.	Sisters Minor of the Mary Immaculate	[]
S.M.M.S.	Society of Mary Missionary Sisters	[]
S.M.P.	Sisters of Mary of the Presentation	[2450]
S.M.P.	Daughters of Our Mother of Peace	[]
S.M.P.	Society of Our Mother of Peace	[]
S.M.R.	Society of Mary Reparatrix	[2560]
S.M.S.H.	Sisters of Saint Marthe (of St. Hyacinthe)	[3940]
S.M.S.M.	Marist Missionary Sisters	[2420]
S.N.D.	Sisters of Notre Dame	[2990]
S.N.D.deN.	Sisters of Notre Dame de Namur	[3000]
S.N.J.M.	Sisters of the Holy Names of Jesus and Mary	[1990]
S.O.L.M.	Sisters of Our Lady of Mercy	[2670]
S.O.L.P.H.	Sisters of Our Lady of Perpetual Help	[]
S.O.L.T.	Our Lady of the Most Holy Trinity Convent	[3105]
S.P.	Sisters of Providence	[3340]
S.P.	Sisters of Providence	[3350]
S.P.	Sisters of Providence of Saint Mary-of-the-Woods, IN	[3360]
S.P.C.	Sisters of St. Paul of Chartres	[3980]
S.R.	Sisters of Reparation of the Sacred Wounds of Jesus	[3475]
S.R.C.	Servants of Our Lady, Queen of Clergy	[3650]
S.R.C.M.	Sisters of Reparation of the Congregation of Mary	[3470]
S.S.A.	Sisters of St. Ann	[3718]
S.S.A.	Sisters of St. Anne	[3720]
S.S.C.	Missionary Sisters of St. Columban	[2880]
S.S.C.	Sisters of St. Casimir	[3740]
S.S.C.	Society of the Sisters of the Church	[]
SS.CC.	Congregation of the Sacred Hearts and of Perpetual Adoration	[3690]
S.S.Ch.	Sisters of St. Chretienne	[3750]
S.S.C.J.	Servants of the Most Sacred Heart of Jesus	[3630]
S.S.C.J.	Sisters of the Sacred Heart of Jesus of Saint Jacut	[3670]
S.S.C.K.	Sisters Servants of Christ the King	[3510]
S.S.C.M.	Servants of the Holy Heart of Mary	[3520]
SS.C.M.	Sisters of Saints Cyril and Methodius	[3780]
S.S.D.	Institute of the Sisters of St. Dorothy	[3790]
S.S.E.	Sisters of St. Elizabeth	[3800]
S.S.F.	Congregation of the Sisters of the Holy Family	[1950]
S.S.H.	Sisters Servants of the Most Sacred Heart	[]
S.S.H.J.P.	Servants of the Sacred Heart of Jesus and of the Poor	[3660]
S.S.J.	Servants of St. Joseph	[3595]
S.S.J.	Sisters of St. Joseph (Buffalo)	[3830-06]
S.S.J.	Sisters of St. Joseph (Burlington)	[3830-07]
S.S.J.	Sisters of St. Joseph (Erie)	[3830-09]
S.S.J.	Sisters of St. Joseph (Kalamazoo, Nazareth)	[3830-11]
S.S.J.	Sisters of St. Joseph (Ogdensburg)	[3830-12]
S.S.J.	Sisters of St. Joseph (Rochester)	[3830-14]
S.S.J.	Sisters of St. Joseph, (Springfield, MA)	[3830-16]
S.S.J.	Sisters of St. Joseph (Wheeling, Eng)	[3830-17]
S.S.J.	Sisters of Saint Joseph of Chestnut Hill, Philadelphia	[3893]
S.S.J.	Sisters of St. Joseph of St. Augustine, Florida	[3900]
S.S.J.C.	Sisters of St. Joseph Benedict Cottolengo	[]
S.S.J.-T.O.S.F.	Sisters of St. Joseph of the Third Order of St. Francis	[3930]
S.S.L.	Congregation of the Sisters of St. Louis, Juilly-Monaghan	[3935]
S.S.LOG.	Seton Sisters of Our Lady of Guadalupe, Tucson	[]
S.S.M.	Sisters of the Sorrowful Mother (Third Order of St. Francis)	[4100]
S.S.M.I.	Sisters Servants of Mary Immaculate	[3610]
S.S.M.I.	Sisters Servants of Mary Immaculate	[3620]
S.S.M.N.	Sisters of Saint Mary of Namur	[3950]
S.S.M.O.	Sisters of St. Mary of Oregon	[3960]
S.S.N.D.	School Sisters of Notre Dame	[2970]
S.S.P.C.	Missionary Sisters of St. Peter Claver	[3990]
S.Sp.S.	Missionary Sisters Servants of the Holy Spirit	[3530]
S.Sp.S.deA.P.	Sister Servants of the Holy Spirit of Perpetual Adoration	[3540]
S.S.S.	Servants of the Blessed Sacrament	[3500]
S.S.S.	Sisters of Social Service of Los Angeles, Inc.	[4080]
S.S.S.	Sisters of Social Service	[4090]
S.S.S.F.	School Sisters of St. Francis	[1680]
S.S.T.V.	Congregation of Sisters of St. Thomas of Villanova	[4030]
S.T.J.	Society of St. Teresa of Jesus	[4020]
S.U.	Society of St. Ursula	[4040]
S.U.S.C.	Sisters of the Holy Union	[2070]
S.V.M.	Sisters of the Visitation of the Congregation of the Immaculate Heart of Mary	[4200]
V.D.C.	Verbum Dei Community	[]
V.H.M.	Visitation Nuns	[4190]
V.S.	Vestiarski Sisters	[]
V.S.C.	Vincentian Sisters of Charity	[4160]
V.S.C.	Vincentian Sisters of Charity	[4170]
V.Z.	Sisters of Charity of St. Vincent de Paul	[0630]
X.M.M.	Xaverian Missionary Society of Mary, Inc.	[4230]
X.S.	Catholic Mission Sisters of St. Francis Xavier	[3810]

A USER'S GUIDE TO *THE OFFICIAL CATHOLIC DIRECTORY*

Each year the editors of ***The Official Catholic Directory*** seek added ways of serving their subscribers. Although the book may never answer every question, this is the conscientious goal; its format, arrangement and editorial features are directed toward the convenience and needs of the public. Comments and suggestions are welcome.

GENERAL PLAN

For the benefit of the subscriber and a more efficient use of *The Official Catholic Directory* and its cross references, a summary of the contents and their meaning follows:

Ecclesiastical forms of address recognized in the United States. Formal forms of address for correspondence with the clergy in the United States.

***The Official Catholic Directory* Glossary**
A listing of some of the ecclesiastical terms and organizations found in the *Directory.*

Religious Order Initials for Men and **Religious Order Initials for Women**
Indexes of abbreviations relevant to the religious institute name and the applicable identification number.

Part I: The Governing Bodies in Vatican City
A chronological table of the **Supreme Roman Pontiffs**; the **Pope**, and an alphabetical list of the **College of Cardinals**; the duties of each of the agencies of the **Roman Curia**, and other commissions and institutions associated with the Holy See, along with their officers; a list of the **Seminaries** and **National Colleges** in Rome; the **Apostolic Nunciature** and the **Permanent Observer Mission to the United Nations**, with their staff. As foreign organizations, these entities are not included in the USCC group tax exemption ruling ("Group Ruling").

Part II: Alphabetical Places List
The cities, towns, and villages where there is a church with a resident priest, or a Catholic institution, or both, together with the abbreviations of the archdiocese or diocese to which it belongs. A key to the (arch)diocesan abbreviations precedes the *Religious Order Initials for Men* section and the *Alphabetical List of Diocesan and Religious Priests of the U.S.*

The Catholic Church in the United States
(Provinces)
The archdioceses and dioceses of the United States arranged under the provinces to which they belong, listed with their active archbishops and bishops.

U.S. Cardinals, Archbishops, Bishops, Archabbots and Abbots
An alphabetical list of Cardinals, Archbishops, Bishops, Archabbots and Abbots, arranged within their specific title. Also listed is their address and status, followed by a hierarchical/chronological list by year.

National Conference of Catholic Bishops [NCCB]
The national body of bishops, with headquarters in Washington, D.C. A listing of the NCCB offices and committees, with their officers.

United States Catholic Conference [USCC]
The coordinating body of the American Catholic bishops, with their committees and officers. Also included are the **National Organizations** approved by the USCC and a brief description of their function, and the **National Association of State Catholic Conference Directors.**

Dioceses and Archdioceses
(in alphabetical sequence)
The most detailed information on the Catholic Church in the United States, including the Military Services, Eastern Churches, Personal Prelatures, and Apostolates to the Hungarians and Lithuanians. Listings are in alphabetical order according to the name of the diocese/archdiocese and include the diocesan curia and administrative offices; a parish-by-parish listing of clergy, churches, missions, and parochial schools; information on institutions, and the religious institutes of men and women located in the diocese/archdiocese; and a statistical profile for each diocese/archdiocese.

United States Territorial Sees
This section contains information on U.S. territories similar to that found in the preceding section.

Part III: The Catholic Church in Canada and Mexico
A brief listing of the provinces, archdioceses, dioceses, and administrative organizations in Canada and Mexico. As

foreign organizations, these entities are not included in the USCC Group Ruling.

American Foreign Missions

This section highlights the Religious working specifically in foreign countries. Each Province lists their U.S. members and the countries they serve in. For specific address requests, contact the mission office listed.

Missionary Activities

Organizations involved in missionary work in the U.S. and foreign countries.

United States Conference of Secular Institutes

An alphabetical list of secular organizations and their purposes.

U.S. Catholic Mission Association

An alphabetical list of countries served by the U.S. Catholic Mission Association, detailing the number and religious order or laity personnel working there.

Mission Churches

A list, by city, of mission churches in the U.S. and the parishes to which they are attached.

Religious Institutes of Men and Women

An alphabetical list of religious institutes of men and of women, using a P.J. Kenedy identification number. Each listing contains the general headquarters, provinces, provincialates, a summary of legal titles and holdings taken from the individual archdioceses and dioceses within the *Directory*, various forms of ministry and works, statistical data of personnel, and representation in the U.S. dioceses and archdioceses.

Colleges and Universities

An alphabetical list of colleges and universities by state and diocese, including detailed information on administrative officers, religious and lay faculty, and student body.

Hospitals

An alphabetical list of hospitals by state and diocese, including information on executive and administrative officers, religious and lay professional staff, bed capacity, and number of patients assisted annually.

Special Care Facilities

An alphabetical list of special care facilities by state and diocese, including administrators, type of care, religious and lay staff, beds, patients assisted annually, outpatients and residents.

Diocesan and Religious Priests

An alphabetical list of diocesan and religious priests denoting their year of ordination, the archdiocese or diocese they are assigned to or work in, and the church or institution with which they are affiliated.

Necrology of U.S. Cardinals, Archbishops, Bishops, Archabbots, Abbots, and Priests

An alphabetical list of the U.S. hierarchy and priests who have died since the last issue of the *Directory*, along with their date of death and last assignment.

The General Summary

A 40+ page general summary of statistics arranged alphabetically by state, listing the archdiocese first within each state, followed by the dioceses. This information, extracted from the Statistical Overview of each diocese/archdiocese, pertains to personnel, parishes, health and welfare, education, and specific sacramental figures, as well as Catholic and total population figures for each diocese/archdiocese. U.S. territories and Eastern Church statistics are also included.

Map of Catholic Diocesan and Province Boundaries in the United States

Map defining the diocesan, archdiocesan, provincial, and state boundaries.

Products & Services Guide

Includes a diverse array of products and services offered to the Catholic community.

***The Official Catholic Directory* Part II**

Provides a comprehensive listing of archdioceses and dioceses of the world. Also contains mid-year updates to the U.S. (arch)dioceses. More information on *The OfficialCatholic Directory* Part II can be obtained from the publisher.

SPECIAL NOTATIONS USED IN THE DIRECTORY

An asterisk (*) denotes a tax-exempt organization that has its own IRS exemption status and is not covered by the USCC Group Ruling. The Group Ruling allows for the exemption from federal income tax of all Catholic institutions listed in *The Official Catholic Directory* for that year. The exemption was established in 1946 and has been extended every year since then.

[CEM] in a parish listing indicates that a cemetery is connected to the parish.

[JC] indicates a joint cemetery, which is a cemetery being utilized by more than one parish. A number following [CEM] or [JC] indicates the number of cemeteries owned by the parish or joint cemeteries shared with other parishes.

A dagger † next to a name in the Necrology denotes a deceased priest. A Maltese cross ✠ denotes a deceased member of the hierarchy.

THE GENERAL SUMMARY

Certain terms used in the General Summary may need additional explanation.

Extern Priests are priests who have not been incardinated into the diocese in which they are currently working and residing.

Health Care Centers include ancillary care systems, medical centers, sanitoriums, and hospices.

Specialized Homes refers to institutions which provide aid to abused children or adults, halfway homes, AIDS patients, ARC patients, ex-offenders, pregnant women, adjudicated delinquents, or runaway youths.

Special Centers for Social Services are institutions or services that provide assistance, such as hotline centers, food banks, homeless centers, legal aid services, or counseling services.

Residential Care of Children refers to orphanages, as opposed to day care centers.

Non-residential Schools for Handicapped are day schools which provide regular and religious education for physically and/or mentally handicapped students.

Received into Full Communion is used to describe people who have been baptized earlier in life and have now been received into full communion in the Catholic Church.

ECCLESIASTICAL FORMS OF ADDRESS RECOGNIZED IN THE UNITED STATES

These are the formal forms of address used in correspondence:

CARDINALS:
Address on envelope: His Eminence (Christian name) Cardinal (Surname)
Salutation: Your Eminence:
Concluding a letter: I have the honor to be, Your Eminence, *etc.*

ARCHBISHOPS:
Address on envelope: Most Reverend N_______ N_______
Salutation: Your Excellency:
Concluding a letter: I have the honor to be, Your Excellency, *etc.*

BISHOPS:
Address on envelope: Most Reverend N_______ N_______
Salutation: Your Excellency:
Concluding a letter: I have the honor to be, Your Excellency, *etc.*

ABBOTS:
Address on envelope: Right Reverend N_______ N_______ *(add religious order initials)*
Salutation: Right Reverend Abbot:
Concluding a letter: I have the honor to be, Right Reverend Abbot, *etc.*

PROTONOTARIES APOSTOLIC:
Address on envelope: Rev. Msgr. N_______ N_______
Salutation: Rev. Msgr.:
Concluding a letter: I am, Rev. Msgr., *etc.*

PRELATE OF HONOR OF HIS HOLINESS:
Address on envelope: Rev. Msgr. N_______ N_______
Salutation: Rev. Msgr.:
Concluding a letter: I am, Rev. Msgr., *etc.*

CHAPLAIN TO HIS HOLINESS:
Address on envelope: Rev. Msgr. N_______ N_______
Salutation: Rev. Msgr.:
Concluding a letter: I am, Rev. Msgr., *etc.*

SECULAR PRIESTS:
Address on envelope: Rev. N_______ N_______
Salutation: Dear Reverend Father:
Concluding a letter: I am, Reverend Father, *etc.*

RELIGIOUS ORDER PRIESTS:
Address on envelope: Rev. N_______ N_______ *(add religious order initials)*
Salutation: Dear Reverend Father:
Concluding a letter: I am, Reverend Father, *etc.*

DEACONS:
Address on envelope: Rev. Mr. N_______
Salutation: Dear Deacon N_______
Concluding a letter: I am, Respectfully yours, *etc.*

BROTHERS:
Address on envelope: Brother N_______
Salutation: Dear Brother N_______
Concluding a letter: I am, Respectfully yours, *etc.*

SISTERS:
Address on envelope: Sister N_______
Salutation: Dear Sister N_______
Concluding a letter: I am, Respectfully yours, *etc.*

THE OFFICIAL CATHOLIC DIRECTORY GLOSSARY

Abbot
The superior of an autonomous community of men religious. He has general and sacramental jurisdiction over his community. The head of a prominent monastery or a congregation consisting of several monasteries is an *archabbot*.

Advocate
An ecclesiastical advocate is someone approved by Church authority to safeguard the rights of a party in a canonical process by arguments regarding the law and the facts of the case. [Cf. c. 1481 and CLSA Comm., p. 967]

Apostolate
Apostolate is the mission of Christ and participation in it. Its object is to bring Christ to others, its goal is the greater glory of God, its scope is universal. The work is carried out by every human agency by which the life of grace may be given or increased in the soul. A mandate from the Church is essential to the Catholic apostolate.

Archbishop
A bishop of a main or metropolitan diocese in an ecclesiastical province. The term is equivalent to *metropolitan* in the Western Church. It may also be granted to other ordinaries and non-residential bishops, and to the ordinary of a diocese outside a province.

Auditor
An official of a diocesan court, who gathers evidence and testimony and draws up a record of an ecclesiastical case.

Bishop
A bishop, by divine institution, carries on the work of the apostles. By reason of episcopal consecration, he shares in the triple apostolic function of teacher of doctrine, priest of sacred worship, and minister of church government. Bishops are responsible for the pastoral care of their dioceses. In addition, bishops have a responsibility to act in council to guide the Church. The term *eparch* is used in Eastern-rite churches.

The bishop to whom a particular or local church is entrusted is called a *diocesan bishop* or a *residential bishop.* All other bishops receive *Titular Sees* over which they exercise no pastoral authority.

When the pastoral needs of a diocese or archdiocese warrant, an *auxiliary bishop* may be assigned to aid the residential bishop in governing his diocese. An auxiliary bishop is assigned when the residential bishop needs assistance in carrying out his duties because of ill health, advanced age, or amount of work. An auxiliary bishop does not have the right of succession within his diocese.

In special circumstances, such as the advanced age or ill health of a diocesan bishop, a *coadjutator bishop* may be appointed to assist the principal bishop of a diocese. Coadjutator bishops have the *right of succession* in the diocese of their appointment from the time the See becomes vacant upon the death or retirement of its bishop.

Brother
A man who is a member of a religious order, but is not ordained or studying for the priesthood.

Cana Conference
A Catholic family movement, originally designed to aid married couples and families in their spiritual and interpersonal relationships. The program is now divided into *Pre-Cana,* for couples engaged to be married, and *Cana Conferences,* programs for married people.

Censor Librorum
A theologian empowered by a bishop to judge a book's soundness in regard to Church teaching before publication.

Chancellor
The office of the chancellor (or the *chancery*) evolved from the practice in the early Church of appointing an official to sign and preserve the letters of the bishop. The first function of the chancellor in the present day is gathering, arranging, and safeguarding the acts of the diocesan curia. Dispensations and other official documents also originate from the chancery. In many dioceses, the chancellor continues to exercise ordinary jurisdiction as delegated by the diocesan bishop. He or she may be assisted by a separate official, the *vice-chancellor.*

Chapter
The *general chapter* of a religious order is an assembly of elected or appointed members and provincials. General chapters are convened for the election of officers, amendments to the constitution, and discussion and legislation of matters of concern to members and the order as a whole.

A *provincial chapter* conducts elections and handles legislation on a provincial level. The assembly is comprised of superiors and representatives of the religious.
A *chapter of canons* is a group of diocesan priests, appointed by the bishop of a diocese, with assigned authority or responsibilities.

College of Cardinals
The College of Cardinals is made up of the cardinals of the Church, who advise the Pope, assist in the central administration of the Church, head the various curial offices

and congregations, administer the Holy See during a vacancy, and elect a new Pope. There are three ranks in the College of Cardinals, corresponding to the historical origins of cardinals in the Roman Catholic Church. All cardinals are bishops, but their rank within the College of Cardinals is characterized by one of the hierarchical ranks of bishop, priest, or deacon. Cardinals are given honorary title to churches in the city of Rome. [CF. c. 350; CLSA Comm., pp. 288-289]

1. Cardinal Bishops
There are two types of Cardinal Bishops: 1) those appointed by the Pope as titular bishops to one of the six suburban dioceses of Rome, and 2) Eastern-rite Patriarchs who are heads of Sees with apostolic origins that have been assigned to the College of Cardinals.

2. Cardinal Priests
Heads of Sees outside the city of Rome are assigned a "titular church," one of the churches in Rome. They have no pastoral authority over their titular church.

3. Cardinal Deacons
Cardinals of diaconal rank are bishops without Sees who head the various departments, offices, congregations, committees, and the Secretariat of State of the Roman Curia.

Confraternity of Christian Doctrine [CCD]
A lay organization established for religious education throughout a person's entire life. The term is currently used to describe Catholic parish-based religious education of children from kindergarten through high school. At the diocesan level, the offices are now more commonly known as offices of *religious education* or *Christian formation.* Nationally, the confraternity's religious education component has been taken over by the USCC's Department of Education. It still exists as a separate entity under the USCC Administrative Board, with responsibility for licensing religious and spiritual literature.

Consolidated School
The term, as used in the *Directory,* may refer to a school that takes students from more than one parish, or a school that was formed by the consolidation of two or three other schools. In both cases, it is a means of keeping a Catholic school in a given area open by taking students from the surrounding areas, regardless of parish boundaries.

Convent
In common usage, the term refers to a house of women religious. Originally, it referred to a building where members of religious institutes lived, and was not restricted to communities of women.

Cursillo
The *cursillo de cristianidad*, or "little course in Christianity," is a three-day program for achieving spiritual renewal or spiritual awakening. It seeks to convey a new sense of individual and organized apostolic action. The program, conducted by priests and laypeople, consists of a three-day weekend focused on prayer, study, and Christian action, and a follow-up program known as the *post-cursillo.*

Deacons
The diaconate is the first order or grade in ordained ministry. Its origins are in early apostolic times, when deacons preached and baptized under the direction of the presbyters or bishops. Any man who is to be ordained to the priesthood must first be ordained as a *transitional deacon.* Deacons serve in the ministry of liturgy, of the word, and of charity.

In 1967, Pope Paul VI reinstituted the *Permanent Diaconate* for men who do not plan to become ordained priests. Although men ordained as permanent deacons are sometimes referred to as "married deacons," the permanent diaconate is open to both married and unmarried men, with the understanding that after ordination, they may not marry even after the death of a spouse. Under the authority of the diocesan bishop, they perform the same functions as the transitional deacons while, at the same time, retaining their roles in society as family and business men.

Dean/Vicar Forane
The title of a priest appointed by the bishop to aid him in administering the parishes in a certain vicinity, called a "deanery," or "vicariates forane." The function of a dean, or vicar forane, involves promotion, coordination, and supervision of the common pastoral activity within the deanery or vicariate.

Defender of the Bond
A member of a diocesan tribunal, either a cleric or a lay person, holding a graduate degree in canon law, who is appointed by the diocesan bishop for cases concerning the nullity of sacred ordination or the nullity or dissolution of the marriage bond. The defender of the bond is responsible for a review of the evidence, scrutiny of the briefs, examination of witnesses, and maintenance of proper procedures during the trial. The defender also deals with some situations concerning the content of the litigation rather than the legal procedures.

Diocesan Consultors
An advisory council of diocesan priests, as appointed by a diocesan bishop, that assists in the administrative affairs of the diocese.

Diocesan Curia
The personnel and offices assisting the diocesan bishop in directing the pastoral activity, administration, and the exercise of judicial power of his diocese. The curia includes among its officers laity and religious as well as clergy. Principal officers of a diocesan curia are the vicar general of the diocese, the chancellor, officials of the diocesan tribunal, examiners, consultors, auditors, the promoter of justice and the defender of the bond.

Diocese
The standard term for a territorial division of the Church, entrusted to a bishop who rules in his own name as local ordinary, and not as a delegate of another. The chief diocese of a province is an *archdiocese.* It is headed by an archbishop. A diocese is usually limited to a definite territory so that it comprises all the faithful who inhabit

that territory. [Cf. cc. 369 and 372, #1] In Eastern-rite churches, the term eparchy is used.

Eastern-rite [Oriental] Church
The term used to describe the Catholic churches which developed in Eastern Europe, Asia, and Africa. The Eastern-rite churches have their own distinctive liturgical and organizational systems. Each is considered equal to the Latin rite within the Church.

Ecumenism/Ecumenical Movement
A movement for spiritual understanding and unity among Christians and their churches. The term is also extended to apply to efforts toward greater understanding and cooperation between Christians and members of other faiths.

Exarch/Exarchy
A church jurisdiction, similar to a diocese, established for Eastern-rite Catholics living outside their native land. The head of an exarchy, usually a bishop, is an *exarch.*

Hierarchy
In general, the term refers to the ordered body of clergy, divided into bishops, priests, and deacons. In Catholic practice, the term refers to the bishops of the world or of a particular region.

Holy Name Society
A lay organization which seeks to aid its members in living a genuinely Christian life. The society organizes retreats and other spiritual and devotional exercises.

Holy See
The term refers to the diocese of Rome. Used in reference to the governance of the Church, it refers to the Pontiff, the Roman Curia, and the Sacred College.

Legion of Mary
A lay organization established to assist the clergy in the sanctification of its members' souls, and the spread of the Christian faith and spiritual service to others. Members participate in almost every form of social service and Catholic action, including evangelization. The organization was founded in 1921.

Metropolitan
The archbishop of an archdiocese in a province. He has limited supervisory powers and influence over the other dioceses and bishops in the province.

Military Ordinariate [Archdiocese for the Military Services, U.S.A.]
A nonterritorial diocese for American Catholics and their dependents who are in the military or affiliated with the armed forces. Personnel employed by or engaged in diplomatic missions for the U.S. government in countries where U.S. military forces are stationed also belong to the Military Ordinariate.

Mission
A mission, or *quasi-parish,* is a parish which has not been established because it lacks one or more of the following qualifications: a resident pastor; necessary financial resources; territorial boundaries; or a natural grouping by way of rite, nationality, or language. Missions are attached to some parishes under the care of their pastors.

Moderator of the Curia
A bishop or priest, appointed by the diocesan bishop, who is concerned primarily with administrative matters and with supervising those working in the curia.

Monastery
An autonomous community house of a religious order, which may or may not be a monastic order. The term is used more specifically to refer to a community house of men religious or women religious in which they lead a contemplative life separate from the world.

Monsignor
An honorary ecclesiastical title granted by the Pope to some diocesan priests. In the United States, the title is given to the vicar general of a diocese. In Europe, the title is also given to bishops.

National Conference of Catholic Bishops [NCCB]
The episcopal conference of U.S. bishops. The membership is comprised of diocesan bishops and their associate bishops. The conference decides matters of ecclesiastical law and issues policy statements on political and social issues.

Newman Apostolate
An apostolate to the Catholic college and university community, now commonly known as "campus ministry."

Notary
An elected or appointed ecclesiastical official who acts as a secretary in formal church proceedings. The notary records the minutes, testimony, etc., of the proceedings.

Opus Dei
A personal prelature dedicated to spreading through society an awareness of the call to Christian virtue, awareness, and witness in one's life and work. The organization was founded in 1928 and in 1950, it received Vatican approval as a secular institution. In 1982, it was designated a personal prelature, the *Prelature of the Holy Cross and Opus Dei.* Members are not members of a religious order, do not take vows, and do not live in community.

Ordinary
Diocesan bishops, religious superiors, and certain other diocesan authorities with jurisdiction over the clergy in a specific geographical area, or the members of a religious order.

Ordination/Ordain
The sacramental rite by which a "sacred order" is conferred (diaconate, priesthood, episcopacy).

Papal Audience
Request for attendance at papal audiences and similar functions may be addressed to: Bishops' Office for United States Visitors to the Vatican. Postal address: North American College, Via dell 'Umilta 30, 00187 Rome, Italy. Tel.: 06-690-011; Fax: 011-39-06-679-1448. Rev. Msgr. Roger C. Roensch.

Papal Representatives
There are three types of representatives of the Roman Pontiff:
1) those who represent him to particular churches;
2) those who represent him to particular churches and civil government;
3) those who represent him in international organizations or at various conferences and meetings. [Cf. c. 363; CLSA Comm., p. 302]

1. Legate
An individual appointed by the Pope to be his personal representative to a nation, international conference, or local church. The legate may be chosen from the local clergy of a country.

2. Apostolic Pro-Nuncio
In the United States, the papal representative is sent by the Pope to both the local church and to the government. His title is Apostolic Pro-Nuncio. Although he holds the title of ambassador, in U.S. law he is not accorded the special privilege of being the dean of the diplomatic corps.

3. Permanent Observer to the United Nations
The Apostolic See maintains permanent legates below the ambassadorial level to several world organizations. Since the Papal Legate does not enjoy the right to vote within the organization, his title at the United Nations is that of *Observer*.

Parish
A specific community of the Christian faithful within a diocese, which has its own church building, under the authority of a *pastor* who is responsible for providing them with ministerial service. Most parishes are formed on a geographic basis, but they may be formed along national or ethnic lines.

Parish Coordinator
A deacon, religious, or lay person who is responsible for the pastoral care of parish. The parish coordinator is in charge of the day-to-day life of the parish in the areas of worship, education, pastoral service and administration.

Pastor
A priest in charge of a parish or congregation. He is responsible for administering the sacraments, instructing the congregation in the doctrine of the Church, and other services to the people of the parish.

Pastoral Associate
A member of the laity who is part of a parish ministry team.

Pastoral Council
A consultative body which the pastor or bishop consults concerning the pastoral activity within the diocese. Its members include laity, religious, and clergy. The pastoral council's purpose is to study practical situations, difficulties and problems, and make concrete recommendations and proposals to the diocesan bishop. The pastoral council is always subject to the final authority of the pastor or bishop.

Patriarch
The Pope is the traditional "Patriarch of the West." All other bishops in the Latin Rite, even those with the honorary title of "Patriarch," are subject to him. Similarly, patriarchs within nations have only an honorary title unless special provisions are made otherwise. Eastern-rite Patriarchs are subject to the Pope while serving as heads of the faithful belonging to their rites throughout the world.

Personal Prelature
In addition to the territorial arrangement of the Church into particular or local churches or dioceses, canon law also provides for non-territorial areas of religious jurisdiction, incorporating secular clergy and deacons. Membership is also open to lay persons. These *prelatures* are established to meet specific pastoral or missionary needs at the regional, national, or international level without infringing on the rights of the local bishops. A prelature is presided over by a *personal prelate,* who is an ordinary with the right to establish seminaries and ordain priests as members of the prelature.

Canon law also allows for laity to be associated in the works of prelatures without being withdrawn from the jurisdiction of their own diocesan bishop.

Presbyteral Council
Also known as the *priests' council,* the presbyteral council is the principal consultative body mandated by the Code of Canon Law to advise the diocesan bishop in matters of pastoral governance. It consists of bishops and priests serving the diocese.

Propagation of the Faith
An organization, headquartered in Rome, which distributes aid to Catholic missions and organizes the work of missionaries all over the world. The organization has responsibility for fostering missionary vocations, assigning

missionaries to field work, defining ecclesiastical boundaries and assigning clergy to them, and encouraging training and installation of native-born clergy.

Promoter of Justice
A cleric or lay person, holding a graduate degree in canon law, who is appointed by the diocesan bishop to serve in the role of a "prosecuting attorney" in trials of crimes against church law and of other judicial litigations in the diocese. A promoter of justice may be appointed for a specific case by the bishop.

Province
A defined geographic area containing an archdiocese, or *Metropolitan See,* and at least one diocese, or *Suffragen See.* The archbishop of the archdiocese has no direct powers over the Suffragen Sees, but does have limited advisory and appellate authority and obligations. The term also refers to a territorial grouping of particular churches or communities, or a territory of a religious order.

Provincial
The superior of the communities of a religious order that constitute a province.

Provincial Council
An assembly of the bishops of an ecclesiastical province, called by the metropolitan archbishop. The term is also used in reference to the provincial superior of a province, along with his or her chief advisors.

Receptions into the Church
Can take two forms: baptism of those not previously validly baptized, or "reception into full communion" with the Church for those who have already been baptized, in which case a profession of faith affects the reception.

Religious Priest/Diocesan Priest
Religious, or regular, priests are those who are professed members of a religious order or institute. Religious clergy live according to the rule of their respective orders. In pastoral ministry, they are under the jurisdiction of their local bishop, as well as the superiors of their order. Diocesan, or secular, priests are under the direction of their local bishop. They commit to serving their congregations and other institutions.

Retreat
A period of time spent in meditation and religious exercise. Retreats may take various forms, from traditional closed forms, to open retreats, which do not disengage the participants from day-to-day life. Both clergy and lay people of all ages participate in retreats. Houses and centers providing facilities for retreats are *retreat houses.*

Rite of Christian Initiation of Adults [RCIA]
The liturgical book containing the norms and rituals of the Catholic Church for people who wish to join the Church. Part of the book is intended for baptized Christians who wish to become Catholics. The term is used in a general sense to refer to the process of entering the Catholic Church.

Roman Curia
The official collective name for the administrative agencies and courts, and their officials, who assist the Pope in governing the Church. Members are appointed and granted authority by the Pope.

St. Vincent DePaul Society
Originally known as the *Conference of Charity,* this is an organization of lay people who serve the poor through spiritual and material works of mercy. The society operates stores, rehabilitation workshops, food centers, shelters, criminal justice and other programs.

Scholastic
A member of a religious order who has completed his novitiate, but has not yet been ordained.

Scholastic Teaching
Usually refers to Scholastic Philosophy, which is the basis for much Catholic Theology. It comes from the canonical "schools" of the 12th-13th centuries, St. Thomas Aquinas, St. Bonaventure, St. Albert the Great, etc., who developed "scholasticism" based mainly on Aristotle. It is the semi-official philosophy of the Church.

Secular Institute
Canonically erected institute of consecrated life for single laity and clerics who strive for the perfection of charity and work for the sanctification of the world while remaining in a lifestyle within the world.

See
The word is taken from the Latin word "sedes" ("seat"), and is used to denote a diocese or ecclesiastical district. The term *Holy See* is reserved to the diocese of Rome whose bishop is the Pope.

Seminary
An educational institution for men preparing for *Holy Orders*. The term originates from the time of St. Augustine, when those preparing for the priesthood were educated in the "cathedral school." During the Middle Ages, the clergy were educated in a university setting where faculties of philosophy, theology, and canon law existed. Eventually individual dioceses or provinces came to establish their own schools for educating their clerical students. Traditional seminaries date from the Council of Trent in the 16th century.

A school for the spiritual, academic, and pastoral education and formation of priesthood candidates is known as a *major seminary* in which the focus is on philosophical and theological education. To prepare for entrance into a major seminary, a period of study is set aside for the required courses in the humanities and the sciences in institutions called *minor seminaries*.

Serra Club
Local units of *Serra International,* an organization which promotes vocations to the priesthood and religious life, and offers instruction to lay leaders.

Sister
The term, in the strictest sense, refers to women religious who belong to institutes which have professed simple vows. However, in everyday usage, the term is used for any woman religious.

Sodality
A group of laity established for the promotion of Christian life and worship, or some other religious purpose.

Special Centers for Social Services
This would seem to overlap with Specialized Homes. Some of the categorization is fairly arbitrary. Catholic Charities might have its own proper distinctions for government or private funding purposes.

Specialized Homes
Includes such institutions as homes for handicapped (e.g., Misericordia Homes), youth homes (e.g., Maryville, Mercy Boys and Girls, Homes), homes for battered women, drug rehab centers, homes for unwed mothers, etc.

Superior
The head of a religious order or congregation. He or she may be the head of a province, or an individual house.

Synod
A gathering of designated officials and representatives of a church, that has legislative and policy-making powers.

1. Synod of Bishops
The Synod of Bishops is a consultative body, unless explicitly stated otherwise by His Holiness, expressing the communion of the hierarchy. A synod of bishops meets in general assembly, either in "Ordinary" or "Extraordinary" session, when the matter for treatment concerns the whole Church and in "Special Assembly" when the matter deals directly with a definite region or regions.

2. Synod of Oriental Churches
The synods of the Oriental Churches enjoy various prerogatives including the right to elect bishops, regulate discipline and exercise pastoral authority in their respective churches.

3. Diocesan Synod
A diocesan synod is an expression of the communion of the particular church. A diocesan synod enjoys the participation of priests, women and men religious and laypersons; the bishop is the sole legislator.

Theologate
An institution which provides the last four years of study for candidates for the priesthood.

Titular See
A former diocese which no longer physically or geographically exists. Titular Sees are given as an honorary title to any bishop not serving as a chief pastor of a diocese, i.e., auxiliary bishops, papal representatives, and bishops of the Roman Curia.

Tribunal
A tribunal (court) is the name given to the person or persons who exercise the Church's judicial powers. By its very nature, this procedure involves the determination of a legal controversy. A major concern of tribunals is conducting the process leading to the dissolution or annulment of marriages. In ecclesiastical matters, definite procedural norms for conducting a trial are found in the Code of Canon Law to settle disputes. There are various grades of tribunals, including diocesan tribunals, the first court of trial for most cases; regional and metropolitan tribunals, located in an archdiocese, the appellate court for all cases tried within the province; and the tribunals of the Holy See, which act as the Church's central appellate court, try cases reserved to the Holy See, deal with questions of procedure and jurisdiction of the other courts, and act as the Church's supreme court.

United States Catholic Conference [USCC]
The civil corporation and executive agency of the National Conference of Catholic Bishops. The USCC acts as the national public policy organization of the NCCB. Its purpose is to organize and promote Catholic activity in the U.S. and abroad, and to carry out the religious and social action of the Catholic Church in the U.S. The major departments are education, communication, and social development and world peace.

Vicar
The appointment of a priest or a bishop as an *episcopal vicar* is an option given to a diocesan bishop when he needs a deputy for governing a specific territory within the diocese, a group of persons or a specific rite, or a type of apostolic work within the diocese.

By Church law, the diocesan bishop is the judge of all cases in the diocesan tribunal of first trial. He must appoint a priest with ordinary power to judge cases not reserved to the bishop himself. This priest must have a graduate degree in canon law. He is called the *judicial vicar,* and is sometimes referred to as the chief judge or officialis. He may be given another priest as an assistant with the title of *adjutant judicial vicar*.

A bishop or priest appointed to participate in the executive (administrative) governance of the diocese with executive jurisdiction as a deputy of the diocesan bishop is a *vicar general*. The appointment of a vicar general is mandatory for every diocese. This office is designed to facilitate and unify diocesan administration.

Vicar for Religious
A priest appointed by a bishop to act as his representative in dealing with the religious communities in his diocese.

Information for this glossary was taken from the *Catholic News Service's Stylebook on Religion,* the *Modern Catholic Dictionary,* published by Doubleday and Company, Inc., the *Concise Oxford Dictionary of the Christian Church,* published by Oxford University Press, and the *Encyclopedic Dictionary of Religion,* published by the Sisters of St. Joseph of Philadelphia. The publishers of the *Official Catholic Directory* also wish to thank the Vice Chancellors of the Archdiocese of Chicago for their work in the preparation of this glossary.

The Supreme Roman Pontiffs

St. Peter of Bethsaida in Galilee, Prince of the Apostles, who received from Jesus Christ the Supreme Pontifical Power to be transmitted to his Successors, resided first at Antioch, then at Rome for twenty-five years where he was martyred in the year 64, or 67 of the common reckoning.

	END OF PONTIFICATE, A.D.
St. Linus	76
St. Anacletus or Cletus	88
St. Clement I	97
St. Evaristus	105
St. Alexander I	115
St. Sixtus I	125
St. Telesphorus	136
St. Hyginus	140
St. Pius I	155
St. Anicetus	166
St. Soterus	175
St. Eleuterius	189
St. Victor I	199
St. Zephyrinus	217
St. Callistus I	222
St. Urban I	230
St. Pontian	235
St. Anterus	236
St. Fabian	250
St. Cornelius	253
St. Lucius I	254
St. Stephen I	257
St. Sixtus II	258
St. Dionysius	268
St. Felix I	274
St. Eutychian	283
St. Caius	296
St. Marcellinus	304
St. Marcellus I	309
St. Eusebius	309
St. Melchiades	314
St. Sylvester I	335
St. Mark	336
St. Julius I	352
Liberius	366
St. Damasus I	384
St. Siricius	399
St. Anastasius I	401
St. Innocent I	417
St. Zozimus	418
St. Boniface I	422
St. Celestine I	432
St. Sixtus III	440
St. Leo I (the Great)	461
St. Hilary	468
St. Simplicius	483
St. Fclix III or II	492
St. Gelasius I	496
Anastasius II	498
St. Symmacus	514
St. Hormisdas	523
St. John I	526
St. Felix IV or III	530
Boniface II	532
John II	535
St. Agapitus	536
St. Silverius	537
Vigilius	555
Pelagius I	561
John III	574
Benedict I	579
Pelagius II	590
St. Gregory I (the Great)	604
Sabinianus	606
Boniface III	607
St. Boniface IV	615
St. Deusdeditus or Adeodatus I	618
Boniface V	625
Honorius I	638
Severinus	640
John IV	642
Theodore I	649
St. Martin I	655
St. Eugene I	657
St. Vitalian	672
Adeodatus II	676
Donus I	678
St. Agathonus	681
St. Leo II	683
St. Benedict II	685
John V	686
Conon	687
St. Sergius I	701
John VI	705
John VII	707
Sisinnius	708
Constantine	715
St. Gregory II	731
St. Gregory III	741
St. Zachary	752
Stephen III	757
St. Paul I	767
Stephen IV	772
Adrian I	795
St. Leo III	816
Stephen V	817
St. Paschal I	824
Eugene II	827
Valentine	827
Gregory IV	844
Sergius II	847
St. Leo IV	855
Benedict III	858
St. Nicholas I (the Great)	867
Adrian II	872
John VIII	882
Marinus I	884
St. Adrian III	885
Stephen VI	891
Formosus	896
Boniface VI	896
Stephen VII	897
Romanus	897
Theodore II	897
John IX	900
Benedict IV	903
Leo V	903
Sergius III	911
Anastasius III	913
Landus	914
John X	928
Leo VI	928
Stephen VIII	931
John XI	935
Leo VII	939
Stephen IX	942
Marinus II	946
Agapitus II	955
John XII	964
Leo VIII	965
Benedict V	966
John XIII	972
Benedict VI	974
Benedict VII	983
John XIV	984
John XV	996
Gregory V	999
Sylvester II	1003
John XVII	1003
John XVIII	1009
Sergius IV	1012
Benedict VIII	1024
John XIX	1032
Benedict IX	1044
Benedict IX	1045
Sylvester III	1045
Gregory VI	1046
Clement II	1047
Benedict IX	1048
Damasus II	1048
St. Leo IX	1054
Victor II	1057
Stephen X	1058
Nicholas II	1061
Alexander II	1073
St. Gregory VII	1085
B. Victor III	1087
B. Urban II	1099
Paschal II	1118
Gelasius II	1119
Callistus II	1124
Honorius II	1130
Innocent II	1143
Celestine II	1144
Lucius II	1145
B. Eugene III	1153
Anastasius IV	1154
Adrian IV	1159
Alexander III	1181
Lucius III	1185
Urban III	1187
Gregory VIII	1187
Clement III	1191
Celestine III	1198
Innocent III	1216
Honorius III	1227
Gregory IX	1241
Celestine IV	1241
Innocent IV	1254
Alexander IV	1261
Urban IV	1264
Clement IV	1268
B. Gregory X	1276
B. Innocent V	1276
Adrian V	1276
John XXI	1277
Nicholas III	1280
Martin IV	1285
Honorius IV	1287
Nicholas IV	1292
St. Celestine V	1296
Boniface VIII	1303
B. Benedict XI	1304
Clement V	1314
John XXII	1334
Benedict XII	1342
Clement VI	1352
Innocent VI	1362
B. Urban V	1370
Gregory XI	1378
Urban VI	1389
Boniface IX	1404
Innocent VII	1406
Gregory XII	1415
Martin V	1431
Eugene IV	1447
Nicholas V	1455
Callistus III	1458
Pius II	1464
Paul II	1471
Sixtus IV	1484
Innocent VIII	1492
Alexander VI	1503
Pius III	1503
Julius II	1513
Leo X	1521
Adrian VI	1523
Clement VII	1534
Paul III	1549
Julius III	1555
Marcellus II	1555
Paul IV	1559
Pius IV	1565
St. Pius V	1572
Gregory XIII	1585
Sixtus V	1590
Urban VII	1590
Gregory XIV	1591
Innocent IX	1591
Clement VIII	1605
Leo XI	1605
Paul V	1621
Gregory XV	1623
Urban VIII	1644
Innocent X	1655
Alexander VII	1667
Clement IX	1669
Clement X	1676
B. Innocent XI	1689
Alexander VIII	1691
Innocent XII	1700
Clement XI	1721
Innocent XIII	1724
Benedict XIII	1730
Clement XII	1740
Benedict XIV	1758
Clement XIII	1769
Clement XIV	1774
Pius VI	1799
Pius VII	1823
Leo XII	1829
Pius VIII	1830
Gregory XVI	1846
Pius IX	1878
Leo XIII	1903
St. Pius X	1914
Benedict XV	1922
Pius XI	1939
Pius XII	1958
John XXIII	1963
Paul VI	1978
John Paul I	1978
John Paul II	now reigning.

PART I
Hierarchy of the Catholic Church

The Hierarchy, as the supreme governing body of the Catholic Church, consists of the Roman Pontiff, the successor of Peter, and the Bishops joined together with him and never without him (canons 330,331,336) in one apostolic college to provide for the common good of the Church. The Roman Pontiff in the exercise of his office is assisted by the College of Cardinals, and further by the departments also called "dicasteries" of the Roman Curia. The bishops, of whom some bear the titles of Patriarch and Archbishop, are united with the Roman Pontiff in the governance of the whole Church; the bishops, when assigned to particular Sees, are individually responsible for the teaching, sanctification and governance of their particular Church. Apostolic Vicars and Prefects together with certain Abbots and other Prelates are also joined in this work.

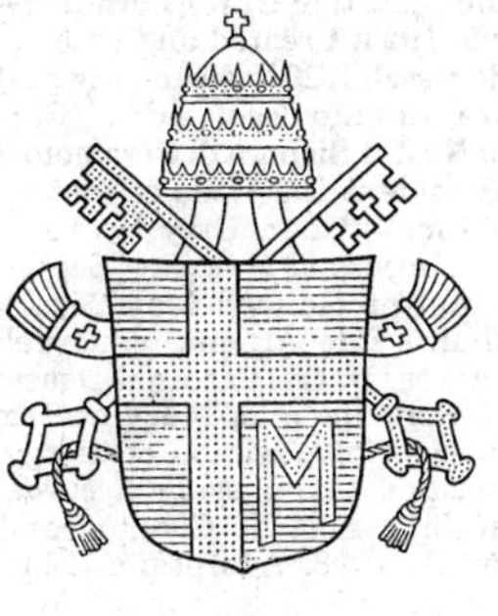

HIS HOLINESS THE POPE

Bishop of Rome and Vicar of Jesus Christ,
Successor of St. Peter, Prince of the Apostles,
Supreme Pontiff of the Universal Church.
Patriarch of the West
Primate of Italy.
Archbishop and Metropolitan of the Roman Province,
Servant of the Servants of God
Sovereign of Vatican City State.

JOHN PAUL II

KAROL WOJTYLA

The present successor of St. Peter was born in Wadowice, Diocese of Krakow, May 18, 1920; ordained Priest, November 1, 1946; appointed Titular Bishop of Ombi July 4, 1958; Promoted to Archbishop of Krakow, January 13, 1964; Proclaimed and created Cardinal June 26, 1967. Elected Pope, October 16, 1978; installed October 22, 1978.

VATICAN CITY

Vatican City is the smallest state in the world, occupying 108.7 acres, of which about one third is covered with buildings and is situated on the right side of the Tiber river. Vatican City has territory, population, and sovereignty. This territory, limited as it is, suffices to guarantee the spiritual and temporal independence needed for the exercise of the Holy See's spiritual mission. In 1870 the Kingdom of Italy seized all Vatican possessions which for several centuries had constituted the papal temporal domain. But even after 1870 the Holy See continued to regard itself as a separate entity in international law, and was recognized as such by numerous states with which it retained normal diplomatic relations. After long discussions the Holy See and the then Kingdom of Italy signed the Lateran Pacts on February 11, 1929, so that the complete and independent authority of the Vatican State was and is recognized by the Italian state.

The Sovereign of this small state is His Holiness, the Pope.

The government presently is administered by a Pontifical Commission of which His Eminence Edmund Casimir Cardinal Szoka is President.

THE COLLEGE OF CARDINALS

The Cardinals constitute a special college and they assist the Roman Pontiff collegially when they are called together to deal with questions of major importance; they do so individually when they assist the Pope especially in the daily care of the universal Church by means of the different offices which they perform (canons 349-350). The Cardinals who are under eighty years of age elect his successor.

The College of Cardinals is divided into three ranks: Cardinal-Bishops, Cardinal-Priests, and Cardinal-Deacons. The College of Cardinals, when complete formerly consisted of 70 members: 6 Cardinal Bishops, 50 Cardinal Priests and 14 Cardinal Deacons, but the late Pontiffs, Pope John XXIII and Pope Paul VI enlarged the College of Cardinals. At the moment the maximum number of Cardinal electors (those under 80 years of age) must not exceed 120.

The Cardinal Bishops (except the Patriarch-Cardinals of the Oriental Rites), have as Titular Sees the Suburban Sees of Rome, which are: Porto Santa Rufina, Albano, Palestrina, Sabina, Frascati, Velletri, Segni. The Cardinal Dean has united to his See the See of Ostia . The Cardinal Priests take their title from the Titular Churches to which they are appointed: the Cardinal Deacons are appointed to other Churches called Deaconries. The first Cardinal Bishop is Dean ; the first Cardinal Priest is First Priest ; and the first Cardinal Deacon is First Deacon of the Sacred College. The Dean has the right of ordaining the new Pope if he is not already a bishop; the First Deacon the right of proclaiming him and investing him with the sacred Pallium. On the death of the Pontiff, the Cardinal Camerlengo has the Administration of the affairs of the Holy See.

Sometimes the Roman Pontiff promotes a person to the dignity of Cardinal but does not make public his name and keeps it in pectore. Upon the publication of his name, this Cardinal enjoys his right of precedence from the day on which his n ame was reserved in pectore by the Pope (cfr. Can. 351¶ 3).

The Cardinals of the Holy Roman Church

Listed in Alphabetical Order

Agnelo, Geraldo Majella (Cardinal Priest), Titular of San Gregorio Magno alla Magliana Nuova, Archbishop of Sao Salvador da Bahia; born in Juiz de Fora, October 19, 1933. Created and proclaimed February 21, 2001. Address: Rua Martin Afonso de Souza 270, 40100-050 Salvador, BA, Brazil.

Agre, Bernard (Cardinal Priest), Titular of San Giovanni Crisostomo a Monte Alto, Archbishop of Abidjan; born in Monga, Archdiocese of Abidjan, March 2, 1926. Created and proclaimed February 21, 2001. Address: Archeveche, av. Jean Paul II, 01, B.P. 1287, Abidjan 01, Cote D'Ivoire.

Agustoni, Gilberto (Cardinal Deacon) Deacon of Ss. Urbano e Lorenzo a Primaporta, Prefect Emeritus of the Supreme Tribunal of the Apostolic Signatura; born in Schaffhausen, Switzerland, Diocese of Basel, July 26, 1922. Created and proclaimed November 26, 1994. Address: 00120 Vatican City State, Europe.

Alvarez Martinez, Francisco (Cardinal Priest), Titular of Santa Maria Regina Pacis a Monte Verde, Archbishop of Toledo; born in Santa Eulalia de Ferrones Llanera, Archdiocese of Oviedo, July 14, 1925. Created and proclaimed February 21, 2001. Address: Arco de Palacio 3, 45002 Toledo, Spain.

Ambrozic, Aloysius Matthew (Cardinal Priest), Titular of Sts. Marcellinus and Peter, Archbishop of Toronto, Canada; born in Gabrje, Archdiocese of Ljubljana, January 27, 1930. Created and proclaimed February 21, 1998. Address: Chancery Office, 1155 Yonge St., Toronto, M4T 1W2 Ontario, Canada.

Angelini, Fiorenzo (Cardinal Deacon), Deacon of S. Spirito in Sassia; President Emeritus of the Pontifical Council for Pastoral Assistance to Health Care Workers; born in Rome, Italy, August 1, 1916. Created and proclaimed June 28, 1991. Address: 00120 Vatican City State, Europe.

Antonetti, Lorenzo (Cardinal Deacon), Deacon of Saint Agnes in Agony; President Emeritus of the Administration of the Patrimony of the Apostolic See; born in Romagnano Sesia, diocese of Novara, July 31, 1922. Created and proclaimed February 21, 1998. Address: 00120 Vatican City State, Europe.

Aponte Martinez, Luis (Cardinal Priest), Titular of S. Maria Madre della Provvidenza a Monte Verde, Archbishop Emeritus of San Juan; born in Lajas, diocese of Mayaguez, August 4, 1922. Created and proclaimed March 5, 1973. Address: Arzobispado, Apartado S-1967, Calle del Cristo 50, San Juan, PR 00902.

Aramburu, Juan Carlos (Cardinal Priest), Titular of San Giovanni Battista dei Fiorentini, Archbishop Emeritus of Buenos Aires; born in Reduccion, Diocese of Villa de la Concepcion del Rio Cuarto, February 11, 1912. Created and proclaimed May 24, 1976. Address: La Pampa 4022, 1430 Buenos Aires, Argentina.

Arinze, Francis (Cardinal Priest), Titular of San Giovanni della Pigna; President of the Pontifical Council for Inter-Religious Dialogue; born in Eziowelle, Archdiocese of Onitsha, November 1, 1932. Created and proclaimed May 25, 1985. Address: Largo del Colonnato 3, 00193 Rome, Italy.

Arns, Paul Evaristo, o.f.m. (Cardinal Priest), Titular of S. Antonio da Padova in Via Tuscolana, Archbishop Emeritus of Sao Paulo; born in Forquilhinha, Diocese of Tubarao, September 14, 1921. Created and proclaimed March 5, 1973. Address: Rua Antonietta Altenfelder 1000, 0217-170, Sao Paulo, SP, Brazil.

Backis, Audrys Juozas (Cardinal Priest), Titular of Nativita di Nostro Signore Gesu Cristo a Via Gallia, Archbishop of Vilnius; born in Kaunas, February 1, 1937. Created and proclaimed February 21, 2001. Address: Sventaragio 4, 2001 Vilnius, Lithuania.

Bafile, Corrado (Cardinal Priest), Titular of Santa Maria in Portico; born in L'Aquila, July 4, 1903. Created and proclaimed May 24, 1976. Address: Via P. Pancrazio Pfeiffer 10, 00193 Rome, Italy.

Baum, William Wakefield (Cardinal Priest), Titular of Santa Croce in Via Flaminia, Penitenziere Maggiore; born in Dallas, Texas, November 21, 1926. Created and proclaimed, May 24, 1976. Address: Via Rusticucci 13, 00193 Rome, Italy.

Bergoglio, Jorge Mario, S.J. (Cardinal Priest), Titular of San Roberto Bellarmino, Archbishop of Buenos Aires; born in Buenos Aires, December 17, 1936. Created and proclaimed February 21, 2001. Address: Arzobispado, Rivadavia 415, 1002 Buenos Aires, Argentina.

Bertoli, Paolo (Cardinal Bishop), Titular Bishop of the suburbicarian church of Frascati; born in Poggio Garfagnana, Archdiocese of Lucca, February 1, 1908. Created and proclaimed April 28, 1969. Address: Piazza San Pietro in Vincoli 8, 00184 Rome, Italy.

Bevilacqua, Anthony J. (Cardinal Priest), Titular of Ss. Redentore e S. Alfonso in Via Merulana, Archbishop of Philadelphia; born in Brooklyn, New York, June 17, 1923. Created and proclaimed June 28, 1991. Address: 222 N. 17th St., Philadelphia, PA 19103-1299, U.S.A.

Biffi, Giacomo (Cardinal Priest), Titular of Ss. Giovanni Evangelista e Petronio, Archbishop of Bologna; born in Milan, June 13, 1928. Created and proclaimed May 25, 1985. Address: Arcivescovado, Via Altabella 6, 40126 Bologna, Italy.

Billé, Louis-Maarie (Cardinal Priest), Titular of San Pietro in Vincoli, Archbishop of Lyon; born in Fleury-les-Aubrais, Diocese of Orleans, February 18, 1938. Created and proclaimed February 21, 2001. Address: 1 Place de Fourviere, 69321 Lyon Cedex 05, France.

Cacciavillan, Agostino (Cardinal Deacon), Deacon of Santi Angeli Custodi a Citta Giardino, President of Administration of the Patrimony of the Apostolic See; born in Novale, Diocese of Vincenza, August 14, 1926. Created and proclaimed February 21, 2001. Address: 00120 Vatican City State, Europe.

Canestri, Giovanni (Cardinal Priest), Titular of St. Andrea della Valle, Archbishop Emeritus of Genoa; born in Castelspina, Diocese of Alessandria, September 30, 1918. Created and proclaimed June 28, 1988. Address: Via Cernaia 9, 00185 Rome, Italy.

Caprio, Giuseppe (Cardinal Priest), Titular of S. Maria della Vittoria; born in Lapio, Archdiocese of Benevento, November 15, 1914. Created and proclaimed June 30, 1979. Address: 00120 Vatican City State, Europe.

Carles Gordo, Ricardo Maria (Cardinal Priest), Titular of S. Maria Consolatrice al Tiburtino, Archbishop of Barcelona, Spain; born in Valencia, September 24, 1926. Created and proclaimed November 26, 1994, Address: Arzobispado, Carrer del Bisbe 5, 08002 Barcelona, Spain.

Carter, Gerald Emmett (Cardinal Priest), Titular of S. Maria in Traspontina, Archbishop Emeritus of Toronto; born in Montreal, March 1, 1912. Created and proclaimed June 30, 1979. Address: 1155 Yonge Street, Toronto, Ont., M4T 1W2, Canada.

Cassidy, Edward I. (Cardinal Deacon), Deacon of S. Maria in Via Lata, President of the Pontifical Council for Promoting Christian Unity; born in Sydney, Australia, July 5, 1924. Created and proclaimed June 28, 1991. Address: 00120 Vatican City State, Europe.

Castillo Lara, Rosalio Jose, s.d.b. (Cardinal Priest), Titular of Nostra Signora di Coromoto in S. Giovanni di Dio, President Emeritus of the Pontifical Commission for Vatican City State; born in San Casimiro, Diocese of Maracay, September 4, 1922. Created and proclaimed May 25, 1985. Address: San Casimiro, Edo. Aragua, Venezuela.

Castrillon Hoyos, Dario (Cardinal Deacon), Deacon of the Most Holy Name of Mary at Trajan's Forum, Prefect of the Congregation of Clergy & President of the Pontifical Commission Ecclesia Dei ; born in Medellin July 4, 1929. Created and proclaimed February 21, 1998. Address: 00120 Vatican City State, Europe.

Ce', Marco (Cardinal Priest), Titular of S. Marco, Patriarch of Venice; born in Izano, Diocese of Crema, July 8, 1925. Created and proclaimed June 30, 1979. Address: S. Marco 318, 30124 Venezia, Italy.

Cheli, Giovanni (Cardinal Deacon), Deacon of Ss. Cosmos and Damian at Via Sacra, President Emeritus of the Pontifical Council for the Pastoral Care of Migrants and Itinerant People; born in Torino, October 4, 1918. Created and proclaimed February 21, 1998. Address: Piazza S. Calisto 16, 00153 Rome, Italy.

Cipriani Thorne, Juan Luis (Cardinal Priest), Titular of San Camillo di Lellis, Archbishop of Lima; born in Lima, December 28, 1943. Created and proclaimed February 21, 2001. Address: Arzobispado, Plaza de Armas s/n, Apartado 1512, Lima 100, Peru.

Clancy, Edward Bede (Cardinal Priest), Titular of S. Maria in Vallicella, Archbishop of Sydney; born in Lithgow, Diocese of Bathurst, December 13, 1923. Created and proclaimed June 28, 1988. Address: St. Mary Cathedral, St. Mary and College Sts., Sydney, NSW 2000, Australia.

Colasuonno, Francesco (Cardinal Deacon), Deacon of St. Eugenio; born in Grumo Appula, Archdiocese of Bari-Bitonte January 2, 1925. Created and proclaimed February 21, 1998. Address: 00120 Vatican City State, Europe.

Connell, Desmond (Cardinal Priest), Titular of San Silvestro in Capite, Archbishop of Dublin; born in Dublin, March 24, 1926. Created and proclaimed February 21, 2001. Address: Archbishop's House, Drumcondra, Dublin 9, Ireland.

Corripio Ahumada, Ernesto (Cardinal Priest), Titular dell'Immacolata al Tiburtino, Archbishop Emeritus of Mexico City; born in Tampico, June 29, 1919. Address: Calle 5 n.54, Colonia Ampliacion Tepepan, 16029, Mexico, D.F. Mexico.

da Cruz Policarpo, José (Cardinal Priest), Titular of Sant' Antonio in Campo Marzio, Patriarch of Lisbon; born in Alvorninha, Patriarchate of Lisbon, February 26, 1936. Created and proclaimed February 21, 2001. Address: Mosteiro de Sao Vicente de For a, Campo de Santa Clara, 1100-473 Lisbon, Portugal.

Daly, Cahal Brendan (Cardinal Priest), Titular of S. Patrizio, Archbishop Emeritus of Armagh; born in Loughguile, Diocese of Down and Connor, October 1, 1917. Created and proclaimed June 28, 1991. Address: Ard Mhacha, 23 Rosetta Avenue, Belfast BT7 3HG, Ireland.

Danneels, Godfried (Cardinal Priest), Titular of S. Anastasia, Archbishop of Malines-Bruxelles; born in Kanegem, Diocese of Brugge, June 4, 1933. Created and proclaimed February 2, 1983. Address: Aartsbisdom, Wollemarkt 15, B-2800 Mechelen, Belgium.

Daoud, Ignace Moussa I (Cardinal Bishop), Prefect of the Congregation for the Oriental Churches; born in Meskane, Archeparchy of Homs of the Syrians, September 18, 1930. Created and proclaimed February 21, 2001. Address: 00120 Vatican City State, Europe.

Darmaatmadja, Julius Riyadi, s.j. (Cardinal Priest), Titular of S. Cuore di Maria, Archbishop of Jakarta, Indonesia; born in Muntilan, Archdiocese of Semarang, December 20, 1934. Created and proclaimed November 26, 1994. Address: Keuskupan Agung, Jl. Katedral 7, Jakarta 10710, Indonesia.

De Giorgi, Salvatore (Cardinal Priest), Titular of S. Maria in Ara Coeli, Archbishop of Palermo; born in Vernole, Archdiocese of Lecce, September 6, 1930. Created and proclaimed February 21, 1998. Address: Corso Vittorio Emanuele 461, 90134 Palermo, Italy.

Degenhart, Johannes Joachim (Cardinal Priest), Titular of San Liborio, Archbishop of Paderborn; born in Schwelm, Diocese of Essen, January 31, 1926. Created and proclaimed February 21, 2001. Address: Erzbischofliches Generalvikariat, Domplatz 3, D-33098 Paderborn, Germany.

Deskur, Andrzej Maria (Cardinal Priest), Titular of S. Cesareo in Palatio; born in Sancygniow, Diocese of Kielce, February 29, 1924. Created and proclaimed May 25, 1985. Address: 00120 Vatican City State, Europe.

Dias, Ivan (Cardinal Priest), Titular of Spirito Santo alla Ferratella, Archbishop of Bombay; born in Mumbai, April 14, 1936. Created and proclaimed February 21, 2001. Address: 21 Nathalal Parekh Marg, Mumbai-400001, India.

do Nascimento, Alexandre (Cardinal Priest), Titular of San Marco in Agro Laurentino, Archbishop Emeritus of Luanda; born in Malanje, Angola, March 1, 1925. Created and proclaimed February 2, 1983. Address: Arcebispado, C.P. 87, 1230-C. Luanda, Angola.

Dulles, Avery, S.J. (Cardinal Deacon), Deacon of Santissimi Nomi di Gesu e Maria in Via Lata; born in Auburn, Archdiocese of New York, August 24, 1918. Created and proclaimed February 21, 2001. Address: Fordham University, 441 E. Fordham Rd., Bronx, NY 10458.

Egan, Edward M. (Cardinal Priest), Titular of Santi Giovanni e Paolo, Archbishop of New York; born in Oak Park, Archdiocese of Chicago, February 4, 1932. Created and proclaimed February 21, 2001. Address: 1011 First Ave., New York, NY 10022.

Errázuriz Ossa, Francisco Javier (Cardinal Priest), Titular of Santa Maria della Pace, Archbishop of Santiago de Chile; born in Santiago de Chile, September 4, 1933. Created and proclaimed February 21, 2001. Address: Casilla 30-D, Erasmo Escala 1884, Santiago, Chile.

Etchegaray, Roger (Cardinal Bishop), Titular of the suburbicarian church of Porto-Santa Rufina, President of the Central Committee for the Great Jubilee of the Year 2,000; born in Espelette, Diocese of Bayonne, September 25, 1922. Created and proclaimed June 30, 1979. Address: Piazza San Calisto 16, 00153 Rome, Italy.

Etsou-Nzabi-Bamungwabi, Frederic, C.I.C.M. (Cardinal Priest), Titular of S. Lucia a Piazza d'Armi, Archbishop of Kinshasa; born in Mazalonga, Diocese of Lisala, December 3, 1930. Created and proclaimed June 28, 1991. Address: Archeveche, B.P. 8431, Kinshasa 1, Democratic Republic of Congo.

Eyt, Pierre (Cardinal Priest), Titular of Ss. Trinita al Monte Pincio, Archbishop of Bordeaux, France; born in Laruns, Diocese of Bayonne, June 4, 1934. Created and proclaimed November 26, 1994. Address: Archeveche, B.P. 79, 183 cours de la Somme, 33034 Bordeaux Cedex, France.

Falcao, Jose Freire (Cardinal Priest), Titular of S. Luca a Via Prenestina, Archbishop of Brasilia; born in Erere, Diocese of Limoeiro do Norte, October 23, 1925. Created and proclaimed June 28, 1988. Address: QL 12-Cj12, Lote 1, Lago Sul, 71630-325 Brasilia, D.F., Brazil.

Felici, Angelo (Cardinal Priest), Titular of Ss. Biagio e Carlo ai Catinari, President Emeritus of the Pontifical Commission Ecclesia Dei ; born in Segni, July 27, 1919. Created and proclaimed June 28, 1988. Address: Piazza della Citta Leonina 9, 00193 Rome, Italy.

Fernandes de Araujo, Serafim (Cardinal Priest), Titular of S. Luigi Maria Grignion de Monzfort, Archbishop of Belo Horizonte, Brazil; born in Minas Novas, Diocese of Aracuai, August 13, 1924. Created and proclaimed February 21, 1998. Address: Metropolitan Curia, Av. Brazil 2079, C.P. 494, 30140-002 Belo Horizonte, MG, Brazil.

Fresno Larrain, Juan Francisco (Cardinal Priest), Titular of S. Maria Immacolata di Lourdes a Boccea, Archbishop Emeritus of Santiago de Chile; born in Santiago de Chile on July 26, 1914. Created and proclaimed May 25, 1985. Address: Echaurren 4, Casilla 13520, Correo 21, Santiago, Chile.

Furno, Carlo (Cardinal Deacon), Deacon of S. Cuore di Cristo Re, Grand Master of the Equestrian Order of the Holy Sepulchre of Jerusalem, Pontifical Delegate for the Patriarchal Basilica of St. Francis in Assisi,

Archpriest of the Patriarchal Liberian Basilica of St. Mary Major; born in Bairo Canavese, Diocese of Ivrea, December 2, 1921. Created and proclaimed November 26, 1994. Address: Piazza della Citta Leonina 1, 00193 Rome, Italy.

Gagnon, Edouard, p.s.s. (Cardinal Priest), Titular of S. Marcello; President of the Pontifical Committee for International Eucharistic Congresses; born in Port-Daniel, Diocese of Gaspe, January 15, 1918. Created and proclaimed May 25, 1985. Address: Via di Porta Angelica 31, 00193 Rome, Italy.

Gantin, Bernardin (Cardinal Bishop), Titular of the suburbicarian church of Palestrina, Dean of the College of Cardinals, Prefect Emeritus Congregation for the Bishops and President Emeritus of the Pontifical Commission for Latin America; born in Toffo, Archdiocese of Cotonou, May 8, 1922. Created and proclaimed June 27, 1977. Address: 00120 Vatican City State, Europe.

George, Francis E., o.m.i. , (Cardinal Priest) Titular of S. Bartolomeo all'Isola, Archbishop of Chicago; born in Chicago, Illinois, U.S.A., January 16, 1937. Created and proclaimed February 21, 1998. Address: Post Office Box 1979, Chicago, IL 60690.

Ghattas, Stéphanos II, C.M. (Cardinal Bishop), Patriarch of Alexandria of the Copts; born in Cheikh Zein-el-Dine, Eparchy of Sohag, January 16, 1920. Created and proclaimed February 21, 2001. Address: Patriarcat Copte Catholique, B.P. 69, 34 Rue Ibn Sandar, Pont de Koubbeh, 11712 Le Caire, Egypt.

Giordano, Michele (Cardinal Priest), Titular of S. Gioacchino ai Prati di Castello, Archbishop of Naples; born in S. Arcangelo, Diocese of Tursi-Lagonegro, September 26, 1930. Created and proclaimed June 28, 1988. Address: Largo Donnaregina 23, 80138 Napoli, Italy.

Glemp, Jozef (Cardinal Priest), Titular of S. Maria in Trastevere, Archbishop of Warsaw; born in Inowroclaw, Archdiocese of Gniezno, December 18, 1929. Created and proclaimed February 2, 1983. Address: ul. Miodowa 17-19, 00-246 Warsaw, Poland.

Gonzalez Martin, Marcelo (Cardinal Priest), Titular of S. Agostino, Archbishop Emeritus of Toledo; born in Villanubla, Archdiocese of Valladolid, January 16, 1918. Created and proclaimed March 5, 1973. Address: Residencia Madre Genoveva, Avda. de Francia 6, 45005 Toledo, Spain.

González Zumárraga, Antonio José (Cardinal Priest), Titular of Santa Maria in via, Archbishop of Quito; born in Pujili, Diocese of Latacunga, March 18, 1925. Created and proclaimed February 21, 2001. Address: Apartado 17-01-00106, Calle Chile 1140, Quito, Ecuador.

Grocholewski, Zenon (Cardinal Deacon), Deacon of San Nicola in Carcere, Prefect of the Congregation for Catholic Education; born in Brodki, Archdiocese of Poznan, October 11, 1939. Created and proclaimed February 21, 2001. Address: 00120 Vatican City State, Europe.

Groer, Hans Hermann, o.s.b. (Cardinal Priest), Titular of Ss. Gioacchino ed Anna al Tuscolano, Archbishop Emeritus of Vienna; born in Vienna, October 13, 1919. Created and proclaimed June 28, 1988. Address: Priorat St. Josef, Marienplatz 2, A-2041 Maria Roggendorf, Austria.

Gulbinowicz, Henryk Roman (Cardinal Priest), Titular dell'Immacolata Concezione di Maria a Grottarossa, Archbishop of Wroclaw; born in Sukiskes, Archdiocese of Vilnius, October 17, 1928. Created and proclaimed May 25, 1985. Address: ul. Katedralna 11, 50-328 Wroclaw, Poland.

Hickey, James Aloysius (Cardinal Priest), Titular of Maria Madre del Redentore a Tor Bella Monaca, Archbishop Emeritus of Washington; born in Midland, Michigan, Diocese of Saginaw, October 11, 1920. Created and proclaimed June 28, 1988. Address: Archdiocesan Pastoral Center, 5001 Eastern Ave., P.O. Box 29260, Washington, DC 20017, U.S.A.

Honoré, Jean (Cardinal Priest), Titular of Santa Maria della Salute a Primavalle, Archbishop Emeritus of Tours; born in Saint-Brice-en-Cogles, Archdiocese of Rennes, August 13, 1920. Created and proclaimed February 21, 2001. Address: 1 Allee de la Rocaille, 37390 La Membrolle-sur-Choisille, France.

Hummes, Claudio, O.F.M. (Cardinal Priest), Titular of Sant' Antonio da Padova in Via a Merulana, Archbishop of Sao Paolo; born in Montenegro, Archdiocese of Portoalegre, August 8, 1934. Created and proclaimed February 21, 2001. Address: Avenida Higienopolis 890, 01238-908 Sao Paulo, SP, Brazil.

Husar, Lubomyr, M.S.U. (Cardinal Priest), Titular of Santa Sofia a Via Boccea, Major Archbishop of Lviv of the Ukrainians; born in Lviv, February 26, 1933. Created and proclaimed February 21, 2001. Address: Ploscha Sviatoho Jura 5, 290000 Lviv, Ukraine.

Innocenti, Antonio (Cardinal Priest), Titular of S. Maria in Aquiro, born in Poppi, Diocese of Fiesole, August 23, 1915. Created and proclaimed May 25, 1985. Address: Piazza della Citta Leonina 9, 00193 Rome, Italy.

Javierre Ortas, Antonio Maria, s.d.b. (Cardinal Priest), Titular of S. Maria Liberatrice a Monte Testaccio, Prefect Emeritus of Congregation for Divine Worship and the Discipline of the Sacraments; born at Sietamo, Diocese of Huesca, February 21, 1921. Created and proclaimed June 28, 1988. Address: Via Rusticucci 13, 00193 Rome, Italy.

Kasper, Walter (Cardinal Deacon), Deacon of Ognissanti in Via Appia Nuova, Secretary of the Pontifical Council for Promoting Christian Unity; born in Heidenheim/Brenz, Diocese of Rottenburg-Stuttgart, March 5, 1933. Created and proclaimed February 21, 2001. Address: 00120 Vatican City State, Europe.

Keeler, William Henry (Cardinal Priest), Titular of S. Maria degli Angeli, Archbishop of Baltimore; born in San Antonio, Texas, March 4, 1931. Created and proclaimed November 26, 1994. Address: 320 Cathedral Street, Baltimore, Maryland 21201. U.S.A.

Kim, Stephen Sou Hwan (Cardinal Priest), Titular of S. Felice da Cantalice a Centocelle, Archbishop Emeritus of Seoul; born in Tae Gu, May 8, 1922. Created and proclaimed April 28, 1969. Address: Episcopal Residence, Seoul Catholic University, 90-1 Hyehwa-dong, Chongro-Ku, Seoul 110-758, Korea.

Kitbunchu, Michael Michai (Cardinal Priest), Titular of S. Lorenzo in Panisperna, Archbishop of Bangkok; born in Samphran, Archdiocese of Bangkok, January 29, 1929. Created and proclaimed February 2, 1983. Address: Assumption Cathedral, 51 Oriental Ave., Bangkok 10500, Thailand.

Konig, Franz (Cardinal Priest), Titular of S. Eusebio, Archbishop Emeritus of Vienna; born in Rabenstein, Diocese of St. Poelten, August 3, 1905. Created and proclaimed December 15, 1958. Address: Wollzeile 2, A-1010 Wien, Austria.

Korec, Jan Chryzostom, s.j. , (Cardinal Priest), Titular of Ss. Fabiano e Venanzio a Villa Fiorelli, Bishop of Nitra; born in Bosany, Diocese of Nitra, January 22, 1924. Created and proclaimed June 28, 1991. Address: Biskupsky urad, post. schranka 46A, 950 50 Nitra, Slovakia.

Kozlowiecki, Adam, s.j. , (Cardinal Priest), Titular of S. Andrea of Quirinale; born in Huta Komorowska, Diocese of Sandomierz, April 1, 1911. Created and proclaimed February 21, 1998. Address: P.O. Box 80858, Kabwe, Zambia.

Kuharic, Franjo (Cardinal Priest), Titular S. Girolamo dei Croati, Archbishop Emeritus of Zagreb; born in Pribic, Archdiocese of Zagreb, April 15, 1919. Created and proclaimed February 2, 1983. Address: Kaptol 31, p.p. 553, 10000, Zagreb, Croatia.

Laghi, Pio (Cardinal Deacon), Proto-deacon of S. Maria Ausiliatrice in Via Tuscolana, Prefect Emeritus of the Congregation for Catholic Education; born in Castiglione, Diocese of Forli-Bertinoro, May 21, 1922. Created and proclaimed June 28, 1991. Address: Piazza della Citta Leonina 1, 00193 Roma, Italy, Europe.

Law, Bernard Francis (Cardinal Priest), Titular of S. Susanna, Archbishop of Boston; born in Torreon, November 4, 1931. Created and proclaimed May 25, 1985. Address: 2101 Commonwealth Ave., Brighton, MA 02135, U.S.A.

Lehmann, Karl (Cardinal Priest), Titular of San Leone I, Bishop of Mainz; born in Sigmaringen, Archdiocese of Freiburg im Breisgau, May 16, 1936. Created and proclaimed February 21, 2001. Address: Bischofliches Ordinariat, Postfach 1560, Bischofsplatz 2, D-55005 Mainz, Germany.

Lopez Rodriguez, Nicolas de Jesus (Cardinal Priest), Titular of S. Pio X alla Balduina, Archbishop of Santo Domingo; born in Barranca, Diocese of La Vega, October 31, 1936. Created and proclaimed June 28, 1991. Address: Arzobispado, Apartado 186, Calle Isabel la Catolica 55, Santo Domingo, Dominican Republic.

Lopez Trujillo, Alfonso (Cardinal Priest), Titular of S. Prisca, President of the Pontifical Council for the Family; born in Villahermosa, Diocese of Libano-Honda, November 8, 1935. Created and proclaimed February 2, 1983. Address: Piazza S. Calisto 16, 00153 Rome, Italy.

Lorscheider, Aloisio, o.f.m. (Cardinal Priest), Titular of San Pietro in Montorio, Archbishop of Aparecida; born in Estrela, Archdiocese of Porto Alegre, October 8, 1924. Created and proclaimed May 24, 1976. Address: Curia Metropolitana, Rua Barao do Rio Branco 412, Centro, C.P. 82, 12570-000, Aparecida, S.P., Brazil.

Lourdusamy, D. Simon (Cardinal Priest), Titular of S. Maria delle Grazie alle Fornaci fuori Porta Cavalleggeri; born in Kalleri, Archdiocese of Pondicherry and Cuddalore, February 5, 1924. Created and proclaimed May 25, 1985. Address: Via dei Corridori 64, 00193 Rome, Italy.

Lustiger, Jean-Marie (Cardinal Priest), Titular of S. Luigi dei Francesi, Archbishop of Paris; born in Paris, September 17, 1926. Created and proclaimed February 2, 1983. Address: 8 rue de la Ville l'Eveque, 75384 Paris, Cedex 08, France.

Macharski, Franciszek (Cardinal Priest), Titular of S. Giovanni a Porta Latina, Archbishop of Krakow; born in Krakow, May 20, 1927. Created and proclaimed June 30, 1979. Address: ul. Franciszkanska 3, 31-004 Krakow, Poland.

Mahony, Roger M. (Cardinal Priest), Titular of Ss. Quattro Coronati, Archbishop of Los Angeles; born in Hollywood, California, Archdiocese of Los Angeles, February 27, 1936. Created and proclaimed June 28, 1991. Address: 3424 Wilshire Blvd,. Los Angeles, CA 90010-2241, U.S.A.

Maida, Adam Joseph (Cardinal Priest), Titular of Ss. Vitale, Valeria, Gervasio e Protasio, Archbishop of Detroit; born in East Vandergrift, Pennsylvania, Diocese of Greensburg, March 18, 1930. Created and proclaimed November 26, 1994. Address: 1234 Washington Blvd., Detroit, Michigan 48226, U.S.A.

Margeot, Jean (Cardinal Priest), Titular of S. Gabriele Arcangelo all' Acqua Traversa, Bishop Emeritus of Port-Louis; born at Quatre-Bornes, Diocese of Port Louis, February 3, 1916. Created and proclaimed June 28, 1988. Address: Bonne-Terre, Vavoas, Ile Maurice.

Martinez Somalo, Eduardo (Cardinal Priest), Titular of SS. Nome di Gesu', Prefect of the Congregation for Institutes of Consecrated Life and for Societies of Apostolic Life, Chamberlain of the Holy Roman Church; born at Banos de Rio Tobia, Diocese of Calahorra y La Calzada-Logrono, March 3, 1927. Created and proclaimed June 28, 1988. Address: 00120 Vatican City State, Europe.

Martini, Carlo Maria, s.j. (Cardinal Priest), Titular of S. Cecilia, Archbishop of Milan; born in Turin, February 15, 1927. Created and proclaimed February 2, 1983. Address: Palazzo Arcivescovile, Piazza Fontana 2, 20122 Milan, Italy.

Mayer, Paul Augustin, o.s.b. (Cardinal Priest), Titular of S. Anselmo all' Aventino; born in Altotting, Diocese of Passau, May 23, 1911. Created and proclaimed May 25, 1985. Address: Via Rusticucci 13, 00193 Rome, Italy.

McCarrick, Theodore E. (Cardinal Priest), Titular of Santi Nereo e Achilleo, Archbishop of Washington; born in New York, July 7, 1930. Created and proclaimed February 21, 2001.Address: P.O. Box 29260, Washington, DC 20017.

Medina Estevez, Jorge Arturo (Cardinal Deacon), Deacon of St. Saba, Prefect of the Congregation for Divine Worship and the Discipline of the Sacraments; born in Santiago de Chile, December 23, 1926. Created and proclaimed February 21, 1998. Address: 00120 Vatican City State, Europe.

Meisner, Joachim (Cardinal Priest), Titular of S. Pudenziana, Archbishop of Cologne; born in Breslau, December 25, 1933. Created and proclaimed February 2, 1983. Address: Kardinal-Frings-Strasse 10, D-50668 Koln 1, Germany.

Mejía, Jorge María (Cardinal Deacon), Deacon of San Girolamo della Carita, Bibliotecary and Archivist of the Holy Roman Church; born in Buenos Aires, January 31, 1923. Created and proclaimed February 21, 2001. Address: 00120 Vatican City State, Europe.

Monduzzi, Dino (Cardinal Deacon), Deacon of S. Sebastiano al Palatino, Prefect Emeritus of the Papal Household; born in Brisighella, Diocese of Faenza-Modigliana, April 2, 1922. Created and proclaimed February 21, 1998. Address: 00120 Vatican City State, Europe.

Murphy-O'Connor, Cormac (Cardinal Priest), Titular of Santa Maria sopra Minerva, Archbishop of Westminster; born in Reading, Diocese of Portsmouth, August 24, 1932. Created and proclaimed February 21, 2001. Address: Ambrosden Avenue, Westminster, London SW1P 1QJ England.

Napier, Wilfrid Fox, O.F.M. (Cardinal Priest), Titular of San Francesco d'Assisi ad Acilia, Archbishop of Durban; born in Swartberg, Diocese of Kokstad, March 8, 1941. Created and proclaimed February 21, 2001. Address: 154 Gordon Rd., P.O. Box 47489, Greyville 4023, South Africa.

Neves, Lucas Moreira, o.p. (Cardinal Bishop), Titular of the suburbicarian church of Sabina Poggio Mirteto, Prefect Emeritus of the Congregation for Bishops; born in Sao Joao Del Rei, September 16, 1925. Created and proclaimed June 28, 1988. Address: 00120 Vatican City State, Europe.

Nguyen Van Thuan, François Xavier (Cardinal Deacon), Deacon of Santa Maria della Scala, President of the Pontifical Council for Justice and Peace; born in Hue, April 17, 1928. Created and proclaimed February 21, 2001. Address: 00120 Vatican City State, Europe.

Noe', Virgilio (Cardinal Deacon), Deacon of S. Giovanni Bosco, Vicar General of His Holiness for Vatican City State, Archpriest of St. Peter Basilica; born in Zelata di Bereguardo, Diocese of Pavia, March 30, 1922. Created and proclaimed June 28, 1991. Address: 00120 Vatican City State, Europe.

Obando Bravo, Miguel, s.d.b. (Cardinal Priest), Titular of S. Giovanni Evangelista a Spinaceto, Archbishop of Managua; born in La Libertad, Diocese of Juigalpa, February 2, 1926. Created and proclaimed May 25, 1985. Address: Arzobispado, Apartado 3058, Managua, Nicaragua.

Oddi, Silvio (Cardinal Priest), Titular of S. Agata de' Goti; born in Morfasso, Diocese of Piacenza-Bobbio, November 14, 1910. Created and proclaimed April 28, 1969. Address: Via delle Grazie 3, 00193 Rome, Italy.

Ortega y Alamino, Jaime Lucas (Cardinal Priest), Titular of Ss. Aquila e Priscilla, Archbishop of San Cristobal de La Habana, Cuba; born in Jaguey Grande, Diocese of Matanzas, October 18, 1936. Created and proclaimed November 26, 1994. Address: Calle Habana 152, Apartado 594, La Habana, 10100 Cuba.

Otunga, Maurice Michael (Cardinal Priest), Titular of San Gregorio Barbarigo, Archbishop Emeritus of Nairobi; born in Chebukwa, Diocese of Kakamega, January 1923. Created and proclaimed March 5, 1973. Address: Archbishop's House, P.O. Box 14231, Nairobi, Kenya.

Palazzini, Pietro (Cardinal Priest), Titular of S. Girolamo della Carita'; born in Piobbico, Archdiocese of Urbino-Urbania-Sant' Angelo in Vado, May 19, 1912. Created and proclaimed March 5, 1973. Address: Via Proba Petronia 83, 00136 Rome, Italy.

Pappalardo, Salvatore (Cardinal Priest), Titular of S. Maria Odigitria dei Siciliani, Archbishop Emeritus of Palermo; born in Villafranca Sicula, Diocese of Agrigento, September 23, 1918. Created and proclaimed March 5, 1973. Address: Casa Diocesana, Piazza Baida 1, 90136 Palermo, Italy.

Paskai, Laszlo, o.f.m. (Cardinal Priest), Titular of S. Teresa al Corso d'Italia, Archbishop of Esztergom-Budapest; born at Szeged, May 8, 1927. Created and proclaimed June 28, 1988. Address: Uri utca 62, H-1014 Budapest, Hungary.

Pengo, Polycarp (Cardinal Priest), Titular of Nostra Signora de La Salette, Archbishop of Dar-es-Salaam, Tanzania; born in Mwazye, Diocese of Sumbawanga, August 5, 1944. Created and proclaimed February 21, 1998. Address: Archbishop's House, P.O. Box 167, Dar-es-Salaam, Tanzania.

Pham Dinh Tung, Paul Joseph (Cardinal Priest), Titular of S. Maria Regina Pacis in Ostiamare, Archbishop of Ha Noi, Viet Nam; born in Binh Hoa, Diocese of Phat Diem, June 15, 1919. Created and proclaimed November 26, 1994. Address: Toa Tong Giam Muc, 40 Pho Nha Chung, Ha Noi, Viet Nam.

Pimenta, Simon Ignatius (Cardinal Priest), Titular of S. Maria Regina Mundi a Torre Spaccata, Archbishop Emeritus of Bombay; born in Marol, Archdiocese of Bombay, March 1, 1920. Created and proclaimed June 28, 1988. Address: Archbishop's House, 21 Nathalal Parekh Marg, Mumbai-400001, India.

Piovanelli, Silvano (Cardinal Priest), Titular of S. Maria delle Grazie a Via Trionfale, Archbishop of Florence; born in Ronta di Mugello, Archdiocese of Florence, February 21, 1924. Created and proclaimed May 25, 1985. Address: Arcivescovado, Piazza S. Giovanni 3, 50129 Firenze, Italy.

Poggi, Luigi (Cardinal Deacon), Deacon of S. Maria in Dominica, Librarian Emeritus and Archivist Emeritus of the Holy Roman Church; born in Piacenza, Italy, November 25, 1917. Created and proclaimed November 26, 1994. Address: 00120 Vatican City State, Europe.

Poletto, Severino (Cardinal Priest), Titular of San Giuseppe in Via Trionfale, Archbishop of Turin; born in Salgareda, Diocese of Treviso, March 18, 1933. Created and proclaimed February 21, 2001. Address: Via Arcivescovado 12, 10121, Turin, Italy.

Pompedda, Mario Francesco (Cardinal Deacon), Deacon of Annunciazione della B.V.M. in Via Ardeatina, Prefect of the Supreme Tribuanl of the Apostolic Signatura; born in Ozieri, April 18, 1929. Created and proclaimed February 21, 2001. Address: 00120 Vatican City State, Europe.

Poupard, Paul (Cardinal Priest), Titular of S. Prassede, President of the Pontifical Council of Culture; born in Bouzille, Diocese of Angers, August 30, 1930. Created and proclaimed May 25, 1985. Address: Piazza San Calisto 16, 00153 Rome, Italy.

Primatesta, Raul Francisco (Cardinal Priest), Titular of S. Maria Vergine Addolorata a Piazza Buenos Aires, Archbishop Emeritus of Cordoba; born in Capilla del Senor, Diocese of Zarate-Campana, April 14, 1919. Created and proclaimed March 5, 1973. Address: Caseros 160 2o Piso, 5000 Cordoba, Argentina.

Pujats, Janis (Cardinal Priest), Titular of Santa Silvia, Archbishop of Riga; born in Nautreni, Archdiocese of Riga, November 14, 1930. Created and proclaimed February 21, 2001. Address: Metropolijas Kurija, Maza Pils iela 2/a, 1050 riga, Latvia.

Puljic, Vinko (Cardinal Priest), Titular of S. Chiara a Vigna Clara, Archbishop of Vrhbosna, Bosnia-Hercegovina; born in Prijecani, Diocese of Banja Luka, September 8, 1945. Created and proclaimed November 26, 1994. Address: Nadbiskupski Ordinarijat, Kaptol 7, 71000 Sarajevo, Bosnia Hercegovina.

Ratzinger, Joseph (Cardinal Bishop), Titular of the suburbicarian church of Velletri-Segni, Prefect of the Congregation for the Doctrine of the Faith, President of the Pontifical Bible Commission and Vice-Dean of the College of Cardinals; born in Marktl am Inn, Diocese of Passau, April 16, 1927. Created and proclaimed June 27, 1977. Address: 00120 Vatican City State, Europe.

Razafindratandra, Armand Gaetan (Cardinal Priest), Titular of Ss. Silvestro e Martino ai Monti, Archbishop of Antananarivo, Madagascar; born in Ambohimalaza, Archdiocese of Antananarivo, August 7, 1925. Created and proclaimed November 26, 1994. Address: Archeveche, Andohalo, B.P. 5159 Antanarivo 101, Madagascar.

Re, Giovanni Battista (Cardinal Priest), Titular of Santi XII Apostoli, Prefect of the Congregation for Bishops; born in Borno, Diocese of Brescia, January 30, 1934. Created and proclaimed February 21, 2001. Address: 00120 Vatican City State, Europe.

Righi-Lambertini, Egano (Cardinal Priest), Titular of S. Maria in Via; born in Casalecchio di Reno, Archdiocese of Bologna, February 22, 1906. Created and proclaimed June 30, 1979. Address: Piazza della Citta Leonina 9, 00193 Rome, Italy.

Rivera Carrera, Norberto (Cardinal Priest), Titular of S. Francesco d' Assisi a Ripa Grande, Archbishop of Mexico City; born in Tepehuanes, Archdiocese of Durango, June 6, 1942. Created and proclaimed February 21, 1998. Address: Apartado Postal 24-433, Durango 90, Col. Roma, 06700 Mexico D.F., Mexico.

Rodríguez Maradiaga, Oscar Andrés (Cardinal Priest), Titular of Santa Maria della Speranza, Archbishop of Tegucigalpa; born in Tegucigalpa, December 29, 1942. Created and proclaimed February 21, 2001. Address: Apartado 106, 3 y 2 Av. 1113 Tegucigalpa, Honduras.

Rossi, Opilio (Cardinal Priest), Titular of S. Lorenzo in Lucina; born in New York, May 14, 1910. Created and proclaimed May 24, 1976. Address: Via della Scrofa, 70, 00186 Rome, Italy.

Rouco Varela, Antonio Maria (Cardinal Priest), Titular of S. Lorenzo in Damaso, Archbishop of Madrid, Spain; born in Villalba Diocese of Mondonedo-Ferrol, August 24, 1936. Created and proclaimed February 21, 1998. Address: Bailen 8, 28071 Madrid, Spain.

Rubiano Sáenz, Pedro (Cardinal Priest), Titular of Trasfigurazione di Nostro Signore Gesu Cristo, Archbishop of Bogotáborn in Cartago, September 13, 1932. Created and proclaimed February 21, 2001. Address: Carrera & N. 10-20, Santafe de Bogota, Colombia.

Ruini, Camillo (Cardinal Priest), Titular of S. Agnese, Vicar General of His Holiness for the Diocese of Rome, Archpriest of the Patriarchal Lateran Basilica, Grand Chancellor of the Pontifical Lateran University; born in Sassuolo, Diocese of Reggio Emilia-Guastalla, February 19, 1931. Created and proclaimed June 28, 1991. Address: Piazza San Giovanni in Laterano 4, 00184 Rome, Italy.

Sabattani, Aurelio (Cardinal Priest), Titular of S. Apollinare alle Terme Neroniane-Alessandrine; born in Casal Fiumanese, Diocese of Imola, October 18, 1912. Created and proclaimed February 2, 1983. Address: Palazzo del Tribunale, Piazza S. Marta, 00120 Vatican City State, Europe.

Saldarini, Giovanni (Cardinal Priest), Titular of S. Cuore di Gesu' a Castro Pretorio, Archbishop Emeritus of Torino; born in Cantu, Archdiocese of Milan, December 11, 1924. Created and proclaimed June 28, 1991. Address: Corso Monforte 1, 20122 Milano, Italy.

Sales, Eugenio de Araujo (Cardinal Priest), Titular of S. Gregorio VII, Archbishop of Sao Sebastiao do Rio de Janeiro; born in Acari, Diocese of Caico, November 8, 1920. Created and proclaimed April 28, 1969. Address: Rua da Gloria, 446, C.P. 1362, 20241-150 Rio de Janeiro, R.J., Brazil.

Sanchez, Jose T. (Cardinal Deacon), Deacon of St. Pio V, Prefect Emeritus of the Congregation for the Clergy; born in Pandan, Diocese of Virac, March 17, 1920. Created and proclaimed June 28, 1991. Address: 00120 Vatican City State, Europe.

Sandoval Iniguez, Juan (Cardinal Priest), Titular of Nostra Signora di Guadalupe e S. Filippo Martire in Via Aurelia, Archbishop of Guadalajara, Mexico; born in Yahualica, Diocese of San Juan de los Lagos, March 28, 1933. Created and proclaimed November 26, 1994. Address: Arzobispado, Apartado Postal 1-331, Liceo 17, 44100 Guadalajara, Jal., Mexico.

Santos, Alexandre Jose Maria dos, o.f.m. (Cardinal Priest), Titular of S. Frumenzio ai Prati Fiscali, Archbishop of Maputo; born in Zavala, Diocese of Inhambane, March 18, 1924. Created and proclaimed June 28, 1988. Address: Paco Arquiepiscopal, Avenida Eduardo Mondlane 1448, C.P. 258, Maputo, Mozambique.

Saraiva, Martins, José, C.M.F. (Cardinal Deacon), Deacon of Nostra Signora del Sacro Cuore, Prefect of the Congregation for the Causes of Saints; born in Gagos, Diocese of Guarada, January 6, 1932. Created and proclaimed February 21, 2001. Address: 00102 Vatican City State, Europe.

Scheffczyk, Leo (Cardinal Deacon), Deacon of San Francesco Saverio alla Garbatella; born in Beuthen, Archdiocese of Wroclaw, February 21, 1920. Created and proclaimed February 21, 2001. Address: Germany.

Schonborn, Christoph, o.p., (Cardinal Priest), Titular of Gesu' Divin Lavoratore, Archbishop of Vienna, Austria; born in Skalsko, Diocese of Litomerice, January 22, 1945. Created and proclaimed February 21, 1998. Address: Wollzeile 2, A-1010 Vienna, Austria.

Schotte, Jan P., c.i.c.m. (Cardinal Deacon), Deacon of S. Giuliano dei Fiamminghi, General Secretary of the Synod of Bishops and President of the Office of Labor of the Apostolic See; born in Beveren-Leie, Diocese of Brugge, April 20, 1928. Created and proclaimed November 26, 1994. Address: Palazzo del Bramante, Via della Conciliazione, 34, 00193 Rome, Italy.

Schwery, Henri (Cardinal Priest), Titular of Ss. Protomartiri a Via Aurelia Antica, Bishop Emeritus of Sion; born in Saint Leonard, Diocese of Sion, June 14, 1932. Created and proclaimed June 28, 1991. Address: C.P. 2334, CH-1950 Sion 2, Switzerland.

Sebastiani, Sergio (Cardinal Deacon), Deacon of Sant' Eustachio, President of the Prefecture for the Economic Affairs of the Holy See; born in Montemonaco, Diocese of San Benedetto del Tronto-Ripatransone-Montalto, April 11, 1931. Created and proclaimed February 21, 2001. Address: 00120 Vatican City State, Europe.

Sensi, Giuseppe Maria (Cardinal Priest), Titular of Regina Apostolorum; born in Cosenza, May 27, 1907. Created and proclaimed May 24, 1976. Address: Piazza S. Calisto, 16, 00153 Rome, Italy.

Sepe, Crescenzio (Cardinal Deacon), Deacon of Dio Padre Misericordioso, Secretary General of the Committee for the Great Jubilee of the Holy Year 2000; born in Carinaro, Diocese of Aversa, June 2, 1943. Created and proclaimed February 21, 2001. Address: 00120 Vatican City State, Europe.

Sfeir, Nasrallah Pierre (Cardinal Bishop), Patriarch of Antioch of the Maronites, Lebanon; born in Reyfoun, Lebanon, Eparchy of Sarba of the Maronites, May 15, 1920. Created and proclaimed November 26, 1994. Address: Patriarcat Maronite, Bkerke, Lebanon.

Shan Kuo-hsi, Paul, s.j., (Cardinal Priest), Titular of S. Crisogono, Bishop of Kaohsiung, Taiwan; born in Puyang, Diocese of Taming, December 3, 1923. Created and proclaimed February 21, 1998. Address: Bishop's House, 125 Szu-wei 3rd Rd., Kaohsiung 80203, Taiwan.

Shirayanagi, Peter Seiichi (Cardinal Priest), Titular of S. Emerenziana a Tor Fiorenza, Archbishop Emeritus of Tokyo, Japan; born in Hachioji, Archdiocese of Tokyo, June 17, 1928. Created and proclaimed November 26, 1994. Address: Archbishop's House, Sekiguchi 3-16-15, Bunkyo-ku, Tokyo, 112-0014, Japan.

Silvestrini, Achille (Cardinal Priest), Titular of S. Benedetto fuori Porta S. Paolo, Prefect Emeritus of the Congregation for Oriental Churches; born in Brisighella, Diocese of Faenza-Modigliana, October 25,

1923. Created and proclaimed June 28, 1988. Address: Palazzina della Zecca, 00120 Vatican City State, Europe.

Simonis, Adrianus Johannes (Cardinal Priest), Titular of S. Clemente, Archbishop of Utrecht; born in Lisse, Diocese of Rotterdam, November 26, 1931. Created and proclaimed May 25, 1985. Address: Aartsbisdom, P.B. 14019, 3508 SB Utrecht, Netherlands.

Sin, Jaime L. (Cardinal Priest), Titular of Santa Maria ai Monti, Archbishop of Manila; born in New Washington, Diocese of Kalibo, August 31, 1928. Created and proclaimed May 24, 1976. Address: P.O. Box 132, 1099 Manila, Philippines.

Sodano, Angelo, (Cardinal Bishop), Titular of the suburbicarian church of Albano, Secretary of State; born in Isola d'Asti, Diocese of Asti, November 23, 1927. Created and proclaimed June 28, 1991. Address: 00120 Vatican City State, Europe.

Stafford, James Francis (Cardinal Deacon), Deacon of Gesu' Buon Pastore alla Montagnola, President of the Pontifical Council for the Laity. Born in Baltimore, Maryland, U.S.A., July 26, 1932. Created and proclaimed February 21, 1998. Address: 00120 Vatican City State, Europe.

Sterzinsky, Georg M. (Cardinal Priest), Titular of S. Giuseppe all' Aurelio, Archbishop of Berlin; born in Warlack, Diocese of Warmia, February 9, 1936. Created and proclaimed June 28, 1991. Address: Wundstrasse 48-50, 14057 Berlin, Germany.

Stickler, Alfons Maria, s.d.b. (Cardinal Priest), Titular of S. Giorgio in Velabro; born in Neunkirchen, Archdiocese of Vienna, August 23, 1910. Created and proclaimed May 25, 1985. Address: Piazza del S. Uffizio 11, 00193 Rome, Italy.

Suarez Rivera, Adolfo Antonio (Cardinal Priest), Titular of Nostra Signora di Guadalupe a Monte Mario, Archbishop of Monterrey in Mexico; born in San Cristobal de las Casas, January 9, 1927. Created and proclaimed November 26, 1994. Address: Apartado Postal 7, Loma Larga 2429 con Sierra Madre, 64000 Monterrey, N.L., Mexico.

Suquia Goicoechea, Angel (Cardinal Priest), Titular of Gran Madre di Dio, Archbishop Emeritus of Madrid; born in Zaldivia, Diocese of San Sebastian, October 2, 1916. Created and proclaimed May 25, 1985. Address: Javier Barcaiztegui 7-3, 20010 San Sebastian, Spain.

Swiatek, Kazimierz (Cardinal Priest), Titular of S. Gerardo Maiella, Archbishop of Minsk-Mohilev, Apostolic Administrator of Pinsk, Belarus; born in Walga, Ap. Adm. of Estonia, October 21, 1914. Created and proclaimed November 26, 1994. Address: pl. Swobody 9, 220030 Minsk, Belarus.

Szoka, Edmund Casimir (Cardinal Priest), Titular of Ss. Andrea e Gregorio al Monte Celio, President of the Pontifical Commission for Vatican City State; born in Grand Rapids, Michigan, September 14, 1927. Created and proclaimed June 28, 1988. Address: 00120 Vatican City State, Europe.

Taofinu'u, Pio, s.m. (Cardinal Priest), Titular of S. Onofrio, Archbishop of Samoa-Apia; born in Falealupo, Archdiocese of Samoa-Apia, December 9 1923. Created and proclaimed March 5, 1973. Address: Archbishop's House, P.O. Box 532, Apia, Western Samoa, Oceania.

Terrazas Sandoval, Julio, C.S.S.R. (Cardinal Priest), Titular of San Giovanni Battista de' Rossi, Archbishop of Santa Cruz de la Sierra; born in Valle Grande, Archdiocese of Santa Cruz de la Sierra, March 7, 1936. Created and proclaimed February 21, 2001. Address: Arzobispado, Casilla 25, Calle Ingavi 49, Santa Cruz, Bolivia.

Tettamanzi, Dionigi (Cardinal Priest), Titular of Ss. Ambrogio e Carlo, Archbishop of Genoa, Italy; born in Renate, Archdiocese of Milan, March 14, 1934. Created and proclaimed February 21, 1998. Address: Piazza Matteotti 4, 16123 Genoa, Italy.

Thiandoum, Hyacinthe (Cardinal Priest), Titular of Santa Maria del Popolo, Archbishop Emeritus of Dakar; born in Poponguine, Archdiocese of Dakar, February 2, 1921. Created and proclaimed May 24, 1976. Address: B.P. 1908, Villa Les Badamiers, Dakar-Fann, Senegal.

Todea, Alexandru (Cardinal Priest), Titular of S. Atanasio, Archbishop Emeritus of Fagaras and Alba Julia; born in Teleac, Archdiocese of Fagaras and Alba Julia, June 5, 1912. Created and proclaimed June 28, 1991. Address: Str. P.P. Aron 2, RO-3175 Blaj, A.B., Romania.

Tomko, Jozef (Cardinal Priest), Titular of S. Sabina, Prefect of the Congregation for the Evangelization of Peoples; born in Udavske, Archdiocese of Kosice, March 11, 1924. Created and proclaimed May 25, 1985. Address: Via della Conciliazione 44, 00193 Rome, Italy.

Tonini, Ersilio (Cardinal Priest), Titular of Ss. Redentore a Val Melaina, Archbishop Emeritus of Ravenna-Cervia, Italy; born in Centovera di San Giorgio Piacentino, Diocese of Piacenza-Bobbio, July 20, 1914. Created and proclaimed November 26, 1994. Address: Via Santa Teresa 8, 48100 Ravenna, Italy.

Tucci, Roberto, S.J. (Cardinal Deacon), Deacon of Sant' Ignazio di Loyola a Campo Marzio, President of the Coordinating Committee of Vatican Radio; born in Naples, Italy, April 19, 1921. Created and proclaimed February 21, 2001. Address: 00120 Vatican City State, Europe.

Tumi, Christian Wiyghan (Cardinal Priest), Titular of Ss. Martiri dell' Uganda a Poggio Ameno, Archbishop of Douala; born in Kikaikelaki, Diocese of Kumbo, October 15, 1930. Created and proclaimed June 28, 1988. Address: Archeveche, B.P. 179, Douala, Cameroon.

Turcotte, Jean-Claude (Cardinal Priest), Titular of Nostra Signora del Ss. Sacramento e Santi Martiri Canadesi, Archbishop of Montreal, Canada; born in Montreal, June 26, 1936. Created and proclaimed November 26, 1994. Address: 1071 rue de la Cathedrale, Montreal, P.Q. H2B 2V4, Canada.

Tzadua, Paulos (Cardinal Priest), Titular of Ss. Nome di Maria a Via Latina, Archbishop Emeritus of Addis Abeba; born in Addifini, Eparchy of Asmara, August 25, 1921. Created and proclaimed May 25, 1985. Address: P.O. Box 2141, Addis Abeba, Ethiopia.

Ursi, Corrado (Cardinal Priest), Titular of S. Callisto, Archbishop Emeritus of Naples; born in Andria, July 26, 1908. Created and proclaimed June 26, 1967. Address: Via Capodimonte 13, 80136 Napoli, Italy.

Vachon, Louis-Albert (Cardinal Priest), Titular of S. Paolo della Croce a Corviale, Archbishop Emeritus of Quebec; born in Saint Frederic-de-Beauce, Archdiocese of Quebec, February 4, 1912. Created and proclaimed May 25, 1985. Address: 1 rue des Remparts, Quebec PQ, G1R 5L7, Canada.

Velasco García, Ignacio Antonio, S.D.B. (Cardinal Priest), Titular of Santa Maria Domenica Mazzarello, Archbishop of Caracas; born in Acarigua, Diocese of Guanare, January 17, 1929. Created and proclaimed February 21, 2001.Address: Arzobispado, Apartado 954, Plaza Bolivar, Caracas 1010-A, Venezuela.

Vidal, Ricardo J. (Cardinal Priest), Titular of Ss. Pietro e Paolo a Via Ostiense, Archbishop of Cebu; born in Mogpoc, Diocese of Boac, February 6, 1931. Created and proclaimed May 25, 1985. Address: D. Jakosalem Str., P.O. Box 52, 6000 Cebu City, Philippines.

Vithayathil, Varkey, C.SS.R. (Cardinal Priest), Titular of San Bernardo alle Terme, Major Archbishop of Emakulam-Angamaly of the Syro-Malabar; born in Parur, Archeparchy of Emakulam-Angamaly of the Syro-Malabar, May 29, 1927. Created and proclaimed February 21, 2001. Address: P.O. Box 2580, Kochi-682031, Kerala, India.

Vlk, Miloslav (Cardinal Priest), Titular of S. Croce in Gerusalemme, Archbishop of Prague, Czech Republic; born in Lisnice-Sepekov, Diocese of Ceske Budejovice, May 17, 1932. Created and proclaimed November 26, 1994. Address: Arcibiskupska Kurie, Hradcanske nam. 16, 119 02, Praha 1, Czech Republic.

Wamala, Emmanuel (Cardinal Priest), Titular of S. Ugo, Archbishop of Kampala, Uganda; born in Kamaggwa, Diocese of Masaka, December 15, 1926. Created and proclaimed November 26, 1994. Address: Archbishop's House, P.O. Box 14125, Mengo, Kampala, Uganda.

Wetter, Friedrich (Cardinal Priest), Titular of S. Stefano al Monte Celio, Archbishop of Munich und Freising; born in Landau, Diocese of Speyer, February 20, 1928. Created and proclaimed May 25, 1985. Address: Kardinal-Faulhaber Str., 7, D-80079 Munchen, Germany.

Willebrands, Johannes (Cardinal Priest), Titular of S. Sebastiano alle Catacombe; born in Bovenkarspel, Diocese of Haarlem, September 4, 1909. Created and proclaimed April 28, 1969. Address: Pontificio Collegio Olandese, Via Ercole Rosa 1, 00153 Rome, Italy.

Williams, Thomas Stafford (Cardinal Priest), Titular of Gesu' Divin Maestro alla Pineta Sacchetti, Archbishop of Wellington; born in Wellington, March 20, 1930. Created and proclaimed February 2, 1983. Address: Archbishop's House, P.O. Box 1937, Wellington 6015, New Zealand.

Winning, Thomas Joseph (Cardinal Priest), Titular of S. Andrea delle Fratte, Archbishop of Glasgow, Scotland; born in Wishaw, Diocese of Motherwell, June 3, 1925. Created and proclaimed November 26, 1994. Address: 40 Newlands Road, Glasgow G43 2JD, Scotland, Great Britain.

Wu Cheng-Chung, John Baptist (Cardinal Priest), Titular of Beata Vergine Maria del Monte Carmelo a Mostacciano, Bishop of Hong Kong; born in Shui-Tsai, Diocese of Kaying, March 26, 1925. Created and proclaimed June 28, 1988. Address: Caritas House, 2 Caine Rd., Hong Kong.

Patriarchs

Alexandria (Egypt), *Coptic Rite* — His Beatitude Stephanos II Ghattas, born January 16, 1920 in Cheikh Zein-el-Dine; ordained March 25, 1944; elected to Luqsor of the Copts June 9, 1967; consecrated June 16, 1967; elected Patriarch June 9, 1986. Address: B.P. 69, 11712 Le Caire, Egypt.

Antioch (Syria), *Syriac Rite* — His Beatitude Gregoire III, B.S., elected Patriarch November 29, 2000. Address: Rue Damas, Beyrouth, Lebanon. Maronite Rite His Beatitude Nasrallah Peter Cardinal Sfeir; born in Reyfoun, May 15, 1920; elected Patriarch April 19, 1986. Rev. Msgr. Jean Assaad Haddad, Apostolic Admin. Address: Patriarcat Maronite Bkerke, Lebanon.

Melkite Greek Catholic — Vacant See. Address: B.P. 22249, Damascus, Syria.

Jerusalem (Israel) — His Beatitude Michel Sabbah, born in Nazareth, Israel, March 19, 1933; elected Patriarch of Jerusalem of the Latins December 11, 1987; consecrated January 6, 1988. Address: Patriarcat Latin, P.O. Box 14152, 91141 Jerusalem (Old City).

Babylon of the Chaldeans — His Beatitude Raphael I Bidawid; born in Mossul, April 17, 1922; elected Patriarch, May 21, 1989. Address: Patriarcat Chaldeen Catholique, P.O. Box 6112, Al-Mansour, Baghdad, Iraq.

Cilicia of the Armenians — His Beatitude Nerses Bedros XIX Tarmouni. Address: Patriarcat Armenien Catholique, Rue de L'Hopital Orthodoxe, Jeitaoui, 2400 Beyrouth, Lebanon.

East Indies — Most Rev. Raul Nicholau Gonsalves; born in Bambolim, Archdiocese of Goa, June 15, 1927; promoted Archbishop January 30, 1978. Address: Paco Patriarcal, Panaji, Goa-403001, India.

Lisbon, (Portugal) — Most Reverend Jose da Cruz Policarpo, born in Alvorninha, Patriarchate of Lisbon, February 26, 1936; consecrated June 29, 1978; appointed Coadjutor Archbishop of the Patriarchate of Lisbon March 7, 1997; promoted Patriarch March 24, 1998. Address: Mosteiro de Sao Vicente De Fora, Campo de Santa Clara 1100-473 Lisbon, Portugal.

Venice, (Italy) — His Eminence Cardinal Marco Ce', born in Izano, Diocese of Crema, July 8, 1925; ordained March 27, 1948; elected Titular Bishop of Vulturia April 22, 1970; Patriarch December 7, 1978. Created and proclaimed Cardinal in the Consistory of June 30, 1979. Address: Curia Patriarcale, S. Marco 320/a, 30124 Venice, Italy.

Synod of Bishops

Synodus Episcoporum President: The Holy Father. Secretary General: His Eminence Jan Cardinal Schotte, C.I.C.M. General Secretariat: Palazzo del Bramante, Via della Conciliazione, 34, 00193 Rome, Italy. Tel: 69.88.48.21 or 69.88.43.24. Fax: 69.88.33.92.

Office of Labor of the Apostolic See

Officium Laboris Apostolicae Sedia President: His Eminence Jan Cardinal Schotte, C.I.C.M. Vice President: Most Rev. Archbishop Giovanni De Andrea. Assessor of the Presidency: Prof. Matteo Dell'Olio. Assessor of the Presidency: Prof. Gian Carlo Perone. Office: Via della Conciliazione, 1, 00193 Rome, Italy. Tel: 69.88.44.49. Fax: 69.88.38.00.

The Roman Curia

The present norms regarding the Roman Curia were publicly announced June 28, 1988, in the Pastor Bonus - Constitutio Apostolica de Romana Curia, and published in A.A.S. LXXX/1988, Commentarium Officiale; pp. 841-934. The Supreme Pontiff usually conducts business of the universal Church by means of the Roman Curia, which fulfills its duty in his name and by his authority for the good and the service of the Churches; it consists of the Secretariat of State or the Papal Secretariat, congregations, tribunals and other institutions, whose structure and competency are defined in special law (can. 360). The Roman curia is the complex of departments and institutes which assist the Roman Pontiff in the exercise of his supreme pastoral function for the good and service of the universal Church and of the particular churches, by which the unity of faith and communion of the people of God is strengthened and the mission is promoted which is proper to the Church in the world.

I. THE SECRETARIAT OF STATE TO HIS HOLINESS

The Secretariat of State

The Secretariat of State closely assists the Supreme Pontiff in the exercise of his supreme function. The cardinal secretary of state presides over it. It includes two sections, namely the section for general affairs under the immediate direction of the substitute, assisted by an assessor, and the section for relations with states under the direction of its own secretary, with the assistance of a subsecretary. Attached to this latter section is a body of cardinals and some bishops.

Secretary of State: His Eminence Angelo Cardinal Sodano.

Office: Apostolic Palace, 00120 Vatican City State, Europe. Tel: 69.88.34.38; Fax: 69.88.50.88.

First Section: for General Affairs

The first section handles anything entrusted to it by the Holy Father, as well as matters of daily business which do not fall within the competence of other dicasteries. It fosters relations with these departments, with the bishops, and with the diplomatic missions of the Holy See.

Substitute: Archbishop Leonardo Sandri

Assessor: Rev. Msgr. Pedro Lopez Quintana.

Second Section: for Relations with States

The second section of the Secretariat of State handles all matters pertaining to civil governments, fostering diplomatic relations with nations, and maintaining contact with all the diplomatic missions of the Holy See. It takes care also of what concerns the presence and activity of the Holy See in international institutes.

Secretary: Archbishop Jean-Louis Tauran.

Under-Secretary: Rev. Msgr. Celestino Migliore.

II. THE CONGREGATIONS

By the name of "department" (dicasteria) is understood: the congregations, tribunals, councils and offices, namely the Apostolic Camera, the Administration of the Patrimony of the Apostolic See, and the Prefecture of Economic Affairs of the Holy See. The departments are juridically equal among themselves. Attached to the institutes of the Roman Curia are the Prefecture of the Papal Household and the Office of Liturgical Celebrations of the Supreme Pontiff.

The Congregation for the Doctrine of the Faith

The proper function of the Congregation on the Doctrine of the Faith is to promote and safeguard the doctrine of faith and morals in the whole Catholic world; therefore, those things belong to it which touch this matter in any way. Fulfilling the function of promoting doctrine, it fosters studies in order that the understanding of the faith might grow and that a response can be prepared under the light of faith for new questions arising from developments in science and human culture. It is a help to bishops, whether individually or gathered in assemblies, in the exercise of the function by which they are constituted authentic teachers and doctors of the faith as well as the office by which they are held to safeguard and promote the integrity of that faith. This Sacred Congregation reproves doctrines opposed to the principles of the faith after the interested Bishops of a region have been heard. It studies the books referred to it and, if necessary, reproves them after the author has been heard and has had an opportunity to defend himself and after the Ordinary has been forewarned. It also examines whatever concerns "the privilege of the faith" whether in law and in fact. It is competent to pass judgement on errors about the faith according to the norms of an ordinary process. It safeguards the dignity of the sacrament of Penance. The Congregation proceeds administratively or judicially according to the nature of the question to be treated.

Cardinal Prefect: His Eminence Joseph Cardinal Ratzinger.

Secretary: Most Rev. Archbishop Tarcisio Bertone, S.D.B.

Office: Piazza del S. Uffizio 11, 00193 Rome, Italy. Tel: 69.88.33.57; 69.88.34.13; Fax: 69.88.34.09.

The Congregation for the Causes of Saints

The Congregation for the Causes of Saints is competent in all matters which in any way pertain to the Beatification of Servants of God or to the Canonization of the Blessed or to the Preservation of Relics.

This Congregation is divided into three offices.

Prefect: Most Rev. Archbishop Jose Saraiva Martins, C.M.F.

Secretary: Most Rev. Archbishop Edward Nowak.

Office: Piazza Pio XII 10, 00193 Rome, Italy. Tel: 011 39 06 69.88.42.47. Fax: 011 39 06 6988 1935.

The Congregation for the Oriental Churches

This Congregation considers those matters, whether regarding persons or things, which touch on the Eastern Catholic Churches. It treats all questions which pertain either to persons, or to discipline, or to the rites of the Oriental Churches, even if they are mixed in that by the nature of the thing or of persons they involve Latins. Territories in which a major part of the Christians belong to Oriental rites are subject only to this Congregation. Even in Latin territories it carefully supervises the faithful of Oriental rites and provides as much as possible for their spiritual needs even by the establishment of their own hierarchy if the number of faithful and circumstances require this.

Prefect: His Beatitude Ignace Moussa I. Daoud

Secretary: Most Rev. Archbishop Miroslav Stefan Marusyn, Titular Archbishop of Cadi.

Office: Via della Conciliazione 34, 00193 Rome, Italy. Tel: 69.88.42.82; Fax: 69.88.43.00.

The Congregation for Bishops

This congregation examines what pertains to the constitution and provision of particular churches as well as the exercise of the episcopal function in the Latin Church, except for the competence of the Congregation for the Evangelization of Peoples. It belongs to the Congregation for Bishops to propose to the Roman Pontiff, for approval, the constitution of new dioceses, provinces and regions; to divide, unite and realign them after consulting the interested Episcopal Conferences; it deals also with the erection of the military ordinariates and, after consulting the Episcopal Conference, prelacies for special pastoral ministries for various regions or social groups. This Congregation provides also for the naming of bishops, apostolic administrators, coadjutors and auxiliaries of bishops, military and other vicars and prelates enjoying personal jurisdiction.

It is competent for all things that have to do with bishops and publishes norms which, through the Episcopal Conference, provide for the more urgent needs of the faithful.

Prefect: His Eminence Giovanni Battista Cardinal Re

Secretary: Most Rev. Archbishop Francesco Monterisi

Office: Piazza Pio XII 10, 00193 Rome, Italy. Tel: 69.88.42.17; Fax: 69.88.53.03.

Pontifical Commission for Latin America

(Directly responsible to Congregation for Bishops)

President: His Eminence Giovanni Battista Cardinal Re.

Vice President: Most Rev. Bishop Cipriano Calderon Polo.

The Congregation for Divine Worship and the Discipline of the Sacraments

This congregation does those things which pertain to the Apostolic See as to the moderation and promotion of the sacred liturgy, especially the sacraments, with due regard for the competence of the Congregation on Doctrine of the Faith. It fosters and safeguards the discipline of the sacraments, especially what pertains to their valid and licit celebration; moreover, it concedes favors and dispensations for matters which are not contained in the facilities of diocesan bishops in this line. It alone examines the non-consummation of a marriage and the presence of causes for the granting of a dispensation and everything connected with them. It has competence with regard to the obligations connected with major orders and it examines questions about the validity of sacred ordination.

Prefect: His Eminence Jorge Cardinal Arturo Medina Estevez.

Secretary: Most Rev. Archbishop Francesco Pio Tamburrino, O.S.B.

Office: Piazza Pio XII 10, 00193 Rome, Italy. Tel: 69.88.43.16; Fax: 69.88.34.99.

The Congregation for the Evangelization of Peoples or for the Propagation of the Faith

It belongs to this congregation to direct and coordinate throughout the world the work of the evangelization of peoples itself and missionary cooperation, while respecting the competence of the Congregation for Eastern Churches. It is competent for those things which pertain to all the missions established for the spread of the Kingdom of Christ throughout the world and therefore for whatever is connected with the assignment and transferral of the necessary ministers, for describing ecclesiastical boundaries and proposing those who will govern them. It encourages also the development of an indigenous clergy. The congregation sponsors missionary initiatives and promotes missionary vocations and spirituality. In the territories subject to it, the Congregation has charge of all that pertains to the holding of synods and councils, to the establishing of episcopal conferences and to the review of their statutes and decrees. The Congregation has a Supreme Council for the direction of Pontifical Missionary Works, on which depend the general Councils of the Missionary Union of the Clergy, the Society for the Propagation of the Faith, the Society of St. Peter the Apostole, and the Society of the Holy Childhood.

Cardinal Prefect: His Eminence Jozef Cardinal Tomko.

Secretary: Most Rev. Archbishop Marcello Zago, O.M.I.

Adjunct Secretary: Most Rev. Archbishop Charles A. Schleck, C.S.C.

Office: Palazzo di Propaganda Fide, Piazza di Spagna 48, 00187 Rome, Italy. Tel: 011 39 06 6987 9299; Fax: 011 39 06 6988 01 18.

The Congregation for Institutes of Consecrated Life and for Societies of Apostolic Life

The principal function of this congregation is to promote and supervise, in the whole Latin Church, the practices of the evangelical counsels as they are exercised in approved forms of consecrated life and at the same time the activities of societies of apostolic life. The Congregation takes care of Religious Institutes of Consecrated Life and Secular Institutes.

Religious Institutes: the Congregation is entrusted with the affairs of all religious institutes of the Latin Rite and their members. It is also competent in matters which pertain to societies of common life, whose members live like religious, or to Third Orders as such.

Secular Institutes: the Congregation is competent in the same way, all else being equal, for Apostolic Societies which, although not religious, make a true and complete profession of the evangelical counsels in the world.

Cardinal Prefect: His Eminence Eduardo Cardinal Martinez Somalo.

Secretary: Most Rev. Archbishop Piergiorgio Silvano Nesti, C.P.

Office: Piazza Pio XII 3, 00193 Rome, Italy. Tel: 69.88.41.28; Fax: 69.88.45.26.

The Congregation for the Clergy

With due regard for the rights of bishops and their conferences, this congregation examines those things which concern priests and deacons of the secular clergy with regard to their persons, pastoral ministry, matters which are in support of the exercise of these things, and in all this provides opportune assistance to the bishops. The Congregation has many functions: studies, proposes and urges the means and aids by which priests strive for sanctity. This office also has charge of everything which concerns the work and discipline of the diocesan clergy. Particularly it promotes the preaching of the Word of God and the works of the apostolate and organization of catechesis, evaluates and approves pastoral and catechetical directories, fosters national and international Catechetical Congresses and indicates the opportune norms for religious instruction of children, young people and adults. The Congregation looks also to the preservation and administration of the temporal goods of the Church without prejudice to the other Congregations which have temporal goods committed to their vigilance.

Prefect: His Eminence Dario Cardinal Castrillon Hoyos.

Secretary: Most Rev. Archbishop Csaba Ternyak.

Office: Piazza Pio XII 3, 00193 Rome, Italy. Tel: 69.88.41.51; Fax: 69.88.48.45.

The Congregation for Catholic Education (of Seminaries and Institutes of Studies)

This Congregation expresses and exercises the Apostolic See's solicitude for the formation of those who are called to holy orders as well as for the promotion and organization of Catholic education. It is competent for all that pertains to the formation of clerics and the Catholic education both of clerics and of the laity.

The Congregation has many functions and is charged with the direction, discipline and temporal administration of seminaries and whatever touches the education of the diocesan clergy and the scientific formation of religious and secular institutes.

The Congregation oversees universities, faculties, athenaea and any institute of higher learning which has the name "Catholic" in so far as they depend on the authority of the Church, not excluding those directed by religious or the laity.

The Congregation cares for the establishment of parochial and diocesan schools; watches over all Catholic schools below the level of a university and faculty, as well as all institutes of instruction or education dependent on the authority of the Church.

Also within the Congregation is located the Pontifical Work for Vocations, which is charged with coordinating and promoting the work of fostering all ecclesiastical vocations.

Prefect: Most Rev. Archbishop Zenon Grocholewski.

Secretary: Most Rev. Archbishop Giuseppe Pittau, S.J.

Office: Piazza Pio XII 3, 00193 Rome, Italy. Tel: 69 88 41 67; Fax: 69 88 41 72.

III. TRIBUNALS

Apostolic Penitentiary

The competence of this Tribunal is concerned with those matters which pertain to the internal forum, for both the sacramental and non-sacramental internal forum. It is competent in matters pertaining to the granting and use of indulgences.

Major Penitentiary: His Eminence William Cardinal Baum.

Regent: Most Rev. Bishop Luigi De Magistris.

Office: Piazza della Cancelleria 1, 00186 Rome, Italy. Tel: 011 39 06 6988 75 26; Fax: 011 39 06 6988 75 57.

Supreme Tribunal of the Apostolic Signatura

This department, in addition to the function which it exercises as Supreme Tribunal, consults that justice may be correctly administered in the Church.

With the many functions, the Apostolic Signatura judges the matters assigned to it in the Code of Canon Law; it prorogues the competence of tribunals; it extends the forum for strangers in Rome to cases of matrimonial nullity in extraordinary circumstances and for grave reasons; it supervises the proper administration of justice; it provides for the establishment of regional and interregional tribunals; it enjoys the rights assigned to it in concordats between the Holy See and the various nations.

The Tribunal settles questions about the exercise of administrative ecclesiastical power which are referred to it. It also passes on conflicts of competence among the departments of the Holy See; it examines administrative matters referred to it by the Congregations of the Roman Curia as well as questions committed to it by the Holy Father.

Prefect: Most Rev. Archbishop Mario Francesco Pompedda.

Secretary: Most Rev. Bishop Francesco Saverio Salerno.

Office: Piazza della Cancelleria 1, 00186 Rome, Italy. Tel: 69.88.75.20; Fax: 69.88.75.53.

Tribunal of the Roman Rota

This tribunal acts as a higher instance at the Apostolic See, usually in the grade of appeal, for safeguarding rights in the Church; it fosters the unity of jurisprudence and, through its own sentences, is a help to lower tribunals. It is also a court of first instance for cases specified in the law and for others committed to the Rota by the Roman Pontiff. The greater part of its decisions concern the nullity of marriage. In such cases its competence includes marriages between two Catholics, between a Catholic and non-Catholic, and between two non-Catholic parties whether one or both of the baptized parties belongs to a Latin or Oriental Rite.

Dean: Rev. Monsignor Rafaello Funghini.

Office: Piazza della Cancelleria 1, 00186 Rome, Italy. Tel: 69.88.75.02; Fax: 69.88.75.54.

IV. PONTIFICAL COUNCILS

Pontifical Council for the Laity

This council is competent in those matters which pertain to the Apostolic See in promoting and coordinating the apostolate of the lay persons and, generally, in those things which look to the Christian life of lay persons as such. The norms were published in the apostolic letter, "Catholicam Christi Ecclesiam" of January 6, 1967 (A.A.S., LIX, pp. 25-28).

President: His Eminence J. Francis Cardinal Stafford.

Secretary: Most Rev. Bishop Stanislaws Rylko.

Office: Piazza S. Calisto 16, 00153 Rome, Italy. Tel: 69.88.73.22; Fax: 69.88.72.14.

Pontifical Council for Promoting Christian Unity

The function of this Council is to concentrate in an appropriate way on initiatives and ecumenical activities for the restoration of unity among Christians. It has charge of relations with those of other communities; considers the correct interpretation and observance of the principles of ecumenism; promotes Catholic groups and coordinates the efforts at unity, both on the national and international levels; institutes colloquies on ecumenical questions and activities with Churches and ecclesial communities separated from the Holy See; deputes Catholic observers for Christian congresses; invites to Catholic gatherings observers of the separated brethren; orders into practice conciliar decrees on ecumenical matters. Furthermore, it is competent for all questions concerning religious relations with Judaism.

President: His Eminence Edward Cardinal Cassidy.

Secretary: Most Rev. Bishop Walter Kasper.

Office: Via dell' Erba 1, 00193 Rome, Italy. Tel: 6988 4083; Fax: 6988 53 65.

Pontifical Council for the Family

This Council promotes the pastoral care of families and fosters their rights and dignity in the Church and in civil society, in order that they might ever more suitably fulfill their own functions.

President: His Eminence Alfonso Cardinal Lopez Trujillo.

Secretary: Most Rev. Bishop Francisco Gil Hellin.

Office: Piazza S. Calisto 16, 00153 Rome, Italy. Tel: 69.88.72.43; Fax: 69.88.72.72.

Pontifical Council for Justice and Peace

This Council looks to those things which will promote justice and peace in the world according to the Gospel and the social teaching of the Church.

President: Most Rev. Archbishop Francois Xavier Nguyen Van Thuan.

Secretary: Most Rev. Bishop Diarmuid Martin.

Office: Piazza S. Calisto 16, 00153 Rome, Italy. Tel: 69.88.71.91; Fax: 69.88.72.05.

Pontifical Council "Cor Unum"

This Council shows the solicitude of the Catholic Church toward the needy, in order that human fraternity might be fostered and the charity of Christ be made manifest.

President: Most. Rev. Archbishop Paul Josef Cordes.

Secretary: Rev. Msgr. Karel Kasteel.

Office: Piazza S. Calisto 16, 00153 Rome, Italy. Tel: 69.88.73.31; Fax: 69.88.73.01.

Pastoral Council for the Pastoral Care of Migrants and Itinerant People

This Council directs the pastoral concern of the Church toward the special needs of those who are forced to leave their own native land or who perhaps lack one; it also sees that there is appropriate study of the questions which touch on this matter.

President: Most Rev. Archbishop Stephen Fumio Hamao.

Secretary: Most Rev. Archbishop Francesco Gioia, O.F.M.Cap.

Under-Secretary: Rev. Father Michael V. Blume, S.V.D.

Office: Piazza S. Calisto 16, 00153 Rome, Italy. Tel: 69.88.71.93; Fax: 69.88.71.11.

Pontifical Council for the Pastoral Assistance to Health Care Workers

This Council shows the solicitude of the Church for the sick by aiding those who carry out a ministry toward the sick and suffering, in order that the apostolate of mercy, which they carry out, may ever more suitably respond to new needs.

President: Most Rev. Archbishop Javier Lozano Barragan.

Secretary: Most Rev. Bishop Jose Luis Redrado Marchite, O.H.

Office: Via della Conciliazione, 00193 Rome, Italy. Tel: 69.88.31.38; Fax: 69.88.31.39.

Pontifical Council for the Intepretation of Legislative Texts

The function of this Council consists especially in interpreting the Church's laws.

President: Most Rev. Archbishop Julian Herranz.

Secretary: Most Rev. Bishop Bruno Bertagna.

Office: Palazzo delle Congregazioni Piazza Pio XII 10, 00193 Rome, Italy. Tel: 69.88.40.08; Fax: 69.88.47.10.

Pontifical Council for Inter-Religious Dialogue

This Council fosters and moderates relations with members and bodies of religions which do not carry the name of Christian, as well as with those who in any way possess a religious spirit. It fosters studies and promotes relations with non-Christians to bring about an increase in mutual respect and seeks ways to establish a dialogue with them; it receives and carefully weighs the wishes of the Ordinaries; it provides for the formation of those who participate in dialogue.

President: His Eminence Francis Cardinal Arinze.

Secretary: Most Rev. Bishop Michael Louis Fitzgerald. *Office:* Via dell' Erba 1, 00193 Rome, Italy. Tel: 69.88.43.21; Fax: 69.88.44.94.

Pontifical Council for Culture

The Council embodies the Church's pastoral concern over the relationship between faith and cultures. Its tasks include: studying unbelief and religious indifference, as present in different cultures; supporting the Church's inculturation of the Gospel; promoting initiatives of dialogue between faith and culture, as well as dialogue with those who do not believe in God. Its activities include seminars, intercultural exchanges, and coordinating the activities of Pontifical Academies and the Pontifical Commission for the Cultural Patrimony of the Church. An important hope of the Council is to show faith as the inspiration of science, literature and the arts.

President: His Eminence Paul Cardinal Poupard.
Secretary: Rev. Bernard Ardura, O.Praem.
Office: Piazza S. Calisto 16, 00153 Rome, Italy. Tel: 69.88.73.21; Fax: 69.88.73.68.

Pontifical Council for Social Communications

This Council is involved in questions touching on the instruments of social communication so that the proclamation of salvation and human progress might be promoted even through them in order to foster civil culture.

President: Most Rev. Archbishop John Foley.
Secretary: Most Rev. Bishop Pierfranco Pastore.
Office: Palazzo S. Carlo, 00120 Vatican City State, Europe. Tel: 69.88.31.97; Fax: 69.88.53.73.

V. OFFICES

Apostolic Camera

The Apostolic Camera is presided over by the cardinal chamberlain of the Holy Roman Church, assisted by the vice-chamberlain together with certain prelates chamberlain. It chiefly exercises the function which is given to it in the special law on the vacancy of the Apostolic See.

Camerlengo: His Eminence Eduardo Cardinal Martinez Somalo.

Prefecture of the Papal Household

The Prefecture looks after the internal order of the pontifical household and supervises everything which pertains to discipline and service either by clergy or laity who constitute the pontifical chapel and family. It is in charge of the Apostolic Palace and is at the service of the Holy Father, both there and wherever he goes. It arranges audiences with His Holiness and supervises papal ceremonies other than the strictly liturgical.

Prefect: Most Reverend Bishop James M. Harvey.
Adjunct Prefect: Most Reverend Bishop Stanislaw Dziwisz.

Administration of the Patrimony of the Apostolic See

This Office is competent to administer the goods proper to the Holy See, the income from which is destined to support the expenditures necessary for the functions of the Roman Curia.

Extraordinary Section: Handles the duties committed to it by the Sovereign Pontiff.

President: Most Rev. Archbishop Agostino Cacciavillan.
Secretary: Most Rev. Archbishop Claudio Maria Celli.
Office: 00120 Vatican City State, Europe. Tel: 011 39 06 6988 4306; Fax: 011 39 06 6988 31 41.

Central Office of Statistics of the Church

This Office gathers and organizes the data which seems necessary or useful for a better understanding of the state of the Church and for assistance to its Bishops.

Director: Rev. Msgr. Vittorio Formenti.

Prefecture of the Economic Affairs of the Holy See

The Prefecture has the function of supervising and governing the administration of goods which belong to the Holy See or which it is in charge of, no matter what kind of autonomy they may perhaps enjoy. This is directed by a Commission of three Cardinals and coordinates and watches over the administration of the possessions of the Holy See. It receives the reports on the receipts and disbursements of the Church's goods and the various budgets.

President: Most Rev. Archbishop Sergio Sebastiani.
Secretary: Most Rev. Bishop Franco Croci.
Office: Largo del Colonnato 3, 00193 Rome, Italy. Tel: 69.88.42.63; Fax: 69.88.50.11.

Office of the Liturgical Celebrations of the Supreme Pontiff

This Office prepares whatever is necessary for liturgical and other sacred celebrations which are carried out by the Supreme Pontiff or in his name and, in keeping with existing prescription of liturgical law, to supervise them.

Master of Ceremonies: Most Rev. Bishop Piero Marini.

Archives of the Second Vatican Council

Director: Rev. Msgr. Vincenzo Carbone.

VI. COMMISSIONS AND COMMITTEES

Pontifical Commission for the Cultural Heritage of the Church

President: Most Rev. Archbishop Francesco Marchisano.
Secretary: Rev. Carlo Chenis, S.D.B.

Pontifical Commission for Sacred Archeology

President: Most Rev. Archbishop Francesco Marchisano.
Secretary: Prof. Fabrizio Bisconti.

Pontifical Commission "Ecclesia Dei"

President: His Eminence Dario Cardinal Castrillon Hoyos.

Council of Cardinals for the Study of Organizational and Economic Problems of the Apostolic See

American Member: His Eminence Roger M. Cardinal Mahony.

International Theological Commission

President: His Eminence Joseph Cardinal Ratzinger.
General Secretary: Rev. Georges Cottier, O.P.

Commission of Cardinals for the Pontifical Shrines of Pompei, Loreto, and Bari

President: His Eminence Virgilio Cardinal Noe.

Pontifical Biblical Commission

President: His Eminence Joseph Cardinal Ratzinger.
Secretary: Rev. P. Albert Vanhoye, S.J.

Pontifical Committee for the International Eucharistic Congresses

President: His Eminence Edouard Cardinal Gagnon.

Pontifical Commission for the Revision and Emendation of the Vulgate

Director: Rev. Jean Mallet, O.S.B.

Pontifical Commission for the Vatican City State

President: His Eminence Edmund Casimir Cardinal Szoka.

Pontifical Committee for Historical Sciences

President: Rev. Msgr. Walter Brandmuller
Secretary: Rev. Vittorino Grossi, O.S.A.

Central Committee of the Great Jubilee of the Year 2000

President: His Eminence Cardinal Roger Etchegaray.
Secretary: Most Rev. Archbishop Crescenzio Sepe.

VII. INSTITUTIONS CONNECTED WITH THE HOLY SEE

Vatican Secret Archives

Archivist: Most Rev. Archbishop Jorge Maria Mejia.
Prefect: Rev. Sergio B. Pagano.

Vatican Apostolic Library

Librarian: Most Rev. Archbishop Jorge Maria Mejia.
Prefect: Rev. Raffaele Farina, S.D.B.

Pontifical Academy of Sciences

President: Prof. Nicola Cabibbo.

Pontifical Academy of Social Sciences

President: Prof. Edmond Malinvaud.

Pontifical Academy for Life

President: Prof. Juan de Dios Vial Correa.
Vice President: Most Rev. Bishop Elio Sgreccia.

Vatican Radio

President of the Coordinating Committee: Rev. Roberto Tucci, S.J.
Director General: Rev. Pasquale Borgomeo, S.J.

Vatican Television Centre

President of the Administrative Council: Dr. Emilio Rossi.
Director General: Rev. Msgr. Ugo Moretto

Fabric of St. Peter's

President: His Eminence Virgilio Cardinal Noe.

Office of Papal Charities

Almoner: Most Rev. Archbishop Oscar Rizzato.

Vatican Polyglot Press

Director General: Rev. Elio Torrigiani, S.D.B.
Administrative Director: Mr. Giacomo Bonassoli, S.D.B.

Vatican Publishing House

President: Most Rev. Archbishop Giovanni De Andrea.
Director: Rev. Nicolo' Suffi, S.D.B.

Institute for Works of Religion

Director General: Dr. Lelio Scaletti.
Prelate: Vacant.

L'Osservatore Romano

Director: Prof. Mario Agnes.
Secretary: Dr. Carlo DeLucia.
English Language Weekly - Contact Person: Rev. Msgr. Robert Dempsey.
Translations of English, French, Spanish, German, Portuguese, and Polish editions available.

Press Office of the Holy See

Director: Dr. Joaquin Navarro-Valls.

VIII. AMERICANS WORKING IN THE ROMAN CURIA

Secretariat of State I—Section for General Affairs: Rev. Msgr. William Millea; Rev. Reginald Foster, O.C.D.; Rev. Msgr. Steven Zak; Sr. Yvonne Mary Loucks, R.S.M.; Sr. Ruth Aubrey, A.S.C.J.; Sr. Rose Mary Wolak, C.S.S.F. *II. Section for Relations with States:* Rev. Msgr. Timothy Broglio; Rev. Msgr. Joseph Marino; Rev. Msgr. Michael Banach.
Congregation for the Doctrine of the Faith: Rev. Msgr. Michael O. Jackels; Rev. Charles Brown.
Congregation for the Oriental Churches: Rev. William Corcoran.
Congregation for Divine Worship and the Discipline of the Sacraments: Rev. Thomas Fucinaro; Rev. Michael K. Magee.
Congregation for Causes of Saints: Rev. Msgr. Robert Sarno.
Congregation for Bishops: Rev. Msgr. Daniel Thomas; Rev. James D. Conley.

Congregation for the Evangelization of Peoples: Most Rev. Archbishop Charles Schleck, C.S.C.; Rev. Joseph McCabe, M.M.
Congregation for the Clergy: Rev. Msgr. Anthony McDaid.
Congregation for The Institutes of Consecrated Life and for Societies of Apostolic Life: Sr. Sharon Holland, I.H.M.
Congregation for Catholic Education: Rev. Msgr. Walter J. Edyvean; Rev. Msgr. Robert Zapfel.
Apostolic Penitentiary: William Cardinal Baum; Rev. Msgr. James Gillen.
Supreme Tribunal of the Apostolic Signatura: Rev. Msgr. Joseph Punderson; Rev. Msgr. Salvatore Cordileone.
Tribunal of the Roman Rota: Rev. Msgr. Kenneth Boccafola; Rev. Msgr. Robert Sable.
Pontifical Council For the Laity: His Eminence J. Francis Cardinal Stafford.
Pontifical Council For Promoting Christian Unity: Rev. Msgr. John Radano.
Pontifical Council for the Family: Ms. Joan E. Collemacine-Parenti, Ph.D.
Pontifical Council for Justice and Peace: Sr. Marjorie Keenan, R.S.C.M.
Pontifical Council - Cor Unum: Rev. Msgr. Frank Dewane.
Pontifical Council for the Interpretation of Legislative Texts: Rev. Msgr. Bernard Hebda.
Pontifical Council for Social Communications: Most Rev. Archbishop John Foley; Dr. Marjorie Weeke.
Administration for the Patrimony of the Apostolic See: Sr. Catherine Danovich, O.S.B.M.; Sr. Judith Zoebelein, F.S.E.
Prefecture of the Papal Household: Prefect: Most Rev. Bishop James M. Harvey.
Pontifical Commission for Vatican City State: His Eminence Edmund Cardinal Szoka; Rev. Todd J. Lajiness.
L'Osservatore Romano: Rev. Msgr. Robert Dempsey, Editor. For subscription information for North America please contact: The Cathedral Foundation, Inc., 320 Cathedral St., Baltimore, MD 21201. Tel: 410-547-5380; Fax: 410-385-0113.
Synod of Bishops: Rev. Msgr. John Abruzzese.
Pontifical Commission Ecclesia Dei: Rev. Msgr. Arthur Calkins.
Residence for American Diocesan Priests working in the Roman Curia: Villa Stritch, Via della Nocetta 63, 00164 Rome, Italy. Tel: 011 39 06 6616 2662; or 6616 2676; Fax: 011 39 06 6616 2700.

INSTITUTES OF GRADUATE STUDIES IN ROME

Pontifical Gregorian University, with which are associated the Pontifical Biblical Institute and the Pontifical Oriental Institute—Constituted in 1552. Address: Piazza della Pilotta 4, 00187 Rome, Italy. Grand Chancellor: Most Rev. Zenon Grocholewski; Vice Chancellor: Rev. Peter-Hans Kolvenbach, S.J.; Rector: Rev. Franco Imoda, S.J.; Rector of the Biblical Institute: Rev. Robert O'Toole, S.J.; Rector of the Oriental Institute: Rev. Hector Vall, S.J.
Pontifical Lateran University—Founded in 1824. Address: Piazza S. Giovanni in Laterano 4, 00184 Rome, Italy. Grand Chancellor: Camillo Cardinal Ruini; Rector: Most Rev. Bishop Angelo Scola.
Patristic Institute Augustinianum at the Pontifical Lateran University—Founded in 1969. Address: Via Paolo VI 25, 00193 Rome, Italy. Rev. Angelo Di Berardino, O.S.A., Pres.
Pontifical Urban University—Founded in 1627. Address: Via Urbano VIII 16, 00165 Rome, Italy. Grand Chancellor: Jozef Cardinal Tomko; Rector: Rev. Ambrogio Spreafico.
Pontifical University of St. Thomas Aquinas—Founded in 1580. Address: Largo Angelicum 1, 00184 Rome, Italy. Grand Chancellor: Very Rev. Timothy Radcliffe, Master General of the Order of Preachers; Rector: Very Rev. Edward Kaczynski, O.P.
Pontifical Atheneum of St. Anselm—Founded in 1687. Address: Piazza Cavalieri di Malta 5, 00153 Rome, Italy. Tel: (06) 57.9.11. Grand Chancellor: Very Rev. Marcel Rooney, Abbot Primate; Rector: Rev. Albert Schmidt, O.S.B.
Pontifical Salesian University—Founded in 1940. Address: Piazza Ateneo Salesiano 1, 00139 Rome, Italy. Grand Chancellor: Rev. Juan Edmundo Vecchi. Rector: Rev. Michele Pellerey.
Pontifical Atheneum Antonianum—Founded in 1933. Address: Via Merulana 124, 00185 Rome, Italy. Grand Chancellor: Very Rev. Giacomo Bini, O.F.M., Minister General of the Order of Friars Minor; Rector: Rev. Marco Nobile, O.F.M.
Pontifical Institute of Sacred Music—Founded in 1911. Address: Via di Torre Rossa 21, 00165, Rome, Italy. Grand Chancellor: Most Rev. Zenon Grocholewski; President: Rev. Msgr. Valentin Miserachs Grau.
Pontifical Institute of Christian Archeology—Founded in 1925. Address: Via Napoleone III 1, 00185 Rome, Italy. Grand Chancellor: Most Rev. Zenon Grocholewski; Rector: Prof. Philippe Pergola.
Pontifical Theological Faculty of St. Bonaventure—Erected in 1935. Address: Via del Serafico 1, 00142 Rome, Italy. Grand Chancellor: Very Rev. Gianfranco Gardin, O.F.M.Conv., Minister General of the Order of Friars Minor Conventual; President: Rev. Orlando Todisco, O.F.M.Conv.
Pontifical Theological Faculty "Teresianum"—Founded in 1935. Address: Piazza S. Pancrazio 5-A, 00152 Rome, Italy. Grand Chancellor: Very Rev. Camilo Maccise, O.C.D., Prepositor General of the Discalced Carmelites; President: Rev. Bruno Moriconi, O.C.D.
Pontifical Theological Faculty "Marianum"—Founded in 1955. Address: Viale 30 Aprile 6, 00153 Rome, Italy. Grand Chancellor: Rev. Hubert Moons, Prior General of the Servites; President: Very Rev. Ignacio M. Calabuig Adan.
Pontifical University of the Holy Cross—Erected on January 9, 1990. Address: Piazza S. Apollinare 49, 00186, Rome, Italy. Grand Chancellor: Most Rev. Bishop Javier Echevarria Rodriguez; Rector: Rev. Lluis Clavell Ortiz-Repiso.

SEMINARIES AND NATIONAL COLLEGES IN ROME

Pontifical Roman Major Seminary—Founded in 1565 by Pius IV. Address: Piazza S. Giovanni in Laterano 4, 00184 Rome, Italy. Rev. Msgr. Pietro Fragnelli, Rector.
Pontifical Roman Minor Seminary—Address: Viale Vaticano 42, 00165 Rome, Italy. Rev. Msgr. Paolo Selvadagi, Rector.
French Seminary (Pontifical)—Founded on October 2, 1853. Address: Via di S. Chiara 42, 00186, Rome, Italy. Rev. Bernard Tenailleau, Rector.
Lombard Seminary of SS. Ambrose and Charles (Pontifical)—Founded in 1863. Address: Piazza S. Maria Maggiore 5, 00185 Rome, Italy. Rev. Msgr. Diego Coletti, Rector.
North American College (Pontifical)—Corporate Title: *The American College of the Roman Catholic Church of the United States*. A Maryland Corporation. Founded in 1859 by Pope Pius IX. Postal Address: Via del Gianicolo 14, 00120 Vatican City State, Europe. Rev. Msgr. Timothy M. Dolan, Rector. (See AMERICAN COLLEGES ABROAD on the next page for further details.)
Armenian College (Pontifical)—Founded on March 1, 1883. Address: Salita S. Nicola da Tolentino 17, 00187 Rome, Italy. Rev. Elia Yeghiayan, Rector.
Beda College (Pontifical)—Founded in 1852; separated from the English College in 1917. Address: Viale San Paolo 18, 00146 Rome, Italy. Rev. Charles R. Strange, Rector.
Belgian College (Pontifical)—Founded in 1844. Rev. Address: Via G.B. Pagano 35, 00167 Rome, Italy. Rev. Johan Bonny, Rector.
Canadian College (Pontifical)—Founded in 1888. Address: Via Crescenzio 75, 00193 Rome, Italy. Rev. Martin Belanger, P.S.S., Rector.
Capranica College (Almo)—Founded in 1457 by Cardinal Capranica. Address: Piazza Capranica 98, 00186 Rome, Italy. Rev. Msgr. Michele Pennisi, Rector.
Ethiopian College (Pontifical)—Founded on October 1, 1919. Address: 00120 Citta del Vaticano, Europe. Rev. P. Teodoro Ghebretensae, Rector.
German-Hungarian College (Pontifical)—Founded on October 28, 1552. Address: Via S. Nicola da Tolentino 13, 00187 Rome, Italy. Rev. Gerwin Komma, S.J., Rector.
Greek College (Pontifical)—Founded on January 13, 1577. Address: Via del Babuino 149, 00187 Rome, Italy. Very Rev. Ambrogio Dolfini, O.S.B., Rector.
English College (Venerabile)—Founded on April 23, 1578. Address: Via Monserrato 45, 00186 Rome, Italy. Rev. Msgr. Patrick Michael Kilgarriff, Rector.
Irish College (Pontifical)—Founded in 1628. Address: Via dei Ss. Quattro 1, 00184 Rome, Italy. Rev. Msgr. John Fleming, Rector.
Lithuanian College (Pontifical)—Founded in 1946. Address: Via Casalmonferrato 20, 00182 Rome, Italy. Rev. Msgr. Antanas Algimantas Bartkus, Rector.
Maronite College—Founded on June 17, 1584. Address: Via Porta Pinciana 14, 00187 Rome, Italy.
Nepomucene College (Pontifical)—Address: Via Concordia 1, 00183 Rome, Italy. Rev. Jan Mraz, Rector.
Philippine College (Pontifical)—Founded on June 29, 1961. Address: Via Aurelia 490, 00165 Rome, Italy. Rev. Msgr. Ruperto C. Santos, Rector.
Pius XI Dutch College (Pontifical)—Founded on October 26, 1930. Address: Via Ercole Rosa 1, 00153 Rome, Italy. Rev. Rudolphus Smit, Rector.
Brazilian College (Pontifical)—Founded in 1934 by Pius XI. Address: Via Aurelia 527, 00165 Rome, Italy. Very Rev. Matias Martinho Lenz, S.J., Rector.
Latin American College (Pio Latino Americano) (Pontifical)—Founded in 1858. Address: Via Aurelia Antica 408, 00165 Rome, Italy. Rev. Luis Palomera, S.J., Rector.
Polish College (Pontifical)—Founded on March 9, 1866. Address: Piazza Remuria 2-A, 00153 Rome, Italy. Rev. Msgr. Marian Rola, Rector.
Portuguese College (Pontifical)—Founded on October 28, 1900. Address: Via Nicolo V 3, 00165 Rome, Italy. Rev. Msgr. Jose Tomas Amandio, Rector.
Russian College of S. Theresa of the Child Jesus (Pontifical)—Founded on August 15, 1929. Address: Via Carlo Cattaneo 2, 00185 Rome, Italy. Rev. Richard Cemus, S.J., Rector.
Ukrainian College of Saint Josephat (Pontifical)— Founded in 1897. Address: Passeggiata del Gianicolo 7, 00165 Rome, Italy. Rev. Genesio Viomar, O.S.B.M., Rector.
College of St. Jerome of the Croatians (Pontifical)—Founded on August 1, 1901. Address: Via Tomacelli 132, 00186 Rome, Italy. Rev. Msgr. Jure Bogdan.
St. Thomas Aquinas—Founded in 1948. Address: Via Degli Ibernesi 20, 00184 Rome, Italy. Very Rev. Glenn Morris, O.P., Rector.
Scots College (Pontifical)—Founded on December 5, 1600. Address: Via Cassia 481, 00189 Rome, Italy. Rev. Christopher Joseph McElroy, Rector.
Spanish College (Pontifical)—Founded on April 1, 1892. Address: Via Di Torrerrossa 2, 00165 Rome, Italy. Rev. Lope Rubio Parrado, Rector.
Teutonic College (S. Maria dell'Anima)—Founded in 1859. Address: Via della Pace 20, 00186 Rome, Italy. Rev. Msgr. Richard Mathes, Rector.
Teutonic College (S. Maria in Camposanto), for the study of Sacred Archaeology and Ecclesiastical History—Founded on November 21, 1876. Address: Via della Sagrestia 17, 00120 Citta del Vaticano, Europe. Rev. Msgr. Erwin Gatz, Rector.
Polish Ecclesiastical Institute (Pontifical)—Founded in 1910. Address: Via Pietro Cavallini 38, 00193 Rome, Italy. Rev. Zbigniew Kiernikowski, Rector.
American Church. Santa Susanna—Address: Via Venti Settembre 15, Postal Address: Via Antonio Salandra 6, 00187 Rome, Italy. Tel: 011 39 6 488.2748; Fax: 011 39 6 474.0236. Very Rev. Paul G. Robichaud, C.S.P., Rector; Rev. Gregory Apparcel, C.S.P., Vice Rector; Rev. Dennis W. Hickey, C.S.P., Vice Rector.

AMERICAN COLLEGES ABROAD

American College. Louvain, Belgium. Corporate title: The American College of the Immaculate Conception, Catholic University of Louvain, a corporation of the District of Columbia. Founded in 1857, the American College is the oldest national seminary operated under the auspices of a special committee of the National Conference of Catholic Bishops. Most Rev. Edward Braxton, S.T.D., Ph.D., Chairman. Postal Address: Naamsestraat 100, B-3000 Leuven, Belgium. Tel: 32.16.32.00.11; Fax: 32.16.32.00.12.

Faculty and Staff: Very Rev. David E. Windsor, C.M., Psy. D., Rector/Pres.; Rev. Michael Nash, S.T.B., J.C.L., Vice Rector-Recruitment; Rev. Kevin A. Codd, S.T.B., M.A., Vice Rector-Formation; Mr. Stephen Zavesky, Vice Pres.-Finance; Rev. Francis Reilly, S.T.B., M.A., Dir.-Spiritual Formation; Rev. Aurelius Boberek, O.S.B., S.T.B., M.A., Dir.-Liturgy and Homiletics; Rev. P. Wallace Platt, C.S.B., M.A., LesL., Ph.D., Dir.-Pastoral Formation & Admissions; Rev. Jan Lambrecht, S.J., S.T.D., Theological Advisor; Rev. Stephen Banet, S.T.B., M.A., Pastor-Our Lady of Mercy Parish, Brussels.

The American College operates four major programs, all in the English language, in conjunction with the Institute of Philosophy, the Faculty of Theology and the Faculty of Canon Law of the Katholieke Universiteit te Leuven (K.U. Leuven) and of the Universite Catholique de Louvain (U.C.L.). These are The Seminary Program of Priestly Formation both on the level of Philosophy, Pre-theology and Theology; The Graduate Studies Programs in Canon Law, Theology and Philosophy; monthly and semester Sabbatical Programs and a summer session for ministerial renewal.

Office for Development and Recruitment for the American College of Louvain—Postal Address: The Americal College, USCC/NCCB 3211 Fourth St., N.E., Washington, DC 20017-1194. Tel: 202-541-3108; Fax: 202-541-3133. E-mail: admissions@acl.be or szavesky@acl.be

The American College founded and remains associated with the English-speaking Parish of Our Lady of Mercy in the Brussels area. Parish Postal Address: 64 Avenue Reine Astrid 1410, Waterloo, Belgium. Tel: 32.2.354.5343; Fax: 32.2.351.2314.

North American College, Rome, Italy. (Pontifical)— Corporate Title: *The American College of the Roman Catholic Church of the United States.* A Maryland Corporation. Operates under the auspices of a special committee of the National Conference of Catholic Bishops. Chairman: Most Reverend Donald A. Cronin. Founded in 1859 by Pope Pius IX, the express purpose being to bring American seminarians and student priests into close association with the Holy See. Seminarians live and take their priestly formation at the College, while studying at the theological universities in Rome. Three major departments: Seminary, Graduate and Institute for Continuing Theological Education.

Postal Address: North American College, 00120 Vatican City State, Europe. Rev. Msgr. Timothy M. Dolan, Rector; Rev. Msgr. Kevin C. McCoy, Vice Rector for Administration.

Seminary Department: Postal Address: North American College, 00120 Vatican City State, Europe. Tel: (011 39 06) 684-931; Fax: (011 39 06) 686-7561; E-mail: pnac@nac.it; Student Fax: (011 39 06) 686-9665. Rev. Msgr. Timothy M. Dolan, Rector; Rev. William J. Waltersheid, Vice Rector for Community Life; Rev. Michael J. Curran, Dir.-Studies & Admissions; Rev. Msgr. James P. Cassidy, Dir.-Counseling; Rev. Thomas H. Radloff, S.J., Spiritual Dir.; Rev. Patrick S. Brennan, Spiritual Dir.; Rev. Joseph C. Henchey, C.S.S., Spiritual Dir.; Rev. Msgr. Charles W. Elmer, Spiritual Dir.; Rev. Gabriel O'Donnell, O.P., Spiritual Dir. & Dir.-Liturgy & Music; Rev. Msgr. J. Mark Williams, Dir.-Homiletics & Asst. Vice Rector; Rev. Thomas A. Milota, Dir.-Pastoral & Apostolic Formation; Sr. Rebecca Abel, O.S.B., Librarian; Sr. Benedicta Clauss, O.S.B., Speech Tutor; Rev. Msgr. Daniel E. Thomas, in residence. Students 175, representing 76 Dioceses and Archdioceses.

Institute for Continuing Theological Education: Postal Address: North American College, 00120 Vatican City State, Europe. Tel: (011 39 06) 687-1529; Fax: (011 39 06) 686-7561; E-mail: romeshabat@pcn.net. Rev. Msgr. Mark A. Svarczkopf, Dir. Fall & Spring 12-week sabbatical sessions for priests. Participants 38.

Graduate Department: Casa Santa Maria, Postal Address: Via dell'Umilta 30, 00187 Rome, Italy. Tel: (011 39 06) 690-011; Fax: (011 39 06) 69-00-18-23. Residence of North American College for post-graduate priests from the United States. Rev. Msgr. Steven J. Raica, Supr.; Rev. Msgr. Richard Mahowald, P.A., Spiritual Dir.; Sr. Mary Carol Kinghorn, Librarian. Graduate priests 80, representing 55 Dioceses and Archdioceses.

Bishops' Office for United States Visitors to the Vatican: Postal Address: Via dell'Umilta 30, 00187 Rome, Italy. Tel: (011 39 06)690-011; Fax: (011 39 06)679-1448. Request for attendance at Papal audiences and similar functions may be addressed to this office. Rev. Msgr. Roger C. Roensch, Dir.

Office for Development of the North American College: Postal Address: 3211 Fourth St., N.E., Washington, DC 20017-1194. Tel: 202-541-5403; Fax: 202-722-8804. E-mail: Nacrome@aol.com. Ms. Tricia Morrin, Dir.-Development.

The Apostolic Nunciature

Established As Apostolic Delegation January 24, 1893; Nunciature January 10, 1984.

Address: 3339 Massachusetts Ave., N.W., Washington, DC 20008-3687. Tel: 202-333-7121. Fax: 202-337-4036.

APOSTOLIC NUNCIO TO THE UNITED STATES

His Excellency
The Most Reverend

GABRIEL MONTALVO, J.C.D.
Titular Archbishop of Celene
Apostolic Nuncio

Born in Santafe de Bogota, Colombia, January 27, 1930; ordained a priest for the Archdiocese of Santafe de Bogota, January 18, 1953. Entered the diplomatic service of the Holy See in 1957; served in Bolivia, Argentina, and El Salvador; from 1964 through 1974 he served at the Secretariat of State, section for Eastern European Countries. On June 14, 1974, he was appointed Apostolic Nuncio to Nicaragua and to Honduras. Received the Episcopal Ordination by His Holiness Pope Paul VI on June 30, 1974. He was named in 1980 Apostolic Pro-Nuncio in Algeria and Tunisia and Apostolic Delegate in Libya. In 1982 he was chosen as a Member of the Papal Mediation Office for resolving the controversy between Argentina and Chile, and then to head the same Office. On June 12, 1986 he was appointed Apostolic Pro-Nuncio to Yugoslavia and remained in Belgrade until May 1996. In the meantime he was named as the first Apostolic Nuncio to Belarus on April 17, 1993. On March 20, 1993 he was appointed President of the Pontifical Ecclesiastical Academy. On December 7, 1998, Pope John Paul II appointed him Apostolic Nuncio to the United States and Permanent Observer of the Holy See to the Organization of American States.

Rev. Msgr. Angelo Becciu, J.C.D., S.T.L. *First Counselor*; Rev. Msgr. Francis Cao Minh-Dung, S.T.D., J.C.L., *Counselor*; Rev. Msgr. Peter G. Magee, J.C.D., S.T.L., *Counselor*.

Rev. Msgr. Salvatore R. Matano, PA, S.T.L., J.C.D., *Secretary*; Rev. Msgr. John H. Maksymowicz, S.T.L., *Secretary*; Rev. Thomas F. Petrillo, M.A., Ed.D.Cand., *Secretary.*

Former Apostolic Delegates:

His Eminence Francesco Cardinal Satolli	1893-1896
His Eminence Sebastiano Cardinal Martinelli	1896-1902
His Eminence Diomede Cardinal Falconio	1902-1911
His Eminence Giovanni Cardinal Bonzano	1911-1922
His Eminence Pietro Cardinal Fumasoni-Biondi	1922-1933
His Eminence Amleto G. Cardinal Cicognani	1933-1958
His Eminence Egidio Cardinal Vagnozzi	1958-1967
His Eminence Luigi Cardinal Raimondi	1967-1973
His Excellency Most Reverend Jean Jadot	1973-1980
His Eminence Pio Cardinal Laghi	1980-1984

Apostolic Pro-Nuncios:

His Eminence Pio Cardinal Laghi	1984-1990
His Eminence Agostino Cardinal Cacciavillan	1990-1998

Apostolic Nuncios:

His Excellency Most Reverend Gabriel Montalvo	1998—

The Permanent Observer Mission of the Holy See to the United Nations

Established January 26, 1964

Address: 25 E. 39th St., New York, NY 10016-0903. 212-370-9614. Fax: 212-370-9622. E-mail: hsmisson@holyseemission.org.

PERMANENT OBSERVER OF THE HOLY SEE TO THE UNITED NATIONS

His Excellency
The Most Reverend

RENATO R. MARTINO, J.C.D., D.D.
Titular Archbishop of Segerme
Apostolic Nuncio

Born in Salerno, Italy on November 23, 1932; ordained for the Archdiocese of Salerno, June 20, 1957; Entered the diplomatic service of the Holy See July 1, 1962; Served in Nicaragua 1962-64; Philippines 1964-66; Lebanon 1966-70; Canada 1975-78; Brazil 1978-80; From 1970 to 1975, he was head of the Department for International Organizations in the Vatican Secretariat of State. Appointed Apostolic Pro-Nuncio to Thailand and named Titular Archbishop of Segerme September 14, 1980. Ordained a Bishop on December 14, 1980. Served as Apostolic Pro-Nuncio to Thailand from 1980-86 and also as Apostolic Delegate to Singapore, Malaysia, Laos and Brunei. Apostolic Pro-Nuncio to Singapore June 24, 1981. Appointed Permanent Observer of the Holy See to the United Nations December 3, 1986. Office Address: 25 East 39th St., New York, NY 10016-0903. Tel: 212-370-7885; Fax: 212-370-9622. E-mail: hsmisson@holyseemission.org. Residential Address: 20 East 72nd St., New York, NY 10021-4196. Tel: 212-734-2900; Fax: 212-988-3633.

Rev. Msgr. Francis Chullikatt, S.S.D., S.T.L., L.C.L., *Counsellor;* Rev. Msgr. Marek Zalewski, S.T.D., *1st Secretary*; Rev. Msgr. James M. Reinert, Ph.D, *Attache*; Rev. Msgr. Anthony R. Frontiero, M.A., S.T.L., S.T.D. Cand., *Attache;* Mr. Karol Krcmery, *Attache*; Ms. Olivetta Danese, *Attache*; Ms. Ikuji Yo, *Attache*.

Former Permanent Observers:

Rev. Msgr. Alberto Giovannetti, J.C.D.	1964-1973
His Eminence Giovanni Cardinal Cheli	1973-1986

PART II
Alphabetical List of Places in the United States

This comprehensive list includes all cities and towns in the United States in which a Catholic Institution is located.

The abbreviations identify each city or town to the corresponding Diocese or Archdiocese.

Abbeville, LA	LAF
SC	CHR
Abbotsford, WI	LC
Abbott, TX	FWT
Abbottstown, PA	HBG
Aberdeen, ID	B
MD	BAL
MS	JKS
SD	SFS
WA	SEA
Abilene, KS	SAL
TX	SAN
Abingdon, IL	PEO
MD	BAL
VA	RIC
Abington, MA	BO
PA	PH
Abiquiu, NM	SFE
Abita Springs, LA	NO
Abrams, WI	GB
Absecon, NJ	CAM
Ackley, IA	DUB
Acme, MI	GAY
Acoma, NM	GLP
Acosta, PA	ALT
Acton, MA	BO
Acushnet, MA	FR
Ada, MI	GR
MN	CR
OH	COL
OK	OKL
Adair, IA	DM
Adams, MA	SPR
MN	WIN
NY	OG
WI	LC
Adamstown, MD	BAL
Addison, IL	JOL
NY	ROC
Adel, IA	DM
Adelanto, CA	SB
Adell, WI	MIL
Adelphi, MD	WDC
Adena, OH	STU
Adjuntas, PR	PCE
Adona, AR	LR
Adrian, MI	LAN
MN	WIN
Advance, MO	SPC
Affton, MO	STL
Afton, IA	DM
MI	GAY
Agana, GU	AGN
Agana Heights, GU	AGN
Agat, GU	AGN
Agawam, MA	SPR
Agoura Hills, CA	LA
Agua Dulce, TX	CC
Aguada, PR	MGZ
Aguadilla, PR	MGZ
Aguas Buenas, PR	CGS
Aguilar, CO	PBL
Aguirre, PR	PCE
Ahmeek, MI	MAR
Ahoskie, NC	R
Aibonito, PR	CGS
Aiea, HI	HON
Aiken, SC	CHR
Ainsworth, NE	GI
Aitkin, MN	DUL
Ajo, AZ	TUC
Akeley, MN	CR
Akron, CO	DEN
IA	SC
NY	BUF
OH	CLV
OH	NTN
OH	PRM
OH	SJP
Alakanuk, AK	FBK
Alameda, CA	OAK
Alamo, TX	BWN
Alamogordo, NM	LSC

Alamosa, CO	PBL
Albany, GA	SAV
KY	L
LA	BR
MN	SCL
NY	ALB
OR	P
TX	FWT
WI	MAD
Albee, MI	SAG
Albemarle, NC	CHL
Albers, IL	BEL
Albert Lea, MN	WIN
Alberta, AL	MOB
Albertville, MN	STP
Albia, IA	DAV
Albion, IN	FTW
MI	KAL
NE	OM
NY	BUF
PA	E
Albuquerque, NM	SFE
NM	VNN
Alburg, VT	BUR
Alcoa, TN	KNX
Alden, NY	BUF
Alden Station, PA	PHU
Aledo, IL	PEO
Aleppo, KS	WCH
Aleppo Township, PA	PIT
Alexander, IL	SFD
Alexander City, AL	BIR
Alexandria, IN	LFT
KY	COV
LA	ALX
MN	SCL
SD	SFS
VA	ARL
Alexandria Bay, NY	OG
Alexis, IL	PEO
Alfred, ME	PRT
NY	BUF
Algoma, WI	GB
Algona, IA	SC
Algonac, MI	DET
Algonquin, IL	RCK
Alhambra, CA	LA
Alhambra, Ponce, PR	PCE
Alice, ND	FAR
TX	CC
Aliquippa, PA	PBR
PA	PIT
PA	SJP
Aliso Viejo, CA	ORG
Allegan, MI	KAL
Allegany, NY	BUF
Allegany State Park, NY	BUF
Allen, TX	DAL
Allen Park, MI	DET
MI	PRM
Allendale, NJ	NEW
Allenspark, CO	DEN
Allenstown, NH	MAN
Allenton, MI	DET
WI	MIL
Allentown, NJ	TR
PA	ALN
PA	PHU
PA	PSC
Alliance, NE	GI
OH	ROM
OH	Y
Allison, IA	DUB
Allison Park, PA	PIT
Alma, KS	KCK
MI	SAG
MN	CR
NE	LIN
WI	LC
Alma Center, WI	LC
Almena, WI	SUP
Almond, NY	BUF
WI	LC

Aloha, OR	P
Aloys, NE	OM
Alpena, MI	GAY
Alpha, MI	MAR
NJ	MET
Alphareta, GA	ATL
Alpharetta, GA	ATL
Alpine, AZ	GLP
CA	SD
MI	GR
TX	ELP
Alsip, IL	CHI
Alta Loma, CA	SB
Alta Vista, IA	DUB
Altadena, CA	LA
Altamont, IL	SFD
NY	ALB
Altamonte Springs, FL	ORL
Altdorf, WI	LC
Alton, IA	SC
IL	SFD
NH	MAN
TX	BWN
Altona, NY	OG
Altoona, IA	DM
PA	ALT
PA	SJP
WI	LC
Altura, MN	WIN
Alturas, CA	SAC
Altus, AR	LR
OK	OKL
Alva, FL	VEN
OK	OKL
Alvada, OH	TOL
Alverno, MI	GAY
WI	GB
Alvin, TX	GAL
Alviso, CA	SJ
Ama, LA	NO
Amargosa Valley, NV	LAV
Amarillo, TX	AMA
Amberg, WI	GB
Ambler, PA	PH
Amboy, IL	RCK
Ambridge, PA	PBR
PA	PIT
PA	SJP
Amelia, LA	HT
OH	CIN
VA	RIC
Amenia, NY	NY
American Canyon, CA	SR
American Falls, ID	B
American Fork, UT	SLC
Americus, GA	SAV
Amery, WI	SUP
Ames, IA	DUB
TX	BEA
Amesbury, MA	BO
Amherst, MA	SPR
NY	BUF
NY	PSC
OH	CLV
VA	RIC
WI	LC
Amite, LA	BR
Amity, OR	P
Amityville, NY	BRK
NY	RVC
Ammannsville, TX	VIC
Amory, MS	JKS
Amsterdam, NY	ALB
NY	STF
OH	STU
Anaconda, MT	HEL
Anacortes, WA	SEA
Anacostia, Washington, DC	WDC
Anadarko, OK	OKL
Anaheim, CA	OLL
CA	ORG
CA	VNN
Anahuac, TX	BEA

Anamoose, ND	FAR
Anamosa, IA	DUB
Anasco, PR	MGZ
Anchorage, AK	ANC
AK	VNN
Anchorville, MI	DET
Andale, KS	WCH
Andalusia, AL	MOB
IL	PEO
Anderson, CA	SAC
IN	LFT
SC	CHR
TX	GAL
Andice, TX	AUS
Andover, MA	BO
NJ	PAT
NY	BUF
OH	Y
SD	SFS
Andrew, IA	DUB
Andrews, NC	CHL
TX	SAN
Aneta, ND	FAR
Angelica, NY	BUF
Angels Camp, CA	STO
Angelus, KS	SAL
Angleton, TX	GAL
Angola, IN	FTW
NY	BUF
Aniak, AK	FBK
Anita, IA	DM
PA	E
Aniwa, WI	GB
Ankeny, IA	DM
Ann Arbor, MI	LAN
MI	OLL
Anna, IL	BEL
Annandale, MN	STP
VA	ARL
VA	PSC
Annapolis, MD	BAL
Annawan, IL	PEO
Anniston, AL	BIR
Annville, PA	HBG
Anoka, MN	STP
Anselmo, NE	GI
Anson, TX	LUB
Ansonia, CT	HRT
CT	STF
Antelope, CA	SAC
Anthon, IA	SC
Anthony, KS	WCH
NM	LSC
Antigo, WI	GB
Antioch, CA	OAK
IL	CHI
TN	NSH
Antlers, OK	TLS
Anton Chico, NM	SFE
Antonino, KS	SAL
Antwerp, OH	TOL
Anza, CA	SB
Apache Junction, AZ	TUC
Apalachicola, FL	PT
Apalachin, NY	ROC
Apex, NC	R
Apison, TN	KNX
Apollo, PA	GBG
Apopka, FL	ORL
FL	SJP
Apple Creek, MO	STL
Apple River, IL	RCK
Apple Valley, CA	SB
Applegate, CA	SAC
Appleton, MN	NU
WI	GB
Appomattox, VA	RIC
Aptos, CA	MRY
Aquadilla, PR	MGZ
Arabi, LA	NO
Aragon, NM	GLP
Aransas Pass, TX	CC
Arbor Vitae, WI	SUP

Arcade, NY	BUF
Arcadia, CA	LA
FL	VEN
IA	SC
PA	PBR
WI	LC
Arcata, CA	SR
Archbald, PA	SCR
Archbold, OH	TOL
Arco, ID	B
Arcola, IL	SFD
IN	FTW
Arden, NC	CHL
Ardmore, OK	OKL
PA	PH
Ardoch, ND	FAR
Ardon, IA	DAV
Ardsley, NY	NY
PA	PH
Arecibo, PR	ARE
Arenzville, IL	SFD
Argo, IL	CHI
Argonne, WI	GB
Argusville, ND	FAR
Argyle, MI	SAG
MN	CR
MO	JC
WI	MAD
Arkadelphia, AR	LR
Arkansas City, KS	WCH
Arkansaw, WI	LC
Arleta, CA	LA
Arlington, IL	PEO
MA	BO
MN	NU
OR	BAK
SD	SFS
TX	FWT
VA	ARL
VT	BUR
WA	SEA
Arlington Heights, IL	CHI
Arma, KS	WCH
Armada, MI	DET
Armonk, NY	NY
Armour, SD	SFS
Armstrong, IA	SC
WI	MIL
Armstrong Creek, WI	GB
Arnaudville, LA	LAF
Arnheim, OH	CIN
Arnold, MO	STL
PA	GBG
Arpin, WI	LC
Arroyo, PR	PCE
Arroyo Grande, CA	MRY
Arroyo Seco, NM	SFE
Artesia, CA	LA
NM	LSC
Artesian, SD	SFS
Arvada, CO	DEN
Arvin, CA	FRS
Asan, GU	AGN
Asbury, NJ	MET
Asbury Park, NJ	TR
Ashburn, VA	ARL
Ashburnham, MA	WOR
Asheboro, NC	CHL
Asherton, TX	LAR
Asheville, NC	CHL
Ashford, CT	NOR
WI	MIL
Ashkum, IL	JOL
Ashland, AL	BIR
IL	SFD
KS	DOD
KY	LEX
MA	BO
ME	PRT
MT	GF
NE	LIN
NH	MAN
OH	CLV
OR	P
PA	ALN
VA	RIC
WI	SUP
Ashland City, TN	NSH
Ashley, ND	FAR
PA	SCR
Ashtabula, OH	PBR
OH	Y
Ashton, IA	SC
WI	MAD
Ashville, PA	ALT
Askeaton, WI	GB
Aspen, CO	DEN
Aspinwall, PA	PIT
Assinins, MI	MAR
Assonet, MA	FR
Assumption, IL	SFD

OH	TOL
Aston, PA	PH
Astoria, NY	BRK
NY	ROM
OR	P
Atascadero, CA	MRY
Atchison, KS	KCK
Atco, NJ	CAM
Athens, AL	BIR
GA	ATL
GA	SCR
IL	SFD
NY	ALB
OH	STU
PA	SCR
TN	KNX
TX	TYL
WI	LC
WV	WH
Atherton, CA	SFR
Athol, MA	WOR
SD	SFS
Athol Springs, NY	BUF
Atkins, AR	LR
Atkinson, IL	PEO
NE	OM
Atlanta, GA	ATL
GA	NTN
GA	SAM
MI	GAY
TX	TYL
Atlantic, IA	DM
Atlantic Beach, FL	STA
Atlantic City, NJ	CAM
Atlantic Highlands, NJ	TR
Atmore, AL	MOB
Attica, IN	LFT
NY	BUF
OH	TOL
Attleboro, MA	FR
Attleboro Falls, MA	FR
Atwater, CA	FRS
Atwood, KS	SAL
Au Sable Forks, NY	OG
Auburn, AL	MOB
CA	SAC
IA	SC
IL	SFD
IN	FTW
MA	WOR
ME	PRT
MI	SAG
NE	LIN
NH	MAN
NY	ROC
NY	STF
NY	SY
WA	SEA
WI	MIL
Auburn Hills, MI	DET
Auburndale, WI	LC
Audubon, IA	DM
NJ	CAM
PA	PH
AuGres, MI	SAG
Augusta, GA	NTN
GA	SAV
IA	DAV
KS	WCH
KY	COV
ME	PRT
MO	STL
WI	LC
Ault, CO	DEN
Auriesville, NY	ALB
Aurora, CO	DEN
IL	JOL
IL	RCK
IL	ROM
IN	IND
KS	SAL
KY	OWN
MN	DUL
MO	SPC
NE	LIN
NY	ROC
OH	Y
SD	SFS
WI	GB
Austin, MN	WIN
TX	AUS
TX	OLL
Austintown, OH	SJP
OH	Y
Ava, IL	BEL
MO	SPC
Avalon, CA	LA
NJ	CAM
PA	PIT
Avella, PA	PBR
PA	PIT

Avenal, CA	FRS
Avenel, NJ	MET
Avenue, MD	WDC
Averill Park, NY	ALB
Avilla, IN	FTW
Aviston, IL	BEL
Avoca, IA	DM
PA	SCR
WI	MAD
Avon, CT	HRT
MA	BO
MN	SCL
NJ	TR
NY	ROC
OH	CLV
Avon Lake, OH	CLV
Avon Park, FL	VEN
Avondale, AZ	PHX
CO	PBL
LA	NO
Avonmore, PA	GBG
Awak, FM	CI
Awak, Pohnpei, FM	CI
Axtel, KY	OWN
Axtell, KS	KCK
Ayer, MA	BO
Aztec, NM	GLP
Azusa, CA	LA
Babbitt, MN	DUL
Babcock, WI	LC
Babeldaob, FM	CI
Babylon, NY	BRK
NY	RVC
Bad Axe, MI	SAG
Baden, MD	WDC
PA	PIT
Badger, MN	CR
Bagdad, AZ	PHX
Bagley, MN	CR
Bailey, CO	COS
Baileys Harbor, WI	GB
Baileyville, KS	KCK
ME	PRT
Bainbridge, GA	SAV
NY	SY
Bainbridge Island, WA	SEA
Bairdford, PA	PIT
Baker, LA	BR
MT	GF
OR	BAK
Baker City, OR	BAK
Bakersfield, CA	FRS
Bakerton, PA	ALT
Bakerville, WI	LC
Bal Harbour, FL	MIA
Bala Cynwyd, PA	PH
Baldwin, KS	KCK
LA	LAF
MI	GR
NY	RVC
Baldwin Boro, PA	PIT
Baldwin Park, CA	LA
Baldwinsville, NY	SY
Baldwinville, MA	WOR
Balfour, ND	FAR
Ball Club, MN	DUL
Ballinger, TX	SAN
Ballouville, CT	NOR
Ballston Lake, NY	ALB
Ballston Spa, NY	ALB
Balltown, IA	DUB
Ballwin, MO	STL
Bally, PA	ALN
Balmorhea, TX	ELP
Balsam Lake, WI	SUP
Balta, ND	FAR
Baltic, CT	NOR
Baltimore, MD	BAL
MD	PHU
MD	PSC
Bancroft, IA	SC
NE	OM
Bandera, TX	SAT
Bandon, OR	P
Bangall, NY	NY
Bangor, ME	PRT
MI	KAL
PA	ALN
WI	LC
Bankston, IA	DUB
Banning, CA	SB
Bannister, MI	SAG
Bantam, CT	HRT
Bapchule, AZ	PHX
Baptistown, NJ	MET
Bar Harbor, ME	PRT
Baraboo, WI	MAD
Baraga, MI	MAR
Barbeau, MI	MAR
Barberton, OH	CLV
OH	PRM

Barbourville, KY	LEX
Barceloneta, PR	ARE
Barclay, IA	DUB
Bardonia, NY	NY
Bardstown, KY	L
Bardwell, KY	OWN
Barefoot Bay, FL	ORL
Baring, MO	JC
Bark River, MI	MAR
Barker, NY	BUF
Barling, AR	LR
Barnegat, NJ	TR
Barnesboro, PA	ALT
Barnesville, MD	WDC
MN	CR
OH	STU
PA	ALN
Barneveld, WI	MAD
Barnum, IA	SC
Barranquitas, PR	CGS
Barre, MA	WOR
VT	BUR
Barrenspot, VI	STV
Barrett Station, TX	GAL
Barrigada, GU	AGN
Barrington, IL	CHI
NJ	CAM
RI	PRO
Barrio Bairoa, PR	CGS
Barrio Hormigas, PR	CGS
Barrio Rio Canas, PR	CGS
Barron, WI	SUP
Barrow, AK	FBK
Barry, IL	SFD
MN	NU
Barrytown, NY	NY
Barryville, NY	NY
Barstow, CA	SB
Bartelso, IL	BEL
Bartlesville, OK	TLS
Bartlett, IL	CHI
Barton, OH	STU
VT	BUR
Bartonville, IL	PEO
Bartow, FL	ORL
Basalt, CO	DEN
Bascom, OH	TOL
Basehor, KS	KCK
Basile, LA	LAF
Basking Ridge, NJ	MET
Bass Lake, CA	FRS
Bassfield, MS	BLX
Bastress, PA	SCR
Bastrop, LA	SHP
TX	AUS
Batavia, IL	RCK
NY	BUF
OH	CIN
Batchtown, IL	SFD
Batesburg, SC	CHR
Batesville, AR	LR
IN	IND
MS	JKS
Bath, ME	PRT
NY	ROC
NY	STF
PA	ALN
Bathgate, ND	FAR
Baton Rouge, LA	BR
LA	OLL
Battle Creek, MI	KAL
NE	OM
Battle Ground, WA	SEA
Battle Lake, MN	SCL
Battle Mountain, NV	RNO
Baudette, MN	CR
Bauer, IA	DAV
Baxter Springs, KS	WCH
Bay City, MI	PRM
MI	SAG
TX	VIC
Bay Head, NJ	TR
Bay Mills, MI	MAR
Bay Minette, AL	MOB
Bay Point, CA	OAK
Bay St. Louis, MS	BLX
Bay Settlement, WI	GB
Bay Shore, MI	GAY
NY	RVC
Bay Village, OH	CLV
Bayamon, PR	SJN
Bayard, IA	DM
NM	LSC
Bayfield, WI	SUP
Bayonne, NJ	NEW
NJ	PHU
NJ	PSC
Bayou Black, LA	HT
Bayou George, FL	PT
Bayou LaBatre, AL	MOB
Bayou Pigeon, LA	BR

Bayou Vista, LA	LAF
Bayport, MN	STP
Bayside, NY	BRK
Baytown, TX	GAL
Bayville, NJ	TR
NY	RVC
Beach, ND	BIS
Beachwood, OH	CLV
Beacon, NY	NY
Beacon Falls, CT	HRT
Beal City, MI	SAG
Beans Cove, PA	ALT
Bear, DE	WIL
Bear Creek, WI	GB
Bear Creek Township, PA	SCR
Bear Valley, WI	LC
Beardsley, KS	SAL
MN	NU
Beardstown, IL	SFD
Beasley, TX	GAL
Beatrice, NE	LIN
Beattie, KS	KCK
Beattyville, KY	LEX
Beaufort, SC	CHR
Beaulieu, MN	CR
Beaumont, CA	SB
TX	BEA
Beaver, KS	DOD
MI	SAG
PA	PBR
PA	PIT
Beaver Crossing, NE	LIN
Beaver Dam, KY	OWN
WI	MIL
Beaver Falls, PA	PIT
Beaver Island, MI	GAY
Beaver Meadows, PA	ALN
PA	PSC
Beaver Prairie, IL	BEL
Beavercreek, OH	CIN
Beaverdale, PA	ALT
PA	PBR
Beaverton, OR	P
Beaverville, IL	JOL
Bechyn, MN	NU
Bechyne, ND	FAR
Beckemeyer, IL	BEL
Becker, MN	SCL
Beckley, WV	WH
Bedford, IA	DM
IN	IND
MA	BO
NH	MAN
NY	NY
OH	CLV
OH	PRM
PA	ALT
TX	FWT
VA	RIC
Bedford Heights, OH	CLV
Bedford Village, NY	NY
Beech Bottom, WV	WH
Beech Grove, IN	IND
Beechview, PA	PIT
Beemer, NE	OM
Beeville, TX	CC
Bejou, MN	CR
Bel Air, MD	BAL
Belchertown, MA	SPR
Belcourt, ND	FAR
Belding, MI	GR
Belen, NM	SFE
Belfast, ME	PRT
NY	BUF
Belfield, ND	BIS
ND	STN
Belgique, MO	STL
Belgium, WI	MIL
Belgrade, MN	NU
MN	SCL
Belington, WV	WH
Bell City, LA	LKC
Bell Gardens, CA	LA
Bella Vista, AR	LR
Bellaire, MI	GAY
OH	STU
Belle, MO	JC
WV	WH
Belle Chasse, LA	NO
Belle Creek, MN	STP
Belle Fontaine, AL	MOB
Belle Fourche, SD	RC
Belle Glade, FL	PMB
Belle Plaine, IA	DUB
MN	STP
Belle Prairie, MN	SCL
Belle River, MN	SCL
Belle Rose, LA	BR
Belle Valley, OH	STU
Belle Vernon, PA	GBG
Belleair Bluffs, FL	SP

Bellechester, MN	STP
Belledeau, LA	ALX
Bellefontaine, OH	CIN
Bellefontaine Neighbors, MO	STL
Bellefonte, DE	WIL
PA	ALT
Bellengham, WA	SEA
Belleview, FL	ORL
IL	SFD
Belleville, IL	BEL
KS	SAL
MI	DET
NJ	NEW
WI	MAD
Bellevue, IA	DUB
KY	COV
MI	LAN
NE	OM
OH	TOL
PA	PIT
WA	SEA
Bellflower, CA	LA
Bellingham, MA	BO
WA	SEA
Bellmawr, NJ	CAM
Bellmore, NY	RVC
Bellows Falls, VT	BUR
Bellport, NY	RVC
Bellville, TX	GAL
Bellwood, IL	CHI
NE	LIN
PA	ALT
Belmar, NJ	TR
Belmond, IA	DUB
Belmont, CA	SFR
MA	BO
MI	GR
NC	CHL
NH	MAN
NY	BUF
WI	MAD
Beloit, KS	SAL
WI	MAD
WI	MIL
Belpre, KS	DOD
OH	STU
Bel-Ridge, MO	STL
Belt, MT	GF
Beltmont, NC	CHL
Belton, MO	KC
TX	AUS
Beltrees, IL	SFD
Beltsville, MD	PSC
MD	WDC
Belvidere, IL	RCK
NJ	MET
Belzoni, MS	JKS
Bement, IL	PEO
Bemidji, MN	CR
Bemus Point, NY	BUF
Ben Avon, PA	PIT
Benavides, TX	CC
The Bend, OH	TOL
Bend, OR	BAK
Bendena, KS	KCK
Benedict, MD	WDC
Benedicta, ME	PRT
Benet Lake, WI	MIL
Benicia, CA	SAC
Benkelman, NE	LIN
Benld, IL	SFD
Bennington, NH	MAN
VT	BUR
Bennington Center, NY	BUF
Bensalem, PA	PH
Bensenville, IL	JOL
Benson, AZ	TUC
IL	PEO
MN	NU
VT	BUR
Bentley Creek, PA	SCR
Bentleyville, PA	PIT
Benton, AR	LR
IL	BEL
MO	SPC
WI	MAD
Benton City, WA	YAK
Benton Harbor, MI	KAL
Bentonville, AR	LR
Benwood, MN	CR
WV	WH
Berea, KY	LEX
OH	CLV
Beresford, SD	SFS
Bergen, NY	BUF
Bergenfield, NJ	NEW
Berger, MO	STL
Berkeley, CA	OAK
MO	STL
Berkeley Heights, NJ	NEW
Berkeley Springs, WV	WH

Berkley, MI	DET
Berlin, MA	WOR
NH	MAN
NJ	CAM
NY	ALB
WI	MAD
Berlinsville, PA	ALN
Bernalillo, NM	SFE
Bernardsville, NJ	MET
Beroun, MN	DUL
Berryville, AR	LR
VA	ARL
Bertha, MN	SCL
Bertram, TX	AUS
Berwick, LA	LAF
ME	PRT
PA	HBG
PA	PHU
Berwyn, IL	CHI
PA	PH
Besancon, IN	FTW
Bessemer, AL	BIR
MI	MAR
PA	PIT
Bethalto, IL	SFD
Bethany, IL	SFD
MO	KC
WV	WH
Bethany Beach, DE	WIL
Bethel, AK	FBK
CT	BGP
OH	CIN
VT	BUR
Bethel Park, PA	PIT
Bethesda, MD	WDC
Bethlehem, CT	HRT
OH	TOL
PA	ALN
PA	PHU
PA	PSC
Bethpage, NY	RVC
Bettendorf, IA	DAV
Beulah, ND	BIS
Bevent, WI	LC
Beverly, MA	BO
NJ	TR
OH	STU
Beverly Hills, CA	LA
FL	SP
MI	DET
Beverly Shores, IN	GRY
Bicknell, IN	EVN
Biddeford, ME	PRT
Biehle, MO	STL
Big Bear Lake, CA	SB
Big Bend, SD	SFS
WI	MIL
Big Clifty, KY	OWN
Big Elbow Lake, MN	CR
Big Lake, LA	LKC
MN	SCL
TX	SAN
Big Long Lake, IN	FTW
Big Pine Key, FL	MIA
Big Rapids, MI	GR
Big River, WI	LC
Big Sandy, MT	GF
Big Spring, TX	SAN
Big Stone City, SD	SFS
Big Stone Gap, VA	RIC
Big Sur, CA	MRY
Big Timber, MT	GF
Big Wells, TX	LAR
TX	SAT
Bigelow, AR	LR
Bigfork, MN	DUL
MT	HEL
Billerica, MA	BO
Billings, MO	SPC
MT	GF
Biloxi, MS	BLX
Bingham, ME	PRT
Binghamton, NY	PSC
NY	SY
Birch Coolie, MN	NU
Birch Run, MI	SAG
Birchwood, WI	SUP
Bird City, KS	SAL
Bird Island, MN	NU
Birdsboro, PA	ALN
Birmingham, AL	BIR
AL	NTN
AL	OLL
MI	DET
Birnamwood, WI	GB
Bisbee, AZ	TUC
ND	FAR
Bishop, CA	FRS
TX	CC
Bishop Creek, IL	SFD
Bismarck, ND	BIS

Bismark, OH	TOL
Bison, OK	OKL
SD	RC
Bissell Hills, MO	STL
Biwabik, MN	DUL
Bixby, OK	TLS
Black Brook, NY	OG
Black Canyon City, AZ	PHX
Black Creek, WI	GB
Black Diamond, WA	SEA
Black Eagle, MT	GF
Black Jack, IL	SFD
Black River, MI	GAY
NY	OG
Black River Falls, WI	LC
Blackduck, MN	CR
Blackfoot, ID	B
Blacksburg, VA	RIC
Blackstone, IL	PEO
MA	WOR
VA	RIC
Blackwell, OK	OKL
Blackwood, NJ	CAM
Bladensburg, MD	WDC
Blaine, KS	KCK
MN	STP
OH	STU
Blair, NE	OM
WI	LC
Blairstown, IA	DUB
NJ	MET
Blairsville, GA	ATL
PA	GBG
Blakely, GA	SAV
Blakeslee, OH	TOL
PA	SCR
Blanchardville, WI	MAD
Blanchester, OH	CIN
Blanco, NM	GLP
TX	AUS
Blasdell, NY	BUF
Blauvelt, NY	NY
Blawnox, PA	PIT
Blenker, WI	LC
Blessing, IA	DUB
TX	VIC
Bliss, NY	BUF
Blissfield, MI	LAN
Bloomer, WI	LC
Bloomfield, CT	HRT
IA	DAV
IN	EVN
NE	OM
NJ	NEW
NM	GLP
Bloomfield Hills, MI	DET
Blooming Prairie, MN	WIN
Bloomingdale, IL	JOL
NY	OG
OH	STU
Bloomington, CA	SB
IL	PEO
IN	IND
MN	STP
TX	VIC
WI	MAD
Bloomsburg, PA	HBG
Bloomsbury, NJ	MET
Bloomsdale, MO	STL
Bloomville, WI	SUP
Blossburg, PA	SCR
Blossom, NY	BUF
Blountstown, FL	PT
Blue Anchor, NJ	CAM
Blue Creek, OH	CIN
Blue Earth, MN	WIN
Blue Grass, IA	DAV
Blue Island, IL	CHI
Blue Point, NY	RVC
Blue Rapids, KS	KCK
Blue Ridge, GA	ATL
Blue Ridge Summit, PA	HBG
Blue Springs, MO	KC
Bluefield, WV	WH
BlueGrass, MN	SCL
Bluffs, IL	SFD
Bluffton, IA	DUB
IN	FTW
MN	SCL
OH	TOL
SC	CHR
Blunt, SD	SFS
Blythe, CA	SB
Blytheville, AR	LR
Boardman, OH	PBR
OH	Y
OR	BAK
Bobtown, PA	PIT
Boca Grande, FL	VEN
Boca Raton, FL	PMB
Bode, IA	SC

Boerne, TX	SAT
Bogalusa, LA	NO
Bogota, NJ	NEW
Bohemia, NY	RVC
Boise, ID	B
Bokeelia, FL	VEN
Bolingbrook, IL	JOL
Bolivar, MO	SPC
NY	BUF
OH	COL
TN	MEM
Boliver, PA	GBG
Bolton, CT	NOR
MA	WOR
Bolton Landing, NY	ALB
Bombay, NY	OG
Bondsville, MA	SPR
Bonesteel, SD	RC
Bonham, TX	DAL
Bonifay, FL	PT
Bonita, CA	LA
CA	SD
Bonita Springs, FL	VEN
Bonne Terre, MO	STL
Bonneauville, PA	HBG
Bonner, MT	HEL
Bonners Ferry, ID	B
Bonnots Mill, MO	JC
Bono, OH	TOL
Boone, IA	SC
NC	CHL
Booneville, AR	LR
MS	JKS
Boonton, NJ	PAT
Boonville, IN	EVN
MO	JC
NY	SY
Boothbay Harbor, ME	PRT
Boothwyn, PA	PH
Bordelonville, LA	ALX
Bordentown, NJ	TR
Borger, TX	AMA
Boron, CA	FRS
Borrego Springs, CA	SD
Boscobel, WI	MAD
Bossier City, LA	SHP
Boston, IN	ROM
MA	ARM
MA	BO
MA	NTN
MA	STF
NY	BUF
Boswell, PA	ALT
Bothell, WA	SEA
Botkins, OH	CIN
Bottineau, ND	FAR
Boulder, CO	DEN
MT	HEL
Boulder City, NV	LAV
Boulder Creek, CA	MRY
Boulder Junction, WI	SUP
Boulevard, CA	SD
Bound Brook, NJ	MET
Bountiful, UT	SLC
Bourbon, MO	JC
Bourbonnais, IL	JOL
Bourg, LA	HT
Bovard, PA	GBG
Bovina, TX	AMA
Bow Valley, NE	OM
Bowbells, ND	BIS
Bowdle, SD	SFS
Bowie, MD	WDC
TX	FWT
Bowling Green, KY	OWN
OH	TOL
Bowlus, MN	SCL
Bowman, ND	BIS
Bowmansville, NY	BUF
Boyce, LA	ALX
Boyceville, WI	LC
Boyd, WI	LC
Boyers, PA	PIT
Boyertown, PA	ALN
Boyes Hot Springs, CA	SR
Boylston, MA	WOR
Boyne City, MI	GAY
Boyne Falls, MI	GAY
Boynton Beach, FL	PMB
Boys Town, NE	OM
Bozeman, MT	HEL
Brackett, WI	LC
Brackettville, TX	SAT
Braddock, PA	PBR
PA	PIT
Braddock Hills, PA	PIT
Bradenton, FL	VEN
Bradenville, PA	PBR
Bradford, IL	PEO
IN	IND
NY	ROC
OH	CIN
PA	E
VT	BUR
Bradley, IL	JOL
ME	PRT
Bradley Beach, NJ	TR
Bradshaw, MD	BAL
Brady, TX	SAN
Brady's Bend, PA	GBG
Braham, MN	SCL
Braidwood, IL	JOL
Brainard, NE	LIN
Brainerd, MN	DUL
Braintree, MA	BO
Branchdale, PA	ALN
Branchville, NJ	PAT
Brandamore, PA	PH
Brandenburg, KY	L
Brandon, FL	SP
MN	SCL
MS	JKS
SD	SFS
VT	BUR
WI	MIL
Brandy Camp, PA	E
Brandywood, DE	WIL
Branford, CT	HRT
FL	STA
Branson, MO	SPC
Brant, NY	BUF
Brant Beach, NJ	TR
Brasher Falls, NY	OG
Brattleboro, VT	BUR
Brawley, CA	SD
Brazil, IN	IND
Brazoria, TX	GAL
Brea, CA	ORG
Breaux Bridge, LA	LAF
Breckenridge, CO	DEN
MN	SCL
TX	FWT
Brecksville, OH	CLV
OH	PRM
Breda, IA	SC
Breese, IL	BEL
Bremen, IN	FTW
ND	FAR
OH	COL
Bremerton, WA	SEA
Bremond, TX	AUS
Brenham, TX	AUS
Brennyville, MN	SCL
Brentwood, CA	OAK
MO	STL
NY	BRK
NY	RVC
PA	PIT
TN	NSH
Brevard, NC	CHL
Brewer, ME	PRT
MO	STL
Brewerton, NY	SY
Brewster, MA	FR
MN	WIN
NY	NY
OH	Y
WA	SPK
Brewton, AL	MOB
Briarcliff Manor, NY	NY
Briarwood, NY	BRK
Brick, NJ	TR
Brick Town, NJ	TR
Bridal Veil, OR	P
Bridge City, LA	NO
TX	BEA
Bridgehampton, NY	RVC
Bridgeport, CT	BGP
CT	PSC
CT	STF
IL	BEL
MI	SAG
NE	GI
NY	SY
OH	STU
PA	PH
PA	PHU
TX	FWT
WA	YAK
WV	WH
Bridger, MT	GF
Bridgeton, MO	SFD
MO	STL
NJ	CAM
Bridgeview, IL	CHI
Bridgeville, PA	PIT
Bridgewater, MA	BO
NJ	MET
SD	SFS
Bridgman, MI	KAL
Bridgton, ME	PRT
Brigantine, NJ	CAM
Briggsville, WI	MAD
Brigham City, UT	SLC
Bright, IN	IND
Brighton, CO	DEN
IL	SFD
MA	BO
MI	LAN
WI	MIL
Brilliant, OH	STU
Brillion, WI	GB
Brimfield, IL	PEO
MA	SPR
Brimley, MI	MAR
Brinkley, AR	LR
Brinktown, MO	JC
Bristol, CT	HRT
IN	FTW
NH	MAN
PA	PH
PA	PHU
RI	PRO
SD	SFS
VA	RIC
VT	BUR
WI	MIL
WI	PRM
Bristow, VA	ARL
Britt, IA	DUB
Britton, SD	SFS
Broad Brook, CT	HRT
Broad Run, VA	ARL
Broadalbin, NY	ALB
Broadus, MT	GF
Broadview Heights, OH	CLV
Broadwater, NE	GI
Brocket, ND	FAR
Brockport, NY	ROC
Brockton, MA	BO
MA	LIT
MA	SAM
PA	ALN
PA	PSC
Brockway, PA	E
Brocton, IL	SFD
NY	BUF
Brodhead, WI	MAD
Brodheadsville, PA	SCR
Broken Arrow, OK	TLS
Broken Bow, NE	GI
Bronson, MI	KAL
Bronx, NY	NY
NY	STF
Bronxville, NY	NY
Brook Park, OH	CLV
Brookeville, MD	WDC
Brookfield, CT	BGP
IL	CHI
MA	WOR
MO	JC
WI	MIL
Brookhaven, MS	JKS
PA	PH
Brookings, OR	P
SD	SFS
Brooklandville, MD	BAL
Brooklawn, NJ	CAM
Brookline, MA	BO
MA	NTN
PA	PH
Brooklyn, CT	NOR
IA	DAV
MI	LAN
NY	ARM
NY	BRK
NY	LIT
NY	NTN
NY	PSC
NY	SAM
NY	STF
OH	CLV
OH	NTN
Brooklyn Center, MN	STP
Brooklyn Park, MN	STP
Brookneal, VA	RIC
Brooks, MN	CR
WI	LC
Brooksville, FL	SP
KY	COV
MS	JKS
Brookville, IN	IND
KS	SAL
NY	RVC
PA	E
Broomall, PA	PH
Broomfield, CO	DEN
Brooten, MN	SCL
Brouillette, LA	ALX
Broussard, LA	LAF
Browerville, MN	SCL
Brown Deer, WI	MIL
Brown's Valley, KY	OWN
MN	SCL
Brownfield, TX	LUB
Browning, MT	HEL
Browns Mills, NJ	TR
Browns Valley, MN	SCL
Brownsburg, IN	IND
Brownsdale, MN	WIN
Brownstown, IN	IND
Brownsville, MN	WIN
PA	GBG
PA	PBR
TN	MEM
TX	BWN
Brownville, NY	OG
Brownville Junction, ME	PRT
Brownwood, TX	SAN
Bruce, MS	JKS
WI	SUP
Bruno, NE	LIN
Brunswick, GA	SAV
MD	BAL
ME	PRT
MI	GR
MO	JC
OH	CLV
OH	PRM
Brush, CO	DEN
Brushton, NY	OG
Brusly, LA	BR
Brussels, IL	SFD
WI	GB
Bryan, OH	TOL
TX	AUS
Bryant, IA	DAV
IN	LFT
SD	SFS
Bryantown, MD	WDC
Bryn Mawr, PA	PH
Bryson City, NC	CHL
Buchanan, MI	KAL
ND	FAR
NY	NY
Buchanan Valley, PA	HBG
Buchtel, OH	STU
Buckeye, AZ	PHX
Buckeye Lake, OH	COL
Buckeystown, MD	BAL
Buckhannon, WV	WH
Buckingham, PA	PH
VA	RIC
Buckley, WA	SEA
Bucklin, KS	DOD
Buckman, MN	SCL
Buckner, MO	KC
VA	RIC
Bucksport, ME	PRT
Bucyrus, OH	TOL
Buda, TX	AUS
Budd, IL	PEO
Budd Lake, NJ	PAT
Buena Park, CA	ORG
Buena Vista, CO	COS
WI	LC
Buffalo, IA	DAV
IL	SFD
MN	STP
MO	SPC
ND	FAR
NY	BUF
NY	STF
SD	RC
TX	TYL
WI	MAD
WY	CHY
Buffalo Center, IA	DUB
Buffalo Grove, IL	CHI
Buford, GA	ATL
Buhl, ID	B
Bulger, PA	PIT
Bullhead City, AZ	PHX
Buna, TX	BEA
Bunker Hill, IL	SFD
Bunkerville, NV	LAV
Bunkie, LA	ALX
Bunnell, FL	STA
Buras, LA	NO
Burbank, CA	LA
IL	CHI
Burdett, KS	DOD
Burgaw, NC	R
Burgettstown, PA	PIT
Burkburnett, TX	FWT
Burke, NY	OG
SD	RC
VA	ARL
Burkettsville, OH	CIN
Burkhart, OH	STU
Burleson, TX	FWT
Burley, ID	B
Burlingame, CA	SFR
Burlington, CA	SB

CO	COS
IA	DAV
KS	KCK
KY	COV
MA	BO
NC	R
ND	BIS
NJ	TR
VT	BUR
WA	SEA
WI	MIL
Burnet, TX	AUS
Burney, CA	SAC
Burnham, IL	CHI
Burns, KS	WCH
OR	BAK
Burnstad, ND	FAR
Burnsville, MN	STP
Burr Ridge, IL	JOL
Burrillville,	PRO
RI	PRO
Burt Lake, MI	GAY
Burton, MI	LAN
OH	PRM
Burtonsville, MD	WDC
Burwell, NE	GI
Bushnell, FL	ORL
IL	PEO
Bushton, KS	WCH
Bushwood, MD	WDC
Butler, AL	MOB
MN	SCL
MO	KC
NJ	PAT
PA	PBR
PA	PIT
TN	KNX
WI	MIL
Butte, MT	HEL
NE	OM
Butternut, WI	SUP
Buttonwillow, CA	FRS
Buttonwood, PA	SCR
Buxton, NC	R
Buzzards Bay, MA	FR
Byers, CO	DEN
Byesville, OH	STU
Byron, CA	OAK
IL	RCK
MN	WIN
WI	MIL
Byron Center, MI	GR
MI	KAL
Cabery, IL	JOL
Cable, WI	SUP
Cabo Rojo, PR	MGZ
Cabot, PA	PIT
Cadet, MO	STL
Cadillac, MI	GAY
Cadiz, KY	OWN
OH	STU
Cadogan, PA	GBG
Cadott, WI	LC
Cadyville, NY	OG
Caguas, PR	CGS
Cahokia, IL	BEL
Cairo, IL	BEL
NY	ALB
Calais, ME	PRT
Calamine, WI	MAD
Caldwell, ID	B
KS	WCH
NJ	NEW
OH	STU
TX	AUS
Caledonia, MI	GR
MN	WIN
NY	ROC
WI	MIL
Calexico, CA	SD
Calhan, CO	COS
Calhoun, GA	ATL
KY	OWN
Caliente, NV	LAV
Califon, NJ	MET
California, KY	COV
MO	JC
PA	PIT
Calimesa, CA	SB
Calipatria, CA	SD
Calistoga, CA	SR
Callahan, FL	STA
Callaway, MN	CR
Callicoon, NY	NY
Calmar, IA	DUB
Calumet, MI	MAR
OK	OKL
PA	GBG
Calumet City, IL	CHI
Calumet Park, IL	CHI
Calvary, KY	L
Calvert, TX	AUS
Calvert City, KY	OWN
Camanche, IA	DAV
Camarillo, CA	LA
Camas, WA	SEA
Cambria, CA	MRY
Cambridge, MA	BO
MD	WIL
MN	SCL
NE	LIN
NY	ALB
OH	STU
VT	BUR
WI	MAD
Cambridge City, IN	IND
Cambridge Springs, PA	E
Camden, AL	MOB
AR	LR
ME	PRT
MS	JKS
NJ	CAM
NY	SY
OH	CIN
SC	CHR
TN	MEM
WV	WH
Camdenton, MO	JC
Cameron, LA	LKC
MO	KC
TX	AUS
WI	SUP
WV	WH
Camillus, NY	SY
Camp Douglas, WI	LC
Camp Grove, IL	PEO
Camp Hill, PA	HBG
Camp Point, IL	SFD
Camp Springs, KY	COV
MD	WDC
Camp Verde, AZ	PHX
Campbell, CA	SJ
NE	LIN
OH	PBR
OH	Y
Campbellsport, WI	MIL
Campbellsville, KY	L
Campti, LA	ALX
Campus, IL	PEO
Camuy, PR	ARE
Canaan, CT	HRT
VT	BUR
Canadensis, PA	SCR
Canadian, TX	AMA
Canajoharie, NY	ALB
Canal Fulton, OH	Y
Canal Winchester, OH	COL
Canandaigua, NY	ROC
Canaseraga, NY	BUF
Canastota, NY	SY
Canby, MN	NU
OR	P
Candia, NH	MAN
Candler, FL	ORL
Cando, ND	FAR
Caney, KS	WCH
Canfield, OH	Y
Canisteo, NY	ROC
Cankton, LA	LAF
Cannelburg, IN	EVN
Cannelton, IN	IND
Cannon Falls, MN	STP
Canoga Park, CA	LA
Canon City, CO	PBL
Canonsburg, PA	PBR
PA	PIT
Canovanas, PR	SJN
Cantera, PR	SJN
Canterbury, CT	NOR
Canton, GA	ATL
IL	PEO
MA	BO
MI	DET
MN	WIN
MO	JC
MS	JKS
NY	OG
OH	ROM
OH	SJP
OH	Y
OK	OKL
PA	SCR
SD	SFS
TX	TYL
Cantonment, FL	PT
Canutillo, TX	ELP
Canyon, TX	AMA
Canyon Lake, TX	SAT
Capac, MI	DET
Capaldo, KS	WCH
Cape Charles, VA	RIC
Cape Coral, FL	VEN
Cape Elizabeth, ME	PRT
Cape Girardeau, MO	SPC
Cape May, NJ	CAM
Cape May Court House, NJ	CAM
Cape May Point, NJ	CAM
Cape Vincent, NY	OG
Capistrano Beach, CA	ORG
Capitola, CA	MRY
Capulin, CO	PBL
Carbondale, IL	BEL
PA	SCR
Cardale, PA	GBG
Cardington, OH	COL
Carefree, AZ	PHX
Carencro, LA	LAF
Carey, OH	TOL
Caribou, ME	PRT
Carle Place, NY	RVC
Carleton, MI	DET
Carlin, NV	RNO
Carlinville, IL	SFD
Carlisle, AR	LR
IA	DM
KY	LEX
MA	BO
OH	STU
PA	HBG
Carlsbad, CA	SD
NM	LSC
TX	SAN
Carlton, MN	DUL
Carlyle, IL	BEL
Carmel, CA	MRY
IN	LFT
NY	NY
Carmel Valley, CA	MRY
Carmi, IL	BEL
Carmichael, CA	SAC
Carmichaels, PA	PIT
Carnegie, PA	PIT
PA	SAM
PA	SJP
Carney's Point, NJ	CAM
Caro, MI	SAG
Carol Stream, IL	JOL
Carolina,PR	SJN
Caroline County, VA	RIC
Carpentersville, IL	RCK
Carpinteria, CA	LA
Carrick, PA	PIT
Carrington, ND	FAR
Carrizo Springs, TX	LAR
Carrizozo, NM	LSC
Carroll, IA	SC
Carrollton, GA	ATL
IL	SFD
KY	COV
MI	SAG
MO	KC
OH	STU
TX	DAL
TX	FWT
Carrolltown, PA	ALT
Carson, CA	LA
ND	BIS
Carson City, MI	GR
NV	RNO
Carter Lake, IA	DM
Carteret, NJ	MET
NJ	PHU
NJ	PSC
Cartersville, GA	ATL
Carterville, IL	BEL
Carthage, IL	PEO
MO	SPC
MS	JKS
NY	OG
TX	TYL
Carthagena, OH	CIN
Caruthersville, MO	SPC
Carver, MA	BO
MN	STP
Carverton, PA	SCR
Cary, IL	RCK
NC	PSC
NC	R
Casa Grande, AZ	TUC
Cascade, CO	COS
IA	DUB
NH	MAN
WI	MIL
Casco, ME	PRT
WI	GB
Caseville, MI	SAG
Casey, IA	DM
IL	SFD
Caseyville, IL	BEL
Cashion, AZ	PHX
Cashmere, WA	YAK
Cashton, WI	LC
Casper, WY	CHY
Caspian, MI	MAR
Cass City, MI	SAG
Cass Lake, MN	DUL
Cassadaga, NY	BUF
Cassandra, PA	ALT
Cassel, WI	LC
Casselberry, FL	ORL
Cassella, OH	CIN
Casselton, ND	FAR
Cassopolis, MI	KAL
Cassville, MO	SPC
WI	MAD
Castaner, PR	PCE
Castine, ME	PRT
Castle Grove, IA	DUB
Castle Hayne, NC	R
Castle Rock, CO	COS
WA	SEA
WI	MAD
Castle Shannon, PA	PIT
Castleton, KS	WCH
NY	ALB
VT	BUR
Castleton-on-Hudson, NY	ALB
Castlewood, SD	SFS
Castro Valley, CA	OAK
Castroville, CA	MRY
TX	SAT
Catahoula, LA	LAF
Catano, PR	SJN
Catasauqua, PA	ALN
Catawba, WI	SUP
Catawissa, MO	STL
Catharine, KS	SAL
Cathedral City, CA	SB
Cato, NY	ROC
Catonsville, MD	BAL
Catskill, NY	ALB
Cattaraugus, NY	BUF
Cavalier, ND	FAR
Cavour, SD	SFS
Cawker City, KS	SAL
Cayey, PR	CGS
Cayucos, CA	MRY
Cayuga, ND	FAR
Cazenovia, NY	SY
WI	LC
Cecil, OH	TOL
PA	PIT
WI	GB
Cecilia, KY	L
LA	LAF
Cedar, MI	GAY
MN	STP
Cedar City, UT	SLC
Cedar Falls, IA	DUB
Cedar Grove, IN	IND
NJ	NEW
WI	MIL
Cedar Knolls, NJ	PAT
Cedar Lake, IN	GRY
MN	STP
Cedar Park, TX	AUS
Cedar Rapids, IA	DUB
NE	OM
Cedar Vale, KS	WCH
Cedarburg, WI	MIL
Cedarhurst, NY	RVC
Cedartown, GA	ATL
Cedarville, NJ	CAM
Ceiba, PR	CGS
Celestine, IN	EVN
Celina, OH	CIN
Centennial, CO	DEN
Center, CO	PBL
ND	BIS
TX	TYL
Center Harbor, NH	MAN
Center Moriches, NY	RVC
Center Ossipee, NH	MAN
Center Ridge, AR	LR
Center Square, PA	PH
Center Township, PA	PIT
Center Valley, PA	ALN
Centereach, NY	RVC
Centerline, MI	DET
Centerport, NY	BRK
NY	RVC
Centerville, IA	DAV
LA	LAF
MA	FR
MN	STP
MO	STL
MT	GF
NY	NY
OH	CIN
SD	SFS
TN	NSH
Central City, IA	DUB
KY	OWN
NE	OM

PA	ALT
Central Falls, RI	PRO
Central Islip, NY	RVC
Central Point, OR	P
Central Square, NY	SY
Centralia, IL	BEL
MO	JC
PA	HBG
PA	PHU
WA	SEA
Centreville, IL	BEL
MD	WIL
Centuria, WI	SUP
Ceres, CA	STO
Cerrillos, NM	SFE
Cestohowa, TX	SAT
Chacahoula, LA	HT
Chackbay, LA	HT
Chadds Ford, PA	PH
Chadron, NE	GI
Chadwicks, NY	SY
Chaffee, MO	SPC
Chagrin Falls, OH	CLV
Chalan Kanoa Village, MP	CHK
Chalan Pago, GU	AGN
Chalfont, PA	PH
Chalmette, LA	NO
Chama, NM	SFE
Chamberino, NM	LSC
Chamberlain, SD	SFS
Chambers Island, WI	GB
Chambersburg, PA	HBG
Chamblee, GA	ATL
Chamois, MO	JC
Champaign, IL	PEO
Champion, MI	MAR
OH	Y
WI	GB
Champlain, NY	OG
Chandler, AZ	PHX
OK	OKL
Chandlerville, IL	SFD
Chanhassen, MN	STP
Channahon, IL	JOL
Channelview, TX	GAL
Channing, MI	MAR
TX	AMA
Chantilly, VA	ARL
Chanute, KS	WCH
Chapel Hill, NC	R
Chapel Point, MD	WDC
Chapin, SC	CHR
Chapman, KS	SAL
Chappaqua, NY	NY
Chapparal, NM	LSC
Chappell, NE	GI
Chappell Hill, TX	AUS
Chaptico, MD	WDC
Chardon, OH	CLV
Charenton, LA	LAF
Chariton, IA	DM
Charleroi, PA	PBR
PA	PIT
Charles City, IA	DUB
Charles Town, WV	WH
Charlesburg, WI	GB
Charleston, AR	LR
IL	SFD
MO	SPC
MS	JKS
SC	CHR
WV	WH
Charlestown, IN	IND
MA	BO
NH	MAN
RI	PRO
WI	GB
Charlevoix, MI	GAY
Charlotte, IA	DAV
MI	LAN
NC	CHL
TX	SAT
VT	BUR
Charlottesville, VA	RIC
Charlton City, MA	WOR
Charter Oak, IA	SC
Chase, KS	WCH
WI	GB
Chaska, MN	STP
Chasm Falls, NY	OG
Chassell, MI	MAR
Chastang, AL	MOB
Chataignier, LA	LAF
Chatawa, MS	JKS
Chateaugay, NY	OG
Chatfield, MN	WIN
Chatham, IL	SFD
MA	FR
NJ	PAT
NY	ALB
Chatham Township, NJ	PAT
Chatom, AL	MOB
Chatsworth, CA	LA
IL	PEO
Chattahoochee, FL	PT
Chattanooga, TN	KNX
Chaumont, NY	OG
Chauncey, OH	STU
Chauvin, LA	HT
Chazy, NY	OG
Cheat Lake, WV	WH
Chebanse, IL	JOL
Cheboygan, MI	GAY
Cheek, TX	BEA
Cheektowaga, NY	BUF
Chefornak, AK	FBK
Chehalis, WA	SEA
Chelan, WA	YAK
Chelmsford, MA	BO
Chelsea, IA	DUB
MA	BO
MI	LAN
SD	SFS
WI	SUP
Cheltenham, PA	PH
Chenango Forks, NY	SY
Cheney, NE	LIN
WA	SPK
Cheneyville, LA	ALX
Chenoa, IL	PEO
Cheraw, SC	CHR
Cherokee, IA	SC
KS	WCH
OK	OKL
Cherokee Village, AR	LR
Cherry, IL	PEO
Cherry Creek, NY	BUF
Cherry Hill, NJ	CAM
NJ	PHU
Cherry Mound, IA	DUB
Cherry Valley, CA	SB
NY	ALB
Cherryvale, KS	WCH
Chesaning, MI	SAG
Chesapeake, OH	STU
VA	RIC
Chesapeake City, MD	PHU
Cheshire, CT	HRT
MA	SPR
Chest Springs, PA	ALT
Chester, CT	NOR
IA	DUB
IL	BEL
MT	GF
NJ	PAT
NY	NY
PA	PH
PA	PHU
SC	CHR
VT	BUR
WV	WH
Chester Heights, PA	PH
Chester, Kent Island, MD	WIL
Chesterfield, MO	STL
Chesterland, OH	CLV
OH	ROM
Chesterton, IN	GRY
Chestertown, MD	WIL
NY	ALB
Chestnut Hill, MA	BO
Chetek, WI	SUP
Chetopa, KS	WCH
Chevak, AK	FBK
Cheverly, MD	WDC
Chevy Chase, MD	WDC
Chewelah, WA	SPK
Cheyenne, WY	CHY
Cheyenne Wells, CO	COS
Chicago, IL	CHI
IL	EST
IL	LIT
IL	PRM
IL	ROM
IL	STN
Chicago Heights, IL	CHI
Chicago Ridge, IL	CHI
Chichiltah, NM	GLP
Chickasaw, AL	MOB
OH	CIN
Chickasha, OK	OKL
Chico, CA	SAC
Chicopee, KS	WCH
MA	SPR
Chicora, PA	PIT
Chiefland, FL	STA
Childress, TX	AMA
Childs, MD	WIL
Chili, WI	LC
Chillicothe, IL	PEO
MO	KC
OH	COL
Chillum, MD	WDC
Chiloquin, OR	BAK
Chilton, WI	GB
Chimayo, NM	SFE
China, TX	BEA
China Spring, TX	AUS
Chincoteague, VA	RIC
Chinle, AZ	GLP
Chino, CA	SB
Chino Hills, CA	SB
Chinook, MT	GF
Chipley, FL	PT
Chippewa Falls, WI	LC
Chippewa Lake, OH	CLV
Chippewa Township, PA	PIT
Chisholm, MN	DUL
Chittenango, NY	SY
Chittenden, VT	BUR
Chokio, MN	SCL
Choteau, MT	HEL
Chowchilla, CA	FRS
Chrisney, IN	EVN
Christiansburg, VA	RIC
Christiansted, VI	STV
Christopher, IL	BEL
Christoval, TX	SAN
Chubbuck, ID	B
Chula Vista, CA	SD
Church Point, LA	LAF
Church Rock, NM	GLP
Churchill Borough, PA	PIT
Churchtown, OH	STU
Churchville, IA	DM
NY	ROC
Churdan, IA	SC
Churubusco, IN	FTW
NY	OG
Chuuk, FM	CI
Ciales, PR	ARE
Cibecue, AZ	GLP
Cicero, IL	CHI
IN	LFT
NY	SY
Cidra, PR	CGS
Cimarron, NM	SFE
Cincinnati, OH	CIN
OH	OLL
Cinnaminson, NJ	TR
Circle, MT	GF
Circleville, OH	COL
Cisco, TX	FWT
Cistern, TX	VIC
Citronelle, AL	MOB
Citrus Heights, CA	SAC
Citrus Springs, FL	SP
Claflin, KS	DOD
Clairton, PA	PBR
PA	PIT
Clam Lake, WI	SUP
Clara City, MN	NU
Clare, IA	SC
MI	SAG
Claremont, CA	LA
MN	WIN
NH	MAN
Claremore, OK	TLS
Clarence, MO	JC
NY	BUF
PA	ALT
PA	PBR
Clarence Center, NY	BUF
Clarendon, TX	AMA
Clarendon Hills, IL	JOL
Clarinda, IA	DM
Clarion, IA	DUB
PA	E
Clarissa, MN	SCL
Clark, NJ	NEW
SD	SFS
Clark Mills, NY	SY
Clarkesville, GA	ATL
Clarkfield, MN	NU
Clarklake, MI	LAN
Clarks, NE	OM
Clarks Green, PA	SCR
Clarks Mills, WI	GB
Clarks Summit, PA	PSC
PA	SCR
Clarksburg, CA	SAC
WV	WH
Clarksdale, MS	JKS
Clarkson, KY	OWN
MI	DET
NE	OM
Clarkston, MI	DET
WA	B
WA	SPK
Clarksville, AR	LR
IN	IND
MD	BAL
PA	PIT
TN	NSH
TX	TYL
VA	RIC
Claudell, KS	SAL
Clawson, MI	DET
Claxton, GA	SAV
Clay Center, KS	SAL
Claymont, DE	WIL
Clayton, DE	WIL
MO	STL
NJ	CAM
NM	SFE
NY	OG
WA	SPK
Clayville, NY	SY
Cle Elum, WA	YAK
Clear Creek, IA	DAV
Clear Lake, IA	DUB
IN	FTW
MN	SCL
SD	SFS
WI	SUP
Clearfield, PA	E
SD	RC
Clearlake, CA	SR
Clearwater, FL	SP
MN	STP
Clearwater Beach, FL	SP
Cleburne, TX	FWT
Clements, MN	NU
Clementsville, KY	L
Clemmons, NC	CHL
Clemson, SC	CHR
Clermont, FL	ORL
IA	DUB
Clermont Harbor, MS	BLX
Cleveland, MN	STP
MS	JKS
NY	SY
OH	CLV
OH	OLL
OH	PRM
OH	ROM
OH	SJP
OK	TLS
TN	KNX
TX	BEA
WI	GB
Cleveland Heights, OH	CLV
Clewiston, FL	VEN
Cliffside Park, NJ	NEW
NJ	NTN
Clifton, AZ	TUC
IL	JOL
KS	SAL
NJ	PAT
TX	FWT
VA	ARL
Clifton Forge, VA	RIC
Clifton Heights, PA	PH
PA	PHU
Clifton Park, NY	ALB
Clifton Springs, NY	ROC
Clint, TX	ELP
Clinton, CT	NOR
IA	DAV
IL	PEO
IN	IND
KY	OWN
MA	WOR
MD	WDC
MI	LAN
MN	NU
MO	KC
MS	JKS
NC	R
NJ	MET
NY	SY
OH	CLV
OK	OKL
SC	CHR
TN	KNX
WI	MAD
Clinton Heights, NY	ALB
Clinton Township, MI	DET
Clinton Twp., MI	DET
Clintonville, WI	GB
Clintwood, VA	RIC
Clio, MI	LAN
Clonmel, KS	WCH
Clontarf, MN	NU
Cloquet, MN	DUL
Closter, NJ	NEW
Cloutierville, LA	ALX
Clover Bottom, MO	STL
Cloverdale, CA	SR
OH	TOL
Cloverport, KY	OWN
Clovis, CA	FRS
NM	SFE
Clute, TX	GAL
Clutier, IA	DUB

Clyde, KS	SAL
MO	KC
NY	ROC
OH	TOL
WI	MAD
Clyman, WI	MIL
Clymer, PA	GBG
PA	PBR
Coachella, CA	SB
Coal City, IL	JOL
Coal Run, PA	PBR
Coal Township, PA	HBG
Coal Valley, IL	PEO
Coaldale, PA	ALN
Coalgate, OK	TLS
Coalinga, CA	FRS
Coalport, PA	E
Coalton, WV	WH
Coamo, PR	PCE
Coates, MN	STP
Coatesville, PA	PH
PA	PSC
Cobden, IL	BEL
Cobleskill, NY	ALB
Cockeysville, MD	BAL
Cocoa, FL	ORL
Cocoa Beach, FL	ORL
Coconut Creek, FL	MIA
FL	PSC
Coconut Grove, FL	MIA
Cody, WY	CHY
Coeur D'Alene, ID	B
Coffeen, IL	SFD
Coffeyville, KS	WCH
Coffman, MO	STL
Coggon, IA	DUB
Cogswell, ND	FAR
Cohasset, MA	BO
Cohocton, NY	ROC
Cohoes, NY	ALB
NY	STF
Colbert, WA	SPK
Colby, KS	SAL
WI	LC
Colchester, CT	NOR
CT	STF
VT	BUR
Cold Spring, KY	COV
MN	SCL
Cold Spring-on-Hudson, NY	NY
Colden, NY	BUF
Coldwater, KS	DOD
MI	KAL
OH	CIN
Colebrook, NH	MAN
Coleman, MI	SAG
TX	SAN
Coleman/Klondike, WI	GB
Colerain, OH	STU
Coleraine, MN	DUL
Coleridge, NE	OM
Colesburg, IA	DUB
KY	L
Colesville, PA	ALN
Colfax, CA	SAC
IA	DAV
IL	PEO
LA	ALX
WA	SPK
College Park, MD	WDC
College Point, NY	BRK
College Station, TX	AUS
Collegeville, MN	SCL
PA	PH
Colleyville, TX	FWT
Collierville, TN	MEM
Collingdale, PA	PH
Collings Lakes, NJ	CAM
Collingswood, NJ	CAM
Collins Center, NY	BUF
Collinsville, CT	HRT
IL	SFD
OK	TLS
Collyer, KS	SAL
Colma, CA	SFR
Colman, SD	SFS
Colo, IA	DUB
Cologne, MN	STP
Colome, SD	RC
Colon, NE	LIN
Colona, IL	PEO
Colonia, NJ	MET
NJ	NEW
Colonia, Yap, FM	CI
Colonial Beach, VA	ARL
Colonial Heights, VA	RIC
Colonie, NY	ALB
The Colony, TX	FWT
TX	STN
Colorado City, TX	SAN
Colorado Springs, CO	COS

CO	VNN
Colstrip, MT	GF
Colton, CA	SB
NY	OG
WA	SPK
Colts Neck, NJ	TR
Columbia, CT	NOR
IL	BEL
KY	L
MD	BAL
MO	JC
MO	OLL
MS	BLX
PA	HBG
SC	CHR
TN	NSH
VA	RIC
Columbia City, IN	FTW
Columbia Falls, MT	HEL
Columbia Heights, MN	STP
Columbia Station, OH	CLV
Columbiana, OH	Y
Columbus, GA	SAV
IN	IND
KS	WCH
MI	DET
MS	JKS
MT	GF
NE	OM
OH	COL
OH	NTN
OH	OLL
OH	PRM
TX	VIC
WI	MAD
Columbus Grove, OH	TOL
Columbus Junction, IA	DAV
Colusa, CA	SAC
Colver, PA	ALT
Colville, WA	SPK
Colwich, KS	WCH
Comanche, TX	FWT
Combined Locks, WI	GB
Comerio, PR	CGS
Comfort, TX	SAT
Comfrey, MN	NU
Commack, NY	BRK
NY	RVC
Commerce, TX	DAL
Commerce City, CO	DEN
Compton, CA	LA
Conception, MO	KC
Conception Junction, MO	KC
Concho, AZ	GLP
Concord, CA	OAK
MA	BO
MI	LAN
NC	CHL
NH	MAN
Concord Hill, MO	STL
Concord Twp., OH	CLV
Concord Village, MO	STL
Concordia, KS	SAL
Conde, SD	SFS
Condon, OR	BAK
Conejos, CO	PBL
Conemaugh, PA	ALT
PA	PBR
Conewago Township, PA	HBG
Congers, NY	NY
Conifer, CO	DEN
Conklin, MI	GR
Conneaut, OH	Y
Conneaut Lake, PA	E
Conneautville, PA	E
Connell, WA	SPK
Connellsville, PA	GBG
Connersville, IN	IND
Conrad, MT	HEL
Conroe, TX	GAL
Conshohocken, PA	PH
Constable, NY	OG
Constableville, NY	OG
Constance, NE	OM
Continental, OH	TOL
Convent, LA	BR
Convent Station, NJ	PAT
Converse, TX	SAT
Conway, AR	LR
MI	GAY
MO	SPC
ND	FAR
PA	PIT
SC	CHR
Conway Springs, KS	WCH
Conyers, GA	ATL
GA	SJP
Conyngham, PA	SCR
Cook, MN	DUL
Cookeville, TN	NSH
Cooks, MI	MAR

Cooks Valley, WI	LC
Coolidge, AZ	TUC
Coon Rapids, IA	SC
MN	STP
Coon Valley, WI	LC
Coopersburg, PA	ALN
Cooperstown, ND	FAR
NY	ALB
WI	GB
Coopersville, MI	GR
NY	OG
Coos Bay, OR	P
Copake Falls, NY	ALB
Copemish, MI	GAY
Copenhagen, NY	OG
Copiague, NY	RVC
Coplay, PA	ALN
Copley, OH	CLV
Coppell, TX	DAL
Copperas Cove, TX	AUS
Copperhill, TN	KNX
Copperopolis, CA	STO
Copperton, UT	SLC
Coquille, OR	P
Coral, PA	GBG
Coral Gables, FL	MIA
Coral Springs, FL	MIA
Coram, NY	RVC
Coraopolis, PA	PIT
Corbin, KY	LEX
Corcoran, CA	FRS
MN	STP
Cordele, GA	SAV
Cordova, AK	ANC
TN	MEM
Corfu, NY	BUF
Corinth, MS	JKS
NY	ALB
Cornelius, OR	P
Cornell, WI	LC
Corning, CA	SAC
IA	DM
KS	KCK
NY	ROC
OH	COL
Cornucopia, WI	SUP
Cornwall, NY	NY
PA	HBG
Cornwall Bridge, CT	HRT
Cornwall-on-Hudson, NY	NY
Corona, CA	SB
Coronado, CA	SD
Corozal, PR	ARE
Corozal-Padilla, PR	ARE
Corozal-Palmarito, PR	ARE
Corozal-Palos Blancos, PR	ARE
Corpus Christi, TX	CC
Corrales, NM	SFE
Corralitos, CA	MRY
Corrigan, TX	BEA
Corry, PA	E
Corsicana, TX	DAL
Cortaro, AZ	TUC
Cortez, CO	PBL
Cortland, NE	LIN
NY	SY
OH	Y
Cortlandt Manor, NY	NY
Corvalis, OR	P
Corwith, IA	DUB
Corydon, IA	DM
IN	IND
Cosgrove, IA	DAV
Coshocton, OH	COL
Costa Mesa, CA	ORG
Cotati, CA	SR
Coteau, LA	LAF
Coteau Holmes, LA	LAF
Coto Laurel, PR	PCE
Cottage Grove, MN	STP
OR	P
WI	MAD
Cottleville, MO	STL
Cottonport, LA	ALX
Cottonwood, AZ	PHX
ID	B
MN	NU
Cotulla, TX	LAR
Coudersport, PA	E
Coulee Dam, WA	SPK
Coulterville, IL	BEL
Council, ID	B
Council Bluffs, IA	DM
Council Grove, KS	WCH
Country Club Hills, IL	CHI
Countryside, IL	CHI
Coupon, PA	ALT
Courtenay, ND	FAR
Coushatta, LA	SHP
Coventry, CT	NOR
RI	PRO

Covina, CA	LA
Covington, GA	ATL
IN	LFT
KY	COV
LA	NO
OH	CIN
TN	MEM
VA	RIC
WA	SEA
Cow Island, LA	LAF
Coweta, OK	TLS
Cowiche, WA	YAK
Coxsackie, NY	ALB
Coylesville, PA	PIT
Cozad, NE	GI
Crabtree, PA	GBG
Crafton, PA	PIT
Craig, AK	JUN
CO	DEN
Cranberry Prairie, OH	CIN
Cranberry Township, PA	PIT
Cranbury, NJ	MET
Crandon, WI	GB
Crane, TX	SAN
Cranford, NJ	NEW
Cranston, RI	PRO
Crawford, NE	GI
Crawfordsville, IN	LFT
Creighton, NE	OM
PA	PIT
Creole, LA	LKC
Cresaptown, MD	BAL
Crescent, NY	ALB
OH	STU
Crescent City, CA	SR
FL	STA
Crescent Lake, WI	SUP
Crescent Springs, KY	COV
Cresco, IA	DUB
PA	SCR
Cresskill, NJ	NEW
Cresson, PA	ALT
Crested Butte, CO	PBL
Crestline, CA	SB
OH	TOL
Creston, IA	DM
Crestone, CO	PBL
Crestview, FL	PT
Crestwood, IL	CHI
KY	L
MO	STL
NY	NY
Crete, IL	JOL
NE	LIN
Creve Coeur, IL	PEO
MO	STL
Crewe, VA	RIC
Crittenden, NY	BUF
Crivitz, WI	GB
Crocker, MO	JC
Crockett, CA	OAK
TX	TYL
Crofton, MD	BAL
NE	OM
Croghan, NY	OG
Cromwell, CT	NOR
Crookston, MN	CR
Crooksville, OH	COL
Crosby, MN	DUL
ND	BIS
TX	GAL
Cross Plains, WI	MAD
Cross Village, MI	GAY
Crossett, AR	LR
Crossingsville, PA	E
Crosslake, MN	DUL
Crossville, TN	KNX
Croswell, MI	SAG
Croton Falls, NY	NY
Croton-on-Hudson, NY	NY
Crow Agency, MT	GF
Crow Hill, ND	FAR
Crowell, TX	FWT
Crowley, LA	LAF
TX	FWT
Crown, PA	E
Crown Butte, ND	BIS
Crown Point, IN	GRY
LA	NO
NY	OG
Crownpoint, NM	GLP
Croydon, PA	PH
Crozet, VA	RIC
Cruz Bay, VI	STV
Crystal, MN	STP
ND	FAR
Crystal City, MO	STL
TX	LAR
Crystal Falls, MI	MAR
Crystal Lake, IL	RCK
Crystal River, FL	SP

Crystal Springs, MS	JKS
Cuba, KS	SAL
MO	JC
NM	GLP
NY	BUF
OH	TOL
Cuba City, WI	MAD
Cudahy, CA	LA
WI	MIL
Cuero, TX	VIC
Culbertson, MT	GF
Culebra, PR	CGS
Cullman, AL	BIR
Cullom, IL	PEO
Culpeper, VA	ARL
Culver, IN	FTW
Culver City, CA	LA
Culvertown, KY	L
Cumberland, IA	DM
KY	LEX
MD	BAL
RI	PRO
WI	SUP
Cumbola, PA	ALN
Cumming, GA	ATL
IA	DM
Cunningham, KS	WCH
Cupertino, CA	SJ
Curdsville, KY	OWN
Curlew, WA	SPK
Currie, MN	WIN
Curtis, NE	LIN
Curtis Bay, MD	PHU
Curwensville, PA	E
Cushing, OK	TLS
Cusick, WA	SPK
Custar, OH	TOL
Custer, MI	GR
SD	RC
WI	LC
Cut Bank, MT	HEL
Cutchogue, NY	RVC
Cutler, CA	FRS
Cut-Off, LA	HT
Cuyahoga Falls, OH	CLV
Cuyahoga Heights, OH	CLV
Cyclone, TX	AUS
Cygnet, OH	TOL
Cynthiana, KY	COV
Cypress, CA	ORG
Czestochowa, WI	LC
D'Hanis, TX	SAT
Dacada, WI	MIL
Dade City, FL	SP
Daggett, MI	MAR
Daguscahonda, PA	E
Dahlgren, IL	BEL
Dahlonega, GA	ATL
Daigle, ME	PRT
Daingerfield, TX	TYL
Dakota, MN	WIN
Dakota Dunes, SD	SFS
Dale, IN	EVN
Dale City, VA	ARL
Dalhart, TX	AMA
Dallas, OR	P
PA	SCR
TX	DAL
Dallastown, PA	HBG
The Dalles, OR	BAK
Dalton, GA	ATL
MA	SPR
PA	SCR
Dalton City, IL	SFD
Daly City, CA	SFR
Dalzell, IL	PEO
Damar, KS	SAL
Damascus, MD	WDC
Damiansville, IL	BEL
Damon, TX	GAL
Dana Point, CA	ORG
Danbury, CT	BGP
CT	NTN
CT	PSC
CT	SAM
IA	SC
TX	GAL
WI	SUP
Dane, WI	MAD
Dania, FL	MIA
Danielson, CT	NOR
Dannemora, NY	OG
Dansville, NY	ROC
Dante, SD	SFS
Danvers, MA	BO
MN	NU
Danville, CA	OAK
IL	PEO
IN	IND
KS	WCH
KY	LEX

OH	COL
PA	HBG
VA	RIC
Daphne, AL	MOB
Darboy, WI	GB
Darby, PA	PH
Dardanelle, AR	LR
Dardenne, MO	STL
Darien, CT	BGP
IL	JOL
Darien Center, NY	BUF
Darlington, NJ	NEW
PA	PIT
WI	MAD
Darnestown, MD	WDC
Darrow, LA	BR
Darwin, MN	NU
Dauby, WI	SUP
Dauphin, PA	HBG
Dauphin Island, AL	MOB
Davenport, CA	MRY
IA	DAV
WA	SPK
Daveport, IA	DAV
Davey, NE	LIN
David City, NE	LIN
Davidsonville, MD	BAL
Davidsville, PA	ALT
Davie, FL	MIA
Davis, CA	SAC
Davis Park, NY	RVC
Davison, MI	LAN
Dawson, MN	NU
NE	LIN
Dawson Springs, KY	OWN
Dayton, IA	SC
KY	COV
MN	STP
NV	RNO
NY	BUF
OH	CIN
OH	OLL
OH	PRM
TN	KNX
TX	BEA
WA	SPK
WI	MAD
WY	CHY
Daytona Beach, FL	ORL
Dayville, CT	NOR
Dazey, ND	FAR
De Forest, WI	MAD
De Funiak Springs, FL	PT
De Graff, MN	NU
De Kalb Junction, NY	OG
De Land, FL	ORL
De Leon, TX	FWT
De Motte, IN	LFT
De Pere, WI	GB
De Queen, AR	LR
De Quincy, LA	LKC
De Ridder, LA	LKC
De Smet, SD	SFS
De Soto, MO	STL
WI	LC
De Witt, MI	LAN
Deadwood, SD	RC
Deal, NJ	TR
Dearborn, MI	DET
MI	ROM
MI	STN
Dearborn Heights, MI	DET
MI	STN
DeBary, FL	ORL
Decatur, AL	BIR
GA	ATL
IL	SFD
IN	FTW
MI	KAL
TX	FWT
Decherd, TN	NSH
Decorah, IA	DUB
Dededo, GU	AGN
Dedham, IA	SC
MA	BO
Deep River, CT	NOR
Deephaven, MN	STP
Deer Lodge, MT	HEL
Deer Park, NY	RVC
TX	GAL
WA	SPK
Deer River, MN	DUL
Deerbrook, WI	GB
Deerfield, IL	CHI
KS	DOD
MI	LAN
MN	WIN
Deerfield Beach, FL	MIA
Deferiet, NY	OG
Defiance, IA	DM
OH	TOL

DeKalb, IL	RCK
Del Mar, CA	SD
Del Norte, CO	PBL
Del Rey, CA	FRS
Del Rio, TX	SAT
Delafield, WI	MIL
Delair, NJ	CAM
Delancey, PA	E
Delano, CA	FRS
MN	STP
Delanson, NY	ALB
Delavan, IL	PEO
MN	WIN
WI	MIL
Delaware, OH	COL
Delaware City, DE	WIL
Delcambre, LA	LAF
Delevan, NY	BUF
Delhi, IA	DUB
NY	ALB
Delia, KS	KCK
DeLisle, MS	BLX
Dell Rapids, SD	SFS
Delmar, IA	DAV
NY	ALB
Delmont, PA	GBG
Delphi, IN	LFT
PA	PH
Delphos, KS	SAL
OH	TOL
Delran, NJ	TR
Delray Beach, FL	NTN
FL	PMB
Delta, CO	PBL
Delta Junction, AK	FBK
Delton, MI	KAL
Deltona, FL	ORL
Demarest, NJ	NEW
Deming, NM	LSC
Demopolis, AL	BIR
Denham Springs, LA	BR
Denison, IA	SC
TX	DAL
Denmark, WI	GB
Dennison, OH	COL
Densmore, KS	SAL
Dent, MN	SCL
Denton, NE	LIN
TX	FWT
Denver, CO	DEN
CO	OLL
CO	STN
CO	VNN
NC	CHL
Denver City, TX	LUB
Denville, NJ	PAT
Depew, NY	BUF
Deposit, NY	SY
Deptford, NJ	CAM
Depue, IL	PEO
Derby, CT	HRT
KS	WCH
NY	BUF
Derby Line, VT	BUR
Derry, NH	MAN
PA	GBG
Derwood, MD	WDC
Des Allemands, LA	NO
Des Moines, IA	DM
WA	SEA
Des Peres, MO	STL
Des Plaines, IL	CHI
Descanso, CA	SD
Desert Hot Springs, CA	SB
Deshler, OH	TOL
DeSmet, ID	B
Desoto, TX	DAL
Destin, FL	PT
Destrehan, LA	NO
DeTour, MI	MAR
Detroit, MI	ARM
MI	DET
MI	EST
MI	OLL
MI	PRM
MI	ROM
MI	STN
Detroit Lakes, MN	CR
Deville, LA	ALX
Devils Lake, ND	FAR
Devine, TX	SAT
Devon, PA	PH
Dewey, OK	TLS
DeWitt, IA	DAV
MI	LAN
Dewitt, NY	SY
Dexter, ME	PRT
MI	LAN
MO	SPC
NM	LSC
Diamond, LA	NO

Diamond Bar, CA	LA
Diboll, TX	TYL
Dickey, ND	FAR
Dickeyville, WI	MAD
Dickinson, ND	BIS
TX	GAL
Dickson, TN	NSH
Dickson City, PA	SCR
Dieterich, IL	SFD
Dighton, KS	DOD
MA	FR
Dike, IA	DUB
Dilley, TX	SAT
Dillingham, AK	ANC
Dillon, MT	HEL
SC	CHR
Dillonvale, OH	STU
Dilly, WI	LC
Dilworth, MN	CR
Dime Box, TX	AUS
Dimmitt, TX	AMA
Dimock, SD	SFS
Dimondale, MI	LAN
Dinuba, CA	FRS
Dittmer, MO	STL
Divernon, IL	SFD
Dix Hills, NY	RVC
Dixon, CA	SAC
IL	RCK
MO	JC
NM	SFE
Dobbs Ferry, NY	NY
Dobie, WI	SUP
Dodge, NE	OM
Dodge Center, MN	WIN
Dodge City, KS	DOD
Dodgeville, IA	DAV
WI	MAD
Dodson Prairie, TX	FWT
Doland, SD	SFS
Dolgeville, NY	ALB
Dominican Republic, VA	ARL
Dona Ana, NM	LSC
Donaldson, IN	FTW
Donaldsonville, LA	BR
Donegal, PA	GBG
Doniphan, KS	KCK
MO	SPC
NE	LIN
Donna, TX	BWN
Donnelly, MN	SCL
Donora, PA	PBR
PA	PIT
Dorado, PR	SJN
Doraville, GA	ATL
Dorchester, IA	DUB
MA	BO
WI	LC
Dorothy, MN	CR
Dorr, MI	KAL
Dorrance, KS	SAL
PA	SCR
Dos Palos, CA	FRS
Dothan, AL	MOB
Dotyville, WI	MIL
Dougherty, IA	DUB
Douglas, AZ	TUC
GA	SAV
MI	KAL
WY	CHY
Douglas Co., NE	OM
Douglaston, NY	BRK
Douglasville, GA	ATL
Dousman, WI	MIL
Dover, DE	WIL
IN	IND
MA	BO
NH	MAN
NH	SAM
NJ	PAT
OH	COL
TN	NSH
Dover Plains, NY	NY
Dover-Foxcroft, ME	PRT
Dow City, IA	SC
Dowagiac, MI	KAL
Downers Grove, IL	JOL
Downey, CA	LA
Downieville, CA	SAC
Downingtown, PA	PH
Downs, IL	PEO
KS	SAL
Doylesburg, PA	HBG
Doylestown, OH	CLV
PA	PH
WI	MAD
Dracut, MA	BO
Drake, ND	FAR
Draper, UT	SLC
Drayton, ND	FAR
Dresden, OH	COL

Drexel Hill, PA	PH
Dripping Springs, TX	AUS
Drummond, MT	HEL
Drums, PA	SCR
Dryden, MI	DET
NY	ROC
Drywood, WI	LC
Du Bois, PA	E
PA	PBR
Du Quoin, IL	BEL
Duarte, CA	LA
Dublin, CA	OAK
GA	SAV
OH	COL
TX	FWT
Dubois, IL	BEL
IN	EVN
Dubuque, IA	DUB
KS	DOD
Dudley, MA	WOR
PA	ALT
Due West, SC	CHR
Duelm, MN	SCL
Dufur, OR	BAK
Duluth, GA	ATL
MN	DUL
Dumas, AR	LR
TX	AMA
Dumont, IA	DUB
MN	SCL
NJ	NEW
Dunbar, PA	GBG
WV	WH
Duncan, IA	DUB
NE	OM
OK	OKL
SD	SFS
Duncan Mills, CA	SR
Duncansville, PA	ALT
Duncanville, TX	DAL
Duncombe, IA	SC
Dundee, IL	RCK
MI	DET
MN	WIN
Dunedin, FL	SP
Dunellen, NJ	MET
NJ	PSC
Dungannon, OH	Y
Dunkirk, IN	LFT
MD	BAL
MD	WDC
NY	BUF
Dunlap, IA	DM
IL	PEO
TN	KNX
Dunlo, PA	ALT
PA	PBR
Dunmore, PA	PSC
PA	SCR
Dunn, NC	R
Dunnellon, FL	ORL
Dunnington, IN	LFT
Dunseith, ND	FAR
Dunsmuir, CA	SAC
Dunwoody, GA	ATL
Dupo, IL	BEL
Dupont, LA	ALX
PA	SCR
Duquesne, PA	PBR
PA	PIT
Duralde, LA	LAF
Durand, IL	RCK
MI	LAN
WI	LC
Durango, CO	PBL
Durant, OK	TLS
Durham, CT	NOR
NC	R
NH	MAN
Durhamville, NY	SY
Durward's Glen, WI	MAD
Duryea, PA	SCR
Dushore, PA	SCR
Duson, LA	LAF
Dutton, MT	HEL
Dutzow, MO	STL
Duxbury, MA	BO
Dwight, IL	PEO
NE	LIN
Dyckesville, WI	GB
Dyer, IN	GRY
Dyersburg, TN	MEM
Dyersville, IA	DUB
Dysart, IA	DUB
Eagan, MN	STP
Eagle, CO	DEN
ID	B
WI	MIL
Eagle Butte, SD	RC
Eagle Center, IA	DUB
Eagle Grove, IA	DUB

Eagle Harbor, MI	STN
Eagle Lake, ME	PRT
TX	VIC
Eagle Pass, TX	LAR
Eagle River, AK	ANC
WI	SUP
Eagle Township, IL	PEO
Earl Park, IN	LFT
Earlimart, CA	FRS
Earling, IA	DM
Earlington, KY	OWN
Earlville, IA	DUB
IL	PEO
Early, IA	SC
Earth City, MO	STL
East Alton, IL	SFD
East Arcade, NY	BUF
East Aurora, NY	BUF
East Bay, NY	ROC
East Berlin, CT	HRT
East Bernard, TX	VIC
East Bethany, NY	BUF
East Bloomfield, NY	ROC
East Boston, MA	BO
East Brady, PA	E
East Bridgewater, MA	BO
East Bristol, WI	MAD
East Brookfield, MA	WOR
East Brunswick, NJ	MET
NJ	PSC
East Carbon, UT	SLC
East Chain, MN	WIN
East Chicago, IL	GRY
IN	GRY
IN	PRM
IN	ROM
East Cleveland, OH	CLV
East Dorset, VT	BUR
East Douglas, MA	WOR
East Dubuque, IL	RCK
East Eden, NY	BUF
East Elmhurst, NY	BRK
East Falmouth, MA	FR
East Freetown, MA	FR
East Gary, IN	GRY
East Goshen, PA	PH
East Grand Forks, MN	CR
East Greenbush, NY	ALB
East Greenwich, RI	PRO
East Hampton, CT	NOR
NY	RVC
East Hanover, NJ	NEW
NJ	PAT
East Hartford, CT	HRT
East Haven, CT	HRT
East Helena, MT	HEL
East Islip, NY	RVC
East Jordan, MI	GAY
East Kingston, NY	NY
East Lansdowne, PA	PH
East Lansing, MI	LAN
East Liverpool, OH	Y
East Longmeadow, MA	SPR
East Lyme, CT	NOR
East McKeesport, PA	PIT
East Meadow, NY	RVC
East Millinocket, ME	PRT
East Millstone, NJ	MET
East Moline, IL	PEO
East Newark, NJ	NEW
East Northport, NY	RVC
East Orange, NJ	NEW
East Palestine, OH	Y
East Palo Alto, CA	SFR
East Patchogue, NY	RVC
East Pembroke, NY	BUF
East Peoria, IL	PEO
East Pittsburgh, PA	PBR
PA	PIT
East Pleasant Plain, IA	DAV
East Providence, RI	PRO
East Rochester, NY	ROC
East Rockaway, NY	RVC
East Rutherford, NJ	NEW
East St. Louis, IL	BEL
East Stroudsburg, PA	SCR
East Syracuse, NY	SY
East Taunton, MA	FR
East Tawas, MI	GAY
East Templeton, MA	WOR
East Troy, WI	MIL
East Vandergrift, PA	GBG
East Walpole, MA	BO
East Wenatchee, WA	YAK
East Windsor, CT	HRT
Eastgate, TX	BEA
Easthampton, MA	SPR
Eastlake, OH	CLV
Eastland, TX	FWT
Eastman, WI	LC
Easton, CA	FRS

CT	BGP
KS	KCK
MA	FR
MD	WIL
MN	WIN
MO	KC
PA	ALN
PA	SAM
Eastpointe, MI	DET
Eastport, ME	PRT
NY	RVC
Eaton, OH	CIN
WI	GB
Eaton Rapids, MI	LAN
Eatonton, GA	ATL
Eatontown, NJ	TR
Eau Claire, WI	LC
Eau Galle, WI	LC
Ebensburg, PA	ALT
Ebeye, MH	MI
Echo, LA	ALX
Ecorse, MI	DET
Edcouch, TX	BWN
Eddystone, PA	PH
Eddyville, IA	DAV
KY	OWN
Eden, NC	CHL
NY	BUF
SD	SFS
TX	SAN
WI	MIL
Eden Prairie, MN	STP
Eden Valley, MN	NU
MN	SCL
Edenton, NC	R
Edgar, WI	LC
Edgard, LA	NO
Edgartown, MA	FR
Edgefield, SC	CHR
Edgeley, ND	FAR
Edgerton, KS	KCK
OH	TOL
WI	MAD
Edgewater, MD	BAL
NJ	NEW
Edgewood, IA	DUB
IL	SFD
KY	COV
MD	BAL
Edina, MN	STP
MO	JC
Edinboro, PA	E
Edinburg, TX	BWN
Edinburgh, IN	IND
Edison, NJ	MET
NJ	PSC
Edisto Island, SC	CHR
Edmond, OK	OKL
Edmonds, WA	SEA
Edmonton, KY	L
Edmore, MI	GR
Edna, TX	VIC
Edson, WI	LC
Edwards, CO	DEN
NY	OG
Edwardsburg, MI	KAL
Edwardsville, IL	SFD
PA	PHU
PA	SCR
Effingham, IL	SFD
KS	KCK
Ege, IN	FTW
Egg Harbor, WI	GB
Egg Harbor City, NJ	CAM
Egg Harbor Township, NJ	CAM
Eggertsville, NY	BUF
Egypt, OH	CIN
Ehrenfeld, PA	ALT
El Cajon, CA	EST
CA	NTN
CA	SD
El Campo, TX	VIC
El Centro, CA	SD
El Cerrito, CA	OAK
El Dorado, AR	LR
KS	WCH
El Dorado Hills, CA	SAC
El Dorado Springs, MO	SPC
El Mirage, AZ	PHX
El Monte, CA	LA
El Paso, IL	PEO
TX	ELP
TX	OLL
El Reno, OK	OKL
El Rito, NM	SFE
El Segundo, CA	LA
CA	NTN
El Sobrante, CA	OAK
El Toro, CA	ORG
Eland, WI	GB
Elba, MN	WIN

NY	BUF
WI	MIL
Elberon, NJ	TR
Elberta, AL	MOB
Elbow Lake, MN	SCL
Elburn, IL	RCK
Elcho, WI	GB
Eldon, IA	DAV
MO	JC
Eldora, IA	DUB
Eldorado, IL	BEL
TX	SAN
WI	MIL
Eldred, PA	E
Eldridge, IA	DAV
Electra, TX	FWT
Elgin, IL	RCK
NE	OM
OK	OKL
OR	BAK
TX	AUS
Elizabeth, IL	RCK
MN	SCL
NJ	NEW
NJ	PHU
NJ	PSC
PA	PIT
Elizabeth City, NC	R
Elizabethton, TN	KNX
Elizabethtown, IL	BEL
KY	L
NY	OG
PA	HBG
Elk, TX	AUS
Elk City, OK	OKL
Elk Grove, CA	SAC
WI	MAD
Elk Grove Village, IL	CHI
Elk Mound, WI	LC
Elk Point, SD	SFS
Elk Rapids, MI	GAY
Elk River, MN	SCL
Elkader, IA	DUB
Elkhart, IA	DM
IL	PEO
IN	FTW
KS	DOD
Elkhart Lake, WI	MIL
Elkhorn, NE	OM
WI	MIL
Elkins, WV	WH
Elkins Park, PA	PH
Elkland, PA	SCR
Elko, NV	RNO
Elkton, FL	STA
KY	OWN
MD	WIL
SD	SFS
VA	RIC
Elkview, WV	WH
Ellenburg, NY	OG
Ellenburg Center, NY	OG
Ellendale, MN	WIN
ND	FAR
Ellengowan, PA	ALN
Ellensburg, WA	YAK
Ellenville, NY	NY
Ellicott City, MD	BAL
Ellicottville, NY	BUF
Ellington, CT	NOR
MO	SPC
Ellinwood, KS	DOD
Ellis, KS	SAL
Ellis Grove, IL	BEL
Ellisville, MO	STL
Ellsworth, KS	SAL
ME	PRT
MN	WIN
PA	PIT
WI	LC
Ellwood City, PA	PIT
Elm Creek, NE	GI
Elm Grove, WI	MIL
Elma, IA	DUB
NY	BUF
WA	SEA
Elmdale, MN	SCL
Elmendorf, TX	SAT
Elmer, NJ	CAM
Elmhurst, IL	JOL
NY	BRK
PA	LIT
PA	SCR
Elmira, MI	GAY
NY	ROC
Elmira Heights, NY	ROC
NY	STF
Elmo, KS	SAL
Elmont, NY	RVC
Elmora, PA	ALT
Elmsford, NY	NY

Elmwood, IL	PEO
WI	LC
Elmwood Park, IL	CHI
NJ	NEW
Elon College, NC	R
Eloy, AZ	TUC
Elrama, PA	PIT
Elrosa, MN	SCL
Elroy, WI	LC
Elsa, TX	BWN
Elsberry, MO	STL
Elsmere, DE	WIL
KY	COV
Elton, LA	LKC
Eltopia, WA	SPK
Elverson, PA	PH
Elwood, IN	LFT
Ely, MN	DUL
NV	LAV
Elyria, NE	GI
OH	CLV
Elyria Township, OH	CLV
Elysburg, PA	HBG
Elysian, MN	STP
Emeigh, PA	ALT
Emerald, KS	KCK
Emerson, NE	OM
NJ	NEW
Emery, SD	SFS
Emeryville, CA	OAK
Emily, MN	DUL
Emlenton, PA	E
Emmaus, PA	ALN
Emmetsburg, IA	SC
Emmett, ID	B
KS	KCK
MI	DET
Emmitsburg, MD	BAL
Emmonak, AK	FBK
Empire, MI	GAY
Emporia, KS	KCK
VA	RIC
Emporium, PA	E
Emsworth, PA	PIT
Encinal, TX	LAR
Encinitas, CA	SD
Encino, CA	LA
Enderlin, ND	FAR
Enders Island, CT	NOR
Endicott, NY	PSC
NY	SY
Endwell, NY	SY
Enfield, CT	HRT
IL	BEL
NH	MAN
Engadine, MI	MAR
Engelberg, AR	LR
Englewood, CO	DEN
FL	VEN
NJ	NEW
OH	CIN
Englewood Cliffs, NJ	NEW
Englishtown, NJ	TR
Enhaut, PA	HBG
Enid, OK	OKL
Ennis, TX	DAL
Enochsburg, IN	IND
Enola, PA	HBG
Enosburg Falls, VT	BUR
Ensenada, PR	PCE
Enterprise, AL	MOB
OR	BAK
Enumclaw, WA	SEA
Ephraim, UT	SLC
Ephrata, PA	HBG
WA	YAK
Epiphany, SD	SFS
Epping, NH	MAN
Epworth, IA	DUB
Equality, IL	BEL
Erath, LA	LAF
Erie, CO	DEN
KS	WCH
MI	DET
PA	E
PA	PBR
Erin, WI	SUP
Erlanger, KY	COV
Ernest, PA	GBG
PA	PBR
Esbon, KS	SAL
Escalon, CA	STO
Escanaba, MI	MAR
Escobares, TX	BWN
Escondido, CA	SD
Eskridge, KS	KCK
Esmond, ND	FAR
Esopus, NY	NY
Espanola, NM	SFE
Essex, CT	NOR
MA	BO

NY	OG
Essex Center, VT	BUR
Essex Junction, VT	BUR
Essexville, MI	SAG
Essington, PA	PH
Estacada, OR	P
Estate Elizabeth, VI	STV
Estate Tutu, VI	STV
Estelline, SD	SFS
Estes Park, CO	DEN
Estherville, IA	SC
Ethan, SD	SFS
Etna, PA	PIT
Ettrick, WI	LC
Euclid, MN	CR
OH	CLV
OH	PRM
Eudora, KS	KCK
Eufaula, AL	MOB
Eugene, OR	P
Eunice, LA	LAF
Eureka, CA	SR
IL	PEO
KS	WCH
MO	STL
MT	HEL
NV	RNO
SD	SFS
UT	SLC
Eureka Springs, AR	LR
Eustis, FL	ORL
Eutaw, AL	BIR
Evangeline, LA	LAF
Evans City, PA	PIT
Evans Mills, NY	OG
Evansdale, IA	DUB
Evanston, IL	CHI
WY	CHY
Evansville, IL	BEL
IN	EVN
WI	MAD
Evart, MI	GR
Eveleth, MN	DUL
Everett, MA	BO
PA	ALT
WA	SEA
Evergreen, CO	DEN
LA	ALX
Evergreen Park, IL	CHI
Everson, PA	GBG
Evesham Township, NJ	TR
Ewa, HI	HON
Ewa Beach, HI	HON
Ewen, MI	MAR
Ewing, MO	JC
NE	OM
Excelsior Springs, MO	KC
Excelsior, Lake Minnetonka, MN	STP
Exeter, CA	FRS
NE	LIN
NH	MAN
PA	SCR
RI	PRO
Exira, IA	DM
Export, PA	GBG
Exton, PA	PH
Eynon, PA	SCR
Eyota, MN	WIN
Fabens, TX	ELP
Fair Haven, NJ	TR
VT	BUR
Fair Lawn, NJ	NEW
Fair Oaks, CA	SAC
Fairbank, IA	DUB
Fairbanks, AK	FBK
Fairborn, OH	CIN
Fairbury, IL	PEO
NE	LIN
Fairchance, PA	GBG
Fairchild, WI	LC
Fairdale, KY	L
Fairfax, CA	SFR
DE	WIL
IA	DUB
MN	NU
OK	TLS
SD	RC
VA	ARL
VT	BUR
Fairfax Station, VA	ARL
Fairfield, AL	BIR
CA	SAC
CT	BGP
IA	DAV
IL	BEL
KY	L
ME	PRT
MT	HEL
ND	STN
NJ	NEW
OH	CIN

PA	HBG
TX	TYL
VT	BUR
Fairfield Bay, AR	LR
Fairfield Glade, TN	KNX
Fairhaven, MA	FR
Fairhope, AL	MOB
Fairlawn, OH	CLV
OH	OLL
Fairless Hills, PA	PH
Fairmont, MN	WIN
WV	WH
Fairmont City, IL	BEL
Fairmount, ND	FAR
NY	SY
Fairmount Springs, PA	SCR
Fairpoint, OH	STU
Fairport, NY	ROC
Fairport Harbor, OH	CLV
OH	PRM
Fairview, NJ	NEW
PA	E
TN	NSH
WI	LC
Fairview Heights, IL	BEL
Fairview Park, OH	CLV
OH	PRM
Faith, SD	RC
Fajardo, PR	CGS
Falconer, NY	BUF
Falfurrias, TX	CC
Fall Creek, WI	LC
Fall River, MA	FR
MA	SAM
MA	STF
Fallbrook, CA	SD
Fallentimber, PA	ALT
Fallon, NV	RNO
Falls Church, VA	ARL
Falls City, NE	LIN
TX	SAT
Falls Creek, PA	E
Fallsington, PA	PH
Fallston, MD	BAL
Falmouth, KY	COV
MA	FR
ME	PRT
Falun, MN	CR
Fancher, WI	LC
Fancy Farm, KY	OWN
Fannett, TX	BEA
Far Hills, NJ	MET
Fargo, ND	FAR
Faribault, MN	STP
Farley, IA	DUB
Farmer, SD	SFS
Farmer City, IL	PEO
Farmersville, CA	FRS
IL	SFD
Farming, MN	SCL
Farmingdale, NJ	TR
NY	BRK
NY	RVC
Farmington, CT	HRT
IA	DAV
IL	PEO
ME	PRT
MI	DET
MN	STP
MO	STL
NH	MAN
NM	GLP
PA	GBG
WI	MIL
WI	SUP
WV	WH
Farmington Hills, MI	DET
MI	OLD
Farmingville, NY	RVC
Farmville, NC	R
VA	RIC
Farnham, NY	BUF
Farrell, PA	E
Farwell, NE	GI
Faulkner, MD	WDC
Faulkton, SD	SFS
Faxon Township, MN	NU
Fayette, AL	BIR
IA	DUB
MO	JC
MS	JKS
OH	TOL
Fayette City, PA	GBG
Fayetteville, AR	LR
GA	ATL
IL	BEL
NC	R
NC	SAM
NY	SY
OH	CIN
TN	NSH

TX	AUS
Feasterville, PA	PH
Federal Way, WA	SEA
Feeding Hills, MA	SPR
Fefan, FM	CI
Felicity, OH	CIN
Fellsmere, FL	PMB
Felton, CA	MRY
MN	CR
Fennimore, WI	MAD
Fenton, LA	LKC
MI	LAN
MO	STL
Ferdinand, ID	B
IN	EVN
Fergus Falls, MN	SCL
Ferguson, MO	STL
Fernandina Beach, FL	STA
Ferndale, CA	SR
MI	DET
WA	SEA
Fernley, NV	RNO
Ferriday, LA	ALX
Ferris, TX	DAL
Fertile, MN	CR
Fessenden, ND	FAR
Festina, IA	DUB
Festus, MO	STL
Fidelity, KS	KCK
Fieldon, IL	SFD
Fife, WA	SEA
Fife Lake, MI	GAY
Fifield, WI	SUP
Fifth Ward, LA	ALX
Fillmore, CA	LA
IA	DUB
NY	BUF
Fincastle, VA	RIC
Findlay, OH	TOL
Fingal, ND	FAR
Finley, KY	L
ND	FAR
Finleyville, PA	PIT
Firebaugh, CA	FRS
Fish Creek, WI	GB
Fish Lake, IN	GRY
Fisher, MN	CR
Fishers, IN	LFT
Fishers Island, NY	NOR
Fisherville, MI	SAG
Fishkill, NY	NY
Fiskdale, MA	WOR
Fitchburg, MA	WOR
Flagler Beach, FL	STA
Flagstaff, AZ	PHX
Flaherty, KY	L
Flambeau, WI	SUP
Flanders, NJ	PAT
NJ	PSC
Flandreau, SD	SFS
Flasher, ND	BIS
Flat Rock, MI	DET
Flatonia, TX	VIC
Fleming, NY	ROC
Flemingsburg, KY	COV
Flemington, NJ	MET
Flensburg, MN	SCL
Flint, MI	LAN
MI	OLL
MI	STN
Flint Hill, MO	STL
Flintville, WI	GB
Floodwood, MN	DUL
Flora, IL	BEL
Flora Vista, NM	GLP
Floral Park, NY	BRK
NY	RVC
Florence, AL	BIR
AZ	TUC
CO	PBL
KS	WCH
KY	COV
NJ	TR
NY	SY
OR	P
SC	CHR
SD	SFS
WI	GB
Floresville, TX	SAT
Florham Park, NJ	PAT
Florian, MN	CR
Florida, NY	NY
PR	ARE
Florissant, LA	NO
MO	STL
Flossmoor, IL	CHI
Flourtown, PA	PH
Floydada, TX	LUB
Flush, KS	KCK
Flushing, MI	LAN
MI	PRM

NY	BRK
OH	STU
Foley, AL	MOB
MN	SCL
Folk, MO	JC
Follansbee, WV	WH
Folsom, CA	SAC
LA	NO
Fond du Lac, WI	MIL
Fonda, IA	SC
NY	ALB
Fontana, CA	SB
CA	VNN
WI	MIL
Footedale, PA	GBG
Footville, WI	MAD
Forbes Road, PA	GBG
Force, PA	E
Ford, WA	SPK
Ford City, PA	GBG
PA	SJP
Fords, NJ	MET
Fordsville, KY	OWN
Fordyce, AR	LR
NE	OM
Forest, MS	JKS
Forest City, IA	DUB
MN	NU
NC	CHL
PA	PSC
PA	SCR
Forest Grove, OR	P
Forest Hill, LA	ALX
Forest Hills, NY	BRK
PA	PIT
Forest Lake, MN	STP
Forest Park, IL	CHI
Forestburgh, NY	NY
Foreston, MN	SCL
Forestport, NY	SY
Forestville, CT	HRT
MD	WDC
NY	BUF
Forked River, NJ	TR
Forks, WA	SEA
Forman, ND	FAR
Forney, TX	DAL
Forrest City, AR	LR
Forsyth, MO	SPC
MT	GF
Fort Ann, NY	ALB
Fort Ashby, WV	WH
Fort Atkinson, IA	DUB
WI	MAD
Fort Bend Co., TX	GAL
Fort Benton, MT	GF
Fort Bragg, CA	SR
Fort Branch, IN	EVN
Fort Calhoun, NE	OM
Fort Collins, CO	DEN
Fort Covington, NY	OG
Fort Davis, TX	ELP
Fort Defiance, AZ	GLP
Fort Dodge, IA	SC
Fort Edward, NY	ALB
Fort Fairfield, ME	PRT
Fort Hancock, TX	ELP
Fort Jennings, OH	TOL
Fort Jones, CA	SAC
Fort Kent, ME	PRT
Fort Lauderdale, FL	MIA
Fort Leavenworth, KS	KCK
Fort Lee, NJ	NEW
Fort Loramie, OH	CIN
Fort Lupton, CO	DEN
Fort Madison, IA	DAV
Fort McClellan, AL	BIR
Fort Mitchell, KY	COV
Fort Monroe, VA	RIC
Fort Morgan, CO	DEN
Fort Myers, FL	VEN
Fort Myers Beach, FL	VEN
Fort Oglethorpe, GA	ATL
Fort Pierce, FL	PMB
FL	PSC
Fort Pierre, SD	RC
Fort Plain, NY	ALB
Fort Recovery, OH	CIN
Fort Riley, KS	SAL
Fort Scott, KS	WCH
Fort Shaw, MT	GF
Fort Smith, AR	LR
Fort Stockton, TX	SAN
Fort Sumner, NM	SFE
Fort Thomas, KY	COV
Fort Thompson, SD	SFS
Fort Tbtten, ND	FAR
Fort Tbtten Reservation, ND	FAR
Fort Walton Beach, FL	PT
Fort Washington, MD	WDC
PA	PH
Fort Wayne, IN	FTW
Fort Wingate, NM	GLP
Fort Worth, TX	FWT
Fort Yates, ND	BIS
Fortuna, CA	SR
Fortville, IN	IND
Forty Fort, PA	SCR
Fosston, MN	CR
Foster, RI	PRO
Foster City, CA	SFR
Fostoria, OH	TOL
Fountain, CO	COS
FL	PT
MN	WIN
Fountain City, WI	LC
Fountain Hill, PA	ALN
Fountain Hills, AZ	PHX
Fountain Valley, CA	ORG
Four Corners, LA	LAF
Fowler, CA	FRS
IN	LFT
KS	DOD
MI	LAN
Fowlerville, MI	LAN
Fox Chase Manor, PA	PH
PA	PHU
Fox Lake, IL	CHI
WI	MIL
Fox Point, WI	MIL
Foxborough, MA	BO
Foxholm, ND	BIS
Foxhome, MN	SCL
Frackville, PA	ALN
PA	PHU
Framingham, MA	BO
Francesville, IN	LFT
Francis Creek, WI	GB
Frankenmuth, MI	SAG
Frankenstein, MO	JC
Frankfort, IL	JOL
IN	LFT
KS	KCK
KY	LEX
MI	GAY
NY	ALB
SD	SFS
Franklin, IL	SFD
IN	IND
KY	OWN
LA	LAF
MA	BO
MN	NU
NC	CHL
NH	MAN
NJ	PAT
OH	CIN
PA	E
TN	NSH
TX	AUS
VA	RIC
WI	MIL
WV	WH
Franklin Furnace, OH	STU
Franklin Lakes, NJ	NEW
Franklin Park, IL	CHI
Franklin Park Borough, PA	PIT
Franklin Square, NY	RVC
Franklinton, LA	NO
Franklinville, NJ	CAM
NY	BUF
Fraser, MI	DET
Frazee, MN	CR
Frazier Park, CA	FRS
Frederic, WI	SUP
Frederick, CO	DEN
MD	BAL
OK	OKL
Fredericksburg, TX	SAT
VA	ARL
Fredericktown, MO	SPC
PA	PIT
Frederiksted, VI	STV
Fredonia, KS	WCH
NY	BUF
WI	MIL
Free Soil, MI	GR
Freeburg, IL	BEL
MO	JC
Freedom, PA	PIT
WI	GB
Freehold, NJ	TR
Freeland, MI	SAG
PA	PSC
PA	SCR
Freeport, FL	PT
IL	RCK
MN	SCL
NY	RVC
OH	STU
PA	GBG
TX	GAL
Freer, TX	CC
Frelsburg, TX	VIC
Fremont, CA	OAK
MI	GR
NE	OM
OH	TOL
Fremont Center, IL	CHI
French Creek, NY	BUF
French Lick, IN	IND
French Settlement, LA	BR
Frenchburg, KY	LEX
Frenchtown, IN	IND
MT	HEL
OH	CIN
OH	TOL
PA	E
Frenchville, ME	PRT
PA	E
Frenstat, TX	AUS
Fresh Meadows, NY	BRK
NY	STF
Fresno, CA	FRS
CA	VNN
Frewsburg, NY	BUF
Friday Harbor, WA	SEA
Fridley, MN	STP
Fried, ND	FAR
Friend, NE	LIN
Friendship, NY	BUF
Friendsville, PA	SCR
Friendswood, TX	GAL
Friona, TX	AMA
Frisco, TX	DAL
Front Royal, VA	ARL
Frontenac, KS	WCH
MN	STP
MO	STL
Frostburg, MD	BAL
Fruita, CO	PBL
Fruitland, ID	B
Fryburg, OH	CIN
PA	E
Frydek, TX	GAL
Fulda, IN	IND
MN	WIN
ND	FAR
OH	STU
Fullerton, CA	ORG
ND	FAR
NE	OM
Fulton, IL	RCK
KS	WCH
KY	OWN
MD	BAL
MO	JC
NY	SY
Fuquay-Varina, NC	R
Gackle, ND	FAR
Gadsden, AL	BIR
Gaffney, SC	CHR
Gagetown, MI	SAG
Gagil-Tomil, FM	CI
Gahanna, OH	COL
Gaines, MI	LAN
Gainesville, FL	STA
GA	ATL
TX	FWT
Gaithersburg, MD	WDC
Galena, AK	FBK
IL	RCK
KS	WCH
MD	WIL
Galena Park, TX	GAL
Gales Ferry, CT	NOR
Galesburg, IL	PEO
Galesville, WI	LC
Galeton, PA	E
Galion, OH	TOL
Gallatin, TN	NSH
Galliano, LA	HT
Gallipolis, OH	STU
Gallitzin, PA	ALT
Galloway, WI	LC
Gallup, NM	GLP
Galt, CA	SAC
Galva, IL	PEO
Galveston, TX	GAL
Gamaliel, KY	L
Gambrills, MD	WDC
Ganado, AZ	GLP
TX	VIC
Garapan Village, MP	CHK
Garber, IA	DUB
Garberville, CA	SR
Garden, MI	MAR
Garden City, KS	DOD
MI	DET
NY	RVC
SC	CHR
Garden Grove, CA	ORG
Garden Plain, KS	WCH
Garden Valley, ID	B
Gardena, CA	LA
Gardendale, AL	BIR
Gardenville, MO	STL
Gardiner, ME	PRT
NY	NY
Gardner, CO	PBL
KS	KCK
MA	WOR
Gardnerville, NV	RNO
Garfield, NJ	NEW
NM	LSC
Garfield Heights, OH	CLV
Garfield Park, DE	WIL
Garland, TX	DAL
Garnavillo, IA	DUB
Garner, IA	DUB
NC	R
Garnerville, NY	NY
Garnett, KS	KCK
Garretson, SD	SFS
Garrett, IN	FTW
Garrett Park, MD	WDC
Garrettsville, OH	Y
Garrison, MN	DUL
ND	BIS
NY	NY
Garryowen, IA	DUB
SD	SFS
Garwin, IA	DUB
Garwood, NJ	NEW
Gary, IN	GRY
SD	SFS
WV	WH
Gary-New Duluth, MN	DUL
Garyville, LA	NO
Gas City, IN	LFT
Gasport, NY	BUF
Gassaway, WV	WH
Gastonia, NC	CHL
Gate City, VA	RIC
Gates Mills, OH	CLV
Gatesville, TX	AUS
Gatlinburg, TN	KNX
Gautier, MS	BLX
Gaylord, MI	GAY
MN	NU
Gays Mills, WI	LC
Geddes, SD	SFS
Genesee, ID	B
Genesee Depot, WI	MIL
Geneseo, IL	PEO
ND	FAR
NY	ROC
Geneva, IA	DUB
IL	RCK
IN	FTW
MN	WIN
NE	LIN
NY	ROC
OH	Y
Genoa, IL	RCK
NE	OM
OH	TOL
WI	LC
Gentilly, MN	CR
George West, TX	CC
Georgetown, CA	SAC
CT	BGP
DE	WIL
IA	DAV
IL	PEO
KY	LEX
MA	BO
MN	CR
OH	CIN
SC	CHR
TX	AUS
WI	SUP
Gering, NE	GI
Germantown, IL	BEL
MD	WDC
NY	ALB
OH	CIN
WI	LC
WI	MIL
Gervais, OR	P
Gettysburg, PA	HBG
SD	SFS
Getzville, NY	BUF
Gheens, LA	HT
Ghent, MN	NU
Gibbon, MN	NU
Gibbsboro, NJ	CAM
Gibbstown, NJ	CAM
Gibraltar, MI	DET
Gibson, LA	HT
Gibson City, IL	JOL
Gibsonburg, OH	TOL
Gibsonia, PA	PBR
Giddings, TX	AUS

Gig Harbor, WA	SEA
Gila Bend, AZ	PHX
Gilbert, AZ	PHX
AZ	VNN
IA	DUB
MN	DUL
Gilbertville, IA	DUB
MA	WOR
Gildehaus, MO	STL
Gilford, NH	MAN
Gillespie, IL	SFD
Gillett, WI	GB
Gillette, WY	CHY
Gills Pier, MI	GAY
Gilman, IL	JOL
MN	SCL
WI	SUP
Gilmanton Iron Works, NH	MAN
Gilmer, TX	TYL
Gilmore City, IA	SC
Gilroy, CA	SJ
Girard, IL	SFD
KS	WCH
OH	Y
PA	E
PA	PBR
Girardville, PA	ALN
Glade Mills, PA	PIT
Gladstone, MI	MAR
MO	KC
NJ	PAT
Gladwin, MI	SAG
Gladwyne, PA	PH
Glandorf, OH	TOL
Glasco, KS	SAL
NY	NY
Glasgow, DE	WIL
KY	L
MO	JC
MT	GF
Glasgow Village, MO	STL
Glassboro, NJ	CAM
Glassport, PA	PIT
Glastonbury, CT	HRT
CT	STF
Glen Allen, VA	SAM
Glen Burnie, MD	BAL
Glen Campbell, PA	GBG
Glen Carbon, IL	SFD
Glen Cove, NY	RVC
NY	STF
Glen Dale, WV	WH
Glen Ellyn, IL	JOL
Glen Falls, NY	ALB
Glen Haven, WI	MAD
Glen Head, NY	RVC
Glen Lyon, PA	PHU
PA	PSC
PA	SCR
Glen Owen, MO	STL
Glen Rock, NJ	NEW
Glen Rose, TX	FWT
Glen Spey, NY	STF
Glen Ullin, ND	BIS
Glenbeulah, WI	MIL
Glenburn, ND	BIS
Glencoe, MN	NU
MO	STL
Glendale, AZ	PHX
CA	ARM
CA	LA
CO	DEN
NY	BRK
Glendale Heights, IL	JOL
Glendive, MT	GF
Glendora, CA	LA
MS	JKS
Glenfield, NY	OG
Glenmora, LA	ALX
Glenmore, WI	GB
Glennallen, AK	ANC
Glennie, MI	GAY
Glennonville, MO	SPC
Glenns Ferry, ID	B
Glenolden, PA	PH
Glenrock, WY	CHY
Glens Falls, NY	ALB
Glenshaw, PA	PIT
Glenside, PA	PH
Glenview, IL	CHI
Glenville, NY	ALB
WV	WH
Glenwood, IA	DM
IL	CHI
MN	SCL
Glenwood City, WI	SUP
Glenwood Springs, CO	DEN
Glidden, WI	SUP
Globe, AZ	TUC
Glocester, RI	PRO
Gloucester, MA	BO

NJ	CAM
VA	RIC
Glouster, OH	STU
Gloversville, NY	ALB
Gloverville, SC	CHR
Glyndon, MD	BAL
Glynwood, OH	CIN
Gobles, MI	KAL
Goddard, KS	WCH
Godfrey, IL	SFD
Goetzville, MI	MAR
Goffstown, NH	MAN
Gold Hill, OR	P
Golden, CO	DEN
Golden Gate, FL	VEN
Golden Meadow, LA	HT
Golden Valley, MN	STP
Goldendale, WA	YAK
Goldenrod, FL	ORL
Goldsboro, NC	R
Goldthwaite, TX	AUS
Goleta, CA	LA
Goliad, TX	VIC
Gonic, NH	MAN
Gonzales, CA	MRY
LA	BR
TX	SAT
Good Hart, MI	GAY
Good Thunder, MN	WIN
Gooding, ID	B
Goodland, IN	LFT
KS	SAL
Goodman, MS	JKS
WI	GB
Goodrich, IL	JOL
MI	LAN
Goodridge, MN	CR
Goodyear, AZ	PHX
Goose Creek, SC	CHR
Gordon, NE	GI
PA	ALN
WI	SUP
Gordonsville, VA	ARL
Gorham, KS	SAL
ME	PRT
NH	MAN
Goshen, CA	FRS
CT	HRT
IN	FTW
KY	L
MA	SPR
NY	NY
Gouldsboro, PA	SCR
Gouverneur, NY	OG
Gowanda, NY	BUF
Graceville, MN	NU
Graettinger, IA	SC
Graford, TX	FWT
Grafton, IL	SFD
MA	WOR
ND	FAR
NE	LIN
NY	ALB
OH	CLV
WI	MIL
WV	WH
Graham, TX	FWT
Grainfield, KS	SAL
Grambling, LA	SHP
Gramercy, LA	BR
Grampian, PA	E
Granada Hills, CA	LA
Granbury, TX	FWT
Granby, CT	HRT
MA	SPR
Grand Bay, AL	MOB
Grand Blanc, MI	LAN
Grand Caillou, LA	HT
Grand Canyon, AZ	PHX
Grand Chain, IL	BEL
Grand Chenier, LA	LKC
Grand Coteau, LA	LAF
Grand Coulee, WA	YAK
Grand Forks, ND	FAR
Grand Haven, MI	GR
Grand Island, NE	GI
NY	BUF
Grand Isle, LA	HT
ME	PRT
Grand Junction, CO	PBL
IA	SC
Grand Lake, CO	DEN
Grand Ledge, MI	LAN
Grand Marais, MI	MAR
MN	DUL
Grand Meadow, MN	WIN
Grand Mound, IA	DAV
Grand Prairie, LA	LAF
TX	DAL
Grand Rapids, MI	GR
MI	STN

MN	DUL
Grand River, IA	DM
Grand Rivers, KY	OWN
Grand Ronde, OR	P
Grand Terrace, CA	SB
Grandview, ID	B
MO	KC
WA	YAK
Grandville, MI	GR
Granger, IA	DM
IN	FTW
TX	AUS
WA	YAK
Grangeville, ID	B
Granite City, IL	SFD
IL	STL
Granite Falls, MN	NU
Graniteville, VT	BUR
Grant, NE	LIN
Grant Town, WV	WH
Grantfork, IL	SFD
Grants, NM	GLP
Grants Pass, OR	P
Grantsburg, WI	SUP
Grants-Milan, NM	GLP
Grantsville, MD	BAL
Grantwood, MO	STL
Granville, IA	SC
IL	PEO
ND	FAR
NY	ALB
NY	PSC
OH	COL
Grapevine, TX	FWT
Grass Lake, MI	LAN
Grass Valley, CA	SAC
Gratiot, WI	MAD
Gray, ME	PRT
Grayling, MI	GAY
Graymoor, NY	NY
Grayslake, IL	CHI
Grayson, KY	LEX
Grayson Springs, KY	OWN
Great Barrington, MA	SPR
Great Bend, KS	DOD
PA	SCR
Great Falls, MT	GF
VA	ARL
Great Meadows, NJ	MET
NJ	PHU
Great Mills, MD	WDC
Great Neck, NY	RVC
Greater Cincinnati, OH	CIN
Greeley, CO	DEN
IA	DUB
KS	KCK
NE	GI
PA	SCR
Green, OH	CLV
Green Bay, WI	GB
Green Cove Springs, FL	STA
Green Creek, IL	SFD
Green Island, NY	ALB
Green Isle, MN	NU
Green Lake, WI	MAD
Green Pond, NJ	PAT
Green River, WY	CHY
Green Springs, OH	TOL
Green Tree, PA	PIT
Green Valley, AZ	TUC
MN	NU
Greenbelt, MD	WDC
Greenbrae, CA	SFR
Greenburgh, NY	NY
Greenbush, KS	WCH
MN	CR
Greencastle, IN	IND
PA	HBG
Greencreek, ID	B
Greendale, WI	MIL
Greene, IA	DUB
NY	SY
Greene County, VA	RIC
Greeneville, TN	KNX
Greenfield, CA	MRY
IA	DM
IL	SFD
IN	IND
MA	SPR
OH	CIN
WI	MIL
Greenfield Center, NY	ALB
Greenlawn, NY	RVC
Greenleaf, KS	SAL
MN	NU
WI	GB
Greenport, NY	RVC
Greensboro, GA	ATL
NC	CHL
Greensburg, IN	IND
KS	DOD

KY	L
PA	GBG
PA	PBR
Greenup, IL	SFD
Greenville, AL	MOB
DE	WIL
IL	SFD
ME	PRT
MI	GR
MS	JKS
NC	R
NH	MAN
NY	ALB
OH	CIN
PA	E
SC	CHR
TX	DAL
WI	GB
Greenwald, MN	SCL
Greenwell Springs, LA	BR
Greenwich, CT	BGP
NY	ALB
Greenwood, IN	IND
MS	JKS
SC	CHR
WI	LC
Greenwood Lake, NY	NY
Greer, SC	CHR
Gregory, SD	RC
TX	CC
Grenada, MS	JKS
Grenora, ND	BIS
Grenville, SD	SFS
Gresham, OR	P
WI	GB
Gretna, LA	NO
NE	OM
Grey Eagle, MN	SCL
Greybull, WY	CHY
Gridley, CA	SAC
Griffin, GA	ATL
Griffith, IN	GRY
Griggsville, IL	SFD
Grindstone, PA	GBG
Grinnell, IA	DAV
KS	SAL
Griswold, CT	NOR
IA	DM
Groom, TX	AMA
Grosse Ile, MI	DET
Grosse Pointe, MI	DET
Grosse Pointe Farms, MI	DET
Grosse Pointe Park, MI	DET
Grosse Tete, LA	BR
Groton, CT	NOR
MA	BO
NY	ROC
SD	SFS
Grove, OK	TLS
Grove City, FL	VEN
OH	COL
PA	E
Grove Hill, AL	MOB
Groveland, MA	BO
Groveport, OH	COL
Grover, SD	SFS
Groves, TX	BEA
Groveton, NH	MAN
Grulla, TX	BWN
Grundy Center, IA	DUB
Gruver, TX	AMA
Grygla, MN	CR
Guadalupe, AZ	PHX
CA	LA
Guanica, PR	PCE
Guasti, CA	SB
Guayama, PR	PCE
Guayanilla, PR	PCE
Guaynabo, PR	SJN
Guckeen, MN	WIN
Guerneville, CA	SR
Guernsey, WY	CHY
Gueydan, LA	LAF
Guilderland, NY	ALB
Guilford, CT	HRT
Gulf Breeze, FL	PT
Gulf Shores, AL	MOB
Gulfport, FL	SP
MS	BLX
Gull Lake, MI	KAL
Gun Barrel City, TX	TYL
Gunnison, CO	PBL
Guntersville, AL	BIR
Gurabo, PR	CGS
Gurnee, IL	CHI
IL	JOL
Gustine, CA	FRS
Guthrie, KY	OWN
OK	OKL
Guthrie Center, IA	DM
Guttenberg, IA	DUB

NJ	NEW
Guymon, OK	OKL
Gwinn, MI	MAR
Gwinner, ND	FAR
Gwynedd Valley, PA	PH
Gypsum, KS	SAL
Hacienda Heights, CA	LA
Hackberry, LA	LKC
Hackensack, MN	DUL
NJ	NEW
Hackettstown, NJ	MET
Haddon Heights, NJ	CAM
Haddon Township, NJ	CAM
Haddonfield, NJ	CAM
Hadley, MA	SPR
Hagaman, IL	SFD
NY	ALB
Hagerman, ID	B
Hagerstown, MD	BAL
Hague, ND	BIS
NY	ALB
Hahnville, LA	NO
Haiku, HI	HON
Hailey, ID	B
Haines, AK	JUN
Haines City, FL	ORL
Haines Falls, NY	ALB
Hainesport, NJ	TR
Hainesville, NJ	PAT
Halbur, IA	SC
Halder, WI	LC
Hale, MI	GAY
Hale Center, TX	LUB
Haledon, NJ	PAT
Hales Corners, WI	MIL
Half Moon Bay, CA	SFR
Halifax, MA	BO
Hallandale, FL	MIA
Hallettsville, TX	VIC
Halliday, ND	BIS
Hallock, MN	CR
Hallowell, ME	PRT
Halstad, MN	CR
Halstead, KS	WCH
Ham Lake, MN	STP
Hamburg, AR	LR
IA	DM
IN	IND
MI	LAN
NJ	PAT
NY	BUF
PA	ALN
Hamden, CT	HRT
Hamel, MN	STP
Hamilton, AL	BIR
GA	SAV
KS	WCH
MA	BO
MO	KC
MT	HEL
NJ	TR
NY	SY
OH	CIN
TX	AUS
VA	ARL
Hamilton Square, NJ	TR
Hamler, OH	TOL
Hamlet, IN	GRY
NC	CHL
Hamlin, ME	PRT
NY	ROC
Hammond, IN	GRY
IN	NTN
LA	BR
MN	WIN
NY	OG
WI	SUP
Hammondsport, NY	ROC
Hammondsville, OH	STU
Hammonton, NJ	CAM
Hampden, MA	SPR
ME	PRT
Hampshire, IL	RCK
Hampstead, NC	R
NH	MAN
Hampton, IA	DUB
MN	STP
NH	MAN
NJ	MET
VA	RIC
Hampton Bays, NY	RVC
Hampton Beach, NH	MAN
Hamptonburgh, NY	STF
Hamptonville, NC	CHL
Hamtramck, MI	DET
MI	STN
Hana, HI	HON
Hancock, MD	BAL
MI	MAR
NY	ALB
Hancock Township, MN	STP

Hanford, CA	FRS
Hankinson, ND	FAR
Hannah, MI	GAY
Hannastown, PA	PBR
Hannibal, MO	JC
NY	SY
Hanover, IA	DUB
IL	RCK
KS	SAL
MA	BO
NH	MAN
PA	HBG
Hanover Park, IL	CHI
Hansboro, ND	FAR
Hanson, MA	BO
Hanston, KS	DOD
Hapeville, GA	ATL
Happy, TX	AMA
Harahan, LA	NO
Harbor Beach, MI	SAG
Harbor Springs, MI	GAY
Harborcreek, PA	E
Hardin, IL	SFD
MT	GF
Harding, MN	SCL
PA	SCR
Hardinsburg, KY	OWN
Hardwick, VT	BUR
Harker Heights, TX	AUS
Harlan, IA	DM
KY	LEX
Harleigh, PA	SCR
Harlingen, TX	BWN
Harlowton, MT	HEL
Harmarville, PA	PIT
Harmon, IL	RCK
Harmony, MN	WIN
Harper, IA	DAV
KS	WCH
TX	SAT
Harper Woods, MI	DET
Harpers Ferry, IA	DUB
WV	WH
Harrah, OK	OKL
Harrietta, MI	GAY
Harriettsville, OH	STU
Harriman, NY	NY
TN	KNX
Harrington, WA	SPK
Harrington Park, NJ	NEW
Harris Hill, NY	BUF
Harrisburg, IL	BEL
PA	HBG
PA	PSC
Harrison, AR	LR
MI	SAG
NJ	NEW
NY	NY
WI	SUP
Harrison City, PA	GBG
Harrison Twp., MI	DET
Harrisonburg, VA	RIC
Harrisonville, MO	KC
Harrisville, MI	GAY
NH	MAN
NY	OG
WV	WH
Harrodsburg, KY	LEX
Harrold, SD	SFS
Harsens Island, MI	DET
Hart, MI	GR
Hartford, AR	LR
CT	HRT
CT	STF
KS	KCK
KY	OWN
MI	KAL
SD	SFS
WI	MIL
Hartford City, IN	LFT
Hartington, NE	OM
Hartland, IL	RCK
MI	LAN
WI	MIL
Hartline, WA	YAK
Hartsdale, NY	NY
Hartshorne, OK	TLS
Hartsville, SC	CHR
Hartwell, GA	ATL
Harvard, IL	RCK
MA	WOR
NE	LIN
Harvey, IL	CHI
LA	NO
ND	FAR
Harvey Cedars, NJ	TR
Harveys Lake, PA	SCR
Harwichport, MA	FR
Harwick, PA	PIT
Harwinton, CT	HRT
Harwood Heights, IL	CHI

Hasbrouck Heights, NJ	NEW
Haskell, NJ	PAT
Hassan Township, MN	STP
Hastings, MI	KAL
MN	STP
NE	LIN
PA	ALT
Hastings-on-Hudson, NY	NY
Hatboro, PA	PH
Hatch, NM	LSC
Hatfield, MA	SPR
PA	PH
Hathaway Manor, MO	STL
Hatillo, PR	ARE
Hatley, WI	LC
Hato Rey, PR	SJN
Hattiesburg, MS	BLX
Haubstadt, IN	EVN
Haugen, WI	SUP
Hauppauge, NY	RVC
Havana, IL	PEO
Havelock, NC	R
Haverford, PA	PH
Haverhill, IA	DUB
MA	BO
Haverstraw, NY	NY
Havertown, PA	PH
Havre, MT	GF
Havre de Grace, MD	BAL
Hawaiian Gardens, CA	LA
Hawarden, IA	SC
Hawesville, KY	OWN
Hawi, HI	HON
Hawk Point, MO	STL
Hawk Run, PA	PBR
Hawkeye, IA	DUB
Hawkins, WI	SUP
Hawley, MN	CR
PA	SCR
Haworth, NJ	NEW
Hawthorne, CA	LA
NJ	PAT
NV	RNO
NY	NY
Hayden, AZ	TUC
Haydenville, MA	SPR
Hayfield, MN	WIN
Hayneville, AL	MOB
Hays, KS	SAL
MT	GF
Haysville, KS	WCH
Hayward, CA	OAK
WI	SUP
Hazard, KY	LEX
Hazel Crest, IL	CHI
Hazel Green, WI	MAD
Hazel Park, MI	DET
Hazelton, ND	BIS
Hazelwood, MN	STP
MO	STL
Hazen, ND	BIS
Hazlehurst, GA	SAV
Hazlet, NJ	TR
Hazleton, IA	DUB
PA	PHU
PA	PSC
PA	SCR
Healdsburg, CA	SR
Healy, AK	FBK
Hearne, TX	AUS
Heart Butte, MT	HEL
Heath, OH	COL
Hebbronville, TX	CC
TX	LAR
Hebron, CT	NOR
IN	GRY
ND	BIS
NE	LIN
Hecker, IL	BEL
Heckscherville, PA	ALN
Hecla, SD	SFS
Hector, MN	NU
Heffron, WI	LC
Hegbert, MN	NU
Heidelberg, MN	STP
Heilwood, PA	GBG
Helena, AR	LR
MI	SAG
MT	HEL
Helenwood, TN	KNX
Hellertown, PA	ALN
Helmetta, NJ	MET
Helmville, MT	HEL
Helotes, TX	SAT
Helper, UT	SLC
Hemet, CA	SB
Hemingford, NE	GI
Hemlock, MI	SAG
Hemphill, TX	TYL
Hempstead, NY	RVC
NY	STF

TX	GAL
Henderson, KY	OWN
LA	LAF
MN	NU
NC	R
NV	LAV
TX	TYL
Hendersonville, NC	CHL
TN	NSH
Hennepin, IL	PEO
Hennessey, OK	OKL
Henniker, NH	MAN
Henning, MN	SCL
Henrietta, NY	ROC
TX	FWT
Henry, IL	PEO
LA	LAF
SD	SFS
Henryetta, OK	TLS
Henryville, IN	IND
Henshaw, KY	OWN
Heppner, OR	BAK
Herculaneum, MO	STL
Hercules, CA	OAK
Hereford, AZ	TUC
TX	AMA
Herington, KS	SAL
Herkimer, NY	ALB
Herman, MN	SCL
PA	PIT
Hermann, MO	JC
Hermansville, MI	MAR
Herminie, PA	GBG
PA	PBR
Hermiston, OR	BAK
Hermitage, MO	JC
PA	E
PA	PBR
Hermosa, SD	RC
Hermosa Beach, CA	LA
Hernando, MS	JKS
Herndon, KS	SAL
VA	ARL
Heron Bay, AL	MOB
Heron Lake, MN	WIN
Herreid, SD	SFS
Herrin, IL	BEL
Herron, MI	GAY
Herscher, IL	JOL
Hershey, PA	HBG
Hesperia, CA	SB
Hessmer, LA	ALX
Hettinger, ND	BIS
Heun, NE	OM
Heuvelton, NY	OG
Hewitt, NJ	PAT
WI	LC
Hewlett, NY	RVC
Hialeah, FL	MIA
Hialeah Gardens, FL	MIA
Hiawatha, IA	DUB
KS	KCK
Hibbing, MN	DUL
Hickman, KY	OWN
Hickory, MD	BAL
NC	CHL
Hickory Hills, IL	CHI
Hicksville, NY	RVC
OH	TOL
Hidalgo, TX	BWN
Higganum, CT	NOR
Higgins Lake, MI	GAY
Higginsville, MO	KC
High Bridge, NJ	MET
High Hill, TX	VIC
High Point, NC	CHL
High Ridge, MO	STL
High Springs, FL	STA
Highbridge, WI	SUP
Highgate Center, VT	BUR
Highland, CA	SB
IL	SFD
IN	GRY
MI	DET
NY	NY
WI	MAD
Highland Beach, FL	PMB
Highland Falls, NY	NY
Highland Heights, KY	COV
OH	CLV
Highland Lakes, NJ	PAT
Highland Mills, NY	NY
Highland Park, IL	CHI
MI	DET
NJ	MET
PA	PH
Highland Springs, VA	RIC
Highlands, NJ	TR
TX	GAL
Highlands Ranch, CO	COS
Highmore, SD	SFS

Hightstown, NJ	TR
Highwood, IL	CHI
Hilbert, WI	GB
Hill City, KS	SAL
MN	DUL
SD	RC
Hillcrest Heights, MD	WDC
Hilliard, OH	COL
Hillje, TX	VIC
Hillman, MI	GAY
MN	DUL
MN	SCL
Hills, IA	DAV
Hillsboro, IL	SFD
MO	STL
ND	FAR
NH	MAN
OH	CIN
OR	P
TX	FWT
WI	LC
Hillsborough, NC	R
NJ	MET
Hillsborough Township, NJ	PSC
Hillsdale, MI	LAN
NJ	NEW
Hillside, IL	CHI
IL	OLL
NJ	NEW
NJ	PHU
Hillsville, PA	PIT
Hilltop, MD	WDC
Hilltown, PA	PH
PA	PSC
Hilmar, CA	FRS
Hilo, HI	HON
Hilton, NY	ROC
Hilton Head Island, SC	CHR
Hinckley, MN	DUL
NY	SY
OH	CLV
Hinesburg, VT	BUR
Hinesville, GA	SAV
Hingham, MA	BO
Hinsdale, IL	JOL
MA	SPR
NH	MAN
NY	BUF
Hinton, WV	WH
Hirlingen, MO	KC
Hitchcock, OK	OKL
TX	GAL
Hobart, IN	GRY
Hobbs, NM	LSC
Hobe Sound, FL	PMB
Hoboken, NJ	NEW
Hobson, TX	SAT
Hockessin, DE	WIL
Hodge, LA	SHP
Hodgenville, KY	L
Hofa Park, WI	GB
Hoffman Estates, IL	CHI
Hogansburg, NY	OG
Hohenwald, TN	NSH
Hohokus, NJ	NEW
Hoisington, KS	DOD
Hokah, MN	WIN
Holbrook, AZ	GLP
IA	DAV
MA	BO
NY	RVC
Holden, MO	KC
WV	WH
Holdenville, OK	TLS
Holdingford, MN	SCL
Holdrege, NE	LIN
Holgate, OH	TOL
Holiday, FL	SP
Holiday Park, PA	PIT
Holland, MI	GR
NY	BUF
PA	LIT
PA	PH
Holland Patent, NY	SY
Hollandale, WI	MAD
Hollandtown, WI	GB
Holley, NY	BUF
Hollidaysburg, PA	ALT
Hollister, CA	MRY
Holliston, MA	BO
Holloway, MN	NU
Holly, CO	PBL
MI	DET
Holly Springs, MS	JKS
Hollywood, CA	SFR
FL	MIA
MD	WDC
Holmdel, NJ	TR
Holmen, WI	LC
Holmes Beach, FL	VEN
Holstein, IA	SC

Holton, KS	KCK
Holts Summit, MO	JC
Holtville, CA	SD
Holy Cross, AK	FBK
IA	DUB
KY	L
WI	MIL
Holy Hill, WI	MIL
Holy Trinity, AL	MOB
Holyoke, CO	DEN
MA	SPR
Holyrood, KS	SAL
Homedale, ID	B
Homer, AK	ANC
NY	SY
Homer City, PA	PBR
Homestead, FL	MIA
PA	PIT
Hometown, IL	CHI
Homewood, IL	CHI
Homosassa, FL	SP
Honaunau, HI	HON
Hondo, TX	SAT
Honeoye, NY	ROC
Honeoye Falls, NY	ROC
Honesdale, PA	SCR
Honey Brook, PA	PH
Honokaa, HI	HON
Honolulu, HI	HON
Hood River, OR	BAK
Hooksett, NH	MAN
Hoonah, AK	JUN
Hoopa, CA	SR
Hooper, NE	OM
Hooper Bay, AK	FBK
Hoopeston, IL	PEO
Hooppole, IL	PEO
Hoosick Falls, NY	ALB
Hooversville, PA	ALT
Hopatcong, NJ	PAT
Hope, AR	LR
KS	SAL
ND	FAR
Hope Mills, NC	R
Hopedale, MA	WOR
OH	STU
Hopewell, NJ	TR
VA	RIC
Hopewell Junction, NY	NY
Hopewell Township, PA	PIT
Hopkins, MN	STP
Hopkins Park, IL	JOL
Hopkinsville, KY	OWN
Hopkinton, IA	DUB
MA	BO
NY	OG
RI	PRO
Hoquiam, WA	SEA
Horicon, WI	MIL
Horizon City, TX	ELP
Hormigueros, PR	MGZ
Hornell, NY	ROC
Hornick, IA	SC
Horseheads, NY	ROC
Horseshoe Bay, TX	AUS
Horseshoe Bend, AR	LR
ID	B
Horsham, PA	PH
Horton, KS	KCK
Hortonville, WI	GB
Hoschton, GA	ATL
Hosmer, SD	SFS
Hospers, IA	SC
Hostyn, TX	VIC
Hostyn Hill, TX	AUS
Hot Springs, AR	LR
NC	CHL
SD	RC
VA	RIC
Hot Springs National Park, AR	LR
Hot Springs Village, AR	LR
Houck, AZ	GLP
Houghton, IA	DAV
MI	MAR
Houghton Lake, MI	GAY
Houlton, ME	PRT
Houma, LA	HT
Housatonic, MA	SPR
House Springs, MO	STL
Houseville, NY	OG
Houston, MN	WIN
MO	SPC
TX	GAL
TX	OLL
TX	PBR
TX	STN
Houtzdale, PA	E
Hoven, SD	SFS
Howard, SD	SFS
WI	GB
Howard City, MI	GR

Howardstown, KY	L
Howell, MI	LAN
Howell Township, NJ	TR
Howells, NE	OM
Howes, SD	RC
Howland, ME	PRT
Hoxie, KS	SAL
Hoyt Lakes, MN	DUL
Hubbard, OH	Y
Hubbardston, MI	GR
Hubbell, MI	MAR
Hubertus, WI	MIL
Hudson, FL	SP
MA	BO
MI	LAN
NH	MAN
NY	ALB
NY	STF
OH	CLV
PA	SCR
WI	SUP
Hudson Falls, NY	ALB
Huffman, TX	GAL
Hughestown, PA	SCR
Hughson, CA	STO
Hugo, MN	STP
OK	TLS
Hugoton, KS	DOD
Hulbert, OK	TLS
Hull, MA	BO
Humacao, PR	CGS
Humacao Playa, PR	CGS
Humble, TX	GAL
Humboldt, IA	SC
KS	WCH
SD	SFS
TN	MEM
WI	GB
Humbolt, WI	GB
Hume, IL	SFD
Humphrey, NE	OM
NY	BUF
Hungerford, TX	VIC
Hunt Valley, MD	BAL
Hunter, ND	FAR
NY	STF
Huntersville, NC	CHL
Huntimer, SD	SFS
Huntingburg, IN	EVN
Huntingdon, PA	ALT
TN	MEM
Huntingdon Valley, PA	PH
Huntington, CT	BGP
IN	FTW
MA	SPR
NY	RVC
WV	WH
Huntington Beach, CA	ORG
Huntington Park, CA	LA
Huntington Station, NY	RVC
Huntingtown, MD	WDC
Huntley, IL	RCK
Huntsville, AL	BIR
AR	LR
OH	CIN
TX	GAL
UT	SLC
Hurdsfield, ND	FAR
Hurley, NM	LSC
NY	NY
WI	SUP
Huron, CA	FRS
OH	TOL
SD	SFS
Hurricane, WV	WH
Hurt, VA	RIC
Hurtsboro, AL	MOB
Hutchinson, KS	WCH
MN	NU
Huttonsville, WV	WH
Hyannis, MA	FR
Hyattsville, MD	WDC
Hyde Park, NY	NY
Hydes, MD	BAL
Ida, MI	DET
Ida Grove, IA	SC
Idabel, OK	TLS
Idaho City, ID	B
Idaho Falls, ID	B
Idaho Springs, CO	DEN
Idalou, TX	LUB
Idyllwild, CA	SB
Idylwilde, SD	SFS
Ignacio, CO	PBL
Ilasco, MO	JC
Iliff, CO	DEN
Ilion, NY	ALB
Illiopolis, IL	SFD
Imlay City, MI	DET
Immaculata, PA	PH
Immokalee, FL	VEN

Imogene, IA	DM
Imperial, CA	SD
MO	STL
NE	LIN
PA	PIT
Imperial Beach, CA	SD
Inarajan, GU	AGN
Inchelium, WA	SPK
Incline Village, NV	RNO
Independence, IA	DUB
KS	WCH
KY	COV
LA	BR
MO	KC
OH	CLV
OR	P
WI	LC
Indialantic, FL	ORL
Indian Creek, IL	CHI
MO	JC
WI	LC
Indian Grove, MO	JC
Indian Head, MD	WDC
Indian Island, ME	PRT
Indian Lake, NY	OG
Indian Orchard, MA	SPR
Indian River, MI	GAY
Indian Rocks Beach, FL	SP
Indian Township, ME	PRT
Indiana, PA	GBG
Indiana Harbor Co., IN	PRM
Indianapolis, IN	IND
IN	PRM
Indianola, IA	DM
MS	JKS
NE	LIN
Indiantown, FL	PMB
Indio, CA	SB
Industry, PA	PIT
Inez, TX	VIC
Ingalls, KS	DOD
Ingleside, IL	CHI
TX	CC
Inglewood, CA	LA
Ingram, PA	PIT
Inkerman, PA	SCR
Inkster, MI	DET
Inlet, NY	OG
Ino, WI	SUP
Institute, WI	GB
Interlachen, FL	STA
Interlaken, NY	ROC
International Falls, MN	DUL
Inver Grove Heights, MN	STP
Inverness, FL	SP
IL	CHI
Inwood, NY	RVC
WV	WH
Iola, KS	WCH
Iona, MN	WIN
Ione, CA	SAC
OR	BAK
WA	SPK
Ionia, IA	DUB
MI	GR
Iota, LA	LAF
Ioueldoab, FM	CI
Iowa, LA	LKC
Iowa City, IA	DAV
Iowa Falls, IA	DUB
Iowa Park, TX	FWT
Ipswich, MA	BO
SD	SFS
Ipwutek, FM	CI
Ireland, IN	EVN
Irish Settlement, IA	DM
Iron Mountain, MI	MAR
Iron River, MI	MAR
WI	SUP
Irons, MI	GR
Ironton, MO	SPC
OH	STU
Ironwood, MI	MAR
Iroquois, SD	SFS
Irvine, CA	ORG
KY	LEX
Irving, TX	DAL
TX	PBR
Irvington, KY	OWN
NJ	NEW
Irvington-on-the-Hudson, NY	NY
Irwin, IL	JOL
PA	GBG
Irwindale, CA	LA
Isaar, WI	GB
Isabela, PR	ARE
Isanti, MN	SCL
Iselin, NJ	MET
PA	GBG
Ishpeming, MI	MAR
Island Falls, ME	PRT

Island Grove, IL	SFD
Island Park, NY	RVC
Island Pond, VT	BUR
Isle Brevelle, LA	ALX
Isle La Motte, VT	BUR
Isleta, NM	SFE
Isleton, CA	SAC
Islip, NY	RVC
Islip Terrace, NY	RVC
Issaquah, WA	SEA
Issue, MD	WDC
Itasca, IL	JOL
Ithaca, MI	SAG
NY	ROC
Ivanhoe, MN	NU
Ivesdale, IL	PEO
Jackman, ME	PRT
Jacksboro, TX	FWT
Jackson, CA	SAC
GA	ATL
KY	LEX
MI	LAN
MN	WIN
MO	SPC
MS	JKS
NE	OM
NJ	MET
NJ	TR
OH	COL
PA	SCR
TN	MEM
WY	CHY
Jacksonport, WI	GB
Jacksonville, AL	BIR
AR	LR
FL	OLD
FL	PSC
FL	SAM
FL	STA
IL	SFD
NC	R
TX	TYL
Jacksonville Beach, FL	STA
Jacob's Prairie, MN	SCL
Jacumba, CA	SD
Jaffrey, NH	MAN
Jal, NM	LSC
Jamaica, IA	DM
NY	BRK
NY	NY
Jamaica Estates, NY	BRK
NY	NY
Jamaica Plain, MA	BO
MA	SAM
Jamesburg, NJ	MET
Jamestown, KS	SAL
KY	L
ND	FAR
NY	BUF
OH	CIN
RI	PRO
Jamesville, NY	SY
Jamison, PA	PH
Jamul, CA	SD
Janesville, MN	WIN
WI	MAD
Jarrell, TX	AUS
Jasonville, IN	EVN
Jasper, AL	BIR
IN	EVN
MN	WIN
TX	BEA
Java Center, NY	BUF
Jay, ME	PRT
Jayuya, PR	PCE
Jeanerette, LA	LAF
Jeannette, PA	GBG
PA	SJP
Jeffers, MN	WIN
Jefferson, GA	ATL
IA	SC
LA	NO
MA	WOR
NC	CHL
OH	Y
SD	SFS
TX	TYL
WI	MAD
Jefferson Boro, PA	PIT
Jefferson City, MO	JC
TN	KNX
Jeffersontown, KY	L
Jeffersonville, IN	IND
NY	NY
Jellico, KY	LEX
Jemez Pueblo, NM	SFE
Jemez Springs, NM	SFE
Jena, LA	ALX
Jenison, MI	GR
Jenkins, KY	LEX
Jenkintown, PA	PH

PA	PHU
Jennings, LA	LKC
MO	STL
Jensen Beach, FL	PMB
Jericho, WI	GB
Jermyn, PA	SCR
Jerome, AZ	PHX
ID	B
PA	PBR
Jersey City, NJ	NEW
NJ	PHU
NJ	PSC
Jersey Shore, PA	SCR
Jerseyville, IL	SFD
Jessenland, MN	NU
Jessie, ND	FAR
Jessup, MD	BAL
PA	PSC
PA	SCR
Jesup, GA	SAV
IA	DUB
Jetmore, KS	DOD
Jewell, IA	DUB
Jewett, OH	STU
Jewett City, CT	NOR
Jim Falls, WI	LC
Jim Thorpe, PA	ALN
Joanna, SC	CHR
Joelton, TN	NSH
Johannesburg, MI	GAY
John Day, OR	BAK
Johns Island, SC	CHR
Johnsburg, IL	RCK
MN	WIN
WI	MIL
Johnson, KS	DOD
Johnson City, NY	STF
NY	SY
TN	KNX
Johnson Creek, WI	MAD
Johnsonburg, PA	E
Johnsonville, NY	ALB
Johnston, IA	DM
RI	PRO
Johnston City, IL	BEL
Johnstown, CO	DEN
NY	ALB
OH	COL
PA	ALT
PA	PBR
PA	SJP
Joliet, IL	JOL
IL	PRM
Jolon, CA	MRY
Jones, OK	OKL
Jonesboro, AR	LR
GA	ATL
Jonesburg, MO	JC
Jonestown, TX	AUS
Joplin, MO	SPC
Joppa, MD	BAL
Jordan, MN	STP
NY	SY
OR	P
Jordan Valley, OR	BAK
Josephville, MO	STL
Joshua Tree, CA	SB
Jourdanton, TX	SAT
Juana Diaz, PR	PCE
Judice, LA	LAF
Julesburg, CO	DEN
Julian, CA	SD
Jump River, WI	SUP
Juncos, PR	CGS
Junction, OH	TOL
TX	SAN
Junction City, KS	SAL
OH	COL
OR	P
WI	LC
Juneau, AK	JUN
WI	MIL
Juno Beach, FL	PMB
Jupiter, FL	PMB
Justice, IL	CHI
Kadoka, SD	RC
Kahoka, MO	JC
Kahuku, HI	HON
Kahului, HI	HON
Kailua, HI	HON
Kailua-Kona, HI	HON
Kalaheo, HI	HON
Kalamazoo, MI	KAL
Kalaupapa, HI	HON
Kalida, OH	TOL
Kalispell, MT	HEL
Kalkaska, MI	GAY
Kaltag, AK	FBK
Kamiah, ID	B
Kampsville, IL	SFD
Kamuela, HI	HON

Kanab, UT	SLC
Kandiyohi, MN	NU
Kane, PA	E
Kaneohe, HI	HON
Kankakee, IL	JOL
Kanopolis, KS	SAL
Kansas, OH	TOL
Kansas City, KS	KCK
MO	KC
Kansas City North, MO	KC
Kansasville, WI	MIL
Kapaa, HI	HON
Kaplan, LA	LAF
Karlsruhe, ND	FAR
Karlstad, MN	CR
Karnes City, TX	SAT
Kaskaskia, IL	BEL
Kasson, MN	WIN
Katonah, NY	NY
Katy, TX	GAL
Kaufman, TX	DAL
Kaukauna, WI	GB
Kaunakakai, HI	HON
Kawkawlin, MI	SAG
Kayenta, AZ	GLP
Keams Canyon, AZ	GLP
Keansburg, NJ	TR
Kearney, MO	KC
NE	GI
Kearneysville, WV	WH
Kearns, UT	SLC
Kearny, AZ	TUC
NJ	NEW
Keaukaha, Hilo, HI	HON
Keene, NH	MAN
NY	OG
Keeseville, NY	OG
Keewatin, MN	DUL
Keizer, OR	P
Kekaha, HI	HON
Kelayres, PA	ALN
Keller, TX	FWT
WA	SPK
Kelley's Island, OH	TOL
Kelliher, MN	CR
Kellnersville, WI	GB
Kellogg, ID	B
MN	WIN
Kelly, KS	KCK
Kelso, MO	SPC
WA	SEA
Kemmerer, WY	CHY
Kenai, AK	ANC
Kendall, NY	BUF
WI	LC
Kendall Park, NJ	MET
Kendallville, IN	FTW
Kenedy, TX	SAT
Kenel, SD	RC
Kenesaw, NE	LIN
Kenilworth, NJ	NEW
Kenmare, ND	BIS
Kenmore, NY	BUF
NY	STF
Kennebec, SD	RC
Kennebunk, ME	PRT
Kennebunkport, ME	PRT
Kennedy Township, PA	PIT
Kenner, LA	NO
Kennesaw, GA	ATL
Kennett, MO	SPC
Kennett Square, PA	PH
PA	WIL
Kennewick, WA	YAK
Kenosha, WI	MIL
WI	PRM
Kensal, ND	FAR
Kensington, CA	OAK
CT	HRT
MD	WDC
MN	SCL
Kent, CT	HRT
MN	SCL
OH	Y
PA	GBG
WA	SEA
Kentfield, CA	SFR
Kentland, IN	LFT
Kenton, KY	COV
OH	COL
Kenton Hills, KY	COV
Kenyon, MN	STP
Keokuk, IA	DAV
Keota, IA	DAV
Kerhonkson, NY	STF
Kerman, CA	FRS
Kermit, TX	ELP
WV	WH
Kernersville, NC	CHL
Kerrville, TX	SAT
Kersey, PA	E

Keshena, WI	GB
Keswick, IA	DAV
Ketchikan, AK	JUN
Kettle Falls, WA	SPK
Keuterville, ID	B
Kew Gardens, NY	BRK
Kewanee, IL	PEO
Kewanna, IN	LFT
Kewaskum, WI	MIL
Kewaunee, WI	GB
Key Biscayne, FL	MIA
Key Largo, FL	MIA
Key West, FL	MIA
IA	DUB
Keyesville, WI	LC
Keyport, NJ	TR
Keyser, WV	WH
Keystone Heights, FL	STA
Kickapoo, IL	PEO
Kiel, WI	GB
Kieler, WI	MAD
Kihei, HI	HON
Kilgore, TX	TYL
Kilkenny, MN	STP
Killdeer, ND	BIS
Killeen, TX	AUS
Killingworth, CT	NOR
Kilmarnock, VA	ARL
Kiln, MS	BLX
Kimball, MN	SCL
NE	GI
SD	SFS
Kimberling City, MO	SPC
Kimberly, WI	GB
Kimberton, PA	PH
Kimeo, KS	SAL
Kimmswick, MO	STL
Kincaid, IL	SFD
Kinde, MI	SAG
Kinder, LA	LKC
Kindred, ND	FAR
King, WI	GB
King City, CA	MRY
King Ferry, NY	ROC
King of Prussia, PA	PH
Kingfisher, OK	OKL
Kingman, AZ	PHX
KS	WCH
Kings Park, NY	RVC
Kingsburg, CA	FRS
Kingsford, MI	MAR
Kingsford Heights, IN	GRY
Kingsland, TX	AUS
Kingsley, IA	SC
Kingsport, TN	KNX
Kingston, MA	BO
NY	NY
PA	PSC
PA	SCR
WI	MAD
Kingstree, SC	CHR
Kingsville, OH	Y
TX	CC
Kingwood, TX	GAL
WV	WH
Kinloch, MO	STL
Kinmundy, IL	BEL
Kinnelon, NJ	PAT
Kinross, IA	DAV
Kinsley, KS	DOD
Kinsman, IL	JOL
OH	Y
Kinston, NC	R
Kintyre, ND	FAR
Kiowa, KS	DOD
Kirby, OH	TOL
TX	SAT
Kirbyville, TX	BEA
Kirkland, WA	SEA
Kirksville, MO	JC
Kirkwood, MO	STL
NY	SY
Kirtland, OH	CLV
Kissimmee, FL	ORL
Kittanning, PA	GBG
Kittery, ME	PRT
Kitty Hawk, NC	R
Klacking Creek, MI	GAY
Klamath Falls, OR	BAK
Klondike, WI	GB
Kloten, WI	GB
Knapp Creek, NY	BUF
Knights Landing, CA	SAC
Knightstown, IN	IND
Knottsville, KY	OWN
Knowlton, WI	LC
Knox, IN	GRY
ND	FAR
Knox City, TX	FWT
Knoxville, IA	DAV
TN	KNX

Kodiak, AK	ANC
Koerth, TX	VIC
Kohler, WI	MIL
Kokomo, IN	LFT
Koloa, HI	HON
Kolonia, FM	CI
Kolonia, Pohnpei, FM	CI
Konawa, OK	OKL
Koppel, PA	PIT
Korona, FL	STA
Koror, FM	CI
Koror, Palau, PW	CI
Kosciusko, MS	JKS
Kosciuszko, TX	SAT
Kossuth, WI	GB
Kotlik, AK	FBK
Kotzebue, AK	FBK
Kountze, TX	BEA
Kouts, IN	GRY
Kovar, TX	AUS
Koyukuk, AK	FBK
Kraemer, LA	HT
Krakow, MO	STL
NE	OM
WI	GB
Kranzburg, SD	SFS
Krebs, OK	TLS
Kremmling, CO	DEN
Krok, WI	GB
Krotz Springs, LA	LAF
Kula, HI	HON
Kulpmont, PA	HBG
Kutztown, PA	ALN
Kwajalein, MH	MI
Kyle, SD	RC
TX	AUS
L'Anse, MI	MAR
La Canada Flintridge, CA	LA
La Crescent, MN	WIN
La Crescenta, CA	ARM
CA	LA
La Crosse, WI	LC
La Feria, TX	BWN
La Grande, OR	BAK
La Grange, IL	CHI
TX	AUS
TX	VIC
La Grange Park, IL	CHI
La Habra, CA	ORG
La Jolla, CA	SD
La Joya, NM	SFE
TX	BWN
La Junta, CO	PBL
La Marque, TX	GAL
La Mesa, CA	SD
NM	LSC
La Mirada, CA	LA
La Motte, IA	DUB
La Moure, ND	FAR
La Pine, OR	BAK
La Place, LA	NO
La Plata, MD	WDC
La Porte, IN	GRY
TX	GAL
La Porte City, IA	DUB
La Pryor, TX	LAR
La Puente, CA	LA
La Quinta, CA	SB
La Rue, OH	COL
La Salle, IL	PEO
La Valle, WI	MAD
La Verne, CA	LA
La Vernia, TX	SAT
Labadieville, LA	BR
LaBelle, FL	VEN
Lac du Flambeau, WI	SUP
LaCenter, KY	OWN
Lacey, WA	SEA
Laceyville, PA	SCR
Lackawanna, NY	BUF
NY	STF
Lacombe, LA	NO
Lacon, IL	PEO
Lacona, IA	DM
NY	SY
Laconia, NH	MAN
LaConner, WA	SEA
LaCoste, TX	SAT
LaCrosse, KS	DOD
Lacrosse, WA	SPK
LaCygne, KS	KCK
Ladd, IL	PEO
Ladue, MO	STL
Lady Lake, FL	ORL
Ladysmith, WI	SUP
Lafargeville, NY	OG
Lafayette, CA	OAK
CO	DEN
IN	LFT
LA	LAF
LA	OLL
MN	NU
NJ	PAT
NY	SY
OR	P
TN	NSH
Lafayette Hill, PA	PH
Lafferty, OH	STU
Lafitte, LA	NO
Laflin, PA	SCR
LaFollette, TN	KNX
Lago Vista, TX	AUS
LaGrange, GA	ATL
IN	FTW
KY	L
TX	AUS
LaGrange Park, IL	CHI
Lagro, IN	FTW
Laguna, NM	GLP
Laguna Beach, CA	ORG
Laguna Hills, CA	ORG
Laguna Niguel, CA	ORG
Lagunitas, CA	SFR
Lahaina, HI	HON
Laingsburg, MI	LAN
Lajas, PR	MGZ
Lake Andes, SD	SFS
Lake Ariel, PA	SCR
Lake Arrowhead, CA	SB
Lake Arthur, LA	LKC
Lake Benton, MN	NU
Lake Charles, LA	LKC
LA	OLL
Lake City, FL	STA
IA	SC
MI	GAY
MN	WIN
SC	CHR
SD	SFS
Lake Clear, NY	OG
Lake Crystal, MN	WIN
Lake Dallas, TX	FWT
Lake Elmo, MN	STP
Lake Elsinore, CA	SB
Lake Eunice Township, MN	CR
Lake Five, WI	MIL
Lake Forest, CA	ORG
IL	CHI
Lake Gaston, VA	RIC
Lake Geneva, WI	MIL
Lake George, NY	ALB
Lake Harmony, PA	ALN
Lake Havasu City, AZ	PHX
Lake Henry, MN	SCL
Lake Hopatcong, NJ	PAT
Lake Itasca, MN	CR
Lake Jackson, TX	GAL
Lake Katrine, NY	NY
Lake Leelanau, MI	GAY
Lake Lillian, MN	NU
Lake Linden, MI	MAR
Lake Luzerne, NY	ALB
Lake Mills, IA	DUB
WI	MAD
Lake Milton, OH	Y
Lake Nebagamon, WI	SUP
Lake Odessa, MI	GR
Lake Orion, MI	DET
Lake Oswego, OR	P
Lake Ozark, MO	JC
Lake Park, MN	CR
Lake Placid, FL	VEN
NY	OG
Lake Pleasant, NY	OG
Lake Providence, LA	SHP
Lake Reno, MN	SCL
Lake Ridge, VA	ARL
Lake Ronkonkoma, NY	RVC
Lake St. Croix Beach, MN	STP
Lake St. Louis, MO	STL
Lake San Marcos, CA	SD
Lake Silkworth, PA	SCR
Lake Station, IN	GRY
Lake Tamarisk, CA	SB
Lake Tomahawk, WI	SUP
Lake Travis, TX	AUS
Lake View, NY	BUF
Lake Villa, IL	CHI
Lake Village, AR	LR
IN	LFT
Lake Wales, FL	ORL
Lake Williams, ND	FAR
Lake Wilson, MN	WIN
Lake Winola, PA	SCR
Lake Worth, FL	PMB
FL	PSC
Lake Zurich, IL	CHI
Lakefield, MN	WIN
Lakehurst, NJ	TR
Lakeland, FL	ORL
GA	SAV
LA	BR
NY	SY
Lakeport, CA	SR
MI	DET
NH	MAN
Lakeside, CA	SD
Lakeview, MI	GR
OR	BAK
Lakeville, CT	HRT
IN	FTW
MA	BO
MN	STP
Lakewood, CA	LA
CO	DEN
NJ	TR
NY	BUF
OH	CLV
OH	PRM
WA	SEA
WI	GB
Lakewood Club, MI	GR
Lakin, KS	DOD
Lakota, ND	FAR
Lamar, CO	PBL
MO	SPC
Lamberton, MN	NU
Lambertville, NJ	MET
Lame Deer, MT	GF
Lamesa, TX	LUB
Lamoille, MN	WIN
Lamont, CA	FRS
IA	DUB
Lampasas, TX	AUS
Lanai City, HI	HON
Lanark, WI	LC
Lanark Village, FL	PT
Lancaster, CA	LA
KY	LEX
MA	WOR
MN	CR
NH	MAN
NY	BUF
NY	STF
OH	COL
PA	HBG
SC	CHR
TX	DAL
WI	MAD
Lancing, TN	KNX
Land O'Lakes, FL	SP
Landeck, OH	TOL
Lander, WY	CHY
Landisville, NJ	CAM
Land-O'-Lakes, WI	SUP
Landover Hills, MD	WDC
Lanesboro, MA	SPR
MN	WIN
Lanesville, IN	IND
Lanett, AL	BIR
Langdon, ND	FAR
Langford, NY	BUF
Langhorne, PA	PH
PA	PHU
Langlade, WI	GB
Langley, OK	TLS
WA	SEA
Lanham, MD	WDC
Lanham-Seabrook, MD	WDC
Lankin, ND	FAR
Lansdale, PA	PH
PA	PHU
Lansdowne, PA	PH
Lansford, PA	ALN
PA	PSC
Lansing, IA	DUB
IL	CHI
KS	KCK
MI	LAN
MI	NTN
NY	ROC
Lantana, FL	PMB
Laona, WI	GB
Lapeer, KS	KCK
MI	DET
LaPointe, WI	SUP
Laporte, MN	CR
Lapwai, ID	B
Laramie, WY	CHY
Larchmont, NY	NY
Larchwood, IA	SC
Laredo, TX	CC
TX	LAR
Lares, PR	ARE
Largo, FL	SP
MD	WDC
Larimore, ND	FAR
Larks Lake, MI	GAY
Larkspur, CA	SFR
Larksville, PA	SCR
Larned, KS	DOD
Larose, LA	HT
Las Animas, CO	PBL
Las Cruces, NM	LSC
NM	VNN
Las Marias, PR	MGZ
Las Piedras, PR	CGS
Las Vegas, NM	SFE
NV	LAV
NV	OLL
NV	VNN
Lastrup, MN	SCL
Latham, NY	ALB
Latium, TX	AUS
Laton, CA	FRS
Latrobe, PA	GBG
PA	SJP
Lattimer Mines, PA	SCR
Laughlin, NV	LAV
LaUnion, NM	LSC
Laurel, MD	BAL
MD	WDC
MS	BLX
MT	GF
NE	OM
Laurence Harbor, NJ	MET
Laurens, IA	SC
Laurie, MO	JC
Laurinburg, NC	R
Lavallette, NJ	TR
Laveen, AZ	PHX
Laverock, PA	PH
Lawler, IA	DUB
Lawrence, KS	KCK
MA	BO
MA	NTN
MA	SAM
NE	LIN
PA	PIT
Lawrenceburg, IN	IND
KY	LEX
TN	NSH
Lawrenceton, MO	STL
Lawrenceville, GA	ATL
IL	BEL
NJ	TR
Lawtell, LA	LAF
Lawton, OK	OKL
Layton, UT	SLC
Le Center, MN	STP
Le Claire-Princeton, IA	DAV
Le Mars, IA	SC
Le Roy, MN	WIN
NY	BUF
WI	MIL
Le Sueur, MN	STP
Lead, SD	RC
Leadore, ID	B
Leadville, CO	COS
League City, TX	GAL
Leander, TX	AUS
Leavenworth, KS	KCK
MN	NU
WA	YAK
Leawood, KS	KCK
Lebanon, CT	NOR
IL	BEL
IN	LFT
KY	L
MO	SPC
NH	MAN
OH	CIN
OR	P
PA	HBG
TN	NSH
VA	RIC
Lebanon Junction, KY	L
Lebanon Township, WI	GB
Lebeau, LA	LAF
Lecanto, FL	SP
Leckrone, PA	GBG
Lecompte, LA	ALX
Ledyard, IA	SC
Lee, IL	RCK
MA	SPR
Lee Center, NY	SY
Lee's Summit, MO	KC
Leechburg, PA	GBG
Leeds, AL	BIR
MA	SPR
ND	FAR
Leesburg, FL	ORL
VA	ARL
Leesville, LA	ALX
Leetonia, OH	Y
Lefor, ND	BIS
Leggett, CA	SR
Lehigh Acres, FL	VEN
Lehighton, PA	ALN
Leicester, MA	WOR
NY	ROC
Leigh, NE	OM
Leipsic, OH	TOL
Leisenring, PA	GBG

PA	PBR
Leisure City, FL	MIA
Leitchfield, KY	OWN
Leland, MS	JKS
Lemay, MO	STL
Lemhi, ID	B
Lemmon, SD	RC
Lemon Grove, CA	SD
Lemont, IL	CHI
IL	LIT
Lemoore, CA	FRS
Lena, IL	RCK
WI	GB
Lenexa, KS	KCK
Lenni, PA	PH
Lennox, SD	SFS
Lenoir, NC	CHL
Lenoir City, TN	KNX
Lenox, IA	DM
MA	SPR
Lenox Dale, MA	SPR
Leo, MN	CR
Leola, SD	SFS
Leominster, MA	WOR
Leon, IA	DM
Leon Springs, TX	SAT
Leonardtown, MD	WDC
Leone, AS	SPP
Leonia, NJ	NEW
Leonore, IL	PEO
Leonville, LA	LAF
Leopold, IN	IND
MO	SPC
Leopolis, WI	GB
Leoti, KS	DOD
Leoville, KS	SAL
Lepua, AS	SPP
Lepuapua, AS	SPP
Leroy, LA	LAF
ND	FAR
LeRoy, NY	BUF
Les Cayes, Haiti	MAN
Leslie, MI	LAN
Lester Prairie, MN	NU
Lesterville, SD	SFS
Letcher, SD	SFS
Levelland, TX	LUB
Levittown, NY	RVC
PA	PH
PA	PSC
Lewis Center, OH	COL
Lewis Run, PA	E
Lewisburg, PA	HBG
TN	NSH
Lewisport, KY	OWN
Lewiston, ID	B
ME	PRT
MI	GAY
MN	WIN
NY	BUF
Lewistown, IL	PEO
MT	GF
PA	HBG
Lewisville, TX	FWT
TX	OLL
Lexington, KY	LEX
MA	ARM
MA	BO
MI	SAG
MN	STP
MO	KC
MS	JKS
NC	CHL
NE	GI
OH	TOL
OK	OKL
SC	CHR
TN	MEM
TX	AUS
VA	RIC
Lexington Park, MD	WDC
Libby, MT	HEL
Liberal, KS	DOD
Liberty, IL	SFD
IN	IND
KS	WCH
MO	KC
NY	NY
OH	TOL
TN	NSH
TX	BEA
Liberty Boro, PA	PIT
Liberty Township, OH	CIN
Libertytown, MD	BAL
Libertyville, IL	CHI
Lidderdale, IA	SC
Lidgerwood, ND	FAR
Liebenthal, KS	DOD
Liftwood, DE	WIL
Lighthouse Point, FL	MIA
Ligonier, IN	FTW
PA	GBG
Liguori, MO	STL
Lihue, HI	HON
Lilburn, GA	ATL
Lillian, AL	MOB
Lillis, KS	KCK
Lilly, PA	ALT
Lillyville, IL	SFD
Lily, SD	SFS
Lima, NY	ROC
OH	TOL
WI	LC
WI	MIL
Lime Ridge, WI	MAD
Lime Rock, NY	BUF
Limeport, PA	ALN
Limerick, ME	PRT
Limestone, ME	PRT
NY	BUF
Limon, CO	COS
Lincoln, CA	SAC
IL	PEO
KS	SAL
MA	BO
ME	PRT
NE	LIN
NE	STN
NH	MAN
RI	NTN
RI	PRO
WI	GB
Lincoln City, OR	P
Lincoln Park, MI	DET
NJ	PAT
Lincolndale, NY	NY
Lincolnton, NC	CHL
Lincroft, NJ	TR
Lind, WA	SPK
Lindale, TX	TYL
Linden, CA	STO
NJ	NEW
NJ	PSC
Lindenhurst, NY	RVC
Lindenwold, NJ	CAM
Lindsay, CA	FRS
NE	OM
TX	FWT
Lindsborg, KS	WCH
Lindstrom, MN	STP
Linesville, PA	E
Linfield, PA	PH
Linn, MO	JC
Lino Lakes, MN	STP
Linthicum, MD	BAL
Linthicum Heights, MD	BAL
Linton, IN	EVN
ND	BIS
Linwood, MA	WOR
MI	SAG
NJ	CAM
PA	PH
Lisbon, ME	PRT
ND	FAR
NH	MAN
NY	OG
OH	Y
Lisbon Falls, ME	PRT
Lisle, IL	JOL
Lismore, MN	WIN
Litchfield, CT	HRT
IL	SFD
MN	NU
OH	CLV
Litchfield Park, AZ	PHX
Lithia Springs, GA	ATL
Lithonia, GA	ATL
Lititz, PA	HBG
Litomysl, MN	WIN
Little Canada, MN	STP
Little Chute, WI	GB
Little Compton, RI	PRO
Little Falls, MN	SCL
NJ	PAT
NY	ALB
NY	STF
Little Ferry, NJ	NEW
Little Kohler, WI	MIL
Little Meadows, PA	SCR
Little River, KS	WCH
Little Rock, AR	LR
Little Suamico, WI	GB
Little Turkey, IA	DUB
Little Valley, NY	BUF
Little York, NJ	MET
Littlefield, TX	LUB
Littlefork, MN	DUL
Littleport, IA	DUB
Littlestown, PA	HBG
Littleton, CO	DEN
MA	BO
NH	MAN
Live Oak, FL	STA
Lively Grove, IL	BEL
Livermore, CA	OAK
IA	SC
KY	OWN
Liverpool, NY	SY
Livingston, AL	BIR
CA	FRS
IL	SFD
MT	GF
NJ	NEW
TX	BEA
Livingston Manor, NY	NY
Livonia, LA	BR
MI	DET
MI	PRM
NY	ROC
Livonia Center, NY	ROC
Llano, TX	AUS
Lock Haven, PA	ALT
Lockbourne, OH	COL
Lockeford, CA	STO
Lockhart, TX	AUS
Lockport, IL	JOL
IL	PRM
LA	HT
NY	BUF
Lockport South, IL	JOL
Locust Gap, PA	HBG
Locustdale, PA	HBG
Lodge Grass, MT	GF
Lodi, CA	STO
NJ	NEW
OH	CLV
WI	MAD
Logan, IA	DM
KS	SAL
OH	COL
UT	SLC
WV	WH
Logansport, IN	LFT
Lohrville, IA	SC
Loiza, PR	SJN
Loma, NE	LIN
Loma Linda, CA	SB
Lombard, IL	JOL
Lometa, TX	AUS
Lomice, ND	FAR
Lomira, WI	MIL
Lomita, CA	LA
Lompoc, CA	LA
Lonaconing, MD	BAL
London, KY	LEX
OH	COL
Londonderry, NH	MAN
Lone Pine, CA	FRS
Lone Rock, WI	LC
Lone Tree, IA	DAV
Lonedell, MO	STL
Long Beach, CA	LA
MS	BLX
NY	RVC
Long Branch, NJ	TR
Long Grove, IA	DAV
Long Island City, NY	BRK
NY	NY
NY	STF
Long Lake, MN	STP
NY	OG
WI	GB
Long Prairie, MN	SCL
Long Valley, NJ	PAT
Longboat Key, FL	VEN
Longmeadow, MA	SPR
Longmont, CO	DEN
Longport, NJ	CAM
Longview, TX	TYL
WA	SEA
Longville, MN	DUL
Longwood, FL	ORL
Lonsdale, AR	LR
MN	STP
Loogootee, IN	EVN
Lookout Mountain, GA	ATL
Loomis, CA	SAC
Loose Creek, MO	JC
Lopez, PA	PSC
Lorain, OH	CLV
OH	PRM
OH	ROM
OH	SJP
Lords Valley, PA	SCR
Lordsburg, NM	LSC
Lore City, OH	STU
Loreauville, LA	LAF
Loreto, WI	MAD
Loretto, IL	PEO
KS	DOD
KY	L
MN	STP
PA	ALT
TN	NSH
Los Alamitos, CA	ORG
Los Alamos, NM	SFE
Los Altos, CA	SJ
Los Altos Hills, CA	SJ
Los Angeles, CA	ARM
CA	LA
CA	OLL
CA	ROM
CA	SB
CA	STN
Los Banos, CA	FRS
Los Fresnos, TX	BWN
Los Gatos, CA	MRY
CA	SJ
CA	VNN
Los Lunas, NM	SFE
Los Nietos, CA	LA
Los Ojos, NM	SFE
Los Osos, CA	MRY
Losoya, TX	SAT
Lost Creek, PA	ALN
Lost Lake, WI	MIL
Lost Nation, IA	DAV
Lostant, IL	PEO
Lott, TX	AUS
Loudonville, NY	ALB
OH	CLV
Louisa, KY	LEX
LA	LAF
Louisburg, KS	KCK
NC	R
Louisiana, MO	JC
Louisville, CO	DEN
KY	L
KY	OLL
MS	JKS
NY	OG
OH	Y
Loup City, NE	GI
Lourdes, IA	DUB
Loveland, CO	DEN
OH	CIN
Lovell, WY	CHY
Lovelock, NV	RNO
Loves Park, IL	RCK
Lovilia, IA	DAV
Loving, NM	LSC
Lovingston, VA	RIC
Lovington, IL	SFD
NM	LSC
Lowell, IN	GRY
MA	BO
MI	GR
OH	STU
Lowellville, OH	Y
Lower Brule, SD	RC
Lower Burrell, PA	GBG
Lower Makefield, PA	PH
Lowville, NY	OG
Loyal, OK	OKL
WI	LC
Lubbock, TX	LUB
Lubec, ME	PRT
Lubeck, WV	WH
Lublin, WI	SUP
Lucan, MN	NU
Lucerne, IN	LFT
Lucerne Valley, CA	SB
Lucernemines, PA	GBG
Lucinda, PA	E
Ludington, MI	GR
Ludlow, KY	COV
MA	SPR
MA	STF
VT	BUR
Luebbering, MO	STL
Lufkin, TX	TYL
Lukachukai, AZ	GLP
Lukunor, FM	CI
Luling, LA	NO
TX	AUS
Lumberton, MS	BLX
NC	R
NM	GLP
TX	BEA
Lunenburg, MA	WOR
Luquillo, PR	SJN
Luray, VA	ARL
Lusk, WY	CHY
Lutherville, MD	BAL
Luverne, MN	WIN
Luxemburg, IA	DUB
MN	SCL
WI	GB
Luzerne, PA	SCR
Lycurgus, IA	DUB
Lydia, LA	LAF
Lyford, TX	BWN
Lykens, PA	HBG
Lyle, MN	WIN

Lyman, ME	PRT
Lynbrook, NY	RVC
Lynch, KY	LEX
NE	OM
Lynchburg, VA	RIC
Lynden, WA	SEA
Lyndhurst, NJ	NEW
OH	CLV
Lyndon Station, WI	LC
Lyndonville, NY	BUF
VT	BUR
Lyndora, PA	PBR
PA	PIT
PA	SJP
Lynn, MA	BO
Lynnfield, MA	BO
Lynnwood, WA	SEA
Lynwood, CA	LA
CA	SJ
Lyon Mountain, NY	OG
Lyons, IL	CHI
KS	WCH
NE	OM
NY	ROC
OH	TOL
WI	MIL
Lyons Point, LA	LAF
Lytle, TX	SAT
Mabel, MN	WIN
Mableton, GA	ATL
Mabton, WA	YAK
Macclenny, FL	STA
Macdona, TX	SAT
Macedon, NY	ROC
Macedonia, OH	CLV
Machias, ME	PRT
NY	BUF
Mackinac Island, MI	MAR
Mackinaw City, MI	GAY
Mackville, WI	GB
Macomb, IL	PEO
MI	DET
Macon, GA	SAV
IL	SFD
MO	JC
Madawaska, ME	PRT
Maddock, ND	FAR
Madelia, MN	WIN
Madera, CA	FRS
Madison, AL	BIR
CT	HRT
FL	PT
IL	SFD
IL	STN
IN	IND
KS	WCH
ME	PRT
MN	NU
MS	JKS
MT	HEL
NE	OM
NJ	PAT
OH	CLV
SD	SFS
TN	NSH
TX	TYL
VA	ARL
WI	MAD
WV	WH
Madison Heights, MI	DET
Madison Lake, MN	WIN
Madisonville, KY	OWN
LA	NO
TN	KNX
TX	TYL
Madonnaville, IL	BEL
Madras, OR	BAK
Madrid, IA	SC
NY	OG
Magee, MS	JKS
Maggie Valley, NC	CHL
Magna, UT	SLC
Magnolia, AR	LR
DE	WIL
NJ	CAM
TX	GAL
Magnolia Springs, AL	MOB
Mahanoy City, PA	ALN
PA	PHU
PA	PSC
Mahanoy Plane, PA	ALN
Mahnomen, MN	CR
Mahomet, IL	PEO
Mahopac, NY	NY
Mahtomedi, MN	STP
Mahwah, NJ	NEW
NJ	PSC
Maina, GU	AGN
Maine, MN	SCL
NY	SY
Maizeville, PA	ALN
PA	PHU
Majuro, MH	MI
Makakilo, HI	HON
Makawao, HI	HON
Malaeloa, AS	SPP
Malaga, NJ	CAM
Malden, MA	BO
MO	SPC
Malibu, CA	LA
Mallard, IA	SC
Mallet, LA	LAF
Malojlo, GU	AGN
Malone, NY	OG
Maloy, IA	DM
Malta, MT	GF
Malvern, AR	LR
OH	STU
PA	PH
Malverne, NY	RVC
Mamaroneck, NY	NY
Mammoth, AZ	TUC
Mammoth Lakes, CA	STO
Mamou, LA	LAF
Man, WV	WH
Manahawkin, NJ	TR
Manalapan, NJ	TR
Manannah, MN	NU
Manasquan, NJ	TR
Manassas, VA	ARL
VA	PHU
Manati, PR	ARE
Manawa, WI	GB
Mancelona, MI	GAY
Manchaug, MA	WOR
Manchester, CT	HRT
IA	DUB
KY	LEX
MD	BAL
MI	LAN
MI	LIT
MO	STL
NH	MAN
NH	NTN
NH	STF
OH	CIN
PA	PIT
Manchester by the Sea, MA	BO
Manchester Center, VT	BUR
Mancos, CO	PBL
Mandan, ND	BIS
Mandaree, ND	BIS
Manderson, SD	RC
Mandeville, LA	NO
Mangilao, GU	AGN
Mangum, OK	OKL
Manhasset, NY	RVC
Manhattan, IL	JOL
KS	SAL
Manhattan Beach, CA	LA
Manheim, PA	HBG
Manilla, IA	SC
Manistee, MI	GAY
Manistique, MI	MAR
Manitou Beach, MI	LAN
Manitowish Waters, WI	SUP
Manitowoc, WI	GB
WI	MIL
Mankato, KS	SAL
MN	WIN
Manley, NE	LIN
Manlius, NY	SY
Manly, IA	DUB
Manning, IA	SC
Mannington, WV	WH
Manoa, PA	PH
Manor, TX	AUS
Manorhaven, NY	RVC
Manorville, NY	RVC
Mansfield, LA	SHP
MA	FR
MO	SPC
OH	TOL
PA	SCR
TX	FWT
Manson, IA	SC
Mansura, LA	ALX
Mantador, ND	FAR
Manteca, CA	STO
Manteno, IL	JOL
Manton, MI	GAY
Mantua, NJ	CAM
OH	Y
Manvel, ND	FAR
TX	GAL
Manville, NJ	MET
NJ	PHU
Many, LA	SHP
Maple City, MI	GAY
Maple Glen, PA	PH
Maple Grove, MI	SAG
MN	STP
WI	GB
Maple Heights, OH	CLV
Maple Hill, KS	KCK
Maple Lake, MN	STP
Maple Mount, KY	OWN
Maple Park, IL	RCK
Maple River, IA	SC
Maple Shade, NJ	TR
Mapleton, IA	SC
MI	GAY
MN	WIN
WI	MIL
Maplewood, MN	STP
MO	STL
NJ	NEW
WI	GB
Maquoketa, IA	DUB
Marak, TX	AUS
Marana, AZ	TUC
Marathon, FL	MIA
NY	SY
Marathon City, WI	LC
Marble, MN	DUL
Marble Falls, TX	AUS
Marblehead, MA	BO
OH	PRM
OH	TOL
Marbury, AL	MOB
Marceline, MO	JC
Marcellus, NY	SY
Marchand, WI	GB
Marco Island, FL	VEN
Marcus, IA	SC
Marcus Hook, PA	PH
Marengo, IA	DAV
IL	RCK
Marfa, TX	ELP
Margaretville, NY	ALB
Margate, FL	MIA
NJ	CAM
Marguerite, PA	GBG
Maria Stein, OH	CIN
Mariah Hill, IN	EVN
Marianna, AR	LR
FL	PT
Maricao, PR	MGZ
Marienthal, KS	DOD
Marietta, GA	ATL
OH	STU
PA	HBG
Marina, CA	MRY
Marina Del Rey, CA	LA
Marine, IL	SFD
Marine City, MI	DET
Marine on St. Croix, MN	STP
Marinette, WI	GB
Maringouin, LA	BR
Marion, IA	DUB
IL	BEL
IN	LFT
KS	WCH
KY	OWN
MA	FR
MI	GR
ND	FAR
NY	ROC
OH	COL
SD	SFS
VA	RIC
WI	GB
Marion Heights, PA	HBG
PA	PHU
Marionville, MO	SPC
Mariposa, CA	FRS
Marked Tree, AR	LR
Markesan, WI	MAD
Markham, IL	CHI
Marks, MS	JKS
Marksville, LA	ALX
Marlboro, MA	BO
NJ	PHU
NJ	TR
NY	NY
Marlborough, CT	HRT
MA	BO
NH	MAN
Marlette, MI	SAG
Marlin, TX	AUS
Marlinton, WV	WH
Marlton, NJ	TR
Marmora, NJ	CAM
Marne, MI	GR
Marquette, MI	MAR
Marrero, LA	NO
Marriottsville, MD	BAL
Mars, PA	PIT
Mars Hill, ME	PRT
NC	CHL
Marseilles, IL	PEO
Marshall, AK	FBK
IL	SFD
MI	KAL
MN	NU
MO	JC
TX	TYL
WI	MAD
Marshalltown, IA	DUB
Marshfield, MA	BO
MO	SPC
WI	LC
Martin, KY	LEX
SD	RC
TN	MEM
Martindale, TX	AUS
Martinez, CA	OAK
TX	SAT
Martins Creek, PA	ALN
Martins Ferry, OH	STU
Martinsburg, MO	JC
WV	WH
Martinsville, IN	IND
NJ	MET
VA	RIC
WI	MAD
Martinton, IL	JOL
Marty, SD	SFS
Marvin, SD	SFS
Mary Esther, FL	PT
Mary's Home, MO	JC
Marydale, IL	BEL
Marydel, MD	WIL
Marygrove, OH	TOL
Maryhill, IA	SC
Maryknoll, NY	NY
Maryland Heights, MO	STL
Marylhurst, OR	P
Marysburg, MN	STP
Marysdale, OH	TOL
Marystown, MN	STP
Marysville, CA	SAC
KS	KCK
MI	DET
OH	COL
PA	HBG
WA	SEA
Marytown, WI	MIL
Maryville, IL	SFD
MO	KC
Marywood, OH	TOL
Masaryktown, FL	SP
Mascoutah, IL	BEL
Mashpee, MA	FR
Mason, MI	LAN
OH	CIN
TX	AUS
Mason City, IA	DUB
Masontown, PA	GBG
WV	WH
Masonville, IA	DUB
Massapequa, NY	RVC
Massapequa Park, NY	RVC
Massena, IA	DM
NY	OG
Massillon, OH	Y
Mastic Beach, NY	RVC
Masury, OH	Y
Matamoras, PA	SCR
Matawan, NJ	PSC
NJ	TR
Matherville, IL	PEO
Mathews, VA	RIC
Mathis, TX	CC
Mattapoisett, MA	FR
Mattawa, WA	YAK
Mattawan, MI	KAL
Mattese, MO	STL
Matteson, IL	CHI
Mattoon, IL	SFD
WI	GB
Mattydale, NY	SY
Mauldin, SC	CHR
Maumee, OH	TOL
Maunabo, PR	CGS
Maurice, LA	LAF
Mauriceville, TX	BEA
Mauston, WI	LC
Maximo, OH	Y
Maxwell, CA	SAC
PA	GBG
May's Lick, KY	COV
Mayaguez, PR	MGZ
Mayaquez, Mayaguez	MGZ
PR	MGZ
Maybee, MI	DET
Maybrook, NY	NY
Mayetta, KS	KCK
Mayfield, KY	OWN
PA	SCR
SD	SFS
Mayhew Lake, MN	SCL
Maynard, MA	BO
OH	STU

Mays Landing, NJ	CAM
Maysel, WV	WH
Maysville, KY	COV
Maytown, IL	RCK
Mayville, MI	SAG
ND	FAR
NY	BUF
WI	MIL
Maywood, CA	LA
IL	CHI
NJ	NEW
Mazeppa, MN	WIN
Mazomanie, WI	MAD
McAdoo, PA	ALN
PA	PHU
PA	PSC
McAfee, NJ	PAT
McAlester, OK	TLS
McAllen, TX	BWN
McBain, MI	GAY
McCall, ID	B
McCamey, TX	SAN
McCartyville, OH	CIN
McCloud, CA	SAC
McClusky, ND	FAR
McComb, MS	JKS
McConchie, MD	WDC
McConnellsburg, PA	ALT
McConnelsville, OH	STU
McCook, NE	LIN
TX	BWN
McCool Junction, NE	LIN
McCracken, KS	DOD
McDonald, OH	Y
PA	PIT
McDonough, GA	ATL
McDowell, KS	SAL
McEwen, TN	NSH
McFarland, CA	FRS
WI	MAD
McGehee, AR	LR
McGrath, AK	FBK
McGregor, IA	DUB
MN	DUL
MN	STP
TX	AUS
McHenry, IL	RCK
ND	FAR
McIntire, IA	DUB
McIntosh, SD	RC
McKean, PA	E
McKees Rocks, PA	PBR
PA	PIT
PA	SJP
McKeesport, PA	PBR
PA	PIT
PA	ROM
PA	SJP
McKenzie Bridge, OR	P
McKinleyville, CA	SR
McKinney, TX	DAL
McLaughlin, SD	RC
McLean, VA	ARL
VA	NTN
VA	WDC
McLeansboro, IL	BEL
McLoud, OK	OKL
McMechen, WV	WH
McMinnville, OR	P
TN	NSH
McNair, TX	GAL
McNary, AZ	GLP
McPherson, KS	WCH
McQuady, KY	OWN
McRae, GA	SAV
McSherrystown, PA	HBG
Mead, NE	LIN
Meade, KS	DOD
Meadowbrook, PA	PH
Meadowlands, PA	PIT
Meadville, PA	E
Mecca, CA	SB
Mechanic Falls, ME	PRT
Mechanicsburg, OH	CIN
PA	HBG
Mechanicsville, IA	DAV
MD	WDC
VA	RIC
Mechanicville, NY	ALB
Medart, FL	PT
Medaryville, IN	LFT
Medfield, MA	BO
Medford, MA	BO
MN	WIN
NJ	TR
NY	RVC
OK	OKL
OR	P
WI	SUP
Media, PA	PH
Mediania Alta Ward, Loiza, PR	SJN
Medical Lake, WA	SPK
Medicine Lodge, KS	DOD
Medina, ND	FAR
NY	BUF
OH	CLV
Medley's Neck, MD	WDC
Medora, IL	SFD
Medway, MA	BO
Meeker, CO	DEN
Megargel, TX	FWT
Mehlville, MO	STL
Meire Grove, MN	SCL
Melbourne, FL	ORL
KY	COV
Melbourne Beach, FL	ORL
Melcher, IA	DAV
Mellen, WI	SUP
Mellette, SD	SFS
Melrose, IA	DAV
MA	BO
MN	SCL
WI	LC
Melrose Park, IL	CHI
Melville, LA	LAF
NY	RVC
Melvindale, MI	DET
Memphis, MI	DET
MO	JC
TN	MEM
TX	AMA
Mena, AR	LR
Menahga, MN	SCL
Menands, NY	ALB
Menard, TX	SAN
Menasha, WI	GB
Mendham, NJ	PAT
Mendocino, CA	SR
Mendon, IL	SFD
MA	WOR
MI	KAL
NY	ROC
Mendota, CA	FRS
IL	PEO
MN	STP
Mendota Heights, MN	STP
Menlo Park, CA	SFR
CA	SJ
Menoken, ND	BIS
Menominee, IL	RCK
MI	MAR
NE	OM
Menomonee Falls, WI	MIL
Menomonie, WI	LC
Mentor, MN	CR
OH	CLV
Mentor-on-the-Lake, OH	PRM
Mentz, TX	VIC
Meppen, IL	SFD
Mequon, WI	MIL
Meraux, LA	NO
Merced, CA	FRS
Mercedes, TX	BWN
Mercer, PA	E
WI	SUP
Mercer Island, WA	SEA
Merchantville, NJ	CAM
Meredith, KS	SAL
NH	MAN
Meriden, CT	HRT
CT	PSC
KS	KCK
Meridian, ID	B
MS	JKS
PA	PIT
Merion, PA	PH
Merion Station, PA	PH
Merizo, GU	AGN
Mermentau, LA	LAF
Merrick, NY	RVC
Merrill, IA	SC
MI	SAG
OR	BAK
WI	SUP
Merrillville, IN	GRY
IN	PRM
Merrimac, MA	BO
WI	MAD
Merrimack, NH	MAN
Merriman, NE	GI
Merritt Island, FL	ORL
Mesa, AZ	PHX
ID	B
Mescalero, NM	LSC
Meshoppen, PA	SCR
Mesilla, NM	LSC
Mesilla Park, NM	LSC
Meta, MO	JC
Metairie, LA	NO
Metaline Falls, WA	SPK
Metamora, IL	PEO
Methuen, MA	BO
MA	NTN
Metropolis, IL	BEL
Metuchen, NJ	MET
Metz, MI	GAY
Mexia, TX	AUS
Mexico, ME	PRT
MO	JC
NY	SY
Mexico Beach, FL	PT
Meyer, IA	DUB
Meyersdale, PA	ALT
Meyersville, TX	DAL
TX	VIC
Miami, AZ	TUC
FL	MIA
FL	NTN
FL	PSC
FL	SAM
FL	SJP
OK	TLS
Miami Beach, FL	MIA
Miami Lakes, FL	MIA
Miami Shores, FL	MIA
Miami Springs, FL	MIA
Miamisburg, OH	CIN
Michael, IL	SFD
Michigan, ND	FAR
Michigan Center, MI	LAN
Michigan City, IN	GRY
Middle Lake, MN	NU
Middle Ridge, WI	LC
Middle River, MN	CR
Middle Village, NY	BRK
NY	NY
Middleborough, MA	BO
Middlebranch, OH	Y
Middleburg, FL	STA
VA	ARL
Middleburg Heights, OH	CLV
Middleburgh, NY	ALB
Middlebury, CT	HRT
VT	BUR
Middlefield, CT	NOR
OH	CLV
Middleport, NY	BUF
PA	PHU
Middlesboro, KY	LEX
Middlesex, NJ	MET
Middlesex County, VA	RIC
Middleton, MA	BO
WI	MAD
Middletown, CA	SR
CT	NOR
DE	WIL
MD	BAL
NJ	TR
NY	NY
NY	STF
OH	CIN
PA	HBG
RI	PRO
Middletown Springs, VT	BUR
Midland, MD	BAL
MI	SAG
PA	PIT
SD	RC
TX	SAN
Midland Park, NJ	NEW
Midlothian, IL	CHI
Midvale, UT	SLC
Midway City, CA	ORG
Miesville, MN	STP
Mifflintown, PA	HBG
Mikado, MI	GAY
Milaca, MN	SCL
Milan, IL	PEO
IN	IND
MI	LAN
MO	JC
NM	GLP
OH	TOL
TN	MEM
WI	LC
Milbank, SD	SFS
Mildred, PA	SCR
Miles, TX	SAN
Miles City, MT	GF
Milford, CT	HRT
DE	WIL
IA	SC
IN	FTW
MA	WOR
MI	DET
NH	MAN
NJ	MET
OH	CIN
PA	SCR
UT	SLC
Mililani Town, HI	HON
Mill Creek, WI	LC
WI	MAD
Mill Valley, CA	SFR
Milladore, WI	LC
Millbrae, CA	OLL
CA	SFR
Millbrook, AL	MOB
NY	NY
Millbury, MA	WOR
Milledgeville, GA	ATL
Millen, GA	SAV
Miller, SD	SFS
Miller City, OH	TOL
Miller Heights, PA	ALN
Millers Falls, MA	SPR
Millersburg, OH	COL
PA	HBG
Millersville, MD	BAL
OH	TOL
PA	HBG
Millerville, MN	SCL
Millhousen, IN	IND
Millinocket, ME	PRT
Millis, MA	BO
Millstadt, IL	BEL
Milltown, NJ	MET
Millvale, PA	PIT
Millville, MA	WOR
NJ	CAM
NJ	PHU
OH	CIN
Millwood, MO	STL
Milmont Park, PA	PH
Milnor, ND	FAR
Milpitas, CA	SJ
Milroy, MN	NU
Milstadt, IL	BEL
Milton, FL	PT
LA	LAF
MA	BO
ND	FAR
NY	NY
PA	HBG
VT	BUR
WI	MAD
Milton Freewater, OR	BAK
Miltonsburg, OH	STU
Miltonvale, KS	SAL
Milwaukee, WI	MIL
WI	NTN
WI	STN
Milwaukie, OR	P
Mims, FL	ORL
Minatare, NE	GI
Minden, LA	SHP
NE	LIN
Mineola, NY	RVC
TX	TYL
Mineral, VA	RIC
Mineral City, OH	COL
Mineral Point, WI	MAD
Mineral Ridge, OH	Y
Mineral Wells, TX	FWT
Minersville, PA	ALN
PA	PHU
PA	PSC
Minerva, OH	STU
Minetto, NY	SY
Mineville, NY	OG
Mingo Junction, OH	PBR
OH	STU
Minneapolis, KS	SAL
MN	OLL
MN	PRM
MN	STN
MN	STP
Minneiska, MN	WIN
Minneota, MN	NU
Minnesota City, MN	WIN
Minnesota Lake, MN	WIN
Minnetonka, MN	STP
Minnewaukan, ND	FAR
Minoa, NY	SY
Minocqua, WI	SUP
Minong, WI	SUP
Minonk, IL	PEO
Minooka, IL	JOL
Minot, ND	BIS
Minotola, NJ	CAM
Minster, OH	CIN
Minto, ND	FAR
Minturn, CO	DEN
Mio, MI	GAY
Miramar, FL	MIA
Mire, LA	LAF
Miriam, MI	GR
Mishawaka, IN	FTW
IN	STN
Mishicot, WI	GB
Mission, KS	KCK
SD	RC
TX	BWN
Mission Hills, CA	LA

Mission San Jose, CA	OAK
Mission Viejo, CA	ORG
Missoula, MT	HEL
Missouri City, TX	GAL
Missouri Valley, IA	DM
Mitchell, IN	IND
NE	GI
SD	SFS
WI	MIL
Mitchellville, MD	WDC
Moab, UT	SLC
Moberly, MO	JC
Mobile, AL	MOB
Mobridge, SD	SFS
Moca, PR	MGZ
Mocanaqua, PA	SCR
Mocksville, NC	CHL
Modesto, CA	STO
Modoc, IL	BEL
Mohall, ND	BIS
Mohawk, NY	ALB
Mohnton, PA	ALN
Mokane, MO	JC
Mokena, IL	JOL
Molalla, OR	P
Moline, IL	PEO
KS	WCH
Momence, IL	JOL
Mon Luis Island, AL	MOB
Monaca, PA	PIT
Monahans, TX	ELP
Monarch, MT	GF
Monches, WI	MIL
Moncks Corner, SC	CHR
Mondamin, IA	DM
Mondovi, WI	LC
Monee, IL	JOL
Monessen, PA	GBG
PA	PBR
Moneta, VA	RIC
Monett, MO	SPC
Mongmong, GU	AGN
Monmouth, IL	PEO
Monmouth Beach, NJ	TR
Monmouth Junction, NJ	MET
Monona, IA	DUB
Monongah, WV	WH
Monongahela, PA	PBR
PA	PIT
Monroe, CT	BGP
GA	ATL
LA	SHP
MI	DET
NC	CHL
NY	NY
OH	CIN
OR	P
UT	SLC
WA	SEA
WI	MAD
Monroe City, MO	JC
Monroeville, AL	MOB
IN	FTW
OH	TOL
PA	PBR
PA	PIT
Monrovia, CA	LA
Monsey, NY	NY
Monson, MA	SPR
Mont Belvieu, (1991)	BEA
Mont Clare, PA	PSC
Montague, MI	GR
NJ	PAT
TX	FWT
Montauk, NY	RVC
Montclair, CA	SB
NJ	NEW
Montdale, PA	SCR
Monte Rio, CA	SR
Monte Vista, CO	PBL
Montebello, CA	LA
Montecito, CA	LA
Montegut, LA	HT
Montello, WI	MAD
Monterey, CA	MRY
IN	LFT
NE	OM
Monterey Park, CA	LA
Montevallo, AL	BIR
Montevideo, MN	NU
Montezuma, IN	IND
NY	ROC
OH	CIN
Montfort, WI	MAD
Montgomery, AL	MOB
IN	EVN
MN	STP
NY	NY
WV	WH
Montgomery City, MO	JC
Monti, IA	DUB

Monticello, AR	LR
FL	PT
IA	DUB
IL	PEO
IN	LFT
KY	LEX
MN	STP
NY	NY
UT	SLC
Montoursville, PA	SCR
Montpelier, IN	LFT
OH	TOL
VA	RIC
VT	BUR
WI	GB
Montreal, WI	SUP
Montrose, CA	ARM
CA	LA
CO	PBL
IA	DAV
IL	SFD
MI	LAN
MO	KC
NY	NY
PA	SCR
SD	SFS
Montvale, NJ	NEW
Montville, CT	NOR
NJ	PAT
Monument, CO	COS
Moodus, CT	NOR
Moody, TX	AUS
Mooers, NY	OG
Mooers Forks, NY	OG
Moon Township, PA	PIT
Moonachie, NJ	NEW
Mooney Creek, KS	KCK
Moore, OK	OKL
Moore Haven, FL	VEN
Moorefield, WV	WH
Moorestown, NJ	TR
Mooresville, IN	IND
NC	CHL
Mooreton, ND	FAR
Moorhead, MN	CR
Moorland, IA	SC
Moorpark, CA	LA
Moose Lake, MN	DUL
Moosup, CT	NOR
Moquah, WI	SUP
Mora, MN	SCL
NM	SFE
Moraga, CA	OAK
Moran, MI	MAR
MN	SCL
Moravia, NY	ROC
Moreauville, LA	ALX
Morehead, KY	LEX
Morehead City, NC	R
Morenci, AZ	TUC
Moreno Valley, CA	SB
Morgan, MN	NU
TX	FWT
Morgan City, LA	HT
Morgan Hill, CA	SJ
Morganfield, KY	OWN
Morganton, NC	CHL
Morgantown, KY	OWN
WV	PBR
WV	WH
Morganza, LA	BR
MD	WDC
Morges, OH	STU
Moriarty, NM	SFE
Morongo Valley, CA	SB
Morovis, PR	ARE
Morrice, MI	LAN
Morrill, MN	SCL
Morrilton, AR	LR
Morris, IL	JOL
IN	IND
MN	SCL
NY	ALB
Morris Plains, NJ	PAT
Morrisdale, PA	E
Morrison, IL	RCK
MO	JC
Morrison Bluff, AR	LR
Morrisonville, IL	SFD
NY	OG
Morristown, NJ	PAT
NY	OG
SD	RC
TN	KNX
Morrisville, NY	SY
PA	PH
VT	BUR
Morro Bay, CA	MRY
Morrow, LA	LAF
OH	CIN
Morrowville, KS	SAL

Morse, LA	LAF
Morse Bluff, NE	LIN
Morton, IL	PEO
MN	NU
PA	PH
TX	LUB
WA	SEA
Morton Grove, IL	CHI
Moscow, ID	B
PA	PHU
PA	SCR
TN	MEM
Moselle, MO	STL
Moses Lake, WA	YAK
Mosinee, WI	LC
Moss Beach, CA	SFR
Moss Bluff, LA	LKC
Moss Point, MS	BLX
Motley, MN	SCL
Mott, ND	BIS
Moulton, AL	BIR
TX	VIC
Moultrie, GA	SAV
Mound, MN	STP
Mound Bayou, MS	JKS
Mound City, IL	BEL
KS	KCK
Moundsville, WV	WH
Mount Airy, NC	CHL
Mt. Angel, OR	P
Mount Arlington, NJ	PAT
Mt. Ayr, IA	DM
Mount Calvary, WI	MIL
Mount Carbon, PA	ALN
Mount Carmel, IA	SC
IL	BEL
ND	FAR
OH	CIN
PA	HBG
PA	PHU
Mount Carroll, IL	RCK
Mount Clemens, MI	DET
Mount Dora, FL	ORL
Mount Ephraim, NJ	CAM
Mount Holly, NJ	TR
Mount Hope, NJ	PAT
WI	MAD
Mount Horeb, WI	MAD
Mount Jewett, PA	E
Mount Joy, PA	HBG
Mt. Kisco, NY	NY
Mount Laurel, NJ	TR
Mt. Lebanon, PA	PIT
Mount Morris, MI	LAN
NY	ROC
Mount Olive, IL	SFD
Mount Orab, OH	CIN
Mount Pleasant, IA	DAV
MI	SAG
PA	GBG
TX	TYL
Mt. Pleasant, VI	STV
Mount Pocono, PA	SCR
Mt. Prospect, IL	CHI
Mount Rainier, MD	WDC
Mount Repose, OH	CIN
Mount Saint Francis, IN	IND
Mount Savage, MD	BAL
Mount Shasta, CA	SAC
Mount Sinai, NY	RVC
Mount Sterling, IL	SFD
Mt. Sterling, KY	LEX
Mount Union, PA	ALT
Mt. Upton, NY	SY
Mount Vernon, AL	MOB
IA	DUB
IL	BEL
IN	EVN
KS	WCH
KY	LEX
MO	SPC
NY	NY
OH	COL
SD	SFS
TX	TYL
WA	SEA
Mount Washington, KY	L
Mt. Zion, IL	SFD
Mountain City, TN	KNX
Mountain Grove, MO	SPC
Mountain Home, AR	LR
ID	B
TX	SAT
Mountain Home Air Force Base, ID	B
Mountain Lakes, NJ	PAT
Mountain View, CA	SJ
HI	HON
MO	SPC
Mountain Village, AK	FBK
Mountainair, NM	SFE
Mountainside, NJ	NEW

Mountaintop, PA	SCR
Mountlake Terrace, WA	SEA
Moville, IA	SC
Mowata, LA	LAF
Moweaqua, IL	SFD
Moxee City, WA	YAK
Muenster, TX	FWT
Mukwonago, WI	MIL
Mulberry, KS	WCH
Muleshoe, TX	LUB
Mullen, NE	GI
Mullens, WV	WH
Mullica Hill, NJ	CAM
Mulvane, KS	WCH
Muncie, IN	LFT
Muncy, PA	SCR
Mundelein, IL	CHI
Munden, KS	SAL
Mundys Corner, PA	ALT
Munger, MI	SAG
Munhall, PA	PBR
PA	PIT
Munich, ND	FAR
Munising, MI	MAR
Munjor, KS	SAL
Munnsville, NY	SY
Munster, IN	GRY
IN	PRM
IN	STN
Murdo, SD	RC
Murdock, FL	VEN
MN	NU
Murfreesboro, TN	NSH
Murphy, NC	CHL
Murphy Village, SC	CHR
Murphysboro, IL	BEL
Murray, KY	OWN
UT	OLL
UT	SLC
Murray City, OH	COL
Murrayville, IL	SFD
Murrieta, CA	SB
Murrysville, PA	GBG
Muscatine, IA	DAV
Muscoda, WI	MAD
Muse, PA	PIT
Muskegan, MI	GR
Muskego, WI	MIL
Muskegon, MI	GR
Muskegon Heights, MI	GR
Muskogee, OK	TLS
Mustang, OK	OKL
Myerstown, PA	HBG
Myrtle Beach, SC	CHR
Myrtle Creek, OR	P
Mystic, CT	NOR
IA	DAV
Naalehu, HI	HON
Nabob, WI	MIL
Naches, WA	YAK
Nacogdoches, TX	TYL
Nada, TX	VIC
Nadeau, MI	MAR
Naguabo, PR	CGS
Nahant, MA	BO
Nahma, MI	MAR
Nampa, ID	B
Namur, WI	GB
Nanakuli, HI	HON
Nanticoke, PA	PHU
PA	PSC
PA	SCR
Nantucket, MA	FR
Nanty-Glo, PA	ALT
PA	PBR
Nanuet, NY	NY
Napa, CA	SR
Napanee, IN	FTW
Naperville, IL	JOL
Naples, FL	VEN
NY	ROC
Napoleon, IN	IND
ND	FAR
OH	TOL
Napoleonville, LA	BR
Naranja, FL	MIA
Naranjito, PR	CGS
Narberth, PA	PH
Narragansett, RI	PRO
Narrowsburg, NY	NY
Nashua, IA	DUB
NH	MAN
Nashville, IL	BEL
IN	IND
TN	NSH
Nashwauk, MN	DUL
Nassau, MN	NU
NY	ALB
Natchez, MS	JKS
Natchitoches, LA	ALX
Natick, MA	BO

National City, CA	SD
National Park, NJ	CAM
Natrona, PA	PIT
Natrona Heights, PA	PIT
Naugatuck, CT	HRT
Nauvoo, IL	PEO
Navajo, NM	GLP
Navarino, WI	GB
Navarre, FL	PT
OH	Y
Navasota, TX	GAL
Navilleton, IN	IND
Naytahwaush, MN	CR
Nazareth, KY	L
MI	KAL
PA	ALN
TX	AMA
Nebish, MN	CR
Nebraska City, NE	LIN
Necedah, WI	LC
Neche, ND	FAR
Nederland, TX	BEA
Needham, MA	BO
Needles, CA	SB
Needville, TX	GAL
Neenah, WI	GB
Neenah/Menasha, WI	GB
Neepwukos, FM	CI
Neepwukos, Chuuk, FM	CI
Neffs, OH	STU
Negaunee, MI	MAR
Neier, MO	STL
Neillsville, WI	LC
Nekoma, ND	FAR
Nekoosa, WI	LC
Neligh, NE	OM
Nelsonville, OH	STU
Nemacolin, PA	PIT
Nemar, FM	CI
Nenana, AK	FBK
Nenno, WI	MIL
Neodesha, KS	WCH
Neoga, IL	SFD
Neola, IA	DM
Neopit, WI	GB
Neosho, MO	SPC
WI	MIL
Neptune, IA	SC
NJ	TR
Nerinx, KY	L
Nesbit, MS	JKS
Nesconset, NY	RVC
Neshannock, PA	PIT
Neshkoro, WI	MAD
Nespelem, WA	SPK
Nesquehoning, PA	ALN
PA	PSC
Ness City, KS	DOD
Netcong, NJ	PAT
Neva, WI	GB
Nevada, IA	DUB
MO	KC
Nevada City, CA	SAC
Nevis, MN	CR
New Albany, IN	IND
MS	JKS
OH	COL
New Albin, IA	DUB
New Alexandria, PA	GBG
PA	SJP
New Almelo, KS	SAL
New Alsace, IN	IND
New Athens, IL	BEL
New Auburn, WI	LC
New Baden, IL	BEL
New Baltimore, MI	DET
PA	ALT
New Bavaria, OH	TOL
New Bedford, MA	FR
MA	SAM
PA	PIT
New Berlin, IL	SFD
NY	SY
WI	MIL
New Bern, NC	R
New Bethlehem, PA	E
New Bloomfield, PA	HBG
New Boston, IN	EVN
MI	DET
OH	COL
TX	TYL
New Braunfels, TX	SAT
New Bremen, OH	CIN
New Brighton, MN	STP
PA	PIT
New Britain, CT	HRT
CT	PSC
CT	STF
New Brunswick, NJ	MET
NJ	PHU
NJ	PSC
New Buffalo, MI	KAL
New Canaan, CT	BGP
New Caney, TX	GAL
New Carlisle, IN	FTW
OH	CIN
New Castle, DE	WIL
IN	IND
PA	PIT
PA	SAM
New Chicago, IN	GRY
New City, NY	NY
New Cleveland, OH	TOL
New Cumberland, PA	HBG
WV	WH
New Cuyama, CA	LA
New Denmark, WI	GB
New Derry, PA	GBG
New Douglas, IL	SFD
New Effington, SD	SFS
New Egypt, NJ	TR
New England, ND	BIS
New Fairfield, CT	BGP
New Franken, WI	GB
New Freedom, PA	HBG
New Garden Township, PA	PH
New Hamburg, MO	SPC
New Hampton, IA	DUB
New Harmony, IN	EVN
New Hartford, CT	HRT
IA	DUB
NY	SY
New Haven, CT	HRT
CT	STF
IA	DUB
IN	FTW
KY	L
MI	DET
MO	STL
New Holland, PA	HBG
New Holstein, WI	GB
New Hope, KY	L
MN	STP
PA	PH
New Hyde Park, NY	RVC
New Iberia, LA	LAF
New Ipswich, NH	MAN
New Kensington, PA	GBG
PA	SJP
New Lebanon, NY	ALB
New Lenox, IL	JOL
New Lexington, OH	COL
New Lisbon, WI	LC
New London, CT	NOR
NH	MAN
NY	SY
OH	TOL
WI	GB
New Madrid, MO	SPC
New Marion, IN	IND
New Market, MN	STP
New Martinsville, WV	WH
New Melle, MO	STL
New Melleray, IA	DUB
New Miami, OH	CIN
New Middletown, IN	IND
OH	Y
New Milford, CT	HRT
NJ	NEW
New Monmouth, NJ	TR
New Munich, MN	SCL
New Munster, WI	MIL
New Orleans, LA	NO
LA	OLL
LA	PBR
New Oxford, PA	HBG
New Paltz, NY	NY
New Paris, OH	CIN
New Philadelphia, OH	COL
PA	ALN
New Plymouth, ID	B
New Port Richey, FL	PSC
FL	SP
New Post, WI	SUP
New Prague, MN	STP
New Providence, NJ	NEW
New Richland, MN	WIN
New Richmond, OH	CIN
WI	SUP
New Riegel, OH	TOL
New Ringgold, PA	ALN
New Roads, LA	BR
New Rochelle, NY	NY
New Rockford, ND	FAR
New Salem, ND	BIS
PA	GBG
PA	PBR
New Shoreham, RI	PRO
New Smyrna Beach, FL	ORL
New Taiton, TX	VIC
New Town, ND	BIS
New Trier, MN	STP
New Ulm, MN	NU
New Underwood, SD	RC
New Vernon, NJ	PAT
New Vienna, IA	DUB
OH	CIN
New Village, NJ	MET
New Washington, OH	TOL
New Waverly, TX	GAL
New Windsor, NY	NY
New York, NY	ARM
NY	BUF
NY	NY
NY	PSC
NY	STF
New York Mills, NY	SY
Newald, WI	GB
Newark, CA	OAK
DE	WIL
NJ	NEW
NJ	OLD
NJ	PHU
NJ	PSC
NY	ROC
OH	COL
Newark Valley, NY	ROC
Newaygo, MI	GR
Newberg, OR	P
Newberry, MI	MAR
SC	CHR
Newberry Springs, CA	VNN
Newburg, MD	WDC
WI	MIL
Newburgh, IN	EVN
NY	NY
Newbury, OH	CLV
Newbury Park, CA	LA
Newburyport, MA	BO
Newcastle, ME	PRT
NE	OM
WY	CHY
Newcomb, NY	OG
TN	KNX
Newcomerstown, OH	COL
Newell, SD	RC
Newfane, NY	BUF
Newfield, NJ	CAM
Newhall, IA	DUB
Newington, CT	HRT
Newkirk, OK	OKL
Newman, CA	STO
Newmarket, NH	MAN
Newnan, GA	ATL
Newport, AR	LR
IA	DAV
KY	COV
MD	WDC
MI	DET
NH	MAN
NY	ALB
OH	CIN
OR	P
RI	PRO
TN	KNX
VT	BUR
WA	SPK
Newport Beach, CA	ORG
Newport News, VA	RIC
Newry, PA	ALT
Newtok, AK	FBK
Newton, IA	DAV
IL	SFD
KS	WCH
MA	BO
NC	CHL
NH	MAN
NJ	PAT
Newton Falls, OH	PBR
OH	Y
Newton Grove, NC	R
Newtown, CT	BGP
PA	ALN
PA	PH
Newtown Square, PA	PH
PA	SAM
Newtowne, MD	WDC
Nezperce, ID	B
Niagara, WI	GB
Niagara Falls, NY	BUF
NY	STF
Niagara University, NY	BUF
Niantic, CT	NOR
IL	SFD
Niceville, FL	PT
Nicholasville, KY	LEX
Nichols, IA	DAV
Nicholson, PA	SCR
Nicktown, PA	ALT
Nicollet, MN	NU
Nicoma Park, OK	OKL
Nightmute, AK	FBK
Niland, CA	SD
Niles, IL	CHI
KS	SAL
MI	KAL
OH	Y
Nine Mile, MI	SAG
Nipomo, CA	MRY
Niskayuna, NY	ALB
Nitro, WV	WH
Nix Settlement, IN	FTW
Nixon, TX	SAT
Noble, LA	SHP
Noblesville, IN	LFT
Nocona, TX	FWT
Nogales, AZ	TUC
Nokomis, FL	VEN
IL	SFD
Nolan Settlement, IA	DAV
Nome, AK	FBK
Norbeck, MD	WDC
Norco, CA	SB
LA	NO
Norcross, GA	ATL
Norfolk, CT	HRT
MA	BO
NE	OM
NY	OG
VA	RIC
Norge, VA	RIC
Normal, IL	PEO
Norman, OK	OKL
WI	GB
Normandy, MO	STL
Normandy Beach, NJ	TR
Norridge, IL	CHI
Norris, SD	RC
TN	KNX
Norristown, PA	PH
North Adams, MA	SPR
North Andover, MA	BO
North Arlington, NJ	NEW
North Arm, IL	SFD
North Attleboro, MA	FR
North Auburn, OH	TOL
North Augusta, SC	CHR
North Aurora, IL	RCK
North Baltimore, OH	TOL
North Bangor, NY	OG
North Bay, NY	SY
North Beach, MD	WDC
North Bend, NE	OM
OR	P
North Bennington, VT	BUR
North Bergen, NJ	NEW
North Bethesda, MD	WDC
North Branch, MI	DET
MN	STP
North Branford, CT	HRT
North Brookfield, MA	SAM
MA	WOR
North Brunswick, NJ	MET
North Buena Vista, IA	DUB
North Caldwell, NJ	NEW
North Canton, OH	Y
North Cape May, NJ	CAM
North Chicago, IL	CHI
North Chili, NY	ROC
North Collins, NY	BUF
North Conway, NH	MAN
North Creek, NY	ALB
OH	TOL
WI	LC
North Dartmouth, MA	FR
North Dighton, MA	FR
North East, PA	E
North Easton, MA	FR
North Ellinwood, KS	DOD
North English, IA	DAV
North Evans, NY	BUF
North Falmouth, MA	FR
North Fond du Lac, WI	MIL
North Fort Myers, FL	PSC
North Grafton, MA	WOR
North Greenbush, NY	ALB
North Grosvenordale, CT	NOR
North Guilford, CT	HRT
North Haledon, NJ	PAT
North Haven, CT	HRT
North Highlands, CA	SAC
North Hills, CA	LA
North Hollywood, CA	EST
CA	LA
CA	NTN
CA	OLD
North Huntingdon, PA	GBG
PA	PBR
North Jackson, OH	OLL
OH	Y
North Java, NY	BUF
North Judson, IN	GRY
North Kingstown, RI	PRO
North Kinsley, KS	DOD

North Lake, WI	MIL
North Las Vegas, NV	LAV
North Lauderdale, FL	MIA
North Lawrence, NY	OG
North Lewisburg, OH	CIN
North Lima, OH	Y
North Little Rock, AR	LR
North Manchester, IN	FTW
North Mankato, MN	NU
North Merrick, NY	RVC
North Miami, FL	MIA
North Miami Beach, FL	MIA
North Muskegon, MI	GR
North Myrtle Beach, SC	CHR
North Oakland, PA	PIT
North Olmsted, OH	CLV
North Oxford, MA	WOR
North Palm Beach, FL	PMB
North Plainfield, NJ	MET
North Plains, OR	P
North Platte, NE	GI
NE	LIN
North Pole, AK	FBK
North Port, FL	SJP
FL	VEN
North Prairie, MN	SCL
North Providence,	PRO
RI	PRO
North Reading, MA	BO
North Ridgeville, OH	CLV
North Riverside, IL	CHI
North Rochester, PA	PIT
North Royalton, OH	CLV
OH	PRM
North St. Paul, MN	STP
North Smithfield, RI	PRO
North Star, OH	CIN
North Stonington, CT	NOR
North Stratford, NH	MAN
North Syracuse,	SY
NY	SY
North Tarrytown, NY	NY
North Tonawanda, NY	BUF
North Topsail Beach, NC	R
North Troy, VT	BUR
North Vassalboro, ME	PRT
North Vernon, IN	IND
North Wales, PA	PH
North Walpole, NH	MAN
North Washington, IA	DUB
North Wildwood, NJ	CAM
North Wilkesboro, NC	CHL
Northampton, MA	SPR
PA	ALN
PA	PHU
Northboro, MA	WOR
Northbridge, MA	WOR
Northbrook, IL	CHI
Northeast Harbor, ME	PRT
Northeim, WI	GB
Northern Cambria, PA	ALT
PA	PBR
PA	SJP
Northfield, IL	CHI
MA	SPR
MN	STP
NJ	CAM
OH	CLV
VT	BUR
Northford, CT	HRT
Northglenn, CO	DEN
Northhampton, PA	ALN
Northlake, IL	CHI
IL	NTN
Northome, MN	DUL
Northport, MI	GAY
NY	RVC
WA	SPK
Northridge, CA	LA
Northumberland, PA	HBG
Northvale, NJ	NEW
Northville, MI	DET
NY	ALB
Northwood, OH	PRM
Norton, KS	SAL
MA	FR
OH	CLV
VA	RIC
Nortonville, KS	KCK
ND	FAR
Norwalk, CA	LA
CT	BGP
OH	TOL
WI	LC
Norway, IA	DUB
ME	PRT
MI	MAR
Norwell, MA	BO
Norwich, CT	NOR
NY	SY
Norwood, MA	BO

MN	STP
NJ	NEW
NY	OG
PA	PH
Notre Dame, IN	FTW
Novato, CA	SFR
Novi, MI	DET
Nulato, AK	FBK
Nunda, NY	ROC
Nutley, NJ	NEW
Nyack, NY	NY
Nyssa, OR	BAK
O'Donnell, TX	LUB
O'Fallon, IL	BEL
MO	STL
O'Hara Township, PA	PIT
O'Neill, NE	OM
Oak Bluffs, MA	FR
Oak Brook, IL	JOL
Oak Creek, CO	DEN
WI	MIL
Oak Forest, IL	CHI
IN	IND
Oak Grove, KY	OWN
LA	SHP
Oak Harbor, OH	TOL
WA	SEA
Oak Hill, WV	WH
Oak Lawn, IL	CHI
Oak Park, IL	CHI
MI	DET
MI	EST
Oak Ridge, MN	WIN
NJ	PAT
TN	KNX
Oak Ridge-Milton, NJ	PAT
Oakbrook Terrace, IL	JOL
Oakdale, CA	STO
CT	NOR
LA	LKC
MN	STP
NE	OM
NY	RVC
PA	PIT
Oakes, ND	FAR
Oakesdale, WA	SPK
Oakfield, NY	BUF
WI	MIL
Oakland, CA	NTN
CA	OAK
MD	BAL
ME	PRT
NJ	NEW
Oakland City, IN	EVN
Oakley, CA	OAK
KS	SAL
MI	SAG
Oaklyn, NJ	CAM
Oakmont, PA	PIT
Oakridge, OR	P
Oakville, CA	SR
CT	HRT
MO	STL
Oakwood, ND	FAR
Oberlin, KS	SAL
LA	LKC
OH	CLV
Obernburg, NY	NY
Oblong, IL	SFD
Ocala, FL	ORL
Occidental, CA	SR
Occum, CT	NOR
Ocean Beach, NY	RVC
Ocean City, MD	WIL
NJ	CAM
Ocean Shores, WA	SEA
Ocean Springs, MS	BLX
Oceanside, CA	SD
NY	RVC
Oconee, IL	SFD
Oconomowoc, WI	MIL
Oconto, WI	GB
Oconto Falls, WI	GB
Odanah, WI	SUP
Odebolt, IA	SC
Odell, IL	PEO
Odem, TX	CC
Odenton, MD	BAL
Odessa, MO	KC
NY	ROC
TX	SAN
WA	SPK
Odin, KS	DOD
Oelwein, IA	DUB
Offerle, KS	DOD
Ogallala, NE	GI
Ogden, IA	SC
KS	SAL
UT	SLC
Ogdensburg, NJ	PAT
NY	OG

Ogema, MN	CR
Ogilvie, MN	SCL
Oglala, SD	RC
Oglesby, IL	PEO
Ogletown, DE	WIL
Ohio, IL	PEO
Oil City, PA	E
Oildale, CA	FRS
Ojai, CA	LA
Okanogan-Omak, WA	SPK
Okarche, OK	OKL
Okawville, IL	BEL
Okeechobee, FL	PMB
Okeene, OK	OKL
Okemos, MI	LAN
Oklahoma City, OK	OKL
OK	PBR
Oklee, MN	CR
Okmulgee, OK	TLS
Olathe, KS	KCK
Olcott, NY	BUF
Old Bridge, NJ	MET
Old Fields, WV	WH
Old Forge, NY	OG
PA	PSC
PA	SCR
Old Hickory, TN	NSH
Old Lyme, CT	NOR
Old Mines, MO	STL
Old Monroe, MO	STL
Old Orchard Beach, ME	PRT
Old Saybrook, CT	NOR
Old Tappan, NJ	NEW
Old Town, ME	PRT
Old Washington-on-the Brazos, TX	AUS
Old Westbury, NY	RVC
Oldenburg, IN	IND
Oldham, SD	SFS
Olean, NE	OM
NY	BUF
NY	PSC
NY	SAM
Olema, CA	SFR
Olfen, TX	SAN
Olga, ND	FAR
Olive Branch, MS	JKS
Olive Hill, KY	LEX
Olivia, MN	NU
Olmitz, KS	DOD
Olmsted Falls, OH	CLV
Olmstedville, NY	OG
Olney, IL	BEL
MD	WDC
TX	FWT
Olpe, KS	KCK
Olympia, WA	SEA
WA	VNN
Olympia Fields, IL	CHI
Olyphant, PA	PHU
PA	SCR
Omaha, NE	OM
NE	STN
Omak, WA	SPK
Omer, MI	PRM
Omro, WI	GB
Ona, WV	WH
Onaga, KS	KCK
Onaka, SD	SFS
Onalaska, WI	LC
Onamia, MN	SCL
Onatrio, CA	SB
Onawa, IA	SC
Onaway, MI	GAY
Oneida, NY	SY
WI	GB
Oneida Township, WI	GB
Onekama, MI	GAY
Oneonta, AL	BIR
NY	ALB
Onida, SD	SFS
Onley, VA	RIC
Onondaga Hill, NY	SY
Onset, MA	FR
Onsted, MI	DET
Ontario, CA	SB
NY	ROC
OR	BAK
Ontonagon, MI	MAR
Opa Locka, FL	MIA
Opelika, AL	MOB
Opelousas, LA	LAF
Opole, MN	SCL
Oquossoc, ME	PRT
Oradell, NJ	NEW
Oran, MO	SPC
Orange, CA	ORG
CT	HRT
MA	SPR
NJ	NEW
TX	BEA

VA	ARL
Orange Beach, AL	MOB
Orange Cove, CA	FRS
Orange Grove, TX	CC
Orange Park, FL	STA
Orange Village, OH	CLV
Orangeburg, NY	NY
SC	CHR
Orangefield, TX	BEA
Orangevale, CA	SAC
Orchard Lake, MI	DET
Orchard Park, NY	BUF
Ord, NE	GI
Ordot, GU	AGN
Oreana, ID	B
Orefield, PA	ALN
Oregon, IL	RCK
OH	TOL
WI	MAD
Oregon City, OR	P
Oreland, PA	PH
Orient, IA	DM
SD	SFS
Oriental, NC	R
Orinda, CA	OAK
Orion, IL	PEO
Orion Township, MI	DET
Oriska, ND	FAR
Oriskany, NY	SY
Oriskany Falls, NY	SY
Orland, CA	SAC
Orland Hills, IL	CHI
Orland Park, IL	CHI
Orlando, FL	ORL
FL	PSC
FL	SAM
Orleans, MA	FR
NE	LIN
VT	BUR
Ormond Beach, FL	ORL
FL	PSC
Orocovis, PR	ARE
Orofino, ID	B
Orono, ME	PRT
Oroville, CA	SAC
WA	SPK
Orr, MN	DUL
Orrin, ND	FAR
Orrville, AL	MOB
OH	CLV
Ortonville, MI	DET
MN	NU
Orwell, OH	Y
VT	BUR
Orwigsburg, PA	ALN
Osage, IA	DUB
Osage Bend, MO	JC
Osage City, KS	KCK
Osakis, MN	SCL
Osawatomie, KS	KCK
Osborne, KS	SAL
Osceola, AR	LR
IA	DM
NE	LIN
WI	SUP
Oscoda, MI	GAY
Osgood, IN	IND
OH	CIN
Oshkosh, WI	GB
Oskaloosa, IA	DAV
Oslo, MN	CR
Osman, WI	GB
Osmond, NE	OM
Osnabrock, ND	FAR
Ossian, IA	DUB
Ossineke, MI	GAY
Ossining, NY	NY
Ost, KS	WCH
Osterville, MA	FR
Oswego, IL	JOL
KS	WCH
NY	SY
Othello, WA	SPK
Otis, IN	GRY
Otis Orchards, WA	SPK
Otisville, MI	LAN
NY	NY
Otsego, MI	KAL
Ottawa, IL	PEO
KS	KCK
OH	TOL
Ottenheim, KY	LEX
Otter Creek, IA	DUB
Otter River, MA	WOR
Otterbein, IN	LFT
Ottoville, OH	TOL
Ottsville, PA	PH
Ottumwa, IA	DAV
Otway, OH	COL
Ouray, CO	PBL
Overbrook, PA	PH

PA	PIT
Overgaard, AZ	GLP
Overland, MO	STL
Overland Park, KS	KCK
Overton, NV	LAV
Ovid, MI	LAN
NY	ROC
Owasso, OK	TLS
Owatonna, MN	WIN
Owego, NY	ROC
Owen, WI	LC
Owensboro, KY	OWN
Owensville, MD	BAL
MO	JC
OH	CIN
Owingsville, KY	LEX
Owosso, MI	LAN
Oxford, CT	HRT
IA	DAV
IN	LFT
KS	WCH
MA	WOR
MI	DET
MS	JKS
NJ	MET
NY	SY
OH	CIN
PA	PH
Oxford Junction, IA	DUB
Oxnard, CA	LA
Oxon Hill, MD	WDC
Oyens, IA	SC
Oyster Bay, NY	RVC
Ozark, AL	MOB
AR	LR
MO	SPC
Ozona, TX	SAN
Ozone Park, NY	BRK
NY	STF
Ozora, MO	STL
Pacific, MO	STL
Pacific City, OR	P
Pacific Grove, CA	MRY
Pacific Palisades, CA	LA
Pacifica, CA	SFR
Pacoima, CA	LA
Paden City, WV	WH
Paderborn, IL	BEL
Padua, MN	SCL
Paducah, KY	OWN
Page, AZ	GLP
ND	FAR
Pagedale, MO	STL
Pago Pago, AS	SPP
Pagosa Springs, CO	PBL
Pahala, HI	HON
Pahoa, HI	HON
Pahokee, FL	PMB
Pahrump, NV	LAV
Paia, HI	HON
Paincourtville, LA	BR
Painesville, OH	CLV
Painted Post, NY	ROC
Paintsville, KY	LEX
Pala, CA	SD
Pala Indian Missions, CA	SD
Palacios, TX	VIC
Palatine, IL	CHI
IL	STN
Palatka, FL	STA
Palau, PW	CI
Palenville, NY	ALB
Palestine, TX	TYL
Palikir, FM	CI
Palisades Park, NJ	NEW
Palm Bay, FL	ORL
Palm Beach, FL	PMB
Palm Beach Gardens, FL	PMB
Palm City, FL	PMB
Palm Coast, FL	STA
Palm Desert, CA	SB
Palm Harbor, FL	SP
Palm Springs, CA	SB
CA	VNN
Palmdale, CA	LA
Palmer, AK	ANC
MA	SPR
PA	GBG
Palmerton, PA	ALN
PA	PHU
PA	PSC
Palmerton-Slatington, PA	ALN
Palmetto, FL	VEN
Palms, MI	SAG
Palmyra, IL	SFD
MO	JC
NE	LIN
NY	ROC
PA	HBG
VA	RIC
WI	MAD
Palo Alto, CA	SJ
Palo Cedro, CA	SAC
Palos Heights, IL	CHI
Palos Hills, IL	CHI
Palos Park, IL	CHI
IL	STN
Pampa, TX	AMA
Pana, IL	SFD
Panama, IA	DM
IL	SFD
NY	BUF
Panama City, FL	PT
Panama City Beach, FL	PT
Panhandle, TX	AMA
Panna Maria, TX	SAT
Panora, IA	DM
Panorama City, CA	LA
Paola, KS	KCK
Paoli, IN	IND
PA	PH
WI	MAD
Paonia, CO	PBL
Papaaloa, HI	HON
Papaikou, HI	HON
Papillion, NE	OM
Paradis, LA	NO
Paradise, CA	SAC
MI	DET
Paradox, NY	ALB
Paragould, AR	LR
Paramount, CA	LA
Paramus, NJ	NEW
Parchment, MI	KAL
Pardeesville, PA	SCR
Pardeeville, WI	MAD
Paris, AR	LR
IL	SFD
KY	LEX
TN	MEM
TX	TYL
WI	MIL
Parish, NY	SY
Parisville, MI	SAG
Park, KS	SAL
Park City, UT	SLC
Park Falls, WI	SUP
Park Forest, IL	CHI
IL	JOL
Park Hills, MO	STL
Park Rapids, MN	CR
Park Ridge, IL	CHI
NJ	NEW
Park River, ND	FAR
Parker, AZ	TUC
CO	COS
PA	GBG
SD	SFS
Parkers Prairie, MN	SCL
Parkersburg, IA	DUB
WV	WH
Parkesburg, PA	PH
Parkland, FL	MIA
Parkman, OH	CLV
Parks, LA	LAF
Parkston, SD	SFS
Parkton, MD	BAL
Parlier, CA	FRS
Parlin, NJ	MET
Parma, ID	B
OH	CLV
OH	PRM
OH	SJP
Parma Heights, OH	CLV
Parmelee, SD	RC
Parnell, IA	DAV
MI	GR
MO	KC
Parrish, FL	VEN
Parshall, ND	BIS
Parsippany, NJ	PAT
Parsons, KS	WCH
Pasadena, CA	LA
MD	BAL
TX	GAL
Pasadina, CA	LA
Pascagoula, MS	BLX
Pasco, WA	SPK
Pascoag, RI	PRO
Paso Robles, CA	MRY
Pass Christian, MS	BLX
Passaic, NJ	PAT
NJ	PHU
NJ	PSC
Patagonia, AZ	TUC
Pataskala, OH	COL
Patch Grove, WI	MAD
Patchogue, NY	RVC
Paterson, NJ	ARM
NJ	PAT
Patillas, PR	PCE
Patterson, CA	STO
LA	LAF
NY	NY
Pattison/Brookshire, TX	GAL
Patton, PA	ALT
PA	PBR
Paul, NE	LIN
Paulding, MS	JKS
OH	TOL
Paulina, LA	BR
Pauls Valley, OK	OKL
Paulsboro, NJ	CAM
Pavilion, NY	BUF
Paw Paw, MI	KAL
Pawcatuck, CT	NOR
Pawhuska, OK	TLS
Pawleys Island, SC	CHR
Pawling, NY	NY
Pawnee, IL	SFD
OK	TLS
Pawnee Rock, KS	DOD
Pawtucket, RI	PRO
RI	SAM
Paxico, KS	KCK
Paxton, IL	JOL
MA	WOR
Payette, ID	B
Payne, OH	TOL
Paynesville, MN	SCL
Payneville, KY	L
Payson, AZ	TUC
UT	SLC
Pe Ell, WA	SEA
Peabody, MA	BO
Peachtree City, GA	ATL
Peaks Island, ME	PRT
Peapack, NJ	MET
Pearisburg, VA	RIC
Pearl, MI	KAL
MS	JKS
Pearl City, HI	HON
Pearl Lake, MN	SCL
Pearl River, LA	NO
NY	NY
Pearland, TX	GAL
Pearlington, MS	BLX
Pearsall, TX	SAT
Pecatonica, IL	RCK
Peckville, PA	SCR
Pecos, NM	SFE
TX	ELP
Peebles, OH	CIN
Peekskill, NY	NY
NY	PSC
Peetz, CO	DEN
Pekin, IL	PEO
Pelham, NH	MAN
NY	NY
Pelham Manor, NY	NY
Pelican Lake, WI	SUP
Pelican Rapids, MN	SCL
Pell City, AL	BIR
Pell Lake, WI	MIL
Pella, IA	DAV
Pellston, MI	GAY
Pembina, ND	FAR
Pembine, WI	GB
Pembroke, MA	BO
Pembroke Pines, FL	MIA
Pen Argyl, PA	ALN
Pena Blanca, NM	SFE
Penacook, NH	MAN
Penasco, NM	SFE
Pence, WI	SUP
Pender, NE	OM
Pendleton, NY	BUF
OR	BAK
Penelope, TX	FWT
Penfield, IL	PEO
NY	ROC
Peninsula, OH	CLV
Penn, ND	FAR
PA	GBG
Penn Hills, PA	PIT
Penn Valley, PA	PH
Penn Yan, NY	ROC
Penndel, PA	PH
Penngrove, CA	SR
Pennington, MN	CR
NJ	TR
Pennington Gap, VA	RIC
Penns Grove, NJ	CAM
Penns Valley, PA	ALT
Pennsauken, NJ	CAM
Pennsburg, PA	PH
Pennsville, NJ	CAM
Pensacola, FL	PT
Pensacola Beach, FL	PT
Penuelas, PR	PCE
Peonia, KY	OWN
Peoria, AZ	PHX
IL	OLL
IL	PEO
Peoria heights, IL	PEO
Peosta, IA	DUB
Peotone, IL	JOL
Peplin, WI	LC
Pepper Pike, OH	CLV
Pepperell, MA	BO
Pequannock, NJ	PAT
Pequot Lakes, MN	DUL
Peralta, NM	SFE
Perezville-Tamuning, GU	AGN
Perham, MN	SCL
Perkins, MI	MAR
Perris, CA	SB
Perronville, MI	MAR
Perry, FL	PT
GA	SAV
IA	DM
KS	KCK
ME	PRT
MO	JC
NY	BUF
OH	CLV
OK	OKL
WI	MAD
Perryopolis, PA	GBG
PA	PBR
Perrysburg, NY	BUF
OH	TOL
Perrysville, PA	PIT
Perryton, TX	AMA
Perryville, MD	WIL
MO	STL
Perth Amboy, NJ	MET
NJ	PHU
NJ	PSC
Peru, IL	PEO
IN	LFT
NY	OG
OH	TOL
Peshabestown, MI	GAY
Peshtigo, WI	GB
Pesotum, IL	PEO
Petal, MS	BLX
Petaluma, CA	SFR
CA	SR
Peterborough, NH	MAN
Peters Township, PA	PIT
Petersburg, AK	JUN
IA	DUB
IL	SFD
IN	EVN
NE	OM
TX	LUB
VA	RIC
WV	WH
Petersham, MA	SAM
MA	WOR
Peterstown, IL	PEO
Petersville, IA	DAV
Petoskey, MI	GAY
Pevely, MO	STL
Pewamo, MI	GR
Pewaukee, WI	MIL
Pewee Valley, KY	L
Pfeifer, KS	SAL
Pflugerville, TX	AUS
Pharr, TX	BWN
Phelan, CA	SB
Phelps, NY	ROC
WI	SUP
Phenix City, AL	MOB
Philadelphia, MS	JKS
PA	ARM
PA	HBG
PA	PH
PA	PHU
PA	PSC
PA	SAM
Philip, SD	RC
Philippi, WV	OLL
WV	WH
Philipsburg, MT	HEL
PA	ALT
Phillips, WI	SUP
Phillipsburg, KS	SAL
NJ	MET
NJ	PSC
Philmont, NY	ALB
Philo, IL	PEO
Philothea, OH	CIN
Philpot, KY	OWN
Phlox, WI	GB
Phoenicia, NY	NY
Phoenix, AZ	NTN
AZ	OLL
AZ	PHX
AZ	STN
AZ	VNN
NY	SY
Phoenixville, PA	PH

PA	PHU
Picayune, MS	BLX
Pickens, SC	CHR
Pickerington, OH	COL
Pico Rivera, CA	LA
Piedmont, CA	OAK
MO	SPC
OK	OKL
SD	RC
Piedmont-Black Hawk, SD	RC
Pierce, NE	OM
Pierce City, MO	SPC
Pierceton, IN	FTW
Piermont, NY	NY
Pierre, SD	SFS
Pierre Part, LA	BR
Pierron, IL	SFD
Pier-Willow, WI	SUP
Pierz, MN	SCL
Piffard, NY	ROC
Pigeon, MI	SAG
Pikeville, KY	LEX
Pilot Grove, MO	JC
Pilot Knob, MO	SPC
Pilot Point, TX	FWT
Pilot Rock, OR	BAK
Pilot Station, AK	FBK
Pilsen, KS	WCH
Pin Oak, TX	AUS
Pinckney, MI	LAN
Pinckneyville, IL	BEL
Pinconning, MI	SAG
Pine Apple, AL	MOB
Pine Bluff, AR	LR
WI	MAD
Pine Bluffs, WY	CHY
Pine Bush, NY	NY
Pine City, MN	DUL
NY	ROC
Pine Creek, WI	LC
Pine Grove, OH	STU
PA	SCR
WI	GB
Pine Hill, NJ	CAM
Pine Island, MN	STP
NY	NY
Pine Lawn, MO	STL
Pine Plains, NY	NY
Pine Prairie, LA	LAF
Pine Ridge, SD	RC
Pine River, MN	DUL
Pinedale, WY	CHY
Pinehaven, NM	GLP
Pinehurst, NC	R
Pinellas Park, FL	SP
Pinetop, AZ	GLP
Pineville, LA	ALX
MS	BLX
WV	WH
Piney Fork, OH	STU
Pingree, ND	FAR
Pinnebog, MI	SAG
Pinole, CA	OAK
Pinon, AZ	GLP
Piopolis, IL	BEL
Piper City, IL	JOL
Pipestone, MN	WIN
Piqua, KS	WCH
OH	CIN
Pirtleville, AZ	TUC
Piscataway, MD	WDC
NJ	MET
Pisek, ND	FAR
Pismo Beach, CA	MRY
Pitcairn, PA	PIT
Piti, GU	AGN
Pitman, NJ	CAM
Pittsburg, CA	OAK
KS	WCH
TX	TYL
Pittsburgh, PA	PBR
PA	PIT
PA	SJP
Pittsfield, IL	SFD
MA	SPR
MA	STF
ME	PRT
NH	MAN
Pittsford, NY	ROC
VT	BUR
Pittsgrove, NJ	CAM
Pittston, PA	PSC
PA	SCR
Pittstown, NJ	MET
NY	ALB
Pittsville, WI	LC
Placentia, CA	NTN
CA	ORG
Placerville, CA	SAC
Placid, IA	DUB
Plain, WI	MAD
Plain City, OH	COL
Plainfield, CT	NOR
IL	JOL
IN	IND
NJ	NEW
WI	GB
Plains, KS	DOD
MT	HEL
PA	SCR
Plainsboro, NJ	MET
Plainview, MN	WIN
NE	OM
NY	RVC
TX	LUB
Plainville, CT	HRT
KS	SAL
MA	BO
Plaisance, LA	LAF
Plaistow, NH	MAN
Planada, CA	FRS
Plankinton, SD	SFS
Plano, IL	JOL
TX	DAL
Plant City, FL	SP
Plantation, FL	MIA
Plantersville, TX	GAL
Plantsville, CT	HRT
Plaquemine, LA	BR
Plateau, AL	MOB
Platte, SD	SFS
Platte Center, NE	OM
Plattekill, NY	NY
Plattenville, LA	BR
Platteville, CO	DEN
WI	MAD
Plattsburg, MO	KC
Plattsburgh, NY	OG
Plattsmouth, NE	LIN
Plaucheville, LA	ALX
Playa De Ponce, PR	PCE
Playa Del Rey, CA	LA
Playa Ponce, PR	PCE
Pleasant City, OH	PBR
Pleasant Hill, CA	OAK
Pleasant Hills, PA	PIT
Pleasant Mount, PA	SCR
Pleasant Point, ME	PRT
Pleasant Prairie, WI	MIL
Pleasant Valley, NY	NY
Pleasanton, CA	OAK
NE	GI
TX	SAT
Pleasantville, NJ	CAM
NY	NY
Pleasure Ridge Park, KY	L
Plentywood, MT	GF
Plover, WI	LC
Plum, PA	PIT
TX	VIC
Plum City, WI	LC
Plummer, MN	CR
Plymouth, IA	DUB
IN	FTW
MA	BO
MI	DET
MI	LAN
MI	NTN
MN	STP
NC	R
NH	MAN
OH	TOL
PA	PHU
PA	SCR
WI	MIL
Plymouth Meeting, PA	PH
Plymouth Rock, IA	DUB
Pocahontas, AR	LR
IA	SC
IL	SFD
VA	RIC
Pocasset, MA	FR
Pocatello, ID	B
Pocomoke City, MD	WIL
Pocono Pines, PA	SCR
Pohnpei, FM	CI
Poinciana, FL	ORL
Point Arena, CA	SR
Point Lookout, NY	RVC
Point Marion, PA	GBG
Point Pleasant, NJ	TR
WV	WH
Point Pleasant Beach, NJ	TR
Point Richmond, CA	OAK
Pointe a la Hache, LA	NO
Pointe-Aux-Chenes, LA	HT
Pojoaque, NM	SFE
Poland, OH	Y
Polo, IL	RCK
SD	SFS
Polonia, WI	LC
Polson, MT	HEL
Pomeroy, IA	SC
OH	STU
WA	SPK
Pomfret, CT	NOR
MD	WDC
Pomona, CA	LA
NJ	CAM
Pompano Beach, FL	MIA
Pompey, NY	SY
Pompton Lakes, NJ	PAT
Pompton Plains, NJ	PAT
Ponca, NE	OM
Ponca City, OK	OKL
Ponce, PR	PCE
Ponchatoula, LA	BR
LA	NO
Pond Settlement, IL	BEL
Poniatowski, WI	LC
Ponsford, MN	CR
Ponte Vedra Beach, FL	STA
Pontiac, IL	PEO
MI	DET
Poolesville, MD	WDC
Poplar, MT	GF
Poplar Bluff, MO	SPC
Poplar Springs, MD	BAL
Poquonock, CT	HRT
Porcupine, SD	RC
Porrassapw, FM	CI
Port Allegany, PA	E
Port Allen, LA	BR
Port Angeles, WA	SEA
Port Aransas, TX	CC
Port Arthur, TX	BEA
Port Austin, MI	SAG
Port Barre, LA	LAF
Port Bolivar, TX	GAL
Port Carbon, PA	ALN
Port Charlotte, FL	VEN
Port Chester, NY	NY
Port Clinton, OH	TOL
Port Edwards, WI	LC
Port Ewen, NY	NY
Port Gibson, MS	JKS
Port Henry, NY	OG
Port Hudson, MO	STL
Port Huron, MI	DET
Port Isabel, TX	BWN
Port Jefferson, NY	RVC
Port Jefferson Station, NY	RVC
Port Jervis, NY	NY
Port Lavaca, TX	VIC
Port Leyden, NY	OG
Port Murray, NJ	MET
Port Neches, TX	BEA
Port Orange, FL	ORL
Port Orchard, WA	SEA
Port Reading, NJ	MET
Port Richey, FL	SP
Port St. Joe, FL	PT
Port St. Lucie, FL	PMB
Port Sanilac, MI	SAG
Port Sulphur, LA	NO
Port Tobacco, MD	WDC
Port Townsend, WA	SEA
Port Vue, PA	PIT
Port Washington, NY	RVC
WI	MIL
Port Wentworth, GA	SAV
Portage, IN	GRY
MI	KAL
PA	ALT
PA	PBR
WI	MAD
Portage Des Sioux, MO	STL
Portageville, MO	SPC
NY	BUF
Portales, NM	SFE
Porterville, CA	FRS
Portland, CT	NOR
IN	LFT
ME	PRT
MI	GR
OR	OLL
OR	P
OR	VNN
TX	CC
Portola, CA	SAC
Portola Valley, CA	SFR
Portsmouth, IA	DM
NH	MAN
OH	COL
RI	PRO
VA	RIC
Portville, NY	BUF
Posen, IL	BEL
IL	CHI
MI	GAY
Poseyville, IN	EVN
Post, TX	LUB
Post Falls, ID	B
Postville, IA	DUB
Poteau, OK	TLS
Poteet, TX	SAT
Poth, TX	SAT
Potlatch, ID	B
Potomac, MD	WDC
Potomac Falls, VA	ARL
Potosi, MO	STL
Potsdam, NY	OG
Pottstown, PA	PH
PA	PHU
PA	PSC
Pottsville, PA	ALN
Poughkeepsie, NY	NY
Poulsbo, WA	SEA
Poultney, VT	BUR
Poway, CA	SD
Powell, OH	COL
WY	CHY
Powhatan, LA	ALX
VA	RIC
WV	WH
Powhatan Point, OH	STU
Poy Sippi, WI	GB
Poynette, WI	MAD
Praga, MI	GAY
Prague, NE	LIN
OK	OKL
Praha, TX	VIC
Prairie, IA	DUB
Prairie du Chien, WI	LC
Prairie du Rocher, IL	BEL
Prairie du Sac, WI	MAD
Prairie View, TX	GAL
Prairie Village, KS	KCK
Prairieburg, IA	DUB
Prairieville, LA	BR
Pratt, KS	DOD
Prattville, AL	MOB
Premont, TX	CC
Prentice, WI	SUP
Prescott, AZ	PHX
MI	GAY
WI	LC
Prescott Valley, AZ	PHX
Presho, SD	RC
Presidio, TX	ELP
Presque Isle, ME	PRT
WI	SUP
Preston, CT	NOR
IA	DUB
MN	WIN
Prestonsburg, KY	LEX
Price, UT	SLC
Prichard, AL	MOB
Priest River, ID	B
Primos, PA	PH
Prince Frederick, MD	WDC
Prince George County, VA	RIC
Princess Anne, MD	WIL
Princeton, IL	PEO
IN	EVN
KY	OWN
MA	WOR
MN	SCL
NJ	TR
WI	MAD
WV	WH
Princeville, IL	PEO
Prineville, OR	BAK
Prior Lake, MN	STP
Proctor, MN	DUL
VT	BUR
Progreso, TX	BWN
Prophetstown, IL	RCK
Prospect, CT	HRT
PA	PIT
Prospect Heights, IL	CHI
Prospect Park, NJ	PAT
Prosser, WA	YAK
Protivin, IA	DUB
Protovin, IA	DUB
Providence, KY	OWN
OH	TOL
RI	PRO
Provincetown, MA	FR
Provo, UT	SLC
Prudenville, MI	GAY
Pryor, MT	GF
OK	TLS
Pueblo, CO	PBL
Puerta De Tierra, PR	SJN
Puerto Nuevo, PR	SJN
Pukwana, SD	SFS
Pulaski, NY	SY
TN	NSH
WI	GB
Pulaskifield, MO	SPC
Pullman, WA	SPK
Punta Gorda, FL	VEN
Punxsutawney, PA	E

PA	PBR
Purcell, KS	KCK
OK	OKL
Purcellville, VA	ARL
Purchase, NY	NY
Put-In-Bay, OH	TOL
Putnam, CT	LIT
CT	NOR
IL	LIT
Putney, VT	BUR
Puyallup, WA	SEA
Pylesville, MD	BAL
Quaker Hill, CT	NOR
Quakertown, PA	PH
Quanah, TX	FWT
Quarryville, PA	HBG
Quebradillas, PR	ARE
Queens, NY	BRK
Queens Village, NY	BRK
Queensbury, NY	ALB
Quemado, NM	GLP
Questa, NM	SFE
Quincy, CA	SAC
FL	PT
IL	SFD
MA	BO
WA	YAK
Quinebaug, CT	NOR
Quinnesec, MI	MAR
Quinton, VA	RIC
Raceland, LA	HT
Racine, WI	MIL
Radcliff, KY	L
Raddle, IL	BEL
Radford, VA	RIC
Radisson, WI	SUP
Radnor, PA	ARM
PA	PH
Radom, IL	BEL
Raeford, NC	R
Raeville, NE	OM
Rahway, NJ	NEW
NJ	PSC
Rainelle, WV	WH
Rainier, OR	P
Raleigh, NC	R
ND	BIS
Ralls, TX	LUB
Ralston, NE	OM
Rambin, LA	SHP
Ramey, PA	E
PA	SJP
Ramona, CA	SD
CA	VNN
SD	SFS
Ramsay, MI	MAR
Ramsey, IL	SFD
NJ	NEW
NJ	PHU
Ranchito, TX	BWN
Rancho Cordova, CA	SAC
Rancho Cucamonga, CA	SB
Rancho Dominguez, CA	LA
Rancho Palos Verdes, CA	LA
CA	ORG
Rancho Santa Fe, CA	SD
Rancho Santa Margarita, CA	ORG
Ranchos De Taos, NM	SFE
Randall, MN	SCL
Randallstown, MD	BAL
Randolph, MA	BO
NE	OM
NJ	PAT
NY	BUF
VT	BUR
WI	MIL
Randolph Township, OH	Y
Random Lake, WI	MIL
Rangely, CO	DEN
Ranger, TX	FWT
Rankin, PA	PBR
PA	PIT
Ranshaw, PA	HBG
Ransom, IL	PEO
KS	DOD
Ransomville, NY	BUF
Rantoul, IL	PEO
Rapid City, SD	RC
Rapid River, MI	MAR
Rapids City, IL	PEO
Rapson, MI	SAG
Raquette Lake, NY	OG
Raritan, IL	PEO
NJ	MET
Ratcliff, AR	LR
Rathbun, IA	DAV
Rathdrum, ID	B
Raton, NM	SFE
Ravena, NY	ALB
Ravenna, KY	LEX
MI	GR
NE	GI
OH	Y
Ravenswood, WV	WH
Rawlins, WY	CHY
Raymond, IA	DUB
IL	SFD
LA	LKC
MN	NU
MS	JKS
WA	SEA
Raymondville, NY	OG
TX	BWN
Rayne, LA	LAF
Raynham, MA	FR
Raytown, MO	KC
Rayville, LA	SHP
Raywick, KY	L
Raywood, TX	BEA
Reading, KS	KCK
MA	BO
PA	ALN
PA	PHU
Readsboro, VT	BUR
Reardan, WA	SPK
Red Bank, NJ	TR
Red Bluff, CA	SAC
Red Brush, IN	EVN
Red Bud, IL	BEL
Red Cliff, WI	SUP
Red Cloud, NE	LIN
Red Creek, NY	ROC
Red Feathers Lakes, CO	DEN
Red Hook, NY	NY
Red Lake, MN	CR
Red Lake Falls, MN	CR
Red Lodge, MT	GF
Red Oak, IA	DM
Red Wing, MN	STP
Redding, CA	SAC
CT	BGP
Redfield, SD	SFS
Redford, MI	DET
NY	OG
Redford Township, MI	DET
Redgranite, WI	GB
Redland, OR	P
Redlands, CA	SB
CA	VNN
Redmond, OR	BAK
WA	SEA
Redondo Beach, CA	LA
Redwood, NY	OG
Redwood City, CA	SFR
CA	SJ
Redwood Falls, MN	NU
Redwood Valley, CA	STN
Reed, KY	OWN
OH	TOL
Reed City, MI	GR
Reedley, CA	FRS
Reedsburg, WI	MAD
Reedsport, OR	P
Reedsville/Maple Grove, WI	GB
Reese, MI	SAG
Reeseville, WI	MIL
Refugio, TX	CC
Regal, MN	NU
Regent, ND	BIS
Rego Park, NY	BRK
Rehoboth, DE	WIL
Reidsville, NC	CHL
Reinbeck, IA	DUB
Reliance, SD	RC
Remington, IN	LFT
Remsen, IA	SC
Remus, MI	GR
Renault, IL	BEL
Reno, NV	RNO
Renovo, PA	ALT
Rensselaer, IN	LFT
NY	ALB
Renton, WA	SEA
Renville, MN	NU
Republic, MI	MAR
MO	SPC
OH	TOL
PA	GBG
WA	SPK
Reseda, CA	LA
Reserve, LA	NO
WI	SUP
Reserve Township, PA	PIT
Reston, VA	ARL
Revere, MA	BO
Revillo, SD	SFS
Revloc, PA	ALT
PA	SJP
Rexmere, LA	ALX
Rexville, NY	ROC
Reynolds, IN	LFT
ND	FAR
Reynoldsburg, OH	COL
Reynoldsville, PA	E
Rhine, OH	CIN
Rhinebeck, NY	NY
Rhineland, MO	JC
TX	FWT
Rhinelander, WI	SUP
Rhodelia, KY	L
Rhodell, WV	WH
Rhodes, IA	DUB
Rialto, CA	SB
Rib Lake, WI	SUP
Ribera, NM	SFE
Rice, MN	SCL
Rice Lake, WI	SUP
Riceville, IA	DUB
Rich Fountain, MO	JC
Richard, LA	LAF
Richardson, TX	DAL
Richardton, ND	BIS
Richboro, PA	PH
Richeyville, PA	PIT
Richfield, MN	STP
OH	CLV
WI	MIL
Richfield Center, OH	TOL
Richfield Springs, NY	ALB
Richford, VT	BUR
Richland, IA	DAV
MO	JC
NJ	CAM
NY	SY
OR	BAK
WA	YAK
Richland Center, WI	LC
Richland Township, PA	PIT
Richlands, VA	RIC
Richmond, CA	OAK
IA	DAV
IL	RCK
IN	IND
KS	KCK
KY	LEX
ME	PRT
MI	DET
MN	SCL
MO	KC
OH	STU
TX	GAL
VA	PHU
VA	RIC
VT	BUR
Richmond Heights, MO	STL
Richmond Hill, GA	SAV
Richwood, TX	GAL
WV	WH
Richwoods, MO	STL
Rickardsville, IA	DUB
Ridge, MD	WDC
Ridge Manor, FL	SP
Ridgecrest, CA	FRS
Ridgefield, CT	BGP
NJ	NEW
Ridgefield Park, NJ	NEW
Ridgeland, SC	CHR
Ridgeley, WV	WH
Ridgely, MD	WIL
Ridgeway, WI	MAD
Ridgewood, NJ	NEW
NY	BRK
Ridgway, IL	BEL
PA	E
Ridley Park, PA	PH
Riegelsville, PA	PH
Riegelwood, NC	R
Rifle, CO	DEN
Riggsville, MI	GAY
Rincon, PR	MGZ
Rindge, NH	MAN
Ringtown, PA	ALN
Ringwood, NJ	PAT
Rio, WI	MAD
Rio Bravo, TX	LAR
Rio Grande, NJ	CAM
OH	STU
PR	SJN
Rio Grande City, TX	BWN
Rio Hondo, TX	BWN
Rio Piedras, PR	SJN
Rio Rancho, NM	SFE
Rio Rico, AZ	TUC
Rio Vista, CA	SAC
Ripley, MS	JKS
NY	BUF
OH	CIN
Ripon, CA	STO
WI	MIL
Rising Sun, WI	LC
Rittman, OH	CLV
Ritzville, WA	SPK
River Aux Vases, MO	STL
River Edge, NJ	NEW
River Falls, WI	SUP
River Forest, IL	CHI
River Grove, IL	CHI
River Ridge, LA	NO
River Rouge, MI	DET
River Vale, NJ	NEW
Riverbank, CA	STO
Riverdale, CA	FRS
GA	ATL
IL	CHI
MD	WDC
NY	NY
Riverhead, NY	RVC
NY	STF
Riverside, CA	SB
CT	BGP
IA	DAV
IL	CHI
NJ	TR
Riverton, IL	SFD
NJ	TR
WY	CHY
Riverview, FL	SP
MI	DET
Riverview Gardens, MO	STL
Riviera Beach, FL	PMB
Roanoke, IL	PEO
IN	FTW
VA	RIC
VA	SAM
Roanoke Rapids, NC	R
Roaring Creek, PA	HBG
Roaring Spring, PA	ALT
Robbinsdale, MN	STP
Robert's Cove, LA	LAF
Robertsdale, AL	MOB
Robesonia, PA	ALN
Robinson, IL	SFD
Robinson Township, PA	PIT
Robinsonville, WI	GB
Robstown, TX	CC
Rochdale, MA	WOR
Rochelle, IL	RCK
Rochelle Park, NJ	NEW
Rochester, IL	SFD
IN	LFT
MA	BO
MI	DET
MN	WIN
NH	MAN
NY	NTN
NY	ROC
NY	STF
PA	PIT
Rochester Hills, MI	DET
Rock Creek, OH	Y
Rock Falls, IL	RCK
WI	LC
Rock Hill, SC	CHR
Rock Island, IL	PEO
Rock Lake, ND	FAR
PA	SCR
Rock Rapids, IA	SC
Rock Springs, WY	CHY
Rock Valley, IA	SC
Rockaway, NJ	PAT
NY	BRK
OR	P
Rockaway Park, NY	BRK
Rockaway Township, NJ	PAT
Rockdale, IL	JOL
TX	AUS
Rockford, IA	DUB
IL	RCK
MI	GR
OH	CIN
WA	SPK
Rockland, MA	BO
ME	PRT
MI	MAR
Rockledge, FL	ORL
Rocklin, CA	SAC
Rockne, TX	AUS
Rockport, IN	EVN
MA	BO
TX	CC
Rocksprings, TX	SAT
Rockville, CT	NOR
IN	IND
MD	WDC
MN	SCL
VA	RIC
Rockville Centre, NY	RVC
Rockwall, TX	DAL
Rockwell, IA	DUB
Rockwell City, IA	SC
Rockwood, MI	DET
Rocky Ford, CO	PBL
Rocky Hill, CT	HRT
Rocky Mount, NC	R

VA	RIC
Rocky Point, NY	RVC
Rocky River, OH	CLV
Rodeo, CA	OAK
Roebling, NJ	PSC
NJ	ROM
NJ	TR
Roeland Park, KS	KCK
Rogers, AR	LR
CT	NOR
MN	STP
TX	AUS
Rogers City, MI	GAY
Rogersville, TN	KNX
Roggen, CO	DEN
Rohnert Park, CA	SR
Rohrerstown, PA	HBG
Rolesville, NC	R
Rolette, ND	FAR
Rolfe, IA	SC
Rolla, MO	JC
ND	FAR
Rolling Ground, WI	LC
Rolling Meadows, IL	CHI
Rolling Prairie, IN	GRY
Rollingstone, MN	WIN
Rollinsford, NH	MAN
Roma, TX	BWN
Rome, GA	ATL
KY	OWN
NY	STF
NY	SY
Rome City, IN	FTW
Romeo, MI	DET
Romeoville, IL	JOL
Romney, WV	WH
Romulus, MI	DET
Ronan, MT	HEL
Ronceverte, WV	WH
Ronkonkoma, NY	RVC
Roosevelt, NY	RVC
UT	SLC
Rootstown, OH	Y
Rosalia, WA	SPK
Rosamond, CA	FRS
Rosario, PR	MGZ
Rosaryville, MD	WDC
Rosati, MO	JC
Roscoe, MN	SCL
PA	PIT
SD	SFS
Roscommon, MI	GAY
Rose Creek, MN	WIN
Roseau, MN	CR
Rosebud, SD	RC
TX	AUS
Roseburg, OR	P
Rosebush, MI	SAG
Rosedale, MS	JKS
NY	BRK
Roseland, NE	LIN
NJ	NEW
Roselle, IA	SC
IL	JOL
NJ	NEW
Roselle Park, NJ	NEW
Rosemead, CA	LA
Rosemont, PA	PH
Rosemont-Des Plaines, IL	CHI
Rosemount, MN	STP
Rosen, MN	NU
Rosenberg, TX	GAL
Rosencrans, IL	CHI
Rosendale, NY	NY
Rosenhayn, NJ	CAM
Roseto, PA	ALN
Roseville, CA	SAC
IA	DUB
MI	DET
MN	STP
Rosholt, SD	SFS
WI	LC
Rosiere, NY	OG
WI	GB
Roslyn, NY	RVC
PA	PH
WA	YAK
Rosman, NC	CHL
Ross Township, PA	PIT
Rossford, OH	SJP
OH	TOL
Rossiter, PA	GBG
Rossville, KS	KCK
Rostraver, PA	GBG
Roswell, GA	ATL
GA	PSC
NM	LSC
OH	COL
Rota, MP	CHK
Rotan, TX	LUB
Rothbury, MI	GR
Rothschild, WI	LC
Rotterdam, NY	ALB
Rotterdam Junction, NY	ALB
Roulette, PA	E
Round Lake, IL	CHI
Round Rock, TX	AUS
Roundup, MT	GF
Rouses Point, NY	OG
Rouseville, PA	E
Rowena, TX	SAN
Rowland Heights, CA	LA
Rowlett, TX	DAL
Rowley, IA	DUB
MA	BO
Roxboro, NC	R
Roxbury, WI	MAD
Roy, NM	SFE
OR	P
Royal, IA	SC
PA	SCR
Royal City, WA	YAK
Royal Oak, MI	DET
Royal Palm Beach, FL	PMB
Royalton, MN	SCL
Royalton-Zeigler, IL	BEL
Royersford, PA	PH
Rozellville, WI	LC
Rubicon, WI	MIL
Ruby, AK	FBK
Rudolph, WI	LC
Rudyard, MI	MAR
Rugby, ND	FAR
Ruidoso, NM	LSC
Rulo, NE	LIN
Ruma, IL	BEL
Rumford, ME	PRT
Rumson, NJ	TR
Runge, TX	SAT
Runnemede, NJ	CAM
Running Springs, CA	SB
Rupert, ID	B
Rush, NY	ROC
Rush City, MN	STP
Rush Lake, MN	SCL
Rushford, MN	WIN
NY	BUF
Rushville, IL	PEO
IN	IND
Ruskin, FL	SP
Russell, KS	SAL
MA	SPR
Russells Point, OH	CIN
Russellton, PA	PIT
Russellville, AL	BIR
AR	LR
KY	OWN
MO	JC
Russia, OH	CIN
Ruston, LA	SHP
Ruth, MI	SAG
Rutherford, NJ	NEW
NJ	PHU
Ruthven, IA	SC
Rutland, IL	PEO
MA	WOR
VT	BUR
Rutten, ND	FAR
Ryan, IA	DUB
MI	SAG
Rydal, PA	PH
Rye, CO	PBL
NY	NY
Rye Beach, NH	MAN
Rynella, LA	LAF
Sabana Grande, PR	MGZ
Sabattus, ME	PRT
Sabetha, KS	KCK
Sabin, MN	CR
Sabinal, TX	SAT
Sabine Pass, TX	BEA
Sabula, IA	DUB
Sac City, IA	SC
Sackets Harbor, NY	OG
Saco, ME	PRT
Sacramento, CA	NTN
CA	SAC
CA	STN
CA	VNN
Saddle Brook, NJ	NEW
Saddle River, NJ	NEW
Saddle River Borough, NJ	NEW
Safety Harbor, FL	SP
Safford, AZ	TUC
Sag Harbor, NY	RVC
Sagamore, PA	GBG
PA	PBR
Saginaw, MI	SAG
St. Agatha, ME	PRT
St. Albans, ME	PRT
VT	BUR
WV	WH
St. Albans Bay, VT	BUR
St. Amant, LA	BR
St. Ann, MO	STL
St. Anna, MN	SCL
WI	GB
St. Anne, IL	JOL
IN	IND
St. Ansgar, IA	DUB
St. Anthony, IA	DUB
ID	B
IN	EVN
MN	SCL
MO	JC
ND	BIS
OH	CIN
St. Augusta, MN	SCL
St. Augustine, FL	STA
IL	PEO
PA	ALT
St. Augustine Shores, FL	STA
St. Benedict, IA	SC
KS	KCK
LA	NO
MN	STP
OR	P
St. Bernard, LA	NO
St. Bonaventure, NY	BUF
St. Boniface, PA	ALT
St. Bonifacius, MN	STP
St. Catharine, KY	L
St. Catherine, IA	DUB
St. Cecilia, IA	DUB
St. Charles, IL	RCK
MI	SAG
MN	WIN
MO	STL
NE	OM
St. Clair, MI	DET
MN	WIN
MO	STL
Saint Clair, PA	ALN
St. Clair, PA	PHU
PA	PSC
St. Clair Shores, MI	DET
St. Clairsville, OH	STU
St. Clement, MO	JC
St. Cloud, FL	ORL
MN	SCL
WI	MIL
St. Columbans, NE	OM
St. Croix, IN	IND
VI	STV
St. David, AZ	TUC
St. Denis, IN	IND
St. Donatus, IA	DUB
St. Edward, NE	OM
St. Elizabeth, MO	JC
St. Elmo, IL	SFD
St. Francis, KS	SAL
KY	L
ME	PRT
MN	SCL
SD	RC
WI	MIL
St. Francisville, IL	BEL
LA	BR
St. Gabriel, LA	BR
St. George, IL	JOL
UT	SLC
WI	MIL
St. Hedwig, TX	SAT
St. Helen, MI	GAY
Saint Helena, CA	SR
St. Helena, NE	OM
St. Helena Island, SC	CHR
St. Helens, OR	P
St. Henry, MN	STP
OH	CIN
St. Ignace, MI	MAR
St. Ignatius, MT	HEL
St. Inigoes, MD	WDC
St. Jacob, IL	SFD
St. James, LA	BR
MI	GAY
MN	WIN
MO	JC
NE	OM
NY	RVC
St. Joe, WI	MIL
Saint John, IN	GRY
St. John, KS	DOD
KY	L
ME	PRT
ND	FAR
NE	OM
TX	VIC
WA	SPK
WI	GB
St. Johns, AZ	GLP
MI	LAN
St. Johnsbury, VT	BUR
St. Johnsville, NY	ALB
St. Joseph, FL	SP
IN	EVN
IN	IND
KS	SAL
KY	L
KY	OWN
LA	ALX
MI	KAL
MN	SCL
MO	KC
MO	STN
OH	CIN
Saint Joseph, TN	NSH
St. Joseph Hill, IN	IND
Saint Joseph Ridge, WI	LC
St. Joseph Settlement, WV	WH
St. Kilian, MN	WIN
WI	MIL
St. Lawrence, PA	ALT
TX	SAN
WI	MIL
Saint Leo, FL	SP
St. Leo, FL.	SP
KS	WCH
MN	NU
St. Leon, IN	IND
St. Libory, IL	BEL
NE	GI
St. Louis, KS	KCK
MI	SAG
MO	JC
MO	OLL
MO	PRM
MO	STL
MO	STN
OR	P
St. Louis County, MO	STL
St. Louis Park, MN	STP
St. Lucas, IA	DUB
Saint Maries, ID	B
St. Mark, IN	IND
St. Mark's, KS	WCH
St. Martin, MN	SCL
Saint Martin, OH	CIN
St. Martin, WI	MIL
St. Martins, MO	JC
St. Martinville, LA	LAF
St. Mary, KS	DOD
KY	L
MO	STL
St. Mary's City, MD	WDC
Saint Mary's Ridge, WI	LC
St. Mary-of-the-Knobs, IN	IND
St. Mary-of-the-Rock, IN	IND
St. Mary-of-the-Woods, IN	IND
St. Marys, AK	FBK
GA	SAV
IA	DM
KS	KCK
OH	CIN
PA	E
WV	WH
St. Mathias, MN	DUL
St. Maurice, IN	IND
St. Meinrad, IN	IND
St. Michael, AK	FBK
MN	STP
ND	BIS
ND	FAR
PA	ALT
WI	MIL
St. Michael's Ridge, OH	TOL
St. Michaels, AZ	GLP
St. Nazianz, WI	GB
St. Nicholas, IN	IND
MN	SCL
St. Paris, OH	CIN
St. Patrick, KS	KCK
MO	JC
OH	CIN
St. Paul, IA	DAV
KS	WCH
KY	OWN
MN	OLL
MN	STN
MN	STP
MO	STL
NE	GI
OR	P
VA	RIC
St. Paul Park, MN	STP
St. Pete Beach, FL	SP
St. Peter, IN	IND
KS	SAL
MN	NU
WI	MIL
St. Peters, MO	STL
St. Petersburg, FL	PSC
FL	SJP
FL	SP

St. Pius, IN	IND
Saint Regis Falls, NY	OG
St. Rosa, MN	SCL
St. Rose, IL	BEL
OH	CIN
St. Sebastian, IL	BEL
OH	CIN
St. Simons Island, GA	SAV
St. Stephen, MN	SCL
OH	TOL
St. Stephens, WY	CHY
St. Theresa, IA	DUB
St. Thomas, KY	L
MN	STP
MO	JC
ND	FAR
VI	STV
St. Vincent, AR	LR
St. Vincent de Paul, IN	IND
St. Wendel, MN	SCL
St. Wendelin, OH	CIN
St. Xavier, MT	GF
Saipan, MP	CHK
Salado, TX	AUS
Salamanca, NY	BUF
Salem, IL	BEL
IN	IND
MA	BO
MA	STF
MO	SPC
NH	MAN
NJ	CAM
NY	ALB
OH	Y
OR	P
SD	SFS
VA	RIC
WV	WH
Salem Twp., OH	TOL
Salida, CO	COS
Salina, KS	SAL
Salinas, CA	MRY
PR	PCE
Saline, MI	LAN
Salineville, OH	Y
Salisbury, MA	BO
MD	WIL
MO	JC
NC	CHL
Salix, IA	SC
Sallisaw, OK	TLS
Salmon, ID	B
Salt Lake City, UT	SLC
UT	VNN
Saltaire, NY	RVC
Saltsburg, PA	GBG
Salyersville, KY	LEX
Sam Rayburn, TX	BEA
Sammamish, WA	SEA
Samuels, KY	L
San Andreas, CA	STO
San Angelo, TX	SAN
San Anselmo, CA	SFR
San Antonio, FL	SP
TX	OLL
TX	SAT
San Antonio Village, District 6, MP	CHK
San Benito, TX	BWN
San Bernardino, CA	NTN
CA	SB
San Bruno, CA	SFR
San Carlos, AZ	TUC
CA	SFR
TX	BWN
San Clemente, CA	ORG
San Diego, CA	OLD
CA	OLL
CA	SB
CA	SD
CA	STN
CA	VNN
TX	CC
San Dimas, CA	LA
San Elizario, TX	ELP
San Fernando, CA	LA
San Fidel, NM	GLP
San Francisco, CA	SFR
CA	STN
San Gabriel, CA	LA
San German, PR	MGZ
San Isidro, TX	BWN
San Jacinto, CA	SB
San Jose, CA	EST
CA	NTN
CA	SJ
San Jose Village, MP	CHK
San Juan, CA	MRY
P.R.	SJN
PR	SJN
TX	BWN
San Juan Bautista, CA	MRY
San Juan Capistrano, CA	ORG
San Juan Pueblo, NM	SFE
San Leandro, CA	OAK
San Lorenzo, CA	OAK
PR	CGS
San Luis, AZ	TUC
CO	PBL
San Luis Obispo, CA	MRY
CA	VNN
San Luis Rey, CA	SD
San Manuel, AZ	TUC
San Marcos, CA	SD
TX	AUS
San Marino, CA	LA
San Mateo, CA	SFR
CA	VNN
NM	GLP
San Miguel, CA	MRY
NM	LSC
San Pablo, CA	OAK
San Patricio, NM	LSC
San Pedro, CA	LA
San Pierre, IN	GRY
San Rafael, CA	SFR
NM	GLP
San Ramon, CA	OAK
San Roque Village, District 9, MP	CHK
San Saba, TX	AUS
San Sebastian, PR	MGZ
San Vicente Village, District 10, MP	CHK
San Ysidro, CA	SD
Sanborn, IA	SC
MN	NU
ND	FAR
WI	SUP
Sanbornville, NH	MAN
Sand Lake, MI	GR
Sand Springs, OK	TLS
Sanderson, TX	SAN
Sandia, TX	CC
Sandoval, IL	BEL
Sandpoint, ID	B
Sandstone, MN	DUL
Sandusky, MI	SAG
OH	TOL
Sandwich, IL	RCK
MA	FR
Sandy, OR	P
UT	SLC
Sandy Hook, KY	LEX
Sanford, FL	ORL
ME	PRT
MI	SAG
NC	R
Sanger, CA	FRS
Sanibel, FL	VEN
Sanitaria Springs, NY	SY
Santa Ana, CA	ORG
Santa Barbara, CA	LA
Santa Clara, CA	SJ
CA	STN
NM	LSC
Santa Clarita, CA	LA
Santa Claus, IN	EVN
Santa Cruz, CA	MRY
NM	SFE
Santa Fe, NM	SFE
Santa Fe Springs, CA	LA
Santa Isabel, PR	PCE
Santa Margarita, CA	MRY
Santa Maria, CA	LA
Santa Monica, CA	LA
Santa Paula, CA	LA
Santa Rita, GU	AGN
Santa Rosa, CA	SR
NM	SFE
TX	BWN
Santa Rosa Beach, FL	PT
Santa Ynez, CA	LA
Santa Ysabel, CA	SD
Santa Ysabel Indian Missions, CA	SD
Sante Fe, NM	SFE
Santee, CA	SD
Santurce, PR	SJN
Sappington, MO	STL
Sapulpa, OK	TLS
Saranac, MI	GR
Saranac Lake, NY	OG
Sarasota, FL	VEN
Saratoga, CA	SJ
NY	ALB
WY	CHY
Saratoga Springs, NY	ALB
Sarcoxie, MO	SPC
Sardinia, NY	BUF
OH	CIN
Sardis, OH	STU
Sarita, TX	CC
Sarona, WI	SUP
Sarpy Co., NE	OM
Sartell, MN	SCL
Satanta, KS	DOD
Satin, TX	AUS
Saugerties, NY	NY
Saugus, MA	BO
Sauk Centre, MN	SCL
Sauk City, WI	MAD
Sauk Rapids, MN	SCL
Sauk Village, IL	CHI
Saukville, WI	MIL
Sault Sainte Marie, MI	MAR
Sausalito, CA	SFR
Savage, MN	STP
Savanna, IL	RCK
Savannah, GA	SAV
MO	KC
Savannah	SAV
TN	MEM
Saxon, WI	SUP
Saxonville, MA	BO
Sayner, WI	SUP
Sayre, PA	PHU
PA	SCR
Sayreville, NJ	MET
Sayville, NY	RVC
Scales Mound, IL	RCK
Scammon, KS	WCH
Scammon Bay, AK	FBK
Scappoose, OR	P
Scarborough, ME	PRT
NY	NY
Scarsdale, NY	NY
Schaffer, MI	MAR
Schaghticoke, NY	ALB
Schaller, IA	SC
Schaumburg, IL	CHI
Scheller, IL	BEL
Schenectady, NY	ALB
Schererville, IN	GRY
Schertz, TX	SAT
Schiller Park, IL	CHI
Schnellville, IN	EVN
Schoenchen, KS	SAL
Schoharie, NY	ALB
School Hill, WI	GB
Schooley's Mountain, NJ	PAT
Schriever, LA	HT
Schroon Lake, NY	OG
Schulenburg, TX	VIC
Schulte, KS	WCH
Schuyler, NE	OM
Schuylerville, NY	ALB
Schuylkill Haven, PA	ALN
Scio, NY	BUF
OR	P
Sciota, NY	OG
Scipio, KS	KCK
Scipio Center, NY	ROC
Scituate, MA	BO
RI	PRO
Scobey, MT	GF
Scotch Plains, NJ	NEW
Scotia, CA	SR
NY	ALB
Scotland, SD	SFS
TX	FWT
Scott, LA	LAF
Scott AFB, IL	BEL
Scott City, KS	DOD
MO	SPC
Scott Township, PA	PIT
Scottdale, PA	GBG
PA	PBR
Scotts Valley, CA	MRY
Scottsbluff, NE	GI
Scottsboro, AL	BIR
Scottsburg, IN	IND
Scottsdale, AZ	EST
AZ	PHX
Scottsville, KY	OWN
NY	ROC
VA	RIC
Scottville, MI	GR
Scranton, AR	LR
IA	SC
KS	KCK
PA	NTN
PA	PHU
PA	PSC
PA	SAM
PA	SCR
Sea Cliff, NY	BRK
NY	RVC
Sea Girt, NJ	TR
Sea Isle City, NJ	CAM
Seabrook, NH	MAN
Seaford, DE	WIL
NY	RVC
Seaforth, MN	NU
Seahurst, WA	SEA
Seal Beach, CA	ORG
Sealy, TX	GAL
Searcy, AR	LR
Searles, MN	NU
Seaside, CA	MRY
OR	P
Seaside Heights, NJ	TR
Seaside Park, NJ	TR
Seat Pleasant, MD	WDC
Seattle, WA	SEA
WA	VNN
Seaview, WA	SEA
Sebastian, FL	PMB
Sebastopol, CA	SR
Sebewaing, MI	SAG
Seboyeta, NM	GLP
Sebree, KY	OWN
Sebring, FL	VEN
OH	Y
Secane, PA	PH
Secaucus, NJ	NEW
Secretary, MD	WIL
Security, CO	COS
Sedalia, CO	COS
MO	JC
Sedan, KS	WCH
MN	SCL
Sedona, AZ	PHX
Sedro Woolley, WA	SEA
Seekonk, MA	FR
Seelyville, IN	IND
Seffner, FL	SP
Seguin, KS	SAL
TX	SAT
Seinwar, FM	CI
Selah, WA	YAK
Selby, SD	SFS
Selden, KS	SAL
NY	RVC
Selfridge, ND	BIS
Seligman, AZ	PHX
Selinsgrove, PA	HBG
Sellersburg, IN	IND
Sellersville, PA	PH
Selma, AL	MOB
CA	FRS
TX	SAT
Selmer, TN	MEM
Selz, ND	FAR
Seminole, FL	SP
OK	OKL
TX	LUB
Semmes, AL	MOB
Senatobia, MS	JKS
Seneca, IL	PEO
KS	KCK
MO	SPC
SD	SFS
WI	LC
Seneca Falls, NY	ROC
Sentinel Butte, ND	BIS
Sepulveda, CA	LA
Sequim, WA	SEA
Sereno, MO	STL
Sesser, IL	BEL
Setauket, NY	RVC
Seven Hills, OH	CLV
Severn, MD	BAL
Severna Park, MD	BAL
Seville-Creston, OH	CLV
Seward, AK	ANC
KS	DOD
NE	LIN
PA	GBG
Sewickley, PA	PIT
Seymour, CT	HRT
IL	PEO
IN	IND
TN	KNX
TX	FWT
WI	GB
WI	MAD
Shade Gap, PA	ALT
Shady Cove, OR	P
Shadyside, OH	STU
Shafter, CA	FRS
Shaker Heights, OH	CLV
Shakopee, MN	STP
Shallotte, NC	R
Shallowater, TX	LUB
Shamokin, PA	HBG
PA	PHU
Shandon, OH	CIN
Shannon, IL	RCK
Sharon, CT	HRT
KS	DOD
MA	BO
PA	E
PA	ROM
WI	MIL
Sharon Hill, PA	PH

Sharon Springs, KS	SAL
Sharpsburg, OH	CIN
PA	PIT
Sharpsville, PA	E
Shavertown, PA	SCR
Shaw, MS	JKS
OR	P
Shaw Island, WA	SEA
Shawano, WI	GB
Shawnee, KS	KCK
OH	COL
OK	OKL
Shawneetown, IL	BEL
Sheboygan, WI	MIL
Sheboygan Falls, WI	MIL
Sheffield, IL	PEO
MA	SPR
OH	CLV
PA	E
PA	PBR
Sheffield Lake, OH	CLV
Shelbina, MO	JC
Shelbourne, VT	SAM
Shelburne, VT	BUR
Shelburne Falls, MA	SPR
Shelby, IN	GRY
MI	GR
MS	JKS
MT	HEL
NC	CHL
NE	LIN
OH	TOL
Shelby Twp., MI	DET
Shelbyville, IL	SFD
IN	IND
KY	L
TN	NSH
Sheldon, IA	SC
ND	FAR
NY	BUF
WI	SUP
Sheldon Springs, VT	BUR
Shell Knob, MO	SPC
Shell Lake, WI	SUP
Shell Rock, IA	DUB
Shelter Island, NY	RVC
Shelter Island Heights, NY	RVC
Shelton, CT	BGP
WA	SEA
Shenandoah, IA	DM
PA	ALN
PA	PHU
Shepherd, MI	SAG
Shepherdstown, WV	WH
Shepherdsville, KY	L
Sheppton, PA	ALN
PA	PSC
Sherborn, MA	BO
Sherburn, MN	WIN
Sherburne, NY	SY
Sheridan, AR	LR
NY	BUF
OR	P
WY	CHY
Sherman, CT	BGP
IL	SFD
NY	BUF
TX	DAL
Sherman Oaks, CA	LA
Sherrill, IA	DUB
NY	SY
Sherwood, AR	LR
OR	P
Sherwood Park, DE	WIL
Sherwood/St. John, WI	GB
Shevlin, MN	CR
Shields, MI	SAG
Shieldsville, MN	STP
Shillington, PA	ALN
Shiloh, IL	BEL
Shiner, TX	VIC
Shinglehouse, PA	E
Shinnston, WV	WH
Shiocton, WI	GB
Shipman, IL	SFD
Shippensburg, PA	HBG
Shiprock, NM	GLP
Shirley, MA	BO
Shoal Creek, AR	LR
Shoals, IN	EVN
Shohola, PA	SCR
Shoreham, NY	RVC
Shoreview, MN	STP
Short Hills, NJ	NEW
Shortsville, NY	ROC
Shoshone, ID	B
Show Low, AZ	GLP
Shreveport, LA	SHP
Shrewsbury, MA	WOR
MO	STL
Shrub Oak, NY	NY

Shullsburg, WI	MAD
Shumway, IL	SFD
Siberia, IN	IND
Sibley, IA	SC
Sicklerville, NJ	CAM
Sidney, MT	GF
NE	GI
NY	ALB
OH	CIN
Sierra Blanca, TX	ELP
Sierra Madre, CA	LA
Sierra Vista, AZ	TUC
Sigel, IL	SFD
SD	SFS
WI	LC
Signal Mountain, TN	KNX
Sigourney, IA	DAV
Sikeston, MO	SPC
Siler City, NC	R
Siloam Springs, AR	LR
Silsbee, TX	BEA
Silver Bay, MN	DUL
Silver City, NM	LSC
Silver Creek, MI	KAL
NE	OM
NY	BUF
Silver Lake, MN	NU
MO	STL
Silver Spring, MD	BAL
MD	PHU
MD	WDC
Silver Springs, NY	BUF
Silverado, CA	ORG
Silverton, CO	PBL
OR	P
Silvis, IL	PEO
Simi, CA	LA
Simi Valley, CA	LA
Simmesport, LA	ALX
Simpson, PA	PHU
PA	SCR
Simpsonville, SC	CHR
Simsbury, CT	HRT
Sinajana, GU	AGN
Sinclair, ME	PRT
Sinclairville, NY	BUF
Sinking Spring, PA	ALN
Sinsinawa, WI	MAD
Sinton, TX	CC
Sioux City, IA	SC
Sioux Falls, SD	SFS
Sioux Rapids, IA	SC
Sisseton, SD	SFS
Sister Bay, WI	GB
Sisters, OR	BAK
Sistersville, WV	WH
Sitka, AK	JUN
Skagway, AK	JUN
Skaneateles, NY	SY
Skiatook, OK	TLS
Skidmore, TX	CC
Skidway Lake, MI	GAY
Skillman, NJ	MET
Skokie, IL	CHI
Skowhegan, ME	PRT
Slater, MO	JC
Slatington, PA	ALN
Slaton, TX	LUB
Slayton, MN	WIN
Sleepy Eye, MN	NU
Sleepy Hollow, NY	NY
Slickville, PA	GBG
Slidell, LA	NO
Slinger, WI	MIL
Slingerlands, NY	ALB
Slippery Rock, PA	PIT
Sloan, NY	BUF
Sloatsburg, NY	NY
NY	STF
Slovak, AR	LR
Slovan, WI	GB
Smethport, PA	E
Smiley, TX	SAT
Smith Center, KS	SAL
Smithfield, NC	R
OH	STU
RI	PRO
VA	RIC
Smithton, IL	BEL
PA	GBG
Smithtown, NY	PSC
NY	RVC
Smithville, MO	KC
TN	NSH
TX	AUS
Smock, PA	GBG
Smyrna, DE	WIL
GA	ATL
TN	NSH
Sneedville, TN	KNX
Snellville, GA	ATL

Snohomish, WA	SEA
Snoqualmie, WA	SEA
Snow Shoe, PA	ALT
Snowflake, AZ	GLP
Snowmass, CO	DEN
Snyder, NE	OM
NY	BUF
TX	LUB
Sobieski, MN	SCL
WI	GB
Soboba Indian Reservation, CA	SB
Socorro, NM	SFE
Soda Springs, ID	B
Soddy Daisy, TN	KNX
Sodus, NY	ROC
Sokehs, FM	CI
Solana Beach, CA	SD
Soldotna, AK	ANC
Soledad, CA	MRY
Solomon, AZ	TUC
KS	SAL
Solomons, MD	WDC
Solon, IA	DAV
OH	CLV
OH	PRM
OH	SJP
Solon Springs, WI	SUP
Solvang, CA	LA
Solvay, NY	SY
Somerdale, NJ	CAM
Somers, NY	NY
Somers Point, NJ	CAM
Somerset, KY	LEX
MA	FR
NJ	MET
NJ	PSC
NJ	SAM
OH	COL
PA	ALT
TX	SAT
WI	SUP
Somersville, CT	NOR
Somersworth, NH	MAN
Somerton, AZ	TUC
Somerville, MA	BO
NJ	MET
TN	MEM
TX	AUS
Somonauk, IL	RCK
Songsong Village, MP	CHK
Sonoita, AZ	TUC
Sonoma, CA	SR
Sonora, CA	STO
TX	SAN
Soquel, CA	MRY
Sorgho, KY	OWN
Sorrento, LA	BR
Sound Beach, NY	RVC
Sour Lake, TX	BEA
South Amboy, NJ	MET
South Amherst, OH	CLV
South Ashburnham, MA	WOR
South Barre, MA	WOR
South Beloit, IL	RCK
South Bend, IN	FTW
IN	NTN
South Berwick, ME	PRT
South Boston, MA	BO
VA	RIC
South Bound Brook, NJ	MET
South Branch, WI	GB
South Burlington, VT	BUR
South Byron, NY	BUF
South Charleston, OH	CIN
WV	WH
South Coventry, PA	PH
South Dartmouth, MA	FR
South Dayton, NY	BUF
South Deerfield, MA	SPR
MA	STF
South Easton, MA	FR
South El Monte, CA	LA
South Euclid, OH	CLV
South Fork, PA	ALT
PA	PBR
South Garryowen, IA	DUB
South Gate, CA	LA
South Glastonbury, CT	HRT
South Glens Falls, NY	ALB
South Grafton, MA	WOR
South Hadley, MA	PSC
MA	SPR
South Haven, MI	KAL
South Heart, ND	BIS
South Hero, VT	BUR
South Hill, VA	RIC
South Holland, IL	CHI
South Houston, TX	GAL
South Huntington, NY	RVC
South Kingstown, RI	PRO
South Kortright, NY	ALB

South Lake Tahoe, CA	SAC
South Lyon, MI	DET
South Mantoloking, NJ	TR
South Meriden, CT	HRT
South Milwaukee, WI	MIL
South Mountain, PA	HBG
South Onondaga, NY	SY
South Orange, NJ	NEW
South Ozone Park, NY	BRK
South Park, PA	PIT
South Pasadena, CA	LA
South Pittsburg, TN	KNX
South Plainfield, NJ	MET
South Portland, ME	PRT
South Range, MI	MAR
South River, NJ	MET
South St. Paul, MN	STP
South San Francisco, CA	SFR
South Sioux City, NE	OM
South Union, KY	OWN
South Waverly, PA	SCR
South Wayne, WI	MAD
South Williamsport, PA	SCR
South Wilmington, IL	JOL
South Windsor, CT	HRT
South Yarmouth, MA	FR
Southampton, NY	RVC
PA	PH
Southborough, MA	WOR
Southbridge, MA	WOR
Southbury, CT	HRT
Southeastern Portage County, WI	LC
Southern Pines, NC	R
Southfield, MI	DET
MI	EST
Southgate, KY	COV
MI	DET
Southhaven, MS	JKS
Southington, CT	HRT
Southold, NY	RVC
Southport, NC	R
Southwick, MA	SPR
Spalding, MI	MAR
NE	GI
Spanaway, WA	SEA
Spangler, PA	ALT
Spanish Lake, MO	STL
Sparkill, NY	NY
Sparks, MD	BAL
NV	RNO
Sparta, IL	BEL
MI	GR
NJ	PAT
TN	NSH
WI	LC
Spartanburg, SC	CHR
Spaulding-City Point, WI	LC
Spearfish, SD	RC
Spearman, TX	AMA
Spearville, KS	DOD
Speigletown, NY	ALB
Spencer, IA	SC
IN	IND
MA	WOR
NE	OM
OH	CLV
SD	SFS
WI	LC
WV	WH
Spencer-Farmer, SD	SFS
Spencerport, NY	ROC
Spencerville, OH	TOL
Spicer, MN	NU
Spillville, IA	DUB
Spirit Lake, IA	SC
Splendora, TX	GAL
Spokane, WA	SPK
WA	VNN
Spokena, WA	SPK
Spooner, WI	SUP
Spotswood, NJ	MET
Spotsylvania, VA	ARL
Sprague, WA	SPK
Spreckels, CA	MRY
Spring, TX	GAL
Spring Branch, TX	SAT
Spring City, PA	PH
Spring Green, WI	MAD
Spring Grove, IL	RCK
PA	HBG
Spring Hill, FL	SJP
FL	SP
MN	SCL
Spring House, PA	PH
Spring Lake, MI	GR
NJ	TR
Spring Valley, CA	SD
IL	PEO
MN	WIN
NY	NY
NY	STF

WI	LC
Springbrook, IA	DUB
NY	BUF
Springdale, AR	LR
PA	PIT
WA	SPK
Springer, NM	SFE
Springerville, AZ	GLP
Springfield,	SFD
CO	PBL
IL	SFD
KY	L
MA	SAM
MA	SPR
MN	NU
MO	SPC
NE	OM
NJ	NEW
OH	CIN
OR	P
OR	STN
PA	PH
SD	SFS
TN	NSH
VA	ARL
VT	BUR
WI	LC
Springfield Gardens, NY	BRK
Springvale, ME	PRT
WI	MIL
Springville, IA	DUB
NY	BUF
Spruce, WI	GB
Spruce Creek, IA	DUB
Spruce Pine, NC	CHL
Spur, TX	LUB
Stacyville, IA	DUB
Stafford, VA	ARL
Stafford Springs, CT	NOR
Stamford, CT	BGP
CT	STF
NY	ALB
TX	LUB
Stamps, AR	LR
Stanberry, MO	KC
Standing Rock, SD	RC
Standish, ME	PRT
MI	SAG
Stanford, CA	SJ
MT	GF
Stangelville, WI	GB
Stanley, KY	OWN
ND	BIS
NY	ROC
WI	LC
Stanton, CA	ORG
MI	GR
NE	OM
TX	SAN
WI	SUP
Stanwood, WA	SEA
Staples, MN	SCL
Stapleton, NE	GI
Star City, AR	LR
IN	LFT
WV	WH
Star Lake, NY	OG
Starford, PA	GBG
Stark, WI	GB
Starke, FL	STA
Starkville, MS	JKS
Starkweather, ND	FAR
Starlight, IN	IND
State Center, IA	DUB
State College, PA	ALT
Staten Island, NY	BRK
NY	NY
NY	STF
Statesboro, GA	SAV
Statesville, NC	CHL
Staunton, IL	SFD
VA	RIC
Stayton, OR	P
Ste. Genevieve, MO	STL
Ste. Marie, IL	SFD
Stead, NV	RNO
Steamboat Springs, CO	DEN
Stebbins, AK	FBK
Steele, ND	FAR
Steelton, PA	HBG
Steelville, MO	JC
Steger, IL	CHI
IL	JOL
Steinauer, NE	LIN
Stella Niagara, NY	BUF
Stephan, SD	SFS
Stephen, MN	CR
Stephenson, MI	MAR
Stephensville, WI	GB
Stephenville, TX	FWT
Sterling, CO	DEN
IL	RCK
MA	WOR
VA	ARL
Sterling Heights, MI	DET
MI	PRM
Stetsonville, WI	SUP
Steubenville, OH	STU
Stevens Point, WI	LC
Stevenson, MD	BAL
Stevensville, MT	HEL
Stewart, MN	NU
Stewartville, MN	WIN
Stickney, IL	CHI
SD	SFS
Stiles, WI	GB
Still River, MA	WOR
Stillwater, MN	STP
NY	ALB
OK	TLS
Stirling, NJ	PAT
Stirum, ND	FAR
Stockbridge, MA	SPR
WI	GB
Stockdale, TX	SAT
Stockholm, ME	PRT
NJ	PAT
Stockton, CA	STO
CA	VNN
IL	RCK
KS	SAL
Stone Bank, WI	MIL
Stone Harbor, NJ	CAM
Stone Lake, WI	SUP
Stone Mountain, GA	ATL
Stoneboro, PA	E
Stonefort, IL	BEL
Stoneham, CO	DEN
MA	BO
Stonelick, OH	CIN
Stonewall, TX	SAT
Stonewood, WV	WH
Stonington, CT	NOR
IL	SFD
ME	PRT
Stony Point, NY	NY
TX	AUS
Storm Lake, IA	SC
Storrs, CT	NOR
Stottville, NY	ALB
Stoughton, MA	BO
WI	MAD
Stoutsville, MO	JC
Stow, MA	BO
OH	CLV
Stowe, PA	PH
VT	BUR
Strafford, PA	PH
Strasburg, ND	BIS
OH	COL
Stratford, CT	BGP
NJ	CAM
TX	AMA
WI	LC
Stratton, CO	COS
Strawberry Point, IA	DUB
Strawn, TX	FWT
Streamwood, IL	CHI
Streator, IL	PEO
Streetsboro, OH	Y
Strickland, WI	SUP
String Prairie, IA	DAV
TX	AUS
Stringtown, IL	BEL
Strong City, KS	WCH
Strongsville, OH	CLV
Stroudsburg, PA	SCR
Struble, IA	SC
Struthers, OH	Y
Stryker, OH	TOL
Strykersville, NY	BUF
Stuart, FL	PMB
IA	DM
NE	OM
Studio City, CA	LA
Sturgeon Bay, WI	GB
Sturgis, KY	OWN
MI	KAL
SD	RC
Sturtevant, WI	MIL
Stuttgart, AR	LR
Stuyvesant, NY	ALB
Stuyvesant Falls, NY	ALB
Suamico, WI	GB
Subiaco, AR	LR
Sublette, IL	RCK
Sublimity, OR	P
Succasunna, NJ	PAT
Sudbury, MA	BO
Suffern, NY	NY
Suffield, CT	HRT
Suffolk, VA	RIC
Sugar Camp, WI	SUP
Sugar Creek, IA	DAV
MO	KC
MO	PRM
Sugar Grove, OH	COL
Sugar Island, MI	MAR
Sugar Land, TX	GAL
Sugar Notch, PA	SCR
Sugarloaf, PA	PSC
Suitland, MD	WDC
Sulligent, AL	BIR
Sullivan, IL	SFD
IN	EVN
MO	STL
WI	MAD
Sulphur, LA	LKC
OK	OKL
Sulphur Springs, TX	TYL
Summerfield, KS	KCK
Summerhill, PA	ALT
Summersville, WV	WH
Summerton, SC	CHR
Summerville, SC	CHR
Summit, IL	CHI
NJ	NEW
NY	ALB
WI	LC
Summit Hill, PA	ALN
Summitville, OH	Y
Sumner, IA	DUB
WA	SEA
Sumter, SC	CHR
Sun City, AZ	PHX
CA	SB
Sun City Center, FL	SP
Sun City West, AZ	PHX
Sun Lakes, AZ	PHX
Sun Prairie, WI	MAD
Sun Valley, CA	LA
ID	B
NV	RNO
Sunbury, OH	COL
PA	HBG
Suncook, NH	MAN
Sunfish, KY	OWN
Sunland, CA	LA
Sunland Park, NM	LSC
Sunny Hills, FL	PT
Sunnyside, WA	YAK
Sunnyvale, CA	SJ
Sunrise, FL	MIA
Sunset, LA	LAF
Sunset Hills, MO	STL
Sunsites, AZ	TUC
Superior, AZ	TUC
NE	LIN
WI	SUP
Surf City, NC	R
Suring, WI	GB
Surprise, AZ	PHX
Susanville, CA	SAC
Susquehanna, PA	SCR
Sussex, NJ	PAT
Sutersville, PA	GBG
Sutherland, IA	SC
NE	GI
Sutherlin, OR	P
Sutter Creek, CA	SAC
Sutton, MA	WOR
NE	LIN
Suttons Bay, MI	GAY
Swainsboro, GA	SAV
Swainton, NJ	CAM
NJ	TR
Swaledale, IA	DUB
Swampscott, MA	BO
Swan Lake, MN	NU
MT	HEL
Swan Valley, MT	HEL
Swannanoa, NC	CHL
Swansboro, NC	R
Swansea, MA	FR
Swanton, OH	TOL
VT	BUR
Swanville, MN	SCL
Swarthmore, PA	PH
Swartswood, NJ	PAT
Swartz Creek, MI	LAN
Swedesboro, NJ	CAM
Swedesburg, PA	PH
Sweeny, TX	GAL
Sweet Home, OR	P
TX	VIC
Sweetwater, TX	SAN
Swissvale, PA	PIT
Switzerland, FL	STA
Swormville, NY	BUF
Swoyersville, PA	PSC
PA	SCR
Sybertsville, PA	PSC
Sycamore, IL	RCK
OH	TOL
Sykeston, ND	FAR
Sykesville, MD	BAL
PA	E
PA	PBR
Sylacauga, AL	BIR
Sylmar, CA	LA
Sylva, NC	CHL
Sylvania, GA	SAV
OH	TOL
Sylvia, IA	DUB
Syosset, NY	BRK
NY	RVC
Syracuse,	SY
IN	FTW
KS	DOD
NE	LIN
NY	STF
NY	SY
Tabb, VA	RIC
Taberg, NY	SY
Tabernacle, NJ	TR
Tabor, MN	CR
SD	SFS
Tacoma, WA	SEA
Taft, CA	FRS
TX	CC
Taftville, CT	NOR
Tahlequah, OK	TLS
Tahoe City, CA	SAC
Tai, GU	AGN
Takoma Park, MD	WDC
Talkeetna, AK	ANC
Talladega, AL	BIR
Tallahassee, FL	PT
Tallassee, AL	MOB
Tallmadge, OH	CLV
Tallulah, LA	ALX
Talofofo, GU	AGN
Tamaqua, PA	ALN
Tamarac, FL	MIA
Tamaroa, IL	BEL
Tama-Toledo, IA	DUB
Tamoroi, FM	CI
Tampa, FL	SP
KS	WCH
Tampico, IL	RCK
Tamuning, GU	AGN
Tanana, AK	FBK
Tanapag Village, District 8, MP	CHK
Taneytown, MD	BAL
Tannersville, PA	SCR
Taos, MO	JC
NM	SFE
Tappahannock, VA	RIC
Tappan, NY	NY
Tappan Lake, OH	STU
Tappen, ND	FAR
Tarboro, NC	R
Tarentum, PA	PBR
PA	PIT
Tariffville, CT	HRT
Tarkio, MO	KC
Tarnov, NE	OM
Tarpon Springs, FL	SP
Tarrytown, NY	NY
Taunton, MA	FR
MN	NU
Tavernier, FL	MIA
Tawas City, MI	GAY
Taycheedah, WI	MIL
Taylor, MI	DET
MI	PRM
PA	PSC
PA	SCR
TX	AUS
Taylor Mill, KY	COV
Taylors, SC	CHR
Taylors Falls, MN	STP
Taylorsville, UT	SLC
Taylorville, IL	SFD
Tazewell, TN	KNX
VA	RIC
Tea, SD	SFS
Teaneck, NJ	NEW
Techny, IL	CHI
Tecumseh, MI	LAN
NE	LIN
Tehachapi, CA	FRS
Tekamah, NE	OM
Tekoa, WA	SPK
Tell City, IN	IND
Teller, AK	FBK
Telluride, CO	PBL
Temecula, CA	NTN
CA	SB
Tempe, AZ	PHX
Temperance, MI	DET
Temperanceville, OH	STU
Temple, TX	AUS
Temple City, CA	LA

Temple Hill, IA	DUB
Temple Terrace, FL	SP
Templeton, IA	SC
Tenafly, NJ	NEW
Tennessee Ridge, TN	NSH
Tennyson-Potosi, WI	MAD
Tequesta, FL	PMB
Terre Haute, IN	IND
Terrebonne, MN	CR
Terrell, TX	DAL
Terrytown, LA	NO
Terryville, CT	HRT
CT	STF
Teutopolis, IL	SFD
Tewksbury, MA	BO
Texarkana, AR	LR
TX	TYL
Texas City, TX	GAL
Thatcher, AZ	TUC
Theilman, MN	WIN
Theresa, WI	MIL
Theriot, LA	HT
Thermal, CA	SB
Thermopolis, WY	CHY
Thibodaux, LA	HT
Thief River Falls, MN	CR
Thiensville, WI	MIL
Thiry Daems, WI	GB
Thomas, WV	WH
Thomasboro, IL	PEO
Thomaston, CT	HRT
Thomasville, GA	SAV
NC	CHL
Thompson, CT	LIT
CT	NOR
ND	FAR
OH	CLV
WI	MIL
Thompson (Erin), WI	MIL
Thompson Falls, MT	HEL
Thomson, GA	ATL
Thoreau, NM	GLP
Thorndike, MA	SPR
ME	PRT
Thornwood, NY	NY
Thorp, WI	LC
Thousand Oaks, CA	LA
Thousand Palms, CA	SB
Three Bridges, NJ	MET
Three Forks, MT	HEL
Three Lakes, WI	SUP
Three Oaks, MI	KAL
Three Rivers, CA	FRS
MA	SPR
MI	KAL
TX	CC
Throckmorton, TX	FWT
Throop, PA	SCR
Thunderbolt, GA	SAV
Thurmont, MD	BAL
Tiburon, CA	SFR
Tickfaw, LA	BR
Ticonderoga, NY	OG
Tidioute, PA	E
Tierra Amarilla, NM	SFE
Tiff, MO	STL
Tiffin, OH	TOL
Tifton, GA	SAV
Tigard, OR	P
Tiger Point, FL	PT
Tigerton, WI	GB
Tijeras, NM	SFE
Tilden, NE	OM
WI	LC
Tillamook, OR	P
Tillman's Corner, AL	MOB
Tilton, NH	MAN
Tiltonsville, OH	STU
Timber Lake, SD	RC
Timken, KS	DOD
Timonium, MD	BAL
Tinaja, NM	GLP
Tinley Park, IL	CHI
Tintah, MN	SCL
Tioga, LA	ALX
ND	BIS
Tipp City, OH	CIN
Tipton, CA	FRS
IA	DAV
IL	BEL
IN	LFT
KS	SAL
MO	JC
Tisch Mills, WI	GB
Tiskilwa, IL	PEO
Titusville, FL	ORL
PA	E
Tiverton,	PRO
RI	PRO
Tivoli, NY	NY
TX	CC

Toa Alta, PR	SJN
Toa Baja, PR	SJN
Tobyhanna, PA	SCR
Toccoa, GA	ATL
Todd's Mill, IL	BEL
Tohatchi, NM	GLP
Tok, AK	FBK
Tokio, ND	FAR
Toksook Bay, AK	FBK
Tol, FM	CI
Tol, Chuuk, FM	CI
Toledo, OH	OLL
OH	TOL
WA	SEA
Tolland, CT	NOR
Tolleson, AZ	PHX
Tolna, ND	FAR
Tolono, IL	PEO
Tolowas, FM	CI
Toluca, IL	PEO
Tomah, WI	LC
Tomahawk, WI	SUP
Tomales, CA	SFR
Tomball, TX	GAL
Tombstone, AZ	TUC
Tome, NM	SFE
Toms River, NJ	PHU
NJ	PSC
NJ	TR
Tonasket, WA	SPK
Tonawanda, NY	BUF
Tonet, WI	GB
Tonganoxie, KS	KCK
Tonkawa, OK	OKL
Tonopah, NV	LAV
Tontitown, AR	LR
Tony, WI	SUP
Tooele, UT	SLC
Topawa, AZ	TUC
Topeka, KS	KCK
Toppenish, WA	YAK
Topsfield, MA	BO
Toronto, IA	DAV
OH	PBR
OH	STU
Torrance, CA	LA
Torrington, CT	HRT
CT	SAM
WY	CHY
Torun, WI	LC
Toto, GU	AGN
Totowa, NJ	PAT
Totowa Borough, NJ	PAT
Tours, TX	AUS
Towanda, PA	SCR
Tower, MN	DUL
Tower City, PA	ALN
Town and Country, MO	STL
Town of Gates, NY	SY
Towner, ND	FAR
Townsend, MA	BO
MT	HEL
TN	KNX
Towson, MD	BAL
Tracy, CA	STO
MN	NU
Traer, IA	DUB
Trafford, PA	GBG
Tranquillity, CA	FRS
Trappist, KY	L
Trauger, PA	GBG
PA	PBR
Traverse City, MI	GAY
Tremont, PA	ALN
Trempealeau, WI	LC
Trenary, MI	MAR
Trenton, IL	BEL
MI	DET
MO	KC
NE	LIN
NJ	PHU
NJ	PSC
NJ	ROM
NJ	TR
OH	CIN
Tres Pinos, CA	MRY
Tresckow, PA	ALN
Trevorton, PA	HBG
Tri Cities, WA	SPK
Triangle, VA	ARL
Tribes Hill, NY	ALB
Tribune, KS	DOD
Trimont, MN	WIN
Trinidad, CO	PBL
Trinity, TX	TYL
Tripp, SD	SFS
Trona, CA	SB
Trooper, PA	PH
Trout River, NY	OG
Troy, AL	MOB
IL	SFD

IN	IND
KS	KCK
MI	DET
MI	EST
MO	STL
NH	MAN
NY	ALB
NY	SAM
NY	STF
OH	CIN
VT	BUR
Truckee, CA	SAC
Trujillo Alto, PR	SJN
Truman, MN	WIN
WI	MAD
Trumansburg, NY	ROC
Trumbull, CT	BGP
CT	PSC
Truro, MA	FR
Trussville, AL	BIR
Truth or Consequences, NM	LSC
Truxton, NY	SY
Tryon, NC	CHL
Tualatin, OR	P
Tuba City, AZ	GLP
Tubac, AZ	TUC
Tuckahoe, NY	NY
Tucker, GA	ATL
Tuckerton, NJ	TR
Tucson, AZ	STN
AZ	TUC
AZ	VNN
Tucumcari, NM	SFE
Tujunga, CA	LA
Tukwila, WA	SEA
Tulare, CA	FRS
Tularosa, NM	LSC
Tulelake, CA	SAC
Tulia, TX	AMA
Tullahoma, TN	NSH
Tully, NY	SY
Tulsa, OK	TLS
Tum Tum, WA	SPK
Tumon Bay, GU	AGN
Tumwater, WA	SEA
Tunkhannock, PA	SCR
Tunnuk, FM	CI
Tunnuk, Chuuk, FM	CI
Tununak, AK	FBK
Tupelo, MS	JKS
Tupper Lake, NY	OG
Tupper Plains, OH	STU
Turlock, CA	EST
CA	STO
Turner Falls, MA	SPR
Turtle Creek, PA	PIT
Turtle Lake, WI	SUP
Turtle Mountain Reservation, ND	FAR
Turton, SD	SFS
Tuscaloosa, AL	BIR
Tuscarora, PA	ALN
Tuscola, IL	SFD
Tuscumbia, AL	BIR
Tuskegee Institute, AL	MOB
Tustin, CA	ORG
CA	SB
Tutwiler, MS	JKS
Tuxedo, NY	NY
Twain Harte, CA	STO
Twenty Mile Stand, OH	CIN
Twentynine Palms, CA	SB
Twin Falls, ID	B
Twin Lakes, MN	WIN
WI	MIL
Twin Rocks, PA	ALT
Twin Valley, MN	CR
Twinsburg, OH	CLV
Twisp, WA	SPK
Two Harbors, MN	DUL
Two Inlets, MN	CR
Two Rivers, WI	GB
Tybee Island, GA	SAV
Tyler, MN	NU
TX	TYL
Tyndall, SD	SFS
Tyngsboro, MA	BO
Tyngsborough, MA	BO
Tyringham, MA	SPR
Tyrone, GA	ATL
PA	ALT
Ubly, MI	SAG
Udot, FM	CI
Uhland, TX	AUS
Ukiah, CA	SR
CA	STN
Ulithi and Neighboring Islands, FM	CI
Ullin, IL	BEL
Ulysses, KS	DOD
NE	LIN
Uman, FM	CI
Umatac, GU	AGN

Umbarger, TX	AMA
Unadilla, NY	ALB
Unalakleet, AK	FBK
Uncasville, CT	NOR
Underhill Center, VT	BUR
Underwood, ND	BIS
Union, KY	COV
MO	STL
NJ	NEW
OR	BAK
SC	CHR
Union Beach, NJ	TR
Union Center, WI	LC
Union City, CA	OAK
CT	HRT
IN	LFT
NJ	NEW
OK	OKL
PA	E
TN	MEM
Union Gap, WA	YAK
Union Grove, WI	MIL
Union Grove-Gladewater, TX	TYL
Union Hill, MN	STP
Union Springs, NY	ROC
Uniondale, NY	RVC
Uniontown, KY	OWN
OH	Y
PA	GBG
PA	PBR
PA	SAM
WA	SPK
Unionville, CT	HRT
United, PA	GBG
Unity, PA	PIT
Universal, IN	IND
University City, MO	STL
University Heights, OH	CLV
University Park, MD	WDC
PA	ALT
Upland, CA	SB
Upper Darby, PA	PH
Upper Gwynedd, PA	PH
Upper Marlboro, MD	BAL
MD	WDC
Upper Montclair, NJ	NEW
Upper Saddle River, NJ	NEW
Upper St. Clair, PA	PBR
PA	PIT
Upper Sandusky, OH	TOL
Upper Uwchlan, PA	PH
Upsala, MN	SCL
Upton, MA	WOR
Urbana, IL	DUB
IL	PEO
MD	BAL
OH	CIN
Urbandale, IA	DM
Urbank, MN	SCL
Ushers, NY	ALB
Usk, WA	SPK
Utica, IL	PEO
MI	DET
NY	NTN
NY	SAM
NY	STF
NY	SY
OH	COL
Utuado, PR	ARE
Uvalde, TX	SAT
Uxbridge, MA	WOR
Vacaville, CA	SAC
Vacherie, LA	BR
Vail, AZ	TUC
CO	DEN
IA	SC
Val Rico, FL	SP
Valatie, NY	ALB
Valdez, AK	ANC
Valdosta, GA	SAV
Vale, NC	CHL
OR	BAK
Valentine, NE	GI
Valeria, IA	DAV
Valhalla, NY	NY
Valier, MT	HEL
Valinda, CA	LA
Vallejo, CA	SAC
Valley, NE	OM
WA	SPK
Valley Center, CA	SD
Valley City, ND	FAR
OH	CLV
Valley Falls, KS	KCK
Valley Forge, PA	PH
Valley Lee, MD	WDC
Valley Park, MO	STL
Valley Station, KY	L
Valley Stream, NY	RVC
Valley View, TX	FWT
Valmeyer, IL	BEL

Valparaiso, IN	GRY
NE	LIN
Valrico, FL	SP
Valyermo, CA	LA
Van Buren, AR	LR
ME	PRT
Van Etten, NY	ROC
Van Horn, TX	ELP
Van Horne, IA	DUB
Van Nuys, CA	LA
CA	VNN
Van Wert, OH	TOL
Vanceburg, KY	COV
Vancleave, MS	BLX
Vancouver, WA	SEA
Vandalia, IL	SFD
MO	JC
NY	BUF
OH	CIN
Vanderbilt, MI	GAY
TX	VIC
Vandergrift, PA	GBG
Varina, IA	SC
Varysburg, NY	BUF
Vashon, WA	SEA
Vassar, MI	SAG
Vattman, TX	CC
Vaughn, NM	SFE
Veblen, SD	SFS
Vega, TX	AMA
Vega Alta, PR	ARE
Vega-Baja, PR	ARE
Velva, ND	FAR
Veneta, OR	P
Venice, CA	LA
FL	VEN
IL	SFD
Ventnor, NJ	CAM
PA	PH
Ventura, CA	LA
Vera Cruz, OH	CIN
Verboort, OR	P
Verdigre, NE	OM
Verga, NJ	CAM
Vergennes, VT	BUR
Vermilion, OH	TOL
Vermillion, MN	STP
SD	SFS
Vernal, UT	SLC
Verndale, MN	SCL
Vernon, CA	LA
CT	NOR
NY	SY
TX	FWT
Vernon Center, MN	WIN
Vernonia, OR	P
Vero Beach, FL	PMB
Verona, MO	SPC
ND	FAR
NJ	NEW
NY	SY
PA	PIT
WI	MAD
Verplanck, NY	NY
Versailles, CT	NOR
KY	LEX
OH	CIN
PA	PIT
Veseleyville, ND	FAR
Veseli, MN	STP
Vesper, WI	LC
Vesta, MN	NU
Vestaburg, MI	GR
Vestal, NY	SY
Vevay, IN	IND
Vicksburg, MI	KAL
MS	JKS
Victor, IA	DAV
NY	ROC
Victoria, KS	SAL
MN	STP
TX	VIC
Victorville, CA	SB
Vidalia, GA	SAV
LA	ALX
Vidor, TX	BEA
Vienna, IL	BEL
MO	JC
OH	Y
VA	ARL
WV	WH
Vieques, PR	CGS
Villa Grove, IL	SFD
Villa Hills, KY	COV
Villa Maria, PA	PIT
Villa Nova, IA	DAV
Villa Park, IL	JOL
Villa Ridge, IL	BEL
Villalba, PR	PCE
Villanova, PA	PH
Villanueva, NM	SFE
Villard, MN	SCL
Villas, NJ	CAM
Ville Platte, LA	LAF
Villisca, IA	DM
Vina, CA	SAC
Vincennes, IN	EVN
Vincent, KS	SAL
OH	STU
Vine Grove, KY	L
Vineland, CO	PBL
MN	SCL
NJ	CAM
Vineyard Haven, MA	FR
Vining, IA	DUB
Vinita, OK	TLS
Vinita Park, MO	STL
Vinton, IA	DUB
LA	LKC
Violet, LA	NO
TX	CC
Virden, IL	SFD
Virgil, IL	RCK
Virginia, IL	SFD
MN	DUL
Virginia Beach, VA	RIC
Virginia City, NV	RNO
Virginia Dale, CO	DEN
Viroqua, WI	LC
Visalia, CA	FRS
Vista, CA	LA
CA	SD
Vivian, LA	SHP
Vodnany, SD	SFS
Volga, IA	DUB
Volo, IL	CHI
Voluntown, CT	NOR
Von Ormy, TX	SAT
Voorheesville, NY	ALB
Vredenburgh, AL	MOB
Vulcan, MI	MAR
Wabash, IN	FTW
Wabasha, MN	WIN
Wabasso, MN	NU
Wabeno, WI	GB
Waco, TX	AUS
TX 76701-2105	AUS
Waconia, MN	STP
Waddington, NY	OG
Wadena, MN	SCL
Wading River, NY	RVC
Wadsworth, IL	CHI
OH	CLV
Waggaman, LA	NO
Wagner, SD	SFS
WI	GB
Wagon Mound, NM	SFE
Wagoner, OK	TLS
Wahiawa, HI	HON
Wahkon, MN	SCL
Wahoo, NE	LIN
Wahpeton, ND	FAR
Waialua, HI	HON
Waianae, HI	HON
Waihee, HI	HON
Waikane, HI	HON
Wailuku, HI	HON
Waimanalo, HI	HON
Wainwright, OH	COL
Waipahu, HI	HON
Waipio, HI	HON
Waite Park, MN	SCL
Waitsburg, WA	SPK
Waitsfield, VT	BUR
Wake Forest, NC	R
WaKeeney, KS	SAL
Wakefield, MA	BO
MI	MAR
Wakeman, OH	TOL
Wakonda, SD	SFS
Walbridge, OH	TOL
Walden, CO	DEN
NY	NY
Waldorf, MD	WDC
MN	WIN
Waldport, OR	P
Waldron, AR	LR
Wales, ND	FAR
Walford, IA	DUB
Walhain, WI	GB
Walhalla, ND	FAR
Walker, IA	DUB
KS	SAL
MN	DUL
Walkersville, MD	BAL
Walkerton, IN	FTW
Walkerville, MT	HEL
Wall, PA	PBR
SD	RC
TX	SAN
Wall Lake, IA	SC
Walla Walla, WA	SPK
WA	VNN
Wallace, ID	B
KS	SAL
NE	LIN
Wallagrass, ME	PRT
Walled Lake, MI	DET
Wallingford, CT	HRT
PA	PH
VT	BUR
Wallington, NJ	NEW
Wallis, TX	GAL
Walls, MS	JKS
Walnut, CA	LA
IA	DM
IL	PEO
KS	WCH
Walnut Creek, CA	OAK
Walnut Grove, CA	SAC
MN	NU
Walnut Ridge, AR	LR
Walpole, MA	BO
Walsenburg, CO	PBL
Walsh, IL	BEL
WI	GB
Walston, PA	E
Walterboro, SC	CHR
Waltham, MA	BO
Walthill, NE	OM
Walton, IL	RCK
KY	COV
NY	ALB
Wamego, KS	KCK
Wampum, PA	PIT
Wanamie, PA	SCR
Wanatah, IN	GRY
Wanblee, SD	RC
Wanda, MN	NU
Wantagh, NY	RVC
Wapakoneta, OH	CIN
Wapato, WA	YAK
Wapella, IL	PEO
Wapello, IA	DAV
Wappingers Falls, NY	NY
War, WV	WH
Ward, SC	CHR
Ward Springs, MN	SCL
Warden, WA	YAK
Wardsville, MO	JC
Ware, MA	SPR
Wareham, MA	FR
Warminster, PA	PH
Warner, NH	MAN
Warner Robins, GA	SAV
Warners, NY	SY
Warren, IL	RCK
MA	WOR
MI	DET
MI	NTN
MI	OLL
MI	STN
MN	CR
NJ	MET
OH	PBR
OH	Y
PA	E
RI	PRO
Warrens, WI	LC
Warrensburg, MO	KC
NY	ALB
Warrensville Heights, OH	CLV
Warrenton, MO	STL
NC	R
VA	ARL
Warrenville, IL	JOL
Warrington, PA	PH
PA	PHU
Warroad, MN	CR
Warsaw, IL	PEO
IN	FTW
KY	COV
MO	JC
ND	FAR
NY	BUF
Warson Woods, MO	STL
Warwick, NY	NY
RI	PRO
Wasco, CA	FRS
OR	BAK
Waseca, MN	WIN
Washburn, IL	PEO
WI	SUP
Washington, DC	PHU
DC	SAM
DC	WDC
GA	ATL
IA	DAV
IL	PEO
IN	EVN
KS	SAL
LA	LAF
MI	DET
MO	STL
NC	R
NJ	MET
PA	PIT
Washington Court House, OH	COL
Washington Crossing, NJ	TR
Washington Depot, CT	HRT
Washington Park, IL	BEL
Washington Township, NJ	CAM
NJ	NEW
Washingtonville, NY	NY
Washtunca, WA	SPK
Wasilla, AK	ANC
Watauga, SD	RC
Watchung, NJ	MET
NJ	NEW
Water Mill, NY	RVC
Waterbury, CT	HRT
CT	SAM
VT	BUR
Waterflow, NM	GLP
Waterford, CT	NOR
CT	NTN
MI	DET
NJ	CAM
NY	ALB
PA	E
WI	MIL
Waterloo, IA	DUB
IL	BEL
IN	FTW
KS	WCH
NY	ROC
WI	MAD
Watersmeet, MI	MAR
Watertown, CT	HRT
MA	BO
MN	STP
NY	OG
SD	SFS
WI	MAD
Waterville, KS	KCK
ME	PRT
ME	SAM
MN	STP
NY	SY
OH	TOL
WA	YAK
Watervliet, MI	KAL
NY	ALB
NY	STF
Watford City, ND	BIS
Wathena, KS	KCK
Watkins, IA	DUB
MN	NU
Watkins Glen, NY	ROC
Watseka, IL	JOL
Watsonville, CA	MRY
Wattenberg, CO	DEN
Waubay, SD	SFS
Waubun, MN	CR
Wauchula, FL	VEN
Waucoma, IA	DUB
Wauconda, IL	CHI
Waukee, IA	DM
Waukegan, IL	CHI
Waukesha, WI	MIL
Waukon, IA	DUB
Waumandee, WI	LC
Waunakee, WI	MAD
Waupaca, WI	GB
Waupun, WI	MIL
Wauregan, CT	NOR
Wausau, WI	LC
Wausaukee, WI	GB
Wauseon, OH	TOL
Wautoma, WI	GB
Wauwatosa, WI	MIL
Wauzeka, WI	LC
Waveland, MS	BLX
Waverly, IA	DUB
IL	SFD
KS	KCK
KY	OWN
MN	STP
NE	LIN
NY	ROC
OH	COL
SD	SFS
Wax, KY	OWN
Waxahachie, TX	DAL
Waycross, GA	SAV
Wayland, MA	BO
MI	KAL
NY	ROC
Waymart, PA	SCR
Wayne, IL	JOL
MI	DET
NE	OM
NJ	PAT
PA	PH

WI	MIL
WV	WH
Waynesboro, GA	SAV
MS	BLX
PA	HBG
TN	NSH
VA	RIC
Waynesburg, OH	Y
PA	PIT
Waynesville, MO	JC
NC	CHL
OH	CIN
Wayside, NJ	TR
Wayzata, MN	STP
Wea, KS	KCK
Weare Twp., MI	GR
Weatherford, OK	OKL
TX	FWT
Weatherly, PA	ALN
Weaverville, CA	SAC
Webb City, MO	SPC
Webster, MA	WOR
NY	ROC
SD	SFS
WI	SUP
Webster City, IA	DUB
Webster Groves, MO	STL
Webster Springs, WV	WH
Wedron, IL	PEO
Weed, CA	SAC
Weedsport, NY	ROC
Weehawken, NJ	NEW
Weimar, TX	VIC
Weiner, AR	LR
Weingarten, MO	STL
Weir, KS	WCH
Weirton, WV	PBR
WV	WH
Weiser, ID	B
Welch, WV	WH
Weldona, CO	DEN
Weller, IA	DAV
Wellesley, MA	BO
Wellesley Hills, MA	BO
Wellfleet, MA	FR
Wellington, FL	PMB
KS	WCH
OH	CLV
SD	SFS
TX	AMA
Wellman, IA	DAV
Wellpinit, WA	SPK
Wells, ME	PRT
MI	MAR
MN	WIN
NY	OG
Wellsboro, PA	SCR
Wellsburg, WV	WH
Wellston, MO	STL
OH	COL
Wellsville, MO	JC
NY	BUF
OH	Y
Welsh, LA	LKC
Welton, IA	DAV
Wenatchee, WA	YAK
Wendelin, IL	BEL
Wendell, ID	B
NC	R
Wendover, UT	SLC
Wenham, MA	BO
Wenona, IL	PEO
Wentzville, MO	STL
Wernersville, PA	ALN
Weslaco, TX	BWN
Wesley, IA	SC
Wesley Hills, NY	NY
Wessington, SD	SFS
Wessington Springs, SD	SFS
West, TX	AUS
West Albany, MN	WIN
West Aliquippa, PA	PIT
West Allis, WI	MIL
West Alton, MO	STL
West Babylon, NY	RVC
West Bangor, PA	ALN
West Barnstable, MA	FR
West Bend, IA	SC
WI	MIL
West Bethesda, MD	WDC
West Bloomfield, MI	DET
MI	EST
West Boylston, MA	WOR
West Branch, IA	DAV
MI	GAY
West Brandywine Twp., PA	PH
West Brattleboro, VT	LIT
West Bridgewater, MA	BO
West Brookfield, MA	WOR
West Brooklyn, IL	RCK
West Burke, VT	STF
West Burlington, IA	DAV
West Chazy, NY	OG
West Chester, OH	CIN
PA	PH
West Chicago, IL	JOL
West Clarksville, NY	BUF
West Collingswood, NJ	CAM
West Concord, MN	WIN
West Conshohocken, PA	PH
West Covina, CA	LA
West Des Moines, IA	DM
West Duluth, MN	DUL
West Easton, PA	PHU
West Falls, NY	BUF
West Fargo, ND	FAR
West Frankfort, IL	BEL
West Greenwich, RI	PRO
West Grove, PA	PH
West Hartford, CT	HRT
West Harwich, MA	FR
West Haven, CT	HRT
West Hazleton, PA	SCR
West Hempstead, NY	NY
NY	RVC
West Hollywood, CA	LA
FL	MIA
West Hurley-Woodstock, NY	NY
West Hyattsville, MD	WDC
West Islip, NY	RVC
NY	STF
West Jefferson, OH	COL
West Jordan, UT	SLC
West Kewaunee, WI	GB
West Lafayette, IN	LFT
West Lake Forest, IL	CHI
West Lawn, PA	ALN
West Lebanon, NH	MAN
West Leechburg, PA	SJP
West Leyden, NY	OG
West Liberty, IA	DAV
KY	LEX
WV	WH
West Long Branch, NJ	TR
West Memphis, AR	LR
West Middlesex, PA	E
West Mifflin, PA	PIT
West Milford Township, NJ	PAT
West Milton, OH	CIN
West Mineral, KS	WCH
West Monroe, LA	SHP
West New York, NJ	NEW
West Newbury, MA	BO
West Newton, PA	GBG
West Newton Township, MN	NU
West Nyack, NY	NY
West Orange, NJ	NEW
West Overland, MO	STL
West Palm Beach, FL	PMB
FL	SAM
West Park, NY	NY
West Paterson, NJ	NTN
NJ	PAT
West Peoria, IL	PEO
West Pittsburg, PA	PIT
West Pittston, PA	SCR
West Plains, MO	SPC
West Point, IA	DAV
MS	JKS
NE	OM
NY	NY
VA	RIC
West Portsmouth, OH	COL
West Reading, PA	ALN
West Redding, CT	BGP
West Rutland, VT	BUR
West Sacramento, CA	SAC
West St. Paul, MN	STP
West Salem, OH	CLV
WI	LC
West Salisbury, PA	ALT
West Seneca, NY	BUF
West Simsbury, CT	HRT
West Springfield, MA	SPR
West Stewartstown, NH	MAN
West Stockbridge, MA	SPR
West Sunbury, PA	PIT
West Swanzey, NH	MAN
West Taghkanic, NY	ALB
West Terre Haute, IN	IND
West Union, IA	DUB
MN	SCL
OH	CIN
WV	WH
West Valley, NY	BUF
West Valley City, UT	SLC
West View, PA	PIT
West Warren, MA	WOR
West Warwick, RI	PRO
West Willington, CT	NOR
West Windsor, NJ	TR
West Winfield, NY	ALB
West Wyoming, PA	SCR
West Yellowstone, MT	HEL
Westboro, WI	SUP
Westborough, MA	WOR
Westbrook, CT	NOR
ME	PRT
MN	WIN
Westbury, NY	PSC
NY	RVC
Westchester, IL	CHI
Westcliffe, CO	PBL
Westend, WA	SPK
Westerly, RI	PRO
Western Springs, IL	CHI
Westernport, MD	BAL
Westerville, OH	COL
Westfield, IN	LFT
MA	SPR
NJ	NEW
NY	BUF
VT	BUR
WI	MAD
Westford, MA	BO
Westhampton Beach, NY	RVC
Westhope, ND	FAR
Westlake, LA	LKC
OH	CLV
Westlake Village, CA	LA
Westland, MI	DET
Westminster, CA	ORG
CO	DEN
MA	WOR
MD	BAL
Westmont, IL	JOL
NJ	CAM
Westmorland, CA	SD
Weston, CT	BGP
IA	DM
MA	BO
MO	KC
NE	LIN
PA	SCR
VT	BUR
WI	LC
WV	WH
Westover, WV	WH
Westphalia, IA	DM
KS	KCK
MI	LAN
MO	JC
TX	AUS
Westport, CT	BGP
MA	FR
NY	OG
SD	SFS
WI	MAD
Westtown, PA	PH
Westville, IL	PEO
NJ	CAM
Westville Grove, NJ	CAM
Westwego, LA	NO
Westwood, CA	SAC
MA	BO
NJ	NEW
Wethersfield, CT	HRT
Wetmore, KS	KCK
Wever, IA	DAV
Wewahitchka, FL	PT
Wexford, IA	DUB
PA	PIT
Weyauwega, WI	GB
Weyerhaeuser, WI	SUP
Weymouth, MA	BO
Wharton, TX	VIC
What Cheer, IA	DAV
Wheat Ridge, CO	DEN
Wheatfield, IN	LFT
Wheatland, IA	DAV
WY	CHY
Wheaton, IL	JOL
IL	RCK
KS	KCK
MD	WDC
MN	SCL
Wheatville, NY	BUF
Wheelersburg, OH	COL
Wheeling, IL	CHI
WV	OLL
WV	SJP
WV	WH
Whippany, NJ	PAT
NJ	PHU
Whistler, AL	MOB
White, SD	SFS
White Bear Lake, MN	STP
White Castle, LA	BR
White Cloud, MI	GR
White Cypress, MS	BLX
White Deer, TX	AMA
White Earth, MN	CR
White Hall, IL	SFD
White Haven, PA	SCR
White Lake, MI	DET
SD	SFS
WI	GB
White Mills, KY	L
PA	SCR
White Oak Boro, PA	PIT
White Pigeon, MI	KAL
White Pine, MI	MAR
White Plains, NY	NTN
NY	NY
NY	PSC
White Post, VA	ARL
White River, SD	RC
White River Junction, VT	BUR
White Salmon, WA	YAK
White Sulphur Springs, MT	HEL
WV	WH
White Swan, WA	YAK
Whitefield, ME	PRT
NH	MAN
Whitefish, MT	HEL
Whitefish Bay, WI	MIL
Whitehall, LA	BR
MT	HEL
NY	ALB
PA	ALN
PA	PIT
WI	LC
Whitehouse, OH	TOL
TX	TYL
Whitehouse Station, NJ	MET
Whitelaw, WI	GB
Whiteriver, AZ	GLP
Whitesboro, NY	SY
Whitestone, NY	BRK
Whitesville, KY	OWN
NY	BUF
WV	WH
Whitethorn, CA	SR
Whiteville, NC	R
Whitewater, CO	PBL
WI	MIL
Whiting, IN	GRY
IN	PRM
NJ	TR
Whitinsville, MA	WOR
Whitley City, KY	LEX
Whitman, MA	BO
Whitney, PA	GBG
Whitney Point, NY	SY
Whittemore, IA	SC
MI	GAY
Whittier, CA	LA
Whittlesey, WI	SUP
Wichita, KS	WCH
Wichita Falls, TX	FWT
Wickatunk, NJ	TR
Wickenburg, AZ	PHX
Wickliffe, OH	CLV
Wien, MO	JC
Wiggins, CO	DEN
MS	BLX
Wilber, NE	LIN
Wilbraham, MA	SPR
Wilbur, WA	SPK
Wilcox, PA	E
Wild Rice, ND	FAR
Wilder, KY	COV
Wildwood, MO	STL
NJ	CAM
PA	PIT
Wildwood Crest, NJ	CAM
Wilkes-Barre, PA	PHU
PA	PSC
PA	SAM
PA	SCR
Wilkinsburg, PA	PIT
Willacoochee, GA	SAV
Willard, OH	TOL
WI	LC
Willcox, AZ	TUC
Willey, IA	SC
Williams, AZ	PHX
IA	DUB
MN	CR
Williamsburg, IA	DAV
KY	LEX
OH	CIN
PA	ALT
VA	PSC
VA	RIC
Williamson, WV	WH
Williamsport, MD	BAL
PA	SCR
Williamston, MI	LAN
NC	R
Williamstown, KY	COV
MA	SPR
NJ	CAM
NJ	PHU

PA	HBG
PA	PSC
Williamsville, NY	BUF
NY	SAM
Willimantic, CT	NOR
CT	STF
Willingboro, NJ	TR
Williston, FL	STA
ND	BIS
VT	BUR
Williston Park, NY	RVC
Willisville, IL	BEL
Willits, CA	SR
Willmar, MN	NU
Willoughby, OH	CLV
Willoughby Hills, OH	CLV
Willow City, ND	FAR
Willow Grove, PA	PH
Willow Lake, SD	SFS
Willow River, MN	DUL
Willow Springs, IL	CHI
MO	SPC
Willowdale, KS	WCH
Willowick, OH	CLV
Willows, CA	SAC
Wills Creek, OH	COL
Willsboro, NY	OG
Wilmerding, PA	PIT
PA	SJP
Wilmette, IL	CHI
Wilmington, CA	LA
DE	PHU
DE	WIL
IL	JOL
MA	BO
NC	R
OH	CIN
VT	BUR
Wilmington Manor, DE	WIL
Wilmont, MN	WIN
Wilmore, PA	ALT
Wilmot, MI	SAG
SD	SFS
WI	MIL
Wilno, MN	NU
Wilson, KS	SAL
MN	WIN
NC	R
NY	BUF
WI	LC
WI	SUP
Wilsonville, IL	SFD
OR	P
Wilton, CT	BGP
IA	DAV
ME	PRT
MN	CR
ND	BIS
ND	STN
NH	MAN
WI	LC
Wilton Center, IL	JOL
Wimberley, TX	AUS
Wimbledon, ND	FAR
Winamac, IN	LFT
Winburne, PA	E
Winchendon, MA	WOR
Winchester, IL	SFD
IN	LFT
KY	LEX
MA	BO
NH	MAN
VA	ARL
Winchester Center, CT	HRT
Wind Lake, WI	MIL
Windber, PA	ALT
PA	PBR
Winder, GA	ATL
Windham, CT	NOR
ME	PRT
NH	MAN
NY	ALB
OH	Y
Windom, MN	WIN
Windsor, CA	SR

CO	DEN
CT	HRT
ND	FAR
NY	SY
VT	BUR
Windsor Locks, CT	HRT
Windthorst, KS	DOD
TX	FWT
Winfield, AL	BIR
IL	JOL
KS	WCH
Winfield Township, IN	GRY
Winlock, WA	SEA
Winnebago, IL	RCK
MN	WIN
NE	OM
Winneconne, WI	GB
Winnemucca, NV	RNO
Winner, SD	RC
Winnetka, IL	CHI
Winnfield, LA	ALX
Winnie, TX	BEA
Winnsboro, LA	ALX
Winona, MN	WIN
Winooski, VT	BUR
Winslow, AR	LR
AZ	GLP
ME	PRT
Winsted, CT	HRT
MN	NU
Winston-Salem, NC	CHL
Winter, WI	SUP
Winter Garden, FL	ORL
Winter Haven, FL	ORL
Winter Park, CO	DEN
FL	ORL
Winter Springs, FL	ORL
Winterhaven, CA	SD
Winterport, ME	PRT
Winters, CA	SAC
TX	SAN
Winterset, IA	DM
Wintersville, OH	STU
Winthrop, IA	DUB
MA	BO
ME	PRT
MN	NU
Wireton, PA	PIT
Wisconsin Dells, WI	MAD
Wisconsin Rapids, WI	LC
Wishek, ND	FAR
Wisner, NE	OM
Withamsville, OH	CIN
Witherbee, NY	OG
Witt, IL	SFD
Wittenberg, WI	GB
Woburn, MA	BO
Woden, IA	DUB
Wofford Heights, CA	FRS
Wolcott, CT	HRT
NY	ROC
Woleai and Neighboring Islands, FM	CI
Wolf Point, MT	GF
Wolfeboro, NH	MAN
Wolfforth, TX	LUB
Wonder Lake, IL	RCK
Wonewoc, WI	LC
Wood Dale, IL	JOL
Wood River, IL	SFD
NE	GI
Woodbine, IA	DM
NJ	CAM
NJ	PHU
Woodbourne, NY	NY
Woodbridge, CT	HRT
NJ	MET
VA	ARL
Woodburg, NY	BRK
Woodburn, OR	P
Woodbury, CT	HRT
MN	STP
NJ	CAM
NY	RVC
Woodbury Heights, NJ	CAM
Woodcliff Lake, NJ	NEW

Woodcrest, DE	WIL
Woodhaven, MI	DET
Woodhull, IL	PEO
WI	MIL
Woodlake, CA	FRS
Woodland, CA	SAC
WA	SEA
WI	MIL
Woodland Hills, CA	LA
Woodland Park, CO	COS
The Woodlands, TX	GAL
Woodlawn, NY	BUF
VA	RIC
Woodlynne, NJ	CAM
Woodmont, CT	HRT
Woodridge, IL	JOL
Wood-Ridge, NJ	NEW
Woodrow, TX	LUB
Woodruff, WI	SUP
Woods Hole, MA	FR
Woodsboro, TX	CC
Woodsfield, OH	STU
Woodside, CA	SFR
Woodson Terrace, MO	STL
Woodstock, GA	ATL
IL	RCK
MD	BAL
MN	WIN
VA	ARL
VT	BUR
Woodstown, NJ	CAM
Woodsville, NH	MAN
Woodville, FL	PT
MS	JKS
TX	BEA
Woodward, IA	DM
IA	SC
OK	OKL
Woonsocket, RI	NTN
RI	PRO
RI	STF
SD	SFS
Wooster, OH	CLV
Worcester,	WOR
MA	BO
MA	NTN
MA	SAM
MA	WOR
NY	ALB
Worland, WY	CHY
Worth, IL	CHI
Worthing, SD	SFS
Worthington, IA	DUB
MN	WIN
Wrangell, AK	JUN
Wray, CO	DEN
Wrentham, MA	BO
Wright, KS	DOD
Wright Township, MI	GR
Wrightstown, WI	GB
Wrightsville Beach, NC	R
Wrightwood, CA	SB
Wuerzburg, WI	LC
Wurtsboro, NY	NY
Wyalusing, PA	SCR
Wyandanch, NY	RVC
Wyandotte, MI	DET
Wyckoff, NJ	NEW
Wykoff, MN	WIN
Wylie, TX	DAL
Wymore, NE	LIN
Wynantskill, NY	ALB
Wyncote, PA	PH
Wyndmere, ND	FAR
Wyndmoor, PA	PH
Wynne, AR	LR
Wynnewood, PA	PH
Wynot, NE	OM
Wyoming, IL	PEO
MI	GR
PA	SCR
Wytheville, VA	RIC
Xenia, OH	CIN
Yabucoa, PR	CGS
Yakima, WA	YAK

Yakutat, AK	JUN
Yale, MI	DET
Yalesville, CT	HRT
Yamhill, OR	P
Yankton, SD	SFS
Yardley, PA	PH
Yarmouth, ME	PRT
Yates Center, KS	WCH
Yatesboro, PA	GBG
Yauco, PR	PCE
Yazoo City, MS	JKS
Yeadon, PA	PH
Yellow Springs, OH	CIN
Yellowstone, WI	MAD
Yelm, WA	SEA
Yerington, NV	RNO
Yigo, GU	AGN
Yoakum, TX	VIC
Yoder, IN	FTW
Yona, GU	AGN
Yonges Island, SC	CHR
Yonkers, NY	NTN
NY	NY
NY	PSC
NY	STF
Yorba Linda, CA	ORG
York, NE	LIN
PA	HBG
SC	CHR
York Harbor, ME	PRT
York Haven, PA	HBG
Yorktown, TX	VIC
VA	RIC
Yorktown Heights, NY	NY
Yorkville, IN	IND
NY	SY
OH	STU
Yosemite National Park, CA	FRS
Youngstown, NY	BUF
OH	OLL
OH	PBR
OH	ROM
OH	SJP
OH	Y
PA	GBG
Youngsville, LA	LAF
NY	NY
PA	E
Youngwood, PA	GBG
Yountville, CA	SR
Ypsilanti, MI	LAN
Yreka, CA	SAC
Yuba, WI	LC
Yuba City, CA	SAC
Yucaipa, CA	SB
Yucca Valley, CA	SB
Yukon, OK	OKL
PA	GBG
Yulan, NY	NY
Yuma, AZ	TUC
CO	DEN
Zachary, LA	BR
Zaleski, OH	COL
Zanesville, OH	COL
OH	NTN
Zapata, TX	LAR
Zearing, IA	DUB
Zeba, MI	MAR
Zeeland, ND	FAR
Zeigler, IL	BEL
Zelienople, PA	PIT
Zell, MO	STL
SD	SFS
Zenda, KS	WCH
Zephyr Cove, NV	RNO
Zephyrhills, FL	SP
Zillah, WA	YAK
Zilwaukee, MI	SAG
Zimmerman, MN	SCL
Zion-Beach Park, IL	CHI
Zionsville, IN	LFT
Zumbrota, MN	STP
Zuni, NM	GLP
Zurich, KS	SAL
Zwolle, LA	SHP

The Catholic Church in the United States

The organizational structure of the Catholic Church in the United States consists of 33 Provinces with as many Archdioceses (Metropolitan Sees); 149 Suffragan Sees (Dioceses); The Military Archdiocese; four Eastern-Rite jurisdictions immediately subject to the Holy See in Rome. The Eparchies of St. Maron (Maronites), Newton (Melkites), St. Thomas the Apostle of Detroit (Chaldeans) and St. George Martyr of Canton, Ohio (Romanians), St. Thomas of Chicago of the Syro-Malabarians. Each of these jurisdictions is under the direction of an Archbishop and Bishop called an Ordinary, who has apostolic responsibility and authority for the pastoral service of the people in his care.

The structure includes the territorial episcopal conference known as the National Conference of Catholic Bishops. In and through this body, which is strictly ecclesiastical and has defined juridical authority, the Bishops exercise their collegiate pastorate over the Church in the entire country.

Related to the NCCB is the United States Catholic Conference, a civil corporation and operational secretariat through which the Bishops, in cooperation with other members of the Church, act on a wider-than-ecclesiastical scale for the good of the Church and society in the United States.

The following is a list of the thirteen regions in the United States and provinces within those regions.

Region I: Includes the states of Maine, Vermont, New Hampshire, Massachusetts, Rhode Island, and Connecticut. Provinces of Boston and Hartford; Eparchy of Stamford and Eparchy for Melkites.

Region II: Includes the state of New York. Province of New York and Eparchy of St. Maron.

Region III: Includes the states of New Jersey and Pennsylvania. Provinces of Newark and Philadelphia; Archeparchy of Philadelphia, Ukrainian Archeparchy of Pittsburgh, Byzantine Eparchy of Passaic, and Apostolic Exarchate for Armenians.

Region IV: Includes the states of Delaware, District of Columbia, Florida, Georgia, Maryland, North Carolina, South Carolina, Virgin Islands, Virginia and West Virginia. Provinces of Atlanta, Baltimore, Miami, Washington, and the Military Archdiocese.

Region V: Includes the states of Alabama, Kentucky, Louisiana, Mississippi and Tennessee. Provinces of Louisville, Mobile and New Orleans.

Region VI: Includes the states of Michigan and Ohio. Provinces of Cincinnati, Detroit; Eparchy of Parma, Apostolic Exarchate for Chaldeans, and Apostolic Exarchate for Romanians.

Region VII: Includes the states of Illinois, Indiana and Wisconsin. Provinces of Chicago, Indianapolis, Milwaukee; Eparchy of St. Nicholas in Chicago-Ukrainian.

Region VIII: Includes the states of Minnesota, North Dakota and South Dakota. Provinces of St. Paul and Minneapolis.

Region IX: Includes the states of Kansas, Missouri and Nebraska. Provinces of Dubuque, Kansas City in Kansas, Omaha and St. Louis.

Region X: Includes the states of Arkansas, Oklahoma and Texas (excluding El Paso). Provinces of Oklahoma City and San Antonio.

Region XI: Includes the states of California, Hawaii and Nevada. Provinces of Los Angeles and San Francisco (excluding Salt Lake City); Eparchy of Van Nuys.

Region XII: Includes the states of Alaska, Idaho, Montana, Oregon and Washington. Provinces of Anchorage, Portland and Seattle.

Region XIII: Includes the states of Utah, Arizona, New Mexico, Colorado and Wyoming. Provinces of Denver, Santa Fe, part of San Francisco, Salt Lake City, and El Paso.

Please refer to individual Diocesan and Archdiocesan listing for complete and detailed information. The following list does not include the retired Archbishops or retired Bishops.

PROVINCE OF ANCHORAGE

Includes the State of Alaska.

Archdiocese of Anchorage, AK—Most. Rev. Roger L. Schwietz, O.M.I., Archbishop of Anchorage.

Diocese of Fairbanks, AK—Vacant See.

Diocese of Juneau, AK—Most Rev. Michael Warfel.

PROVINCE OF ATLANTA

Includes the States of Georgia, North Carolina and South Carolina.

Archdiocese of Atlanta, GA—Most Rev. John F. Donoghue, Archbishop of Atlanta.

Diocese of Charleston, SC—Most Rev. Robert J. Baker, Bishop of Charleston.

Diocese of Charlotte, NC—Most Rev. William G. Curlin, Bishop of Charlotte.

Diocese of Raleigh, NC—Most Rev. F. Joseph Gossman, Bishop of Raleigh.

Diocese of Savannah, GA—Most Rev. John K. Boland, Bishop of Savannah.

PROVINCE OF BALTIMORE

Includes the States of Maryland (except Montgomery, Prince Charles, St. Mary's, Calvert and Charles Counties), Delaware, Virginia and West Virginia.

Archdiocese of Baltimore, MD—His Eminence William Cardinal Keeler, Archbishop of Baltimore. Most Rev. William Newmann, Auxiliary Bishop. Most Rev. Gordon D. Bennett, S.J., Auxiliary Bishop. Most Rev. William F. Malooly, Auxiliary Bishop.

Diocese of Arlington, VA—Most Rev. Paul S. Loverde, Bishop of Arlington.

Diocese of Richmond, VA—Most Rev. Walter F. Sullivan, Bishop of Richmond.

Diocese of Wheeling-Charleston, WV—Most Rev. Bernard W. Schmitt, Bishop of Wheeling-Charleston.

Diocese of Wilmington, DE—Most Rev. Michael A. Saltarelli, Bishop of Wilmington.

PROVINCE OF BOSTON

Includes the States of Maine, New Hampshire, Vermont and Massachusetts.

Archdiocese of Boston, MA—His Eminence Bernard Cardinal Law, Archbishop of Boston. Most Rev. John P. Boles, Auxiliary Bishop. Most Rev. William F. Murphy, Auxiliary Bishop. Most Rev. Francis X. Irwin, Auxiliary Bishop. Most Rev. Emilio Allue, S.D.B. Most Rev. Richard J. Malone, Auxiliary Bishop.

Diocese of Burlington, VT—Kenneth A. Angell, Bishop of Burlington.

Diocese of Fall River, MA—Most Rev. Sean P. O'Malley, O.F.M.Cap., Bishop of Fall River.

Diocese of Manchester, NH—Most Rev. John B. McCormack, Bishop of Manchester. Most Rev. Francis J. Christian, Auxiliary Bishop.

Diocese of Portland, ME—Most Rev. Joseph Gerry, O.S.B., Bishop of Portland. Most Rev. Michael R. Cote, Auxiliary Bishop.

Diocese of Springfield, MA—Most Rev. Thomas L. Dupre, Bishop of Springfield.

Diocese of Worcester, MA—Most Rev. Daniel P. Reilly, Bishop of Worcester. Most Rev. George Rueger, Auxiliary Bishop.

PROVINCE OF CHICAGO

Includes the State of Illinois.

Archdiocese of Chicago, IL—His Eminence Francis Cardinal George, O.M.I., Archbishop of Chicago. Most Rev. John R. Gorman, Auxiliary Bishop. Most Rev. Thad J. Jakubowski, Auxiliary Bishop. Most Rev. Raymond E. Goedert, Auxiliary Bishop. Most Rev. Gerald F. Kicanas, Auxiliary Bishop. Most Rev. Edwin M. Conway, Auxiliary Bishop. Most Rev. John R. Manz, Auxiliary Bishop. Most Rev. Joseph N. Perry, Auxiliary Bishop. Most Rev. Jerome E. Listecki, Auxiliary Bishop of Chicago.

Diocese of Belleville, IL—Most Rev. Wilton D. Gregory, Bishop of Belleville.

Diocese of Joliet, IL—Most Rev. Joseph L. Imesch, Bishop of Joliet. Most Rev. Roger L. Kaffer, Auxiliary Bishop.

Diocese of Peoria, IL—Most Rev. John J. Myers, Bishop of Peoria.

Diocese of Rockford, IL—Most Rev. Thomas G. Doran, Bishop of Rockford.

Diocese of Springfield, IL—Most Rev. George Lucas, Bishop of Springfield.

PROVINCE OF CINCINNATI

Includes the State of Ohio.

Archdiocese of Cincinnati, OH—Most Rev. Daniel E. Pilarczyk, Archbishop of Cincinnati. Most Rev. Carl K. Moeddel, Auxiliary Bishop.

Diocese of Cleveland, OH—Most Rev. Anthony M. Pilla, Bishop of Cleveland. Most Rev. A. Edward Pevec, Auxiliary Bishop. Most Rev. Alexander James Quinn, Auxiliary Bishop.

Diocese of Columbus, OH—Most Rev. James A. Griffin, Bishop of Columbus.

Diocese of Steubenville, OH—Most Rev. Gilbert I. Sheldon, Bishop of Steubenville.

Diocese of Toledo, OH—Most Rev. James R. Hoffman, Bishop of Toledo. Most Rev. Robert Donnelly, Auxiliary Bishop.

Diocese of Youngstown, OH—Most Rev. Thomas J. Tobin, Bishop of Youngstown.

PROVINCE OF DENVER

Includes the States of Colorado and Wyoming.

Archdiocese of Denver, CO—Most Rev. Charles J. Chaput, O.F.M.Cap., Archbishop of Denver. Most Rev. Jose H. Gomez, Auxiliary Bishop of Denver.

Diocese of Cheyenne, WY—Most Rev. Joseph Hart, Bishop of Cheyenne. Most Rev. David L. Ricken, Coadjutor Bishop of Cheyenne.

Diocese of Colorado Springs, CO—Most Rev. Richard C. Hanifen, Bishop of Colorado Springs.

Diocese of Pueblo, CO—Most Rev Arthur N. Tafoya, Bishop of Pueblo.

PROVINCE OF DETROIT

Includes the State of Michigan.

Archdiocese of Detroit, MI—His Eminence Adam Cardinal Maida, Archbishop of Detroit. Most Rev. Thomas J. Gumbleton, Auxiliary Bishop. Most Rev. Moses B. Anderson, S.S.E., Auxiliary Bishop. Most Rev. Kevin M. Britt, Auxiliary Bishop. Most Rev. John C. Nienstedt, Auxiliary Bishop. Most Rev. Allen H. Vigneron, Auxiliary Bishop. Most Rev. Leonard P. Blair, Auxiliary Bishop.

Diocese of Gaylord, MI—Most Rev. Patrick R. Cooney, Bishop of Gaylord.

Diocese of Grand Rapids, MI—Most Rev. Robert J. Rose, Bishop of Grand Rapids. Most Rev. Joseph C. McKinney, Auxiliary Bishop.

Diocese of Kalamazoo, MI—Most Rev. James A. Murray, Bishop of Kalamazoo.

Diocese of Lansing, MI—Most Rev. Carl F. Mengeling, Bishop of Lansing.

Diocese of Marquette, MI—Most Rev. James H. Garland, Bishop of Marquette.

Diocese of Saginaw, MI—Most Rev. Kenneth E. Untener, Bishop of Saginaw.

PROVINCE OF DUBUQUE

Includes the State of Iowa.

Archdiocese of Dubuque, IA—Most Rev. Jerome G. Hanus, O.S.B., Archbishop of Dubuque.

Diocese of Davenport, IA—Most Rev. William E. Franklin, Bishop of Davenport.

Diocese of Des Moines, IA—Most Rev. Joseph L. Charron, C.P.P.S., Bishop of Des Moines.

Diocese of Sioux City, IA—Most Rev. Daniel N. Dinardo, Bishop of Sioux City.

PROVINCE OF HARTFORD

Includes the States of Connecticut and Rhode Island.

Archdiocese of Hartford, CT—Most Rev. Daniel A. Cronin, Archbishop of Hartford. Most Rev. Peter A. Rosazza, Auxiliary Bishop. Most Rev. Christie A. Macaluso, Auxiliary Bishop.

Diocese of Bridgeport, CT—Most Rev. William E. Lori, Bishop of Bridgeport.

Diocese of Norwich, CT—Most Rev. Daniel A. Hart, Bishop of Norwich.

Diocese of Providence, RI—Most Rev. Robert E. Mulvee, Bishop of Providence.

PROVINCE OF INDIANAPOLIS

Includes the State of Indiana.

Archdiocese of Indianapolis, IN—Most Rev. Daniel M. Buechlein, O.S.B., Archbishop of Indianapolis.

Diocese of Evansville, IN—Most Rev. Gerald A. Gettelfinger, Bishop of Evansville.

Diocese of Fort Wayne-South Bend, IN—Most Rev. John D'Arcy, Bishop of Fort Wayne-South Bend. Most Rev. Daniel R. Jenky, C.S.C., Auxiliary Bishop.

Diocese of Gary, IN—Most Rev. Dale J. Melczek, Bishop of Gary.

Diocese of Lafayette in Indiana, IN—Most Rev. William Higi, Bishop of Lafayette in Indiana.

PROVINCE OF KANSAS CITY, KANSAS

Includes the State of Kansas.

Archdiocese of Kansas City, KS—Most Rev. James P. Keleher, Archbishop of Kansas City.

Diocese of Dodge City, KS—Most Rev. Ronald M. Gilmore, Bishop of Dodge City.

Diocese of Salina, KS—Most Rev. George K. Fitzsimons, Bishop of Salina.

Diocese of Wichita, KS—Most Rev. Eugene J. Gerber, Bishop of Wichita.

PROVINCE OF LOS ANGELES

Includes Southern California and Central California.

Archdiocese of Los Angeles, CA—His Eminence Roger Cardinal Mahony, Archbishop of Los Angeles. Most Rev. Thomas J. Curry, Auxiliary Bishop. Most Rev. Joseph M. Sartoris, Auxiliary Bishop. Most Rev. Gabino Zavala, Auxiliary Bishop. Most Rev. Gerald E. Wilkerson, Auxiliary Bishop. Most Rev. Edward W. Clark, Auxiliary Bishop.

Diocese of Fresno, CA—Most Rev. John T. Steinbock, Bishop of Fresno.

Diocese of Monterey, CA—Most Rev. Sylvester D. Ryan, Bishop of Monterey.

Diocese of Orange, CA—Most Rev. Tod D. Brown, Bishop of Orange. Most Rev. Jaime Soto, Auxiliary Bishop.

Diocese of San Bernardino, CA—Most Rev. Gerald R. Barnes, Bishop of San Bernardino.

Diocese of San Diego, CA—Most Rev. Robert Brom, Bishop of San Diego. Most Rev. Gilbert Chavez, Auxiliary Bishop.

PROVINCE OF LOUISVILLE

Includes the States of Kentucky and Tennessee.

Archdiocese of Louisville, KY—Most Rev. Thomas C. Kelly, O.P., Archbishop of Louisville.

Diocese of Covington, KY—Most Rev. Robert W. Muench, Bishop of Covington.

Diocese of Knoxville, TN—Most Rev. Joseph E. Kurtz, Bishop of Knoxville.

Diocese of Lexington, KY—Most Rev. J. Kendrick Williams, Bishop of Lexington.

Diocese of Memphis, TN—Most Rev. J. Terry Steib, S.V.D., Bishop of Memphis.

Diocese of Nashville, TN—Most Rev. Edward U. Kmiec, Bishop of Nashville.

Diocese of Owensboro, KY—Most Rev. John J. McRaith, Bishop of Owensboro.

PROVINCE OF MIAMI

Includes the State of Florida.

Archdiocese of Miami, FL—Most Rev. John C. Favalora, Archbishop of Miami. Most Rev. Agustin A. Roman, Auxiliary Bishop. Most Rev. Gilberto Fernandez, Auxiliary Bishop. Most Rev. Thomas Wenski, Auxiliary Bishop.

Diocese of Orlando, FL—Most Rev. Norbert Dorsey, C.P., Bishop of Orlando.

Diocese of Palm Beach, FL—Most Rev. Anthony J. O'Connell, Bishop of Palm Beach.

Diocese of Pensacola-Tallahassee, FL—Most Rev. John Ricard, S.S.J., Bishop of Pensacola-Tallahassee.

Diocese of St. Augustine, FL—Vacant See

Diocese of St. Petersburg, FL—Most Rev. Robert N. Lynch, Bishop of St. Petersburg.

Diocese of Venice, FL—Most Rev. John J. Nevins, Bishop of Venice.

PROVINCE OF MILWAUKEE

Includes the State of Wisconsin.

Archdiocese of Milwaukee, WI—Most Rev. Rembert G. Weakland, O.S.B., Archbishop of Milwaukee. Most Rev. Richard J. Sklba, Auxiliary Bishop.

Diocese of Green Bay, WI—Most Rev. Robert Banks, Bishop of Green Bay. Most Rev. Robert F. Morneau, Auxiliary Bishop.

Diocese of La Crosse, WI—Most Rev. Raymond L. Burke, Bishop of La Crosse.

Diocese of Madison, WI—Most Rev. William H. Bullock, Bishop of Madison. Most Rev. George O. Wirz, Auxiliary Bishop.

Diocese of Superior, WI—Most Rev. Raphael M. Fliss, Bishop of Superior.

PROVINCE OF MOBILE

Includes the states of Alabama and Mississippi.

Archdiocese of Mobile, AL—Most Rev. Oscar H. Lipscomb, Archbishop of Mobile.

Diocese of Birmingham, AL—Most Rev. David E. Foley, Bishop of Birmingham.

Diocese of Biloxi, MS—Most Rev. Joseph L. Howze, Bishop of Biloxi.

Diocese of Jackson MS—Most Rev. William R. Houck, Bishop of Jackson.

PROVINCE OF NEWARK

Includes the State of New Jersey.

Archdiocese of Newark, NJ—Vacant See. Most Rev. Dominic A. Marconi, Auxiliary Bishop. Most Rev. David Arias, O.A.R., Auxiliary Bishop. Most Rev. Charles J. McDonnell, Auxiliary Bishop. Most Rev. Paul G. Bootkoski, Auxiliary Bishop. Most Rev. Arthur J. Serratelli, Auxiliary Bishop.

Diocese of Camden, NJ—Most Rev. Nicholas A. DiMarzio, Bishop of Camden.

Diocese of Metuchen, NJ—Most Rev. Vincent DePaul Breen, Bishop of Metuchen.

Diocese of Paterson, NJ—Most Rev. Frank J. Rodimer, Bishop of Paterson.

Diocese of Trenton, NJ—Most Rev. John M. Smith, Bishop of Trenton.

PROVINCE OF NEW ORLEANS

Includes the State of Louisiana.

Archdiocese of New Orleans, LA—Most Rev. Francis B. Schulte, Archbishop of New Orleans. Most Rev. Alfred C. Hughes, Coadjutor Archbishop of New Orleans. Most Rev. Dominic Carmon, Auxiliary Bishop.

Diocese of Alexandria, LA—Most Rev. Sam Jacobs, Bishop of Alexandria.

Diocese of Baton Rouge, LA—Vacant See.

Diocese of Houma-Thibodaux, LA—Most Rev. Michael C. Jarrell.

Diocese of Lafayette, LA—Most Rev. Edward J. O'Donnell, Bishop of Lafayette.

Diocese of Lake Charles, LA—Most Rev. Edward K. Braxton, Bishop of Lake Charles.

Diocese of Shreveport, LA (1986)—Most Rev. William Friend, Bishop of Shreveport.

PROVINCE OF NEW YORK

Includes the State of New York.

Archdiocese of New York, NY—His Eminence Edward Cardinal Egan, Archbishop of New York. Most Rev. Anthony F. Mestice, Auxiliary Bishop. Most Rev. Francisco Garmendia, Auxiliary Bishop. Most Rev. William J. McCormack, Auxiliary Bishop. Most Rev. Robert A. Brucato, Auxiliary Bishop. Most Rev. James F. McCarthy, Auxiliary Bishop.

Diocese of Albany, NY—Most Rev. Howard J. Hubbard, Bishop of Albany.

Diocese of Brooklyn, NY—Most Rev. Thomas Daily, Bishop of Brooklyn. Most Rev. Joseph M. Sullivan, Auxiliary Bishop. Most Rev. Rene A. Valero, Auxiliary Bishop. Most Rev. Ignatius Catanello, Auxiliary Bishop.

Diocese of Buffalo, NY—Most Rev. Henry J. Mansell, Bishop of Buffalo. Most Rev. Edward M. Grosz, Auxiliary Bishop.

Diocese of Ogdensburg, NY—Most Rev. Gerald M. Barbarito, Bishop of Ogdensburg.

Diocese of Rochester, NY—Most Rev. Matthew H. Clark, Bishop of Rochester.

Diocese of Rockville Centre, NY—Vacant See. Most Rev. John C. Dunne, Auxiliary Bishop. Most Rev. Emil A. Wcela, Auxiliary Bishop.

Diocese of Syracuse, NY—Most Rev. James M. Moynihan, Bishop of Syracuse. Most Rev. Thomas J. Costello, Auxiliary Bishop.

PROVINCE OF OKLAHOMA CITY

Includes States of Arkansas and Oklahoma.

Archdiocese of Oklahoma City, OK—Most Rev. Eusebius J. Beltran, Archbishop of Oklahoma City.

Diocese of Little Rock, AR—Most Rev. J. Peter Sartain, Bishop of Little Rock.

Diocese of Tulsa, OK—Most Rev. Edward J. Slattery, Bishop of Tulsa.

PROVINCE OF OMAHA

Includes the State of Nebraska.

Archdiocese of Omaha, NE—Most Rev. Elden F. Curtiss, Archbishop of Omaha.

Diocese of Grand Island, NE—Most Rev. Lawrence J. McNamara, Bishop of Grand Island.

Diocese of Lincoln, NE—Most Rev. Fabian W. Bruskewitz, Bishop of Lincoln.

PROVINCE OF PHILADELPHIA

Includes the State of Pennsylvania.

Archdiocese of Philadelphia, PA—His Eminence Anthony Cardinal Bevilacqua, Archbishop of Philadelphia. Most Rev. Robert P. Maginnis, Auxiliary Bishop. Most Rev. Joseph F. Martino, Auxiliary Bishop.

Diocese of Allentown, PA—Most Rev. Edward P. Cullen Bishop of Allentown.

Diocese of Altoona-Johnstown, PA—Most Rev. Joseph V. Adamec, Bishop of Altoona-Johnstown.

Diocese of Erie, PA—Most Rev. Donald W. Trautman, Bishop of Erie.

Diocese of Greensburg, PA—Most Rev. Anthony G. Bosco, Bishop of Greensburg.

Diocese of Harrisburg, PA—Most Rev. Nicholas Dattilo, Bishop of Harrisburg.

Diocese of Pittsburgh, PA—Most Rev. Donald W. Wuerl, Bishop of Pittsburgh. Most Rev. William J. Winter, Auxiliary Bishop. Most Rev. David A. Zubik, Auxiliary Bishop.

Diocese of Scranton, PA—Most Rev. James C. Timlin, Bishop of Scranton. Most Rev. John M. Dougherty, Auxiliary Bishop.

PROVINCE OF PORTLAND IN OREGON

Includes the States of Oregon, Idaho and Montana.

Archdiocese of Portland, OR—Most Rev. John G. Vlazny, Archbishop of Portland in Oregon. Most Rev. Kenneth D. Steiner, Auxiliary Bishop.

Diocese of Baker, OR—Most Rev. Robert F. Vasa, Bishop of Baker.

Diocese of Boise, ID—Most Rev. Michael P. Driscoll, Bishop of Boise.

Diocese of Great Falls-Billings, MT—Most Rev. Anthony M. Milone, Bishop of Great Falls-Billings.

Diocese of Helena, MT—Most Rev. Robert C. Morlino, Bishop of Helena.

PROVINCE OF ST. LOUIS

Includes the State of Missouri.

Archdiocese of St. Louis, MO—Most Rev. Justin F. Regali, Archbishop of St. Louis. Most Rev. Joseph F. Naumann, Auxiliary Bishop. Most Rev. Michael J. Sheridan, Auxiliary Bishop.

Diocese of Jefferson City, MO—Most Rev. John R. Gaydos, Bishop of Jefferson City.

Diocese of Kansas City-St. Joseph, MO—Most Rev. Raymond J. Boland, Bishop of Kansas City-St. Joseph.

Diocese of Springfield-Cape Girardeau, MO—Most Rev. John J. Leibrecht, Bishop of Springfield-Cape Girardeau.

PROVINCE OF ST. PAUL AND MINNEAPOLIS

Includes the States of Minnesota, South Dakota and North Dakota.

Archdiocese of St. Paul and Minneapolis, MN—Most Rev. Harry J. Flynn, Archbishop of St. Paul and Minneapolis. Most Rev. Frederick F. Campbell, Auxiliary Bishop. Most Rev. Richard E. Pates, Auxiliary Bishop.

Diocese of Bismarck, ND—Most Rev. Paul A. Zipfel, Bishop of Bismarck.

Diocese of Crookston, MN—Most Rev. Victor H. Balke, Bishop of Crookston.

Diocese of Duluth, MN—Most Rev. Dennis M. Schnurr, Bishop of Duluth.

Diocese of Fargo, ND—Most Rev. James Sullivan, Bishop of Fargo.

Diocese of New Ulm, MN—Vacant See.

Diocese of Rapid City, SD—Most Rev. Blase Cupich, Bishop of Rapid City.

Diocese of St. Cloud, MN—Most Rev. John F. Kinney, Bishop of St. Cloud.
Diocese of Sioux Falls, SD—Most Rev. Robert J. Carlson, Bishop of Sioux Falls.
Diocese of Winona, MN—Most Rev. Bernard J. Harrington, Bishop of Winona.

PROVINCE OF SAN ANTONIO

Includes the State of Texas.

Archdiocese of San Antonio, TX—Most Rev. Patrick F. Flores, Archbishop of San Antonio. Most Rev. Thomas J. Flanagan, Auxiliary Bishop. Most Rev. Patrick J. Zurek, Auxiliary Bishop.
Diocese of Amarillo, TX—Most Rev. John W. Yanta, Bishop of Amarillo.
Diocese of Austin, TX— Most Rev. Gregory M. Aymond, Bishop of Austin.
Diocese of Beaumont, TX—Most Rev. Curtis J. Guillory, S.V.D., Bishop of Beaumont.
Diocese of Brownsville, TX—Most Rev. Raymundo J. Pena, Bishop of Brownsville.
Diocese of Corpus Christi, TX—Most Rev. Edmond Carmody, Bishop of Corpus Christi.
Diocese of Dallas, TX—Most Rev. Charles Grahmann, Bishop of Dallas. Most Rev. Joseph A. Galante, Coadjutor Bishop of Dallas.
Diocese of El Paso, TX—Most Rev. Amando Ochoa, Bishop of El Paso.
Diocese of Fort Worth, TX—Most Rev. Joseph P. Delaney, Bishop of Fort Worth.
Diocese of Galveston-Houston, TX—Most Rev. Joseph A. Fiorenza, Bishop of Galveston-Houston.
Diocese of Laredo, TX—Most Rev. James A. Tamayo, Bishop of Laredo.
Diocese of Lubbock, TX—Most Rev. Placido Rodriguez, C.M.F., Bishop of Lubbock.
Diocese of San Angelo, TX—Most Rev. Michael Pfeifer, O.M.I., Bishop of San Angelo.
Diocese of Tyler, TX— Most Rev. Alvaro del Rio Corrada, S.J., Bishop of Tyler.
Diocese of Victoria, TX—Most Rev. David E. Fellhauer, Bishop of Victoria.

PROVINCE OF SAN FRANCISCO

Includes Northern California and the States of Nevada, Utah and Hawaii.

Archdiocese of San Francisco, CA—Most Rev. William J. Levada, Archbishop of San Francisco. Most Rev. John Charles Wester, Auxiliary Bishop.
Diocese of Honolulu, HI—Most Rev. Francis X. DiLorenzo, Bishop of Honolulu.
Diocese of Las Vegas, NV—Vacant See.
Diocese of Oakland, CA—Most Rev. John S. Cummins, Bishop of Oakland.
Diocese of Reno, NV—Most Rev. Phillip F. Straling, Bishop of Reno.
Diocese of Sacramento, CA—Most Rev. William K. Weigand, Bishop of Sacramento. Most Rev. Richard J. Garcia, Auxiliary Bishop.
Diocese of Salt Lake City, UT—Most Rev. George H. Niederauer, Bishop of Salt Lake City.
Diocese of San Jose, CA—Most Rev. Patrick J. McGrath, Bishop of San Jose.
Diocese of Santa Rosa, CA— Most Rev. Daniel F. Walsh, Bishop of Santa Rosa.
Diocese of Stockton, CA—Most Rev. Stephen E. Blaire, Bishop of Stockton.

PROVINCE OF SANTA FE

Includes the States of New Mexico, and Arizona.

Archdiocese of Santa Fe, NM—Most Rev. Michael Sheehan, Archbishop of Santa Fe.
Diocese of Gallup, NM—Most Rev. Donald E. Pelotte, S.S.S., Bishop of Gallup.
Diocese of Las Cruces, NM—Most Rev. Ricardo Ramirez, C.S.B., Bishop of Las Cruces.
Diocese of Phoenix, AZ—Most Rev. Thomas J. O'Brien, Bishop of Phoenix.
Diocese of Tucson, AZ—Most Rev. Manuel D. Moreno, Bishop of Tucson.

PROVINCE OF SEATTLE

Includes the State of Washington.

Archdiocese of Seattle, WA—Most Rev. Alexander J. Brunett, Archbishop of Seattle. Most Rev. George L. Thomas, Auxiliary Bishop.
Diocese of Spokane, WA—Most Rev. William S. Skylstad, Bishop of Spokane.
Diocese of Yakima, WA—Most Rev. Carlos Sevilla, S.J., Bishop of Yakima.

PROVINCE OF WASHINGTON

Includes the District of Columbia, and Montgomery, Prince Georges, Charles, Calvert and St. Mary's Counties in Maryland, also Virgin Islands.

Archdiocese of Washington, DC—His Eminence Cardinal Theodore McCarrick, Archbishop of Washington. Most Rev. Leonard Olivier, S.V.D., Auxiliary Bishop.
Diocese of St. Thomas, V.I.—Most Rev. George V. Murry, S.J., Bishop of St. Thomas, Virgin Islands.
Military Archdiocese—Most Rev. Edwin F. O'Brien, Archbishop for the Military Services. Most Rev. Francis X. Roque, Auxiliary Bishop. Most Rev. Joseph J. Madera, M.Sp.S., Auxiliary Bishop. Most Rev. John J. Glynn, Auxiliary Bishop. Most Rev. John J. Bachmann, Auxiliary Bishop. Most Rev. John J. Kaising, Auxiliary Bishop.

EASTERN CATHOLIC JURISDICTIONS

ANTIOCHENE TRADITION

Maronite Rite—
Diocese of Saint Maron of Brooklyn—Most Rev. Hector Doueihi, Bishop St. Maron.
Diocese of Our Lady of Lebanon—Most Rev. Robert J. Shaheen, Bishop of Our Lady of Lebanon.

ARMENIAN TRADITION

Armenian Catholic Exarchate of U.S.A. and Canada—Most Rev. Manuel Batakian, Apostolic Exarch for the Armenians.

CHALDEAN TRADITION

Eparchy of St. Thomas the Apostle—Most Rev. Ibrahim Ibrahim, Eparch of St. Thomas the Apostle.

CONSTANTINOPOLITAN TRADITION

Melkite - Greek Rite—
Diocese of Newton—Most Rev. John A. Elya, B.S., Bishop of Newton. Most Rev. Nicholas J. Samra, Auxiliary Bishop.
Romanian Rite—
Diocese of St. George's in Canton—Most Rev. John M. Botean, Eparch of St. George's in Canton.
Ruthenian Rite—
Metropolitan Archdiocese of Pittsburgh—Most Rev. Judson M. Procyk, Archbishop of Pittsburgh Byzantine Rite.
Diocese of Parma—Most Rev. Basil Schott,o.f.m., Bishop of Parma
Diocese of Passaic—Most Rev. Andrew Pataki, Bishop of Passaic.
Diocese of Van Nuys—Vacant See
Russian Rite—
Two parishes—
Ukrainian Rite—
Metropolitan Archdiocese of Philadelphia—Most Rev. Stefan Soroka, Archbishop of Philadlephia for Ukrainian Catholics.
Diocese of St. Josaphat in Parma—Most Rev. Robert Moskal, Bishop of St. Josaphat in Parma.
Diocese of St. Nicholas—Vacant See
Diocese of Stamford—Most Rev. Basil Losten, Bishop of Stamford.
Syrian Rite
Diocese of Our Lady of Deliverance of Newark—Most Rev. Joseph Younan, Bishop of Our Lady of Deliverance.
Syro-Malabar—
Eparchy of St. Thomas of Chicago of the Syro-Malabarians and Permanent Apostolic Visitator in Canada—Most Rev. Jacob Angadiath, Bishop of St. Thomas of Chicago.

AN ALPHABETICAL LIST OF THE

Cardinals, Archbishops, Bishops, Archabbots & Abbots of the United States

CARDINALS

His Eminence Luis Cardinal Aponte Martinez, Archbishop of San Juan, P.O. Box S-1967, San Juan, PR 00903.
His Eminence William Cardinal Baum, Prefect of Sacred Congregation for Catholic Education, Piazza Pio XII, 00120 Vatican City State, Europe.
His Eminence Anthony Cardinal Bevilacqua, Archbishop of Philadelphia, 222 N. 17th St., Philadelphia, PA 19103.
His Eminence Edward Cardinal Egan, Archbishop of New York, 1011 First Ave., New York, NY 10022.
His Eminence Francis Cardinal George, *o.m.i.*, Archbishop of Chicago, 155 E. Superior St., Chicago, IL 60611.
His Eminence James Cardinal Hickey, Retired Archbishop of Washington DC, P.O. Box 29260, Washington, DC 20017.
His Eminence William Cardinal Keeler, Archbishop of Baltimore, 320 Cathedral St., Baltimore, MD 21201.
His Eminence Bernard Cardinal Law, Archbishop of Boston, 2101 Commonwealth Ave., Boston, MA 02135.
His Eminence Roger Cardinal Mahony, Archbishop of Los Angeles, 3424 Wilshire Blvd., Los Angeles, CA 90010-2241.
His Eminence Adam Cardinal Maida, Archbishop of Detroit, 1234 Washington Blvd., Detroit, MI 48226.
His Eminence Theodore Cardinal McCarrick, Archbishop of Washington DC, P.O. Box 29260, Washington, DC 20017.
His Eminence Francis Cardinal Stafford, President - Pontifical Council for the Laity, Piazza San Calisto 16, Vatican City State, Europe 00120.
His Eminence Edmund Cardinal Szoka, President Pontifical Commission, 00120 Vatican City State, Europe.

ARCHBISHOPS

His Excellency,
The Most Reverend

Apuron, Anthony Sablan, *o.f.m.cap.*, Archbishop of Agana, Cuesta San Ramon Agana, Guam 96910.
Beltran, Eusebius J., Archbishop of Oklahoma City, P.O. Box 32180, Oklahoma City, OK 73123.
Borders, William D., Retired Archbishop of Baltimore, 320 Cathedral St., Baltimore, MD 21201.
Brunett, Alexander J., Archbishop of Seattle, 910 Marion St., Seattle, WA 98104.
Buechlein, Daniel, *o.s.b.*, Archbishop of Indianapolis, 1400 N. Meridian St., P.O. Box 1410, Indianapolis, IN 46206.
Chaput, Charles J., *o.f.m.cap.*, Archbishop of Denver, 1300 Steele St., Denver, CO 80210.
Cronin, Daniel A., Archbishop of Hartford, 134 Farmington Ave., Hartford, CT 06105.
Curtiss, Elden F., Archbishop of Omaha, 100 N. 62nd St., Omaha, NE 68132-2795.
Dimino, Joseph T., Retired Archbishop of Military Services, P.O. Box 4469, Washington, DC 20017.
Donoghue, John F., Archbishop of Atlanta, 680 W. Peachtree St., N.W., Atlanta, GA 30308.
Favalora, John C., Archbishop of Miami, 9401 Biscayne Blvd., Miami Shore, FL 33138.
Flores, Patrick F., Archbishop of San Antonio, 2600 W. Woodlawn Ave., San Antonio, TX 78228.
Flynn, Harry J., Archbishop of St. Paul and Minneapolis, 226 Summit Ave., St. Paul, MN 55102.
Foley, John P., Archbishop, President of the Pontifical Council for Social Communications, 00120 Vatican City State, Europe.
Gerety, Peter Leo, Retired Archbishop of Newark, 31 Mulberry St., Newark, NJ 07102.
Gonzalez, Roberto O., *o.f.m.*, Archbishop of San Juan, P.O. Box S-1967, San Juan, PR 00903.
Hannan, Philip M., Retired Archbishop of New Orleans, FOCUS Worldwide Television Network, 106 Metairie Lawn Dr., Metairie, LA 70001-5449.
Hanus, Jerome, *o.s.b.*, Archbishop of Dubuque, 1229 Mt. Loretto Ave., P.O. Box 479, Dubuque, IA 52004-0479.
Hughes, Alfred C., Coadjutor Archbishop of New Orleans, and Diocesan Administrator of Baton Rouge, 1800 South Acadian Thruway, P.O. Box 2028, Baton Rouge, LA 70821-2028.
Hunthausen, Raymond G., Retired Archbishop of Seattle, 910 Marion St., Seattle, WA 98104.
Hurley, Francis T., Archbishop Emeritus of Anchorage, P.O. Box 2239, Anchorage, AK 99510.
Keleher, James P., Archbishop of Kansas City, Kansas, 12615 Parallel Parkway, Kansas City, KS 66109.
Kelly, Thomas, *o.p.*, Archbishop of Louisville, 212 E. College St., Louisville, KY 40201.
Kucera, Daniel W., *o.s.b.*, Retired Archbishop of Dubuque, 13952 E. Marina Dr. -#612, Aurora, CO 80014.
Levada, William J., Archbishop of San Francisco, One Peter York Way, San Francisco, CA 94109.
Lipscomb, Oscar H., Archbishop of Mobile, 400 Government St., Mobile, AL 36633.
Marcinkus, Paul C., Working Outside Chicago Archdiocese, Vatican City State, Europe.
McCarthy, Edward A., Retired Archbishop of Miami, St. John Vianney College Seminary, 2900 S.W. 87th Ave., Miami, FL 33138.
McDonough, Thomas J., Retired Archbishop of Louisville, St. Francis Country Home, 1412 Lansdowne Ave., Darby, PA 19023.
O'Brien, Edwin F., Archbishop of the Military Services USA, P.O. Box 4469, Washington, DC 20017.

His Excellency,
The Most Reverend

Pilarczyk, Daniel E., Archbishop of Cincinnati, 100 E. 8th St., Cincinnati, OH 45202.
Procyk, Judson M., Archbishop of Pittsburgh Byzantine, 66 Riverview Ave., Pittsburgh, PA 15214.
Quinn, John R., Retired Archbishop of San Francisco, 322 Middlefield Rd., Menlo Park, CA 94025.
Rigali, Justin F., Archbishop of St. Louis, 4445 Lindell Blvd., St. Louis, MO 63108.
Roach, John R., Retired Archbishop of St. Paul-Minneapolis, 226 Summit Ave., St. Paul, MN 55102.
Salatka, Charles A., Retired Archbishop of Oklahoma City, Box 23205, Oklahoma City, OK 73123.
Sanchez, Robert F., Former Archbishop of Santa Fe, Catholic Center, St. Joseph's Pl., N.W., Albuquerque, NM 87120.
Schwietz, Roger L., *o.m.i.*, Archbishop of Anchorage, P.O. Box 2239, Anchorage, AK 99510.
Schleck, Charles A., *c.s.c.*, Titular Archbishop of Africa, Congregation for Evangelization, Palazzo di Propaganda Fide, Piazza di Spagna 48, 00187 Rome, Italy.
Schulte, Francis B., Archbishop of New Orleans, 7887 Walmsley Ave., New Orleans, LA 70125-3496.
Sheehan, Michael J., Archbishop of Santa Fe, Catholic Center, 4000 Saint Joseph's Place, N.W., Albuquerque, NM 87120.
Soroka, Stefan, Archbishop of the Ukrainian Catholic Archeparchy of Philadelphia, 827 N. Franklin St., Philadelphia, PA 19123.
Strecker, Ignatius J., Retired Archbishop of Kansas City in Kansas, 3408 Minnesota Ave., Kansas City, KS 66102.
Sulyk, Stephen, Archbishop Emeritus of Philadelphia Ukrainian, 827 N. Franklin St., Philadelphia, PA 19123.
Vlazny, John G., Archbishop of Portland Oregon, 2838 E. Burnside St., Portland, OR 97214-1895.
Weakland, Rembert G., *o.s.b.* Archbishop of Milwaukee, 3501 S. Lake Dr., St. Francis, WI 53235-3703.
Zayek, Francis M., Retired Archbishop and Former Eparch (Bishop) of St. Maron of Brooklyn, 4010 Galt Ocean Dr.-Apt. 1230, Fort Lauderdale, FL 33308.

BISHOPS

His Excellency,
The Most Reverend

Adamec, Joseph V., Bishop of Altoona-Johnstown, 126 Logan Blvd., Hollidaysburg, PA 16648.
Ahern, Patrick V., Retired Auxiliary Bishop of New York, St. Thomas More, 65 E. 89th St., New York, NY 10128.
Allue, Emilio, *s.d.b.*, Auxiliary Bishop of Boston, 327 Gorham St., Lowell, MA 01852-3310.
Anderson, Moses B., *s.s.e.*, Auxiliary Bishop of Detroit, 13305 Grove, Detroit, MI 48235-4296.
Angadiath, Jacob, Bishop of Eparchy of St. Thomas of Chicago of the Syro-malabarians, Mar Thoma Shleeha Center, 5000 St. Charles Rd., Bellwood, IL 60104.
Angell, Kenneth A., Bishop of Burlington, 351 North Ave.-P.O. Box 526, Burlington, VT 05402-0526.
Arias, David, *o.a.r.*, Auxiliary Bishop of Newark, St. Joseph of the Palisade Rectory, 6401 Palisade Ave., West New York, NJ 07093.
Arzube, Juan, Retired Auxiliary Bishop of Los Angeles, Sacred Heart Church, 2889 N. Lincoln Ave., Altadena, CA 91001.
Aymond, Gregory M., Bishop of Austin, 1600 N. Congress Ave.-P.O. Box 13327, Austin, TX 78711.

His Excellency,
The Most Reverend

Baker, Robert J., Bishop of Charleston, 119 Broad St., -P.O. Box 818, Charleston, SC 29402.
Balke, Victor, Bishop of Crookston, 1200 Memorial Dr., Crookston, MN 56716.
Baltakis, Paul A., *o.f.m.*, Titular Bishop of Egara & Lithuanian Catholics, 361 Highland Blvd., Brooklyn, NY 11207.
Banks, Robert J., Bishop of Green Bay, 1910 S. Webster Ave.-P.O. Box 23825, Green Bay, WI 54305-3825.
Barbarito, Gerald, Bishop of Ogdensburg, 622 Washington St.-P.O. Box 369 Ogdensburg, NY 13669.
Barnes, Gerald R., Bishop of San Bernardino, 1201 E. Highland Ave., San Bernardino, CA 92405.
Batakian, Manuel, Apostolic Exarch for Armenian Catholics in the U.S. and Canada, 110 E. 12th St., New York, NY 10003-5395.
Begley, Michael J., Retired Bishop of Charlotte, 1315 Greensboro Rd., High Point, NC 27260.
Bennett, Gordon D., *s.j.*, Auxiliary Bishop of Balitmore, Pres.-Loyola High School, 320 Cathedral St., Baltimore, MD 21201.
Blair, Leonard P., Auxiliary Bishop of Detroit, 1234 Washington Blvd., Detroit, MI 48226.
Blaire, Stephen E., Bishop of Stockton, 1125 N. Lincoln St., Stockton, CA 95203.
Boland, J. Kevin, Bishop of Savannah, 601 E. Liberty St., Savannah, GA 31401.
Boland, Raymond J., Bishop of Kansas City-St. Joseph, P.O. Box 419037, Kansas City, MO 64141-6037.
Boles, John P., Auxiliary Bishop of Boston, 307 Bowdoin St., Dorchester, MA 02122.
Bootkoski, Paul G., Auxiliary Bishop of Newark, Sacred Heart, 89 Ridge St., Newark, NJ 01704.
Bosco, Anthony G., Bishop of Greensburg, 723 E. Pittsburgh St., Greensburg, PA 15601.
Botean, John M., Bishop of St. George's in Canton, P.O. Box 7189, Canton, OH 44705-0189.
Braxton, Edward K., Bishop of Lake Charles, 414 Iris St., Lake Charles, LA 70602.
Breen, Vincent DePaul, Bishop of Metuchen, Ten Library Pl., Metuchen, NJ 08840.
Breitenbeck, Joseph M., Retired Bishop of Grand Rapids, 660 Burton St., S.E., Grand Rapids, MI 49507.
Britt, Kevin M., Auxiliary Bishop of Detroit, 1234 Washington Blvd., Detroit, MI 48226.
Broderick, Edwin B., Former Bishop of Albany, 900 Park Ave., New York, NY 10021.
Brom, Robert H., Bishop of San Diego, P.O. Box 85728, San Diego, CA 92186-5728.
Brown, Tod D., Bishop of Orange, Marywood Center, 2811 E. Villa Real Dr., Orange, CA 92867.
Brucato, Robert A., Auxiliary Bishop of New York, 1011 First Ave., New York, NY 10022.
Bruskewitz, Fabian W., Bishop of Lincoln, 5301 A Street, Lincoln, NE 68510.
Bullock, William H., Bishop of Madison, 3577 High Point Rd., -P.O. Box 44983, Madison, WI 53744-4983.
Burke, Raymond L., Bishop of La Crosse, 3710 East Avenue, S., Box 4004, La Crosse, WI 54602-4004.
Buswell, Charles A., Retired Bishop of Pueblo, Villa Pueblo Towers, 111 Bonforte Blvd., #210, Pueblo, CO 81001-1837.
Camacho, Tomas A., Bishop of Chalan Kanoa, Our Lady of Mt. Carmel, P.O. Box 745, Saipan, MP 9695.
Campbell, Frederick F., Auxiliary Bishop of St. Paul and Minneapolis, 226 Summit Ave., St. Paul, MN 55102.

His Excellency,
The Most Reverend

Carlson, Robert J., Bishop of Sioux Falls, 523 N. Duluth Ave., Sioux Falls, SD 57104.

Carmody, Edmond, Bishop of Corpus Christi, 620 Lipan St.,-P.O. Box 2620 Corpus Christi, TX 78403-2620.

Carmon, Dominic, *s.v.d.*, Auxiliary Bishop of New Orleans, P.O. Box 641000, Kenner, LA 70064-1000.

Casiano-Vargas, Ulises, Bishop of Mayaguez, P.O. Box 2272, Mayaguez, PR 00708.

Catanello, Ignatius, Auxiliary Bishop of Brooklyn, 175-20 74th Ave., Brooklyn, NY 11202.

Charron, Joseph L., *c.pp.s.*, Bishop of Des Moines, P.O. Box 1816, 601 Grand Ave., Des Moines, IA 50306-5071.

Chavez, Gilbert E., Auxiliary Bishop of San Diego, 2020 Alaquinas Dr., San Ysidro, CA 92073.

Chedid, John, Retired Bishop of Our Lady of Lebanon of Los Angeles, 333 S. San Vicente Blvd., Los Angeles, CA 90048.

Christian, Francis J., Auxiliary Bishop of Manchester, St. Joseph Cathedral, 145 Lowell St., Manchester, NH 03105.

Clark, Edward W., Auxiliary Bishop of Los Angeles, Our Lady of the Angels Pastoral Region, 2636 South Mansfield Ave., Los Angeles, CA 90016-3512.

Clark, Matthew H., Bishop of Rochester, 1150 Buffalo Rd., Rochester, NY 14624.

Clinch, Harry A., Retired Bishop of Monterey, 3400 Paul Sweet Rd., #C-119, Santa Cruz, CA 95065.

Connolly, Thomas J., Former Bishop of Baker, P.O. Box 5999, Bend, OR 97708.

Conway, Edwin M., Auxiliary Bishop of Chicago, 1651 W. Diversey, Chicago, IL 60614.

Cooney, Patrick R., Bishop of Gaylord, 611 North St., Gaylord, MI 49735-8349.

Corrada del Rio, Alvaro, *s.j.*, Bishop of Tyler, 1015 E.S.E. Loop 323, Tyler, TX 75701-9663.

Costello, Thomas J., Auxiliary Bishop of Syracuse, P.O. Box 511, Syracuse, NY 13201.

Cote, Michael R., Auxiliary Bishop of Portland in Maine, 510 Ocean Ave., P.O. Box 11559, Portland, OR 04104-7559.

Crowley, Joseph R., Retired Auxiliary Bishop of Fort Wayne-South Bend, 1240 Honan Dr., South Bend, IN 46614.

Cullen, Edward P., Bishop of Allentown, P.O. Box F., 4029 W. Tilghman St., Allentown, PA 19103.

Cummins, John S., Bishop of Oakland, 634 21st St., Oakland, CA 94612.

Cupich, Blase, Bishop of Rapid City, 606 Cathedral Dr., Rapid City, SD 57709.

Curlin, William G., Bishop of Charlotte, P.O. Box 36776, Charlotte, NC 28236.

Curry, Thomas J., Auxiliary Bishop of Los Angeles, Santa Barbara Pastoral Region, 3240 Calle Pinon, Santa Barbara, CA 93105.

Daily, Thomas V., Bishop of Brooklyn, P.O. Box C, Brooklyn, NY 11202.

Daly, James J., Former Auxiliary Bishop of Rockville Centre, 50 N. Park Ave., Rockville Centre, NY 11570-4129.

D'Antonio, Nicholas, *o.f.m.*, Retired Vicar for Latin American Apostolate, Archdiocese of New Orleans, Chateau de Notre Dame, Room 416, 2820 Burdette St., New Orleans, LA 70125.

D'Arcy, John M., Bishop of Fort Wayne-South Bend, P.O. Box 390, Fort Wayne, IN 46801.

Dattilo, Nicholas, Bishop of Harrisburg, 4800 Union Deposit Rd., P.O. Box 2153, Harrisburg, PA 17105.

Delaney, Joseph P., Bishop of Fort Worth, 800 West Loop 820 South, Fort Worth, TX 76108.

DeSimone, Louis A., Former Auxiliary Bishop of Philadelphia, 2422 S. 17th St., Philadelphia, PA 19145.

DiLorenzo, Francis X., Bishop of Honolulu, 1184 Bishop St., Honolulu, HI 96813.

DiMarzio, Nicholas A., Bishop of Camden, 631 Market St., Camden, NJ 08102.

DiNardo, Daniel N. DiNardo, Bishop of Sioux City, 1821 Jackson St. - P.O. Box 3379, Sioux City, IA 51102-3379.

Donnelly, Robert, Auxiliary Bishop of Toledo, 2544 Parkwood Ave., Toledo, OH 43610.

Donovan, Paul V., Retired Bishop of Kalamazoo, 238 Falkirk, Kalamazoo, MI 49006.

Doran, Thomas G., Bishop of Rockford, 1245 North Court St., Rockford, IL 61103.

Dorsey, Norbert L., *c.p.*, Bishop of Orlando, 421 E. Robinson, P.O. Box 1800, Orlando, FL 32802-1800.

Doueihi, Hector, Bishop of the Maronite Eparchy of St. Maron of Brooklyn, Our Lady of Lebanon Cathedral, 109 Remsen St., Brooklyn, NY 11201-4212.

Dougherty, John M., Auxiliary Bishop of Scranton, 300 Wyoming Ave., Scranton, PA 18503.

Driscoll, Michael P., Bishop of Boise, 303 Federal Way, Boise, ID 83705-5925.

Dudick, Michael J., Retired Bishop of Passaic, 32 Lakeview Trail, Sugarloaf, PA 18249-1043.

His Excellency,
The Most Reverend

Dudley, Paul V., Retired Bishop of Sioux Falls, Church of St. Dominic, 116 North Linden, Northfield, MN 55057-1435.

DuMaine, R. Pierre, Former Bishop of San Jose, 20 Willow Rd., - Unit 43, Menlo Park, CA 94025.

Dunne, John C., Auxiliary Bishop of Rockville Centre, P.O. Box 39, Farmingdale, NY 11735-0039.

Dupre, Thomas L., Bishop of Springfield, P.O. Box 1730, Springfield, MA 01105.

Elya, John A. *b.s.o.*, Eparch of Newton, 158 Pleasant St., Brookline, MA 02446.

Fellhauer, David E., Bishop of Victoria, P.O. Box 4070, Victoria, TX 77903.

Fernandez, Gilberto, Auxiliary Bishop of Miami, St. John Vianney College Seminary, 2900 S.W. 87th St., Miami, FL 33165.

Ferrario, Joseph A., Retired Bishop of Honolulu, 45 N. Kalaheo Ave., Kailua, HI 96734.

Fiorenza, Joseph A., Bishop of Galveston-Houston, 1700 San Jacinto, Houston, TX 77002.

Fitzpatrick, John J., Retired Bishop of Brownsville, P.O. Box 2279, Brownsville, TX 78522-2279.

Fitzsimons, George K., Bishop of Salina, P.O. Box 980, Salina, KS 67402-0980.

Flanagan, Thomas J., Auxiliary Bishop of San Antonio, P.O. Box 28410, San Antonio, TX 78228-0410.

Fliss, Raphael M., Bishop of Superior, 1201 Hughitt Ave., P.O. Box 969, Superior, WI 54880.

Foley, David E., Bishop of Birmingham, P.O. Box 12047, Birmingham, AL 35202-2047.

Forst, Marion F., Retired Bishop of Dodge City, Villa St. Francis, 16600 West 126th St., Olathe, KS 66062.

Franklin, William E., Bishop of Davenport, 2761 Scott St., Davenport, IA 52803.

Franzetta, Benedict C., Retired Auxiliary Bishop of Youngstown, 144 W. Wood St., Youngstown, OH 44503.

Frey, Gerard L., Retired Bishop of Lafayette, P.O. Drawer 3387, Lafayette, LA 70502.

Friend, William B., Bishop of Shreveport, 3500 Fairfield Ave., Shreveport, LA 71104-4108.

Galante, Joseph A., Coadjutor Bishop of Dallas, 3725 Blackburn, P.O. Box 190507, Dallas, TX 75219.

Garcia, Richard J., Auxiliary Bishop of Sacramento, 2110 Broadway, Sacramento, CA 95818.

Garland, James H., Bishop of Marquette, 300 Rock St., P.O. Box 550, Marquette, MI 49855.

Garmendia, Francis, Auxiliary Bishop of New York, St. Thomas Aquinas, 1900 Crotona Parkway, Bronx, NY 10460.

Gaydos, John R., Bishop of Jefferson City, Bishop's House, P.O. Box 417, Jefferson City, MO 65102.

Gelineau, Louis E., Retired Bishop of Providence, One Cathedral Square, Providence, RI 02903.

Gendron, Odore J., Retired Bishop of Manchester, St. Joseph Cathedral Rectory, 145 Lowell St., Manchester, NH 03104-6135.

Gerber, Eugene J., Bishop of Wichita, 307 E. Central Ave., Wichita, KS 67202.

Gerry, Joseph J., *o.s.b.*, Bishop of Portland (in Maine), 510 Ocean Ave., Portland, ME 04101.

Gettelfinger, Gerald A., Bishop of Evansville, 3980 Woodcastle, Evansville, IN 47711.

Gilmore, Ronald M., Bishop of Dodge City, 910 Central Ave. - Box 137, Dodge City, KS 67801.

Glynn, John J., Auxiliary Bishop of the Military Services, P.O. Box 4469, Washington, DC 20017-0469.

Goedert, Raymond E., Auxiliary Bishop of Chicago, 155 E. Superior St., Chicago, IL 60690.

Gomez, Jose H., Auxiliary Bishop of Denver, 1300 Steele St., Denver, CO 80210.

Gorman, John R., Auxiliary Bishop of Chicago, 2330 W. 118th St., Chicago, IL 60643.

Gossman, F. Joseph, Bishop of Raleigh, 715 Nazareth, Raleigh, NC 27606.

Gottwald, George J., Retired Auxiliary Bishop of St. Louis, c/o General Delivery, P.O. Box 220, Valles Mines, MO 63087.

Gracida, Rene H., Retired Bishop of Corpus Christi, 620 Lipan St., Corpus Christi, TX 78403-2620.

Grady, Thomas J., Retired Bishop of Orlando, P.O. Box 1800, Orlando, FL 32802-1800.

Grahmann, Charles V., Bishop of Dallas, 3725 Blackburn, P.O. Box 190507, Dallas, TX 75219.

Gregory, Wilton D., Bishop of Belleville, 222 South Third St., Belleville, IL 62220.

Griffin, James A., Bishop of Columbus, 198 E. Broad St., Columbus, OH 43215.

Grosz, Edward M., Auxiliary Bishop of Buffalo, St. Stanislaus Kostka Parish, 2437 Niagara St., Niagara Falls, NY 14303-1925.

Guillory, Curtis J., Bishop of Beaumont, 703 Archie St.- P.O. Box 3948, Beaumont, TX 77704-3948.

His Excellency,
The Most Reverend

Gumbleton, Thomas J., Auxiliary Bishop of Detroit, 4860 15th St., Detroit, MI 48208.

Ham, J. Richard, *m.m.*, Retired Auxiliary Bishop of St. Paul-Minneapolis, St. Teresa's Residence, Maryknoll Headquarters, Ossining, NY 10545.

Hanifen, Richard C., Bishop of Colorado Springs, 29 West Kiowa St., Colorado Springs, CO 80903-1498.

Harrington, Bernard J., Bishop of Winona, 55 W. Sanborn St. - P.O. Box 588, Winona, MN 55987.

Harrison, Frank J., Retired Bishop of Syracuse, 6655 Kirkville Rd., East Syracuse, NY 13057.

Hart, Daniel A., Bishop of Norwich, 201 Broadway, P.O. Box 587, Norwich, CT 06360.

Hart, Joseph H., Bishop of Cheyenne, Box 1468, Cheyenne, WY 82003-1468.

Head, Edward D., Retired Bishop of Buffalo, 77 Oakland Place, Buffalo, NY 14222.

Higi, William L., Bishop of Lafayette in Indiana, 610 Lingle Ave., Lafayette, IN 47902.

Hoffman, James R., Bishop of Toledo, 2544 Parkwood Ave., Toledo, OH 43610.

Hogan, James J., Retired Bishop of Altoona- Johnstown, 126 Logan Blvd., Hollidaysburg, PA 16648.

Houck, William R., Bishop of Jackson, Mailing Address: P.O. Box 2248, Jackson, MS 39225.

Howze, Joseph L., Bishop of Biloxi, P.O. Box 1189, Biloxi, MS 39533.

Hubbard, Howard J., Bishop of Albany, 125 Eagle St., Albany, NY 12203.

Hughes, Edward T., Retired Bishop of Metuchen, 10 Library Pl., Metuchen, NJ 08840.

Hughes, William A., Retired Bishop of Covington, Cathedral Basilica of the Assumption, 1140 Madison Ave., Covington, KY 41011-3116.

Ibrahim, Ibrahim, Bishop-Eparch to St. Thomas the Apostle, 25585 Berg Rd., Southfield, MI 48034.

Imesch, Joseph L., Bishop of Joliet, 425 Summit St., Joliet, IL 60435.

Irwin, Francis X., Auxiliary Bishop of Boston, 2 Gardner St., Peabody, MA 01960-1896.

Jacobs, Sam, Bishop of Alexandria, P.O. Box 7417, Alexandria, LA 71306.

Jakubowski, Thad J., Auxiliary Bishop of Chicago, 6002 W. Berteau Ave., Chicago, IL 60634-7720.

Jarrell, Charles Michael, Bishop of Houma-Thibodaux, P.O. Box 505, 2779 Hwy. 311, Schriever, LA 70395.

Jenky, Daniel R., *c.s.c.*, Auxiliary Bishop of Fort Wayne-South Bend, University of Notre Dame, Fisher Graduate Residences, Notre Dame, IN 46556-5676.

Kaffer, Roger L., Auxiliary Bishop of Joliet, 425 Summit St., Joliet, IL 60435.

Kaising, John J., Auxiliary Bishop of the Archdiocese for the Military Services, P.O. Box 4469, Washington, DC 20017.

Kicanas, Gerald F., Auxiliary Bishop of Chicago, 200 N. Milwaukee, Suite 200, Libertyville, IL 60048-2250.

Kinney, John F., Bishop of St. Cloud, 214 Third Ave., South, Box 1248, St. Cloud, MN 56302-1248.

Kmiec, Edward U., Bishop of Nashville, 2400 Twenty-First Ave., South, Nashville, TN 37212.

Kurtz, Joseph E., Bishop of Knoxville, 805 Northshore Dr., S.W. – P.O. Box 11127, Knoxville, TN 37939-1127.

Kuzma, George M., Retired Bishop of Van Nuys, Byzantine Catholic Eparchy of Van Nuys, 8105 North 16th St., Phoenix, AZ 85020.

Larkin, W. Thomas, Retired Bishop of St. Petersburg, P.O. Box 40200, St. Petersburg, FL 33743.

Leibrecht, John J., Bishop of Springfield-Cape Girardeau, The Catholic Center, 601 S. Jefferson, Springfield, MO 65806-3143.

Lessard, Raymond W., Retired Bishop of Savannah, St. Vincent de Paul Seminary, 10701 S. Military Trail, Boynton Beach, FL 33436-4899.

Listecki, Jerome E., Auxiliary Bishop of Chicago, St. Ignatius Parish, 6559 N. Glenwood, Chicago, IL 60626.

Lohmuller, Martin N., Retired Auxiliary Bishop of Philadelphia, Villa Maria House of Studies, King Rd.- P.O. Box 701, Immaculata, PA 19345.

Lori, William E., Bishop of Bridgeport, 238 Jewett Ave., Bridgeport, CT 06606-2892.

Losten, Basil, Bishop of Stamford, 14 Peveril Rd., Stamford, CT 06902-3019

Lotocky, Innocent, *o.s.b.m.*, Retired Bishop of St. Nicholas in Chicago, 2245 W. Rice St., Chicago, IL 60622.

Loverde, Paul S., Bishop of Arlington, 200 N. Glebe Rd., Arlington, VA 22203.

Lucas, George J., Bishop of Springfield in Illinois, 1615 W. Washington St., Box 3187, Springfield, IL 62708.

Lucker, Raymond A., Retired Bishop of New Ulm, Leo C. Byrne Res., 60 S. Mississippi River Blvd., #318, St. Paul, MN 55105-1052.

Lynch, George E., Retired Auxiliary Bishop of Raleigh, P.O. Box 130, Bronx, NY 10470-0130.

His Excellency,
The Most Reverend

Lynch, Robert N., Bishop of St. Petersburg, P.O. Box 40200, St. Petersburg, FL 33743-0200.
Lyne, Timothy J., Retired Auxiliary Bishop of Chicago, 730 N. Wabash, Chicago, IL 60611.
Macaluso, Christie A., Auxiliary Bishop of Hartford, 134 Farmington Ave., Hartford, CT 06105-3784.
Madera, Joseph J., *m.sp.s.*, Auxiliary Bishop of Military Services, P.O. Box 4469, Washington, DC 20017-0469.
Maguire, Joseph F., Retired Bishop of Springfield, 68 Elliot St., Springfield, MA 01101.
Maginnis, Robert P., Auxiliary Bishop of Philadelphia, St. Colman Rectory, 11 Simpson Rd., Ardmore, PA 19003-2812.
Mahoney, James P., Retired Auxiliary Bishop of New York, Assumption Parish, 131 Union Ave., Peekskill, NY 10566.
Malone, Richard J., Auxiliary Bishop of Boston, 236 Pleasant St., Weymouth, MA 02190.
Maloney, Charles G., Retired Auxiliary Bishop of Louisville, P.O. Box 1073, Louisville, KY 40201.
Malooly, William Francis, Auxiliary Bishop of Baltimore, 320 Cathedral St., Baltimore, MD 21201.
Mansell, Henry J., Bishop of Buffalo, 795 Main St., Buffalo, NY 14203.
Manz, John R., Auxiliary Bishop of Chicago, 1820 S. Leavitt St., Chicago, IL 60608.
Marconi, Dominic A., Auxiliary Bishop of Newark, P.O. Box 1246, Linden, NJ 07036.
Martino, Joseph F., Auxiliary Bishop of Phildelphia, St. Charles Borromeo Seminary, Overbrook, 100 E. Wynnewood Rd., Wynnewood, PA 19096.
Matthiesen, Leroy T., Retired Bishop of Amarillo, P.O. Box 5644, Amarillo, TX 79117.
McAuliffe, Michael F., Retired Bishop of Jefferson City, Bishop's House, P.O. Box 417, Jefferson City, MO 65102.
McCarthy, James F., Auxiliary Bishop of New York, St. Elizabeth Ann Seton, 1377 N. Main St., Shrub Oak, NY 10588.
McCarthy, John E., Bishop Emeritus of Austin, P.O. Box 13327, Austin, TX 78711.
McCormack, John B., Bishop of Manchester, 153 Ash St.- P.O. Box 310, Manchester, NH 03105.
McCormack, William J., Auxiliary Bishop of New York, 142 E. 29th St., New York, NY 10016.
McDonald, Andrew J., Former Bishop of Little Rock, P.O. Box 7565, Little Rock, AR 72217.
McDonnell, Charles J., Auxiliary Bishop of Newark, 34 Maple Ave., Hackensack, NJ 07601.
McDowell, John B., Former Auxiliary Bishop of Pittsburgh, 1817 Red Coach Rd., Allison Park, PA 15101.
McFarland, Norman F., Retired Bishop of Orange, Marywood Center, 2811 E. Villa Real Dr., Orange, CA 92867.
McGann, John R., Former Bishop of Rockville Centre, 50 N. Park Ave., Rockville Centre, NY 11570.
McGrath, Patrick J., Bishop of San Jose, 900 Lafayette St., Suite 301, Santa Clara, CA 95050-4966.
McKinney, Joseph C., Auxiliary Bishop of Grand Rapids, Villa Maria #5110, 1315 Walker Ave., Grand Rapids, MI 49504.
McLaughlin, Bernard J., Retired Auxiliary Bishop of Buffalo, 204 Knoche Rd., Tonawand, NY 14150.
McNamara, John R., Former Auxiliary Bishop of Boston, Regina Cleri-60 William Cardinal O'Connell Way, Boston, MA 02114.
McNamara, Lawrence J., Bishop of Grand Island, P.O. Box 1531, Grand Island, NE 68802.
McManus, Robert J., Auxiliary Bishop of Providence, Diocese of Providence, One Cathedral Square, Providence, RI 02903-3695.
McRaith, John J., Bishop of Owensboro, 501 W. Fifth St., Owensboro, KY 42301.
Medina, Ruben Antonio Gonzalez, *c.m.f.*, Bishop of Caguas.
Melczek, Dale J., Bishop of Gary, 9292 Broadway, Merrillville, IN 46410.
Mengeling, Carl F., Bishop of Lansing, 300 West Ottawa St., Lansing, MI 48933.
Mestice, Anthony F., Auxiliary Bishop of New York, Resurrection, 910 Boston Post Rd., Rye, NY 10580.
Michaels, James E., *s.s.c.*, Resigned Auxiliary Bishop of Wheeling-Charleston, 7500 Woodmont Ave.-Apt. 522, Bethesda, MD 20814.
Mikloshazy, Attila, *s.j.*, Bishop to Hungarians, St. Augustine's Seminary, 2661 Kingston Rd., Scarborough, Ontario, Canada, M1M 1M3.
Milone, Anthony M., Bishop of Great Falls- Billings, 2825 4th Ave., N. Great Falls, MT 59401-2911.
Moeddel, Carl K., Auxiliary Bishop of Cincinnati, 100 East 8th St., Cincinnati, OH 45202.
Montrose, Donald, Bishop of Stockton, 1105 N. Lincoln St., Stockton, CA 95204-0237.
Moreno, Manuel D., Bishop of Tucson, 192 S. Stone Ave., Tucson, AZ 85702.

His Excellency,
The Most Reverend

Morlino, Robert C., Bishop of Helena, 515 N. Ewing St., P.O. Box 1729, Helena, MT 59624-1729.
Morneau, Robert F., Auxiliary Bishop of Green Bay, 1910 S. Webster, P.O. Box 23825, Green Bay, WI 54305-3825.
Moskal, Robert M., Bishop of St. Josaphat in Parma, 5720 State Rd., Parma, OH 44134.
Moynihan, James M., Bishop of Syracuse, 240 East Onondaga St. -P.O. Box 511, Syracuse, NY 13201.
Muench, Robert W., Bishop of Covington, P.O. Box 18548, Erlanger, KY 41018.
Mulvee, Robert E., Bishop of Providence, One Cathedral Sq., Providence, RI 02903.
Murphy, Michael J., Retired Bishop of Erie, 130 E. Fourth St., Erie, PA 16507.
Murphy, William F., Auxiliary Bishop of Boston, 2121 Commonwealth Ave., Brighton, MA 02135.
Murray, James A., Bishop of Kalamazoo, 215 N. Westnedge Ave., Kalamazoo, MI 49007-3760.
Murry, George V., *s.j.*, Bishop of St. Thomas, Virgin Islands, P.O. Box 301825, Charlotte Amalie, VI 00803.
Myers, John Joseph, Bishop of Peoria, 607 N.E. Madison, Peoria, IL 61603.
Naumann, Joseph F., Auxiliary Bishop of St. Louis, 8900 Clayton Rd., Richmond Heights, MO 63117.
Nevins, John J., Bishop of Venice, P.O. Box 2006, Venice, FL 34284.
Newman, William C., Auxiliary Bishop of Baltimore, 6536 Cherry Hill Rd., Baldwin, MD 21013.
Neylon, Martin J., *s.j.*, Retired Bishop of The Caroline Islands, P.O. Box 250, Truk, Caroline Islands 96942.
Niederauer, George H., Bishop of Salt Lake City, 27 C St., Salt Lake City, UT 84103.
Niedergeses, James D., Retired Bishop of Nashville, 2400 Twenty-First Ave., South, Nashville, TN 37212.
Nienstedt, John C., Auxiliary Bishop of Detroit, 1234 Washington Blvd., Detroit, MI 48226.
Ochoa, Armando, Bishop of El Paso, 499 St. Matthews St., El Paso TX 79907.
O'Brien, Thomas J., Bishop of Phoenix, 48 E. Wagon Wheel Dr., Phoenix, AZ 85020.
O'Connell, Anthony J., Bishop of Palm Beach, P.O. Box 109650 - 9995 N. Military Trail, Palm Beach Gardens, FL 33410-9650.
O'Donnell, Edward J., Bishop of Lafayette, P.O. Box Drawer 3387, Lafayette, LA 70502.
O'Leary, Edward C., Retired Bishop of Portland (in Maine), 510 Ocean Ave., Portland, ME 04102.
Olivier, Leonard J., *s.v.d.*, Auxiliary Bishop of Washington, 3340 St. Peter's Dr., Waldorf, MD 20601-2359.
O'Malley, Sean, *o.f.m.cap.*, Bishop of Fall River, Box 2577, Fall River, MA 02722.
O'Neil, Dennis P., Auxiliary Bishop of San Bernardino, 10900 California Ave., Lynwood, CA 90262-2094.
O'Neill, Arthur J., Retired Bishop of Rockford, 1245 North Court St., Rockford, IL 61103.
Ottenweller, Albert H., Retired Bishop of Steubenville, 609 North Seventh St., Steubenville, OH 43952.
Paska, Walter, Auxiliary Bishop of Philadelphia Ukraine, 827 N. Franklin St., Philadelphia, PA 19123.
Pataki, Andrew, Bishop of Passaic of the Ruthenians, 445 Lackawanna Ave., West Paterson, NJ 07424.
Pates, Richard E., Auxiliary Bishop of St. Paul and Minneapolis, 4125 Woodbury Dr., Woodbury, MN 55129-9627.
Paul, John J., Retired Bishop of La Crosse, P.O. Box 69, La Crosse, WI 54601.
Pelotte, Donald, *s.s.s.*, Bishop of Gallup, 711 S. Puerco Drive, Gallup, NM 87301.
Pena, Raymundo J., Bishop of Brownsville, 1910 E. Elizabeth St., Brownsville, TX 78522-2279.
Perry, Joseph N., Auxiliary Bishop of Chicago, P.O. Box 733, South Holland, IL 60473-0733.
Pevec, A. Edward, Auxiliary Bishop of Cleveland, 28700 Euclid Ave., Wickliffe, OH 44092.
Pfeifer, Michael D., *o.m.i.*, Bishop of San Angelo, P.O. Box 1829, San Angelo, TX 76902.
Pilla, Anthony M., Bishop of Cleveland, 1027 Superior Ave., Cleveland, OH 44114.
Popp, Bernard F., Retired Auxiliary Bishop of San Antonio, 4535 Lord Rd., San Antonio, TX 78220-3543.
Povish, Kenneth J., Retired Bishop of Lansing, 401-A East Madison St., DeWitt, MI 48820.
Puscas, Vasile Louis, Former Apostolic Eparch of St. George Martyr in Canton for Romanian-Byzantine Catholics, 609 N. Lincoln Ave., Aurora, IL 60505-2112.
Quinn, A. James, Auxiliary Bishop of Cleveland, 2500 Elyria Ave., Lorain, OH 44055.
Quinn, Francis A., Retired Bishop of Sacramento, 8840 East 22nd St., Tucson, AZ 85710.
Ramirez, Ricardo, *c.s.b.*, Bishop of Las Cruces, 1280 Med Park Dr., Las Cruces, NM 88005.
Reilly, Daniel P., Bishop of Worcester, 49 Elm St., Worcester, MA 01609.

His Excellency,
The Most Reverend

Reiss, John C., Retired Bishop of Trenton, P.O. Box 5147, Trenton, NJ 08638-0147.
Ricard, John H., *s.s.j.*, Bishop of Pensacola-Tallahassee, 11 N. B St., Pensacola, FL 32501.
Ricken, David L., Coadjutor Bishop of Cheyenne, P.O. Box 1468, Cheyenne, WY 82003-1468.
Riley, Lawrence J., Retired Auxiliary Bishop of Boston, 43 Maple St., Hyde Park, Boston, MA 02136.
Rivera, Enrique Hernandez, Retired Bishop of Caguas, P.O. Box 8698, Caguas, PR 00626.
Rivera, Hector M., Auxiliary Bishop of San Juan, P.O. Box S-1967, San Juan, PR 00603.
Rodimer, Frank J., Bishop of Paterson, 178 Derrom Ave., Paterson, NJ 07504.
Rodriguez, Miguel, *c.ss.r.*, Retired Bishop of Arecibo, P.O. Box 9, Aguadilla, PR 00605-0009.
Rodriguez, Placido, *c.m.f.*, Bishop of Lubbock, P.O. Box 98700 - 4620 4th St., Lubbock, TX 79416.
Roque, Francis X., Auxiliary Bishop Military Services, P.O. Box 4469, Washington, DC 20017-0469.
Roman, Agustin A., Auxiliary Bishop of Miami, 9401 Biscayne Blvd., Miami Shores, FL 33138.
Rosazza, Peter A., Auxiliary Bishop of Hartford, 1450 Chapel St., New Haven, CT 06511.
Rose, Robert J., Bishop of Grand Rapids, 660 Burton St., S.E., Grand Rapids, MI 49507.
Rueger, George E., Auxiliary Bishop of Worcester, 2 High Ridge Rd., Worcester, MA 01602.
Ryan, Daniel L., Former Bishop of Springfield in Illinois, 1615 W. Washington St., Box 3187, Springfield, IL 62705.
Ryan, Sylvester D., Bishop of Monterey, P.O. Box 2048, Monterey, CA 93942-2048.
Saltarelli, Michael A., Bishop of Wilmington, 1925 Delaware Ave., Suite 1-A, Wilmington, DE 19806.
Samo, Amando, Auxiliary Bishop of the Caroline Islands. P.O. Box 250, Truk, Caroline Islands FSM 96942.
Samra, Nicholas J., Auxiliary Bishop of Newton, 8525 Cole St., Warren, MI 48093.
Santana, Hermin Negron, Auxiliary Bishop of San Juan, Calle 6, D-9 Urb. Royal Town, Bayamon, PR 00956.
Sartoris, Joseph M., Auxiliary Bishop of Los Angeles, San Pedro Pastoral Region, 3555 St. Pancratius Plc., Lakewood, CA 90712-1416.
Sartain, J. Peter, Bishop of Little Rock, P.O. Box 7239, Little Rock, AR 72217.
Schad, James L., Retired Auxiliary Bishop of Camden, Neumann House - St. Mary's Home, Suite 102, 1730 Kresson Rd., Cherry Hill, NJ 08003.
Schlarman, Stanley G., Retired Bishop of Dodge City, 16 S. Illinois St., Belleville, IL 62220-2104.
Schmitt, Bernard W., Bishop of Wheeling-Charleston, 1300 Byron St., Box 230, Wheeling, WV 26003.
Schmitt, Mark F., Retired Bishop of Marquette, HC01 Box 159, Marquette, MI 49855.
Schoenherr, Walter J., Retired Auxiliary Bishop of Detroit, 14465 Levan Rd.- Apt. A, Livonia, MI 48154-5022.
Schuster, Eldon B., Retired Bishop of Great Falls, 1325 Smelter Ave., Black Eagle, Great Falls, MT 59414.
Schnurr, Dennis M., Bishop of Duluth, 2830 E. Fourth St., Duluth, MN 55812.
Schott, Basil, *o.f.m.*, Bishop of Parma of the Ruthenians.
Serratelli, Arthur J., Auxiliary Bishop of Newark, Cathedral Basilica of the Sacred Heart, 89 Ridge St., Newark, NJ 07104.
Setian, Nerses M., Former Apostolate Exarch for the Armenian Catholics, c/o Our Lady Queen of Martyrs Church, 1327 Pleasant Ave., Los Angeles, CA 90033.
Sevilla, Carlos, *s.j.*, Bishop of Yakima.
Shaheen, Robert J., Bishop of Our Lady of Lebanon of Los Angeles, 331 S. San Vicente Blvd., Los Angeles, CA 90048.
Sheets, John R., *s.j.*, Retired Auxiliary Bishop of Ft. Wayne-South Bend, 18705 75th St., Omaha, NE 68124-1792.
Sheldon, Gilbert I., Bishop of Steubenville, P.O. Box 969, Steubenville, OH 43952.
Sheridan, Michael J., Auxiliary Bishop of St. Louis.
Sheridan, Patrick J., Retired Auxiliary Bishop of New York, 452 Madison Ave., New York, NY 10022.
Sklba, Richard J., Auxiliary Bishop of Milwaukee, 2491 N. Murray Ave., Milwaukee, WI 53211.
Skylstad, William S., Bishop of Spokane, W. 1023 Riverside Ave., Spokane, WA 99201.
Slattery, Edward J., Bishop of Tulsa, P.O. Box 2009, Tulsa, OK 74101.
Smith, John M., Bishop of Trenton, 701 Lawrenceville (Box 5147) Rd., Trenton, NJ 08638-0147.
Snyder, John J., Retired Bishop of St. Augustine, 35 Treasury St., St. Augustine, FL 32084.
Soens, Lawrence D., Former Bishop of Sioux City, 2501 Jay Ave., Sioux City, IA 51106.

His Excellency,
The Most Reverend

Soto, Jaime, Auxiliary Bishop of Orange, Office of Hispanic Ministry-Marywood Ctr., 2811 Villa Real Dr., Orange, CA 92867.
Speltz, George H., Retired Bishop of St. Cloud, Box 1248, St. Cloud, MN 56301.
Speyrer, Jude, Bishop Emeritus of Lake Charles, P.O. Box 3223, Lake Charles, LA 70602.
Steib, James Terry, *s.v.d.*, Bishop of Memphis, The Catholic Center, P.O. Box 341669, Memphis, TN 38184-1669.
Steinbock, John T., Bishop of Fresno, 1550 N. Fresno St., Fresno, CA 93703-3788.
Steiner, Kenneth D., Auxiliary Bishop of Portland in Oregon, 10955 S.E. 25th Ave., Milwaukie, OR 97222.
Straling, Phillip F., Bishop of Reno, 290 S. Arlington Ave., Ste. 200, Reno, NV 89501.
Sullivan, James S., Bishop of Fargo, Box 1750, Fargo, ND 58107.
Sullivan, Joseph M., Auxiliary Bishop of Brooklyn, 378 Clermont Ave., Brooklyn, NY 11238.
Sullivan, Walter F., Bishop of Richmond, 800 Cathedral Place, Richmond, VA 23220.
Surinach-Carreras, Ricardo, Bishop of Ponce, Obispado de Ponce, Carretera Estatal 504 P.R., Glenview Gardens hacia Rio Chiquito, Ponce, PR 00731.
Symons, J. Keith, Former Bishop of Palm Beach, P.O. Box 7, Alma MI 48801-0007.
Tafoya, Arthur N., Bishop of Pueblo, 1001 N. Grand Ave., Pueblo, CO 81003.
Tamayo, James A., Bishop of Laredo, Laredo Pastoral Center, 1901 Corpus Christi St., Laredo, TX 78044.
Tertzakian, Hovhannes, *o.m.ven.*, Apostolic Exarch Emeritus for Armenian Catholics in the United States and Canada, 110 E. 12th St., New York, NY 10003-5395.
Thomas, Elliot G., Bishop of St. Thomas, in the Virgin Islands, P.O. Box 301825, Charlotte Amalie, VI 00803.
Thomas, George, Auxiliary Bishop of Seattle, 910 Marion St., Seattle, WA 98104.
Thompson, David B., Former Bishop of Charleston, 4479 Downing Plc., Mount Pleasant, SC 29466.
Timlin, James C., Bishop of Scranton, 300 Wyoming Ave., Scranton, PA 18503.
Tobin, Thomas J., Bishop of Youngstown, 144 W. Wood St., Youngstown, OH 44503.
Torres Oliver, Fremiot, Bishop Emeritus of Ponce, Obispado de Ponce, Carretera Estatal 504 P.R., Glenview Gardens hacia Rio Chiquito, Ponce, PR 00731.
Trautman, Donald W., Bishop of Erie, 205 West 9th St., Erie, PA 16501.
Tschoepe, Thomas, Retired Bishop of Dallas, 3915 Lemmon Ave, Box 19507, Dallas, TX 75219.
Txertudi, Inaki Mallona, *c.p.* , 206 Dr. Salas St. - Box 616, Arecibo, PR 00613-0616.
Untener, Kenneth E., Bishop of Saginaw, 5800 Weiss St., Saginaw, MI 48603.
Valero, Rene, Auxiliary Bishop of Brooklyn, 34-43 93rd St., Jackson Heights, NY 11372.
Vasa, Robert Francis, Bishop of Baker, P.O. Box 5999, Bend, OR 97708.
Vigneron, Allen H., Auxiliary Bishop of Detroit, Sacred Heart Major Seminary, 2701 Chicago Blvd., Detroit, MI 48206.
Walsh, Daniel F., Bishop of Santa Rosa, 3336 Hermit Way, Santa Rosa, CA 95405.
Ward, John J., Former Auxiliary Bishop of Los Angeles, 3424 Wilshire Blvd., Los Angeles, CA 90010-2241.
Warfel, Michael, Bishop of Juneau, 419 6th St., Suite 200, Juneau, AK 99801.
Watters, Loras J., Retired Bishop of Winona, 618 Forest, Apt. D., Pacific Grove, CA 93950.
Wcela, Emil A., Auxiliary Bishop of Rockville Centre, Eastern Vicariate, P.O. Box 780, Riverhead, NY 11901.
Webster, John C., Auxiliary Bishop of San Francisco, One Peter Yorke Way, San Francisco, CA 94109.
Weigand, William K., Bishop of Sacramento, Pastoral Center, 2110 Broadway, Sacramento CA 95818-2541.
Weitzel, John Quinn, *m.m.*, Bishop of Samoa-Pago Pago, Fatuoaiga P.O. Box 596, Pago Pago, American Samoa 967.
Welsh, Thomas J., Retired Bishop of Allentown, 1325 Prospect Ave., Bethlehem, PA 18018.
Wenski, Thomas G., Auxiliary Bishop of Miami, Catholic Relief Services, 9401 Biscayne Blvd., Miami, FL 33138.
Wester, John Charles, Auxiliary Bishop of San Francisco, 445 Church St., San Francisco, CA 94114.
Whelan, Robert L., *s.j.*, Retired Bishop of Fairbanks, Regis Community, 1107 N. Astor, Spokane, WA 99202.
Wilkerson, Gerald E., Auxiliary Bishop of Los Angeles, P.O. Box 7608, Mission Hills, CA 91346.
Williams, James Kendrick, Bishop of Lexington, 1310 West Main St., Lexington, KY 40508-2040.
Winter, William J., Auxiliary Bishop of Pittsburgh, Sacred Heart Church, 310 Shady Ave., Pittsburgh, PA 15206-4389.

His Excellency,
The Most Reverend

Wirz, George O., Auxiliary Bishop of Madison, 3577 S. High Point Rd., Madison WI 53719-4999.
Wuerl, Donald W., Bishop of Pittsburgh, 111 Blvd. of the Allies, Pittsburgh, PA 15222-1618.
Wycislo, Aloysius J., Retired Bishop of Green Bay, 1910 S. Webster, P.O. Box 23835, Green Bay, WI 54305-3825.
Yanta, John W., Bishop of Amarillo, P.O. Box 5644, Amarillo, TX 79117-5644.
Younan, Joseph, Bishop of Our Lady of Deliverance of Newark of the Syrians, P.O. Box 8366, Union City, NJ 07087-8262.
Zavala, Gabino, Auxiliary Bishop of Los Angeles, San Gabriel Pastoral Region, 16009 East Cypress Ave., Irwindale, CA 91706-2122.
Ziemann, G. Patrick, Former Bishop of Santa Rosa, 320 10th St., Santa Rosa, CA 95401.
Zipfel, Paul A., Bishop of Bismarck, 420 Raymond St., Bismarck, ND 58502-1575.
Zubik, David A., Auxiliary Bishop of Pittsburgh, 111 Blvd. of the Allies, Pittsburgh, PA 15222-1618.
Zurek, Patrick J., Auxiliary Bishop of San Antonio, P.O. Box 28410, San Antonio, TX 78228-0410.

U.S. HIERARCHY SERVING IN OTHER COUNTRIES

Adams, Edward J., Archbishop Apostolic Nuncio in Bangladesh, P.O. Box 6003, Dhaka, Bangladesh.
Boyle, Paul M., *c.p.*, Apostolic Vicar of Mandeville, Jamaica, West Indies.
De Paoli, Ambrose, Apostolic Nuncio to Japan: 9-2 Sanban-cho, Chiyodku, Tokyo.
Dion, George E., *o.m.i.*, Retired Bishop of Jolo, Oblates of Notre Dame Motherhouse, Sinsuat Ave., 9600 Cotabato City, Philippines.
Harvey, James M., Titular Bishop of Memfi, Bishop/ Prefect of the Papal Household, 00120 Vatican City State, Europe.
McGarry, Urban E., *t.o.r.*, Bishop of Bhagalpur, Chancery Office: Nawab Colony, P.O. Box 61, Bhagalpur 812001, Bihar, India.
McNaughton, William J., *m.m.*, Bishop of Inchon, 3 Tap Tong, P.O. Box 19, Chung Ku, Inchon 400-600, Korea.
Pelletier, Donald L., Bishop of Morondava Madagascar, Bishop's House, P.O. Box 132, Morondava 619, Madagascar.
Schmitz, Paul Evin, *o.f.m.cap.*, Vicariate Apostolic of Bluefields, Apartado Postal 8, Bluefields, R.A.A.S., Nicaragua, C.A.
Smith, Philip Francis, *m.m.*, Archbishop of Cotabato, Residence, P.O. Box 186, Sinsuat Ave., Cotabato City 9600, Philippines.

OTHER HIERARCHY RESIDING IN THE UNITED STATES

Comber, John W., *m.m.*, Former Superior & Bishop of Maryknoll, 141 E. 43rd St., New York, NY 10017.
DePalma, Joseph A., *s.c.j.* Former Bishop of De Aar, South Africa, Sacred Heart Residence, 6701 82nd Ave., N., Pinellas Park, FL 34665.
Durning, Dennis V., *c.s.sp.*, Bishop Emeritus of Arusha Tanzania, East Africa, Holy Ghost Provincialate, 6230 Brush Run Rd., Bethel Park, PA 15102.
Kung, Ignatius Cardinal, Our Lady Queen of the Clergy Home, 128 Strawberry Hill Ave., Stamford, CT 06904.
Meeking, Basil, Retired Bishop from New Zealand, 4635 S.W. 148th Ave., Beaverton, OR 97007.
Nolker, Bernard J., *c.ss.r.*, Retired Bishop of Paranagua Brazil, 600 S. Conkling St., Baltimore, MD 21224.
Pearce, George H., *s.m.*, Former Archbishop of Suva, 30 Fenner St., Providence, RI 02903. Dominican Republic, 1545 Tremont St., Roxbury, MA 02120.
Schmidt, Firmin, *o.f.m.cap.*, Former Bishop of Papua, New Guinea, c/o Diocese of Salina, 103 N. Ninth, Salina, KS 67402-0980.
Veigle, Adriano J., *t.o.r.*, Retired Bishop of Borba, Brazil, Mount Assisi Monastery, Loretto, PA 15940.

ARCHABBOTS

The Right Reverend

Knaebel, Bonaventure, *o.s.b.*, Resigned. St. Meinrad Archabbey, St. Meinrad, IN 47577.
Maher, Paul R., *o.s.b.*, (Resigned) St. Vincent Archabbey, 300 Fraser Purchase Rd., Latrobe, PA 15650-2686.
Nowicki, Douglas R., *o.s.b.*, St. Vincent Archabbey, 300 Fraser Purchase Rd., Latrobe, PA 15650-2686.
Reilly, Lambert, *o.s.b.*, St. Meinrad Archabbey, St. Meinrad, IN 47577.

ABBOTS

Abdo, Michael, *o.c.s.o.*, St. Benedict Monastery, 1012 Monastery Rd., Snowmass, CO 81654.
Anderson, Hugh R., *o.s.b.*, St. Procopius Abbey, 5601 College Rd., Lisle, IL 60532.
Augustine, Dom, *o.c.s.o.*, Retired. Monastery of the Holy Spirit, Inc., 2625 Hwy. 212 S.W., Conyers, GA 30094.
Balsavich, Marion E., *o.s.b.*, Retired. St. Bede Abbey, Peru, IL 61354.
Bamberger, John E., *o.c.s.o.*, Abbey of Genesee, Piffard, NY 14533.
Barnes, Robert, *o.c.s.o.*, Abbey of Our Lady of the Holy Cross, 901 Cool Spring Ln., Berryville, VA 22611-2700.
Bataille, Vincent, *o.s.b.*, Marmion Abbey, Butterfield Rd., Aurora, IL 60504.
Benedict, Francis, *o.s.b.*, St. Andrew's Abbey, 31001 N. Valyermo Rd., Valyermo, CA 93563.
Benkert, Gerald, *o.s.b.*, Resigned. Marmion Abbey, Butterfield Rd., Aurora, IL 60504.
Berndt, Alan, *o.s.b.*, Retired. Blue Cloud Abbey, P.O. Box 98, Marvin, SD 57252.
Berning, Philip, *o.s.b.*, Retired. St. Gregory Abbey, Shawnee, OK 74801.
Bock, David R., *o.c.s.o.*, Retired. New Melleray Abbey, 6500 Melleray Circle, Peosta, IA 52068.
Boultwood, Alban, *o.s.b.*, St. Anselm Abbey, 4501 S. Dakota Ave., N.E., Washington, DC 20017.
Boyle, Joseph, *o.s.b.*, St. Benedict Monastery, 1012 Monastery Rd., Snowmass, CO 81654.
Buergler, Luke, *o.s.b.*, Corpus Christi Abbey, HCR #2, Box 6300, Sandia, TX 78383.
Burne, Martin J., *o.s.b.*, Retired. St. Mary Abbey, Delbarton, Mendham Rd., Morristown, NJ 07960.
Burnett, Oscar, *o.s.b.*, Retired. Belmont Abbey, 100 Belmont-Mount Holly Rd., Belmont, NC 28012-2795.
Burns, Flavian, o.c.s.o., Abbey of Our Lady of the Holy Cross, Rt. 2, Box 3870, Berryville, VA 22611.
Campbell, Edward C., *o.s.b.*, Retired. Glastonbury Abbey, 16 Hull St., Hingham, MA 02043.
Carr, Christian Aidan, *o.c.s.o.*, Retired. Our Lady of Mepkin Abbey, HC 69, Box 800, Moncks Corner, SC 29461. Serving as chaplain in Africa.
Cassell, Leonard G., *o.s.b.*, Retired. St. Mary Abbey, Delbarton, Mendham Rd., Morristown, NJ 07960.
Chassagne, M. Anthony, *o.c.s.o.*, Retired. Abbey of Our Lady of Mepkin, HC 69, Box 800, Moncks Corner, SC 29461.
Clark, Victor J., *o.s.b.*, St. Bernard Abbey, 1600 St. Bernard Dr., Cullman, AL 35055.
Clarke, Brian H., *o.s.b.*, St. Mary Abbey, Delbarton, Mendham Rd., Morristown, NJ 07960.
Cole, Edwin J., *o.s.b.*, St. Anselm Church, 530 S. Mason Rd., St. Louis, MO 63141.
Confroy, Thomas J., *o.s.b.*, St. Mary's Abbey, Delbarton, Morristown, NJ 07960.
Connor, James, *o.c.s.o.*, Retired. Assumption Abbey, Rte 5 - Box 1056, Ava, MO 65660.
Corpus, Roger, *o.s.b.*, St. Bede Abbey, Peru, IL 61354.
Cyr, David J., *o.s.b.*, Marmion Abbey, Butterfield Rd., Aurora, IL 60504.
Dagher, George, *b.s.o.*, American Headquarters, 30 East St., Methuen, MA 01844.
Davis, Thomas X., *o.c.s.o.*, Our Lady of New Clairvaux Abbey, P.O. Box 80, Vina, CA 96092.
De Wane, Thomas E., *o.praem.*, St. Norbert Abbey, 1016 N. Broadway, De Pere, WI 54115-2697.
Dimitrijevich, Nicholas, Our Lady of the Valley, P.O. Box 419, Gloverville, SC 29828.
Dosch, Leander, *o.c.s.o.*, Abbey of the Holy Trinity, 1250 South 9500 East, Huntsville, UT 84317.
Driscoll, William J., *o.mar.*, Monastery of the Most Holy Trinity, 67 Dugway Rd., Petersham, MA 01366.
Dzikowicz, Justin E., *o.s.b.*, Retired. St. Paul Abbey, Newton, NJ 07860.
Eberle, Peter, *o.s.b.*, Mount Angel Abbey, St. Benedict, OR 97373.
Ehringer, Claude, *o.s.b.*, Prince of Peace Abbey, Oceanside, CA 92054.
Eidenschink, John, *o.s.b.*, Chaplain. Mother of Mercy Nursing Home & Retirement Center, Albany, MN 56307.
Farkasfalvy, Denis, *o.cist.*, Abbey of Our Lady of Dallas, 1 Cistercian Rd., Irving, TX 75039.
Flaherty, Malachy, *o.c.s.o.*, Abbey of Our Lady of the Holy Trinity, 1250 S. 9500 E., Huntsville, UT 84317.
Freeman, Brendan J., *o.c.s.o.*, Abbey of Our Lady of New Melleray, 6500 Melleray Circle, Peosta, IA 52068.
Frerking, Thomas, *o.s.b.*, Abbey of St. Mary and St. Louis, 500 S. Mason Rd., St. Louis, MO 63141.
Fuez, Blaise J. *o.cist.*, Our Lady of Spring Bank Abbey, Rt. 3, Box 211, Sparta, WI 54656.
Galvin, Anselm, *o.s.b.*, Resigned, Mt. Angel Abbey, St. Benedict, OR 97373.
Garber, Andrew V., *o.s.b.*, Resigned. St. Benedict Abbey, Benet Lake, WI 53102.
Geraets, David, *o.s.b.*, Our Lady of Guadalupe Abbey, Pecos, NM 87552.

Gibbs, Gabriel, *o.s.b.*, St. Benedict Abbey, 252 Still River Rd., P.O. Box 67, Still River (Harvard), MA 01467.
Gries, Roger, *o.s.b.*, St. Andrew Abbey, 10510 Buckeye Rd., Cleveland, OH 44104.
Hacker, Louis, *o.s.b.*, Corpus Christi Abbey, HCR 2, Box 6300, Sandia, TX 78383.
Harrison, Cyprian, *o.c.s.o.*, Assumption Abbey, Rt. 5, Box 1056, Ava, MO 65608.
Havlik, Thomas J., *o.s.b.*, St. Procopius Abbey, 5601 College Rd., Lisle, IL 60532.
Hayes, Eugene, *o.praem.*, St. Michael Abbey, 19292 El Toro Rd., Silverado, CA 92676-9710.
Heidgen, Warren J., *o.s.b.*, Retired. Holy Cross Abbey, P.O. Box 1510, Canon City, CO 81215-1510.
Hein, Kenneth, *o.s.b.*, Abbot, Holy Cross Abbey, P.O. Box 1510, Canon City, CO 81215-1510.
Hess, Gilbert, *o.s.b.*, Retired. Blue Cloud Abbey, P.O. Box 98, Marvin, SD 57251.
Hillenbrand, Thomas, *o.s.b.*, Blue Cloud Abbey, P.O. Box 98, Marvin, SD 57251.
Hinches, Augustine J., *o.s.b.*, Resigned. St. Paul Abbey, Newton, NJ 07860.
Hoenig, Alfred, *o.s.b.*, Retired. Corpus Christi Abbey, HCR No. 2, P.O. Box 6300, Sandia, TX 78383.
Jones, James, *o.s.b.*, Retired. Conception Abbey, Conception, MO 64433.
Keating, Thomas, *o.c.s.o.*, Contemplative Outreach, Chrysalis House, 21 Ball Rd., Warwick, NY 10990.
Kelly, Timothy, *o.s.b.*, St. John's Abbey, P.O. Box 2015, Collegeville, MN 56321-2015.
Kerndt, James J., *o.c.s.o.*, Retired. New Melleray Abbey, 6500 Melleray Circle, Dubuque, IA 52068.
Kline, Francis, *o.c.s.o.*, Our Lady of Mepkin Abbey, HC 69, Box 800, Moncks Corner, SC 29461.
Kodell, Jerome, *o.s.b.*, New Subiaco Abbey, Subiaco, AR 72865.
Koehler, Ralph, *o.s.b.*, Retired. St. Benedict's, Abbey, Atchison, KS 66002.
Kostrzanski, Hubert, *o.cist.*, Retired. Cistercian Fathers Our Lady Mother of Church, 8121 Archer Rd., Willow Springs, IL 60480-1501.
Lawrence, Philip, *o.s.b.*, Monastery of Christ in the Desert, Abiquiu, NM 87510.
Leavy, Matthew K., *o.s.b.*, St. Anselm Abbey, Manchester, NH 03102.
Liprie, James, *o.s.b.*, Abbot of Our Lady of Guadalupe Abbey, Pecos, NM 87552.
Logan, John M., *o.praem.*, Daylesford Abbey, 220 S. Valley Rd., Paoli, PA 19301.
Lugo, Martin, *o.s.b.*, St. Gregory's Abbey, Shawnee, OK 74804.
Luykx, Boniface, Holy Transfiguration Monastery, 17001 Tomki Rd., Redwood Valley, CA 95470.
Mackin, Benjamin T., *o.praem.*, Retired, St. Norbert Abbey, 1016 N. Broadway, De Pere, WI 54115-2697.
Massoth, Charles, *o.s.b.*, Retired. St. Gregory Abbey, Shawnee, OK 74801.
Matter, Robert, *o.c.s.o.*, Retired. Assumption Abbey, Rt. 5, Box 1056, Ava, MO 65608.
McCarthy, Peter, *o.c.s.o.*, The Cistercian (Trappist) Abbey of Our Lady of Guadalupe, Lafayette, OR 97127.
McCorkell, Edward, *o.c.s.o.*, Retired. Abbey of Our Lady of the Holy Cross, Rt. 2, Box 3870, Berryville, VA 22611.
Macrae, Maurus, *o.s.b.*, Westminster Abbey Mission, British Columbia, Canada V2V 4J2.
Macul, Joel P., *o.s.b.*, St. Paul's Abbey, Newton, NJ 07860.
McDermott, Benedict, *o.s.b.*, Mary Mother of Church Abbey, 12829 River Rd., Richmond, VA 23221.
McGonigle, Kevin, *o.s.b.*, Retired. Conception Abbey, Conception, MO 64433.
McVeigh, Bernard, *o.c.s.o.*, Our Lady of Guadalupe Abbey, Lafayette, OR 97127.
Meagher, Cletus D., *o.s.b.*, St. Bernard Abbey, Cullman, AL 35055.
Moore, Augustine J., *o.c.s.o.*, Retired. Monastery of the Holy Spirit, 2625 Hwy. 213 S.W., Conyers, GA 30208.
Moore, Patrick, *o.s.b.*, Assumption Abbey, P.O. Box A, Richardton, ND 58652.
Morcone, Nicholas J., *o.s.b.*, Glastonbury Abbey, 16 Hull St., Hingham, MA 02043.
Neitzel, John E., *o.praem.*, Retired. Daylesford Abbey, 220 S. Valley Rd., Paoli, PA 19301.
O'Connor, Philip J., *o.c.s.o.*, Retired. New Melleray Abbey, 6500 Melleray Circle, Peosta, IA 52068.
Odenbrett, Stephen, *o.s.b.*, Our Lady of Guadalupe Abbey, Pecos, NM 87552.
Parcher, Adrian, *o.s.b.*, Retired. St. Martin's Abbey, 5300 Pacific Ave. S.E., Lacey, WA 98503.
Parker, Ladislaus K., *o.praem.*, Retired, St. Michael Abbey, 19292 E. Toro Rd., Silverado, CA 92676-9710.
Pennington, M. Basil, *o.c.s.o.*, Monastery of the Holy Spirit, 2625 Hwy. 212 S.W., Conyers, GA 30208.
Polan, Gregory, *o.s.b.*, Abbot of Conception Abbey, Conception, MO 64433.
Purcell, Owen, *o.s.b.*, Retired. St. Benedict's Abbey, Atchison, KS 66002.
Quinkert, Denis, *o.s.b.*, Blue Cloud Abbey, P.O. Box 98, Marvin, SD 57251.
Rausch, Conrad, *o.s.b.*, Retired. St. Martin's Abbey, 5300 Pacific Ave. S.E., Lacey, WA 98503.
Regan, Patrick, *o.s.b.*, St. Joseph Abbey, St. Benedict, LA 70457.
Rigby, Luke, *o.s.b.*, Abbey of St. Mary and St. Louis, 500 S. Mason Rd., St. Louis, MO 63141.
Roberts, Augustine, *o.c.s.o.*, St. Joseph Abbey, Spencer, MA 01562.
Rodriguez-Santiago, Jose M., *o.s.b.*, Abbey of San Antonio, Box 729, Humacao, PR 00661.
Roettger, Gregory J., *o.s.b.*, Retired. St. Bernard Abbey, 1600 St. Bernard Dr., Cullman, AL 35055.
Rooney, Marcel, *o.s.b.*, Conception Abbey, Conception, MO 64433.
Roth, Neal G., *o.s.b.*, St. Martin's Abbey, 5300 Pacific Ave. S.E., Lacey, WA 98503.
Ryska, Leo M., *o.s.b.*, St. Benedict's Abbey and Retreat Center, Benet Lake, WI 53102.
Schoofs, Robert, *o.s.b.*, St. Benedict Abbey, Benet Lake, WI 53102.
Senecal, Barnabas, *o.s.b.*, St. Benedict's Abbey, Atchison, KS 66002.
Serna, Dom Mark, *o.s.b.*, Abbey of St. Gregory, Cory's Ln., Portsmouth, RI 02871.
Shea, Aidan, *o.s.b.*, St. Anselm Abbey, 4501 S. Dakota, N.E., Washington, DC 20017.
Shelton, Patrick, *o.s.b.*, St. Leo Abbey, St. Leo, FL 33574.
Solari, Placid D. *o.s.b.*, Belmont Abbey 100 Belmont-Mount Holly Rd., Belmont, NC 28012-1802.
Spillane, M. Emmanuel, *o.c.s.o.*, Retired. Abbey of Our Lady of the Trinity, 1250 S. 9500 E. Huntsville, UT 84317.
Stark, Matthew, *o.s.b.*, Abbey of St. Gregory the Great, Cory's Ln., Portsmouth, RI 02871.
Thompson, Damien, *o.s.c.o.*, Abbey of Gethsemani, Trappist, KY 40051.
Tremel, Jerome G., *o.praem.*, Admin.- Daylesford Abbey Norbertine Canonry, 220 S. Valley Rd., Paoli, PA 19301-1900.
Valvano, Melvin J., *o.s.b.*, Newark Abbey, 528 Dr. Martin Luther King Jr. Blvd., Newark, NJ 07102.
Veilleux, Armand J., *o.s.c.o.*, Monastery of the Holy Spirit, 2625 Hwy. 213 S.W., Conyers, GA 30208.
Vollmer, Edward J., *o.s.b.*, Retired. Holy Cross Abbey, P.O. Box 1510, Canon City, CO 81215-1510.
Vorderlandwehr, Adrian R., *o.s.b.*, Retired. St. Gregory Abbey, Shawnee, OK 74801.
Wagner, Lawrence, *o.s.b.*, Retired. Assumption Abbey, P.O. Box A, Richardton, ND 58652.
Walsh, Raphael, *o.s.b.*, Mt. Michael Abbey, Elkhorn, NE 68022.
Wechter, David L., *o.s.c.o.*, Retired. New Melleray Abbey, 6500 Melleray Circle, Peosta, IA 52068.
West, Robert, o.s.b., Retired. Assumption Abbey, P.O. Box A, Richardton, ND 58652.
Wiseman, James, *o.s.b.*, Resigned. St. Anselm Abbey, 4501 S. Dakota Ave., N.E., Washington, DC 20017.
Wolff, Theodore, *o.s.b.*, Mount Michael Abbey, 22520 Mount Michael Rd., Elkhorn, NE 68022.
Wood, Joseph, *o.s.b.*, Mt. Angel Abbey, St. Benedict, OR 97373.
Wright, Charles, *o.s.b.*, Prince of Peace Abbey, 650 Benet Hill Rd., Oceanside, CA 92054.

A LIST OF CARDINALS IN THE UNITED STATES IN THE ORDER OF THEIR SENIORITY

CARDINALS

His Eminence Luis Cardinal Aponte Martinez, San Juan
His Eminence William Cardinal Baum, Vatican City State
His Eminence Bernard Cardinal Law, Boston
His Eminence James Cardinal Hickey, Washington
His Eminence Edmund Cardinal Szoka, Vatican City State
His Eminence Roger Cardinal Mahony, Los Angeles
His Eminence Anthony Cardinal Bevilacqua, Philadelphia
His Eminence William Cardinal Keeler, Baltimore
His Eminence Adam Cardinal Maida, Detroit
His Eminence Francis Cardinal Stafford, Vatican City State
His Eminence Francis Cardinal George, O.M.I., Chicago
His Eminence Avery Cardinal Dulles
His Eminence Edward Cardinal Egan, New York
His Eminence Theodore Cardinal McCarrick, Washington

A CHRONOLOGICAL LIST OF CARDINAL, ARCHBISHOP & BISHOP ACTIVITY BY YEAR

1954

Bishop

Maloney, Charles G., Appointed Dec. 30, Ordained Dec. 8, 1937. Retired Auxiliary Bishop of Louisville.

1956

Bishops

Clinch, Harry A., Appointed Dec. 5, Ordained June 6, 1936. Auxiliary Bishop of Monterey-Fresno.

Hannan, Philip M., Appointed June 16, Ordained Dec. 8, 1939. Auxiliary Bishop of Washington.

1959

Bishops

Buswell, Charles A., Appointed Aug. 8, Ordained July 9, 1939. Retired Bishop of Pueblo.

Hogan, James J., Appointed Nov. 27, Ordained Dec. 8, 1937. Auxiliary Bishop of Trenton.

1960

Bishops

Aponte Martinez, Luis, Appointed July 23, Ordained April 10, 1950. Auxiliary of Ponce.

Forst, Marion F., Appointed Jan. 2, Ordained June 10, 1934. Former Bishop of Dodge City.

Wycislo, Aloysius J., Appointed Oct. 17, Ordained April 7, 1934. Auxiliary Bishop of Chicago.

1961

Bishops

Gottwald, George J., Appointed June 20, Ordained June 9, 1940. Retired Auxiliary Bishop of St. Louis.

Salatka, Charles A., Appointed Dec. 9, Ordained Feb. 24, 1945. Auxiliary Bishop of Grand Rapids.

1962

Bishops

Hunthausen, Raymond G., Appointed July 8, Ordained June 1, 1946. Bishop of Helena.

Strecker, Ignatius J., Appointed April 7, Ordained Dec. 19, 1942. Bishop of Springfield-Cape Girardeau.

Zayek, Francis M., Appointed May 30, Ordained March 17, 1946. Titular Bishop of Callinicum.

1963

Bishops

Aponte Martinez, Luis, Appointed Nov. 18, Ordained April 10, 1950. Coadjutor Bishop of Ponce.

D'Antonio, Nicholas, Appointed Dec. 31, Ordained June 7, 1942. Bishop of Olancho, Honduras.

Speltz, George H., Appointed Feb. 13, Ordained June 2, 1940. Auxiliary Bishop of Winona.

Ward, John J., Appointed Oct. 16, Ordained May 4, 1946. Auxiliary Bishop of Los Angeles.

1964

Archbishop

Aponte Martinez, Luis, Appointed Nov. 11, Ordained April 10, 1950. Archbishop of San Juan.

Bishop

Torres, Juan Fremiot, Appointed Nov. 4, Ordained April 10, 1950. Bishop of Ponce.

1965

Archbishop

Hannan, Philip M., Appointed Sept. 29, Ordained Dec. 8, 1939. Retired Archbishop of New Orleans.

Bishops

Breitenbeck, Joseph M., Appointed Oct. 18, Ordained May 30, 1942. Auxiliary Bishop of Detroit.

McCarthy, Edward A., Appointed April 21, Ordained May 29, 1943. Auxiliary Bishop of Cincinnati.

Watters, Loras J., Appointed June 23, Ordained June 7, 1941. Auxiliary Bishop of Dubuque.

1966

Bishops

Gerety, Peter L., Appointed March 4, Ordained June 29, 1939. Coadjutor Bishop of Portland (in Maine).

Hogan, James J., Appointed May 23, Ordained Dec. 8, 1937. Retired Bishop of Altoona-Johnstown.

Michaels, James, *s.s.c.*, Appointed Feb. 15, Ordained Dec. 21, 1951. Resigned Auxiliary Bishop of Wheeling-Charleston.

McDowell, John B., Appointed July 18, Ordained Nov. 4, 1945. Auxiliary Bishop of Pittsburgh.

Schad, James L., Appointed Oct. 18, Ordained April 10, 1943. Auxiliary Bishop of Camden.

Speltz, George H., Appointed April 4, Ordained June 2, 1940. Coadjutor Bishop of St. Cloud.

Tschoepe, Thomas, Appointed Jan. 12, Ordained May 30, 1943. Retired Bishop of Dallas.

1967

Bishops

Broderick, Edwin B., Appointed March 4, Ordained May 30, 1942. Auxiliary Bishop of New York.

Clinch, Harry A., Appointed Dec. 14, Ordained June 6, 1936. Retired Bishop of Monterey.

Frey, Gerard L., Appointed May 31, Ordained April 2, 1938. Bishop of Savannah.

Gerety, Peter L., Appointed Feb. 18, Ordained June 29, 1939. Apostolic Administrator of Portland (in Maine).

Grady, Thomas J., Appointed June 21, Ordained April 23, 1938. Auxiliary Bishop of Chicago.

Ham, J. Richard *m.m.*, Appointed Nov. 28, Ordained June 12, 1948. Auxiliary Bishop of Guatemala.

Hickey, James A., Appointed April 14, Ordained June 15, 1946. Auxiliary Bishop of Saginaw.

Quinn, John R., Appointed Oct. 21, Ordained July 19, 1953. Auxiliary Bishop of San Diego.

Reiss, John C., Appointed Oct. 21, Ordained May 31, 1947. Auxiliary Bishop of Trenton.

Whelan, Robert L., *s.j.*, Appointed Dec. 6, Ordained June 17, 1944. Coadjutor Bishop of Fairbanks.

1968

Bishops

Borders, William D., Appointed May 8, Ordained May 18, 1940. Bishop of Arlington.

Cronin, Daniel A., Appointed June 10, Ordained Dec. 20, 1952. Auxiliary Bishop of Boston.

Dudick, Michael J., Appointed Aug. 21, Ordained Nov. 13, 1945. Bishop of Passaic.

Fitzpatrick, John J., Appointed June 24, Ordained Dec. 13, 1942. Auxiliary Bishop of Miami.

Gossman, F. Joseph, Appointed July 15, Ordained Dec. 17, 1955. Auxiliary Bishop of Baltimore.

Gumbleton, Thomas J., Appointed March 8, Ordained June 2, 1956. Auxiliary Bishop of Detroit.

McKinney, Joseph C., Appointed July 24, Ordained Dec. 20, 1953. Auxiliary Bishop of Grand Rapids.

McLaughlin, Bernard J., Appointed Dec. 28, Ordained Dec. 21, 1935. Retired Auxiliary Bishop of Buffalo.

O'Neill, Arthur J., Appointed Aug. 19, Ordained March 27, 1943. Bishop of Rockford.

Salatka, Charles A., Appointed Jan. 10, Ordained Feb. 24, 1945. Bishop of Marquette.

Schoenherr, Walter J., Appointed March 8, Ordained Oct. 27, 1945. Auxiliary Bishop of Detroit.

Shea, Robert L., *s.j.*, Succeeded to See Nov. 30, Retired Bishop of Fairbanks.

Speltz, George H., Succeeded to See Jan. 31, Retired Bishop of St. Cloud.

Wycislo, Aloysius J., Appointed March 8, Ordained April 7, 1934. Retired Bishop of Green Bay.

1969

Archbishop

Strecker, Ignatius J., Appointed Sept. 10, Ordained Dec. 19, 1942. Archbishop of Kansas City in Kansas.

Bishops

Breitenbeck, Joseph, Appointed Oct. 15, Ordained May 30, 1942. Retired Bishop of Grand Rapids.

Broderick, Edwin B., Appointed March 19, Ordained May 30, 1942. Former Bishop of Albany.

Gerety, Peter L., Succeeded to See Sept. 15. Bishop of Portland (in Maine).

Lynch, George E., Appointed Oct. 20, Ordained May 29, 1943. Retired Auxiliary Bishop of Raleigh.

McAuliffe, Michael F., Appointed July 2, Ordained May 31, 1945. Bishop of Jefferson City.

McCarthy, Edward A., Appointed Aug. 25, Ordained May 29, 1943. Bishop of Phoenix.

Neylon, Martin J., *s.j.*, Appointed Oct. 2, Ordained June 18, 1950. Titular Bishop of Libertina.

Tshoepe, Thomas, Appointed Aug. 27, Ordained May 30, 1943. Retired Bishop of Dallas.

Watters, Loras J., Appointed Jan. 8, Ordained June 7, 1941. Retired Bishop of Winona.

1970

Bishops

Ahern, Patrick V., Appointed Feb. 3, Ordained Jan. 27, 1945. Auxiliary Bishop of New York.

Baum, William, Appointed Feb. 18, Ordained May 12, 1951. Bishop of Springfield-Cape Girardeau.
Bosco, Anthony G., Appointed May 14, Ordained June 7, 1952. Auxiliary Bishop of Pittsburgh.
Cronin, Daniel A., Appointed Oct. 30, Ordained Dec. 20, 1952. Bishop of Fall River.
Flores, Patrick F., Appointed March 18, Ordained May 26, 1956. Auxiliary Bishop of San Antonio.
Head, Edward D., Appointed Jan. 27, Ordained Jan. 27, 1945. Auxiliary Bishop of New York.
Hurley, Francis T., Appointed Feb. 4, Ordained June 16, 1951. Auxiliary Bishop of Juneau.
Lohmuller, Martin N., Appointed Feb. 11, Ordained June 3, 1944. Auxiliary Bishop of Philadelphia.
McFarland, Norman F., Appointed June 5, Ordained June 15, 1946. Auxiliary Bishop of San Francisco.
McGann, John R., Appointed Nov. 12, Ordained June 3, 1950. Auxiliary Bishop of Rockville Centre.
O'Leary, Edward C., Appointed Nov. 17, Ordained June 15, 1946. Auxiliary Bishop of Portland (in Maine).
Povish, Kenneth J., Appointed July 28, Ordained June 3, 1950. Bishop of Crookston.
Schmitt, Mark F., Appointed May 5, Ordained May 22, 1948. Auxiliary Bishop of Green Bay.
Sullivan, Walter F., Appointed Oct. 20, Ordained May 9, 1953. Auxiliary Bishop of Richmond.
Welsh, Thomas J., Appointed Feb. 18, Ordained May 30, 1946. Auxiliary Bishop of Philadelphia.

1971

Bishops

Arzube, Juan, Appointed Feb. 9, Ordained May 5, 1954. Auxiliary Bishop of Los Angeles.
Begley, Michael J., Appointed Nov. 30, Ordained May 26, 1934. Retired Bishop of Charlotte.
Connolly, Thomas J., Appointed May 4, Ordained April 8, 1947. Bishop of Baker.
Crowley, Joseph R., Appointed June 16, Ordained May 1, 1953. Retired Auxiliary Bishop of Fort Wayne-South Bend.
Donovan, Paul V., Appointed June 15, Ordained May 20, 1950. Bishop of Kalamazoo.
Fitzpatrick, John J., Appointed April 21, Ordained Dec. 13, 1942. Retired Bishop of Brownsville.
Gelineau, Louis E., Appointed Dec. 6, Ordained June 5, 1954. Bishop of Providence.
Gracida, Rene H., Appointed Dec. 6, Ordained May 23, 1959. Auxiliary Bishop of Miami.
Harrison, Frank J., Appointed March 1, Ordained June 4, 1937. Auxiliary Bishop of Syracuse.
Hurley, Francis T., Appointed July 20, Ordained June 16, 1951. Bishop of Juneau.
Losten, Basil, Appointed March 15, Ordained June 10, 1957. Auxiliary Bishop of Philadelphia Ukrainian.
Lucker, Raymond A., Appointed July 12, Ordained June 7, 1952. Auxiliary Bishop of St. Paul-Minneapolis.
Maguire, Joseph F., Appointed Dec. 1, Ordained June 29, 1945. Auxiliary Bishop of Boston.
Neylon, Martin J., *s.j.*, Appointed Sept. 20, Ordained June 18, 1950. Vicar Apostolic of The Carolines-Marshalls.
Riley, Lawrence J., Appointed Dec. 7, Ordained Sept. 21, 1940. Retired Auxiliary Bishop of Boston.
Roach, John R., Appointed July 12, Ordained June 8, 1946. Auxiliary Bishop of St. Paul-Minneapolis.
Szoka, Edmund, Appointed June 15, Ordained June 5, 1954. Bishop of Gaylord.
Zayek, Francis M., Appointed Nov. 11, Ordained March 17, 1946. Eparch of St. Maron.

1972

Archbishop

Quinn, John R., Appointed Dec. 13, Ordained July 19, 1953. Archbishop of Oklahoma City.

Bishops

Frey, Gerard L., Appointed Nov. 7, Ordained April 2, 1938. Retired Bishop of Lafayette.
Howze, Joseph L., Appointed Nov. 8, Ordained May 7, 1959. Auxiliary Bishop of Jackson.
Mahoney, James P., Appointed July 25, Ordained May 19, 1951. Auxiliary Bishop of New York.
McDonald, Andrew J., Appointed July 4, Ordained May 8, 1948. Bishop of Little Rock.
Snyder, John J., Appointed Dec. 19, Ordained June 9, 1951. Auxiliary Bishop of Brooklyn.
Sullivan, James S., Appointed July 25, Ordained June 4, 1955. Auxiliary Bishop of Lansing.

1973

Cardinal

Aponte Martinez, Luis Cardinal, Created March 5. Archbishop of San Juan.

Archbishop

Baum, William, Appointed May 9, Ordained May 12, 1951. Archbishop of Washington.

Bishops

Head, Edward D., Appointed Jan. 17, Ordained Jan. 27, 1945. Bishop of Buffalo.
Imesch, Joseph L., Appointed Feb. 8, Ordained Dec. 16, 1956. Auxiliary Bishop of Detroit.
Law, Bernard, Appointed Oct. 22, Ordained May 21, 1961. Bishop of Springfield-Cape Girardeau.
Lessard, Raymond W., Appointed March 5, Ordained Dec. 16, 1956. Bishop of Savannah.
Mestice, Anthony F., Appointed March 5, Ordained June 4, 1949. Auxiliary Bishop of New York.
Sullivan, Walter F., Appointed April 30, Ordained May 9, 1953. Apostolic Administrator of Richmond.

1974

Archbishops

Borders, William D., Appointed March 25, Ordained May 18, 1940. Retired Archbishop of Baltimore.
Gerety, Peter Leo, Appointed April 2, Ordained June 29, 1939. Retired Archbishop of Newark.
Sanchez, Robert F., Appointed June 1, Ordained Dec. 20, 1959. Archbishop of Santa Fe.

Bishops

Angell, Kenneth A., Appointed Aug. 9, Ordained May 26, 1956. Auxiliary Bishop of Providence.
Chavez, Gilbert E., Appointed April 19, Ordained March 19, 1960. Auxiliary Bishop of San Diego.
Cummins, John S., Appointed Feb. 26, Ordained Jan. 24, 1953. Auxiliary Bishop of Sacramento.
Daily, Thomas V., Appointed Dec. 31, Ordained Jan. 10, 1952. Auxiliary Bishop of Boston.
D'Arcy, John M., Appointed Dec. 31, Ordained Feb. 2, 1957. Auxiliary Bishop of Boston.
Gendron, Odore J., Appointed Dec. 12, Ordained May 31, 1947. Retired Bishop of Manchester.
Grady, Thomas J., Appointed Nov. 9, Ordained April 23, 1938. Retired Bishop of Arlington.
Hanifen, Richard C., Appointed July 6, 1974. Ordained June 6, 1959. Auxiliary Bishop of Denver.
Hickey, James A., Appointed June 4, Ordained June 15, 1946. Bishop of Cleveland.
Hughes, William A., Appointed July 23, Ordained April 6, 1946. Auxiliary Bishop of Youngstown.
McFarland, Norman F., Appointed Dec. 6, Ordained June 15, 1946. Apostolic Administrator of Reno-Las Vegas.
O'Leary, Edward C., Appointed Dec. 4, Ordained June 15, 1946. Retired Bishop of Portland (in Maine).
Ottenweller, Albert H., Appointed April 17, Ordained June 19, 1943. Auxiliary Bishop of Toledo.
Pilarczyk, Daniel E., Appointed Nov. 12, Ordained Dec. 20, 1959. Auxiliary Bishop of Cincinnati.
Rodriguez, Miguel, *c.ss.r.*, Appointed Jan. 21, Ordained June 22, 1958. Retired Bishop of Arecibo.
Sullivan, Walter F., Succeeded to See June 6. Bishop of Richmond.
Welsh, Thomas J., Appointed June 4. Bishop of Arlington.

1975

Archbishops

Hunthausen, Raymond G., Appointed Feb. 25, Ordained June 1, 1946. Archbishop of Seattle.
Roach, John R., Appointed May 21, Ordained June 8, 1946. Archbishop of St. Paul-Minneapolis.

Bishops

Fitzsimons, George K., Appointed May 27, Ordained March 18, 1961. Auxiliary Bishop of Kansas City-St. Joseph.
Gracida, Rene H., Appointed Oct. 1, Ordained May 23, 1959. Bishop of Pensacola-Tallahassee.
Gossman, F. Joseph, Appointed April 8, Ordained Dec. 17, 1955. Bishop of Raleigh.
Lucker, Raymond A., Appointed Dec. 23, Ordained June 7, 1952. Bishop of New Ulm.
Mahony, Roger M., Appointed Jan. 7, Ordained May 1, 1962. Auxiliary Bishop of Fresno.
Niedergeses, James D., Appointed April 8, Ordained May 20, 1944. Bishop of Nashville.
Povish, Kenneth J., Appointed Oct. 21, Ordained June 3, 1950. Bishop of Lansing.
Reilly, Daniel P., Appointed June 17, Ordained May 30, 1953. Bishop of Norwich.
Surinach Carreras, Ricardo, Appointed May 26, Ordained April 13, 1957. Auxiliary Bishop of Ponce.

1976

Cardinal

Baum, William Cardinal, Created May 24. Prefect of Sacred Congregation for Catholic Education, Vatican.

Archbishops

Hurley, Francis T., Appointed May 4, Ordained June 16, 1951. Archbishop of Anchorage.
McCarthy, Edward A., Appointed Sept. 17, Ordained May 29, 1943. Coadjutor Archbishop of Miami.

Bishops

Balke, Victor, Appointed July 7, Ordained May 24, 1958. Bishop of Crookston.
Broderick, Edwin B., Appointed June 3. Exec. Dir. Catholic Relief Services.
Casiano-Vargas, Ulises, Appointed March 4, Ordained May 30, 1967. Bishop of Mayaguez.
Curtiss, Elden F., Appointed March 4, Ordained May 24, 1958. Bishop of Helena.
Dudley, Paul V., Appointed Nov. 16, Ordained June 2, 1951. Auxiliary Bishop of St. Paul-Minneapolis.
Forst, Marion F., Appointed Oct. 16, Ordained June 10, 1934. Retired Auxiliary Bishop of Kansas City in Kansas.
Gerber, Eugene J., Appointed Oct. 16, Ordained May 19, 1959. Bishop of Dodge City.
Harrison, Frank J., Appointed Nov. 16, Ordained June 4, 1937. Retired Bishop of Syracuse.
Hart, Daniel A., Appointed Aug. 30, Ordained Feb. 2, 1953. Auxiliary Bishop of Boston.
Hart, Joseph H., Appointed July 1, Ordained May 1, 1956. Bishop of Cheyenne.
Hughes, Edward T., Appointed June 14, Ordained May 31, 1947. Auxiliary Bishop of Philadelphia.
Kinney, John F., Appointed Nov. 16, Ordained Feb. 2, 1963. Auxiliary Bishop of St. Paul-Minneapolis.
Losten, Basil H., Appointed June 8, Ordained June 10, 1957. Apostolic Administrator Philadelphia Ukrainian.
Maguire, Joseph F., Appointed April 3, Ordained June 29, 1945. Coadjutor Bishop of Springfield.
Marconi, Dominic A., Appointed May 3, Ordained May 30, 1953. Auxiliary Bishop of Newark.
McFarland, Norman F., Appointed Feb. 10, Ordained June 15, 1946. Bishop of Reno-Las Vegas.
McGann, John R., Appointed May 3, Ordained June 3, 1950. Bishop of Rockville Centre.
Moreno, Manuel D., Appointed Dec. 20, Ordained April 25, 1961. Auxiliary Bishop of Los Angeles.
Murphy, Michael J., Appointed April 20, Ordained Feb. 28, 1942. Auxiliary Bishop of Cleveland.
Pena, Raymundo, Appointed Oct. 16, Ordained May 25, 1957. Auxiliary Bishop of San Antonio.
Sheldon, Gilbert I., Appointed April 20, Ordained Feb. 28, 1953. Auxiliary Bishop of Cleveland.
Stafford, J. Francis, Appointed Jan. 27, Ordained Dec. 15, 1957. Auxiliary Bishop of Baltimore.
Timlin, James C., Appointed Aug. 3, Ordained July 16, 1951. Auxiliary Bishop of Scranton.

1977

Archbishops

McCarthy, Edward A., Succeeded to See July 26. Archbishop of Miami.
Quinn, John R., Appointed Feb. 22, Ordained July 19, 1953. Archbishop of San Francisco.
Salatka, Charles A., Appointed Sept. 27, Ordained Feb. 24, 1945. Archbishop of Oklahoma City.
Weakland, Rembert, *o.s.b.*, Appointed Sept. 20, Ordained June 24, 1951. Archbishop of Milwaukee.

Bishops

Cummins, John S., Appointed May 3, Ordained Jan. 24, 1953. Bishop of Oakland.
Daly, James J., Appointed Feb. 28, Ordained May 22, 1948. Auxiliary Bishop of Rockville Centre.
D'Antonio, Nicholas, *o.f.m.*, Appointed Aug. 22. Retired Vicar for Spanish-speaking, New Orleans.
Ferrario, Joseph A., Appointed Nov. 8, Ordained May 19, 1951. Auxiliary Bishop of Honolulu.
Garmendia, Francis, Appointed May 24, Ordained June 28, 1947. Auxiliary Bishop of New York.
Howze, Joseph L., Appointed March 1, Ordained May 7, 1959. Bishop of Biloxi.
Hubbard, Howard J., Appointed Feb. 1, Ordained Dec. 18, 1963. Bishop of Albany.
Kelly, Thomas C., *o.p.*, Appointed July 12, Ordained June 5, 1958. Auxiliary Bishop of Washington.
Kucera, Daniel W., *o.s.b.*, Appointed June 6, Ordained May 26, 1949. Auxiliary Bishop of Joliet.
Losten, Basil H., Appointed Sept. 20, Ordained June 10, 1957. Bishop of Stamford.

Maguire, Joseph F., Succeeded to See Nov. 4. Bishop of Springfield.
McCarrick, Theodore E., Appointed May 24, Ordained May 31, 1958. Auxiliary Bishop of New York.
Mulvee, Robert E., Appointed Feb. 15, Ordained June 30, 1957. Auxiliary Bishop of Manchester.
Ottenweller, Albert H., Appointed Oct. 11, Ordained June 19, 1943. Retired Bishop of Steubenville.
Paul, John J., Appointed May 17, Ordained Jan. 24, 1943. Titular Bishop of Lambese.
Rodimer, Frank J., Appointed Dec. 13, Ordained May 19, 1951. Bishop of Paterson.
Skylstad, William, Appointed Feb. 22, Ordained May 21, 1960. Bishop of Yakima.
Steiner, Kenneth, Appointed Dec. 6, Ordained May 19, 1962. Auxiliary Bishop of Portland in Oregon.
Wirz, George O., Appointed Dec. 20, Ordained May 31, 1952. Auxiliary Bishop of Madison.

1978

Bishops

Beltran, Eusebius J., Appointed Feb. 28, Ordained May 14, 1960. Bishop of Tulsa.
Costello, Thomas J., Appointed Jan. 10, Ordained June 5, 1954. Auxiliary Bishop of Syracuse.
Dudley, Paul V., Appointed Sept. 26, Ordained June 2, 1951. Bishop of Sioux Falls.
DuMaine, R. Pierre, Appointed April 28, Ordained June 5, 1957. Auxiliary Bishop of San Francisco.
Flores, Patrick F., Appointed April 4, Ordained May 26, 1956. Bishop of El Paso.
Hoffman, James R., Appointed April 18, Ordained July 28, 1957. Auxiliary Bishop of Toledo.
McNamara, Lawrence J., Appointed Jan. 10, Ordained May 30, 1953. Bishop of Grand Island.
Morneau, Robert F., Appointed Dec. 19, Ordained May 28, 1966. Auxiliary Bishop of Green Bay.
Murphy, Michael J., Appointed Nov. 28, Ordained Feb. 28, 1942. Coadjutor Bishop of Erie.
Quinn, Francis A., Appointed April 28, Ordained June 15, 1946. Auxiliary Bishop of San Francisco.
Rosazza, Peter A., Appointed Feb. 28, Ordained June 29, 1961. Auxiliary Bishop of Hartford.
Schmitt, Mark F., Appointed March 21, Ordained May 22, 1948. Bishop of Marquette.
Straling, Phillip F., Appointed July 18, Ordained March 19, 1959. Bishop of San Bernardino.

1979

Archbishop

Flores, Patrick F., Appointed Aug. 28, Ordained May 26, 1956. Archbishop of San Antonio.

Bishops

Clark, Matthew H., Appointed May 2, Ordained Dec. 19, 1962. Bishop of Rochester.
Fiorenza, Joseph A., Appointed Sept. 4, Ordained May 29, 1954. Bishop of San Angelo.
Fliss, Raphael M., Appointed Nov. 6, Ordained May 26, 1956. Coadjutor Bishop of Superior.
Friend, William B., Appointed Aug. 31, Ordained May 7, 1959. Auxiliary Bishop of Alexandria-Shreveport.
Griffin, James A., Appointed June 30, Ordained May 28, 1960. Auxiliary Bishop of Cleveland.
Houck, William R., Appointed March 28, Ordained May 19, 1951. Auxiliary Bishop of Jackson.
Hughes, William A., Appointed April 13, Ordained April 6, 1946. Bishop of Covington.
Imesch, Joseph L., Appointed June 30, Ordained Dec. 16, 1956. Bishop of Joliet.
Keeler, William H., Appointed July 24, Ordained July 17, 1955. Auxiliary Bishop of Harrisburg.
Larkin, W. Thomas, Appointed April 24, Ordained May 15, 1947. Retired Bishop of St. Petersburg.
Madera, Joseph J., *m.sp.s.*, Appointed Dec. 18, Ordained June 15, 1957. Coadjutor Bishop of Fresno.
McCarthy, John E., Appointed Jan. 23, Ordained May 26, 1956. Auxiliary Bishop of Galveston-Houston.
Nevins, John J., Appointed Feb. 6, Ordained June 6, 1959. Auxiliary Bishop of Miami.
Neylon, Martin J., *s.j.*, Appointed May 3, Ordained June 18, 1950. Bishop of The Carolines-Marshalls.
Pilla, Anthony M., Appointed June 30, Ordained May 23, 1959. Auxiliary Bishop of Cleveland.
Quinn, Francis A., Appointed Dec. 18, Ordained June 15, 1946. Bishop of Sacramento.
Rivera, Enrique Hernandez, Appointed June 11, Ordained June 8, 1968. Auxiliary Bishop of San Juan.
Rivera, Hector M., Appointed June 11, Ordained June 12, 1966. Auxiliary Bishop of San Juan.
Roman, Agustin A., Appointed Feb. 6, Ordained July 5, 1959. Auxiliary Bishop of Miami.
Schlarman, Stanley G., Appointed March 13, Ordained July 13, 1958. Auxiliary Bishop of Belleville.
Sklba, Richard J., Appointed Nov. 6, Ordained Dec. 20, 1959. Auxiliary Bishop of Milwaukee.
Snyder, John J., Appointed Oct. 2, Ordained June 9, 1951. Bishop of St. Augustine.

1980

Archbishops

Hickey, James A., Appointed June 17, Ordained June 15, 1946. Archbishop of Washington.
Lipscomb, Oscar H., Appointed July 29, Ordained July 15, 1956. Archbishop of Mobile.
Sulyk, Stephen, Appointed Dec. 29. Archbishop of Philadelphia Ukrainian.

Bishops

Bevilacqua, Anthony, Appointed Oct. 7, Ordained June 11, 1949. Auxiliary Bishop of Brooklyn.
Bullock, William H., Appointed June 3, Ordained June 7, 1952. Auxiliary Bishop of St. Paul-Minneapolis.
Chedid, John, Appointed Oct. 28, Ordained Dec. 21, 1951. Auxiliary Bishop of St. Maron.
Franzetta, Benedict C., Appointed July 29, Ordained April 29, 1950. Auxiliary Bishop of Youngstown.
Ham, J. Richard, *m.m.*, Appointed Oct. 7, Ordained June 12, 1948. Retired Auxiliary Bishop of St. Paul-Minneapolis.
Hoffman, James R., Appointed Dec. 16, Ordained July 28, 1957. Bishop of Toledo.
Kucera, Daniel W., *o.s.b.*, Appointed March 11, Ordained May 26, 1949. Bishop of Salina.
Madera, Joseph J., *m.sp.s.*, Succeeded to See July 1. Bishop of Fresno.
Mahony, Roger M., Appointed Feb. 26, Ordained May 1, 1962. Bishop of Stockton.
Matthiesen, Leroy T., Appointed March 25, Ordained March 10, 1946. Bishop of Amarillo.
Pena, Raymundo J., Appointed April 29, Ordained May 25, 1957. Bishop of El Paso.
Pilla, Anthony M., Appointed Nov. 18, Ordained May 23, 1959. Bishop of Cleveland.
Reiss, John C., Appointed March 4, Ordained May 31, 1947. Bishop of Trenton.
Speyrer, Jude, Appointed Jan. 29, Ordained July 25, 1953. Bishop of Lake Charles.
Sullivan, Joseph M., Appointed Oct. 7, Ordained June 2, 1956. Auxiliary Bishop of Brooklyn.
Tafoya, Arthur N., Appointed July 1, Ordained May 12, 1962. Bishop of Pueblo.
Untener, Kenneth E., Appointed Oct. 4, Ordained June 1, 1963. Bishop of Saginaw.
Valero, Rene, Appointed Oct. 7, Ordained June 2, 1956. Auxiliary Bishop of Brooklyn.
Weigand, William K., Appointed Sept. 3, Ordained May 25, 1963. Bishop of Salt Lake City.

1981

Archbishops

Kelly, Thomas C., *o.p.*, Appointed Dec. 29, Ordained June 5, 1958. Archbishop of Louisville.
Marcinkus, Paul C., Appointed Sept. 26, Ordained May 3, 1947. Titular Archbishop of Orta, Vatican City State.
Szoka, Edmund C., Appointed March 28, Ordained June 5, 1954. Emeritus Archbishop of Detroit.

Bishops

Delaney, Joseph P., Appointed July 10, Ordained Dec. 18, 1960. Bishop of Fort Worth.
DeSimone, Louis A., Appointed June 27, Ordained May 10, 1952. Auxiliary Bishop of Philadelphia.
Dumaine, Pierre, Appointed Jan. 27, Ordained June 5, 1957. Bishop of San Jose.
Grahmann, Charles V., Appointed June 30, Ordained March 17, 1956. Auxiliary Bishop of San Antonio.
Hughes, Alfred C., Appointed July 21, Ordained Dec. 15, 1957. Auxiliary Bishop of Boston.
Lotocky, Innocent, *o.s.b.m.*, Appointed Jan. 29, Ordained Nov. 24, 1940. Bishop of St. Nicholas Chicago.
McCarrick, Theodore E., Appointed Nov. 24. Bishop of Metuchen.
Milone, Anthony M., Appointed Nov. 10, Ordained Dec. 15, 1957. Auxiliary Bishop of Omaha.
Moskal, Robert M., Appointed Aug. 3, Ordained March 25, 1963. Bishop of St. Josaphat in Parma.
O'Brien, Thomas J., Appointed Nov. 24. Ordained May 7, 1961. Bishop of Phoenix.
Ramirez, Ricardo, *c.s.b.*, Appointed Oct. 27, Ordained Dec. 10, 1966. Auxiliary Bishop of San Antonio.
Rivera, Enrique Hernandez, Appointed Feb. 13, Ordained June 8, 1968. Bishop of Caguas.
Rose, Robert J., Appointed Oct. 13, Ordained Dec. 21, 1955. Bishop of Gaylord.
Ryan, Daniel L., Appointed Aug. 14, Ordained May 3, 1956. Auxiliary Bishop of Joliet.
Santana, Hermin Negron, Appointed June 30, Ordained May 30, 1969. Auxiliary Bishop of San Juan.
Schulte, Francis B., Appointed June 27, Ordained May 10, 1952. Auxiliary Bishop of Philadelphia.
Setian, Nerses Mikael, Appointed July 3, Ordained April 13, 1941. Bishop of Armenian Catholic Exarchate of U.S.A. and Canada.
Symons, J. Keith, Appointed Jan. 16, Ordained May 18, 1958. Auxiliary Bishop of St. Petersburg.
Walsh, Daniel F., Appointed June 30, Ordained March 30, 1963. Auxiliary Bishop of San Francisco.

1982

Archbishops

Pilarczyk, Daniel E., Appointed Nov. 2, Ordained Dec. 20, 1959. Archbishop of Cincinnati.
Zayek, Francis M., Appointed Dec. 22, Ordained March 17, 1946. Archbishop of St. Maron, Brooklyn.

Bishops

Anderson, Moses B., *s.s.e.*, Appointed Dec. 3, Ordained May 30, 1958. Auxiliary Bishop of Detroit.
Cooney, Patrick, R., Appointed Dec. 7, Ordained Dec. 20, 1959. Auxiliary Bishop of Detroit.
Ferrario, Joseph A., Appointed May 13, Ordained May 13, 1951. Bishop of Honolulu.
Friend, William B., Appointed Nov. 23. Bishop of Alexandria-Shreveport.
Gerber, Eugene J., Appointed Nov. 23, Ordained May 19, 1959. Bishop of Wichita.
Grahmann, Charles V., Appointed April 14, Ordained March 17, 1956. Bishop of Victoria.
Kinney, John F., Appointed June 28, Ordained Feb. 2, 1963. Bishop of Bismarck.
Kmiec, Edward V., Appointed Aug. 26, Ordained Dec. 20, 1961. Auxiliary Bishop of Trenton.
McRaith, John J., Appointed Oct. 23, Ordained Feb. 21, 1960. Bishop of Owensboro.
Melczek, Dale J., Appointed Dec. 3, Ordained June 6, 1964. Auxiliary Bishop of Detroit.
Moreno, Manuel D., Appointed Jan. 12, Ordained April 25, 1961. Bishop of Tucson.
Murphy, Michael J., Succeeded to See July 16. Bishop of Erie.
Pevec, Edward A., Appointed April 13, Ordained April 29, 1950. Auxiliary Bishop of Cleveland.
Puscas, Louis, Appointed Dec. 4, Ordained May 14, 1942. Eparch of Romanian Diocese of Canton.
Ramirez, Ricardo, *c.s.b.*, Appointed Aug. 31, Ordained Dec. 10, 1966. Bishop of Las Cruces.
Stafford, J. Francis, Appointed Nov. 16, Ordained Dec. 15, 1957. Bishop of Memphis.

1983

Archbishop

Kucera, Daniel, Appointed Dec. 20. Archbishop of Dubuque.

Bishops

Apuron, Anthony, *o.f.m.cap.*, Appointed Dec. 8. Auxiliary Bishop of Agana.
Arias, David, *o.a.r.*, Appointed Jan. 25. Auxiliary Bishop of Newark.
Bevilacqua, Anthony, Appointed Oct. 7. Bishop of Pittsburgh.
Brom, Robert, Appointed March 25. Bishop of Duluth.
Carlson, Robert, Appointed Nov. 22. Auxiliary Bishop of St. Paul-Minneapolis.
Dimino, Joseph, Appointed March 29. Auxiliary Bishop of Military Services.
Gracida, Rene, Appointed May 19. Bishop of Corpus Christi.
Gregory, Wilton, Appointed Oct. 31. Auxiliary Bishop of Chicago.
Griffin, James, Appointed Feb. 7. Bishop of Columbus.
Hanifen, Richard, Appointed Nov. 10. Bishop of Colorado Springs.
Keeler, William, Appointed Nov. 10. Bishop of Harrisburg.
Levada, William, Appointed March 29. Auxiliary Bishop of Los Angeles.
Lyne, Timothy, Appointed Oct. 31. Auxiliary Bishop of Chicago.
Maida, Adam, Appointed Nov. 8. Bishop of Green Bay.
Montrose, Donald, Appointed March 25. Auxiliary Bishop of Los Angeles.
Moskal, Robert, Appointed Dec. 5. Bishop of St. Josaphat in Parma.
O'Donnell, Edward, Appointed Dec. 6. Auxiliary Bishop of St. Louis.
Pataki, Andrew, Appointed May 30. Auxiliary Bishop of Passaic.

Paul, John J., Appointed Oct. 18. Bishop of LaCrosse.
Popp, Bernard, Appointed June 7. Auxiliary Bishop of San Antonio.
Quinn, A. James, Appointed Oct. 14. Auxiliary Bishop of Cleveland.
Rodriguez, Placido, *c.m.f.*, Appointed Oct. 31. Auxiliary Bishop of Chicago.
Roque, Francis, Appointed March 29. Auxiliary Bishop of Military Services.
Ryan, Daniel, Appointed Nov. 22. Bishop of Springfield in Illinois.
Schlarmann, Stanley, Appointed March 1. Bishop of Dodge City.
Sheehan, Michael, Appointed March 29. Bishop of Lubbock.
Soens, Lawrence, Appointed June 15. Bishop of Sioux City.
Steib, J. Terry, *s.v.d.*, Appointed Dec. 6. Auxiliary Bishop of St. Louis.
Symons, J. Keith, Appointed Sept. 29. Bishop of Pensacola-Tallahassee.
Vlazny, John, Appointed Oct. 31. Auxiliary Bishop of Chicago.
Welsh, Thomas, Appointed Feb. 8. Bishop of Allentown.

1984

Archbishops

Foley, John, Appointed April 9. Archbishop to the Pontifical Commission for Social Communication.
Law, Bernard, Appointed Jan. 24. Archbishop of Boston.

Bishops

Baltakis, Paul, Appointed June 1. Bishop for the Lithuanian Apostolate.
Camacho, Tomas A., Appointed Nov. 8. Bishop of Chalan Kanoa.
Daily, Thomas, Appointed July 17. Bishop of Palm Beach.
Donnelly, Robert, Appointed March 20. Auxiliary Bishop of Toledo.
Donoghue, John, Appointed Nov. 6. Bishop of Charlotte.
Fiorenza, Joseph, Appointed Dec. 18. Bishop of Galveston-Houston.
Fitzsimons, George, Appointed March 22. Bishop of Salina.
Garland, James, Appointed June 25. Auxiliary Bishop of Cincinnati.
Higi, William, Appointed April 7. Bishop of Lafayette in Indiana.
Houck, William, Appointed April 24. Bishop of Jackson.
Keleher, James, Appointed Oct. 23. Bishop of Belleville.
Leibrecht, John, Appointed Oct. 23. Bishop of Springfield-Cape Girardeau.
Nevins, John, Appointed July 17. Bishop of Venice.
Newman, William, Appointed July 2. Auxiliary Bishop of Baltimore.
O'Malley, Sean, *o.f.m.cap.*, Appointed May 30. Coadjutor Bishop of St. Thomas Virgin Islands.
Pataki, Andrew, Appointed June 19. Bishop of Parma.
Ricard, John, *s.s.j.*, Appointed May 29. Auxiliary Bishop of Baltimore.
Steinbock, John, Appointed May 29. Auxiliary Bishop of Orange.
Timlin, James, Appointed April 24. Bishop of Scranton.
Williams, J. Kendrick, Appointed April 15. Auxiliary Bishop of Covington.

1985

Cardinals

Law, Bernard Cardinal, Created May 25. Archbishop of Boston.
Mahony, Roger, Appointed July 16. Archbishop of Los Angeles.

Bishops

Apuron, Anthony S., *o.f.m.cap.*, Appointed Oct. 27. Apostolic Administrator of Agana.
Banks, Robert J., Appointed June 26. Auxiliary Bishop of Boston.
Corrada, Alvaro, *s.j.*, Appointed Aug. 4. Auxiliary Bishop of Washington.
D'Arcy, John M., Appointed Feb. 26. Bishop of Fort Wayne-South Bend.
Egan, Edward M., Appointed April 1. Auxiliary Bishop of New York.
Fliss, Raphael M., Succeeded to See June 27. Bishop of Superior.
Ibrahim, Ibrahim, Appointed Sept. 14. Eparch of St. Thomas the Apostle.
Kaffer, Roger L., Appointed April 25. Auxiliary Bishop of Joliet.
McCarthy, John E., Appointed Dec. 24. Bishop of Austin.
Montrose, Donald, Appointed Dec. 19. Bishop of Stockton.
Mulvee, Robert E., Appointed Feb. 16. Bishop of Wilmington.
O'Malley, Sean, *o.f.m.cap.*, Succeeded to See Oct. 16. Bishop of St. Thomas in the Virgin Islands.
Pfeifer, Michael, *o.m.i.*, Appointed July 26. Bishop of San Angelo.
Schulte, Francis B., Appointed June 4. Bishop of Wheeling-Charleston.
Sullivan, James S., Appointed April 2. Bishop of Fargo.
Trautman, Donald W., Appointed Feb. 27. Auxiliary Bishop of Buffalo.
Wuerl, Donald, Appointed Dec. 3. Auxiliary Bishop of Seattle.

1986

Archbishops

Apuron, Anthony S., *o.f.m.cap.*, Succeeded to See May 11. Archbishop of Agana.
Levada, William J., Appointed July 1. Archbishop of Portland in Oregon.
McCarrick, Theodore, Appointed June 1. Archbishop of Newark.
Stafford, J. Francis, Appointed June 3. Archbishop of Denver.

Bishops

Dorsey, Norbert, *c.p.*, Appointed Jan. 10. Auxiliary Bishop of Miami.
Elya, John A., *b.s.o.*, Appointed April 2. Auxiliary Bishop of Newton.
Favalora, John C., Appointed June 16. Bishop of Alexandria.
Flynn, Harry, Appointed April 19. Coadjutor Bishop of Lafayette.
Foley, David, Appointed May 3. Auxiliary Bishop of Richmond.
Friend, William, Appointed June 1. Bishop of Shreveport.
Gerry, Joseph, *o.s.b.*, Appointed April 21. Auxiliary Bishop of Manchester.
Hughes, Edward, Appointed Dec. 11. Bishop of Metuchen.
Kuzma, George M., Appointed Nov. 11. Auxiliary Bishop of Passaic.
McCormack, William J., Appointed Dec. 23. Auxiliary Bishop of New York.
McFarland, Norman F., Appointed Dec. 29. Bishop of Orange.
Ochoa, Armando, Appointed Dec. 29. Auxiliary Bishop of Los Angeles.
Pelotte, Donald E., *s.s.s.*, Appointed Feb. 24. Coadjutor Bishop of Gallup.
Watters, Loras J., Appointed Oct. 14. Apostolic Administrator of Winona.
Weitzel, John Q., *m.m.*, Appointed Oct. 29. Bishop of Samoa-Pago Pago.
Ziemann, G. Patrick, Appointed Dec. 29. Auxiliary Bishop of Los Angeles.

1987

Bishops

Adamec, Joseph V., Appointed March 12. Bishop of Altoona-Johnstown.
Bosco, Anthony G., Appointed April 14. Bishop of Greensburg.
Buechlein, Daniel, *o.s.b.*, Appointed Jan. 20. Bishop of Memphis.
Bullock, William, Appointed Feb. 10. Bishop of Des Moines.
Franklin, William, Appointed Jan. 29. Auxiliary Bishop of Dubuque.
Guillory, Curtis, Appointed Dec. 29. Auxiliary Bishop of Galveston-Houston.
Hanus, Jerome, *o.s.b.*, Appointed July 6. Bishop of St. Cloud.
Milone, Anthony G., Appointed Dec. 14. Bishop of Great Falls-Billings.
Myers, John J., Appointed July 14. Coadjutor Bishop of Peoria.
Rueger, George, Appointed Jan. 19. Auxiliary Bishop of Worcester.
Samo, Amando, Appointed May 10. Auxiliary Bishop of The Carolines-Marshalls.
Smith, John M., Appointed Dec. 1. Auxiliary Bishop of Newark.
Steinbock, John, Appointed March 31. Bishop of Santa Rosa.
Vlazny, John, Appointed May 19. Bishop of Winona.
Walsh, Daniel F., Appointed June 9. Bishop of Reno-Las Vegas.

1988

Cardinals

Hickey, James Cardinal, Created June 29. Archbishop of Washington.
Szoka, Edmund Cardinal, Created June 29. Pres. Prefecture for Economic Affairs of the Holy See, Vatican.

Archbishops

Bevilacqua, Anthony J., Appointed Feb. 11. Archbishop of Philadelphia.
Schulte, Francis B., Appointed Dec. 13. Archbishop of New Orleans.

Bishops

Boland, Raymond J., Appointed Feb. 2. Bishop of Birmingham.
Brown, Tod D., Appointed Dec. 27. Bishop of Boise.
Carmody, Edmond, Appointed Nov. 8. Auxiliary Bishop of San Antonio.
Chaput, Charles, *o.f.m.cap.*, Appointed April 11. Bishop of Rapid City.
Curlin, William G., Appointed Dec. 20. Auxiliary Bishop of Washington.
DiLorenzo, Francis, Appointed Jan. 26. Auxiliary Bishop of Scranton.
Dunne, John C., Appointed Oct. 21. Auxiliary Bishop of Rockville Centre.
Egan, Edward, Appointed Nov. 8. Bishop of Bridgeport.
Gerry, Joseph, *o.s.b.*, Appointed Dec. 27. Bishop of Portland (in Maine).
Gonzalez, Roberto, *o.f.m.*, Appointed July 19. Auxiliary Bishop of Boston.
Gorman, John R., Appointed Feb. 16. Auxiliary Bishop of Chicago.
Jakubowski, Thaddeus J., Appointed Feb. 16. Auxiliary Bishop of Chicago.
Loverde, Paul S., Appointed Feb. 3. Auxiliary Bishop of Hartford.
McGrath, Patrick, Appointed Dec. 6. Auxiliary Bishop of San Francisco.
O'Connell, Anthony J., Appointed June 7. Bishop of Knoxville.
Olivier, Leonard J., *s.v.d.*, Appointed Dec. 20. Auxiliary Bishop of Washington.
Schmitt, Bernard W., Appointed May 31. Auxiliary Bishop of Wheeling-Charleston.
Sevilla, Carlos A., *s.j.*, Appointed Dec. 6. Auxiliary Bishop of San Francisco.
Wcela, Emil A., Appointed Oct. 21. Auxiliary Bishop of Rockville Centre.
Williams, J. Kendrick, Appointed March 2. Bishop of Lexington.
Winter, William J., Appointed Dec. 27. Auxiliary Bishop of Pittsburgh.
Wuerl, Donald, Appointed Feb. 11. Bishop of Pittsburgh.

1989

Archbishop

Keeler, William, Appointed April 6. Archbishop of Baltimore.

Bishops

Brom, Robert, Appointed April 22. Coadjutor Bishop of San Diego.
Charron, Joseph L., *c.pp.s.*, Appointed Nov. 6. Auxiliary Bishop of St. Paul-Minneapolis.
Cooney, Patrick, Appointed Nov. 21. Bishop of Gaylord.
Datillo, Nicholas, Appointed Nov. 21. Bishop of Harrisburg.
Driscoll, Michael P., Appointed Dec. 19. Auxiliary Bishop of Orange.
Favalora, John, Appointed March 7. Bishop of St. Petersburg.
Flynn, Harry J., Succeeded to the See May 13. Bishop of Lafayette.
Gettelfinger, Gerald A., Appointed March 11. Bishop of Evansville.
Grahmann, Charles V., Appointed Dec. 18. Coadjutor Bishop of Dallas.
Grosz, Edward, Appointed Nov. 22. Auxiliary Bishop of Buffalo.
Jacobs, Sam, Appointed July 1. Bishop of Alexandria.
Mikloshazy, Attila, *s.j.*, Appointed Aug. 12. Bishop for the Apostolate to the Hungarians.
Rose, Robert J., Appointed July 11. Bishop of Grand Rapids.
Samra, Nicholas J., Appointed June 29. Auxiliary Bishop of Newton.
Schmitt, Bernard W., Appointed March 30. Bishop of Wheeling-Charleston.
Schwietz, Roger L., *o.m.i.*, Appointed Dec. 12. Bishop of Duluth.
Thompson, David B., Appointed May 9. Coadjutor Bishop of Charleston.
Zipfel, Paul A., Appointed May 16. Auxiliary Bishop of St. Louis.

1990

Archbishop

Maida, Adam J., Appointed June 11. Archbishop of Detroit.

Bishops

Banks, Robert J., Appointed Oct. 16. Bishop of Green Bay.
Blaire, Stephen E., Appointed Feb. 17. Auxiliary Bishop of Los Angeles.
Brom, Robert H., Succeeded to the See July 10. Bishop of San Diego.
Daily, Thomas V., Appointed Feb. 20. Bishop of Brooklyn.
Dorsey, Norbert M., *c.p.*, Appointed March 20. Bishop of Orlando.
Dupre, Thomas L., Appointed April 19. Auxiliary Bishop of Springfield in Massachusetts.
Fellhauer, David E., Appointed April 19. Bishop of Victoria.
George, Francis E., *o.m.i.*, Appointed July 10. Bishop of Yakima.
Grahmann, Charles V., Succeeded to See July 14. Bishop of Dallas.
Kuzma, George M., Appointed Oct. 23. Bishop of Van Nuys.
Muench, Robert W., Appointed May 8. Auxiliary Bishop of New Orleans.
Myers, John J., Succeeded to See Jan. 23. Bishop of Peoria.
Pelotte, Donald E., *s.s.s.*, Succeeded to See March 20. Bishop of Gallup.
Ryan, Sylvester D., Appointed Feb. 17. Auxiliary Bishop of Los Angeles.
Saltarelli, Michael A., Appointed June 12. Auxiliary Bishop of Newark.
Sheridan, Patrick J., Appointed Dec. 12. Auxiliary Bishop of New York.
Skylstad, William S., Appointed April 17. Bishop of Spokane.
Symons, J. Keith, Appointed June 2. Bishop of Palm Beach.
Thompson, David B., Succeeded to See Feb. 22. Bishop of Charleston.
Trautman, Donald W., Appointed July 16. Bishop of Erie.

1991

Cardinals

Bevilacqua, Anthony Cardinal, Created June 28. Archbishop of Philadelphia.
Mahony, Roger Cardinal, Created June 28. Archbishop of Los Angeles.

Archbishops

Cronin, Daniel A., Appointed Dec. 9. Archbishop of Hartford.
Dimino, Joseph T., Succeeded to the See June 21. Archbishop of the Military Services.

Bishops

Glynn, John J., Appointed Dec. 10. Auxiliary Bishop of the Military Services.
Goedert, Raymond E., Appointed July 8. Auxiliary Bishop of Chicago.
Madera, Joseph J., *m.sp.s.*, Appointed May 28. Auxiliary Bishop of the Military Services.
Sheets, John R., *s.j.*, Appointed May 14. Auxiliary Bishop of Fort Wayne-South Bend.
Smith, John M., Appointed June 24. Bishop of Pensacola-Tallahassee.
Steinbock, John T., Appointed October 15. Bishop of Santa Rosa.

1992

Archbishops

Beltran, Eusebius J., Appointed November 24. Archbishop of Oklahoma City, from Bishop of Tulsa.
Buechlein, Daniel M., *o.s.b.*, Appointed July 14. Archbishop of Indianapolis, from Bishop of Memphis.

Bishops

Angell, Kenneth A., Appointed October 10. Bishop of Burlington, from Auxiliary Bishop of Providence.
Barnes, Gerald R., Appointed January 28. Auxiliary Bishop of San Bernardino.
Boles, John P., Appointed April 14. Auxiliary Bishop of Boston.
Bruskewitz, Fabian W., Appointed March 24. Bishop of Lincoln.
Carmody, Edmond, Appointed March 24. Bishop of Tyler, from Auxiliary Bishop of San Antonio.
Carmon, Dominic, *s.v.d.*, Appointed December 16. Auxiliary Bishop of New Orleans.
Galante, Joseph A., Appointed October 13. Auxiliary Bishop of San Antonio.
Garland, James H., Appointed October 10. Bishop of Marquette, from Auxiliary Bishop of Cincinnati.
Jarrell, Michael Charles, Appointed December 29. Bishop of Houma-Thibodaux.
Kmiec, Edward Urban, Appointed October 13. Bishop of Nashville, from Auxiliary Bishop of Trenton.
McNamara, John R., Appointed April 14. Auxiliary Bishop of Boston.
Mansell, Henry J., Appointed November 24. Auxiliary Bishop of New York.
O'Malley, Sean P., *o.f.m.cap.*, Appointed July 16. Bishop of Fall River, from Bishop of St. Thomas Virgin Islands.
Paska, Walter, Appointed January 26. Auxiliary Bishop of Philadelphia Ukrainian.
Ryan, Sylvester D., Appointed January 21. Bishop of Monterey, from Auxiliary Bishop of Los Angeles.
Sheldon, Gilbert I., Appointed January 28. Bishop of Steubenville, from Auxiliary Bishop of Cleveland.
Tobin, Thomas J., Appointed November 3. Auxiliary Bishop of Pittsburgh.
Ziemann, G. Patrick, Appointed July 14. Bishop of Santa Rosa, from Auxiliary Bishop of Los Angeles.

1993

Archbishops

Curtiss, Elden F., Appointed May 4. Archbishop of Omaha, from Bishop of Helena.
Donoghue, John F., Appointed June 22. Archbishop of Atlanta, Bishop of Charlotte.
Keleher, James P., Transferred Sept. 8. Archbishop of Kansas City in Kansas, from Bishop of Belleville.
Sheehan, Michael J., Appointed April 6. Archbishop of Santa Fe.

Bishops

Boland, Raymond J., Appointed June 22. Bishop of Kansas City St. Joseph, from Bishop of Birmingham.
Britt, Kevin M., Appointed November 23. Auxiliary Bishop of Detroit.
Bullock, William H., Appointed April 13. Bishop of Madison, from Bishop of Des Moines.
Charron, Joseph L., *c.pp.s.* Appointed November 12. Bishop of Des Moines, from Auxiliary Bishop of St. Paul and Minneapolis.
Elya, John A., *b.s.o.* Appointed December 7. Bishop of Newton from Auxiliary Bishop of Newton.
Franklin, William E., Appointed November 12. Bishop of Davenport, from Auxiliary Bishop of Dubuque.
Gregory, Wilton, Appointed December 29. Bishop of Belleville from Auxiliary Bishop of Chicago.
Harrington, Bernard J., Appointed November 23. Auxiliary Bishop of Detroit.
Hughes, Alfred C., Appointed September 7. Bishop of Baton Rouge, from Auxiliary Bishop of Boston.
Loverde, Paul S., Appointed November 11. Bishop of Ogdensburg, from Auxiliary Bishop of Hartford.
Moeddel, Carl K., Appointed June 15. Auxiliary Bishop of Cincinnati.
Slattery, Edward J., Appointed November 11. Bishop of Tulsa.
Steib, James Terry, *s.v.d.* Appointed March 23. Bishop of Memphis, from Auxiliary Bishop of St. Louis.
Tamayo, James A., Appointed January 26. Auxiliary Bishop of Galveston-Houston.
Thomas, Elliot G., Appointed October 10. Bishop of St. Thomas, Virgin Islands.
Weigand, William K., Appointed November 3. Bishop of Sacramento from Bishop of Salt Lake City.
Wiwchar, Michael, *c.ss.r.* Appointed July 15. Bishop of St. Nicholas in Chicago for Ukrainians.

1994

Cardinals

Keeler, William Cardinal, Created November 26. Archbishop of Baltimore.
Maida, Adam Cardinal, Created November 26. Archbishop of Detroit.

Archbishops

Favalora, John C., Appointed November 3. Archbishop of Miami.
Flynn, Harry J., Appointed February 2. Coadjutor Archbishop of St. Paul-Minneapolis.
Hanus, Jerome, *o.s.b.* Appointed August 23. Coadjutor Archbishop of Dubuque.
Procyk, Judson M., Appointed November 15. Archbishop of Pittsburgh Byzantine.
Rigali, Justin F., Appointed January 25. Archbishop of St. Louis.

Bishops

Barbarito, Gerald, Appointed June 28. Auxiliary Bishop of Brooklyn.
Brunett, Alexander J., Appointed April 19. Bishop of Helena.
Burke, Raymond L., Appointed December 10. Bishop of La Crosse.
Carlson, Robert J., Appointed January 13. Bishop Coadjutor of Sioux Falls, from Auxiliary Bishop of St. Paul-Minneapolis.
Catanello, Ignatius, Appointed June 28. Auxiliary Bishop of Brooklyn.
Chedid, John G., Appointed March 1. First Bishop of Our Lady of Lebanon in Los Angeles, from Auxiliary Bishop of St. Maron of Brooklyn.
Cullen, Edward P., Appointed February 8. Auxiliary Bishop of Philadelphia.
Curlin, William G., Appointed February 22. Bishop of Charlotte, from Auxiliary Bishop of Washington.
Curry, Thomas J., Appointed February 8. Auxiliary Bishop of Los Angeles.
Doran, Thomas G., Appointed April 19. Bishop of Rockford.
DiLorenzo, Francis X., Appointed October 4. Bishop of Honolulu.
Foley, David E., Appointed March 22. Bishop of Birmingham, from Auxiliary Bishop of Richmond.
Galante, Joseph A., Appointed April 5. Bishop of Beaumont, from Auxiliary Bishop of San Antonio.
McDonnell, Charles J., Appointed March 15. Auxiliary Bishop of Newark.
Niederauer, George H., Appointed November 3. Bishop of Salt Lake City.
O'Donnell, Edward J., Appointed November 8. Bishop of Lafayette (Louisiana).
Reilly, Daniel P., Appointed October 27. Bishop of Worcester.
Rodriguez, Placido, *c.m.f.*, Appointed April 5. Bishop of Lubbock, from Auxiliary Bishop of Chicago.
Sartoris, Joseph M., Appointed February 8. Auxiliary Bishop of Los Angeles.
Yanta, John W., Appointed October 27. Auxiliary of San Antonio.
Zavala, Gabino, Appointed February 8. Auxiliary Bishop of Los Angeles.

1995

Archbishops

Flynn, Harry J., Appointed September 8. From Coadjutor to Archbishop of St. Paul-Minneapolis.
Hanus, Jerome G., *o.s.b.*, Succeeding as Archbishop of Dubuque from status of Coadjutor.
Levada, William J., Succeeding as Archbishop of San Francisco December 1995.
Schleck, Charles A., *c.s.c.*, Appointed February 10. Titular Archbishop of Africa, Adjunct Secretary of the Congregation for the Evangelization of Peoples.

Bishops

Barnes, Gerald R., Appointed December 28, 1995. Bishop of San Bernardino, from Auxiliary of same Diocese.
Boland, J. Kevin, Appointed February 7, 1995. Bishop of Savannah.
Braxton, Edward K., Appointed March 28. Auxiliary Bishop of St. Louis.
Carlson, Robert J., Succeeding as Bishop of Sioux Falls in March, from status of Coadjutor.
Conway, Edwin M., Appointed January 24. Auxiliary Bishop of Chicago.
Cote, Michael R., Appointed May 9. Auxiliary Bishop of Portland in Maine.
Dougherty, John M., Appointed February 7, 1995. Auxiliary Bishop of Scranton.
Dupre, Thomas L., Appointed March 14. Bishop of Springfield, from Auxiliary Bishop of Springfield.
Gonzalez, Roberto O., *o.f.m.*, Appointed May 16. Coadjutor Bishop of Corpus Chrisit, from Auxiliary Bishop of Boston.
Hart, Daniel A., Appointed September 12. Bishop of Norwich, from Auxiliary Bishop of Boston.
Kicanas, Gerald F., Appointed January 24. Auxiliary Bishop of Chicago.
Kinney, John F., Appointed May 8. Bishop of St. Cloud from Bishop of Bismarck.
Lori, William E., Appointed February 27. Auxiliary Bishop of Washington.
Lynch, Robert N., Appointed Bishop of St. Petersburg December 4, 1995.
McCormack, John B., Appointed November Auxiliary Bishop of Boston.
Mansell, Henry J., Appointed April 18, installed June 12. Bishop of Buffalo, from Auxiliary Bishop of New York.
Melczek, Dale J., Named Coadjutor Bishop of Gary November 9.

Mengeling, Carl F., Appointed November Bishop of Lansing.
Moynihan, James M., Appointed April 29, installed May 29. Bishop of Syracuse.
Mulvee, Robert Edward, Appointed February 7. Coadjutor Bishop of Providence from Bishop of Wilmington.
Murphy, William F., Appointed November Auxiliary Bishop of Boston.
Murry, George V., *s.j.* Appointed January 24. Auxiliary Bishop of Chicago.
Pataki, Andrew, Appointed Bishop of Passaic November, from Bishop of Parma.
Pena, Raymundo J., Appointed May 23. Bishop of Brownsville, from Bishop of El Paso.
Saltarelli, Michael A., Appointed Bishop of Wilmington, from Auxiliary of Newark.
Smith, John M., Named Coadjutor of Trenton from Bishop of Pensacola-Tallahassee.
Straling, Phillip F., Appointed March 21. Bishop of Reno, from former Bishop of San Bernadino.
Tertzakian, Hovhannes, *o.m.ven.*, Appointed January 6, ordained April 29. Apostolic Exarch for Armenian Catholics in the United States and Canada.
Tobin, Thomas J., Appointed Bishop of Youngstown, from Auxiliary of Pittsburgh.
Walsh, Daniel F., Appointed March 21. Bishop of Las Vegas, formerly Bishop of Reno-Las Vegas.

1996

Archbishop

George, Francis, *o.m.i.*, Appointed Archbishop of Portland in Oregon from Bishop of Yakima.

Bishops

Allue, Emilio, *s.d.b.*, Appointed Auxiliary Bishop of Boston July 24.
Aymond, Gregory M., Appointed Auxiliary Bishop of New Orleans November 19.
Botean, John Michael, Appointed Bishop of Romanian Catholic Diocese of St. George in Canton.
DiMarzio, Nicholas A., Appointed Auxiliary Bishop of Newark September.
Doueihi, Hector, Appointed Bishop of St. Maron of Brooklyn.
Irwin, Francis X., Appointed Auxiliary Bishop of Boston July 24.
O'Brien, Edwin F., Appointed Auxiliary Bishop of New York.
Manz, John R., Appointed Auxiliary Bishop of Chicago January 23.
Maginnis, Robert P., Appointed Auxiliary Bishop of Philadelphia January 23.
Martino, Joseph F., Appointed Auxiliary Bishop of Philadelphia, January 23.
Muench, Robert W., Bishop of Covington from Auxiliary Bishop of New Orleans.
Nienstedt, John C., Appointed Auxiliary Bishop of Detroit June 11.
Ochoa, Armando, Appointed Bishop of El Paso from Auxiliary Bishop of Los Angeles.
Sevilla, Carlos A., *s.j.* Appointed Bishop of Yakima from Auxiliary Bishop of San Francisco December 31.
Schott, Basil, o.f.m., Bishop of Parma (Ruthenians).
Steiner, Kenneth, Appointed Auxiliary Bishop of Portland in Oregon.
Vigneron, Allen H., Appointed Auxiliary Bishop of Detroit June 11.
Warfel, Michael, Appointed Bishop of Juneau November 19.
Younan, Joseph, Appointed Bishop of Our Lady of Deliverance of Newark.
Zipfel, Paul A., Appointed Bishop of Bismarck from Auxiliary Bishop of Saint Louis December 31.

1997

Archbishops

Chaput, Charles J., *o.f.m.cap.*, Appointed Archbishop of Denver February 18, 1997, from Bishop of Rapid City.
George, Francis, *o.m.i.*, Appointed Archbishop of Chicago from Archbishop of Portland in Oregon from Bishop of Yakima.
O'Brien, Edwin F., Appointed Archbishop for the Military Services from Auxiliary Bishop of New York.

Bishops

Bootkoski, Paul G., Appointed Auxiliary Bishop for the Archdiocese of Newark, July.
Breen, Vincent DePaul, Appointed Bishop of Metuchen, July 8.
Brucato, Robert A., Appointed Auxiliary Bishop for the Archdiocese of New York, July.
Cullen, Edward P., Appointed Bishop of Allentown from Auxiliary Bishop of Philadelphia, December.
Fernandez, Gilberto, Appointed Auxiliary Bishop for the Archdiocese of Miami, June 23.
Garcia, Richard J., Appointed Auxiliary Bishop of Sacramento, November.
Gaydos, John R., Appointed June 24. Bishop of Jefferson City.
Gonzalez, Roberto, Appointed Bishop of Corpus Christi March 31.
Jenky, Daniel R., *c.s.c.*, Appointed Auxiliary Bishop of Fort Wayne-South Bend,
Macaluso, Christie A., Appointed Auxiliary Bishop of Hartford March 18.
Mulvee, Robert E., Succeeds as Bishop of Providence from Coadjutor Bishop of Providence, June.
Murray, James A., Appointed Bishop of Kalamazoo November.
Naumann, Joseph F., Appointed Bishop of St. Louis, July.
Ricard, John H., *s.s.j.*, Appointed Bishop of Pensacola-Tallahassee January.
Sheridan, Michael J., Appointed Auxiliary Bishop of St. Louis, July.
Smith, John M., Succeeds as Bishop of Trenton from Coadjutor Bishop of Trenton, July.
Wenski, Thomas G., Appointed Auxiliary Bishop for the Archdiocese of Miami, June 23.
Wilkerson, Gerald E., Appointed Auxiliary Bishop of Los Angeles, November 5.
Yanta, John W., Appointed Bishop of Amarillo, from Auxiliary of San Antonio in January.
Zubik, David A., Appointed Auxiliary Bishop of Pittsburgh February 18, 1997.

1998

Cardinals

George, Francis Cardinal, *o.m.i.*, Archbishop of Chicago.
Stafford, Francis Cardinal, Pres.-Pontifical Council for the Laity, Vatican.

Bishops

Brown, Tod D., Appointed Bishop of Orange, from Bishop of Boise.
DiNardo, Daniel N., Appointed Bishop of Sioux City in December.
Gilmore, Ronald M., Appointed Bishop of Dodge City in May.
Harrington, Bernard J., Appointed Bishop of Winona, from Auxiliary Bishop of Detroit in November.
Harvey, James M., Bishop and Prefect of the Papal Household March.
Murry, George V., *s.j.*, Appointed Coadjutor to St. Thomas Virgin Islands May.
Perry, Joseph N., Appointed Auxiliary Bishop of Chicago May.
McCormack, John B., Appointed Bishop of Manchester from Auxiliary of Boston.

1999

Bishops

Baker, Robert J., appointed Bishop of Charleston July 12.
Barbarito, Gerald M., Appointed Bishop of Ogdensburg, from Auxiliary Bishop of Brooklyn.
Blair, Leonard P., Appointed Auxiliary Bishop of Detroit.
Blaire, Stephen E., Appointed Bishop of Stockton, from Auxiliary Bishop of Los Angeles, September.
DiMarzio, Nicholas A., Appointed Bishop of Camden.
Driscoll, Michael P., Appointed Bishop of Boise, from Auxiliary Bishop of Orange.
Galante, Joseph A., Appointed Coadjutor Bishop of Dallas, from Bishop of Beaumont, November 23.
Kurtz, Joseph E., Appointed Bishop of Knoxville.
Loverde, Paul S., Appointed Bishop of Arlington, from Bishop of Ogdensburg January.
Lucas, George J., Appointed Bishop of Springfield, Illinois, October 19.
McHugh, James T., Succeeded to Bishop of Rockville Centre, from Coadjutor.
McGrath Patrick J., Succeeded to Bishop of San Jose, from Coadjutor, November 27.
Morlino, Robert C. Morlino, appointed Bishop of Helena.
Murry, George V., *s.j.*, Appointed Bishop to St. Thomas Virgin Islands, June 30.
O'Connell, Anthony J., Appointed Bishop of Palm Beach, from Bishop of Knoxville.
Olmsted, Thomas J., Appointed Coadjutor Bishop of Wichita, February.
Ricken, David L., Appointed Coadjutor Bishop of Cheyenne, December.
Sartain, J. Peter, Appointed Bishop of Little Rock, December.
Thomas, George, Appointed Auxiliary Bishop of Seattle, November 19.
Vasa, Robert F., Appointed Bishop of Baker, November 19.

2000

Archbishop

Egan, Edward M., appointed Archbishop of New York, from Bishop of Bridgeport in June.
Gonzalez, Robert O., *o.f.m.*, Archbishop of San Juan.
Schwietz, Roger L., *o.m.i.*, Coadjutor Archbishop of Anchorage from Bishop of Duluth.
Soroka, Stephen, appointed Archbishop of the Ukrainian Archeparchy of Philadelphia.

Bishops

Aymond, Gregory M., Coadjutor Bishop of Austin, June.
Braxton, Edward K., Bishop of Lake Charles-December 11, 2000.
Carmody, Edmond, Appointed Bishop of Corpus Christi, from Bishop of Tyler February 2.
Corrada del Rio, Alvaro, *s.j.* from Auxiliary Bishop of Washington; Administrator of Caguas to Bishop of Tyler.
Guillory, Curtis J., Bishop of Beaumont, June.
Kaising, John J., Appointed Auxiliary Bishop to the Archdiocese for the Military Services February.
Listecki, Jerome E., appointed November 7th Auxiliary Bishop of Chicago.
Malone, Richard J., Appointed as Auxiliary Bishop for the Archdiocese of Boston, February.
Malooly, William Frances, Auxiliary Bishop of Baltimore December 11.
McCarthy, James F., Appointed Auxiliary Bishop for the Archdiocese of New York.
Serratelli, Arthur J., appointed Auxiliary Bishop of Newark.
Shaheen, Robert J., Eparch of Our Lady of Lebanon December 4.
Soto, Jaime, appointed Auxiliary Bishop of Orange, March 23
Surinach-Carreras, Ricardo, appointed November, Bishop of Ponce, from Auxiliary Bishop of Ponce.
Tamayo, James A., Bishop of Laredo.
Walsh, Daniel F., appointed Bishop of Santa Rosa, from Bishop of Las Vegas.

2001

Cardinals

Egan, Edward Cardinal, Archbishop of New York.
McCarrick, Theodore Cardinal, Archbishop of Washington

Archbishops

Hughes, Alfred C., Coadjutor Archbishop of New Orleans from Bishop of Baton Rouge.
McCarrick, Theodore E., to Archbishop of Washington from Archbishop of Newark.
Schwietz, Roger L., *o.m.i.*, Archbishop of Anchorage from Coadjutor Archbishop of Anchorage.

Bishops

Angadiath, Jacob, appointed March 12, Bishop of Eparchy of St. Thomas of Chicago of the Syro-Malabarians.
Aymond, Gregory M., Coadjutor Bishop of Austin to Bishop of Austin.
Clark, Edward W., appointed Auxiliary Bishop of Los Angeles January 16.
Gomez, Jose H., appointed Auxiliary Bishop of Denver January 22.
Lori, William E., Bishop of Bridgeport from Auxiliary Bishop of San Bernardino January 16.
Medina, Ruben Antonio Gonzalez, *c.m.f.,* Bishop of Caguas.
O'Neil, Dennis P., appointed Auxiliary Bishop of San Bernardino January 16.
Pates, Richard E., Auxiliary Bishop of St. Paul and Minneapolis.
Schnurr, Dennis M., appointed Bishop of Duluth January 18.

National Conference of Catholic Bishops

Address—3211 Fourth St., Washington, DC 20017-1194. Tel: 202-541-3000.

The National Conference of Catholic Bishops (NCCB) is a canonical entity operating in accordance with the Conciliar Decree *Christus Dominus*. Its purpose is to foster the Church's mission by providing the Bishops of the United States of America with an opportunity to exchange views and insights of prudence and experience and to exercise in a joint manner their pastoral office. (cf. *Christus Dominus*, # 38). The NCCB is the successor to the Annual Meeting of the Bishops of the United States, approved in the brief "Communes" issued by Pope Benedict XV, April 10, 1919 and in a special letter of Pius XI issued on August 10, 1927. The present NCCB statutes with some slight amendment are those originally approved by the Sacred Consistorial Congregation in a decree issued on June 22, 1922.

The National Conference of Catholic Bishops is composed of every Bishop, residential or titular, who serves the Church in the United States, its territories or possessions. Each Bishop has an active and passive voice in the Conference. Under certain conditions, enunciated in conciliar legislation, the National Conference of Catholic Bishops can initiate actions that are juridically binding on all the bishops of the country.

The National Conference of Catholic Bishops is presided over by a president who is elected by the general membership. Other officers of the organization are a vice president, secretary, treasurer and general secretary. The National Conference of Catholic Bishops is a distinct entity from the United States Catholic Conference. Its relationship to the USCC is that of a sponsoring organization.

NCCB OFFICES AND COMMITTEES

I. Officers

President—Bishop Joseph A. Fiorenza
Vice President—Bishop Wilton D. Gregory
Treasurer—Bishop Henry J. Mansell
Secretary—Bishop William B. Friend

II. NCCB General Secretariat

General Secretary—Rev. Msgr. William P. Fay
Associate General Secretary—Mr. Bruce E. Egnew
Associate General Secretary—Rev. Msgr. David J. Malloy
Associate General Secretary—Sr. Lourdes Sheehan, R.S.M.

III. Staff Offices

Finance—Mr. Kenneth Korotky, Dir.
Accounting—Ms. Sharon Heinle, Dir.
General Counsel—Mr. Mark E. Chopko, Esq.
Associate General Counsel—Ms. Deirdre A. Halloran
General Services—Mr. Douglas Cissel, Dir.
Printing & Mailing—Mr. Ronald D. Gibson, Dir.
Government Liaison—Mr. Frank J. Monahan, Dir.
Human Resources—Ms. Linda Hunt, Dir.
Library Services—Ms. Anne LeVeque
Management Information Systems—Mr. William Kissane, Dir.
Office of Public and Promotion Services—Mr. Paul Henderson, Dir.

NCCB COMMITTEES

I. Executive Level

Administrative Committee

Chairman—Bishop Joseph A. Fiorenza
Members—William Cardinal Keeler
Bernard Cardinal Law
Roger Cardinal Mahony
Adam Cardinal Maida (Region VI)
Archbishop Daniel A. Cronin
Archbishop Oscar H. Lipscomb
Archbishop John G. Vlazny
Archbishop Roger L. Schwietz, O.M.I.
Bishop Victor Balke (Region VIII)
Bishop Gordon D. Bennett, O.S.B.
Bishop Stephen E. Blaire
Bishop J. Kevin Boland (Region IV)
Bishop Edward K. Braxton
Bishop Tod D. Brown
Bishop Edmond Carmody
Bishop John S. Cummins
Bishop Thomas J. Curry
Bishop Nicholas A. DiMarzio
Bishop Daniel N. DiNardo (Region IX)
Bishop William B. Friend
Coadjutor Bishop Joseph A. Galante
Bishop Richard J. Garcia (Region XI)
Bishop John R. Gaydos
Bishop Wilton D. Gregory
Bishop Curtis J. Guillory, S.V.D.
Bishop Joseph H. Hart
Bishop William R. Houck (Region V)
Bishop Howard J. Hubbard (Region II)
Bishop Joseph L. Imesch (Region VII)
Bishop Gerald F. Kicanas
Bishop John J. Leibrecht
Bishop Basil H. Losten
Bishop Henry J. Mansell
Bishop John J. McRaith
Bishop Manuel D. Moreno (Region XIII)
Bishop William F. Murphy (Region I)
Bishop George H. Niederauer
Bishop Anthony J. O'Connell
Bishop Sean P. O'Malley O.F.M.Cap.
Bishop A. James Quinn
Bishop John H. Ricard, S.S.J.
Bishop Peter A. Rosazza
Bishop Carlos A. Sevilla, S.J. (Region XII)
Bishop William S. Skylstad
Bishop John M. Smith (Region III)
Bishop J. Terry Steib, S.V.D.
Bishop Arthur N. Tafoya
Bishop Donald W. Trautman
Bishop Michael W. Warfel
Bishop Donald W. Wuerl
Bishop Paul A. Zipfel
Bishop Patrick J. Zurek (Region X)
Alternate (Region I): Bishop John B. McCormack
Alternate (Region II): Bishop James M. Moynihan
Alternate (Region III): Bishop Joseph F. Martino
Alternate (Region IV): (Vacant)
Alternate (Region V): Bishop Edward U. Kmiec
Alternate (Region VI): Bishop Gilbert I. Sheldon
Alternate (Region VII): Bishop Edwin M. Conway
Alternate (Region VIII): Bishop John F. Kinney
Alternate (Region IX): Bishop Michael J. Sheridan
Alternate (Region X): Bishop John W. Yanta
Alternate (Region XI): Bishop Gerald E. Wilkerson
Alternate (Region XII): Bishop George L. Thomas
Alternate (Region XIII): Bishop Donald E. Pelotte, S.S.S.

Executive Committee

Chairman—Bishop Joseph A. Fiorenza
Vice President—Bishop Wilton D. Gregory
Treasurer—Bishop Henry J. Mansell
Secretary—Bishop William B. Friend
Ex-Officio—Bishop John J. Leibrecht
Staff—Rev. Msgr. William P. Fay

Committee on Budget and Finance

Chairman—Bishop Henry J. Mansell
Members—Bishop John J. McRaith
Bishop George H. Niederauer
Bishop John H. Ricard, S.S.J.
Rev. Msgr. William P. Fay
Staff—Mr. Kenneth Korotky

Committee on Personnel

Chairman—Bishop Wilton D. Gregory
Members—Bishop Anthony J. O'Connell
Bishop J. Terry Steib, S.V.D.
Rev. Msgr. William P. Fay
Staff—Mr. Bruce E. Egnew
Ms. Linda Hunt

Committee on Priorities and Plans

Chairman—Bishop Joseph A. Fiorenza
Vice-President—Bishop Wilton D. Gregory
Treasurer—Bishop Henry J. Mansell
Past President—Bishop Anthony M. Pilla
Members—Bishop Stephen E. Blaire
Bishop Anthony J. O'Connell
Rev. Msgr. William P. Fay
Staff—Sr. Lourdes Sheehan, R.S.M.

II. General Membership Level

Standing Committees

African American Catholics

Chairman—Bishop J. Terry Steib, S.V.D.
Members—Archbishop Harry J. Flynn
Bishop Dominic Carmon, S.V.D.
Bishop Curtis J. Guillory, S.V.D.
Bishop George V. Murry, S.J.
Bishop Joseph N. Perry
Bishop John H. Ricard, S.S.J.
Consultants—Francis Cardinal George, O.M.I.
James Cardinal Hickey
Rev. James Goode, O.F.M.
Staff—Ms. Beverly A. Carroll, Exec. Dir.
Ms. Stephanie Greenhouse, Program Coord.

American Bishops' Overseas Appeal

Chairman—Bishop Joseph A. Fiorenza
Members— Administrative Committee Members

American College Louvain

Chairman—Bishop Edward K. Braxton
Members by Region—
Region I Bishop Francis J. Christian
Region II Bishop Matthew H. Clark
Region III Bishop Nicholas A. DiMarzio
Region IV Bishop John J. Nevins
Region V Archbishop Francis B. Schulte
Region VI Bishop James A. Murray
Region VII Bishop Robert F. Morneau
Region VIII Bishop Frederick F. Campbell
Region IX Bishop Edward K. Braxton
Region X Bishop James A. Tamayo
Region XI Bishop Sylvester D. Ryan
Region XII Bishop William S. Skylstad
Region XIII Bishop Thomas J. O'Brien
Consultants—Bishop Charles A. Buswell
Bishop Benedict C. Franzetta
Staff—Rev. David E. Windsor, Rector
Rev. Michael P. Nash, Vice Rector-Recruitment
Mr. Stephen C. Zavesky, Vice Pres.-Finance

Boundaries of Dioceses and Provinces

Chairman—Bishop Joseph A. Fiorenza
Members by Region—
Region I Bishop Robert J. McManus
Region II Bishop Thomas V. Daily
Region III Bishop Dominic A. Marconi
Region IV Bishop Walter F. Sullivan
Region V Archbishop Thomas C. Kelly, O.P.
Region VI Bishop James A. Griffin
Region VII Bishop Raymond E. Goedert
Region VIII Bishop Bernard J. Harrington
Region IX Bishop Joseph L. Charron, C.PP.S.
Region X Bishop J. Peter Sartain
Region XI Roger Cardinal Mahony
Region XII Bishop Thomas J. Connolly
Region XIII Bishop Joseph H. Hart
Staff—Rev. Msgr. William P. Fay

Canonical Affairs

Chairman—Bishop A. James Quinn
Members—Bishop Gerald M. Barbarito
Bishop Michael R. Cote
Bishop Thomas G. Doran
Bishop David E. Fellhauer
Coadjutor Bishop Joseph A. Galante
Bishop Gabino Zavala
Consultants—Sr. Sharon A. Euart, R.S.M.
Ms. Barbara Anne Cusack
Rev. Robert T. Kennedy
Rev. Lawrence G. Wrenn
Staff—Rev. Msgr. David J. Malloy

Church in Latin America

Chairman—Bishop Edmond Carmody
Members—Archbishop Eusebius J. Beltran
Archbishop John F. Donoghue
Archbishop James P. Keleher
Bishop Gerald R. Barnes

Bishop Thomas V. Daily
Bishop Thomas G. Wenski
Staff—Rev. John W. Swope, S.J., Exec. Dir.
Mr. Daniel Lizarraga, Asst. Dir.

Consecrated Life

Chairman—Bishop Sean P. O'Malley, O.F.M.Cap.
Members—Bishop Raymond L. Burke
Bishop Alvaro Corrada del Rio, S.J.
Bishop George V. Murry, S.J.
Coadjutor Bishop Thomas J. Olmsted
Staff—Sr. Lourdes Sheehan, R.S.M.
Rev. Msgr. William P. Fay

Diaconate

Chairman—Bishop Gerald F. Kicanas
Members—Bishop Gregory M. Aymond
Bishop Gordon D. Bennett, S.J.
Bishop Howard J. Hubbard
Bishop John B. McCormack
Bishop Michael J. Sheridan
Consultants—Adam Cardinal Maida
Bishop Richard J. Garcia
Bishop Donald W. Wuerl
Staff—Deacon Gerard Wilson

Doctrine

Chairman—Bishop Donald W. Trautman
Members—Bishop Edward K. Braxton
Bishop James A. Griffin
Bishop Gerald F. Kicanas
Bishop William E. Lori
Bishop Robert J. McManus
Bishop Emil A. Wcela
Consultants—Avery Cardinal Dulles, S.J.
William Cardinal Keeler
Bishop Francis X. DiLorenzo
Rev. Michael R. Carey, O.P.
Rev. Joseph A. Komonchak
Staff—Rev. Msgr. John Strynkowski, O.P., Exec. Dir.
Ms. Siobhan M. Verbeek, Assoc. Dir.
Dr. James LeGrys, Theological Advisor

Ecumenical and Interreligious Affairs

Chairman—Bishop Tod D. Brown
Members—William Cardinal Keeler
Archbishop Rembert G. Weakland, O.S.B.
Bishop Joseph J. Gerry, O.S.B.
Bishop Donald E. Pelotte, S.S.S.
Bishop Placido Rodriguez, C.M.F.
Bishop Nicholas J. Samra
Bishop William S. Skylstad
Bishop John J. Snyder
Bishop J. Kendrick Williams
Consultants—Archbishop Alexander J. Brunett
Archbishop Oscar H. Lipscomb
Bishop Patrick R. Cooney
Bishop Howard J. Hubbard
Bishop John H. Ricard, S.S.J.
Bishop Richard J. Sklba
Bishop James C. Timlin
Staff—Rev. John F. Hotchkin, Exec. Dir.
Dr. John Borelli, Assoc. Dir.
Eugene Fisher, Ph.D., Assoc. Dir.
Bro. Jeffrey Gros, F.S.C., Assoc. Dir.
Rev. Ronald G. Roberson, C.S.P., Assoc. Dir.
Ms. Ann Riggs, Asst. to the Dir.

Subcommittee on Interreligious Dialogue

Chairman—Bishop Joseph J. Gerry, O.S.B.
Members—William Cardinal Keeler
Theodore Cardinal McCarrick
Bishop Ibrahim N. Ibrahim
Bishop Joseph F. Martino
Consultants—Bishop Kevin M. Britt
Bishop Ignatius A. Catanello
Bishop Donald E. Pellotte, S.S.S.
Staff—Dr. John Borelli, Assoc. Dir.

Evangelization

Chairman—Bishop Michael W. Warfel
Members—Bishop Edward K. Braxton
Bishop Joseph F. Martino
Bishop Armando X. Ochoa
Bishop Basil Schott, O.F.M.
Bishop Gabino Zavala
Bishop Patrick J. Zurek
Consultants—Mr. Mark Berchem
Rev. Kenneth Boyack, C.S.P.
Rev. Frank DeSiano, C.S.P.
Rev. Larry Esposito
Mrs. Annette Mandley-Turner
Staff—Rev. John E. Hurley, C.S.P., Exec. Dir.
Ms. Iris Brown, Administrative Sec.

Hispanic Affairs

Chairman—Bishop Arthur N. Tafoya
Members—Theodore Cardinal McCarrick
Archbishop Michael J. Sheehan
Archbishop John G. Vlazny
Bishop Gilberto Fernandez
Bishop Joseph N. Perry
Bishop Placido Rodriguez, C.M.F.
Bishop James A. Tamayo
Bishop Gabino Zavala
Consultants—Sr. Maria Elena Gonzalez, R.S.M.
Sr. Ana Maria Pineda, R.S.M.
Staff—Mr. Ronaldo M. Cruz, Exec. Dir.
Mr. Alejandro Aguilera-Titus, Assoc. Dir.
Ms. Rosalva Castaneda, Program Specialist
Ms. Leonor Castro, Bilingual Sec.

Home Missions

Chairman—Bishop Paul A. Zipfel
Members—Bishop John A. Elya, B.S.O.
Bishop Bernard J. Harrington
Bishop Joseph F. Naumann
Bishop Joseph N. Perry
Bishop James A. Tamayo
Bishop Daniel F. Walsh
Consultants—Bishop Sam G. Jacobs
Staff—Dr. David M. Byers, Exec. Dir.
Ms. Margit Serenyi, Mission Support Specialist
Dr. David J. Suley, Resource Development Coord.
Mrs. Carliss Parker-Smith, Admin. Asst.

Laity

Chairman—Bishop John J. McRaith
Members—Bishop Kevin M. Britt
Bishop Joseph P. Delaney
Bishop Robert P. Maginnis
Bishop Michael A. Saltarelli
Bishop Gerald E. Wilkerson
Bishop Gabrino Zavala
Staff—Dr. H. Richard McCord, Exec. Dir.
Ms. Ana Villamil, Assoc. Dir.

SubCommittee on Lay Ministry

Chairman—Bishop Joseph P. Delaney
Members—Bishop Gerald R. Barnes
Bishop John C. Dunne
Bishop Gerald F. Kicanas
Bishop Kenneth E. Untener
Bishop Emil A. Wcela
Consultants—Archbishop William J. Levada
Archbishop Daniel E. Pilarczyk
Ms. Zoila Diaz
Dr. Zeni Fox
Rev. Msgr. Phil J. Murnion
Sr. Elissa Rinere, C.P.
Staff—Dr. H. Richard McCord, Exec. Dir.
Ms. Ana Villamil, Assoc. Dir.
Sr. Amy Hoey, R.S.M., Project Coord.

SubCommittee on Youth and Young Adults

Chairman—Bishop Kevin M. Britt
Members—Bishop Gordon D. Bennett, S.J.
Bishop Blase J. Cupich
Bishop Gerald A. Gettelfinger
Bishop Daniel R. Jenky, C.S.C.
Bishop Ricardo Ramirez, C.S.B.
Staff—Dr. H. Richard McCord, Exec. Dir.
Ms. Ana Villamil, Assoc. Dir.
Ms. Michelle Miller, Project Specialist

Liturgy

Chairman—Archbishop Oscar H. Lipscomb
Members—Archbishop Daniel E. Pilarczyk
Archbishop Justin F. Rigali
Bishop Tod D. Brown
Bishop Blase J. Cupich
Bishop Donald W. Trautman
Bishop Allen H. Vigneron
Consultants—Francis Cardinal George, O.M.I.
Bernard Cardinal Law
Roger Cardinal Mahony
Bishop George V. Murry, S.J.
Bishop Carlos A. Sevilla, S.J.
Rev. Sam Aquila
Rev. Virgil Funk
Rev. John D. Laurence, S.J.
Rev. Heliodoro Lucatero
Mrs. Delores Martinez
Bro. Joseph Rocco, S.C.
Rev. Michael Spillane
Staff—Rev. James P. Moroney, Exec. Dir.
Rev. Kenneth J. Martin, Assoc. Dir.
Mr. Dennis D. McManus, Assoc. Dir.
Ms. Sharon Washington, Staff Asst.
Sr. Clelia Cecchetti, S.P., Administrative Sec.

Marriage and Family Life

Chairman—Bishop Anthony J. O'Connell
Members—Bishop Edmond Carmody
Bishop John C. Dunne
Bishop Carl K. Moeddel
Bishop Joseph F. Naumann
Bishop Anthony M. Pilla
Bishop Placido Rogriguez, C.M.F.
Consultants—Mrs. Terri Lyke
Mr. Andrew Lyke, Jr.
Mr. Bill Coffin
Ms. Gail Risch
Ms. Susan Vogt
Staff—Mr. H. Richard McCord, Exec. Dir.
Ms. Sheila Garcia, Asst. Dir.

Migration

Chairman—Bishop Nicholas A. DiMarzio
Members—Adam Cardinal Maida
Bishop John S. Cummins
Bishop Michael P. Driscoll
Bishop Richard J. Garcia
Bishop John R. Manz
Bishop Thomas G. Wenski
Consultants—Theodore Cardinal McCarrick
Bishop Robert A. Brucato
Bishop Joseph L. Howze
Bishop Peter A. Rosazza
Bishop Phillip F. Staling
Bishop James C. Timlin
Bishop John W. Yanta
Bishop Joseph Younan
Staff—Mr. Mark Franken, Exec. Dir.
Mr. Kevin Appleby, Dir., Migration and Refugee Policy
Dr. Patricia Maloof, Dir., Refugee Programs
Rev. Anthony McGuire, Dir., Pastoral Care for Migrants and Refugees
Rev. John Jamnicky, Coord. for Mobility Apostolates

North American College Rome

Chairman—Archbishop Daniel A. Cronin
Members—
Region I Archbishop Daniel A. Cronin
Region II Bishop Henry J. Mansell
Region III Bishop Donald W. Wuerl
Region IV Archbishop Edwin F. O'Brien
Region V Archbishop Oscar H. Lipscomb
Region VI Bishop John C. Nienstedt
Region VII Bishop Richard J. Sklba
Region VIII Bishop Robert J. Carlson
Region IX Bishop John R. Gaydos
Region X Coadjutor Bishop Joseph A. Galante
Region XI Archbishop William J. Levada
Region XII Archbishop John G. Vlazny
Region XIII Coadjutor Bishop David L. Ricken
Staff—Rev. Msgr. David J. Malloy

Pastoral Practices

Chairman— Bishop Stephen E. Blaire
Members —Bishop Robert J. Carlson
Bishop Joseph L. Imesch
Bishop Daniel P. Reilly
Bishop Phillip F. Straling
Bishop James A. Tamayo
Bishop George L. Thomas
Consultants—Bishop J. Terry Steib, S.V.D.
Staff —Rev. Msgr. John Strynkowski, Exec. Dir.
Ms. Siobhan M. Verbee, Assoc. Dir.

Priestly Formation

Chairman —Bishop George H. Niederauer
Members —Archbishop Edwin F. O'Brien
Bishop Gregory M. Aymond
Coadjutor Bishop Thomas J. Olmsted
Bishop Daniel F. Walsh
Bishop Gabino Zavala
Bishop David A. Zubik
Consultants —Rev. Ronald D. Witherup, S.S.
Staff —Rev. Edward J. Burns, Exec. Dir.

Priestly Life and Ministry

Chairman—Bishop John R. Gaydos
Members—Bishop Robert J. Baker
Bishop John F. Kinney
Bishop George J. Lucas
Bishop Daniel P. Reilly
Bishop Robert F. Vasa
Bishop David A. Zubik
Staff—Rev. Cletus Kiley, Exec. Dir.

Pro-Life Activities

Chairman—William Cardinal Keeler
Members—Adam Cardinal Maida
Archbishop Daniel Buechlein, O.S.B.

Bishop Robert N. Lynch
Bishop Andrew Pataki
Bishop John H. Ricard, S.S.J.
Bishop William K. Weigand
Consultants—Anthony Cardinal Bevilacqua
Francis Cardinal George, O.M.I.
James Cardinal Hickey
Bernard Cardinal Law
Roger Cardinal Mahony
Coadjutor Bishop Joseph A. Galante
Bishop Alfred C. Hughes
Bishop Ricardo Ramirez, C.S.B.
Ms. Helen Alvare
Mr. Virgil C. Dechant
Mr. John M. Haas
Ms. Frances X. Hogan, Esq.
Mr. John Huebscher
Rev. Michael Place
Staff—Ms. Gail P. Quinn, Exec. Dir.
Ms. Cathleen Cleaver, Dir. Information & Planning
Mr. Richard Doerflinger, Assoc. Dir. Policy Devel.
Mrs. Susan Wills, Asst. Dir. Programming
Ms. Theresa Notare, Spec. Asst. Natural Family Planning

Relationship Between Eastern and Latin Catholic Churches

Chairman—Bishop Basil H. Losten
Members—Bernard Cardinal Law
Archbishop Alexander J. Brunett
Archbishop Edwin F. O'Brien
Archbishop Judson M. Procyk
Archbishop John G. Vlazny
Bishop Tod D. Brown
Bishop Stephen Hector Doueihi
Bishop John A. Elya, B.S.O.
Staff—Rev. Msgr. David J. Malloy

Science and Human Values

Chairman—Bishop John S. Cummins
Members—Edward Cardinal Egan
Bishop Robert J. Banks
Bishop Francis J. Christian
Bishop Francis X. DiLorenzo
Bishop Thomas G. Doran
Bishop John C. Nienstedt
Consultants—Bishop R. Pierre DuMaine
Bishop John C. Dunne
Bishop William B. Friend
Bishop Sylvester D. Ryan
Dr. Eric Fisher
Dr. John E. Haught
Rev. James Salmon, S.J.
Dr. Phillip Sloan
Dr. Robert J. White
Staff—Dr. David M. Byers, Ph.D., Exec. Dir.

Selection of Bishops

Chairman—Bishop Joseph A. Fiorenza
Members—
Region I Bishop Robert J. McManus
Region II Bishop Thomas V. Daily
Region III Bishop Dominic A. Marconi
Region IV Bishop Walter F. Sullivan
Region V Archbishop Thomas C. Kelly, O.P.
Region VI Bishop James A. Griffin
Region VII Bishop Raymond E. Goedert
Region VIII Bishop Bernard J. Harrington
Region IX Bishop Joseph L. Charron, C.PP.S.
Region X Bishop J. Peter Sartain
Region XI Roger Cardinal Mahony
Region XII Bishop Thomas J. Connolly
Region XIII Bishop Joseph H. Hart
Staff—Rev. Msgr. William P. Fay

Vocations

Chairman—Archbishop Roger L. Schwietz, O.M.I.
Members—
Archbishop Charles J. Chaput, O.F.M.Cap.
Archbishop Judson M. Procyk
Bishop Gregory M. Aymond
Bishop Kevin M. Britt
Bishop Richard J. Garcia
Bishop Curtis J. Guillory, S.V.D.
Consultants—Sr. Catherine Bertrand, S.S.N.D.
Mrs. Dorothy Foss
Mr. James B. O'Hanlon
Ms. Patricia Skarda
Staff—Rev. Edward J. Burns, Exec. Dir.

Women in Society and in the Church

Chairman—Archbishop John G. Vlazny
Members—Bishop Thomas G. Doran
Bishop R. Pierre DuMaine
Bishop Gilberto Fernandez
Bishop Curtis J. Guillory, S.V.D.
Bishop Howard J. Hubbard
Bishop John J. McRaith
Consultants—Ms. Leodia Gooch
Mrs. Joann Hillebrand
Sr. Ana Maria Pineda, R.S.M.
Ms. Nancy Werner
Staff—Dr. H. Richard McCord, Exec. Dir.
Ms. Sheila Garcia, Asst. Dir
Sr. Amy Hoey, R.S.M., Project Coord.

World Missions

Chairman—Bishop Curtis J. Guillory, S.V.D.
Members—Francis Cardinal George, O.M.I.
Theodore Cardinal McCarrick
Bishop Gregory M. Aymond
Bishop Thomas V. Daily
Bishop John R. Gaydos
Bishop Arthur N. Tafoya
Bishop Michael Warfel
Consultants—Bishop Norbert M. Dorsey, C.P.
Bishop William E. Lori
Bishop William J. McCormack
Bishop Thomas G. Wenski
Sr. Barbara Anne Gooding, R.S.M.
Rev. Ted Keating, S.M.
Mr. James Lindsay
Sr. Rosanne Rustemeyer, S.S.N.D.
Sr. Janet Stolba, R.J.M.
Rev. Francis Wright, C.S.Sp.
Staff—Dr. David M. Byers, Exec. Dir.

Agricultural Issues

Chairman—Bishop William S. Skylstad
Members—Bishop Raymond L. Burke
Bishop Nicholas A. DiMarzio
Bishop Richard J. Garcia
Bishop Charles V. Grahmann
Constultants—Bro. David Andrews, National Rural Life Conference
Staff—Mr. Mark Franken, Exec. Dir.-Migration Refugee Services
Mr. John Carr, Sec.-Social Development & World Peace
Mr. Frank J. Monahan, Dir.-Government Liaison

Aid to the Church in Central and Eastern Europe

Chairman—Adam Cardinal Maida
Members—Theodore Cardinal McCarrick
Archbishop Judson M. Procyk
Archbishop Justin F. Rigali
Archbishop Francis B. Schulte
Bishop John J. Myers
Staff—Rev. Msgr. R. George Sarauskas, Exec. Dir.
Mr. James H. O'Beirne, Deputy Dir.
Ms. Dimitra C. Bolger, Staff Asst.

Bishops' Life and Ministry

Chairman Bishop William S. Skylstad
Members—Bishop John Michael Botean
Bishop Joseph F. Maguire
Bishop Robert E. Mulvee
Bishop Leonard J. Olivier, S.V.D.
Bishop Ricardo Ramirez, C.S.B.
Bishop Thomas J. Tobin
Staff—Rev. Msgr. William P. Fay

Catholic Charismatic Renewal

Chairman—Bishop Sam G. Jacobs
Members—Archbishop Harry J. Flynn
Bishop Thomas J. Flanagan
Bishop Francisco Garmendia
Bishop Edward U. Kmiec
Bishop Joseph C. McKinney
Bishop Augustin A. Roman
Staff—Rev. Msgr. David J. Malloy

Catholic Health Care Issues and the Church

Chairman—Bishop Joseph L. Charron, C.P.P.S.
Members—Archbishop Justin F. Rigali
Bishop Henry J. Mansell
Bishop William F. Murphy
Bishop Joseph M. Sullivan
Staff—Rev. Msgr. John Strynkowski
Dr. James LeGrys

Diocesan Audits

Chairman—Bishop Joseph P. Delaney
Members—Bishop Robert J. Banks
Bishop Norman F. McFarland
Bishop Donald W. Trautman
Bishop Daniel F. Walsh
Staff—Mr. Bruce E. Egnew
Mr. Kenneth Korotky

Economic Concerns of the Holy See

Chairman—Archbishop James P. Keleher
Members—James Cardinal Hickey
Bernard Cardinal Law
Roger Cardinal Mahony
Archbishop Oscar H. Lipscomb
Archbishop John G. Vlazny
Bishop Roger L. Schwietz, O.M.I.
Bishop Tod D. Brown
Bishop Edmond Carmody
Bishop Anthony J. O'Connell
Bishop J. Terry Steib, S.V.D.
Bishop Arthur N. Tafoya
Bishop Donald W. Wuerl
Staff—Mr. Bruce E. Egnew

Mandatum

Chairman—Archbishop Daniel E. Pilarczyk
Members—Anthony Cardinal Bevilacqua
Bishop Edward K. Braxton
Bishop Thomas G. Doran
Bishop Donald W. Wuerl
Consultants—Sr. Maureen Fay, O.P.
Rev. James Conn, S.J.
Dr. Daniel Finn
Dr. Terrence W. Tilley
Staff—Rev. Msgr. John Strynkowski

Native American Catholics

Chairman—Bishop Donald E. Pelotte, S.S.S.
Members—
Archbishop Alexander J. Brunett
Archbishop Charles J. Chaput, O.F.M.Cap.
Bishop Blase J. Cupich
Bishop Anthony M. Milone
Consultants—Rev. Raymond Bucko, S.J.
Rev. John Hatcher, S.J.
Rev. Msgr. Paul Lenz
Sr. Kateri Mitchell
Staff—Sr. Lourdes Sheehan, R.S.M.
Mr. Daniel Mulhall

Nomination of Conference Offices

Chairman—Archbishop Jerome G. Hanus, O.S.B.
Members—
Region I Bishop Michael R. Cote
Region II Bishop Thomas J. Costello
Region III Bishop Paul G. Bootkoski
Region IV (Vacant)
Region V Bishop Sam G. Jacobs
Region VI Bishop Carl F. Mengeling
Region VII Bishop John J. Myers
Region VIII Bishop Frederick F. Campbell
Region IX Archbishop Jerome G. Hanus, O.S.B.
Region X Bishop Gregory M. Aymond
Region XI Bishop John C. Wester
Region XII Bishop Robert C. Morlino
Region XIII Bishop Armando X. Ochoa
Staff—Rev. Msgr. William P. Fay

Oversee the Use of the Catechism

Chairman—
Archbishop Daniel M. Buechlein, O.S.B.
Members—Francis Cardinal George, O.M.I.
Archbishop William J. Levada
Bishop Robert J. Banks
Bishop Alfred C. Hughes
Bishop Donald W. Wuerl
Consultant—Rev. John Pollard
Staff—Rev. Daniel Kutys, Exec. Dir.
Mr. Brian Keane, Coord.-Assessment

Publishing and Promotion Services

Chairman—Bishop James A. Griffin
Members—Bishop Robert J. Banks
Bishop Wilton D. Gregory
Bishop Robert N. Lynch
Bishop Edward J. O'Donnell
Staff—Mr. Paul Henderson
Mr. Bruce E. Egnew

Review of Scripture Translations

Chairman—Bishop Richard J. Sklba
Members—Archbishop John R. Quinn
Bishop Edward K. Braxton
Bishop Michael J. Murphy
Bishop Arthur J. Serratelli
Bishop Donald W. Trautman
Bishop Emil A. Wcela
Staff—Rev. Msgr. John Strynkowski
Ms. Siobhan M. Verbeek

Sexual Abuse

Chairman—Bishop John B. McCormack
Members—Coadjutor Bishop Joseph A. Galante

Bishop John R. Gaydos
Bishop George H. Niederauer
Bishop A. James Quinn
Staff—Rev. J. Cletus Kiley
Rev. Msgr. Francis Maniscalco
Mr. Mark Chopko, Esq.

Shrines

Chairman—Archbishop James P. Keleher
Members—Francis Cardinal George, O.M.I.
Archbishop Charles J. Chaput, O.F.M.Cap.
Archbishop John G. Vlazny
Bishop John J. Myers
Bishop Sean P. O'Malley, O.F.M.Cap.
Staff—Rev. James P. Moroney

Stewardship

Chairman—Bishop Sylvester D. Ryan
Members—Archbishop James P. Keleher
Bishop Robert J. Baker
Bishop Ronald M. Gilmore
Bishop Joseph L. Imesch
Bishop John J. McRaith
Bishop John J. Snyder
Staff—Mr. Bruce E. Egnew

United States Catholic Conference

Address—3211 Fourth St., N.E., Washington, DC 20017-1194. Tel: 202-541-3000.

The United States Catholic Conference (USCC) is a civil entity of the American Catholic Bishops assisting them in their service to the Church in the United States of America by uniting the People of God where voluntary, collective action on a broad diocesan level is needed. The USCC provides an organizational structure and the resources needed to insure coordination, cooperation, and assistance in the public, educational, and social concerns of the Church at the national, regional, state, interdiocesan and, as appropriate, diocesan levels.

I. Officers

President—Bishop Joseph A. Fiorenza
Vice President—Bishop Wilton D. Gregory
Treasurer—Bishop Henry J. Mansell
Secretary—Bishop William B. Friend

II. NCCB General Secretariat

General Secretary—Rev. Msgr. William P. Fay
Associate General Secretary—Mr. Bruce E. Egnew
Associate General Secretary—Rev. Msgr. David J. Malloy
Associate General Secretary—Sr. Lourdes Sheehan, R.S.M.

III. Staff Offices

Finance—Mr. Kenneth Korotky, Dir.
Accounting—Ms. Jennifer McGowan, Dir.
Business Systems—Ms. Sharon Heinle, Dir.
General Counsel—Mr. Mark E. Chopko
Associate General Counsel—Ms. Deirdre A. Dessingue
General Services—Mr. Douglas Cissel, Dir.
Printing & Mailing Services—Mr. Ronald D. Gibson, Mgr.
Government Liaison—Mr. Frank J. Monahan, Dir.
Human Resources—Ms. Linda Hunt, Dir.
Library Services—Ms. Anne LeVeque, Dir.
Management Information Systems—Mr. William Kissane, Dir.
Office of Public & Promotional Services—Mr. Paul Henderson, Dir.

USCC COMMITTEES

EXECUTIVE LEVEL

Administrative Board

Chairman—Bishop Joseph A. Fiorenza
Members—William Cardinal Keeler; Bernard Cardinal Law; Roger Cardinal Mahony; Adam Cardinal Maida (Region VI); Archbishop Daniel A. Cronin; Archbishop John G. Vlazny; Archbishop Roger L. Schwietz; Bishop Victor Balke (Region VIII); Bishop Gordon D. Bennett, S.J.; Bishop Stephen E. Blaire; Bishop J. Kevin Boland, (Region IV); Bishop Edward K. Braxton; Bishop Tod D. Brown; Bishop Edmond Carmody; Bishop John S. Cummins; Bishop Thomas J. Curry; Bishop Nicholas A. DiMarzio; Bishop Daniel N. DiNardo (Region IX); Bishop Joseph A. Galante; Bishop Richard J. Garcia (Region XI); Bishop John R. Gaydos; Bishop Wilton D. Gregory; Bishop Curtis J. Guillory, S.V.D.; Bishop Joseph H. Hart; Bishop William R. Houck (Region V); Bishop Howard J. Hubbard (Region II); Bishop Joseph L Imesch (Region VII); Bishop Gerald F. Kicanas; Bishop John F. Kinney; Bishop John J. Leibrecht; Bishop Basil H. Losten; Bishop Robert N. Lynch; Bishop Henry J. Mansell; Bishop John J. McRaith; Bishop Manuel D. Moreno (Region XIII); Bishop William F. Murphy (Region I); Bishop Anthony J. O'Connell; Bishop Sean P. O'Malley, O.F.M.Cap.; Bishop A. James Quinn; Bishop John H. Ricard, S.S.J.; Bishop Peter A. Rosazza; Bishop Carlos A. Sevilla, S.J., (Region XII); Bishop William S. Skylstad; Bishop John M. Smith (Region III); Bishop J. Terry Steib, S.V.D.; Bishop Arthur N. Tafoya; Bishop Donald W. Trautman; Bishop Michael W. Warfel; Bishop Donald W. Wuerl; Bishop Paul A. Zipfel; Bishop Patrick J. Zurek (Region X)

Executive Committee

Chairman—Bishop Joseph A. Fiorenza
Vice President—Bishop Wilton D. Gregory
Treasurer—Bishop Henry J. Mansell
Secretary—Bishop William B. Friend
Staff—Rev. Msgr. William P. Fay

Committee on Budget and Finance

Chairman—Bishop Henry J. Mansell
Members—Bishop John J. McRaith; Bishop George H. Niederauer; Bishop John H. Ricard, S.S.J.; Rev. Msgr. William P. Fay
Staff—Mr. Kenneth Korotky

Committee on Personnel

Chairman—Bishop Wilton D. Gregory
Members—Bishop Anthony J. O'Connell; Bishop J. Terry Steib, S.V.D.; Rev. Msgr. William P. Fay
Staff—Ms. Linda Hunt, Dir.; Mr. Bruce E. Egnew

Committee on Priorities and Plans

Chairman—Bishop Joseph A. Fiorenza
Vice President—Bishop Wilton D. Gregory
Treasurer—Bishop Henry J. Mansell
Past President—Bishop Anthony A. Pilla
Members—Bishop Stephen E. Blaire; Bishop Anthony J. O'Connell; Rev. Msgr. William P. Fay
Staff—Sr. Lourdes Sheehan, R.S.M.

DEPARTMENTAL LEVEL

Campaign for Human Development

Chairman—Bishop John J. Leibrecht
Members—Bishop Norbert M. Dorsey, C.P.; Bishop Joseph H. Hart; Bishop Howard J. Hubbard; Bishop Sean P. O'Malley, O.F.M.Cap.; Bishop Raymundo J. Pena; Bishop Joseph N. Perry; Bishop Carlos A. Sevilla, S.J.; Ms. Donna M. Hanson; Ms. Kerry A. Robinson; Ms. Delena Stephens; Ms. Kathleen Maas Weigert
Staff—Rev. Robert J. Vitillo, Exec. Dir.; Mr. Timothy Collins, Deputy Dir.; Mr. Douglas M. Lawson, Assoc. Dir.- Program; Ms. Barbara Stephenson, Assoc. Dir.- Communications.

COMMUNICATIONS

Chairman—Bishop Joseph A. Galante
Chairman-Elect—Bishop Thomas J. Curry
Members—Archbishop Michael J. Sheehan; Bishop J. Kevin Boland; Bishop Thomas J. Costello; Bishop Blasé J. Cupich; Bishop John R. Gaydos; Bishop Daniel R. Jenky, C.S.C.; Bishop John B. McCormack; Bishop John C. Nienstedt; Mr. Charles Robert Carner; Mr. Edward Murray; Ms. Christine Bonahoom-Nix; Mr. Frank DeRosa; Mr. Richard Dowling; Ms. Karen M. Franz; Ms. Annette Gonzales Taylor; Mrs. Mary Jeffcoat; Rev. Msgr. James Lisante; Mr. Frank Morock
Consultant—William Cardinal Keeler
Staff—Rev. Msgr. Francis J. Maniscalco, Dir. for Communications; Ms. Patricia R. Garcia, Dir.- Catholic Communication Campaign Distribution; Ms. Ellen McCloskey, Dir.-Catholic Communication Productions; Ms. Gerri Pare, Dir.-Film and Broadcasting; Mr. Ramon E. Rodriguez, Dir. Catholic Communication Campaign Development; Mr. Thomas N. Lorsung, Dir. & Editor-in-Chief Catholic News Service.

DOMESTIC POLICY

Chairman—Roger Cardinal Mahony
Members—Bishop Edwin M. Conway; Bishop Michael P. Driscoll; Bishop Carlos A. Sevilla, S.J.; Bishop William S. Skylstad; Bishop J. Terry Steib, S.V.D.; Bishop Joseph M. Sullivan; Rev. Dennis J. Dease; Mr. W. Shepherdson Abell; Ms. Nancy Bernstine; Sr. Mary Roch Rocklage, R.S.M.; Mr. Gerry Shea; Mr. John Sweeney

Department of Social Development and World Peace

Secretary-Social Development & World Peace—Mr. John Carr
Outreach Coordinator—Mr. Richard Fowler
Office of Domestic Social Development
Director—Ms. Nancy Wisdo
Policy Advisor-Health & Welfare Issues—Ms. Kathleen Curran
Policy Advisor-Food, Agriculture & Rural Devel.—Mr.Daniel Misleh
Policy Advisor-Urban & Economic Issues—Mr. Thomas Shellabuger

INTERNATIONAL POLICY

Chairman—Bernard Cardinal Law
Members—Archbishop Theodore E. McCarrick; Bishop Edward K. Braxton; Bishop John J. Glynn; Bishop Ibrahim Ibrahim; Bishop William F. Murphy; Bishop Ricardo Ramirez, C.S.B.; Bishop Peter A. Rosazza; Mr. J. Brian Benestad; Mr. Bob Craves; Dr. Mary Ann Glendon; Sr. Doris Gottemoeller, R.S.M.; Mr. Paul Michael Kennedy; Dr. Maryann Cusimano Love; Mr. John Steinbruner; Mr. Anthony C. E. Quainton

Department of Social Development and World Peace

Secretary for Social Development and World Peace—Mr. John L. Carr
Outreach Coordinator—Mr. Richard Fowler

Office of International Justice and Peace

Director for International Justice and Peace—Mr. Gerard Powers
Policy Advisor, Europe and Security Policies—Mr. Walt Grazer
Policy Advisor, Europe and Security Policies—Ms. Frances Horner
Policy Advisor, African Affairs—Rev. Michael Perry, O.F.M.
Policy Advisor, Latin American, Caribbean, and Asian Affairs—Mr. Thomas Quigley
Manager, Environmental Justice Project—Mr. Walt Grazer

EDUCATION

Chairman—Bishop Donald W. Wuerl
Members—Mr. Edmund F. Gordon; Bishop Gordon D. Bennett, S.J.; Bishop Vincent D. Breen; Bishop Paul S. Loverde; Bishop Richard J. Malone; Bishop John C. Nienstedt; Bishop Gambino Zavala; Rev. John Pollard; Sr. Sr. Ann Dominic Roach, O.P.; Rev. Thomas T. Toale, Ph.D.; Rev. Dennis Dease; Ms. Carol Obrokta
Staff—Rev. Msgr. John Strynkowski, Exec. Dir; Rev. William Davis, O.S.F.S., Asst. Sec. for Catholic School & Public Policy; Sr. Maureen Shaughnessy, S.C., Asst. Sec. For Catechesis & Leadership Formation; Mr. Daniel Mulhall, Asst. Sec. for Catechesis and Inculturation; Mrs. Mary Ellen Russell, Asst. Sec. For Catholic Schools Parental Rights

Advisory Committee on Public Policy and Catholic Schools

Chairman—Bishop Donald W. Wuerl
Members—Bishop Gordon D. Bennett, S.J.; Sr. Kathryn Ann Connelly, S.C.; Mr.George Corwell; Sr. Mary Elizabeth Galt; Mr. George Henry; Rev. David F. McCauley; Sr. Dale McDonald, P.B.V.M.; Mr. Robert O'Hara; Sr. Dominica Rocchio, S.C.; Dr. Leonard DeFiore (NCEA)

Committee of Bishops and Catholic College and University Presidents

Chairman—Bishop Donald W. Wuerl

Members—Bishop John P. Boles; Bishop Paul G. Bootkoski; Bishop John M. D'Arcy; Bishop James R. Hoffman; Bishop James R. Hoffman; Bishop George H. Niederauer

Presidents—Rev. Dennis Dease, University of St. Thomas; Dr. Marilou Eldred, St. Mary's College; Bro. James Gaffney, F.S.C., Lewis University; Dr. Alice B. Hayes, University of San Diego; Rev. William Leahy, S.J., Boston College; Rev. David M. O'Connell, C.M., The Catholic University of America

COMMITTEE ON CATECHESIS

Chairman—Bishop Donald W. Wuerl

Members—Bishop Gordon D. Bennett, S.J.; Bishop Daniel N. DiNardo; Bishop William E. Lori; Sr. Alice Molina, R.S.H.M.; Rev. Kris Stubna; Rev. John Kachuba; Sr. Eva Lumas, S.S.S.; Ms. Catherine Minkiewicz; Dr. Chris Villapando

Staff—Sr. Maureen Shaughnessy, S.C., Asst. Sec.-Catechesis and Leadership Formation; Mr. Daniel Mulhall, Asst. Sec.-Catechesis and Inculturation

SAPIENTIA CHRISTIANA

Chairman—Bishop John P. Boles

Members—Bishop Donald W. Trautman; Bishop Donald W. Wuerl

USCC Department of Education

Assistant Secretary for Catholic Schools and Public Policy—Rev. William Davis, O.S.F.S.

Assistant Secretary for Catechesis and Inculturation—Mr. Daniel Mulhall

Assistant Secretary for Catholic School Parent Rights—Mrs. Mary Ellen Russell

Assistant Secretary for Catechesis and Leadership Formation—Sr. Maureen Shaughnessy, S.C.

NATIONAL ADVISORY COUNCIL

Chairman—Mr. Henry W. Dwyer

Chairman-Elect— Mr. Sidney S. Simmons, II

Secretary— Mrs. Julie French

Members—Bishop Joseph H. Hart; Bishop Gerald F. Kicanas; Bishop Paul A. Zipfel; Bishop Patrick J. Zurek

Diocesan Priests—Rev. Timothy F. Babcock; Rev. Msgr. W. Ronald Jameson; Rev. James F. Kuhns; Rev. Msgr. Arturo Meza; Rev. Steven Verhelst; Rev. Richard E. Zajac

Religious Men—Rev. Michael Higgins, C.P.; Rev. Arthur M. Johnson, S.A.

Religious Women— Sr. Joanne M. Hanrahan, S.S.N.D.; Sr. Julia Jamink, S.J.H.; Sr. Linda Werthman, R.S.M.

Regional Representatives—

Region I: Mr. Marcos Brizuela; Ms. Mercedes Rojas

Region II: Mr. Henry W. Dwyer; Ms. Mary E. Thompson.

Region III: Ms. Ann Burgmeyer; Deacon Frank C. Pregler

Region IV: Ms. Joanna Martin

Region V: Mrs. Patty Gaines; Mr. Sidney Shaw

Region VI: Mr. Brian Corbin; Ms. Adriana Vlasic

Region VII: Mr. John F. Rogan; Mrs. Donna L. Hansen

Region VIII: Mr. Richard L. Thompson; Mrs. Lois P. Anderson

Region IX: Mr. Duane J. Gross; Mrs. Betty Frommelt

Region X: Ms. Charlotte Davis; Mr. Charles Kaler, Jr.

Region XI: Ms. Rosalina Domondon

Region XII: Mrs. Julie French

Region XIII: Mr. Ernest D. Tsosie, Jr.; Mrs. Barbara C. Kozeliski

RELATED ORGANIZATIONS

*** Catholic Legal Immigration Network, Inc. (CLINIC)**

Theological College, National Office,401 Michigan Ave. N.E., First Flr., Washington, DC 20017. Tel: 202-635-2556; Fax: 202-635-2649.

Staff—Most Rev. Thomas G. Wenski, Chm.; Mr. Donald Kerwin, Sec. & Chief Operating Officer; Most Rev. George V. Murry, S.J., Treas.

Members—Most Revs. Emilio Allue, S.D.B.; Stephen E. Blaire; Nicolas A. DiMarzio; Michael P. Driscoll; Thomas J. Flanagan; Thomas J. Olmsted; John H. Ricard, S.S.J.; James A. Tamayo; Mr. Mark Franken Sr. Lourdes Sheehan, R.S.M.; Ms. Jane Golden Belford, Esq.; Sr. Raymonda Duvall; Mr. Austin Fragomen.

CLINIC was incorporated in 1988 as a non profit tax-exempt subsidiary of the National Conference of Catholic Bishops. It is a unique legal services corporation charged with the mandate to serve as a national support and resource center and to assist diocesan programs in the provision of immigration services to their indigent and low-income clients, regardless of race, nationality, ethnicity, political or religious beliefs.

Catholic Relief Services—

CRS World Headquarters, 209 W. Fayette St., Baltimore, MD 21201. Tel: 410-625-2220; Fax: 410-685-1635. Mr. Kenneth F. Hackett, Exec. Dir. Each diocese has a local CRS diocesan director listed in this book.

Catholic Relief Services Board of Directors:

Chairman—Most Rev. John H. Ricard, S.S.J.

Members—Most Revs. Roger L. Schwietz, O.M.I.; Gerald R. Barnes; Joseph L. Charron, C.P.P.S.; Joseph L. Imesch; John B. McCormack; Dale J. Melczek; William C. Newman; Donald E. Pelotte, S.S.S.; Michael A. Saltarelli; J. Terry Steib, S.V.D.; John W. Yanta; Rev. Msgr. William P. Fay.

Catholic Relief Services-USCC The official overseas relief and development agency of U.S. Catholics; it is a separately incorporated organization of the U.S. Catholic Conference.

CRS was founded in 1943 by the bishops of the United States to assist the poor and disadvantaged outside this country.

CRS maintains programs and projects in over 80 countries around the world. Help is given to all those in need regardless of race, creed or political affiliation.

In addition to its highly acclaimed disaster relief work, CRS carries on community development and social justice programs throughout the developing world. These include health projects, school feeding programs, agricultural development, water resource management, income-generating projects, and community promotion and are designed to help people help themselves and to raise the standard of living of families and entire communities.

CRS operations are funded, in part, from the proceeds of an annual collection - American Bishops Overseas Appeal (also known as the Bishop's Welfare Emergency Fund) - held during the Lenten season in more than 18,000 Catholic churches in the U.S. - Support is also received from Operation Rice Bowl, Catholic Relief Services Lenten program of prayer, fasting, learning and giving, and from individuals, church and school groups, foundations and corporations. Assistance from the federal government takes several forms: food available under Title II of Public Law 480; defrayment of ocean freight costs on U.S. government-donated foods and relief supplies generated by CRS itself; grants for some emergency operations.

In addition to Operation Rice Bowl, Catholic Relief Services' Church Outreach programs, such as Work of Human Hands and Food Fast, involve schools and parishes in global solidarity and the work of social justice. Educational materials as well as other Catholic Relief Services brochures, newsletters, and information on planned giving programs, including wills/bequests, and annuities, are available upon request.

In the year ending Dec. 31, 1998, Catholic Relief Services' global program in 80 countries had a total value of 248 million dollars.

CTNA Telecommunications, Inc.

3211 Fourth St. N.E., Washington, DC 20017-1194. Tel: 202-541-3200. Rev. Msgr. Francis J. Maniscalco, Pres.; Rev. Msgr. William P. Fay, Chm.-Board of Directors.

National Religious Retirement Office

3211 Fourth St., N.E., Washington, DC 20017-1194. Tel: 202-541-3215. Sr. Andree Fries, C.P.P.S., Exec. Dir.

The USCC Commission on Certification and Accreditation

3195 S. Superior St. –Rm. 317S Milwaukee, WI 53207-3074. Tel: 414-486-0139; Fax: 414-489-0006. Mary T. O'Neill, Board Chm.; Sr. Kay L. Sheskaitis, I.H.M., Exec. Dir.

Established by the Administrative Board of the United States Catholic Conference in 1983, the USCC/CCA accredits post-secondary programs that offer pastoral formation or education for persons preparing for ministry. These programs may be offered or sponsored by colleges, dioceses, health institutions, retreat centers, universities, or other institutions that are authorized to conduct post-secondary programs and whose programs are in compliance with the USCC/CCA standards, accreditation policies, and procedures established by the Commission.

The Commission also approves certification standards for national organizations of specialized ministers and certification procedures of dioceses utilizing the certification standards of national organizations and procedures established by the Commission.

NATIONAL ORGANIZATIONS

Listing in this category is not related to classification under Canon Law as a public juridic person.

American Catholic Correctional Chaplains Association—

13934 Lemoli Ave., Hawthorne, CA 90250. Tel: 310-676-2038. Most Rev. J. Kendrick Williams, D.D., Episcopal Advisor; Rev. Mark Santo, Pres.; Rev. John Wilkinson, O.M.I., Vice Pres. & Treas.; Edward Bryon, Sec.

The Board of Directors include the Episcopal Advisor, Elected Officers, Regional Vice Presidents, and Past Presidents. Address all Communications to the President or Secretary.

A non profit organization for the purposes of unifying and implementing the Church's corrective and rehabilitative efforts for the spiritual welfare of persons committed to the Catholic Chaplains' care, and to foster a Catholic approach to the problems and study of the correctional field in accord with the principles of Sacred Scriptures, Catholic philosophy and theology. Affiliated with the Social Development and World Peace Department, U.S. Catholic Conference, Inc., American Correctional Association, American Correctional Chaplains Assocation, National Council on Crime and Delinquency and Catholic University of America, it was established with approval of the American Bishops. Grants USCC recognized certification to qualified members.

Publication: *The Chap-lett.*

American Catholic Historical Association (1919)—

The Catholic University of America, Washington, DC 20064. Tel: 202-319-5079; Fax: 202-319-5079. E-mail: CUA-chracha@CUA.edu. Patrick W. Carey, Pres.; Rev. Msgr. Robert Trisco, Sec. & Treas.

A membership organization, founded to promote the study of church history understood in the broad sense and to assist American Catholics and other members in all fields of history.

The American College of the Roman Catholic Church of the United States—North American College (1859)—

3211 Fourth St., N.E., Washington, DC 20017-1194. Tel: 202-541-5403; Fax: 202-722-8804. His Eminence Edward Cardinal Egan, Chm.; Rev. Msgr. Timothy M. Dolan, Rector, 00120, Vatican City, Europe. Ms. Tricia Morrin, Dir. Office for Devel. & Public Rels.

The College is owned and operated by the Bishops of the United States and is incorporated under the laws of the State of Maryland.

Association of Catholic Diocesan Archivists—

Archdiocese of Chicago Archives & Record Ctr., 711 W. Monroe, Chicago, IL 60661. Tel: 312-831-0711. His Eminence Roger Cardinal Mahony, Episcopal Moderator; Lisa May, Pres.; Marc F. Lerman, Vice Pres.; John J.(Jac) Treanor, Treas.; Bernice M. Mooney, Sec.

The Association of Catholic diocesan archivists first met in 1979 and formally organized the Association of Catholic Diocesan Archivists in 1982. The organization promotes professionalism in the management of diocesan archives in the United States and Canada, and fosters cooperation between diocesan archivists and others on regional, national and international levels. Membership information is available through the above address and telephone number.

Catholic Association of Teachers of Homiletics (CATH)—

St. Francis Seminary, 3257 South Lake Dr., St. Francis, WI 53235.

Officers—Rev. Stephen DeLeers, Pres.; Sr. Mary Ann Wiesemann-Mills, O.P., Vice-Pres.; Patricia Hughes Baumer, Sec./Treas.

Catholic Campus Ministry Association—
Executive Office, 300 College Park, Dayton, OH 45469-2515. Tel: 937-229-4648; Fax: 937-229-4024. Edmund L. Franchi, Exec. Dir.

Founded in 1969 by campus ministers, the association promotes the mission of the Church in higher education and implements the 1985 Pastoral Letter on Campus Ministry through educational programs and services, leadership, the development of cooperative relationships with other organizations and development activities. Membership is open to individuals interested in campus ministry.

Publication: *Crossroads*, bi monthly publication; *The Catholic Campus Ministry Directory.*

Catholic Charities USA—
1731 King St., Ste. 200, Alexandria, VA 22314. Tel: 703-549-1390; Fax: 703-549-1656. Most Rev. Joseph M. Sullivan, Episcopal Liaison; Ms. Kathleen McGowan, Chm.; Rev. Fred Kammer, S.J., Pres.

Catholic Charities USA is a national network of more than 1,200 agencies and institutions as well as thousands of concerned individuals who are dedicated to serving the most vulnerable members of American society. The nation's largest network of private, independent social service organizations aims to support families, strengthen communities, and reduce poverty.

Diocesan Catholic Charities agencies provide shelter, food, counseling and a host of other services to children, teen parents, adults, and the elderly. The services are offered to people of all religious, national, racial, social, and economic backgrounds. Each year, millions of people turn to Catholic Charities for everything from a hot meal at a soup kitchen to a new family through adoption.

The organization was founded in 1910 as the National Conference of Catholic Charities by the Most Rev. Thomas J. Shahan and Rt. Rev. Msgr. William J. Kerby in cooperation with lay leaders of the Society of St. Vincent de Paul. Today the network has several hundred thousand volunteers and staff members who provide services to people in need, advocate for justice in social structures, and call the entire Church and other people of good will to do the same.

Catholic Charities USA serves members through national and regional meetings and networking, training, literature, and social policy advocacy on the national level. It is commissioned by the U.S. Catholic Conference to represent the Catholic community when disasters strike in the United States. Catholic Charities USA's president represents North America before Caritas International, the international conference of Catholic Charities, and thus maintains contact with the Catholic Charities Movement throughout the world.

Publications: quarterly membership magazine, *Charities USA;* annual report, *Directory of Catholic Charities, Agencies; Annual Survey of Catholic Charities* services nationwide; various books, pamphlets and studies.

The Catholic Communications Foundation (CCF)—
PMB# 12611420 U.S. Hwy One, North Palm Beach, FL 33408. Tel: 561-776-5733. Most Rev. Anthony G. Bosco, Chm; Most Rev. Daniel A. Cronin, Pres.; Bernard J. Lengerman, Exec. Vice Pres.; James R. Bastis, Sec.

The Catholic Communications Foundation was established and is supported by Catholic Fraternal Benefit Societies. Its mission is to assist the communications apostolates of the Catholic Church in the United States, with particular emphasis at the diocesan level. The Foundation awards religious communications training scholarships.

The Catholic Health Association of the United States (1919)—
Headquarters, 4455 Woodson Rd., St. Louis, MO 63134. Tel: 314-427-2500; Fax: 314-427-0029. Web Site: www.chausa.org. Rev. Michael D. Place, S.T.D., Pres. & CEO; Timothy J. Eckels, Sr. Vice Pres. Planning & Policy Devel.; Cal Smith, Vice Pres. Exec. & Admin. Services; Sr. Beverly McGuire, R.S.M., Vice. Pres., Sponsorship & Mission Services; Maureen H. McCullough, Vice Pres.-Public Policy and Advocacy; Rhonda Mueller, Financial Controller; J. Fred Caesar, Dir. Public Affairs; Joanne Elden Beale, Sr. Assoc. Sponsor Services/Dir.-Assembly; Theresa Van Schaik, Mgr. Editorial Services.

CHA represents the combined strength of its members, more than 2,000 Catholic healthcare sponsors, systems, facilities, and related organizations. Founded in 1915, CHA unites members to advance selected strategic issues that are best addressed together rather than as individual organizations. It strengthens the Church's health ministry in the United States by advocating for a just healthcare system, convening leaders to share ideas and foster collaboration, and uniting the ministry voice on critical issues. Presents annual awards recognizing contribution to the health ministry by organizations and individuals. Sponsors continuing education for healthcare personnel. Conducts surveys; compiles statistics.

Service Areas: Planning and Policy Development, Public Policy and Advocacy, Communications, Sponsorship and Mission Services. Annual Assembly: Annual assembly and membership meeting for 2001 will be held in Atlanta, GA, June 10-13. San Francisco, CA. June 10-13. The 2002 annual assembly will be held in Chicago, IL, August 4-7.

Publications: 6 times-year, *Health Progress*; bi monthly *Catholic Health World*; annual, *Guidebook of Catholic Health Care Facilities*; booklets, books & audio-visual on healthcare, Church-related subjects.

CHA's Web Site, CHA Online, can be found at http:\\www.chusa.org.

Catholic Kolping Society of America (1849)—
9 East 8th St., Clifton, NJ 07011-1101. (Please direct all correspondence to the National Administrator.) Edward Farkas, Natl. Admin.

The Society was founded by Rev. Adolph Kolping in Cologne, Germany, and established in the United States in 1856. The Catholic Kolping Society of America is a part of the world-wide Kolping movement and belongs to the International Kolping Society. There are 12 branches in principal cities of the United States with a combined membership of approximately 2,500. The membership is open to men and women of all ages. The Society's mission statement reads: We, the members of the Catholic Kolping Society of America, extend the vision of our founder, Blessed Adolph Kolping, by promoting the development of the individual and family; we foster a sense of belonging and friendship through our program of spiritual, educational, charitable and social activities.

Catholic Network Of Volunteer Service—
1410 Q St., N.W., Washington, DC 20009. Tel: 202-332-6000; 800-543-5046; Fax: 202-332-1611. Most Rev. John J. Snyder, Episcopal Advisor; James G. Lindsay, Exec. Dir.

Catholic Network of Volunteer Service promotes, recruits and refers volunteers to missions in the United States and overseas. We represent nearly 200 faith-based volunteer programs worldwide and work with the U.S. dioceses, religious communities and the private sector to determine their needs for help. Catholic Network of Volunteer Service (CNVS) is committed to the goal that every Catholic man and woman be invited to consider a period of service in the missions, as a vital and important manifestation of the baptismal call of all Catholic people. Currently, 6,500 men and women are serving in CNVS member mission programs offering their gifts and abilities in full-time service to people in need and living their Catholic faith more fully than many had imagined possible. These volunteers are serving domestically for a summer, six months, a year or more, and they are serving internationally for two or more years at a time. They are single and married, recent college graduates and early retirees, doctors and teachers, parish ministers and social workers, community organizers, computer programmers, legal aides and more. Gatherings: Annual Conference; Formation Workshops, Training Seminars.

Publications: annual, *Response: Directory of Volunteer Opportunities;* biweekly, *How Can I Help?*; quarterly, *Lay Mission Handbook.*

Awards: The Father George Mader Award, given annually during the Fall meeting of the NCCB to honor organizations and individuals who promote the value of lay mission service.

The Catholic Press Association of the United States and Canada, Inc.—
Attn: Owen McGovern, 3555 Veterans Memorial Hwy.-Unit O, Ronkonkoma, NY 11779. Tel: 631-471-4730. Most Rev. Joseph A. Galante, Honorary Pres.; Ms. Karen Franz, Pres.; Mr. Owen McGovern, Exec. Dir. Web Site: http//www.catholicpress.org; E-mail address: CathoJourn@aol.com.

The Catholic Press Association of the United States and Canada, Inc., is the trade and professional association of Catholic newspapers, magazines, and general publishers in the U.S. and Canada and their staff personnel. The CPA was established in 1911. It serves a professional Catholic press market of nearly 2,000 persons working in more than 600 publications with a wide promotion and representation of Catholic press interests in legal, postal, tax and professional matters.

The Catholic Theological Society of America
Attn: Dolores L. Christie, Ph.D, Exec. Sec. John Carroll University, 20700 North Park Blvd., University Hgts., OH 44118. Tel: 216-751-5419; Fax: 216-752-5841. Kenneth R. Himes, Pres., Washington, DC; Peter C. Phan, Pres.-elect Washington, DC; Jon Nilson, Vice Pres., Chicago, IL; Mary Ann Hinsdale, Sec., Worcester, MA; Roger McGrath, Treas., Cherry Hill, NJ; Mary Ann Donovan, Past Pres., Berkeley, CA. Board Members: Bradford Hinze, Milwaukee, WI; Robert P. Imbelli, Chestnut, MA; Sandra M. Schneiders, Berkeley, CA; Susan Wood, Collegeville, MN; Dolores Christie, Exec. Sec., University Hgts., OH; Michael Downey, Editor of New Proceedings, Camarillo, CA.

An association of professional theologians. Its purpose is to promote studies and research in theology within the Roman Catholic tradition, to relate theological science to current problems, and to foster a more effective theological education by providing a forum for an exchange of views among theologians and with scholars in other disciplines.

Conference for Catholic Facility Management—
P.O. Box 177, Bowie, MD 20719-0177. Tel: 202-541-3333; Fax: 202-541-3322. E-mail address: dcissel@nccbuscc.org. Most Rev. Carl K. Moeddel, Episcopal Moderator; Doug Cissel, Exec. Dir.

Mindful of their special ministry in the Roman Catholic Church in facility and real estate matters, the members of the CCFM united to be of service to the Church in ministry of facility and real estate concerns. In particular, this organization promotes the spiritual growth of its membership; promotes facility and real estate knowledge and expertise in service to the local and national Church, facilitates the exchange of ideas and information through personal contacts, quarterly newsletters and annual meetings.

Conference of Diocesan Coordinators of Health Affairs—
1031 Superior Ave.-Rm. 327, Cleveland OH 44114. Tel: 216-429-8307; Fax: 216-429-8033. Rev. Frank Godic, Chm.

Membership in this Conference is by direct appointment and authority from the Ordinary of the appointee and gives members an opportunity of maintaining mutually helpful relationships with the Catholic Health Association, with one another, and with all religious, professional and governmental organizations in the health and hospital field.

The Conference of Major Religious Superiors of Men's Institutes of the United States, Inc.—
8808 Cameron St., Silver Spring, MD 20910. Tel: 301-588-4030; Fax: 301-587-4575. Rev. Ted Keating, S.M., Exec. Dir.; Bro. Stephen Glodek, S.M., Pres.; Rev. Kurt Hartrich, O.F.M., Vice Pres.; Rev. John Libens, S.J., Sec. & Treas.

An association of the major superiors of religious communities and institutes of men for the purpose of promoting the spiritual and apostolic welfare of priests and brothers.

The Confraternity of Christian Doctrine, Inc.—
3211 Fourth St. N.E., Washington, DC 20017. Tel: 202-541-3098; Fax: 202-541-3089. Mary Elizabeth Sperry, Permissions Mgr.

The Confraternity is a distinct entity, separately incorporated and directed by a Board of Trustees from the United States Catholic Conference. The purpose of the Corporation is to foster and promote the teachings of Christ as understood and handed down by the Roman Catholic Church. To this end it licenses use of the Lectionary for Mass and the New American Bible, translations made from the original languages.

Council of Major Superiors of Women Religious in the United States of America—
1211 Lawrence St., N.E.- P.O. Box 4467, Washington, DC 20017-0467. Tel: 202-832-2575; Fax: 202-832-6325. Mother Mary McGreevy, R.S.M., Chm.

A canonically erected conference of Major Superiors of women's religious communities established in 1992 to promote mutual support among them and to foster coordination and cooperation with the Bishops' conference and individual Bishops.

Federation of Diocesan Liturgical Commissions—
National Office, 415 Michigan Ave., N.E., Suite 70, Washington, DC 20017. Tel: 202-635-6990; Fax: 202-529-2452. Revs. Michael Spillane, Exec. Dir.; John H. Burton, Chm.; Ms. Joan A. Workmaster; Vice Chm.; Mr. David Reilly, Treas.; Rev. James Field, Delegate-at-Large; Ms. Carolyn Lassek, Delegate-at-Large.

The FDLC is a voluntary association of all diocesan liturgical commissions/offices from the United States. Two members of each diocesan liturgical commission/office serve as diocesan representatives to the FDLC. From this membership are elected 24 representatives (two from each of the 12 episcopal regions) to serve as the National Board of Directors. The day-to-day activities of the FDLC are directed by the Executive Director. The FDLC relates closely to the Bishops because its membership consists of their appointees. The Federation serves the Bishops and local commissions in matters of ongoing liturgical renewal. It also serves through education and other coordinated services requested by individual commissions or through consultation and voting at national meetings. The FDLC is organized and operated exclusively for religious and educational purposes.

Diocesan Fiscal Management Conference—
National Office, P.O. Box 199, Waterville, OH 43566-0199. Tel: 800-709-3362; 419-878-3146; Fax: 419-878-7265. Most Rev. Donald W. Trautman, S.T.D., S.S.L., Episcopal Moderator; Rev. Robert J. Yeager, Ed.D., Exec. Dir.; Kevin J. Heffernan, Pres.; Deacon Ronald D. Henderson, Vice Pres.; Sheila R. Murray, Sec. & Treas.

Mindful of their special ministry in the Roman Catholic Church as the extension of the Diocesan Bishop in fiscal matters, the members of the DFMC unite to be of service to the Church in the ministry of fiscal management.

In particular, this organization promotes the spiritual growth of its members; promotes financial and administrative knowledge and expertise in service to the local and national Church; facilitates the free exchange of ideas and information, and serves as a liaison among the fiscal managers of the Dioceses and Archdioceses of the Church.

Instituto de Liturgia Hispana—
P.O. Box 29387, Washington, DC 20017-0387. Tel: 202-319-6450; Fax: 202-319-6449. Rev. Heliodoro Lucatero, Pres.; Sr. Marilu Covani, S.P., Vice Pres.; Mrs. Maria Perez Rudisill, Sec.; Ms. Sylvia Sanchez, Treas.; Sr. Doris Mary Turek, S.S.N.D., Exec. Dir.

The Instituto is a national organization committed to meeting the liturgical needs of Hispanic Catholic communities. Its aim is to study, reflect and celebrate more authentically our Catholic faith from the perspective of our religious traditions and in the light of the teachings of the Church. Its members cooperate and assist in national, regional, diocesan, and parish groups with regard to Hispanic liturgical needs and concerns. They give lectures, publish in Spanish and in bilingual editions, and translate liturgical materials. Membership is open to all persons and institutions interested in liturgy. Committees: Art and Environment, Music, Popular Religiosity, Sacraments and Sacramentals, and Texts. The Instituto sponsors a national conference every two years on liturgical topics. The members meet annually.

International Catholic Migration Commission (ICMC) & ICMC, Inc.—
ICMC, Inc. Headquarters, 1319 F St., N.W., Washington, DC 20004. Prof. Stefano Zamagni, Pres.; William A. Canny, Sec. Gen.

Provides technical assistance and coordination in area of service to migrants and refugees. Non-profit New York Corporation.

Jesuit Conference, Inc.—
1616 P St., N.W., Washington, DC 20036-1405. Tel: 202-462-0400; Fax: 202-328-9212. Revs. Bradley M. Schaeffer, S.J., Pres.; James A. Casciotti, S.J., Exec. Sec.

Ladies of Charity of the United States of America (LCUSA)—
P.O. Box 31697, St. Louis, MO 63131-0697. Mrs. Alma Arredondo, Pres.; Most Rev. Howard J. Hubbard, Episcopal Chm.; Spiritual Advisors: Revs. Fred Kammer, S.J.; Richard Gielow.

LCUSA Service Center, Ladies of Charity in the United States of America, whose 17,500 members give personal service to the illiterate, needy, sick (especially the poor sick), underprivileged, handicapped and elderly, and also assist the clergy in pastoral care. They also strive for social justice. LCUSA encourages activities of the current Associations and promotes the organization of new Associations. The Board of Directors is the governing body of LCUSA. Organizational information is provided to members and Bishops through its official publication ""Servicette," published four times annually and through contact with the President. They also affiliate with the Association of International Charities of St. Vincent de Paul (AIC). Ladies of Charity was founded in 1617 by St. Vincent de Paul and has continued in existence longer than any other church-oriented volunteer group of lay persons. They work closely with the Daughters of Charity. Annual National meetings.

Leadership Conference of Women Religious in the United States of America—
Office, 8808 Cameron St., Silver Spring, MD 20910. Tel: 301-588-4955; Fax: 301-587-4575. Sr. Mary Christine Fellerhoff, C.S.A., Exec. Dir.; Sr. Nancy Sylvester, I.H.M., Past Pres.; Sr. Mary Mollison, C.S.A., Pres.; Sr. Kathleen Pruitt, C.S.J.P., Vice Pres.; Sr. Mary Bernadette McNulty, C.S.J., Treas.

A conference of leaders of U.S. women religious congregations, founded in 1956, canonically approved in 1959 with a name change in 1972 and canonical approval of revised by-laws in 1972 and 1989, to promote a developing understanding and living of religious life, to assist members to carry out more collaboratively their service of leadership, to provide a vehicle for dialogue with the Bishops' Conference and other ecclesiastical authority, and to collaborate with other groups concerned with the needs of society in continuing the mission of Christ in the world today.

Legal Resource Center for Religious, Inc.—
8812 Cameron St., Silver Spring, MD 20910. Tel: 301-589-8143; Fax: 301-589-2897. Daniel J. Ward, O.S.B., Exec. Dir.

Lithuanian Roman Catholic Federation of America—
4545 W. 63rd St., Chicago, IL 60629. Tel: 312-585-9500. Most Rev. Paulius Baltakis, O.F.M., Episcopal Advisor; Rev. Msgr. Joseph Prunskis, Spiritual Advisor; Saulius V. Kuprys, Pres., 150 S. Wacker Dr., Ste. 1050, Chicago, IL 60606. Tel: 312-346-5275; 708-243-0416; Fax: 312-346-5640; 708-243-0418.

A not-for-profit corporation founded in 1906 in Wilkes-Barre, PA, to promote and coordinate religious, educational and charitable activities among Lithuanian American Catholics, their organizations, institutions, religious communities, and parishes (for detailed information regarding religious institutions please refer to the Apostolate for Lithuanians).

Mariological Society of America (1949)—
Secretariat: Marian Library, University of Dayton, Dayton, OH 45469-1390. Tel: 937-229-4294; Fax: 937-229-4258. Rev. Thomas A. Thompson, S.M., Exec. Sec.; Most Rev. Austin B. Vaughan, Episcopal Chm.

The objects and purposes of this organization are to promote interest and research in the theology of the Virgin Mary. Professional and associate membership. Proceedings of annual meeting published in Marian Studies. Annual convention in late May or early June.

The Mexican American Cultural Center (1972)—
3115 West Ashby Plc., San Antonio, TX 78228. Tel: 210-732-2156. Most Rev. Patrick F. Flores, Chm.; Sr. Maria Elena Gonzalez, R.S.M., Pres.

The Mexican American Cultural Center (MACC) is a National Catholic Institute for Pastoral Leadership and Language Studies for Hispanic ministry. MACC researches and responds to the religious and social needs of the Hispanic community in light of the Gospel and the social teachings of the Roman Catholic Church in light of the Gospel. MACC programs include: *Hispanic Pastoral Ministry*: A program that offers a creative response to the need for preparation for U.S. Hispanic ministry. Dates: January-April and September-December. *Mini-Pastoral*: An intense three-week preparation to meet the challenges of U.S. Hispanic Ministry. Dates: January (in English), June (in English), July (in Spanish), and August (in English). Intensive Pastoral Spanish: A language program that concentrates on the needs of persons engaged in Hispanic ministry. *Intensive Pastoral English* for those whose first language is other than English; Cooperative Seminary Program, Masters degree in cooperation with Universities throughout the United States; Workshops and Weeks of Study. By Request, MACC faculty members serve dioceses, parishes and other groups by offering courses and workshops throughout the United States.

National Apostolate for Inclusion Ministry (1997) NAFIM—
Mailing Address, P.O. Box 218, Riverdale, MD 20738-0218. Tel: 800-736-1280; 301-699-9500; Fax: 240-220-8374. E-mail: qnafim@aol.com; Web site: www.nafim.org. Most Rev. John J. Snyder, Episcopal Moderator; Charles M. Luce, Pres.; Barbara J. Lampe, Exec. Dir.

Established in 1968 to promote the full participation and inclusion of Catholics with mental retardation in the life of their church community. Formerly known as National Apostolate with Persons with Mental Retardation (NAPMR) 1992-1997, National Apostolate with Mentally Retarded Persons (NAMRP) 1974-1992 and National Apostolate for the Mentally Retarded (NAMR) 1968-1974.

Publication: quarterly journal; newsletter; pamphlets; training materials.

Religious Brothers Association—
National Office, 1337 W. Ohio St., Chicago, IL 60622-6490. Tel: 312-829-8525; Fax: 312-829-8915. Bros. G. Timothy Smyth, C.F.C., Pres.; Dennis Wermert, S.C., Past Pres.; William D. Wright, G.H.M., Vice Pres.; David Turmel, C.S.C., Treas.; Tim Raible, M.M., Sec.; Leo Shea, F.M.S., Coord.

The National Association of Religious Brothers is a membership organization of brothers from all religious orders in the U.S., Canada and around the world.

Publication: bi monthly, *Brothers' Voice.*

National Association for Treasurers of Religious Institutes, Inc. (NATRI) (1981)—
8824 Cameron St., Silver Spring, MD 20910. Tel: 301-587-7776; Fax: 301-589-2897. Sr. Laura Reicks, R.S.M., Exec. Dir.

Serving finance officers and staffs of religious institutes by assisting them in fulfilling their stewardship responsibilities. An annual national conference, seminar for new personnel in financial offices, and a consulting service are key program components. All roman Catholic religious institutes are eligible for membership in NATRI and currently approximately 585 belong.

Publication: annual membership and service directories and other miscellaneous publications 5 times a year, *Accounting and Financial Management.*

National Assembly of Religious Women (NARW)—
National Office, 529 S. Wabash, Rm. 404, Chicago, IL 60605. Tel: 312-663-1980; Fax: 312-663-9161. Sr. Judith Vaughan, C.S.J., Natl. Coord.

A grassroots organization of Catholic women with a commitment to work inclusively for systemic change. NARW members commit themselves to a Ministry of Justice by the continuous use of their organized power for the liberation of all peoples from oppression; to work actively to promote respect for and dignity of all, and to ensure effective participation of people in decisions which affect their own lives. Their challenging and supportive action is based on Gospel values. NARW publishes books, periodicals, and other educational materials; sponsors training conferences and workshops; and collaborates with groups addressing similar issues, particularly but not exclusively, those of justice for women in society, the Church and the world.

National Association of African American Catholic Deacons, Inc.—
Office of the President, 1418 Glenview Dr. - P.O. Box 106, Yellow Springs, OH 45387. Tel: 937-767-2848 or 767-5381; Fax: 937-767-7465. Deacons Paul E. Richardson, Pres.; Ralph Cyrus, Vice Pres., Ft. Washington, MD; Ron Ealey, Sec., Wichita, KS.; Jerry Lett, Treas., Lithonia, GA.

To establish an organization of Permanent deacons of African American heritage ordained in the Roman Catholic Church. To promote unity among African American deacons by facilitating an effective communication network on a national regional, and diocesan level. To be a pro-active organization in promoting and contributing to the future of the African American family with emphasis on African American men. To promote justice, peace, equality; and end to racism, and the sharing of resources among all peoples in light of the social teachings of the Roman Catholic Church.

National Association of Catholic Chaplains—
National Office, P.O. Box 070473, Milwaukee, WI 53207-0473. Tel: 414-483-4898; Fax: 414-483-6712. Most Rev. Thomas Kelly, O.P., Episcopal Liaison; Rev. Richard M. Leliaert, O.S.C., Pres.; Rev. Joseph J. Driscoll, Exec. Dir.

The mission of this association is to promote professional development and support services for its members who share in the Church's mission of healing. Membership includes those who minister to the sick and dying, the mentally retarded, the aged, the incarcerated and confined; the families of the above and all who are a part of the faith and/or service communities in which the members serve in both public and private institutions. Certification as Chaplain and Supervisor is granted by the authority of the United States Catholic Conference.

Continuing education programs are presented on a national and a regional basis.
Publication: 10 times-year, journal-newsletter, *Vision.*

The National Association of Catholic Family Life Ministers—
Univ. of Dayton, 300 College Park, Dayton, OH 45469-2512. Mary Ann Paulukonis, Pres.; Scottie Foley, Sec.

The National Association of Church Personnel Administrators (NACPA)—
Headquarters, 100 E. Eighth St., Cincinnati, OH 45202. Tel: 513-421-3134; Fax: 513-421-3085. Rev. Paul Jaroszeski, Pres.; Sr. Ellen Doyle, O.S.U., Exec. Dir.
The National Association of Church Personnel Administrators (NACPA) is a membership association of lay, religious and clergy Personnel Directors, Assistant Directors, and Personnel Board Members serving dioceses, religious congregations and other church-related institutions. The purpose of the Association is to identify skills and competencies for human resource managers, develop personnel systems which integrate management and pastoral values, and advocate standards of just treatment for Church Personnel.

National Association of Deacon Organizations—
4410 89th St., Kenosha, WI 53142-2452. Tel: 262-694-9143; Fax: 262-694-8394. E-mail address: rlesjak@execpc.com. Deacon Ron Lesjak, Exec. Sec.; Deacon Bill Brown, Pres.

National Association of Diocesan Directors of Campus Ministry—
305 Michigan Ave., Detroit, MI 48226. Tel: 313-237-5962. Ms. Krista Bajoka, Contact Person.

National Association of Diocesan Ecumenical Officers (NADEO)—
8003 Mobud, Houston, TX 77036-6403. Tel: 713-774-0097; Fax: 713-774-0320. Ms. Garland Pohl, Pres.; Rev. Joseph Witmer, Vice Pres.; Sr. Maryanne Guertin, S.S.J., Treas.; Rev. Gary Reller, Sec.
The purposes of NADEO are to stimulate an exchange of ideas, experiences and evaluations among the ecumenical officers of the (Arch)Dioceses in union with Rome; to promote programs which further the work of Christian unity and of interreligious cooperation; and to cooperate with the Bishops' Committee for Ecumenical and Interreligious Affairs of the National Conference of Catholic Bishops, and with other ecumenical and interreligious agencies.
Publication: quarterly Newsletter; annual booklets on various ecumenical topics, *Handbook for Catholic Ecumenical Officers.*

National Association of Pastoral Musicians—
National Office, 225 Sheridan St., N.W., Washington, DC 20011. Tel: 202-723-5800; Fax: 202-723-2262. Rev. Virgil C. Funk, Exec. Dir.
A national membership organization for the improvement of music within the parish, with special emphasis on liturgical music. Membership includes parish musicians and parish clergy simultaneously, with a unique interest in the practical issues facing the practicing musician and parish clergy.
Publications: six times a year with membership, *Pastoral Music;* bi monthly with membership, *Pastoral Music Notebook.*
Services: NPM Conventions—national and regional gatherings for clergy and musicians. Director of Music Ministries Division (DMMD)—division for members who are full-time, salaried music staff in a parish or diocese and have responsibility for managing the overall liturgical music program. NPM-ME—division for music educators working in Catholic schools. NPM Hotline assists musicians seeking positions, and parishes looking for musicians. Resources for Association members are issued under the name, NPM Publications. NPM Board and NPM Council: Dr. J. Michael McMahon, Chm.
The Association has Sections for Clergy, Choir Directors, Organists, Cantors, Seminary Music Educators, Military Musicians, Campus Ministers, Young Musicians, Hispanic Musicians and Musicians serving African-American parishes. The NPM Council provides committee leadership in each of these areas. National Training programs: annually, for Choir Directors, Organists, Guitarists and Cantors with emphasis on developing musical skills, leadership abilities and ministerial skills.

National Association of Diaconate Directors (1977)—
National Office, 1204 N. Church St., Rockford, IL 61103. Tel: 815-965-0075. Deacon Thomas C. Welch, Exec. Dir.; Deacon Patrick DeLozier, Pres.; Deacon Richard Santello, Pres.-Elect.
Directors, vicars of deacons, and others responsible for the formation of candidates and the ongoing growth and development of deacons in the U.S. Promotes communication and facilitates the exchange of information and resources among members. Seeks to develop professional expertise among members through research, dialogue, formation and self-evaluation procedures. Proposes ways and means for effective implementation of solutions to national and regional issues relating to the diaconate. Maintains library on related issues.

National Black Catholic Clergy Caucus—
Office, 321 N. Walnut St., P.O. Box 1088, Opelousas, LA 70571-1088. Tel: 318-942-2392; Fax: 318-942-9201. Rev. Albert J. McKnight, C.S.Sp., Exec. Dir.

National Catholic Cemetery Conference—
National Office, 710 North River Rd., Des Plaines, IL 60016. Tel: 847-824-8131. Mrs. Irene K. Pesce, Exec. Dir.; Most Rev. John G. Vlazny, D.D., Episcopal Moderator.
The Conference is an organization of Diocesan Directors of Cemeteries and parish cemetery administrators from throughout the United States, Canada, Australia and Guam. Guided by the principle: "That burial of the dead is one of the Corporal Works of Mercy," the Conference promotes high standards of Catholic cemetery management, development, operation and maintenance consistent with Christian service to the Catholic community; and fosters and promotes the religious, charitable and educational interests of Catholic cemeteries and the people they serve.
Publications: monthly magazine, *Catholic Cemetery;* various booklets on cemetery management & evaluation services; funeral liturgy at the cemetery. Annual Convention; Summer Seminar on Leadership.

National Catholic Conference of Airport Chaplains (NCCAC)—
P.O. Box 2220, Newark, NJ 07114. Tel: 973-961-0260; Fax: 973-961-0260. Rev. David J. Baratelli, Pres., (Newark International Airport); Rev. James T. Devine, Vice Pres., (Kennedy International Airport); Deacon James A. O'Malley, Treas., (Chicago O'Hare International Airport); Deacon Donald A. Kelsey, Sec., (Atlanta Hartsfield International Airport); Most Rev. James C. Timlin, Bishop of Scranton, Episcopal Liaison.
This Conference provides support and communication for all Catholics performing pastoral ministry to airport & airline workers, and travelers; in affiliation with the Bishop's Committee on Migration of the National Conference of Catholic Bishops.

National Catholic Conference for Seafarers—
1500 Jefferson Dr., Port Arthur, TX 77642. Tel: 409-982-5111; Fax: 409-985-5111. E-mail: Sinclair Oubre@compuserve.com. Rev. Sinclair Oubre, J.C.L., Pres.; Deacon Glen Teske, Vice Pres.; Ms. Diane Bentley, Sec.; Rev. James P. Keating, Treas.
An association of Catholic maritime chaplains, pastoral associates, seafarers and associates serving in the pastoral care of seafarers in the ports of the U.S. in affiliation with the Apostleship of the Sea in the United States.

National Catholic Committee on Scouting Executive Committee (1934)—
1325 W. Walnut Hill Lane, P.O. Box 152079, Irving, TX 75015-2079. Fax: 972-580-7870. Most Rev. Gerald A. Gettelfinger Bishop of Evansville, IN, Episcopal Liaison; Robert Oldowski, Chm., (Bloomington, MN); Edward Gargiulo, Chm. Elect, (Wilmington, DE); William Davies, Vice Chm., (Minneapolis, MN); Joseph DeStefano, Vice Chm., (Providence, RI); John Ribar, Vice Chm., (Louisville, KY); John Hammerschmidt, Vice Chm., (O'Fallon, MO); Bray B. Barnes, Vice Chm., (Red Bank, NJ); Revs. Dennis O'Rourke, Natl. Chap., (Chandler, AZ); Donald Hummel, Assoc. Chap., (Westfield, NJ); Randy Cuevas, Past Natl. Chap., (Donaldson, LA).
A voluntary organization of clergy and laymen, members include a chaplain and lay chairman from all of the dioceses in the United States Conferences. It serves as an advisory committee to the Boy Scouts of America. It has the responsibility of promoting and guiding cooperative contracts between the proper authorities of the Catholic Church in the United States and the Boy Scouts of America.

National Catholic Conference for Total Stewardship, Inc. (NCCTS)—
Mailing Address, 1633 N. Cleveland Ave., Chicago, IL 60614. Tel: 413-464-3666 & 701-280-0418; Fax: 701-298-3834. Websites: www.steward.org and www.citrn.org. Rev. Francis A. Novak, C.SS.R., Pres.; Richard Kluzak, Admin.
The goal of this organization is to provide parishes and dioceses with a Total Stewardship Process called THE CHRISTIAN CELEBRATION OF LIFE (CCL), an integrated, comprehensive, systematically carried out formation of laity and clergy in Evangelization, Discipleship and Stewardship. The NCCTS achieves its goal by conducting Schools of Evangelization in parishes and via its websites on the Internet. The Schools form laity and clergy in sound spirituality especially those belonging to *"Small Ecclesial Faith Communities"*; train Home Visitors to evangelize the lapsed and alienated; promoted under *"Stewardship of Eucharist"* are belief in the mystery of Eucharist, quality celebration that dignifies the Mass, and reverence for the real presence; *"Giving in Thanksgiving*: centers on church-giving and tithing as an act of worship. Homily Guides for Clergy and Spiritual Formation Sessions for Laity in liturgical years A,B and C are accessible.

National Catholic Council on Alcoholism and Related Drug Problems, Inc.—
Headquarters, 1550 Hendrickson St., Brooklyn, NY 11234-3514. Tel: 718-951-7177; Fax: 718-951-7233. Mr. Thomas A. Russell, Exec. Dir.; Mr. Leo Miller, Pres.; Sr. M. Damien Adams, C.S.J., Vice Pres.; Rev. Msgr. Kieran Martin, Treas.; Sr. Janet Jeffers, I.H.M., Sec.; His Eminence Anthony Cardinal Bevilacqua, Episcopal Moderator.
N.C.C.A. is an agency of the Church which is dedicated to the promotion of adequate treatment for all clergy, men and women religious, and laity who are suffering from alcoholism and other drug dependencies. N.C.C.A. also provides educational programs, especially through and an annual symposium and publication of the Blue Book, to reach all those engaged in pastoral ministry and (or) education concerning the problems associated with the use, misuse and abuse of alcohol and other drugs in our society.

National Catholic Development Conference (1968)—
86 Front St., Hempstead, NY 11550. Tel: 516-481-6000. Sr. Georgette Lehmuth, O.S.F., Admin. Rev. Joseph M. Hertel, O.F.M., Chm.; Sr. Kathleen Lunsmann, I.H.M., Vice Chm.; Ms. Sally Pietrofitta, Sec.; Victor L. Ottenlips, Treas.; Most Rev. Robert F. Morneau, D.D., Episcopal Advisor.
Members, of one of the nation's largest association of religious fund raising organizations, include religious orders, colleges, high schools, hospitals, Catholic social service organizations and other institutions engaged in raising funds to support their activities. The function of the NCDC is to assist its members in developing effective, professional, ethical methods of raising funds. Members of the NCDC have subscribed to a code of ethics called Precepts of Stewardship. The national office serves as a center of information, issues special interest bulletins, conducts an annual conference and numerous seminars, workshops and regional meetings, maintains a library, follows and reports on legislative matters, conducts a special public information program, Giving is an Act of Faith, and maintains relations with a number of associations and organizations in related fields.
Publications: *Dimensions,* frequently issued; Monitor on postal, regulatory and tax issues, *A Guide for Preparing a Statement of Accountability.*

National Catholic Educational Association (1904)—
National Headquarters, 1077-30th St. N.W., Ste. 100, Washington, DC 20007. Tel: 202-337-6232; Fax: 202-333-6706. Most Rev. Robert J. Banks, D.D., Chm.; Dr. Leonard DeFiore, Pres.
The National Catholic Educational Association (NCEA) has been providing leadership and service to American Catholic educators since 1904. NCEA's institutional and individual memberships represent Catholic education at all levels and in a variety of settings: preschools, elementary and secondary schools, parish catechetical/religious education programs, diocesan offices, colleges, universities and seminaries. The Association advances the educational and catechetical mission of the Church; provides leadership and service to its members; articulates the contribution of Catholic education to the Church and society; proclaims the uniqueness of Catholic schools; advocates recognition of and support for Catholic education in parish, school, college and university communities; enhances and supports leadership among the members; and fosters local, national and international collaboration.

National Catholic Office for the Deaf (1971)—
NCOD Office, 7202 Buchanan St., Landover Hills, MD 20784-2236. Tel: 301-577-1684 (Voice); 301-577-4184

(TTY only); Fax: 301-577-1690. Arvilla Rank, Exec. Dir.

The NCOD, established by the Catholic pastoral workers of the deaf in 1971 at Trinity College, Washington, DC is devoted to coordinating the Church's pastoral ministry to deaf and hard-of-hearing persons at the national level; developing special liturgies, catechetical texts and materials; organizing workshops, leadership programs, cursillos and marriage encounters, and national and regional pastoral workers meetings; coordinating a training program for ministers with the deaf; and serving as an information and referral center for all those involved in this special ministry as well as members of the deaf community and their families. Policy is established by a board of directors elected by the members.

Publication: pastoral journal, *Vision.*

National Catholic Office for Persons with Disabilities (NCPD) (1982)—

415 Michigan Ave., N.E.-Suite 240, Washington, DC 20017-1557. Tel: 202-529-2933 (TTY 202-529-2934); Fax: 202-529-4678. Website: www.ncpd.org. Mary Jane Owen, Exec. Dir.; Kent A. Peters, Chm.

Established to foster and facilitate the challenges of "Pastoral Statement of U.S. Catholic Bishops on People with Disabilities." Provides resources and enhances visibility of diocesan offices addressing access and inclusion; works with NCCB/USCC staff and other national Catholic organizations in advocating for disability involvement and concerns; collaborates with other ministries of the church to enhance meaningful participation; affirms the culture of life through promoting the giftedness of all people with assorted disabilities at all stages of the life cycle. Mission is promoted through appropriate media, consultation, lectures, workshops and regional gatherings.

National Catholic Rural Life Conference—

National Headquarters, 4625 Beaver Ave., Des Moines, IA 50310-2199. Tel: 515-270-2634; Fax: 515-270-9447. E-mail address: ncrlc@aol.com; Website: www.ncrlc.com. Bro. David G. Andrews, Esq., C.S.C., Exec. Dir.; Most Rev. Raymond Burke, Bishop of LaCrosse, Pres. of the Bd. of Directors of the National Catholic Rural Life Conference.

The National Catholic Rural Life Conference is a membership organization grounded in a spiritual tradition which brings together the Church, care for creation and care for community. The NCRLC fosters programs of direct service and systemic change. As an educator in the faith, the NCRLC seeks to relate religion to the rural world; develops support services for rural pastoral ministers; serves as a prophetic voice and as a catalyst and convener for social justice.

National Catholic Stewardship Council, Inc.—

National Office, 1275 K St. N.W., Ste. 980, Washington, DC 20005. Tel: 202-289-1093; Fax: 202-682-9018. Most Rev. James P. Keleher, S.T.D.; Archbishop of Kansas City, KS, Episcopal Moderator; Mr. Matthew R. Paratore, Natl. Dir.

Through its Annual conference, Stewardship and Development Institute, events and printed and audio materials, the NCSC allows people committed to Christian stewardship to gather, share ideas, and learn from each other. At one with the universal church, NCSC takes seriously its role of fostering a solidarity of stewardship with parishes and dioceses all over the world. Membership in NCSC is extended to several categories of Christian stewards: (arch)dioceses, parishes, Catholic associations, religious congregations, Catholic colleges/universities and professional firms. NCSC encourages the growing professionalism of diocesan development procedures and programs, as well as the development of parish-centered stewardship programs aimed at increasing monies and personal service on the basis of the principles of stewardship as outlined in the 1992 NCCB Pastoral Letter: Stewardship: *A Disciple's Response.*

Publication: newsletter, *Commitment*; journal, *Resource* guide for pastoral leaders; *Stewardship: Disciples Respond;* publications available for parish and diocesan use through Liturgical Press; Stewardship Kit; For a complete list of services and publications contact the National Office. Membership information available on request.

National Catholic Student Coalition (1988)—

6801 N. Yates Rd.-Box 90A, Milwaukee, WI 53217. Tel: 414-410-4251; Fax: 414-410-4252. Ms. Judy Devine Smies, Exec. Dir.

The National Catholic Student Coalition (NCSC) is a national coalition of Catholic student communities in institutes of higher education. The coalition provides a platform for Catholic students to reflect, speak, and act on issues within the university, the Church and society. The NCSC promotes the development of campus ministry and Catholic lay and religious leaders for the Church and society. The NCSC is a member of the International Movement of Catholic Students. Membership is open to groups or individuals associated with Catholic student groups in higher education. The NCSC holds an annual leadership conference.

Publication: *The Catholic Collegian.*

The National Center for Urban Ethnic Affairs (1971)—

National Office, P.O. Box 20, Cardinal Station, Washington, DC 20064. Tel: 202-232-3600; 635-5128. Dr. John A. Kromkowski, Pres.; Rev. George F. McLean, Sec.; Rev. Msgr. Salvatore Polizzi, Chm.; Ruth Dee, Treas.

"The great task incumbent on all men of good will is to restore the relations of the human family in truth, in justice, in love, and in freedom." (Pope John XXIII, *Peace on Earth.*) The independent program of this non profit organization has evolved from the efforts initiated by the former Task Force on Urban Problems of the United States Catholic Conference. Its aims and purposes are to continue the expression of the Catholic Church's concern for the problems facing our urban society. NCUEA promotes the celebration of cultural pluralism in America and bridges the gaps between groups of various ethnic and cultural traditions. The Center disseminates information, conducts research, develops and supports programs concerned with ethnic Americans and urban society. The Center in association with various community and church groups develops workshops, conferences and programs related to the quality of human life, national priorities and the development of an urban mission strategy. The Center is also associated with public and private agencies in developing urban economic, social, and intercultural programs, etc.

The National Conference for Catechetical Leadership (NCCL)—

3021 Fourth St. N.E., Washington, DC 20017-1102. Tel: 202-636-3826; Fax: 202-832-2712. Mrs. Sue Grenough, Pres.; Mr. Neil Parent, Exec. Dir.

A voluntary organization composed of diocesan catechetical personnel, including vicars and secretaries of education, catechetical office directors and staff; academics specializing in religious education; representatives of diocesan parish DRE organizations and various associate and affiliated members, including publishers of catechetical texts. The Conference operates on three levels: national, regional and provincial. The purpose of the Conference is to assist its members in their roles as leaders in the Church's catechetical ministry through networking, resource development, research, training, consultation and advocacy. The Conference is also committed to collaboration with other national groups concerned with catechesis/religious education.

National Council for Catholic Evangelization (1983)—

905 E. 166th St., P.O. Box 1260, South Holland, IL 60473-2420. Tel: 1-800-786-NCCE; Fax: 1-708-596-4039. Sr. Priscilla Lemire, R.J.M., Pres., San Diego, CA; Sr. Rita Wenzlick, O.P., Vice Pres., Lansing, MI; Ms. Sandra Wilson, Sec., St. Louis, MO; Bro. Douglas Zlatis, C.F.C., Treas., Lisle, IL; Mr. John Simon, Exec. Dir., South Holland, IL; Most Rev. Michael J. Sheehan, Episcopal Liaison, Albuquerque, NM.

Established at the request of the Bishops' Committee on Evangelization, NCCE is an independent membership association which brings together (Arch)Dioceses, organizations, religious congregations, parishes and individuals to promote evangelization as the primary and essential mission of the Church. NCCE sponsors an Annual Conference and Evangelization Training Workshops and Seminars.

Publications: ten issues a year, *Newsletter; Resource Review; Resources: printed materials, audio and video tapes. Memberships are available to (Arch)Dioceses, religious congregations, organizations, parishes and individuals.*

National Council of the Catholic Men—

5664 Midforest Ln., Cincinnati, OH 45233. Mr. Ferd Niehaus, Pres.

The NCCM, a federation of Catholic organizations of men, has pioneered in promoting parish councils and diocesan renewal.

National Council of Catholic Women—

1275 K St. N.W., Ste. 975, Washington, DC 20005. Tel: 202-682-0334; Fax: 202-682-0338. E-mail: nccw@us.net; Website: www.nccw.org. K. LaVerne Redden, Pres.; Annette Kane, Exec. Dir.

The NCCW is a federation of Catholic women's organizations in the United States, numbering 6,000 local, diocesan and national organizations. It programs through its six commissions, Church, Family Concerns, Community Concerns, International Concerns, Legislation and Organization. The program of the Council is furthered through leadership training institutes and national conventions.

Publication: bimonthly, *Catholic Woman.*

National Federation of Catholic Physicians' Guilds (1932)—

P.O. Box 757, Pewaukee, WI 53072. Tel: 262-523-6201; 877-CATHDOC; Fax: 262-523-6211. E-mail address: cathmed@cathmed.com; Website: www.cathmed.com.

Officers 1999-2000: Michael R. Aiello, M.D., Pres., Lake Placid, NY; Charles P. Prezzia M.D., Pres. Elect, Pittsburgh, PA; Robert J. Saxer, M.D., Vice Pres., Ft. Walton Beach, FL; Dennis M. Doody, M.D., Sec., Columbus, OH; John D. Lane, M.D., Treas., Philadelphia, PA; Most. Rev. Edwin O'Brien, S.T.D. D.D., Episcopal Advisor, Yonkers, NY; Richard A. Watson, M.D., Past Pres., Mountainside, NJ; Robert H. Herzog, Exec. Dir.

Upholding the principles of the Catholic faith and morality as related to the science and practice of medicine.

National Federation for Catholic Youth Ministry, Inc. (NFCYM) (1981)—

415 Michigan Ave., N.E. – Ste. 40, Washington, DC 20017. Tel: 202-636-3825. Most Rev. Matthew H. Clark, Episcopal Liaison; Mr. Robert J. McCarty, Exec. Dir.; Sr. Jude Ruggeri, A.S.C.J., Chm.; Ms. Kathleen Carver, Assoc. Dir.; Mr. Scott Miller, Assoc. Dir.; Ruby Mikell, Admin. Dir.; Mr. Mark Moitoza, Germany Project Coord.

A membership association of diocesan youth offices, founded after a reorganization of the USCC Department of Education and the National CYO Federation (now defunct). The stated purpose is "In light of the Gospel message, the Federation will foster the development of youth ministry in the United States to, with, by, and for youth." Members of the Federation work through diocesan, regional and national structures to provide national leadership, support and direction for adults and youth in youth ministry. The biennial National Conference on Catholic Youth Ministry (a conference for adults working with youth); the biennial National Catholic Youth Conference (for teenagers and their adult chaperones); the writing and distributing of resource booklets for parish workers; religious recognitions for Catholic Girl Scouts/Camp Fire; position papers on current topics and issues in youth ministry; and regional and diocesan consultations.

National Foundation for Catholic Youth—

415 Michigan Ave., N.E., Washington, DC 20017. Tel: 202-636-3825. Mr. Robert J. McCarty, Exec. Dir.; Mrs. Irene Friend, Pres. of Board.

National Office for Black Catholics (1972)—

The Paulist Center, 3025 Fourth St., N.E., Washington, DC 20017. Tel: 202-635-1778. Walter T. Hubbard, Exec. Dir.

The National Office for Black Catholics, organized in 1970, is a central agency with the general purpose of promoting active and full participation by Black Catholics in the Church and of making more effective the presence and ministry of the Church in the Black community. Its operations support the aspirations of Black Catholics for objectives that include: representation and voice among Bishops and other leaders of the Church; promotion of vocations to the priesthood and religious life; sponsorship of programs of evangelization, pastoral ministry, education and liturgy on national and regional levels; recognition of Black heritage in liturgy, community life, theology and education; and establishment of an Institute for Leadership Training Formation and Development.

National Organization for Continuing Education of Roman Catholic Clergy, Inc.—

1337 W. Ohio St., Chicago, IL 60622-6490. Tel: 312-226-1890; Fax: 312-829-8915. Revs. Francis S. Tebbe, O.F.M., Pres.; Michael J. Cronin, O.F.M. Exec. Dir.

A professional organization of those involved in the continuing education/formation of priests in the Catholic Church. Dioceses and religious communities in the U.S. are full members. Institutions and organizations that are concerned with continuing education/formation of priests are associate members. Dioceses and provinces outside the U.S. may be associate members. NOCERCC was founded in 1973 through the efforts of the National Federation of Priests Councils. It is governed by a Board of Directors that involves a president elected by the membership, elected members from the 13 NCCB Regions and two elected religious members. Its services include an Annual Convention, training for new and experienced directors, regional meetings, consultations and service to regional and interdiocesan programs.

Publications: *NewsNotes, Sabbatical Programs, Handbook for Continuing Formation of Priests*, other print and video resources.

National Pastoral Center for the Chinese Apostolate, Inc.—

344 6th St., Jersey City, NJ 07302. Tel: 201-795-0837 or 795-0120; Fax: 201-795-1389. Rev. Msgr. Joseph Chiang, Dir.

National Pastoral Life Center—

Headquarters, 18 Bleecker St., New York, NY 10012-2404. Tel: 212-431-7825; Fax: 212-274-9786. Rev. Msgr. Philip J. Murnion, Dir.; Ms. Karen Sue Smith, Editorial Dir.; Donna Ciangio, O.P., Project Dir.; Catherine Patten, R.S.H.M., Coord.-Catholic Common Ground Initiative; Jeffry Korgen, Coord.-The Roundtable.

The Center is an information, training, and consulting resource for diocesan and parish leaders. The Center conducts and staffs educational and training programs for pastors and others in ministry. It also sponsors pastoral ministry conventions, conducts pastoral research, and serves as a resource and referral center for church ministers.

Publications: magazine, *Church Magazine; Center Papers* and other publications.

North American Pastoral Center for Czech Catholics—

c/o Bishop Peter Esterka, 300 E. Taft Ave., Orange, CA 92865-4330. Tel: 714-998-0251; Fax: 714-637-0201. Most Rev. Peter Esterka, Pres.

The Papal Foundation—

Office, Attn: Rev. Msgr. Thomas J. Benestad, Exec. Dir., 222 North 17th St., Philadelphia, PA 19103. Tel: 215-587-2491. Rev. Msgr. Thomas J. Benestad, Vice Pres.-Admin.; Rev. Milton B. Jordan, Vice Pres.-Devel.

Board of Trustees: Anthony Cardinal Bevilacqua, Chm.; Francis Cardinal George, O.M.I.; Bernard Cardinal Law; James Cardinal Hickey; Roger Cardinal Mahony; William Cardinal Keeler; Adam Cardinal Maida; Trustees: Theodore Cardinal McCarrick, Pres.; Mr. Arthur Birtcher; Mr. Geoffrey T. Boisi; Mr. John Brennan; Mr. William F. Connell; Mr. Thomas J. Flatley; Most Rev. Harry J. Flynn; Most Rev. Charles V. Grahmann; Mr. E. F. Hansen; Most Rev. William J. Levada; Mr. Frank J. Lynch; Mr. William A. McIntosh; Mr. Robert J. Morrissey; Mr. Edward J. Piszek; Mr. Gerald A. Rauenhorst; Most Rev. Justin Rigali; Mr. John V. Saeman; Most Rev. Francis B. Schulte; Mr. Francis J. Sehn; Mr. Daniel J. Donohue, Trustee Emeritus.

The Parish Evaluation Project—

3195 South Superior St., Milwaukee, WI 53207. Tel: 414-483-7370; Fax: 414-483-7380. Rev. Thomas P. Sweetser, S.J., Dir.; Sr. Peg Bishop, O.S.F., Assoc. Dir.

The Parish Evaluation Project is a non profit organization under the laws of Wisconsin, whose purpose is to provide religious and educational services to Catholic parishes in the United States in the areas of surveying, needs assessment, leadership skills, goal setting, evaluation techniques, staff development, pastoral council formation and other resources helpful in parish planning and renewal.

Pax Christi U.S.A., National Catholic Peace Movement—

532 W. 8th St., Erie, PA 16502-1343. Tel: 814-453-4955; Fax: 814-452-4784. Mr. Etienne de'Jonghe, Intl. Sec.; Most Rev. Walter F. Sullivan, Pres.; Thomas Cordaro, Chm.; Kathleen Phelan, O.P., Treas.

Pax Christi has as its primary objective to develop alternatives to violence always witnessing to the peace of Christ. The movement of 14,000 members is rooted in a gospel vision of peace. It asks its members to ground their peacemaking in prayer, study and action. Pax Christi keeps as its priorities the Christian vision of spirituality, nonviolence and peacemaking, disarmament, demilitarization, reconciliation with justice, human rights and global restoration, and economic and interracial justice in the United States.

Publications: quarterly newspaper and peace education materials.

Religious Formation Conference—

National Office, 8820 Cameron St., Silver Spring, MD 20910-4152. Tel: 301-588-4938; Fax: 301-585-7649. Sr. Janet Mock, C.S.J., Exec. Dir.; Sr. Phyllis Giroux, S.C., Assoc. Dir.; Board Co-Chm.: Sr. Mary Foley, S.S.N.D.; Sr. Amedee Maxwell, S.B.S.

A national organization which assists women and men Religious who are engaged in the ministry of intial and on-going formation in their congregations.

Retreats International, Inc.—

National Office, Box 1067, Notre Dame, IN 46556. Tel: 219-631-5320; Fax: 219-631-6968. Anne M. Luther, Exec. Dir.; Most Rev. Robert Morneau, Bishop Advisor; Sr. Mary Elizabeth Imler, O.S.F., Pres.; Ms. S. Marion Renkens, Vice Pres.; Geri Eitter, Sec. & Treas.; Trustees: Sr. Catherine Cahill, O.S.F.; Ms. Mary Ann Lewis; Mr. Richard Wray; Tom Grant; Carolyn Glynn; Sarah Morgan; Rev. Ted Haag, O.F.M.

Created in 1928 under the guidance of the Archbishops and Bishops of the United States. The national headquarters for information and all phases of the retreat movement in the United States.

The Slovak Catholic Federation (1911)—

915 Cornell St., Youngstown, OH 44502. Tel: 330-788-5082; FAX: 330-788-2383. Rev. Msgr. Peter M. Polando, Pres.; Most Rev. Joseph V. Adamec, Episcopal Advisor; Rev. Andrew S. Hvozdovic, Spiritual Dir.; Mrs. Bernadette J. Demechko, Sec. & Treas.

Founded by Father Joseph Murgas at Wilkes-Barre, Pennsylvania as a non profit corporation to promote and coordinate religious activities among Slovak Catholic fraternal societies, religious communities, and Slovak ethnic parishes in their effort to address themselves to the pastoral needs of Slovak Catholics in the United States and Canada.

UNDA-USA National Catholic Association for Communicators—

National Office: 901 Irving Ave., Dayton, OH 45409-2316. Tel: 937-229-2303; Fax: 937-229-2300. Mr. Frank Morock, Pres.; Ms. Rose Hammes, 1st Vice Pres.; Sr. Rose Pacatte, F.S.P., 2nd Vice Pres.; John E. Kearns, Jr., Treas.; Rev. James Gardiner, S.A., Sec.

UNDA-USA, the national Catholic association of communicators, includes more than 400 individual and organizational members: diocesan directors of communications, professional broadcasters, editors of regional and national publications, educators, religious community communications personnel, directors of closed-circuit educational television (ITFS) systems and staffs, and syndicators of national Catholic radio and television programs. UNDA-USA has on its Board of Directors representatives of local, regional and national Catholic communications agencies, including the Catholic Television Network (dioceses having ITFS systems), the Association of Catholic Television and Radio Syndicators and the U.S. Catholic Conference Department of Communications. UNDA-USA, organized in 1972 as successor to the Catholic Broadcasters Association (CBA), is a member of the international Catholic association for radio and television known as UNDA International (the Latin word for ""Wave," symbolic of air waves of communication). UNDA-USA is dependent on annual individual and organizational membership fees for its operating expenses. Principal activities of UNDA-USA: annual General Assembly for all members, consisting of professional communication sessions; previews and ministry-related activities; annual Gabriel Awards for excellence in broadcasting on local and national levels.

Publication: quarterly newsletter, *White Papers.*

United States Catholic Mission Association—

3029 Fourth St. N.E., Washington, DC 20017. Tel: 202-832-3112; Fax: 202-832-3688. Sr. Christine Beckett, G.H.M.S., Pres; Sr. Rosanne Rustemeyer, S.S.N.D., Exec. Dir.

The USCMA was juridically established September 1, 1981. Its members include U.S. missioners, mission organizations, diocesan mission offices, and others concerned about the mission of the Church and global solidarity. The Association seeks to help missioners to stay up-to-date on mission and world trends, to promote greater global awareness, sensibility, and solidarity in the U.S., and periodically to be a voice for U.S. missioners speaking out in defense of the poor and oppressed throughout the world. USCMA activities include a national conference and regional seminars that highlight specific mission themes and issues, liaison and cooperation with missionary bodies of other Christian churches. The USCMA is responsible for gathering statistical data on the U.S. missionary personnel, which is published bi-annually.

Publications: quarterly newsletter, *Mission Update;* reports, *U.S. Catholic Missionary Statistics,* and education programs on mission and global awareness.

NATIONAL ORGANIZATIONS WITH INDIVIDUAL I.R.S. RULINGS

The Beginning Experience—

International Ministry Center, 1247 171st Place., Hammond, IN 46324. Tel: 219-989-8915; Fax: 219-989-8916. Most Rev. A. Edward Pevec, Episcopal Moderator; Kathleen Murphy, Pres.; Dorothy Van Poppel-Ray, Vice Pres.; Wilma Ofstad, Sec. & Treas.

The Beginning Experience is a copyrighted weekend program to help divorced, separated and widowed persons, as well as their families, work through the trauma of the loss of their spouse and make a new beginning in life. The program was designed by and for Catholics and has its roots in soundCatholic tradition and the sacramental life of the Church. True to the ecumenical spirit in the Church since Vatican II, it has been open to persons of all faiths from the beginning. The BE Weekend was originated in 1974 by Sr. Josephine Stewart of Fort Worth, TX. It has spread throughout the United States as well as other countries. Trained teams make the Beginning Experience Weekend available on a regular basis. It also serves as an informational and materials resource for the establishment of support groups to minister to the needs of the divorced, separated and widowed and their families at various points in their growth process.

Canon Law Society of America—

Catholic University, Washington, DC 20064. Tel: 202-269-3491; Fax: 202-319-5719. Rev. Arthur J. Espelage, O.F.M., Exec. Coord.; Rev. Msgr. Robert P. Deeley, Pres., Boston, MA; Rev. Kevin E. McKenna, Vice Pres., Rochester, NY; Sr. Margaret Stallmeyer, C.D.P., Treas., Melbourne, KY; Rev. Patrick R. Lagges, Sec., Chicago, IL.

A membership association of Bishops, Clergy, Religious and Laity for the purpose of promoting research and professional collaboration in the area of Canon Law.

Catholic Coalition on Preaching, Inc.—

Madonna University, 36600 Schoolcraft Rd., Livonia, MI 48150-1173. Tel: 734-432-5538. Rev. Francis S. Tebbe, O.F.M., Pres.

Catholic Engaged Encounter, Inc.—

143 Reed St., Lower Burrell, PA 15068. Tel: 1-800-339-9790. Mr. George Ziringer; Mrs. Pat Ziringer; Rev. Peter Horton.

Catholic Library Association—

100 North Street, Ste 224, Pittsfield, MA 01201-5109. Tel: 413-443-2252 (2CLA); Fax: 413-442-2252. E-mail: cla@vgernet.net; Website: http://www.cathla.org. Sr. Jean R. Bostley, S.S.J., Exec. Dir.

The Catholic Mutual Relief Society of America—

4223 Center St., Omaha, NE 68105. Tel: 402-551-8765. Mr. Joseph T. Beveridge, Pres. & CEO; Mr. Michael A. Intrieri, Exec. Vice Pres. & Chief Oper. Officer.

The Catholic Relief Insurance Company of America—

4223 Center St., Omaha, NE 68105. Tel: 402-551-8765. Mr. Joseph T. Beveridge, Pres. & CEO; Mr. Michael A. Intrieri, Exec. Vice Pres. & Chief Oper. Officer.

Conference for Pastoral Planning and Council Development—

12545 Olive Blvd. #175, St. Louis, MO 63141. Tel: 314-579-9577. E-mail: info@cppcd.org Website: www.cppcd.org. David R. Spotanski, Chm.; Maria Rodgers O'Rourke, Exec Dir.

National Association for Lay Ministry (NALM)—

National Office, 5420 S. Cornell Ave., Ste. 103, Chicago, IL 60615-5604. Tel: 773-241-6050; Fax: 773-241-6061. E-mail: nalm@nalm.org Website: www.nalm.org. Sr. Louise Bond, S.N.J.M., Exec. Dir.; Marti Jewell, Chm.; Dennis Beeman Vice Chm.; Graziano Marcheschi, Sec./Treas.

NALM is a professional organization that supports, educates and advocates for lay ministers and promotes the development of lay ministry in the Catholic Church. In accomplishing its mission, NALM is committed to: 1)the Gospel of Jesus Christ and the Mission of the Catholic Church; 2) Faith that the richness that results from diversity; 4) ongoing conversion of persons and structures; 5) Collaboration in ministry and participative Church leadership; 6) The life experiences lay ministers bring to ministry from their unique relationships and responsibilities as family members, workers, and citizens.

Publications: bimonthly, *Lay Ministry; National Competency-Based Standards for Pastoral Ministers, Pastoral Associates, Parish Life Coordinators; No Turning Back: A Lay Perspective on Ministry in the Catholic Church of the United States; Formation of Laity for Ecclesial Ministry; More Than Manna; Ministry Formation Self-Assessment Instrument; NALM Chapter Manual; Pastoral Ministers' Association Models; The Journey of the Laity Since Vatican II Annual Conference—19998 "A New Heaven and A New Earth; Exploring a Spirituality of Ministry". Research, Chapters, Affiliations, Networking.*

National Catholic Conference for Interracial Justice NCCIJ (1959)—

Office, 1200 Varnum St., N.E., Washington, DC 20017-2796. Tel: 202-529-6480; Fax: 202-526-1262. Co-Chm., Most Rev. Charles J. Chaput, O.F.M.; Hon. Lindy Boggs; Deacon Joseph M. Conrad, Jr., Exec. Dir.

Established to implement the teaching of the Catholic Church on cultural and racial justice and to promote the church's vision of multicultural, multiracial understanding, mutual respect and collaboration.

National Catholic Risk Retention Group, Inc.—

National Office, 801 Warrenville Rd.-Suite 175, Lisle, IL 60532-4334. Tel: 630-725-0986; 877-486-2774; Fax: 630-725-1374. Most Rev. Raymond J. Boland, Episcopal Moderator; Mr. Michael J. Bemi, Pres. & CEO; Rev. Edward J. Arsenault, Chm. Bd.; Mr. William H. Hinkes, Vice Chm.; Mr. Joseph Frank, Vice. Pres.; Rev. Jay C. Haskin, Sec.; Mr. John J. Maxwell, Treas.

The Company is wholly owned by 56 Catholic (Arch)Dioceses and one Catholic Risk Pooling Trust. It underwrites excess liability insurance for Dioceses and other Church organizations listed in the Official Catholic Directory. Coverage is always subject to a minimum self-insured retention or underlying coverage of $250,000. Maximum limits of coverage available are $5 million. The company has the capability to underwrite insurance in all states, Territories and Possessions of the U.S.

National Catholic Young Adult Ministry Association, Inc.—

Membership Office, 1185 Van Buren Ave., St. Paul, MN 55104. Tel: 888-629-2621. James Breen, Pres.; Paul Combest, Treas.; Christine Zirker, Sec.

Founded in 1982, NCYAMA is an organization for young adults (single or married, late teens, twenties or thirties) and those who are ministering to and with young adults in an intentional way. NCYAMA is dedicated to the development of ministerial competence among our members, encouraging and providing opportunities for mutual support in professional and faith journeys, advocating for young adults with the Church and society, constantly striving to research and develop new avenues of outreach to young adults and interpreting to Church constituencies the contemporary needs, concerns hopes and insights of young adults.

Publication: quarterly, *The Cutting Edge.*

National Conference of Diocesan Vocation Directors (1962)—

National Office: P.O. Box 1570, Little River, SC 29566. Tel: 843-280-7191. Revs. William Kubacki, Pres.; John Desocio, Vice Pres.; Anthony Vercellone, Sec./Treas. Members at Large: Revs. David Hulshof; Mark O'Donnell; Mrs. Dorothy Foss, Exec. Dir.

NCDCD is the professional organization that serves all diocesan vocation offices associated with the National Conference of Catholic Bishops NCCB in the United States, and some dioceses in Canada, England, Australia and Ireland. NCNCN provides support education and resources for diocesan vocation personnel.

Publications: four times a year, *Newsletter;* annual, Vocation Journal; documents of interest & training institutes; Meetings annually for Regional Conferences and a National Convention.

The National Federation of Priests' Councils(1968)—

National Office, 1337 W. Ohio, Chicago, IL 60622. Tel: 312-226-3334; Fax: 312-829-8915. E-mail: nfpc@nfpc.org Website: www.nfpc.org. Rev. Robert Silva, Pres.; Bro. Bernard F. Stratman, S.M., Exec. Dir.

The NFPC was organized to promote priestly fraternity by facilitating communication among priests' councils, to provide a forum for priests to discuss pastoral matters, to enable priests' councils to speak with a common voice, to promote and collaborate on programs of pastoral research, to further the spiritual renewal of priestly life, to collaborate with national lay and religious groups in ways that promote renewal in the Church, to collaborate with the NCCB in addressing the needs of the Church in the U.S.A., to encourage priests' councils to promote justice in light of the social teachings of the Church, and to participate in developing a national and universal perspective of church and ministry.

The NFPC represents 123 priests' councils, priests' associations and religious communities. Elected delegates of member councils meet annually to set policy, and a national executive board meets regularly to carry out the work of the NFPC, assisted by standing committees. Member councils represent approximately 26,000 priests.

Publications: quarterly newsletter, *Touchstone;* bimonthly; *NFPC Update;* books; occasional papers and studies concerned with various aspects; of ministry, the ministerial priesthood and the spiritual renewal of priests.

National Institute for the Word of God—

Headquarters, 487 Michigan Ave. N.E., Washington, DC 20017. Tel: 202-529-0001. Episcopal Advisory Board: Most Rev. John R. Quinn; Most Rev. David E. Foley; Most Rev. Patrick R. Cooney; Most Rev. William G. Curlin; Staff: Rev. John Burke, O.P., Exec. Dir.; Mr. William H. Graham, Assoc. Dir.; Rev. George P. M. Schommer, O.P., Assoc. Dir.; Mary C. Graham, Sec.; Very Rev. Joseph P. Allen, O.P., Treas. Board of Advisors: Rev. Msgr. Raymond East; Revs. James Patrick Moroney; Rutilio J. del Riego; James Walsh; Martha Fernandez; Carol Graham Lehan; Mary Ann McGuire; Michael M. McGuire.

The Institute is an unaffiliated nonprofit organization incorporated under the laws of the District of Columbia, whose purpose is to promote, support, conduct and assist in any way whatsoever educational, liturgical, and remedial programs and activities, public and private, through the use of any and all media, to further effective communication of the revealed word of God, as the primary pastoral work of the Church. Ongoing efforts include the dissemination of scriptural, theological and pastoral aids such as books, films and tape albums, and the conducting of parish missions, conferences and retreats for clergy and laity.

National Service Committee of the Catholic Charismatic Renewal of the United States Inc.—

P.O. Box 628, Locust Grove, VA 22508-0628. Rev. Patsy Iaquinta, Chm.; Mr. Walter Matthews, Dir.

Our focus is to foster baptism in the Holy Spirit in the life of the Church in the United States and throughout the world, to broaden and deepen the understanding that baptism in the Holy Spirit is the Christian inheritance of all, and to strengthen the Catholic Charismatic Renewal. The National Service Committee has established and supported numerous programs to help further our mission. Some of the activities and programs include the establishment of Chariscenter USA, which serves as the national headquarters for our committee and a national office for the Catholic Charismatic Renewal.

Publications: *The NSC* offers a national newsletter, a *Catholic Charismatic Renewal Directory* and leadership training materials as well as an annual national conference, outreach to youth, and evangelization training. The NSC has supported the International Catholic Charismatic Renewal Office in Rome.

The North American Forum on the Catechumenate—

3033 Fourth St., N.E., Washington, DC 20017-1102. Tel: 202-529-9493; Fax: 202-529-9497. James M. Schellman, Exec. Dir.; Sr. Sheila O'Dea, R.S.M., Assoc. Dir.

The North American Forum on the Catechumenate is an international network committed to the implementation of the Rite of Christian Initiation of Adults. The work of FORUM is overseen by a Board of Directors of seven elected representatives. A variety of institutes are offered in co-sponsorship with a hosting diocese to serve the local Church. FORUM networks with other U.S., Canadian and international groups, promotes research into issues raised by Christian Initiation (including outreach to the inactive through a process of Re-Membering Church), and provides a newsletter which focuses on the impact of Christian Initiation on the Church as well as key issues related to its implementation.

Worldwide Marriage Encounter (1969)—

National Office, 2210 E. Highland Ave., Ste. 106, San Bernardino, CA 92404. Tel: 909-863-9963; Fax: 909-863-9986. Secretariat Team: Rev. Gerry Bolduc, O.M.I.; Lee Kremer; Janet Kremer.

Organized to foster a program of Christian information to instruct married couples in the means to find God's plan and matrimony in their lives, for their own spiritual development and the betterment of all humankind; and to develop, foster and disseminate an adult catechesis supporting, furthering and building upon such instruction. Worldwide Marriage Encounter offers the marriage encounter weekend experience in 150 dioceses in the United States as well as in 88 foreign countries. In the United States over 1,500,000 couples and over 5,000 priests and bishops have experienced the Worldwide weekend.

Publication: quarterly; *Matrimony - A Sign of Our Church.*

MISCELLANEOUS

Catholic Committee for Refugees & Children—

3211 Fourth St. N.E., Washington, DC 20017-1194. Fax: 202-722-8755. Mr. Mark Franken, Pres.

In operation since January 4, 1937, and incorporated since 1954, the Catholic Committee for Refugees and Children was founded to counsel and cooperate with European refugees during and after World War II. Since that time its mission has been expanded to include service to refugees worldwide. It has a special mandate from the bishops concerning its work with children through international child welfare, child care or placement, and international adoption. The NCCB Committee on Migration serves as the Board of Directors for CCRC.

National Association of State Catholic Conference Directors

An Association of the Directors of the State Catholic Conferences, organized in 1968 to facilitate and encourage the exchange of information among its members pertaining to the activities, programs and organization of the Conferences. A State Catholic Conference is a Church agency composed of the dioceses within a state to provide for the coordination of the public policy concerns of the Church. Thus a Conference of the Church communicates with state government, other Church Agencies, non-Catholic churches and secular agencies. Bishops, priests, religious and lay persons are involved in the work of the State Conferences. National Association: NCCB-USCC, 3211 4th St., N.E., Washington, DC 20017-1194.

ALASKA

Alaska Catholic Conference.
225 Cordova, Anchorage AK 99501. Tel: 907-297-7738; Fax: 907-297-3885.
Contact Person: Mr. Robert Flint

ARIZONA

Arizona Catholic Conference.
400 E. Monroe St., Phoenix AZ 85004-2376. Tel: 602-257-5597; Fax: 602-256-1356.
Chairman: Bishop Manuel D. Moreno
Executive Director: Rev. Msgr. Edward J. Ryle, M.A., M.S.W.

CALIFORNIA

California Catholic Conference.
Cathedral Square, 1119 K St.-2nd Fl., Sacramento, CA 95814. Tel: 916-443-4851; Fax: 916-443-5629.
President: Bishop Sylvester D. Ryan
Vice President: Bishop William K. Weigand
Secretary-Treasurer: Bishop Stephen Blaire
Executive Director: Mr. Edward E. Dolejsi
Associate Director for Public Policy: Mr. David A. Pollard
Associate Director for Education: Mr. Robert Teegarden
Associate Director for Communications & Pastoral Projects: Mrs. Carol Hogan
Executive Director of Catholic Charities of California, Inc.: Mr. Richard Mockler

COLORADO

Colorado Catholic Conference.
Catholic Pastoral Center, 1300 S. Steele St., Ste. 303, Denver, CO 80210-2599. Tel: 303-715-3206; Fax: 303-715-2042.
Executive Director: Mr. James P. Tatten

CONNECTICUT

Connecticut Catholic Conference.
134 Farmington Ave., Hartford, CT 06105. Tel: 860-524-7882; Fax: 860-525-0750; E-mail: Lobby134@aol.com.
President and Chairman of the Board: Archbishop Daniel A. Cronin
Secretary: Bishop Daniel A. Hart
Executive Director: Dr. Marie T. Hilliard, Ph.D., R.N.

FLORIDA

Florida Catholic Conference.
313 S. Calhoun St., Tallahassee, FL 32301. Tel: 850-222-3803; Fax: 850-681-9548.
President: Archbishop John Clement Favalora
Executive Director: D. Michael McCarron, Ph.D.

GEORGIA

Georgia Catholic Conference.
Office Building, 3200 Deans Bridge Rd., Augusta, GA 30906. Tel: 404-798-1719; Fax: 706-798-6037.
Executive Director: Mr. Cheatham E. Hodges, Jr.

HAWAII

Hawaii Catholic Conference.
St. Stephen Diocesan Center, 6301 Pali Hwy., Kaneohe, HI 96744-5298. Tel: 808-263-8844, ext. 548; Fax: 808-261-7022; Email: hcc@pono.net.
Program Director: Errol J. Christian

ILLINOIS

Catholic Conference of Illinois.
65 East Wacker Place, Suite 1620, Chicago, IL 60601. Tel: 312-368-1066 and 108 E. Cook, Springfield, IL 62701. Tel: 217-528-9200.
Chairman: His Eminence Francis Cardinal George, O.M.I.
Executive Director: Mr. Doug Delaney
Associate Directors: Joan McKinney; Robert F. Gilligan

INDIANA

Indiana Catholic Conference.
1400 N. Meridian St., P.O. Box 1410, Indianapolis, IN 46206. Tel: 317-236-1455; Fax: 317-236-1456.
General Chairman: Archbishop Daniel M. Buechlein, O.S.B., D.D.
Executive Chairman: Bishop William L. Higi, D.D.
Executive Director: Dr. M. Desmond Ryan, Ph.D.

IOWA

Iowa Catholic Conference.
505 5th Ave., Ste. 818, Des Moines, IA 50309-2393. Tel: 515-243-6256; Fax: 515-243-6257; E-mail: iacathconf@aol.com.
President: Archbishop Jerome Hanus, O.S.B.
Vice President: Bishop William E. Franklin
Secretary-Treasurer: Bishop Joseph Charron, C.PP.S.
Executive Director: Dr. Thomas Feld

KANSAS

Kansas Catholic Conference.
6301 Antioch, Merriam, KS 66202. Tel: 913-722-6633.
Chairman: Archbishop James P. Keleher
Executive Director: Mr. Michael P. Farmer
Associate Director for Education: Mrs. Beatrice Swoopes

KENTUCKY

Catholic Conference of Kentucky.
1042 Burlington Ln., Frankfort, KY 40601. Tel: 502-875-4345; Fax: 502-875-2841.
Chairman: Archbishop Thomas C. Kelly, O.P.
Executive Director: Mrs. Jane J. Chiles

LOUISIANA

Louisiana Catholic Conference.
3423 Hundred Oaks Ave., Baton Rouge, LA 70808. Tel: 225-344-7120; Fax: 225-383-9591.
Chairman: Archbishop Francis B. Schulte
Executive Director: Mr. Kirby J. Ducote
Assistant Director for Administrative Services: Mrs. Barbara Bovard

MARYLAND

Maryland Catholic Conference.
188 Duke of Gloucester St., Annapolis, MD 21401-2515. Tel: 410-269-1155.
Chairman: His Eminence William Cardinal Keeler
Executive Director: Richard J. Dowling, Esq.

MASSACHUSETTS

Massachusetts Catholic Conference.
150 Staniford St.-West End Pl., Boston, MA 02114-2511. Tel: 617-367-6060.
Executive Director: Mr. Gerald D. D'Avolio, Esq.

MICHIGAN

Michigan Catholic Conference.
505 N. Capitol Ave., Lansing, MI 48933. Tel: 517-372-9310; Fax: 517-372-3940.
Chairman: His Eminence Adam Cardinal Maida
Vice Chairman: Bishop Robert J. Rose
President & CEO: Sr. Monica Kostielney, R.S.M.
Secretary-Treasurer: Bishop Patrick R. Cooney

MINNESOTA

Minnesota Catholic Conference.
475 University Ave., W., Ste. B, St. Paul, MN 55103-1959. Tel: 651-227-8777; Fax: 651-227-2675.
President: Archbishop Harry J. Flynn
Secretary / Treasurer: Bishop Frederick Campbell
Executive Director: Rev. David F. McCauley
Social Concerns Department Director: Mr. Thomas (Toby) J. Pearson
Education Department Director: Dr. Peter Noll

MISSOURI

Missouri Catholic Conference.
600 Clark Ave., P.O. Box 1022, Jefferson City, MO 65102. Tel: 573-635-7239; Fax: 573-635-7431.
General Chairman: Archbishop Justin Rigali
Executive Chairman: Bishop John R. Gaydos
General Counsel Executive Director: Lawrence A. Weber
Assistant Director: Mike Hoey
Administrative Assistant: Josetta M. Forck

MONTANA

Montana Catholic Conference.
P.O. Box 1708, Helena, MT 59624. Tel: 406-442-5761; Fax: 406-442-9047.
President: Sr. Mary Jo McDonald, S.C.L.
Vice President: Linda McCauley
Treasurer: Kim Larsen
Executive Director: Sharon Hoff-Brodowy

NEBRASKA

Nebraska Catholic Conference.
215 Centennial Mall South, Ste. 410, Lincoln, NE 68508-1890. Tel: 402-477-7517.
President: Archbishop Elden Francis Curtiss
Director: Bishop Fabian W. Bruskewitz
Director: Bishop Lawrence J. McNamara
Executive Director: James R. Cunningham

NEVADA

Nevada Catholic Conference.
290 South Arlington Ave. – Ste. 200, Reno NV 89501-1713. Tel: 775-326-9416; Fax: 775-348-8619.
Executive Director: Mr. Bob Payant

NEW JERSEY

New Jersey Catholic Conference.
211 N. Warren St., Trenton, NJ 08618. Tel: 609-599-2110.
Executive Director: William F. Bolan, Jr. , J.D.

NEW YORK

New York State Catholic Conference.
465 State St., Albany, NY 12203. Tel: 518-434-6195.
President: His Eminence Edward Cardinal Egan
Vice President: Bishop Henry J. Mansell
Secretary- Treasurer: Bishop Thomas V. Daily
Chairman—Public Policy Committee: Bishop Howard J. Hubbard
Executive Director: John M. Kerry

NORTH DAKOTA

North Dakota Catholic Conference.
227 W. Broadway, Ste. 2, Bismarck, ND 58501. Tel: 701-223-2519; Fax: 701-223-6075.
President: Bishop James S. Sullivan
Vice-President: Bishop Paul A. Zipfel
Secretary-Treasurer: Tracey Wold Frei
Executive Director: Christopher T. Dodson

OHIO

Catholic Conference of Ohio.
9 East Long St. , Suite 201, Columbus, OH 43215. Tel: 614-224-7147.
President: Archbishop Daniel E. Pilarczyk
Vice President: Bishop Anthony M. Pilla
Secretary-Treasurer: Bishop James A. Griffin
Executive Director: Timothy V. Luckhaupt

OREGON

Oregon Catholic Conference.
2838 E. Burnside St., Portland, OR 97214. Tel: 503-233-8387; Fax: 503-235-2630.
President: Archbishop John G. Vlazny
Vice President: Bishop Robert F. Vasa
Secretary-Treasurer: Rev. Dennis O'Donovan
General Counsel & Executive Director: Mr. Robert J. Castagna

PENNSYLVANIA

Pennsylvania Catholic Conference.
223 North St., P.O. Box 2835, Harrisburg, PA 17105. Tel: 717-238-9613; Fax: 717-238-1473.
Chairman: His Eminence Anthony Cardinal Bevilacqua
President: Bishop Nicholas C. Dattilo
Vice President: Rev. Msgr. Joseph G. Quinn
Secretary: Bishop David A. Zubik
Executive Director: Dr. Robert J. O'Hara, Jr.
Treasurer: Rev. Msgr. Michael E. Servinsky

TEXAS

Texas Catholic Conference.
1625 Rutherford Ln., Bldg. D, Austin, TX 78754-5105. Tel: 512-339-9882.
Chairman: Archbishop Patrick F. Flores
Executive Director: Bro. Richard Daly, C.S.C.
Associate Director: Rev. Msgr. William L. Broussard
Associate Director for Education: Mr. George Solana
Co-Directors, Volunteers for Education and Social Services: Jody Hart, Jill Seidenberger
Director, Catholic Archives of Texas: Mrs. Kinga Perzynska

WASHINGTON

Washington State Catholic Conference.
508 2nd Avenue West, Seattle, WA 98119. Tel: 206-301-0556; Fax: 206-301-0558.
President: Archbishop Alex J. Brunett, Ph.D.
Executive Director: Sr. Sharon Park, O.P.
Administrative Assistant: JoAnn St. Peirre
Legislative Coordinator: Michael Whitley

WEST VIRGINIA

West Virginia State Catholic Conference.
1300 Byron St., P.O. Box 230, Wheeling, WV 26003. Tel: 304-233-0880, ext. 242; Fax: 304-233-0890.
Director: Very Rev. John R. Gallagher, V.G.

WISCONSIN

Wisconsin Catholic Conference.
30 W. Mifflin St., Room 302, Madison, WI 53703-2579. Tel: 608-257-0004; Fax: 608-257-0376.
Chairman: Archbishop Rembert G. Weakland, O.S.B.
Vice Chairman: Bishop William H. Bullock
Executive Director: John A. Huebscher
Associate Director Respect Life: Kathy M. Markeland
Associate Director Education: M. Colleen Wilson

Diocesan Abbreviations

ARCHDIOCESES AND DIOCESES

(ALB)	Albany (New York)
(ALN)	Allentown (Pennsylvania)
(ALT)	Altoona-Johnstown (Pennsylvania)
(ALX)	Alexandria (Louisiana)
(AGN)	Agana (Guam)
(AMA)	Amarillo (Texas)
(ANC)	Anchorage (Alaska)
(ARE)	Arecibo (Puerto Rico)
(ARL)	Arlington (Virginia)
(ARM)	Armenian Catholic Exarchate (Pennsylvania)
(ATH)	Apostolate To Hungarians (Washington, DC)
(ATL)	Atlanta (Georgia)
(AUS)	Austin (Texas)
(B)	Boise (Idaho)
(BAK)	Baker (Oregon)
(BAL)	Baltimore (Maryland)
(BEA)	Beaumont (Texas)
(BEL)	Belleville (Illinois)
(BGP)	Bridgeport (Connecticut)
(BIR)	Birmingham (Alabama)
(BIS)	Bismarck (North Dakota)
(BLX)	Biloxi (Mississippi)
(BO)	Boston (Massachusetts)
(BR)	Baton Rouge (Louisiana)
(BRK)	Brooklyn (New York)
(BUF)	Buffalo (New York)
(BUR)	Burlington (Vermont)
(BWN)	Brownsville (Texas)
(CAM)	Camden (New Jersey)
(CC)	Corpus Christi (Texas)
(CGS)	Caguas (Puerto Rico)
(CHI)	Chicago (Illinois)
(CHK)	Chalan Kanoa
(CHL)	Charlotte (North Carolina)
(CHR)	Charleston (South Carolina)
(CHY)	Cheyenne (Wyoming)
(CI)	Caroline Islands
(CIN)	Cincinnati (Ohio)
(CLV)	Cleveland (Ohio)
(COL)	Columbus (Ohio)
(COS)	Colorado Springs (Colorado)
(COV)	Covington (Kentucky)
(CR)	Crookston (Minnesota)
(DAL)	Dallas (Texas)
(DAV)	Davenport (Iowa)
(DEN)	Denver (Colorado)
(DET)	Detroit (Michigan)
(DM)	Des Moines (Iowa)
(DOD)	Dodge City (Kansas)
(DUB)	Dubuque (Iowa)
(DUL)	Duluth (Minnesota)
(E)	Erie (Pennsylvania)
(ELP)	El Paso (Texas)
(EST)	Eparchy of Saint Thomas the Apostle
(EVN)	Evansville (Indiana)
(FAR)	Fargo (North Dakota)
(FBK)	Fairbanks (Alaska)
(FgM)	Foreign Mission Section
(FR)	Fall River (Massachusetts)
(FRS)	Fresno (California)
(FTW)	Fort Wayne-South Bend (Indiana)
(FWT)	Fort Worth (Texas)
(GAL)	Galveston-Houston (Texas)
(GAY)	Gaylord (Michigan)
(GB)	Green Bay (Wisconsin)
(GBG)	Greensburg (Pennsylvania)
(GF)	Great Falls-Billings (Montana)
(GI)	Grand Island (Nebraska)
(GLP)	Gallup (New Mexico)
(GR)	Grand Rapids (Michigan)
(GRY)	Gary (Indiana)
(HBG)	Harrisburg (Pennsylvania)
(HEL)	Helena (Montana)
(HON)	Honolulu (Hawaii)
(HRT)	Hartford (Connecticut)
(HT)	Houma-Thibodaux (Louisiana)
(IND)	Indianapolis (Indiana)
(JC)	Jefferson City (Missouri)
(JKS)	Jackson (Mississippi)
(JOL)	Joliet in Illinois
(JUN)	Juneau (Alaska)
(KAL)	Kalamazoo (Michigan)
(KC)	Kansas City-St. Joseph (Missouri)
(KCK)	Kansas City in Kansas
(KNX)	Knoxville (Tennessee)
(L)	Louisville (Kentucky)
(LA)	Los Angeles (California)
(LAF)	Lafayette (Louisiana)
(LAN)	Lansing (Michigan)
(LAR)	Laredo (Texas)
(LC)	La Crosse (Wisconsin)
(LEX)	Lexington (Kentucky)
(LFT)	Lafayette in Indiana
(LIN)	Lincoln (Nebraska)
(LIT)	Lithuanian Apostolate for Lithuanian Catholics
(LKC)	Lake Charles (Louisiana)
(LR)	Little Rock (Arkansas)
(LSC)	Las Cruces (New Mexico)
(LUB)	Lubbock (Texas)
(LAV)	Las Vegas (Nevada)
(MAD)	Madison (Wisconsin)
(MAN)	Manchester (New Hampshire)
(MAR)	Marquette (Michigan)
(MEM)	Memphis (Tennessee)
(MET)	Metuchen (New Jersey)
(MGZ)	Mayaguez (Puerto Rico)
(MI)	Marshall Islands
(MIA)	Miami (Florida)
(MIL)	Milwaukee (Wisconsin)
(MO)	Military Services (Maryland)
(MOB)	Mobile (Alabama)
(MRY)	Monterey in California
(NEW)	Newark (New Jersey)
(NO)	New Orleans (Louisiana)
(NOR)	Norwich (Connecticut)
(NSH)	Nashville (Tennessee)
(NTN)	Newton (Melkite, United States)
(NU)	New Ulm (Minnesota)
(NY)	New York (New York)
(OAK)	Oakland (California)
(OG)	Ogdensburg (New York)
(OKL)	Oklahoma City (Oklahoma)
(OLD)	Our Lady of Deliverance Syriac (Union City, New Jersey)
(OLL)	Our Lady of Lebanon of Los Angeles (California)
(OM)	Omaha (Nebraska)
(ORG)	Orange in California
(ORL)	Orlando (Florida)
(OWN)	Owensboro (Kentucky)
(P)	Portland in Oregon
(PAT)	Paterson (New Jersey)
(PBL)	Pueblo (Colorado)
(PBR)	Pittsburgh Byzantine (Pennsylvania)
(PCE)	Ponce (Puerto Rico)
(PEO)	Peoria (Illinois)
(PH)	Philadelphia (Pennsylvania)
(PHU)	Philadelphia Ukrainian (Pennsylvania)
(PHX)	Phoenix (Arizona)
(PIT)	Pittsburgh (Pennsylvania)
(PMB)	Palm Beach (Florida)
(PP)	Personal Prelatures
(PRM)	Parma Byzantine (Ohio)
(PRO)	Providence (Rhode Island)
(PRT)	Portland (Maine)
(PSC)	Passaic Byzantine (New Jersey)
(PT)	Pensacola-Tallahassee (Florida)
(R)	Raleigh (North Carolina)
(RC)	Rapid City (South Dakota)
(RCK)	Rockford (Illinois)
(RIC)	Richmond (Virginia)
(RNO)	Reno (Nevada)
(ROC)	Rochester (New York)
(ROM)	Romanian (Byzantine) (Ohio)
(RVC)	Rockville Centre (New York)
(SAC)	Sacramento (California)
(SAG)	Saginaw (Michigan)
(SAL)	Salina (Kansas)
(SAM)	St. Maron of Brooklyn (U.S.A.)
(SAN)	Eparchy of San Angelo (Texas)
(SAT)	San Antonio (Texas)
(SAV)	Savannah (Georgia)
(SB)	San Bernadino (California)
(SC)	Sioux City (Iowa)
(SCL)	St. Cloud (Minnesota)
(SCR)	Scranton (Pennsylvania)
(SD)	San Diego (California)
(SEA)	Seattle (Washington)
(SFD)	Springfield in Illinois
(SFE)	Santa Fe (New Mexico)
(SFR)	San Francisco (California)
(SFS)	Sioux Falls (South Dakota)
(SHP)	Shreveport (Louisiana)
(SJ)	San Jose in California
(SJN)	San Juan (Puerto Rico)
(SJP)	St. Josaphat in Parma (Ohio)
(SLC)	Salt Lake City (Utah)
(SP)	St. Petersburg (Florida)
(SPC)	Springfield-Cape Girardeau (Missouri)
(SPK)	Spokane (Washington)
(SPP)	Samoa-Pago Pago
(SPR)	Springfield in Massachusetts
(SR)	Santa Rosa in California
(STA)	St. Augustine (Florida)
(STF)	Stamford Ukrainian (Connecticut)
(STL)	St. Louis (Missouri)
(STN)	St. Nicholas in Chicago Ukrainian
(STO)	Stockton (California)
(STP)	St. Paul and Minneapolis (Minnesota)
(STU)	Steubenville (Ohio)
(STV)	St. Thomas, Virgin Islands
(SUP)	Superior (Wisconsin)
(SY)	Syracuse (New York)
(TLS)	Tulsa (Oklahoma)
(TOL)	Toledo (Ohio)
(TR)	Trenton (New Jersey)
(TUC)	Tucson (Arizona)
(TYL)	Tyler (Texas)
(VEN)	Venice (Florida)
(VIC)	Victoria in Texas
(VNN)	Van Nuys Byzantine (California)
(WCH)	Wichita (Kansas)
(WDC)	Washington (District of Columbia)
(WH)	Wheeling-Charleston (West Virginia)
(WIL)	Wilmington (Delaware)
(WIN)	Winona (Minnesota)
(WOR)	Worcester (Massachusetts)
(Y)	Youngstown (Ohio)
(YAK)	Yakima (Washington)

Diocese of Albany

(Dioecesis Albanensis)

Most Reverend

HOWARD J. HUBBARD, D.D.

Bishop of Albany; ordained December 18, 1963; appointed February 1, 1977; ordained and installed March 27, 1977. *Res., 125 Eagle St., Albany, NY, 12202.* Tel.: 518-462-3804.

Chancery Office: Pastoral Center, 40 N. Main Ave., Albany, NY, 12203. Tel.: 518-453-6600; Fax: 518-453-6793.

Web site address: www.rcda.org

E-mail address: chancery@rcda.org

ESTABLISHED APRIL 23, 1847.

Square Miles 10,419.

(Incorporated by a special act of the Legislature of the State of New York, April 12, 1941, with the title "The Roman Catholic Diocese of Albany, New York.")

Comprises the entire Counties of Albany, Columbia, Delaware, Fulton, Green, Montgomery, Otsego, Rensselaer, Saratoga, Schenectady, Schoharie, Warren and Washington and that part of Herkimer and Hamilton Counties, south of the northern line of the townships of Ohio and Russia, as existing in 1872 in the State of New York.

For legal titles of parishes and diocesan institutions, consult the Chancery Office.

STATISTICAL OVERVIEW

Personnel	
Bishop	1
Retired Bishops	1
Priests: Diocesan Active in Diocese	198
Priests: Active Outside Diocese	14
Priests: Retired, Sick or Absent	80
Number of Diocesan Priests	292
Religious Priests in Diocese	77
Extern Priests in Diocese	7
Ordinations:	
Diocesan Priests	1
Permanent Deacons	81
Permanent Deacons in Diocese	90
Total Brothers	94
Total Sisters	946
Parishes	
Parishes	184
With Resident Pastor:	
Resident Diocesan Priests	144
Resident Religious Priests	12
Without Resident Pastor:	
Administered by Priests	20
Administered by Deacons	1
Administered by Women Religious	9
Administered by Lay People	1
Missions	34
Professional Ministry Personnel:	
Brothers	2
Sisters	100
Lay Ministers	1,327
Welfare	
Catholic Hospitals	4
Total Assisted	668,100
Health Care Centers	15
Total Assisted	51,000
Homes for the Aged	10
Total Assisted	1,314
Day Care and Extended Day Care Centers	7
Total Assisted	517
Specialized Homes	12
Total Assisted	1,250
Special Centers for Social Services	25
Total Assisted	175,000
Residential Care of Disabled	7
Total Assisted	225
Other Institutions	9
Total Assisted	625
Educational	
Diocesan Students in Other Seminaries	7
Total Seminarians	7
Colleges and Universities	3
Total Students	4,000
High Schools, Diocesan and Parish	4
Total Students	1,194
High Schools, Private	3
Total Students	870
Elementary Schools, Diocesan and Parish	37
Total Students	8,555
Elementary Schools, Private	2
Total Students	12,181
Catechesis/Religious Education:	
High School Students	9,273
Elementary Students	31,211
Total Students Under Catholic Instruction	67,291
Teachers in the Diocese:	
Priests	6
Brothers	17
Sisters	65
Lay Teachers	898
Vital Statistics	
Receptions into the Church:	
Infant Baptism Totals	4,623
Adult Baptism Totals	143
Received into Full Communion	324
First Communions	5,298
Confirmations	2,963
Marriages:	
Catholic	1,242
Interfaith	517
Total Marriages	1,759
Deaths	5,232
Total Catholic Population	400,000
Total Population	1,386,200

Former Bishops—His Eminence JOHN CARDINAL MCCLOSKEY, D.D., appt. Bishop of Axiere and Coadjutor to the Bishop of New York, Nov. 21, 1843; cons. March 10, 1844; transferred to Albany, May 21, 1847; promoted to New York, May 6, 1864; created Cardinal Priest of the Holy Roman Church, March 15, 1875, under the title Sanctae Mariae supra Minervam; died Oct. 10, 1885.—Rt. Rev. JOHN J. CONROY, appt. Bishop July 7, 1865; cons. Oct. 15, 1865; resigned Oct. 16, 1877; transferred to the See of Curium, March 22, 1878; died Nov. 20, 1895.—Rt. Rev. Msgr. FRANCIS MCNEIRNY, D.D., appt. Bishop of Rhesina and Coadjutor to the Bishop of Albany, Dec. 22, 1871; cons. April 21, 1872; appt. Administrator of the Diocese of Albany, Jan. 18, 1874; Bishop of Albany, by right of succession, Oct. 16, 1877; died Jan. 2, 1894.—Rt. Rev. Msgr. THOMAS M. A. BURKE, D.D., preconized May 18, 1894; cons. July 1, 1894; died Jan 20, 1915.—Rt. Rev. Msgr. THOMAS F. CUSACK, D.D., cons. Titular Bishop of Themiscyra and Auxiliary to the Archbishop of New York, April 25, 1904; transferred to Albany, July 5, 1915; died July 12, 1918.—Most Rev. EDMUND F. GIBBONS, D.D., appt. Bishop, Feb. 1, 1919; cons. March 25, 1919; resigned Nov. 10, 1954; transferred to See of Verbe; died June 19, 1964.—Most Rev. WILLIAM A. SCULLY, D.D., appt. Coadjutor Bishop "cum jure successionis," Aug. 21, 1945; cons. Oct. 24, 1945; succeeded to See, Nov. 10, 1954; died Jan. 5, 1969.—Most Rev. EDWIN B. BRODERICK, D.D., appt. Titular Bishop of Tizica and Auxiliary of New York, March 8, 1967; cons. April 21, 1967; transferred Albany, March 19, 1969; resigned June 2, 1976; appt. Exec. Dir. Catholic Relief Services, June 3, 1976; retired September, 1985.

Chancery Office—Pastoral Center, 40 N. Main Ave., Albany, 12203. Tel: 518-453-6600; Fax: 518-453-6793. Office Hours: Mon.-Fri. 8:30-4:30.

Vicars General—Rev. LEO P. O'BRIEN, *900 Madison Ave., Albany, 12208.* Tel: 518-489-5408. Rev. MICHAEL A. FARANO, *23 Crumite Rd., Loudonville, 12211.*

Chancellors—Pastoral Center, 40 N. Main Ave., Albany, 12203. Rev. KENNETH DOYLE, Chancellor Public Information. Tel: 518-453-6612. Sr. KATHLEEN TURLEY, R.S.M., Chancellor, Planning & Pastoral Svcs. Tel: 518-453-6612.

Chief Financial Officer—RICHARD FARRELL, *40 N. Main Ave., Albany, 12203.* Tel: 518-453-6640.

Insurance Office—RONALD WATERS, Dir., *40 N. Main Ave., Albany, 12203.* Tel: 518-453-6790.

Office of Human Resources—Sr. MARILYN K. MURRAY, R.S.M., Dir., *40 N. Main Ave., Albany, 12203.* Tel: 518-453-6635. FRANK DUCHARME, Asst. Dir., Human Resources. Tel: 518-453-6681. MARY JO HELNARSKI, Personnel Asst. Tel: 518-453-6635. Sr. NOLA BRUNNER, Spec. Projects. Tel: 518-453-6662.

Pastoral Planning—Sr. KATHLEEN TURLEY, R.S.M., Dir., *40 N. Main Ave., Albany, 12203.* Tel: 518-453-6661.

Archivist—KAY HEWIG, *40 N. Main Ave., Albany, 12203.* Tel: 518-453-6633.

Office of Canonical Services—40 N. Main Ave., Albany, 12203. Tel: 518-453-6620; Fax: 518-453-6778. Office Hours: 8:30-4:30 (By appointment only).

Vicar Judicial—Rev. JAMES I. DONLON, J.C.D.

Adjutant Vicar Judicial—Rev. PETER J. SULLIVAN, III, J.C.L.

Judges—Revs. DAVID BERBERIAN, J.C.L.; JAMES I. DONLON, J.C.L.; PETER J. SULLIVAN, III, J.C.L.

Defender of the Marriage Bond in First Instance—Sr. MARY ANN HAYES, C.S.J., J.C.L.

Promoter of Justice—Rev. ALMERICO F. DICERBO, J.C.D.

Advocates—Revs. THOMAS KRUPA; THOMAS BERARDI; JAMES LEFEBVRE; JOSEPH O'BRIEN; JOHN MOYNA; ARTHUR BECKER; FRANK GILCHRIST.

Bishop's Delegate for Marriage Dispensations—Revs. JAMES I. DONLON, J.C.D.; PETER J. SULLIVAN, III, J.C.L.; DAVID V. BERBERIAN, J.C.L.

Notaries—JOANNE MONAHAN; MARTHA MCEWAN; MARY FIORILLO.

Inter Diocesan Tribunal for the Province of NY—(Second Instance Appeal Court), Rev. Msgr. WALTER F. KENNY, Vicar Judicial; Sr. AILEEN KELLY, Admin. & Chief Exec. Sec., *201 Seminary Ave., Yonkers, 10704-1852.* Tel: 914-968-4301; 800-293-6598; Fax: 914-968-4466.

Presbyteral Council—Most Rev. HOWARD J. HUBBARD, Pres.; Revs. ANTHONY LIGATO, Chm. DOMINIC ISOPO, Vice Chm. KENNETH SWAIN, Sec. JOSEPH BUSH; THOMAS CHEVALIER; GEORGE FLEMING; R. ADAM FORNO; JAMES LEFEBVRE; ROBERT LONGOBUCCO; JACK MOLYN; JAMES O'BLANEY, C.SS.R; DAVID TRESSIC. Ex Officio: Revs. KENNETH DOYLE; JAMES I. DONLON; MICHAEL A. FARANO; RICHARD FARRELL; LEO P. O'BRIEN.

Diocesan Board of Consultors—Revs. JOSEPH BUSH; GEORGE FLEMING; THOMAS CHEVALIER; R. ADAM FORNO; DOMINIC ISOPO; JAMES LEFEBVRE; ANTHONY LIGATO; ROBERT LONGOBUCCO; JACK MOLYN; JAMES O'BLANEY, C.SS.R.; KENNETH SWAIN; DAVID TRESSIC; JAMES I. DONLON, Canonical Consultant to the Board.

Deans—Rev. ROBERT J. HOHENSTEIN, V.F., Albany Co.-City; Rev. LAWRENCE MCTAVEY, V.F., Northern; Rev. JOHN WALDRON, Suburban; Rev. GARY GELFENBEIN, V.F., Colombia; Rev. ROBERT PURCELL, V.F., Delaware; Rev. DONALD CZELUSNIAK, V.F., Fulton; Rev. JEREMIAH NUNAN, V.F., Greene; Rev. JOSEPH BENINTENDE, Herkimer; Rev. JAMES GULLEY, Montgomery; Rev. PAUL ROMAN, Otsego; Rev. DONALD OPHALS, Rensselaer Co.-Northern; Rev. GEORGE G. ST. JOHN, Southern; Rev. ANTHONY DIACETIS, Saratoga; Rev. LOUIS DEIMEKE, Schenectady Co.; Rev. THOMAS BERARDI, Schoharie; Rev. JOSEPH ANSELMENT, Warren; Rev. BARRY LONERGAN, Washington.

Diocesan Offices and Directors

All Diocesan Offices and Directors are located at The Pastoral Center, 40 N. Main Ave., Albany, 12203. Tel: 518-453-6600; Fax: 518-453-6793 unless otherwise indicated

Office of Real Property—NOEL A. OLSEN, Dir. Tel: 518-453-6623.

Receptionists—Ms. SUZANNE SECOR; Ms. ZOE BOPP; Ms. JEANNE MCGARRY.

Administrative Review Board (Due Process)—Rev. DAVID BERBERIAN, J.C.L., Chm. Tel: 518-453-6620.

Apostleship of Prayer—Rev. JOHN J. PARET, S.J., *Auriesville, 12016.* Tel: 518-853-3153.

Korean Catholic Apostolate—Rev. PIUS BIO JUNG, *10 Lodge St., Albany, 12207.*

Bishop's Appeal—JOHN MANNING, Dir. Tel: 518-453-6680.

Black Apostolate—Rev. KOFI NTSIFUL-AMISSAH, Admin., *St. George's Church, 50 Thornton St., Albany, 12206.* Tel: 518-462-9604.

Campus Ministry—Sr. MAUREEN O'LEARY, F.S.P., Diocesan Dir., *SUNY at Albany, P.O. Box 22225, Albany, 12222.* Tel: 518-489-8573.

Albany Diocesan Media Office (In-house TV/Audio Production Office)—KATHERINE MALLE, Dir., Media Office, *40 N. Main Ave., Albany, 12203.* Tel: 518-453-6690; Fax: 518-453-6793.

Catholic Deaf Ministry—Rev. JAMES E. CLARK, Chap., *St. Jude the Apostle Parish, 42 Dana Ave., P.O. Box 347, Wynantskill, 12198-0347.* Tel: 518-283-1162; Fax & TDD: 518-286-2808.

Cemeteries—RICHARD TOUCHETTE, Dir., *Albany Diocesan Cemeteries, 48 Cemetery Ave., Menands, Albany, 12204.* Tel: 518-432-4953.

Censores Librorum—Rev. JOHN R. ROOS, J.C.D.

Catholic Office for Motion Pictures—Rev. ANTHONY D. GULLEY, Diocesan Dir., *Res., 607 Central Ave., Albany, 12205.* Tel: 518-482-3375.

Architecture and Building Commission—Rev. THOMAS PHELAN, Chm. CAROL FITZGERALD, Coord. Tel: 518-453-6622.

Public Information—Rev. KENNETH DOYLE, Chancellor. Tel: 518-453-6612. KATHERINE MALLE, Dir. Media Office. Tel: 518-453-6690.

Cursillos in Christianity Diocese of Albany—Rev. VINCENT CIOTOLI, *St. Patrick's Church, 21 Main St., Ravena, 12143.* Tel: 518-756-3145. Deacon MICHAEL MELANSON, *27 Kyle Dr., Scotia, 12302.* Tel: 518-399-1425.

Diocesan Service Committee for Charismatic Renewal—Deacon JERRY GRIGAITIS; MARIE GRIGAITIS, *7 Granada Dr., Clifton Park, 12065.* Tel: 518-371-7911. JAMES B. RYAN, Communications, *707 Pleasantview Ave., Scotia, 12302.* Tel: 518-374-6891.

Diocesan Stewardship Office—JOHN MANNING. Tel: 518-453-6680.

Department of Information Resources—Vacant, Dir. Tel: 518-453-6685; Fax: 518-453-6779.

Catholic Charities of Diocese of Albany, Inc.; St. Vincent's Child Care Society, Inc.—Sr. MAUREEN JOYCE, R.S.M., CEO & Sec. to the Bishop for Health & Social Svcs. Tel: 518-453-6650; Fax: 518-453-6792. Sr. MAUREEN JOYCE, R.S.M., Sec., St. Vincent's Child Care Society, Inc. RICHARD MARINI, CFO. Assoc. Exec. Directors: WILLIAM J. PRZYLUCKI; KAREN DEHAIS; JOSEPH WALKER; JOSEPH BUTTIGIEG; JOSEPH PROFIT, Developer Long Term Care Campus/Sr. Housing.

Catholic Charities Agencies—LINDA BONESTEEL, Dir., Catholic Charities of Albany & Rensselaer Counties, *100 Slingerland St., Albany, 12202.* Tel: 518-426-3511. ALBERT TURO, Dir., Catholic Charities of Montgomery County, *One Kimball St., Amsterdam, 12010.* Tel: 518-842-4202. AGNES DONLON, Dir., Catholic Charities of Colombia & Greene Counties, *431 E. Allen St., Hudson, 12534.* Tel: 518-828-8660. JOHN NASSO, Dir., Catholic Charities of Fulton County, *208 W. State St., Johnstown, 12095.* Tel: 518-762-8313. DAVID BRUCE, Dir., Catholic Charities of Herkimer County, *61 West St., Ilion, 13357.* Tel: 315-894-9917. KATHIE GREENBLATT, Dir., Catholic Charities of Delaware & Otsego Counties, *9-11 S. Main St., Oneonta, 13820.* Tel: 607-432-0061. Sr. CHARLA COMMINS, C.S.J., Dir., Catholic Charities of Saratoga, Warren & Washington Counties, *142 Regent St., Saratoga, 12866.* Tel: 518-587-5000. JOHN D. STEELE, Dir., Catholic Charities of Schenectady County, *818 Union St., Schenectady, 12308.* Tel: 518-372-5667. THOMAS MAYER, Dir., Family & Community Svcs. of Schoharie County, *41 W. Main St., Cobleskill, 12043.* Tel: 518-234-3581.

Diocesan-wide Agencies and Commissions—Sr. SERENA BRANSON, D.C., Exec. Sec., Commission on Aging. Tel: 518-453-6650. BARBARA DITOMMASO, Dir., Commission on Peace & Justice. Tel: 518-453-6650. MARTHA HAASE, Dir., Caregivers Program of Catholic Charities, *100 Slingerland St., Albany, 12202.* Tel: 518-449-2001. Sr. MARY ANN LOGIUDICE, R.S.M., Dir., Community Maternity Svcs., *27 N. Main Ave., Albany, 12203.* Tel: 518-482-8836. GARY SIEGEL, Dir., Catholic Charities Disabilities Svcs., *15 Avis Dr., Latham, 12210.* Tel: 518-783-1111. DEBORAH DAMM O'BRIEN, Dir., Diocesan Housing and Property Management Services, *41 N. Main Ave., Albany, 12203.* Tel: 518-459-0183. Sr. CLAUDETTE HARRIS, C.S.J., Dir., Sunnyside Center, *P.O. Box 1410, Troy, 12180.* Tel: 518-274-5986. Sr. ANNE TRANELLI, C.S.J., Dir., Hispanic Outreach Svcs., *40 N. Main Ave., Albany, 12203.* Tel: 518-453-6655. JOSEPH KERWIN, Catholic Charities Diocesan AIDS Svcs., *100 Slingerland St., Albany, 12202.* Tel: 518-449-3581. JAMES J. MCCORMACK, Ph.D., Health Care Coord., *Diocesan Community Health Alliance, 40 N. Main Ave., Albany, 12203.* Tel: 518-453-6650. Bro. LARRY BACKUS, C.S.C., Dir. Diocesan Jail Ministry, *St. Joseph's Center, Valatie, 12184.* Tel: 518-784-9481.

Catholic Campaign for Human Development—
Catholic Charities of the Diocese of Albany—Tel: 518-453-6650.

Catholic Relief Services—Catholic Charities of the Diocese of Albany. Tel: 518-453-6650.

Disaster Relief Services—Catholic Charities of the Diocese of Albany. Tel: 518-453-6650.

Health and Hospitals Office—Sr. MAUREEN JOYCE, R.S.M., Bishop's Rep. Tel: 518-453-6650.

Catholic Women's Service League—BERNICE I. LEYDEN, Pres., *c/o LaSalle, 391 Western Ave., Albany, 12203.* Tel: 518-242-4731.

Ladies of Charity—MARY ESMAY, *4 Denny Rd., Guilderland, 12084.* Tel: 518-456-8606.

Society of St. Vincent de Paul—EDWARD NARE, Diocesan Central Council Pres., *202 S. Ballston Ave., Scotia, 12302.* Tel: 518-374-2548. EMMET J. LYNCH, Pres. Emeritus; Rev. RICHARD DOWNS, Spiritual Dir., *12 Rosemont St., Albany, 12203.* Tel: 518-489-8197.

Consultation Center of the Diocese of Albany—A non-profit Mental Health Center which provides quality professional psychological counseling services and educational programs in the area of mental health to individuals and groups.

Office—Rev. ANTHONY J. CHIARAMONTE, Ph.D., Dir.; Sr. MARY FRANCES BECK, S.N.J.M., Admin. Dir.; Rev. JOHN J. MALECKI, Ph.D., Psychologist; KATHLEEN STIFFEN, Sec., *790 Lancaster St., Albany, 12203.* Tel: 518-489-4431; Fax: 518-489-5189.

Psychological Counseling—Provides individual therapy, marriage and couples counseling, psychological testing and consultative services to individuals and groups in matters calling for psychological expertise.

Group Therapy—Provides a variety of different kinds of therapy groups.

Educational Programs—Offers lectures and workshops in the area of mental health and personal growth. The Center also offers specialized workshops and training programs to meet the needs of various groups.

Spiritual Direction—Provides a program of individual spiritual direction for any person interested in developing a deeper relationship with God.

Counseling for Laity—Sr. ANNE BRYAN SMOLLIN, C.S.J., Ph.D., Exec. Dir. ETTA JONES, Admin. Asst. Tel: 518-453-6625. Provides individual and group psychological counseling-therapy by certified trained therapists. The staff provides services for the Young Married program and assessments for second marriages. Consultation and training programs are offered upon request.

Diocesan Pastoral Care Association—BARBARA DUGAN LILLY, Head of Leadership Team, *St. Mary's Church, 39 Walnut St., Oneonta, 13820.* Tel: 607-432-3920.

Diocesan Pastoral Council—PATRICIA MOUSAW, Staff; Mrs. MARGARET KANE, Chm.; Mrs. MARY MCGINTY, Vice Chm.; Mr. HENRY DIGESER, Sec. Tel: 518-453-6661.

Prevention Services - Catholic Schools Office—CATHY GOLAS, Prog. Dir. Tel: 518-453-6771; Fax: 518-453-6667. Services students, faculty and parents of Catholic schools in the diocese.

Ecumenical and Interreligious Affairs of the Roman Catholic Diocese of Albany, Commission for—Mrs. AUDREY HUGHES; Deacons WILLIAM GAFFNEY; EARLE FLATT; RAYMOND SULLIVAN; Mr. DAVID AMICO; JOAN HOLMAN; JOAN LIPSCOMB; Rev. THOMAS PHELAN; Sr. MARY GEN SMYTH, R.C.S.J.; Mrs. JOAN DUNHAM; Sr. ELIZABETH HOYE, R.C.S.J.; Mr. FRANK M. PELL; Revs. JAMES BELOGI; PHILIP CIOPPA; MAURICE DROWN; JAMES KANE, Dir. DAVID MICKIEWICZ; Mrs. PENNY MEADE, Sec. Tel: 518-453-6660.

"The Evangelist"—Diocesan Newspaper *Albany Catholic Press Assoc., Inc.,* JAMES P. BREIG, Editor. Tel: 518-453-6688; Fax: 518-453-8448.

Family Life Office—MEG BERGH, Dir. Assoc. Directors: MARY MORIARTY; MARTHA ARENAS-FENN; PEG FURLONG MALOY, Consultant NFP; KAREN FONTANELLI, Admin. Asst. Tel: 518-453-6677. Bereavement Ministry; Catholic Singles; Family Perspective; Gay/Lesbian Ministry; Hispanic Ministry; Marriage & Remarriage Preparation; Marriage & Family Enrichment; Natural Family Planning; Parenting; Respect Life; Separated, Divorced & Widowed; Young Adult Ministry.

Education Sites for Natural Family Planning—HELENE WALLINGFORD, *St. Peter's Hospital, 315 S. Manning Blvd., Albany, 12208.* Tel: 518-525-1388. ELIZABETH SMITKA, *St. Mary's Hospital, 380 Guy Park Ave., Amsterdam, 12010.* Tel: 518-841-7423.

Holy Name Societies—Rev. WILLIAM W. CRANDALL, Dir., *St. Joseph Rectory, 181 Main St., Worcester, 12197.* Tel: 607-397-9373.

Initial & Ongoing Formation Cluster—Tel: 518-453-6670. C. ELIZABETH ROWE, Dir. Formation for Ministry Program. Tel: 518-453-6670. Rev. JOSEPH COTUGNO, Dir. Formation for Diaconate. Tel: 518-453-6670.

Formation for Priesthood / Vocation Awareness—Sr. KATHERINE HANLEY, C.S.J.; Revs. JAMES WALSH; THOMAS KONOPKA. Tel: 518-453-6670.

Legion of Mary—Deacon WILLIAM J. BRETT, *197 Woods Edge Ct., Voorheesville, 12186.* Tel: 518-765-4654.

Office of Evangelization and Catechesis—JEANNE SCHREMPF, Diocesan Dir.; Sr. PATRICIA CONRON, C.S.J., Assoc. Dir., Catechist Formation; PATRICIA TAAFFE, Resource Library Coord. DAVID G. AMICO, Assoc. Dir., Persons with Developmental Disabilities/Special Needs; Vacant, Assoc. Dir., Adult/Young Adult Faith Formation; Deacon WILLIAM GAFFNEY, Deacon Assoc. - Evangelization; MARY HARRISON, Assoc. Dir., Youth Ministry; JOYCE SOLIMINI, Assoc. Dir., Sacramental and Family Catechesis; Rev. ANTHONY MAIONE, Clergy Assoc., Youth Ministry.

Permanent Diaconate Office—Co-Directors: Deacons FRANK LUKOVITS; TIMOTHY MCAULIFFE. Tel: 518-453-6612.

Catholic Foundation—Most Rev. HOWARD J. HUBBARD, Pres. JOHN MANNING, Exec. Dir. Tel: 518-453-6680.

Office of Prayer & Worship—ELIZABETH SIMCOE, Dir., *40 N. Main Ave., Albany, 12203.* Tel: 518-453-6645; Fax: 518-453-6793.

Administrative Advocate for Priests—Rev. L. EDWARD DEIMEKE. Tel: 518-453-6643.

Priests Placement Committee—Revs. L. EDWARD DEIMEKE, Chm. JOHN BRADLEY; LEO MARKERT; ARTHUR TOOLE; JAMES WALSH.

Priestly Life and Ministry Council—Rev. RONALD MENTY, Chm.

Ongoing and Continuing Education for Priests—Rev. PHILIP M. CIOPPA, Chm.

Ministry to Priests—Revs. GEORGE BRUCKER; FRANCIS GILCHRIST.

Priests Retirement Board—Revs. JOHN F. CONNOLLY, Chm. Tel: 518-453-6640. JOSEPH E. ANSELMENT; JOSEPH BARKER; PAUL COX; JOSEPH DAVORAK; JOHN T. PROVOST; ROBERT ROOS; ERWIN SCHWEIGART; Mr. RICHARD FARRELL. Tel: 518-453-6612.

Priests' Retirement Plan Board—Rev. JOHN CONNOLLY. Tel: 518-453-6640.

Propagation of the Faith-Pontifical Society—Revs. MICHAEL A. FARANO, Dir. JAMES MACKEY, Assoc. Dir. Tel: 518-453-6675.

Schools: Diocesan School Board—DEBORAH O'BRIEN, Chm. Tel: 518-459-0183.

Diocesan School Office—Sr. MARY JANE HERB, I.H.M., Ph.D., Supt. of Schools. Tel: 518-453-6602. THOMAS FITZGERALD, Ph.D., Asst. Supt., Admin. Svcs. Tel: 518-453-6666. EDITH TOOHEY, Asst. Supt. for Instructional Svcs. Tel: 518-453-6666. CATHY GOLAS, Preventative Svcs. Program. Tel: 518-453-6771. CURTIS A. MCEWAN, Business Mgr. Tel: 518-453-6604. SAL CARBONE, Safety Coord. Tel: 518-853-4001. DARLENE CARDILLO, Dir. Educational Technology. Tel: 518-453-6666. JOANNE GUILMETTE, Dir., Pub. Rels. Tel: 518-453-6666.

Scouting—Rev. JOSEPH SCHUCK, Diocesan Chap., *c/o Gilead House of Prayer, 1101 State Hwy. 7, Unadilla, 13849-3120.* Tel: 607-369-2317.

St. Bernard's Institute/Albany—JOSEPH R. PICCOLINO, Ed.D., Dir. Tel: 518-453-6760; Fax: 518-453-6793.

Vicar for Religious—Sr. NOLA BRUNNER, C.S.J. Tel: 518-453-6662. Rev. JOHN ROOS, Asst. Vicar, *Res., St. Mary Rectory, 31 Elm St., Cooperstown, 13326.* Tel: 607-547-2213.

Vocations and Vocation Awareness Program—Sr. KATHERINE HANLEY, C.S.J.; Revs. JAMES WALSH; THOMAS KONOPKA. Tel: 518-453-6670.

CLERGY, PARISHES, MISSIONS AND PAROCHIAL SCHOOLS

CITY OF ALBANY
(Albany County)

1—CATHEDRAL OF THE IMMACULATE CONCEPTION, Rev. William H. Pape, Rector. In res., Most Rev. Howard J. Hubbard Tel: 518-462-3804.
Rectory Office: 125 Eagle St., 12202. Tel: 518-463-4447; Fax: 518-436-5177.
Religious Education Office—Tel: 518-436-7918.
Cathedral Social Services—Tel: 518-463-2279.
Convent—93 Park Ave., 12202. Tel: 518-436-7697. Sisters 9.

2—ST. JOHN-ST. ANN, Rev. John Kirwin; Deacon Russell J. Kratz.
Office: 157 Franklin St., 12202. Tel: 518-472-9091; Fax: 518-427-5983.

3—BLESSED SACRAMENT, Revs. John J. Bradley; Patrick J. Winslow; Sr. Mary Coons, R.S.M., Pastoral Assoc.; Deacon William Fitzgerald. In res., Rev. Anthony D. Gulley.
Res., 607 Central Ave., 12206. Tel: 518-482-3375; Fax: 518-482-3376.
School—605 Central Ave., 12206. Tel: 518-438-5854; Fax: 518-438-1532. Sr. Jane Somerville, Prin.
Sisters of Mercy 2; Lay Teachers 18; Students 248.

4—ST. CASIMIR (Polish). Attended by Our Lady of Angels. Rev. Alvin Somerville, O.F.M.Conv., Admin. In res., Revs. Francis A. O'Connor; Francis J. Gilchrist.
Res., 324 Sheridan Ave., 12206. Tel: 518-463-7147; Fax: 518-463-7147.
School—Tel: 518-434-4264. James Leveskas, Prin.
Sisters of the Resurrection 3; Lay Teachers 13; Students 122.
Convent—315 Sheridan Ave., 12206. Tel: 518-463-5440.

5—ST. CATHERINE OF SIENA, Rev. Kennth Doyle; Deacon Gerald Ladouceur. In res., Revs. John A. Keefe; Joseph Romano; Robert J. Donnelly; John Tallman.
Res., 40 Collins Pl., 12208. Tel: 518-489-3204; Fax: 518-482-3721.
School—35 Hurst Ave., 12208. Tel: 518-439-3111; Fax: 518-439-3111. Theresa L. Ewell, Prin.
Lay Teachers 17; Students 245.

6—ST. GEORGE (African-American), Rev. Kofi Amissah, Admin. & Dir. Black Apostolate.
Res., 50 Thornton St., 12206. Tel: 518-462-9604.

7—CHURCH OF THE HOLY CROSS, Revs. Daniel J. Maher; Peter J. Sullivan, III; Sr. Helen Charles, Spiritual Growth Coord.
Res., 12 Rosemont St., 12203. Tel: 518-489-8197.
School—Rosement St., 12203. Tel: 518-438-0066. Sr. Mary Ellen Owens, Prin.
Sisters 1; Lay Teachers 16; Students 291.

8—ST. JAMES, Rev. Dominic Ingemie; Deacon Gerald DeMauro. Pastoral Assocs.: Sr. Mary Ellen Holohan, S.N.J.M.; Sr. Patricia Houlihan, C.S.J.; Loretta Putorti. In res., Revs. Joseph Cotugno; Anthony Sidoti, Pastor Emeritus.
Res., 391 Delaware Ave., 12209. Tel: 518-434-4028; Fax: 518-434-1097.
School—50 Summit Ave., 12209. Tel: 518-465-1973; Fax: 518-465-3879. Mrs. Elizabeth Barton-Rubinstein, Prin.
Sisters 3; Lay Teachers 16; Students 196.
Convent—58 Summit Ave., 12209. Tel: 518-449-7993.
Mission—Albany, Albany Co., Child's Hospital & Eden Park Nursing Home.

9—ST. JOSEPH. Records are kept at Sacred Heart of Jesus, Albany.
Parish Office: 31 Walter St., 12204. Tel: 518-463-3286; Fax: 518-462-0506.

10—ST. MARGARET MARY, Rev. Thomas H. Chevalier; Deacon J. Neil Hook. In res., Rev. David Berberian.
Parish Office: 1168 Western Ave., 12203. Tel: 518-482-4497; Fax: 518-482-4719.

11—ST. MARY, Rev. James Lefebvre; Deacon George Witko; Rev. Lloyd Rebeyro. In res., Rev. Pius-Bio Jung.
Res., 10 Lodge St., 12207. Tel: 518-462-4254; Fax: 518-462-4255.
Chapel—111 Washington Ave., 12203.

12—OUR LADY OF ANGELS, Revs. Alvin Somerville, O.F.M.Conv.; Nicholas Weiss, O.F.M.Conv. In res., Revs. Rufino Maloney, O.F.M.Conv., Guardian; Salvatore Pantano, O.F.M.Conv.; Giles Van Wormer, O.F.M.Conv.; Germain Williams, O.F.M.Conv.; Bro. Leo Merriman, O.F.M.Conv.
Res., 183 Central Ave., 12206. Tel: 518-463-3262; Fax: 518-463-3264. [CEM]

13—OUR LADY HELP OF CHRISTIANS (German), Very Rev. Robert J. Hohenstein, V.F.
Res., 74 Second Ave., 12202. Tel: 518-463-7338; 434-4868. [CEM]

14—ST. PATRICK, Rev. Francis A. O'Connor.
Office: 283 Central Ave., 12206. Tel: 518-465-3685.

15—SACRED HEART OF JESUS, Deacon William A. Gorman, D.Min., Ph.D., Admin.
Res., 33 Walter St., 12204. Tel: 518-463-3286; Fax: 518-462-0506.

16—ST. TERESA OF AVILA, Rev. Thomas M. Powers. In res., Revs. John L. Close; John L. Jones, (Retired).
Res., 435 New Scotland Ave., 12208. Tel: 518-438-7851; Fax: 518-489-6401.
Schools—(Grades PreK-4) 433 New Scotland Ave., 12208. Tel: 518-438-5268.; (Grades 5-8) 8 Hollywood Ave., 12208. Tel: 518-482-3736; Fax: 518-482-3745. Sr. Patricia Houlihan, R.S.M., Prin.
Sisters of Mercy 4; Lay Teachers 15; Students 207.
Convent—401 New Scotland Ave., 12208. Tel: 518-482-8901.
Mission—Albany, Albany Co., Albany Medical Center.

17—ST. VINCENT DE PAUL, Rev. Leo P. O'Brien; Deacon William Gaffney.
Parish Office: 900 Madison Ave., 12208. Tel: 518-489-5408; Fax: 518-489-5474.
Res., 35 Colonial Ave., 12203. Tel: 518-489-0563.

OUTSIDE THE CITY OF ALBANY

Altamont, Albany Co., St. Lucy, Rev. Paul Smith; Sr. Mary Lou Liptak, R.S.M., Parish Life Dir.
Parish House: 109 Grand St., 12009. Tel: 518-861-8770.
Mission—Berne, Albany Co., St. Bernadette, 1763 Helderberg Trail, Berne, 12023. Tel: 518-872-1131.

Amsterdam, Montgomery Co.,

1—ST. CASIMIR, (Lithuanian), Rev. Stanislaus J. Swierzowski; Sr. Roberta O'Rourke, C.S.T., Pastoral Assoc.
Res., 260 E. Main St., 12010. Tel: 518-842-5481; Fax: 518-842-5481. [CEM]

2—ST. JOHN THE BAPTIST, (Polish), Rev. Stanislaus J. Swierzowski.
Res., 40 Van Derveer St., 12010. Tel: 518-842-6851. [CEM]

3—ST. JOSEPH-ST. MICHAEL-OUR LADY OF MOUNT CARMEL. Canonically merged parishes in 1980. Rev. Lawrence J. Decker.
Mailing Address: P.O. Box 699, 12010.
Office: 39 St. John St. & 58 Grove St., 12010. Tel: 518-843-3250; Fax: 518-843-4070.
Res., 35 St. John St., 12010.

4—ST. JOSEPH. Canonically merged in 1980 into St. Joseph-St. Michael-Our Lady of Mount Carmel. All inquiries should be directed to the listed address, 39 St. John St. & 58 Grove St., Amsterdam, NY 12010.

5—ST. MICHAEL THE ARCHANGEL. Canonically merged in 1980 into St. Joseph-St. Michael-Our Lady of Mount Carmel. All inquiries should be directed to the listed address, 39 St. John St. & 58 Grove St., Amsterdam, NY 12010.

6—OUR LADY OF MT. CARMEL, (Italian). Canonically merged in 1980 into St. Joseph-St. Michael-Our Lady of Mount Carmel. All inquiries should be directed to the listed address, 39 St. John St. & 58 Grove St., Amsterdam, NY 12010.

7—ST. MARY, Rev. James Gulley.
Res., 156 E. Main St., 12010. Tel: 518-842-4500; Fax: 518-842-4529. [CEM]
School—St. Mary Institute, Upper Church St., 12010. Tel: 518-842-4100; Fax: 518-842-0217.
Sisters 1; Lay Teachers 45; Students 350.

8—ST. STANISLAUS, (Polish), Revs. Walter Czechowicz; Edward Sipperly.
Res., 73 Reid St., 12010. Tel: 518-842-2771; Fax: 518-842-2771. [CEM]
School—42-44 Cornell St., 12010. Tel: 518-842-6710; Fax: 518-842-3339. Sr. M. Bernice, C.S.S.F., Prin.
Felician Sisters 3; Lay Teachers 7; Students 167.
Convent—46 Cornell St., 12010. Tel: 518-842-2621.

Athens, Greene Co., St. Patrick, Rev. Richard J. Doyle.
Res., 19 N. Franklin St., 12015. Tel: 518-945-1656.

Averill Park, Rensselaer Co., St. Henry, Rev. Brian Raiche; Deacons Frank Lukovits; John W. Novak; Robert Pasquarelli.
Res., Crystal Lake Rd., P.O. Box 550, 12018. Tel: 518-674-3818; Fax: 518-674-1043. [CEM 2]

Ballston Lake, Saratoga Co., Our Lady of Grace, Rev. Anthony C. Diacetis.
Res., 73 Midline Rd., 12019. Tel: 518-399-5713; Fax: 518-399-5713.

Ballston Spa, Saratoga Co., St. Mary, Revs. John F. French; James McDevitt.
Res., 167 Milton Ave., 12020. Tel: 518-885-7411; Fax: 518-885-6863. [CEM]
School—40 Thompson St., 12020. Tel: 518-885-7300; Fax: 518-855-7378. Sr. Ranah Phelan, C.S.J., Prin.
Sisters 1; Lay Teachers 13; Students 218.

Berlin, Rensselaer Co., Sacred Heart, Rev. Kenneth Gregory; Sr. Kenan McGowan, R.S.M., Parish Life Dir.
Res., P.O. Box 243, 12022. Tel: 518-279-4803, 658-2780 (Office); Fax: 518-279-3055.

Bolton Landing, Warren Co., Blessed Sacrament, Rev. Peter G. Young.
Res., Goodman Ave., P.O. Box 266, 12814. Tel: 518-644-3861. [CEM]

Broadalbin, Fulton Co., St. Joseph, Rev. Timothy Mangan, S.S.S.
Res., 7 North St., P.O. Box 538, 12025. Tel: 518-883-3774; Fax: 518-883-3774.
Mission—Galway, St. Mary. [CEM]

Cairo, Greene Co., Sacred Heart, Revs. Jeremiah Nunan; Sean McMahon.
Res., Mountain Ave., 12413. Tel: 518-622-3319; Fax: 518-622-0131.
Missions—East Durham, Greene Co., Our Lady of Knock Shrine, P.O. Box 223, 12423. Tel: 518-634-7448; East Durham, Greene Co., St. Mary.

Cambridge, Washington Co., St. Patrick, Revs. Thomas E. Konopka; Liam Condon; Sr. Anne Sheridan, C.S.J., Parish Life Dir.
Res., 17 S. Park St., 12816-1248. Tel: 518-677-2757; Fax: 518-677-2810. [CEM]

Canajoharie, Montgomery Co., St. Peter's and Paul's, Rev. William J. Gaffigan.
Res., 100 Cliff St., 13317-1199. Tel: 518-673-3333. [CEM]

Castleton-on-Hudson, Rensselaer Co., Sacred Heart, Rev. Thomas J. Krupa.
Res., 3 Catholic Way, 12033-1543. Tel: 518-732-2155; Fax: 518-732-4906. [CEM 2]
Missions—Schodack Landing, Assumption of B.V.M.; Schodack Landing, Shrine of St. Jude.

Catskill, Greene Co., St. Patrick, Rev. John J. Murphy. In res., Rev. Richard Jacobs.
Res., 157 Bridge St., 12414. Tel: 518-943-3150.
School—80 Woodland Ave., 12414. Tel: 518-943-2952.
Franciscan Sisters of Allegany 1; Lay Teachers 10; Students 188.
Convent—82 Woodland Ave., 12414. Tel: 518-943-5341.
Mission—Leeds, St. Bridget.

Chatham, Columbia Co., St. James, Rev. Gary Paul Gelfenbien; Deacon Peter Trawinski.
Res., 129 Hudson Ave., 12037. Tel: 518-392-4991; Fax: 518-392-9205.

Cherry Valley, Otsego Co., St. Thomas the Apostle, Rev. Donald Vittengl, Admin.
Res., 24 Maple Ave., 13320. Tel: 607-264-3779.
Mission—Springfield Center, Blessed Sacrament.

Chestertown, Warren Co., St. John the Baptist, Rev. George Fleming, Admin.
Res., Riverside Dr., P.O. Box 471, 12817. Tel: 518-494-2617; Fax: 518-494-2617.

Clifton Park, Saratoga Co., St. Edward the Confessor, Revs. John L. Cairns; John R. Lanese; Deacons Jerry Grigaitis; Walter MacKinnon.
Office: Tel: 518-371-7372; Fax: 518-371-1206.
Res., 569 Clifton Park Center Rd., 12065-4838. Tel: 518-371-9595.

Clinton Heights, Rensselaer Co., St. Mary, Rev. Jerome R. Gingras.
Res., 163 Columbia Tpke., East Greenbush, 12144-3521. Tel: 518-449-2232; Fax: 518-449-2234.
School—Tel: 518-449-2498; Fax: 518-465-1850. Sr. Patricia Lynch, R.S.M., Supr.
Lay Teachers 14; Students 158.

Cobleskill, Schoharie Co., St. Vincent de Paul, Rev. Thomas F. Berardi; Deacon Gary Surman.
Res., One Washington Heights, 12043. Tel: 518-234-2892. [CEM]
Mission—Sharon Springs, St. Mary.

Cohoes, Albany Co.,

1—HOLY TRINITY, Rev. Arthur Becker; Deacons Albert Schrempf; Konrad Raup.
Res., 122 Vliet Blvd., 12047-1842. Tel: 518-237-2373; Fax: 518-238-9427.
School—Cohoes Consolidated Schools. See separate listing.

2—ST. AGNES-ST. PATRICK. Merged with St. Marie, Cohoes to form Holy Trinity, Cohoes.

3—ST. BERNARD, Revs. Lawrence G. McTavey; Marc L. Touchette; Deacon Walter MacKinnon; Sr. Margaret Totten, C.S.J., Pastoral Assoc.
Res., 107 Canvass St., P.O. Box 137, 12047. Tel: 518-237-2721; Fax: 518-237-7980.

4—ST. JOSEPH, (French), Rev. Joseph S. Robitaille.
Res., 65 Congress St., 12047. Tel: 518-237-4241. [CEM]
School—Cohoes Consolidated Catholic Schools. See separate listing.

5—ST. MARIE. Merged with St. Agnes-St. Patrick, Cohoes to form Holy Trinity, Cohoes.

6—ST. MICHAEL, (Polish), Rev. Richard W. Dybas.
Res., 36 Page Ave., 12047. Tel: 518-237-5151; Fax: 518-233-9381. [CEM]

7—ST. RITA-SACRED HEART, Rev. John Facci, S.A.C.
Res., 50 St. Rita Ln., 12047. Tel: 518-237-4444.
Mission—Cohoes, Sacred Heart of Jesus.

Colonie, Albany Co., Our Lady of Mercy, Rev. John F. Waldron.
Res., 424 Shaker Run, 12205. Tel: 518-456-8269.
Parish Center: 26 Wilson Ave., 12205. Tel: 518-459-1272; Fax: 518-459-1285.

St. Clare, Rev. Michael T. Schmitt; Deacon George Nahm. In res., Rev. Louis Deimeke.
Res., 1947 Central Ave., 12205-4299. Tel: 518-456-3112; Fax: 518-456-1072.

Cooperstown, Otsego Co., St. Mary, Rev. John P. Rosson.
Res., 31 Elm St., 13326. Tel: 607-547-2213; Fax: 607-547-5742. [CEM 2]

Copake Falls, Columbia Co., St. Bridget, Rev. Peter Russo; Deacon Martin Stosiek.
Res., 8074 State Rte. 22, 12517. Tel: 518-329-4711; Fax: 518-329-4240. [CEM]

Corinth, Saratoga Co., Immaculate Conception, Rev. Owen F. Shanley.
Res., 409 Palmer Ave., 12822. Tel: 518-654-2113. [CEM]

Coxsackie, Greene Co., St. Mary, Rev. John L. Moyna.
Res., 80 Mansion St., 12051. Tel: 518-731-8800; Fax: 518-731-8505. [CEM]

Crescent, Saratoga Co., St. Mary, Rev. Thomas J. Hayes.
Parish Center: 86 Church Hill Rd., Waterford, 12188. Tel: 518-371-9632; Fax: 518-371-7235.

Delanson, Schenectady Co., Our Lady of Fatima, Revs. David William Mickiewicz, Admin.; Joseph Romano.
Res., 1735 Alexander Rd., P.O. Box 219, 12053-0219. Tel: 518-895-2788; Fax: 518-895-2788.

Delhi, Delaware Co., St. Peter, Rev. Joseph Manerowski.
Res., 8 Franklin St., 13753. Tel: 607-746-2503.

Delmar, Albany Co., St. Thomas the Apostle, Revs. James D. Daley; Michael Flannery; Deacon Alfred Manzella.
Res., 35 Adams Pl., 12054. Tel: 518-439-4951; Fax: 518-439-0108.
School—42 Adams Pl., 12054. Tel: 518-439-5573; Fax: 518-439-0108. Mr. Thomas Kane, Prin.
Lay Teachers 22; Students 235.

Dolgeville, Herkimer Co., St. Joseph, Rev. Leo F. Potvin; Deacon Peter Manno.
Res., 31 N. Helmer Ave., 13329. Tel: 315-429-8338. [CEM 2]

East Greenbush, Rensselaer Co., Holy Spirit, Rev. George G. St. John; Deacon William Dringus. In res., Rev. Joseph M. Siniskey.
Res., 667 Columbia Tpke., 12061. Tel: 518-477-7925.
School—Highland Dr., 12061. Tel: 518-477-5739; Fax: 518-477-5743. Sr. Maureen Moffitt, C.S.J., Prin.
Sisters 1; Lay Teachers 16; Students 252.

Fonda, Montgomery Co., St. Cecilia, Revs. Augustine Kapinus, O.F.M.Conv.; Kevin Kenny, O.F.M.Conv. In res., Rev. Kirk Holland, O.F.M.Conv.; Bro. Kenneth Lucas, O.F.M.Conv.
Res., 26 Broadway, P.O. Box 837, 12068. Tel: 518-853-4195. [CEM]

Fort Ann, Washington Co., St. Ann, Rev. William A. Gorman.
Res., 85 George St., P.O. Box 226, 12827. Tel: 518-639-5218; Fax: 518-639-4073.
Mission—South Hartford, St. Philip.

Fort Edward, Washington Co., St. Joseph, Rev. James Rosch; Deacon Donald Webster. In res., Rev. Edward N. Leroux.
Res., 164 Broadway, 12828. Tel: 518-747-5117; Fax: 518-747-3444. [CEM]

Fort Plain, Montgomery Co., St. James, Rev. Kenneth J. Swain.
Parish Office: Tel: 518-993-3822.
Res., 119 Reid St., P.O. Box 287, 13339-0287. Tel: 518-993-5523; Fax: 518-993-2105.

Frankfort, Herkimer Co., Our Lady Queen of Apostles (1995), Rev. John Yanas.
Res., 414 Frankfort St., 13340. Tel: 315-894-2025; 894-2360; Fax: 315-894-2025. [CEM]

St. Mary. Merged with SS. Peter & Paul, Frankfort, to form Our Lady Queen of Apostles, Frankfort, Jan. 8, 1995.

SS. Peter & Paul. Merged with St. Mary, Frankfort, to form Our Lady Queen of Apostles, Frankfort, Jan. 8, 1995.

Germantown, Columbia Co., Resurrection, Rev. Theodore Gerken.
Res., 9 Church Ave., P.O. Box 96, 12526. Tel: 518-537-6136; Fax: 518-537-3621. [CEM]
Mission—Linlithgo, Nativity of Our Lord.

Glens Falls, Warren Co., St. Alphonsus, Rev. George Gagnon; Deacon William F. Bazinet.
Res., 4 Crandall St., P.O. Box 2088, 12801. Tel: 518-792-1574; Fax: 518-792-6049. [CEM]
School—Merged with St. Mary's Academy to form St Mary's/St. Alphonsus Regional School.

St. Mary, Deacon F. David Powers. In res., Rev. Bernard Turner.
Res., 62 Warren St., 12801. Tel: 518-792-0989; Fax: 518-792-0251.
School—St. Mary's/St. Alphonsus Regional School, Tel: 518-792-3178; Fax: 518-792-6056.

Glenville, Schenectady Co., Immaculate Conception, Revs. J. Thomas Connery; R. Mansfield Starks, Pastor Emeritus; Anthony Ligato; Deacons August Van Patten; Michael Melanson.
Res., 400 Saratoga Rd., 12302. Tel: 518-399-9168; Fax: 518-384-3278.

Gloversville, Fulton Co., St. Mary. Canonically merged with Our Lady of Mount Carmel in 1990. See St. Mary of Mount Carmel.

St. Mary of Mt. Carmel. Consolidated from Our Lady of Mount Carmel and St. Mary in 1990. Rev. Donald Czelusniak.
Res., 149 S. Main St., 12078. Tel: 518-725-3143; Fax: 518-725-7245. [CEM]
Mission—Caroga Lake, St. Barbara.

Sacred Heart, Rev. David L. Tressic.
Res., 189 Kingsboro Ave., 12078. Tel: 518-725-9375; Fax: 518-773-3341.

Grafton, Rensselaer Co., St. John Francis Regis, Sr. Mary Kenan McGowan, R.S.M., Parish Life Dir.; Rev. Kenneth Gregory, Sacramental Min.
Mailing Address: P.O. Box 234, 12082. Tel: 518-279-4943; Fax: 518-279-4943.

Granville, Washington Co., Roman Catholic Community of Granville. Consolidated St. Mary's, All Saints, and Our Lady of Mount Carmel. Rev. Thomas Zelker.
Res., 23 Bulkley Ave., 12832. Tel: 518-642-1262.
Parish Center: All Saints House, Morrison Ave., 12832.

St. Mary. Closed. For inquiries for parish records contact the Chancery.

Greenfield Center, Saratoga Co., St. Joseph, Rev. John Weyand.
Res., 3159 Rte. 9N, P.O. Box 168, 12833. Tel: 518-893-7680.
Mission—Rock City Falls, St. Paul, Tel: 518-885-4877.

Green Island, Albany Co., St. Joseph, Rev. Donald Kelly.
Res., 131 George St., 12183. Tel: 518-273-3552.

Greenville, Greene Co., St. John the Baptist, Rev. William M. Bauer; Deacon Peter Sedlmeir.
Mailing Address: P.O. Box 340, 12083.
Office: Rte. 81, 12083. Tel: 518-966-8317; Fax: 518-966-4652.

Greenwich, Washington Co., St. Joseph, Rev. Thomas E. Konopka; Deacon Herbert Howley.
Res., 36 Bleecker St., 12834. Tel: 518-692-2159; Fax: 518-692-8706.

Guilderland, Albany Co., Christ the King, Rev. Patrick J. Butler; Deacons Timothy McAuliffe; Joseph Markham.
Res., 20 Sumpter Ave., Albany, 12203. Tel: 518-456-1644; Fax: 518-456-4696.
School—Tel: 518-456-5400. Mr. Thomas F. Gould, Prin.
Lay Teachers 14; Students 190.

St. Madeleine Sophie, Rev. James Belogi; Deacon Earle Flatt. In res., Rev. James Hayes.
Res., 3500 Carman Rd., Schenectady, 12303. Tel: 518-355-0421; Fax: 518-355-0412.
School—3510 Carman Rd., Schenectady, 12303. Tel: 518-355-3080. Miss Teresa Kovarovic, Prin.
Lay Teachers 13; Students 186.
Convent—3514 Carman Rd., Schenectady, 12303. Tel: 518-355-8052.

Hagaman, Montgomery Co., St. Stephen, Rev. Ronald Matulewicz.
Res., 51 Pawling, 12086. Tel: 518-843-2951. [CEM]

Hague, Warren Co., Blessed Sacrament, Rev. George Fleming, Admin.
Res., Hague Rd., P.O. Box 529, 12836. Tel: 518-543-8828.
Mission—Brant Lake, Warren Co., St. Teresa of Avila.

Haines Falls, Greene Co., Immaculate Conception, Rev. Anthony Motta.
Res., Mountain House Rd., 12436. Tel: 518-589-5577. [CEM]
Missions—Elka Park, Greene Co., St. Francis de Sales; Haines Falls, Greene Co., Wayside Shrine.

Hancock, Delaware Co., St. Paul the Apostle, Rev. Stephen P. Morris, Admin.
Res., 60 W. Main St., 13783. Tel: 607-637-2571; Fax: 607-637-3203. [CEM 2]

Herkimer, Herkimer Co., St. Anthony-St. Joseph, Rev. Robert Shinos. Pastoral Assocs.: Deacon Dennis Jones, Parish Operations; Ms. Christine Jones, Liturgy.
Res., 228 S. Main St., 13350. Tel: 315-866-2892; 866-6373 (Parish Office); Fax: 315-867-6186.

St. Francis de Sales, Rev. Mark Cunningham.
Parish Center: 219 N. Bellinger St., 13350. Tel: 315-866-4282; Fax: 315-866-9043.
Res., 25 Park Pl. S., 13350. Tel: 315-866-7301. [CEM]
School—220 Henry St., 13350. Tel: 315-866-4831. Sr. Rosalie Kelly, C.S.J., Prin.
Sisters of St. Joseph of Carondolet 3; Lay Teachers 10; Students 190.
Convent—One Park Pl., 13350. Tel: 315-866-4492.

Hoosick Falls, Rensselaer Co., Immaculate Conception, Rev. Philip M. Cioppa.
Res., 67 Main St., Box 269, 12090. Tel: 518-686-5064; Fax: 518-686-1625. [CEM]
School—St. Mary Academy, 4 Parsons Ave., 12090. Tel: 518-686-4314; Fax: 518-686-5957. Ms. Carol Hayes, Prin.
Lay Teachers 11; Students 164.

Hudson, Columbia Co., Church of St. Mary. Canonically merged with Our Lady of Mount Carmel and Our Lady of Perpetual Help-Sacred Heart in 1991. Rev. Winston L. Bath; Deacon Charles O'Neill. In res., Rev. Edward F. Cantwell.
Mailing Address: P.O. Box 323, 12534.
Res., 429 E. Allen St., 12534. Tel: 518-828-1334; Fax: 518-828-2783.

Our Lady of Mt. Carmel. Canonically merged with Church of St. Mary in 1991. All inquiries should be directed to P.O. Box 323, Hudson, NY 12534. Tel: 518-828-1334.

Our Lady of Perpetual Help-Sacred Heart (Polish). Canonically merged with Church of St. Mary in 1991. All inquiries should be directed to P.O. Box 323, Hudson, NY 12534. Tel: 518-828-1334.

Hudson Falls, Washington Co., Church of St. Mary's/St. Paul's (Sandy Hill). The Roman Catholic Community of Hudson Falls/Kingsbury. Rev. James B. Lonergan, V.F. In res., Rev. George Gagnon.
Res., 11 Wall St., 12839. Tel: 518-747-4823; Fax: 518-747-2265. [CEM 2]

Immaculate Heart of Mary (Sandy Hill) (French). Canonically merged with St. Paul, Hudson Falls. Now called Church of St. Mary's/St. Paul's, Roman Catholic Community of Hudson Falls/Kingsbury.

St. Paul (Sandy Hill) (French). Canonically merged with Immaculate Heart of Mary parish, Hudson Falls. Now called Church of St. Mary's/St. Paul's, Roman Catholic Community of Hudson Falls/Kingsbury.

Ilion, Herkimer Co., Annunciation, Rev. Joseph Benintende.
Res., 109 West St., 13357. Tel: 315-894-3766; Fax: 315-894-1550. [CEM]

Johnsonville, Rensselaer Co., St. Monica's Church, Rev. Gregory S. Weider; Deacon Walter Rehder.
Mailing Address: P.O. Box 300, Schaghticoke, 12154. Tel: 518-753-4554.
Res., 55 N. Lake Ave., Troy, 12180. Tel: 518-273-7602.

Johnstown, Fulton Co., St. Anthony (Slovak), Rev. James T. Fitzmaurice.
Res., 4 Nicholas St., 12095. Tel: 518-762-8176; Fax: 518-762-6920. [CEM]
Immaculate Conception (Italian), Rev. Joseph F. DiMaggio.
Res., One Warren St., 12095. Tel: 518-762-3272. [CEM]
St. Patrick, Rev. James T. Fitzmaurice.
Res., 205 Glebe St., 12095. Tel: 518-762-8775; Fax: 518-736-1775. [CEM]

Lake George, Warren Co., Sacred Heart, Revs. Joseph O'Brien; James I. Donlon.
Res., 50 Mohican St., 12845. Tel: 518-668-2046; Fax: 518-668-4377.
Mission—Queensbury, Warren Co., Our Lady of the Assumption, Ridge Rd., 12804. Tel: 518-668-2046.

Lake Luzerne, Warren Co., Holy Infancy, Rev. Charles A. Gaffigan.
Res., 323 Lake Ave., P.O. Box 470, 12846. Tel: 518-696-2625; Fax: 518-696-2625. [JC]

Latham, Albany Co., Our Lady of the Assumption, Revs. Geoffrey D. Burke; David LeFort.
Res., 498 Watervliet-Shaker Rd., 12110. Tel: 518-785-0234; Fax: 518-785-0420.
St. Ambrose, Revs. Francis J. DuBois; John P. Bertolucci; Deacon Helmut Neurohr. In res., Rev. George Phillips.
Res., 347 Old Loudon Rd., 12110. Tel: 518-785-1351; Fax: 518-785-8370.
School—Tel: 518-785-6453. Sr. Mary Presentation, P.B.V.M., Prin.
Sisters 9; Lay Teachers 10; Students 355.

Little Falls, Herkimer Co.,

1—St. Joseph. Consolidated with St. Mary and Sacred Heart to form Holy Family Parish, Little Falls.

2—St. Mary. Consolidated with St. Joseph and Sacred Heart to form Holy Family Parish, Little Falls.

3—Sacred Heart, (Polish). Consolidated with St. Joseph and St. Mary to form Holy Family Parish, Little Falls.

4—Holy Family, Rev. Charles R. Celeste; Sr. Marilyn Hayes, C.S.J., Pastoral Assoc.; Deacon Joseph DeLorenzo.
Office: 763 E. Main St., 13365. Tel: 315-823-3410; 823-3319; Fax: 315-823-2701. [CEM]

Loudonville, Albany Co., St. Pius X, Revs. Michael A. Farano, V.G.; James J. Walsh.
Res., 2 Fairview Rd., 12211. Tel: 518-462-1336; Fax: 518-462-1338.
School—Upper Loudon Rd., 12211. Tel: 518-465-4539. Nicholas Audi, Prin.
Sisters 3; Lay Teachers 19; Students 316.
Convent—Upper Loudon Rd., 12211. Tel: 518-449-1658.
St. Francis de Sales (1972), Rev. David E. Noone.
Church & Offices: One Maria Dr., 12211. Tel: 518-489-8386; Fax: 518-489-6910.
Res., 15 Exchange St., Albany, 12205. Tel: 518-489-8386.
Old Church—15 Exchange St., Albany, 12205.

Margaretville, Delaware Co., Sacred Heart, Rev. Robert H. Purcell, V.F.
Res., Academy St., 12455. Tel: 914-586-2665.
Missions—Andes, St. Ann; Roxbury, Our Lady of Good Counsel.

Mechanicville, Saratoga Co., Assumption-St. Paul, Revs. William A. Recchuti, O.S.A.; David Kelley, O.S.A. In res., Rev. Joseph Getz, O.S.A.; Deacon Arthur Canary.
Res., 52 William St., P.O. Box 308, 12118. Tel: 518-664-6196; Fax: 518-664-6782.
Convent—77 Viall Ave., 12118. Tel: 518-664-4053. Sisters of St. Joseph

Menands, Albany Co., St. Joan of Arc, Rev. William F. Jillisky; Deacon Andy Cohen.
Parish Office & Res.: 76 Menand Rd., 12204. Tel: 518-463-0378; 462-2496; Fax: 518-463-0489.

Middleburgh, Schoharie Co., St. Catherine, Rev. Thomas Holmes, Admin.
Res., 24 Wells Ave., 12122. Tel: 518-827-5132.

Mohawk, Herkimer Co., Blessed Sacrament, Rev. James Steuer.
Res., 54 E. Main St., 13407. Tel: 315-866-1752.

Morris, Otsego Co., Holy Cross, Rev. John Burns.
Res., 43 W. Main St., P.O. Box 118, 13808. Tel: 607-263-5143.
Mission—Edmeston, Nativity of B.V.M.

Nassau, Rensselaer Co., St. Mary, Rev. Antone Kandrac, O.F.M.Conv.; Deacon John Skelly.
Res., 26 Church St., P.O. Box 435, 12123. Tel: 518-766-2701; Fax: 518-766-7535. [CEM]

New Lebanon, Columbia Co., Immaculate Conception, Rev. John Close.
Church—Church and Shrine of Our Lady of Lourdes, U.S. Rte. 20, 12125. Tel: 518-794-7651; 766-5651. [CEM]
Mission—Stephentown, St. Joseph's.

Newport, Herkimer Co., St. John the Baptist, Rev. Leo F. Potvin.
Res., Main St., Box 475, 13416. Tel: 315-845-8017.
Mission—Middleville, St. Mary of the Assumption. [CEM]

North Creek, Warren Co., St. James, Rev. George Fleming.
Res., Main St., 12853. Tel: 518-251-2518. [CEM]
Mission—Pottersville, St. Pius X.

Northville, Fulton Co., St. Francis of Assisi, Rev. Robert Powhida.
Mailing Address: P.O. Box 126, 12134.
Res., 501 Bridge St., 12134. Tel: 518-863-4736; Fax: 518-863-4736.

Oneonta, Otsego Co., St. Mary, Revs. Paul A. Roman; Robert Longobucco; Mrs. Barbara Dugan Lilly, Pastoral Ministry; Susan Nesbitt, Campus Ministry.
Res., 39 Walnut St., 13820. Tel: 607-432-3920; Fax: 607-432-6437. [CEM]
School—38 Walnut St., 13820. Tel: 607-432-1450; Fax: 607-432-4826. Sr. Mary Christopher Comproski, C.R., Prin.
Religious 2; Lay Teachers 14; Students 225.
Convent—10 Irving Pl., 13820. Tel: 607-433-2220.

Palenville, Greene Co., Sacred Heart, Rev. Kieran Monahan, O.F.M.
Mailing Address: Rte. 32 A, Box 40, 12463. Tel: 518-678-9937.

Philmont, Columbia Co., Sacred Heart, Rev. Raymond Ethier.
Res., 141 Main St., 12565. Tel: 518-672-4655; Fax: 518-672-4714. [CEM]
Mission—Philmont, Pine Haven Home.

Pittstown, Rensselaer Co., St. George, Rev. John F. Riley.
Res., 134 Factory Hollow Rd., Valley Falls, 12185-2904. Tel: 518-663-8378.

Queensbury, Warren Co., Our Lady of the Annunciation, Rev. Joseph Anselment.
Res., 448 Aviation Rd., 12804. Tel: 518-793-9677; Fax: 518-793-9678.

Ravena, Albany Co., St. Patrick, Rev. Vincent J. Ciotoli.
Res., 21 Main St., 12143. Tel: 518-756-3145. [CEM]

Rensselaer, Rensselaer Co., St. John the Evangelist, Rev. R. Adam Forno; Sr. M. Andre, R.S.M., Pastoral Assoc.
Res., 20 Lawrence St., 12144. Tel: 518-465-2209; Fax: 518-449-7088. [CEM]
Parish Office: P.O. Box 256, 12144. Tel: 518-465-0482.
Convent—20 Lawrence St., 12144. Tel: 518-465-1514. Sr. M. Kathleen Turley, R.S.M., Coord. Sisters 15.
St. Joseph (1915), Rev. R. Adam Forno.
Office: 1620 Third St., 12144. Tel: 518-463-4401; Fax: 518-463-3194.
School—St. Joseph-St. John, 1641 Third St., 12144. Tel: 518-465-1151. Sr. Kathleen Pritty R.S.M., Prin.
Lay Teachers 16; Students 155.
Catechesis / Religious Programs—Students 165.

Richfield Springs, Otsego Co., St. Joseph, Rev. Terence Healy; Sr. Patricia Woolheater, C.S.J., Parish Life Dir.
Res., 35 Canadarago St., 13439-0791. Tel: 315-858-1682. [CEM]

Rotterdam, Schenectady Co., St. Gabriel the Archangel, Revs. Leo F. Markert; Michael Cournoyer, 98; Deacon Kenneth Baechel.
Res., 3040 Hamburg St., Schenectady, 12303. Tel: 518-355-6600; Fax: 518-355-6604.

Rotterdam Junction, Schenectady Co., St. Margaret of Cortona, Rev. Dennis Murphy, Admin.
Res., 2 Putnam St., 12150. Tel: 518-887-5288.

St. Johnsville, Montgomery Co., St. Patrick, Sr. Dolores Stevens, Parish Life Dir.
Res., 30 Center St., 13452. Tel: 518-568-7418.

Salem, Washington Co., Holy Cross, Rev. Liam Condon.
Res., 26 N. Main St., 12865. Tel: 518-854-7626. [CEM]

Saratoga Springs, Saratoga Co., St. Clement, Revs. James O'Blaney, C.SS.R.; James Cannon, C.SS.R.; Francis E. Sullivan, C.SS.R.; Arthur Tuttle, C.SS.R. Pastoral Assocs.: Deacons Larry Willette; Arthur Turcotte; Lee Hanson.
Res., 231 Lake Ave., 12866. Tel: 518-584-6122; Fax: 518-584-2644.
School—Lake Ave., 12866. Tel: 518-584-7350; Fax: 518-587-2623. Dr. Thaddeus Obloy, Prin.
Lay Teachers 25; Students 398.
Chapel—Gansevoort, St. Therese, Tel: 518-587-3180. Deacon Danny Boyd.
St. Peter, Rev. Robert J. LeFevre Tel: 518-584-6113.
Res., 241 S. Broadway, 12866. Tel: 518-584-2375; Fax: 518-584-5471. [CEM]

Schaghticoke, Rensselaer Co., St. John the Baptist, Rev. Gregory S. Weider; Deacon Walter Rehder.
Mailing Address: P.O. Box 300, 12154. Tel: 518-753-4554.
Res., 55 N. Lake Ave., Troy, 12180. [CEM]
Mission—Valley Falls, Our Lady of Good Counsel.

Schenectady, Schenectady Co.,

1—Church of St. Adalbert, (Polish), Rev. Carl A. Urban; Sr. Bernadette Filter, C.R., Pastoral Assoc. for Elderly.
Res., 550 Lansing St., 12303-1195. Tel: 518-346-4204; Fax: 518-346-0348. [CEM]

2—St. Anthony, (Italian), Revs. John M. Medwid; Anthony DeFranco, Pastor Emeritus; Sr. Maria Rose Querini, M.P.V., Pastoral Assoc.
Parish Office: 331 Seward Pl., 12305. Tel: 518-374-4591; Fax: 518-377-5245.
School—1840 Van Vranken Ave., 12305. Tel: 518-372-5961; Fax: 518-372-7337. Sr. Elisa Brasili, M.P.V., Prin.
Venerini Sisters 2; Lay Teachers 10; Students 168.
Convent—1834 Van Vranken Ave., 12305. Tel: 518-346-2060.

3—Sacred Heart-St. Columba, Rev. Michael Hogan; Deacon Ramon Tapia; Mr. George Vielkind, Admin. Pastoral Assocs.: Sr. Rosemary Endres, C.S.J.; Sr. Joseph Andrew Dunham, C.S.J., Coord. of Food Pantry; Sr. Norina Mastro, M.P.V.; Sr. M. Therese Van de Mosselaer, I.C.M., Parish Visitor; Judy Fitzner-Atchinson, Artist-in-Residence.
Res., 801 Stanley St., 12307. Tel: 518-377-8559; 346-0261; Fax: 518-393-9265.

4—SS. Cyril and Methodius. Closed. For inquiries for parish records contact Our Lady of Mount Carmel, Schenectady.

5—St. Helen, Rev. James J. Kane.
Res., 1803 Union St., 12309. Tel: 518-346-6137; Fax: 518-346-5390.
School—1801 Union St., 12309. Tel: 518-382-8225; Fax: 518-382-2226. Sr. Anne Marie, P.B.V.M., Prin.
Sisters of Presentation 4; Lay Teachers 15; Students 204.
Convent—40 Ray St., 12309. Tel: 518-374-7055.

6—Holy Cross, Rev. John T. Provost.
Mailing Address: and Res.: 19 N. College St., 12305. Tel: 518-374-1551; Fax: 518-372-0992.

7—Immaculate Conception, Rev. O. Robert De Martinis.
Res., 523 Thompson St., 12306. Tel: 518-382-0451; Fax: 518-382-3243.
School—Marian Academy, 520 Bradt St., 12306. Tel: 518-377-7470; Fax: 518-370-1089. Marjorie Edgar, Prin.
Religious 1; Lay Teachers 11; Students 160.

8—St. John the Baptist, Revs. Michael Hogan; Ken Tunney.
Res., 427 Franklin St., 12305. Tel: 518-374-9148; Fax: 518-374-9149. [CEM]

9—St. John the Evangelist, Revs. John T. Provost; Anthony Curran. In res., Revs. Anthony DeFranco; James R. Joslin.
Res., 802 Union St., 12308. Tel: 518-377-9607; Fax: 518-372-0992.
Office: 816 Union St., 12308. Tel: 518-372-3381; Fax: 518-372-0992.
School—806 Union St., 12308. Tel: 518-393-5331; Fax: 518-374-4663. Marie Keenan, Prin.
Lay Teachers 20; Students 267.

10—St. Joseph, (German), Rev. Michael Hogan.
Res., 225 Lafayette St., 12305. Tel: 518-374-4466; Fax: 518-374-4466. [CEM 2]

11—St. Luke, Revs. Dominic Isopo; Howard F. Manny, Pastor Emeritus.
Res., 1241 State St., 12304. Tel: 518-346-3405; Fax: 518-346-3406.
School—1252 Albany St., 12304. Tel: 518-377-7330; Fax: 518-377-7330. Sr. Ann Christi Brink, C.S.J., Prin.
Sisters of St. Joseph of Carondelet 2; Lay Teachers 13; Students 223.
Convent—1252 Albany St., 12304. Tel: 518-372-2182.
Mission—Schenectady, Schenectady Co., St. Teresa Carmelite Monastery, 428 Duane Ave., 12304.

12—St. Mary, (Polish), Rev. John T. Provost. In res., Rev. Michael W. Zakens, Pastor Emeritus.
Res., 828 Eastern Ave., 12308. Tel: 518-374-2423;. [CEM]

13—Our Lady of the Assumption, Rev. Richard A. Carlino.
Res., 3034 Ford Ave., 12306. Tel: 518-346-4926; Fax: 518-374-5670.

14—Our Lady of Fatima, Rev. Alan D. Jupin.
Res., 2216 Rosa Rd., 12309. Tel: 518-370-3136; Fax: 518-370-5137.

15—Our Lady of Mt. Carmel, (Italian), Rev. Joseph A. Mancuso.
Res., 1255 Pleasant St., 12303. Tel: 518-393-4109;

Fax: 518-393-4100.
Our Lady of Mt. Carmel Center—1274 Pleasant St., 12303. Tel: 518-372-0336.

16—ST. PAUL THE APOSTLE, Revs. George W. Brucker; Peter Pagones; Deacon Owen South. In res., Revs. Kenneth J. Tunny; Brian Cronin.
Res., 2777 Albany St., 12304. Tel: 518-377-8886; Fax: 518-377-8887.
School—16 Van Zandt St., 12304. Tel: 518-377-0506. Mr. Mark Reilly, Prin.
Lay Teachers 15; Students 130.

17—ST. THOMAS THE APOSTLE. Closed. For inquires for parish records please see Our Lady of Mt. Carmel, Schenectady.

Schoharie, Schoharie Co., St. Joseph, Rev. Thomas Holmes; Sr. Joan Curley, C.S.J., Parish Life Dir.
Res., P.O. Box 514, 12157. Tel: 518-295-8923.

Schuylerville, Saratoga Co., Notre Dame-Visitation, Rev. Joseph McKay.
Res., 18 Pearl St., 12871. Tel: 518-695-3391; Fax: 518-695-4651. [CEM 2]
Convent—127 Pearl St., 12871. Tel: 518-695-3318.
Visitation of the Blessed Virgin Mary. Closed. For inquiries for parish records contact Notre Dame de Lourdes Parish, Schuylerville.

Scotia, Schenectady Co., St. Joseph, Rev. Ronald A. Menty; Deacons Robert R. Brady; John P. Crane.
Res., 231 Second St., 12302. Tel: 518-346-4960.
Parish Center: 45 MacArthur Dr., 12302. Tel: 518-346-2316; Fax: 518-374-3383.

Sidney, Delaware Co., Sacred Heart, Revs. Gordon Polenz; Joseph J. Schuck; Deacons Thomas E. Luby; Michael R. Donnell.
Res., 15 Liberty St., 13838. Tel: 607-563-1591.
Missions—Unadilla, Otsego Co., St. Ambrose; Franklin, Delaware Co., St. Paul.

South Glens Falls, Saratoga Co., St. Michael the Archangel, Rev. Robert Nugent.
Res., 80 Saratoga Ave., 12803. Tel: 518-792-5859; Fax: 518-792-5850.

South Kortright, Delaware Co., Church of the Most Precious Blood of Jesus. Merged with Sacred Heart, Stamford.

Speigletown, Rensselaer Co., St. Bonaventure, Rev. Salvatore A. Rodino.
Res., Hillview Dr., Troy, 12182. Tel: 518-235-0337; Fax: 518-235-8726.

Stamford, Delaware Co., Sacred Heart, Rev. Joseph S. Cebula; Louise Evan, Pastoral Assoc.
Res., 27 Harper St., P.O. Box 38, 12167. Tel: 607-652-7170. [CEM]
Mission—Grand Gorge, Delaware Co., St. Philip Neri.

Stillwater, Saratoga Co., St. Peter the Apostle, Rev. James O'Neill.
Res., 271 N. Hudson Ave., 12170. Tel: 518-664-3354. [CEM]
Mission—Saratoga Lake, Saratoga Co., St. Isaac Jogues. (Summer).

Stottville, Columbia Co., Holy Family, Rev. William H. Kennedy.
Res., 2824 Atlantic Ave., 12172. Tel: 518-828-1889; Fax: 518-822-9238.

Stuyvesant, Columbia Co., Nativity of the Blessed Virgin Mary. Unassigned.
1820 Rte. 9, 12173.

Stuyvesant Falls, Columbia Co., St. Mary/Nativity, Rev. Martin De Rose.
Church—1820 Rte. 9, Stuyvesant, 12173. Tel: 518-799-5411; Fax: 518-799-3144. [CEM]

Summit, Schoharie Co., St. Anna, Rev. Edward Golding, Admin.
Res., Main St., P.O. Box 124, 12175. Tel: 518-287-1553.
Missions—Camp Summit, N.Y.S. Correctional Facility; Camp Summit, S.U.N.Y. Cobleskill College.

Tribes Hill, Montgomery Co., Sacred Heart, Rev. Augustine Kapinus, O.F.M.Conv.
Res., Box 264 Third Ave., 12177. Tel: 518-829-7301.

Troy, Rensselaer Co.,

1—ST. ANTHONY OF PADUA, (Italian), Revs. Bonaventure Bionda, O.F.M.; Giles Barreda, O.F.M.; Deacon Gerald Christiano.
Res., Friary, 28 State St., 12180-3916. Tel: 518-273-8622; Fax: 518-273-2731.
Center—107 Fourth St., 12180-3916. Tel: 518-273-8351; Fax: 518-270-0579.

2—ST. AUGUSTINE, Revs. James Spenard, O.S.A.; Joseph D. Keffer, O.S.A.; Edward J. Dixey, O.S.A.
Res., 25 115th St., 12182. Tel: 518-235-3861; Fax: 518-233-0284.
School—525 Fourth Ave., 12182. Tel: 518-235-7287; Fax: 518-237-7943. Ms. Elizabeth Allard, Prin.
Lay Teachers 12; Students 151.

3—ST. FRANCIS DE SALES, Rev. Donald J. Ophals. In res., Rev. John Lysogorski.
Res., 316 Congress St., 12180. Tel: 518-274-4232.

4—HOLY TRINITY, (Polish), Rev. Romaeus Cooney, O.Carm., Admin.
Mailing Address: St. Joseph's Priory, 416 Third St., 12180. Tel: 518-274-6720; Fax: 518-272-6503.

5—ST. JOSEPH, Revs. Romaeus Cooney, O.Carm.; Albert Pavlik, O.Carm.
Res., 416 Third St., 12180. Tel: 518-274-6720; Fax: 518-272-6503. [CEM]

6—ST. LAWRENCE. Closed. For inquiries for parish records contact St. Joseph Parish, Troy.

7—ST. MARY, Rev. Harry Donaghy.
Res., 196 Third St., 12180. Tel: 518-272-5820.

8—ST. MICHAEL THE ARCHANGEL, Rev. James M. Mackey; Deacons Frank Yankowski; Dan Ackerson.
Res., 26 Bridle Pl., East Greenbush, 12061. Tel: 518-477-5656.
Church—175 Williams Rd., 12180. Tel: 518-283-6110; Fax: 518-283-3938.
Missions—North Greenbush, Rensselaer Co., Van Rensselaer Manor, County Welfare Home; Troy, Rensselaer Co., Hallmark Nursing Home.

9—OUR LADY OF VICTORY, Revs. Randall P. Patterson; Guy A. Childs. In res., Rev. Gregory Weider.
Res., 55 N. Lake Ave., 12180. Tel: 518-273-7609; 273-7602 (Office); Fax: 518-273-0310.
School—451 Marshland Ct., 12180. Tel: 518-274-6202. Ms. Karen Snyder, Principal.
Lay Teachers 15; Students 173.

10—ST. PATRICK, Revs. Thomas J. Kelly; Cyril F. Pereira.
Res., 3027 Sixth Ave., 12180. Tel: 518-272-4666; Fax: 518-272-4666.
School—762 River St., 12180. Tel: 518-274-6502.
Sisters 2; Lay Teachers 7; Students 72.

11—ST. PAUL THE APOSTLE, Rev. James McNerney. In res., Revs. William Turnbull; Joseph Halloran.
Res., 138 Twelfth St., 12180. Tel: 518-274-4083; Fax: 518-274-4289.

12—ST. PETER, Rev. James McNerney.
Res., 2310 Fifth Ave., 12180. Tel: 518-272-2750. [CEM]

13—SACRED HEART, Revs. Gary Mercure; James Vaughan, Pastor Emeritus.
Res., 310 Spring Ave., 12180. Tel: 518-274-1363; Fax: 518-274-8720.
School—308 Spring Ave., 12180. Tel: 518-274-3655; Fax: 518-274-8270. Susan Holland, Prin.
Sisters 2; Lay Teachers 20; Students 278.

14—ST. WILLIAMS, Rev. Gary Mercure; Sr. Rita Duggan, C.S.J., Admin.
Parish Office: 310 Spring Ave., 12180. Tel: 518-273-1680.

Ushers, Saratoga Co., Corpus Christi, Revs. Edward C. Pratt; Christopher Welch; Deacons Michael Sheppeck; John Tierney; Frank Herlihy.
Mailing Address: P.O. Box 628, Round Lake, 12151-0628.
Res., 10 Southwood Dr., Ballston Lake, 12019-1302. Tel: 518-877-8506 (Office); Fax: 518-877-5620 (Office).

Valatie, Columbia Co., St. John the Baptist, Rev. John Molyn.
Res., 1025 Kinderhook St., 12184. Tel: 518-758-9401; Fax: 518-758-9409. [CEM]

Voorheesville, Albany Co., St. Matthew, Rev. Arthur A. Toole.
Res., 31 Mountain View St., 12186. Tel: 518-765-2805; Fax: 518-765-3701.

Walton, Delaware Co., St. John the Baptist, Rev. Eugene F. Willis.
Mailing Address: P.O. Box 315, 13856-0315.
Res., 15 Benton Ave., 13856-0315. Tel: 607-865-4720; 865-7394 (Office).
Mission—Downsville, Delaware Co., Holy Family.

Warrensburg, Warren Co., St. Cecilia, Rev. Joseph O'Brien; Sr. Linda Hogan, C.S.J., Parish Life Dir.
Res., 3802 Main St., 12885-1629. Tel: 518-623-3021; Fax: 518-623-3021. [CEM]

Waterford, Saratoga Co., St. Anne, Rev. Daniel J. Menihane, O.S.A.
Res., 75 Grace St., 12188. Tel: 518-237-5211; Fax: 518-233-8292.
St. Mary of the Assumption, Rev. Marshall J. Halphen, O.S.A. In res., Rev. J. Riley Havener, O.S.A.
Res., 119 Broad St., 12188-2397. Tel: 518-237-3131; Fax: 518-237-9625. [CEM]
School—St. Mary's Catholic School, 12 Sixth St., 12188. Tel: 518-237-0652; Fax: 518-233-0898. Mr. John E. Houlihan, Prin.
Lay Teachers 21; Students 327.

Watervliet, Albany Co.,

1—ST. BRIGID, Rev. Joseph Busch.
Res., 695 Fifth Ave., 12189. Tel: 518-273-2913.
School—(Regional) 700 Fifth Ave., 12189. Tel: 518-273-3321; Fax: 518-273-9355. Patricia Eldridge, Prin.
Sisters 3; Lay Teachers 18; Students 278.

2—IMMACULATE CONCEPTION, (Polish), Rev. Paul J. Antos. In res., Rev. Boleslaus M. Watroba, Pastor Emeritus.
Res., 2420 Seventh Ave., 12189. Tel: 518-273-3173. [CEM]
Convent—2425 Seventh Ave., 12189. Tel: 518-273-4423.

3—OUR LADY OF MT. CARMEL, (Italian), Rev. Emery Parillo, O.F.M.
Res., 410 23rd St., 12189. Tel: 518-273-2932.

4—ST. PATRICK, Rev. Erwin H. Schweigardt. In res., Rev. James I. Donlon.
Res., 515 19th St., Box 388, 12189. Tel: 518-273-2971; Fax: 518-273-2972.

5—SACRED HEART OF MARY, Rev. John J. Rooney.
Res., 1511 Sixth Ave., 12189. Tel: 518-273-6252.

West Taghkanic, Columbia Co., Holy Cross, Rev. Raymond Ethier, Admin.
Res., 880 Rte. 82, Elizaville, 12523. Tel: 518-851-7577.

West Winfield, Herkimer Co., St. Joseph, Rev. Terence P. Healy; Deacon Richard Brown.
Res., 305 W. Main St., P.O. Box 360, 13491-0360. Tel: 315-822-3191. [CEM]

Whitehall, Washington Co., Notre Dame des Victoires. Merged with Our Lady of Angels, Whitehall to form Our Lady of Hope, Whitehall.
Our Lady of Angels. Merged with Notre Dame des Victoires, Whitehall to form Our Lady of Hope, Whitehall.
Our Lady of Hope, Rev. William A. Gorman.
Res., 9 Wheeler Ave., 12887. Tel: 518-499-1656; Fax: 518-499-1656.
Mission—Huletts Landing, Washington Co., Our Lady of Assumption.

Windham, Greene Co., St. Theresa of Child Jesus, Revs. Donald E. Doyle; John G. O'Grady.
Res., 2 Boardman St., Whitehall, 12887. Tel: 518-499-1656; Fax: 518-499-1597. [CEM]
Res., Main St., 12496. Tel: 518-734-3352.
Mission—Ashland, St. Joseph's Chapel.

Worcester, Otsego Co., St. Joseph, Rev. Edward Golding.
Res., 181 Main St., 12197. Tel: 607-397-9373.
Mission—Schenevus, Otsego Co., St. Mary. [CEM]

Wynantskill, Rensselaer Co., St. Jude the Apostle, Rev. James E. Clark.
Res., 6 Schuyler Ct., P.O. Box 347, 12198. Tel: 518-283-1162; Fax: 518-286-2808.
School—Brookside Ave., 12198. Tel: 518-283-0333; Fax: 518-283-0475. Mrs. Barbara A. Bennett, Admin.
Lay Teachers 15; Students 153.

Chaplains of Public Institutions

ALBANY. *Albany County Jail*. Rev. Richard Broderick.
Albany County Nursing Home. Deacon Gerard O'Connor.
Albany Medical Center Hospital. Revs. David Mickiewicz; Kenneth Gregory; Michael Cournoyer; Robert Hohenstein.
Capital District Psychiatric Center. Rev. James R. Joslin.
Columbia County Jail. Rev. Theodore Gerken.
Memorial Hospital. Rev. John T. Kelly.
New York State Department of Corrections. Rev. James Hayes, Chief of Chaplains.
St. Peter's Hospital. Chaplains: Rev. John Tallman; Sr. Joyce Houle, S.N.J.M.; Sr. Patricia Mills, S.N.J.M.; Sr. Gail Waring, R.S.M.; Mr. Younas Azad; Ms. Sally Conklin.
University Heights Nursing Home. Sr. Jane Carr, R.S.M., Chap.
Veterans' Administration Hospital. Rev. John Minkler.

COMSTOCK. *Great Meadows Correctional Institution*. Rev. Michael Miller.

COXSACKIE. *Coxsackie Correctional Facility*. Rev. Richard Shaw.
Greene Correctional Facility. Rev. Joseph Romano.
Regional Medical Unit. Rev. John L. Moyna.

GLENS FALLS. *Glens Falls Hospital*. Chaplains: Rev. O. Robert DeMartinis; Sr. Helen LeClerc, C.S.J.
Hudson Correctional Facility. Rev. Edward F. Cantwell, Chap.

SCHENECTADY. *Ellis Hospital*. Rev. John Varno, Chap.
Hallmark Nursing Home. Deacon Earle Flatt, Chap.
Schenectady County Nursing Home. Sr. Clare Pelkey, C.S.J., Chap.; Deacon Robert Brady.

TROY. *Samaritan Hospital*. Rev. Anthony Maione; Deacons Frank Lukovits; Dana Ackerson.
Seton Health. Rev. William Turnbull.
Van Rensselaer Manor. Rev. James M. Mackey; Deacon Dana Ackerson, Chap.

WILTON. *Mount McGregor Correctional Facility*. Rev. Richard Severson.

Special Assignment:
Most Rev.—
Broderick, Edwin B., 900 Park Ave., New York, NY 10021
Reverend Fathers—
Berberian, David, Tribunal, 40 N. Main Ave., Albany, NY 12203
Broderick, Richard J., Prison Chap., 2431 22nd St., Troy, NY 12180
Cantwell, Edward F., Chap., Brookwood and Hudson Correctional Facility, 429 E. Allen St., Hudson, NY 12534
Chiaramonte, Anthony, Consultation Center, 790 Lancaster St., Albany, NY 12203
Connolly, John, Retirement Board, Liason to Retired Clergy, Pastoral Consultant to Diocesan Cemeteries
Cotugno, Joseph, Dir. Diaconate, 40 N. Main Ave., Albany, NY 12203
DeGiovine, Christopher, College of St. Rose, 432 Western Ave., Albany, NY 12203
Deimeke, L. Edward, Administrative Advocate for Priests, 40 N. Main Ave., Albany, NY 12203
Donlon, James I., Judicial Vicar, Tribunal, Pastoral Center, 40 N. Main Ave., Albany, NY 12203
Donnolly, Robert, Chap. Sisters of Mercy, St. Catherine of Siena, 40 Collins Pl., Albany, NY 12208
Dworak, Joseph J., Chap., St. Mary's Hospital, 427 Guy Park Ave., Amsterdam, NY 12010
Falletta, Joseph, Hispanic/Latino Apostolate, One William St., P.O. Box 512, Kinderhook, NY 12106
Farano, Michael A., Vicar Gen. & Dir. Society of the Propagation of Faith, 2 Fairview Rd., Loudonville, NY 12211
Fisher, Martin, (On Sabbatical), 465 State St., Albany, NY 12203
Gregory, Kenneth, Chap., Albany Medical Center, Albany, NY 12208
Gulley, Anthony D., Prof. College of St. Rose, 607 Central Ave., Albany, NY 12206
Hayes, James, Chief of Chaplains NYS Dept. of Corrections, St. Madeline Sophie, 3500 Carmen Rd., Schenectady, NY 12303
Joslin, James R., Chap. Capitol District Psychiatric Center, St. John Evangelist, 802 Union St., Schenectady, NY 12308
Jung, Pius-Bio, Korean Apostolate, 10 Lodge St., Albany, NY 12207-2196
Kacerguis, Edward, Slavin House, 2008 19th St., Troy, NY 12181
Kampfer, Gerald D., Altamont Program/North Country Ministry, Sonoma Pt., Loon Lake, Chestertown, NY 12817
Kane, James J., Dir., Pastoral Center, Ecumenical & Interreligious Affairs, 40 N. Main Ave., Albany, NY 12203
Kelly, John T., Chap. Memorial Hospital, 600 N. Blvd., Albany, NY 12010
Konopka, Thomas E., Vocations Office, 40 N. Main Ave., Albany, NY 12203
Leskovar, Richard J., Chap. St. Clare's Hospital, 600 McClellan St., Schenectady, NY 12304
Lysogorski, John, AIDS Ministries/Albany Med., 39 Grandview Dr., Latham, NY 12110
Maione, Anthony J., Chap. Samaritan Hospital, 465 State St., Albany, NY 12203
Malecki, John, Chap., Teresian House, 200 Washington Ave. Extension, Albany, NY 12203
Marbury, Cabell B., Vice Prin. Bishop Maginn High School, 99 Slingerland St., Albany, NY 12202
McCloskey, Francis, Charismatic Ministry, Box 63, Copake Falls, NY 12517
McDevitt, James, Seton Health, 1300 Massachusetts Ave., Troy, NY 12180
Mickiewicz, David, Chap., Albany Medical Hospital, New Scotland Ave., Albany, NY 12208
Miller, Michael, Prison Chap., 9 Wheeler Ave., Whitehall, NY 12887
Minkler, John, Chap. Veterans Administration Hospital, 113 Holland Ave., Albany, NY 12208
Ntsiful-Amissah, Kofi, Black Apostolate, 50 Thornton St., Albany, NY 12206
O'Brien, Leo P., Vicar Gen., 900 Madison Ave., Albany, NY 12208
Pereira, Cyril F., 3027 Sixth Ave., Troy, NY 12180
Phelan, Thomas, RPI (Christ Sun of Justice), 5 Whitman Ct., Troy, NY 12180
Romano, Joseph R., St. Catherine, 40 Collins Pl., Albany, NY 12208
Severson, Richard, Chap., Mt. McGregor Correctional Facility, P.O. Box 2264, Wilton, NY 12866
Shaw, Richard, Chap. Green Correctional Facility, St. Helen's Rectory, 1803 Union St., Schenectady, NY 12309
Shuck, Joseph J., Scouting Chap., 1011 State Hwy. 7, Unadilla, NY 13849
Smith, Paul, Sacramental Min., St. Lucy's, Altamount, 37 Parkwood St. E., Albany, NY 12203
Sullivan, Peter J., III, Adjutant Vicar Judicial Tribunal, Pastoral Center, 40 N. Main Ave., Albany, NY 12203
Tallman, John, Chap. St. Peter's Hospital, St. Catherine of Siena, 40 Collins Pl., Albany, NY 12208
Testa, Richard, 512 Third Ave., Troy, NY 12182
Tunny, Kenneth J., St. Paul's Rectory, 277 Albany St., Schenectady, NY 12304
Varno, John N., Chap. Ellis Hospital, 1011 Nott St., Schenectady, NY 12308
Vosko, Richard, Liturgical Design Consultant, 4611 Foxwood Dr., P.O. Box 2217, Clifton Park, NY 12605
Walsh, James J., Vocation Office, 40 Main Ave., Albany, NY 12203

On Duty Outside the Diocese:
Reverend Fathers—
Allie, Stanley J., Sacred Heart Church, 1201 Bogard Rd., Wasilla, AK 99654-6523
Casey, Liam C., St. Francis Hospital, 114 Woodland St., Hartford, CT 06105
Fragomeni, Richard, 5401 S. Cornell Ave., Chicago, IL 60615-5698
Hurst, Thomas, S.S., 820 Gale Dr., Campbell, CA 95008
Kostek, John, Our Lady of Victory Church, 60 William St., New York, NY 10005
Nusbaum, Daniel C., Mt. St. Mary College, Emmitsburg, MD 21727
O'Grady, John F., Barry University, 11300 N.E. Second Ave., Miami, FL 33161
Polewczak, Michael J., Holy Trinity Parish, 2161 Griffith Dr., Orangeburg, SC 29118
Redmond, Paul V., Mt. St. Mary College, Emmitsburg, MD 21727
Testa, David, Holy Spirit Monastery, Ave Maria College, 300 W. Forest Ave., Ypsilanti, MI 48197

Military Chaplains:
Reverend Fathers—
Estabrook, Joseph, Fleet Chap. (NOIC), Commander-in-Chief, Capt., CHC, USN, Pacific Fleet, Pearl Harbor, HI 96860-7000
Minkler, John, Chaplain's Office, V.A. Hospital, Holland Ave., Albany, NY 12208
O'Keeffe, L. Joseph, 66 Birch Hill Dr., Fort Richardson, AK 99505
Rutherford, Donald L., 301 Marshall Rd., Carlisle, PA 17013

Unassigned:
Reverend Fathers—
Bentley, David, 40 N. Main Ave., Albany, NY 12203

Leave of Absence:
Reverend Fathers—
Allman, Mark
Harrison, Timothy
Rossi, Desmond

Retired:
Reverend Monsignors—
Jones, John L., St. Teresa's Rectory, 435 New Scotland Ave., Albany, NY 12208-2397
Manny, Howard F., St. Luke's Rectory, 1241 State St., Schenectady, NY 12304
Reverend Fathers—
Ahern, Bernard, 4418 Poppy Tree Ln., Jacksonville, FL 32223
Amato, Joseph, 5320 53rd St. E. V-16 Windmill Manor, Bradenton, FL 34203
Baniak, Walter, 540 Second St., Troy, NY 12180
Barker, Joseph, 316 Congress St., Troy, NY 12180
Bondi, Paul, 167 Milton Ave., Ballston Spa, NY 12020
Caldara, John N., 3028 Myrtle Ave., Schenectady, NY 12306
Campagnone, Nicholas, Wesley Health Care Center, 131 Lawrence St., Hathorn Residence, Room 117, Saratoga Springs, NY 12866
Ciani, Francis P., 856 Warner Rd., Valley Stream, NY 11580
Ciulek, Joseph, c/o Konik, 126 2nd Ave., Gloversville, NY 12078
Clemente, Michael, 4906 Brittany Dr. S., Apt. #613, St. Petersburg, FL 33715
Clune, Gerald F., 9466 Navajo Tr., Morongo Valley, CA 92256
Cox, Paul, P.O. Box 134, Kattskill Bay, NY 12844
Crandall, William, 9 King St., Waterford, NY 12188
Cyvas, Matthew, 555 68th Ave., St. Petersburg Beach, FL 33706
D'Agostino, Joseph, 6 Bircher Ave., Poughkeepsie, NY 12601
De Caprio, John, 105 Florida Ave., Amsterdam, NY 12010
De Franco, Anthony, 802 Union St., Schenectady, NY 12308
De Pascale, Daniel, CDR, 2750 Blarrita Ct., Ponte Vedra Beach, FL 32802
Delos, Bernard M., 4044 N.W. 19th St., G 109, Lauderhill, FL 33313
Di Cerbo, Almerico F., Teresian House, 200 Washington Ave. Ext., Albany, NY 12203
Douglas, Louis, 1880 Superfine Ln., #8, Wilmington, DE 19802
Downs, Richard J., 77 Crescent Dr., Albany, NY 12208
Dunbar, Francis, 20 1/2 Williams St., Whitewall, NY 12887
Dwyer, Morris, Holy Cross, 43 W. Main St., P.O. Box 118, Morris, NY 13808
Engel, Paul, P.O. Box 506, Schoharie, NY 12157
Esmond, William, Ledgewood Village, Rte. 149, 17 Ledgewood Dr., Lake George, NY 12845
Fitzpatrick, Edward, 32 Joseph St., Saratoga Springs, NY 12866
Flanigan, Thomas, 2310 5th Ave., Troy, NY 12180
Gilchrist, Francis J., St. Casimir, 324 Sheridan Ave., Albany, NY 12206
Girzone, Joseph, 8 Leesome Ln., Altamont, NY 12209
Grabys, Joseph, Matularitis Nursing Home, 10 Thurber Rd., Putnam, CT 06260
Halloran, Joseph, St. Paul the Apostle Rectory, 138 12th St., Troy, NY 12180
Husselbeck, Francis E., Our Lady of Mercy Life Center, 2 Mercy Ln., Guilderland, NY 12084
Ianotti, Pascal, 15 Steadwell Ave., Amsterdam, NY 12010
Jonaitis, Peter, 217 N. Kingsboro Ave., Gloversville, NY 12078
Keefe, John A., 40 Collins Pl., Albany, NY 12208
Kelly, James, 30 Allouette Way, Carson City, NV 89701
Keyrouze, Joseph, 321 W. Sand Lake Rd., Rte. 150, Wynantskill, NY 12198
Klementowicz, Chester, 30 William St., Amsterdam, NY 12010
Konisky, Edward, 64 Parkwin Dr., Delmar, NY 12054
Kranch, Peter V., Teresian House, 200 Washington Ave. Ext., Albany, NY 12203
Lamanna, Alfred, The Prospect Inn, 20 N. Prospect St., Apt. J, Herkimer, NY 13350
Lemoyne, William, 29 Burgoyne St., Schuylerville, NY 12871
Leroux, Edward N., 8 Clark St., South Glens Falls, NY 12803
Lynch, Patrick J., P.O. Box 68, Lansingburgh Sta., Troy, NY 12182
Malecki, John, Teresian House, 200 Washington Ave. Ext., Albany, NY 12203
Manny, Howard, St. Luke's Rectory, 1241 State St., Schenectady, NY 12304
McNamara, John, Our Lady of Hope Residence, One Jeanne Jugan Ln., Latham, NY 12110
Morrill, Giles, P.O. Box 6566, Delray Beach, FL 33482-6566
Mulcahy, Howard J., McAuley Residence, 308 S. Manning Blvd., Albany, NY 12208
Mulhall, J. Gregory, Our Lady of Hope, One Jeanne Jugan Ln., Latham, NY 12110
Nabozny, Peter, 9 Morley Dr., Apt. F, Ballston Spa, NY 12020
Nowak, Vincent A., 4025 N. Federal Hwy., Apt. 119A, Ft. Lauderdale, FL 33308-5501
Phillips, George, 347 Old Loudon Rd., Latham, NY 12110
Phillips, John, Teresian House, 200 Washington Ave. Ext., Room 240B, Albany, NY 12203
Piechocki, Raymond S., Mt. Loretto Rest Home, 301 Swart Hill Rd., Amsterdam, NY 12010
Roos, John, 90 Elm St., Apt. 7, Cobleskill, NY 12043
Roos, Robert E., 10 Stewart St., Albany, NY 12205
Ryan, Edward, P.O. Box 277, Stamford, NY 12094
Sidoti, Anthony, 496 Delaware Ave., Albany, NY 12209
Siniskey, Joseph M., 667 Columbia Tpke., East Greenbush, NY 12061
Sise, John, 64 Pioneer St., Apt. C., Box 293, Cooperstown, NY 13346
Starks, R. Mansfield, 400 Saratoga Rd., Scotia, NY 12302
Stone, Carl, P.O. Box Owlshead, Owlshead, NY 12969
Tartaglia, Paul, (June-Nov.), 465 State St., Albany, NY 12203
Titta, Santino, 19 Juniper Pl., Grant City, NY 10306
Tremblay, Nellis, P.O. Box 134, Kattskill Bay, NY 12844
Vail, Thomas, 76 Moreland St., Little Falls, NY 13365
Vaughan, James, 310 Spring Ave., Troy, NY 12180
Watroba, Boleslaus M., 2420 Seventh Ave., Watervliet, NY 12189

Whalen, John P., 1614 Pacham Rd., Silver Spring, MD 20903
Whalen, William F., Beverwyck Apartments, 40 Autumn Dr., Apt. 147, Slingerlands, NY 12159
Zakens, Michael W., St. Mary's Church, 828 Eastern Ave., Schenectady, NY 12308

Permanent Deacons:
Ackerson, Dana J., Van Rensselaer Manor Nursing Facility; St. Francis de Sales, Troy
Baechel, Kenneth, St. Gabriel, Rotterdam & Office of Prayer and Worship
Bazinet, William, St. Alphonsus, Glens Falls
Beck, Gary, Leave of Absence
Beckman, Martin L., Nativity/St. Mary's, Stuyvesant
Beuerman, David, Outside Diocese
Bickmore, Henry, (Retired)
Boyd, Danny S., St. Therese Mission, Gansevoort
Brady, Robert, Glendale Nursing Home & St. Joseph, Scotia
Brett, William, Chap., Our Lady of Mercy Center, Guilderland; Legion of Mary
Brown, Richard Dr., St. Joseph, West Winfield
Canary, Arthur, Assumption-St. Paul, Mechanicville
Carbone, Michael S., St. Joseph, West Winfield
Christiano, Gerald, (Retired)
Cioppa, Richard, Leave of Absence
Cohen, Andrew, St. Joan of Arc, Menands
Crane, John, St. Joseph, Scotia; Glendale Nursing Home
Culkin, John J., Sr., Holy Cross, St. Mary & St. John the Evangelist, Schenectady
DeLorenzo, Joseph, Holy Family, Little Falls
DeMauro, Gerald, Family Life Office; St. James, Albany
Desormeaux, David, Leave of Absence
Devine, Patrick, (On Duty Outside Diocese)
Donnell, Michael, Sacred Heart, Sidney
Dringus, William, Holy Spirit Church, East Greenbush
Fitzgerald, William, Blessed Sacrament, Albany
Flatt, Earle, St. Madeleine Sophie & Hallmark Nursing Home, Rotterdam
Gaffney, William, St. Vincent de Paul, Albany
Gallipeo, Paul, St. Mary, Glens Falls
Garcia, Angel, St. Patrick's Hispanic Community
Gaul, William H., Jr., Diocesan Office of Scouting; St. John Newman Residence, Saratoga Springs
Gil, Joseph, St. Patrick, Albany; Hispanic Outreach Services
Glennon, Dr. John E., Health Care Advocate for HIV/AIDS, Great Meadow Correctional Facility; St. Mary's, Granville
Gorman, William A., Admin., Sacred Heart, Albany
Grigaitis, Jerry, St. Edward the Confessor, Clifton Park
Hall, Charles H., Capitol District Psychiatric Center, Albany
Hanson, Lee, Saratoga Hospital Nursing Home; St. Celement's, Saratoga
Herlihy, Frank, Ministry of Service and Liturgy; Corpus Christi, Ushers; Ministry of Liturgy, Sacred Heart, Lake George
Hewitt, William, St. Peter's, Saratoga
Hook, J. Neil, St. Margaret Mary, Albany
Howley, Herbert J., St. Joseph's, Greenwich
Jones, Dennis, St. Anthony and St. Joseph, Herkimer
Kratz, Russell J., Educational/Sacramental Preparation, St. John's/St. Ann's, Albany
Ladouceur, Gerald, St. Catherine of Siena, Albany
Lavin, Cyril, (On Duty Outside the Diocese)
Leonard, Mark J., St. Madeleine Sophie, Schenectady
Luby, Thomas T., Rural Ministry, Sacred Heart, Sidney
Lukovits, Frank, St. Henry, Averill Park & Dir. Deacon Personnel
MacKinnon, Walter, St. Edward, Clifton Park
Manno, Peter, St. Joseph's, Dolgeville
Mansfield, E. Gregory, St. Paul's, Mechanicville
Manzella, Alfred R., St. Thomas, Delmar
Markham, Joseph, Christ the King, Albany
McAuliffe, Timothy, Holy Cross, Albany; Dir. Deacon Administration
McGarry, Frank, Leave of Absence
McNamara, Eugene, Outside Diocese
Melanson, Michael, Immaculate Conception, Glenville
Monscko, Walter G., (Retired)
Nahm, George H., St. Clare's, Colonie
Neurohr, Helmut N., St. Ambrose, Latham
Novak, John W., (Retired)
O'Connell, Thomas, St. Peter's, Delhi
O'Neill, Charles, St. Mary's, Hudson
Pasquarelli, Robert, St. Henry's, Averill Park
Picher, Gary, Holy Infancy, Lake Luzerne
Powers, David F., St. Mary's, Glen Falls
Pudney, E. Jack, Leave of Absence
Quinn, Peter, Immaculate Conception, New Lebanon
Raup, Konrad, Holy Trinity, Cohoes
Rehder, Walter, St. John the Baptist, Schaghticoke; St. Monica, Johnsonville
Roemer, Paul W., St. Patrick's, Catskill
Rucinski, Robert, (Retired)
Salamone, Samuel, Our Lady Queen of Apostles, Frankfort
Santana, Richard, (On Leave of Absence)
Schickel, Frank, Holy Cross, St. Mary and St. John the Evangelist, Schenectady
Schrempf, Albert G., Holy Trinity, Cohoes; Seton Health, Troy
Sedlmeir, Peter, St. John the Baptist, Greenville
Sheehan, George D., Rural Preaching, Delaware County; St. Peter, Delhi
Sheppeck, Michael, Corpus Christi, Ushers
Skelly, John, St. Mary, Nassau & Our Lady of Mercy Center
Solar, Richard, St. Anthony, Johnstown
South, Owen D., St. Paul the Apostle, Schenectady
Stosiek, Martin, St. Bridget, Copake Falls; Rural Affairs Coord., Diocese of Albany
Sullivan, Raymond, Cathedral of the Immaculate Conception, Albany
Surman, Dr. Gary, St. Vincent, Cobleskill
Szarejko, Walter, St. John the Baptist, Newport
Tapia, Raymon, Sacred Heart, Schenectady
Tierney, John, Corpus Christi, Ushers; County and State Prison
Trawinski, Peter, St. James, Chatham
Turcotte, Arthur W., St. Clement, Saratoga Springs
Vaillancourt, Leonard, Outside Diocese
VanPatten, August, Immaculate Conception, Glenville
Webster, Donald, St. Joseph, Fort Edward
Whalen, Charles, Outside Diocese
Willette, Lawrence, St. Clement, Saratoga Springs
Witko, George, St. Mary, Albany
Yankowski, Frank, Eden Park Nursing Home & St. Michael, Troy
Zoltowski, Gregory, Our Lady of Grace, Ballston Lake

INSTITUTIONS LOCATED IN THE DIOCESE

[A] SEMINARIES, RELIGIOUS OR SCHOLASTICATES

CATSKILL. *St. Anthony Friary*, 24 Harrison St., P.O. Box 487, 12414. Tel: 518-943-3451. Order of Friars Minor. Revs. Steven M. Sysol, O.F.M., Guardian, Dir. Novices; Owen Angeloni, O.F.M.; Francis Solanus DeLorenzo, O.F.M., Vicar; Frederick Fusco, O.F.M.; Kieran Mohahan, O.F.M., Dir. Health Care; John B. Frisoli, O.F.M.; Benedict Carrozza, O.F.M.; Reginald Semiraro, O.F.M.; Bros. Thomas Hollowood, O.F.M., Assoc. Dir. Novices; John Golisano, O.F.M.; Emery Kish, O.F.M.; Lawrence Stumpo, O.F.M. Novices: Bros. Stephen Alimonti, O.F.M.; Amelio Lautieri, O.F.M.; Bert Hanthey, O.F.M.; Joel Mroz, O.F.M.; Orlando Ruiz, O.F.M.; Joseph Samoska, III, O.F.M.; Jose Yatko, O.F.M.

RENSSELAER. *Conventual Franciscan Friars.* Immaculate Conception Province, Provincialate, Office of the Treasurer, P.O. Box 629, 12144. Tel: 518-472-1016; Fax: 518-472-1013.
E-mail: BJJDolan@aol.com
Web site: conventualfranciscanfriars.com
(Corporate Name: Order Minor Conventuals). 517 Washington Ave., 12144. Friars Minor Conventual. Tel: 518-472-1000; Fax: 518-472-1013. In res. Revs. Canice Connors, O.F.M.Conv., Minister Prov.; Paul Lininger, O.F.M.Conv., Treas.; Bros. Andre Picotte, O.F.M.Conv.; John Joseph Dolan, O.F.M.Conv., Guardian & Prov. Sec.; Stephen Merrigan, O.F.M.Conv., Archivist, Elder Care Dir. Priests 2; Brothers 3.

[B] COLLEGES AND UNIVERSITIES

ALBANY. *The College of Saint Rose*, 432 Western Ave., 12203. Tel: 518-454-5111; 800-657-8556; Fax: 518-458-5447
For a complete listing, refer to the Colleges and Universities section.

Maria College, 700 New Scotland Ave., 12208
For a complete listing, refer to the Colleges and Universities section.

St. Bernard's Institute at Albany, 40 N. Main Ave., 12203. Tel: 518-453-6760; Fax: 518-453-6793.
E-mail: stbernardsinstitute@rcda.org
For a complete listing, refer to the Colleges and Universities section.

LOUDONVILLE. *Siena College*, 12211. Tel: 518-783-2300; Fax: 518-783-4293.
Web site: www.siena.edu
For a complete listing, refer to the Colleges and Universities section.

[C] HIGH SCHOOLS, DIOCESAN

ALBANY. *Bishop Maginn High School*, 99 Slingerland St., 12202. Tel: 518-463-2247; Fax: 518-463-9880.
E-mail: maginn@capital.net
Web site: www.capital.net/~Maginn
Mr. Joseph Grasso, Prin.; Rev. Cabell B. Marbury, Vice Prin. Priests 1; Sisters 3; Lay Teachers 28; Students 450.

AMSTERDAM. *Bishop Scully High School*, Upper Church St., 12010. Tel: 518-842-4100.

GLENS FALLS. *St. Mary-St. Alphonsus Regional Catholic School*, 10-12 Church St., 12801. Tel: 518-792-3178; Fax: 518-792-6056.
E-mail: albsmsa@rcdaschools.org
Pastors: Revs. Martin Fisher; George Gagnon. Lay Teachers 26; Students 315.

SARATOGA SPRINGS. *Saratoga Central Catholic High School*. (Grades 7-12), 247 S. Broadway, 12866. Tel: 518-587-7070; Fax: 518-587-0678.
E-mail: albscc@rcdaschools.org
Web site: www.saratogacatholichigh.org
Mr. Edwin Hammond, Jr., Prin.; Rev. Christopher Welch, Chap. Sisters 1; Lay Teachers 24; Students 255.

SCHENECTADY. *Notre Dame-Bishop Gibbons School*. (Coed Grades 6-12), 2600 Albany St., 12304. Tel: 518-393-3131; Fax: 518-370-3817.
E-mail: info@ndbg.org
Bro. Paul Beaudin, C.F.C., Prin. Conducted by the Congregation of Christian Brothers. Brothers 3; Sisters 2; Lay Teachers 30; Students 392.

TROY. *Catholic Central High School*. (Grades 7-12), 625 Seventh Ave., 12182. Tel: 518-235-7100; Fax: 518-237-1796.
E-mail: albcchs@rcdaschools.org
Web site: www.cchstroy.org
Sr. Carolyn Schanz, C.S.J., Pres.; Sr. Katherine Arseneau, C.S.J., Prin. Sisters 5; Lay Teachers 48; Students 575.

[D] HIGH SCHOOLS, PRIVATE

ALBANY. *Academy of the Holy Names Upper, Middle and Lower Schools*, 1073 New Scotland Rd., 12208. Tel: 518-438-7895. Sr. Constance Casey, S.N.J.M., Pres. (PreK-12); Ms. Mary Anne Vigliante, Prin. (Grades 9-12); Sr. Virginia Dunn, S.N.J.M., Prin. (Grades PreK-8); Rev. Paul Smith. Sisters 9; Lay Teachers 50; Students 480.

The Christian Brothers' Academy of Albany, 12 Airline Dr., 12205. Tel: 518-452-9809; Fax: 518-452-9804.
Web site: www.cba-albany.org
Brothers of the Christian Schools. Mr. David McGuire, Prin. JROTC College Prep. Program. Brothers 8; Lay Teachers 38; Students 482.

The Doane Stuart School. (Grades Nursery-12). Ecumenical Day School. Coed., 12202. Tel: 518-465-5222; Fax: 518-465-5230.
Web site: www.doanstuart.org
Religious of the Sacred Heart and the Episcopal Diocese of Albany. Faculty 30; Students 245.

Mercy High, Private School for Girls, c/o 40 N. Main Ave., 12203.

TROY. *LaSalle Institute*, 174 Williams Rd., 12180. Tel: 518-283-2500; Fax: 518-283-6265.
E-mail: info@lasalleinstitute.org
Web site: lasalleinstitute.org
Brothers of the Christian Schools. Bro. Christopher Belleman, F.S.C., Prin. Brothers 9; Lay Teachers 49; Students 609.

[E] ELEMENTARY SCHOOLS, PRIVATE

LOUDONVILLE. *Saint Gregory's School*, 121 Old Niskayuna Rd., 12211-1399. Tel: 518-785-6621; Fax: 518-782-1364. Francis X. Foley, Jr., Headmaster. An independent Catholic day school for boys staffed by laity (Nursery-8). Girls admitted in Nursery and Kindergarten classes. Lay Teachers 22; Students 199.

[F] CONSOLIDATED ELEMENTARY SCHOOLS

ALBANY. *Cathedral Academy*, 75 Park Ave., 12202. Tel: 518-449-5232.

COHOES. *Cohoes Catholic School*, One St. Marie's Ln., 12047. Tel: 518-235-5202; Fax: 518-235-8568.
E-mail: albccs@rcdaschools.org
Mrs. Sally Jovell, Prin. Sisters 1; Lay Teachers 9; Students 158.

GLEN FALLS. *St. Mary's/St. Alphonsus Regional Catholic School.* 12 Brookwood Dr., Queensbury, 12804. Tel: 518-792-3178; Fax: 518-792-6056.
E-mail: albsmsa@rcdaschools.org
Mr. Roger Marcy, Prin.

WATERFORD. *St. Mary's School.* (Grades K-8), 12 Sixth St., 12188. Tel: 518-237-0652; Fax: 518-233-0898.
E-mail: wccs@rcdaschools.org
Jack Houlihan, Prin. Lay Teachers 20; Students 327.

[G] RESIDENTIAL INSTITUTIONS FOR CHILDREN & ADOLESCENTS

ALBANY. *LaSalle School, Inc.*, 391 Western Ave., 12203. Tel: 518-242-4731; Fax: 518-242-4747.
E-mail: information@lasalle-school.org
Web site: www.lasalle-school.org
For a complete listing, refer to the Special Care Facilities section.

Saint Anne Institute, 160 N. Main Ave., 12206. Tel: 518-437-6500; Fax: 518-437-6555
For a complete listing, refer to the Special Care Facilities section.

Saint Catherine's Center for Children, 40 N. Main Ave., 12203. Tel: 518-453-6700; Fax: 518-453-6712.
Web site: www.st-cath.org
For a complete listing, refer to the Special Care Facilities section.

WATERVLIET. *St. Colman's Home*, 12189. Tel: 518-273-4911; Fax: 518-273-3312
For a complete listing, refer to the Special Care Facilities section.

[H] GENERAL HOSPITALS

ALBANY. *Mercycare Corporation, St. Peter's Hospital*, 315 S. Manning Blvd., 12208. Tel: 518-454-1540
For a complete listing, refer to the Hospitals section.

St. Peter's Health Care Services, 315 S. Manning Blvd., 12208. Tel: 518-454-1084; Fax: 518-454-1520.
E-mail: sboyle@stpetersburghealthcare.org
For a complete listing, refer to the Hospitals section.

AMSTERDAM. *St. Mary's Hospital*, 427 Guy Park Ave., 12010. Tel: 518-842-1900; Fax: 518-842-0107.
E-mail: capobiancop@SMHA.org
For a complete listing, refer to the Hospitals section.

SCHENECTADY. *St. Clare's Holding Company, Inc.*, 600 McClellan St., 12304. Tel: 518-347-5660; Fax: 518-347-5522.
E-mail: jowens@stclares.org
Web site: stclares.org
For a complete listing, refer to the Hospitals section.

St. Clare's Hospital, 600 McClellan St., 12304. Tel: 518-382-2000; Fax: 518-347-5522.
E-mail: jowens@stclares.org
Web site: stclares.org
For a complete listing, refer to the Hospitals section.

TROY. *Seton Health System, Inc.*, 1300 Massachusetts Ave., 12180. Tel: 518-268-5000; Fax: 518-268-5257.
E-mail: info@setonhealth.org
Web site: setonhealth.org
For a complete listing, refer to the Hospitals section.

[I] SERVICES FOR ELDERLY

ALBANY. *St. Peter's Licensed Home Care Agency*, 310 S. Manning, 12208. Tel: 518-525-6000. Sr. Jean McGinty, R.S.M.

SMILE, Independent Living Services, Inc. at Catholic Charities, 100 Slingerland St., 12202. Tel: 518-432-0089. James McCaffrey, Dir.

GERMANTOWN. *Carmelite System for the Aged and Infirm, Inc.*, 646 Woods Rd., 12526-5617. Tel: 518-537-7500. Reverend Mother Mary Suzanne Sapa, O.Carm., Chair.

[J] NURSING AND AGED HOMES

ALBANY. *McAuley Living Services*, 310 S. Manning Blvd., 12208. Tel: 518-437-8400; Fax: 518-437-8418.
E-mail: mhulihan@stpetershealthcare.org
For a complete listing, refer to the Special Care Facilities section.

Teresian House, (1974) 200 Washington Ave. Ext., 12203. Tel: 518-456-2000; Fax: 518-456-1142.
E-mail: info@teresianhouse.com
Web site: www.teresianhouse.com
For a complete listing, refer to the Special Care Facilities section.

Villa Mary Immaculate, 301 Hackett Blvd., 12208. Tel: 518-482-3363; Fax: 518-482-8136.
E-mail: rcassano@mercycare.com
For a complete listing, refer to the Special Care Facilities section.

AMSTERDAM. *Mt. Loretto Nursing Home*, 302 Swart Hill Rd., 12010. Tel: 518-842-6790; Fax: 518-843-5993
For a complete listing, refer to the Special Care Facilities section.

CASTLETON. *Resurrection Nursing Home*, 12033. Tel: 518-732-7617; Fax: 518-732-4211.
E-mail: rnh@ix.netcom.com
For a complete listing, refer to the Special Care Facilities section.

CATSKILL. *St. Joseph's Villa*, 38 Prospect Ave., 12414. Tel: 518-943-5701; Fax: 518-943-5033
For a complete listing, refer to the Special Care Facilities section.

GERMANTOWN. *Avila Institute of Gerontology, Inc.*, 600 Woods Rd., 12526. Tel: 518-537-5000; Fax: 518-537-4579
For a complete listing, refer to the Special Care Facilities section.

LATHAM. *Our Lady of Hope Residence* Little Sisters of the Poor, Jeanne Jugan Ln., 12110. Tel: 518-785-4551; Fax: 518-785-3331.
For a complete listing, refer to the Special Care Facilities section.

TROY. *St. Mary's Woodland Village, Inc.*, Upper Tibbits Ave., 12180. Tel: 518-273-2040; Fax: 518-273-1542
For a complete listing, refer to the Special Care Facilities section.

[K] APARTMENTS FOR ELDERLY

ALBANY. *Bishop Broderick Apartments Housing Development Fund Co., Inc.*, 50 Prescott St., 12205. Tel: 518-869-7441; Fax: 518-869-0443
For a complete listing, refer to the Special Care Facilities section.

C.S.C. Housing Development Fund Co., Inc., dba Sanderson Court Senior Apts./ De Paul Housing Management.
E-mail: mkscsa@aol.com 6 Carondelet Dr. Watervliet, 12189. Tel: 518-459-0185; 782-1123; Fax: 518-782-1125.
For a complete listing, refer to the Special Care Facilities section.

Cusack Community Service Corporation, 40 N. Main Ave., 12203. Tel: 518-453-6650
For a complete listing, refer to the Special Care Facilities section.

DePaul Housing Management Corp., 41 N. Main Ave., 12203. Tel: 518-459-0183; Fax: 518-459-0202.
E-mail: ddobdep@aol.com
For a complete listing, refer to the Special Care Facilities section.

St. Vincent Apartments Housing Development Fund Co., Inc., 475 Yates St., 12208. Tel: 518-482-8915; Fax: 518-489-1220
For a complete listing, refer to the Special Care Facilities section.

CLIFTON PARK. *Halfmoon Housing Development Fund Co., Inc.*, 54 Katherine Dr., 12065. Tel: 518-383-2705; Fax: 518-383-6350.
E-mail: jmsbhsa@aol.com
For a complete listing, refer to the Special Care Facilities section.

NORTH GREENBUSH. *S.J. Housing Development Fund Company, Inc. dba St. Jude's Apartments* 50 Dana Ave. Wynantskill, 12198. Tel: 518-283-5690; Fax: 518-283-5893.
For a complete listing, refer to the Special Care Facilities section.

RENSSELAER. *East Greenbush Housing Development Fund Co., Inc. dba Branson Manor Senior Apartment*, 3 Grandview Dr., 12144. Tel: 518-283-8280; Fax: 518-283-8292
For a complete listing, refer to the Special Care Facilities section.

SLINGERLANDS. *Marie-Rose Manor HDFCI*, 100 Marquis Dr., 12159. Tel: 518-459-0204; Fax: 518-459-0527
For a complete listing, refer to the Special Care Facilities section.

WATERVLIET. *Carondelet Commons Senior Apartments*, 2 Carondelet Dr., 12189. Tel: 518-783-0444; Fax: 518-783-0456
For a complete listing, refer to the Special Care Facilities section.

Fontbonne Manor Housing Development Fund Company, Inc., c/o DePaul Management, 10 Carodelet Dr., 12189. Tel: 518-782-2780; Fax: 518-782-2778
For a complete listing, refer to the Special Care Facilities section.

Italian-American Housing Development Fund Co., Inc. dba Cabrini Acers Senior Apts., 4 Carondelet Dr., 12189. Tel: 518-785-0050; Fax: 518-785-0110
For a complete listing, refer to the Special Care Facilities section.

[L] MONASTERIES AND RESIDENCES OF PRIESTS AND BROTHERS

ALBANY. *Vincentian Fathers Residence*, 110 Menands Rd., 12204-1499. Tel: 518-433-1003. Revs. Stephen J. India, C.M., Supr.; Alfred R. Pehrsson, C.M. Priests 2.

LAKE GEORGE. *St. Mary of the Lake*, P.O. Box 31, 12845. Tel: 518-668-5594. c/o 40 N. Main Ave., Albany, 12203. Rev. Ken McGuire, Dir. Summer retreat of the Paulist Fathers.

RENSSELAER. *Franciscan Mission House*, Washington Ave., 12144. Tel: 518-465-0062; Fax: 518-465-3673.
E-mail: fmhbj@aol.com
Web site: www.thefma.org
Promotion Center for Order's Missions. Bro. James Amrhein, O.F.M.Conv., Dir. & Guardian; Revs. Antone Kandrac, O.F.M.Conv.; Simon Mohr, O.F.M.Conv.; Angelus Netzer, O.F.M.Conv.

Provincialate, Immaculate Conception Friary - Order of Friars Minor Conventual (1872). (Immaculate Conception Province), P.O. Box 629, 12144. Tel: 518-472-1000; Fax: 518-472-1013.
E-mail: bjjdolan@aol.com
Web site: conventualfranciscanfriars.com
Revs. Canice Connors, O.F.M.Conv., Min. Prov.; Paul Lininger, O.F.M.Conv., Treas.; Bros. Stephen Merrigan, O.F.M.Conv., Archivist, Elder Care Dir.; John Joseph Dolan, O.F.M.Conv., Guardian & Prov. Sec. (Asst. Provincial); Andre Picotte, O.F.M.Conv.
(Corporate Name: Order Minor Conventuals, Inc.).

SARATOGA SPRINGS. *St. John Neumann Residence*, 233 Lake Ave., 12866-2729. Tel: 518-584-7500; Fax: 518-581-8421. Redemptorist Priests and Brothers of the Baltimore Province. Most Rev. Bernard Nolker, D.D.; Very Rev. Arthur P. Gildea, C.SS.R., Rector; Revs. George H. Bridge, C.SS.R.; Robert Gaugler, C.SS.R.; Joseph Oberle, C.SS.R.; Alfred C. Rush, C.SS.R.; Thomas F. O'Toole, C.SS.R.; Richard Knappik, C.SS.R.; John McGuire, C.SS.R.; John Guiniven, C.SS.R.; Bernard Power, C.SS.R.; James Lacey, C.SS.R.; John Salamon, C.SS.R.; Charles Fehrenbach; James Ferris, C.SS.R.; Edward Tardiff, C.SS.R.; Joseph Ellison, C.SS.R.; Francis Freel, C.SS.R.; George Deimel, C.SS.R.; William Heanue, C.SS.R.; Mark Knoll, C.SS.R.; John Ruef, C.SS.R.; William Biffar, C.SS.R.; Charles Gildea, C.SS.R.; Bros. Nelson (Louis) Hoerner, C.SS.R.; John Bosco Hammond, C.SS.R.; David Skarda, C.SS.R.; Gilbert Hunter, C.SS.R.; William Fritsch, C.SS.R.

VALATIE. *St. Joseph.* Residence for retired Holy Cross Brothers and Priests. 495 Maple Ln., 12184. Tel: 518-784-9481; Fax: 518-784-9494.
E-mail: broffssley@hotmail.com
Bros. Francis Feeley, C.S.C., Supr.; Peter A. Martin, C.S.C., Admin.; Rev. Gregory R. Roy, S.J., Chap.

[M] CONVENTS AND RESIDENCES FOR SISTERS

ALBANY. *Convent of the Sacred Heart*, Kenwood, 799 S. Pearl St., 12202-1027. Tel: 518-465-3341; Fax: 518-465-3663.
E-mail: pmeier@kenwoodconvent.com
Convent and Retirement Center for Religious of the Sacred Heart. Sr. Marie Buonato, R.S.C.J., Area Dir.; Sr. Loretta Somerville, R.S.C.J., Coord. of the Pax Christi Community; Sr. Priscilla Meier, R.S.C.J., Campus Admin.; Rev. Christopher DeGiovine, Chap. (Corporate Name: Female Academy of the Sacred Heart of Albany). Sisters 80.

Franciscan House, Mill Hill Sisters. Regional House, 1006 Madison Ave., 12208-2600. Tel: 518-482-1991; Fax: 518-482-8320. Sr. Joan Kerley, F.M.S.J. Sisters 5.

Franciscan Sisters of Mary, 4 Katherine St., 12801-3839. Tel: 518-761-0976.

Sisters of Mercy of the Americas Albany Regional Community, 310 S. Manning Blvd., 12208. Tel: 518-437-3000; Fax: 518-437-3030.
E-mail: bhines@mercycare.com
Administrative Offices of Sisters of Mercy. Sr. Margaret J. Straney, R.S.M., Pres.; Sr. Helen Dillon, R.S.M., Councilor; Sr. Peg Sullivan, R.S.M., Councilor; Rev. Robert J. Donnelly, Chap. Sisters 159.

Sisters of the Holy Names of Jesus and Mary, Province Center, 1061 New Scotland Ave., 12208-1198. Tel: 518-489-5469; Fax: 518-489-5804.
E-mail: snjmny@aol.com
(Corporate Name: Sisters of the Holy Names of Jesus and Mary of the New York Province, Inc.). Sr. Grace Diaz, S.N.J.M., Province Dir.

Academy of the Holy Names of New York, 1075 New Scotland Ave., 12208. Tel: 518-438-7895; Fax: 518-438-7368.

CASTLETON-ON-HUDSON. *Provincial House, Juniorate and Novitiate of the Sisters of Resurrection*, 35 Boltwood Ave., 12033-1011. Tel: 518-732-2226; Fax: 518-732-2898.
E-mail: crsister@ix.netcom.com
Web site: www.resurrectionsisters.org
Sr. Jeanne Marie Harla, Prov. Supr.; Sr. M. Krystyna, C.R., Local Supr.; Sr. Dolores Palermo, C.R., Dir. Novices. Sisters 24. Chaplain's Residence: 34 Boltwood Ave. Tel: 518-732-7831.

CLIFTON PARK. *Sisters of Charity of St. Louis Convent*, Blue Spruce Apartments, 706 Solomon Ave., 12065-3725. Tel: 518-371-0247; Fax: 518-371-1206.

GERMANTOWN. *St. Teresa's Motherhouse*, Avila on the Hudson, 600 Woods Rd., 12526-5617. Tel: 518-537-5000; Fax: 518-537-5226. Motherhouse and Novitiate. Carmelite Sisters for the Aged and Infirm. Mother M. Suzanne Sapa, O.Carm., Supr. Gen.; Rev. Joseph E. Finch, Chap. Sisters 27; Novices 2; Postulants 1.

Postulation Office. Tel: 518-537-5000; Fax: 518-537-5226. Mother M. Angeline Teresa, O.Carm., Servant of God; Rev. Mario Esposito, O.Carm.; Sr. M. Gabriel, O.Carm., Coord. of the Cause.

GLEN FALLS. *Franciscan Sisters of Mary*, 4 Katherine St., 12801-3839. Tel: 518-761-0976.

LATHAM. *Provincial House of the Sisters of St. Joseph of Carondelet (Albany Province)*, 12110-4799. Tel: 518-783-3500; Fax: 518-783-5209.
Web site: csjalb.org
Rev. Geoffrey D. Burke, Chap. Province Leadership Team: Sr. Lauren Vandermark, C.S.J.; Sr. Danielle Bonetti, C.S.J.; Sr. Laura Anne Bufano, C.S.J.; Sr. Mary Catherine Ryan, C.S.J.; Sr. Miriam Dorothy Ukeritis, C.S.J.; Sr. Christine Partisano, C.S.J.; Sr. Rita Duggan, C.S.J.; Sr. Mary O'Brien, C.S.J.; Sr. Miriam Ukeritis, C.S.J.; Sr. Lauren Van Dermark, C.S.J. Sisters 561.

MENANDS. *De Paul Provincial House*. (Corporate Name: Daughters of Charity of St. Vincent de Paul, N.E. Prov.), 96 Menands Rd., 12204. Tel: 518-462-5593; Fax: 518-462-5024.
E-mail: dcinfo@dc-northeast.org
Web site: wwww.dc-northeast.org
Sr. Louise Gallahue, D.C., Prov. Supr.; Rev. James E. Smith, C.M., Prov. Dir.

SCHENECTADY. *Monastery of St. Teresa of Jesus of Discalced Carmelites*, 428 Duane Ave., 12304. Mother Mary St. John of the Cross, O.C.D., Prioress. Professed Sisters 12.

WATERVLIET. *St. Colman's Convent*, 12189. Tel: 518-273-4911; Fax: 518-273-3312. Motherhouse and Novitiate of Sisters of the Presentation of the B.V.M. Mother M. Carmel, P.B.V.M., Mother Gen.; Rev. Kenneth Gregory, Chap.

[N] HOUSES OF PRAYER AND RETREAT HOUSES

ALBANY. *Abba House of Prayer*. A nonprofit corporation. 647 Western Ave., 12203. Tel: 518-438-8320.

AURIESVILLE. *Jesuit Retreat House at Aurissville*. Tel: 518-853-3033; Fax: 518-853-3051.
E-mail: jesuit@martyrshrine.org
Web site: www.martyrshrine.org
Mailing Address: Shrine of Our Lady of Martyrs, c/o Rev. John G. Marzolf, S.J., 12016.

Shrine of Our Lady of Martyrs, 12016. Tel: 518-853-3033; Fax: 518-853-3051.
E-mail: jesuit@martyrshrine.org
Web site: www.martyrshrine.org
National Shrine of the Jesuit Martyrs of North America. Revs. John G. Marzolf, S.J., Supr. & Dir.; John J. Paret, S.J., Asst. Dir. & Vice-Postulator Cause of Kateri Tekakwitha; John M. Doolan, S.J. Priests 3.

CHESTERTOWN. *The Priory*, 12817. Tel: 518-494-3733; Fax: 518-494-3733. Sr. Constance M. Messitt, C.S.J., Dir.; Sr. Francis Anne Gilchrist, C.S.J., Co-Dir.

FONDA. *Blessed Kateri Guest House*, Rte. 5, P.O. Box 627, 12068. Tel: 518-853-3646; Fax: 518-853-3371. Rev. Kevin Kenny, O.F.M.Conv., Dir.

GLENS FALLS. *Wellsprings*. A Program for Christian Ministers. 93 Maple St., 12801. Tel: 518-792-3183; Fax: 518-792-3184.
E-mail: info@wsprings.org
Web site: www.wsprings.org
Holistic Sabbatical/Renewal/Retreat Center. Sr. Margaret Picha, S.S.N.D., Dir.; Michael Laratonda, F.M.S., Assoc. Dir.

MIDDLEBURGH. *Bethany Ministries*, 26C Mill Ln., P.O. Box 420, 12212. Tel: 518-827-4699.
E-mail: bethmin@midtel.net
Web site: www.midtel.net/~bethmin

PARADOX. *Pyramid Life Center*. Corporation name: Albany Catholic Youth Association, Inc., 12858. Tel: 518-585-7545.
E-mail: monphy@juno.com
Web site: pyramidlife.com
Summer, fall and winter retreat house, located at Pyramid Lake.

SCHENECTADY. *Dominican Spiritual Life Center*. Corporation Name: Dominican Congregation of St. Catherine De Ricci. 1945 Union St., 12309. Tel: 518-393-4169; Fax: 518-393-4525.
E-mail: dslc@acmenet.net
Jeanne Qualters, Admin. Residence Facilities for 45; Non-resident Facilities for 90 to 100.

STILLWATER. *Still Point House of Prayer*, Rte. 423, Box 53, 12170. Tel: 518-587-4967; Fax: 518-587-4967.
E-mail: stillpt423@aol.com
House of Prayer operated by The Community of Still Point, Inc. Year-round hermitages, retreats, sabbaticals, holistic and interfaith programs. Sr. Lillian Needham, S.S.J., Dir.; Sr. Mary Ellen Curtin, C.S.J., Assoc. Dir.

UNADILLA. *Gilead, Inc.*, 1011 State Hwy. 7, 13849. Tel: 607-563-3713.
E-mail: tngilead@aol.com
Web site: www.gilead.org
Eucharistic Community.

VALATIE. *St. Joseph Spiritual Life Center*, 495 Maple Ln., 12184. Tel: 518-784-9481; Fax: 518-784-9494.
Web site: bpmcsc.berk.com
Bros. Francis Feeley, Dir.; Peter Martin, Admin.

[O] SHELTERS FOR WOMEN

ALBANY. *Arbor House*, 302 Western Ave., 12203. Tel: 518-489-6030
For a complete listing, refer to the Special Care Facilities section.

[P] YOUTH TREATMENT FACILITIES

ALBANY. *Hospitality House Therapeutic Community Inc.*, 271 Central Ave., 12206. Tel: 518-434-6468; Fax: 518-434-6302.
E-mail: timber2@alephia.com
A private, not-for-profit, residential treatment program for young people, 16 to 35 years old, with a history of drug and/or substance abuse.

ALTAMONT. *Bernard and Caroline Cobb Memorial School*. Day Care Center for infants through 12 years old and special education day program for students 5-21 years. Sisters of the Presentation Day Care Center, 100-300 Mt. Presentation Way., 12009. Tel: 518-861-6446; Fax: 518-861-5228.
E-mail: cobbschool@aol.com

[Q] SHRINES

ALTAMONT. *La Salette Shrine*, Leesome Ln., P.O. Box 680, 12009-0680. Tel: 518-861-8159; Fax: 518-861-7052.
Web site: www.lasalette.com
Rev. Jeffrey L'Arche, M.S., Dir; Bro. Anthony Casso, M.S., Asst. Dir.
Corporate Titles: Missionaries of Our Lady of La Salette Inc., Altamont, NY; La Salette Shrine, Altamont, NY.

FONDA. *The National Shrine of Blessed Kateri Tekakwitha and Friary*, P.O. Box 627, 12068. Tel: 518-853-3646; Fax: 518-853-3371.
E-mail: kkenny@klink.net
Web site: klink.net~kkenny
Rev. Kevin Kenny, O.F.M.Conv., Shrine Dir. & Guardian; Bro. Kenneth Lucas, O.F.M.Conv., Assoc. Dir.; Rev. Augustine Kapinus, O.F.M.Conv., Local Pastor. In res. Rev. Kirk Holland, O.F.M.Conv.

[R] CAMPUS MINISTRY

ALBANY. *New York State University at Albany*. (Albany Collegiate Interfaith Center, Inc.) with offices at Albany-Chapel House. 1400 Washington Ave., 12222. Tel: 518-489-8573; Fax: 518-489-8573.
E-mail: sroleary@concentric.net
Sr. Maureen O'Leary, F.S.P., Chap.

COBLESKILL. *State University of New York College of Agricultural & Technology at Cobleskill*, Main St., P.O. Box 124, 12175. Rev. Thomas F. Berardi.

DELHI. *State University of New York College of Agricultural & Technology at Delhi*, St. Peter Rectory, 8 Franklin St., 13753. Tel: 607-746-2503. Rev. Joseph Manerowski.

GLENS FALLS. *Adirondack Community College*. c/o 40 N. Main Ave., Albany, 12203. Tel: 518-793-9677.

HUDSON. *Columbia-Greene Community College*, P.O. Box 1000, 12534. Tel: 518-828-4181.

LOUDONVILLE. *Siena College*, 12211. Tel: 518-783-2332; Fax: 518-783-4293.
Web site: www.siena.edu
Rev. James Sabak, O.F.M., Chap. Assoc. Campus Ministers: Bro. Michael J. Harlan, O.F.M.; Laura Graeber; Rev. Kenneth Cox, Protestant Min.; Ms. Claire Morgan, Vol. Coord.; Ms. Judy Dougherty, Sec.

ONEONTA. *New York State University at Oneonta and Hartwick College*. Corporate Title: Oneonta Newman Foundation. Newman House, 77 Spruce St., 13820. Tel: 607-432-4400; Fax: 607-432-4400.
E-mail: newman@dmcom.net
Web site: www.dmcom.net/newmanhouse/
Susan Nesbitt, Campus Min. Tel: 607-432-4400; Maureen DeBonis, Pres. of Foundation, Bd. of Dir.; Rev. Robert Longobucco, Sacramental Min.; Joan Hale, Admin. & Sec.

SARATOGA. *Skidmore College*, 815 N. Broadway, 12866. Tel: 518-580-5682; Fax: 518-580-5555. Rev. Christopher Welch, Sacramental Min.; Sr. Rosemary J. Sqroi, r.s.m., Chap.

SCHENECTADY. *Union College, Catholic Campus Ministry*, 12308. Tel: 518-388-6087.
E-mail: forsheyg@union.edu
Mr. George Forshey, Chap. Religious Programs Office of Union College, Silliman Hall.

TROY. *Hudson Valley Community College*, 80 Vandenburgh Ave., 12180. Tel: 518-629-7168.
E-mail: cuneoros@hvcc.edu
Sr. Rosemary Ann Cuneo, C.R., Campus Min.

Rensselaer Polytechnic Institute. Tel: 518-276-6518; Fax: 518-276-2040.
E-mail: phelan@rpi.edu
Web site: www.rpi.edu/dept/chaplains/public
Office of the Resident Catholic Chaplain, Rm. 3514 Rensselaer Union, 12180. Tel: 518-276-6518; Fax: 518-274-5945. Chaplains: Rev. Edward Kacerguis; Margaret Leathem.

The Rensselaer Newman Foundation, Rm. 3514 Rensselaer Union, 12180. Tel: 518-276-6518; Fax: 518-274-5945. Michael Duffy, Pres.

University Parish of Christ Sun of Justice. Rev. Thomas Phelan, Chapel & Cultural Center, 2008 19th St., 12180. Tel: 518-274-7793; Fax: 518-274-5945. William McQuiston, Dir.

Russell Sage College, Campus Ministry Office, Rm. #304 Student Center, 12180. Tel: 518-244-4507.
E-mail: cuneor@sage.edu
Sr. Rosemary Ann Cuneo, C.R.

[S] MISCELLANEOUS LISTINGS

ALBANY. *Birthright of Albany*, 586 Central Ave., 12206. Tel: 518-438-2978; Fax: 518-438-2978.

Burke Community Service Corp., Inc., 40 N. Main Ave., 12203. Tel: 518-453-6623; Fax: 518-453-6792.
E-mail: noel.olsen@rcda.org

The Cathedral Restoration Corp., 40 N. Main Ave., 12203. Tel: 518-463-4447. Rev. William Pape, Sec. & Treas.

Diocesan HIV/AIDS Services, 100 Slingerlands St., 12202. Tel: 518-449-3581; Fax: 518-426-3662. Joseph Kerwin, Exec. Dir.; Rev. John Lysogorski, Pastoral Care.

Emmaus House. Albany Catholic Worker Community, 35 N. Main Ave., 12203.

Family Rosary Albany Office. Sponsored by Congregation of Holy Cross (Eastern Prov.). 16 Cornell Ave., 12207. Tel: 518-452-3082; Fax: 518-452-3956.
E-mail: mission@familyrosary.org
Web site: www.familyrosary.org
Laetitia Rhatigan, Albany Mission Dir.

Crusade for Family Prayer, Inc. Sponsored by Congregation of Holy Cross (Eastern Prov.). P.O. Box 1527, Guilderland, 12084. Tel: 518-452-3082; Fax: 518-452-3956. Rev. John P. Phalen, C.S.C., Pres.

The Foundation of the Roman Catholic Diocese of Albany, New York, Inc., 40 N. Main Ave., 12203. Tel: 518-453-6680; Fax: 518-453-6793. Mr. Jack Manning, Dir.

Kenwood Braille Association, Inc., Kenwood Convent of the Sacred Heart, 799 S. Pearl St., 12202. Tel: 518-465-3341. Sr. Marie Buonato, R.S.C.J.

LaSalle Albany, Inc., De La Salle Rd., 12208. Bros. Michael Corry, F.S.C., Chm.; Stephen McCabe, F.S.C., Vice Chm.; E. James Stolz, F.S.C., Sec.

LSC Housing Development Fund Company, Inc., 41 N. Main Ave., 12203. Tel: 518-452-2552. Charles J. Tobin, III Esq.

The Marillac-N.E. Charitable Trust, 96 Menands Rd., 12204-1499. Tel: 518-462-5596; Fax: 518-462-5192.
E-mail: patbouza@yahoo.com

McCloskey Community Service Corporation, 40 N. Main Ave., 12203. Tel: 518-453-6683; Fax: 518-453-6792. Phyllis Hathaway, Exec. Dir.

New York State Catholic Conference, 465 State St., 12203. Tel: 518-434-6195; Fax: 518-434-9796.
E-mail: info@nyscatholicconference.org
Web site: www.nyscatholicconference.org
John M. Kerry, Exec. Dir.

New York State Catholic Healthcare Council, 465 State St., 12203. Tel: 518-434-6195; Fax: 518-434-9796.
E-mail: info@nyscatholicconference.org
Web site: www.nyscatholicconference.org
Ronald Guglielmo, Exec. Sec.

New York State Council of Catholic Charities Directors, 465 State St., 12203. Tel: 518-434-3482; Fax: 518-434-9796.
E-mail: dhamilton@nyscatholicconference.org
Web site: www.nyscatholicconference.org
David Hamilton, Exec. Sec.

New York State Council of Catholic School Superintendents. New York State Council of Diocesan Directors of Religious Education. 465 State St., 12203. Tel: 518-434-6195; Fax: 518-434-9796.
E-mail: jcultrara@nyscatholicconference.org
Web site: www.nyscatholicconference.org
James D. Cultrara, Exec. Sec.

Noonan Community Service Corporation, 40 N. Main Ave., 12203-1422. Rev. Paul Roman, Contact Person.

St. Francis Chapel, Wolf Road Shoppers Park, 145A Wolf Rd., 12205. Tel: 518-783-4156; Fax: 518-783-4195. Order of Friars Minor Province of the Most Holy Name of Jesus.

St. Yon Charitable Trust, 391 Western Ave., 12203-1401. Tel: 518-242-4731. Bro. James Martino, F.S.C.

Sisters of the Holy Names of Jesus & Mary of the New York Province, Inc. Continuing Support Charitable Trust to provide for the needs of the Tutwiler Clinic, Tutwiler, Mississippi. 1061 New Scotland Ave., 12208-1198. Tel: 601-345-8334; Fax: 518-489-5804.
E-mail: snjmny@aol.com

Sisters of the Holy Names of Jesus and Mary. Community Support Charitable Trust. 1061 New Scotland Ave., 12208-1198. Tel: 518-489-5469; Fax: 518-489-5804.
E-mail: snjmny@aol.com

Support Fund Trust of the Province of St. Thomas of Villanova, c/o 40 N. Main Ave., 12203.

CASTLETON-ON-HUDSON. *C.C.M. of Schodack, Inc.,* 92 S. Main St., 12033.

COHOES. *Apostolate for the Suffering,* c/o St. Rita Rectory, 50 St. Rita Pl., 12047. Tel: 518-237-4444. Rev. Mario Pacini, S.A.C.

GERMANTOWN. *Oneness in Peace Center, Inc.,* 49 Main St., 12526. Tel: 518-537-5678. Co-Directors: Sr. Vergilia Jim, O.S.F.; Claire Langie.

LATHAM. *The Sister M. Athanasia Gurry Trust Fund of the Sisters of St. Joseph,* 385 Watervliet-Shaker Rd., 12110-4799. Tel: 518-783-3538; Fax: 518-783-1123.

NISKAYUNA. *Villa Fusco Child Day Care Center,* 955 Balltown Rd., 12309. Tel: 518-377-1613; Fax: 518-377-1613.
E-mail: villafusco@juno.com
Sr. Josephine Alderuccio, D.C.P.B., Supr. Daughters of Charity of the Most Precious Blood. Capacity 14.

RENSSELAER. *Franciscorps, Inc.,* 517 Washington Ave., 12144. Tel: 518-472-1000.

Order of Friars Minor Conventual Immaculate Conception Province Charitable Trust. (Established 1990), P.O. Box 629, 12144. Tel: 518-472-1000; Fax: 518-472-1013.
E-mail: plininger@aol.com
Web site: conventualfranciscanfriars.com
Rev. Paul Lininger, O.F.M.Conv., Trustee.

SCHENECTADY. *St. Luke's Guild,* c/o St. Clare Hospital, 600 McClellan St., 12304. Tel: 518-347-5760.

Secular Order of Discalced Carmelites, 428 Duane Ave., 12304-2691. David W. Phelan, Pres.

TROY. *Catholic School Administrators' Association of New York State,* 406 Fulton St., Ste. 512, 12180. Tel: 518-273-1205; Fax: 518-273-1206.
E-mail: nysadm@aol.com
Web site: www.csaanys.org
Sr. Carol Cimino, S.S.J., Exec. Dir.

[T] SUMMER CAMPS

ALBANY. *Camp Scully,* 100 Slingerland St., 12202. Tel: 518-426-3511; 283-1617 (Snyders Lake); Fax: 518-426-3662. Summer Address, 24 Camp Scully Way, Wynantskill, 12198. Tel: 518-283-1617; Fax: 518-286-1943. A program of Catholic Charities of Albany and Rensselaer Counties. Summer Residential Camp for children 7-14. Under direction of Catholic Charities of the Diocese of Albany. Financed by local Youth Bureaus, the Albany Catholic Diocese, USDA Summer Program and by contributions. Capacity 110 per week for 7 weeks.

TROY. *Troy CYO Day Camp,* Box 867, 237 Fourth St., 12180. Tel: 518-274-2630. Sponsored by Troy Youth Organization, Inc. for Boys and Girls, ages 5-12 yrs. Raymond R. Piscitelli, Exec. Dir.; Mara A. Wager, Prog. Dir.; Jeanne Mailloux, Exec. Sec.

RELIGIOUS INSTITUTES OF MEN REPRESENTED IN THE DIOCESE

For further details refer to the corresponding bracketed number in the Religious Institutes of Men or Women section.

[0140]—*The Augustinians.*—O.S.A.
[0330]—*Brothers of the Christian Schools.* (New York Prov.).—F.S.C.
[0600]—*Brothers of the Congregation of Holy Cross.* (Eastern Prov.).—C.S.C.
[0270]—*Carmelite Fathers & Brothers.*—O.Carm.
[0310]—*Congregation of Christian Brothers.* (Eastern US).—C.F.C.
[0220]—*Congregation of the Blessed Sacrament.*—S.S.S.
[1330]—*Congregation of the Mission.* (Eastern Prov.).—C.M.
[0480]—*Conventual Franciscans.* (Prov. of Immaculate Conception).—O.F.M.Conv.
[0520]—*Franciscan Friars.* (Most Holy Name Prov.).—O.F.M.
[0690]—*Jesuit Fathers and Brothers.* (New York Prov.).—S.J.
[0720]—*The Missionaries of Our Lady of La Salette.* (Prov. of Our Lady of Seven Dolors).—M.S.
[1030]—*Paulist Fathers.* (New York).—C.S.P.
[0610]—*Priests of the Congregation of Holy Cross.* (Eastern Prov.).—C.S.C.
[1070]—*Redemptorist Fathers.* (Baltimore Prov.).—C.SS.R.
[0990]—*Society of the Catholic Apostolate.*—S.A.C.

RELIGIOUS INSTITUTES OF WOMEN REPRESENTED IN THE DIOCESE

[0330]—*Carmelite Sisters for the Aged and Infirm.*—O.Carm.
[2980]—*Congregation of Notre Dame.*—C.N.D.
[0760]—*Daughters of Charity of St. Vincent de Paul.*—D.C.
[0740]—*Daughters of Charity of the Most Precious Blood.*—D.C.P.B.
[0420]—*Discalced Carmelite Nuns.*—O.C.D.
[1070-17]—*Dominican Sisters - Congregation of St. Catherine de Ricci.*—O.P.
[1105]—*Dominican Sisters of Hope.*—O.P.
[1170]—*Felician Sisters.*—C.S.S.F.
[1180]—*Franciscan Sisters of Allegany, New York.*—O.S.F.
[1415]—*Franciscan Sisters of Mary.*—F.S.M.
[1425]—*Franciscan Sisters of Peace.*—F.S.P.
[1190]—*Franciscan Sisters of the Atonement.*—S.A.
[2340]—*Little Sisters of the Poor.*—L.S.P.
[1410]—*Mill Hill Sisters (Franciscan Missionaries of St. Joseph).*—F.M.S.J.
[2750]—*Missionary Sisters of the Immaculate Heart.*
[1830]—*Religious of the Good Shepherd - RGS of Mary.*—I.C.M.
[2070]—*Religious of the Holy Union of the Sacred Hearts.*—S.U.S.C.
[3430]—*Religious Teachers Filippini.*—M.P.F.
[4180]—*Religious Venerini Sisters.*—M.P.V.
[2970]—*School Sisters of Notre Dame.*—S.S.N.D.
[0620]—*Sisters of Charity of St. Louis.*—S.C.S.L.
[2560]—*Sisters of Mary Reparatrix.*—S.M.R.
[2575]—*Sisters of Mercy of the Americas.* (Albany).—R.S.M.
[2990]—*Sisters of Notre Dame.*—S.N.D.
[1660]—*Sisters of St. Francis of the Providence of God.*—O.S.F.
[3840]—*Sisters of St. Joseph of Carondelet.*—C.S.J.
[0150]—*Sisters of the Assumption.*—S.A.S.V.
[2980]—*Sisters of the Congregation de Notre Dame.*—C.N.D.
[1990]—*Sisters of the Holy Names of Jesus and Mary.*—S.N.J.M.
[3320]—*Sisters of the Presentation of the B.V.M.*—P.B.V.M.
[3480]—*Sisters of the Resurrection.*—C.R.
[1490]—*Sisters of the Third Franciscan Order.*—O.S.F.
[4070]—*Society of the Sacred Heart.*—R.S.C.J.

DIOCESAN CEMETERIES

COHOES. *St. Agnes Cemetery,* St. Agnes Hwy., 12047. Tel: 518-463-0134.

GLENVILLE. *St. Anthony Cemetery,* Glenridge Rd., 12325. Tel: 518-374-5319.

MENANDS. *St. Agnes Cemetery,* 48 Cemetery Ave. Tel: 518-463-0134.

ROTTERDAM. *Holy Cross Cemetery.* Tel: 518-374-5319.

SCHENECTADY. *Most Holy Redeemer Cemetery,* 2501 Troy Rd.

St. Cyril & St. Methodius Cemetery. Tel: 518-374-5319.

TROY. *St. Jean Baptiste Cemetery,* 968 Spring Ave., 12180. Tel: 518-272-0931.

St. John Cemetery. Tel: 518-272-0931.

St. Mary's Cemetery of Troy, Inc., Brunswick Rd., 12180. Tel: 518-272-0931.

WATERVLIET. *St. Patrick Cemetery,* Troy Rd., 12189. Tel: 518-463-0134.

NECROLOGY

✠ Ryan, Most Rev. Joseph T., (Retired). —Died Oct. 9, 2000.
† Guillaume, Lionel, (Retired). —Died May 2, 2000.
† Halpin, Raymond, (Retired). —Died April 24, 2000.
† Hart, Rev. Msgr. James G., (Retired). —Died Jan. 13, 2000.
† Hiney, Thomas, (Retired). —Died Nov. 20, 1999.
† Keefe, John W, Latham, NY Our Lady of Hope. —Died Oct. 30, 2000.
† Mallon, John F., (Retired). —Died Nov. 11, 2000.
† Mullen, John. —Died April 5, 2000.
† Nowakowski, Francis, (Retired). —Died Oct. 1, 2000.
† O'Grady, John G., (Retired). —Died May 31, 2000.

Diocese of Alexandria

(Dioecesis Alexandrina in Louisiana)

Most Reverend

SAM G. JACOBS, D.D.

Bishop of Alexandria; ordained June 6, 1964; appointed Bishop of Alexandria July 1, 1989; ordained and installed August 24, 1989. *Mailing Address: P.O. Box 7417, Alexandria, LA, 71306.*

Chancery Office: 2618 Vandenburg Dr., P.O. Box 7417, Alexandria, LA, 71306. Tel.: 318-445-2401; Fax: 318-448-6121.

Web site address: www.diocesealex.org

E-mail address: info@diocesealex.org

Erected as Diocese of Natchitoches July 29, 1853.

Square Miles 22,212.

Transferred to Alexandria August 6, 1910 and became Diocese of Alexandria.

Redesignated Diocese of Alexandria-Shreveport on January 12, 1977; split, forming two Dioceses, the Diocese of Alexandria and the Diocese of Shreveport as of June 16, 1986.

Square Miles 11,116.

Comprises the counties (parishes) of Rapides, Avoyelles, Concordia, Catahoula, LaSalle, Grant, Natchitoches, Vernon, Tensas, Caldwell, Winn, Franklin and Madison.

For legal titles of parishes and diocesan institutions, consult the Chancery Office.

STATISTICAL OVERVIEW

Personnel	
Bishop	1
Priests: Diocesan Active in Diocese	35
Priests: Active Outside Diocese	5
Priests: Retired, Sick or Absent	23
Number of Diocesan Priests	63
Religious Priests in Diocese	16
Extern Priests in Diocese	9
Ordinations:	
Transitional Deacons	2
Permanent Deacons in Diocese	6
Total Brothers	3
Total Sisters	49
Parishes	
Parishes	48
With Resident Pastor:	
Resident Diocesan Priests	26
Resident Religious Priests	17
Without Resident Pastor:	
Administered by Priests	4
Administered by Women Religious	1
Missions	24
Pastoral Centers	1
Professional Ministry Personnel:	
Brothers	1
Sisters	8
Lay Ministers	15
Welfare	
Catholic Hospitals	2
Total Assisted	108,490
Homes for the Aged	2
Total Assisted	164
Special Centers for Social Services	18
Total Assisted	92,215
Residential Care of Disabled	1
Total Assisted	152
Educational	
Diocesan Students in Other Seminaries	17
Total Seminarians	17
High Schools, Diocesan and Parish	3
Total Students	669
Elementary Schools, Diocesan and Parish	9
Total Students	2,501
Catechesis/Religious Education:	
High School Students	1,366
Elementary Students	2,649
Total Students Under Catholic Instruction	7,202
Teachers in the Diocese:	
Brothers	2
Sisters	13
Lay Teachers	211
Vital Statistics	
Receptions into the Church:	
Infant Baptism Totals	753
Adult Baptism Totals	156
Received into Full Communion	283
First Communions	792
Confirmations	603
Marriages:	
Catholic	188
Interfaith	105
Total Marriages	293
Deaths	722
Total Catholic Population	48,050
Total Population	401,211

Former Bishops—Rt. Rev. Augustus M. Martin, cons. Nov. 30, 1853; died Sept. 29, 1875.—Rt. Rev. Francis Xavier Leray, cons. Bishop of Natchitoches, April 22, 1877; named Bishop of Janopolis, Coadjutor of New Orleans, and Administrator of Natchitoches, Oct. 23, 1879; promoted to the See of New Orleans, Dec. 1883; died Sept. 23, 1887.—Rt. Rev. Anthony Durier, D.D., cons. March 19, 1885; died Feb. 28, 1904.—Most Rev. Cornelius Van de Ven, cons. Nov. 30, 1904; made assistant at the Pontifical Throne, Nov. 12, 1929; died May 8, 1932.—Most Rev. Daniel Francis Desmond, D.D., cons. Bishop of Alexandria Jan. 5, 1933; died Sept. 11, 1945.—Most Rev. Charles P. Greco, D.D., cons. Feb. 25, 1946; retired May 22, 1973; died Jan. 20, 1987.—Most Rev. Lawrence P. Graves, D.D., J.C.L., cons. April 25, 1969; installed Bishop of Alexandria, Sept. 18, 1973; retired July 14, 1982; died Jan. 15, 1994.—Most Rev. William B. Friend, D.D., ord. Oct. 30, 1979; installed Bishop of Alexandria-Shreveport Jan. 11, 1983 then after Diocese of Alexandria-Shreveport was split into two dioceses June 16, 1986; installed Bishop of Shreveport July 30, 1986.—Most Rev. John C. Favalora, D.D., ord. Dec. 20, 1961; appt. Bishop of Alexandria June 16, 1986; ord. and installed July 29, 1986; installed Bishop of St. Petersburg May 16, 1989; installed Archbishop of Miami Dec. 20, 1994.

Vicar General—Rev. Msgr. Ronald C. Hoppe, *P.O. Box 7417, Alexandria, 71306.* Tel: 318-445-2401.

Chancery Office—P.O. Box 7417, Alexandria, 71306. Tel: 318-445-2401; Fax: 318-448-6121. Office Hours: Mon.-Fri. 8-12 & 1-4:30.

Moderator of the Curia—Rev. Msgr. Ronald C. Hoppe, V.G.

Chancellor—Rev. Msgr. Joseph M. Susi.

Ecclesiastical Notaries—Rev. Msgr. Joseph M. Susi; Ms. Addie Butler; Ms. Deborah Deorosan; Mrs. Patricia LaCaze; Mrs. Etta Ohrt; Mrs. Patricia Thomas.

Diocesan Tribunal—P.O. Box 7417, Alexandria, 71306. Tel: 318-445-2401.

Judicial Vicar—Rev. Bruce Miller, J.C.L.

Judges—Most Rev. Sam G. Jacobs, D.D.; Rev. Bruce Miller, J.C.L.

Defenders of the Bond and Promoters of Justice—Rev. James A. Ferguson, J.C.L.

Chief Auditors—Ms. Addie Butler; Mrs. Patricia Thomas.

College of Consultors—Rev. Msgr. Ronald C. Hoppe, V.G.; Rev. Msgr. Joseph M. Susi; Rev. Msgr. Steve J. Testa, V.F.; Revs. Gerard M. Foley, V.F.; H. Gerald Bordelon, V.F.; Vincent Manuel, V.F.; Russell J. Lemoine.

Finance Council—Mr. Robert Chappuis; Mr. Sherman Cook; Mr. Darrell Dubroc; Mr. Norman Olson; Mrs. Dorothy Pugh; Mr. Gus Voltz, Jr.; Rev. Msgr. Ronald C. Hoppe, V.G.; Rev. Msgr. Joseph M. Susi; Rev. Msgr. Steve J. Testa.

Building Review Committee—Mr. George C. Adams; Mr. C. Keith Capdepon; Mr. Donald A. Mansour; Mr. G. Lynn McCain; Mr. Finley L. Ponthie; Mr. Rex L. Ponthie; Mr. Willie Pugh, Jr.; Mr. William O. Rollins; Mr. Joseph T. Simms, Jr.; Mr. William J. Thevenote.

Priests Council—Revs. Daniel P. O'Connor, Chm. Victor P. Vead, Vice Chm. Rusty Rabalais, Sec.; Rev. Msgr. Ronald C. Hoppe, V.G.; Rev. Msgr. Joseph M. Susi; Rev. Msgr. Steve J. Testa, V.F.; Revs. Gerard Foley, V.F.; H. Gerald Bordelon, V.F.; Angelo Messina; Russell J. Lemoine; Vincent Manuel, V.F.; James A. Ferguson; Kenneth J. Michiels; George Krosfield; Scott Chemino; Craig Scott.

Retirement Board—Rev. Msgr. Frederick J. Lyons; Rev. Msgr. John M. Timmermans; Rev. Gerard Foley, V.F.; Dr. Vincent Vincent.

Rural Deans—Rev. Msgr. Steve J. Testa, V.F.; Revs. H. Gerald Bordelon, V.F.; Gerard M. Foley, V.F.; Vincent Manuel, V.F.

The Catholic Foundation of North-Central Louisiana, Inc.—P.O. Box 8021, Alexandria, 71306. Tel: 318-487-9222. Joseph L. Hebert, Pres.-Treas.; Mrs. Betty Chop, Corp. Sec.

Diocesan Offices and Directors

Archivist—Rev. Msgr. Joseph M. Susi, *P.O. Box 7417, Alexandria, 71306-0417.* Tel: 318-445-2401.

Black Affairs—Rev. James Moran, C.O., Chm., *Our Lady of Prompt Succor Church, P.O. Box 67, Mansura, 71350-0067.*

Business Affairs—Mr. David Brook, Dir., *P.O. Box 7417, Alexandria, 71306-0417.* Tel: 318-445-2401.

Campaign for Human Development—Sr. MARY BORDELON, C.D.P., Dir., *P.O. Box 7417, Alexandria, 71306-0417.* Tel: 318-445-2401.

Campus Ministry—Rev. PATRICK X. BRAQUET, Dir., *LSU-A, 8100 Hwy. 71-S, Alexandria, 71302-9633.* Tel: 318-473-6494.

Catholic Community Services—Sr. MARY BORDELON, C.D.P., Dir., *P.O. Box 7417, Alexandria, 71306-0417.* Tel: 318-445-2401.

Catholic Relief Services—Sr. MARY BORDELON, C.D.P., Dir., *P.O. Box 7417, Alexandria, 71306-0417.* Tel: 318-445-2401.

Cemeteries—Rev. Msgr. JOHN M. TIMMERMANS, Coord., *238 Mon Borde St., Moreauville, 71355.* Tel: 318-985-1774.

Charismatic Movement—Rev. H. GERALD BORDELON, V.F., Diocesan Liaison, *P.O. Box 40, Cloutierville, 71416-0040.* Tel: 318-379-2231.

Church Financial Development—Mrs. ANN MASDEN, Dir., *P.O. Box 7417, Alexandria, 71301.* Tel: 318-445-2401.

Church Vocations Board—Most Rev. SAM G. JACOBS, D.D.; Revs. PATRICK X. BRAQUET; KENNETH J. MICHIELS; GEORGE KROSFIELD; Mr. TOMMY RIGMAIDEN; Ms. GAIL BRODNAX.

Clergy and Religious—Vacant.

Communications—Mr. AL NASSIF, Print Media; Mrs. ANN MASDEN, Electronic Media, *P.O. Box 7417, Alexandria, 71306-0417.* Tel: 318-445-2401.

Continuing Formation of the Clergy—Rev. THOMAS M. JEZAK, *4052 Hwy. 452, Marksville, 71351-3530.* Tel: 318-253-9237.

Ecumenical—Rev. S. SCOTT CHEMINO, Liaison, *401 21st St., Alexandria, 71301-6500.* Tel: 318-445-3693.

Eucharistic League, Priests—Rev. Msgr. JOSEPH M. SUSI, Dir., *P.O. Drawer 7417, Alexandria, 71306-0417.* Tel: 318-445-2401.

Evangelization—Rev. CRAIG SCOTT, Chm., *P.O. Box 9, Plancheville, 71362-0009.* Tel: 318-922-3131.

Family Life Ministry—Sr. MARY BORDELON, C.D.P., Dir., *P.O. Box 7417, Alexandria, 71306-0417.* Tel: 318-445-2401.

Fiscal Management—Mr. DAVID BROOK, Dir. Business Affairs, *P.O. Box 7417, Alexandria, 71306-0417.* Tel: 318-445-2401.

Hispanic Apostolate—Rev. PEDRO J. SIERRA-POSADA, *P.O. Box 7417, Alexandria, 71306-0417.* Tel: 318-445-2401.

Holy Childhood Association—Rev. Msgr. STEVE J. TESTA, V.F., Dir., *P.O. Box 7417, Alexandria, 71306-0417.* Tel: 318-445-2401.

Liturgy Committee—Rev. JOSE A. ROBLES-SANCHEZ, *P.O. Box 31, Bordelonville, 71320-0031.* Tel: 318-997-2151.

Maryhill Renewal Center—Mr. TODD MARYE, Dir., *600 Maryhill Rd., Pineville, 71360.* Tel: 318-640-1378.

Newspaper "The Church Today"—Mr. AL NASSIF, Editor, *P.O. Box 7417, Alexandria, 71306-0417.* Tel: 318-445-2401.

Permanent Deacons—Rev. D. MATHEW WOOLLETT, *P.O. Box 1123, Cottonport, 71327-1123.* Tel: 318-876-3681.

Personnel/Property Management—Mr. LONNIE DUFOUR, Dir., *P.O. Box 7417, Alexandria, 71306-0417.* Tel: 318-445-2401.

Print Media—("The Church Today" and "Digest of the News")—Mr. AL NASSIF, Dir. & Editor, *P.O. Box 7417, Alexandria, 71306-0417.* Tel: 318-445-2401.

Propagation of the Faith and Foreign Mission Education—Rev. Msgr. STEVE J. TESTA, Dir., *P.O. Box 7417, Alexandria, 71306-0417.* Tel: 318-445-2401.

Public Affairs—Mrs. ANN MASDEN, Dir., *P.O. Box 7417, Alexandria, 71306-0417.* Tel: 318-445-0417.

Religious, Coordinator for—Bro. ANDRE M. LUCIA, F.S.E., *P.O. Box 25, Plaucheville, 71362.* Tel: 318-922-3630.

Religious Education—Sr. MARY ELLEN THERIOT, S.S.N.D., Dir., *P.O. Box 7417, Alexandria, 71306-0417.* Tel: 318-445-2401.

Renew—Mr. TOM WEBB, Dir., *P.O. Box 7417, Alexandria, 71306-0417.* Tel: 318-445-2401.

Rural Life Ministry—Rev. JAMES ROY, Coord., *P.O. Box 66, Hessmer, Alexandria, 71341.* Tel: 318-563-4550.

Schools—Sr. MARICE ELVEKROG, S.S.N.D., Supt., *P.O. Box 7417, Alexandria, 71306-0417.* Tel: 318-445-2401.

Scouting—Rev. CHARLES MORGAN, Area 5 Chap., *1712 West St., Winnsboro, 71295.* Tel: 318-435-5658. Rev. STEPHEN J. BRANDOW, Diocesan & Attakapas Council Chap., *P.O. Box 39, Tioga, 71477.* Tel: 318-473-0010.

Seminarians—Rev. PATRICK X. BRAQUET, Dir., *P.O. Box 7417, Alexandria, 71306-0417.* Tel: 318-445-7120.

Social Ministry—Sr. MARY BORDELON, C.D.P., Admin., *P.O. Box 7417, Alexandria, 71306-0417.* Tel: 318-445-2401.

School Food Service—Ms. ERMA DAVIS, Food and Nutrition Supvr., *P.O. Box 7417, Alexandria, 71306-0417.* Tel: 318-445-2485.

The Beginning Experience—Rev. BRUCE MILLER, J.C.L., *P.O. Box 7417, Alexandria, 71306-0417.* Tel: 318-445-2401.

Vocations Recruitment—Rev. PATRICK X. BRAQUET, Dir., *P.O. Box 7417, Alexandria, 71306-0417.* Tel: 318-445-7120.

Youth Ministry—Mrs. SID MCDANIEL, Dir., *P.O. Box 7417, Alexandria, 71306-0417.* Tel: 318-445-2401.

CLERGY, PARISHES, MISSIONS AND PAROCHIAL SCHOOLS

CITY OF ALEXANDRIA
(Rapides Parish)

1—ST. FRANCIS XAVIER CATHEDRAL (1834), Revs. Edwin Rodriguez, Rector; Jason E. Gootee. In res., Rev. Pedro J. Sierra-Posada (Colombia).
Res., 626 Fourth St., 71301-8424. Tel: 318-445-1451; Fax: 318-445-1433.

2—OUR LADY OF PROMPT SUCCOR (1947), Revs. Stephen Scott Chemino; Marc A. Noel. In res., Rev. Jacob Thomas (India).
Res., 401 21st St., 71301-7022. Tel: 318-445-3693; Fax: 318-445-8471.
School—Tel: 318-487-1862; Fax: 318-473-9321.
Sisters of Divine Providence 2; Lay Teachers 30; Students 524.

3—ST. FRANCES XAVIER CABRINI (1947), Rev. Msgr. Ronald C. Hoppe, V.G.; Rev. Jose L. Del Toro, T.O.R.
Office: 2211 E. Texas Ave., 71301-4207. Tel: 318-445-4588; Fax: 318-443-7156.
Res., 2012 Wedgewood Ave., 71301. Tel: 318-487-4413; Fax: 318-443-7156.
School—Tel: 318-448-3333; Fax: 318-448-3343.
Sisters of Charity of the Incarnate Word 1; Lay Teachers 20; Students 299.

4—ST. JAMES MEMORIAL (1911), Rev. Vincent Manuel, S.A.C., V.F. (India).
Mailing Address: 900 Daspit St., 71302-5343. Tel: 318-445-6700; Fax: 318-445-9826.
Church: 714 Winn St., 71301. Tel: 318-487-9512; Fax: 318-445-9826.

5—ST. JULIANA (1959), Rev. Vincent Manuel, S.A.C.,V.F. (India).
Res., 900 Daspit St., 71302-5343. Tel: 318-445-6700; Fax: 318-445-9826.

6—ST. RITA (1940), Revs. S. Bruce Miller, J.C.L.; Rickey J. Gremillion.
Res., 214 N. 17th St., P.O. Box 7056, 71306-0056. Tel: 318-445-7120; Fax: 318-448-0704.
School—Tel: 318-473-0538; Fax: 318-473-0403.
Lay Teachers 19; Students 261.

OUTSIDE THE CITY OF ALEXANDRIA

Belledeau, Avoyelles Parish, St. Martin of Tours (1950), Rev. Timothy R. Marceau, O.S.B.
Res., 1981 Hwy. 114, Hessmer, 71341-4234. Tel: 318-563-4533; Fax: 318-563-4385. [CEM]

Bordelonville, Avoyelles Parish, St. Peter (1903), Rev. Jose A. Robles-Sanchez (Puerto Rico).
Res., P.O. Box 31, 71320-0031. Tel: 318-997-2151; Fax: 801-991-6959. [CEM]

Boyce, Rapides Parish, St. Margaret (1936), Rev. John W. Andries.
Res., 402 Ryan St., 71409. Tel: 318-793-8811; Fax: 318-793-8815.
Missions—Flatwoods, St. Cyril; Gorum, St. Margaret Mary.

Brouillette, Avoyelles Parish, St. Genevieve (1953), Rev. Thomas M. Jezak.
Res., 4052 Hwy. 452, Marksville, 71351-3530. Tel: 318-253-9237; Fax: 318-253-0703. [CEM]

Bunkie, Avoyelles Parish, St. Anthony of Padua (1904), Rev. Msgr. Steve J. Testa, V.F.
Res., 409 St. John St., P.O. Box 719, 71322-0719. Tel: 318-346-7274; Fax: 318-346-7475. [CEM]
School—Tel: 318-346-2739; Fax: 318-346-9191.
Daughters of Divine Providence 1; Lay Teachers 12; Students 234.

Campti, Natchitoches Parish, Nativity of The Blessed Virgin Mary (1831), Rev. Daniel A. Cook.
Res., 119 Tally St., P.O. Box 439, 71411-0439. Tel: 318-476-2116; Fax: 318-476-2815. [CEM 3]
Missions—Trichel, St. Joseph; Black Lake, Our Lady of the Holy Rosary.

Cheneyville, Rapides Parish, St. Joseph (1966), Rev. Msgr. Julius G. Walle.
Res., P.O. Box 446, 71325-0446. Tel: 318-279-2394; Fax: 318-279-2394. [CEM]

Cloutierville, Natchitoches Parish, St. John the Baptist (1816), Rev. H. Gerald Bordelon, V.F.
Res., P.O. Box 40, 71416-0040. Tel: 318-379-2231. [CEM]
Missions—Emmanuel, Holy Rosary; Monet Ferry, Holy Family.

Colfax, Grant Parish, St. Joseph (1897), Rev. James A. Foster.
Res., 801 Third St., P.O. Box 243, 71417-0243. Tel: 318-627-5442.
Mission—Montgomery, St. Patrick, P.O. Box 243, 71417.

Cottonport, Avoyelles Parish, St. Mary Assumption (1889), Rev. D. Mathew Woollett.
Res., P.O. Box 1123, 71327-1123. Tel: 318-876-3681; Fax: 318-876-2816. [CEM 3]
School—Tel: 318-876-3651.
Sisters 1; Lay Teachers 10; Students 208.

Deville, Rapides Parish, St. John the Baptist (1942), Rev. Joseph F. Pellettieri, C.SS.R.
Res., P.O. Box 7, 71328-0007. Tel: 318-466-5587; Fax: 318-466-5265. [CEM 2]
Missions—Kolin, Sts. Francis and Anne; Effie, St. Winifred.

Dupont, Avoyelles Parish, Immaculate Conception (1945), Rev. Cyriac Kizhakkedath, C.M.I. (India).
Res., P.O. Box 385, 71329-0385. Tel: 318-922-3243. [CEM]

Echo, Rapides Parish, St. Francis de Sales (1894), Rev. Raphael Karekatt, M.S.F.S. (India).
Res., P.O. Box 37, 71330-0037. Tel: 318-563-4530; Fax: 318-563-4530. [CEM]

Evergreen, Avoyelles Parish, Little Flower (1928), Rev. James Nellikunnell, C.M.I.
Res., P.O. Box 20, 71333-0020. Tel: 318-346-2840; Fax: 318-346-2840. [CEM 2]
Mission—Goudeau, St. Charles.

Ferriday, Concordia Parish, St. Patrick (1952), Revs. Paul Kunnumpuram, M.S.F.S. (India); Anthony Dharmaraj, M.S.F.S. (India).
Res., P.O. Box 369, 71334. Tel: 318-757-3834. [JC]
Mission—Jonesville, St. Gerard, P.O. Box 863, Jonesville, 71343. Tel: 318-339-6143.

Fifth Ward, Avoyelles Parish, Our Lady of Lourdes (1948), Rev. Rusty P. Rabalais.
Res., 1315 Eggbend Rd., 71351-4223. Tel: 318-253-9936; Fax: 318-253-6300. [CEM 4]
Mission—Moncla, St. John the Baptist.

Glenmora, Rapides Parish, St. Louis (1941), Rev. Msgr. Ronald C. Hoppe, V.G.; Revs. Jacob Thomas (India); Pedro J. Sierra-Posada (Colombia). In res., Sr. Marie T. Brogan, S.S.N.D., Parish Life Coord.
Res., 826 8th St., P.O. Box 636, 71433-0636. Tel: 318-748-8324; Fax: 318-748-8324. [CEM]
Missions—Elmer, St. Peter; Sieper, St. Jude.

Hessmer, Avoyelles Parish, St. Alphonsus (1898), Rev. James Roy.
Res., P.O. Box 66, 71341-0066. Tel: 318-563-4550; Fax: 318-563-8395. [CEM]

Isle Brevelle, Natchitoches Parish, St. Augustine's (1856), Rev. Victor P. Vead.
Res., 2262 Hwy. 484, Natchez, 71456-3622. Tel: 318-379-2521; Fax: 318-379-6085. [CEM]
Missions—Bermuda, St. Charles; Old River, St. Anne.

Jena, LaSalle Parish, St. Mary (1949), Rev. George Pookkattu, C.M.I. (India).
Mailing Address: P.O. Box 669, Pollock, 71467-0669. Tel: 318-765-3798.
Mission—Fishville, St. Edward.

Lecompte, Rapides Parish, St. Martin (1860), Rev. David J. Braquet.
Res., P.O. Box 459, 71346-0459. Tel: 318-776-9480; Fax: 318-776-9485. [CEM]
Mission—Woodworth, Mary, Mother of Jesus.

Leesville, Vernon Parish, St. Michael (1946), Rev. Angelo Messina.
Res., 604 S. Fifth St., P.O. Box 240, 71496-0240. Tel: 318-239-2656; Fax: 318-239-2657.

Mansura, Avoyelles Parish, Our Lady of Prompt Succor (1937), Rev. James Moran, C.O.
Res., Escude St., P.O. Box 67, 71350-0067. Tel: 318-964-2654; Fax: 318-964-5469.
St. Paul the Apostle (1796), Rev. Russell J. Lemoine.
Res., P.O. Box 130, 71350-0130. Tel: 318-964-2921. [CEM]

Marksville, Avoyelles Parish, Holy Ghost (1919), Rev. D. Jamie Medina-Cruz, S.T.L. In res., Rev. Thomas Paithottiyil, C.M.I.
Res., 121 S. Preston St., 71351-3034. Tel: 318-253-7131; Fax: 318-253-7131. [CEM 2]
Mission—Hickory Hill, St. Richard.
St. Joseph's (1869), Revs. James A. Ferguson, J.C.L.; D. Jamie Medina-Cruz, S.T.L.

Res., 141 S. Washington, 71351-3025. Tel: 318-253-5610; 253-7561 (Office); Fax: 318-253-8871. [CEM 2]

Moreauville, Avoyelles Parish, Our Lady of Sorrows (1944), Rev. George Kallumkalkudiyil, C.M.I. (India).
Res., P.O. Box 247, 71355-0247. Tel: 318-985-2968. [CEM]

Sacred Heart (1860), Rev. George Krosfield (India).
Res., 9986 Bayou Des Glaises St., 71355-9702. Tel: 318-985-2774; Fax: 318-985-2397. [CEM]
School—Tel: 318-985-2772; Fax: 318-985-2164.
Sisters of Our Lady of Sorrows 3; Lay Teachers 15; Students 224.

Natchitoches, Natchitoches Parish, Holy Cross (1968), Rev. Daniel P. O'Connor.
Res., 129 Second St., P.O. Box 211, Nachitoches, 71458-0211. Tel: 318-352-2615; Fax: 318-352-8989.

Immaculate Conception (1728), Rev. Kenneth J. Roy.
Res., 145 Church St., P.O. Box 13, Nachitoches, 71458-0013. Tel: 318-352-3422. [CEM]
School—St. Mary, (Grades PreK-8) 1101 E. Fifth St., P.O. Box 2070, 71458-2070. Tel: 318-352-8394; Fax: 318-352-5798.
Lay Teachers 18; Students 264.
High School—Lay Teachers 27; Students 238.

St. Anthony (1935), Rev. Norbert Rosso, C.S.Sp.
Res., 911 Fifth St., P.O. Box 432, Nachitoches, 71458-0432. Tel: 318-352-2559. [JC]

Pineville, Rapides Parish, Sacred Heart (1933), Rev. Terry E. Allen.
Res., 600 Lakeview, P.O. Drawer 3009, 71361-3009. Tel: 318-445-2496; Fax: 318-443-0808.

Plaucheville, Avoyelles Parish, Mater Dolorosa (1879), Rev. Michael Craig Scott.
Res., P.O. Box 9, 71362-0009. Tel: 318-922-3131; Fax: 318-922-3545. [CEM]
School—Tel: 318-922-3401; Fax: 318-922-3776.
Brothers of the Holy Eucharist 1; Marianites of the Holy Cross 1; Lay Teachers 10; Students 199.
High School—Sisters 2; Lay Teachers 6; Students 97.

Powhatan, Natchitoches Parish, St. Francis of Assisi (1952), Rev. Michael Manase, O.C.D.
Res., P.O. Box 82, 71066-0082. Tel: 318-352-8819; Fax: 318-352-8008.
Mission—Spanish Lake, St. Anne. [CEM]

Rexmere, Avoyelles Parish, St. Michael (1964), Rev. Jose A. Robles-Sanchez (Puerto Rico).
Res., P.O. Box 31, Bordelonville, 71320-0031. Tel: 318-997-2151; Fax: 801-991-6959. [CEM]

St. Joseph, Tensas Parish, St. Joseph (1940), Rev. Antony Aelavanthara (India).
Res., P.O. Box 198, 71366-0198. Tel: 318-766-3565; Fax: 318-766-3560. [CEM]
Mission—Waterproof, St. Francis of Assisi, P.O. Box 198, 71366.

Simmesport, Avoyelles Parish, Christ the King (1935), Rev. Daniel Corkery (Ireland).
Res., P.O. Box 186, 71369-0186. Tel: 318-941-2381. [CEM]

Tallulah, Madison Parish, St. Edward (1936), Rev. Ferreolus D'Cruz (India).
Res., Hwy. 80 E., P.O. Box 1308, 71282-1308. Tel: 318-574-1677.

Tioga, Rapides Parish, Immaculate Heart of Mary (1971), Rev. Gerard M. Foley, V.F.
Res., P.O. Box 687, 71477-0687. Tel: 318-640-5314; 640-9446 (Office); Fax: 318-640-3864.

Vidalia, Concordia Parish, Our Lady of Lourdes (1887), Revs. Paul Kunnumpuram, M.S.F.S. (India); Anthony Dharmaraj, M.S.F.S. (India).
Res., 503 Texas St., P.O. Box 460, 71373. Tel: 318-336-5450; Fax: 318-336-9770. [JC]

Winnfield, Winn Parish, Our Lady of Lourdes (1988), Rev. Peter J. Grant (South Africa).
Res., P.O. Box 1412, 71483-1412. Tel: 318-628-2561; Fax: 318-648-2288.
Mission—Olla, St. William.

Winnsboro, Franklin Parish, St. Mary (1945), Rev. Charles J. Morgan.
Res., 1712 West St., 71295-3240. Tel: 318-435-5658; Fax: 318-435-2002.
Mission—Columbia, St. John, 1712 West St., 71295.

Chaplains of Public Institutions

PINEVILLE. *Central Louisiana State Hospital* W. Shamrock Ave., P.O. Box 5031, 71361. Tel: 318-484-6357; 484-6352. Rev. J. Ronald Mathews.
Veterans Administration Medical Center Shreveport Hwy., 71360. Tel: 318-473-0010. Rev. Stephen J. Brandow.

Special Assignment:
Reverend Monsignors—
Susi, Joseph M., Chancellor

On Duty Outside the Diocese:
Reverend Monsignors—
Bordelon, Roland, USCC Relief Services, New York, NY
Reverend Fathers—
Hasieber, Joseph S., St. Joseph, Coatesville, PA
LaPalme, Paul M., St. Joseph Church, Webster, MA
Viviano, Nino, St. Michael Church, Clearwater, FL

Military Chaplains:
Reverend Fathers—
Fey, Thomas J., U.S.A.F.

Absent on Leave:
Reverend Fathers—
Deevy, Edward
Head, Joseph G.
Mathews, Kenneth M.
Roy, Sheldon L.

Retired:
Reverend Monsignors—
Anderson, Marcel
Early, Thomas C.
Lyons, Frederick J.
Murphy, Patrick J. (Ireland)
Susi, Joseph M.
Timmermans, John
Wakeman, John J.
Walle, Julius G.
Reverend Fathers—
Cunningham, John H.
Engelen, R. J.
Gagnard, Louis
Glasnovic, Serafin
Horacek, Mark
Montalbano, Joseph E.
Ryan, John
Thompson, August L.
Van-Hoorn, Leo
Voorhies, Louis

Permanent Deacons:
Daigrepont, William, Avoyelles Prison Ministry
Foster, John, (Retired)
Giaco, Vincent, Chap., Rapides Regional Medical Center
Gremillion, Norman, Immaculate Conception, Dupont
Jones, Charles A., (Retired)
Peltier, Joseph, St. Augustine, Isle Brevelle

INSTITUTIONS LOCATED IN THE DIOCESE

[A] HIGH SCHOOLS, DIOCESAN

ALEXANDRIA. *Holy Savior Menard Central*, 4603 Coliseum Blvd., 71303. Tel: 318-445-8233; Fax: 318-448-8170.
E-mail: hsmenard@centuryinter.net
Junior & High School. Mr. Dale Skinner, Prin. Sisters 1; Lay Teachers 34; Students 501.

[B] ELEMENTARY SCHOOLS, INTERPAROCHIAL

MARKSVILLE. *Holy Ghost Catholic School*, 322 E. Mark St., 71351. Tel: 318-253-6932; 253-7440; Fax: 318-240-8154.
E-mail: mcslib@kricket.com
Rev. Kenneth J. Michiels, Prin. Priests 1; Handmaids of the Holy Child Jesus 2; Lay Teachers 10; Students 121.

[C] GENERAL HOSPITALS

ALEXANDRIA. *Christus Health Central Louisiana dba St. Frances Cabrini Hospital*, 3330 Masonic Dr., 71301. Tel: 318-487-1122; Fax: 318-448-6754.
Web site: www.cabrini.org
For a complete listing, refer to the Hospitals section.
The Dubuis Hospital for Continuing Care, 3330 Masonic Dr., 71301. Tel: 318-448-4960; Fax: 318-448-4941
For a complete listing, refer to the Hospitals section.

[D] PROTECTIVE INSTITUTIONS

ALEXANDRIA. *Our Lady of Sorrows Community Homes*, 347 Browns Bend Rd., 71303. Tel: 318-487-8897; Fax: 318-487-9987
For a complete listing, refer to the Special Care Facilities section.
St. Mary's Residential Training School, Inc., P.O. Box Drawer 7768, 71306. Tel: 318-445-6443; Fax: 318-449-8520.
E-mail: A2greco@aol.com
For a complete listing, refer to the Special Care Facilities section.

[E] HOMES FOR AGED

ALEXANDRIA. *Our Lady's Manor, Inc.*, 402 Monroe St., 71301. Tel: 318-473-2560; Fax: 318-443-2449
For a complete listing, refer to the Special Care Facilities section.

MOREAUVILLE. *St. John's Village*, 116 Beridon St., 71355-3004. Tel: 318-985-2948
For a complete listing, refer to the Special Care Facilities section.

[F] RESIDENCES OF PRIESTS AND BROTHERS

PLAUCHEVILLE. *Brothers of the Holy Eucharist*, P.O. Box 25, 71362. Tel: 318-922-3630. Bro. Andre M. Lucia, F.S.E., Supr. Brothers 3.

[G] CONVENTS AND RESIDENCES FOR SISTERS

ALEXANDRIA. *Congregation of the Marianites of Holy Cross*, St. Rita Convent, 1717 Ashley Ave., 71301. Tel: 318-448-8001. Sisters 2.
Congregation of the Sisters of Charity of the Incarnate Word, St. Francis Cabrini Hospital Convent, 3330 Masonic Dr., 71301. Tel: 318-487-1122; Fax: 318-448-6974.
E-mail: sr.perpetua@centurytel.net
Sisters 6.
Congregation of the Sisters of Charity of the Incarnate Word, Nazareth Community, 340 Park Pl., 71301-3942. Tel: 318-443-5520. Sisters 3.
Disciples of the Lord Jesus Christ, 4609 Coliseum Blvd., 71303. Tel: 318-443-4495; Fax: 318-443-4495-5**.
E-mail: dljcalex@juno.com
Sisters 2.
Sisters of Divine Providence of San Antonio, Texas, Our Lady of Prompt Succor Convent, 580 Chester St., 71301-6516. Tel: 318-442-3315. Sisters 5.
Sisters of Our Lady of Sorrows, St. Mary's Convent, P.O. Box 7768, 71306. Tel: 318-445-6461; Fax: 318-445-7124.
E-mail: corianousa@aol.com
Sisters 3.
Sisters of Our Lady of Sorrows, St. Joseph Convent, 440 Browns Bend Rd., 71303. Tel: 318-443-4688; Fax: 318-443-0994.
E-mail: stjoe@aol.com
Sisters 4.

BUNKIE. *Daughters of Divine Providence*, St. Anthony Convent, 114 Knoll St., 71322. Tel: 318-346-4481; Fax: 318-346-4481.
E-mail: sisters@kricket.net
Sisters 4.

COTTONPORT. *Congregation of Marianites of Holy Cross*, Holy Cross Convent, P.O. Box 1062, 71327-1062. Tel: 318-876-3794; Fax: 318-876-2816. Sisters 1.

GLENMORA. *School Sisters of Notre Dame*, Miryam House, P.O. Box 636, 71433. Tel: 318-748-8324.
E-mail: sis2ters@juno.com
Sisters 2.

MARKSVILLE. *The Sisters of the Handmaids of the Holy Child Jesus (of Nigeria, Africa)*, 304 E. Mark St., 71351. Tel: 318-240-8527. Sisters 2.

MOREAUVILLE. *Sisters of Our Lady of Sorrows*, Sacred Heart Convent, P.O. Box 179, 71355. Tel: 318-985-2772. Sisters 4.

[H] RETREAT HOUSES

PINEVILLE. *Maryhill Renewal Center*, 600 Maryhill Rd., 71360. Tel: 318-640-1378; Fax: 318-640-8604.
E-mail: maryhill@iamerica.net
Web site: www.diocesealex.org
Rev. Harold Imamshah, Spiritual Dir.& Chap.; Mr. Todd J. Marye, M.P.S., Exec. Dir.; Mr. Leland G. McCullough, III, D.Min.

[I] CATHOLIC COMMUNITY SERVICES

ALEXANDRIA. *Catholic Community Services*, 4400 Coliseum Blvd., P.O. Box 7417, 71306. Tel: 318-445-2401; Fax: 318-448-6121.
E-mail: info@diocesealex.org
Web site: www.diocesealex.org
Sr. Mary Bordelon, C.D.P., Dir.

[J] NEWMAN CENTERS

ALEXANDRIA. *Louisiana State University at Alexandria*, Catholic Student Center, 8100 Hwy. 71-S, 71302-9633. Tel: 318-473-6494.
E-mail: pbraquet@juno.com
Rev. Patrick X. Braquet, Dir.

NATCHITOCHES. *Northwestern State University*, Catholic Student Center, 129 Second St., P.O. Box 211, 71458. Tel: 318-352-2615. Rev. Daniel P. O'Connor, Chap.

[K] MISCELLANEOUS

ALEXANDRIA. *Kuumba Center*, 1407 Eighth St., 71301. Tel: 318-792-1641 (Office); 442-0494 (Center).
E-mail: sote@iamerica.net
Sr. Linda Anne Ranard, A.S.C., Dir. Center for Creative Formation.

St. Joseph House of Formation, 415 Elliott St., 71301-8114. Tel: 318-449-1421. Rev. Patrick X. Braquet, Dir.

FOREST HILL. *Our Lady of Guadlupe Mission*, 10 Butter Cemetary Rd., 71430. Mailing Address: 4400 Coliseum Blvd., Alexandria, 71303. Franciscan Religious of Our Lady of Refuge 3.

HESSMER. *Magnificat - Central Louisiana Chapter of the Diocese of Alexandria*, P.O. Box 37, 71341. Tel: 318-563-8213. M. Sue Dauzat, Coord.

RELIGIOUS INSTITUTES OF MEN REPRESENTED IN THE DIOCESE

For further details refer to the corresponding bracketed number in the Religious Institutes of Men or Women section.

[0200]—*Benedictine Monks.* (Lisle, IL).—O.S.B.
[0620]—*Brothers of the Holy Eucharist.*—F.S.E.
[0275]—*Carmelites of Mary Immaculate.*—C.M.I.
[0260]—*Discaled Carmelite Friars.*—O.C.D.
[0650]—*Holy Ghost Fathers.* (Western Prov.).—C.S.Sp.
[]—*Missionaries of St. Francis de Sales (of India).*—M.S.F.S.
[0950]—*Oratorians.*—C.O.
[1070]—*Redemptorist Fathers.*—C.Ss.R.
[0990]—*Society of the Catholic Apostolate.*—S.A.C.
[0560]—*Third Order Regular of St. Francis.* (Prov. of the Most Sacred Heart of Jesus).—T.O.R.

RELIGIOUS INSTITUTES OF WOMEN REPRESENTED IN THE DIOCESE

[0100]—*Adorers of the Blood of Christ.*—A.S.C.
[]—*Congregation of the Franciscan Religious of Our Lady of Refuge.* (Guadalajara, Mexico).—R.F.R.
[2410]—*Congregation of the Marianites of Holy Cross.* (Louisiana Prov.).—M.S.C.
[0470]—*Congregation of the Sisters of Charity of the Incarnate Word.*—C.C.V.I.
[0800]—*Daughters of Divine Providence.*—F.D.P.
[0965]—*Disciples of the Lord Jesus Christ.*—D.L.J.C.
[1070]—*Dominican Sisters.*—O.P.
[]—*Handmaids of the Holy Child Jesus of Nigeria, Africa.*—H.H.C.J.
[2970]—*School Sisters of Notre Dame.*—S.S.N.D.
[1010]—*Sisters of Divine Providence of San Antonio, Texas.*—C.D.P.
[3120]—*Sisters of Our Lady of Sorrows.*—O.L.S.
[4070]—*Society of the Sacred Heart.*—R.S.C.J.

DIOCESAN CEMETERIES

PINEVILLE. *Maryhill Cemetery for Clergy.*

NECROLOGY

† Beckers, Rev. Msgr. Henry F., (Retired). —Died Jan. 5, 2000.
† Deasy, Edward, (Retired). —Died Feb. 13, 2000.
† Fortier, Harvey J, Evergreen, LA Little Flower of Jesus. —Died Dec. 10, 1999.

Diocese of Allentown

(Dioecesis Alanopolitana)

Most Reverend

EDWARD P. CULLEN, D.D.

Bishop of Allentown; ordained May 19, 1962; appointed Auxiliary Bishop of Philadelphia and Titular Bishop of Paria in Preconsilare February 8, 1994; consecrated April 14, 1994; appointed Bishop of Allentown December 16, 1997; installed Third Bishop of Allentown February 9, 1998. *Office: 4029 W. Tilghman St., Allentown, PA, 18104. Mailing Address: Bishop's Office, P.O. Box F, Allentown, PA, 18105-1538.*

Most Reverend

THOMAS J. WELSH, D.D., J.C.D.

Retired Bishop of Allentown; ordained May 30, 1946; appointed Titular Bishop of Scattery Island and Auxiliary Bishop of Philadelphia on February 18, 1970; consecrated April 2, 1970; appointed as First Bishop of Arlington on June 4, 1974; installed on August 13, 1974; appointed Bishop of Allentown February 8, 1983; installed Second Bishop of Allentown on March 21, 1983; resigned December 16, 1997. *Mailing Address: 1325 Prospect Ave., Bethlehem, PA, 18018.*

ESTABLISHED JANUARY 28, 1961.

Square Miles 2,773.

Comprises the Counties of Berks, Carbon, Lehigh, Northampton and Schuylkill in the State of Pennsylvania.

Chancery Office: 4029 W. Tilghman St., Allentown, PA, 18104. Mailing Address: P.O. Box F, Allentown, PA, 18105-1538. Tel.: 610-437-0755; Fax: 610-433-7822.

STATISTICAL OVERVIEW

Personnel	
Bishop	1
Retired Bishops	1
Priests: Diocesan Active in Diocese	185
Priests: Active Outside Diocese	13
Priests: Diocesan in Foreign Missions	1
Priests: Retired, Sick or Absent	45
Number of Diocesan Priests	244
Religious Priests in Diocese	66
Extern Priests in Diocese	5
Ordinations:	
Diocesan Priests	3
Transitional Deacons	2
Permanent Deacons	24
Permanent Deacons in Diocese	100
Total Sisters	505
Parishes	
Parishes	153
With Resident Pastor:	
Resident Diocesan Priests	114
Resident Religious Priests	5
Without Resident Pastor:	
Administered by Priests	34
Missions	9
Welfare	
Catholic Hospitals	3
Total Assisted	962,822
Health Care Centers	1
Total Assisted	32,940
Homes for the Aged	10
Total Assisted	694
Day Care and Extended Day Care Centers	39
Total Assisted	1,593
Specialized Homes	2
Total Assisted	2,444
Special Centers for Social Services	14
Total Assisted	74,010
Residential Care of Disabled	11
Total Assisted	68
Educational	
Diocesan Students in Other Seminaries	24
Total Seminarians	24
Colleges and Universities	2
Total Students	3,305
High Schools, Diocesan and Parish	9
Total Students	4,140
Elementary Schools, Diocesan and Parish	53
Total Students	13,749
Non-residential Schools for the Disabled	3
Total Students	138
Catechesis/Religious Education:	
High School Students	1,444
Elementary Students	17,700
Total Students Under Catholic Instruction	40,500
Teachers in the Diocese:	
Priests	11
Sisters	78
Lay Teachers	910
Vital Statistics	
Receptions into the Church:	
Infant Baptism Totals	3,658
Adult Baptism Totals	175
First Communions	4,056
Confirmations	4,270
Marriages:	
Catholic	693
Interfaith	476
Total Marriages	1,169
Deaths	3,210
Total Catholic Population	264,373
Total Population	1,125,349

Former Bishops—Most Rev. JOSEPH MCSHEA, appt. Titular Bishop of Mina and Auxiliary Bishop of Philadelphia Feb. 9, 1952; cons. March 19, 1952; appt. Bishop of Allentown Feb. 15, 1961; installed April 11, 1961; retired Feb. 8, 1983; died Nov. 28, 1991.—Most Rev. THOMAS J. WELSH, D.D., J.C.D., appt. Titular Bishop of Scattery Island and Auxiliary Bishop of Philadelphia, Feb. 18, 1970; cons. April 2, 1970; appt. First Bishop of Arlington, June 4, 1974; installed Aug. 13, 1974; appt. Bishop of Allentown, Feb. 8, 1983; installed Second Bishop of Allentown, March 21, 1983; resigned Dec. 16, 1997.

Vicar General—Rev. Msgr. ALFRED A. SCHLERT, J.C.L., V.G., *4029 W. Tilghman St., Allentown, 18105., P.O. Box F, Allentown, 18105-1538.* Tel: 610-437-0755; Fax: 610-433-7822.

Chancellor—Rev. Msgr. JOHN B. MCCANN, S.T.L., L.S.W., *4029 W. Tilghman St., Allentown, 18105., P.O. Box F, Allentown, 18105-1538.* Tel: 610-437-0755; Fax: 610-433-7822.

Secretary to the Bishop—Rev. Msgr. JOHN B. MCCANN, S.T.L., L.S.W., *4029 W. Tilghman St., Allentown, 18105., P.O. Box F, Allentown, 18105-1538.* Tel: 610-437-0755; Fax: 610-433-7822.

Diocesan Tribunal—Rev. Msgr. RONALD W. GAINER, M.Div., J.C.L., Judicial Vicar, *202 N. 17th St., Allentown, 18104.* Tel: 610-434-3200; Fax: 610-433-3104.

Judges—Rev. Msgr. DAVID J. MORRISON, J.C.D., M.A.; Rev. Msgr. NEVIN J. KLINGER, J.C.L., M.A.; Revs. JAMES J. WARD, M.Div.; JOHN PAUL, M.S.C., S.T.L., J.C.D.

Promoter of Justice—Rev. DAVID J. KOZAK, J.C.L.

Defenders of the Bond—Revs. DAVID J. KOZAK, J.C.L.; MICHAEL S. LAWRENCE, M.Div.; Rev. Msgr. ALFRED A. SCHLERT, J.C.L., V.G.

Secretary—Deacon EUGENE J. WYRWA.

Advocates—Revs. VICTOR F. FINELLI, M.Div., Th.M.; THOMAS P. KOONS; JOHN A. KRIVAK, Ed.D.; Deacon EUGENE J. WYRWA.

Notaries—Mrs. JUDY CHUSS; Mrs. PATRICIA ECHTERNACH; Mrs. DIANE SELDOMRIDGE; Mrs. COLETTE SNYDER.

Vicar for Religious—Rev. Msgr. THOMAS E. HOBAN, V.R., *St. Ann Rectory, 415 S. 6th St., Emmaus, 18094.* Tel: 610-965-2426; Fax: 610-967-1099.

Vicars Forane—Rev. Msgr. JOHN G. CHIZMAR, V.F., Carbon Deanery: Rev. Msgr. ALFRED R. OTT, V.F., Lehigh Deanery: Rev. Msgr. JAMES A. TRESTON, V.F., Berks Deanery: Rev. Msgr. MICHAEL J. CHABACK, V.F., Northampton Deanery: Very Rev. EDWARD S. ZEMANIK, V.F., North Schuylkill Deanery: Rev. Msgr. WILLIAM E. JONES, V.F., South Schuylkill Deanery:

Secretariat for Clergy—Rev. Msgr. JOHN B. MCCANN, S.T.L., L.S.W., Sec., *P.O. Box F, Allentown, 18105-1538.* Tel: 610-437-0755; Fax: 610-433-7822.

Priest Personnel Office—Rev. Msgr. JOHN B. MCCANN, S.T.L., L.S.W., Dir., *P.O. Box F, Allentown, 18105-1538.* Tel: 610-437-0755; Fax: 610-433-7822.

Holy Family Villa for Priests—Rev. JOSEPH J. CAMPION, M.Div., Rector, *1325 Prospect Ave., Bethlehem, 18018.* Tel: 610-694-0395; Fax: 610-694-9990.

Permanent Diaconate Office—Rev. Msgr. JAMES J. MULLIGAN, S.T.L., Dir., *2145 Madison Ave. at Dewberry Ave., Bethlehem, 18018.* Tel: 610-866-0581; Fax: 610-867-8702., *P.O. Box 20607, Lehigh Valley, 18002-0607.*

Vocations Office—Rev. FRANCIS A. NAVE, Dir., *4029 W. Tilghman St., Allentown, 18105.* Tel: 610-437-0755; Fax: 610-433-7822.

Priestly Life and Ministry Office—Rev. Msgr. JAMES J. MULLIGAN, S.T.L., Dir., *Mary Immaculate Center, 300 Cherryville Rd., Northampton, 18067-0027.* Tel: 610-262-1885; Fax: 610-262-6766.

Secretariat for Catholic Life and Evangelization—Rev. Msgr. RONALD W. GAINER, M.Div., J.C.L., Sec., *900 S. Woodward St., Allentown, 18103.* Tel: 610-289-8900; Fax: 610-289-7917.

Ecumenical and Interreligious Affairs Office—Rev. RICHARD J. FORD, Dir., *510 Union St., Allentown, 18101-2307.* Tel: 610-439-0111; Fax: 610-439-6048.

Office of Worship—Rev. Msgr. EDWARD J. COYLE, M.A., Th.M., Dir.; Mrs. CAROLE C. CHUK, M.A., Asst. Dir., *900 S. Woodward St., Allentown, 18103-4179.* Tel: 610-289-8900; Fax: 610-289-7917.

Catechumenate Office—Mrs. CAROLE C. CHUK, M.A., Dir., *900 S. Woodward St., Allentown, 18103-4179.* Tel: 610-289-8900; Fax: 610-289-7917.

Institute for the Evangelization of Spanish Speaking People—Rev. GEORGE R. WINNIE, M.A., Dir., *900 S. Woodward St., Allentown, 18103-4179.* Tel: 610-289-8900; Fax: 610-289-7917.

Office of Communications—MATTHEW T. KERR, Dir., *2141 Downyflake Ln., Allentown, 18103-4724.* Tel: 610-797-3845; Fax: 610-797-3941.

The A.D. Times—Mrs. JILL M. CARAVAN, Editor, *2141 Downyflake Ln., Allentown, 18103-4724.* Tel: 610-797-3330; Fax: 610-797-3941.

Campus Ministry Office—Rev. JOHN A. KRIVAK, Ed.D., Dir., *The Newman Center, 2339 Liberty St., Allentown, 18104.* Tel: 610-821-3122; Fax: 610-821-3123.

Youth Ministry Office—Rev. WILLIAM F. GLOSSER, *St. Francis Center, 900 W. Market St., Orwigsburg, 17961-1006.* Tel: 570-366-1405; Fax: 570-366-1426.

Social Action Bureau—Mrs. MARY ANN HAMMER, Dir., *900 S. Woodward St., Allentown, 18103-4179.* Tel: 610-289-8900; Fax: 610-289-7917.

Pro-Life Office—Mrs. MARYANN W. DUNN, M.S., Dir., *900 S. Woodward St., Allentown, 18103-4179.* Tel: 610-289-8900; Fax: 610-289-7917.

Adult Formation—Rev. E. MICHAEL CAMILLI, M.S.C., S.T.L., H.E.L., Ph.D., Dir., *900 S. Woodward St., Allentown, 18103-4179.* Tel: 610-289-8900; Fax: 610-289-7917.

Secretariat for Temporal Affairs—FRED A. WILLIAMS, Sec. & CFO, *1101 W. Hamilton St., P.O. Box F, Allentown, 18105-1538.* Tel: 610-871-5200; Fax: 610-871-5211.

Financial Administration—RONALD J. JACOBS, SPHR, Dir.

Accounting Services—DARLENE F. HERTZOG, Dir.

Parish Support—NEIL BENTZ, Dir.

Elementary and Secondary Schools Support Services—PAUL CHARLTON, Dir.

Information Systems—NANCY A. TORO, Dir.

Cemeteries Office—Rev. Msgr. WILLIAM F. BAVER, Dir., *1101 W. Hamilton St., P.O. Box F, Allentown, 18105-1538.* Tel: 610-871-5200; Fax: 610-871-5211.

Human Resources Office—RONALD J. JACOBS, SPHR, Dir., *1101 W. Hamilton St., P.O. Box F, Allentown, 18105-1538.* Tel: 610-871-5200; Fax: 610-871-5211.

Diocesan Benefit Programs—Mrs. CAROLE SARMIR, Dir.

Insurance and Real Estate—KELLY BRUCE, Dir.

Development Office—1101 W. Hamilton St., P.O. Box F, Allentown, 18105-1538. Tel: 610-871-5200; Fax: 610-871-5211.

Planned Giving Office—ROBERT H. DESILVER, JR., ChFC, Dir., *1101 W. Hamilton St., P.O. Box F, Allentown, 18105-1538.* Tel: 610-871-5200; Fax: 610-871-5211.

Government Affairs Office—FRANK C. GODINO, M.P.A., CFRE, Dir., *1101 W. Hamilton St., P.O. Box F, Allentown, 18105-1538.* Tel: 610-871-5200; Fax: 610-871-5211.

Secretariat for Catholic Education—Dr. JAMES J. CUSIMANO, J.D., Sec., *2145 Madison Ave., Bethlehem, 18017.* Tel: 610-866-0581; Fax: 610-867-8702.

Elementary School Religious Education—BARBARA PENGITORE, Dir.

Religious Education—BARBARA PENGITORE, Dir.

Curriculum, Supervision and Professional and Development (Elementary/Secondary Schools)—MARIANNE WHELAN, Asst. Supt.

Personnel (Elementary and Secondary)—PHILIP J. FROMUTH, M.Ed., Asst. Supt.

Early Childhood Education—MARIANNE WHELAN, Asst. Supt.

Secondary Schools—Rev. JOHN S. MRAZ, M.A., M.Ed., Asst. Supt.

Government Programs and Technology—JOHN R. CLARK, Asst. Supt.

Marketing and Public Relations—CHRISTINE M. CHEW, Dir.

Media Library—SUZANNE M. MELLO, Librarian.

Board of Education—Rev. ALBERT J. BYRNE, Pres., *St. Benedict Rectory, 2020 Chestnut Hill Rd., Mohnton, 19540-9755.* Tel: 610-856-1006; Fax: 610-856-1035.

Secretariat for Catholic Human Services—BARBARA W. MURPHY, M.S.W., Sec., *2141 Downyflake Ln., Allentown, 18103-4774.* Tel: 610-791-3888; Fax: 610-791-1878.

Catholic Social Agency—BARBARA W. MURPHY, Exec. Dir., *2141 Downyflake Ln., Allentown, 18103-4774.* Tel: 610-791-3888; Fax: 610-791-1878.

Family Life Ministries—Dr. WILLIAM F. URBINE, D.Min.

Berks County Office—Mrs. CATHERINE MOORE, County Supvr., *2147 Perkiomen Ave., Reading, 19606.* Tel: 610-370-3378; Fax: 610-370-3378.

Lehigh-Northampton County Office—Mr. ROBERT NICOLELLA, County Supvr., *530 Union Blvd., Allentown, 18109-3230.* Tel: 610-435-1541; Fax: 610-435-4367.

Schuylkill-Carbon County Office—Sr. MIRIAM DENIS, County Supvr., *900 W. Market St., Orwigsburg, 17961-1006.* Tel: 570-366-1403; Fax: 570-366-7311.

Ministry with Persons with Disabilities—Sr. JANICE MARIE JOHNSON, R.S.M., M.A., *2141 Downyflake Ln., Allentown, 18103-4774.* Tel: 610-791-3888; Fax: 610-791-1878.

Holy Family Manor, Inc.—Rev. Msgr. DENNIS A. RIGNEY, M.Div., M.S.W., L.S.W., A.C.S.W., N.H.A., Pres. & CEO, *1200 Spring St., Bethlehem, 18018.* Tel: 610-865-5595; Fax: 610-865-5866.

Residential Services, Inc.—Rev. Msgr. DENNIS A. RIGNEY, M.Div., M.S.W., L.S.W., A.C.S.W., N.H.A., Pres. & CEO; Mr. R. JAMES POLASKI, Dir., *1200 Spring St., Bethlehem, 18018.* Tel: 610-865-5595; Fax: 610-865-5866.

Collaborative Residential Services—Seton Manor, 1000 Seton Dr., Orwigsburg, 17961. Tel: 570-366-0400; Fax: 570-366-1970., *Covenant Home Care, 1510 Hwy. 61 S., Pottsville, 17901-8409.* Tel: 570-385-5522; 800-726-8761; Fax: 570-385-5287.

Diocesan Health Affairs Office—Rev. Msgr. JAMES J. MULLIGAN, S.T.L., Dir., *Mary Immaculate Center, 300 Cherryville Rd., Northampton, 18067-0027.* Tel: 610-262-1885; Fax: 610-262-6766.

Censor of Books—Rev. Msgr. JAMES J. MULLIGAN, S.T.L., *Mary Immaculate Center, 300 Cherryville Rd., Northampton, 18067-0027.* Tel: 610-262-1885.

Council of Priests/Diocesan Consultors—4029 W. Tilghman St., P.O. Box F, Allentown, 18105. Tel: 610-437-0755; Fax: 610-433-7822.

College of Consultors—Rev. Msgr. ALFRED A. SCHLERT; Rev. Msgr. JOHN B. MCCANN; Rev. Msgr. RONALD W. GAINER; Revs. JOSEPH J. CAMPION; JOSEPH A. DESANTIS; Rev. Msgr. JOHN P. MURPHY; Rev. JOHN M. GIBBONS; Rev. Msgr. GERALD E. GOBITAS; Rev. STEPHEN J. RADOCHA; Rev. Msgr. JAMES J. REICHERT; Rev. Msgr. EDWARD R. SACKS; Rev. Msgr. JOSEPH P.T. SMITH.

Ex Officio Members—Rev. Msgr. ALFRED A. SCHLERT, J.C.L., V.G.; Rev. Msgr. JOHN B. MCCANN; Rev. Msgr. RONALD W. GAINER.

Elected Members—Rev. Msgr. JOSEPH P.T. SMITH; Revs. BRUNO M. TUCCI; STEPHEN J. RADOCHA; Rev. Msgr. EDWARD R. SACKS; Revs. JOHN M. GIBBONS; EDWARD J. O'CONNOR; MICHAEL J. STONE; ADAM C. SEDAR; ERIC J. GRUBER; JAMES G. PRIOR, C.M.; MICHAEL J. BRIGGMAN; HENRY E. STRASSNER; FRANS J. BERKHOUT; JOSEPH T. WHALEN; E. MICHAEL CAMILLI.

Appointed Members—Rev. Msgr. JAMES J. REICHERT; Rev. Msgr. JOHN P. MURPHY; Revs. JOSEPH J. CAMPION; JOSEPH A. DESANTIS; Rev. Msgr. GERALD E. GOBITAS; Revs. DENNIS T. HARTGEN; RONALD V. JANKAITIS.

Finance Committee—Rev. Msgr. ALFRED A. SCHLERT, J.C.L., V.G., Bishop's Delegate, *4029 W. Tilghman St., P.O. Box F, Allentown, 18105-1538.* Tel: 610-437-0755. Very Rev. DANIEL G. GAMBET, O.S.F.S.; CARL FEICHTEL; JOHN F. HORRIGAN, JR.; MARIANNE S. LAVELLE, ESQ.; CARL S. FRENSKY; BERNARD F. MULLIGAN; Rev. Msgr. ALFRED R. OTT; THOMAS F. TRAUD, ESQ.; ALBERT BOVA; FRED A. WILLIAMS.

Affiliated Organizations

American Catholic Overseas Aid Fund—Rev. RICHARD J. FORD, Diocesan Dir., *510 Union St., Allentown, 18101-2307.* Tel: 610-439-0111; Fax: 610-439-6048.

Apostleship of Prayer—Rev. EUGENE W. JUNG, M.S.C., Dir., *55 Rothermel St., Reading, 19605.* Tel: 610-929-2025.

Beginning Experience—Rev. Msgr. RONALD W. GAINER, M.Div., J.C.L., Diocesan Spiritual Dir., *Diocesan Tribunal, 202 N. 17th St., Allentown, 18104.* Tel: 610-434-3200.

Blue Army of Our Lady of Fatima—Mrs. PATRICIA HODGES, Pres.; Rev. DOMINIC THAO PHAM, Spiritual Dir., *4102 S. Lee St., Whitehall, 18052.* Tel: 610-262-0947.

Catholic Daughters of the Americas—Rev. FLOYD CAESAR, JR., Diocese Committee Chap.

Charismatic Renewal—Rev. LARRY J. HESS, Bishop's Liaison, *Our Lady of Good Counsel Rectory, 218 W. Biddle St., Gordon, 17936-9999.* Tel: 570-875-0774; Fax: 570-875-2443.

Courage—P.O. Box F, Allentown, 18105-1538. Tel: 610-797-3546.

Cursillo Movement—Rev. ROBERT J. REED, Dir., *730 W. Broad St., Bethlehem, 18018-5295.* Tel: 610-866-5582.

Father Walter Ciszek Prayer League, Inc. (The)—Most Rev. THOMAS J. WELSH, Pres., *The Ciszek Center, 231 N. Jardin St., Shenandoah, 17976-1642.* Tel: 570-462-2270; Fax: 570-462-2274.

Holy Childhood Association—Rev. Msgr. JOHN P. MURPHY, Dir., *1040 Flexer Ave., Allentown, 18103-5520.* Tel: 610-433-7413; Fax: 610-433-2308.

Holy Name Societies—Deacon STEPHEN ANDRUSISIAN, Dir., *516 N. Front St., Minersville, 17954-1421.* Tel: 570-544-5339.

Knights of Columbus—

St. Peter the Fisherman Council #10772, Lake Harmony—ANTHONY CARANGELO, Grand Knight, *P.O. Box 1257, Albrightsville, 18210-3012.* Tel: 570-722-1576.

St. Joseph the Worker Council #10921, Orefield—JAMES POLICARE, Grand Knight, *5663 Cetronia Rd., Allentown, 18106.* Tel: 610-398-3548.

St. Paul Council #10922, Allentown—JOHN M. LEVCHAK, Grand Knight, *2437 S. 5th St., Allentown, 18103.* Tel: 610-791-4876.

Calvary Council #528, Allentown—JOHN PHILAPAVAGE, Grand Knight, *1530 W. Pennsylvania St., Allentown, 18102.* Tel: 610-434-1580.

Sarto Council #1322, Ashland—THOMAS P. COLIHAN, Grand Knight, *75 S. Hoffman Blvd., Ashland, 17921-1951.* Tel: 570-875-2091.

Father DeNisco Council #3862, Bangor—RONALD CESARE, Grand Knight, *1646 Alpine Dr., Pen Argyl, 18072.* Tel: 610-863-4053; 6205.

Trinity Council #313, Bethlehem—ROBERT W. CURZI, Grand Knight, *2028 Country Place, Bethlehem, 18018.* Tel: 610-867-7183.

Holy Cross Council #4754, Bethlehem—ROBERT J. NAVIN, Grand Knight, *1713 Budd Ave., Bethlehem, 18018-4601.* Tel: 610-865-1639.

Union Council #345, Easton—ROBERT FREDERICK, Grand Knight, *3105 Val Vista Dr., Easton, 18045.*

Rev. James A. Hogan Council #2580, Frackville—SAMUEL BENDER, Grand Knight, *56 N. Center St., Frackville, 17931.* Tel: 570-874-1438.

Damien Council #598, Jim Thorpe—MICHAEL A. HEERY, Grand Knight, *68 White Pine Ln., Lehighton, 18235-9612.* Tel: 570-386-2297.

Archbishop Ryan Council #1552, Lansford—FRANK SERINA, Grand Knight, *107 W. Bertsch St., Lansford, 18232-1908.* Tel: 570-645-5221.

Mahanoy City Council #549, Mahanoy City—GEORGE J. GAYDOSH, Grand Knight, *407 W. Pine St., Mahanoy City, 17948-2515.* Tel: 570-773-2844.

Our Lady of the Sacred Heart Council #4282, Nazareth—JOSEPH M. INHOFF, Grand Knight, *156 W. Mountain Ave., Wind Gap, 18091-9730.* Tel: 610-759-3184; Fax: 610-746-3553.

Queenship of Mary Council #4050, Northampton—JOSEPH A. PALKOVITS, Grand Knight, *217 E. 10th St., Northampton, 18067.* Tel: 610-262-5778.

Lafayette Council #2522, Palmerton—GEORGE KATTNER, Grand Knight, *203 Howard Ave., Palmerton, 18071-1222.* Tel: 610-823-6336.

Schuylkill Council #431, Pottsville—EMIL RUSHANAN, Grand Knight, *110 Arlene St., Minersville, 17954.* Tel: 570-544-6931.

Reading Council #793, Reading—WM. R. FOREMAN, Grand Knight, *413 Brookline St., Reading, 19611-1651.* Tel: 610-375-4616.

Holy Eucharist Council #4198, Reading—EDWARD W. KOSAK, Grand Knight, *210 Fairway Dr., Reading, 19606-3667.* Tel: 610-370-0739.

Francis Cardinal Brennan Council #618, Shenandoah—ALBERT KORNAK, Grand Knight, *301 W. Cherry St., Shenandoah, 17976.* Tel: 570-462-3622.

Holy Name Council #7179, Shillington—ANTHONY G. FARINA, Grand Knight, *114 New Kirk Ave., Shillington, 19607.* Tel: 610-777-7133.
Light of Christ Council #8726, Sinking Spring—RICHARD WEINHOFFER, Grand Knight, *37 Wellington Blvd., Wyomissing Hills, 19610.*
Father Henry Baker Council #2711, Tamaqua—WILLIAM SOMMERS, Grand Knight, *RR 1, Box 329, Tamaqua, 18252-9474.*

Legion of Mary, Reading Curia—Mrs. ELIZABETH PAOLINI, Pres., *414 Douglass St., Reading, 19601.* Tel: 610-374-0557.

Marriage Encounter—Rev. ROBERT A. DRESSLER, Dir., *Holy Family Villa, 1325 Prospect Ave., Bethlehem, 18018.* Tel: 610-861-8049.

National Shut-In Visitation Society—Rev. Msgr. FELIX A. LOSITO, Natl. Dir., *237 Franklin St., Reading, 19602-1099.* Tel: 610-374-2930.

Operation Rice Bowl—Rev. Msgr. JOHN P. MURPHY, Dir., *1040 Flexer Ave., Allentown, 18103-5520.* Tel: 610-433-7413; Fax: 610-433-2308.

Our Lady's Missionaries of the Eucharist—Most Rev. THOMAS J. WELSH, A Public Association of Christ's Faithful. *Magnificat House, 4530 Vera Cruz Rd., Center Valley, 18034.* Tel: 610-797-1950; Fax: 610-797-1715.

Pontifical Society for the Propagation of the Faith—Rev. Msgr. JOHN P. MURPHY, Dir., *1040 Flexer Ave., Allentown, 18103-5520.* Tel: 610-433-7413; Fax: 610-433-2308.

Saint Vincent De Paul Society—Rev. FRANCIS P. STRAKA, Spiritual Advisor; Mr. RONALD PLOCINIK, Pres. Diocesan Council, *251 1st St., Coaldale, 18218-1602.* Tel: 570-645-2848.

Secular Franciscan Order—*St. Francis Friary and Retreat House, 3918 Chipman Rd., Easton, 18042.* Tel: 610-258-3053; Fax: 610-258-2412. Mrs. MICHELLE MACKEY, S.F.O., Min., *845 Centre St., Easton, 18042.* Tel: 610-252-4768.

Serra Clubs—
Serra Club of Bethlehem—Rev. Msgr. ROBERT F. KOZEL, Chap. JOSEPH SULINSKI, Pres., *1717 Carlisle St., Bethlehem, 18017.* Tel: 610-882-9643.
Forks of the Delaware Serra—Rev. JOSEPH A. SHEEHAN, Chap. JOSEPH DAGON, II, Pres., *136 E. St. Joseph St., Easton, 18042.* Tel: 610-252-3340.
Serra Club of Allentown—Rev. Msgr. ALFRED R. OTT, V.F., Chap. ROBERT FLEMING, Pres., *3830 Oakwood Dr., Allentown, 18103.* Tel: 610-435-6059.
Reading Serra—Rev. Msgr. JAMES J. REICHERT, Chap. ROBERT LEPIANE, Pres., *1906 Meadow Lane, Wyomissing, 19610.* Tel: 610-775-2166.

Third Order Dominican Chapter—Dr. FELICIDAD QUILO, Moderator, *Expectation of Blessed Virgin Mother Chapter, 4290 Vassar Ave., Bethlehem, 18017.* Tel: 610-691-6761.

Miscellaneous Affiliated Organizations

Catholic Men of Good News (CMOGN)—Rev. LARRY J. HESS, *Our Lady of Good Counsel, 220 W. Biddle St., Gordon, 17936-9999.* Tel: 570-875-0774; Fax: 570-875-2443.

Dayspring Homes, Inc.—Sr. FRANCIS BISLAND, C.P.S., Dir., *P.O. Box 172, Reading, 19607.* Tel: 610-374-9036; Fax: 610-374-9086.

Mary's Shelter—Sr. JOANNA MONTICELLO, M.S.C., Admin., *325 S. 12th St., Reading, 19602-2021.* Tel: 610-376-1973; Fax: 610-376-5391.

U.S. Province Director's Offices—*460 St. Bernardine St., Reading, 19607-1737.* Tel: 610-777-4174; Fax: 610-777-3973.
Office of Communication—Sr. ROSE JAMESON, Dir. Tel: 610-777-4174; Fax: 610-777-3973.
Office of Development—Sr. DOLORICE DOMIN, Dir. Tel: 610-796-8970; Fax: 610-777-3973.
Office of Finance—Sr. ANTOINETTE KEISER, Dir.; Sr. MARIE JANEEN OBARA, Sec.; Vacant, Bookkeeper. Tel: 610-777-2967; 800-777-1894; Fax: 610-777-3973.
Health Benefits Office—Sr. JANET TAPHORN, O.S.F. Tel: 800-777-1894; 610-777-2967.
Office of Formation—Sr. CLAUDE MARIE JABLONSKI, Dir., Initial Formation and Vocations/Assocs. Tel: 610-796-7713.
Office of Justice, Peace, Earthcare—Sr. ROSE MACDERMOTT, Dir., *2627 W. Ninth St., Chester, 19013-2115.* Tel: 610-497-3641; Fax: 610-497-3434.
Office of Personnel—Sr. KATERI PEAKE, Dir. Tel: 610-796-8972.
Office of Retirement—Vacant.
Office of Vocations / Associates—JENNIFER GLASS, Asst. Vocations/Assoc. Dir. Tel: 610-796-8971.

CLERGY, PARISHES, MISSIONS AND PAROCHIAL SCHOOLS

CITY OF ALLENTOWN
(Lehigh County)

1—CATHEDRAL OF ST. CATHARINE OF SIENA (1919), Rev. Msgr. Alfred R. Ott, V.F.; Revs. Robert J. George; David L. James; Deacon William Hassler. In res., Rev. Msgr. Alfred A. Schlert, V.G., J.C.L.
Res., 1825 Turner St., 18104. Tel: 610-433-6461; Fax: 610-433-5452.
School—(Grades K-8) 210 N. 18th St., 18104. Tel: 610-435-8981; Fax: 610-437-7951. Mrs. H. Jacqueline Greco, Prin.
Lay Teachers 30; Students 472.
Catechesis / Religious Programs—Tel: 610-432-7655. Sr. Laura Berryman, S.C.S., D.R.E. Students 231.

2—ST. FRANCIS OF ASSISI (1928), Rev. Msgr. Dennis A. Rigney; Revs. Paul L. Rothermel; Peter Jurcik; Deacon Eugene M. Flanley, Jr.
Res., 801 N. 11th St., 18102-1304. Tel: 610-434-8776; Fax: 610-434-6972.
School—(Grades PreK-8) 1035 Washington St., 18102. Tel: 610-435-0364; Fax: 610-435-2666.
Sisters of St. Francis of Philadelphia 2; Lay Teachers 14; Students 422.
Parish Center—1046 W. Cedar St., 18102. Tel: 610-433-6102.
Catechesis / Religious Programs—Tel: 610-434-8299.
Students 220.

3—IMMACULATE CONCEPTION (1857). (Declared National Shrine of Our Lady of Guadalupe, Mother of the Americas 1974). Rev. Harold F. Dagle; Deacon Brian J. Monahan. In res., Rev. Msgr. John B. McCann.
Res., 501 Ridge Ave., 18102. Tel: 610-433-4404; Fax: 610-433-8401. [CEM]
School—Holy Spirit Regional Catholic Elementary School, Allentown. See separate listing. Tel: 610-434-4044; Fax: 610-434-5458.
Catechesis / Religious Programs—Located at Holy Spirit Elementary School, Allentown.
Convent—508 Ridge Ave., 18102. Tel: 610-432-0838.

4—ST. JOHN THE BAPTIST (Slovak), Rev. Msgr. Francis J. Zavodny.
Res., 924 N. Front St., 18102-1999. Tel: 610-432-0034; Fax: 610-432-2776. [CEM]
School—Holy Spirit Regional Catholic Elementary School, Allentown. See separate listing.
Convent—920 N. Front St., 18102. Tel: 610-434-1471.

5—OUR LADY HELP OF CHRISTIANS (1927), Revs. Daniel J. Yenushosky; Frans J. Berkhout; Deacon Charles Coyle.
Res., 444 N. Jasper St., 18109. Tel: 610-432-9384; Fax: 610-782-9297.
School—934 Hanover Ave., 18109. Tel: 610-433-1592.
Sisters of Christian Charity 1; Lay Teachers 9; Students 176.
Catechesis / Religious Programs—Students 76.
Convent—922 Hanover Ave., 18103. Tel: 610-433-4915.

6—OUR LADY OF MT. CARMEL (1911) (Italian), Rev. Msgr. Joseph R. Sobiesiak; Deacon Dominick F. Amedeo.
Res., 336 N. 4th St., 18102-5478. Tel: 610-434-5171; Fax: 610-434-2441. [CEM]
School—Sacred Heart Regional Catholic Elementary School, Allentown. See separate listing. Tel: 610-437-3031; Fax: 610-437-1310.
Catechesis / Religious Programs—Located at Sacred Heart, Allentown. Sr. Kathleen Brown, I.H.M., D.R.E.

7—ST. PAUL (1928), Rev. Msgr. Robert M. Forst; Revs. Francis J. Fromholzer; Luigi Palmieri; Deacons Daniel A. Thomson; Gary Granato. In res., Rev. Michael S. Lawrence.
Res., 920 S. Second St., 18103. Tel: 610-797-9733; Fax: 610-797-9742;9537.
Church—Second St. & Susquehanna St., 18103.
School—(Grades K-8) 219 W. Susquehanna St., 18103. Tel: 610-797-5321. Rita Curran, Prin.
Lay Teachers 12; Students 245.
Catechesis / Religious Programs—Students 150.

8—SS. PETER AND PAUL (Polish), Rev. Ladislaus J. Dudek.
Res., 1065 Fullerton Ave., 18102. Tel: 610-432-2252; Fax: 610-432-0247.
School—Holy Spirit Regional Catholic Elementary School, Allentown. See separate listing.

9—SACRED HEART OF JESUS (1869) (German-Spanish), Rev. Msgr. Joseph R. Sobiesiak; Rev. Andrew N. Gehringer; Deacons Victor M. Quiles; Alfonso Solis; Dominic Amadeo. In res., Rev. George R. Winne.
Res., 336 N. Fourth St., 18102. Tel: 610-434-5171; Fax: 610-434-2441. [CEM]
School—(Grades PreK-8) 321 N. Fourth St., 18102. Tel: 610-437-3031; Fax: 610-437-1310. James Krupka, Prin.
Lay Teachers 10; Students 170.
High School—Tel: 610-437-4601; Fax: 610-437-6760. Rev. Frans J. Berkhout, Prin.
Catechesis / Religious Programs—Parish Center, 417 Pine St., 18102. Tel: 610-434-5171. Sr. Kathleen Brown, I.H.M., D.R.E.
Students 320.

10—ST. STEPHEN OF HUNGARY (1915) (Hungarian), Rev. Richard J. Ford.
Res., 510 Union St., 18101-2307. Tel: 610-439-0111; Fax: 610-439-6048.
School—Sacred Heart Regional Catholic Elementary School, Allentown. See separate listing.

11—ST. THOMAS MORE (1966), Rev. Msgr. John P. Murphy; Rev. Eric R. Arnout, Jr.; Deacons James R. Duncan; Thomas J. Mullins. In res., Rev. John S. Mraz.
Res., 1040 Flexer Ave., 18103. Tel: 610-433-7413; Fax: 610-433-2308.
School—Tel: 610-432-0396; Fax: 610-432-1395.
Bernardine Sisters 2; Lay Teachers 37; Students 640.
Catechesis / Religious Programs—Tel: 610-437-3491.
Students 493.
Convent—992 Flexer Ave., 18103. Tel: 610-437-9520.

OUTSIDE CITY OF ALLENTOWN

Ashland, Schuylkill Co., St. Joseph (1856), Rev. Floyd Caesar; Deacon Robert McManus.
Res., 1100 Walnut St., 17921. Tel: 570-875-1521; Fax: 570-875-2635. [CEM]
School—Immaculate Heart Regional Catholic Elementary School, Girardville. See separate listing. Tel: 717-276-6568.
Catechesis / Religious Programs—Students 60.
Convent—1123 Walnut St., 17921. Tel: 717-875-3553.
St. Mauritius (1856) (German), Rev. Floyd Caesar; Deacon Robert McManus.
Res., 802 Pine St., 17921. Tel: 570-875-2990; Fax: 570-875-2635. [CEM]
School—Immaculate Heart Regional Catholic Elementary School, Girardville. See separate listing. Tel: 570-276-6568.
Catechesis / Religious Programs—Students 60.
Mission—Lavelle, Schuylkill Co., St. Elizabeth, Main St., Lavelle, 17943.

Bally, Berks Co., Most Blessed Sacrament (1741), Rev. Msgr. Edward J. Coyle; Revs. Michael J. Briggman, Pastor Emeritus; Robert Freed; Deacon Thomas J. Murphy.
Res., 610 Pine St., Box C, 19503. Tel: 610-845-2460; Fax: 610-845-2660. [CEM]
School—St. Francis Academy, Bally. See separate listing. Tel: 610-845-7364; Fax: 610-845-2223.
Catechesis / Religious Programs—Barbara A. Seaman, D.R.E.
Students 325.

Bangor, Northampton Co., Our Lady of Good Counsel (1915), Rev. John B. Fitzgerald, C.M.
Res., 436 S. Second St., 18013. Tel: 610-588-5445; Fax: 610-599-8811. [CEM]
School—Our Lady of Mt. Carmel Regional Catholic Elementary School, Roseto. See separate listing. Tel: 610-588-2629.
Catechesis / Religious Programs—Fax: 610-588-8811. Elizabeth Thompson, D.R.E.
Students 105.
Mission—Portland, Northampton Co., St. Vincent de Paul, Church St., Portland, 18351.

Barnesville, Schuylkill Co., St. Richard (1950), Rev. Paul G. Puza.
Res., Park Crest, R.R. 2, Box 221, 18214-9747. Tel: 570-467-2315; Fax: 570-467-3803.
Catechesis / Religious Programs—Tel: 570-773-3687. Marcella Gill, D.R.E.
Students 19.

Bath, Northampton Co., Sacred Heart (1920), Revs. Gregory J. Tauber, S.T.L.; Dominic Pham, M.Div.; Deacon John Hanni.
Res., 210 E. Northampton St., 18014. Tel: 610-837-7874; Fax: 610-837-4570. [CEM]
School—(Grades PreK-8) 115 Washington St., 18014. Tel: 610-837-6391; Fax: 610-837-2469. Louise Glass, Prin.
Lay Teachers 9; Students 250.
Catechesis / Religious Programs—Mrs. Helen Browne, D.R.E.
Students 396.

Beaver Meadows, Carbon Co., St. Mary (1841), Rev. John J. Duminiak.
Res., 121 Berwick St., P.O. Box 235, 18216. Tel: 570-455-2613; Fax: 570-455-3125. [CEM]
Catechesis / Religious Programs—Students 47.

Berlinsville, Northampton Co., St. Nicholas, Rev. Edward W. McElduff.
Res., 1152 Oak Rd., Walnutport, 18088-9728. Tel: 610-767-3107; Fax: 610-760-8384.
School—St. John Neumann Regional Catholic Elementary School, Palmerton-Slatington. See separate listing.

Bethlehem, Northampton Co.,

1—ST. ANNE, (1929), Rev. Msgr. Robert F. Kozel; Rev. John M. Gibbons; Deacons Francis Cosgrove; Richard G. Scrak; Sr. Kathleen Mackerer, S.S.J., Pastoral Assoc. In res., Rev. Stephen L. Maco.
Res., 450 Washington Ave., 18017. Tel: 610-867-5039; Fax: 610-882-4094.
School—(Grades PreK-8) Easton Ave. & Hickory St., 18017. Tel: 610-868-4182; Fax: 610-868-8709. Mrs. Norma Romberger, Prin.
Lay Teachers 20; Students 451.
Catechesis/Religious Programs—Tel: 610-868-7514. Mrs. Stephanie Tomko, D.R.E.
Students 186.

2—SS. CYRIL AND METHODIUS, (1891) (Slovak), Rev. Msgr. Michael J. Chaback, S.T.D.; Deacons Frank J. Danyi, Jr.; Jeffrey R. Trexler.
Res., 617 Pierce St., 18015. Tel: 610-866-3391; Fax: 610-866-6490. [CEM]
School—(Grades K-8) 551 Thomas St. & Pierce St., 18015. Tel: 610-866-0042. Mrs. Joan M. West, Prin.
Lay Teachers 9; Students 105.
Catechesis/Religious Programs—Students 41.
Convent—520 Buchanan St., 18015. Tel: 610-866-0275.

3—HOLY GHOST, (1871) (German), Rev. Msgr. William F. Baver, M.Th.; Deacon Franklin J. Chiles. In res., Rev. Ai Ba Do (Vietnam).
Res., 417 Carlton Ave., 18015. Tel: 610-867-9382; Fax: 610-867-6839. [CEM]
School—Holy Child Regional Catholic Elementary School, Bethlehem. See separate listing. Tel: 610-865-0861.
Convent—427 Carlton Ave., 18015. Tel: 610-867-3364.

4—HOLY INFANCY, (1861), Rev. Msgr. Robert J. Biszek; Rev. David J. Kozak; Deacons Nicasio Rodriguez; Roberto DeJesus; Victor M. Quiles. In res., Rev. Jose Nunes Santos, Portugese Apostolate.
Res., 312 E. Fourth St., 18015-1706. Tel: 610-866-1121; Fax: 610-866-7094. [CEM]
School—(Grades PreK-8) 202 E. Fourth St., 18015. Tel: 610-868-2621. Sr. Joyce Valese, Prin.
Sisters of St. Joseph 4; Sisters of St. Francis 1; Lay Teachers 8; Students 285.
Catechesis/Religious Programs—Stephanie Rivera, D.R.E.
Students 160.
Convents—Tel: 610-867-7384. Poor Sisters of St. Joseph; Casa Belen, 305 E. Fourth St., 18015. Tel: 610-867-4030.

5—ST. JOHN CAPISTRANO, (1903) (Hungarian), Rev. Edward C. Bolez.
Res., 910 E. Fourth St., 18015. Tel: 610-866-2714; Fax: 610-317-8026.
School—SS. Cyril and Methodius Regional Catholic Elementary School, Bethlehem. See separate listing. Tel: 610-866-0042; Fax: 610-866-6490.
Catechesis/Religious Programs—Students 8.

6—ST. JOSEPH, (1913) (Slovenian), Rev. Joseph N. Galic, O.F.M.
Res., 416 E. Fifth St., 18015-1893. Tel: 610-866-4102; Fax: 610-866-4258.
School—SS. Cyril and Methodius Regional Catholic Elementary School, Bethlehem. See separate listing. Tel: 610-866-0042.

7—NOTRE DAME OF BETHLEHEM, Lehigh Co., (1954), Rev. Msgr. William E. Handges; Revs. Joseph D. Hulko; Gregory Karpyn; Deacons Lemuel Von Leer; Richard Sewald. In res., Rev. Bernard J. Ezaki.
Res., 1861 Catasauqua Rd., 18018-1298. Tel: 610-866-4371; Fax: 610-866-9065.
School—(Grades K-8) 1835 Catasauqua Rd., 18018. Tel: 610-866-2231; Fax: 610-866-4374. Sr. Patricia A. Cullen, S.S.J., Prin.
Sisters of St. Joseph 1; Lay Teachers 24; Students 469.
Catechesis/Religious Programs—Tel: 610-866-1418. Mrs. Stephanie Kalavoda, D.R.E.
Students 335.
Convent—1823 Catasauqua Rd., 18018. Tel: 610-866-4310.

8—OUR LADY OF PERPETUAL HELP, (1963), Rev. Msgr. Edward R. Sacks; Rev. Martin F. Kern; Deacons Bernard J. Salabsky, Jr.; George Kelly. In res., Rev. Msgr. David J. Morrison.
Res., 3219 Santee Rd., 18020. Tel: 610-867-8409; Fax: 610-867-4870.
School—3221 Santee Rd., 18020. Tel: 610-868-6570; Fax: 610-868-7941.
Lay Teachers 12; Students 295.
Catechesis/Religious Programs—Students 546.

9—OUR LADY OF POMPEII, (1902) (Italian), Rev. Msgr. Paul B. della Picca.
Res., 826 E. Fourth St., 18015. Tel: 610-691-0719; Fax: 610-691-0719.
School—SS. Cyril and Methodius Regional Catholic Elementary School, Bethlehem. See separate listing. Tel: 610-866-0042; Fax: 610-866-6490.
Catechesis/Religious Programs—Located at SS. Cyril and Methodius School, Bethlehem.

10—SS. SIMON AND JUDE, Lehigh Co., (1917), Revs. Robert J. Reed; Victor F. Finelli.
Res., 730 W. Broad St., 18018. Tel: 610-866-5582; Fax: 610-866-2992.
School—(Grades K-8) 6th Ave. & North St., 18018. Tel: 610-867-9530. Sr. Lisa Ann Golden, I.H.M., Prin.
Sisters of the Immaculate Heart of Mary 2; Lay Teachers 12; Students 195.
Catechesis/Religious Programs—Tel: 610-861-7507.
Students 210.
Convent—714 W. Broad St., 18018. Tel: 610-867-9546.

11—ST. STANISLAUS, (1906) (Polish), Rev. Frederick Przydzial.
Res., 429 Hayes St., 18015. Tel: 610-867-9323.
School—SS. Cyril and Methodius Regional Catholic Elementary School, Bethlehem. See separate listing.
Catechesis/Religious Programs—Students 11.

Birdsboro, Berks Co., Immaculate Conception (1916), Rev. Msgr. Nevin J. Klinger, J.C.L., M.A.
Res., 640 Main St., 19508. Tel: 610-582-2411. [CEM 2]
School—St. Catharine of Siena Regional Catholic Elementary School, Reading, PA. See separate listing. Tel: 610-779-5810; Fax: 610-779-6888.
Catechesis/Religious Programs—Tel: 610-582-3880; Fax: 610-404-2609.
Students 330.

Boyertown, Berks Co., St. Columbkill (1921), Revs. Robert C. Quinn; Edward Essig.
Res., 200 Indian Spring Rd., 19512. Tel: 610-367-2371; Fax: 610-369-0242.
School—St. Francis Academy, Bally. See separate listing. Tel: 610-845-7364; Fax: 610-845-2223.
Catechesis/Religious Programs—Tel: 610-367-5975. D.R.E. Sr. Nancy Kramer, S.S.J.; Constance Boyer.
Students 695.

Branchdale, Schuylkill Co., St. Mary Star of the Sea (1886), Rev. Leo J. Maletz.
Res., State Rd., 17923. Tel: 570-544-2592; Fax: 570-544-5742. [CEM]
School—Good Shepherd Regional Catholic Elementary School, Minersville. See separate listing. Tel: 570-544-3766.

Brockton, Schuylkill Co., St. Bartholomew (1846), Rev. Francis M. Grundowski.
Res., 214 Green St., Box 292, 17925. Tel: 570-668-1500; Fax: 570-668-5487. [CEM]
School—St. Jerome Regional Catholic Elementary, Tamaqua. See separate listing.
Catechesis/Religious Programs—Located at St. Jerome Regional, Tamaqua. Tel: 570-668-4416.

Catasauqua, Northampton Co., St. Andrew (1902) (Slovak), Rev. Stephen J. Radocha; Deacon Gregory J. Bankos, Sr.
Mailing Address: c/o 2174 Lincoln Ave., Northampton, 18067. Tel: 610-262-2559; Fax: 610-262-1613. [CEM]
Church—Third St. & Cypress St., North Catasauqua, 18032. Tel: 610-264-0612.
School—Our Lady of Hungary Regional Catholic Elementary School, Northampton. See separate listing. Tel: 610-262-9171; Fax: 610-262-2202.
Catechesis/Religious Programs—Located at Assumption B.V.M., Northampton. Tel: 610-262-7343.

Annunciation B.V.M. - St. Mary's, Lehigh Co., (1857) (German), Rev. Francis T. Gillespie.
Res., 122 Union St., 18032-1923. Tel: 610-264-0332; Fax: 610-264-5271. [CEM]
Catechesis/Religious Programs—Tel: 610-264-9383.
Students 156.

St. Lawrence (Lehigh Co.) (1858), Rev. William T. Baker.
Res., 1001 Second St., 18032. Tel: 610-264-1972; Fax: 610-264-2105. [CEM 2]

Coaldale, Schuylkill Co., SS. Cyril and Methodius (1920) (Slovak), Rev. John J. Pavlosky.
Res., 41 E. Ruddle St., 18218-1206. Tel: 570-645-4647; Fax: 570-645-4849. [CEM]
School—Our Lady of the Angels Academy, Lansford. See separate listing. Tel: 570-645-7170.

St. John the Baptist (1914) (Lithuanian), Rev. John J. Pavlosky, M.Div.
Res., 41 E. Ruddle St., 18218-1206. Tel: 570-645-4647; Fax: 570-645-4849. [JC]
School—Our Lady of the Angels Academy, Lansford. See separate listing. Tel: 570-645-7170.

St. Mary of the Assumption (1892), Rev. John J. Pavlosky, M.Div.
Res., 41 E. Ruddle St., 18218-1206. Tel: 570-645-4647; Fax: 570-645-4849.
School—Our Lady of the Angels Academy, Lansford. See separate listing.
Convent—231 Second St., 18218. Tel: 570-645-2310.

Colesville, Lehigh Co., Assumption B.V.M. (1927), Rev. Msgr. John J. Martin; Rev. James P. Finnegan, O.S.F.S.; Patricia Herbst, Pastoral Min.; Deacons Bernard M. Wisser; Richard Thoden.
Res., 4101 Old Bethlehem Pike, Bethlehem, 18015. Tel: 610-867-7424; Fax: 610-867-8301.
School—St. Michael the Archangel Regional Catholic Elementary School, Colesville-Limeport. See separate listing.
Catechesis/Religious Programs—Tel: 610-814-0712. Christina Bigatel Durback, D.R.E.
Students 256.

Coplay, Lehigh Co., St. Peter (1927) (Austrian-Hungarian), Revs. Paul L. Bader; Francis J. Opps; Deacon Stephen F. Nemeth.
Res., 4 S. Fifth St., 18037. Tel: 610-262-2417; Fax: 610-262-2652. [CEM]
School—Christ the King Regional Catholic Elementary School, Coplay, Whitehall. See separate listing. Tel: 610-262-5822; Fax: 610-262-5632.
Catechesis/Religious Programs—Deacon Stephen F. Nemeth, D.R.E.
Students 89.

Cumbola, Schuylkill Co., St. Anthony of Padua (1907) (Polish), Rev. Ronald J. Yarrosh.
Parish Office: 41 Clay St., New Philadelphia, 17959. Tel: 570-277-6815; Fax: 570-277-0528. [CEM]
Market St., 17930.
Catechesis/Religious Programs—Students 2.

Easton, Northampton Co.,

1—ST. ANTHONY OF PADUA, (1909) (Italian), Revs. William T. Campion; David W. Karns; Robert R. Fagan; Deacon Charles A. DeBellis.
Res., 900 Washington St., 18042. Tel: 610-253-7188; Fax: 610-253-6184. [CEM]
Nursery School—138 E. Nesquehoning St., 18042. Tel: 610-242-4033.
School—Easton Catholic School, Easton. See separate listing. Tel: 610-252-1393.
Catechesis/Religious Programs—Mrs. Karen Donato, D.R.E.
Students 206.
Convent—770 Washington St., 18042. Tel: 610-258-7792; Fax: 610-258-7792.
Chapel—South Easton, St. Mary's.

2—ST. BERNARD, (1829), Revs. John J. Grabish; Richard W. Campo; Deacons Henry Fleck, Jr.; Thomas C. Reichard.
Res. and Parish Center: 132 S. Fifth St., 18042. Tel: 610-252-7381; Fax: 610-252-6757. [CEM][JC]
School—Easton Catholic School, Easton. See separate listing. Tel: 610-252-1393; Fax: 610-253-6184.
Catechesis/Religious Programs—Karen Corpora, D.R.E.
Students 304.

3—ST. JANE FRANCES DE CHANTAL, (1925), Rev. Msgr. Gerald Gobitas; Revs. Edward Domin; Joseph Elamparayil, O.C.D.; Deacon Robert W. Rodgers.
Res., 1918 Washington Blvd., 18042. Tel: 610-253-3553; Fax: 610-253-5711. [JC]
Church—19th St. & Washington Blvd., 18042.
School—(Grades PreK-8) 1946 Washington Blvd., 18042. Tel: 610-253-8442.
Sisters of the Immaculate Heart of Mary 3; Lay Teachers 18; Students 540.
Catechesis/Religious Programs—Tel: 610-253-7794.
Students 458.
Convent—Tel: 610-253-4912.

4—ST. JOSEPH, (1852) (German), Rev. Joseph A. Sheehan.
Res., 129 Davis St., 18042-6295. Tel: 610-252-0242; Fax: 610-253-7558. [CEM 2]
School—Easton Catholic School, Easton. See separate listing.
Catechesis/Religious Programs—Students 105.

5—ST. MICHAEL, (1915) (Lithuanian), Rev. John J. Grabish; Deacons Thomas C. Reichard; Henry Fleck, Jr.
Res., 132 S. Fifth, 18042. Tel: 610-252-7381; Fax: 610-252-6757. [CEM]
School—Easton Catholic School, Easton. See separate listing. Tel: 610-252-1393; Fax: 610-253-6184.
Catechesis/Religious Programs—Students 2.

Ellengowan, Schuylkill Co., St. Aidan. Closed. Parish from November 1919 to July 9, 1948. Records at the Annunciation B.V.M. Church, Shenandoah.

Emmaus, Lehigh Co., St. Ann (1931), Rev. Msgr. Thomas E. Hoban; Rev. Thomas P. Koons; Deacons Richard B. Close; Gerald R. Schmidt.

Res., 415 S. Sixth St., 18049. Tel: 610-965-2426; Fax: 610-967-1099. [CEM]
School—(Grades PreK-8) 570 Wood St., 18049. Tel: 610-965-9220. Loretta Chapin, Prin.
Sisters 2; Lay Teachers 13; Students 370.
Catechesis/Religious Programs—Tel: 610-965-6888. Angela Faidley, D.R.E.
Students 540.
Convent—526 Fairview St., 18049. Tel: 610-965-6818.

Fountain Hill, Lehigh Co., St. Ursula (Bethlehem P.O.) (1919), Rev. Vincent P. York; Deacon Joseph G. Buragino. In res., Rev. Frederick F. Sattler.
Res., 1300 Broadway, 18015. Tel: 610-867-5122; Fax: 610-867-6569.
School—Holy Child Regional Catholic Elementary School, Bethlehem. See separate listing. Tel: 610-865-0861; Fax: 610-997-0180.
Catechesis/Religious Programs—Students 168.

Frackville, Schuylkill Co., St. Ann (1924) (Polish), Rev. Dominik P. Kalata, M.Ed.; Deacon John A. Setlock.
Res., 7 S. Broad Mountain Ave., 17931. Tel: 570-874-0842; Fax: 570-874-2265.
School—Holy Family Regional Catholic Elementary School, Frackville. See separate listing. Tel: 570-874-0285.
Catechesis/Religious Programs—Located at St. Joseph, Frackville. Tel: 570-874-0610.

Annunciation B.V.M. (1917) (Lithuanian), Rev. Dominik P. Kalata, M.Ed.; Deacon John A. Setlock.
Res., 7 S. Broad Mountain Ave., 17931. Tel: 570-874-0842; Fax: 570-874-2265. [CEM]
School—Holy Family Regional Catholic Elementary School, Frackville. See separate listing. Tel: 570-874-0285.
Catechesis/Religious Programs—Located at St. Joseph, Frackville.
Convent—25 S. Broad Mountain Ave., 17931. Tel: 570-874-0351.

St. Joseph (1909), Rev. Joseph A. DeSantis; Deacon Joseph Burda.
Res., 14 N. Nice St., 17931. Tel: 717-874-0610; Fax: 717-874-0969. [CEM]
School—Holy Family Regional Catholic Elementary School, Frackville. See separate listing. Tel: 717-874-0285.
Catechesis/Religious Programs—Clustered with St. Ann and Annunciation BVM, Frackville.

Girardville, Schuylkill Co., St. Joseph (1870), Rev. Robert J. Kuzmann, M.S., M.A., M.Div.
Res., 211 W. Main St., 17935. Tel: 570-276-6239; Fax: 570-276-1444. [CEM]
School—Immaculate Heart Regional Catholic Elementary School, Girardville. See separate listing. Tel: 570-276-6568; Fax: 570-276-6568.
Catechesis/Religious Programs—Students 86.

St. Vincent de Paul (1907) (Lithuanian), Rev. David M. Liebner.
Res., 260 N. Second St., 17935. Tel: 570-276-6033. [CEM]
School—Immaculate Heart Regional Catholic Elementary School, Girardville. See separate listing. Tel: 570-276-6568.
Catechesis/Religious Programs—Students 10.

Gordon, Schuylkill Co., Our Lady of Good Counsel (1922), Rev. Larry J. Hess.
Res., 220 W. Biddle St., 17936. Tel: 570-875-0774; Fax: 570-875-2443.
School—Immaculate Heart Regional Catholic Elementary School, Girardville. See separate listing. Tel: 570-276-6568.
Catechesis/Religious Programs—Students 32.

Hamburg, Berks Co., St. Mary (1854), Rev. Joseph M. Braudis; Deacon Henry G. Gordon.
Res., 766 State St., 19526. Tel: 610-562-4251; Fax: 610-562-0379. [CEM]
Catechesis/Religious Programs—Parish Hall, 501 State St., 19526. Tel: 610-562-8110. Sr. Michele Fisher, C.S.F.N., D.R.E.
Students 268.
Station—Hamburg State School and Hospital, Tel: 610-562-6063.

Heckscherville, Schuylkill Co., St. Kieran (1857), Rev. Walter J. Hall.
Res., 225 Church Rd., Pottsville, 17901-9171. Tel: 570-544-4857; Fax: 570-544-4854. [CEM]
School—Good Shepherd Regional Catholic School, Minersville. See separate listing. Tel: 570-544-4360.
Catechesis/Religious Programs—Located at St. Vincent de Paul, Minersville.

Hellertown, Northampton Co., St. Theresa of the Child Jesus (1925), Rev. Msgr. Raymond F. Merman; Rev. Clifton E. Bishop, Jr.
Res., 1408 Easton Rd., 18055. Tel: 610-838-7045; Fax: 610-838-0932.
School—(Grades PreK-8) 300 Leonard St., 18055. Tel: 610-838-8161; Fax: 610-838-1915. Mrs. Elizabeth Smith, Prin.
Lay Teachers 9; Students 156.
Catechesis/Religious Programs—Tel: 610-838-7645.
Students 145. Sister Servants of the Immaculate Heart of Mary.
Convent—255 Wilson Ave., 18055.

Jim Thorpe, Carbon Co., Immaculate Conception (1848), Rev. Msgr. John G. Chizmar, V.F., M.Div.
Res., 180 W. Broadway, 18229. Tel: 570-325-2791; Fax: 570-325-2427. [CEM]
School—St. Joseph Regional Academy, Jim Thorpe. See separate listing. Tel: 570-325-3186.

St. Joseph (1871), Rev. Francis J. Baransky.
Res., 526 North St., 18229. Tel: 570-325-3731; Fax: 570-325-2523. [CEM]
School—St. Joseph Regional Academy, Jim Thorpe. See separate listing. Tel: 570-325-3186; Fax: 570-325-9451.
Catechesis/Religious Programs—Nicole Brasavage, D.R.E.
Students 222.
Convent—27 W. Sixth St., 18229. Tel: 570-325-2212.

Kelayres, Schuylkill Co., Immaculate Conception (1899) (Italian), Very Rev. Edward S. Zemanik. In res., Rev. Richard C. Brensinger, M.Div.
17 N. Cleveland St., McAdoo, 18237. [CEM]
School—McAdoo Regional Catholic Elementary School, McAdoo. See separate listing. Tel: 570-929-1442; Fax: 570-929-3016.
Catechesis/Religious Programs—Students 53.

Kutztown, Berks Co., St. Mary (1919), Rev. Msgr. Walter T. Scheaffer.
Res., 14833 Kutztown Rd., 19530. Tel: 610-683-7443; 683-7466 (Church); Fax: 610-683-7625.
Catechesis/Religious Programs—44 Rose Alley, 19530. Tel: 610-683-3797.
Students 371.

Lake Harmony, Carbon Co., St. Peter the Fisherman (1982), Rev. Msgr. John A. Auchter; Deacon John F. Thompson.
Res., Lake Dr., P.O. Box 237, 18624-0237. Tel: 570-722-2034; Fax: 570-722-1348.
Catechesis/Religious Programs—Students 155.

Lansford, Carbon Co., St. Ann, Rev. Stephen J. Halabura.
Res., 8 E. Bertsch St., 18232-2001. Tel: 570-645-2575; Fax: 570-645-3723.
School—Our Lady of the Valley Regional Catholic Elementary School, Lansford-Summit Hill. See separate listing.
Convent—30 E. Bertsch St., 18232. Tel: 570-645-2750.

St. Michael (1891) (Slovak), Rev. Thomas A. Derzack.
Res., 124 E. Abbott St., 18232-2012. Tel: 570-645-2282; Fax: 570-645-2754. [CEM]
School—Our Lady of the Angels Academy, Lansford. See separate listing. Tel: 570-645-7101;7170; Fax: 570-645-5278.

SS. Peter and Paul (Polish). Attended by St. Ann's Church. Rev. Stephen J. Halabura.
Mailing Address: 8 E. Bertsch St., 18232-2001.
Church—225 W. Phillip St., Coaldale, 18218. Tel: 570-645-7605. [CEM]
School—St. Michael Regional Catholic Elementary School, Lansford. See separate listing.

Lehighton, Carbon Co., SS. Peter and Paul (1885) (German), Rev. Philip F. Rodgers; Deacon William J. Wagner.
Res., 260 N. Third St., 18235-1595. Tel: 610-377-3690; Fax: 610-377-8881. [CEM]
School—307 Coal St., 18235. Tel: 610-377-4466. Mrs. Antoinette Collier, M.A., Prin.
Lay Teachers 6; Students 123.
Catechesis/Religious Programs—Students 105.

Limeport, Lehigh Co., St. Joseph (1926), Rev. Thomas R. Buckley; Deacon James F. Giltrap, III.
Res., 5050 St. Joseph's Rd., P.O. Box 178, 18060-0178. Tel: 610-965-2877; Fax: 610-965-8317. [CEM]
School—St. Michael the Archangel Regional Catholic Elementary School, Colesville-Limeport. See separate listing. Tel: 610-965-4441; Fax: 610-965-1030.
Catechesis/Religious Programs—Tel: 610-965-0590.
Students 192.

Lost Creek, Schuylkill Co., St. Mary Magdalen (1879), Rev. Edward J. O'Connor. In res., Rev. Charles J. Dene.
Res., 218 W. Cherry St., Shenandoah, 17976. Tel: 570-462-1916. [JC]
School—Father Walter J. Ciszek Elementary School, Shenandoah. See separate listing. Tel: 570-462-9666.

McAdoo, Schuylkill Co.,

1—St. Kunegunda, (Polish), Very Rev. Edward S. Zemanik.
Res., 36 E. Washington St., 18237. Tel: 570-929-2341; Fax: 570-929-2158. [CEM]
School—McAdoo Regional Catholic Elementary School, McAdoo. See separate listing. Tel: 570-929-1442.

2—St. Mary, (1893) (Slovak), Rev. Joseph Martinkovic (Slovakia).
Res., 101 E. Grant St., 18237-1905. Tel: 570-929-1061; Fax: 570-929-3707. [CEM]
School—McAdoo Regional Catholic Elementary School, McAdoo. See separate listing.

3—St. Patrick, (1869) (Irish), Rev. Edward S. Zemanik. In res., Rev. Richard C. Brensinger, M.Div.
Res., 17 N. Cleveland St., 18237. Tel: 570-929-1073; Fax: 570-929-4155. [CEM]
School—McAdoo Regional Catholic Elementary School, McAdoo. See separate listing. Tel: 570-929-1442; Fax: 570-929-3016.

4—St. Stephen of Hungary, (Hungarian). Attended by St. Kunegunda, McAdoo, 36 E. Washington St., 18237 Tel: 570-929-2341.

Mahanoy City, Schuylkill Co.,

1—Assumption B.V.M., (1892) (Slovak), Rev. Lawrence J. Bukaty.
Res., 728 W. Centre St., 17948. Tel: 570-773-1990; Fax: 570-773-1990. [CEM]
School—Mahanoy City Regional Catholic Elementary School, Mahanoy City. See separate listing.

2—St. Canicus, (1862), Rev. William F. Glosser; Deacon Ted Koval.
Res., 22 S. Catawissa St., 17948. Tel: 570-773-0550; Fax: 570-775-0668. [CEM]
School—Academy of the Blessed Virgin Mary, Mahanoy City. See separate listing. Tel: 570-773-2668; Fax: 570-773-2015.
Catechesis/Religious Programs—Students 200.

3—St. Casimir, (1893) (Polish), Rev. Lawrence J. Bukaty.
Res., 113 S. Catawissa St., 17948. Tel: 570-773-2461; Fax: 570-773-0610. [CEM]
School—Academy of the Blessed Virgin Mary, Mahanoy City. See separate listing. Tel: 717-773-2668.

4—St. Fidelis, (1863) (German), Rev. William F. Glosser; Deacon Ted Koval.
Res., 22 S. Catawissa St., 17948. Tel: 570-773-2850; Fax: 570-773-0668. [CEM]
School—Academy of the Blessed Virgin Mary, Mahanoy City. See separate listing. Tel: 570-773-2668; Fax: 570-773-2015.
Catechesis/Religious Programs—Clustered with St. Canicus, Mahanoy.

5—St. Joseph, (Lithuanian), Rev. Msgr. Anthony F. Wassel.
Res., 614 W. Mahanoy Ave., 17948-2416. Tel: 570-773-2771; Fax: 570-773-1937. [CEM]
School—Mahanoy City Regional Catholic Elementary School, Mahanoy City. See separate listing.

6—Sacred Heart, (Italian), Rev. Lawrence J. Bukaty.
Res., 728 W. Centre St., 17948. Tel: 570-773-1990; Fax: 570-773-1990. [CEM]
School—Mahanoy City Regional Catholic Elementary School, Mahanoy City. See separate listing.

Mahanoy Plane, Schuylkill Co., Holy Rosary. Closed. 1988. Parish records at St. Joseph's, Girardville.

Maizeville, Schuylkill Co., Our Lady of Siluva (Gilberton P.O.) (1907) (Lithuanian). (Formerly St. Louis) Administered by St. Joseph, Frackville. Rev. Joseph A. DeSantis; Deacon Joseph Costa.
Res., c/o 14 N. Nice St., Frackville, 17931. Tel: 717-874-0610; Fax: 717-874-0969. [CEM]
Catechesis/Religious Programs—Clustered with Assumption B.V.M., Mahanoy City. Tel: 717-773-1990; Fax: 717-773-1990.

Martins Creek, Northampton Co., St. Rocco (1937), Rev. Msgr. Joseph P. Dooley; Kathleen M. Edwards, Pastoral Assoc.
Res., 6658 School St., Box 421, 18063-0010. Tel: 610-258-9059; Fax: 610-258-4780.
School—Immaculate Conception Regional Catholic Elementary School, Pen-Argyl. See separate listing. Tel: 610-863-4816; Fax: 610-863-8158.
Catechesis/Religious Programs—Students 143.

Miller Heights, Northampton Co., Sacred Heart of Jesus (1936), Rev. Thomas J. King; Deacon Hugh E. McShane. In res., Rev. Patrick H. Lamb.
Res., 1817 First St., Bethlehem, 18017. Tel: 610-865-5042; Fax: 610-865-1912.
School—(Grades K-8). Tel: 610-867-0221; Fax: 610-867-8351. John Schulte, Prin.
Lay Teachers 11; Students 211.
Catechesis/Religious Programs—Students 180.

Minersville, Schuylkill Co.,

1—St. Barbara, (1913) (Italian), Rev. David C. Liebner; Deacon James Henninger.
Res., 320 Spruce St., 17954. Tel: 570-544-2234; Fax: 570-544-5043. [CEM]
School—Good Shepherd Regional Catholic Elementary School, Minersville. See separate listing under Regional Catholic Elemetary Schools, Diocesan.

Tel: 570-544-4360 (Grades PreK-3); 544-3766 (Grades 4-8); Fax: 570-544-4870 (Grades PreK-8).
Catechesis/Religious Programs—Tel: 570-544-6288. Mary Sacavage, D.R.E.
Students 20.

2—ST. FRANCIS OF ASSISI, (1895) (Lithuanian), Rev. David C. Liebner; Deacon James Henninger.
Res., 320 Spruce St., 17954. Tel: 570-544-2234; Fax: 570-544-5043. [CEM]
School—Good Shepherd Regional School, (Grades PreK-3). No longer Holy Redeemer Regional Catholic Elementary School. Merged to form Good Shepherd Regional School, Minersville. 538 Sunbury St., 17954. Tel: 570-544-4360; Fax: 570-544-4870.
(Grades 4-8) 301 St. Francis St., 17954. Tel: 717-544-3766. Ms. Rosalie Novack, Prin.
Catechesis/Religious Programs—Mary Sacavage, D.R.E., Tel: 570-544-6288.
Students 65.
Convent—300 Oak St., 17954. Tel: 570-544-4534. Sisters of St. Casimir

3—OUR LADY OF MOUNT CARMEL, (1855) (German), Rev. John W. Bambrick.
Res., 519 School St., 17954-1331. Tel: 570-544-2031; Fax: 570-544-4978. [CEM]
School—Good Shepherd Regional School, (Grades PreK-3) 538 Sunbury St., 17954. Tel: 570-544-4560.
(Grades 4-8) 301 St. Francis St., 17954. Tel: 570-544-3766. Ms. Rosalie Novack, Prin.
Catechesis/Religious Programs—Students 350.

4—ST. STANISLAUS KOSTKA, (1905) (Polish), Rev. Leo J. Maletz.
Res., 139 Spruce St., 17954-1652. Tel: 570-544-2211; Fax: 570-544-2317. [CEM 2]
School—Good Shepherd Regional School, (Grades PreK-3) 538 Sunbury St., 17954. Tel: 570-544-4360.
(Grades 4-8) 301 St. Francis St., 17954. Tel: 570-544-3766; Fax: 570-544-4870. Ms. Rosalie Novack, Prin.
Catechesis/Religious Programs—Tel: 570-544-6288.
Students 42.

5—ST. VINCENT DE PAUL, (1842), Rev. Msgr. John S. Campbell.
Res., 541 Sunbury St., 17954. Tel: 570-544-4741; Fax: 570-544-4742. [CEM 2]
School—Good Shepherd Regional Catholic School, Minersville. See separate listing under Regional Catholic Elementary Schools, Diocesan.
Catechesis/Religious Programs—Students 295.
Convent—534 Sunbury St., 17954. Tel: 570-544-2016. Sisters of St. Joseph

Mohnton, Berks Co., St. Benedict's (1955), Rev. Albert J. Byrne.
Res., 2020 Chesnut Hill Rd., 19540. Tel: 610-856-1006; Fax: 610-856-1035.
School—LaSalle Academy, Shillington. See separate listing. Tel: 610-777-7392.
Catechesis/Religious Programs—Tel: 610-370-0199; 856-5146. Ms. Valerie Christo, D.R.E.
Students 254.

Mount Carbon, Schuylkill Co., St. Francis de Sales (Pottsville P.O.), Rev. Edward B. Connolly.
Res., 49 Main St., Pottsville, 17901. Tel: 570-622-8270.
School—All Saints Regional Catholic Elementary School, Pottsville. See separate listing.

Nazareth, Northampton Co., Holy Family (1908), Revs. Jacob Welle, M.S.C.; John P. Kavcik, M.S.C.; Deacon Michael P. McGouldrick.
Res., 23 Forest Dr., 18064-1326. Tel: 610-759-0870; Fax: 610-746-2026. [CEM 2]
School—(Grades PreK-8) 17 Convent Ave., 18064. Tel: 610-759-5642. Ms. Barbara Amabile, Prin.
Lay Teachers 22; Students 362.
Catechesis/Religious Programs—Tel: 610-759-7467. D.R.E.: Jeanine Breault; Eileen Boligitz.
Students 560.

Nesquehoning, Carbon Co., Immaculate Conception of B.V.M. (1914) (Slovak), Rev. Bruno M. Tucci.
Mailing Address: 140 W. Mill St., 18240.
Res., 15 E. Garibaldi Ave., 18240. Tel: 570-669-6321; Fax: 570-669-9440.
School—Our Lady of the Angels Academy, Lansford. See separate listing. Tel: 570-645-7101;7170.
Catechesis/Religious Programs—Students 22.

Our Lady of Mount Carmel (1913) (Italian), Rev. Bruno M. Tucci.
Res., 15 E. Garibaldi Ave., 18240. Tel: 570-669-6321; Fax: 570-669-9440. [CEM]
School—Our Lady of the Angels Academy, Lansford. See separate listing. Tel: 570-645-7101;7170.
Catechesis/Religious Programs—140 W. Mill St., 18240.
Students 53.

Sacred Heart (1839), Revs. Paul P. Welkie, Pastor Emeritus; Edward W. Coleman.
Res., 81 W. High St., 18240. Tel: 570-669-9008; Fax: 570-669-5091. [CEM]
School—Our Lady of the Angels Academy, Lansford. See separate listing. Tel: 717-645-4700.
Catechesis/Religious Programs—Students 69.
Mission—Lake Hauto, Sacred Heart Chapel.

New Philadelphia, Schuylkill Co., Holy Family (1866) (Irish), Rev. Ronald J. Yarrosh.
Res. and Mailing Address: 41 Clay St., 17959. Tel: 570-277-6800; Fax: 570-277-0528. [CEM]
101 Valley St., 17959.
Catechesis/Religious Programs—Holy Cross, Tel: 570-277-6815.
Students 31.

Sacred Heart (1895) (Lithuanian), Rev. Ronald J. Yarrosh.
Res., 41 Clay St., 17959. Tel: 570-277-6815; Fax: 570-277-0528. [CEM]
Catechesis/Religious Programs—Holy Cross.
Students 26.
Mission—Middleport, Schuylkill Co., Immaculate Heart of Mary Chapel, Washington St., Middleport, 17953.

Newtown, Schuylkill Co., Sacred Heart (1896) (German), Rev. Edmund J. Brennan.
Res., State Rd., Branchdale, 17923. Tel: 570-544-2592; Fax: 570-544-5742. [CEM]
School—Good Shepherd Regional School, (Grades PreK-3) 538 Sunbury St., Minersville, 17954. Tel: 570-544-4560.
(Grades 4-8) 301 St. Francis St., Minersville, 17954. Tel: 570-544-3766. Ms. Rosalie Novack, Prin.

Northampton, Northampton Co., Assumption of the Blessed Virgin Mary (1922) (Slovak), Rev. Stephen J. Radocha; Deacon Gregory J. Bankos, Sr.
Res., 2174 Lincoln Ave., 18067. Tel: 610-262-2559; Fax: 610-262-1613. [CEM]
School—Our Lady of Hungary Regional Catholic Elementary School, Northampton. See separate listing. Tel: 610-262-9171; Fax: 610-262-2202.
Catechesis/Religious Programs—22nd & Washington Ave., 18067. Tel: 610-262-7343. Mrs. Linda Santucci, D.R.E.
Students 166.

St. Michael (1914) (Polish), Rev. Edwin V. Schwartz.
Res., 829 Main St., 18067. Tel: 610-262-2472; Fax: 610-261-4736. [JC]
School—Our Lady of Hungary Regional Catholic Elementary School, Northampton. See separate listing.
Catechesis/Religious Programs—Students 12.

Our Lady of Hungary (German-Magyar), Revs. Edwin V. Schwartz; John J. L. Little. In res., Rev. Msgr. James J. Mulligan.
Res., 1324 Newport Ave., 18067. Tel: 610-262-2227; Fax: 610-262-4192. [CEM]
School—Our Lady of Hungary Regional Catholic Elementary School, Northampton. See separate listing.
Convent—1314 Newport Ave., 18067. Tel: 610-262-2427.

Orefield, Lehigh Co., St. Joseph The Worker (1948), Rev. Msgr. Robert J. Wargo; Rev. Luis Angel Bonilla; Sr. Mary Kathryn Quinn, S.S.J., Pastoral Assoc.; Deacons Anthony T. Campanell; Daniel F. Metzker.
Res., 1879 Applewood Dr., 18069-9507. Tel: 610-395-2876; Fax: 610-395-2616.
Preschool—Program for 3 & 4 year old children. Tel: 610-395-4010. Mrs. Stacy Gowell, Dir.
Students 90.
School—(Grades K-8) 1858 Applewood Dr., 18069. Tel: 610-395-7221; Fax: 610-395-7904. Mrs. Patricia L. Johnson, Prin.
Students 416.
Catechesis/Religious Programs—Tel: 610-395-4920. Charlane Faught, D.R.E.
Students 940.

Palmerton, Carbon Co., Sacred Heart (1908), Rev. James J. Ward; Deacons William P. Pitts; Andrew J. Mihalik.
Res., 243 Lafayette Ave., 18071-1511. Tel: 610-826-2335; Fax: 610-826-5360. [CEM]
School—St. John Neumann Regional Catholic Elementary School, Palmerton-Slatington. See separate listing.
Annex—252 Lafayette Ave., 18071. Tel: 610-826-2849.

Pen Argyl, Northampton Co., St. Elizabeth of Hungary (1929), Rev. Richard A. Schware. In res., Rev. Donald J. Schaible.
Res., 300 W. Babbitt Ave., P.O. Box 126, 18072-0126. Tel: 610-863-4777; Fax: 610-863-7449. [CEM]
School—Immaculate Conception Regional Catholic Elementary School, Pen Argyl. See separate listing. Tel: 610-863-4816.
Catechesis/Religious Programs—Students 120.
Convent—111-115 Lobb Ave., 18072. Tel: 610-863-9214.

Port Carbon, Schuylkill Co., St. Stephen (1847), Rev. John J. McNamara.
Res., 218 Valley St., 17965. Tel: 717-622-6600. [CEM]
School—214 Valley St., 17965. Tel: 570-622-9817.
Sisters of the Immaculate Heart of Mary 4; Lay Teachers 8; Students 183.
Catechesis/Religious Programs—Tel: 570-622-1461.
Students 120.
Convent—Tel: 717-622-1461.

Pottsville, Schuylkill Co.,

1—ST. JOHN THE BAPTIST, (1841) (German), Rev. David J. Loeper; Sr. Barbara J. Wojnicki, C.S.N.F., Pastoral Assoc.; Deacon Luis R. Visot.
Res., 913 Mahantongo St., 17901. Tel: 570-622-5470; Fax: 570-622-4589. [CEM 3]
School—All Saints Regional Catholic Elementary School, Pottsville. See separate listing. Tel: 570-622-0106.
Catechesis/Religious Programs—Lucilla Kochol, D.R.E.
Students 135.

2—ST. JOSEPH, (Italian), Rev. Edward B. Connolly.
Res., 321 W. Howard Ave., 17901. Tel: 570-622-3081; Fax: 570-622-3084. [CEM]
School—All Saints Regional Catholic Elementary School, Pottsville. See separate listing.

3—MARY QUEEN OF PEACE, (1920), Revs. Bernard A. Flanagan; Charles L. McNulty, Pastor Emeritus; Deacon Stephen Andrusisian.
Res., 728 N. Centre St., 17901. Tel: 570-622-7004; Fax: 570-622-4287.
School—All Saints Regional Catholic Elementary School, Pottsville. See separate listing. Tel: 570-622-0106; Fax: 570-627-4737.
Catechesis/Religious Programs—Peterine Wojcik, D.R.E.
Students 73.

4—ST. PATRICK, (1827), Rev. Msgr. William E. Jones, V.F.; Revs. William J. Nahn; James F. Gaffney, M.A. In res., Rev. Joseph T. Whalen, M.Div.
Res., 319 Mahantongo St., 17901. Tel: 570-622-1802; Fax: 570-622-2593. [CEM 3]
Catechesis/Religious Programs—Students 195.
Convent—825 Mahantongo St., 17901. Tel: 570-622-0203.
Chapel—St. John Neumann, 2051 W. Norwegian St., 17901.

Reading, Berks Co.,

1—ST. ANTHONY, (Lithuanian). Attended by St. Peter, 322 S. Fifth St., 16902. Tel.: 610-372-9652.

2—ST. ANTHONY OF PADUA, (1914) (Polish), Rev. Richard E. Nachajski; Sr. Mary Joy Wasnesky, O.S.F., Pastoral Assoc.
Res., 501 Summit Ave., 19611. Tel: 610-374-1539; Fax: 610-374-0263.
School—LaSalle Academy & Early Childhood Center, Shillington. See separate listing. Tel: 610-777-7392; Fax: 610-777-1280.
Catechesis/Religious Programs—Students 46.
Convent—234 Grace St., 19611. Tel: 610-372-8578.

3—ST. CATHARINE OF SIENA, (1925), Rev. Msgr. Joseph P.T. Smith; Revs. Anthony M. Drouncheck; Paul A. DaDamio; Deacons George J. Faller; Richard A. Horst; Craig A. Fry.
Res., 2427 Perkiomen Ave., 19606. Tel: 610-779-4005; Fax: 610-779-0859.
Church—4975 Boyertown Pike, 19606. Tel: 610-779-4090.
School—St. Catharine of Siena Regional Catholic Elementary School, Reading. See separate listing. Tel: 610-779-5810; Fax: 610-779-6888.
Catechesis/Religious Programs—Tel: 610-779-8535.
Students 570.
Convent—2328 Perkiomen Ave., 19606. Tel: 610-779-5583.

4—SS. CYRIL AND METHODIUS, (1895) (Slovak), Rev. Charles S. Sperlak; Deacon John J. Allison.
Res., 449 S. Sixth St., 19602. Tel: 610-373-0627; Fax: 610-371-9532.
Catechesis/Religious Programs—Students 37.
Convent—502 S. Sixth St., 19602. Tel: 610-375-8001.

5—HOLY GUARDIAN ANGELS, (1929), Revs. Dennis T. Hartgen; John S. Pendzick; James J. Maranki.
Res., 3121 Kutztown Rd., 19605. Tel: 610-921-2729; Fax: 610-921-8886.
School—(Grades PreK-8) 3125 Kutztown Rd., 19605. Tel: 610-929-4124; Fax: 610-929-1623. Mrs. Maureen Wallin, Prin.
Lay Teachers 9; Students 307.
Catechesis/Religious Programs—Tel: 610-929-1416. Mrs. Rose Quaglia, D.R.E.
Students 341.
Mission—Temple, Berks Co., St. Anthony, 8th & Columbia, Temple, 19560.

6—Holy Rosary, (1904) (Italian), Rev. Msgr. Felix A. Losito; Deacon Lawrence A. Dudeck. In res., Rev. John P. Conte.
Res., 237 Franklin St., 19602. Tel: 610-373-5579; Fax: 610-372-0130.
School—Cabrini Academy, (Grades PreK-8) 240 Franklin St., 19602. Tel: 610-374-8483; Fax: 610-374-0369.
Sisters 4; Lay Teachers 9; Students 232.
Catechesis/Religious Programs—Students 80.
Convent—234 Franklin St., 19602. Tel: 610-375-9072; Fax: 610-375-4895.
Mission—Reading, Berks Co., Holy Rosary Chapel, Schuylkill Ave., 19601. Tel: 610-376-4383.

7—St. Joseph, (1891), Rev. Richard Clement; Deacon Peter LaFata.
Res., 1018 N. Eighth St., 19604. Tel: 610-376-2976; Fax: 610-376-2825.
School—(Grades K-8) 1040 N. Eighth St., 19604. Tel: 610-374-2951; Fax: 610-375-4889. Sr. Cecilia Didonato, I.H.M., Prin.
Sisters of the Immaculate Heart of Mary 1; Lay Teachers 8; Students 130.
Catechesis/Religious Programs—Students 36.
Convent—Tel: 610-372-1302.

8—St. Margaret, (1920), Rev. Francis P. Schoenauer; Deacons John P. Konopelski; Jose Trejo.
Res., 925 Centre Ave., 19601. Tel: 610-376-2919; Fax: 610-376-2462.
School—(Grades PreK-8) 233 Spring St., 19601. Tel: 610-375-1882. Sr. Diane Licordare, Prin.
Servants of Immaculate Heart of Mary 2; Lay Teachers 12; Students 235.
Catechesis/Religious Programs—Tel: 610-376-4584. William Davis, D.R.E.
Students 70.
Convent—233 Spring St., 19601. Tel: 610-372-1302.

9—St. Mary, (1888) (Polish), Rev. Leo S. Stajkowski.
250 S. 12th St., 19602. Tel: 610-376-6321; Fax: 610-376-1378. [CEM]
School—1200 Spruce St., 19602. Tel: 610-375-9311; Fax: 610-375-1298.
Lay Teachers 12; Students 98.
Catechesis/Religious Programs—Students 10.

10—St. Paul, (1860) (German), Revs. Andrew A. Ulincy; Theodore S. Macunas; Aram Berard, S.J.
Res., 151 N. 9th St., 19601. Tel: 610-372-1531; Fax: 610-372-7478. [CEM]
Catechesis/Religious Programs—Students 23.

11—St. Peter, (1752) (Spanish American), Revs. Charles A. Marciano; Christopher L. Wakefield, Vicar; Gabriel Vargas, Vicar; Deacons Jesus Centeno; Mariano Torres; Julio Colon; Fernando L. Torres; Leopoldo Alvarado; Francisco Najera. In res., Rev. Thomas J. Orsulak.
Res., 322 S. Fifth St., 19602. Tel: 610-372-9652; Fax: 610-374-3351. [CEM]
School—218 S. Fifth St., 19602. Tel: 610-374-2447.
Sisters of the Immaculate Heart of Mary 5; Lay Teachers 7; Students 200.
Catechesis/Religious Programs—Tel: 610-378-1947.
Students 450.
Convent—Tel: 610-373-6185.

Ringtown, Schuylkill Co., St. Mary (1923), Rev. Victor J. Anselmi.
Mailing Address: 18 E. Oak St., Shenandoah, 17976. Tel: 570-889-3850; Fax: 570-462-1747.
Res., 86 N. Center St., 17967. Tel: 570-889-3850; Fax: 570-462-1747. [CEM]
School—Father Walter J. Ciszek Elementary School, Shenandoah. See separate listing. Tel: 570-462-3927; Fax: 570-462-4603.
Catechesis/Religious Programs—Students 57.

Robesonia, Berks Co., St. Francis de Sales (1982), Rev. David J. Devlin, O.S.F.S.; Sr. Mary Heffron, I.H.M., Pastoral Assoc.
Res., 321 N. Church St., 19551. Tel: 610-693-5851; Fax: 610-693-5852.
Catechesis/Religious Programs—Students 218.

Roseto, Northampton Co., Our Lady of Mt. Carmel (1897) (Italian), Revs. Thomas W. Prior, C.M.; James G. Prior, C.M.
Res., P.O. Box 422, 18013. Tel: 610-588-2183; Fax: 610-588-6973. [CEM 2]
School—Our Lady of Mt. Carmel Regional Catholic Elementary School, Roseto. See separate listing. Tel: 610-588-2629; Fax: 610-588-3423.
Catechesis/Religious Programs—Students 199.

Saint Clair, Schuylkill Co.,

1—St. Boniface, (1854) (German), Rev. Kevin P. Gallagher.
Parish Office: Tel: 570-429-0370; Fax: 570-429-0630.
Res., 250 E. Hancock St., 17970. Tel: 570-429-0701; Fax: 570-429-0630. [CEM]
School—St. Stephen Regional Catholic School, Port Carbon. See separate listing. Tel: 570-622-3063; Fax: 570-622-3689.
Catechesis/Religious Programs—Located at St. Mary's, St. Clair. Tel: 570-429-1621.

2—St. Casimir, (Lithuanian), Rev. Ronald V. Jankaitis.
Res., 441 S. Nichols St., 17970-9998. Tel: 570-429-2400. [CEM]
School—Saint Clair Regional Catholic Elementary School, Saint Clair. See separate listing.

3—Immaculate Conception, (1905) (Slovak), Rev. Paul E. Masiar.
Res., Caroline Ave., Diener's Hill, 17970-1361. Tel: 570-429-1315; Fax: 570-429-0369. [CEM]
Catechesis/Religious Programs—Located at St. Mary's Hall, St. Clair. Tel: 717-429-0370; Fax: 717-429-0630.

4—St. Mary, (1864), Rev. Kevin P. Gallagher; Deacon John F. Pogash.
Parish Office: Tel: 570-429-0370; Fax: 570-429-0630.
Res., 250 E. Hancock St., 17970. Tel: 570-429-0701. [CEM 2]
School—St. Stephen Regional Catholic School, Port Carbon. See separate listing. Tel: 570-622-3063; Fax: 570-622-3689.
Catechesis/Religious Programs—Tel: 570-429-1621.
Students 56.

5—SS. Peter and Paul, (1918) (Polish), Rev. Kevin P. Gallagher.
Res., 250 E. Hancock St., 17970. Tel: 570-429-0701 (Res.); 570-429-0370 (Parish Office); Fax: 570-429-0630. [CEM]
School—St. Stephen Regional Catholic School, Port Carbon. See separate listing. Tel: 717-622-3063; Fax: 717-622-3689.
Catechesis/Religious Programs—Located at St. Mary's, St. Clair. Tel: 570-429-1621.

Schuylkill Haven, Schuylkill Co., St. Ambrose (1851), Revs. Michael J. Stone; Eric J. Gruber; Deacon Richard K. Braun.
Res., 201 Randel St., 17972. Tel: 570-385-1031; Fax: 570-385-1035. [CEM]
School—(Grades PreK-8) 302 Randel St., 17972. Tel: 570-385-2377; Fax: 570-385-2387. Mary Lou Michaels, Prin.
Lay Teachers 10; Students 209.
Catechesis/Religious Programs—Tel: 570-385-2472. Sr. Dolorita C.S.F.N., D.R.E.
Students 375.
Station—Schuylkill County Hospital and Home for Aged.

Shenandoah, Schuylkill Co.,

1—Annunciation, (1870), Revs. Edward J. O'Connor; Robert T. Finlan.
Res., 218 W. Cherry St., 17976. Tel: 570-462-1916; Fax: 570-462-1245. [CEM]
School—Father Walter J. Ciszek Elementary School, Shenandoah. See separate listing. Tel: 570-462-3927.
Convent—229 W. Cherry St., 17976. Tel: 570-462-1024.

2—St. Casimir, (1872) (Polish), Rev. Msgr. Edward W. Sarzynski.
Res., 108 W. Cherry St., 17976-2207. Tel: 570-462-1968; Fax: 570-462-1388. [CEM]
School—Father Walter J. Ciszek School, Shenandoah. See separate listing. Tel: 570-462-3927.
Convent—233 N. Jardin St., 17976. Tel: 570-462-0877.

3—St. George, (1891) (Lithuanian), Revs. Robert J. Potts; Deogratias Rwegasira, A.J. In res., Rev. Paul O. Gaggawala, A.J.
Res., 129 S. Jardin St., 17976. Tel: 570-462-1989; Fax: 570-462-1980. [CEM 5]
School—Father Walter J. Ciszek Elementary School, Shenandoah. See separate listing.

4—Holy Family, (1870-1934). Closed. Records kept at Annunciation, Shenandoah.

5—Our Lady of Mt. Carmel, (1914) (Italian), Revs. Robert J. Potts; Deogratias Rwegasira, A.J.
Res., 129 S. Jardin St., 17976. Tel: 570-462-1989; Fax: 570-462-1980. [CEM]
School—Father Walter J. Ciszek Elementary School, Shenandoah. See separate listing.

6—St. Stanislaus, (1898) (Polish), Rev. Msgr. Edward W. Sarzynski.
Res., 108 W. Cherry St., 17976. Tel: 570-462-1968; Fax: 570-462-1388. [CEM]
School—Father Walter J. Ciszek Elementary School, Shenandoah. See separate listing. Tel: 570-462-3927.

7—St. Stephen, (1899) (Slovak), Rev. Victor J. Anselmi.
Res., 18 E. Oak St., 17976. Tel: 717-462-0331; Fax: 717-462-1747. [CEM]
School—Father Walter J. Ciszek Elementary School, Shenandoah. See separate listing. Tel: 570-462-3927; Fax: 570-462-4603.
Catechesis/Religious Programs—Located at Fr. Ciszek School, Shenandoah.

Sheppton, Schuylkill Co., St. Joseph (1894), Rev. Raymond P. Slezak.
Res., 14 E. Oak St., P.O. Box 118, 18248-0118. Tel: 570-384-4102; Fax: 570-384-4757. [CEM][JC]
Catechesis/Religious Programs—Students 18.
Mission—Oneida, Schuykill Co., St. John the Baptist, P.O. Box 118, 18248.

Shillington, Berks Co., St. John Baptist de la Salle (1948), Rev. Msgr. Thomas J. Birch, Pastor Emeritus; Revs. David C. Gillis; Michael E. Ahrensfield; Sr. Katherine O'Donnell, R.S.M., Pastoral Assoc.; Deacon Sylvester F. Simchick.
Res., 420 Holland St., 19607. Tel: 610-777-1697; Fax: 610-777-4468.
School—LaSalle Academy, Shillington. See separate listing. Tel: 610-777-1697; Fax: 610-777-4468.
Catechesis/Religious Programs—Bernadette H. Yohn, D.R.E.
Students 337.

Sinking Spring, Berks Co., St. Ignatius Loyola (1965), Rev. Msgr. James A. Treston, V.F.; Revs. Adam C. Sedar; Francis J. McNelis; Deacons John A. Coffin; John W. Murphy, Jr.
Res., 2810 St. Alban's Dr., 19608-1028. Tel: 610-678-3767; Fax: 610-678-4483.
School—(Grades PreK-8). Tel: 610-678-0111; Fax: 610-670-5795. Mrs. Janice Bayerle, Prin.
Sisters of the Third Order of St. Francis 2; Lay Teachers 33; Students 619.
Catechesis/Religious Programs—2710 St. Alban's Dr., Reading, 19609. Tel: 610-678-0676.
Students 695.
Convent—2601 St. Alban's Dr., West Lawn, 19609. Tel: 610-678-2769.

Slatington, Lehigh Co., Assumption B.V.M. (1883), Rev. Joseph L. Grembocki, M.Div.
Res., 633 W. Washington St., 18080. Tel: 610-767-2214; Fax: 610-767-2702. [CEM]
School—St. John Neumann Regional Catholic Elementary School, Palmerton-Slatington. See separate listing. Tel: 610-767-2935; Fax: 610-767-2948.
Catechesis/Religious Programs—Students 173.

Summit Hill, Carbon Co., St. Joseph (1850), Rev. James M. Torpey; Sr. Mary Florence, R.S.M., Pastoral Assoc.
Res., 118 N. Market St., 18250. Tel: 570-645-2664; Fax: 570-645-5655. [CEM 3]
School—Our Lady of the Angels Academy, Lansford. See separate listing. Tel: 570-645-7101.
Catechesis/Religious Programs—Students 89.

St. Stanislaus (1924) (Polish), Rev. James M. Torpey; Sr. Mary Florence, R.S.M., Pastoral Assoc.
Res., 118 N. Market St., 18250. Tel: 717-645-3037; Fax: 717-645-5655.
School—Our Lady of the Angels Academy, Lansford. See separate listing. Tel: 570-645-7101.
Catechesis/Religious Programs—Students 5.

Tamaqua, Schuylkill Co., St. Jerome (1833), Revs. Anthony P. Mongiello; Henry E. Strassner.
Res., 266 W. Broad St., 18252. Tel: 570-668-2301; Fax: 570-668-4406.
School—250 W. Broad St., 18252. Tel: 570-668-2757.
Sisters of the Immaculate Heart of Mary 2; Lay Teachers 8; Students 195.
Catechesis/Religious Programs—Tel: 570-668-4416.
Students 215.
Convent—Tel: 570-668-2730.
Mission—Coaldale, Schuylkill Co., St. Patrick (Seek), Miner St., Coaldale, 18218. [CEM][JC 2]

SS. Peter and Paul (1911) (Lithuanian), Rev. William J. Linkchorst.
Res., 307 Pine St., 18252. Tel: 570-668-1150; Fax: 570-668-6933. [CEM][JC]
Catechesis/Religious Programs—Tel: 570-668-4416.
Students 48.

Tower City, Schuylkill Co., SS. Peter and Paul (1896), Rev. James J. Burdess, Th.M.
Res., 825 E. Grand Ave., 17980. Tel: 717-647-9472; Fax: 717-647-7174. [CEM]
School—St. Elizabeth Ann Seton Regional Catholic Elementary School, Minersville. See separate listing.
Catechesis/Religious Programs—Students 52.

Tremont, Schuylkill Co., Immaculate Conception (1853), Revs. James R. Brady, Pastor Emeritus; James J. Burdess; Deacon William Ahrensfield.
Res., 113 Cherry St., P.O. Box 35, 17981. Tel: 570-695-3648; Fax: 570-695-2275. [CEM]
School—Good Shepherd Regional School, (Grades PreK-3) 538 Sunbury St., Minersville, 17954. Tel: 570-544-4560.
(Grades 4-8) 301 St. Francis St., Minersville, 17954. Tel: 570-544-3766. Ms. Rosalie Novack, Prin.
Catechesis/Religious Programs—Ann Starr, D.R.E.
Students 56.

Tresckow, Carbon Co., St. Bartholomew (1917) (Italian), Rev. Thomas Shanfelt.
Res., 25 E. Maple St., P.O. Box 238, 18254-0238. Tel: 570-455-0922.
School—McAdoo Regional Catholic Elementary School, McAdoo. See separate listing. Tel: 570-929-3016; Fax: 570-929-3016.
St. Michael (1908), Rev. Thomas Shanfelt.
Res., 14 S. Chestnut St., 18254-0236. Tel: 570-454-2802; Fax: 570-454-1765. [CEM]
School—McAdoo Regional Catholic Elementary School, McAdoo. See separate listing. Tel: 570-929-1442; Fax: 570-929-3016.

Tuscarora, Schuylkill Co., St. Bertha (1922), Rev. Francis M. Grundowski.
Res., 214 Green St., Brockton, 17925. Tel: 570-668-1500; Fax: 570-668-5487. [CEM]
Church—710 Broad St., P.O. Box 245, 17982.
School—St. Jerome Regional Catholic Elementary School, Tamaqua. See separate listing.
Catechesis/Religious Programs—Located at St. Jerome Regional, Tamaqua. Tel: 570-668-4416.

Weatherly, Carbon Co., St. Nicholas (1874), Rev. James C. Bechtel; Deacon Raymond W. Wilkinson.
Res., 318 Plane St., 18255. Tel: 570-427-4123; Fax: 570-427-4615. [CEM 2][JC]
School—McAdoo Regional Catholic Elementary School, McAdoo. See separate listing. Tel: 717-929-1442; Fax: 717-929-3016.
Catechesis/Religious Programs—Students 65.
Station—Weatherwood, Carbon County District Home, Tel: 717-427-8683; Fax: 717-427-4988.

West Bangor, Northampton Co., St. Roch (1937), Rev. Msgr. Charles T. Moss.
Res., 1141 Verona Dr., Pen Argyl, 18072. Tel: 610-863-9055; Fax: 610-863-5971. [CEM]
School—Immaculate Conception Regional Catholic Elementary School, Pen Argyl. See separate listing. Tel: 610-863-4876.
Catechesis/Religious Programs—Located at Immaculate Conception, Pen Argyl.

West Reading, Berks Co., Sacred Heart (1917) (German), Rev. Msgr. James J. Reichert; Rev. Francis P. Straka; E. Jerry Yoder, Business Admin.; Deacons William R. Kase; John E. DeTurck. In res., Rev. David J. Fick.
Res., Lakeview Dr. and Cherry St., P.O. Box 6217, Reading, 19610. Tel: 610-372-4010; Fax: 610-372-4926.
School—701 Franklin St., 19611. Tel: 610-373-3316. Thomas Frey, Prin.
Lay Teachers 12; Students 211.
Catechesis/Religious Programs—Tel: 610-374-5430. Valerie Christo, D.R.E.
Students 178.

Whitehall, Lehigh Co., Holy Trinity (1928), Rev. Thomas D. Baddick, M.Th.; Deacons Eugene J. Wyrwa; Michael J. Laroche. In res., Rev. John A. Frink, M.Div.
Res., 4102 S. Church St., 18052. Tel: 610-262-9315; Fax: 610-261-3576.
School—Christ the King Regional Catholic Elementary School, Coplay, Whitehall. See separate listing. Tel: 610-262-4177; Fax: 610-262-5632.
Catechesis/Religious Programs—Mrs. Barbara Majkowski, D.R.E.
Students 293.
St. Elizabeth (1941), Rev. Msgr. Anthony D. Muntone; Revs. Francis A. Nave; Joseph J. Kweder; Deacon Alexander L. Maggitti, Sr.
Res., 618 Fullerton Ave., 18052. Tel: 610-266-0695; Fax: 610-266-1548.
School—(Grades PreK-8) 431 Pershing Blvd., 18052. Tel: 610-264-0143. Sr. Bonita Smith, R.S.M., Prin.
Sisters of Mercy 1; Lay Teachers 15; Students 245.
Catechesis/Religious Programs—Mrs. Carol O'Connor, D.R.E.
Students 160.
St. John the Baptist (1927), Rev. Francis J. Schuster, K.H.S.
Res., 3024 S. Ruch St., 18052. Tel: 610-262-2260; Fax: 610-262-1935. [CEM]
School—Christ the King Regional Catholic Elementary School, Coplay, Whitehall. See separate listing.
Catechesis/Religious Programs—Tel: 610-262-4177. Sr. Mary Dolora, D.R.E.
Students 62.

Chaplains of Public Institutions

ALLENTOWN. *Good Shepherd Home and Rehabilitation Hospital*. (St. Paul). Deacon Daniel A. Thomson.
Lehigh County Prison. (Sacred Heart).
Lehigh Valley Hospital at 17th St. (St. Catharine of Siena).
Lehigh Valley Hospital at Cedar Crest. (St. Thomas More). Rev. Joseph P. Becker, O.S.F.S.; Deacon Richard B. Close.
Liberty Nursing Center. (St. Catharine of Siena).
Luthercrest. (St. Joseph, Orefield).
Phoebe Devitt Home. (St. Catharine of Siena).
St. Luke's Hospital. (St. Catharine of Siena) Allentown Campus.
State Hospital. (Our Lady Help of Christians).
Westminster Village. (Our Lady Help of Christians).

ASHLAND. *Ashland State Hospital*. Administered by St. Mauritius, Ashland; St. Joseph, Ashland; St. Joseph, Girardville; St. Vincent de Paul, Girardville; Our Lady of Good Counsel, Gordon.

BETHLEHEM. *Lutheran Manor*. (Notre Dame of Bethlehem).
Manor Care Nursing and Rehabilitation Centers I and II. (Notre Dame of Bethlehem).
Muhlenberg Medical Center. (Notre Dame of Bethlehem).
Muhlenberg Rehab Center. (Notre Dame of Bethlehem).

COALDALE. *Miners Memorial Medical Center*. Administered by SS. Cyril & Methodius, St. John the Baptist, St. Mary of the Assumption, Coaldale; St. Michael, Lansford; St. Stanislaus, St. Joseph, Summit Hill; SS. Peter and Paul, Lansford.

EASTON. *Easton Hospital*. (Priests of Easton Area).
Northampton County Prison. (St. Bernard).

FOUNTAIN HILL. *Cedarbrook*. (Lehigh County Home) St. Ursula.
St. Luke's Hospital. (St. Ursula).

FRACKVILLE. *SCI-Mahoney*. Rev. John T. Whalen.

HAMBURG. *Hamburg State School and Hospital*. (St. Mary).

LEHIGHTON. *Gnaden Huetten Memorial Hospital*. (SS. Peter and Paul).
Gnaden Huetten Nursing Home. (SS. Peter & Paul).
Mahoning Valley Nursing Home. (SS. Peter & Paul).

MINERSVILLE. *FCI-Schuylkill, Federal Correctional Institute*. Rev. Charles J. Dene.

NAZARETH. *Gracedale*. (Northampton County Home) Holy Family. Deacon Michael P. McGouldrick.

NEW TRIPOLI. *Zimmerman Country Homestead*. (St. Joseph, Orefield).

ORWIGSBURG. *Orwigsburg Manor*. (St. Ambrose, Schuylkill Haven).

PALMERTON. *Palmerton Hospital*. (Sacred Heart).

PINEBROOK. *Personal Care Center*. (St. Ambrose, Schuylkill Haven).

POTTSVILLE. *Leader Nursing Home*. (Mary, Queen of Peace).
Pottsville Hospital and Warne Clinic. Sr. Marjorie Sweeney, S.S.J., Chap.
Schuylkill County Prison. (Mary, Queen of Peace).

READING. *Community Hospital*. (St. Peter).
Reading Hospital. (Sacred Heart). Rev. David J. Fick, Chap.; Deacon John P. Konopelski.

SCHUYLKILL HAVEN. *Rest Haven County Home*. (St. Ambrose).

TREXLERTOWN. *Mosser Nursing Home*. (St. Joseph, Orefield).

WEATHERWOOD. *Carbon County District Home*. (St. Nicholas, Weatherly).

WERNERSVILLE. *Berks County Prison*. (St. Ignatius Loyola, Reading; St. Joseph, Reading; St. Peter, Reading).
Berks-Heim. (Berks County Home; St. Ignatius Loyola, Reading).
State Hospital. Deacons Richard A. Horst; John J. Allison.

WESCOSVILLE. *Lehigh County Home*. (Cedarbrook) St. Catharine of Siena, Allentown.

On Duty Outside the Diocese:
Reverend Monsignors—
Baker, Andrew R., St. Charles Borromeo Seminary, 100 E. Wynnwood Rd., Wynnewood, PA 19096-3099
Bartkus, Algimantas A., Pontificio Collegio Lituano, Via Casal Monferrato, Rome, 00182 Italy
Benestad, Thomas J., The Papal Foundation, 222 N. 17th St., Philadelphia, PA 19103
Callaghan, Aloysius R., Moderator of the Curia & Chancellor, Archdiocese for the Military Services, P.O. Box 4469, Washington, DC 20017-0469
Reverend Fathers—
Beers, John Michael, S.S.L., Ph.D., Annecy House, P.O. Box 176, Berkley Springs, WV 25411
Fanti, Joseph J.
Jurcik, Peter
Kessler, Thomas J., St. Dorothy Rectory, 601 N. Grove St., P.O. Box 1718, Lincolnton, NC 28093
McConaghy, Robert J., Archdiocese of Manila, Phillipines

Military Chaplains:
Reverend Fathers—
Connolly, James M., Lt., 464 Lake Havasu Dr., Virginia Beach, VA 23454-3979
Czartorynski, David F., Chap. Maj. USAF, PSC 80, Box 13377, APO, AP 96367
Dermott, William, Our Lady Help of Christians, 444 N. Jasper St., Allentown, PA 18109
Medve, A.A., Chap. Lt, CHC, USNR, 3rd Marine Div., Headquarters BN, Camp Courtney, FMF-PAC Unit 35801 Chap, FPO, AP 96602-5801
Thomas, James J., Chap. Lt. Col., PSC 1, Unit 604, Scott AFB, IL 62225

Unassigned:
Reverend Fathers—
Bender, Thomas J.
Brennan, Edmund J.
Cofenas, Robert G.
Czaus, Joseph C.
Donahue, Edward J.
Galko, Joseph
Hilferty, John G.
Kean, Joseph H.
Kerestus, Thomas J.
Milhalak, James J.
Onushco, William J.
Soderlund, David

Retired:
Reverend Monsignors—
Barrett, Francis X., Saw Creek Estates, #89, Bushkill, PA 18324
Birch, Thomas J., 1315 Penn Forest Streams, Jim Thorpe, PA 18229
Coll, Robert J., P.O. Box 1363, Marco, FL 34145
Loeper, Richard J., Immaculate Conception Rectory, 640 E. Main St., Birdsboro, PA 19508
Messaros, Michael F., Fairways at Brookside, 2866 Whitemarsh Pl., Macungie, PA 18062
Morrison, David J., J.C.D., Our Lady of Perpetual Help Parish Center, 3219 Santee Rd., Bethlehem, PA 18020
Reverend Fathers—
Barnes, Joseph A., Holy Family Villa, 1325 Prospect Ave., Bethlehem, PA 18018
Brady, James J., Immaculate Conception, 113 Cherry St., Tremont, PA 17981-0035
Briggman, Michael J., Holy Family Villa, 1325 Prospect Ave., Bethlehem, PA 18018
Carroll, Joseph D., Holy Family Villa, 1325 Prospect Ave., Bethlehem, PA 18018
Cervella, Albert T., Holy Family Villa, 1325 Prospect Ave., Bethlehem, PA 18018
Dressler, Robert A., Holy Family Villa, 1325 Prospect Ave., Bethlehem, PA 18018
Edwards, Thomas L., Seton Manor, 1000 Seton Dr., Orwigsburg, PA 17961
Flynn, Stephen F.X., Holy Family Manor, 1200 Spring St., Bethlehem, PA 18018
Graff, Edward R., P.O. Box 47, Silverton, TX 79257
Horan, Thomas A., 125 E. Main St., Girardville, PA 17935
Iacono, Leonardo, Via Casa Mattera 31, Panza S'Ischia, Napoli, Italia 80070
Jones, William P., Holy Family Villa, 1325 Prospect Ave., Bethlehem, PA 18018
Lofton, James J., 25 Blueberry Ln., Nesquehoning, PA 18240-2006
Maslar, William J., c/o Assumption BVM Rectory, 728 W. Centre St., Mahanoy City, PA 17948
McGarr, Joseph M., 1432-1 Catasauqua Rd., Bethlehem, PA 18017
McKenna, F. Charles, Holy Family Villa, 1325 Prospect Ave., Bethlehem, PA 18018
McNulty, Charles L., Seton Manor, 1000 Seton Rd., Orwigsburg, PA 17961
Nave, Francis R., Holy Family Villa, 1325 Prospect Ave., Bethlehem, PA 18018
O'Donnell, William J., Holy Family Villa, 1325 Prospect Ave., Bethlehem, PA 18018
Ondic, John L., Holy Family Villa, 1325 Prospect Ave., Bethlehem, PA 18018
Oranczak, Ronald J., Holy Family Villa, 1325 Prospect Ave., Bethlehem, PA 18018
Paskowicz, Marian, 611 Caroline Dr., Norristown, PA 19401
Sheridan, John F., Holy Family Villa, 1325 Prospect Ave., Bethlehem, PA 18018
Sweeney, James E., 1817 First St., Miller Heights, PA 18017
Vandergeest, Peter J., 1008 Hemlock Pl., Huntington Valley, PA 19006
Welkie, Paul P., Lake Hauto, R.R.1 Lake Dr., P.O. Box 34, Nesquehoning, PA 18240-0034

Permanent Deacons:
Ahrensfield, William L., Immaculate Conception, Tremont
Allison, John J., Wernersville State Hospital & SS. Cyril and Methodius, Reading
Alvarado, Leopoldo, Spanish Apostolate, Berks County & St. Peter, Reading
Amedeo, Dominick F., Sacred Heart & Our Lady of Mt. Carmel, Allentown

Andrusisian, Stephen, Mary, Queen of Peace, Pottsville
Bankos, Gregory J., Assumption B.V.M., Northampton, St. Andrew, Catasauqua, & Pro-Life Office, Bethlehem
Bogusky, Joseph H., Annunciation B.V.M., Catasauqua
Buragino, Joseph G., St. Ursula, Bethlehem
Burda, Joseph R., St. Joseph, Frackville
Cain, Leonard, St. Francis de Sales, Robesonia
Centeno, Jesus, Hispanic Apostolate, Berks Co. & St. Peter, Reading
Chiles, Franklin J., Holy Ghost, Bethlehem
Chin-Fatt, Arthur L., (On Duty Outside the Diocese)
Close, Richard B., Lehigh Valley Hospital Center, Allentown & St. Ann, Emmaus
Coffin, John A., St. Ignatius Loyola, Sinking Spring
Colon, Francisco De La Gracia, (On Duty Outside the Diocese)
Colon, Julio, Hispanic Apostolate, Berks Co. & St. Peter, Reading
Cosgrove, Francis J., Office of the Permanent Diaconate & St. Anne, Bethlehem
Costa, Joseph J., Our Lady of Siluva, Gilberton
Coyle, Charles A., Our Lady Help of Christians, Allentown
Cummings, John D., (On Duty Outside the Diocese)
Danyi, Frank J., SS. Cyril and Methodius, Bethlehem
De Bellis, Charles A., St. Anthony of Padua, Easton
De Jesus, Jaime
De Jesus, Roberto, Hispanic Apostolate, Northampton County & Holy Infancy, Bethlehem
DeTurck, John E., Sacred Heart, Reading
Dudeck, Lawrence A., Holy Rosary, Reading; Allentown State Hospital & Our Lady Help of Christians, Allentown
Duncan, James R., St. Thomas More, Allentown
End, Gerard Edward, Jr., Immaculate Conception, Birdsboro
Faller, George J., St. Catharine of Siena, Mt. Penn
Flanagan, Eugene M., Jr., St. Francis of Assisi, Allentown
Flanagan, Michael D., St. Mary, Kutztown
Fleck, Henry, Jr., St. Bernard, Easton
Fry, Craig A., St. Catharine of Siena, Reading
Giltrap, James F., St. Joseph, Limeport
Godiska, Joseph F., Our Lady of Hungary, Northampton
Gonzalez, Jose
Gordon, Henry G., Jr., St. Mary, Hamburg
Gousie, Joseph N., Sr., St. Joseph, Reading
Granato, Gary J., St. Paul, Allentown
Hanni, John A., Sacred Heart, Bath
Hassler, William R., Cathedral of St. Catharine of Siena, Allentown
Henninger, James P., St. Francis of Assisi, Minersville
Hernandez, Saul, Hispanic Apostolate Lehigh County and Sacred Heart, Allentown
Horst, Richard A., St. Catharine of Siena, Reading & Wernersville State Hospital, Wernersville
Hunkele, Thomas H.
Jaccodine, Ralph J., St. Thomas More, Allentown
Kase, William R., Holy Name High School, Reading & Sacred Heart, West Reading
Keenan, Leo F., Jr.
Kelly, George C., Our Lady of Perpetual Help, Bethlehem
Konopelski, John P., Reading Hospital & St. Margaret, Reading
Koval, Edward P., State Correctional Facility, Frackville & St. Canicus and St. Fidelis, Mahanoy City
Lafata, Peter M., St. Joseph, Reading
Laroche, Michael J., Holy Trinity, Whitehall
Maggitti, Alexander L., Sr., St. Elizabeth, Whitehall
Matos, Rodoberto, Hispanic Apostolate, Northampton Co. and St. Bernard, Easton
McGouldirck, Michael P., Gracedale County Home & Holy Family, Nazareth
McManus, Robert J., St. Mauritius & St. Joseph, Ashland
McShane, Hugh E., Sacred Heart, Miller Heights
Metzker, Daniel F., Cathedral of Catharine of Siena, Allentown; St. Joseph the Worker, Orefield
Mihalik, Andrew J., Jr., Sacred Heart, Palmerton
Monahan, Brian J., Immaculate Conception, Allentown
Morales, Edison
Mullins, Thomas J., St. Thomas More, Allentown
Murphy, John W., Jr., St. Ignatius Loyola, Sinking Spring
Murphy, Thomas J., Most Blessed Sacrament & St. Francis Academy, Bally
Najera-Ramirez, Francisco, Hispanic Apostolate, Berks County and St. Peter, Reading
Nemeth, Stephen F., St. Peter, Coplay
Paschall, Joseph L., St. Columbkill, Boyertown
Pitts, William P., Sacred Heart, Palmerton
Pogash, John F., SS. Peter and Paul & St. Mary, St. Clair
Quiles, Victor M., Hispanic Apostolate, Lehigh Co. & Holy Infancy, Allentown
Quirk, John E., St. Patrick, Pottsville
Reichard, Thomas C., St. Bernard & St. Michael, Easton
Rodgers, Robert W., St. Jane Frances de Chantal, Wilson Borough
Rodriguez, Nicasio, Hispanic Apostolate, Northampton Co. & Holy Infancy, Bethlehem
Roos, Carl J.
Salabsky, Bernard J., Jr., Our Lady of Perpetual Help, Bethlehem
Schmidt, Gerald R., St. Ann, Emmaus
Scrak, Richard G., Catholic Social Agency, Ecumenical Soup Kitchen, Allentown & St. Anne, Bethlehem
Setlock, John A., Annunciation & St. Ann, Frackville
Sewald, Richard T., Notre Dame of Bethlehem, Bethlehem
Simchick, Sylvester F., St. John Baptist de la Salle, Shillington
Solis, Alfonso D., Hispanic Apostolate, Lehigh Co. & Sacred Heart, Allentown
Thoden, Richard M., Jr., Assumption B.V.M., Bethlehem
Thompson, John F., St. Peter the Fisherman, Lake Harmony
Thomson, Daniel, Good Shepherd Home and Rehabilitation Hospital & St. Paul, Allentown
Torres, Fernando L., Hispanic Apostolate, Berks Co. & St. Peter, Reading
Torres, Mariano, Hispanic Apostolate, Berks Co. & St. Peter, Reading
Trejo, Jose N. Rodriguez, St. Margaret, Reading
Trexler, Jeffrey R., SS. Cyril and Methodius, Bethlehem
Tyson, Robert J.
Vanzino, William C., St. Jane Frances de Chantal, Wilson Borough
Visot, Luis R., M.D., St. John the Baptist, Pottsville
VonLeer, Lemuel, Office of Life Ministries, Marriage Preparation Program, Allentown & Notre Dame, Bethlehem
Wagner, William J., S.S. Peter and Paul, Lehighton
Wilkinson, Raymond, St. Nicholas, Weatherly
Wisser, Bernard M., Assumption B.V.M., Colesville
Wyrwa, Eugene, Holy Trinity, Whitehall; Diocesan Tribunal, Allentown

INSTITUTIONS LOCATED IN THE DIOCESE

[A] SEMINARIES, RELIGIOUS OR SCHOLASTICATES

CENTER VALLEY. *Missionaries of the Sacred Heart*, 3300 Station Ave., P.O. Box 9, 18034-0009. Tel: 610-282-1415; Fax: 610-282-0610. Revs. Thomas Cain, M.S.C., Supr.; E. Michael Camilli, M.S.C.; Robert Cell, M.S.C.; Raymond Costello, M.S.C.; Walter Downs, M.S.C.; Joseph Gaspar, M.S.C.; Stephen Geusic, M.S.C.; Michael J. Vasti, M.S.C.; Jacob Welle, M.S.C.; Philip Yandrisevits, M.S.C.; Bros. Edward Baker, M.S.C.; Richard Kuhl, M.S.C.; John Peralta, M.S.C.; Lawrence Viele, M.S.C.

NORTHAMPTON. *Mary Immaculate Center*, 300 Cherryville Rd., 18067-9548. Tel: 610-262-7866; Fax: 610-262-6766. Conducted by the Archdiocese of Philadelphia as a seminary for the Spirituality Year Program for seminarians and for the ongoing formation of priests, and as a house of prayer and retreat for priests, religious, and laity. Rev. Joseph P. Gentili, M.Div., S.T.D., Dir. for Continuing Formation of Diocesan Priests; Bro. John P. McErlean, F.S.C., Admin., Spirituality Year Program. Tel: 610-262-9674; Fax: 610-262-7810. Revs. John M. Savinski, M.A., M.Div., Dir.; Anthony J. Costa, S.T.L., M.A., M.Div., Assoc. Priests 2; Brothers 1; Lay Staff 10.

WERNERSVILLE. *Jesuit Center*, N. Church Rd., Box 223, 19565-0223. Tel: 610-678-8085; Fax: 610-678-8747.
E-mail: jescntsec@talon.net
Web site: jesuitcenter.webjump.com
Revs. Joseph A. Panuska, S.J., Rector; James A. Borbely, S.J., Admin.; George A. Aschenbrenner, S.J., Dir. Spiritual Center; Mr. Joseph Rodolff, Treas. In res. Revs. George A. Aschenbrenner, S.J.; John P. Barron, S.J.; James A. Borbely, S.J.; Frederick A. Brew, S.J.; Bro. Joseph M. Connor, S.J.; Revs. Robert J. Dullahan; Henry J. Erhart, S.J.; Bros. John T. Gibbons, S.J.; Joseph E. Grega, S.J.; Revs. Joseph B. Hanzely, S.J.; Joseph Henry, S.J.; Harold J. Hocking, S.J.; John J. Keenan, S.J.; Bro. Thomas S. Kretz, S.J.; Rev. Thomas J. Kuller, S.J.; Bro. Robert A. Larouere, S.J.; Revs. Clarence A. Martin, S.J.; Robert J. McAllister, S.J.; John T. McCaslin, S.J.; Joseph A. Newell, S.J.; Richard W. Norman, S.J.; Joseph A. Panuska, S.J.; Eugene J. Power, S.J.; Edwin J. Sanders, S.J.; Joseph P. Sanders; William E. Schaffner; William J. Sneck, S.J.; Bro. William J. Sudzina, S.J.; Revs. D. Gilbert Sweeney, S.J.; Francis A. Wallner, S.J.; George S. Williams, S.J. Priests 29; Brothers 6.

[B] COLLEGES AND UNIVERSITIES

CENTER VALLEY. *Desales University*, 2755 Station Ave., 18034-9568. Tel: 610-282-1100; Fax: 610-282-2255.
E-mail: admiss@desales.edu
Web site: www.desales.edu
For a complete listing, refer to the Colleges and Universities section.

READING. *Alvernia College*, 19607. Tel: 610-796-8200; Fax: 610-796-8324.
E-mail: mazzela@alvernia.edu
Web site: www.alvernia.edu
For a complete listing, refer to the Colleges and Universities section.

[C] HIGH SCHOOLS, DIOCESAN

ALLENTOWN. *Allentown Central Catholic High School*, 301 N. Fourth St., 18102-3098. Tel: 610-437-4601; Fax: 610-437-6760.
E-mail: altlcchs@impresso.com
Web site: www.acchs.pvt.k12.pa.us
Rev. Msgr. Joseph R. Sobiesiak, Dir.; Rev. Frans J. Berkhout, M.Div., M.Ed., Prin.; Mr. William F. Tielman, Vice Prin.; Rev. Msgr. Francis C. Revak; Rev. John A. Frink. Priests 5; Sisters 2; Lay Teachers 48; Students 930.

ASHLAND. *Cardinal Brennan Jr./Sr. High School*, 130 Academy Ln., 17921. Tel: 570-874-3921; Fax: 570-874-2239.
E-mail: altscbhs@impresso.com
Web site: www.pottsville.com/cardinalbrennan/
Rev. Robert T. Finlan, Prin.; Mr. Paul Brutto, Dir. Studies. Sisters 1; Lay Teachers 17; Students 229.

BANGOR. *Pius X High School*, 580 Third Ave., 18013-1399. Tel: 610-588-3291; Fax: 610-599-3048.
E-mail: altnpxhs@impresso.com
Mr. Leonard D. Litzi, Jr., Prin.; Rev. Donald J. Schaible, M.Div., M.A., M.S., Vice Prin. & Dir. Spiritual Activities. Priests 1; Lay Teachers 22; Students 278.

BETHLEHEM. *Bethlehem Catholic High School*, 2133 Madison Ave., 18017-4699. Tel: 610-866-0791; Fax: 610-866-9892.
E-mail: altnbchs@impresso.com
Founded as two-year commercial high school, 1897. Founded as four-year comprehensive high school, 1925. Mr. Richard B. Culver, M.Ed., Prin.; Sr. Marjorie Keenan, S.S.J., Vice Prin.; Mr. Richard F. Mazza, Dir. Studies; Revs. Stephen L. Maco, Dir. Spiritual Activities; Bernard J. Ezaki. Sisters of St. Joseph 4; Lay Teachers 40; Students 790.

EASTON. *Notre Dame High School*, 3417 Church Rd., 18042. Tel: 610-868-1431; Fax: 610-868-6710.
E-mail: altnndhs@impresso.com
Mr. Joseph R. Kramer, Prin.; Revs. Patrick H. Lamb; Wayne E. Killian. Priests 1; Sisters 7; Lay Teachers 33; Students 518.

POTTSVILLE. *Nativity B.V.M. High School*, One Lawtons Hill, 17901. Tel: 570-622-8110; Fax: 570-622-0454.
E-mail: altsnhs@impresso.com
Web site: www.pottsville.com/nativity/index.htm
Rev. Msgr. Ronald V. Jankaitis; Revs. Wayne E. Killian; Ronald V. Jankaitis. Sisters 4; Lay Teachers 16; Students 300.

READING. *Central Catholic High School of Berks County*, 1400 Hill Rd., 19602-1499. Tel: 610-373-4178; Fax: 610-375-4898.
E-mail: admins@cchsbc.pvt.k12.pa.us
Web site: www.cchsbc.pvt.k12.pa.us
Rev. Msgr. Ronald C. Bocian, Prin.; Thomas P. Mirabella, Asst. Prin. Sisters 4; Lay Teachers 27; Administrators 2; Students 400.

Holy Name High School, 955 E. Wyomissing Blvd., 19611. Tel: 610-374-8361; Fax: 610-374-4309.
E-mail: altbhnhs@impresso.com
Sr. Joseph Eleanor Murphy, I.H.M., Prin.; Deacon William R. Kase, Vice Prin.; Rev. Thomas J. Orsulak, Dir. of Spiritual Activities. Priests 1; Sisters 2; Lay Teachers 35; Students 530.

TAMAQUA. *Marian Catholic High School*, R.D. 4, Box 446, 18252. Tel: 570-467-3335; Fax: 570-467-0186.
E-mail: mrcc2@ptd.net
Web site: xxhome.ptd.net/~mrcc2
Sr. Bernard Agnes, I.H.M., Prin.; Mr. Paul Coombe, Vice Prin.; Rev. Richard C. Brensinger. Priests 1; Servants of the Immaculate Heart of Mary 3; Lay Teachers 27; Students 349.

[D] REGIONAL CATHOLIC ELEMENTARY SCHOOLS, DIOCESAN

ALLENTOWN. *Holy Spirit School*. Serving St. John the Baptist, Immaculate Conception, SS. Peter and Paul, Allentown. Enrollment 200 (Grades PreK-8).
Primary School. (Grades PreK-3), Front St. & Bridge St., 18102. Tel: 610-820-0220.
Middle School. (Grades 4-8), 508 Ridge Ave., 18102. Tel: 610-434-4044. Sr. Catherine Bones, S.S.J., Prin. Tel: 610-434-4044.
Sacred Heart School, 325 N. Fourth St., 18102. Tel: 610-437-3031; Fax: 610-437-1310.
E-mail: altlsh@impresso.com
Mr. James Krupka, Prin. Lay Teachers 10; Students 163.
Serving Sacred Heart, Our Lady of Mt. Carmel, St. Stephen, Allentown.

BALLY. *St. Francis Academy*, 668 Pine St., 19503. Tel: 610-845-7364.
E-mail: sfacademy@aol.com
Deacon Thomas J. Murphy, Prin. Lay Teachers 10; Students 273.
Serving Most Blessed Sacrament, Bally, and St. Columbkill, Boyertown.

BETHLEHEM. *Holy Child School*. (Grades K-8), 1301 Sioux St., 18015-4400. Tel: 610-865-0861; Fax: 610-997-0180. Sr. Marie John Holland, O.S.F., Prin. Sisters 2; Lay Teachers 10; Students 175.
Serving Holy Ghost, St. Ursula, Bethlehem.
St. Michael the Archangel School. Primary Bldg. & Main Office. (Grades K-4), St. Joseph's Rd., Limeport, 18060. Tel: 610-965-4441; Fax: 610-965-1030. Middle School. (Grades PreK & 5-8), 4121 Old Bethlehem Pike, 18015. Tel: 610-867-8422; Fax: 610-865-2098. Carol Sonon, Prin. Priests 2; Lay Teachers 16; Students 399.
Serving Assumption B.V.M., Colesville; St. Joseph, Limeport.
SS. Cyril and Methodius Regional Catholic Elementary School. (Grades PreK-8), 551 Thomas St., 18015. Tel: 610-866-0042. Mrs. Joan M. West, Prin. Lay Teachers 10; Students 105.
Serving SS. Cyril and Methodius, St. Joseph, St. John Capistrano, Our Lady of Pompeii, St. Stanislaus.

EASTON. *Easton Catholic Elementary School*. (Grades K-3), Primary Bldg., 283 W. St. Joseph St., 18042. Tel: 610-253-0651. Middle Bldg. (Grades 4-8), 841 Washington St., 18042. Tel: 610-252-1393. Mary Frances Haluska, Prin. Lay Teachers 12; Students 200.
Serving St. Anthony, St. Joseph, St. Michael, St. Bernard.

FRACKVILLE. *Holy Family School*. (Grades PreK-6), 29 S. Broad Mountain Ave., 17931. Tel: 570-874-0285; Fax: 570-874-3193.
E-mail: altshf@impresso.com
Mrs. Dolores Bartashus, Prin. Sisters 1; Lay Teachers 6; Students 107.
Serving Annunciation, B.V.M., St. Joseph, St. Ann.

GIRARDVILLE. *Immaculate Heart Elementary School*. (Grades PreK-6), Main St. & Richard St., 17935. Tel: 717-276-6568; Fax: 717-276-6568.
E-mail: altsih@impresso.com
Web site: www.geocities.com/athens/acropolis/4136
Sr. Helene Joseph Kollar, I.H.M., Prin. Religious 1; Lay Teachers 7; Students 157.
Serving St. Joseph, St. Mauritius, Ashland; St. Joseph, St. Vincent, Girardville; Our Lady of Good Counsel, Gordon.

JIM THORPE. *St. Joseph Regional Academy*. (Grades K-8), Sixth St. & School St., 18229. Tel: 570-325-3186; Fax: 570-325-9451.
E-mail: altcsjra@impresso.com
Sr. Joanne Marie Aumand, S.C.C., Prin. Sisters 2; Lay Teachers 7; Students 233.
Serving St. Joseph, Immaculate Conception and St. Peter the Fisherman.

LANSFORD. *Our Lady of the Angels Academy*. (Grades K-5), 123 E. Water St., 18232-2001. Tel: 570-645-7170. (Grades 6-8), 30 E. Bertsch St., 18232. Tel: 570-645-7101; Fax: 570-645-5278.
E-mail: altcola@impresso.com
Sr. Susan Joseph, I.H.M., Prin. Sisters 1; Lay Teachers 14; Students 275.
Serving St. Joseph, St. Stanislaus, Summit Hill; St. Ann, St. Michael, SS. Peter & Paul, Lansford; Immaculate Conception, Our Lady of Mt. Carmel, Sacred Heart, Nesquehoning; St. John the Baptist, St. Mary, SS. Cyril & Methodius, Coaldale.

MAHANOY CITY. *Academy of the Blessed Virgin Mary*. (Grades K-8), 29 S. Catawissa St., 17948. Tel: 570-773-2668; Fax: 570-773-2015. E. Marilyn Baluh, Prin. Lay Teachers 7; Students 76.
Serving St. Canicus, St. Casimir, St. Joseph, Our Lady of Silva, St. Richard, and St. Mary Byzantine.

MCADOO. *McAdoo Catholic Elementary School*. (Grades K-8), 35 N. Cleveland St., 18237. Tel: 570-929-1442; Fax: 570-929-3016. Sr. Anne Francine Windle, I.H.M., Prin. Sisters 3; Lay Teachers 9; Students 205.
Serving St. Patrick, St. Kunegunda, St. Mary, McAdoo; St. Bartholomew, St. Michael, Tresckow; Immaculate Conception, Kelayres; St. Nicholas, Weatherly; St. Mary, Beaver Meadows.

MINERSVILLE. *Good Shepherd Regional School*. (Grades PreK-3), 538 Sunbury St., 17954. Tel: 570-544-4360.
E-mail: altsgsr@impresso.com
Web site: www.pottsville.com/goodshep/
(Grades 4-8), 301 Heffner St., 17954. Tel: 570-544-3766; Fax: 570-544-4870. Ms. Rosalie Novack, Prin. Lay Teachers 10; Students 185.
Serving St. Kieran, Heckscherville; St. Mary, Star of the Sea, Branchdale; Sacred Heart, Newtown; Immaculate Conception, Tremont; SS. Peter and Paul, Tower City; St. Barbara, St. Francis of Assisi, St. Stanislaus Kostka, St. Vincent de Paul, Our Lady of Mt. Carmel, Minersville.

NORTHAMPTON. *Our Lady of Hungary Regional School*, 1300 Newport Ave., 18067. Tel: 610-262-9171; Fax: 610-262-2202.
E-mail: altnolh@impresso.com
Mrs. Barbara J. Sullivan, M.Ed., Prin. Sisters 3; Lay Teachers 18; Students 400.
Serving Our Lady of Hungary, Assumption B.V.M., St. Michael, Northampton; St. Lawrence and St. Andrew, Catasauqua.

PALMERTON-SLATINGTON. *St. John Neumann Regional School*. Tel: 610-826-2354; Fax: 610-826-6444.
E-mail: altcsjn@impresso.com
(Grades K-3), 641-645 W. Washington St., Slatington, 18080. Tel: 610-767-2935; Fax: 610-767-2948. (Grades 4-8), 259 Lafayette Ave., Palmerton, 18071. Tel: 610-826-2354; Fax: 610-826-6444. Mrs. Mary Ellen Chuss-Mirro, M.Ed., Prin. Lay Teachers 9; Students 175.
Serving St. Nicholas, Berlinsville; Sacred Heart, Palmerton; Assumption B.V.M., Slatington.

PEN ARGYL. *Immaculate Conception School*. (Grades K-6), Babbitt Ave. & Heller Ave., 18072. Tel: 610-863-4816; Fax: 610-863-8158.
E-mail: altnics@impresso.com
Sr. Maria Luz, O.P., Prin. Sisters 6; Lay Teachers 2; Students 155.
Serving St. Elizabeth, Pen Argyl; St. Rocco, Martins Creek; St. Roch, West Bangor.

PORT CARBON. *St. Stephen Regional School*. (Grades PreK-8), 214 Valley St., 17965. Tel: 570-622-3063; Fax: 570-622-3689.
E-mail: stss@pottsville.infi.net
Web site: www.pottsville.com/st_stephen
Sr. Mary Anne Hoesle, I.H.M., Prin. Sisters 1; Lay Teachers 10; Students 212.
Serving the following parishes: St. Stephen, Port Carbon; St. Mary, Immaculate Conception & St. Casimir, Ss. Peter & Paul & St. Boniface, St. Clair; Sacred Heart, Holy Family, New Philadelphia; St. Anthony, Cumbola.

POTTSVILLE. *All Saints Elementary School*. (Grades K-8), 112 S. Seventh St., 17901. Tel: 570-622-0106; 622-1765; Fax: 570-622-4737.
E-mail: altsase@impresso.com
Web site: www.pottsville.com/allsaints/
Sr. Mary Jane Hahner, C.S.F.N., Prin. Sisters 1; Lay Teachers 14; Students 243.
Serving St. Patrick, St. John the Baptist, Mary, Queen of Peace, St. Joseph and St. Francis.
Little Saints Preschool, 2051 W. Norwegian St., 17901. Tel: 570-622-1073. Sr. M. Leonore Bauer, S.S.J., Dir. Sisters 1; Lay Teachers 1; Students 60.
Serving the Pottsville area.

READING. *St. Catharine of Siena School*, 2330 Perkiomen Ave., 19606. Tel: 610-779-5810; Fax: 610-779-6888.
Web site: www.scrschool.aol
Sr. Mary Ellen Tennity, I.H.M., Prin. Sisters 1; Lay Teachers 22; Students 605.
Serving St. Catharine of Siena, Reading, and Immaculate Conception, Birdsboro.

ROSETO. *Our Lady of Mt. Carmel School*, 80 Ridge St., 18013. Tel: 610-588-2629; Fax: 610-588-3423.
E-mail: altnolmc@impresso.com
Mr. Joseph Yannuzzi, Prin. Lay Teachers 7; Students 200.
Serving Our Lady of Mt. Carmel, Roseto, and Our Lady of Good Counsel, Bangor.

SHENANDOAH. *Father Walter J. Ciszek Elementary School*. (Grades PreK-6), 233 W. Cherry St., 17976. Tel: 570-462-3927; Fax: 570-462-4603.
E-mail: altsfwc@impresso.com
Web site: www.ces-msa.org/registry.html
Sr. Catherine Danielle LeTourneau, I.H.M., Prin. Religious 1; Lay Teachers 10; Students 209.
Serving Annunciation, St. Casimir, St. George, Our Lady of Mt. Carmel, St. Stanislaus, St. Stephen, Shenandoah; St. Mary Magdalen, Lost Creek; St. Mary, Ringtown.

SHILLINGTON. *La Salle Academy and Early Childhood Center*. (Grades PreK-8), 440 Holland St., 19607. Tel: 610-777-7392; Fax: 610-777-1280.
E-mail: altblsa@impresso.com
Miss Geraldine M. Williams, M.Ed., Prin. Lay Teachers 17; Students 430.
Serving St. John Baptist de La Salle, Shillington; St. Benedict, Plowville; St. Anthony, Millmont.

SINKING SPRING. *St. Ignatius Loyola School*. (Grades PreK-8), 2700 St. Alban's Dr., 19609. Tel: 610-678-0111; Fax: 610-670-5795.
E-mail: albsil@impresso.com
Web site: www.stignatiusreading.org/
Mrs. Janice E. Bayerle, Prin. Sisters 1; Lay Teachers 33; Students 619.
Serving St. Ignatius Loyola, Sinking Spring; St. Francis de Sales, Robesonia.

TAMAQUA. *St. Jerome Regional School*, 250 W. Broad St., 18252. Tel: 570-668-2757; Fax: 570-668-6101.
E-mail: sjrsoffc@ptd.prolog.net
Sr. Donna Ariente, I.H.M., Prin. Sisters 1; Lay Teachers 8; Students 200.
Serving St. Jerome, SS. Peter and Paul, Tamaqua; St. Bartholomew, Brockton; St. Bertha, Tuscarora.

WHITEHALL. *Christ the King School*, Primary Bldg., 3008 Ruch St., 18052. Tel: 610-262-4177; Fax: 610-262-5632. Middle Bldg., 22 S. Fifth St., Coplay, 18037. Tel: 610-262-5822. Mrs. Irene M. Griffaton, Prin. Lay Teachers 14; Students 315.
Preschool, 40 S. Fifth St., Coplay, 18037. Tel: 610-262-4064.
Serving St. Peter, Coplay; St. John the Baptist, Whitehall; Holy Trinity, Egypt.
St. Elizabeth School, 433 Pershing Blvd., 18052. Tel: 610-264-0143; Fax: 610-264-1563.
E-mail: stelizabeth1@enter.net
Web site: www.enter.net/~stelizabeth
Sr. Bonita Smith, R.S.M., Prin. Religious 1; Lay Teachers 9; Students 245.
Serving St. Elizabeth, Whitehall; Annunciation, Catasauqua.

[E] SPECIAL SCHOOLS

ALLENTOWN. *Mercy Special Learning Center*, 830 S. Woodward St., 18103-3440. Tel: 610-797-8242; Fax: 610-797-9092.
E-mail: altlmslc@impresso.com
Mrs. Heidi Fritts, Prin. Ages: Newborn to 21. Lay Teachers 9; Students 90.

BETHLEHEM. *The Aquinas Program*, SS. Cyril & Methodius School, 551 Thomas St., 18015. Tel: 610-866-0042. Sr. Janice Marie Johnson, R.S.M., Supvr., Learning Disabilities. Lay Teachers 2; Students 14.
St. Francis Academy Kindergarten, Monocacy Manor, 395 Bridle Path Rd., 18017. Tel: 610-866-5030. Sr. Roseann Velas, O.S.F., Prin. Sisters 2; Students 7.
St. Francis Day Care, Monocacy Manner, 395 Bridle Path Rd., 18017. Tel: 610-866-5030.
E-mail: stfrandc@enter.net
Sr. Roseann Velas, O.S.F., Dir. Sisters 3; Lay Staff 7; Students 70.

POTTSVILLE. *St. Joseph Center*, 2075 W. Norwegian St., 17901. Tel: 570-622-4638; Fax: 570-622-3420.
E-mail: principalsjc@hotmail.com
Web site: www.pottsville.com/stjosephctr
Mr. Richard L. Webb, Prin. Lay Teachers 3; Students 22.

READING. *Alvernia Montessori School*. (Grades PreK-K), Mt. Alvernia, 19607. Tel: 610-775-0250; Fax: 610-777-6029. Sr. Ann Marie Coll, Dir. Sisters 3; Students 66.

WEST READING. *John Paul II Center for Special Learning*, 200 Reading Ave., 19611. Tel: 610-373-5687; Fax: 610-373-5699. Lay Teachers 3; Students 29.

[F] CATHOLIC CHARITIES AND SOCIAL AGENCIES

ALLENTOWN. *Catholic Social Agency-Catholic Charities Administrative Office*, 2141 Downyflake Ln., 18103-4774. Tel: 610-791-3888; Fax: 610-791-1878.
E-mail: csa1admin@worldnet.att.net
Mrs. Barbara W. Murphy, M.S.W., Exec. Dir. of Catholic Social Agency.
Branch Offices:
Branch Office, 530 Union Blvd., 18109-3230. Tel: 610-435-1541; Fax: 610-435-4367. (For Lehigh and Northampton Cos.).
Adult Outreach Center, 310 E. Mahanoy Ave., Mahanoy City, 17948-2727. Tel: 570-773-2010.
St. Francis Center, 900 W. Market St., Orwigsburg, 17961-1006. Tel: 570-366-1403; Fax: 570-366-7311. (For Schuylkill and Carbon Cos.).
Operation Plus, 913 Howard Ave., Pottsville, 17901-3421. Tel: 570-622-6010; Fax: 570-622-6019. Day Treatment Center and Partial Hospitalization for Adolescents.
Berks County Branch Office, 2147 Perkiomen Ave., Reading, 19606. Tel: 610-370-3378; Fax: 610-370-3378.
Pastoral Visitor, 218 W. Cherry St., Shenandoah, 17976-2209. Tel: 570-462-1154.
Pregnancy Crisis Center. (24-Hour Hotline). Tel: 1-800-CARE-002. Mt. Bethel. Tel: 570-897-6060. Easton. Tel: 610-253-3373. Bangor. Tel: 610-588-8400. Parish-Based Counseling Centers: Our Lady

of Mt. Carmel, Bangor; Sacred Heart, Palmerton; St. Fidelis, Mahanoy City; St. Joseph, Summit Hill; St. Columbkill, Boyertown; St. Jerome, Tamaqua; SS. Peter & Paul, Lehighton & Easton Area Neighborhood Center, Easton.

[G] GENERAL HOSPITALS

ALLENTOWN. *Sacred Heart Hospital*, 421 Chew St., 18102-3490. Tel: 610-776-4500; Fax: 610-776-5141. Web site: shh.org
For a complete listing, refer to the Hospitals section.

POTTSVILLE. *Good Samaritan Regional Medical Center*, 700 E. Norwegian St., 17901. Tel: 717-621-4000; Fax: 717-622-7950
For a complete listing, refer to the Hospitals section.

READING. *Bornemann Health Corporation*, c/o Saint Joseph Hospital, 12th St. & Walnut St., P.O. Box 316, 19603-0316. Tel: 610-358-4269; Fax: 610-358-4299
For a complete listing, refer to the Hospitals section.

Community Campus of St. Joseph Medical Center, 215 N. 12th St., Box 316, 19603. Tel: 610-358-4215
For a complete listing, refer to the Hospitals section.

Saint Joseph Medical Center, 215 N. 12th St., P.O. Box 316, 19603. Tel: 610-378-2000; Fax: 610-378-2798.
E-mail: bridgetmcnamara@chi-east.org
For a complete listing, refer to the Hospitals section.

[H] SKILLED NURSING FACILITIES

BETHLEHEM. *Holy Family Manor*, 1200 Spring St., 18018. Tel: 610-865-5595; Fax: 610-865-5866
For a complete listing, refer to the Special Care Facilities section.

ORWIGSBURG. *Holy Family Home Health and Hospice Care*, Schuylkill County and Admin. Office, 900 W. Market St., 17961. Tel: 570-366-2912
For a complete listing, refer to the Special Care Facilities section.

[I] HOMES AND SERVICES FOR THE ELDERLY AND CONVALESCENT

BETHLEHEM. *Grace Mansion Assisted Living Residence of Holy Family Manor*, 1200 Spring St., 18018. Tel: 610-865-6748
For a complete listing, refer to the Special Care Facilities section.

Holy Family Apartments, 330-338 13th Ave., 18018. Tel: 610-866-4603; Fax: 610-866-1622.
E-mail: hfabeth@nni.com
For a complete listing, refer to the Special Care Facilities section.

Trexler Pavilion, Assisted Living Residence of Holy Family Manor, 1220 Prospect Ave., 18018. Tel: 610-868-7776
For a complete listing, refer to the Special Care Facilities section.

EASTON. *Antonian Towers*, 2405 Hillside Ave., 18042. Tel: 610-258-2033; Fax: 610-258-6541.
E-mail: antonian@nni.com
For a complete listing, refer to the Special Care Facilities section.

NEW PHILADELPHIA. *Holy Family Apartments*, Valley St. & Clay St., 17959. Tel: 570-429-0699; Fax: 570-429-2368
For a complete listing, refer to the Special Care Facilities section.

ORWIGSBURG. *Holy Family Adult Day Care at St. Francis Center*, 900 W. Market St., 17961. Tel: 570-366-2924; Fax: 570-366-2301
For a complete listing, refer to the Special Care Facilities section.

Holy Family Assisted Living Residence, 900 W. Market St., 17961. Tel: 570-366-2912; Fax: 570-366-7781
For a complete listing, refer to the Special Care Facilities section.

POTTSVILLE. *Queen of Peace Apartments*, 777 Water St., 17901. Tel: 570-628-4504; Fax: 570-628-4712.
E-mail: qpeace@voicenet.com
For a complete listing, refer to the Special Care Facilities section.

READING. *Queen of Angels Apartment*, 22 Rothermel St., Hyde Park, 19605. Tel: 610-921-3115; Fax: 610-921-8576.
E-mail: qangels@voicenet.com
For a complete listing, refer to the Special Care Facilities section.

SAINT CLAIR. *Neumann Apartments*, 25 N. Nichols St., 17970. Tel: 570-429-0699; Fax: 570-429-2368
For a complete listing, refer to the Special Care Facilities section.

[J] HOMES FOR PRIESTS

BETHLEHEM. *Holy Family Villa*, 1325 Prospect Ave., 18018. Tel: 610-694-0395; Fax: 610-694-9777. Rev. Msgr. Dennis A. Rigney, M.Div., L.S.W., A.C.S.W., Diocesan Dir.; Rev. Joseph J. Campion, Rector. In res. Revs. Joseph A. Barnes; Michael J. Briggman, S.T.B.; Joseph D. Carroll; Albert T. Cervella; Robert A. Dressler; Stephen Flynn; William P. Jones; Thomas J. Kerestus; F. Charles McKenna; James J. Mihalak; Francis R. Nave; William J. O'Donnell; John Ondic; Ronald Oranczak; Francis C. Revak; Joseph A. Rock, Chap.; John Rusek; John F. Sheridan; James E. Sweeney; Peter J. Vandergeest; Most Rev. Thomas J. Welsh, Retired Bishop.

[K] MONASTERIES AND RESIDENCES OF PRIESTS AND BROTHERS

BETHLEHEM. *The Barnabite Fathers Barnabite Spiritual Center*, R.D. 1, 4301 Hecktown Rd., 18020. Tel: 610-691-8648; Fax: 610-691-8649.
E-mail: gp00@msl.allencol.edu
Web site: http://www.catholic-church.org/barnabites
Revs. Anthony M. Bianco, C.R.S.P., M.A., Local Supr., Moderator of Spiritual Center & House Sec.; Richard M. Delzingaro, C.R.S.P., M.A., Local Vicar, Prefect of Sacristy, Provincial Counselor & NACC Chap.; Gabriel M. Patil, C.R.S.P., M.A., S.T.L., S.S.L., Theology College Professor & House Treasurer; Peter M. Calabrese, C.R.S.P., Fatima Shrine Basilica, Youngstown, NY.

CENTER VALLEY. *Oblates of St. Francis de Sales*, Wills Hall, 2755 Station Ave., 18034-9568. Tel: 610-282-3300; Fax: 610-282-2254.
E-mail: pjl1@desale.edu
Web site: www.desales.edu
In res. Very Rev. Bernard F. O'Connor, O.S.F.S., Ph.D.; Revs. Joseph P. Becker, O.S.F.S., M.A.; Douglas C. Burus, O.S.F.S., M.A.; Thomas F. Dailey, O.S.F.S., Ph.D.; Joseph A. DiMauro, O.S.F.S., M.A.; Bernard F. Donahue, O.S.F.S., Ph.D.; James P. Finnegan, O.S.F.S., S.T.D.; Daniel G. Gambet, O.S.F.S., Ph.D.; John F. Harvey, O.S.F.S., S.T.D.; Christopher J. Hudgin, O.S.F.S., M.A.; Peter J. Leonard, O.S.F.S., Ph.D., Supr.; A. Robert McGilvary, O.S.F.S., Ph.D.; John F. McGinley, O.S.F.S., M.Ed.; Alexander T. Pocetto, O.S.F.S., Ph.D.; Gerard H. Schubert, O.S.F.S., Ph.D.; Robert M. Rutledge, O.S.F.S., Graduate Studies. Total in Residence 13.

EASTON. *St. Francis Friary*, 3918 Chipman Rd., 18045. Tel: 610-258-3053; Fax: 610-258-2412. Franciscan Vice Province of the Holy Savior. Revs. William Reisteter, O.F.M.; Charles Smiech, O.F.M., Guardian; Bros. Marcel Groth, O.F.M.; Edward Skutka, O.F.M. Total in Residence 4. Brothers 2.

NEW RINGGOLD. *Cistercian Conventual Priory, St. Mary's Priory*, R.D. 1, Box 206, 17960. Tel: 570-943-2645; Fax: 570-943-3035. Very Rev. Luke Anderson, S.O.Cist., Th.M., Ph.D., Prior; Revs. Hugh Montague, S.O.Cist., M.A., Th.M.; Alphonsus Lachapelle, S.O.Cist., M.A., Th.M. Fathers 3.

READING. *Missionaries of the Sacred Heart*, 55 Rothermel St., 19605-2680. Tel: 610-929-2025; Fax: 610-929-4397.
E-mail: wperr7777@aol.com
Very Rev. John J. Paul, M.S.C., Supr.; Revs. William Gies, M.S.C.; Eugene Jung, M.S.C.; Robert Tobolski, M.S.C.; Lawrence H. Wildonger, M.S.C.; Bro. Warren Perrotto, M.S.C.; Rev. Philip DeRea, M.S.C., 4401 14th St., N.E., Washington, D.C., 20017. Tel: 202-526-6482.

[L] CONVENTS AND RESIDENCES OF SISTERS

ALLENTOWN. *Villa Maria Convent*, 303 N. Sixth St., 18102. Tel: 610-433-3567. Faculty house of Sisters, Servants of the Immaculate Heart of Mary, who teach at Allentown Central Catholic High School and staff Centro Parroquial Sacred Heart Parish. Tel: 610-434-5171 (Rectory at Sacred Heart). Sisters 5.

BETHLEHEM. *Casa Belen*, 305 E. Fourth St., 18015. Tel: 610-867-4030. Sr. Irma N. Candelaria, P.S.S.J., Supr. Residence of the Poor Sisters of St. Joseph who minister to the Spanish speaking people of the area. Sisters 4.

Monocacy Manor, 395 Bridle Path Rd., 18017. Tel: 610-866-2597; Fax: 610-861-7478.
E-mail: monocacy@enter.net
Web site: www.catholic-church.org/stfrancis-cfn
Provincialate and Novitiate of the School Sisters of the Third Order Regular of St. Francis (Bethlehem Prov.). Sr. M. Rosaria Shina, O.S.F., Prov. Supr. Professed Sisters 28; Retreat Center Total Staff 7.

St. Joseph Convent, 2133 Madison Ave., 18017-4699. Tel: 610-865-4691; Fax: 610-866-9892.
E-mail: ssj2133@aol.com
Sisters of St. Joseph 15; Immaculate Heart Sisters (Scranton) 1.

Ss. Cyril & Methodius Convent, 520 Buchanan St., 18015-3449. Tel: 610-866-0275. Sisters 4.

COOPERSBURG. *Carmelite Monastery*. St. Therese of the Child Jesus and St. Mary Magdalen de Pazzi, St. Therese's Valley. 3551 Lanark Rd., 18036-9324. Tel: 610-797-3721. Carmelite Nuns of the Ancient Observance. Mother Marie Charlette, O.Carm., Prioress; Rev. Michael S. Lawrence, Chap. Professed Nuns 11.

EMMAUS. *Transfiguration Monastery* (1998), 526 Fairview St., 18049-3837. Tel: 610-965-6818. Benedictine Sisters. Sr. Martina Revak, O.S.B., Supr. Charter Members 3. Ministries in the fields of education, pastoral ministry, hospitality and spirituality.

MAHANOY CITY. *St. Joseph Convent*, 536 W. South St., 17948. Tel: 570-773-1420. Missionaries of Charity. Sisters 4.

NESQUEHONING. *Our Lady of Perpetual Help House of Prayer*, 140 W. Mill St., 18240. Tel: 570-669-9858. Sister Servants of the Immaculate Heart of Mary. Sr. Elizabeth Ann Brooks, I.H.M., Supr. Sisters 4.

PEN ARGYL. *Dominican Daughters of the Immaculate Mother*, 115 Lobb Ave., 18072. Tel: 610-863-9214; Fax: 610-863-9214. Sr. Marie Luz, O.P., Supr. Sisters 6.

POTTSVILLE. *Sisters House*, 700 E. Norwegian St., 17901. Tel: 570-621-4000; 621-4651.
E-mail: healing@pottsville.infi.net
Res. of the Daughters of Charity of St. Vincent de Paul, Northeast Province, who staff Good Samaritan Regional Medical Center, Nativity and Cardinal Brennan High Schools. Sr. Helen Gertrude Carroll, D.C., Supr. Sisters 8.

READING. *Daughters of Divine Zeal, Inc.*, 1526 Hill Rd., 19602. Tel: 610-375-1738; 375-9072; Fax: 610-375-2188; 375-4895.
E-mail: srdivinezeal@hotmail.com
Sr. M. Alodia, Contact Person. Tel: 610-796-8331. Sisters 4.

House of Nazareth (Casa Nazaret), 532 Spruce St., 19602. Tel: 610-378-1947. Sr. Maria Gonzalez, Supr. Residence of the Poor Sisters of St. Joseph who work in Spanish Apostolate of Berks County. Sisters 4.

MSC Province Center, 2811 Moyers Ln., 19605. Tel: 610-929-5944; Fax: 610-929-3634.
E-mail: mscprovusa@juno.com
Sr. Marie Clark, M.S.C., Prov. Sisters 4.

Neumann Convent Sisters of St. Francis of Philadelphia (Glen Riddle). Tel: 610-374-4974.
E-mail: sistersofs@cs.com
Mailing Address: 1235 Elm St., 19604. Tel: 610-374-4974. Sisters 9.

Our Lady of the Angels Convent - Alvernia College, 19607. Tel: 610-796-8333.
E-mail: alodisr@alvernia.edu
Web site: www.alvernia.edu
Residence for Bernardine Sisters on college faculty. Sr. M. Pacelli, Local Min. Tel: 610-796-8329. Total in Residence 4.

Our Lady of the Assumption Convent, 1500 Eckert Ave., 19602. Tel: 610-373-8203. Faculty House of Sisters of Christian Charity, teaching in Central Catholic High School. Sr. Ida Heinzmann, S.C.C., Supr. Sisters 5.

Precious Blood Convent, 1094 Welsh Rd.P.O. Box 97, 19607-0097. Tel: 610-777-1624; Fax: 610-777-3359.
E-mail: cpspa@aol.com; missioncps@aol.com
Web site: http://members.aol.com/cpspa/index.html
Residence for Missionary Sisters of the Precious Blood and Novitiate. Sr. Theresa Bringazi, C.P.S., Supr. Sisters 25.

Sacred Heart Convent, Mt. Alvernia, 460 St. Bernardine St., 19607-1737. Tel: 610-777-6111; Fax: 610-777-6029.
E-mail: shconvent@aol.com
Web site: www.bfranciscan.org
Residence for Bernardine Sisters of Third Order of St. Francis. Sr. Mary Maxine, O.S.F., Admin. Tel: 610-777-7221; Sr. Rosemary McGowan, O.S.F., Contact Person; Sr. Anna Suszek, O.S.F., Care Giver; Rev. Msgr. Ronald C. Bocian, Chap.
U.S. Province Offices. Total Staff 10. Professed Sisters 40.

St. Clare Convent, 465 St. Bernardine St., 19607-1736. Tel: 610-777-4590; Fax: 610-777-3973. Bernardine Franciscan Sisters. Sr. Claude Marie Jablonski, O.S.F., Local Min.; Sr. Ann Marie Coll, O.S.F., Contact Person. Sisters 4.

St. Joseph Villa, 464 Bernardine St., 19607. Tel: 610-777-5556; Fax: 610-777-5545.
E-mail: jeananthony44@aol.com
Home of the Retired Bernardine Sisters of the Third Order of St. Francis. Sr. Jean Anthony Rodgers, O.S.F., Admin.; Sr. Josandra Ciucci, O.S.F., Sisters Care Coord.; Rev. Robert Reece, O.S.F.S., Chap. Sisters 95.

St. Michael Convent, 19605. Tel: 610-929-5751; Fax: 610-929-0762. Missionary Sisters of the Sacred Heart of Jesus. Sr. Joanne Leblanc, M.S.C., Coord., Motherhouse Community; Sr. Mary Seibert, M.S.C., Coord., Retirement Center Community.
Attended by M.S.C. Fathers from Sacred Heart Monastery, Hyde Park. Professed Sisters 80.

Sisters of St. Francis Residence, 502 S. Sixth St., 19602. Tel: 610-375-8001. Convent of the Sisters of St. Francis of Philadelphia who are on the staffs at Central Catholic High School and SS. Cyril and Methodius Parish. Sisters 2.

WEST LAWN. *Saint Ignatius Convent,* 2601 St. Alban Dr., 19609-1132. Tel: 610-678-2769. Sisters 2.

WHITEHALL. *Sisters for Christian Community / Poor Servants,* Two Maryland Cir.-120, 18052. Tel: 610-437-4463; Fax: 610-437-8843.
E-mail: learnclub@aol.com
Web site: www.learningclub.org
Sisters 2.

[M] RETREAT HOUSES

BETHLEHEM. *St. Francis Center for Renewal (Monocacy Manor),* 395 Bridle Path Rd., 18017. Tel: 610-867-8890; Fax: 610-861-7478.
E-mail: peace@enter.net
Web site: www.catholic-church.org/stfrancis-cfn
School Sisters of St. Francis. Sr. M. Anita Kuchera, O.S.F., Dir. Weekend retreats (68) and days of recollection (150); retreats for men and women, marriage encounter; engaged encounters; parish retreats; workshops; youth groups; weekends; privately directed retreats; private retreats. Total Staff 4.

EASTON. *St. Francis Retreat House,* 3918 Chipman Rd., 18045. Tel: 610-258-3053; Fax: 610-258-2412. Rev. William Reisteter, O.F.M., Dir. of Retreat Development. Houses of Religious Men: Total in Residence 6; Total Staff 8; Retreat Centers: Total in Residence 6; Total Staff 10. Retreatants 80.

NORTHHAMPTON. *Mary Immaculate Center,* 300 Cherryville Rd., 18067-9548. Tel: 610-262-7866; Fax: 610-262-6766. Bro. John P. McErlean, F.S.C., Admin. Seminarians 15; Total Staff 13.

ORWIGSBURG. *St. Francis Center,* 900 W. Market St., 17961-1006. Tel: 570-366-1016; Fax: 570-366-1017. Deacon Alex L. Maggitti, Dir.
Diocesan Agencies with Facilities in the St. Francis Center:
Office for Youth & Young Adult Ministry. Tel: 570-366-1405; Fax: 570-366-1426. Mary Ellen Johns, Dir.
Adult & Youth Retreats. Tel: 570-366-1405; Fax: 570-366-1426.
E-mail: oyyak@ptbprolog.net
Total Staff 6. Overnight retreats, day retreats, weekend retreats and workshops.
Catholic Social Agency. (Schuykill & Carbon Branch Office). Tel: 570-366-1403; Fax: 570-366-7311. Sr. Miriam Denis, S.S.J., M.B.A., County Supvr.
Holy Family Adult Day Care. Tel: 570-366-2924; Fax: 570-366-2301. Mrs. Linda Herb, Dir. Total Assisted Average 25/Day; Total Staff 5.
Holy Family Residence. Tel: 570-366-2912; Fax: 570-366-7781. Mr. James Polaski, Admin.

READING. *Mariawald Renewal Center,* 1094 Welsh Rd., P.O. Box 97, 19607. Tel: 610-777-0135; Fax: 610-777-3359.
E-mail: mariawald@aol.com
For women, men and mixed groups. Sr. Theresa Bringazi, C.P.S., Supr.; Ida Fantauzzi, Admin. Total Staff 8; Total in Residence 2.

[N] CENTERS FOR SPIRITUAL GROWTH

WERNERSVILLE. *Jesuit Center for Spiritual Growth,* 19565. Tel: 610-678-8085; Fax: 610-678-8747.
E-mail: jescntsec@talon.net
Web site: jesuitcenter.webjump.com
Rev. George A. Aschenbrenner, S.J., Dir.; Kathryn M. Fitzgerald, Acting Dir.; Revs. John P. Barron, S.J.; William J. Sneck, S.J.; George S. Williams, S.J.; Susan Bowers; Bernadette Duross; Maria McCoy; Bro. Renatus Foldenauer, C.S.C. Directed retreats, programs in prayer, discernment, psychology and spirituality.

[O] NEWMAN CENTERS

ALLENTOWN. *The Newman Center,* 2339 Liberty St., 18104. Tel: 610-821-3122; Fax: 610-821-3123. Rev. John A. Krivak, Diocesan Dir., Campus Ministry.
Albright College (Reading), Holy Guardian Angels, 3121 Kutztown Rd., Reading, 19605. Tel: 610-921-2729; Fax: 610-921-8886. Rev. John S. Pendzick.
Allentown College of St. Francis de Sales (Center Valley). Oblates of St. Francis de Sales, 2755 Station Ave., Center Valley, 18034-9568. Tel: 610-282-1100; Fax: 610-282-3798.
Alvernia College, Dept. of Campus Ministry, 400 St. Bernardine St., Reading, 19607. Tel: 610-796-8300; Fax: 610-796-8378.
Cedar Crest College (Allentown), Catholic Chaplaincy Center, 2400 Chew St., 18104-5586. Tel: 610-821-3122; Fax: 610-821-3123. Rev. John A. Krivak, Ed.D.
Kutztown University (Kutztown), Christopher House, 15207 Kutztown Rd., Kutztown, 19530. Tel: 610-683-8380; Fax: 610-683-8457.
E-mail: frbill26@aol.com
Rev. William N. Seifert.
Lafayette College (Easton), 119 McCartney St., Easton, 18042-7647. Tel: 610-253-5044; Fax: 610-253-1391.
E-mail: normanc@lafayette.edu
Rev. Charles Norman, O.S.F.S.
Lehigh University (Bethlehem), Newman Center at Lehigh University, Bldg. 41, 661 Taylor St., Bethlehem, 18015-3127. Tel: 610-758-4148; 866-0581; Fax: 610-758-6392. Rev. Wayne E. Killian.
Moravian College (Bethlehem), Koinonia House, 1130 Monocacy St., Bethlehem, 18018-6650. Tel: 610-861-3936; Fax: 610-253-1391.
E-mail: normac@moravian.edu
Rev. Charles Norman, O.S.F.S.
Muhlenberg College (Allentown), Newman Center, 2339 Liberty St., 18104-5586. Tel: 610-821-3122; Fax: 610-821-3123. Rev. John A. Krivak, Ed.D.
Penn State University (Berks Center), St. Ignatius Loyola, 2810 St. Alban Dr., Sinking Spring, 19608. Tel: 610-678-3767.
Penn State University (Schuylkill Haven Center, Schuylkill Haven), St. Ambrose Rectory, 201 Randel St., Schuylkill Haven, 17972. Tel: 570-385-1031. Rev. Eric J. Gruber.

[P] MISCELLANEOUS

BETHLEHEM, PA. *Third Order Dominican Chapter,* 4290 Vassar Ave., 18017. Tel: 610-691-6761.

EASTON, PA. *Secular Franciscan Fraternity, Secular Franciscan Order,* c/o St. Francis Retreat House, 3918 Chipman Rd., 18042. Tel: 610-258-3053.
E-mail: kaysfo@aol.com
Web site: www.catholic-church.org/stfran-retreat

ORWIGSBURG, PA. *Seton Manor, Inc.,* 1000 Seton Dr., 17961. Tel: 570-366-0400; Fax: 570-366-1970. Raymond Dee, Chm.; Rev. Msgr. Dennis A. Rigney, M.Div, M.S.W., L.S.W., A.C.S.W., N.H.A., Vice Chm.; Mary Ann Chaklos, Admin.
Board of Directors: Daniel Kochie, C.P.A., Treas.; Gino J. Pazzaglini, FACHE; Rev. Msgr. William E. Jones, V.F.; Robert S. Carl, Jr., FACHE; Rev. Michael J. Stone. Total Staff 172; Beds 120; Total Assisted 180.

POTTSVILLE, PA. *Covenant Home Care,* 1510 Hwy. 61 S., 17901. Tel: 570-385-5522; Fax: 570-385-5287.
E-mail: holyfmly@ptd.net

READING, PA. *Mary's Shelter,* 325 S. 12th St., 19602. Tel: 610-376-1973; Fax: 610-376-5391.
E-mail: mshelter@juno.com
Sr. M. Joanna Monticello, M.S.C., Admin. A residence for homeless unwed pregnant women.

SHENANDOAH, PA. *Apostles of Jesus,* P.O. Box 215, 17976-0215. Tel: 570-462-2104; Fax: 570-462-2321.
E-mail: apostles@shen-heightsaccess.net
Rev. Paul O. Gaggawala, A.P., Coord.

WHITEHALL, PA. *Blue Army of Our Lady of Fatima,* 4102 S. Lee St., 18052.

RELIGIOUS INSTITUTES OF MEN REPRESENTED IN THE DIOCESE

For further details refer to the corresponding bracketed number in the Religious Institutes of Men or Women section.

[]—*Apostles of Jesus.*—A.J.

[0330]—*Brothers of the Christian Schools.*—F.S.C.

[]—*Cistercian Monks of the Strict Observance.*—O.Cist.

[0160]—*Clerics Regular of St. Paul.* (Bernabite Fathers).—C.R.S.P.

[1330]—*Congregation of the Mission.* (Eastern Prov.).—C.M.

[0520]—*Franciscan Friars.* (Custody of the Most Holy Savior; Croatian Custody of the Holy Family).—O.F.M.

[0690]—*Jesuit Fathers and Brothers.* (Maryland Prov.).—S.J.

[]—*Missionaries of the Queen of the Angels.*—M.I.S.R.A.

[1110]—*Missionaries of the Sacred Heart.* (U.S. Prov.).—M.S.C.

[0920]—*Oblates of St. Francis de Sales.*—O.S.F.S.

RELIGIOUS INSTITUTES OF WOMEN REPRESENTED IN THE DIOCESE

[0120]—*Angelic Sisters of St. Paul.*—A.S.S.P.

[1810]—*Bernardine Sisters of the Third Order of St. Francis.*—O.S.F.

[0320]—*Carmelite Nuns of the Ancient Observance.*—O.Carm.

[]—*Congregation of Sisters of Holy Family Nazareth.*—C.S.F.N.

[]—*Congregation of St. Agnes.*—C.S.A.

[0760]—*Daughters of Charity of St. Vincent de Paul.*—D.C.

[0795]—*Daughters of Divine Zeal.*—F.D.Z.

[1065]—*Dominican Daughters of the Immaculate Mother.*—O.P.

[2710]—*Missionaries of Charity.*—M.C.

[]—*Missionary Sisters of the Most Sacred Heart of Jesus.*—M.S.C.

[2850]—*Missionary Sisters of the Precious Blood.*—C.P.S.

[3250]—*Poor Sisters of St. Joseph.*—P.S.S.J.

[1700]—*School Sisters of the Third Order of St. Francis.* (Bethlehem Prov.).—O.S.F.

[0660]—*Sisters of Christian Charity.*—S.C.C.

[]—*Sisters of Mercy.* (Merion).—R.S.M.

[3780]—*Sisters of Saints Cyril and Methodius.*—SS.C.M.

[3700]—*Sisters of St. Benedict.*—O.S.B.

[3740]—*Sisters of St. Casimir.*—S.S.C.

[]—*Sisters of St. Francis of Philadelphia.* (Glen Riddle).—O.S.F.

[3830]—*Sisters of St. Joseph.*—S.S.J.

[2170]—*Sisters, Servants of the Immaculate Heart of Mary.*—I.H.M.

DIOCESAN CEMETERIES

ALLENTOWN. *Resurrection,* 547 N. Krocks Rd., 18106-9732. Tel: 610-395-3819.

BETHLEHEM. *Holy Saviour,* 2575 Linden St., 18017-3842. Tel: 610-866-2372; 866-9177; Fax: 610-866-9277.

NECROLOGY

† Fox, Francis J., (Retired). —Died Feb. 23, 2000.

† Shields, William J., (Retired). —Died Aug. 27, 2000.

† Sosnowski, Rev. Msgr. Stanley, Emmaus, PA St. Ann. —Died April 6, 2000.

Diocese of Altoona-Johnstown

(Dioecesis Altunensis-Johnstoniensis)

Most Reverend

JOSEPH V. ADAMEC, D.D., S.T.L.

Bishop of Altoona-Johnstown; ordained July 3, 1960; appointed Bishop of Altoona-Johnstown March 17, 1987; ordained and installed May 20, 1987. *Mailing Address: Chancery Office, 126 Logan Blvd., Hollidaysburg, PA, 16648.*

Most Reverend

JAMES J. HOGAN, D.D.

Retired Bishop of Altoona-Johnstown; ordained December 8, 1937; appointed Titular Bishop of Philomelium and Auxiliary of Trenton November 27, 1959; consecrated February 25, 1960; appointed to the See of Altoona-Johnstown May 23, 1966; installed July 6, 1966; retired October 17, 1986. *Office: 126 Logan Blvd., Hollidaysburg, PA, 16648.*

ESTABLISHED DIOCESE OF ALTOONA, MAY 27, 1901.

REDESIGNATED DIOCESE OF ALTOONA-JOHNSTOWN, OCTOBER 9, 1957.

Square Miles 6,674.

Comprises the Counties of Bedford, Blair, Cambria, Centre, Clinton, Fulton, Huntingdon and Somerset in the State of Pennsylvania.

For legal titles of parishes and diocesan institutions, consult the Chancery Office.

The Chancery: 126 Logan Blvd., Hollidaysburg, PA, 16648. Tel.: 814-695-5579; Fax: 814-695-8894.

Web site address: www.diocesealtjtn.org

E-mail address: dajreply@diocese.org

STATISTICAL OVERVIEW

Personnel	
Bishop	1
Retired Bishops	1
Priests: Diocesan Active in Diocese	112
Priests: Active Outside Diocese	5
Priests: Retired, Sick or Absent	37
Number of Diocesan Priests	154
Religious Priests in Diocese	62
Ordinations:	
Diocesan Priests	1
Religious Priests	2
Transitional Deacons	2
Permanent Deacons	6
Permanent Deacons in Diocese	30
Total Brothers	6
Total Sisters	89
Parishes	
Parishes	103
With Resident Pastor:	
Resident Diocesan Priests	84
Resident Religious Priests	12
Without Resident Pastor:	
Administered by Priests	7
Missions	5
Closed Parishes	7
Welfare	
Catholic Hospitals	1
Total Assisted	115,851
Health Care Centers	1
Total Assisted	200
Homes for the Aged	3
Total Assisted	267
Special Centers for Social Services	2
Total Assisted	57,449
Educational	
Diocesan Students in Other Seminaries	4
Total Seminarians	4
Colleges and Universities	2
Total Students	3,993
High Schools, Diocesan and Parish	3
Total Students	1,221
Elementary Schools, Diocesan and Parish	29
Total Students	4,733
Catechesis/Religious Education:	
High School Students	4,328
Elementary Students	9,066
Total Students Under Catholic Instruction	23,345
Teachers in the Diocese:	
Priests	6
Sisters	17
Lay Teachers	561
Vital Statistics	
Receptions into the Church:	
Infant Baptism Totals	1,512
Adult Baptism Totals	133
Received into Full Communion	229
First Communions	1,750
Confirmations	1,818
Marriages:	
Catholic	428
Interfaith	319
Total Marriages	747
Deaths	1,656
Total Catholic Population	110,651
Total Population	641,763

Former Bishops—Rt. Rev. EUGENE A. GARVEY, D.D., ord. Sept. 22, 1869; cons. Sept. 8, 1901; died Oct. 22, 1920.—Most Rev. JOHN JOSEPH MCCORT, D.D., ord. Oct. 14, 1883; cons. Titular Bishop of Azotus and Auxiliary to the Archbishop of Philadelphia, Sept. 17, 1912; appt. Coadjutor cum jure successionis to the Bishop of Altoona, Jan. 27, 1920; appt. Bishop of Altoona, Oct. 22, 1920; appt. Assistant at the Pontifical Throne, Oct. 5, 1933; died April 21, 1936.—Most Rev. RICHARD T. GUILFOYLE, D.D., ord. June 2, 1917; appt. Aug. 8, 1936; cons. Nov. 30, 1936; died June 10, 1957.—Most Rev. HOWARD J. CARROLL, D.D., ord. April 2, 1927; appt. Dec. 5, 1957; cons. Jan. 2, 1958; died March 21, 1960.—Most Rev. J. CARROLL MCCORMICK, D.D., ord. July 10, 1932; cons. April 20, 1947; appt. June 25, 1960; transferred to See of Scranton March 4, 1966; retired Feb. 15, 1983; died Nov. 2, 1996.—Most Rev. JAMES J. HOGAN, D.D., ord. Dec. 8, 1937; appt. Titular Bishop of Philomelium and Auxiliary of Trenton, Nov. 27, 1959; cons. Feb. 25, 1960; appt. to the See of Altoona-Johnstown May 23, 1966; retired Oct. 17, 1986.

Diocesan Officials

Bishop—Most Rev. JOSEPH V. ADAMEC, D.D., S.T.L., *126 Logan Blvd., Hollidaysburg, 16648.* Tel: 814-695-5579; Fax: 814-695-8894.

Secretary to the Bishop—Rev. LUBOMIR STRECOK, *126 Logan Blvd., Hollidaysburg, 16648.* Tel: 814-695-5579; Fax: 814-695-8894.

Retired Bishop—Most Rev. JAMES J. HOGAN, D.D., J.C.D., *126 Logan Blvd., Hollidaysburg, 16648.* Tel: 814-696-0278.

Chancellor—Rev. Msgr. DENNIS R. BOGGS, *126 Logan Blvd., Hollidaysburg, 16648.* Tel: 814-695-5579; Fax: 814-695-8894.

Vicars General—Rev. Msgr. STANLEY B. CARSON, V.G., Admin. (Secretariats), *126 Logan Blvd., Hollidaysburg, 16648.* Tel: 814-695-5579; 943-8553 (Res.); Fax: 814-695-8894. Rev. Msgr. GEORGE B. FLINN, V.G., S.T.L., Pastoral Life and Ministry, *126 Logan Blvd., Hollidaysburg, 16648.* Tel: 814-695-5579; 536-0117 (Res.); Fax: 814-695-8894.

Judicial Vicar—Rev. Msgr. MICHAEL E. SERVINSKY, S.T.L., J.C.L., *126 Logan Blvd., Hollidaysburg, 16648.* Tel: 814-695-5579; 943-8464 (Res.); Fax: 814-695-8894.

Bishop's Vicar for Religious—Rev. MICHAEL HIGGINS, T.O.R., *St. Francis Friary, P.O. Box 600, Loretto, 15940.* Tel: 814-472-3362.

Secretary for Communications—Sr. MARY PARKS, C.S.J., *126 Logan Blvd., Hollidaysburg, 16648.* Tel: 814-695-5579; Fax: 814-695-8894.

Vicars Forane

Allegheny Deanery—Rev. Msgr. JOHN R. SASWAY, V.F., *Our Lady of the Alleghenies, Lilly.*

Altoona Deanery—Very Rev. PAUL E. TURNBULL, V.F., *St. John the Evangelist Parish, Altoona (Lakemont).*

Cambria Deanery—Very Rev. LEONARD E. VOYTEK, V.F., *St. John Cantius and St. Mary Parishes, Windber.*

Johnstown Deanery—Rev. Msgr. JOSEPH R. KINIRY, P.A., V.F., *St. Benedict Parish, Johnstown.*

Juniata Deanery—Very Rev. CLEMENT G. GARDNER, V.F., *St. Michael Parish, Hollidaysburg.*

Northern Deanery—Rev. Msgr. DENNIS R. BOGGS, V.F., *Immaculate Conception Parish, Lock Haven.*

Prince Gallitzin Deanery—Rev. Msgr. TIMOTHY J. SWOPE, V.F., *St. Michael the Archangel Parish, Loretto, Minor Basilica.*

Southern Deanery—Rev. Msgr. SAMUEL J. TOMASELLI, V.F., *St. Peter Parish, Somerset.*

Diocesan Offices

Adult Formation & Lay Ministry—Ms. CONNIE STOWE, Dir.; Mr. PAUL VOELKER, Asst. Dir., *124 Logan Blvd., Hollidaysburg, 16648.* Tel: 814-693-9605; Fax: 814-695-8894.

Building Commission—Mr. JERRY KINIRY. Tel: 814-288-2663.

Campus Ministry—(For further details regarding Campus Ministries please refer to Institutions Located in the Diocese.).

Catholic Social Service—Rev. Msgr. ROBERT J. SALY, Dir., Sr. CAROL JEAN CZYRNIK, Intake Worker, *1300 12th Ave., P.O. Box 1349, Altoona, 16603.* Tel: 814-944-9388; Fax: 814-941-2677.

Johnstown Offices—741 Railroad St., Johnstown, 15901. Tel: 814-535-6538; Fax: 814-535-2235.

State College Offices—276 W. Hamilton Ave., P.O. Box 680, State College, 16801. Tel: 814-238-4937; Fax: 814-238-4207.

"The Catholic Register"—Rev. TIMOTHY P. STEIN, Editor, *P.O. Box 413, Hollidaysburg, 16648.* Tel: 814-695-7563; Fax: 814-695-7517.

Communications—Sr. MARY PARKS, C.S.J., *126 Logan Blvd., Hollidaysburg, 16648.* Tel: 814-695-5579; Fax: 814-695-8894.

Cemetery Commission—Rev. DAVID H. ROESCH, *St. Joseph Rectory, 623 E. Third St., Bellwood, 16617.* Tel: 814-742-7075.

Chancery—Rev. Msgr. DENNIS R. BOGGS, Chancellor, *126 Logan Blvd., Hollidaysburg, 16648.* Tel: 814-695-5579; Fax: 814-695-8894.

Christian Initiation—Mrs. JEANNE THOMPSON, *126A Logan Blvd., Hollidaysburg, 16648.* Tel: 814-695-5579; Fax: 814-695-8894.

Computer Systems—RONALD MULDOON, Dir., Sr. DONNA MARHEFKA, Asst., *126 Logan Blvd., Hollidaysburg, 16648.* Tel: 814-695-5579; Fax: 814-695-8894.

Comptroller—HERMAN NAGLE, *126 Logan Blvd., Hollidaysburg, 16648.* Tel: 814-695-5579; Fax: 814-695-8894.

Development & Stewardship Office—Mr. JOSEPH M. SCIALABBA, Dir., Mr. CHRIS RINGKAMP, Asst. Dir., Mrs. LORI HARTNETT, H.S. Devel. Dir., ERIC ZEIGLER, Penn St. Catholic Comm. Dir., *P.O. Box 409, Hollidaysburg, 16648.* Tel: 814-696-4389; Fax: 814-695-8894.

Diaconal Formation—Deacon JOHN J. CONCANNON, *124 Logan Blvd., Hollidaysburg, 16648.* Tel: 814-695-5579; Fax: 814-695-8894.

Diocesan Shrines—Rev. MICHAEL BECKER, *Prince Gallitzin Chapel House, P.O. Box 99, Loretto, 15940.* Tel: 814-472-5441; Fax: 814-472-5446.

Education—Mr. CHARLES J. KOREN, Dir., *126A Logan Blvd., Hollidaysburg, 16648.* Tel: 814-695-5579; Fax: 814-695-8894. Asst. Directors: CHARLEEN BLUM, Religious Ed., Sr. MARK PLESCHER, C.S.A., Elementary, Mr. THOMAS MCCONNELL, Campus/Youth Ministry.

Ecumenical Minister—Rev. HAROLD N. BILLER, *609 Park Ave., Johnstown, 15902.* Tel: 814-539-2186.

Family Life Office—Mrs. SUSAN STITH, Dir., *5379 Portage St., Lilly, 15938.* Tel: 814-886-5551; Fax: 814-886-7697. Mrs. KIM CURTIS, Prog. Coord. *Divorced/Separated & Bereaved Ministries; Parent & Marriage Preparation Ministries.* Programs: *Persons with Disabilities Ministry; Natural Family Planning; Respect Life.*

Finance Office—LARRY R. SUTTON, Dir., *126 Logan Blvd., Hollidaysburg, 16648.* Tel: 814-695-5579; Fax: 814-695-8894.

Holy Childhood Association—Rev. ROBERT J. KELLY, Dir., *124 Logan Blvd., Hollidaysburg, 16648.* Tel: 814-695-5579; Fax: 814-695-8894.

Interfaith Minister—Rev. Msgr. ROY KLINE, *P.O. Box 88, Duncansville, 16635.* Tel: 814-695-2337.

Liturgical Commission—Vacant. Tel: 814-693-9870.

Liturgy & Worship—Rev. ROBERT C. MAZUR, *124 Logan Blvd., Hollidaysburg, 16648.* Tel: 814-695-5579; Fax: 814-695-8894.

Mission - Carmelite Community of the Word—110 S. Third St., McConnellsburg, 17233. Tel: 717-485-5917; Fax: 717-485-3856.

Ongoing Formation Clergy—Rev. ALAN THOMAS, Dir., *P.O. Box 99, Loretto, 15940.* Tel: 814-472-5441; Fax: 814-472-5446.

Permanent Deacons—Deacon JOHN J. CONCANNON, *124 Logan Blvd., Hollidaysburg, 16648.* Tel: 814-695-5579; Fax: 814-695-8894.

Peace & Justice Commission—Mr. CHARLES LEIDEN, *306 Coleridge Ave., Altoona, 16602.* Tel: 814-946-9291.

Presbyteral Council—Rev. MARTIN D. MCCAMLEY, Chm., *820 Westerly Pkwy., State College, 16801.* Tel: 814-237-7832.

Priests' Personnel Board—Rev. Msgr. GEORGE B. FLINN, V.G., S.T.L., *126 Logan Blvd., Hollidaysburg, 16648.* Tel: 814-695-5579; Fax: 814-695-8894.

Priests' Residence - Dmitri Manor—Rev. Msgr. GEORGE B. FLINN, Dir., *St. Mary's Lane, Hollidaysburg, 16648.* Tel: 814-944-9338.

Retreat & Conference Center—St. John the Baptist Retreat Center, P.O. Box 10, New Baltimore, 15553. Tel: 814-733-2210; Fax: 814-733-2966.

Scouting—Rev. JOSEPH ORR, *406 W. 11th St., Tyrone, 16686.* Tel: 814-684-1480.

Self Insurance Program—JOSEPH WATT, *Gallagher Bassett Insurance - Berkshire Center, Ste. 302, Greensburg, 15601.* Tel: 800-831-3247; Fax: 412-836-8684.

Society for the Propagation of the Faith—Rev. ROBERT J. KELLY, Dir., *124 Logan Blvd., Hollidaysburg, 16648.* Tel: 814-695-5579; Fax: 814-695-8894.

St. Vincent de Paul Society—Deacon JOHN E. SROKA, Exec. Dir., *566 Vine St., Johnstown, 15901.* Tel: 814-535-4357; Fax: 814-536-6690.

Tribunal Office—Rev. Msgr. MICHAEL E. SERVINSKY, S.T.L., J.C.L., *126 Logan Blvd., Hollidaysburg, 16648.* Tel: 814-695-5579; Fax: 814-695-8894.

Vocation Office—Rev. MICHAEL A. BECKER, *Prince Gallitzin Chapel House, P.O. Box 99, Loretto, 15940.* Tel: 814-472-5441; Fax: 814-472-5446.

CLERGY, PARISHES, MISSIONS AND PAROCHIAL SCHOOLS

CITY OF ALTOONA
(Blair County)

1—CATHEDRAL OF THE BLESSED SACRAMENT (1851), Revs. Robert C. Mazur, Rector; Josef Kovacik; Brian R. Saylor; Rev. Msgr. Thomas E. Madden, P.A., (Retired); Deacon James F. Leap.
Res., 1331 13th Ave., P.O. Box 33, 16603. Tel: 814-944-4603.
School—Cathedral of the Blessed Sacrament. (Altoona Central Catholic School) See Elementary Diocesan Schools under Institutions Located in the Diocese. 1304 13th Ave., 16601. Tel: 814-943-7423. Mr. Anthony Consiglio, Prin.
A.C.C.S. Bus. Office: 1400 Fourth Ave., 16602. Tel: 814-944-1250.
Catechesis/Religious Programs—Tel: 814-949-4794. Mrs. Jeanne Thompson, D.R.E.
Students 105.

2—IMMACULATE CONCEPTION (1860). (St. Mary's). Revs. Robert G. Neugebauer; John D. Byrnes.
Res., 1405 Fifth Ave., 16602. Tel: 814-942-2416. [CEM]
School—Immaculate Conception. (Altoona Central Catholic School) See Elementary Diocesan Schools under Institutions Located in the Diocese. 1400 Fourth Ave., 16602. Tel: 814-944-1250.
Lay Teachers 7; Students 109.
Catechesis/Religious Programs—Tel: 814-944-1250. Mrs. Sheridan Luke, D.R.E.
Students 149.

3—ST. MARK'S (1889), Rev. James B. Coveney; Deacon John E. Rys. In res., Revs. John Neugebaur; Robert Reese.
Res., 416 Sixth Ave., 16602. Tel: 814-942-0364.
Catechesis/Religious Programs—Students 105.
Chapel—Valley View Home for the Aged, Tel: 814-944-0845.

4—SACRED HEART (1890), Rev. Msgr. Stanley B. Carson, V.G. In res., Rev. Leo A. Lynch.
Res., 511 20th St., 16602. Tel: 814-943-8553; Fax: 814-943-1556.
Formation Center—2009 Sixth Ave., 16602. Tel: 814-944-3922.
Catechesis/Religious Programs—Students 165.

5—HOLY ROSARY (1901), Revs. Carl A. Spishak; Edward J. Dabcosky.
Res., 900 N. Fourth St.-Juniata, 16601. Tel: 814-944-6676; Fax: 814-946-9207.
Catechesis/Religious Programs—Tel: 814-944-4611. Mrs. Margaret M. McCulloch, D.R.E.
Students 142.

6—OUR LADY OF FATIMA (1995) (Irish-Polish), Rev. Anthony J. Pollack.
Res., 2010 12th Ave., 16601. Tel: 814-942-0371. [CEM]
School—Altoona Central Catholic School Our Lady of Fatima Site. See Elementary Diocesan Schools under Institutions Located in the Diocese. Tel: 814-943-7423.
Catechesis/Religious Programs—1304 13th Ave., 16603. Tel: 814-943-7423.
Students 28.

7—OUR LADY OF MT. CARMEL (1905) (Italian), Revs. Frank Scornaienchi, T.O.R.; William Santre, T.O.R.; Seraphin Conley, T.O.R. In res., Rev. Louis J. Secondo, T.O.R.
Res., 806 11th St., 16602. Tel: 814-942-8501; Fax: 814-944-2208.
School—Our Lady of Mount Carmel. (Altoona Central Catholic School) 1012 8th Ave., 16602. Tel: 814-943-5931; Fax: 814-943-1837. Mrs. Susan Curfman, Prin.
Franciscan Sisters of the Immaculate Conception 2; Lay Teachers 9; Students 99.
Catechesis/Religious Programs—Tel: 814-941-4960. Mr. Ronald Petak, D.R.E.
Students 167.
Convent—Tel: 814-942-8964.
Mission—Pleasant Valley, Blair Co., Our Lady of the Assumption, (1925) 15 1/2 Pierce St., Pleasant Valley, 16602.

8—ST. LEO THE GREAT (1911). Merged with SS. Peter & Paul to form Our Lady of Fatima, Altoona.

9—SS. PETER AND PAUL (1911) (Polish). Merged with St. Leo the Great to form Our Lady of Fatima, Altoona.

10—ST. JOHN THE EVANGELIST (1921), Very Rev. Paul E. Turnbull, V.F.; Deacon Gene Neral.
Res., 309 Lotz Ave., Lakemont, Altoona, 16602. Tel: 814-942-5503; Fax: 814-942-4514.
School—Tel: 814-943-4966; Fax: 814-943-8832. Gary Evangelisto, Prin.
Lay Teachers 9; Students 112.
Catechesis/Religious Programs—Tel: 814-943-4966. Ms. Joan Price, D.R.E.
Students 181.

11—OUR LADY OF LOURDES (1923), Revs. Dennis M. Kurdziel; Edward L. Eckenrod.
Res., 2716 Broad Ave., 16601. Tel: 814-943-6185; Fax: 814-943-1968.
School—2713 W. Chestnut Ave., 16601. Tel: 814-942-3421. Mrs. Catherine M. DiSabato, Prin.
Lay Teachers 6; Students 94.
Catechesis/Religious Programs—Tel: 814-943-1685. Colleen Sheehan, D.R.E.
Students 75.

12—ST. ROSE OF LIMA (1924), Revs. James F. Crookston; James M. Dugan.
Res., 5514 Roselawn Ave., 16602. Tel: 814-944-8509; Fax: 814-942-8345 (Call first).
School—5519 Sixth Ave., 16602. Tel: 814-942-7835; Fax: 814-942-1095. Jennifer Long, Prin.
Lay Teachers 13; Students 206.
Catechesis/Religious Programs—Students 195.

13—ST. THERESE OF THE CHILD JESUS (1927), Rev. Msgr. Anthony B. Little.
Res., 2301 5th St., 16601. Tel: 814-942-4479; Fax: 814-942-1873.
School—Altoona Central Catholic Middle School, 424 Wopsononock Ave., 16601. Tel: 814-944-3751; Fax: 814-944-8283. Sr. Mary Kevin Breen, O.S.F., Prin.
Lay Teachers 10; Students 190.
Catechesis/Religious Programs—Andrew Callaghan, D.R.E.
Students 109.

CITY OF JOHNSTOWN
(Cambria County)

1—ST. JOHN GUALBERT CATHEDRAL (1835), Rev. Msgr. George B. Flinn, V.G., Rector; Revs. John F. Brezovec; Alan E. Thomas; Clarence S. Bridges; Deacon John J. Concannon.
Res., 117 Clinton St., P.O. Box 807, 15907. Tel: 814-536-0117; Fax: 814-535-6771. [CEM 2]
School—Central Catholic Elementary. See Elementary Diocesan Schools under Institutions Located in the Diocese. Tel: 814-536-1532; Fax: 814-536-0493.
Catechesis/Religious Programs—St. Anthony School, 124 Maple Ave., 15901. Tel: 814-535-4228.
Students 50.

2—ST. JOSEPH'S (1852) (German). Merged with Our Lady of Mercy to form St. John Gualbert Cathedral, Johnstown.
School—Central Catholic Elementary. See Elementary Diocesan Schools under Institutions Located in the Diocese. Tel: 814-536-1532.

3—IMMACULATE CONCEPTION (1859) (German), Rev. Francis P. Balestino.
Res., 308 Broad St., 15906. Tel: 814-535-4407. [CEM]
School—West End Catholic. See Elementary Diocesan Schools under Institutions Located in the Diocese. Tel: 814-536-4722.
Catechesis/Religious Programs—Students 12.

4—SS. CASMIR & EMERICH (1997) (Polish-Hungarian), Rev. John J. Marshall.
Res., 501 Power St., 15906. Tel: 814-535-2139; Fax:

814-539-1942. [CEM][JC]
School—West End Catholic. See Elementary Diocesan Schools under Institutions Located in the Diocese. Tel: 814-536-4722.
Catechesis/Religious Programs—Students 51.

5—ST. CLARE OF ASSISI, Revs. Gererd M. Connolly, T.O.R.; Terrence Smith, T.O.R. In res., Rev. Adalbert Wolski, T.O.R.
Office: 218 Maple Ave., 15901.
Res., 124 Maple Ave., 15901. Tel: 814-535-4228; Fax: 814-535-1664. [CEM 8]
School—Central Catholic Elementary. See Elementary Diocesan Schools under Institutions Located in the Diocese. Tel: 814-536-1532.
Catechesis/Religious Programs—Students 59.

6—ST. COLUMBA'S (1888), Rev. Benjamin Dykas.
Res., 916 Broad St., 15906. Tel: 814-535-1627; Fax: 814-534-0031. [CEM]
School—West End Catholic. See Elementary Diocesan Schools under Institutions Located in the Diocese. Tel: 814-536-4722.
Catechesis/Religious Programs—Students 27.

7—ST. STEPHEN, FIRST KING OF HUNGARY (1891) (Slovak), Rev. Andrew C. Stanko.
Res., 414 Fourth Ave., 15906. Tel: 814-539-6334; Fax: 814-539-6334. [CEM]
School—West End Catholic. See Elementary Diocesan Schools under Institutions Located in the Diocese. Tel: 814-536-4722.
Catechesis/Religious Programs—Tel: 814-539-6334.
Students 72.

8—ST. ROCHUS (1900) (Croatian), Rev. Charles M. Amershek, Jr., V.F.; Sr. Nancy Spence, C.C.W., Pastoral Min.
Res., 314 Eighth Ave., 15906. Tel: 814-539-1520; Fax: 814-539-8845. [CEM]
School—West End Catholic. See Elementary Diocesan Schools under Institutions Located in the Diocese. Tel: 814-536-4722.
Catechesis/Religious Programs—Tel: 814-535-5409. Theresa Marcus, D.R.E.
Students 209.

9—ST. PATRICK'S (1904), Rev. Harold N. Biller; Deacon Leo A. Kist, P.D.
Res., 609 Park Ave., 15902. Tel: 814-539-2186; Fax: 814-539-2410.
School—617 Park Ave., 15902. Tel: 814-535-2926. Dr. Kevin J. Moran, Prin.
Lay Teachers 11; Students 165.
Catechesis/Religious Programs—Students 68.

10—ST. EMERICH'S (1905) (Hungarian). Merged with St. Casimir's, Johnstown to form Saints Casimir & Emerich's, Johnstown.

11—ST. ANTHONY'S (1905) (Italian). Merged with SS. Peter & Paul, Johnstown to form St. Clare of Assisi, Johnstown.

12—ST. MICHAEL'S (1910) (German), Rev. Francis P. Balestino.
Res., 180 Gilbert St., 15906. Tel: 814-535-4407.
Catechesis/Religious Programs—Tel: 814-535-5409.
Students 33.

13—SS. PETER AND PAUL'S (1918). Merged with St. Anthony, Johnstown to form St. Clare of Assisi, Johnstown.

14—OUR MOTHER OF SORROWS (1920), Rev. Msgr. Thomas K. Mabon; Revs. George M. Gulash; Allen Zeth.
Res., 415 Tioga St., 15905. Tel: 814-535-7646; Fax: 814-536-7850.
School—430 Tioga St., 15905. Tel: 814-539-5315. Mr. John Skubak, Prin.
Lay Teachers 20; Students 370.
Catechesis/Religious Programs—Tel: 814-255-1264. Mrs. Karen Fink, D.R.E.
Students 145.

15—OUR LADY OF MERCY (1921). Merged with St. Joseph to form St. John Gualbert Cathedral, Johnstown.

16—ST. FRANCIS OF ASSISI (1922) (Slovak), Rev. Martin A. Cingle; Deacon Thomas Lemmon.
Res., 120 Barron Ave., 15906. Tel: 814-539-1632; Fax: 814-539-1632. [CEM]
School—West End Catholic. See Elementary Diocesan Schools under Institutions Located in the Diocese. Tel: 814-536-4722.
Catechesis/Religious Programs—Students 60.

17—VISITATION OF THE B.V.M. (1927), Rev. Richard D. Clark; Deacon John E. Sroka.
Res., 1127 McKinley Ave., 15905. Tel: 814-526-6110; Fax: 814-536-3709.
Catechesis/Religious Programs—Students 59.

18—ST. THERESE OF THE CHILD JESUS (1929) (Slovenian), Rev. Bernard Karmanocky, O.F.M.
Res., 536 Decker Ave., 15906. Tel: 814-539-7633; Fax: 814-539-7633. [CEM]
School—West End Catholic. See Elementary Diocesan Schools under Institutions Located in the Diocese. Tel: 814-536-4722.
Mission—Moxham, Cambria Co., St. Anne's, (1935) 533 Woodland Ave., Moxham, 15902. Tel: 814-539-7633.
Catechesis/Religious Programs—Tel: 814-536-2287.
Students 51.

19—ST. CLEMENT'S (1956), Rev. William E. Rosenbaum; Very Rev. Robert Radasky.
Res., 114 Lindberg Ave., 15905. Tel: 814-255-4422; Fax: 814-255-2623.
School—110 Lindberg Ave., 15905. Tel: 814-255-1964. A. Ernest Papinchak, Prin.
Lay Teachers 10; Students 192.
Catechesis/Religious Programs—Ms. Mary Drager, D.R.E.
Students 177.

20—ST. ANDREW'S (1956), Rev. Barry J. Baroni; Deacon Samuel Cammarata. In res., Rev. Leo F. Arnone.
Res., 1621 Ferndale Ave., 15905. Tel: 814-288-4324; Fax: 814-288-6750.
School—(Grades PreK-8) 1629 Ferndale Ave., 15905. Tel: 814-288-1854.
Lay Teachers 15; Students 224.
Catechesis/Religious Programs—Students 326.

21—ST. GREGORY'S (1919), Rev. Daniel J. O'Neill; Deacon Thomas M. Papinchak.
Res., 120 Boltz St., 15902. Tel: 814-536-6818; Fax: 814-534-0651.
Catechesis/Religious Programs—Clustered with St. Barnabas, Johnstown.
Students 120.

22—ST. BARNABAS (1954) (Slovenian), Rev. Daniel J. O'Neill; Deacon Thomas M. Papinchak.
Res., 120 Boltz St., 15902. Tel: 814-536-6818; Fax: 814-534-0651. [CEM]
Catechesis/Religious Programs—Clustered with St. Gregory, Johnstown.

23—ST. BENEDICT'S (1930), Rev. Msgr. Joseph R. Kiniry, P.A., V.F.; Revs. Peter J. Kuligowski; David S. Peles.
Res., 2310 Bedford St., 15904. Tel: 814-266-9718; Fax: 814-269-4220.
School—2306 Bedford St., 15904. Tel: 814-266-3837; Fax: 814-266-7718. Ms. Lois A. Paul, Prin.
Lay Teachers 24; Students 448.
Catechesis/Religious Programs—Tel: 814-266-2105. Dianne Brandle, D.R.E.
Students 590.

OUTSIDE THE CITIES OF ALTOONA AND JOHNSTOWN

Acosta, Somerset Co., St. John the Baptist's (1912). Merged with St. Joseph, Boswell, and St. Stanislaus, Boswell, to form All Saints Church, Boswell.

Ashville, Cambria Co., St. Thomas Aquinas (1889), Rev. James F. Bunn.
Res., 16613. Tel: 814-944-5615; 674-5416. [CEM]
Catechesis/Religious Programs—Mr. Robert Sutton, D.R.E.
Students 119.

Bakerton, Cambria Co., Sacred Heart (1904). Merged with St. Patrick, Spangler, to form St. Jude, Elmora.

Barnesboro, Cambria Co., Christ the King (1993). Merged with St. Stanislaus Kostka, Barneboro; St. John the Baptist, Northern Cambria; Our Lady of Mt. Carmel, Northern Cambria; Holy Cross, Northern Cambria to form Prince of Peace, Northern Cambria.
St. Stanislaus Kostka (1906) (Polish). Merged with Christ the King, Barnesboro; St. John the Baptist, Northern Cambria; Our Lady of Mt. Carmel, Northern Cambria; Holy Cross, Northern Cambria to form Prince of Peace, Northern Cambria.

Beans Cove, Bedford Co., Seven Dolors B.V.M. (1878). Unassigned.
Mailing Address: 2174 Beans Cove Rd., Clearville, 15535-7901. Tel: 814-767-9522; Fax: 814-767-8158.
Res., 215 E. Penn St., Bedford, 15522. Tel: 814-623-5526; Fax: 814-623-1741. [CEM]
Catechesis/Religious Programs—Students 9.

Beaverdale, Cambria Co., St. Joseph's (1904) (Slovak). Merged with St. Agnes, Beaverdale, and Corpus Christi, Dunlo, to form Holy Spirit Church, Beaverdale.
St. Agnes (1909). Merged with St. Joseph, Beaverdale, and Corpus Christi, Dunlo, to form Holy Spirit Church, Beaverdale.
Holy Spirit (1995), Rev. Anthony J. Legarski.
Mailing Address: 802 Cameron Ave., P.O. Box 616, 15921. Tel: 814-487-5633; 487-5653 (office); Fax: 814-487-5773. [CEM 2]
Catechesis/Religious Programs—Students 111.

Bedford, Bedford Co., St. Thomas (1816), Rev. John C. Vago.
Res., 215 E. Penn St., 15522. Tel: 814-623-5526; Fax: 814-623-1741. [CEM 2]
School—129 W. Penn St., 15522. Tel: 814-623-8873; Fax: 814-623-1208. Joyce Wityk, Prin.
Lay Teachers 7; Students 50.
Catechesis/Religious Programs—Tel: 814-623-9525. Mrs. Debbie Will, D.R.E.
Students 162.

Bellefonte, Centre Co., St. John the Evangelist's (1828), Revs. D. Timothy Grimme; James M. Foster; Deacon Joseph F. Mazurkiewicz.
Res., 134 E. Bishop St., 16823. Tel: 814-355-3134; Fax: 814-355-4820. [CEM 2]
School—(Grades PreK-8) 116 E. Bishop St., 16823. Tel: 814-355-7859; Fax: 814-355-2939. Mrs. Carol Gouty, Prin.
Lay Teachers 14; Students 203.
Catechesis/Religious Programs—Students 240.

Bellwood, Blair Co., St. Joseph's (1890), Rev. David H. Roesch.
Res., 623 E. Third St., 16617. Tel: 814-742-7075.
Catechesis/Religious Programs—Tel: 814-742-7894.
Students 129.

Boswell, All Saints (1995), Rev. Martin Breski, O.F.M.Conv.
Res., 325 Quemahoning St., 15531. Tel: 814-629-5551; Fax: 814-629-5677. [CEM 3]
Catechesis/Religious Programs—Students 115.
St. Stanislaus, Somerset Co., (1901) (Polish). Merged with St. John the Baptist, Acosta to form All Saints Church, Boswell.

Carrolltown, Cambria Co., St. Benedict's (1840), Revs. Vincent E. Zidek, O.S.B.; Jeremy J. Bolha, O.S.B.
Res., 15722. Tel: 814-344-6548; Fax: 814-344-8656. [CEM 3]
School—119 S.Church St., 15722. Tel: 814-344-6512; Fax: 814-344-8530.
Religious 1; Lay Teachers 12; Students 210.
Catechesis/Religious Programs—Peggy J. Bowser, D.R.E.
Students 270.

Cassandra, Cambria Co., St. Agnes (1909), Rev. Robert L. Ruston.
Res., P.O. Box 56, 15925. Tel: 814-736-8314.
Catechesis/Religious Programs—Students 24.

Central City, Somerset Co., Sacred Heat of Jesus (1914) (Polish). Merged with St. John the Baptist, Central City to form Our Lady Queen of Angels, Central City.
St. John the Baptist (1917) (Slovak). Merged with Sacred Heart of Jesus, Central City to form Our Lady Queen of Angels, Central City.
Our Lady Queen of Angels (1999), Rev. Charles F. Bodziak.
Res., 738 Sunshine Ave., 15926. Tel: 814-754-5224; Fax: 814-754-1480. [CEM 2]
Catechesis/Religious Programs—Fax: 814-754-1481.
Students 93.

Chest Springs, Cambria Co., St. Monica's (1859), Rev. Timothy P. Stein.
Res., 3037 Colonel Drake Hwy., 16624. Tel: 814-674-3712. [CEM]
Catechesis/Religious Programs—Tel: 814-674-5064.
Students 61.

Clarence, Centre Co., St. Michael's (1900) (Slovak), Rev. Sylvester J. Bendzella.
Res., 102 Church St., 16829. Tel: 814-387-6762. [CEM]
Catechesis/Religious Programs—Students 66.

Colver, Cambria Co., Holy Family (1912) (Polish), Rev. Bernard F. Grega.
Res., 562 Fifth St., 15927. Tel: 814-748-7054. [CEM]
Catechesis/Religious Programs—Sr. Anna Marie, S.A., D.R.E.
Students 59.

Conemaugh, Cambria Co., Sacred Heart (1902), Rev. Robert C. Hall.
Res., 340 Second St., 15909. Tel: 814-535-6432. [CEM]
Catechesis/Religious Programs—Tel: 814-535-2250.
Students 85.
Assumption of B.V.M. (1910) (Polish), Rev. Robert C. Hall. In res., Rev. Bernard V. Grattan.
Res., 340 Second St., 15909. Tel: 814-535-6432. [CEM]
Catechesis/Religious Programs—219 Oak St., 15909. Tel: 814-535-2250, Ext. 203.
Students 62.

Coupon, Cambria Co., St. Joseph's (1855), Rev. Msgr. Michael E. Servinsky.
Res., 16629. Tel: 814-943-8464. [CEM 2]
Catechesis/Religious Programs—Students 55.

Cresson, Cambria Co., St. Aloysius (1838), Rev. William E. Mullen.
Res., 7911 Admiral Peary Hwy., 16630. Tel: 814-886-2235. [CEM]

School—All Saints Catholic. See Elementary Diocesan Schools under Institutions Located in the Diocese. Tel: 814-886-7942; Fax: 814-886-7942.
Catechesis/Religious Programs—Tel: 814-886-2669. Marcia E. Hammond, D.R.E.
Students 181.

St. Francis Xavier (1908), Rev. Angelo J. Patti. In res., Rev. David R. Rizzo.
Res., 211 Powell Ave., 16630. Tel: 814-886-2374. [CEM]
School—All Saints Catholic. See Elementary Diocesan Schools under Institutions Located in the Diocese. Tel: 814-886-7942; Fax: 814-886-7942.
Catechesis/Religious Programs—Tel: 814-886-2374. Mrs. Barbara Ferazzi, D.R.E.
Students 135.

Davidsville, Somerset Co., St. Anne (1911), Rev. Michael Lewandowski, O.F.M.Conv.
Mailing Address: 205 Woodstown Hwy., P.O. Box 500, 15928. Tel: 814-479-2664; Fax: 814-479-7702. [CEM 2]
Catechesis/Religious Programs—Students 76.

Dudley, Huntingdon Co., Immaculate Conception (1856), Rev. Patrick R. Leahey.
Res., P.O. Box 188, 16634. Tel: 814-635-2919. [CEM]
Catechesis/Religious Programs—Students 35.

Duncansville, Blair Co., St. Catherine of Siena (1963), Rev. Msgr. Roy F. Kline.
Res., 49 Woodland Terr., 16635. Tel: 814-695-2337.
Catechesis/Religious Programs—P.O. Box 88, 16635. Tel: 814-696-0616. Debra Terchanik, D.R.E.
Students 129.

Dunlo, Cambria Co., Corpus Christi (1903). Merged with St. Agnes and St. Joseph, Beaverdale to form Holy Spirit Church, Beaverdale.

Ebensburg, Cambria Co., Holy Name (1816), Rev. Msgr. Arnold L. Gaus; Rev. Richard B. Tomkosky.
Res., 500 N. Julian St., 15931. Tel: 814-472-7244; Fax: 814-472-7249. [CEM]
School—Tel: 814-472-8817. Sr. Jean Uzupis, Prin.
Sisters 1; Lay Teachers 21; Students 341.
Catechesis/Religious Programs—Students 619.

Ehrenfeld, Cambria Co., Our Lady of Mt. Carmel (1892). Merged with St. James and St. Anthony's, South Fork to form Most Holy Trinity, South Fork.

Elmora, St. Jude (1995). Closed. For inquiries for parish records contact the Chancery.

Emeigh, Cambria Co., Most Precious Blood. See Christ the King, Barnesboro.

Everett, Bedford Co., St. John the Evangelist (1971), Rev. Norman P. Imgrund.
Res., 161 E. First Ave., 15537. Tel: 814-652-5854.
Church—163 E. First Ave., 15537.
Catechesis/Religious Programs—Students 44.

Fallentimber, Cambria Co., St. Mary Magdalen's (1889). Merged with St. Richard's Mission, Blandburg to form St. Joan of Arc Church, Fallentimber. Rev. James F. Bunn.
Res., 692 Glendale Valley Blvd., 16639. Tel: 814-943-5437.
Catechesis/Religious Programs—Students 57.

St. Joan of Arc (1995), Rev. James F. Bunn.
Res., 692 Glendale Valley Blvd., 16639. Tel: 814-943-5437.
Catechesis/Religious Programs—Mrs. Nancy Francisco, D.R.E.
Students 52.

Gallitzin, Cambria Co., St. Demetrius (2000), Rev. Msgr. Bernard A. Przybocki.
Res., 811 Church St., 16641. Tel: 814-886-7941. [CEM 2]
School—825 Church St., 11641. Tel: 814-886-8772. Mrs. Helen Saylor, Prin.
Lay Teachers 5; Students 66.
Catechesis/Religious Programs—Students 196.

Our Lady of Czestochowa (1903) (Polish). Merged with St. Patrick, Gallitzin to form St. Demetrius, Gallitzin.

St. Patrick's (1850). Merged with Our Lady of Czestochowa, Gallitzin to form St. Demetrius, Gallitzin.

Hastings, Cambria Co., St. Bernard (1890), Rev. Joachim R. Fatora, O.S.B.
Res., Beaver St., P.O. Box 497, 16646. Tel: 814-247-6558; Fax: 814-247-8522. [CEM 2]
Catechesis/Religious Programs—Tel: 814-674-5841. Mrs. Aileen Ropp, D.R.E.
Students 157.
Mission—St. Boniface, Cambria Co., St. Boniface Chapel, 1278 Main St., 16675.

Hollidaysburg, Blair Co., St. Mary's (1841), Rev. John J. Palko; Deacon John A. Tiernan.
Res., 312 Clark St., P.O. Box 317, 16648. Tel: 814-695-0622; Fax: 814-696-9609. [CEM 2]
School—Hollidaysburg Consolidated Catholic Elementary. See Elementary Diocesan Schools under Institutions Located in the Diocese. Tel: 814-695-6112; Fax: 814-696-8960.
Catechesis/Religious Programs—Tel: 814-695-5678. Mrs. Connie Curfman, D.R.E.
Students 285.

St. Michael's (1862) (German), Rev. Clement Gardner.
Res., 301 Spruce St., 16648. Tel: 814-695-0912; Fax: 814-693-9820. [CEM]
School—Hollidaysburg Consolidated Catholic Elementary. See Elementary Diocesan Schools under Institutions Located in the Diocese. Tel: 814-695-6112; Fax: 814-695-1215.
Catechesis/Religious Programs—Tel: 814-695-9735. Susan M. Teske, D.R.E.
Students 351.

Hooversville, Somerset Co., Holy Family (1911), Rev. Romulus Roslowski, O.F.M. Conv.
Res., 15936. Tel: 814-798-2933; Fax: 814-798-8601. [CEM]
Catechesis/Religious Programs—Students 70.

Huntingdon, Huntingdon Co., Most Holy Trinity (1826), Rev. David J. Arseneault.
Res., 524 Mifflin St., 16652. Tel: 814-643-0160; Fax: 814-643-0160. [CEM]
Catechesis/Religious Programs—Students 273.

Lilly, Cambria Co., St. Brigid's (1883). Merged with Our Lady of Mount Carmel, Lilly to form Our Lady of the Alleghenies, Lilly. Rev. Msgr. John R. Sasway.
Res., 608 Main St., 15938. Tel: 814-866-2504. [CEM]
Catechesis/Religious Programs—Tel: 814-886-2161. Barbara Pysher, D.R.E.
Students 172.

Our Lady of Mt. Carmel (1910) (Polish). Merged with St. Brigid, Lilly to form Our Lady of the Alleghenies, Lilly.

Our Lady of the Alleghenies (1995), Rev. Msgr. John R. Sasway; Deacon Bernard J. Zernick.
Res., 608 Main St., 15938. Tel: 814-886-2504. [CEM 2]
Catechesis/Religious Programs—Tel: 814-886-2161.
Students 182.

Lock Haven, Clinton Co., Immaculate Conception (1852), Rev. Msgr. Dennis R. Boggs.
Res., 310 W. Water St., 17745. Tel: 717-748-4535; Fax: 717-748-1674. [CEM]
School—Lock Haven Catholic School, Tel: 717-748-7252. Sr. Mary Joan Gibson, O.P., Prin.
Sisters of Sinsinawa Dominicans 3; Lay Teachers 18; Students 192.
Catechesis/Religious Programs—Tel: 717-748-4828; Fax: 570-893-8229.
Students 99.

St. Agnes (1873), Rev. Neil R. Dadey.
Res., 3 E. Walnut St., 17745. Tel: 717-748-4594; Fax: 570-893-8229. [CEM]
School—Lock Haven Catholic School. See Immaculate Conception for details. Tel: 717-742-7252.
Catechesis/Religious Programs—Tel: 717-748-4282.
Students 99.

Loretto, Cambria Co., Basilica of St. Michael the Archangel (1799), Very Rev. Msgr. Timothy J. Swope, V.F. In res., Rev. Michael Becker.
Res., 15940. Tel: 814-472-8551; Fax: 814-471-4959. [CEM]
School—Tel: 814-472-9117; Fax: 814-472-9117. Judy M. Noel, Prin.
Lay Teachers 8; Students 96.
Catechesis/Religious Programs—Tel: 814-472-2332. D.R.E.: Maggie Biter, (Elementary), Tel: 717-472-6064; Betty Seymour, (High School), Tel: 717-472-6279.
Students 186.

McConnellsburg, Fulton Co., St. Stephen's (1962), Rev. David R. Becker.
Res., 303 Lincoln Way E., 17233. Tel: 717-485-3723.
Catechesis/Religious Programs—Students 45.

Meyersdale, Somerset Co., SS. Philip and James (1850), Rev. Donald W. Dusza.
Res., 247 High St., 15552. Tel: 814-634-8150. [CEM 2]
Catechesis/Religious Programs—Students 62.
Mission—MacDonaldton, Somerset Co., St. Gregory, (1907) 247 High St., 15552. Tel: 814-634-8150.

Mount Union, Huntingdon Co., St. Catherine's (1912), Rev. Elwood F. Figurelle.
Res., 205 W. Market St., 17066. Tel: 814-542-4582; Fax: 814-542-4582. [CEM]
Catechesis/Religious Programs—Students 43.

Mundys Corner, Cambria Co., St. John Vianney's (1950), Rev. Paul M. Robine.
Res., 3513 William Penn Ave., Johnstown, 15909. Tel: 814-322-4789; Fax: 814-322-3799.
Catechesis/Religious Programs—Tel: 814-322-1149. Yvonne Allbaugh.
Students 202.

Nanty-Glo, Cambria Co., St. Mary's (1902), Rev. Msgr. John J. Little; Deacon Thomas M. Buige.
Res., 1020 Caroline St., 15943. Tel: 814-749-9103. [CEM]
School—1005 Caroline St., 15943. Tel: 814-749-9031. Mrs. Rosemary Conzo, Prin.
Sisters of St. Agnes 1; Lay Teachers 9; Students 87.
Catechesis/Religious Programs—D.R.E.: Mrs. Patricia LaMantia; Mrs. Mary Frances Shedlock.
Students 103.

New Baltimore, Somerset Co., St. John the Baptist (1829), Rev. Mark S. Begly.
Res., 15553. Tel: 814-733-2210; Fax: 814-733-2966. [CEM]
Catechesis/Religious Programs—Students 101.

Newry, Blair Co., St. Patrick's (1816), Rev. William A. Rosensteel.
Res., P.O. Box 398, 16665. Tel: 814-695-3413; Fax: 814-695-5274. [CEM 2]
School—Tel: 814-695-3819. Sr. Pauline Kastoski, C.C.W., Prin.
Sisters 2; Lay Teachers 8; Students 133.
Catechesis/Religious Programs—Tel: 814-695-3819. Mrs. Linda Guiffre, D.R.E.
Students 95.

Nicktown, Cambria Co., St. Nicholas (1861), Rev. Claude W. Pollak, O.S.B.
Res., 15762. Tel: 814-948-9614. [CEM]
School—Northern Cambria Catholic. See Elementary Diocesan Schools under Institutions Located in the Diocese. Tel: 814-948-8900; Fax: 814-948-8720.
Catechesis/Religious Programs—Tel: 814-948-8900. Nancy McKee, D.R.E.
Students 158.

Northern Cambria, Cambria Co.,

1—HOLY CROSS, (1893). Merged with St. Stanislaus Kostka, Barneboro; Christ the King, Barnesboro; St. John the Baptist, Northern Cambria; Our Lady of Mt. Carmel, Northern Cambria to form Prince of Peace, Northern Cambria.

2—ST. JOHN THE BAPTIST, (1896) (Slovak). Merged with St. Stanislaus Kostka, Barnesboro; Christ the King, Barensboro; Holy Cross, Northern Cambria; Our Lady of Mt. Carmel, Northern Cambria to form Prince of Peace, Northern Cambria.

3—OUR LADY OF MT. CARMEL, (1908) (Italian). Merged with St. Stanislaus Kostka, Barnesboro; Christ the King, Barnesboro; Holy Cross, Northern Cambria; St. John the Baptist to form Prince of Peace, Northern Cambria.

4—PRINCE OF PEACE, (2000), Rev. Msgr. Robert J. Saly; Rev. Lawrence L. Lacovic.
Res., 811 Chestnut Ave., 15714. Tel: 814-948-6842; Fax: 814-948-7533. [CEM 5]
School—See Elementary Diocesan Schools under Institutions Located in the Diocese. Tel: 814-948-8900.
Catechesis/Religious Programs—Tel: 814-948-6622. Sr. Karen C.C.W., D.R.E.
Students 500.

Patton, Cambria Co., Our Lady of Perpetual Help (1892). Merged with St. George, Patton, and St. Lawrence to form Queen of Peace, Patton. Revs. Joseph Gerg, O.S.B.; Robert Roche, O.S.B.
Res., 907 Sixth Ave., 16668. Tel: 814-674-8983. [CEM]
Catechesis/Religious Programs—Tel: 814-674-8938. D.R.E.: Michelle Kirk; Rita Horne.
Students 222.

Queen of Peace (1995), Revs. Joseph Gerg, O.S.B.; Robert Roche, O.S.B.
Res., 907 Sixth Ave., 16668. Tel: 814-674-8983; Fax: 814-674-8805. [CEM]
Catechesis/Religious Programs—Tel: 814-674-5591. Joanne VanOrmer, D.R.E.
Students 211.

St. George (1907) (Slovak). Merged with Our Lady of Perpetual Help, Patton and St. Lawrence to form Queen of Peace, Patton.

Penns Valley, Centre Co., Blessed Kateri Tekakwitha (1986), Rev. William S. Crouse.
Res., R.D. No. 1, Box 245A, Spring Mills, 16875. Tel: 814-422-8983. [JC]
Catechesis/Religious Programs—Students 72.

Philipsburg, Centre Co., SS. Peter and Paul (1868), Rev. Robert J. Kelly.
Res., 400 S. Fourth St., 16866. Tel: 814-342-1700; Fax: 814-342-5480. [CEM][JC]
Catechesis/Religious Programs—William J. Slother, Jr., D.R.E.
Students 208.

Portage, Cambria Co.,

1—ST. JOSEPH'S, (1898), Rev. Walter J. Moll, Jr.; Deacon James J. Janosik.
Res., 509 Caldwell Ave., 15946. Tel: 814-736-4279; Fax: 814-736-4764.

Catechesis/Religious Programs—Tel: 814-736-9214. Mary E. Heinrich, D.R.E.
Students 188.

2—ASSUMPTION B.V.M., (1907) (Slovak). Merged with Sacred Heart of Jesus to form Our Lady of the Sacred Heart, Portage.

3—SACRED HEART OF JESUS, (1909) (Polish). Merged with Assumption of the Blessed Virgin Mary, Portage to form Our Lady of the Sacred Heart, Portage.

4—ST. JOHN THE BAPTIST, (1923) (Hungarian), Rev. Ronald B. Yogus.
Res., 900 Johnson Ave., 15946. Tel: 814-736-9747. [CEM]
Catechesis/Religious Programs—812 Orchard St., 15946.
Students 28.

5—OUR LADY OF THE SACRED HEART, (1999) (Polish-Slovak), Rev. Ronald V. Osinski.
Res., 601 Mountain Ave., 15946. Tel: 814-736-4239; Fax: 814-736-9285. [CEM 2]
School—(Grades PreK-K) 812 Orchard St., 15946. Tel: 814-736-3588. Sr. M. Margaret, S.S.C.J., Prin.
Students 23.
Catechesis/Religious Programs—Tel: 814-736-4239.
Students 141.
Convent—803 Orchard St., 15946. Tel: 814-736-3875.

Renovo, Clinton Co., St. Joseph's (1869), Rev. Donald E. Boslett.
Res., 925 Huron Ave., 17764. Tel: 570-923-0172. [CEM 2]
Catechesis/Religious Programs—Judy M. Kurutz, D.R.E.
Students 126.

Revloc, Cambria Co., Most Holy Redeemer (1920), Rev. William J. Kovach.
Res., 553 Cambria Ave., 15948. Tel: 814-472-7928.
Catechesis/Religious Programs—Students 16.

Roaring Spring, Blair Co., St. Thomas More (1969), Rev. Msgr. William E. Shultz.
Res., 825 Williams St., 16673. Tel: 814-224-4522.
Catechesis/Religious Programs—Students 56.

St. Augustine, Cambria Co., St. Augustine (1847), Rev. Joseph W. Fleming.
Res., 803 St. Augustine Rd., Dysart, 16636. Tel: 814-674-8550. [CEM]
Catechesis/Religious Programs—Students 113.

St. Boniface, Cambria Co., St. Boniface Chapel (1859). Merged to form St. Bernard, Hastings.

St. Lawrence, Cambria Co., St. Lawrence's (1853). Merged with Our Lady of Perpetual Help and St. George Patton, to form Queen of Peace, Patton.

St. Michael, Cambria Co., St. Michael's (1913), Rev. George J. Valko.
Res., Box 103, 15951. Tel: 814-495-9640. [CEM]
Catechesis/Religious Programs—Students 176.

Shade Gap, Huntingdon Co., St. Mary's (1840), Rev. George D. Koharchik.
Res., Shade Gap, H.C. 62, Box 696, 17255. Tel: 814-447-3172; Fax: 814-447-9030. [CEM 2]
Catechesis/Religious Programs—Students 47.

Snow Shoe, Centre Co., St. Mary's (1865) (Irish), Rev. Sylvester J. Bendzella.
Res., 522 Fourth St., 16874. Tel: 814-387-6793. [CEM]
Catechesis/Religious Programs—Students 36.

Somerset, Somerset Co., St. Peter's (1920), Rev. Msgr. Samuel J. Tomaselli; Rev. Sean A. Code; Deacon Frederick F. Weaver.
Res., 433 W. Church St., 15501. Tel: 814-443-6574; Fax: 814-445-7766. [CEM]
School—Tel: 814-445-6662. Mrs. Karen Ferry, Prin.
Lay Teachers 7; Students 119.
Catechesis/Religious Programs—Tel: 814-443-6574.
Students 331.

St. Peter in Chains (1995),
Mailing Address: S.C.I.-Somerset, 1590 Walters Mill Rd., 15501-0001. Tel: 814-443-8100.

South Fork, Cambria Co., Most Holy Trinity (1995), Rev. Louis J. Mulvehill.
Res., 550 Main St., 15956. Tel: 814-495-4419; Fax: 814-495-4419. [CEM 2]
Catechesis/Religious Programs—Tel: 814-495-4028. Mrs. Betty Rosmus, D.R.E.
Students 84.

St. Anthony's (1905) (Polish). Merged with St. James, South Fork and Our Lady of Mt. Carmel, Ehrenfeld to form Most Holy Trinity, South Fork.

St. James (1906). Merged with St. Anthony, South Fork and Our Lady of Mt. Carmel, Ehrenfeld to form Most Holy Trinity, South Fork.

Spangler, Cambria Co., St. Patrick's (1902). Merged with Sacred Heart, Bakerton to form St. Jude, Elmora.

State College, Centre Co., Good Shepherd (1989), Rev. Philip M. Bender; Deacons Robert A. Killoren, Jr. Tel: 814-867-5657; Michael A. Ondik Tel: 814-237-1857. In res., Rev. Joseph G. Hlubik.
Res., 867 Gray's Woods Blvd., P.O. Box 8186, 16803. Tel: 814-238-7463.
Church—Tel: 814-238-2110; Fax: 814-238-3484.
Catechesis/Religious Programs—Tel: 814-238-0649. Dorothy Kardohely, D.R.E.
Students 430.

Our Lady of Victory (1908), Revs. Martin Dugan McCamley; Frantisek A. Halka; James D. Zatalava; Deacons David Lapinski; Anthony Wagner.
Res., 820 Westerly Pkwy., 16801. Tel: 814-237-7832; Fax: 814-237-6709.
PreSchool—Tel: 814-238-6616.
Lay Teachers 6; Students 74.
School—Tel: 814-238-1592; Fax: 814-238-4553. Kathleen Bechdel, Prin.
Lay Teachers 16; Students 339.
Catechesis/Religious Programs—Tel: 814-234-3315. Shannon Jones, D.R.E.
Students 661.

Summerhill, Cambria Co., St. John (1903), Rev. Eric T. Vogt, O.S.B.
Res., 538 Main St., P.O. Box 248, 15958. Tel: 814-495-5241. [CEM]
Mission—New Germany, Cambria Co., Immaculate Conception, (1855) 1640 New Germany Rd., P.O. Box 248, Summerhill, 15958.
Catechesis/Religious Programs—Students 233.

Twin Rocks, Cambria Co., St. Charles (1917). Merged with Immaculate Conception Mission, Vintondale to form SS. Timothy & Mark Church, Twin Rocks & SS. Timothy & Mark Chapel, Vintondale.

SS. Timothy & Mark (1995),
Mailing Address: P.O. Box 275, 15960. Tel: 814-749-9331; Fax: 814-749-8000. [CEM]
Catechesis/Religious Programs—Students 61.
Mission—Vintondale, Cambria Co., SS. Timothy & Mark Chapel, 314 4th St., Vintondale, 15961.

Tyrone, Blair Co., St. Matthew's (1853), Rev. Joseph T. Orr.
Res., 406 W. 11th St., 16686. Tel: 814-684-1480; Fax: 814-684-7969. [CEM]
School—1107 Cameron Ave., 16686. Tel: 814-684-3510. Mrs. Jamie DiDomenico, Prin.
Lay Teachers 5; Students 59.
Catechesis/Religious Programs—Tel: 814-684-4808. Mary Boscaino, D.R.E.
Students 131.

West Salisbury, Somerset Co., St. Michael's (1887), Rev. Albert J. Anselmi.
Res., 15565. Tel: 814-662-2958. [CEM 2]
Mission—Pocahontas, Somerset Co., St. Mary's, (1906) P.O. Box 31, 15565. Tel: 814-662-2958.
Catechesis/Religious Programs—Students 22.

Williamsburg, Blair Co., St. Joseph (1861), Rev. Bernard L. White.
Res., 628 W. First St., 16693. Tel: 814-832-2137; Fax: 814-832-1025. [CEM 2]
Catechesis/Religious Programs—Students 50.

Wilmore, Cambria Co., St. Bartholomew's (1840), Rev. Robert L. Ruston.
Res., P.O. Box 96, 15962. Tel: 814-495-5360; 736-8314. [CEM]
Catechesis/Religious Programs—Tel: 814-495-5360.
Students 97.

Windber, Somerset Co.,

1—ST. JOHN CANTIUS, (1898) (Polish), Rev. Leonard E. Voytek; Deacon Thaddeus Janisko.
Res., 605 Graham Ave., 15963-1398. Tel: 814-467-7191; Fax: 814-467-1621. [CEM]
Catechesis/Religious Programs—D.R.E.: Paul Banjak, (High School), Tel: 814-467-8443; Sr. Evangelista Strohmier, (Elementary), Tel: 814-467-9670.
Students 140.

2—SS. CYRIL AND METHODIUS, (1906) (Slovak), Rev. Matthew Misurda.
Res., 604 Graham Ave., 15963. Tel: 814-467-7042; Fax: 814-467-0183. [CEM 2]
Catechesis/Religious Programs—600 Graham Ave., 15963. Tel: 814-467-9670.
Students 61.

3—ST. ANTHONY OF PADUA, (1908) (Italian), Revs. Blase R. Romano, T.O.R.; Adrian Tirpak, T.O.R.; Mark Reifel, T.O.R.; Deacon Joseph R. Dalla Valle.
Res., 2201 Graham Ave., 15963. Tel: 814-467-7292; Fax: 814-467-9182. [CEM]
Schools—St. Benedict School, Tel: 814-266-3837; Fax: 814-266-7718.
Students 15; St. Andrew School, Tel: 814-288-2811; Fax: 814-288-6750.
Students 1; St. Clement School, Tel: 814-255-1964; Fax: 814-255-2623.
Catechesis/Religious Programs—Tel: 814-467-9670. D.R.E.: Sr. Evangelista R.S.M.; Roxann Newcomer.
Students 164.

4—ST. MARY'S, (1914) (Hungarian), Rev. Leonard E. Voytek; Deacon Thaddeus Janisko.
Res., 605 Graham Ave., 15963-1398. Tel: 814-467-7191; Fax: 814-467-1621. [CEM]
Catechesis/Religious Programs—D.R.E.: Sr. Evangelista Strohmier, (Elementary), Tel: 814-467-9670; Paul Banjak, (High School), Tel: 814-467-8443.
Students 54.

5—HOLY CHILD JESUS, (1921) (Irish), Rev. Charles F. Leonardis.
Res., 913 Graham Ave., 15963. Tel: 814-467-7097. [JC]
Catechesis/Religious Programs—Tel: 814-467-9670.
Students 30.

Chaplains of Public Institutions

ALTOONA. *Altoona Hospital* Howard Ave. & Seventh St., 16601. Tel: 814-946-2011. Chaplains: Revs. Edward L. Eckenrod Tel: 814-943-6185; Brian Saylor Tel: 814-943-4603.

Veterans Medical Center 2907 Pleasant Valley Blvd., 16602. Tel: 814-943-8164. Rev. Edward J. Dabcosky, Chap.

JOHNSTOWN. *Conemaugh Memorial Medical Center* 1083 Franklin St., 15905. Tel: 814-533-9000; 536-0117 (Res.). Chaplains: Revs. Adalbert Walski, T.O.R.; Bernard V. Grattan.

UPMC Lee Hospital 320 Main St., 15901. Tel: 814-533-0123; 536-0117 (Res.). Chaplains: Rev. Msgr. David Lockard; Revs. Adalbert Walski, T.O.R.; Bernard V. Grattan.

BELLEFONTE. *State Correctional Institution* Our Lady of the Mount, Box A, 16823. Tel: 814-355-4874; 422-8983 (Res.). Rev. William S. Crouse.

CRESSON. *State Correctional Institution* P.O. Box A, 16630. Tel: 814-886-8181; 736-9747 (Res.). Rev. Ronald B. Yogus, Chap.

EBENSBURG. *Laurel Crest Rehabilitation & Special Care Center* 429 Manor Dr., 15931. Tel: 814-472-8100. Sr. Mary Brenda Helis, S.C.

HUNTINGDON. *State Correctional Institution* St. Dismas, Drawer R, 16652. Tel: 814-643-5250; 447-3172 (Res.). Revs. George D. Koharchik; Bernard White Tel: 814-832-2137.

LAURAL HIGHLANDS. *State Correctional Institution* 5706 Glades Pike Rd., P.O. Box 631, Tel: 814-445-6501. Deacon Pasquale Valerio, Chap.

LORETTO. *Federal Correctional Institution* P.O. Box 1000, 15940. Tel: 814-472-4140; 472-9363 (Res.). Sr. Mary Ann Palko, C.C.W., Chap.

SMITHFIELD. *State Correctional Institution*. 1120 Pike St., Huntingdon, 16652. Tel: 814-643-6520; 832-2137 (Res.). Rev. Bernard L. White.

SOMERSET. *State Correctional Institution* St. Peter in Chains, 1590 Walters Mill Rd., 15510. Tel: 814-443-8100. Deacon Pasquale Valerio, Chap.

On Duty Outside the Diocese:
Reverend Monsignors—
Lenz, Paul A., Black and Indian Mission Office, 2021 H St., N.W., Washington, DC 20006. Tel: 202-331-8542
Reverend Fathers—
Ledoux, Albert H., St. Mary's Seminary, Emmittsburg, MD. Tel: 301-447-5809
Mancini, Nicholas, St. Paul, 1459 Superior Ave., N.E., Canton, OH 44705

On Special or Other Diocesan Assignment:
Reverend Fathers—
Strecok, Lubomir, Diocese of Altoona-Johnstown, 126 Logan Blvd., Hollidaysburg, PA 16648

Military Chaplains:
Reverend Fathers—
Gergel, Stephen J., U.S. Navy
Gomulka, Eugene T., U.S. Navy

Absent on Leave:
Reverend Fathers—
Braman, Dennis J.
Christiana, Nicholas M.
Cronauer, David W.
Karr, Raymond E.
Mascherino, Alphonse T.
Mazurkiewicz, Joseph
Norcavage, Albert R.
Petracca, Anthony

Retired:
Reverend Monsignors—
Ackerson, Francis A., 723 Mifflin St., Huttingdon, PA 16652. Tel: 814-643-3582

Fleming, Joseph H., 14408 Gallagher Rd., Delray Beach, FL 33445. Tel: 561-498-7646
Fleming, Patrick V., FL 33445. Tel: 561-498-7646
Lafferty, John J., Dmitri Manor, 3 St. Mary's Ln., Hollidaysburg, PA 16648
Madden, Thomas E., P.O. Box 33, Altoona, PA 16603
McCaa, Francis B., 311 Lincoln Dr., Martinsburg, WV 25401
O'Toole, Anthony J., Dmitri Manor, 6 St. Mary's Ln., Hollidaysburg, PA 16648
O'Toole, Joseph M., Garvey Manor Nursing Home, 128 Logan Blvd., Hollidaysburg, PA 16648
Panza, Paul D., P.A., Dmitri Manor, 1 St. Mary's Ln., Hollidaysburg, PA 16648
Pier, Joseph, 1776 Clapboard Run Rd., Johnstown, PA 15904
Saylor, Philip, Mid Town Square, 310 S. Allen St., State College, PA 16801
Wadas, Ignatius C., 221 Luray Ave., Johnstown, PA 15904. Tel: 814-266-8415
Walsh, Richard J., 1254 Lincoln Ave., P.O. Box 197, Tyrone, PA 16686. Tel: 814-684-2505

Reverend Fathers—
Boyle, John J., P.O. Box 159, Mill Hall, PA 17751
Crosser, Raymond G., 100 Beckman Dr., 6F, Altoona, PA 16602
Ellias, John J.
George, J. Clark, Dmitri Manor, 2 St. Mary's Ln., Hollidaysburg, PA 16648
Greiner, Kenneth A., REAR 319 Cherry Ave., Altoona, PA 16601
Inman, Leonard T., 1029 Johnson Ave., Portage, PA 15946
Joly, Henry L., P.O. Box 705, Hollidaysburg, PA 16648
Knapik, Andrew G., P.O. Box 111, Bellefonte, PA 16823
Mattiello, Lucian C., 121 E. 25th Ave., Altoona, PA 16601
Michaels, Emmett T., Box 94, Accomac, VA 23301
Myers, Regis F., Dmitri Manor, 10 St. Mary's Ln., Hollidaysburg, PA 16648
Orlando, John V., Garvey Manor Nursing Home, 128 Logan Blvd., Hollidaysburg, PA 16648
Ream, Gerard J., P.O. Box 5002, Johnstown, PA 15906
Stange, Henry A., P.O. Box 1133, Altoona, PA 16603
Strittmatter, J. Joseph, Dmitri Manor, 8 St. Mary's Ln., Hollidaysburg, PA 16648
Thomas, Paul, Garvey Manor Nursing Home, 128 Logan Blvd., Hollidaysburg, PA 16648

Permanent Deacons:
Buige, Thomas M., St. Mary, Nanty Glo
Cammarata, Samuel M., St. Andrew, Johnstown
Concannon, John, St. John Gualbert, Johnstown
Condor, Michael, Jr., Basilica of St. Michael, Loretto
Dalla Valle, Joseph R., St. Anthony, Windber
Gibson, Philip, Immaculate Conception, Lock Haven
Gillan, Garth, Blessed Kateri, Penns Valley
Ivantis, Laszlo P., Penn State Catholic Community
Janisko, Thaddeus J., St. John Cantius/St. Mary, Windber
Janosik, James, St. Joseph, Portage
Killoran, Bernard J., Good Shepherd, State College
Kist, Leo A., St. Patrick, Johnstown
Lapinski, David C., Our Lady of Victory, State College
Leap, James F., Blessed Sacrament Cathedral, Altoona
Lemmon, Thomas M., St. Francis of Assisi, Johnstown
Lux, Herman J., Holy Spirit, Beaverdale
Marchu, James F., SS. Timothy & Mark, Twin Rocks
Mazurkiewicz, Joseph F., Sr., St. John Evangelist, Bellefonte
Neral, Gene, St. John the Evangelist, Lakemont
Ondik, Michael A., Good Shepherd, State College
Papinchik, Thomas M., St. Gregory/St.Barnabas, Johnstown
Rys, John E., St. Mark, Altoona
Schuette, Carl F., St. Thomas Apostle, Bedford
Sroka, John, Visitation, Johnstown
Tiernan, John A., St. Mary, Holidaysburg
Valerio, Pat N., St. Peter in Chains, SCI, Somerset
Wagner, Anthony E., Our Lady of the Mount, SCI, Rockview; Our Lady of Victory, State College
Weaver, Frederick F., St. Peter, Somerset
Zernick, Bernard J., Lady of Alleghenies. Lilly

INSTITUTIONS LOCATED IN THE DIOCESE

[A] COLLEGES AND UNIVERSITIES
(NON-DIOCESAN)

CRESSON. *Mount Aloysius College*, 7373 Admiral Peary Hwy., 16630. Tel: 814-886-4131; Fax: 814-886-2978.
E-mail: cmiller@mtaloy.edu
Web site: www.mtaloy.edu
For a complete listing, refer to the Colleges and Universities section.

LORETTO. *St. Francis College*, P.O. Box 600, 15940-0600. Tel: 814-472-3000; Fax: 814-472-3044.
Web site: www.sfcpa.edu
For a complete listing, refer to the Colleges and Universities section.

[B] HIGH SCHOOLS, DIOCESAN

ALTOONA. *Bishop Guilfoyle High School*, 2400 Pleasant Valley Blvd., 16602. Tel: 814-944-4014; Fax: 814-944-8695.
E-mail: bghsl@penn.com
Web site: www.users.penn.com/~bghsl/index.htm
Rev. Leo A. Lynch, Prin.; Sr. Beverly Hmel, I.H.M., Asst. Prin. Priests 1; Lay Teachers 26; Students 380.

JOHNSTOWN. *Bishop McCort High School*, 25 Osborne St., 15905. Tel: 814-536-8991; Fax: 814-535-4118.
E-mail: mccort@third-wave.com
Sr. Donna Marie Leiden, S.C., Prin.; Rev. Leo F. Arnone, Chap. Priests 1; Deacons 1; Lay Teachers 35; Students 513.

EBENSBURG. *Bishop Carroll High School*, 15931. Tel: 814-472-7500; Fax: 814-472-8020.
E-mail: Bishopcarroll@USA.net
Web site: diocesealtjtn.org
Mrs. Deborah L. Meckey, Prin.; Rev. David Rizzo, Chap. Priests 1; Sisters 2; Lay Teachers 19; Students 328.

[C] ELEMENTARY DIOCESAN SCHOOLS

ALTOONA. *Altoona Central Catholic School Site*. (Grades PreK-8), 1400 4th Ave., 16602. Tel: 814-944-1250; Fax: 814-942-0894.
E-mail: stmarys@aasdcat.com

Cathedral of the Blessed Sacrament. (Grades K-5), 1304 13th Ave., 16601. Tel: 814-943-7423; Fax: 814-743-7609.
E-mail: cathedral@aasdcat.com
Anthony Consiglio, Prin. Lay Teachers 78; Students 124.

Our Lady of Mount Carmel. (Grades K-5), 1012 8th Ave., 16602. Tel: 814-943-5931; Fax: 814-943-1837.
E-mail: mtcarmel@aasdcat.com
Susan Curfman, Prin. Lay Teachers 6; Students 99.

St. Mary. (Grades K-5), 1400 4th Ave., 16602. Tel: 814-944-1250; Fax: 814-942-0894.
E-mail: stmarys@aasdcat.com
Diana Fanale, Prin. Lay Teachers 6; Students 109.

Altoona Central Catholic Middle School. (Grades 6-8), 424 Wopsononock Ave., 16601. Tel: 814-944-3751; Fax: 814-944-8283.
E-mail: ccmidsch@aasdcat.com
Sr. Mary Kevin Breen, O.S.F., Prin. Lay Teachers 11; Students 200. Sisters 1; Lay Teachers 29; Students 530.

JOHNSTOWN. *Central Catholic Elementary School*. (Grades K-8), 751 Railroad St., 15901. Tel: 814-536-1532; Fax: 814-536-0493.
E-mail: centralcath@Lenzlink.net
Mrs. Lois Ryan, Prin.
Consolidation of the following parishes: St. Clare of Assisi and St. John Gualbert. Lay Teachers 9; Students 127.

West End Catholic School. (Grades K-8), 317 Power St., 15906. Tel: 814-536-4722. Mr. Louis Bennese, Prin.
Consolidation of the following parishes: St. Casimir; St. Columba; St. Emerich; St. Francis of Assisi; Immaculate Conception; St. Rochus; St. Stephen; St. Therese. Sisters 1; Lay Teachers 10; Students 161.

CRESSON. *All Saints Catholic School*. (Grades K-8), 220 Powell Ave., 16630. Tel: 814-886-7942; Fax: 814-886-7942. Mrs. Susan Glass, Prin.
Consolidation of the following parishes: St. Francis Xavier; St. Aloysius; St. Agnes; Our Lady of the Alleghenies; St. Thomas Aquinas; St. Joseph. Sisters 1; Lay Teachers 8; Students 157.

HOLLIDAYSBURG. *Hollidaysburg Consolidated Catholic Elementary School*. (Grades PreK-8), Spruce & Wayne Sts., P.O. Box 599, 16648. Tel: 814-695-6112; Fax: 814-696-8960.
E-mail: salo416@aol.com
Web site: www.nb.net/~hcs/
Mr. Edward DiSabato, Prin.
Consolidation of the following parishes: St. Michael's; St. Mary's. Lay Teachers 9; Students 205.

NICKTOWN. *Northern Cambria Catholic School*, P.O. Box 249, Rte. 271S, 15762. Tel: 814-948-8900; Fax: 814-948-8720.
E-mail: nccs@northerncambria.org
Sr. Mary Carol Kardell, C.S.S.F., Prin.
Consolidation of the following parishes: St. Nicholas & Prince of Peace. Sisters 2; Lay Teachers 9; Students 140.

[D] GENERAL HOSPITALS
(NON-DIOCESAN)

ALTOONA. *Bon Secours - Holy Family Regional Health System*, 2500 Seventh Ave., 16602. Tel: 814-944-1681; Fax: 814-949-5880.
E-mail: Davecuz@aol.com
Web site: www.bonsecoursholyfamily.org
For a complete listing, refer to the Hospitals section.

JOHNSTOWN. *Good Samaritan Medical Center*, 1020 Franklin St., 15905. Tel: 814-533-1000; Fax: 814-539-0264.
E-mail: stucker@conemaugh.org
For a complete listing, refer to the Hospitals section.

[E] HOMES FOR AGED
(NON-DIOCESAN)

HOLLIDAYSBURG. *Garvey Manor*, 128 Logan Blvd., 16648. Tel: 814-695-5571; Fax: 814-695-8516
For a complete listing, refer to the Special Care Facilities section.

St. Leonard's Home, Inc., 601 N. Montgomery St., 16648. Tel: 814-695-9581; Fax: 814-695-2606
For a complete listing, refer to the Special Care Facilities section.

(DIOCESAN)

HOLLIDAYSBURG. *Dmitri Manor Priests' Residence*, St. Mary's Ln., 16648. Tel: 814-696-4698
For a complete listing, refer to the Special Care Facilities section.

[F] MONASTERIES AND RESIDENCES OF PRIESTS AND BROTHERS
(NON-DIOCESAN)

HOLLIDAYSBURG. *St. Joseph Friary*, 501-503 Walnut St., 16648. Tel: 814-695-5802. Bro. Bernard Dougherty, T.O.R., Supr.; Very Rev. Canon Aloysius Hankinson, T.O.R.; Rev. Domenic R. Aversa, T.O.R.; Very Rev. Adalbert Wolski, T.O.R.

LORETTO. *Mount Assisi Friary*, P.O. Box 40, 15940. Tel: 814-472-5324; Fax: 814-472-3349. Revs. Marianus D. Lieb, T.O.R.; Damian L. Noel, T.O.R.; Bro. Mark McBride, T.O.R., Prov. Econome & Vicar Min.; Revs. Ronald Bodenschatz, T.O.R.; John J. Wilger, T.O.R.; Vincent R. Negherbon; Daniel Mulkern, T.O.R.; Simon Engler, T.O.R.; Kenneth Flaherty, T.O.R.; Nicholas Polichnowski, T.O.R., Local Min. Tel: 814-472-5324 Ext. 302; Andre Strittmatter, T.O.R.; Edward Stafford, T.O.R.; Francis Moyher, T.O.R.; Laurence Uhlman, T.O.R.; Richard Davis, T.O.R.; Thomas Carapella, T.O.R.; Bros. Callistus Gerardi, T.O.R.; Damien W. Koehler, T.O.R. Priests 15; Brothers in Solemn Vows 3.

St. Bonaventure Friary, P.O. Box 155, 15940-0155. Tel: 814-472-9422; Fax: 814-472-3878. Revs. Laurence R. Uhlman, T.O.R., Dir. Novices; Richard L. Davis, T.O.R., Dir. Vocations. Priests 2; Novices 3.

St. Francis Friary, Third Order Regular of St. Francis of Penance. Province of the Most Sacred Heart of Jesus. P.O. Box 600, 15940. Tel: 814-472-3360. Revs. Christian R. Oravec, T.O.R., Pres., St. Francis College; Michael Higgins, T.O.R.; Bede F. Hines, T.O.R.; Emil C. Resconich, T.O.R.; Oliver J. Hebert, T.O.R.; John Mark Klaus, T.O.R.; Patrick Donahoe, T.O.R.; David Morrier, T.O.R.; Bro. Shaun Roberson, T.O.R. Total in Residence 9.

NEWRY. *St. Bernardine Monastery*, P.O. Box 208, 16665. Tel: 814-695-3992; 695-8991; Fax: 814-695-1611.
E-mail: broalexis@aol.com
Web site: www.penn.com/francisanstor
Revs. Alexis Nagle, T.O.R., Local Min.; Eugene Kubina, T.O.R., Vicar; Martin D. Brady, T.O.R.; Camillus Angle, T.O.R.; Kenneth La Pan, T.O.R.; Alan Polimine, T.O.R.; Bro. Stephen Baker, T.O.R. Priests 6; Brothers 2.

Novitiate of the Immaculate Conception Province of the T.O.R. of St. Francis. Tel: 814-695-3992; Fax: 814-695-1611. Franciscan Development Office, P.O. Box 139, Hollidaysburg, 16648. Tel: 814-695-3802; Fax: 814-695-1611.
E-mail: anagle1@penn.com
Rev. Alexis Nagle, T.O.R., Dir. Devel. & Mass Association, Province Econome's Office, P.O. Box 117, Hollidaysburg, 16648. Tel: 814-696-3321; Fax: 814-695-1611. Rev. Eugene Kubina, T.O.R., Province Econome.

[G] CONVENTS AND RESIDENCES FOR SISTERS
(NON-DIOCESAN)

ALTOONA. *Carmelite Community of the Word*, Ss. Peter & Paul Convent, 1906 19th St., 16601. Tel: 814-942-5747; Fax: 814-942-8052.
E-mail: lindaccw@cs.com
Total in Residence 4.

Our Lady of Perpetual Help Convent, 601 North Sixth Ave., 16601. Tel: 814-942-3819. Sisters, Servants of the Immaculate Heart of Mary. Total in Residence 2; Total Staff 2.

JOHNSTOWN. *Carmelite Community of the Word*, St. Joseph's Convent, 741 Railroad St., 15901. Tel: 814-535-7118; Fax: 814-535-7118.
E-mail: newsccw@aol.com
Total in Residence 2.

Sisters of Mercy, Mercy Convent, 972 Fritz St., 15905. Tel: 814-536-2610. Sr. Vincent de Paul Gibbon, R.S.M., Coord. Sisters 3.

CRESSON. *McAuley Hall*, 4 College Dr., 16630-1900. Tel: 814-886-4159. Institute of the Sisters of Mercy of the Americas (Silver Spring, MD). Sr. Ruth Hollen, R.S.M., Coord. Total in Residence 16; Total Staff 9.

Sisters Servants of the Sacred Heart, Provincial House, 866 Cambria St., 16630-1713. Tel: 814-886-4223; Fax: 814-886-4735.
E-mail: sscjusa@nb.net
Web site: www.nb.net/~sscjusa
Sr. Theresa Marie, S.S.C.J., Provincial Supr.

Personal Care Home. Tel: 814-536-4546. Total in Residence 18; Total Staff 7.

EBENSBURG. *Carmelite Community of the Word*, St. Therese Convent, 218 W. Lloyd St., 15931. Tel: 814-472-9457; Fax: 814-472-5105. Total in Residence 2.

Mount St. Ann Retreat House and Novitiate, P.O. Box 328, 15931. Tel: 814-472-9354; Fax: 814-472-9354. Sisters of St. Ann. Sr. Melany Pereira, S.S.A., Supr. Total in Residence 4.

GALLITZIN. *Carmelite Community of the Word Administration Center*, 394 Bem Rd., 16641. Tel: 814-886-4098; Fax: 814-886-4098.
E-mail: Genadccw@aol.com
Sr. Marilyn Welch, C.C.W., General Admin. Total in Residence 6.

Little Sisters of Jesus, 347 Tunnel Hill St., 16641. Tel: 814-886-4679. Sr. Anne Beth Boucher, Supr. Total in Residence 3.

LILLY. *Family Life Office*, 5379 Portage St., 15938. Tel: 814-886-5551; Fax: 814-886-7697.
E-mail: famlifaj@aol.com
Web site: www.diocesealtjtn.org
Susan Stith, Family Life Dir. Total Staff 5; Total Assisted 13,200.

LORETTO. *Carmel of St. Therese of Lisieux Monastery*, P.O. Box 57, 15940. Tel: 814-472-8620. Mother John of the Cross, O.C.D., Prioress. Discalced Carmelite Nuns. Nuns with Solemn Vows 10; Extern Professed 1; Nuns with Simple Vows 1; Novices 1; Candidates 1.

Our Lady of Loretto, 139 St. Ann St., Box 36, 15940. Tel: 814-472-2332. Sisters of Mercy. Total in Residence 3.

McCONNELLSBURG. *Carmelite Community of the Word*, Fulton County Mission, 110 S. Third St., 17223. Tel: 717-485-5917; 485-0661; Fax: 717-485-3855.
E-mail: fccm@cun.net
Total in Residence 2.

PORTAGE. *Sisters Servants of the Sacred Heart Novitiate*, Sacred Heart Novitiate, 1872 Munster Rd., 15946. Tel: 814-886-7785. Sr. Jacinta Miryam, S.S.C.J., Novice Mistress.

[H] CAMPUS MINISTRY

HOLLIDAYSBURG. *Campus Ministry*, Altoona-Johnstown Diocese, 126A Logan Blvd., 16648. Mr. Thomas J. McConnell, Dir.

Juniata College, 17th & Moore St., Huntington, 16652. Tel: 814-641-3362 (Office). Rev. David J. Arseneault, Chap.; Cheryl Smith, Campus Min.

Lock Haven University (Lock Haven), Newman Center, 445 W. Main St., Lock Haven, 17745. Tel: 717-748-8592. Rev. Neil R. Dadey; Marianne Mitchell, M.A., Campus Min.

Mount Aloysius College (Cresson), 7373 Admiral Peary Hwy., Cresson, 16630. Tel: 814-886-6498. Sr. Benedict Joseph Watters, R.S.M., M.S., Dir.; Rev. John J. Slovikovski, Chap.

Penn State University - Altoona Campus, 3000 Ivyside Park, Altoona, 16601. Tel: 814-949-5137. Rev. James B. Coveney, Chap.

St. Francis College (Loretto), Loretto, 15940. Tel: 814-472-7000. Campus Ministers: Revs. Terrence Henry, T.O.R.; John Mark Klaus, T.O.R.; David Morrier, T.O.R. Tel: 814-472-3318; Edward Stafford, T.O.R.; Bro. Shawn Roberson.

University of Pittsburgh at Johnstown, 450 Schoolhouse Rd., Johnstown, 15904. Tel: 814-269-2007. Rev. David R. Rizzo, Chap.; Sr. Corinne Kirsch, C.S.J., Campus Min.

[I] NEWMAN CENTERS
(NON-DIOCESAN)

UNIVERSITY PARK. *Penn State Catholic Community*, 207A Helen Eakin Eisenhower Chapel, 16802. Tel: 814-865-4281; Fax: 814-863-7251.
E-mail: catholic@psu.edu
Web site: http://www.psu.edu/catholic
Campus Ministers: Revs. Conan E. Feigh, O.S.B.; Frederick Byrne, O.S.B.; Joseph G. Hlubik; Deacon Laszlo Ivantis. Total in Residence 3; Total Staff 7. Catholic Students attending Penn State University 10,000.

[J] MISCELLANEOUS LISTINGS
(NON-DIOCESAN)

BEDFORD. *St. Mary's House of Greater Solitude*, Passionist Community, 2970 Imlertown Rd., 15522-8101. Tel: 814-623-1796; Fax: 814-623-2457. Revs. Silvan Rouse, C.P., Supr.; Malachy McGill, C.P.; Howard Chirdon, C.P.; Albert Cabrera, C.P.; Theophane McEwen, C.P.

HOLLIDAYSBURG. *Conference of Slovak Clergy*, 126 Logan Blvd., 16648. Tel: 814-695-5579; Fax: 814-695-8894.
E-mail: lubomir@dioceseaj.org
Most Rev. Joseph V. Adamec, Chm.; Rev. Msgr. Michael J. Chaback, Vice Chm.; Rev. Lubomir J. Strecok, Sec.

LORETTO. *American Parish Youth Center, Inc.*, P.O. Box 40, 15940. Tel: 814-472-9632; Fax: 814-472-5089.

Prince Gallitzin Chapel House (Diocesan). Tel: 814-472-5441; Fax: 814-472-5446.
E-mail: mbecker253@aol.com
Mailing Address: P.O. Box 99, 15940. Tel: 814-472-5441.

Office of Vocations.
Office of Ongoing Formation of Clergy.

NEW BALTIMORE. *St. John The Baptist Retreat Center*, P.O. Box 10, 15553. Tel: 814-733-2210; Fax: 814-733-2966. Total in Residence 1; Total Staff 7.

RELIGIOUS INSTITUTES OF MEN REPRESENTED IN THE DIOCESE

For further details refer to the corresponding bracketed number in the Religious Institutes of Men or Women section.

[0200]—*Benedictine Monks.*—O.S.B.
[0470]—*The Capuchin Friars.*—O.F.M.Cap.
[1000]—*Congregation of the Passion.*—C.P.
[0480]—*Conventual Franciscans.* (St. Anthony of Padua Prov.).—O.F.M.Conv.
[0520]—*Franciscan Friars.*—O.F.M.
[0560]—*Third Order Regular of Saint Francis.* (Provs. of Sacred Heart, Immaculate Conception).—T.O.R.

RELIGIOUS INSTITUTES OF WOMEN REPRESENTED IN THE DIOCESE

[0100]—*Adorers of the Blood of Christ.*—A.S.C.
[0315]—*Carmelite Community of the Word.*—C.C.W.
[0330]—*Carmelite Sisters for the Aged and Infirm.*—O.Carm.
[3710]—*Congregation of the Sisters of Saint Agnes.*—C.S.A.
[0420]—*Discalced Carmelite Nuns.*—O.C.D.
[1070-03]—*Dominican Sisters.*—O.P.
[1170]—*Felician Sisters.*—C.S.S.F.
[2330]—*Little Sisters of Jesus.*—L.S.J.
[3630]—*Servants of the Most Sacred Heart of Jesus.*—S.S.C.J.
[0570]—*Sisters of Charity of Seton Hill, Greensburg, Pennsylvania.*—S.C.
[2575]—*Sisters of Mercy of the Americas.*—R.S.M. (Dallas Regional Community).
[1620]—*Sisters of Saint Francis of Millvale, Pennsylvania.*—O.S.F.
[3780]—*Sisters of Ss. Cyril and Methodius.*—SS.C.M.
[3718]—*Sisters of St. Ann.* (Italy).—S.S.A.
[3830]—*Sisters of St. Joseph.*—C.S.J.
[1970]—*Sisters of the Holy Family of Nazareth.*—C.S.F.N.
[3260]—*Sisters of the Precious Blood (Ohio).*—C.PP.S.
[2160]—*Sisters, Servants of the Immaculate Heart of Mary.* (Scranton, PA).—I.H.M.
[4160]—*Vincentian Sisters of Charity.*—V.S.C.

NECROLOGY

† Beiter, Rev. Msgr. Lambert M., (Retired). —Died Dec. 2, 1999.
† Bender, Joseph J., (Retired). —Died Aug. 7, 2000.
† Burkardt, Rev. Msgr. Harold J, Newry, PA St. Patrick. —Died March 17, 2000.
† Maher, Rev. Msgr. Thomas J, Loretto, PA Basilica of St. Michael the Archangel. —Died Dec. 31, 1999.
† Malloy, Rev. Msgr. Faber J, Ebensburg, PA Holy Name. —Died June 1, 2000.

Diocese of Amarillo

(Dioecesis Amarillensis)

Most Reverend

JOHN W. YANTA, D.D.

Bishop of Amarillo; ordained March 17, 1956; appointed Titular Bishop of Naratcata and Auxiliary Bishop of San Antonio October 27, 1994; consecrated December 30, 1994; appointed Bishop of Amarillo January 21, 1997.

Most Reverend

LEROY T. MATTHIESEN, D.D., M.A., LITT.D.

Retired Bishop of Amarillo; ordained March 10, 1946; appointed March 25, 1980; ordained May 30, 1980; retired January 21, 1997. *Mailing Address: P.O. Box 5644, Amarillo, TX, 79117-5664.*

ERECTED A DIOCESE BY POPE PIUS XI, AUGUST 25, 1926.

Square Miles Approximately 25,800.

Comprises that part of the State of Texas known as the Panhandle, and extending thence southward; bounded on the east by Oklahoma, and by the eastern county line of Childress and by the southern lines Childress, Hall, Briscoe, Swisher, Castro and Parmer Counties; the western boundary is the New Mexico state line from the southern line of Parmer County, Texas, northward to the northwestern corner of the Panhandle of Texas. There are 26 counties.

For legal titles of parishes and diocesan institutions, consult the Chancery Office.

Diocesan Pastoral Center: 1800 N. Spring St., P.O. Box 5644, Amarillo, TX, 79117-5644. Tel.: 806-383-2243; Fax: 806-383-8452.

STATISTICAL OVERVIEW

Personnel	
Bishop	1
Retired Bishops	1
Priests: Diocesan Active in Diocese	37
Priests: Active Outside Diocese	4
Priests: Retired, Sick or Absent	23
Number of Diocesan Priests	64
Religious Priests in Diocese	6
Extern Priests in Diocese	1
Ordinations:	
Diocesan Priests	1
Permanent Deacons in Diocese	45
Total Sisters	132
Parishes	
Parishes	35
With Resident Pastor:	
Resident Diocesan Priests	26
Resident Religious Priests	4
Without Resident Pastor:	
Administered by Priests	3
Administered by Deacons	2
Missions	13
Professional Ministry Personnel:	
Sisters	4
Lay Ministers	8
Welfare	
Catholic Hospitals	1
Total Assisted	22,300
Health Care Centers	1
Total Assisted	750
Homes for the Aged	1
Total Assisted	56
Day Care and Extended Day Care Centers	3
Total Assisted	170
Specialized Homes	2
Total Assisted	550
Special Centers for Social Services	4
Total Assisted	35,000
Other Institutions	1
Total Assisted	4
Educational	
Diocesan Students in Other Seminaries	6
Total Seminarians	6
High Schools, Diocesan and Parish	1
Total Students	118
Elementary Schools, Diocesan and Parish	7
Total Students	1,085
Catechesis/Religious Education:	
High School Students	1,718
Elementary Students	4,380
Total Students Under Catholic Instruction	7,307
Teachers in the Diocese:	
Sisters	8
Lay Teachers	87
Vital Statistics	
Receptions into the Church:	
Infant Baptism Totals	1,230
Adult Baptism Totals	111
Received into Full Communion	146
First Communions	1,363
Confirmations	1,617
Marriages:	
Catholic	216
Interfaith	59
Total Marriages	275
Deaths	264
Total Catholic Population	54,208
Total Population	401,261

Former Bishops—Most Rev. RUDOLPH ALOYSIUS GERKEN, D.D., ord. June 10, 1917; cons. April 26, 1927; installed Bishop of Amarillo, April 28, 1927; elevated to the Metropolitan See of Santa Fe, NM, June 2, 1933; died March 2, 1943.—Most Rev. ROBERT E. LUCEY, ord. May 14, 1916; cons. May 1, 1934; installed May 16, 1934; elevated to the Metropolitan See of San Antonio, Jan. 22, 1941.—Most Rev. LAURENCE J. FITZSIMON, D.D., ord. May 17, 1921; cons. Oct. 22, 1941; installed Nov. 5, 1941; died July 2, 1958.—Most Rev. JOHN L. MORKOVSKY, appt. Auxiliary of Amarillo, Dec. 22, 1955; named Bishop of Amarillo, Aug. 18, 1958; transferred as Coadjutor Bishop of Galveston-Houston *"cum jure successionis"*, April 16, 1963.—Most Rev. LAWRENCE M. DEFALCO, D.D., ord. June 11, 1942; appt. April 16, 1963; cons. May 30, 1963; installed June 13, 1963; retired Aug. 28, 1979; died Sept. 22, 1979.—Most Rev. LEROY T. MATTHIESEN, D.D., M.A., LITT.D, ord. March 10, 1946; appt. March 25, 1980; ord. Bishop, May 30, 1980; retired Jan. 21, 1997.

Diocesan Officials

Diocesan Pastoral Center—1800 N. Spring St., Amarillo, 79107. Tel: 806-383-2243; Fax: 806-383-8452., *P.O. Box 5644, Amarillo, 79117-5644.*

Vicar General—Very Rev. Msgr. JOSEPH E. BIXENMAN.

Vicar of Clergy—Rev. Msgr. HAROLD L. WALDOW.

Vicar of Catholic Schools—Rev. Msgr. RAYMOND CROSIER.

Vicars Forane—Rev. Msgr. ORVILLE BLUM, South Deanery; Rev. Msgr. HAROLD WALDOW, Central Deanery; Rev. JOHN VALDEZ, East Deanery; Rev. JIM MCGHEE, North Deanery.

Diocesan Tribunal—

Judicial Vicar—Very Rev. PHU T. PHAN, J.C.L.

Defender of the Bond—Rev. Msgr. JAMES GURZYNSKI, J.C.L.

Advocates—Rev. Msgr. JOSEPH TASH; Rev. Msgr. HAROLD WALDOW.

Notaries—Ms. CAROL SANFORD; Ms. SUSAN GARNER.

Chancellor—Rev. MICHAEL COLWELL, J.C.L.

Diocesan Advisory Councils

Presbyteral Council—Revs. SCOTT RAEF; DENNIS BOYLAN; JOHN SALAZAR-JIMENEZ; JOSE GOMEZ, Bishop's Appointee; POLYCARP DUCTHUAN, C.M.C., Bishop's Appointee; ROBERT BUSCH, Ph.D.; Rev. Msgr. ORVILLE R. BLUM; Very Rev. PHU T. PHAN, J.C.L.; Rev. Msgr. HAROLD WALDOW, Bishop's Appointee. Ex Officio: Revs. MICHAEL COLWELL; JOHN VALDEZ; Rev. Msgr. HAROLD WALDOW; Very Rev. Msgr. JOSEPH E. BIXENMAN.

College of Consultors—Revs. NEAL DEE; POLYCARP DUCTHUAN, C.M.C.; JOHN SALAZAR-JIMENEZ; MICHAEL COLWELL, J.C.L.; PHU PHAN, J.C.L.; Rev. Msgr. HAROLD WALDOW; Rev. Msgr. ARTURO MEZA; Very Rev. Msgr. JOSEPH E. BIXENMAN.

Diocesan Pastoral Council—Rev. Msgr. HAROLD WALDOW, Liaison to Diocesan Pastoral Council.

Vocation Development Team—Revs. MICHAEL COLWELL, Dir. PHU PHAN; JOHN VALDEZ; SCOTT RAEF; ROBERT BUSCH; JUAN CARLOS BARRAGAN.

Deacon Director—Deacon BLAINE WESTLAKE.

Diocesan Departments

Vicar of Youth—Rev. SCOTT RAEF, Dir. PETE GALAN, Coord.; Deacon JESSIE GUERRERO, Conferences.

Office for the Catholic Schools—Dr. WILLIAM REENTS, Supt.

Christian Formation Commission—BERNICE NOGGLER, Dir.

Department of Communications—CATHY LEXA, Dir. Information & Editor "The West Texas Catholic".

Department of Finances and Ecclesiastical Properties—Fiscal Manager—JOSEPH INGRAHAM.

Director of Administrative Services—PATSY GRAHAM.

Office of Development and Stewardship—NANCY KOONS, Dir., *P.O. Box 1011, Canyon, 79015.* Tel: 806-655-2556.

United Catholic Appeal—NANCY KOONS.

General Auxiliary Pastoral Services

Diocesan Attorney—FREDERICK J. GRIFFIN, *504 S. Polk, Amarillo, 79101.*

Vicar for Canonical Affairs—(see Tribunal).

Coalition for Catholic Social Services - CCSS—Rev. KEN KELLER, Chm.

Catholic Historical Society—EDITH DANILE, Pres. MARGARET FERENCE, Museum Cur.

Diocesan Liturgical Commission—Rev. Msgr. ARTURO MEZA, Coord.; Very Rev. PHU T. PHAN, J.C.L.; Revs. JOHN VALDEZ; PATRICK CARATHERS.

Rural Life Director—Rev. DARRYL BIRKENFELD.

Holy Childhood Association—Rev. Msgr. RICHARD F. VAUGHAN.

Propagation of the Faith—Rev. Msgr. ORVILLE BLUM.

Office of Worship—Rev. ARTURO MEZA, Coord.

Rite of Christian Initiation of Adults Commission—Coordinators: Rev. Msgr. HAROLD WALDOW; BERNICE NOGGLER.

Auxiliary Pastoral Services for the Laity

Institute for Pastoral Ministry—Rev. ROBERT BUSCH, Ph.D., Dir., *2610 4th Ave., Canyon, 79015.* Tel: 806-655-4345.

Diocesan Council of Catholic Women—Rev. Msgr. FRANCIS A. SMYER, Moderator, *1200 S. Washington, Amarillo, 79102.*

Engaged Encounter—Directors:: BLAIN WESTLAKE; LOUISE WESTLAKE. Contact Couple: JENNY BALLARD; AGNES BALLARD. Tel: 806-353-0907.

Beginning Experience—BECKY SONDERSON. Tel: 806-364-5813.

Catholic Student Center at West Texas A & M University—Rev. ROBERT BUSCH, Dir.-Chap., *2614 Fourth Ave., Canyon, 79015.* Tel: 806-655-4345.

Scouting—Deacon ROBERT SMITH.

Serra Club—DANIEL MARTINEZ, Pres.

Natural Family Planning—Certified Teaching Couples: GERALD MARNELL; DENISE MARNELL, *Rte. 5, Box 117-A, Hereford, 79045.* JOHN BRADICICH; CALEY BRADICICH.

Cursillo Movement—Rev. Msgr. HAROLD WALDOW; FELIPE PORTILLO, Lay Director.

Family Life Commission—RITA DILLER; ANNETTE VILLA.

Vicar for Religious—Co-Vicars: Rev. NICOLAS PEREZ, O.F.M.; Sr. THERESA ROZGA, S.C.S.J.A.

Office for the Permanent Diaconate—Deacon BLAINE WESTLAKE, Coord.

Continuing Education of Clergy—Rev. Msgr. HAROLD L. WALDOW.

Priests' Retirement—PATSY GRAHAM.

CLERGY, PARISHES, MISSIONS AND PAROCHIAL SCHOOLS

CITY OF AMARILLO
(Potter County)

1—SACRED HEART CATHEDRAL. Closed. This parish ceased to exist 1/19/75. For inquiries contact the Diocese of Amarillo: P.O. Box 5644, Amarillo, TX 79117-5644. Tel: 806-383-2243.

2—ST. LAURENCE CATHEDRAL, Revs. Rosendo Herrera; Patrick Hoffman; Rev. Msgr. Arturo Meza, Mod. Pastoral Team; Deacons Leo Ramos; Pete Valdez.
Res., 2300 N. Spring St., 79107. Tel: 806-383-2261; Fax: 806-383-2266.
Child Development Center—.
Lay Teachers 3; Students 36.
Catechesis/Religious Programs—Students 263.

3—BLESSED SACRAMENT, Rev. Msgr. Harold L. Waldow; Deacon Mark Seidlitz.
Res., 4112 S.E. 25th St., 79103. Tel: 806-374-1132; Fax: 806-372-3631.
Catechesis/Religious Programs—Ignacio Rosas, D.R.E.
Students 142.

4—OUR LADY OF GUADALUPE, Rev. Msgr. Rex Nichol; Deacon Hector Gallegos. In res., Rev. Rosendo Herrera.
Res., 1210 E. 11th Ave., 79102. Tel: 806-372-1128; Fax: 806-372-2225.
School—See Elementary Schools, City-Wide under Institutions Located in the Diocese.
Catechesis/Religious Programs—Martha Loza, D.R.E.
Students 614.

5—OUR LADY OF VIETNAM, Rev. Polycarp Ducthuan, C.M.C., Pastor.
Res., 2001 N. Grand, 79107. Tel: 806-383-0467.
Catechesis/Religious Programs—Students 100.

6—ST. FRANCIS, Rev. Theodore E. Podson, Sch.P.
Res., 5005 Klinke Rd., 79108-9628. Tel: 806-335-1872.
Catechesis/Religious Programs—Evelyn Detten, D.R.E.
Students 51.

7—ST. HYACINTH'S, Revs. Patrick Carathers; Bert Horvath; Deacon Belvin Dollins; Sr. Hilary Decker, O.S.B., Pastoral Assoc.
Res., 4500 W. Hills Tr., 79106. Tel: 806-358-1351; Fax: 806-467-1708.
Catechesis/Religious Programs—Students 75.

8—ST. JOSEPH'S, Rev. Msgr. Raymond Crosier; Deacons Richard Riley; Bill Jordon; Robert Smith.
Res., 4122 Bonham St., 79110. Tel: 806-355-5621; Fax: 806-355-5622.
School—See Elementary Schools, City-Wide under Institutions Located in the Diocese.
St. Joseph Day Care Center—4108 Bonham, 79110. Tel: 806-359-1604.
Students 124.
Catechesis/Religious Programs—Mrs. Rosie Sisneros, D.R.E.
Students 205.

9—ST. MARTIN DE PORRES MISSION, Rev. John Hickey.
Res., P.O. Box 5053, 79117. Tel: 806-376-8871.

10—ST. MARY'S, Very Rev. Msgr. Joseph E. Bixenman; Rev. Msgr. Francis Smyer, Pastor Emeritus; Rev. Ken Keller.
Res., 1200 Washington St., 79102. Tel: 806-376-7204; Fax: 806-376-4314.
School—See Elementary Schools, City-Wide under Institutions Located in the Diocese.
Catechesis/Religious Programs—Sara Walsh, D.R.E.
Students 255.

11—ST. THOMAS THE APOSTLE, Rev. Msgr. Joseph T. Tash; Deacons Terry Pevehouse; Timothy Reid; Blain Westlake. In res., Rev. Robert Busch.
Res., 4100 Coulter Dr., 79109. Tel: 806-358-2461; Fax: 806-358-2529.
Catechesis/Religious Programs—Eileen Dolan, D.R.E.
Students 550.

OUTSIDE THE CITY OF AMARILLO

Borger, Hutchinson Co., St. John the Evangelist, Rev. Msgr. Norbert Kuehler; Rev. Juan Carlos Barragan; Deacon Zeferino Jimenez.
Res., 201 St. John's Rd., 79007. Tel: 806-274-7064; Fax: 806-274-7065.
School—Bret Parker, Prin. Sisters 3; Lay Teachers 3; Students 31.
Catechesis/Religious Programs—Loriann Chavez, D.R.E.
Students 225.
Convent—Tel: 806-274-6504.
Mission—Stinnett, St. Ann's.

Bovina, Parmer Co., St. Ann's, Rev. Juan Carlos Barragan.
Res., Box 657, 79009. Tel: 806-238-1511.
Catechesis/Religious Programs—Nancy Schwertner, D.R.E.
Students 80.

Canadian, Hemphill Co., Sacred Heart, Rev. Guillermo Morales; Deacon Jose Jesus Gutierrez.
Res., 721 Main, P.O. Box 786, 79014. Tel: 806-323-9705.
Catechesis/Religious Programs—Students 150.
Mission—Wheeler, Collingsworth Co., St. Mary.

Canyon, Randall Co., St. Ann's, Rev. Phu T. Phan; Deacons August Hesse, III; Mauro Hernandes; Gabriel Rivas; Bill Dorsey.
Mailing Address: P.O. Box 59, 79015.
Res., 605 38th St., 79015. Tel: 806-655-3302; Fax: 806-655-3384.
Catechesis/Religious Programs—Carol Sanford, D.R.E.
Students 392.

Childress, Childress Co., Holy Angels, Rev. Dennis Boylan.
Res., 308 Ave. B, S.W., P.O. Box 608, 79201. Tel: 940-937-3946; Fax: 940-937-3946.
Catechesis/Religious Programs—Students 60.

Clarendon, Donley Co., St. Mary's, Deacon John Nino.
Res., 815 McClelland St., P.O. Drawer C, 79226. Tel: 806-874-3910.

Dalhart, Dallam Co., St. Anthony's, Rev. James E. McGhee; Deacon Ronald Hein.
Res., 411 Texas Blvd., Box 1029, 79022. Tel: 806-244-4128; Fax: 806-244-7128.
School—1302 Oak St., 79022. Tel: 806-244-4811; Fax: 806-244-4811. Sr. Peter Marie Rieigliano, Prin.
School Sisters of the Third Order of St. Francis 3; Lay Teachers 4; Students 67.
Mission—Texline, Dallum Co., St. Mary's.

Dimmitt, Castro Co., Immaculate Conception, Rev. Fern Couture, s.P.; Deacons Joseph Ortega; John Nino; Jose Luis Velo.
Res., 710 W. Halsell St., 79027. Tel: 806-647-4219 (Church); 647-0105 (Office).
Catechesis/Religious Programs—Students 220.
Mission—Hart, Castro Co., St. John's.

Dumas, Moore Co., SS. Peter and Paul, Rev. Richard D. Scully; Deacons Joseph Schwertner; Vacilio Anaya.
Res., Box 503, 79029. Tel: 806-935-5002; Fax: 806-934-3382.
Catechesis/Religious Programs—Eva Gresham, D.R.E.
Students 290.
Missions—Sunray, Moore Co., Christ the King, Box 503, Dumas, 79029. Deacon Wayne Norrell.; Cactus, Our Lady of Guadalupe, Box 28, Stratford, 79084. Tel: 806-396-5687.

Friona, Parmer Co., St. Teresa of Jesus, Rev. Edward Sweeney.
Res., HCR 2, Box B, 79035-0381. Tel: 806-247-2871; Fax: 806-247-2871.
Catechesis/Religious Programs—D.R.E.: Diana Santella; Lisa Alaniz.
Students 250.

Groom, Carson Co., Immaculate Heart of Mary, Rev. Neal Dee.
Res., 411 Ware Ave., P.O. Box 130, 79039. Tel: 806-248-7584. [CEM]
Catechesis/Religious Programs—Students 70.

Gruver, Cristo Redentor, Rev. Scott Raef; Deacon Jesus Favela.
Res., 603 Main St., P.O. Box 238, 79040. Tel: 806-733-5236.
Catechesis/Religious Programs—Elena Salazar, D.R.E.
Students 51.

Happy, Swisher Co., Holy Name of Jesus, Rev. Peter Otto; Deacon Amadeo Perez.
Res., 317 W. Main, P.O. Box 128, 79042. Tel: 806-558-2871. [CEM]
Catechesis/Religious Programs—Students 40.

Hereford, Deaf Smith Co., St. Anthony's, Rev. Msgr. Orville Blum; Deacon Jonny Cloud; Charlotte Paetzold, Pastoral Asst.
Res., 115 N. 25 Mile Ave., 79045. Tel: 806-364-6150; 364-6152; Fax: 806-364-0969.
School—120 W. Park Ave., 79045. Tel: 806-364-1952. Nancy Neusch, Prin.
Franciscan Sisters of Mary Immaculate 2; Lay Teachers 2; Students 109.
Catechesis/Religious Programs—Students 297.
Convent—114 Sunset, 79045. Tel: 806-364-3344.

San Jose, Revs. Nicholas Perez, O.F.M.; Aldalberto Ramirez, O.F.M.; Leobardo Heredia Olivo, O.F.M.; Deacons Emilio Fuentes; Vicente Garcia; Jessie Guerrero.
Res., 735 Brevard, 79045. Tel: 806-364-5053; Fax: 806-364-2880.
Preschool—.
Catechesis/Religious Programs—Tel: 806-364-5053.
Students 399.

Memphis, Hall Co., Sacred Heart, Deacon John Nino.
Mailing Address: 213 N. Third St., P.O. Box 239, 79245. Tel: 806-259-2178.
Catechesis/Religious Programs—Mrs. Juanita Garza, D.R.E.
Students 32.

Nazareth, Castro Co., Holy Family, Rev. Peter Otto; Deacons Jerome Brockman; Alfonse Mauer.
Res., 210 St. Joseph, P.O. Box 100, 79063. Tel: 806-945-2616; Fax: 806-945-2564.
Catechesis/Religious Programs—Gladys Fortenberry, D.R.E.
Students 161.

Pampa, Gray Co., St. Vincent de Paul, Revs. John Valdez; Francisco Perez.
Res., 810 W. 23rd St., 79065. Tel: 806-665-8933; Fax: 806-665-2840.
School—2300 N. Hobart, 79065. Tel: 806-665-5665.
Students 100.
Catechesis/Religious Programs—Students 155.

Panhandle, Carson Co., St. Theresa, Rev. Jim Hutzler.
Res., P.O. Box 366, 79068. Tel: 806-537-3677.
Catechesis/Religious Programs—Karen Berry, D.R.E.
Students 80.

Perryton, Ochiltree Co., Immaculate Conception, Rev. Jose Gomez.
Res., 1000 S.W. 15th Ave., 79070. Tel: 806-435-3802.
Catechesis/Religious Programs—Daryla Allred, D.R.E.
Students 225.
Mission—Booker, St. Peter.

Spearman, Hansford Co., Sacred Heart, Rev. Scott Raef.
Res., 901 S. Roland, P.O. Box 127, 79081. Tel: 806-659-2166; Fax: 806-659-1042.
Catechesis/Religious Programs—Ms. Shawn Thompson, D.R.E.
Students 155.
Mission—Gruver, Hansford Co., Cristo Redentor, P.O. Box 238, Gruver, 79040.

Stratford, Sherman Co., St. Joseph's, Rev. Darryl Birkenfeld; Deacon Willie Artho.
Mailing Address: Box 28, 79084. Tel: 806-366-5687.
Catechesis/Religious Programs—Johnny Garza, D.R.E.
Students 70.

Tulia, Swisher Co., Church of the Holy Spirit, Rev. John Salazar-Jimenez. Pastoral Assocs.: Mary Lou Moreno; Ventura Ramos.
Res., 513 S. Austin, P.O. Box 25, 79088. Tel: 806-995-3191; Fax: 806-995-3286.
Catechesis/Religious Programs—D.R.E.: Sara Basaldua; Delia Gonzales.
Students 221.
Missions—Silverton, Briscoe Co., Our Lady of Loreto, P.O. Box 47, Silverton, 79257. Rev. Ed Graff, Parochial Admin.; Kress, Swisher Co., St. Paul the Apostle, P.O. Box 231, Kress, 79052. Tel: 806-823-2548. Ampara Becerra, Pastoral Assoc.
Station—Quitaque. Lupe Reyes, Pastoral Asst.

Umbarger, Randall Co., St. Mary's, Rev. Robert A. Busch, Ph.D.
Res., P.O. Box 105, 79091. Tel: 806-499-3531. [CEM]
Catechesis/Religious Programs—Students 75.

Vega, Oldham Co., Immaculate Conception, Revs. Patrick Carathers; Bert Horvath.
Res., P.O. Box 250, 79092. Tel: 806-267-2343.
Catechesis/Religious Programs—Patty Frerich, D.R.E.
Students 70.

Wellington, Collingsworth Co., Our Mother of Mercy, Rev. Cal Stalter.
Church—1108 Floydada, P.O. Box 686, 79095. Tel: 806-256-5358; Fax: 806-256-2829.
Mission—Shamrock, St. Patrick. Rev. Cal Stalter, Admin.

White Deer, Carson Co., Sacred Heart, Rev. Msgr. Kevin Hand, (Retired).
Res., Box 427, 79097. Tel: 806-883-4781.
Catechesis/Religious Programs—Ben Rapstine, D.R.E.
Students 67.

Absent on Leave:
Reverend Fathers—
Alvarez, Xavier
Castillo, Domingo
Contreras, David
Guidry, Dale
Jaramillo, Peter
Lindley, Philip
Rosolen, Emil
Wood, Michael

On Duty Outside the Diocese:
Reverend Fathers—
Afunugo, Emmanuel, D.D.
Greka, David
Madrigal, Hector

Retired:
Rev.—
Stortz, Mario, Rte. 1, Box 174, Tulia, TX 79088
Reverend Monsignors—
Brahears, Bill, 1505 Rusk, Amarillo, TX 79102
Corcoran, Clifton J., P.O. Box 1179, Panhandle, TX 79068
Erpen, B. A., 318 S.E. Fifth, Tulia, TX 79088
Gurzynski, James C., 2229 Loucust, Amarillo, TX 79109
Hand, Kevin
Malner, Matthew
Sonderman, James W., P.O. Box 1179, Panhandle, TX 79068
Vaughan, Richard, P.O. Box 1179, Panhandle, TX 79068
Reverend Fathers—
Chen, Raphael, 9170 Graham, Cypress, CA 90630
Choong, Norbert, 6303 Butte Ave., New Port Richey, FL 34653
Kieferle, Norbert
Kieran, Edward, Ireland
Pawlak, Ed, 5431 Denise Ave., Orlando, FL 32810-3609
Sherry, Brendan, Ireland
Stein, Jerry, P.O. Box 159, Nazareth, TX 79063

Permanent Deacons:
Ambs, James R., Prison Ministry
Anaya, Vacilio, Sts. Peter and Paul Church, Dumas
Artho, Kenneth, Inactive
Artho, Willie F., St. Joseph's Church, Stratford
Blunt, Orvel Ray, On Leave
Brockman, Jerome, Holy Family Church, Nazareth
Campos, Tony, (On Leave of Absence)
Castillo, Esteban, (On Leave of Absence)
Cloud, Jonny E., St. Anthony Church, Hereford
Dollins, Belvin G., St. Hyacinth's
Dorsey, Bill, St. Ann's, Canyon
Frausto, Joseph, Inactive
Fuentes, Emilio, Sr., San Jose Church, Hereford
Gallegos, Hector, Our Lady of Guadalupe Church, Amarillo
Garcia, Vicente H., San Jose Church, Hereford
Gonzales, Roberto, On Leave
Grossman, Jerry, On Leave
Guerrero, Jesse, San Jose Church, Hereford
Gutierrez, Jose Jesus, Sacred Heart Church, Canadian
Gutierrez, Robert, Sick Leave
Hein, Ronald, St. Anthony's Church, Dalhart
Hernandez, Mauro, St. Ann's Church, Canyon
Hesse, August, III, St. Ann's Church, Canyon
Jimenez, Zeferino, St. John's Church, Borger
Jordan, Bill, St. Joseph's Church, Amarillo
Keller, Robert C., Diocese of Galveston-Houston
Maurer, Alfons A., Holy Family Nazareth
Nino, John, Sacred Heart, Memphis
Norrell, Wayne, Christ the King Church, Sunray
Ortega, Joseph, (Retired)
Perez, Amadeo, Holy Name Church, Happy
Pevehouse, Terry, St. Thomas the Apostle Church, Amarillo
Ramos, Leo, St. Laurence Cathedral, Amarillo
Reid, Timothy, St. Thomas Church, Amarillo
Riley, Richard D., St. Joseph's Church, Amarillo
Rivas, Gabriel, St. Ann's Church, Canyon
Ruiz, Jesse P., Diocese of Fort Worth
Schwertner, Joseph A., SS. Peter & Paul Church, Dumas
Seidlitz, Mark, Blessed Sacrament Church, Amarillo
Smith, Robert, St. Joseph's Church, Amarillo
Thiele, William E., Sick Leave
Valdez, Pete, St. Laurence Cathedral, Amarillo
Velo, Joe, Immaculate Conception Church, Dimmitt
Westlake, Blain, St. Thomas Church, Amarillo

INSTITUTIONS LOCATED IN THE DIOCESE

[A] HIGH SCHOOLS, CITY-WIDE

AMARILLO. *Holy Cross Catholic Academy.* (Coed), 4114 S. Bonham, 79110-1113. Tel: 806-355-9637; Fax: 806-353-9520.
E-mail: holyc@arn.net
Rev. John Dalton, Chap.; Sr. Ann Gorman, R.S.M., Prin., 4110 S. Bonham, 79110-1113.
High School. Lay Teachers 13; Students 42.
Middle School. Lay Teachers 15; Students 120.

[B] ELEMENTARY SCHOOLS, CITY-WIDE

AMARILLO. *Our Lady of Guadalupe School,* 1103 S. Houston, 79102. Tel: 806-372-2629. Dr. Bill Reents, Prin. Lay Teachers 4; Students 51. 1108 S. Houston, 79102.
St. Joseph's School, 4118 Bonham St., 79110. Tel: 806-359-1604; Fax: 806-355-5622.
E-mail: mfkeller@arn.net
Mrs. Betty Keller, Prin. Priests 1; Sisters 2; Lay Teachers 6; Students 125.
St. Laurence Cathedral School. (Temporarily Suspended), 2300-B N. Spring St., 79107. Tel: 806-383-7155; Fax: 806-383-2266. Thomas Salzar, Prin. Lay Teachers 3; Students 32.
St. Mary School and St. Mary's Montessori Preschool, 1200 S. Washington, 79102. Tel: 806-376-9112; Fax: 806-376-9112.
E-mail: caltman@stmarys-ama.com
Chris Altman, Prin. Sisters 1; Lay Teachers 28; Students 297.

[C] CATHOLIC CHILDREN'S DEVELOPMENT CENTERS

AMARILLO. *Amarillo Catholic Children's Development Centers.*
St. Joseph Campus, 4108 Bonham St., P.O. Box 19726, 79114. Tel: 806-383-4411. Theresa Pigott, Dir. Teachers 5; Caregivers 11; Students 120.
St. Laurence Campus, 2300-B N. Spring St., 79107. Tel: 806-383-4411. Lisa Martinez, Dir. Lay Teachers 5; Students 100.
San Jose Preschool, 725 Brevard, Hereford, 79045. Tel: 806-364-5053; Fax: 806-364-2880. Alice Medina, Dir. & Teacher.

[D] HOMES FOR THE AGED

PANHANDLE. *St. Ann's Nursing Home,* P.O. Box 1179, 79068. Tel: 806-537-3194; Fax: 806-537-3003
For a complete listing, refer to the Special Care Facilities section.
St. Joseph's Home for Retired Priests, P.O. Box 1179, 79068
For a complete listing, refer to the Special Care Facilities section.

[E] COALITION OF CATHOLIC SOCIAL SERVICES

AMARILLO.
Catholic Family Service, Inc., 200 S. Tyler, 79101. Tel: 806-376-4571; Fax: 806-345-7911.
E-mail: cfs@arn.net
Web site: www.webtex.com/cfs
Mailing Address: Box 15127, 79105-5127. Al Bednorz, Dir.
Morning Star Hostel and Mark Schupp Center, 2501 W. Sixth, 79102. Tel: 806-371-0373. Rev. Terence Burke, Dir.
Downtown Women's Center and Abba House, Inc., P.O. Box 1985, 79105. Tel: 806-372-3625. Sr. Mary Virginia Clarke, D.C., Dir.
Another Chance Houses, Inc., 209 S. Jackson, 79101. Tel: 806-372-3344. Dale Botts, Dir.

[F] GENERAL HOSPITALS

AMARILLO. *Baptist St. Anthony's Health System,* 1600 Wallace Blvd., 79106. Tel: 806-212-2000; Fax: 806-212-2277.
E-mail: loark@bsahs.org
For a complete listing, refer to the Hospitals section.

[G] SPECIAL HOSPITALS

AMARILLO. *St. Anthony's Hospice and Life Enrichment Center,* 600 N. Tyler, P.O. Box 950, 79176. Tel: 806-378-6777; Fax: 806-378-5031
For a complete listing, refer to the Hospitals section.

[H] RETREAT HOUSE

AMARILLO. *Bishop DeFalco Retreat Center,* 2100 N. Spring St., 79107. Tel: 806-383-1811; Fax: 806-383-6919.
E-mail: bdrc@ls.net
Web site: www.bdrc.org
Sr. M. Theresa Rozga, S.C.S.J.A., Dir.; Rev. Msgr. Arturo Mesa; Deacon Robert Smith, Business Mgr.
Bishop DeFalco Retreat Center Foundation.

CHANNING. *Prayer Town Emmanuel Retreat House,* P.O. Box 17, 79018-0017. Tel: 806-534-2312; Fax: 806-534-2223. The Disciples of the Lord Jesus Christ. Sr. Joan Rodriguez, Coord.

[I] CONVENTS AND RESIDENCES FOR SISTERS

AMARILLO. *Daughters of Charity of St. Vincent de Paul,* 1104 S. Washington, 79102. Tel: 806-374-7812. Sisters 3.
Madres Clarisas Capuchinas, Capuchin Nuns of St. Clare, 4201 N.E. 18th Ave., 79107.
Convent of the Blessed Sacrament and Our Lady of Guadalupe. Mother Theresa Cortes, O.S.C., Abbess. Professed Nuns 12; Apostulants 3; Novices 1.
St. Francis Convent, Novitiate and U.S. Provincial House, 4301 N.E. 18th, 79107. Tel: 806-383-5769; Fax: 806-383-6545. Franciscan Sisters of Mary Immaculate of the Third Order of St. Francis. Sr. Geraldine Duran, F.M.I., Prov. Supr.; Rev. Bert Horvath, Chap. Sisters 40.
St. Francis Mission Community, O.S.F., LaVerna Convent, 203 S. Avondale, 79106. Tel: 806-352-2981. Sr. Mary Jane Alaniz, O.S.F., Provincial, Lubbock House. Sisters 5.

CANYON. *St. Benedict's Monastery,* 17825 S. Western, 79015. Tel: 806-655-9317; Fax: 806-655-9736. Sr. Mary Hawkins, O.S.B., Supr. Sisters 5.

CHANNING. *Disciples of the Lord Jesus Christ,* P.O. Box 17, 79018-0017. Tel: 806-534-2312; Fax: 806-534-2223.
Web site: www.disciples-of-the-lord-jesus-christ.org
Sr. Bernadette Beamsley, Supr. Gen.

DALHART. *St. Anthony's Convent,* 1301 Oak Ave., 79022. Tel: 806-244-2390. School Sisters of St. Francis. Sisters 3.

HEREFORD. *St. Anthony's Convent,* 114 Sunset Dr., 79045. Tel: 806-364-3344. Franciscan Sisters of Mary Immaculate. Sisters 3.

PANHANDLE. *Sancta Maria Convent (North American Region and Novitiate),* P.O. Box 906, 79068-0906. Tel: 806-537-3182; Fax: 806-537-3479.
E-mail: schsrs@amaonline.com
Web site: www.members.amaonline/schsrspanhandle

School Sisters of the Third Order of St. Francis. Mother Bernadette Black, Regl. Supr. Sisters 24.

[J] CAMPUS MINISTRY

CANYON. *Catholic Student Center at West Texas A & M University*, 2610 Fourth Ave., 79015. Tel: 806-655-4345; Fax: 806-655-0534.
E-mail: cscwtamu@arn.net
Web site: www.wtcsc.org
Rev. Robert Busch, Ph.D., Chap. & Dir.; Amy Reid, Assoc. Dir.

[K] MISCELLANEOUS LISTINGS

AMARILLO. *Amarillo Catholic Education Foundation*, 1800 N. Spring St., 79107. Tel: 806-383-2243; Fax: 806-383-8452.

Amarillo Catholic School System, 1800 N. Spring St., 79109. Tel: 806-383-2243; Fax: 806-383-8452.
E-mail: amacathschof@connectInc.com

Amarillo Scholarship Endowment and Assistance Fund, 1800 N. Spring St., 79107. Tel: 806-383-2243; Fax: 806-383-8452.

The Catholic Foundation of the Texas Panhandle 1985, 1800 N. Spring, 79107. Tel: 806-383-2243; Fax: 806-383-8452.
E-mail: joel02946@dellnet.com
Trustees: Most Rev. John W. Yanta, D.D.; Robert Neslage; Ed Wieck; Frank Walsh; Ed Lewis; Daniel Martinez; Dr. Anh My Do.

Engaged Encounter, 3600 Torre, 79109. Tel: 806-352-2607. Directors: Blain Westlake; Louise Westlake. Contact Couple: Jenny Ballard. Tel: 806-353-0907; Agnes Ballard.

Marriage Encounter, 1800 N. Spring, 79107.
E-mail: pvkrat@msn.com
Rev. Michael Colwell. Ecclesastucal Team: Patrick Kratochvil; Virginia Kratochvil.

Monsignor B.A. Erpen Trust Fund (1985), Diocese of Amarillo, 1800 N. Spring, 79107. Tel: 806-383-2243; Fax: 806-383-8452.
E-mail: joelo2046@dellnet.com
Joe Ingraham, C.F.O. Trustees: Rev. Msgr. B.A. Erpen, Chm.; Most Rev. John W. Yanta; Rev. Msgr. Kevin Hand; Rev. Msgr. Harold L. Waldow.

RELIGIOUS INSTITUTES OF MEN REPRESENTED IN THE DIOCESE

For further details refer to the corresponding bracketed number in the Religious Institutes of Men or Women section.

[]—*Congregation of Mother Coredemptrix*.—C.M.C.

[1040]—*Piarist Fathers*.—SCH.P.

[]—*Provincia de los SS. Francisco and Santiago*. (Mexico).—A.R.

[1230]—*Servants of Paraclete*.—s.P.

RELIGIOUS INSTITUTES OF WOMEN REPRESENTED IN THE DIOCESE

[0230]—*Benedictine Sisters of Pontifical Jurisdiction*. (Little Rock, AR).—O.S.B.

[0460]—*Congregation of the Sisters of Charity of the Incarnate Word*.—C.C.V.I.

[0760]—*Daughters of Charity of St. Vincent De Paul*.—D.C.

[0965]—*Disciples of the Lord Jesus Christ*.—D.L.J.C.

[1500]—*Franciscan Sisters of Mary Immaculate of the Third Order of St. Francis of Assisi*.—F.M.I.

[]—*Franciscan Sisters of Perpetual Adoration*.—F.F.P.A.

[]—*Missionary Catechist Sisters of St. Joseph*. (Mexico).—O.F.M.

[]—*St. Clare Capuchin Sisters*.—C.P.C.

[1695]—*School Sisters of the Third Order of St. Francis, (Panhandle, Texas)*.—O.S.F.

[]—*Sisters for Christian Community*.—S.F.C.C.

[2575]—*Sisters of Mercy of the Americas*.—R.S.M.

[3670]—*Sisters of the Sacred Heart of Jesus of St. Jacut*.—S.S.C.J.

[1705]—*Sisters of the Third Order of St. Francis of Assisi*.—O.S.F.

NECROLOGY

(No Deaths)

Archdiocese of Anchorage

(Archidioecesis Ancoragiensis)

Most Reverend

FRANCIS T. HURLEY, D.D.

Archbishop of Anchorage; ordained June 16, 1951; appointed Titular Bishop of Daimlaig and Auxiliary of Juneau February 4, 1970; consecrated March 19, 1970; appointed Bishop of Juneau July 20, 1971; installed September 8, 1971; appointed Archbishop of Anchorage May 4, 1976; installed July 8, 1976.

Most Reverend

ROGER L. SCHWIETZ, O.M.I., D.D.

Coadjutor Archbishop of Anchorage; ordained December 20, 1967; appointed Bishop of Duluth December 12, 1989; consecrated and installed Bishop of Duluth February 2, 1990; appointed Coadjutor Archbishop of Anchorage January 2000.

ESTABLISHED FEBRUARY 9, 1966.

Comprises the Third Judicial Division of Alaska.

Square Miles 138,985.

For legal titles of parishes and archdiocesan institutions, consult the Chancery Office.

Chancery Office: 225 Cordova St., Anchorage, AK, 99501. Tel.: 907-297-7700; Fax: 907-279-3885.

Web site address: www.archdioceseofanchorage.org

E-mail address: archdiocese@caa-ak.org

STATISTICAL OVERVIEW

Personnel	
Archbishop	2
Priests: Diocesan Active in Diocese	11
Priests: Diocesan in Foreign Missions	1
Priests: Retired, Sick or Absent	6
Number of Diocesan Priests	18
Religious Priests in Diocese	12
Extern Priests in Diocese	10
Permanent Deacons in Diocese	18
Total Brothers	1
Total Sisters	42
Parishes	
Parishes	19
With Resident Pastor:	
Resident Diocesan Priests	10
Without Resident Pastor:	
Administered by Women Religious	3
Administered by Lay People	3
Administered by Pastoral Teams, etc.	1
Completely Vacant	1
Missions	8
Professional Ministry Personnel:	
Sisters	10
Lay Ministers	28
Welfare	
Catholic Hospitals	3
Total Assisted	403,479
Health Care Centers	2
Total Assisted	462
Homes for the Aged	1
Total Assisted	60
Specialized Homes	6
Total Assisted	3,705
Special Centers for Social Services	5
Total Assisted	22,091
Educational	
Diocesan Students in Other Seminaries	6
Total Seminarians	6
High Schools, Private	1
Total Students	115
Elementary Schools, Diocesan and Parish	2
Total Students	348
Elementary Schools, Private	1
Total Students	79
Catechesis/Religious Education:	
High School Students	938
Elementary Students	3,145
Total Students Under Catholic Instruction	4,625
Teachers in the Diocese:	
Sisters	2
Lay Teachers	48
Vital Statistics	
Receptions into the Church:	
Infant Baptism Totals	614
Adult Baptism Totals	71
Received into Full Communion	70
First Communions	614
Confirmations	571
Marriages:	
Catholic	100
Interfaith	76
Total Marriages	176
Deaths	151
Total Catholic Population	32,364
Total Population	370,376

Former Bishop—Most Rev. JOSEPH T. RYAN, D.D., Archbishop of Anchorage; ord. June 3, 1939; cons. March 25, 1966; installed April 14, 1966; transferred as Coadjutor Military Vicar of U.S. Armed Forces Dec. 13, 1975; appt. First Archbishop of the Archdiocese for the Military Services, U.S.A., March 16, 1985; died Oct. 9, 2000.

Vicar General—Rev. STEVEN C. MOORE.

Chancery Office—225 Cordova St., Anchorage, 99501. Tel: 907-297-7700; Fax: 907-279-3885.

Chancellor—Vacant.

Assistant to Archbishop—Rev. TIMOTHY M. CROWLEY.

Secretary to Archbishop—FRANCIS T. HURLEY.

Secretary to Archbishop Roger L. Schwietz—DELORES MALZAHN.

Office of Stewardship/Development—Mr. JAMES CALDAROLA.

Tribunal—225 Cordova St., Box 102239, Anchorage, 99510-2239. Tel: 907-297-7728.

Judicial Vicar—Rev. J. MICHAEL HORNICK, S.T.B., J.C.L.

Defenders of the Bond—Deacon WILLIAM FINNEGAN, J.C.L.; MIRIAM DONOHUE.

Notaries—MIRIAM DONOHUE; EILEEN T. KRAMER.

Diocesan Consultors—Revs. STEVEN C. MOORE, Ex Officio; ALFRED W. GIEBEL; LEO DESSO; RICHARD D. TERO; FRED BUGARIN; DANIEL J. HEBERT.

Representatives for Pastoral Adminstrators—Sr. MARIE ANN BRENT, S.H.F.; Sr. JOYCE ROSS, R.S.M.

Archdiocesan Offices and Directors

Apostleship of the Sea—Port Chaplains: SALLY BOSTWICK, Anchorage; Mrs. SHARON FROST, Cordova; Rev. FRED BUGARIN, Kodiak; Rev. RICHARD STRASS, C.SS.R., Seward.

Archdiocesan Newspaper—"Catholic Anchor"; Mr. JOHN ROSCOE, Editor, *c/o Chancery Office.* Tel: 907-297-7707.

A.R.E.A./RENEW Coordinator—Vacant, *c/o Chancery Office.*

Campaign for Human Development—Ms. ANNETTE JOHNSON; Mrs. ANGELA LISTON, *c/o Chancery Office.*

Catholic Social Services—KARLEEN JACKSON, Exec. Dir. CHERYL SHELDON, Dir. Program Operations; Ms. KELLY FERHMAN, Dir. Human Resources; Mrs. SANDY ADAMS, Dir. Fund Devel., *225 Cordova St., Anchorage, 99501.* Tel: 907-297-7742; Fax: 907-272-7370.

Board Members—DAVID GOTTSTEIN; JAMES PALMER; Mrs. SUSAN ELLIOTT; Mr. CHRIS SWALLING; ANGELA DIRKS; Mr. JOE MORAN; REBECCA PARKER; AL LEVY; BARBARA DONATELLI; TOM HARRIS; Rev. LEO WALSH; PENNY WELLS; JIM CLOUD.

Communications—Bro. CHARLES MCBRIDE, C.S.C., *c/o Chancery Office.*

Hispanic Ministry—Sr. VERONICA RIVAS, M.C.D.P., *c/o Our Lady of Guadalupe Parish, 3900 Wisconsin St., Anchorage, 99517.*

Korean Ministry—Rev. SUNG HAK LAURENTIUS CHO; Sr. HOY SOON CLARA CHOI, S.P.C.; Sr. SUK HEE GEMMA

KIM, S.P.C., *St. Anthony's Parish, 825 S. Klevin St., Anchorage, 99508.* Tel: 907-337-5307.
Ministry Team—Sr. ARLENE BOYD, R.S.M., Catechetical Formation; Mrs. DONNA GUM, Events Coord., *c/o Chancery Office.*
Native Ministry—Sr. M. VICTOR NEGRETE, S.H.F., *c/o Chancery Office.*
Office of Finance—Mr. ROBERT B. FLINT, C.F.O.; Mr. THOMAS RODDA, Treas., *c/o Chancery Office.*
Permanent Diaconate—Rev. TIMOTHY M. CROWLEY, *c/o Chancery Office.*
Propagation of the Faith—JAMES CALDAROLA, Dir., Stewardship and Development, *c/o Chancery Office.*
Retreats—Rev. PAUL MACKE, S.J., Dir., *Holy Spirit Center, 10980 Hillside Dr., Anchorage, 99516.* Tel: 907-346-2343.
Superintendent of Schools—Sr. DIANE BARDOL, G.N.S.H., *St. Mary's School, 2932 Mill Bay Rd., Kodiak, 99615.* Tel: 907-486-3513.
Vocations—Rev. STEVEN MOORE, *c/o Chancery Office.*
Youth—Vacant, *c/o Chancery Office.*

CLERGY, PARISHES, MISSIONS AND PAROCHIAL SCHOOLS

CITY OF ANCHORAGE

1—HOLY FAMILY CATHEDRAL, Revs. Joseph Sergott, O.P.; Alejandro Crosthwaite, O.P.; Bryan Kromholtz, O.P. Pastoral Assocs.: Sr. Victor Negrete, S.H.F.; Sr. Barbara Scanlon, C.S.J.; Deacon Gerald Grewe. In res., Rev. Urban M. Bates, O.P.
Mailing Address: 811 W. 6th Ave., 99501-2093. Tel: 907-276-3455; Fax: 907-258-9785. [JC]
Catechesis/Religious Programs—Mrs. Theresa Lutes, D.R.E.
Students 324.

2—ST. ANTHONY, Revs. Gangarapu Balasawamy; Sung hak Laurentius Cho; Deacon Theodore W. Greene, Pastoral Assoc.
Res., 825 S. Klevin St., 99508-2698. Tel: 907-333-5544; Fax: 907-338-3864.
Catechesis/Religious Programs—Students 235.

3—ST. BENEDICT, Rev. Alfred W. Giebel.
Res., 8110 Jewel Lake Rd., 99502. Tel: 907-243-2195; Fax: 907-243-0088.
Catechesis/Religious Programs—Students 440.

4—ST. ELIZABETH ANN SETON, Rev. Scott Medlock; Sr. Loretta Luecke, C.PP.S., Dir. Parish Life; Deacon Kenneth Donohue.
Res., 2901 E. Huffman Rd., 99516. Tel: 907-345-4466; Fax: 907-345-6361.
Catechesis/Religious Programs—Kathryn Gallagher, D.R.E.
Students 617.

5—HOLY CROSS, Rev. Ernest H. Muellerleile; Sr. Joan Oberle, C.PP.S., Pastoral Assoc.; Deacon William Finnegan.
Res., 8147 Medellin Cir., 99507. Tel: 907-349-3910; Fax: 907-349-3910.
Catechesis/Religious Programs—Mrs. Janine Redding, D.R.E.
Students 258.

6—OUR LADY OF GUADALUPE, Rev. Daniel Hebert. In res., Rev. Timothy Crowley (LAN).
Res., 3900 Wisconsin St., 99517. Tel: 907-248-2000; Fax: 907-245-1600.
Guadalupe Centre—Tel: 907-243-2657.
Catechesis/Religious Programs—Students 176.

7—ST. PAUL MIKI. Closed. For inquiries for parish records contact St. Elizabeth Ann Seton Parish, Anchorage.

8—ST. PATRICK, Very Rev. Steven C. Moore, V.G.; Rev. Paul Rajareegam.
Res., 2111 Muldoon Rd., 99504-3699. Tel: 907-337-1538; Fax: 907-337-5460.
Catechesis/Religious Programs—Martha Rogers, D.R.E.
Students 335.

OUTSIDE THE CITY OF ANCHORAGE

Cordova, St. Joseph, Mrs. Sharon Frost, Pastoral Admin.
Res., 220 Adams Ave., P.O. Box 79, 99574. Tel: 907-424-3637; Fax: 907-424-3637.

Dillingham, Holy Rosary, Rev. James F. Kelley.
Res., P.O. Box 810, 99576. Tel: 907-842-5581; Fax: 907-842-5581.
Missions—Naknek, St. Theresa, P.O. Box 73, Naknek, 99633. Tel: 907-246-6652; Unalaska, St. Christopher, P.O. Box 405, Unalaska, 99685. Tel: 907-581-4022; Fax: 801-382-1197. Ms. Annemiek Brunklaus, Pastoral Admin.

Eagle River, St. Andrew, Rev. Leo Walsh; Sr. Camilla Menting, S.S.S.F., Pastoral Assoc. & D.R.E.; Deacon James Hostman.
Res., 16601 Artillery Rd., 99577. Tel: 907-694-2170; Fax: 907-694-1385.
Catechesis/Religious Programs—Students 555.

Glennallen, Holy Family, Mrs. Tami Jindra, Pastoral Admin.
Res., P.O. Box 126, 99588. Tel: 907-822-3442; Fax: 907-822-3442.

Homer, St. John the Baptist, Mrs. Henrietta Leger, Pastoral Admin.
Res., 238 Jenny Way, 99603. Tel: 907-235-8436; Fax: 907-235-5251.
Missions—Seldovia, St. James the Apostle, Tel: 907-234-7478; Ninilchik, St. Peter, Box 39290, Ninilchik, 99639. Tel: 907-567-3490.
Catechesis/Religious Programs—Ms. Maria Walli, D.R.E.
Students 126.

Kenai, Our Lady of the Angels, Sr. Joyce Ross, R.S.M., Admin.; Sr. Joan Barina, M.M.S., Pastoral Assoc.
Res., 225 S. Spruce Rd., 99611. Tel: 907-283-4555; Fax: 907-283-4555.
Catechesis/Religious Programs—Ms. Valarie Kwietniak, D.R.E.
Students 117.

Kodiak, St. Mary's of Kodiak and the Islands, Rev. Fred Bugarin; Mrs. Delores Ossowski, Parish Admin.
Res., 2934 Mill Bay Rd., 99615. Tel: 907-486-5411.
School—Tel: 907-486-3513. Sr. Diane Bardol, G.N.S.H., Prin. & D.R.E.
Sisters 1; Lay Teachers 13; Students 161.
Catechesis/Religious Programs—Students 62.

Palmer, St. Michael, Rev. Leo Desso.
Res., 432 E. Fireweed Ave., 99645. Tel: 907-745-3229; Fax: 907-746-7040.
Catechesis/Religious Programs—Mrs. Joanne Rousculp, D.R.E.
Students 232.

Seward, Sacred Heart, Rev. Richard Strass, C.Ss.R.
Res., 409 Fifth Ave., P.O. Box 207, 99664. Tel: 907-224-5414; Fax: 907-224-5093.
Catechesis/Religious Programs—Mrs. Diane Elhard, D.R.E.
Students 48.
Mission—Cooper Landing, St. John Neumann Church, P.O. Box 737, Cooper Landing, 99572. Tel: 907-595-1300.

Soldotna, Our Lady of Perpetual Help, Rev. Richard D. Tero.
Res., 222 Redoubt Ave., 99669. Tel: 907-262-4749; Fax: 907-262-5542.
Catechesis/Religious Programs—Marlys Verba, D.R.E.
Students 160.

Talkeetna, St. Bernard. Unassigned.
Res., P.O. Box 510, 99676. Tel: 907-733-2442.
Missions—Trapper Creek, St. Philip Benizi, Trapper Creek, 99683.; Willow, St. Christopher, Willow, 99688.

Valdez, St. Francis Xavier, Sr. Marie Ann Brent, S.H.F., Pastoral Admin.
Res., 341 Pioneer Dr., P.O. Box 908, 99686. Tel: 907-835-4556; Fax: 907-835-4556.
Catechesis/Religious Programs—Carla Oster, D.R.E.
Students 80.

Wasilla, Sacred Heart, Rev. Kasparaj Mallavarapu.
Res., 1201 Bogard Rd., 99654-6523. Tel: 907-376-5087; Fax: 907-373-1156.
Catechesis/Religious Programs—Students 185.
Mission—Big Lake, Our Lady of the Lake, P.O. Box 520769, Big Lake, 99652-0769. Tel: 907-892-6492; Fax: 907-892-6497. Kathy Bishop, Admin.

On Duty Outside Archdiocese:
Reverend Fathers—
Means, David (STL), Magadan, Russia
Shields, Michael, Magadan, Russia

Retired:
Reverend Monsignors—
Lunney, John A., 9100 Centennial Dr., Anchorage, AK 99504
Murphy, Francis A., P.O. Box 1625, Cuba, NM 87013
Reverend Fathers—
Abele, Alan Carl, 340 N. Worthy, Marblehead, OH 43440
Daley, Neil, 100 4th Ave., Shalimar, FL 32579
Houck, Peter, 4611 Kupreanof St., Anchorage, AK 99507
Marx, John, 2200 First Ave. N., Apt. 208, Seattle, WA 98109

Permanent Deacons:
Albert, Merle, Milan, NH
Allor, Raymond W., Albany, OR
Cable, Jay, Wasilla
Corrigan, Walter, Seward
Donohue, Kenneth, St. Elizabeth Ann Seton, Anchorage
Finnegan, William, Anchorage
Foreman, Dennis, Anchorage
Frost, William, Cordova
Gnerich, Otto, Anchorage
Greene, Theodore, St. Anthony Church, Anchorage
Greve, Gerald, Anchorage
Hoffman, Louis, Our Lady of the Lake, Big Lake
Hostman, James, St. Andrew, Eagle River
Larroque, Robert, Portland, OR
Lee, Jim, Eagle River
Maguire, Felix M., Cathedral, Anchorage
Schutt, David E., Wasilla
Vance, Herb, Wasilla

INSTITUTIONS LOCATED IN THE ARCHDIOCESE

[A] GRADE SCHOOLS, PAROCHIAL

ANCHORAGE. *St. Elizabeth Ann Seton School*, 2901 E. Huffman Rd., 99516. Tel: 907-345-3712; Fax: 907-345-2910.
E-mail: admin@akseas.com
Web site: www.akseas.com
Mr. Jerry Balisteri, Prin. Lay Teachers 15; Students 165.

KODIAK. *St. Mary's*, 2932 Mill Bay Rd., 99615. Tel: 907-486-3513.
E-mail: dbardol@kodiak.alaska.edu
Sr. Diane Bardol, G.N.S.H., Prin. Sisters 1; Lay Teachers 13; Students 161.

[B] PRIVATE SCHOOLS

ANCHORAGE. *Holy Rosary Academy.* (Grades K-12), 1010 W. Fireweed Ln., 99503. Tel: 907-276-5822; Fax: 907-258-1055. Sr. Marianna Alpha, Headmaster.
Lumen Christi Jr./Sr. High School, 8110 Jewel Lake Rd., 99502. Tel: 907-245-9231; Fax: 907-245-9232. Mrs. Pat Wagner, Prin.

[C] GENERAL HOSPITALS

ANCHORAGE. *Providence Alaska Medical Center*, 3200 Providence Dr., P.O. Box 196604, 99519. Tel: 907-562-2211; Fax: 907-261-3041
For a complete listing, refer to the Hospitals section.

[D] NURSING HOMES

ANCHORAGE. *Providence Extended Care Center*, 4900 Eagle St., 99503. Tel: 907-562-2281
For a complete listing, refer to the Special Care Facilities section.

[E] HOMES FOR AGED

ANCHORAGE. *Mary Conrad Center*, 9100 Centennial Dr., 99504. Tel: 907-333-8100; Fax: 907-338-6789
For a complete listing, refer to the Special Care Facilities section.

[F] CATHOLIC SOCIAL SERVICES

ANCHORAGE. *Brother Francis Shelter*, 1021 E. Third Ave., 99501. Tel: 907-277-1731. Mr. Jeff Bealles, Dir. Overnight shelter for homeless men and women.
Brother Francis Shelter, 411 Cedar St., P.O. Box 3421, Kodiak, 99615. Tel: 907-486-5610. Monte Hawver, Dir.
Catholic Social Services Center, Administrative Office, 225 Cordova St., Bldg. B, 99501. Tel: 907-297-7742. Mrs. Karleen Jackson, Exec. Dir., Catholic Social Services Center, 3710 E. 20th Ave., 99508. Tel: 907-276-5590. Ms. Robin Bronen, Dir., Immigration & Refugee Svcs.; Ms. Marilyn Moreno, Pregnancy Support & Adoption Dir.; Ms. Stephanie Wheeler, Dir., Beyond Shelter Prog., St. Francis House; Lynn Caswell, Dir., Special Needs Respite Prog.
Clare House, 420 W. 54th Ave., 99518. Tel: 907-563-4545. Ms. Linda McDivitt, Dir. Temporary shelter for homeless women and women with children.
McAuley Manor, 3015 Yale Dr., 99508. Ms. Linda McDivitt, Dir. Residence for homeless teenage girls.

[G] MONASTERIES AND RESIDENCES OF PRIESTS AND BROTHERS

ANCHORAGE. *Holy Spirit Center*, 10980 Hillside Dr., 99516. Tel: 907-346-2343; Fax: 907-346-2140. Revs. Robert H. Fitzgerald, S.J.; J. Michael Hornick; William T. Burke, S.J.
Jesuit House, 1500 Birchwood, 99508. Tel: 907-279-4389. Revs. Paul B. Macke, S.J.; Vincent Beuzer, S.J.; Robert V. Paskey, S.J. Alaska Region of OR Prov.

[H] CONVENTS AND RESIDENCES FOR SISTERS

ANCHORAGE. *Convent of Mercy*, 2627 Redwood St., 99508. Tel: 907-258-7802. Sisters 3.

Convent of the Daughters of Charity, 3424 E. 15th St., 99508. Tel: 907-569-6279. Sisters 4.

Marian House / Guadalupe Arms Apartments, 3005-7 W. 34th Ave., 99517. Priests 2; Sisters 3; Brothers 1.

Sisters of Perpetual Adoration, 2645 E. 72nd Ave., 99507. Tel: 907-344-3330; Fax: 907-522-2945. Mother Maria de las Victorias Amezcua, A.P., Supr. Sisters 6.

Sisters of St. Paul de Chartres, 825 S. Klevin St., 99508. Tel: 907-258-3273. Sisters 2.

KENAI. *Kenai Convent*, 1122 Walnut St., 99611. Tel: 907-283-6466. Sisters 2.

KODIAK. *St. Mary's Convent*, 2932 Mill Bay Rd., 99615. Tel: 907-486-5214. Sisters 4.

[I] RETREAT HOUSES

ANCHORAGE. *Holy Spirit Center*, 10980 Hillside Dr., 99516. Tel: 907-346-2343; Fax: 907-346-2140. Rev. Paul Macke, S.J., Dir.

[J] CAMPS

ANCHORAGE. *St. Theresa's Camp, Inc.*, 225 Cordova St., 99501. Tel: 907-297-7700.

[K] MISCELLANEOUS

ANCHORAGE. *Alaska Catholic Conference*, 225 Cordova, 99501. Tel: 907-297-7738; Fax: 907-279-3885. E-mail: archdiocesegeneraldelivery@caa-ak.org Robert Flint, Contact Person.

Archdiocese of Anchorage Priests Pension Trust, 225 Cordova St., 99501.

Catholic Foundation of Alaska, 225 Cordova St., 99501.

Catholic Retreat House Ministries, Inc., 225 Cordova St., 99501.

Covenant House Alaska, 609 F St., 99501. Tel: 907-272-1255. Ms. Deirdre Phayer, Exec. Dir. Crisis center for homeless and runaway youth.

Providence Alaska Foundation, 3200 Providence Dr., P.O. Box 196604, 99519. Tel: 907-261-3600; Fax: 907-261-3048. Rebecca Parker, Pres.

Providence Horizon House, 4140 Folker Ave., 99508. Tel: 907-261-4140.

St. Vincent de Paul Society, Holy Family Cathedral, 811 W. 6th Ave., 99501. Tel: 907-258-9785.

RELIGIOUS INSTITUTES OF MEN REPRESENTED IN THE ARCHDIOCESE

For further details refer to the corresponding bracketed number in the Religious Institutes of Men or Women section.

[0600]—*Brothers of the Congregation of Holy Cross.*—C.S.C.

[0690]—*Jesuit Fathers and Brothers.* (Oregon Prov.).—S.J.

[0430]—*Order of Preachers-Dominicans.* (Oakland Prov.).—O.P.

[0610]—*Priests of the Congregation of Holy Cross.*—C.S.C.

[1070]—*Redemptorist Fathers.* (Oakland Prov.).—C.Ss.R.

RELIGIOUS INSTITUTES OF WOMEN REPRESENTED IN THE ARCHDIOCESE

[0760]—*Daughters of Charity of St. Vincent DePaul.*—D.C.

[1070-03]—*Dominican Sisters.*—O.P.

[1840]—*Grey Nuns of the Sacred Heart.*—G.N.S.H.

[2575]—*Institute of the Sisters of Mercy of the Americas.* (Albany, NY; Merion, PA; Providence, RI).—R.S.M.

[2330]—*Little Sisters of Jesus.*—L.S.J.

[2490]—*Medical Mission Sisters.*—M.M.S.

[2690]—*Missionary Catechists of Divine Providence.*—M.C.D.P.

[3190]—*Nuns of Perpetual Adoration of the Blessed Sacrament.* (Mexico).—A.P.

[1680]—*School Sisters of St. Francis.*—O.S.F.

[3350]—*Sisters of Providence.*—S.P.

[3830-01]—*Sisters of St. Joseph.* (Boston, MA).—C.S.J.

[3840]—*Sisters of St. Joseph of Carondelet.*—C.S.J.

[3890]—*Sisters of St. Joseph of Peace.* (Bellevue).—C.S.J.P.

[3980]—*Sisters of St. Paul de Chartres, South Korea.*—S.P.C.

[1960]—*Sisters of the Holy Family.*—S.H.F.

[3270]—*Sisters of the Most Precious Blood.* (O'Fallon, MO).—C.PP.S.

[4110]—*Ursuline Nuns.*—O.S.U.

NECROLOGY

† Cowgill, Rev. Msgr. Francis, Anchorage, AK St. Anthony. —Died Oct. 16, 2000.

Diocese of Arlington

(Dioecesis Arlingtonensis)

Most Reverend

PAUL S. LOVERDE, D.D., S.T.L., J.C.L.

Bishop of Arlington; ordained December 18, 1965; appointed Titular Bishop of Ottabia and Auxiliary Bishop of Hartford February 3, 1988; consecrated April 12, 1988; appointed Bishop of Ogdensburg November 11, 1993; installed as Eleventh Bishop of Ogdensburg January 17, 1994; appointed Bishop of Arlington January 25, 1999; installed as Third Bishop of Arlington March 25, 1999.

The Chancery: Ste. 914, 200 N. Glebe Rd., Arlington, VA, 22203. Tel.: 703-841-2500; Fax: 703-524-5028.

ESTABLISHED AUGUST 13, 1974.

Square Miles 6,541.

Comprises the following 21 Counties in Northern Virginia: Arlington, Clarke, Culpeper, Fairfax, Fauquier, Frederick, King George, Lancaster, Loudoun, Madison, Northumberland, Orange, Page, Prince William, Rappahannock, Richmond, Shenandoah, Spotsylvania, Stafford, Warren and Westmoreland and the 7 independent cities of Alexandria, Fairfax City, Falls Church, Fredericksburg, Manassas, Manassas Park and Winchester.

For legal titles of parishes and diocesan institutions, consult the Chancery Office.

STATISTICAL OVERVIEW

Personnel	
Bishop	1
Abbots	1
Retired Abbots	3
Priests: Diocesan Active in Diocese	130
Priests: Active Outside Diocese	6
Priests: Diocesan in Foreign Missions	2
Priests: Retired, Sick or Absent	16
Number of Diocesan Priests	154
Religious Priests in Diocese	80
Extern Priests in Diocese	19
Ordinations:	
Diocesan Priests	4
Transitional Deacons	7
Permanent Deacons in Diocese	41
Total Brothers	17
Total Sisters	171
Parishes	
Parishes	66
With Resident Pastor:	
Resident Diocesan Priests	55
Resident Religious Priests	11
Missions	5
New Parishes Created	1
Professional Ministry Personnel:	
Sisters	43
Lay Ministers	190
Welfare	
Special Centers for Social Services	8
Total Assisted	38,624
Educational	
Diocesan Students in Other Seminaries	34
Total Seminarians	34
Colleges and Universities	4
Total Students	4,935
High Schools, Diocesan and Parish	3
Total Students	3,474
High Schools, Private	2
Total Students	576
Elementary Schools, Diocesan and Parish	34
Total Students	13,585
Elementary Schools, Private	1
Total Students	191
Non-residential Schools for the Disabled	1
Total Students	100
Catechesis/Religious Education:	
High School Students	5,122
Elementary Students	30,618
Total Students Under Catholic Instruction	58,635
Teachers in the Diocese:	
Priests	9
Brothers	3
Sisters	16
Lay Teachers	1,065
Vital Statistics	
Receptions into the Church:	
Infant Baptism Totals	7,103
Adult Baptism Totals	848
Received into Full Communion	552
First Communions	7,072
Confirmations	5,392
Marriages:	
Catholic	1,090
Interfaith	859
Total Marriages	1,949
Deaths	1,463
Total Catholic Population	353,367
Total Population	2,317,773

Former Bishops—Most Rev. THOMAS J. WELSH, D.D., J.C.D., appt. Titular Bishop of Scattery Island and Auxiliary Bishop of Philadelphia on Feb. 18, 1970; cons. April 2, 1970; appt. as 1st Bishop of Arlington on June 4, 1974; installed on Aug. 13, 1974; transferred to the See of Allentown, Feb. 8, 1983; resigned Dec. 16, 1997; appt. Diocesan Administrator; retired Feb. 9, 1998.—Most. Rev. JOHN R. KEATING, D.D., J.C.D., ord. Dec. 20, 1958; appt. Second Bishop of Arlington on June 7, 1983; cons. and installed on Aug. 4, 1983; died March 22, 1998.

The Chancery

The Chancery—200 N. Glebe Rd., Ste. 914, Arlington, 22203. Tel: 703-841-2500; Fax: 703-524-5028. Office Hours: Mon.-Fri. 8:30-4:30. Address all official business to this office.

Bishop—Most Rev. PAUL S. LOVERDE, *200 N. Glebe Rd., Ste. 914, Arlington, 22203.* Tel: 703-841-2511.

Vicar General—Rev. Msgr. R. ROY COSBY, V.G., *13752 Mary's Way, Woodbridge, 22191.* Tel: 703-494-2444.

Secretary to the Bishop—Bro. DAVID EDDY, C.F.X., *200 N. Glebe Rd., Ste. 914, Arlington, 22203.* Tel: 703-841-2511; Fax: 703-524-5028.

Moderator of the Curia & Episcopal Vicar for Pastoral Services—Rev. MARK S. MEALEY, O.S.F.S., J.C.D., Ph.D., *200 N. Glebe Rd., Ste. 914, Arlington, 22203.*

Chancellor—Rev. ROBERT J. RIPPY, J.C.L., *The Chancery, 200 N. Glebe Rd., Ste. 914, Arlington, 22203.* Tel: 703-841-2508.

Episcopal Vicar for Parish Development—Rev. Msgr. JAMES W. MCMURTRIE, V.F., *200 N. Glebe Rd., Arlington, 22203.* Tel: 703-841-2500.

Bishop's Delegate for Clergy—Rev. ROBERT E. AVELLA, *200 N. Glebe Rd., Ste. 914, Arlington, 22203.* Tel: 703-841-2508.

Episcopal Vicar for Finance—Rev. DANIEL J. MAHER, *200 N. Glebe Rd., Ste. 914, Arlington, 22203.* Tel: 703-841-2577.

Diocesan Fiscal Manager—SUSAN D. HANDLON, C.P.A., Fiscal Mgr., *200 N. Glebe Rd., Ste. 914, Arlington, 22203.* Tel: 703-841-2577.

Director of Diocesan Charities—Rev. CHARLES C. MCCOART, *200 N. Glebe Rd., Ste. 506, Arlington, 22203.* Tel: 703-841-2544.

Deans—Rev. Msgr. JAMES W. MCMURTRIE, V.F.; Revs. ROBERT J. RIPPY, V.F.; DANIEL E. HAMILTON, V.F.; WILLIAM F. RUEHL, V.F.; FRANK J. READY, V.F.

Vicar for Religious—Vacant.

The Tribunal

The Tribunal—200 N. Glebe Rd., Ste. 524, Arlington, 22203. Tel: 703-841-2555.

Judicial Vicar—Rev. MARK S. MEALEY, O.S.F.S., J.C.D., Ph.D.

Adjutant Judicial Vicar—Rev. LEE R. ROOS, J.C.L.

Diocesan Judges—Revs. ROBERT C. BROOKS; J. STEWART CULKIN, M.A.; JOHN C. CREGAN; PAUL F. DELADURANTAYE, S.T.D.; HORACE H. GRINNELL; PATRICK HOLROYD; JOSE EUGENIO HOYOS; MARK S. MEALY, O.S.F.S., J.C.D., Ph.D.; LEE R. ROOS, J.C.L.; STEPHEN A. ROSZEL, J.C.L.; DAVID A. WHITESTONE, J.C.L.; LEO J. ZONNEVELD, C.I.C.M., Ph.D.

Defenders of the Bond—Revs. ROBERT E. AVELLA; ROBERT C. CILINSKI; Rev. Msgr. R. ROY COSBY, M.A., V.G.; Revs. PAUL M. EVERSOLE; THOMAS P. FERGUSON, J.C.L.; DANIEL E. HAMILTON, V.F.; THOMAS J. LEHNING, S.T.L., Ph.D.; DANIEL L. MODE; RICHARD A. MULLINS; PETER W. NASSETTA; Deacon CHARLES A. COUTU.

Promoter of Justice—Rev. ROBERT J. RIPPY, J.C.L.

Advocates—Revs. ALEXANDER R. DRUMMOND; JOHN H. MELMER; RONALD S. ESCALANTE; RONALD J. GRIPSHOVER, JR.; DANIEL J. MAHER; JOHN P. MOSIMANN; MATTHEW H. ZUBERHUELER.

Notaries—Revs. PAUL A. BERGHOUT; KEVIN J. BERES; JOHN C. DE CELLES; BRIAN G. BASHISTA; FRANCIS M. DEROSA; PAUL M. GRANKAUSKAS; MATTHEW CARR; ANDREW J. FISHER; STEPHEN HOLMES; JOHN M. O'DONOHUE; JAMES C. HUDGINS; MARK F. CARRIER; TERRY A. CRAMER; CHRISTOPHER D. MURPHY; CHRISTOPHER J. POLLARD; MICHAEL J. DOBBINS; PAUL D. SCALIA; JOSEPH R. KENNA; EDWIN T. TEWES; J. EDWIN THAYER TEWES; JERRY A. WOOTON; JOHN ZIEGLER.

Diocesan Offices

Diocesan Offices—Unless otherwise noted, all offices are located at, 200 N. Glebe Rd., Arlington, 22203.

Accounting Office—CLARE M. FARISS, Mgr., *Ste. 602.* Tel: 703-841-2582.

Archives—MAGGIE O'CONNOR, *80 N. Glebe Rd., Arlington, 22203.* Tel: 703-524-2124.

Arlington Catholic Herald, Inc.—MICHAEL F. FLACH, Editor & Gen. Mgr., *Ste. 607.* Tel: 703-841-2590.

Audio-Visual—MAGGIE O'CONNOR, Coord., *Ste. 517.* Tel: 703-841-2530.

Bishop's Lenten Appeal—JUANITA PADGETT, Coord., *Ste. 617.* Tel: 703-841-2570.

Campaign for Human Development—Rev. CHARLES C. MCCOART, Diocesan Dir., *Ste. 506.* Tel: 703-841-2531.

Campus Ministry—Rev. CURTIS L. CLARK, JR., Bishop's Liaison, *Ste. 619.* Tel: 703-841-2514.

Catholic Charities of the Diocese of Arlington—Rev. CHARLES C. MCCOART, Exec. Dir. MICHAEL J. O'ROURKE, Assoc. Dir. Finance & Admin. ELIANA V. TURINA, Assoc. Dir. Community Services, *200 N. Glebe Rd., Ste. 506, Arlington, 22203.* Tel: 703-841-2531. HELEN P. MUDD, M.S.W., A.C.S.W., Assoc. Dir. Social Svcs., *Ste. 506.* Tel: 703-841-2531.

Catholic Charities Fredericksburg Office—DIANN KELLISON, M.S.W., Prog. Dir., *612 Lafayette Blvd., Ste. 50, Fredericksburg, 22401.* Tel: 540-371-1124.

Catholic Charities Winchester Office—ELAINA M. ANDREW, M.S.W., Prog. Dir., *1011 Berryville Ave., Ste. 1, Winchester, 22601.* Tel: 540-667-7940.

Children's Services—Vacant, Prog. Dir., *5294 Lyngate Ct., Burke, 22015.* Tel: 703-425-0100.

Christ House—ROSEMARIE LAROCCA, M.Ed., Prog. Dir., *131 S. West St., Alexandria, 22314.* Tel: 703-549-8644.

Communications—CAROLINE E. ALBRIGO, Coord., *Ste. 506.* Tel: 703-841-2531.

Development—DORIS M. DEMAY, Prog. Dir., *Ste. 506.* Tel: 703-841-2531.

Elderly Services—CAROL AUGUSTINE, M.A., Prog. Dir., *St. Martin de Porres Senior Center, 4650 Taney Ave., Alexandria, 22304.* Tel: 703-751-2766.

Emergency Assistance—ROSE MARIE LAROCCA, M.S., Prog. Dir., *131 S. West St., Alexandria, 22314.* Tel: 703-548-4227.

Family Services—DAVID CAVANAUGH, M.S.W., Prog. Dir., *3838 N. Cathedral Ln., Arlington, 22203.* Tel: 703-841-2531.

Hogar Hispano-Assistance to Immigrants—NANCY SHESTACK, Esq., Prog. Dir., *6201 Leesburg Pike, Ste. 307, Falls Church, 22044.* Tel: 703-534-9805.

Parish Social Ministry—ANNE MURPHY, Prog. Dir., *Ste. 506.* Tel: 703-841-2531.

Prison Ministry—ANNE MURPHY, Prog. Dir., *Ste. 506.* Tel: 703-841-2531.

Services for Disabled Persons—HARRY BURKE, Prog. Dir., *3838 N. Cathedral Ln., Arlington, 22203.* Tel: 703-841-2531.

Catholic Education, Office of Catechetics—Rev. PAUL F. DELADURANTAYE, Sec. for Religious Education and Sacred Liturgy, *Ste. 503.* Tel: 703-841-2554. MAGGIE O'CONNOR, Coord., Audio-Visual Materials, *Ste. 517.* Tel: 703-841-2530. Mrs. PROVIE RYDSTROM, Coord. Pastoral Ministry for the Hearing Impaired. Tel: 703-978-7997 (V-TTD).; Mrs. NADINE HALLUMS, Dir., Special Religious Education (SPRED). Tel: 703-569-2428.

Office of Catholic Schools—TIMOTHY J. MCNIFF, Ed.D., Supt. of Schools., *Ste. 503.* Tel: 703-841-2519. Sr. PATRICIA HELENE EARL, I.H.M., Asst. Supt. for Secondary Education & Professional Educational Personnel. Tel: 703-841-2519. Sr. KARL ANN HOMBERG, S.S.J., Asst. Supt. for Elementary Education. Tel: 703-841-2519.

Catholic Relief Services—Rev. CHARLES C. MCCOART, Dir., *Ste. 506.* Tel: 703-841-2531.

Central Purchasing—JOAN CANAN, Purchasing Agent, *Ste. 618.* Tel: 703-841-2571.

Communications Office—LINDA SHOVLAIN, S.T.L., Dir., *Ste. 914.* Tel: 703-841-2767; Fax: 703-524-5028.

Development Office—ROBERT P. MUELLER, Dir., *Ste. 914.* Tel: 703-841-2545; Fax: 703-524-5028.

Management Information Systems—WILFREDO MALDONADO, Dir., *Ste. 606.* Tel: 703-841-2585.

Construction Management, Office of—*Ste. 625.* Tel: 703-841-2572. Construction Supervisors: PETER B. FISHER; PAUL E. MAY; MOON C. KIM.

Ecumenical Affairs—Rev. Msgr. R. ROY COSBY, Coord., *Our Lady of Angels, Woodbridge, 22191.* Tel: 703-494-2444.

Employee Benefits—LINDA HENNESSEY, C.E.B.S., Mgr., *Ste. 611.* Tel: 703-841-2588.

Family Life Office—Mr. ROBERT E. LAIRD, Dir., *Ste. 523.* Tel: 703-841-2550. Vacant, Asst. Dir.

Marriage Preparation—Conferences for the Engaged. Tel: 703-841-2550.

Natural Family Planning—Tel: 703-841-2550.

Project Rachel Post-Abortion Counseling—*814.* Tel: 703-276-0373; 888-456-HOPE.

Respect Life / Pro-Life Activities—Tel: 703-841-2550.

Young Adult Programs—ANDREA KING. Tel: 703-841-2550.

General Information—COLETTE IUSI, *Ste. 617.* Tel: 703-841-2517; Fax: 703-841-4786.

Liturgy, Office of Sacred—Rev. PAUL F. DELADURANTAYE, Sec. for the Liturgy, *Ste. 503.* Tel: 703-841-2554. RICHARD GIBALA, Chm., Diocesan Music Committee. Tel: 703-524-2815.

Permanent Diaconate—Rev. ROBERT E. AVELLA, *Ste. 914.* Tel: 703-841-2500.

Propagation of the Faith—Rev. WILLIAM J. SCHOPPS, Dir., *Ste. 524.* Tel: 703-841-2762.

Publications / List Maintenance—OLGA A. HRYCAJ, Coord., *Ste. 617.* Tel: 703-841-2516; Fax: 703-841-4786.

Spanish Apostolate—Rev. OVIDIO PECHARROMAN, Dir., *80 N. Glebe Rd., Arlington, 22203.* Tel: 703-524-2122.

Office of Resettlement—DAVID HERRMANN, Refugee Program Coord., *80 N. Glebe Rd., Arlington, 22203.* Tel: 703-524-2154.

Stewardship and Development, Office of—ROBERT P. MUELLER, Dir., *Ste. 914.* Tel: 703-841-2545; Fax: 703-524-5028.

Vocations, Office of—Revs. CURTIS L. CLARK, Dir. DANIEL L. MODE, Promoter; OVIDIO PECHARROMAN, Coord. Spanish Speaking Vocations, *Ste. 619.* Tel: 703-841-2514.

Youth Activities, Office of—Rev. MICHAEL G. TAYLOR, Dir., *Ste. 519.* Tel: 703-841-2559.

Scouting & Camp Fire, Diocesan Committee on—Mrs. MARGARET MATARESE, Chm., *20 Hickory Ridge Dr., Falmouth, 22405-1440.* Tel: 540-371-8093.

Consultative Bodies

Clergy Personnel Board—Rev. ROBERT E. AVELLA, Chm., *St. Mary, Alexandria, 22314.* Tel: 703-836-4100.

Diaconal Committee—Deacon CHARLES A. COUTU, Coord. Tel: 540-937-4709. Deacon WILLIAM D. PIVARNIK, Coord. Tel: 703-519-7424.

Diocesan Consultors—Rev. Msgr. JAMES W. MCMURTRIE, V.F.; Rev. ROBERT C. CILINSKI; Rev. Msgr. R. ROY COSBY, V.G.; Revs. FRANKLYN M. MCAFEE; J. STEWART CULKIN; RICHARD J. LEY; MARK S. MEALEY, O.S.F.S.; FRANK J. READY, V.F.; ROBERT J. RIPPY, V.F.; WILLIAM P. SAUNDERS; MICHAEL G. TAYLOR.

Diocesan Finance Committee—Most Rev. PAUL S. LOVERDE, D.D., S.T.L., J.C.L., Chm. Tel: 703-841-2511. Rev. DANIEL J. MAHER, Episcopal Vicar for Finance. Tel: 703-841-2577.

Diocesan School Board—MOLLIE ROY, Chm. Tel: 703-255-4623.

Priests' Council—Revs. ROBERT C. CILINSKI; CURTIS L. CLARK; Rev. Msgr. R. ROY COSBY, V.G.; Revs. GERARD CREEDON; J. STEWART CULKIN; DANIEL N. GEE; JAMES R. GOULD; HORACE H. GRINNELL; Rev. Msgr. JOHN P. HANNAN; Revs. DENNIS W. KLEINMANN; THOMAS J. LEHNING; DAVID L. MARTIN; Rev. Msgr. JAMES W. MCMURTRIE, V.F.; Revs. MARK S. MEALEY, O.S.F.S.; JOHN M. O'NEILL, O.S.F.S.; FRANK J. READY, V.F.; ROBERT J. RIPPY, V.F.; PAUL D. SCALIA; MICHAEL G. TAYLOR.

Sisters' Council—Sr. LOUISE DOWGIALLO, O.S.B., Pres., *St. Benedict Monastery, Bristow, 20136.* Tel: 703-361-0106. Sr. ANNETTE MATTLE, R.C., Vice Pres., *The Cenacle House, 1033 Riva Ridge Dr., Great Falls, 22066.* Tel: 703-759-6901.

CLERGY, PARISHES, MISSIONS AND PAROCHIAL SCHOOLS

COUNTY OF ARLINGTON

1—CATHEDRAL OF ST. THOMAS MORE (1938), Revs. Dominic P. Irace, Rector; Ronald J. Gripshover, Jr.; Deacons Samuel M. Taub; Claudio F. Benedi. In res., Revs. Paul F. deLadurantaye; Daniel J. Maher.

Res., 3901 Cathedral Ln., 22203. Tel: 703-525-1300; 525-0450; Fax: 703-528-5760.

School—105 N. Thomas St., 22203. Tel: 703-528-6781; 528-1547; Fax: 703-528-5040. Mrs. Kathleen H. Swinehart, Prin.

Lay Teachers 24; Students 425.

Catechesis / Religious Programs—Tel: 703-528-7104. Sr. Maria Angelica I.H.M., D.R.E. Students 245.

2—ST. AGNES (1936), Revs. Robert L. Ruskamp; Thomas P. Vander Woude; Deacon William J. Donovan. In res., Rev. Msgr. John T. Cilinski; Rev. Msgr. Thomas P. Scannell; Rev. David J. Murungi.

Res., 1914 N. Randolph St., 22207. Tel: 703-525-1166; Fax: 703-243-2840.

School—2024 N. Randolph St., 22207. Tel: 703-527-5423; Fax: 703-527-6325. Ms. Sheila Tomlinson, Prin.

Sisters 2; Lay Teachers 29; Students 393.

Catechesis / Religious Programs—Tel: 703-522-7045. Sr. Mary Margaret Ann Schlather, S.N.D., D.R.E.

Students 346.

Convent—Tel: 703-527-3276. Sisters of Notre Dame

3—ST. ANN (1947), Revs. William B. Schardt; Michael T. Orlowsky; Deacon Eduardo Ramirez.

Res., 5312 10th St. N., 22205. Tel: 703-528-6276; Fax: 703-522-4758.

School—980 N. Frederick St., 22205. Tel: 703-525-7599; Fax: 703-525-2687. Mrs. Marlene Tennier, Prin.

Sisters of Notre Dame of Cleveland, Ohio 1; Lay Teachers 19; Students 267.

Catechesis / Religious Programs—Tel: 703-524-8377. Sr. Theresa Sullivan, S.N.D., D.R.E.

Students 241.

Convent—5307 N. Fairfax Dr., 22205. Tel: 703-525-8395.

4—ST. CHARLES BORROMEO (1909), Revs. Gerard Creedon; Francisco Mendez de Dios; Deacon John B. Mallon.

Res., 3304 N. Washington Blvd., 22201. Tel: 703-527-5500; Fax: 703-527-5505. In res., Rev. Charles C. McCoart.

School—Tel: 703-527-0608; Fax: 703-526-0262. Sr. Benedict Kesock, O.S.B., Prin.

Sisters of St. Benedict 1; Lay Teachers 14; Students 240.

Catechesis / Religious Programs—Tel: 703-527-5500, Ext. 19. Mrs. Anne Marie Kauffman, M.R.E., D.R.E.

Students 216.

Convent—3299 N. Fairfax Dr., 22201. Benedictine Sisters of Virginia

5—HOLY MARTYRS OF VIETNAM (1979) (Vietnamese), Revs. Anthony Tien Minh Dinh, O.P.; John Baptist Vuong Due Nguyen, O.P.; Deacon Pham Minh Kien, D.R.E.

Res., 915 S. Wakefield St., 22204. Tel: 703-553-0370; Fax: 703-553-4326.

Catechesis / Religious Programs—Tel: 703-553-4326; Fax: 703-0371.

Students 366.

6—OUR LADY OF LOURDES (1946), Revs. Robert J. Rippy, V.F.; Francis M. deRosa; Deacon James F. Ambury. In res., Rev. Joseph J. Loftus, (Retired).

Res., 830 S. 23rd St., 22202. Tel: 703-684-9261; 684-9211; Fax: 703-684-6342.

Catechesis / Religious Programs—Sr. Mary Brady, S.N.D., D.R.E., Tel: 703-534-9805.

Students 23.

7—OUR LADY, QUEEN OF PEACE (1945), Rev. Jeffrey T. Duaime, C.S.Sp.; Deacon Eugene D. Betit. In res., Rev. Leonard Tuozzolo, C.S.Sp.

Res., 2700 S. 19th St., 22204. Tel: 703-979-5580; Fax: 703-979-5590.

Catechesis / Religious Programs—Adolphe Gervais, D.R.E.

Students 92.

OUTSIDE THE COUNTY OF ARLINGTON

Alexandria

1—BLESSED SACRAMENT (1946), Revs. John C. Cregan; Matthew Zuberbueler; Michael J. Dobbins. In res., Rev. Msgr. Edward P. Browne; Rev. Tarsicio Buitrago (Colombia).

Church—1427 W. Braddock Rd., 22302. Tel: 703-998-6100; Fax: 703-671-3219.

Res., 1407 W. Braddock Rd., 22302.

School—1417 W. Braddock Rd., 22302. Tel: 703-998-4170. Valerie Garcia, Prin.

Lay Teachers 19; Students 363.

Catechesis / Religious Programs—Tel: 703-998-6100; Fax: 703-671-3219. Colette Ellis, D.R.E.

Students 354.

2—GOOD SHEPHERD (1965), Revs. George J. Griffin; Ronald S. Escalante; Deacon Thomas G. White. In res., Rev. Jesus Navarrette (Spain).

Church & Mailing Address—8710 Mount Vernon Hwy., 22309. Tel: 703-780-4055; Fax: 703-360-5385.

Res., 3321 Wessynton Way, 22309.

Catechesis / Religious Programs—Sue Ivory, D.R.E.

Students 908.

3—QUEEN OF APOSTLES (1963), Revs. Salvator L. Ciullo; James C. Hudgins; Frank Holscher, C.I.C.M.

Res., 4329 Sano St., 22312. Tel: 703-354-8711; Fax: 703-354-0766.

School—4409 Sano St., 22312. Tel: 703-354-0714; Fax: 703-354-1820. Mary L. West, Prin.

Lay Teachers 16; Students 279.

Catechesis / Religious Programs—Tel: 703-354-4360. James K. Ward, D.R.E.

Students 136.

4—ST. JOSEPH'S (1915), Rev. John J. McBrearty, S.S.J.

Res., 711 N. Columbus St., 22314. Tel: 703-836-3725; Fax: 703-837-9066.

Catechesis / Religious Programs—Tel: 301-839-3095. Mrs. Wilma Anderson, D.R.E.

Students 80.

5—ST. LAWRENCE (Franconia) (1967), Revs. William J. Erbacher; James Haley; Deacon Richard Caporiccio. In res., Rev. Anthony J. Carbone.

Res., 6222 Franconia Rd., 22310. Tel: 703-971-4378; Fax: 703-971-0331.

Catechesis/Religious Programs—Tel: 703-971-8541. James H. Drennan, D.R.E.
Students 246.

6—ST. LOUIS (1949), Revs. John J. Riley; Matthew Paul Richardson; Terrence R. Staples; Deacon Paul J. Plaisance.
Res., 2907 Popkins Ln., 22306. Tel: 703-765-4421; Fax: 703-765-1750.
School—2901 Popkins Ln., 22306. Tel: 703-768-7732; Fax: 703-768-3836. Mrs. Noreen M. Gilmour, Prin.
Lay Teachers 27; Students 458.
Catechesis/Religious Programs—Tel: 703-765-6600.
Students 469.

7—ST. MARY'S (1795), Revs. Robert E. Avella; Dennis W. Kleinmann; Stefan Starzynski; Christian Connelly; Deacon William D. Pivarnik.
Res., 310 Duke St., 22314. Tel: 703-549-3603; 836-4100; Fax: 703-549-3605. [CEM]
School—400 Green St., 22314. Tel: 703-549-1646; Fax: 703-519-0840. Mrs. Kathleen Dolan, Prin.
Sisters 2; Lay Teachers 36; Students 689.
Catechesis/Religious Programs—Tel: 703-548-6833.
Students 199.
Convent—309 S. Royal St., 22314. Tel: 703-548-3545. Sisters of the Holy Cross

8—ST. RITA'S (1914), Revs. Denis M. Donahue; Mark E. Moretti.
Res., 3815 Russell Rd., 22305. Tel: 703-836-1640; Fax: 703-836-7825.
School—3801 Russell Rd., 22305. Tel: 703-548-1888. Mrs. Mary Pat Schlickenmaier, Prin.
Sisters of St. Joseph 1; Lay Teachers 12; Students 214.
Catechesis/Religious Programs—Tel: 703-836-1356. John Heil, D.R.E.
Students 190.
Convent—231 W. Glebe Rd., 22305. Tel: 703-683-1929. Sisters of St. Joseph

Annandale, Fairfax Co., Holy Spirit (1964), Revs. Frank J. Ready, V.F.; Andrew Tu Minh Nguyen; Matthew A. Carr; John M. O'Donohue. In res., Rev. Msgr. Francis L. Bradican, (Retired).
Res., 5121 Woodland Way, 22003. Tel: 703-978-8074; Fax: 703-978-9671.
School—8800 Braddock Rd., 22003. Tel: 703-978-7117; Fax: 703-978-7438. Mrs. Deborah Mohney, Prin.
Lay Teachers 27; Students 490.
Catechesis/Religious Programs—Tel: 703-978-8925; Fax: 703-978-7438. Mrs. Margaret Whitehead, D.R.E.
Students 725.

St. Ambrose (1966), Revs. Richard J. Ley; Michael C. Kelly; Deacon Roger T. Ostrom.
Res., 3901 Woodburn Rd., 22003. Tel: 703-280-4400; Fax: 703-280-1123.
School—Tel: 703-698-7171; Fax: 703-698-7170. Mrs. Virginia Connell, Prin.
Lay Teachers 15; Students 231.
Catechesis/Religious Programs—Tel: 703-280-1122. Mr. John Mallory, D.R.E.
Students 234.

St. Michael's (1953), Revs. Jerome R. Daly; Michael R. Duesterhaus; Alexander R. Drummond; Deacon David S. McCaffrey. In res., Rev. Lee R. Roos.
Res., 7401 St. Michael's Ln., 22003. Tel: 703-256-7822; Fax: 703-256-0446.
School—Tel: 703-256-1222. Sr. Dorothy Mayer, I.H.M., Prin.
Servants of the Immaculate Heart of Mary 6; Lay Teachers 24; Students 490.
Catechesis/Religious Programs—Tel: 703-941-9403. Mr. William Duffy, D.R.E.
Students 407.
Convent—7421 St. Michael's Ln., 22003. Tel: 703-256-2130. Sisters, Servants of the Immaculate Heart of Mary

Ashburn, St. Theresa (1991), Rev. Msgr. James W. McMurtrie, V.F.; Rev. Richard A. Mullins.
Mailing Address: P.O. Box 526, 20146-0526. Tel: 703-729-2287.
Rectory—43313 Dovetail Pl., 20147. Tel: 703-729-9036.
Church—21370 St. Theresa Ln., 20147. Tel: 703-729-2287.
School—Tel: 703-729-3577. Mrs. Jacqueline MacKenzie, Prin.
Lay Teachers 21; Students 440.
Catechesis/Religious Programs—Tel: 703-729-3714. Ms. Janet Healy, D.R.E.
Students 1,032.

Burke, Fairfax Co., Church of the Nativity (W. Springfield) (1973), Revs. Richard B. Martin; Kevin J. Larsen; Deacon Wilson I. Korpi.
Mailing Address: 6400 Nativity Ln., 22015. Tel: 703-455-2400; Fax: 703-455-6832.
Res., 9523 Lyra Ct., 22015. Tel: 703-913-2306.
School—6398 Nativity Ln., 22015. Tel: 703-455-2300; Fax: 703-569-8109. Mrs. Patricia V. Beeks, Prin.
Lay Teachers 17; Students 254.
Catechesis/Religious Programs—Tel: 703-455-0372. D.R.E.: Sr. Donatella Merulla, A.R., M.R.E.; Sr. Mary Attilia Todaro, A.R., M.R.E.
Students 1,490.
Convent—6300 Capella Ave., 22015. Tel: 703-455-4180. Handmaids of Reparation of the Sacred Heart of Jesus

Chantilly, Fairfax Co., St. Timothy (1969), Revs. Gerald Weymes; J. Edwin Thayer Tewes; Wilhelm Ettner; Terry A. Cramer; Deacons David E. Conroy; William J. Pyrek.
Res., 13807 Poplar Tree Rd., 20151. Tel: 703-378-7461; 378-7646; Fax: 703-378-7552.
School—13809 Poplar Tree Rd., 20151. Tel: 703-378-6932; Fax: 703-378-1273. Mrs. Marilyn Valatka, Prin.
Lay Teachers 32; Students 633.
Catechesis/Religious Programs—Tel: 703-378-9143; Fax: 703-378-7552. Maria Garvey, D.R.E.
Students 1,322.

Clifton, Fairfax Co., St. Andrew the Apostle (1989), Revs. Jerome W. Fasano; David C. Rahn; John C. De Celles. In res., Rev. Julius J. Cilinski, (Retired).
Res., 6720 Union Mill Rd., 20124. Tel: 703-817-1770; Fax: 703-817-0928.
School—Tel: 703-817-1774. Mrs. Phyllis Hammang, Prin.
Lay Teachers 15; Students 253.
Catechesis/Religious Programs—Tel: 703-817-1773. Mrs. Delores Nelson, D.R.E.
Students 1,400.

St. Claire of Assisi (1981), Rev. Paul L. Dudzinski.
Mailing Address: 7616 Maple Branch Rd., 20124. Tel: 703-266-1310; Fax: 703-266-7011.
Church—12409 Henderson Rd., 20124. Tel: 703-266-1310; Fax: 703-266-7011.
Catechesis/Religious Programs—George Alexa, D.R.E.
Students 176.

Colonial Beach, Westmoreland Co., St. Elizabeth (1906), Revs. Vincent P. Bork; John H. Melmer; Deacons Robert Baker; Edward Cleary.
Res., 21 Irving Ave. S., P.O. Box 275, 22443. Tel: 804-224-7221; Fax: 804-224-7221. [JC]
Catechesis/Religious Programs—Students 154.
Mission—King George, King George Co., St. Anthony's, P.O. Box 275, 22443. [CEM]

Culpeper, Culpeper Co., Precious Blood (1880), Rev. Leo J. Zonneveld, C.I.C.M.
Res., 114 E. Edmondson St., 22701. Tel: 540-825-8945; Fax: 540-825-8987. [CEM]
Catechesis/Religious Programs—Tel: 540-825-1339. Ms. Patricia Reed, D.R.E.
Students 286.
Mission—Washington, Rappahannock Co., St. Peter, P.O. Box 27, Washington, 22747. Tel: 540-675-3432; Fax: 540-675-1053. Rev. Jerry J. Pokorsky; Deacon Charles A. Coutu.

Dale City, Prince William Co., Holy Family (1970), Revs. Stephen F. Leva; Carroll L. Oubre; Tren Dinh Nhi; Deacons Gerald J. Moore; Vincent Einsmann; Frederick J. Romanski. In res., Revs. Andrew W.P. Krafcik, (Retired); Joseph Howard.
Res., 14160 Ferndale Rd., 22193. Tel: 703-670-8161; Fax: 703-670-8323.
School—Darlene Hilton, Prin.; Judi Peacott, PreK Dir., (PreK-4). Lay Teachers 8; Students 135.
Catechesis/Religious Programs—Joyce Stark Franklin, D.R.E.
Students 1366.

Fairfax, Fairfax Co., St. Leo's (1957), Revs. John D. Kelly; Donald J. Rooney; Mark F. Carrier. In res., Rev. Terry W. Specht.
Res., 3700 Old Lee Hwy., 22030. Tel: 703-273-5369; Fax: 703-273-2371.
School—3704 Old Lee Hwy., 22030. Tel: 703-273-1211; Fax: 703-273-6913. Mrs. Diane Drews, Prin.
Lay Teachers 25; Students 545.
Catechesis/Religious Programs—Tel: 703-273-4868.
Students 397.
Station—Fairfax Nursing Home, Tel: 703-273-7705.

St. Mary of Sorrows (1858), Revs. Donald C. Greenhalgh; Stephen Holmes; Brian G. Bashista; Deacons John M. Ligon; Nicholas LaDuca. In res., Rev. David A. Whitestone.
Mailing & Parish Center Address—5222 Sideburn Rd., 22032-2640. Tel: 703-978-4141; Fax: 703-978-2568.
Historic Church—5612 Ox Rd., Fairfax Station, 22039.
Res., 11112 Fairfax Station Rd., Fairfax Station, 22039. [CEM]
Preschool—Tel: 703-978-9656. Elena Quartuccio, Dir.
Catechesis/Religious Programs—Tel: 703-978-4283. D.R.E.: Maureen Kelly, (PreK-6); William Gavin, (7-12).
Students 1,341.

St. Paul Chung (1996) (Korean), Revs. Francis X. Soon-Sin Park (Wonju); Gregorius Young-Geun Choi; Deacon Paul Lee.
Res., 4708 Rippling Pond Dr., 22033. Tel: 703-818-9707; Fax: 703-968-3013.
Church and Mailing Address: 4712 Rippling Pond Dr., 22033-5077. Tel: 703-968-3010.
Catechesis/Religious Programs—Moon C. Kim, D.R.E., Tel: 703-841-2572.
Students 460.

Fairfax Station, St. Raymond of Penafort (1997), Rev. James R. Gould.
Res., 8900 Triple Ridge Rd., 22039. Tel: 703-690-6650; Fax: 703-690-7399.
Catechesis/Religious Programs—D.R.E.: Bob Ward; Beverly Ward.
Students 309.

Falls Church, Fairfax Co., St. Anthony's (1952), Revs. Horace H. Grinnell; Jose E. Hoyos; Paul A. Berghout; Deacon Mario Mendoza. In res., Revs. Ben M. Opara (Nigeria); William J. Schopps.
Res., 3305 Glen Carlyn Rd., 22041. Tel: 703-820-7111; Fax: 703-379-9195.
Catechesis/Religious Programs—Tel: 703-820-2158. Mary Lou Miller, D.R.E.
Students 1,156.

St. James (1892), Rev. Cornelius O'Brien; Rev. Msgr. Frank E. Mahler; Rev. J. Kevin O'Keefe; Deacons James A. Fishenden; Thomas M. Bello. In res., Revs. Daniel L. Mode; Roberto Orihuela; Kevin B. Walsh.
Res., 905 Park Ave., 22046. Tel: 703-532-8815; Fax: 703-533-7644. [CEM]
School—830 W. Broad St., 22046. Tel: 703-533-1182; Fax: 703-532-8316. Sr. Teresa Ballisty, I.H.M., Prin.
Sisters, Servants of the Immaculate Heart of Mary 7; Lay Teachers 26; Students 625.
Catechesis/Religious Programs—Tel: 703-532-4344. Sr. Joseph Michele, I.H.M., D.R.E.
Students 303.
Convent—101 N. Spring St., 22046. Tel: 703-532-2388. Sisters, Servants of the Immaculate Heart of Mary

St. Philip (1963), Revs. Daniel S. Spychala; Robert J. DeMartino; Deacon Noel Vivaldi. In res., Revs. Ovidio Pecharroman; John W. Rea, (Retired).
Res., 7500 St. Philip's Ct., 22042. Tel: 703-573-3808; Fax: 703-560-2832.
Catechesis/Religious Programs—Tel: 703-573-1899; Fax: 703-573-6832.
Students 200.

Fredericksburg, St. Mary (1858), Revs. Daniel E. Hamilton, V.F.; Christopher J. Mould; Francis J. Peffley; Deacon Donald K. McAskill.
Res., 1009 Stafford Ave., 22401-5418. Tel: 540-373-6491; 373-6663; Fax: 540-371-0251.
Catechesis/Religious Programs—Tel: 540-373-7770. Diane K. McFall, D.R.E.
Students 823.
Convent—1104 Augustine Ave., 22401. Tel: 540-371-1652; Fax: 540-371-1672. Oblate Sisters of St. Francis de Sales, St. Mary Convent

St. Patrick's (1983), Revs. Philip S. Majka; Paul D. Scalia; Deacons David Conroy; David J. Geary.
Res., 12023 Tee Side Dr., 22407. Tel: 540-785-9328; Fax: 540-785-5692.
Church—9151 Ely's Ford Rd., 22407. Tel: 540-785-5299.
School—9151 Ely's Ford Rd., 22407. Tel: 540-786-2277; Fax: 540-785-2213. Mr. George Elliott, Prin.
Lay Teachers 11; Students 232.
Catechesis/Religious Programs—Tel: 540-785-7857; Fax: 540-785-5758. Philip Camill, D.R.E.
Students 505.

Front Royal, Warren Co., St. John the Baptist (1884), Rev. William F. Ruehl, V.F.; Deacon Richard Demers.
Res., 123 W. Main St., 22630. Tel: 540-635-3780; Fax: 540-635-2683.
Catechesis/Religious Programs—Tel: 540-635-9493. Dr. Eleanor Kelly, D.R.E.
Students 220.

Gordonsville, Orange Co., St. Mark's (1972), Rev. David L. Martin.
Mailing Address: P.O. Box 124, 22942.
Res., 317 Main St., 22942. Tel: 540-832-3062.

Great Falls, Fairfax Co., St. Catherine of Siena (1979), Revs. Franklyn M. McAfee; Richard M. Guest; Deacon Joseph G. Benin. In res., Rev. Robert Schreiner (CR).
Mailing Address: 1020 Springvale Rd., 22066. Tel: 703-759-4350; Fax: 703-759-3753.
Catechesis/Religious Programs—Tel: 703-759-3530. Mr. Peter Savva, D.R.E.
Students 576.

Herndon, Fairfax Co., St. Joseph (1950), Revs. David C. Bonarrigo, T.O.R.; Christopher Dobson, T.O.R.; James Angert, T.O.R.; Ronald J. Mohnickey, T.O.R.
Res., 750 Peachtree St., 20170. Tel: 703-437-3737; Fax: 703-437-8745.
School—Tel: 703-437-3014; Fax: 703-437-0765. Mrs. Joan Cargill, Prin.
Lay Teachers 24; Students 586.
Catechesis/Religious Programs—Students 1,171.

St. Veronica (1999), Rev. Marcus A. Pollard. In res., Rev. Christopher M. Buckner.
3300 Dairy Lou Dr., 20171. Tel: 703-689-4409; Fax: 703-689-4410.

Kilmarnock, Lancaster Co., St. Francis de Sales (1966), Rev. James C. Bruse.
Res., 151 E. Church St., P.O. Box 759, 22482-0759. Tel: 804-435-0568; Fax: 804-435-2362. [CEM 2]
Catechesis/Religious Programs—Tel: 804-580-8213; Fax: 804-436-9614. Anna Marie Rundall, D.R.E.
Students 77.
Mission—Hague, Westmoreland Co., St. Paul.

Lake Ridge, Prince William Co., St. Elizabeth Ann Seton (1976), Revs. James S. Barkett; Jerry A. Wooton; Deacon Emil P. Myskowski.
Mailing Address: 12805 Valleywood Dr., 22192. Tel: 703-494-4008; Fax: 703-494-1995.
Catechesis/Religious Programs—Tel: 703-494-4008. Jackie Ezersky, D.R.E.
Students 1,003.

Leesburg, Loudoun Co., St. John the Apostle (1926), Revs. Robert C. Brooks; Sean K. Rousseau.
Mailing Address: 101 Oakcrest Manor Dr., N.E., 20176-2221. Tel: 703-777-1317; Fax: 703-771-9016. [CEM]
Res., 302 N. King St., N.E., 20176.
Catechesis/Religious Programs—Tel: 703-777-3891. Mrs. Kathleen A. Fridley, D.R.E.
Students 595.

Luray, Page Co., Our Lady of the Valley (1954), Rev. Christopher Lemme, T.O.R.
Mailing Address: 200 Collins Ave., P.O. Box 462, 22835. Tel: 540-743-4919; Fax: 540-743-2490.
Catechesis/Religious Programs—Susie Temple, D.R.E.
Students 50.

McLean, Fairfax Co., St. John's (1913), Revs. Edward C. Hathaway; John F. Heisler. In res., Rev. Anthony G. Percy.
Res., 6420 Linway Ter., 22101. Tel: 703-356-7916; Fax: 703-356-4517.
School—6422 Linway Ter., 22101. Tel: 703-356-7554; Fax: 703-448-3811. Mrs. Christine Wells, Prin.
Lay Teachers 18; Students 284.
Catechesis/Religious Programs—Tel: 703-356-5275. Ms. Laura Pennefather, D.R.E.
Students 338.

St. Luke's (1961), Revs. Martin McGuill; Thomas P. Ferguson. In res., Rev. Curtis L. Clark.
Res., 7001 Georgetown Pike, 22101. Tel: 703-356-1255; Fax: 703-442-0848.
School—7005 Georgetown Pike, 22101. Tel: 703-356-1508; Fax: 703-356-1141. Mrs. Margaret Cahill, Prin.
Lay Teachers 20; Students 251.
Catechesis/Religious Programs—Tel: 703-356-8419; Fax: 703-356-3543. Carol Mournighan, D.R.E.
Students 730.

Madison, Madison Co., Our Lady of the Blue Ridge (1974), Rev. John F. Morel, C.I.C.M.
Res., H.C.R. 4, Box 28, 22727. Tel: 540-948-4144; Fax: 540-948-3325.
Catechesis/Religious Programs—Tel: 540-547-3850. Jayne Machleit, D.R.E.
Students 80.

Manassas, Prince William Co., All Saints (1929), Revs. Robert C. Cilinski; Paul M. Grankauskas; John P. Mosimann; Joseph R. Kenna; Deacons John W. Eberlein; Richard O'Connell.
Res., 9300 Stonewall Rd., 20110. Tel: 703-368-4500; Fax: 703-257-9299.
School—9294 Stonewall Rd., 20110. Tel: 703-368-4400; Fax: 703-393-2157. Mr. David E. Conroy, Jr., Prin.; Mrs. Judy Fisher, Asst. Prin.
Lay Teachers 27; Students 500.
Catechesis/Religious Programs—Tel: 703-393-2142. D.R.E.: Mrs. Marie Riley, (Elementary); Mary Pat Maher, (Junior-Senior Education).
Students 1,457.

Sacred Heart (1984), Revs. Thomas J. Lehning; Joseph J. Clark; Deacon Thomas W. Wolter.
Mailing Address: 12975 Purcell Rd., 20112-3217. Tel: 703-590-0030; Fax: 703-590-0141.
Res., 6258 Terrapin Dr., 20112. Tel: 703-791-5131. [CEM]
Catechesis/Religious Programs—Tel: 703-590-0030.
Students 500.

Middleburg, Loudoun Co., St. Stephen the Martyr (1975), Rev. Joseph P. Biniek.
Mailing Address: P.O. Box 474, 20118-0474. Tel: 540-687-6433; Fax: 540-687-5170.
Res., 23309 Sam Fred Rd., 20117. Tel: 540-687-6433.
Church—Intersection Rte. 50 & Sam Fred Rd., 20117.
Catechesis/Religious Programs—Tel: 703-754-8567. D.R.E.: Julia Neely; Marilyn Krause.
Students 159.

Orange, Orange Co., St. John's (1946), Rev. David L. Martin (ARL).
Res., 108 W. Nelson St., P.O. Box 350, 22960. Tel: 703-672-4933; Fax: 703-672-7416.
Catechesis/Religious Programs—Nancy Schleser, D.R.E.
Students 77.

Potomac Falls, Loudoun Co., Our Lady of Hope (2000), Rev. William P. Saunders.
Res., 20648 Belwood Ct., 20165. Tel: 703-430-5702; Fax: 703-430-5727.
Catechesis/Religious Programs—D.R.E.: Sally Girardi; Phil Girardi.
Students 622.

Purcellville, Loudoun Co., St. Francis de Sales (1967), Rev. Msgr. Thomas J. Cassidy; Rev. Stephen A. Roszel.
Res., 37730 St. Francis Ct., 20132. Tel: 540-338-6381; Fax: 540-338-6431.
Catechesis/Religious Programs—D.R.E.: Rebecca Sparks-LaPointe; Janice Rees.
Students 601.

Reston, Fairfax Co., St. John Neumann (1979), Revs. Robert A. Brown, O.S.F.S.; Joseph T. Brennan, O.S.F.S.; Patrick T. O'Connor, O.S.F.S.
Res., 11900 Lawyers Rd., 20191-4299. Tel: 703-860-8510; Fax: 703-860-2136.
Catechesis/Religious Programs—Tel: 703-860-2815. Susan Merkel Hayden, M.R.E.
Students 1,700.

St. Thomas a Becket (1970), Rev. Patrick Holroyd.
Res., 1421 Wiehle Ave., 20190. Tel: 703-437-7113; Fax: 703-689-3814.
Catechesis/Religious Programs—Tel: 703-689-3816. Kathleen McCabe, D.R.E.
Students 521.

Spotsylvania, Spotsylvania Co., St. Matthew (1999), Revs. David P. Meng; John P. Peterson; Deacon Edward Whelan.
8200 Robert E. Lee Dr., 22553. Tel: 540-582-5575; Fax: 540-582-8639.
Convent—8208 Robert E. Lee Dr., 22553. Tel: 540-582-2653. Daughters of Charity of St. Vincent de Paul (Emmitsburg, MD) Sr. Gloria Gilman, D.C., Supr.
Sisters 3.
Catechesis/Religious Programs—Joanne Wittaker, D.R.E.
Students 297.

Springfield, Fairfax Co., St. Bernadette's (1959), Revs. John J. Hughes; Michael G. Taylor; Kevin J. Beres; John T.B. Trong.
Res., 7600 Old Keene Mill Rd., 22152-2022. Tel: 703-451-8576; Fax: 703-451-6893.
School—7602 Old Keene Mill Rd., 22152-2099. Tel: 703-451-8696; Fax: 703-451-8221. Mrs. Catherine M. Gilbride, Prin.
Priests 2; Lay Teachers 24; Students 512.
Catechesis/Religious Programs—Tel: 703-569-0512. D.R.E.: Karen Murphy; Claudia Fiebig.
Students 1,013.
Convent—7676 Tiverton Dr., 22152. Daughters of Wisdom

Stafford, Stafford Co., St. William of York (1971), Revs. Charles W. Merkle, III; Andrew J. Fisher; Deacon Richard P. Smith. In res., Rev. Anthony J. Pinizzotto, O.S.F.S.
Mailing Address: P.O. Box 116, 22555. Tel: 540-659-1102; Fax: 540-659-5637.
Res., 3130 Jefferson Davis Hwy., 22554. Tel: 540-659-9190.
School—(Grades PreK-8). Tel: 540-659-5207. Mrs. Claire Dougherty, Admin.
Franciscan Missionary Sisters of the Infant Jesus 3; Lay Teachers 9; Students 196.
Catechesis/Religious Programs—Tel: 540-659-5705; 288-0201. Sr. Claire V. Sabini, F.M.I.J., D.R.E.
Students 704.
Convent—13 Emerson Ct., 22554. Tel: 540-288-0201. Franciscan Missionary Sisters of the Infant Jesus

Sterling, Loudoun Co., Christ the Redeemer (1972), Revs. C. Donald Howard, S.A.; William F. Schmidt, S.A.; Deacon Joseph R. Singer. In res., Revs. Natividad Menjivar (Honduras); Michael A. Daniel, S.A.
Res., 512 N. York Rd., 20164. Tel: 703-430-1686.
Church—46833 Harry Byrd Hwy., 20164. Tel: 703-430-0811; Fax: 703-430-1590.
Catechesis/Religious Programs—Tel: 703-430-0813. Mrs. Marie Kordes, D.R.E.
Students 1,036.

Triangle, Prince William Co., St. Francis of Assisi (1957), Revs. John F. O'Connor, O.F.M.; Robert Menard, O.F.M.; Gene B. Pistacchio, O.F.M.
Res., 18825 Fuller Heights Rd., 22172. Tel: 703-221-4575.
Church—Tel: 703-221-4044; Fax: 703-221-3246.
School—Tel: 703-221-3868; Fax: 703-221-0700. Dr. Tricia Barber, Prin.
Lay Teachers 16; Students 356.
Catechesis/Religious Programs—Mrs. Margaret Bruni, D.R.E.
Students 867.

Vienna, Fairfax Co., Our Lady of Good Counsel (1956), Revs. John M. O'Neill, O.S.F.S.; Raymond G. Collins, O.S.F.S.; James M. Turner, O.S.F.S.; Paul G. Dechant; William J. Metzger, O.S.F.S. In res., Revs. Mark S. Mealey, O.S.F.S.; Francis W. Danella, O.S.F.S.
Office and Mailing Address: P.O. Box 97, 22183. Tel: 703-938-2828; Fax: 703-938-2828.
Res., 8601 Wolftrap Rd., 22182.
School—Tel: 703-938-3600; Fax: 703-255-1543. Mr. Austin Poole, Prin.
Lay Teachers 32; Students 536.
Catechesis/Religious Programs—Tel: 703-938-2553, Ext. 19; Fax: 703-938-2828. Ms. Patricia Jones, D.R.E.
Students 414.

St. Mark's (1965), Revs. J. Stewart Culkin; Christopher J. Pollard; Deacon Lawrence L. Ziemianski.
Res., 9970 Vale Rd., 22181. Tel: 703-281-9100; Fax: 703-281-0675. [CEM]
Catechesis/Religious Programs—Tel: 703-938-1948. D.R.E.: Sue Long; Patricia Wheatley.
Students 943.

Warrenton, Fauquier Co., St. John the Evangelist (1874), Revs. Michael J. Bazan; Christopher D. Murphy; Deacons W. Bernard Ragan; Richard A. Cronican.
Res., 271 Winchester St., 22186. Tel: 540-347-2922; Fax: 540-347-1274.
School—111 King St., 22186. Tel: 540-347-2458; Fax: 540-349-8007. Elizabeth Roach, Prin.
Lay Teachers 9; Students 245.
Catechesis/Religious Programs—Michelle Leary, D.R.E.
Students 730.

Winchester, Frederick Co., Sacred Heart of Jesus (1870), Revs. Stanley J. Krempa; John A. Ziegler; Deacon Edward L. Christianson.
Res., 130 Keating Dr., 22601-2806. Tel: 540-662-5858; Fax: 540-667-6156. [CEM]
School—110 Keating Dr., 22601-2806. Tel: 540-662-7177. Mrs. Kathleen Weiss, Prin.
School Sisters of Notre Dame 1; Lay Teachers 15; Students 190.
Catechesis/Religious Programs—Tel: 540-665-1975. Sr. Bernadette Melling, S.S.N.D., D.R.E.
Students 448.
Convent—140 Keating Dr., 22601. Tel: 540-662-6687. School Sisters of Notre Dame
Mission—Berryville, Clarke Co., St. Bridget of Ireland, 130 Keating Dr., Winchester, 22601. Tel: 540-662-5858; Fax: 540-667-6156.

Woodbridge, Prince William Co., Our Lady of Angels (1959), Revs. Robert A. Lange; Lawrence M. Violette; Daniel N. Gee; Deacons Danny E. Johnson; Jose I. Pardo; Stephen F. McGraw. In res., Rev. Msgr. R. Roy Cosby, V.G.
Res., 13752 Mary's Way, 22191. Tel: 703-494-2444; 494-5015; Fax: 703-494-0005.
Catechesis/Religious Programs—Tel: 703-494-3696; Fax: 703-494-3605.
Students 729.

Woodstock, Shenandoah Co., St. John Bosco (1888), Rev. William M. Aitcheson. In res., Rev. Joseph A. Salazar, M.S.A.
Res., 315 N. Main St., 22664. Tel: 540-459-4448; Fax: 540-459-4448.
Catechesis/Religious Programs—Tel: 540-459-8334. Hugh Owen, D.R.E.
Students 155.
Mission—Basye, Shenandoah Co., Our Lady of the Shenandoah, 240 Fretzel Way, Basye, 22810. Tel: 540-856-2411. Rev. Clarence M. Trinkle.

DIOCESAN MISSION PARISH

Dominican Republic, San Francisco de Asis, Banica, Revs. Patrick L. Posey; John T. O'Hara.
Mailing Address: c/o Lynx Air, P.O. Box 407052, Fort Lauderdale, FL 33340. Tel: 011-874-761-879-153; Fax: 011-874-761-879-154.

San Jose, Pedro Santana, Revs. Patrick L. Posey; John T. O'Hara.
Mailing Address: c/o Lynx Air, P.O. Box 407052,

Fort Lauderdale, FL 33340. Tel: 011-874-761-879-153; Fax: 011-874-761-879-154.

Special Assignment:
Reverend Fathers—
Nassetta, Peter W., George Mason University, Fairfax

On Duty Outside the Diocese:
Reverend Fathers—
Albertson, Eric J., Chap. Maj., Fort Meade, MD
Eversole, Paul M., Basilica of the National Shrine of the Immaculate Conception, Washington, D.C.
Gross, Lee W., Mount St. Mary's Seminary, Emmitsburg, MD
Mercer, James G., Priestly Fraternity of St. Peter, Elmhurst, PA
O'Hara, John T.
Pilon, Mark A.
Planty, Donald J., Nunziature Apostolica in Ethiopa
Posey, Patrick L., St. Joseph Parish, Pedro Santana and Banica, Dominican Republic

Military Chaplains:
Reverend Fathers—
Albertson, Eric J., Maj., Fort Meade, MD

Retired:
Reverend Monsignors—
Bradican, Francis L., Holy Spirit, Annandale
Browne, Edward P., Blessed Sacrament, Alexandria
Cilinski, John T., St. Agnes, Arlington
Cosby, R. Roy, V.G., Our Lady of Angels, Woodbridge
Hannan, John P., Gainsville
Hendrick, Frank J., Southern Pines, NC
Scannell, Thomas P., St. Agnes, Arlington
Reverend Fathers—
Cilinski, Julius J., St. Andrew the Apostle, Clifton
Dair, Richard J., Fairfax
Gerloff, Charles W., Virginia Beach
Kollar, Edmund, Life Care Center of Citrus Co., Lecanto, FL
Krafcik, Andrew W., Holy Family, Dale City
Loftus, Joseph J., Our Lady of Lourdes, Arlington
Muldowney, James D., Our Lady of Perpetual Help Retired Community, Virginia Beach, VA
Rea, John W., St. Philip, Falls Church
Slivonik, Stanley, Lovettsville
Watkins, Clarence N., Falls Church

Permanent Deacons:
Ambury, James F., Our Lady of Lourdes, Arlington
Arquette, Lester K., Leave of Absence
Bayne, James L., Leave of Absence
Bello, Thomas M., St. James, Falls Church
Benedi, Claudio F., Cathedral of St. Thomas More, Arlington
Benin, Joseph G., St. Catherine, Great Falls
Betit, Eugene D., Our Lady Queen of Peace, Arlington
Bosch, Joseph L., Leave of Absence
Braun, Richard L., Leave of Absence
Burrell, Richard L., Leave of Absence
Canonica, Donald A., St. Mary, Opelika, AL
Christianson, Edward L., Sacred Heart, Winchester
Conroy, David E., St. Timothy, Chantilly; St. Patrick, Chancellorsville
Coutu, Charles A., St. Peter Mission, Washington
Curtin, Robert J., (Retired)
de Ladurantaye, Robert E., Leave of Absence
Demers, Richard L., St. John the Baptist, Front Royal
Donovan, William J., St. Agnes, Arlington
Dunn, Darryl A., Leave of Absence
Eberlein, John W., All Saints, Manassas
Einsmann, W. Vincent, Holy Family, Dale City
Fishenden, James A., St. James, Falls Church
Frank, John L., Leave of Absence
Galvez, Rene A., Annunciation, West Hollywood, FL
George, Paul J., Leave of Absence
Henry, Lawrence B., Leave of Absence
Johnson, Danny E., Our Lady of Angels, Woodbridge
Kenski, Frank G., Prince of Peace, Steelton, PA
Korpi, Wilson I., Nativity, Burke
La Duca, Nicholas J., St. Mary of Sorrows, Fairfax
Lee, Jea Duck, Leave of Absence
Lee, Paul, St. Paul Chung, Fairfax
Ligon, Jack M., St. Mary of Sorrows, Fairfax
Malinowski, Leonard P., Our Lady of Good Counsel, Vienna
Mallon, John B., St. Charles Borromeo, Arlington
Melvin, Gerald A., Leave of Absence
Mendoza, Mario L., St. Anthony, Falls Church
Moore, Gerald J., Holy Family, Dale City
Myskowski, Emil P., St. Elizabeth Ann Seton, Lake Ridge
Nickle, Dennis E., Leave of Absence
O'Connell, Richard T., All Saints, Manassas
Ostrom, Roger T., St. Ambrose, Annandale
Pardo, Jose I., Our Lady of Angels, Woodbridge
Pham, Kien Minh, Holy Martyrs of Vietnam, Arlington
Pivarnik, William D., St. Mary, Alexandria
Prien, Richard K., Leave of Absence
Pyrek, William J., St. Timothy, Chantilly
Ragan, W. Bernard, St. John the Evangelist, Warrenton
Ramirez, Eduardo A., St. Ann, Arlington
Rees, Paul J., Leave of Absence
Resendes, Daniel F., (Retired)
Singer, Joseph R., Christ the Redeemer, Sterling
Smith, Richard P., St. William of York, Stafford
Soutuyo, Francisco R., Leave of Absence
Taub, Samuel M., Cathedral of St. Thomas More, Arlington
Vivaldi, Noel, St. Philip, Falls Church
Ward, Albert P., (Retired)
White, Thomas G., Good Shepherd, Alexandria
Wilbur, Carl A., Catholic Chapel, National Institute of Health
Wolter, Thomas W., Sacred Heart, Manassas

INSTITUTIONS LOCATED IN THE DIOCESE

[A] COLLEGES AND UNIVERSITIES

ARLINGTON. *Marymount University*, 2807 N. Glebe Rd., 22207. Tel: 703-522-5600; Fax: 703-522-0349.
E-mail: admissions@marymount.edu
Web site: www.marymount.edu
For a complete listing, refer to the Colleges and Universities section.

FRONT ROYAL. *Christendom College*, 134 Christendom Dr., 22630. Tel: 540-636-2900; Fax: 540-636-1655
For a complete listing, refer to the Colleges and Universities section.

[B] CATECHETICAL INSTITUTE

ALEXANDRIA. *Notre Dame Graduate School of Christendom College*, 4407 Sano St., 22312. Tel: 703-658-4304; Fax: 703-658-2318. Rev. William P. Saunders, Ph.D., Dean; Sr. M. Timothy Prokes, F.S.E., Ph.D., Dean of Students; Luther P. Niehoff, Admin. Dir. Priests 1; Sisters 1; Lay Teachers 3; Total Enrollment 300.

[C] CORRESPONDENCE SCHOOL

HAMILTON. *The Catholic Distance University fka The Catholic Home Study Institute*, 120 E. Colonial Hwy., 20158-9012. Tel: 540-338-2700; Fax: 540-338-4788.
E-mail: cdu@cdu.edu
Web site: http://www.cdu.edu
Accredited Catechetical Institute for Adults; Catechetical Diploma; Continuing Education; and Optional College credit, Masters in Religious Studies. All programs through distance learning. Most Rev. Thomas J. Welsh, D.D., Bd. Chm., Pres. & Chancellor; Marianne Evans Mount, Exec.Vice Pres. Priests 2; Adjunct Faculty 20; Staff 13; Total Staff 33; Total Students 700.

[D] HIGH SCHOOLS, DIOCESAN

ARLINGTON. *Bishop Denis J. O'Connell High School*, 6600 Little Falls Rd., 22213. Tel: 703-237-1400; Fax: 703-237-1465.
E-mail: ee.cua.edu/~oconnell
Web site: www.ee.cua.edu/oconnell
Mr. Alward V. Burch, Prin. Asst. Principals: Sr. Marie laReine, I.H.M.; Mr. John J. Gutter; Mr. Richard J. Martin; Rev. Daniel L. Mode, Spiritual Dir.; Mr. Thomas McNichol, Guidance Dir. Priests 1; Sisters 10; Teachers 89; Total Staff 100; Sisters Servants of the Immaculate Heart of Mary 1; Lay Teachers 89; Students 1,457.

ALEXANDRIA. *Bishop Ireton High School*, 201 Cambridge Rd., 22314. Tel: 703-751-7606; Fax: 703-212-8173. (See separate listing for Oblates of St. Francis de Sales Residence). Revs. Kevin M. Nadolski, O.S.F.S., Prin.; Matthew J. Hillyard, O.S.F.S., Chap.; Edward J. Roszko, O.S.F.S., B.A. Oblates of St. Francis de Sales 5; Brothers 1; Sisters 2; Lay Teachers 56; Students 820.

FAIRFAX. *Paul VI High School*, 10675 Lee Hwy., 22030. Tel: 703-352-0925; Fax: 703-273-9845.
E-mail: paulVI@erols.com
Philip V. Robey, Prin. Asst. Principals: Mr. David DiPippa; Mrs. Helen Brewer; Mrs. Marie Powell; Rev. Terry W. Specht, Chap. Lay Teachers 89; Students 1,215.

[E] HIGH SCHOOLS, PRIVATE

MIDDLEBURG.
Notre Dame Academy Inc., 35321 Notre Dame Ln., 20117. Tel: 540-687-5581; Fax: 540-687-3103.
E-mail: nda@mnsinc.com
Web site: www.rc.net/arlington/nda
Sr. Cecilia Liberatore, S.N.D., Head of School. Sisters of Notre Dame 3; Lay Teachers 27; Students 230.

[F] ELEMENTARY SCHOOLS, PRIVATE

BRISTOW. *Linton Hall*, 9535 Linton Hall Rd., 20136. Tel: 703-368-3157; Fax: 703-368-3036.
E-mail: lintonhall@aol.com
Web site: www.intonhall.edu
Robert Manning, Prin. Benedictine Sisters of Virginia 7; Lay Teachers 14; Students 191.

[G] INTERPAROCHIAL SCHOOLS

CULPEPER. *Epiphany School*. (Grades PreK-6), Precious Blood, 114 E. Edmondson St., 22701. Tel: 540-825-9017; Fax: 540-825-8987.
E-mail: pbcc@erols.com
Web site: www.diws.com/epiphany
Sponsoring parishes: Precious Blood, Culpeper; Our Lady of the Blue Ridge, Madison; St. John, Orange; St. Mark, Gordonsville and St. Peter Mission, Washington, VA. Mrs. Barbara Terry, Prin. Lay Teachers 13; Students 149.

FALLS CHURCH. *Corpus Christi School*. (Grades 1-8), 3301 Glen Carlyn Rd., 22041. Tel: 703-820-7450; Fax: 703-820-9635.
E-mail: corpusc@mnsinc.com
Web site: www.corpuschristischool.org
Sponsoring parishes: St. Anthony and St. Philip. Mr. George Chiplock, Prin. Lay Teachers 24; Students 471.

FREDERICKSBURG. *Holy Cross Academy*. (Grades K-8), 250 Stafford Lakes Pkwy., 22406. Tel: 540-286-1600; Fax: 540-286-1625.
E-mail: holycrossacademy@erols.com
Sponsoring parish: St. Mary, Fredericksburg. Sr. Susan Louise Eder, O.S.F.S. Oblate Sisters of St. Francis de Sales 3; Lay Teachers 24; Students 491.

WOODBRIDGE. *Aquinas School*. (Grades K-8), 13750 Mary's Way, 22191. Tel: 703-491-4447; Fax: 703-492-8828.
E-mail: aquinas@erols.com
Sponsoring parishes: Our Lady of Angels, Woodbridge; Holy Family, Dale City; St. Elizabeth Ann Seton, Lake Ridge; and Sacred Heart, Manassas. Sr. Dominie Mary, O.P., Prin. Dominican Sisters, Congregation of St. Cecilia 2; Lay Teachers 21; Students 540.

[H] DAY CARE AND CHILD LEARNING CENTERS

ARLINGTON. *Holy Martyrs of Vietnam Child Enrichment Day Care Center*. (Children 2 1/2-5 years), 915 S. Wakefield St., 22204. Tel: 703-920-1049. Lay Teachers 5; Students 40.

ALEXANDRIA. *Blessed Sacrament Early Childhood Center*. (Grades PreK). (Children 3-5 years), 1417 W. Braddock Rd., 22302. Tel: 703-998-4170; Fax: 703-671-3219.
Web site: www.BlessedSacramentcc.org
Mrs. Valerie Garcia, Coord. Lay Teachers 25; Students 363.

St. Gabriel's. (Children 2-5 years), 4319 Sano St., 22312. Tel: 703-354-0395; Fax: 703-354-0395. Poor Sisters of St. Joseph (Buenos Aires). Sr. Marta Munoz, P.S.S.J., Local Supr. Sisters 6; Students 90.

FALLS CHURCH. *Corpus Christi Early Childhood Center*. (Children 3-5 years), 7506 St. Philip's Ct., 22042. Tel: 703-573-4570. Mr. George Chiplock, Prin.; Mrs. allis Hanley, Dir.; Mrs. Mary Stevens, Daycare Dir. Sponsoring Parishes: St. Anthony and St. Philip. Lay Teachers 8; Students 170.

St. Joseph's Day Nursery & Kindergarten. (Children 2-6 years), 203 N. Spring St., 22046. Tel: 703-533-8441. Servants of St. Joseph (Salamanca, Spain). Sr. Jacinta Salazar, S.S.J., Dir. Sisters 3; Lay Teachers 7; Students 80.

[I] SCHOOLS FOR EXCEPTIONAL CHILDREN

ALEXANDRIA.
Saint Coletta of Greater Washington Inc., 207 S. Peyton St., 22314. Tel: 703-683-3686; Fax: 703-683-9888. Ms. Sharon Raimo, Prin. Private, Non-residential School providing education and vocational training for students and young adults with mental retardation, autism and secondary disabilities ages 4 through 22. Medicaid waivered day program for adults, age 22 and up. Religious 1; Teachers 14; Teacher Aides 48; Speech Pathologists 5; Physical Therapists 3; Occupational Therapists 3; Music Teachers 1; Adaptive Physical Education Instructors 1; LCSW 1; Adult Program Instructors 3; Students 127.

FALLS CHURCH. *Seton Centers, Inc.*, 115 Hillwood Ave., 22046. Tel: 703-533-7670; Fax: 703-533-7678.
E-mail: stnctr@erols.com
Elementary & High School Programs/Services for children with learning disabilities in diocesan schools. Mary K. Doherty, Dir. Teachers 8; Students 100.

[J] MONASTERIES AND RESIDENCES OF PRIESTS AND BROTHERS

ARLINGTON. *Missionary Servants of the Most Holy Trinity, S.T.*, 1215 N. Scott St., 22209-3097. Tel: 703-276-8646; Fax: 703-522-2656.
E-mail: stgeneral@aol.com
Web site: www.mssst.org
Generalate of the Missionary Servants of the Most Holy Trinity. Revs. Austin Walsh, S.T., Gen. Custodian; Jesus Rivera, S.T., Gen. Councilor; Gary Banks, S.T., Gen. Councilor; Bro. Steven Vesely, S.T., Sec. Gen. Legal Titles: *Missionary Servants Charitable Trust.; Father Judge Charitable Trust.*

Missionhurst, C.I.C.M.-Central House and Provincialate, 4651 N. 25th St., 22207. Tel: 703-528-3800; Fax: 703-528-5355.
E-mail: provincial@missionhurst.org
Web site: www.missionhurst.org
Congregation of the Immaculate Heart of Mary foreign and home missions. Legal Titles: *American I.H.M. Province, Inc.; Immaculate Heart Missions, Inc.; Missionhurst, Inc.* Revs. William G. Quigley, C.I.C.M., Prov. Supr.; Joseph Giordano, C.I.C.M., Rector; William Wyndaele, C.I.C.M., Editor of Missionhurst Magazine & Dir. Mission Ctr.; His Eminence Jan Cardinal Schotte, C.I.C.M.; Revs. Howard Picard, C.I.C.M.; Frank Holscher, C.I.C.M.; Roger Van Cauwenbergh, C.I.C.M.; Joseph Dewaele, C.I.C.M.; Jerome Meersman, C.I.C.M.; Charles Denys, C.I.C.M.; Marcel Van Thillo, C.I.C.M.; Robert A. Timperman, C.I.C.M.; Paul DeWolf, C.I.C.M.

ALEXANDRIA. *Oblates of St. Francis de Sales Residence*, 101 Cambridge Rd., 22314. Tel: 703-751-7606; Fax: 703-370-0238. (See separate listing for Bishop Ireton High School regarding staff.). Revs. John W. Crossin, O.S.F.S., Supr.; Charles R. Chamberlain; Matthew J. Hillyard; Kevin Nadolski; Edward J. Roszko, O.S.F.S.

BERRYVILLE. *Cistercian Abbey of Our Lady of the Holy Cross*, Rte. 2, Box 3870, 22611-9526. Tel: 540-955-1425; Fax: 540-955-1356.
E-mail: HolyCross@shentel.net
Web site: www.MonasteryFruitcake.org
Order of Cistercians of the Strict Observance (Trappist). Rt. Revs. Robert T. Barnes, O.C.S.O., Abbot; Flavian Burns, O.C.S.O., Retired Abbot & Chap., Our Lady of the Angels, Crozet; Edward McCorkell, O.C.S.O., Retired Abbot; Mark Delery, O.C.S.O., Retreat House Counsellor & Retired Abbot; Revs. Edmund Flynn, O.C.S.O., Treas.; Paschal Balkan, O.C.S.O.; Andrew Gries, O.C.S.O.; Vincent Collins, O.C.S.O.; Maurice Flood, O.C.S.O.; Joseph Wittstock, O.C.S.O., Prior; James Orthmann, O.C.S.O., Novice Master & Vocation Dir.; Malachy Marrion, O.C.S.O.; Bro. Stephen Maguire, O.C.S.O., Guest Master. Community 25; Residents 23; Priests 12; Solemnly Professed Non-priest Monks 10; Novices 2; Temporarily Professed 1.

WHITE POST. *Sacred Heart Friary*, P.O. Drawer B, 22663. Tel: 540-869-1599; Fax: 540-869-0106. Third Order Regular of St. Francis. Revs. Aidan Mullaney, T.O.R., Local Min.; Marion Deck, T.O.R.; Francis McKinney, T.O.R.; Christopher Petrosky, T.O.R.; James Cleary, T.O.R.; Jude Ventiquattro, T.O.R.; Canice Crawford, T.O.R.; Fabian McNichol, T.O.R.; Theodore Midile, T.O.R.; Bros. Bernard Nicolosi, T.O.R., Vicar; Stephen Liebal, T.O.R.; Norman McNelis, T.O.R.; John Carosella, T.O.R. Professed Brothers 3.

[K] CONVENTS AND RESIDENCES FOR SISTERS

ARLINGTON. *Religious of the Sacred Heart of Mary*, 2807 N. Glebe Rd., 22207-4299. Tel: 703-284-1495; Fax: 703-284-1685.
E-mail: sister.bloomingdale@marymount.edu.
Web site: www.rshm.org
Sr. Mary Louise Bloomingdale, R.S.H.M., Coord. Sisters 11.

Sisters Servants of the Immaculate Heart of Mary, 6600 Little Falls Rd., 22213. Tel: 703-237-1410.
E-mail: SCVOD@yahoo.com
Sr. Christine Virginia O'Donnell, I.H.M., Supr.; Sr. St. Kathleen Blaston; Sr. Charles Borromeo Harvey; Sr. Claudine Hagerty; Sr. Marie la Reine Spain; Sr. Mary Joanne McKelvey; Sr. Clare Dolores McFadden; Sr. Maureen Chistopher Dusterhoff; Sr. Rose Lawrence Harlan; Sr. Elizabeth Ann Goltman; Sr. Janice Urbanec; Sr. Patricia McCormack; Sr. Marie Diane Mollica; Sr. Regina Joseph Ryan; Sr. Ruth Bolarte. Sisters 15.

ALEXANDRIA. *Poor Clare Monastery of Mary, Mother of the Church*, 2505 Stonehedge Dr., 22306. Tel: 703-768-4918; Fax: 703-765-2985. Observing the Primitive Rule of St. Clare. Solemnly Professed 13; Junior Professed 2; Novices 2; Postulants 1.

St. Gabriel Convent, 4319 Sano St., 22312. Tel: 703-354-0395; Fax: 703-354-0395. Mother Maria Dolores Gonzalez, P.S.S.J., Delegate Gen.; Sr. Marta Munoz, P.S.S.J., Local Supr. Poor Sisters of St. Joseph's Buenos Aires Regional House and Novitiate 6.

Sisters of the Holy Cross, 5582 First Statesman Ln., 22312. Tel: 703-658-9519. Legal Title: *Sisters of the Holy Cross, Inc.* Sisters 2.

BRISTOW. *St. Benedict Monastery*, Benedictine Pastoral Center, 9535 Linton Hall Rd., 20136-1217. Tel: 703-361-0106; Fax: 703-361-0254.
E-mail: osbva@erols.com
Sr. Andrea Verchuck, O.S.B., Prioress. Tel: 703-368-4848. B.E.A.C.O.N.: Benedictine Educational Assistance Community Outreach to Neighbors. Professed Sisters 38; Sisters in Temporary Commitment 2; Sisters Resident at Motherhouse 33.

FAIRFAX. *Adorers of the Holy Cross*, 10917 Marilta Ct., 22030. Tel: 703-591-0862; Fax: 703-591-0862. Sr. Mary Nguyen Thi Trinh, M.T.G., Supr.

FALLS CHURCH. *Holy Family House Convent, S.S.J.*, 3438 Charles St., 22041. Tel: 703-820-9785. Sisters 3.

Servants of St. Joseph Convent, 203 N. Spring St., 22046. Tel: 703-533-8441; Fax: 703-538-5165. Sr. Augustina Temprano, S.S.J., Supr. Tel: 703-534-9549; Sr. Prudencia Gonzalo, S.S.J.; Sr. Josefina Laguno, S.S.J.; Sr. Jacinta Salazar, S.S.J.; Sr. Filomena Gajate, S.S.J. Sisters 5.

FRONT ROYAL. *Pax Christi Institute*, 118 Jamestown Rd., 22630. Tel: 540-635-7690; Fax: 540-635-9139.
E-mail: pax@rma.edu
Sr. Teresa Diaz, P.C.I., Supr. Sisters 6.

WOODBRIDGE. *Dominican Sisters Convent.* (Congregation of St. Cecilia), 2655 Falmouth Ct., 22192. Tel: 703-494-4488; Fax: 703-491-4407.
E-mail: aquinasconvent@starpower.net
Dominican Sisters. Sr. Henry-Suso, O.P., Supr. Sisters 3.

[L] RETREAT HOUSES

BERRYVILLE. *Retreat House, Holy Cross Abbey*, Rte. 2, Box 3870, 22611. Tel: 540-955-3124; Fax: 540-955-1356. Retreat Masters: Rt. Rev. Mark Delery, O.C.S.O., Retreat Dir.; Bro. Stephen Maguire, O.C.S.O., Guest Master.

MCLEAN. *Dominican Retreat House*. Accommodations for 41 persons. 7103 Old Dominion Dr., 22101-2799. Tel: 703-356-4243; Fax: 703-893-4502. Dominican Sisters of St. Catherine De Ricci. Sisters 4.

[M] CAMPUS MINISTRY

ARLINGTON. *Marymount University*. Campus Ministry, 2807 N. Glebe Rd., 22207. Tel: 703-284-1607; Fax: 703-284-3850.
E-mail: fatherkevin@marymount.edu
Web site: www.marymount.edu
Rev. Kevin B. Walsh, Chap. & Dir. Campus Ministry.

FAIRFAX. *George Mason University, Catholic Campus Ministry House*, 4521 Roberts Rd., 22032. Tel: 703-425-0022; Fax: 703-425-0753.
E-mail: pnassett@gmu.edu
Web site: www.gmu/org/ccm
Rev. Peter W. Nassetta, Chap. & Dir. Campus Ministry.

St. Robert Bellarmine Chapel. Catholic Campus Ministry. George Mason University, 4515 Roberts Rd., 22032. Tel: 703-425-0022; Fax: 703-425-0753. Rev. Peter W. Nassetta; Ms. Nora Collins, Assoc. Campus Min.

FREDERICKSBURG. *Mary-Washington College*, 1614 College Ave., 22401. Tel: 540-373-6746; Fax: 540-373-4875.
E-mail: FatherJ@mwc.edu
Rev. John P. Peterson, Chap.

[N] MISCELLANEOUS

ARLINGTON. *Youth Apostles Institute, An Association of Christian Faithful.* 1600 Carlin Ln., McLean, 22101-4100. Tel: 703-556-0914; Fax: 703-556-9455.
E-mail: yas@erols.com
Web site: www.youthapostles.org

ALEXANDRIA. *St. Paul Books & Media Center (Daughters of St. Paul)*, 1025 King St., 22314. Tel: 703-549-3806; 683-1741 (Convent); Fax: 703-683-2568.
E-mail: alexandria@pauline.org
Web site: www.pauline.org
Sr. Mary Lea Hill, F.S.P. An international congregation of women religious who serve the church with the communications media.

BROAD RUN. *National Association of Catholic Home Educators (NACHE)*, 6102 Saints Hill Ln., 20137. Tel: 540-349-4314; Fax: 540-347-7345.
E-mail: lpayne@cts.com
Web site: www.nache.org
Mr. Bill Bales, Pres.

FALLS CHURCH. *Cardinal Newman Society*, 207 Park Ave., Ste. B-2, 22046. Tel: 703-536-9585; Fax: 703-532-3094.
E-mail: cardnewman@erols.com
Web site: www.newmansociety.org
Patrick J. Reilly, Exec. Dir.

FRONT ROYAL. *Seton Home Study School*, 1350 Progress Dr., 22630. Tel: 540-636-9990; Fax: 540-636-1602.
E-mail: info@setonhome.org
Web site: www.setonhome.org
Dr. Mary K. Clark, Dir.

SPOTSYLVANIA. *St. Francis Catholic Worker West*, 9631 Peppertree Rd., 22553. Tel: 540-972-3218. Mr. John Mahoney. Total in Residence 2.

STAFFORD. *American Life League, Inc.*, P.O. Box 1350, 22555. Tel: 540-659-4171; Fax: 540-659-2586.
E-mail: jbrown@all.org
Web site: www.all.org
Mrs. Judie Brown, Pres.

VIENNA. *Mount Tabor Society, Inc.*, 2363 Hunter Mill Rd., 22181. Tel: 703-938-2564. A House of Prayer and Christian Community. Rev. Paul G. Wynants, C.I.C.M., Dir.

WOODBRIDGE. *Apostolate for Family Consecration*, St. Damien Center, 1410 Harrison St., 22191-2215. Tel: 703-491-6544. Jerome F. Coniker, Exec. Dir.

RELIGIOUS INSTITUTES OF MEN REPRESENTED IN THE DIOCESE

For further details refer to the corresponding bracketed number in the Religious Institutes of Men or Women section.

[1350]—*Brothers of St. Francis Xavier.*—C.F.X.
[0350]—*Cistercians Order of the Strict Observance.* (Trappists).—O.C.S.O.
[0520]—*Franciscan Friars.* (Holy Name Prov.).—O.F.M.
[0530]—*Franciscan Friars of the Atonement.*—S.A.
[0650]—*Holy Ghost Fathers.*—C.S.Sp.
[0840]—*Missionary Servants of the Most Holy Trinity.*—S.T.
[0860]—*Missionhurst Congregation of the Immaculate Heart of Mary.*—C.I.C.M.
[0920]—*Oblates of St. Francis de Sales.* (Wilmington-Philadelphia Prov.).—O.S.F.S.
[0700]—*St. Joseph's Society of the Sacred Heart.* (Baltimore, MD).—S.S.J.
[0560]—*Third Order Regular of Saint Francis.* (Sacred Heart Prov.).—T.O.R.
[]—*Vietnamese Dominican Fathers.* (Calgary, Alberta, Canada).—O.P.

RELIGIOUS INSTITUTES OF WOMEN REPRESENTED IN THE DIOCESE

[4155]—*Adorers of the Holy Cross.*—M.T.G.
[0230]—*Benedictine Sisters of Virginia.*—O.S.B.
[3110]—*Congregation of Our Lady of the Retreat in the Cenacle.*—R.C.
[1920]—*Congregation of the Sisters of the Holy Cross.*—C.S.C.
[0760]—*Daughters of Charity of St. Vincent de Paul.* (Emmitsburg Province).—D.C.
[0960]—*Daughters of Wisdom.*—D.W.
[1070-17]—*Dominican Sisters Congregation of St. Catherine deRicci.*—O.P.
[1070-07]—*Dominican Sisters Congregation of St. Cecilia.*—O.P.
[1365]—*Franciscan Missionary Sisters of the Infant Jesus.*—F.M.I.J.
[1880]—*Handmaidens of Reparation of the Sacred Heart of Jesus.*—A.R.
[3060]—*Oblate Sisters of St. Francis de Sales.*—O.S.F.S.
[3760]—*Order of St. Clare (Cloistered).*—P.C.C.
[]—*Pax Christi Institute.* (Corpus Christi, TX).—P.C.I.
[0950]—*Pious Society of Daughters of St. Paul.*—F.S.P.
[3250]—*Poor Sisters of St. Joseph.*—P.S.S.J.
[3465]—*Religious of the Sacred Heart of Mary.* (Eastern North Amer. Prov.).—R.S.H.M.
[2970]—*School Sisters of Notre Dame.*—S.S.N.D.
[3595]—*Servants of St. Joseph.* (Salamanca, Spain).—S.S.J.
[2990]—*Sisters of Notre Dame.*—S.N.D.
[3893]—*Sisters of St. Joseph of Chestnut Hill* . (Philadelphia).—S.S.J.
[2170]—*Sisters, Servants of the Immaculate Heart of Mary.*—I.H.M.

NECROLOGY

† Kollar, Edmund V., (Retired). —Died Aug. 1, 2000.
† Snella, Adolp A., (Retired). —Died May 4, 2000.

Archdiocese of Atlanta

(Archidioecesis Atlantensis)

Most Reverend

JOHN FRANCIS DONOGHUE, D.D.

Archbishop of Atlanta; ordained June 4, 1955; appointed Bishop of Charlotte November 6, 1984; appointed Archbishop of Atlanta June 22, 1993; installed August 18, 1993.

Catholic Center Archdiocese of Atlanta: 680 W. Peachtree St., N.W., Atlanta, GA, 30308. Tel.: 404-888-7802; Fax: 404-885-7494.

Web site address: www.archatl.com/

ESTABLISHED JULY 2, 1956.

CANONICALLY ERECTED NOVEMBER 8, 1956; CREATED AN ARCHDIOCESE FEBRUARY 21, 1962.

Square Miles 21,445.

Comprises the 69 Counties in the northern part of the State of Georgia, north of and including the following counties: Lincoln, McDuffie, Warren, Hancock, Baldwin, Putnam, Jasper, Monroe, Upson, Meriwether and Troup.

PATRONS OF THE ARCHDIOCESE: I. Our Blessed Lady under the title of the Immaculate Heart of Mary; II. Saint Pius X.

For legal titles of parishes and archdiocesan institutions, consult the Archbishop's Office.

STATISTICAL OVERVIEW

Personnel	
Archbishop	1
Abbots	1
Retired Abbots	2
Priests: Diocesan Active in Diocese	127
Priests: Active Outside Diocese	10
Priests: Diocesan in Foreign Missions	1
Priests: Retired, Sick or Absent	8
Number of Diocesan Priests	146
Religious Priests in Diocese	70
Extern Priests in Diocese	11
Ordinations:	
Diocesan Priests	12
Transitional Deacons	6
Permanent Deacons in Diocese	137
Total Brothers	1
Total Sisters	119
Parishes	
Parishes	77
With Resident Pastor:	
Resident Diocesan Priests	62
Resident Religious Priests	15
Without Resident Pastor:	
Administered by Priests	1
Administered by Pastoral Teams, etc.	5
Missions	21
Pastoral Centers	1
New Parishes Created	2
Professional Ministry Personnel:	
Brothers	1
Sisters	21
Lay Ministers	119
Welfare	
Catholic Hospitals	2
Total Assisted	244,723
Health Care Centers	2
Total Assisted	20,176
Homes for the Aged	5
Total Assisted	275
Specialized Homes	1
Total Assisted	106
Special Centers for Social Services	33
Total Assisted	40,000
Educational	
Diocesan Students in Other Seminaries	55
Total Seminarians	55
High Schools, Diocesan and Parish	3
Total Students	1,479
High Schools, Private	1
Total Students	1,028
Elementary Schools, Diocesan and Parish	15
Total Students	5,309
Elementary Schools, Private	2
Total Students	860
Catechesis/Religious Education:	
High School Students	5,942
Elementary Students	27,216
Total Students Under Catholic Instruction	41,889
Teachers in the Diocese:	
Priests	12
Brothers	2
Sisters	2
Lay Teachers	412
Vital Statistics	
Receptions into the Church:	
Infant Baptism Totals	7,865
Adult Baptism Totals	617
Received into Full Communion	1,192
First Communions	5,211
Confirmations	3,701
Marriages:	
Catholic	1,079
Interfaith	853
Total Marriages	1,932
Deaths	975
Total Catholic Population	250,999
Total Population	5,241,325

Former Bishops—Most Rev. FRANCIS E. HYLAND, D.D., J.C.D., appt. Titular Bishop of Gomphi and Auxiliary Bishop of Savannah-Atlanta, Oct. 15, 1949; cons. Dec. 21, 1949; First Bishop of Atlanta, July 17, 1956; installed on Nov. 8, 1956; resigned and appointed Titular Bishop of Bisica, Oct. 11, 1961; died Jan. 31, 1968.—Most Rev. PAUL J. HALLINAN, D.D., appt. Bishop of Charleston, Sept. 9, 1958; cons. Oct. 28, 1958; elevated to the Archiepiscopal dignity, Feb. 21, 1962; installed First Archbishop of Atlanta, March 29, 1962; died March 27, 1968.—Most Rev. JOSEPH L. BERNARDIN, D.D., appt. Auxiliary of Atlanta, March 9, 1966; cons. April 26, 1966; appt. Gen. Sec. U.S.C.C., April 5, 1968.—Most Rev. THOMAS A. DONNELLAN, appt. Bishop of Ogdensburg, March 4, 1964; cons. April 9, 1964; appt. to Atlanta, May 29, 1968; installed July 16, 1968; died Oct. 15, 1987.—Most Rev. EUGENE A. MARINO, S.S.J., D.D., appt. Auxiliary of Washington, July 15, 1974; appt. Archbishop of Atlanta, March 14, 1988; installed May 5, 1988; resigned July 10, 1990; died Nov. 12, 2000.—Most Rev. JAMES P. LYKE, O.F.M., Ph.D., appt. Auxiliary Bishop of Cleveland and Titular Bishop of Fornos Maggiore, June 30, 1979; cons. Aug. 1, 1979; appt. Apostolic Administrator Archdiocese of Atlanta, July 10, 1990; appt. Archbishop of Archdiocese of Atlanta, April 30, 1991; installed June 24, 1991 Palium conferred June 29, 1991; died Dec. 27, 1992.

Moderator of Religious—Sr. MARY PRINISKI, O.P., *235 E. Ponce de Leon Ave., Ste. 226, Decatur, 30030.*

Vicar for Clergy—Rev. Msgr. HENRY C. GRACZ.

Associate Vicar for Clergy—Rev. RICHARD MORROW.

Archdiocesan Offices and Directors

Catholic Center Archdiocese of Atlanta—680 W. Peachtree St., N.W., Atlanta, 30308.

Catholic Information—Tel: 404-888-7801.

Archbishop's Office—Tel: 404-888-7804; Fax: 404-885-7230.

Vicars General—Rev. Msgr. R. DONALD KIERNAN, Pastoral Ministries; Very Rev. PAUL H. REYNOLDS, Curia.

Chancellor—Rev. DAVID P. TALLEY. Tel: 404-888-7844.

Director of Operations—BETTI KNOTT. Tel: 404-888-7804.

Secretariat for Finance & Administration—Tel: 404-888-7808. MICHAEL J. MCNAMARA, Sec. & Chief Financial Officer.

Secretariat for Education—Tel: 404-888-7833; 7835. DONAL T. SASSO, Sec. Education.

Continuing Education in Ministry—Rev. JAMES A. SCHILLINGER. Tel: 404-636-7237.

Secretariat for Catholic Charities—JAMES E. KANTNER, Ph.D. Tel: 404-881-6571. See separate listing for detailed information.

Office for Black Catholic Ministry—Tel: 404-888-7848; Fax: 404-885-7494. CHARLES PREJEAN, Dept. Head (Secretariat Supvr. & Operations).

Office Of Communications—Tel: 404-888-7832; Fax: 404-888-7849. KATHI STEARNS.

"The Georgia Bulletin"—KATHI STEARNS, Asst. Publisher; GRETCHEN KEISER, Editor.

Media Relations—KATHI STEARNS. Tel: 404-888-7805; Fax: 404-885-7230.

Metropolitan Tribunal—Tel: 404-888-7815.

Judicial Vicar—Rev. Msgr. LOUIS NAUGHTON, J.C.L., S.T.B., M.A.

Director—KIM M. DANIEL.

Court Administrator—Deacon WHITNEY F. ROBICHAUX, B.S., M.A., M.P.S.

Auditors—Rev. RICHARD A. ZIVIC, M.Div., J.C.L. (Cand.); Sr. FRANCES WHITMAN, G.N.S.H., M.A.

Archdiocesan Judges—Rev. STEPHEN T. CHURCHWELL, J.C.D., M.Div.; Rev. Msgr. EDWARD J. DILLON, J.C.D.; Revs. DAVID P. TALLEY, J.C.D., M.Div., B.A., M.S.W.; TIMOTHY A. GADZIALA, M.A., M.Div., J.C.L. (Cand.).

Defender of the Bond—Rev. MICHAEL ONYEKURU, J.C.L.; ROBERT J. KAMPINE, J.C.L., S.T.B., B.A.; ROBERT G. WESSELMANN, J.C.L., S.T.L.

Notaries—WENDY A. ABRAHAM; MARGARITA RICE, B.A.; TERRY B. BROWN; JEAN M. SMITH; SARAH J. ENGE.

Court of Appeals-Province of Atlanta—Tel: 404-888-7813; Fax: 404-885-7494.

Judicial Vicar—Very Rev. PAUL J. HACHEY, S.M., J.C.L.

Administrator—Sr. MARIE BREITENBECK, O.P., J.C.D.

Defenders of the Bond—Rev. Msgr. PETER A. DORA, M.Div.; Revs. JOHN R. HENLEY, M.Div.; DANIEL J. MCCORMICK, B.A.; LUIS ZARAMA, J.C.L.

Judges—Sr. MARIE BREITENBECK, O.P. J.C.D.; Revs. GREGORY D. GOOLSBY, M.Div., J.D.; ALBERT W. JOWDY, M.Div.; Rev. Msgr. R. DONALD KIERNAN, P.A., D.P.A., Ph.D.; Very Rev. JAMES A. MICELI, M.Div.; Rev. RICHARD B. MORROW, B.A.; Very Rev. PAUL H. REYNOLDS; Rev. JAMES A. SCHILLINGER, S.T.L.

Notary—DOROTHY WESSELMANN, M.S.Ed.

Promoter of Justice—Rev. DANIEL J. MCCORMICK, B.A.

Office of Vocations—Rev. DAVID P. TALLEY, Dir. Tel: 404-888-7844.

Vice Chancellor - Special Projects—KATHI STEARNS.

Office for Permanent Diaconate—Deacons ALFRED MITCHELL, Dir. LORIS SINANIAN, Dir. of Formation; Rev. DAVID P. TALLEY.

Office for Pro-Life—MARY BOYERT, Dir. (Secretariat Supvr. & Operations).

Office of Family Concerns—Tel: 404-888-7819. MARY ELLEN HUGHES, Dir. (Secretariat Supvr./Catholic Charities).

Office of Hispanic Apostolate—Tel: 404-888-7839. GONZALO SALDANA, Dir. (Chancery).

Development Office—

Director—ANSLEY DAVIS, Dir. (Secretariat Supvr. & Oper.). Tel: 404-888-7802.

Director of the Archdiocesan Annual Appeal and Archdiocesan Stewardship—ANSLEY DAVIS.

Archives—Mrs. AMIE BRITTON, Dir. (Chancery). Tel: 404-888-7802.

Other Archdiocesan Offices

AACCW—JOANN RIEGER, *1430 Woodcraft Dr., Roswell, 30075.* Tel: 770-992-7085. Rev. PAUL W. BERNY, Spiritual Moderator. Tel: 770-992-7085.

Apostleship of Prayer—Rev. VINCENT R. MALATESTA, S.J., *Ignatius House, 6700 Riverside Dr., N.W., Atlanta, 30328.* Tel: 404-255-0503.

Girl and Boy Scouts—Deacon BRUCE C. PUBLICOVER, *P.O. Box 78, Woodstock, 30188.* Tel: 770-591-9200.

Cana Conferences—MARY ELLEN HUGHES, *680 W. Peachtree St., N.W., Atlanta, 30308.* Tel: 404-888-7819.

Consultors—Rev. Msgr. R. DONALD KIERNAN; Very Rev. PAUL H. REYNOLDS,Very Rev. Deans and Vicar for Clergy, Presbyteral Council Pres. & Chancellor.

Cursillo—Sr. MARGARET MCANOY, I.H.M., Dir., *3731 Embry Circle, Atlanta, 30341.* Tel: 770-455-1500.

Deans—Very Rev. JAMES J. FENNESSY, V.F., Northeast Metro; Very Rev. JAMES D. CAFFERY, M.S., Northwest Metro; Very Rev. RICHARD P. WISE, V.F., South Metro; Very Rev. DANIEL STACK, V.F., Northeast Rural; Very Rev. WILLIAM G. HOFFMAN, V.F., Northwest Rural; Very Rev. LEO P. HERBERT, V.F., South Rural.

Georgia Catholic Conference—CHEATHAM E. HODGES, JR., Exec. Sec., *Office Bldg., 3200 Deans Bridge Rd., Augusta, 30906.* Tel: 706-798-1719.

Campus Ministry—Mr. LLOYD SUTTER, *680 W. Peachtree St., N.W., Atlanta, 30308.* Tel: 404-888-7804.

Council of Priests—Rev. JAMES A. SCHILLINGER, Pres., *Catholic Center at Emory University, 1753 N. Decatur Rd., N.E., Atlanta, 30307.* Tel: 404-636-7237.

Atlanta Conference of Sisters—Sr. MARY PRINISKI, O.P., Pres., *978 Eden Ave., S.E., Atlanta, 30316.*

Archdiocesan Councils, Boards, Commissions, and Committees

Boards—

Education—DONALD SASSO, Sec., *680 W. Peachtree St., N.W., Atlanta, 30308.* Tel: 404-888-7833; 7835.

Catholic Charities—JAMES E. KANTNER, Ph.D., Sec., *680 W. Peachtree St., N.W., Atlanta, 30308.* Tel: 404-881-6571.

Clergy Retirement—Rev. Msgr. R. DONALD KIERNAN, P.A., *2443 Mt. Vernon Rd., Dunwoody, 30338.* Tel: 404-393-3255.

Commissions—

Liturgical—Rev. Msgr. LOUIS NAUGHTON, Sec., *680 W. Peachtree St., N.W., Atlanta, 30308.* Tel: 404-888-7815.

CLERGY, PARISHES, MISSIONS AND PAROCHIAL SCHOOLS

CITY OF ATLANTA
(Fulton County)

1—CATHEDRAL OF CHRIST THE KING (1936), Rev. Msgr. Thomas Kenny, Rector; Revs. Richard B. Morrow, (Retired); Brian J. Higgins; Fabio Sotelo-Pena; Thony R. Jean; Deacons Whitney Robichaux; Harold Gourgues. In res., Rev. Msgr. Louis Naughton.
Res., 2699 Peachtree Rd., N.E., 30305. Tel: 404-233-2145; 233-0524; Fax: 404-233-9711.
School—46 Peachtree Way, 30305. Tel: 404-233-0383; Fax: 404-266-0704. Mrs. Peggy Warner, Prin.
Lay Teachers 39; Students 564.
Catechesis/Religious Programs—Tel: 404-267-3694; Fax: 404-233-4984.
Students 530.

2—HOLY CROSS (1964), Revs. Paul Fogarty; Alvaro D. Avendano; Peter Duc Vu; Darragh Griffith; Deacons Lou Hettel; Sam Mure; Cece Reimer; Dick Suever; Tom Silvestri.
Res., 3175 Hathaway Ct., 30341. Tel: 770-939-3501; Fax: 770-723-7013.
Catechesis/Religious Programs—Tel: 770-934-5757. Barbara Mancuso, D.R.E.
Students 620.

3—HOLY SPIRIT (1964), Rev. Msgr. Edward J. Dillon; Rev. Victor A. Galier; Deacon Thomas Shuler. In res., Revs. Paul Burke; John C.K. Fallon.
Church & Res.: 4465 Northside Dr., N.W., 30327. Tel: 404-252-4513; Fax: 404-252-1162.
Catechesis/Religious Programs—Tel: 404-252-2764.
Students 457.

4—IMMACULATE HEART OF MARY (1958), Revs. Alfred W. Wendel; James H. Sexstone; Jose Refugio Onate-Melendez; Deacons James Stewart; Thomas McGrane. In res., Rev. Carlos E. Garcia-Carreras, S.J.
Res., 2855 Briarcliff Rd., N.E., 30329. Tel: 404-636-1418; Fax: 404-636-4394.
School—Tel: 404-636-4488; Fax: 404-636-1853. Karen Russ, Prin.
Lay Teachers 36; Students 500.
Catechesis/Religious Programs—Tel: 404-321-3175; Fax: 404-321-0071. Sr. Marietta Jansen, A.C.J., D.R.E.
Students 320.
Mission—Doraville, Dekalb Co., Our Lady of the Americas, 5918 New Peachtree Rd., Doraville, 30340. Tel: 770-454-8437; Fax: 770-454-4885. Rev. Richard K. Young.

5—MOST BLESSED SACRAMENT (1960), Rev. Bruce W. Wilkinson. In res., Rev. Raymond F. Horan.
Church and Mailing Address: 2971 Butner Rd., S.W., 30331. Tel: 404-349-0176; Fax: 404-349-0178.
Res., 1926 Austin Rd., 30331. Tel: 404-349-1406.
Catechesis/Religious Programs—Students 45.

6—OUR LADY OF THE ASSUMPTION (1951), Revs. James F. McGoldrick, S.M.; James D. Duffy, S.M.; Deacons Bill Bevacqua; Robert Gresher; Michael O'Brien; William Pond; John Shell.
Office: 1350 Hearst Dr., N.E., 30319. Tel: 404-261-7181; Fax: 404-364-1913.
Res., 1406 Hearst Dr., N.E., 30319. Tel: 404-365-0508; 365-0510.
School—1320 Hearst Dr., N.E., 30319. Tel: 404-364-1902; Fax: 404-364-1914. Mrs. Joan Tiernan, Prin.
Lay Teachers 36; Students 490.
Catechesis/Religious Programs—Fax: 404-364-1913.
Students 115.
Chapels—Marist School, Tel: 404-457-7201; Fax: 404-457-8402; St. Joseph's Hospital, Tel: 404-851-7001; Fax: 404-851-5901; Sisters of Mercy Convent at St. Joseph's Hospital, Tel: 404-255-6427.

7—OUR LADY OF LOURDES (1912), Rev. John S. Adamski.
Res., 25 Boulevard, N.E., 30312. Tel: 404-522-6776; Fax: 404-222-0202.
School—29 Boulevard, N.E., 30312. Tel: 404-581-0643; Fax: 404-581-0707.
Lay Teachers 17; Students 118.
Catechesis/Religious Programs—Students 80.

8—SACRED HEART OF JESUS (1880), Revs. Stephen T. Churchwell; Craig David; Deacons Wayne D. Smith; Enrique Galvis. In res., Rev. Msgr. Walter J. Donovan, (Retired); Revs. Richard A. Zivic; Jose Duvan Gonzalez-Florez.
Res., 353 Peachtree St., N.E., 30308. Tel: 404-522-6800; Fax: 404-524-5440.
Catechesis/Religious Programs—Tel: 404-522-6800.
Students 256.
Mission—Atlanta, Fulton Co., San Felipe de Jesus, 402 McDonough Blvd., S.E., 30315. Tel: 404-627-0821.

9—ST. ANTHONY OF PADUA (1903) (African American), Rev. Thomas J. Meehan; Deacon Joseph Barker.
Res., 928 Ralph David Abernathy Blvd., S.W., 30310. Tel: 404-758-8861; Fax: 404-755-6755.
School—953 Ralph David Abernathy Blvd., S.W., 30310. Tel: 404-755-8869; Fax: 404-755-8871.
Lay Teachers 17; Students 95.
Catechesis/Religious Programs—Tel: 404-753-0787; Fax: 404-755-6755.
Students 133.

10—ST. JUDE (1960), Rev. Msgr. Daniel J. O'Connor; Revs. Pedro Poloche-Rodriguez; Robert A. Frederick, Jr. In res., Rev. Gabriel Byong-Young Je, S.J.
Res., 7171 Glenridge Dr. N.E., 30328. Tel: 770-394-3896; Fax: 770-399-7866.
School—Tel: 770-394-2880; Fax: 770-804-9248.
Lay Teachers 50; Students 498.
Catechesis/Religious Programs—Tel: 770-394-4588; Fax: 770-804-2733.
Students 250.

11—ST. PAUL OF THE CROSS (1954) (African American), Rev. Melvin Shorter, C.P.; Deacons Joseph P. Goolsby; Hilliard M. Lee, Jr.; Benjamin Petty, (Retired). In res., Rev. Joseph A. Fahy, C.P.
Res., 551 Harwell Rd. N.W., 30318. Tel: 404-696-6704; Fax: 404-696-4735.
Catechesis/Religious Programs—Students 77.

12—SHRINE OF THE IMMACULATE CONCEPTION (1848), Revs. Joseph J. Chaloux; Michael Campbell; Deacon William Payne.
Res., 48 Martin Luther King, Jr. Dr., S.W., 30303-3599. Tel: 404-521-1866.

OUTSIDE CITY OF ATLANTA

Alpharetta, Fulton Co., St. Brigid, Rev. W. Joseph Corbett.
3400 Old Alabama Rd., 30022. Tel: 678-393-0060; Fax: 678-393-0071.

St. Thomas Aquinas (1972), Revs. Albert W. Jowdy; Daniel J. Fleming; Jesus D. Trujillo-Luna; Deacons William W. Keeling; Edmund LaHouse; Donald N. Nadeau; John Strachan.
Res., 535 Rucker Rd., 30004. Tel: 770-475-4501; Fax: 770-772-0355.
Catechesis/Religious Programs—Tel: 770-475-4508.
Students 2,394.

Athens, Clarke Co., St. Joseph's (1873), Revs. Victor J. Reyes; Joy Nellissery; Deacons Don Marchildon; Bill Lakin; Jim Gaudin.
Res., 134 Prince Ave., 30601. Tel: 706-548-6332; Fax: 706-354-1783.
School—Tel: 706-543-1621; Fax: 706-543-0149. Sr. Mary Glackin, Prin.
Servants of the Immaculate Heart of Mary 4; Missionary Sisters of the Sacred Heart 5; Lay Teachers 29; Students 387.
Catechesis/Religious Programs—Tel: 706-548-5487; Fax: 706-548-5487.
Students 463.
Chapels—St. Mary's Hospital, Tel: 706-548-7581; Fax: 706-355-7274; Catholic Student Center at The University of Georgia, Tel: 706-543-2293; Fax: 706-543-2541. Rev. John McDowell, O.F.M.

Blairsville, Union Co., St. Francis of Assisi (1966), Rev. Balappa Selvaraj; Deacons Lawrence Casey; William Diehl; Loris Sinanian.
Res., 2839 Young Harris Hwy., 30512. Tel: 706-745-6400; Fax: 706-745-1468. [CEM]
Catechesis/Religious Programs—Tel: 706-781-3671.
Students 37.
Mission—Cleveland, White Co., St. Paul the Apostle, 1397 Helen Hwy., Cleveland, 30528. Tel: 706-865-4474; Fax: 706-219-3009.

Blue Ridge, Fannin Co., St. Anthony's (1976), Rev. Christopher Williamson; Deacon John Stanley.
Res., 967 E. Main St., P.O. Box 1448, 30513. Tel: 706-632-5970; Fax: 706-632-2120. [CEM]
Catechesis/Religious Programs—Students 13.
Mission—Ellijay, Gilmer Co., Good Samaritan, (1982) 25 Church St., Ellijay, 30540. Tel: 706-636-2772.

Buford, Gwinnett Co., Prince of Peace (1978), Revs. John R. Anderson; Sergio M. Calle-Perez; Deacons Michael R. Jones; William Speed.
Mailing Address: 4300 S. Lee St., 30618. Tel: 770-945-2244 (Office); 945-0200 (Rectory); Fax: 770-945-4599.
Res., 4300 S. Lee St., 30518. Tel: 770-945-0200.
Catechesis/Religious Programs—Students 733.

Calhoun, Gordon Co., St. Clements (1958) (Spanish), Rev. Thad B. Rudd, Admin.
Mailing Address: 875 Hwy. 53 W., 30701. Tel: 706-629-2345; Fax: 706-625-5219.
Catechesis/Religious Programs—Students 72.

Canton, Cherokee Co., Our Lady of LaSalette (1984), Revs. Neil G. Jones, M.S.; Denis Kolumber, M.S.
Mailing Address: P.O.Box 1146, 30114.
Res., 2942 Sam Nelson Rd., P.O. Box 1146, 30114. Tel: 770-479-8923; Fax: 770-479-8923.
Catechesis/Religious Programs—Students 204.
Mission—Jasper, Pickens Co., Our Lady of the Mountains, Hwy. 108 & Refuge Rd., P.O. Box 1146, Canton, 30114. Tel: 706-692-3078.

Carrollton, Carroll Co., Church of Our Lady of Perpetual Help (1962), Rev. John P. Farrelly; Deacon David Higgins.
Res., 210 Old Center Point Rd., 30117. Tel: 770-832-8977; Fax: 770-832-1666. [CEM]
Newman Center West Georgia College—Rev. John P. Farrely, Catholic Campus Min.
Catechesis/Religious Programs—Students 250.

Cartersville, Bartow Co., St. Francis of Assisi (1969), Bro. Robert Russell, M.S., Admin.
Res., 57 Pine Grove Rd., P.O. Box 2048, 30120. Tel: 770-386-7811; Fax: 770-382-4506. [JC]
850 Douthit Ferry Rd., 30120. Tel: 770-382-4549.
Catechesis/Religious Programs—Students 186.

Cedartown, Polk Co., St. Bernadette's (1941), Rev. Jaime Barona; Deacon William Rusmisel.
Res., 101 S. College St., 30125. Tel: 770-748-1517; Fax: 770-748-1568.
Catechesis/Religious Programs—Students 198.

Clarkesville, Habersham Co., St. Mark (1964), Rev. Luis Zarama; Deacon John F. Thompson.
Mailing Address: 5410 Hwy. 197 S., 30523. Tel: 706-754-4518; Fax: 706-754-9751.
Res., 151 Salome Dr., 30523. Tel: 706-754-6504.
Church—5410 Hwy. 197 S., 30523-9542.
Catechesis/Religious Programs—Students 130.
Mission—Clayton, Rabun Co., St. Helena, P.O. Box 534, Clayton, 30525. Tel: 706-782-5152.

Conyers, Rockdale Co., St. Pius X Catholic (1974), Revs. John C. Kieran; Charles J. Kerscher, (Retired); Michael B. Heninger.
Res., 2621 Hwy. 20, S.E., 30013-2424. Tel: 770-483-3660; Fax: 770-483-7006.
Catechesis/Religious Programs—Tel: 770-929-1017.
Students 787.

Covington, Newton Co., St. Augustine Church (1977), Rev. John T. Howren.
Res., 11524 Hwy. 278 E., 30014. Tel: 770-787-1064; Fax: 770-787-0871.
Catechesis/Religious Programs—Tel: 770-787-0685.
Students 158.
Mission—Madison, Morgan Co., St. James, 562 Vine St., Madison, 30650. Tel: 706-342-9661. Rev. Msgr. Peter A. Dora, Admin.

Cumming, Forsyth Co., Good Shepherd (1975), Revs. Peter J. Rau; John T. Conway.
Church—3740 Holtzclaw Rd., 30041. Tel: 770-887-9861; Fax: 770-887-2241.
Catechesis/Religious Programs—Tel: 770-887-9861, Ext. 16; Fax: 770-887-9861, Ext. 16.
Students 485.

St. Brendan, Rev. William M. Hickey, Admin.
4633 Shiloh Rd., 30040. Tel: 770-205-7969; Fax: 770-205-5040.

Dahlonega, Lumpkin Co., St. Luke Catholic (1960), Rev. Edward A. Danneker.
Catholic Center—75 Park St. N., 30533. Tel: 706-864-4779; Fax: 706-864-2568.
Res., 75 Park St. N., 30533.
Catechesis/Religious Programs—Tel: 706-864-2331.
Students 102.
Mission—Dawsonville, Dawson Co., Christ Redeemer, P.O. Box 506, Dawsonville, 30534. Tel: 706-265-1361.
Station—Dahlonega, North Georgia College (Newman Club).

Dalton, Whitfield Co., St. Joseph's (1941), Revs. William G. Hoffman; Abel Guerrero-Orta.
Res., 1775 Old Haig Mill Rd., 30720. Tel: 706-278-3107; Fax: 706-278-6902. [JC]
Catechesis/Religious Programs—Students 600.

Decatur, DeKalb Co., Sts. Peter and Paul (1959) (African American), Revs. Richard P. Wise; Michael Onyekuru; Deacons Jerry Lett; Alfred Mitchell.
Res., 2372 Collier Dr., 30032. Tel: 404-241-5862; Fax: 404-241-5839. [JC]
School—2560 Tilson Rd., 30032. Tel: 404-241-3063; Fax: 404-241-4382. Queen Grady, Prin.
Daughters of Mary Mother of Mercy 3.
Catechesis/Religious Programs—Tel: 404-243-8333; Fax: 404-241-5839. Sr. Gloria George Patrick, D.R.E.
Students 140.

St. Thomas More (1949), Revs. Francis X. Richardson; Augustine Hoa T. Tran.
Res., 624 W. Ponce de Leon Ave., 30030. Tel: 404-378-4588; Fax: 404-378-0506.
School—Tel: 404-373-8456; Fax: 404-377-8554. Mrs. Gail M. Sezane, Prin.
Lay Teachers 30; Students 476.
Catechesis/Religious Programs—Students 285.

Douglasville, Douglas Co., St. Theresa (1985), Rev. Stewart A. Wilber; Deacon Paul Dietz; Mrs. Pam Cates, Office Mgr.
Res., 3194 S. Elizabeth Dr., 30135.
Church—4401 Prestley Mill Rd., 30135. Tel: 770-489-7115; Fax: 770-489-4873.
Catechesis/Religious Programs—Tel: 770-942-9765; Fax: 770-942-9462.
Students 416.

Duluth, Fulton Co., St. Benedict (1987), Revs. Hugh M. Marren; Luis Guillermo Cordoba Isaza; Daniel Rogaczewski; Deacons John Stroop; William Monahan; Michael Esper; William Lange.
Office & Mailing Address: 11045 Parsons Rd., 30097. Tel: 770-442-5903; Fax: 770-442-0744.
Res., 11085 Parsons Rd., 30097. Tel: 770-664-5099.
Catechesis/Religious Programs—Students 2,340.

Catholic Church Of St. Monica, Gwinnett Co., (1994), Revs. Gregory Goolsby; Nathan C. Calhoun; Deacon John Koppenaal.
Res., 1700 Buford Hwy., 30097. Tel: 770-495-9829; Fax: 678-584-9760.
Catechesis/Religious Programs—Tel: 678-584-9947.
Students 1,030.

Dunwoody, DeKalb Co., All Saints Catholic (1977), Rev. Msgr. R. Donald Kiernan, P.A., V.G.; Revs. Daniel J. McCormick; David M. Dye; Karl J. Duggan; Deacon Raymond F. Egan.
Res., 2443 Mount Vernon Rd., 30338-3099. Tel: 770-393-3255; Fax: 770-913-0140.
Catechesis/Religious Programs—Students 675.
Mission—Norcross, Gwinnett Co., Mary, Our Queen, 6260 The Corners Pkwy., Norcross, 30092. Tel: 770-416-0002; Fax: 770-416-1846.

Eatonton, Putnam Co., Christ Our Savior Mission (1993). Merged with Christ Our King, Greensboro to form Christ Our King and Saviour, Greensboro.

Fayetteville, Fayette Co., St. Gabriel (1993), Rev. Daniel R. Toof; Deacons Al C. McHugh; I. Carl McBride; T.C. Meuninck; Tom Zaworski.
Office: 135 Antioch Rd., 30215-5702. Tel: 770-461-0492; Fax: 770-461-0374.
Catechesis/Religious Programs—Tel: 770-461-0493.
Students 346.

Fort Oglethorpe, Catoosa Co., St. Gerard Majella (1952), Rev. Michael J. Redden.
Res., 3049 LaFayette Rd., 30742. Tel: 706-861-9410; Fax: 706-866-0574.
Catechesis/Religious Programs—Tel: 706-861-0563.
Students 100.

Gainesville, Hall Co., St. Michael's (1945), Revs. Serge E. Ward; Jorge Christancho; Joseph Liem Nguyen; Deacon Michael Kennedy.
Office: 1440 Pearce Cir. N.E., 30501-2457. Tel: 770-534-3338; Fax: 770-535-2440.
Catechesis/Religious Programs—Students 613.

Greensboro, Greene Co., Christ Our King and Savior (1992). Consolidation of Christ Our Savior, Eatonton, and Christ Our King, Greensboro. Rev. William M. Williams; Bro. Curt Kedley.
Office, Res. & Church Address: 6341 Lake Oconee Pkwy., 30642. Tel: 706-453-7292; 485-0102; 453-1584 (Res.); Fax: 706-453-7095.
Catechesis/Religious Programs—Students 61.

Griffin, Spalding Co., Sacred Heart (1941), Revs. Paul D. Williams, Jr.; Thomas J. Hennessy; Deacons James Hedderman, (Retired); Felix Marrero.
Res., 1323 MacArthur Dr., 30223. Tel: 770-227-2378; Fax: 770-227-6440.
Missions—Thomaston, Upson Co., St. John the Baptist, 2969 McCorkle's Curve Rd., Thomaston, 30286. Tel: 706-648-2599; Barnesville, Lamar Co., St. Ann, Redbud Rd. & Hwy. 341, Barnesville, 30204. Tel: 706-358-0635.

Hapeville, DeKalb Co., St. John the Evangelist (1950), Revs. Vincent J. Douglass, C.Ss.R.; Thomas Burke, C.Ss.R.; Jerome Chavarria, C.Ss.R.; Deacons Richard Beckman; Henry Akers; Michael K. Mobley.
Mailing Address: 230 Arnold St., 30354-1530. Tel: 404-768-5647 (Church); Fax: 404-767-6416.
Res., 3370 Sunset Ave., 30354.
School—240 Arnold St., 30354. Tel: 404-767-4312; Fax: 404-767-0359.
Lay Teachers 18; Students 282.
Catechesis/Religious Programs—Tel: 404-767-5877; Fax: 404-767-6416. Mrs. Daphny Keel, D.R.E.
Students 150.

Hartwell, Hart Co., Sacred Heart of Jesus (1977), Rev. Terence Kane; Deacon Jerry Korte.
Res., 1009 Benson St., 30643. Tel: 706-376-4112; Fax: 706-376-1695.
Catechesis/Religious Programs—Students 70.

Jonesboro, Clayton Co., St. Philip Benizi (1965), Revs. Gregory J. Hartmayer, O.F.M.Conv.; John P. Krzyzanski, O.F.M.Conv.; Vincent A. Rubino, O.F.M.Conv.; Vincent Gluc, O.F.M.Conv.; Deacon Joseph C. Anzalone.
Res., 591 Flint River Rd., 30238-3452. Tel: 770-478-0178; Fax: 770-471-2079.
Catechesis/Religious Programs—Tel: 770-471-2881. Mary M. Mauldin, D.R.E.
Students 835.

Kennesaw, Cobb Co., St. Catherine of Siena (1981), Revs. James Harrison; Martin-Ralph Kalu (Nigeria); Adrian C.H. Pleus; Hieu Minh Ha (Vietnam); Deacon Pat O'Connor.
Res., 1620 Overlook Ct., 30144. Tel: 770-419-9112.
Church—1618 Ben King Rd., N.W., 30144. Tel: 770-428-7139; Fax: 770-428-0131.
Catechesis/Religious Programs—Tel: 770-428-7440. D.R.E.: Rita Bek; Catherine Hackney; Bill Schreiner; Maureen Ingalls; Rose Robbins.
Students 1,450.

LaGrange, Troup Co., St. Peter's (1936), Rev. Larry P. Niese.
Res., 200 LaFayette Pkwy., 30241. Tel: 706-884-0887 (Rectory); 884-4224 (Church); Fax: 706-884-1624.
Catechesis/Religious Programs—Students 307.
Mission—Warm Springs, Meriwether Co., St. Elizabeth Seton, P.O. Box 638, Warm Springs, 31830. Tel: 706-846-5223.

Lawrenceville, Gwinnett Co., St. Lawrence (1971), Revs. Anthony T. Curran; Stanislaw Drzal, S.Ch.; Joseph Mullakkara, M.S.F.S.; Deacons A.B. King; Richard Johnson; Walter T. Bedard, Sr.
Res., 319 Grayson Hwy., 30045. Tel: 770-963-8992; Fax: 770-963-1710.
Catechesis/Religious Programs—Tel: 770-962-2765.
Students 1,170.

St. Marguerite D'Youville (1994), Revs. Brendan Doyle; Isaac Sobhasundar.
Res., 85 Gloster Rd., 30044. Tel: 770-381-7337; Fax: 770-381-6568.
Catechesis/Religious Programs—Tel: 770-381-6982.
Students 410.

Lilburn, Gwinnett Co., St. John Neumann (1977), Revs. James J. Fennessy; John F. Durkin, Jr.; Norberto Mateus; Deacons Rafael Cintron; Jim O'Brien; Gary Womack.
Church—801 Tom Smith Rd., 30047-2299. Tel: 770-923-6633; Fax: 770-381-7856.
School—(Grades K-8). (Regional) 791 Tom Smith Rd., 30047. Tel: 770-381-0557; Fax: 770-381-0276. Terri Lonergan, Prin.
Lay Teachers 35; Students 571.
Catechesis/Religious Programs—Students 1,375.

St. Stephen the Martyr (1999), Rev. Patrick H.M. Donaghey.
Church—5373 Wydella Rd., 30047.
Res., 382 Rockbridge Rd., 30047. Tel: 770-381-7488; Fax: 770-923-8061.
Catechesis/Religious Programs—Students 261.

Lithia Springs, Douglas Co., St. John Vianney (1958), Rev. Carl Zdancewicz, O.F.M. Conv.; Deacon William Lyday. In res., Revs. Linus DeSantis, O.F.M.Conv.; Gerald Waterman, O.F.M.Conv.
Mailing Address: 1920 Skyview Dr., 30122. Tel: 770-941-2807; Fax: 770-941-5821.
Catechesis/Religious Programs—Students 220.
Mission—Dallas, Paulding Co., St. Vincent de Paul, 680 W. Memorial Dr., Dallas, 30132. Tel: 770-443-1533.

Lithonia, DeKalb Co., Christ Our Hope (1984), Rev. Paul A. Flood.
Res., 1786 Wellborn Rd., 30058. Tel: 770-482-5017; Fax: 770-482-9476.
Catechesis/Religious Programs—Tel: 770-482-5894.
Students 141.

Lookout Mountain, Walker Co., Our Lady of the Mount (1947), Rev. Adam Z. Ozimek.
Res., (Memorial Garden For Ashes) 1227 Scenic Hwy., P.O. Box 214, 30750. Tel: 706-820-0680; Fax: 706-820-2797. [JC]
Catechesis/Religious Programs—Students 130.

Mableton, Cobb Co., St. Francis De Sales (1999), Rev. Mark F. Fisher, F.S.S.P.
Res., 584 Landers Dr., 30126. Tel: 770-948-6888; Fax: 917-477-6274.
587 Landers Dr., 30126.

McDonough, Henry Co., St. James The Apostle (1979), Rev. Msgr. Henry C. Gracz; Rev. Austin Fogarty; Deacons Robert Rich; Robert Readdy.
Res., Georgia Hwy. 155, P.O. Box 32, 30253. Tel: 770-957-5441; Fax: 770-957-0383.
Catechesis/Religious Programs—Tel: 770-957-2990.
Students 677.
Mission—Jackson, Butts Co., St. Mary's, P.O. Box 901, Jackson, 30233. Tel: 770-775-4162; Fax: 770-775-4174.

Marietta, Cobb Co.,
1—HOLY FAMILY, (1973), Revs. Edward Thein; Juan de la Cruz; Dennis Ramesh Juan; Liam A. Coyne; Deacons Fred Jones; Al Gallagher.
Res., 3401 Lower Roswell Rd., 30068. Tel: 770-973-0038; Fax: 770-578-0475.

Catechesis/Religious Programs—Tel: 770-973-7400.
Students 615.

2—CHURCH OF ST. ANN, (1978), Revs. Robert F. Susann, M.S.; Raymond G. Cadran, M.S.; Leo B. Cummings, M.S.; Deacons Edmund M. Grabowy; J. Nicholas Morning. In res., Revs. Joseph J. Nolan, M.S.; James P. Hurley, M.S.
Res., 4905 Roswell Rd., N.E., 30062. Tel: 770-552-6400; Fax: 770-552-6420.
Catechesis/Religious Programs—Tel: 770-552-6400, Ext. 6044; Fax: 770-552-6421.
Students 2,300.

3—ST. JOSEPH, (1952), Revs. Paul W. Berny; Hernan Quevedo-Rodriguez; Kevin J. Hargaden; Sylvester Nwadgu; Deacon Thomas Shaver.
Res., 87 Lacy St., N.W., 30060. Tel: 770-422-5633; Fax: 770-422-1148.
School—Tel: 770-428-3328; Fax: 770-424-2960. Ms. Laura Riley, Prin.
Lay Teachers 30; Students 480.
Catechesis/Religious Programs—Tel: 770-428-1833; Fax: 770-422-1472. Linda Hughey, D.R.E.
Students 988.

4—CHURCH OF THE TRANSFIGURATION, (1977), Revs. Patrick A. Bishop; Raphael A. Castano-Fernandez; Eric J. Hill; Deacons Bruce Publicover; Tom Coffey. Pastoral Assocs.: Sr. Celeste Schoppy, I.H.M.; Sr. Theresa Okiyi, D.M.M.M.; Sr. Mary Uzonna Ife, D.M.M.M.
Res., 1815 Blackwell Rd., N.E., 30066-2911. Tel: 770-977-1442; Fax: 770-578-1415.
Catechesis/Religious Programs—D.R.E.: Melissa Engels; Rick Fehrenbach; Joyce Guris.
Students 2,500.

Milledgeville, Baldwin Co., Sacred Heart of Jesus (1874), Rev. Michael L. McWhorter.
Res., 110 N. Jefferson St., P.O. Box 754, 31061. Tel: 478-452-2421; Fax: 478-454-1110.
Catechesis/Religious Programs—Students 104.
Chapel—Milledgeville, Central State Hospital.

Monroe, Walton Co., St. Anna's (1951), Rev. Daniel Stack; Deacons Jerry F. Connell; Herbert Berding.
Res., 836 E. Spring St., 30655. Tel: 770-267-7637; Fax: 770-267-0465.
Catechesis/Religious Programs—Tel: 770-267-0420.
Students 110.

Newnan, Coweta Co., St. George's (1952), Very Rev. Leo P. Herbert, V.F.; Rev. Stephen J. Lyness; Deacons Ben Gross; John Myers.
Res., 771 Roscoe Rd., 30263. Tel: 770-253-0512; Fax: 770-251-2053. [JC]
Catechesis/Religious Programs—Tel: 770-254-9933.
Students 295.

Norcross, Gwinnett Co., Saint Patrick's (1968), Revs. John F. Tiernan, M.S.F.S.; Abraham Mullenkuzhy, M.S.F.S.; Matthew Thayil, M.S.F.S.; Deacons Jose Narvaez; Bob Tipton; Edwin Martinez; Rich Mickle.
Res., 2140 Beaver Ruin Rd., 30071. Tel: 770-446-2041.
Church—Beaver Ruin Rd., 30071. Tel: 770-448-2028; Fax: 770-448-7046.
Catechesis/Religious Programs—Tel: 770-448-6386.
Students 594.

Peachtree City, Fayette Co., Holy Trinity Catholic (1972), Revs. Fernando Molina-Restrepo; John P. Walsh; Kevin T. Peek; Joseph E. Morris; Deacons Don Kelsey; Anthony F. Cuomo.
Res., 101 Walt Banks Rd., P.O. Box 2121, 30269. Tel: 770-487-7672; Fax: 770-486-9152.
Catechesis/Religious Programs—Tel: 770-487-0175. Mary Ann Cox, D.R.E.
Students 1,650.
Mission—Sharpsburg, Coweta Co., 4046 Lower Fayetteville Rd., Sharpsburg, 30277. Tel: 770-253-1888.

Riverdale, Clayton Co., Our Lady of Vietnam (1989) (Vietnamese), Rev. Msgr. Francis Pham Van Phuong; Rev. Tuan Quoc Tran.
Res., 91 Valley Hill Rd., 30274. Tel: 770-471-8453; Fax: 770-473-5211. [JC]
Catechesis/Religious Programs—Students 320.

Rome, Floyd Co., St. Mary's (1930), Very Rev. James A. Miceli, V.F.; Deacon Ronald A. Comeau.
Res., 911 N. Broad St., 30161. Tel: 706-290-9000; Fax: 706-295-1717.
School—401 E. 7th St., 30161. Tel: 404-234-4953; Fax: 706-234-4455. Mrs. Janet Byington, Prin.
Lay Teachers 15; Students 200.
Catechesis/Religious Programs—Students 179.

Roswell, Fulton Co., St. Andrew (1981), Revs. John Murphy; John C. Druding; Deacons William Keen; Robert Smith.
Res., 115 River Lake Ct., 30075. Tel: 770-552-0485; 641-9720; Fax: 770-641-8584 (Office).
Catechesis/Religious Programs—Tel: 770-641-0261; Fax: 770-641-8584.
Students 750.
St. Peter Chanel, Rev. Francis G. McNamee.
1455 Jones Rd., 30075. Tel: 678-277-9424; Fax: 678-277-9423.

Smyrna, Cobb Co., St. Thomas the Apostle (1966), Revs. James Caffery, M.S., V.F.; Eugene Barrette, M.S.; Jaime Molina Juarez, M.N.M.; Jaroslaw Topolewski, M.S.
Res., 4300 King Springs Rd., 30082. Tel: 770-432-8579; Fax: 770-432-8570.
Catechesis/Religious Programs—Tel: 770-432-5296; Fax: 770-432-5296.
Students 543.

Snellville, Gwinnett Co., St. Oliver Plunkett (1978), Revs. Thomas J. Carroll, M.S.; Michael J. Flanagan, M.S.; Clifford Hasler, M.S.; Deacons Michael Cappoza; William Jindrich.
Church & Mailing Address: 3200 Brooks Dr., 30078. Tel: 770-979-2500; Fax: 770-985-6590.
Res., 1318 Summit Chase Dr., 30078. Tel: 770-979-3827; Fax: 770-985-6590.
Catechesis/Religious Programs—Tel: 770-978-6751.
Students 981.

Stone Mountain, DeKalb Co., Corpus Christi (1971), Revs. Gregory D. Kenny, C.M.F.; Milton Alvarez, C.M.F.; Severino Lopez, C.M.F.; John Molyneux, C.M.F.; Deacons Will MacDonald; Eugene Whitmeyer.
Res., 600 Mountain View Dr., 30083. Tel: 770-469-0395; Fax: 770-469-6822. [JC]
Catechesis/Religious Programs—Tel: 770-469-0597.
Students 338.

Thomson, McDuffie Co., Queen of Angels (1955), Rev. Edward O'Connor.
Res., 1326 Washington Rd., 30824. Tel: 706-595-2913; Fax: 706-595-2913.
Catechesis/Religious Programs—Students 75.

Toccoa, Stephens Co., St. Mary's (1956), Rev. Richard K. Tibbett.
Res., 6388 Rothell Rd. Ext., 30577. Tel: 706-886-2819; Fax: 706-886-8770. [JC]
Catechesis/Religious Programs—Students 77.
Mission—Commerce, Jackson Co., St. Catherine Laboure, 708 State St., Commerce, 30529. Tel: 706-335-2622.

Tyrone, Fulton Co., St. Matthew's (1979), Rev. Leo C. Holleran, M.S.
Church—215 Kirkley Rd., P.O. Box 970, 30290. Tel: 770-964-5804; Fax: 770-964-1228.
Catechesis/Religious Programs—Students 57.

Washington, Wilkes Co., St. Joseph's (1840), Rev. G. Philip Ryan.
Res., P.O. Box 632, U.S. Hwy. 78, 30673. Tel: 706-678-2110; Fax: 706-678-3353. [CEM]
Catechesis/Religious Programs—Students 20.
Missions—Elberton, Elbert Co., St. Mary's, Forest Ave., Elberton, 30635.; Sharon, Talifero Co., Purification, Hwy. 47, Sharon, 30631.

Winder, Barrow Co., St. Matthew (1999), Rev. Guyma Noel.
25 Wilkins Rd., S.W., 30680-1009. Tel: 770-867-4876; Fax: 770-867-6034.; Rectory: 124 2nd St. Apt. 45, 30680. Tel: 770-867-0605.
Catechesis/Religious Programs—Students 200.

Woodstock, Cherokee Co., St. Michael the Archangel (1995), Revs. Patrick J. Kingery; Michael S. Sherliza; Deacon Jim Eastwood.
Res., 490 Arnold Mill Rd., 30188. Tel: 770-516-0009; Fax: 770-516-4664.
Catechesis/Religious Programs—Tel: 770-516-9699; Fax: 770-516-4664.
Students 678.

Chaplains of Public Institutions

ATLANTA. *Atlanta Veterans Administration Hospital.* Augustine Hoa Trung Tran Tel: 404-378-4588.
Cobb County Jail. Rev. Eric Hill.
Dobbins Air Force Base. Vacant. 94 AW/HC, 1311 Patrol Rd., Dobbins Air Force Base, 30069-5003. Tel: 404-919-4955; 4956.
Fort McPherson. Office of the Garrison Chaplain, Vacant. Bldg. 51, Fort McPherson, 30330-5000. Tel: 404-752-2616. Office of the FORSCOM Chap., Vacant 1777 Hardee Ave., S.W., Fort McPherson, 30330. Tel: 404-464-6030.
Prison Apostolate. Rev. John C. Fallon, Chap.
U.S. Penitentiary. Deacon Richard P. Tolcher.

JACKSON. *Georgia Diagnostic & Classification Center.* Deacon Thomas O. Silvestri, Chap.

Special or Other (Arch)Diocesan Assignment:
Reverend Monsignors—
Kiernan, Donald R., Vicar Gen. for Pastoral Min.
Naughton, Louis, Judicial Vicar, Court of Appeals
Reverend Fathers—
Hachey, Paul J., S.M., Judicial Vicar, Court of Appeals
Reynolds, Paul H., Vicar Gen. in Curia
Talley, David P., Vocations Dir. & Chancellor

Released from Archdiocesan Assignment:
Reverend Fathers—
Lacey, Mark W.
Sidler, Gordon L.

On Duty Outside the Archdiocese:
Reverend Monsignors—
Kenny, Donald A.
Reverend Fathers—
Adams, James P., The Chinandega 2001 Foundation Carretera Chinandega, P.O. Box 103, Chinandega, Nicaragua, Central America
Atkins, James P., Monastery of Our Savior, 711 North St., Steubenville, OH 43952
Kinast, Robert L., Center for Theological Reflection, P.O. Box 726, Indian Rocks Beach, FL 34635
McBrearity, Gerald D., S.S., Assumption Seminary, 2600 W. Woodlawn Ave., San Antonio, TX 78226-5196
Patterson, David L., Diocese of Savannah, GA
Sanches, Joseph A., Diocese of Nashville, TN
Scherer, James F., Diocese of Charlotte, NC
Woods, Michael A., Diocese of Knoxville, TN

Graduate Studies:
Reverend Fathers—
Gadziala, Timothy A., The Catholic University of America, Washington, DC

Military Chaplains:
Reverend Fathers—
Dillmann, Alan M., 409th BSB, CAMR 411, Box 1197, APO, AE 09112
McCormick, Patrick J., PSC 473, Box 10, FPO, AP 96349-1102. Tel: 011-81-311-741-4500

Sabbatical:
Reverend Monsignors—
Young, Terry W.

On Sick Leave:
Reverend Fathers—
Kieran, Richard A.
Mulhern, Patrick J.

Retired:
Reverend Fathers—
Dillman, Alan M., 409 th BSB, CAMR 411, Box 1197, APO, AE 09112
Donovan, Walter J., Sacred Heart Church, 353 Peachtree St., Atlanta, GA 30308
Drohan, Joseph W.
Dullea, Denis
Foley, Walter W.
Henley, John R.
Kerscher, Charles J.
Morrow, Richard B.
Ware, Joseph F., St. Francis Cabrini, 11500 Middleground Rd., Savannah, GA 31419

Permanent Deacons:
Akers, Henry, St. John the Evangelist, Hapeville
Anderson, Douglas J., St. Francis De Sales, Mableton
Angelich, George D., Unassigned
Anzalone, Joseph C., St. Philip Benizi, Jonesboro
Anzalone, Joseph S., On Duty Outside of the Diocese
Barker, Joseph J., Leave of Absence
Bathea, Val, On Duty Outside of the Diocese
Beckman, Richard F., St. John the Evangelist, Hapeville
Bedard, Walter T., St. Lawrence, Lawrenceville
Beers, Steven (Steve), St. George, Newnan
Berding, Herbert C., (Retired)
Bevacqua, Bill J., Our Lady of the Assumption, Atlanta
Borsavage, Charles T., St. Patrick's, Norcross
Bradach, Daniel D., (Retired)
Briesch, Forrest R., On Duty Outside the Diocese
Burke, Clayton, (Retired)
Capozza, Michael A., St. Oliver Plunkett, Snellville
Casal, Matias A., St. Philip Benizi, Jonesboro
Casey, Lawrence B., St. Francis of Assisi, Blairsville
Cintron, Rafael, St. John Neumann, Lilburn
Coffey, Thomas A., Church of the Transfiguration
Comeau, Ronald A., St. Mary's, Rome
Connell, Jerry F., St. Anna's, Monroe
Cosme, Felix, St. Michael's, Gainsville
Coughlin, Frank F., Unassigned
Cuomo, Anthony F., Holy Trinity, Peachtree City
De Sandre, Bart R., Unassigned
Diehl, William P., St. Francis of Assisi, Blairsville

Dietz, Paul E., St. Theresa, Douglasville
Easterwood, James M., St. Michael the Archangel, Canton
Egan, Raymond F., All Saints, Dunwoody
Esper, Michael L., St. Benedict, Duluth
Gallagher, Alexander S., Holy Family, Marietta
Galvis, Enrique L., Sacred Heart, Atlanta
Garcia-Carreras, Evelio, St. Stephen the Martyr, Lilburn
Gaudin, James M., Jr., St. Joseph's, Athens
Gillespie, Patrick (Pat) J., St. James, McDonough
Goolsby, Joseph B., St. Paul of the Cross, Atlanta
Gourgues, Harold W., Jr., Christ the King
Grabowdy, Edmund M., St. Ann's, Marietta
Gresher, Robert C., Our Lady of the Assumption, Atlanta
Gross, Benedict, St. George, Newnan
Hampton, William (Bill) L., St. Matthew's, Tyrone
Hedderman, James J., Sr., (Retired)
Henrich, Robert A., Unassigned
Hettel, Louis A., Holy Cross, Atlanta
Higgins, David J., Our Lady of Perpetual Help, Carrollton
Huynh, Hung Viet (Vic), Our Lady of Vietnam, Riverdale
Jansen, John C., St. Pius X, Conyers
Jimenez, Arturo P., Leave of Absence
Jindrich, William L., St. Oliver Plunkett, Snellville
Johnson, Richard M., St. Lawrence, Lawrenceville
Jones, Frederick T., Holy Family, Marietta
Jones, Michael R., Prince of Peace, Buford
Keeling, William W., St. Thomas Aquinas, Alpharetta
Keen, William, St. Andrew's, Roswell
Kelsey, Donald A., Holy Trinity, Peachtree City
Kennedy, Michael L., St. Michael's, Gainesville
King, A.B., III, St. Lawrence, Lawrenceville
Kirksey, Timothy K., St. Mathew's Mission Winder
Koppenaal, John A., St. Monica, Duluth
Korte, Jerry R., Sacred Heart of Jesus, Hartwell
La House, Edmund J., St. Thomas Aquinas, Alpharetta
Lakin, William P., St. Joseph's, Athens
Lampe, Martin J., St. Peter Chanel Mission, Roswell
Lange, William G., St. Brigid Mission, Alpharetta
Lee, Hilliard M., Jr., St. Paul of the Cross, Atlanta
Lett, Jerry M., Sts. Peter & Paul, Decatur
Lyday, William E., St. John Vianney, Lithia Springs
Mac Donald, Will, (Retired)
Mackin, Thomas F., (Retired)
Marchildon, Donald W., St. Joseph's, Athens
Marrero, Felix, Sacred Heart, Griffin
Martinez, Edwin N., St. Patrick's, Norcross
Martorell, Gerardo G., (Retired)
Mc Bride, I. Carl, St. Gabriel's, Fayetteville
Mc Carthy, Kevin J., On Duty Outside of the Diocese
Mc Carthy, William F., Holy Spirit, Atlanta
Mc Grane, Thomas J., Immaculate Heart of Mary, Atlanta
Mc Hugh, Al C., St. Gabriel's, Fayetteville
Meuninck, Tilton C., St. Gabriel's, Fayetteville
Mickle, Richard (Rich) A., St. Patrick's, Norcross
Miller, Paul M., (Retired)
Mitchell, Alfred, Sts. Peter & Paul, Decatur
Mobley, Michael K., St. John the Evangelist, Hapeville
Moenk, Jean R., Deacon Emeritus, St. Matthew, Tyrone
Monahan, William J., St. Brendan Mission, Cumming
Morning, J. Nicholas, St. Ann, Marietta
Mulligan, M. Robert, (Retired)
Mure, Samuel M., Holy Cross, Atlanta
Myers, John W., St. George's, Newnan
Nadeau, Donald N., St. Thomas Aquinas, Alpharetta
Narey, Richard D., (Retired)
Narvaez, Jose A., St. Patrick's, Norcross
O'Brien, James M., St. John Neumann, Lilburn
O'Brien, Michael J., Our Lady of Assumption, Atlanta
O'Connor, D. Patrick, St. Catherine of Siena, Kennesaw
O'Neill, Robert A., (Retired)
Patterson, Clay, Immaculate Heart of Mary, Atlanta
Payne, William E., Jr., Shrine of the Immaculate Conception, Atlanta
Petty, Benjamin R., (Retired)
Pond, Billy, Our Lady of Assumption, Atlanta
Prawdzik, Stanley T., Unassigned
Publicover, Bruce C., Archdiocesan Scout Chap., Transfiguration, Marietta
Readdy, Robert G., St. James the Apostle, McDonough
Reimer, Cecil R., Holy Cross, Atlanta
Rich, Robert M., St. James the Apostle, McDonough
Rivera, Prudencio I., Shrine of the IMMAC-CONC., San Felipe de Jesus Mission
Robichaux, Whitney F., Jr., Cathedral of Christ the King, Atlanta
Rusmisel, William O., St. Bernadette, Cedartown
Russell, Robert, Pastoral Assoc., St. Francis of Assisi, Cartersville
Sambrone, Fred J., Jr., Atlanta Catholic University Center
Santiago, Rigoberto A., St. St. Francis de Sales, Mableton
Shaver, Thomas R., St. Joseph's, Marietta
Shell, John B., Our Lady of the Assumption, Atlanta
Shoemaker, John W., Sacred Heart, Milledgeville
Shuler, Thomas B., Holy Spirit, Atlanta
Silvestri, Thomas D., Holy Cross, Atlanta; Chap., Georgia Diagnostic and Correctional Center, Jackson
Sinanian, Loris R., Dir. Diaconate Formation, St. Francis of Assisi, Blairsville
Smith, Robert B., St. Andrew's, Roswell
Smith, Wayne D., Sacred Heart, Atlanta
Speed, William (Bill) E., Prince of Peace, Buford
Stagg, James A., Leave of Absence
Stanley, John C., St. Anthony's, Blue Ridge
Stewart, James M., Immaculate Heart of Mary, Atlanta
Stives, Edward C., Unassigned
Stone, James E., Mary Our Queen, Norcross
Strachan, John S., St. Thomas Aquinas, Alpharetta
Stroop, John, St. Benedict's, Duluth
Suever, Richard M., Holy Cross, Atlanta
Thompson, John F., St. Mark's, Clarkesville
Timme, William G., (Retired)
Tipton, Robert F., St. Patrick's, Norcross
Tolcher, Richard P., Chap., Federal Prison, Atlanta; St. Philip Benizi, Jonesboro
Weeks, Jim G., St. Matthew's, Fairburn
Weiss, James (Jim), Dr., Holy Cross, Atlanta
Whitmeyer, J. Eugene, Corpus Christi, Stone Mountain
Womack, Gary D., St. John Neumann, Lilburn
Zaworski, Thomas E., St. Gabriel's, Fayetteville

INSTITUTIONS LOCATED IN THE ARCHDIOCESE

[A] SEMINARIES, RELIGIOUS OR SCHOLASTICATES

ATLANTA. *Aquinas Center of Theology at Emory University*, 1703 Clifton Rd., F-5, 30322. Tel: 404-727-8860; Fax: 404-727-8862.
E-mail: aqinasc@emory.edu
Victor A. Kramer, Dir. Total Staff 5.

[B] HIGH SCHOOLS, ARCHDIOCESAN

ATLANTA. *St. Pius X Catholic High School*. (Coed), 2674 Johnson Rd., N.E., 30345. Tel: 404-636-3023; Fax: 404-633-8387. Mr. Stephen W. Spellman. Priests 2; Lay Teachers 76; Students 1,060.

[C] HIGH SCHOOLS, PRIVATE

ATLANTA. *Marist School*. (Grades 7-12), 3790 Ashford-Dunwoody, N.E., 30319-1899. Tel: 770-457-7201; 451-1316 (Res.); Fax: 770-457-8402.
E-mail: marist@marist.com
Web site: www.marist.com
A Private Catholic School. College Preparatory Day School conducted by The Marists. Corporate Title: Marist School, Inc. Revs. Joel M. Konzen, S.M., Prin.; Richmond J. Egan, S.M., Dir., Mission Implementation; Paul Cabrita, S.M.; Francis J. Kissel, S.M.; Ralph F. Olek, S.M., Supr.; James L. Hartnett, S.M., Pres.; Ronald J. Nikodem, S.M., Chap.; Bro. Timothy McCoy, S.M. In res. Revs. Paul J. Hachey, S.M., Court of Appeals; Charles A. Girard, S.M., Provincial Archivist; Thomas D. O'Donnell, S.M., (Retired); Lawrence R. Schmuhl, S.M., (Retired). Priests 7; Brothers 1; Lay Faculty 97; Total Staff 105; Students 1,028.

[D] ELEMENTARY SCHOOLS, PRIVATE

ATLANTA. *The Donnellan School*, 4820 Long Island Dr., 30342-2570. Tel: 404-255-0900; Fax: 404-255-0914.
E-mail: jarthur@donellan.org
Web site: www.donnellan.org
Gary Delneo, Middle School Prin.; Jamie Arthur, Lower School Interim Prin. Lay Teachers 37; Total Staff 60; Students 430.

CUMMING. *Pinecrest Academy*, 955 Peachtree Pkwy., 30041. Tel: 770-888-4477; Fax: 770-888-0404.
E-mail: info@pinecrestacademy.org
Web site: www.pinecrestacademy.org
Ms. Arlene Gannon, Middle School Coord.; Dr. Brian A. Tierney, Prin. Priests 1; Brothers 1; Lay Teachers 44; Students 525.

[E] REGIONAL CATHOLIC ELEMENTARY SCHOOLS

ALPHARETA. *Holy Redeemer*, 3380 Old Alabama Rd., 30022. Tel: 770-410-4056; Fax: 770-410-1454. Mary Reiling, Prin. Lay Teachers 29; Students 478.

ROSWELL. *Queen of Angels*, 11340 Woodstock Rd., 30075. Tel: 770-518-1804; Fax: 770-518-0945.
E-mail: Pclune@QA.Cathsch.org
Web site: www.catholicedga.org/queenofangels
Sr. Patricia Clune, C.S.J., Prin. Lay Teachers 29; Students 503; Total Staff 51.

TYRONE. *Our Lady of Victoria*, 211 Kirkley Rd., 30290. Tel: 770-306-9026; Fax: 770-306-0323. Sallie McQuaid, Prin. Lay Teachers 18; Students 200.

[F] RESIDENTIAL TREATMENT CENTER

ATLANTA. *Village of St. Joseph*. (Children & Adolescents, Ages 5-18), 1961 N. Druid Hills Rd., Ste. 205-B, 30329. Tel: 404-321-2900; Fax: 404-321-2911. Charles L. Bright, M.A.Ed. Therapists 5; Total Staff 6.

[G] CATHOLIC CHARITIES

Departmental Agencies

ATLANTA. *Catholic Charities*, 680 W. Peachtree St., N.W., 30308-1984. Tel: 404-881-6571. James E. Kantner, Ph.D., Dir.
Catholic Personal Care Homes, Inc., 3409 Washington Rd., East Point, 30344. Tel: 404-669-0143. Mrs. Regina Harris, Dir.
Marian Manor, 2801 Briarcliff Rd., N.E., 30329. Tel: 404-982-0606.
St. Thomas Manor, 3409 Washington Rd., East Point, 30344. Tel: 404-669-0143.
St. Teresa Manor, 227 Medical Way, Riverdale, 30244. Tel: 770-996-8707.
Catholic Housing Initiatives, Inc., 3409 Washington Rd., East Point, 30344. Tel: 404-669-0143. Mrs. Regina Harris, Dir.
Catholic Retirement Facilities, Inc., 680 W. Peachtree St., N.W., 30308. Tel: 404-885-7212. James E. Kantner, Ph.D., Dir.
Catholic Social Services, Inc., 680 W. Peachtree St., N.W., 30308-1984. Tel: 404-881-6571.
Counseling Services, Pregnancy, Parenting & Adoption, Immigration Services, Multicultural Services & Parish Social Ministry, Branch Offices outside the city of Atlanta:
Parish Social Ministry/Community Connections. Tel: 404-881-6571.
Pregnancy, Parenting & Adoption Services. Tel: 404-881-6571. Noreen Horrigan, Prog. Dir.
Immigration Services. Tel: 404-885-7454. Sue Colussy, Esq., Prog. Dir.
Multicultural Services. Tel: 404-885-7465.
Community Centers:
Tri-Cities, 532 Cleveland Ave., 30315. Tel: 404-766-5553.
Grant Park, 570D Burroughs St., 30315. Tel: 404-624-9329.
Cobb Multicultural Center, 4300 Kingspring Rd., Smyrna, 30082. Tel: 770-432-6068.
CSS at Doraville, 5918 New Peachtree Rd., Doraville, 30082. Tel: 770-432-6880.
CSS/Athens, 160 Winston Dr., Ste. 1, Athens, 30607. Tel: 706-548-9421. Margaret Portillo Bell, Prog. Dir.
Office of Family Concerns, 680 W. Peachtree St., N.W., 30308. Tel: 404-888-7819. Mary Ellen Hughes, Dir.
Village of St. Joseph, Inc., 1961 N. Druid Hills, N.E., Ste. 204B, 30319. Tel: 404-349-2400. Charles I. Bright, M.A.Ed., Dir. Residential Child Care for Emotionally Disturbed Children.

[H] GENERAL HOSPITALS

ATLANTA. *Saint Joseph's Hospital of Atlanta, Inc.*, 5665 Peachtree Dunwoody Rd., N.E., 30342. Tel: 404-851-7001; Fax: 404-851-5770.
Web site: www.st.josephsatlanta.org
For a complete listing, refer to the Hospitals section.

ATHENS. *St. Mary's Hospital*, 1230 Baxter St., 30606-3791. Tel: 706-354-3033; Fax: 706-354-3197.
E-mail: efechtel@stmarysathens.org
Web site: www.stmarysathens.com
For a complete listing, refer to the Hospitals section.

[I] SPECIAL HOSPITALS

ATLANTA. *Our Lady of Perpetual Help Home*, 760 Pollard Blvd., S.W., 30315. Tel: 404-688-9515; Fax: 404-588-9568
For a complete listing, refer to the Special Care Facilities section.
Saint Joseph's Mercy Care Services, 60 Eleventh St., 30309-3970. Tel: 404-249-8600
For a complete listing, refer to the Special Care Facilities section.

ROME. *Mercy Senior Care, Inc.*, 212 W. Third St., 30165. Tel: 706-291-0100; Fax: 706-295-5953.
E-mail: rlawler@sjha.org
For a complete listing, refer to the Special Care Facilities section.

[J] MONASTERIES AND RESIDENCES OF PRIESTS

ATLANTA. *Legionaries of Christ*, 2595 Spalding Ln., 30350. Tel: 770-394-2158; 393-3688; Fax: 770-393-0934. Revs. Scott Reilly, L.C., Supr.; John Hopkins, L.C.; Patrick Murphy, L.C., Promotion, Retreats; Peter Devereux; Timothy Mulcahey, L.C.; Bros. Paul Campbell, L.C.; Jason Koch, L.C.; Daniel Brey, L.C. Total In Residence 8.

Marist Provincial Office, Society of Mary - Washington Province. Mailing Address: P.O. Box 81144, 30366. 3790 Ashford-Dunwoody Rd., N.E., 30319-1899. Tel: 770-458-1435; Fax: 770-458-1044.
E-mail: dennisjsteik@aol.com
Web site: www.maristsociety.org
Res., 1485 Ashford Pl., 30319. The Marists Provincial Headquarters of the San Francisco, Washington D.C., and Atlanta Province of the Society of Mary, Marist Fathers and Brothers. Very Rev. Dennis J. Steik, S.M., Provincial.

CONYERS. *The Monastery of the Holy Spirit*, 2625 Hwy. 212 S.W., 30094. Tel: 770-483-8705; Fax: 770-760-0989.
E-mail: monastery@trappist.net
Web site: www.trappist.net
Rt. Revs. Dom M. Basil Pennington, O.C.S.O., Abbot; Augustine J. Moore, O.C.S.O., Retired Abbot; Bro. Mark Dohle, O.C.S.O., Prior; Revs. Richard Donarski, O.C.S.O., Sub Prior; Methodius Telnack, O.C.S.O., Procurator; Deacon Alberic Farbolin, Novice Master; Revs. James Stephen Behrens, O.C.S.O.; Clarence J. Biggers, O.C.S.O.; Edmund H. Brand, O.C.S.O.; Malachy Corley, O.C.S.O.; Philip R. Dehner, O.C.S.O.; Anthony Delisi, O.C.S.O.; Corentine J. Finnegan, O.C.S.O.; Gerard Gross, O.C.S.O.; Jerome J. Hickey, O.C.S.O.; Francis X. Kavanagh, O.C.S.O.; Luke C. Kot, O.C.S.O.; Edward T. Morley, O.C.S.O.; John M. O'Brien, O.C.S.O.; Robert L. Pearson, O.C.S.O.; Eduardo Rodriguez, O.C.S.O.; Thomas F. Skonny, O.C.S.O.; Thomas F. Smith, O.C.S.O.; Francis Michael Stiteler, O.C.S.O.; Lawrence Swartz, O.C.S.O.; Matt G. Torpey, O.C.S.O.; Damian C. Turk, O.C.S.O.; Joseph F. Tynan, O.C.S.O.; Charles Felix Zell, O.C.S.O.
Located Elsewhere: Rev. George J. Evans, O.C.S.O., (Retired), San Antonio, TX; Rt. Rev. Dom Bernard Johnson, O.C.S.O., (Retired), Our Lady of Clairvaux Abbey, P.O. Box 80, Vina, CA, 96092-0080. Priests 28; Professed Brothers 18; Novices 2.

LAWRENCEVILLE. *The Missionaries of St. Francis De Sales*, Villa Luyet, 109 Johnson Rd., 30045-5521. Tel: 770-963-3774.
Web site: www.msfs@mindspring.com
Rev. C. John Devore, M.S.F.S.

[K] CONVENTS AND RESIDENCES OF SISTERS

ATLANTA. *Missionaries of Charity*, 995 St. Charles Ave., N.E., 30306-4211. Tel: 404-892-5111. Sr. M. Gaynel, M.C., Supr.; Sr. M. Fidelia, M.C.; Sr. Celine John, M.C.; Sr. M. Annunciella, M.C. Sisters 4; Total Assisted 122.

CHAMBLEE. *Missionary Sisters of the Sacred Heart "Ad Gentes"*, 3152 Terramar Dr., 30341. Tel: 770-934-8939. To serve the Hispanic community. Sr. Gudelia Ramos Tapia, M.A.G., Supr., Atlanta Community. Sisters 5.

SNELLVILLE. *Monastery of the Visitation* (Maryfield), 2055 Ridgedale Dr., 30278. Tel: 770-972-1060. Strictly cloistered contemplative Office of First Federation. Private retreats for women, no more than 3 at a time. Mother Mary Jozefa Kowalewski, V.H.M., Supr. Maryfield. U.S. Professed Sisters 13; Novices 1.

[L] RETREAT HOUSES

ATLANTA. *Ignatius House*, 6700 Riverside Dr., N.W., 30328-2710. Tel: 404-255-0503; Fax: 404-256-0776.
E-mail: rethouse@mindspring.com
Revs. John L. Vessels, S.J., Dir.; James C. Babb, S.J., Assoc. Dir.; Vincent R. Malatesta, S.J., Assoc. Dir.; Thomas D. Stegman, S.J., Assoc. Dir.; Bro. Claude Ory, S.J. Total In Residence 5; Total Staff 10.

Maisha House of Prayer, Inc., 520 Parkway Dr., N.E., 30308. Tel: 404-872-0096; Fax: 404-872-7925. Sr. Loretta McCarthy, Pres. Total in Residence 2; Total Staff 2.

CONYERS. *Monastery of the Holy Spirit*, 2625 Hwy. 212, S.W., 30094. Tel: 770-760-0959; Fax: 770-760-0989.
E-mail: rhouse@trappist.net
Web site: www.trappist.net
Purpose: Private retreats for men and women.

GAINESVILLE. *Cedar Hill Enrichment Center, Inc.*, 5735 Dawsonville Hwy., 30506. Tel: 770-887-0051; Fax: 770-844-1371.
E-mail: cedarhillenrichment@juno.com
Web site: www.cedarhillenrichment.org
Sr. June Racicot, O.P., Dir.; Sr. Kathrine Cliatt, O.P., Co-Dir. Total Staff 3; Total In Residence 2.

HOSCHTON. *Sisters of the Cenacle*, 5913 Jackson Trail Rd., 30548. Tel: 706-654-3460; Fax: 706-654-1459. Sr. Susan Arcaro, r.c.; Sr. Barbara Young, r.c. Congregation of Our Lady of the Retreat in the Cenacle. Retreat Ministry, Spiritual Development Programs, Spiritual Direction, and Other Forms of Spiritual Ministry. Sisters 2.

[M] CAMPUS MINISTRY CENTERS

ATLANTA. *Campus Ministry*, 680 W. Peachtree St., N.W., 30308. Tel: 404-888-7804.

The Catholic Center at Atlanta University Complex, 809 Beckwith St., S.W., 30314-3720. Tel: 404-755-2646; Fax: 404-755-3460. Rev. Edward B. Branch.

Berry College. 3487 Frey Lake Rd., Kennesaw, 30144. Tel: 770-423-9909; Fax: 770-423-9605. Rev. Linus De Santis, O.F.M.Conv.

Emory University, Agnes Scott College, 1753 N. Decatur Rd., N.E., 30307. Tel: 404-636-7237; Fax: 404-636-6099. Rev. James Schillinger.

Georgia Institute of Technology, 172 4th St., N.W., 30313. Tel: 404-892-6759; Fax: 404-829-6759. Rev. Mario Di Lella, O.F.M.

Oglethorpe University, 4484 Peachtree Rd., N.E., 30319. Tel: 404-261-1441. Our Lady of the Assumption Catholic Church, 1350 Hearst Dr., N.E., 30319. Tel: 404-261-7181; Fax: 404-364-1913. Rev. James F. McGoldrick, S.M.

Catholic Student Center - University of Georgia. (Athens), 1344 S. Lumpkin St., Athens, 30605. Tel: 706-543-2293; Fax: 706-543-2541. Rev. John McDowell, O.F.M., Dir.

West Georgia College. (Carrollton), Church of Our Lady of Perpetual Help, Center Point Rd., Rte. 5, Box 100, Carrollton, 30117. Tel: 706-832-8977; Fax: 770-832-1666. Rev. John P. Farrelly.

North Georgia College. (Dahlonega). St. Luke the Evangelist Church, 301 Hawkins St., Dahlonega, 30533. Tel: 706-864-2568; Fax: 706-864-4294. Rev. Edward A. Danneker.

Dalton Junior College. (Dalton). Church of St. Joseph, 623 S. Thornton Ave., Dalton, 30720. Tel: 706-278-3107; Fax: 706-278-6902. Rev. William Hoffman.

Brenau College. (Gainesville), St. Michael's Catholic Church - 1440 Pearce Cir., N.E., Gainesville, 30501-2457. Tel: 706-534-3338; Fax: 706-535-2440. Rev. Serge E. Ward.

Kennesaw State University. (Kennesaw), 3487 Frey Lake Rd., Kennesaw, 30144. Tel: 770-423-9909; Fax: 770-423-9605. Rev. Linus DeSantis, O.F.M.Conv.

LaGrange Jr. College. (LaGrange), 200 LaFayette Pkwy., LaGrange, 30240. Tel: 706-884-4224; Fax: 706-884-1624. Rev. Lawrence P. Niese.

Georgia College. (Milledgeville). Sacred Heart Church, 110 N. Jefferson St., Milledgeville, 31061. Tel: 912-452-2421; Fax: 478-454-1110. Rev. Michael L. McWhorter.

Shorter College. (Rome). St. Mary's Church, 911 N. Broad St., Rome, 30161. Tel: 706-295-7014; Fax: 706-295-1717. Rev. James A. Miceli.

Dekalb Community College. (Stone Mountain). Corpus Christi Church, 600 Mountain View Dr., Stone Mountain, 30083. Tel: 770-469-0395; Fax: 770-469-6822. Rev. Gregory D. Kenny, C.M.F.

[N] MISCELLANEOUS LISTINGS

ATLANTA. *The Catholic Charismatic Renewal in Atlanta*, Sabra Tower, 3300 Buckeye Rd., Ste. 811, P.O. Box 54672, 30341. Catholic Church of St. Gabriel, 135 Antioch Rd., Fayettevile, 30215-5072. Tel: 770-461-0492; Fax: 770-461-0374.
E-mail: frhep@aol.com
Rev. Timothy M. Hepburn, Liaison; Paul A. Grutsch, Ph.D., Coord.

Catholic Construction Services, Inc., 688 W. Peachtree St, N.W., 30308-1984. Tel: 404-888-7838; Fax: 404-885-7299. George Barrie, Pres. & CEO; Donna L. Worley, Office Mgr., Real Estate Acquisitions; Richard Jansen, Field Rep. - Quality Control; Chris Knott, Field Rep. - Quality Control; Rachel Brockington, Admin. Asst.; Allen Kronenberger, Dir. of Facilities. Project Managers: Carl Trevathan; Dennis W. Kelly.

Catholic Education of North Georgia, Inc., 680 W. Peachtree St., N.W., 30308. Tel: 404-888-7835; Fax: 404-885-7494.

Catholic Foundation of North Georgia, Inc., 680 W. Peachtree St., N.W., 30308-1984. Tel: 404-888-7804; Fax: 404-885-7230.
E-mail: bdnott@archatl.com
Rev. Msgr. Edward J. Dillon.

Good Shepherd Services of Atlanta, Inc. (Incorporated as Good Shepherd Corporation). Main Office, 2430 Shallowford Terr., Chamblee, 30341. Tel: 770-455-1230; Fax: 770-455-4776.
E-mail: goodshepherd@mindspring.com
Nancy Stanton, Exec. Dir. Tel: 770-455-1230.

Good Shepherd Outreach Center, 2426 Shallowford Ter., Chamblee, 30341. Tel: 770-455-9379; Fax: 770-455-4776. Sr. Barbara Beasley, Pres. Sisters 4.

Greater Northeast Atlanta Serra Club #875, Dist. #169, 680 W. Peachtree St., N.W., 30308. Tel: 770-945-6577. Phillip Grant, Pres.; Joseph J. Krygiel, Governor. Tel: 770-565-7792.

Home and Family, Inc., 2595 Spalding Dr., 30350. Tel: 770-394-2158; Fax: 770-393-0934. Revs. Scott Reilly, L.C., Supr.; John Hopkins, L.C.; Patrick Murphy, L.C.; Timothy Mulcahey; Peter Devereux, L.C.; Bros. Paul Campbell, L.C.; Jason Koch, L.C.; Daniel Ray, L.C.

National Catholic Association of Diocesan Directors for Hispanic Ministry, Inc., 680 W. Peachtree St., N.W., 30308. Tel: 404-888-7839; Fax: 404-885-7494.
E-mail: gsaldana@archatl.com
Gonzalo Saldana, Pres. Total Staff 11; Total Assisted 6,500.

Renovacion Carismatica Catolica Hispana De Atlanta, 3234 Henderson Mill Rd., Apt. 7, 30341. Tel: 770-938-3009. Ms. Anais Arias.

Saint Joseph's Health System, Inc., 1100 Johnson Ferry Rd., Ste. 150, 30342. Tel: 404-851-5700; Fax: 404-851-5770.
E-mail: sjgerety@sjha.org
Web site: www.stjosephsatlanta.org
Ronald P. Hogan, Pres. & CEO; Sr. Jane Gerety, R.S.M., Senior Vice Pres. for Sponsorship.
Sponsorship. Holding Company Sponsored by Sisters of Mercy of Americas, Baltimore Regional Community, which operates: Saint Joseph's Hospital of Atlanta, Inc.; Saint Joseph's Mercy Foundation, Inc.; Saint Joseph's Mercy Care Services, Inc.; Saint Joseph's Care Management Corporation and Saint Joseph's Service Corporation.

Saint Joseph's Mercy Foundation, 1100 Johnson Ferry Rd., N.E., Ste. 150, 30342. Tel: 404-851-5710; Fax: 404-851-4986.
E-mail: pmazzara@sjha.org
Phil Mazzara, Pres.

Serra Club #120, Dist. 169. Metro Atlanta, 680 W. Peachtree St., N.W., 30308. David R. Dorries, Pres. Tel: 404-872-8653; Joseph J. Krygiel. Tel: 770-565-7792.

Serra Club #684, Dist. 169. North Metro Atlanta, 680 W. Peachtree St., N.W., 30308. Patricia Carden, Pres. Tel: 678-290-1444; Joseph J. Krygiel. Tel: 770-565-7792.

CHAMBLEE. *Atlanta Particular Council, St. Vincent de Paul Society, Inc.*, 2050 Chamblee - Tucker Rd., Ste. C, 30341. Tel: 770-457-2920; 458-5415; Fax: 770-457-3021.
E-mail: sbissonnette@svdpatl.org
Web site: www.mindspring.com/~sudp
Ms. Sheila Bissonnette, Exec. Dir. Total Assisted 68,000; Total Staff 29; Thrift Stores 8.

DORAVILLE. *Korean Martyrs Pastoral Center*, 6003 Buford Hwy., N.E., 30340. Tel: 770-455-1380; Fax: 770-455-4262.
E-mail: kmccga@hotmail.com
Rev. Msgr. Donald Kiernan; Rev. Gabriel Byong-Young Je, S.J., Chap.

JACKSON. *Magnificat - Joyful Visitation Chapter, Inc.*, 198 Harris Rd., 30233. Tel: 770-775-3783; Fax: 770-504-8703.
E-mail: olgam@earthlink.net
Olga Myers, Coord.

JEFFERSON. *Catholic Home Educators of Georgia, Inc.*, 74 Williamson St., 30549. Tel: 706-367-2437. Karen Donaldson, Dir.; Jack O'Neill, Sec.; Julie Wilborn, Treas.; Petra Raville, Membership Dir.; Kim McDonald, Newsletter Liason.

TUCKER. *Faith Enrichment Institute, Inc.*, 3776 Lavista Rd., Ste. 250, 30084. Tel: 404-329-125- Fax: 404-248-9335.
E-mail: dsmlaw@avana.net
Mr. Dennis S. Mackin, Contact Person.

RELIGIOUS INSTITUTES OF MEN REPRESENTED IN THE ARCHDIOCESE

For further details refer to the corresponding bracketed number in the Religious Institutes of Men or Women section.

[0350]—*Cistercians Order of the Strict Observance-Trappists*.—O.C.S.O.

[0360]—*Claretian Missionaries*. (Eastern Province).—C.M.F.

[1000]—*Congregation of the Passion*. (Prov. of St. Paul of the Cross).—C.P.

[0480]—*Conventual Franciscans*. (Prov. of St. Anthony of Padua, Baltimore).—O.F.M.Conv.

[0520]—*Franciscan Friars*. (Prov. of the Most Holy Name of Jesus).—O.F.M.

[0690]—*Jesuit Fathers and Brothers*. (New Orleans Prov.).—S.J.

[0730]—*Legionaries of Christ.*—L.C.

[0780]—*Marist Fathers.* (San Francisco-Washington Prov.).—S.M.

[0720]—*The Missionaries of Our Lady of La Salette.*—M.S.

[]—*Missionaries of St. Francis de Sales.* (Annecy, France).—M.S.F.S.

[1065]—*The Priestly Fraternity of St. Peter.*—F.S.S.P.

[1070]—*Redemptorist Fathers.* (Baltimore Prov.).—C.SS.R.

RELIGIOUS INSTITUTES OF WOMEN REPRESENTED IN THE ARCHDIOCESE

[3110]—*Congregation of Our Lady of the Retreat in the Cenacle.*—R.C.

[]—*Daughters of Mary, Mother of Mercy.*—D.M.M.M.

[1070-13]—*Dominican Sisters (Adrian, MI).*—O.P.

[1070-03]—*Dominican Sisters (Sinsinawa, WI).*—O.P.

[1070-23]—*Dominican Sisters of St. Rose of Lima (Hawthorne, NY).*—O.P.

[]—*Franciscan Sisters of Our Lady of Refuge.*—R.F.R.

[1840]—*Grey Nuns of the Sacred Heart (Yardley, PA).*—G.N.S.H.

[1870]—*Handmaids of the Sacred Heart of Jesus (Philadelphia, PA).*—A.C.J.

[2575]—*Institute of the Sisters of Mercy of the Americas.* (Merion, PA; Rochester, NY; Baltimore, MD).—R.S.M.

[2710]—*Missionaries of Charity.*—M.C.

[2800]—*Missionary Sisters of the Most Sacred Heart of Jesus of Hiltrup.*—M.S.C.

[]—*Missionary Sisters of the Sacred Heart.* (Mexico).—M.A.G.

[]—*Sisters for Christian Community.*—S.F.C.C.

[0650]—*Sisters of Charity of St. Vincent de Paul.* (New York).—S.C.

[0430]—*Sisters of Charity of the Blessed Virgin Mary.*—B.V.M.

[1580]—*Sisters of St. Francis (Sylvania, OH).*—O.S.F.

[1570]—*Sisters of St. Francis of the Holy Family (Dubuque, IA).*—O.S.F.

[3830-01]—*Sisters of St. Joseph (Boston, MA).*—C.S.J.

[3840]—*Sisters of St. Joseph of Carondelet (St. Louis, MO).*—C.S.J.

[3830-15]—*Sisters of St. Joseph of Concordia (Concordia, KS).*—C.S.J.

[0260]—*Sisters of the Blessed Sacrament.*—S.B.S.

[1830]—*The Sisters of the Good Shepherd (Silver Spring, MD).*—R.G.S.

[1990]—*Sisters of the Holy Names of Jesus and Mary (Albany, NY.*—S.N.J.M.

[4190]—*Sisters of the Visitation.*—V.H.M.

[2170]—*Sisters, Servants of the Immaculate Heart of Mary (Immaculata, PA).*—I.H.M.

[2150]—*Sisters, Servants of the Immaculate Heart of Mary (Monroe, MI).*—I.H.M.

ARCHDIOCESAN CEMETERIES

ATLANTA. *Locust Grove.*

NECROLOGY

✠ Marino, Most Rev. Eugene A., D.D., S.S.J. —Died Nov. 12, 2000.

Diocese of Austin

(Dioecesis Austiniensis)

Most Reverend

GREGORY M. AYMOND, D.D.

Coadjutor Bishop of Austin; ordained May 10, 1975; appointed Titular Bishop of Acolla and Auxiliary Bishop of New Orleans November 19, 1996; appointed Coadjutor Bishop of Austin June 1, 2000. *Office: P.O. Box 13327, Austin, TX, 78711.*

Most Reverend

JOHN E. McCARTHY, D.D.

Retired Bishop of Austin; ordained May 26, 1976; appointed Titular Bishop of Pedena and Auxiliary Bishop of Galveston-Houston January 15, 1979; appointed Bishop of Austin December 19, 1985.

ERECTED 1948.

Square Miles 19,511.

Comprises the Counties of Mills, Hamilton, San Saba, Lampasas, Coryell, McLennan, Limestone, Bell, Falls, Robertson, Mason, Llano, Burnet, Williamson, Milam, Brazos, Blanco, Travis, Bastrop, Lee, Burleson, Washington, Hays, Caldwell and the part of Fayette County north of the Colorado River in the State of Texas.

For legal titles of parishes and diocesan institutions, consult the Chancery Office.

Chancery Office: 1600 N. Congress Ave., P.O. Box 13327, Austin, TX, 78711. Tel.: 512-476-4888; Fax: 512-469-9537.

Web site address: www.austindiocese.org

E-mail address: info@austindiocese.org

STATISTICAL OVERVIEW

Personnel	
Bishop	1
Retired Bishops	1
Priests: Diocesan Active in Diocese	105
Priests: Active Outside Diocese	5
Priests: Diocesan in Foreign Missions	2
Priests: Retired, Sick or Absent	19
Number of Diocesan Priests	131
Religious Priests in Diocese	93
Extern Priests in Diocese	10
Ordinations:	
Diocesan Priests	1
Permanent Deacons	33
Permanent Deacons in Diocese	181
Total Brothers	43
Total Sisters	107
Parishes	
Parishes	101
With Resident Pastor:	
Resident Diocesan Priests	80
Resident Religious Priests	21
Without Resident Pastor:	
Administered by Priests	26
Missions	26
Pastoral Centers	1
New Parishes Created	1
Professional Ministry Personnel:	
Sisters	12
Lay Ministers	112
Welfare	
Catholic Hospitals	4
Total Assisted	587,487
Health Care Centers	4
Total Assisted	80,054
Homes for the Aged	2
Total Assisted	445
Residential Care of Children	1
Total Assisted	4,000
Day Care and Extended Day Care Centers	4
Total Assisted	200
Specialized Homes	1
Total Assisted	300
Special Centers for Social Services	1
Total Assisted	240
Residential Care of Disabled	1
Total Assisted	3,250
Educational	
Diocesan Students in Other Seminaries	18
Total Seminarians	18
Colleges and Universities	1
Total Students	3,669
High Schools, Diocesan and Parish	2
Total Students	274
High Schools, Private	2
Total Students	461
Elementary Schools, Diocesan and Parish	15
Total Students	3,400
Elementary Schools, Private	3
Total Students	625
Catechesis/Religious Education:	
High School Students	3,200
Elementary Students	17,000
Total Students Under Catholic Instruction	28,647
Teachers in the Diocese:	
Priests	4
Brothers	2
Sisters	13
Lay Teachers	379
Vital Statistics	
Receptions into the Church:	
Infant Baptism Totals	7,337
Adult Baptism Totals	629
Received into Full Communion	992
First Communions	5,958
Confirmations	4,167
Marriages:	
Catholic	1,183
Interfaith	531
Total Marriages	1,714
Deaths	1,712
Total Catholic Population	266,838
Total Population	2,027,192

Former Bishops—Most Rev. LOUIS J. REICHER, D.D., ord. Dec. 6, 1918; appt. first Bishop of Austin Nov. 29, 1947; cons. April 14, 1948; died Feb. 23, 1984.—Most Rev. VINCENT M. HARRIS, D.D., ord. March 19, 1938; appt. Bishop of Beaumont July 4, 1966; cons. Sept. 28, 1966; transferred to Austin April 21, 1971; succeeded to the See Nov. 16, 1971; retired Feb. 25, 1986; died March 31, 1988.

Vicar-General—Rev. Msgr. EDWARD C. MATOCHA, P.A.

Moderator of the Curia—Rev. Msgr. DONALD J. FRUGE, J.C.D.

Chancery Office—1600 N. Congress Ave., P.O. Box 13327, Austin, 78711. Tel: 512-476-4888; Fax: 512-469-9537. Office Hours: Mon.-Fri. 8:30-5.

Deans—Rev. Msgr. LONNIE REYES, Central Austin; Rev. ELMER HOLTMAN, North Austin; Rev. JOHN KORCSMAR, C.S.C., South Austin; Rev. MICHAEL SIS, Brazos Valley; Rev. EDWARD DOKUPIL, Southern; Rev. LOUIS PAVLICEK, Temple; Rev. ISIDORE ROZYCKI, Northern; Rev. Msgr. HARRY MAZURKIEWICZ, Eastern; Rev. JOSEPH NISARI, Central; Rev. HILARIO GUAJARDO, Western.

Presbyteral Council—Rev. Msgr. EDWARD MATOCHA; Rev. Msgr. FRED BOMAR; Rev. Msgr. EDWARD JORDAN; Rev. Msgr. BEN MAZURKIEWICZ; Rev. Msgr. LOUIS WOZNIAK; Revs. DANIEL GARCIA; WILLIAM DONAHUE, C.S.C.; KIRBY GARNER; VICTOR GOERTZ; THOMAS FRANK; JOHN KORCSMAR, C.S.C.; LONNIE URBAN; DEAN WILHELM; MICHAEL SIS; THOMAS FOLEY, C.S.P.; ALBERT RUIZ; RICHARD O'ROURKE, M.S.C.

Consultors—Rev. Msgr. FRED BOMAR; Rev. Msgr. LONNIE REYES; Rev. Msgr. MARK DEERING; Rev. Msgr. HARRY MAZURKIEWICZ; Revs. KIRBY GARNER; ALBERT RUIZ.

Diocesan Tribunal—1625 Rutherford Ln., Austin, 78754. Tel: 512-832-0313; Fax: 512-832-0316; 832-0016. Direct all inquiries concerning marriage nullity, dispensation and permissions to this address.

Judicial Vicar—Rev. RONNY E. JENKINS, M.A., S.T.L., J.C.D.

Adjutant Judicial Vicars—Revs. JOZEF MUSIOL, S.D.S. J.C.D.

Diocesan Judges—Rev. Msgr. DONALD J. FRUGE, J.C.D.; Revs. GILES AMARASEKERA; ROBERT KINCL, J.C.L.; Deacons FRANK MONROE; PETER SCHWAB.

Defenders of the Bond—Rev. Msgr. EDWARD C. MATOCHA; Rev. KIRBY GARNER; Ms. TAMMY EDGERLY, J.C.L.; Mrs. MEG ROMANO-HOGAN, J.C.L.

Administrator—Mr. CHARLES M. COLLINS.

Secretary to the Tribunal—Miss KIM THOMPSON.

Notaries—Ms. PEGGY LEAZER; Mr. CHARLES COLLINS; Ms. KIM THOMPSON.

Advocates—Ms. MYRTLE WILHELM; Sr. AGNES MURRAY; Sr. NANCY PEWTERBAUGH; Ms. CAROLYN RUFFINO; Ms. JAMIE CREECH,Including also priests or deacons exercising their ministry in the diocese.

Finance Office—Rev. Msgr. DONALD J. FRUGE, J.C.D., Finance Officer; MICHAEL LAWSON, Business Mgr., *P.O. Box 13327, Austin, 78711.* Tel: 512-476-4888; Fax: 512-469-9537.

Finance Council—Rev. Msgr. DONALD J. FRUGE, J.C.D.; DON E. COX; SWITZER DEASON; CAMPBELL MCGINNIS; MICHAEL LAWSON; ROBERT GREENWOOD; JIM SMOLIK.

Catholic Archives—KINGA PERZYNSKA, Archivist; SUSAN EASON, Archives Asst., *P.O. Box 13124, Austin, 78711-3124.* Tel: 512-476-6296; Fax: 512-476-3715.

Black Ministry—Mr. JOHNNY DORSEY, Dir., *P.O. Box 13327, Austin, 78711.* Tel: 512-388-1320; 472-3741.

Building Commission—Rev. Msgr. EDWARD C. MATOCHA, *P.O. Box 13327, Austin, 78711.* Tel: 512-476-4888; Fax: 512-469-9537.

Catholic Campaign for Human Development—Rev. JOHN KORCSMAR, C.S.C., *1111 Montopolis Dr., Austin, 78741.* Tel: 512-385-4333.

Campus Ministry—Rev. LEON STRIEDER, Dir., *9845 Memorial Dr., Houston, 77024.* Tel: 713-682-4629.

Catholic Charities of Central Texas—Mrs. CHRIS KAZEN-ATTAL, Interim Dir., *P.O. Box 13327, Austin, 78711-3327.* Tel: 512-476-4888; Fax: 512-478-5962.

Catholic Schools Office—Sr. THECLA CAIN, O.S.F., Supt., *1625 Rutherford Ln., Austin, 78754.* Tel: 512-873-7771; Fax: 512-873-8338.

Catholic Services Appeal—LEANN POWERS, Dir., *P.O. Box 13327, Austin, 78711.* Tel: 512-476-4888; Fax: 512-476-5341.

"Catholic Spirit"—HELEN OSMAN, Editor, *P.O. Box 13327, Austin, 78711.* Tel: 512-476-4888; Fax: 512-476-5341.

Office of Youth Ministry—LAURIE KISH, Dir., *1625 Rutherford Ln., Austin, 78754.* Tel: 512-873-7771; Fax: 512-873-8338.

Young Adult Ministry—ANNA HUTH, Dir., *1625 Rutherford Lane, Austin, 78754.* Tel: 512-873-7771; Fax: 512-873-8338.

Cemeteries—Rev. Msgr. JOHN MALINOWSKI, *P.O. Box 3931, Bryan, 77805-3931.* Tel: 409-776-3777, Ext. 2010.

Charismatic Renewal—JESSE MARTINEZ, Dir., *1104 Turtle Creek, Austin, 78745.* Tel: 512-447-8977.

Communications—HELEN OSMAN, Dir., *P.O. Box 13327, Austin, 78711.* Tel: 512-476-4888.

Continuing Education Priests—Rev. MICHAEL MULVEY, *2700 E. University Ave., Georgetown, 78626.* Tel: 512-863-3041.

Council of Catholic Women—MILDRED FAZZINO, Pres., *P.O. Box 445, Calvert, 77837.* Tel: 979-279-5449.

Cursillo—Our Lady of Guadalupe Cursillo Center, Jarrell, 76537. Tel: 512-746-2041. Spanish: LOUIS RUIZ, Pres., *3201 Shady Hill, Temple, 76502.* Tel: 254-773-5905. English: ADOLFO ALVAREZ, Pres., *P.O. Box 142486, Austin, 78714-2486.* Tel: 512-784-7964. Young Adults: Deacon WILLIE CORTEZ, *1816 E. Sixth St., Austin, 78762.* Tel: 512-322-0632.

Deaf Ministry—Sr. DENISE MARIE HACKETT, C.S.C., Dir., *St. Ignatius Church, 2309 Euclid St., Austin, 78704.* Tel: 512-444-5330.

Diaconate—Deacon JEROME KLEMENT, Dir., *St. Luke's, 2807 Oakdale, Temple, 76502.* Tel: 254-773-1561.

Diocesan Pastoral Center—Sr. LOIS PAHA, O.P., Dir., *1625 Rutherford Ln., Austin, 78754.* Tel: 512-873-7771; Fax: 512-873-8338.

Ecumenism—Rev. CHARLES L. COVINGTON, Dir., *St. Louis Church, 7601 Burnet Rd., Austin, 78757.* Tel: 512-454-0384. Rev. HARRY DEAN, Assoc. Dir., *P.O. Box 13327, Austin, 78711.* Tel: 512-476-4888.

Mission/Evangelization—ANNA HUTH, *1625 Rutherford Ln., Austin, 78754.* Tel: 512-873-7771; Fax: 512-873-8338.

Family Life Office—Coordinators: JULIE ALEXANDER; GREG ALEXANDER, *Diocesan Pastoral Center, 1625 Rutherford Ln., Austin, 78754.* Tel: 512-873-7771; Fax: 512-873-8338.

Health Care—Rev. Msgr. WILLIAM BROUSSARD, Dir., *1625 Rutherford Ln., Austin, 78754.* Tel: 512-339-1157.

Holy Childhood—Rev. Msgr. EDWARD MATOCHA, *P.O. Box 13327, Austin, 78711-3327.* Tel: 512-476-4888.

Criminal Justice Ministry—Deacon E. GENERES (DOOTS) DUFOUR, Dir., *P.O. Box 13327, Austin, 78711.* Tel: 512-476-4888.

Knights of Columbus—PHIL FREDERICKS, Diocesan Deputy, *R.R. 1, Box 76-B, Red Rock, 78662.* Tel: 512-303-2012.

Lifeline—THERESA WARE, Dir., *2026 Guadalupe St., Austin, 78705.* Tel: 512-477-1092.

Catholic Adult Formation Office—CHARLENE O'CONNELL, Dir., *1625 Rutherford Ln., Austin, 78754.* Tel: 512-873-7771; Fax: 512-873-8338.

Mission Council—Rev. LOUIS PAVLICEK, Chm., *St. Luke's, 2807 Oakdale, Temple, 76502.* Tel: 254-773-4541; Fax: 254-774-7044.

Natural Family Planning—Co-Directors: RANDY MCCASLIN; NANCY MCCASLIN, *2026 Guadalupe St., Austin, 78705.* Tel: 512-474-2757.

Office of Hispanic Ministry—Rev. ALBERT RUIZ, *1625 Rutherford Lane, Austin, 78754.* Tel: 512-873-7771; Fax: 512-873-8338.

Parish Social Ministries—CHRIS ATTAL, Coord., *2811 E. Second, Austin, 78702.* Tel: 512-324-4921; Fax: 512-324-4929.

Propagation of the Faith—Rev. Msgr. EDWARD MATOCHA, *P.O. Box 13327, Austin, 78711-3327.* Tel: 512-476-4888.

Catechetical Office—CHARLENE O'CONNELL, Dir., *1625 Rutherford Ln., Austin, 78754.* Tel: 512-873-7771; Fax: 512-873-8338.

Respect Life—ANN BIERSCHENK, *590 Young Ranch Rd., Georgetown, 78628.* Tel: 512-931-2663; Fax: 512-868-5591.

Rural Life—Rev. STEVEN KANA, *306 S. Parker, Bryan, 77803.* Tel: 979-823-8145.

Serra Clubs—Rev. WALTER CARR, Chap.-Austin; JAMES HICKS, Pres., *8615 Rockwood, Apt. 107, Austin, 78757.* Tel: 512-346-0934.

Special Collections—LEANN POWERS, Dir., *P.O. Box 13327, Austin, 78711.* Tel: 512-476-4888; Fax: 512-476-5341.

Stewardship—LEANN POWERS, Dir., *P.O. Box 13327, Austin, 78711-3327.* Tel: 512-476-4888; Fax: 512-476-5341.

Vicar for Religious—Sr. MARIE ANDRE WALSH, I.H.M., *3001 S. Congress Ave., Austin, 78704.* Tel: 512-448-8617.

Vocations—Rev. EDWARD KARASEK, Vocation Dir., *P.O. Box 276, West, 76691-0276.* Tel: 254-826-3705. Rev. DANIEL GARCIA, Assoc. Tel: 512-918-8356. Rev. DAVID KONDERLA, Assoc. Tel: 409-846-5717. LYNN JOHNSON, Vocation Office Coord. Tel: 512-873-7771.

Worship Office & Liturgical Commission—Sr. LOIS PAHA, O.P., Dir., *1625 Rutherford Ln., Austin, 78754.* Tel: 512-873-7771; Fax: 512-873-8338.

Foundations, Endowments and Trusts

Charitable Trusts—

Father Bernard C. Goertz Scholarship Trust Fund—Sacred Heart Church, 4045 FM 535, Bastrop, 78602.

John J. Kearns Memorial Charitable Trust Fund—P.O. Box 5040, Waco, 78708.

Clerical Endowment Fund—Rev. Msgr. HARRY MAZURKIEWICZ, *Sacred Heart Church, P.O. Box 548, LaGrange, 78945.* Tel: 409-968-3430.

Sts. Cyril & Methodius School Endowment—Rev. JOSEPH NISARI, *Sts. Cyril & Methodius, P.O. Box 201, Granger, 76530.*

Clergy Medical and Retirement Trust of the Diocese of Austin and the Diocese of Austin Pension Plan Committee—Most Rev. JOHN E. MCCARTHY, D.D., Chm., Diocesan Presbyteral Council.

Seton Fund of the Daughters of Charity of St. Vincent De Paul—ALLAN SHIVERS, JR., Chm., *1201 W. 38th St., Austin, 78705.*

St. Joseph's Foundation of Bryan—MILTON L. DARE, Exec., *2801 Franciscan Dr., Bryan, 77802.* Tel: 409-774-4087.

St. Jude Foundation, Inc.—1306 N. Park, Brenham, 77833.

St. Joseph's School Memorial Endowment Fund—Rev. JOHN A. MCCAFFREY, *St. Joseph, 600 E. 26th St., Bryan, 77803.*

CLERGY, PARISHES, MISSIONS AND PAROCHIAL SCHOOLS

CITY OF AUSTIN
(Travis County)

1—ST. MARY'S CATHEDRAL (1852), Rev. Glynn (Bud) Roland, Admin. Pastoral Assocs.: Rev. Jerry A. Smith; Rev. Msgr. Edward C. Matocha, P.A., Rector Emeritus; Rev. Lawrence J. Stehling; Deacons Willie Cortez; Ron Walker.
Res., 203 E. 10th St., 78701. Tel: 512-476-6182; Fax: 512-476-8799.
School—Tel: 512-476-1480; Fax: 512-476-9922. Cecilia Abbott, Prin.
Lay Teachers 19; Students 203.
Catechesis/Religious Programs—Tel: 512-476-4801; Fax: 512-476-8799. Mary Cortez, D.R.E. Students 240.

2—ST. ALBERT THE GREAT (1987), Rev. William C. Brooks; Deacon Patrick Kennedy.
Res., 12041 Bittern Hollow, 78758. Tel: 512-837-7825; Fax: 512-834-2377.
Rectory: 1800 Montana Sky, 78727. Tel: 512-251-3355. [CEM]
Catechesis/Religious Programs—Students 489.

3—CRISTO REY (1950) (Hispanic), Rev. Lawrence Mattingly, O.F.M.Conv.; Bro. Kerry Guillory, O.F.M.Conv.; Deacon Lupe Medrano.
Res., 2110 E. 2nd St., 78702. Tel: 512-474-6376; Fax: 512-474-8417.
Catechesis/Religious Programs—Tel: 512-477-1099. Sr. Guadalupe Medina, F.M.A., D.R.E.
Students 798.

4—EMMAUS CATHOLIC CHURCH (1963), Rev. Msgr. Richard McCabe; Deacons Boyce Foreman; John Hill; Jesse Martinez.
Mailing Address: & Res.: 1700 Lohman's Crossing, Lakeway, 78734. Tel: 512-261-8500; Fax: 512-261-8200. [CEM][JC]
Catechesis/Religious Programs—Students 315.
Stations—Apache Shores, 1104 Turtle Creek, 78745.; Briarcliff.

5—HOLY CROSS (1936) (African American), Rev. Isidore Ndagizimana.
Res., 1610 E. 11th St., 78702. Tel: 512-472-3741; Fax: 512-472-3783.
Catechesis/Religious Programs—Tel: 512-244-3642. Debbie Juhlke, D.R.E.
Students 110.

6—HOLY VIETNAMESE MARTYRS (1990) (Vietnamese), Rev. Joe Van Anh Nguyen.
Res., 1107 E. Yager Ln., 78753. Tel: 512-834-8483.
Catechesis/Religious Programs—Tel: 512-836-6632.
Students 250.

7—OUR LADY OF GUADALUPE (1907) (Hispanic), Rev. William Elliott, O.M.I. In res., Deacon Mario Renteria.
Res., 1206 E. 9th St., 78702. Tel: 512-478-7955; Fax: 512-478-8377.
Catechesis/Religious Programs—Rosemary Pardo, D.R.E.
Students 298.

8—NUESTRA SENORA DE DOLORES (1952) (Hispanic), Rev. John S. Korcsmar, C.S.C.; Deacons Hector Rosales; Manuel Montalvo.
Res., 1111 Montopolis Dr., 78741. Tel: 512-385-4333; Fax: 512-385-6116.
Catechesis/Religious Programs—Tel: 512-385-4333. Sr. Rose Moreno, D.R.E.
Students 500.
Convent—Tel: 512-385-5090. Hijas De La Misericordia
Sisters 5.

9—SACRED HEART (1958), Revs. Robert Becker; Harry Dean; Deacons Jesse M. Garza; Robert Martinez; William Vela; Michael Wright; Nelson Fahlund. In res., Rev. Robert Bradley, S.J.
Res., 5909 Reicher Dr., 78723. Tel: 512-926-2552; Fax: 512-926-5138.
School—Tel: 512-926-0687. Sr. Mary Jean Olsovsky, Prin.
Sisters of St. Dominic 1; Lay Teachers 17; Students 210.
Catechesis/Religious Programs—Tel: 512-926-2116. Angelica Mishoe, D.R.E.
Students 535.
Convent—5911 Reicher Dr., 78723. Tel: 512-926-0687.

10—SANTA BARBARA (1991) (Hispanic), Rev. Bernard C. Goertz; Mr. Joe Arellano, Admin.; Deacon Cruz Banda, Jr.
Mailing Address: 13713 FM 969, 78724. Tel: 512-276-7718; Fax: 512-276-7718.
Catechesis/Religious Programs—Students 67.

11—ST. AUSTIN (1908), Revs. Patrick Johnson, C.S.P.; Thomas Foley, C.S.P.; Alan Oakes, C.S.P. In res., Revs. Ruben Patino, C.S.P.; Robert Michele, C.S.P.; Edward Philip O'Hern, C.S.P.; Robert Scott, C.S.P.; David Farnum.
Res., 2026 Guadalupe St., 78705. Tel: 512-477-9471; Fax: 512-477-9430.
School—1911 San Antonio St., 78705. Tel: 512-477-3751; Fax: 512-477-3079. John Steven Cisneros, Prin.
Lay Teachers 19; Students 225.
Catechesis/Religious Programs—Students 195.

12—ST. CATHERINE OF SIENA (1979), Rev. Oliver F. Johnson; Pam Neumann, Pastoral Assoc.; Deacons W. J. Ham; Jim Berg; Larry Terrell.
Church—4800 Convict Hill Rd., 78749. Tel: 512-892-2420; Fax: 512-892-0488.
Res., 4916 Flaming Oak, 78749. Tel: 512-892-1799.
Catechesis/Religious Programs—Tel: 512-892-2426.
Students 1,525.

13—St. Ignatius Martyr (1937), Revs. Jeffrey Allison, C.S.C.; Harold G. Zink, C.S.C.; Harold Essling, C.S.C.; Deacon Patrick Murray; Joe Juranek, Parish Admin. In res., Rev. John T. Payne, C.S.C.
Res., 2309 Euclid Ave., 78704. Tel: 512-442-3602; Fax: 512-373-4631.
School—Tel: 512-442-8547. Lynn Parra, Prin.
Lay Teachers 14; Students 245.
Catechesis/Religious Programs—Tel: 512-442-8586. D.R.E.: Sr. M. Adelaide Cannon, C.S.C.; Sr. Judith Hallock, C.S.C.; Sr. Denise Hackett, C.S.C.; Sr. Agnes Murray, I.H.M.
Students 236.

14—St. John Neumann (1984), Rev. Msgr. Edward Jordan; Deacons Douglas Morris; D. Mark Hamlet; Mike Gesch.
Res., 101 Westlake Dr., 78746. Tel: 512-328-3220; Fax: 512-328-3226.
Rectory: Tel: 512-415-0700.
Catechesis/Religious Programs—102 Westlake Dr., 78746. Tel: 512-328-8856; Fax: 512-328-3226.
Students 771.

15—St. Julia (1957), Rev. Msgr. Lonnie C. Reyes; Deacons Alfred Vasquez; Ralph Arevalo, Jr.; Jose Chavez.
Res., 3010 Lyons Rd., 78702. Tel: 512-926-4186; Fax: 512-926-8821.
Catechesis/Religious Programs—Tel: 512-928-3381.
Students 511.

16—St. Louis (1952), Revs. Larry Covington; Kevin Manion; Edilberto Mesias, M.F.; Deacons Rob Embry; Alejandro Lara; Donald Turner; Tony Pynes.
Res., 7601 Burnet Rd., 78757. Tel: 512-454-0384; Fax: 512-454-2010.
School—Tel: 512-454-0384, Ext. 242; Fax: 512-454-7252. Robert Lewis, Prin.
Sisters 1; Lay Teachers 24; Students 414.
Catechesis/Religious Programs—Tel: 512-454-0384, Ext. 225. D.R.E.: Betty Danner, Childhood Ministries; Anette Phinney, Middle School; Eric Garza, Youth Ministries; Charles Balsam, Adult Ministries.
Students 746.

17—St. Margaret of Scotland (1984). Closed. For inquiries for parish records contact the Chancery.

18—St. Patrick, Rev. Andrew Gunn.
P.O. Box 143477, 78714-3477. Tel: 512-278-0763.

19—St. Paul's (1989) (Hispanic), Rev. Paul F. McCallum; Deacons Richard Larner; W. Kent Parks.
Res., 10000 David Moore Rd., 78748. Tel: 512-280-4460; Fax: 512-280-7219.
Catechesis/Religious Programs—Tel: 512-280-5777; Fax: 512-280-7219. Joyce Gerold, D.R.E.
Students 715.

20—St. Peter the Apostle (1962), Rev. Msgr. Fred Bomar; Deacon Oswaldo Nira.
Res., P.O. Box 17575, 4600 E. Ben White Blvd., 78760. Tel: 512-442-0655.
Catechesis/Religious Programs—Tel: 512-444-7477.
Students 209.

21—St. Theresa (1968), Revs. Gregory A. Romanski; Gregory A. McLaughlin; Deacons Ray James; John O'Neill; Ray Sanders; George Zacek.
Res., 4311 Small Dr., 78731. Tel: 512-451-5121; Fax: 512-453-6824.
School—(Grades PreK-6). Tel: 512-451-7105; Fax: 512-451-8808.
Lay Teachers 19; Students 278.
Catechesis/Religious Programs—Tel: 512-451-2940; Fax: 512-453-6824. Dee Dee Schoenberger, D.R.E.
Students 640.

22—St. Thomas More (1978), Revs. Elmer E. Holtman; Keith Koehl; Deacons Peter Schwab; Thomas Mallinger; Edward Holicky; Thomas Johnson; Daniel Wright; Gregory Hipskind.
Office: 10205 Ranch Rd., 620 N., 78726. Tel: 512-258-1161; Fax: 512-258-8812.
Catechesis/Religious Programs—Cynthia Klaer, D.R.E.
Students 1,681.

23—St. Thomas More Chapel (1958). Unassigned.
Chancery Building: 1600 N. Congress Ave., 78701. Tel: 512-476-4888; Fax: 512-469-9537.

24—St. Vincent de Paul (1995), Rev. Daniel E. Garcia; Deacon Allen Desorcie.
Mailing Address: 9500 Neenah Ave., 78717. Tel: 512-918-8356; Fax: 512-918-0598.
Rectory: 13007 Partridge Bend, 78729. Tel: 512-249-1549; Fax: 512-918-0598.
Catechesis/Religious Programs—Students 311.

25—San Francisco (1941) (Hispanic), Rev. Miguel Paredes, Admin.; Deacons Rudy Rios; Johnny Ojeda.
Res., 9110 Hwy. 183 S., 78747. Tel: 512-243-1404; Fax: 512-243-2995.
Catechesis/Religious Programs—Tel: 512-243-1899. D.R.E.: Sr. Jacinta Amengual, F.H.M.; Sr. Martha Cupido, F.H.M.
Students 381.

26—San Jose (1939) (Hispanic), Revs. Kirby D. Garner; Ernesto Elizondo; George Joseph, Jr.; Deacons Joe Gutierrez; Elias Moran; John Rivera; Enrique Saenz; Romeo Sanchez; Richard Botello; Alfred Benavides.
Res., 2435 Oak Crest, 78704. Tel: 512-444-7587; Fax: 512-443-1212.
Catechesis/Religious Programs—Tel: 512-444-4664. Anna Singleton, D.R.E.
Students 1,200.

OUTSIDE CITY OF AUSTIN

Andice, Williamson Co., Santa Rosa (1937), Rev. Walter F. Carr.
Mailing Address: P.O. Box 20176, 78628. Tel: 254-863-3041; Fax: 512-863-8558. [CEM]
Catechesis/Religious Programs—Students 80.

Bastrop, Bastrop Co., Ascension (1911), Rev. Edward J. Dokupil.
Res., P.O. Drawer W, 78602. Tel: 512-321-2452; Fax: 512-303-6539.
Catechesis/Religious Programs—Tel: 512-321-5511. Laura Geer, D.R.E.
Students 285.

Belton, Bell Co., Christ the King (1969), Rev. Richard Hudson; Deacons Armando Aguirre; Jose Jimenez; William Shoemake; Ronnie Lastovica.
Res., 310 E. 24th Ave., 76513. Tel: 254-939-0806; 939-6109 (Rectory).
Catechesis/Religious Programs—Students 300.

Bertram, Burnet Co., Holy Cross (1941) (Hispanic). Attended by Our Mother of Sorrows, Burnet. Rev. Joseph DeVliegher, C.S.C.; Deacon Joe Ruiz.
Mailing Address: P.O. Box 94, 78605. Tel: 512-355-2972.
Catechesis/Religious Programs—Hope Ruiz, D.R.E.
Students 102.

Blanco, Blanco Co., St. Ferdinand's (1940), Rev. John Finn, M.S.C. (Ireland).
Res., Rte. 1, Box 1, 78606. Tel: 830-833-5227; Fax: 830-833-2235. [CEM]
Catechesis/Religious Programs—Tel: 830-833-5227.
Students 87.
Missions—Johnson City, Blanco Co., Good Shepherd, P.O. Box 528, Johnson City, 78636. Tel: 830-868-0370; Twin Sisters, Blanco Co., Our Lady Help of Christians, 78606.

Bremond, Robertson Co., St. Mary's (1879), Rev. Celso A. Yu, M.F (Philippines).
Res., Rte. 1, Box 58, 76629. Tel: 254-746-7789; Fax: 254-746-7280. [CEM]
Catechesis/Religious Programs—Tel: 254-746-7789.
Students 140.

Brenham, Washington Co., St. Mary of the Immaculate Conception (1870), Rev. David Williams; Deacon Bill Januszewski.
Res., 701 Church St., 77833. Tel: 979-836-4441; Fax: 979-836-9383. [CEM]
Catechesis/Religious Programs—Tel: 979-830-8331.
Students 530.

Bryan, Brazos Co., St. Joseph's (1873), Rev. John A. McCaffrey; Deacons Ray Sis; Gilbert Wilson; Abraham Orozco; Gary Nelson.
Res., 600 E. 26th St., 77803. Tel: 979-822-2721; Fax: 979-779-3120. [CEM 2]
School—Tel: 979-822-6641; Fax: 979-779-2810. Mr. Tim Luza, Prin.; Mr. Tom Deming, Asst. Prin.
Lay Teachers 35; Students 403.
Catechesis/Religious Programs—Tel: 979-823-5568; Fax: 979-779-3120. D.R.E.: Becky Luza; Lisa Storemski.
Students 526.

St. Anthony's (1896) (Italian), Rev. Steven Kana.
Mailing Address: 401 S. Parker, 77803.
Res., 306 S. Parker, 77803. Tel: 979-823-8145; Fax: 979-823-6001. [JC]
Catechesis/Religious Programs—Students 515.
Mission—Bryan, Brazos Co., San Salvador, 77803.

Santa Teresa's (1940), Rev. Victor G. Robles; Deacon Louis Garcia.
Res., 1212 Lucky, 77803. Tel: 979-822-2932; Fax: 979-822-6957.
Catechesis/Religious Programs—Tel: 979-822-5557. Nickie Rodriguez, D.R.E.
Students 505.

Buda, Hays Co., Santa Cruz (1941) (Hispanic), Rev. Joseph Deane; Deacons Richard Bigelow; Rodolfo Gonzalez.
Res., P.O. Box 187, 78610. Tel: 512-312-2520; Fax: 512-295-2034.
Catechesis/Religious Programs—Rose M. Luera, D.R.E.
Students 308.

Burnet, Burnet Co., Our Mother of Sorrows (1941), Rev. Joseph DeVliegher, C.S.C.; Deacon Eugene Montag.
Res., 507 Buchanan Dr., 78611-2304. Tel: 512-756-4410; Fax: 512-756-2323.
Catechesis/Religious Programs—Tel: 512-756-2323. D.R.E.: Betty Buratti; Hope Ruiz.
Students 170.
Mission—Bertram, Burnet Co., Holy Cross, P.O. Box 94, 78605. Tel: 512-355-2972. Deacon Jose Ruiz.

Caldwell, Burleson Co., St. Mary's (1895) (Hispanic), Rev. Dimitrij Colankin; Deacon John Young.
Res., 509 N. Thomas, 77836. Tel: 979-567-3667; Fax: 979-567-3667. [CEM]
Catechesis/Religious Programs—Students 272.
Mission—Caldwell, Burleson Co., Holy Rosary. [CEM]

Calvert, Robertson Co., St. Mary (1876) (Hispanic). Attended by St. Mary's Church, Hearne. Rev. Scott Mikkelson.
Mailing Address: 402 W. First St., Hearne, 77859.
Res., 505 Logan St., 77837. Tel: 409-279-2233; Fax: 409-279-9606. [CEM]

Cameron, Milam Co., St. Monica's (1883), Rev. Thomas J. Hanus; Deacon Juan Garza.
Mailing Address: P.O. Box 673, 76520. Tel: 254-697-2107; Fax: 254-697-3334. [CEM]
Church—306 S. Nolan, 76520.
Catechesis/Religious Programs—Tel: 254-697-4544. Merri Trdy, D.R.E.
Students 260.

Cedar Park, Williamson Co., St. Margaret Mary (1942), Revs. William Benish; Le-Minh Pham.
Mailing Address: P.O. Box 2410, 78630-2410. Tel: 512-259-3126; Fax: 512-259-9658.
Res., 1101 W. New Hope Dr., 78630-2410.
Catechesis/Religious Programs—Tel: 512-259-9050. Robin Anthony, D.R.E.
Students 522.

Chappell Hill, Washington Co., St. Stanislaus (1889) (Polish), Rev. Eugene Sheherd.
Mailing Address: 9175 FM 1371, 77426. Tel: 979-836-3030; Fax: 979-836-7170. [CEM]
Res., 9175 FM 1371, 77426. Tel: 979-836-8545.
Catechesis/Religious Programs—Students 53.

China Spring, McLennan Co., St. Philip (1996), Deacon Joseph Weynand, Pastoral Admin.
Mailing Address: P.O. Box 430, 76633. Tel: 254-836-4321.
Res., 1581 Bend of the Bosque, P.O. Box 327, 76633.
Catechesis/Religious Programs—Students 17.

College Station, Brazos Co., St. Mary's (1926), Revs. Michael J. Sis; David A. Konderla; Deacons Bill Scott, Jr.; David Reed.
Res., 603 Church Ave., 77840. Tel: 979-846-5717; Fax: 979-846-4493.

St. Thomas Aquinas (1982), Rev. Dean E. Wilhelm; Deacon Theodore Baker. In res., Rev. Msgr. John C. Malinowski.
Res., 2541 Earl Rudder Fwy S., 77845. Tel: 979-696-3284; 693-6994 (Office); Fax: 979-260-4502.
Catechesis/Religious Programs—Tel: 979-693-7551. Becky Surovik, D.R.E.
Students 597.

Copperas Cove, Coryell Co., Holy Family (1963), Rev. William H. Donahue, C.S.C.; Deacons Weldon Bowling; David Cardona; John Consentino. In res., Rev. Charles Van Winkle, C.S.C.
Res., 1001 Georgetown Rd., 76522. Tel: 254-547-3735; Fax: 254-547-3735. [JC]
Catechesis/Religious Programs—Tel: 254-542-7626. Leslie Noel, D.R.E.
Students 410.

Cyclone, Bell Co., St. Joseph's (1902) (Czech-German), Rev. Walter J. Matus.
Mailing Address: 20120 FM 485, Burlington, 76519. Tel: 254-985-2280.
Res., Farm Rd. 485, Tel: 254-985-2280. [CEM]
Catechesis/Religious Programs—1201 S. St. Joseph Rd. #400, Burlington, 76519. Tel: 817-985-2257.
Students 80.
Mission—Marak, Milam Co., Ss. Cyril & Methodius, FM 485, Burlington, 76519. Tel: 254-985-2280.

Dime Box, Lee Co., St. Joseph's (1902), Rev. Msgr. Emilian Foltyn.
Res., Rte. 1, Box 5A, 77853. Tel: 979-884-3100. [CEM]
Church—Farm-Market Rd. 141, 77853.
Catechesis/Religious Programs—Students 34.
Mission—Lexington, Lee Co., Holy Family, (1990) P.O. Box 541, Lexington, 78947. Tel: 949-773-2244.

Dripping Springs, Hays Co., St. Martin de Porres (1974), Rev. James L. Evans; Deacons Philip Krotzer; Edward Rositas; Gene Davis; Paul Lavallee; Joe Syring.
Mailing Address: P.O. Box 1062, 78620. Tel: 512-858-5667; Fax: 512-858-1467.
Res., County Rd. 360, off Ranch Rd. 12, 78620.
Catechesis/Religious Programs—Mary Carder, D.R.E.
Students 257.

Elgin, Bastrop Co., Sacred Heart (1908) (Hispanic), Rev. John G. Boiko; Deacons John Franklin; Sam Santa Ana.
Res., 302 W. 11th St., 78621. Tel: 512-281-3536; Fax: 512-281-2527. [JC]
Catechesis/Religious Programs—Students 237.
Mission—McDade, Bastrop Co., St. Christopher's, P.O. Box 655, McDade 78650. Tel: 512-273-2543. Deacon Cleo Cruz.

Elk, McLennon Co., St. Joseph's (1925). Attended by St. Martin, Tours.
Res., 301 St. Martins Church Rd., West, 76691. Tel: 254-822-1145; Fax: 254-822-0171. [CEM]
Catechesis/Religious Programs—Tel: 254-863-5919; Fax: 254-822-0171. Mary Mann, D.R.E.
Students 88.

Fayetteville, Fayette Co., St. John's (1872) (Czech), Rev. Msgr. Benedict J. Mazurkiewicz.
Mailing Address: P.O. Box 57, 78940. Tel: 979-378-2277; Fax: 979-378-4407. [CEM]
Res., 205 E. Bell St., 78940.
Catechesis/Religious Programs—Tel: 979-378-2275. Sr. Euphrosine Honc, D.R.E.
Students 136.
Convent—Tel: 979-378-2275. Sisters of Divine Providence
Missions—Hostyn Hill, Fayette Co., St. Mary's, 78940.; Warrenton, Fayette Co., St. Martin's, 78940.

Franklin, Robertson Co., St. Francis of Assisi (1997), Rev. Joseph Frazer; Deacon Luis Dariocourt, Pastoral Admin.
Mailing Address: P.O. Box 543, 77856. Tel: 979-828-3719 (Rectory);828-1269 (Office); Fax: 979-828-1269.
Catechesis/Religious Programs—Students 55.

Frenstat, Burleson Co., Holy Rosary (1888) (Czech). Attended by St. Mary's, Caldwell. Rev. Dimitrij Colankin.
Mailing Address: RR 4 Box 86, Caldwell, 77836-9306. Tel: 979-567-4994; Fax: 979-596-2857. [CEM 2]
Rectory: 509 N. Thomas, Caldwell, 77836. Tel: 409-567-3667.
Catechesis/Religious Programs—RR 4 Box 177, Caldwell, 77836. Tel: 409-535-7557.
Students 49.

Gatesville, Coryell Co., Our Lady of Lourdes (1946), Rev. Hilario Guajardo; Deacon James Gallagher.
Res., 1108 W. Main St., 76528-1123. Tel: 254-865-6710.
Catechesis/Religious Programs—Deborah Grmela, D.R.E.
Students 130.

Georgetown, Williamson Co., St. Helen's (1932), Revs. Wm. Michael Mulvey; Albert Ruiz; Deacons Victor Droll; Joe Ruiz; Tony Smerke; Vern Dawson; Joli Esping, Parish Bus. Admin.
Res., 2700 E. University Ave., 78626. Tel: 512-863-3041; Fax: 512-863-8558.
Catechesis/Religious Programs—Tel: 512-863-0799. Richard Phillips, D.R.E.
Students 515.

Giddings, Lee Co., St. Margaret (1944) (German-Hispanic), Rev. Juan A. Maravilla, F.M.M. (El Salvador); Deacon Edward J. Hoefling.
Res., 526 S. Grimes St., 78942. Tel: 979-542-3380; Fax: 979-542-4186. [JC]
Catechesis/Religious Programs—Tel: 979-542-2091.
Students 94.
Mission—Pin Oak, Bastrop Co., St. Mary's, Hwy 2104, 78942.

Goldthwaite, Mills Co., St. Peter's (1885). Attended by St. Mary's, Lampasas. Revs. Kevin Blade, M.S.C.; Vincent Chacko; Deacon Richard Menchaca, Pastoral Admin.
Res., P.O. Box 352, 76844. Tel: 915-648-3732. [JC]
Catechesis/Religious Programs—Tel: 915-938-5441. Tani Menchaca, D.R.E.
Students 65.

Granger, Williamson Co., SS. Cyril and Methodius (1891) (Czech), Rev. Joseph Sadiq Nisari (Pakistan). In res., Rev. Msgr. John Frizelle.
Res., 300 W. Davilla, P.O. Box 608, 76530. Tel: 512-859-2223; Fax: 512-859-2030. [CEM 2]
School—Tel: 512-859-2927; Fax: 512-859-2649. Ivan R. Leschber, Prin.
Sisters 1; Lay Teachers 9; Students 99.
Catechesis/Religious Programs—Tel: 512-859-2634. Cara Finn, D.R.E.
Students 210.

Hamilton, Hamilton Co., St. Thomas (1965), Deacon Victor Beltran, Pastoral Admin.
Res., 707 N. Nicholson Ave., 76531. Tel: 254-386-5513. [JC]
Catechesis/Religious Programs—Students 8.

Harker Heights, Bell Co., St. Paul Chong Hasang (1986), Revs. Richard O'Rourke, M.S.C. (Ireland); Francis Chung, S.J. (Korea); Deacon Peter Kim; Ms. Margaret Hunt, Pastoral Assoc.
Mailing Address: P.O. Box 2414, 76548.
Res., 1000 E. FM Rd. 2410, 76548. Tel: 254-698-4110; 698-4338; Fax: 254-698-4608.
Catechesis/Religious Programs—Tel: 254-699-6855. Ms. Olga Touchet, D.R.E.
Students 230.

Hearne, Robertson Co., St. Mary's (1872) (Italian & Mexican-American), Rev. Scott Mikkelson.
Res., 402 W. First St., 77859. Tel: 409-279-2233; Fax: 409-279-9606. [CEM]
Catechesis/Religious Programs—Tel: 979-279-2259. Linda Rios, D.R.E.
Students 175.
Mission—Calvert, Robertson Co., St. Mary, 505 Logan St., 77837. Tel: 979-279-2222.

Horseshoe Bay, Burnet Co, St. Paul the Apostle (1982), Rev. William J. Dougherty, C.S.P.
Mailing Address: P.O. Box 8019, 78657. Tel: 830-598-8342; Fax: 830-598-6350.
Res., 201 Dalton Cir., 78657.
Catechesis/Religious Programs—Students 30.

Hostyn Hill, Fayette Co., St. Mary's (1855) (Czech). Attended by St. John's, Fayetteville. Rev. Msgr. Ben J. Mazurkiewicz.
Mailing Address: P.O. Box 57, Fayetteville, 78940. Tel: 979-378-2277; Fax: 979-378-4407. [CEM]
Catechesis/Religious Programs—209 E. Bell St., Fayetteville, 78940.
Students 40.

Jarrell, Williamson Co., Holy Trinity (1889) (Czech-German), Rev. Msgr. Arthur Michalka.
Res., 8626 FM 1105, 76537. Tel: 512-863-3020. [CEM]
Catechesis/Religious Programs—Tel: 512-746-5118. Susan Klepac, D.R.E.
Students 110.

Killeen, Bell Co., St. Joseph (1954), Revs. Raphael Clancy; Giles Amasekera; Deacon Eugene Morse.
Res., 2903 E. Rancier Ave., 76543. Tel: 254-634-7878; 634-7844; Fax: 254-634-1508.
School—(Grades PreK-5). Tel: 254-634-7272; Fax: 254-634-1224.
Lay Teachers 9; Students 129.
Catechesis/Religious Programs—Tel: 254-634-7878, Ext. 107.
Students 375.

Kingsland, Llano Co., St. Charles Borromeo (1965), Rev. Joseph Mitrano, C.S.B.; Deacons Larry Crochet; Dr. George Lillard.
Mailing Address: P.O. Box 1748, 78639.
Church—205 Trinity Dr., 78639.
Rectory: 1927 Hwy. 1431, 78639. Tel: 915-388-3742; Fax: 915-388-2567.
Catechesis/Religious Programs—Students 78.
Mission—Sunrise Beach, Burnet Co., Our Lady of the Lake, 233 Deer Dr., Sunrise Beach, 78643. Tel: 512-598-8342.

Kovar, Bastrop Co., Sts. Peter and Paul (1909) (Czech). Attended by St. Paul's, Smithville. Rev. Karel Fink.
Mailing Address: 204 Mills St., Smithville, 78957. Tel: 512-237-2179. [CEM 2][JC]
Mission—Smithville, St. Paul the Apostle.

Kyle, Hays Co., St. Anthony Marie De Claret (1909) (Hispanic), Rev. Howard Goertz; Deacons John Peca; John Lawrence; Joe Flores.
Res., 801 N. Burleson St., P.O. Box 268, 78640. Tel: 512-268-5312; 268-5311 (Office); Fax: 512-268-5311.
Catechesis/Religious Programs—Tel: 512-268-5311; Fax: 512-268-5311.
Students 532.
Mission—Stoney Point, Travis Co., Blessed Juan Diego, 200 Janzet Dr., Kyle, 78640. Tel: 512-312-0357. Deacon Richard Duecker.

Lago Vista, Travis Co., St. Mary, Our Lady of the Lake (1970), Rev. Msgr. Joseph J. Schmitt.
Mailing Address: 6100 Lohman Ford Rd., 78645. Tel: 512-267-2644; Fax: 512-267-2649.
Rectory: 6502 Avenida Ann, 78645. Tel: 512-267-1336.
Catechesis/Religious Programs—Tel: 512-267-2644.
Students 90.

La Grange, Fayette Co., Sacred Heart of Jesus (1886), Rev. Msgr. Harry C. Mazurkiewicz; Deacon Mike Meismer.
Res., Box 548, 78945. Tel: 979-968-3430; Fax: 979-968-5740. [JC]
School—Tel: 979-968-3223. Elmer Faykus, Prin.
Lay Teachers 19; Students 198.
Catechesis/Religious Programs—Tel: 979-968-3377. Sr. Elizabeth Agnes Gabriel, C.V.I., D.R.E.
Students 206.

Lampasas, Lampasas Co., St. Mary's (1885), Rev. Kevin Blade, M.S.C.; Deacon Carlos Jasso.
Mailing Address: P.O. Box 866, 76550-0866. Tel: 512-556-5544; Fax: 512-556-6967.
Church—701 N. Key Ave., Lampassas, 76550.
Catechesis/Religious Programs—Tel: 512-556-6203. D.R.E.: Emily Young; Teresa Dimas.
Students 162.
Missions—Lometa, Lampasas Co., Good Shepherd Catholic Church, (1927) 500 W. Main St., Lometa, 76853.; Goldthwaite, Mills Co., St. Peter's, (1885) P.O. Box 352, Goldthwaite 78644. Tel: 915-648-3732.

Latium, Washington Co., Sacred Heart (1872) (Polish & Czech). Attended by St. Mary's, Brenham.
701 Church St., Brenham, 77833. Tel: 979-836-4441. [CEM]

Leander, Williamson Co., St. Andrew Kim Taegon Korean Catholic Church (1995) (Korean), Rev. Francis Chung, S.J.
Mailing Address: Oak Grove Apt. 115, 3625 S. 1st St., Austin, 78704. Tel: 512-259-3463.
Church—311 S. Hwy. 183, 78646. Tel: 512-448-1705.
Catechesis/Religious Programs—Students 21.

Lexington, Lee Co., Holy Family (1990). Mission of St. Joseph, Dime Box. Rev. Msgr. Emilian Foltyn.
Res., Rte. 1, Box 5A, Dime Box, 77853. Tel: 979-884-3100. [JC]
Catechesis/Religious Programs—Students 24.

Llano, Llano Co., Holy Trinity (1890), Rev. Jack Maddux, Jr.; Deacon Richard Larner.
Mailing Address: P.O. Box 673, 78643. Tel: 915-247-4481; Fax: 915-247-4481.
Catechesis/Religious Programs—Tel: 915-793-6885.
Students 80.
Mission—Mason, Mason Co., St. Joseph, Box 1572, Mason, 76856. Tel: 915-347-6932.

Lockhart, Caldwell Co., St. Mary's (1887), Rev. Adam Martinez; Deacons Guadalupe Aguilar; William Long; William Haywood; Patrick Venglar.
Res., 205 W. Pecan, 78644. Tel: 512-398-4649; 376-3634; Fax: 512-398-2285. [CEM 2]
Catechesis/Religious Programs—Tel: 512-398-3506. Eva Mendez, D.R.E.
Students 611.

Lometa, Lampasas Co., Good Shepherd (1927). Attended by St. Mary's, Lampasas. Rev. Kevin Blade, M.S.C.; Deacon Carlos Jasso.
Mailing Address: P.O. Box 866, Lampasas, 76550-0866. Tel: 512-556-5544; Fax: 512-556-6967.
Res., 500 W. Main St., 76853.
Catechesis/Religious Programs—Clustered with St. Mary's, Lampasas.

Lott, Falls Co., Sacred Heart (1905). Attended by St. Joseph's, Marlin. Rev. E. Peter Royal.
Mailing Address: P.O. Box 371, Marlin, 76661. Tel: 254-883-2016. [CEM]
Res., 6th St. & Hackberry St., 76656.

Luling, Caldwell Co., St. John the Evangelist (1879), Rev. Jesse Euresti; Deacon Wilfred Dub Hargraves.
Res., 500 E. Travis St., 78648. Tel: 830-875-5354; Fax: 830-875-3533. [CEM]
Catechesis/Religious Programs—Tel: 830-875-3901. Sr. Mary Frances Bartsch, O.L.V.M., D.R.E.
Students 282.

Manor, Travis Co., St. Joseph's (1876) (Hispanic), Rev. Robert Mahoney; Deacons Roy Barkley; James Fuller.
Mailing Address: P.O. Box 389, 78653. Tel: 512-272-4004; Fax: 512-272-9272. [JC]
Catechesis/Religious Programs—Tel: 512-272-5466.
Students 150.

Marak, Milam Co., SS. Cyril and Methodius (1903) (Czech). Attended from St. Joseph's, Cyclone.
20120 FM 485, Burlington, 76519. Tel: 254-985-2280. [CEM][JC]
Catechesis/Religious Programs—Students 75.

Marble Falls, Burnet Co., St. John the Evangelist (1961), Rev. Jairo Lopez; Deacon Eraclio Solarzano.
Church—105 Hwy. 1431 E., 78654. Tel: 830-693-5134; Fax: 830-798-9574.
Catechesis/Religious Programs—Students 168.

Marlin, Falls Co., St. Joseph's (1876), Rev. E. Peter Royal; Deacon Julian Tyboroski.
Mailing Address: Box 371, 76661. Tel: 254-883-2016; Fax: 254-883-2099.
Church—311 Oakes St., 76661.
Catechesis/Religious Programs—Mr. Eddie Roberts, D.R.E.
Students 144.

Mission—Lott, Falls Co., Sacred Heart, 6th & Hackberry, Lott, 76656. [CEM]

Martindale, Caldwell Co., Immaculate Heart of Mary (1908) (Hispanic), Rev. Dan Drinan, C.M.F.; Ofelia Cervantez, Admin.
Mailing Address: P.O. Box 117, 78655. Tel: 512-357-6573; Fax: 512-357-2933.
Church—310 Lockhart St., 78655.
Catechesis/Religious Programs—Tel: 512-357-9076. Becky Oliva, D.R.E.
Students 242.

Mason, Mason Co., St. Joseph's (1873) (Hispanic). Attended by Holy Trinity, Llano. Rev. Jack Maddux, Jr.; Deacons Joe Rabke Tel: 915-347-5105; George Kellen Tel: 915-347-5678.
Mailing Address: P.O. Box 1572, 76856. Tel: 915-347-6932.
Church—216 Ave. B, 76856.
Catechesis/Religious Programs—Tel: 915-347-5327. D.R.E.: Aida Dominguez Tel: 915-347-6176; Gladys Garner Tel: 915-347-5327.
Students 90.

McGregor, McLennan Co., St. Eugene (1958) (Hispanic), Rev. Martin Rabbitte; Deacon David Morales.
Res., 207 N. Johnson Dr., 76657. Tel: 254-840-3174. [JC]
Catechesis/Religious Programs—Tel: 254-666-0021.
Students 115.
Mission—Moody, McLennan Co., Our Lady of San Juan, 207 N. Johnson Dr., 76657. Tel: 254-853-9011.

Mexia, Limestone Co., St. Mary's (1886), Rev. Carlo Benjamin Magnaye, M.F.; Deacon Daniel Ramirez.
Mailing Address: 506 E. Sumpter, 76667. [JC]
Res., 606 N. Bonham, 76667. Tel: 254-562-3619; Fax: 254-562-2690.
Catechesis/Religious Programs—Students 163.

Moody, McLennan Co., Our Lady of San Juan (1991) (Hispanic). Attended by Mission of St. Eugene, McGregor. Rev. Martin Rabbitte.
Mailing Address: 207 N. Johnson Dr., McGregor, 76657. Tel: 254-840-3174.
Church—2nd & Ave. A, 76557. Tel: 254-853-9011.
Catechesis/Religious Programs—Tel: 254-853-9011.
Students 35.

Old Washington-on-the Brazos, Washington Co., Blessed Virgin Mary (1849) (African American). Attended by St. Ann's, Somerville. Rev. Sunny Sebastian; Deacon Limas Sweed, Sr.
Mailing Address: 333 Thornberry Dr., Somerville, 77879.
Catechesis/Religious Programs—Students 15.

Pflugerville, Travis Co., St. Elizabeth (1932), Revs. Tom Frank; Kevin Rai; Deacon Marc Washburne.
Mailing Address: P.O. Box 524, 78691-0524. Tel: 512-251-9838; Fax: 512-251-9868.
Res., 304 S. 8th St., Tel: 512-251-9866.
Catechesis/Religious Programs—Tel: 512-251-9842.
Students 900.

Pin Oak, Bastrop Co., St. Mary's (1866) (German). Attended by St. Margaret's, Giddings.
Church—Hwy. 2104, Giddings, 78942. Fax: 979-542-4186.
526 S. Grimes, Giddings, 78942. Tel: 979-542-3380. [CEM]
Catechesis/Religious Programs—Students 6.

Rockdale, Milam Co., St. Joseph's (1880), Rev. Robert Herald; Deacon Donald Sims.
Mailing Address: P.O. Box 548, 76567. Tel: 512-446-2049; Fax: 512-446-0411.
Rectory: 521 E. Davilla St., 76567. Tel: 512-446-2196.
Church—234 San Gabriel St., 76567.
Catechesis/Religious Programs—Bonnie Holub, D.R.E.
Students 216.

Rockne, Bastrop Co., Sacred Heart (1876) (German), Rev. Jozel Musiol, S.D.S. (Poland); Deacon Roger Muehr.
Mailing Address: 4045 FM 535, Bastrop, 78602. Tel: 512-321-7991; Fax: 512-303-2723. [CEM]
Church—Farm-Market Rd., 78602.
Catechesis/Religious Programs—Carol Kadura, D.R.E.
Students 250.
Mission—String Prairie, Bastrop Co., Assumption of the Blessed Virgin Mary, Tel: 512-839-4580. [CEM]

Rogers, Bell Co., St. Matthew (1991). Attended by St. Luke's, Temple. Rev. Louis Paulicek.
Mailing Address: P.O. Box 366, 76569.
Church—Tel: 817-642-3450.

Rosebud, Falls Co., St. Ann's (1915), Rev. Andrew Alberic Lipinski, S.O.Cist.
Mailing Address: P.O. Drawer 85, Burlington, 76519. Tel: 254-869-2525. [CEM]
Church—Stalworth St. & Rowena St., Burlington, 76519.
Catechesis/Religious Programs—Tel: 254-583-4624.
Students 117.
Mission—Burlington, Milam Co., St. Michael's, (1879) P.O. Box 85, Burlington, 76519.

Round Rock, Williamson Co., St. John Vianney (1997), Rev. Samuel Hose; Deacon Channing Fell, Jr.
Res., 3201 Sunrise, 78664. Tel: 512-218-1183; Fax: 512-218-8272.
Catechesis/Religious Programs—Tel: 512-671-6519; Fax: 512-218-8272.
Students 245.

St. William's (1956), Revs. Joel D. McNeil; Pedro Alfonso Castillo Aguillon; Deacons Concho Castillo; Juan Gonzalez, Jr.; Richard Kotrola; Beverly Collin, Pastoral Assoc.
Mailing Address: & Office: 1000 McNeil Rd., 78681. Tel: 512-255-4473; Fax: 512-255-8126.; Rectory: 1700 St. William's St., 78681. Tel: 512-255-3825.
Catechesis/Religious Programs—Tel: 512-255-9118.
Students 1,267.

Salado, Bell Co., St. Stephen (1989), Rev. Charles Davis.
Mailing Address: P.O. Box 662, 76571. Tel: 254-947-8037; Fax: 254-947-8091.
Rectory: 601 FM 2268, 76751.
Church—FM 2268 (Holland Rd.), 76751.
Catechesis/Religious Programs—Tel: 254-947-0144. Terre Slima, D.R.E.
Students 104.

San Marcos, Hays Co., St. John the Evangelist (1883), Revs. Brian Culley, C.M.F.; Richard Wozniak, C.M.F.; Daryl Olds, C.M.F. Pastoral Assocs.: Deacons Lalo Duran; Domingo Vargas; Louis Endris; Jesse Mojica.
Res., 624 E. Hopkins, 78666. Tel: 512-353-8969; Fax: 512-396-7522.
Catechesis/Religious Programs—Tel: 512-353-5065. D.R.E.: Sr. Adelina Esquivel, M.C.M.; Sr. Roseann Castilleja, M.C.M.
Students 630.
Convent—964 Field St., 78666. Tel: 512-396-5333.
Mission—San Marcos, Hays Co., Guadalupe Chapel, Corner of Roosevelt & Churchill, 78666.

San Saba, San Saba Co., St. Mary's (1967) (Hispanic), Rev. Vincent V. Chacko, I.M.S.; Deacon Richard Menchaca.
Mailing Address: P.O. Box 415, 76877. Tel: 915-372-3679. [JC]
504 W. Wallace, 76877.
Catechesis/Religious Programs—D.R.E.: Tani Menchaca, (Goldthwaite); Colleen Womack, (San Saba).
Students 105.

Satin, Satin Falls Co., Santa Rita Shrine (1921) (Hispanic). Attended by St. Francis, Waco.
Mailing Address: 301 Jefferson Ave., Waco, 76701. Tel: 817-752-8434; Fax: 817-752-2415.

Smithville, Bastrop Co., St. Paul the Apostle (1896), Rev. Karel Fink.
Res., 204 Mills St., 78957. Tel: 512-237-2179.
Catechesis/Religious Programs—512-237-3299
Students 109.
Mission—Kovar, Bastrop Co., Sts. Peter and Paul.

Somerville, Burleson Co., St. Ann's (1913), Rev. Sunny Sebastian.
Mailing Address: P.O. Box 99, 77879. Tel: 979-596-1966; Fax: 979-596-2857.
Church—Thornberry Rd., 77879.
Catechesis/Religious Programs—Theresa Perez, D.R.E.
Students 75.
Mission—Old Washington, Washington Co., Blessed Virgin Mary Chapel, (1849) 17370 Sweed Rd., Washington, 77880. Fax: 409-836-9389.

Stony Point, Travis Co., Blessed Juan Diego (1987). Attended by St. Anthony, Kyle. Rev. Howard Goertz; Deacon Richard Duecker, Pastoral Admin.
Mailing Address: 200 Janzet Dr., Kyle, 78640.
Church—No. 22 & 43 Stoney Point Dr., Del Valle, 78617. Tel: 512-247-2476; 312-0357 (Parish Hall).
Catechesis/Religious Programs—Students 65.

String Prairie, Bastrop Co., St. Mary's of the Assumption (1876) (German). Attended by Sacred Heart, Rockne. Rev. Jozef Musiol, S.D.S. (Poland).
Mailing Address: 4045 FM 535, Bastrop, 78602. Tel: 512-839-4580. [CEM]
405 St. Mary's Rd., Bastrop, 78602.
Catechesis/Religious Programs—Fax: 512-471-8808. Sharon Evans, D.R.E.
Students 44.

Taylor, Williamson Co.

1—St. Mary's (1877), Rev. Lonnie A. Urban; Deacon Dan Ozuna.
Res., 408 Washburn St., 76574. Tel: 512-352-2175; Fax: 512-365-5313. [CEM]
School—Tel: 512-352-2313. Jacqueline C. Horton, Prin.
Sisters 2; Lay Teachers 16; Students 187.
Catechesis/Religious Programs—Tel: 512-352-2133. Mrs. Belinda Ozuna, D.R.E.
Students 187.
Convent—317 E. 4th St., 76574. Tel: 512-352-2144.

2—Our Lady of Guadalupe (1914) (Hispanic), Rev. Tom Chamberlain; Deacon Alfredo Torres.
Res., 113 Dickey St., 76574. Tel: 512-365-2380; Fax: 512-365-1733. [CEM]
Catechesis/Religious Programs—Students 242.

Temple, Bell Co., St. Mary's (1883), Rev. Steven Nesrsta; Deacon John Petter.
Res., 1018 S. 7th St., 76504. Tel: 254-773-4541; Fax: 254-774-7044. [JC]
School—Tel: 254-778-8141; Fax: 254-778-1396. David Peterson, Ph.D., Prin.
Lay Teachers 20; Students 194.
Catechesis/Religious Programs—Tel: 254-773-1980. Loris Edwards, D.R.E.
Students 249.
Rectory—1004 S. 7th St., 76504. Tel: 254-773-3238.

St. Luke's (1969), Revs. Louis Pavlicek; Larry Heimsoth; Deacons Jerome J. Klement; Willie Luna; James Madsen; Switzer Deason.
Res., 2807 Oakdale, 76502. Tel: 254-773-1561; Fax: 254-773-4623. [JC]
Catechesis/Religious Programs—Tel: 254-773-2330; Fax: 254-773-2643.
Students 428.
Mission—Rogers, Bell Co., St. Matthew, Hwy. 190, Rogers 76569.

Our Lady of Guadalupe (1952) (Hispanic), Rev. Ricardo Aguilar; Deacons J. Margarito Alvarado; Jose Cruz Perez; Joseph Vela.
Res., 708 S. 6th St., 76504. Tel: 254-773-6779; Fax: 254-773-5469.
Catechesis/Religious Programs—Students 235.

Tours, McLennan Co., St. Martin (1870) (German-Czech), Rev. Isidore Rozycki.
Res., 301 St. Martin's Church Rd., West, 76691-2135. Tel: 254-822-1145; Fax: 254-822-0171. [CEM]
Catechesis/Religious Programs—Tel: 254-822-1026. Dorothy Middleton, D.R.E.
Students 118.
Mission—Elk, McLennon Co., St. Joseph, 76691.

Uhland, Hays Co., St. Michael's (1924) (Hispanic), Rev. Dan Drinan, C.M.F.; Deacon Lalo Duran, Pastoral Coord.
Church and Mailing Address: 80 S. Old Spanish Tr., 78640. Tel: 512-398-7475. [CEM][JC]
Catechesis/Religious Programs—Tel: 512-398-5720. Ofelia Cervantez, D.R.E.
Students 70.

Waco, McLennan Co.,

1—Sacred Heart, (1957) (Spanish), Rev. Lawrence Soler, T.O.R.; Deacon Lorenzo Garcia.
Res., 2621 Bagby Ave., 76711. Tel: 254-756-2656; Fax: 254-756-6302.
Catechesis/Religious Programs—Tel: 254-756-2390.
Students 264.

2—St. Francis on the Brazos, (1924) (Hispanic), Revs. Anthony P. Ferrer, T.O.R.; Fernando Hernandez, T.O.R. (Mexico); Deacons Antonio Arocha; Jessie C. Garza.
Res., 301 Jefferson Ave., 76701. Tel: 254-752-8434; Fax: 254-752-2415. [JC]
School—Tel: 254-753-5565; Fax: 254-753-6816. Sr. Barbara Herrera, Prin.
Sisters 5; Lay Teachers 7; Students 147.
Nursery & Kindergarten—612 N. 3rd St., 76701. Fax: 254-757-0537.
Catechesis/Religious Programs—Tel: 254-752-1159.
Students 550.
Convent—612 N. 3rd St., 76701. Tel: 254-753-5565.
Mission—Satin, Satin Falls Co., Santa Rita.

3—St. Jerome, (1982), Rev. Don Loftin; Deacons Douglas Wuenchel; Jordan Pfuntner; Joseph Potter; Rae Carter; Greg George.
Res., 9820 Chapel Rd., 76712. Tel: 254-666-7722; Fax: 254-666-4848.
Catechesis/Religious Programs—Tel: 254-666-3555. Lisa Sanders, D.R.E.
Students 550.

4—St. John the Baptist, (1953) (African American). Attended by St. Mary's, Waco. Deacons Alton Hithe, Pastoral Admin.; Louie Hawkins.
Mailing Address: P.O. Box 585, 76704-0585.
Res., 1312 Dallas St., 76704-0585. Tel: 254-753-6742.
Catechesis/Religious Programs—Students 950.
Mission—Waco.

5—ST. JOSEPH, (1950), Rev. Timothy V. Vaverek.
Res., 1011 Boston St., 76705. Tel: 254-799-2531.
Catechesis/Religious Programs—Tel: 254-799-6646. Brenda Fetsch, D.R.E.
Students 200.

6—ST. LOUIS, (1964), Rev. David Leibham. In res., Rev. Melvin Dornak.
Res., 2001 N. 25th St., P.O. Box 5040, 76708. Tel: 254-754-1221; Fax: 254-754-4019.
School—Tel: 254-754-2041; Fax: 254-754-2091. John Vasek, Prin.
Lay Teachers 24; Students 375.
Catechesis/Religious Programs—Tel: 254-754-2041. Sally Rue, D.R.E.
Students 120.

7—ST. MARY OF THE ASSUMPTION, (1870), Rev. Angelo Bertini; Deacons Frank Jasek; David Morales; Sidney Prewitt.
Mailing Address: 1401 Washington Ave., 76701. Tel: 254-753-0146; Fax: 254-753-5100. [JC]
Church—205 N. 14th St., 76701.
School—Tel: 254-754-1622; Fax: 254-756-6365. Sr. M. Kenneth Regan, C.S.C., Prin.
Sisters 1; Lay Teachers 15; Students 116.
Catechesis/Religious Programs—Tel: 254-756-0548. Terri Bukowski, D.R.E.
Students 70.
Convent—224 N. 14th St., 76701. Tel: 254-756-0548.
Mission—Waco, McLennan Co., St. John the Baptist, 1312 Dallas St., Waco 76704.

West, McLennan Co., Assumption (1892) (Czech), Rev. Edward Karasek; Deacons Cecil Friend; Buddy Shieldes.
Mailing Address: P.O. Box 276, 76691. Tel: 254-826-3705; Fax: 254-826-5497. [CEM]
Church—303 S. Harrison.
School—Tel: 254-826-5991; Fax: 254-826-7047. Joe Gough, Prin.
Lay Teachers 12; Students 201.
Catechesis/Religious Programs—D.R.E.: Mrs. Charlotte Klaus; Mrs. Edwina Deiterman.
Students 388.

Westphalia, Falls Co., Visitation (1883), Rev. Reinhold Schmitt, C.M.M.; Deacons Bill Smetana; Charley Wright.
Res., 144 County Rd. 3000, Lott, 76656-3827. Tel: 254-584-4983; Fax: 254-584-7063. [CEM]
Catechesis/Religious Programs—Tel: 254-584-4407. Linda Lorenz, D.R.E.
Students 151.

Wimberley, Hays Co., St. Mary (1956), Rev. Everett Trebtoske; Deacons John C. Maher; Frank Monroe.
Res., 14711 Ranch Rd. 12, 78676. Tel: 512-847-9181 (Church); Fax: 512-847-5573. [CEM]
Catechesis/Religious Programs—Minerva Martinez, D.R.E.
Students 87.

Chaplains of Public Institutions

AUSTIN. *Brackenridge Hospital* Tel: 512-324-7480; 324-7106. Rev. Don Oliver Weerakkody.
St. David's Hospital 2010 Guadalupe, 78705. Tel: 512-477-9471. Rev. Robert Michele, C.S.P.
School for the Blind 7601 Burnet Rd., 78757. Tel: 512-454-0384. Rev. Larry Covington.
School for the Deaf. Served by St. Ignatius Catholic Church. 2309 Euclid St., 78704. Tel: 512-442-3602.
Seton Hospital 1201 W. 38th, 78705. Tel: 512-324-1000. Rev. Richard J. Tijerina.
State Hospital 4110 Guadalupe, 78751. Tel: 512-419-2573. Rev. Lawrence J. Stehling.
State School 2010 Guadalupe, 78705. Tel: 512-477-9471. Rev. Patrick Johnson, C.S.P.

BASTROP. *Federal Correctional Institute*. Vacant.

GATESVILLE. *Texas Department of Criminal Justice* P.O. Box 665, 76528. Deacon James Gallagher, Chap.

GIDDINGS. *State School*. Attended by St. Margaret, Giddings. Tel: 409-542-3380.

MARLIN. *V.A. Hospital* P.O. Box 371, 76661. Rev. E. Peter Royal.

MEXIA. *State School* 606 N. Bonham, 76667. Tel: 254-562-3619. Rev. Carlo Benjamin Magnaye, M.F.

TEMPLE. *V.A. Hospital* 1901 S. First St., 76501. Tel: 254-778-4811, Ext. 4879. Rev. Richard Beyer.

WACO. *V.A. Hospital* 4800 Memorial Dr., 76711. Tel: 254-752-6581. Revs. Thomas J. Niemira; Richard Beyer.

Special Assignments:
Reverend Monsignors—
Fruge, Donald J. (GAL), Finance Officer
Matocha, Edward C., Vicar General
Reverend Fathers—
Goertz, Bernard C., Rte. 2, Box 129, Cedar Creek, TX 78612
Goertz, Victor, Cedarbrake Renewal Center, P.O. Box 58, Belton, TX 76513

On Duty Outside the Diocese:
Reverend Monsignors—
Elmer, Charles, North American College, Casa Maria, Via dell' Umilta, 30, Rome, 00187 Italy
Reverend Fathers—
Chalupa, Fred, Diocese of Galveston-Houston, P.O. Box 907, Houston, TX 77001
Garcia, Pedro, Parroquia de San Isidro Labrador, Hidalgo 204, Apdo. 24, Arteaga, Coahuila C.P. 25350 Mexico
Kincl, Robert L., Spiritual Dir., Christendon College, 134 Christendon Dr., Front Royal, VA 22630. Tel: 540-636-2900
Mahoney, Bernard, 1722 Chippendale, Houston, TX 77108
Strieder, Leon, St. Mary's Seminary, 9845 Memorial Dr., Houston, TX 77024

Military Chaplains:
Reverend Fathers—
Moss, Donald G., Naval Chaplain's School, Mailing Address: Code 8EOOOO, 1 Administration Circle, China Lake, CA 93555

On Leave:
Reverend Fathers—
O'Connor, James, P.O. Box 667, Austin, TX 78767
Olnhausen, James Robert, St. Thomas More, 510 Bayshore Dr., Pensacola, FL 32507. Tel: 850-456-2543

Retired:
Reverend Monsignors—
Brennan, Ralph, Brother Vincent Pieau Residence, 921 St. Edward's Dr., Austin, TX 78704. Tel: 512-493-0122
Deering, Mark, 4700 Westchester, Waco, TX 76710. Tel: 254-772-5263
Frizelle, John D.
Fuchs, Robert A., Rte. 2, Box 48A, Rosebud, TX 76570
Fuchs, Sylvester, Lost Prairie Villa, 9901 FM Rd. 2086, Temple, TX 76501-3528
Miller, Frank, Rte. 2, Box 46-E, Abbott, TX 76621
Stram, Gideon, Rte. 1, Box 138-N, Jarrell, TX 76537. Tel: 512-746-2028
Tydlacka, George, 874 Burleson-Manor Rd., Manor, TX 78653
Wozniak, Louis, 2212 Rifle Bend Dr., Georgetown, TX 78626. Tel: 512-864-1907
Reverend Fathers—
Collins, Robert, 3003 Maplelawn Cir., Austin, TX 78723
Conrad, Stanley, Rte. 1, Box 56A, Bremond, TX 76629. Tel: 254-754-7788
Hand, Chester, Jr., 400 Austin Ave., Waco, TX 76703
Leddy, Leonard, Western Hill Village, 3000 W. Adams Ave. #314, Temple, TX 76504
Maddox, Edward, 7902 Avellano, San Antonio, TX 78250. Tel: 210-523-8995
Palermo, Albert, 1104 Huntridge Circle, Austin, TX 78758
Tzanakas, George M., 4701 Staggerbrush, #115, Austin, TX 78749. Tel: 512-892-8293
Willemsen, Andrew J., Eindhovenseweg 32, 5524 AR Steensel, Holland

---

Permanent Deacons:
Abraham, Ellis, St. Anthony's, Bryan
Adam, Klaus, Ft. Hood Cath. Comm., Killeen
Aguilar, Guadalupe, St. Mary's, Lockhart
Aguirre, Armando, Christ the King, Belton
Alvarado, J. Margarito, Our Lady of Guadalupe, Temple
Arellano, Joe, Santa Barbara, Hornsby Bend
Arevalo, Ralph, St. Julia's, Austin
Arocha, Antonio, St. Francis, Waco
Baker, Ted, St. Thomas Aquinas, College Station
Banda, Cruz, Jr., Santa Barbara, Hornsby Bend
Barkley, Roy, St. Joseph's, Manor
Behr, Roger L., Sacred Heart, Austin
Beltran, Victor, St. Thomas, Hamilton
Benavides, Alfred, San Jose, Austin
Berg, James R., St. Catherine of Siena, Austin
Bigelow, Richard, Santa Cruz, Buda
Botello, Richard, San Jose, Austin
Bowling, Weldon, Holy Family, Copperas Cove
Burleson, Don, St. John Vianney, Round Rock
Cardona, David, Holy Family, Copperas Cove
Carter, Rae, St. Jerome's, Waco
Castillo, Concepcion, St. Williams, Round Rock
Cepak, Benny, Seminarian and St. Joseph's, Waco
Chavez, Jose, Cristo Rey, Austin
Cochran, Lee, St. Anthony's, Bryan
Collins, Roger, Santa Rosa, Andice
Consentino, John, Holy Family, Copperas Cove
Cortez, Willie, St. Mary's Cathedral
Crochet, Larry, St. Charles Borromeo, Kingsland
Crowley, Joe, Our Lady's Maronite, Austin
Cruz, Cleo, St. Christopher's, McDade
Davis, Gene, St. Martin de Porres, Dripping Springs
Dawson, Vern, St. Helen's, Georgetown
Deason, Switzer, St. Luke's. Temple
Desorcie, Allen, St. Vincent de Paul, Austin
Doriocourt, Luis, St. Francis de Assisi, Franklin
Droll, Victor, St. Helen's, Georgetown
Duecker, Richard, Blessed Juan Diego, Stoney Point
Dufour, Generes "Doots", Diocesan Prison Ministry
Dunne, Larry, Sacred Heart, Elgin
Duran, Everardo "Lalo", St. Michael's, Uhland
Embry, Rob, St. Louis, Austin
Endris, Lou, St. John the Evangelist, San Marcos
Fahlund, Nelson, Sacred Heart, Austin
Fansler, Lyman C., St. Joseph's, Killeen
Fell, Channing, St. John Vianney, Round Rock
Flores, Joe, St. Anthony's, Kyle
Foreman, Boyce A., Emmaus, Lakeway
Franklin, John, Sacred Heart, Elgin
Friend, Cecil, Church of the Assumption, West
Fuller, James, St. Joseph's, Manor
Gallagher, James, Our Lady of Lourdes, Gatesville
Garcia, Lorenzo, Sacred Heart, Waco
Garcia, Louis, Santa Teresa, Bryan
Garza, Jesse M., Sacred Heart, Austin
Garza, Jessie C., St. Francis, Waco
Garza, Juan, St. Monica's, Cameron
George, Gregory, St. Jerome's, Waco
Gesch, Michael, St. John Neumann, Austin
Gonzales, Gumisindo, St. John's, Rochester, MN
Gonzalez, John, St. William, Round Rock
Gonzalez, Rodolfo, St. John's, San Marcos
Gutierrez, Joe, San Jose, Austin
Ham, W. J., St. Catherine's, Austin
Hamlet, Mark, St. John Neumann, Austin
Hansen, Clarence
Hargraves, Wilfred (Dub), St. John, Luling
Harper, Steve
Hawkins, Louie, St. John's, Waco
Haywood, Daryl, St. Mary's, Lockhart
Hill, John, Jr., Emmaus, Lakeway
Hipskind, Gregory, St. Thomas More, Austin
Hithe, Alton, St. John's, Waco
Hoefling, Ed, St. Margaret, Giddings
Holicky, Edward, Jr., St. Thomas More, Austin
James, Ray, St. Theresa's, Austin
Januszewski, Bill, St. Mary's, Brenham
Jasek, Frank, St. Mary of Assumption, Waco
Jasso, Carlos, St. Mary's, Lampasas
Jimenez, Jose, Christ the King, Belton
Johnson, Tom, St. Thomas More, Austin
Keller, George, St. Joseph's, Mason
Kennedy, Pat, St. Albert, Austin
Kim, Peter, St. Paul Chong Hasang, Harker Heights
Klement, Jerry, St. Luke's, Temple; Dir. of Diaconal Ministry
Kotrola, Richard, St. William's, Round Rock
Krotzer, Philip, St. Martin de Porres, Dripping Springs
Lara, Alejandro, St. Louis, Austin
Larner, Richard, Holy Trinity, Llano
Lastovia, Ronnie, Christ the King, Belton
Lavallee, Paul, St. Martin de Porres, Dripping Springs
Lawrence, John, St. Anthony's, Kyle
Lilliard, George, St. Charles, Kingsland
Long, Bill, St. Mary's, Lockhart
Lopez, Juan, Cristo Rey, Austin
Luna, Conception, St. Mary's, Hearne
Luna, Willie, St. Luke's, Temple
Madsen, James, St. Luke's, Temple
Mallinger, Thomas, St. Thomas More, Austin
Martinez, Jesse, Apache Shores; Evangelization
Martinez, Roberto, Sacred Heart, Austin
Medrano, Lupe, Cristo Rey, Austin
Meismer, Mike, Sacred Heart, La Grange
Menchaca, Richard, St. Mary's, San Saba
Moat, Jim, Queretaro, Qro., Mexico
Mojica, Jessie, St. John's, San Marcos
Monroe, Frank, St. Mary's, Wimberley
Montag, Eugene J., Our Mother of Sorrows, Burnet
Montalvo, Manuel, Dolores, Austin
Moore, Ray, Santa Rosa, Andice
Morales, David, St. Mary of Assumption, Waco
Moran, Elias, San Jose, Austin
Morris, Douglas, St. John Neumann, Austin
Morse, Eugene, St. Joseph, Killeen
Muehr, Roger, Sacred Heart, Rockne
Murray, Patrick, St. Ignatius, Austin
Murrell, Jack, Good Shepherd, Johnson City
Nelson, Gary, St. Joseph's, Bryan
Nira, Oswaldo, St. Peter the Apostle, Austin
Nowak, Dan, St. Stanislaus, Chappell Hill
O'Neill, John, St. Theresa's, Austin
Ojeda, Johnny, San Francisco Javier, Creedmoor
Orton, Dick, St. Edward's University, Austin
Ozuna, Dan, St. Mary's, Taylor
Parks, Kent, St. Paul's, Austin
Peca, John M., St. Anthony's, Kyle
Perez, Jose Cruz, Our Lady of Guadalupe, Temple
Petter, John, St. Mary's, Temple

Pfuntner, Jordan, St. Jerome's, Hewitt
Potter, Joseph, St. Jerome's, Hewitt
Prewitt, Sidney, St. Mary's, Waco
Pynes, Tony, St. Louis, Austin
Rabke, Joseph, St. Joseph's, Mason
Ramirez, Daniel, St. Mary's, Mexia
Ramsey, Jess
Reed, David, St. Mary's, College Station
Renteria, Mario, Our Lady of Guadalupe, Austin
Rios, Rudy, San Francisco Javier, Creedmoor
Rivera, John, San Jose, Austin
Rodriguez, J. Paul, St. Margaret Mary, Cedar Park
Rosales, Hector, Dolores, Austin
Rositas, Edward, St. Martin de Porres, Dripping Springs
Ruiz, Joe, Holy Cross, Bertram
Ruiz, Joe, St. Helen's, Georgetown
Saenz, Enrique, San Jose, Austin
Sanchez, Romeo, San Jose, Austin
Sanders, Raymond, Jr., St. Theresa's, Austin
Santa Ana, Sam, Sacred Heart, Elgin
Scarmardo, Bill, St. Anthony's, Bryan
Schwab, Peter, St. Thomas More, Austin
Scott, Bill, St. Mary's, College Station
Shieldes, George, Church of the Visitation, West, TX
Shoemake, William, Christ the King, Belton
Sims, Donald, St. Joseph's, Rockdale
Sis, Ray, St. Joseph's, Bryan
Smerke, Tony, St. Helen's, Georgetown
Smetana, Bill, Visitation, Westphalia
Solarzano, Eraclio, St. John the Evangelist, Marble Falls
Sweed, Limas, Blessed Virgin Mary, Washington
Syring, Joe, St. Martin de Porres, Dripping Springs
Terrell, John Larry, St. Catherine of Sienna, Austin
Thornton, Johnnie, Sts. Cyril & Methodius, Granger
Torres, Alfredo, Our Lady of Guadalupe, Taylor
Turner, Donald, St. Louis, Austin
Tyboroski, Julian, St. Joseph's, Marlin
Vargas, Domingo, St. John's, San Marcos
Vasquez, Alfredo, St. Julia's, Austin
Vela, Joe, Our Lady of Guadalupe, Temple
Vela, William, Sacred Heart, Austin
Venglar, Patrick, St. Mary's, Lockhart
Walker, Ron, St. Mary's Cathedral, Austin
Washburne, Marc, St. Elizabeth, Pflugerville
Wearden, Glen, St. Joseph's, Dime Box
Weilert, Otto, Diocesan Pastoral Center
Weynand, Joe, St. Philip's, China Spring
Wilson, Gilbert, St. Jospeh's, Bryan
Wright, Charlie, Visitation, Westphalia
Wright, Dan, St. Thomas More, Austin
Wright, Michael, Sacred Heart, Austin
Wuenchel, Douglas, St. Jerome's, Waco
Young, John, St. Mary's, Caldwell
Zacek, George, St. Theresa's, Austin

INSTITUTIONS LOCATED IN THE DIOCESE

[A] COLLEGES AND UNIVERSITIES

AUSTIN. *St. Edward's University*, 3001 S. Congress Ave., 78704-6489. Tel: 512-448-8400; Fax: 512-448-8492.
E-mail: seu.admit@admin.stedwards.edu
Web site: www.stedwards.edu
For a complete listing, refer to the Colleges and Universities section.

[B] HIGH SCHOOL, DIOCESAN

WACO. *Reicher Catholic High School*, 2102 N. 23rd St., 76708. Tel: 254-752-8349; Fax: 254-752-8408.
E-mail: kcaspersen@esc12.net
Web site: www.reicher
Kevin H. Caspersen, Ph.D., Prin. Campus Ministry: Revs. Kevin Duggan, S.M.; John Ulrich, S.M. Priests 2; Sisters 3; Lay Teachers 20; Students 230.

[C] HIGH SCHOOL, PRIVATE

AUSTIN. *St. Michaels's Catholic Academy*, 3000 Barton Creek Blvd., 78735. Tel: 512-328-2323; Fax: 512-328-2327.
E-mail: jkennedy@stmichaelsacademy.org
Web site: www.stmichaelsacademy.org
Mr. John (Jack) T. Kennedy, II, Head of School. Priests 2; Sisters 1; Lay Teachers 29; Students 412.

TEMPLE. *Holy Trinity Catholic High School*, 2807 Oakdale Dr., 76502. Tel: 254-771-0787; Fax: 254-771-2285.
E-mail: holytrin@vvm.com
Susan Terry, Prin.

[D] ELEMENTARY SCHOOL, PRIVATE

AUSTIN. *Dominican Academy*. (Grades K-5), 12475 Trail Driver, 78737. Tel: 512-288-4266; Fax: 512-301-4213. Sr. Barbara Ann Cernosek, O.P.; Sr. Stephen Anne Zawacki, O.P. Sisters 2; Lay Teachers 5; Students 58.

St. Gabriel's Catholic School. (Legal name: Southwest Austin Catholic School Inc.), 2500 Wimberly Ln., 78735. Tel: 512-512-327-7755; Fax: 512-327-4335. Mr. Greg Wesely, Prin. Lay Teachers 44; Students 409.

[E] MATERNITY AND ADOPTION PROGRAM

AUSTIN. *Marywood Children & Family Services*, 510 W. 26th St., 78705. Tel: 512-472-9251; Fax: 512-472-4829.
E-mail: marywood@eden.com
Web site: marywood.org
Total in Residence 29; Staff 30. Capacity 35.

[F] GENERAL HOSPITALS

AUSTIN. *Seton McCarthy Community Health Center*, 2811 E. Second St., 78702. Tel: 512-324-4929; Fax: 512-324-4948
For a complete listing, refer to the Hospitals section.

Seton Medical Center, 1201 W. 38th St., 78705. Tel: 512-324-1000; Fax: 512-459-5629.
E-mail: mdigenan@seton.org
Web site: www.goodhealth.com
For a complete listing, refer to the Hospitals section.

Seton Northwest Hospital, 11113 Research Blvd., 78759. Tel: 512-324-6000; Fax: 512-324-6924.
E-mail: cdurant@seton.org
Web site: www,goodhealth.com
For a complete listing, refer to the Hospitals section.

Seton South Community Health Center, 3706 S. First St., 78704. Tel: 512-324-4940
For a complete listing, refer to the Hospitals section.

Seton Topfer Community Clinic, 8913 Collingfield Dr., 78758. Tel: 512-324-6850
For a complete listing, refer to the Hospitals section.

BRENHAM. *Trinity Community Medical Center of Brenham*, 700 Medical Pkwy., 77833. Tel: 979-836-6173; Fax: 979-830-2277.
Web site: trinitymed.org
For a complete listing, refer to the Hospitals section.

BRYAN. *Burleson St. Joseph Health Center of Caldwell, Texas*, 2801 Franciscan Dr., 77802. Tel: 409-776-2599; Fax: 409-774-4590.
E-mail: info@mail.st-joseph.org
Web site: www.st-joseph.org
For a complete listing, refer to the Hospitals section.

St. Joseph Regional Health Center, 2801 Franciscan Dr., 77802. Tel: 979-776-3777; Fax: 979-774-4590.
E-mail: dbuch@mail.st-joseph.org
Web site: http://www.st-joseph.org
For a complete listing, refer to the Hospitals section.

St. Joseph Services Corp., 2801 Franciscan Dr., 77802. Tel: 979-776-3777; Fax: 979-774-4590.
E-mail: info@mail.st-joseph.org
Web site: http://www.st-joseph.org
For a complete listing, refer to the Hospitals section.

WACO. *Providence Health Center*, 6901 Medical Pkwy., P.O. Box 2589, 76702-2589. Tel: 254-751-4764; Fax: 254-751-4769.
E-mail: kkeahey@phn-waco.org
Web site: prov-waco.org
For a complete listing, refer to the Hospitals section.

[G] SPECIAL HOSPITAL

WACO. *DePaul Center*, 301 Londonderry Dr., 76712. Tel: 254-776-5970; 1-800-777-5043
For a complete listing, refer to the Special Care Facilities section.

[H] MONASTERIES AND RESIDENCES OF PRIESTS AND BROTHERS

AUSTIN. *Brother Andre House*, 2113 Brackenridge St., 78704. Tel: 512-462-3540; Fax: 512-416-1216. Bro. Thomas G. Krieter, C.S.C.; Rev. Richard S. Teall, C.S.C.

Brothers of the Congregation of Holy Cross. Brother John Baptist Province Center, 1101 St. Edward's Dr., 78704-6512. Tel: 512-442-7856; Fax: 512-444-3133.
E-mail: jmclaug@acad.stedwards.edu
Web site: www.stedwards.edu/holycross/home.htm
Bros. Richard Critz, C.S.C., Prov. Supr.; Stephen Walsh, C.S.C., Asst. Provinicial; Harold Ehlinger, C.S.C., Steward; William Nick, C.S.C., Councilor; Michael Brickman, C.S.C., Councilor; Johnny Juno, C.S.C., Asst. Steward; Carl Smith, C.S.C., Receptionist; Joel Giallanza, C.S.C., Sec.; Kelly Lahare, C.S.C., Accounting/Computers. Total in Province 116.

Brother Vincent Pieau Residence, 921 St. Edward Dr., 78704. Tel: 512-493-0121. Bro. Michael Brickman, Dir.

Congregation of Holy Cross - Southern Province, Provincial House, 2111 Brackenridge St., 78704. Tel: 512-443-3886; Fax: 512-416-1216.
Web site: southerncsc.org
Revs. John R. Birkmeyer, C.S.C., (Retired); Leon J. Boarman, C.S.C., (Retired); Jeremiah R. Buttomer, C.S.C., (Retired); Barry E. Cabell, C.S.C.; Leonard J. Collins, C.S.C.; Joseph F. Geniesse; John S. Korcsmar, C.S.C., Prov.; Paul B. Rankin, C.S.C., (Retired); Joseph W. Rehage, C.S.C., (Retired); Richard S. Teall, C.S.C.; Joseph A. Tomei, C.S.C.; Charles E. Van Winkle, C.S.C.; Bro. Thomas G. Krieter, C.S.C., Asst. Prov., Prov. Steward.

Dominican Friars of Austin, 2502 Comburg Castle Way, 78748-5258. Tel: 512-282-3908; Fax: 512-280-9011.
E-mail: chiefop@austin.rr.com
Revs. James A. McDonough, O.P., Supr.; Gerardo Guerra-Mayaudon, O.P. Tel: 512-292-3381; Bro. Angel Mendez Montoya, O.P., 6008 Club Terrace, 78741. Tel: 512-385-1719; Fax: 512-280-9011. Rev. Ralph Rogawski, O.P.

Moreau House, St. Edward University #1069, 3001 S. Congress, 78704. Tel: 512-448-8595; Fax: 512-448-8549.
E-mail: larrya@admin.stedwards.edu
Bros. Lawrence Atkinson, C.S.C., Dir.; Michael Winslow, C.S.C.

St. Joseph Hall, St. Edward University, 3001 S. Congress Ave., 78704. Tel: 512-442-4534; Fax: 512-442-0589. Bro. Edwin Reggio, C.S.C., Supr. In res. Rev. John C. Tiba Kunirwa. Total in Residence 19; Brothers 19.

Steiner Lodge Retreat, 3117 Westlake Dr., 78746. Tel: 512-328-0459. Revs. Harold W. Essling, C.S.C.; Edwin J. Kadzielawski, C.S.C.

BLANCO. *Missionaries of the Sacred Heart, M.S.C.* (Irish Providence), Rte. 1, Box 1, 78606. Tel: 830-833-5227; Fax: 830-833-2235.
E-mail: stferd@moment.net
Revs. James Dudley, M.S.C.; Richard O'Rourke, M.S.C.; Kevin Blade, M.S.C.

BREMOND. *Clerical Congregation Missionaries of Faith*, St. Mary's Catholic Church, Rte. 1, Box 58, 76629. Tel: 254-746-7789; Fax: 254-746-7280. Rev. Celso A. Yu, M.F., Supr.

BRENHAM. *Order of Friars Minor*, St. Francis Friary, 9539 FM 2193, 77833-0139. Tel: 409-830-1554; Fax: 409-836-9652. Rev. Curt C. Lanzrath, O.F.M. Total in Residence 1.

JONESTOWN. *Hermitage*, 17818 Sandy Ln., 78645-3134. Tel: 512-267-1443. Rev. Francis Chruma.

WACO. *Marist Community*, 4501 Scottwood Dr., 76708. Revs. Kevin Duggan, S.M.; John Ulrich, S.M.

[I] CONVENTS AND RESIDENCES FOR SISTERS

AUSTIN. *Adrian Dominican Sisters*, 1943 Dapplegrey Ln., 78727-4590. Tel: 512-834-9620.
E-mail: loispaha@juno.com

Daughters of Charity of St. Vincent De Paul, 1018 W. 31st St., 78705-2002. Tel: 512-453-9655; Fax: 512-459-5629.
E-mail: DC31st@aol.com
Sisters 5.
Other Address: 5803 Fairlane Dr., 78757-4414. Tel: 512-452-8980; Fax: 512-459-5629.
E-mail: DCFairlane@aol.com
Sisters 3.
Other Address: 3404 Medical Pkwy., 78705-1017. Tel: 512-324-4906; Fax: 512-324-7051. Sisters 4.
Other Address: 11402 Pencewood Dr., 78750-2555. Tel: 512-336-2986; Fax: 512-324-7051.
E-mail: pencewood@usa.net
Sisters 3.

Daughters of Mary Help of Christians (Salesian Sisters of St. John Bosco), St. Mary Mazzarello Convent, 747 Cherico, 78702. Tel: 512-385-9122; Fax: 512-389-2677.
E-mail: fmasuoau@ix.netcom.com
Sr. M. Guadalupe Medina, F.M.A.; Sr. Silvia Castillo, F.M.A.; Sr. Emma Stefanoni, F.M.A. Sisters 3.

Dominican Sisters of Houston, 5911 Reicher Dr., 78723. Tel: 512-926-0687; Fax: 512-926-5138. Sr. Mary Jean Olsovsky, O.P., 12505 B Traildriver, 78737. Tel: 512-301-3911. Sr. Stehen Anne, O.P.; Sr. Barbara Ann Cernosek, O.P.

Franciscan Sisters Daughters of Mercy (Hermanas Franciscanas Hijas de la Misericordia), Dolores Convent, 1111 Montopolis Dr., 78741. Tel: 512-385-4333; 385-5090; Fax: 512-385-6116.
E-mail: sr.rose@doloreschurch.org
House of Formation. Sr. Rose Moreno, F.H.M., Regional Supr. Sisters 4; Novices 1; Postulants 1. St. Francis Convent, 612 N. 3rd St., Waco, 76701. Tel: 817-753-6816; Fax: 254-757-0537. Sisters 5.

Franciscan Sisters of Our Lady of Perpetual Help. (St. Louis, MO), 1300 S. Pleasant Valley Rd., #133, 78741. Tel: 512-912-0047. Sr. Ann Francis Monedero, Contact Person.

Missionary Cathechists of Divine Providence, 1943 Dapplegrey Ln., 78727. Tel: 512-837-7562; 873-7771; Fax: 512-873-8338.
E-mail: sr_celia_ann_cavazos@austindiocese.org
Sr. Celia Ann Cavazos, M.C.D.P.

Missionary Sisters of the Immaculate Conception of the Mother of God, 4211-B Shoalwood, 78756. Tel: 512-451-2890. Sr. Joan Reisch, S.M.I.C.; Sr. Ruthanne Steiner, S.M.I.C. Sisters 2.

Secular Institute of Schoenstatt Sisters of Mary, 12304 Indian Mound Dr., 78758. Tel: 512-837-4467.
E-mail: schoenstattsrs@cs.com
Sr. Christa Marie Hamilton, I.S.S.M.; Sr. Amalia Mata, I.S.S.M.; Sr. Brigid Schneider, I.S.S.M. Total in Residence 3.

Sinsinawa Dominican Sisters, 11200 A Parkfield Dr., 78758. Tel: 512-836-6424; Fax: 512-324-7116.
E-mail: ssimlik@seton.org
Web site: www.sisinawa.org
Sr. Sigrid Simlik, O.P., 6008 Club Terr., 78741. Tel: 512-385-1719. Sr. Helen Raycraft, O.P.; Sr. Guadalupe Soria, O.P. Sisters 3.

Sisters of Mercy of New Jersey, R.S.M. (Watchung, NJ), 2600 Cockburn Dr., 78745. Tel: 512-707-8199. Sr. Linda Chebro, Contact Person.

Sisters of St. Francis of Dubuque, 1943 Dapplegrey Ln., 78727-4590. Tel: 512-834-9793; Fax: 512-873-8338.
E-mail: sr_thecla_cain@austindiocese.org
Web site: www.austindiocese.org
Sr. Thecla Cain, O.S.F.

Sisters of the Holy Cross, La Casa Convent, 2213 Euclid Ave., 78704. Tel: 512-441-6693. Sr. Judith Hallock, C.S.C.

Sisters of the Holy Cross, Loretto Convent, 2301 E. Side Dr., 78704-5214. Tel: 512-441-3850. Sisters 3.

Sisters of the Holy Cross, Our Lady of Victory Convent, 2215 Euclid Ave., 78704-5214. Tel: 512-441-3850. Sisters 3.

Sisters, Servants of the Immaculate Heart of Mary, 3300 Parker Ln., #134, 78741. Tel: 512-447-1335; Fax: 512-448-8492.
E-mail: mariew@admin.stedwards.edu
Web site: www.austindiocese.org
Sr. Marie Andre Walsh, I.H.M., Contact Person, 3311 Parker Ln., #235, 78741. Tel: 512-326-8239; Fax: 512-448-8492. Sr. Anne Crane, 3001 S. Congress, #1030, 78704. Tel: 512-442-5295; Fax: 512-448-8492. Sr. Madeleine Sophie Weber, 1508 South Port #229, 78704. Tel: 512-442-1124; Fax: 512-373-4631. Sr. Agnes Murray, 5508 N. Hwy 317, Belton, 76513. Tel: 254-780-1739; Fax: 254-780-2684. Sr. Jean Burbo.

Ursuline Sisters - Roman Union, O.S.U. (Crystal City, MO), 4921 Crestway, 78731. Tel: 512-452-6070. Sr. Carla Dolce, Contact Person.

BRENHAM. *Monastery of St. Clare*, 9300 Hwy. 105, 77833. Tel: 409-836-2444; Fax: 409-836-9652.
E-mail: chandler@phoenix.net
Rev. Curt C. Lanzrath, O.F.M., Chap. Sisters 8. Res., 9300 Hwy. 105, 77833. Tel: 409-836-2444. Sr. Mary Angela Chandler, O.S.C., Abbess.

Sisters of St. Francis of Our Lady of Lourdes (O.S.F.). Tel: 979-836-2106; 836-9481; Fax: 979-830-2277. 605 Church St. A, 77833. Sr. Nathaniel Eisel. Tel: 979-836-9481(h); 830-2276 (w); Sr. Kathleen Skog. Tel: 979-836-9481(h); 830-2276(w), 605 Church St. B, 77833. Sr. Geraldine Paluszak. Tel: 979-836-2106 (h); 830-2275(w); Sr. Winifred Templin. Tel: 979-836-2106(h); 836-9770 (w), 2819 Foster Ln., #F235, Austin, 78757. Tel: 512-453-0808; Fax: 512-454-2010. Sr. Josetta Konopka, 6801 Tennyson #206, Waco, 76710. Tel: 254-741-1312. Sr. Mary Patricia Zielinski.

BRYAN. *Sisters of St. Francis of Our Lady of Lourdes*, 2801 Franciscan Dr., 77802. Tel: 409-776-2599; Fax: 409-774-4590.
E-mail: info@mail.st-joseph.org
Web site: http://www.st-joseph.org
Sisters 8.

BURNET. *Sisters of the Holy Cross / Council Creek Village*, Star Route, 78611. Tel: 512-756-2997. Sr. Mary Elizabeth, C.S.C., Contact Person.

FAYETTEVILLE. *Sisters of Divine Providence*, St. John's Convent, 209 E. Bell, 78940-5500. Tel: 409-378-2275. Sr. Euphrosine Honc, C.D.P.

LA GRANGE. *Sisters of the Incarnate Word and Blessed Sacrament*, Sacred Heart Convent, 570 E. Pearl St., 78945. Tel: 409-968-3370; Fax: 409-968-5740.
E-mail: sreagnesgabriel@hotmail.com
Sr. Elizabeth Agnes Gabriel, C.V.I.

LULING. *Our Lady of Victory Missionary Sisters*, 500 E. Travis, 78648. Tel: 512-875-5354. Sr. Mary Francis Bartsch.

SAN MARCOS. *Cordi-Marian Sisters*, 964 Field St., St. Anthony Claret Mission House, 78666. Tel: 512-396-5333. Sr. Adelina Esquivel; Sr. Rose Ann Castilleja. Sisters 2.

SOMERVILLE. *Missionary Ecumenical*, P.O. Box 367, 77879. Tel: 979-595-1494; Fax: 979-596-1494.

TAYLOR. *Dominican Sisters of Houston*, St. Mary Convent, 317 E. Fourth St., 76574-3624. Tel: 512-352-2144; Fax: 512-365-1431.
E-mail: stmaryspastor@austin.rr.com
Sr. Paschal Hoelscher; Sr. Mary V. Hugger. Sisters 2.

Sisters of St. John Bosco, St. John's Convent, 1101 Symes, 76574. Tel: 512-352-2802. Sr. Joseph Moreno.

WACO. *Congregation of the Sisters of the Incarnate Word, C.C.V.I.*, 6901 Medical Pkwy., 76702. Tel: 817-751-4000. Sr. Rosemary Burke, C.C.V.I.

Daughters of Charity of St. Vincent De Paul, 2416 Colcord, 76707. Tel: 254-753-3817.
E-mail: dcswaco@email.com
Sr. Cecile Matushek; Sr. Natalie Marengo; Sr. Brigid O'Donoghue. Sisters 3. 213 Bonham Dr., 76643. Tel: 254-666-0611.
E-mail: hewittdc@aol.com
Sr. Mary Teresa Fox; Sr. Rebecca Hite. Sisters 2.

Franciscan Sisters Daughters of Mercy. (Franciscanas Hijas de la Misericordia), 612 N. Third St., 76701. Tel: 817-753-5565. 1111 Montopolis Dr., Austin, 78741. Sisters 4.

Marist Missionary Sisters, S.M.S.M. (Waltham, MA), 1600 Lakeshore Dr., 76708. Tel: 254-753-0445. Sr. Philothea Blake, Contact Person.

Sisters of Charity of the Incarnate Word, 717 Cardinal, 76712. Tel: 254-776-2707; Fax: 254-754-0133. Sr. Stephen Guiry, C.C.V.I.

Sisters of the Holy Cross, St. Mary's Convent, 224 N. 14th St., 76701-1109. Tel: 254-756-0548. Sr. Kenneth Regan, C.S.C.

[J] HOMES FOR THE AGED & HANDICAPPED

BRENHAM. *Trinity Care Center*, 400 E. Sayles, 77833. Tel: 979-836-9770.
E-mail: fjulian@mail.st-joseph.org
Web site: TRINITYMED.ORG
For a complete listing, refer to the Special Care Facilities section.

BRYAN. *St. Joseph Manor*, 2801 Franciscan Dr., 77802. Tel: 979-821-7590
For a complete listing, refer to the Special Care Facilities section.

CALDWELL. *Burleson St. Joseph Manor*, 1022 Presidential Corridor, Hwy. 21E, 77836. Tel: 979-821-7590; Fax: 979-567-4811.
E-mail: hcottrell@mail.st-joseph.org
For a complete listing, refer to the Special Care Facilities section.

WACO. *CHRISTUS, The Regis Retirement Home & St. Elizabeth Nursing Home*, 400 Austin Ave., P.O. Box 1909, 76703. Tel: 254-756-5441; Fax: 254-754-0133.
E-mail: doug35@aol.com
Web site: members.aol.com/regisst
For a complete listing, refer to the Special Care Facilities section.

[K] MISSION CENTERS

SOMERVILLE. *St. Ann Mission Center*, P.O. Box 367, 77879. Tel: 979-596-1696; Fax: 979-596-1496. Missionary Ecumenical. Sr. M. John DellaMorte, M.E., Supr. Kindergarten Students 20; Total Staff 1.

WACO. *St. Francis Mission Center*, 612 N. Third St., 76701. Tel: 817-753-5565. Franciscan Sisters Daughters of Mercy. Sr. Catherine Vallespir, F.H.M., Catechetical, Kindergarten & Nursery; Sr. Barbara Herrera, F.H.M., Supr. Total Staff 11. Sisters 4.

[L] RENEWAL CENTERS

BELTON. *Cedarbrake Renewal Center*, P.O. Box 58, 76513-0058. Tel: 254-780-2436; Fax: 254-780-2684.
E-mail: sr_jean_burbo@austindiocese.org
Sr. Jean Burbo, I.H.M., Dir. Total in Residence 4; Total Staff 11.

[M] NEWMAN APOSTOLATE

AUSTIN. *University Catholic Center*, 2010 University Ave., 78705. Tel: 512-476-7351; Fax: 512-476-7377.
E-mail: terry@utcatholic.org
Web site: http://www.utexas.edu/students/univcath
Serving the Catholic community at the University of Texas. Rev. Ruben Patino, C.S.P., Dir. Campus Ministers: Sr. Martha Ann Burch, D.C.; Michelle Goodwin; Rev. David Farnum, C.S.P.; Terry M. Martin, Admin.

BRENHAM. *Blinn College Catholic Student Union*, Blinn College, 77833. For Catholic students attending Blinn Jr. College. Mr. John Dujka, Sponsor. Tel: 409-830-4249; Deacon William Januszewski, Campus Minister. Tel: 409-836-9329.

COLLEGE STATION. *St. Mary's Catholic Center*, 603 Church Ave., 77840. Tel: 979-846-5717; Fax: 979-846-4493.
E-mail: info@aggiecatholic.org
Web site: http://www.aggiecatholic.org
Campus ministry at Texas A & M University. Revs. Michael J. Sis; David A. Konderla; Deacons Bill Scott, Jr.; David Reed. Total in Residence 2; Total Staff 25.

SAN MARCOS. *Catholic Student Center*, 100 Concho St., 78666. Tel: 512-392-5925; Fax: 512-392-5922.
E-mail: catholic-studentcenter@swt.edu
Catholic Students attending Southwest Texas State University. Rev. Daryl Olds, C.M.F.

WACO. *Catholic Student Center at Baylor University*, 1415 S. 9th St., P.O. Box 6060, 76706-6060. Tel: 254-757-0636; Fax: 254-454-3042.
E-mail: catholic@texnet.net
Web site: www.baylor.edu/~catholic/
For Catholic students attending Baylor University. Mr. Mervyn S. Pacheco, Dir.; Revs. John Ulrich, S.M., Campus Min.; Kevin Duggan, S.M., Campus Min.; James Deaconson, Chap.

[N] FOUNDATIONS, ENDOWMENTS & TRUSTS

AUSTIN. *Holy Family School Foundation*, P.O. Box 201975, 78720-1975. Tel: 512-244-3119.
E-mail: hfcs@holyfamily.pvt.k12.tx.us
Clarence J. Kellerman, Contact Person.

BRYAN. *St. Joseph Memorial Endowment Fund*, St. Joseph's, 600 E. 26th, 77803. Tel: 979-822-2721; Fax: 979-779-3120.
E-mail: frjohn@stjosephbcs.org
Web site: ww.stjosephbcs.org
Rev. John A. McCaffrey.

[O] MISCELLANEOUS

AUSTIN. *Blue Ladies Minerals, Inc.*, 1206 W. 38th St., Ste. 4200, 78705-1056. Tel: 512-324-1990. Gene Attal, Contact Person.

Brothers of Holy Cross, South-West Province, Charitable Trust, 3001 S. Congress Ave., #1046, 78704. Tel: 512-442-7856; Fax: 512-444-3133.
Trustees: Bros. Donald Blauvelt, C.S.C.; Harold Ehlinger, C.S.C., Chm.; Ralph Kuder, C.S.C.; Patrick Sopher, C.S.C.

Catholic Archives of Texas, N. Congress & W. 16th St., P.O. Box 13124, 78711-3124. Tel: 512-476-6296; Fax: 512-476-3715.
E-mail: cat@onr.com
Web site: www.onr.com/user.cat
Kinga L. Perzynska, Archive Dir.; Susan Eason, Archives Asst. Historical collection of the Church in the Southwest and Texas from 1519.

Catholic Family Fraternal of Texas. KJZT, P.O. Box 1884, 78767-1844. Tel: 512-444-9586. Mrs. Geraldine Nekuza, Pres.; Loretta Shal, Vice Pres.

Catholic Southwest, 1625 Rutherford Ln., Bldg. D, 78754-5105. Tel: 512-339-9882; Fax: 512-339-8670. Patrick Foley, Ph.D., Editor; Jesus F. de la Teja, Ph.D., Mng. Editor.

Children's Hospital Foundation of Austin, 601 E. 15th St., 78701-1996. Tel: 512-324-8420; Fax: 512-324-8435.
E-mail: mstromain@seton.org
Ms. Martha St. Romain, Contact Person.

Christ Child Society of Austin, 3226 Stratford Hills Ln., 78746. Tel: 512-347-0655; Fax: 512-347-0708. Nancy Jamial, Pres.

Holy Family Catholic School, P.O. Box 201975, 78720-1975. Tel: 512-246-4455; Fax: 512-246-4454.
E-mail: hfcs@holyfamily.pvt.k12.tx.us
Web site: www.holyfamily.pvt.k12.tx.us
Mrs. Falba F. Turner, Prin.

Juan Diego Missionary Society, Inc., P.O. Box 6067, 78762. Tel: 512-731-8434; Fax: 512-441-3778. Elias and Christina Limon, Directors.

Ladies of Charity of Austin, TX, 510 W. 26th St., 78705. Tel: 512-472-9251; Fax: 512-335-5713. Nicky Mercado, Pres.

North Central Catholic School Corporation, 13729 Research Blvd., #610-147, P.O. Box 201975, 78720-4454. Tel: 512-219-8914; Fax: 512-246-4454.

Our Lady's Family Center, 1817 E. Sixth St., P.O. Box 6453, 78762. Tel: 512-322-0632; Fax: 512-322-0632.
E-mail: ourlady@austinfreenet.com
Web site: afn-neighbor.net/eacn/orgeaml
Deacon Willie J. Cortez, Dir. Patients Assisted 200; Total Staff 2.

The Seton Cove - A Spirituality Center, 3708 Crawford St., 78731. Tel: 512-451-0272; Fax: 512-451-0784.
E-mail: setoncove@seton.org
Web site: seton. net
Total Staff 7.

Society of St. Vincent de Paul, 6503 Wolfcreek Pass, 78749-1825. Tel: 512-288-3370; Fax: 512-288-9130.
E-mail: svdpaus@aol.com
Deacon Michael B. Wright, Spiritual Advisor; Raymond DuPont, Pres.; Frederick L. Gale, Vice Pres.; Jeannine DuPont, Treasurer; Esther L. Barrientes, Sec.; Bobby L. Sherry, Dir.

Texas Catholic Conference, 1625 Rutherford Ln., Bldg. D, 78754-5105. Tel: 512-339-9882; Fax: 512-339-8670. Bro. Richard Daly, C.S.C., Exec. Dir.

Texas Catholic Historical Society, c/o Texas Catholic Conference, 1625 Rutherford Ln. Bldg. D, 78704-5105. Tel: 512-339-9882; Fax: 512-339-8670. Rev. Jose Roberto (Beto) Juarez, Pres.

Texas Conference of Catholic Health Facilities, 1625 Rutherford Ln., Bldg. D, 78754-5105. Tel: 512-339-1157; Fax: 512-339-8670.
E-mail: tcchf@airmail.net
Web site: www.techf.org
Rev. Msgr. William L. Broussard, Exec. Dir.

VESS, Volunteers for Educational and Social Services, 1625 Rutherford Ln., Bldg. D, 78754-5105. Tel: 512-339-7123; 1-800-771-5677; Fax: 512-339-8670.
E-mail: info@vess.org
Web site: www.vess.org
Directors: Jill Seidenberger; Jody Hart.

BASTROP. *Ladies of Charity of Bastrop, TX*, P.O. Drawer W, 78602. Tel: 512-321-9819; Fax: 512-321-1647. Presidents: Putzie Martin; Kay Condit.

HARKER HEIGHTS. *Ladies of Charity of Harker Heights*, 1005-A S. Ann Blvd., 76548. Tel: 254-680-7970.
E-mail: alponce@juno.com
Debra Ponce, Pres.

LAGRANGE. *Catholic Union of Texas, The K.J.T.*, P.O. Box 297, 78945-0297. Tel: 979-968-5877; Fax: 979-968-5823.
E-mail: kjt@cvtv.net
Elo J. Goerig, Pres. KJT NEWS, official publication.

LAKE TRAVIS. *Ladies of Charity*, P.O. Box 340026, 78734. Tel: 512-261-7018. Mary Lee Baker, Pres.

WACO, TX 76701-2105. *CHRISTUS Health Waco*, 106 S. 5th St.
Ladies of Charity of Waco, TX, 622 N. 36th St., 76710-5429. Tel: 254-753-5059.
E-mail: Lbb622@aol.com
Web site: Lbb622@aol.com
Lorraine Brooks, Pres.

RELIGIOUS INSTITUTES OF MEN REPRESENTED IN THE DIOCESE

For further details refer to the corresponding bracketed number in the Religious Institutes of Men or Women section.

[0170]—*Basilian Fathers.* (Galveston-Houston, TX).—C.S.B.
[0600]—*Brothers of the Congregation of Holy Cross.* (Southwest Province).—C.S.C.
[0360]—*Claretian Missionaries.* (Rome, Italy).—C.M.F.
[0750]—*Congregation of Marian Hill Missionaries.* (Dearborn Heights, MI).—C.M.M.
[0480]—*Conventual Franciscans.* (Mt. Francis, IN).—O.F.M.Conv.
[0520]—*Franciscan Friars.* (Cincinnati Prov.).—O.F.M.
[0690]—*Jesuit Fathers and Brothers.* (Detroit, MI).—S.J.
[0780]—*Marist Fathers.* (Washington, DC).—S.M.
[1110]—*Missionaries of the Sacred Heart.* (San Antonio, TX).—M.S.C.
[0910]—*Oblates of Mary Immaculate.* (San Antonio, TX).—O.M.I.
[]—*Order of Cistercian.* (Poland).—O.S.Cist.
[0430]—*Order of Preachers-Dominicans.* (New Orleans, LA).—O.P.
[1030]—*Paulist Fathers.* (Jamaica Estates, NY).—C.S.P.
[0610]—*Priests of the Congregation of Holy Cross.* (Southern Prov.; Austin, TX).—C.S.C.
[1200]—*Society of the Divine Savior.* (Milwaukee, WI).—S.D.S.
[0560]—*Third Order Regular of Saint Francis of Waco, TX.* (Vice-Province of Santa Maria de Guadalupe, Mexico).—T.O.R.

RELIGIOUS INSTITUTES OF WOMEN REPRESENTED IN THE DIOCESE

[2190]—*Congregation of the Incarnate Word and Blessed Sacrament.* (Houston, TX).—C.V.I.
[0470]—*Congregation of the Sisters of Charity of the Incarnate Word.* (Houston, Texas).—C.C.V.I.
[0460]—*Congregation of the Sisters of Charity of the Incarnate Word.* (San Antonio, TX).—C.C.V.I.
[1920]—*Congregation of the Sisters of the Holy Cross.* (Notre Dame, IN).—C.S.C.
[]—*Cordi-Marian Sisters.* (San Antonio, TX).—M.C.M.
[0760]—*Daughters of Charity of St. Vincent de Paul.* (St. Louis, MO).—D.C.
[0850]—*Daughters of Mary Help of Christian.* (San Antonio, TX).—F.M.A.
[1070-13]—*Dominican Sisters.* (Adrian, MI).—O.P.
[1070-19]—*Dominican Sisters.* (Houston, TX).—O.P.
[1070-03]—*Dominican Sisters.* (Sinsinawa, WI).—O.P.
[1235]—*Franciscan Sisters Daughters of Our Lady of Mercy (Franciscanas Hijas de la Misericordia).* (U.S. delegation: Waco, TX).—F.H.M.
[1430]—*Franciscan Sisters of Our Lady of Perpetual Help*
[2420]—*Marist Missionary Sisters.* (Waltham, MA).—S.M.S.M.
[2690]—*Missionary Catechists of Divine Providence.* (San Antonio, TX).—M.C.D.P.
[]—*Missionary Ecumenical.* (Rome, Italy).—M.E.
[2760]—*Missionary Sisters of the Immaculate Conception of the Mother of God.* (Paterson, NJ).—S.M.I.C.
[3760]—*Order of St. Clare.* (Brenham, TX).—O.S.C.
[3130]—*Our Lady of Victory Missionary Sisters.* (Huntington, IN).—O.L.V.M.
[2970]—*School Sisters of Notre Dame.* (St. Louis, MO; Dallas, TX).—S.S.N.D.
[]—*Secular Institute of Schoenstatt Sisters of Mary.* (Southern Prov., Rockport, TX).—I.S.S.M.
[2575]—*Sister of Mercy of New Jersey.* (Watchung, NJ).—R.S.M.
[1010]—*Sisters of Divine Providence.* (San Antonio, TX).—C.D.P.
[3000]—*Sisters of Notre Dame de Namur.* (Cincinnati, OH).—S.N.D.deN.
[1530]—*Sisters of St. Francis of the Congregation of Our Lady of Lourdes.* (Sylvania, OH).—O.S.F.
[1570]—*Sisters of St. Francis of the Holy Family.* (Dubuque, IA).—O.S.F.
[]—*Sisters of St. John Bosco.* (Taylor, TX).—S.J.B.
[2150]—*Sisters, Servants of the Immaculate Heart of Mary.* (Monroe, MI).—I.H.M.
[4110]— *Ursuline Sisters - Roman Union.* (Crystal City, MO).—O.S.U.

NECROLOGY

(No Deaths)

Diocese of Baker

(Dioecesis Bakeriensis)

Most Reverend

ROBERT FRANCIS VASA

Bishop of Baker; ordained May 22, 1976; appointed November 19, 1999; consecrated and installed January 26, 2000.

Most Reverend

THOMAS J. CONNOLLY, D.D., J.C.D.

Retired Bishop of Baker; ordained April 8, 1947; appointed May 4, 1971; consecrated June 30, 1971; retired January 2000. *Res., P.O. Box 5999, Bend, OR, 97708.*

ESTABLISHED JUNE 19, 1903.

Square Miles 66,826.

Comprises the counties of Baker, Crook, Deschutes, Gilliam, Grant, Harney, Hood River, Jefferson, Klamath, Lake, Malheur, Morrow, Sherman, Umatilla, Union, Wallowa, Wasco and Wheeler in the State of Oregon.

For legal titles of parishes and diocesan institutions, consult the Chancery Office.

Diocesan Pastoral Office: P.O. Box 5999, Bend, OR, 97708. Tel.: 541-388-4004; Fax: 541-388-2566.

Web site address: users.bendnet.com/diocbakr/

E-mail address: diocbakr@bendnet.com

STATISTICAL OVERVIEW

Personnel	
Bishop	1
Retired Bishops	1
Priests: Diocesan Active in Diocese	22
Priests: Active Outside Diocese	2
Priests: Diocesan in Foreign Missions	1
Priests: Retired, Sick or Absent	12
Number of Diocesan Priests	37
Religious Priests in Diocese	6
Extern Priests in Diocese	10
Ordinations:	
Diocesan Priests	1
Permanent Deacons	8
Permanent Deacons in Diocese	15
Total Brothers	1
Total Sisters	28
Parishes	
Parishes	36
With Resident Pastor:	
Resident Diocesan Priests	25
Resident Religious Priests	2
Without Resident Pastor:	
Administered by Priests	9
Missions	27
Professional Ministry Personnel:	
Sisters	9
Lay Ministers	13
Welfare	
Catholic Hospitals	5
Total Assisted	276,384
Homes for the Aged	1
Total Assisted	110
Day Care and Extended Day Care Centers	3
Total Assisted	286
Special Centers for Social Services	7
Total Assisted	25,218
Educational	
Diocesan Students in Other Seminaries	5
Total Seminarians	5
Elementary Schools, Diocesan and Parish	3
Total Students	644
Catechesis/Religious Education:	
High School Students	1,417
Elementary Students	2,395
Total Students Under Catholic Instruction	4,461
Teachers in the Diocese:	
Sisters	1
Lay Teachers	36
Vital Statistics	
Receptions into the Church:	
Infant Baptism Totals	776
Adult Baptism Totals	182
Received into Full Communion	145
First Communions	932
Confirmations	338
Marriages:	
Catholic	137
Interfaith	100
Total Marriages	237
Deaths	326
Total Catholic Population	36,179
Total Population	425,650

Former Bishops—Rt. Rev. CHARLES J. O'REILLY, D.D., ord. June 29, 1890; appt. June 24, 1903; cons. Bishop of Baker City, Aug. 25, 1903; transferred to the See of Lincoln March 20, 1918; died Feb. 4, 1923.—Most Rev. LEO F. FAHEY, D.D., ord. May 29, 1926; appt. Titular Bishop of Ipsus and Coadjutor "cum jure successionis" March 13, 1948; cons. May 26, 1948; died March 31, 1950.—Most Rev. JOSEPH F. MCGRATH, D.D., assistant at the Pontifical Throne, Bishop of Baker City; ord. Dec. 21, 1895; appt. Dec. 21, 1918; cons. March 25, 1919; died April 12, 1950.—Most Rev. FRANCIS P. LEIPZIG, D.D., ord. April 14, 1920; appt. Bishop of Baker July 18, 1950; cons. Sept. 12, 1950; retired May 4, 1971; died Jan. 17, 1981.—Most Rev. THOMAS J. CONNOLLY, D.D., J.C.D., ord. April 8, 1947; appt. May 4, 1971; cons. June 30, 1971; retired Nov. 19, 1999.

Vicar General—Rev. Msgr. MATTHEW M. CROTTY, J.C.D.

Vicar of Canonical Affairs—Very Rev. W. THOMAS FAUCHER, J.C.L.

Chancellor—Rev. JAMES P. LOGAN, J.C.L.

Diocesan Pastoral Office—Mailing Address: P.O. Box 5999, Bend, 97708. Tel: 541-388-4004; Fax: 541-388-2566. *911 S.E. Armour, Bend, 97702.*

Receptionist and Secretary—VIRGINIA MOHR.

Diocesan Tribunal—Tel: 541-388-4010.

Judicial Vicar and Chief Judge—Very Rev. W. THOMAS FAUCHER, J.C.L.

Judge—Rev. Msgr. MATTHEW M. CROTTY, J.C.D.

Defender of the Bond and Promoter of Justice—Revs. LEO F. WECKERLE, J.C.L.; MATTHEW PU, J.C.D.; JAMES P. LOGAN, J.C.L.

Coordinator and Notary—DOLORES FRIBERG.

Council of Priests and Diocesan Consultors—Most Rev. ROBERT F. VASA, Pres., Ex Officio; Very Rev. W. THOMAS FAUCHER, Chm.; Revs. JOSEPH KELBEL; CHARLES V. DREISBACH; JAMES RADLOFF; RICHARD O. FISCHER; RAYMOND HOPP; TODD UNGER; Rev. Msgr. MATTHEW M. CROTTY, V.G.

Priestly Life and Ministry—Revs. RICHARD O. FISCHER; CHARLES U. DREISBACH; RAYMOND HOPP.

Deans—Central: Rev. LEO F. WECKERLE, J.C.L., Eastern: Rev. RAYMOND JARBOE, Northern: Rev. DENNIS STRACHOTA, Southern: Rev. CHARLES V. DREISBACH, Western: Rev. TODD UNGER.

Diocesan Offices and Directors

Board of Education—Most Rev. ROBERT F. VASA; Revs. TODD UNGER; MARTIN HAGGINS, O.F.M.Cap.; W. RAYMOND JARBOE,Principals of Schools and Representatives from each Parish School Board.

Building Committee—Rev. Msgr. MATTHEW M. CROTTY; Rev. RONALD E. MAAG.

Campus Ministry Apostolate—Rev. W. RAYMOND JARBOE, *829 S.W. Second Ave., Ontario, 97914.* Tel: 541-889-8469.

Catholic Services—MARGUERITE REED, *P.O. Box 563, Baker City, 97814.* Tel: 541-523-2902.

Church Property, Administration of—Most Rev. ROBERT F. VASA, Pres.; Rev. Msgr. MATTHEW M. CROTTY, Sec. JOSEPH LA CASSE, Realtor.

DeSales Program of Adult Education—Direct Inquiries to:Tel: 800-488-0488. Direct Orders to: *St. Anthony Messenger Press, 1615 Republic St., Cincinnati, OH, 45210;* Fax: 513-241-1197.

Diocesan Attorney—Vacant.

Diocesan Development Office—JOHN SCHIEMER, *P.O. Box 5999, Bend, 97708.* Tel: 541-388-4004.

Diocesan Finance Minister—HOPE BURKE.

Diocesan Financial Board—Rev. CHARLES V. DREISBACH.

Diocesan Historian Emeritus—Rev. Msgr. WILLIAM S. STONE, *P.O. Box 41, The Dalles, 97058.* Tel: 541-296-3426.

Diocesan Superintendent of Schools—Sr. MARY CATHERINE PERKINS, O.P., *P.O. Box 5999, Bend, 97708.* Tel: 541-385-1865.

Director of Campaign for Human Development—Rev. RONALD E. MAAG, *St. Mary Church, P.O. Box 693, Hood River, 97031.* Tel: 541-386-3373.

Director of Catholic Hospitals—Rev. TODD UNGER, *St. Peter Church, P.O. Box 41, The Dalles, 97058.* Tel: 541-296-2026.

Friends of the Catholic University of America—Rev. Msgr. WILLIAM S. STONE, *P.O. Box 41, The Dalles, 97058.* Tel: 541-296-3426.

Health and Retirement Board—Most Rev. ROBERT F. VASA, Pres.; Revs. TODD UNGER, Sec. & Treas. FRANKLIN BUCKMAN; CHARLES V. DREISBACH, Chm. LEO F. WECKERLE, J.C.L.; ROBERT C. IRWIN.

Office of Worship and Spirituality—Very Rev. W. THOMAS FAUCHER, J.C.L., *Pastoral Office, P.O. Box 5999, Bend, 97708.* Tel: 541-388-4004.

Natural Family Planning—Vacant, Dir., *P.O. Box 5999, Bend, 97708.* Tel: 541-383-8928; 388-4004.

Office of Faith Development and Ministry—P.O. Box 9250, Bend, 97708. 911 S.E. Armour St., Bend, 97702. Sr. PEGGY GLYNN, O.P., Rel. Educ. Tel: 541-388-3991. Sr. MARY CATHERINE PERKINS, O.P., Adult Education. Tel: 541-385-1865.

Office of Hispanic Ministry—Sr. MARIE VIANNEY BILGRIEN, S.S.N.D., Dir., *P.O. Box 5999, Bend, 97708.* Tel: 541-388-4004.

Priests' Continuing Education Committee—Most Rev. ROBERT F. VASA; Revs. DENNIS J. STRACHOTA, Chm. ROBERT GREINER; ROBERT C. IRWIN; RAYMOND JARBOE.

R.C.I.A. Office—Rev. DENNIS STRACHOTA, Dir., *800 S.E. Court Ave., Pendleton, 97801.* Tel: 541-276-3615.

Diocesan Scout Director—TED YAROSH, *5160 S. Etna St., Klamath Falls, 97603.* Tel: 541-882-4611.

Vocations—Rev. RICHARD O. FISCHER, *Holy Family Church, 685 N. Fairview, Burns, 97720.* Tel: 541-573-2613.

CLERGY, PARISHES, MISSIONS AND PAROCHIAL SCHOOLS

BAKER CITY
(County of Baker)

1—CATHEDRAL OF ST. FRANCIS DE SALES (1871), Revs. Robert C. Irwin, Rector; John R. Jasper.
Res., 2235 First St., 97814. Tel: 541-523-4521; Fax: 541-523-8362. [CEM]
Catechesis/Religious Programs—Tamara Skidmore, D.R.E.
Students 140.
Missions—Halfway, St. Therese; Unity, St. Joseph's; North Powder, St. Anthony.

OUTSIDE BAKER CITY

Arlington, Gilliam Co., St. Francis (1931), Rev. Livinus Obioha, Admin.
Mailing Address: P.O. Box 485, Condon, 97823. Tel: 541-384-5271; Fax: 541-384-5271.

Bend, Deschutes Co., St. Francis of Assisi (1904), Revs. Martin Haggins, O.F.M.Cap.; Michael Walsh, O.F.M.Cap.; Brian McKenna, O.F.M.Cap.; Sr. Patricia Rayburn, O.S.F., Pastoral Assoc.; Deacon Bob Walling.
Office: 2450 N.E. 27th St., 97701. Tel: 541-382-3631; Fax: 541-385-8879.
School—(Grades PreK-8). Tel: 541-382-4701; Fax: 541-312-9111. Sr. Kathleen Cordes, S.H.C.J., Prin.
Lay Teachers 26; Students 302.
Day Care—Tel: 541-389-3906.
Students 20.
Catechesis/Religious Programs—Duke Johnson, D.R.E.
Students 515.
Diocese of Baker - El Programa de Ayuda—Tel: 541-382-4366.

Boardman, Morrow Co., Our Lady of Guadalupe, Rev. Gregory Okorobia.
Mailing Address: P.O. Box 1277, 97818. Tel: 541-481-2024.

Burns, Harney Co., Holy Family (1899), Rev. Richard O. Fischer.
Res., 685 N. Fairview Ave., 97720. Tel: 541-573-2613.
Catechesis/Religious Programs—620 N. Egan Ave., 97720. Mary Lemos, D.R.E.
Students 90.
Missions—Drewsey, Our Lady of Loretto; Crane, St. Thomas.

Chiloquin, Klamath Co., Our Lady of Mt. Carmel (1927), Rev. Ronald J. Warren.
Res., 503 W. Chocktoot, P.O. Box 396, 97624. Tel: 541-783-2411.
Catechesis/Religious Programs—Students 18.
Mission—Bly, St. James the Apostle.

Condon, Gilliam Co., St. John's (1925), Rev. Livinus Obioha, Admin.
Res., P.O. Box 485, 97823. Tel: 541-384-5271; Fax: 541-384-5271.
Mission—Fossil, St. Catherine.

Dufur, Wasco Co., St. Alphonsus (1911), Rev. Anselm Fister, O.S.B., Admin.
Res., P.O. Box 395, 97021. Tel: 541-467-2580.
Catechesis/Religious Programs—Students 32.
Mission—Maupin, St. Mary's.

Elgin, Union Co., St. Mary (1966). Attended by Our Lady of the Valley, La Grande. Deacon Joseph Garlitz.
Res., P.O. Box 97, 97827. Tel: 541-437-8101.
Catechesis/Religious Programs—Sharon Woody, D.R.E.
Students 30.

Enterprise, Wallowa Co., St. Katherine's (1923), Rev. Peter Fernando, Admin.
Res., 301 E. Garfield St., P.O. Box 370, 97828. Tel: 541-426-3043.
Parish Office: Tel: 541-426-4008.
Catechesis/Religious Programs—Students 35.
Mission—Wallowa, St. Pius X, South Pine St., 97885. Tel: 541-886-3165.

Heppner, Morrow Co., St. Patrick's (1887), Rev. Gerald W. Condon.
Res., 525 Gale St., P.O. Box 633, 97836. Tel: 541-676-9462.
Catechesis/Religious Programs—D.R.E.: Mike Armato; Kim Armato.
Students 45.

Hermiston, Umatilla Co., Our Lady of Angels (1910), Revs. Joseph Reinig; William Kalin; Kay Edwards, Parish Mgr.
Res., 565 Hermiston Ave., 97838. Tel: 541-567-5812; Fax: 541-564-0933.
Catechesis/Religious Programs—Tel: 541-567-3825. Martha Chartres, D.R.E.
Students 293.

Hood River, Hood River Co., Immaculate Conception (1906), Rev. Ronald E. Maaq; Deacon Lou DeSitter, Pastoral Assoc.
Res., 1501 Belmont Ave., P.O. Box 693, 97031. Tel: 541-386-3373; Fax: 541-386-1451. [CEM]
Catechesis/Religious Programs—Tel: 541-387-6797. D.R.E.: Maria Ramirez, (Spanish); Holly Holmes, (English).
Students 190.

Ione, Morrow Co., St. William, Rev. Gerald W. Condon.
Mailing Address: P.O. Box 633, Heppner, 97836. Tel: 541-676-9462.
Church—110 Main St., 97843.
Catechesis/Religious Programs—Jeri Mc Elligott, D.R.E.
Students 27.

John Day, Grant Co., St. Elizabeth's (1939), Rev. Robert Van Sickler.
Res., 111 S.W. 2nd St., P.O. Box 189, 97845. Tel: 541-575-1459.
Catechesis/Religious Programs—Tel: 541-575-0415. Mary Ann Vidourek, D.R.E.
Students 35.
Missions—Monument, St. Anne; Seneca, St. Charles; Longcreek, St. Katherine.

Jordan Valley, Malheur Co., St. Bernard's (1915), Rev. Matthew C. Pu.
Res., P.O. Box 186, 97910. Tel: 541-586-2266; Fax: 541-586-2448.
Catechesis/Religious Programs—Lily Garrard, D.R.E.
Students 8.
Mission—Arock, Holy Family, Arock Rd., 97902.

Klamath Falls, Klamath Co., Sacred Heart (1904), Rev. Charles V. Dreisbach; Deacon P. Kenneth Morton, Pastoral Assoc.
Res., 815 High St., 97601. Tel: 541-884-4566; Fax: 541-882-0472.
Catechesis/Religious Programs—Tel: 541-882-4864. Vicki Bauer, D.R.E.
Students 191.

St. Pius X (1957), Rev. Franklin J. Buckman (ORG) Admin.
Res., 4880 Bristol Ave., 97603. Tel: 541-884-4242; Fax: 541-885-8724. [CEM]
Catechesis/Religious Programs—Tel: 541-882-7593; Fax: 541-882-7593. Deacon James R. Roy, D.R.E.
Students 169.

La Grande, Union Co., Our Lady of the Valley (1914). (Under the title of the Immaculate Conception). Rev. Louis Henry Albrecht.
Parish Office: 1002 L Ave., 97850. Tel: 541-963-7341; Fax: 541-963-7341.
Res., 1101 4th St., 97850. Tel: 541-963-0006.
Catechesis/Religious Programs—Tel: 541-963-0861; Fax: 541-963-0861. Charlene Storoe, D.R.E.
Students 211.

La Pine, Deschutes Co., Holy Redeemer (1983), Rev. James A. Radloff.
Res., 16137 Burgess Rd., P.O. Box 299, 97739. Tel: 541-536-3571; Fax: 541-536-5647.
Catechesis/Religious Programs—Tel: 541-536-9213. Rosemary Kim, D.R.E.
Students 42.
Missions—Gilchrist, Our Lady of the Snows; Christmas Valley, Holy Family; Sun River, Deschutes Co., Holy Trinity, 18143 Cottonwood, Sun River, 97707.

Lakeview, Lake Co., St. Patrick's (1912), Rev. Raymond Hopp.
Res., 12 G St. N., P.O. Drawer 29, 97630. Tel: 541-947-2741; Fax: 541-947-2756.
Catechesis/Religious Programs—185 S. G St., Tel: 541-947-3875.
Students 95.
Missions—Adel, St. Richard; Plush, St. Thomas; Paisley, St. John the Apostle.

Madras, Jefferson Co., St. Patrick's (1955), Rev. James Stephens.
Res., 341 S.W. J St., P.O. Box 786, 97741. Tel: 541-475-2936; Fax: 541-475-2444.
Catechesis/Religious Programs—Tel: 541-475-2444. Elouise Kirsch, D.R.E.
Students 156.
Mission—Warm Springs, Jefferson Co., Blessed Kateri Tekakwitha. (Indian Reservation) P.O. Box 764, Warm Springs, 97761. Tel: 541-553-1235. Sr. Pauline Igoe, O.P., Dir. Native American Affairs.

Merrill, Klamath Co., St. Augustine (1939), Rev. Robert Simard.
Res., 905 E. Front St., P.O. Box 340, 97633. Tel: 541-798-5823.
Catechesis/Religious Programs—Tel: 530-667-5566. Tricia Plass, D.R.E.
Students 78.
Mission—Bonanza, St. Frances Cabrini, Tel: 541-545-6002.
Catechesis/Religious Programs—Students 18.

Milton Freewater, Umatilla Co., St. Francis of Assisi (1940), Rev. Lawrence C. Bower.
Res., 925 Vining, 97862. Tel: 541-938-5436.
Catechesis/Religious Programs—Students 35.
Mission—Athena, Sacred Heart, 5th St. & College St., Athena, 97813.

Nyssa, Malheur Co., St. Bridget of Kildare (1951), Rev. Robert M. Greiner.
Res., 504 Locust, 97913-3235. Tel: 541-372-3133.
Catechesis/Religious Programs—Students 90.
Mission—Adrian, Our Lady of Guadalupe. 2nd St. & Owyhee St.

Ontario, Malheur Co., Blessed Sacrament (1911), Rev. W. Raymond Jarboe; Mrs. Frances A. Schaffer, Pastoral Assoc.
Res., 829 S.W. Second Ave., 97914-2695. Tel: 541-889-8469; Fax: 541-889-8483.
School—Saint Peter, (Grades K-8) 98 S.W. Ninth St., 97914. Tel: 541-889-7363; Fax: 541-889-2852. Sr. Linda Riggers, S.N.J.M., Prin.
Religious Teacher 1; Lay Teachers 9; Students 142.
Catechesis/Religious Programs—Tel: 541-889-8404. D.R.E.: Tim Cables; Virginia Crow.
Students 150.
Mission—Huntington, St. Joachim, 455 Lincoln Ave., Huntington, 97907. [CEM]

Pendleton, Umatilla Co., St. Andrew's Indian Mission (1847), Rev. Michael J. Fitzpatrick, S.J.
Res., 48022 St. Andrews Rd., 97801. Tel: 541-276-6155; Fax: 541-276-0767. [CEM]
Catechesis/Religious Programs—Tel: 541-276-0767. Lillian Moses, D.R.E.
Students 35.

St. Mary's (1902), Revs. Dennis Strachota; Hyacinth Okwara; Deacons Martin Omar Tores; Daniel Martinez.
Res., 800 S.E. Court Ave., 97801. Tel: 541-276-3615; Fax: 541-276-7484. [CEM]
Catechesis/Religious Programs—Tel: 541-276-6163. Mrs. Darlene Ledbetter, D.R.E.
Students 272.

Pilot Rock, Umatilla Co., St. Helen (1930). Attended by St. Mary's, Pendleton.
Res., 740 S.W. Birch, P.O. Box V, 97868. Tel: 541-443-3151;276-3615.
Catechesis/Religious Programs—Students 35.

Prineville, Crook Co., St. Joseph's (1943), Rev. James P. Logan.
Res., 150 E. First, P.O. Box 1315, 97754. Tel: 541-447-6475; Fax: 541-416-9141.
Catechesis/Religious Programs—200 E. First St., P.O. Box 721, 97754. Tel: 541-447-1227; 389-0888. Jennie Bachman, D.R.E.
Students 65.

Redmond, Deschutes Co., St. Thomas (1941), Rev. Leo F. Weckerle.
Res., 526 S. 12th, P.O. Box 247, 97756. Tel: 541-923-3390; Fax: 541-548-6630.
Catechesis/Religious Programs—535 S. 11th St., 97756. Tel: 541-923-0597. Mary Lehnertz, D.R.E. Students 197.

Sisters, Deschutes Co., St. Edward (1984), Very Rev. W. Thomas Faucher.
Res., 123 Trinity Way, P.O. Box 489, 97759-0489. Tel: 541-549-0751 (Rectory); 549-9391 (Office); Fax: 541-549-1057.
Catechesis/Religious Programs—David Brehm, D.R.E.
Students 55.

The Dalles, Wasco Co., St. Peter's (1848), Revs. Todd Unger; Joseph Kelbel. In res., Rev. Msgr. William Stone.
Res., 1222 W. 10th St., P.O. Box 41, 97058. Tel: 541-296-2026; Fax: 541-296-5835. [CEM]
School—St. Mary, (Grades PreK-8) 1112 Cherry Heights Rd., Tel: 541-296-6004; Fax: 541-296-7858. Jacqueline Pajda, Prin.
Lay Teachers 13; Students 199.
Catechesis/Religious Programs—1111 W. 10th, P.O. Box 41, 97058.
Students 170.

Union, Union Co., Sacred Heart (1905). Attended by Our Lady of the Valley, La Grande.
Church—340 S. 10th St., P.O. Box 473, 97883. Tel: 541-562-6285.
Catechesis/Religious Programs—Tel: 541-562-5486. Willard Bertrand, D.R.E.
Students 21.

Vale, Malheur Co., St. Patrick's (1946), Rev. Richard Saksons, O.Praem., Admin.
Res., P.O. Box J, 97918. Tel: 541-473-3906; Fax: 541-473-2687.
Catechesis/Religious Programs—Tel: 541-473-3848. Susan Seals, D.R.E.
Students 85.
Mission—Juntura, St. Charles.
Station—Harper, St. John the Beloved.

Wasco, Sherman Co., St. Mary's (1954), Rev. Anselm Fister, O.S.B.
Res., 807 Barnett St., P.O. Box 14, 97065. Tel: 541-442-5496.
Catechesis/Religious Programs—Molly Belshe, D.R.E.
Students 30.
Missions—Antelope, St. Mary's; Grass Valley, St. John the Baptist.

Special Assignment:
Reverend Monsignors—
Crotty, Matthew M., Vicar Gen., 1011 S.E. 15th, #31, Bend, OR 97702

On Duty Outside the Diocese:
Reverend Fathers—
Hickie, J. Noel, Sacred Heart General Hospital, 1305 Willagillespie Rd., Eugene, OR 97401
Kiely, Cornelius, Iglesia La Immaculada Concepcion, Puerto Lopez, Manabi, Ecuador
Miles, Michael, St. Nicholas Ukrainian Catholic Cathedral, 2238 W. Rice St., Chicago, IL 60622
Reeves, Joseph, 12223 N.W. Cornell Rd., Apt. 306, Portland, OR 97229

Absent on Leave:
Reverend Fathers—
Holmes, Dennis

Retired:
Reverend Monsignors—
Beard, Raymond, P.O. Box 57, Athena, OR 97813
Keating, Bernard A., P.O. Box 861, Redmond, OR 97756
Stone, William S., P.O. Box 41, The Dalles, OR 97058
Reverend Fathers—
Collins, Timothy, Pendleton House, Avondale House, Kilrush Rd., Ennis, Co. Clare, Ireland
Conway, Richard J., 950 Pomona, #166, The Dalles, OR 97058
Cribbin, Austin J., 220 Newcastle Rd., Klamath Falls, OR 97601
Fisher, A. J., 1200 W. Dimond #14105, Anchorage, AK 99515
Gillen, C. H., Milton-Freewater, OR
Quigley, Martin J., 3564 E. 2nd, Sp. 72, The Dalles, OR 97058
Scanlan, Thomas R., 11055 S.W. Summerfield Dr., #7, Tigard, OR 97224
Simard, Robert, 298 E. 1st, Prineville, OR 97754

INSTITUTIONS LOCATED IN THE DIOCESE

[A] GENERAL HOSPITALS

BAKER CITY. *St. Elizabeth Health Services, Inc.*, 3325 Pocahontas Rd., 97814. Tel: 541-523-6461 (Hospital); 523-4452 (Nursing Care); Fax: 541-523-1794.
E-mail: johnperushek@chiwest.com
For a complete listing, refer to the Hospitals section.

BEND. *St. Charles Medical Center*, 2500 N.E. Neff Rd., 97701. Tel: 541-382-4321; Fax: 541-388-7723.
Web site: www.scmc.org
For a complete listing, refer to the Hospitals section.

HOOD RIVER. *Providence Hood River Memorial Hospital*, 811 13th St., 97031. Tel: 541-386-3911; Fax: 541-387-6462.
E-mail: gyoung@providence.org
Web site: www.providence.org
For a complete listing, refer to the Hospitals section.

ONTARIO. *The Dominican Sisters of Ontario, Inc. dba Holy Rosary Medical Center*, 351 S.W. Ninth St., 97914. Tel: 541-881-7000; Fax: 541-881-7184.
Web site: holyrosary-ontario.org
For a complete listing, refer to the Hospitals section.

PENDLETON. *St. Anthony Hospital*, 1601 S.E. Court Ave., 97801. Tel: 541-276-5121; Fax: 541-278-3227.
E-mail: usimonton@chiwest.com
For a complete listing, refer to the Hospitals section.

[B] MONASTERIES AND RESIDENCES FOR PRIESTS AND BROTHERS

LA PINE. *Monastery of Annunciation Hermitage*, 146640 Hwy. 97, 97739-9127. Tel: 541-433-2903; Fax: 520-441-2051.
E-mail: hermitage@usa.com
Bro. Bruno Wilson, Anchorite.

[C] CONVENTS AND RESIDENCES FOR SISTERS

BAKER CITY. *St. Clare Convent*, 2365 4th St., #B-3, 97814. Tel: 541-523-6770. Sisters 2.

[D] MISCELLANEOUS

BEND. *Saint Vincent de Paul Society - District Council of Central Oregon*, P.O. Box 1011, 97709. Tel: 541-389-5117; Fax: 541-389-5093.
E-mail: svdp@bendnet.com
Wes Colbo, Pres. Bd. Directors; Judy Mackel, Exec. Dir. Tel: 541-389-5117.

Bend Social Services Conference, 950 S.E. 3rd St. Tel: 541-389-6643; Fax: 541-389-5093.

Distribution Center, 1223 N.E. 1st St., 97701. Tel: 541-389-3325; Fax: 541-312-6385.

Thrift Store, 401 N.E. 2nd, 97701.

Thrift Store, 950 S.E. 3rd St., 97702.

THE DALLES. *Saint Vincent de Paul Society - The Dalles Conference*, 315 W. 3rd St., 97058. Tel: 541-298-7837; Fax: 541-298-7940.
E-mail: svdp@gorge.net
David Lutgens, Chm.

HERMISTON. *Hermiston Our Lady of Angels Conference of St. Vincent de Paul*, 565 W. Hermiston Ave., 97838. Tel: 541-567-5812. Ronald Schenk, Pres.

LA PINE. *La Pine Conference*, P.O. Box 1008, 97739. Tel: 541-536-1956; Fax: 541-536-6135. Arlene Mura, Pres.

PRINEVILLE. *Saint Vincent de Paul Society - Prineville Conference*, 150 E. 1st St., 97754. Tel: 541-447-4565. John Solitz, Pres.

REDMOND. *Saint Vincent de Paul Society - Redmond Conference*, 1114 S.W. Evergreen, 97756. Tel: 541-923-5264. Robert Haack, Pres.

Thrift Store, 2014 S. Hwy. 97, 97756. Tel: 541-548-3055.

RICHLAND. *North American Conference of Separated & Divorced Catholics*, P.O. Box 360, 97870. Tel: 541-893-6089; Fax: 541-893-6089, Ext. 51.
E-mail: nacsdc@pinetel.com
Web site: www.eoni.com/~nacsdc
Krista Dennis, Office Mgr., Contact for future mailings.

RELIGIOUS INSTITUTES OF MEN REPRESENTED IN THE DIOCESE

For futher details refer to the corresponding bracketed number in the Religious Institutes of Men or Women section.

[0200]—*Benedictine Monks.* (Benet Hills, CA).—O.S.B.
[0900]—*Canons Regular of Premontre, England.*—O.Praem.
[0470]—*The Capuchin Friars.*—O.F.M.Cap.
[0690]—*Jesuit Fathers and Brothers.* (California, Oregon Provs.).—S.J.

RELIGIOUS INSTITUTES OF WOMEN REPRESENTED IN THE DIOCESE

[1070-25]—*Dominican Sisters of Kenosha, WI.*—O.P.
[1070-03]—*Dominican Sisters of Sinsinawa, WI.*—O.P.
[1070-20]—*Dominican Sisters of St. Thomas Aquinas.*—O.P.
[2470]—*Maryknoll Sisters of St. Dominic.*—M.M.
[2970]—*School Sisters of Notre Dame.*—S.S.N.D.
[3000]—*Sisters of Notre Dame de Namur.*—S.N.D.deN.
[1630]—*Sisters of St. Francis of Penance and Christian Charity.*—O.S.F.
[1650]—*Sisters of St. Francis of Philadelphia.*—O.S.F.
[3830]—*Sisters of St. Joseph.*—C.S.J.
[3960]—*Sisters of St. Mary of Oregon.*—S.S.M.O.
[1990]—*Sisters of the Holy Names of Jesus and Mary.*—S.N.J.M.
[4060]—*Society of the Holy Child Jesus.*—S.H.C.J.

NECROLOGY

† Phelan, Rev. Msgr. John F., (Retired). —Died Nov. 22, 1999.

Archdiocese of Baltimore

(Archidioecesis Baltimorensis)

His Eminence

WILLIAM CARDINAL KEELER, D.D., J.C.D.

Archbishop of Baltimore; ordained July 17, 1955; appointed Titular Bishop of Ulcinium and Auxiliary Bishop of Harrisburg July 24, 1979; ordained Bishop September 21, 1979; appointed Bishop of Harrisburg November 10, 1983; installed January 4, 1984; appointed Archbishop of Baltimore April 6, 1989; installed as Fourteenth Archbishop of Baltimore May 23, 1989; created Cardinal Priest November 26, 1994. *Office: 320 Cathedral St., Baltimore, MD, 21201.* Tel.: 410-547-5437.

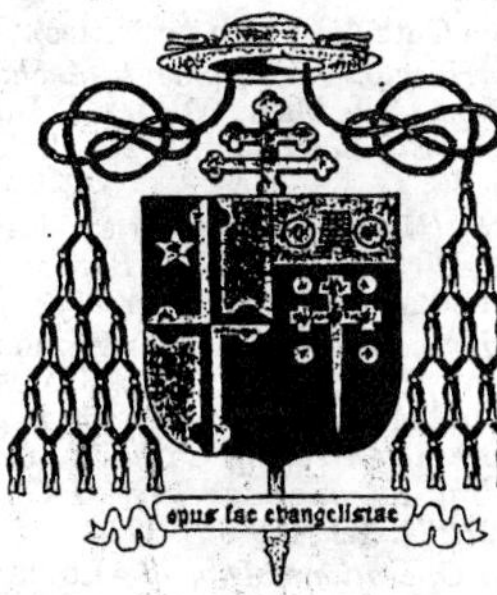

Chancery Office: 320 Cathedral St., Baltimore, MD, 21201. Tel.: 410-547-5446; Fax: 410-727-8234.

Web site address: www.archbalt.org

E-mail address: chancery@archbalt.org

Most Reverend

WILLIAM DONALD BORDERS, D.D.

Retired Archbishop of Baltimore; ordained May 18, 1940; appointed Bishop of Orlando May 2, 1968; consecrated June 14, 1968; appointed Archbishop of Baltimore March 25, 1974; installed June 26, 1974; retired April 6, 1989. *Office: 320 Cathedral St., Baltimore, MD, 21201.* Tel.: 410-547-5439.

Most Reverend

WILLIAM C. NEWMAN, D.D., V.G.

Auxiliary Bishop of Baltimore, Eastern Vicar and Titular Bishop of Numluli; ordained May 29, 1954; ordained Bishop July 2, 1984. *Office: 320 Cathedral St., Baltimore, MD, 21201.* Tel.: 410-547-5438. *Res., 5300 N. Charles St., Baltimore, MD, 21201.*

Most Reverend

GORDON D. BENNETT, S.J., D.D., V.G.

Auxiliary Bishop of Baltimore and Titular Bishop of Nesqually; ordained June 14, 1975; ordained Bishop March 3, 1998. *Office: 320 Cathedral St., Baltimore, MD, 21201.* Tel.: 410-547-5453.

Most Reverend

WILLIAM FRANCIS MALOOLY

Auxiliary Bishop of Baltimore; ordained May 7, 1970; appointed Auxiliary Bishop December 12, 2000; ordained Auxiliary Bishop March 1, 2001

ESTABLISHED A DIOCESE NOVEMBER 6, 1789; ESTABLISHED AN ARCHDIOCESE APRIL 8, 1808.

Square Miles 4,801.

Comprises the City of Baltimore and Allegany, Anne Arundel, Baltimore, Carroll, Frederick, Garrett, Harford, Howard and Washington Counties.

By a Decree of the Sacred Congregation of the Propaganda, July 19, 1858, approved by His Holiness, Pius IX, July 25, 1858, "Prerogative of Place" was conferred on the Archdiocese of Baltimore. By the explicit words of said decree of the Holy See, the Archbishop of Baltimore takes precedence over all Archbishops of the United States (not Cardinals) in Councils, gatherings and meetings of whatever kind of the Hierarchy (in concillis, coetibus et comitiis quibuscumque) regardless of the seniority of other Archbishops in promotion or ordination. Decree signed by Cardinal Barnabo, August 15, 1858.

For legal titles of parishes and archdiocesan institutions, consult the Chancery Office.

STATISTICAL OVERVIEW

Personnel	
Cardinal	1
Archbishop	1
Retired Archbishops	1
Bishop	4
Auxiliary Bishops	2
Priests: Diocesan Active in Diocese	212
Priests: Active Outside Diocese	11
Priests: Diocesan in Foreign Missions	2
Priests: Retired, Sick or Absent	76
Number of Diocesan Priests	301
Religious Priests in Diocese	304
Extern Priests in Diocese	25
Ordinations:	
Diocesan Priests	7
Transitional Deacons	5
Permanent Deacons	179
Permanent Deacons in Diocese	184
Total Brothers	74
Total Sisters	1,233
Parishes	
Parishes	155
With Resident Pastor:	
Resident Diocesan Priests	107
Resident Religious Priests	37
Without Resident Pastor:	
Administered by Priests	5
Administered by Women Religious	3
Administered by Lay People	1
Completely Vacant	2
Missions	9
Closed Parishes	1
Welfare	
Catholic Hospitals	6
Total Assisted	1,251,895
Homes for the Aged	21
Total Assisted	1,828
Day Care and Extended Day Care Centers	4
Total Assisted	251
Special Centers for Social Services	44
Total Assisted	721,081
Other Institutions	1
Total Assisted	12,000
Educational	
Seminaries, Diocesan	2
Students from This Diocese	20
Students from Other Diocese	211
Diocesan Students in Other Seminaries	8
Total Seminarians	28
Colleges and Universities	3
Total Students	11,049
High Schools, Diocesan and Parish	23
Total Students	10,510
High Schools, Private	12
Total Students	7,265
Elementary Schools, Diocesan and Parish	73
Total Students	23,374
Elementary Schools, Private	9
Total Students	1,866
Non-residential Schools for the Disabled	1
Total Students	129
Catechesis/Religious Education:	
High School Students	3,184
Elementary Students	25,317
Total Students Under Catholic Instruction	82,722
Teachers in the Diocese:	
Priests	17
Brothers	24
Sisters	156
Lay Teachers	3,069
Vital Statistics	
Receptions into the Church:	
Infant Baptism Totals	8,051
Adult Baptism Totals	676
First Communions	8,216
Confirmations	5,684
Marriages:	
Catholic	1,529
Interfaith	1,061
Total Marriages	2,590
Deaths	5,315
Total Catholic Population	486,607
Total Population	2,870,150

Former Bishops—Most Rev. JOHN CARROLL, D.D., cons. Aug. 15, 1790; Archbishop, April 8, 1808; died Dec. 3, 1815.—Most Rev. LEONARD NEALE, D.D., cons. Coadjutor, Dec. 7, 1800; acceded Dec. 3, 1815; died June 18, 1817.—Most Rev. AMBROSE MARECHAL, S.S., D.D., cons. Dec. 14, 1817; died Jan. 29, 1828.—Most Rev. JAMES WHITFIELD, D.D., cons. May 25, 1828; died Oct. 19, 1834.—Most Rev. SAMUEL ECCLESTON, S.S., D.D., cons. Sept. 14, 1834; died April 22, 1851.—Most Rev. FRANCIS PATRICK KENRICK, D.D., cons. June 6, 1830; Coadjutor Bishop of Philadelphia; promoted to Aug. 19, 1851; died July 8, 1863.—Most Rev. MARTIN JOHN SPALDING, D.D., cons. Sept. 10, 1848; Coadjutor Bishop of Louisville; promoted to May 6, 1864; died Feb. 7, 1872.—Most Rev. JAMES ROOSEVELT BAYLEY, D.D., cons. Oct. 30, 1853; Bishop of Newark; promoted to July 30, 1872; died Oct. 3, 1877.—His Eminence JAMES CARDINAL GIBBONS, cons. Vicar Apostolic of North Carolina, Aug. 16, 1868; transferred to See of Richmond, July 30, 1872; promoted to See of Baltimore, Oct. 3, 1877; created Cardinal Priest of S. Maria in Trastevere, June 7, 1886; died March 24, 1921.—Most Rev. MICHAEL J. CURLEY, D.D., cons. Bishop of St. Augustine, June 30, 1914; promoted to Aug. 10, 1921; died May 16, 1947.—Most Rev. FRANCIS P. KEOUGH, D.D., cons. Bishop of Providence, May 22, 1934; promoted to Nov. 29, 1947; died Dec. 8, 1961.—His Eminence LAWRENCE CARDINAL SHEHAN, cons. Auxiliary Bishop of Baltimore, Dec. 12, 1945; transferred to Diocese of Bridgeport, Aug. 25, 1953; appt. Coadjutor Archbishop of Baltimore, July 10, 1961; acceded Dec. 8, 1961; created Cardinal Priest of S. Clemente, Feb. 22, 1965; retired March 25, 1974; died Aug. 26, 1984.—Most Rev. WILLIAM DONALD BORDERS, D.D., appt. Bishop of Orlando, May 2, 1968; cons. June 14, 1968; promoted to March 25, 1974; installed June 26, 1974; retired April 6, 1989.

Vicars General—Most Rev. WILLIAM C. NEWMAN, D.D., V.G.; Most Rev. GORDON D. BENNETT, S.J., D.D., V.G.; Rev. Msgr. W. FRANCIS MALOOLY, V.G.

Archbishop, Office of the—Rev. LAWRENCE A. WAUDBY, JR., Secretary to the Cardinal. Tel: 410-547-5303., *320 Cathedral St., Baltimore, 21201.* Tel: 410-547-5437; Fax: 410-727-8234.

Office of the Former Archbishop—Most Rev. WILLIAM D. BORDERS, *320 Cathedral St., Baltimore, 21201.* Tel: 410-547-5437.

Chancery Office—*320 Cathedral St., Baltimore, 21201.* Tel: 410-547-5446; Fax: 410-727-8234. Office Hours: Mon.-Fri. 9-5; Closed holidays.

Chancellor—Rev. Msgr. W. FRANCIS MALOOLY, V.G.

Vice Chancellor—Rev. Msgr. JEREMIAH F. KENNEY.

Assistant Chancellor—Rev. LAWRENCE A. WAUDBY, JR.

Canonical Adviser, Office of—Rev. JAMES J. CONN, S.J., Canonical & Theological Consultant to the Archbishop. Tel: 410-864-3600.

Consultors—Most Rev. WILLIAM C. NEWMAN, D.D., V.G.; Most Rev. GORDON D. BENNETT, S.J., V.G.; Rev. Msgr. PAUL G. COOK; Rev. Msgr. ROBERT ARMSTRONG; Rev. Msgr. W. FRANCIS MALOOLY, V.G.; Rev. Msgr. JAMES MCGOVERN; Rev. Msgr. GEORGE MOELLER; Rev. Msgr. G. MICHAEL SCHLEUPNER; Rev. Msgr. VICTOR GALEONE; Rev. Msgr. ARTHUR VALENZANO; Rev. Msgr. RICHARD WOY.

Eastern Vicar, Office of the—Most Rev. WILLIAM C. NEWMAN, D.D., V.G., Vicar; Sr. EDITHANN KANE, S.N.D., Asst., *320 Cathedral St., Baltimore, 21201.* Tel: 410-547-5438; Fax: 410-727-5432.

Interdiocesan Tribunal of Appeals of the Province of Baltimore—*320 Cathedral St., Baltimore, 21201.* Tel: 410-576-6924.

Judicial Vicar—Rev. Msgr. JEREMIAH F. KENNEY.

Interdiocesan Judges—Rev. Msgr. JOHN P. HANNAN; Rev. Msgr. CHARLES A. KELLY; Rev. Msgr. JOSEPH REBMAN; Rev. Msgr. THOMAS F. SHREVE; Revs. FREDERICK P. ANNIE; JOHN A. BARRES; THOMAS BAUERNFEIND; FREDERICK J. FEUSAHRENS; GEORGE J. GRIFFIN; CHRISTIAN J. HAYDINGER; MARK R. LANE; JOHN S. LEDFORD; MARTIN MCGUILL; CHRISTOPHER P. MOORE; WILLIAM J. NOLTE, JR.; EUGENE S. OSTROWSKI; RICHARD A. REISSMANN; JOHN E. RIDGELL; RICHARD W. SHODA; EUGENE J. WEBER; Deacon ROBERT GRAHAM.

Defenders of the Bond—Rt. Rev. BENEDICT MCDERMOTT, O.S.B.; Revs. CHARLES DILLINGHAM; JAMES F. KAUFFMAN; RICHARD T. MOONEY; GILBERT J. SEITZ, JR.; JOHN B. WARD; GERALD T. WEYMES.

Notaries—Mrs. RENA BOWMAN; Revs. CHRISTIAN T. CONNELLY; EDWARD C. HATHAWAY; JOANNE D'SURNEY; JOANN KUBASKO; BARBARA A. LEE; BERTHA GOODMAN.

Metropolitan Tribunal—*320 Cathedral St., Baltimore, 21201.* Tel: 410-576-6920.

Cardinal's Delegate for Tribunal Canonical Administration—Rev. Msgr. JEREMIAH F. KENNEY, J.V.

Judicial Vicar—Rev. Msgr. G. MICHAEL SCHLEUPNER.

Adjutant Judicial Vicar—Rev. WILLIAM A. COLLINS.

Judges—Revs. JAMES H. BRENNAN, S.S.; MICHAEL J. CARRION; JAMES DITILLO, S.J.; THOMAS J. GOLUEKE; Deacons RAY BRITT; HARRY ST. A. O'NEILL.

Defenders of the Bond—Rev. Msgr. ROBERT A. ARMSTRONG; Rev. ALBAN HARMON, C.P.; LUCY LEE; WILLIAM Q. SIMMS.

Promoter of Justice—Rev. JAMES CONN, S.J.

Advocates and Procurators—Rev. Msgr. RICHARD W. WOY; Revs. BERNARD BAK; MICHAEL J. CALLAGHAN; PATRICK M. CARRION; E. JOSEPH COTE; RICHARD E. CRAMBLITT; MARTIN E. FEILD; WILLIAM FOLEY; JAMES HANNON; ROBERT HARTNETT; C. LOU MARTIN; EDWARD MILLER; KEVIN MUELLER; G. EUGENE NICKOL; MITCHELL ROZANSKI; C. DOUG KENNEY; Deacons JOHN ABELL; ALPHONSE C. BANKARD; ALBERT COSLA; NICHOLAS FEURER; HERMAN GRABENSTEIN; JOHN MCKENNA; ROBERT LEHR; JOHN MARTELLE; HUGH MILLS, JR.; DONALD MURRAY; WILLIAM NAIRN; STANLEY G. PIET; JOHN RAFTER; GERALD RAIBLE; FRANK RONGIONE; WALTER SHIPLEY; FREDDY WENDT; Sr. KATHERINE BELL, R.S.M.; Sr. REGINA BURGAN, S.S.N.D.; Sr. AGNESINE CONNORS, S.S.N.D.; Sr. MARIETTA CULHANE, O.S.F.; Sr. CAROL CZYZEWSKI, F.S.S.J.; Sr. FRANCES DEMARCO, R.S.M.; Sr. JOAN BASTRESS, I.H.M.; Sr. SUSAN ENGEL, M.H.S.H.; Sr. JOYCE HOLDEN, M.H.S.H.; Sr. ELIZABETH KANE, O.S.F.; Sr. PATRICIA MCALPIN, O.S.F.; Sr. MARTINA MARIE WAGNER, S.S.N.D.; Sr. JOAN MINELLA, S.S.N.D.; Sr. NANCY STILES, S.U.S.C.; ANDREW BAUER; STEPHEN R. BEARD; MARY JOYCE BLESSING; LOUIS CASHIOLA; JOHN W. FISHER; ROBERT NICHOLSON; JOHN SAUER; JOHN KUTZ.

Notaries—PATRICIA FREUND; CHRISTINA MAKOWIECKI; CLARA JULIAO.

Urban Vicar, Office of the—Most Rev. GORDON D. BENNETT, S.J., V.G.; Deacon PAUL WEBER, Asst. to Urban Vicar. Tel: 410-547-5486., *320 Cathedral St., Baltimore, 21201.* Tel: 410-547-5452; Fax: 410-727-5432.

Western Vicar, Office of the—*320 Cathedral St., Baltimore, 21201.* Tel: 410-547-5447; Fax: 410-727-5432.

Archdiocesan Offices and Directors

African American Ministries, Archdiocesan Office of—THERESE WILSON FAVORS, Dir., *320 Cathedral St., Baltimore, 21201.* Tel: 410-625-8472; Fax: 410-727-5432.

Apostleship of Prayer—Rev. JAMES A. CASCIOTTI, S.J., Dir., *5704 Roland Ave., Baltimore, 21210-1399.* Tel: 410-332-1412.

Archdiocesan Directory—PATTI MEDINGER, Project Mgr., *320 Cathedral St., Baltimore, 21201.* Tel: 410-547-5324. Official directory of the Archdiocese of Baltimore. Published annually by *The Catholic Review.* $27 per copy.

Archdiocesan Gay-Lesbian Outreach (AGLO)—Rev. JOSEPH HUGHES, Coord., *2034 Park Ave., Baltimore, 21217.* Tel: 410-728-2638.

Archdiocesan Pastoral Council—(See Pastoral Council Archdiocesan).

Archives-Archivist—Rev. PAUL K. THOMAS, *320 Cathedral St., Baltimore, 21201.* Tel: 410-547-5443 (By appointment).

Boy Scouts—(See Catholic Youth Activities).

Campaign For Human Development, Archdiocese of Baltimore, Inc.—Rev. Msgr. WILLIAM F. BURKE, Dir., *320 Cathedral St., Baltimore, 21201.* Tel: 410-235-5136; 547-5446.

Campus Ministry (Newman Apostolate)—Rev. ROBERT E. ALBRIGHT, Dir., *7909 York Rd., Baltimore, 21204.* Tel: 410-828-0622; Fax: 410-828-4825.

The Cathedral Foundation, Inc.—His Eminence WILLIAM H. KEELER, D.D., J.C.D., Pres. JAMES CURRAN, Vice Pres. Publishers of *The Catholic Review, Official Archdiocesan Directory, Catholic International* and *Cathedral Foundation Press. P.O. Box 777, Baltimore, 21203.* Tel: 410-547-5380.

Catholic Center Operations, Div. of—LOUIS WILLETT, Facilities Mgr., *320 Cathedral St., Baltimore, 21201.* Tel: 410-547-5312; Fax: 410-783-5993.

Catholic Charities Fund, Inc.—*320 Cathedral St., Baltimore, 21201.*

Catholic Education Ministries, Department of—Dr. RONALD J. VALENTI, Sec., *320 Cathedral St., Baltimore, 21201.* Tel: 410-547-5383; Fax: 410-547-5566.

Catholic Relief Services—MARY D'AMBROGI, Archdiocesan Dir., *320 Cathedral St., Baltimore, 21201.* Tel: 410-547-5548.

"The Catholic Review"—His Eminence WILLIAM H. KEELER, D.D., J.C.D., Publisher; DANIEL L. MEDINGER, Assoc. Publisher & Editor; CHRISTOPHER GAUL, Mng. Editor, *320 Cathedral St., P.O. Box 777, Baltimore, 21203.* Tel: 410-547-5380. Newspaper of the Archdiocese of Baltimore. Established 1913. Published every Thursday by the Cathedral Foundation, Inc.

Catholic Schools, Division of—Dr. RONALD J. VALENTI, Supt., *320 Cathedral St., Catholic Center, Baltimore, 21201.* Tel: 410-547-5391; Fax: 410-547-5566.

Catholic Students Mission Crusade—See Propagation of the Faith.

New Cathedral Cemetery—*4300 Old Frederick Rd., Baltimore, 21229.* Tel: 410-566-7770; Fax: 410-566-0709.

Censor Librorum—Rev. Msgr. CARROLL E. SATTERFIELD, S.T.D., *363 Homeland Southway, Apt. 1-A, Baltimore, 21212.* Tel: 410-433-6517.

Clergy Personnel, Division of—Rev. J. BRUCE JARBOE, Div. Dir. Tel: 410-547-5428. Rev. PATRICK M. CARRION, Assoc. Dir. Tel: 410-547-5558. Mrs. CAROL PURWIN, Admin. Asst. Tel: 410-547-5427. Mrs. AMBER GREGG, Sec. Tel: 410-547-5550., *320 Cathedral St., Rm. 620, Baltimore, 21201.*

Commission for Ecumenical and Inter-Religious Affairs—Rev. RICHARD H. TILLMAN, Chm., *10431 Twin Rivers Rd., Columbia, 21044.* Tel: 410-964-1425; Fax: 410-730-9253.

Deacon Personnel Board—Deacon ANTHONY GRILLO; Mrs. COCO LOPATA; Deacon CHARLES HIEBLER; Mrs. DELORES KRYSIAK; Deacons DONALD MILLER; PAUL MANN; GEORGE WACHTER; FRED D. WENDT; MICHAEL MCCOY; JOHN MCKENNA; MIGUEL SAINZ.

Facilities Management, Division of—LOUIS F. BAIRD, Dir. LOUIS WILLETT, Facilities Mgr. ROBERT CLANCY, Facilities Specialist III, *320 Cathedral St., Baltimore, 21201.* Tel: 410-547-5366.

Financial Administration, Board of—His Eminence WILLIAM CARDINAL KEELER, D.D., J.C.D., Chm. MICHAEL BATZA, Vice Chm.; Rev. Msgr. RICHARD W. WOY, Sec., *320 Cathedral St., Baltimore, 21201.*

Fiscal Services—JOSEPH A. SPADARO, C.P.A., CFO, *320 Cathedral St., Baltimore, 21201.* Tel: 410-547-5300; Fax: 410-332-8233.

Fund Development, Department of—THOMAS J. SONNI, Exec. Dir. Devel. GEORGE E. REED, III, Dir. Devel. - Western Vicariate; JAMES EDWARDS, Dir. Devel. - Eastern Vicariate; ROBERT BROWN, Dir. Devel. - Urban Vicariate; JENNIFER HAMMOND, Dir. Major Gifts; PATRICIA RILEY, Mktg. & Communications Specialist; NANCY MCDOWELL, Exec. Asst. SHERRY TAITT-BLAND, Devel. Asst. LYNNE BOERI, Information Mgmt. Coord., *320 Cathedral St., Baltimore, 21201.* Tel: 410-547-5356; Fax: 410-625-8485.

Gay and Lesbian Ministries, Office of—Deacon PAUL WEBER, Dir., *320 Cathedral St., Baltimore, 21201.* Tel: 410-547-5486.

Hispanic Ministries, Office of—MARIA T.P. JOHNSON, Dir., *320 Cathedral St., Baltimore, 21201.* Tel: 410-547-5363.

Holy Childhood Association—Rev. Msgr. VICTOR GALEONE, Dir., *320 Cathedral St., Baltimore, 21201.*

Human Resources, Department of—SHEILA A. KELLY, S.P.H.R., Exec. Dir., *320 Cathedral St., Baltimore, 21201.* Tel: 410-547-5556; Fax: 410-234-2953.

Human Resources Committee—LEONARD STROM, Chm. SHEILA KELLY, Staff, *320 Cathedral St., Baltimore, 21201.*

Human Resource Services, Division of—MICHELLY B. MERRICK, Dir., *320 Cathedral St., Baltimore, 21201.* Tel: 410-547-5448; Fax: 410-234-2953.

Information Systems, Division of—WILLIAM A. GLOVER, Dir., *320 Cathedral St., Baltimore, 21201.* Tel: 410-547-5539; Fax: 410-332-8233.

Insurance, Division of—PETRA PHELPS, Dir., *320 Cathedral St., Baltimore, 21201.* Tel: 410-547-5317; Fax: 410-783-5993.

Insurance Committee—WILLIAM FRANEY, Chm. PETRA PHELPS, Sec., *320 Cathedral St., Baltimore, 21201.* Tel: 410-547-5317; Fax: 410-783-5993.

Lay Employees Retirement Board—JAYNE MCGEEHAN, Chm. PETRA PHELPS, Sec., *320 Cathedral St., Baltimore, 21201.* Tel: 410-547-5317; Fax: 410-783-5993.

League of the Little Flower—Rev. Msgr. PAUL G. COOK, Dir., *320 Cathedral St., Baltimore, 21201.* Tel: 410-547-5361.

Leadership Development, Division of—M. BARBARA CLAGETT, Coord. Church Leadership Institute, *320 Cathedral St., Baltimore, 21201.* Tel: 410-547-5470; Fax: 410-234-2953.

Management Services, Department of—Rev. Msgr. RICHARD W. WOY, M.S., Exec. Dir. JOSEPH A. SPADARO, C.P.A., CFO, *320 Cathedral St., Baltimore, 21201.* Tel: 410-547-5587; Fax: 410-332-8233.

Maryland Catholic Conference—RICHARD J. DOWLING, ESQ., Exec. Dir., *188 Duke of Gloucester St., Annapolis, 21401.* Tel: 410-269-1155 (Bal.); 301-261-1979 (Wash.); Fax: 410-269-1790.

Office of Diaconate—Revs. J. BRUCE JARBOE, Dir. PATRICK M. CARRION, Assoc. Dir. Tel: 410-547-5558. Mrs. CAROL PURWIN, Admin. Asst.; Mrs. AMBER GREGG, Sec., *320 Cathedral St., Rm 620, Baltimore, 21201.* Tel: 410-547-5427.

Office of Pastoral Service for Senior and Retired Clergy—Rev. JOHN C. COLLOPY, Dir., *320 Cathedral St., Baltimore, 21201.* Tel: 410-547-5427; 252-4500, Ext. 286.

Clergy Personnel, Division of—Revs. J. BRUCE JARBOE, Dir. PATRICK M. CARRION, Assoc. Dir.; Mrs. CAROL PURWIN, Admin. Asst.; Mrs. AMBER GREGG, Sec., *320 Cathedral St., Baltimore, 21201.* Tel: 410-547-5427; Fax: 410-234-2953.

Pastoral Council, Archdiocesan—*320 Cathedral St., Baltimore, 21201.* Tel: 410-547-5455.

Permanent Deacon Formation Program—Rev. PATRICK M. CARRION, Dir., *320 Cathedral St., Baltimore, 21201.* Tel: 410-547-5558.

Research, Planning and Collegial Services, Division of—ROBERT W. JACOBS, Dir. KATHLEEN SWANSON, Consultant, Parish & Pastoral Planning; LINDSAY THOMPSON, Ph.D., Consultant Collegial Svcs. JENNIFER WINDERS, Admin. Asst. Tel: 410-547-5455; Fax: 410-783-5993.

Priests' Council—Rev. Msgr. LLOYD AIKEN, Vice Chm.; Revs. RICHARD TILLMAN, Sec. WILLIAM AU; Rev. Msgr. THOMAS BEVAN; Revs. MELVIN BLANCHETTE, S.S.; KEITH BOISVERT; JAMES FARMER; GERARD FRANCIK; J. KEVIN FARMER; DOMINIC MARUCA, S.J.; JAY O'CONNOR; Rev. Msgr. ROBERT PASSARELLI; Revs. SYLVESTER PETERKA, C.M.; THOMAS PHILLIPS; WILLIAM REMMEL, S.D.S.; JOSEPH SIMMONS; RICHARD TILLMAN; WILLIAM WATTERS, S.J., *320 Cathedral St., Baltimore, 21201.* Tel: 410-547-5455.

Ex Officio—His Eminence WILLIAM CARDINAL KEELER, D.D., J.C.D.; Most Rev. GORDON D. BENNETT, S.J., V.G.; Rev. Msgr. W. FRANCIS MALOOLY, Chancellor; Most Rev. WILLIAM C. NEWMAN, D.D., V.G. Consultors: Rev. Msgr. ROBERT ARMSTRONG; Rev. Msgr. PAUL G. COOK; Rev. Msgr. VICTOR GALEONE; Rev. Msgr. JAMES O. MCGOVERN; Rev. Msgr. GEORGE B. MOELLER; Rev. Msgr. G. MICHAEL SCHLEUPNER; Rev. Msgr. ARTHUR VALENZANO; Rev. Msgr. RICHARD W. WOY.

Priest Personnel Board—Rev. Msgr. VICTOR GALEONE, Chm.; Rev. Msgr. ARTHUR VALENZANO, Vice Chm.; Rev. Msgr. JOHN MCCALL; Rev. Msgr. JOSEPH LUCA; Rev. Msgr. JAMES MCGOVERN; Rev. Msgr. ROBERT

Passarelli; Rev. Msgr. James Cronin; Rev. Msgr. Dennis Tinder; Revs. William Au; Richard Bozzelli; William Frankin; Wayne Funk; Mitchell Rozanski; John Auer; Dominic Cieri; Raymond Harris; Eugene Nickol; Jay O'Connor; Kevin Schenning; Alfred Smith; Richard Smith; Samuel Young.

Propagation of the Faith, Home and Foreign Mission Society—His Eminence William Cardinal Keeler, D.D., J.C.D., Gen. Dir.; Rev. Msgr. Victor Galeone, Dir., *320 Cathedral St., Baltimore, 21201.* Tel: 410-576-6926; Fax: 410-576-6932.

Communications Office—Raymond P. Kempisty, Dir. Communications; Matthew Lane, Communications Assoc., *320 Cathedral St., Baltimore, 21201.* Tel: 410-547-5379; Fax: 410-625-8480.

Religious Education, Division of—Carol A. Augustine, Dir., *320 Cathedral St., Baltimore, 21201.* Tel: 410-547-5403; Fax: 410-347-7896.

Senior Priests Retirement Board—Rev. Msgr. James McGovern, Chm. Petra Phelps, Sec., *320 Cathedral St., Baltimore, 21201.* Tel: 410-547-5317; Fax: 410-783-5993.

Urban Affairs, Archdiocesan Office—320 Cathedral St., Baltimore, 21201. Tel: 410-547-5486; Fax: 410-727-5432.

St. Vincent de Paul Society—Baltimore Council: His Eminence William Cardinal Keeler, D.D., J.C.D., Honorary Pres.; Rev. Msgr. Jeremiah F. Kenney, Spiritual Dir. Barbara H. Medcalf, Pres. John J. Schiavone, Exec. Dir., *320 Cathedral St., Baltimore, 21201.* Tel: 410-547-5377.

Vocation Office—Rev. James Barker, Dir. Tel: 410-547-5426; Fax: 410-234-2953. Rev. Gerard Francik, Assoc. Dir. Tel: 410-547-5354.

Youth and Young Adult Ministry, Division of—Mark Pacione, Dir., *320 Cathedral St., Baltimore, 21201.* Tel: 410-547-5372; Fax: 410-625-8481.

Associated Catholic Charities, Inc

Catholic Charities—Associated Catholic Charities, Inc. (Catholic Charities) is the largest private provider of human services in Maryland, meeting the needs of men, women, and children without regard to religion, race, or other circumstances. Headquartered in Baltimore, the 77 year old agency operates in the city and in nine Maryland counties under auspices of the Roman Catholic Archdiocese of Baltimore. The agency operates 88 programs providing: Community services, services for the aging, housing services, child and family services, services for the developmentally disabled. For more information on Catholic Charities and its programs please contact: *Catholic Charities, 320 Cathedral St., 3rd Fl., Baltimore, 21201-4421.* Tel: 410-261-5800. For detailed information on specific Catholic Charities and its programs, please refer to the Institution Section.

Executive Director—Harold A. Smith, *Associated Catholic Charities, Inc., 320 Cathedral St., 3rd Fl., Baltimore, 21201-4421.* Tel: 410-547-5497; Fax: 410-752-7260.

CLERGY, PARISHES, MISSIONS AND PAROCHIAL SCHOOLS

METROPOLITAN BALTIMORE
(Baltimore City and Baltimore County)

1—Cathedral of Mary Our Queen (1954), Rev. Msgr. Robert A. Armstrong, Rector; Revs. Richard B. Hilgartner, Jr.; Thomas A Rydzewski; Deacon Brian P. Nolan. In res., Most Rev. William C. Newman, D.D.; Rev. Joseph F. Breighner.
Res., 5300 N. Charles St., 21210-2023. Tel: 410-433-8800; Fax: 410-433-4909. [CEM]
School—111 Amberly Way, 21210. Tel: 410-433-6204; Fax: 410-433-7678. Sr. Eileen Weisman, S.S.N.D., Prin.
Lay Teachers 34; Students 450.
Catechesis/Religious Programs—115 Amberly Way, 21210. Tel: 410-435-1921. Sr. Geraldine Majerowicz, D.R.E.
Students 311.
Parish & Family Ministry—115 Amberly Way, 21210. Tel: 410-532-5269. Mrs. Judith Ann Hvisc, Dir.
Youth Ministry—5300 N. Charles St., 21210. Tel: 410-433-3894; Fax: 410-433-4909. Mr. David Huber, Dir.

2—Basilica of the National Shrine of the Assumption of the Blessed Virgin Mary (1795). (Co-Cathedral). Corporate Title: The Trustees of the Catholic Cathedral Church of Baltimore (The Basilica); Basilica of the Assumption Historic Trust, Inc. Established for the Preservation of the Basilica as a National Landmark of American Architecture. Cathedral & Mulberry St. Rev. Msgr. James V. Hobbs, Rector.
The Cardinal's Residence: 408 N. Charles St., 21201. Tel: 410-727-3564; Fax: 410-539-0407. His Eminence William H. Keeler, D.D., J.C.D.; Parish Office: 408 N. Charles St., 21201. Tel: 410-727-3565.

3—St. Agnes (Catonsville) (1852), Rev. Msgr. Victor B. Galeone; Rev. Msgr. Francis W. Fortenbaugh, Pastor Emeritus; Rev. Larry G. Rock.
Res., 5422 Old Frederick Rd., 21229. Tel: 410-744-2900; Fax: 410-744-8304. [CEM]
School—603 St. Agnes Ln., 21229. Tel: 410-747-4070; Fax: 410-747-0138. Sr. Anne Mary Smith, I.H.M., Prin.
Students 490.
Catechesis/Religious Programs—Tel: 410-747-9073.
Students 221.

4—The New All Saints (1912) (African American), Rev. Donald A. Sterling; Deacons Paul D. Shelton; Malcolm Thompson.
Res., 4408 Liberty Heights Ave., 21207. Tel: 410-542-0445; Fax: 410-542-8852.
School—(Grades 4-8) 3510 Eldorado Ave., 21207. Tel: 410-664-9433; Fax: 410-664-9434. Mr. Henry Fortier, Prin.
Lay Teachers 10; Students 125.
Catechesis/Religious Programs—Tel: 410-367-3791.
Students 71.

5—St. Alphonsus, Shrine of (1842), Rev. Msgr. Arthur W. Bastress; Rev. William F. Spacek; Deacon Hugh H. Mills, Jr. In res., Rev. Lawrence A. Waudby, Jr.
Res., 114 W. Saratoga St., 21201. Tel: 410-685-6090; Fax: 410-244-1670.
School—125 W. Saratoga St., 21201. Tel: 410-837-7310; Fax: 410-837-6948.
Lay Teachers 17; Students 214.

6—St. Ambrose (1907), Pastoral Ministry: Rev. John Pfannenstiel, O.F.M.Cap.
Res., 4502 Park Heights Ave., 21215. Tel: 410-367-9918; Fax: 410-542-6056.
School—4506 Park Heights Ave., 21215. Tel: 410-664-2373; Fax: 410-664-0857. Ms. Joanne Rojas, Prin.
Lay Teachers 24; Students 310.
Catechesis/Religious Programs—Pat West, D.R.E.
Students 95.
Outreach Center—3445 Park Heights Ave., 21215. Tel: 410-225-0870. Sr. Charmaine Krohe, S.S.N.D., Dir.

7—St. Andrew. Closed 1974. Parish records available at the Chancery. Tel: 410-547-5446.

8—St. Ann (1873). Twinned with St. Wenceslaus, Baltimore. Rev. Peter A. Lyons, T.O.R.; Deacon James E. Bee; Sr. Jeanne Barasha, S.S.N.D., Pastoral Admin. In res., Rev. Earl Jennings, T.O.R.
Res., 528 E. 22nd St., 21218. Tel: 410-235-8169; Fax: 410-235-8253.
Catechesis/Religious Programs—Students 47.

9—Annunciation (1968), Revs. William P. Foley; Joseph Breighner; Sr. Susan Engel, M.H.S.H., Pastoral Assoc.; Deacons Frederick X. Schoennagel, Jr.; Herman S. Wilkins. In res., Rev. Salvatore J. Livigni.
Res., 5212 McCormick Ave., 21206. Tel: 410-866-4020; Fax: 410-866-2754.
Catechesis/Religious Programs—Tel: 410-866-4706. Mrs. Marylou Hare, D.R.E.
Students 193.

10—St. Anthony of Padua (1884). Twinned with Most Precious Blood. Rev. C. Lou Martin; Deacons Joseph C. Krysiak; Joseph Schultz; Dr. Gloria R. Carpeneto, Pastoral Assoc. In res., Most Rev. Gordon D. Bennett, S.J.; Rev. William Fitzgerald.
Res., 4414 Frankford Ave., 21206. Tel: 410-488-0400; Fax: 410-488-0032.
School—4410 Frankford Ave., 21206. Tel: 410-488-4848; Fax: 410-325-3766. Mrs. Elizabeth Phelan, Prin.
Lay Teachers 25; Students 254.
Catechesis/Religious Programs—Students 20.

11—Ascension (Halethorpe) (1913), Revs. Manuel R. Roman; E. Gerard Huesman, Pastor Emeritus; Conan H. Timoney; Basil Stockmeyer, C.P.; Sr. Mary Catherine Lewandowski, O.S.F., Pastoral Assoc.
Res., 4603 Poplar Ave., 21227. Tel: 410-242-2292; Fax: 410-242-6807.
School—(Grades PreK-8). Tel: 410-242-2020. Ms. Rita Ann Swift, M.S., Prin.
Sisters 1; Lay Teachers 17; Students 249.
Catechesis/Religious Programs—Students 220.

12—St. Athanasius (1891), Rev. Robert A. DiMattei, Jr.
Res., 4708 Prudence St., Curtis Bay, 21226. Tel: 410-355-5740; Fax: 410-355-8122.
Catechesis/Religious Programs—April Dietrich, D.R.E.
Students 89.

13—St. Augustine (Elkridge) (1844), Revs. Gerard J. Bowen; Frank Ernst, S.J.
Res., 5976 Old Washington Rd., Elkridge, 21075. Tel: 410-796-8150; Fax: 410-796-8172. [CEM]
School—5990 Old Washington Rd., Elkridge, 21075. Tel: 410-796-3040. Sr. Rita Dorn, S.S.N.D, Prin.
School Sisters of Notre Dame 4; Lay Teachers 9; Students 321.
Catechesis/Religious Programs—Tel: 410-796-8150.
Students 352.

14—St. Barnabas. Closed 1931. Parish records available at St. Pius V Church. Tel: 410-523-1930.

15—St. Benedict (1876), Rt. Rev. Paschal A. Morlino, O.S.B.; Revs. James Miles; Michael McKay, O.S.B.; Sr. Beatrice Wise, D.C., Pastoral Assoc.; Deacon Duc Duong. In res., Rev. George Kallampally.
Res., 2612 Wilkens Ave., 21223. Tel: 410-947-4988; Fax: 410-947-6009.
Catechesis/Religious Programs—Sr. Eva Fitzgerald, D.R.E.
Students 38.

16—St. Bernard (Korean). Closed. For parish records prior to 1989 contact the chancery office. For parish records past 1989 contact Holy Korean Martyrs, Baltimore.

17—St. Bernardine (1928), Revs. Edward M. Miller; John A. Delclos; Deacons Phillip W. Harcum; Charles Knight.
Res., 3812 Edmondson Ave., 21229. Tel: 410-362-8664; Fax: 410-945-0459.
School—3601 Old Frederick Rd., 21229. Tel: 410-624-5088; Fax: 410-947-5439.
Lay Teachers 17; Students 251.
Catechesis/Religious Programs—Tel: 410-362-8978. Delores Hawthorne, D.R.E.
Students 203.

18—Blessed Sacrament Church (1911), Rev. P. Edward Kenny, Jr.; Sr. Marie Mack, S.S.N.D., Pastoral Admin.
Res., 4103 Old York Rd., 21218. Tel: 410-323-0424; Fax: 410-323-4478. [CEM]
Catechesis/Religious Programs—Students 25.

19—St. Brigid (1854), Rev. Joseph G. Bochenek; Bette Brocato, Pastoral Assoc.
Res., 911 S. Ellwood Ave., 21224. Tel: 410-563-1717; Fax: 410-563-1776.
School—Bishop John Newman. See separate listing.
Catechesis/Religious Programs—Students 50.

20—St. Casimir (1902), Revs. Ross Syracuse, O.F.M.Conv.; Vincent Gluc, O.F.M.Conv. In res., Rev. Timothy Kulbicki, O.F.M.Conv.
Res., 2736 O'Donnell St., 21224. Tel: 410-276-1981; Fax: 410-732-7436.
School—Father Kolbe School. See separate listing. Tel: 410-342-2681; Fax: 410-342-5715.

21—St. Cecilia (1902). (Twinned with Immaculate Conception, Baltimore.). Rev. Sylvester Peterka, C.M.; Bro. William Stover, C.M., Pastoral Assoc.
Res., 3300 Clifton Ave., 21216. Tel: 410-624-3600; Fax: 410-945-0157.
Catechesis/Religious Programs—Irene Mallory, D.R.E.
Students 39.

22—St. Charles Borromeo (Pikesville) (1848), Rev. E. Joseph Cote; Rev. Msgr. Martin A. Schwalenberg, Pastor Emeritus; Rev. Thomas Gillo, Admin.
Res., 101 Church Ln., 21208. Tel: 410-486-5400; Fax: 410-486-5421. [CEM]
Catechesis/Religious Programs—Sr. Marylita Friia, S.S.N.D., D.R.E.
Students 87.

23—Christ the King (Dundalk) (1957), Rev. Richard P. Wojciechowski.
Res., 335 Sollers Point Rd., 21222. Tel: 410-288-3629; 285-0604; Fax: 410-285-1126.
Catechesis/Religious Programs—Students 24.

24—St. Clare (Essex) (1956), Rev. Michael Thornsberry; Deacon Fred Miller. In res., Rev. Patrick M. Carrion.
Res., 714 Myrth Ave., 21221-4898. Tel: 410-687-6011; Fax: 410-687-3054.
School—Tel: 410-687-7787; Fax: 410-687-2715. Mrs. Dorothy Williams, Prin.
Sisters 3; Lay Teachers 22; Students 284.
Catechesis/Religious Programs—Tel: 410-686-7693.
Students 230.

25—St. Clement (Lansdowne) (1891), Revs. Steven P. Girard; Joseph A. Kenney, Pastor Emeritus; Deacons John I. McKenna; Thomas J. Yannuzzi.

Res., 2700 Washington Ave., 21227. Tel: 410-242-1025; Fax: 410-536-0636.
School—139 First Ave., 21227. Tel: 410-242-3432; Fax: 410-242-3433. Mrs. Mary Garmer, Headmistress.
Lay Teachers 9; Students 184.
Catechesis/Religious Programs—Tel: 410-242-2230.
Students 137.

26—ST. CLEMENT MARY HOFBAUER (Rosedale) (1925), Revs. Richard Florek, O.F.M.Conv.; Justin Ratajczak, O.F.M.Conv.; Santo Cricchio, O.F.M.Conv.; Deacons Nicholas Feurer, Pastoral Min.; Walter Shipley; Francis Zeiler.
Res., 1220 Chesaco Ave., 21237. Tel: 410-686-6188; Fax: 410-686-6198.
School—1216 Chesaco Ave., 21237. Tel: 410-686-3316. Sr. Michael Kathleen, O.S.F., Prin.
Sisters of St. Francis of Philadelphia 2; Lay Teachers 24; Students 428.
Catechesis/Religious Programs—Tel: 410-391-5028.
Students 126.

27—CORPUS CHRISTI (1881), Rev. Richard J. Bozzelli; Deacon Frank Hodges.
Res., 110 W. Lafayette Ave., 21217. Tel: 410-523-4161; Fax: 410-523-5745.
Catechesis/Religious Programs—Students 49.

28—ST. DOMINIC (1906), Revs. George Loskarn; Robert F. Lentz; Deacon Anthony Maranto.
Res., 5302 Harford Rd., 21214. Tel: 410-426-0360; Fax: 410-444-6963.
School—5304 Harford Rd., 21214. Tel: 410-426-0797; Fax: 410-426-3190. Patricia Larkin, Prin.
Lay Teachers 15; Students 274.
Catechesis/Religious Programs—Students 105.

29—ST. EDWARD (1880), Rev. Samuel Lupico; Sr. Anita B. Smith, O.S.F.; Deacons Joseph Neale; Carl A. Anderson.
Res., 901 Poplar Grove St., 21216. Tel: 410-362-2000; Fax: 410-945-7113.

30—ST. ELIZABETH OF HUNGARY (1895), Rev. Daniel Sinisi, T.O.R.; Bro. Finbar Gallagher, T.O.R.; Deacon Richard Morris. In res., Rev. Gerard Gordon, T.O.R.
Mailing & Office Address: 2 N. Belnord Ave., 21224. Tel: 410-675-8260; Fax: 410-675-8262.
Res., 2638 E. Baltimore St., 21224. Tel: 410-675-7771; Fax: 410-675-2530.
School—27 N. Lakewood Ave., 21224. Tel: 410-276-2253. Ms. Cathy Marshall, Prin.
Lay Teachers 12; Students 232.
Catechesis/Religious Programs—Students 27.

31—FOURTEEN HOLY MARTYRS. Closed 1964. Parish records available at St. Martin Church. Tel: 410-947-1242.

32—ST. FRANCIS OF ASSISI (1927), Rev. Msgr. William F. Burke; Rev. Joseph J. Bonadio, S.S.; Sr. Katherine Bell, R.S.M., Pastoral Assoc.
Res., 3615 Harford Rd., 21218. Tel: 410-235-5136; Fax: 410-467-9503.
School—3617 Harford Rd., 21218. Tel: 410-467-1683.
Sisters of Mercy 1; Lay Teachers 19; Students 304.
Catechesis/Religious Programs—Sr. Katherine M. Bell, D.R.E.
Students 45.

33—ST. FRANCIS XAVIER (1793), Rev. Alfred A. Dean, S.S.J.; Deacons Russell Matthews; Charles Mercer; Walton Smith. In res., Rev. Joseph C. Verretti, S.S.J.
Res., 1501 E. Oliver St., 21213. Tel: 410-727-3103; 3104; Fax: 410-625-9587.
Catechesis/Religious Programs—Tel: 410-837-0556.
Students 122.

34—ST. GABRIEL (1997). Formerly St. Lawrence and Our Lady of Perpetual Help, Woodlawn. Rev. Thomas L. Phillips; Deacons John J. Codd; Paul T. Mann, Pastoral Assoc.
Parish Office: 6950 Dogwood Rd., 21244. Tel: 410-298-8888; Fax: 410-944-7409.
School—John Paul Regional School. See separate listing.

35—ST. GREGORY THE GREAT (1883), Rev. Damien Nalepa; Sr. M. Assisi Jackson, O.S.P., Pastoral Assoc.
Res. & Church: 1542 N. Gilmor St., 21217. Tel: 410-523-0061; 523-0063; Fax: 410-669-1385.
Catechesis/Religious Programs—Rev. Louise G. Tildon, D.R.E.
Students 41.

36—HOLY CROSS (1858) (German), Rev. Thomas R. Malia. In res., Rev. Msgr. John L. Reinsfelder.
Res., 110 E. West St., 21230. Tel: 410-752-8498; Fax: 410-752-2703. [CEM]
School—Catholic Community School of South Baltimore. See separate listing. Tel: 410-685-6155; Fax: 410-685-0692.
Catechesis/Religious Programs—Students 100.

37—HOLY KOREAN MARTYRS (1972) (Korean), Rev. Joseph Y. Kim.
Res., 5801 Security Blvd., 21207. Tel: 410-265-8885; Fax: 410-265-1655. [CEM]
Catechesis/Religious Programs—Students 95.

38—HOLY ROSARY (1887) (Polish), Rev. Ronald Pytel; Rev. Msgr. Chester J. Mieczkowski, Pastoral Emeritus; Rev. Tomasz Kozub, S.Ch. In res., Revs. Francis Okroy, S.Ch.; Thomas Ryan.
Res., 408 S. Chester St., 21231. Tel: 410-732-3960; Fax: 410-675-4917. [CEM]
Catechesis/Religious Programs—Sr. Theresa Leimbach, D.R.E.
Students 43.

39—ST. IGNATIUS (1856), Revs. William J. Watters, S.J.; Francis P. Ernst, S.J.; Francis H. McGauley, S.J.
Church—740 N. Calvert St., 21202. Tel: 410-727-3848; Fax: 410-727-1573.
Jesuit Community of St. Ignatius Parish: 102 E. Madison St., 21202. Tel: 410-727-8729.
Catechesis/Religious Programs—Students 25.
St. Ignatius Social Services Self-Help—Tel: 410-625-4509. Rev. Robert J. Braunreuther, S.J., Dir.

40—IMMACULATE CONCEPTION (1850) (African American). (Twinned with St. Cecilia, Baltimore.). Rev. Sylvester Peterka, C.M.; Bro. William Stover, C.M.
Mailing Address: P.O. Box 16570, 21217.
Res., 1512 Druid Hill Ave., 21217. Tel: 410-523-0809; Fax: 410-945-0157.
Catechesis/Religious Programs—Karen Sullivan, D.R.E.
Students 26.

41—IMMACULATE CONCEPTION (Towson) (1883), Rev. Msgr. F. Dennis Tinder; Rev. Msgr. Edward J. Lynch, Pastor Emeritus; Revs. Paul Sparklin; Raymond Lee Harris, Jr.; John T. Carter. In res., Rev. Msgr. Jeremiah F. Kenney; Rev. James Reusing; Deacon John C. Gramling.
Res., 200 Ware Ave., 21204. Tel: 410-823-6175; Fax: 410-823-3936. [CEM]
School—(Grades PreK-8) 112 Ware Ave., Towson, 21204. Tel: 410-337-5222. Mrs. Marie Ann Cote, Prin.
High School—Towson Catholic, 114 Ware Ave., 21204. Tel: 410-823-8400; Fax: 410-823-8404. Mr. Thomas Peri, Prin.
Catechesis/Religious Programs—School of Religion, 701 Baltimore Ave., 21204. Tel: 410-821-8287. Ms. Lisa E. Padian, Dir.
Students 227.
Convent—112 Ware Ave., 21204. Tel: 410-823-3470. Sisters of St. Francis

42—IMMACULATE HEART OF MARY (Baynesville) (1948), Revs. Michael W. Carrion; Joseph L. McManus, Pastor Emeritus; George I. Jakopac; Edgar Graham, S.J.; James Risacher; Deacons Jack Martin; Ken Pivec.
Res., 8501 Loch Raven Blvd., 21286. Tel: 410-668-7935; Fax: 410-661-6560.
School—Tel: 410-668-8466; Fax: 410-668-6171. Mrs. Wilma Short, Prin.
Sisters of Mercy 2; Lay Teachers 25; Students 562.
Catechesis/Religious Programs—Tel: 410-661-3820; Fax: 410-661-3838.
Students 200.

43—ST. ISAAC JOGUES (1968), Rev. H. Martin Hammond; Rev. Msgr. James J. Cronin, Pastor Emeritus; Deacons Alan Rose; Arthur L. Micozzi; James Westwater.
Church Office—9215 Old Harford Rd., 21234. Tel: 410-661-4888; Fax: 410-882-1484.
Res., 9400 Old Harford Rd., 21234. Tel: 410-661-4888; Fax: 410-882-1484.
Catechesis/Religious Programs—Tel: 410-665-2561. D.R.E.: Sr. John Francis Kearney, S.S.N.D.; Barbara Anderson.
Students 538.

44—ST. JAMES AND ST. JOHN. Closed 1986. Parish records available at the Chancery. Tel: 410-547-5446.
School—Queen of Peace Elementary Cluster. See separate listing.

45—ST. JEROME (1887), Revs. John D. Harvey, O.F.M. Cap.; Kevin Thompson, O.F.M.Cap.; Deacon Gerald Anthony Roberts. Pastoral Assocs.: Sr. Eleanor Casey, D.C.; Sr. Suzanne Baumgartner, D.C.
Res., 775 W. Hamburg St., 21230. Tel: 410-727-0430; Fax: 410-727-0431.
Catechesis/Religious Programs—Students 34.
Headstart & Social Hall—765 W. Hamburg St., 21230. Tel: 410-539-2429.

46—ST. JOHN GERMAN CATHOLIC CHURCH. Closed 1841. Original records, stored at The Catholic Center, are available to researchers on microfilm at the Maryland State Archives in Annapolis.

47—ST. JOHN THE EVANGELIST. Closed 1966. Parish records available at the Chancery. Tel: 410-547-5446.

48—ST. JOSEPH. Closed 1962. Parish records available at Holy Cross Rectory. Tel: 410-752-8498.

49—ST. JOSEPH (Fullerton) (1850) (German), Rev. Msgr. George B. Moeller; Revs. Stephen R. Sutton; John A. Eckard; Deacons William J. DeAngelis; Vincent J. Perticone; Charles A. Baynes; William S. Albaugh.
Res., 8420 Belair Rd., 21236. Tel: 410-256-1630; Fax: 410-529-2990. [CEM]
School—Tel: 410-256-8026; Fax: 410-529-7234. Mrs. Joyce Thaler, Prin.
Lay Teachers 26; Students 524.
Catechesis/Religious Programs—Tel: 410-256-8235.
Students 723.

50—ST. JOSEPH PASSIONIST MONASTERY PARISH (1868), Rev. William Murphy, C.P.; Pat Skarupa, Pastoral Assoc.
Res., 251 S. Morley St., 21229. Tel: 410-566-0877; Fax: 410-233-4974.
Catechesis/Religious Programs—Gloria Rinky, D.R.E.
Students 48.

51—ST. JUDE SHRINE (1873) (Italian), Rev. Frank S. Donio, S.A.C. In res., Revs. Flavian Bonifazi, S.A.C.; John G. Biermann, S.A.C.
Res., 308 N. Paca St., P.O. Box 1455, 21203. Tel: 410-685-6026; 685-3497; Fax: 410-244-5728.
St. Jude Shrine Corp.—Tel: 410-685-6026.

52—ST. KATHARINE OF SIENNA. Closed 1986. Parish records available at St. Wenceslaus Church. Tel: 410-675-7304.

53—ST. LAWRENCE (1962). Merged with The Shrine of Our Lady of Perpetual Help, Baltimore, to form St. Gabriel Parish, Baltimore. Records available at St. Gabriel Parish.

54—ST. LEO (1881) (Italian), Rev. Michael Salerno, S.A.C. In res., Rev. Nicholas Rinaldi, S.A.C.
Res., 227 S. Exeter St., 21202. Tel: 410-675-7275; Fax: 410-675-8291.
School—Father Kolbe Interparochial. See separate listing. Tel: 410-342-2681.

55—LITTLE FLOWER, SHRINE OF (1926), Rev. Michael J. Orchik; Deacon Henry L. Siarkowski. In res., Revs. Thomas J. Bauernfeind; James C. Miles.
Res., 2854 Brendan Ave., 21213. Tel: 410-483-1700; Fax: 410-488-6482.
School—(Grades PreK-8) 2800 Brendan Ave., 21213. Tel: 410-488-1483; Fax: 410-488-0929. Mr. Richard G. Gatto, Prin.
Sisters of St. Francis of Philadelphia 2; Lay Teachers 15; Students 258.
Catechesis/Religious Programs—Students 41.

56—ST. LUKE (Edgemere) (1888), Rev. Joseph S. Lizor, Jr.
Res., 7517 Northpoint Blvd., 21219-1499. Tel: 410-477-5200; Fax: 410-477-5996.
School—Our Lady of Hope/St. Luke's School, Tel: 410-288-2793.
Catechesis/Religious Programs—Doris Lundin, D.R.E.
Students 131.

57—ST. MARK (Cantonsville) (1888), Revs. Christopher Whatley; Jason C. Worley; John W. Bowen, S.S.; Sr. Kathleen Martin, M.H.S.H., Pastoral Assoc. In res., Rev. Msgr. Henry F. Zerhusen; Rev. Ross A. Laporta, Pastor Emeritus.
Res., 27 Melvin Ave., 21228. Tel: 410-744-6560; Fax: 410-747-3182.
School—26 Melvin Ave., 21228. Tel: 410-747-6613; Fax: 410-747-3188. Sr. Raymond Marie Lorenzen, S.S.N.D., Prin.
Catechesis/Religious Programs—Tel: 410-788-6211.
Students 438.

58—ST. MARTIN (1865), Revs. John D. Harvey, O.F.M.Cap.; Kevin Thompson, O.F.M.Cap.; Deacon Tony Roberts. Pastoral Assocs.: Sr. Suzanne Baumgartner, D.C.; Sr. Eleanor Casey, D.C.
Res., 31 N. Fulton Ave., 21223. Tel: 410-947-1242; Fax: 410-625-2406.
Catechesis/Religious Programs—Students 82.

59—ST. MARY OF THE ASSUMPTION (1849), Rev. P. Edward Kenny, Jr.; Deacon Miguel Sainz. In res., Deacon Rochus Vu Dinh Hoat.
Res., 5502 York Rd., 21212. Tel: 410-435-5900; Fax: 410-435-4879. [CEM]
School—Tel: 410-435-5850. Mrs. Elaine Reed, Prin.
Lay Teachers 16; Students 158.
Catechesis/Religious Programs—Students 61.

60—ST. MARY, STAR OF THE SEA (1868), Rev. Thomas R. Malia.
Res., 110 E. West St., 21230. Tel: 410-685-2255; Fax: 410-332-4036.
School—Catholic Community School of South Baltimore. See separate listing. Tel: 410-685-6155; Fax: 410-685-0692.

Catechesis/Religious Programs—Tel: 410-752-8498; Fax: 410-752-2703.
Students 100.
Convent—1410 Riverside Ave., 21230. Tel: 410-752-4344; Fax: 410-685-0692. Sisters of St. Joseph

61—ST. MATTHEW (1949), Rev. Joseph L. Muth.
Res., 5401 Loch Raven Blvd., 21239. Tel: 410-433-2300; Fax: 410-433-5263.
School—Cardinal Shehan School. See separate listing. Tel: 410-433-2775; Fax: 410-323-6131.
Catechesis/Religious Programs—Students 41.

62—ST. MICHAEL (Broadway) (1852) (Hispanic). Merged with St. Patrick 1995. Revs. James-Santiago W. Gilmour, C.SS.R.; Andrew Carr, C.SS.R.; Bro. John Bosco Hammond, C.SS.R.; Sr. Sonia-Marie Fernandez, M.H.S.H., Pastoral Assoc.; Deacons Rafael Villagaray; Pablo Osorio; Richard Novak. In res., Rev. Reginald Andrietta.
Res., 7 S. Wolfe St., 21231-1913. Tel: 410-276-1646; Fax: 410-522-0789.

63—ST. MICHAEL (Overlea) (1913), Revs. Christopher M. Carney; J. James Purvey. In res., Rev. James M. Barker; Deacons Henry Davis; Kevin Brooksbank.
Res., 2 Willow Ave., 21206. Tel: 410-665-1054; Fax: 410-665-4024.
School—10 Willow Ave., 21206. Tel: 410-668-8797; Fax: 410-668-8797. Mrs. Patricia Rohde Kelly, Prin.
Lay Teachers 30; Students 428.
Catechesis/Religious Programs—Tel: 410-882-8120.
Students 237.

64—ST. MILDRED CHURCH. Closed 1967. Parish records available at Our Lady of Hope Rectory. Tel: 410-284-6600.

65—ST. MONICA. Closed 1959. Parish records available at the Chancery. Tel: 410-547-5446.

66—MOST PRECIOUS BLOOD (1948). (Twinned with St. Anthony of Padua, Baltimore.). Revs. C. Lou Martin; William Fitzgerald; Dr. Gloria R. Carpeneto, Pastoral Assoc.; Deacons Joseph C. Krysiak; Joseph Schultz. In res., Most Rev. Gordon D. Bennett, S.J.
Office: 4414 Frankford Ave., 21206. Tel: 410-488-0400; Fax: 410-488-0032.
Church—5010 Bowleys Ln., 21206.

67—OUR LADY OF THE ANGELS CATHOLIC COMMUNITY (Catonsville) (1993), Rev. Leo J. Larrivee, S.S. Pastoral Assocs.: Sr. Victoria Kessler, S.S.N.D.; Sr. Eileen McFadden, S.S.N.D.
Mailing Address: 711 Maiden Choice Ln., Catonsville, 21228. Tel: 410-247-4779; Fax: 410-737-8826.

68—OUR LADY OF FATIMA (1951), Revs. Michael D. Sergi, C.SS.R.; Francis A. Poux, C.SS.R.; Richard K. Poetzel, C.SS.R.; Patrick Flynn, C.SS.R.; Gerard Chylko, C.SS.R.; Bro. DeSales Zimpfer, C.SS.R., Pastoral Assoc.; Sr. Julianne Hau, M.H.S.H., Pastoral Assoc.; Deacon Alphonse Bankard, III. Missionaries: Rev. Gerard Chylko, C.SS.R.
Res., 6420 E. Pratt St., 21224. Tel: 410-633-9393; Fax: 410-631-7239.
School—6400 E. Pratt St., 21224. Tel: 410-633-5882; Fax: 410-633-5268.
Lay Teachers 3; Students 242.
Catechesis/Religious Programs—Tel: 410-633-6256.
Students 103.

69—OUR LADY OF GOOD COUNSEL (1889), Rev. Raymond D. Martin.
Office: 1532 E. Fort Ave., 21230. Tel: 410-752-0205; Fax: 410-576-0929.
School—Catholic Community School of South Baltimore. See separate listing. Tel: 410-685-6155.
Catechesis/Religious Programs—Students 80.

70—OUR LADY OF HOPE (1967), Revs. John B. Ward; Paul G. Witthauer.
Res., 1727 Lynch Rd., 21222. Tel: 410-284-6600; Fax: 410-282-9361.
School—(Grades PreK-8) 8003 N. Boundary Rd., 21222. Tel: 410-288-2793.
School Sisters of Notre Dame 3; Lay Teachers 24; Students 396.
Catechesis/Religious Programs—8003 N. Boundary Rd., Tel: 410-282-3120; Fax: 410-282-9361.
Students 275.

71—OUR LADY OF LOURDES. Closed 1995. Parish records available at The New All Saints Church. Tel: 410-542-0445.

72—OUR LADY OF MOUNT CARMEL (Middle River) (1887), Revs. Robert L. Hartnett; Kevin Mueller; Leo Patalinghug; Sr. Betty Kane, O.S.F., Pastoral Assoc.
Res., 1704 Old Eastern Ave., 21221. Tel: 410-686-4972; Fax: 410-574-8785.
School—1702 Old Eastern Ave., 21221. Tel: 410-686-0859; Fax: 410-686-4916. Mrs. Kathleen Sipes, Prin.
Sisters of St. Francis of Philadelphia 2; Lay Teachers 28; Students 532.
High School—1706 Old Eastern Ave., 21221. Tel: 410-686-1023. Mrs. Kathleen Sipes, Prin.
Lay Teachers 22; Students 220.
Catechesis/Religious Programs—Tel: 410-686-9016; Fax: 410-574-8785.
Students 241.

73—OUR LADY OF PERPETUAL HELP (1936). Merged with St. Lawrence, Baltimore, to form St. Gabriel Parish, Baltimore. Records available at St. Gabriel.

74—OUR LADY OF POMPEI (1924), Revs. Luigi Esposito; Gilberto Leboroni-Pierozzi; Deacon Thom Kuhl.
Res., 3600 Claremont St., 21224. Tel: 410-675-7790; Fax: 410-563-9067.
School—201 S. Conkling St., 21224. Tel: 410-276-6534; Fax: 410-276-6915. Ms. Angela Rebbert, Prin.
Lay Teachers 10; Students 193.
High School—Tel: 410-276-4503. Mr. Christopher Russo, Prin.
Priests 1; Lay Teachers 7; Students 142.

75—OUR LADY OF SORROWS. Closed 1935. Parish records available at Holy Cross Rectory. Tel: 410-752-8498.

76—OUR LADY, QUEEN OF PEACE (1953), Revs. Brian Zielinski, O.Praem.; Mark Falcone, O.Praem.; Deacons George Jenkins; Robert Hacher.
Res., 10003 Bird River Rd., 21220. Tel: 410-686-3085; Fax: 410-687-1916.
School—10001 Bird River Rd., 21220. Tel: 410-687-8513; Fax: 410-687-1916. Ms. Cynthia Stewart, Prin.
Lay Teachers 17; Students 155.
Catechesis/Religious Programs—Dennis Gerber, D.R.E.
Students 155.

77—OUR LADY OF VICTORY (Arbutus) (1952), Deacon William Jauquet.
Res., 4414 Wilkens Ave., 21229. Tel: 410-242-0131; 0180; Fax: 410-242-6963.
School—4416 Wilkens Ave., 21229. Tel: 410-242-3688; Fax: 410-242-8867. Thomas E. Riddle, Prin.; Deborah Reese, Asst. Prin.
Lay Teachers 21; Students 516.
Catechesis/Religious Programs—Students 77.

78—ST. PATRICK (Broadway) (1792) (Hispanic). Twinned with St. Michael (Wolfe St.) 1995. Revs. James W. Gilmour, C.SS.R.; Andrew Carr, C.SS.R.; Bro. John Bosco Hammond, C.SS.R.; Sr. Sonia Marie Fernandez, M.H.S.H., Pastoral Assoc.; Deacons Richard Novak; Pablo Osorio; Rafael Villagary. In res., Rev. Reginald Andrietta.
Res., 7 S. Wolfe St., 21231. Tel: 410-276-1646; Fax: 410-522-0789.

79—ST. PAUL'S (1888). Closed. Parish records available at St. Francis Xavier. Tel: 410-727-3103.

80—ST. PETER THE APOSTLE (1842), Revs. John D. Harvey, O.F.M.Cap.; Kevin Thompson, O.F.M.Cap.; Sr. Kenneth McGuire, R.S.M., Parish Mgr. Pastoral Assocs.: Sr. Eleanor Casey, D.C.; Sr. Suzanne Baumgartner, D.C.; Deacon Tony Roberts.
Res., 848 Hollins St., 21201. Tel: 410-685-5044; Fax: 410-625-2406.
Catechesis/Religious Programs—Students 49.

81—ST. PETER CLAVER (1888) (African American), Revs. Raymond Woodka, S.S.J., Pastoral Admin.; Henry Harper, S.S.J.; Joseph Del Vecchio, S.S.J.; Deacon John Briscoe.
Res., 1546 N. Fremont Ave., 21217. Tel: 410-669-0512; Fax: 410-383-8227.
School—Father Charles A. Hall Lower and Middle School, (Grades PreK-8) 1546 N. Fremont Ave., 21217. Tel: 410-225-7555; Fax: 410-225-7721. M. Kathleen Filippelli, Prin.
Lay Teachers 10; Students 156.
Catechesis/Religious Programs—Students 52.
Convent—1526 N. Fremont Ave., 21217. Tel: 410-383-1288.

82—SS. PHILIP AND JAMES (1897), Rev. William A. Au; Deacons D. Vincent Provenza; Chester J. Jakowski.
Res., 2801 N. Charles St., 21218. Tel: 410-235-2294; Fax: 410-243-5262.

83—ST. PIUS V (1878) (African American), Rev. Cletus C.U. Udoh, M.S.P.
Res., 521 N. Schroeder St., 21223. Tel: 410-523-1930; Fax: 410-523-8164. [JC]

84—ST. PIUS X (1957), Revs. Thomas J. Golueke; Louis M. Reitz, S.S.; Mrs. Pat Howlett, Parish Admin.
Res., 6428 York Rd., 21212. Tel: 410-377-7440; Fax: 410-377-2651.
School—6432 York Rd., 21212. Tel: 410-377-9738; Fax: 410-372-0552. Geri Morrison, Prin.
Lay Teachers 23; Students 448.
Catechesis/Religious Programs—Tel: 410-377-0722. Mrs. Pinky Howard, D.R.E.
Students 291.

85—ST. RITA (1922), Revs. William J. Remmel, S.D.S.; Bogdan Palka, S.D.S.; Deacons John Martelle; George T. Evans.
Res., 2907 Dunleer Rd., 21222. Tel: 410-284-0388; Fax: 410-284-3998.
School—2905 Dunleer Rd., 21222. Tel: 410-284-3580; Fax: 410-284-1971. Sr. Mary Mark Carnes, I.H.M., Prin.
Lay Teachers 13; Students 189.
Catechesis/Religious Programs—Tel: 410-284-7355. Kathleen M. McLhinney, D.R.E.
Students 135.

86—ST. ROSE OF LIMA (1914), Rev. Joseph M. O'Meara; Sr. Kathleen White, O.S.B., Pastoral Assoc.
Res., 3803 4th St., 21225. Tel: 410-355-8515; 8516; Fax: 410-355-1938.
School—410 Jeffrey St., 21225. Tel: 410-355-1050; Fax: 410-355-2408. Madeleine Hobik, Prin.
Lay Teachers 15; Students 226.
Catechesis/Religious Programs—Elise Buchner, D.R.E.
Students 77.

87—SACRED HEART OF JESUS (1873), Revs. Thomas B. Loftus, C.SS.R.; John Drum, C.SS.R.; William Harbison, C.SS.R.; Edwin G. Foley, C.SS.R.; Deacon Leo Nuedling. In res., Revs. Gerard Kurek; John Farrell, C.SS.R.; Joseph Freund, C.SS.R.; Bros. Raphael Rock, C.SS.R.; Barnabas Hipkins, C.SS.R.
Res., 600 S. Conkling St., 21224-4294. Tel: 410-342-4336; Fax: 410-522-2022.
School—Bishop John Neumann School. See separate listing. Tel: 410-675-6271; Fax: 410-327-1543.
Catechesis/Religious Programs—Students 48.
Missions—Baltimore, Baltimore Co., Holy Redeemer Chapel, 800 S. Oldham St., 21224. Tel: 410-342-0151; Baltimore, Baltimore Co., St. Gerard's Chapel, Charlotte & Cardiff Aves., 21224. Tel: 410-633-9515.

88—SACRED HEART OF MARY (1925), Rev. Msgr. Richard E. Parks; Revs. Leon Warczynski, Pastor Emeritus; David Kruse; Bro. William Ciganek, C.F.X., Pastoral Assoc.
Res., 6736 Youngstown Ave., 21222-1097. Tel: 410-633-2828; Fax: 410-633-0349. [CEM]
School—6726 Youngstown Ave., 21222-1098. Tel: 410-633-7040; Fax: 410-633-7644. Mrs. Helen Roby, Prin.
Lay Teachers 18; Students 261.
Catechesis/Religious Programs—Michael Demski, D.R.E.
Students 123.

89—SHRINE OF THE SACRED HEART (Mt. Washington) (1867), Rev. Richard E. Cramblitt; Sr. Mary Margaret Savage, S.S.J., Pastoral Assoc.
Res., 1701 Regent Rd., 21209. Tel: 410-466-6884; 6885; Fax: 410-664-0523.
School—5800 Smith Ave., 21209. Tel: 410-542-7406; Fax: 410-664-1463. Martha Pierorazio, Prin.
Lay Teachers 14; Students 200.
Catechesis/Religious Programs—Tel: 410-466-6884, Ext. 15.
Students 168.

90—ST. STANISLAUS KOSTKA (1880) (Polish). Closed. For inquiries for parish records please contact St. Casimir, Baltimore. Tel: 410-276-1981; 732-7436 (fax).

91—ST. THOMAS AQUINAS (1867), Rev. James Farmer; Sr. Alice Joseph Rohe, O.S.F., Pastoral Assoc. In res., Revs. George Restrepo, S.J.; William Simms.
Res., 1008 W. 37th St., 21211. Tel: 410-366-4488; Fax: 410-366-8352.
School—(Grades PreK-8) 3710 Roland Ave., 21211. Tel: 410-889-4618; Fax: 410-889-1956.
School Sisters of Notre Dame 3; Lay Teachers 12; Students 232.
Catechesis/Religious Programs—Tel: 410-366-4488; Fax: 410-366-8352. Susan Sousa, D.R.E.
Students 31.

92—ST. THOMAS MORE (1960), Rev. John P. Cunningham; Sr. Mary Small, S.S.J., Pastoral Assoc.; Deacons Michael P. McCoy; James L. Mann, Jr. In res., Rev. Msgr. Francis W. Malooly.
Parish Center & Mailing Address—6806 McClean Blvd., 21234. Tel: 410-444-6500; Fax: 410-444-6502.
School—Cardinal Shehan School. See separate listing. Tel: 410-433-2775; Fax: 410-323-6131.
Catechesis/Religious Programs—Tel: 410-444-4563. Susan Keating, D.R.E.
Students 39.

93—ST. URSULA (Parkville) (1934), Rev. Msgr. A. Thomas Baumgartner; Rev. Msgr. Myles McGowan, Pastor Emeritus; Revs. Gerald Hynes, C.P.; Paul Holthaus; Sr. Anne Mooney, S.S.N.D., Pastoral Min.; Deacons Robert Keenan; Frank Rongione, Sr.
Res., 8801 Harford Rd., 21234. Tel: 410-665-2111; Fax: 410-665-0758.
School—8900 Harford Rd., 21234. Tel: 410-665-3533; Fax: 410-661-1620. Sr. Joan Kelly, S.N.D., Prin.
Catechesis/Religious Programs—Tel: 410-655-4106.
Students 400.

94—St. Veronica (1945) (African American), Rev. Donald M. Fest, S.S.J.; Deacons Jhan Harris; Williard Pinkney, Jr.; Alexander Smith.
Res., 806 Cherry Hill Rd., 21225. Tel: 410-355-7466; Fax: 410-355-7741.

95—St. Vincent de Paul (1840), Rev. Richard T. Lawrence.
Res., 120 N. Front St., 21202. Tel: 410-962-5078; Fax: 410-962-8427. [CEM]
St. Vincent de Paul Church Historic Trust, Inc.—Tel: 410-962-5078.
Jonestown Planning Council, Inc.—Tel: 410-962-5078.
Catechesis/Religious Programs—Students 32.

96—St. Wenceslaus (1872), Rev. Peter A. Lyons, T.O.R. In res., Rev. Earl Jennings, T.O.R.
Res., 2111 Ashland Ave., 21205. Tel: 410-675-7304; Fax: 410-675-5746.
School—Queen of Peace Elementary Cluster. See separate listing.
Catechesis/Religious Programs—Students 25.

97—St. William of York (1914), Rev. Martin H. Demek; Deacons Donald Miller; John Langmead.
Res., 600 Cooks Ln., 21229. Tel: 410-566-2140; Fax: 410-362-5475.
School—Tel: 410-945-1442; Fax: 410-945-4036.
Lay Teachers 14; Students 217.
Catechesis/Religious Programs—Students 63.

OUTSIDE METROPOLITAN BALTIMORE

Aberdeen, Harford Co., St. Joan of Arc (1920), Rev. Samuel V. Young, Parish Admin.; Fred Koenig, Business Mgr.; Deacon Daniel Kopczyk. In res., Rev. Msgr. James J. Cronin.
Office: 222 S. Law St., 21001. Tel: 410-272-4535; 575-6909; Fax: 410-272-9025.
Res., 257 S. Law St., 21001.
School—230 S. Law St., 21001. Tel: 410-272-1387; Fax: 410-272-1959. Dr. Jane Towery, Prin.
Lay Teachers 21; Students 241.
Catechesis/Religious Programs—Tel: 410-272-6944. Rosemarie Homberg, D.R.E.
Students 179.

Abingdon, Harford Co., St. Francis de Sales (1866), Rev. Msgr. G. Michael Schleupner; Deacon Richard Stine.
Res., 1450 Abingdon Rd., 21009. Tel: 410-676-5119; 679-4555; Fax: 410-676-7520. [CEM]
Catechesis/Religious Programs—Tel: 410-676-3354; Fax: 410-676-7520.
Students 535.

Annapolis, Anne Arundel Co., St. Andrew by the Bay (Cape St. Claire) (1981), Revs. Jay O'Connor; Edward S. Szymanski; Deacons R. Paul Woofter; James C. Monaghan, Jr.
Parish Center—701 College Pkwy., 21401. Tel: 410-974-4366; Fax: 410-974-4339.
Catechesis/Religious Programs—Students 684.

St. Mary (1853), Revs. John Sodomora, C.SS.R.; John G. Tizio, C.SS.R.; Denis J. Sweeney, C.SS.R.; Alphonsus Olive, C.SS.R.; John Lavin, C.SS.R.; Theodore Heyburn, C.SS.R.; E. Patrick Lynch, C.SS.R.; Deacons Leroy S. Moore; Anthony F. Norcio. In res., Revs. Bernard Baumgartner, C.SS.R.; Francis X. Murphy, C.SS.R.; Sr. M. Mark Tippett, S.S.N.D., Pastoral Assoc.
Res., 109 Duke of Gloucester St., 21401. Tel: 410-263-2397; 269-6092; Fax: 410-263-3027. [CEM]
School—111 Duke of Gloucester St., 21401. Tel: 410-263-2869; Fax: 410-269-6513. Timothy Lynch, Prin.
Lay Teachers 37; Students 915.
High School—113 Duke of Gloucester St., 21401. Tel: 410-263-3294; Fax: 410-269-7843. Sr. Franchita Hobbs, S.S.N.D., Prin.
School Sisters of Notre Dame 2; Lay Teachers 36; Students 580.
Catechesis/Religious Programs—Tel: 410-268-5834; Fax: 410-263-7381.
Students 625.
Convent—4 Shipwright St., 21401. Tel: 410-269-0568.
School Sisters of Notre Dame 5.
Mission—Annapolis, Anne Arundel Co., St. John Neuman, 620 N. Bestgate Rd., 21401. Tel: 410-266-2499.

Bel Air, Harford Co., St. Margaret (1905), Revs. Francis X. Callahan; C. Douglas Kenney; Timothy Kulbicki; Patrick Carrion; Karen Saccenti, Pastoral Assoc.; Deacons Paul Ciesla; Patrick Goles; J. Donald MacKnew.
Res., 141 Hickory Ave., 21014. Tel: 410-838-6969; Fax: 410-879-2518.
School—205 Hickory Ave., 21013. Tel: 410-879-1113. Ms. Amelia Mike, Prin.
Lay Teachers 29; Students 599.
Catechesis/Religious Programs—Tel: 410-838-4224. Bridgit Cupp, D.R.E.
Students 1,438.
Mission—Bel Air, Harford Co., St. Mary Magdalen, 1716 Churchville Rd., 21015. Tel: 410-838-6969.

Bradshaw, Baltimore Co., St. Stephen (1863), Revs. Lawrence F. Kolson; Paul Breczinski; Deacons Gilbert Hartlieb; Robert Schott; Frank R. Laws.
Res., 8030 Bradshaw Rd., 21021. Tel: 410-592-7071; Fax: 410-592-6803. [CEM]
School—8028 Bradshaw Rd., 21021. Tel: 410-592-7617; Fax: 410-592-7330. Mrs. Helena K. Scher, Prin.
Catechesis/Religious Programs—Tel: 410-592-8666. Sr. Angela DeFontes, O.S.F., D.R.E.
Students 490.

Brunswick, Frederick Co., St. Francis of Assisi (1893), Rev. Lawrence Gesy.
Res., 113 First Ave., 21716. Tel: 301-834-9185; Fax: 301-834-4162. [JC]
Catechesis/Religious Programs—Students 108.
Mission—Petersville, Frederick Co., St. Mary's.

Buckeystown, Frederick Co., St. Joseph-on-Carrollton Manor (1811), Revs. Lawrence K. Frazier; Paul J. Iaia, Pastor Emeritus; Deacon Robert M. Balderas.
Mailing Address: P.O. Box 33, 21717. Tel: 301-663-0907; Fax: 301-663-6525.
Res., 5843 Manor Woods Rd., Frederick, 21703. [CEM]
Catechesis/Religious Programs—Tel: 301-663-0907, Ext. 12.
Students 388.

Clarksville, Howard Co., St. Louis (1855), Rev. Msgr. Joseph L. Luca; Revs. Gregory J. Ferri; Erik J. Arnold.
Res., P.O. Box 155, 21029. Tel: 410-531-6040; Fax: 410-531-6191. [CEM]
School—Rte. 108, 21209. Tel: 410-531-6664. Mrs. Terry Weiss, Prin.
Sisters 1; Lay Teachers 22; Students 496.
Catechesis/Religious Programs—Tel: 410-531-6688. Mrs. Rhonda Milauskas, D.R.E.
Students 1,531.

Cockeysville, Baltimore Co., St. Joseph (1852), Rev. Msgr. Paul G. Cook; Revs. John Jicha; Charles Wible; Deacon Edward Sulivan. Pastoral Assocs.: Sr. Rose Lindner, S.S.N.D.; Ann LaRocque.
Res., 101 Church Ln., 21030. Tel: 410-666-1619; Fax: 410-628-2956. [CEM]
School—105 Church Ln., 21030. Tel: 410-666-0393; Fax: 410-628-6814. Sr. Anne O'Donnell, R.S.M., Prin.
Lay Teachers 25; Students 455.
Catechesis/Religious Programs—40 Church Ln., 21030. Tel: 410-666-8840.
Students 729.

Columbia, Howard Co., St. John the Evangelist (1967), Revs. Richard H. Tillman; James P. Kiesel; Deacon George Martin.
Res., 21044.
Interfaith Centers—(Wilde Lake) 10431 Twin Rivers Rd., 21044. Tel: 410-964-1425; Fax: 410-730-9253.
(Oakland Mills) 5885 Robert Oliver Pl., 21045. Tel: 410-964-1434; Fax: 410-740-9323.
Catechesis/Religious Programs—Tel: 410-964-1437.
Students 720.

Cresaptown, Allegany Co., St. Ambrose (1887), Rev. Marvin Justi, O.F.M.Cap.; Ms. Margaret Gaughan, Pastoral Assoc.
Res., P.O. Box 5130, 21505-5130. Tel: 301-729-2790; Fax: 301-729-2436. [CEM]
Catechesis/Religious Programs—Students 117.

Crofton, Anne Arundel Co., St. Elizabeth Ann Seton (1976), Rev. Edward C. Connelly; Sr. Joan Bunty, O.S.F., Pastoral Assoc.; Deacon Frederick Seibold.
Office: 1800 Seton Dr., 21114. Tel: 410-721-5770; Fax: 410-721-5508.
School—Arthur Slade Regional Catholic School. See separate listing.
Catechesis/Religious Programs—Tel: 410-721-5774.
Students 700.

Cumberland, Allegany Co., St. Mary (1900) (Italian), Rev. Milton A. Hipsley; Bro. James T. Kirkpatrick, F.S.C., Pastoral Assoc.; Deacon David A. Conley.
Res., 300 E. Oldtown Rd., 21502. Tel: 301-777-2990; Fax: 301-777-1108. [CEM]
School—St. John Neumann, (Grades K-5). See separate listing.
High School—Bishop Walsh, (Grades 6-12).

St. Patrick (1790) (Irish), Rev. Thomas R. Bevan; Deacons Gerald A. Raible; Paul H. Dignan, Sr.; Loren Mooney; Francis L. Werner, Jr.
Res., 201 N. Centre St., 21502. Tel: 301-777-1750; Fax: 301-777-2669. [CEM]
Neumann Early Childhood Center—See separate listing. 209 N. Centre St., 21502. Tel: 301-724-4055.
Catechesis/Religious Programs—Loren L. Mooney, D.R.E.
Students 101.

SS. Peter and Paul (1848) (German), Rev. Vernon Busch, O.F.M.Cap.; Deacon Herman Grabenstein.
Res., 109 N. Smallwood St., 21502-2992. Tel: 301-777-3131; Fax: 301-759-3568. [CEM]
School—St. John Neumann. See separate listing. Tel: 301-724-4055; Fax: 301-724-4827.
Catechesis/Religious Programs—Students 151.

Davidsonville, Anne Arundel Co., Holy Family (1929), Rev. Joseph F. Barr.
Res., 826 W. Central Ave., P.O. Box 130, 21035-0130. Tel: 410-269-0586; 301-261-7399; Fax: 410-798-5315.
Catechesis/Religious Programs—Tel: 410-798-5680.
Students 467.

Edgewater, Anne Arundel Co., Our Lady of Perpetual Help (1976), Rev. Frank J. Brauer; Deacon Stephen Cooley.
Res., 515 Loch Haven Rd., 21037. Tel: 410-956-2883; Fax: 410-798-0076.
Catechesis/Religious Programs—Mary Ellen Fisher, D.R.E.
Students 269.

Edgewood, Harford Co., Prince of Peace (1975), Revs. Stephen D. Gosnell; William J. Lee, S.S.
Office Address: 2600 Willoughby Beach Rd., 21040. Tel: 410-679-5912; Fax: 410-679-6715.
Catechesis/Religious Programs—Students 150.

Ellicott City, Howard Co., Our Lady of Perpetual Help (1893), Revs. Richard E. Smith; Isaac Karoor; Deacon Raymond Crawford; Sr. Mary McFadden, S.N.D., Pastoral Assoc.
Res., 4795 Ilchester Rd., 21043. Tel: 410-747-4334; Fax: 410-747-4339. [CEM]
School—4801 Ilchester Rd., Ellicott City, 21043. Tel: 410-744-4251; Fax: 410-788-5210.
Lay Teachers 21; Students 259.
Catechesis/Religious Programs—Tel: 410-747-0131; Fax: 410-788-8905.
Students 1,042.

Resurrection (1974), Revs. James O. McGovern; Timothy J. Fell; J. Bryan Hehir; Joseph Donders, M.Afr.; M. Stephen Barrett, S.S.; Deacon Ray Britt.
Office: 3175 Paulskirk Dr., 21042. Tel: 410-461-9111; Fax: 410-203-9419.
School—Resurrection/St. Paul, Tel: 410-465-8746; Fax: 410-461-8621. Sr. Joan Elias, G.N.S.H., Prin.
Grey Nuns of the Sacred Heart 2; Lay Teachers 22; Students 326.
Catechesis/Religious Programs—Tel: 410-461-9111, Ext. 221.
Students 1,000.

St. Paul (1838), Rev. Thomas J. Donaghy.
Res., 3755 St. Paul St., 21043. Tel: 410-465-1670; Fax: 410-313-8551. [CEM]
Catechesis/Religious Programs—Tel: 410-465-0622.
Students 220.

Emmitsburg, Frederick Co., St. Anthony Shrine (1805), Revs. Leo R. Tittler; Edward T. Sargus, Pastor Emeritus; Sr. Carol C. Czyzewski, F.S.S.J., Pastoral Assoc., Tel: 301-271-7300; Sr. M. Valenta Rusin, F.S.S.J., Pastoral Min., Tel: 301-271-7300.
Res., 16150 St. Anthony Rd., 21727. Tel: 301-447-6294; 447-2367 (Office); Fax: 301-447-3618 (Office). [CEM]
Res., 18 Altamont Ave., Thurmond, 21788.
Catechesis/Religious Programs—Students 30.

St. Joseph (1793), Revs. James O. Kiernan, C.M.; Stephen Trzecieski, C.M.; John Buckley, C.M. In res., Revs. William Goff, C.M.; Michael J. Kennedy, C.M.; Walter F. Menig, C.M.; Louis B. Storms, C.M.
Res., 47 DePaul St., 21727. Tel: 301-447-2326; Fax: 301-447-3579. [CEM 2]

Fallston, Harford Co., St. Mark (1887), Rev. Edward B. Hemler; Deacons T. Russell Gibson; Charles Hicks; Eugene Miller.
Res., 812 Reckord Rd., 21047. Tel: 410-879-9110; 877-9750; Fax: 410-877-0576.
Catechesis/Religious Programs—Tel: 410-879-1706; 877-1692.
Students 762.

Frederick, Frederick Co., St. John the Evangelist (1763), Revs. Wayne G. Funk; Keith W. Boisvert; Robert J. Jaskot; Deacons Daniel C. Roff; James F. Casey; J. Michael Zusi.
Res., 116 E. Second St., 21701. Tel: 301-662-8288; Fax: 301-698-1832. [CEM]
School—St. John Regional Catholic School. See separate listing. Tel: 301-662-6722; Fax: 301-695-7024.
Catechesis/Religious Programs—Tel: 410-662-8495; Fax: 301-695-7024.
Students 958.
Mission—Frederick, New Frederick County Mission.

Frostburg, Allegany Co., St. Michael (1850), Revs. Paul A. Byrnes; William J. Moody; Deacons Bertrand O. Michael; Lou Concordia; Joseph Keating.
Res., 44 E. Main St., P.O. Box 402, 21532. Tel: 301-689-6767; Fax: 301-689-6411. [CEM]

School—56 E. Main St., 21532. Tel: 301-689-2155. Lay Teachers 12; Students 147.
Catechesis/Religious Programs—Tel: 301-689-2898.
Students 151.

Fulton, Howard Co., St. Francis of Assisi (1988), Rev. Dennis P. Diehl; Deacon Joseph McKenna.
Office: 11305 Rte. 216, 20759. Tel: 410-792-0470; Fax: 410-792-0472.
Res., 10681 Glen Hannah Dr., Laurel, 20723. Tel: 410-880-3068.
Catechesis/Religious Programs—D.R.E.: Barbara Anderson; Kathy Airel.
Students 786.

Glen Burnie, Anne Arundel Co., Crucifixion, Church of the (1972), Rev. Dale Picavella; Sr. Marlene Cunningham, S.N.D., Pastoral Assoc.
Rectory: 100 Scott Ave., 21060. Tel: 410-768-4880; Fax: 410-768-5025.
Catechesis/Religious Programs—Students 79.

Church of the Good Shepherd (1972), Revs. John L. Kelly; Joseph V. Messer, (Retired).
Res., 1451 Furnace Ave., 21060. Tel: 410-761-4607; Fax: 410-761-6019.
School—Arthur Slade Regional Catholic School. See separate listing. Tel: 410-766-7130; Fax: 410-787-0594.
Catechesis/Religious Programs—Students 78.

Holy Trinity (1919), Revs. G. Eugene Nickol; Brandon Carr; Sydney Griffith; Phil Cover; Joseph McDonough; Deacons John Boscoe; Edward Gardner; Robert Herzog.
Res., 7436 Baltimore-Annapolis Blvd., 21061. Tel: 410-766-1213; Fax: 410-760-6738.
Parish Center—126 Dorsey Rd., 21061. Tel: 410-766-5070; Fax: 410-766-5071.
School—Arthur Slade Regional Catholic School. See separate listing. Tel: 410-766-7130; Fax: 410-787-0594.
Catechesis/Religious Programs—Tel: 410-768-3890; Fax: 410-760-6738. Sr. Vera Green, D.R.E.
Students 693.

Glyndon, Baltimore Co., Sacred Heart (1873), Revs. Lloyd E. Aiken; James D. Proffitt; Deacon James A. Ryan. Pastoral Assocs.: Sr. Judith Cianfrogna, S.S.J.; Mr. Lyle K. Weiss.
Res., 65 Sacred Heart Ln., 21071. Tel: 410-833-1696; Fax: 410-833-2676.
School—Tel: 410-833-0857; Fax: 410-833-0914. Anne H. Price, Prin.; Patricia E. Balcerzak, Asst. Prin. Sisters 1; Lay Teachers 30; Students 712.
Catechesis/Religious Programs—Tel: 410-833-8515. Sr. Nancy Stiles, S.U.S.C, D.R.E.
Students 946.

Grantsville, Northern Garrett Co., St. Ann (1976), Sr. Joan Minella, S.S.N.D., Pastoral Life Dir.
Res., 12814 New Germany Rd., 21536. Tel: 301-895-5877; Fax: 301-895-4353.
Catechesis/Religious Programs—Students 41.

Hagerstown, Washington Co., St. Ann (1966), Rev. Msgr. Edward W. Manalis; Rev. Michael Jendrek; Deacons William Nairn; Richard Kunkel.
Res., 1525 Oak Hill Ave., 21742. Tel: 301-733-0410; Fax: 301-733-6218.
Church—1525 Oak Hill Ave., 21742.
School—Saint Maria Goretti High School. See Separate Listing. Tel: 301-739-4266; Fax: 301-739-4261.
Catechesis/Religious Programs—Tel: 301-733-0411. Patricia Rogers, D.R.E.
Students 588.

St. Joseph (1793), Rev. Christopher P. Moore.
Res., 17630 Virginia Ave., 21740. Tel: 301-797-9435; Fax: 301-797-2490.
Catechesis/Religious Programs—Students 119.

St. Mary (1790), Rev. George A. Limmer; Rev. Msgr. Robert S. Passarelli, Pastor Emeritus; Rev. Robert Morey.
Res., 224 W. Washington St., 21740. Tel: 301-739-0390; Fax: 301-739-7082.
School—218 Washington St., Hagertown, 21740. Tel: 301-733-1184; Fax: 301-745-4997.
School Sisters of Notre Dame 3; Lay Teachers 14; Students 260.
Catechesis/Religious Programs—Tel: 301-790-2444.
Students 208.
Mission—Boonsboro, Washington Co., St. James, c/o 224 W. Washington St., Hagerstown, 21740. Tel: 410-432-2887.

Hancock, Washington Co., St. Peter's (1834). Unassigned.
Res. & Mailing Address: 16 E. High St., 21750. Tel: 301-678-6339; Fax: 301-678-7578. [CEM]
Mission—Little Orleans, Allegany Co., St. Patrick's, (1860) 12517 St. Patrick Rd., S.E., Little Orleans, 21766. [CEM]

Havre de Grace, Harford Co., St. Patrick's (1847), Rev. William J. O'Brian, III; Sr. Frances Schimiushel, O.S.F., Pastoral Assoc.
Res., 615 Congress Ave., 21078. Tel: 410-939-2525; 575-6741; Fax: 410-575-6490. [CEM]
Catechesis/Religious Programs—Tel: 410-939-2547.
Students 194.

Hickory, Harford Co., St. Ignatius (1792), Revs. Kenneth Farabaugh; Fernando Christancho; Deacons Robert Lehr; Ralph Trautwein.
Res., 533 E. Jarrettsville Rd., Forest Hill, 21050. Tel: 410-879-1926; Fax: 410-879-1352. [CEM]
Catechesis/Religious Programs—Tel: 410-879-9390.
Students 1,201.

Hunt Valley, Baltimore Co., St. Francis Xavier (1988), Rev. Jeffrey S. Dauses; Rev. Msgr. Thomas J. Donellan, Pastor Emeritus.
13717 Cuba Rd., P.O. Box 407, 21030. Tel: 410-785-0356; Fax: 410-785-1628.
Res., 19 Rainflower Path #204, Sparks, 21152. Tel: 410-472-4836.
Catechesis/Religious Programs—Joan Carlson, D.R.E.
Students 168.

Hydes, Baltimore Co., St. John the Evangelist (1822), Rev. William F. Franken; Rev. Msgr. Martin R. Strempeck, Pastor Emeritus; Rev. Msgr. John C. Collopy; Rev. Msgr. Charles F. Meisel; Deacon J. Donald Murray.
Res., 13305 Long Green Pike, 21082. Tel: 410-592-6206; Fax: 410-817-4432. [CEM]
School—13311 Long Green Pike, 21082. Tel: 410-592-9585, Ext. 120; Fax: 410-817-4548. Mrs. Genevieve Delcher, Prin.
Lay Teachers 30; Students 355.
Catechesis/Religious Programs—M. Colleen Sisolak, D.R.E.
Students 631.

Jessup, Anne Arundel Co., St. Lawrence (1866), Rev. William J. Axe, O.SS.T. In res., Rev. Stanley W. DeBoe, O.SS.T.
Res., 7669 Clark Rd., Hanover, 21076. Tel: 410-799-1970; Fax: 410-799-4425. [CEM]
School—Arthur Slade Regional Catholic School. See separate listing.
Catechesis/Religious Programs—St. Lawrence School of Religion, P.O. Box 1188, 20794. Tel: 410-799-7790.
Students 117.

Joppa, Harford Co., Church of the Holy Spirit (1963), Rev. Joseph C. Simmons.
Res., 540 Joppa Farm Rd., 21085. Tel: 410-679-2191.
Office: Tel: 410-679-0377; Fax: 410-679-2874.
Catechesis/Religious Programs—Joanne Haney, D.R.E.
Students 168.

Laurel, Anne Arundel Co., Resurrection of Our Lord (1963), Revs. John T. Wielebski; Joseph F. Kitko, Pastor Emeritus. Pastoral Assocs.: Deacon Larry Wilson; Sr. Eileen Dolak, S.S.J. In res., Rev. Robert Llanos.
Res., 8402 Brock Bridge Rd., 20724. Tel: 410-792-7982; Fax: 410-792-8337.
Catechesis/Religious Programs—Students 187.

Libertytown, Frederick Co., St. Peter (1823), Rev. John A. Dietzenbach; Deacon Michael Misulia.
Res., 9207 A Church St., 21762. Tel: 301-898-5111(Office); 898-9069 (Rectory); Fax: 301-898-0465. [CEM]
Catechesis/Religious Programs—Anne Mason, D.R.E.
Students 713.

Linthicum Heights, Anne Arundel Co., St. Philip Neri (1964), Rev. Msgr. Francis X. Zorbach; Rev. John L. Lippold; Deacon Robert Keeley.
Res., 6405 S. Orchard Rd., 21090-2628. Tel: 410-859-0571; Fax: 410-859-5047.
School—6401 Orchard Rd., 21090. Tel: 410-859-1212. Teresa Baker, Prin.
Lay Teachers 26; Students 576.
Catechesis/Religious Programs—Tel: 410-859-0249.
Students 369.

Lonaconing, Allegany Co., St. Mary of the Annunciation (1865), Sr. Marietta Culhane, O.S.F., Pastoral Life Dir.
Res., 16102 St. Mary Church Ter., 21539. Tel: 301-463-2514; Fax: 301-463-6729. [CEM]
Catechesis/Religious Programs—Students 42.

Manchester, Carroll Co., St. Bartholomew (1965), Rev. Michael J. Roach.
Mailing Address: & Parish Center: 3071 Park Ave., P.O. Box 448, 21102. Tel: 410-239-8881.
Res., 2940 Park Ave., P.O. Box 448, 21102-0448. Tel: 410-239-8207; Fax: 410-239-3216. [CEM]
Catechesis/Religious Programs—Lynn Szymanski.
Students 473.

Middletown, Frederick Co., Holy Family Catholic Community (1986), Rev. John Charles Moore; Deacon P. Gregory Rausch.
Mailing Address: 7321 Burkittsville Rd., 21769.
Res., 3240 Old National Pike, 21769. Tel: 301-371-3239.
Church—7321 Burkittsville Rd., 21769. Tel: 301-473-4800; Fax: 301-371-6810.
Catechesis/Religious Programs—Students 565.

Midland, Allegany Co., St. Joseph (1891) (Irish), Sr. Joan Maenner, Pastoral Life Dir.
Mailing Address: 19925 Church St., P.O. Box 1, 21542. Tel: 301-777-7060; Fax: 301-463-6729. [CEM]
Catechesis/Religious Programs—Students 42.

Millersville, Anne Arundel Co., Our Lady of the Fields (1903), Revs. John J. Auer; Andrew Aaron; Michael J. Callaghan; Deacons James L. Awalt; Anthony Grillo; Edward Stoops; Albert Kosla; G. William Walker.
Res., 1070 Cecil Ave. S., 21108. Tel: 410-923-3133; 987-1551; Fax: 410-987-9723. [CEM]
School—Arthur Slade Regional Catholic School. See separate listing.
Catechesis/Religious Programs—Tel: 410-923-2195. Carole Katrivie, D.R.E.
Students 831.
Mission—Millersville, Waugh Chapel Mission Community Inc., Tel: 410-729-8592.

Mount Savage, Allegany Co., St. Patrick (1863), Sr. Joan Minella, S.S.N.D., Pastoral Life Dir.; Sr. Eileen Carney, O.S.U., Pastoral Assoc.; Deacon Robert Lilly.
Mailing Address: P.O. Box 577, 21545. Tel: 301-264-3521; Fax: 301-264-3603. [CEM]
Shipping Address:—15706 St. Patrick Church Rd., 21545.
Catechesis/Religious Programs—Students 77.

Oakland, Garrett Co., St. Peter the Apostle (1851), Rev. Donald J. Parson; Deacon James L. Comfort, Sr.
Res., 208 S. Fourth St., P.O. Box 186, 21550. Tel: 301-334-2202; Fax: 301-334-9006. [CEM]
Catechesis/Religious Programs—Students 88.
Mission—Kitzmiller, Garrett Co., Immaculate Conception, P.O. Box 186, 21550.

Odenton, Anne Arundel Co., St. Joseph (1924), Revs. William L. Viola; Modesto Martinez Navarro, T.C. (Hispanic); Guillermo Casa Ferrer, T.C. (Hispanic); Deacons David A. Page; Richard C. Swann.
Mailing Address: & Church: 1283 Odenton Rd., P.O. Box 172, 21113-0172. Tel: 410-551-9238; Fax: 410-674-4761.
School—Arthur Slade Regional Catholic School. See separate listing. Tel: 410-766-7130; Fax: 410-787-0594.
Catechesis/Religious Programs—Dottie Campbell, D.R.E.
Students 448.

Owensville, Anne Arundel Co., Our Lady of Sorrows (1880), Rev. Mark Logue; Deacon John H. Abell, Jr.
Res., 101 Owensville Rd., West River, 20778. Tel: 410-867-2059; 269-6803; Fax: 410-867-8276. [CEM]
Catechesis/Religious Programs—Students 309.

Parkton, Baltimore Co., Our Lady of Grace (1974), Rev. Msgr. Nicholas P. Amato; Deacon Charles Hiebler, Jr.
Res., 425 Everett Rd., P.O. Box 517, Monkton, 21111. Tel: 410-329-2102.
Parish Center—18310 Middletown Rd., P.O. Box 360, 21120. Tel: 410-329-6826; Fax: 410-329-6830.
Catechesis/Religious Programs—Students 479.

Pasadena, Anne Arundel Co., St. Jane Frances de Chantal (Riviera Beach) (1946), Rev. Msgr. Thomas J. Fannon, Pastor Emeritus; Revs. Kevin T. Schenning; John A. Williamson; Joseph J. Cosgrove; Deacons Fred Wendt; Melvin Baranoski; John Rafter.
Res., 8499 Virginia Ave., 21122. Tel: 410-255-4646; Fax: 410-437-5191.
School—8513 Saint Jane Dr., 21122. Tel: 410-255-4750; Fax: 410-360-6720. Ronald Burinsky, Prin.
Lay Teachers 23; Students 640.
Catechesis/Religious Programs—Tel: 410-437-4727. Mary Beth Barnes, D.R.E.
Students 565.

Our Lady of the Chesapeake (1979), Revs. Brian M. Rafferty; Walter J. Paulits, Ph.D., Pastor Emeritus; Deacon Donald Latrick.
Church—8325 Ventnor Rd., 21122. Tel: 410-255-3677; Fax: 410-437-7527.
School—See separate listing. Tel: 410-766-7130; Fax: 410-787-0594.
Catechesis/Religious Programs—Tel: 410-255-3677; Fax: 410-437-7527. Timothy Janiszewski, D.R.E.
Students 445.

Poplar Springs, Howard Co., St. Michael (1879), Revs. Michael J. Ruane; Stanley Janaites; Ed Wagner, O.SS.T.; Deacon Gary L. Fulmer.

Res., 1125 St. Michael's Rd., Mount Airy, 21771-3299. Tel: 410-489-4211; 442-2845; Fax: 410-442-1486. [CEM]
Parish Center—Tel: 410-489-7667;442-1717; Fax: 410-442-1486.
Catechesis/Religious Programs—Trenna Brody, D.R.E.
Students 838.

Pylesville, Harford Co., St. Mary (1853), Rev. A. Henry Kunkel, III; Deacons Simon Driesen; John R. Simpson, Jr.
Res., 1021 St. Mary's Rd., 21132. Tel: 410-838-7471; 879-4015; Fax: 410-452-8493. [CEM]
Catechesis/Religious Programs—Tel: 410-838-7471. Veronica Lux, D.R.E.
Students 467.

Randallstown, Baltimore Co., Holy Family (1876), Revs. Edward J. Bayer; Walter J. McGovern, Senior Priest; John J. Lombardi; Deacon Richard W. Montalto, Admin. In res., Rev. William A. Collins.
Res., 9533 Liberty Rd., 21133. Tel: 410-521-3800; Fax: 410-922-3804. [CEM]
Office: Tel: 410-922-3800; Fax: 410-922-3804.
School—9535 Liberty Rd., 21133. Tel: 410-922-3677; Fax: 410-521-9764. Laura Hamilton, Prin.
Lay Teachers 17; Students 230.
Catechesis/Religious Programs—9531 Liberty Rd., 21133. Tel: 410-922-2805.
Students 133.

Severn, Anne Arundel Co., St. Bernadette (1969), Rev. Domenic L. Cieri; Ann McDonald, Pastoral Assoc.
Res., 801 Stevenson Rd., 21144. Tel: 410-969-2783; Fax: 410-969-2789.
School—Arthur Slade Regional Catholic School. See separate listing. Tel: 410-766-7130; Fax: 410-787-0594.
Catechesis/Religious Programs—Tel: 410-969-2786. Andrea Montrose, D.R.E.
Students 277.

Severna Park, Anne Arundel Co., St. John the Evangelist (1959), Revs. Mitchell T. Rozanski, Temp. Admin.; John J. Kucharczyk; McLean A. Cummings; Deacons John Naughton, (Retired); Dean Lopata.
Res., 689 Ritchie Hwy., S.E., 21146. Tel: 410-647-4884; Fax: 410-544-3047.
School—669 Ritchie Hwy., 21146. Tel: 410-647-2283; Fax: 410-431-5438. Sr. Linda Larsen, S.S.J., Prin.
Sisters of St. Joseph, Chestnut Hill 7; Lay Teachers 38; Students 596.
Catechesis/Religious Programs—Tel: 410-647-4892.
Students 760.
Convent—Tel: 410-647-2041.

Sykesville, Carroll Co., St. Joseph (1868), Revs. Patrick J. Tonry, S.M.; Paul A. Reich, S.M.; Joseph M. Marshall, S.M.
Office: 915 Liberty Rd., Eldersburg, 21784. Tel: 410-795-7838; Fax: 410-795-7516.
Res., 7620 Mellor Ave., P.O. Box 384, 21784. Tel: 410-795-2722. [CEM]
Catechesis/Religious Programs—Tel: 410-552-5402.
Students 1,127.

Taneytown, Carroll Co., St. Joseph (1797), Revs. Martin Eugene Feild; Paul F. Dolan, Pastor Emeritus; Deacon Darrell W. Smith.
Res., 44 Frederick St., 21787. Tel: 410-756-2500; Fax: 410-756-1260. [CEM]
Catechesis/Religious Programs—Tel: 410-876-8108.
Students 173.

Thurmont, Frederick Co., Our Lady of Mount Carmel (1856), Rev. Leo R. Tittler; Sr. Carol C. Czyzewski, F.S.S.J., Pastoral Assoc., Tel: 301-271-7300; Sr. M. Valenta Rusin, F.S.S.J., Pastoral Min., Tel: 301-271-7300.
Office: 16150 St. Anthony Rd., Emmitsburg, 21727. Tel: 301-447-6294. [CEM]
Res., 18 Altamont Ave., 21788. Fax: 301-447-3628.
Church—Church St., 21788. Tel: 301-447-2367; Fax: 301-447-3618.
Catechesis/Religious Programs—Tel: 301-271-4099; Fax: 301-271-7127.
Students 80.

Timonium, Baltimore Co., Church of the Nativity (1968), Rev. Michael J. White.
Office: 20 E. Ridgely Rd., 21093. Tel: 410-252-6080; Fax: 410-252-2657.
Res., Tel: 410-252-0345.

Urbana, Frederick Co., St. Ignatius Loyola (1879), Rev. Thomas Polk.
Res., 3523 Urbana Pike, Frederick, 21704. Tel: 301-695-8845; Fax: 301-695-0259.
School—St. John Regional School. See separate listing. Tel: 301-662-6722.
Catechesis/Religious Programs—Tel: 301-695-8879.
Students 251.

Walkersville, Frederick Co., St. Timothy (1985), Rev. Richard J. Murphy; Deacon John L. Manley.
Res., 200 Glade Blvd., 21793. Tel: 301-845-8028; Fax: 301-845-0332.
Catechesis/Religious Programs—Tel: 301-845-8025. Sandra Maxel, D.R.E.
Students 252.

Westernport, Allegany Co., St. Peter (1854), Rev. James W. Hannon.
Res., 127 Church St., 21562. Tel: 301-359-3055; Fax: 301-359-0657. [CEM]
School—Tel: 301-359-9832.
Lay Teachers 8; Students 53.
Catechesis/Religious Programs—Students 93.
Mission—Barton, St. Gabriel.

Westminster, Carroll Co., St. John (1852), Rev. Msgr. Arthur F. Valenzano; Revs. John V. DoBranski; Andrew Mohl; Gerard Steffenes; Deacons John Coster; Robert Malinowski; John Robbins.
Res., 43 Monroe St., 21157. Tel: 410-848-4744; 876-2248; Fax: 410-857-1519. [CEM]
School—45 Monroe St., Westminister, 21157. Tel: 410-848-7455; Fax: 410-848-2822.
Lay Teachers 24; Students 522.
Catechesis/Religious Programs—Fax: 410-857-1519. Theresa Greene, D.R.E.
Students 1,016.

Williamsport, Washington Co., St. Augustine (1854), Rev. Alfred E. Smith; Deacon Andrew Komarinski, (Retired).
Res., 32 E. Potomac St., 21795. Tel: 301-223-7959; Fax: 301-223-9506. [CEM]
Catechesis/Religious Programs—Students 46.
Mission—Clear Spring, Washington Co., St. Michael.

Woodstock, Baltimore Co., St. Alphonsus Rodriguez (1869), Rev. Joseph P. Lacey, S.J.; Dee Papania, Pastoral Assoc.; Deacon William Fallon. In res., Rev. Richard P. McHugh, S.J.
Res., 10800 Old Court Rd., 21163. Tel: 410-461-5267; Fax: 410-750-7286. [CEM]
Catechesis/Religious Programs—Students 160.

Shrines

1—NATIONAL SHRINE OF ST. ELIZABETH ANN SETON, 333 S. Seton Ave., 21727. Tel: 301-447-6606; Fax: 301-447-6061. Sr. Cecilia Rose, D.C., Admin.

Chaplains of Public Institutions

BALTIMORE. *Baltimore City Correctional Center, Baltimore Pre-Release Unit*. Bob Lashinsky.
Baltimore City Jail. Rev. Damien Nalepa, Chap.
Baltimore City Jail, Women's Detention Center. Sr. Patricia Ash, Chap.
Carroll County Detention Center. St. John Westminister, Lay Coord.
Charles H. Hickey School. Deacon Russell Matthews, Chap.
Dismas House.
Francis Scott Key Medical Center. Staffed by Our Lady of Fatima Parish.
Franklin Square Hospital. Covered on rotating basis by Annunciation, St. Clement Mary Hoffbauer, Our Lady Queen of Peace, Our Lady of Mt. Carmel, St. Clare, Our Lady of Hope, St. Joseph-Fullerton, St. Anthony of Padua, St. Michael the Archangel-Overlea. Deacons Nicholas F. Feurer; Daniel R. Kopczyk; Walter Shipley.
Greater Baltimore Medical Center. Immaculate Conception, Towson.
Harbor Hospital. Covered on rotating basis by Holy Cross, St. Mary Star of the Sea, Our Lady of Good Counsel, St. Veronica, St. Rose and St. Athanasius parish staff. Rev. Charles Klein.
Johns Hopkins Medical Institutions. Rev. Salvatore J. Livigni.
Maryland Correctional Adjustment Center. Our Lady of Fatima. Rev. Charles J. Canterna, Chap.
Maryland Penitentiary. Bob Lashinsky.
Rosewood State Hospital. Vacant.
Spring Grove Center Hospital. Rev. F. Philip Vogel, S.D.S.
University of Maryland Hospital. Revs. Lawrence Schulmeister, O.F.M.; William F. Spacek.
Veterans Hospital, Baltimore. Rev. Conan H. Timoney, C.P., Chap.
Veterans Hospital, Fort Howard. Rev. Conan H. Timoney, C.P., Chap.

CROWNSVILLE. *Crownsville Hospital Center*. Staffed by St. Mary's Parish, Annapolis.

HAGERSTOWN. *Maryland Correctional Institution*. Sr. Dolores Chepiga, S.S.J.
Maryland Correctional Training Center. Sr. Dolores Chepiga, S.S.J.
Roxbury Correctional Institution. Sr. Dolores Chepiga, S.S.J.

JESSUP. *Brockbridge Pre-Release Unit*. Jim Sanders, Lay Coord.
Maryland Correctional Institution. Mary Dunn, Lay Coord.
Maryland Correctional Institution for Women. Jim Sanders, Catholic Coord.
Maryland House of Correction & Annex. Jim Sanders, Lay Coord.
Patuxent Institute. Jim Sanders, Lay Coord.
Perkins Hospital. Jim Sanders, Lay Coord.

SYKESVILLE. *Springfield Hospital Center*. Rev. Stanley Janaites, Chap.; Deacon George C. Wachter, Chap.
Sykesville Laundry Facility. Bryan Masterson, Lay Coord.; Richard Horwitt, Lay Coord.

Special Assignment:
Reverend Monsignors—
Collopy, John C., Dir. Senior & Retired Priests
Kenney, Jeremiah F., Tribunal, 320 Cathedral St., Baltimore, MD 21201
Madden, Denis J., Neareast Welfare, NY
Malooly, Francis W., Chancellor, 320 Cathedral St., Baltimore, MD 21201
Woy, Richard, Exec. Dir., Dept. Mgmt. Svcs.
Reverend Fathers—
Abrahams, John J., St. Martin Home for the Aged
Albright, Robert E., Campus Ministry, Towson, MD 21204
Barker, James M., Vocation Dir., 320 Cathedral St., Baltimore, MD 21201
Bergquist, Patrick, Missionary Work, Fairbanks, AK
Breighner, Joseph F., Special Ministry
Buttner, Michael, Special Ministry
Byrne, Glenn, St. Anthony Church, Allston, MA 02134
Canterna, Charles J., Chap., Baltimore City Jail & Maryland Penitentiary
Carey, David M., Special Ministry, Chap. Villa Assumpta
Carlsen, Jeffrey, Chap., Maryland House of Correction & Annex
Carrion, Patrick M., Assoc. Dir. Division of Clergy Personnel
Chase, Raymond, Gallagher Center
Collins, William A., Tribunal, 320 Cathedral St., Baltimore, MD 21201
Farmer, J. Kevin, Dir., Msgr. O'Dwyer Retreat House, Sparks
Francik, Gerard, Asst. Dir. of Vocations, 320 Cathedral St., Baltimore, MD 21201
Harris, Raymond L., Chap., Mt. St. Mary's College, Emmitsburg, MD
Hendricks, Edward S., Campus Minister, Frostburg, MD
Henry, Paul, Spiritual Dir., VA Hospital, Perryville
Janaites, Stanley, Chap., Springfield Hospital
Jarboe, J. Bruce, Dir. Division of Clergy Personnel
Johnson, Lawrence M., Chap., Cardinal Sheehan Center
Lesnick, John F., Chap., St. Elizabeth Center for Nursing Care
Livigni, Salvatore J., Chap., Johns Hopkins Hospital
Lobert, Richard C., Teaching, MI
Martin, Joseph C., S.S., 103 Foxridge Dr., Havre de Grace, MD 21078
O'Brien, John E., Chap., Calvert HCV
Raum, Blair, Dir., Project Rachel
Reusing, James M., Chap., Good Samaritan Hospital, Baltimore, MD
Riepe, Charles K., Chap., John Hopkins Univ., Newman Apostolate, Baltimore, MD
Seitz, Gilbert J., Archdiocese Tribunal, 320 Cathedral St., Baltimore, MD 21201
Simms, William, Archdiocesan Tribunal, 320 Cathedral St., Baltimore, MD 21201
Spacek, William F., Chap., University Hospital
Spillane, Michael, Washington, DC
Thomas, Paul, Archdiocesan Archivist
Waudby, Lawrence, Asst. Chancellor, Sec. to the Cardinal

On Duty Outside the Archdiocese:
Reverend Fathers—
Hoffman, David, Immaculate Heart Hermitage, Big Sur, CA
Obrimski, Paul G.
Warman, William C.

Graduate Studies:
Reverend Fathers—
Parker, Adam, Rome, Italy

Military Chaplains:
Reverend Fathers—
Spencer, F. Richard, U.S. Army, ISB-MFO- Unit 31520, APO, AE, 09832
Wilson, Stuart T., (Retired)
Zeller, Leonard H., U.S.A.F., Wright Patterson AFB, OH

Sabbatical:
Reverend Monsignors—
Fitzgerald, John L.
Reverend Fathers—
Cummings, Carl

Absent on Leave:
Reverend Fathers—
Blackwell, Maurice J.
Bonderenko, Thomas S.
Cox, Brian
Dowdy, James H.
Le Fevre, Francis J.
Mahon, Matthew Shawn
Mannion, William
Maskell, A. Joseph
Messina, John
Pietropaoli, David
Smith, David G.

Absent on Sick Leave:
Reverend Fathers—
Carter, John T.
Fullen, John N.
Zoubek, Ronald J.

Retired:
Most Rev.—
Borders, William Donald, 13th Archbishop of Baltimore, 320 Cathederal St., Baltimore, MD 21201
Reverend Monsignors—
Bozel, Robert A., St. Elizabeth Hall M-201, 2300 Dulaney Valley Rd., Timonium, MD 21093
Broderick, Gerard W., St. John Hall, Long Crandon, 2300 Dulaney Valley Rd., Timonium, MD 21093
Collopy, John C., St. John Hall, Long Crandon, 2300 Dulaney Valley Rd., Timonium, MD 21093
Cronin, James J., St. Joan of Arc, 257 S. Law St., Aberdeen, MD 21001
Donellen, Thomas J., Hampton House, 204 E. Joppa Rd., Baltimore, MD 21204
Fannon, Thomas J., St. Elizabeth Hall F 210, 2300 Dulaney Valley Rd., Timonium, MD 21093
Fortenbaugh, Francis W., St. Agnes Rectory, 5422 Old Frederick Rd., Baltimore, MD 21228
McGowan, Myles, 3 Baratra Ct., Apt. 204, Timonium, MD 21093
Meisel, Charles F., St. Elizabeth Hall, Apt. W 301, 2300 Dulaney Valley Rd., Timonium, MD 21093
Mieczkowski, Chester J., 3215 Fleet St., Baltimore, MD 21224
Passarelli, Robert S., 27 First St., Frostburg, MD 21532
Phillips, Hugh J., Mount St. Mary's College, Emmitsburg, MD 21727
Reinsfelder, John L., Holy Cross Rectory, 110 E. West St., Baltimore, MD 21230
Satterfield, Carroll E., 363 Homeland Southway, Apt. 1, Baltimore, MD 21212
Schwalenberg, Martin, 8465 Meadow Ln., Riviera Beach, MD 21122
Strempeck, Martin R., St. Margaret, 141 Hickory Ave., Bel Air, MD 21014
Tewes, Thomas, 5905 Walther Ave., Baltimore, MD 21206
Reverend Fathers—
Altmann, George, 32 Carrolls Tract Rd., Fairfield, PA 17320
Bak, Bernard, 1857 Portship Rd., Baltimore, MD 21222
Barbernitz, John P., St. Martin's Home for the Aged, Baltimore, MD
Bauernfeind, Thomas J., Shrine of the Little Flower, 2854 Brendan Ave., Baltimore, MD 21213
Bowling, Frederick T., Keswick Multi-Care Center, 700 40th St., Baltimore, MD 21211
Buettner, George, 600 Light St., Apt. 351, Baltimore, MD 21230
Carney, John, 9000 Briarcroft Ln., Laurel, MD 20708
Coyne, Patrick J., Eastpoint Nursing Care, Baltimore, MD 21222
Dolan, Paul F., St. John Hall, Long Crandon, 2300 Dulaney Valley Rd., Timonium, MD 21093
FitzGerald, William, St. Anthony of Padua, 4414 Frankford Ave., Baltimore, MD 21206 Egypt
Gallagher, Joseph J., 3838 Roland Ave., #1302, Baltimore, MD 21211
Gies, Norman J., 2453 Brazilia Dr., Apt. 21, Clearwater, FL 21163
Hill, Edward T., U.S.N., 4614 Eugene Ave., Baltimore, MD 21206
Hisky, William G., 1400 Dalmation Pl., Apt. T1, Belcamp, MD 21017
Hopkins, Robert F., 941 Bishop Walsh Rd., Cumberland, MD 21502
Hughes, Joseph B., 2034 Park Ave., Baltimore, MD 21217
Iaia, Paul P., 967 A. Tortoise St., Bethany Beach, DE 19930
Kaiser, Joseph A., St. John Hall, Long Crandon, 2300 Dulaney Valley Rd., Timonium, MD 21093
Kelmartin, John J., 9050 Waltham Woods Rd., Apt. C, Baltimore, MD 21234
Kenney, Joseph A., Stella Maris Hospice, 2300 Dulaney Valley Rd., Timonium, MD 21093
Kitko, Joseph F., Our Lady of Mt. Carmel, 1706 Old Eastern Ave., Baltimore, MD 21221
Klein, Charles R., Harbor Hospital Center, 3001 S. Hanover St., Baltimore, MD 21225
Krach, Joseph W., 805 Union Ave., Baltimore, MD 21211
La Porta, Gerald, 4136 Fairway Dr., Little River, SC 29566
La Porta, Ross A., 4136 Fairway Dr., Little River, SC 29566
McGovern, Walter J., Holy Family Parish, Randallstown, MD
McManus, Joseph, 6127 Windsong Ln., Ct. 10, Unit 1019, Stewart, FL 34997
Messer, Joseph V., Good Shepherd Rectory, 1451 Furnace Ave., Glen Burnie, MD 21061
Moody, William, 86 Mt. Pleasant St., Frostburg, MD 21532
Muller, Kennard, 7 Joppawood Ct. A-1, Baltimore, MD 21236
Muller, Myles, St. John Hall, Long Cramdon, 2300 Dulaney Valley Rd., Timonium, MD 21093
Paulits, Walter J., Ph.D., 513 Sylview Dr., Pasadena, MD 21222
Peterson, Casimir M., 3601 Greenway, Apt. 704, Baltimore, MD 21218
Quinn, Charles H., St. John Hall, Long Crandon, 2300 Dulaney Valley Rd., Timonium, MD 21093
Rose, Alphonse G., 5510 Woodlawn Rd., Baltimore, MD 21210
Sargus, Edward T., Lawn Acres, 420 S. 57 St., Hollywood, FL 33023
Shaum, David W., Mount St. Mary's College, P.O. Box 246, Emmitsburg, MD 21727
Snouffer, Philip T., 8820 Walther Blvd., Apt. 1401, Baltimore, MD 21234
Stroup, Edmund F., 36 E. Drumbed Rd., Villas, NJ 08251
Vu, Hoat Dinh, St. Mary Rectory, 5502 York Rd., Baltimore, MD 21212
Warczynski, Leon, 3316 Beverly Rd., Baltimore, MD 21214
Wenderoth, Joseph R.
West, Gerald, Franciscan Sisters of Baltimore Generalate, 3725 Ellerslie Ave., Baltimore, MD 21218
Wilson, Stuart T., 5269 North Spring Pointe Pl., Tucson, AZ 85749

Permanent Deacons:
Abell, John H., Jr., Our Lady of Sorrows, Owensville
Albaugh, William S., St. Joseph, Fullerton
Anderson, Carl A., St. Edward, Baltimore
Antczak, George, St. Thomas Aquinas, Baltimore
Awalt, James L., Our Lady of the Fields, Millersville
Bankard, Alphonse, Our Lady of Fatima, Baltimore
Baynes, Charles A., Our Lady of Mt. Carmel, Middle River
Bee, James E., St. Ann, Baltimore
Beimel, Leroy W., Holy Trinity, Glen Burnie
Boscoe, John, Holy Trinity, Glen Burnie
Briscoe, John, St. Peter Claver
Britt, Ray, Resurrection, Ellicott City
Bullinger, Raymond A., (Retired)
Carpenter, Harry G., (Retired)
Casey, J. Faherty, St. John the Evangelist, Frederick
Chesnavage, Albert W., (Retired)
Ciesla, Paul R., St. Margaret, Bel Air
Codd, John J., Sr., St. Gabriel, Woodlawn
Colson, Norman E., (Retired)
Comfort, James L., Sr., St. Peter the Apostle, Oakland
Concordia, Louis, St. Michael, Frostburg
Conley, David, St. Mary, Cumberland
Cook, Charles E., (Retired)
Cooley, Stephen, Our Lady of Perpetual Help, Edgewater (Diocese of Joliet)
Coster, John E., St. John, Westminster
Crawford, Raymond C., Our Lady of Perpetual Help, Ellicott City
Davis, Henry, St. Michael the Archangel, Overlea
DeAngelis, William J., St. Joseph, Fullerton
Derouaux, Bert, (Retired)
Dignan, Paul H., St. Patrick, Cumberland
Driesen, Simon, St. Mary, Pylesville
Evans, George T., St. Rita, Baltimore
Fallon, William L., Prison Ministry and St. Alphonsus Rodriguez
Feurer, Nicholas E., St. Clement and Franklin Square Hospital, Rosedale
Fitzpatrick, T. Kelly, (Out of Diocese)
Fulmer, Gary Lee, St. Michael, Poplar Springs
Fulton, Watson, Jr., St. Ambrose, Baltimore
Gardner, Edward L., Sr., Holy Trinity, Glen Burnie
Gibson, T. Russell, (Retired)
Goles, Patrick J., St. Margaret, Bel Air
Grabenstein, Herman J., (Retired)
Graham, Robert L., Spencer, TN
Gramling, John C., Immaculate Conception, Towson
Grape, William F., (Retired)
Grillo, Anthony, Our Lady of the Fields, Millersville
Gross, Theodore C., (Retired)
Hacker, Robert, Hospital Ministry, Baltimore
Harcum, Philip W., St. Bernardine, Baltimore
Harris, Jhan M., St. Veronica, Baltimore
Hartlieb, Gilbert J., (Retired)
Hayden, Dennis L., Our Lady of the Fields, Millersville
Herzog, Robert, Holy Trinity, Glenburnie
Hicks, Charles, St. Mark, Fallston
Hiebler, Charles H., Jr., Our Lady of Grace, Parkton
Hodges, Frank P., Corpus Christi, Baltimore
Jakowski, Chester J., SS. Philip & James, Baltimore
Jauquet, William, Our Lady of Victory, Baltimore
Jenkins, George, Our Lady Queen of Peace, Baltimore
Jensen, Joseph E., Education Ministry
Johe, Richard, (Retired)
Keating, Joseph J., (Retired)
Keeley, Robert L., St. Philip Neri, Linthicum Heights
Keenan, Robert G., St. Ursula, Baltimore
Kempf, William J., Jr., Unassigned
Kent, James R., Sr., (Retired)
Knight, Charles, St. Bernardine, Baltimore
Komarinski, Andrew, (Retired)
Kopczyk, Daniel R., St. Joan of Arc, Aberdeen
Kosla, Albert F., Our Lady of the Fields, Millersville
Krysiak, Joseph C., St. Anthony Padua and Most Precious Blood, Baltimore
Kuhl, Thomas, Our Lady of Pompei, Baltimore
Kunkel, Richard, (Retired)
Lambert, Francis E., Out of State
Langbehn, Eugene
Langmead, John T., St. William of York, Baltimore
Latrick, Donald P., Holy Family Ukrainian Catholic Church
Laws, Francis R., St. Stephen, Bradshaw
Lehr, Robert I., St. Ignatius, Hickory
Lilly, Robert B., Diocese of Wheeling, Charleston
Lopata, Dean M., St. John, Severna Park
Lynne, Robert O., SS. Philip and James, Baltimore
MacKnew, J. Donald, St. Margaret, Bel Air
Malinowski, Robert, St. John, Westminster
Manley, John L., St. Timothy, Walkersville
Mann, James L., Sr., St. Thomas More, Baltimore
Mann, Paul T., St. Gabriel, Woodlawn
Maranto, Anthony S., St. Dominic, Baltimore
Martelle, John T., St. Rita and Church Hospital, Dundalk
Martin, George W., St. John, Columbia
Martin, John, Immaculate Heart of Mary, Baltimore
Matthews, Russell, St. Francis Xavier and Maryland Training School for Boys, Baltimore
McAndrews, George F., (Out of Diocese)
McCoy, Michael, St. Thomas More, Baltimore
McKenna, John I., St. Clement I, Lansdowne
McKenna, Joseph, St. Francis of Assisi, Fulton
Mercer, Charles S., St. Francis Xavier, Baltimore
Michael, Bertrand O., St. Michael, Frostburg
Micozzi, Arthur L., St. Isaac Jogues, Baltimore
Miller, Donald, St. William of York, Baltimore
Miller, Eugene, Jr., St. Mark, Fallston
Miller, Ferdinand G., (Retired)
Mills, Hugh, Jr., St. Alphonsus, Baltimore
Misulia, Michael, (Retired)
Monaghan, James, St. Andrew by the Bay, Annapolis
Montalto, Richard W., Holy Family, Randallstown
Mooney, Loren, St. Patrick, Cumberland
Moore, LeRoy S., St. Mary, Annapolis
Moritz, Francis X., (Retired)
Morris, Richard F., St. Elizabeth of Hungary, Baltimore
Murphy, Lawrence, On Duty Outside the Diocese
Murray, Donald, St. John the Evangelist, Hydes
Nairn, William P., St. Ann, Hagerstown
Naughton, John F., (Retired)
Neale, Joseph L., St. Edward, Baltimore
Norcio, Anthony F., St. Mary, Annapolis
Novak, Richard D., St. Michael & St. Patrick, Baltimore
Nuedling, Leo, Sacred Heart of Jesus, Baltimore
O'Neill, Harry St. A., (Retired)
Oliver, Robert W.
Osorio-Carmona, Pablo E., Spanish Ministry
Page, David A., St. Joseph, Odenton

Parrish, John N., Church of Resurrection, Laurel
Perticone, Vincent, Jr., St. Joseph, Fullerton
Petrosino, Victor R., St. Margaret, Bel Air
Piet, Stanley G., (Retired)
Pinkney, Willard A., Jr., (Retired)
Pivec, J. Kenneth, Immaculate Heart of Mary, Baltimore
Provenza, Vincent, (Retired)
Rafter, John J., Jr., St. Jane Frances de Chantal, Pasadena
Raible, Gerald A., St. Patrick, Cumberland
Rausch, Paul G., Holy Family, Middletown
Reinsfelder, Edward, On Duty Outside the Diocese
Resh, Michael K., Leave of Absence
Roberts, Gerald A., Univ. of Maryland Hospital & St. Jerome, Baltimore
Roff, Daniel, St. John the Evangelist, Frederick
Rongione, Frank, St. Ursula, Baltimore
Rose, Alan, Prison Ministry and St. Isaac Jogues, Baltimore
Roy, Americus M., (Retired)
Ryan, James A., Sacred Heart,Glyndon
Sainz, Miguel E., St. Mary Govans and Spanish Apostolate
Schoennagel, Frederick, Annunciation, Baltimore
Schott, Robert G., St. Stephen, Bradshaw
Schultz, Joseph L., St. Anthony of Padua/Most Precious Blood, Baltimore
Seibold, Frederick, St. Elizabeth Ann Seton, Crofton
Shelton, Paul D., All Saints, Baltimore
Shipley, Walter R., Jr., (Retired)
Siarkowski, Henry L., Shrine of the Little Flower, Baltimore
Simpson, John R., St. Mary, Pylesville
Smith, Alexander, St. Veronica, Baltimore
Smith, Darrell, St. Joseph, Taneytown
Smith, Earl A., (Retired)
Smith, Walton, St. Francis Xavier, Baltimore
Spytkowski, Daniel, St. William of York, Baltimore
Stine, Richard J., St. Francis de Sales, Abingdon
Stoops, Edward, Our Lady of the Fields, Millersville
Stretmater, Daniel, Jr., (Retired)
Sullivan, Edward C., St. Joseph, Cockeysville
Swann, C. Richard, (Retired)
Swanson, James V., (Out of Diocese)
Teixeira, Lawrence, St. Louis, Clarksville
Thompson, Malcolm, All Saints, Baltimore
Trautwein, Ralph, St. Ignatius, Hickory
Vassie, Frederick, On Duty Outside the Diocese
Vaughan, William E., (Retired)
Villagaray, Rafael F., Hispanic Ministry
Wachter, George C., Springfield Hospital Center, Sykesville
Walker, George W., Jr., (Out of Diocese)
Wendt, Fred, St. Jane Frances de Chantal, Riviera Beach
Werner, Francis L., St. Patrick, Cumberland
Westwater, James, St. Isaac Jogues, Baltimore
Wiedel, Verdaw P., (Retired)
Wilkins, Herman, Church of Annunciation, Baltimore
Wilson, Larry L., Resurrection, Laurel
Wise, Stanley L., (Retired)
Woofter, R. Paul, St. Andrew by the Bay, Cape St. Claire
Wright, James, Leave of Absence
Yannuzzi, Thomas J., St. Clement I, Lansdowne
Yorkshire, Thomas X., St. Gregory, Baltimore
Zeiler, Francis, St. Clement, Rosedale

INSTITUTIONS LOCATED IN THE ARCHDIOCESE

[A] SEMINARIES, ARCHDIOCESAN

BALTIMORE. *St. Mary's Seminary and University*, 5400 Roland Ave., 21210. Tel: 410-864-4000; Fax: 410-864-4278.
E-mail: pgrega@stmarys.edu
Web site: stmarys.edu
Legal Title: *St. Mary's Seminary and University.* His Eminence William Cardinal Keeler, D.D., J.C.D., Archbishop of Baltimore, Chancellor, Chm. Board of Trustees.
Officers of the Administration: Revs. Robert F. Leavitt, S.S., S.T.D., Pres.-Rector; Thomas J. Burke, O.SS.T., S.T.M., S.T.D., Candidate & Vice Rector; Timothy Kulbicki, O.F.M.Conv., S.T.B., H.E.D., Dean, School of Theology; John W. Bowen, S.S., Alumni News Editor; Richard G. Childs, M.B.A., Vice Pres. for Admin. & Finance; Michael J. Gorman, Ph.D., Dean, Ecumenical Institute of Theology; Mr. Edward McCormack, Ph.D., Candidate, Dir. Field Education; Christa R. Klein, Ph.D., Dean, Center for Continuing Formation; Mrs. Kathleen P. Mignini, Dir. Institutional Svcs.; Mrs. Patricia Grega, Univ. Registrar and Dir. of Information Svcs.; Joyce Williams, M.S., Financial Aid Officer; Sr. Ian Stewart, S.S.N.D., M.L.S., Acting Dir., Library Svcs.; Mrs. Elizabeth L. Visconage, B.S., Vice Pres. Institutional Advancement.
Faculty: Revs. Michael L. Barre, S.S., S.T.L., Ph.D.; Melvin C. Blanchette, S.S., M.A., S.T.B., Ph.D.; Thomas J. Burke, O.SS.T., S.T.M.; James J. Conn, S.J., M.A., M.Div., J.C.D., J.D; Daniel J. Doherty, M.Div.; Corbin Eddy, S.T.L., M.A.; Michael J. Gorman, M.Div., Ph.D.; Daniel P. Haggerty, M.A., Ph.D., Candidate; Patricia A. Lamoureux, Ph.D.; Revs. Philip S. Keane, S.S., S.T.D.; Robert F. Leavitt, S.S., S.T.D.; Dominic W. Maruca, S.J., M.A., Ph.L., S.T.L., S.T; Anthony R. Perez, S.S., M.Div., S.T.D.; Charles J.T. Talar, M.A., Ph.D., S.T.D.; Paul Zilonka, C.P., M.A., S.S.L., S.T.D.
Adjunct Academic Faculty: Mr. Martin Becker; Mr. Peter Culman, B.A.; Mr. Christopher Dreisbach, Ph.D.; Ms. Sylvia P. Moore, B.S.; Mr. Stephen J. Vicchio, Ph.D.; Haydee M. Rodriguez, B.A., J.D., Candidate; Revs. Richard B. Hilgartner, Jr.; Daniel M. Ruff, S.J., M.A., M.Div., S.T.M.; Thomas R. Ulshafer, S.S., S.T.L., Ph.D; Joseph J. Bonadio, S.S., S.T.B., S.T.L., M.Ed., D.Min. Diocesan Seminarians 93; Diocesan Seminarians on Pastoral Leave 4; Others Studying 6; Priests 19; Lay Teachers 12. Ecumenical Institute of Theology, 5400 Roland Ave., 21210. Tel: 410-864-4200; Fax: 410-864-4205. Michael J. Gorman, M.Div., Ph.D. Students 204.

EMMITSBURG. *Mount St. Mary's Seminary*, 21727-7797. Tel: 301-447-5295; Fax: 301-447-5636.
E-mail: semweb@msmary.edu
Legal Title: *An integral part of the corporation known as Mount St. Mary's College and Seminary.* Administration: His Eminence William Cardinal Keeler, Chancellor and Chm. of Seminary Committee; Mr. George R. Houston, Pres.; Sr. Paula Marie Buley, I.H.M., M.B.A., Ed.D., Treas.; Very Rev. Kevin C. Rhoades, S.T.L., J.C.L. (HBG), Rector; Rev. Msgr. Paul J. Langsfeld, S.T.D. (WDC), Vice Rector & Dean Formation; Revs. Lee W. Gross, M.Div. (ARL), Dean of Students & Dir. Liturgy; J. Daniel Mindling, O.F.M.Cap., S.T.D., Academic Dean; Paul S. Coakley, S.T.L. (WCH), Dir. Spiritual Formation; Salvatore R. Lamendola, M.Div. (GBG), Dir. Pastoral Field Education; Sr. Ann Miriam Gallagher, R.S.M, Ph.D., Dir. Seminary Research & Planning; Dr. D. Stephen Rockwood, Ph.D., M.L.S., Dir. Library; Mrs. Amelia Y. Rodriguez, Seminary Registrar & Asst. to the Academic Dean; Mrs. Rosemary S. Mick, Admin. Asst. to Rector, (Admissions, Formation, Finance).
Full Time Faculty: Very Rev. Kevin C. Rhoades, S.T.L., J.C.L. (HBG); Rev. Msgr. Paul J. Langsfeld, S.T.D. (WDC); Revs. Paul S. Coakey, S.T.L. (WCH); Lee W. Gross, M.Div. (ARL); Salvatore R. Lamendola, M.Div (GBG); Albert H. Ledoux, M.A., Ph.D Cand. (ALT); J. Daniel Mindling, O.F.M.Cap., S.T.D.; Mark A. Pilon, S.T.D (ARL); William D. Virtue, S.T.D. (PEO); Michael G. Wensing, S.T.L. (SFS); Robert V. Zylla, O.S.C., S.T.L.; Sr. Joan Gormley, Ph.D.; Sr. Elizabeth McDonough, O.P., J.C.D.; Robert D. Miller, II, S.F.O., Ph.D.
Part Time Faculty: Rev. Msgr. Aloysius Callaghan, S.T.L., J.C.D. (ALN); Revs. James J. Conn, S.J., J.D., J.C.L.; Ronald Gillis, S.T.L., J.C.D. (WDC); Daniel C. Nusbaum, Ph.D. (ALB); Anthony R. Perez, S.S., S.T.D.; Michael J. Roach, M.A. (BAL); Sr. Ann Miriam Gallagher, R.S.M., Ph.D.; Theresa H. Farnan, Ph.D.; Dr. Carol L. Houghton, S.T.D., J.C.D.; Dr. Germain Grisez, Ph.D.; Dr. Charles J. Merrill, Ph.D.; Andrew B. Rosenfield, D.M.A.; Deborah Wentling. Priests 17; Sisters 4; Lay Teachers 7; Lay Administrators 4; Support Staff 2; Total Staff 34; Diocesan Seminarians 203; Religious Seminarians 4; Others 9; Total Enrollment 216.

[B] COLLEGES AND UNIVERSITIES

BALTIMORE. *College of Notre Dame of Maryland*, 4701 N. Charles St., 21210. Tel: 410-435-0100; Fax: 410-532-5791.
Web site: www.ndm.edu
For a complete listing, refer to the Colleges and Universities section.

Loyola College in Maryland, 4501 N. Charles St., 21210. Tel: 410-617-2000; Undergraduate Admissions: Ext 5012; Fax: 410-617-2176.
Web site: www.loyola.edu
For a complete listing, refer to the Colleges and Universities section.

EMMITSBURG. *Mount Saint Mary's College*, (1808), 21727. Tel: 301-447-6122; Fax: 301-447-5755.
E-mail: communications@msmary.edu
Web site: www.msmary.edu
For a complete listing, refer to the Colleges and Universities section.

[C] HIGH SCHOOLS, DIOCESAN

BALTIMORE. *Archbishop Curley High School*, 3701 Sinclair Ln., 21213. Tel: 410-485-5000; Fax: 410-483-2545.
E-mail: dgrzymsk@curley.loyola.edu
Web site: www.curley.loyola.edu
Administered by Order of Friars Minor Conventual, St. Anthony of Padua Province (USA). Revs. Donald Grzymski, O.F.M.Conv., Pres. & Guardian; Michael Heine, O.F.M.Conv.; Thomas E. Walsh, O.F.M.Conv., Vicar; Ignatius M. Piatek, O.F.M.Conv.; Michael Martin, O.F.M.Conv., Prin. Seminarian 1; Priests 5; Lay Teachers 37; Students 547; Total Staff 60.

The Seton Keough High School, 1201 Caton Ave., 21227-1092. Tel: 410-646-4444; Fax: 410-368-1591.
E-mail: danielle@setonkeough.com
Web site: setonkeough.com
Sr. Marie Danielle Amspacher, S.S.N.D., Pres.; Donna M. Stadler, Prin.; Ms. Marge Critcher, Asst. Prin. Sisters 8; Lay Teachers 38; Students 450.

SEVERN. *Archbishop Spalding High School*, 8080 New Cut Rd., 21144. Tel: 410-969-9105; Fax: 410-969-1026. Rev. Thomas Ryan, Chap.; John E. Abrahms, Prin. Lay Teachers 65; Students 418.

[D] HIGH SCHOOLS, PRIVATE

BALTIMORE. *Calvert Hall*, 8102 La Salle Rd., 21286. Tel: 410-825-4266; Fax: 410-825-6826.
E-mail: chc@calverthall.com
Web site: www.calverthall.com
Conducted by the Brothers of the Christian Schools (F.S.C.). Bros. Kevin Strong, F.S.C., Pres.; Kevin Stanton, F.S.C., Prin.; Rev. John E. O'Brien, Chap.; Mr. Louis Heidrick, Asst. Prin. Academic Affairs; Mr. Charles Stembler, Asst. Prin. Student Affairs. Priests 1; Brothers 11; Lay Teachers 76; Students 1,103.

The Catholic High School of Baltimore, 2800 Edison Hwy., 21213. Tel: 410-732-6200; Fax: 410-732-7639.
E-mail: chsb@tchs.loyola.edu
Web site: www.tchs.loyola.edu
Sisters of St. Francis of Philadelphia. Sisters 6; Lay Teachers 32; Students 400; Total Staff 60.

Institute of Notre Dame (1847), 901 Aisquith St., 21202. Tel: 410-522-7800; Fax: 410-522-7810.
Web site: indofmd.org
Legal Title: *Institute of Notre Dame, Inc.* Mary Fitzgerald, S.S.N.D., Pres.; Ann Seeley, Prin. Sisters 6; Lay Teachers 27; Lay Employees 26; Counselors 3; Students 432.

Loyola Blakefield, P.O. Box 6819, 21285-6819. Tel: 410-823-0601. Revs. John M. Dennis, S.J., M.Ed., Pres.; F. Joseph Michini, S.J., Chap.; Joseph Lingan, S.J., Supr.; D. Bradley Murray, S.J.; Robert B. Cullen, S.J.; James Bradley, S.J.; Lloyd George, S.J.; John Weetenkamp, Headmaster. Priests 5; Brothers 2; Lay Teachers 93; Students 953.

Mercy High School, 1300 E. Northern Pkwy., 21239. Tel: 410-433-8880; Fax: 410-323-8816.
E-mail: mhischo@archbalt.org
Web site: www.mercyhighschool.com
Sisters of Mercy of the Americas. Sr. Carol E. Wheeler, R.S.M., Prin. Sisters 5; Lay Teachers 50; Students 455; Total Staff 81.

Mount de Sales Academy, 700 Academy Rd., 21228. Tel: 410-744-8498; Fax: 410-747-5105.
E-mail: jwarthen@mountdesales.org
Web site: www.mountdesales.org
Sr. Mary Reginald, O.P., Headmistress. Priests 2; Sisters 3; Lay Teachers 42; Students 461.

Mt. St. Joseph College High School, 4403 Frederick Ave., 21229. Tel: 410-644-3300; Fax: 410-646-6221.
E-mail: barry@admin.msjnet.edu
Web site: www.msjnet.edu
Xaverian Brothers. Mr. Barry J. Fitzpatrick, Prin. & Acting Pres. Priests 1; Brothers 2; Lay Teachers 81; Students 1,094; Total Staff 131.

St. Frances Academy. (Coed), 501 E. Chase St., 21202. Tel: 410-539-5794; Fax: 410-685-2650.
E-mail: sfa@sfacademy.org
Web site: www.sfal.sfacademy.org
Oblate Sisters of Providence. Sr. John Francis Schilling, O.S.P., Pres. & Prin.; Ms. Mary Butler, Asst. Prin.; Fred A. Lee, Asst. Prin.; Mrs. Judy Treadwell, Dir. Guidance. Brothers 4; Sisters 7; Lay Teachers 15; Students 275.

BEL AIR. *The John Carroll School*, 703 Churchville Rd., 21014. Tel: 410-879-2480; Fax: 410-836-8514.
E-mail: jcs@techcord.loyola.edu
Web site: techcord.loyola.edu
Mr. Gary Scholl, Prin.; Mrs. Patti Murphy, Campus Min. Priests 1; Sisters of St. Joseph Chestnut Hill 3; Lay Teachers 57; Students 817; Total Staff 61.

CUMBERLAND. *Bishop Walsh Middle-High School*. (Grades 6-12), 700 Bishop Walsh Rd., 21502. Tel: 301-724-5360; Fax: 301-722-0555.
E-mail: spartans@miworld.net
Web site: www.miworld.net/bishopwalsh/

Brothers of the Christian Schools, School Sisters of Notre Dame. Sr. Phyllis McNally, S.S.N.D., Prin. Brothers 4; Sisters 1; Lay Teachers 25; Students 300.

FREDERICK. *St. John's Literary Institution at Prospect Hall* (1841). (Coed), 889 Butterfly Ln., 21703. Tel: 301-662-4210; Fax: 301-662-5166.
E-mail: sjph@erols.com
Web site: www.asd.com
Mr. Richard E. Fairley, Headmaster; Mr. Robert Boyer, Academic Dean. Priests 1; Lay Teachers 30; Students 270; Total Staff 45.

HAGERSTOWN. *St. Maria Goretti High School.* (Coed), 1535 Oak Hill Ave., 21742. Tel: 301-739-4266; Fax: 301-739-4261.
E-mail: goretti@goretti.org
Web site: www.goretti.org
Mr. Christopher Siedor, Prin. Lay Teachers 20; Students 214; Total Staff 30.

[E] MIDDLE/HIGH SCHOOLS, DIOCESAN

BALTIMORE. *Cardinal Gibbons School for Boys* (1962). (Grades 6-12), 3225 Wilkens Ave., 21229-4286. Tel: 410-644-1770; Fax: 410-525-3757.
E-mail: CGsch@archbalt.org
Web site: nmc.loyola.edu/cardinalgibbons/
Mr. Gary T. Meyerl, Prin. Lay Teachers 28; Students 301.

[F] MIDDLE/HIGH SCHOOLS, PRIVATE

BROOKLANDVILLE. *Maryvale Preparatory School* 6-12. (Girls), 21022-1490. Tel: 410-252-3366; Fax: 410-561-1826.
E-mail: maquire@maryvale.com
Web site: info@maryvale.com
Sr. Shawn Marie Maguire, S.N.D., Prin. Sisters of Notre Dame de Namur 2; Lay Teachers 40; Students 343; Total Staff 70.

TOWSON. *Notre Dame Preparatory School.* (Grades 6-12), 815 Hampton Ln., 21286. Tel: 410-825-6202; Fax: 410-832-2625.
Web site: www.notredameprep.com
Legal Title: *Notre Dame Preparatory School, Inc.* Sr. Christine Mulcahy, S.S.N.D., Headmistress. Sisters 2; Lay Teachers 73; Students 692; Total Staff 112.

[G] ELEMENTARY/MIDDLE SCHOOLS, PRIVATE

BALTIMORE. *John Paul Regional Catholic School, Inc.* (Grades PreK-8), 6946 Dogwood Rd., 21244. Tel: 410-944-0367. Dr. Nancy Gilroy, Prin., 5801 Security Blvd., 21207. Mrs. Joann Callahan, Dir. Early Childhood Program. Tel: 410-265-7454. Lay Teachers 28; Students 318.

WOODSTOCK. *Woodmont Academy*, 10817 Davis Ave., 21163. Tel: 410-203-0619; Fax: 410-465-9162.
E-mail: woodmontacademy.org
Mr. Keith Laser, Prin. Lay Teachers 18; Students 208.

[H] ELEMENTARY/MIDDLE SCHOOLS, REGIONAL AND COMMUNITY

BALTIMORE. *Catholic Community School of South Baltimore.* (Grades PreK-8), 300 E. Gittings St., 21230. Tel: 410-685-6155; Fax: 410-685-0692.
E-mail: jwagoner@archbalt.org
Web site: www.archnet.edu
Sr. Josephann Wagoner, S.S.N.D., Prin. Sisters 2; Lay Teachers 11; Students 250. Res. Sisters of St. Joseph, 1410 Riverside Ave., 21230-4695. Tel: 410-752-4344.
Consolidation of the following parishes: Holy Cross; Our Lady of Good Counsel; St. Mary, Star of the Sea.

[I] ELEMENTARY SCHOOLS, PRIVATE

BALTIMORE. *Mother Seton Academy*, 724 S. Ann St., 21231. Tel: 410-563-2833; Fax: 410-563-7353.
E-mail: mbader@archbalt.org
Innovative Middle School for Inner City Youth. Sisters 7; Brothers 2; Lay Teachers 9; Lay Volunteers 1; Students 70.

ELLICOTT CITY. *Trinity School*, 4985 Ilchester Rd., P.O. Box 299, 21041. Tel: 410-744-1524; Fax: 410-744-3617.
E-mail: faltrin@aol.com
Web site: trinitynews.org
Sr. Catherine Phelps, Pres.; Frangiska Lewis, Prin. Sisters of Notre Dame de Namur 2; Lay Teachers 26; Students 388.

EMMITSBURG. *Mother Seton School*, 100 Creamery Rd., 21727. Tel: 301-447-3161; Fax: 301-447-3914.
E-mail: office@mothersetonschool.org
Web site: www.mothersetonschool.org
Sr. Mary Catherine Conway, Prin. Daughters of Charity of St. Vincent de Paul 1; Sisters 2; Lay Teachers 17; Students 421.

FREDERICK. *Academy of the Visitation*, 200 E. 2nd St., 21701. Tel: 301-662-3322; 662-2814; Fax: 301-695-8549. Dr. Bernadette Emerson, Prin. Sisters of the Visitation 6; Lay Teachers 18; Students 228.

[J] ELEMENTARY SCHOOLS, REGIONAL AND COMMUNITY

BALTIMORE. *Bishop John Neumann School.* (Grades PreK-8), 3500 Foster Ave., 21224. Tel: 410-675-6271; Fax: 410-327-1543.
E-mail: bjnschool@archbalt.org
Web site: www.bjnschool.com
Mrs. Phyllis Karko, Prin. Lay Teachers 16; Students 213; Total Staff 20.

Cardinal Shehan School, 5407 Loch Raven Blvd., 21239-2996. Tel: 410-433-2775.
E-mail: csspeace@aol.com
Serving St. Matthew and St. Thomas More Parishes. Sr. Rita Michelle Proctor, O.S.P., Interim Prin. Lay Teachers 34; Sisters 3; Total Staff 37; Students 442.

Holy Spirit School, 932 Gorsuch Ave., 21218. Tel: 410-889-0679. Pauline Tobias-Jones, Prin. Lay Teachers 10; Students 204.

Queen of Peace Elementary Cluster, St. James and St. John School. (Grades PreK-5), 1012 Somerset St., 21202. Tel: 410-342-3222; Fax: 410-732-1323. Mrs. LaUanah King-Cassell, Prin. Sisters 2; Lay Teachers 14; Students 323.

St. Katherine of Sienna School, 1201 N. Rose St., 21213. Tel: 410-327-4738. Mr. Kirk Gaddy, Prin. Lay Teachers 10; Students 272.

St. Ignatius Loyola Academy, 740 N. Calvert St., 21202. Tel: 410-539-8268; Fax: 410-539-4821.
E-mail: jsindler@saintignatius.org
Revs. William J. Watters, S.J., Pres.; Robert J. Braunreuther, S.J., Chap.; Jeffrey Sindler, Headmaster. Middle School for underprivileged boys. Lay Teachers 11; Students 66.

Southeast Baltimore Catholic Academy (SEBCA) - Father Kolbe Campus, 1035 S. Kenwood Ave., 21224. Tel: 410-342-2681; Fax: 410-342-5715.
E-mail: kolbesch@archbalt.org
Serving the parishes of St. Casimir, St. Leo and St. Stanislaus. Sr. Barbara Ann Brzeczko, F.S.S.J., Prin. Franciscan Sisters of St. Joseph 1; Lay Teachers 15; Students 206.

Southeast Baltimore Catholic Academy, Inc. (SEBCA). Main Office, 440 South Chester St., 21231. Tel: 410-327-5134; Fax: 410-327-5137. Harry Schrader, Contact Person. Includes five elementary and one high school campus located in the Patterson Park Area of Southeast Baltimore.
Elementary/Middle School Campuses:
Our Lady of Pompei E.S., 201 S. Conkling St., 21224. Tel: 410-276-6534. Angela Rebbert, Prin. Students 175; Total Laystaff 23.
Our Lady of Fatima E.S., 6400 E. Pratt St., 21224. Tel: 410-633-5882. Jean Wimmer, Prin. Students 237; Total Laystaff 21.
Fr. Kolbe E.S., 1035 S. Kenwood Ave., 21224. Tel: 410-342-2681. Sr. Barbara Breczko. Students 185; Total Laystaff 16.
St. Elizabeth of Hungary E.S., 27 N. Lakewood Ave., 21224. Tel: 410-276-6344. Catherine Marshall, Prin. Students 205; Total Laystaff 19.
Bishop John Neumann E.S., 3500 Foster Ave., 21224. Tel: 410-675-6271. Phyllis Karko, Prin. Students 215; Total Laystaff 23.
High School Campus:
Our Lady of the Rosary High School, 420 S. Chester St., 21231. Tel: 410-327-0600. Mary Louise Kolb, Prin. Students 138; Total Laystaff 17. SEBCA Total Enrollment 1,155; Total Laystaff 119.

CUMBERLAND. *St. John Neumann School.* (Grades K-5), 151 Fayette St., 21502. Tel: 301-724-4055; Fax: 301-724-4827.
E-mail: SJNsch@archbalt.org
Sr. Kathleen F. Jancuk, S.S.N.D., Prin. Sisters 1; Lay Teachers 18; Students 294.
Bishop Walsh Middle-High School. (See listing under High Schools, Private).

FREDERICK. *St. John Regional Catholic School.* (Grades K-8), 114 E. Second St., 21701. Tel: 301-662-6722; Fax: 301-695-7024.
E-mail: sjrcs@fred.net
Ms. Joyce Connelly, Prin. Lay Teachers 26; Students 525.

GLEN BURNIE. *Arthur Slade Regional Catholic School*, 120 Dorsey Rd., 21061. Tel: 410-766-7130.
E-mail: asrcs@aol.com
Serving Glen Burnie, Millersville, Pasadena, Odenton, Crofton, Hanover and Severn Parishes. Mrs. Janice McIntosh, Prin. Lay Teachers 41; Students 848.

[K] SPECIAL EDUCATION

BALTIMORE. *St. Elizabeth School, Inc.*, 801 Argonne Dr., 21218-1998. Tel: 410-889-5054; Fax: 410-889-2356.
Web site: www.stelizabeth-school.org
Christine Manlove, Ed.D., Exec. Dir. & Prin. Franciscan Sisters of Baltimore 4; Lay Teachers 26; Other Lay Staff 35; Aides 53; Children 126.

St. Peter's Adult Learning Center, 13 S. Poppleton St., 21201. Tel: 410-685-7340; Fax: 410-625-4696.
E-mail: klnrsm@erols.com
Program for developmentally disabled persons(sheltered workshop/supported employment). Sr. Katherine Nueslein, R.S.M., Dir. Sisters 1; Lay Teachers 11; Students 40.

TIMONIUM. *Villa Maria School.* (Main Campus), 2300 Dulaney Valley Rd., 21093. Tel: 410-252-6343; Fax: 410-560-1347. Revanette Gilmore, Dir. Education. Non-public (Level V and VI) special education for children with emotional disabilities, ages 3-13. Lay Teachers 22; Teacher Aides 20; Children 112.
Villa Maria School at St. Vincent's, 2600 Pot Spring Rd., 21093. Tel: 410-252-3725; Fax: 410-561-8109. Lay Teachers 7; Teacher Aides 9; Children 40.
Villa Maria School at Seton Keough, 1201 S. Caton Ave., Baltimore, 21227. Tel: 410-644-3792; Fax: 410-644-3796. Lay Teachers 6; Teacher Aides 4; Children 35.
Villa Maria- Children in Need of Services Program, 1301 Continental Dr., Ste. 101, Abingdon, 21009-2338. Tel: 410-676-1220; Fax: 410-538-3376.
Villa Maria- Landsowne Therapeutic After School Program, 500 3rd Ave., Baltimore, 21227-3218. Tel: 410-536-1205; Fax: 410-536-1831.

[L] CHILD CARE CENTERS

BALTIMORE. *Good Shepherd Center*, 4100 Maple Ave., 21227. Tel: 410-247-2770; Fax: 410-247-3242.
E-mail: gsc@goodshepherdcenter.org
Web site: www.goodshepherdcenter.com
Legal Titles: *House of the Good Shepherd.*; *Sisters of the Good Shepherd, A Corporation.* Sr. Mary Rosaria Baxter, R.G.S., Admin.; Sr. Mary Catherine Massei, R.G.S., Supr. Residential psychiatric treatment for adolescent girls with emotional and behavioral problems. Sisters 15; Capacity 105; Residents 98; Total Assisted 181; Total Staff 260.

Mount Providence Child Development Center, 701 Gun Rd., 21227. Tel: 410-247-0449. Oblate Sisters of Providence. Sr. Mary Concetta Melton, O.S.P., Dir. Sisters 2; Students 80; Total Assisted 9; Total Staff 13.

St. Frances Outreach Center, 1026 Brentwood Ave., 21202. Tel: 410-685-1975; Fax: 410-832-1299. Sr. Brenda Motte, O.S.P., Dir. Total Assisted 50 Families; Total Staff 3.

St. Veronica's Headstart Center. For additional information please see the Associated Catholic Charities section.

Sisters Servants of Mary Immaculate Day Nursery & Convent, 100-104 S. Patterson Park Ave., 21231. Tel: 410-276-2630. Sr. Lydia Eugenia Ziecina, Supr. Total Assisted 50.

Villa Louise Family Resource Center, St. Agnes Hospital, DePaul Bldg., 900 Caton Ave., 21229. Tel: 410-368-2060. Legal Title: *Associated Catholic Charities, Inc.* Bon Secours Community Support Center, 26 N. Fulton Ave., 21223. Tel: 410-362-3168. Harriet Bachman, Dir. Total Staff 14; Total Assisted 200.

CUMBERLAND. *Neumann Early Childhood Center, Inc.*, 209 N. Centre St., 21502. Tel: 301-777-1166. Mrs. G. Louise Elliott, Dir. Total Assisted 106; Total Staff 10.

TIMONIUM. *Francis X. Gallagher Services*, 2520 Pot Spring Rd., 21093. Tel: 410-252-4005; Fax: 410-560-3495.
Web site: www.catholiccharities-md.org/programs/gallagher
Mark J. Schulz, Admin.
Residential, day habilitation and medical day programs for the developmentally disabled. Residential Capacity 207; Day Capacity 245; Total Assisted 256; Total Staff 300.

St. Vincent's Center. For additional information please see the Associated Catholic Charities section.

Villa Maria Treatment Center, 2300 Dulaney Valley Rd., 21093. Tel: 410-252-4700; Fax: 410-252-3040.
E-mail: jhackbar@catholiccharities-md.org
Web site: www.catholiccharities-md.org
Mark Greenberg, Admin.; Rev. Raymond Chase, Chap.
We operate a full continuum of 14 different mental health and special education programs for children and their families. Children 650; Total Staff 425.

[M] GENERAL HOSPITALS

BALTIMORE. *Bon Secours Baltimore Health Corporation, Inc.*, 2000 W. Baltimore St., 21223. Tel: 410-362-3000; Fax: 410-362-3126.
E-mail: phyllis_reese@bshsi.com
Web site: www.bonsecours.org
For a complete listing, refer to the Hospitals section.

Good Samaritan Hospital of Maryland Inc., 320 Cathedral St., 21201
For a complete listing, refer to the Hospitals section.

Mercy Health Services Inc., 301 St. Paul Pl., 21202. Tel: 410-332-9000; Fax: 410-962-1303.
E-mail: srmanella@mercymed.com
Web site: www.mercymed.com
For a complete listing, refer to the Hospitals section.
St. Agnes HealthCare, Inc., 900 Caton Ave., 21229-5299. Tel: 410-368-6000; Fax: 410-368-2109.
E-mail: info@stagnes.org
Web site: www.stagnes.org
For a complete listing, refer to the Hospitals section.
CUMBERLAND. *Sacred Heart Hospital of the Western Maryland Health System*, 900 Seton Dr., 21502. Tel: 301-723-4200; Fax: 301-723-5583.
E-mail: webmaster@wmhs.com
Web site: www.wmhs.com
For a complete listing, refer to the Hospitals section.
TOWSON. *St. Joseph Medical Center, Inc.*, 7601 Osler Dr., 21204. Tel: 410-337-1000; Fax: 410-337-1024.
E-mail: nancyconner@chi-east.org
Web site: www.sjmcmd.org
For a complete listing, refer to the Hospitals section.

[N] NURSING HOMES (SKILLED) AND REHABILITATION CENTERS

BALTIMORE. *Dismas House East*, 1415 N. Caroline St., 21213. Tel: 410-539-2520
For a complete listing, refer to the Special Care Facilities section.
Dismas House West, 105 S. Mount St., 21223-0435. Tel: 410-566-9400; Fax: 410-233-1622
For a complete listing, refer to the Special Care Facilities section.
Good Samaritan Nursing Center Inc., 320 Cathedral St., 21201
For a complete listing, refer to the Special Care Facilities section.
St. Elizabeth Rehabilitation and Nursing Center, 3320 Benson Ave., 21227-1035. Tel: 410-644-7100; Fax: 410-644-2154.
E-mail: info@catholiccharities-md.org
Web site: www.catholiccharities-md.org
For a complete listing, refer to the Special Care Facilities section.
ELLICOTT CITY. *St. Agnes Nursing and Rehabilitation Center*, 3000 N. Ridge Rd., 21043. Tel: 410-461-7577; Fax: 410-461-6695.
Web site: stagnes.org
For a complete listing, refer to the Special Care Facilities section.
EMMITSBURG. *Villa St. Catherine, Inc.*, 331 S. Seton Ave., 21727. Tel: 301-447-7000; Fax: 301-447-7015
For a complete listing, refer to the Special Care Facilities section.

[O] HOMES FOR AGED

BALTIMORE. *St. Charles Villa*, 603 Maiden Choice Ln., 21228. Tel: 410-747-1211; Fax: 410-747-2460.
E-mail: wtokss@aol.com
For a complete listing, refer to the Special Care Facilities section.
St. Joseph's Nursing Home, 1222 Tugwell Dr., 21228. Tel: 410-747-0026; Fax: 410-747-0386
For a complete listing, refer to the Special Care Facilities section.
St. Martin's Home for Aged, Little Sisters of the Poor, 601 Maiden Choice Ln., 21228. Tel: 410-744-9367; Fax: 410-747-0835
For a complete listing, refer to the Special Care Facilities section.
TIMONIUM. *Stella Maris*, 2300 Dulaney Valley Rd., 21093. Tel: 410-252-4500; 560-9675 (Admissions); Fax: 410-560-9675.
E-mail: STELLA@erols.com
Web site: www.stellamarisinc.com
For a complete listing, refer to the Special Care Facilities section.

[P] SOCIAL SERVICES

BALTIMORE. *Franciscan Center*, 101 W. 23rd St., 21218. Tel: 410-467-5340; Fax: 410-467-4559.
E-mail: franciscen@aol.com
Franciscan Sisters of Baltimore. Sr. Kathleen DeLancey, Dir. Total Assisted 150,000; Total Staff 18.
House of Mercy, Inc., 901 Hollins St., 21223. Tel: 410-244-6220; Fax: 410-244-6237. Sr. Margaret Downing, R.S.M., Dir.
Mount Providence Reading Center, 701 Gun Rd., 21227. Tel: 410-247-0448, 242-8500. Oblate Sisters of Providence. Sr. M. Constance Fenwick, O.S.P., Dir. Students 200; Total Assisted 200; Total Staff 10.
Trinitarian Counseling Services, Inc., 8400 Park Heights Ave. P.O. Box 5719, 21282. Tel: 410-476-5764; Fax: 410-486-0614.
E-mail: tburke@stmarys.edu
Rev. Thomas J. Burke, O.SS.T., Dir. Total Assisted 183; Total Staff 2.
EMMITSBURG. *Seton Center, Inc.*, 16840 S. Seton Ave., 21727. Tel: 301-447-6102; Fax: 301-447-1748.
E-mail: seton@clark.net
Social Service; Outreach; Thrift Shop. Daughters of Charity. Sr. Dorothy A. Pyle, Admin. Total Assisted 22,154; Total Staff 11.
PASADENA. *Mary's Center*, P.O. Box 1804, 21123-1804. Tel: 410-761-8082. Pregnancy Support Services. Mary Albero, Dir. Total Assisted 860; Total Staff 32.

[Q] ASSOCIATED CATHOLIC CHARITIES

BALTIMORE. *Associated Catholic Charities, Inc. (Catholic Charities).*
For more information on Catholic Charities and its programs please contact: Catholic Charities, 320 Cathedral St., 3rd Floor, 21201-4421. Tel: 410-261-5800.
E-mail: info@catholiccharities-md.org
Web site: www.catholiccharities-mdorg
Associated Catholic Charities. Inc. (Catholic Charities) is the largest private provider of human services in Maryland, meeting the needs of men, women, and children without regard to religion, race, or other circumstances. Headquartered in Baltimore, the 76-year-old agency operates in the city and in nine Maryland counties under auspices of the Roman Catholic Archdiocese of Baltimore. The agency operates 88 separate programs providing: community services, services for the aging, housing services, child and family services, and services for the developmentally disabled. Management Team: Harold A. Smith, Exec. Dir., Associated Catholic Charities Inc., 320 Cathedral St., 3rd Floor, 21201-4421. Tel: 410-547-5497; Fax: 410-752-7260. James Gabriel, Assoc. Dir., Chief Fin. Officer, Associated Catholic Charities, Inc., 320 Cathedral St., 3rd. Floor, 21201-4421. Tel: 410-547-5459; Fax: 410-752-7260. Angela Boer, Dir., Community Svcs. Div., Associated Catholic Charities Inc., 2305 N. Charles St., 3rd Floor, 21218-5128. Tel: 410-261-6774; Fax: 410-889-0203. Stevenson W. Close, Jr., Dir., Devel. and Communications Div., Associated Catholic Charities Inc., 320 Cathedral St., 3rd Floor, 21201-4421. Tel: 410-547-5481; Fax: 410-576-2179. S. Rebecca Galloway, Dir., SeniorLife Svcs. Div., Associated Catholic Charities Inc., 3220 Benson Ave., 21227-1035. Tel: 410-646-6501; Fax: 410-646-0500. Dale R. McArdle, Dir., Housing Svcs. Div., Associated Catholic Charities Inc., 320 Cathedral St., 3rd Floor, 21201-4421. Tel: 410-547-5544; Fax: 410-576-0987. Kathleen H. Mills, Dir., Human Resources Div., Associated Catholic Charities Inc., 2305 N. Charles St., 21218-5128. Tel: 410-261-5839; Fax: 410-889-9243. John D. Rusinko, Children's Svcs. Div., Associated Catholic Charities Inc., 2300 Dulaney Valley Rd., Timonium, 21093-2739. Tel: 410-252-4700, Ext. 101; Fax: 410-252-3040.
661 Corporation, 320 Cathedral St., 21201. Mark P. Keener, Resident Agent.
The Jenkins Fund, Inc.
Children's Services Division: 2300 Dulaney Valley Rd., Timonium. Tel: 410-252-3040; Fax: 410-252-3040. John D. Rusinko, Dir.
Catholic Charities Early Head Start, Harford County, 1301 Continental Dr., Abingdon, 21009-2338. Tel: 410-538-3388; Fax: 410-538-3376.
Catholic Charities Head Start, Carroll County, #9 Westminster Shopping Center, Rte. 140 and Englar Rds., Westminster, 21157. Tel: 410-871-2450; Fax: 410-871-2452.
Center for Family Services/International Adoption Services, 19 W. Franklin St., 21201-5005. Tel: 410-659-4050; Fax: 410-659-4060.
Center for Family Services/Pregnancy, Parenting, and Adoption Services, 19 W. Franklin St., 21201-5005. Tel: 410-659-4050; Fax: 410-659-4060.
Center for Family Services/Treatment Foster Care, 11 E. Mount Royal Ave., 21202-2714. Tel: 410-685-2363; Fax: 410-685-2364.
Center for Family Services/Young Parents Program, 900 S. Caton Ave., 21229. Tel: 410-368-2060; Fax: 410-368-2554.
Chara House, 4203 Belvieu Ave., 21215-4812. Tel: 410-367-1191; Fax: 410-367-3039.
Child Safe Program, 2600 Pot Spring Rd., Timonium, 21093-2732. Tel: 410-252-4000; Fax: 410-561-8109.
Damascus Career Center, 806 Cherry Hill Rd., Brooklyn, 21225-1314. Tel: 410-354-7507; Fax: 410-354-0271.
Herring Run Head Start, 5010 Bowleys Ln., 21206-6744. Tel: 410-485-1010; Fax: 410-485-1009.
Our Friends' Place, 775 W. Hamburg St., 21230-2539. Tel: 410-837-6870; Fax: 410-659-4022.
St. Jerome's Head Start, 915 Sterrett St., 21230-2502. Tel: 410-685-1700; Fax: 410-659-3921.
St. Veronica's Head Start, 2920 Joseph Ave., Brooklyn, 21225-1139. Tel: 410-354-0220; Fax: 410-354-4785.
St. Vincent's Center, 2600 Pot Spring Rd., Timonium, 21093-2732. Tel: 410-252-4000, Ext. 1601; Fax: 410-561-8109.
School Counseling Program, 2600 Pot Spring Rd., Timonium, 21093-2732. Tel: 410-252-4000; Fax: 410-561-8109.
Villa Maria Residential Treatment Center (Villa Maria, Inc.) (Friends of Villa Maria Inc.), 2300 Dulaney Valley Rd., Timonium, 21093-2739. Tel: 410-252-4700; Fax: 410-252-3040.
Villa Maria- Baltimore Children and Adolescent Response System, 2041 E. Fayette St., Ste. 102, 21231. Tel: 410-558-2212; Fax: 410-558-2244.
Villa Maria- Child & Family Counseling Services, 2300 Dulaney Valley Rd., Timonium, 21093-2739. Tel: 410-252-4700; Fax: 410-252-3040.
Villa Maria- Children in Need of Services Program, 1301 Continental Dr., Abingdon, 21009-2338. Tel: 410-676-4002; Fax: 410-538-3376.
Villa Maria- In-Home Intervention Program, 2300 Dulaney Valley Rd., Timonium, 21093-2739. Tel: 410-252-4700; Fax: 410-252-3040.
Villa Maria- Lansdowne Therapeutic After School Program, 500 3rd Ave., 21227-3218. Tel: 410-536-1205; Fax: 410-536-1831.
Villa Maria- Project PrePARE (Predelinquency Prevention, Advocacy, Responsibility, and Empowerment), 1301 Continental Dr., Abingdon, 21109-2338. Tel: 410-676-4002; Fax: 410-676-7365.
Villa Maria- Respite Program, 2300 Dulaney Valley Rd., Timonium, 21093-2739. Tel: 410-252-4700; Fax: 410-252-3040.
Villa Maria- Home Based Respite, 2300 Dulaney Rd., Timonium, 21093-2739. Tel: 410-252-4700; Fax: 410-252-3040.
Villa Maria- Return and Diversion Services, 455 Bow St., Elkton, 21921-5476. Tel: 410-620-9849; Fax: 410-620-9849.
Villa Maria- Safe Start, 1301 Continental Dr., Abingdon, 21109-2338. Tel: 410-676-4002; Fax: 410-676-7365.
Villa Maria School, 2300 Dulaney Valley Rd., Timonium, 21093-2799. Tel: 410-252-6343; Fax: 410-560-1347.
Villa Maria School at St. Vincent's, 2600 Pot Spring Rd., Timonium, 21093-2732. Tel: 410-252-3725; Fax: 410-453-9712.
Villa Maria School at Seton Keough, 1201 S. Caton Ave., 21227-1092. Tel: 410-644-3792; Fax: 410-644-3796.
Villa Maria Therapeutic Group Home, 1422 Gibsonwood Rd., Catonsville, 21228-2523. Tel: 410-788-9440; Fax: 410-788-9440.
Villa Maria- Timonium Therapeutic After School Program, 2300 Dulaney Valley Rd., Timonium, 21093-2739. Tel: 410-252-4700; Fax: 410-252-3040.
Community Services Division: 2305 N. Charles St., 21218. Tel: 410-261-6774; Fax: 410-889-0203. Angelo Boer, Dir.
Anna's House, P.O. Box 88, Bel Air, 21014-0088. Tel: 410-638-1479; Fax: 410-638-1753.
Apostolado Hispano/Hispanic Apostolate, 430 S. Broadway, 21231-2410. Tel: 410-522-2668; Fax: 410-675-1451.
Auburne Center, 5500 Old Frederick Rd., 21229-2302. Tel: 410-744-8961; Fax: 410-744-4831.
Catholic Charities Employment Services, 2305 N. Charles St., 21218-5128. Tel: 410-261-5800; Fax: 410-889-0203.
Catholic Charities, Frederick County, 303 W. Lincoln Ave., Emmitsburg, 21727-9179. Tel: 301-898-1940; Fax: 301-694-6654.
Catholic Charities, Washington County, 229 N. Potomac St., Hagerstown, 21740-3812. Tel: 301-733-5858; Fax: 301-733-5858.
Cherry Hill Town Center (Cherry Hill Town Center, Inc.), 2305 N. Charles St., 21218-5128. Tel: 410-261-6760; Fax: 410-889-0203.
Christopher Place Employment Academy, 709 E. Eager St., 21202-4234. Tel: 410-576-0066; Fax: 410-576-0914.
Emmanus (Shelter & Care), 123 W. Mulberry St., 21201-3619. Tel: 410-727-3523; Fax: 410-727-1611.
Immigration Legal Services, 430 S. Broadway, 21231-2410. Tel: 410-534-8015; Fax: 410-675-1451.
My Sister's Place, 123 W. Mulberry St., 21201-3619. Tel: 410-727-3523; Fax: 410-727-1611.
My Sister's Place Lodge, 111 W. Mulberry St., 21201-3619. Tel: 410-528-9002; Fax: 410-528-9004.
Our Daily Bread, 411 Cathedral St., 21201-4449. Tel: 410-659-4000; Fax: 410-659-4014.
Parish Relations, 2305 N. Charles St., 21218-5128. Tel: 410-261-5800; Fax: 410-889-0203.
Project FRESH Start (Family Relocation, Empowerment, and Self-Help), 2305 N. Charles St., 21218-5128. Tel: 410-261-5800; Fax: 410-889-0203.
Project SERVE (Service and Education through Residential Volunteer Experience), 2305 N. Charles St., 21218-5128. Tel: 410-261-5800; Fax: 410-889-0203.
Samaritan Center, 411 Cathedral St., 21201-4147. Tel: 410-659-4000; Fax: 410-659-4059.

Sarah's House, 2015 20th St., Fort Meade, 20755-1301. Tel: 410-551-7722; Fax: 410-551-7279.

SHARE-Baltimore (Self-Help and Resource Exchange), 808 Barkwood Ct., Linthicum, 21090-1424. Tel: 410-636-9615; Fax: 410-636-9629.

Social Concerns, 2305 N. Charles St., 21218-5128. Tel: 410-261-5800; Fax: 410-889-0203.

Up County Family Center, 303 W. Lincoln Ave., Emmitsburg, 21727-9179. Tel: 301-447-2810; Fax: 301-447-6325.

Western Maryland Catholic Charities, P.O. Box 1916, Cumberland, 21502-1916. Tel: 301-777-8685; Fax: 301-722-0197.

Housing Services Division: 320 Cathedral St., 3rd Floor, 21201-4421. Tel: 410-547-5544; Fax: 410-576-0987.

Arundel Woods Apartments (Glen Burnie Senior Housing, Inc.), 403 W. Ordinance Rd., Glen Burnie, 21061.

Basilica Place Apartments (The Catholic Charities Housing, Inc.), 124 W. Franklin St., 21201-4576. Tel: 410-539-0418; Fax: 410-752-6207.

Coursey Station Apartments (Coursey Station Apartments, Inc.), 200 First Ave., Halethorpe, 21227-3031. Tel: 410-242-6167; Fax: 410-242-3459.

Friendship Station Senior Housing (Odenton Senior Housing, Inc.). Friendship Station Senior Housing is a senior living facility in western Anne Arundel County. 1212 Odenton Rd., Odenton, 21113. Tel: 410-519-6085; Fax: 410-519-6092.

Holden Hall, 761 W. Hamburg St., 21230-2539. Tel: 410-347-9830; Fax: 410-347-9831.

Home Ownership Program, 4367 Hollins Ferry Rd., Ste. 3D, 21227-3400. Tel: 410-737-8374; Fax: 410-737-8378.

St. Charles House Apartments (St. Charles House, Inc.), 11 Church Ln., Pikesville, 21208-6607. Tel: 410-484-6125; Fax: 410-242-3459.

St. Luke's Place Apartments (St. Luke's Apartments, Inc.), 2825 Lodge Farm Rd., Sparrows Point, 21219-1347. Tel: 410-477-3661; Fax: 410-477-0199.

St. Mark's Apartments, 19 Winters Ln., Catonsville, 21228-4499. Tel: 410-788-0972; Fax: 410-242-3459.

Stamer Hill Apartments (Backbone Housing, Inc.), P.O. Box 489, Grantsville, 21536-0489. Tel: 301-895-5842; Fax: 301-895-3762.

Trinity House Apartments (Trinity House Apartments, Inc.), 409 Virginia Ave., Towson, 21286-5372. Tel: 410-825-5288; Fax: 410-825-5592. Senior Life Services Division, 3320 Benson Ave., 21227-1035. Tel: 410-646-6501; Fax: 410-646-0500.

Answers for the Aging, 3320 Benson Ave., 21227-1035. Tel: 410-646-0100; Fax: 410-646-0500.

Cherry Hill Senior Life Center, 606 Cherry Hill Rd., Ste. 201, 21225-1229. Tel: 410-354-5101; Fax: 410-354-5103.

Congregate Housing Services, 3449 Wilkens Ave., 21229-2409. Tel: 410-644-0845; Fax: 410-644-0950.

DePaul House (DePaul House, Inc.), 3300 Benson Ave., 21227-1030. Tel: 410-644-8484; Fax: 410-644-1334.

Everall Gardens Senior Housing, 6100 Everall Ave., 21206-1946. Tel: 410-444-5850; Fax: 410-444-0190.

Hosanna House, 2829 Lodge Farm Rd., Sparrows Point, 21219-1315. Tel: 410-388-9030; Fax: 410-477-0199.

Joseph Center, 430 S. Broadway, 21231-2409. Tel: 410-732-5000; Fax: 410-675-1451.

Kessler Park Senior Housing, 4230 Hollins Ferry Rd., 21227-3440. Tel: 410-247-9244; Fax: 410-242-3459.

Reistertown Village Senior Housing (Reistertown Village Senior Housing, Inc.), 320 Cathedral St., 21201-4421. Tel: 410-547-5483.

St. Ann Adult Day Services, 3329 Benson Ave., 21227-1001. Tel: 410-646-0320; Fax: 410-644-0840.

St. Elizabeth Rehabilitation and Nursing Center (Jenkins Memorial Nursing Home, Inc.), 3320 Benson Ave., 21227-1035. Tel: 410-644-7100; Fax: 410-644-2154.

St. Joachim House (St. Joachim House, Inc.), 3310 Benson Ave., 21227-1075. Tel: 410-644-8269; Fax: 410-525-9227.

Senior Center Plus at the Joseph Center, 430 S. Broadway, 21231-2409. Tel: 410-732-5000; Fax: 410-675-1451.

Independent Programs:

Francis X. Gallagher Services (Gallagher Services Auxillary, Inc.). (The Father Raymond W. Gribbin Activity Center, Inc.), 2520 Pot Spring Rd., Timonium, 21093-2795. Tel: 410-252-4005; Fax: 410-560-3495.

Group homes constructed and operated under the Dept. of Housing and Urban Development's Section 202-8 Program:

The Bethany Community, Inc. 3731 Ellerslie Ave., 21218. Tel: 410-366-5002. 2421 Pot Spring Rd., 21093. Tel: 410-561-5733. 2292 Dulaney Valley Rd., 21093. Tel: 410-252-7875. 18314 Middletown Rd., 21120. Tel: 410-343-2536.

St. Francis Housing Corporation. 3400 Benson Ave., 21227. Tel: 410-368-3890. 8240 Jumpers Hole Rd., 21108. Tel: 410-544-0838. 4607 Mountain Rd., 21122. Tel: 410-360-5125.

St. Martha's Housing, Inc. 2560 Pot Spring Rd., 21093. Tel: 410-561-5744. 501 Belfast Rd., 21152. Tel: 410-472-3066. 4605 Mountain Rd., 21122. Tel: 410-360-5126.

St. Mary's Housing, Inc. 751 Argonne Dr., 21218. Tel: 410-467-7540. 47 Church Rd., 21012. Tel: 410-974-4356. 1925 Rockhaven Ave., 21228. Tel: 410-719-0681.

Project AWARE, 320 Cathedral St., 21201-4421. Tel: 410-547-5521; Fax: 410-576-2179.

Additional Related Corporation:

The Children's Fund, Inc.

[R] RETREAT HOUSES FOR MEN, WOMEN AND YOUTH

BALTIMORE. *Holy Trinity Spiritual Center*, 8400 Park Heights Ave., P.O. Box 5719, 21282. Tel: 410-486-5171; Fax: 410-486-0614.
Web site: trinitarians.org
Rev. Thomas Morris, O.SS.T., Dir. Spirituality Center. Total Assisted 1,113; Total Staff 7; Total in Residence 7.

St. Mary's Spiritual Center, 600 N. Paca St., 21201-1995. Tel: 410-728-6464; Fax: 410-669-8140.
E-mail: SMSCBalto@aol.com
Rev. John E. McMurry, S.S., Dir. Adjunct Staff 13; Auxiliary Staff 3.

ADAMSTOWN. *Christian Brothers Spiritual Center*, 2535 Buckeystown Pike, P.O. Box 29, 21710. Tel: 301-874-5180; Fax: 301-874-3757. Bro. Richard W. Breese, F.S.C., Admin. Brothers 3.

CATONSVILLE. *Our Lady of Guadalupe Renewal Center*, 1903 Norhurst Way N., 21228. Tel: 410-788-8821. Spiritual Life and Renewal Programs for Religious and Laity. Sr. Anne Colette Potthast, S.N.D., Dir. Total in Residence 2; Total Staff 2; Pastoral Team 13.

EMMITSBURG. *Seton Retreat Center*, 333 S. Seton Ave., 21727. Tel: 301-447-6021; Fax: 301-447-6038.
E-mail: srvincen@doc.org
Daughters of Charity. Sr. Vincentia Goeb, D.C., Dir.; Joan Little, Retreat Coord.

MARRIOTTSVILLE. *Bon Secours Spiritual Center*, 1525 Marriottsville Rd., 21104-1301. Tel: 410-442-1320; Fax: 410-442-8219.
E-mail: bssc@bshsi.com
Web site: www.bonsecours.org/bssc
Sisters of Bon Secours. Sr. Carol J. Marozzi, S.S.J., Dir. Total Staff 35.

SPARKS. *Msgr. Clare J. O'Dwyer Retreat House*, 15523 York Rd., 21152. Tel: 410-666-2400; Fax: 410-472-3281.
E-mail: odwyer@clark.net
Rev. J. Kevin Farmer, Dir. Total Staff 16.

[S] MONASTERIES AND RESIDENCES OF PRIESTS AND BROTHERS

BALTIMORE. *Ferdinand Wheeler Jesuit Community*, 3048 Guilford Ave., 21218. Tel: 410-338-1296. Revs. Mark F. Horak, S.J., Supr.; James R. Stormes, S.J.; Theodore E.A. Brady, S.J.; Charles P. Costello, S.J.; Thomas P. Gaunt, S.J.; Joachim Nthawie, S.J.; Miller Lamothe, S.J.; William Walsh, S.J.; Bro. James Horan, S.J. Priests 8; Brothers 1.

Holy Trinity Monastery, Prov. Admin. P.O. Box 5742, 21282. Tel: 410-486-5171; Fax: 410-486-0614.
E-mail: provtreas.@aol.com
Web site: trinitarians.org
Office, 8400 Upper Park Heights Ave., P.O. Box 5719, 21282-0742. Tel: 410-486-5764; Fax: 410-486-0614. In res. Revs. Raul P. Rendon, O.SS.T., Min. Prov.; John Dorn, O.SS.T., Vicar Prov.; Thomas A. Morris, O.SS.T., Min. Conventual, Dir. Spiritual Center, Sec. Prov.; Timothy Murphy, O.SS.T.; Edward Wagner, O.SS.T., Chap.; Joseph T. Gross, O.SS.T, Historian; Bros. Eric Beardsley, O.SS.T.; Christopher Doyle, O.SS.T.; Daniel Montemarano, O.SS.T. Priests 6; Brothers 3.

Assigned But Serving Elsewhere: Rev. Matthew Maniamkerry, O.SS.T., Holy Trinity Ashram, P.O. Aranattukara, Kerala State, Trichur, 680618. Tel: 011-91-80-487-360379; Fax: 011-91-80-487-361596. Rev. Luke Mennella, O.SS.T., General Council, The Trinitarians, Via Massimi, 114C, Rome, Italy, 00136. Tel: 011-39-063-542-0529; Fax: 011-39-063-534-1673. Rev. Joseph C. Gidaro, O.SS.T., St. Bridgid Church, 119 Ave. B, New York, NY, 10009. Tel: 212-228-5400; Fax: 212-677-5210. Rev. Aaron M. Dowdell, O.SS.T., St. Bridgid Church, 119 Ave. B, New York, NY, 10009. Tel: 212-228-5400; Fax: 212-254-0334. Rev. Jose T. Narlaly, O.SS.T., Mt. St. Joseph, P.O., Bannerghatta Road, Bangalore 560-076/Karnataka, India. Tel: 011-91-80-658596; Fax: 011-91-80-658596. Rev. Damon Geiger, O.SS.T., Trinity House, 1511E. Commercial, Victoria, TX, 77901-7021. Tel: 361-573-7059. Rev. David Colella, O.SS.T, St. Clare Church, 321 Calumet St., Dallas, TX, 75211. Tel: 214-337-3936; Fax: 214-333-9148. Rev. Armand Iavarone, O.SS.T., St. Joseph's Church, 333 Sneden Pl. W., Spring Valley, NY, 10977-3943. Tel: 914-356-0311; Fax: 914-352-8126. Rev. Weston J. Lamb, O.SS.T., 1048 E. Cherry St., Jesup, GA, 31546. Tel: 912-427-9239; Fax: 912-427-9238. Rev. J. Edward Owens, O.SS.T., St. John's Seminary, 5012 Seminary Rd., Camarillo, CA, 93012-2598. Tel: 805-482-2755; Fax: 805-484-4074. Rev. Carl Pfeiffer, O.SS.T., 410 Ferncliffe Rd., Elgin, SC, 29045. Tel: 803-865-5091. Rev. Claude Gravel, O.SS.T., St. Ann Church, 357 Dorrance St., P.O. Box 1175, Bristol, PA, 19007-1175. Tel: 215-788-2128; Fax: 215-781-9782. Rev. Thomas Dymcwski, O.SS.T., Assumption Seminary, 2600 W. Woodlawn Ave., San Antonio, TX, 78228-5122. Tel: 210-732-6752; Fax: 210-734-2324. The Trinitarian Community, 8636 Trail View Dr., Ellicott City, 21043. Tel: 410-203-3135; Fax: 410-203-2117. In res. Revs. Thomas J. Burke, O.SS.T.; William J. Moorman, O.SS.T., The Trinitarian Community, 8612 Laverne Dr., Adelphi, 20783. Tel: 301-422-0155; Fax: 301-422-0070. In res. Revs. Lawrence C. Hernandez, O.SS.T.; William Sullivan, O.SS.T.

Redeemer House, 1401 Battery Ave., 21230-4603. Tel: 410-576-9565. In res. Bros. Thomas Janeczko; Richard J. Micka, Prog. Dir. & Trinitarian-In-Charge; David Nash, Treas. Brothers 3; Total Staff 3.

Immaculate Heart of Mary Friary, 4220 Erdman Ave., 21213. Tel: 410-485-5511; Fax: 410-483-2545.
E-mail: dgrzmsk@curley.loyola.edu
Residence of Franciscan Friars, O.F.M.Conv., conducting Archbishop Curley High School. Revs. Joseph Grzybowski, O.F.M.Conv.; Michael Martin, O.F.M.Conv.; Michael Heine, O.F.M.Conv.; Ignatius M. Piatek, O.F.M.Conv.; Donald Grzymski, O.F.M.Conv., Pres. & Guardian; Thomas E. Walsh, O.F.M.Conv., Vicar; Callistus Juras, O.F.M.Conv.; Thomas Hunt, O.F.M.Conv. Seminarian 1; Priests 7; Total Staff 1.

Jesuit Community of Loyola College, Inc., Loyola College, 4603 Millbrook Rd., 21212-4721. Tel: 410-617-2318; Fax: 410-617-2125. Revs. Eugene M. Geinzer, S.J., Rector; Ronald J. Anton, S.J.; Jeffrey P. Baerwald, S.J.; Michael L. Braden, S.J.; Timothy B. Brown, S.J.; John L. Brunett, S.J.; Edwin H. Convey, S.J.; Michael D. French, S.J.; C. Kevin Gillespie, S.J.; Teodulo P. Gonzales, S.J.; Edgar Graham, S.J.; Frank R. Haig, S.J.; Gregory C. Hartley, S.J.; Francis G. Hilton, S.J.; Joseph M. Kennedy, S.J.; William K. McGroarty, S.J.; Francis G. McManamin, S.J.; Francis J. Nash, S.J.; Harold E. Ridley, S.J.; Joseph S. Rossi, S.J.; Daniel M. Ruff, S.J.; Peter F. Ryan, S.J.; James F. Salmon, S.J.; Rony Kusnadi; Bro. Claude L. Ory, S.J. Total in Residence 26.

Jesuit Fathers and Brothers Maryland Provincial Curia, 5704 Roland Ave., 21210. Tel: 410-532-1400; Fax: 410-532-1419.
E-mail: marprvsj@vax.loyola.edu
Web site: www.marprovincejesuits.org
Legal Title: *Corporation of the Roman Catholic Clergymen*. Very Rev. James R. Stormes, S.J.; Revs. J. Donald Freeze, Supr. & Treas.; James J. Ditillo, S.J., Min.; Thomas P. Gaunt, S.J., Asst. for Formation and Studies; David G. Allen, S.J.; William A. Dawson, S.J.; James H. Donahoe, S.J.; James M. English, S.J.; Francis P. Ernst, S.J.; Hugh A. Kennedy, S.J., Asst. Sec.; Liborio J. LaMartina, S.J., Res. Archivist; William F. Lamm, S.J., Asst. Treas. & Asst. Sec.; Joseph R. Lerch, S.J.; Joseph E. Lingan, S.J., Exec. Sec.; Thomas P. Martin, S.J., Asst. Treas.; Francis X. Metzbower, S.J.; Bradley Murray, S.J.; Clement J. Petrik, S.J., Asst. for Pastoral Ministries. Total in Residence 15. Military Chaplains: Revs. E. Paul Betowski, S.J., White Sands Missile Range, NM. Tel: 505-678-2740; Paul J. Shaughnessy, S.J., Naval Station Pearl Harbor, 850 Ticonderoga St., Ste. 100, Pearl Harbor, HI 96860-5102. Tel: 808-473-3971.

Priests of the Province Serving Abroad: Rev. Michael J. Kuchera, S.J., Pont. Ist Orientale, Piazza S. Maria Maggiore 7, Rome, Italy, 00185. Tel: 011-39-06-446-5589; Fax: 011-39-06-446-5576. Rev. Philip J. Rosato, S.J., Pont. Univ. Greg., Piazza della Pilotta 4, Rome, Italy, 00187. Tel: 011-39-06-6701-5353; Fax: 011-39-06-6701-5413. Rev. J. Allan Loftus, S.J., 15 St. Mary St., Toronto, Canada, M4Y 2R5. Tel: 416-922-5474; Fax: 416-922-2898. Rev. Vincent J. Capuano, S.J., Parroq. San Jose Obrero, Juan Larrea 1161, Barrio San Jose, Salta, Argentina, 4400. Tel: 011-54-387-423-5519. Rev. Jeffrey G.L. Chang, S.J., c/o Bank of the Orient, 25 Xing, Huli Industrial District, Xiamen, Fujian, China, 361006. Tel: 011-86-592-203-9322; Fax: 011-86-592-225614 (bank). Rev. John J. O'Donnell, S.J., 56 Bentinck St., Kelvingrove, Glasgow, Scotland, G3 7TT. Tel: 011-44-141-339-9406. Rev. Jerome M. Hall, S.J., Pont Univ. Greg, Piazza della Pilotta 4,

Rome, Italy, 00187. Tel: 011-39-06-6701-5367; Fax: 011-39-06-6701-5413. Rev. John T. Kelly, S.J., Kolleg St. Georgen, Offenbacher Landstrasse 224, Frankfurt, Germany, D-60599. Tel: 011-49-69-6061-391; Fax: 011-49-69-6061-330. Rev. Thomas M. McCoog, S.J., Jesuit Historical Institute, C.P. 6139, Rome Prati, Italy, 00195. Tel: 011-39-06-689-77695; Fax: 011-39-06-686-8214. Rev. Donald M. Ward, S.J., Airport parish, P.O. Box 1079, Dodoma, Tanzania. Tel: 011-255-61-302-813; Fax: 011-255-61-24-515. Rev. Francis M. O'Connor, S.J., P.O. Box 854, Benin City, Edo State, Nigeria. Tel: 011-234-52-253926; Fax: 011-234-52-253926. Rev. Thomas E. Roach, S.J., Liceum Jezuitow, ul. Tatrzanska 35, Gdynia, Poland, 81-313. Tel: 011-48-58-620-6909; Fax: 011-48-58-621-0350. Rev. Robert D. Wiesenbaugh, S.J., Comunidad Arnoldo Gutierrez, Calle Venezuela 68, Casilla 227, Potosi, Bolivia. Tel: 011-591-62-42737; Fax: 011-591-62-42737. Rev. Eugene J. Barber, S.J., Resid. S. Pedro Claver, Casilla 452, Arica, Chile. Tel: 011-56-58-22-9402; Fax: 011-56-58-22-9402. Rev. John K. Bingham, S.J., Kirey Hotel, 105 Beijing East Rd., Lhasa, Tibet, China, 850000. Tel: 011-86-891-633-4133. Rev. William J. Currie, S.J., SJ House, Kioicho 7-1, Chiyoda-ku, Tokyo (102), Japan. Tel: 011-81-3-3238-5182; Fax: 011-81-3-3238-5056. Rev. Edgar J. Debany, S.J., P.O. Box 341, Surulere, Lagos, Nigeria. Tel: 011-234-1-526517. Rev. James M. Desjardins, S.J., P.O. Box "Inigo", 630051 Novosibirsk, Russia. Tel: 011-7-3832-77-2013; Fax: 011-7-3832-77-2013. Rev. Edward C.A. Dougherty, S.J., Jesuit House of Studies, 4 Baron Rd., Merrivale, Natal 3291, Republic of South Af. Tel: 011-27-332-306274; Fax: 011-27-332-307929. Rev. John F. Guidera, S.J., DWSC, Post Box 47, Dhanbad, Bihar, India, 326-001; Fax: 011-91-326-203214. Rev. George A. Hess, S.J., Xavier Institute of Management, Bhubaneswar 751 013, India. Tel: 011-91-674-441571; Fax: 011-91-674-440995. Rev. F. Scott Howell, S.J., SJ House, Kioicho 7-1, Chiyoda-ku, Tokyo (102), Japan. Tel: 011-81-3-3238-5196; Fax: 011-81-3-3238-5056. Rev. Gerard S. Barry, S.J., SJ House, Kioicho 7-1, Chiyoda-ku, Tokyo (102), Japan. Tel: 011-81-3-3238-5027; Fax: 011-81-3-3238-5056. Rev. Edward J. Brady, S.J., Loyola House, P.O. Box 21399, Nairobi, Kenya. Tel: 011-254-2-570436; Fax: 011-254-2-566873. Rev. Robert F. Currie, S.J., Apartado A-90, Managua 11, Nicaragua. Tel: 011-505-278-4108. Rev. Angelo D'Agostino, S.J., Loyola House, Box 21399, Nairobi, Kenya. Tel: 011-254-2-716829; Fax: 011-254-2-718711. Rev. John J. Deeney, S.J., Claver Bhavan, Amda PO, West Singbhum Dt. 833 101, India. Tel: 011-91-6583-4314. Rev. Carl L. Dincher, S.J., Jesu Bhavan, Old Purulia Rd., Mango, Jamshedpur, 831 012 Bihar, India. Tel: 011-91-657-460340. Rev. Thomas M. Gavin, S.J., Casa Ejercicios, Casilla 1, Padre Hurtado, Chile. Tel: 011-56-2-811-1241; Fax: 011-56-2-811-1123. Rev. Robert E. Hamm, S.J., P.O. Box 854, Benin City, Edo State, Nigeria. Tel: 011-234-52-245610. Rev. John F. Henry, S.J., Resid. S. Pedro Claver, Casilla 452, Arica, Chile. Tel: 011-56-58-22-9402; Fax: 011-56-58-22-9402. Rev. Richard A. Kenna, S.J., Loyola Hall, PB 153, Jamshedpur, Bihar 831 001, India. Tel: 011-91-657-231842. Rev. Sigmund J. Laschenski, S.J., Saeng Tham Coll., 20 Moo 6, Tha Kham, Nakorn Pathom, Thailand, 73110. Tel: 011-662-429-0820; Fax: 011-662-429-0100. Rev. Edward H. Nash, S.J., St. Xavier's High School, P B 10, Lupungutu, Chaibasa 833 201, India, 833 201. Tel: 011-91-6582-52513. Rev. George W. Quickley, S.J., P.O. Box 854, Benin City, Edo State, Nigeria. Tel: 011-234-52-253926; Fax: 011-234-52-253926. Rev. Eugene M. Rooney, S.J., San Ignacio, Casilla 597, Santiago, Chile. Tel: 011-56-2-695-5014; Fax: 011-56-2-672-2117. Rev. Dominic J. Totaro, S.J., P.O. Box 854, Benin City, Edo State, Nigeria. Tel: 011-234-52-245610. Rev. Charles E. Wolf, S.J., P.O. Box 257, U.P. Post Off., 1144 Quezon City, PI, 1099. Tel: 011-63-2-426-6430; Fax: 011-63-2-426-5967. Rev. Edward H. McGrath, S.J., Human Life Centre, Vivekananda Marg, Balasore 756 001, India. Tel: 011-91-6782-65627; Fax: 011-91-6782-62056. Rev. John J. Nissel, S.J., Immaculate Heart College, Tbso 4-22-1, Kagoshima, Japan, 890-0081. Tel: 011-81-992-57-5220; Fax: 011-81-992-54-5247. Rev. Eugene A. Welch, S.J., Loyola Hall, P B 153, Jamshedpur, Bihar 831 001, India. Tel: 011-91-657-231842.

Priests of the Province Serving Elsewhere: Rev. Patrick T. Brannan, S.J., Sacred Heart Seminary, 2701 Chicago Blvd., Detroit, MI, 48206. Tel: 313-883-8500. Rev. Thomas J. Brennan, S.J., Bea House, 176 Commonwealth Ave., Chestnut Hill, MA, 02167. Rev. Stephen W. Planning, S.J., Miguel Pro Jesuit Community, 1611 S. Allport St., Chicago, IL, 60608-2131. Tel: 312-738-1812; Fax: 312-226-2915. Rev. Paul A. Donovan, S.J., 3681 Ashford St., San Diego, CA, 92111-4312. Tel: 858-715-8115. Rev. Bernard J. Dooley, S.J., 302-A Sea Oats Dr., Juno Beach, FL, 33408. Tel: 407-775-3810; Fax: 407-622-6471. Rev. Bernard G. Filmyer, S.J., 9784 Guisante Ter., San Diego, CA, 92124. Tel: 619-278-1027. Rev. Gerard J. McGlone, S.J., 1607 Cable St., San Diego, CA, 92107-3313. Tel: 619-224-2868; Fax: 619-222-6324. Rev. Joseph C. Sands, S.J., 66 Witherspoon St., #110, Princeton, NJ, 08542. Tel: 609-514-1631. Rev. Willy DeCraemer, S.J., Park Towne W. 1808, 2200 Benjamin Franklin Pkwy., Philadelphia, PA, 19130. Tel: 215-567-0284. Rev. James N. Gelson, S.J., St. Lucy Church, Highland Beach, 33487-3326. Tel: 561-272-4409; Fax: 561-278-8509. Rev. Leigh A. Fuller, S.J., St. Mary's Hospital, 2900 First Ave., Huntington, WV, 25702. Tel: 304-526-1342. Rev. Joseph F. Monaghan, S.J., St. Joseph's Hospital, 1600 W. Girard Ave., Philadelphia, PA, 19130. Tel: 215-787-9013. Rev. A. Richard Sotelo, S.J., P.O. Box 972141, El Paso, TX, 79997-2141. Tel: 915-541-9076. Rev. David L. Ungerleider, S.J., P.O. Box 434648, San Ysidro, CA, 92143-4648. Tel: 526-680-1825.

On Leave: Revs. Daniel S. Cutrara, S.J.; Daniel C. Doherty, S.J.; Michael A. McElwee, S.J.

Marianist Community, 738 S. Beechfield Ave., 21229. Tel: 410-242-5159.
E-mail: cjjsm@netzero.net
Bros. Stephen Glodek, S.M.; Charles J. Johnson, S.M., Dir.; Francis P. Mullan, S.M.; Steven O'Neil, S.M.; Norbert Sturm, S.M. Brothers 5; Total in Residence 5; Total Staff 5.

Pallottine Center for Apostolic Causes, 512 W. Saratoga St., 21201. Tel: 410-685-3063; Fax: 410-234-1459. Promotional Center for St. Jude Shrine. Legal Title: *St. Jude Shrine-Pallottine Missions; Pallottine Center for Apostolic Causes, Inc.* Peter T. Sticco, S.A.C., Dir.

St. Charles Villa, 603 Maiden Choice Ln., 21228. Tel: 410-747-1211; Fax: 410-747-2460.
E-mail: wtokss@aol.com
Home for Retired Sulpicians supervised by the Little Sisters of the Poor. Revs. William T. O'Keeffe, S.S. (CLV), Dir. & Supr.; Raymond F. Hesler, S.S. (ALB), Assoc. Dir.; Lawrence A. Bender, S.S. (WDC); John W. Bowen, S.S. (BAL); James H. Brennan, S.S. (BAL); Charles P. Dillon, S.S. (TOL); Claude H. Dukehart, S.S. (BAL); James J. Healy, S.S. (MAN); William J. Lee, S.S. (CLV); John F. Mattingly, S.S. (BAL); Vincent deP. McMurry, S.S. (NSH); William S. Morris, S.S. (NY); John H. Oliver, S.S. (MAR); John A. Ward, S.S. (DET); J. Paul Welch, S.S. (SEA); Joseph L. White, S.S. (BAL). Priests 16; Total Staff 10.

St. Joseph Society of the Sacred Heart House of Central Administration, 1130 N. Calvert St., 21202. Tel: 410-727-3386; Fax: 410-727-1006.
E-mail: josephite1@aol.com
Web site: www.josephite.com
Very Revs. Robert M. Kearns, S.S.J., Supr. Gen.; Edward J. Chiffriller, S.S.J., Vicar Gen.; Joseph C. Verrett, S.S.J., Consultor Gen.; Nelson A. Moreira, S.S.J., Treas. & Rector; Revs. Peter E. Hogan, S.S.J., Archivist; Peter J. Kenney, S.S.J., Historian and Asst. Rector; Joseph L. Waters, S.S.J., Historian; Eugene P. McManus, S.S.J., Dir. Public Rels.; Earle A. Newman, S.S.J.; Joseph C. Verrett, S.S.J., Editor, The Josephite Harvest & Dir. Mission Office; John F. Byrne, S.S.J., Asst. to Admin.; Raymond A. Woodka, S.S.J., Asst. to Admin.; Armand J. Manuel, S.S.J., Asst. to Admin.; Mrs. Bernice Jones, Asst. Archivist. Priests 15. Retired: Revs. John J. Conlon, S.S.J.; N. Wilfrid DesRosiers, S.S.J.; Dominic A. Marchese, S.S.J.; Ralph R. Ransom, S.S.J.; Joseph R. Murphy, S.S.J.; Paul A. Ortner, S.S.J.; William A. Richardson, S.S.J.; Joseph J. Rimshaw, S.S.J.; W. Dayton Salisbury, S.S.J.; Louis R. Saporito, S.S.J.; James P. Schappert, S.S.J.

St. Joseph's Manor. (Josephite Fathers and Brothers), 911 W. Lake Ave., 21210. Tel: 410-323-3829. Very Revs. Edward J. Mullowney, S.S.J., Rector; Matthew J. O'Rourke, S.S.J., Vice Rector; Revs. John C. Crotty, S.S.J.; Daniel H. Cassidy, S.S.J.; Rupert A. MacDonald, S.S.J.; Eugene J. McKenna, S.S.J.; Robert J. O'Connell, S.S.J.; John J. Rawlins, S.S.J.; Joseph Calamari, S.S.J.; Bros. Andrew Hogya, S.S.J.; Peter J. McLaughlin, S.S.J.; Charles Douglas, S.S.J. Priests 9; Brothers 3.

St. Joseph's Passionist Community, 251 S. Morley St., 21229. Tel: 410-566-3750; Fax: 410-233-4974. Congregation of the Most Holy Cross and Passion of Our Lord Jesus Christ. Revs. Basil Stockmeyer, C.P.; Alban Harmon, F.N., C.P.; Eustace McDonald, C.P.; William Murphy, C.P.; Simon Wood, C.P. Priests 5.

Society of Mary (Marianists). (Province of New York), Marianist Provincial House, 4301 Roland Ave., 21210-2793. Tel: 410-366-1300; Fax: 410-889-5743. Revs. George J. Cerniglia, S.M., Asst. Prov.; Robert J. Backherms, S.M.; Bros. Stephen Glodek, S.M., Prov.; Howard L. Hughes, S.M.; Frank O'Donnell, S.M. In res. Rev. Robert Nugent, S.D.S.; Bros. Mark Anokwuru, F.M.S.; Brendan Geary, F.M.S.; Nee Wayoe, C.S.C. Priests 3; Brothers 6; Total in Residence 9; Total in Province 76.

Sulpician Provincial House. (Associated Sulpicians of the United States), 5408 Roland Ave., 21210. Tel: 410-323-5070; Fax: 410-433-6524.
E-mail: RWitherup@sulpicians.org
Web site: sulpicians.org
Very Rev. Ronald D. Witherup, S.S., U.S. Prov. of the Society of St. Sulpice; Revs. Thomas R. Ulshafer, S.S., Prov. Sec. & Dir. Discernment & Admissions; Gerald D. McBrearity, S.S., Dir. Formation; Charles J.T. Talar, S.S., Prov. Treas.; Mr. Joseph M. Reynolds, Exec. Asst. to Prov.; Laura Tester, Finance Dir. & Business Mgr.
Members and Candidates on Individual Assignments: Rev. Joseph J. Bonadio, S.S., St. Francis of Assisi Church, 3615 Harford Rd., 21218-3196. Tel: 410-235-5136. Revs. Patrick Simutowe; Cornelius Hankomoone, Emmaus Spirituality Center, P.O. Box 320084 Woodlands, Lusaka, Zambia, 157101. Tel: 011-260-126-3354; Fax: 011-260-126-3404. Rev. Vincent D. Bui, S.S., Catholic University of America, c/o Theological College, 401 Michigan Ave, N.E., Washington, D.C., 20064. Tel: 202-756-4923; Fax: 202-756-4909. Rev. Jeremiah P. Farrell, S.S., Santa Clara University, c/o St. Anthony's, 20101 McKean Rd., San Jose, CA, 95120. Tel: 408-997-4800; Fax: 408-997-4801. Rev. William E. Hartgen, S.S., 634 E. St., N.E., Washington, DC, 20002. Tel: 202-543-1075. Rev. Joseph C. Martin, S.S., 4006 York Dr., Havre De Grace, 21078-2100. Tel: 410-273-6600; Fax: 410-272-5617. Rev. Robert P. Waznak, S.S., 5 Buttercharm Ct., Silver Spring, 20905-5738. Tel: 202-541-5259; Fax: 202-541-5244. Rev. John J. Kselman, S.S., 7 Kirkland Rd., Cambridge, MA, 02138-3012. Tel: 617-492-1960. Rev. Addison G. Wright, S.S., 24 Killian Ave., Trumbull, CT, 06611-4118. Tel: 203-268-3610. Rev. Thomas Doyle, S.S., 1248 Brentwood Pointe, Brentwood, TN, 37027-2945. Tel: 615-377-3009. Rev. Thomas R. Hurst, S.S., St. Dominic's Major Seminary, P.O. Box 320-191 Woodlands, Lusaka, Zambia, Central Africa, 157101. Tel: 011-260-126-4997; Fax: 011-260-126-1482. Rev. Cale J. Crowley, S.S., St. Augustine's Major Seminary, P.O. Box 81011, Kabwe, Zambia, Central Africa, 157101. Rev. John L. Bitterman, S.S., Rector, Emmaus Spirituality Center, P.O. Box 32-0084, Woodlands, Lusaka, Zambia, Central Africa, 157101. Tel: 011-260-126-3354; Fax: 011-260-126-3404. Rev. Gerald V. Lardner, S.S., Emmaus Spirituality Center, P.O. Box 32-0084, Woodlands, Lusaka, Zambia, Central Africa, 157101. Tel: 011-260-126-3354; Fax: 011-260-126-3404. Rev. David Mellott, S.S., Studies, 800 Peachtree St., Apt. 8331, Atlanta, GA, 30308. Tel: 404-875-7397; Fax: 404-815-0985.

Xaverian Brothers Generalate, 4409 Frederick Ave., 21229. Tel: 410-644-0034; Fax: 410-644-2762.
E-mail: mburke@xavbros.msjnet.edu
Web site: www.angelfire.com/ma/xb
Bros. Matthew Burke, C.F.X., Supr. Gen.; Cornelius Hubbuch, C.F.X., Vicar Gen.; Lawrence Harvey, C.F.X., Dir. Xaverian Sponsored Schools; John Fox, C.F.X., Assoc. Xaverian Sponsored Schools; Richard Mazza, C.F.X., Dir. Pastoral Care; Thomas Morrissey, C.F.X., Dir. Development; Alice Hession, Dir. Staff Formation, Xaverian Sponsored Schools; Michael Naccarato, Chief Financial Officer.
Legal Titles and Schools Sponsored: Xaverian Brothers USA, Inc.;(f/k/a The American Central Province of the Xaverian Brothers Inc., The American Northeast Province of the Xaverian Brother, Inc., and the Working Boys Home, Inc.); St. Mary's-Ryken High School, Inc.; Our Lady of Good Counsel High School, Inc.; St. Xavier High School, Inc.; Xaverian High School, Inc.; Holy Family High School, Inc.; Mt. St. Joseph High School, Inc.; Xaverian Brothers Auxiliary; St. Michael's High School Alumni Association; Nazareth Regional High School, Inc.; St. John's Preparatory School, Inc.; St. John's High School, Inc.; Xaverian Brothers High School, Inc.; Malden Catholic High School, Inc.; Xavier High School, Inc.; Isidore Charitable Trust. Brothers 255.

ADAMSTOWN. *Christian Brothers Provincialate*, P.O. Box 29, 21710. Tel: 301-874-5188; Fax: 301-847-5674.
E-mail: fscl845@ix.netcom.com
Web site: delasallebrothers.org
Legal Title: *Christian Brothers of Frederick, Inc.* Brothers of the Christians Schools, Baltimore Province. Bros. Benedict Oliver, F.S.C., Prov.; Timothy J. Froehlich, F.S.C., Dir. Finance; Kevin M. Dalmasse, F.S.C., Asst. Prov. Brothers 3; Total 187; Total Staff 4.

ANNAPOLIS. *Saint Mary Rectory*, 109 Duke of Gloucester St., 21401. Tel: 410-263-2397;269-6092; Fax: 410-263-3027.
Web site: www.stmaryschurch.org

Residence of the Redemptorist Fathers and Brothers. Very Rev. Denis Sweeney, C.SS.R.; Revs. Theodore Heyburn, C.SS.R.; John Lavin, C.SS.R.; Edward Lynch, C.SS.R.; John Sodomora, C.SS.R.; John G. Tizio, C.SS.R.; Sr. M. Mark Tippett, S.S.N.D., Pastoral Assoc.; Deacons J. Larry Wilson; Leroy Moore; Anthony F. Norcio. In res. Revs. Bernard Baumgartner, C.SS.R.; Francis X. Murphy, C.SS.R.; Joseph Oppitz, C.SS.R. Total in Residence 11.

CUMBERLAND. *SS. Peter and Paul Friary*, 109 N. Smallwood St., 21502. Tel: 301-777-3131; 301-777-3137; Fax: 301-759-3568.
E-mail: ppaul@archbalt.org
Legal Title: *Province of St. Augustine of the Capuchin Order*. Revs. Vernon Busch, O.F.M.Cap., Guardian & Assoc. Pastor; Jerome Dunn, O.F.M.Cap.; Marvin Justi, O.F.M.Cap., Pastor, St. Ambrose, Cresaptown. Priests 4.

ELLICOTT CITY. *Friary of St. Joseph Cupertino*, 12290 Folly Quarter Rd., 21042. Tel: 410-531-2800; Fax: 410-531-2801. Companions of St. Anthony. Tel: 410-988-9833; Fax: 410-988-9705. Secular Franciscans. Tel: 410-531-9136. Conventual Franciscan Friars. Revs. Gregory Moore, O.F.M.Conv., Guardian; Bart Karwacki, O.F.M.Conv.; Rick Deptula, O.F.M.Conv.; Jude Winkler, O.F.M.Conv.; Romuald Meograssi, O.F.M.Conv.; Francis Lombardo, O.F.M.Conv.; Bro. Thaddeus Grzankowski, O.F.M.Conv.

Order of Friars Minor Conventual, 12300 Folly Quarter Rd., 21042-1419. Tel: 410-531-9200; Fax: 410-531-4881.
E-mail: saprovsec@aol.com
Very Revs. Mark L. Curesky, O.F.M.Conv., Min. Prov.; Gregory Moore, O.F.M.Conv., Vicar Prov.; Revs. Robert Twele, O.F.M.Conv., Sec. & Treas.; Martin Kobos, O.F.M.Conv., Dir. Devel. (Franciscan Devel. Office); Bro. Brian Newbigging, O.F.M.Conv.
On Assignment Outside the U.S.A.: Very Rev. Joachin Giermek, O.F.M.Conv., Asst. General; Rev. Matteo Luo, O.F.M.Conv., Curia Generale dei Frati Minori Conventualli, Piazza Ss. Apostoli 51, Rome, Italy, 00187. Tel: 011-39-06-699-571; Fax: 011-39-06-699-57321. Bro. Daniel Geary, O.F.M.Conv., Piazza Inferiore di S Francesco, 06082 Assisi Santuario (PG), Assisi, Italy. Tel: 011-36-075-819-001; Fax: 011-39-075-819-0035. Rev. Donald Kos, O.F.M.Conv., Convento S. Antonio Baccelli, 56, Via del Serafico, 1, Rome, Italy, 00153. Tel: 011-39-06-572-993-41; Fax: 011-39-06-572-993-42. Rev. Bernard Przewozny, O.F.M.Conv., Seraphicum, Via del Serafico, 1, Rome, Italy, 00142. Tel: 011-39-06-5192-007; Fax: 011-39-06-5192-067. Rev. David Blowey, O.F.M.Conv., P.O. Box 24177, Nairobi, Kenya. Tel: 011-254-2-884481; Fax: 011-254-2-88420. Rev. Timothy Dore, O.F.M.Conv., Convento San Francisco, Apartado 358 (Moravia), San Jose, Costa Rica. Tel: 011-506-235-9021; Fax: 011-506-240-9672. Rev. Jerome Lukaszewski, O.F.M.Conv., St. Mary's Catholic Church, 16-8 Furuta-cho, Naze-shi 894, Japan. Tel: 011-81-997-520-061; Fax: 011-81-992-520-309. Rev. Ronald Roll, O.F.M.Conv., Parroquia Santa Ana Central America, Campamento, Olancho, Honduras. Rev. Vincent Lachendro, O.F.M.Conv., San Augustin Parish/Village Metro Manila, Novaliches Post Office, P.O. Box 186, Paranaque, Phillipines. Rev. Dominic Slemba, O.F.M.Conv., St. Francis of Assisi Friary West Africa, P.O. Box 238, Saltpond, Ghana. Tel: 011-233-42-34555. Rev. Giles Zakowicz, O.F.M.Conv., St. Francis of Assisi Friary West Africa, P.O. Box 238, Saltpond, Ghana. Tel: 011-233-42-34555. Rev. Nicholas Swiatek, O.F.M. Conv., St. Mary's Catholic Church, 16-8 Furuta-cho, Naze-shi 894, Japan. Tel: 011-81-997-520-061; Fax: 011-81-997-520-309. Bro. Mitchell Sawicki, O.F.M.Conv., St. Bonaventure Friary, P.O. Box 3, Achimota, Accra, Ghana, West Africa. Tel: 011-233-21-304718; Fax: 011-233-27-540376. Rev. Daniel Pietrzak, O.F.M.Conv., St. Joseph Cupertino Friary, 10 Dimar Ct., Dingley, Victoria, Australia, 3172. Tel: 011-6139-551-7136; Fax: 011-6139-551-7579.
Individual Assignment Within the U.S.A.: Rev. Henry Karwel, O.F.M.Conv., St. Mary's Parish, 60 South St., Ware, MA, 01082-1619. Tel: 413-967-5913; Fax: 413-967-4679. Rev. Thomas Gwozdz, O.F.M.Conv., (Retired), Pope John Paul II Center, 33 Lincoln Ave., Danbury, CT, 06810. Tel: 203-790-9071. Revs. Brad Heckathorne, O.F.M.Conv.; Robert Schlageter, O.F.M.Conv.; Michael Englert, O.F.M.Conv., Catholic University of America, Campus Ministry Office - Calwell Hall, Washington, DC, 20064. Tel: 202-238-1653; Fax: 202-319-4431. Rev. Paul Duzinski, O.F.M.Conv., Sts. Mary and Joseph Home, 4291 Richmond Rd. - #102, Cleveland, OH, 44122-6103. Tel: 216-464-1222, Ext. 138. Rev. Clement Jarnot, O.F.M.Conv., St. Mary of Czetochova Parish, 79 S. Main St., Middletown, CT, 06457-3606. Tel: 860-347-2365; Fax: 860-347-2110. Rev. Michael Zielke, O.F.M.Conv., Western Connecticut State University, Neuman Center, Danbury, CT. Tel: 203-790-9071. Rev. Patrick Rolak, O.F.M.Conv., (Retired), Sacred Heart Home, 4520 Ransom Rd., Clarence, NY, 14031. Rev. Ronald Sermak, O.F.M.Conv., Chaplain's Office, 5286 South Park Ave., Hamburg, NY, 14075-1596. Tel: 716-649-1205; Fax: 716-646-0971. Rev. John Bambol, O.F.M.Conv., (Retired), Mater Dolorosa Friary, 71 Maple St., Holyoke, MA, 01040-4698. Tel: 413-798-2933; Fax: 413-538-6754.
Military Chaplains: Rev. Blase Wegierski, O.F.M.Conv., U.S.S. Nimitz, Newport News, VA, Res., 507 Wrought Iron Bend, Yorktown, VA, 23693. Tel: 757-688-4381; Fax: 757-865-6195. Total in Residence 185.

St. Joseph Cupertino Friary, Friars Minor Conventual of St. Francis of Assisi, 12290 Folly Quarter Rd., 21042. Tel: 410-531-2800; Fax: 410-531-2801. Corporate Title: Franciscan Fathers Minor Conventuals of MD, Inc. Secular Franciscans. Tel: 410-531-9136. Revs. Gregory Moore, O.F.M.Conv., Guardian & Vicar Prov.; Bart Karwacki, O.F.M.Conv., Spiritual Asst. for Secular Franciscan Order; Rick Deptula, O.F.M.Conv.; Francis Lombardo, O.F.M.Conv.; Romuald Meograssi, O.F.M.Conv.; Jude Winkler, O.F.M.Conv.; Bro. Thaddeus Grzankowski, O.F.M.Conv.

EMMITSBURG. *Vincentian House*, P.O. Box 376, 21727. Tel: 301-447-2326; Fax: 301-447-3579. Revs. James O. Kiernan, C.M., Pastor, Supr.; Michael J. Kennedy, C.M., Chap.; William P. Goff, C.M.; Louis B. Storms, C.M.; Walter J. Menig, C.M., Chap.; Stephen P. Trzecieski, C.M., Assoc. Pastor, Asst. Supr. Priests 6.

[T] CONVENTS AND RESIDENCES FOR SISTERS

BALTIMORE. *Carmelite Communities Assoc.*, 1318 Dulaney Valley Rd., 21286-1399. Tel: 410-823-7415.

Carmelite Sisters of Baltimore, 1318 Dulaney Valley Rd., 21286-1399. Tel: 410-823-7415; Fax: 410-823-7418.
E-mail: carmelit@erols.com
Web site: www.geocities.com/baltimorecarmel
Discalced Carmelite Nuns. Sr. Colette Ackerman, Prioress. Professed Sisters 14; Novices 2.

Chesapeake Province of the Sisters of Notre Dame de Namur, Provincial Offices, 305 Cable St., 21210-2511. Tel: 410-243-1993; Fax: 410-243-2279.
E-mail: chesprv@aol.com
Web site: www.sndden.org
Legal Title: *Chesapeake Province of the Sisters of Notre Dame de Namur, Inc.*
Administrative Team: Sr. Margaret Shawn Scanlan, S.N.D.deN.; Sr. Louann Sciubba, S.N.D.deN. Sisters in Province 79; Sisters in Baltimore Diocese 33.

Daughters of Charity, 900 Caton Ave., 21229. Tel: 410-368-2104; Fax: 410-368-2109. Sr. Ellen Eisenberger, Sister Servant. Total in Residence 11.

Franciscan Sisters of Baltimore-General Motherhouse and Novitiate, 3725 Ellerslie Ave., 21218. Tel: 410-235-0139; Fax: 410-243-2569.
E-mail: srmtwhite@aol.com
Legal Titles: *Franciscan Sisters of Baltimore City.*; *Declaration of Trust of the Franciscan Sisters of Baltimore, Inc.* Sr. Mary Therese White, O.S.F., Gen. Supr.; Rev. Gerald West, Chap. Sisters 44.

Little Sisters of Jesus-Regional Residence, 400 N. Streeper St., 21224-1230. Tel: 410-327-7863.
E-mail: littlesisters@juno.com
Sr. Anne-Marie Boucher, Rgnl. Supr. Sisters 3.

Little Sisters of the Poor-Provincial Residence, 601 Maiden Choice Ln., 21228-3698. Tel: 410-744-9367; Fax: 410-747-0601. Sr. Mary Bernard Du St. Esprit, L.S.P., Prov.; Sr. Patricia Mary Metzgar, L.S.P., Supr. Sisters 22; Total Assisted 104; Total Staff 133.

Maria Health Care Center, Inc., 6401 N. Charles St., 21212. Tel: 410-377-3011; Fax: 410-377-6042. Sr. Grace Sciamanna, S.S.N.D., Admin. Health Center for School Sisters of Notre Dame.

Mission Helper Center, 1001 W. Joppa Rd., 21204-3787. Tel: 410-823-8585; Fax: 410-825-6355.
E-mail: csbmhsh@aol.com
Sr. M. Judith Waldt, Pres.; Sr. Patricia McCulloch, Treas.; Sr. Natalie DeLuca, Asst.; Sr. Mary Louise Zaworski, Mgr. Sisters 25; Sisters in Diocese 51; Total Staff 9.

Mission Helpers of the Sacred Heart-Our Lady of Pompei Convent, 225 S. Conkling St., 21224. Tel: 410-675-6034.
E-mail: mdjaxon1@juno.com
Sisters 2.

Missionaries of Charity, Gift of Hope Convent, 818 N. Collington Ave., 21205. Tel: 410-732-6056. Sr. M. Lumen, M.C., Supr. Sisters 4; Total Assisted 300; Total Staff 5.

Our Lady of Mt. Providence Convent-Motherhouse, 701 Gun Rd., 21227. Tel: 410-242-8500; Fax: 410-242-4963. Sr. Mary Clarice, Proctor, Motherhouse; Sr. Mary Crescentia, Proctor, Motherhouse; Sr. Rita Michelle, Proctor, Convent. Oblate Sisters of Providence. Sisters in the Motherhouse 68; Sisters in the Diocese 77; Total in Residence 104; Total Assisted 60; Total Staff 39.
Attended by Sulpician Fathers and Josephite Fathers.

The School Sisters of Notre Dame in the City of Baltimore (Baltimore Prov.), 6401 N. Charles St., 21212. Tel: 410-377-7774; Fax: 410-377-5363.
E-mail: jamohan@aol.com
Web site: www.ssnd.org
Sr. Jane Burke, S.S.N.D., Prov. Leader; Rev. David M. Carey, Chap. Sisters 104; Sisters in Province 389; Sisters in Diocese 287.

Sisters of Mercy, Mercy Center, 1322 E. Northern Pkwy., 21239-1998. Tel: 410-435-4400; Fax: 410-433-8868.
E-mail: som@qis.net
Web site: www.mercysistersbalt.com
Sisters of Mercy of the Americas, Baltimore Regional Community. Sr. Barbara Wheeley, R.S.M., Pres. Sisters in Community 219; Sisters in Diocese 115.

Sisters of St. Francis of Philadelphia.
Web site: www.osfphila.org
Congregational Office - Our Lady of Angels Convent, 609 S. Convent Rd., Aston, PA, 19014. Tel: 610-459-4125; Fax: 610-459-0195.
Web site: www.osfphila.org
Convents in the Diocese: Shrine of the Little Flower Convent, 2851 Kentucky Ave., 21213. Tel: 410-483-3484. Our Lady of Mt. Carmel Convent, 37 Seaford Ave., 21221. Tel: 410-687-5335. St. Clement Convent, 1212 Chesaco Ave., 21237. Tel: 410-687-4433. St. Joseph Medical Center, 7601 Osler Dr., Towson, 21204. Tel: 410-337-1100. St. Stephen Convent, 8020 Bradshaw Rd., P.O. Box 62, Bradshaw, 21021-0062. Tel: 410-592-9433. Immaculate Conception Convent, 112 Ware Ave., Towson, 21204. Tel: 410-823-3470. Bethany House, 2618 Erdman Ave., 21213. Tel: 410-235-4767. St. Joseph Convent, Box 1, Midland, 21542. Tel: 301-463-2248. Franciscan Residence, 18 Treeway Ct., 4-A, Towson, 21286. Tel: 410-825-4189. St. Anthony Convent, 4500 Frankford Ave., 21206. Tel: 410-488-0054. Sisters of St. Francis, 34 Acorn Cir. #202, 21286. Tel: 410-832-1858. Sisters of St. Francis, 806D Cinnamon Ridge Pl., Cockeysville, 21030. Tel: 410-683-1427. Sisters of St. Francis, 3020-D Autumn Branch Ln., Ellicott City, 21043. Tel: 410-418-8823. Sisters of St. Francis, 11 Peroba Ct., 21234. Tel: 410-882-3212. Sisters of St. Francis, 3303 Northway Dr., 21234. Tel: 410-426-0085. Sisters of St. Francis, John Carroll Faculty House, 701 Churchville Rd., Bel Air, 21014. Tel: 410-838-8610. Sisters of St. Francis, 303 Commerce St., Apt. 2, Havre de Grace, 21078. Tel: 410-942-0841. Genesis House, 9 Skidmore Ct., Towson, 21204. Tel: 410-296-8071. Total in Residence 82.

Sisters of the Good Shepherd, 4100 Maple Ave., 21227-4099. Tel: 410-247-2770; Fax: 410-242-5890.
E-mail: mcatheri@goodshepherdcenter.org
Sr. Mary Catherine Massei, R.G.S., Supr. Sisters 16; Total Staff 2.

Sisters of the Good Shepherd-St. Joseph Residence, 4130 Maple Ave., 21227-4099. Tel: 410-247-3898; 247-2770, Ext. 232; Fax: 410-242-5890. Infirmary and Retirement Center for Washington Province. Sisters 15; Total Staff 30.

Sisters Servants of Mary Immaculate, Inc. Convent and Novitiate. 1220 Tugwell Dr., 21228. Tel: 410-747-1353; Fax: 410-747-0386. Sr. Bernadetta Kozyra, Prov. Sisters 16.

The Villa, 6806 Bellona Ave., 21212-1299. Tel: 410-377-2450; Fax: 410-377-2501. Suzanne L. Carson, Admin. Convent for Retired Sisters of Mercy and Mission Helpers of the Sacred Heart. Legal Title: *Joint Retirement Convent, Inc.-The Villa.* Sisters 70; Total Staff 60.

EMMITSBURG. *Daughters of Charity of St. Vincent de Paul, Emmitsburg Province*, 21727. Tel: 301-447-3121; Fax: 301-447-6038.
Web site: www.setonhs.org/Eburg/eburg.htm
(St. Joseph's Provincial House). Legal Title: *Sisters of Charity of St. Joseph's, Emmitsburg, MD.* Sr. Elyse Staab, D.C., Prov. Sisters at Provincial House 42; Sisters in Diocese 158; Sisters in Province 247.

Villa St. Michael-St. Joseph's Provincial House, 333 S. Seton Ave., 21727-9299. Tel: 301-447-3121; Fax: 301-447-7082. Retirement Home of Daughters of Charity of St. Vincent de Paul. Martha Coleman, Admin., Pro-tem. Sisters 45; (D.C.); Sisters 10; (S.N.D.).

FREDERICK. *Visitation Monastery of Frederick, MD*, 200 E. Second St., 21701. Tel: 301-662-3322; Fax: 301-695-8549. Mother Marguerite Therese Leary, V.H.M., Supr. Cloistered Community with Apostolate of Teaching (Grades PreK-8). Sisters 6.

LUTHERVILLE. *Emmanuel Monastery*, 2229 W. Joppa Rd., 21093. Tel: 410-821-5792; Fax: 410-296-9560.
E-mail: emmanuelosb@juno.com
Web site: members.tripod.lycos.com/emmanuelosb
Benedictine Sisters of Baltimore.
Ministering in Education, Pastoral Ministry and

Counseling, Retreats and Spiritual Direction, Social Services, Justice Ministry, Hospital Ministry, and Business Admin. Sisters 16.

MARRIOTTSVILLE. *Sisters of Bon Secours, C.B.S., Provincial House*, 21104. Tel: 410-442-1333; Fax: 410-442-1394.
Web site: www.bonsecours.org
Sr. Anne Marie Mack, Pres. Retired Sisters 9; Total in Residence 42; Total Staff 63.

STEVENSON. *Maryland Province Center*, 1531 Greenspring Valley Rd., 21153. Tel: 410-486-5599; Fax: 410-486-5466.
E-mail: sndmd@aol.com
Web site: www.sndden.org
Maryland Province of the Sisters of Notre Dame de Namur. Legal Titles: *Baltimore Province of the Sisters of Notre Dame de Namur, Inc.*; *Trinity School, Inc.*; *Maryvale Preparatory School, Inc.*; *Academy of Notre Dame de Namur, Inc.*; *Sisters of Notre Dame de Namur, Maryland Province, Charitable Trust*.
Additional Projects Sponsored: Maryland Province Center of Stevenson, MD; Villa Julie at Seven Oaks of Stevenson, MD; Notre Dame Educ. Center, Washington, DC.
Additional Projects Co-Sponsored: The Development Office, a joint project of the Maryland, Chesapeake & Notre Dame Base Communities Provinces; Director: Mr. Gil A. Van Schoor. Sr. Marian Schaechtel, Prov. Moderator; Sr. Jeanne McGlone, Prov. Leadership; Sr. Patricia Loome, Prov. Leadership. Sisters in Province 139; Sisters in Diocese 70; Total Staff 14.

Villa Julie at Seven Oaks (Maryland Province), 1531 Greenspring Valley Rd., 21153. Tel: 410-486-6946; Fax: 410-484-6930.
E-mail: sndvilla@aol.com
Web site: www.sndden.org
Assisted Living Home for Sisters of Notre Dame and Staff Residence. Sisters 25.

St. Catherine Nursing Home, 333 S. Seton Ave., Emmitsburg, 21727-9200. Tel: 301-447-3121. Sisters of Notre Dame 20.

Stella Maris, 2300 Dulaney Valley Rd., Baltimore, 21204. Tel: 410-252-4500. Sisters of Notre Dame 6.

TIMONIUM. *Sisters of the Visitation-Stella Maris Hospice*, 2300 Dulaney Valley Rd., 21093. Tel: 410-252-9598. Legal Title: *Visitation Monasteries, Inc.* Total in Residence 11.

[U] NEWMAN CENTERS

BALTIMORE. *Archdiocesan Office-Newman Center*, 7909 York Rd., 21204. Tel: 410-828-0622; Fax: 410-828-4825.
E-mail: albright@towson.edu
Rev. Robert E. Albright, Archdiocesan Dir. Total in Residence 3; Total Staff 5.

Johns Hopkins University, Newman House, 2941 N. Charles St., 21218. Tel: 410-243-7066; Fax: 410-877-2841. Rev. Charles K. Riepe.

Morgan State University, St. Matthew Church, 5401 Loch Raven Blvd., 21239. Tel: 410-433-2300.

Towson University, Newman Center, 7909 York Rd., 21204. Tel: 410-828-0622; Fax: 410-828-4825. Rev. Robert E. Albright, Dir.

University of Maryland-Baltimore County, 5401 Wilkens Ave., 21228. Tel: 410-828-0622; Fax: 410-828-4825.

Hood College, St. John Church, Rosemont Ave., Frederick, 21701. Tel: 301-662-8288; 410-828-0622; Fax: 410-828-4825.

Frostburg State University, Osborne Center, 130 S. Broadway, Frostburg, 21532. Tel: 301-689-5041; Fax: 301-689-8910. Rev. Edward S. Hendricks.

Western Maryland College. Contact St. John Church, Westminster, 21157. Tel: 410-848-4744. Tel: 410-876-2248.

[V] FOUNDATIONS, FUNDS AND TRUSTS

BALTIMORE. *Archdiocesan Priests Post-Retirement Benefits Plan Trust Fund*, 320 Cathedral St., 21201. Tel: 410-547-5317; Fax: 410-783-5993.
E-mail: pphelps@archbalt.org
Petra R. Phelps, Contact Person.

Baltimore Mercy Health Foundation, Inc., 301 St. Paul Pl., 21201. Thomas R. Mullen, Dir.

Bon Secours Baltimore Health Corp., Inc., 2000 W. Baltimore St., 21223. Tel: 410-362-3000.

Bon Secours Housing, Inc.

Bon Secours Housing II, Inc.

Bon Secours Facilities, Inc.

Bon Secours of Maryland Foundation, Inc.

Unity Properties, Inc.

The Urban Medical Institute Foundation, Inc.

The Catholic Family Foundation of the Archdiocese of Baltimore, Inc., 320 Cathedral St., 21201. Tel: 410-547-5381. Thomas Sonni, Contact Person.

Chancery Office. For further information and additional listings, please see Associated Catholic Charities Section. 320 Cathedral St., 21201. Tel: 410-547-5444; Fax: 410-727-8234.

Archbishop of Baltimore Annual Appeal Trust. Tel: 410-547-5439; Fax: 410-727-8234.

Archdiocesan Health Plan Trust Fund Agreement. Tel: 410-547-5317; Fax: 410-783-5993.

Archdiocesan General Insurance Program Trust. Tel: 410-547-5317; Fax: 410-783-5993.

Basilica of the Assumption Historic Trust, Inc. Tel: 410-727-3564; Fax: 410-539-0407.

Cemetery Continuing Care Trust. St. Patrick's Havre de Grace, Cemetery Continuing Care Trust; Holy Cross Cemetery Continuing Care Trust; St. Joseph, Fullerton, Cemetery-Continuing Care Trust Agreement; St. Mary of the Assumption, Govans, Cemetery Continuing Care Trust; St. Mary's, Pylesville Cemetery, Continuing Care Trust.

Christian Brothers Community Support Charitable Trust. Tel: 410-539-3321.

Corpus Christi Jenkins Memorial Trust, Inc. Tel: 410-523-4161; Fax: 410-523-5745.

Dart, Inc.

The Dr. Charles J. Foley Sr. and Mildred H. Foley Memorial Endowment Trust. Tel: 410-547-5322; Fax: 410-332-8233.

Franciscan Sisters of Baltimore, Inc., Trust. Tel: 410-235-2496; Fax: 410-243-2569.

The Gallagher Family Fund, 320 Cathedral St., 21201. Tel: 410-547-5322; Fax: 410-332-8233.

G S Housing, Inc.

G S Properties, Inc.

St. Joachim House, Inc. Tel: 410-547-5495.

John Carroll Foundation of the Roman Catholic Archdiocese of Baltimore. Tel: 410-547-5300; Fax: 410-332-8233.

John Paul II Regional School, Inc. Tel: 410-944-0367; Fax: 410-265-5316.

St. Joseph's Texas, School Endowment Trust. Tel: 410-666-0393; Fax: 410-628-6814.

Marian House, Inc. Tel: 410-467-4121.

The Marion Burk Knott Scholarship Fund, Educational Trust. Tel: 301-603-9501.

Marianist Charitable Trust. Tel: 410-366-1300; Fax: 410-889-5743.

Maryvale Educational Fund, Inc. Tel: 410-252-3366; Fax: 410-561-1826.

Mercy Primary Care Group, Inc. Tel: 410-332-9000; Fax: 410-962-1303.

The National Black Catholic Congress, Inc. Tel: 410-547-8496; Fax: 410-752-3958.

Neumann Early Childhood Center, Inc. Tel: 410-547-5495.

Our Lady of Good Counsel Historic Trust, Inc. Tel: 410-752-0205; Fax: 410-576-0929.

Pallottine Charitable, Educational and Apostolic Ministry Trust. Tel: 301-422-3777.

Plan of Self-Insurance Trust. Tel: 410-547-5317; Fax: 410-783-5993.

The Priests Continuing Education and Formation Endowment Trust. Tel: 410-547-5317; Fax: 410-783-5993.

Prime E.A.P., Inc. Tel: 410-547-5317; Fax: 410-783-5993.

St. Agnes Clinical Practice Group, Inc. Tel: 410-368-6000.

St. Gregory the Great Housing Committee, Inc. Tel: 410-523-0061; Fax: 410-669-1385.

St. Agnes Hospital Foundation, Inc. Tel: 410-368-3155; Fax: 410-368-3533.

St. Augustine School Education Endowment Trust. Tel: 301-796-3040; Fax: 410-579-1165.

St. Jane Frances Educational Endowment Trust. Tel: 410-255-4750; Fax: 410-350-6720.

St. Jerome Housing Corporation, Inc. Tel: 410-547-5527.

St. John Neumann Regional School, Inc. Tel: 301-724-4055; Fax: 301-724-4827.

St. Jude Shrine Corporation. Tel: 410-685-6026; Fax: 410-244-5728.

St. Luke Parish Endowment Trust. Tel: 410-477-5200; Fax: 410-477-5996.

St. Mark's Parish School Endowment Trust. Tel: 410-747-6613; Fax: 410-747-3188.

St. Peter's Cemetery Restoration Fund, Inc. Tel: 410-547-5300; Fax: 410-332-8233.

St. Peter's, Westernport, School Endowment Trust. Tel: 301-359-0892; Fax: 301-359-0657.

St. Pius V Housing Committee, Inc. Tel: 410-523-1930; Fax: 410-523-8164.

St. Stephen School Endowment Trust. Tel: 410-592-7617; Fax: 410-592-7330.

St. Vincent De Paul Historic Trust, Inc. Tel: 410-547-5377; Fax: 410-625-8483.

Sacred Heart Community Health Services, Inc. Tel: 301-723-5222.

Sacred Heart Foundation, Inc. Tel: 301-723-5222.

Sacred Heart Hospital of the Sisters of Charity, Inc. Tel: 410-723-5222.

The SS. Peter & Paul Parish Endowment Trust. Tel: 301-777-3131; Fax: 301-759-3568.

School Sisters of Notre Dame in the City of Baltimore Charitable Trust, Inc. Tel: 410-377-7774; Fax: 410-377-5363.

The Seton Keough High School Endowment Trust. Tel: 410-646-4444; Fax: 410-368-1591.

Sisters of Notre Dame de Namur Charitable Trusts. Tel: 410-255-1577.

Sisters of Notre Dame de Namur, Maryland Province, Charitable Trust. Tel: 410-486-5382; Fax: 410-486-5466.

The Thomas O'Neill Catholic Health Care Fund, Inc. Women's Auxiliary Board.

Mercy Health Foundation, Inc., 301 St. Paul Pl., 21201. Tel: 410-332-9521. Thomas R. Mullen, Dir.

St. Luke Parish Education Endowment Trust, 7517 N. Point Rd., 21219. Tel: 410-477-5200; Fax: 410-477-5996.
E-mail: stluk@archbalt.org
Purpose: to support the youth of the parish who attend catholic schools. Total Assisted 50; Total Staff 1.

The Seton Keough High School Endowment Trust, 1201 Caton Ave., 21227.

BRADSHAW. *St. Stephen School Endowment Trust*, 8030 Bradshaw Rd., 21201.

CUMBERLAND. *The SS. Peter & Paul Parish Endowment Trust*, 109 N. Smallwood St., 21502-2992. Tel: 301-777-3131; Fax: 301-759-3568.
E-mail: ppaul@archbalt.org

ELLICOTT CITY. *St. Agnes Care Services, Inc.*, 300 N. Ridge Rd., 21043.

The St. Paul's Parish Endowment Trust, 3755 St. Paul St., 21043. Tel: 410-465-1670. Rev. Thomas J. Donaghy, Ph.D.

FROSTBURG. *St. Michael School Endowment Trust*, 44 E. Main St., P.O. Box 402, 21532. Tel: 301-689-6767. Rev. Paul A. Byrnes.

GLEN BURNIE. *The Church of the Good Shepherd Parish Endowment Trust*, 1451 Furnace Ave., 21060. Tel: 410-761-4607. Rev. John L. Kelly.

MARRIOTTSVILLE. *Bon Secours Health System, Inc.*, 1505 Marriottsville Rd., 21104. Tel: 410-442-5511; Fax: 410-442-3256.
Web site: www.bonsecours.org/bshsi
Sr. Patricia A. Eck, C.B.S., Chm. & Board of Directors; Christopher M. Carney, CEO & Pres.

Bon Secours Baltimore Health Corporation. Tel: 410-362-3000; Fax: 410-362-3450.

Bon Secours, Inc., 1525 Marriottsville Rd., 21104. Tel: 410-442-1333; Fax: 410-442-1394.

Bon Secours Providers, Inc. under Bon Secours Health System, Inc.

PASADENA. *St. Jane Frances Educational Endowment Trust*, 8499 Virginia Ave., 21122. Tel: 410-255-4646; Fax: 410-437-5191.
E-mail: postmaster@stjane.org
Web site: stjane.org

TOWSON. *The Immaculate Conception Elementary School Endowment Trust*, 200 Ware Ave., 21204. Tel: 410-823-6175. Rev. Msgr. Edward J. Lynch, Contact Person.

[W] MISCELLANEOUS

BALTIMORE. *Alhambra, International Order of*, Supreme Headquarters, 4200 Leeds Ave., 21229. Tel: 410-242-0660; Fax: 410-536-5729.
E-mail: salaamone@worldnet.att.net
Web site: www.OrderAlhambra.org
Nonprofit organization dedicated to assisting the developmentally disabled.

Apostles in the Marketplace (A.I.M.), 320 Cathedral St., 21201.

Apostleship of the Sea (Baltimore), 3048 Guilford Ave., 21218. Tel: 410-338-1296. Bro. Jim Horan, S.J., Port Chap.
Member of a 100 year old International Catholic organization.
Christian hospitality services in the Catholic tradition with spiritual, temporal, and emotional support for seafarers and their families. Also, transportation to and from ships for their crew members to the local Stella Maris Maritime Center and the city.

Bon Secours Community Health Services, Inc., 2000 W. Baltimore St., 21223. Tel: 410-362-3148.

Cardijn Associates, Inc., 1806 Lancaster St., 21231. Tel: 410-563-3190. Ms. Nancy Lee Conrad, Pres.

The Caroline Center, 900 Somerset St., 21202. Tel: 410-563-1303; Fax: 410-563-1302.
E-mail: carolctr@erols.com
Web site: Caroline-Center.org
Legal Title: *The Caroline Freiss Center, Inc.* Sr. Patricia McLaughlin, S.S.N.D., Exec. Dir. Total Assisted 120; Total Staff 18. Employment counseling center for women.

Cathedral Library, 5200 N. Charles St., 21210. Tel: 410-464-4041. Laura M. Perry, Library Chm.
Staffed by the Catholic Evidence League. Total Staff 15.

Catholic Alumni Club, P.O. Box 22305, 21203-2305. Tel: 410-580-1250.
E-mail: cac-skipjack@yahoo.com
Web site: www.caci.org/cac/CACBwebpage.html

Catholic Community at Relay, 5025 Cedar Ave., 21227. Tel: 410-247-4033; Fax: 410-247-2557.
E-mail: ccr247@clark.net
Rev. Nwaka Chris Egbulem, O.P. Total Staff 2.

Catholic Deaf of Baltimore, 2744 Pelham Ave., 21213. Tel: 410-483-2563. Thelma Breighnor, Pres.

Catholic Evidence League, 5200 N. Charles St., 21210. Tel: 410-435-8140; Fax: 410-435-8381.
E-mail: lpodles@compuserve.com

Catholic Fraternity. Incorporated 1910. 951 Rosedale Ave., 21237. Tel: 410-687-8787.

Catholic Relief Services, U.S.C.C. World Headquarters, 209 W. Fayette St., 21201. Tel: 410-625-2220; Fax: 410-685-1635. Kenneth Hackett, Exec. Dir.

Catholic Single Again Council of Baltimore, 1300 E. Northern Pkwy., 21239. Tel: 410-433-8880; Fax: 410-323-8816.
E-mail: mhsalum@clark.net
Sr. Joannes Clifford, R.S.M., Contact Person.

Catholic War Veterans, Inc., 5226 Millfield Rd., 21237. Tel: 410-433-5161. Rev. Conan H. Timoney, C.P., State Chap.; John A. Jarosinski, Commander; Elizabeth Kruger, Auxiliary Pres.

Central Maryland Catholic Charities, Inc. For additional information please see the Assocoiated Catholic Charities section. 320 Cathedral St., 21201.

Christ Child Society of Baltimore, 6003 Lakehurst Dr., #14, 21210. Tel: 410-377-8147. Olivia E. Chatard, Contact Person.

Cursillo Movement. Rev. Edward J. Bayer, Spiritual Dir. Tel: 410-922-3800; Deacon Albert Kosla, Spiritual Dir., 1311 St. Stephen's Church Rd., Churchville, 21032. Tel: 410-721-2612. Sr. Virginie Fish, O.S.P., Spiritual Dir., 701 Gun Rd., 21227. Tel: 410-242-8500. Sherry Rhoades, Lay Dir., 916 Bernadette Rd., Forest Hill, 21050. Tel: 410-879-2543.

Division of Leadership Development, 320 Cathedral St., 21201.

Efharisto Studio, Inc., 5130 N. Franklintown Rd., 21207-6598. Tel: 410-448-1711; Fax: 410-448-3259.
E-mail: fharisto@charm.net
Web site: www.efharistostudio.org
Sr. Stephana Toomey, O.P., Pres.
Services to advance the Roman Catholic religion by charitable, religious, and educational efforts in pursuing a nonprofit ministry of preaching by developing colorful worship areas and art forms to communicate visual meditations and services for the liturgy.

Food for Thought, Inc., 1625 E. Baltimore, 21231. Tel: 410-563-0081. Sr. Mary Ann Hartnett, S.S.N.D., Dir. Tutorial program for children & adult literacy.

Francis House, Inc., 2226 Maryland Ave., 21218-5625. Tel: 410-235-2588; Fax: 410-243-6125.
E-mail: pmcalpin@aol.com
Sr. Patricia McAlpin, O.S.F., Dir. Total in Residence 12; Total Staff 3.

Holy Name Society (Union), P.O. Box 12032, 21281. Rev. Msgr. Jeremiah E. Kenney, Archdiocesan Dir.

Ignatian Lay Volunteer Corps, 801 St. Paul St., 21202. Tel: 410-752-4686; Fax: 410-752-8480.
E-mail: JRConroy@ILVC.org
Rev. James R. Conroy, S.J., Exec. Dir. Co-Directors: Rev. Charles P. Costello, S.J.; Barbara Castellano; Eileen Capshaw, Dir. Development & Communications.

International Federation of Catholic Alumnae, Maryland Chapter, 1409 Union Ave., 21211-1906. Tel: 410-235-0406; Fax: 410-235-0406.
E-mail: rerug@juno.com
Marian Birck, Governor. Total Staff 79. Benefits & other fund raising activities are held to accumulate funds which are rewarded to members catholic schools in the archdiocese, for scholarships & financial assistance to students.

Jesuit Educational Association of Maryland, Inc., 5704 Roland Ave., 21210. Tel: 410-532-1400; Fax: 410-532-1419.
E-mail: dlahart@gonzaga.org
Web site: www.marprovincejesuits.org
Rev. Daniel K. Lahart, S.J., Pres.

Jesuit Jamshedpur Mission Society, Inc., 7400 York Rd., Ste. 401, 21204-7531. Tel: 410-825-2360; Fax: 410-825-2365.
E-mail: iap@ignatianpartners.org
Web site: www.ignatianpartners.org
Rev. Joseph M. Kennedy, S.J., Dir.

Jesuit Mission Bureau, Maryland Province, Inc., 7400 York Rd., Ste. 401, 21204. Tel: 410-825-2360; Fax: 410-825-2365.
E-mail: iap@ignatianpartners.org
Web site: www.ignatianpartners.org
Mr. Kevin O'Brien, Dir.; Ms. Susan Geaney, Dir. Devel.; Rev. Joseph M. Kennedy, S.J., Assoc. Dir.

Jesuit Seminary Guild, Maryland Province, Inc., 7400 York Rd., Ste. 401, 21204. Tel: 410-825-2360; Fax: 410-825-2365.
E-mail: iap@ignatianpartners.org
Web site: www.ignatianpartners.org
Mr. Kevin O'Brien, Dir.; Ms. Suzanne Geaney, Dir. Devel.; Rev. Joseph M. Kennedy, S.J., Asst. Dir.

Johns Hopkins Hospital Apostolate. Rev. Salvatore J. Livigni.
Chaplain's Office, Johns Hopkins Medical Center, 600 N. Wolfe St., 21287-4170. Tel: 410-955-5842; Fax: 410-550-6765. Total in Residence 800; Total Staff 20.

Ladies of Charity, 19 Maple Ave., 21206. Tel: 410-665-8876; Fax: 410-529-2042. Rev. Casimir M. Peterson, Spiritual Dir.; Sr. Claire Debes, D.C., Moderator & Vincentian Collaboration Coord.; Charlotte Casserly, Pres.

Legion of Mary. 3229 Birchmede Dr., Ellicott City, 21042. Tel: 410-465-1355.
E-mail: jamessaboejimbo@aol.com
Rev. Msgr. John Reinsfelder, Spiritual Dir.; Mr. Jim Saboe, Pres.
Baltimore Comitium, governing body for the Legion of Mary in the Baltimore archdiocese.

Marianist Conference, 4301 Roland Ave., 21210. Tel: 410-366-1300; Fax: 410-889-5743.
E-mail: georgejcer@aol.com
Rev. George J. Cerniglia, S.M., Pres. Purpose: a vehicle of interprovincial communication, coordination and networking.

Maryland Catholic Health Care Consortium, Inc., Holy Cross Hospital of Silver Spring, Inc., 1500 Forest Glen Rd., 20910.

Mercy Family Care, Inc., 301 St. Paul Pl., 21202. Tel: 410-332-9313. John Topper, Contact Person.

Mercy Health Services, Inc., 301 St. Paul Pl., 21202. Tel: 410-332-9202; Fax: 410-962-1303.
E-mail: tmullen@mercymed.com
Web site: www.mercymed.com
Thomas R. Mullen, Pres. & CEO.

Mercy Home Health Services, Inc., 102 E. Pleasant St., 21202. Tel: 410-332-9784. Sr. Ann Laidlaw, M.P.H., R.N., Dir.

Mission Helper Productions, Inc. (non-profit full-service video production studio), 1001 W. Joppa Rd., 21204-3787. Tel: 410-823-8585, Ext. 240; Fax: 410-825-6355.
E-mail: mhproducer@aol.com
Sr. Anne Guinan, M.H.S.H., Contact Person.

Mother Seton House on Paca Street, Inc., 600 N. Paca St., 21201. Tel: 410-523-3443.

The Mount Saint Agnes Theological Center for Women, Inc., P.O. Box 10484, 21209. Tel: 410-435-7500; Fax: 410-435-9522.
E-mail: msawomen@aol.com
Web site: msawomen.org
Sr. Mary Aquin O'Neill, R.S.M., Dir. Total Staff 5.

Parish Social Ministry Outreach, 1512 Druid Hill Ave., 21217. Tel: 410-523-3256.
Immaculate Conception Parish, Baltimore. Sr. Genevieve Noonan, D.C., Staff.

Radio Mass of Baltimore, Inc., St. Ignatius Church, 740 N. Calvert St., 21202. Tel: 410-539-7812. Rev. William J. Watters, S.J., Dir.
Mass is broadcast every Sunday morning from St. Ignatius Church at 9:30 A.M., WBAL, 1090 AM Radio Dial.

St. Agnes Clinical Practice Group, Inc. (inactive at this time), 900 S. Caton Ave., 21229. Tel: 410-368-6000; Fax: 410-368-3594.
E-mail: info@stagnes.org
Web site: www.stagnes.org
Robert W. Adams, Pres. & CEO.

SS. Matthew and Thomas More Religious Education and Youth Ministry Center, Inc., 6806 McClean Blvd., 21234. Tel: 410-444-4563; Fax: 410-444-6502.
E-mail: skeating@archbalt.org

Serra Club Vocation Office, 320 Cathedral St., 21201. Tel: 410-547-5431. Rev. James M. Barker, Chap.

Vietnamese Catholic Community at Baltimore (VC-CAB), 1314 Old Eastern Ave., 21221. Tel: 410-238-7870.

The Young Christian Workers, Inc., P.O. Box 6052, 21231-0052. Tel: 410-563-3281; Fax: 410-563-3281.
E-mail: ycwus@aol.com
Web site: www.jociycw.net
Total in Residence 2; Total Staff 2.

CATONSVILLE. *St. Thomas More Society of Maryland*. The local branch of the National Society of Catholic Lawyers. 14 N. Rolling Rd., 21228. Tel: 410-744-4967; Fax: 410-744-8936. Administrative Office, Box 4764, Timonium, 21228. Nancy West, Pres.

CUMBERLAND. *Catholic Education Ministries of Western Maryland*.
Web site: www.mindspring.com/~catholicwmd/cem
Bishop Walsh Middle/High School, 700 Bishop Walsh Rd., 21502. Tel: 301-777-9082; Fax: 301-722-6114.
E-mail: catholicwmd@mindspring.com
Margaret Meyers, Area Coord.

DUNKIRK. *Family of the Americas Foundation, Inc.*, P.O. Box 1170, 20754-1170. Tel: 301-627-3346; 800-443-3395; Fax: 301-627-0847.
E-mail: family@upbeat.com

ELLICOTT CITY. *Christlife, Inc.*, 12290-A Folly Quarter Rd., 21042. Tel: 410-531-7701; Fax: 410-531-7702.
E-mail: info@christlife.org
Web site: www.christlife.org
Mr. Dave Nodar, Dir.

Conventual Franciscan Friars, St. Anthony of Padua Province USA, 12300 Folly Quarter Rd., 21042. Tel: 410-531-9200; Fax: 410-531-4881. Legal Title: *Order of Friars Minor Conventual, St. Anthony of Padua Province, U.S.A., Inc.; Franciscan Minor Conventuals of Maryland, Inc. of Ellicott City, MD.; The Franciscan Fathers, Minor Conventuals, of St. Stanislaus Church of Baltimore City, Inc.; Franciscan Friars, St. Anthony of Padua Province, Education Fund, Inc.; Franciscan Friars, St. Anthony of Padua Province, Fund for the Aged and Infirm Friars, Inc.; St. Francis of Assisi Community, Inc., Companions of St. Anthony; St. Stanislaus Cemetery, Inc.* Total in Residence 5.

LINTHICUM. *Catholic Daughters of the Americas*, 6420 Wilben Rd., 21090. Tel: 410-859-5206. Rev. Alphonse G. Rose, State Chap.; Most Rev. William Newman, Clergy Consultant; Mrs. Anne Nelson, State Regent.

Daughters of Charity National Health System East, Inc., 891 Elkridge Landing Rd., Ste. 400, 21090-1025. Tel: 410-850-9000; Fax: 410-859-3459. James E. Small, Regl. Exec.

MARRIOTTSVILLE. *Bon Secours Health System, Inc.*, 1505 Marriottsville Rd., 21104. Tel: 410-442-5511; Fax: 410-442-3256.
Web site: www.bonsecours.org/bshsi
Sr. Patricia A. Eck, C.B.S., Chm., Board of Directors; Christopher M. Carney, CEO & Pres.

MILLERSVILLE. *Disciples Now Ministries Inc.*, P.O. Box 1063, 21108. Tel: 410-724-1501; Fax: 410-729-1502. Paul Raspa, Jr., Contact Person.

PASADENA. *Reparation Society of the Immaculate Heart of Mary, Inc.*, 8006 Caliburn Ct., 21122-6348. Tel: 410-360-1817. Rev. Casimir M. Peterson, S.T.L., J.C.D., Dir. Volunteers 3; Total in Residence 1.

SILVER SPRING. *Christian Life Community Regional Information Center*, 201 E. Wayne Ave., 20901. Tel: 301-495-2969; Fax: 301-495-7318.
E-mail: bfleone@erols.com
Web site: www.world.std.com/uclcusa
Mr. Fred C. Leone, Regl. Rep.

UPPER MARLBORO. *Knights of Columbus*, 9305 Southmoor Ct., 20772. Tel: 301-856-2158. Rev. James A. Finan, State Chap.; John J. Glynn, State Deputy.

WESTMINSTER. *Dominican Pastoral Counseling Center*, 187 E. Main St., 21157. Tel: 410-876-8315; Fax: 410-876-8315.
E-mail: dolorespfeiffer@maxinter.net
Sr. Dolores A. Pfeiffer, O.P., M.A., M.S., Dir. Total Assisted 309 (Counseling Hrs.); Total Staff 1.

RELIGIOUS INSTITUTES OF MEN REPRESENTED IN THE ARCHDIOCESE

For further details refer to the corresponding bracketed number in the Religious Institutes of Men or Women Section.

[0200]—*Benedictine Monks (Latrobe, PA)*.—O.S.B.
[1350]—*Brothers of St. Francis Xavier*.—C.F.X.
[0330]—*Brothers of the Christian Schools*. (Baltimore Prov.).—F.S.C.
[0470]—*The Capuchin Friars*. (Prov. of St. Augustine).—O.F.M.Cap.
[1330]—*Congregation of the Mission*. (Eastern Prov.).—C.M.
[1000]—*Congregation of the Passion*. (Prov. of St. Paul of the Cross).—C.P.
[0480]—*Conventual Franciscans*. (Ellicott City, MD).—O.F.M.Conv.
[0400]—*Crosier Fathers*.—O.S.C.
[0520]—*Franciscan Friars (Most Holy Name)*.—O.F.M.
[0690]—*Jesuit Fathers and Brothers*. (Maryland Prov.).—S.J.
[0730]—*Legionaries of Christ*.—L.C.
[0854]—*Missionary Society of St. Paul of Nigeria*.
[]—*Norbertine Fathers*. (Immaculate Conception Priory, DE).—O.Praem.
[1310]—*Order of the Most Holy Trinity, Immaculate Heart of Mary Province*.—O.SS.T.
[1070]—*Redemptorist Fathers*. (Baltimore Prov.).—C.SS.R.
[0700]—*St. Joseph's Society of the Sacred Heart*.—S.S.J.
[1260]—*Society of Christ*.—S.Ch.
[0760]—*Society of Mary*.—S.M.
[0990]—*Society of the Catholic Apostolate*. (Immaculate Conception Prov.).—S.A.C.
[1200]—*Society of the Divine Saviour*.—S.D.S.
[1290]—*Society of the Priests of St. Sulpice*.—S.S.

[]—*Sulpicians.*—S.S.
[0560]—*Third Order Regular of St. Francis.*—T.O.R.

RELIGIOUS INSTITUTES OF WOMEN REPRESENTED IN THE ARCHDIOCESE

[0230]—*Benedictine Sisters of Pontifical Jurisdiction.* (Baltimore).—O.S.B.
[0270]—*Congregation of Bon Secours.*—C.B.S.
[3270]—*Congregation of the Sisters of the Most Precious Blood.*—C.PP.S.
[0760]—*Daughters of Charity of St. Vincent de Paul.*—D.C.
[0420]—*Discalced Carmelite Nuns.*—O.C.D.
[1070-03]—*Dominican Sisters.*—O.P.
[1070-07]—*Dominican Sisters.*—O.P.
[1070-13]—*Dominican Sisters.*—O.P.
[1200]—*Franciscan Sisters of Baltimore.*—O.S.F.
[1470]—*Franciscan Sisters of St. Joseph.*—F.S.S.J.
[1840]—*Grey Nuns of the Sacred Heart.* (Pennsylvania).—G.N.S.H.
[2575]—*Institute of the Sisters of the Mercy of the Americas.* (Baltimore, Merion).—R.S.M.
[2330]—*Little Sisters of Jesus.*
[2340]—*Little Sisters of the Poor.*—L.S.P.
[2470]—*Maryknoll Sisters.* (New York).—M.M.
[2490]—*Medical Missionary Sisters.* (Pennsylvania).—M.M.S.
[2720]—*Mission Helpers of the Sacred Heart.*—M.H.S.H.
[2710]—*Missionaries of Charity.* (New York).—M.C.
[3040]—*Oblate Sisters of Providence.*—O.S.P.
[]—*Oblates of St. Martha.*
[2070]—*Religious of the Holy Union of the Sacred Hearts.*—S.U.S.C.
[3465]—*Religious of the Sacred Heart of Mary.* (New York).—R.S.H.M.
[2970]—*School Sisters of Notre Dame.*—S.S.N.D.
[0640]—*Sisters of Charity.* (Halifax).—S.C.
[3000]—*Sisters of Notre Dame de Namur.*—S.N.D.deN.
[4080]—*Sisters of Social Service.*
[1650]—*Sisters of St. Francis of Philadelphia.*—O.S.F.
[]—*Sisters of St. Francis of Rochester.* (Minnesota).—O.S.F.
[3893]—*Sisters of St. Joseph.*—S.S.J.
[3890]—*Sisters of St. Joseph of Peace.*
[1030]—*Sisters of the Divine Savior.*—S.D.S.
[1830]—*Sisters of the Good Shepherd.* (Mid North-American Prov.).—R.G.S.
[1920]—*Sisters of the Holy Cross.*
[1990]—*Sisters of the Holy Names of Jesus and Mary.*
[3610]—*Sisters Servants of Mary Immaculate.*—S.S.M.I.
[2160]—*Sisters, Servants of the Immaculate Heart of Mary.*—I.H.M.
[4120]—*Ursuline Nuns, of the Congregation of Kentucky.*—O.S.U.
[4190]—*Visitation Nuns.*—V.H.M.

ARCHDIOCESAN CEMETERIES

BALTIMORE. *New Cathedral.*

NECROLOGY

† Byrd, Thomas, (Retired). —Died Jan. 5, 2000.
† Coady, Edward L., (Retired). —Died Aug. 15, 2000.
† Glick, George W, Hancock, MD St. Peter. —Died May 15, 2000.
† Kaczkowski, Leon, (Retired). —Died Feb. 5, 2000.
† Pugevicius, Casimir, (Retired). —Died Feb. 29, 2000.
† Reed, Robert A., (Retired). —Died Dec. 11, 1999.
† Spraker, Rev. Msgr. Gerard W., (Retired). —Died March 3, 2000.
† Staub, Rev. Msgr. Edward F, Severna Park, MD St. John the Evangelist. —Died May 12, 2000.
† Wisnieski, Rev. Msgr. Theodore, (Retired). —Died Feb. 1, 2000.

Diocese of Baton Rouge

(Dioecesis Rubribaculensis)

ESTABLISHED JULY 20, 1961.

Square Miles 5,513.

Comprises the civil parishes (counties) of Ascension, Assumption, East Baton Rouge, West Baton Rouge, Iberville, Pointe Coupee, East Feliciana, West Feliciana, St. Helena, Tangipahoa, Livingston and St. James in the State of Louisiana.

For legal titles of parishes and diocesan institutions, consult the Chancery Office.

(Vacant See)

Chancery Office: Catholic Life Center, 1800 S. Acadian Thruway, P.O. Box 2028, Baton Rouge, LA, 70821-2028. Tel.: 225-387-0561; Fax: 225-336-8789.

Web site address: www.diobr.org

E-mail address: chancery@diobr.org

STATISTICAL OVERVIEW

Personnel	
Priests: Diocesan Active in Diocese	64
Priests: Active Outside Diocese	1
Priests: Retired, Sick or Absent	14
Number of Diocesan Priests	79
Religious Priests in Diocese	42
Extern Priests in Diocese	5
Ordinations:	
Diocesan Priests	2
Religious Priests	1
Transitional Deacons	1
Permanent Deacons in Diocese	26
Total Brothers	12
Total Sisters	114
Parishes	
Parishes	70
With Resident Pastor:	
Resident Diocesan Priests	52
Resident Religious Priests	10
Without Resident Pastor:	
Administered by Priests	7
Administered by Lay People	1
Professional Ministry Personnel:	
Brothers	3
Sisters	14
Lay Ministers	81
Welfare	
Catholic Hospitals	2
Total Assisted	212,012
Homes for the Aged	3
Total Assisted	604
Specialized Homes	6
Total Assisted	251
Special Centers for Social Services	6
Total Assisted	123,285
Educational	
Diocesan Students in Other Seminaries	7
Seminaries, Religious	7
Total Seminarians	7
Colleges and Universities	1
Total Students	1,047
High Schools, Diocesan and Parish	6
Total Students	2,713
High Schools, Private	2
Total Students	1,665
Elementary Schools, Diocesan and Parish	25
Total Students	12,406
Non-residential Schools for the Disabled	1
Total Students	34
Catechesis/Religious Education:	
High School Students	5,170
Elementary Students	11,530
Total Students Under Catholic Instruction	34,572
Teachers in the Diocese:	
Brothers	2
Sisters	23
Lay Teachers	1,002
Vital Statistics	
Receptions into the Church:	
Infant Baptism Totals	3,043
Adult Baptism Totals	208
Received into Full Communion	412
First Communions	3,030
Confirmations	2,831
Marriages:	
Catholic	700
Interfaith	307
Total Marriages	1,007
Deaths	1,702
Total Catholic Population	215,929
Total Population	831,478

Former Bishops—Most Rev. ROBERT E. TRACY, D.D., LL.D., appt. Titular Bishop of Sergentza and Auxiliary of Lafayette March 18, 1959; cons. May 19, 1959; appt. first Bishop of Baton Rouge Aug. 10, 1961; retired March 21, 1974; died April 4, 1980.—Most Rev. JOSEPH V. SULLIVAN, S.T.D., appt. Titular Bishop of Tagamuta and Auxiliary to the Bishop of Kansas City-St. Joseph March 3, 1967; cons. April 3, 1967; appt. Second Bishop of Baton Rouge August 5, 1974; died September 4, 1982.—Most Rev. STANLEY JOSEPH OTT, S.T.D., appt. Titular Bishop of Nicives and Auxiliary Bishop of New Orleans May 24, 1976; cons. June 29, 1976; appt. Third Bishop of Baton Rouge January 18, 1983; died November 28, 1992.

Vicar General & Moderator of the Curia—Very Rev. JOHN CARVILLE, S.T.D., V.G.

Chancery Office—Catholic Life Center, 1800 S. Acadian Thruway, P.O. Box 2028, Baton Rouge, 70821-2028. Tel: 225-387-0561; Fax: 225-336-8789. Office Hours: Mon.-Fri. 8:30-4:30.

Chancellor—Rev. Msgr. ROBERT H. BERGGREEN, M.Ed.

Vice-Chancellors—Very Rev. PAUL D. COUNCE, J.C.L., M.C.L.; Rev. MARTIN A. HERNANDEZ, J.C.L., M.C.L.

Diocesan Tribunal—Catholic Life Center, 1800 S. Acadian Thruway, P.O. Box 1087, Baton Rouge, 70821-1087. Tel: 225-387-0561; Fax: 225-336-8789.

Judicial Vicar—Very Rev. PAUL D. COUNCE, J.C.L., M.C.L.

Promoter of Justice—Very Rev. VINCENT J. DUFRESNE, S.T.L., J.C.L., V.F.

Judges—Rev. Msgr. WILLIAM L. GREENE; Rev. Msgr. GERALD M. LEFEBVRE; Revs. FRANK M. UTER; MICHAEL J. MORONEY; DEAN J. MARTIN, J.C.L.

Defenders of the Bond—Very Rev. VINCENT J. DUFRESNE, S.T.L., J.C.L., V.F.; Revs. GARLAND T. BELSOME; THAN N. VU, S.T.L.; MARTIN A. HERNANDEZ, J.C.L., M.C.L.; JOSEPH X. STEFFES, C.SS.R.; SHELTON J. FABRE; GERARD R. MARTIN.

Notaries—Mrs. JOSIE C. ZGANJAR; Mrs. PATRICIA F. SONIAT.

College of Consultors—Very Rev. JOHN CARVILLE, S.T.D., V.G.; Rev. Msgr. ROBERT H. BERGGREEN; Revs. THAN N. VU, S.T.L.; GERARD F. YOUNG; MICHAEL J. SCHATZLE; SHELTON J. FABRE.

Diocesan Pro-Vicar—

Pro-Vicar for Women Religious—Sr. DIANNE HEINRICH, C.D.P.

Diocesan Corporation (The Roman Catholic Church of the Diocese of Baton Rouge)—Most Rev. ALFRED C. HUGHES, S.T.D., Pres.; Very Rev. JOHN CARVILLE, S.T.D., V.G., Vice Pres.; Rev. Msgr. ROBERT H. BERGGREEN, M.Ed., Sec.; Mr. J. ERROL GAUTREAU, Treas.

Diocesan Offices and Directors

Apostolate to the Deaf—Mr. WILLIAM G. DUGAS, Dir., *2585 Brightside Ln., Baton Rouge, 70820-3504.* Tel: 225-766-9320; 769-0223; Fax: 225-766-9320.

Archives—Mrs. RENEE RICHARD, *P.O. Box 2028, Baton Rouge, 70821-2028.* Tel: 225-387-0561; Fax: 225-242-0299.

Black Catholics—Rev. SHELTON J. FABRE, *P.O. Box 8, Grosse Tete, 70740-0008.* Tel: 225-648-2420.

Campus Ministry—Rev. THAN N. VU, S.T.L., *P.O. Box 25131, Baton Rouge, 70894-5131.* Tel: 225-383-1574; Fax: 225-344-1920.

Catholic Charismatic Renewal—Rev. HENRY W. GAUTREAU, *13281 Hwy. 644, Vacherie, 70090-9716.* Tel: 225-265-3953; Fax: 225-265-2507.

Catholic Community Services—Ms. DEBORAH A. ROE, M.S.W., Exec. Dir., Office: *1900 S. Acadian Thruway, P.O. Box 1668, Baton Rouge, 70821-1668.* Tel: 225-336-8770; Fax: 225-336-8745.

Catholic Social Services Dept.—Ms. JANICE ALLEN, M.S.W., *1900 S. Acadian Thruway, P.O. Box 1668, Baton Rouge, 70821-1668.* Tel: 225-336-8770; Fax: 225-336-8745.

Social Responsibility Dept.—Ms. PEGGY STUART.

Family Life Dept.—Mr. WARREN DAZZIO, Dir., Office: *1900 S. Acadian Thruway, P.O. Box 1668, Baton Rouge, 70821-1668.* Tel: 225-336-8770; 387-0561; Fax: 225-336-8745.

Cemeteries—Rev. FRANK M. UTER, *P.O. Drawer 1501, Gramercy, 70052-1501.* Tel: 225-869-5324; Fax: 225-869-5325.

Ecumenical Affairs—Rev. MICHAEL J. MORONEY, *445 Marquette Ave., Baton Rouge, 70806-4497.* Tel: 225-926-1883; Fax: 225-923-0448.

Communications—Deacon ROBERT FURLOW, *P.O. Box 2028, Baton Rouge, 70821-2028.* Tel: 225-387-0561; 383-0880; Fax: 225-383-0924.

Continuing Formation for the Clergy—Rev. PATRICK J. MASCARELLA, Dir., *P.O. Box 25131, Baton Rouge, 70894-5131.* Tel: 225-383-1574; Fax: 225-344-1920.

Development—Mr. MARK J. BLANCHARD, Dir., *P.O. Box 2028, Baton Rouge, 70821-2028.* Tel: 225-336-8790; Fax: 225-336-8710.

Finance—Mr. J. ERROL GAUTREAU, Fiscal Officer (Oeconomus), *P.O. Box 2028, Baton Rouge, 70821-2028.* Tel: 225-387-0561; Fax: 225-336-8789.

Christian Formation—Mrs. BETTY BOURGEOIS, *P.O. Box 2028, Baton Rouge, 70821-2028.* Tel: 225-336-8760; Fax: 225-336-8765.

Hispanic Apostolate—Rev. RAPHAEL JUANTORENA, S.T.L., Ph.D., Dir., *5850 Florida Blvd., Ste. B, Baton Rouge, 70806-4247.* Tel: 225-927-8700; Fax: 225-927-8787.

Newspaper "The Catholic Commentator"—Mrs. LAURA G. DEAVERS, Exec. Editor & Gen. Mgr., Office: *Catholic Life Center, 1800 S. Acadian Thruway, Baton Rouge, 70821-1668., Mailing Address: P.O. Drawer 14746, Baton Rouge, 70898-4746.* Tel: 225-387-0983; Fax: 225-336-8710.

Permanent Diaconate Office—Deacon ALBERT R. ELLIS, JR., Dir., *7808 St. George Dr., Baton Rouge, 70809-4699.* Tel: 225-293-2212; Fax: 225-291-8063.

Presbyteral Council—Rev. Msgr. ROBERT H. BERGGREEN; Very Rev. JOHN CARVILLE, S.T.D., V.G.; Very Rev. PAUL D. COUNCE, J.C.L.; Revs. JULES A. BRUNET; CHARLES R. LANDRY; PAUL A. MCDUFFIE; ROBERT F. STINE; SHELTON J. FABRE; MATTHEW C. DUPRE; SAMUEL C. MARANTO, C.SS.R.; MICHAEL J. SCHATZLE; N. JOHN NUTTER; LOUIS T. OUBRE; THAN N. VU, S.T.L.; ROBERT U. PERRY, O.P.; GERARD F. YOUNG.

Propagation of the Faith and Association of Holy Childhood—Rev. N. JOHN NUTTER, Dir.; Mrs. BETTY LOU STOKES, Office Mgr., *P.O. Box 2028, Baton Rouge, 70821-2028.* Tel: 225-387-0561; Fax: 225-242-0343.

Religious Education—Ms. CAROLE OBROKTA, *P.O. Box 2028, Baton Rouge, 70821-2028.* Tel: 225-336-8730; Fax: 225-336-8731.

Catholic Schools—Sr. MARY MICHAELINE GREEN, O.P., Supt.; Dr. JACQUELINE C. LEWIS, Ed.D., Asst. Supt.; Mr. JOSEPH M. SCIMECA, Asst. Supt., *P.O. Box 2028, Baton Rouge, 70821-2028.* Tel: 225-336-8735; Fax: 225-336-8711.

Scouting—Rev. PAUL A. MCDUFFIE, Chap., *P.O. Box 349, Independence, 70443-0349.* Tel: 504-878-9639; Fax: 504-878-6260.

Separated and Divorced—Rev. FRED YOUNGS, Dir., *5657 Thomas Rd., Baton Rouge, 70811-7356.* Tel: 225-775-8850; Fax: 225-775-7072.

Serra Clubs—Rev. M. JEFFREY BAYHI, Spiritual Advisor, *P.O. Box 2028, Baton Rouge, 70821-2028.* Tel: 225-336-8778; Fax: 225-336-8710.

Society of St. Vincent De Paul—Mr. MICHAEL J. ACALDO, Exec. Dir.; Rev. MICHAEL A. MICELI, Spiritual Advisor, *P.O. Box 127, Baton Rouge, 70821-0127.* Tel: 225-383-7837.

Vietnamese Apostolate—Rev. HUNG VIET NGUYEN, I.C.M., Dir., *2580 Tecumseh St., Baton Rouge, 70805-7999.* Tel: 225-357-4787; Fax: 225-355-9794.

Vocations—Rev. M. JEFFREY BAYHI, Dir.; Sr. DIANNE HEINRICH, C.D.P., Assoc. Dir., *P.O. Box 2028, Baton Rouge, 70821-2028.* Tel: 225-336-8778; Fax: 225-336-8710.

Worship, Office of—Rev. THOMAS C. RANZINO, Dir., *P.O. Box 2028, Baton Rouge, 70821-2028.* Tel: 225-387-0561; Fax: 225-336-8789.

Youth Ministry—Mr. CHARLES JUMONVILLE, Dir., *P.O. Box 2028, Baton Rouge, 70821-2028.* Tel: 225-336-8751; Fax: 225-336-8765.

CLERGY, PARISHES, MISSIONS AND PAROCHIAL SCHOOLS

CITY OF BATON ROUGE
(East Baton Rouge Parish)

1—ST. JOSEPH CATHEDRAL (1792), Revs. Gerard F. Young; William Minj (India); Deacon Robert Furlow.
Res., 412 North St., 70802-5496. Tel: 225-387-5928; Fax: 225-387-5929.

2—ST. AGNES (1917), Rev. Msgr. Robert H. Berggreen. In res., Revs. M. Jeffrey Bayhi; J. Daniel Walsh, C.S.C.
Res., 749 East Blvd., 70802-6398. Tel: 225-383-4127; Fax: 225-383-4154.

3—ST. ALOYSIUS (1955), Revs. Gerald H. Burns; Valerian Nazareth (India).
Mailing Address: 2025 Stuart Ave., 70808-3998. Tel: 225-343-6657; Fax: 225-344-6847.
School—Tel: 225-383-3871; Fax: 225-383-4500. Mr. John L. Bennett, Prin.
Daughters of Jesus 3; Lay Teachers 49; Students 902.

4—ST. ANTHONY OF PADUA (1920) (Vietnamese), Rev. Hung Viet Nguyen, I.C.M. (Vietnam).
Res., 2580 Tecumseh St., 70805-7999. Tel: 225-357-4800; Fax: 225-354-0611.

5—ST. CHARLES BORROMEO (1964), Very Rev. Maynard E. Hurst, Jr., M.S.N., M.Ed., V.F.; Revs. Thomas P. Duhe; Joseph Steffes, C.SS.R.
Res., 3852 E. Brookstown Dr., 70805-4791. Tel: 225-356-2527; Fax: 225-356-2528.

6—CHRIST THE KING (1980), Revs. Than N. Vu, S.T.L.; Matthew Dupre.
Mailing Address: P.O. Box 25131, 70894-5131.
Res., Highland Rd. & Dalrymple Dr., 70803. Tel: 225-344-8595; 383-1574; Fax: 225-344-1920.

7—ST. FRANCIS DE SALES PARISH (1979). (Center for Hearing Impaired). Mr. William G. Dugas, Exec. Dir.; Rev. Richard A. Luberti, C.SS.R.
Res., 2585 Brightside Dr., 70820-3504. Tel: 225-766-9320; 769-0223 (Voice/TDD); Fax: 225-766-9320.

8—ST. FRANCIS XAVIER (1918), Rev. Michael K. Saah-Buckman, S.S.J.
Res., 1143 S. 11th St., 70802-4997. Tel: 225-383-3479; Fax: 225-343-4259.
School—(Grades PreK-8). Tel: 225-387-6639. Dr. Alvin DeCuir, Prin.
Lay Teachers 15; Students 179.

9—ST. GEORGE (1908), Revs. Thomas C. Ranzino; Joey F. Angeles; Deacons Albert R. Ellis; Guy E. Decker.
Office: 7808 St. George Dr., 70809-4699. Tel: 225-293-2212; Fax: 225-291-8063. [CEM]
School—7880 St. George Dr., 70809-4699. Tel: 225-293-1298. Mrs. Ann Bertsch, Prin.
Lay Teachers 36; Students 823.

10—ST. GERARD MAJELLA (1944), Rev. Samuel Maranto, C.SS.R. In res., Rev. Joseph Steffes, C.SS.R.; Bro. Clement J. Furno, C.SS.R.
Res., 3808 Gerard St., 70805-2834. Tel: 225-355-2553; Fax: 225-356-7472.
School—3655 St. Gerard Ave., 70805-2898. Tel: 225-355-1437. Joanie Hudson, Prin.
Lay Teachers 17; Students 167.

11—IMMACULATE CONCEPTION (1953), Rev. Hilton L. Rivet, S.J. In res., Rev. Francis R. Brou, S.J.
Res., 1565 Curtis St., 70807-4906. Tel: 225-775-7067; Fax: 225-775-0775.

12—ST. JEAN VIANNEY (1975), Very Rev. Donald V. Blanchard, V.F.; Rev. Anthony J. Russo; Deacons Thomas M. Robinson; Brent Duplessis.
Res., 16166 S. Harrell's Ferry Rd., 70816-3199. Tel: 225-753-7950; Fax: 225-753-7965.
School—(Grades K-8) 16266 S. Harrell's Ferry Rd., 70816-3103. Tel: 225-751-1831; Fax: 225-752-8774. Mrs. Lorry Perry, Prin.
Lay Teachers 32; Students 531.
Preschool—Tel: 225-752-5356. Ms. Kathy Simoneaux, Dir.
Lay Teachers 16; Students 128.

13—ST. JUDE THE APOSTLE (1966), Revs. David E. Allen; Francis E. Lonakutty, I.M.S. (India).
Res., 9150 Highland Rd., 70810-4096. Tel: 225-766-2431; Fax: 225-766-0722.
School—(Grades PreK-8). Tel: 225-769-2344; Fax: 225-769-0671. Mrs. Karen Jackuback, Prin.
Lay Teachers 33; Students 653.

14—ST. LOUIS, KING OF FRANCE (1966), Very Rev. Maynard E. Hurst, Jr., M.S.W., V.F.
Res., 2121 N. Sherwood Forest Dr., 70815-1998. Tel: 225-275-7280; Fax: 225-275-5845.
School—(Grades K-8) 2311 N. Sherwood Forest Dr., 70815-1997. Tel: 225-273-3932; Fax: 225-273-3978. Mrs. Mary Clare Polito, Prin.
Lay Teachers 25; Students 390.
Early Learning Center—Tel: 225-272-6438; Fax: 225-275-5845. Diane Blouin, Dir.
Lay Teachers 10; Students 85.

15—MOST BLESSED SACRAMENT (1979), Revs. Michael J. Collins; Miles D. Walsh, S.T.L.
Res., 7853 Broker Ave., 70817-6002. Tel: 225-752-6230; Fax: 225-756-5014.
School—(Grades K-8). Tel: 225-751-0273; Fax: 225-753-7259.
Lay Teachers 26; Students 56.

16—OUR LADY OF MERCY (1947), Revs. Michael J. Moroney; Arun John, I.M.S. (India); Victor G. Messina; Rafael Juantorena, Ph.D., S.T.L (Honduras).
Office: 445 Marquette Ave., 70806-4497. Tel: 225-926-1883; Fax: 225-923-0448.
Res., 450 Marquette Ave., 70806-4497. Tel: 225-927-7106.
School—400 Marquette Ave., 70806-4498. Tel: 225-924-1054; Fax: 225-923-2201. Mrs. Carolyn Guidry, Prin.
Lay Teachers 42; Students 844.

17—ST. PATRICK (1974), Rev. Myles J. Kearney; Deacon J. Peter Walsh.
Res., 12424 Brogdon Ln., 70816-4801. Tel: 225-753-5750; Fax: 225-756-9636.

18—ST. PAUL THE APOSTLE (1960), Rev. Joseph I. Guidry, S.V.D.
Res., 3912 Gus Young Ave., 70802-1727. Tel: 225-383-2537; Fax: 225-383-3702.

19—ST. PIUS X (1963), Rev. Jon C. Koehler.
Res., 6380 Hooper Rd., 70811-2499. Tel: 225-357-5935; Fax: 225-357-6005.

20—SACRED HEART OF JESUS (1928), Rev. Kenneth A. Smith. In res., Rev. Msgr. Donald J. Songy; Revs. Francis V. Ferrier, S.J.; Michael Jung, O.S.B.
Res., 2250 Main St., 70802-3198. Tel: 225-387-6671; Fax: 225-387-6674.
School—Tel: 225-383-7481; Fax: 225-383-1810. Sr. Patricia Sullivan, C.S.J., Prin.
Sisters of St. Joseph 6; Lay Teachers 34; Students 501.

21—ST. THOMAS MORE (1959), Very Rev. John Carville, S.T.D., V.G.; Rev. Gerard R. Martin. In res., Rev. Patrick Rice, S.J. (Malta). Pastoral Assocs.: Sr. Jane Louise Arbour, C.S.J.; Sr. Dianne Heinrich, C.D.P.; Deacon Clayton Hollier, Ph.D.
Office: 11441 Goodwood Blvd., 70815-6299. Tel: 225-275-3940; Fax: 225-275-1407.
School—Tel: 225-275-2820; Fax: 225-275-0376. Mr. Steve Ketcham, Prin.
Lay Teachers 50; Students 1,070.
Preschool—Tel: 225-272-3477; Fax: 225-272-0468. Ms. Angie Ducote, Dir.
Lay Teachers 15; Students 135.

OUTSIDE THE CITY OF BATON ROUGE

Albany, Livingston Parish, St. Margaret Queen of Scotland (1910), Rev. Msgr. Leo Guillot, V.F.; Deacon Warren Fortenberry, Ed.D.
Res., P.O. Box 100, 70711-0100. Tel: 225-567-3573; Fax: 225-567-2031. [CEM]
Chapel—Springfield, St. Thomas.

Amite, Tangipahoa Parish, St. Helena (1868), Rev. N. John Nutter.
Res., P.O. Box 685, 70422-0685. Tel: 504-748-9057; Fax: 504-748-9094.
Chapels—Greensburg, St. Jude.; Kentwood, St. Elizabeth.

Baker, East Baton Rouge Parish, St. Isidore the Farmer (1958), Rev. Fred Youngs; Deacon Bruno Rizzo.
Res., 5657 Thomas Rd., Baton Rouge, 70811-7356. Tel: 225-775-8850 (Office); Fax: 225-775-7072.
School—Tel: 225-775-3336; Fax: 225-775-3351.
Lay Teachers 25; Students 442.

Bayou Pigeon, Iberville Parish, St. Joan of Arc (1965), Rev. Joseph M. Camilleri.
Res., 39315 Hwy. 75, Plaquemine, 70764-9629. Tel: 225-545-8213; Fax: 225-545-2456.
Chapel—Bayou Sorrel, St. Catherine Laboure.

Belle Rose, Assumption Parish, St. Jules (1912), Rev. Garland T. Belsome.
Res., P.O. Box 38, 70341-0038. Tel: 225-473-8569; Fax: 225-473-2950. [CEM 2]
Chapel—Brusly/St. Martin, St. Martin.

Brusly, West Baton Rouge Parish, St. John the Baptist (1835), Rev. Eric V. Gyan.
Res., P.O. Box 248, 70719-0248. Tel: 225-749-2189; 687-8363; Fax: 225-749-1921.

Convent, St. James Parish, St. Michael the Archangel (1812), Revs. Mariano J. Rizzuto, S.M.; Ed Fuss, S.M.; Deacon Alfred Adams, Sr. In res., Rev. Albert Hebert, S.M.
Res., P.O. Box 65, 70723-0065. Tel: 225-562-3211; Fax: 225-562-3213. [CEM 2]

Darrow, Ascension Parish, St. Anthony of Padua (1962), Rev. Mansueto "Chito" P. Palang.
Mailing Address: P.O. Box 9, Sorrento, 70778. Tel: 225-675-8126; Fax: 225-675-6150.

Denham Springs, Livingston Parish, Immaculate Conception (1960), Revs. Cleo J. Milano, S.T.L.; Michael A. Miceli; Deacon Peter Schlette.
Mailing Address: P.O. Box 1609, 70727-1609.
Res., 865 Hatchell Ln., 70726. Tel: 225-665-5359; Fax: 225-665-4422.
Chapel—Livingston, Sacred Heart of Jesus, Tel: 225-686-7322.

Donaldsonville, Ascension Parish, Ascension of Our Lord Jesus Christ (1772), Rev. Randy M. Cuevas, S.T.L. In res., Rev. Joseph U. Goss, O.P.
Res., P.O. Box 508, 70346-0508. Tel: 225-473-3176; Fax: 225-473-3256. [CEM]

St. Catherine of Siena (1924), Rev. George W. Burden, S.S.J.
Res., P.O. Box 428, 70346-0428. Tel: 225-473-8350; Fax: 225-473-9978.

St. Francis of Assisi (1884), Rev. Michael A. Galea.
Res., 818 W. Tenth St., 70346-9501. Tel: 225-473-8302; Fax: 225-474-0348. [CEM]

French Settlement, Livingston Parish, St. Joseph (1849), Rev. James A. Kinkead; Deacon James A. Little.
Res., 15710 Louisiana Hwy. 16, 70733-9802. Tel: 225-698-3110; Fax: 225-698-3110. [CEM]
Chapels—Head of Island, Our Lady of Perpetual Help.; Port Vincent, St. William.

Gonzales, Ascension Parish, St. Theresa of Avila (1918), Revs. Philip F. Spano; Gregory J. Daigle.
Res., 1022 N. Burnside Ave., 70737-2551. Tel: 225-647-6588; Fax: 225-647-2223.
School—212 E. New River St., 70737-2499. Tel: 225-647-2803; Fax: 225-647-7814. Mr. Jay L. Sullivan, Prin.
Sisters 6; Lay Teachers 24; Students 601.
St. Mark (1973), Rev. J. Joel LaBauve.
Res., 42021 Hwy. 621, 70737-9354. Tel: 225-647-8461; Fax: 225-647-5125.

Gramercy, St. James Parish, Most Sacred Heart of Jesus (1961), Rev. Frank M. Uter. In res., Rev. Louis A. Poche, S.J.
Res., P.O. Box 1501, 70052-1501. Tel: 225-869-5324; Fax: 225-869-5325.

Greenwell Springs, East Baton Rouge Parish, St. Alphonsus Liguori (1962), Rev. Thomas P. Duhe'; Deacon J. Phillip BeJeaux.
Res., 14040 Greenwell Springs Rd., 70739-3302. Tel: 225-261-4650; Fax: 225-261-5650.
School—Tel: 225-261-5299; Fax: 225-261-2795. Sr. Mary Esther Hulin, C.S.J., Prin.
Lay Teachers 28; Students 650.

Grosse Tete, Iberville Parish, St. Joseph (1904), Rev. Shelton J. Fabre.
Res., P.O. Box 8, 70740-0008. Tel: 225-648-2420; Fax: 225-648-2506. [CEM]

Hammond, Tangipahoa Parish, Holy Ghost (1902), Revs. Robert U. Perry, O.P.; Christopher T. Eggleton, O.P.; Jamie A. Diaz, O.P.; Deacon Wallace Gainey, Jr. In res., Rev. Gerald D. Coverdale, O.P.
Res., 601 North Oak St., 70401-2529. Tel: 504-345-3360; Fax: 504-542-4191.
School—506 N. Magnolia St., 70401-2598. Tel: 504-345-0977; Fax: 504-542-6545. Mr. Thomas W. O'Neill, Jr., Prin.
Lay Teachers 39; Students 789.

Independence, Tangipahoa Parish, Mater Dolorosa (1908), Rev. Paul A. McDuffie (CHR); Deacon M. J. Schanzbach.
Res., P.O. Box 349, 70443-0349. Tel: 504-878-9639; Fax: 504-878-6260.
School—P.O. Box 380, 70443-0380. Tel: 504-878-4295; Fax: 504-878-4888. Mrs. Helen Adams, Prin.
Lay Teachers 14; Students 181.
Chapel—Husser, St. Dominic.

Labadieville, Assumption Parish, St. Philomena (1847), Very Rev. Vincent J. Dufresne, S.T.L., J.C.L., V.F.
Res., P.O. Box 11, 70372-0011. Tel: 504-526-4247; Fax: 504-526-4128. [CEM]
School—120 Convent St., 70732-9760. Tel: 504-526-8508; Fax: 504-526-4128. Mr. Rodney P. Bergeron, Prin.
Lay Teachers 11; Students 178.

Lakeland, Pointe Coupee Parish, Immaculate Conception (1859), Very Rev. Matthew P. Lorrain, V.F.
Res., P.O. Box 158, 70752-0158. Tel: 225-627-5124; Fax: 225-627-5125. [CEM 2]

Livonia, Pointe Coupee Parish, St. Frances Xavier Cabrini (1955), Rev. Joseph Thai-Doan Nguyen.
Res., P.O. Box 128, 70755-0128. Tel: 225-637-2396; Fax: 225-637-2390. [CEM]
Chapel—Fordoche, St. Catherine of Siena.

Maringouin, Iberville Parish, Immaculate Heart of Mary (1964), Rev. Shelton J. Fabre.
Res., 11140 Hwy. 77, 70757-9703. Tel: 225-625-2438; Fax: 225-625-3513. [CEM]

Morganza, Pointe Coupee Parish, St. Ann (1872), Rev. Howard B. Hall.
Res., P.O. Box 128, 70759-0128. Tel: 225-694-3781; Fax: 225-694-3711. [CEM 2]
Chapel—Innis, St. Vincent De Paul.

Napoleonville, Assumption Parish, St. Anne (1874), Rev. Caye A. Nelson.
Res., P.O. Box 99, 70390-0090. Tel: 504-369-6656; Fax: 504-369-9718. [CEM 2]
St. Benedict the Moor (1911), Rev. Emmanuel Agbor, M.S.P.
Res., P.O. Box 220, 70390-0220. Tel: 504-369-7225; Fax: 504-369-2772. [CEM 2]
Chapel—Klotzville, St. Augustine.

New Roads, Pointe Coupee Parish, St. Augustine (1923), Rev. Anthony Nwachukwu-Udaku, S.S.J. In res., Rev. Philip Tarallo, S.S.J.; Deacon Norman Christophe.
Res., P.O. Box 548, 70760-0548. Tel: 225-638-7553; Fax: 225-638-2947.
St. Mary of False River, Pointe Coupe'e Parish, (1865), Rev. Michael J. Schatzle; Deacon Norman Christophe.
Res., 348 W. Main St., 70760-3587. Tel: 225-638-9665; Fax: 225-638-6346. [CEM 2]
Chapel—Pointe Coupee, St. Francis.

Paincourtville, Assumption Parish, St. Elizabeth (1840), Rev. Garland T. Belsome.
Mailing Address: P.O. Box 1, 70391-0001.
Res., 6057 St. Elizabeth St., 70391. Tel: 504-369-7398; Fax: 504-369-9892. [CEM]

Paulina, St. James Parish, St. Joseph (1900), Rev. Frank M. Uter.
Res., P.O. Box 129, 70763-0129. Tel: 225-869-5751; Fax: 225-869-4166. [CEM]
Chapel—Lutcher, Our Lady of Prompt Succor.

Pierre Part, Assumption Parish, St. Joseph the Worker (1858), Rev. Clarence J. Waguespack.
Res., P.O. Box 190, 70339-0190. Tel: 504-252-6008; Fax: 504-252-8011. [CEM 2]

Plaquemine, Iberville Parish, St. Clement of Rome (1964), Revs. Dean J. Martin, J.C.L.; Jerome A. Dugas; Sr. Cecile Poitras, S.S.J., Pastoral Assoc.
Res., 58725 St. Clement Ave., 70764-3535. Tel: 225-687-3337; 687-1227; 336-9584; Fax: 225-687-3658.
St. John the Evangelist (1850), Revs. Dean J. Martin, J.C.L.; Jerome A. Dugas.
Office: 57805 Main St., 70764-2531.
Res., 57810 Plaquemine St., 70764-2538. Tel: 225-687-2402; Fax: 225-687-1587. [CEM]

Plattenville, Assumption Parish, Assumption of the Blessed Virgin Mary (1793), Rev. Caye A. Nelson.
Mailing Address: P.O. Box 99, Napoleonville, 70390-0099. Tel: 504-369-6656; Fax: 504-369-9718.
Church—L.A. Hwy. 308. [CEM]

Ponchatoula, Tangipahoa Parish, St. Joseph (1875), Rev. Justin R. Kauchak, O.P.; Deacon Larry Melancon.
Res., P.O. Box 368, 70454-0368. Tel: 504-386-3749; Fax: 504-386-4188. [CEM]
School—(Grades PreK-8) 175 N. Eighth St., 70454-3306. Tel: 504-386-6421; Fax: 504-386-0560. Mrs. Shirley Bougere, Prin.
Lay Teachers 21; Students 300.

Port Allen, West Baton Rouge Parish, Holy Family (1920), Rev. Henry C. Vavasseur.
Res., P.O. Box 290, 70767-0290. Tel: 225-383-1838; Fax: 225-383-1839.
School—(Grades K-8) 335 N. Jefferson Ave., 70767-2798. Tel: 225-344-4100; Fax: 225-344-1928. Sr. Joel Miller, M.S.C., Prin.
Marianites of Holy Cross 1; Lay Teachers 24; Students 499.
Preschool—415 N. Jefferson Ave., 70767-2727. Tel: 225-343-6541. Mrs. Diane Harkins, Dir.
Lay Teachers 4; Students 53.

Prairieville, Ascension Parish, St. John the Evangelist (1919), Revs. Martin A. Hernandez, J.C.L., M.C.L.; Vicente Panaligan (Philippines); Deacon Reese Wiggins.
Res., 15208 Hwy. 73, 70769-3507. Tel: 225-673-8307; Fax: 225-673-8680.

St. Amant, Ascension Parish, Holy Rosary (1905), Very Rev. Robert F. Stine, V.F.; Rev. Gregory J. Daigle; Sr. Mary John Hotard, C.S.J., Pastoral Assoc.
Res., 44450 Hwy. 429, 70774-4597. Tel: 225-647-5321; Fax: 225-647-5322. [CEM 2]
Chapel—Lake, Sacred Heart.

St. Francisville, West Feliciana Parish, Our Lady of Mount Carmel (1874), Rev. Charles R. Landry.
Res., P.O. Box 67, 70775-0067. Tel: 225-635-3630; Fax: 225-383-5219.
Chapels—Jackson, Our Lady of Perpetual Help.; Angola State Penitentiary, Tel: 225-655-4411, Ext. 2028. [CEM]

St. Gabriel, Iberville Parish, St. Gabriel (1769), Rev. Rubin R. Reynolds; Deacon Vernon J. Melancon.
Res., 3625 Hwy. 75, 70776-9411. Tel: 225-642-8441; Fax: 225-642-8491. [CEM]

St. James, St. James Parish, St. James (1757), Rev. Louis T. Oubre; Deacon Henry Zeringue.
Res., 6613 Hwy. 18, 70086-9054. Tel: 225-265-4210; Fax: 225-265-4225. [CEM]

Sorrento, Ascension Parish, St. Anne (1963), Rev. Mansueto "Chito" P. Palang; Deacon Jerry Braud.
Res., P.O. Box 9, 70778-0009. Tel: 225-675-8126; Fax: 225-675-6150.

Tickfaw, Tangipahoa Parish, Our Lady of Pompeii (1973), Rev. Robert U. Perry, O.P.
Res., P.O. Box 276, 70466-0276. Tel: 504-345-8957; Fax: 504-542-1585.

Vacherie, St. James Parish, Our Lady of Peace (1864), Rev. Henry W. Gautreau, Jr.
Res., 13281 Hwy. 644, 70090-3102. Tel: 225-265-3953; Fax: 225-265-2507. [CEM]
St. Philip (1873), Rev. David M. Chauvin; Deacon Francis Waguespack.
Res., 1175 Hwy. 18, 70090-9527. Tel: 225-265-4085; Fax: 225-265-9348. [CEM]

White Castle, Iberville Parish, Our Lady of Prompt Succor (1899), Rev. Jules A. Brunet.
Res., P.O. Box 249, 70788-0249. Tel: 225-545-3635; Fax: 225-545-8615. [CEM 2]
Chapel—Bayou Goula, St. Paul.

Whitehall, Livingston Parish, St. Stephen the Martyr (1964), Rev. Keun-Soo Lee, Ph.D.
Res., 22494 Hwy. 22, Maurepas, 70449-3404. Tel: 225-695-6310; Fax: 225-695-6039.
Chapel—Bear Island, St. Mary.

Zachary, East Baton Rouge Parish, St. John the Baptist (1964), Rev. Kenneth W. Laird.
Res., 4727 McHugh Dr., 70791-3935. Tel: 225-654-5778; Fax: 225-654-5796.
Chapel—Clinton, Our Lady of the Assumption.

Chaplains of Public Institutions

BATON ROUGE. *Baton Rouge General Medical Center* P.O. Box 3611, 70821-3611. Tel: 225-387-7000. Rev. Michael Jung, O.S.B., Chap.
Dixon Correctional Institute. Deacon J. Phillip BeJeaux, Chap., Mailing Address:Mailing Address: 18367 Ednie Ln., Greenwell Springs, 70739. Tel: 225-261-4650 (Office); 261-5906.
Jetson Correctional Institution For Youth. Deacon J. Peter Walsh, Chap., Mailing Address:Mailing Address: 12424 Brogdon Ln., 70816-4801. Tel: 225-753-5750.

ANGOLA. *Louisiana State Penitentiary*. St. Augustine Chapel. Rev. J. Joel Labauve, Mailing Address:Mailing Address: P.O. Box 428, 70712-0428. Tel: 225-655-4411; 655-3243.

CARVILLE. *National Hansen's Disease Center* Gillis Long Memorial Hospital. Rev. Reynolds Garland, O.F.M., Chap., 5445 Point Clair Rd., 70721-9607. Tel: 225-642-5533.

JACKSON. *East Feliciana Chronic Disease Hospital and Rehabilitation Center*. Rev. J. Daniel Walsh, C.S.C., Chap., P.O. Box 438, 70748-0438.

ST. GABRIEL. *Hunt Correctional Institute*. (Vacant). Mailing Address:Mailing Address: P.O. Box 174, 70776-0174. Tel: 225-642-3306.
LA Correctional Institute For Women. Deacon Joseph Mamou, Chap., Mailing Address:Mailing Address: P.O. Box 26, 70726-0026. Tel: 225-642-5529, Ext. 240.

Special Assignment:
Reverend Fathers—
Crifasi, Peter D., Chap., Nursing homes not under Catholic auspice., 6824 Ozark St., Baton Rouge, LA 70805-6248. Tel: 225-336-8708; 357-9562
Ferrier, Francis V., S.J., Nursing homes not under Catholic auspice., 2250 Main St., Baton Rouge, LA 70802-3198. Tel: 225-387-6671
McCue, Will, S.C., 855 Hearthstone Dr., Baton Rouge, LA 70806-5599. Tel: 225-383-0381
Seynaeve, Jaak, M.Afr., S.T.D., 2187 Olive St., Baton Rouge, LA 70806-6621. Tel: 225-336-9867
Very Rev.—
Counce, Paul D., J.C.L., M.C.L., Diocesan Tribunal, P.O. Box 1087, Baton Rouge, LA 70821-1087. Tel: 225-387-0561; 225-383-4370; Fax: 225-336-8789

On Leave:
Reverend Fathers—
DeBenedetto, David J.
Lemoine, Daniel P.
Maggio, J. Mark
Moran, Salvador N.

Military Chaplains:
Reverend Fathers—
Rodriguez, Aloysius M.

Retired:
Reverend Monsignors—
Frey, Andrew F., P.O. Box 2458, Bay St. Louis, MS 39521-2458. Tel: 228-467-4382; Fax: 228-466-6477
Greene, William L., 3111 Kleinert Ave., Baton Rouge, LA 70806-6833. Tel: 225-336-0903
Lefebvre, Gerald M., P.O. Box 84126, Baton Rouge, LA 70884-4126. Tel: 225-925-8241
Songy, Donald J., 2250 Main St., Baton Rouge, LA 70802-3198. Tel: 225-387-6671; Fax: 225-387-6672
Reverend Fathers—
Caballero, Lloyd C., 24546 Louand Dr., Lacombe, LA 70445-9801. Tel: 504-626-7765; Fax: 504-626-7765
Clement, James P., St. Clare Manor, 7435 Bishop Ott Dr. #113-A, Baton Rouge, LA 70806-8930. Tel: 225-216-1596
Faschan, Matthew, Oakwood Village, 4400 McHugh Rd., Zachary, LA 70791. Tel: 225-654-2133

Hewson, William J., 24546 Louand Dr., Lacombe, LA 70445-9801. Tel: 504-626-7765; Fax: 504-626-7765
Ibanez, Rodolfo, Domingo Sautu, 15, Murguia, Alava 01130 Spain
Kersey, Walter L., 501 N. Pacific St., #21, Oceanside, CA 92054. Tel: 619-966-0515
Marcell, Robert G., P.O. Box 80783, Baton Rouge, LA 70898-0783. Tel: 225-346-8258
McDonald, A. John, 333 Lee Dr., #134, Baton Rouge, LA 70808-4974. Tel: 225-767-8237
Rocheleau, Raymond, Carestone at River Center, 6665 E. River Rd., Tucson, AZ 85747-2043. Tel: 520-615-1448
Termini, Mario, 38860 LA Hwy. 75, Plaquemine, LA 70764-7729. Tel: 225-545-3608

Permanent Deacons:
Adams, Alfred P., St. Michael the Archangel, Convent
BeJeaux, J. Phillip, St. Alphonsus Liguori Church, Greenwell Springs; Dixon Correctional Institute, Baton Rouge
Braud, Jerry W., St. Anne Church, Sorrento
Christophe, Norman (OKL), St. Mary of False River and St. Augustine, New Roads
Decker, Guy E., St. George Parish, Baton Rouge
Duplessis, W. Brent, Immaculate Conception, Denham Springs
Ellis, Albert R., Jr., St. George Church, Baton Rouge; Diocesan Permanent Diaconate Office
Fortenberry, Warren D., St. Margaret, Albany
Furlow, Robert E., Jr., Diocesan Communications Office and St. Joseph Cathedral, Baton Rouge
Gainey, Wallace L., Jr., Holy Ghost, Hammond
Hollier, Clayton A., St. Thomas More Church, Baton Rouge
Lacoste, Ronald J., On Leave
Little, James A., St. Joseph Church, French Settlement
Mamou, Joseph (NO), Chap., LA Correctional Institute For Women, St. Gabriel
Melancon, Larry, St. Joseph Church, Ponchatoula
Melancon, Vernon J., St. Gabriel Church, St. Gabriel
Rizzo, Bruno, St. Isidore the Farmer Church, Baker
Robinson, Thomas H., St. Jean Vianney Church, Baton Rouge
Schanzbach, Dr. Milton, St. Joseph Church, Ponchatoula
Waguespack, Francis, Jr., St. Philip Church, Vacherie
Walsh, J. Peter, St. Patrick Church and Jetson Correctional Institution For Youth, Baton Rouge
Wax, James E., Our Lady of Mercy, Baton Rouge
Wiggins, Reese, St. John the Evangelist, Prairieville
Zeringue, Henry J., St. James Church, St. James

INSTITUTIONS LOCATED IN THE DIOCESE

[A] COLLEGES AND UNIVERSITIES

BATON ROUGE. *Our Lady of the Lake College*, 5345 Brittany Dr., 70808-4398. Tel: 225-768-1710; Fax: 225-768-1726.
E-mail: msmith@ololcollege.edu
Web site: www.ololcollege.edu
For a complete listing, refer to the Colleges and Universities section.

[B] DIOCESAN HIGH SCHOOLS, INTERPAROCHIAL

BATON ROUGE. *Bishop Joseph V. Sullivan Diocesan Regional Catholic High School.*
E-mail: jwray@bishopsullivanhigh.org
Mailing Address: P.O. Box 86110, 70879-6110. 17521 Monitor Ave., 70817-2640. Tel: 225-753-9782; Fax: 225-753-0605. Mr. Joseph A. Wray, Prin. Sisters 1; Lay Teachers 56; Students 738.
Redemptorist High School, 4000 St. Gerard Ave., 70805-2999. Tel: 225-357-0936; Fax: 225-357-4555.
E-mail: redempths@aol.com
Mr. John C. Fabre, Prin. Lay Teachers 59; Students 824.
Serving parishes in Baton Rouge, Baker, Brusly, Denham Springs, Greenwell Springs, Lakeland, New Roads, Gonzales, Port Allen, St. Gabriel, Zachary, Plaquemine, Maringouin, Prairieville and Clinton.

DONALDSONVILLE. *Ascension Catholic Interparochial High School*, 311 St. Vincent St., 70346-2697. Tel: 225-473-7486; Fax: 225-473-8559. Dr. Lou Campomenosi, Prin. Lay Teachers 21; Students 266.
Serving parishes in Donaldsonville, St. James, Belle Rose, Vacherie, White Castle, Darrow, Gonzales, Convent, Paincourtville and Plattenville.

HAMMOND. *St. Thomas Aquinas Regional Catholic High School*, 14520 Voss Dr., 70401-9801. Tel: 504-542-7662; Fax: 504-542-4010.
E-mail: stthomas@i-55.com
Web site: www.i-55.com/falcon.
Dominican Sisters, Springfield, IL. Sr. Judith Anne Haase, O.P., Prin. Sisters 2; Lay Teachers 28; Students 325.

NEW ROADS. *Catholic High School of Pointe Coupee*, 504 Fourth St., 70760-3499. Tel: 225-638-3469; Fax: 225-638-6471.
E-mail: cispc@gateway.net
Mrs. Marsha M. Langlois, Prin. Lay Teachers 30; Students 411.
Serving parishes in Lakeland, Livonia, Morganza, New Roads and Maringouin.

PLAQUEMINE. *St. John Interparochial High School*, 24250 Regina St., 70764-3598. Tel: 225-687-3056; Fax: 225-687-3658.
E-mail: info@stjohnschool.org
Mr. Lester Bourg, Admin.; Mrs. Mary T. Moran, Prin. Lay Teachers 15; Students 218.
Serving parishes in Plaquemine, Brusly, Port Allen, Grosse Tete and White Castle.

[C] HIGH SCHOOLS, PRIVATE

BATON ROUGE. *Catholic High School*, 855 Hearthstone Dr., 70806-5599. Tel: 225-383-0397; Fax: 225-383-0381.
E-mail: gbrandao@catholichigh.org
Web site: www.catholichigh.org
Dr. Gregory Brandao, Prin..Brothers of the Sacred Heart 6; Lay Teachers 65; Boys 892.
St. Joseph's Academy, 3015 Broussard St., 70808-1198. Tel: 225-383-7207; Fax: 225-344-5714.
Web site: www.sjabr.org
Sr. Judith Brun, C.S.J., Prin..Sisters of St. Joseph 4; Lay Teachers 59; Girls 773.

[D] DIOCESAN ELEMENTARY SCHOOLS, INTERPAROCHIAL

DONALDSONVILLE. *Ascension Catholic Interparochial School*, 311 St. Vincent St., 70346-3499. Tel: 225-473-9227. Mrs. Janice M. Burns, Prin. Lay Teachers 26; Students 425.
Serving parishes in Donaldsonville, St. James, Belle Rose, Vacherie, White Castle, Darrow, Gonzales, Convent, Paulina, Paincourtville, and Plattenville.

NEW ROADS. *Catholic Elementary School of Pointe Coupee*, 304 Napoleon St., 70760-3527. Tel: 225-638-9313; Fax: 225-638-9953.
E-mail: catholicelemofpc@csobr.org
Carrie S. Maillet, Prin. Sisters of St. Joseph 1; Lay Teachers 20; Students 440.
Serving parishes in Lakeland, Livonia, Morganza, New Roads and Maringouin.

PAINCOURTVILLE. *St. Elizabeth Interparochial.* (Grades PreK-8), P.O. Drawer M, 70391-0420. Tel: 504-369-7402; Fax: 504-369-1527.
E-mail: St.Elizabeth@csobr.org
Mrs. Liane Landry, Prin. Lay Teachers 10; Students 239.
Serving parishes in Belle Rose, Bertrandville, Napoleonville, Paincourtville, Pierre Part and Plattenville.

PAULINA. *St. Peter Chanel Interparochial School*, 2590 LA Hwy. 44, 70763. Tel: 225-869-5778; Fax: 225-869-8131.
E-mail: StPeterChanel@csobr.org
Web site: www.stpchanel.org
Ms. Cassie D. Bourgeois, Prin. Lay Teachers 24; Students 416.
Serving parishes in Paulina, Gramercy, Convent, Vacherie, St. James and Grand Point.

PLAQUEMINE. *St. John Interparochial Elementary / Middle School*, 58645 St. Clement Ave., 70764-3599. Tel: 225-687-6616; Fax: 225-687-6280.
E-mail: info@stjohnschool.org
Web site: www.stjohnschool.org
Ms. Ruth H. Larpenteur, Prin. Lay Teachers 32; Students 615.
Serving parishes in Plaquemine, Brusly, Grosse Tete, White Castle, Baton Rouge, St. Gabriel, Maringouin, Bayou Pigeon, and Donaldsonville.

[E] SCHOOL, EXCEPTIONAL CHILDREN

BATON ROUGE. *Department of Special Education.* Guardian Angels Center (7-14 yrs.) and Redemptorist Center (15-21 yrs.). P.O. Box 2028, 70821-2028. Tel: 225-383-3066; Fax: 225-242-0344.
E-mail: deptspecialed@csobr.org
Mrs. Gail Campo, Admin. Housed on St. Gerard Elementary Campus and at Redemptorist High School. Sisters 1; Teachers 8; Speech Therapist 1; Students 54.

[F] GENERAL HOSPITALS

BATON ROUGE. *Our Lady of the Lake Regional Medical Center*, 5000 Hennessy Blvd., 70808-4398. Tel: 225-765-6565; Fax: 225-766-5645
For a complete listing, refer to the Hospitals section.

GONZALES. *St. Elizabeth Hospital*, 1125 W. Hwy. 30, 70737-5000. Tel: 225-647-5071
For a complete listing, refer to the Hospitals section.

[G] HOMES AND SPECIAL CARE FACILITIES

BATON ROUGE. *Elderly Housing of Our Lady of the Lake Medical Center*, 5000 Hennessy Blvd., 70808-4398. Tel: 225-765-6565
For a complete listing, refer to the Special Care Facilities section.
Ollie Steele Burden Manor, 4250 Essen Ln., 70809-2196. Tel: 225-926-0091; Fax: 225-926-4937
For a complete listing, refer to the Special Care Facilities section.

[H] MONASTERIES AND RESIDENCES OF PRIESTS OR BROTHERS

BATON ROUGE. *Brothers of the Sacred Heart*, 855 Hearthstone Dr., 70806-5599. Tel: 225-383-7117. Bro. Francis David, S.C., Supr.; Rev. Will McCue, S.C., Chap. Brothers 8.
Franciscan Residence, 4155 Essen Ln. #4, 70809-2115. Tel: 225-924-3836. Rev. Anthony Walter, O.F.M.
Incarnatio Consecratio Mission. (Vietnamese Institute.), 2305 Choctaw Dr., 70805-7999. Tel: 225-357-1204; Fax: 225-354-0611.
E-mail: nvhung@bellsouth.net
Revs. Hung Viet Nguyen, I.C.M., Dir.; Joseph Lien To, I.C.M.; Martin Thanh Nguyen, I.C.M.; Thomas Tranh Dinh, I.C.M.
The Redemptorist Education and Formation, P.O. Box 53900, 70892-3900. Tel: 225-355-2600; Fax: 225-355-6200. Rev. Joseph Pelletieri, C.Ss.R.
Redemptorist Vice Province. Mailing Address: P.O. Box 53900, 70892-3900. Tel: 225-355-2600; Fax: 225-355-6200. Very Rev. Thomas D. Picton, C.Ss.R., Vice Prov.; Bro. Steven E. Fruge, C.Ss.R., Vice Pres. & Sec. In res. Rev. Eugene J. Staub, C.Ss.R. Priests 5.
Priests of Vice Province in Residences not listed elsewhere: Revs. John C. Vargas, C.Ss.R., Redemptorist Generalate, Rome; Robert O. Curry, C.Ss.R.

[I] CONVENTS AND RESIDENCES FOR SISTERS

BATON ROUGE. *Baton Rouge / Southwest Regional Office*, P.O. Box 65105, 70896-5105. Tel: 225-383-3475. Sr. Carolyn Brady, C.S.J., Development Dir.
Maryville Novitiate and Provincial House, 4200 Essen Lane, 70809-2196. North American Province, 4200 Essen Ln., 70809-2196. Tel: 225-927-7481; 926-1627; Fax: 225-925-5268. Sr. Brendan Mary Ronayne, O.S.F., Prov. Supr. Temporary Professed 1; Final Vows 25.
St. Joseph Convent, 3080 Kleinert Ave., 70806-6899. Tel: 225-344-1517; Fax: 225-343-0261.
E-mail: stjosephsbr@juno.com
Sr. Ursula Harelson, C.S.J., Local Coord. Sisters of St. Joseph 10.

TICKFAW. *Our Lady Queen Contemplative Monastery*, 50352 Antioch Rd., 70466-9747. Tel: 504-345-2630; Fax: 504-345-2630. Benedictine Nuns. Very Rev. Mary Herbert Walsh, O.S.B., Prioress; Revs. Marion C. Walsh, O.S.B. (IND), Chap.; Frederick P. Walsh, O.S.B. (IND), (Retired); Joachim E. Walsh, O.S.B. (IND), (Retired). Nuns 6.

[J] RETREAT HOUSES

BATON ROUGE. *Bishop Robert E. Tracy Center.* Mailing Address: P.O. Box 2028, 70821-2028. Tel: 225-336-8750; Fax: 225-336-8765. 3300 Hundred Oaks Ave., 70808-1599. Mr. Charles Jumonville, Admin.

CONVENT. *Manresa House of Retreats*, Office, P.O. Box 89, 70723-0089. Tel: 225-562-3596; 800-782-9431; Fax: 225-562-3147.
E-mail: manresa@stargazer.net
Rev. Anthony H. Ostini, S.J., Dir. Assoc. Directors: Revs. Thomas J. Cronin, S.J.; Hacker J. Fagot, S.J.; Edward J. Romagosa, S.J.

PONCHATOULA. *Rosaryville / Spirit Life Center*, 39003 Rosaryville Rd., 70454-9580. Tel: 225-294-5039; 800-627-9183; Fax: 225-294-3510. Sr. M. Edmund Gibson, O.P., Dir.; Rev. William J. Aldridge, O.P., Chap. Dominican Sisters 2.

[K] CAMPUS MINISTRY

BATON ROUGE. *Christ the King Parish and Catholic Student Center*, Louisiana State University, P.O. Box 25131, 70894-5131. Tel: 225-344-8595; 383-1574; Fax: 225-344-1920.
E-mail: lsucsc@unix1.sncc.lsu.edu
Web site: www.lsu.edu/guests/lsucsc

Revs. Than N. Vu, S.T.L.; Matthew C. Dupre, Highland Rd. & Dalrymple Dr., 70803. Total Catholic Students 16,000.

Martin Luther King, Jr. Student Center, St. Joseph Chapel, Southern University, 586 Harding Blvd., 70807-5301. Tel: 225-775-8691; 775-1301; Fax: 225-775-7067. Rev. Francis R. Brou, S.J., Chap. & Dir. Total Catholic Students 3,270.

HAMMOND. *St. Albert the Great Catholic Student Center*, 409 W. Dakota St., 70401-2517. Tel: 504-345-7206; Fax: 504-345-7223.
E-mail: stalbert@i-55.com
Web site: www.i-55/~stalbert
Serving Southeastern Louisiana University. Rev. Sean O. Sheehy, Ed.D., Dir. Total Students 15,600.

[L] MISCELLANEOUS

BATON ROUGE. *Bishop Stanley J. Ott Shelter Program*. Mailing Address: P.O. Box 127, 70821-0127. Tel: 225-383-7343; Fax: 225-383-6623. Mr. Michael Acaldo, Exec. Dir.

Catholic Community Services, 1900 S. Acadian Thruway, 70808-1688. Tel: 225-336-8770; Fax: 225-336-8745.
E-mail: droe@ccsbr.org
Web site: www.ccsbr.org
Mailing Address: P.O. Box 1668, 70821-1668. Ms. Deborah Roe, M.S.W., Exec. Dir.

Catholic-Presbyterian Apts., Inc., 655 North St., 70802-5420. Tel: 225-383-5551; Fax: 225-383-0050.
E-mail: flash@intersurf.com
Mr. Gordon D. McDowell, Exec. Dir.

Counseling, Maternity & Adoption, 1900 S. Acadian Thruway, 70808. Tel: 225-336-8708; Fax: 225-336-8703.
E-mail: adopt@ccsbr.org
Web site: www.adoptbatonrouge.com
Mailing Address: P.O. Box 4785, 70821-4785.

FMOL Health Systems, Inc., 4200 Essen Ln., 70809-2196. Tel: 225-923-2701; 926-0708; Fax: 225-926-4846.
E-mail: jfinan@ololrmc.com
Mr. John J. Finan, Jr., Pres. & CEO.

Haiti Project, Inc., 4200 Essen Ln., 70809-2196. Tel: 225-926-1627; Fax: 225-925-5268. Mailing Address: P.O. Box 80376, 70898-0376. Sr. Brendan Mary Ronayne, O.S.F., Pres.
Organized and under the supervision of the Franciscan Missionaries of Our Lady, North American Province.

MAGNIFICAT-Baton Rouge Chapter, 4307 Lake Lawrence Cir., 70816-4423. Tel: 225-291-2550. A Ministry to Catholic Women. Mrs. Carol Dazzio, Coord.

Myriam's House, Inc. Mailing Address: 3027 Nicholson Dr., 70802-8432. Ms. Mary McClure, Pres.; Ms. Yolanda P. Perrilloux, Exec. Dir. (Sponsored in part by Sisters of St. Joseph). Facility for homeless women, providing temporary housing, assistance with job placement and other needed services.

Queen of Peace Home and Soup Kitchen, 749 East Blvd., 70802-6399. Tel: 225-383-4127; 383-8367. Missionaries of Charity.

St. Michael's Home. (Vietnamese), 2305 Choctaw Dr., 70805-7999.
E-mail: nvhung@bellsouth.net
Rev. Hung Viet Nguyen, I.C.M., Dir. Tel: 225-357-1204; Fax 225-354-0611.

St. Vincent DePaul Dining Room. Mailing Address: P.O. Box 127, 70821-0127. Tel: 225-383-7837; 383-7439; Fax: 225-383-6623. Mr. Michael J. Acaldo, Exec. Dir.

St. Vincent DePaul Stores. Mailing Address: P.O. Box 127, 70821-0127. Tel: 225-356-5158; Fax: 225-383-6623. Mr. Al St. Pierre, Mgr. Tel: 225-356-5158; Mr. Michael J. Acaldo, Exec. Dir. Tel: 225-383-7837.

Sisters of St. Joseph - St. Paul Center, 3920 Gus Young Ave., 70802-1727. Tel: 225-344-8590; Fax: 225-387-5169.
E-mail: spalc@juno.com
Sr. Kathleen Bahlinger, C.S.J., Dir.

St. Vincent DePaul Community Pharmacy, Inc. Mailing Address: P.O. Box 127, 70821-0127. Tel: 225-383-7450; Fax: 225-383-6623. Mr. Michael J. Acaldo, Exec. Dir.

U.S. Federation of Sisters of St. Joseph, 1841 Glenmore Ave., 70808-1234. Tel: 225-927-0273; Fax: 225-927-2735.
E-mail: phyllisFed@aol.com
Web site: www.nd.edu/csjus.html
Sr. Phyllis Manda, C.S.J., Exec. Dir.

Unwed Mothers Home, 715 East Blvd., 70802-6399. Tel: 225-343-2138. Missionaries of Charity.

[M] FOUNDATIONS, FUNDS AND TRUSTS

BATON ROUGE. *Baton Rouge Chancery Office*. Mailing Address: P.O. Box 2028, 70821-2028. 1800 S. Acadian Thruway, 70808-1698. Tel: 225-387-0561; Fax: 225-336-8789.
E-mail: chancery@diobr.org
Ascension Catholic Interparochial School Endowment Fund, Donaldsonville.
Bishop Stanley J. Ott Works of Mercy Trust.
Diocese of Baton Rouge Clergy Retirement Plan.
Diocese of Baton Rouge Lay Retirement Plan.
Diocese of Baton Rouge Trust Fund.
Nim Pecquet Holy Family School Foundation.
Our Lady of Perpetual Help Trust.
Pamphile and Mabyn Donaldson Trust for St. Louis King of France Church.
Pointe Coupee Catholic Interparochial School Endowment Fund, New Roads.
Sacred Heart Parish Endowment Fund.
St. Aloysius School Endowment Fund.
St. Joseph Cathedral Cemetery Fund.
St. Joseph Cathedral Trust.
St. Theresa of Avila Catholic School Educational Foundation, Gonzales.
St. Thomas More School Endowment Trust.
Sherri Lyn Shaffer Trust for St. Thomas More Church.
Veritas Foundation, Hammond.
Brothers of the Sacred Heart Foundation of the New Orleans Province, Inc., 720 Hearthstone Dr., 70806-5599. Tel: 225-338-0034; Fax: 225-336-0505. Rev. Will McCue, S.C., Pres.
CHS Foundation, 855 Hearthstone Dr., 70806-5599. Tel: 225-389-0978; Fax: 225-389-0983. Bro. Aquin Gauthier, S.C., Pres.
Our Lady of the Lake Foundation, 5000 Hennessy Blvd., 70808-9907. Tel: 225-765-5000.

CONVENT. *Hynes Fund*, 5858 Hwy. 44, 70723-0089. Tel: 504-821-0334. Mailing Address: P.O. Box 89, 70723-0089. Legal Title: *The Administrators of the Rev. John W. Hynes, S.J., Manresa Memorial Endowment Fund, Inc.* Bro. Lawrence J. Lundin, S.J., Treas.

RELIGIOUS INSTITUTES OF MEN REPRESENTED IN THE DIOCESE

For further details refer to the corresponding bracketed number in the Religious Institutes of Men or Women section.

[0200]—*Benedictine Monks.* (St. Meinrad Archabbey).—O.S.B.
[0200]—*Benedictine Monks.* (St. Joseph Abbey, St. Benedict, LA).—O.S.B.
[1100]—*Brothers of the Sacred Heart.* (New Orleans Prov.).—S.C.
[0470]—*The Capuchin Friars.*—O.F.M.Cap.
[1070]—*Congregation of the Most Holy Redeemer-Redemptorists.* (New Orleans Vice Prov.).—C.Ss.R.
[0520]—*Franciscan Friars.* (Prov. of St. John the Baptist).—O.F.M.
[]—*Incarnatio Consecratio Missionaries.*—I.C.M.
[0850]—*Missionaries of Africa.*—M.Afr.
[]—*Missionaries of St. Paul.*—M.S.P.
[0430]—*Order of Preachers-Dominicans.* (Prov. of St. Martin de Porres).—O.P.
[0610]—*Priests of the Congregation of Holy Cross.* (Southern Prov.).—C.S.C.
[0700]—*St. Joseph's Society of the Sacred Heart-Josephites.*—S.S.J.
[0690]—*Society of Jesus.* (New Orleans Prov.).—S.J.
[0760]—*Society of Mary-Marists.* (American Prov.).—S.M.
[0420]—*Society of the Divine Word.* (Southern Prov.).—S.V.D.

RELIGIOUS INSTITUTES OF WOMEN REPRESENTED IN THE DIOCESE

[0233]—*Benedictine Nuns.*—O.S.B.
[0760]—*Daughters of Charity of St. Vincent de Paul.* (West Central Prov.).—D.C.
[0840]—*Daughters of Jesus.*—F.I.
[1070-08]—*Dominican Sisters.*—O.P.
[1070-10]—*Dominican Sisters.*—O.P.
[1140]—*Eucharistic Missionaries of St. Dominic.*
[1380]—*Franciscan Missionaries of Our Lady.*—O.S.F.
[2410]—*Marianites of Holy Cross.*—M.S.C.
[2710]—*Missionaries of Charity.*—M.C.
[1070-03]—*Sinsinawa Dominican Congregation of the Most Holy Rosary.*—O.P.
[0500]—*Sisters of Charity of Nazareth.* (Southern Region).—S.C.N.
[0430]—*Sisters of Charity of the Blessed Virgin Mary.*—B.V.M.
[0990]—*Sisters of Divine Providence.*—C.D.P.
[2570]—*Sisters of Mercy of Philadelphia.*—R.S.M.
[2630]—*Sisters of Mercy of the Holy Cross.*—S.C.S.C.
[3880]—*Sisters of St. Joseph of Medaille.*—C.S.J.
[3830-16]—*Sisters of St. Joseph of Springfield, Mont Marie.*—S.S.J.
[1950]—*Sisters of the Holy Family.*—S.S.F.
[2940]—*Sisters of the Most Holy Sacrament.*—M.H.S.
[4070]—*Society of the Sacred Heart.*—R.S.C.J.

NECROLOGY

† Weber, Rev. Msgr. John A., (Retired). —Died Feb. 22, 2000.

Diocese of Beaumont

(Dioecesis Bellomontensis)

Most Reverend

CURTIS JOHN GUILLORY, S.V.D., D.D.

Bishop of Beaumont; ordained December 16, 1972; appointed Titular Bishop of Stagno and Auxiliary Bishop of Galveston-Houston December 29, 1987; consecrated February 19, 1988; appointed Bishop of Beaumont June 2, 2000; installed July 28, 2000. *Mailing Address: P.O. Box 3948, Beaumont, TX, 77704-3948. Office: 703 Archie St., Beaumont, TX, 77701.* Tel.: 409-838-0451, Ext. 130; Fax: 409-838-4511.

Diocesan Pastoral Office: 703 Archie St., P.O. Box 3948, Beaumont, TX, 77704-3948. Tel.: 409-838-0451; Fax: 409-838-4511.

Web site address: www.dioceseofbmt.org

E-mail address: chancery@dioceseofbmt.org

ESTABLISHED SEPTEMBER 29, 1966.

Square Miles 7,878.

Comprises the counties of Chambers, Hardin, Jasper, Jefferson, Liberty, Newton, Orange, Polk and Tyler.

For legal titles of parishes and diocesan institutions, consult the Diocesan Pastoral Office.

STATISTICAL OVERVIEW

Personnel	
Bishop	1
Priests: Diocesan Active in Diocese	31
Priests: Active Outside Diocese	4
Priests: Retired, Sick or Absent	11
Number of Diocesan Priests	46
Religious Priests in Diocese	28
Extern Priests in Diocese	8
Ordinations:	
Diocesan Priests	1
Transitional Deacons	1
Permanent Deacons	30
Permanent Deacons in Diocese	30
Total Brothers	4
Total Sisters	41
Parishes	
Parishes	44
With Resident Pastor:	
Resident Diocesan Priests	25
Resident Religious Priests	18
Without Resident Pastor:	
Administered by Priests	1
Missions	9
Professional Ministry Personnel:	
Sisters	3
Lay Ministers	42
Welfare	
Catholic Hospitals	3
Total Assisted	386,358
Health Care Centers	1
Total Assisted	80,000
Special Centers for Social Services	2
Total Assisted	53,854
Educational	
Diocesan Students in Other Seminaries	14
Total Seminarians	14
High Schools, Diocesan and Parish	1
Total Students	567
Elementary Schools, Diocesan and Parish	6
Total Students	1,286
Catechesis/Religious Education:	
High School Students	2,303
Elementary Students	6,287
Total Students Under Catholic Instruction	10,457
Teachers in the Diocese:	
Sisters	5
Lay Teachers	130
Vital Statistics	
Receptions into the Church:	
Infant Baptism Totals	1,480
Adult Baptism Totals	126
Received into Full Communion	310
First Communions	1,408
Confirmations	1,085
Marriages:	
Catholic	196
Interfaith	160
Total Marriages	356
Deaths	809
Total Catholic Population	95,397
Total Population	588,265

Former Bishops—Most Rev. VINCENT M. HARRIS, D.D., ord. March 19, 1938; appt. Bishop of Beaumont, July 4, 1966; cons. Sept. 28, 1966; installed as First Bishop of Beaumont, Sept. 29, 1966; appt. Titular Bishop of Rotaria and Coadjutor with right of succession to the Bishop of Austin, TX, April 21, 1971; succeeded to as Second Bishop of Austin, Nov. 16, 1971; died March 31, 1988.—Most Rev. WARREN L. BOUDREAUX, J.C.D., D.D., ord. May 30, 1942; appt. Titular Bishop of Calynda and Auxiliary Bishop of Lafayette, LA, May 19, 1962; cons. July 25, 1962; appt. second Bishop of Beaumont, June 4, 1971; installed Aug. 25, 1971; appt. first Bishop of Houma-Thibodaux, March 2, 1977; installed as first Bishop of Houma-Thibodaux, June 5, 1977; died Oct. 6, 1997.—Most Rev. BERNARD J. GANTER, D.D., ord. May 22, 1952; appt. first Bishop of Tulsa, Dec. 19, 1972; cons. and installed, Feb. 7, 1973; appt. third Bishop of Beaumont, Oct. 3, 1977; installed Dec. 13, 1977; died Oct. 9, 1993.—Most Rev. JOSEPH A. GALANTE, D.D., J.C.D., ord. May 16, 1964; cons. Dec. 11, 1992; appt. Bishop of Beaumont, April 5, 1994; installed Bishop of Beaumont, May 9, 1994; appt. Coadjutor Bishop of Dallas, Nov. 23, 1999.

Pastoral Center—703 Archie St., P.O. Box 3948, Beaumont, 77704-3948. Tel: 409-838-0451; Fax: 409-838-4511. Office Hours: 8:30-5:00.

Vicar General and Moderator of the Curia—Rev. Msgr. MICHAEL A. JAMAIL, J.C.D., Ed.D., *P.O. Box 3948, Beaumont, 77704-3948.* Tel: 409-838-0451, Ext. 123; 835-9902 (Res.); Fax: 409-838-4511.

Episcopal Vicars—Central Vicariate: Rev. Msgr. FRANCIS BURLTON, S.T.L., *Our Lady of the Assumption, 4445 Ave. A, Beaumont, 77705.* Eastern Vicariate: Very Rev. SEVERIANO FERNANDEZ, O.S.A., *Our Lady of Lourdes Church, 1600 N. Main, Vidor, 77662-3014.* Northern Vicariate: Very Rev. RONALD B. FOSHAGE, M.S., *St. Michael, P.O. Box 239, Jasper, 75951.* Southern Vicariate: Very Rev. DON GOLASINSKI, *Immaculate Conception Church, P.O. Box 967, Groves, 77619.* Western Vicariate: Very Rev. FRANK PADUCH, *Immaculate Conception Church, 411 Milam, Liberty, 77575-4730.*

Diocesan College of Consultors and Presbyteral Council—Rev. Msgr. RICHARD DESTEFANO; Rev. Msgr. MICHAEL A. JAMAIL; Revs. WILLIAM MANGER; RONALD FOSHAGE, M.S.; FRANCIS CONROY; ANDREW MOORE; BENNIE PATILLO, M.A.; DAN MALAIN; JOHN HUGHES, Chm. TELESFORO BLANCO, O.S.A.; JOSEPH P. DALEO; LUONG QUANG TRAN, J.C.L.

Chancellor—Sr. ESTHER DUNEGAN, I.W.B.S., J.C.L., *Diocesan Offices, P.O. Box 3948, Beaumont, 77704-3948.* Tel: 409-838-0451, Ext. 124; Fax: 409-838-4511.

Chief Financial Officer/Controller—RUSSELL J. CHIMENO, C.P.A., *Diocesan Pastoral Office, P.O. Box 3948, Beaumont, 77704-3948.* Tel: 409-838-0451, Ext. 134; Fax: 409-838-4511.

Tribunal—703 Archie St., P.O. Box 3948, Beaumont, 77704-3948. Tel: 409-838-0451, Ext. 140; Fax: 409-838-4511.

Judicial Vicar—Rev. LUONG QUANG TRAN, M.A., J.C.L.

Diocesan Judges—Rev. LUONG QUANG TRAN, M.A., J.C.L., Judicial Vicar; Rev. Msgr. KENNETH R. GREIG, M.Th.; Rev. JOSEPH KHANH HO, S.T.L., J.C.L.; Rev. Msgr. SIDNEY J. MARCEAUX, J.C.D.; Revs. ART MORGAN, J.C.L., El Paso; KEVIN BADEAUX, J.C.L., S.T.L.; JOSEPH THUC NGUYEN, J.C.L.; SINCLAIR OUBRE, S.T.B., J.C.L.; BENNIE PATILLO, M.Ed.; Sr. ESTHER DUNEGAN, I.W.B.S., J.C.L.; Sr. ROSEMARY SMITH, S.C., J.C.D.

Promoter of Justice—Rev. Msgr. FRANCIS H. BURLTON, S.T.L.

Defenders of Bond—Rev. Msgr. MICHAEL A. JAMAIL, J.C.D., Ed.D., V.G.; Rev. Msgr. FRANCIS BURLTON, S.T.L.; Rev. JOSEPH STRATMAN, M.Th.

Psychologists for the Tribunal—RAY COXE, Ph.D.; Rev. Msgr. MICHAEL A. JAMAIL, J.C.D., Ed.D.; Mr. PATRICK BRADY, M.A., C.H.

Secretary-Notary—MARILYN PRICE; Sr. BARBARA ANNE OSTERHAUS, C.V.I., Sec.

Diocesan Officers and Directors

Apostleship of the Sea—Beaumont Port: Rev. SINCLAIR OUBRE, J.C.L., *c/o P.A.C.E. 4-23, 1500 Jefferson Dr., Port Arthur, 77642.* Tel: 409-982-5111; Fax: 409-982-5111.

African American Advisory Committee, Diocesan—Ms. JOSIE CURTIS, Chm., *P.O. Box 3948, Beaumont, 77704-3948.* Tel: 409-838-0451; Fax: 409-838-4511.

Boy Scouts—Rev. MICHAEL BALUYOT, *St. Charles Borromeo Church, 211 Hardy Ave., Nederland, 77627.*

Building Commission, Diocesan—Rev. Msgr. RICHARD DESTEFANO, Chm., *1975 Sams Way, Beaumont, 77706.* Tel: 409-866-3562; Fax: 409-866-3562.

Catholic Charities—Mr. DEAN M. TERREBONNE, Dir., *Mailing Address: P.O. Box 829, Beaumont, 77704-0829. 1410 North St., Beaumont, 77704-0829.* Tel: 409-835-7118; Fax: 409-832-0145.

Catholic Clerical Student Fund—P.O. Box 3948, Beaumont, 77704-3948.

Diocesan Finance Council—RUSSELL J. CHIMENO, C.F.O., *P.O. Box 3948, Beaumont, 77704-3948.*

Office of Lifelong Catholic Formation/Education—LORRAINE S. DELUCA, Ed.D., Dir., *P.O. Box 3948, Beaumont, 77704-3948.* Tel: 409-838-0451, Ext. 144; Fax: 409-838-4511.

Office of Catholic Schools—RITA LEGER, B.S., M.Ed., Supt., *P.O. Box 3948, Beaumont, 77704-3948.* Tel: 409-838-0451; Fax: 409-838-4511.

Catholic Daughters of America—CATHERINE LAUZON, District Deputy, *2215 Link Ave., Orange, 77630.* Tel: 409-883-2668.

Catholic Women, Council of—Very Rev. DONALD GOLASINSKI, Moderator, *Immaculate Conception Church, P.O. Box 967, Groves, 77619-0967.*

Charismatic Prayer Renewal—Rev. WILLIAM MANGER, Group Liaison, *St. Anne Church, P.O. Box 3429, Beaumont, 77704-3429.*

Communication, Information & Diocesan Press—Rev. JAMES VANDERHOLT, D.Min., Exec. Dir., *1019 Colorado, Beaumont, 77705.* Tel: 409-832-3944; Fax: 409-832-4129., *P.O. Box 3948, Beaumont, 77704-3948.*

Continuing Education of Religious and Clergy, Office of—Rev. JAMES VANDERHOLT, D.Min., Dir., *P.O. Box 3948, Beaumont, 77704-3948.* Tel: 409-832-3944.

Diaconate, Permanent Diaconate—Rev. JEREMIAH MCGRATH, D.Min., Vicar, *St. Anthony Cathedral, P.O. Box 3309, Beaumont, 77704-3309.* Tel: 409-833-6433; Fax: 409-833-6688. Rev. KEVIN BADEAUX, S.T.L., J.C.L., Dir. Diaconate Formation, *Diocese of Beaumont, P.O. Box 3948, Beaumont, 77704-3948.* Deacon JOSEPH SCHEURICH, Dir., *310 Summerwood St., Beaumont, 77706.* Tel: 409-892-6990; Fax: 409-896-5230.

Diocesan Development & Stewardship, Office of—ANNE STEINMAN, Dir., *P.O. Box 3948, Beaumont, 77704.* Tel: 409-838-0451, Ext. 138; Fax: 409-838-4511.

Hispanic Ministry, Diocesan Office of—Sr. PILAR DALMAU, A.C.J., *P.O. Box 3948, Beaumont, 77704-3948.* Tel: 409-838-0451; Fax: 409-838-4511.

Holy Childhood—Ms. ANNE STEINMAN, *P.O. Box 3948, Beaumont, 77704-3948.* Tel: 409-838-0451, Ext. 138; Fax: 409-838-4511.

Master of Ceremonies, Diocesan—Rev. PATRICK A. TURNER.

Office of African American Ministry—Ms. JOSIE CURTIS, Dir., *P.O. Box 3948, Beaumont, 77704-3948.* Tel: 409-838-0451; Fax: 409-838-4511.

Office of Worship; Liturgical Commission; Diocesan Choir—Mrs. ROSALIND SANCHEZ, Dir., *P.O. Box 3948, Beaumont, 77704-3948.* Tel: 409-838-0451; Fax: 409-838-4511.

R.C.I.A. Commission—LORRAINE S. DELUCA, Ed.D, Dir., *P.O. Box 3948, Beaumont, 77704-3948.*

Diocese of Beaumont Retirement Committee—JOE BROUSSARD, IV, J.D., Chm., *P.O. Box 3948, Beaumont, 77704-3948.* Tel: 409-838-0451; Fax: 409-838-4511.

Priests' Personnel Board—Rev. BENNIE PATILLO, Chm., *P.O. Box 3948, Beaumont, 77704-3948.*

Propagation of the Faith; Mission Coop—Ms. ANNE STEINMAN, *P.O. Box 3948, Beaumont, 77704-3948.* Tel: 409-838-0451, Ext. 138; Fax: 409-838-4511.

Family Life Office & Respect Life Liaison—Mr. RON GOUGENHEIM, M.Ed., Dir., *P.O. Box 3948, Beaumont, 77704-3948.* Tel: 409-838-0451; Fax: 409-838-4511.

Office of Criminal Justice Ministry—Deacon AL O'BRIEN, Dir., *P.O. Box 3948, Beaumont, 77704-3948.* Tel: 409-866-3002; Fax: 409-866-3002.

Diocesan School Board—MIKE MCILHERAN, Pres. LEW SHEFFLER, Vice Pres.

Director of Seminarians—Rev. JOHN HUGHES, *St. Jude Thaddeus Church, 6825 Gladys Ave., Beaumont, 77706.* Tel: 409-866-5088; Fax: 409-866-1866.

Vocations—Rev. ANDREW MOORE, Dir., *P.O. Box 10095 L.U.S., Beaumont, 77710.* Tel: 409-835-5037.

Office of Youth & Campus Ministry—TOMMY CHATLOSH, Dir. GINA DECUIR, Sec. & Coord. Campus Activities, *P.O. Box 10095 L.U.S., Beaumont, 77710.* Tel: 409-835-3972.

CLERGY, PARISHES, MISSIONS AND PAROCHIAL SCHOOLS

CITY OF BEAUMONT
(Jefferson County)

1—ST. ANTHONY CATHEDRAL (1879), Rev. Jeremiah McGrath. In res., Revs. Chrysostom Plavunikunnathil, C.M.I.; George Manchapilly, C.M.I.; Antony Paulose, C.M.I.
Res., 700 Jefferson St., P.O. Box 3309, 77704-3309. Tel: 409-833-6433; Fax: 409-833-8996.
School—Sisters 2; Lay Teachers 22; Students 248.

2—ST. ANNE (1937), Revs. William Manger; Andrew Moore; Deacon Joseph Scheurich. In res., Rev. Msgr. Michael Jamail.
Res., Calder Ave. & 11th, P.O. Box 3429, 77704-3429. Tel: 409-832-9963; Fax: 409-832-9964.
School—(Formerly St. Anne Tri-Parish School). Lay Teachers 40; Students 635.

3—BLESSED SACRAMENT (1915) (African American), Rev. Rodney J. Armstrong, S.S.J.
Res., 780 Porter St., 77701-7198. Tel: 409-833-6089; Fax: 409-833-6091. [CEM]

4—CRISTO REY (1951) (Hispanic), Rev. Luis Urriza, O.S.A.
Res., 767 Ave. A, 77701. Tel: 409-835-7788; Fax: 409-835-7788.

5—ST. JOSEPH (1905) (Italian-Vietnamese), Rev. Thuc Nguyen (Vietnam) Admin.
Res., 1115 Orange St., 77701-4392. Tel: 409-835-5662; Fax: 409-832-7717.

6—OUR LADY OF THE ASSUMPTION (1951), Rev. Msgr. Francis H. Burlton. In res., Rev. Joseph Stratman.
Res., 4445 Ave. A, 77705-4998. Tel: 409-835-5343; Fax: 409-835-5344.

7—OUR MOTHER OF MERCY (1937) (African American), Revs. David Frueh, S.S.J.; Emmanuel Madu (Nigeria); Sidney Speaks, S.S.J.
Res., 3390 Sarah St., 77705-3098. Tel: 409-842-5533; Fax: 409-842-4710.
School—Sisters 3; Lay Teachers 10; Students 185.
Convent—3380 Sarah St., Tel: 409-842-2940. Sisters of the Holy Spirit and Mary Immaculate & Handmaids of the Holy Child Jesus

8—ST. PIUS X (1954), Rev. Francis X. Conroy; Deacon Robert Gros. In res., Rev. Jos Alukal, C.M.I.
Res., 5075 Bigner Rd. at East Lucas, 77708-5299. Tel: 409-892-3316; Fax: 409-892-8916.

9—ST. JUDE THADDEUS (1978), Revs. John Hughes; Sebastian Abraham, C.M.I.; Deacon Alfred J. O'Brien.
Res., 6825 Gladys, 77706-3239. Tel: 409-866-5088; Fax: 409-866-1866.

OUTSIDE THE CITY OF BEAUMONT

Ames, Liberty Co., Our Mother of Mercy (1903) (African American), Rev. Raphael Asika, M.S.P.
Res., P.O. Box 264, Liberty, 77575. Tel: 409-336-3004; Fax: 409-336-5955. [CEM]

Anahuac, Chambers Co., Our Lady of Light (1938), Rev. Louis J. Villarreal, O.M.I.; Deacon E. R. LeBlanc.
Res., Rte. 2, Box 1-F, 77514-9001. Tel: 409-267-3158; Fax: 409-267-3158.

Bridge City, Orange Co., St. Henry (1948), Rev. James McClintock; Deacons Eddie Blankenstein; Hazen Kenney.
Mailing Address: P.O.Box 427, 77611-0427.
Res., 475 W. Round Bunch Rd., 77611-2448. Tel: 409-735-2422; Fax: 409-738-2158.

Buna, Jasper Co., St. Francis of Assisi Mission (1968), Rev. Paul Sumler.
Mailing Address: P.O. Box 1688, 77612-1688. Tel: 409-994-3456; Fax: 409-994-2923.

Cheek, Jefferson Co., St. Martin de Porres Mission (1972) (African American), Rev. George Kalappura, C.M.I.
Mailing Address: 9894 Gilbert, Beaumont, 77705. Tel: 409-794-2548; Fax: 409-794-3411.

China, Jefferson Co., Our Lady of Sorrows (1918), Rev. Luong Quang Tran.
Res., P.O. Box 38, 77613-0038. Tel: 409-752-3571; Fax: 409-752-5134. [CEM]

Cleveland, Liberty Co., St. Mary (1950), Rev. Joseph Malayampuram, C.M.I.
Res., P.O. Box 816, 77328-0816. Tel: 281-592-2985; Fax: 281-592-7247.

Corrigan, Polk Co., St. Martin de Porres Mission (1971), Rev. Roger Thibodeaux; Deacon Rudy Cockburn.
Mailing Address: P.O. Box 930, Livingston, 77351. Tel: 409-967-8385; Fax: 409-967-8385, Ext. 51. Hwy. 287, 75939.

Dayton, Liberty Co., St. Joseph the Worker (1945), Rev. Thomas E. Phelan.
Res., P.O. Box 640, 77535-0640. Tel: 936-258-5735; Fax: 936-258-7220. [CEM]

Eastgate, Liberty Co., St. Anne Mission (1918), Rev. Thomas E. Phelan.
Mailing Address: P.O. Box 640, Dayton, 77535-0640. Tel: 936-258-5735; Fax: 936-258-7220.

Fannett, Jefferson Co., St. Mary (1964). Formerly St. Mary, Hamshire (1899). Rev. George Kalappura, C.M.I.
Res., 9894 Gilbert Rd., Beaumont, 77705-9696. Tel: 409-794-2548; Fax: 409-794-3411.

Groves, Jefferson Co., Immaculate Conception (1928), Rev. Donald J. Golasinski.
Res., 6248 Washington, P.O. Box 967, 77619-0967. Tel: 409-962-0255; Fax: 409-963-3464.

St. Peter the Apostle (1972), Rev. Msgr. Kenneth R. Greig.
Res., 2049 Taft Ave., 77619-4953. Tel: 409-962-8365; Fax: 409-962-8366.

Jasper, Jasper Co., St. Michael (1951), Rev. Ronald Foshage, M.S.; Deacons John Charnisky; David Luther.
Res., P.O. Box 239, 75951-0239. Tel: 409-384-2447; Fax: 409-384-2447.
Station—Toledo Village.

Kirbyville, Jasper Co., Our Lady of La Salette Mission (1948), Rev. Ronald Foshage, M.S.
Mailing Address: P.O. Box 239, Jasper, 75951-0239. Tel: 409-384-2447; Fax: 409-384-2447.

Kountze, Hardin Co., Holy Spirit Mission (1986), Rev. Paul E. Sumler.
470 Monroe, 77625. Tel: 409-246-4457 (Office); Fax: 409-246-4623.

Liberty, Liberty Co., Immaculate Conception (1756), Rev. Frank Paduch; Deacon Luther Wells.
Res., 411 Milam, 77575-4730. Tel: 936-336-7267; Fax: 936-336-9740. [CEM]

Livingston, Polk Co., St. Joseph (1970), Rev. Roger Thibodeaux; Deacon Rudy Cockburn.
Res., P.O. Box 930, 77351-0930. Tel: 936-967-8385; Fax: 936-967-8385.

Lumberton, Hardin Co., Infant Jesus (1948), Rev. Paul E. Sumler.
Res., P.O. Box 8180, 77657-0180. Tel: 409-755-1734; Fax: 409-755-2833.

Mauriceville, Orange Co., St. Maurice (1966), Rev. Delphyn J. Meeks.
Res., P.O. Box 940, 77626-0940. Tel: 409-745-4060; Fax: 409-745-4272.

Mont Belvieu, Chambers Co., Holy Trinity Mission, Rev. Louis J. Villarreal, O.M.I.
Mailing Address: Rte. 2, Box 1-F, Anahuac, TX 77514-9001. Tel: 409-267-3158; Fax: 409-267-3158.

Nederland, Jefferson Co., St. Charles Borromeo (1923), Revs. Dan Malain; Michael Baluyot; Deacons Vernon Drummond; Dallas Broussard.
Res., 130 Hardy Ave., 77627-7326. Tel: 409-722-3413; Fax: 409-722-2020.

Orange, Orange Co., St. Mary (1880), Rev. Joseph P. Daleo; Deacon Melvin Payne.
Res., 912 W. Cherry St., 77630-5017. Tel: 409-883-2883; Fax: 409-883-3547. [CEM]
School—2600 Bob Hall Rd., 77630-2418. Tel: 409-883-8913.
Sisters 1; Lay Teachers 21; Students 311.

St. Therese (1924) (African American), Rev. Patrick Otor, M.S.P.; Deacon Julian Richard.
Res., 1409 N. Sixth St., 77630-3927. Tel: 409-883-3783; Fax: 409-883-4918.

St. Francis of Assisi (1978), Rev. Kevin Badeaux; Deacons Harvey Dubois; Stronnie McBride.
Church—4300 Meeks Dr., 77632-4508. Tel: 409-883-9153; Fax: 409-883-9154.

Orangefield, Orange Co., St. Helen (1938), Rev. Patrick Turner; Deacons Morris Smith; Glen Hebert.
Res., 8105 FM 1442, Orange, 77630. Tel: 409-735-2200 (Office); Fax: 409-735-7786.

Port Arthur, Jefferson Co.,

1—OUR LADY OF GUADALUPE, (1927) (Hispanic), Rev. Telesforo R. Blanco, O.S.A.; Deacon Jimmy Bourgeois.
Res., 3648 S. Sgt. Lucian Adams Dr., 77642-6100. Tel: 409-962-6777; Fax: 409-963-0669.

2—QUEEN OF VIETNAM, (1977) (Vietnamese), Revs. Michael Mai Tran, C.M.C.; Louis Ha Pham, C.M.C.
Res., 801 Ninth Ave., 77642-3329. Tel: 409-983-7676; Fax: 409-982-1212.
Convent—1148 Ninth Ave., 77642. Tel: 409-985-5102.
Dominican Sisters 6.

3—SACRED HEART, (1915) (African American), Rev. Larry Leduff-Gutierrez, S.S.J.
Res., 920 Booker Washington Ave., 77640-4923. Tel: 409-985-5104; Fax: 409-982-0106.

4—ST. CATHERINE OF SIENA, (1954), Revs. Joseph J. Romero; Duc Quang Duong; Deacon Jim Gard.
Res., 3706 Woodrow Dr., 77642-2320. Tel: 409-962-5715; Fax: 409-962-4775. [CEM]
School—Lay Teachers 18; Students 243.
Convent—3949 Woodrow St., 77642-2320.

5—ST. JAMES, (1929), Revs. James Vanderholt; Philip Payyappilli, C.M.I. In res., Rev. Sinclair Oubre.
Res., 3503 Gulfway Dr., 77642-3693. Tel: 409-985-8865; Fax: 409-985-3847.

6—ST. JOHN, (1951) (African American), Rev. Louis Delarue; Deacon W. B. Goudeau, Jr.
Res., 620 53rd St., 77640-2351. Tel: 409-985-8010; Fax: 409-982-2589.

7—St. Joseph, (1951), Rev. D. Stephen McCrate. In res., Rev. Vidal Robles (Curacao).
Res., 4600 Procter St., 77642-1365. Tel: 409-982-6409; Fax: 409-983-5383.

8—St. Mary, (1903) (African American), Rev. Oliver Obele, M.S.P.; Deacon Roy Cormier, Sr.
Office: 545 Savannah Ave., 77640-6026. Tel: 409-985-9661; Fax: 409-985-9691.

9—St. Therese the Little Flower of Jesus, (1928), Rev. Antony Moozhikuzhy, C.M.I.
Res., 6412 Garnet Ave., 77640-1308. Tel: 409-736-1536; Fax: 409-736-1537.

Port Neches, Jefferson Co., St. Elizabeth (1922), Rev. Bennie J. Patillo.
Res., 2006 Nall St., 77651-3714. Tel: 409-727-8874; Fax: 409-727-8875.

Raywood, Liberty Co., Sacred Heart (1952) (African American), Rev. Raphael Asika, M.S.P.
Res., P.O. Box 429, 77582. Tel: 409-587-4631; Fax: 409-587-1012. [CEM]

Sabine Pass, Jefferson Co., St. Paul Mission (1955), Rev. James Vanderholt.
Mailing Address: 3503 Gulfway Dr., Port Arthur, 77642-3693. Tel: 409-985-8865; Fax: 409-985-3847.

Sam Rayburn, Jasper Co., St. Raymond Mission (1970), Rev. Ronald Foshage, M.S.
Mailing Address: P.O. Box 239, Jasper, 75951-0239. Tel: 409-384-2447.

Silsbee, Hardin Co., St. Mark the Evangelist (1940), Rev. Charles Sellars, O.M.I.; Deacon Nolen Landry.
Res., 905 N. Ninth St., 77656. Tel: 409-385-4498; 385-5631; Fax: 409-385-0806.

Sour Lake, Hardin Co., Our Lady of Victory (1906), In res., Rev. Martin Lester Nelson.
Res., 210 E. Barkley St., P.O. Box 1359, 77659. Tel: 409-287-3287; Fax: 409-287-3287.

Vidor, Orange Co., Our Lady of Lourdes (1938), Rev. Severiano Fernandez, O.S.A.
Res., 1600 N. Main, 77662. Tel: 409-769-2865; Fax: 409-769-4577.

Winnie, Chambers Co., St. Louis (1947), Rev. Joseph Khanh Ho.
Res., Rte. 1, Box 354, 77665-9711. Tel: 409-296-4200; Fax: 409-296-9715.

Woodville, Tyler Co., Our Lady of the Pines (1950), Rev. Egidio Vecchio, M.S.; Deacon Paul Rachal.
Res., P.O. Box 2029, 75979-2029. Tel: 409-283-5367; Fax: 409-283-2219.
Station—Wildwood

Chaplains of Public Institutions

Beaumont. *Memoral Hermann Baptist Hospital*. Rev. Jos Alukal, C.M.I.

Port Arthur. *Convalescent Home Ministry*. Rev. Chrysostom Plavunikunnathil, C.M.I.

Prisons

Beaumont. *Federal Correctional Complex-Penitentiary*. Revs. Ed O'Reily (NY) Low Security; Vidal Robles (Curacao) Medium Security.
Federal Work Camp & U.S. Penitentiary. Rev. James Cong Ba Do (Vietnam) Chap.
Larry Gist State Jail. Rev. Lawrence D. Mello (SAN) Chap.
Mark Stiles Unit, TDCJ. (Vacant).

Dayton. *Plane State Jail*. Ms. Glory Siller, Chap.

Livingston. *Terrell Unit*. Deacon John Stanley, Chap.

Special Assignment:
Reverend Fathers—
Colbert, John, 7455 Calder #22, Beaumont, TX 77706-5705
Scolozzi, Angelo, Hispanic Ministry, P.O. Box 327, Cleveland, TX 77327. Tel: 409-592-5446

On Duty Outside the Diocese:
Reverend Fathers—
Deeter, Timothy, Archdiocese of Perth, Australia
DeFrancisco, Joseph, St. Ambrose Univ., Davenport, IA

Military Chaplains:
Reverend Monsignors—
Marceaux, Sidney J., Chap. Col., U.S.A., CMR451, Noc273, APO, AE 09708
Reverend Fathers—
Beck, Robert P., Chap., Capt. U.S.A.F., 6700 Oakshore Dr. #207, Panama City, FL 32404

Absent On Leave:
Reverend Fathers—
Sumler, Kevin

Retired:
Reverend Monsignors—
Culotta, Salvador J.
DeStefano, Richard
DiStefano, John
Fee, Paul A.
Reverend Fathers—
Bertrand, Joseph
Dempsey, James
Iglesias, Clement
Montondon, Walter, Chap. Col.
Mudd, Earl
Stratman, Joseph

Permanent Deacons:
Blankenstein, Ed, St. Henry, Bridge City
Bourgeois, Jimmy, Our Lady of Guadalupe, Port Arthur
Broussard, Dallas, St. Charles, Nederland
Charnisky, John, St. Michael, Jasper
Cockburn, Rudy, St. Martin de Porres, Corrigan
Cormier, Roy, Sr., St. Mary, Port Arthur
Davis, Harry, (Unassigned)
Drummond, Vernon, St. Charles Borromeo, Nederland
Dubois, Harvey, St. Francis, Orange
Gard, Jim, St. Catherine of Siena, Port Arthur
Goudeau, W. B., Jr., St. John, Port Arthur
Gros, Robert, St. Pius X, Beaumont
Hebert, Glen, St. Helen, Orangefield
Kenny, Hazen, St. Henry, Bridge City
Landry, Nolen, St. Mark the Evangelist, Silsbee
LeBlanc, E. R., Holy Trinity Mission, Mont Belvieu; Our Lady of Light, Anahuac
Luther, David, St. Michael, Jasper; Our Lady of LaSalette, Kirbyville; St. Raymond, Rayburn
McBride, Stronnie, St. Francis of Assisi and Southeast Texas Hospice, Orange
McKinney, Tom (GAL), TDCJ, Huntsville
O'Brien, Alfred J., Diocesan Dir. Office of Jail & Prison Ministry
Payne, Melvin, St. Mary, Orange
Rachal, Paul, Our Lady of the Pines, Woodville
Richard, Julian, St. Therese, Orange
Rudolph, William, (Retired)
Scheurich, Joseph, St. Anne and Dir. of Permanent Diaconate, Beaumont
Smith, Morris, St. Helen, Orangefield
Stanley, John, TDCJ, Terrell Unit, Livingston
Wells, Luther, Immaculate Conception, Liberty
Wycliff, Wilbert, (Retired)
Wynn, Dow, (Retired)

INSTITUTIONS LOCATED IN THE DIOCESE

[A] HIGH SCHOOLS, DIOCESAN

Beaumont. *Monsignor Kelly Catholic High School*, 5950 Kelly Dr., 77707. Tel: 409-866-2351; Fax: 409-866-0917.
E-mail: llambright@kelly.beaumont.tx.us
Web site: www.kelly.beaumont.tx.us
Mr. Emile Fair, Prin.; Rev. Martin Lester Nelson, Chap. Sisters 1; Lay Teachers 46; Students 567.

[B] ELEMENTARY SCHOOLS, DIOCESAN

Port Arthur. *Sr. Thea Bowman Academy*. (Formerly Central Catholic Parochial School), 3617 Gulfway Dr., 77642. Tel: 409-982-4140; Fax: 409-982-1850. Mrs. Patricia Gougenheim, Dir. Sisters 1; Lay Teachers 4; Students 94.

[C] GENERAL HOSPITALS

Beaumont. *CHRISTUS St. Elizabeth Hospital*, 2830 Calder Ave., P.O. Box 5405, 77726-5405. Tel: 409-892-7171; Fax: 409-899-8191
For a complete listing, refer to the Hospitals section.

Jasper. *CHRISTUS Jasper Memorial Hospital*, 1275 Hancock Dr., 75951
For a complete listing, refer to the Hospitals section.

Port Arthur. *CHRISTUS St. Mary Hospital*, 3600 Gates Blvd., P.O. Box 3696, 77643. Tel: 409-985-7431; Fax: 409-985-9404
For a complete listing, refer to the Hospitals section.

[D] MONASTERIES AND RESIDENCES OF PRIESTS AND BROTHERS

Beaumont. *Holy Cross Brothers Residence*, 2520 Liberty, 77702-1912. Tel: 409-835-1699.

[E] NEWMAN CENTERS

Beaumont. *Lamar University-Catholic Student Center*, 1010 E. Virginia, P.O. Box 10095, 77710. Tel: 409-835-3972. Mr. Tommy Chatlosh, Dir.; Ms. Gina DeCuir, Sec. & Coord. of Campus Activities.

[F] RETREAT CENTERS

Beaumont. *Holy Family Retreat Center*, 9920 N. Major Dr., 77713-7618. Tel: 409-899-5617; Fax: 409-899-3161. Rev. Peter C. Funk, Dir.; Bro. Michael Gallagher, Asst. Dir.; Sr. Carletta LaCour, O.P., B.A., Asst. Dir.

[G] MISCELLANEOUS

Beaumont. *Charismatic Diocesan Renewal Center*. (Abiding Place), 4440 Chaison, 77705. Tel: 409-839-8788; Fax: 409-839-8788. Ms. Nita Chavis, Dir.
Diocese of Beaumont School Foundation, Inc., P.O. Box 3948, 77704-3948.
Family Practice Center, 830 N. 11th St., 77702. Tel: 409-899-8160; Fax: 409-899-8184.
Monsignor Kelly Catholic High School Foundation, Inc., 5950 Kelly Dr., 77707. Tel: 409-866-2351; Fax: 409-866-0917.
E-mail: adavis@kelly.beaumont.tx.us
Web site: www.kelly.beaumont.tx.us
Angela Davis, Dir.
Rev. Herman Vincent Scholarship Fund Nederland, 130 Hardy St., 77627. Tel: 409-722-3413; Fax: 409-722-2020. Rev. Dan Malain, Admin.
St. Anne's Catholic School Foundation, 375 N. 11th St., 77702.
St. Anthony Cathedral School Foundation, 850 Forsythe St., 77701-2890. Tel: 409-832-3481; Fax: 409-838-9051. Marianne Mechura, Prin.
St. Thomas More Society of Southeast Texas, P.O. Box 26005, 77720-6005. Tel: 800-765-5801; Fax: 409-833-8236.
E-mail: rmqlaw@aol.com
Mr. Richard Clarkson, Pres.; Rev. Luong Quang Tran, Chap.

Orange. *St. Mary School Foundation*, 912 Cherry, 77630. Tel: 409-883-2883; Fax: 409-883-3547.

Port Arthur. *Hospitality Center of Catholic Charities, Inc.*, 3959 Gulfway Dr., 77642. Tel: 409-982-4842; Fax: 409-982-4842.
St. Catherine School Foundation, 3840 Woodrow Dr., 77642.
St. Mary Hospital Foundation of Port Arthur, 3619 Professional Dr., 77642. Tel: 409-983-5065; Fax: 409-983-5780.
E-mail: cmnset@exp.net
Brenda Drago, Exec. Dir.

RELIGIOUS INSTITUTES OF MEN REPRESENTED IN THE DIOCESE

For further details refer to the corresponding bracketed number in the Religious Institutes of Men or Women section.

[0140]—*The Augustinians*. (Prov. of Castile, Spain).—O.S.A.

[0600]—*Brothers of the Congregation of Holy Cross*. (Southwest Prov.).—C.S.C.

[0275]—*Carmelites of Mary Immaculate*. (Chanda, India).—C.M.I.

[]—*Carmelites of Mary Immaculate*. (Kerala, India).—C.M.I.

[]—*Carmelites of Mary Immaculate*. (Kalmassery, India).—C.M.I.

[]—*Congregation of the Mother Coredemptrix*. (Missouri).—C.M.C.

[]—*Missionaries of Charity, Third Order*.—M.C.III.O.

[0720]—*The Missionaries of Our Lady of La Salette*. (Prov. of Mary Queen).—M.S.

[]—*Missionaries of St. Paul*.—M.S.P.

[0910]—*Oblates of Mary Immaculate*. (Southern Prov.).—O.M.I.

[0700]—*St. Joseph's Society of the Sacred Heart*. (Baltimore).—S.S.J.

RELIGIOUS INSTITUTES OF WOMEN REPRESENTED IN THE DIOCESE

[1010]—*Congregation of Divine Providence*. (San Antonio).—C.D.P.

[2190]—*Congregation of the Incarnate Word and Blessed Sacrament*. (Houston, TX).—C.V.I.

[2200]—*Congregation of the Incarnate Word and Blessed Sacrament*. (Victoria).—I.W.B.S.

[0470]—*Congregation of the Sisters of Charity of the Incarnate Word*. (Houston, TX).—C.C.V.I.

[1070-03]—*Dominican Sisters*.—O.P.

[1070-19]—*Dominican Sisters*.—O.P.

[1140]—*Eucharistic Missionaries of St. Dominic*. (New Orleans).—O.P.

[]—*Handmaids of the Holy Child Jesus.*—H.H.C.J.
[1870]—*The Handmaids of the Sacred Heart of Jesus.* (U.S. Prov.).—A.C.J.
[]—*Sisters of the Eucharistic Covenant.*—S.E.C.
[]—*Sisters of the Holy Cross.* (Notre Dame, ID).—C.S.C.
[2050]—*Sisters of the Holy Spirit and Mary Immaculate.*—S.H.Sp.
[2205]—*Sisters of the Incarnate Word and Blessed Sacrament.* (Corpus Christi).—I.W.B.S.
[4100]—*Sisters of the Sorrowful Mother.* (U.S./Caribbean Prov.).—S.S.M.
[]—*Vietnamese Dominican Sisters.* (Houston).—O.P.

NECROLOGY

† O'Connell, Rev. Msgr. Patrick Hayes, (Retired). —Died Oct. 16, 2000.

Diocese of Belleville

(Dioecesis Bellevillensis)

Most Reverend

WILTON D. GREGORY, S.L.D.

Bishop of Belleville; ordained May 9, 1973; appointed Auxiliary Bishop of Chicago and Titular Bishop of Oliva October 31, 1983; consecrated December 13, 1983; appointed Bishop of Belleville December 29, 1993; installed February 10, 1994. *Mailing Address: Chancery Office, 222 S. Third St., Belleville, IL, 62220.* Tel.: 618-277-8181.

ERECTED JANUARY 7, 1887.

Square Miles 11,678.

Comprises Illinois south of the northern limits of the counties of St. Clair, Clinton, Marion, Clay, Richland and Lawrence.

For legal titles of parishes and diocesan institutions, consult the Chancery Office.

Chancery Office: 222 S. Third St., Belleville, IL, 62220-1985. Tel.: 618-277-8181; 397-1279; Fax: 618-277-0387.

Web site address: www.diobelle.org

E-mail address: belvchan@impresso.com

STATISTICAL OVERVIEW

Personnel	
Bishop	1
Retired Bishops	1
Priests: Diocesan Active in Diocese	88
Priests: Active Outside Diocese	4
Priests: Retired, Sick or Absent	43
Number of Diocesan Priests	135
Religious Priests in Diocese	34
Extern Priests in Diocese	3
Ordinations:	
Transitional Deacons	2
Permanent Deacons in Diocese	32
Total Brothers	13
Total Sisters	241
Parishes	
Parishes	124
With Resident Pastor:	
Resident Diocesan Priests	81
Resident Religious Priests	1
Without Resident Pastor:	
Administered by Priests	33
Administered by Deacons	2
Administered by Women Religious	3
Administered by Lay People	4
Missions	1
Closed Parishes	1
Professional Ministry Personnel:	
Sisters	24
Lay Ministers	30
Welfare	
Catholic Hospitals	8
Total Assisted	705,498
Homes for the Aged	4
Total Assisted	466
Day Care and Extended Day Care Centers	6
Total Assisted	395
Specialized Homes	1
Total Assisted	128
Special Centers for Social Services	3
Total Assisted	41,074
Educational	
Diocesan Students in Other Seminaries	15
Total Seminarians	15
High Schools, Diocesan and Parish	3
Total Students	1,729
Elementary Schools, Diocesan and Parish	37
Total Students	6,978
Catechesis/Religious Education:	
High School Students	1,290
Elementary Students	7,166
Total Students Under Catholic Instruction	17,178
Teachers in the Diocese:	
Sisters	9
Lay Teachers	403
Vital Statistics	
Receptions into the Church:	
Infant Baptism Totals	1,540
Adult Baptism Totals	275
Received into Full Communion	283
First Communions	1,685
Confirmations	2,025
Marriages:	
Catholic	337
Interfaith	339
Total Marriages	676
Deaths	1,422
Total Catholic Population	107,425
Total Population	849,925

Former Bishops—Most Rev. JOHN JANSSEN, D.D., ord. Nov. 19, 1858; cons. April 25, 1888; died July 2, 1913.—Most Rev. HENRY J. ALTHOFF, D.D., ord. July 26, 1902; appt. Dec. 4, 1913; cons. Feb. 24, 1914; died July 3, 1947.—Most Rev. ALBERT R. ZUROWESTE, D.D., ord. June 8, 1924; appt. Nov. 29, 1947; cons. Jan. 29, 1948; retired Sept. 3, 1976; died March 28, 1987.—Most Rev. WILLIAM M. COSGROVE, D.D., ord. Dec. 18, 1943; Auxiliary Bishop of Cleveland June 19, 1968; cons. Sept. 3, 1968; appt. Bishop of Belleville Sept. 3, 1976; installed Oct. 28, 1976; retired May 19, 1981; died Dec. 11, 1992.—Most Rev. JOHN N. WURM, S.T.D., Ph.D., ord. April 3, 1954; Auxiliary Bishop of St. Louis June 25, 1976; cons. Aug. 17, 1976; appt. Bishop of Belleville Sept. 19, 1981; installed Nov. 4, 1981; died April 27, 1984.—Most Rev. JAMES P. KELEHER, S.T.D., M.Ed., ord. April 12, 1958; appt. Bishop of Belleville Oct. 23, 1984; cons. Dec. 11, 1984; transferred to Kansas City, KS Sept. 8, 1993.

Diocese of Belleville Chancery Office—222 S. Third St., Belleville, 62220-1985. Tel: 618-277-8181; 397-1279; Fax: 618-277-0387.

Diocesan Pastoral Center—2620 Lebanon Ave., Belleville, 62221. Tel: 618-235-9601; Fax: 618-235-7416.

Vicar General—Rev. Msgr. JAMES E. MARGASON, V.G., M.Div., J.C.L.

Moderator of the Curia—Rev. Msgr. JAMES E. MARGASON, V.G., M.Div., J.C.L.

Chancellor—Rev. KENNETH J. YORK, J.C.L.

Vice-Chancellor—DAVID R. SPOTANSKI.

Secretary to the Bishop—Mrs. PATRICIA SCHILLING.

Archivist—Sr. MARY KENAN WOLFF, S.S.N.D., *220 W. Lincoln St., Belleville, 62220.* Tel: 618-234-3157.

Diocesan Tribunal—Diocesan Pastoral Center, 2620 Lebanon Ave., Belleville, 62221. Tel: 618-235-9601. Address all rogatory commissions to the Chancellor at the Chancery Office.

Judicial Vicar—Very Rev. JAMES M. NALL, J.C.L.

Adjutant Judicial Vicar—Rev. PAUL R. WIENHOFF, J.C.L.

Judges—Rev. Msgr. JAMES E. MARGASON, V.G., M.Div., J.C.L.; Sr. MARY KATHLEEN KUENSTLER, P.H.J.C., J.C.D.

Promoter Justitiae—Rev. PAUL WIENHOFF, J.C.L.

Defensores Vinculi—Rev. PAUL WIENHOFF, J.C.L.

Advocates—Rev. JOHN T. MYLER; Rev. Msgr. DONALD W. EICHENSEER.

Notaries—RENEE QUIRIN; JACQUELINE MATT.

Diocesan Consultors—Rev. Msgr. JAMES E. MARGASON, V.G., M.Div., J.C.L.; Rev. Msgr. THEODORE J. BAUMANN; Rev. Msgr. JAMES A. BLAZINE; Rev. Msgr. JEROME D. HARTLEIN; Rev. Msgr. WILLIAM J. HITPAS; Rev. Msgr. KENNETH J. SCHAEFER; Revs. BRIAN BARKER; JOHN T. MYLER; JAMES M. NALL; PATRICK N. PETER; EUGENE H. WOJCIK.

Diocesan Deans—Rev. Msgr. CARL E. SCHERRER, V.F., Belleville Deanery; Very Rev. GERALD HECHENBERGER, V.F., East St. Louis Deanery; Very Rev. DONALD E. ABELL, V.F., East Deanery; Very Rev. DAVID M. DARIN, V.F., North Central Deanery; Very Rev. THOMAS STOUT, V.F., West Deanery; Rev. Msgr. WILLIAM P. MCGHEE, South Deanery.

Diocesan Finance Office—WILLIAM J. KNAPP, CFO; DAVID WAELTZ, Comptroller, *Chancery Office.* Tel: 618-277-8181; Fax: 618-277-0819.

Diocesan Finance Council—DEBI EDWARDS, Chm.; Rev. Msgr. JAMES E. MARGASON, V.G., M.Div., J.C.L.; WILLIAM J. KNAPP; J. ROY DEE, III; ARTHUR HAMPTON; IRENE KRUSE; Rev. Msgr. THOMAS MILLER; Rev. Msgr. DONALD W. EICHENSEER; JEFF RENNER; Sr. JAN RENZ, A.S.C.; JACKIE SETTLES; JOHN SMITH; JAY TEBBE.

Diocesan Pastoral Council—MARGARET SPEZIA, Chm. JOE HERMES, Vice Chm. ROSE HOGAN, Sec. Tel: 618-277-8181; Fax: 618-277-0387.

Building Commission, Chancery Office—Rev. Msgr. JEROME D. HARTLEIN, Chm. WILLIAM JOHNSON.

Campaign for Human Development—Rev. J. CLYDE GROGAN, Dir., *771 Vogel Pl., East St. Louis, 62205.* Tel: 618-874-5025.

Catholic Social Service—LESTER C. HIMSTEDT, Exec. Dir., Office: *8601 W. Main St., Ste. 201, Belleville, 62223.* Tel: 618-394-5900; Fax: 618-394-5909., Branch Offices: *216 S. University, Carbondale, 62901.* Tel: 618-351-0743., *1 Doctor's Park Rd., Ste. H, Mt. Vernon, 62864.* Tel: 618-244-0344., *120 W. Fifth St., P.O. Box 23, Mt. Carmel, 62863.* Tel: 618-263-3863., *509 N. Second St., Breese, 62230.* Tel: 618-526-2267.

Catholic Urban Programs—JOSEPH P. HUBBARD, Co-ord., *771 Vogel Pl., East St. Louis, 62205.* Tel: 618-398-5616; Fax: 618-274-4659.

Holy Angels Shelter—PATRICIA LEWIS, Dir., *1410 N. 37th St., East St. Louis, 62204.* Tel: 618-874-4079.
Griffin Center—Sr. JULIA HUISKAMP, D.C., Dir., *2630 Lincoln Ave., East St. Louis, 62204.* Tel: 618-874-2500.
Griffin Center Sites—De Shields Center: *1235 McCasland, East St. Louis, 62201.* Tel: 618-874-0637. Roosevelt Center: *400 Bunkum Rd., East St. Louis, 62204.* Tel: 618-271-9859. ORR-Weathers Center: *1400 Missouri Ave., D-1 Bldg., East St. Louis, 62201.* Tel: 618-875-0535.
Family Center—Sr. CAROL LEHMKUHL, O.P., *705 Summit, East St. Louis, 62201.* Tel: 618-875-7295.
St. Regis Center After School Program—GLENDA DREW, Dir., After School Prog., *3500 Market St., East St. Louis, 62207.*
CYO—COLETTE KENNETT, Dir.; Rev. BERNARD C. GOEDDE, JR., Spiritual Moderator; JAMES KEIM, Athletic Dir., *Diocesan Pastoral Center.*
Cemeteries—JOSEPH P. HUBBARD, Dir., *Chancery Office.*
Clergymen's Aid Society—Rev. Msgr. ALBERT L. JEROME, Pres., *305 N. Front St., Box 106, Okawville, 62271.* Tel: 618-243-6236.
Conciliation and Arbitration Board—THOMAS E. PRICE, Chm., *740 Market St., Mt. Carmel, 62863.* Tel: 618-263-6591.
Council of Women Religious—Vacant.
Diocesan Development Office—MARTIN LEIFELD, *Chancery Office.* Tel: 618-277-8181; Fax: 618-277-0387.
Diocesan Liturgical Commission—DOUGLAS BOYER, Chm. Tel: 618-397-3725.
Diocesan Outreach Apostolate—Serving Alexander and Pulaski Counties. Daystar Community Program, *909 Washington Ave., Cairo, 62914.* Tel: 618-734-0178. JOHN KLEIN, Dir. SHERRY MILLER, Assoc. Dir.
Diaconate, Office of Permanent—Rev. Msgr. MARVIN C. VOLK, Vicar for Deacons; Deacon RONALD KARCHER, Assoc. Vicar for Deacons, *Diocesan Pastoral Center.*
Diocesan Council of Catholic Women—Rev. Msgr. ALBERT L. JEROME, Diocesan Moderator, *305 Front St., P.O. Box 106, Okawville, 62271.* Tel: 618-243-6236. JULIA "BETTY" VAHLKAMP, Pres., *Diocesan Pastoral Center.*
Ecumenical and Interreligious Affairs—Rev. ROBERT B. FLANNERY, *303 S. Poplar St., Carbondale, 62901.* Tel: 618-457-4556.
Formation of Priests—Rev. JAMES R. DEITERS, Chm., *205 W. Third St., O'Fallon, 62269.* Tel: 618-632-3562.
Office of Education—THOMAS H. POSNANSKI, Dir., *Diocesan Pastoral Center.*
Department of Elementary Education—Sr. KATHLEEN KOENEN, S.S.N.D., Dir.
Religious Education and Catechesis—MARK MARKULY, Assoc. Dir.
Diocesan Board of Education—SUE TAYLOR, Pres., *44 Glenview Dr., Belleville, 62203.*
Guatemala Mission Society—VIRGINIA KOCH, Chm., *One Park Ln., Centralia, 62801.* Tel: 618-533-4005.
Hispanic Ministry—Carbondale Area: Rev. FEDERICO HIGUERA, *101 Centennial St., Box 237, Cobden, 62920.* Tel: 618-893-2276. Fairmont City Area: Vacant.
Holy Childhood Association—Very Rev. KENNETH J. YORK, Dir., *Chancery.*
Hospitals—Rev. EUGENE J. NEFF, Delegate, *Ministry to Sick and Aged, 2620 Lebanon Ave., Belleville, 62221.* Tel: 618-235-9991.
Human Resource Office—ROBERT OTREMBIAK, Dir., *Chancery Office, 222 S. Third St., Belleville, 62220.* Tel: 618-277-8181; Fax: 618-277-0387.
Insurance Commission—WILLIAM J. KNAPP, Dir., *Chancery Office.*
Catholic Mutual Group—WILLIAM P. JOHNSON, Claims/Risk Mgr., *Diocesan Pastoral Center.* Tel: 618-233-1090.
Pastoral Services—Deacon BILL DITEWIG, Dir., *Diocesan Pastoral Center.*
Natural Family Planning—*Catholic Social Services, 617 S. Belt W., Belleville, 62220-2414.* Tel: 618-277-9200.
Newman Center—JOHN SCARANO, Diocesan Dir. & Campus Min., *715 S. Washington St., Carbondale, 62901.* Tel: 618-529-3311. Rev. GREGORY JONES, C.S.V., Chaplain; MARY MERTZLUFFT, Campus Min.
Newman Auxiliary—MARGE MANGAN, Pres., *9741 Stilley's Mill Dr., Marion, 62959.* Tel: 618-982-2218.
Newspaper, "The Messenger"—LIZ QUIRIN, Editor, *Diocesan Pastoral Center.*
Ondessonk, Camp—Diocese of Belleville, Department of Outdoor Education: PATRICK R. HIGGINS, Exec. Dir., *3760 Ondessonk Rd., Ozark, 62972.* Tel: 618-695-2489; Fax: 618-695-3593.
Priests Organizations—
Confraternity of Catholic Clergy—Vacant.
Southern Illinois Association of Priests—Co-Chm.: Revs. WALTER M. BARR; GEORGE A. MAUCK, *1171 Jefferson, Carlyle, 62231.* Tel: 618-594-2225.
Pro-Life Office—ANN POLKA, Chm., *Diocesan Pastoral Center.*
Propagation of the Faith—Very Rev. KENNETH J. YORK, J.C.L., Dir., *Chancery.*
Office for Professional Fitness Review—PATRICIA KIEVLAN KEELEY, *220 W. Lincoln St., #407, Belleville, 62220.* Tel: 618-236-1812.
Rural Life Conference—Rev. Msgr. JOSEPH A. LAWLER, Dir., *R.R. 3, P.O. Box 170-Piopolis, McLeansboro, 62859.* Tel: 618-648-2490.
St. Vincent DePaul Society—RAY BERKEL, Admin., *3718 State St., East St. Louis, 62205.* Tel: 618-397-3113.
Sick and Aged (Ministry)—Rev. EUGENE J. NEFF, Dir., *Diocesan Pastoral Center.* Tel: 618-235-9991.
Vocation Office—Rev. EUGENE H. WOJCIK, Dir., *Diocesan Pastoral Center.*

CLERGY, PARISHES, MISSIONS AND PAROCHIAL SCHOOLS

CITY OF BELLEVILLE
(St. Clair County)

1—CATHEDRAL OF ST. PETER (1842), Rev. Msgr. James A. Buerster, Rector; Rev. Larry Lemay; Deacons Robert Becker; Joseph Stock; Donald Deitz.
Res., 200 W. Harrison, 62220. Tel: 618-234-1166; Fax: 618-234-2957. [CEM]
School—Cathedral School, 200 S. Second St., 62220. Tel: 618-233-6414; Fax: 618-233-3587. Sr. Ruth Ann Klauser, S.S.N.D., Prin.
School Sisters of Notre Dame 3; Lay Teachers 20; Students 320.
Catechesis/Religious Programs—D.R.E.: Sr. Theresa Markus, S.S.N.D.; Mrs. Cheryl Neu.
Students 140.
Convent—300 S. Second St., 62220. Tel: 618-233-3580.

2—BLESSED SACRAMENT (1927), Rev. Msgr. Marvin C. Volk; Deacon Douglas Boyer.
Res., 8707 W. Main St., 62223. Tel: 618-397-2287; Fax: 618-397-2269.
School—8801 W. Main St., 62223. Tel: 618-397-1111; Fax: 618-397-8431. Ms. Claire Hatch, Prin.
School Sisters of Notre Dame 2; Lay Teachers 14; Students 200.
Catechesis/Religious Programs—Students 66.
Convent—8901 W. Main St., 62233. Tel: 618-397-0039.

3—OUR LADY QUEEN OF PEACE (1955), Rev. John W. McEvilly.
Res., 5923 N. Belt W., 62223. Tel: 618-234-6196; Fax: 618-234-6217.
School—5915 N. Belt W., 62223. Tel: 618-234-1206; Fax: 618-234-6123. Mrs. Frances Smith, Prin.
Lay Teachers 19; Students 315.
Catechesis/Religious Programs—Students 48.

4—ST. AUGUSTINE OF CANTERBURY (1955), Rev. Andrew J. Knopik.
Res., 1910 W. Belle, 62226. Tel: 618-233-3813; Fax: 618-233-3946.
School—1900 Canterbury Dr., 62226. Tel: 618-234-4958; Fax: 618-234-3360. Sr. Ann Marie Bonvie, S.S.N.D., Prin.
Lay Teachers 18; Students 232.
Catechesis/Religious Programs—Students 50.

5—ST. HENRY (1925), Rev. Msgr. Bernard L. Voss. In res., Rev. Robert D. Gore.
Res., 5315 W. Main St., 62223. Tel: 618-233-2423; Fax: 618-233-9879.
School—5303 W. Main St., 62223. Tel: 618-234-6061; Fax: 618-234-6801. Mr. Ronald Karcher, Prin.
Lay Teachers 10; Students 139.
Catechesis/Religious Programs—Students 75.

6—ST. LUKE (1883), Rev. Msgr. James E. Margason, V.G., M.Div., J.C.L.; Sr. Grace Marie Mueller, S.S.N.D., Pastoral Assoc., Tel: 618-236-1839; Fax: 618-236-1839; Deacon Robert Lanter.
Res., 301 N. Church St., 62220. Tel: 618-236-1124; Fax: 618-236-1134.
Catechesis/Religious Programs—Tel: 618-236-1839.
Students 70.

7—ST. MARY (1893), Rev. John T. Myler, D.Min.
Res., 1706 W. Main St., 62226. Tel: 618-233-2391; Fax: 618-233-9201.
School—1722 W. Main St., 62226. Tel: 618-234-2476; Fax: 618-234-0267. Mrs. Claudia Dougherty, Prin.
Sisters 2; Lay Teachers 10; Students 194.
Catechesis/Religious Programs—Mrs. Lucille Sautman, D.R.E.
Students 96.

8—ST. TERESA OF THE CHILD JESUS (1926). (Little Flower). Rev. Msgr. Donald W. Eichenseer; Rev. Joseph S. Schrage.
Res., 1201 Lebanon Ave., 62221. Tel: 618-233-3500; Fax: 618-233-9703.
School—1108 Lebanon Ave., 62221. Tel: 618-235-4066; Fax: 618-235-7930. Mr. Leo Hodapp, Prin.
Lay Teachers 20; Students 360.
Catechesis/Religious Programs—Tel: 618-233-3550.
Students 121.

9—CHAPEL OF ST. JOHN CHILDREN'S HOME, Rev. Msgr. James E. Margason, V.G., M.Div., J.C.L.
Mailing Address: Chancery Office, 222 S. Third St., 62220. Tel: 618-277-8181; Fax: 618-277-0387. [CEM]

OUTSIDE THE CITY OF BELLEVILLE

Albers, Clinton Co., St. Bernard (1908), Rev. Louis A. Koehr.
Res., 62215. Tel: 618-248-5112; Fax: 618-248-5112. [CEM]
Catechesis/Religious Programs—Sr. Joan Stoverink, A.S.C., D.R.E.
Students 120.

Anna, Union Co., St. Mary (1857), Rev. Msgr. Thomas W. Miller; Sr. Joan Backes, S.S.N.D., Pastoral Assoc. & D.R.E.
Res., 402 Freeman, 62906. Tel: 618-833-5835.
Catechesis/Religious Programs—Tel: 618-833-3131.
Students 112.

Ava, Jackson Co., St. Elizabeth (1890), Rev. Leo J. Hayes.
Res., 606 W. George St., P.O. Box 157, 62907. Tel: 618-426-3321; Fax: 608-426-3321.
Catechesis/Religious Programs—Students 9.

Aviston, Clinton Co., St. Francis of Assisi (1865), Rev. Daniel L. Friedman; Deacons Gerald E. Stockman; Charles Litteken.
Res., 251 S. Clinton, Box 93, 62216. Tel: 618-228-7219; Fax: 618-228-7320. [CEM]
Catechesis/Religious Programs—Tel: 618-228-7245; Fax: 618-228-7320.
Students 236.

Bartelso, Clinton Co., St. Cecilia (1885), Rev. Henry J. Fischer.
Res., 304 S. Washington St., P.O. Box 176, 62218. Tel: 618-765-2162; Fax: 618-765-2264.
Catechesis/Religious Programs—Tel: 618-765-2163. Sr. Mary Benedict Hayden, A.S.C., D.R.E.
Students 184.

Beaver Prairie, Clinton Co., St. Felicitas (1883), Sr. Diane M. Turner, S.S.N.D., Pastoral Life Coord.; Rev. Lawrence M. Nickels, O.F.M.; Very Rev. David M. Darin.
Mailing Address: 13322 Church Rd., Carlyle, 62231. Tel: 618-594-3040. [CEM]
Catechesis/Religious Programs—Students 27.

Beckemeyer, Clinton Co., St. Anthony (1905), Rev. Steven F. Poole; Deacon Robert Lippert.
Res., P.O. Box 305, 62219. Tel: 618-227-8236; Fax: 618-227-8630. [CEM]
Catechesis/Religious Programs—Students 63.

Benton, Franklin Co., St. Joseph (1910), Rev. Joseph L. Trapp.
Res., 506 W. Main, 62812. Tel: 618-438-9941; Fax: 618-438-9941. [CEM]
Catechesis/Religious Programs—Tel: 618-438-0009.
Students 53.

Breese, Clinton Co., St. Augustine (1912), Rev. Steven F. Poole; Deacon Robert Lippert.
Res., 525 S. Third St., 62230. Tel: 618-526-4362; Fax: 618-526-4362. [CEM]
Catechesis/Religious Programs—Students 44.
St. Dominic (1857), Rev. Patrick N. Peter.
Res., 493 N. Second St., 62230. Tel: 618-526-7746; Fax: 618-526-7755. [CEM]
Catechesis/Religious Programs—Tel: 618-526-8144. Mrs. Sue Darr, D.R.E.
Students 100.

Bridgeport, Lawrence Co., Immaculate Conception (1856), Rev. Thomas Barrett.
Mailing Address: 1006 Collins, Lawrenceville, 62439. Tel: 618-943-5255; Fax: 618-943-3147. [CEM]
Catechesis/Religious Programs—Students 12.

Cahokia, St. Clair Co., Holy Family (1699), Very Rev. Gerald R. Hechenberger, V.F.
Res., 116 Church St., 62206. Tel: 618-337-4548; Fax: 618-332-1699. [CEM 3]
School—Tel: 618-337-2880. Cynthia Cramer, Prin.
Lay Teachers 10; Students 120.
Catechesis/Religious Programs—Students 15.
St. Catherine Laboure (1959), Rev. Mark D. Reyling.
Res., 913 Rome Ln., 62206. Tel: 618-337-4173; Fax: 618-337-1231.
School—1820 Jerome Ln., 62208. Tel: 618-337-4448; Fax: 618-337-1231. Joseph Morice, Prin.
Lay Teachers 9; Students 140.

Day Care—1826 Jerome Ln., 62208. Tel: 618-337-3555.
Catechesis/Religious Programs—Students 210.

Cairo, Alexander Co., St. Patrick (1838), Rev. Jerome D. Fortenberry, C.M.
Res., 312 Ninth St., 62914. Tel: 618-734-2061. [CEM]
School—St. Joseph, Tel: 618-734-4182; Fax: 618-734-4205. Louis Fortenberry, Prin.
Lay Teachers 5; Students 50.

Carbondale, Jackson Co., St. Francis Xavier (1900), Rev. Robert B. Flannery. In res., Rev. Peter Amponsah.
Res., 303 S. Poplar St., 62901. Tel: 618-457-4556; Fax: 618-457-7368.
Catechesis/Religious Programs—Toni Intravaia, D.R.E.
Students 185.

Carlyle, Clinton Co., St. Mary (1853). (Immaculate Conception). Rev. George A. Mauck.
Res., 12th St. & Jefferson St., Box 179, 62231. Tel: 618-594-2225; Fax: 618-594-4638. [CEM]
Catechesis/Religious Programs—Tel: 618-594-2284; Fax: 618-594-4638. Sr. Geraldine Neier, S.S.N.D., D.R.E.
Students 240.

Carmi, White Co., St. Polycarp (1847), Rev. Stephen A. Rudolphi.
Res., 209 Fourth St., 62821. Tel: 618-382-7732. [CEM]
Catechesis/Religious Programs—Students 34.

Carterville, Williamson Co., Church of the Holy Spirit (1974), Russell Peterson, Parish Life Coord.; Rev. Msgr. William McGhee; Rev. Peter Amponsah.
216 Pine St., P.O. Box 93, 62918. Tel: 618-985-2900; 985-2570; Fax: 618-985-3952.
Catechesis/Religious Programs—Tel: 618-985-6929.
Students 129.

Caseyville, St. Clair Co., St. Stephen (1893), Rev. Joseph C. Rascher; Sue Huett, Pastoral Assoc.; Deacon William DeWolf.
Res., 901 S. Main St., P.O. Box 458, 62232. Tel: 618-397-0666; Fax: 618-397-4430.
Catechesis/Religious Programs—Students 30.

Centralia, Marion Co., St. Mary (1857), Very Rev. David M. Darin.
Res., 424 E. Broadway, 62801. Tel: 618-532-5041. [CEM]
Church Office: 424 E. Broadway, 62801. Tel: 618-532-6291; Fax: 618-532-4758.
School—Tel: 618-532-3473. Sr. Jacklyn Pritchard, C.D.P., Prin.
Sisters 1; Lay Teachers 8; Students 143.
Catechesis/Religious Programs—Mrs. Dolores Sanders, D.R.E.
Students 60.

Centreville, St. Clair Co., Immaculate Conception (1858), James Byrd, Parish Life Coord.; Rev. Mark D. Reyling.
Res., 6210 Church Rd., 62207. Tel: 618-337-5682; 337-7493; Fax: 618-337-7493. [CEM]

Chester, Randolph Co., St. Mary Help of Christians (1842), Rev. Msgr. Dennis R. Schaefer.
Res., 911 Swanwick St., 62233. Tel: 618-826-2444; Fax: 618-826-3486. [CEM]
School—Tel: 618-826-3120; Fax: 618-826-3486. Sr. Cindy Weber, S.S.N.D., Prin.
Sisters 2; Lay Teachers 12; Pre-School 35; K-8 90.
Catechesis/Religious Programs—Tel: 618-826-2526. Cheryl Gross, D.R.E.
Students 46.

Christopher, Franklin Co., St. Andrew (1905), Rev. Walter M. Barr.
Res., 412 E. Washington St., 62822. Tel: 618-724-4114. [CEM]
Catechesis/Religious Programs—Elaine Polbinski, D.R.E.
Students 71.

Cobden, Union Co., St. Joseph, Rev. Federico Higuera; Deacon Patrick Patterson.
Res., 101 Centennial St., P.O. Box 237, 62920. Tel: 618-893-2276. [CEM]
Catechesis/Religious Programs—Tel: 618-893-2368.
Students 69.

Columbia, Monroe Co., Immaculate Conception of the B.V.M. (1846), Rev. John C. Iffert, Admin.; Deacon John DuPrey.
Res., 117 E. Madison, 62236. Tel: 618-281-5105; Fax: 618-281-6848. [CEM]
School—Tel: 618-281-5353; Fax: 618-281-6044. Michael Kish, Prin.
Lay Teachers 19; Students 339.
Catechesis/Religious Programs—Students 158.

Coulterville, Randolph Co., St. Anthony. Closed. For inquiries for parish records contact the Chancery.

Dahlgren, Hamilton Co., St. John Nepomucene (1893), Rev. Msgr. Joseph A. Lawlor.
Church—7th & Main Sts., P.O. Box 220, 62828. Tel: 618-736-2879; 643-3552; Fax: 618-643-3112. [CEM]
Res., Rte. 3, Box 170, McLeansboro, 62859.
Catechesis/Religious Programs—Tel: 618-643-3552. Rita Rapp, D.R.E.
Students 70.

Damiansville, Clinton Co., St. Damian (1861), Rev. Louis A. Koehr, Pastor.
One W. Main St., 62215. Tel: 618-248-5134; Fax: 618-248-5134. [CEM]
Res., 202 N. Broadway, Albers, 62215.
Catechesis/Religious Programs—Students 111.

Dubois, Washington Co., St. Charles Borromeo (1877), Rev. Msgr. Melvin Vandeloo.
Res., P.O. Box 6, 62831. Tel: 618-787-2781; Fax: 618-787-2781. [CEM]
Catechesis/Religious Programs—Students 75.

Dupo, St. Clair Co., Sacred Heart of Jesus (1914), Very Rev. Gerald R. Hechenberger, V.F.; Kathleen Cafferata, Pastoral Assoc.
100 S. 3rd St., 62239. Tel: 618-286-3224; Fax: 618-286-5484.
Catechesis/Religious Programs—Tel: 618-286-4373.
Students 64.

Du Quoin, Perry Co., Sacred Heart of Jesus (1863), Rev. Msgr. Harry J. Jerome.
Res., 17 N. Walnut St., 62832. Tel: 618-542-3423. [CEM]
School—Tel: 618-542-2335; Fax: 618-542-2329. Bonnie L. Paszkiewicz, Prin.
Lay Teachers 5; Students 55.
Catechesis/Religious Programs—Students 26.

East St. Louis, St. Clair Co.,

1—IMMACULATE CONCEPTION, (1895) (Lithuanian), Very Rev. Kenneth J. York, Admin.
1509 Baugh Ave., 62205. Tel: 618-874-0162.

2—ST. JOHN FRANCIS REGIS, (1901), Rev. J. Clyde Grogan.
3500 Market Ave., 62207. Tel: 618-874-5025.

3—ST. JOSEPH, (1902), Rev. James A. Voelker.
Res., 408 Columbia Pl., 62205. Tel: 618-274-0655.
Catechesis/Religious Programs—Nicole Younge, D.R.E.
Students 21.

4—ST. PATRICK, (1861), Rev. James Clyde Grogan; Deacon John Coates.
Res., 771 Vogel Pl., 62205. Tel: 618-874-5025; Fax: 618-274-4659. [CEM]

5—ST. PHILIP, (1841), Rev. James A. Voelker, Pastor.
Res., 408 Columbia Pl., 62205. Tel: 618-274-0655. [CEM]
Church—8313 Church Ln., 62203. Tel: 618-397-1860.

Eldorado, Saline Co., St. Mary (1900), Very Rev. Donald E. Abell.
Res., 1158 N. 2nd St., 62930. Tel: 618-273-6947; Fax: 618-273-3147. [CEM]
Catechesis/Religious Programs—Students 89.

Elizabethtown, Hardin Co., St. Joseph (1897), Rev. Tadeusz Gegotek.
Res., IL 146-185 E Rd., Box 140, 62931-9711. Tel: 618-285-3332. [CEM]
Catechesis/Religious Programs—Tel: 618-287-4824.
Students 25.

Ellis Grove, Randolph Co., Divine Maternity of the B.V.M. (1933), Deacon Omer E. DuBois.
Res., 7362 Shawneetown Trail, 62241. Tel: 618-859-3541.
Catechesis/Religious Programs—Students 42.

Enfield, White Co., St. Patrick (1830), Rev. Stephen A. Rudolphi, Admin.
St. Polycarp Church: 209 Fourth St., Carmi, 62821. Tel: 618-963-2013. [CEM]
Catechesis/Religious Programs—Students 20.

Equality, Gallatin Co., St. Joseph (1873), Rev. Mark D. Stec.
Mailing Address: P.O. Box 99, 62934. Tel: 618-276-4252; Fax: 618-272-5400.
Res., P.O. Box 190, Ridgway, 62979. Tel: 618-272-7059; Fax: 618-272-5400. [CEM]
Catechesis/Religious Programs—Students 60.

Evansville, Randolph Co., St. Boniface (1860), Rev. John J. Joyce.
Res., 1007 Olive St., 62242. Tel: 618-853-4453; Fax: 618-853-4453. [CEM]
Catechesis/Religious Programs—Students 24.

Fairfield, Wayne Co., St. Edward (1881), Rev. Henry R. Engelhart.
Res., 300 N.W. 5th St., 62837. Tel: 618-847-7931; Fax: 618-842-7393.
Catechesis/Religious Programs—Peggy Garrison, D.R.E.
Students 40.

Fairmont City, St. Clair Co., Holy Rosary (1922), Rev. David M. Wilke, Pastor.
Res., 2716 N. 42nd St., 62201. Tel: 618-274-3486; Fax: 618-274-1814.
School—Tel: 618-271-8600; Fax: 618-271-7041. Mrs. Shirley Kurre, Prin.
Lay Teachers 8; Students 129.
Catechesis/Religious Programs—Students 40.

Fairview Heights, St. Clair Co., Our Lady of the Assumption (1965), Rev. James H. Jansen; Deacon Dennis C. Rickert.
Res., 9950 Bunkum Rd., 62208. Tel: 618-397-0121.
Catechesis/Religious Programs—Students 77.

St. Albert the Great (1951), Rev. James T. Long; Deacons Thomas Underwood; David Bigham.
Res., 15 E. Lincoln Hwy., 62208. Tel: 618-632-5334; Fax: 618-632-0903.
School—Tel: 618-632-4937. Robert Bigham, Prin.
Sisters 3; Lay Teachers 13; Students 205.
Catechesis/Religious Programs—Tel: 618-632-8577.
Students 155.

Fayetteville, St. Clair Co., St. Pancratius (1837), Margaret Heil, Parish Life Coord.; Very Rev. Kenneth J. York.
Res., 2213 N. 2nd St., 62258. Tel: 618-677-2717. [CEM]

Flora, Clay Co., St. Stephen (1854), Rev. Hyacinth Mazuchowski.
Res., 812 N. Main St., 62839. Tel: 618-662-6261. [CEM]
Catechesis/Religious Programs—Tel: 618-662-8121.
Students 66.

Freeburg, St. Clair Co., St. Joseph (1857), Rev. Msgr. Theodore J. Baumann.
Res., 9 N. Alton St., 62243. Tel: 618-539-3209. [CEM]
School—Tel: 618-539-3930. Jeffrey Humes, Prin.
Sisters 1; Lay Teachers 10; Students 150.
Catechesis/Religious Programs—Tel: 618-539-3209.
Students 146.

Germantown, Clinton Co., St. Boniface (1837), Rev. Stephen J. Humphrey.
Res., 402 Munster St., Box 280, 62245. Tel: 618-523-4271; Fax: 618-523-4263. [CEM]
Catechesis/Religious Programs—Students 327.

Grand Chain, Pulaski Co., St. Catherine (1891), Rev. Msgr. William P. McGhee; Sr. Nancy Flamm, S.S.N.D., Pastoral Assoc.
517 N. Walnut St., Box 67, Mound City, 62963. Tel: 618-748-9113; Fax: 618-748-9639. [CEM]
Catechesis/Religious Programs—Students 21.

Harrisburg, Saline Co., St. Mary (1906), Very Rev. Donald E. Stallings.
Res., 2000 W. Poplar St., 62946. Tel: 618-253-7408; Fax: 618-252-7874. [CEM]
Catechesis/Religious Programs—Tel: 618-252-7874.
Students 71.

Hecker, Monroe Co., St. Augustine of Canterbury (1824), Rev. Joseph D. Hansmann.
Res., 310 N. Main St., P.O. Box 126, 62248. Tel: 618-473-2217; Fax: 618-473-9141. [CEM]
Catechesis/Religious Programs—340 N. Main, 62248.
Students 31.

Herrin, Williamson Co., Our Lady of Mount Carmel (1901), Rev. Msgr. Kenneth J. Schaefer.
Res., 316 W. Monroe St., 62948. Tel: 618-942-3114; Fax: 618-988-1375. [CEM]
School—Tel: 618-942-4484; Fax: 618-942-2864. Mr. Terry Hughes, Prin.
Lay Teachers 14; Students 263.
Catechesis/Religious Programs—Students 65.

Johnston City, Williamson Co., St. Paul (1904), Rev. Msgr. William P. McGhee, V.F.; Sr. Catherine Wellinghoff, A.S.C., Parish Life Coord.; Rev. Kenneth Schaefer.
1103 Washington St., 62951. Tel: 618-983-5073.
Catechesis/Religious Programs—Students 37.

Kaskaskia, Randolph Co., Immaculate Conception (1675). (Independent Mission).
Mailing Address: 6450 Klein Lane, St. Mary's, MO 63673. Tel: 618-366-2633.

Kinmundy, Marion Co., St. Elizabeth Ann Seton (1878), Rev. Jon O'Guinn.
Mailing Address: 812 W. Main St., Salem, 62881. Tel: 618-548-0899; Fax: 618-548-0269.
Catechesis/Religious Programs—N. Madison St., 62854. Tel: 618-245-6221.
Students 10.

Lawrenceville, Lawrence Co., St. Lawrence (1909), Rev. Thomas Barrett, Pastor.
Res., 1006 Collins, 62439. Tel: 618-943-5255; Fax: 618-943-3147. [JC]
Catechesis/Religious Programs—Students 47.

Lebanon, St. Clair Co., St. Joseph (1862), Rev. Msgr. James E. Margason, V.G., M.Div., J.C.L.; Mrs. Brenda Pehle, Parish Life Coord. In res., Rev. Eugene J. Neff.
Res., 901 N. Alton St., 62254. Tel: 618-537-2575. [CEM]
Catechesis/Religious Programs—Students 72.

Lively Grove, Washington Co., St. Anthony (1868), Rev. Dennis F. Voss Tel: 618-768-4921.
Church—6101 St. Anthony Church Rd., Oakdale, 62268. Tel: 618-824-6271; Fax: 618-824-6200. [CEM]
Catechesis/Religious Programs—Tel: 618-824-6271.
Students 55.

Madonnaville, Monroe Co., Immaculate Conception (1921), Rev. Edwin H. Hustedde.
Mailing Address: 101 S. Meyer St., Valmeyer, 62295. Tel: 618-939-6618; 935-2247.

Marion, Williamson Co., St. Joseph (1940), Rev. Richard G. Mohr.
Res., 600 N. Russell St., P.O. Box 1679, 62959. Tel: 618-993-3194; Fax: 618-997-9391.
Catechesis/Religious Programs—Tel: 618-997-7373; Fax: 618-997-9391. Sr. Anastasia Wehner, S.S.N.D., D.R.E.
Students 213.

Marydale, Clinton Co., St. Teresa of Avila (1919), Sr. Mary Catherine Clark, A.S.C., Parish Life Coord.; Very Rev. David M. Darin; Rev. Lawrence M. Nickels, O.F.M.
18021 Marydale Rd., Carlyle, 62231. Tel: 618-594-3266.
Catechesis/Religious Programs—Students 35.

Mascoutah, St. Clair Co., Holy Childhood of Jesus (1857), Rev. Msgr. Jerome D. Hartlein.
Res., 104 N. Independence St., P.O. Box 160, 62258. Tel: 618-566-2958; Fax: 618-566-4447. [CEM]
School—Tel: 618-566-2922; Fax: 618-566-7720. Kelly Koishor, Prin.
Lay Teachers 16; Students 199.
Catechesis/Religious Programs—Tel: 618-566-2922.
Students 81.

McLeansboro, Hamilton Co., St. Clement (1881), Rev. Msgr. Joseph A. Lawler.
Res., 103 N. Hancock, 62859. Tel: 618-643-3552; Fax: 618-643-3112. [CEM]
Catechesis/Religious Programs—Tel: 618-643-3628.
Students 80.

Metropolis, Massac Co., St. Rose of Lima (1872), Rev. Tadeusz Gegotek.
Res., 315 E. Third St., 62960-2229. Tel: 618-524-9006; Fax: 618-524-9006.
Catechesis/Religious Programs—Office:, 405 E. Third St., 62960. Tel: 618-524-8202. Marjorie J. Hawes, D.R.E.
Students 37.

Millstadt, St. Clair Co., St. James (1851), Rev. Bernard C. Goedde, Jr.; Deacon Ronald Karcher.
Res., 405 W. Madison St., 62260. Tel: 618-476-3513; Fax: 618-476-3513 (call ahead). [CEM]
School—Tel: 618-476-3510; Fax: 618-476-3510 (Call first). Sr. Barbara Hudock, A.S.C., Prin.
Sisters 2; Lay Teachers 9; Students 145.
Catechesis/Religious Programs—Tel: 618-476-1923.
Students 93.

Modoc, Randolph Co., St. Leo, Rev. Richard J. Weidert, Admin.
Res., #1 Pioneer Ln., Red Bud, 62278. Tel: 618-282-3176. [CEM]

Mound City, Pulaski Co., Church of the Immaculate Conception-St. Mary (1863), Rev. Msgr. William P. McGhee; Sr. Nancy Flamm, S.S.N.D., Pastoral Assoc.
Res., 517 N. Walnut St., Box 67, 62963. Tel: 618-748-9113; Fax: 618-748-9639. [CEM]
Catechesis/Religious Programs—Students 19.

Mount Carmel, Wabash Co., St. Mary (1836), Rev. William J. Rowe; Deacon Charles Speaks.
Res., 125 W. Fifth St., 62863. Tel: 618-262-5337; Fax: 618-262-5333. [CEM]
School—Tel: 618-263-3183; Fax: 618-263-3596. Mrs. Alice Wirth, Prin.
Lay Teachers 13; Students 177.
Catechesis/Religious Programs—Students 72.

Mount Vernon, Jefferson Co., St. Mary (1871), Rev. Daniel J. Jurek.
Res., 115 N. 14th St., 62864. Tel: 618-244-1559; Fax: 618-242-5365. [CEM]
School—Tel: 618-242-5353; Fax: 618-242-5365. Susan Cunningham, Prin.
Lay Teachers 8; Students 117.
Catechesis/Religious Programs—Students 144.

Murphysboro, Jackson Co., St. Andrew (1868), Rev. Gary P. Gummersheimer; Deacons Michael Dougherty; Joseph Teaff.
Res., 724 Mulberry St., 62966. Tel: 618-687-2012; Fax: 618-684-3431. [CEM]
School—Tel: 618-687-2013; Fax: 618-684-4969. Marilyn Johnson, Prin.
Lay Teachers 14; Students 155.
Catechesis/Religious Programs—Tel: 618-684-6364; Fax: 618-684-3431. Mr. Bill Harper, D.R.E.
Students 130.

Nashville, Washington Co., St. Ann (1874), Rev. Paul R. Wienhoff, Admin.
Res., 631 S. Mill St., 62263. Tel: 618-327-3232; Fax: 618-321-4904. [CEM]
School—Tel: 618-327-8741. Laurie Klostermann, Prin.
Lay Teachers 9; Students 139.
Catechesis/Religious Programs—Tel: 618-327-3232.
Students 96.
Convent—695 S. Mill St., 62263.

New Athens, St. Clair Co., St. Agatha (1870), Rev. Richard Daly.
Res., 205 S. Market St., 62264. Tel: 618-475-2331. [CEM]
School—Tel: 618-475-2170; Fax: 618-475-3177. Mrs. Charlotte Newbold, Prin.
Lay Teachers 5; Students 45.
Catechesis/Religious Programs—Tel: 618-295-2686.
Students 70.

New Baden, Clinton Co., St. George (1894), Rev. Msgr. James A. Blazine.
Res., 200 N. 3rd St., 62265. Tel: 618-588-4323. [CEM]
Catechesis/Religious Programs—Tel: 618-588-3504. Martha Kruchten, D.R.E.
Students 167.

O'Fallon, St. Clair Co., St. Clare (1867), Rev. James E. Deiters.
Res., 205 W. 3rd St., 62269. Tel: 618-632-3562; Fax: 618-632-9036. [CEM]
School—214 W. 3rd St., 62269. Tel: 618-632-6327; Fax: 618-632-5587. Mr. Ken Pajares, Prin.
Lay Teachers 25; Students 425.
Catechesis/Religious Programs—Tel: 618-632-4281. Mrs. Cindy Doil, D.R.E.
Students 162.

St. Nicholas (1982), Rev. Msgr. William J. Hitpas; Deacon Richard H. Olson.
Res., 900 N. Smiley, 62269. Tel: 618-632-1997; Fax: 618-632-7703.
Church and Office: 625 St. Nicholas Dr., 62269. Tel: 618-632-1797; Fax: 618-632-7703.
Catechesis/Religious Programs—Tel: 618-632-1007. Barbara Furdek, D.R.E.
Students 273.

Okawville, Washington Co., St. Barbara (1867), Rev. Msgr. Albert Jerome.
Res., 305 N. Front St., 62271. Tel: 618-243-6236; Fax: 618-243-5270. [CEM]
Catechesis/Religious Programs—Tel: 618-243-6236.
Students 90.

Olney, Richland Co., St. Joseph (1857), Rev. Jerry E. Wirth.
Res., 215 S. Elliott St., 62450. Tel: 618-392-8181; Fax: 618-395-8500. [CEM]
School—Tel: 618-395-3081; Fax: 618-395-8500. John Stephenson, Prin.
Lay Teachers 12; Students 192.
Catechesis/Religious Programs—Students 66.

Paderborn, St. Clair Co., St. Michael (1843), Rev. Joseph D. Hansmann.
Church—4576 Buss Branch Rd., Waterloo, 62298. Tel: 618-473-2798; Fax: 618-473-2798. [CEM]
Catechesis/Religious Programs—Tel: 618-473-2915. Jackie Billings, D.R.E.
Students 79.

Pinckneyville, Perry Co., St. Bruno (1872), Rev. John L. Venegoni.
Res., 204 N. Gordon Ave., 62274. Tel: 618-357-5510; Fax: 618-357-6050. [CEM]
School—Tel: 618-357-8276; Fax: 618-357-6425. Sr. Rose Huelsmann, Prin.
Lay Teachers 10; Students 113.
Catechesis/Religious Programs—Tel: 618-357-8278. Sr. Joyce Engle, S.S.N.D., D.R.E.
Students 85.

Piopolis, Hamilton Co., St. John the Baptist (1841), Rev. Msgr. Joseph A. Lawler; Deacon Gary D. Walsh.
Res., Rte. 3, P.O. Box 170, McLeansboro, 62859. Tel: 618-648-2490. [CEM]
Catechesis/Religious Programs—Tel: 618-648-2586. Jewell Wilson, D.R.E.
Students 75.

Pond Settlement, Gallatin Co., St. Patrick (1842), Rev. Mark D. Stec.
Mailing Address: P.O. Box 579, Shawneetown, 62984. Tel: 618-269-3318; Fax: 618-272-5400.
Catechesis/Religious Programs—Students 21.

Posen, Washington Co., Our Lady of Perpetual Help (1901), Rev. James R. Van Oss.
Res., 19824 Posen Rd., Nashville, 62263. Tel: 618-327-3556. [CEM]

Prairie du Rocher, Randolph Co., St. Joseph (1721), Rev. Albert E. Kreher.
Res., 802 Middle St., 62277. Tel: 618-284-3314. [CEM]
Catechesis/Religious Programs—Students 35.

Raddle, Jackson Co., St. Ann (1875), Rev. Leo J. Hayes. 606 W. George St., P.O. Box 157, Ava, 62907. Tel: 618-426-3321; Fax: 618-426-3321.
Catechesis/Religious Programs—Students 11.

Radom, Washington Co., St. Michael (1874), Rev. Jerome H. Hibner.
Res., 52 S. Third St., 62876. Tel: 618-485-2265; Fax: 618-485-2272. [CEM]
School—Tel: 618-485-6461. Mr. Ray Albu, Prin.
Lay Teachers 5; Students 56.
Catechesis/Religious Programs—Students 56.

Red Bud, Randolph Co., St. John the Baptist (1862), Very Rev. Thomas Stout.
Res., 515 Locust St., 62278. Tel: 618-282-3222; Fax: 618-282-6867. [CEM]
School—Tel: 618-282-3215; Fax: 618-282-6790. Sr. Aquinas Kurtz, O.S.F., Prin.
Lay Teachers 9; Students 180.
Catechesis/Religious Programs—Students 70.

Renault, Monroe Co., Our Lady of Good Counsel (1879), Rev. Roger R. Karban, Admin.
Res., P.O. Box 98, 62279. Tel: 618-458-7710; Fax: 618-458-7710. [CEM]

Ridgway, Gallatin Co., St. Joseph (1870), Rev. Mark D. Stec.
Res., 205 W. South St., P.O. Box 190, 62979. Tel: 618-272-7059; Fax: 618-272-5400. [CEM]
Catechesis/Religious Programs—Students 108.

Royalton-Zeigler, Franklin Co., St. Aloysius/Sacred Heart (1919), Rev. Brian Barker; Sr. Laura Reynolds, Pastoral Assoc.
Res., 212 Pecan St., P.O. Box 100, Royalton, 62983. Tel: 618-984-2146. [CEM]
Catechesis/Religious Programs—Students 15.

Ruma, Randolph Co., St. Patrick (1818), Rev. Richard J. Weidert, Admin.
Res., #1 Pioneer Ln., Red Bud, 62278. Tel: 618-282-3176. [CEM]
Catechesis/Religious Programs—Students 34.

St. Francisville, Lawrence Co., St. Francis Xavier (1836), Rev. Thomas M. Barrett.
Mailing Address: 1006 Collins St., Lawrenceville, 62439. Tel: 618-943-5255. [CEM]
Catechesis/Religious Programs—Students 14.

St. Libory, St. Clair Co., St. Liborius (1838), Rev. Dennis F. Voss; Deacon Andrew Lintker.
Res., P.O. Box 331, 62282. Tel: 618-768-4921; Fax: 618-768-4207. [CEM]
Catechesis/Religious Programs—Tel: 618-768-4207. Donna Dressler, D.R.E.
Students 113.

St. Rose, Clinton Co., St. Rose (1868), Rev. Edward F. Schaefer.
Res., 18010 St. Rose Rd., 62230-2506. Tel: 618-526-4118; Fax: 618-526-0004. [CEM]
Catechesis/Religious Programs—Tel: 618-526-4886. Sr. Justina Schaefer, A.S.C., D.R.E.
Students 210.

St. Sebastian, Wabash Co., St. Sebastian (1871), Rev. Henry R. Engelhart.
Mailing Address: 300 N.W. Fifth St., Fairfield, 62837. Tel: 618-847-7931; Fax: 618-872-7393. [CEM]
Catechesis/Religious Programs—Students 44.

Salem, Marion Co., St. Theresa of Avila (1868), Rev. Jon O'Guinn.
Res., 812 W. Main St., 62881. Tel: 618-548-0899; Fax: 618-548-0269. [CEM]
School—Tel: 618-548-3492. Sr. Ruth Chausse, S.S.N.D., Prin.
School Sisters of Notre Dame 1; Lay Teachers 6; Students 81.
Catechesis/Religious Programs—Tel: 618-548-6316.
Students 66.

Sandoval, Marion Co., St. Lawrence (1871), Rev. Charles W. Tuttle.
Church—311 W.M St., P.O. Box 278, 62882. Tel: 618-247-3300. [CEM]
Res., P.O. Box 189, Breese, 62230. Tel: 618-594-2131.

Catechesis/Religious Programs—Students 62.

Scheller, Jefferson Co., St. Barbara (1898), Rev. Jerome Hibner.
Res., 62883. Tel: 618-279-7207.
Catechesis/Religious Programs—Students 29.

Sesser, Franklin Co., St. Mary (1909), Rev. Edward Balestrieri.
Res., 100 N. Poplar St., P.O. Box 568, 62884. Tel: 618-625-5053; Fax: 618-625-5053.
Catechesis/Religious Programs—Students 31.

Shawneetown, Gallatin Co., St. Mary (1842), Rev. Mark D. Stec.
Mailing Address: 655 W. Marshall St., P.O. Box 579, 62984. Tel: 618-269-3318; Fax: 618-272-5400. [CEM]
Catechesis/Religious Programs—Students 45.

Shiloh, St. Clair Co., Corpus Christi (1913), Rev. Msgr. Carl E. Scherrer.
Res., 206 Rasp St., O'Fallon, 62269. Tel: 618-632-5631; Fax: 618-632-7614.
Catechesis/Religious Programs—Tel: 618-632-7614.
Students 70.

Smithton, St. Clair Co., St. John the Baptist (1867), Very Rev. Kenneth J. York, J.C.L.; Deacon Donald R. Deitz.
Res., 10 S. Lincoln St., 62285-1614. Tel: 618-234-2068; Fax: 618-234-0179. [CEM]
School—Tel: 618-233-0581; Fax: 618-233-0581. Stephen Boyer, Prin.
Lay Teachers 7; Students 110.

Sparta, Randolph Co., Our Lady of Lourdes (1897), Rev. William F. Rensing; Deacon J. Richard Downen.
Res., 611 W. Broadway, 62286. Tel: 618-443-2811.
Catechesis/Religious Programs—Tel: 618-443-2878. Lila Lehnherr, D.R.E.
Students 120.

Stonefort, Williamson Co., St. Francis de Sales (1879), Rev. Jose Ancheril.
Mailing Address: 2020 State Rte. 146E., Vienna, 62995. Tel: 618-658-4501.

Stringtown, Richland Co., St. Joseph (1841), Rev. David L. Braun.
6342 N. Stringtown Rd., Olney, 62450. Tel: 618-752-5671 (Wendelin Rectory). [CEM]
Catechesis/Religious Programs—Tel: 618-395-2862. Barbara Ochs, D.R.E.
Students 72.

Tamaroa, Perry Co., Immaculate Conception (1904), Rev. Msgr. Melvin Vandeloo.
Res., 533 W. 2nd North St., 62888. Tel: 618-496-5867.
Catechesis/Religious Programs—Tel: 618-787-2361.
Students 30.

Tipton, Monroe Co., St. Patrick (1850), Rev. Eugene J. Wojcik.
Res., 5675 LL Rd., Waterloo, 62298. Tel: 618-458-6875; Fax: 618-458-6875[*]51. [CEM]

Todd's Mill, Perry Co., St. Mary Magdalen (1868), Rev. James R. Van Oss.
Res., 5047 Todd's Mill Rd., Pinckneyville, 62274. Tel: 618-336-5414. [CEM]

Trenton, Clinton Co., St. Mary (1858), Rev. James R. Dougherty; Sr. Angela J. Schrage, A.S.C., Pastoral Assoc. & D.R.E.; Deacon John P. Dilley, (Retired).
Res., 215 W. Kentucky St., 62293. Tel: 618-224-9335; Fax: 618-224-9346. [CEM]
Catechesis/Religious Programs—Students 237.

Ullin, Pulaski Co., Our Lady of Fatima (1949), Rev. Msgr. William P. McGhee; Sr. Nancy Flamm, S.S.N.D., Pastoral Assoc.
517 N. Walnut St., Box 67, Mound City, 62963. Tel: 618-748-9113; Fax: 618-748-9639. [CEM]
Catechesis/Religious Programs—Students 1.

Valmeyer, Monroe Co., Seven Dolors of the B.V.M. (1921), Rev. Edwin H. Hustedde.
Res., 101 Meyer Dr., P.O. Box 206, 62295. Tel: 618-939-6618; 935-2247.
Catechesis/Religious Programs—Tel: 618-935-2521. Mrs. Caryl Sondag, D.R.E.
Students 79.

Vienna, Johnson Co., St. Paul (1895), Rev. Jose Ancheril.
Res., 2020 State Rte. 146 E., 62995. Tel: 618-658-4501.
Catechesis/Religious Programs—Tel: 618-658-4701.
Students 31.

Walsh, Randolph Co., St. Pius (1905), Rev. John J. Joyce.
7681 Walsh Rd., P.O. Box 32, 62297. Tel: 618-853-4404.
Catechesis/Religious Programs—Students 21.

Washington Park, St. Clair Co., St. Martin of Tours. Closed. For inquiries for parish records contact the Chancery.

Waterloo, Monroe Co., SS. Peter and Paul (1843), Rev. Msgr. Thomas D. Flach.
Res., 204 W. Mill St., 62298. Tel: 618-939-6426; Fax: 618-939-2011. [CEM]
School—Tel: 618-939-7217; Fax: 618-939-5994. Miss Kristine Hill, Prin.
Lay Teachers 22; Students 413.
Catechesis/Religious Programs—Sr. Mary Essner, S.S.N.D., D.R.E.
Students 215.

Wendelin, Clay Co., Holy Cross (1870), Rev. David L. Braun.
Res., P.O. Star Rte., Newton, 62448. Tel: 618-752-5671. [CEM]
Catechesis/Religious Programs—Students 166.

West Frankfort, Franklin Co., St. John the Baptist (1916), Rev. Brian Barker.
Res., 703 E. Main St., 62896. Tel: 618-932-2828; Fax: 618-932-2828. [CEM]
School—Tel: 618-937-2017; Fax: 618-937-2017. Mr. Joseph Bierbaum, Prin.
Franciscan Sisters of Our Lady of Perpetual Help 2; Lay Teachers 8; Students 85.
Catechesis/Religious Programs—Peggy DeMaretti, D.R.E.
Students 15.

Willisville, Perry Co., St. Joseph (1903), Rev. Leo J. Hayes.
Mailing Address: 606 George St., P.O. Box 157, Ava, 62907. Tel: 618-426-3321; Fax: 618-426-3321. [CEM]
Catechesis/Religious Programs—Tel: 618-497-8115.
Students 18.

Zeigler, Franklin Co., Sacred Heart. Merged with St. Aloysius, Royalton to form St. Aloysius/Sacred Heart, Royalton-Zeigler.

Sacramental Records Located In Chancery Archives:

1—St. John's Orphanage, Belleville, St. Anthony, Coulterville.
2—Holy Angels Church, East St. Louis,
3—Sacred Heart Church, East St. Louis,
4—St. Adalbert Church, East St. Louis,
5—SS. Cyril and Methodius Church, East St. Louis,
6—St. Elizabeth Church, East St. Louis,
7—St. Henry Church, East St. Louis,
8—St. Mary Church, East St. Louis,
9—St. Thomas Church, Millstadt,
10—St. Augustine Church, East St. Louis,
11—St. Joseph Church, Wetaug, St. Anthony, Coulterville. St. Martin of Tours, Washington Park.

Chaplains of Correctional Institutions and State Hospitals

Anna. *Anna State Hospital.* Attended from St. Mary Church, Anna. Rev. Msgr. Thomas W. Miller, Chap., Tel: 618-833-5835.

Centralia. *Centralia Correctional Center* P.O. Box 1266, 62801. Rev. George A. Mauck.

Chester. *Chester Mental Health Center* P.O. Box 31, 62233. Tel: 618-826-4571. 310 N. Main St., Hecker, 62248. Tel: 618-473-2217. Rev. Ralph L. Haas, Chap.

Harrisburg. *Illinois Youth Center.* (Vacant) P.O. Box 300, 62946.

Ina. *Big Muddy River Correctional Center.* (Vacant).

Marion. *Federal Maximum Security Prison* P.O. Box 2000, 62959. Deacon Pat Patterson, Chap., Tel: 618-964-1441.
Veterans Hospital. Attended from St. Joseph, Marion.

Menard. *Menard Correctional Center* P.O. Box 711, 62259. Rev. Leo J. Hayes, Chap., Tel: 618-826-5071.

Vienna. *Dixon Springs Work Camp* 62995. Rev. Msgr. Thomas W. Miller, Contact.
Shawnee Correctional Center Box 400, 62995. Rev. Msgr. Thomas W. Miller, Chap.
Vienna Correctional Center. Attended from Anna. Rev. Msgr. Thomas W. Miller, Chap., Tel: 618-833-5835.

Military Chaplains:
Reverend Fathers—
Voelker, David A., U.S.A.F.

Special Assignment:
Reverend Fathers—
Geller, Charles H., Fort Stockton, TX
Schultz, C. Ray, Las Vegas, NV
Thoonkuzhy, Joseph, Tulsa, OK

Leave of Absence:
Reverend Monsignors—
Schwaegel, Joseph R.
Reverend Fathers—
Chlopecki, Robert J.
Crook, David G.
Harbaugh, Paul E.
Kownacki, Raymond F.
Linnemann, Eugene C.
Peterson, Louis P.
Ruppert, Alan E.
Sebescak, Gary
Unverferth, Steven R.
Witte, Steven D.

Retired:
Most Rev.—
Schlarman, Stanley G., Meredith Home, 16 S. Illinois, Belleville, IL 62220. Tel: 618-277-6814
Reverend Monsignors—
Dobkowski, Paulin J., Hincke Residence for Priests, 2620 Lebanon Ave., Belleville, IL 62221
Driscoll, Maurice F., 228 River Bend Dr., Mobile, AL 36605-3198
Fellner, John V., Breese Nursing Home, 1155 N. 1st St., Breese, IL 62230
Haselhorst, Vincent, Hincke Residence, 2620 Lebanon Ave., Belleville, IL 62221
Kuhl, Urban B., Hincke Residence for Priests, 2620 Lebanon Ave., Belleville, IL 62221
Lombardo, Angelo J., Hincke Residence for Priests, 2620 Lebanon Ave., Belleville, IL 62221
Nebel, Charles A., Hincke Residence for Priests, 2620 Lebanon Ave., Belleville, IL 62221
Stallings, John E., 644 S. Spring St., Apt. A, Cape Girardeau, MO 63703
Reverend Fathers—
Arnold, J. Ralph, Hincke Residence for Priests, 2620 Lebanon Ave., Belleville, IL 62221
Bertsche, Conrad J., 6451 Fairlynn Blvd., Yorba Linda, CA 92686
Dollar, Robert J., 2175 Woods Creek Rd., Robertsville, MO 63072
Frerker, Jack W., 7315 Henderson S.E., Olympia, WA 98501
Haas, Melvin B., 801 E. Palmer Ave., Apt. 223, Glendale, CA 91205
Haas, Ralph L., 9 S. 51st St., Belleville, IL 62223
Hays, Joseph C., Sense Residence, 2620 Lebanon Ave., Belleville, IL 62221
Hentschel, Cletus B., 5315 W. Main St., Belleville, IL 62223
Hsu, Peter, 123 S. Pine, Ziegler, IL 62999
Iffert, Wilbert J., 147 Juniper Dr., Oak Grove Terrace, Mount Vernon, IL 62864
Kastner, Edwin H., 222 S. Third St., Belleville, IL 62220
Kopff, Herbert C., 4419 Taft, St. Louis, MO 63116
Kribs, Charles R., Jefferson Town Homes, 2686 Elkhill Dr., St. Louis, MO 63125
Lenzini, Donald J., Hincke Residence for Priests, 2620 Lebanon Ave., Belleville, IL 62221
Lopardo, Vito R., Hincke Residence for Priests, 2620 Lebanon Ave., Belleville, IL 62221
MacPherson, Walter E., 222 S. Third St., Belleville, IL 62220
Malec, Raymond S., Hincke Residence for Priests, 2620 Lebanon Ave., Belleville, IL 62221
Maughan, Michael, S.M.A., Hincke Residence for Priests, 2620 Lebanon Ave., Belleville, IL 62221
Meskenas, Vincent A., St. Isidore Church, 222 Clark Ave., Yuba City, CA 95991
Miriani, Gerald C., 7158 E. Charro Cir., Tuscan, AZ 85715
Misho, Lloyd P., Sense Residence, 2620 Lebanon Ave., Belleville, IL 62221
O'Shea, Robert J., Sense Residence, 2620 Lebanon Ave., Belleville, IL 62221
Perjak, Edmond J., 210 Pelham Rd., Pier 1, Apt. 108-B, Fort Walton Beach, FL 32547
Ratermann, Jerome B., 303 Hillcrest Dr., Belleville, IL 62286-1203
Reinhardt, Leo S., Hincke Residence for Priests, 2620 Lebanon Ave., Belleville, IL 62221
Stauder, Paul W., Hincke Residence for Priests, 2620 Lebanon Ave., Belleville, IL 62221
Vonnahmen, Robert J., 222 S. Third St., Belleville, IL 62220

Permanent Deacons:
Becker, Robert H.
Bigham, David
Boyer, Douglas
Cerneka, Peter
Coates, John
DeWolf, William
Dietz, Donald
Dilley, John P.
Dougherty, Michael
Downen, J. Richard
DuBois, Omer E.
Duff, James P., (On Sick Leave)
DuPrey, John L.
Hempen, John
Karcher, Ronald

Kirchgraber, Robert B., (Retired)
Kronenberger, Ken, (Retired)
Lanter, Robert
Lintker, Andrew
Lippert, Robert
Litteken, Charles
Munie, George J.
Olson, Richard H.
Patterson, Pat
Rickert, Dennis
Speaks, Charles
Stock, Joseph E.
Stockmann, Gerald E.
Teaff, Joseph
Theis, Francis D., (On Leave of Absence)
Underwood, Thomas
Walsh, Gary D.

INSTITUTIONS LOCATED IN THE DIOCESE

[A] HIGH SCHOOLS, DIOCESAN

BELLEVILLE. *Althoff Catholic High School*, 5401 W. Main St., 62226-4796. Tel: 618-235-1100; Fax: 618-235-9535.
E-mail: althoff@norcom2000.com
Web site: www.althoff.net
Sr. Jan Renz, A.S.C., Prin..Sisters 2; Lay Teachers 50; Students 765.

BREESE. *Mater Dei High School*, 900 N. Mater Dei Dr., 62230. Tel: 618-526-7216; Fax: 618-526-8310.
E-mail: mda@lcls.org
Web site: www.materdei.breese.il.us/mdhs
Central Catholic High School for Clinton Co. Curt L. Winter, Prin.; Sr. Virginia Kampwerth, P.H.J.C., Asst. Prin., Academics; Dennis Litteken, Asst. Prin., Student Affairs; Rev. Charles W. Tuttle. Priests 1; Sisters 3; Lay Teachers 40; Students 594.

WATERLOO. *Gibault Catholic High School*, 501 Columbia Ave., 62298. Tel: 618-939-3883; Fax: 618-939-7215.
E-mail: dbruegg@hTc.neT
Web site: gibaulTonline.com
Mr. Daniel J. Brueggeman, Prin.; Revs. Edwin H. Hustedde, Dir. of Devel.; Roger R. Karban..Priests 2; Sisters 3; Lay Teachers 25; Students 370.

[B] ELEMENTARY SCHOOLS

BREESE. *All Saints Academy*. (Grades PreK-8), 295 N. Clinton St., 62230. Tel: 618-526-4323; Fax: 618-526-2547.
E-mail: Belvalsnts@impresso.com
Consolidated schools of Saint Augustine, Saint Dominic parishes, Breese, IL, and St. Anthony Parish, Beckemeyer, IL. Teri Voss, Prin. Sisters 1; Lay Teachers 24; Students 431.

EAST ST. LOUIS. *Sister Thea Bowman Catholic School*, 8213 Church Ln., 62203. Tel: 618-397-0316; Fax: 618-397-0337.
E-mail: belvsthea@impresso.com
Alice Gardner, Prin.; Cynthia Rivera, Asst. Prin-..Sisters 2; Lay Teachers 13; Students 260.

FAIRVIEW HEIGHTS. *Elizabeth Ann Seton Catholic School*, 9940 Bunkum Rd., 62208. Tel: 618-398-3011; Fax: 618-398-3421.
E-mail: belveseton@impresso.com
Consolidated schools of St. Stephen Parish, Caseyville, IL, and Our Lady of the Assumption Parish, Fairview Heights, IL. Sr. Patricia Gravemann, S.S.N.D., Prin. Sisters 2; Lay Teachers 12; Students 180.

[C] DAY CARE CENTERS

BELLEVILLE. *Don Bosco Home Children's Center*, 300 N. Church St., 62220. Tel: 618-277-7055; Fax: 618-277-7084. Michele Dain, Dir. Administrative Office, 305 N. Charles St., 62220.

St. Henry Day Care Center, 5301 W. Main St., 62223. Tel: 618-233-3454.
E-mail: sthdaycare@peaknet.net
Coordinators: Judy Shovlin; Linda Moyer. Children 107.

St. John Children's Home, 2620 Lebanon Ave., 62221. Rev. Msgr. James E. Margason, V.G., M.Div., J.C.L., Chancery Office, 222 S. Third St., 62220. Tel: 618-277-8181.

St. John Day Care Center, 2620 Lebanon Ave., 62221. Tel: 618-235-6717; Fax: 618-235-6717. Ida Louise Pierce, Dir. Lay Women 11; Children 62.

EAST ST. LOUIS. *Catholic Day Care Center*, 617 Summit Ave., 62201. Tel: 618-874-7178. Nursery and Kindergarten. Conducted by the Cordi-Marian Sisters. Sr. Gema Juarez, M.C.M., Dir.; Sr. Henrietta Torres, M.C.M., Supr., 2417 Ridge Ave., 62205. Tel: 618-875-1447. Brothers 2; Sisters 3; Lay Teachers 13; Children 90.

[D] GENERAL HOSPITALS

BELLEVILLE. *St. Elizabeth Hospital*, 211 S. Third St., 62220-1998. Tel: 618-234-2120; Fax: 618-222-4650.
Web site: www.steliz.org
For a complete listing, refer to the Hospitals section.

BREESE. *St. Joseph Hospital*, 9515 Holy Cross Ln., 62230. Tel: 618-526-4511; Fax: 618-526-8022.
Web site: www.stjoebreese.com
For a complete listing, refer to the Hospitals section.

CENTRALIA. *St. Mary's Hospital*, 400 N. Pleasant Ave., 62801. Tel: 618-532-6731
For a complete listing, refer to the Hospitals section.

EAST ST. LOUIS. *St. Mary's Hospital*, 129 N. 8th St., 62201. Tel: 618-274-1900; Fax: 618-482-7015.
E-mail: ascott@ancilla.org
Web site: www.ancilla.org/stmaryesl.htm
For a complete listing, refer to the Hospitals section.

HARRISBURG. *Harrisburg Medical Center*, 100 Hospital Dr., P.O. Box 428, 62946. Tel: 618-253-7671; Fax: 618-252-7274.
E-mail: cchatt@intrnet.net
Web site: www.harrisburgmedicalcenter.com
For a complete listing, refer to the Hospitals section.

MOUNT VERNON. *Good Samaritan Regional Health Center*, 605 N. 12th St., 62864. Tel: 618-242-4600
For a complete listing, refer to the Hospitals section.

MURPHYSBORO. *St. Joseph Memorial Hospital*, 2 S. Hospital Dr., 62966. Tel: 618-684-3156; Fax: 618-684-6243.
Web site: www.sih.net
For a complete listing, refer to the Hospitals section.

RED BUD. *St. Clement Health Services*, One St. Clement Blvd., 62278. Tel: 618-282-3831; Fax: 618-282-6101
For a complete listing, refer to the Hospitals section.

[E] HOMES FOR SENIOR CITIZENS

BELLEVILLE. *Charles and Bertha Hincke Residence for Priests and Sense Residence*, 2620 Lebanon Ave., 62221. Tel: 618-234-5722; Fax: 618-234-5792
For a complete listing, refer to the Special Care Facilities section.

Meredith Memorial Home, 16 S. Illinois St., 62220. Tel: 618-233-8780; Fax: 618-233-9602
For a complete listing, refer to the Special Care Facilities section.

Our Lady of the Snows Apartment Community Retirement Home, 726 Community Dr., 62223. Tel: 618-397-6700; Fax: 618-394-9051
For a complete listing, refer to the Special Care Facilities section.

RED BUD. *Maria Care*, 350 W. South First St., 62278. Tel: 618-282-3891; Fax: 618-282-4070
For a complete listing, refer to the Special Care Facilities section.

[F] MONASTERIES AND RESIDENCES OF PRIESTS AND BROTHERS

BELLEVILLE. *Missionary Oblates of Mary Immaculate - St. Henry's Oblate Residence*, 200 N. 60th St., 62223. Tel: 618-233-2991. Revs. Michael S. Deis, O.M.I.; Andrew G. Chalkey, O.M.I.; James Donovan, O.M.I.; Rene DuFour, O.M.I.; John Ettensohn, O.M.I.; Vincent Fitzgerald, O.M.I.; Urban Figge, Supr. Oblate Community; Elmar Mauer, O.M.I; Robert Morin, O.M.I.; James E. Taylor, O.M.I.; Boniface Wittenbrink, O.M.I.; James J. Wynne, O.M.I.; Charles Zachman, O.M.I.; Bros. David Schell, O.M.I.; Andrew Lawlor, O.M.I.; William Lundberg, O.M.I.; Francis Sullivan, O.M.I. Priests 13; Brothers 4.

Shrine of Our Lady of the Snows, 442 S. DeMazenod Dr., 62223. Tel: 618-397-6700; Fax: 618-398-6549.
E-mail: mami@oblateusa.org
Web site: www.snows.org
Missionary Oblates of Mary Immaculate. Revs. Allen Maes, O.M.I., Area Supr.; Louis B. Studer, O.M.I., Dir.; Floyd B. Boeckman, O.M.I.; Gregory Gallagher, O.M.I., Voc. Dir., Supr.; Gabriel Biondolillo, O.M.I.; Zygmunt Dzierzek, O.M.I.; Joseph Pitts, O.M.I.; Robert Braun, O.M.I.; Anthony Wroblewski, O.M.I.; Leonard Baldus, O.M.I.; Eugene Glaub, O.M.I.; Leo Miller, O.M.I.; Robert Olson, O.M.I.; Raul Salas, O.M.I.; Bro. Lorenzo Williams.

[G] CONVENTS AND RESIDENCES FOR SISTERS

BELLEVILLE. *Hospital Sisters of St. Francis*, 1036 Rutledge Dr., 62221. Tel: 618-235-5486; Fax: 618-235-5486. Sisters 4.

Hospital Sisters of St. Francis, 1000 Royal Heights Rd., Apt. 58, 62226. Tel: 618-233-1687; Fax: 618-233-1687.
E-mail: SISTER T@peaknet.net
Sisters 2.

Motherhouse and Novitiate of Ursuline Sisters of Belleville, 1026 N. Douglas Ave., 62220-4198. Tel: 618-235-3444; Fax: 618-235-3444.
E-mail: OSUBELL@Juno.com
Sr. Dorothy Helbling, O.S.U., Community Leader. Total Membership of Congregation 15.

Poor Clare Monastery of Our Lady of Mercy, 300 N. 60th St., 62223. Tel: 618-235-4407; Fax: 618-235-4426.
Web site: www.poorclare.org/belleville
Mother Mary Therese, P.C.C., Abbess; Rev. Robert D. Gore, Chap. Tel: 618-233-2423..Sisters 8.

CAIRO. *Mary Katherine Convent, Poor Handmaids of Jesus Christ*, 725 22nd St., 62914. Tel: 618-734-0778; Fax: 618-734-0778.
E-mail: mkccairo@onemain.com
Sisters 3.

EAST ST. LOUIS. *St. Mary Convent, Poor Handmaids of Jesus Christ*, 5727 Warren St., 62204. Tel: 618-875-7570.
E-mail: estlouis@Juno.com
Sisters 3.

MOUNT VERNON. *Franciscan Sisters of Mary Convent*, 4235 Lincolnshire Dr., #3-C, 62864-2164. Tel: 618-244-3091. Sisters 2.

RUMA. *Province Center, Adorers of the Blood of Christ, United States Province*, 2 Pioneer Ln., 62278. Tel: 618-282-3848; Fax: 618-282-3266.
E-mail: rumacent@htc.net
Web site: Adorers.org
Sr. Barbara Jean Franklin, A.S.C., Provincial; Sr. Celine Birk, A.S.C., Local Admin. Chaplains: Revs. Richard J. Weidert; Joseph Nassal, C.P.P.S. Sisters 81; Total Membership of the Province 488.

[H] RETREAT HOUSES

BELLEVILLE. *King's House Retreat and Renewal Center*, 700 N. 66th St., 62223-3949. Tel: 618-397-0584; Fax: 618-397-5123.
E-mail: Knghsebv@peaknet.net
Rev. Robert Aaron, O.M.I.; Bro. William Johnson, O.M.I., Team Mod.; Rev. David Kraus, O.M.I.; Bros. Victor Capek, O.M.I.; Edward Driggins, O.M.I.

[I] NEWMAN CENTERS

CARBONDALE. *The Newman Center*, Southern Illinois University, 715 S. Washington, 62901. Tel: 618-529-3311; Fax: 618-549-9401.
E-mail: jscarano@siu.edu
Web site: http://www.siu.edu/~newman
Mr. John Scarano, Diocesan Dir.; Rev. C. Gregory Jones, C.S.V., Chap.; Ms. Mary Mertzlufft, Campus Min.

[J] MISCELLANEOUS LISTINGS

BELLEVILLE. *Althoff Catholic High School Educational Endowment Trust*, 5401 W. Main St., 62226-4796. Tel: 618-235-1100; Fax: 618-235-9535.
E-mail: Belvalthoff@impresso.com
Web site: www.althoff.net
Sr. Jan Renz, A.S.C., Contact Person.

Ancient Order of Hibernians. 1303 Edgewood Dr., Fairview Heights, 62208. Tel: 618-397-6494. Charles Herr, Pres.

Ancient Order of Hibernians (LAOH). P.O. Box 23193, 62223. Tel: 618-398-1948. Stephanie Feist, Pres.

Catholic Committee on Scouting of the Diocese of Belleville. 19824 Posen Rd., Nashville, 62263. Tel: 618-336-5414. Rev. James R. Van Oss, Chap.

Catholic Community Foundation for the Diocese of Belleville, 222 South 3rd St., 62220-1985. Tel: 618-277-8181.
E-mail: MLeifeld@diobelle.org
Martin Leifeld, Executive Dir.

Catholic Daughters of the Americas. 805 S. Jesse, Christopher, 62822. Tel: 618-724-4364. Mrs. Frances Furlin, Diocesan Chm.

The Catholic Diocese of Belleville Custodial Fund, 222 S. Third St., 62220. Tel: 618-277-8181; Fax: 618-277-0819. Most Rev. Wilton D. Gregory, Pres.; Rev. Msgr. James E. Margason, V.G., M.Div., J.C.L., Sec.; William Knapp, C.P.A., CFO.

The Catholic Diocese of Belleville Deposit and Loan Fund, 222 S. Third St., 62220. Tel: 618-277-8181; Fax: 618-277-0819. Most Rev. Wilton D. Gregory, Pres.; Rev. Msgr. James E. Margason, V.G., M.Div., J.C.L., Sec.; William Knapp, C.P.A., CFO.

The Catholic Diocese of Belleville Group Health Insurance Fund, 222 S. Third St., 62220. Tel: 618-277-8181; Fax: 618-277-0819. Most Rev. Wilton D. Gregory, Pres.; Rev. Msgr. James E. Margason, V.G., M.Div., J.C.L., Sec.; William Knapp, C.P.A., CFO.

The Catholic Diocese of Belleville Ministry Formation Fund, 222 S. Third St., 62220. Tel: 618-277-8181; Fax: 618-277-0819. Most Rev. Wilton D. Gregory, Pres.; Rev. Msgr. James E. Margason, V.G., M.Div., J.C.L., Sec.; William Knapp, C.P.A., CFO.

The Catholic Diocese of Belleville Property Insurance Fund, 222 S. Third St., 62220. Tel: 618-277-8181; Fax: 618-277-0819. Most Rev. Wilton D. Gregory, Pres.; Rev. Msgr. James E. Margason, V.G., M.Div., J.C.L., Sec.; William Knapp, C.P.A., CFO.

Catholic Fraternal Life, P.O. Box 327, 62222. Tel: 618-233-0286; Fax: 618-277-8257.
E-mail: JohnL@cfllife.com
Web site: www.cfllife.com

Catholic Social Service, 8601 W. Main St., Suite 201, 62223. Tel: 618-394-5900; Fax: 619-394-5909.
Web site: www.cssil.org

Catholic War Veterans, Hincke Residence for Priests, 2620 Lebanon Ave., 62221. Tel: 618-257-1584. Rev. Msgr. Urban B. Kuhl, Chap.

Cursillos in Christianity. Belleville Diocese, 703 S. Jackson, 62220. Tel: 618-234-0456; Fax: 618-234-3168.
E-mail: jbassett@icss.net
John R. Bassett, Lay Dir.

Engaged Encounter, 221 S. 17th St., 62226. Tel: 618-277-1652. Gerry Bach, Coord.; Ann Bach, Co-ord.

Health Care Endowment Fund of the Reverend Oblate Fathers, 726 Community Dr., 62223. Tel: 618-397-6700; Fax: 618-394-9051.
Oblate Fathers and Trustees. D. Robert McCardle, Admin. & Contact Person. Legal Title: *Health Care Endowment Fund of the Reverend Oblate Fathers at the Shrine of Our Lady of the Snows.*

Missionary Association of Mary Immaculate-Missionary Oblates of Mary Immaculate. Serving the missions of the Missionary Oblates, the National Shrine of Our Lady of the Snows, and the Tekakwitha Indian Missions. 9480 N. De Mazenod Dr., 62223-1160. Tel: 618-398-4848; Fax: 618-398-8788.
E-mail: mami@oblatesusa.org
Web site: www.oblatesusa.org
Rev. Louis B. Studer, O.M.I., Oblate Dir.; Mr. William J. Nixon, Exec. Dir.; Mr. William P. O'Connor, Planned Giving Dir. Planned Giving Associates: Revs. Floyd B. Boeckman, O.M.I.; James E. Taylor, O.M.I.; Mrs. Rosalee Cavataio; Mr. C. Duke Hynek.

Oblate Preaching Team, 200 N. 60th St., 62223. Tel: 618-233-2991; Fax: 618-233-9855. Specializing in Parish Missions. Revs. William Mason, O.M.I.; Robert Morin, O.M.I.

Radio Information Service for Blind and Print Handicapped, 9541 Church Circle Dr., 62223. Tel: 618-394-6221; Fax: 618-394-6438.
E-mail: Radioinfo@server.stl.unitedway.org
Closed Circuit Radio for the blind and print handicapped. Mr. Joseph E. Kasperek, Exec. Dir.

St. Francis Thrift Shop, 800 E. Main St., 62220. Tel: 618-233-6998. Mrs. Catherine Heap, Mgr.

Serra Club of St. Clair County, P.O. Box 23017, Dutch Hollow Sta., 62223. Tel: 618-234-2773. Chaplains: Rev. Msgr. Leonard A. Bauer, 16 S. Illinois St., 62220. Rev. Msgr. Bernard L. Voss, 5315 W. Main St., 62223. Tel: 618-233-2423.

TEC (Teens Encounter Christ), 2620 Lebanon Ave., 62221.
E-mail: Blulym@norcom2000.com
Web site: www.bellevilletec.com
Kyle Holtgrave, Chairperson.

Victorious Missionaries, 442 S. DeMazenod Dr., 62223-1097. Tel: 618-394-6281 (Voice/TDD); Fax: 618-397-1210.
Web site: www.vmusa.org
Spiritual Support Network for people with disabilities, chronic illness, and those who want to share the journey. Bro. Francis Sullivan, O.M.I., Natl. Dir.

Western Catholic Union, Br. No. 59, 405 Southgate, 62223. Tel: 618-277-2892. Mrs. Marion Mueth, Pres.

World Apostolate of Fatima, The Blue Army, U.S.A., c/o 222 South 3rd St., 6220-1985. Rev. John T. Myler, D.Min., Spiritual Advisor. Tel: 618-233-2391.

BREESE. *Daughters of Isabella.* Precious Blood Circle #718, 248 W. Elm, Aviston, 62216. Tel: 618-526-7590. Jeanette Benhoff, Diocesan Chairperson.

CARBONDALE. *Worldwide Marriage Encounter*, 105 Archelle Dr., 62901. Tel: 618-549-9450.
E-mail: seaborn@accessus.net
Executive Couple: Scott & Karen Seaborn.

CARLYLE. *Carlyle Priest Center.* Contact the Chancery, Tel: 618-277-8181. 17440 Highline Rd., 62231.

EAST ST. LOUIS. *St. Mary Hospital of East St. Louis, Illinois Volunteers*, 129 N. 8th St., 62201. Tel: 618-274-1900; Fax: 618-482-7015.
E-mail: ascott@ancill.org
Web site: www.ancilla.org/stmaryesl.htm
Richard Mark, Pres. & CEO.

St. Mary's Hospital Health Foundation, 129 N. 8th St., 62201. Tel: 618-482-7093; Fax: 618-482-7014.
E-mail: mgerth@ancilla.org
Web site: www.ancilla.org/stmaryesl.htm

MILSTADT. *Secular Franciscan Order*, 7 Concord Dr., 62260-1701. Tel: 618-234-1166; Fax: 618-234-2957.
E-mail: Fransfo@aol.com
Rev. Bradley Dunn, S.F.O., Min. St. Peter Fraternity.

O'FALLON. *ASC Health Services*, 6 Eagle Center, Ste. 4, 62269. Tel: 618-632-1284; Fax: 618-632-8063.
E-mail: mldegenhart@compu-type.net
Sr. Mary Louise Degenhart, A.S.C., Exec. Dir.

Couple to Couple League, 338 Amy Dr. Tel: 618-628-7759; Fax: 618-624-0902. Mike & Denise Terneus, Teaching Couple.

SCOTT AFB. *Scott Air Force Base*, Scott AFB Chapel, 375 AW/HC, 320 J St., Bldg. 1620, 62225-5256. Tel: 618-256-3303; Fax: 618-256-2319. Revs. Carlo Montecaldo, Ch. Col., Command Chap.; James P. Thomas, Ch. Lt. Col., Senoir Catholic Chap.

INCORPORATED CEMETERIES

BELLEVILLE. *Green Mount Catholic Cemetery of the Cathedral Congregation of Belleville.*

BREESE. *St. Dominic Roman Catholic Cemetery of Breese.*

EAST ST. LOUIS. *Holy Cross Cemetery of St. Henry Roman Catholic Church of East St. Louis.*

Mount Carmel Cemetery of St. Patrick Roman Catholic Church.

FAIRVIEW HEIGHTS. *St. Adalbert Association (An Illinois Religious Corporation).*

O'FALLON. *Mount Calvary Cemetery of St. Clare Roman Catholic Congregation.*

VILLA RIDGE. *Calvary Cemetery of St. Patrick Roman Catholic Church of Cairo.*

NECROLOGY

† Arentsen, Edwin F., (Retired). —Died Jan. 3, 2000.

† Dunn, Rev. Msgr. Meinrad M., (Retired). —Died May 15, 2000.

Diocese of Biloxi

(Dioecesis Biloxiiensis)

Most Reverend

JOSEPH LAWSON HOWZE, D.D.

Bishop of Biloxi; ordained May 7, 1959; appointed Titular Bishop of Maxita and Auxiliary of Natchez-Jackson November 8, 1972; ordained Bishop January 28, 1973; appointed Bishop of Biloxi March 1, 1977; installed June 6, 1977. *Mailing Address: P.O. Box 1189, Biloxi, MS, 39533.*

Chancery Office: 120 Reynoir St., P.O. Box 1189, Biloxi, MS, 39533. Tel.: 601-374-0222; Fax: 601-435-7949.

Legal Title: "Catholic Diocese of Biloxi".

ESTABLISHED MARCH 1, 1977.

Square Miles 9,653.

Comprises 17 counties in southern Mississippi: Jackson, Harrison, Hancock, George, Stone, Pearl River, Greene, Perry, Forrest, Lamar, Marion, Walthall, Wayne, Jones, Covington, Jefferson Davis and Lawrence.

For legal titles of parishes and diocesan institutions, consult the Chancery Office.

STATISTICAL OVERVIEW

Personnel	
Bishop	1
Retired Bishops	1
Priests: Diocesan Active in Diocese	42
Priests: Active Outside Diocese	1
Priests: Diocesan in Foreign Missions	1
Priests: Retired, Sick or Absent	14
Number of Diocesan Priests	58
Religious Priests in Diocese	24
Extern Priests in Diocese	14
Ordinations:	
Diocesan Priests	2
Permanent Deacons in Diocese	19
Total Brothers	32
Total Sisters	59
Parishes	
Parishes	44
With Resident Pastor:	
Resident Diocesan Priests	35
Resident Religious Priests	7
Without Resident Pastor:	
Administered by Priests	2
Missions	15
Professional Ministry Personnel:	
Brothers	1
Sisters	10
Lay Ministers	7
Welfare	
Homes for the Aged	7
Total Assisted	7,656
Special Centers for Social Services	4
Total Assisted	62,325
Other Institutions	4
Total Assisted	11,302
Educational	
Diocesan Students in Other Seminaries	7
Total Seminarians	7
High Schools, Diocesan and Parish	4
Total Students	1,185
High Schools, Private	1
Total Students	571
Elementary Schools, Diocesan and Parish	14
Total Students	3,331
Catechesis/Religious Education:	
High School Students	2,238
Elementary Students	3,384
Total Students Under Catholic Instruction	10,716
Teachers in the Diocese:	
Brothers	11
Sisters	20
Lay Teachers	444
Vital Statistics	
Receptions into the Church:	
Infant Baptism Totals	821
Adult Baptism Totals	406
Received into Full Communion	236
First Communions	1,246
Confirmations	619
Marriages:	
Catholic	206
Interfaith	203
Total Marriages	409
Deaths	789
Total Catholic Population	68,043
Total Population	748,433

Office of the Bishop—1790 Popps Ferry Rd., P.O. Box 6489, Biloxi, 39532-6489. Tel: 228-702-2111.

Vicar General—Rev. Msgr. ANDREW MURRAY, J.C.L., *1790 Popps Ferry Rd., P.O. Box 6489, Biloxi, 39532-6489.* Tel: 228-702-2112.

Chancery Office—1790 Popps Ferry Rd., P.O. Box 6489, Biloxi, 39532-6489. Tel: 228-702-2100; Fax: 228-702-2125. Office Hours: Mon.-Fri. 8:30-5 All Offices are at this address unless otherwise noted.

Chancellor—Rev. Msgr. ANDREW MURRAY, J.C.L. Tel: 228-374-2112.

Vice Chancellor—Rev. JOHN R. MCGRATH, J.C.L. Tel: 228-702-2116.

Office for Planning and Development—Deacon ROBERTO JIMENEZ, Dir. Tel: 228-702-2113.

Marriage Tribunal—

Judicial Vicar—Rev. JOHN R. MCGRATH, J.C.L. Tel: 228-702-2116.

Director of the Tribunal—Mr. RICK S. CONASON, J.C.L.

Promoter of Justice—Rev. Msgr. JAMES J. HANNON, J.C.D.

Defenders of the Bond—Rev. Msgr. RONALD P. HERZOG; Rev. Msgr. JAMES P. MCGOUGH, J.C.D.; Rev. Msgr. ANDREW MURRAY, J.C.L.; Rev. THOMAS CONWAY.

Pro-Synodal Judges—Rev. Msgr. JAMES J. HANNON, J.C.D.; Rev. Msgr. JAMES P. MCGOUGH, J.C.D.; Rev. JAMES B. TAYLOR.

Advocates—Revs. LOUIS LOHAN; PATRICK MOCKLER; Deacons MARTIN FINNEGAN; LUCIEN MORAGAS; AL STOCKERT.

Canonical Ecclesiastical Notary—Mrs. CLAIRE D. JONES.

Deans—Rev. JOHN NOONE, West Coast Deanery; Rev. Msgr. JAMES P. MCGOUGH, J.C.D., Central Coast Deanery; Rev. PATRICK MCDERMOTT, East Central Coast Deanery; Rev. GERARD M. CLEARY, East Coast Deanery; Rev. THOMAS CONWAY, Northern Deanery.

Diocesan Attorney—KEVIN J. NECAISE, *P.O. Box 636, Gulfport, 39502.* Tel: 228-586-0933.

Department of Administration and Finance Comptroller—TAMMY W. DILORENZO, C.P.A.; MARJORIE GILL, Chief Accountant. Tel: 228-702-2100.

Diocesan Risk Management for Property and Medical—Mr. A. J. SCARDINO, Contact Person. Tel: 228-702-2119; 452-3014.

Catholic Foundation of the Diocese of Biloxi, Inc.—Deacon ROBERTO JIMENEZ, Exec. Dir. Tel: 228-702-2123.

Mission Office—Rev. Msgr. ANDREW MURRAY. Tel: 228-702-2112.

Department of Communications—

"Gulf Pine Catholic Newspaper"—SHIRLEY HENDERSON, Editor. Tel: 228-702-2126; 2127.

Radio & Television—SHIRLEY HENDERSON. Tel: 228-702-2126; 2127.

Department of Education—

Office of Superintendent of Catholic Schools—Dr. LANNY ACOSTA. Tel: 228-702-2130; 2129., *Res., 12446 Windance Dr., Gulfport, 39503.* Tel: 228-831-1928.

Office of Resource Center—Dr. LANNY ACOSTA, Dir.; Mrs. ELIZABETH ECKERT, Coord. Tel: 228-702-2134.

Office of Special Education—Dr. LANNY ACOSTA.

Office of Religious Education—Sr. JANE WALKER, O.P., Dir., *Res., 164 E. Beach Blvd., Apt. 201, Gulfport, 39507.* Tel: 228-863-6263.

Office of Youth Ministry—BRAGG MOORE, Dir. Tel: 228-702-2142.

Catholic Boy Scouts—ERNEST J. FALGO, JR., *3511 Magnolia St., Pascagoula, 39567.* Tel: 228-762-8174.

Campus Ministry—Rev. THOMAS CONWAY, Dir., *3117 W. Fourth St., Hattiesburg, 39401.* Tel: 601-264-5192.

Priests' Continuing Education and Retreat Programs—Rev. CUTHBERT O'CONNELL, *P.O. Box 10, Bassfield, 39421-0010.* Tel: 601-943-5104.

Ecumenical & Interreligious Affairs—Sr. JANE WALKER, O.P., Contact Person. Tel: 228-702-2131.

Liturgy, Office of—Rev. Msgr. RONALD P. HERZOG, Dir., *Immaculate Conception Church, 833 West Sixth, Laurel, 39440-3436.* Tel: 601-426-3473.

Department of Social and Community Services—1790 Popps Ferry Rd., P.O. Box 6489, Biloxi, 39532-6489. Tel: 228-702-2137. All offices at this address unless otherwise noted. Legal Title: Catholic Social and Community Services, Inc. Sr. REBECCA RUTKOWSKI, A.C.S.W., Exec. Dir.

Hattiesburg Regional Office—2410 O'Ferral St., Hattiesburg, 39401. Tel: 601-545-1616. VICKI TAYLOR, L.M.S.W., Dir. POLLY SUMRALL, Office Mgr.

Pascagoula Regional Office—3512 Magnolia St., Pascagoula, 39567-3113. Tel: 228-769-8283; 769-8151. GAYLE OAKES, Dir.

Council of the St. Vincent de Paul Society—Dr. PETER PAVLOV, Pres. Tel: 228-875-5230.

Counseling Services—DENNIS CENAC, L.S.W.

Adoption Services—JENNIFER WILLIAMS, L.S.W., *1790 Popps Ferry Rd., P.O. Box 6489, Biloxi, 39532-6489.* Tel: 228-702-2137.

Emergency Assistance—DELANE KRAUSE; DIANNE PURSER, *P.O. Box 1457, Biloxi, 39533-1457.* Tel: 228-432-0045. JANNIE GREENE FUNCHESS, *2410 O'Ferral St., Hattiesburg, 39401.* Tel: 601-545-1616.

Morning Star Pregnancy Care Center—(Unplanned pregnancy services); NANCY LOFTUS, Maternity Caseworker; ANN RIVERA, Office Mgr., *2204 24th Ave., Gulfport, 39503.* Tel: 228-864-4221.

Respect Life Office—BETH RILEY, Dir. Tel: 228-702-2137.

12 Baskets Food Bank—SHIRLEY HEGGINS, Dir. Tel: 228-374-6884.

Refugee Resettlement—Mrs. MAGDA LELEAUX, Dir., *P.O. Box 1457, Biloxi, 39533-1457.* Tel: 228-374-6507.

Family Life Office—Tel: 228-702-2137.

Catholic Charities Housing Association of Biloxi, Inc.

Santa Maria Retirement Apartments; Villa Maria Retirement Apartments—Most Rev. JOSEPH L. HOWZE, D.D., Pres. Tel: 228-702-2100. Sr. REBECCA RUTKOWSKI, A.C.S.W., Contact Person. Tel: 228-702-2137.

Samaritan Housing, Inc.—Most Rev. JOSEPH L. HOWZE, D.D., Pres. Tel: 228-702-2100. Sr. REBECCA RUTKOWSKI, A.C.S.W., Contact Person. Tel: 228-702-2137.

Notre Dame de la Mer, Inc.—Most Rev. JOSEPH L. HOWZE, D.D., Pres. Tel: 228-702-2100. Sr. REBECCA RUTKOWSKI, A.C.S.W. Tel: 228-702-2137.

Gabriel Manor, Inc.—Most Rev. JOSEPH L. HOWZE, D.D., Pres. Tel: 228-702-2100. Sr. REBECCA RUTKOWSKI, A.C.S.W. Tel: 228-702-2137.

Caritas Manor, Inc.—Most Rev. JOSEPH L. HOWZE, D.D., Pres. Tel: 228-702-2100. Sr. REBECCA RUTKOWSKI, A.C.S.W. Tel: 228-702-2137.

Carlow Manor—Most Rev. JOSEPH L. HOWZE, D.D., Pres. Tel: 228-702-2100. Sr. REBECCA RUTKOWSKI, A.C.S.W. Tel: 228-702-2137.

Gabriel Manor II, Inc.—Most Rev. JOSEPH L. HOWZE, D.D., Pres. Tel: 228-702-2100. Sr. REBECCA RUTKOWSKI, A.C.S.W. Tel: 228-702-2137.

Apostleship of the Sea—Deacon CHARLES L. WALKER; HAROLD SEAMEN, JR.

Vietnamese Apostolate—Rev. DOMINIC PHAN, *St. Michael Church, P.O. Box 523, Biloxi, 39533.* Tel: 228-435-5578.

Prison Apostolate—Deacon VICTOR BAGLIONI, Dir. Tel: 228-475-5437. Jackson County Jails: Deacon THOMAS MILLER,Harrison County Jails: Tel: 228-388-5467. South Mississippi Correctional Facility: Rev. CHARLES C. VENUS, JR.

Diocesan Boards and Committees—

Association of Priests (Diocese of Biloxi and Jackson)—Most Rev. JOSEPH L. HOWZE, D.D., Bishop of Biloxi & Co-Chm.; Most Rev. WILLIAM R. HOUCK, Bishop of Jackson & Co-Chm.; Rev. PATRICK FARRELL, Pres.; Rev. THOMAS CONWAY, Sec. & Treas. Trustees: Rev. Msgr. ANDREW MURRAY; Revs. KENNETH RAMON-LANDRY; ELVIN SUNDS; JEFFREY WALDREP.

Building and Real Estate Committee—LEONARD COLLINS; EDWARD CRAIG; WILLIAM H. CRAIG; H. F. FOUNTAIN, JR.; GERALD HOPKINS; GERALD PORCHE; MARK SEYMOUR; BOB SLAUGHTER.

Catholic Foundation-Diocese of Biloxi—Most Rev. JOSEPH L. HOWZE, D.D., Pres.; Rev. Msgr. ANDREW MURRAY, Vice Pres.; Deacon ROBERTO JIMENEZ, Exec. Dir.; Dr. HARRY SCHMIDT, JR., Chm. CHARLES HEWES; JOSEPH HUDSON; TED LONGO; DAVID LORD; ALFRED PARKER; MICHAEL PELA; ROBERT TUCEI.

Catholic Housing Board—Most Rev. JOSEPH L. HOWZE, D.D., Pres.; Sr. REBECCA RUTKOWSKI, A.C.S.W., Chm.; Rev. Msgr. ANDREW MURRAY; Rev. BERNARD FARRELL; TAMMY W. DILORENZO; SALVADOR DOMINO; GEORGE WATSON; GERALD HOPKINS.

Diocesan Counsultors—Rev. JOHN NOONE; Rev. Msgr. JAMES P. MCGOUGH, J.C.D.; Rev. Msgr. ANDREW MURRAY; Rev. PATRICK MCDERMOTT; Revs. THOMAS CONWAY; GERARD M. CLEARY.

Finance Council—Most Rev. JOSEPH L. HOWZE, D.D.; WILLIAM PENEGUY, Chm.; Rev. Msgr. FRANCIS FARRELL; Rev. Msgr. ANDREW MURRAY; RICHARD ECKERT; RAYMOND HUDACHEK; JOSEPH P. HUDSON; DAVID L. LORD; STEVE MONTAGNET; JOHN P. MYERS; A. J.M. OUSTALET, JR.; DAVID A. TRUETEL.

Insurance Committee—Most Rev. JOSEPH L. HOWZE, D.D.; Dr. LANNY ACOSTA; Mrs. HARRIET BELLONE; Rev. Msgr. RONALD P. HERZOG; Sr. REBECCA RUTKOWSKI, A.C.S.W.; STEVE MONTAGNET; Mr. PAT SANQUINETTI; Rev. Msgr. ANDREW MURRAY. Advisors: TAMMY W. DILORENZO; A. J. SCARDINO, JR.

Mission Board—Most Rev. JOSEPH L. HOWZE, D.D.; Rev. Msgr. ANDREW MURRAY.

Personnel Board—Rev. Msgr. FRANCIS FARRELL; Rev. Msgr. JOSEPH MERCIER; Rev. Msgr. ANDREW MURRAY; Rev. Msgr. JAMES M. RUSSELL; Rev. KENNETH RAMON-LANDRY.

Presbyteral Council—Most Rev. JOSEPH L. HOWZE, D.D., Pres.; Revs. GERARD M. CLEARY; PATRICK MCDERMOTT; Rev. Msgr. JAMES P. MCGOUGH, J.C.D.; Rev. THOMAS CONWAY; Rev. Msgr. ANDREW MURRAY; Revs. JOHN NOONE; ANTHONY ARGUELLES; DENNIS CARVER; BERNARD FARRELL; PATRICK HAYES; WILLIAM KELLEY, S.V.D.; LOUIS LOHAN; PATRICK MOCKLER; CUTHBERT O'CONNELL; MICHAEL SNYDER.

Vocations Committee—Most Rev. JOSEPH L. HOWZE, D.D.; Rev. Msgr. JOSEPH MERCIER; Revs. I. ANTHONY ARGUELLES; LOUIS LOHAN; GREGORY M. BARRAS.

Miscellaneous Apostolates—

Campaign for Human Development—Rev. IVAN J. WEIS, Dir., *27074 St. Matthew Church Rd., Perkinson, 39573.*

Catholic Relief Services—Sr. REBECCA RUTKOWSKI, A.C.S.W., *P.O. Box 6489, Biloxi, 39532-6489.*

Catholic University, Friends of—Rev. Msgr. ANDREW MURRAY, *P.O. Box 6489, Biloxi, 39532-6489.*

Charismatic Renewal—Rev. GEORGE KITCHIN, Dir., *4900 Riley Rd., Ocean Springs, 39564.*

Cursillo and Retreats—Rev. ANTHONY DOAN TRAN, *14595 Vidalia Rd., Pass Christian, 39571.* Tel: 228-255-7560.

Deaf and Disabled, Office of the—RODNEY W. WOODS, Ph.D., Dir., *de l'Epee Deaf Center, Inc., 1450 North St., Gulfport, 39507., Mailing Address: P.O. Box 6918, Gulfport, 39506-6918.* Tel: 228-897-2280 (Voice-TDD); Fax: 228-897-2462.

Latin American Apostolate—Mission-Saltillo, Mexico, co-sponsored with Diocese of Jackson. Rev. Msgr. MICHAEL THORNTON, *Parroquia San Miguel Arcangel, Apdo. 52 Sucursal "A", 25000 Saltillo, Coah, Mexico.*

Legion of Mary—Deacon VICTOR A. BAGLIONI, *3855 Riverpine Dr., Moss Point, 39563.*

Permanent Diaconate Program—Deacon MARTIN FINNEGAN, Dir., *5713 Belle Fontaine Dr., Ocean Springs, 39564.* Assoc. Directors: Deacons VICTOR BAGLIONI, (Formation); THOMAS LEBLANC, (Continuing Education & Formation).

Pontifical Association of the Holy Childhood—Rev. Msgr. ANDREW MURRAY, Dir., *P.O. Box 6489, Biloxi, 39532-6489.*

Propagation of the Faith—Rev. Msgr. ANDREW MURRAY, Dir., *P.O. Box 6489, Biloxi, 39532-6489.* Tel: 228-374-0222.

Vocations—Rev. DENNIS CARVER, Dir., *P.O. Box 548, Pass Christian, 39571.* Tel: 228-452-4586.

CLERGY, PARISHES, MISSIONS AND PAROCHIAL SCHOOLS

CITY OF BILOXI
(Harrison County)

1—CATHEDRAL OF THE NATIVITY OF THE BLESSED VIRGIN MARY (1843), Revs. I. Anthony Arguelles, Rector; Greg Barras; Deacons Rene J. Moniot; Ray DeRosier; Sr. Mary Riordan, R.S.M., Pastoral Assoc. & D.R.E.
Res., 870 Howard Ave., P.O. Box 367, 39533. Tel: 228-374-1717; Fax: 228-374-1773.
School—(Grades K-6). Tel: 228-432-2269; Fax: 228-432-9421. Sr. Mary Jo Mike, O.S.F., Prin.
Nativity 1; Lay Teachers 20; Students 280.
Catechesis/Religious Programs—Students 215.

2—CHURCH OF THE VIETNAMESE MARTYRS, MS, Rev. Dominic Phan.
Res., 163 Oak St., 39530.

3—OUR LADY OF FATIMA (1957), Rev. Peter F. Mockler. In res., Rev. Msgr. Francis Farrell, (Retired).
Res., 2090 Pass Rd., 39531. Tel: 228-388-3887; Fax: 228-388-7069.
School—(Grades PreK-6) 320 Jim Money Rd., 39531. Tel: 228-388-3602; Fax: 228-385-1140. Sr. Mary Ann Peltier, M.S.C., Prin.
Religious Teachers 1; Lay Teachers 14; Students 269.
Catechesis/Religious Programs—Tel: 228-388-5737. Mr. Richard Belvel, D.R.E.
Students 201.

4—OUR MOTHER OF SORROWS (1914) (African American), Rev. Peter O. Quinn (JKS).
Res., 803 Division St., 39530. Tel: 228-436-6503.

5—SACRED HEART (1921), Rev. Patrick M. McDermott. In res., Rev. Denis Harlow.
Res., 10446 Le Moyne Blvd., 39532. Tel: 228-392-4526; Fax: 228-396-3270.
School—(Grades PreK-6). Tel: 228-392-4180; Fax: 228-392-4859. Sr. Joan Landry, R.S.M., Prin.
Sisters of Mercy 3; Lay Teachers 21; Students 216.
Catechesis/Religious Programs—Tel: 228-392-4180. Sr. Julia Marie Burke, R.S.M., D.R.E.
Students 517.

6—ST. JOHN (1922), Rev. Michael E. Snyder.
Res., 724 Bradford St., 39530. Tel: 228-374-0117; 0118.

7—ST. LOUIS (1957), Rev. Michael E. Snyder. In res., Rev. Msgr. Kevin Bambrick.
Res., 425 Division St., 39530. Tel: 228-432-7735.
Catechesis/Religious Programs—Students 4.

8—ST. MARY (1973), Rev. Thomas White.
Res., 8343 Woolmarket Rd., 39532. Tel: 228-392-7500; Fax: 228-392-1999.
Catechesis/Religious Programs—Tel: 228-392-1999.
Students 172.

9—ST. MICHAEL (1917), Revs. Patrick O'Shaughnessy; Dominic Phan, Dir. Vietnamese Apostolate.
Res., 177 First St., P.O. Box 523, 39533. Tel: 228-435-5578; Fax: 228-435-5579.

OUTSIDE THE CITY OF BILOXI

Bassfield, Jefferson Davis Co., St. Peter (1904) (Irish), Rev. Cuthbert O'Connell; Deacon Robert Everard.
Res., P.O. Box 10, 39421. Tel: 601-943-5104. [CEM 2][JC 2]
Catechesis/Religious Programs—Tel: 601-943-6259. Mrs. Mary E. Coulter, D.R.E.
Students 119.
Missions—Carson, Jefferson Davis Co., St. Elizabeth; Prentiss, Jefferson Davis Co., St. Mary's; Monticello, Lawrence Co., St. Lawrence, P.O. Box 16, Monticello, 39654.

Bay St. Louis, Hancock Co., Our Lady of the Gulf (1847), Rev. Michael Tracey (Ireland). In res., Rev. John T. O'Brien, (Retired).
Res., 228 S. Beach Blvd., P.O. Box 208, 39520-0208. Tel: 228-467-6509; Fax: 228-467-6509. [CEM]
School—Bay St. Louis Catholic Elementary, (Grades PreK-6). Tel: 228-467-5158; Fax: 228-467-9742. Mrs. Charlene Cherota, Prin.
Lay Teachers 20; Students 395.
High School—Tel: 228-467-7048; Fax: 228-467-1666. Sr. Donella Hartman, Prin.
Sisters 3; Lay Teachers 19; Students 245.
Catechesis/Religious Programs—Students 145.
Mission—Bay St. Louis, Hancock Co., St. Joseph's Chapel, Dunbar & Blakemore, 39520.

St. Rose De Lima (1924) (African American), Rev. A. Francis Theriault, S.V.D.; Deacon George Gromley, Pastoral Assoc.
Res., 301 S. Necaise Ave., 39520. Tel: 228-467-7347; Fax: 228-467-7740.
Catechesis/Religious Programs—Tel: 228-466-2769. Mrs. Joan Thomas, D.R.E.
Students 107.

Clermont Harbor, Hancock Co., St. Ann (1915), Rev. John J. Kelly.
Res., 5858 Lower Bay Rd., P.O. Box 1037, Lakeshore, 39558-1037. Tel: 228-467-4746; Fax: 228-467-4746. [CEM]
Catechesis/Religious Programs—Sheryl Colson, D.R.E.
Students 85.
Mission—Lakeshore, Hancock Co., St. John, P.O. Box 1037, Lakeshore, 39558.

Columbia, Marion Co., Most Holy Trinity (1959), Rev. Michael Nance, Admin.
Res., 1429 N. Park Ave., 39429. Tel: 601-736-3136.
Catechesis/Religious Programs—Tel: 601-736-8787. D.R.E.: Heather Rhodes, (Holy Trinity); Betty Smet, (St. Paul the Apostle).
Students 98.
Mission—Tylertown, Walthall Co., St. Paul the Apostle, 702 Union Rd., Tylertown, 39667. Tel: 228-876-6422.

DeLisle, Harrison Co., The Catholic Church in DeLisle (1874), Rev. John E. Ford, S.T.; Deacon Regis Brennan, S.T., Pastoral Assoc.
Res., 25220 St. Stephen Rd., 39571. Tel: 228-255-1294; Fax: 228-255-7479.
Catechesis/Religious Programs—Sr. Catherine Murray, M.S.B.T., D.R.E.
Students 180.
Missions—Dubuisson, Harrison Co., St. Ann, Vidalia Rd., 39571.; Rotten Bayou, Harrison Co., St. William, Edwin Ladner Rd., 39571.

Gautier, Jackson Co., St. Mary (1968), Rev. Patrick Hayes.
Res., 809 De La Pointe Rd., 39553. Tel: 228-497-2364; Fax: 228-497-5887.
Catechesis/Religious Programs—Donna Harper, D.R.E.
Students 235.

Gulfport, Harrison Co.,

1—ST. ANN, (1939), Rev. Fintan J. Kilmurray.
Res., 23529 Hwy. 53, 39503. Tel: 228-832-2560.
Catechesis/Religious Programs—Tel: 228-831-9452. Robert Earl Lizana, D.R.E.
Students 121.
Mission—Delmas Dedeaux, Harrison Co., Our Lady of Chartres.

2—St. James, (1898), Rev. Msgr. James P. McGough; Rev. Joseph Truong Quang Trinh; Deacon John R. Henderson.
Res., 366 Cowan Rd., P.O. Box 7267, 39506. Tel: 228-896-6059; Fax: 228-896-5498. [CEM]
School—(Grades PreK-6). Tel: 228-896-6631. Sr. Rita Murray, R.S.M., Prin.
Sisters of Mercy (Ennis, Ireland) 5; Lay Teachers 13; Students 264.
Catechesis/Religious Programs—Tel: 228-896-4579; Fax: 228-896-6095. Mr. Robert Russo, D.R.E. Students 135.

3—St. John the Evangelist, (1900), Rev. Msgr. Andrew Murray.
Res., 2414 17th St., P.O. Box 970, 39501. Tel: 228-864-2272; Fax: 228-864-2273.
School—(Grades PreK-6). Tel: 228-863-1606; Fax: 228-863-9677. Mary Ruspoli, Prin.
Lay Teachers 18; Students 241.
High School—Tel: 228-863-8343; Fax: 228-864-2788. Sr. Jacqueline Howard, R.S.M., Prin.
Lay Teachers 28; Students 320.
Catechesis/Religious Programs—D.R.E.: Sr. Mary Kealy, P.B.V.M.; Amber Romano.
Students 48.

4—St. Joseph Catholic Church, (Northwood Hills) (1966), Rev. Antone J. Lynch.
Res., 12290 DePew Rd., 39503. Tel: 228-832-3244; 832-1166; Fax: 228-832-1166.
Catechesis/Religious Programs—Mrs. Bernice Engel, D.R.E.
Students 135.

5—St. Therese, (1932) (African American), Rev. Raymond P. Carignan, S.S.J.
Res., 3521 19th St., 39501. Tel: 228-863-0624; Fax: 228-863-2531.
Catechesis/Religious Programs—Tel: 228-863-7719. D.R.E.: Sr. Carmelita Mulry, S.H.Sp.; Ms. Cynthia Graham.
Students 87.

Hattiesburg, Forrest Co., Holy Rosary (1949) (African American), Rev. William Vollor.
Res., 900 Dabbs St., 39401. Tel: 601-584-6528; Fax: 601-584-9533.

Sacred Heart (1900), Rev. George Murphy.
Res., 313 Walnut St., P.O. Box 1027, 39401. Tel: 601-583-9404; Fax: 601-583-9486.
School—(Grades PreK-8). Tel: 601-583-8683; Fax: 601-583-8684. Sr. Sharon Friedrich, M.S.C., Prin.
Lay Teachers 15; Students 322.
Catechesis/Religious Programs—Tel: 601-583-9404; Fax: 601-583-9486. Sr. Mary Anne Poeschl, R.S.M., D.R.E.
Students 224.

St. Thomas Aquinas (1968). (University of Southern Mississippi-Student Parish). Rev. Thomas Conway.
Res., 3117 W. Fourth St., 39401. Tel: 601-264-5192; Fax: 601-264-0834.
Catechesis/Religious Programs—Tel: 601-271-2919. Angie Box, D.R.E.
Students 147.
Station—Danforth Chapel, U.S.M. (University of Southern Mississippi-Student Parish).

Kiln, Hancock Co., Annunciation (1869), Rev. Henry McInerney; Deacon Lucien Moragas.
Res., P.O. Box 97, 39556. Tel: 228-255-1800; Fax: 228-255-1894.
Catechesis/Religious Programs—Tel: 228-255-1869. Ms. Jean Bruneau, D.R.E.
Students 250.

Laurel, Jones Co., Immaculate Conception (1887), Rev. Msgr. Ronald P. Herzog; Mrs. Suzie Middleton, Youth Min.
Res., 833 W. Sixth St., 39440. Tel: 601-426-3473; Fax: 601-426-3890.
School—(Grades PreK-6). Tel: 601-428-0129; Fax: 601-428-2056. Sr. Jacqueline Tarrant, R.S.M., Prin.
Religious 1; Lay Teachers 14; Students 86.
Catechesis/Religious Programs—Tel: 601-426-3473.
Students 107.
Convent—803 W. 6th St., 39440. Tel: 601-422-0557.

Long Beach, Harrison Co., St. Thomas the Apostle (1903), Revs. Louis Lohan; Michael Paul Austin; Sr. Consilio Buckley, Pastoral Assoc.; Deacon Bob Jones.
Res., 720 E. Beach Blvd., 39560. Tel: 228-863-1610; Fax: 228-868-6068.
School—(Grades PreK-6). Tel: 228-863-6876; Fax: 228-863-9537. Mrs. Elizabeth Fortenberry, Prin.
Lay Teachers 12; Students 200.
Catechesis/Religious Programs—Tel: 228-868-3774. Mrs. Myrna Jordan, D.R.E.
Students 601.

Lumberton, Lamar Co., Our Lady of Perpetual Help (1922) (German), Rev. Ken Ramon-Landry; Mrs. Katie Murphy, Pastoral Assoc.
Res., 379 W. Seneca Rd., 39455-7728. Tel: 601-796-3051 (Office); 769-3053 (Rectory); Fax: 601-796-3023. [CEM]
Catechesis/Religious Programs—Students 111.
Mission—Poplarville, Pearl River Co., St. Joseph, P.O. Box 202, Poplarville, 39470. Tel: 601-795-4471.

Moss Point, Jackson Co., St. Joseph (1950), Rev. Dominick Fullam; Deacons Victor A. Baglioni; Emery E. Elder.
Res., 4114 First St., P.O. Box 8549, 39562-8549. Tel: 228-475-0777; Fax: 228-475-3672.
Catechesis/Religious Programs—D.R.E.: Mrs. Triss Elder, (St. Joseph), Tel: 228-475-3449; Mrs. Dianne Stewart, (St. Ann), Tel: 228-641-3937.
Students 130.
Mission—Hurley, Jackson Co., St. Ann, P.O. Box 8549, 39562-8549.

Ocean Springs, Jackson Co., St. Alphonsus (1860), Revs. Bernard Farrell; Martin Joseph Gillespie; Deacon Thomas Miller.
Res., 502 Jackson Ave., 39564. Tel: 228-875-5419.
School—(Grades PreK-6). Tel: 228-875-5329; Fax: 228-875-3584. Sherrie McAllister, Prin.
Lay Teachers 22; Students 380.
Catechesis/Religious Programs—Tel: 228-872-2652. Sr. Eileen Lowney, D.R.E.
Students 344.

St. Elizabeth Ann Seton (1975), Rev. George Kitchin; Deacon Tom Le Blanc, Pastoral Assoc.
Res., 4900 Riley Rd., 39564. Tel: 228-875-0654; Fax: 228-875-6852.
Catechesis/Religious Programs—Deacon Martin Finnegan, D.R.E.
Students 224.

Pascagoula, Jackson Co., Our Lady of Victories (1855), Rev. Gerard Cleary.
Res., 510 Convent St., P.O. Box 368, 39568. Tel: 228-762-1653; Fax: 228-762-1663.
Catechesis/Religious Programs—Tel: 228-762-1227. Michele Hill, D.R.E.
Students 118.

Sacred Heart (1963), Rev. Michael Kelleher; Deacon Warren Goff. In res., Rev. James B. Taylor, (Retired).
Mailing Address: P.O. Box 2190, 39569. Tel: 228-762-1837.
Res., 3702 Quinn Dr., 39581. Tel: 228-762-1837.
School—Resurrection School-Elementary, (Grades PreK-5) 3709 Quinn Dr., 39581-2356. Tel: 228-762-7207; Fax: 228-762-0611. Elizabeth Benefield, Prin.
Lay Teachers 14; Students 262.

St. Peter the Apostle (1907) (African American), Rev. Robert Sullivan, S.S.J.
Res., 1715 Telephone Rd., P.O. Box 876, 39567. Tel: 228-762-1759; Fax: 228-762-1759. [CEM]
School—(Grades K-6). Tel: 228-762-3766; Fax: 228-762-4642. Sr. Bernadette McNamara, S.H.Sp., Prin.
Servants of the Holy Spirit 3; Lay Teachers 9; Students 130.
Catechesis/Religious Programs—Tel: 228-762-1759. Mrs. Angela Ashford, D.R.E.
Students 97.

Pass Christian, Harrison Co., Our Mother of Mercy (1911) (African American), Rev. Batholomew Enslow, S.S.J.
Res., 222 E. Railroad Ave., 39571. Tel: 228-452-4514; Fax: 228-452-4514. [JC]
Catechesis/Religious Programs—Tel: 228-452-4002.
Students 106.
Convent—251 Saucier Ave., P.O. Box 157, 39571.

Sacred Heart (Dedeaux) (1967), Rev. Anthony Doan Tran; Deacon Roberto Jiminez.
Res., 14595 Vidalia Rd., 39571. Tel: 228-255-7453; Fax: 228-255-7560.
Catechesis/Religious Programs—Students 190.
Station—Cursillo Center, Tel: 228-255-7560.
Students 190.

St. Paul (Dedeaux) (1847), Rev. Dennis J. Carver. In res., Rev. James M. Russell, (Retired).
Res., 140 E. Beach Blvd., P.O. Box 548, 39571. Tel: 228-452-4686; Fax: 228-452-5488. [CEM]
School—(Grades PreK-6). Tel: 228-452-7359. Mr. Jack Clark, Prin.
Lay Teachers 12; Students 128.
Catechesis/Religious Programs—Students 160.

Pearlington, Hancock Co., St. Joseph (1939), Rev. Dominic Cangemi, S.T., Ph.D.
Mailing Address: P.O. Box 39, 39572. Tel: 228-533-7968. [JC]

Picayune, Pearl River Co., St. Charles Borromeo (1950), Rev. John Noone.
Res., 321 Juniper St., 39466. Tel: 601-798-4779; Fax: 601-798-4779.
Catechesis/Religious Programs—Tel: 601-798-7574; Fax: 601-798-4749. Dorothy Ducote, D.R.E.
Students 369.

Pineville, Harrison Co., Our Lady of Lourdes (Pass Christian) (1973), Rev. Thaddeus Searles, S.T.
Mailing Address: P.O. Box 508, Pass Christian, 39571. Tel: 228-452-7132.
Res., 22342 Evangeline Rd., Pass Christian, 39571. Tel: 228-452-7132.
Catechesis/Religious Programs—Students 32.

Vancleave, Jackson Co., Holy Spirit Catholic Church (1980), Rev. John R. McGrath.
Res., P.O. Box 5032, 39565. Tel: 228-826-4008.
Catechesis/Religious Programs—Students 227.
Mission—Latimer, Jackson Co., Christ the King, 10601 Daisy Vestry, Latimer, 39565. Tel: 228-392-0340.

Waveland, Hancock Co., St. Clare (1919), Rev. Noel Fannon.
Res., 236 S. Beach Blvd., P.O. Box 500, 39576. Tel: 228-467-9275.
School—Tel: 228-467-7071; Fax: 228-467-0584. Ms. Harriet Bellone, Prin.
Lay Teachers 8; Students 190.
Catechesis/Religious Programs—Ms. Harriet Bellone, D.R.E.
Students 80.

Waynesboro, Wayne Co., St. Bernadette (1977), Rev. Msgr. Ronald P. Herzog.
Res., 401 Mississippi Dr., 39367. Tel: 601-735-9420. [JC 2]
Catechesis/Religious Programs—Students 13.
Mission—Leakesville, Perry Co., Holy Trinity, P.O. Box 896, 39451. Tel: 601-394-4745.

White Cypress, Hancock Co., St. Matthew the Apostle (1982), Rev. Ivan Weis.
Res., 27074 St. Matthew Church Rd., Perkinston, 39573. Tel: 228-255-7720; Fax: 228-586-0389.
Catechesis/Religious Programs—Students 90.

Wiggins, Stone Co., St. Francis Xavier (1961), Rev. Patrick J. Mockler.
Res., 1206 E. Central Ave., 39577. Tel: 601-928-2182; Fax: 601-928-2182. [JC]
Church—Tel: 601-947-9756.
Catechesis/Religious Programs—Students 70.
Mission—Lucedale, George Co., St. Lucy, CB6308, Lucedale, 39452. Tel: 601-947-9968. Deacon Caruba L. Merrill.
Station—Perkinston Junior College.

Chaplains of Public Institutions

Biloxi. *Biloxi Regional Hospital, Gulf Coast Community Hospital*. Rev. Denis Harlow.
Keesler Airforce Base. Revs. Steve Booth, Maj.; George George, Capt.
V.A. Center. Revs. Frank Popeleski; Joseph Dilettuso.

Columbia. *Industrial and Training School*. Rev. Michael Nance.

Gulfport. *Naval Const. Bn. Center*. Rev. Robert P. McClanahan, Jr., Cdr.
U.S. Naval Home. Rev. James Julius.
V.A. Hospital. Revs. Frank Popeleski; Joseph Dilettuso.

Hattiesburg. *University of Southern Mississippi*. Rev. Thomas Conway.

Leakesville. *South Mississippi Correctional Institution*. Rev. Charles C. Venus, Jr.

Special Assignment:
Reverend Fathers—
Dilettuso, Joseph, Veterans Affairs Hospital, Biloxi, MS 39531

Military Chaplains:
Reverend Fathers—
Higginbotham, Robert, U.S.A.F.

Retired:
Reverend Monsignors—
Bambrick, Kevin
Hannon, James J.
Johnson, Gregory
Mercier, Joseph
Russell, James M.
Reverend Fathers—
Filipich, Nicholas
Izral, John
Kozak, Remigius A.
O'Brien, John
Scott, Francis
Taylor, James B.

Permanent Deacons:
Baglioni, Victor A., St. Joseph, Moss Point
Brennan, Regis S.T., DeLisle
DesRosier, Raymond, Nativity B.V.M. Cathedral, Biloxi
Elder, Emery, St. Joseph, Moss Point
Everard, Robert, St. Peter, Bassfield

Finnegan, Martin, St. Elizabeth Seton, Ocean Springs

Gaule, Harold, Our Lady of Perpetual Help, Lumberton

Goff, Warren P., Sr., Sacred Heart, Pascagoula

Henderson, John R., St. James, Gulfport

Hunter, Jack, St. Joseph, Gulfport

Jimenez, Roberto, Sacred Heart, Pass Christian

Jones, Bob, St. Thomas, Long Beach

LeBlanc, Tom, St. Elizabeth Seton, Ocean Springs

Merrill, Caruba L., St. Lucy, Lucedale

Miller, Thomas M., St. Alphonsus, Ocean Springs

Moniot, Rene Joseph, Nativity of the Blessed Virgin Mary, Biloxi

Moragas, Lucien F., Jr., Annunciation, Kiln

Stockert, Al, Catholic Church of the Holy Spirit, Vancleave

Walker, Charles L., St. John the Evangelist, Gulfport

INSTITUTIONS LOCATED IN THE DIOCESE

[A] SEMINARIES, RELIGIOUS OR SCHOLASTICATES

BAY ST. LOUIS. *St. Augustine's*, 199 Seminary Dr., 39520. Tel: 228-467-6414; Fax: 228-466-4393. St. Augustine's Retreat Center. Tel: 228-467-9837; Fax: 228-466-4393. Very Rev. Raymond Lennon, S.V.D., Rector; Bro. Richard Chambers, S.V.D., Fin. Admin.; Rev. William Kelley, S.V.D., Retreat Dir., Media Production Center. Tel: 228-467-1097; Fax: 228-466-5640. Rev. James Pawlicki, S.V.D., Dir. Media Production Center. In res. Revs. George Artis, S.V.D.; Thaddeus Boucree, S.V.D.; William Kelley, S.V.D.; Robert Kelly, S.V.D.; John Kersten, S.V.D.; Raymond Lennon, S.V.D.; James Pawlicki, S.V.D.; Stephen Schuler, S.V.D.; Pete Smits, S.V.D.; Charles Heskamp, S.V.D. Priests 10. Bros. Joachim Brignac, S.V.D.; Richard Chambers, S.V.D.; Michael Decker, S.V.D.; James Heeb, S.V.D.; Paul Lengyel, S.V.D.; Lawrence Morton, S.V.D. Priests 10; Brothers 6.

[B] HIGH SCHOOLS, INTERPAROCHIAL

BILOXI. *Mercy Cross Inter-Parochial High School*. (Grades 7-12). (Coed; includes junior high school), 390 Crusader Dr., 39530. Tel: 228-374-4145; Fax: 228-374-8119.
E-mail: mercycross@mercycross.com
Pat Sanguinetti, Prin. Lay Teachers 30; Students 409.

BAY ST. LOUIS. *Our Lady Academy*. (Grades 7-12). (Girls), 222 S. Beach Blvd., 39520-4320. Tel: 228-467-7048; Fax: 228-467-1666.
E-mail: OLASTAFF@datasync.com
Web site: http://www.datasync.com/~ola
Sr. Mary Donella Hartman, R.S.M., Prin. Sisters of Mercy 3; Lay Teachers 20; Students 270.

GULFPORT. *St. John Inter-Parochial High School*. (Coed), 620 Pass Rd., 39501-6494. Tel: 228-863-8141; Fax: 228-864-2788. Sr. Jacqueline Howard, R.S.M., Prin. Lay Teachers 26; Students 320.

PASCAGOULA. *Resurrection School-Jr. / Sr. School*. (Coed), 520 Watts Ave., 39567. Kathleen Carr, Ed.D., Prin. Religious 1; Lay Teachers 19; Students 177.

[C] HIGH SCHOOLS AND ELEMENTARY SCHOOLS, DIOCESAN

BAY ST. LOUIS. *St. Stanislaus College*, 304 S. Beach Blvd., 39520. Tel: 228-467-9057; Fax: 228-466-2972.
E-mail: ssc@ststan.com
Web site: http://www.ststan.com
Boys boarding and day school, secondary and elementary. Brothers of the Sacred Heart. Bros. Ronald Talbot, S.C., Pres.; Ronald Hingle, S.C., Prin.; Dolores Richmond, Dir. Admissions. Brothers 14; Lay Teachers 50; Students 571.

[D] HOUSING FOR THE ELDERLY

BILOXI. *Gabriel Manor*, 2321 Atkinson Rd., 39531. Tel: 228-388-1013; Fax: 228-388-1176.
E-mail: gab.apt@worldnet.att.net
For a complete listing, refer to the Special Care Facilities section.

Santa Maria Retirement Apartments, 674 Beach, 39530. Tel: 228-432-1289; Fax: 228-435-0380.
E-mail: santamar@datasync.com
For a complete listing, refer to the Special Care Facilities section.

BAY ST. LOUIS. *Notre Dame de la Mer Retirement Apartments*, 292 Hwy. 90, 39520. Tel: 228-467-2885; Fax: 228-466-6300
For a complete listing, refer to the Special Care Facilities section.

GULFPORT. *Carlow Manor*, 15195 Barbara Dr., 39503. Tel: 228-539-0707; Fax: 228-539-0704.
E-mail: carlowmanor@digiscape.com
For a complete listing, refer to the Special Care Facilities section.

OCEAN SPRINGS. *Samaritan House*, 642 Jackson Ave., 39564. Tel: 228-875-1087; Fax: 228-872-9500.
E-mail: samhouse@ametro.net
For a complete listing, refer to the Special Care Facilities section.

Villa Maria Retirement Apartments, 921 Porter Ave., 39564. Tel: 228-875-8811; Fax: 228-875-8889.
E-mail: villacindy@aol.com
For a complete listing, refer to the Special Care Facilities section.

PETAL. *Caritas Manor*, 145 W. 10th Ave., 39465. Tel: 601-545-7744; Fax: 601-545-7740
For a complete listing, refer to the Special Care Facilities section.

[E] MONASTERIES AND RESIDENCES OF PRIESTS AND BROTHERS

BILOXI. *St. John Neumann Residence*, 1044 Beach Blvd., 39530. Tel: 228-374-1800; Fax: 228-374-1829. Redemptorists. Revs. Joseph Armshaw, C.Ss.R., Supr.; Albert Babin, C.Ss.R., Local Supr.; Warren Drinkwater, C.Ss.R.; Joseph Elworthy, C.Ss.R.; Edward C. Cosgrove, C.Ss.R.; Earl Toups, C.Ss.R.

BAY ST. LOUIS. *Media Production Center "In A Word"*, 199 Seminary Dr., 39520. Tel: 228-467-1097; Fax: 228-466-4393.
E-mail: editor@inaword.com
Web site: http:www.inaword.com
Rev. James Pawlicki, S.V.D., Dir. & Editor.

Saint Stanislaus Community, 109 Bookter St., 39520. Tel: 228-467-9102.
E-mail: bxw@ststan.com
Brothers of the Sacred Heart. Bros. Xavier Werneth, S.C., Dir.; Albert Ledet, S.C.; Canisius Schell, S.C., (Retired); Chris Sweeney, S.C.; Donnan Berry, S.C., (Retired); Eduardo Baldioceda, S.C.; Francis Fleming, S.C.; Gunther Aucoin, S.C., (Retired); Harold Harris, S.C.; James Burns, S.C.; Joseph Donovan, S.C.; Loyola Mattingly, S.C.; Malcolm Melcher, S.C.; Mark Thornton, S.C., (Retired); Noel Lemmon, S.C.; Ramon Daunis, S.C.; Raymond Sylve, S.C.; Roy Reinecke, S.C., (Retired). Total in Residence 18.

Southern Province of St. Augustine - Provincial Residence, 201 Ruella Ave., 39520. Tel: 228-467-4322; Fax: 228-466-5618.
E-mail: clabbe1005@aol.com
Society of the Divine Word. Very Rev. Clifton Labbe, S.V.D., Prov.; Rev. Thomas James, S.V.D., Prov.; Bro. Richard Chambers, S.V.D., Treas.

Province Development Office. Tel: 228-467-3815; Fax: 228-466-5618. Rev. Robert Kelly, S.V.D., Dir.

Retreats. Tel: 228-467-9837; Fax: 228-466-4393. Rev. William Kelley, S.V.D. Priests 50; Brothers 8; Parishes 24; Mission Stations 4; Elementary schools 5.

WAVELAND. *Brothers of the Sacred Heart*, 126 Bienville Dr., 39576. Tel: 228-463-0282; Fax: 228-466-2972.
E-mail: gaudina@ststan.com
Bros. Adrian Gaudin, S.C., Dir.; Charles Schilling, S.C.; Ronald Hingle, S.C.; Ronald Talbot, S.C. Total in Residence 4.

[F] CONVENTS AND RESIDENCES FOR SISTERS

BILOXI. *Our Lady of Fatima Convent*, 314 Jim Money Rd., 39531. Tel: 228-388-8912; Fax: 228-385-1140.
E-mail: maryanne.peltier@juno.com
Marianite of Holy Cross 2; Total Staff 2.

Sisters of Mercy Convent, 11454 Spring Ln., 39532. Tel: 228-392-2575; Fax: 228-392-2582. Sr. Kim Marie Lajoie, R.S.M., Contact Person. Religious Sisters of Mercy of the Americas 4.

GULFPORT. *Eucharistic Missionaries of St. Dominic*, 164 E. Beach Blvd., Apt. 201, 39507. Tel: 228-863-6263. Other Address: Seashore Manor, 1450 Beach Blvd., Apt. 221, Biloxi, 39530. Tel: 228-432-8698. Sr. Dorothy Trosclair, O.P., Pres.

HATTIESBURG. *Sisters For Christian Community*, #4 North Ln., 39402. Tel: 601-264-9307.

LONG BEACH. *Congregation of the Holy Rosary*. (Vietnamese), 5122 N. Gates Ave., 39560. Tel: 228-863-3045. Sisters 5; Aspirants 14.

Presentation Sisters, 18091 Commission Rd., 39560. Tel: 228-864-8418. Union of the Sisters of the Presentation of the Blessed Virgin Mary.

PASCAGOULA. *Emmaus Community*, 1917 Arizona St., #5, 39581. Tel: 228-762-8401; Fax: 228-769-1226.
E-mail: sbmssnd@datasync.com
School Sisters of Notre Dame.

St. Peter the Apostle Convent, 1703 Telephone Rd., 39567. Tel: 228-762-3766; Fax: 228-762-4642.
E-mail: Sstpeter13@aol.com
Sisters of the Holy Spirit and Mary Immaculate Consensus Community Sisters 3; Total Staff 3; Total in Residence 3.

[G] NEWMAN CENTERS

HATTIESBURG. *University of Southern Mississippi*, St. Thomas Aquinas Chapel, 3117 W. Fourth St., 39401. Tel: 601-264-5192; Fax: 601-264-0834.
E-mail: sainttho@netdoor.com
Web site: www.stthomas.usm.org
Rev. Tommy Conway, Chap.

[H] MISCELLANEOUS

BILOXI. *Gabriel Manor II, Inc.*, c/o The Catholic Diocese of Biloxi, P.O. Box 1189, 39533. Tel: 228-702-2136; Fax: 228-702-2125.
E-mail: srrebecca@biloxidiocese.org
Most Rev. Joseph Lawson Howze, D.D., Pres.; Sr. Rebecca Rutkowski, A.C.S.W., Contact Person.

Magnificat - Mississippi Gulf Coast Chapter, P.O. Box 4344, 39531. Tel: 228-435-5911; Fax: 228-374-4157. Mrs. Gay T. Hopkins, Contact Person.

BAY ST. LOUIS. *St. Stanislaus College*, 304 S. Beach Blvd., 39520. Tel: 228-467-9057; 800-517-6257; Fax: 228-466-2972.
E-mail: ssc@ststan.com
Web site: http://www.ststan.com
Bro. Ronald Talbot, S.C., Pres. Day and resident Catholic boys school grades 6-12.

Camp Stanislaus. Boys' summer program for ages 9-15. Tel: 228-467-9057; 800-517-6257; Fax: 228-466-2972.

RELIGIOUS INSTITUTES OF MEN REPRESENTED IN THE DIOCESE

For further details refer to the corresponding bracketed number in the Religious Institutes of Men or Women section.

[1100]—*Brothers of the Sacred Heart.*—S.C.

[1330]—*Congregation of the Mission (Southern Prov.).*—C.M.

[0840]—*Missionary Servants of the Most Holy Trinity.*—S.T.

[1070]—*Redemptorist Fathers.*—C.Ss.R.

[0700]—*St. Joseph's Society of the Sacred Heart.*—S.S.J.

[0420]—*Society of the Divine Word.*—S.V.D.

RELIGIOUS INSTITUTES OF WOMEN REPRESENTED IN THE DIOCESE

[2410]—*Congregation of the Marianites of Holy Cross.*—M.S.C.

[1920]—*Congregation of the Sisters of the Holy Cross.*—C.S.C.

[]—*Daughters of Our Lady of the Holy Rosary.*—F.M.S.R.

[1070-11]—*Dominican Sisters.*—O.P.

[1140]—*Eucharistic Missionaries of St. Dominic.*—O.P.

[2575]—*Institute of the Sisters of Mercy of the Americas.*—R.S.M.

[2790]—*Missionary Servants of the Most Blessed Trinity.*—M.S.B.T.

[3530]—*Missionary Sisters Servants of the Holy Spirit.*—S.Sp.S.

[3280]—*Presentation of the Blessed Virgin Mary Sisters.*—P.B.V.M.

[3450]—*Religious of Jesus-Mary.*—R.J.M.

[2970]—*School Sisters of Notre Dame.*—S.S.N.D.

[]—*Sisters for Christian Community.*—S.F.C.C.

[0430]—*Sisters of Charity of the Blessed Virgin Mary.*—B.V.M.

[2560]—*Sisters of Mercy (Killaloe).*

[1510]—*Sisters of St. Francis.*—O.S.F.

[2040]—*Sisters of the Holy Spirit.*—S.H.S.

[2350]—*Sisters of the Living Word.*—S.L.W.

[2940]—*Sisters of the Most Holy Sacrament.*—M.H.S.

NECROLOGY

(No Deaths)

Diocese of Birmingham

(Dioecesis Birminghamiensis)

Most Reverend

DAVID E. FOLEY, D.D.

Bishop of Birmingham; ordained May 26, 1956; appointed Titular Bishop of Ottaba and Auxiliary Bishop of Richmond May 3, 1986; consecrated June 27, 1986; appointed Bishop of Birmingham 1994; installed May 13, 1994.

Chancery Office: Catholic Life Center, P.O. Box 12047, Birmingham, AL, 35202-2047. Tel.: 205-838-8322; Fax: 205-836-1910.

E-mail address: Chancery@bhmdiocese.org

ESTABLISHED JUNE 28, 1969.

Square Miles 28,091.

Comprises the Counties of North Alabama in an irregular line between the Counties (west to east) of Sumter and Choctaw and following the base of the following Counties: Marengo, Perry, Chilton, Coosa, Tallapoosa and Chambers or comprising the Counties of: Bibb, Blount, Calhoun, Chambers, Cherokee, Chilton, Clay, Clebourne, Colbert, Coosa, Cullman, DeKalb, Etowah, Fayette, Franklin, Greene, Hale, Jackson, Jefferson, Lamar, Lauderdale, Lawrence, Limestone, Madison, Marengo, Marion, Marshall, Morgan, Perry, P.ickens, Randolph, St. Clair, Shelby, Sumter, Talladega, Tallapoosa, Tuscaloosa, Walker and Winston

Legal Title: *The Catholic Bishop of Birmingham in Alabama, a Corporation Sole.*

For legal titles of institutions, consult the Chancery Office.

STATISTICAL OVERVIEW

Personnel	
Bishop	1
Abbots	1
Retired Abbots	2
Priests: Diocesan Active in Diocese	49
Priests: Active Outside Diocese	3
Priests: Diocesan in Foreign Missions	1
Priests: Retired, Sick or Absent	14
Number of Diocesan Priests	67
Religious Priests in Diocese	41
Extern Priests in Diocese	1
Ordinations:	
Diocesan Priests	1
Religious Priests	1
Transitional Deacons	3
Permanent Deacons	18
Permanent Deacons in Diocese	48
Total Brothers	33
Total Sisters	143
Parishes	
Parishes	57
With Resident Pastor:	
Resident Diocesan Priests	37
Resident Religious Priests	14
Without Resident Pastor:	
Administered by Priests	1
Administered by Deacons	2
Administered by Women Religious	2
Administered by Lay People	1
Missions	18
Professional Ministry Personnel:	
Sisters	22
Lay Ministers	57
Welfare	
Catholic Hospitals	1
Total Assisted	167,189
Health Care Centers	1
Total Assisted	242,431
Special Centers for Social Services	9
Total Assisted	59,539
Educational	
Diocesan Students in Other Seminaries	15
Students Religious	5
Total Seminarians	20
High Schools, Diocesan and Parish	4
Total Students	1,491
High Schools, Private	1
Total Students	133
Elementary Schools, Diocesan and Parish	20
Total Students	5,224
Elementary Schools, Private	1
Total Students	147
Non-residential Schools for the Disabled	1
Total Students	126
Catechesis/Religious Education:	
High School Students	1,965
Elementary Students	6,402
Total Students Under Catholic Instruction	15,508
Teachers in the Diocese:	
Sisters	21
Lay Teachers	503
Vital Statistics	
Receptions into the Church:	
Infant Baptism Totals	1,678
Adult Baptism Totals	237
Received into Full Communion	561
First Communions	1,488
Confirmations	1,239
Marriages:	
Catholic	201
Interfaith	246
Total Marriages	447
Deaths	408
Total Catholic Population	90,590
Total Population	2,769,842

Former Bishops—Most Rev. JOSEPH G. VATH, ord. June 7, 1941; appt. Auxiliary Bishop of Mobile-Birmingham March 25, 1966; cons. May 26, 1966; transferred to the Diocese of Birmingham Dec. 9, 1969; died July 14, 1987.—Most Rev. RAYMOND J. BOLAND, D.D., ord. June 16, 1957; appt. Bishop of Birmingham Feb. 2, 1988; cons. March 25, 1988; transferred to Kansas City-St. Joseph Sept. 9, 1993.—Most Rev. DAVID E. FOLEY, D.D., ord. May 26, 1956; appt. Titular Bishop of Ottaba and Auxiliary Bishop of Richmond, May 3, 1986; cons. June 27, 1986; appt. Bishop of Birmingham in Alabama, March 22, 1994; installed May 13, 1994.

Chancery Office—P.O. Box 12047, Birmingham, 35202-2047. Catholic Life Center, *8131 Fourth Ave. S., Birmingham, 35206.* Tel: 205-838-8322; Fax: 205-836-1910. Address all Diocesan Correspondence to the above Post Office Box unless otherwise indicated. Telephones listed below.

Office of the Bishop—ELAINE WILLIS, Sec. Tel: 205-838-8318. GERRY NABORS, Exec. Asst. Tel: 205-833-0175.

Chancellor—Vacant.

Priests' Council—Most Rev. DAVID E. FOLEY, D.D., Pres.; Rev. JOSEPH CULOTTA, Chm. Tel: 256-353-2667. Rev. MARK HYDE, S.D.B., Vice Chm. Members: Rev. Msgr. MICHAEL SEXTON, V.G.; Revs. KEVIN COOKE; RAYMOND DUNMYER; BRIAN EGAN, V.A.; JOHN FALLON; LOUIS GIARDINO; GERALD HOLLOWAY; JAMES NAUGHTON, S.D.B.; VERNON HUGULEY; FRANK MUSCOLINO; PAUL ROHLING, V.C.; ROBERT SULLIVAN; JERRY DEASY.

Diocesan College of Consultors—Rev. Msgr. MICHAEL SEXTON, V.G.; Revs. GREGORY BITTNER; JOSEPH CULOTTA; RAYMOND DUNMYER; BRIAN EGAN; JOHN FALLON; LOUIS GIARDINO; ROBERT SULLIVAN; PAUL ROHLING.

Diocesan College of Vicars—Rev. Msgr. MICHAEL SEXTON, Vicar General-Vicar for Northwest Deanery. Tel: 205-764-3303. Revs. GREGORY BITTNER, Judicial Vicar. Tel: 205-838-8307. PAUL ROHLING, Vicar for Clergy. Tel: 205-871-1153. BRIAN EGAN, Vicar for Admin. Tel: 205-838-8309. RAYMOND MURRIN, Vicar for West Birmingham Deanery. Tel: 205-798-5326. PATRICK SULLIVAN, Vicar for Central Birmingham Deanery. Tel: 205-822-4480. EUGENE O'CONNOR, Vicar for East Birmingham Deanery. Tel: 205-833-0334. LOUIS GIARDINO, Vicar for Northeast Deanery. Tel: 205-881-4781. JOHN FALLON, Vicar for Southwest Deanery. Tel: 205-553-9733. RICHARD DONOHOE, Vicar for Southeast Deanery. Tel: 205-237-3011.

Diocesan Pastoral Council—Most Rev. DAVID E. FOLEY, D.D., Pres. Members include lay representatives of the Diocesan Deaneries, four Vicars for Deaneries, four religious and a staff representative.

Diocesan Finance Council—Most Rev. DAVID E. FOLEY, D.D., Pres.; Rev. BRIAN EGAN, Vicar for Admin. THOMAS CURTIN, Chm. Members: Rev. GREGORY BITTNER; PAUL J. SHARBEL; LOUIS R. FORTIER; SHEILA BLAIR; JIM FRANKLIN; JOHN DEWITT, C.P.A.; RAY G. DYER, JR., C.P.A.; STAN MACKIN, JR.; MARY ELLEN PETERS; YOLANDA N. SULLIVAN, C.P.A. Staff Members: ROBERT M. SELLERS, JR., Finance Admin.

Tribunal—Rev. GREGORY T. BITTNER, J.C.L., Judicial Vicar. Tel: 205-838-8307; 838-8320. CYWILLA FABIJANIC, Sec., Notary & Case Mgt.; Rev. KEVIN COOKE, Trial Advocate.

Judges—Revs. RICHARD DONOHOE; LOUIS GIARDINO; PAUL ROHLING; PAUL J. HACHEY, S.M., J.C.L.; JAMES MULVANNEY; MARGARET POLL.

Defenders of the Bond—Rev. BRIAN EGAN; Sr. LYNN MCKENZIE, O.S.B., J.C.L.; Rev. KEVIN HAMMON, O.F.M.Conv.,Please address all Rogatory Commissions to the Office of the Tribunal, *Catholic Life Center.* Tel: 205-838-8307.

Catholic Social Services—Dr. MARIO G. MARTINEZ, Chm. Tel: 205-979-7676. ALBERT MANZELLA, Exec. Dir. Tel: 205-838-8316.

Catholic Family Services—TOM COOK, D.S.W., Dir., *2164 11th Ave. S., Birmingham, 35205.* Tel: 205-324-6561.

Catholic Family Services Offices—LAURA DINWIDDIE, Dir., *1010 Church St., Huntsville, 35804.* Tel: 256-536-0073., *733 37th St. E., Tuscaloosa, 35405.* Tel: 205-553-9045. ELLEN BEADLE, Dir., *1111 E. College St., Florence, 35630.* Tel: 256-768-1550.

Catholic Centers of Concern—Birmingham; Anniston; Gadsden; Hamilton; Huntsville; Eutaw; Winfield; Sulligent; Fayette.

Apostolate to the Aged—AL GERMANN, *369 Midwood Ave., Birmingham, 35228.* Tel: 205-923-7108.

Engaged Encounter—PAM DIPIAZZA; ANTHONY DIPIAZZA, *1932 Crossvine Rd., Birmingham, 35244.* Tel: 205-987-0977.

Natural Family Planning—HAROLD GRAY; CATHY GRAY, *613 Bienville Ln., Birmingham, 35213.* Tel: 205-879-2042.

Department of Education—FRANK X. SAVAGE, Dir., Catholic Education & Lifelong Learning.

Catholic Schools—Sr. M. LEANNE WELCH, P.B.V.M., Supt. Tel: 205-838-8303.

Religious Education—Bro. HENRY WERNER, F.S.C., Dir. Tel: 205-838-8312.

Apostolate with Mentally Retarded Persons—Rev. PATRICK CULLEN; Sr. MARY VERNON GENTLE, R.S.M., *The Nazareth House, 2120 Third Ave. N., Birmingham, 35202.* Tel: 205-251-1279 (Voice or TDD).

Catholic Youth Ministry—DONALD SCHWARZHOFF, Dir. Tel: 205-838-8301.

Campus Ministry—Rev. ANDREW SULLIVAN, Dir., *St. Francis University Parish, 811 Fifth Ave., Tuscaloosa, 35401.* Tel: 205-758-5672.

Catholic Scouting—DONALD SCHWARZHOFF, Dir. Tel: 205-838-8301.

Toy Bowl Association—MICHAEL CAMMARATA, Dir., *222 73rd St. N., Birmingham, 35202.* Tel: 205-838-2112.

Board of Education—DAN FLEMMING, Chm. Tel: 800-292-4847 (Office); 205-956-9300 (Res.).

Finance Office and Administration—

Diocesan Finance Administrator—ROBERT M. SELLERS, JR. Tel: 205-833-0173.

Annual Catholic Charities Appeal, Campaign for Human Development, Catholic Relief Services, and National and Special Collections—Very Rev. BRIAN EGAN, Dir. Tel: 205-838-8309.

Office of Pastoral Services—

Beginning Experience—HELEN BOWERS. Tel: 205-802-6216; 969-8509 (Voice Mail).

Development—BARBARA SHELTON. Tel: 205-838-8328.

Children's Beginning Experience—JEANNETTE CAMPISI, *c/o St. Peter Church, 2061 Patton Chapel Rd., Bham, 35216.* Tel: 205-822-4480.

Cursillo Program—Directors: DICK SWEENEY; JANE SWEENEY. Tel: 205-987-8038.

Hispanic Ministries—BRENDA BULLOCK, Dir. Tel: 205-838-8306.

Lay Ministries Program—Sr. MARIE LEONARD, O.S.B., Dir. Tel: 205-838-8300.

Marriage Encounter—DEL FISHER; NANCY FISHER. Tel: 205-556-6471.

Black Catholic Ministry—LINDA DUHON, Dir. Tel: 205-838-8313.

Pro-Life Activities—Vacant.

Propagation of the Faith and Holy Childhood—Rev. RAYMOND MURRIN, Dir. CATHY SCARVEY, Asst. Dir. Tel: 205-838-8306.

Serra Club of Birmingham—Dr. THOMAS O. JAMES, Pres. Tel: 205-426-3557.

Vocations—TERESA RUSHWORTH, Coord. Tel: 205-838-2184.

"One Voice"—Diocesan weekly; MARY ALICE CROCKETT, Mng. Editor. Tel: 205-838-8305. SAMUEL A. CIULLA, Advertising; ANN LANZI, Circulation; DAVID SAN MIGUEL, Photojournalist, *The Birmingham Catholic Press, Inc., P.O. Box 10822, Birmingham, 35202.* Tel: 205-838-8305; Fax: 205-838-8319.

Assembly of Religious—Sr. MARY RUTH COFFMAN, O.S.B., Chm., *Sacred Heart Monastery, P.O. Box 2040, Cullman, 35056.* Tel: 256-734-2199.

Retrouvaille of Alabama, Inc.—Coordinators: FRAN HINES; LEE HINES. Tel: 205-967-3458.

Diocesan Council of Catholic Women—RUTH MAYS, Pres., *2409 Old Creek Trail, Decatur, 35603.* Tel: 256-353-7899.

Priests' Retirement Fund—Rev. LOUIS GIARDINO, Chm., *625 Airport Rd., S.W., Huntsville, 35802.* Tel: 256-881-4781.

RENEW 2000—Sr. MADELINE CONTORNO, O.S.B., Coord. ARLENE DEL BUENO, Sec., *P.O. Box 12047, Birmingham, 35202-2047.* Tel: 205-838-8323; Fax: 205-836-1910.

CLERGY, PARISHES, MISSIONS AND PAROCHIAL SCHOOLS

CITY OF BIRMINGHAM
(Jefferson County)

1—ST. PAUL'S CATHEDRAL (1871), Rev. Patrick P. Cullen; Deacon Hugh O'Brien. In res., Most Rev. David E. Foley, D.D.; Rev. Desmond Regan.
Mailing Address: P.O. Box 10044, 35202-0044. Tel: 205-251-1279; Fax: 205-251-1284.
Res., 2120 Third Ave. N., 35203.
School—Tel: 205-251-9345; Fax: 205-322-7265. Gladys J. McGee, Prin.
Lay Teachers 11; Students 150.

2—ST. ANTHONY'S (1900). Closed. For inquiries for parish records contact St. Paul Cathedral, Birmingham.

3—ST. BARNABAS (1908), Very Rev. Eugene O'Connor, V.F.
Mailing Address: P.O. Box 610304, 35261.
Res., 7921 First Ave. N., 35206. Tel: 205-833-0334; 833-5695; Fax: 205-833-0272.
School—7901 First Ave. N., 35206. Tel: 205-836-5385; Fax: 205-833-0272. Tillie S. Barnhill, Prin.
Lay Teachers 14; Students 195.
Mailing Address: P.O. Box 610347, 35261.
Catechesis/Religious Programs—Tel: 205-836-4567. Rosemary Gagliano, D.R.E.
Students 37.

4—ST. BERNARD'S (Inglenook) (1928). Closed. For inquiries for parish records contact St. Paul Cathedral, Birmingham.

5—BLESSED SACRAMENT (1910), Very Rev. Gregory Bittner, J.C.L. In res., Rev. Charles V. Cross; Deacon Sam Anzalone.
Res., 1460 Pearson Ave., S.W., P.O. Box 110006, 35211. Tel: 205-785-9840. [CEM]

6—ST. FRANCIS XAVIER (1953), Very Rev. Paul Rohling, V.C.; Sr. Jane Bishop, O.S.B., Pastoral Min.; Deacon George Mickwee; Sr. Janet Flemming, O.S.B., Adult Ed. In res., Bro. Henry Werner, F.S.C.
Res., P.O. Box 130669, 35213. Tel: 205-871-1153; Fax: 205-871-9831.
School—Tel: 205-871-1687. Sr. Judith Dianne McGowan, R.S.M., Prin.
Sisters 1; Lay Teachers 15; Students 208.
Catechesis/Religious Programs—Sr. Therese Francis Walker, M.S.B.T., D.R.E.
Students 313.

7—HOLY FAMILY (1938) (African American), Revs. Philip Paxton, C.P.; Robert Crossmeyer, C.P.; Ray McDonough, C.P.; Deacon Benjamin Jett.
Res., 1910 19th St., 35218. Tel: 205-780-3440; Fax: 205-780-5272.
School—1916 19th St., Ensley, 35218. Tel: 205-785-5858; Fax: 205-785-2666. Sr. M. DePorres Collier, C.S.S.F., Prin.
Sisters 1; Lay Teachers 15; Students 205.
Catechesis/Religious Programs—Fax: 205-780-3440.
Students 423.
Mission—Fairfield, Jefferson Co., St. Mary's, (1943) 6101 Dr. Martin Luther King Dr., Fairfield, 35064. Tel: 205-923-0202 (Office); 780-3440 (Res.); Fax: 205-923-2276.
School—6124 Myron Massey Blvd., Fairfield, 35064. Tel: 205-923-5161; Fax: 205-923-5166. Ms. Mary Collins, Prin.
Lay Teachers 14; Students 160.

8—HOLY ROSARY (Gate City) (1889). (See St. John Bosco, Birmingham for details.).

9—ST. JOHN BOSCO (1973), Rev. Mark Hyde, S.D.B. In res., Rev. Sean Rooney, S.D.B.
Mailing Address: P.O. Box 321576, 35232. Tel: 205-595-1009; Fax: 205-591-1547.
Res., 5224 First Ave. N., 35212.
Mission—Birmingham, Jefferson Co., Holy Rosary (Gate City), (1889) 7414 Georgia Rd., 35212. Tel: 205-595-0652; Fax: 205-595-3091. Revs. Mark Hyde, S.D.B.; Anthony D'Angelo, S.D.B.; Gregory Fishel, S.D.B.; Bro. Charles Todel, S.D.B.

10—ST. JOSEPH'S (1921) (Italian), Rev. Crescenzio Defavio; Deacon Al Germann.
Res., 3020 Avenue K, 35218. Tel: 205-788-5721; Fax: 205-788-7146.
Convent—1100-31st St., 35218. Tel: 205-787-1517.

11—KOREAN CATHOLIC COMMUNITY, ST. LUKE HWANG (1995) (Korean), Rev. Francesco Choi.
Res., 460 Park Ter., 35226. Tel: 205-879-1703.

12—ST. MARGARET'S. Closed. 1986. For inquiries for parish records contact Blessed Sacrament Parish, Birmingham.

13—ST. MARK'S (1904). Closed. For inquiries for parish records contact the Chancery.

14—ST. MARK THE EVANGELIST, Jefferson Co., Rev. Patrick P. Collen.
Church—1115 Meadow Dr., #1115, 35242. Tel: 205-980-1810; Fax: 205-980-9207.
Catechesis/Religious Programs—Mary Kay Gubenski, D.R.E.
Students 184.

15—OUR LADY OF FATIMA (1905), Rev. Paul Oberg, S.S.J.; Deacon Willie Moore.
Res., 708 First St. S., 35205. Tel: 205-322-1205; Fax: 205-714-5056.
School—630 First St. S., 35205. Tel: 205-251-8395. Sr. Rita Radloff, S.B.S., Prin.
Sisters of Notre Dame of Covington, KY 3; Lay Teachers 14; Students 220.
Catechesis/Religious Programs—Tel: 205-251-8395. D.R.E.: Sr. Mary Carleta, S.N.D.; Mrs. Theresa Nalls.
Students 90.

16—OUR LADY OF LOURDES (1959), Rev. Andrew Kennedy.
Res., 980 Huffman Rd., 35215.
Office: Tel: 205-836-2274; Fax: 205-836-5436.
Catechesis/Religious Programs—Robin Barron, D.R.E., Tel: 205-836-2274; Fax: 205-836-5436.
Students 209.

17—OUR LADY OF SORROWS (1887), Revs. Martin M. Muller; James Thomas Ackerman, Jr. In res., Very Rev. Brian Egan, V.A.; Rev. Emmanuel Iheaka.
Mailing Address: P.O. Box 59447, 35259. Tel: 205-871-8121; Fax: 205-871-8180.
Res., (Homewood) 1728 Oxmoor Rd., 35209.
School—Tel: 205-879-3237; Fax: 205-879-9332. Deborah White, Prin.
Lay Teachers 32; Students 503.
Catechesis/Religious Programs—Tel: 205-871-1431; Fax: 205-871-1487. D.R.E.: Barbara Bess; Sr. Joan Harrington, C.S.J.
Students 444.

18—OUR LADY OF THE VALLEY (1974), Rev. Michael MacMahon.
Res., 5514 Double Oak Ln., 35242. Tel: 205-991-6288; Fax: 205-991-5181.
Church—Tel: 205-991-5488; Fax: 205-991-5181.
School—Tel: 205-991-5692; Fax: 205-991-1251. Mrs. Sandra Roden, Prin.
Lay Teachers 36; Students 515.
Catechesis/Religious Programs—Tel: 205-991-5489; Fax: 205-991-5181. Deacon Dan Whitaker, D.R.E.
Students 385.

19—OUR LADY QUEEN OF THE UNIVERSE (1955) (African American), Rev. Vernon Huguley.
Res., 961 Center St. N., 35204. Tel: 205-328-7729; Fax: 205-328-7703.
Mission—Collegeville, Jefferson Co., Sacred Heart, 3401 27th Ct. N., 35207. Tel: 205-252-8909.

20—ST. PATRICK'S (1983), Rev. Raymond J. Murrin; Sr. Maura Sampson, P.B.V.M., Pastoral Min. & D.R.E.
Res., 301 Shamrock Tr., Adamsville, 35005. Tel: 205-674-1426. Sr. Maura Sampson, P.B.V.M., Pastoral Min. & D.R.E., Tel: 205-787-1517.
Church—Tel: 205-798-5326; Fax: 205-798-5330.
Catechesis/Religious Programs—Tel: 205-798-5326; Fax: 205-798-5330.
Students 201.
Family Life Center—Tel: 205-798-0372.

21—ST. PETER THE APOSTLE (1962), Very Rev. Patrick J. Sullivan, V.F.; Rev. Joseph M. Palathingal; Sr. Virginia Rohling, O.S.B., Pastoral Assoc. In res., Rev. John Robinson.
Res., 2061 Patton Chapel Rd., 35216. Tel: 205-822-4480; Fax: 205-822-4534.
Catechesis/Religious Programs—Tel: 205-823-6324; Fax: 205-822-4534. Rebecca Sullivan, D.R.E.
Students 520.

22—PRINCE OF PEACE (1984), Rev. John Fallon; Deacons Frank Iovino; Jerry Motherway.
Church & Mailing Address—4600 Moss Creek Blvd., Birmingham (Hoover), 35226. Tel: 205-822-9125; Fax: 205-822-9127.
Res., 614 Valley St., 35226. Tel: 205-822-7397.
School—Connie Angstadt, Prin. Students 150.
Catechesis/Religious Programs—Tel: 205-822-9125; Fax: 205-822-9127. Kathleen Dunne, D.R.E.
Students 613.

23—SACRED HEART (1955). (See Our Lady Queen of the Universe, Birmingham for details.).

24—ST. STANISLAUS (1914), Rev. Crescenzio DeFazio; Sr. Mary Humphries, P.B.V.M., Pastoral Admin.
Mailing Address: 904 Indiana St., 35224. Tel: 205-785-9625.
Catechesis/Religious Programs—Students 14.
Convent—Tel: 205-744-8698.

25—ST. STEPHEN THE MARTYR (1991), Rev. Frank J. Muscolino; Mr. Michael Hansell, Pastoral Assoc.
Res., 1515 12th Ave. S., 35205. Tel: 205-933-2500; Fax: 205-939-1500.
Catechesis/Religious Programs—Students 22.

26—ST. THERESA'S. Closed. For inquiries for parish records contact St. Paul's Cathedral, Birmingham.

OUTSIDE THE CITY OF BIRMINGHAM

Alexander City, Tallapoosa Co., St. John the Apostle (1948), Rev. Robert J. Stone, C.M.
Res., 454 N. Central St., 35010. Tel: 256-234-3631; Fax: 256-234-3789.
Catechesis/Religious Programs—Tel: 205-329-2592. Marty Rittman, D.R.E.
Students 44.
Mission—Ashland, Clay Co., St. Mark, (1994) 460 Country Club Rd., Ashland, 36251. Tel: 256-354-3598; Fax: 256-354-3599. In res., Revs. Bruce J. Krause, C.M., Admin.; Thomas J. Hynes, C.M., Hispanic Min.

Anniston, Calhoun Co., Sacred Heart of Jesus (1886), Very Rev. Richard E. Donohoe, V.F.; Deacon William Taffee.
Res., 3005 Woodbridge Dr., 36207. Tel: 256-237-3011; Fax: 256-241-2048.
School—16 Morton Rd., Fort McClellan, 36205. Tel: 256-237-4231; Fax: 256-241-2353. Robin Woolsey, Prin.
Lay Teachers 14; Students 205.
Catechesis/Religious Programs—Tel: 256-237-3011. Mary Zielinski, D.R.E.
Students 100.
Mission—Anniston, Calhoun Co., All Saints, c/o Dianne Greene, P.O. Box 4862, 36204. Tel: 256-237-9230.

All Saints. (See Sacred Heart, Anniston for details.).

Ashland, Clay Co., St. Mark's. (See St. John the Apostle, Alexander City for details.).

Athens, Limestone Co., St. Paul's (1959), Rev. Joseph C. Allen.
Mailing Address: P.O. Box 998, 35612.
Res., 1900 Hwy. 72 W., 35611. Tel: 256-232-4191.
Catechesis/Religious Programs—Tel: 256-232-4191. Ruth Southers, D.R.E.
Students 172.

Bessemer, Jefferson Co., St. Aloysius Church (1886), Rev. Raymond A. Dunmyer; Stephanie Gerson, Pastoral Assoc.
Mailing Address: P.O. Box 1570, 35021. Tel: 205-424-2984; Fax: 205-426-5753.
Res., 204 Westwood Dr., 35022. Tel: 205-424-1839.
School—Tel: 205-425-0045; Fax: 205-425-0046. Mrs. Lisa Corona, Prin.
Lay Teachers 16; Students 225.
Catechesis/Religious Programs—Tel: 205-425-3448.
Students 58.

St. Francis of Assisi (1940) (African American), Rev. Noel Danielewicz, O.F.M.Conv.
Res., 2400 Seventh Ave. N., 35020. Tel: 205-425-0984; Fax: 205-428-4758.
School—2410 Seventh Ave. N., 35020. Tel: 205-428-1684; Fax: 205-428-4751. Jewel Adiele-Burge, Prin.
Franciscan Friars 1; Lay Teachers 5; Students 52.

Cullman, Cullman Co., Sacred Heart (1877) (German), Revs. Kevin D. McGrath, O.S.B.; John O'Donnell, O.S.B.; Deacon William Roberson.
Res., 217 Second St. S.E., P.O. Box 1085, 35056. Tel: 256-734-3730; Fax: 256-734-3476. [CEM]
School—Tel: 256-734-4563; Fax: 256-734-5882. Sr. Tneresa Johnson, O.S.B., Prin.
Sisters 2; Lay Teachers 9; Students 201.
Catechesis/Religious Programs—Mary Merritt, D.R.E.
Students 73.
Mission—Hanceville, Cullman Co., St. Boniface, P.O. Box 1085, Hanceville, 35056. Tel: 256-734-3730; Fax: 256-734-3476. [CEM]

Decatur, Morgan Co., St. Ann's (1870), Rev. Joseph Culotta.
Res., 250 Johnston St. S.E., 35601. Tel: 256-353-2667; Fax: 256-353-8994. [JC]
School—Tel: 256-353-6543. Janet Jensen, Prin.
Lay Teachers 10; Students 200.
Catechesis/Religious Programs—Joan Sowell, D.R.E.
Students 219.
Mission—Hartselle, Morgan Co., Holy Family, P.O. Box 783, Hartselle, 35640. Tel: 256-773-5701.

Demopolis, Marengo Co., St. Leo (1936), Revs. Robert J. Sullivan; Mathew Thottiyil.
Res., 307 Main Ave., P.O. Box 937, 36732. Tel: 334-289-2767; Fax: 334-289-0544.
Catechesis/Religious Programs—Students 40.
Missions—Greensboro, Hale Co., Our Lady of Lourdes, 8 Erwin Woods Dr., Greensboro, 37644.; Eutaw, Greene Co., St. Mary, (1948). (African American) 274 Wilson Ave., Eutaw 35462.

Eutaw, Greene Co., St. Mary (1948) (African American). (See St. Leo, Demopolis for details.).

Fairfield, Jefferson Co., St. Mary (1943). (See Holy Family, Birmingham for details.).

Florence, Lauderdale Co., St. Joseph's (1898), Rev. David Buchanan; Gena Wade, Pastoral Min.
Res., 1111 E. College St., 35630. Tel: 256-764-3303; 767-9069 (Rectory); Fax: 256-718-0208.
School—Tel: 256-766-1923; 766-1955; Fax: 256-766-1713. Cathy Lennartz, Prin.
Lay Teachers 20; Students 222.
Catechesis/Religious Programs—Students 165.

St. Michael (1873), Rt. Rev. Victor J. Clark, O.S.B.
Res., 2751 County Rd. 30, 35634. Tel: 256-764-1885; Fax: 256-764-8933. [CEM]
Catechesis/Religious Programs—D.R.E.: Karen Holden, (High School); Ron Smith, (Elementary).
Students 43.

Gadsden, Etowah Co., St. James (1912), Rev. Kevin Cooke.
Mailing Address: P.O. Box 38, 35902.
Res., 225 Carleen St., 35901. Tel: 256-546-2975; Fax: 256-546-2930.
Church—622 Chestnut St., 35901. Tel: 256-546-2975; Fax: 256-546-2930.
School—Tel: 256-546-0132; Fax: 256-546-0134. Sr. M. Cecilia MacDermott, O.S.B., Prin.
Lay Teachers 13; Students 139.
Catechesis/Religious Programs—Judy Ritter, D.R.E.
Students 297.

St. Martin de Porres. Closed. For inquiries for parish records contact St. James, Gadsden.

Gardendale, Jefferson Co., St. Elizabeth Ann Seton (1976), Rev. Ray W. Keiser.
Mailing Address: 334 Main St., P.O. Box 1027, 35071. Tel: 205-631-9398 (Office); Fax: 205-631-5781.
Res., 105 Powell Dr., P.O. Box 1027, 35071. Tel: 205-631-8582.
Catechesis/Religious Programs—Fax: 205-631-5781. Michael Brasher, D.R.E.
Students 110.
Mission—Warrior, Jefferson Co., St. Henry, 211 5th St., Warrior, 35180. Tel: 205-647-7740. [CEM]

Guntersville, Marshall Co., St. William's (1952), Revs. Thomas M. Kelly; George Dyer, O.P., Hispanic Min.; Deacon Hector Garcia.
Res., 929 Gunter Ave., 35976. Tel: 256-571-9905; 582-4245 (Office); Fax: 256-571-9906.
Catechesis/Religious Programs—Ms. Carol Miller, D.R.E.
Students 160.

Huntsville, Madison Co.,

1—Good Shepherd, (1981), Rev. Philip N. O'Kennedy; Deacons Ron Puent; Helmut Sassenfeld. In res., Rev. Joseph Arul, S.V.D. India.
Res., P.O. Box 4447, 35815-4447. Tel: 256-882-1844; Fax: 256-882-1841.
Catechesis/Religious Programs—Tel: 256-822-1844. Katherine Maxwell, D.R.E.
Students 549.

2—St. Mary of the Visitation, (1861), Rev. William M. Kelly, S.D.S.
Res., 222 N. Jefferson St., 35801. Tel: 256-536-6349; Fax: 256-536-6349.
Catechesis/Religious Programs—Tel: 256-536-6760. Mrs. Evelyn Jaap, D.R.E.
Students 59.

3—St. Joseph's, (1952), Rev. Roman Mueller, S.D.S. In res., Rev. Robert Wagner, S.D.S.
Res., 2300 Beasley Ave., N.W., 35816. Tel: 256-534-8459; Fax: 256-534-8450.
School—Holy Family School, Tel: 256-539-5221; Fax: 256-533-0747. Mary Tomaine, Prin.
Sisters of the Divine Savior 1; Lay Teachers 16; Students 189.
Catechesis/Religious Programs—Tel: 256-534-1310; Fax: 256-534-8450. Carmen Amato, D.R.E.
Students 142.

4—Holy Spirit, (1965), Very Rev. Louis Giardino, V.F.; Rev. Gerald Holloway; Deacon Lee Roy Hoekenschnieder, Sr.; Bro. Benedict Stoegbauer, S.D.S.
Res., 625 Airport Rd., 35802. Tel: 256-881-4781; Fax: 256-881-5510.
School—Tel: 256-881-4852; Fax: 256-881-4904. James Bell, Prin.
Lay Teachers 23; Students 419.
Catechesis/Religious Programs—Tel: 256-881-0345. Mrs. Carolyn Brunty, D.R.E.
Students 372.

5—Our Lady Queen of the Universe, (1965), Rev. Albert Fisher.
Mailing Address: P.O. Box 3268, 35810.
Res., 3701 Grizzard, 35810. Tel: 256-852-0788.
Church—2421 Shady Lane Dr., N.W., 35810. Fax: 256-852-0199.
Catechesis/Religious Programs—Susan Turner, D.R.E.
Students 98.

Jacksonville, Calhoun Co., St. Charles (1964), Rev. William Lucas.
Church—308 Seventh St. N.E., 36265. Tel: 256-435-3238; Fax: 256-435-4942.
Res., 400 Seventh St. N.E., 36265. Tel: 256-435-1307.
Mission—Piedmont, Calhoun Co., St. Joachim, 308 7th St. N.E., Jacksonville, 36265.

Jasper, Walker Co., St. Cecilia (1964), Rev. Henry McDaid.
Res., 906 Shady Ln., 35503. Tel: 205-384-4800 (Office); Fax: 205-384-1009.
Mailing Address: P.O. Box 3638, 35502.
Catechesis/Religious Programs—Beth McCandless, D.R.E.
Students 60.
Mission—Haleyville, Winston Co., Our Lady of Guadalupe, P.O. Box 3638, 35502. Tel: 205-486-9691.

Lanett, Chambers Co., Holy Family (1915), Rev. Martin McGeough, C.M.
Res., 705 N. Third Ave., 36863-0325. Tel: 334-644-4405; Fax: 706-645-6783. [CEM]
Catechesis/Religious Programs—Katie Roberts, D.R.E.
Students 20.
Mission—Roanoke, Randolph Co., Immaculate Conception, 1256 Main St., Roanoke, 36274. Fax: 334-863-4418.

Leeds, Jefferson Co., St. Theresa's (1951), Rev. James Naughton, S.D.B.
Res., P.O. Box 525, 35094. Tel: 205-699-8534. [CEM]
Catechesis/Religious Programs—Students 41.

Livingston, Sumter Co., St. Francis of Assisi (1972). Administered by The Catholic Church in West Central Alabama. Revs. Robert J. Sullivan; Mathew Thottiyil.
Mailing Address: P.O. Box 937, Demopolis, 36732. Tel: 334-289-2767; Fax: 334-289-0544.
Church—Hwy. 28 E., 35470. Tel: 205-652-7742.

Madison, Madison Co., St. John the Baptist (1973), Rev. Msgr. Michael Sexton, V.G.; Rev. Alan C. Mackey; Deacons Dan Laurita; Darrell Diem; Carmello Graffagnini; Terry Thompson, Pastoral Asst. & D.R.E.
Res., 1055 Hughes Rd., 35758. Tel: 256-722-0130; Fax: 256-722-0303.
School—1057 Hughes Rd., 35758. Tel: 256-722-0772; Fax: 256-722-0151. Tommy Bridges, Prin.
Lay Teachers 21; Students 393.
Catechesis/Religious Programs—Tel: 256-722-8590.
Students 667.

Montevallo, Shelby Co., St. Thomas the Apostle (1951), Rev. Raymond J. Remke; Sr. Pat Hinton, O.S.F., Pastoral Assoc.
Res. & Mailing Address: 80 St. Thomas Way, 35115. Tel: 205-663-3936; Fax: 205-663-3929.
Catechesis/Religious Programs—Students 212.
Mission—Clanton, Chilton Co., Church of the Resurrection, P.O. Box 735, Clanton, 35046. Tel: 205-755-5498; Fax: 205-755-0715.
Catechesis/Religious Programs—Sr. Mariadina Puddu, M.C., Pastoral Admin.
Students 117.

Moulton, Lawrence Co., Resurrection Catholic Chapel (1993), Deacon Robert Laremore, Pastoral Coord.
Res., 7363 Alabama Hwy. 33, 35650. Tel: 256-292-3333; Fax: 256-292-3333 (Call First).

Oneonta, Blount Co., Corpus Christi (1983), Deacon Al Girodo, Admin.
Res., 216 Lakeshore Dr., 35121. Tel: 205-274-7372.
Church—32015 State Hwy. 75, 35121. Tel: 205-625-6078.
Catechesis/Religious Programs—Students 20.

Pell City, St. Clair Co., Our Lady of the Lake (1969), Rev. Matthew Brennan.
Mailing Address: Hwy. 231 S., P.O. Box 388, 35125.
Res., 117 Ingram Lane, Cropwell, 35054. Tel: 205-525-4711; 525-5161 (Church); Fax: 205-525-5161.
Catechesis/Religious Programs—Students 73.

Russellville, Franklin Co., Good Shepherd Church (1973), Rev. Bruce Bumbarger, M.SS.CC.
Res., 1700 N. Jackson Ave., P.O. Box 630, 35653. Tel: 256-332-0095; Fax: 256-332-4861. [JC]
Catechesis/Religious Programs—Students 46.

Scottsboro, Jackson Co., St. Jude (1971), Rev. Edmund G. Fay, O.P.; Deacon Jerome P. Raispis.
Res., P.O. Box 971, 35768. Tel: 205-259-2520.
Catechesis/Religious Programs—Tel: 205-574-6156. Laura Page, D.R.E.
Students 68.

Sylacauga, Talladega Co., St. Jude (1947), Rev. Joy Chalissery; Sr. Rose Mae Rausch, O.S.F., Pastoral Admin.
Res., 306 W. Bay St., P.O. Box 111, 35150. Tel: 256-245-7741; Fax: 256-245-7741. [JC]
Catechesis/Religious Programs—Students 59.
Mission—Childersburg, Talladega Co., Holy Name of Jesus, 4th St., N.W., Childersburg, 35044.

Talladega, Talladega Co., St. Francis of Assisi (1951), Rev. Joy Chalissery.
Res., 722 S. East St., P.O. Box 1142, 35160. Tel: 256-362-5372; Fax: 256-362-5372.
Catechesis/Religious Programs—Students 34.

Trussville, Jefferson Co., Holy Infant of Prague (1941), Rev. Patrick O'Donoghue. Pastoral Ministers: Sr. Marie Carolyn Cutcliff, R.S.M., D.R.E.; Terry Pruet; Deacon Ed Pruet. In res., Rev. John Owens.
Res., 215 Hewitt St., P.O. Box 43, 35173. Tel: 205-655-2541; Fax: 205-661-9231.
Catechesis/Religious Programs—Students 272.

Tuscaloosa, Tuscaloosa Co., Holy Spirit (1961), Very Rev. Jeremiah Deasy, V.F.
Res., 733 37th St. E., 35405. Tel: 205-553-9733; Fax: 205-553-7014.

School—711 37th St., 35405. Tel: 205-553-9630; Fax: 205-553-8880.
Lay Teachers 48; Students 696. Principals: Ana MacCrone, (Grades PreK-6); Steve Calabro, (Grades 7-12), Tel: 205-553-5606.
Catechesis/Religious Programs—Students 80.
Mission—Tuscaloosa, Tuscaloosa Co., St. John, c/o Rev. Jeremiah Deasy at Holy Spirit, 8th & Lurleen Wallace Blvd., 35401.

St. Francis of Assisi University Parish (1929), Rev. Andrew A. Sullivan; Sr. Helene Higgins, C.S.J., Campus Co-Min.
Res., 811 Fifth Ave., 35401. Tel: 205-758-5672; Fax: 205-758-5673.
Catechesis/Religious Programs—Nancy Woodbury, D.R.E.
Students 115.
Mission—Reform, Pickens Co., St. Robert, Hwy. 175, Reform, 35481. Tel: 205-375-8140.

Tuscumbia, Colbert Co., Our Lady of the Shoals (1869), Very Rev. Patrick J. Tierney, V.F.
Church & Res.: 200 N.E. Commons, 35674. Tel: 256-383-7207 (Church); 381-2699 (Res.); Fax: 256-383-7883. [CEM]
Catechesis/Religious Programs—Carolyn Wilson, D.R.E.
Students 133.

Winfield, Marion Co., Holy Spirit (1965), Rev. Michael Kerin, Glmy.
Catechesis/Religious Programs—Tel: 205-487-3616.
Students 51.
Mission—Fayette, Fayette Co., Holy Family, 423 19th St. N.W., Fayette, 35555. Tel: 205-932-6242.

On Special or Other Diocesan Assignment:
Reverend Fathers—
Egan, Brian, Catholic Charities Appeal, Birmingham, AL
O'Donnell, John, O.S.B., 112 Second Ave., S.E., Cullman, AL 35055

On Duty Outside the Diocese:
Reverend Monsignors—
Marino, Joseph, Secretariat of State, Second Section, Vatican City, Rome, EVR 120 Italy. Tel: 39-6-698-83122 (Office); 688-97301(Res)
Reverend Fathers—
Klauck, Michael, 6802 Edinborough Ct., Rapid City, S.D. 57702
Reynolds, Jeffrie S., P.O. Box 51, Perry Point, MD 21902. Tel: 410-642-2411 Ext. 5601 (Res) 939-1548
Walsh, Edward P., DVAMC Dayton (552) Dept. of Chaplains, P.O. Box 28171, Dayton, OH 45428-9937. Tel: 937-268-6511, Ext. 2903

Absent on Leave:
Reverend Fathers—
Cairns, Thomas
Summitt, James A.
Ventura, John

Retired:
Reverend Fathers—
Blazak, Camillus, St. Jude Church, P.O. Box 971, Scottsboro, AL 35768. Tel: 256-259-2520
Bordenca, Charles, P.O. Box 933, Fairhope, AL 36533. Tel: 334-990-9860 (Office)
DeFazio, Crescenzio, 2400 Rocky Ridge Rd., Birmingham, AL 35216. Tel: 205-824-8732
Donnelly, Paul J., 112 Fairway Blvd., Apt. 206, Panama City, FL 32407. Tel: 904-234-0659
Hill, Timothy, #4 Annville, 13 Ballinlough Rd., Cork, Ireland
Kula, Joseph, St. John Vianney Villa, 1464 Green Trails Dr., Naperville, IL 60540-83. Tel: 630-548-3953 (Office)
Mulvaney, James J., 1321 Santa Maria, Lady Lake, FL 32159. Tel: 904-750-4284
O'Connor, Thomas, O.S.B., Prior, St. Bernard Abbey, 1600 St. Bernard Dr., S.E., Cullman, AL 35055. Tel: 205-934-8291
O'Sullivan, Robert, 1500 S.W. 66th Ave., Boca Raton, FL 33428. Tel: 407-488-6147
Owen, John J., P.O. Box 259, Trussville, AL 35173. Tel: 205-655-9092
Regan, Desmond, Cathedral of St. Paul, P.O. Box 10044, Birmingham, AL 35202. Tel: 205-324-0237 (Private)
Sheehan, J. Peter, 653 S.E. Lakeview Dr., Sebring, FL 33870. Tel: 813-471-0378
Thorsen, Henry, 700 Connell Dr., Pensacola, FL 32507. Tel: 904-469-0919
Underwood, Joseph, 6520 Court K, Birmingham, AL 35228. Tel: 205-925-8329
White, Michael J., 4616 Lake Valley Dr., Birmingham, AL 35244. Tel: 205-733-8328

Permanent Deacons:
Anzalone, Sam, Blessed Sacrament, Birmingham
Ash, Donald J., St. Joachim, Piedmont
Bodine, James G., St. Ann, Decatur
Bufano, Ralph, Our Lady of the Shoals, Tuscumbia
Canonica, Donald, Holy Family, Lanett
Cova, Michael A., Sacred Heart of Jesus, Anniston
Dias, Sam A., Holy Spirit, Huntsville
Diem, Darrell, St. John the Baptist, Madison
Dunn, James A., St. Aloysius, Bessemer
Garcia, Hector, St. William, Guntersville
Germann, Aloysius A., St. Joseph, Birmingham
Girodo, Albert, Admin., Corpus Christi Church, Oneonta
Graffagnini, Carmello, St. John the Baptist, Madison
Henderson, Walter J., St. Mary, Fairfield
Hoekenschnieder, Lee Roy, Holy Spirit, Huntsville
Iovino, Frank, Prince of Peace, Birmingham
Jett, Benjamin, Holy Family, Birmingham
Joly, Walter Jerome, On Leave
Kelly, Alfred, (Retired)
Laremore, Robert, Glenmary Ministries, Moulton
Laurita, Dan, St. John the Baptist, Madison
Macey, James R., Archdiocese for the Military Services
Machos, Paul, (Retired)
Melchior, Daniel R., Our Lady, Queen of the Universe, Huntsville
Mickwee, George, St. Francis Xavier, Birmingham
Moore, William
Motherway, Gerald, Prince of Peace, Hoover
O'Brien, Hugh A., Cathedral of St. Paul, Birmingham
Pruett, Ed, Holy Infant of Prague, Trussville
Puent, Ron, Good Shepherd, Huntsville
Raispis, Jerome P., St. Jude, Scottsboro
Ritchey, Seraphim, St. George the Great Martyr
Roberson, William, Sacred Heart, Cullman
Robinson, E. Lee, Sr., Holy Infant of Prague, Trussville
Rosko, Christopher J., St. Mark the Evangelist, Birmingham
Rumore, Terrence L., Our Lady of the Lake, Pell City
Sassenfeld, Helmut, Good Shepherd, Huntsville
Slapikas, Frank R., Holy Spirit, Tuscaloosa
Stephens, Joseph R., Jr.
Straley, J. Adrian, St. Francis University, Tuscaloosa
Sullivan, Paul Mark, St. John the Apostle, Alexander City
Taffee, William Francis, Jr., Sacred Heart of Jesus, Anniston
Vazquez, Jose R., Prince of Peace, Birmingham
Viselli, Francis N., Jr., Holy Spirit, Tuscaloosa
Whitaker, Dan, Our Lady of the Valley, Birmingham
Yancey, Paul V., Our Lady of Lourdes, Birmingham
Zieverink, Edward Walter, Jr., Cathedral of St. Paul, Birmingham

INSTITUTIONS LOCATED IN THE DIOCESE

[A] HIGH SCHOOLS, DIOCESAN

BIRMINGHAM. *John Carroll Catholic High School*, 300 Lakeshore Pkwy., P.O. Box 19907, 35219. Tel: 205-940-2400; Fax: 205-945-7429.
E-mail: LWFisher@usit.net
Mr. Lee W. Fisher, Prin.; Revs. Gregory Fishel, S.D.B.; James Thomas Ackerman, Jr..Priests 2; Sisters 2; Lay Teachers 70; Students 920.

HUNTSVILLE. *Catholic High School*, 4810 Bradford Dr., 35805. Tel: 256-430-1760; Fax: 256-430-1766.
E-mail: vaquila@chsfalcons.net
Web site: www.chsfalcons.net
Vince Aquila, Interim Prin.; Revs. Gerald Holloway; Alan C. Mackey..Priests 2; Lay Teachers 19; Students 164.

TUSCALOOSA. *Holy Spirit High School*, 601 37th St. E., 35405. Tel: 205-553-5606; Fax: 205-556-7103.
E-mail: office@holyspiritschool.org
Web site: www.holyspiritschool.org
Steve Calabro, Prin..Lay Teachers 24; Students 237.

[B] HIGH SCHOOLS, PRIVATE

BIRMINGHAM. *Holy Family High School*, 2001 19th St., 35218. Tel: 205-787-9937; Fax: 205-787-8530.
E-mail: pbeckwith@holyfamilykhs.org
Web site: www.schoolsinsites.com
Passionist Community of Chicago, IL. Patricia Beckwith, Prin. Priests 1; Lay Teachers 13; Students 170.

CULLMAN. *St. Bernard Preparatory School Educational Foundation*, 1600 St. Bernard Dr., SE, 35055. Tel: 256-739-6682; Fax: 256-734-2925.
E-mail: sbprep@hiwaay.net
Web site: www.st.bernardprep.com
Revs. Marcus J. Voss, O.S.B., Pres.; Joel W. Martin, O.S.B., Headmaster..Priests 4; Sisters 2; Brothers 2; Lay Teachers 12; Students 133.

[C] ELEMENTARY SCHOOLS, PRIVATE

BIRMINGHAM. *St. Rose of Lima Academy*. (Grades K-8), 1401 S. 22nd St., 35219. Tel: 205-933-0549; Fax: 205-933-8847.
E-mail: strose.bham@mindspring.com
Sr. Mary Andrew, O.P., Prin. Dominican Sisters of Nashville, TN. Sisters 7; Lay Teachers 7; Students 247.

[D] GENERAL HOSPITALS

BIRMINGHAM. *St. Vincent's Hospital*, P.O. Box 12407, 35202-2407. Tel: 205-939-7000; Fax: 205-930-2157.
E-mail: apurdy@stv.org
Web site: www.stv.org
For a complete listing, refer to the Hospitals section.
Seton Health Corporation of North Alabama, P.O. Box 12407, 35202-2407. Tel: 205-939-8600
For a complete listing, refer to the Hospitals section.

[E] MONASTERIES AND RESIDENCES OF PRIESTS AND BROTHERS

BIRMINGHAM. *Franciscan Missionaries of the Eternal Word, A Public Association of the Christian Faithful*, 5821 Old Leeds Rd., 35210. Tel: 205-271-2937; Fax: 205-271-2931.
Web site: www.ewtn.com/mfva
Revs. Joseph M. Wolfe, M.F.V.A., Father Guardian; Augustine Mary Hedderman, M.F.V.A.; Francis Mary Stone, M.F.V.A.; Anthony Mary Stelten, M.F.V.A..Professed 17; Novices 1; Total in Residence 17.

CULLMAN. *St. Bernard Abbey*. (Corporate Title: Benedictine Society of Alabama, Inc.), 1600 St. Bernard Dr., 35055. Tel: 256-734-8291; Fax: 256-734-2925.
E-mail: cdmosb@hiwaay.net
Rt. Revs. Cletus D. Meagher, O.S.B., Abbot; Victor J. Clark, O.S.B., Retired Abbot; Gregory J. Roettger, O.S.B., J.U.D., Retired Abbot; Very Rev. Thomas J. O'Connor, O.S.B., Prior; Revs. Thomas J. Schnurr, O.S.B.; Roger R.S. Lott, O.S.B.; Francis M. Reque, O.S.B.; Edward P. Markley, O.S.B.; Ignatius B. Kane, O.S.B.; Howard R. Moussier, O.S.B.; Marcus J. Voss, O.S.B.; Kevin D. McGrath, O.S.B.; Jose Ramon Mascareno, O.S.B.; John O'Donnell, O.S.B.; Joel W. Martin, O.S.B..Total Priests of Abbey 15; Brothers 11.

[F] CONVENTS AND RESIDENCES OF SISTERS

BIRMINGHAM. *Our Lady of the Angels Monastery, Inc.*, 5817 Old Leeds Rd., 35210. Tel: 205-271-2917; Fax: 205-271-2927. Mother M. Angelica, P.C.P.A., Abbess & Pres. Poor Clare Nuns of Perpetual Adoration. Sisters 33; Novices 4; Postulants 3.
Sister Servants of the Eternal Word, Casa Maria Retreat House, 3721 Belmont Rd., 35210. Tel: 205-956-6760; Fax: 205-951-0386. Mother Mary Gabriel, Supr.

CULLMAN. *Sacred Heart Monastery*, P.O. Box 2040, 35056. Tel: 256-734-4622; 734-2199; Fax: 256-734-3835.
E-mail: shmon@highwaay.net
Web site: fly.hiwaay.net/~shmon
Sr. Veronica Ryan, O.S.B., Prioress. Benedictine Sisters. Professed Sisters 61.

[G] DIOCESAN SOCIAL SERVICE

BIRMINGHAM. *Catholic Center of Concern*. (Div. of Catholic Charities), 712 Fourth Ct. W., 35204. Tel: 205-786-4388; Fax: 205-786-6321. Sr. Adelangela Paita, M.C. Total Staff 5; Total Assisted 32,000. Consolata Missionary Sisters.
Catholic Family Services, 2164 11th Ave. S., 35205. Tel: 205-324-6561; Fax: 205-323-0475.
E-mail: cfsbham@bellsouth.net
Thomas Cook, Dir. Total Staff 6; Total Assisted 1,073.

ANNISTON. *All Saints Interfaith Center of Concern*, 1029 W. 15th St., 36201. Tel: 256-236-7793; Fax: 256-236-7793. Sr. Mary Roy, D.H.S., Dir. Tel: 256-238-1365. Total Staff 2; Total Assisted 4,466.

EUTAW. *Consolata Apostolate*, 331 Boligee St., P.O. Box 538, 35462. Tel: 205-372-3497; Fax: 205-372-2413. Sr. Zelita M. Bragagnolo, M.C., Dir. Total Staff 3; Total Assisted 9,155.

FAYETTE. *Christian Center of Concern*. Mailing Address: P.O. Box 952, 35555. 210 1st St, N.W., 35555. Tel: 205-932-3218. Rev. Gerald Peterson, Glmy., Dir. Tel: 205-487-3616. Staff 10; Total Assisted 5,259.

FLORENCE. *Catholic Family Services*, 1111 E. College St. P.O. Box 3633, 35630. Tel: 256-768-1550; Fax:

256-768-1551. Ellen Beadle, Social Worker.

GADSDEN. *Catholic Center of Concern (C/O St. James Church)*, 912 Chestnut St., 35901. Tel: 256-546-0028; Fax: 256-546-2930. Bryan Utter, Dir. Total Assisted 5,827.

HAMILTON. *Christian Center of Concern*, P.O. Box 973, 35570. Tel: 205-921-3470. Co-Directors: Sonja Leonelli; Janis Griffin. Total Assisted 1,238.

HUNTSVILLE. *Catholic Center of Concern*, 1010 Church St., N.W., P.O. Box 745, 35804. Tel: 256-536-0041; Fax: 256-534-3141. Cindy M. Whalen, Dir. Total Assisted 3,987.

Catholic Family Services, 1010 Church St., N.W., P.O. Box 745, 35804. Tel: 256-536-0073; Fax: 256-534-3141.
E-mail: hsvcfs@bellsouth.com
Laura Dinwiddie, Dir..Total Served 199.

SULLIGENT. *Christian Center of Concern*, P.O. Box 1154, 35584. Tel: 205-698-7197. Martha Richards, Dir. Staff 8; Total Assisted 858.

TUSCALOOSA. *Catholic Family Services*, 733 37th St. E., 35405. Tel: 205-553-9045; Fax: 205-554-0136.
E-mail: cfs.c@mindspring.com
Carly McRae, Dir..Total Assisted 356.

WINFIELD. *Christian Center of Concern*, 197 State Hwy. 253, 35594. Tel: 205-487-6230. Marie Weeks, Dir. Total Assisted 1,465.

[H] CAMPUS MINISTRY

BIRMINGHAM. *St. Stephen the Martyr Catholic Church and Catholic Campus Center*, 1515 12th Ave. S., 35205. Tel: 205-933-2500; Fax: 205-939-1500.
E-mail: saintst@bellsouth.com
Rev. Frank J. Muscolino. Total Staff 2; Students 300.

FLORENCE. *University of North Alabama*, St. Joseph's Church, 1111 E. College St., 35630. Tel: 256-764-3303; Fax: 256-718-0208.
E-mail: stjoseph@traveller.com
Rev. David Buchanan.

JACKSONVILLE. *Jacksonville State University*, St. Charles Church, 308 Seventh St., N.E., 36265. Tel: 256-435-3238; Fax: 256-435-4942.
E-mail: stcharleschurch@aol.com
Rev. William Lucas. Total Staff 2; Total in Program 25.

MONTEVALLO. *University of Montevallo*, St. Thomas the Apostle Catholic Campus Ministry, 80 St. Thomas Way, 35115. Tel: 205-665-7379.
E-mail: pastthomas@juno.com
Rev. Raymond J. Remke.

TALLADEGA. *Talladega College Catholic Campus Ministry*, St. Francis of Assisi, P.O. Box 1142, 35160. Tel: 256-362-5372; Fax: 256-362-5372.
E-mail: prassisi@earthlink.net
Dr. Trellie Jeffers.

TUSCALOOSA. *Diocesan Campus Ministry Office*, St. Francis University Parish, 811 Fifth Ave., 35401. Tel: 205-758-5672; Fax: 205-758-5673.
E-mail: stfrant@dbtech.net
Web site: welcome.to/search.retreat
Rev. Andrew A. Sullivan. Total Staff 1; Total in Residence 1.

University of Alabama in Tuscaloosa, St. Francis University Parish, 811 Fifth Ave., 35401. Tel: 205-758-5672; Fax: 205-758-5673.
E-mail: stfrant@dbtech.net
Web site: welcome.to/search.retreat
Campus Ministers: Rev. Andrew A. Sullivan; Sr. Helene Higgins, C.S.J. Total Staff 2; Total in Residence 1.

[I] MISCELLANEOUS LISTINGS

BIRMINGHAM. *Agape Institute of St. Teresa of Jesus*, 3528 Deerfield Dr., 35226. Tel: 205-823-5773. Co-Founders: Bob Tevebaugh; Rita Tevebaugh; Very Rev. Paul Rohling, V.C., Moderator. Members 29.

Bruno Family's Catholic Diocesan Trust, P.O. Box 12047, 35202-2047. Tel: 205-838-8318.

Casa Maria Rereat House, 3721 Belmont Rd., 35210. Tel: 205-956-6760. Mother Mary Gabriel, Dir.

Catholic Horizons, Inc., 2828 Crestwood Blvd., 35210. Tel: 205-956-1053; 1-888-266-5701; Fax: 205-956-1950.
E-mail: cathhori@bellsouth.net
George Hackney, Advisory Board Chm. Diocesan book, gift, & information center.

Catholic Housing of Birmingham, Inc., P.O. Box 12047, 35202. Tel: 205-838-8309. 8131 Fourth Ave. S., 35206. Very Rev. Brian Egan, Vice Pres.& Sec.; William M. Moran, Pres.

Congregation of the Passion: Holy Family Community, Inc. (House of Religious Men), 1910 19th St., Ensley, 35218. Tel: 205-780-3440; Fax: 205-780-5272.
E-mail: rcrossmyer@aol.com
Corporation for Holy Family Church, and Holy Family Elementary, Birmingham, and St. Mary's Church, Fairfield, St. Mary Elementary, Fairfield. Rev. Robert Crossmyer, C.P., Local Supr.

Contemplative Outreach Birmingham. Sacred Heart Monastery, P.O. Box 2040, Cullman, 35056. Tel: 256-736-5820.
E-mail: smmcgehee@hotmail.com
Sr. Mary McGehee, O.S.B., Coord.; Aloysius Golden, Area Contact Person. Tel: 205-592-3930.

The Fatima Educational Foundation, 708 First St. S., 35205. Tel: 205-251-8395; Fax: 205-251-8393.
E-mail: ritaad@bellsouth.net
Sr. Rita Radloff, S.N.D., Prin.

Holy Family Educational Foundation, 1910 19th St., 35218. Tel: 205-780-3440; Fax: 205-782-5272.
E-mail: rcrossmyer@aol.com
Web site: www.passionist.org

Holy Name of Jesus Hospital Trust. (Senior Citizen Housing), c/o Regions Bank, P.O. Box 10247, 35202. Tel: 205-326-7219; Fax: 205-326-7052.
E-mail: sroebuck@regionsbank.com
Sidney O. Roebuck, Jr., Trustee, Vice Pres. & Senior Trust Officer, Regions Bank..Total Assisted 231.

John Carroll Catholic Education Foundation, Inc., 300 Lakeshore Pkwy., 35209. Tel: 205-940-2400; Fax: 205-945-7429.
E-mail: lwfisher@usit.net

Magnificat: Mary, Woman of Faith Chapter, 1341 Forest Ridge Ct., 35226. Tel: 205-941-0144; Fax: 205-941-0144.
E-mail: carolynwright@msn.com
Carolyn Mathis Wright, Coord.

Our Lady of Sorrows Educational School Foundation, 1728 Oxmoor Rd., 35209. Tel: 205-871-8121; Fax: 205-871-8180.

Our Lady of the Valley Educational Foundation, 5514 Double Oak Ln., 35242. Tel: 205-991-5488; Fax: 205-991-5181.
E-mail: olvchurch@worldnet.att.net

St. Barnabas Regional School Educational Foundation, 7921 First Ave. N., 35206. Tel: 205-833-0334; Fax: 205-833-0270.
E-mail: tbarnhil@gte.net

St. Francis Xavier Catholic School Education Foundation, P.O. Box 130669, 35213. Tel: 205-871-1153; Fax: 205-871-1674.
E-mail: srjdmcgowan@juno.com
Sr. Judith Dianne McGowan, R.S.M., Prin. & Contact Person.

St. Paul Cathedral School Education Foundation, P.O. Box 370104, 35237. Tel: 205-251-9345; Fax: 205-251-9668.

St. Peter's Endowment Foundation, 2061 Patton Chapel Rd., 35216. Total Assisted 197; Total Staff 37.

St. Vincent's Foundation, P.O. Box 12407, 35202-2407. Tel: 205-939-7825; Fax: 205-930-2525.
E-mail: stvfoundation.org
Barbara Traylor, Dir. Devel.; William M. Moran, Exec. Dir.; Nita Rayburn, Exec. Asst.; Sr. Mary Cecilia Schlebecker, D.C., Special Project Asst.

Villa Maria, 500 82nd St. S., 35206. Tel: 205-836-7839. Violet Ashworth, Mgr. Total Staff 7; Total in Residence 63.

BESSEMER. *St. Aloysius Educational Foundation*, P.O. Box 1570, 35021. Tel: 205-424-2981; Fax: 205-426-5753.
E-mail: aloysiusst@aol.com
Rev. Raymond A. Dunmyer. Total Assisted Monthly 220.

CULLMAN. *Benedictine Manor Retirement Home, Inc.*, 200 Janeway Dr., 35055. Tel: 256-739-2853; Fax: 256-734-8300 (Call First).
E-mail: shmon@hiwaay.net
Web site: fly.hiwaay.net/~shmon
Sr. Bertha True, O.S.B., Dir..Lay Administrator 1; Resident Capacity 40-50.

Benedictine Spirituality and Conference Center, P.O. Box 2040, 35056-2040. Tel: 256-734-8302; Fax: 256-734-8302 (Call First).
E-mail: shmon@hiwaay.net
Web site: www.shmon.org
Sr. Eleanor Harrison, O.S.B., Dir. Beds 72; Total Staff 5.

St. Bernard Foundation, 101 St. Bernard Dr., S.E., 35055. Tel: 256-739-6682; Fax: 256-734-2295.
E-mail: sbprep@hiwaay.net
Rev. Marcus Voss, O.S.B., Pres.

DECATUR. *St. Ann's Educational Foundation*, 240 Johnson St. S.E., 35601. Tel: 256-353-6543; Fax: 256-353-8994.
E-mail: stann@hiwaay.net
Web site: freeyellow.com/members8/stannschool/indev.htm/
Janet Jensen.

FLORENCE. *St. Joseph School Foundation, Florence*, 115 Plum St., 35630. Tel: 256-766-1923.

Society of St. Vincent de Paul, St. Joseph Conference, 659 S. Poplar St., 35630. Tel: 256-718-0901; Fax: 256-718-0208.
E-mail: svdpts@hiwaay.net
Rev. David Buchanan, Spiritual Advisor; Donald J. O'Brien, Pres.; Peter A. Goudreau, Sec.

FORT MCCLELLAN. *Gertrude C. Luther, M.D. Charitable Trust*, 16 Morton Rd., 36205. Tel: 256-237-4231; Fax: 256-237-4281.
E-mail: robin@sacredheartanniston.org

Sacred Heart of Jesus Charitable Trust, 16 Morton Rd., 36205. Tel: 256-237-4231; Fax: 256-237-4231.
E-mail: robin@sacredheartanniston.org

GADSDEN. *St. James Educational Foundation*, 700 Albert Rains Blvd., 35901. Tel: 256-546-0132; Fax: 256-546-0134. Total Staff 18.

HUNTSVILLE. *Holy Family Regional School Foundation*, 2300 Beasley Ave., 35816-4004. Total Staff 3; Total Assisted 5.

Holy Spirit Regional School Foundation, 625 Airport Rd., 35802. Tel: 205-881-4781; Fax: 205-881-4904.
E-mail: cbev@hiwaay.net

Society of St. Vincent dePaul, P.O. Box 16070, 35802. Tel: 256-882-0040.
E-mail: bakerhd@mindspring.com
David J. Baker, Pres.

MADISON. *St. John's Educational Foundation*, 1055 Hughes Rd., 35758. Tel: 256-722-0130. Rev. Msgr. Michael Sexton.

TUSCALOOSA. *The Harrison Family Endowment Trust for the Benefit of Holy Spirit School*, 711 37th St. E., 35405. Tel: 205-553-9630; Fax: 205-553-8880.
E-mail: hselem@dbtech.net
Rev. Jeremiah Deasy.

RELIGIOUS INSTITUTES OF MEN REPRESENTED IN THE DIOCESE

For further details refer to the corresponding bracketed number in the Religious Institutes of Men or Women section.

[0910]—*Oblates of Mary Immaculate*—O.M.I.
[0200]—*Benedictine Monks.*—O.S.B.
[0330]—*Brothers of the Christian Schools.*—F.S.C.
[1330]—*Congregation of the Mission.* (Eastern Prov.).—C.M.
[1000]—*Congregation of the Passion.*—C.P.
[0480]—*Conventual Franciscans.* (Prov. of St. Anthony of Padua).—O.F.M.Conv.
[]—*Franciscan Missionaries of the Eternal Word.*—M.F.V.A.
[0570]—*Glenmary Home Missioners.* (Cincinnati, OH).
[0700]—*St. Joseph's Society of the Sacred Heart.* (Baltimore, MD).—S.S.J.
[1190]—*Salesians of Don Bosco.*—S.D.B.
[1200]—*Society of the Divine Savior.*—S.D.S.
[]—*Society of the Divine Word.*—S.V.D.

RELIGIOUS INSTITUTES OF WOMEN REPRESENTED IN THE DIOCESE

[0230]—*Benedictine Sisters of Pontifical Jurisdiction.*—O.S.B.
[0260]—*Blessed Sacrament Sisters.*—S.B.S.
[0720]—*Consolata Missionary Sisters.*—M.C.
[0760]—*Daughters of Charity of St. Vincent de Paul.*—D.C.
[0820]—*Daughters of the Holy Spirit.*—D.H.S.
[1070-03]—*Dominican Sisters.* (Adrian, MI).—O.P.
[1070-07]—*Dominican Sisters.* (Nashville, TN).—O.P.
[1070-13]—*Dominican Sisters.* (Sinsinawa, WI).—O.P.
[1170]—*Felician Sisters.*—C.S.S.F.
[1310]—*Franciscan Sisters.* (Little Falls, MN).—O.S.F.
[2720]—*Mission Helpers of the Sacred Heart*—M.H.S.H.
[2790]—*Missionary Servants of the Most Blessed Trinity.*—M.S.B.T.
[3210]—*Poor Clares of Perpetual Adoration.*—P.C.P.A.
[0850]—*Salesian Sisters, Daughters of Mary, Help of Christians (Salesian Sisters).*—F.M.A.
[2970]—*School Sisters of Notre Dame.*—S.S.N.D.
[]—*Sister Servants of the Eternal Word.*—S.S.E.W.
[2575]—*Sisters of Mercy of the Americas.*—R.S.M.
[2990]—*Sisters of Notre Dame.*—S.N.D.
[1650]—*Sisters of St. Francis of Philadelphia.*—O.S.F.
[3840]—*Sisters of St. Joseph of Carondelet.*—C.S.J.
[1030]—*Sisters of the Divine Savior.*—S.D.S.
[3320]—*Sisters of the Presentation of the B.V.M.*—P.B.V.M.
[4048]—*Society of Sisters Faithful Companions of Jesus.*—F.C.J.
[4190]—*Visitation Nuns.*—V.H.M.

NECROLOGY

† Burns, Timothy L, Huntsville, AL Our Lady, Queen of the Universe. —Died Jan. 1, 1999.
† Igoe, John T, Birmingham, AL St. Joseph. —Died Jan. 13, 2000.
† Inkel, Roland, (Retired). —Died Sept. 24, 2000.
† MacCarthy, Peter, Leeds, AL St. Theresa. —Died Aug. 23, 2000.
† Murphy, Patrick J, Birmingham, AL St Mark the Evangelist. —Died Sept. 16, 2000.

Diocese of Bismarck

(Dioecesis Bismarckiensis)

Most Reverend

PAUL A. ZIPFEL, D.D.

Bishop of Bismarck; ordained March 18, 1961; appointed Titular Bishop of Walla Walla and Auxiliary Bishop of St. Louis May 16, 1989; consecrated June 29, 1989; appointed Bishop of Bismarck December 31, 1996; installed February 20, 1997.

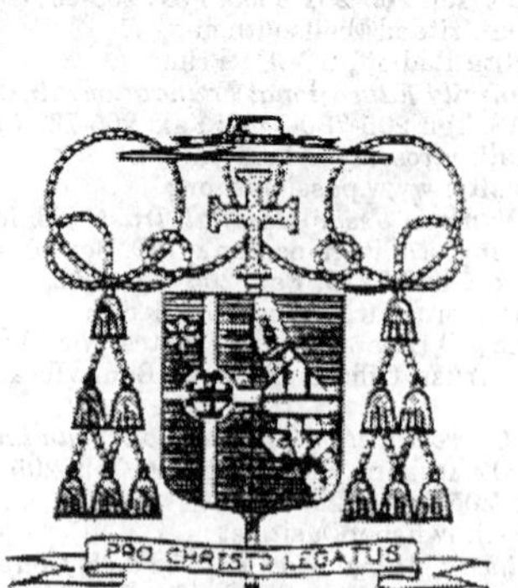

Chancery Office: 420 Raymond St., Box 1575, Bismarck, ND, 58502-1575. Tel.: 701-223-1347; Fax: 701-223-3693.

ESTABLISHED DECEMBER 31, 1909.

Square Miles 34,268.

Comprises the Counties of Adams, Billings, Bowman, Burke, Burleigh, Divide, Dunn, Emmons, Golden Valley, Grant, Hettinger, McKenzie, McLean, Mercer, Morton, Mountrail, Oliver, Renville, Sioux, Slope, Stark, Ward and Williams in the State of North Dakota.

For legal titles of parishes and diocesan institutions, consult the Chancery Office.

STATISTICAL OVERVIEW

Personnel	
Bishop	1
Abbots	1
Retired Abbots	2
Priests: Diocesan Active in Diocese	47
Priests: Active Outside Diocese	4
Priests: Retired, Sick or Absent	20
Number of Diocesan Priests	71
Religious Priests in Diocese	27
Extern Priests in Diocese	5
Ordinations:	
Diocesan Priests	6
Transitional Deacons	1
Permanent Deacons in Diocese	59
Total Brothers	24
Total Sisters	142
Parishes	
Parishes	62
With Resident Pastor:	
Resident Diocesan Priests	41
Resident Religious Priests	9
Without Resident Pastor:	
Administered by Priests	10
Administered by Deacons	2
Missions	38
Professional Ministry Personnel:	
Brothers	1
Sisters	4
Lay Ministers	35
Welfare	
Catholic Hospitals	4
Total Assisted	208,350
Homes for the Aged	4
Total Assisted	495
Specialized Homes	1
Total Assisted	169
Other Institutions	1
Total Assisted	8
Educational	
Diocesan Students in Other Seminaries	13
Students Religious	1
Total Seminarians	14
Colleges and Universities	1
Total Students	2,343
High Schools, Diocesan and Parish	3
Total Students	1,143
Elementary Schools, Diocesan and Parish	12
Total Students	1,656
Catechesis/Religious Education:	
High School Students	3,260
Elementary Students	7,320
Total Students Under Catholic Instruction	15,736
Teachers in the Diocese:	
Priests	5
Sisters	7
Lay Teachers	163
Vital Statistics	
Receptions into the Church:	
Infant Baptism Totals	1,047
Adult Baptism Totals	145
Received into Full Communion	147
First Communions	1,190
Confirmations	1,325
Marriages:	
Catholic	306
Interfaith	208
Total Marriages	514
Deaths	685
Total Catholic Population	68,484
Total Population	254,426

Former Bishops—Most Rev. VINCENT DE PAUL WEHRLE, O.S.B., D.D., appt. Bishop of Bismarck, April 9, 1910; cons. May 19, 1910; retired Dec. 11, 1939; named Titular Bishop of Teos by Pope Pius XII; died Nov. 2, 1941.—Most Rev. VINCENT J. RYAN, D.D., LL.D., appt. March 19, 1940; cons. May 28, 1940; died Nov. 10, 1951.—Most Rev. LAMBERT A. HOCH, D.D., L.L.D., appt. Jan. 23, 1952; cons. March 25, 1952; transferred to Diocese of Sioux Falls, Dec. 5, 1956; died June 27, 1990.—Most Rev. HILARY B. HACKER, D.D., appt. Bishop, Dec. 29, 1956; retired June 28, 1982; died Nov. 6, 1990.—Most Rev. JOHN F. KINNEY, D.D., J.C.D., appt. June 28, 1982; Episcopal Ord. Jan. 25, 1977; installed Aug. 23, 1982; transferred to Diocese of St. Cloud, July 6, 1995.

Vicar General—Rev. THOMAS E. KRAMER.

Chancery Office—420 Raymond St., Box 1575, Bismarck, 58502-1575. Tel: 701-223-1347; Fax: 701-223-3693.

Chancellor—Sr. JOANNE GRAHAM, O.S.B., J.C.L.

Center for Pastoral Ministry Office—520 N. Washington St., P.O. Box 1137, Bismarck, 58502-1137. Tel: 701-222-3035.

Diocesan Tribunal—520 N. Washington St., P.O. Box 1137, Bismarck, 58502-1137. Tel: 701-222-3035.

Judicial Vicar—Rev. GENE E. LINDEMANN, J.C.L.

Defensor Vinculi—Revs. LEONARD A. ECKROTH; DAVID L. ZIMMER, J.C.L.

Pro-Synodal Judges—Revs. PHILLIP BROWN, J.C.D.; GEORGE A. DUKART; MARVIN J. KLEMMER; BRUCE D. KREBS; THOMAS E. KRAMER; MICHAEL T. KRANK; ALBERT R. LEARY; EDWIN P. WEHNER; GERALD RUELLE, O.S.B.; Rev. Msgr. GERALD J. WALSH.

Procurator / Advocates—RUTH MOERICKE.

Notary—HELEN GOLDADE.

Presbyteral Council—Revs. THOMAS E. KRAMER, Chm. DAVID ZIMMER; BRUCE D. KREBS; THOMAS J. RICHTER, Sec. CHRIS B. WALTER; C. ROBERT KAVANEY; AUSTIN VETTER, Vice Chm.; Rt. Rev. PATRICK MOORE, O.S.B.

Diocesan Corporate Board—Most Rev. PAUL A. ZIPFEL, Pres.; Revs. THOMAS E. KRAMER, Vice Pres. PAUL D. BECKER; JAMES B. BRAATEN; Sr. JOANNE GRAHAM, O.S.B., J.C.L., Sec.

Diocesan Finance Council—Most Rev. PAUL A. ZIPFEL; Revs. THOMAS E. KRAMER, Chm. JAMES B. BRAATEN; PAUL D. BECKER; Mr. RICHARD F. WHITE; ERNEST B. BORR; MIKE SCHWINDT; MARVIN HEINERT; JEFFRY TESCHER; Sr. JOANNE GRAHAM, O.S.B., J.C.L.; RON SCHATZ.

Diocesan Offices and Directors

Archives—KENNETH SMALL, *Box 1137, Bismarck, 58502-1137.* Tel: 701-222-3035.

Boy Scouts—KEN ROETHLER, Chm., *1210 N. 18th St., Bismarck, 58501.*

Campaign For Human Development—Sr. JOANNE GRAHAM, O.S.B., J.C.L., Dir., *P.O. Box 1575, Bismarck, 58502-1575.* Tel: 701-223-1347.

Catholic Family Service—PAUL GRIFFIN, Exec. Dir., *2537 University Dr. S., Fargo, 58103.* Tel: 701-235-4457., Other Locations: *1223 S. 12th, Bismarck, 58504.* Tel: 701-255-1793., *400-22nd Ave., N.W., Minot, 58703.* Tel: 701-852-2854.

Catholic Relief—Sr. JOANNE GRAHAM, O.S.B., J.C.L., Dir., *P.O. Box 1575, Bismarck, 58502-1575.* Tel: 701-223-1347.

Office of Vocations—Rev. DENNIS SCHAFER, Dir., *P.O. Box 1137, Bismarck, 58502-1137.* Tel: 701-222-3035.

Vicar for Presbyters—Rev. MARVIN J. KLEMMER, *P.O. Box 1137, Bismarck, 58502-1137.* Tel: 701-222-3035.

Office of Worship—Vacant, *P.O. Box 1137, Bismarck, 58501.* Tel: 701-222-3035.

Continuing Education for Clergy—Rev. JOHN G. GUTHRIE, *P.O. Box K, Williston, 58802-1115.* Tel: 701-572-2116.

Ecumenism—Rev. MARVIN J. KLEMMER, *1902 S. Third St., Bismarck, 58504.* Tel: 701-223-3606.

Holy Childhood—Sr. JOANNE GRAHAM, O.S.B., J.C.L., Dir., *P.O. Box 1575, Bismarck, 58502-1575.* Tel: 701-223-1347.

Newspaper—"Dakota Catholic Action", MARGE GROSZ, Editor, *P.O. Box 1137, Bismarck, 58502-1137.* Tel: 701-222-3035.

North Dakota Catholic Conference—CHRISTOPHER DODSON, *227 W. Broadway, Ste. 2, Bismarck, 58501.* Tel: 701-223-2519; Fax: 701-223-6075.

Permanent Diaconate Office—

Vicar for Deacons—Rev. AUSTIN VETTER.

Director of Deacons—Deacon STEPHEN B. MAYS.

Director of Formation Program—Deacon ALVIN W. SCHWINDT, *P.O. Box 1137, Bismarck, 58502-1137.* Tel: 701-222-3035.

Priests' Benefit Association—Most Rev. PAUL A. ZIPFEL, Pres.; Revs. WILLIAM J. FAHNLANDER; JAMES B. BRAATEN, Chm. DAVID MORMAN; C. ROBERT KAVANEY; PHILLIP BROWN; EDWIN P. WEHNER.

Priests' Personnel Board—Revs. ALBERT R. LEARY, Chm.

PATRICK A. SCHUMACHER; DENNIS R. SCHAFER; MARVIN J. KLEMMER, Ex Officio; JEFFREY A. ZWACK; GENE E. LINDEMANN, Vice Chm.

Propagation of the Faith—Sr. JOANNE GRAHAM, O.S.B., J.C.L., *P.O. Box 1575, Bismarck, 58502-1575.* Tel: 701-223-1347.

Communications Office—Deacon ROBERT P. SCHULLER, Dir., *P.O. Box 1137, Bismarck, 58502-1137.* Tel: 701-222-3035; Fax: 701-221-9795.

Office of Catechesis—Sr. KATHLEEN ATKINSON, O.S.B., *Box 1137, Bismarck, 58502-1137.* Tel: 701-222-3035.

Pro-Life—MARGE GROSZ, Dir., *P.O. Box 1137, Bismarck, 58502-1137.* Tel: 701-222-3035; Fax: 701-673-3178.

Office of Education—ROMAN WEILER, Dir., *P.O. Box 1137, Bismarck, 58502-1137.* Tel: 701-222-3035.

Social Concerns—ANNETTA SUTTON, Dir., *Box 1137, Bismarck, 58502-1137.* Tel: 701-222-3035.

Stewardship and Resource Development Office—RONALD SCHATZ, Dir., *Box 1137, Bismarck, 58502-1137.* Tel: 701-222-3035.

Directors for Office of Religious—Rev. DANIEL MALONEY, O.S.B., *Annunciation Priory, 7520 University Dr., Bismarck, 58504-9653.* Tel: 701-255-1520. Sr. JOANNE GRAHAM, O.S.B., J.C.L., *P.O. Box 1575, Bismarck, 58502-1575.* Tel: 701-223-1347.

Youth Ministry—KENNETH H. ROSHAU, Dir., *Box 1137, Bismarck, 58502-1137.* Tel: 701-222-3035.

Search Program—KENNETH H. ROSHAU, *Box 1137, Bismarck, 58502-1137.* Tel: 701-222-3035.

CLERGY, PARISHES, MISSIONS AND PAROCHIAL SCHOOLS

CITY OF BISMARCK
(Burleigh County)

1—CATHEDRAL OF THE HOLY SPIRIT (1947), Revs. Thomas E. Kramer; David A. Richter; Deacons Wilfred Wolf; Ralph von Reuden; Richard Fettig.
Res., 519 Raymond St., 58501. Tel: 701-223-1033; Fax: 701-223-1438. [JC]
School—Tel: 701-223-5484; Fax: 701-223-5485. Elizabeth Gross, Prin.
Sisters of St. Benedict 2; Lay Teachers 17; Students 282.
Catechesis/Religious Programs—Tel: 701-222-2259. Marie Gabel, D.R.E.
Students 306.

2—ASCENSION (1974), Rev. Marvin J. Klemmer; Deacons Steve Brannan; John Lamontagne; Ray Grabar; Al Schwindt.
Res., 1905 S. Third St., 58504-7118. Tel: 701-223-3606; Fax: 701-223-5783. [JC]
Catechesis/Religious Programs—Tel: 701-258-5692. Cheryle Gagner, D.R.E.
Students 735.

3—CORPUS CHRISTI (1964), Rev. Stephen R. Zastoupil; Sr. Ivo Schoch, Pastoral Assoc.; Deacons Lynn Clancy; Harry M. Deichert; Joseph J. Mathern; Rex McDowell; Robert Schuller; John Tharaldsen; Leonard Baenen, Admin.
Res., 1936 N. Second St., 58501. Tel: 701-255-4620; Fax: 701-255-4616. [JC]
Catechesis/Religious Programs—Tel: 701-255-3104. D.R.E.: Patricia Clark; Mary Kay Vetter; Patrick Hall.
Students 706.

4—ST. ANNE (1957), Rev. Edwin P. Wehner; Betty E. Greff, Pastoral Assoc.; Edward Hartwig, Parish Admin.; Deacons Alvin Schmitz; Ed Wesolowski; Wayne Jundt; Joe Krupinsky.
Res., 1321 Braman Ave., 58501. Tel: 701-223-1549; Fax: 701-250-9214. [JC]
School—(Grades PreK-8). Tel: 701-223-3373. Mrs. Darlene Reinarts, Prin.
Lay Teachers 15; Students 200.
Catechesis/Religious Programs—Tel: 701-224-0847. Mrs. Frances I. Roehrich, D.R.E.
Students 400.

5—ST. MARY (1877), Rev. Charles A. Heidt; Steve Braus, Admin.; Deacons Tony Dworshak; Kenneth Klein. Pastoral Ministers: Sr. Kristi Gray; Sr. Colette Wolfe, O.S.B.; Liz Braus; Audrey Uhrich.
Res., 806 E. Broadway, 58501. Tel: 701-223-5562; Fax: 701-530-0864. [JC]
School—Tel: 701-223-0225; Fax: 701-250-9918. Gwyn Marback-Tschosik, Prin.
Lay Teachers 15; Students 179.
Catechesis/Religious Programs—Students 164.

OUTSIDE THE CITY OF BISMARCK

Beach, Golden Valley Co., St. John the Baptist (1909), Rev. David G. Morman; Deacons Samuel Larson; Donald Nistler; James Wosepka.
Res., Box 337, 58621. Tel: 701-872-4153; Fax: 701-872-4695. [CEM 2]
Catechesis/Religious Programs—D.R.E.: Karen Wojahn; Swenda Braden.
Students 184.
Mission—Golva, Golden Valley Co., St. Mary, P.O. Box 337, 58621. [CEM 2]

Belfield, Stark Co., St. Bernard (1910), Rev. Thomas J. Richter.
Res., P.O. Box 38, 58622. Tel: 701-575-4295. [CEM]
Catechesis/Religious Programs—Tel: 701-575-4099. Diane Procive, (High School).
Students 157.
Mission—Medora, Billings Co., St. Mary, Box 356, Medora, 58645. Tel: 701-623-4817.

Beulah, Mercer Co., St. Joseph (1915) (German-Russian), Rev. Charles Zins.
Res., P.O. Box 146, 58523. Tel: 701-873-5397; Fax: 701-873-5614. [CEM]
Catechesis/Religious Programs—Tel: 701-873-5006; 873-5622. Julie Knodel, D.R.E.
Students 248.

Bowbells, Burke Co., St. Joseph (1905) (German-Scandinavian), Rev. Berchmans Konnully (India); Deacon Edmund Morgel.
Res., P.O. Box 339, 58721. Tel: 701-377-2611.
Catechesis/Religious Programs—Tel: 701-377-2766. D.R.E.: Clarice Corey; Mary Hawbaker.
Students 19.
Mission—Portal, Burke Co., St. John the Baptist, P.O. Box 31, Portal, 58772. Tel: 701-926-4621. [CEM]

Bowman, Bowman Co., St. Charles (1910), Rev. Jeffrey Zwack.
Res., 58623. Tel: 701-523-5292. [CEM][JC 2]
Catechesis/Religious Programs—Tel: 701-523-5415. Kari Janvrin, D.R.E. (Grades 1-12).
Students 132.
Missions—Rhame, Bowman Co., St. Mel, P.O. Box 709, 58623. Tel: 701-523-5292; Marmarth, Slope Co., Immaculate Heart of Mary, P.O. Box 709, 58623.

Burlington, Ward Co., St. Francis of Assisi. Closed. For inquiries for parish records contact the Chancery. (Quasi-Parish).

Carson, Grant Co., St. Theresa the Child Jesus (1920), Rev. Gary Benz.
Res., 421 Court St., Flasher, 58535-7216. Tel: 701-597-3570; 597-3228. [JC]
Catechesis/Religious Programs—Tel: 701-597-3228.
Students 49.

Center, Mercer Co., St. Martin (1914), Rev. Roger A. Synek.
Res., P.O. Box 2766, 58530. Tel: 701-794-3329; Fax: 701-794-3601. [CEM][JC 2]
Catechesis/Religious Programs—Tel: 701-794-3191. D.R.E.: Judith McNulty; Alice Henderscheid.
Students 110.
Mission—Washburn, Mercer Co., St. Edwin.

Crosby, Divide Co., St. Patrick (1912), Rev. Norman J. Dukart.
Res., P.O. Box 89, 58730. Tel: 701-965-6537. [CEM 3][JC 2]
Catechesis/Religious Programs—Students 59.
Mission—Noonan, Divide Co., St. Luke, 304 Main St., Noonan, 58765.

Crown Butte, Morton Co., St. Vincent (1896), Deacon Robert Olson; Loretta Olson, Pastoral Assoc. & D.R.E.
Mailing Address: 3180 36th St., Mandan, 58554.
Res., 1703 1/2 N.E. Second, Mandan, 58554. Tel: 701-663-2544. [CEM]
Catechesis/Religious Programs—Students 14.

Dickinson, Stark Co.,

1—QUEEN OF PEACE CHURCH, (1973), Rev. James W. Ryan.
Office: 725 12th St. W., 58601-3516. Tel: 701-483-2134; 483-2991 (Res.). [JC]
Catechesis/Religious Programs—Tel: 701-483-9894. Dickie Jo Boespflug, D.R.E.
Students 249.

2—ST. JOSEPH, (1902) (German-Russian), Rev. Kenneth Phillips; Deacon Ralph Stockert.
Res., 240 E. Broadway, 58601. Tel: 701-225-2222.
School—Tel: 701-225-6162.
Sisters 1; Lay Teachers 7; Students 78.
Catechesis/Religious Programs—Marlene Reisenauer, D.R.E.
Students 218.

3—ST. PATRICK, (1885), Revs. Austin Vetter; Claude Seeberger, O.S.B.; Deacons Joe Kappel; Anton Wanner.
Res., 229 Third Ave. W., 58601. Tel: 701-483-6700; Fax: 701-483-6702.
School—St. Patrick Queen of Peace, 145 Third Ave. West, 58601. Tel: 701-225-8094; Fax: 701-225-5325. Patricia Hardy, Prin.
Lay Teachers 10; Students 165.
Catechesis/Religious Programs—Tel: 701-225-8831. Mary Agostini, D.R.E.
Students 112.

4—ST. PIUS. Closed. For inquiries for parish records contact the Chancery.

5—ST. WENCESLAUS, (1912) (Bohemian), Revs. Phillip Brown; Christopher J. Kadrmas; Deacons Eugene F. Morman; Raymond Jilek.
Res., 525 Third St. E., 58601. Tel: 701-225-3972; Fax: 701-225-0474. [JC]
School—Tel: 701-225-9463. Sr. Dorothy Zeller, S.S.N.D., Prin.
Lay Teachers 9; Students 158.
Catechesis/Religious Programs—Tel: 701-225-3972. Gini Zent, D.R.E.
Students 266.
Mission—New Hradec, Dunn Co., SS. Peter and Paul.

Flasher, Morton Co., St. Lawrence (1912), Rev. Gary Benz.
Res., 421 Court St., 58535-7216. Tel: 701-597-3570. [CEM]
Catechesis/Religious Programs—Tel: 701-597-3228.
Students 99.

Fort Yates, Sioux Co., St. Peter - Catholic Indian Mission (1878) (Native American). (Standing Rock Indian Reservation). Revs. Casimir A. Paluck; Terrance R. Wipf.
Res., P.O. Box 394, 58538. Tel: 701-854-3473; Fax: 701-854-3474. [CEM]
School—St. Bernard Mission School, Tel: 701-854-7413. Sr. Julie Brandt, S.S.N.D., Prin.
Sisters 2; Lay Teachers 4; Students 71.
Catechesis/Religious Programs—Tel: 701-854-3447. Sr. Frances M. Voigt, D.R.E.
Students 21.
Missions—Cannon Ball, Sioux Co., St. Elizabeth, P.O. Box 394, 58538. Tel: 701-854-3474. [CEM]
Porcupine, Sioux Co., St. James, P.O. Box 394, Porcupine, 58538. [CEM]

Foxholm, Ward Co., St. Mary, Rev. Paul D. Becker.
Res., 17901 128th Ave. N.W., 58718-9643. Tel: 701-852-8575. [JC]
Catechesis/Religious Programs—Tel: 701-468-5648.
Students 38.
Mission—Berthold, Ward Co., St. Ann, Berthold, 58718. Tel: 701-453-3660.

Garrison, McLean Co., St. Nicholas (1905), Rev. Hugo L. Blotsky, O.S.B.
Res., 235 Second St. N.E., P.O. Box 870, 58540. Tel: 701-463-2327; Fax: 701-463-2323. [JC 8]
Catechesis/Religious Programs—Tel: 701-463-2197. Kim Rensch, D.R.E.
Students 202.
Missions—Max, McClean Co., Immaculate Conception; Garrison, St. Nicholas, White Shield, Sacred Heart, 58540.

Glenburn, Renville Co., St. Philomena (1948) (German-Scandinavian), Rev. Jacob Konath.
Res., 302 Raymond St., Box 68, 58740. Tel: 701-362-7571; Fax: 701-362-7571. [CEM]
Catechesis/Religious Programs—1627 - 76th St., North Deering, 58731. Tel: 701-362-7367; 362-7419. Darla Johnson, D.R.E.
Students 28.
Mission—Lansford, Bottineau Co., St. John, Rte. 2, Box 3, Lansford, 58750. Tel: 701-784-5421.

Glen Ullin, Morton Co., Sacred Heart of Jesus (1883) (German-Russian), Rev. Sebastian Schmidt, O.S.B.
Res., Box 609, 58631. Tel: 701-348-3518. [CEM 2]
Catechesis/Religious Programs—Tel: 701-348-3527. Mrs. Kathy Schirado, D.R.E.
Students 141.
Mission—Glen Ullin, Grant Co., St. Joseph, 58631-0609.

Grenora, Williams Co., St. Boniface (1912), Rev. Raymond A. Aydt.
Church—P.O. Box 37, 58845. Tel: 701-694-3743.
Res., 118 Fifth St. W., Williston, 58801. Tel: 701-572-6732. [CEM 2][JC]
Catechesis/Religious Programs—Peggy Degele, D.R.E.
Students 11.

Hague, Emmons Co., St. Mary (1890) (German-Russian), Rev. Leonard A. Eckroth.
Church—P.O. Box 156, 58542. Tel: 701-336-7119.
Res., Box 322, Strasburg, 58573. Tel: 701-336-2603; 336-7172. [CEM 2]
Catechesis/Religious Programs—Tel: 701-336-7102. Kathleen J. Dosch, D.R.E.
Students 35.

Halliday, Dunn Co., St. Paul (1952). (Quasi-Parish). Rev. Gerald Ruelle, O.S.B.
Res., P.O. Box 299, Killdeer, 58640. Tel: 701-764-5357. [CEM][JC]
Catechesis/Religious Programs—Tel: 701-938-4504. Vickie Clarys, D.R.E.
Students 51.

Hazelton, Emmons Co., St. Paul (1905), Revs. Bruce Krebs; Frank J. Schuster, Jr.; Deacon Kenneth Wolbaum.
Res., 372 Harold St., 58544. Tel: 701-254-4588.
Catechesis/Religious Programs—Tel: 701-782-6281. Charlotte Beastrom, D.R.E.
Students 62.
Mission—Braddock, Emmons Co., St. Katherine, 613 N. Broadway, Linton, 58552-7311. [CEM 2]

Hazen, Mercer Co., St. Martin (1914), Rev. Charles Zins.
P.O. Box 387, 58545.
Res., P.O. Box 146, Beulah, 58523. [CEM]
Catechesis/Religious Programs—Tel: 701-748-2121. D.R.E.: Peg Rahn; LuAnn Woeste.
Students 198.

Hebron, Morton Co., St. Ann (1906) (German), Rev. Francis dos Remedios, O.S.B.
Res., P.O. Box 12, 58638. Tel: 701-878-4658. [CEM 3]
Catechesis/Religious Programs—Tel: 701-878-4972. Jean Wanner, D.R.E.
Students 86.
Mission—Haymarsh, Morton Co., St. Clement, P.O. Box 12, 58638.

Hettinger, Adams Co., Holy Trinity (1916) (German), Rev. John Mathai.
Res., 405 3rd St. N., 58639. Tel: 701-567-2772; Fax: 701-567-2772. [CEM][JC]
Catechesis/Religious Programs—Tel: 701-567-2766. Grace Meier, D.R.E.
Students 157.
Missions—Reeder, Adams Co., Sacred Heart, 405-3rd St. N., 58639. Tel: 701-853-2920; Scranton, Bowman Co., Sacred Heart, 405-3rd St. N., 58639. Tel: 701-275-8778.

Kenmare, Ward Co., St. Agnes (1901), Rev. Kenneth Wald.
Res., P.O. Box 488, 58746. Tel: 701-385-4311. [CEM]
Catechesis/Religious Programs—Tel: 701-386-2403. Evan and Deb Zeltinger, D.R.E.
Students 98.
Mission—Donnybrook, Ward Co., St. Anthony, 58734. [CEM]

Killdeer, Dunn Co., St. Joseph (1917), Rev. Gerald Ruelle, O.S.B.; Deacons Edward J. Ziman; Herman Dukart.
Res., P.O. Box 299, 58640. Tel: 701-764-5357. [CEM][JC 2]
Catechesis/Religious Programs—Tel: 701-548-8068. Candice Benz, D.R.E.
Students 138.

Lefor, Stark Co., St. Elizabeth (1898), Rev. Lawrence L. Wagner, O.S.B.
Res., 18401 168th Ave. S.E., 58641-5010. Tel: 701-483-3376. [CEM][JC 3]
Catechesis/Religious Programs—Rev. Lawrence L. Wagner, O.S.B., D.R.E.
Students 39.
Mission—Gladstone, Stark Co., St. Thomas the Apostle, 309 Cliff, Gladstone, 58630.

Linton, Emmons Co., St. Anthony (1909), Revs. Bruce Krebs; Frank J. Schuster, Jr.; Deacon Martin Schumacher.
Res., 613 N. Broadway, 58552-7311. Tel: 701-254-4588. [CEM]
Catechesis/Religious Programs—Tel: 701-254-4646; Fax: 701-254-4646. LuAnn Hanson, D.R.E.
Students 275.

Mandan, Morton Co., Christ the King (1957), Revs. Albert R. Leary; Daniel J. Berg; Deacons Ward Johnson; Emil Riehl.
Res., 505-10th Ave., N.W., 58554-2599. Tel: 701-663-8842; Fax: 701-667-1730. [CEM]
School—Tel: 701-663-6200; Fax: 701-667-1730. Rev. Albert R. Leary, Supt.
Lay Teachers 13; Students 126.
Catechesis/Religious Programs—Julie Schatz, D.R.E.
Students 167.
Missions—Huff, Morton Co., St. Martin; St. Anthony, Morton Co., St. Anthony.

St. Joseph (1881), Rev. Patrick A. Schumacher, S.T.L.; Deacons Peter Hoffman; Larry Dorrheim.
Res., 108 Third St. N.E., P.O. Box 603, 58554. Tel: 701-663-9562; Fax: 701-663-6522. [CEM]
School—(Grades K-6). Tel: 701-663-9563.
Lay Teachers 10; Students 117.
Catechesis/Religious Programs—D.R.E.: Al Shreve, (Grades K-8); Randy Frohlich, (Confirmation Dir.).
Students 159.

Spirit of Life (1978), Rev. Cyprian T. Meier; Deacon David Vaughn.
Mailing Address: Box 247, 58554.
Res., 801 First St. S.E., 58554. Tel: 701-663-1660; Fax: 701-667-2021.
Catechesis/Religious Programs—Jim Fritzhuspen, D.R.E.
Students 477.

Mandaree, Dunn Co., St. Anthony (Native American), Rev. Stephen Kranz, O.S.B.
Res., Fr. Berthold Reservation, 9385 BIA Rte. 12, 58757-9269. Tel: 701-759-3412; Fax: 701-759-3412 (Call first). [CEM]
Catechesis/Religious Programs—Students 196.
Mission—Twin Buttes, Dunn Co., St. Joseph, 58757.

Menoken, Burleigh Co., St. Hildegard (1949), Rev. George A. Dukart.
Res., 17200 Hwy. 10, 58558-9604. Tel: 701-673-3177; Fax: 701-673-3178. [JC]
Catechesis/Religious Programs—Tel: 701-673-3452. Janice Aberle, D.R.E.
Students 55.

Minot, Ward Co.,

1—Minot Air Force Base Chapel, (1954), Rev. Peter S. Lambert.
Res., 5 BW/HC, 230 Missile Ave., 58505-5003. Tel: 701-723-2456; Fax: 701-723-3052.
Catechesis/Religious Programs—Students 219.

2—Our Lady of Grace, (1959), Rev. Gene E. Lindemann, J.C.L.
Res., 715 16th Ave., S.W., 58701. Tel: 701-839-6834;852-3002; Fax: 701-837-1080.
Catechesis/Religious Programs—D.R.E.: Darlene Demars, (Grades K-5); Bev Cushing, (Grades 6-12).
Students 407.

3—St. John the Apostle, (1961), Rev. Henry W. Schneider; Deacons M. Stephen Mays; Charles Kramer.
Res., 109-25th St. N.W., 58703-2862. Tel: 701-839-7076. [JC]
Catechesis/Religious Programs—Tel: 701-838-0769. Carol Mays, D.R.E.
Students 245.

4—St. Leo, (1886) (German), Revs. Chris B. Walter; Keith N. Streifel.
Res., 305 First St. S.E., 58701. Tel: 701-838-1026; Fax: 701-852-4683. [CEM]
Catechesis/Religious Programs—Tel: 701-838-1026. Rosie Workman, D.R.E.
Students 363.

5—St. Theresa, the Little Flower, (1954), Rev. Paul L. Cervinski; Deacon Pat Cunningham.
Res., 800 University Ave. W., 58703. Tel: 701-838-1520; Fax: 701-838-1520. [JC]
School—See separate listing under Institutions Located in the Diocese. Tel: 701-839-5882.
Catechesis/Religious Programs—Tel: 701-839-8567. Becky O'Shea, D.R.E.
Students 127.

Mohall, Renville Co., St. Jerome (1906), Rev. James B. Braaten.
P.O. Box 457, 58761.
Res., 303 E. Main St., 58761. Tel: 701-756-6601. [CEM]
Catechesis/Religious Programs—Students 85.
Mission—Sherwood, Renville Co., St. James, Mohall, 58761. Tel: 701-756-6601.

Mott, Hettinger Co., St. Vincent de Paul (1907), Rev. Kuriakose Nediakala, M.C.B.S.; Deacon Ervin Schneider.
Res., 408 Iowa Ave., 58646. Tel: 701-824-2651; Fax: 701-824-2651. [CEM]
Catechesis/Religious Programs—Maureen Kautzman, D.R.E.
Students 121.
Mission—New Leipzig, Grant Co., St. John the Baptist, New Leipzig, 58562.

New England, Hettinger Co., St. Mary (1910), Rev. William P. Cosgrove.
Res., 437 Main St., P.O. Box 369, 58647. Tel: 701-579-4312; Fax: 701-579-4874.
Catechesis/Religious Programs—Lynn Dvorak, D.R.E.
Students 109.
Mission—Regent, Hettinger Co., St. Henry's, P.O. Box 155, Regent, 58650. Tel: 701-563-4595. [CEM]

New Salem, Morton Co., St. Pius V (1912), Rev. David L. Zimmer.
Res., P.O. Box C, 58563. Tel: 701-843-7144. [CEM]
Catechesis/Religious Programs—Tel: 701-843-7061. D.R.E.: Mary Kreidt; Sharon Wetzel.
Students 168.
Mission—Almont, Morton Co., St. Mary, Queen of Peace, Almont, 58520.

New Town, Mountrail Co., St. Anthony (1954) (Native American), Rev. C. R. Kavaney; Deacon Daniel Barone.
Res., P.O. Box 715, 58763. Tel: 701-627-4423. [CEM 4][JC]
Catechesis/Religious Programs—Tel: 701-627-3420; Fax: 701-627-3297. D.R.E.: Nancy Carda; Julie Herbal.
Students 57.

Parshall, Mountrail Co., St. Bridget (1917) (German-Norwegian), Rev. Leonard Savelkoul.
Res., 12 First St., N.E., Box 519, 58770-0519. Tel: 701-862-3484. [CEM 4][JC 3]
Catechesis/Religious Programs—Claudia Schneider, D.R.E.
Students 32.
Missions—Plaza, Mountrail Co., Sacred Heart, 58770-0519.; Makoti, Ward Co., St. Elizabeth, 58770-0519.

Raleigh, Grant Co., St. Gertrude (1913), Rev. Gary Benz.
Res., 421 Court St., Flasher, 58535-7216. Tel: 701-597-3570. [CEM]
Catechesis/Religious Programs—Tel: 701-597-3228.
Students 32.

Regent, Hettinger Co., St. Henry (1913), Rev. William P. Cosgrove.
Res., P.O. Box 155, 58650-0155. Tel: 701-563-4595. [JC]
Catechesis/Religious Programs—Tel: 701-563-4543. Karen Kouba, D.R.E.
Students 57.

Richardton, Stark Co., St. Mary (1895), Rev. Brian Wangler, O.S.B.
Res., P.O. Box A, 58652. Tel: 701-974-3569. [CEM]
Catechesis/Religious Programs—Dennise Miller, D.R.E. (Grades K-11).
Students 144.
Mission—Richardton, Stark Co., St. Stephen, Box A, 58652. Tel: 701-974-3332.

St. Anthony, Morton Co., St. Anthony (1897) (German-Russian), Rev. Dennis R. Schafer.
Res., P.O. Box 45, 58566. Tel: 701-445-7373. [CEM]
Catechesis/Religious Programs—Students 36.
Mission—Huff, Morton Co., St. Martin, 58566-0045. Tel: 701-445-7373.

St. Michael, Emmons Co., St. Michael's. Closed. For inquiries for parish records contact the Chancery.

Selfridge, Sioux Co., St. Philomena (1919) (German-Russian), Revs. Casimir A. Paluck; Terrance R. Wipf.
Res., P.O. Box 394, Fort Yates, 58538. Tel: 701-854-3473; Fax: 701-854-3474. [CEM]
Catechesis/Religious Programs—Sr. Frances Marie Voigt, D.R.E.
Students 28.
Mission—Fort Yates, Sioux Co., Sacred Heart, Box 394, Fort Yates, 58538.

South Heart, Stark Co., St. Mary (1923), Rev. Thomas J. Richter.
Res., P.O. Box 189, 58655. Tel: 701-677-5886; Fax: 701-677-5886. [CEM]
Catechesis/Religious Programs—Students 103.

Stanley, Mountrail Co., Queen of the Most Holy Rosary (1908), Rev. Wayne Sattler.
Res., P.O. Box 159, 58784. Tel: 701-628-2323. [JC]
Catechesis/Religious Programs—Karen Fritel, D.R.E.
Students 78.
Mission—Powers Lake, Burke Co., St. James, 8334 Hwy. 50, Powers Lake, 58773. Tel: 701-464-5771. [CEM][JC]

Strasburg, Emmons Co., Sts. Peter and Paul (1889) (German-Russian), Rev. Leonard A. Eckroth.
Res., Box 322, 58573. Tel: 701-336-2603; 336-7172. [CEM]
Catechesis/Religious Programs—Tel: 701-336-4607. Kathleen J. Dosch, D.R.E.
Students 125.

Tioga, Williams Co., St. Thomas (1914), Rev. Johnson Kuriappilly (India).
Res., P.O. Box 667, 58852. Tel: 701-664-2445. [CEM][JC]
Catechesis/Religious Programs—Students 71.
Mission—Ray, Williams Co., St. Michael, Ray, 58849. Tel: 701-568-2252.

Underwood, McLean Co., St. Bonaventure (1913), Rev. Ed Korte.
Res., P.O. Box 700, 58576. Tel: 701-442-5229.
Catechesis/Religious Programs—Tel: 701-442-3412.
Students 81.
Mission—Turtle Lake, McLean Co., St. Catherine, Main St., Turtle Lake, 58575. Tel: 701-488-9289. [CEM][JC]

Watford City, McKenzie Co., Epiphany (1915), Rev. John M. Pfeifer.
Res., 112 6th Ave. N.E., P.O. Box 670, 58854. Tel: 701-842-3505.
Catechesis/Religious Programs—Tel: 701-842-3791; 842-2483. Carol Garman, D.R.E.
Students 114.

Missions—Alexander, McKenzie Co., Our Lady of Consolation, R.R. 1, Box 58, Alexander, 58831. Tel: 701-586-3720; Grassy Butte, McKenzie Co., St. Peter Canisius, HCO2, Box 27, Grassy Butte, 58634. Tel: 701-863-6759.

Williston, Williams Co., St. Joseph (1901), Revs. John G. Guthrie; Frederick R. Harvey, Jr.
Res., 124 Sixth St. W., P.O. Box K, 58802. Tel: 701-572-6731; Fax: 701-572-4203. [JC]
School—Tel: 701-572-6384; Fax: 701-774-0998. Debbie Johnson, Prin.
Lay Teachers 13; Students 109.
Catechesis/Religious Programs—Tel: 701-572-0201. Ida Kirchmeier, D.R.E.
Students 400.
Mission—Trenton, Williams Co., St. John the Baptist, P.O. Box K, 58802. Tel: 701-572-6731; Fax: 701-572-0987.

Wilton, McLean Co., Sacred Heart (1908), Deacon James Nistler.
Res., P.O. Box 128, 58579. Tel: 701-734-6384; Fax: 701-734-6377. [CEM][JC]
Catechesis/Religious Programs—Tel: 701-734-8136; 734-6377. Debbie Smith, D.R.E.
Students 38.

Chaplains of Public Institutions

BISMARCK. *North Dakota State Penitentiary* 2905 Winnipeg Dr., 58501. Tel: 701-258-7566. Deacon John Tharaldsen.
North Dakota Youth Correctional Center 1045 Tacoma Ave., Apt. 113, 58504-7462. Tel: 701-667-1400. Steve Brannan; Nancy Brannan.

On Duty Outside the Diocese:
Reverend Fathers—
Allen, Joseph A., 14207-63rd St., N.E., Grafton, ND 58237
Deichert, Joseph, PSC 41-Box 138, APO AE, 09464
Hill, Donald, Chap., Army National Guard, 807 N. Howard St., #114, Alexandria, VA 22304
Kuss, Allen R., Office of the Chaplain, 10 Fabbri Green, Suite 715, Winter Harbor, ME 04693

Retired:
Reverend Monsignors—
Walsh, Gerald J., 3037 W. Avenida Destino, Tucson, AZ 85746-8268
Reverend Fathers—
Backes, Hugo G., 1050 N. 28th St., Bismarck, ND 58501-3193
Bova, Eugene R., 360 Pinon Rd., Bailey, CO 80421
Cook, Blaine, 1021 N. 26th St., Bismarck, ND 58501
Fahnlander, William J., Emmaus Place, 1020 N. 26th St., Bismarck, ND 58501
Frank, Eugene G., St. Benedict's Health Center, 851 4th Ave. E., Dickinson, ND 58601
Gustin, Theodore F., Emmaus Place, 1020 N. 26th St., Bismarck, ND 58501
Krank, Michael T., P.O. Box 745, Dickinson, ND 58602
Kuhn, John H., 1020 N. 26th St., Bismarck, ND 58501
O'Leary, John P., 1006 N. 28th St. #314, Bismarck, ND 58501
Owens, John J., 520 N. Washington St., P.O. Box 1137, Bismarck, ND 58502-1137
Rushford, William A., 1020 N. 26th St., Bismarck, ND 58501
Schumacher, Jacob J., Emmaus Place, 1020 N. 26th St., Bismarck, ND 58501
Spain, P. Arnold, 2881 B Warwick Loop, Bismarck, ND 58504
Sullivan, Thomas, 1555 118th Lane, N.W., Apt. 221, Coon Rapids, MN 55418-7503

Permanent Deacons:
Barone, Daniel, St. Anthony, New Town
Berg, Melvin J., (Retired)
Brannan, Steve M., Ascension, Bismarck
Bunce, Donald A., St. Leo, Minot
Clancy, Lynn, Corpus Christi, Bismarck
Cunningham, Patrick M., Little Flower, Minot
Dean, Dennis L., St. John, Lansford
Deichert, Harry M., (Retired)
Dorrheim, Larry L., St. Joseph, Mandan
Dukart, Herman, St. Joseph, Killdeer
Dworshak, Anton T., (Retired)
Fettig, Richard H., Cathedral of the Holy Spirit, Bismarck
Grabar, Ray A., (Retired)
Hibl, Albert W., (Retired)
Hoffman, Peter, (Retired)
Jilek, Raymond, St. Wenceslaus, Dickinson
Johnson, Ed J., Sr., Rolla, ND
Johnson, Ward A., (Retired)
Jundt, Wayne M., St. Anne, Bismarck
Kappel, Joseph, (Retired)
Klein, Kenneth M., St. Mary, Bismarck
Knopik, Martin, (Retired)
Kordonowy, Leonard J., Ukranian Church of St. Demetrius, Fairfield
Kramer, Charles L., St. John the Apostle, Minot
Krupinsky, Joseph M., St. Anne, Bismarck
Kuss, Leroy M., Colorado Springs, CO
Lamontagne, John H., Ascension, Bismarck
Larson, Samuel, St. John the Baptist, Beach
Lupo, Joseph G., Epiphany, Watford City
Martin, Morris E., (Retired)
Mathern, Joseph J., Corpus Christi, Bismarck
Mattson, Joseph M., Holy Trinity, Hettinger
Mays, Stephen B., St. John, Minot
McDowall, Rexford R., Corpus Christi, Bismarck
Morgel, Edmund D., (Retired)
Morman, Eugene F., St. Wenceslaus, Dickinson
Nistler, Donald R., St. Mary, Golva
Nistler, James A., Coordinator, African Mission, Wilton
Olson, Robert C., St. Vincent De Paul, Crown Butte
Ressler, James V., (Retired)
Riehl, Emil J., (Retired)
Rustand, Gerald T., St. Joseph, Williston
Schmitz, Alvin R., (Retired)
Schneider, Ervin H., St. Vincent de Paul, Mott
Schuller, Robert P., (Retired)
Schumacher, Martin, (Retired)
Schwindt, Alvin W., Ascension, Bismarck
Stockert, Ralph F., (Retired)
Streitz, Steven F., Our Lady of Grace, Minot
Tharaldsen, John, Corpus Christi, Bismarck
Vaughn, David L., Spirit of Life, Mandan
Von Ruden, Ralph, Cathedral of the Holy Spirit, Bismarck
Wanner, Anton, Jr., St. Patrick, Dickinson
Wesolowski, Edwin A., St. Anne, Bismarck
Wolbaum, Kenneth J., St. Katherine, Braddock
Wolberg, Ronald R., Queen of Peace, Dickinson
Wolf, Wilfred P., (Retired)
Wosepka, James, St. John the Baptist, Beach
Ziman, Edward J., (Retired)

INSTITUTIONS LOCATED IN THE DIOCESE

[A] SEMINARIES, RELIGIOUS OR SCHOLASTICATES

RICHARDTON. *Assumption Abbey*, P.O. Box A, 58652. Tel: 701-974-3315; Fax: 701-974-3317.
E-mail: monks@assumptionabbey.com
Web site: www.assumptionabbey.com
Rt. Revs. Patrick Moore, O.S.B., Abbot; Robert West, O.S.B., Retired Abbot; Lawrence Wagner, O.S.B., Retired Abbot; Very Rev. Valerian Odermann, O.S.B., Prior; Bro. Basil Kirsch, O.S.B., Subprior; Revs. David Wolf, O.S.B., Business Mgr.; Eugene Hornstein, O.S.B.; Claude Seeberger, O.S.B.; Gerald Ruelle, O.S.B.; Wilfrid J. Splonskowski, O.S.B.; Raymond Dietlein, O.S.B.; John Odermann, O.S.B. (FAR); Stephen Kranz, O.S.B.; Damian Dietlein, O.S.B. (IND); Raphael Stovik, O.S.B.; Sebastian Schmidt, O.S.B.; Denis Fournier, O.S.B.; Francis Wehri, O.S.B., (Overseas); Terrence Kardong, O.S.B.; Victor Feser, O.S.B.; Odo Muggli, O.S.B.; Daniel Maloney, O.S.B.; Brian Wangler, O.S.B.; Philip Vanderlin, O.S.B., (Overseas); Francis dos Remedios, O.S.B.; Carlos Suarez, O.S.B., (Overseas); Julian Nix, O.S.B.; Hugo L. Blotsky, O.S.B.; Efraim Villegas, O.S.B., (Overseas); Boniface Muggli, O.S.B.; Gonzalo Blanco, O.S.B., (Overseas); Thomas Wordekemper, O.S.B.; Nicolas Cano, O.S.B., (Overseas); Milton Martinez, O.S.B., (Overseas); James Kilzer, O.S.B. Priests 34; Brothers 23; Novices 5.

[B] COLLEGES AND UNIVERSITIES

BISMARCK. *University of Mary*, 7500 University Dr., 58504-9652. Tel: 701-255-7500; Fax: 701-255-7687.
E-mail: marauder@umary.edu
Web site: www.umary.edu
For a complete listing, refer to the Colleges and Universities section.

[C] HIGH SCHOOLS, INTERPAROCHIAL AND PARISH

BISMARCK. *St. Mary's Central High School*, 1025 N. Second St., 58501. Tel: 701-223-4113; Fax: 701-223-8629.
E-mail: smchs@smchs.org
Web site: www.smchs.org
Steve Brannan, Supt.; Tom Eberle, Prin. Priests 1; Sisters 2; Lay Teachers 30; Students 396.

DICKINSON. *Trinity High School*, 810 Empire Rd., P.O. Box 1177, 58602-1177. Tel: 701-483-6081; Fax: 701-483-1450.
E-mail: tquintus@sendit.nodak.edu
Web site: www.trinity@sendit.nodak.edu
Terry Quintus, Supt.; Rod Torgerson, Prin. Priests 1; Lay Teachers 25; Students 349.

MINOT. *Bishop Ryan High School*, 316 11th Ave. N.W., 58701. Tel: 701-852-4004; Fax: 701-839-4651.
E-mail: bunce@BRHS.com
Don Bunce, Supt.; Patrick McNally, Prin. Priests 1; Lay Teachers 28; Students 396.

[D] GENERAL HOSPITALS

BISMARCK. *St. Alexius Medical Center*, P.O. Box 5510, 58506-5510. Tel: 701-530-7000; Fax: 701-530-7284.
Web site: www.st.alexius.org
For a complete listing, refer to the Hospitals section.

DICKINSON. *St. Joseph's Hospital and Health Center*, 30 W. Seventh St., 58601. Tel: 701-264-4271; Fax: 701-264-4800.
Web site: stjoeshospital.org
For a complete listing, refer to the Hospitals section.

GARRISON. *Garrison Memorial Hospital*, P.O. Box 39, 58540. Tel: 701-463-2275; Fax: 701-463-2886.
E-mail: dgoebel@primecare.org
For a complete listing, refer to the Hospitals section.

WILLISTON. *Mercy Medical Center - Affiliate of Catholic Health Initiatives*, 1301 15th Ave. W., 58801. Tel: 701-774-7400; Fax: 701-774-7479
For a complete listing, refer to the Hospitals section.
Mercy Medical Foundation, 1301 15th Ave. W., 58801. Tel: 701-774-7404; Fax: 701-774-7479.
E-mail: dougblack@chi-midwest.org
For a complete listing, refer to the Hospitals section.

[E] SPECIAL CARE FACILITIES

DICKINSON. *St. Benedict's Health Center*, 851 Fourth Ave. E., 58601. Tel: 701-456-7242; Fax: 701-456-7250.
E-mail: jefrantsvog@bhshealth.org
Web site: www.stbens.org
Operated by Benedictine Living Communities, Inc. Jon Frantsvog, Admin. Bed Capacity 180; Total Staff 245; Total Assisted 180.

GARRISON. *Benedictine Living Center of Garrison fka Garrison Nursing Center*, 609 4th Ave., N.E., P.O. Box 219, 58540. Tel: 701-463-2226; Fax: 701-463-2650.
E-mail: blc@ndak.net
Operated by Benedictine Health System Long Term Care, Inc. Bed Capacity 71; Total Staff 82.

[F] PROTECTIVE INSTITUTIONS

SENTINEL BUTTE. *Home On The Range*, 16351 I-94, 58654-9500. Tel: 701-872-3745; Fax: 701-872-3748.
E-mail: hotr@beach.midstate.net
For a complete listing, refer to the Special Care Facilities section.

[G] HOMES FOR AGED

BISMARCK. *Emmaus Place*, 1020 N. 26th St., 58501. Tel: 701-258-2618
For a complete listing, refer to the Special Care Facilities section.
Marillac Manor, 1016 N. 28th St., 58501. Tel: 701-258-8702; Fax: 701-223-3127.
E-mail: phoebeosb@hotmail.com
For a complete listing, refer to the Special Care Facilities section.
St. Vincent's Care Center, Inc., 1021 N. 26 St., 58501-3199. Tel: 701-223-6888; Fax: 701-223-3015.
E-mail: lblakeman@att.global.net
For a complete listing, refer to the Special Care Facilities section.

[H] CONVENTS AND RESIDENCES FOR SISTERS

BISMARCK. *Annunciation Monastery*, 7520 University Dr., 58504-9653. Tel: 701-255-1520; Fax: 701-255-1440.
Web site: www.rc.net/bismarck/am
Sr. Susan Berger, O.S.B., Prioress; Rev. Daniel Maloney, O.S.B., Res. Chap. Motherhouse and Novitiate of the Benedictine Sisters of the Annunciation, B.M.V. Professed Sisters 89.

RICHARDTON. *Sacred Heart Monastery*, P.O. Box 364, 58652. Tel: 701-974-2121; Fax: 701-974-2124.
E-mail: home@sacredheartmonastery.com
Web site: www.rc.net/bismarck/shm
Sr. Paula Larson, O.S.B., Prioress. Motherhouse and Novitiate of the Sisters of the Order of St. Benedict. Professed Sisters 38.

[I] NEWMAN CENTERS

DICKINSON. *Catholic Student Center*, 238 Eighth Ave. W., 58601. Tel: 701-225-6210. Louise A. Oleson, Dir. Total Staff 1.

MINOT. *Catholic Student Center*, 409 University Ave., N.W., 58703-2212. Tel: 701-838-2815. Louise A. Oleson, Dir. Total Staff 1.

[J] MISCELLANEOUS

DICKINSON. *Subiaco Manor*, 2441 10th Ave. W., 58601. Tel: 701-483-2350.
E-mail: renee_branigan@dsu.nodak.edu
Sponsored by the Benedictine Sisters of Sacred Heart Monastery in Richardton. Sr. Renee Branigan, O.S.B., Res. Mgr. Total Staff 3; Total in Residence 11.

MINOT. *Minot Catholic Schools Corporation*, 316 11th Ave., N.W., 58703-2299. Tel: 701-852-4004; Fax: 701-839-4651.
E-mail: bunce@BRHS.com
Don Bunce, Supt. Total Staff 3; Total Assisted 5,600.
Bishop Ryan High School, 316 11th Ave., N.W., 58703-2299. Tel: 701-852-4004; Fax: 701-839-4651. Patrick McNally, Prin. Priests 1; Lay Teachers 27; Students 396.
Little Flower School, 800 University Ave. W., 58703. Tel: 701-839-5882; Fax: 701-839-8567. Diane Zander, Prin. Lay Teachers 10; Students 126.
St. Leo's School, 305 First St., S.E., 58701. Tel: 701-838-2597. Patricia Herbel, Prin. Lay Teachers 11; Students 174.

RICHARDTON. *Sacred Heart Benedictine Foundation*, P.O. Box 364, 58652-0364. Tel: 701-974-2121; Fax: 701-974-2124.
E-mail: sacredheartmonastery.com
Web site: www.rc.net/bismarck/shm

SENTINEL BUTTE. *Home On The Range Foundation*, 16351 I-94, 58654. Tel: 701-872-3745; Fax: 701-872-3748.
E-mail: hotr@beach.midstate.net
Rev. David G. Morman, Pres.

RELIGIOUS INSTITUTES OF MEN REPRESENTED IN THE DIOCESE

For further details refer to the corresponding bracketed number in the Religious Institutes of Men or Women section.

[0200]—*Benedictine Monks.* (Richardton, ND) .—O.S.B.
[]—*Missionary Congregation of the Blessed Sacrament.* (Kerala, India).—M.C.B.S.
[1200]—*Society of the Divine Savior.* (Milwaukee, WI).—S.D.S.

RELIGIOUS INSTITUTES OF WOMEN REPRESENTED IN THE DIOCESE

[0230]—*Benedictine Sisters of Pontifical Jurisdiction.* (Bismarck; Richardton, ND; Watertown, SD; Yankton, SD; Cottonwood, ID; Duluth, MN).—O.S.B.
[2970]—*School Sisters of Notre Dame.* (Mankato Prov.; St. Louis, MO).—S.S.N.D.
[0990]—*Sisters of Divine Providence.* (Allison Park, PA).—C.D.P.
[]—*Sisters of Mary of the Presentation.* (Valley City, ND).—S.M.P.
[1630]—*Sisters of St. Francis of Penance and Christian Charity.* (Denver, CO).—O.S.F.
[]—*Sisters of St. Francis of the Holy Family.* (Dubuque, IA).—OSF.

NECROLOGY

(No Deaths)

Diocese of Boise

(Dioecesis Xylopolitana)

Most Reverend

MICHAEL P. DRISCOLL, M.S.W., D.D.

Bishop of Boise; ordained May 1, 1965; appointed Titular Bishop of Massita and Auxiliary Bishop of Orange December 19, 1989; consecrated March 6, 1990; appointed Bishop of Boise January 18, 1999; installed March 18, 1999. *Res., 303 Federal Way, Boise, ID, 83705-5925.*

ESTABLISHED AS A VICARIATE-APOSTOLIC MARCH 3, 1868.

ERECTED A DIOCESE BY HIS HOLINESS POPE LEO XIII, AUGUST 26, 1893.

Square Miles 83,557.

Legal Title: "Roman Catholic Diocese of Boise".

Comprises the State of Idaho, with a Total Population of 1,258,700.

For legal titles of parishes and diocesan institutions, consult the Chancery Office.

Chancery Office: 303 Federal Way, Boise, ID, 83705-5925. Tel.: 208-342-1311; Fax: 208-342-0224.

E-mail address: jbowen@rcdb.org

STATISTICAL OVERVIEW

Personnel	
Bishop	1
Priests: Diocesan Active in Diocese	50
Priests: Active Outside Diocese	10
Priests: Retired, Sick or Absent	26
Number of Diocesan Priests	86
Religious Priests in Diocese	13
Extern Priests in Diocese	6
Ordinations:	
Diocesan Priests	3
Permanent Deacons in Diocese	34
Total Brothers	4
Total Sisters	92
Parishes	
Parishes	57
With Resident Pastor:	
Resident Diocesan Priests	48
Without Resident Pastor:	
Administered by Priests	7
Administered by Deacons	1
Administered by Women Religious	1
Missions	32
Pastoral Centers	24
Professional Ministry Personnel:	
Sisters	8
Lay Ministers	73
Welfare	
Catholic Hospitals	5
Total Assisted	613,998
Day Care and Extended Day Care Centers	4
Total Assisted	143
Special Centers for Social Services	15
Total Assisted	68,015
Educational	
Diocesan Students in Other Seminaries	14
Total Seminarians	14
High Schools, Diocesan and Parish	1
Total Students	672
Elementary Schools, Diocesan and Parish	13
Total Students	2,478
Catechesis/Religious Education:	
High School Students	3,164
Elementary Students	7,465
Total Students Under Catholic Instruction	13,793
Teachers in the Diocese:	
Sisters	1
Lay Teachers	162
Vital Statistics	
Receptions into the Church:	
Infant Baptism Totals	2,652
Adult Baptism Totals	402
Received into Full Communion	241
First Communions	2,184
Confirmations	1,288
Marriages:	
Catholic	372
Interfaith	230
Total Marriages	602
Deaths	727
Total Catholic Population	130,500
Total Population	1,310,000

Former Bishops—Rt. Rev. LOUIS LOOTENS, D.D., appt. first Vicar-Apostolic of Idaho, March 3, 1868; cons. Bishop of Castabala, Aug. 9, 1868; resigned July 16, 1876; died Jan. 13, 1898.—Rt. Rev. ALPHONSE JOSEPH GLORIEUX, D.D., appt. second Vicar-Apostolic of Idaho, Feb. 27, 1885; cons. Titular Bishop of Apolonia, April 19, 1885; appt. first Bishop of the Diocese of Boise, Aug. 26, 1893; died Aug. 25, 1917.—Rt. Rev. DANIEL MARY GORMAN, D.D. LL.D., cons. May 1, 1918; died June 9, 1927.—Most Rev. EDWARD JOSEPH KELLY, D.D., cons. March 6, 1928; died April 21, 1956.—Most Rev. JAMES J. BYRNE, D.D., S.T.D., ord. June 3, 1933; appt. Titular Bishop of Etenna and Auxiliary of St. Paul, July 2, 1947; cons. July 2, 1947; transferred to Boise June 16, 1956; appt. Archbishop of Dubuque, March 19, 1962; retired Aug. 23, 1983; died Aug. 2, 1996.—Most Rev. SYLVESTER WILLIAM TREINEN, D.D., ord. June 11, 1946; appt. May 19, 1962; cons. July 25, 1962; retired Aug. 17, 1988; died Sept. 30, 1996.—Most Rev. TOD D. BROWN, D.D., ord. May 1, 1963; appt. Dec. 27, 1988; ord. and installed April 3, 1989; appt. Bishop of Orange, June 30, 1998.

Executive Secretary to Bishop/Administration—BARBARA BIRD.

Moderator of the Curia—Rev. DENNIS WASSMUTH, V.G.

Administrative Assistant to Moderator of the Curia—SHARON RHODES.

Vicar for Religious—Rev. DENNIS WASSMUTH, V.G.

Vicar for Administration—Rev. DENNIS WASSMUTH, V.G.

Office of Ethnic Ministries—JOHN HITCHMAN, Dir. ELEANOR SMITH, Sec. Programs Facilitator, *303 Federal Way, Boise, 83705-5925.* Tel: 208-342-1311.

Chancery Office—303 Federal Way, Boise, 83705-5925. Tel: 208-342-1311; Fax: 208-342-0224.

Chancellor—Deacon GERALD D. PERA.

Notary—LODICE GRANT.

Diocesan Tribunal—303 Federal Way, Boise, 83705-5925. Tel: 208-344-1344; Fax: 208-342-0224. (Direct all correspondence here.).

Director—Dr. DIANE L. BARR, J.C.D.

Judicial Vicar—Very Rev. HENRY CARMONA, J.C.L.

Adjutant Judicial Vicars—Revs. JOSEPH F. MCDONALD, III; WILLIAM CROWLEY; GERALD FUNKE.

Promoter of Justice—Dr. DIANE L. BARR.

Notaries—Rev. DENNIS WASSMUTH, V.G.; Deacon GERALD D. PERA; Dr. DIANE L. BARR; LISA WILLIAMS; MARK RAPER; COLLEEN CUNNINGHAM.

Judges—Revs. JOHN W. MORGAN; WILLIAM C. CROWLEY; SIMEON VAN DE VOORD, O.S.B.; SEAN CAULFIELD; JOSEPH MCDONALD, III, J.C.L.; GERALD FUNKE; Very Rev. HENRY CARMONA; Rev. GEORGE KING; Sr. ANN MARGUERITE SOUZA, C.S.J.

Defenders of the Bond—Dr. DIANE L. BARR; Rev. ANDREW SCHUMACHER; Sr. BERNICE WESSELS, O.S.B.

College of Consultors—Revs. WILLIAM CROWLEY; ROGER LACHANCE; JOHN MORGAN; JOHN KOELSCH; JOSEPH SCHMIDT; MICHAEL ST. MARIE; ENRIQUE TERRIQUEZ; GERALD FUNKE; OSCAR JARAMILLO; DENNIS WASSMUTH, V.G.

Deans—Revs. ROGER LACHANCE, Northern Deanery; WILLIAM CROWLEY, Eastern Deanery; OSCAR JARAMILLO, Western Deanery; DENNIS WASSMUTH, West Central Deanery; JOHN MORGAN, Southern Deanery; JOSEPH F. SCHMIDT, North Central Deanery.

Presbyteral Council—See College of Consultors.

Priest Personnel Commission—Revs. DENNIS WASSMUTH, V.G.; WILLIAM GOULD; HENRY CARMONA; RICHARD HALDANE; JOSEPH MUHA; ANDREW SCHUMACHER; RON WEKERLE; STEVE RUKAVINA.

Finance Council—Rev. DENNIS WASSMUTH, V.G., Chm. JAMES BRUCE; LARRY HELLHAKE; STANLEY WELSH; CHARLES HUMMEL; SUSAN COPPLE; T. STEVE JOYCE; Deacon GERALD PERA; PATRICK CRISLER, C.P.A., Finance Office Consultant.

Building Commission—Deacon GERALD D. PERA, Chm.; Rev. CALVIN BLANKINSHIP; MARILYN SCANLAN; DAVID DAVIES; BRIAN ELLSWORTH; MICHAEL JONES; ROBERT PETERS; ROY CROWDER.

Priest Retirement Committee—Revs. DENNIS WASSMUTH, V.G., Chm. JOHN KOELSCH; ROBB KELLER; DONALD RIFFLE; JOHN MORGAN; JOSEPH DA SILVA, *303 Federal Way, Boise, 83705.* Tel: 208-342-1311.

Diocesan Offices and Directors

Apostleship of Prayer—Vacant.

Bureau of Information—"Idaho Catholic Register", 303 Federal Way, Boise, 83705-5925.

Campaign for Human Development—Deacon GERALD D. PERA, *303 Federal Way, Boise, 83705-5925.*

Catholic Communications Center—Vacant.

Catholic Relief Services—Deacon GERALD D. PERA, *303 Federal Way, Boise, 83705-5925.*

Catholic Scouts—Rev. ROGER LACHANCE, Chap., *St. Pius X, 625 E. Haycraft, Coeur d'Alene, 83815.* Tel: 208-765-5108.

Catholic Daughters of the Americas—BONNIE WISSEL, State Regent, *224 S. Canyon, Nampa, 83686.* Tel: 208-467-4825.

Catholic Schools—BOB SOBOTTA, Coord., *303 Federal Way, Boise, 83705-5925.*

Catholic Hospitals—Rev. MARK R. SCHMACHER, *St. Augustine's Catholic Center, P.O. Box 3457, Moscow, 83843.* Tel: 208-882-4613.

Catholic Liturgical Commission—Deacon RICK BONNEY; JOHN ANNEN; Rev. RONALD WEKERLE; MARCIA

BECKMAN; LARRY HARRISON; Rev. LEN MACMILLAN, Chm., *303 Federal Way, Boise, 83705*. Tel: 208-342-1311.

Censor Librorum—Rev. ANDREW SCHUMACHER, *P.O. Box 425, Cottonwood, 83522*.

Charismatic Renewal—Rev. ROBB KELLER, *152 7th Ave. E., Twin Falls, 83301*.

Priest Retirement Plan—Direct Inquiries to the Chancery, *303 Federal Way, Boise, 83705*.

Cursillo Movement—Rev. JOHN KOELSCH, Spiritual Dir., *P.O. Box 5127, Boise, 83705*. Rev. MAURICIO MEDINA, Hispanic Dir., *584 W. Sexton, Blackfoot, 83221*.

Development/Stewardship Office—Rev. DONALD J. RIFFLE.

Ecumenical Commission—Rev. JOHN KOELSCH, *P.O. Box 5127, Boise, 83705*.

Education Ministries Office—JACK CRAVEN, Dir. PATRICIA THOMAS, Sec. & Events Coord., *303 Federal Way, Boise, 83705*. Tel: 208-342-1311.

Coordinator of Schools—BOB SOBOTTA.

Coordinator Child and Family Catechesis,—Sr. CLARISSA GOECKNER, O.S.B.

Coordinator Youth Ministry—KEN COOK.

Coordinator of Adult Education—DAN MCGILL.

Resource Center Manager—GLORIA PETTINGER.

Finance Officer—PATRICK CRISLER, C.P.A.

Idaho Council of Catholic Women—KATHLEEN SORGE, Pres., *2532 N. Edgewood, Eagle, 83616*.

Knights of Columbus—RUDOLPH WILSON, State Deputy, *2165 Ridgeway Way, Boise, 83712-8408*. Rev. ROBB KELLER, State Chap.

Legislative Liaison—TIMOTHY BRENNAN.

Campus Ministry—CHARLES L. SKORO, *1915 University Dr., Boise, 83706*.

Newspaper—"Idaho Catholic Register"; Most Rev. MICHAEL P. DRISCOLL, Publisher; COLETTE COWMAN, Exec. Editor; LEONARD GEORGE, Advertising/Business/Circulation; BARBARA HAMILTON, Artist Production, *303 Federal Way, Boise, 83705*. Tel: 208-342-1311.

Deacons, Director—Deacon RICHARD BONNEY, *804 N. 9th St., Boise, 83702*. Tel: 208-342-3511.

Deacon Council President—Deacon RALPH FLAGER, *5152 Burlington Dr., Boise, 83704*. Tel: 208-375-2459.

Deacon Formation Director—Sr. GRAYCE ROSS, S.N.J.M., *4450 N. Five Mile Rd., Boise, 83713*. Tel: 208-376-5787.

Prison Ministry—Rev. JESUS CAMACHO, *322 S. Manville St., Boise, 83705*. Tel: 208-429-9196.

Propagation of Faith—Deacon GERALD PERA, *303 Federal Way, Boise, 83705*.

Respect Life Program—Deacon RALPH FLAGER, Dir., *5152 Burlington Dr., Boise, 83704*. Tel: 208-375-2459.

St. Vincent de Paul Society—Rev. RAUL COVARRUBIAS, Diocesan Spiritual Dir., *P.O. Box 310, Mountain Home, 83647*. Tel: 208-587-3046. Deacon GERALD PERA, Diocesan Liaison, *303 Federal Way, Boise, 83705*. Tel: 208-342-1311.

State Trustee—MARGO HENNING, *3717 Ticonderoga, Boise, 83706*. Tel: 208-344-0702.

Vocations—Rev. JAIRO RESTREPO, Dir., *P.O. Box 87, Weiser, 83672*. Tel: 208-549-0088.

CLERGY, PARISHES, MISSIONS AND PAROCHIAL SCHOOLS

CITY OF BOISE
(Ada County)

1—CATHEDRAL OF ST. JOHN THE EVANGELIST, Revs. Joseph F. McDonald; Rogation Urasa, A.L.C.P.; Deacons Richard Bonney, Pastoral Assoc.; Richard Henning; Ken Hiner.
Res., 804 N. 9th St., 83702. Tel: 208-342-3511; 3512; Fax: 208-342-1564.
School—St. Joseph's School. Mrs. Kathleen Crowley, Prin.
Lay Teachers 15; Students 266.
Catechesis/Religious Programs—Kelley Kolpitcke, D.R.E.
Students 420.

2—ST. MARK'S, Revs. Leonard MacMillan; Steven Rukavina; Deacons Ralph Pierce; James Bowen.
Res., 7503 Northview St., 83704. Tel: 208-375-6651; Fax: 208-375-3211.
School—Dan Maloney, Prin. Lay Teachers 11; Students 262.
Catechesis/Religious Programs—Students 730.

3—ST. MARY'S, Revs. Joseph F. Donald; Patrick Dennis; Deacon William Petzak.
Res., 2612 W. State St., 83702. Tel: 208-344-2597; Fax: 208-344-9337.
School—2620 W. State St., 83702. Tel: 208-342-7476; Fax: 208-345-5154. Marcia Beckman, Prin.
Lay Teachers 11; Students 230.
Catechesis/Religious Programs—Students 180.

4—OUR LADY OF THE ROSARY, Rev. Dennis Wassmuth, V.G.; Deacon Michael Dessert.
Res., 1500 E. Wright, 83706. Tel: 208-343-9041; Fax: 208-343-2644.
Catechesis/Religious Programs—Rosie Skoro, D.R.E. Students 412.
Chapels—Idaho City, St. Joseph's.; Boise, St. Paul's Student Center.

5—RISEN CHRIST CATHOLIC COMMUNITY, Rev. Joseph da Silva; Deacon Michael Eisenbeiss.
Res., 11511 W. Lake Hazel Rd., 83709. Tel: 208-362-6584; Fax: 208-362-9545.
Catechesis/Religious Programs—Students 180.

6—SACRED HEART, Rev. John W. Koelsch; Deacons Alan Shaber; James Kelly.
Mailing Address: P.O. Box 5127, 83705-0127. Tel: 208-344-8311; Fax: 208-343-1876.
School—3901 Cassia St., 83705. Tel: 208-344-9738; Fax: 208-343-1939. John Loffer, Prin.
Sisters 1; Lay Teachers 12; Students 230.
Catechesis/Religious Programs—Deborah Fischer, D.R.E.
Students 162.

7—ST. PAUL'S. Closed. See Our Lady of the Rosary, Boise for details.

OUTSIDE THE CITY OF BOISE

Aberdeen, Bingham Co., Blessed Sacrament. Merged with St. Mary, American Falls to form Presentation of the Lord, Aberdeen.

Presentation of the Lord, Rev. Carlos A. Perez.
Res., Hwy. 39 & S. 4th W., P.O. Box 833, 83210. Tel: 208-397-7036; Fax: 208-397-3061.
Catechesis/Religious Programs—D.R.E.: Carla Gonzales; Kathy Barkdull.
Students 185.
Chapels—Pingree, St. John.; St. Mary, P.O. Box 117, American Falls, 83211. Tel: 208-226-5217; Fax: 208-226-1125; Aberdeen, Blessed Sacrament.

American Falls, Power Co., St. Mary. Merged with Blessed Sacrament, Aberdeen to form Presentation of the Lord, Aberdeen.

Arco, Butte Co., St. Ann's. See St. Charles, Salmon for details.

Blackfoot, Bingham Co., St. Bernard's, Rev. Mauricio Medina.
Res., 584 W. Sexton St., 83221. Tel: 208-785-1935; Fax: 208-785-1935.
Catechesis/Religious Programs—Students 137.
Chapel—Blessed Kateri Tekakwitha, Sheepskin Rd., Fort Hall, 83203.

Bonners Ferry, Boundary Co., St. Ann's, Rev. David Riffle.
Res., 6712 El Paso, 83805. Tel: 208-267-2852; Fax: 208-267-8222.
Catechesis/Religious Programs—Annette Sturmans, D.R.E.
Students 65.

Buhl, Twin Falls Co., Immaculate Conception, Rev. John Worster.
Res., 1701 Poplar, Box 626, 83316. Tel: 208-543-5136; Fax: 208-543-5714.
Catechesis/Religious Programs—Christine Welch, D.R.E.
Students 150.
Station—Hagerman, St. Catherine's.

Burley, Cassia Co., St. Theresa, Rev. Juan Maria Garatea.
Res., 1550 Oakley, Box 1223, 83318. Tel: 208-678-5453; Fax: 208-678-5479.
Catechesis/Religious Programs—Karen Carlisle, D.R.E.
Students 145.

Caldwell, Canyon Co., St. Mary, Revs. Enrique Terriquez; Arnold J. Miller, Jr.
Office: 616 Dearborn, P.O. Box 399, 83606. Tel: 208-459-3653; Fax: 208-454-8789.
Catechesis/Religious Programs—Students 825.
Chapel—Marsing, Good Shepherd.

Chubbuck, Bannock Co., St. Paul's, Rev. Joseph Muha.
Res., 820 W. Chubbuck, Box 5367, 83202. Tel: 208-237-7167; Fax: 208-237-2724.
Catechesis/Religious Programs—Diana Calabro, D.R.E.
Students 75.

Coeur D'Alene, Kootenai Co., St. Pius X, Rev. Roger LaChance; Deacons Gary McSwain; Leonard Trueworthy.
Res., 625 E. Haycraft, 83715. Tel: 208-765-5108; Fax: 208-664-5325.
Catechesis/Religious Programs—Deacon Gary McSwain, D.R.E.
Students 270.

St. Thomas, Rev. James Rodenspiel.
Res., 919 Indiana Ave., 83814. Tel: 208-664-9259; Fax: 208-667-8321.
Catechesis/Religious Programs—Carol White, D.R.E.
Students 122.

Cottonwood, Idaho Co., St. Mary's, Rev. Andrew J. Schumacher.
Mailing Address: P.O. Box 425, 83522-0425. Tel: 208-962-3214; Fax: 208-962-5477.
Res., 503 Garrett St., 83522.
Catechesis/Religious Programs—Mary Jane Arnzen, D.R.E.
Students 121.
Chapel—Keuterville, Holy Cross.

Council, Adams Co., St. Jude Station. See St. Agnes, Weiser for details.

DeSmet, Benewah Co., Sacred Heart, Revs. Thomas Connolly, S.J.; Andrew L. Maddock, S.J.; Sr. Dolores Ellwart, S.P., Pastoral Assoc.
Res., Box 306, 83824. Tel: 208-274-5871; Fax: 208-274-3015.
Stations—Plummer, Our Lady of Perpetual Help.; Worley, St. Michael's.

Eagle, Ada Co., St. Matthew. Merged with Holy Spirit, Meridian to form Holy Apostles, Meridian.

Emmett, Gem Co., Sacred Heart, Rev. Marcellus Fernandez.
Res., 211 E. First, 83617. Tel: 208-365-4320; Fax: 208-365-0754.
Catechesis/Religious Programs—Students 130.
Station—Garden Valley, St. Jude.

Ferdinand, Idaho Co., Assumption, Rev. Andrew Schumacher.
Mailing Address: P.O. Box 112, 83526. Tel: 208-962-5220; Fax: 208-962-3726.
Catechesis/Religious Programs—Mary Jane Arnzen, D.R.E.
Students 35.

Fruitland, Payette Co., Corpus Christi, Revs. Jairo Restrepo; Nondier Zuleta; Jorge Garcia.
Mailing Address: P.O. Box 818, Payette, 83661.
Res., 1212 1st Ave., S. Payette, 83661. Tel: 208-642-2261; Fax: 208-642-1099.
Catechesis/Religious Programs—Students 230.
Chapels—New Plymouth, St. Aloysius.; Payette, Holy Family.

Garden Valley, Boise Co., St. Jude's. See Sacred Heart, Emmett for details.

Genesee, Latah Co., St. Mary Station. See St. Mary's, Moscow for details. In res., Rev. Robert Finucane.
Res., 138 N. Jackson, P.O. Box 36, 83832. Tel: 208-285-1218; Fax: 208-285-1139.
Catechesis/Religious Programs—Connie Esser, D.R.E.
Students 40.

Glenns Ferry, Elmore Co., Our Lady of Limerick Station. See Our Lady of Good Counsel, Mountain Home for details. In res., Rev. Eugene Esch, O.S.B.
Res., 113 W. Arthur St., Box 216, 83623. Tel: 208-366-7721.
Catechesis/Religious Programs—Natalie Lehman, D.R.E.
Students 80.

Gooding, Gooding Co., St. Elizabeth's, Rev. Paul Wander.
Res., 1515 California St., Box 147, 83330. Tel: 208-934-5634; Fax: 208-934-5634.
Catechesis/Religious Programs—Jane Woodland, D.R.E.
Students 155.
Station—Wendell, St. Anthony's.

Grandview, Owyhee Co., St. Henry Chapel. See Our Lady of Good Counsel, Mountain Home for details.

Grangeville, Idaho Co., SS. Peter and Paul, Rev. Thomas Loucks.
Res., 318 S. B St., 83530. Tel: 208-983-0403; Fax: 208-983-1152.
School—Tel: 208-983-2182. Milton Baelocher, Prin.
Lay Teachers 4; Students 62.
Catechesis/Religious Programs—Students 30.
Station—Nez Perce, Holy Trinity.

Greencreek, Idaho Co., St. Anthony's, Rev. Andrew Schumacher.
Res., Rte. 1, Box 90, 83533. Tel: 208-962-3565; Fax: 208-962-3726.
Catechesis/Religious Programs—Mary Jane Arnzen, D.R.E.
Students 45.

Hagerman, Gooding Co., St. Catherine's. See Immaculate Conception, Buhl for details.

Hailey, Blaine Co., St. Charles Borromeo, Rev. John W. Morgan, Admin.; Sr. M. Arlene Ellis, S.S.C., Pastoral Assoc.
Res., 311 S. 1st. Ave. E, Box 789, 83333. Tel: 208-788-3024; Fax: 208-788-0726.
Catechesis/Religious Programs—Students 65.
Chapel—Fairfield, Immaculate Conception.

Homedale, Owyhee Co., St. Hubert, Rev. Oscar Jaramillo.
Res., 115 E. Owyhee St., Box 186, 83628. Tel: 208-337-3153; Fax: 208-337-3153.
Catechesis/Religious Programs—Lynne Tiddens, D.R.E.
Students 102.

Horseshoe Bend, Boise Co., Our Lady Queen of Angels Chapel. See Holy Apostle, Meridian for details.

Idaho City, Boise Co., St. Joseph's Chapel. See Our Lady of the Rosary, Boise for details.

Idaho Falls, Bonneville Co., Holy Rosary, Revs. Michael St. Marie; Carlos Felipe Velez; Deacon Richard Kelso.
Res., 145 Ninth St., 83404-6392. Tel: 208-522-4366; Fax: 208-523-3827.
School—161 Ninth St., 83404. Tel: 208-522-7781. Gerald Chouinard, Prin.
Lay Teachers 10; Students 200.
Catechesis/Religious Programs—Sue Clark, D.R.E. Students 435.
Stations—Roberts, St. Anthony's.; Mud Lake, St. Ann's.

Christ the King, Rev. William Crowley; Deacon Charles Solbrig.
Res., 1690 E. 17th St., 83404. Tel: 208-529-8170; Fax: 208-528-9164.
Catechesis/Religious Programs—Susan Clark, D.R.E.
Students 250.
Chapel—Shelley, Our Lady of Guadalupe.

Jerome, Jerome Co., St. Jerome's, Rev. Ron Wekerle; Deacons William Last; John Baumbach; Marino Perea.
Res., 216 2nd Ave. E., Box 169, 83338. Tel: 208-324-8794; Fax: 208-324-4141.
Catechesis/Religious Programs—Theresa May, Pastoral Assoc.
Students 220.

Kamiah, Lewis Co., St. Catherine's of Siena, Rev. George L. King.
Res., 407 7th St., Box 685, 83536. Tel: 208-935-2130; Fax: 208-935-2984.
Catechesis/Religious Programs—Students 26.

Kellogg, Shoshone Co., St. Rita's, Rev. Mel Sprute; Deacon David Beverman.
Res., 27 Kellogg Ave., 83837-2626. Tel: 208-784-7361; Fax: 208-784-7361.

Keuterville, Idaho Co., Holy Cross. Merged with St. Mary's, Cottonwood.

Lapwai, Nez Perce Co., Sacred Heart Station. See Our Lady of Lourdes, Lewiston for details.

Leadore, Lemhi Co., St. Joseph's Chapel. See St. Charles, Salmon for details.

Lewiston, Nez Perce Co., St. Stanislaus, Sr. Margie Schmidt, O.S.B., Parish Life Coord.
Res., 633 5th Ave., 83501. Tel: 208-743-7331; Fax: 208-746-7134.
School—Tri-Parish School. Marcia Ney, Prin.
Lay Teachers 10; Students 146.
Catechesis/Religious Programs—Students 75.

Our Lady of Lourdes, Rev. Leslie P. Kish.
Church & Res.—2015 13th Ave., 83501. Tel: 208-743-3238; 743-6101 (Church); Fax: 208-743-5301.
Catechesis/Religious Programs—Students 200.

St. James, Rev. Richard S. Haldane.
Office: 1519 Ripon Ave., 83501. Tel: 208-743-8231; Fax: 208-798-8407.
Catechesis/Religious Programs—Students 110.
Station—Lapwai, Sacred Heart.

McCall, Valley Co., Our Lady of the Lake, Rev. Donald D. Fraser.
Res., 501 Cross Rd., Box 821, 83638. Tel: 208-634-5474.
Catechesis/Religious Programs—Students 45.
Station—Cascade, St. John the Baptist.
Chapel—Riggins, St. Jerome's.

Meridian, Ada Co., Holy Spirit. Merged with St. Matthew, Eagle to form Holy Apostles, Meridian.

Holy Apostles, Revs. Timothy M. Ritchey; Donald J. Riffle; Deacons Ralph Flager; Jack Pelowitz, Pastoral Assoc.; Gerald Pera; Charles Rasmussen.
Res., Box 708, 83680. Tel: 208-888-1182; Fax: 208-884-1800.
Catechesis/Religious Programs—Mary Ossenkop, D.R.E.
Students 800.
Chapels—Meridian, Holy Spirit.; Eagle, St. Matthew.; Horseshoe Bend, Our Lady Queen of Angels.

Moscow, Latah Co., St. Mary's, Rev. Joseph F. Schmidt.
Res., 618 E. First St., Box 9106, 83843. Tel: 208-882-4813; Fax: 208-883-0608.
School—412 N. Monroe, 83843. Tel: 208-882-2121. Sr. Margaret Johnson, O.S.U., Prin.
Lay Teachers 10; Students 168.
Kindergarten & Preschool, St. Rose—Owned by the Ursuline Nuns, affiliated with St. Mary's School. 412 N. Howard, 83843. Tel: 208-882-4014; Fax: 208-882-0970.
Catechesis/Religious Programs—Students 155.
Station—Genessee, St. Mary's.

St. Augustine's. (Catholic Center). Rev. Mark R. Schumacher; Deacon Verne Geidl.
Res., 628 Deakin St., P.O. Box 3457, 83843. Tel: 208-882-4613; Fax: 208-882-2823.
Station—Potlatch, St. Mary's.

Mountain Home Air Force Base, Elmore Co., St. Mary's, Rev. John A. Kovalcin.
Res., 366 Wing/HC, 420 Gunfighter Ave., 83648. Tel: 208-828-6417; Fax: 208-828-4570.

Mountain Home, Elmore Co., Our Lady of Good Counsel, Rev. Raul R. Covarrubias.
Res., 115 N. 4th St. E., Box 310, 83647. Tel: 208-587-3046; Fax: 208-587-5114.
Catechesis/Religious Programs—Barbara Faneuf, D.R.E.
Students 280.
Stations—Bruneau, St. Bridget.; Glenn's Ferry, Our Lady of Limerick.
Chapel—Grandview, St. Henry's.

Nampa, Canyon Co., St. Paul's, Revs. Gerald J. Funke; Francisco Q. Flores; Sr. Ramona Negrette, O.S.F., Pastoral Assoc.
Res., 1515 8th St. S., 83651. Tel: 208-466-7031; Fax: 208-467-7203.
School—Tel: 208-467-3601. MaryAnn VandeBrake, Prin.
Lay Teachers 12; Students 254.
Catechesis/Religious Programs—Students 660.
Station—Melba, St. Joseph.
Chapels—Silver City, Our Lady of Tears.; Oreana, Queen of Heaven.

Our Lady of Guadalupe Chapel. Closed. See St. Paul's, Nampa for details.

New Plymouth, Payette Co., St. Aloysius. Merged with Holy Family, Payette to form Corpus Christi, Fruitland.

Nezperce, Lewis Co., Holy Trinity. See SS. Peter and Paul, Grangeville for details. In res., Rev. Kenneth Arnzen.
Res., 506 Willow St., Box 65, 83543. Tel: 208-937-2300.
Catechesis/Religious Programs—Students 65.

Oreana, Owyhee Co., Queen of Heaven Chapel. See St. Paul's, Nampa for details.

Orofino, Clearwater Co., St. Theresa's, Rev. George L. King; Sr. Petronilla Lieser, O.S.B., Pastoral Assoc.
Res., 446 Brown Ave., Box 1169, 83544. Tel: 208-476-5121.
Catechesis/Religious Programs—Students 64.
Chapel—Pierce, Our Lady of Woodland.

Parma, Canyon Co., Sacred Hearts of Jesus and Mary, Rev. Oscar Jaramillo.
Mailing Address: P.O. Box 777, 83660.
Res., 101 E. Owyhee St., P.O. Box 186, Homedale, 83628. Tel: 208-337-3153.
Catechesis/Religious Programs—Students 65.

Payette, Payette Co., Holy Family. Merged with St. Aloysius, New Plymouth to form Corpus Christi, Fruitland.

Pocatello, Bannock Co., St. Joseph's, Revs. Joseph Muha; Camillus Temba, A.L.C.P.; Deacon Mel Hardy.
Res., 455 N. Hayes, P.O. Box 757, 83204. Tel: 208-232-1470; Fax: 208-232-0586.
Catechesis/Religious Programs—Ann Hysell, D.R.E.
Students 91.

St. Anthony's, Revs. Joseph Muha; Camillus Temba, A.L.C.P.; Deacon Mel Hardy.
Res., 524 N. 7th Ave., 83205. Tel: 208-232-1196; Fax: 208-234-1624.
School—540 N. 7th Ave., 83205. Tel: 208-232-5763. Steve Anderson, Prin.
Lay Teachers 14; Students 191.
Catechesis/Religious Programs—Sr. Mary Paul Moeller, F.S.E., D.R.E.
Students 125.
Chapel—St. John's Catholic Student Center, 920 E. Lovejoy St., I.S.U., Box 8129, 83209. Tel: 208-233-0880; Fax: 208-233-5745.

St. John's Catholic Student Center. Closed. See St. Anthony, Pocatello for details.

Post Falls, Kootenai Co., St. George's, Revs. William R. Gould; Colman J. Molan, S.T.
Res., 2003 N. William St., Box 10, 83877-0010. Tel: 208-773-4715; Fax: 208-777-1549.
Catechesis/Religious Programs—Megan Rounds, D.R.E.
Students 255.
Chapels—Rathdrum, St. Stanislaus.; Spirit Lake, St. Joseph.

Potlatch, Latah Co., St. Mary's Station. See St. Augustine's, Moscow for details.

Priest River, Bonner Co., St. Catherine's, Deacon Richard S. Hamm, Admin.
Res., 206 Summit Blvd., Box 445, 83856. Tel: 208-448-2127.
Catechesis/Religious Programs—Students 10.
Station—Priest Lake, St. Blanche.

Rathdrum, Kootenai Co., St. Stanislaus Chapel. See St. George, Post Falls for details.

Rupert, Minidoka Co., St. Nicholas, Rev. Henry Carmona; Deacon Pete Rodriquez.
Res., 802 F St., Box 115, 83350. Tel: 208-436-3781; Fax: 208-436-0628.
School—P.O. Box 26, 83350. Tel: 208-436-6320. Suzette Miller, Prin.
Lay Teachers 6; Students 120.
Catechesis/Religious Programs—Students 240.

St. Anthony, Fremont Co., Mary Immaculate, Rev. Gabriel Vargas.
Res., 328 W. First N., Box 527, 83445. Tel: 208-624-7459.
Catechesis/Religious Programs—Holly Woodcock, D.R.E.
Students 29.
Stations—Rexburg, St. Patrick's.; Driggs, Good Shepherd.; Island Park, Chapel of the Pines.

Saint Maries, Benewah Co., St. Mary's, Rev. William Taylor.
Res., 921 Jefferson St., Box 335, 83861. Tel: 208-245-2977.
Catechesis/Religious Programs—Shannon Shepherd, D.R.E.
Students 70.
Station—Harrison, Our Lady of Perpetual Help.

Salmon, Lemhi Co., St. Charles, Revs. Alan B. Cox; Gordon A. Taylor; Peter Bourne.
Res., 505 Hope Ave., 83467. Tel: 208-756-2432; Fax: 208-756-1190.
Catechesis/Religious Programs—Mary Vander Schaaf, D.R.E.
Students 109.
Stations—Arco, St. Ann.; Challis, St. Louise.; Mackay, St. Barbara.
Chapel—Leadore, St. Joseph.

Sandpoint, Bonner Co., St. Joseph's, Rev. Dennis C. Day; Deacon Ralph Arndt, (Retired).
Res., 621 Oak St., P.O. Box 279, 83864-0279. Tel: 208-263-3720; Fax: 208-265-4974.
Catechesis/Religious Programs—Irene Sundquist, D.R.E.
Students 195.
Chapel—Clark Fork, Sacred Heart.

Shoshone, Lincoln Co., St. Peter's, Rev. Paul Wander; Deacon Dee Aslett.
Res., 215 W. B St., Box 336, 83352. Tel: 208-886-2002; 934-5634; Fax: 208-886-2030.
Catechesis/Religious Programs—Students 20.

Soda Springs, Caribou Co., St. Mary's, Rev. Calvin Blankinship, Jr., Admin.
Res., 99 W. Center, 83276. Tel: 208-547-3200; Fax: 208-547-3200.
Catechesis/Religious Programs—Students 60.
Stations—Montpelier, Blessed Sacrament.; Malad City, St. Paul's.; Preston, St. Peter's.; Lava Hot Springs, Our Lady of Lourdes.

Sun Valley, Blaine Co., Our Lady of the Snows, Rev. John W. Morgan; Sr. Elizabeth Kugi, O.P., Pastoral Assoc.
Res., Sun Valley Rd., Box 1650, 83353. Tel: 208-622-3432; Fax: 208-622-4348.
Catechesis/Religious Programs—Students 80.

Twin Falls, Twin Falls Co., St. Edward's. Merged with Our Lady of Guadalupe, Twin Falls to form St. Edward The Confessor, Twin Falls.

Our Lady of Guadalupe. Merged with St. Edward's, Twin Falls to form St. Edward The Confessor, Twin Falls.

St. Edward The Confessor, Revs. Robb Keller; Ernie Anderson, (Retired); Dominic Nguyen; Deacons John McKinley; Lloyd LeClair; Robert Sass.
Res., 630 Falls Ave., 83301-3300. Tel: 208-734-2327; Fax: 208-734-4145.
School—Tel: 208-734-3872; Fax: 208-734-1214. Denise Hart, Prin.
Lay Teachers 8; Students 142.
Catechesis/Religious Programs—Jean Thompson, D.R.E.
Students 300.
Chapel—Our Lady of Guadalupe.

Wallace, Shoshone Co., St. Alphonsus, Rev. Mel Sprute, Admin.; Deacon David Beuerman.
Res., 214 Pine St., Box 970, 83873. Tel: 208-752-3551.
Chapel—Mullan, St. Michael's.

Weiser, Washington Co., St. Agnes, Revs. Jairo Restrepo; Nondier Zuleta; Deacon Francis Wander.
Res., 214 E. Liberty, P.O. Box 87, 83672. Tel: 208-549-0088; Fax: 208-549-1080.
Catechesis/Religious Programs—Students 165.
Stations—Cambridge, Holy Rosary.; Council, St. Jude the Apostle.

Wendell, Gooding Co., St. Anthony's. See St. Elizabeth's, Gooding for details.

Chaplains of Public Institutions

BOISE. *Chateau de Boise Retirement Center* 7250 Poplar St., 83704. Tel: 208-372-0257. Rev. Patrick Russell.

Elks Rehabilitation. 9th St., Boise, ID, 83702. Tel: 208-342-3511. 204 Fort Pl., 83702. Rev. Simeon Van De Voord, O.S.B.

St. Luke's Medical Center. Attended by St. John Cathedral, 804 N. 9th St., Boise, ID, 83702. Tel: 208-342-3511. Vacant. 190 E. Bannock, 83712.

VA Hospital. Attended by St. John Cathedral, 804 N. 9th St., Boise, ID, 83702. Tel: 208-342-3511. Vacant. 5th St. & Fort St., 83401.

COTTONWOOD. *Monastery of St. Gertrude* HC 3 Box 121, 83522. Tel: 208-962-3224. Rev. Meinrad Schallenberger, O.S.B.

On Duty Outside the Diocese:
Reverend Fathers—
Dolan, Raymond, Box 217, M.H. Station, Staten Island, NY 10303
Faucher, W. Thomas, St. Edward's, 68817 Trinity Way, P.O. Box 489, Sisters, OR 97759
Legerski, John, Marist High School, 1900 Kingsley Rd., Eugene, OR 97401
O'Toole, Timothy L., Cathedral of St. Ignatius Loyola, 9999 N. Military Tr., Palm Beach Gardens, FL 33410
Pu, Matthew C., St. Bernard's, P.O. Box 186, Jordan Valley, OR 97910
Segatta, Bruno, Gonzaga in Florence, Piazza Antinori No. 3, Florence, Italy
Stravinskas, Peter M.J., 21 Fairview, Mt. Pocono, PA 18344

Retired:
Reverend Monsignors—
Falk, Dennis G., 324 S. Manville, Boise, ID 83705
Hallissey, James T., 855 Galena Ct., Box 370, Mountain Home, ID 83647
Hughes, Nicholas V., Rosemount, Kilkenny, Johnston Co., Ireland
Simmons, Donald W., 2612 E. 44th St., Spokane, WA 99223

Reverend Fathers—
Carroll, William, 569 Fairview Dr., Hamilton, MT 59840
Caulfield, Sean, 606 17th Ave. #B, Lewiston, ID 83501
Daws, Dominic, 511 3rd Ave. E., Twin Falls, ID 83301
DiLoreto, Anthony, 524 N. 7th Ave., Pocatello, ID 83201
Dodds, Perry W., P.O. Box 264, Twin Falls, ID 83303
Dohman, William, J.C.L., 5972 Via Casitas Ave., Carmichael, CA 95608
Donoghue, John F., P.O. Box 5773, Boise, ID 83705
Dulberg, Albert V., P. O. Box 943, Post Falls, ID 83877
Gebhardt, Joseph M., 3060 S.E. Stark St., Portland, OR 97214
Hebert, Francis, 465 W. Linden Way, Heppner, OR 97836
McGoldrick, John T., 106 N. 12th St., #4C, Payette, ID 83661
McNeill, Malachy, 6 Dublin Rd., Drogheda, Co. Louth, Ireland
O'Donovan, Timothy John, 1802 W. Ontario St., Sand Point, ID 83864
O'Sullivan, John, 700 E. Fairview, #116, Meridian, ID 83642
Peterson, Francis A., Karcher Estates, 1127 Caldwell Blvd., Apt. 247, Nampa, ID 83651
Riffle, Douglas H., P.O. Box 456, Meridian, ID 83680
Scarcello, Michael S., 3247 W. Scarcello Rd., Rathdrum, ID 83858
Shinnick, James F., 1520 N. Fillmore, Jerome, ID 83338
Steinhoff, Henry, P.O. Box 626, Eureka, MT 59917
Taylor, Gordon A., P.O. Box 161, Arco, ID 83213
Van De Voord, Simeon, O.S.B., 1915 University Dr., Boise, ID 83706
Waldmann, Robert J., P.O. Box 112, Ferdinand, ID 83526
Wilson, James R., 4335 Rose Hill Ct., Boise, ID 83705

Permanent Deacons:
Arndt, Ralph, (Retired)
Aslett, Devon H., St. Peter, Shoshone
Baumbach, John, St. Jerome's, Jerome
Beuerman, David, St. Alphonsus, Wallace
Bonney, Richard James, St. John's Cathedral, Boise
Booth, Charles
Bowen, James E., St. Mark, Boise
Dessert, Michael, Our Lady of the Rosary, Boise
Eisenbeiss, Michael, Risen Christ Catholic Community, Boise
Flager, Ralph, Holy Apostles, Meridian
Geidl, Verne, St. Augustine Catholic Center, Moscow
Hamm, Richard, St. Catherine of Siena, Priest River
Hardy, Melvin, St. Anthony's, Pocatello
Henning, Richard, St. John Cathedral, Boise
Hiner, Kenneth, St. John Cathedral, Boise
Jackson, Walter, (Retired)
Kelly, James, Sacred Heart, Boise
Kelso, Richard, Holy Rosary, Idaho Falls
Kreilcamp, Ben, (Retired)
Last, William, St. Jerome, Jerome
Le Clair, Lloyd, St. Edward, Twin Falls
McKinley, John D., Jr., St. Edward, Twin Falls
McSwain, Gary, St. Pius X, Coeur d'Alene
Pelowitz, Jack, Holy Apostles, Meridian
Pera, Gerald D., Holy Apostles, Meridian
Perea, Marino, St. Jerome, Jerome
Petzak, William, St. Mary, Boise
Pierce, Ralph, St. Mark, Boise
Rasmussen, Charles, Holy Apostles, Meridian
Rodriguez, Pete, St. Nicholas, Rupert
Sass, Robert, (Retired)
Shaber, Alan, Sacred Heart, Boise
Solbrig, Charles W., Christ the King, Idaho Falls
Trueworthy, Leonard, St. Pius X, Coeur d' Alene
Wander, Francis, St. Agnes, Weiser

INSTITUTIONS LOCATED IN THE DIOCESE

[A] HIGH SCHOOLS, INTER-PAROCHIAL

BOISE. *Bishop Kelly High School*, 7009 Franklin Rd., 83709-0998. Tel: 208-375-6010; Fax: 208-375-3626. Dr. David Lachiondo, Prin. Lay Teachers 39; Students 672.

COEUR D'ALENE. *Holy Family Catholic School of Coeur d'Alene*, 406 N. Tenth, 83814. Tel: 208-765-4327; Fax: 208-664-2903. Karen Durgin, Prin. Lay Teachers 8; Students 175.

[B] GENERAL HOSPITALS

BOISE. *St. Alphonsus Regional Medical Center, Inc.*, 1055 N. Curtis Rd., 83706. Tel: 208-378-2121
For a complete listing, refer to the Hospitals section.

COTTONWOOD. *St. Mary's Hospital*, 701 N. Lewiston St., P.O. Box 137, 83522. Tel: 208-962-3251; Fax: 208-962-3722
For a complete listing, refer to the Hospitals section.

JEROME. *St. Benedict's Family Medical Center*, 709 N. Lincoln, 83338. Tel: 208-324-4301; Fax: 208-324-3878
For a complete listing, refer to the Hospitals section.

LEWISTON. *St. Joseph Regional Medical Center*, 415 6th St., P.O. Box 816, 83501. Tel: 208-743-2511
For a complete listing, refer to the Hospitals section.

NAMPA. *Mercy Medical Center*, 1512 12th Avenue Rd., 83686. Tel: 208-467-1171
For a complete listing, refer to the Hospitals section.

[C] MONASTERIES AND RESIDENCES OF PRIESTS AND BROTHERS

JEROME. *Monastery of the Ascension*, 541 East, 100 South, 83338. Tel: 208-324-2377; Fax: 208-324-2377. Order of St. Benedict. Revs. Boniface Lautz, O.S.B., Prior; Norbert Novak, O.S.B., Subprior; Meinrad Schallberger, O.S.B.; Jude Anderson, O.S.B.; Andrew Baumgartner, O.S.B.; Hugh Feiss, O.S.B.; Joel Kehoe, O.S.B.; Eugene Esch, O.S.B.; Simeon VanDeVoord, O.S.B.; Bros. Sylvester Sonnen, O.S.B.; Tobiah Urrutia, O.S.B.; Inigo Echanove, O.S.B.

LEMHI. *Hermitage of St. Joseph*, Box 37, 83465. Hermits of Mt. Carmel. Rev. Peter Bourne, H.M.C., Prior; Bro. Maurice Mansfield, H.M.C.

[D] CONVENTS AND RESIDENCES OF SISTERS

BOISE. *St. Alphonsus Regional Medical Center Convent-Sisters of Holy Cross*, 2480 N. Westminster Ln., 83704. Tel: 208-367-2121. Legal Title: *Sisters of the Holy Cross, Inc.* Sisters 2.

COTTONWOOD. *Monastery of St. Gertrude, Motherhouse and Novitiate*, HC3 Box 121, 83522-9408. Tel: 208-962-3224; Fax: 208-962-7212. Sr. Jean LaLande, O.S.B., Prioress; Sr. Meg Sass, O.S.B., Asst. Prioress. Sisters of St. Benedict 61.

MESA. *Marymount Hermitage, Inc., Hermit Sisters of Mary*, 2150 Hermitage Ln., 83643-5005. Tel: 208-256-4354 (msg. only). Sr. Rebecca Mary Bonnell, H.S.M., Supr.; Rev. Robert E. Griffin, S.J., Chap. Sisters 2.

[E] RETREAT HOUSES

BOISE. *Nazareth*, 4450 N. Five Mile Rd., 83713-2709. Tel: 208-375-2932; Fax: 208-376-5787. Sr. Grayce E. Ross, S.N.J.M., Exec. Dir.
Advisory Council: Mr. James Ballantyne; Mr. Cornelius O'Keeffe; Mrs. Greta Pate; Rev. Joseph DaSilva.

[F] CAMPUS MINISTRY

BOISE. *Boise State University, St. Paul's Catholic Center*, 1915 University Dr., 83706. Tel: 208-343-2128; Fax: 208-343-2142. Charles L. Skoro, Dir.

CALDWELL. *Albertson's College of Idaho*, c/o St. Mary, 616 Dearborn, Box 399, 83606. Tel: 208-459-3653; Fax: 208-454-8789. Rev. Enrique Terriquez.

COEUR D'ALENE. *North Idaho College*, St Pius X, 625 E. Haycraft, 83815. Tel: 208-765-5108; Fax: 208-664-5325. Rev. Roger LaChance.

LEWISTON. *Lewis and Clark State College*, St. Stanislaus, 633 5th Ave., 83501. Tel: 208-743-7331; Fax: 208-746-7134. Sr. Margie Schmidt, O.S.B.

MOSCOW. *St. Augustine Catholic Center*. (Serving University of Idaho.), 628 Deakin, Box 3457, 83843-1911. Tel: 208-882-4613; Fax: 208-882-2823. Rev. Mark R. Schumacher.

POCATELLO. *Idaho State University, St. John's Catholic Student Center*, 920 E. Lovejoy, I.S.U. Box 8129, 83209. Tel: 208-233-0880; Fax: 208-233-5745. Fawndora Neeser, Dir.

TWIN FALLS. *College of Southern Idaho*. Attended by St. Edward the Confessor, Twin Falls, 630 Falls Ave., 83301-3300. Tel: 208-734-2327; Fax: 208-734-4145. Rev. Ernie Anderson.

[G] MISCELLANEOUS

BOISE. *The Catholic Migrant Farmworker Network, Inc.*, 1915 University Dr., 83706-3022. Tel: 208-384-1778; Fax: 208-384-1879. Celine Caufield, Exec. Dir.

St. Vincent de Paul Society. St. Francis of Assisi Conference. 6464 W. State St., 83703. Tel: 208-853-4921; Fax: 208-853-4935. Charles Nilles, Exec. Dir.

St. Vincent de Paul Society. St. John's Conference. 5645 Hallmark Ct., 83703. Tel: 208-344-3302. Francis McDonnell, Pres.

St. Vincent de Paul Society. Risen Christ Conference. 5059 Silverspur, 83709. Tel: 208-362-3778. Karen Knotts, Pres.

St. Vincent de Paul Society. Sacred Heart Conference. 314 Jackson, 83705. Tel: 208-344-6947. Ida Fisk, Pres.

Southwest Idaho District Council, 3717 Ticonderoga, 83706. Tel: 208-344-0702; Fax: 208-331-1047. Margo Henning, Pres.

BLACKFOOT. *St. Vincent de Paul Thrift Store*. St. Bernard Conference. 206 S. Spruce, 83221. Tel: 208-785-0353; 785-0423; Fax: 208-782-0224. Brian Cornett, Pres.

CALDWELL. *Society of St. Vincent de Paul*. St. Vincent de Paul of Canyon County Conference. 3719 E. Cleveland Blvd., 83605. Tel: 208-454-2132. Jerry Phillips, Store Mgr.

CLARKSTON, WA. *Lewis and Clark District Council of St. Vincent de Paul*. St. Stanislaus Conference. 604 2nd St., 99403. Mary Ropp, Pres., 422 15th Ave., Lewiston, ID, 83501. Tel: 208-746-2329.

COEUR D'ALENE. *St. Vincent de Paul Store*. St. Thomas Conference. 108 E. Walnut, 83814. Tel: 208-664-3095; Fax: 208-664-1772. Lynn Peterson, Exec. Dir.

IDAHO FALLS. *St. Vincent de Paul Society of Idaho Falls*, 433 May St., 83404-2619. Tel: 208-528-9979; Fax: 208-522-6280. Corbett Jonker, Mgr.

KELLOGG. *Society of St. Vincent de Paul*. St. Rita Conference. 104 E. Riverside, 83837. Tel: 208-783-5551. Gary Strope, Pres.

MERIDIAN. *St. Vincent Thrift Store*, 213 E. First St., 83642. Tel: 208-888-9101. Charles Nilles, Exec. Dir.

MOUNTAIN HOME. *St. Vincent de Paul Society*. Our Lady of Good Counsel Conference. P.O. Box 310, 83647. Tel: 208-587-3046; Fax: 208-587-5114. Kathleen M. Hiler, Pres.

NAMPA. *Mercy Housing Idaho, Inc.*, 1512 12th Avenue Rd., 83686. Tel: 208-463-5858; Fax: 208-463-5859. Mary W. Pridmore, Vice Pres. Housing & Community Devel.
Mercy Properties II, Inc.
Mercy Affordable Housing, Inc.
Mercy Idaho Properties, Inc.
Mercy Twin Falls, Inc.
Mercy Moscow, Inc.
Mercy Southeast Idaho, Inc.

POCATELLO. *PortNeuf Valley Conference (St. Vincent de Paul)*, 335 N. Main, 83204-8359. Tel: 208-233-2555; Fax: 208-478-8359. Rilla James, Mgr.

TWIN FALLS. *St. Michael Conference (St. Vincent de Paul)*, 244 Main Ave. S., 83301. Tel: 208-734-9143. Mary Nutting, Pres.; Rick Mesaros, Store Mgr.

RELIGIOUS INSTITUTES OF MEN REPRESENTED IN THE DIOCESE

For further details refer to the corresponding bracketed number in the Religious Institutes of Men or Women section.

[]—*Apostolic Life Community of Priests.*—A.L.C.P.

[0200]—*Benedictine Monks.*—O.S.B.

[0690]—*Jesuit Fathers.* (Oregon Prov.).—S.J.

[0840]—*Missionary Servants of the Most Holy Trinity.*—S.T.

[1070]—*Redemptorist Fathers.* (Oakland Prov.).—C.SS.R.

RELIGIOUS INSTITUTES OF WOMEN REPRESENTED IN THE DIOCESE

[0230]—*Benedictine Sisters of Pontifical Jurisdiction.*—O.S.B.

[1920]—*Congregation of the Sisters of the Holy Cross.*—C.S.C.

[1780]—*Congregation of the Sisters of the Third Order of St. Francis of Perpetual Adoration.*—F.S.P.A.

[1070-21]—*Dominican Sisters.*—O.P.

[]—*Hermit Sisters of Mary.*—H.S.M.

[1250]—*Institute of the Franciscan Sisters of the Eucharist.*—F.S.E.

[2575]—*Institute of the Sisters of Mercy of the Americas.*—R.S.M.

[3340]—*Sisters of Providence.*—S.P.

[1705]—*Sisters of St. Francis of Assisi.* (Milwaukee, WI).—O.S.F.

[3830]—*Sisters of St. Joseph.*—C.S.J.

[1990]—*Sisters of the Holy Names of Jesus and Mary.*—S.N.J.M.

[]—*Society of Sisters of the Church.*—S.S.C.

[4110]—*Ursuline Nuns.* (Western Prov.).—O.S.U.

NECROLOGY

† Aresserial, Xavier, Pocatello, ID St. Anthony. —Died Feb. 2, 2000.

† Hughes, Martin, (Retired). —Died Dec. 28, 1999.

† Later, Morse, (Retired). —Died June 1, 2000.

† Lustig, Victor, (Retired). —Died March 18, 2000.

Archdiocese of Boston

(Archidioecesis Bostoniensis)

His Eminence

BERNARD CARDINAL LAW, D.D.

Archbishop of Boston; ordained priest May 21, 1961; ordained bishop of Springfield-Cape Girardeau December 5, 1973; appointed Archbishop of Boston March 23, 1984; named Cardinal Priest of Santa Susanna on May 25, 1985. *Office and Residence: 2101 Commonwealth Ave., Boston, MA, 02135-3192.* Tel.: 617-782-2544; Fax: 617-782-8358.

Chancery Office: 2121 Commonwealth Ave., Boston, MA, 02135-3193. Tel.: 617-254-0100; Fax: 617-783-4564.

Web site address: www.rcab.org

Most Reverend

WILLIAM FRANCIS MURPHY, D.D., S.T.D.

Auxiliary Bishop of Boston, Titular Bishop of Saia Maior, Vicar General and Moderator of the Curia; ordained December 16, 1964; ordained Bishop December 27, 1995. *Office and Residence: 2121 Commonwealth Ave., Boston, MA, 02135-3193.* Tel.: 617-254-0100; Fax: 617-783-2947.

Most Reverend

JOHN PATRICK BOLES, D.D., PH.D.

Auxiliary Bishop of Boston, Titular Bishop of Nova Sparsa Vicar General and Regional Bishop-Central; ordained February 2, 1955; ordained Bishop May 21, 1992. *Office: 307 Bowdoin St., Boston, MA, 02122-2245.* Tel.: 617-436-3113; Fax: 617-436-7619. *Res., St. Gregory Rectory, 2223 Dorchester Ave., Boston, MA, 02124-5671.*

Most Reverend

FRANCIS XAVIER IRWIN, D.D., A.C.S.W.

Auxiliary Bishop of Boston, Titular Bishop of Ubaza, Vicar General and Regional Bishop-North; ordained February 2, 1960; ordained Bishop September 17, 1996. *Office and Residence: 2 Gardener St., Peabody, MA, 01960-1896.* Tel.: 978-531-1013; Fax: 978-531-5312.

Most Reverend

EMILIO SIMEON ALLUE, S.D.B., D.D., PH.D.

Auxiliary Bishop of Boston, Titular Bishop of Croe, Vicar General and Regional Bishop-Merrimack. *Office and Residence: 827 Gorham St., Lowell, MA, 01852.* Tel.: 978-459-4082; Fax: 978-452-5584.

Most Reverend

RICHARD JOSEPH MALONE, D.D., S.T.L., TH.D.

Auxiliary Bishop of Boston, Titular Bishop of Aptuca, Vicar General and Regional Bishop-South; ordained priest May 20, 1972; ordained Bishop March 1, 2000. *Office: 236 Pleasant St., Weymouth, MA, 02190-2509.* Tel.: 781-337-4413; Fax: 781-337-3625. *Res., Holy Ghost Rectory, 518 Washington St., Whitman, MA, 02382.*

Most Reverend

LAWRENCE JOSEPH RILEY, D.D., S.T.D.

Auxiliary Bishop Emeritus of Boston and Titular Bishop of Daimlaig; ordained priest September 21, 1940; ordained bishop February 2, 1972; named Assistant at the Pontifical Throne January 1987; resigned January 16, 1990. *Office and Residence: Most Precious Blood Rectory, 43 Maple St., Boston, MA, 02136-2738.* Tel.: 617-364-9500; Fax: 617-364-2590.

Most Reverend

JOHN RICHARD McNAMARA, D.D.

Auxiliary Bishop Emeritus of Boston and Titular Bishop of Risinium; ordained priest January 10, 1952; ordained bishop May 21, 1992; resigned October 12, 1999. *Office and Residence: Regina Cleri Residence, 60 William Cardinal O'Connell Way, Boston, MA, 02114.* Tel.: 617-523-1861; Fax: 617-720-0585.

ERECTED APRIL 8, 1808; MADE METROPOLITAN ARCHDIOCESE FEBRUARY 12, 1875.

Square Miles 2,465.

Comprises the Counties of Essex, Middlesex, Norfolk, Suffolk and Plymouth (excepting the towns of Marion, Mattapoisetts and Wareham) in the Commonwealth of Massachusetts.

For legal titles of parishes and archdiocesan institutions, consult the Chancery Office.

STATISTICAL OVERVIEW

Personnel	
Cardinal	1
Auxiliary Bishops	5
Retired Bishops	2
Abbots	1
Priests: Diocesan Active in Diocese	560
Priests: Active Outside Diocese	46
Priests: Diocesan in Foreign Missions	14
Priests: Retired, Sick or Absent	312
Number of Diocesan Priests	932
Religious Priests in Diocese	842
Extern Priests in Diocese	23
Ordinations:	
Diocesan Priests	8
Permanent Deacons	22
Permanent Deacons in Diocese	190
Total Brothers	105
Total Sisters	2,877
Parishes	
Parishes	369
With Resident Pastor:	
Resident Diocesan Priests	336
Resident Religious Priests	27
Without Resident Pastor:	
Administered by Priests	6
Pastoral Centers	2
New Parishes Created	1
Closed Parishes	5
Welfare	
Catholic Hospitals	10
Total Assisted	833,311
Health Care Centers	6
Total Assisted	4,181
Homes for the Aged	11
Total Assisted	2,748
Residential Care of Children	1
Total Assisted	430
Day Care and Extended Day Care Centers	11
Total Assisted	1,675
Specialized Homes	22
Total Assisted	1,656
Special Centers for Social Services	43
Total Assisted	203,792
Residential Care of Disabled	8
Total Assisted	199
Other Institutions	3
Total Assisted	29,647
Educational	
Seminaries, Diocesan	4
Students from This Diocese	45
Students from Other Diocese	139
Seminaries, Religious	4
Students Religious	152
Total Seminarians	197
Colleges and Universities	7
Total Students	21,457
High Schools, Diocesan and Parish	15
Total Students	5,941
High Schools, Private	20
Total Students	11,159
Elementary Schools, Diocesan and Parish	119
Total Students	36,329
Elementary Schools, Private	9
Total Students	2,626
Non-residential Schools for the Disabled	3
Total Students	343
Catechesis/Religious Education:	
High School Students	31,128
Elementary Students	125,954
Total Students Under Catholic Instruction	234,937
Teachers in the Diocese:	
Priests	6
Brothers	33
Sisters	468
Lay Teachers	3,092
Vital Statistics	
Receptions into the Church:	
Infant Baptism Totals	29,301
Adult Baptism Totals	575
Received into Full Communion	383
First Communions	24,735
Confirmations	15,748
Marriages:	
Catholic	6,027
Interfaith	1,507
Total Marriages	7,534
Deaths	18,847
Total Catholic Population	2,038,032
Total Population	3,857,751

Former Bishops—His Eminence JOHN LEFEVRE CARDINAL DE CHEVERUS, ord. Dec. 18, 1790; appt. first Bishop of Boston, Apr. 8, 1808; ord. Nov. 1, 1810; transferred to Montauban, Jan. 15, 1823, then to Bordeaux, Oct. 2, 1826; appt. Cardinal Archbishop of Bordeaux, Oct. 2, 1826; died July 19, 1836.—Most Rev. BENEDICT J. FENWICK, S.J., ord. June 11, 1808; appt. second Bishop of Boston, May 10, 1825; ord. Nov. 1, 1825; died Aug. 11, 1846.—Most Rev. JOHN BERNARD FITZPATRICK, ord. June 13, 1840; appt. Titular Bishop of Callipolis and Coadjutor of Boston, Nov. 21, 1843; ord. March 24, 1844; appt. third Bishop of Boston, Aug. 11, 1846; died Feb. 13, 1866.—Most Rev. JOHN JOSEPH WILLIAMS, D.D., ord. May 17, 1845; appt. Titular Bishop of Tripolis and Coadjutor of Boston, Jan. 8, 1866; ord. fourth Bishop of Boston, March 11, 1866; named first Archbishop of Boston, Feb. 12, 1875; died Aug. 30,

1907.—His Eminence WILLIAM CARDINAL O'CONNELL, ord. June 7, 1884; appt. third Bishop of Portland, Maine, Feb. 8, 1901; ord. May 19, 1901; appt. Titular Archbishop of Constantia and Coadjutor with right of succession to the Archbishop of Boston, Feb. 8, 1906; appt. fifth Bishop and second Archbishop of Boston, April 30, 1907; named Cardinal, Nov. 27, 1911, Titular Church, San Clemente; died April 22, 1944.—His Eminence RICHARD CARDINAL CUSHING, ord. May 26, 1921; appt. Titular Bishop of Mela and Auxiliary of Boston, June 10, 1939; ord. June 29, 1939; appt. sixth Bishop and third Archbishop of Boston, Sept. 25, 1944; named Cardinal December 15, 1958, Titular Church, Santa Susanna; died Nov. 2, 1970.—His Eminence HUMBERTO CARDINAL MEDEIROS, ord. June 15, 1946; appt. second Bishop of Brownsville, April 14, 1966; ord. June 9, 1966; named seventh Bishop and fourth Archbishop of Boston, Sept. 8, 1970; named Cardinal March 5, 1973, Titular Church, Santa Susanna; died Sept. 17, 1983.

Regional Bishops—Central Region: Most Rev. JOHN P. BOLES, D.D., Ed.D., Bishop's Office: *307 Bowdoin St., Dorchester, 02122-2245.* Tel: 617-436-3113; Fax: 617-436-7619. Merrimack Region: Most Rev. EMILIO S. ALLUE, S.D.B., D.D., S.T.L., Ph.D., Bishop's Office and Residence: *827 Gorham St., Lowell, 01852.* Tel: 978-459-4082; Fax: 978-452-5584. North Region: Most Rev. FRANCIS X. IRWIN, D.D., A.S.C.W., Bishop's Office and Residence: *2 Gardner St., Peabody, 01960-1896.* Tel: 978-531-1013; Fax: 978-531-5312. South Region: Most Rev. RICHARD J. MALONE, D.D., Th.D., S.T.L., Bishop's Office: *236 Pleasant St., Weymouth, 02190-2599.* Tel: 781-337-4413; Fax: 781-337-3625. West Region:; Vacant, Bishop's Office and Residence: *248 School St., Watertown, 02472-1495.* Tel: 617-926-2117; Fax: 617-926-2160.

Vicars General—Most Rev. JOHN P. BOLES; Most Rev. FRANCIS X. IRWIN; Most Rev. EMILIO S. ALLUE, S.D.B.; Most Rev. WILLIAM F. MURPHY; Most Rev. RICHARD J. MALONE.

Vicars—

Central Region—CENTRAL REGION: Most Rev. JOHN P. BOLES, Regl. Bishop, *Regional Bishop's Office, Boston.* Tel: 617-436-3113. Rev. Msgr. CHARLES J. BOURQUE, V.F., Vicariate I, Pastor, *Our Lady of Lourdes Rectory, Jamaica Plain.* Tel: 617-524-0434. Very Rev. DANIEL J. RILEY, V.F., Vicariate II, Pastor, *St. William Rectory, Dorchester.* Tel: 617-265-0100. Very Rev. HUGH H. O'REGAN, V.F., Vicariate III, Pastor, *St. James the Greater, Boston.* Tel: 617-542-8498. Very Rev. ARTHUR F. WRIGHT, V.F., Vicariate IV, Pastor, *Immaculate Conception, Cambridge.* Tel: 617-547-3455. *MERRIMACK REGION: Most Rev.* EMILIO S. ALLUE, S.D.B., D.D., S.T.L., Ph.D., *Regional Bishop's Office, Lowell.* Tel: 978-459-4082. Very Rev. RICHARD J. CRAIG, V.F., Chelmsford Vicariate, Pastor, *St. John the Evangelist, Chelmsford.* Tel: 978-251-8571. Very Rev. MARK S. SHEEHAN, V.F., Concord Vicariate, Pastor, *St. Michael Rectory, Bedford.* Tel: 781-275-6318. Very Rev. JAMES M. CARROLL, V.F., Haverhill Vicariate, Pastor, *St. Mary, Georgetown.* Tel: 978-352-2024. Vacant, Lawrence Vicariate; Very Rev. JOHN F. HANLEY, O.M.I., V.F., Lowell Vicariate, Parochial Vicar, *Immaculate Conception, Lowell.* Tel: 978-458-1474. *NORTH REGION: Most Rev.* FRANCIS X. IRWIN, Regl. Bishop, *Regional Bishop's Office, Peabody.* Tel: 978-531-1013. Very Rev. JOHN E. FARRELL, V.F., Gloucester Vicariate, Pastor, *Our Lady of the Assumption, Lynnfield.* Tel: 781-598-4313. Very Rev. BRIAN M. FLATLEY, V.F., Medford Vicariate, Pastor, *St. Agnes, Arlington.* Tel: 781-648-0220. Rev. Msgr. PAUL V. GARRITY, V.F., Salem Vicariate, Pastor, *St. Mary, Lynn.* Tel: 781-598-2088. Very Rev. VINCENT P. MELLONE, V.F., Stoneham Vicariate, Pastor, *St. Barbara, Woburn.* Tel: 781-933-4130. *SOUTH REGION: Most Rev.* RICHARD J. MALONE, D.D., Th.D., S.T.L., Regl. Bishop, *Regional Bishop's Office, Weymouth.* Tel: 781-337-4413. Very Rev. JOSEPH H. MANNING, V.F., Brockton Vicariate, Pastor, *Our Lady of Lourdes, Brockton.* Tel: 508-586-4715. Very Rev. JOHN A. DOOHER, V.F., Norwood Vicariate, Pastor, *St. Mary, Dedham.* Tel: 781-326-0550. Rev. Msgr. FREDERICK J. RYAN, V.F., Plymouth Vicariate, Pastor, *St. Joseph, Kingston.* Tel: 781-585-6679. Very Rev. DANIEL M. GRAHAM, V.F., Quincy Vicariate, Pastor, *St. Joseph, Quincy.* Tel: 617-479-7810. Very Rev. JAMES J. RAFFERTY, V.F., Weymouth Vicariate, Pastor, *St. Paul, Hingham.* Tel: 781-749-0587. *WEST REGION: Very Rev.* ROBERT C. FICHTNER, Interim Regl. Vicar, *Regional Bishop's Office, Watertown.* Tel: 617-926-2117. Rev. Msgr. FRANCIS V. STRAHAN, V.F., Framingham Vicariate, Pastor, *St. Bridget, Framingham.* Tel: 508-875-5959. Very Rev. MICHAEL J. BOVA CONTI, V.F., Marlborough Vicariate, Pastor, *Our Lady of Fatima, Sudbury.* Tel: 978-443-2647. Rev. Msgr. JOSEPH G. LIND, V.F., Natick Vicariate, Pastor, *St. Paul, Wellesley.* Tel: 781-235-1060. Rev. Msgr. ROGER J. BRADY, V.F., Newton Vicariate, Pastor, *St. Luke Parish, Belmont.* Tel: 617-484-1996.

Archdiocesan Consultative Bodies—

Presbyteral Council—His Eminence BERNARD CARDINAL LAW, Pres.; Most Rev. EMILIO S. ALLUE, S.D.B.; Most Rev. JOHN P. BOLES; Most Rev. FRANCIS X. IRWIN; Most Rev. JOHN R. MCNAMARA; Most Rev. RICHARD J. MALONE; Most Rev. WILLIAM F. MURPHY; Most Rev. LAWRENCE J. RILEY; Rev. Msgr. PETER V. CONLEY; Rev. Msgr. THOMAS J. DALY; Rev. Msgr. WILLLIAM A. GRANVILLE; Rev. Msgr. FRANCIS H. KELLEY; Rev. Msgr. FRANCIS D. KELLY; Rev. Msgr. RICHARD G. LENNON; Very Rev. ROBERT C. FICHTNER; Revs. ROBERT L. CONNORS; RICHARD S. DEVEER; ROBERT C. FICHTNER; OSCAR J. PRATT; G. MICHAEL BERCIK, O.F.M.; JAMES BERTELLI; ROBERT W. BULLOCK; WALTER A. CARREIRO; THOMAS F. CLARK, S.J.; PAUL T. CLIFFORD; ARNOLD F. COLLETTI; ARTHUR M. COYLE; JAMES D. FOLEY; MICHAEL S. FOSTER; JOHN W. GENTLEMAN; PAUL K. HURLEY; WILLIAM P. JOY; ROBERT T. KICKHAM; CAMILLO LANDO, C.S.; JOHN E. MACINNIS; STEPHEN J. MADDEN; JUSTINIAN MANNING, C.P.; JOHN P. MCGINTY; PATRICK J. MCLAUGHLIN; WILLIAM O'DONNELL, O.M.I.; GREGORY SHORT, O.M.V.; JOHN P. TACKNEY; GEORGE D. VARTZELIS; WALTER WAGNER, O.P.; WILLIAM F. WALTERS, O.S.A.

Archdiocesan College of Consultors—His Eminence BERNARD CARDINAL LAW; Most Rev. EMILIO S. ALLUE, S.D.B.; Most Rev. JOHN P. BOLES; Most Rev. FRANCIS X. IRWIN; Most Rev. JOHN R. MCNAMARA; Most Rev. RICHARD J. MALONE; Most Rev. WILLIAM F. MURPHY; Most Rev. LAWRENCE J. RILEY; Very Rev. ROBERT C. FICHTNER; Revs. ROBERT L. CONNORS; RICHARD S. DEVEER; OSCAR J. PRATT.

Finance Council—His Eminence BERNARD CARDINAL LAW, Pres. Members: Most. Rev. WILLIAM F. MURPHY; Ms. REGINA E. CAINES; Mr. JOHN CUNNINGHAM; Mr. THOMAS J. FLATLEY; Sr. THERESE HIGGINS, C.S.J.; Mr. JOHN A. KANEB; Mr. PETER S. LYNCH; Mr. WILLIAM F. MCCALL; Mr. JOHN A. MCNIECE; Mr. JAMES MOONEY; Mr. ROBERT J. MORRISSEY; Mr. GILES MOSHER; Mr. GERALD T. REILLY; Mrs. MICHAEL A. VALERIO; Mr. FRANCIS M. WARD.

Archdiocesan Pastoral Council—His Eminence BERNARD CARDINAL LAW, Pres. Ex officio: Most. Rev. WILLIAM F. MURPHY; Most Rev. JOHN R. MCNAMARA; Most Rev. JOHN P. BOLES; Most Rev. FRANCIS X. IRWIN; Most Rev. EMILIO S. ALLUE, S.D.B.; Most Rev. RICHARD J. MALONE; Most Rev. LAWRENCE J. RILEY; Rev. Msgr. FRANCIS D. KELLY; Rev. Msgr. RICHARD G. LENNON; Very Rev. ROBERT C. FICHTNER; Rev. ARTHUR M. COYLE; Mr. GERALD T. REILLY. Appointed: Rev. Msgr. PAUL B. MCINERNY; Revs. WALLACE E. BLACKWOOD; BRIAN CLARY; JOHN CULLOTY; JOSE FERRIERA; MICHAEL FOSTER; ROBERT LEVENS, S.J.; MICHAEL W. MACEWAN; CHRISTOPHER O'CONNOR; LAWRENCE PRATT; PETER UGLIETTO; Deacons ROBERT JOHNSON; RICHARD MCLAUGHLIN; Sr. MARY ANNE DOYLE, C.S.J.; Sr. GERMANA SANTOS, F.S.P.; FRANK J. ANGIULO; PATRICK ARMANO; CATHERINE A. BACOTE; IRENE BONNER; E. THOMAS BOULETTE; LAURA CHAN; JOAN COLLUPY; FRANCIS L. COLPOYS; KATHLEEN COVEYOU; SHIRLEY T. CYR; LINDA DECRISTOFORO; PATRICIA E. DELANEY; MICHAEL FARMA; KATHLEEN HECK; STEVEN A. KRUEGER; RUTH LEBRUN; ROGER LEMIRE; MARIANNE LUTHIN; MICHAEL MANZI; GARY MARTIN; SUSAN MATTUCHIO; JOHN P. MCGONAGLE; GEORGE W. PACHECO; LEONARD PEPE; THERESA PERRY; CARA RYAN; EDWARD W. SANTOS; WILLIAM J. SAWYER; CAROLE ANNE SCOTT; ALVIN SHIGGS; CLAIRE M. SOULNIER; LORI A. SOUSA; JOHN STEWART; TED WOODWARD; TER YANG; Dr. PAUL Y. YIN.

Vicar General and Moderator of the Curia—Most Rev. WILLIAM F. MURPHY, *2121 Commonwealth Ave., Boston, 02135-3193.* Tel: 617-254-0100; Fax: 617-783-2947.

Assistant to the Moderator of the Curia for Administrative Affairs—Vacant.

Assistant to the Moderator of the Curia for Canonical Affairs—Rev. JAMES M. DIPERRI, *2121 Commonwealth Ave., Boston, 02135-3193.* Tel: 617-254-0100; Fax: 617-746-5754.

Development—ROBERT X. CHANDLER, *2121 Commonwealth Ave., Boston, 02135-3193.* Tel: 617-254-0100; Fax: 617-783-6366.

Holy Childhood Association—Rev. Msgr. ANDREW F. CONNELL, *49 Franklin St., Boston, 02110-1382.* Tel: 617-542-1771; Fax: 617-542-1778.

Planning and Research—Rev. ROBERT MCMILLAN, S.J., *2121 Commonwealth Ave., Boston, 02135-3193.* Tel: 617-254-0100; Fax: 617-746-5754.

Propagation of the Faith—Rev. Msgr. ANDREW F. CONNELL, *49 Franklin St., Boston, 02110-1382.* Tel: 617-542-1776; Fax: 617-542-1778.

Society of St. Peter the Apostle—Rev. Msgr. ANDREW F. CONNELL, *49 Franklin St., Boston, 02110-1382.* Tel: 617-542-1771; Fax: 617-542-1778.

Synod Office—Vacant, Exec. Dir., *2121 Commonwealth Ave., Boston, 02135-3193.* Tel: 617-254-0100; Fax: 617-746-5754.

Cabinet Secretaries

Secretary for Central Services—GERALD T. REILLY, *2121 Commonwealth Ave., Boston, 02135-3193.* Tel: 617-254-0100; Fax: 617-783-4564.

Secretary for Community Relations—JOHN B. WALSH, *2121 Commonwealth Ave., Boston, 02135-3193.* Tel: 617-254-0100; Fax: 617-782-8358.

Secretary for Education, Acting—Sr. CLARE BERTERO, O.S.F., *One Lake St., Boston, 02135-3800.* Tel: 617-254-4425; Fax: 617-782-0213.

Secretary for Health Care Services—MICHAEL F. COLLINS, M.D., *736 Cambridge St., Boston, 02135-2997.* Tel: 617-789-2500; Fax: 617-789-2124.

Secretary for Ministerial Personnel—Rev. PAUL E. MICELI, *2121 Commonwealth Ave., Boston, 02135-3193.* Tel: 617-254-0100; Fax: 617-783-2947.

Secretary for Pastoral Services—Rev. PAUL B. O'BRIEN, *2121 Commonwealth Ave., Boston, 02135-3193.* Tel: 617-254-0100; Fax: 617-783-2947.

Secretary for Social Services—Dr. JOSEPH DOOLIN, *75 Kneeland St., Boston, 02111-1931.* Tel: 617-482-5440; Fax: 617-451-0337.

Delegate for Religious—Sr. ROBERTA MARIE BROWN, C.S.J., *2121 Commonwealth Ave., Boston, 02135-3193.* Tel: 617-254-0100; Fax: 617-783-2947.

Chancery Office—2121 Commonwealth Ave., Boston, 02135-3193. Tel: 617-254-0100; Fax: 617-783-4564. Office Hours: Mon.-Fri. 9-5.

Chancellor—GERALD T. REILLY, *2121 Commonwealth Ave., Boston, 02135-3193.* Tel: 617-254-0100; Fax: 617-783-4564.

Archdiocesan Counsel—WILSON D. ROGERS, Esq., *2121 Commonwealth Ave., Boston, 02135-3193.* Tel: 617-254-0100; Fax: 617-783-2947.

Archivist—ROBERT JOHNSON-LALLY, *2121 Commonwealth Ave., Boston, 02135-3193.* Tel: 617-254-0100; Fax: 617-783-5642.

Secretaries to the Cardinal and Masters of Ceremonies—Rev. Msgr. PAUL B. MCINERNY; Rev. MICHAEL W. MACEWEN, *Cardinal's Residence, 2101 Commonwealth Ave., Boston, 02135-3192.* Tel: 617-782-2544; Fax: 617-782-8358.

Metropolitan Tribunal—One Lake St., Boston, 02135-3800. Tel: 617-746-5900; Fax: 617-783-2423. Office Hours: Mon.-Fri. 9-5.

Judicial Vicar—Rev. MICHAEL S. FOSTER, J.C.D.

Promoter of Justice—Rev. Msgr. RICHARD G. CUNNINGHAM, J.C.D.

Defender of the Bond—Rev. JAMES G. BURKE, J.C.L.

Secretary to the Tribunal—JOANNE M. CURRY, M.A.

Archdiocesan Judges—Rev. Msgr. RICHARD G. CUNNINGHAM, J.C.D.; Rev. Msgr. ROBERT P. DEELEY, J.C.D.; Rev. Msgr. PAUL B. MCINERNY, J.C.L.; Revs. JAMES G. BURKE, J.C.L.; RODNEY J. COPP, J.C.L.; MICHAEL S. FOSTER, J.C.D.; JAMES A. O'DONOHOE, J.C.D.; Sr. MARGARET L. SULLIVAN, C.S.J., J.C.L.

Judge Auditor—Rev. JAMES W. DEADDER, S.T.D., Ph.D., J.D.

Court Advocates—Rev. PETER G. GORI, O.S.A., J.C.D.

Advocates—Rev. Msgr. FRANCIS H. KELLEY; Revs. JOSEPH A. ANTONELLIS; JAMES J. BARRY; MICHAEL J. BOVA CONTI; JOHN E. BUCKLEY; JAMES M. CARROLL; PETER J. CASEY; DISMAS CENTRELLA, O.F.M.; HENRY G. CHAMBERS; WILLIAM D. COUGHLIN; JOHN A. DOOHER; PAUL J. FINEGAN; PAUL R. E. FRANCIS, J.C.B., S.T.D.; MICHAEL HARKINS; GEORGE G. HOGAN; THOMAS A. KOPP; JAMES F. LANERGAN; VICTOR C. LAVOIE; JOHN F. LEONARD; ANTONIO MEDEIROS; BRIAN F. MANNING; DENNIS J. NASON; PETER J. O'HARA; JAMES E. O'LEARY; LEONARD F. O'MALLEY; GERALD J. OSTERMAN; PETER F. QUINN; THOMAS J. REILLY; FRANK J. SILVA; THOMAS J. WALSH; ROBERT A. WARD.

Psychological Consultants—Family Counseling & Guidance Centers, Inc., NEIL J. CRONIN, L.I.C.S.W., Clinical Dir. JOSEPH DOHERTY, Ed.D.; CHARLES J. FERRO, M.Ed.; MARGARET L. HAGER, L.I.C.S.W.; THOMAS F. HIGGINS, Ed.D.; CHARLES H. HOGAN, Psy.D.; FRANCIS J. KELLY, L.I.C.S.W., M.S.W.; HELEN O'MEARA, L.I.C.S.W.; CLAIRE O'ROURKE; MICHAEL ST. CLAIR, M.A., Ph.D.; JOSEPH LIFTIK, Ph.D.; THOMAS H. KELLEY, Ph.D.; KERNAN T. MANION, M.D.; PAUL MCCORMICK, M.Div., Ph.D.; A. EUGENE NEWMAN, Ph.D.; DANIEL J. QUINN, L.I.C.S.W.

Ecclesiastical Notaries—LAURA M. CELLUCCI; M. CONNIE MURPHY.

Seminaries—

Pope John XXIII National Seminary—Rev. Msgr. FRANCIS D. KELLY, S.T.D., Rector, *558 South St., Weston, 02493-2699.* Tel: 781-899-5500; Fax: 781-899-9057.

St. John Seminary School of Theology—Rev. Msgr. RICHARD G. LENNON, Rector, *Lake St., Boston, 02135-3898.* Tel: 617-254-2610; Fax: 617-787-2336.

St. John Seminary College of Liberal Arts—Rev. ROBERT W. FLAGG, Dean, *127 Lake St., Boston, 02135-3898.* Tel: 617-254-2610; Fax: 617-787-2336.

Continuing Education and Spiritual Enrichment of Priests—Rev. ARTHUR J. COYLE, *5 Lake St., Boston, 02135-3899.* Tel: 617-254-2610.

Central Services

Central Services—GERALD T. REILLY, Cabinet Sec., *2121 Commonwealth Ave., Boston, 02135-3193.* Tel: 617-254-0100; Fax: 617-783-4564.

Cemeteries—Deacon ANTHONY RIZZUTO, *175 Broadway, Malden, 02148-6097.* Tel: 888-919-7926; Fax: 781-322-3801.

Planning Office for Urban Affairs—Rev. Msgr. MICHAEL F. GRODEN, Dir., *185 Devonshire St., Boston, 02110-1407.* Tel: 617-350-8885; Fax: 617-350-8889.

Volunteer Resources—Mrs. ANN LALLY, *2121 Commonwealth Ave., Boston, 02135-3193.* Tel: 617-254-0100; Fax: 617-783-4564.

Community Relations—JOHN B. WALSH, Cabinet Sec., *2121 Commonwealth Ave., Boston, 02315-3193.* Tel: 617-254-0100; Fax: 617-562-1104.

Boston Catholic Directory—Rev. Msgr. PETER V. CONLEY, Editor; Rev. ROBERT M. O'GRADY, Assoc. Editor, *141 Tremont St., Boston, 02111-1209.* Tel: 617-542-8393; Fax: 617-542-9547.

Campaign for Human Development—Rev. WILLIAM F. JOY, *St. Angela Parish, 1548 Blue Hill Ave., Boston, 02126-2187.* Tel: 617-298-0080; Fax: 617-298-2388.

Communications—JOHN WALSH, Dir., *2121 Commonwealth Ave., Boston, 02135-3193.* Tel: 617-254-0100; Fax: 617-562-1104.

Labor Guild—Rev. EDWARD F. BOYLE, S.J., Dir., *883 Hancock St., Quincy, 02170-3860.* Tel: 617-786-1822; Fax: 617-472-2486.

Liaison for Catholic-Jewish Relations—Rev. DAVID C. MICHAEL, *St. Mary Rectory, 133 School St., Waltham, 02451.* Tel: 781-891-1730; Fax: 781-642-0604.

Massachusetts Catholic Conference—GERALD D'AVOLIO, Exec. Dir., *West End Place, 150 Staniford St., Boston, 02114-2511.* Tel: 617-367-6060; Fax: 617-367-2767.

The Pilot—Rev. Msgr. PETER V. CONLEY, Editor in Chief; Rev. ROBERT M. O'GRADY, Asst. to the Editor, *141 Tremont St., Boston, 02111-1209.* Tel: 617-482-4316; Fax: 617-482-5647.

Radio Apostolate—Rev. ROBERT P. REED, *Holy Ghost Parish, 518 Washington St., Whitman, 02382.* Tel: 781-447-4421; Fax: 781-447-1375.

TV Apostolate—Rev. Msgr. FRANCIS T. MCFARLAND, *55 Chapel St., P.O. Box 9109, Newton, 02158-9109.* Tel: 617-965-0050; Fax: 617-965-6587.

Boston Catholic Television Center, Inc.—55 Chapel St., P.O. Box 9109, Newton, 02158-9109. Tel: 617-965-0050; Fax: 617-965-6587.

Education

Education—Sr. CLARE BERTERO, O.S.F., Acting Cabinet Sec., *One Lake St., Boston, 02135-3800.* Tel: 617-254-4425; Fax: 617-782-0213.

Campus Ministry—Dr. JEANNE LAMARCHE, Dir., *68 St. Stephen St., Boston, 02115-4302.* Tel: 617-266-2635; Fax: 617-266-6148.

Catholic School Office—Sr. KATHLEEN CARR, C.S.J., Supt., Schools, *2200 Dorchester Ave., Boston, 02124-5607.* Tel: 617-298-6555; Fax: 617-298-6622.

Ecumenical and Interreligious Affairs—Rev. EDWARD M. O'FLAHERTY, S.J., Dir., *2121 Commonwealth Ave., Boston, 02135-3193.* Tel: 617-254-0100; Fax: 617-562-1104.

Religious Education—Sr. CLARE BERTERO, O.S.F., Dir., *One Lake St., Boston, 02135-3800.* Tel: 617-254-4425; Fax: 617-782-0213.

Social Justice—Rev. WILLIAM P. JOY, Dir., *St. Angela Merici Parish, 1548 Blue Hill Ave., Boston, 02126-2187.* Tel: 617-298-0080; Fax: 617-298-2388.

Health Care Services

Caritas Christi Health Care System—MICHAEL F. COLLINS, M.D., Pres. & C.E.O., *736 Cambridge St., Boston, 02135-2997.* Tel: 617-789-2500; Fax: 617-789-2124. - The Carney Hospital, Boston - Holy Family Hospital, Inc., Methuen - St. Elizabeth Medical Center, Boston - St. John of God Hospital, Boston - Good Samaritan Hospice, Inc., Boston - Good Samaritan Medical Center, Inc., Brockton & Stoughton - Caritas Christi Support Services, Inc., Boston - Holy Family Hospital Foundation, Inc., Methuen - Valley Regional Health System, Inc., Methuen - Valley Regional Support Services, Inc., Methuen - Metropolitan Boston Dialysis Center, Waltham Archdiocesan Liaison with all other Catholic Hospitals in the Archdiocese - Franciscan Children's Hospital & Rehabilitation Center, Boston - Sancta Maria Hospital, Cambridge - Youville Hospital, Cambridge - Bethany Hospital, Framingham - Saints Memorial Medical Center, Inc., Lowell.

Council of Nurses—ANNETTA L. ROMANO, R.N., Pres., *9 Nancia St., Boston, 02128-1261.* Tel: 617-569-1726.

Guild of St. Luke—GERALD P. CORCORAN, M.D., *87 Chestnut St., Needham, 02492-2514.* Tel: 781-444-5515; Fax: 781-444-1866.

Ministerial Personnel

Ministerial Personnel—Rev. PAUL E. MICELI, Cabinet Sec., *2121 Commonwealth Ave., Boston, 02135-3193.* Tel: 617-254-0100; Fax: 617-783-2947.

Assistant Secretary for Ministerial Personnel and Delegate of the Archbishop—Rev. CHARLES J. HIGGINS, *2121 Commonwealth Ave., Boston, 02135-3193.* Tel: 617-254-0100; Fax: 617-783-2947.

Clergy Personnel—Rev. RICHARD W. FITZGERALD, *One Lake St., Boston, 02135-3800.* Tel: 617-779-3685; Fax: 617-254-8407.

Delegate of the Archbishop—Rev. CHARLES J. HIGGINS, Delegate. Co-Delegates: Rev. JOHN A. DOOHER; Sr. RITA MCCARTHY, C.S.J., *2121 Commonwealth Ave., Boston, 02135-3193.* Tel: 617-254-0100; Fax: 617-783-2947.

Delegate for Religious—Sr. ROBERTA MARIE BROWN, C.S.J., *2121 Commonwealth Ave., Boston, 02135-3193.* Tel: 617-254-0100; Fax: 617-783-2947.

Lay Volunteer Program—PATRICK MARCHAN, *Pallotti Center, 159 Washington St., Boston, 02135.* Tel: 617-783-3924.

Pastoral Ministries—BARBARA A. SHINE, Dir.; Sr. DOROTHEA MASURET, C.S.J., *One Lake St., Boston, 02135-3800.* Tel: 617-782-6675; Fax: 617-254-8407.

Pastoral Support for Priests—Rev. EDWARD M. O'FLAHERTY, S.J., *5 Lake St., Boston, 02135-3899.* Tel: 617-254-2610.

Permanent Diaconate—Deacon LEO J. DONOGHUE, Dir.; Rev. ALVARO SILVA, Assoc. Dir. for Hispanic Deacons; Sr. CLARE O'KEEFE, S.C.H., Asst. Dir., *2121 Commonwealth Ave., Boston, 02135-3193.* Tel: 617-746-5648; Fax: 617-746-5699.

Priests Recovery Program—Rev. ROBERT P. BEALE, Dir., *287 Highland St., Milton, 02186-4413.* Tel: 617-696-0593.

Regina Cleri, Inc.—Rev. Msgr. JAMES E. TIERNEY, *60 William Cardinal O'Connell Way, Boston, 02114.* Tel: 617-523-1861; Fax: 617-720-0585.

Senior Priests—Rev. JAMES L. MCCUNE, Dir., *Regina Cleri, 60 William Cardinal O'Connell Way, Boston, 02114.* Tel: 617-523-1861; Fax: 617-720-0585.

Sisters Senate—Sr. MARY RITA GRADY, C.S.J., *72 Cresent Ave., Newton, 02459-2198.* Tel: 617-630-9057.

Society of St. James the Apostle—Rev. JOSEPH F. SHIELDS, Dir., *24 Clark St., Boston, 02109-1127.* Tel: 617-742-4715; Fax: 617-723-7389.

Vocation Information Center—Revs. ROBERT W. FLAGG; ROBERT M. BLANEY, *127 Lake St., Boston, 02135-3898.* Tel: 617-254-2610; Fax: 617-787-2336.

Pastoral Services

Pastoral Services—Rev. PAUL B. O'BRIEN, Cabinet Sec., *2121 Commonwealth Ave., Boston, 02135-3193.* Tel: 617-254-0100; Fax: 617-783-2947.

Black Catholics—MEYER CHAMBERS, *2121 Commonwealth Ave., Boston, 02135-3193.* Tel: 617-254-0100; Fax: 617-783-5642.

Charismatic Renewal—DAVID THORP, *20 Pond St., Waltham, 02451-4514.* Tel: 781-891-3592; Fax: 781-891-3593.

Courage—Rev. KEVIN F. MULLEN, O.F.M., Dir., *100 Arch St., Boston, 02107-2278.* Tel: 617-542-6440; Fax: 617-542-4225.

Cursillo—Rev. JOHN A. SASSANI, Spiritual Dir.; Mrs. MARY ANN MCLAUGHLIN, Dir., *2121 Commonwealth Ave., Boston, 02135-3193.* Tel: 617-783-1510.

Deaf Apostolate—Rev. MICHAEL J. MEDAS, *2121 Commonwealth Ave., Boston, 02135-3193.* Tel: 617-254-0100.

Ethnic Apostolates—Rev. VINCENZO ROSATO, C.S., Coord.; Sr. PEGGY LOFTUS, S.N.D.; Sr. CHARLOTTE KANE, S.N.D., *2121 Commonwealth Ave., Boston, 02135-3193.* Tel: 617-746-5805; Fax: 617-783-5642.

Asian Indian Apostolate—Rev. THOMAS D'SOUZA. Tel: 617-631-3443.

Brazilian Apostolate—Rev. ROBERT BOUFFIER, S.M. Tel: 617-354-5008.

Cambodian Apostolate—Rev. ANTHONY GIANG NGUYEN. Tel: 617-889-2774. Sr. PEGGY CUMMINS, S.N.D. Tel: 508-454-7663.

Cameroon Apostolate—Sr. MARILYN GIGNAC. Tel: 508-458-8862.

Cape Verdean Apostolate—Vacant. Tel: 617-445-7645.

Chinese Apostolate (Mandarin)—Rev. DENIS R. COMO, S.J. Tel: 617-482-2949.

Croatian Apostolate—JOYCE GALANTIC. Tel: 617-484-2619.

Ethiopian/Eritrean Apostolate—Rev. HABTAMARIAN KETEMA. Tel: 617-289-1234.

Laotion Apostolate—Sr. EILEEN BURNS, S.N.D. Tel: 508-599-7750.

Filipino Apostolate—Rev. JOHN COSS, F.M.S.I. Tel: 508-879-6711.

French Apostolate—Office for Ethnic Apostolates. Tel: 617-254-0100.

Ghanaian Apostolate—Rev. PETER AYOROGO. Tel: 617-325-1404.

German Apostolate—Rev. Msgr. FREDERICK J. MURPHY. Tel: 617-542-5682.

Haitian Apostolate—Rev. JOHN MORIN, O.M.I. Tel: 617-298-0080.

Hmong Apostolate—PAULE VERDET. Tel: 617-965-2499.

Irish Apostolate—Rev. DANIEL FINN. Tel: 617-288-2367.

Italian Apostolate—Rev. PRIMO PISCITELLO, O.F.M. Tel: 617-523-2110.

Japanese Apostolate—Sr. FEDRE TANNO, P.D.D.M. Tel: 617-482-0978.

Khmhu Laotian Apostolate—Rev. JOHN FAGAN, S.J. Tel: 617-445-1524.

Korean Apostolate—Rev. PAUL RI. Tel: 617-899-9947. Dr. KYU KIM. Tel: 508-835-6947.

Liberian Apostolate—Rev. JAMES CALLAHAN, S.M.A. Tel: 617-329-4774.

Lithuanian Apostolate—Rev. ALBERT CONTONS. Tel: 617-268-0353.

Nigerian Apostolate—Rev. GERALD OSTERMAN. Tel: 617-442-1431.

Polish Apostolate—Rev. Msgr. STANISLAUS SYPEK. Tel: 617-361-0565.

Portuguese Apostolate—Rev. JOSE S. FERREIRA. Tel: 617-547-5593.

Rwanda Apostolate—Rev. BASILE BAZINE. Tel: 617-229-6884.

Ugandan Apostolate—Dr. ALOYSIUS LUGIRA. Tel: 617-729-9245.

Vietnamese Apostolate—Rev. EPHREM VU KIEM CUNG, C.M.C. Tel: 617-265-2479.

Zaire Apostolate—Rev. BASILE BAZINE. Tel: 617-229-6884.

Family Life Apostolate—Ms. LINDA MANTERNACH, Dir., *2121 Commonwealth Ave., Boston, 02135-3193.* Tel: 617-746-5800; Fax: 617-783-5642.

Health Care Ministry—KELLY L. DUNN, *St. Elizabeth Medical Center, 736 Cambridge St., Boston, 02135-2997.* Tel: 617-789-2456; Fax: 617-789-2573.

Hispanic Apostolate—Rev. JAMES F. GAUDREAU, Dir., *2121 Commonwealth Ave., Boston, 02135-3193.* Tel: 617-746-5816; Fax: 617-783-5642.

Holy Name Society—Rev. JOHN MCLAUGHLIN, *25 Arlington St., Somerville, 02145-3342.* Tel: 617-625-0029; Fax: 617-666-5944.

Juvenile Court Chaplain—Rev. JAMES F. FRATUS, *601 Broadway, Chelsea, 02150-2998.* Tel: 617-889-2774; Fax: 617-889-2854.

League of Catholic Women—Rev. MARTIN J. CONNOR, Spiritual Dir., *St. John Seminary, 127 Lake St., Boston, 02135-3898.* Tel: 617-254-2610; Fax: 617-783-2336.

Legion of Mary—Rev. JOHN KILMARTIN, F.D.P., *Madonna Queen National Shrine, 111 Orient Ave., Boston, 02128-3063.* Tel: 617-569-2100; Fax: 617-569-8701.

Liturgical Commission—Rev. SEAN M. MCCARTHY, Chm., *St. Elizabeth of Hungary Parish, 89 Arlington St., Acton, 01720-4305.* Tel: 978-263-4305; Fax: 978-263-9014.

Marian Devotions—Rev. WILLIAM R. CARROLL, *24 Medford St., Arlington, 02174-3197.* Tel: 781-648-0220; Fax: 781-643-8955.

Pilgrimages—Rev. WALTER H. CUENIN, Coord., *573 Washington St., Newton, 02158-1494.* Tel: 617-527-7560; Fax: 617-527-1338.

Prison Ministry Office—Deacon WILLIAM F. KANE, Dir., *2121 Commonwealth Ave., Boston, 02135-3193.* Tel: 617-254-0100; Fax: 617-783-2947.

Seaport of Boston—Waterfront Chapel, Rev. PHILIP LAPLANTE, S.M., *27 Isabella St., Boston, 02116-5262.* Tel: 617-482-5495; Fax: 617-268-8100.

Spiritual Development—Rev. JOHN E. SASSANI, *2121 Commonwealth Ave., Boston, 02135-3193.* Tel: 617-254-1040; Fax: 617-254-6469.

Worship—Rev. JAMES F. FIELD, *2121 Commonwealth Ave., Boston, 02135-3193.* Tel: 617-746-5880; Fax: 617-787-8144.

Young Adult Ministry—JAMES J. BREEN, *2121 Commonwealth Ave., Boston, 02135-3193.* Tel: 617-254-0100; Fax: 617-783-5642.

Youth Ministry—Rev. THOMAS A. DUNNE, S.D.B., *139 Crescent St., Quincy, 02169-4040.* Tel: 617-472-0333; Fax: 617-479-6298.

Social Services

Social Services—Dr. JOSEPH DOOLIN, Cabinet Sec., *75 Kneeland St., Boston, 02111-1431.* Tel: 617-482-5440; Fax: 617-451-0337.

Catholic Social Services, Inc.—Dr. JOSEPH DOOLIN, Pres., *75 Kneeland St., Boston, 02111-1431.* Tel: 617-482-5440; Fax: 617-451-0337.

Catholic Charitable Bureau of the Archdiocese of Boston, Inc.—Dr. JOSEPH DOOLIN; Pres., *75 Kneeland St., Boston, 02111-1431.* Tel: 617-482-5440; Fax: 617-451-0337.

Catholic Charities Brockton—SANDRA WIXTED, Dir.

Catholic Charities Greater Boston - Somerville—ELISABETH ZWEIG, Dir.

Catholic Charities Merrimack Valley - Lowell, Lawrence—PATRICIA KIRWIN, Dir.

Catholic Charities North - Lynn, Peabody, Salem—Sr. LINDA O'ROURKE, Dir.

Catholic Charities West - Framingham—PATRICIA DUNN, Dir.

El Centro Del Cardenal - Boston—RUTH RUBALCAVA, Dir.

Laboure Center - South Boston—Sr. MARYADELE ROBINSON, Dir.

Haitian Multi-Service Center - Dorchester—PIERRE IMBERT, Dir.

Catholic Charities Behavioral Health Division - Brockton—VIVIAN SOPER, Dir.

Catholic Charities Child Care Division - Jamaica Plain—MARY ANN ANTHONY, Dir.

Catholic Charities Parish Social Ministries Division - Framingham & Franklin—PATRICIA DUNN, Dir.

Life Resources—WILLIAM CHIARADONNA, Pres., *140 Adams St., Braintree, 02184-0907.* Tel: 781-848-5510; Fax: 781-380-3901.

Nazareth—Sr. THERESA MARIE O'LEARY, R.G.S., Pres., *75 Kneeland St., Boston, 02111-1431.* Tel: 617-482-5440; Fax: 617-451-0337.

Pro-Life Activities—BARBARA THORP, Dir., *159 Washington St., Boston, 02135.* Tel: 617-783-5410; Fax: 617-787-7797.

St. Ann Home, Inc.—Mr. DENIS GRANDBOIS, Pres., *100-A Haverhill St., Methuen, 01844-4297.* Tel: 978-682-5276; Fax: 978-688-4932.

Society of St. Vincent de Paul—ALBERT CROCKER, Dir., *1280 Washington St., Boston, 02118-2109.* Tel: 617-542-0883; Fax: 617-542-3610., *Mailing Address: P.O. Box 180359, Boston, 02118-2109.*

CLERGY, PARISHES, MISSIONS AND PAROCHIAL SCHOOLS

BOSTON
(Suffolk County)

1—CATHEDRAL OF THE HOLY CROSS (1788), Rev. Msgr. Frederick J. Murphy, Rector; Rev. Terence J. Moran; Rev. Msgr. William H. Roche; Deacon Luis Casillas; Sr. M. Celeste Burgos, M.H.S.H., Pastoral Assoc. In res., Bro. Steven B. Wang, F.M.S.
Res., 75 Union Park St., 02118. Tel: 617-542-5682; Fax: 617-542-5926.
School—Tel: 617-422-0042.
Sisters 3; Lay Teachers 7; Students 191.

2—ST. ADALBERT (1913) (Polish), Rev. Msgr. Stanislaus T. Sypek.
Res., 1450 River St., Hyde Park, 02136-2150. Tel: 617-361-0565; Fax: 617-361-0565.

3—ALL SAINTS (1894). Closed. For inquiries for parochial records contact St. Joseph, Roxbury.

4—ST. AMBROSE (1914), Rev. Vincent P. Von Euw; Sr. Mary Damien Powers, O.S.M., Pastoral Assoc.; Deacon Macio Fonseca. In res., Rev. J. Joseph Kierce.
Res., 240 Adams St., Dorchester, 02122-1380. Tel: 617-265-5302; Fax: 617-265-0886.
School—Tel: 617-825-9400.
Sisters 5; Lay Teachers 9; Students 250.

5—ST. ANDREW (1918). Unassigned.
Res., 40 Walk Hill St., Forest Hills, 02130-4196. Tel: 617-522-1222; Fax: 617-522-0489.
School—Tel: 617-524-7733.
Sisters 6; Lay Teachers 3; Students 226.

6—ST. ANGELA (1907), Revs. William Joy; John Morin, O.M.I.; Sr. Paula Coelho, S.U.S.C., Pastoral Assoc.
Res., 1548 Blue Hill Ave., Mattapan, 02126. Tel: 617-298-0080; Fax: 617-298-2388.
School—Tel: 617-296-1161.
Lay Teachers 7; Students 222.

7—ST. ANN (1889), Revs. Walter F. Keymont; John F. Reardon. In res., Rev. Joseph F. Hennessey.
Res., 243 Neponset Ave., Dorchester, 02122-3239. Tel: 617-825-6180; Fax: 617-825-7869.
School—Tel: 617-825-6262.
Religious 5; Lay Teachers 12; Students 328.

8—ST. ANN (1945), Rev. Paul E. Kilroy. Pastoral Assocs.: Sr. Rosemary Mulvihill, R.S.M., Northeastern Univ.; Sr. Ann Pennick, Emerson College.
68 St. Stephen St., 02115. Tel: 617-266-2635; Fax: 617-266-9015.

9—ST. ANNE (1919), Rev. William F. Joyce. In res., Rev. Paul J. Bolduc.
Res., 79 W. Milton St., Readville, 02136-1929. Tel: 617-361-3443; Fax: 617-361-6690.
School—Tel: 617-361-3563.
Lay Teachers 11; Students 225; Religious 1.

10—ST. ANTHONY (1896), Revs. Daniel P. Hegarty; Robert Bouffier, S.M.; Glen F. Byrne; Bros. Michael Galvin, S.M.; Michael Kraszewski, S.M.
Res., 43 Holton St., Allston, 02134-1397. Tel: 617-782-0775; Fax: 617-782-2008.
School—Tel: 617-782-7170.
Lay Teachers 8; Students 119.

11—ST. AUGUSTINE (1868), Rev. Msgr. Thomas J. McDonnell; Rev. James H. Lane.
Res., 9 F St., South Boston, 02127-2898. Tel: 617-268-1230; Fax: 617-269-2233.
School—Tel: 617-269-2233.
Sisters 2; Lay Teachers 9; Students 249.

12—BLESSED SACRAMENT (1891), Rev. Michael F. McLellan; Deacon Luciano Herrera.
Res., 365 Centre St., Jamaica Plain, 02130-1240. Tel: 617-522-0650; Fax: 617-983-1407.
School—Tel: 617-522-1870.
Sisters 2; Lay Teachers 7; Students 198.

13—ST. BRENDAN (1929), Revs. Ronald D. Coyne; Stephen S. Josoma. In res., Rev. Timothy E. Linehan.
Res., 15 Rita Rd., Dorchester, 02124. Tel: 617-436-0310; Fax: 617-436-1386.
School—Tel: 617-282-3388.
Sisters 2; Lay Teachers 9; Students 245.

14—ST. BRIGID (1908), Revs. Robert E. Casey; Joseph S. McCarthy. In res., Revs. Richard F. Clancy; Daniel F. Sheehan.
Res., 841 E. Broadway, South Boston, 02127-2397. Tel: 617-268-2122; Fax: 617-268-2666.
School—Tel: 617-268-2326.
Sisters 2; Lay Teachers 7; Students 275.

15—ST. CATHERINE OF SIENA (1887), Rev. Paul M. Parker.
Res., 49 Vine St., Charlestown, 02129. Tel: 617-242-1750; Fax: 617-242-1899.
School—Tel: 617-242-0169.
Lay Teachers 8; Students 161.

16—ST. CECILIA (1888), Rev. Msgr. Michael F. Groden. In res., Revs. Thomas Grenham, S.P.S.; Todd Nolan.
Res., 30 St. Cecilia St., 02115-3132. Tel: 617-536-4548; Fax: 617-536-1781.

17—ST. CHRISTOPHER (1956), Rev. George A. Carrigg, Admin.
Res., 263 Mt. Vernon St., Dorchester, 02125-3182. Tel: 617-436-7273; Fax: 617-436-7273.

18—ST. COLUMBKILLE (1871), Revs. Richard J. Shmaruk; Lawrence J. Borges; James J. O'Rourke; Deacon Eddy Montes. In res., Rev. Carney E. Gavin.
Res., 321 Market St., Brighton, 02135-2199. Tel: 617-782-5126; 782-5774; Fax: 617-782-7283.
School—Tel: 617-254-3110.
Sisters 2; Lay Teachers 6; Students 200.

19—ST. FRANCIS DE SALES-ST. PHILIP (1867), Rev. Thomas F. Clark, S.J. Pastoral Assocs.: Sr. Mary Hart, R.G.S.; Mr. James Atkins; Mr. Tipp Harris. In res., Rev. Robert G. McMillan, S.J.
Res., One Warwick St., Roxbury, 02120-2415. Tel: 617-445-8915; Fax: 617-445-6522.

20—ST. FRANCIS DE SALES (1859), Rev. Daniel J. Mahoney. In res., Revs. William J. McConnell; Celestino V. Pascual.
Res., 303 Bunker Hill St., Charlestown, 02129-1826. Tel: 617-242-0147; Fax: 617-242-3026.

21—ST. GABRIEL (1934), Rev. Justinian Manning, C.P. In res., Revs. Brendan Breen, C.P.; Roger Gannon, C.P.; Bernardine Grande, C.P.; John O'Brien, C.P.; Sr. Catherine O'Brien, S.N.D., Pastoral Assoc.
Res., 139 Washington St., Brighton, 02135-4325. Tel: 617-254-6582; Fax: 617-783-1766.

22—GATE OF HEAVEN (1862), Revs. Alexander J. Keenan; Richard A. Uftring; A. Paul White; Deacon Richard C. Martin.
Res., 606 E. 4th St., South Boston, 02127-3092. Tel: 617-268-3344; Fax: 617-269-4299.
School—Tel: 617-268-8431.
Sisters 3; Lay Teachers 17; Students 483.

23—ST. GREGORY (1863), Rev. Msgr. Paul T. Ryan; Revs. James M. Larner; John F. O'Donnell. In res., Most Rev. John P. Boles.
Res., 2223 Dorchester Ave., Dorchester, 02124. Tel: 617-298-2460; Fax: 617-298-9232.
School—Tel: 617-296-1210.
Sisters 2; Lay Teachers 8; Students 495.

24—HOLY FAMILY (1995), Rev. Msgr. William C. Francis; Deacon Francisco Guerrios; Sr. Rita Brereton, Pastoral Assoc.
Mailing Address: One Lingard St., Dorchester, 02125-2732. Tel: 617-445-9553; Fax: 617-445-2417.
School—516 Columbia Rd., Dorchester, 02125. Tel: 617-825-3883.

25—HOLY NAME (1927), Rev. Msgr. George F. Carlson; Revs. Wayne A. Cavalier, O.P.; Anthony V. Luongo, S.D.B.; Mark A. Mahoney; Deacon Charles O. Leslie.
Res., 1689 Centre St., West Roxbury, 02132-1292. Tel: 617-325-4865; Fax: 617-327-6122.
School—Tel: 617-325-9338.
Sisters 10; Lay Teachers 19; Students 639.

26—HOLY TRINITY (1844) (German), Very Rev. Hugh H. O'Regan, Admin.
Res., 140 Shawmut Ave., 02118-2227. Tel: 617-426-6142; Fax: 617-426-6142.

27—ST. JAMES THE GREATER (1854), Very Rev. Hugh H. O'Regan. In res., Revs. Joseph J. Baggetta; Paul B. O'Brien.
Mailing Address: Box 1538, 02205-1538. Tel: 617-542-5044; 542-8489; Fax: 617-542-2708.
Res., 135 Harrison Ave., 02111.

28—ST. JOHN BAPTIST (1921) (Portuguese). Closed. For inquiries for sacramental records contact Sacred Heart, East Boston.

29—ST. JOHN CHRYSOSTOM (1952), Revs. Paul A. Phinn; Charles B. Flaherty, S.S.C.; Sr. Maureen Taaffe, S.C.N., Pastoral Assoc.
Res., 4740 Washington St., West Roxbury, 02132-2199. Tel: 617-323-4410; Fax: 617-323-0423.

30—ST. JOHN-ST. HUGH (1901), Rev. Gerald J. Osterman.
Church—517 Blue Hill Ave., Roxbury, 02121.
Res., 26 Lawrence Ave., Dorchester, 02121. Tel: 617-442-1431; Fax: 617-442-2965.

31—ST. JOSEPH (1845), Revs. Walter J. Waldron; Russell W. Best. Pastoral Assocs.: Sr. Gerard Ndagano, I.H.M.R.; Sr. Marie Mullane, R.C.
Res., 85 Regent St., Roxbury, 02119-1990. Tel: 617-442-0900; Fax: 617-442-0900.
School—18 Hulbert St., Roxbury, 02119. Tel: 617-442-2675.
Lay Teachers 9; Students 159; Religious 1.

32—ST. JOSEPH (1862), Rev. Gabriel Troy. In res., Revs. Philip E. McGaugh; Vincent Daily.
Res., 68 Cardinal O'Connell Way, 02114. Tel: 617-523-4342; Fax: 617-523-8459.

33—ST. JOSEPH (1938), Rev. William H. McLaughlin.
Res., 21 Chapel Rd., Hyde Park, 02136. Tel: 617-361-1314; Fax: 617-364-7129.

34—ST. JOSEPH-ST. LAZARUS (1891), Rev. John Kilmartin, F.D.P. In res., Rev. Mirek Kowalczyk, F.D.P.
Res., 59 Ashley St., East Boston, 02128. Tel: 617-569-0406; Fax: 617-569-8212.

35—ST. KEVIN (1945). Closed. For inquiries for parochial records contact Holy Family, Dorchester.

36—ST. LAZARUS (1892). Merged with St. Joseph to form St. Joseph-St. Lazarus, East Boston.

37—ST. LEO (1902). Closed. For inquiries for sacramental records contact St. Matthew, Dorchester.

38—ST. LEONARD OF PORT MAURICE (1873) (Italian), Revs. Michael Nappo, O.F.M.; Dismas Centrella, O.F.M.; Matthias Rendon, O.F.M.
Res., 14 N. Bennet St., 02113. Tel: 617-523-2110; Fax: 617-367-0456.
Chapel—St. Mary, 150 Endicott St., 02113.

39—ST. MARGARET (1893), Revs. Nicholas Ciccone; Raymond P. Benoit; Deacon Ricardo Mesa. Pastoral Assocs.: Sr. Catherine Therese Barrett, S.C.H.; Sr. Nancy Duffy, S.N.D.
Res., 800 Columbia Rd., Dorchester, 02125-1750. Tel: 617-436-2190; Fax: 617-282-5428.
School—Tel: 617-282-5621.
Sisters of Charity 8; Lay Teachers 9; Students 316.
High School—Msgr. Ryan Memorial High School, Tel: 617-282-2818.
Sisters 7; Lay Teachers 1; Girls 227.

40—ST. MARK (1905), Revs. Daniel J. Finn; Robert T. Kickham.
Res., 20 Roseland St., Dorchester, 02124. Tel: 617-825-2852; Fax: 617-825-0514.
School—Tel: 617-282-2577.
Sisters 7; Lay Teachers 15; Students 512.

41—ST. MARY. Closed. For inquiries for parochial records contact St. Leonard of Port Maurice, Boston.

42—ST. MARY (1828), Revs. James B. Canniff; Paul E. McCarthy.
Res., One Monument Sq., Charlestown, 02129-3499. Tel: 617-242-4664; Fax: 617-242-0016.

43—ST. MARY OF THE ANGELS (1904), Rev. John E. Fagan, S.J. In res., Revs. Joseph J. Bruce, S.J.; David Gill, S.J.
Res., 377 Walnut Ave., Roxbury, 02119. Tel: 617-445-1524:800-439-0183 (TTY); Fax: 617-442-6455.

44—ST. MARY, STAR OF THE SEA (1864), Rev. Robert R. Kennedy.
Res., 63 Moore St., East Boston, 02128-1547. Tel: 617-567-0056; Fax: 617-569-8440.
School—Tel: 617-567-6609.
Lay Teachers 10; Students 266.

45—ST. MATTHEW (1900), Rev. Msgr. Leandre Jeannot. Pastoral Assocs.: Michael Bolivar; Immacula Bernard.
Res., 33 Stanton St., Dorchester, 02124-3716. Tel: 617-436-3590; Fax: 617-822-0407.
School—Tel: 617-825-7955.
Sisters 2; Lay Teachers 10; Students 247.

46—ST. MONICA (1907), Rev. Msgr. Thomas J. McDonnell; Rev. James H. Lane.
Res., 70 Devine Way, South Boston, 02127-3536. Tel: 617-269-6760; Fax: 617-269-3654.

47—MOST HOLY REDEEMER (1844), Rev. Robert F. Hennessey; Deacon Antonio M. Perea.
Res., St. Agnes Building, 65 London St., East Boston, 02128-1924. Tel: 617-567-3227; Fax: 617-569-6950. Member Central Catholic School of East Boston.

48—MOST PRECIOUS BLOOD (1880), Rev. Peter P. Nolan, C.S.Sp. In res., Most Rev. Lawrence J. Riley; Rev. Raymond Barry, C.S.Sp.
Res., 43 Maple St., Hyde Park, 02136-2738. Tel: 617-364-9500; Fax: 617-364-2590.
School—Tel: 617-361-2162.
Sisters 2; Lay Teachers 6; Students 187.

49—OUR LADY OF THE ASSUMPTION (1869), Rev. Adelard J. Gagnon.
Res., 404 Sumner St., East Boston, 02128. Tel: 617-567-1223; Fax: 617-561-6319. Member East Boston Central Catholic School Consortium.

50—OUR LADY OF CZESTOCHOWA (1893) (Polish), Revs. Andrew Sujka, O.F.M.Conv.; Miroslaw Podymniak, O.F.M.Cap. In res., Revs. Stephen Majewski, O.F.M.Conv.; Germain Kopaczynski, O.F.M. Conv.
Res., 655 Dorchester Ave., South Boston, 02127-3551. Tel: 617-268-4355; Fax: 617-268-4599.
School—Tel: 617-268-3766.
Felician Sisters 3; Lay Teachers 6; Students 202.
Convent—666 Dorchester Ave., 02127.

51—OUR LADY OF LOURDES (1908), Rev. Msgr. Charles J. Bourque, V.F.; Deacon Leonard F. De Coste. In res., Revs. Michael F. McLellan; Marco Reyes.
Res., 46 Brookside Ave., Jamaica Plain, 02130-2370. Tel: 617-524-0434; Fax: 617-524-1888.
School—Tel: 617-524-6136.
Sisters 3; Lay Teachers 8; Students 220.

52—OUR LADY OF MT. CARMEL (1905) (Italian), Revs. Francis de Sales Paolo, O.F.M.; Kenneth Garofalo, O.F.M.; Aubert Marie Picardi, O.F.M.
Res., 128 Gove St., East Boston, 02128. Tel: 617-567-3215; Fax: 617-569-0552. Member East Boston Central Catholic School.

53—OUR LADY OF PERPETUAL HELP (1868), Revs. Kevin Milton, C.SS.R.; Vincent J. Kelly, C.SS.R.; Lawrence J. Buckley, C.SS.R.; Richard Bennett, C.SS.R.; John Furey, C.SS.R.; Joseph Adamec, C.SS.R.; John Devin, C.SS.R.; Joseph E. Manton, C.SS.R.; Edward McDonough, C.SS.R.; John E. Doherty, C.SS.R.; Philip A. Cabasino, C.SS.R.; John J. Ryan, C.SS.R.; George W. Drew, C.SS.R.; Paul Henderson, C.SS.R.; Robert Lennon, C.SS.R.; Kevin MacDonald, C.SS.R.; John J. Hennessey, C.SS.R.; Michael Barrett, C.SS.R.
Res., 1545 Tremont St., Roxbury, 02120-2996. Tel: 617-445-2600; Fax: 617-445-1857.
School—(Grades 1-6). Tel: 617-442-2660.
Sisters 4; Lay Teachers 3; Students 152.

54—OUR LADY OF THE PRESENTATION (1909), Rev. William F. Salmon. In res., Rev. Joseph K. Coleman.
Res., 676 Washington St., Brighton, 02135-1612. Tel: 617-782-6260; 6261; Fax: 617-782-3303.
School—Tel: 617-782-8670.
Sisters 1; Lay Teachers 9; Students 226.

55—OUR LADY OF VICTORIES (1880) (French), Revs. Philip Laplante, S.M.; Albert Dilanni, S.M.; Armand Robichaud, S.M.; John Meade, S.M.; Romeo Yuchung, S.M.; Antoine Charest, S.M.; Armand Thibault, S.M.; Kenneth Thibodeau, S.M.; Lucien Chasse, S.M.; Bros. Gregory Theriault, S.M.; Roland Bernier, S.M.; Leonard Haley, S.M.
Res., 27 Isabella St., 02117. Tel: 617-426-4448; Fax: 617-482-1570.

56—ST. PATRICK (1836), Revs. Walter J. Waldron; Russell W. Best; Terence J. Moran; Zachary Grant; Bernardo Vaschetto, O.F.M.Cap. Pastoral Assocs.: Sr. Mary Andreas, S.B.S.; Sr. M. Matthias Gallagher, S.B.S.; Sr. Mary Hurley, S.B.S.; Sr. Maria Macedo, F.I.C.; Sr. Mary Thomasine Twomey, M.S.B.T.; Sr. Luisa Vasconcelos, F.I.C.; Sr. Domingas Baptista, F.I.C.
Res., 10 Magazine St., Roxbury, 02119-2797. Tel: 617-445-7645; Fax: 617-445-6166.
School—Tel: 617-427-3881.
Sisters 2; Lay Teachers 14; Students 349.

57—ST. PAUL (1907). Closed. For inquiries for parochial records contact Holy Family, Dorchester.

58—ST. PETER (1872), Revs. John L. Doyle; Michael Do Quang Chinh, C.M.C.; Mark Doan Quang Bau, C.M.C.; John Bosco Pham Trung Thuc, C.M.C.; Deacon Jesus Ortiz. Pastoral Assocs.: Sr. Sally McLaughlin, S.C.H.; Sr. Glenna Connors, S.C.H.
Res., 309 Bowdoin St., Dorchester, 02122-1834. Tel: 617-265-1132; Fax: 617-265-0463.
School—Tel: 617-282-8573.
Sisters 3; Lay Teachers 5; Students 210.

59—ST. PETER (1904) (Lithuanian), Rev. Stephen P. Zukas.
Res., 50 Orton-Marotta Way, South Boston, 02127-2006. Tel: 617-268-0353; Fax: 617-268-2588.
School—Tel: 617-268-0750.
Sisters 3; Lay Teachers 8; Students 260.

60—SS. PETER AND PAUL (1844). Closed. For inquiries for parochial records contact St. Vincent de Paul, South Boston.

61—ST. PHILIP. Merged with St. Francis de Sales to form St. Francis de Sales-St. Philip, Roxbury.

62—ST. RICHARD. Closed. For inquiries for parochial records contact St. Joseph's, Roxbury.

63—SACRED HEART (1873), Rev. Brian J. McHugh.
Res., 303 Paris St., East Boston, 02128-3063. Tel: 617-567-5776; Fax: 617-567-3042.
School—Member East Boston Catholic School Consortium.
Sisters 1; Brothers 3; Lay Teachers 8; Students 229.

64—SACRED HEART (1888) (Italian), Rev. Vincenzo Rosato, C.S. In res., Revs. Mario Tardivo, C.S.; Peter Bortolazzo, C.S.; Deacon Mario Lopriore.
Res., 12 North Sq., 02113-2498. Tel: 617-523-5638; Fax: 617-227-4552.
School—St. John's School, Tel: 617-227-3143.
Lay Teachers 11; Students 171.

65—SACRED HEART (1893), Rev. Msgr. Francis H. Kelley; Revs. John J. Mendicoa; John J. Graham; Deacon Francisco Quiles. Pastoral Assocs.: Sr. Virginia Bobrowski, S.S.N.D.; Mr. John Scanlon.
Res., 169 Cummins Hwy., Roslindale, 02131-3739. Tel: 617-325-3322; Fax: 617-325-2145.
School—Tel: 617-323-2500.
Sisters 2; Lay Teachers 15; Students 464.

66—ST. THERESA OF AVILA (1895), Rev. Msgr. William M. Helmick; Revs. Charles J. Higgins; Richard S. Bradford. In res., Revs. Raymond G. Helmick, S.J.; James M. DiPerri.
Res., 10 St. Theresa Ave., West Roxbury, 02132-3499. Tel: 617-325-1300; Fax: 617-325-0380.
School—Tel: 617-323-1050.
Sisters 2; Lay Teachers 20; Students 589.

67—ST. THOMAS AQUINAS (1869), Rev. Gerald D. Perno.
Res., 97 South St., Jamaica Plain, 02130-3899. Tel: 617-524-0240; Fax: 617-524-1840.

68—ST. VINCENT DE PAUL (1872), Rev. Richard E. Cannon. In res., Rev. Msgr. Andrew F. Connell; Janet Powers, Pastoral Assoc.
Res., 55 W. Broadway, South Boston, 02127. Tel: 617-268-0710; Fax: 617-268-1277.

69—ST. WILLIAM (1909), Revs. Daniel J. Riley; Joseph Chinh Nguyen; Sr. Margaret Lannen, S.N.D., Pastoral Assoc.; Deacon Stanley Pugsley. In res., Rev. Stephen Duffin.
Res., 1048 Dorchester Ave., Dorchester, 02125-1750. Tel: 617-265-0100; Fax: 617-265-5464.
School—Tel: 617-265-7110.
Lay Teachers 9; Students 193.

OUTSIDE THE CITY OF BOSTON

Abington, Plymouth Co., St. Bridget (1863), Revs. Allan L. Butler; Thomas C. Boudreau. In res., Rev. Michael J. Regan.
Res., 455 Plymouth St., 02351-1841. Tel: 781-878-0900; Fax: 781-878-6566.
School—Tel: 617-878-8482.
Lay Teachers 11; Students 249.
St. Nicholas (1964), Revs. Joseph L. Welsh; Robert B. Costello.
Res., 127 N. Quincy St., 02351-1073. Tel: 781-857-2461; 2462; Fax: 781-857-2923.

Acton, Middlesex Co., St. Elizabeth of Hungary (1945), Revs. Walter J. Woods; Sean M. McCarthy; Edmond L Parker; Sharon Laronga, Pastoral Assoc.; Deacons Alexander J. Patrick; Eugene A. Counihan; Howard P. Hardin; John E. Bortz, s.P.
Res., 89 Arlington St., 01720. Tel: 978-263-4305; Fax: 978-263-9014.

Amesbury, Holy Family (1998), Team Ministry: Revs. Thomas J. Buckley; John W. Gentleman. In res., Rev. John D. Silk; Hilde Champion, Pastoral Assoc.
School and Friend St., 01913. Tel: 978-388-0330; Fax: 978-388-1451. [CEM]
Parish Office: 6 Allen's Ct., 01913-2302.
Res., 9 Sparhawk St., 01913.
St. Joseph, Essex Co. Closed. For inquiries for parochial records contact Holy Family, Amesbury.
Sacred Heart, Essex Co. Closed. For inquiries for parochial records contact Holy Family, Amesbury.

Andover, Essex Co., St. Augustine (1866), Revs. Alfred J. Ellis, O.S.A.; Richard L. Foley, O.S.A.; Harry J. Erdlen, O.S.A.; Deacon John J. Capomaccio. In res., Rev. George R. Morgan, O.S.A.
Res., 43 Essex St., 01810-3779. Tel: 978-475-0050; Fax: 978-475-3078. [CEM]
School—Tel: 508-475-2414.
Sisters 2; Lay Teachers 21; Students 405.
Mission—Ballardville, St. Joseph's, (1881).
St. Robert Bellarmine (1961), Revs. Arthur J. Driscoll; Francis C. O'Hare; Mrs. Betty Pendergast, Pastoral Assoc.
Res., 198 Haggetts Pond Rd., 01810. Tel: 978-683-8922; Fax: 978-689-8878.

Arlington, Middlesex Co.,

1—ST. AGNES, (1872), Very Rev. Brian M. Flatley; Revs. William R. Carroll; Shawn Allen; Deacon Francis A. Mendoza.
Res., 24 Medford St., 02474. Tel: 781-648-0220; Fax: 781-643-7883.
School—Tel: 617-643-9031.
Religious 1; Lay Teachers 20; Students 426.
High School—Tel: 617-646-7770; Fax: 617-648-8345.
Religious 5; Lay Teachers 24; Students 628.

2—ST. CAMILLUS, (1950), Rev. James E. O'Leary.
Res., 1175 Concord Tpke., 02476-7298. Tel: 781-643-3132; Fax: 781-643-8228.

3—ST. JAMES THE APOSTLE, (1914), Rev. Francis E. Daley. In res., Revs. Kenneth F. McAskill; Robert F. McAuliffe.
Res., 22 Appleton St., 02476-5900. Tel: 781-643-0636; Fax: 781-643-7488.

4—ST. JEROME, (1934), Rev. James L. Publicover.
Res., 201 Lake St., 02474-0298. Tel: 781-648-2506; Fax: 781-648-2126.

Ashland, Middlesex Co., St. Cecilia (1885), Revs. Paul F. Mulligan; John Sheridan; Mrs. Mary Sheedy, Pastoral Assoc.
Res., 54 Esty St., 01721-2126. Tel: 508-881-1107; Fax: 508-881-8606.

Avon, Norfolk Co., St. Michael (1908), Rev. Paul Rouse.
Res., 87 N. Main St., 02322-1286. Tel: 508-586-7210; Fax: 508-586-7211.

Ayer, Middlesex Co., St. Mary (1858), Rev. Richard R. Gosselin.
Res., 31 Shirley St., 01432-1295. Tel: 978-772-2414; Fax: 978-772-0727.

Bedford, Middlesex Co., St. Michael (1931), Very Rev. Mark S. Sheehan, V.F.; Rev. Michael L. Nolan. In res., Rev. Joseph P. Robinson.
Res., 90 Concord Rd., 01730-1596. Tel: 781-275-6318; Fax: 781-271-9879.

Bellingham, Norfolk Co., Assumption (1927), Rev. Brian F. McMahon. In res., Rev. Daniel J. Gilmartin.
Res., 370 Pulaski Blvd., 02019. Tel: 508-883-8226; Fax: 508-883-1713.
St. Blaise (1962), Rev. James H. Connolly.
Res., 1158 S. Main St., 02019-1597. Tel: 508-966-1258; Fax: 508-966-0310.
St. Brendan (1945), Rev. David J. Mullen.
Res., 384 Hartford Ave., 02019. Tel: 508-966-0260; Fax: 508-966-4404.

Belmont, Middlesex Co., St. Joseph (1900), Revs. William C. Burckhart; Timothy A. Harrison. In res., Rev. Richard R. Santerre.
Res., 345 Waverley St., 02478-2418. Tel: 617-484-0279; Fax: 617-489-5445.
St. Luke (1919), Rev. Msgr. Roger J. Brady; Revs. Thomas F. Bouton; Robert M. Blaney; Sr. Ernestine Quealy, C.S.J., Pastoral Assoc.
Res., 132 Lexington St., 02478-1239. Tel: 617-484-1996; Fax: 617-484-7831.
Our Lady of Mercy (1926), Rev. James J. McGowan.
Res., 15 Lawndale St., 02478-3451. Tel: 617-489-1160; Fax: 617-489-9682.

Beverly, Essex Co.,

1—ST. ALPHONSUS, (1917), Rev. Robert W. Kirchmeyer; Robert Tufts, Pastoral Assoc. In res., Rev. Edward D. Cowhig.
Res., 488 Elliott St., 01915-2399. Tel: 978-922-1240; Fax: 978-922-8614.

2—ST. JOHN THE EVANGELIST, (1955), Revs. George J. Butera; Joseph Keville; Sr. Agnes Therrien, S.S.C.H., Pastoral Assoc.
Res., 552 Cabot St., 01915. Tel: 978-922-5542; Fax: 978-921-4563.
School—Tel: 508-922-0048.
Sisters 1; Lay Teachers 8; Students 157.

3—St. Mary Star of the Sea, (1870), Revs. Charles J. Hughes; Edward P. Geary; David J. Barnes; Deacon Joseph Kasenenko. Pastoral Assocs.: Bros. Tamaru Francis; Bisrat Abebe; Sr. Marian Patrice, S.N.D.; Sr. Julie Theresa Kane, S.N.D.
Res., 253 Cabot St., 01915-4597. Tel: 978-922-0113; Fax: 978-922-8501.
School—Tel: 508-927-3259.
Sisters 4; Lay Teachers 6; Students 212.

4—St. Margaret (1905), Rev. James L. Fahey.
Res., 672 Hale St., 01915-2119. Tel: 978-927-0069; Fax: 978-927-8359.

Billerica, Middlesex Co., St. Andrew (1868), Rev. Michael J. Parise. In res., Rev. Francis L. Gallagher.
Res., 45 Talbot Ave., 01862-1414. Tel: 978-663-3624; Fax: 978-670-1433.
St. Mary (1937), Revs. W. James Nyhan; Edward M. McMahon; Deacon Allan R. Shanahan.
Res., 796 Boston Rd., 01821. Tel: 978-663-2215; Fax: 978-663-0127.
St. Theresa of Lisieux (1945), Revs. Eugene D. Tully; John J. McCormick; Michael C. Randone; Deacon Thomas F. Mullins.
Res., 80 Concord Rd., 01821. Tel: 978-663-8816; Fax: 978-663-0577.

Braintree, Norfolk Co., St. Clare (1959), Revs. Paul S. Shugrue; Brian M. Clary; Deacon Michael J. Cavanaugh. In res., Rev. Joseph A. Farrell, M.M.
Res., 1244 Liberty St., 02184-8299. Tel: 781-848-7480; Fax: 781-356-8380.
St. Francis of Assisi (1903), Rev. Kevin M. Sepe. In res., Revs. Charles I. Sheehy; Daniel J. Crowley; Deacon Kenneth Ryan.
Res., 856 Washington St., 02184-6464. Tel: 781-843-1332; Fax: 781-848-0976.
School—Tel: 617-848-0842.
Lay Teachers 8; Students 193.
St. Thomas More (1938), Rev. James J. McCarthy; Deacon Charles P. Webb.
Res., 8 Hawthorn Rd., Box 330, 02184-0330. Tel: 781-843-1980; Fax: 781-843-7110.

Bridgewater, Plymouth Co., St. Thomas Aquinas (1853), Revs. Lawrence J. Drennan; Edward J. McLaughlin; Francine Bell, Pastoral Assoc.
Res., 103 Center St., 02324-1397. Tel: 508-697-9528; Fax: 508-279-1859.

Brockton, Plymouth Co.,

1—St. Casimir, (1898) (Lithuanian), Rev. John P. Prusaitis.
Res., 21 Sawtell Ave., 02402. Tel: 508-586-2226; Fax: 508-559-2761.
School—Tel: 508-587-7367.
Sisters 1; Lay Teachers 5; Students 176.

2—St. Colman of Cloyne, (1910), Revs. John E. Schatzel; David P. O'Donnell. In res., Christine E. Kowalcky, Pastoral Assoc.
Res., 42 Wendell Ave., 02402-3191. Tel: 508-586-1575; Fax: 508-586-9393.

3—St. Edward, (1897), Rev. James A. Flavin; Sr. Mary Lou McCarthy, C.S.J., Pastoral Assoc.
Res., 71 E. Main St., 02401-2461. Tel: 508-586-6491; Fax: 508-587-1796.
School—Tel: 508-583-6231.
Lay Teachers 9; Students 238.

4—St. Margaret, (1902), Rev. Richard C. Conway.
Res., Box 3025, 917 Montello St., 02404-6657. Tel: 508-586-1295; Fax: 508-586-8443.

5—Our Lady of Lourdes, (1931), Very Rev. Joseph H. Manning, V.F.; Rev. James M. Mahony. In res., Revs. Francis G. Goss; David C. Murphy.
Res., 439 West St., 02401-4899. Tel: 508-586-4715; Fax: 508-584-6257.

6—Our Lady of Ostrobrama, (1914) (Polish), Rev. Msgr. John B. Missa.
Res., 696 N. Main St., 02401-2444. Tel: 508-586-4270; Fax: 508-586-7507.

7—St. Patrick, (1856), Rev. Francis J. Cloherty; Jeanne Lafond, Pastoral Assoc. In res., Rev. Msgr. Paul L. Moritz; Rev. Joseph A. Gaudet.
Res., 335 Main St., 02401-5396. Tel: 508-586-4840; Fax: 508-941-0639.

8—Sacred Heart, (1891) (French), Revs. Thomas A. Kopp; Jean Marx Pierre-Louis.
Res., 235 Court St., 02402-4698. Tel: 508-586-1740; Fax: 508-584-8553.
School—Tel: 508-588-4481.
Sisters 3; Lay Teachers 6; Students 228.

Brookline, Norfolk Co.,

1—St. Aidan, (1911). Closed. For inquiries for sacramental records contact St. Mary, Brookline.

2—Infant Jesus, (1938). Merged with St. Lawrence, Brookline to form Infant Jesus-St. Lawrence, Brookline.

3—St. Lawrence, (1898). Merged with Infant Jesus, Brookline to form Infant Jesus-St. Lawrence, Brookline.

4—Infant Jesus-St. Lawrence, (Chestnut Hill) (1999), Rev. James G. Burke; Deacon John J. Mannion. In res., Revs. Christopher J. Kirwin, Jr.; Sylvester Kuubetersuur.
Res., 774 Boylston St., Chestnut Hill, 02467. Tel: 617-566-3131; Fax: 617-738-3330.
Churches—Infant Jesus, 918 W. Roxbury Pkwy., 02467.; St. Lawrence, 774 Boyleston St., Chestnut Hll, 02467.

5—St. Mary of the Assumption, (1852), Revs. John J. Ahern; Joseph T. MacCarthy; Deacon Richard F. Radford. In res., Revs. Charles J. Higgins; Robert Nee.
Res., 5 Linden Pl., 02446-7311. Tel: 617-734-0444; Fax: 617-734-3001.
School—Tel: 617-566-7184.
Sisters 1; Lay Teachers 10; Students 185.

Burlington, Middlesex Co., St. Malachy (1964), Rev. Leonard F. O'Malley; Mr. Ken Meltz, Pastoral Assoc.
Res., 99 Bedford St., 01803. Tel: 781-272-5111; Fax: 781-270-9407.
St. Margaret (1945), Revs. John R. Crispo; John E. Buckley. In res., Rev. Basile Bazina; Deacon Richard F. Bilotta.
Res., 111 Winn St., 01803-3124. Tel: 781-272-3111; Fax: 781-272-9204.

Cambridge, Middlesex Co.,

1—St. Anthony, (1902) (Portuguese), Rev. Jose S. Ferreira. In res., Rev. Victor Okumu.
Res., 400 Cardinal Medeiros Ave., 02141. Tel: 617-547-5593; Fax: 617-547-1505.

2—Blessed Sacrament, (1905), Rev. Paul W. Hurley.
Res., 189 Pearl St., 02139-4087. Tel: 617-547-1669; Fax: 617-547-3220.

3—St. Francis of Assisi, (1917) (Italian), Rev. Norbert DeAmato, O.F.M.; Joan DeGuglielmo, Pastoral Assoc.
Res., 42 Sciarappa St., 02141-1204. Tel: 617-876-6754; Fax: 617-876-6753.

4—St. Hedwig, (1907) (Polish). Closed. For inquiries for parochial records contact the Chancery.

5—Immaculate Conception, (1910) (Lithuanian), Rev. Simeon W. Saulenas.
Res., 432 Windsor St., 02141-1343. Tel: 617-547-1623; Fax: 617-547-0336.

6—Immaculate Conception, (1926), Very Rev. Arthur F. Wright; Sr. Phyllis O'Callaghan, C.S.J., Pastoral Assoc.
Res., 45 Alewife Brook Pkwy., 02140-1098. Tel: 617-547-3456; Fax: 617-354-8052.

7—St. John the Evangelist, (1893), Rev. Charles E. Collins; Joanne Hogan, Pastoral Assoc.
Res., 2254 Massachusetts Ave., 02140-1891. Tel: 617-547-4880; Fax: 617-441-8028.
School—Tel: 617-876-3589. Miss Marian Burns, Prin.
Lay Teachers 10; Students 198.

8—St. Mary of the Annunciation, (1867), Revs. Joseph T. Canavan; Alfred Monsalve; Pedro Foschiatti. In res., Rev. Andres G. Nino, O.S.A.
Res., 134 Norfolk St., 02139-1805. Tel: 617-547-0120; Fax: 617-547-0232.

9—Our Lady of Pity, (1892). Closed. For inquiries for parochial records contact St John the Evangelist, Cambridge.

10—St. Patrick, (1908). Closed. For inquiries for parochial records contact Sacred Heart of Jesus, Cambridge.

11—St. Paul, (1875), Rev. Msgr. Dennis F. Sheehan; Rev. James W. Savage. In res., Revs. George S. Salzmann, O.S.F.S.; J. Bryan Hehir; Thomas Brennan, S.D.B.
Res., 29 Mt. Auburn St., 02138. Tel: 617-491-8400; Fax: 617-354-7092.
School—Tel: 617-868-8658.
Sisters 2; Lay Teachers 4; Students 49.

12—St. Peter, (1848), Rev. William D. Walsh. In res.,
Res., 31 Buckingham St., 02138-2297. Tel: 617-547-4235; Fax: 617-547-1525.
School—Tel: 617-547-0101.
Sisters 5; Lay Teachers 7; Students 201.

13—Sacred Heart of Jesus, (1842), Rev. John P. Tackney. In res., Rev. Paul W. Miceli.
Res., 49 Sixth St., 02141-1594. Tel: 617-547-0399; Fax: 617-441-8648.

Canton, Norfolk Co., St. Gerard Majella (1960), Rev. Bernard P. McLaughlin; Sr. Christiana Cronin, C.S.J., Pastoral Assoc.
Res., 1860 Washington St., 02021-1642. Tel: 781-828-3420; Fax: 781-828-2520.
St. John the Evangelist (1861), Revs. Michael J. Doyle; Raymond P. Kiley; Deacons Edward M. Quigley; John J. Carey. In res., Rev. Robert G. LaBrie.
Res., 700 Washington St., 02021-3036. Tel: 781-828-0090; Fax: 781-828-2480.
School—Tel: 617-828-2130.
Sisters 1; Lay Teachers 11; Students 256.

Carlisle, Middlesex Co., St. Irene (1960), Rev. Thomas P. Donohoe. In res., Rev. Terence Langley, S.C.J.; Deacon Dean Bulpett.
Res., 187 East St., 01741. Tel: 978-369-3940; Fax: 978-287-1440.

Carver, Plymouth Co., Our Lady of Lourdes (1950), Rev. Anthony J. Medairos; Deacon Paul S. Jones; Sr. Elizabeth Brabazon, C.S.J., Pastoral Assoc.
Res., 192 Center St., 02355-0068. Tel: 508-866-4491; Fax: 508-866-5588.
Box 68, 02355-0068.

Chelmsford, Middlesex Co., St. John the Evangelist (1893), Very Rev. Richard J. Craig; Revs. John M. Capuci; Kenneth C. Overbeck; Deacon Joseph A. Donnelly; Joyce Wholey, Pastoral Assoc. In res., Rev. Francis B. Leonard.
Res., 115 Middlesex St., 01863-2037. Tel: 978-251-8571; Fax: 978-251-7873.
St. Mary (1931), Revs. Leo E. Martel; Paul W. Berube; Christopher K. O'Connor; Deacon Dennis Vandi.
Res., 25 North Rd., 01824-2767. Tel: 978-256-2374; Fax: 978-256-0122.

Chelsea, Suffolk Co.,

1—Our Lady of the Assumption, (1907) (French). Closed. For inquiries for sacramental records contact St. Rose of Lima, Chelsea.

2—St. Rose of Lima, (1849), Revs. James F. Fratus; Richard DeVeer; Robert J. Carr; Anthony Nguyen; Deacon Luis Rivera. Pastoral Assocs.: Sr. Innocentia M.S.H.J.; Sr. Digna, M.S.H.J.; Sr. Josepha M.S.H.J. In res., Revs. Ignacio Berrio; John Bosco.
Res., 601 Broadway, 02150-2998. Tel: 617-889-2774; Fax: 617-889-2854.
School—Tel: 617-884-2626.
Sisters 8; Lay Teachers 10; Students 423.

3—St. Stanislaus, (1905) (Polish), Rev. Andrew T. Grelak, Admin.
Res., 163 Chestnut St., 02150. Tel: 617-889-0261; Fax: 617-889-2967.

4—Our Lady of Grace (1913), Rev. James J. Barry; Sr. Ann Kelly, S.N.D., Pastoral Assoc.; Deacon Leo A. Martin.
Res., 59 Nichols St., 02150. Tel: 617-884-0030; Fax: 617-884-0957.
School—Tel: 617-387-8034.
Lay Teachers 7; Students 147.

Cohasset, Norfolk Co., St. Anthony (1873), Rev. John R. Mulvehill.
Res., 129 S. Main St., 02025-2006. Tel: 781-383-0219; Fax: 781-383-2988.

Concord, Middlesex Co., St. Bernard (1863), Rev. John A. Murray; Deacons Alfred Murphy; Francis D'Ambrosio. In res., Revs. Michael B. Medas; Peter J. Murphy.
Res., 70 Monument Sq., 01742. Tel: 978-369-3778; Fax: 978-371-3346.
Our Lady Help of Christians (1907), Rev. Austin H. Fleming; Deacon Charles Clough.
Res., 1004 Main St., 01742-2937. Tel: 978-369-2810; Fax: 978-371-0853.

Danvers, Essex Co., St. Mary of the Annunciation (1871), Revs. Gerard L. Dorgan; William M. Walsh.
Res., 24 Conant St., 01923-2988. Tel: 978-774-0340; Fax: 978-774-9407.
St. Richard (1963), Revs. Bruce G. Flanagan; John Unni; Deacons David Shrader; Norman St. Hilaire.
Res., 90 Forest St., 01923. Tel: 978-774-7575; Fax: 978-774-9543.

Dedham, Norfolk Co., St. Mary (1866), Revs. John J. Dooher; Christopher J. Hickey; Deacon Louis W. Sheedy. In res., Rev. Edward J. Banks, S.J.
Res., 420 High St., 02026-2892. Tel: 781-326-0550; Fax: 781-326-1809.
St. Susanna (1960), Rev. Terence P. Curley; Karen MacDougall, Pastoral Assoc.
Res., 262 Needham St., 02026-0033. Tel: 781-329-9575; Fax: 781-329-5966.

Dover, Norfolk Co., Most Precious Blood (1959), Rev. Joseph P. Fratic.
Res., 30 Center St., Box 33, 02030-0033. Tel: 508-785-0305; Fax: 508-785-0432.

Dracut, Middlesex Co., St. Francis (1963), Revs. Brian P. Kiely; John F. Carmichael; Deacon John C. Hunt.
Res., 110 Percy St., 01826. Tel: 978-452-6611; Fax: 978-452-0772.
St. Mary of the Assumption (1909), Rev. Lucien H. Loiselle. In res., Rev. Arnold E. Kelly.
Res., 1868 Lakeview Ave., 01826. Tel: 978-957-3214; Fax: 978-957-7883.
St. Therese (1927) (French), Revs. Lawrence J. Chane; Paul T. Clifford; Deacon Everett F. Penny.
Res., 1340 Lakeview Ave., 01826-3499. Tel: 978-957-0322; Fax: 978-957-5266.

Duxbury, Plymouth Co., Holy Family (1945), Rev. Msgr. William F. Glynn; Rev. Joseph F. Mozer; Deacons Arthur J. Keefe; Daniel R. Burns.
Church—601 Tremont St., 02332-4450. Tel: 781-934-5055; Fax: 781-934-5796.

East Bridgewater, Plymouth Co., St. John (1902), Rev. John W. Corcoran; Deacons Leo J. Donoghue; Lee A. Beatrice; Brendan Fitzgerald, Pastoral Assoc.
Res., 210 Central St., 02333-1998. Tel: 508-378-4207; Fax: 508-378-7317.

Essex, Essex Co., St. John the Baptist (1931), Rev. Thomas W. Buckley.
Res., 52 Main St., 01929. Tel: 978-768-6284; Fax: 978-768-2533.

Everett, Middlesex Co.,

1—St. Anthony, (1927) (Italian), Revs. Camillo Lando, C.S.; Antonio Carvalho; Samuel Fonseca; Deacon Thomas W. Marchant.
Res., 38 Oakes St., 02149. Tel: 617-387-0310; Fax: 617-387-1229.
School—Tel: 617-389-2448.
Sisters 2; Lay Teachers 8; Students 213.

2—Immaculate Conception, (1885), Rev. Msgr. Edmond J. Sviokla; Rev. Keith LeBlanc.
Res., 489 Broadway, 02149. Tel: 617-389-5660; 5661; Fax: 617-389-2456.
School—Tel: 617-387-8304.
Sisters 3; Lay Teachers 9; Students 270.

3—St. Joseph, (1912), Rev. Philip J. DesRosiers.
Res., 195 Bucknam St., 02149-1297. Tel: 617-387-3343; Fax: 617-389-4733.

4—St. Therese, (1927), Rev. Msgr. William J. Forster; Rev. Roger C. Cormier.
Res., 20 Gledhill Ave., 02149-4605. Tel: 617-389-0412; Fax: 617-387-0052.

Foxborough, Norfolk Co., St. Mary (1859), Revs. Thomas J. Reilly; John R. McLaughlin; Ms. Lenore Danesco, Pastoral Assoc. In res., Rev. John J. Hever.
Res., 83 Central St., 02035. Tel: 508-543-7726; Fax: 508-543-7728.

Framingham, Middlesex Co.,

1—St. Bridget, (1878), Rev. Msgr. Francis V. Strahan, V.F.; Rev. Michael A. Hobson; Mrs. Elizabeth Mingolelli, Pastoral Assoc.
Res., 15 Wheeler Ave., 01702-2902. Tel: 508-875-5959; Fax: 508-875-1270.
School—Tel: 508-875-0181.
Lay Teachers 14; Students 242.

2—St. George, (Saxonville) (1847), Revs. Francis E. O'Brien; Albert C. Hughes; Sr. Ann Marie McAndrews, S.N.D., Pastoral Assoc.; Deacon Neil F. Lacey.
Res., 74 School St., 01701. Tel: 508-877-5130; Fax: 508-877-3080.

3—St. Jeremiah, (1958), Revs. Thomas H. Maguire; John J. Stagnaro.
Res., 41 Brook St., 01701-3996. Tel: 508-877-1428; Fax: 508-788-1592.

4—St. Stephen, (1883), Revs. Albert H. Stankard, Team Ministry; George F. Emerson, Team Ministry; Beverly Good, Pastoral Assoc.; Deacons Guy Spiri; Pedro Torres.
Res., 221 Concord St., 01702. Tel: 508-875-4788; Fax: 508-875-2577.

5—St. Tarcisius, (1907) (Italian), Revs. Joseph A. Scopa, C.S.; Gelso A. Dadalt, C.S.; Deacon Gus Diotalevi.
Res., 35 Cedar St., 01702-6950. Tel: 508-875-8623; Fax: 508-875-6358.
School—Tel: 508-872-8188.

Franklin, Norfolk Co., St. Mary (1877), Revs. Thomas J. Walsh; Carlos C. Kim; David C. Goodrow. In res., Rev. Francis W. Beksha; Deacon Richard P. Delio.
Res., Church Sq., 02038-1896. Tel: 508-528-0020; Fax: 508-528-0020.

Georgetown, Essex Co., St. Mary (1870), Very Rev. James M. Carroll.
Res., 94 Andover St., Box 396, 01833. Tel: 978-352-2024; Fax: 978-352-5513.

Gloucester, Essex Co.,

1—St. Ann, (1855), Revs. Frederick L. Guthrie; James J. O'Driscoll; Deacon Richard Gindel.
Res., 60 Prospect St., 01930. Tel: 978-283-0054; Fax: 978-283-5313.
School—Tel: 508-283-3455.
Sisters 3; Lay Teachers 6; Students 185.
Mission—Magnolia, St. Joseph's Chapel.

2—Our Lady of Good Voyage, (1889) (Portuguese), Rev. Eugene L. Alves.
Res., 142 Prospect St., 01930-3797. Tel: 978-283-1490; Fax: 978-283-0787.

3—St. Peter, (1928), Rev. Thomas J. Fleming. In res., Rev. Richard G. Johnson.
Res., One Brightside Ave., 01930-3299. Tel: 508-283-0874; Fax: 508-283-8223.
Chapel—Eastern Point, St. Anthony-by-the-Sea.

4—Sacred Heart, (1946), Rev. Myron F. Bullock.
Res., 5 High St., 01930-1113. Tel: 978-283-4457; Fax: 978-281-7279.

Groton, Middlesex Co., St. James (1945), Rev. John T. Atwater.
Res., 29 Old Orchard Rd., Box 186, 01472-0186. Tel: 978-448-5513; Fax: 978-448-9308.
Sacred Heart (1907), Rev. John T. Atwater; Ella Kingsley, Pastoral Assoc.
Res., 271 Main St., Box 259, 01450. Tel: 978-448-6633; Fax: 978-448-2732.

Groveland, Essex Co., St. Patrick (1946). Unassigned.
Res., 728 Salem St., 01834. Tel: 978-372-6044; Fax: 978-374-9006.

Halifax, Plymouth Co., Our Lady of the Lake (1945), Rev. Paul G. McPartland. In res., Rev. Charles D. Logue.
Res., 580 Monponsett St., Box 35, 02338-0035. Tel: 781-293-7971; Fax: 781-293-7969.

Hamilton, Essex Co., St. Paul (1922), Rev. Louis D. Bourgeois; Deacons William J. James; James Manzi.
Res., 50 Union St., 01982-2118. Tel: 978-468-2337; Fax: 978-468-6538.

Hanover, Plymouth Co., St. Mary of the Sacred Heart (1907), Revs. Henry F. Doherty; Richard G. Curran; Mrs. Marilyn Zedik, Pastoral Assoc.
Res., 392 Hanover St., 02339-2215. Tel: 781-826-4303; Fax: 781-826-5203.

Hanson, Plymouth Co., St. Joseph the Worker (1956), Rev. John M. Hannon; Deacon Gerald P. Ryan.
Res., One Maquan St., 02341-0714. Tel: 781-293-3581; Fax: 781-294-1052.

Haverhill, Essex Co.,

1—All Saints, (1998), Revs. Dennis T. Nason; Kelvin E. Iguabita-Rodriguez; Deacon Richard R. Bowley.
Res., 120 Bellevue Ave., 01832-4711. Tel: 978-372-7721; Fax: 978-372-2085.
School—St. Joseph, 56 Oak Ter., 01832. Tel: 978-521-4256. Sr. Maria Joseph Foley, Prin.
St. Joseph's Early Childhood Ed. Center—100 Bellevue Ave., 01832. Tel: 978-372-0111.

2—St. George, (1961). Closed. For inquiries for parochial records contact All Saints, Haverhill.

3—St. James, (1859), Revs. Francis X. Mawn; Robert D. Smith. In res., Rev. Edward L. King.
Res., 6 Cottage St., 01830-4999. Tel: 978-372-8537; Fax: 978-373-1505.

4—St. John the Baptist, (1955), Rev. Frederick E. Sweeney.
Res., 110 Lincoln Ave., 01830. Tel: 978-372-2780; Fax: 978-469-0947.

5—St. Joseph, (1876). Closed. For inquiries for parochial records contact All Saints, Haverhill.

6—St. Michael, (1910). Closed. For inquiries for parochial records contact All Saints, Haverhill.

7—St. Rita, (1932). Closed. For inquiries for parochial records contact All Saints, Haverhill.

8—Sacred Hearts, (1908), Revs. Marc A. Piche; James T. Kelly; Deacon Robert J. Gaudreau. In res., Rev. James M. Broderick.
Res., 48 Chestnut St., 01835-7446. Tel: 978-373-1281; Fax: 978-374-3043.
School—Tel: 508-372-5451.
Sisters 1; Lay Teachers 9; Students 247.

Hingham, Plymouth Co., St. Paul (1871), Very Rev. James F. Rafferty, V.F.; Revs. Albert M. Faretra; Joseph D. Flynn; Deacons John W. McHugh; Timothy A. Lawless; Sr. Eleanor Ballantine, S.C., Pastoral Assoc.
Res., 147 North St., 02043-7894. Tel: 781-749-0587; Fax: 781-749-8053.
School—18 Fearing Rd., 02043. Tel: 781-749-2407.
Lay Teachers 9; Students 253; Religious 1.
Resurrection of Our Lord and Saviour Jesus Christ (1957), Rev. Albert J. Sallese; Deacon John Steuterman.
Res., 1057 Main St., 02043-1497. Tel: 781-749-3577; Fax: 781-740-0689.

Holbrook, Norfolk Co., St. Joseph (1887), Revs. Joseph K. Raeke; Louis R. Palmieri.
Res., 153 S. Franklin St., 02343. Tel: 781-767-0605; Fax: 781-767-2563.
School—143 S. Franklin St., 02343. Tel: 781-767-1544.
Sisters 2; Lay Teachers 14; Students 290.

Holliston, Middlesex Co., St. Mary (1870), Revs. William J. Haley; Brian G. Bashand; Deacons Martin Breinlinger; Philip Caruso.
Res., 8 Church St., 01746-1741. Tel: 508-429-4427; Fax: 508-429-3324.

Hopkinton, Middlesex Co., St. John the Evangelist (1866), Revs. James F. Degnan; Joseph Diem; Regina O'Connor, Pastoral Assoc.
Res., 25 Church St., 01748-1836. Tel: 508-435-3313; Fax: 508-435-5651.

Hudson, Middlesex Co., Christ the King (1927). Unassigned.
Res., 12 Florence St., 01749-2098. Tel: 781-562-7662; Fax: 781-562-9762.
St. Michael (1870), Revs. Thomas M. Curran; Antonio L. Andrade; Sr. Yvonne Millman, Pastoral Assoc.
Res., 20 High St., 01749-2391. Tel: 978-562-2552; Fax: 978-568-1761.
School—Tel: 978-562-2917.
Lay Teachers 8; Students 119.
High School—Hudson Catholic, Tel: 978-562-6701.

Hull, Plymouth Co., St. Mary of the Assumption (1938), Revs. William G. Williams; Joseph M. White; Deacon Edward L. Doyle.
Res., 58 Nantasket Ave., 02045. Tel: 781-925-0680; Fax: 781-925-0685.

Ipswich, Essex Co.,

1—Our Lady of Hope, (1997), Rev. Lawrence J. Wetterholm.
Res., One Pineswamp Rd., 01938-2909. Tel: 978-356-3944; Fax: 978-356-9592.

2—St. Joseph, (1889). Closed. For inquiries for parochial records contact Our Lady of Hope, Ipswich.

3—Sacred Heart, (1908) (Polish). Closed. For inquiries for parochial records contact Our Lady of Hope, Ipswich.

4—St. Stanislaus, (1910) (French). Closed. For inquiries for parochial records contact Our Lady of Hope, Ipswich.

Kingston, Plymouth Co., St. Joseph (1908), Rev. Msgr. Frederick J. Ryan; Deacons William V. Nagle; Richard G. Monroe.
Res., 268 Main St., 02364-1922. Tel: 781-585-6679; Fax: 781-585-7104.

Lakeville, Plymouth Co., Saints Martha and Mary (1958), Rev. Thomas J. Naughton; Sr. Carol Flaherty, F.M.M., Pastoral Assoc. In res., Rev. Thomas J. Mooney.
Res., 354 Bedford St., 02347-2107. Tel: 508-947-2107; Fax: 508-947-6543.

Lawrence, Essex Co.,

1—St. Anne. Closed. For inquiries for parochial records contact Sacred Heart, Lawrence.

2—Asuncion de la Virgen Maria, (1993) (Spanish), Revs. Paul G. McManus; Rafael Arango; Orlando Morales. Pastoral Assocs.: Sr. Rufina Carrillo, M.S.P.; Sr. Rosa Martinez, M.S.P.; Sr. Virginia Arrellano, M.S.P.; Deacon Domingo Naveo.
Res., 216 Lawrence St., 01841-1715. Tel: 978-683-1069; Fax: 978-686-4677.

3—St. Augustine, (1935), Revs. Peter G. Gori, O.S.A.; Thomas J. Casey, O.S.A.; Deacons Edward J. Grimley; Steven J. Murphy.
Res., 124 Ames St., 01841. Tel: 978-686-0727; Fax: 978-686-1988.
School—Tel: 978-682-9761.
Sisters of Notre Dame de Namur 1; Lay Teachers 9; Students 226.

4—St. Francis, (1903) (Lithuanian), Rev. Richard J. Brady.
Res., 94 Bradford St., 01840-1003. Tel: 978-687-7356; Fax: 978-687-6480.

5—Holy Rosary, (1904) (Italian), Revs. James J. Ronan; Luis A. Duque; Emilson Aguirre.
Res., 35 Essex St., 01840-1797. Tel: 978-685-1711; Fax: 978-687-9047.

6—Holy Trinity, (1905) (Polish), Revs. Conrad Salach, O.F.M.Conv.; Stanley Sobiech, O.F.M.Conv. In res., Rev. Valerian Czywil, O.F.M.Conv.
Res., 30 Trinity St., 01841. Tel: 978-688-7226; Fax: 978-681-5356.
School—Tel: 978-686-3007.
Sisters 2; Lay Teachers 7; Students 231.

7—St. Mary Immaculate Conception, (1848), Revs. William F. Waters, O.S.A.; Luis M. Madera; Jorge A. Reyes, O.S.A.; Deacons John D. Harrison; Diego Rodriguez. Pastoral Assocs.: Sr. Janet Veno, S.M.S.M.; Sr. Vitolia Moa S.M.S.M.
Res., 300 Haverhill St., 01840-3698. Tel: 978-685-1111; Fax: 978-686-5555.
School—Tel: 978-685-2091.
Sisters 2; Lay Teachers 8; Students 171.

8—St. Patrick, (1872), Revs. Paul O'Brien; James P. Seymour; Sr. Mary O'Connor, S.S.N.D., Pastoral Assoc.; Deacon Paul V. Specht.
Res., 118 S. Broadway, 01843-1427. Tel: 978-683-9416; Fax: 978-681-5808.
School—101 Parker St., 01843. Tel: 978-683-5822.
Sisters 6; Lay Teachers 11; Students 440.

9—SS. Peter and Paul, (1907) (Portuguese), Rev. Albert A. Sylvia; Deacon Richard A. Rocha.
Res., 125 Chestnut St., 01841-3844. Tel: 978-681-9080; Fax: 978-687-4112.

10—Sacred Heart, (1905) (French), Revs. Gerard A. Demers, S.M.; Laurence Ross, S.M.; Clifton W. Moors, S.M.; Roland Lacasse; Deacon Gerard E. Gagne. In res., Rev. Raymond Fournier, S.M.

Res., 321 S. Broadway, 01843-2691. Tel: 978-686-7921; Fax: 978-686-5687.
School—Tel: 978-682-8935.
Sisters 1; Lay Teachers 13; Students 289.

Lexington, Middlesex Co., St. Brigid (1931), Revs. Eugene P. Curtin; William P. Smith; Francine Edwards, Pastoral Assoc.
Res., 2001 Massachusetts Ave., 02173. Tel: 781-862-0335; Fax: 781-862-1409.
Sacred Heart (1931), Rev. Arnold F. Coletti; Sr. Mary Nagle, C.S.J., Pastoral Assoc.
Res., 21 Follen Rd., 02173-5921. Tel: 781-862-4646; Fax: 781-863-5614.

Lincoln, Middlesex Co., St. Joseph (1945), Rev. John G. Kiley.
Res., 142 Lincoln Rd., Box 234, 01773-0234. Tel: 781-259-8364; Fax: 781-259-3332.

Littleton, Middlesex Co., St. Anne (1945), Rev. David P. Callahan.
Res., 75 King St., Box 2246, 01460-3246. Tel: 978-486-4100; Fax: 978-952-6303.

Lowell, Middlesex Co.,

1—St. Anthony, (1901) (Portuguese), Revs. Francis M. Glynn; Mark Ballard; Victor Mello, Pastoral Assoc. In res., Rev. Pedro J. Damazio.
Res., 893 Central St., 01852-3407. Tel: 978-452-1506; Fax: 978-458-9662.

2—Holy Trinity, (1904) (Polish), Rev. Stanislaus Kempa; Joanne Faticanti, Pastoral Assoc.
Res., 340 High St., 01852. Tel: 978-452-2564; Fax: 978-452-4679.
School—St. Stanislaus, Tel: 978-453-2360.
Sisters 2; Lay Teachers 6; Students 224.

3—Immaculate Conception, (1869), Very Rev. John W. Hanley, O.M.I.; Revs. James Erving; Francis Ouelette, O.M.I.; Bro. James H. Lucas, O.M.I.; Claire Couillard, Pastoral Assoc. In res., Rev. John Hogan.
Res., 3 Fayette St., 01852-1298. Tel: 978-458-1474; Fax: 978-446-0790.
School—Tel: 978-454-5339.
Sisters 1; Lay Teachers 8; Students 175.

4—Saint Jeanne d'Arc, (1922), Revs. Donald G. Lozier, O.M.I.; Paul Beauregard, O.M.I.; Normand Fillion. In res., Rev. Adhemar Deveau, O.M.I.
Res., 129 Fourth Ave., 01854-2904. Tel: 978-458-6316; Fax: 978-970-2299.
School—Tel: 978-453-4114.
Sisters 2; Lay Teachers 18; Students 466.

5—St. Jean Baptiste. Closed. For inquiries for parochial records contact St. Louis de France, Lowell.

6—St. Joseph, (1908) (Lithuanian). Closed. For inquiries for sacramental records contact Immaculate Conception, Lowell.

7—St. Louis de France, (1904) (French), Team Ministry: Rev. Leonard E. Pelletier; Deacon Gerard J. Hardy.
Res., 221 W. Sixth St., 01850. Tel: 978-454-0496; Fax: 978-446-7992.
School—Tel: 978-458-7594.
Sisters 5; Lay Teachers 6; Students 275.

8—St. Margaret, (1910), Revs. Joseph A. Ruggeri; Andrew Albert, S.M.
Res., 374 Stevens St., 01851-3695. Tel: 978-454-5143; Fax: 978-458-8472. [CEM]
School—Tel: 978-453-8491.
Sisters 1; Lay Teachers 19; Students 430.

9—St. Marie, (1931) (French), Revs. Roger Lamoreaux, O.M.I.; Gilmond Boucher, O.M.
Res., 80 Chamberlain St., 01852-5523. Tel: 978-453-2134; Fax: 978-446-0324.

10—St. Michael, (1883), Revs. Albert L. Capone; Mario J. Orrigo; Mary T. Carleton, Pastoral Assoc.
Res., 543 Bridge St., 01850. Tel: 978-459-0713; Fax: 978-453-1123.
School—Lay Teachers 9; Students 260.

11—Notre Dame de Lourdes, (1908) (French), Rev. Patrick J. Hollywood, O.M.I.; Joan M. Blazevich, Pastoral Assoc.
Res., 101 Smith St., 01851-2698. Tel: 978-459-2339; Fax: 978-446-0838.

12—Nuestra Senora del Carmen, (1990), Revs. James A. Loiacono, O.M.I.; Terrence E. O'Connell, O.M.I.; James E. Taggart, O.M.I.
Res., 725 Merrimack St., 01854-3978. Tel: 978-459-7829; Fax: 978-446-0442.

13—St. Patrick, (1831), Revs. D. George Spagnolia; Anthony Giang Nguyen; Deacon Peter An Ros.
Res., 282 Suffolk St., 01854-4297. Tel: 978-459-0561; Fax: 978-446-0266.
School—Tel: 978-458-4232.
Sisters 2; Lay Teachers 8; Students 231.

14—St. Peter, (1841). Closed. For inquiries for parochial records contact Sacred Heart, Lowell.

15—St. Rita, (1910), Revs. Daniel M. Magni; Paul R. Soper; Deacon Bob Dzuris.
Res., 158 Mammoth Rd., 01854. Tel: 978-452-4812; Fax: 978-459-8969.

16—Sacred Heart, (1884), Revs. Roger Lamoreaux, O.M.I.; Gilmond Boucher, O.M.I.; Norman Parent, O.M.I. Pastoral Assocs.: Sr. Joan Gregoire, S.N.D.; Mrs. Linda Burns; Mrs. Carol Shepherd.
Res., 159 Moore St., 01852-5099. Tel: 978-453-3962; Fax: 978-454-3466.
School—Tel: 978-453-4751.
Sisters 1; Lay Teachers 8; Students 255.

Lynn, Essex Co.,

1—Holy Family, (1922) (Italian), Rev. Gregory J. Mercurio.
Res., 26 Bessom St., 01902-1205. Tel: 781-599-7200; Fax: 781-599-7201.

2—St. Jean Baptiste, (1886) (French). Closed. For inquiries for parochial records contact St. Mary, Lynn.

3—St. Joseph, (1874), Revs. James E. Gaudreau; Luis Arrioyave.
Res., 40 Green St., 01902-2999. Tel: 781-599-7040; Fax: 781-598-7439.
Convent—.Sisters of St. Joseph 2.

4—St. Mary, (1862), Rev. Msgr. Paul V. Garrity, V.F.; Revs. Michael M. Ferraro; Lamartine Petit-Monsieur; Timothy Kearney; Sr. Eileen Burns, S.N.D., Pastoral Assoc.; Deacon Timothy F. Dempsey.
Res., 8 S. Common St., 01902-4489. Tel: 781-598-4907; Fax: 781-599-2088.
High School—Tel: 781-595-7885.
Lay Teachers 16; Students 291.

5—St. Michael, (1906) (Polish), Rev. Kazimierz Zastawny.
Res., 567 Summer St., 01905-2011. Tel: 781-593-4584; Fax: 781-599-7547.

6—St. Patrick, (1906). Closed. For inquiries for parochial records contact St. Mary, Lynn.

7—St. Pius Fifth, (1912), Team Ministry: Revs. Cornelius J. Mullaney; Joseph M. Rossi. In res., Rev. Msgr. Peter F. Hart; Sr. Kathleen Crowley, S.C.
Res., 215 Maple St., 01904-2799. Tel: 781-595-7487; Fax: 781-595-7270.
School—Tel: 781-593-8292.
Sisters 2; Lay Teachers 8; Students 540.

8—Sacred Heart, (1894), Revs. Jerome F. Gillespie; Oscar J. Pratt; Deacon John W. Hardy.
Res., 571 Boston St., 01905-2160. Tel: 781-593-8047; Fax: 781-599-4040.
School—Tel: 781-592-7581.
Sisters 1; Lay Teachers 8; Students 261.

Lynnfield, Essex Co., Our Lady of the Assumption (1937), Very Rev. John E. Farrell, V.F.; Rev. Mark G. Derrane.
Res., 17 Grove St., 01940-1446. Tel: 781-598-4313; Fax: 781-598-0055.
School—Sisters 1; Lay Teachers 16; Students 457.
St. Maria Goretti (1960), Rev. J. Michael Lawlor.
Res., 112 Chestnut St., 01940. Tel: 781-334-2367; Fax: 781-334-9819.

Malden, Middlesex Co.,

1—Immaculate Conception, (1854), Revs. Richard J. Mehm; Thomas D. Reynolds; Stephen M. Boyle; Deacon Mark E. Romley. Pastoral Assocs.: Sr. Laetitia A. Campbell, O.P.; Mr. Paul Farrell. In res., Rev. Francisco Cruz, C.M.
Res., 10 Fellsway E., 02148. Tel: 781-324-4941; Fax: 781-397-8571.
School—Tel: 781-322-0129.
Sisters 3; Lay Teachers 14; Students 426.

2—St. Joseph, (1902), Revs. John A. Daley; Richard T. Bakker, S.M.A.
Res., 790 Salem St., 02148. Tel: 781-324-0402; Fax: 781-324-1790.

3—Sacred Hearts, (1890), Revs. Daniel J. Hickey; Francis E. Sullivan.
Res., 297 Main St., 02148. Tel: 781-324-0728; Fax: 781-324-2714.
School—Tel: 781-324-6584.
Sisters 2; Lay Teachers 17; Students 463.

4—St. Peter, (1972) (Italian), Rev. John U. Paris, Admin.; Deacon Frank Valeri. In res., Rev. Donald Howard, C.S.P.
Res., 12 Thacher St., 02148. Tel: 781-322-6142; Fax: 781-321-6169.

Manchester by the Sea, Essex Co., Sacred Heart (1905), Rev. James J. Harrington.
Res., 62 School St., 01944. Tel: 978-526-1263; Fax: 978-526-4335.

Marblehead, Essex Co., Our Lady, Star of the Sea (1859), Revs. Dennis J. Burns; Joseph R. Foster; Deacon John E. Whipple.
Res., 85 Atlantic Ave., 01945-3036. Tel: 781-631-0086; Fax: 781-631-5668.

Marlborough, Middlesex Co.,

1—St. Ann, (1921) (Italian), Revs. G. Michael Bercik, O.F.M.; Bruce C. Czapla, O.F.M.; Deacon Richard C. Martino.
Res., 466 Lincoln St., 01752-3036. Tel: 508-485-1968; Fax: 508-481-7255.

2—Immaculate Conception, (1854), Rev. Paul J. McLaughlin; Deacon Douglas Peltak; Yvonne Millman, Pastoral Assoc. In res., Rev. Geraldo Ildeo Franco.
Res., 17 Washington Ct., 01752. Tel: 508-485-0016; Fax: 508-480-9644.
School—Tel: 508-460-3400.
Lay Teachers 14; Students 257.

3—St. Mary, (1870) (French), Rev. Laurier J. Martineau.
Res., 26 Broad St., 01752-4098. Tel: 508-485-0390; Fax: 508-480-9835.

4—St. Matthias, (1963), Rev. John R. Lizio; Deacon Robert I. Hoaglund.
Res., 409 Hemenway St., 01752-6710. Tel: 508-460-9255; Fax: 508-480-8801.

Marshfield, Plymouth Co., St. Ann (1945), Revs. Edward T. Serena; Stephen M. Healy.
Res., 591 Ocean St., P.O. Box 2607, 02065-2607. Tel: 781-834-4953; Fax: 781-834-7472.
St. Christine (1945), Revs. Francis A. Regan; Vincent P. Doolan. Pastoral Assocs.: Mary Doolan; Barbara MacRae.
Res., Rte. 3A, Box 274, 02051-0274. Tel: 781-834-6003; Fax: 781-834-0671.
Mission—Humarock, St. Theresa's.
Our Lady of the Assumption (1949), Rev. Donald P. Clifford.
Res., 40 Canal St., Box 368, 02041-0368. Tel: 781-834-6252; Fax: 781-834-5694.

Maynard, Middlesex Co., St. Bridget (1881), Rev. Kenneth Quinn; Deacon John W. Pepi.
Res., One Percival St., 01754-1699. Tel: 978-897-2171; Fax: 978-897-5358.
St. Casimir (1912) (Polish). Closed. For inquiries for sacramental records contact St. Bridget, Maynard.

Medfield, Norfolk Co., St. Edward the Confessor (1892), Rev. Leroy E. Owens.
Res., 133 Spring St., Box 336, 02052-0003. Tel: 508-359-2633; Fax: 508-359-1846.

Medford, Middlesex Co.,

1—St. Francis of Assisi, (1921), Revs. Joseph F. Scorzello; Paul F. Coughlin; Deacon Henry A. Mariani.
Res., 441 Fellsway W., 02155. Tel: 781-396-3400; Fax: 781-396-3254.
School—Tel: 781-395-9170.
Sisters 4; Lay Teachers 12; Students 347.

2—St. James, (1919), Rev. James F. Darcy, Admin.; Deacon Arthur F. Rogers.
Res., 779 Fellsway, 02155-4953. Tel: 781-396-0025; Fax: 781-396-2161.

3—St. Joseph, (1883), Team Ministry: Revs. Robert J. Fountain; Patrick J. McLaughlin; Deacon Robert P. Amerault. In res., Rev. Msgr. Francis T. McFarland.
Res., 114 High St., 02155-3882. Tel: 781-396-3860; Fax: 781-391-2919.
School—Tel: 781-396-3636.
Sisters 5; Lay Teachers 14; Students 342.

4—St. Raphael, (1905), Rev. Kevin G. Toomey. In res., Revs. Charles T. Duggan, Senior Priest; David M. O'Leary; Deacon David C. McCallum.
Mailing Address: 512 High St., 02155-6722.
Res., 38 Boston Ave., 02155-6722. Tel: 781-488-5444; Fax: 781-483-3375.
School—Sisters of St. Joseph 2; Lay Teachers 11; Students 283.

5—Sacred Heart, (1937), Rev. Robert J. Doherty. In res., Rev. Anthony J. Vasaturo.
Res., 51 Winthrop St., 02155-5324. Tel: 781-396-2232; Fax: 781-396-3731.

Medway, Norfolk Co., St. Joseph (1885), Rev. Msgr. Timothy J. Moran; Revs. Brian E. Mahoney; Kenneth A. LeBlanc.
Res., 2 Barber St., Box 557, 02053-0557. Tel: 508-533-6500; Fax: 508-533-1236.

Melrose, Middlesex Co., Incarnation (1958), Team Ministry: Rev. Lawrence E. Pratt; Deacon John W. Wise; Linda Swett, Pastoral Assoc.
Res., 429 Upham St., 02176-3233. Tel: 781-662-8844; Fax: 781-662-6653.
St. Mary of the Annunciation (1894), Revs. John J. Ronaghan; John M. Sullivan; Bernard J. Shea. In res., Rev. Msgr. Alfonso G. Palladino.
Res., 46 Myrtle St., 02176-3898. Tel: 781-665-0152; Fax: 781-665-2750.
School—4 Myrtle St., 02176. Tel: 781-665-5037.
Lay Teachers 10; Students 198.

Merrimac, Essex Co., Nativity (1891), Rev. Edward F. Sherry.
Res., 4 Green St., 01860. Tel: 978-346-8604; Fax: 978-346-9970.

Methuen, Essex Co.,

1—St. Lucy, (1958), Rev. Angelo P. Loscocco; Sr. Rena Brunetti, P.M., Pastoral Assoc.
Res., 254 Merrimack St., 01844. Tel: 978-686-3311; Fax: 978-686-5343.

2—St. Monica, (1917), Rev. David A. Keene.
Res., 231 Broadway, 01844-3067. Tel: 978-683-1193; Fax: 978-686-0249.
School—Tel: 978-686-1801.
Sisters 4; Lay Teachers 12; Students 522.

3—Our Lady of Mount Carmel, (1937), Revs. Andre Gosselin, S.M.; John Meade, S.M.; Roland Lacasse, S.M.
Res., 78 Union St., 01844-3699. Tel: 978-682-9160; Fax: 978-725-6099.
School—Tel: 978-688-3040.
Sisters 1; Lay Teachers 9; Students 221.

4—St. Theresa, (1936) (French), Revs. George L. Szal, S.M.; Leo Bourdeau, S.M. In res., Rev. Irenee DuPerry, S.M.
Res., 22 Plymouth St., 01844-4299. Tel: 978-686-3984; Fax: 978-686-8300.

Middleborough, Plymouth Co., Sacred Heart (1885), Revs. Richard P. Crowley; Thomas A. Mahoney. In res., Rev. Daniel F. Moran.
Res., 340 Center St., 02346-2102. Tel: 508-947-0444; Fax: 508-947-2364.

Middleton, Essex Co., St. Agnes (1945), Rev. Jon C. Martin; Deacons John M. Bresnahan; Gerald Kaelin.
Res., 22 Boston St., 01949-2199. Tel: 978-774-1958; Fax: 978-774-1964.

Millis, Norfolk Co., St. Thomas the Apostle (1937), Rev. Henry G. Chambers.
Res., 111 Exchange St., 02054-9998. Tel: 508-376-2621; Fax: 508-376-4308.

Milton, Norfolk Co.,

1—St. Agatha, (1922), Revs. Peter J. Casey; Charles E. Salamone; Robert J. Bowers; Sr. Helen Cornelia Lyons, S.N.D., Pastoral Assoc.; Deacon Daniel F. Sullivan. In res., Rev. Msgr. Charles E. Anadore, Senior Priest; Rev. William F. Kenneally.
Res., 432 Adams St., 02186-4399. Tel: 617-698-2439; Fax: 617-698-1517.
School—Tel: 617-696-3548.
Sisters 2; Lay Teachers 15; Students 377.

2—St. Elizabeth, (1946), Revs. Gilbert S. Phinn; Francis X. Gorman, O.M.I.; Aidan Walsh; Sr. Regina Harrington, C.S.J., Pastoral Assoc.; Deacon Joseph P. MacDonald. In res., Rev. Msgr. William R. Coen.
Res., 350 Reedsdale Rd., 02186. Tel: 617-696-6688; Fax: 617-698-4864.

3—St. Mary of the Hills, (1931), Rev. Thomas C. Foley.
Res., 29 St. Mary's Rd., 02186-2024. Tel: 617-696-0120; Fax: 617-696-7044.
School—Tel: 617-698-2464.
Sisters 2; Lay Teachers 14; Students 307.

4—St. Pius Tenth, (1954), Rev. David M. Burke.
Res., 865 Brush Hill Rd., 02186-1299. Tel: 617-333-0401; Fax: 617-333-0191.

Nahant, Essex Co., St. Thomas Aquinas (1902), Rev. Henry H. Cunney.
Res., 248 Nahant Rd., 01908. Tel: 781-581-0023; Fax: 781-598-8860.

Natick, Middlesex Co., St. Linus (1950), Rev. Msgr. J. Robert Giggi; Cynthia Giardina, Pastoral Assoc.
Res., 119 Hartford St., 01760-2497. Tel: 508-653-5505; Fax: 508-655-4577.

St. Patrick (1856), Revs. Daniel F. Twomey; Michael McNamara; Denise Perreault, Pastoral Assoc.
Res., 44 E. Central St., 01760-4639. Tel: 508-653-1093; Fax: 508-650-2922.

Sacred Heart (1891). Unassigned.
Res., 19 Eliot St., 01760-6092. Tel: 508-653-5113; Fax: 508-653-3051.

Needham, Norfolk Co., St. Bartholomew (1952), Rev. Francis D. Garrity.
Res., 1180 Greendale Ave., 02192-4700. Tel: 781-444-3434; Fax: 781-449-7550.

St. Joseph (1917), Rev. Msgr. James J. Haddad; Rev. Stephen Madden; Deacon William J. McCarty. In res., Rev. Msgr. Francis J. McGann.
Res., 1382 Highland Ave., 02192-2694. Tel: 781-444-0245; Fax: 781-444-7713.
School—Tel: 781-444-4459.
Sisters 1; Lay Teachers 18; Students 411.

Newburyport, Essex Co., Immaculate Conception (1848), Revs. Robert L. Connors; Derek J. Borek; John J. Jusseaume.
Res., 7 Court St., 01950-2502. Tel: 978-462-2724; Fax: 978-463-6989.
School—Tel: 978-465-7780.
Sisters 2; Lay Teachers 7; Students 198.
Mission—Plum Island, St. James.

St. Louis de Gonzague (1902) (French). Closed. For inquiries for sacramental records contact Immaculate Conception, Newburyport.

Newton, Middlesex Co.,

1—St. Bernard, (1876), Revs. Gerard D. Barry; Richard S. Moran; Daniel J. Issing, C.S.C.; Sr. Diane Valerio, O.S.F., Pastoral Assoc. In res., Rev. Daniel C. O'Connell.
Res., 1529 Washington St., 02165-4419. Tel: 617-244-0608; Fax: 617-332-4951.

2—Corpus Christi, (1922), Rev. Joseph F. McGlone; Cathi Duffy, Pastoral Assoc. In res., Rev. Vincent H. Poirier.
Res., 45 Ash St., 02166. Tel: 617-244-9110; Fax: 617-558-7515.

3—St. Ignatius, (1926), Revs. Robert F. VerEecke, S.J.; James F. Morgan, S.J.; James A. Benson, S.J.; James Mattaliano, S.J.; Kenneth Loftus, S.J.
Res., 28 Commonwealth Ave., 02167-3849. Tel: 617-332-1104; Fax: 617-244-0488.

4—St. John the Evangelist, (1911). Closed. For inquiries for parochial records contact Our Lady Help of Christians, Newton.

5—Mary Immaculate of Lourdes, (1870), Rev. Stephen A. Koen. In res., Revs. Barry O'Sullivan; Issam Abi-Khalil; Paul Daly.
Res., 270 Elliot St., 02164-203. Tel: 617-244-0558; Fax: 617-965-4815.

6—Our Lady Help of Christians, (1878), Rev. Walter H. Cuenin. Pastoral Assocs.: Mr. Thomas Leahy; Sr. Marie Labollita, S.C.; Mary Ellen Cocks. In res., Revs. Paul E. Kilroy; John E. Sassani; Michael S. Foster.
Res., 573 Washington St., 02158-1494. Tel: 617-527-7560; Fax: 617-527-1338.
High School—Trinity Catholic High School Interparish, Tel: 617-244-1841.
Sisters 2; Lay Teachers 10; Students 152.

7—St. Philip Neri, (1934), Rev. Charles J. McCoy. In res., Revs. Paul Park; Honore Kombo.
Res., 1518 Beacon St., 02168-1530. Tel: 617-244-0590; Fax: 617-558-7522.

8—Sacred Heart, (1890), Rev. John J. Connelly.
Res., 1321 Centre St., 02159-2496. Tel: 617-969-2248; Fax: 617-965-7515.

Norfolk, Norfolk Co., St. Jude (1949), Rev. Msgr. Peter V. Conley. In res., Rev. Robert Rivard, F.M.S.I.
Res., 86 Main St., Box 305, 02056-0305. Tel: 508-528-0170; Fax: 508-528-1470.

North Andover, Essex Co., St. Michael (1900), Revs. Paul T. Keyes; George C. Hogan; John W. Delaney.
Res., 196 Main St., 01845-2598. Tel: 978-686-4050; Fax: 978-606-5408.
School—Tel: 978-686-1862.
Sisters 8; Lay Teachers 8; Students 153.

North Reading, Middlesex Co., St. Theresa (1945), Revs. Thomas M. Gillespie; Thomas J. Powers; Deacon Alfred Balestracci; Paula Frew, Pastoral Assoc.
Res., 63 Winter St., 01864-2264. Tel: 978-664-3412; Fax: 978-276-0034.

Norwell, Plymouth Co., St. Helen (1950), Rev. Richard J. Smith.
Res., 383 Washington St., 02061-2009. Tel: 781-659-2993; Fax: 781-659-7861.

Norwood, Norfolk Co.,

1—St. Catherine of Siena, (1890), Rev. Msgr. Cornelius M. McRae; Revs. James P. Braley; Edward M. Riley; Sr. Frances Sears, C.S.J., Pastoral Assoc. In res., Bro. James Moran, S.J.
Res., 547 Washington St., 02062-0547. Tel: 781-762-6080; Fax: 781-256-9312.
School—Tel: 781-769-5354.
Sisters 1; Lay Teachers 20; Students 472.

2—St. George, (1912) (Lithuanian), Rev. William L. Wolkovich. In res., Rev. William F. Lucey.
Res., 36 St. George Ave., 02062-4420. Tel: 781-762-0979; Fax: 781-762-6389.

3—St. Peter, (1918) (Polish). Closed. For inquiries for parochial records contact the Chancery.

4—St. Timothy, (1963), Rev. John P. Culloty. In res., Rev. James A. Field.
Res., 650 Nichols St., 02062. Tel: 781-769-2522; Fax: 781-769-9362.

Peabody, Essex Co.,

1—St. Adelaide, (1962), Revs. Robert H. Blute; John C. Chaisson; Deacon Anthony Juliano.
Res., 17 Bow St., 01960-3427. Tel: 978-535-1985; Fax: 978-535-4845.

2—St. Ann, (1937), Rev. Wallace E. Blackwood; Deacon Martin J. Walsh.
Res., 136 Lynn St., 01960-6432. Tel: 978-531-1480; Fax: 978-531-6683.

3—St. John the Baptist, (1874), Revs. John E. MacInnis; Francisco J. Anzoategui, S.X.; Rev. Msgr. Francis G. O'Sullivan; Rev. Clifton M. Thuma; Sr. Nancy Rowen, S.N.D., Pastoral Assoc.; Deacon Valentin Rivera.
Res., 17 Chestnut St., 01960-5480. Tel: 978-531-0002; Fax: 978-531-5199.
School—Tel: 978-531-0444.
Sisters 5; Lay Teachers 5; Students 578.

4—St. Joseph, (1927). Closed. For inquiries for parish records contact Our Lady of Hope, Ipswich.

5—Our Lady of Fatima, (1965), Rev. John Mendonca; Sr. Ellen Dabrieo, S.N.D., Pastoral Assoc.
Res., 35 Newcastle Rd., 01960. Tel: 978-532-0272; Fax: 978-977-2991.

Pembroke, Plymouth Co., St. Thecla (1964), Revs. Robert J. Sullivan; Michael J. Harkins; Deacon Thomas F. McMorrow.
Res., 145 Washington St., 02358-0587. Tel: 781-826-9786; Fax: 781-826-3484.

Pepperell, Middlesex Co., St. Joseph (1870), Rev. Robert J. Butler; Sr. Roberta Rzeznik, S.N.D., Pastoral Assoc.
Res., 28 Tarbell St., Box 1486, 01463-3486. Tel: 978-433-5737; Fax: 978-433-9566.

Plainville, Norfolk Co., St. Martha (1953), Rev. John F. Walsh; Deacon Burt Guerin.
Res., 227 South St., Box 1745, 02762-1745. Tel: 508-699-8543; Fax: 508-699-6677.

Plymouth, Plymouth Co.,

1—Blessed Kateri Tekakwitha, (1982), Rev. William T. Kremmell; Deacon Edward F. Creutz.
Res., 126 S. Meadow Rd., 02360-4740. Tel: 508-747-1568; Fax: 508-747-0616.

2—St. Bonaventure, (1950), Revs. Robert J. Deehan; Edward F. Doughty; Deacon Charles H. Bower.
Res., 807 State Rd., Box 996, 02345-0996. Tel: 508-224-3636; Fax: 508-224-5889.
Mission—White Horse Beach, St. Catherine's Chapel.

3—St. Mary, (1915), Rev. Byran K. Parrish. In res., Rev. James F. Lanergan.
Res., 313 Court St., 02360-4336. Tel: 508-746-0426; Fax: 508-747-5886.

4—St. Peter, (1876), Revs. Paul F. Bailey; John J. Shea.
Res., 81 Court St., 02360-3886. Tel: 508-746-0663; Fax: 508-747-1071.

Quincy, Norfolk Co.,

1—St. Ann, (1922), Rev. Msgr. Robert P. Deeley; Revs. Garrett J. Barry; Alvaro Silva.
Res., 757 Hancock St., 02170-2761. Tel: 617-479-5400; Fax: 617-479-0955.
School—St. Ann's Rd., 02170. Tel: 617-471-9071.
Sisters 4; Lay Teachers 8; Students 176.

2—St. Boniface, (1956), Rev. Michael J. Kearney; Deacon John R. Menz.
Res., 26 Shed St., 02169-5923. Tel: 617-479-9200; Fax: 617-479-5766.

3—St. John the Baptist, (1863), Revs. Peter F. Quinn; Gerard Petringa; William H. Mullin. In res., Revs. Theodore L. Fortier, A.A.; William R. McCarthy.
Res., 21 Gay St., 02169-6602. Tel: 617-773-1021; Fax: 617-773-5608.

4—St. Joseph, (1917), Very Rev. Daniel M. Graham; Rev. Robert J. Monagle; Deacon John F. Jennette.
Res., 556 Washington St., 02169-7216. Tel: 617-472-6321; Fax: 617-471-8849.
School—Tel: 617-773-8080.
Sisters 3; Lay Teachers 9; Students 234.

5—St. Mary, (1840), Rev. John M. Rowan; Margaret L. Donaher, Pastoral Assoc.
Res., 115 Crescent St., 02169. Tel: 617-773-0120; Fax: 617-786-9199.
School—Tel: 617-773-5237.
Lay Teachers 10; Students 226.

6—Most Blessed Sacrament, (1915), Revs. William J. English; John P. Carroll; Deacon Paul G. Markey; Maureen C. Simons, Pastoral Assoc.
Res., 1000 Sea St., 02169. Tel: 617-773-0233; Fax: 617-471-7143.

7—Our Lady of Good Counsel, (1938), Rev. William M. MacKenzie; Deacon John Menz, Pastoral Assoc.
Res., 227 Sea St., 02169-2537. Tel: 617-472-1408; Fax: 617-847-3958.

8—Sacred Heart, (1903), Revs. John W. O'Brien; James E. Robertson; Deacon John D. Salenius.
Res., 386 Hancock St., 02171-2414. Tel: 617-328-8666; Fax: 617-773-2522.
School—Tel: 617-328-3830.
Sisters 5; Lay Teachers 16; Students 479.

9—Star of the Sea, (1945), Rev. Frederick L. Barr; Deacon James Little; Sr. Peggy Lowell, C.S.J., Pastoral Assoc.
Res., 107 Bellevue Rd., 02171. Tel: 617-328-0866; Fax: 617-328-8457.

Randolph, Norfolk Co., St. Bernadette (1937), Rev. Paul J. Finegan; Deacons John J. Ego; Francis G. Gates. Res., 1026 N. Main St., 02368-3099. Tel: 781-963-1327; Fax: 781-963-0198.

St. Mary (1851), Revs. Richard L. Harrington; Vincent R. Maffei; Michael K. Harvey; Deacons James Eames; Thomas P. Burke. Res., 211 N. Main St., 02368. Tel: 781-963-4141; Fax: 781-963-0884.

Reading, Middlesex Co., St. Agnes (1904), Revs. Arthur C. Flynn; Edward T. Malone; Carol A. Gaudette, Pastoral Assoc. Res., 186 Woburn St., 01867-3599. Tel: 617-944-0490; Fax: 617-944-4409.

St. Athanasius (1961), Rev. Thomas D. Conway. Res., 306 Haverhill St., 01867-1898. Tel: 781-944-0330; Fax: 781-944-1266.

Revere, Suffolk Co.,

1—St. Anthony of Padua, (1906) (Italian), Revs. F. Dominic Menna; Anthony J. Rebeiro; Mark De Angelis; Deacon Joseph A. Belmonte. Res., 250 Revere St., 02151-4618. Tel: 781-289-1234; Fax: 781-284-7123.

2—Immaculate Conception, (1888), Revs. Joseph A. Antonellis; Paul J. Aveni; Deacon Francis M. Gaffney. Res., 22 Lowe St., 02151-3125. Tel: 781-289-0735; Fax: 781-286-1124. *School*—Tel: 781-284-0519. Sisters 3; Lay Teachers 6; Students 269.

3—St. John Vianney, (1950), Rev. R. Michael Guarino. Res., 7 Harrington Ave., 02151. Tel: 781-289-5268; Fax: 781-289-1950.

4—St. Mary of the Assumption, (1947), Rev. William L. Butler; Ms. Linda Decristoforo, Pastoral Assoc. Res., 670 Washington Ave., 02151. Tel: 781-284-5252; Fax: 781-284-5801.

5—Our Lady of Lourdes, (1905), Rev. Thomas E. Keyes. Res., One Endicott Ave., 02151. Tel: 781-284-0234; Fax: 781-284-0235.

6—St. Theresa, (1937), Rev. Michael Guarino. Res., 500 Revere St., 02151-1536. Tel: 781-289-2404; Fax: 781-286-9256.

Rochester, Plymouth Co., St. Rose of Lima, Rev. John P. Lyons. Res., 282 Vaughan Hill Rd., Box 40, 02770-0040. Tel: 508-763-2244; Fax: 508-763-9877.

Rockland, Plymouth Co., Holy Family (1882), Revs. James F. Hickey; James B. Clark; Sr. Ann Conway, C.S.J., Pastoral Assoc. In res., Rev. Henry F. Barry, Senior Priest. Res., 403 Union St., 02370-1799. Tel: 781-878-0160; Fax: 781-871-6389. *School*—Tel: 781-878-1154. Religious 3; Lay Teachers 14; Students 315.

Rockport, Essex Co., St. Joachim (1870), Rev. Ronald J. Gariboldi; Deacon William F.X. Kane. Res., 9 Broadway Ave., 01966. Tel: 978-546-6756; Fax: 978-546-2272.

Rowley, Essex Co., St. Mary (1945), Rev. James D. Lyons; Deacon Daniel E. McCarthy. Res., Main St., 01969-0737. Tel: 978-948-3344; Fax: 978-948-3356.

Salem, Essex Co.,

1—St. Anne, (1901) (French), Rev. George J. Dufour; Deacon Lewis Warren. Res., 292 Jefferson Ave., 01970-2895. Tel: 978-744-1930; Fax: 978-745-1190.

2—Immaculate Conception, (1826), Rev. Timothy J. Murphy. In res., Rev. Daniel J. Doyle. Res., 15 Hawthorne Blvd., 01970-3709. Tel: 978-745-6303; Fax: 978-744-4382.

3—St. James, (1850), Rev. Daniel E. Flaherty. In res., Rev. Maurice V. Connolly; Deacon George L'Italien. Res., 161 Federal St., 01970-3297. Tel: 978-745-9060; Fax: 978-745-4229.

4—St. John the Baptist, (1903) (Polish), Rev. Stanley Parsieniczyk (Poland). Res., 28 St. Peter St., 01970. Tel: 978-744-1278; Fax: 978-744-2093.

5—St. Joseph, (1873) (French), Revs. Lawrence J. Rondeau; James D. Foley; Deacon Norman P. LaPointe. Res., 135 Lafayette St., 01970-5099. Tel: 978-744-0095; Fax: 978-744-3312. *School*—Tel: 978-744-4773. Sisters 4; Lay Teachers 6; Students 232.

6—St. Mary, (1918) (Italian), Rev. Edward M. Keohan, Admin. Res., 56 Margin St., 01970. Tel: 978-744-0631; Fax: 978-744-4620.

7—St. Thomas the Apostle, (1927), Rev. David J. Bartley; Deacon Richard W. Cordeau. Res., One Margin St., Peabody, 01960-1999. Tel: 978-531-0224; Fax: 978-531-6517.

Salisbury, Essex Co., Star of the Sea (1947), Rev. Thomas B. Morgan. Res., 18 Beach Rd., 01950-2007. Tel: 978-465-3334; Fax: 978-465-5524.

Saugus, Essex Co., Blessed Sacrament (1917), Revs. John F. Mulloy; Paul Flammia; Sr. Mary O'Rourke, C.S.J., Pastoral Assoc. Res., 14 Summer St., 01906-2139. Tel: 781-233-2497; Fax: 781-231-5569.

St. Margaret (1949), Rev. George E. Morin. Res., 431 Lincoln Ave., 01906-3917. Tel: 781-233-1040; Fax: 781-233-7135.

Scituate, Plymouth Co., St. Frances Xavier Cabrini (1960), Rev. Paul V. MacDonald; Mary Fitzgerald, Pastoral Assoc. Res., 78 Mann Hill Rd., 02066-2117. Tel: 781-545-4585; Fax: 781-545-4249.

St. Mary of the Nativity (1921), Rev. Msgr. Eugene P. McNamara; Rev. Kevin J. O'Leary; Deacon C. Michael Hickey. Res., One Kent St., 02066-4215. Tel: 781-545-3335; Fax: 781-545-6538.

Sharon, Norfolk Co., Our Lady of Sorrows (1906), Rev. Robert W. Bullock; Deacon Michael Iwanowicz. Res., 59 Cottage St., 02067-2132. Tel: 781-784-2265; Fax: 781-784-2540.

Sherborn, Middlesex Co., St. Theresa (1945), Rev. Paul E. Ritt; Sr. Pauline Laurence, S.S.A., Pastoral Assoc. Res., 24 S. Main St., Box 176, 01770. Tel: 508-653-6253; Fax: 508-651-1318.

Shirley, Middlesex Co., St. Anthony (1905), Rev. Edmond M. Derosier; Deacon Raymond Gagnon. Res., 12 Phoenix St., Box 595, 01464-0595. Tel: 978-425-4588; Fax: 978-425-2033.

Somerville, Middlesex Co.,

1—St. Ann, (1881), Revs. Gerald J. Fitzgerald; Steven Poitras; Deacons Lawrence J. Bloom; Charles E. Sullivan. Pastoral Assocs.: Sr. Margaret Stinson, C.S.J.; Sr. Mary Gowern, C.S.J. In res., Rev. Antonio Lopez, F.S.C.B. Res., 399 Medford St., 02145-3899. Tel: 617-625-1904; Fax: 617-625-7043. *School*—Tel: 617-625-1108. Sisters 4; Lay Teachers 6; Students 235.

2—St. Anthony, (1915) (Italian), Revs. Moacir Balen, C.S.; Domingos Pergher, C.S. Res., 12 Properzi Way, 02143-3226. Tel: 617-625-4530; Fax: 617-625-2457. *School*—Tel: 617-623-0995. Sisters 5; Lay Teachers 5; Students 204.

3—St. Benedict, (1911), Revs. John E. McLaughlin; David A. Doucet; Joachim Martinez, S.J. In res., Sr. Stephen Marie C.S.J. Res., 25 Arlington St., 02145-3342. Tel: 617-625-0029; Fax: 617-666-5944. *School*—Tel: 617-628-7775. Sisters 5; Lay Teachers 4; Students 196.

4—St. Catherine of Genoa, (1891), Rev. Brian F. Manning. Res., 179 Summer St., 02143-2596. Tel: 617-666-2087; Fax: 617-666-5470. *School*—Tel: 617-666-9116. Sisters 2; Lay Teachers 9; Students 225.

5—St. Clement, (1912), Revs. Dennis A. Dever; James J. O'Driscoll; Deacon Andrew Goldy. Res., 71 Warner St., 02144-1399. Tel: 617-625-0122; Fax: 617-628-7767. *School*—Tel: 617-625-3459. Sisters of St. Joseph 2; Lay Teachers 17; Students 421. *High School*—Sisters 2; Lay Teachers 3; Students 196.

6—St. Joseph, (1869), Revs. Henry J. Jennings; Stephen Brennick. In res., Rev. John P. Kelly, Senior Priest. Res., 264 Washington St., 02143-3313. Tel: 617-666-4140; Fax: 617-628-0557.

7—St. Polycarp, (1927). Closed. For inquiries for sacramental records contact St. Ann, Somerville.

Stoneham, Middlesex Co., St. Patrick (1868), Revs. William T. Schmidt; Ronald A. Barker; Robert M. Browne. Pastoral Assocs.: Sr. Neonilla Barrett, C.S.J.; Sr. Marylou A. Cassidy, C.S.J.; Deacons John R. Turner; Cyril T. O'Neil; Joan Kilday Puleo. Res., 9 Pomeworth St., 02180-2025. Tel: 781-438-0960; Fax: 781-438-6809. *School*—Tel: 781-438-2593. Lay Teachers 10; Students 223.

Stoughton, Norfolk Co., Immaculate Conception (1872), Revs. Joseph P. McDermott; Aristide Z. Arude; Emil Boutin; Deacons Francis X. Heffernan; Charles J. Ferrazzi. Res., 122 Canton St., 02072-2271. Tel: 781-344-2073; Fax: 781-344-2979.

St. James (1962), Rev. John E. Kelly. Res., 560 Page St., 02072. Tel: 781-344-9121; Fax: 781-341-9323.

Our Lady of the Rosary (1958), Rev. Maurice J. O'Connor; Deacon Eugene V. Stenstrom. Res., 39 South St., 02072-3705. Tel: 781-341-6110; Fax: 781-344-3306.

Stow, Middlesex Co., St. Isidore (1961), Rev. Richard J. Butler; Deacon Charles A. Cornell; Shirley Ormsby, Pastoral Assoc. Res., 429 Great Rd., Box 279, 01775-1101. Tel: 978-897-2710; Fax: 978-461-0577.

Sudbury, Middlesex Co., St. Anselm (1963), Rev. John P. Fitzpatrick, Admin.; Deacon Joseph Ramrath; Kathryn Cleary, Pastoral Assoc. Res., 100 Landham Rd., 01776-0916. Tel: 978-443-8981; Fax: 978-443-7032.

Our Lady of Fatima (1955), Very Rev. Michael J. Bova Conti; Sr. Brenda Forry, C.S.J., Pastoral Assoc.; Deacon Walter J. Miles. Res., 160 Concord Rd., Box 916, 01776-0916. Tel: 978-443-2647; Fax: 978-443-6264.

Swampscott, Essex Co., St. John the Evangelist (1907), Revs. Joseph T. Sheehy; Thomas B. Corcoran; Deacon Andrew Acampora. Res., 174 Humphrey St., 01907-2512. Tel: 781-593-2544; Fax: 781-593-3616.

Tewksbury, Middlesex Co., St. William (1935), Revs. William O'Donnell, O.M.I.; Martin Walsh, O.M.I.; Dwight Hoeberechts, O.M.I.; Deacon William Emerson. In res., Revs. Edward Lowney, O.M.I.; William P. Smith. Mailing Address: 1268 Main St., 01876. Res., 1351 Main St., 01876-2098. Tel: 978-851-7331; Fax: 978-858-0544.

Topsfield, Essex Co., St. Rose of Lima (1945), Rev. E. Paul Sullivan. Res., 17 Prospect St., Box 258, 01983-0458. Tel: 978-887-5505; Fax: 978-887-8201.

Townsend, Middlesex Co., St. John (1945), Rev. Clyde H. Chetwynde. Res., One School St., Box 533, 01469-0523. Tel: 978-597-2291; Fax: 978-597-3401.

Tyngsborough, Middlesex Co., St. Mary Magdalen (1959), Revs. Ronald L. St. Pierre; Thomas P. Rossi; Deacon Barry Lloyd. Pastoral Assocs.: Mrs. Carol Gagne; Sr. Linda Greenwood, O.S.F. Res., 93 Lakeview Ave., Box 100, Tyngsboro, 01879. Tel: 978-649-7315; Fax: 978-649-3796.

Wakefield, Middlesex Co., St. Florence (1947), Rev. H. Joseph Murphy. Res., 49 Butler Ave., 01880-5125. Tel: 781-245-2711; Fax: 781-245-4512.

St. Joseph (1854), Revs. Michael J. Steele; David F. Ziomek. Res., 173 Albion St., 01880-3296. Tel: 781-245-5770; Fax: 781-246-2423. *School*—Tel: 781-245-2081. Sisters 1; Lay Teachers 7; Students 167.

Most Blessed Sacrament (1931), Revs. William D. Coughlin; Tinh Van Nguyen; Deacon Robert Hackett. Res., 11 Grove St., 01880-4222. Tel: 781-245-2080; Fax: 781-245-7981.

Walpole, Norfolk Co., Blessed Sacrament (1874), Rev. Timothy J. Kelleher. Pastoral Assocs: Jeanne Remillard; Marie A. Martin. Res., 10 Diamond St., 02081-3408. Tel: 508-668-4700; Fax: 508-668-3554. *School*—Tel: 508-668-2336. Sisters 3; Lay Teachers 17; Students 433.

St. Mary (1931), Rev. Donald R. Delay; Brian Mercier, Pastoral Assoc. Res., 176 Washington St., Box 131, 02032-0131. Tel: 508-668-4974; Fax: 508-668-3083.

Waltham, Middlesex Co.,

1—St. Charles Borromeo, (1909), Rev. Rodney J. Copp; Deacon James C. Callahan. Res., 51 Hall St., 02154-5217. Tel: 781-893-0330; Fax: 781-893-2060.

2—St. Joseph, (1894) (French), Rev. Roger N. Jacques; Deacon Albert J. Aucoin. Res., 519 Main St., 02154-5524. Tel: 781-893-3185; Fax: 781-893-9681.

3—St. Jude, (1949), Rev. Robert J. Waldron; Deacon Alfred E. Santosuosso. Res., 147 Main St., 02154-6622. Tel: 781-893-3100; Fax: 781-893-6635. *School*—Tel: 781-899-3644. Sisters 2; Lay Teachers 8; Students 199.

4—St. Mary, (1839), Revs. Wendell Verrill; Henry M. Yanju; Deacons Francisco Alicea; Teodoro Camacho. In res., Rev. David C. Michael. Res., 133 School St., 02154. Tel: 781-891-1730; Fax: 781-642-0604.

5—OUR LADY, COMFORTER OF THE AFFLICTED, (1930), Rev. Joseph F. Byrne; Deacon William E. MacKenzie.
Res., 857 Trapelo Rd., 02154. Tel: 781-894-3481; Fax: 781-894-0021.
School—Tel: 781-899-0353.
Lay Teachers 8; Students 180.

6—SACRED HEART, (1922), Revs. Dennis F. Wheatley, O.F.M.; Michael A. MacInnis, O.F.M.; Friar Damien J. Johnson, Pastoral Assoc.
Res., 311 River St., 02154. Tel: 781-899-0469; Fax: 781-899-0081.

Watertown, Middlesex Co., St. Patrick (1847), Very Rev. Robert C. Fichtner; Rev. Thomas P. Kelly; Deacon Leo F. LaBrache.
Res., 25 Chestnut St., 02172-2337. Tel: 617-926-9680; Fax: 617-926-3715.
Sacred Heart (1893), Rev. Joseph L. Curran; Sr. Estellyn Ganley, C.S.J., Pastoral Assoc. In res., Rev. Robert M. O'Grady.
Res., 770 Mt. Auburn St., 02172-1567. Tel: 617-924-9110; Fax: 617-926-3341.
St. Theresa of the Child Jesus (1927). Closed. For inquiries for sacramental records contact St. Patrick, Watertown.

Wayland, Middlesex Co., St. Ann (1945), Rev. Frank Silva.
Res., 124 Cochituate Rd., 01778-2610. Tel: 508-358-2985; Fax: 508-358-3415.
St. Zepherin (Cochituate Village) (1889), Rev. Ronald L. Bourgault; Sr. Theresa Regan, S.C., Pastoral Assoc.; Deacon James M. Crump.
Res., 99 Main St., 01778-4936. Tel: 508-653-8013; Fax: 508-655-6948.

Wellesley, Norfolk Co., St. James the Great (1950), Revs. George D. Vertzelis; James F. Power.
Res., 900 Worcester St., 02181. Tel: 781-237-1160; Fax: 781-237-0497.
St. John the Evangelist (1890), Rev. Thomas F. Powers; Sr. Evelyn Ronan, S.N.D., Pastoral Assoc. In res., Rev. Msgr. John J. Philbin; Deacon J. Scott Abercrombie.
Res., 9 Glen Rd., 02181. Tel: 781-235-0045; Fax: 781-235-6990.
School—Tel: 781-235-0300.
Sisters 2; Lay Teachers 5; Students 187.
St. Paul (1922), Rev. Msgr. Joseph G. Lind, V.F.; Rev. Michael C. Harrington. In res., Rev. Richard W. Fitzgerald; Deacon Paul Cloonan.
Res., 502 Washington St., 02181-5907. Tel: 781-235-1060; Fax: 781-235-4620.
School—Tel: 781-235-1510.
Sisters 3; Lay Teachers 7; Students 134.

West Bridgewater, Plymouth Co., St. Ann (1938), Rev. Edward C. McDonagh.
Res., 103 N. Main St., Box 427, 02379-0427. Tel: 508-586-4880; Fax: 508-588-0239.

Westford, Middlesex Co., St. Catherine of Alexandria (1922), Revs. William M. Sullivan; Daniel F. Cronin; Thomas J. Stanton; Deacons Russell Morey; Richard Joy.
Res., 107 N. Main St., 01886-1219. Tel: 978-692-6353; Fax: 978-392-0644.

West Newbury, Essex Co., St. Ann (1945), Rev. John F. Leonard.
Res., 46 Maple St., Box 237, 01985. Tel: 978-363-2303; Fax: 978-363-2046.

Weston, Middlesex Co., St. Julia (1919), Rev. Robert D. Tyrell; Susan Bayard, Pastoral Assoc.
Res., 374 Boston Post Rd., 02193. Tel: 781-899-2611; Fax: 781-899-8046.

Westwood, Norfolk Co., St. Denis (1949), Revs. Edwin D. Condon; Joseph W. Sylva; Deacon Joseph L. Delaney.
Res., 157 Washington St., 02090-1336. Tel: 781-326-5858; Fax: 781-326-1232.
St. Margaret Mary (1931), Rev. T. Joseph Moynihan; Deacons Joseph Holderried; Joseph M. Messina.
Res., 845 High St., Box 386, 02090-0386. Tel: 781-326-1071; Fax: 781-329-1879.

Weymouth, Norfolk Co.,

1—ST. ALBERT THE GREAT, (1950), Rev. John J. Nichols.
Res., 1130 Washington St., 02189-1997. Tel: 781-337-8778; Fax: 781-335-5850.

2—ST. FRANCIS XAVIER, (1851), Revs. Eugene P. Sullivan; Paul L. Ring; Sr. Mary Joan Lofgren, C.S.J., Pastoral Assoc.; Deacons Joseph V. Vitello; Joseph A. Canova. In res., Rev. Charles J. Murphy.
Res., 261 Pleasant St., 02190-2507. Tel: 781-337-2171; Fax: 781-331-4192.
School—Pleasant St., 02190. Tel: 781-335-6868.
Religious 2; Lay Teachers 5; Students 172.

3—IMMACULATE CONCEPTION, (1879), Rev. Msgr. Peter T. Martocchio; Revs. Linh T. Nguyen; Peter J. O'Hara; Deacon Joseph T. Nickley, Pastoral Assoc.
Res., 1199 Commercial St., 02189. Tel: 781-337-0380; Fax: 781-340-3979.

4—ST. JEROME, (1928), Revs. Thomas F. Wyndham; Mark J. Coiro; Deacon Joseph A. Papile.
Res., 632 Bridge St., 02191-1845. Tel: 781-335-2038; Fax: 781-340-7165.
School—Tel: 781-335-1235.
Sisters 1; Lay Teachers 9; Students 234.

5—SACRED HEART, (1871), Revs. John V. Sutton; Richard P. Cornell; Deacon Henry Welch. In res., Rev. Arthur M. Calter.
Res., 55 Commercial St., 02188-2604. Tel: 781-337-6333.
School—Tel: 781-335-6010.
Sisters 2; Lay Teachers 7; Students 165.

Whitman, Plymouth Co., Holy Ghost (1897), Rev. Robert P. Reed; Most Rev. Richard T. Malone; Deacon Gerald P. Ryan. In res., Rev. Paul E. Curran.
Res., 518 Washington St., 02382. Tel: 781-447-4421; Fax: 781-447-1375.

Wilmington, Middlesex Co., St. Dorothy (1954), Rev. Donald S. Abbott.
Res., 11 Harnden St., 01887-3519. Tel: 978-658-3550; Fax: 978-658-2006.
St. Thomas of Villanova (1919), Revs. Philip B. Early; Walter Carreiro; Deacon Clifford D. King; Paul Merullo, Pastoral Assoc.
Res., 126 Middlesex Ave., Box 397, 01887-2723. Tel: 978-658-4665; Fax: 978-658-4670.

Winchester, Middlesex Co., St. Eulalia (1966), Revs. Victor C. Lavoie; John P. McGinty; Sr. Rose Marie Lipke, C.D.P, Pastoral Assoc.
Res., 50 Ridge St., 01890. Tel: 781-729-8220; Fax: 781-729-0919.
Immaculate Conception (1931), Rev. Thomas S. Foley, Admin.
Res., 1004 Main St., 01890-1929. Tel: 781-729-1858; Fax: 781-721-5329.
St. Mary (1876), Revs. Richard C. Messina; Richard C. Beaulieu; Deacon James V. Kerrigan; Mr. Salvatore Caraviello, Pastoral Assoc. In res., Rev. Paul G. Kelley.
Res., 158 Washington St., 01890. Tel: 781-729-0055; Fax: 781-721-6542.
School—Lay Teachers 7; Students 144.

Winthrop, Suffolk Co., Holy Rosary (1953), Rev. Thomas A. DiLorenzo, Admin.
Res., 993 Shirley St., 02152-2535. Tel: 617-846-1210; Fax: 617-539-4402.
St. John the Evangelist (1907), Rev. Charles E. Bourke; Sr. Jane Iannaccone, S.P., Pastoral Assoc.
Res., 320 Winthrop St., 02152. Tel: 617-846-7400; Fax: 617-539-0627.

Woburn, Middlesex Co.,

1—ST. ANTHONY, (1945), Revs. Leo X. Lynch; Hubert E. Desmond.
Res., 80 Elm St., 01801-1855. Tel: 781-933-1323; Fax: 781-937-3233.

2—ST. BARBARA, (1954), Very Rev. Vincent P. Mellone, V.F.; Revs. Thomas J. Reilly; Edward G. Carroll; Deacon William E. Kerns.
Res., 138 Cambridge Rd., 01801-4772. Tel: 781-933-4130; Fax: 781-932-2536.

3—ST. CHARLES, (1862), Revs. Timothy J. Shea; Wayne Belschner; Joseph F. Donahue, S.V.D.; Deacon Philip P. Hardcastle. In res., Rev. Patrick J. Kelly.
Res., 280 Main St., 01801-3294. Tel: 781-933-0300; Fax: 781-932-7581.
School—Tel: 781-935-4635.
Lay Teachers 19; Students 315.

4—ST. JOSEPH, (1906), Rev. Harold E. LeBlanc.
Res., 22 Central St., 01801. Tel: 781-938-0473; Fax: 781-938-7818.

Wrentham, Norfolk Co., St. Mary (1928), Rev. John G. Connolly; Deacon Kenneth W. Oles.
Res., 130 South St., Box 326, 02093-0326. Tel: 508-384-3373; Fax: 508-384-5747.

Special Chaplaincies:
Reverend Fathers—
Bradford, Richard S., Chap., (Anglican Use), 192 Foster St., Brighton, MA 02135-4620
Roy, George O.M.I. (Haiti), Chap., 45 Alewife Brook Pkwy., Cambridge, MA 02140

Chaplains of Public Institutions

BOSTON. *Health Care Ministry* Our Lady Hall, St. Elizabeth Medical Center, 736 Cambridge St., 02135-2997. Tel: 617-789-2457; Fax: 617-789-2573. Ms. Kelly L. Dunn, Dir.

NEWTON. *Office of Prison Ministry*. Vacant. 251 Watertown St., 02158. Tel: 617-244-7544; Fax: 617-244-7891.

Health Care Ministry

BOSTON. *Arbour Hospital*. Attended by Our Lady of Lourdes, Jamaica Plain. 49 Robinwood Ave., 02130. Tel: 617-522-4400.
Beth Israel Deaconess Medical Center 330 Brookline Ave., 02215. Tel: 617-667-4205. Spiritual Care Services: Revs. John R. Carroll Tel: 617-667-4205; Peter Grover, O.M.V.; Bruce Aguilar Tel: 617-632-8103.
Boston Medical Center University Campus, One Medical Center Pl., 02118-2393. Tel: 617-638-6851. Rev. Raymond P. Benoit, Spiritual Care Svcs.
Boston Medical Center Boston City Campus, 818 Harrison Ave., 02118. Tel: 617-534-5336. Special Care Services: Sr. Claire Hayes, C.D.P.; Carmela D'Elia.
Brigham and Women's Hospital 75 Francis St., 02115-6195. Tel: 617-732-7480; Fax: 617-232-2746. Rev. George P. Winchester, S.J., Spiritual Care Svcs.
Children's Hospital 300 Longwood Ave., 02115. Tel: 617-355-4775. Spiritual Care Services: Rev. Mark J. Riley; Sr. Carlotta Gilarde, C.S.J.
Dana Farber Cancer Institute 44 Binney St., 02115. Tel: 617-732-3000. Rev. John E. Doherty, C.SS.R., Spiritual Care Svcs.
Hebrew Rehabilitation Center. Attended by Sacred Heart, Roslindale. 1200 Centre St., 02131. Tel: 617-325-8000.
Jewish Memorial Hospital. Attended by St. Joseph, Roxbury. 59 Townsend St., 02119. Tel: 617-442-8760.
Massachusetts General Hospital 32 Fruit St., 02114. Tel: 617-726-2222; Fax: 617-724-3401. Spiritual Care Services: Revs. Philip E. McGaugh; Felix Ojimba; Michael McElhinny, S.M.
New England Medical Center 750 Washington St., 02111. Tel: 617-636-7500. Spiritual Care Services: Revs. Jan Hernick, O.F.M.Conv.; Dac Tat Tran, O.F.M.; James M. Shaughnessy, S.J.; Amy Edmonds.
St. Elizabeth's Medical Center 736 Cambridge St., 02135-2997. Tel: 617-789-3045; Fax: 617-789-2124. Ms. Kelly L. Dunn, Dir., Our Lady Hall, Spiritual Care Services: Sr. Catherine O'Connor, C.S.B.; Revs. Phillip M. Conroy; Garrett J. Thompson; Yaroslov Nalysnk; Matthew Perumpil, O.S.C.; Sr. Susan Keating; Sr. MaryAnn Gallagher, O.S.F.; Sr. Ivan Cadigan, C.S.J.; Deacon Fran Bogle; Ann Cody; Edna Lezotte, St. Margaret's Center: Martha Sullivan.
Shriners Burn Institute. Attended by St. Joseph, Boston. 51 Blossom St., 02114. Tel: 617-722-3000.
Spaulding Rehabilitation Hospital 125 Nashua St., 02114-1198. Tel: 617-720-6400; Fax: 617-720-6960. Sr. Mary Samson, S.H.C.J., Spiritual Care Svcs.

ARLINGTON. *Medical Center at Symmes*. Attended by St. Agnes, Arlington. Hospital Rd., 02174. Tel: 781-646-1500.

AYER. *Deaconess-Nashoba Hospital*. Attended by St. Mary, Ayer. 200 Groton St., 01432. Tel: 978-772-0200.

BEDFORD. *Veterans Administration Hospital Bedford* 200 Spring Rd., 01730. Tel: 781-687-2384. Spiritual Care Services: Revs. Joseph P. Robinson; Philip Cabasino, C.S.S.R.; Aidan J. Walsh; Deacon John Watson.

BELMONT. *Fernald Developmental Center* Box 150, 02178. Tel: 781-894-3600, Ext. 2117. Spiritual Care Services: Rev. William T. Leonard; Deacon Eugene Counihan.
McLean Hospital. Attended by St. Luke, Belmont. 115 Mill St., 02178. Tel: 617-855-2000.

BEVERLY. *Beverly Hospital* Herrick St., 01915. Tel: 978-922-3000, Ext. 2790. Joan Rossi, Spiritual Care Svcs.

BRAINTREE. *Healthsouth Braintree Hospital*. Attended by St. Francis of Assisi, Braintree. 250 Pond St., 02184. Tel: 781-848-5353.
Massachusetts Respiratory Hospital. Attended by St. Clare, Braintree. 2001 Washington St., 02185. Tel: 781-848-2600.

BRIGHTON. *Franciscan Children's Hospital* 30 Warren St., 02135. Tel: 617-779-1644. Spiritual Care Services: Sr. Helen Mary McGonagle, C.S.J.; Sr. Rena Foley, C.S.J.; Patricia Huff Byrne.
St. John of God Hospital 296 Allston St., 02135. Tel: 617-277-5750. Spiritual Care Services: Rev. Joseph K. Coleman; Sr. Alicia Brennan, D.C.
Vencor Hospital Boston 1515 Commonwealth Ave., 02135. Tel: 617-254-1100. Rev. George Thekkummattathil, C.S.C., Spiritual Care Svcs.

BROCKTON. *Brockton Hospital* 680 Centre St., 02402. Tel: 508-941-7000, Ext. 2550. Spiritual Care Services: Rev. David Murphy; Deacon John Connor.
Good Samaritan Medical Center 235 N. Pearl St., 02401. Tel: 508-427-2376. Spiritual Care Services: Rev. Richard W. Visbisky; Sr. Margaret Crowley, S.C.N.; Sr. George Powell, C.J.C.; Sr. Helen Carpinelli, S.U.S.C.; Sr. Eileen McCarthy, R.N.
Veterans Administration Hospital Brockton-West Roxbury 940 Belmont St., 02402. Tel: 508-583-4500, Ext. 1125. Spiritual Care Services: Revs. Henry P. Nichols; Avelino R. Garcia.

BROOKLINE. *Bournewood Hospital.* Attended by Infant Jesus, Brookline. 300 South St., 02146. Tel: 617-469-0300.

BURLINGTON. *Lahey Hitchcock Medical Center* 41 Mall Rd., 01805. Tel: 781-744-8800. Spiritual Care Services: Rev. Clif Moors, S.M.; William W. Houghton.

CAMBRIDGE. *Cambridge Hospital.* Attended by St. Mary, Cambridge. 1493 Cambridge St., 02139. Tel: 617-498-1000.

Mount Auburn Hospital 330 Mt. Auburn St., 02238. Tel: 617-499-5665, Ext. 4669. Spiritual Care Services: Revs. Lucien A. Sawyer, O.M.I.; Celestino Vasquez Pascual; Sr. Margaret Holleran, S.S.C.

Youville Lifecare, Inc 1575 Cambridge St., 02138-4398. Tel: 617-876-4344, Ext. 333. Spiritual Care Services: Revs. Ronald Paquin; William J. Mulligan, S.J.; Sr. Virginia Murray, C.S.J.; Patricia Kennedy; Elizabeth Walsh; Georgia Gojmerac Leiner.

CANTON. *Massachusetts Hospital School.* Attended by St. Gerard Majella, Canton. Randolph St., 02121. Tel: 781-828-2440.

CHELSEA. *Quigley Memorial Hospital* 91 Crest Ave., 02150. Tel: 617-889-7146. Rev. Lawrence F. Sullivan, O.C.D., Spiritual Care Svcs.

CONCORD. *Emerson Hospital* Rte. 2 ORNAC, P.O. Box 9120, 01742-9120. Tel: 978-287-3015. Joan Horgan, Spiritual Care Svcs.

DORCHESTER. *Carney Hospital* 2100 Dorchester Ave., 02124-5666. Tel: 617-296-4000, Ext. 2187; Fax: 617-296-9513. Spiritual Care Services: Revs. Mikel Satcher; John J. Caskin, S.J.; Sr. Paula Tinlin, S.N.D.; Sr. Lillian McDonald, C.S.J.; Jean Marchant.

EVERETT. *Whidden Memorial Hospital* 103 Garland St., 02149. Tel: 617-389-6270, Ext. 2202. Sr. Agnes Melly, C.S.J., Spiritual Care Svcs.

FRAMINGHAM. *Metro West Medical Center* Framingham Campus, 115 Lincoln St., 01701-9167. Tel: 508-383-1007. Spiritual Care Services: Rev. Robert E. Champagne, S.M.; Sr. Ursula Tisdall, O.S.F.; Deacon Augusto Diotalevi.

GLOUCESTER. *Addison Gilbert Hospital.* Attended by St. Ann, Gloucester. 298 Washington St., 01930. Tel: 978-283-4000.

HAVERHILL. *Hale Hospital.* Attended by St. John the Baptist, Haverhill. 140 Lincoln Ave., 01830. Tel: 978-374-2000.

Whittier Rehabilitation Hospital. Attended by St. Joseph, Haverhill. 76 Summer St., 01830. Tel: 978-372-8000.

JAMAICA PLAIN. *Faulkner Hospital* 1153 Centre St., 02130. Tel: 617-983-7000, Ext. 1556. Deacon Leonard F. DeCoste, Spiritual Care Svcs.

Jamaica Plain 150 S. Huntington Ave., 02130. Tel: 617-232-9500. Revs. Philip Salois; Roger A. Sinclair.

Lemuel Shattuck Hospital 170 Morton St., 02130. Tel: 617-522-8110, Ext. 463. Rev. Leonard J. Tighe, Spiritual Care Svcs.

Veterans Administration Hospital 150 S. Huntington Ave., 02130. Tel: 617-232-9500. Spiritual Care Services: Revs. Philip Salois; Roger A. Sinclair.

LAWRENCE. *Lawrence General Hospital* One General St., 01842. Tel: 978-683-4000, Ext. 2344. Maureen LaBelle, Spiritual Care Svcs.

LOWELL. *Lowell General Hospital* 295 Varnum Ave., 01854. Tel: 978-937-6418. Sr. Eileen Auger, C.S.C., Spiritual Care Svcs.

Saints Memorial Medical Center Hospital Dr. (Box 30), 01852. Tel: 978-458-1411. Spiritual Care Services: Revs. John J. Hogan, O.M.I.; Romeo J. Murphy, O.M.I.; Sr. Doris Brouillette, S.C.O.; Dr. John Giannino; Patricia Hardy.

LYNN. *Atlanticare Medical Center* 500 Lynnfield St., 01904. Tel: 781-581-9200. Deacon Lawrence R. McManus, Spiritual Care Svcs.

MARLBOROUGH. *Marlborough Hospital.* Attended by St. Mary, Marlborough. 57 Union St., 01752. Tel: 508-485-1121.

MEDFIELD. *Medfield State Hospital* 45 Hospital Rd., 02052-2406. Tel: 508-359-7312, Ext. 4371. Rev. John J. Hever, Spiritual Care Svcs.

MEDFORD. *Lawrence Memorial Hospital of Medford* 170 Governor's Ave., 02155. Tel: 781-306-6000. Rosemary Burke, Spiritual Care Svcs.

MELROSE. *Melrose-Wakefield Hospital* 585 Lebannon St., 02176. Tel: 781-979-3011. Sr. Eunice Condrick, C.S.J., Spiritual Care Svcs.

METHUEN. *Holy Family Hospital, Inc* 70 East St., 01844. Tel: 978-687-0151, Ext. 2005. Spiritual Care Services: Sr. Claudia Blanchette, S.N.D.; Rev. John T. Crabb, S.J., Chap.; Martha Byron, Nursing Svcs.

MILTON. *Milton Hospital* 92 Highland St., 02186. Tel: 617-696-4600, Ext. 1801. Sr. Nora O'Connell, S.N.D., Spiritual Care Svcs.

NATICK. *Metro West.* Attended by St. Patrick, Natick Leonard Morse Campus, 67 Union St., 01760. Tel: 508-650-7331.

NEEDHAM. *Deaconess-Glover Hospital.* Attended by St. Joseph, Needham. 148 Chestnut St., 02192. Tel: 781-444-5600.

NEWBURYPORT. *Anna Jacques Hospital.* Attended by Immaculate Conception, Newburyport. Highland Ave., 01950. Tel: 978-462-6601.

NEWTON. *Newton-Wellesley Hospital* 2014 Washington St., 02162. Tel: 617-243-6634. Ann Lomuto, Spiritual Care Svcs.

NORFOLK. *Caritas Southwood Hospital* 111 Dedham St., 02056. Tel: 781-278-6045. Sr. Barbara Lavin, O.P., Spiritual Care Svcs.

NORWOOD. *Caritas Norwood Hospital* 800 Washington St., 02062. Tel: 781-278-6045, Ext. 2012. Spiritual Care Services: Rev. Robert G. LaBrie; Sr. Barbara Lavin, O.P.

PEABODY. *Vencor-Boston Northshore.* Attended by St. John the Baptist, Peabody. 15 King St., 01960. Tel: 978-531-2900.

PLYMOUTH. *Jordan Hospital* 275 Sandwich St., 02360. Tel: 508-746-2000, Ext. 2662. Nan Bouche, Spiritual Care Svcs.

QUINCY. *Quincy Hospital* 114 Whitwell St., 02169. Tel: 617-773-6100, Ext. 5501. Rev. Theodore L. Fortier, A.A., Spiritual Care Svcs.

ROXBURY. *New England Baptist Hospital* 91 Parker Hill Ave., 02120. Tel: 617-754-5160. Rev. Joseph O'Brien, Spiritual Care Svcs.

SALEM. *North Shore Medical Center* 57 Highland Ave., 01970. Tel: Rectory: 978-741-0631; P.C. Dept.: 978-741-1215, Ext. 7698. Spiritual Care Services: Rev. Edward M. Keohan; Jane Korins; Christopher Junker.

SOMERVILLE. *Somerville Hospital.* Attended by St. Catherine, Somerville. 230 Highland Ave., 02143. Tel: 617-666-4400.

SOUTH WEYMOUTH. *South Shore Hospital* 55 Frogg Rd., 02190. Tel: 781-340-8589; 340-8612. Spiritual Care Services: Rev. Daniel Crowley; Mary T. O'Connor.

STOUGHTON. *New England Sinai Hospital* 150 York St., 02072. Tel: 781-344-0600, Ext. 302; Fax: 781-344-3226. Spiritual Care Services: Rev. Msgr. William A. Granville; Rev. William O'Connor; Sr. Ellen Reilly, S.N.D.

TEWKSBURY. *Tewksbury Hospital* East St., 01876. Tel: 978-851-7321, Ext. 288. Spiritual Care Services: Rev. Edward Lowney, O.M.I.; John Carley.

WALTHAM. *Deaconess-Waltham Hospital* Hope Ave., 02154. Tel: 781-647-6573. Spiritual Care Services: Elinor Quill; Arlene Larsen.

WESTWOOD. *Westwood Lodge Hospital.* Attended by St. Margaret Mary, Westwood. 45 Clapboard St., 02090. Tel: 781-762-7764.

WINCHESTER. *Winchester Hospital* 41 Highland Ave., 01890. Tel: 781-729-9000. Sr. Geraldine DeFilippo, R.C.E., Spiritual Care Svcs.

WOBURN. *Healthsouth New England Rehabilitation Hospital.* Attended by St. Barbara, Woburn. Two Rehabilitation Way, 01801. Tel: 617-636-7500.

WRENTHAM. *Wrentham State School* Box 144, 02093. Tel: 508-384-3114. Rev. John Fernz, Spiritual Care Svcs.

Prison Ministry

BRIDGEWATER. *Bridgewater State Hospital & Treatment Center* 12 Administration Rd., 02324. Tel: 617-727-7672. Rev. James F. Lanergan.

Massachusetts Boot Camp 12 Administration Rd., 02324. Tel: 617-727-7672. Deacon John W. McHugh.

Old Colony Correction Center One Administration Rd., 02324. Tel: 617-727-3400. Deacon John W. McHugh.

Southeastern Correctional Center 12 Administration Rd., 02324. Tel: 617-727-7672. Deacon Thomas H. Hanlon.

CARVER. *MCI-Plymouth* Myles Standish State Forest, Box 207, 02355. Tel: 617-727-8938. Deacon John W. McHugh.

CONCORD. *MCI-Concord* 965 Elm St., Box 00, 01742. Tel: 617-727-1950. Rev. Peter J. Murphy.

Northeast Correctional Center Barretts Mill Rd., 01742. Tel: 617-727-0288. Deacon Arthur F. Rogers, Jr.

FRAMINGHAM. *MCI-Framingham* 99 Loring St., 01701. Tel: 617-727-5056. Sr. Maureen Clark, C.S.J.

South Middlesex Correctional Center 135 Western Ave., Box 850, 01701. Tel: 617-727-5676. Sr. Maureen Clark, C.S.J.

JAMAICA PLAIN. *Shattuck Hospital Correctional Unit* 180 Morton St., 02130. Tel: 617-727-6904. Rev. Leonard J. Tighe.

MATTAPAN. *Metropolitan Youth Service Center* 591 Morton St., 02126. Tel: 617-288-9100. Rev. Joseph J. Baggetta.

NORFOLK. *Baystate Correctional Facility* 28 Clark St., Box 73, 02056. Tel: 617-727-8474. Deacon John J. Mannion.

MCI-Norfolk 2 Clark St., Box 43, 02056. Tel: 617-727-1480. Ms. Ruth Raichle; Sr. Kathleen Denevan, O.S.F.; Deacon Gerald Rooney; Ms. Ruth Raichle.

Pondville Correctional Center Box 146, 02056. Tel: 617-727-5203. Ms. Elizabeth Slaney, Catholic Coord.; Sr. Kathleen Denevan, O.S.F.; Ms. Ruth Raichle.

ROSLINDALE. *Judge John J. Connelly Youth Center* 450 Cantebury St., 02131. Tel: 617-288-9100. Rev. Joseph J. Baggetta.

SHIRLEY. *MCI-Shirley* Medium and Minimum Facilities, P.O. Box 1218, 01464. Tel: 978-425-4341. Rev. John Kilmartin, F.D.P.; Deacons Carroll H. Taylor, Medium Facilities Tel: 978-425-4341 Ext. 4818; Arthur F. Rogers, Jr., Minimum Facilities Tel: 978-425-4341 Ext. 2267.

SOUTH WALPOLE. *MCI-Cedar Junction* Rte. 1A, Box 100, 02071. Tel: 617-727-1686. Deacon John Mannion.

County Facilities

BOSTON. *Nashua Street Jail* 200 Nashua St., 02114. Tel: 617-635-1100. Bro. George T. Williams, S.J.

Suffolk County House of Correction at South Bay 20 Brandston St., 02118. Tel: 617-635-1000. Bro. George T. Williams, S.J.

BILERICA. *Middlesex County House of Correction* Treble Pond Rd., 01821. Rev. Msgr. Francis S. Rossiter; Deacon Harold E. Killam.

CAMBRIDGE. *Middlesex County Jail* 40 Thorndike St., 02146. Tel: 617-494-4375. Rev. Msgr. Francis S. Rossiter; Deacon Harold E. Killam.

DEDHAM. *Norfolk County House of Correction* 200 West St., 02026. Tel: 617-696-0593. Rev. Robert P. Beale.

MIDDLETON. *Essex County Correctional Facility* 20 Manning Ave., 01949. Tel: 617-542-2564; 978-750-1900, ext. 503. Rev. Jon C. Martin; Mr. Jack McCauley, Catholic Coord.

PLYMOUTH. *Plymouth County Correctional Facility* 26 Long Pond Rd., 02360. Tel: 508-830-6200. Ms. Loraine Pietrantonio, Catholic Coord.

Absent on Leave:
(For further information contact Tel: 617-254-2085.)
Reverend Fathers—
Crowley, Kevin J.
Daley, James J.
Healy, Thomas C.
Hendricks, Scott B.
Kearns, John P.
Malloy, Stephen J.
Morrissette, Robert H.
Novello, Lawrence E.
O'Brien, Joseph C.
Perillo, Christopher G.
Riley, Mark J.
Schiavone, Christopher F.
Walsh, Martin J.

Emergency Response Group:
(For further information contact Tel: 617-254-2085.)
Reverend Fathers—
Calhoun, Ronald G., (Temporary)
Casey, Richard L.
Charest, Edmund P.
Connolly, John J., (Temporary)
Cordery, Robert J., (Temporary)
Crowley, Kevin J.
Curran, Richard G., M.A., Ed.D., (Temporary), 3 Strawberry Hill Rd., Plymouth, MA 02360
Darcy, James F.
Forry, Thomas P., (Temporary)
Gianni, Vincent J., (Temporary)
Hendricks, Scott B., (Temporary)
Horrigan, Kevin P., (Temporary)
Keane, John F.
Kelleher, Robert N., (Temporary)
LeBlanc, Kenneth A., (Temporary)
McQuade, Richard E.
Swencki, John T.

Graduate Studies:
(For further information contact Tel: 617-254-2085.)
Reverend Monsignors—
McDonough, John P.
Reverend Fathers—
Braley, James E.
Condon, Edwin A.
Connolly, John J.
Daily, Vincent E.
Euvard, Scott A.
Kirwan, Christopher J., Jr.
Laughlin, James J.
Le, Hoang V.
Murphy, William F.
O'Connell, Mark
Thompson, Garrett J.

Health Leave:
(For further information contact Tel: 617-254-2085.)
Reverend Monsignors—
Little, Richard P.
Reverend Fathers—
Bolduc, Paul J.
Brown, Arthur A.
Carroll, Edward G.
Fay, Robert D.
Foley, James J.
Franz, Paul R.
Fraser, Gerald C.
Frost, Peter J.
Jezowski, Anthony C.
Keane, John F.
Kelley, Laurence E.
Malone, Edward T.
McGahey, Charles R.
Meskell, David B.
Sullivan, Brendan J.
Toomey, John M.
Ward, Robert A.

Military & VA Chaplains:
(For further information contact Tel: 617-254-2085.)
Reverend Fathers—
Butler, Timothy A.
Crowley, Francis J.
Cuddy, William F.
Deeley, Kevin J.
Devine, William J.
Donohoe, Stephen S.
Erickson, Richard M.
Girardin, Peter T.
Hurley, Paul K.
Kennedy, William M.
Linehan, Stephen J.
McCabe, Edward D.
Nichols, Henry P.
Pucciarelli, George W.
Raux, Redmond P.
Robinson, Joseph P.
Rock, Stephen B.
Russo, Lawrence J.
Scanlan, William J.

On Duty Outside the Archdiocese:
(For further information contact Tel: 617-254-2085.)
Reverend Monsignors—
Abruzzese, John A.
Edyvean, Walter J.
Fay, William P.
Russell, Paul F.
Reverend Fathers—
Brown, Francis E.
Carrigg, William J.
Donahue, Richard T.
Driscoll, Joseph J.
Galvin, John P.
Hawker, James F.
Hehir, J. Bryan
Kennedy, Arthur L.
McMahon, Gerard T.
McNeil, John R.
Moran, James F.
O'Brien, Richard M.
Picardi, John M.
Sullivan, Robert E.

Permanent Disability:
(For further information contact Tel: 617-254-2085.)
Reverend Fathers—
Barrett, Robert E.
Butler, James P.
DePietro, Arthur J.
DiFruscio, John A.
Driscoll, Nicholas J.
Fraser, Gerald C.
Gomes, Ronald A.
Higgins, Michael J.
Kinsella, Charles R.
McGrade, Kevin M.
Morris, John S.
Motherway, Thomas F.
Regan, Michael J.
Santerre, Richard R.
Tivnan, Paul J.

Senior Priests:
(For further information contact Tel: 617-523-1861.)
Most Rev.—
McNamara, John R.
Riley, Lawrence J.
Rev.—
Thomas, John E.
Reverend Monsignors—
Abucewicz, John A.
Alves, Joseph T.
Anadore, Charles E.
Boyle, Robert J.
Coen, William R.
Collins, Russell J.
Contons, Albert J.
Coppenrath, Leonard
Daly, Thomas J.
Day, John D.
Finnegan, Thomas J.
Forster, William J.
Granville, William A.
Hart, Peter F.
Keilty, John P.
Lawler, John F.
McGann, Francis J.
McManus, Frederick R.
McManus, Paul J.
Moritz, Paul L.
O'Sullivan, Francis G.
Palladino, Alfonso G.
Philbin, John J.
Roche, William H.
Rossiter, Francis S.
Shea, William B.
Sheehan, John J.
Sullivan, Timothy E.
Sullivan, William P.
Reverend Fathers—
Abracinskas, Albert C.
Ahearn, Richard F.
Anderson, William R.
Atwater, John T.
Aubut, Charles E.
Baltrushumas, Anthony P.
Barrett, Daniel J.
Barry, Henry F.
Beksha, Francis W.
Bergeron, Robert E.
Bernatonis, John F.
Bertelli, Ameilio J.
Berube, John J.
Billicky, Louis S.
Boivin, Henry P.
Bonfiglio, David G.
Boucher, Clarence R.
Brennan, Gerard M.
Brennan, James F.
Broderick, James M.
Brudzynski, Peter F.
Bryson, Robert C.
Buchette, Anthony J.
Buckley, Frederick J.
Buckley, John K.
Burke, Leonard J.
Burns, John F.
Burns, William W.
Calter, Arthur M.
Campbell, William W.
Carr, John F.
Carr, Mark V.
Casey, Walter E.
Cedrone, Laurence C.
Clifford, Donald G.
Clougherty, Paul L.
Coffey, James H.
Collins, Frederick J.
Collins, Joseph I.
Commane, William J.
Connolly, Maurice V.
Connor, Robert M.
Cormier, Leo G.
Cormier, Roger C.
Cowhig, Edward D.
Creighton, Gerard E.
Cronin, Daniel F.
Curran, Paul E.
Curtin, James F.
Dailey, Vincent E.
Daley, Joseph D.
Daly, James J.
Daniele, Anthony J.
DeAdder, James W.
Delaney, David F.
Delaney, Francis H.
Donahue, Daniel J.
Donelin, John M.
Donlon, William J.
Donovan, John L.
Donovan, Joseph F.
Doocey, Michael F.
Doonan, John A.
Downey, Joseph J.
Doyle, Daniel J.
Doyle, Lawrence J.
Doyle, Robert M.
Driscoll, Richard A.
Driscoll, Walter L.
Dufour, Louis C.
Duggan, Charles T.
Fallon, John F.
Fallon, John J.
Finn, Alfred E.
Finnegan, John T.
Flynn, John H.
Flynn, Robert G.
Foley, Gerald J.
Foley, John I.
Foley, John T.
Francis, Paul R.
Gagnon, Adelard J.
Gagnon, Henry J.
Gallagher, Edward L.
Gallagher, Francis L.
Gallagher, John E.
Gaudet, Joseph A.
Gaudette, Edward J.
Gibbons, James M.
Gillis, Edward F.
Gilmartin, Daniel J.
Goss, Francis J.
Gosselin, Robert H.
Goulet, Raymond O.
Grant, Frederick A.
Greaney, Francis M.
Guarcello, Russell V.
Guerrette, William A.
Hane, Howard S.
Hanlon, John R.
Hession, James J.
Hughes, Albert C.
Janiunas, Albin F.
Jennings, John J.
Johnson, Harold J.
Johnson, Richard G.
Joyal, Rene J.
Jusseaume, John E.
Keane, Thomas F.
Kelley, Paul G.
Kelly, John P.
Kelly, Patrick J.
Kenneally, William F.
Kierce, J. Joseph
King, Edward L.
King, Philip J.
Kramer, George C.
Lambert, Raymond P.
Lane, Bernard J.
LaRaia, Joseph P.
Laurano, Anthony J.
Lawson, Harold F.
Leonard, Clyde A.
Leonard, Francis B.
Logue, Charles D.
Lucey, William F.
Lucid, Vincent F.
Lukas, Joseph S.
Lynch, Daniel G.
MacDonald, Stirling B.
MacLeod, Thomas E.
Mahoney, James F.
Mahoney, John P.
Mansfield, John L.
Masciarelli, Rudolph
Mason, Albert M.
McAskill, Kenneth F.
McAuliffe, Robert F.
McCarthy, William R.
McConnell, William J.
McConville, Philip G.
McElroy, John W.
McGann, Gerard J.
McGowan, Frederick R.
McMahon, Edward M.
McNulty, Joseph P.
Meade, Henry J.
Meade, Maurice P.
Medeiros, Antonio S.
Meffan, Robert V.
Meskill, David B.
Mooney, Thomas J.
Moran, Daniel F.
Moriarty, Thomas W.
Mottau, Robert S.
Mowatt, John J.
Mulkern, John F.
Murphy, Lawrence F.
Murray, Frederick J.
Murray, Thomas F.
Naguszewski, Edward B.
Noonan, William J.
O'Brien, Frederick W.
O'Connor, William B.
O'Connor, William J.
O'Donohoe, James A.
O'Hara, Francis A.
O'Hare, Francis C.
O'Hearn, Paul V.
O'Leary, Adrian P.
O'Leary, Arthur P.
O'Sullivan, Eugene M.
Oliviera, Joel D.
Ouellette, Lionel P.
Pearsall, Ernest P.
Pearsall, William T.
Perron, Richard J.

Pied, Wilfrid L.
Piscitelli, Vincent J.
Pollis, Robert G.
Powers, Richard J.
Ready, Francis P.
Regan, John J.
Reilly, Joseph L.
Riley, James H.
Ritchie, Francis J.
Rogers, James M.
Ronan, Henry T.
Rothwell, Joseph T.
Ryan, Joseph E.
Rynne, Paul P.
Saunders, John A.
Shakalis, Peter A.
Shanley, Paul R.
Sheehan, Daniel J.
Sheehy, Charles I.
Silk, John D.
Silva, John F.
Slejzer, Ferdinand E.
Smyth, Joseph P.
Soucy, Robert P.
Stocklosa, J. Walter
Sullivan, James L.
Sullivan, John L.
Sullivan, Michael D.
Sullivan, Paul V.
Svirskas, Joseph J.
Thomas, John E.
Toland, Paul L.
Tolland, Cyril E.
Toomey, John M.
Tourigney, Ernest E.
Vasaturo, Anthony J.
Wasnewski, Richard P.
Weber, Charles P.
White, John J.
Whittier, James E.
Williams, George J.
Zuromskis, John D.

Society of St. James the Apostle:
(For further information contact Tel: 617-742-4715.)
Reverend Fathers—
Domurat, Thomas S.
Flynn, George R.
Grimes, John J.
Kirke, Eugene K.
Martin, Joseph I.
McCarthy, Jeremiah J.
O'Meara, Gerard J.
O'Sullivan, Raymond S.
Oates, Thomas F.
Pashby, John J.
Stanley, Charles R.
Thomas, Robert W.
Tynan, Desmond A.
White, David P.

Unassigned:
(For further information contact Tel: 617-254-2085.)
Reverend Fathers—
Berthold, George C.
Buntel, Richard A.
Conole, Robert W.
Conroy, Francis M.
Conte, Denis A.
Gale, Robert V.
German, Kenneth N.
Hickey, Gerald J.
Keefe, Dennis A.
Kelley, Arnold E.
Manning, Paul F.
Matte, Richard O.
Paquin, Ronald A.
Rosenkranz, George J.
Whalan, Thomas J.

Permanent Deacons:
Alicea, Francisco, St. Mary, Waltham
Amerault, Robert P., St. Joseph, Medford
Arsenault, Joseph G., Awaiting Assignment
Aucoin, Albert J., (Retired)
Balestracci, Alfred, St. Theresa, North Reading
Barton, John M., St. Thomas, Peabody
Beatrice, Lee A., St. John, East Bridgewater
Belmonte, Joseph A., St. Anthony, Revere
Bloom, Laurence J., St. Ann, Somerville
Bower, Charles H., St. Bonaventure, Manomet
Bowley, Richard R., Sacred Heart, Amesbury
Breinlinger, Martin, St. Mary's, Holliston
Bresnahan, John M., St. Agnes, Middleton
Bulpett, Dean C., St. Irene, Carlisle
Cabral, John F., Somerville Hospital
Callahan, James C., St. Charles Borromeo, Waltham
Camacho, Teodoro, St. Mary, Waltham
Canoua, Joseph A., St. Anthony, Cohasset
Capomaccio, John J., Sick Leave
Caruso, Philip M., St. Mary, Holliston
Casillas, Luis, Cathedral of the Holy Cross, Boston
Chevarley, Joseph W., (Retired)
Chisholm, Finley H., St. Joseph, Lynn
Clough, Charles I., Our Lady Help of Christians, Concord
Connelly, Milton E., Jr., Immaculate Conception, Newburyport
Connor, John P., Chap., Brockton Hospital, St. Mary of the Hills, Milton
Cordeau, Richard W., St. Jean Baptiste, Lynn
Cornell, Charles A., St. Isidore, Stowe
Counihan, Eugene A., St. Elizabeth, Acton & Fernald School, Waltham
Creutz, Edward F., Blessed Kateri Tekakwitha, Plymouth
Crosby, Herbert W., (Retired)
Crowley, Joseph I, Jr., Children's Hospital, Boston
Crump, James M., Awaiting Assignment
D'Ambrosio, Francis A., M.D., (Retired)
Dacey, Dennis J., Sick Leave
DeCoste, Leonard F., Our Lady of Lourdes, Jamaica Plain
Delaney, Joseph L., St. Denis, Westwood
Dempsey, Timothy F., St. Mary, Lynn
Diotalevi, Augustus J., St. Tarcisius, Framingham
Donnelly, Joseph A., St. John, Chelmsford
Donoghue, Leo J., Dir., Office of Permanent Deaconate, St. John the Evangelist, East Bridgewater
Doyle, Edward L., St. Mary of the Assumption, Hull
Dunn, Daniel A., St. Marie, Lowell
Dzuris, Robert W., St. Mary, Chelmsford
Eames, James H., St. Mary, Randolph
Egan, Thomas F., St. Brendan, Dorchester
Ego, John J., St. Bernadette, Randolph
Elibero, Edward P., St. Pius V, Lynn
Farguheson, Wood Rowe, St. Joseph, Salem
Fenton, Jack H., St. Agnes, Reading
Gaffney, Francis M., Immaculate Conception, Revere
Gagne, Gerard E., Sacred Heart, Lawrence
Gagne, Ronald D., St. Rose of Lima, Topsfield
Gagnon, Raymond A., St. Anthony, Shirley
Gardyna, Henry A., Sick Leave
Gaudreau, Robert J., Sacred Hearts, Haverhill
Geneus, Alfred J., Our Lady of Pity, Cambridge
Gindel, Richard W., St. Ann, Gloucester
Goldy, Andrew J., St. Clement, Somerville
Grimley, Edward J., St. Augustine, Lawrence
Guerin, Bertrand H., Assumption, Bellingham
Guerrini, Patrick E., St. Elizabeth's Medical Center, Brighton
Guerrios, Francisco, Holy Family, Dorchester
Guillet, Andre
Hackett, Robert T., Most Blessed Sacrament, Wakefield
Halloran, John B., St. Paul, Hingham
Hanlon, Thomas H., St. Bridget, Abington & MCI-Bridgewater
Hardcastle, Philip P., St. Charles, Woburn
Hardin, Howard P., St. Elizabeth of Hungary, Acton
Hardy, Gerard J., St. Louis de France, Lowell
Hardy, John W., Sacred Heart, Lynn
Harrison, John D., St. Mary-Immaculate Conception, Lawrence
Heffernan, Francis X., Immaculate Conception, Stoughton
Herrera, Luciano, Blessed Sacrament, Jamaica Plain
Hickey, Charles M., St. Jerome, Weymouth
Hoaglund, Robert, St. Matthias, Marlboro
Holderried, Joseph E., St. Margaret Mary, Westwood
Iwanowicz, Michael A., Our Lady of Sorrows, Sharon
James, William H., St. Paul, Hamilton
Jennette, John F., St. Joseph, Quincy
Johnson, Robert N., Our Lady Help of Christians, Newton
Juliano, Anthony J., St. Adelaide, Peabody
Kaelin, Gerard J., St. Adelaide, Peabody
Kane, William F.X., St. Joachim, Rockport
Kasenenko, Joseph S., St. Mary Star of the Sea, Beverly
Keefe, Arthur J., Holy Family, Duxbury
Kerns, William E., St. Barbara, Woburn
Killam, Harold E., Prison Ministry
King, Clifford D., St. Thomas, Wilmington
Kramich, Robert A., Unassigned
L'Italien, George G., St. James, Salem
LaBrache, Leo F., St. Patrick, Watertown
Lacey, Neil F., St. George, Framingham
LaFargue, John L., St. Joseph, Holbrook
LaPointe, Norman P., St. Joseph, Salem
Lauture, Aubert, St. Leo, Dorchester
Lawless, Timothy, St. Paul, Hingham
LePage, Donald E., (Retired)
Leslie, Charles O., Holy Name, West Roxbury
Little, James B., St. Brendan, Dorchester
Lloyd, Barry V., St. Margaret, Lowell
LoPriore, Mario, Sacred Heart, Boston
MacDonald, Joseph P., St. Elizabeth, Milton
Machicado, Hernan, (Retired)
MacKenzie, William E., Our Lady Comforter of the Afflicted, Waltham
Mandoza, Francis A., St. Agnes, Arlington
Mannion, John J., St. Lawrence, Brookline & MCI-Cedar Junction, Walpole
Marchant, Thomas W., St. Anthony, Everett
Mariani, Henry A., St. Francis of Assisi, Medford
Markey, Paul G., Most Blessed Sacrament, Quincy
Martin, Leo A., Our Lady of Grace, Chelsea
Martin, Richard C., Sr., Gate of Heaven, South Boston
Martinez, Orlando, Asuncion de la Virgen Maria, Lawrence
McCarthy, Daniel E., St. Mary, Rowley
McCarthy, John P., (Retired)
McCarty, William J., St. Joseph, Needham
McDavitt, Thomas S., Regl. Bishop's Office (South)
McDonough, John J., St. Clare, Braintree
McGrail, John S., St. Michael, Lowell
McHugh, John W., Chap., MCI-Bridgewater, St. Paul, Hingham
McLaughlin, Richard B., St. Malachy, Burlington
McManus, Lawrence R., St. Joseph, Lynn
Menz, John R., St. Boniface, Quincy
Messina, Joseph M., St. Margaret Mary, Westwood
Miles, Walter J., Jr., Coord., Office of Prison Ministry, Our Lady of Fatima, Sudbury
Mills, Chester P., Unassigned
Montes, Edward M., St. Columbkille, Brighton
Morey, Russell W., St. Catherine, Westford
Mullins, Thomas F., St. Theresa, Billerica
Murphy, Alfred I., St. Bernard, Concord
Murphy, Steven J., St. Mary-Immaculate Conception, Lawrence
Nagle, William V., St. Joseph, Kingston
Nashawaty, Nicholas, Our Lady of Cedars of Lebanon, Jamaica Plain
Naveo, Jose, Asuncion de la Virgen Maria, Lawrence
Nickley, Joseph T., Jr., Immaculate Conception, Weymouth
O'Neil, Cyril T., St. Patrick, Stoneham
Oles, Kenneth W., St. Mary, Wrentham
Ortiz, Jesus M., St. Peter, Dorchester
Papile, Joseph A., St. John the Baptist, Quincy
Patrick, Alexander J., Jr., St. Elizabeth of Hungary, Acton
Peltak, Douglas P., Immaculate Conception, Marlboro
Penney, Edward F., Jr., St. Mary Magdalene, Tyngsboro
Pepe, John W., St. Bridget, Maynard
Perea, Antonio M., Most Holy Redeemer, East Boston
Pugsley, Stanley G., St. William, Dorchester
Quigley, Edward M., (Retired)
Quiles, Jesus, Blessed Sacrament, Jamaica Plain
Radford, Richard F., Jr., St. Mary, Brookline
Ramey, Allan A., St. Anthony, Lawrence
Ramrath, Joseph R., St. Anselm, Sudbury
Rivera, Louis, St. Rose, Chelsea
Rivera, Valentin, St. John, Peabody
Rizzuto, Anthony P., Sacred Heart, Lexington
Rocha, Richard H., SS. Peter & Paul, Lawrence
Rodriguez, Diego N., St. Mary-Immaculate Conception, Lawrence
Rogers, Arthur F., Jr., St. James, Medford
Rooney, Gerard P., (Retired)
Ros, Peter An, St. Patrick, Lowell
Rosa, Andres, Cathedral of the Holy Cross, Boston
Ryan, Gerald P., Holy Ghost, Whitman
Ryan, John G., (Retired)
Salenius, John D., Sacred Heart, Quincy
Sanchez, Tomas E., St. John the Evangelist, Beverly
Santosuosso, Alfred E., St. Jude, Waltham
Shanahan, Allan R., St. Mary, Billerica
Shrader, David J., St. Richard, Danvers
Sicuso, Anthony C., Absent on Leave
Specht, Paul V., St. Patrick, Lawrence
Spiri, Guy J., St. Stephen, Framingham
Stenstrom, Eugene, Our Lady of the Rosary, Stoughton
Sullivan, Charles E., Resurrection, Hingham
Sullivan, Daniel F., St. Agatha, Milton
Taylor, Carroll H., Prison Ministry
Torres, Pedro Luis, St. Stephen, Framingham
Turner, J. Robert, St. Patrick, Stoneham
Valeri, Frank A., St. Peter, Malden
Vitello, Joseph V., St. Francis Xavier, Weymouth
Walsh, Martin J., St. Ann, Peabody
Warren, Lewis F., St. Anne, Salem
Watson, John W., Jr., VA Medical Center, Bedford
Welch, Henry M., Unassigned
Werner, Robert M., Unassigned
Whipple, John E., Our Lady Star of the Sea, Marblehead
Wildes, William H., (Retired)
Wise, John W., Incarnation, Melrose
Yanikoski, Florian F., (Retired)

INSTITUTIONS LOCATED IN THE ARCHDIOCESE

[A] SEMINARIES, ARCHDIOCESAN

BOSTON. *St. John's Seminary School of Theology.* Tel: 617-254-2610; Fax: 617-787-2336. 127 Lake St., Brighton, 02135. Tel: 617-254-2610; Fax: 617-787-2336. Rev. Msgr. Richard G. Lennon, Rector; Rev. Msgr. Laurence W. McGrath, M.S., M.A.; Rev. Msgr. Richard G. Cunningham, J.C.D.; Revs. Martin P. Connor, S.T.L.; John L. Sullivan, S.S.L.; George P. Evans, M.Div., S.T.D.; Stephen E. Salocks, S.S.L.; Paul E. Ritt, S.T.D.; Thomas F. Nestor, Ph.D.; William B. Palardy, Ph.D.; Romanus Cessario, O.P., S.T.D.; Robert J. Congdon, S.T.D.; Christopher J. Coyne; William T. Kelly, S.T.D.; Mark L. Noonan, Ph.D.; Robert W. Flagg, M.S., S.T.L.; Robin C. Ryan, C.P., Ph.D.; Arthur L. Kennedy, Ph.D.; William F. Murphy, M.Div.; Robert W. Murray, M.Div.; Arthur M. Coyle, M.Div.; Michael L. Nolan, Adjuct Faculty. Priests 21; Lay Teachers 7; Students 113.

BRIGHTON. *St. John's Seminary.* Tel: 617-254-2610. College of Liberal Arts, 127 Lake St., 02135. Tel: 617-254-2610; Fax: 617-746-5499. Revs. Robert W. Flagg, M.Div., M. Ed., M.S., S.T, Dean of College & Admissions; Thomas F. Nestor, Ph.D., Dean of Students; Arthur L. Kennedy, Ph.D.; William F. Murphy, M.Div.; John J. Clabeaux, Ph.D., Academic Dean; Rev. Mark L. Noonan, Ph.D.; Deborah DeChiara-Quenzer, Ph.D.; Jeffrey Hause, Ph.D.; Michael Raiger, Ph.D.; Tracey Stark, Ph.D. Priests 5; Lay Teachers 5; Students 32.

WESTON. *Pope John XXIII National Seminary,* 558 South Ave., 02493. Tel: 781-899-5500; Fax: 781-899-9057. Rev. Msgr. Francis D. Kelly, S.T.L., Ph.D., Rector & Pres.; Revs. Leo M. Manglaviti, S.J., S.T.L., Ph.D.; Thomas F. Schmitt, S.T.L.; Alfred McBride, O.Praem., Ph.D.; Charles J. Healey, S.J., S.T.L., S.T.D.; James Massa, Ph.D.; Peter J. Uglietto, M.Div., S.T.L., S.T.D.; Sr. Rose Clarisse Gadoury, S.S.A., M.A., D.Min.; Leonard Maluf, S.T.D. A Major National Seminary open to men over thirty studying for the diocesan and religious priesthood. Priests 6; Sisters 1; Lay Teachers 1; Students 71.

[B] SEMINARIES, RELIGIOUS OR SCHOLASTICATES

BOSTON. *Oblate Provincialate,* 2 Ipswich St., 02215-3607. Tel: 617-536-7471; 536-4141; Fax: 617-536-7016.
E-mail: omvusaprov@aol.com
Web site: www.oblatesofthevirginmary.org
St. Ignatius Province of the Oblates of the Virgin Mary, Inc. Revs. Timothy Gallagher, O.M.V., Prov.; William M. Brown, O.M.V., Prov. Treas.; Bro. Luigi Falbo, O.M.V., Asst. Treas. Priests of the Province on Special Assignment:
Philippines: Rev. Thomas Haake, O.M.V.
Italy: Rev. Craig MacMahon, O.M.V.
Mexico: Rev. Vincenzo Antolini, O.M.V.
U.S.A.: Revs. Placido Ferracini, O.M.V.; John Ferrara, O.M.V.; Donald Kelpinski, O.M.V.; Bruce Williamson, O.M.V.; Richard Woldum, O.M.V.
Trinidad: Rev. D. Clifford Graham, O.M.V.

Our Lady of Grace Seminary, 1105 Boylston St., 02215-3660. Tel: 617-266-5999; Fax: 617-247-7576.
Web site: www.oblatesofthevirginmary.org
St. Ignatius Province of the Oblates of the Virgin Mary, Inc. Revs. Peter P. Gojuk, O.M.V., Rector; David N. Beauregard, O.M.V., Dean of Students. Formation Staff: Revs. Timothy M. Gallagher, O.M.V.; Thomas Carzon, O.M.V.; Peter Grover, O.M.V.; William M. Brown, O.M.V.; S. Gregory Cleveland, O.M.V.; Bro. Luigi Falba. Priests 7; Lay Teachers 4; Students 12.

BRIGHTON. *Oblate Seminary Residence,* 62 Kirkwood Rd., 02135-5157. Tel: 617-787-0008. Bro. Richard Cote, O.M.I., Dir.

CAMBRIDGE. *Weston Jesuit School of Theology,* 3 Phillips Pl., 02138. Tel: 617-492-1960; Fax: 617-492-5833.
E-mail: rmanning@wjst.edu
Web site: www.wtst.edu
Revs. Robert E. Manning, S.J., Pres.; John R. Sachs, S.J., Dean. Legal Title: *Weston College Corporation.* Priests 16; Sisters 3; Lay Teachers 10; Students 219.

DANVERS. *Xavier Center.* House of Formation. 21 Spring St., 01923. Tel: 508-777-1326. Xaverian Brothers, USA. Bro. John D. Hamilton, C.F.X., Dir. Brothers Professed 3.

FRAMINGHAM. *Sylva Maria,* 567 Salem End Rd., 01702-5599. Tel: 508-879-2541; Fax: 508-879-7667.
E-mail: sonsofmary@prodigy.net
Web site: www.sonsofmary.com
Motherhouse and Novitiate of the Sons of Mary, Health of the Sick. Revs. John Murphy, F.M.S.I.; John Coss, F.M.S.I.; Robert Rivard, F.M.S.I.; John Wallace, F.M.S.I. Priests 5; Brothers 4.

HAVERHILL. *Sons of Divine Providence School for Exceptional Boys,* Groveland Rd., P.O. Box 205, 01835. Tel: 508-373-0461. Rev. Gino Marchesani, F.D.P.

[C] COLLEGES AND UNIVERSITIES

BOSTON. *Emmanuel College,* 400 The Fenway, 02115. Tel: 617-735-9715; Fax: 617-735-9877.
E-mail: johnsonp@emmanuel.edu
Web site: www.emmanuel.edu
For a complete listing, refer to the Colleges and Universities section.

CHESTNUT HILL. *Boston College,* 02467. Tel: 617-552-8000; Fax: 617-522-8828.
Web site: www.bc.edu
For a complete listing, refer to the Colleges and Universities section.

NORTH ANDOVER. *Merrimack College,* 01845. Tel: 978-837-5000.
Web site: www.merrimack.edu
For a complete listing, refer to the Colleges and Universities section.

WESTON. *Regis College,* 235 Wellesley St., 02493-1571. Tel: 781-768-7000; Fax: 781-768-8339.
E-mail: postmaster@regiscollege.edu
Web site: www.regiscollege.edu
For a complete listing, refer to the Colleges and Universities section.

[D] HIGH SCHOOLS, DIOCESAN

BOSTON. Sisters of Notre Dame de Namur. Sr. Mary Murphy, S.N.D.deN., Dir.

Cathedral High School, 74 Union Park St., 02118. Tel: 617-542-2325; Fax: 617-542-1745. Mary Kay Brady, Prin. Brothers 2; Sisters 6; Lay Teachers 19; Staff 10; Students 240.

St. Clare High School, 190 Cummins Hwy., 02131. Tel: 617-323-0966.
E-mail: stclare@stclare.mec.edu
Web site: www.stclare.mec.edu
Donna L. Fiori, Ph.D., Prin. Sisters 8; Lay Teachers 13; Students 205.

BRAINTREE. *Archbishop Williams High School,* 80 Independence Ave., 02184. Tel: 781-843-3636; Fax: 781-843-3782.
Web site: www.awhs.org
Mary Ellen Barnes, Prin.; Rev. John M. Capuci, Chap. Priests 1; Sisters 5; Lay Teachers 37; Students 570.

BRIGHTON. *Archdiocesan Central High Schools, Inc.,* 2121 Commonwealth Ave., 02135. Tel: 617-746-5855; Fax: 617-782-0213. His Eminence Bernard Cardinal Law; Sr. Kathleen Carr, C.S.J.

BROCKTON. *Cardinal Spellman High School,* 738 Court St., 02402. Tel: 508-583-6875; Fax: 508-580-1977.
E-mail: cshs@spellman.pvt.kiz.ma.us
Web site: www.spellman.com
Sisters of St. Joseph. Sr. Thomasine Knowlton, C.S.J., Prin. Brothers 1; Sisters 5; Deacons 1; Lay Teachers 36; Students 560.

CAMBRIDGE. *Matignon High School,* One Matignon Rd., 02140. Tel: 617-876-1212. Mr. Gary R. LeFave, Prin.; Ms. Mary Trahan, Asst. Prin.; Rev. James Nyhan, Chap. College Preparatory. Religious 3; Lay Teachers 38; Students 550.

North Cambridge Catholic High School, 40 Norris St., 02140. Tel: 617-876-6068; Fax: 617-576-1898.
E-mail: sisterellen@hotmail.com
Sr. Ellen Powers, C.S.J., Prin. Sisters 1; Lay Teachers 18; Students 260.

EVERETT. *Pope John XXIII Central High School,* 888 Broadway, 02149. Tel: 617-389-0240; Fax: 617-389-2201.
E-mail: popejohnhs@aol.com
Web site: www.popejohn.mec.edu
Sr. Kristin Hokanson, S.N.D., Prin. Sisters 7; Lay Teachers 29; Students 400.

FRAMINGHAM. *Marian High School,* 273 Union Ave., 01702. Tel: 508-875-7646; Fax: 508-875-0838.
E-mail: ARBOSH78@connectinc.com
Web site: www.marianhigh.net
Mr. Carl DiMaiti, Prin. Priests 1; Sisters 1; Lay Teachers 23; Students 305.

PEABODY. *Bishop Fenwick High School,* 99 Margin St., 01960. Tel: 978-531-8200; Fax: 978-532-9053.
Web site: www.fenwick.org
David J. Marion, Prin. Religious 6; Sisters 2; Lay Teachers 58; Students 902.

[E] HIGH SCHOOLS, PRIVATE

BOSTON. *Boston College High School & Jesuit Community.* 150 Morrissey Blvd., Dorchester, 02125. Tel: 617-436-3900; Fax: 617-282-7503.
E-mail: hanwellsj@bchigh.edu
Web site: www.bchigh.edu./
Revs. Joseph T. Bennett, S.J. Tel: 617-929-9482; Edward F. Boyle, S.J. Tel: 617-929-9483; William J. Hamilton, S.J. Tel: 617-929-9478; John J. Hanwell, S.J., Rector. Tel: 617-929-9413; James J. Hosie, S.J. Tel: 617-929-9488; Daniel C. Lewis, S.J. Tel: 617-929-9456; Joaquin Martinez-Mari, S.J. (Bolivia). Tel: 617-929-9463; Perard C. Monestime, S.J. Tel: 617-929-9424; James W. O'Neil, S.J. Tel: 617-929-9452; Francis J. O'Neill, S.J. Tel: 617-929-9494; Joseph P. O'Neill, S.J. Tel: 617-929-9425; Clement L. Pelletier, S.J. Tel: 617-929-9430; Ignatius F. Pennisi, S.J. Tel: 617-929-9430; George A. Duffy, S.J. Tel: 617-929-9441; Peter D. Hickey, S.J. Tel: 617-929-9495; Stephen F. Dawber, S.J. Tel: 617-929-9423; Joseph R. Laughlin, S.J. Tel: 617-929-9470; John Joseph Walsh, S.J. Tel: 617-929-9462; William R. Campbell, S.J. Tel: 617-929-9442; John R. d'Anjou, S.J. Tel: 617-929-9427; Charles F. Kelley, S.J., Pres. Tel: 617-436-3900; Simon E. Smith, S.J. Tel: 617-929-9429; Bros. Cornelius C. Murphy, S.J. Tel: 617-929-9414; Donald J. Murray, S.J. Tel: 617-436-3900; William C. Swan, S.J., Scholastic. Tel: 617-929-9493; John C. Wronski, S.J., Scholastic. Tel: 617-929-9438. Religious 26; Sisters 1; Brothers 2; Lay Teachers 82; Students 1,278. Jesuit Community. Tel: 617-929-9400; Fax: 617-929-9459.

Catholic Memorial School. (Grades 7-12). (Boys). Tel: 617-323-7373; Fax: 617-325-0888.
E-mail: jmacdona@cath-mem.org
Web site: www.cath-mem.org
235 Baker St., West Roxbury, 02132-4395. Tel: 617-323-7333; Fax: 617-325-0888. Congregation of Christian Brothers. Bro. James J. MacDonald, C.F.C., Pres.; Richard F. Chisholm, C.F.C., Prin. Brothers 7; Lay Teachers 47; Boys 740.

Mt. St. Joseph Academy. 617 Cambridge St., Brighton, 02135. Tel: 617-254-8383 (School Office); 783-4747 (Guidance Office); Fax: 617-254-0240.
E-mail: mtstjoseph@aol.com
Web site: www.msja.mec.edu/
Sisters 3; Lay Teachers 21; Girls 260. Sponsored by Sisters of St. Joseph of Boston. Kathleen Fraser, Prin.

Savio Preparatory High School. Tel: 617-567-2710; Fax: 617-569-6883.
Web site: www.savioprep.org
145 Byron St., East Boston, 02128. Tel: 617-567-2710; Fax: 617-569-6883. Mr. Edward Minor, Exec. Dir.; Revs. John J. Serio, S.D.B., Prin.; John DiFiore, S.D.B., Coord. Youth Min.; Jack Janko, S.D.B.; Angelo Bongiorno, S.D.B. A college preparatory school, sponsored by the Salesians of Don Bosco. Priests 4; Lay Teachers 33; Students 395.

DANVERS. *St. John's Preparatory School,* 01923. Tel: 978-774-1050; Fax: 978-774-5069.
E-mail: wdrinan@stjohnsprep.org
Web site: www.stjohnsprep.org
Day Students. Bro. William Drinan, C.F.X., Headmaster. Brothers 7; Lay Teachers 79; Boys 1,130.

DEDHAM. *Ursuline Academy.* (Grades 7-12), 85 Lowder St., 02026-4299. Tel: 781-326-6161; Fax: 781-326-6161 (call ahead).
E-mail: ursuline@mediaone.net
Web site: www.welcome.to/ursuline
Sr. Mercedes Videira, O.S.U., Prin. Operated by Ursuline Convent. Ursuline Nuns. College Prep School for Girls. Sisters 1; Lay Teachers 21; Total Staff 56; Girls 359.

HINGHAM. *Notre Dame Academy,* 1073 Main St., 02043. Tel: 781-749-5930; Fax: 781-749-8366.
Web site: www.ndahingham.com
Sr. Barbara A. Barry, S.N.D., Prin. Total Staff 76; Girls 562.

KINGSTON. *Sacred Heart High School,* 399 Bishops Hwy., 02364. Tel: 781-585-7511; Fax: 781-585-7063.
E-mail: shhs@adelphia.net
Web site: www.sacredhearths.org
Mrs. Susan Krastin, Prin. Asst. Principals: Mr. John F. Enos; Dr. Thomas Gorsuch, Ph.D. Religious 9; Sisters 5; Lay Teachers 36; Students 583.

LAWRENCE. *Central Catholic High School of Lawrence, Inc.,* 300 Hampshire St., 01841. Tel: 508-682-0260. Bro. Richard J. Carey, F.M.S., Prin. Conducted by the Marist Brothers of the Schools. Religious 9; Lay Teachers 54; Students 984.

LOWELL. *Lowell Catholic High School, Inc.,* 530 Stevens St., 01851. Tel: 978-452-1794.
E-mail: ed2000@tiac.net
Mr. Edward J. Quinn, Prin. Sisters 2; Lay Teachers 18; Students 280.

MALDEN. *Malden Catholic High School,* 99 Crystal St., 02148. Tel: 781-322-3098; Fax: 781-397-0573.
E-mail: greenr@maldencatholic.org
Web site: www.maldencatholic.org
Xaverian Brothers. Bro. Robert J. Green, C.F.X., Headmaster. Sisters 1; Brothers 8; Lay Teachers 45; Boys 723.

METHUEN. *Presentation of Mary Academy,* 209 Lawrence St., 01844. Tel: 978-682-9391; Fax: 978-975-3595.
E-mail: pma@pmamethuen.org
Web site: www.pmamethuen.org
Sisters of the Presentation of Mary. Sr. Rose Marie Dupre, Prin. Sisters 2; Lay Teachers 18; Total Staff 40; Girls 287.

MILTON. *Fontbonne Academy*, 930 Brook Rd., 02186. Tel: 617-696-3241.
Web site: www.mec.edu
Sr. Marilyn McGoldrick, Pres. Sisters of St. Joseph 4; Lay Teachers 52; Students 573.

NEEDHAM. *St. Sebastian's Country Day School, Inc.* (Grades 7-12), 1191 Greendale Ave., 02192. Tel: 617-449-5200; Fax: 617-449-5630.
Web site: www.stsebastians.org
Mr. William L. Burke, III, Headmaster; Revs. John F. Arens; John U. Paris. Priests 2; Lay Teachers 46; Boys 337.

NEWTON. *Country Day School of the Sacred Heart.* (Grades 5-12), 785 Centre St., 02158. Tel: 617-244-4246; Fax: 617-965-5313.
E-mail: postmaster@ncdsnet.net
Web site: www.ncdsnet.net
Sr. Barbara Rogers, R.S.C.J., Prin. Legal Title: *Boston Academy of the Sacred Heart.* Religious of the Sacred Heart 1; Lay Teachers 55; Girls 325.

Mount Alvernia High School. (Grades 7-12), 790 Centre St., 02458. Tel: 617-964-5643 (Convent); 969-2260 (School); Fax: 617-969-4246.
E-mail: mountalverniahs.org
Web site: www.mountalverniahs.org
Missionary Franciscan Sisters of the Immaculate Conception. Mrs. Kathleen Kent, Prin. Sisters 3; Lay Teachers 22; Total Staff 43; Girls 239.

READING. *Austin Preparatory School.* (Grades 6-12), 101 Willow St., 01867. Tel: 781-944-4900; Fax: 781-944-7530.
E-mail: apadmit.@austin.mec.edu
Web site: www.austin.mec.edu
Paul J. Moran, Headmaster; Revs. John D. Harrington (England); Kenneth Healey, S.M.; James Morris. Priests 3; Sisters 1; Lay Teachers 48; Administrators 11; Students 641.

TYNGSBORO. *Academy of Notre Dame*, 01879. Tel: 978-649-7611; Fax: 978-649-2909.
Web site: www.netiplus.com/users/notredame/nda.htm
Sr. Maureen Marr, S.N.D., Prin. Sisters of Notre Dame de Namur 2; Faculty 24; Girls 255.

WAKEFIELD. *Our Lady of Nazareth Academy*, 14 Winship Dr., 01880. Tel: 781-245-5210.
E-mail: mkelley@nazacad.org
Sisters of Charity of Nazareth. Mrs. Molly Kelley, Prin. Lay Teachers 17; Girls 170.

WESTWOOD. *Xaverian Brothers High School*, 800 Clapboardtree St., 02090. Tel: 781-326-6392; Fax: 781-320-0458.
E-mail: admin@xbhs.com
Web site: www.xbhs.com
Xaverian Brothers. Bro. Daniel Skala, C.F.X., Headmaster. Brothers 3; Sisters 1; Lay Teachers 70; Boys 930.

[F] ELEMENTARY SCHOOLS, DIOCESAN

DANVERS. *St. Mary of the Annunciation School*, 14 Otis St., 01923. Tel: 978-774-0307; Fax: 978-750-4852. Mrs. Constance Morency, M.Ed., Prin. (Grades PreK-8 & Extended Day Care). Sisters of Notre Dame de Namur 1; Lay Teachers 25; Students 550.

[G] MONTESSORI SCHOOLS

HAVERHILL. *The Merrimack Montessori School*, 55 Saltonstall Rd., 01830. Tel: 978-374-6103; Fax: 978-469-0730.
E-mail: merrmont@juno.com
Web site: www.merrimacmontessori.org
Juliet Nagle, Prin. (For boys and girls aged 3-6). Lay Teachers 6; Students 128.

MARLBORO. *The St. Anne Montessori School*, 720 Boston Post Rd. E., 01752. Tel: 508-485-3791. Sr. Doreen Scott, S.S.A., Dir. (For boys and girls aged 3-5). Religious 2; Lay Teachers 3; Students 72.

NEWTON. *Walnut Park Montessori School*, 47 Walnut Park, 02158. Tel: 617-969-9208; Fax: 617-969-6408. Sr. Mary Ann Connolly, S.C., Prin. Religious 5; Lay Teachers 5; Students 130.

WENHAM. *Notre Dame Children's Class*, 74 Grapevine Rd., 01984. Tel: 508-468-1340; Fax: 508-468-0166.
E-mail: notredcc@aol.com
Sr. Barbara Beauchamp, S.N.D., Dir.; Sr. Susan Raymo, S.N.D., Co-Dir. Religious 2; Lay Teachers 2; Primary Class 28; Preschool Students 48.

[H] ELEMENTARY SCHOOLS, PRIVATE

BOSTON. *Lt. Joseph P. Kennedy, Jr., Memorial School.* (Under the patronage of Our Lady of Czestochowa.). Tel: 617-364-4975; Fax: 617-361-8820.
E-mail: S.JoanneH@aol.com
Web site: www.rc.net/boston/kennedyschool
17 Hale St., Hyde Park, 02136. Tel: 617-364-4975; 361-1726; Fax: 617-361-8820. Bernardine Sisters of the Third Order of St. Francis of Mass., Inc. Sr. Joanne Helen Grejdus, O.S.F., Prin.; Sr. M. de Lourdes, Okoniewski, O.S.F., Clerk. Sisters 1; Lay Teachers 7; Students 200.

Mother Caroline Academy. (Grades 5-8), 515 Blue Hill Ave., Dorchester, 02121. Tel: 617-427-1177; Fax: 617-427-7788.
E-mail: info@mothercaroline.org
Web site: www.mothercaroline.org
Students 60; Sisters 4; Lay Teachers 10. School Sisters of Notre Dame. Sr. Mary Dooley, S.S.N.D., Exec. Dir.; Sr. Frances Butler, S.S.N.D., Prin. Legal Title: *Mother Caroline Academy for Girls, Inc.*

Nativity Preparatory School. (Grades 5-8). Tel: 617-442-1993; Fax: 617-541-4148.
E-mail: hicks@bchigh.edu
Web site: www.bchigh.edu/nativity/index.htm
30 Raynor Cir., Roxbury, 02120. Tel: 617-442-1993; Fax: 617-541-4148. Legal Title: *Nativity-Boston, Inc.* Revs. William R. Campbell, Exec. Dir.; Alfred J. Hicks, S.J., Prin.; Simon E. Smith, S.J. A Jesuit Middle School. Priests 3; Lay Teachers 10; Scholastics 2; Boys 63.

BRAINTREE. *St. Coletta Day School, Inc.*, 85 Washington St., 02184. Tel: 617-848-6250; Fax: 617-848-0640.
E-mail: PLarson@Coletta.org
Web site: www.Coletta.org
Day School for multiply handicapped, developmentally delayed children, ages 4-22 years. Legal Title: *Braintree St. Coletta Day School.* Lay Teachers 11; Students 57.

GLOUCESTER. *St. Mel Independent Day School*, 12 Edgemoor Rd., 01930. Tel: 978-283-1700; Fax: 978-283-0422.
E-mail: ARBOSE123082@connectinc.com
Web site: www.marina.cove.com/index/stmels
Ms. Maureen J. Kelleher, Prin. Sisters 1; Lay Teachers 8; Students 144.

GROTON. *Country Day School of the Holy Union*, 14 Main St., 01450. Tel: 978-448-5646; Fax: 978-448-2392.
E-mail: cdsgroton@yahoo.com
Sr. Lucille Guay, S.U.S.C., Prin. Sisters of the Holy Union 2; Lay Teachers 9; Students 230.

HANOVER. *Cardinal Cushing School and Training Center, Inc.*, 400 Washington St., 02339. Tel: 781-826-6371; Fax: 781-826-1559. Lawrence Sauer, Exec. Dir. Sisters 7; Lay Staff 276; Students 142.

KINGSTON. *Sacred Heart Elementary School.* (Day School), 329 Bishops Hwy., 02364. Tel: 617-585-2114. Sr. Jeanne Morris, C.D.P., Prin. (Grades 1-6). Sisters of Divine Providence 8; Lay Teachers 17; Students 444.

Sacred Heart Pre-Primary School, 363 Bishops Hwy., 02364-2035. Tel: 781-585-3545; Fax: 781-582-1596. Sr. Angela Provost, C.D.P., Dir. Religious 1; Lay Teachers 3; Students 64.

LOWELL. *Franco-American Private School*, 357 Pawtucket St., 01854. Tel: 978-458-0308; Fax: 978-458-0308.
E-mail: ARBOSE105@connectinc.com
Web site: www.lowellonline.org/fas/
Sr. Lorraine Richard, S.C.Q., Prin.; Sr. Jane Holland, S.C.Q., Asst. Prin. Religious 2; Lay Teachers 18; Students 381.

MARLBORO. *Our Lady Preschool Learning Center*, 197 Pleasant St., 01752. Tel: 508-481-0654; Fax: 508-481-0663.
E-mail: OLPreschool@hotmail.com
Sr. Jeanne Allard, S.S.Ch., Dir. Religious 2; Students 80 (ages 3-5).

NEWTON. *Jackson School Elementary.* (Grades 1-6), 200 Jackson Rd., 02458-1428. Tel: 617-969-1537; Fax: 617-244-8596.
E-mail: info@jacksonschool.org
Mrs. Susan G. Niden, Prin. Sisters 8; Lay Teachers 17; Staff 6; Students 226.

Mount Alvernia Academy. (Grades N-6), 20 Manet Rd., Chestnut Hill, 02467. Tel: 617-527-7540; Fax: 617-527-7995. Sisters 4; Lay Teachers 10. Convent School. Tel: 617-527-7540. Joan T. Sullivan, Prin. Convent. Tel: 617-244-3696. Sisters 3; Lay Teachers 26; Students 362.

TYNGSBORO. *Academy of Notre Dame at Tyngsboro*, 180 Middlesex Rd., 01879. Tel: 978-649-7611; Fax: 978-649-2909.
E-mail: smband@mec.edu
Sr. Marcia Billings, S.N.D., Prin. Sisters of Notre Dame de Namur 2; Lay Teachers 27; Students 482.

[I] SPECIAL SCHOOLS

BOSTON. *Emmanuel House Kindergarten*, 11 Newcomb St., 02118. Tel: 617-445-2037; Fax: 617-445-2479.
E-mail: srestergarcia@compuserve.com
Community Based Agency of Catholic Charitable Bureau of Archdiocese of Boston, Inc. Sr. Kristine Koba, S.A., Dir.; Sr. Esther Garcia, Prin. Franciscan Sisters of the Atonement 3; Lay Teachers 4; Students 44.

Laboure College, Inc., 2120 Dorchester Ave., 02124. Tel: 617-296-8300; Fax: 617-296-7947.
Web site: www.labourecollege.org
Sr. Clarisse Correia, D.C., Pres. Two year college for nursing and allied health. Member of Caritas Christi Health Care System. Priests 1; Sisters 5; Lay Teachers 70; Students 450.

METHUEN. *St. Ann's Home Special Needs School*, 100 A. Haverhill St., 01844. Tel: 978-682-5276; Fax: 978-688-4932.
E-mail: dgrandbois@stannshome.org
Web site: www.st.annshome.org
Denis Grandbois, Exec. Dir. Ungraded special needs school for emotionally disturbed and behaviorally disordered children. Lay Teachers 38; Psychotherapists 20; Counsellors 100; Administrators 11; Staff 23; Residential Students 100; Day Students 66.

PEABODY. *Holy Childhood Nursery & Kindergarten*, 5 Wheatland St., 01960. Tel: 508-531-4733; Fax: 978-531-2468. Sr. Bernadette Zaccardi, Supr.; Sr. Kathleen A. Bettencourt, O.Carm., Co-Dir. Sisters 4; Lay Teachers 8; Students 100.

SWAMPSCOTT. *Marian Court College*, Little's Point Rd., 01907. Tel: 617-595-6768; Fax: 617-595-3560.
E-mail: info@mariancourt.edu
Web site: www.mariancourt.edu
Sr. Joanne Bibeau, R.S.M., Pres. Sisters 1; Lay Teachers 6; Lay Staff 60; Students 300.

WATERTOWN. *Rosary Academy Learning Center*, 2 Rosary Dr., 02172. Tel: 617-923-1935; Fax: 617-923-2993.
E-mail: ROSARY1@erols.com
Preschool & Day Care. Sr. Rosaire Hickey, O.P., Dir. Sisters of St. Dominic (St. Catherine, KY). Sisters 2; Lay Teachers 8; Students 70.

[J] CATHOLIC CHARITIES

BOSTON. *Catholic Charitable Bureau of the Archdiocese of Boston, Inc.*, Central Office, 49 Franklin St., 02110. Tel: 617-482-5440; Fax: 617-451-0337. Dr. Joseph Doolin, Pres. Multi-Service Agency. Total Clients served 144,828.

[K] FAMILY COUNSELING AND GUIDANCE CENTERS

BOSTON. *Family Counseling and Guidance Centers.* A Division of Catholic Charities. Admin. Headquarters, 49 Franklin St., 02110. Tel: 617-482-4355. Mr. Jack E. Mazzotti, III, M.A, Clinic Admin.
Local Clinics:
Metropolitan Boston, 49 Franklin St., 02110. Tel: 617-542-0903.
South Shore Braintree, 40 Independence Ave., Braintree, 02184. Tel: 617-848-7840.
West Area-Framingham, 350 Worcester Rd., Framingham, 01701. Tel: 508-875-0648.
North Shore-Danvers, 6 State Rd., Danvers, 01923. Tel: 508-774-6820.
Plymouth County-Marshfield, 475 School, Marshfield, 02050. Tel: 617-837-1133.

[L] SOCIETY OF ST. VINCENT DE PAUL

BOSTON. *Society of St. Vincent DePaul, Central Office*, 1280 Washington St., P.O. Box 180359, 02118-2109. Tel: 617-542-0883. Mr. Albert N. Crocker, Exec. Dir.

[M] CHILD CARE AGENCIES

BOSTON. *The Laboure Center / Catholic Charities*, 371 & 376 W. Fourth St., 02127. Tel: 617-268-9670. Daughters of Charity of St. Vincent de Paul. Sr. Maryadele Robinson, D.C., Dir., Laboure Center; Mrs. Margaret Kelly, Dir. Early Childhood Services (includes Infant-Toddler, Preschool, Child Care, Special Needs). Sisters 1; Lay Teachers 12; Students 80.

Nazareth Day Care. 19 St. Joseph St., Jamaica Plain, 02130. Tel: 617-522-4040. Pamela J. Penton, Dir. Capacity 83; Total Staff 18. Legal Title: *Nazareth.*

Nazareth Residence for Mothers and Children. 91 Regent St., Roxbury, 02119. Tel: 617-541-0100; Fax: 617-541-8781.
E-mail: CToledo@compuserve.com
Paul Brown, Senior Program Dir. Capacity 8-10 Families; Total Staff 10; Total in Residence 22. Home for mothers and children who are HIV positive.

METHUEN. *St. Ann's Home, Inc.*, 100A Haverhill St., 01844. Tel: 978-682-5276; Fax: 978-688-4932.
E-mail: dgrandbois@st.annshome.org
Web site: www.st.annshome.org
Denis Grandbois, Exec. Dir.; Mrs. Sharon Cutter, Business Mgr. School. Children 135. Residential Treatment Center. Tel: 978-692-5276; Fax: 978-688-4932. Children 85. Total in Residence 100; Day Students 66; Total Staff 192; School Children 145.

[N] SETTLEMENT HOUSES

BOSTON. *Chinese Catholic Pastoral Center*, 78 Tyler St., 02111-1831. Tel: 617-482-2949; Fax: 617-482-2949.
E-mail: comobccc@onebox.com

El Centro Del Cardenal / Catholic Charities, 76 Union Park St., 02118. Tel: 617-542-9292; Fax: 617-542-6912. Ms. Elisabeth Zweig-Snippe.

Emmanuel House / Catholic Charities - Community Social Service Center, 11 Newcomb St., 02118. Tel: 617-445-2037; Fax: 617-445-2479.
E-mail: kkoba@compuserve.com

Sr. Kristine Koba, S.A., Exec. Dir. Community Based Agency of Catholic Charitable Bureau of Archdiocese of Boston, Inc.
Various Child Programs-Multi-Service. Franciscan Sisters of the Atonement 3; Total Assisted 2,377; Total Staff 12.
Haitian Multi-Service Center / Catholic Charitable Bureau of Boston. 12 Bicknell St., Dorchester, 02121. Tel: 617-436-2848. Mr. Jean Marc Jean-Baptiste, Dir. Education and Outreach, Day Care, Counseling and Advocacy.
Salesian Boys & Girls Club. (Central Unit), 189 Paris St., 02128. Tel: 617-567-0508; Fax: 617-567-0418.
E-mail: sbgclub@juno.com
(Orient Heights Unit), 145-150 Bryon St., 02128. Tel: 617-567-6626. Salesians of St. John Bosco. Revs. Richard Crager, S.D.B., Exec. Dir. & Club Admin.; Jack Janko, S.D.B., Ph.D., Rector & Psychologist; Bro. John Robert Metell, S.D.B., Program Dir. Total Assisted 3,000; Total Staff 20.
HULL. *Children's Vacation House / Catholic Charities,* 138 Edgewater Rd., 02045. Tel: 617-925-0710. Conducted by the Catholic Charitable Bureau of Boston. Children 300.

[O] GUIDANCE CENTERS

BOSTON. *Life Resources, Inc.,* 199 State St., Fifth Floor, 02109; Fax: 617-523-1747. Mr. William J. Chiaradonna, L.I.C.S.W., B.C.D., Pres. Tel: 617-227-8766. Total in Residence 252; Total Staff 157; Total Assisted 359.
St. Mary's Women and Infants Center, 90 Cushing Ave., 02125. Tel: 617-436-8600.
E-mail: jbeckler@SMWIC.org
Web site: www.smwic.org
For pregnant & parenting women & their children. Caritas Christi. Judith Beckler, Executive Dir. Patients assisted annually 250; Total Staff 60.
BROCKTON. *Phaneuf Center,* 104 Market St., 02401. Tel: 508-584-0500. Coed emergency shelter for 9 adolescents.
Phaneuf Out-Patient, 792 N. Main St., 02401. Tel: 508-588-2882. Drug and Alcohol outpatient counseling for all ages.
LAKEVILLE. *Bishop Joseph John Ruocco House,* 22 Highland Rd., 02347. Tel: 508-947-2823. Mr. Stephen Folino, Dir. Long term residential group home for 17 male adolescents. To provide comprehensive life skill services to residents and their families.
LITTLETON. *Life Resources / Alpha-Omega,* Four Omega Way, P.O. Box 922, 01460. Tel: 508-486-8919; Fax: 508-486-3990.
E-mail: alphomeg@acunet.net
Web site: www.liferesourcesinc.org
A long term residence for 17 adolescent boys. John C. Comeau, Prog. Dir. Total Staff 20; Total Assisted 30.

[P] INFORMATION - CONFERENCE CENTERS

BOSTON. *Archdiocesan Information Center,* Boston Catholic Directory, 141 Tremont St., 02110-1209. Tel: 617-542-8393; Fax: 617-542-9547. Rev. Msgr. Peter V. Conley, Editor. Assistants to the Editor: Rev. Robert M. O'Grady; Sr. Mary Ellen Sweney, S.N.D.; Sr. Theresa Cunningham, S.N.D.; Mrs. Anita Sweet.
Paulist Center, 5 Park St., 02108. Tel: 617-742-4460; Fax: 617-720-5756.
E-mail: fiveparkst@aol.com
Revs. John B. Ardis, C.S.P., Dir.; Richard J. Colgan, C.S.P., Pastoral Min.; Charles A. Martin, C.S.P., Pastoral Min.; Donna Stiglmeier, Pastoral Min.; Drew Deskur, Dir. Music; Patricia Simpson, Admin.
ANDOVER. *Franciscan Center,* 475 River Rd., 01810. Tel: 978-851-3391; Fax: 978-858-0675.
E-mail: franretc@aol.com
Web site: www.franrcent.org
Order of Friars Minor. Rev. John D. Bavaro, O.F.M., Dir.; Guardian, Retreat Team.
Retreat Team: Revs. John C. DiMauro, O.F.M.; Justin J. Bailey, O.F.M.; Robert J. Caprio, O.F.M.; Michael Travaglione, O.F.M.; Bro. Gabriel Aceto, O.F.M.; Sr. Lorraine Pianka, S.S.N.D.; Mrs. Mildred Sheehan, Sec.; Jerrie Lou Buffo; Margaret McCarthy; Jackie Picken. Total in Residence 8; Total Staff 11.
BROCKTON. *Chapel of Our Savior-Catholic Pastoral and Information Center,* 475 Westgate Dr., 02301-1819. Tel: 508-583-8357; Fax: 508-586-5510. Bro. DePorres Poncia, S.A., Dir.; Revs. Boniface Riedmann, S.A.; Joseph DiMauro, S.A.; Malcolm Martin, S.A.; Bros. Louis Marek, S.A.; Savio McNeice, S.A. Priests 3; Brothers 3.
PEABODY. *Catholic Information Center,* North Shore Shopping Center, 01960. Tel: 978-531-6145; Fax: 978-531-1359. Revs. Charles E. Contie, O.Carm., Prior - Dir.; Kilian Healy, O.Carm.; Alan N. Crowley, O.Carm.; Peter Thomas Sherry, O.Carm.; Lambert Zulkie, O.Carm.; Bro. Damien Chong, O.Carm. Priests 5; Brothers 1.

[Q] GENERAL HOSPITALS

BOSTON. *Daughters of Charity National Health System - Boston, Inc.,* 2100 Dorchester Ave., 02124. Tel: 617-296-4000
For a complete listing, refer to the Hospitals section.
St. Elizabeth's Hospital of Boston 736 Cambridge St. Brighton, 02135. Tel: 617-789-3900.
For a complete listing, refer to the Hospitals section.
BROCKTON. *Good Samaritan Medical Center,* 235 N. Pearl St., 02401. Tel: 508-427-3000; 427-3151
For a complete listing, refer to the Hospitals section.
DORCHESTER. *The Carney Hospital, Inc.,* 2100 Dorchester Ave., 02124-5666. Tel: 617-723-1100
For a complete listing, refer to the Hospitals section.
LOWELL. *Saints Memorial Health System, Inc .* Tel: 978-458-1411; Fax: 978-458-8369.
E-mail: info@stmmc.org
Web site: www.saints-memorial.org
One Hospital Dr., 01852. Tel: 978-458-1411; Fax: 978-458-8369.
For a complete listing, refer to the Hospitals section.
METHUEN. *Holy Family Hospital and Medical Center,* 70 East St., 01844-4597. Tel: 978-687-0151; Fax: 978-688-7689.
Web site: www.holyfamilyhosp.org
For a complete listing, refer to the Hospitals section.

[R] SPECIAL HOSPITALS

BOSTON. *Franciscan Children's Hospital and Rehabilitation Center.* Tel: 617-254-3800; Fax: 617-779-1119 30 Warren St. Brighton, 02135. Tel: 617-254-3800; Fax: 617-779-1119.
For a complete listing, refer to the Special Care Facilities section.
BRIGHTON. *St. John of God Hospital,* 296 Allston St., 02135. Tel: 617-277-5750; Fax: 617-731-3094
For a complete listing, refer to the Special Care Facilities section.
CAMBRIDGE. *Youville Hospital & Rehabilitation Center, Inc.,* 1575 Cambridge St., 02138-4398. Tel: 617-876-4344; Fax: 617-547-5501
For a complete listing, refer to the Special Care Facilities section.

[S] SOCIAL SERVICES

BOSTON. *The Laboure Center / Catholic Charities,* 371 & 376 W. Fourth St., 02127. Tel: 617-268-9670. Sr. Maryadele Robinson, D.C., Dir. Certified Home Health Services, Elderly Social Services, Early Childhood Services, Adult Day Health Program, Substance Abuse and Mental Health Counseling, Family Intervention Services, Emergency Assistance, Afterschool Programs, and Support Groups. Daughters of Charity of St. Vincent de Paul 5.
DORCHESTER. *Little Sisters of the Assumption, Family Health Service, Inc.* (Project Hope), 45 Magnolia St., 02125. Tel: 617-442-1880; Fax: 617-442-1356.
E-mail: mleonard@prohope.org
Web site: www.tiac.net/users/prohope
A community based shelter for homeless families offering food pantry, education, child care and social services. Total Assisted 1,800; Staff 35; Sisters 3.
LEXINGTON. *Grey Nuns Elder Services Inc., dba Adult Day Center at Youville Place,* 10 Pelham Rd., Ste. 1000, 02421-8499. Tel: 781-862-4700; Fax: 781-861-9641.
E-mail: ndrago@sgmlex.org
Sr. June Ketterer, S.G.M., Prov. Supvr.

[T] PROTECTIVE INSTITUTIONS

BOSTON. *St. Mary's Women and Infants Center* 90 Cushing Ave. Dorchester, 02125.
For a complete listing, refer to the Special Care Facilities section.

[U] HOMES FOR AGED-RESIDENTS & NURSING

BOSTON. *Don Orione Nursing Home* 111 Orient Ave. East Boston, 02128-1006. Tel: 617-569-2100; Fax: 617-561-1138.
For a complete listing, refer to the Special Care Facilities section.
Marian Manor, (1954).
Web site: www.marianmanor.org
130 Dorchester St. South Boston, 02127. Tel: 617-268-3333; Fax: 617-268-4589.
For a complete listing, refer to the Special Care Facilities section.
St. Joseph Nursing Care Center 321 Centre St. Dorchester, 02122. Tel: 617-825-6320; Fax: 617-825-7410.
For a complete listing, refer to the Special Care Facilities section.
BROCKTON. *St. Joseph Manor Health Care Inc.,* 215 Thatcher St., 02402-3999. Tel: 508-583-5834; Fax: 508-583-8551.
E-mail: ateri@stjosephmanor.com
For a complete listing, refer to the Special Care Facilities section.
CAMBRIDGE. *Sancta Maria Nursing Facility,* 799 Concord Ave., 02138. Tel: 617-868-2200; Fax: 617-864-2801
For a complete listing, refer to the Special Care Facilities section.
FRAMINGHAM. *Carmel Terrace,* 933 Central St., 01701. Tel: 508-788-8000; Fax: 508-626-1603
For a complete listing, refer to the Special Care Facilities section.
St. Patrick's Manor, Inc., 863 Central St., 01701. Tel: 508-879-8000; Fax: 508-626-1604
For a complete listing, refer to the Special Care Facilities section.
LAWRENCE. *M.I. Adult Day Health Center, Inc.,* 189 Maple St., 01841. Tel: 978-682-7575; Fax: 978-691-5374.
E-mail: lori_barrett@mihs.com
For a complete listing, refer to the Special Care Facilities section.
M.I. Nursing-Restorative Center, Inc., 172 Lawrence St., 01841. Tel: 978-685-6321; Fax: 978-975-0050
For a complete listing, refer to the Special Care Facilities section.
M.I. Residential Community II, Inc., 191 Maple St., 01841. Tel: 978-682-7575; Fax: 978-691-5374
For a complete listing, refer to the Special Care Facilities section.
M.I. Residential Community III, Inc., 193 Maple St., 01841. Tel: 978-682-7575; Fax: 978-691-5374
For a complete listing, refer to the Special Care Facilities section.
M.I. Residential Community, Inc., 189 Maple St., 01841. Tel: 978-682-7575; Fax: 978-691-5374
For a complete listing, refer to the Special Care Facilities section.
M.I. Transportation, Inc., 189 Maple St., 01841. Tel: 978-682-7575; Fax: 978-975-0050
For a complete listing, refer to the Special Care Facilities section.
LOWELL. *D'Youville Manor,* 981 Varnum Ave., 01854. Tel: 978-454-5681; Fax: 978-459-7002.
E-mail: dyouvill@dyouville.com
Web site: www.dyouville.com
For a complete listing, refer to the Special Care Facilities section.
MARLBORO. *Marie Esther Health Center, Inc.,* 720 Boston Post Rd., 01752. Tel: 508-485-3791; Fax: 508-229-2294.
E-mail: mehci@ibm.net
For a complete listing, refer to the Special Care Facilities section.
SOMERVILLE. *Jeanne Jugan Pavilion,* 190 Highland Ave., 02143. Tel: 617-776-4420; Fax: 617-623-0707
For a complete listing, refer to the Special Care Facilities section.
Jeanne Jugan Residence, 186 Highland Ave., 02143. Tel: 617-776-4420; Fax: 617-623-0707
For a complete listing, refer to the Special Care Facilities section.
WALTHAM. *Maristhill Nursing & Rehabilitation Center,* 66 Newton St., 02453-6063. Tel: 781-893-0240; Fax: 781-894-6330
For a complete listing, refer to the Special Care Facilities section.

[V] PERSONAL PRELATURES

CAMBRIDGE. *Opus Dei, Prelature of the Holy Cross and Opus Dei,* 25 Follen St., 02138. Tel: 617-354-3204; Fax: 617-868-0349.
Web site: www.opusdei.org
Rev. Robert P. Bucciarelli.
CHESTNUT HILL. *Opus Dei,* 481 Hammond St., 02167. Tel: 617-738-7348; Fax: 617-868-0349.
Web site: www.opusdei.org
Revs. Michael Geisler; Richard W. Rieman; Raphael Caamano.

[W] MONASTERIES AND RESIDENCES OF PRIESTS AND BROTHERS

BOSTON. *Arrupe House,* 35 Creighton St., 02130. Tel: 617-524-9328. Revs. James A. Gillon, S.J., Supr. & Novice Dir.; William C. Russell, S.J.; John T. Butler, S.J.; Simon E. Smith, S.J. Priests 3; Novices 3.
Assumptionist Center. 330 Market St., Brighton, 02135. Tel: 617-783-0400; Fax: 617-783-8030.
E-mail: sgoguen330@aol.com
Very Rev. John L. Franck, A.A., Prov. Supr.; Bro. Stephen Goguen, A.A., Prov. Treas., Supr.; Rev. Ernest Fortin, A.A.,.Total in Residence 12. St. Patrick's Manor, 863 Central St., Framingham, 01701-4892. Tel: 508-879-8000. Revs. Robert Fortin, A.A.; Joseph Fredette, A.A.; Claude Grenache, A.A.; Norman Meiklejohn, A.A.; Paul O'Connor, A.A.; Richard E. Richards, A.A.; Yvon Dubois, A.A.; George Tavard, A.A.
Assumption Guild, Inc.: Bro. Stephen Goguen, A.A., Dir.
Attached to Province: Rev. Gregory Boisvert, A.A., St. Francis of Assisi Church, P.O. Box 1861, Fairfield Glade, TN, 38558. Tel: 931-484-3628. Rev.

Theodore L. Fortier, A.A., St. John, 21 Gay St., Quincy, 02169. Tel: 617-773-1021. Rev. Gerard Messier, A.A., St. Vincent de Paul Rectory, 116 W. 24th St., New York, NY, 10011. Tel: 212-243-4727. Rev. Anselm Morrison, A.A., 3754 Glenn Haven Cir., Zephyrhills, FL, 33541. Tel: 813-783-9969. Rev. John Martin, A.A., 250 W. 15th St., Apt. 1E, New York, NY, 10011. Tel: 212-242-0448.

Serving Abroad: Rev. Gary Perron, A.A., Parroquia Emperatriz de America, Mercaderes 99, 03900 Mexico D.F., Mexico. Tel: 5-593-2002; Fax: 52-5-651-2000. Rev. Camillus Thibault, A.A., Parroquia de la Emperatriz, Mercaderes 99, Mexico D.F., Mexico. Tel: 5-593-2002; Fax: 52-5-651-2000. Rev. Roger Tougas, A.A., Montmartre Canadien, 1676 Chemin St. Louis, Quebec, QUE GIS 165, Canada. Tel: 418-681-7357; Fax: 418-681-9644. Rev. Robert Fortin, A.A., 836-24 Naebang Dong, Sogu, Korea, 502-250. Revs. Leo Brassard, A.A.; Luc Martel, A.A.; Richard Brunelle, A.A.; Oliver Blanchette, A.A., Assumptionist Community, P.O. Box 58488, Nairobi, Kenya.

Special Situations: Edward Pepka, A.A.; Bro. Paul Henry, A.A.

Carmelite Monastery. 166 Foster St., Brighton, 02135-3902. Tel: 617-787-5056; Fax: 617-783-1396. Priests 9; Brothers 1; Total in Residence 18. Discalced Carmelite Friars. Revs. Giles Dzuban, O.C.D.; Emmanuel Sullivan, O.C.D.; Anthony Haglof, O.C.D.; Paul Trementozzi, O.C.D.; Lawrence F. Sullivan, O.C.D.; Salvatore Sciurba, O.C.D.; Stephen-Joseph Ross, O.C.D.; Bruno Cocuzzi, O.C.D.; Terrence Dougherty, O.C.D.; Bros. Robert Sentman, O.C.D.; Mark DeVelis, O.C.D.

Divine Word Missionaries, 184 Beacon St., 02116. Tel: 617-267-5143; Fax: 617-267-0726. Divine Word Missionaries. Revs. Donald P. Mulrenan, S.V.D., Supr. & Mission Dir.; Casmir Damor, S.V.D. (India); Franz Gassner, S.V.D. (Austria); Vincent Twomey, S.V.D. (Ireland). In res. Rev. Donald Skerry, S.V.D.

Jesuit Urban Center & Immaculate Conception Community, 775 Harrison Ave., 02118-2311. Tel: 617-536-8440; Fax: 617-536-2142.
E-mail: jucboston@aol.com
Revs. Thomas J. Carroll, S.J.; Denis R. Como, S.J.; Jon D. Fuller, S.J.; Thomas J. Gallagher, S.J.; George P. Winchester, S.J. Total in residence 5.

Little Brothers of St. Francis, 785-789 Parker St., 02120. Tel: 617-442-2556. Bro. James Curran, L.B.S.F., Guardian. Regional Fraternity and Novitiate. Legal Title: *Little Brothers of St. Francis Franciscan Fraternity of Peace and Love*. Brothers 4; Novices 1; Postulants 2.

Loyola House, 300 Newbury St., 02115-2801. Tel: 617-267-1008; Fax: 617-267-6672.
E-mail: loybos@aol.com
The Society of Jesus. Revs. Joseph J. Bruce, S.J.; Thomas F. Clark, S.J.; Herbert J. Cleary, S.J.; Charles B. Connolly, S.J., Minister & Tres.; John T. Crabb, S.J.; Charles G. Crowley, S.J.; Joseph D. Devlin, S.J.; William F. Doyle, S.J.; John E. Fagan, S.J.; Norman H. Houle, S.J.; Michael J. Kossak, S.J.; Paul T. Lucey, S.J.; Robert G. McMillan, S.J.; William L. Mulligan, S.J.; Edward J. Murawski, S.J.; Joseph J. Schad, S.J.; James M. Shaughnessy, S.J.; Richard J. Stanley, S.J.; Alfred O. Winshman, S.J.; Bros. Paul J. Geysen, S.J.; James J. Moran, S.J. Priests 19; Brothers 2; Total in Residence 21.

Marist Fathers and Brothers Provincial House, 27 Isabella St., 02116-5216. Tel: 617-426-5297; 426-4448; Fax: 617-482-1570. Very Rev. Kenneth Thibodeau, S.M., Prov.; Rev. Albert DiIanni, S.M., Vicar Prov.

Priests of the Province Not Listed Elsewhere: Rev. Armand Thibault, S.M., 27 Isabella St., 02116-5216. Tel: 617-426-4448. Rev. Frank Reitter, S.M., The Marist House, 518 Pleasant St., Framingham, 01701-2898. Tel: 508-879-1620; Fax: 508-879-1132. Rev. Antoine Charest, S.M., 27 Isabella St., 02116-5216. Tel: 617-426-4448; Fax: 617-482-1570.

Marist Fathers Lourdes Residence, 698 Beacon St., 02215. Tel: 617-262-2271. Revs. Gerard Caron, S.M., Dir.; Michael Pavlick, S.M.; Julian Rondeau, S.M.; Marcel Lajoie, S.M. Priests 4.

Marist Fathers of Our Lady of Victories (Boston Prov.), 27 Isabella St., 02116. Tel: 617-426-4448; Fax: 617-482-1570.
E-mail: rlajoie@aol.com
Revs. Kenneth Thibodeau, S.M.; Lucien Chasse, S.M.; Albert DiIanni, S.M., Supr.; Philip Laplante, S.M.; John Meade, S.M.; Romeo Yu Chang, S.M.; Armand Robichaud, S.M.; Armand Thibault, S.M.; Antoine Charest, S.M.; Bros. Roland Bernier, S.M.; Leonard Haley, S.M.; Jude Roy, S.M.; Gregory Theriault, S.M. Priests 9; Brothers 3; Sisters 6.

Ministry of the Word. Revs. Philip O'Shea, O.F.M.; John Anglin, O.F.M.; James Fitzmaurice, O.F.M.; Bro. Robert Frazzetta, O.F.M.

Paulist Fathers Residence, 5 Park St., 02108-4897. Tel: 617-742-4460; Fax: 617-723-2170.
E-mail: stancsp@aol.com
Revs. Stanley F. MacNevin, C.S.P., Supr.; John B. Ardis, C.S.P., Dir.; John P. Campbell, C.S.P.; Harold J. Foye, C.S.P.; Joseph T. Griffin, C.S.P.; Paul A. Reynolds, C.S.P.; Richard J. Colgan, C.S.P.; Edward J. McDonald, C.S.P.; Frank Sabatte, C.S.P.; Francis M. Sweeney, C.S.P. Total in Residence 10; Total Staff 3.

St. Bonaventure Friary, Franciscan Friars. 284 Foster St., Brighton, 02135. Tel: 617-254-2447.
E-mail: sbonfriary@aol.com
Revs. Rashid Francis, O.F.M., Postulant Dir.; Valerian Faugno, O.F.M., Guardian (Supr.); Bro. Damian Johnson, O.F.M., Vicar.
In Formation: Mr. Aaron Tekin; Mr. Donatello Iocco; Mr. Daniel Langlois; Mr. Ednald Yves; Mr. Juan Luis Rivera; Rev. Sean McEwen. Priests 2; Total Staff 3.

St. Christopher Friary, 18 N. Bennet St., 02113-1913. Tel: 617-742-4190; Fax: 617-725-0343. Revs. Ronald A. Siciliano, O.F.M., Guardian; John Baptist Frisoli, O.F.M.; Claude Scrima, O.F.M. Priests 3.

St. Gabriel Passionist Community. 139 Washington St., Brighton, 02135-4235. Tel: 617-254-6582; Fax: 617-783-1766. Priests 5. The Congregation of the Passion (The Passionists). Rev. Justinian Manning, C.P., Supr. Pastor. In res. Revs. Brendan Breen, C.P.; Roger Gannon, C.P.; Bernadine Grande, C.P.; John O'Brien, C.P.

The Society of Jesus of New England-Provincial Offices, 771 Harrison Ave., 02118-2311. Tel: 617-266-7233; Fax: 617-536-8074.
E-mail: nenprvsj@bc.edu
Revs. Robert J. Levens, S.J., Prov.; John P. Murray, S.J.; David I. Donovan, S.J., Asst. for Formation and Pastoral Ministries; Joseph R. Fahey, S.J., Asst. for Province Finances; James M. Hayes, S.J., Laison for Intl. Ministries, Vocation co-Dir.; William C. McInnes, S.J., Liaison for Continuing Educ.; Thomas P. O'Malley, S.J., Asst. for Devel.; Richard H. Roos, S.J., Liason for Men in Apostolate of Spiritual Exercises; Richard J. Stanley, S.J., Vocation co-Dir.; James F. Walsh, S.J., Liaison for Social Ministries.

Priests of Province on Special Assignment: Revs. Albert A. Agresti, S.J.; Robert J. Araujo, S.J.; Edward J. Banks, S.J.; John J. Begley, S.J.; Aram J. Berard, S.J.; Richard D. Bertrand, S.J.; B. Jeffrey Blangiardi, S.J.; Stephen J. Bonian, S.J.; Richard P. Boyle, S.J.; Robert J. Braunreuther, S.J.; James F. Bresnahan, S.J.; Scott N. Brodeur, S.J.; Joseph J. Bruce, S.J.; John J. Caskin, S.J.; Gregory C. Chisholm, S.J.; Thomas F. Clark, S.J.; Denis R. Como, S.J.; Michael J. Connolly, S.J.; John T. Crabb, S.J.; William J. Cullen, S.J.; Michael J. Doody, S.J.; Robert R. Dorin, S.J.; Robert F. Drinan, S.J.; Raymond V. Dunn, S.J.; John E. Fagan, S.J.; Michael A. Fahey, S.J.; Peter J. Fennessy, S.J.; Gerald F. Finnegan, S.J.; John F. Foley, S.J.; William B. Foley, S.J.; Anthony J. Forte, S.J.; Francois Gick, S.J.; David H. Gill, S.J.; Robert G. Gilroy, S.J.; Julio Giulietti, S.J.; William J. Hamilton, S.J.; John B. Handrahan, S.J.; Robert M. Hanlon, S.J.; G. Simon Harak, S.J.; Paul F. Harman, S.J.; Edward F. Howard, S.J.; Daniel P. Jamros, S.J.; John J. Karwin, S.J.; James M. Keegan, S.J.; John W. Keegan, S.J.; William J. Kennedy, S.J.; Paul C. Kenney, S.J.; Philip S. Kiley, S.J.; James F. Lafontaine, S.J.; Daniel J. Lusch, S.J.; Leo M. Manglaviti, S.J.; Frederic A. Maples, S.J.; Stanley B. Marrow, S.J.; James J. Martin, S.J.; Richard B. McCafferty, S.J.; Peter R. McGrath, S.J.; Frederick G. McLeod, S.J.; Francis J. McManus, S.J.; Robert G. McMillan, S.J.; Ronald A. Mercier, S.J.; John J. Moriarty, S.J.; Francis J. Moy, S.J.; John J. Mullen, S.J.; Joseph E. Mullen, S.J.; John F. Mullin, S.J.; George R. Murphy, S.J.; Thomas R. E. Murphy, S.J.; Eugene F. Orteneau, S.J.; Lawrence J. O'Toole, S.J.; Arthur H. Pare, S.J.; Robert V. Paskey, S.J.; Normand A. Pepin, S.J.; James F.X. Pratt, S.J.; Philip A. Pusateri, S.J.; Robert F. Regan, S.J.; William Reiser, S.J.; Richard W. Rousseau, S.J.; Gregory R. Roy, S.J.; Stephen J Sanford, S.J.; Solomon I. Sara, S.J.; Francis X. Sarjeant, S.J.; John D. Savard, S.J.; Joseph J. Schad, S.J.; Andrew J. Scopp, S.J.; Gregory C. Sharkey, S.J.; James M. Shea, S.J.; John F.X. Sheehan, S.J.; Myles N. Sheehan, S.J.; Thomas J. Sheehan, S.J.; Lester O. Shields, S.J.; Edward J. Small, S.J.; Lawrence C. Smith, S.J.; Walter J. Smith, S.J.; James G. Stinson, S.J.; Paul M. Sullivan, S.J.; Paul J. Tabor, S.J.; Robert F. Taft, S.J.; Timothy E. Toohig, S.J.; David O. Travers, S.J.; James F. Walsh, S.J.; John Joseph Walsh, S.J.; Terrance G. Walsh, S.J.; Robert L. Keane, S.J., Chaplain, Res. Ignatius House, 771 Harrison Ave, 02118-2311. Revs. David I. Donovan, S.J.; John P. Murray, S.J., Executive Asst. & Asst. for Secondary Educ.; Thomas J. Gibbons, S.J.; James M. Hayes, S.J.; Alfred J. Hicks, S.J.; Robert J. Levens, S.J.; James J. Walsh, S.J.; Bros. Edward P. Babinski, S.J.; H. Francis Cluff, S.J.; James P. McDavitt, S.J. Priests 7; Brothers 3.

The Society of St. James the Apostle, Inc., 24 Clark St., 02109. Tel: 617-742-4715; Fax: 617-723-7389.
E-mail: socjames@gte.net
Web site: socstjames.com
Revs. Kevin Hays, Asst. Dir.; Hugh Joseph Shields (Philadelphia), Dir.; Milton Eggerling (OAK).
Founded by His Eminence Richard Cardinal Cushing, in 1958 to recruit Priest volunteers for South America. See American Foreign Missions Section for Diocesan Priests serving in Latin America.

ANDOVER. *St. Francis Friary*, 459 River Rd., 01810. Tel: 978-851-3391; Fax: 978-858-0675.
E-mail: franretc@aol.com
Web site: www.franrcent.org
Rev. John D. Bavaro, O.F.M., Dir., Guardian, Retreat Team. Community: Revs. John C. DiMauro, O.F.M.; Justin J. Bailey, O.F.M.; Robert J. Caprio, O.F.M.; Michael Travaglione, O.F.M.; Deacon Charles Gingerich, O.F.M., Vicar, Vocational Dir.; Bros. Gabriel Aceto, O.F.M.; Charles Trebino, O.F.M., Vocation Office. Total in Residence 8; Total Staff 11.

BROCKTON. *Chapel of Our Saviour*, 475 Westgate Dr., 02301-1819. Tel: 508-583-8357; Fax: 508-586-5510. Franciscan Friars of the Atonement. Bro. DePorres Poncia, S.A., Dir.; Revs. Boniface Riedmann, S.A.; Joseph Di Mauro, S.A.; Malcolm Martin, S.A.; Bros. Savio McNeice, S.A.; Louis Marek, S.A. Priests 3; Brothers 3.

CAMBRIDGE. *Faber House*, 42 Kirkland St., 02138-2031. Tel: 617-497-5564. Revs. Christopher Frechette, S.J. (CA); Kenneth J. Hughes, S.J. (New England); Carlos Quijano, S.J. (CAN); Stephen Chow, S.J. (China); Augustine Tsang, S.J. (California); Ludger Viefhues, S.J. (Germany). Residence for Jesuit Priests and Scholastics.

Weston Jesuit Community, 20 Sumner Rd., 02138. Tel: 617-547-3742; Fax: 617-868-8714. Rev. John A. Privett, S.J., Rector.

Residences of Priests: Rev. John Baldovin, S.J., St. Edmunds House, 15 Avon St., 02138. Tel: 617-492-3908. Rev. Kevin Burke, S.J., Xavier House, 80 Lexington Ave., 02138. Tel: 617-491-0864. Rev. Youngmin Choi, S.J., 40 Kirkland St., 02138. Tel: 617-868-6568. Rev. Stephen Chow, S.J., Faber House, 42 Kirkland St., 02138. Tel: 617-497-5564. Rev. Mark Cieslik, S.J., 2222 Mass Ave., 02140. Tel: 617-868-5032. Rev. William Clark, S.J., 10 Martin St., 02138. Tel: 617-491-2155. Rev. Richard J. Clifford, S.J., 7 Kirkland Rd., 02138. Tel: 617-661-4155. Rev. Carlos Coupeau, S.J., 10 Martin St., 02138. Tel: 617-491-2155. Rev. Lawrence Daka, S.J., 66 Oxford St., 02138. Tel: 617-876-1233. Rev. George Drury, S.J., 40 Kirkland St., 02138. Tel: 617-868-6568. Rev. Peter Dubovsky, S.J., 10 Martin St., 02138. Tel: 617-491-2155. Rev. Peter Fink, S.J., 6 Sumner Rd., 02138. Tel: 617-547-5310. Rev. Manuel Francisco, S.J., 10 Martin St., 02138. Tel: 617-491-2155. Rev. Christopher Frechette, S.J., Faber House, 42 Kirkland St., 02138. Tel: 617-497-5564. Rev. Mikio Conrad Fukuchi, S.J., Faber House, 42 Kirkland St., 02138. Tel: 617-497-5564. Rev. Eric Genilo, S.J., 6 Manassas Ave., 02138. Tel: 617-547-1086. Rev. Roger Haigt, S.J., 7 Kirkland Rd., 02138. Tel: 617-661-4155. Rev. Thomas Hamel, S.J., Faber House, 42 Kirkland St., 02138. Tel: 617-497-5564. Rev. William Ibach, S.J., 15 Hawthorn St., 02138. Tel: 617-497-0164. Rev. Daniel J. Harrington, S.J., 12 Linnaean St., 02138. Tel: 617-547-0931. Rev. Kenneth Hughes, S.J., Faber House, 42 Kirkland St., 02138. Tel: 617-497-5564. Rev. Ignatius Hung, S.J., 40 Kirkland St., 02138. Tel: 617-868-6568. Rev. James Keenan, S.J., 10 Martin St., 617-491-2155. Rev. Stanley B. Marrow, S.J., 3 Phillips Pl., 02138. Tel: 617-492-1960. Rev. Thomas Massaro, S.J., Xavier House, 80 Lexington Ave., 02138. Tel: 617-491-0864. Rev. John W. O'Malley, S.J., 10 Martin St., 02138. Tel: 617-491-2155. Rev. John R. Sachs, S.J., 6 Sumner Rd., 02136. Tel: 617-547-5310. Rev. Edward V. Vacek, S.J., 40 Kirkland St., 02138. Tel: 617-868-6568. Rev. John J. Kselman, S.S., 7 Kirkland Rd., 02138. Tel: 617-661-4155. Rev. Christopher Llanos, 10 Martin St., 02138. Tel: 617-491-2155. Rev. Janos Lukacs, 40 Kirkland Rd., 02138. Tel: 617-868-6568. Rev. Lawrence Madden, 7 Kirkland Rd., 02138. Tel: 617-661-4155. Rev. Patrick Magro, 6 Manassas Ave., 02138. Tel: 617-547-1086. Rev. Robert E. Manning, S.J., 7 Kirkland Rd., 02138. Rev. Masashi Masuda, Faber House, 42 Kirkland St., 02138. Tel: 617-497-5564. Rev. Paul McCarren, Faber House, 42 Kirkland St., 02138. Tel: 617-497-5564. Rev. James McPolin, Faber House, 42 Kirkland St., 02138. Tel: 617-497-5564. Rev. Thomas Melancon, 40 Kirkland St., 02138. Tel: 617-868-6568. Rev. Joseph Michini, 7 Kirkland St., 02138. Tel: 617-661-4155. Rev. Donald Miranda, Xavier House, 80 Lexington Ave., 02138. Tel: 617-491-0864. Rev. Sieu

Cao Nguyen, 6 Manassas Ave., 02138. Tel: 617-547-1086. Rev. Rigobert Nsibu Tona, 6 Manassas Ave., 02138. Tel: 617-547-1086. Rev. Liem Thanh Pham, 6 Sumner Rd., 02138. Tel: 617-547-5310. Rev. Min-Uoc Pham, 66 Oxford St., 02138. Tel: 617-876-1233. Rev. John Privett, 42 Kirkland St., 02138. Tel: 617-497-5564. Rev. Carlos Quijano, Faber House, 42 Kirkland St., 02138. Tel: 617-497-5564. Rev. Jocelyn Rabeson, Xavier House, 80 Lexington Ave., 02138. Tel: 617-491-0864. Rev. M.W. Randriamanantena, 2222 Mass Ave., 02140. Tel: 617-868-5032. Rev. Juan Rueda, 2222 Mass Ave., 02140. Tel: 617-868-5032. Rev. Chak-Long Tong, 2222 Mass Ave., 02140. Tel: 617-868-5032. Rev. Alexander Tortell, 66 Oxford St., 02138. Tel: 617-876-1233. Rev. Augustine Tsang, Faber House, 42 Kirkland St., 02138. Tel: 617-497-5564. Rev. Edwin Vasquez, 10 Martin St., Cambridge St., 02138. Tel: 617-491-2155. Rev. Carlos Sergio Viana, 66 Oxford St., 02138. Tel: 617-876-1233. Rev. Ludger Viefhus, Faber House, 42 Kirkland St., 02138. Tel: 617-497-5564. Rev. Trung Vu, 6 Sumner Rd., 02138. Tel: 617-547-5310. Rev. Kevin White, St. Edmunds House, 15 Avon St., 02138. Tel: 617-492-3908. Priests 58; Brothers 1; Scholastics 41.

CHESTNUT HILL. *The Jesuit Community at Boston College*, 02467. Tel: 617-552-8200; Fax: 617-552-2380.
Web site: www.bc.edu/sj/
Very Rev. Frank R. Herrmann, S.J., Rector; Revs. James M. Collins, S.J., Admin. & Treas. & Asst. Rector; Francis J. Nicholson, S.J., Asst. Rector; Edward M. O'Flaherty, S.J., Asst. Rector; Michael Alosanaya, S.J. (India); Ronald Anderson, S.J.; Joseph A. Appleyard, S.J.; Felipe Bacalso, S.J. (Philippines/China); J. Robert Barth, S.J. (New York); James W. Bernauer, S.J. (New York); Stanley J. Bezuszka, S.J.; Richard Blake, S.J. (NY); Thomas Brennan, S.J. (Wisconsin); Michael Buckley, S.J. (California); John F. Caulfield, S.J.; Richard T. Cleary, S.J.; Francis X. Clooney, S.J. (New York); Walter Conlan, S.J. (BAH); Michael Cook, S.J. (Oregon); William Connolly, S.J.; J. Daniel Daly, S.J. (Missouri); Robert J. Daly, S.J.; Neil F. Decker, S.J.; John F. Devane, S.J.; Terrence P. Devino, S.J.; John A. Dinneen, S.J. (New York); Joseph P. Duffy, S.J.; Harvey D. Egan, S.J.; Frederick Enman, S.J.; James Erps, S.J. (California); Joseph Fahey, S.J.; Wellington Fernando, S.J. (India); Robert Farrell, S.J.; Joseph F. X. Flanagan, S.J.; James Fleming, S.J.; Thomas F. Fleming, S.J.; J. Michael Flynn, S.J.; David H. Gill, S.J.; Joseph A. Glavin, S.J.; Howard Gray, S.J. (Detroit); Gary Gurtler, S.J. (New York); Edward J. Hanrahan, S.J.; Charles J. Healey, S.J.; Raymond G. Helmick, S.J.; David Hollenbach, S.J. (Maryland); John W. Howard, S.J.; John Izzo, S.J. (California); George Karuvelli, S.J. (India); T. Frank Kennedy, S.J.; Kevin Kersten, S.J. (Wisconsin); John Konicek, S.J. (NO); O'myun Kwon, S.J. (Korea); William P. Leahy, S.J. (Wisconsin), Pres.; Francis Liuima, S.J. (Lithuania); Daniel J. Lusch, S.J.; Martin MacDonnell, S.J.; Francis C. Mackin, S.J.; Donald A. MacMillan, S.J.; Arthur R. Madigan, S.J. (New York); Simon Makuru, S.J. (Zambia); James B. Malley, S.J.; Douglas Marcouiller, S.J. (Missouri); James Mattaliano, S.J.; Richard A. McGowan, S.J. (Maryland); William C. McInnes, S.J.; John P. McIntyre, S.J.; Paul McNellis, S.J. (NY); William W. Meissner, S.J. (New York); Paul A. Messer, S.J.; J. Donald Monan, S.J. (New York); John Montag, S.J. (Wisconsin); James F. Morgan, S.J.; Franco Mormando, S.J.; Bruce Morrill, S.J.; Frederick L. Moriarty, S.J.; Mpumelo Moyo, S.J. (ZIM); John F. Mullin, S.J.; Paul A. Nash, S.J.; William B. Neenan, S.J. (Wisconsin); Timothy Ngodcho, S.J. (Philippines); Gerard C. O'Brien, S.J.; James C. O'Brien, S.J.; Joseph M. O'Keefe, S.J.; Martin O'Malley, S.J. (NY); Thomas P. O'Malley, S.J.; Charles Onyango, S.J. (Africa); Protas Opondo, S.J. (Africa); Virgilio Oliveira e.Costa, S.J. (Portugal); Cyril Opeil, S.J. (Maryland); Pyong Gwan Pak, S.J. (Korea); John Paris, S.J.; Frank J. Parker, S.J.; Ai Pham, S.J. (Australia); Sugiyo Pitoyo, S.J. (Indonesia); Donald J. Plocke, S.J.; Jacek Prusak, S.J. (Poland); William J. Richardson, S.J. (New York); Lubos Rojka, S.J. (Slovakia); Patrick J. Ryan, S.J.; Joop Schopman, S.J. (Netherlands); Stephen Schloesser, S.J. (MIL); James W. Skehan, S.J.; David Skelskey, S.J.; John Spencer, S.J.; Francis A. Sullivan, S.J.; Francis W. Sweeney, S.J.; Ronald K. Tacelli, S.J.; Timothy E. Toohig, S.J.; Francis W. Vye, S.J.; James A. Woods, S.J.

COHASSET. *Bellarmine House*, 150 Howard Gleason Rd., 02025. Tel: 781-383-0723; Fax: 781-383-3164. Rev. James M. Collins, S.J., Admin. (Summer Res. for Jesuits of New England Prov.).

DANVERS. *Xavier Center*, 21 Spring St., 01923. Tel: 508-777-1326. Xaverian Brothers, U.S.A. Bro. John D. Hamilton, C.F.X., Dir. of Formation, House of Formation. Brothers Professed 3.

DEDHAM. *African Mission House*. Society of African Missions, Inc. 269-337 Common St., 02026-4030. Tel: 781-326-3288; 326-4670; Fax: 781-326-7627.
E-mail: smausa-d@ix.netcom.com
Web site: www.smafathers.org
Revs. F. Joseph Foley, S.M.A.; Francis B. Gillis, S.M.A.; James B. Hill, S.M.A.; Michael J. Rooney, S.M.A.; Michael J. Feeley, S.M.A. Priests 5.

DOVER. *St. Stephen Priory*, 20 Glen St., Box 370, 02030. Tel: 508-785-0124; Fax: 508-785-1020.
E-mail: thepriory@aol.com
Web site: www.ststephenpriory.org
Revs. Walter C. Wagner, O.P., Prior; John E. Allard, O.P.; E. Henry Gallagher, O.P.; Bruce A. Williams, O.P.; Richard A. Fleck, O.P.; John Stephen Fitzhenry, O.P.; Louis Roy, O.P. (CAN); Romanus Cessario, O.P.; Stephen D. Ryan, O.P.; Michael A. Ciccone, O.P.; Bro. Patrick Foley, O.P. Spiritual Life Center and Retreat Center. Priests 9; Religious Brothers 1; Total Staff 12.

DUXBURY. *Society of the Divine Word*, 121 Parks St., P.O. Box M, 02331-0614. Tel: 781-585-2460; Fax: 781-585-3770.
E-mail: miramarma@aol.com
Revs. Joseph Connolly, S.V.D.; Edward Dudink, S.V.D.; John J. Bergin, S.V.D.; Edward Tuohy, S.V.D.; Robert Mallonee, S.V.D.; Robert Jones, S.V.D., Rector; William Kane, S.V.D.; Bro. Donald Champagne, S.V.D. Priests 6; Brothers 1; Total Staff 16.

EAST BOSTON. *The Salesian Community*, 145 Byron St., 02128. Tel: 617-569-6551; 569-6645; Fax: 617-568-3851.
E-mail: jankoj@prodigy.net

EAST WALPOLE. *Maryknoll Mission Promotion Department*. Tel: 508-668-6831; Fax: 508-660-0252.
E-mail: mklboston@aol.com
80 Emerson Rd., 02032-1349. Tel: 508-668-6831; Fax: 508-668-0252. Revs. James R. Roy, M.M.; Francis J. Breen, M.M.; Gerald E. Kelly, M.M., Dir. Total in Residence 3; Staff 1.

HINGHAM. *Glastonbury Abbey*, 16 Hull St., 02043. Tel: 781-749-2155; Fax: 781-749-6236.
E-mail: office@glastonburyabbey.org
Web site: www.glastonburyabbey.org
Rt. Revs. Nicholas J. Morcone, O.S.B., Abbot; Edward C. Campbell, O.S.B., Retired Abbot; Very Rev. Timothy J. Joyce, Prior; Revs. Andrew M. Quillen; Jonah P. Trombetta, O.S.B.; Gerald T. Leibenguth, O.S.B.; Richard J. Bourgeois, O.S.B.; Thomas J. O'Connor; Roger Nolette; Bros. Damian A. Boucher, O.S.B.; John Mark Carlin, O.S.B.; David K. Coakley, O.S.B.; James Crowley, O.S.B.; Daniel F. Walters, O.S.B. Priests 9; Brothers 5. Retreat Center. Benedictine Monks. Capacity 29. Lincoln School Apartments for the Elderly. Tel: 781-749-2155; Fax: 781-749-6236.
E-mail: office@glastonburyabbey.org
Web site: www.glastonburyabbey.org

HOLLISTON. *Xaverian Missionaries*, 101 Summer St., P.O. Box 5857, 01746-5857. Tel: 508-429-2144; Fax: 508-429-4793.
E-mail: XAVMISSMA@aol.com
Web site: www.sigmaweb.net/xavmissions
Revs. Francis Signorelli, S.X., Supr.; Robert S. Maloney, S.X., Supr.; Gerard Furlan, S.X.; Tony Lalli, S.X.; Eugene Montesi, S.X. Priests 5.

IPSWICH. *Missionaries of Our Lady of LaSalette Corp.* National Shrine of Our Lady of LaSalette. Formation Res., 251 Topsfield Rd., 01938-1195. Tel: 508-356-3151. Total in residence 1.

LAWRENCE. *Marist Brothers Residence*, 12 Sheridan St., 01841. Tel: 508-682-1163. Bros. William Lambert, F.M.S., Dir.; C. Vincent Dinnean, F.M.S.; Ernest Beland, F.M.S.; Richard Carey, F.M.S. Brothers 4.

LOWELL. *Missionary Oblates of Mary Immaculate*, 27 Kirk St., 01852-1004. Tel: 978-937-9594; Fax: 978-459-4146. Andre Garin Retirement Residence. Tel: 978-937-9594; Fax: 978-459-4146. Bro. Charles Gilbert, Dir. Tel: 978-441-1245; Revs. Roland Couture, Asst. Dir.; Anatole Baillargeon; Marcel Bolduc; Paul Beauregard, O.M.I.; Roger Roy, O.M.I.; Bros. Joseph Gagne; Thomas Cruise.

Missionary Oblates of Mary Immaculate. St. Eugene House, 60 Wyman St., 01852-2841. Tel: 978-441-0649; Fax: 978-454-0677.
E-mail: artobin@juno.com
Web site: www.omiusa.org
Revs. Arthur Obin, O.M.I.; Herve Gagnon, O.M.I.; Lucien Richard, O.M.I.; Francis Demers, O.M.I., Preaching Team; George Protopapas, O.M.I.; Richard McAlear, O.M.I.

Missionary Oblates of Mary Immaculate. Northeast Area Office, 60 Wyman St., 01852. Tel: 978-458-9912; Fax: 978-458-7274. Revs. Arthur Obin, O.M.I., Northeast Area Supr.; Marc Boisvert, O.M.I.; Bevil Bramwell; George Brown, O.M.I.; Norman Comtois, O.M.I.; Roger Couture, O.M.I.; Wilfred Harvey, O.M.I.; Roger J. Lamoureux, O.M.I.; Michael Lauze, O.M.I.; Albert Lirette, O.M.I., (Retired); George Roy, O.M.I.; Jean-Joseph Vallieres, O.M.I., (Retired); Bro. Robert Dutil, O.M.I. Priests 105; Brothers 14; Total Staff 1; Serving Abroad 2; Total in Residence 6; Total Membership 119.

LYNN. *Franciscan Community (Province of Immaculate Conception)*, 38 Michigan Ave., 01902. Tel: 617-592-7396; Fax: 617-593-8805. Revs. Alfonse Ferreira, O.F.M., Procurator & Guardian; Bede Ferrara, O.F.M.

"The Listening Place" (Counseling Center), 36 Michigan Ave., 01902. Tel: 781-592-7396; Fax: 781-593-8805. Rev. Alfonse Ferreira, O.F.M., Dir.; Sr. Jane Hogan, O.S.F., Assoc. Dir.

MILTON. *Oblate Residence (St. Joseph House)*, 65 Fr. Carney Dr., 02186-4206. Tel: 617-698-6785; Fax: 617-698-7621.
Web site: www.oblatesofthevirginmary.org
Congregation of the Oblates of the Virgin Mary. Revs. David Kueter, O.M.V.; Robert Lowrey, O.M.V.; James Montanaro, O.M.V.; William Mullen, O.M.V.; James Nibler, O.M.V.; Gregory Short, O.M.V.; Gerald Wright, O.M.V.; Bro. Joseph O'Connor, O.M.V. Priests 8; Brothers 1.

NATICK. *Annunciation Friary*, 29 Purington Ave., 01760. Tel: 508-655-5147; Fax: 508-655-5334. Total in Residence 3.

QUINCY. *St. Columban's Foreign Mission Society*, 310 Adams St., 02169. Tel: 472-1494. Rev. John S. Roche, S.S.C., P.O. Box 227, Humarock, 02047. Rev. Edward A. Roberts, S.S.C., 20 Frisbie Rd., Marshfield, 02050. Rev. James O'Brien, Supr., 310 Adams St., 02169. Rev. Michael Breen, S.S.C., 310 Adams St., 02169. Rev. Charles B. Flaherty, S.S.C., St. John Chrystostom, 4750 Washington St., West Roxbury, 02132. Rev. Joseph L. Crehan, S.S.C., Immaculate Conception, 487 Broadway, Everett, 02149. Rev. Paul O'Malley, S.S.C., Presentation Apts., #54, 309 Church St., Clinton, 01510. Priests 8.

SOMERVILLE. *Brotherhood of Hope*, 194 Summer St., 02143-2525. Tel: 617-623-9592; Fax: 617-625-1837.
E-mail: br-hope@juno.com
Web site: www.brotherhoodofhope.org
Total in Residence 12.

TEWKSBURY. *Oblate Fathers-Office of the Provincial Treasurer*, 486 Chandler St., Box 419, 01876; Fax: 508-858-3661. Rev. Patrick J. Hollywood, O.M.I., Prov. Treas. Legal Title: *Society of Oblate Fathers for Missions Among the Poor*. Total in Residence 27; Total Staff 23.

Oblate World/Missionary Association of Mary Immaculate, 486 Chandler St., Box 680, 01876-0680. Tel: 978-858-0434; Fax: 978-858-3661. Rev. William O'Donnell, O.M.I., Editor & Dir.

WALTHAM. *Stigmatine Fathers & Brothers Provincial House*, 554 Lexington St., 02452. Tel: 718-209-3100; Fax: 781-894-9785. Very Rev. Gregory J. Hoppough, C.S.S., Prov. Supr.; Revs. Anthony Corigliano, C.S.S.; Charles Dolan, C.S.S. (Thailand); Donald Toner, C.S.S. (Brazil); Richard Woodarek, C.S.S. (Thailand); Pius C.W. Murray, C.S.S. (Italy); Joseph Henchey, C.S.S. (Italy). Total Staff 4.

Stigmatine House. Bertoni Hall, 554 Lexington, 02452-3097. Tel: 781-209-3100. Revs. David F. Gallagher, C.S.S.; Francis L. Keefe, C.S.S.; Pius C.W. Murray, C.S.S.; Anthony Penna, C.S.S.; Donald Higgins, C.S.S.; Nicholas Spagnolo, C.S.S.; Robert S. White, C.S.S., S.T.L.; Bro. Richard Spencer, C.S.S.

WESTON. *Campion Health Center, Inc.*, 319 Concord Rd., 02493. Tel: 781-788-6800; Fax: 781-894-5864. Revs. Ronald J. Amiot, S.J., Rector; Ronald E. Wozniak, S.J., Min.; George W. Nolan, S.J., Treas.; David G. Boulton, S.J., Chap.; James T. Sheehan, S.J., Asst. Chap.; Harry W. Ball, S.J.; Robert F. Banks, S.J.; Joseph F. Brennan, S.J.; Eugene C. Brissette, S.J.; John F. Broderick, S.J.; Robert R. Burke, S.J.; Edward K. Cheney, S.J.; Richard J. Coakley, S.J.; John J.L. Collins, S.J.; William A. Connolly, S.J.; Hubert F. Cunniff, S.J.; J. Frank Devine, S.J.; John J. Diskin, S.J.; Thomas P. Donovan, S.J.; James J. Drohan, S.J.; Joseph G. Fennell, S.J.; Paul P. Gilmartin, S.J.; Donald F. Grady, S.J.; William G. Guindon, S.J.; Philip K. Harrigan, S.J.; Alwyn C. Harry, S.J.; Robert J. Higgins, S.J.; Robert F. Hoey, S.J.; Joseph I. Holland, S.J.; Thomas F. Hussey, S.J.; Thomas J. C. Kelly, S.J.; William J. Larkin, S.J.; Robert E. Lindsay, S.J.; George S. Mahan, S.J.; John L. Mahoney, S.J.; James P. McCaffrey, S.J.; Martin F. McCarthy, S.J.; Paul T. McCarty, S.J.; Raymond E. McCluskey, S.J.; Joseph E. McCormick, S.J.; Thomas F. McDermott, S.J.; Francis P. Molloy, S.J.; Henry J. Murphy, S.J.; Edward H. Nowlan, S.J.; William F. O'Connor, S.J.; Richard F. Olson, S.J.; Joseph A. Paquet, S.J.; William J. Power, S.J.; Joseph F. Quane, S.J.; Leo F. Quinlan, S.J.; Martin E. Ryan, S.J.; Joseph S. Scannell, S.J.; William J. Sheehan, S.J.; John J. Sullivan, S.J.; John W. Sullivan, S.J.; Patrick A. Sullivan, S.J.; Robert J. Sullivan, S.J.; Felix F. Talbot, S.J.; Wilfrid J. Vigeant, S.J.; James P. Walsh, S.J.; Maurice b. Walsh, S.J.; Bros. Austin J. Burns, S.J.; Peter J. Gabriel, S.J.; Vincent L Molinaro, S.J.; Edward L. Niziolek, S.J.; Italo A. Parnoff, S.J. Priests 60; Brothers 5.

Campion Jesuit Community, 319 Concord Rd., 02493-1398. Tel: 781-788-6800; Fax: 781-894-5864. Revs. Ronald J. Amiot, S.J., Rector; Ronald E. Wozniak, S.J., Min.; George W. Nolan, S.J., Treas.; David G. Boulton, S.J., Chap.; James T. Sheehan, S.J., Asst. Chap.; Walter M Abbot, S.J.; Edward J. Banks, S.J.; William A Barry, S.J.; John F. Broderick, S.J.; Harry J. Cain, S.J.; Joseph H. Casey, S.J.; John J. Caskin, S.J.; Ned H. Cassem, S.J.; Lawrence E. Corcoran, S.J.; Robert G. Doherty, S.J.; John F. Foley, S.J.; Philip S. Kiley, S.J.; John J. Mandile, S.J.; John J. McGrath, S.J.; John W. Michalowski, S.J.; John J. Moriarty, S.J.; John J. Mullen, S.J.; George B. Murray, S.J.; Lawrence J. O'Toole, S.J.; W. Richard Ott, S.J.; Anthony R. Picariello, S.J.; James F. Talbot, S.J.; E. Corbett Walsh, S.J.; Bros. Vincent M. Brennan, S.J.; William M. Quegan, S.J. Legal Title: *Campion Residence & Renewal Center, Inc.* Priests 28; Brothers 2.

[X] CONVENTS AND RESIDENCES FOR SISTERS

BOSTON. *Bernardine Sisters, O.S.F.* 17 Hale St., Hyde Park, 02136. Tel: 617-361-1726; Fax: 617-361-8820.
E-mail: sdelourdes@aol.com
Sisters 21. Legal Title: *Bernardine Sisters of the Third Order of St. Francis of Mass., Inc.* Sr. M. Laetitia Okoniewski, Local Min.

Cardinal's Residence. Tel: 617-782-2544; Fax: 617-782-8358. 2101 Commonwealth Ave., Brighton, 02135. Tel: 617-782-2101; Fax: 617-782-8358. Sisters of St. Joan of Arc of Quebec 4.

Columban Sisters. Tel: 617-782-5683; Fax: 617-789-3569.
E-mail: columbans@juno.com
73 Mapleton St., Brighton, 02135. Tel: 617-782-5683; Fax: 617-789-3569. Sr. Ruth Duckert, Regl. Coord. Professed Sisters 8. Legal Title: *Missionary Sisters of Saint Columban.*

Daughters of St. Paul Inc. 50 St. Paul's Ave., Jamaica Plain, 02130-3491. Tel: 617-522-8911; Fax: 617-524-8648.
E-mail: prov3rdfl@aol.com
Web site: www.pauline.org
Prov. Community 6; Perpetually Professed Sisters 62; Novices 3; Initial Formation 7. Legal Title: *Daughters of St. Paul, Inc. Novitiate, Juniorate, Provincialate Headquarters, and Technical Apostolate Center for U.S.*

Pauline Book & Media Center, 885 Providence Hwy., Dedham, 02026. Tel: 781-326-5385; Fax: 781-461-1013.

Franciscan Missionary Sisters for Africa. (USA Headquarters and only house.). Tel: 617-254-4343; Fax: 617-787-8007.
E-mail: helenfmsa@aol.com; Rmc172@aol.com
Web site: www.members.aol.com/sisters172/fmsa.html
Serving in Uganda, Kenya, Zambia, Ethiopia, Zimbabwe, And South Africa. Completely a Missionary congregation. 172 Foster St., Box 35095, Brighton, 02135. Tel: 617-254-4343; Fax: 617-787-8007. Sisters 7.

Franciscan Monastery of St. Clare, The, 920 Centre St., 02130. Tel: 617-524-1760; Fax: 617-983-5205.
E-mail: Bostonpoorclares@worldnet.att.net
Web site: www.St.AnthonyShrine.org/PoorClares
Franciscan Poor Clare Nuns. Sr. Teresa Dericks, O.S.C., Abbess.
Solemn Vows. Cloistered Solemnly Professed 18; Extern Sisters 2.

Little Sisters of the Assumption Convent. 65 Magnolia St., Dorchester, 02125. Tel: 617-442-9411. Legal Title: *Little Sisters of the Assumption Family Health Services, Inc., dba Project Hope, Co-Opportunity, Inc.* 45 Magnolia St., Dorchester, 02125. Tel: 617-442-1880; Fax: 617-442-1356. Sisters 5.

Monastery of Discalced Carmelites. Tel: 617-442-1411; Fax: 617-442-0203.
E-mail: bostoncarmel@juno.com
61 Mt. Pleasant Ave., Roxbury, 02119. Tel: 617-442-1411; Fax: 617-442-0203.
E-mail: bostoncarmel@juno.com
Cloistered. Sr. Mary Teresa, O.C.D., Prioress. Professed 9.

Motherhouse of the Sisters of St. Joseph of Boston. Tel: 617-783-9090; Fax: 617-783-8246. 637 Cambridge St., Brighton, 02135. Tel: 617-783-9090; Fax: 617-783-8246.
E-mail: boscsj@aol.com
Web site: www.boscsj.org/
Sr. Joan Duffy, C.S.J. Sisters 62.

Sacred Heart Convent. Tel: 617-542-1143.
E-mail: Joannemhsh@aol.com
Mission Helpers of the Sacred Heart. Legal Title: *Institute of Mission Helpers.* 286 Shawmut Ave., 02118-1613. Tel: 617-542-1143. Sisters 3.

St. Theresa House. 50 Brown Ave., Roslindale, 02131. Tel: 617-323-4644. Sr. Mary. Little Missionaries (A Pious Society) 1; Sisters 1; Lay Associates 12.

Sister Disciples of the Divine Master, Convent and Eucharistic Center, 43 West St., 02111. Tel: 482-0978; 423-2629; Fax: 482-682-3779. Sr. Michelle Hernandez, P.D.D.M., Supr. Sisters 10.

Sisters of Notre Dame de Namur (Boston Province Offices). Tel: 617-387-2500; Fax: 617-387-1303.
E-mail: bosprovctr@aol.com
Web site: www.sndden.org/boston
Mailing Address: 351 Broadway, Everett, 02149-3425. Legal Title: *The Boston Province of the Sisters of Notre Dame de Namur, Inc.*

Sisters of the Good Shepherd. Tel: 617-469-2492; Fax: 617-469-9857.
E-mail: smcgo21188@aol.com
35 Tyndale St., Roslindale, 02131. Tel: 617-469-2492; Fax: 617-469-9857. Sisters 3.

ANDOVER. *Monastery of St. Clare*, 460 River Rd., 01810-4260. Tel: 978-851-6743; Fax: 978-851-2320. Poor Clare Nuns. Sr. Therese Lacroix, O.S.C., Abbess. Cloistered Solemnly Professed 12; Extern Perpetually Professed 2.

BROCKTON. *Our Lady of Sorrows Convent*, 261 Thatcher St., 02302-3997. Tel: 508-588-5070; Fax: 508-580-6770.
E-mail: sr.mary@sisterscjcbrocktonma.org
Web site: www.sisterscjcbrocktonma.org
Sr. Mary Valliere, C.J.C., Gen. Supr. Poor Sisters of Jesus Crucified and the Sorrowful Mother. Sisters 37.

CAMBRIDGE. *Franciscan Missionaries of Mary*, 16 Lancaster St., 02140. Tel: 617-868-8036; Fax: 617-661-1835.
E-mail: fmmvisit@aol.com
Sr. Mary Motte, F.M.M., Prov., 3305 Wallace Ave., Bronx, NY, 10467-6599. Tel: 718-547-4693; Fax: 718-547-4607. Sr. Thesesa Conway, F.M.M.; Sr. Sumiko Maeda, F.M.M.; Sr. Doris McShane, F.M.M.; Sr. Anne Richards, F.M.M.; Sr. Margarida Tavares, F.M.M.; Sr. Patricia Murphy, F.M.M.; Sr. Elizabeth A. Conyers, F.M.M.; Sr. Pauline Williams, F.M.M., Coord.; Sr. Mary Rose Nguyen, F.M.M.

Sancta Maria Convent, 799 Concord Ave., 02138. Tel: 617-868-2200, Ext. 2950.

CHELSEA. *Don Guanella Center, Inc., Daughters of St. Mary of Providence*, 37 Nichols St., 02150. Tel: 617-889-0179; Fax: 617-889-3363.
E-mail: donguanellacenter@worldnet.att.net
Sr. Nancy McLennon, D.S.M.P., Dir. of Center, Family Support Respite for Developmentally Handicapped Ladies (Ages 18-65). Tel: 617-889-0179; Fax: 617-889-3363. Families 100; Total Staff 21. Sisters 2.

DANVERS. *Discalced Carmelite Monastery*, 15 Mt. Carmel Rd., 01923-3796. Tel: 978-774-3008; Fax: 978-774-7409. Mother Michael of Christ the King, O.C.D., Prioress. Total in residence 17.

DEDHAM. *Ursuline Convent*, 65 Lowder St., 02026-4205. Tel: 617-326-3158; Fax: 617-326-4428.
E-mail: nestabeaudoin@msn.com
Sr. M. Aimee Bouffard, O.S.U., Prioress. Sisters 16.

Ursuline Provincialate, 45 Lowder St., 02026-4200. Tel: 781-326-6219; Fax: 781-326-7296.
E-mail: provosu@juno.com
Sr. Angela Krippendorf, O.S.U., Prov. Ursulines of the Roman Union, Northeastern Province 49.

EVERETT. *Pope John XXIII Convent*, 888 Broadway, 02149. Sr. Marjarita, Coord. Sisters 3.

FRAMINGHAM. *Fontbonne Hall*, 85 Bethany Rd., 01702. Tel: 508-879-1295.
E-mail: fontfram@aol.com
Sr. Bernadette Kenney, C.S.J., Admin.; Rev. Henry Bourgeois, C.S.C., Chap. Professed Sisters 60.

HAVERHILL. *Sacred Hearts Convent.*
E-mail: scimsh@juno.com
48 S. Chestnut St., Bradford, 01835. Tel: 978-521-6867. Sr. Cecile Labrecque, Supr. Servants of the Immaculate Heart of Mary. Good Shepherd Sisters of Quebec 5.

IPSWICH. *Sisters of Notre Dame de Namur (Provincial Residence)*, 30 Jeffreys Neck Rd., 01938-1308. Tel: 978-356-4381; Fax: 978-356-9759.
E-mail: prvncoff@aol.com
Web site: www.sndden.org
Sr. Therese Julie Fitzmaurice, S.N.D., Prov. Admin. Legal Title: *Notre Dame Training School, Inc.* Sisters 88; Total Staff 15.

Sisters of Notre Dame de Namur Generalate Office, 30 Jeffrey's Neck Rd., 01938. Tel: 978-356-2159; Fax: 978-356-1034.
E-mail: juanamcc@aol.com

Casa Generalizia di Suore di Nostra Signora di Namur. (Generalate), Via Raffaello Sardiello, 20, Rome, Italy, 00165. Tel: 39-06-6641-8704; Fax: 39-06-6641-8709. Sr. Ellen Gielty, S.N.D.deN., Gen. Mod.

KINGSTON. *Provincial Residence, Sisters of Divine Providence*, Our Lady of Divine Providence Province, 363 Bishops Hwy., 02364. Tel: 781-585-7707; Fax: 781-582-1596.
E-mail: cdpward@rcn.com
Sr. Claudia Ward, C.D.P., Prov.

LEXINGTON. *Congregation of Armenian Catholic Sisters of Immaculate Conception, Inc.*, 6 Eliot Rd., 02173. Tel: 781-863-5962; Fax: 781-862-8479. Sr. Veronica Achikian. Sisters 3.

Grey Nuns Provincial Offices, 10 Pelham Rd., Ste. 1000, 02421-8499. Tel: 781-862-4700; Fax: 781-861-9641.
E-mail: srjunek@sgmlex.org
Web site: www.sgmlex.org/
Headquarters (U.S.A. Province) of the Sisters of Charity of Montreal. "Grey Nuns". General Administration, 138 Rue Saint-Pierre, Montreal, Canada, H2Y 2L7. Tel: 514-842-9411; Fax: 514-842-7855. Sr. June Ketterer, S.G.M., Prov. Supr. Co-Chaplains: Revs. James A. O'Donohoe; John E. Sassani. Sisters 2.

LOWELL. *Convent of the Holy Union Retirement Home*, 142 Chestnut St., 01852. Tel: 978-458-8862; 458-8835; Fax: 978-970-3780. Holy Union Sisters. Sr. Pauline LaRoche, S.U.S.C.; Sr. Daniel Rioux, S.U.S.C. Sisters 28.

Franciscan Sisters of Alleghany, Region II Office, 282 Suffolk St., 01854. Tel: 978-452-2823. Sr. Mary Lou Lafferty, O.S.F., Region II Min.

St. Joseph Provincial House, 975 Varnum Ave., 01854. Tel: 978-453-4993; Fax: 978-453-8708.
E-mail: lowellsco@juno.com
Sisters of Charity of Ottawa (Grey Nuns of the Cross). Sr. Gabrielle Jean, S.C.O., Prov. Supr. Sisters 43.

LYNN. *Sisters of St. Chretienne*, 30 Basset St., 01902-2506. Tel: 781-593-1014. Sisters 4.

MARLBOROUGH. *Sisters of St. Anne, Provincialate*, 720 Boston Post Rd. E., 01752. Tel: 508-481-4934; Fax: 508-481-4934.
E-mail: syd@hotmail.com
Web site: www.anna-maria.edu/ssa www.sistersofsaintanne.org
Headquarters of American Province. Sisters 157.

Community of the Sisters of Saint Anne. Tel: 508-481-4934; Fax: 508-481-4934. St. Anne Convent, 720 Boston Post Rd. E., Marlboro, 01752. Tel: 508-485-3791. Sisters 80.

Sisters of Ste. Chretienne, 197 Pleasant St., 01752-1169. Tel: 508-485-0740; Fax: 508-481-0663.
E-mail: ssch@pop.tiac.net
Sr. Lorraine Michaud, S.S.Ch., Local Coord. House of Retirement. Sisters 34.

Sisters of Ste. Chretienne, 207 Pleasant St., Marlboro, 01752-1169. Tel: 508-229-3505. Sr. Yvette Campbell, S.S.Ch., Local Coord. Sisters 4.

Sisters of the Good Shepherd. Tel: 508-485-8610; Fax: 508-460-6372. 406 Hemenway St., Marlboro, 01752. Tel: 508-485-8610; Fax: 508-460-6372. Superiors: Sr. Lillian Masse, R.G.S. Sisters 31.

METHUEN. *Our Lady of Mount Carmel Convent*, 82 Union St., 01844. Tel: 508-682-4833.
E-mail: mtcarmel6@juno.com
Sr. Elaine Lachance, Supr. Servants of the Immaculate Heart of Mary. Good Shepherd Sisters of Quebec 6.

Provincial House, 209 Lawrence St., 01844. Tel: 978-687-1369; Fax: 978-975-1998.
E-mail: prov@netway.com
Web site: www.presmarymethuen.org
Sr. Helene Bissonnette, Prov. Supr. Presentation of Mary. Sisters 145; Total in Residence 97.

MILTON. *Franciscan Sisters of the Immaculate Conception, St. Mary of the Hills*, 260 Brook Rd., 02186. Tel: 617-698-3141. Sr. Rita Murray, O.S.F., Supr. School. St. Mary of the Hills. (Grades K-8).

Holy Union Sisters, Province Office, P.O. Box 410, 444 Centre St., 02186-0006. Tel: 617-696-8765; Fax: 617-696-8571.
Web site: www.holyunionsisters.org
Province Mission Team: Sr. Mary Catherine Duerr, S.U.S.C.; Sr. Theresa M. Horvath, S.U.S.C.; Sr. Mary Lou Sullivan, S.U.S.C.

Religious of Christian Education, Inc., Generalate Annex, 55 Parkwood Dr., 02186. Tel: 617-696-9405; 282-3471; Fax: 617-282-9107.
E-mail: yvetterce@aol.com
Sr. Yvette Rivard, R.C.E., Gen. Councillor.

NEWTON. *Immaculate Conception Provincialate*, 790 Centre St., 02458-2530. Tel: 617-527-1004; Fax: 617-527-2528.
E-mail: usaprov@aol.com
Missionary Franciscan Sisters of the Immaculate Conception. Sr. M. Michele Craig, M.F.I.C. Total in Residence 5; Total Staff 4.

Mt. Alvernia Convent, 790 Centre St., 02158-2529. Tel: 617-969-4766; Fax: 617-527-2528.
E-mail: usercfinne@aol.com
Sisters 35.

PLAINVILLE. *Jesus and Mary Mission Center*, 92 School St., 02762-2033. Tel: 508-699-4427; Fax: 508-643-4179.
E-mail: thpicard1juno.com
Sr. Therese Picard, R.J.M., Admin. Total in Residence 18.

QUINCY. *Sisters of Charity (Halifax)*. (Boston Branch Office), 26 Phipps St., 02169. Tel: 617-773-6085; Fax: 617-472-7179.
E-mail: emplefk@banet.net
Web site: www.schalifax.ca
Sr. Esther Plefka, Congregational Councillor. Tel: 617-773-6076; Sr. Joan Verner, Congregational Sec.

Sisters of Charity (Halifax) Corporate Mission, Inc., 26 Phipps St., 02169. Tel: 617-773-6085; Fax: 617-472-7179.
E-mail: mlb@schalifax.ca
Web site: www.schalifax.ca
Sr. Mary Louise Brink, Congregational Leader.

Sisters of Charity of Nazareth Regional House, 169 Fenno St., 02170. Tel: 617-479-4909; Fax: 617-786-0767.
E-mail: gwn357@aol.com
Sr. Gwen McMahon, S.C.N., Regional. Legal Title: *Nazareth Literary and Benevolent Institution*.

SALEM. *St. Chretienne Convent*, 12 Pope St., 01970. Tel: 508-744-1228. Sisters 3.

SOMERVILLE. *Medical Missionaries of Mary, Inc.*, Somerville House, 179 Highland Ave., 02143. Tel: 617-666-3223; Fax: 617-666-1877.
E-mail: mmm179@juno.com
Web site: www.mmmusa.org
Congregation of the Medical Missionaries of Mary Motherhouse, Beechgrove, Drogheda, Ireland. Professed Sisters 10.

WAKEFIELD. *Mother Saint Joseph House*, 7 Emerson St., 01880. Tel: 617-387-2500; Fax: 781-224-0582.
E-mail: sndmsjn@aol.com
Sponsored by the Sisters of Notre Dame de Namur. Sr. Lorraine Connell, S.N.D., Pres.

WALTHAM. *Marist Missionary Sisters*. Tel: 781-893-0149; Fax: 781-899-6838.
E-mail: maristsmsm@aol.com
Legal Title: *Missionary Sisters of the Society of Mary, Inc., S.M.S.M.* Provincial Offices, 349 Grove St., 02453-6018. Tel: 781-893-0149; Fax: 781-899-7610. Sr. Mary Jane Kenney, S.M.S.M., Residence for Senior Sisters, 62 Newton St., 02453-6058. Tel: 781-893-3960. Sisters 34.
Other Local Communities: 60 Newton St., 02453-6058. Tel: 781-899-1837. Sisters 4. 21 Beech St., Belmont, 02478-1299. Tel: 617-489-3587. Sisters 10. 4 Craig St., Framingham, 01701-7664. Tel: 508-877-7371. Sisters 3. 357 Grove St., 02453-6018. Tel: 781-899-3839. Sisters 7. 20 Bartlett Ave., Arlington, 02476-6418. Tel: 781-648-4341. Sisters 10. 94 Irene St., Lawrence, 01841. Tel: 978-975-4375. Sisters 2. 193 Maple St., #6E, Lawrence, 01841. Tel: 978-975-2662.

Sisters of the Good Shepherd, 83-85 Lake St., 02451. Tel: 781-894-6183. Sr. Elish McPartland, Contact Person.

WATERTOWN. *Rosary Manor*, One Rosary Dr., 02172. Tel: 617-924-1717; Fax: 617-924-8118.
E-mail: rosarymanor@juno.com
Sr. Eleanor Fabrizi, O.P., Coord. Total in Residence 28; Total Staff 3.

WAYLAND. *Emmanuel House*, Sisters of St. Anne, 17 Forty Acres Dr., 01778. Tel: 508-358-4033.
E-mail: emmanua1@ibm.net
Web site: www.sisterofsaintanne.org
Sisters 8.

WELLESLEY HILLS. *Elizabeth Seton Residence, Inc.*, 125 Oakland St., 02481. Tel: 781-237-2161; Fax: 781-431-2589.
E-mail: Elisabethseton@msn.com
Web site: www.Elizabethseton.org
84 bed Skilled Nursing & Rehab Facility. Medicare-Medicaid Certified. Accredited by Joint Commission on Accreditation of Healthcare Organizations (JCAHO). Sr. Blanche LaRose, S.C., Admin. Sisters of Charity of St. Vincent de Paul, Halifax, Nova Scotia, Canada.

Marillac Residence, Inc., 125 Oakland St., 02481. Tel: 781-237-0236; Fax: 781-237-8152.
E-mail: aregan1211@aol.com
Sr. Ann Regan, S.C., Pres. Sisters of Charity (Halifax).

Mount St. Vincent Retirement Community, 125 Oakland St., 02481. Tel: 781-237-2161; Fax: 781-237-8152. Community Leadership Team: Sr. Ann Marie Barry; Sr. Elizabeth Groome; Sr. Ann Regan. Tel: 781-237-0236. Sisters of Charity (Halifax).

Sisters of Charity (Halifax) Supporting Corporation, 125 Oakland St., 02481-5338. Tel: 781-237-0487; Fax: 781-235-8068. Sr. Mary Louise Brink, Congregational Leader.

WRENTHAM. *Mount St. Mary's Abbey*, 300 Arnold St., 02093. Tel: 508-528-1282; Fax: 508-528-5630.
E-mail: sisters@msmabbey.org
Web site: www.msmabbey.org
Legal Title: *The Cistercians of the Strict Observance in Massachusetts, Inc.* The Cistercian Nuns of the Strict Observance (Trappistines). Mother M. Agnes Day, O.C.S.O., Abbess. Professed Sisters 46; Total in Residence 48.

St. Chretienne Provincialate, 297 Arnold St., 02093-1798. Tel: 508-384-7841; 384-8066; Fax: 508-384-3170.
E-mail: ssch@tiac.net
Sisters of St. Chretienne. Sr. Suzanne Beaudoin, S.S.Ch. Sisters 4; Total in Residence 3.

[Y] RETREAT HOUSES

ANDOVER. *Franciscan Center - Retreat House*, 459 River Rd., 01810. Tel: 978-851-3391; Fax: 978-858-0675.
E-mail: franretc@aol.com
Web site: www.franrcent.org
Order of Friars Minor. Rev. John D. Bavaro, O.F.M., Dir.; Guardian, Retreat Team. Retreat Team: Revs. John C. DiMauro, O.F.M.; Justin J. Bailey, O.F.M.; Robert J. Caprio, O.F.M.; Michael Travaglione, O.F.M.; Sr. Lorraine Pianka, S.S.N.D.; Bro. Gabriel Aceto, O.F.M.; Jerri Lou Buffo; Mrs. Mildred Sheehan, Sec.; Jackie Picken, Youth Ministry. Total in Residence 8; Total Staff 11.

COHASSET. *St. Joseph Villa Retreat Center*, 339 Jerusalem Rd., 02025. Tel: 781-383-6024; 383-6028.
E-mail: csjratctr@mediaone.net
Sisters of St. Joseph 3.

DOVER. *St. Stephen Priory Spiritual Life Center*, 20 Glen St., Box 370, 02030-0370. Tel: 508-785-0124; Fax: 508-785-1020.
E-mail: ThePriory@aol.com
Web site: www.ststephenpriory.org
Revs. Joseph Barranger, O.P., Prior; Stephen Fitzhenry, O.P., Subprior. Co-Directors of Retreat & Renewal: Revs. John E. Allard, O.P.; Joseph Barranger, O.P.; Stephen Fitzhenry, O.P.; Sr. Maureen Casey, S.N.D. Dominican Priests 10; Religious Brother 3; Total in Residence 13; Total Staff 17.

DUXBURY. *Miramar Retreat Center*, 121 Parks St., P.O. Box M, 02331-0614. Tel: 781-585-2460.
E-mail: miramarma@aol.com
Rev. Robert M. Jones, Rector. Total in Residence 7; Total Staff 16.

FRAMINGHAM. *The Marist House*, 518 Pleasant St., 01701. Tel: 508-879-1620; Fax: 508-879-1132. Revs. Raymond J. Arsenault, S.M.; James G. Strasz, S.M., Retreat Dir.& Supr.; Robert E. Champagne, S.M.; Dolor Ginchereau, S.M.; Henry Rancourt, S.M.; Raymond Boulanger, S.M.; Robert Graham, S.M.; Emile Guilmette, S.M.; Frank Reitter, S.M.; Leo Lapointe, S.M.; Bros. Ernie Morasci, S.M.; Camille Rossignol, S.M. Total in Residence 13; Total Staff 4.

GLOUCESTER. *Eastern Point Retreat House*, Gonzaga Hall, 37 Niles Pond Rd., 01930. Tel: 978-283-0013; Fax: 978-282-1989.
E-mail: wgdev@aol.com
Revs. William G. Devine, S.J., Supr. & Dir.; Francis H. Belcher, S.J.; John J. Bresnahan, S.J.; John B. Kerdiejus, S.J.; Joseph B. McHugh, S.J.; Bro. William J. Spokesfield, S.J.; Sr. Mary Boretti, S.N.D. Priests 5; Brothers 1; Sisters 1; Total Staff 8.

HAVERHILL. *Don Orione Center*. Old Groveland Rd., P.O. Box 205, 01835. Tel: 508-373-0461. Rev. Gino Marchesani, F.D.P., Dir.

IPSWICH. *LaSalette Retreat House at Newman Hall*, 251 Topsfield Rd., 01938. Tel: 508-356-3151. Total in residence 1.

SCITUATE. *Foyer of Charity*, 74 Hollett St., 02066. Tel: 781-545-1080; Fax: 240-332-5826.
E-mail: info@foyerofcharity.com
Web site: www.foyerofcharity.com
Rev. Matthew Bradley, Dir. Total in Residence 1; Total Staff 6.

WALTHAM. *Espousal Retreat House and Conference Center*, 554 Lexington St., 02452. Tel: 781-209-3101; Fax: 781-209-0291. Stigmatine Fathers and Brothers. Weekend and Weekly Retreats, Days-Evenings of Recollection. Rev. Robert Masciocchi, C.S.S., Dir. Total in Residence 2; Total Staff 8.

WESTON. *Campion Renewal Center*, 319 Concord Rd., 02493-1398. Tel: 781-788-6810; Fax: 781-894-5864.
E-mail: campionrenewal@yahoo.com
Revs. John W. Michalowski, S.J., Dir.; Robert G. Doherty, S.J.; Joseph F. Brennan, S.J., Staff; Lawrence E. Corcoran, S.J., Staff; James P. Walsh, S.J., Staff. Total in Residence 5; Total Staff 9.

[Z] RETIREMENT RESIDENCES FOR PRIESTS AND BROTHERS

BOSTON. *Regina Cleri, Inc.*, 60 William Cardinal O'Connell Way, 02114. Tel: 617-523-1861; Fax: 617-720-0585.
E-mail: jtierney@reginacleri.org
Rev. Msgr. James E. Tierney, Dir. Residence for Retired Archdiocesan Priests. Priests 50; Sisters 2.

Saint Anthony Residence, 103 Arch St., 02110-1102. Tel: 617-542-6454; 6455; Fax: 617-542-6659. (For Retired Franciscan Friars). Bros. Albert Aldrich, O.F.M., Guardian; Frank Waywood, O.F.M., Vicar; Stephen O'Neil, O.F.M.; Revs. Cormac Dungan, O.F.M.; David J. Fleming, O.F.M.; Remy A. Goudreau, O.F.M.; Cornelius F. Kelly, O.F.M.; Robert B. Lynch, O.F.M.; Martin L. McCormack, O.F.M.; Kenan Morris, O.F.M.; Gordon A. Murphy, O.F.M.; Stephen M. Walsh, O.F.M. Total in Residence 13.

LAWRENCE. *Marist Brothers*, 26 Leeds Ter., 01843. Tel: 978-686-7411; Fax: 978-686-6506. Bros. Kenneth Hogan, F.M.S.; Joseph DiBenedetto, F.M.S.; Richard La Rose, F.M.S.; Jerry Dowsky, F.M.S. Brothers 4.

TEWKSBURY. *Immaculate Heart of Mary Infirmary*, 486 Chandler St., P.O. Box 419, 01876. Tel: 978-851-7258; Fax: 978-851-3558.
E-mail: macomi@aol.com
Revs. John M McHugh, O.M.I., Supr.; F. William Denzel, O.M.I.; Robert F. Kilroy, O.M.I.; Francis P. McCartin, O.M.I.; Joseph O. Stack, O.M.I.; Gerald McCormack, O.M.I.; Raymond Steen, O.M.I.; Joseph A. Ryan, O.M.I.; Patrick F. Healy, O.M.I.; Francis Campbell, O.M.I.; Joseph Murphy, O.M.I.; Donald O'Brien, O.M.I.; Gerald Flater, O.M.I.; Laurence Deery, O.M.I.; Gerald Forkin, O.M.I.; Brendan Hunt, O.M.I.; John J. Savage, O.M.I.; Leo Wetzel, O.M.I.; John Wholey, O.M.I.; Arthur J. King, O.M.I.; Robert Paradis; John Lyons; James Sullivan; Bros. Earl Wetzel, O.M.I.; Patrick O'Neil; Michael F. Holly, O.M.I.; Richard Schaltz, O.M.I. Priests 23; Brothers 4.

WALTHAM. *Stigmatine Fathers and Brothers*, St. Joseph's Hall, 554 Lexington St., 02154. Tel: 781-209-3100; 0006. Revs. Richard Ahern, C.S.S. Tel: 781-209-3100; James Cunningham, C.S.S.; Rocco Leotilo, C.S.S.; Paul Merrill, C.S.S.; John Ford, C.S.S.; Charles Egan, C.S.S.; Henry Linse, C.S.S.; Carlo Bevilacqua, C.S.S.; Vito Cannizzo, C.S.S.; Charles Grady, C.S.S.; Anthony Parcheski, C.S.S.; Dominic Ruscetta, C.S.S.; Joseph Welch, C.S.S.; Samuel Fayad, C.S.S.; Joseph Fellin, C.S.S.; Bro. John E. Fowler, C.S.S. Priests 18; Brothers 1.

[AA] RESIDENCES FOR MEN AND WOMEN

BOSTON. *Our Lady of the Way Residence*. Tel: 617-524-1640; Fax: 617-524-1640. 60-80 Pond St., Jamaica Plain, 02130. Tel: 617-524-1640. Oblate Sisters of the Most Holy Redeemer. Residence for young women. (students, workers, travelers). Sisters 3.

Our Lady's Guild House - Residence for Women, 20 Charlesgate W., 02215. Tel: 617-536-3000; Fax: 617-536-8508. Andrea Beall, Admin. Daughters of Mary of the Immaculate Conception 3; Residents 126.

St. Helena House, 89 Union Park St., 02118. Tel: 617-426-2922; Fax: 617-542-3460. Seniors, low income & disabled persons. Lucille Becker, Property Mgr. Residents 89.

[BB] PUBLIC ORATORIES AND CHAPELS

BOSTON. *Chapel of Our Lady of Lourdes*, 698 Beacon St., 02215. Tel: 617-536-2761. Marist Fathers. Marist Fathers Residence. Tel: 617-262-2271. Revs. Gerard Caron, S.M., Dir.; Michael Pavlick, S.M.; Julian Rondeau, S.M.; Marcel Lajoie, S.M. Priests 4.

Chapel of the Holy Spirit, Paulist Center, 5 Park St., 02108. Tel: 617-742-4460; Fax: 617-720-5756.
E-mail: fiveparkst.@aol.com
Paulist Fathers. Revs. John B. Ardis, C.S.P., Dir.; Richard J. Colgan, C.S.P.; Charles A. Martin, C.S.P.; Patricia Simpson, Admin.; Wayne Lautenslager, Admin. Asst.; Donna Stiglmeier; Drew Deskur, Dir. Music.

Immaculate Conception Church, 775 Harrison Ave., 02118. Tel: 617-536-8440; Fax: 617-536-2142.
E-mail: jucboston@aol.com
(Jesuit Urban Center). Revs. Thomas J. Carroll, S.J.; Thomas J. Gallagher, S.J.; Richard D. Stanley; Mark S. Brown, Pastoral Assoc.; Christa Rakich, Music Ministry; Sr. Jeannette T. Normandin, S.S.A., Pastoral Assoc.

Madonna Queen Shrine. Tel: 617-569-2100; Fax: 617-569-8701.
E-mail: mqnsusa@aol.com
111 Orient Ave., East Boston, 02128. Tel: 617-569-82100; Fax: 617-569-8701.
E-mail: mqnsusa@aol.com
Don Orione Fathers. Rev. John Kilmartin, F.D.P., Rector.

St. Anthony Shrine, 100 Arch St., P.O. Box 2278, 02107-2278. Tel: 617-542-6440; Fax: 617-542-4225.
E-mail: info@StAnthonyShrine.org
Web site: www.StAnthonyShrine.org
Revs. John R. Ullrich, O.F.M., Rector; Donan McGovern, O.F.M., Vice Rector; Stephen Doyle, O.F.M.; Aidan Duffy, O.F.M.; Fergus Healey, O.F.M.; Wilfrid Hept, O.F.M.; Hugh Hines, O.F.M.; Michael Joyce, O.F.M.; John P. Hogan, O.F.M.; Philip Lavere, O.F.M.; Brice Leavins, O.F.M.; Raymond Mann, O.F.M.; John J. Marino, O.F.M.; Gerald T. McCaffrey, O.F.M.; Myron McCormick, O.F.M.; Emeric Meier, O.F.M.; Carmel Miotke, O.F.M.; Gerald R.

Mudd, O.F.M.; Samuel O'Connor, O.F.M.; Colin O'Rourke, O.F.M.; Cyril Seaman, O.F.M.; Brian E. Smail, O.F.M.; Dac Tat Tran, O.F.M.; John R. Ullrich, O.F.M., Guardian/Rector; Bros. Francis Baggan, O.F.M.; Dominic Finneran, O.F.M.; Justus Frazier, O.F.M.; Edward Higgins, O.F.M.; John Jaskowiak, O.F.M.; John Maganzini, O.F.M.; John Mahon, O.F.M.; Thomas McGowan, O.F.M.; Mark J. Murphy, O.F.M.; Frederick Musser, O.F.M. Priests 24; Brothers 10.

St. Clement's Archdiocesan Eucharistic Shrine, 1105 Boylston St., 02215. Tel: 617-266-5999; Fax: 617-247-7576.
E-mail: petergrover@juno.com
Web site: www.oblatesofthevirginmary.org
St. Ignatius Province of the Oblates of the Virgin Mary. Revs. Peter Grover, O.M.V., Dir. of Shrine; David N. Beauregard, O.M.V. Priests 2.

St. Francis Chapel, Prudential Center Plaza, 800 Boylston St., #21, 02199. Tel: 617-437-7117; Fax: 617-437-8420.
Web site: www.oblatesofthevirginmary.org
St. Ignatius Province of the Oblates of the Virgin Mary. Revs. James Nibler, O.M.V., Dir.; Thomas Carzon, O.M.V.; Robert Lowrey, O.M.V.; William Mullen, O.M.V.; Bro. Joseph O'Connor, O.M.V. Priests 4; Brothers 1.

St. Stephen, 24 Clark St., 02109. Tel: 617-523-1230; Fax: 617-723-7389.
E-mail: socjames@gte.net
Revs. Kevin Hays, Asst. Dir.; Milton Eggerling; Hugh Joseph Shields (PH).

St. Thomas More Chapel, 49 Franklin St., 02110. Tel: 617-542-1776. Rev. Msgr. Andrew F. Connell.

BROCKTON. *Chapel of Our Saviour*, 475 Westgate Dr., 02301-1819. Tel: 508-583-8357; Fax: 508-586-5510. Bro. DePorres Poncia, S.A., Dir.; Revs. Malcolm Martin, S.A.; Boniface Riedmann, S.A.; Joseph Di Mauro, S.A.; Bros. Savio McNiece, S.A.; Louis Marek, S.A. Priests 3; Brothers 3.

EAST BOSTON. *Our Lady of the Airways Chapel*, First Floor, Tower Bldg., Logan International Airport, 02128. Tel: 617-567-2800; Fax: 617-569-6950.
E-mail: fatherrichard@assport.com
Rev. Richard A. Uftring.

HOLLISTON. *Our Lady of Fatima Shrine*, 101 Summer St., P.O. Box 5857, 01746-5857. Tel: 508-429-2144. Xaverian Missionaries. Rev. Tony Lalli, S.X., Dir.

IPSWICH. *National Shrine of Our Lady of La Salette*, 251 Topsfield Rd., 01938-1195. Tel: 508-356-3151. Rev. John R. Dolan, M.S., Dir. Total in Residence 1.

LOWELL. *St. Joseph the Worker Shrine*, 37 Lee St., 01853-1276. Tel: 978-458-6346; 459-9522 & 800-287-9522 (Gift Shop); Fax: 978-441-0963; 323-0763 (Gift Shop).
E-mail: stjosephshrine@netzero.net
Web site: www.stjosephshrine.org

St. Joseph the Worker Residence, 29 Kirk St., 01852-1103. Tel: 978-454-6004; Fax: 978-454-8836.

Oblate Justice & Peace Office, 37 Lee St., 01852. Tel: 978-454-9769; Fax: 978-454-8836. Revs. John Cox, O.M.I., Dir.; Charles Beausoleil, O.M.I.; George Croft, O.M.I.; Albert P. Martineau, O.M.I.

PEABODY. *St. Theresa Carmelite Chapel*, North Shore Mall, 01960. Tel: 978-531-6145; Fax: 978-531-1359. Revs. Herbert J. Jones, O.Carm., Prior & Dir.; Kilian Healy, O.Carm.; Alan N. Crowley, O.Carm.; Peter Thomas Sherry, O.Carm.; Mario Lopez, O.Carm.; Bro. Damien Chong, O.Carm. Priests 5; Brothers 1.

SOUTH BOSTON. *Our Lady of Good Voyage Chapel*, 65 Northern Ave., 02110. Tel: 617-268-8100; Fax: 617-268-1277.
E-mail: REC7339@aol.com
Revs. Richard E. Cannon, Admin.; Philip La Plante, S.M., Chap. to Seaport, St. Vincent de Paul Rectory, 363 E St., South Boston, 02127. Tel: 617-268-8100; Fax: 617-268-1277.

[CC] CAMPUS MINISTRY

BOSTON. *The Catholic Center at Boston University*, 211 Bay State Rd., 02215. Tel: 617-353-3632; Fax: 617-353-7331.
E-mail: catholic@bu.edu
Web site: www.bu.edu/CATHOLIC
Rev. Paul D. Helfrich, C.S.P.; Dr. Jane M. LaMarche, D.Min.

Emmanuel College Campus Ministry, 400 The Fenway, 02115. Tel: 617-735-9777. Sr. Patricia McSharry, S.N.D.

St. Ann's University Parish. Catholic Student Center, 68 St. Stephen St., 02115. Tel: 617-266-2635; Fax: 617-266-9015.
E-mail: stann@lynx.neu.edu
Web site: www.dac.neu.edu/st.ann
(Serving Northeastern University and neighbouring Colleges). Rev. Paul E. Kilroy, Pastor & Campus Min., Northeastern Univ. Pastoral Assocs. - Campus Ministers: Sr. Rosemary Mulvihill, R.S.M., Northeastern Univ.; Sr. Mary Walsh, S.U.; Ann Pencik, Emerson College.

University of Massachusetts at Boston Campus Ministry, 02125-3393. Tel: 617-287-5839.
E-mail: sungae.kim@umb.edu
Harbor Campus, Dorchester, 02125. Tel: 617-287-5839. Rev. Richard F. Chancy; Sr. Sungae Kim, R.S.C.J.

BRIDGEWATER. *Bridgewater State College Catholic Center*, 122 Park Ave., 02324. Tel: 508-697-1346; Fax: 508-279-6188. Campus Ministers: Rev. John F. Denning, C.S.C.; Sr. Mary Ellen Dow, S.N.D.

CAMBRIDGE. *Harvard Catholic Student Center*, 20 Arrow St., 02138. Tel: 617-868-6585; Fax: 617-354-7092.
E-mail: dsheehan@fas.harvard.edu
Web site: www.hcs.harvard.edu/~csa
Rev. Msgr. Dennis F. Sheehan, Senior Chap. Chaplains: Revs. Thomas E. Brennan, S.D.B.; George S. Salzmann, O.S.F.S.; Jacqueline L. Landry; Joan Travers, Admin.

Massachusetts Institute of Technology Catholic Community, 40 Massachusetts Ave., W-11, 02139. Tel: 617-253-2981; Fax: 617-253-3260.
E-mail: catholic@mit.edu
Web site: www.web.mit.edu/tcc/
Rev. Paul A. Reynolds, C.S.P.; Cyndi Ross. Total Staff 2.

FRAMINGHAM. *Framingham State College Campus Ministry*, 100 State St., 01701. Tel: 508-626-4610.
E-mail: vpoirier@wellesley.edu
Rev. Vincent H. Poirier.

LOWELL. *The Catholic Center U Mass, Lowell*, 52 Colonial Ave., 01854. Tel: 978-454-0151.
E-mail: casey_murphy@uml.edu
Web site: www.uml.edu/student-services/ministry/catholic/
Rev. Paul R. Soper; Ms. Casey E. Murphy. Total in Residence 7; Total Staff 3.

MEDFORD. *Tufts University Catholic Center*, 58 Winthrop St., 02155. Tel: 781-391-7272; Fax: 781-396-8779.
E-mail: dolear01@tufts.edu
Rev. David M. O'Leary, S.T.L., Ph.D. Total Staff 2; Total Assisted 1,500.

NEWTON. *Boston College Campus Ministry*. Tel: 617-552-3475; Fax: 617-552-3044.
E-mail: ministry@bc.edu
Web site: www.bc.edu/campus-ministry
McElroy 215, Chestnut Hill, 02167. Tel: 617-552-3475; Fax: 617-552-3044. Rev. James Erps, S.J., Dir. Total in Residence 3; Total Staff 11.

NORTH ANDOVER. *Merrimack College Campus Ministry Center*, 303 Gildea Hall, 01845. Tel: 508-837-5450.
E-mail: jfarrell@merrimack.edu
Ms. Dori White Pulizzi. Campus Ministers: Revs. Joseph L. Farrell, O.S.A., Dir.; James Wenzel, O.S.A.; Joseph Gillin, O.S.A.

SALEM. *Salem State College, Catholic Campus Ministry*, 352 Lafayette St., 01970. Tel: 978-542-6074; Fax: 978-744-0581.
E-mail: muriel.lemoine@salem.mass.edu
Sr. Muriel Lemoine, S.A.S.V.

WALTHAM. *Bentley College Spiritual Life Center*, 175 Forest St., 02452-4705. Tel: 781-891-2194; Fax: 781-891-2788.
E-mail: cgrenache@Bentley.edu
Web site: www.bentley.edu
Rev. Claude Grenache, A.A., Dir. Spiritual Life Center.

Brandeis University Campus Ministry, M.S. U5, P.O. Box 549110, 02454-9110. Tel: 781-736-3574; Fax: 781-736-3577.
E-mail: dmichael@brandeis.edu
Rev. David C. Michael.

WELLESLEY. *Babson College Campus Ministry*, 9 Glen Rd., 02181. Tel: 617-235-1200. Sr. Frances Sheehey, O.S.F., Campus Coord.

Wellesley College Campus Ministry, 02181. Tel: 781-283-2688.
E-mail: vpoirier@wellesley.edu
Rev. Vincent H. Poirier.

WESTON. *Regis College Office of Campus Ministry*, 235 Wellesley St., 02493. Tel: 781-768-7027; 7028; 7029; Fax: 781-768-8339.
E-mail: ministry@regiscollege.edu
Mildred Crowley, S.C., Dir.; Joan Collupy, Campus Min.

[DD] FOUNDATIONS, FUNDS & TRUSTS

BOSTON. *The Archdiocese of Boston Self-Insurance Group, Inc.* Tel: 617-746-5740; Fax: 617-746-5421.
E-mail: Art-Powers@rcab.org
2121 Commonwealth Ave., Brighton, 02135. Mr. Arthur W. Powers, Admin.; Mr. Paul Goodrich, Counsel. Board of Directors: Rev. Philip B. Earley, Clerk; Mr. Gerald T. Reilly, Pres.; Mr. David Smith, Treas.; Mr. Steven Fischer; Mr. Paul Sweeney; Mr. Robert Cantwell; Ms. Nancy Drago.

Chancery Office. 2121 Commonwealth Ave., Brighton, 02135. Tel: 617-254-0100; Fax: 617-783-4564.
Web site: www.rcab.org
Also see Miscellaneous Section for additional listings.

The Cardinal Medeiros Trust. Tel: 617-254-0100.

Cardinal Cushing General Hospital Foundation, Brockton.

The Carney Hospital Foundation, Inc. (Formerly The New Caritas Christi Hospital, Inc.), 2100 Dorchester Ave., 02124. Tel: 617-296-1788. J. Barry Driscoll, Pres.; Paul J. Kingston, Vice Pres.; Daniel J. McDevitt, Sec.; William F. Henderson, Exec. Dir.

Catholic Schools Foundation, Inc. (Formerly St. Anthony's Scholarship Fund, Inc.). Tel: 617-254-0100; Fax: 617-783-6366.

Clergy Benefit Trust. Tel: 617-254-0100; Fax: 617-783-2947. Most Rev. William F. Murphy, Sec.

Clergy Fund Society. Tel: 617-254-0100; Fax: 617-783-2947.

Clergy Medical-Hospitalization Trust. Tel: 617-254-0100; Fax: 617-783-2947.

Archdiocese of Boston Clergy Retirement/Disability Trust. Tel: 617-254-0100; Fax: 617-783-2947.

Family Counseling Endowment Fund, Inc., 141 Tremont St., 02111. Tel: 617-482-4355.

Marist Capital Trust Fund. c/o Financial Admin., The Missionary Sisters of the Society of Mary, Inc., 349 Grove St., Waltham, 02154. Tel: 617-893-0149. Sr. Virginia Fornasa, S.M.S.M., Trustee; John E. McCormack.

Metropolitan Boston Dialysis Center, Inc., 736 Cambridge St., Brighton, 02135.

Mission Promotion. Missionary Sisters of the Society of Mary. c/o Mission Promoter, 13 Pelham Rd., Lexington, 02173. Tel: 617-861-6116.

Roman Catholic Archdiocese of Boston Health Benefit Trust. Tel: 617-746-5680; Fax: 617-783-4564. Mr. David W. Smith, Admin.

Roman Catholic Archdiocese of Boston Insurance Trust. Benefit Office. Tel: 617-746-5640; Fax: 617-783-4564. Mr. David W. Smith, Admin.

Roman Catholic Archdiocese of Boston Pension Trust. Benefit Office. Tel: 617-746-5640; Fax: 617-746-4564. Mr. David W. Smith, Admin.

Roman Catholic Archdiocese of Boston Long Term Disability Trust. Tel: 617-746-5640; Fax: 617-783-4564. Mr. David W. Smith, Admin.

Roman Catholic Archdiocese of Boston Common Investment Fund. Tel: 617-746-5680; Fax: 617-783-4564.

Roman Catholic Archdiocese of Boston Fixed Income Investment Fund. Tel: 617-746-5680; Fax: 617-783-4564.

St. Charles Borromeo Educational Foundation, Inc.

Sacred Heart Trust Fund, c/o Society of Jesus, Trustee, 761 Harrison Ave., 02118. Tel: 617-536-5604. Bro. H. Francis Cluff, S.J.

St. Elizabeth's Hospital Foundation, Inc., 159 Washington St., Brighton, 02135.

Holy Family Hospital Foundation, Inc.

Catholic Foundation of the Archdiocese of Boston, 2121 Commonwealth Ave., Brighton, 02135. Tel: 617-746-5621; Fax: 617-783-2947. Mr. James Mooney, Jr., Pres.

The Xaverian Brothers Northeastern Community Support Charitable Trust Fund, 704 Brush Hill Rd., Milton, 02186.

Benefit Trust for Non-Incardinated Priests. Tel: 617-254-0100; Fax: 617-783-2947. Legal Title: *Benefit Trust for Non-Incardinated Priest Duly Assigned for Service in the Archdiocese of Boston*.

Clergy Assistance Trust. Tel: 617-746-5656; Fax: 617-783-4564. 2121Commonwealth Ave., Brighton, 02135.

FRAMINGHAM. *Senior Religious Trust Fund of Marist Fathers of Boston*, 518 Pleasant St., 01701-2898. Tel: 508-879-7223; Fax: 508-879-0719.

HANOVER. *St. Coletta's of Massachusetts, Inc.*, 405 Washington St., 02339. Tel: 617-826-6371.
Web site: www.coletta.org
Mr. Paul J. Hudson, Pres. & CEO.

IPSWICH. *Blin Charitable Trust*, 30 Jeffrey's Neck Rd., 01938. Tel: 978-356-4381; Fax: 978-356-9759.
E-mail: PRVNOFF@aol.com
Sisters of Notre Dame de Namur.

LOWELL. *Saints Memorial Medical Center Foundation*, P.O. Box 367, 01853-0367. Tel: 9784-8334; Fax: 9784-8479.
E-mail: fund.kec@tmmc.org
Web site: www.saints-memorial.org
Thom Clark, Pres. & CEO; Kevin E. Coughlin, Vice Pres.; D. Harold Sullivan, Chm.

METHUEN. *Holy Family Hospital Foundation, Inc.*, 70 East St., 01844-4597. Tel: 978-687-0151; Fax: 978-688-7689.
E-mail: nmallen@cchcs.org
Web site: www.holyfamilyhosp.org
Mrs. Noreen V. Mallen, Exec. Dir.

NEEDHAM. *St. Joseph Parish School Fund, Inc., Needham*, 1382 Highland Ave., 02492. Tel: 781-444-0245; Fax: 781-444-7713. Mr. James S. DiStasio, Treas.

TEWKSBURY. *The Society of Oblate Fathers Continuing Support Fund*, c/o the Society of Oblate Fathers for Missions Among the Poor, 486 Chandler St., 01876; Fax: 508-858-3661. Rev. William Sheehan, O.M.I., Prov.

The Society of Oblate Fathers for Missions Among the Poor Formation Charitable Trust, 486 Chandler St., P.O. Box 419, 01876; Fax: 508-858-3661. Rev. William Sheehan, O.M.I., Prov. Total in Residence 27; Total Staff 22.

[EE] LIFE RESOURCES

BRAINTREE.

Pilgrim Center for Boys, 140 Adams St., P.O. Box 850907, 02185-0907. Tel: 617-848-5510. Total Staff 25; Students 24.

[FF] MISCELLANEOUS

BOSTON. *The Cambridge Center for the Study of Faith and Culture*, 2121 Commonwealth Ave, 02135. Tel: 617-782-2544; Fax: 617-782-5358. Sr. Madonna Murphy, C.S.C., Pres.

Caritas Christi - A Catholic Health Care System. Tel: 617-789-2500; Fax: 617-789-2124. 736 Cambridge St., Brighton, 02135. Tel: 617-789-2500; Fax: 617-789-2124. Michael F. Collins, M.D., Pres. & CEO.

Caritas Christi Support Services, Inc. Tel: 617-789-3187; Fax: 617-789-2124.

Caritas Christi Diagnostic Support Services, Inc. Tel: 617-789-2500; Fax: 617-789-2124.

St. Elizabeth's Realty Corporation. Tel: 617-789-2500; Fax: 617-789-2124.

Good Samaritan Hospice. Tel: 617-566-6242; Fax: 617-566-3055.

The Catholic Lawyers Guild of the Archdiocese of Boston, Inc., One Union St., 02108. Tel: 617-523-2640; Fax: 617-720-4363. Hon. Joseph R. Nolan, Pres.

Catholic Purchasing Services, Inc. Tel: 617-965-4343; Fax: 617-965-5430.
E-mail: RJW@catholicpurchasing.org
Web site: catholicpurchasing.org
580 Washington St., Newton, 02458. Tel: 617-965-4343; Fax: 617-965-5430. Mr. Richard J. Wasilauskas, Pres.

Catholic Social Services, Inc., 49 Franklin St., 02110. Tel: 617-482-5440; Fax: 617-451-0337. Joseph Doolin, Ph.D., Pres. & CEO.

Equestrian Order of the Holy Sepulchre of Jerusalem. Tel: 781-235-6291; Fax: 781-235-6291.
E-mail: DennisJLooney@aol.com
Northeastern Lieutenancy, 27 Southgate Rd., Wellesley, 02482. Tel: 781-235-6291; Fax: 781-235-6291. Dennis J Looney, Jr., KC HS Lt.; Jonathan A Noonan, KC HS Chancellor.

Lanteri Charitable Trust, 1105 Boylston St., 02215-3660. Tel: 617-536-4141; Fax: 617-536-7016. Rev. William M. Brown, O.M.V., Admin.

League of Catholic Women of the Archdiocese of Boston. 127 Lake St., Brighton, 02135. Tel: 617-254-2610; Fax: 617-787-2336. Mrs. Daniel Sullivan, Pres.; Rev. Martin P. Connor, Spiritual Dir.

Lourdes Bureau, 698 Beacon St., 02215. Tel: 617-536-2761. Marist Fathers. Official Representatives in America for the Shrine of Lourdes, France.

Medaille Corporation, 637 Cambridge St., 02135. Tel: 617-783-9090; Fax: 617-783-8246.
E-mail: boscsj@aol.com
Web site: www.boscsj.org
Sr. Joan Duffy, C.S.J., Pres.; Sr. Maureen Doherty, C.S.J., Treas.

MI Management, Inc. Covenant Health Systems. 172 Lawrence St., Lawrence, 01841. Tel: 978-685-6321; Fax: 978-975-0050. Management company for all Mary Immaculate Facilities. Barbara E. Grant, Pres. & CEO.

Ministry of Evangelization and Catechesis, 286 Shawmut Ave., 02118-1613. Tel: 617-542-1143.
E-mail: joannemhsh@aol.com
Legal Title: *Institute of Mission Helpers*. Mission Helpers of the Sacred Heart. Sr. Joanne Frey, M.H.S.H., Local Coord. & Contact Person. Total Staff 3.

Propagation of the Faith and Holy Childhood Association & Society of St. Peter the Apostle, 49 Franklin St., 02110. Tel: 617-542-1776; Fax: 617-542-1778. Rev. Msgr. Andrew F. Connell, K.J., K.H.S., Dir. Total Staff 12.

St. Francis Charities, 2121 Commonwealth Ave., 02135. 159 Washington St., Brighton, 02135. Tel: 617-783-3924; Fax: 617-787-7797. Ms. Carolyn C. Thompson, Dir. Total in Residence 10.

ARLINGTON. *Fidelity House*, 25 Medford St., 02474-3105. Tel: 781-648-2005; Fax: 781-648-4604.
E-mail: Fidelityhouse@rcn.com
Edward F. Woods, Dir.
Purpose: A community center sponsored by the Saint Agnes Parish providing quality services primarily for youth development with flexible and diverse services for people of all ages.

BRIGHTON. *Caritas Christi Retirement Plan and Trust*, 2121 Commonwealth Ave., 02135. Tel: 617-746-5680. David W. Smith, Plan Admin.
Governing Board: His Eminence Bernard Cardinal Law; Most Rev. William F. Murphy; Gerald T. Reilly; Rev. James DiPerri; Anna-Marie Ferraro; John Gianino; Rev. Msgr. Richard Little; Lawrence McManus; Michael Metzler; Wilson D. Rogers, Jr., Esqui; Joseph Schellings; Lynn Wiatrowski.

Corporation for the Sponsored Ministries of the Sisters of St. Joseph of Boston, 637 Cambridge St., 02135-2800. Tel: 617-746-2191.
E-mail: ckschz@aol.com
Charles A. Schuetz, Pres. & Exec. Dir.

CSJ Ministries Connection, Inc., 637 Cambridge St., 02135-2800. Tel: 617-746-2191.
E-mail: ckschz@aol.com
Charles A. Schuetz, Pres.

St. Vincent Pallotti Center for Apostolic Development of Boston, Inc., 159 Washington St., 02135. Tel: 617-783-3924; Fax: 617-787-7797.
E-mail: VolService@aol.com
Web site: www.pallotti.cua.edu

Women Affirming Life, Inc., P.O. Box 35532, 02135. Tel: 617-254-2277; Fax: 617-254-2299.
E-mail: mail@affirmlife.com
Web site: www.affirmlife.com
Marianne Luthin, Exec. Dir.

BRIGHTON/BOSTON. *National Catholic Bioethics Center*, 159 Washington St., 02135. Tel: 617-787-1900; Fax: 617-787-4900.
E-mail: postmaster@NCBCenter.org
Web site: http://www.NCBCenter.org
John M. Haas, Ph.D., S.T.L., Pres.; Rev. Albert S. Moraczewski, O.P., Ph.D., Pres. Emeritus, Distinguished Scholar in Residence; Bro. Ignatius Perkins, O.P., D.N.Sc, M.A.Ed., R.N., Exec. Vice Pres.; Susan P. Jordan, B.A., M.B.A., Vice Pres. for Inst. Rels.; Rev. Germain Kopaczynski, O.F.M.Conv., Ph.D., S.T.D., Dir. Education; Peter J. Cataldo, Ph.D., Dir. of Research; Edward J. Furton, M.A., Ph.D., Dir. Publications; J. Scott Abercrombie, Jr., M.D., Senior Fellow in Medicine & Hospital Admin.; Richard M. Doerflinger, M.A., Adjunct Fellow in Bioethics & Public Policy; Thomas E. Gannoe, Systems Dir.; Donald J. Powers, Chief Fin. Officer; Jeanne L. Burke, Admin. Asst. to Pres.

CAMBRIDGE. *Notre Dame Mission Volunteer Corporation*, 203 Erie St., 02134.
E-mail: ndamercrps@aol.com
Branch Office: 403 Markland Ave., Baltimore, MD, 21212. Tel: 410-532-6864; Fax: 410-532-2812.

The Youville House, Inc., 1575 Cambridge St., 02138-4398. Tel: 617-876-4344.
E-mail: leaheyd@youville.org
Web site: www.youville.org
Mr. T. Richard Quigley, Pres. & CEO; Ms. Marsha V. Whelan, Vice Pres. Mission Integration. Chaplains: Revs. William L. Mulligan, S.J.; Jennifer Casstevens; Ms. Patricia Kennedy, Dir. of Pastoral Care Services; Ms. Elizabeth Walsh.
Member of Youville Lifecare, Inc. Priests 1; Sisters of Charity (Grey Nuns) 3; Assisted Living Units 95.

Youville Lifecare, Inc., 1575 Cambridge St., 02138-4398. Tel: 617-876-4344; Fax: 617-547-5501. Mr. Daniel Leahey, Pres. & CEO.
Member of Covenant Health Systems, Lexington, MA.

DEDHAM. *St. Pauline Book and Media*, 885 Providence Hwy., Rte. 1, 02026. Tel: 781-326-5385; Fax: 781-461-1013.
E-mail: fspdedham@aol.com
Web site: www.pauline.org
Pious Society, Daughters of St. Paul (Missionary Sisters of the Media of Social Communication).

FRAMINGHAM. *Bethany Health Care Center, Inc*., 97 Bethany Rd., 01701. Tel: 508-872-6750; Fax: 508-875-5425.
E-mail: Jmmcc1@fiam.net
Web site: www.Bethanyhcc.org
Skilled Nursing Facility and Health Clinic. Congregation of Sisters of St. Joseph of Boston. Bed Capacity 169.

Bethany Hill School, Inc., 89 Bethany Rd., 01702. Tel: 508-875-1117; Fax: 508-875-2288.
E-mail: dakcsj@aol.com
41 units of educational housing for low-income people with a variety of needs. Sponsored by the Sisters of St. Joseph of Boston.

IPSWICH. *Cuvilly Arts and Earth Center, Inc*., 10 Jeffrey Neck Rd., 01938. Tel: 508-356-4288.
E-mail: cuvilly@shore.net
Sr. Mary Farren, S.N.D., Pres. Total Assisted 95; Total Staff 10.

JAMAICA PLAIN. *Most Holy Name of Jesus Federation of Poor Clare Monasteries in the Eastern Region of the United States*, Monastery of Saint Clare, 920 Centre St., 02130. Tel: 617-524-1760; Fax: 617-983-5205.
E-mail: clarefrancesosc@worldnet.att.net
Web site: www.stanthonyshrine.org/poorclares
Sr. Clare Frances McAvoy, O.S.C., Pres. Solemn Vows 124; Simple Professed 3.

LAWRENCE.

Greater Lawrence Health Center, Inc., 30 General St., 01841. Tel: 978-683-3128, Ext. 2304; Fax: 978-686-7856. Jeffrey Fox, Exec. Dir.

Notre Dame Education Center 1992. (Adult Literacy), 301 Haverhill St., P.O. Box 1012, 01842-9998. Tel: 978-682-6441; Fax: 978-974-8940.
E-mail: ndeclaw@aol.com
Sisters of Notre Dame de Namur. Sr. Maria Delaney, S.N.D., Exec. Dir. ESOL, GED, Diploma, External Diploma, Adult Basic Education, Job COunseling, Case Mangement, Citizenship. Sisters 8; Adults 500; Total Staff 14.

LEXINGTON. *Covenant Health Systems, Inc*., 420 Bedford St., 02173. Tel: 781-862-1634; Fax: 781-862-5477.
E-mail: chealths@aol.com
Web site: www.covenanths.org
David R. Lincoln, Pres. & CEO. Member organizations: Youville Lifecare, Cambridge, MA; St. Joseph Healthcare, Nashua, NH; Sisters of Charity Health System, Lewiston, ME; Marcotte Congregate Housing; St. Marguerite D'Youville Pavilion; St. Mary's Regional Medical Center, Lewiston, M.E.; Mary Immaculate Health/Care Services, Lawrence, MA; Maristhill Nursing Home, Waltham, MA; St. Joseph Manor Health Care, Brockton, MA; Fanny Allen Corp., Colchester, VT; St. Mary Health Care Center, Worcester, MA. Affiliate organizations: Sancta Maria Nursing Facility, Cambridge, MA; Mount Marie Health Care Center, Holyoke, MA; Bethany Health Care Center, Framingham, MA; Notre Dame Long Term Care Center, Worcester, MA; Matulaitis Nursing Home, Putnam, CT.

Youville Place, Inc., 10 Pelham Rd., Ste. 2000, 02421-8408. Tel: 781-861-3535; Fax: 781-862-4289.
E-mail: jscianna@erols.com
Sr. June Ketterer, S.G.M., Pres. Bd. Directors. Assisted Living Facility.

LOWELL. *Oblate Ministry Development Service*, 27 Kirk St., P.O. Box 1401, 01853-1401. Tel: 508-459-1637; Fax: 508-459-4146. Rev. Charles Breault, O.M.I. Legal Title: *Oblate Ministry Development Service*.

Pro Maria Committee, 22 Second Ave., 01854-2808. Tel: 978-453-5281.
E-mail: promaria@aol.com
Miss Doris M. Poisson, Sec.

Saints Memorial Special Service, Inc., Saints Memoiral Medical Center, One Hospital Dr., 01852. Tel: 978-458-1411.
E-mail: fs.soc@stmmc.org
Web site: www.saints_memorial.org
Mr. Stephen O'Connor, Vice Pres. Finance.

MALDEN. *Xaverian Brothers Province Development Office*. (Corporate Title: American Northeastern Province of Xaverian Brothers, Inc. and Working Boy's Home), 99 Crystal St., 02148-5994. Tel: 617-324-8099. Bro. Edward Rice, C.F.X.

METHUEN. *Holy Family Hospital Men's Guild*, 70 East St., 01844-4597. Tel: 978-687-0151, Ext. 2362; Fax: 978-688-7689.
Web site: www.holyfamilyhosp.org

Valley Regional Health System, Inc., 70 East St., 01844-4597. Tel: 978-687-0151; Fax: 978-688-7689.

Holy Family Hospital, Inc. Tel: 978-687-0151; Fax: 978-688-7689.

Holy Family Hospital Auxiliary. Tel: 978-687-0151; Fax: 978-688-7689.

Valley Regional Support Services, Inc. Tel: 978-687-0151; Fax: 978-688-7689.

Holy Family Men's Guild. Tel: 978-687-0151; Fax: 978-688-7689.

NEWTON. *Focolare Movement*, Women's Branch, 189 Jackson Rd., 02458-1427. Tel: 617-965-4879; Fax: 617-965-4879.
E-mail: mcferreira@worldnet.att.net
Web site: www.rc.net/focolare
Total in Residence 5.

KOLBE Association, Inc., 251 Watertown St., 02495-5135. Rev. Michael B. Medas, M.S.W., Contact Person.

QUINCY. *The Good Shepherd: Maria Droste Services*, 1354 Hancock St., Ste. 209, 02169. Tel: 617-471-5686; Fax: 617-471-6622. Legal Title: *Madonna Hall*. Sr. Joanne Westwater, Exec. Dir. Total Staff 6; Volunteers 26; Total Assisted 560.

WALTHAM. *The Gathering Place*, 3 Common St., Ste. 3B, 02451-4401. Tel: 781-647-0012; Fax: 781-647-0055.
E-mail: gather1997@aol.com
Web site: www.hometown.aol.com/gather1997

Marist Missionary Sisters Senior Religious Trust, 349 Grove St., 02453. Tel: 781-893-0149; Fax: 781-899-6838.
E-mail: maristsmsm@aol.com

WORCESTER. *Notre Dame Development Fund, INC.*, 71 Elm St., 01609. Tel: 508-757-5711; Fax: 508-798-9150.
E-mail: SNDNEdev@aol.com
Sr. Therese Julie Fitzmaurice, S.N.D., Pres.; Mrs. Jan Attridge, Dir. Devel.

RELIGIOUS INSTITUTES OF MEN REPRESENTED IN THE ARCHDIOCESE

For further details refer to the corresponding bracketed number in the Religious Institutes of Men or Women section.

[0130]—*Assumptionists*.—A.A.
[1040]—*The Augustinians*. (Villanova, PA).—O.S.A.
[0200]—*Benedictine Monks*.—O.S.B.
[1350]—*Brothers of St. Francis Xavier*.—C.F.X.
[0330]—*Brothers of the Christian Schools*. (Long Island, New England Provs.).—F.S.C.
[0470]—*The Capuchin Friars*. (Prov. of Mary). —O.F.M.Cap.
[0270]—*Carmelite Fathers & Brothers*. (Prov. of Most Pure Heart of Mary).—O.Carm.
[0310]—*Congregation of Christian Brothers*. (Eastern Prov.).—C.F.C.
[1210]—*Congregation of the Missionaries of St. Charles*.—C.S.
[1000]—*Congregation of the Passion*. (St. Paul of the Cross Prov.).—C.P.
[1140]—*Congregation of the Sacred Hearts of Jesus and Mary*.—SS.CC.
[0480]—*Conventual Franciscans*. (Buffalo, NY).—O.F.M.Conv.
[0260]—*Discalced Carmelite Friars*.—O.C.D.
[0520]—*Franciscan Friars*. (Assumption of B.V.M., Holy Name, Immaculate Conception Provs.).—O.F.M.
[0530]—*Franciscan Friars of the Atonement*.—S.A.
[0670]—*Hospitaller Brothers of St. John of God*.—O.H.
[0690]—*Jesuit Fathers and Brother*. (New England Prov.).—S.J.
[0770]—*The Marist Brothers*. (Poughkeepsie, NJ).—F.M.S.
[0780]—*Marist Fathers*. (Boston Prov.).—S.M.
[0800]—*Maryknoll*.—M.M.
[]—*Mekhitarist Fathers*.—C.M.Vd.
[0720]—*The Missionaries of Our Lady of La Salette*. (Eastern Prov.).—M.S.
[0910]—*Oblates of Mary Immaculate*. (Eastern, St. John the Baptist Provs.).—O.M.I.
[0430]—*Order of Preachers-Dominicans*. (Prov. of St. Joseph).—O.P.
[1030]—*Paulist Fathers*.—C.S.P.
[0610]—*Priests of the Congregation of Holy Cross*. (Eastern Prov.).—C.S.C.
[1070]—*Redemptorist Fathers*. (Baltimore Prov.).—C.SS.R.
[1190]—*Salesians of Don Bosco*. (Prov. of St. Philip).—S.D.B.
[0110]—*Society of African Missions*.—S.M.A.
[0420]—*Society of Divine Word*. (Sacred Heart Prov.).—S.V.D.
[0850]—*Society of Missionaries of Africa*.—M.Afr.
[0370]—*Society of St. Columban*. (American Region).—S.S.C.
[0410]—*Sons of Divine Providence*.—F.D.P.
[1270]—*Sons of Mary Missionary Society*.—F.M.S.I.
[1280]—*Stigmatine Fathers and Brothers*. (Rome, Italy).—C.S.S.
[1360]—*Xaverian Missionary Fathers*.—S.X.

RELIGIOUS INSTITUTES OF WOMEN REPRESENTED IN THE ARCHDIOCESE

[1810]—*Bernardine Franciscan Sisters*.—O.S.F.
[0330]—*Carmelite Sisters for the Aged and Infirm*.—O.Carm.
[0670]—*Cistercian Nuns of the Strict Observance*.—O.C.S.O.
[0270]—*Congregation of Bon Secours*.—C.B.S.
[3110]—*Congregation of Our lady of the Retreat in the Cenacle*.—R.C.
[]—*Congregation of the Armenian Catholic Sisters of the Immaculate Conception, Inc.*
[1920]—*Congregation of the Sisters of the Holy Cross*.—C.S.C.
[0760]—*Daughters of Charity of St. Vincent de Paul*.—D.C.
[0860]—*Daughters of Mary of the Immaculate Conception*.—C.M.
[0420]—*Discalced Carmelite Nuns*.—O.C.D.
[1070-01]—*Dominican Sisters*.—O.P.
[1070-03]—*Dominican Sisters*.—O.P.
[1070-13]—*Dominican Sisters*.—O.P.
[1170]—*Felician Sisters*.—C.S.S.F.
[1370]—*Franciscan Missionaries of Mary*.—F.M.M.
[1320]—*Franciscan Missionary Sisters for Africa*. (Co. Louth, Ireland).—O.S.F.
[1180]—*Franciscan Sisters of Allegany, New York*.—O.S.F.
[1470]—*Franciscan Sisters of St. Joseph*.—F.S.S.J.
[1840]—*Grey Nuns of the Sacred Heart*.—G.N.S.H.
[]—*Holy Union Sisters*.—S.U.S.C.
[0410]—*Institute of the Sisters of Our Lady of Mt. Carmel*.—O.Carm.
[2290]—*Little Missionary Sisters of Charity*.—L.M.S.C.
[2310]—*Little Sisters of the Assumption*.—L.S.A.
[2320]—*Little Sisters of the Holy Family*.—P.S.S.F.
[2340]—*Little Sisters of the Poor*.—L.S.P.
[2420]—*Marist Missionary Sisters-Missionary Sisters of the Society of Mary*.—S.M.S.M.
[2470]—*Maryknoll Sisters of St. Dominic*.—M.M.
[2480]—*Medical Missionaries of Mary*.—M.M.M.
[1360]—*Missionary Franciscan Sisters of the Immaculate Conception*.—O.S.F.
[2790]—*Missionary Servants of the Most Blessed Trinity*.—M.S.B.T.
[2880]—*Missionary Sisters of St. Columban*.—S.S.C.
[2800]—*Missionary Sisters of the Most Sacred Heart of Jesus of Hiltrup*.—M.S.C.
[3030]—*Oblates of the Most Holy Redeemer*.—O.SS.R.
[3760]—*Order of St. Clare*.—O.S.C.
[0950]—*Pious Society Daughters of St. Paul*.—D.S.P.
[3240]—*Poor Sisters of Jesus Crucified and the Sorrowful Mother*.—C.J.C.
[3410]—*Religious of Christian Education*.—R.C.E.
[2070]—*Religious of the Holy Union of the Sacred Hearts*.—S.U.S.C.
[2970]—*School Sisters of Notre Dame*.—S.S.N.D.
[3550]—*Servants of the Immaculate Heart of Mary*.—S.C.I.M.
[0980]—*Sisters Disciples of the Divine Master*.—P.D.D.M.
[0490]—*Sisters of Charity of Montreal-Grey Nuns*.—S.G.M.
[0500]—*Sisters of Charity of Nazareth*.—S.C.N.
[0560]—*Sisters of Charity of Quebec-Grey Nuns*.—S.C.Q.
[0590]—*Sisters of Charity of Saint Elizabeth, Convent Station*.—S.C.
[0640]—*Sisters of Charity of St. Vincent de Paul, Halifax*.—S.C.
[0540]—*Sisters of Charity, At Ottawa-Grey Nuns of the Cross*.—S.C.O.
[0990]—*Sisters of Divine Providence*.—C.D.P.
[2580]—*Sisters of Mercy of the Union in the United States of America*.—R.S.M.
[3000]—*Sisters of Notre Dame de Namur*.—S.N.D.deN.
[3360]—*Sisters of Providence of Saint Mary-Of-The-Woods, Indiana*.—S.P.
[3950]—*Sisters of Saint Mary of Namur*.—S.S.M.N.
[3720]—*Sisters of St. Anne*.—S.S.A.
[3750]—*Sisters of St. Chretienne*.—S.S.Ch.
[1650]—*Sisters of St. Francis of Philadelphia*.—O.S.F.
[3830]—*Sisters of St. Joseph*.—C.S.J.
[3815]—*Sisters of Ste. Jeanne D'Arc*.—S.J.A.
[0150]—*Sisters of the Assumption B.V.*—S.A.S.V.
[1830]—*Sisters of the Good Shepherd*.—R.G.S.
[3310]—*Sisters of the Presentation of Mary*.—P.M.
[1490]—*Sisters of the Third Franciscan Order*.—O.S.F.
[1705]—*Sisters of the Third Order of St. Francis of Assisi*.—O.S.F.
[4060]—*Society of the Holy Child Jesus*.—S.H.C.J.
[4070]—*Society of the Sacred Heart*.—R.S.C.J.
[4110]—*Ursuline Nuns*. (Eastern Prov.).—O.S.U.

ARCHDIOCESAN CEMETERIES

BOSTON. *Diocesan Office*. 175 Broadway, Malden, 02148.
ARLINGTON. *St. Paul*.
BEVERLY. *St. Mary*.
CAMBRIDGE. *North Cambridge Catholic*.
CHARLESTOWN. *St. Francis de Sales*.
HAVERHILL. *St. James, St. Joseph & St. Patrick*.
LOWELL. *St. Patrick*.
LYNN. *St. Mary, St. Joseph & St. Jean Baptiste*.
MALDEN. *Holy Cross & St. Mary*.
MARBLEHEAD. *Star of the Sea*.
SALEM. *St. Mary*.
SAXONVILLE. *St. George*.
STONEHAM. *St. Patrick*.
WALTHAM. *Calvary*.
WATERTOWN. *Mount Auburn & St. Patrick*.
WOBURN. *Calvary*.

NECROLOGY

† Broderick, Rev. Msgr. John A., (Retired). —Died Aug. 21, 2000.
† Conroy, Cyril J, Beverly, MA St. Margaret. —Died May 26, 2000.
† Crowley, John D, Cambridge, MA St. Mary of the Annunciation. —Died Nov. 6, 2000.
† Donelin, John M., (Retired). —Died June 2, 2000.
† Fairbairn, Frank E, Boston, MA Society of St. James the Apostle. —Died Sept. 14, 2000.
† Flynn, Joseph D, Hingham, MA St. Paul. —Died Oct. 8, 2000.
† Hart, James P., (Retired). —Died Nov. 20, 2000.
† Herlihy, Charles E, Marlborough, MA Immaculate Conception. —Died Dec. 24, 1999.
† Hogan, Cornelius J., (Retired). —Died Jan. 29, 2000.
† Jansonis, Alphonse B. —Died May 13, 2000.
† Langely, Joseph W., (Retired). —Died April 26, 2000.
† Low, Rev. Msgr. Albert W., (Retired). —Died Aug. 22, 2000.
† Lynch, Daniel G., (Retired). —Died Oct. 25, 2000.
† Maguire, John J., (Retired). —Died March 25, 2000.
† McEntee, Paul H, Watertown, MA Sacred Heart. —Died Oct. 11, 2000.
† Moynihan, Paul V., (Retired). —Died June 24, 2000.
† O'Donovan, Rickard J, Wilmington, MA St. Dorothy. —Died Aug. 7, 2000.
† Ouellette, Lionel P, Marlborough, MA St. Mary. —Died Sept. 4, 2000.
† Palmieri, John A., (Retired). —Died Nov. 17, 2000.
† Pineau, Gerard P, Braintree, MA St. Francis of Assisi. —Died Oct. 20, 2000.
† Puccini, Alfred V, Malden, MA St. Peter. —Died Jan. 18, 2000.
† Riordan, Rev. Msgr. Daniel F., (Retired). —Died May 10, 2000.
† Sennott, Rev. Msgr. Robert J., (Retired). —Died Feb. 19, 2000.

Diocese of Bridgeport

(Dioecesis Bridgeportensis)

Most Reverend

WILLIAM E. LORI, S.T.D.

Bishop of Bridgeport; ordained May 14, 1977; appointed Titular Bishop of Bulla and Auxiliary of Washington April 20, 1995; appointed Bishop of Bridgeport January 23, 2001; installed March 19, 2001. *Office: 238 Jewett Ave., Bridgeport, CT, 06606-2892.*

Chancery: The Catholic Center, 238 Jewett Ave., Bridgeport, CT, 06606-2892. Tel.: 203-372-4301; Fax: 203-371-8698.

ESTABLISHED AUGUST 6, 1953.

Square Miles 633.

Corporate Title: *The Bridgeport Roman Catholic Diocesan Corporation.*

Comprises all of Fairfield County in the State of Connecticut.

For legal titles of parishes and diocesan institutions, consult the Chancery at The Catholic Center.

STATISTICAL OVERVIEW

Personnel	
Bishop	1
Priests: Diocesan Active in Diocese	188
Priests: Active Outside Diocese	21
Priests: Diocesan in Foreign Missions	3
Priests: Retired, Sick or Absent	56
Number of Diocesan Priests	268
Religious Priests in Diocese	67
Extern Priests in Diocese	12
Ordinations:	
Diocesan Priests	3
Religious Priests	1
Transitional Deacons	2
Permanent Deacons	12
Permanent Deacons in Diocese	87
Total Sisters	466
Parishes	
Parishes	87
With Resident Pastor:	
Resident Diocesan Priests	83
Resident Religious Priests	4
Without Resident Pastor:	
Missions	2
Closed Parishes	1
Professional Ministry Personnel:	
Sisters	98
Lay Ministers	161
Welfare	
Catholic Hospitals	1
Total Assisted	167,172
Homes for the Aged	4
Total Assisted	825
Day Care and Extended Day Care Centers	18
Total Assisted	340
Specialized Homes	1
Total Assisted	43
Special Centers for Social Services	24
Total Assisted	11,353
Other Institutions	2
Total Assisted	119
Educational	
Seminaries, Diocesan	1
Students from This Diocese	10
Diocesan Students in Other Seminaries	19
Total Seminarians	29
Colleges and Universities	3
Total Students	11,191
High Schools, Diocesan and Parish	5
Total Students	2,603
High Schools, Private	3
Total Students	1,160
Elementary Schools, Diocesan and Parish	33
Total Students	9,709
Elementary Schools, Private	2
Total Students	507
Non-residential Schools for the Disabled	1
Total Students	8
Catechesis/Religious Education:	
High School Students	3,257
Elementary Students	26,423
Total Students Under Catholic Instruction	54,887
Teachers in the Diocese:	
Priests	19
Brothers	1
Sisters	52
Lay Teachers	992
Vital Statistics	
Receptions into the Church:	
Infant Baptism Totals	6,149
Adult Baptism Totals	154
Received into Full Communion	118
First Communions	5,809
Confirmations	4,275
Marriages:	
Catholic	1,585
Interfaith	300
Total Marriages	1,885
Deaths	3,660
Total Catholic Population	364,685
Total Population	841,334

Former Bishops—His Eminence LAWRENCE J. CARDINAL SHEHAN, D.D., ord. Dec. 23, 1922; cons. Dec. 12, 1945 as Auxiliary Bishop of Baltimore; installed as first Bishop of Bridgeport, Dec. 1, 1953; transferred to Archdiocese of Baltimore, July 10, 1961; created Cardinal, Feb. 22, 1965; died Aug. 26, 1984.—Most Rev. WALTER W. CURTIS, S.T.D., ord. Dec. 8, 1937; appt. Auxiliary Bishop of Newark and Titular Bishop of Bisica in Tunis; cons. Sept. 24, 1957; appt. Bishop of Bridgeport, Sept. 23, 1961; installed Nov. 20, 1961; retired June 28, 1988; died Oct. 18, 1997.—Most Rev. EDWARD M. EGAN, J.C.D., D.D., ord. Dec. 15, 1957; appt. Titular Bishop of Allegheny and Auxiliary Bishop of New York, April 1, 1985; cons. May 22, 1985; appt. Bishop of Bridgeport, Nov. 8, 1988; installed Dec. 14, 1988; appt. Archbishop of New York, May 11, 2000; installed June 19, 2000.

Vicars General—Rev. Msgr. WILLIAM J. SCHEYD, P.A.; Rev. Msgr. THOMAS J. DRISCOLL, *238 Jewett Ave., Bridgeport, 06606-2892.*

Chancery—The Catholic Center, 238 Jewett Ave., Bridgeport, 06606-2892. Tel: 203-372-4301; Fax: 203-371-8698. Office Hours: Sept.-June Mon.-Fri. 9-5; July-Aug. 9-4.

Diocesan Administrator and Chancellor—Rev. Msgr. LAURENCE R. BRONKIEWICZ, S.T.D., *Catholic Center, 238 Jewett Ave., Bridgeport, 06606-2892.* Tel: 203-372-4301.

Vice Chancellor & Secretary to the Bishop—Rev. SAMUEL V. SCOTT.

Episcopal Vicar for Religious—Rev. Msgr. LAURENCE R. BRONKIEWICZ, S.T.D.

Director for Clergy Personnel—Rev. FRANK C. MCGRATH.

Episcopal Vicar for Hispanics—Rev. Msgr. ANICETO VILLAMIDE.

Finance Officer—GARY J. NIELSEN, Interim Officer.

Judicial Vicar—Rev. Msgr. JERALD A. DOYLE, Ph.D., J.C.D.

Diocesan Tribunal—The Catholic Center, 238 Jewett Ave., Bridgeport, 06606-2892. Tel: 203-372-4301.

Judges—Rev. Msgr. WILLIAM A. GENUARIO, P.A., J.C.D.; Rev. Msgr. THOMAS J. DRISCOLL; Rev. Msgr. J. JAMES CUNEO, J.C.D.; Rev. Msgr. GEORGE D. BIRGE; Rev. MICHAEL A. BOCCACCIO; Rev. Msgr. JOHN B. HOSSAN; Rev. Canon ALBERT W. WATTS, J.C.L.; Revs. JOSEPH K. PARAMPATH, J.C.D.; ALBERT W. MCGOLDRICK, J.C.L.; MICHAEL R. MOYNIHAN, J.C.L.

Defenders of the Bond—Revs. RICHARD F. FUTIE, J.C.D.; ALFRED F. PECARIC; WILLIAM F. VERRILLI.

Notaries—MARY A. MOLLOY; KERRY PERILLE.

Promoter of Justice—Rev. G. FRANTZ DESRUISSEAUX, J.C.L.

Diocesan General Counsel—MICHAEL T. DOLAN, ESQ.

Diocesan Censors—Rev. Msgr. LAWRENCE R. BRONKIEWICZ, S.T.D.; Rev. Msgr. THOMAS J. DRISCOLL; Rev. CHRISTOPHER J. WALSH, Ph.D.

Diocesan Consultors—Rev. Msgr. LAURENCE R. BRONKIEWICZ; Rev. Msgr. THOMAS J. DRISCOLL; Rev. Msgr. NICHOLAS V. GRIECO; Rev. Msgr. MARTIN P. RYAN; Rev. ERNEST T. ESPOSITO; Rev. Msgr. WILLIAM J. SCHEYD, P.A.; Revs. WALTER C. ORLOWSKI; ROBERT E. WEISS; Rev. Msgr. ANICETO VILLAMIDE; Rev. Msgr. KEVIN W. WALLIN; Rev. Msgr. JERALD A. DOYLE.

Presbyteral Council—Vacant, Chm.; Rev. Msgr. LAURENCE R. BRONKIEWICZ; Rev. Msgr. JERALD A. DOYLE; Rev. Msgr. WILLIAM J. SCHEYD, P.A., Vice Chm.; Rev. Msgr. JOHN F. JAZOWSKI; Rev. Msgr. J. PETER CULLEN; Rev. Msgr. WILLIAM A. GENUARIO; Rev. Msgr. ANICETO VILLAMIDE; Rev. Msgr. KEVIN W. WALLIN; Rev. Msgr. THOMAS J. DRISCOLL; Rev. Msgr. NICHOLAS V. GRIECO; Rev. Msgr. BLASE M. GINTOLI; Revs. MATTHEW BERNELLI; JAMES D. GROSSO; DAVID W. BLANCHFIELD; LAWRENCE J. CARROLL; NICHOLAS A. CIRILLO; M. JUDE FAY; FRANCIS T. HOFFMANN; FRANK C. MCGRATH; THOMAS W. POWERS; THOMAS P. THORNE; FREDERICK L. SAVIANO; EDWARD SMALL, S.J.; JAMES SMYKA, O.F.M.Conv.; ERNEST T. ESPOSITO; WILLIAM R. MOYNIHAN.

Pastoral Council—Rev. Msgr. WILLIAM J. SCHEYD, P.A.; Rev. G. FRANTZ DESRUISSEAUX; Rev. Msgr. ANICETO VILLAMIDE; Deacons DANIEL J. IANNIELLO; JOHN J. MORANSKI; Mr. TIMOTHY DEVINE; Sr. CHRISTINE KILEY, A.S.C.J.; Sr. MADELINE MCADAM, S.N.D.; THOMAS MULLIGAN, JR., ESQ.; ROBERT SALVESTRINI; HELEN F. CARROLL; NANCY DOLAN; Dr. ROMELEE A. HOWARD, K.S.G.; EILEEN HOWARD; Mrs. ROLAND J. WILSON, JR.; ISRAEL CORTES; MARY LOUISE SEMEDO; STEFAN GAWEL; MARIE WALSH; NICHOLAS PAVIA; ANNE CHATLOS; EMILIO ALICEA; ADRIANA MOLINA.

Finance Council—Rev. Msgr. WILLIAM J. SCHEYD, P.A.; Rev. Msgr. THOMAS J. DRISCOLL; Mr. DIGBY W. BARRIOS; WILLIAM G. MALONEY, K.M., K.H.S.,

Finance Council—Rev. Msgr. WILLIAM J. SCHEYD, P.A.; Rev. Msgr. THOMAS J. DRISCOLL; Mr. DIGBY W. BARRIOS; WILLIAM G. MALONEY, K.M., K.H.S., K.C.S.G.; DONALD T. STUDLEY, C.P.A.; GEORGE TAYLOR; WILLIAM TOTTON.

Parochial Examiners—Rev. Msgr. LOUIS A. DEPROFIO; Rev. Msgr. JOHN E. GILMARTIN; Rev. Msgr. JOHN F. JAZOWSKI; Rev. Msgr. BARTHOLOMEW J. LAURELLO; Rev. MICHAEL C. PALMER; Rev. Msgr. JOSEPH A. SULLIVAN; Rev. Msgr. ANICETO VILLAMIDE.

Territorial Vicars—Vicariate I (Stamford, Darien, Glenbrook, Greenwich, Byram, Riverside): Rev. MICHAEL R. MOYNIHAN, *St. Michael Rectory, 469 North St., Greenwich, 06830.* Tel: 203-869-5421. Vicariate II (Norwalk, New Canaan, Wilton, Weston, Westport): Rev. Msgr. NICHOLAS V. GRIECO, *St. Francis of Assisi Rectory, P.O. Box 1025, 35 Norfield Rd., Weston, 06883.* Tel: 203-227-1341. Vicariate III (Fairfield, Easton, West Bridgeport): Rev. Msgr. BLASE M. GINTOLI, Vicar, *Assumption Rectory, 545 Stratfield Rd., Fairfield, 06432.* Tel: 203-333-9065. Vicariate IV (East Bridgeport, Stratford, Trumbull, Monroe, Shelton): Rev. MATTHEW BERNELLI, *St. Mary Rectory, 25 Sherman St., Bridgeport, 06608.* Tel: 203-334-8811. Vicariate V (Bethel, Brookfield, Danbury, Georgetown, Newtown, New Fairfield, Redding, Ridgefield, Sherman): Rev. JAMES D. GROSSO, *St. Joseph Rectory, 8 Robinson Ave., Danbury, 06810.* Tel: 203-748-8177.

Ministry for Clergy and Religious—Rev. Msgr. LAURENCE R. BRONKIEWICZ, S.T.D., Episcopal Vicar for Clergy; Rev. ERNEST T. ESPOSITO, Asst. Vicar for Religious; Rev. FRANK C. MCGRATH, Dir. Clergy Personnel.

The Catholic Center—238 Jewett Ave., Bridgeport, 06606. Tel: 203-372-4301.

Finance Office—JOHN P. ROONEY, Dir., Parish Accounting & Finance; Mr. GARY J. NIELSEN, C.P.A., Acting Finance Officer, *The Catholic Center, 238 Jewett Ave., Bridgeport, 06606-2892.* Tel: 203-372-4301.

Members of the Clergy Personnel Committee—Rev. Msgr. STANLEY B. ROUSSEAU, Chm.; Rev. KEVIN T. ROYAL; Rev. Msgr. PETER P. DORA.

Office for the Continuing Education of Clergy—Rev. ERNEST T. ESPOSITO, Dir.

Office of Vocations—Rev. CHRISTOPHER J. WALSH, Ph.D., Dir., *St. John Fisher Residence, 894 Newfield Ave., Stamford, 06905.* Tel: 203-322-5331.

Pastors' Vocation Advisory Board—Rev. Msgr. LAURENCE R. BRONKIEWICZ, S.T.D.; Rev. Msgr. LOUIS A. DEPROFIO, P.A.; Rev. Msgr. THOMAS J. DRISCOLL; Rev. Msgr. WILLIAM J. SCHEYD, P.A.; Rev. Msgr. ANICETO VILLAMIDE; Rev. Msgr. FRANCIS C. WISSEL; Revs. ALBERT D. AUDETTE; FRANK C. MCGRATH; MICHAEL R. MOYNIHAN; WALTER C. ORLOWSKI.

Office of the Permanent Diaconate—Deacons ANTHONY J. DETJE, Dir., Formation; JOHN J. MORANSKI, Asst. Dir. Diaconate Formation; RICHARD STENBERG, Dir., Continuing Education; Rev. Msgr. LAURENCE R. BRONKIEWICZ, S.T.D., Spiritual Dir., Formation, *The Catholic Center, 238 Jewett Ave., Bridgeport, 06606-2892.* Tel: 203-372-4301.

Office for Ecumenical and Interreligious Affairs—Rev. Msgr. ALAN F. DETSCHER, S.L.D., Dir., *St. Catherine of Siena Rectory, 4 Riverside Ave., Riverside, 06878.* Tel: 203-637-3661.

Office of Liturgy—Vacant, *The Catholic Center, 238 Jewett Ave., Bridgeport, 06606-2892.* Tel: 203-372-4301.

Diocesan Commission on the Liturgy—Rev. ANDREW G. VARGA, D.Min., Chm., *Res., St. Luke, 84 Long Lots Rd., Westport, 06880-3917.*

Catechesis, Office for—Dr. JOAN M. KELLY, Dir., *The Catholic Center, 238 Jewett Ave., Bridgeport, 06606-2892.* Tel: 203-372-4301.

Catechist Formation—BARBARA D. CROSE, Asst. Dir.

D.R.E. Liaison—Sr. SUSAN CZAPLICKI, S.S.N.D., Asst. Dir. Elementary Educ.

Catechumenate—Mrs. JEAN A. KECHEJIAN, Asst. Dir. Adult Catechesis.

Youth Services—JOHN P. CAMPBELL, Asst. Dir.

Catholic Scouts—Deacon JOSEPH MELITA, Dir.

Office for Education—ARMAND R. FABBRI, Dir. & Supt., Schools; Sr. JOHN VIANNEY ZULLO, S.S.N.D., Asst. Dir. Elementary Educ., *238 Jewett Ave., Bridgeport, 06606-2892.* Tel: 203-372-4301. WILLIAM J. ADAMS, Coord., Federal-State Programs, *238 Jewett Ave., Bridgeport, 06606.* Tel: 203-576-7944.

Special Education—Sr. ELEACE KING, I.H.M., Ed.D., Dir., *The Catholic Center, 238 Jewett Ave., Bridgeport, 06606-2892.* Tel: 203-372-4301, Ext. 330. Sr. NANCY O'NEILL, C.N.D., Coord., Ministry to the Deaf. Tel: 203-372-4301, Ext. 335; 372-4782 (TTY).

Apostolate for the Deaf—Rev. PETER A. DEMARCO, Moderator, *St. Catherine of Siena Rectory, 200 Shelton Rd., Trumbull, 06611.* Tel: 203-459-0484 (TTY).

Catholic Charities of Fairfield County, Inc.—BRIAN A. CRONIN, A.C.S.W., C.I.S.W., Exec. Dir. BENEDICT P. MAZATOS, Comptroller, *Catholic Center, 238 Jewett Ave., Bridgeport, 06606-2892.* Tel: 203-372-4301, Ext. 379; 564; Fax: 203-372-5045.

Diocesan Offices and Directors

Ethnic and Cultural Services—Deacon JOSEPH J. FARLEY, Sec., *238 Jewett Ave., Bridgeport, 06606-2892.* Tel: 203-372-4301.

Aging, Diocesan Task Force—EDIE CASSIDY, Chm., *238 Jewett Ave., Bridgeport, 06606-2892.* Tel: 203-372-4301.

Archives—Rev. Msgr. JOHN V. HORGAN-KUNG, Archivist, *238 Jewett Ave., Bridgeport, 06606-2892.* Tel: 203-372-4301.

African Americans, Apostolate of—Rev. Msgr. JOHN C. SANDERS, Dir., *The Catherine Dennis Keefe Queen of the Clergy Retired Priests' Residence, 274 Strawberry Hill Ave., Stamford, 06902.* Tel: 203-358-9906.

Catholic Lawyers—Rev. Msgr. J. JAMES CUNEO, J.C.D., Spiritual Moderator; JAMES J. RUANE, ESQ., Coord., St. Thomas More Society of Fairfield Co., *238 Jewett Ave., Bridgeport, 06606-2892.* Tel: 203-372-4301.

Catholic Physicians Guild—Dr. THOMAS G. FLYNN, Coord., *39 Old Studio Rd., New Canaan, 06840.* Tel: 203-966-1959.

Catholic Women, Council of—Rev. MICHAEL R. MOYNIHAN, Diocesan Dir., *St. Michaels Rectory, 469 N. St., Greenwich, 06083.* Tel: 203-869-5421. Mrs. HELEN F. CARROLL, Diocesan Pres., *1216 Noble Ave., Bridgeport, 06608.* Tel: 203-335-7468. District Spiritual Directors: Revs. ERNEST T. ESPOSITO, (Bridgeport); MARTIN S. IGOE, (Greenwich); Rev. Msgr. EDWIN F. BURKE, (Norwalk); Rev. ROBERT G. POHLEY, (Stamford).

Cemeteries—RAY CAPO, Dir., *238 Jewett Ave., Bridgeport, 06606-2892.* Tel: 203-372-4301.

Charismatic Renewal—BETTY ANN CASARETTI, *238 Jewett Ave., Bridgeport, 06606-2892.* Tel: 203-372-4301.

Communications—Dr. JOSEPH MCALEER, Editor & Dir., *238 Jewett Ave., Bridgeport, 06606-2892.* Tel: 203-372-4301. Rev. MARK CONNOLLY, Diocesan Dir., Radio & Television, *10 Millbrook Rd. West, Stamford, 06902.* Tel: 203-348-7114.

Connecticut Catholic Conference—Dr. MARIE HILLIARD, Exec. Dir., *134 Farmington Ave., Hartford, 06105.* Tel: 203-524-7882.

Cursillos of Fairfield County, Inc.—Rev. PAUL F. MERRY, Advisor for English Language, *Blessed Sacrament Church, 275 Union Ave., Bridgeport, 06607.* Tel: 203-333-1202. Rev. Msgr. ANICETO VILLAMIDE, Advisor for Spanish Language, *St. Peter Rectory, 695 Colorado Ave., Bridgeport, 06605.* Tel: 203-366-5611.

Deaf, Apostolate for—Rev. PETER A. DEMARCO, Moderator, *Res., St. Catherine of Siena Rectory, 200 Shelton Rd., Trumbull, 06611.* Tel: 203-261-3676; 459-0484 (TTY).

Development, Office of—THOMAS M. SWEENEY, Dir. Planned Giving; Rev. Msgr. KEVIN W. WALLIN, Dir. Inner City Foundation; Mr. THOMAS M. SWEENEY, Dir., Annual Bishop's Appeal, *238 Jewett Ave., Bridgeport, 06606-2892.* Tel: 203-372-4301.

Fairfield Foundation of the Diocese of Bridgeport, Inc.—MICHELLE JONES DELMHORST, Pres. JOHN CROFFY, Exec. Dir., *238 Jewett Ave., Bridgeport, 06606-2892.* Tel: 203-372-4301.

Inner-City Foundation for Charity and Education—Rev. Msgr. KEVIN W. WALLIN, Exec. Dir., *238 Jewett Ave., Bridgeport, 06606-2892.* Tel: 203-372-4301.

Catholic Ministry for the Elderly—Rev. DAVID H. KRAHEL, Chap. (Greenwich, Darien, Stamford), *Our Lady Star of the Sea Rectory, 1200 Shippan Ave., Stamford, 06902.* Tel: 203-357-7956.

Haitian American Catholic Center of Greater Stamford—Rev. JEAN RIDLY JULIEN, Exec. Dir., *93 Hope St., Stamford, 06906.* Tel: 203-323-8391.

Hispanic Apostolate, Episcopal Vicar for—Rev. Msgr. ANICETO VILLAMIDE, Vicar, *The Catholic Center, 238 Jewett Ave., Bridgeport, 06606-2892.* Tel: 203-372-4301.

Insurance Office—JOSEPH G. BURTON, Claims & Risk Mgr., *Catholic Mutual Group, 238 Jewett Ave., Bridgeport, 06606.* Tel: 203-371-8471.

Nurses, Council of Catholic—Rev. STEPHEN J. GLEESON, Dir., *St. Stephen's Rectory, 6949 Main St., Trumbull, 06611.* Tel: 203-268-6217; Fax: 203-268-9861.

Official Newspapers—*"The Fairfield County Catholic"*, (Monthly), Dr. JOSEPH MCALEER, Editor & Dir. Communications, *238 Jewett Ave., Bridgeport, 06606.* Tel: 203-372-4301., *"The Catholic Transcript"*, (Weekly), *785 Asylum Ave., Hartford, 06105.* Tel: 203-527-1175.

Pilgrimages, Office of Diocesan—Rev. Msgr. WILLIAM J. LOUGHLIN, *St. Thomas Rectory, 1719 Post Rd., Fairfield, 06430.* Tel: 203-255-1097.

Pontifical Association of the Holy Childhood—Rev. ROBERT J. MATY, Dir. ELIZABETH SAULNIER, Coord. for Schools; R.E. Programs, *The Catholic Center, 238 Jewett Ave., Bridgeport, 06606-2892.* Tel: 203-372-4301.

Portuguese-Speaking People, Apostolate for—Rev. Msgr. CONSTANTINO R. CALDAS, Dir., *429 Huntington Rd., Bridgeport, 06608.* Tel: 203-333-7575.

Propagation of the Faith—Rev. ROBERT J. MATY, Dir., *The Catholic Center, 238 Jewett Ave., Bridgeport, 06606-2892.* Tel: 203-372-4301.

Boy Scouts and Girl Scouts—Deacon JOSEPH MELITA, Dir., *Catholic Center, 238 Jewett Ave., Bridgeport, 06606-2982.* Tel: 203-372-4301. Rev. STEPHEN J. BALINT, *Res., St. Ladislaus Rectory, 25 Cliff St., South Norwalk, 06854.* Tel: 203-866-1867.

Retired Priests—Rev. Msgr. BERNARD S. SCANLON, Dir., *The Catherine Dennis Keefe Queen of the Clergy Retired Priests' Residence, 274 Strawberry Hill Ave., Stamford, 06904.* Tel: 203-358-9906.

CLERGY, PARISHES, MISSIONS AND PAROCHIAL SCHOOLS

CITY OF BRIDGEPORT
(Fairfield County)

1—ST. AUGUSTINE CATHEDRAL (1842), Revs. Raymond K. Petrucci, Admin.; John Punnakunnel. In res., Revs. Douglas J. Tufaro; Alphonsus Tran Van Dong; Sr. Antoinette Mongkolrutana, S.L.C., Vietnamese Pastoral Assoc., Tel: 203-333-0837; Deacon Timothy Sullivan.

Res., 359 Washington Ave., 06604. Tel: 203-368-6777; Fax: 203-368-6386.

School—See separate listing under Elementary Schools, Regional in the Institution section.

Catechesis/Religious Programs—Students 125.

2—ST. AMBROSE (1928), Revs. Dennis G. Bludnicki; John Paul Long. In res., Rev. Nello A. Barachini, C.M.; Deacons James Volpe; Michael K. Wolfer.

Res., 1596 Boston Ave., 06610. Tel: 203-333-1336; Fax: 203-330-9085.

School—See separate listing under Elementary Schools, Regional in the Institution section.

Stations—Bishop Curtis Homes, Tel: 203-366-4333; Success Park.

3—ST. ANDREW (1961), Revs. Robert J. Crofut; Peter F. Lenox; Deacons Roland Blier; Edward Hendricks.

Res., 435 Anton St., 06606. Tel: 203-374-6171; Fax: 203-372-7709.

School—See separate listing under Elementary Schools, Regional in the Institution section.

Catechesis/Religious Programs—Tel: 203-374-8118; Fax: 203-374-9450. Mrs. Jeanne Bisson, D.R.E.

Students 352.

4—ST. ANN (1922), Revs. Joseph J. Malloy; George F. O'Neill; Mrs. Margaret Daley, Prin.; Deacons John J. Moranski; Nicholas A. Pratt.

Res., 481 Brewster St., 06605. Tel: 203-368-1607; Fax: 203-368-0859.

School—See separate listing under Elementary Schools, Regional in the Institution section.

Catechesis/Religious Programs—Tel: 203-334-5856.

Students 270.

5—ST. ANTHONY OF PADUA. Merged with St. Peter, Bridgeport. See separate listing.

6—BLESSED SACRAMENT (1917), Revs. Paul F. Merry; George M. Karcsinski; Deacons Ricardo Martinez; Donald P. Foust.

Res., 275 Union Ave., 06607. Tel: 203-333-1202; Fax: 203-368-3502.

7—ST. CHARLES (1902), Revs. Joseph J. Saba, Admin.; Gustavo Adolfo Falla, Admin.; Jean-Rony Philippe; Sr. Antoinette Mongkolrutana, S.L.C., Laotian Pastoral Assoc., Tel: 203-333-0837; Deacon Santos Garcia.

Res., 391 Ogden St., 06608. Tel: 203-333-2147; Fax: 203-330-8316.

Catechesis/Religious Programs—Tel: 203-576-1629. Mrs. Mercedes Rojas, D.R.E.

Students 508.

8—SS. CYRIL AND METHODIUS (1907) (Slovak), Rev. Msgr. Joseph W. Pekar.

Res., 79 Church St., 06608. Tel: 203-333-7003.

9—ST. GEORGE (1907), Rev. Jose Rebaque, S.A.C., Admin., Tel: 203-579-1653.

Res., 443 Park Ave., 06604. Tel: 203-335-1797.

10—HOLY ROSARY (1903) (Italian), Rev. Guido G. Montanaro. In res., Rev. Robert J. Maty.

Res., 365 E. Washington Ave., 06608. Tel: 203-334-2447; Fax: 203-335-5334.

11—ST. JOHN NEPOMUCENE. Closed. For inquiries for parish records contact Holy Name of Jesus, Stratford.

12—ST. JOSEPH'S. Closed. May 23, 1988. For inquiries for parish records contact St. Patrick, Bridgeport.

13—ST. MARY (1857), Rev. Matthew Bernelli.
Res., 25 Sherman St., 06608. Tel: 203-334-8811; Fax: 203-334-8574.

14—ST. MICHAEL THE ARCHANGEL (1989) (Polish), Revs. James Smyka, O.F.M.Conv.; Stefan Morawski, O.F.M.Conv.
Res., 310 Pulaski St., 06608. Tel: 203-334-1822; Fax: 203-696-0078.

15—OUR LADY OF FATIMA (1962) (Portuguese), Rev. Joseph De Brito Alves (Portugal) Admin. In res., Rev. Msgr. Constantino R. Caldas; Deacon Gabriel A. Pereira.
Res., 429 Huntington Rd., 06608. Tel: 203-333-7575; Fax: 203-333-7575.
Catechesis/Religious Programs—Students 332.

16—OUR LADY OF GOOD COUNSEL (1955), Rev. Martin J. Nikodem. In res., Rev. Msgr. Gregory M. Smith.
Res., 163 Ortega Ave., 06606. Tel: 203-372-3533.
Catechesis/Religious Programs—Virginia Mora, D.R.E.
Students 41.

17—ST. PATRICK CHURCH (1889), Revs. Andrew G. Marus; Bernardo C. Rodriguez; Sr. Eleanore Studwell, Pastoral Assoc.; Deacons William J. Bissenden; Alix Africot. In res., Rev. Michael J. Bachman.
Res. and Business Office: 170 Thompson St., 06604. Tel: 203-335-0106; Fax: 203-335-0107.
Church—851 North Ave., 06606. Tel: 203-367-4679.
Catechesis/Religious Programs—Sandra Mihalek, D.R.E.
Students 114.
Stations—Connecticut State Correctional Institution.; St. Vincent Medical Center, Tel: 203-576-6000; Northbridge Health Care Center, Tel: 203-336-0232.

18—ST. PETER (1900) (Spanish), Rev. Msgr. Aniceto Villamide; Rev. Greg J. Markey; Deacons Domingo Reveron; Luis Torres. In res., Rev. Jose Rebaque, S.A.C.
Res., 695 Colorado Ave., 06605. Tel: 203-366-5611; Fax: 203-335-1924.
School—See separate listing under Elementary Schools, Regional in the Institution section.
Catechesis/Religious Programs—Tel: 203-334-5681; Fax: 203-333-1590. Sr. Mirta Cruz, D.R.E.
Students 220.

19—ST. RAPHAEL (1925) (Italian), Revs. Carducci S. D'Amico; Grazioso Artuso; Deacon Joseph Melita.
Res., 162 Oak St., 06604. Tel: 203-333-3161; Fax: 203-368-1727.
School—See separate listing under Elementary Schools, Regional in the Institution section.
Catechesis/Religious Programs—Students 338.
Convent—671 Oak St., 06604. Tel: 203-535-9817; Fax: 203-336-9205.
Chapel—St. Margaret's, 2539 Park Ave., 06604. Tel: 203-368-4425.

OUTSIDE THE CITY OF BRIDGEPORT

Bethel, Fairfield Co., St. Mary (1882), Rev. Msgr. Edward B. Karl; Revs. Michael L. Dunn; Andrew W. Walter; Deacon Robert Becker.
Church & Office: 26 Dodgingtown Rd., 06801. Tel: 203-744-5777; Fax: 203-744-3740. [CEM]
School—See separate listing under Elementary Schools, Regional in the Institution section.
Catechesis/Religious Programs—Tel: 203-743-4557. Mary Ferri, D.R.E.
Students 916.
Convent—Tel: 203-743-6985.

Brookfield, Fairfield Co., St. Joseph (1941), Revs. Lawrence J. Carroll; Michael P. Lyons; Deacons William Shaughnessy; Peter Kuhn.
Res., 159 Whisconier Rd., P.O. Box 5072, 06804. Tel: 203-775-1035; Fax: 203-775-1684.
School—See separate listing under Elementary Schools, Regional in the Institution section.
Catechesis/Religious Programs—Tel: 203-775-1035.
Students 651.

St. Marguerite Bourgeoys (1982), Revs. Albert D. Audette; Brian P. Gannon; Deacons Louis F. Howe; Anthony J. Detje.
Res., 138 Candlewood Lake Rd., 06804. Tel: 203-775-5117; Fax: 203-775-9254.
Catechesis/Religious Programs—Tel: 203-775-2644.
Students 225.

Danbury, Fairfield Co.,

1—ST. GREGORY, (1960), Revs. Angelo S. Arrando; John Stronkowski; Raymond M. Scherba; Deacons Robert Blankschen; William D. Murphy; Daniel N. Myott; Donald J. Naiman.
Res., 85 Great Plain Rd., 06811. Tel: 203-797-0222; Fax: 203-743-5464.
School—See separate listing under Elementary Schools, Regional in the Institution section.
Catechesis/Religious Programs—Tel: 203-743-5168. Mrs. Mary Ann Hauser, D.R.E.
Students 839.

2—IMMACULATE HEART OF MARY, (1980) (Portuguese), Rev. Antonio Carvalho de Azevedo, Admin.; Deacon Jose Rodrigues Cabral.
Res., 149 Deer Hill Ave., 06811. Tel: 203-797-1821; Fax: 203-743-9146.
Catechesis/Religious Programs—Students 173.

3—OUR LADY OF GUADALUPE, (1985) (Spanish), Revs. Frederick L. Saviano; Hector Leon.
Res., 29 Golden Hill Rd., 06811-4629. Tel: 203-743-1021; Fax: 203-798-8143.

4—ST. JOSEPH, (1905), Revs. James D. Grosso; John F. Pikulski, Ph.D.; Cyprian P. LaPastina; Deacon David Vaughn.
Res., 8 Robinson Ave., 06810. Tel: 203-748-8177; Fax: 203-748-2010.
School—See separate listing under Elementary Schools, Regional in the Institution section.
Catechesis/Religious Programs—Tel: 203-778-1920.
Students 356.

5—ST. PETER, (1851), Rev. Msgr. Kevin W. Wallin; Rev. Msgr. Pedro D. Diniz (Brazil); Revs. Corey V. Piccinino; Michael J. Madden; Gregg D. Mecca.
Res., 104 Main St., 06810. Tel: 203-743-2707; Fax: 203-794-1928.
School—See separate listing under Elementary Schools, Regional in the Institution section.
Catechesis/Religious Programs—Tel: 203-743-1048; Fax: 203-797-9471. Margaret M. Curran, D.R.E.
Students 290.

6—SACRED HEART, (1925) (Polish), Revs. Maurice Piszczatowski, O.F.M.Conv.; Gerald Waterman, O.F.M.Conv.; Deacon John F. Esterheld. In res., Revs. Michael Zielke, O.F.M.Conv., Campus Min. West Connecticut Univ.; Thomas Gwozdz, O.F.M.Conv.
Res., 12 Cottage St., 06810. Tel: 203-748-9029; Fax: 203-748-9168.
School—See separate listing under Elementary Schools, Regional in the Institution section.
Catechesis/Religious Programs—Students 86.
Convent—46 Stone St., 06810. Tel: 203-743-6406.

Darien, Fairfield Co., St. John (1895), Revs. Michael Jude Fay; Joseph Cervero; Deacon William K. Rowe. In res., Rev. Msgr. Joseph J. Kohut.
Res., 1986 Post Rd., 06820. Tel: 203-655-1145; Fax: 203-655-1048.
Catechesis/Religious Programs—Tel: 203-655-8020. John Cunningham, D.R.E.
Students 610.

St. Thomas More (1966), Revs. J. Barry Furey; Robert J. Post; Sr. Madeline McAdam, S.N.D., Pastoral Assoc.
Res., 384 Middlesex Rd., 06820. Tel: 203-655-3303; Fax: 203-655-8901.
Catechesis/Religious Programs—374 Middlesex Rd., 06820. Tel: 203-655-3077. Ms. Cornelia G. Dinnean, D.R.E.
Lay Teachers 82; Students 907.
Convent—370 Middlesex Rd., 06820. Tel: 203-655-3580.
Sisters of Notre Dame de Namur 2.

Easton, Fairfield Co., Notre Dame of Easton (1956), Rev. Msgr. Thomas J. Driscoll, V.G.; Rev. Xavier F. Renda; Deacons Harold J. Lynch; Gerald F. Sabol.
Res., 640 Morehouse Rd., 06612. Tel: 203-268-5838; Fax: 203-459-4940.
Church—655 Morehouse Rd., 06612. Tel: 203-261-5596.
Catechesis/Religious Programs—Students 590.

Fairfield, Fairfield Co.,

1—ST. ANTHONY OF PADUA, (1927) (Polish), Revs. Innocent Kurkowski, O.F.M.Conv.; Berard Dudek, O.F.M.Conv.
Res., 149 S. Pine Creek Rd., 06430. Tel: 203-259-0358; Fax: 203-259-0358.

2—ASSUMPTION, (1922), Rev. Msgr. Blase M. Gintoli; Revs. John P. Baran; Ernest T. Esposito. In res., Deacon Donald J. Ross, Jr.
Res., 545 Stratfield Rd., 06430. Tel: 203-333-9065; Fax: 203-333-2562.
School—See separate listing under Elementary Schools, Regional in the Institution section.
Catechesis/Religious Programs—Frank Macari, D.R.E.
Students 403.
Convent—605 Stratfield Rd., 06432. Tel: 203-336-3419.

3—ST. EMERY, (1932) (Hungarian). (United with St. Stephen's of Bridgeport 1899-1971). Revs. Louis M. Pintye, O.F.M.; Emeric Szlezak, O.F.M.
Res., 838 King's Hwy. E., 06432. Tel: 203-334-0312; Fax: 203-579-9423.
Convent—105 Biro St., 06432. Tel: 203-334-3913. Congregation of Notre Dame 3.

4—HOLY CROSS, (1913) (Slovenian), Rev. Milan Dimic, Admin.; Deacon Kevin Moore.
Res., 750 Tahmore Dr., 06432. Tel: 203-372-4595; Fax: 203-372-4668.
Catechesis/Religious Programs—Tel: 203-373-0466.
Students 135.

5—HOLY FAMILY, (1938), Revs. William D. Donovan; Eugene R. Szantyr.
Res., 700 Old Stratfield Rd., 06432. Tel: 203-336-1835; Fax: 203-336-0342.
School—See separate listing under Elementary Schools, Regional in the Institution section.
Catechesis/Religious Programs—Tel: 203-579-4540. Stephen Sebestyen, D.R.E.
Students 340.
Convent—70 Laurel St., 06432. Tel: 203-333-3423.

6—ST. PIUS X, (1955), Rev. Msgr. Edward J. Scull; Rev. George Sankoorikal; Deacon Richard Stenberg. In res., Rev. Samuel V. Scott.
Res., 834 Brookside Dr., 06430. Tel: 203-255-6134; Fax: 203-255-5232.
Catechesis/Religious Programs—Tel: 203-259-4800.
Students 501.

7—ST. THOMAS AQUINAS, (1876), Rev. Msgr. William J. Loughlin; Revs. Victor T. Martin; Russell A. Augustine; Deacon Daniel Ianniello.
Res., 1719 Post Rd., 06430. Tel: 203-255-1097; Fax: 203-256-8177. [CEM]
School—See separate listing under Elementary Schools, Regional in the Institution section.
Catechesis/Religious Programs—Tel: 203-255-1984. Sr. Catherine Jemapete, S.S.N.D., D.R.E.
Students 735.

Georgetown, Fairfield Co., Sacred Heart (1881), Revs. M. Joseph Joaquin; Mark E. Grimes.
Res., 30 Church St., Box 388, 06829. Tel: 203-544-8345; Fax: 203-544-1246.
Catechesis/Religious Programs—Tel: 203-544-8423.
Students 315.

Greenwich, Fairfield Co.,

1—ST. MARY, (1874), Rev. Msgr. Frank C. Wissel, D. Min.; Revs. Alfred A. Riendeau; Richard J. Gemza; German Martinez, O.S.B., (Spain) Hispanic Ministry; Deacon Matthew T. Ashe.
Res., 178 Greenwich Ave., 06830. Tel: 203-869-9393; Fax: 203-869-1032.
Catechesis/Religious Programs—Tel: 203-869-9250; Fax: 203-625-4760. Sr. Patricia Wachter, S.S.N.D., D.R.E.
Students 350.

2—ST. MICHAEL THE ARCHANGEL, (1963), Revs. Michael Robert Moynihan; William J. Kennedy, S.J.; Mark Connolly.
Res., 469 North St., 06830. Tel: 203-869-5421; Fax: 203-869-0169.
Catechesis/Religious Programs—Tel: 203-661-3088. Sr. Celine M. Flynn, S.S.N.D., D.R.E.
Students 385.
Mission—Greenwich, Fairfield Co., St. Timothy's, 469 North St., 06830.

3—ST. PAUL, (1902), Rev. Albert W. McGoldrick, J.C.L. In res., Rev. Msgr. Joseph A. Sullivan.
Res., 84 Sherwood Ave., 06831. Tel: 203-531-8741; Fax: 203-532-1414.
Catechesis/Religious Programs—Tel: 203-531-4265. D.R.E.: Dr. Karen Shields-Wright; Michael Baber.
Students 225.

4—ST. ROCH, (1938) (Italian), Revs. Nicholas J. Calabro; William G. Carey.
Res., 10 St. Roch Ave., 06830. Tel: 203-869-4176; Fax: 203-618-0341.
Catechesis/Religious Programs—Jane Kowaleski, D.R.E.
Students 172.

5—ST. AGNES, (1963), Rev. Stephen J. DeLuca.
Res., 247 Stanwich Rd., 06830. Tel: 203-869-5396; Fax: 203-625-0596.
Catechesis/Religious Programs—Mrs. Linda Nardone, D.R.E.
Students 62.

6—SACRED HEART, (1890), Rev. Martin S. Igoe.
Res., 95 Henry St., 06830. Tel: 203-531-8730; Fax: 203-531-8794.
Catechesis/Religious Programs—Tel: 203-531-4772. Sr. Elizabeth Telford, S.A., D.R.E.
Students 219.

Huntington, Fairfield Co., St. Lawrence (1955), Rev. Msgr. Joseph M. Fitzgerald; Revs. Michael F. Dogali; Nicholas A. Cirillo; Deacons James A. Brown; Joseph Filingeri; F. Robert Dwyer; Frank Masso.
Res., 505 Shelton Ave., Shelton, 06484. Tel: 203-929-5355; Fax: 203-929-8939.
School—See separate listing under Elementary Schools, Regional in the Institution section.
Catechesis/Religious Programs—Tel: 203-929-8421. Mrs. Barbara Pekar, D.R.E.
Students 950.

Monroe, Fairfield Co., St. Jude (1973), Rev. Msgr. John B. Sabia; Rev. Joseph J. Karcsinski; Deacon Ian F. Black.
Res., 707 Monroe Tpke., 06468. Tel: 203-261-6404; Fax: 203-261-7507.
School—See separate listing under Elementary Schools, Regional in the Institution section.
Catechesis/Religious Programs—Tel: 203-261-6788. Mrs. Jean Paul, D.R.E.
Students 1,596.

New Canaan, Fairfield Co., St. Aloysius (1896), Rev. Msgr. J. Peter Cullen; Rev. Dariusz J. Zielonka; Deacons John H. Tugman; Joseph L. Rowan.
Res., 40 Maple St., 06840. Tel: 203-966-0020; Fax: 203-972-7691.
School—See separate listing under Elementary Schools, Regional in the Institution section.
Catechesis/Religious Programs—30 Maple St., 06840. Tel: 203-966-4555; Fax: 203-801-0170.
Students 1,032.

New Fairfield, Fairfield Co., St. Edward the Confessor (1954), Rev. Msgr. Martin P. Ryan; Revs. Sylvester Ennin-Essien; Brian M. Gray; William M. Quinlan; Deacon Henry Hein.
Res., P.O. Box 8866, 06812. Tel: 203-746-2200; Fax: 203-746-4856.
Catechesis/Religious Programs—Tel: 203-746-4270. Ms. Joan Marschall, D.R.E.
Students 1,100.

Newtown, Fairfield Co., St. Rose of Lima (1859), Revs. Robert E. Weiss; Lawrence A. Larson; Peter J. Towsley; Deacon Thomas F. Curran.
Res., 46 Church Hill Rd., 06470. Tel: 203-426-1014; Fax: 203-426-6222. [CEM]
School—See separate listing under Elementary Schools, Regional in the Institution section.
Catechesis/Religious Programs—Tel: 203-426-2333. Pam Arsenault, D.R.E.
Students 1,472.

Norwalk, Fairfield Co.,

1—St. Jerome, (1960), Revs. David W. Blanchfield; Joseph Palacino.
Church—23 Half Mile Rd., 06851. Tel: 203-847-5349; Fax: 203-846-0238.
Catechesis/Religious Programs—Tel: 203-846-2111.
Students 400.

2—St. Joseph, (South Norwalk) (1895), Revs. David W. Howell; Gilbert P. D'Souza. In res., Rev. G. Frantz Desruisseaux; Deacon William O. Murphy.
Res., 85 S. Main St., P.O. Box 443, 06856. Tel: 203-838-4171; Fax: 203-899-0007.
Catechesis/Religious Programs—Tel: 203-866-1225. Deacon William O. Murphy, D.R.E.
Students 286.
Convent—14 Chestnut St., 06854. Tel: 203-866-9452.

3—St. Ladislaus, (1907) (Hungarian), Rev. Msgr. Edwin F. Burke. In res., Rev. Stephen J. Balint.
Res., 25 Cliff St., 06854. Tel: 203-866-1867; Fax: 203-866-7830.

4—St. Mary, (1848), Rev. Msgr. John C. Sanders; Revs. Gregory J. Huminski; Otoniel Lizcano; Deacon Stephan A. Genovese. In res., Revs. Paul N. Check; Christopher J. Walsh.
Res., 669 West Ave., 06850. Tel: 203-866-5546; Fax: 203-866-0464.
Catechesis/Religious Programs—Tel: 203-866-7429. Mrs. Deborah Ruffin, D.R.E.
Students 125.

5—St. Matthew, (1957), Revs. Walter C. Orlowski; Otoniel Lizcano; Deacon David M. Sochacki. In res., Rev. John Loftus.
Res., 216 Scribner Ave., 06854. Tel: 203-838-3788; Fax: 203-838-8195.
Catechesis/Religious Programs—Tel: 203-838-0231. Virginia Codeanne, D.R.E.
Students 575.

6—St. Philip, (1964), Revs. Michael A. Boccaccio; Albert G. Pinciaro, III; Deacons Frank J. Chiappetta; Paul J. Reilly.
Res., One Fr. Conlon Pl., 06851. Tel: 203-847-4549 (Office); Fax: 203-847-4148.
Catechesis/Religious Programs—Tel: 203-847-4286. Sr. Mary Ann McPartland, C.N.D., D.R.E.
Students 300.
Convent—23 France St., 06851. Tel: 203-847-1478.

7—St. Thomas the Apostle, (1935), Rev. Msgr. William J. Scheyd, P.A., V.G.; Revs. Michael F. Flynn; Richard Daniel Murphy; Deacon Joseph Gagne.
Res., 203 East Ave., 06855. Tel: 203-866-3141; Fax: 203-866-1219.
Good Counsel's Malta House—5 Prowitt St., 06855. Tel: 203-857-0088; Fax: 203-857-0018.
Catechesis/Religious Programs—Tel: 203-866-1189; Fax: 203-866-1219. Mrs. Patricia Braccio, D.R.E.
Students 350.

Redding, Fairfield Co., St. Patrick (1879), Rev. Msgr. John B. Hossan; Deacon William C. Timmel.
Res., 169 Black Rock Tpke., P.O. Box 119, Redding Ridge, 06876. Tel: 203-938-2253; Fax: 203-938-3396.
Catechesis/Religious Programs—Tel: 203-938-2963. Barbara L. Clarke, D.R.E.
Students 175.

Ridgefield, Fairfield Co., St. Elizabeth Seton (1978), Revs. Joseph A. Prince; Walter J. Seekamp; Deacons Bart Mauceri; Terence Grant.
Res., 520 Ridgebury Rd., 06877. Tel: 203-438-7292; Fax: 203-438-0600.
Catechesis/Religious Programs—Tel: 203-438-9707; Fax: 203-438-7947. Andrea Kennedy, D.R.E.
Students 640.

St. Mary, Fairfield Co, (1882), Revs. Robert P. Morrissey; Patrick J. Mooney; Leszek Szymaszek; Deacon Norman Roos.
Res., 183 High Ridge Ave., 06877. Tel: 203-438-6538; Fax: 203-438-4406. [CEM]
School—See separate listing under Elementary Schools, Regional in the Institution Section.
Catechesis/Religious Programs—Tel: 203-438-7335. Sr. Joan Brennan, D.R.E.
Students 1,525.

Riverside, Fairfield Co., St. Catherine of Siena (1913), Rev. Msgr. William A. Genuario, P.A.; Rev. Msgr. Alan F. Detscher; Revs. Marcel St. Jean; William F. Platt; Deacons Renato Berzolla; Robert Henrey; Vincent Heidenreich.
Res., 4 Riverside Ave., 06878. Tel: 203-637-3661; Fax: 203-637-8934.
Catechesis/Religious Programs—6 Riverside Ave., 06878. Tel: 203-637-3661, Ext. 30; Fax: 203-637-2089. Barbara Glynn, D.R.E.
Students 627.

Shelton, Fairfield Co., St. Joseph (1906), Revs. Francis T. Hoffmann; Colin J. McKenna; Deacon David Munson.
Res., 50 Fairmont Pl., 06484. Tel: 203-924-8611; Fax: 203-924-9446.
School—See separate listing under Elementary Schools, Regional in the Institution section.
Catechesis/Religious Programs—Tel: 203-924-9677. Mrs. Patricia Heller, D.R.E.
Students 510.
Convent—420 Coram Ave., 06484. Tel: 203-924-1545. Sisters of St. Joseph Chambery

St. Margaret Mary (1963), Rev. Msgr. Thomas J. Whalen; Rev. Raymond K. Petrucci; Deacon Matthew Skurat.
Res., 380 Long Hill Ave., 06484. Tel: 203-924-4929; Fax: 203-924-1849.
Catechesis/Religious Programs—Tel: 203-924-2679. Mrs. Carol D'Amico, D.R.E.
Students 335.

Sherman, Fairfield Co., Holy Trinity (1985), Rev. Msgr. George D. Birge.
Res., Rte. 37 & 39, P.O. Box 97, 06784. Tel: 860-354-1414; Fax: 860-355-9439.
Catechesis/Religious Programs—Tel: 860-355-5189; Fax: 860-355-9439. Mrs. Karen Cardillo, D.R.E.
Students 258.

Stamford, Fairfield Co.,

1—St. Benedict, (1930) (Slovak). Merged with Our Lady of Montserrat, Stamford to form Saint Benedict and Our Lady of Montserrat, Stamford.

2—Saint Benedict and Our Lady of Montserrat, (2000), Rev. Vincent J. Veich.
Mailing Address: One St. Benedict Cir., 06902. Tel: 203-327-7250; Fax: 203-327-7251.

3—St. Bridget, (1963), Rev. Gill C. Babeu.
Res., 278 Strawberry Hill Ave., 06902. Tel: 203-324-2910; Fax: 203-363-0135.
Catechesis/Religious Programs—Tel: 203-357-8157. Mrs. Jo Ann Tolla, D.R.E.
Students 145.

4—St. Cecilia, (1926), Revs. David J. Riley; Francis J. Moy, S.J.
Res., 1184 Newfield Ave., 06905. Tel: 203-322-1562; Fax: 203-968-1550.
School—See separate listing under Elementary Schools, Regional in the Institution section.

5—St. Clement, (1928), Revs. Andre R. Dube; David W. Franklin; Carlos Rodrigues; Deacon Paul E. Tupper.
Res., 535 Fairfield Ave., 06902. Tel: 203-348-4206; Fax: 203-316-8131.
Catechesis/Religious Programs—Tel: 203-348-1233; Fax: 203-316-8131.
Students 185.

6—St. Gabriel, (1963), Rev. Robert A. Uzzilio; Deacon Larry Buzzeo.
Res., 914 Newfield Ave., 06905. Tel: 203-322-7426; Fax: 203-968-6266.
School—See separate listing under Elementary Schools, Regional in the Institution section.
Catechesis/Religious Programs—Tel: 203-329-1978. Sr. Ann Marie Strileckis, C.N.D., D.R.E.
Students 218.

7—Holy Name of Jesus, (1903) (Polish), Revs. Sherman W. Gray, Jr., Ph.D.; Stanley Staniszewski, C.M.
Res., 4 Pulaski St., 06902. Tel: 203-323-4967; Fax: 203-327-2229.
Catechesis/Religious Programs—Tel: 203-359-3618; Fax: 203-323-4546. Sr. Donna Shatell, S.M.M.I., D.R.E.
Students 150.

8—Holy Spirit, (1962), Rev. Robert J. Hyl.
Res., 403 Scofieldtown Rd., 06903. Tel: 203-322-3722; Fax: 203-322-0543.
School—See separate listing under Elementary Schools, Regional in the Institution section.
Catechesis/Religious Programs—Tel: 203-357-1094. Linda Dunn, D.R.E.
Students 181.

9—St. John the Evangelist, (1854), Rev. Msgr. Stephen M. Di Giovanni, H.E.D.; Rev. Paul N. Check.
Res., 279 Atlantic St., 06901. Tel: 203-324-1553; Fax: 203-359-2660.
Catechesis/Religious Programs—Students 100.

10—St. Leo, (1960), Rev. Msgr. Benedict F. Tighe; Rev. Norman J. Guilbert; Deacons Joseph J. Farley; Ralph Hammock.
Res., 24 Roxbury Rd., 06902. Tel: 203-322-1669; 329-8884; Fax: 203-461-9761.
Catechesis/Religious Programs—Tel: 203-348-0052; Fax: 203-357-9639. Mrs. Florence Gambino, D.R.E.
Students 695.

11—St. Mary, (1907), Revs. Richard F. Futie; Matthew R. Mauriello; Edicson Orozco.
Res., 566 Elm St., 06902. Tel: 203-324-7321; Fax: 203-323-9407.
Catechesis/Religious Programs—Tel: 203-348-5196. Sr. Theresa Kovacs, D.R.E.
Students 220.

12—St. Maurice, (1935), Revs. Gerald T. Devore; Bernard A. Keefe. In res., Rev. John J. Castaldo.
Res., 358 Glenbrook Rd., 06906-2198. Tel: 203-324-3434; Fax: 203-964-8023.
Catechesis/Religious Programs—Tel: 203-348-8768; Fax: 203-964-8023. Janis Pataky, D.R.E.
Students 198.

13—Our Lady of Montserrat, (1984) (Spanish). Merged with St. Benedict, Stamford to form Saint Benedict and Our Lady of Montserrat, Stamford.

14—Our Lady Star of the Sea, (1964), Rev. Msgr. Edward R. Surwilo. In res., Rev. David H. Krahel.
Res., 1200 Shippan Ave., 06902. Tel: 203-324-4634; Fax: 203-348-9963.
School—See separate listing under Elementary Schools, Regional in the Institution section.
Catechesis/Religious Programs—Students 125.
Convent—1216 Shippan Ave., 06902. Tel: 203-359-1127.

15—Sacred Heart, (1920) (Italian), Revs. Robert G. Pohley; Thomas D. Nicastro; Alfred F. Pecaric; Rufin Kuveikis, O.F.M.Cap.; Deacon Fred Harrity.
Res., 37 Schuyler Ave., 06902. Tel: 203-324-9544; Fax: 203-324-9202.
School—See separate listing under Elementary Schools, Regional in the Institution section.
Catechesis/Religious Programs—Students 187.
Convent—21 Schuyler Ave., 06902. Tel: 203-323-3524.

Stratford, Fairfield Co.,

1—Holy Name of Jesus, (1923) (Slovak), Rev. Msgr. Peter P. Dora; Rev. Msgr. J. James Cuneo; Deacon Thomas Freibott.
Res., 1950 Barnum Ave., 06614. Tel: 203-375-5815; Fax: 203-375-5954.
School—See separate listing under Elementary Schools, Regional in the Institution section.
Catechesis/Religious Programs—Tel: 203-378-7407.
Students 333.
Convent—2 Mary Ave., 06614. Tel: 203-378-1203.

2—St. James, (1886), Revs. Thomas F. Lynch; Frank A. Winn; Louis M. Dytkowski; Deacon John Barton. In res., Rev. Donald A. Guglielmi.
Res., 2110 Main St., 06615. Tel: 203-375-5887; Fax: 203-378-1562.

School—See separate listing under Elementary Schools, Regional in the Institution section.
Catechesis/Religious Programs—Therese LeFever, D.R.E.
Students 491.

3—St. Mark, (1960), Rev. Msgr. Lawrence J. McMahon; Rev. Stanley N. Koziol; Deacons T. Emmet Murray; F. Paul Kurmay; Andrew Dzujna.
Res., 500 Wigwam Ln., 06614. Tel: 203-377-0444; Fax: 203-378-7913.
School—See separate listing under Elementary Schools, Regional in the Institution section.
Catechesis/Religious Programs—Tel: 203-377-3158. Mr. Jon Ribeiro, D.R.E.
Students 510.

4—Our Lady of Grace, (1954), Rev. Msgr. William F. Schultz; Rev. Edward J. Small, S.J. In res., Rev. Msgr. Jerald A. Doyle; Deacon Robert W. McLaughlin.
Res., 497 Second Hill Ln., 06614-2595. Tel: 203-377-0928; Fax: 203-377-5235.
Parish Center—375 Second Hill Ln., 06614-2595. Tel: 203-375-2005.
Catechesis/Religious Programs—Tel: 203-375-2005. Mrs. Denise L. Bartelson, D.R.E.
Students 290.

5—Our Lady of Peace, (1948), Rev. Msgr. John E. Gilmartin. In res., Rev. Frank C. McGrath.
Res., 230 Park Blvd., 06615. Tel: 203-377-4863; Fax: 203-378-5253.
Catechesis/Religious Programs—Tel: 203-378-3053. Sr. Carolyn Stoe, S.S.N.D., D.R.E.
Students 155.

Trumbull, Fairfield Co.,

1—Christ the King, (1962), Revs. Bernard M. Dolan; Lawrence F. Carew; Deacon Frederick A. Harrity.
Res., 4700 Madison Ave., 06611. Tel: 203-268-8695; Fax: 203-268-9265.
Catechesis/Religious Programs—Tel: 203-261-2583.
Students 350.

2—St. Catherine of Siena, (1955), Rev. Msgr. Richard J. Shea; Rev. Peter A. DeMarco. In res., Rev. Peter J. Lynch.
Res., 200 Shelton Rd., 06611. Tel: 203-377-3133; Fax: 203-377-1023.
School—See separate listing under Elementary Schools, Regional in the Institution section. Tel: 203-375-1947; Fax: 203-378-3935.
Convent—14 Great Neck Rd., Shelton, 06484. Tel: 203-925-0458.

3—St. Stephen, (1953), Revs. Stephen J. Gleeson; Nicholas S. Pavia; Edward A. Colohan; Deacons Gary Carpenter; Donald Brunetto; Thomas Mack.
Res., 6948 Main St., 06611. Tel: 203-268-6217; Fax: 203-268-9861.
Catechesis/Religious Programs—Tel: 203-268-6860. Sr. Beth McGlynn, S.S.N.D., D.R.E.
Students 554.

4—St. Theresa, (1934), Rev. Msgr. Louis A. DeProfio; Revs. Thomas W. Powers; Kevin P. Fitzpatrick; Bose Raja Selvaraj; Sr. Joan Flynn, R.S.M., Dir. Pastoral Min.; Deacons H. Paul Herman; Salvatore Clarizio, Ph.D. In res., Rev. William F. Sangiovanni.
Res., 5301 Main St., 06611. Tel: 203-261-3676; Fax: 203-268-8723.
School—See separate listing under Elementary Schools, Regional in the Institution section.
Catechesis/Religious Programs—19 Rosemond Ter., 06611. Tel: 203-261-4706. Sr. Georgiana Miller, S.M.M.I., D.R.E.
Students 953.
Convent—Tel: 203-261-3848.
Sisters Minor of Mary Immaculate 3.

Weston, Fairfield Co., St. Francis of Assisi (1955), Rev. Msgr. Nicholas V. Grieco. In res., Revs. Joseph K. Parampath; Alfred J. Bietighofer; Robert D. Karpinski.
Res., 35 Norfield Rd, P.O. Box 1025, 06883. Tel: 203-227-1341; Fax: 203-226-1154.
Catechesis/Religious Programs—Tel: 203-226-9474.
Students 471.

Westport, Fairfield Co., Assumption (1876), Revs. Thomas P. Thorne; David C. Leopold; Deacons Eugene P. Kamper; John S. Fay. In res., Rev. Msgr. Laurence R. Bronkiewicz; Rev. Robert D. Karpinski.
Res., 98 Riverside Ave., 06880. Tel: 203-227-5161; Fax: 203-227-1206. [CEM]
Catechesis/Religious Programs—Tel: 203-226-5448. Cathy Romano, D.R.E.
Students 339.

St. Luke (1957), Revs. Andrew G. Varga; Paul G. Murphy; Deacons Brian J. Kelly; Lance C. Fredricks.
Res., 84 Long Lots Rd., 06880. Tel: 203-227-7245; Fax: 203-226-8063.
Catechesis/Religious Programs—Tel: 203-226-0729; Fax: 203-226-5446. Jane E. Ferreira, D.R.E.
Students 854.

Wilton, Fairfield Co., Our Lady of Fatima (1953), Revs. Michael C. Palmer; James Breen; Deacons Thomas K. Seith; Thomas J. McManus.
Res., 229 Danbury Rd., 06897. Tel: 203-762-3928; Fax: 203-834-1261.
School—See separate listing under Elementary Schools, Regional in the Institution section.
Catechesis/Religious Programs—Tel: 203-762-9080. Mrs. Kathleen Rooney, D.R.E.
Students 1,200.

Chaplains of Public Institutions

Bridgeport. *Bridgeport Community Correctional Facility* 1106 North Ave., 06604. Tel: 203-579-6131. Deacon Carl M. Vecca Tel: 203-582-6477.
Bridgeport Health Care 600 Bond St., 06610. Tel: 203-384-6400. Rev. Michael A. D'Elia.
Bridgeport Hospital 267 Grant St., 06610. Tel: 203-384-3311. Revs. Nello A. Barachini; Bernardo C. Rodriguez.

Danbury. *Danbury Area Mental Health Authority*. Vacant. 64 West St., 06810. Tel: 203-778-1640, Ext. 247.
Danbury Hospital 24 Hospital Ave., 06810. Tel: 203-797-7000. Revs. John F. Pikulski; Brian M. Gray.
Federal Correctional Institution 06811. Tel: 203-743-6471. Sr. Anne Marie Raftery, O.S.F., Dir. of Pastoral Care.

Greenwich. *Greenwich Hospital* 06830. Tel: 203-863-3000. Revs. William F. Platt; David W. Franklin.

Norwalk. *Norwalk Hospital* 06856. Tel: 203-852-2000. Rev. Rufin Kuveikis, O.F.M.Cap.

Stamford. *Stamford Hospital* 06902. Tel: 203-325-7584. Rev. David W. Franklin.

On Duty Outside the Diocese:
Reverend Monsignors—
Cusack, Andrew T., Dir. National Institute for Clergy Formation, Seton Hall University, 400 S. Orange Ave., South Orange, NJ 07079
Green, Thomas J., Catholic University of America, Department of Canon Law, Washington, DC 20017
Millea, William V., Via della Nocetta 63, Rome, 00164 Italy
Reverend Fathers—
Holbrook, Harold M., Padres De Santiago Apostol, Casilla 1021, Oruro, Bolivia
Loftus, Robert A., St. Ann Rectory, 130 Boston Tpke., Shewsbury, PA 01545
McDevitt, James A., St. Ann, 1220 Northway Rd., Williamsport, PA 17701
McDonough, Roger F., St. Joan of Arc, 370 S.W. Third St., Boca Raton, FL 33432
Mitchell, John C., P.O. Box 701, Carmel, NY 10072
Posluszny, Francis, Parroquia San Juan Apostal, APTO 735, Chiclayo, Peru
Smolko, John F., Catholic University of America, 9808 Dale Dr., Upper Marlboro, MD 20870
Talar, Charles J.T., St. Mary Seminary & University, 5400 Roland Rd., Baltimore, MD 21210
Terentieff, Robert J., Georgian Court College, 900 Lakewood Ave., Lakewood, NJ 08701
Tracy, David W., University of Chicago, The Divinity School, 5521 S. University, Chicago, IL 60637
Verrilli, William F., St. Mary Church, 520 Veirs Mill Rd., Rockville, MD 20852

Graduate Studies:
Reverend Fathers—
Jones, Michael K.

Military Chaplains:
Reverend Fathers—
Carey, William F., U.S. Army
Gay, James A., U.S. Navy
Thompson, William D., U.S. Air Force

Leave of Absence:
Reverend Monsignors—
Stubbs, Charles W.
Reverend Fathers—
Federici, Martin J.
Griffin, Paul D.
Hudanish, Jeffrey A.
Moore, Joseph P.
Yocis, David A.

Retired:
Reverend Monsignors—
Botton, Pierre A.
Caldas, Constantino R.
Campagnone, Francis A.
Hale, Harry L.
Halloran, Edward D.
Horgan-Kung, John V.
Jazowski, John F.
Kohut, Joseph J.
Laurello, Bartholomew J.
Medynski, Francis J.
Methe, Normand A.
Nagle, William A.
Potter, Joseph D.
Sanders, John C.
Scanlon, Bernard S.
Tetreault, Jean C.
Watts, Roger J.
Reverend Fathers—
Brady, Philip W.
Coleman, W. Philip
Coyne, Edwin J.
Dennehy, Martin J.
Dennis, James J.
Fernandez, Jose A.
Fonseca, John
Gregori, Emidio O.
Grise, J. Clifford
Hitchcock, Martin B.
Hribsek, Aloysius J.
Knurek, Dennis A.
Maglione, Joseph J.
Monahan, Richard J.
Morrissey, Philip T.
Onze, Robert E.
Polinsky, John R.
Rarus, Boleslaus J.
Rossitto, Joseph V.
Suwinski, Leo S.
Usenza, Robert J.

Permanent Deacons:
Africot, Alix, St. Patrick, Bridgeport
Ashe, Matthew, St. Mary, Greenwich
Barton, Jack, St. James, Stratford
Becker, Robert, St. Mary, Bethel
Berzolla, Renato L., St. Catherine, Riverside
Bissenden, William J., St. Patrick, Bridgeport
Black, Ian F., St. Jude, Monroe
Blankschen, Robert, St. Gregory, Danbury
Blier, Roland, St. Andrew, Bridgeport
Brown, James, St. Lawrence, Huntington
Brunetto, Donald W., St. Stephen, Trumbull
Buzzeo, Michael L., St. Gabriel, Stamford
Cabral, Jose R., Immaculate Heart of Mary, Danbury
Calabrese, Robert P., St. Anthony Maronite, Danbury
Carpenter, Gary E., St. Stephen, Trumbull
Chiappetta, Frank, St. Philip, Norwalk
Clarizio, Salvatore, St. Theresa, Trumbull
Curran, Thomas F., St. Rose, Newtown
Detje, Anthony, St. Edward the Confessor, New Fairfield
Dwyer, F. Robert, St. Joseph, Shelton
Dzujna, Andrew W., St. Mark, Stratford
Esterheld, John, Sacred Heart, Danbury
Farley, Joseph J., St. Leo, Stamford
Fay, John S., Assumption, Westport
Filingeri, Joseph, St. Lawrence, Huntington
Finch, Dean, St. Jerome, Norwalk
Foust, Donald P., Blessed Sacrament, Bridgeport
Fredricks, Lance C., St. Luke, Westport
Freibott, Thomas, Holy Name, Stratford
Gagne, Joseph, St. Thomas, Fairfield
Garcia, Santos, Florida
Genovese, Stephan, St. Mary, Norwalk
Grant, Terence J., St. Elizabeth Seton, Ridgefield
Hammock, Ralph, St. Leo, Stamford
Harrity, Frederick A., Sacred Heart, Stamford
Heidenreich, Vincent, St. Catherine, Riverside
Hein, Henry R., St. Edward, New Fairfield
Hendricks, Edward R., St. Andrew, Bridgeport
Henrey, Robert, St. Catherine of Siena, Riverside
Herman, H. Paul, St. Teresa, Trumbull
Howe, Louis F., Sacred Heart, Stamford
Ianniello, Daniel, Holy Rosary, Bridgeport
Isidro, Ramon, Our Lady of Montserrat, Stamford
Kamper, Eugene P., Assumption, Westport
Kelly, Brian J., St. Luke, Westport
Kovacs, Edward, Our Lady Star of the Sea, Stamford
Kovacs, Richard, St. Joseph, Brookfield
Kuhn, Peter, St. Joseph, Brookfield
Kurmay, Paul, St. Mark, Stratford
Lynch, Harold, Notre Dame, Easton
Mack, D. Thomas, St. Stephen, Trumbull
Mann, John J., Our Lady Star of the Sea, Stamford
Martinez, Ricardo, Blessed Sacrament, Bridgeport
Masso, Frank J., St. Lawrence, Huntington
Mauceri, Bartholomew, St. Elizabeth Seton, Ridgefield
McLaughlin, Robert, Our Lady of Grace, Stratford
McMarcus, Thomas, Our Lady of Fatima, Wilton
Melita, Joseph, St. Raphael, Bridgeport
Moore, Kevin, Holy Cross, Fairfield
Moranski, John J., St. Ann, Bridgeport
Munson, David D., St. Joseph, Shelton

Murphy, William D., St. Gregory the Great, Danbury
Murphy, William O., St. Joseph, Norwalk
Murray, Emmet, St. Mark, Stratford
Myott, Daniel N., St. Gregory the Great, Danbury
Naiman, Donald, St. Gregory, Danbury
Nelson, Thomas E., Marguerite Bourgeoys, Brookfield
Pereira, Gabriel, Our Lady of Fatima, Bridgeport
Pilkington, Paul, St. Edward, New Fairfield
Pratt, Nicholas, St. Ann, Bridgeport
Reilly, Paul, St. Philip, Norwalk
Reveron, Domingo, St. Peter, Bridgeport
Ross, Donald J., Assumption, Fairfield
Ross, Norman, St. Mary, Ridgefield
Rowan, Joseph L., St. Thomas More, Darien
Rowe, William K., St. John, Darien
Sabol, Gerald, Notre Dame, Easton
Saymon, Richard F., Leave of Absence
Sebestyen, Stephen, Holy Family, Fairfield
Seith, Thomas K., Our Lady of Fatima, Wilton
Shaughnessy, William, St. Joseph, Brookfield
Shine, Mark, St. Matthew, Norwalk
Skurat, Matthew, St. Margaret Mary, Shelton
Sochacki, David, St. Matthew, Norwalk
Stenberg, S. Richard, St. Pius X, Fairfield
Stroud, Kenneth, St. Rose, Newtown
Sullivan, Timothy, St. Augustine Cathedral, Bridgeport
Timmel, William C., St. Patrick, Redding
Torres, Luis, St. Peter, Bridgeport
Tugman, John H., St. Aloysius, New Canaan
Tupper, Paul, St. Clement, Stamford
Vaughn, David J., St. Joseph, Danbury
Volpe, James, St. Ambrose, Bridgeport
Wolfer, Michael K., St. Stephen, Trumbull

INSTITUTIONS LOCATED IN THE DIOCESE

[A] SEMINARIES, DIOCESAN

STAMFORD. *St. John Fisher Seminary Residence*, 894 Newfield Ave., 06905. Tel: 203-322-5331; Fax: 203-461-9876.
E-mail: info@saintjohnfisher.org
Rev. Kevin T. Royal, S.T.L., Rector; Rev. Msgr. Stanley B. Rousseau, S.T.L., M.A., Spiritual Dir.; Christopher J. Walsh, Ph.D., Vocation Dir.

[B] COLLEGES AND UNIVERSITIES

BRIDGEPORT. *St. Vincent's College*, 2800 Main St., 06606. Tel: 203-576-5235; Fax: 203-576-5893.
E-mail: jnolanfaye@aol.com
Web site: www.stvincentscollege.edu
For a complete listing, refer to the Colleges and Universities section.

FAIRFIELD. *Fairfield University*, 1073 N. Benson Rd., 06430-5195. Tel: 203-254-4000; Fax: 203-254-4101.
Web site: www.fairfield.edu
For a complete listing, refer to the Colleges and Universities section.

Sacred Heart University, 5151 Park Ave., 06432-1000. Tel: 203-371-7999; Fax: 203-365-7652.
E-mail: QUINNM@sacredheart.edu
Web site: sacredheart.edu
For a complete listing, refer to the Colleges and Universities section.

[C] HIGH SCHOOLS, DIOCESAN

BRIDGEPORT. *Kolbe-Cathedral High School*, 33 Calhoun Pl., 06604. Tel: 203-335-2554; Fax: 203-335-2556.
E-mail: cjones@kolbecaths.com
Mrs. Jo Anne Jakab, Prin.; Ms. Carol A. Jones, Asst. Prin.; Rev. Donald A. Guglielmi, Spiritual Dir. Priests 1; Sisters 1; Lay Teachers 25; Administrators 2; Students 300.

DANBURY. *Immaculate High School*, 73 Southern Blvd., 06810. Tel: 203-744-1510; Fax: 203-744-1275.
E-mail: immacula@mail1.NAI.NET
Web site: www.immaculatehs.org
Dr. Joseph Gerics, Prin.; Mr. Richard T. Stoops, Asst. Prin.; Rev. Corey V. Piccinino, Spiritual Dir. Priests 2; Sisters 1; Lay Teachers 31; Students 410.

FAIRFIELD. *Notre Dame Catholic High School*, 220 Jefferson St., 06432. Tel: 203-372-6521; Fax: 203-374-0387.
E-mail: info@notredame.org
Web site: www.notredame.org
Rev. William F. Sangiovanni, Prin.; Mr. Carl Philipp, Asst. Prin. Priests 1; School Sisters of Notre Dame 1; Lay Teachers 43; Students 700.

STAMFORD. *Trinity Catholic High School*. (Formerly Stamford Catholic High School), 926 Newfield Ave., 09605. Tel: 203-322-3401; Fax: 203-322-5330.
E-mail: TCHS1@JUNO.COM
Web site: www.trinitycatholic.org
Peter M. Borchetta, Prin.; Robert D'Aquila, Asst. Prin.; Robert Chomiak, Asst. Prin.; Mrs. Connie McGoldrick, Admissions Coord.; Rev. John J. Castaldo, Spiritual Dir.; Mrs. Margaret Mira, Dir. Guidance; Mr. Tracy Nichols, Athletic Dir.; Mrs. Eileen Irving, Dir. Devel. & Alumni Rels.; Mrs. Mary D'Aquila, Reach Out. Priests 2; Sisters 1; Lay Teachers 31; Students 420. Records for Central Catholic High School, Norwich, and St. Mary's High School, Greenwich, located at Trinity.

TRUMBULL. *St. Joseph High School*, 2320 Huntington Tpke., 06611-5099. Tel: 203-378-9378; Fax: 203-378-7306.
E-mail: rbishop@sjhs.put.K12.ct.us
Web site: www.shjs.pvt.k12.ct.us
Mr. Richard A. Bishop, Prin.; Rev. Robert D. Karpinski, Asst. Prin. Academic Affairs; Mrs. Laurene Collins, Asst. Prin. for Student Affairs; Mrs. Suzanne Siano, Dir. of Guidance; Rev. Peter J. Lynch, Spiritual Dir.; Mr. Vito M. Montelli, Dir. Athletics; Mrs. Jackie Carlino, Alumni Relations; Mrs. Maureen Anderson, Coord. for Student Activities; Mr. Kenneth Mayo, Dean of Students; Mrs. Patricia Hayes, Dean of Students; Mrs. Margaret Marino, Admissions Coord.; Sr. Marie E. Iannuccillo, Dir. of Campus Min.; Mr. Gerald DeForge, Registrar; Mrs. Doreen Rafferty, Bursar. Priests 2; Sisters 2; Lay Teachers 52; Students 800.

[D] SPECIAL SCHOOLS, DIOCESAN

BRIDGEPORT. *St. Catherine Academy*. (Grades K-12), 238 Jewett Ave., 06606-2892. Tel: 203-372-1623; Fax: 203-373-0571. Sr. Marilyn Muldoon, O.S.U., Admin.

[E] HIGH SCHOOLS, PRIVATE

FAIRFIELD. *Fairfield College Preparatory School*, N. Benson Rd., 06430. Tel: 203-254-4200; Fax: 203-254-4108.
E-mail: rperrotta@campus.Fairfield.edu
Web site: www.prep.fairfield.edu
A preparatory day school for boys, established in 1942. Society of Jesus of New England. Very Rev. Aloysius P. Kelley, S.J., Pres. Fairfield University; Revs. Michael Boughton, S.J., Pres.; Donald M. Barry, S.J.; James J. Hederman, S.J.; George A. Gallarelli, S.J.; Walter R. Pelletier, S.J.; Ronald V. Perry, S.J.; Lawrence D. Ryan, S.J.; Martin G. Shaughnessy, S.J. Priests 8; Lay Teachers 59; Students 846.

STAMFORD. *Sacred Heart Academy of Stamford*, 200 Strawberry Hill Ave., 06902-2589. Tel: 203-323-3173; Fax: 203-975-7804.
E-mail: sha200adm@aol.com
Web site: www.shastamford.org
Sisters of St. Joseph. Sr. Jeanne Paulella, C.S.J., Prin. Sisters 4; Lay Teachers 19; Students 120.

[F] ELEMENTARY SCHOOLS, REGIONAL

BRIDGEPORT. *Catholic Elementary Schools-Region X*, The Catholic Center, 238 Jewett Ave., 06606. Tel: 203-372-4301, Ext. 233; Fax: 203-372-0020.
E-mail: bcessmgr@aol.com
Mr. Robert P. Gaits, Business Mgr.
St. Ambrose. (Grades PreK-8), 461 Mill Hill Ave., 06610. Tel: 203-368-2835; Fax: 203-366-0599. Sr. Catherine Van Houten, S.S.J., Prin. Servants of the Immaculate of Mary 3; Lay Teachers 12; Students 381. St. Andrew. (Grades K-8), 395 Anton St., 06606. Tel: 203-372-4819; Fax: 203-373-0641. Mr. Michael Fettig, Prin. Lay Teachers 9; Students 227. St. Ann. (Grades PreK-8), 521 Brewster St., 06605. Tel: 203-334-5856; Fax: 203-333-8263. Mrs. Mary Daley, Prin. Daughters of the Holy Spirit 1; Lay Teachers 9; Students 238. St. Augustine Cathedral. (Grades PreK-8), 63 Pequonnock St., 06604. Tel: 203-367-5896; Fax: 203-333-6694. Mrs. Barbara A. Coscio, Prin. Lay Teachers 10; Students 216. St. Peter. (Grades K-8), 659 Beechwood Ave., 06605. Tel: 203-333-2048; Fax: 203-333-2878. Miss Suzanna Zello, Prin. Sisters of the Company of the Savior 2; Lay Teachers 7; Students 241. St. Raphael. (Grades PreK-8), 324 Frank St., 06604. Tel: 203-333-6818; Fax: 203-336-9205. Sr. Kathleen Mary Coonan, A.S.C.J., Prin. Apostles of the Sacred Heart 3; Lay Teachers 8; Students 277.

DANBURY. *Catholic Elementary Schools-Region IX and XI*, Business Office, 3 Tammany Tr., 06811. Tel: 203-744-6248; Fax: 203-748-7603.
Region IX. Tel: 203-744-6248; Fax: 203-748-7603. Rev. Msgr. Martin P. Ryan; Mr. Frank X. Hauser, Business Mgr., St. Gregory the Great. (Grades K-8), 85 Great Plain Rd., 06811. Tel: 203-748-1217; Fax: 203-748-1217, Ext. 51. Sr. Mary John O'Rourke, O.S.U., Prin., Lay Teachers 10; Students 262. St. Joseph. (Grades K-8), 370 Main St., 06810. Tel: 203-748-6615; Fax: 203-748-6508. Mrs. Sharon Quish, Prin., Lay Teachers 15; Students 304. St. Peter, 98 Main St., 06810. Tel: 203-748-2895; Fax: 203-748-5684. Mrs. Josephine P. Ferry, Prin., Lay Teachers 10; Students 235. Sacred Heart. (Grades K-8), 17 Cottage St., 06810. Tel: 203-792-6194; Fax: 203-778-4025.
E-mail: shschool@snet.net
Web site: www.danbury.org
Sr. M. Benilda Nadloski, F.S.S.J., Prin. Franciscan Sisters of St. Joseph 3; Lay Teachers 8; Students 209.
Region XI. St. Mary. (Grades K-8), 24 Dodgingtown Rd., Bethel, 06801. Tel: 203-744-2922; Fax: 203-798-8803. Sr. Anne McCarthy, Prin., Lay Teachers 10; Students 230. St. Joseph. (Grades K-8), Rte. 133, Brookfield, 06804. Tel: 203-775-2774; Fax: 203-775-5810. Mrs. Barbara Blank, Prin., Lay Teachers 9; Students 241. St. Rose. (Grades K-8), 40 Church Hill Rd., Newtown, 06470. Tel: 203-426-5102; Fax: 203-426-5374. Mrs. Donna DeLuca, Prin. Lay Teachers 10; Students 247.

FAIRFIELD. *Catholic Elementary Schools-Region V*, 108 Biro St., P.O. Box 320358, 06432. Tel: 203-334-6327; Fax: 203-334-6497.
E-mail: FERCSjec@aol.com
Mrs. Jean Correa, Business Mgr., Holy Family. (Grades PreK-8), Edison Ave., 06430. Tel: 203-367-5409; Fax: 203-335-7317. Mrs. Mary McCormack. Lay Teachers 15; Students 305. Our Lady of the Assumption. (Grades PreK-8), 591 Stratfield Rd., 06432. Tel: 203-334-6271; Fax: 203-334-1374. Ms. Gerri Desio, Prin. Sisters of St. Dominic of Newburgh 1; Lay Teachers 20; Students 380. St. Thomas Aquinas. (Grades PreK-8), 1719 Post Rd., 06430. Tel: 203-255-0556; Fax: 203-255-0596. Mrs. Mary Frances King, Prin. Lay Teachers 20; Students 455.

GREENWICH. *Catholic Elementary Schools-Region I*. Greenwich Catholic School, 471 North St., 06830. Tel: 203-869-4000; Fax: 203-869-3405.
E-mail: Greencath@aol.com
Web site: www.greenwichcatholic.com.
Mrs. Mary Flume, Business Mgr., Greenwich Catholic School. (Grades PreK-8), 471 North St., 06830. Tel: 203-869-4000. Mrs. Genevieve Madonna, Prin. Lay Teachers 34; Students 469.

NORWALK. *Catholic Elementary Schools-Region III*, All Saints Catholic School, 139 W. Rocks Rd., 06851. Tel: 203-847-3881; Fax: 203-847-3884. Mrs. Jean Nichols, Business Mgr., All Saints Catholic Elementary School. (Grades DayCare-8), 139 W. Rocks Rd., 06851. Tel: 203-847-3881. Sr. Catherine Sheehy, R.S.M., Prin. Lay Teachers 51; Sisters 3; Students 844.

SHELTON. *Catholic Elementary Schools-Region VIII*. St. Lawrence Rectory/Shelton Catholic Regional School, 505 Shelton Ave., 06484. Tel: 203-924-4754; Fax: 203-922-0161.
E-mail: Stlawrence.school@snet.net
Web site: www.ctschool.net/stlawrenceschool
Mrs. Joanne Simpson, Business Mgr., St. Joseph. (Grades PreK-8), 430 Coram Ave., 06484. Tel: 203-924-4669; Fax: 203-922-0161.
E-mail: stjoseph.school@snet.net
Mrs. Cheryl Nelson, Prin. Sisters of St. Joseph of Chambery 2; Lay Teachers 16; Students 442. St. Lawrence. (Grades PreK-8), 503 Shelton Ave., 06484. Tel: 203-929-4422; Fax: 203-929-3669. Mrs. Kathleen Gosart, Prin. Sisters 1; Lay Teachers 12; Students 326.

STAMFORD. *Catholic Elementary Schools-Region II*, Catholic Regional School System, Inc., 926 Newfield Ave., P.O. Box 3127, 06905-0127. Tel: 203-968-2795; Fax: 203-968-2794. Mrs. Kathleen K. Carty, Business Mgr., St. Aloysius. (Grades K-8), 33 South Ave., New Canaan, 06840. Tel: 203-966-0786; Fax: 203-972-6960. Suzanne Dale Wilcox, Prin. Lay Teachers 18; Students 187. Holy Spirit. (Grades PreK-5), 403 Scofieldtown Rd., 06903. Tel: 203-329-1623; Fax: 203-595-0858. Alfred Liotta, Prin. Lay Teachers 12; Students 160. Our Lady Star of the Sea. (Grades PreK-5), 1170 Shippan Ave., 06902. Tel: 203-348-1155; Fax: 203-324-6150. Mrs. Gail Ryan, Prin. Ursuline Sisters 1; Lay Teachers 9; Students 148. Sacred Heart. (Grades PreK-8), One Schuyler Ave., 06902. Tel: 203-323-4844; Fax: 203-359-9859. Sr. Pietrina Mazzola, M.P.F., Prin. Religious Teachers Filippini 2; Lay Teachers 10; Students 175. St. Cecilia. (Grades PreK-5), 1186 Newfield Ave., 06905. Tel: 203-322-6505; Fax: 203-322-6835. Mrs. Joann Borchetta, Prin. Sisters 1; Lay Teachers 16; Students 332. St. Gabriel. (Grades 6-8), 948 Newfield Ave., 06905. Tel: 203-322-7383; Fax: 203-322-4435. Mr. Robert J. Cavaliero, Prin. Religious 1; Lay Teachers 21; Students 266.

STRATFORD. *Catholic Elementary Schools-Region VI*, Stratford Catholic Regional School, St. James Campus, One Monument Pl., 06615. Tel: 203-380-1990; Fax: 203-380-0749.
E-mail: stjames.school.01@snet.net
Mrs. Natalia Zamachaj, Business Mgr., St. James. (Grades K-8), One Monument Pl., 06615. Tel: 203-375-5994; Fax: 203-380-0749. Ms. Carolyn E. Stockdale, Prin.; Sr. Gloria Marie Kascak, S.S.C.M., Asst. Prin. Lay Teachers 28; Students 479. St.

Mark. (Grades K-8), 500 Wigwam Ln., 06614. Tel: 203-375-4291; Fax: 203-386-1955. Mr. Phillip T. Adzima, Prin. Lay Teachers 11; Students 241.

TRUMBULL. *Catholic Elementary Schools-Region VII*, St. Catherine of Siena, 190 Shelton Rd., 06611. Tel: 203-375-1947; Fax: 203-378-3935. Mr. Ray LaLuna, Business Mgr., St. Jude. (Grades PreK-8), 707 Monroe Tpke., Monroe, 06468. Tel: 203-261-3619; Fax: 203-268-8748. Mrs. Linda Dunn, Prin. Lay Teachers 10; Students 261. St. Catherine of Siena. (Grades PreK-8), 190 Shelton Rd., 06611. Tel: 203-375-1947; Fax: 203-378-3935. Sr. Anne Marie Dorff, S.S.N.D., Prin. Lay Teachers 10; Students 294. St. Theresa. (Grades PreK-8), 55 Rosemond Ter., 06611. Tel: 203-268-3236; Fax: 203-268-3236. Sr. Carolyn Mary Cossack, S.M.M.I., Prin. Lay Teachers 11; Students 276.

WILTON. *Catholic Elementary Schools-Region IV*, Our Lady of Fatima School, 225 Danbury Rd., 06897. Tel: 203-762-8100.
Web site: www.wiltonCT.com/Fatima/
Mrs. Mary Gardiner, Business Mgr., Our Lady of Fatima. (Grades PreK-8), 225 Danbury Rd., 06897. Tel: 203-762-8100; Fax: 203-834-0614. Mrs. Mary Ann Bozzuti, Prin. Lay Teachers 22; Students 260. Saint Mary's. (Grades K-4), 183 High Ridge Ave., Ridgefield, 06877. Tel: 203-438-7288; Fax: 203-438-4406. Mrs. Jeannine Ludeke, Prin. Lay Teachers 9; Students 90.

[G] ELEMENTARY SCHOOLS, PRIVATE

GREENWICH. *Convent of the Sacred Heart*. (Grades PreK-12). Day School for Girls, 1177 King St., 06831. Tel: 203-531-6500; Fax: 203-531-5206.
E-mail: sacredheart@cshgreenwich.org
Web site: www.chsgreenwich.org
Sr. Joan Magnetti, R.S.C.J., Headmistress. Students 573.

STAMFORD. *Villa Maria Education Center*, 161 Sky Meadow Dr., 06903. Tel: 203-322-5886; Fax: 203-322-0228. Bernardine Sisters. School for Children with Learning Disabilities. Sr. Carol Ann, O.S.F., Exec. Dir.; Laura LaMura, Educ. Dir. Students 74.

[H] CATHOLIC CHARITIES

BRIDGEPORT. *Catholic Charities of Fairfield County*, Catholic Center, 238 Jewett Ave., 06606-2892. Tel: 203-372-4301, Ext. 379; 564; Fax: 203-372-5045.
E-mail: info@cathcharitiesffldcty.com
Web site: www.cathcharitiesffldcty.org
Brian A. Cronin, A.C.S.W., L.C.S.W., Exec. Dir.; Benedict P. Mazotas, Controller.

Adoption Program. China Identified Adoptions, Traditional Adoptions and Home Studies. 238 Jewett Ave., 06606-2892. Tel: 203-372-4301, ext. 370.
E-mail: ccfcadptn@aol.com
Anne Lyons-Steers, Dir.

Catholic Family Services, Bridgeport, 238 Jewett Ave., 06606-2892. Tel: 203-372-4301, Ext. 348; Fax: 203-373-0835. Michael Tintrup, A.C.S.W., L.C.S.W., District Exec. Dir.

Catholic Family Services, Danbury, 30 Main St., Ste. 503, Danbury, 06810. Tel: 203-743-4412; Fax: 203-744-3500.
E-mail: ccfcdnb@aol.com

Ways to Work Family Loan Program, 30 Main St., Ste. 503, Danbury, 06810.

Catholic Family Services, Norwalk, 7 Chapel St., P.O. Box 2025, Norwalk, 06852. Tel: 203-838-2316; Fax: 203-838-6364.
E-mail: ccfcnwlk@aol.com
Susan Williams, L.C.S.W., District Exec. Dir.

Catholic Family Services, Stamford, 30 Myano Ln., Stamford, 06902. Tel: 203-323-1105; Fax: 203-323-1108.
E-mail: ccfcstmfd@aol.com
Elaine Eichler, A.C.S.W., L.C.S.W., District Exec. Dir.
Catholic Family Services Outreach Offices: 1986 Post Rd., Darien, 06820. Tel: 203-655-2169; Fax: 203-744-3500.
E-mail: ccfcstmfd@aol.com
90 East Ridge, Ridgefield, 06877. Tel: 203-431-8170; Fax: 203-744-3500.
E-mail: ccfcdnb@aol.com
452 Howe Ave., Shelton, 06484. Tel: 203-924-9604. 80 Ferry Blvd., Stratford, 06615. Tel: 203-375-9553; Fax: 203-373-0835.
E-mail: ccfcbpt@aol.com
44 Old Ridgefield Rd., Wilton, 06897. Tel: 203-834-2076; Fax: 203-834-7485.
E-mail: ccfcnwlk@aol.com
Day Care Programs/Room to Grow, 208 East Ave., Norwalk, 06855. Tel: 203-831-8200; Fax: 203-855-0637.
E-mail: ccfcnwlk@aol.com
Susan Williams, L.C.S.W., Interim Dir.

Houses of Hospitality:
New Covenant House of Hospitality (Yerwood Center), 90 Fairfield Ave., Stamford, 06904. Tel: 203-964-8228; Fax: 203-375-0314.
E-mail: ccfcnch@aol.com
Eva L. Colon, M.S., C.E.D., Dir.

Thomas Merton Center, 43 Madison Ave., 06604. Tel: 203-367-9036; Fax: 203-367-8828.
E-mail: ccfctmc@aol.com
Mary Ann Furlong, R.N., Dir.

Family Life Ministry. Please call Rev. Ernest T. Esposito, Exec. Dir., Tel: 203-372-4301, Ext. 314, for the following programs: Ministry to Widows; Bereavement; Job Transition; Post-Abortion Support; Divorced and Separated; Marriage Profile; Marriage Preparation; Marriage Enrichment; and Family Enrichment. Diocesan Office, 238 Jewett Ave., 06606-2892. Tel: 203-372-4301, Ext. 320; Fax: 203-371-8698. Rev. Ernest T. Esposito, D.Min., Dir.

Family Life / Respect Life Catholic Center, 238 Jewett Ave., 06606-2892. Tel: 203-372-4301, Ext. 314.

St. Stephen's Emergency Food Center, 477 Paquonnock St., 06604. Tel: 203-394-6881.

Mental Health Outreach: Danbury, New Heights, 66 West Street, Danbury, 06810. Tel: 203-794-0819; Fax: 203-731-3260.
E-mail: ccfcnh@aol.com
Maria Urban, Program Dir. Case Management Program, 233 White St., Danbury, 06810. Tel: 203-748-0848; Fax: 203-748-4839.
E-mail: ccfcm@aol.com
Web site: www.cathcharitiesffldcty.org
Sandy Cole, Dir.

Homeless Outreach Team, 233 White St., Danbury, 06810. Tel: 203-748-0848; Fax: 203-748-4839.
E-mail: ccfccm@aol.com
Web site: www.cathcharitiesffldcty.org
Eileen Walsh, Dir.

Thresholds. (Shelter for Women & Children), 5 Harmony St., Danbury, 06810. Tel: 203-792-8609; Fax: 203-792-2813.
E-mail: ccfcth@aol.com
Sandy Cerqueria, Prog. Dir.

Nutrition and Aging Services, 30 Myano Ln., Stamford, 06902. Tel: 203-324-6175; Fax: 203-323-1108.
E-mail: ccfcsn@aol.com
Cindy Phelps, Dir.

Table to Table Program, 30 Myano Ln., Ste. 10, Stamford, 06902. Tel: 203-323-3211; Fax: 203-975-1199.
Web site: www.table2table.org
Mary Ryan, Contact Person.

Senior Citizen Outreach, 30 Main St., Ste. 503, Danbury, 06810. Tel: 203-743-4412; Fax: 203-744-3500.
E-mail: ccfcdnb@aol.com
Robin Resin, L.C.S.W., Prog. Coord.

Intensive Outreach and Monitoring. (for adjudicated delinquents 10-16 years), CFS Stamford, 30 Myano Ln., Stamford, 06902. Tel: 203-323-1105; Fax: 203-323-1108.

Intensive Outreach and Monitoring, 96 Catherine St., 06604. Tel: 203-366-0721, Ext. 386; Fax: 203-366-1143.
E-mail: ccfciom@aol.com

Intensive Outreach and Monitoring, 7 Chapel St., Norwalk, 06852-2025. Tel: 203-838-2316; Fax: 203-838-6364.
E-mail: ccfciom@aol.com
Larry O'Brien, B.S.; M.S, Regl. Dir.

Social Issues Advocacy, 238 Jewett Ave., 06606-2892. Tel: 203-372-4301; Fax: 203-372-5045, Ext. 386.
E-mail: ccfcsc@aol.com
Edie Cassidy, R.N., Dir. Health, Aging Issues. Tel: 203-372-4301 Ext. 386.

St. Joseph Center for Poor and Needy, Inc., 238 Jewett Ave., 06606. Tel: 203-372-4301, Ext. 564; Fax: 203-372-5045. Brian A. Cronin, Exec. Dir.

[I] DAY NURSERIES

BRIDGEPORT. *Daughters of Charity of the Most Precious Blood Day Nursery*, 1490 North Ave., 06604. Tel: 203-334-7000. Sr. Theresa Tremblay, Dir.

STAMFORD. *Our Lady of Grace Day Nursery*, 635 Glenbrook Rd., 06906. Tel: 203-348-5531; Fax: 203-324-9638. Little Workers of the Sacred Hearts. Sr. Lillian Cairo, P.O.S.C., Supr.

Stepping Stones Preschool, Inc., Sacred Heart Academy, 200 Strawberry Hill Ave., 06902. Tel: 203-323-3173. Sisters of Saint Joseph.

WILTON. *Notre Dame Child Development Center, Inc.*, 345 Belden Hill Rd., 06897. Tel: 203-762-2814. Sr. Mary Serafine Della Croce, S.S.N.D.

[J] GENERAL HOSPITALS

BRIDGEPORT. *St. Joseph Medical Center Foundation, Inc.*, Diocese of Bridgeport, 238 Jewett Ave., 06606-2852
For a complete listing, refer to the Hospitals section.

St. Vincent's Development Corporation, 2800 Main St., 06606. Tel: 203-576-5459; Fax: 203-576-5345.
Web site: www.stvincents.org
For a complete listing, refer to the Hospitals section.

St. Vincent's Health Services Corporation, 2800 Main St., 06606. Tel: 203-576-5455; Fax: 203-576-5345.
Web site: www.stvincents.org
For a complete listing, refer to the Hospitals section.

St. Vincent's Medical Center, 2800 Main St., 06606. Tel: 203-576-6000; Fax: 203-576-5345.
Web site: www.stvincents.org
For a complete listing, refer to the Hospitals section.

St. Vincent's Medical Center Foundation, 2800 Main St., 06606. Tel: 203-576-5451; Fax: 203-576-5880
For a complete listing, refer to the Hospitals section.

[K] SPECIAL HOSPITALS

BRIDGEPORT. *Bridgeport Diocesan Health Care Corporation*, 238 Jewett Ave., 06606. Tel: 203-372-4301; Fax: 203-372-1817.
E-mail: nygs@aol.com
For a complete listing, refer to the Special Care Facilities section.

The Pope John Paul II Foundation, Inc., 238 Jewett Ave., 06606. Tel: 203-797-9300; Fax: 203-797-9300
For a complete listing, refer to the Special Care Facilities section.

St. Camillus Home Foundation, Inc., 238 Jewett Ave., 06606. Tel: 203-325-0200; Fax: 203-353-0550
For a complete listing, refer to the Special Care Facilities section.

DANBURY. *The Pope John Paul II Center for Health Care, Inc.*, 33 Lincoln Ave., 06810. Tel: 203-797-9300; Fax: 203-790-4645.
E-mail: onedee98@aol,com
For a complete listing, refer to the Special Care Facilities section.

STAMFORD. *St. Camillus Health Center*, 494 Elm St., 06902. Tel: 203-325-0200; Fax: 203-353-0550.
Web site: www.stcamillushealth.org
For a complete listing, refer to the Special Care Facilities section.

[L] HOMES FOR AGED

BRIDGEPORT. *Augustana Homes / Bishop Curtis Homes*, 525 Palisade Ave., 06610. Tel: 203-366-4333; Fax: 203-366-4756
For a complete listing, refer to the Special Care Facilities section.

Augustana Homes / Bishop Curtis Homes, 280 Jewett Ave., 06606. Tel: 203-374-5346
For a complete listing, refer to the Special Care Facilities section.

Augustana Homes / Bishop Curtis Homes - East Bridgeport, 238 Jewett Ave., 06606. Tel: 203-372-4301; Fax: 203-371-8698
For a complete listing, refer to the Special Care Facilities section.

Roncalli Apartments, 430 Grant St., 06610. Tel: 203-384-9984
For a complete listing, refer to the Special Care Facilities section.

BETHEL. *Augustana Homes / Bishop Curtis Homes*, Simeon Rd., 06801. Tel: 203-743-2508
For a complete listing, refer to the Special Care Facilities section.

DANBURY. *Augustana Homes Bishop Curtis Homes - Danbury*, 88 Main St., 06810. Tel: 203-791-8510; Fax: 203-791-8513
For a complete listing, refer to the Special Care Facilities section.

FAIRFIELD. *Augustana Homes / Bishop Curtis Homes*, 1677 Post Rd., 06430
For a complete listing, refer to the Special Care Facilities section.

RIVERSIDE. *Augustana Homes of Greenwich / Bishop Curtis Homes*, 1040 E. Putnam Ave., 06878
For a complete listing, refer to the Special Care Facilities section.

STAMFORD. *Augustana Homes / Bishop Curtis Homes - Glenbrook*, 352 Glenbrook Rd., 06902. Tel: 203-576-0823
For a complete listing, refer to the Special Care Facilities section.

TRUMBULL. *Carmel Ridge*, 6454 Main St., 06611. Tel: 203-261-2229
For a complete listing, refer to the Special Care Facilities section.

St. Joseph's Housing Corporation, Teresian Towers & Carmel Ridge Estates, 6448 Main St., 06611. Tel: 203-261-2229
For a complete listing, refer to the Special Care Facilities section.

St. Joseph's Manor, 6448 Main St., 06611. Tel: 203-268-6204; Fax: 203-268-5271.
E-mail: saint.joseph.manor@snet.net
Web site: www.stjosephsmanor.org
For a complete listing, refer to the Special Care Facilities section.

[M] CONVALESCENT HOMES

NORWALK. *Notre Dame Convalescent Home,* 76 W. Rocks Rd., 06851. Tel: 203-847-5893; Fax: 203-849-1959 *For a complete listing, refer to the Special Care Facilities section.*

[N] SOCIAL PROGRAMS

BRIDGEPORT. *Social Issues Advocate-Parish Social Concerns,* 238 Jewett Ave., 06606. Tel: 203-372-4301. Brian A. Cronin, Campaign for Human Development; Edith Cassidy, Social Concerns Dir.

[O] MONASTIC FOUNDATIONS

WEST REDDING. *The Benedictine Grange,* 06896. Tel: 203-938-3689; Fax: 203-938-3689. Rev. John B. Giuliani, Dir.

[P] RESIDENCES OF PRIESTS AND BROTHERS

BRIDGEPORT. *Provincial Offices of the Priests and Brothers of Holy Cross, Eastern Province.* (Province of Our Lady of Holy Cross), 835 Clinton Ave., 06604. Tel: 203-367-7252; Fax: 203-366-7886.
E-mail: acolgan@hcep.com
Web site: www.stonehill.Edu.HolyCross
Revs. Arthur J. Colgan, C.S.C., Prov.; James T. Preskenis, C.S.C., Asst. Vicar Prov. & Vicar; James Lackenmier, C.S.C., Prov. Steward & Treas.; James J. Doherty, C.S.C., Most Holy Trinity Parish, Saco, ME. Tel: 207-282-3321; Fax: 207-284-2274. Rev. James T. Donohue, C.S.C., 784 Columbus Ave., Apt. 14-C, New York, NY. Tel: 212-360-3948. Holy Cross Residence, Easton, MA. Tel: 508-230-8446. Rev. Robert A. Krieg, C.S.C., University of Notre Dame, Notre Dame, IN. Tel: 219-631-5129; Fax: 219-631-9233. Rev. Jerome R. Lawyer, C.S.C., Holy Cross House, Notre Dame, IN. Tel: 219-631-6337. Rev. James P. Madden, C.S.C., Brothers of Holy Cross, Valatie, NY. Tel: 518-784-9481. Rev. Michael A. Massaro, C.S.C., Holy Cross Church, 'Vero Beach, FL. Tel: 561-231-0671. Rev. James L. Rebeta, C.S.C., Cornell Medical Center, White Plains, NY. Tel: 914-997-5776. Rev. Patrick J. Sullivan, C.S.C., King's College, Wilkes-Barre, PA. Tel: 570-208-5816. Our Lady's House of Prayer, Clearwater, FL. Tel: 727-726-5267; Fax: 727-799-2595. Rev. Frank A. Toste, C.S.C., Union Institute of Cincinnati, Sanbornville, NH; Fax: 603-522-9244. Rev. John L. Young, C.S.C., Whiting Forensic Institute, Middletown. Tel: 860-262-5487; Fax: 860-262-5477. Legal Title: *Congregation of Holy Cross - Eastern Province, Inc.*

FAIRFIELD. *The Fairfield Jesuit Community-Fairfield University,* 06430-5195. Tel: 203-256-2663; Fax: 203-255-5947.
E-mail: jhiggins@Fair1.Fairfield.EDU
Web site: www.faculty.fairfieldedu/faculty/jmac/fjc/fjcomm.htw
Revs. Charles H. Allen, S.J.; Francis R. Allen, S.J.; Donald M. Barry, S.J.; John V. Borgo, S.J.; Michael Boughton, S.J.; Gerhard H. Bowering, S.J. (Germany); James S. Bowler, S.J.; Mark J. Burke, S.J.; Vincent M. Burns, S.J.; Albert A. Cardoni, S.J.; William F. Carr, S.J.; Paul E. Carrier, S.J.; Mark J. Connolly, S.J.; Richard D. Costello, S.J.; William J. Cullen, S.J.; Richard J. Deshaies, S.J.; John W. Elder, S.J.; George A. Gallarelli, S.J.; Andrew J. Garavel, S.J.; Gregg H. Grovenburg, S.J.; Francis T. Hannafey, S.J.; Johannes B. Hari Kustanto, S.J. (Indonesia); James J. Hederman, S.J.; John J. Higgins, S.J.; Aloysius P. Kelley, S.J.; William J. Kennedy, S.J.; Victor F. Leeber, S.J.; Francis W. Lewis, S.J.; Donald D. Lynch, S.J.; Joseph F. MacDonnell, S.J.; James J. Mayzik, S.J.; Francis J. McManus, S.J.; Francis J. Moy, S.J.; W. Laurence O'Neil, S.J.; Walter R. Pelletier, S.J.; Ronald V. Perry, S.J.; Albert F. Reddy, S.J.; Thomas J. Regan, S.J.; Laurence D. Ryan, S.J.; James P. Scull, S.J.; Martin G. Shaughnessy, S.J.; Edward J. Small, S.J.

STAMFORD. *The Catherine Dennis Keefe Queen of the Clergy Retired Priests' Residence.* Home for Retired Priests. 274 Strawberry Hill Ave., 06902. Tel: 203-358-9906; Fax: 203-358-9524. Rev. Msgr. Bernard S. Scanlon; Rev. Msgr. Harry L. Hale; Rev. Msgr. Edward D. Halloran; Rev. Msgr. John V. Horgan-Kung; Rev. Msgr. Normand A. Methe; Rev. Msgr. William A. Nagle; Rev. Msgr. John C. Sanders; Revs. James J. Dennis; Joseph J. Maglione; John R. Polinsky; Boleslaus J. Rarus; Joseph V. Rossito.
St. John Fisher Seminary Residence, 894 Newfield Ave., 06905. Tel: 203-322-5331; Fax: 203-461-9876. Revs. Kevin T. Royal, S.T.L., Rector; Christopher J. Walsh, Ph.D., Vocation Dir.; Rev. Msgr. Stanley B. Rousseau, Spiritual Dir.

[Q] CONVENTS AND RESIDENCES FOR SISTERS

BRIDGEPORT. *Convent of Mary Immaculate, Missionary Sisters of the Blessed Sacrament and Mary Immaculate.* Prov. Headquarters. 1111 Wordin Ave., 06605. Tel: 203-334-5681; Fax: 203-333-1590.
E-mail: mssmi1896@aol.com
Sr. Nirma Rodriguez, Provincial. Assisting the Apostolate to Spanish-Speaking People. Sisters 6.
Daughters of Charity of the Most Precious Blood Convent, 1482 North Ave., 06604. Tel: 203-334-7000. Sr. Theresa Tremblay, Dir.
Holy Spirit Convent, Daughters of the Holy Spirit, 50 Pequonnock St., 06604. Tel: 203-334-6926; Fax: 203-334-6926.
E-mail: sisters.holy.ghost@snet.net
Staffing & ministry work in public health.
Sisters of the Company of the Savior, 820 Clinton Ave., 06604. Tel: 203-368-1875; Fax: 203-368-1875. Spanish-Speaking Apostolate. Mother Araceli Fernandez, Supr.

GREENWICH. *Sacred Heart Convent,* 38 Gold St., 06830. Tel: 203-531-8547. Franciscan Sisters of the Atonement 7.

MONROE. *Provincial House, Immaculate Heart of Mary Province, Sisters of the Holy Family of Nazareth, C.S.F.N.,* 1428 Monroe Tpke., 06468. Tel: 203-268-7646; Fax: 203-452-9947. Sr. M. Agnese Palczynski, C.S.F.N., Prov. Supr.; Rev. James J. Cole, Chap. Professed 55.

NORWALK. *Regional House of Sisters of St. Thomas of Villanova,* 76 W. Rocks Rd., 06851. Tel: 203-847-2885; Fax: 203-847-3740.
E-mail: vocationdirectorsstv@juno.com
Mother Edmond, S.S.T.V., Supr. Notre Dame Convalescent Home; Rev. Albert W. Watts, Chap. Professed 4.

RIDGEFIELD. *Provincial House, Congregation de Notre Dame,* 223 W. Mountain Rd., 06877. Tel: 203-438-5282; Fax: 203-894-9686.
E-mail: provsec@juno.com
Sr. Anne C. Leonard, C.N.D., Prov. Supr.; Sr. Kathleen Murphy, C.N.D., Supr., Local Community. Tel: 203-438-3115; Rev. Michael J. McCarthy, Chap.

STAMFORD. *Heart of Mary Convent (Residence for Bernardine Sisters),* 163 Sky Meadow Dr., 06903. Tel: 203-322-5920; Fax: 203-322-5491.
E-mail: HMCSTAM@aol.com
Sr. M. Dymphna Zakowski, O.S.F., Admin. Tel: 203-322-8721. Bernardine Sisters 8.
Villa Maria Education Center. Tel: 203-322-5886; Fax: 203-322-0228. School for children with learning disabilities (Grades 1-8). Sr. Carol Ann Nawracaj, O.S.F., Exec. Dir.
Monastery of St. Clare, 1954 Long Ridge Rd., 06903-3232. Tel: 203-329-2252; Fax: 603-754-0504.
E-mail: stamfdmsc@aol.com
Web site: www.geocities.com/heartland/hills/8054
Sr. Mary Michael Biosseau, O.S.C., Abbess.
Our Lady of Grace Convent, 635 Glenbrook Rd., 06906. Tel: 203-348-5531; Fax: 203-324-9638. Motherhouse and Novitiate of Little Workers of Sacred Hearts. Sr. Daria Gencarelli, P.O.S.C., Supr.
Sisters Minor of Mary Immaculate, Holy Name of Jesus Convent, 305 Washington Blvd., 06902. Tel: 203-323-4546. Sisters 3.
St. Francis Villa Custody House, Immaculate Conception Custody, 138 Brushy Hill Rd., Danbury, 06810. Tel: 203-744-8041. Sr. Theresa Marie Kovacs, S.M.M.I., Delegate and V.G. Sisters 3.
Villa Divino Amore Convent, Little Workers of the Sacred Hearts of Jesus & Mary, 117 Hope St., 06906. Tel: 203-324-2449. Sr. Giacinta Scaramuzzo, P.O.S.C., Supr.

WILTON. *Lourdes Health Care Center, Inc.,* 345 Belden Hill Rd., 06897-3898. Tel: 203-762-3318, Ext. 361; Fax: 203-762-2144.
E-mail: Hfrostssnd@cs.com
Sr. Mary Henrita Frost, Pres.; Rev. Victor W. Chaupetta, M.S., Res. Chap.
School Sisters of Notre Dame Motherhouse (Northeastern Province), 345 Belden Hill Rd., 06897. Tel: 203-762-3318; Fax: 203-761-9228.
Web site: http://www.SSND.ORG
Sr. Marie Jeannette Blatz, Prov. Supr.; Rev. Victor W. Chaupetta, M.S. Tel: 203-762-3318. Priests 1; Professed 130.

[R] SECULAR INSTITUTES

BRIDGEPORT. *The Society of Our Lady of the Way,* 584 Capitol Ave., Apt. 6, 06606. Tel: 203-579-4531. A secular institute for women. Miss Margaret Gould, Unit Dir.; Rev. Timothy Curtin, S.J.

[S] FOUNDATIONS, TRUSTS AND FUNDS

BRIDGEPORT. *Fairfield Foundation of the Diocese of Bridgeport, Inc.,* 238 Jewett Ave., 06606-2892. Tel: 203-372-4301; Fax: 203-371-8698. Mrs. Michele H. Jones Delmhorst, Pres.; Mr. John Croffy, Exec. Dir.
Inner-City Foundation for Charity & Education, 238 Jewett Ave., 06606-2892. Tel: 203-372-4301; Fax: 203-371-8698.
E-mail: innercity.foundation@snet.net
Rev. Msgr. Kevin W. Wallin, Exec. Dir.

[T] GUEST HOUSES

DARIEN. *Convent of St. Birgitta,* 06820. Tel: 203-655-1068; Fax: 203-655-3496.
E-mail: convent.st.birgitta@snet.net
Sr. M. Sabina Kavanadi, O.SS.S., Supr.; Rev. Richard G. Cipolla, Chap.

[U] HOUSES OF STUDIES

BRIDGEPORT. *St. Peter's Parish, St. Maximillian Kolbe House of Studies,* 535 Colorado Ave., 06605. Tel: 203-335-4992.
E-mail: st.m.kolbe.house@snet.net
Rev. Msgr. Francis C. Wissel, Dir.; Ms. Carmen Serrano, Supr.

[V] RETREAT HOUSES

BRIDGEPORT. *Queen of Saints, The Catholic Center,* 238 Jewett Ave., 06606. Tel: 203-372-4301, Ext. 217. School of Religion and Spirituality and Retreat Facility.
The Urban Center of St. Charles Parish, 1279 E. Main St., 06608. Tel: 203-366-4190; Fax: 203-333-8422.
St. Charles Outreach Program. Sr. Ilona Mensik, S.S.N.D., Dir. of Outreach.

STAMFORD. *Villa Maria Retreat,* 159 Sky Meadow Dr., 06903. Tel: 203-322-0107; Fax: 203-595-0647.
E-mail: villa.maria@juno.com
Retreat center for men & women. Sr. Maria J. Riedel, O.S.F., Exec. Dir., Spiritual Direction; Sr. Joanne Slanga, O.S.F., Retreat/Spiritual Direction; Reiki Master, Myers-Briggs; Sr. Patricia Jamison, C.N.D., Program Devel. Dir., Spiritual Direction, Supervision; Sr. Peggy Riordan, R.S.M., Dir., Spiritual Dir., Reiki Practitioner, Marketing Dir.; Rev. Paul Lalic, Chap. Bernardine Franciscan Sisters 8.

[W] NEWMAN CENTERS

FAIRFIELD. *Newman Centers - Campus Ministry,* 06432-1000. Ms. Patricia Leonard-Pasley, Campus Min.
Sacred Heart University (Fairfield), 5151 Park Ave., 06430-1000. Tel: 203-371-7840. Rev. Michael Zielke, O.F.M.Conv., Dir. Campus Ministry.
Western Connecticut State University (Danbury), P.O. Box 706, Danbury, 06813. Tel: 203-837-9225.
Fairfield University (Fairfield), N. Benson Rd., 06430. Tel: 203-255-4511. Rev. Paul E. Carrier, S.J. Assistant Chaplains: Revs. Joseph J. Shad, S.J.; Richard J. Stanley, S.J.; Mr. Robert W. Canter, S.J.

[X] MISCELLANEOUS LISTINGS

BRIDGEPORT. *Blessed Brother Andre Charitable Trust,* 835 Clinton Ave., 06604. Tel: 203-367-7252; Fax: 203-366-7886.
E-mail: acolgan@hcep.com
Cardinal Shehan Center, Inc., 1494 Main St., 06604. Tel: 203-336-4468; Fax: 203-368-0901.
E-mail: camray93@snet.net
Web site: shehancenter.org
Mr. Terry O'Connor, Exec. Dir.
Caroline House, Inc., 574 Stillman St., 06608. Tel: 203-334-0640; Fax: 203-334-0248.
E-mail: schotzi@aol.com
Sr. Maureen Fleming, S.S.N.D., Dir.; Sr. Brenda Lynch, S.S.N.D., Dir.
The Diocesan Cemetery Care Fund, Inc., 238 Jewett Ave, 06606.
Faith in the Future Fund, Inc., 238 Jewett Ave., 06606. Tel: 203-372-4301; Fax: 203-373-6890.
E-mail: schwipp@ibm.net
Thomas M. Sweeney, Dir. for Devel.
Hispanic Social Ministries of Fairfield County, Inc., 238 Jewett Ave., 06606-9990. Rev. Msgr. Aniceto Villamide, Contact Person.
Needle Fund, Inc., 238 Jewett Ave., 06606.
The Queen's Daughters, c/o Sr. Therese, D.H.S., 50 Pequonnock St., 06604. Tel: 203-334-6924; Fax: 203-334-6926.
E-mail: sisters.holy.ghost@snet.net
Mrs. Mary Mazur, Pres. Sponsoring agency for Holy Spirit Convent. Care of the sick and poor in their homes by Daughters of the Holy Spirit.
St. Catherine Academy, 238 Jewett Ave., 06610. Tel: 203-372-1623; Fax: 203-371-8698. Sr. Marilyn Muldoon, Prin.; Sr. Eleace King, Contact Person.

FAIRFIELD. *The Institute for Religious Education and Pastoral Studies (REAPS),* Sacred Heart University, 5151 Park Ave., 06432-1000. Tel: 203-371-7843; 371-7867; Fax: 203-365-4798.
E-mail: reaps@sacredheart.edu
Web site: www.sacredheart.edu/reaps
Rev. Msgr. Gregory M. Smith, Ed.D., Dir.; Mrs. Patricia A. Murphy, Asst. Dir.; Mr. William G. Joyce, Special Asst. to Dir.; Deacon Daniel Ianniello, Dir. Devel. & Grants; Mrs. Patricia Maurer, Coord. Admissions & Retention; Mr. William Lyons, Coord. Electronic & Technological Learning; Mrs. Catherine Brewer, Admin. Sec.; Mr. Christopher Sheehan, Coord. of Publicity & Grants; Mrs. Florence Wheeler, Data Programmer.

GREENWICH. *Clemons Productions, Inc.* (In association with That's The Spirit Productions, Inc.), P.O. Box 7466, 06836; Fax: 203-316-9396.
Web site: www.spirituality.org
Rev. Mark Connolly, Pres. Tel: 203-316-9394, Spirituality For Today.

NORWALK. *Malta House of Good Counsel*, 5 Prowitt St., 06855-1203. Tel: 203-857-0088; Fax: 203-857-0018.

RIDGEFIELD. *The St. Mary's Endowment Trust*, 183 High Ridge Ave., 06877. Tel: 203-438-6538; Fax: 203-438-4406.
E-mail: stmarysrcc@aol.com
Web site: www.stmarysridgefield.org

SHELTON. *Fr. McKenna St. Vincent de Paul Shoppe*, P.O. Box 271, 06484-0271. Tel: 203-924-4817. Rev. Robert G. Pohley, Chap.; Barbara Samor, Dir.; Sandie Bailie, Asst. Dir.

STAMFORD. *Haitian American Catholic Center of Greater Stamford*, 93 Hope St., 06906. Tel: 203-323-8391. Rev. Jean Ridly Julien, Exec. Dir.

Stamford Catholic Library, 566 Elm St., 06902. Tel: 203-348-4422. Mr. Lawrence Smith, Pres.; Rev. Robert G. Pohley, Chap.; Mary Louise Flowers, Contact Person.

WILTON. *St. Benedict Guild*, Cannondale Depot, 06897. Tel: 203-762-3633. Marion Najamy, Owner.

RELIGIOUS INSTITUTES OF MEN REPRESENTED IN THE DIOCESE

For further details refer to the corresponding bracketed number in the Religious Institutes of Men or Women section.

[0200]—*Benedictine Monks.*—O.S.B.
[0470]—*The Capuchin Friars.* (Prov. of St. Mary).—O.F.M.Cap.
[0270]—*Carmelite Fathers & Brothers.* (St. Elias Prov. New York).—O.Carm.
[0480]—*Conventual Franciscans.* (St. Anthony of Padua Prov.).—O.F.M.Conv.
[0520]—*Franciscan Friars.* (Commissariat of St. Stephen).—O.F.M.
[0650]—*Holy Ghost Fathers.* (Irish Prov.).—C.S.Sp.
[0690]—*Jesuit Fathers and Brothers.* (New England Prov.).—S.J.
[0870]—*Montfort Missionaries.* (Haitian Prov.).—S.M.M.
[0610]—*Priests of the Congregation of Holy Cross.* (Prov. of Our Lady of Holy Cross).—C.S.C.

RELIGIOUS INSTITUTES OF WOMEN REPRESENTED IN THE DIOCESE

[0130]—*Apostles of the Sacred Heart of Jesus.*—A.S.C.J.
[1810]—*Bernardine Sisters of the Third Order of St. Francis.*—O.S.F.
[0280]—*Brigittine Sisters.*—O.SS.S.
[0330]—*Carmelite Sisters for the Aged and Infirm.*—O.Carm.
[0710]—*Company of the Savior.*—C.S.
[4030]—*Congregation of Sisters of St. Thomas of Villanova.*—S.S.T.V.
[0760]—*Daughters of Charity of St. Vincent de Paul.*—D.C.
[0740]—*Daughters of Charity of the Most Precious Blood.*
[0790]—*Daughters of Divine Charity.*—F.D.C.
[0820]—*Daughters of the Holy Spirit.*—D.H.S.
[0960]—*Daughters of Wisdom.*—D.W.
[1070]—*Dominican Sisters.*—O.P.
[1470]—*Franciscan Sisters of St. Joseph.*—F.S.S.J.
[1190]—*Franciscan Sisters of the Atonement.*—S.A.
[2575]—*Institute of the Sisters of Mercy of the Americas.*—R.S.M.
[2345]—*Little Workers of the Sacred Hearts of Jesus & Mary.*—P.O.S.C.
[2780]—*Missionary Sisters of the Most Blessed Sacrament.* (Spain).—M.SS.S.
[3760]—*Order of St. Clare.*—O.S.C.
[3430]—*Religious Teachers Filippini.*—M.P.F.
[2970]—*School Sisters of Notre Dame.*—S.S.N.D.
[]—*Sisters Minor of the Mary Immaculate.*—S.M.M.I.
[0590]—*Sisters of Charity of Saint Elizabeth, Convent Station.*—S.C.
[0620]—*Sisters of Charity of St. Louis.*—S.C.S.L.
[2990]—*Sisters of Notre Dame.*—S.N.D.
[3000]—*Sisters of Notre Dame de Namur.*—S.N.D.deN.
[3780]—*Sisters of Saints Cyril and Methodius.*—SS.C.M.
[3850]—*Sisters of St. Joseph of Chambery.*
[2980]—*Sisters of the Congregation de Notre Dame.*—C.N.D.
[1970]—*Sisters of the Holy Family of Nazareth.*—C.S.F.N.
[3480]—*Sisters of the Resurrection.* (Eastern Prov.).—C.R.
[2160]—*Sisters, Servants of the Immaculate Heart of Mary.*—I.H.M.
[4070]—*Society of the Sacred Heart.*—R.S.C.J.
[4130]—*Ursuline Sisters of the Congregation of Tildonk, Belgium.*—O.S.U.

DIOCESAN CEMETERIES

BRIDGEPORT. *St. Michael's*, 2205 Stratford Ave., 06497. Tel: 203-378-0404.

DANBURY. *St. Peter's*, Lake Ave. Exit, 06810. Tel: 203-743-9626.

GREENWICH. *Putnam*, 35 Parsonage Rd., 06830. Tel: 203-869-4828.

St. Mary's, 399 North St., 06830. Tel: 203-869-7026.

NEWTOWN. *Resurrection*, c/o St. Peter Cemetery, Lake Ave. Exit, 06810. Tel: 203-743-9626.

NORWALK. *St. John's & St. Mary's*, 223 Richards Ave., 06850. Tel: 203-838-4271.

STAMFORD. *Queen of Peace*, c/o St. John Cemetery, 25 Camp Ave., 06820. Tel: 203-322-0455.

St. John's, 25 Camp Ave., 06820. Tel: 203-322-0455.

TRUMBULL. *Gate of Heaven*, c/o St. Michael's, 2205 Stratford Ave., 06497. Tel: 203-378-0404.

WESTPORT. *Assumption Green Farms*, Kings Hwy., c/o St. John Cemetery, 223 Richards Ave., 06850. Tel: 203-838-4271.

NECROLOGY

† Biondino, Joseph Patrick, Schenectady, NY St. Joseph. —Died Jan. 8, 2001.

† D'Elia, Michael Anthony, Chap, Bridgeport, CT Dinan Center. —Died Oct. 29, 2000.

† Pranckus, Rev. Msgr. Francis John, (Retired). —Died Sept. 6, 2000.

Diocese of Brooklyn

(Dioecesis Bruklyniensis)

Most Reverend

THOMAS V. DAILY, D.D.

Sixth Bishop of Brooklyn; ordained January 10, 1952; appointed Auxiliary to the Archbishop of Boston and Titular Bishop of Bladia December 31, 1974; consecrated February 11, 1975; appointed First Bishop of Palm Beach July 17, 1984; appointed Sixth Bishop of Brooklyn February 20, 1990; took possession April 16, 1990; installed April 18, 1990. *Mailing Address: 75 Greene Ave., P.O. Box C, Brooklyn, NY, 11202.*

Chancery Office: 75 Greene Ave., P.O. Box C, Brooklyn, NY, 11202. Tel.: 718-399-5900; Fax: 718-399-5934.

E-mail address: curiabrook@aol.com

Most Reverend

JOSEPH M. SULLIVAN, M.S.W., M.P.A., V.E.

Tenth Auxiliary to the Bishop of Brooklyn; ordained June 2, 1956; appointed Titular Bishop of Suliana October 7, 1980; episcopal ordination November 24, 1980. *Mailing Address: 378 Clermont Ave., Brooklyn, NY, 11238.*

Most Reverend

RENE A. VALERO, M.S.W.

Eleventh Auxiliary to the Bishop of Brooklyn; priestly ordination June 2, 1956; appointed Titular Bishop of Vicus Turris October 7, 1980; episcopal ordination November 24, 1980. *Res., 34-43 93rd St., Jackson Heights, NY, 11372.*

Most Reverend

IGNATIUS A. CATANELLO, PH.D.

Twelfth Auxiliary to the Bishop of Brooklyn; ordained May 28, 1966; appointed Titular Bishop of Deulto June 28, 1994; episcopal ordination August 22, 1994. *Res., 175-20 74th Ave., Flushing, NY, 11366.*

ESTABLISHED JULY 29, 1853.

Square Miles 179.25.

Comprises Kings and Queens Counties in the State of New York.

For legal titles of parishes and diocesan institutions, consult the Chancery Office.

STATISTICAL OVERVIEW

Personnel	
Bishop	1
Auxiliary Bishops	3
Retired Bishops	2
Priests: Diocesan Active in Diocese	416
Priests: Active Outside Diocese	47
Priests: Diocesan in Foreign Missions	1
Priests: Retired, Sick or Absent	185
Number of Diocesan Priests	649
Religious Priests in Diocese	78
Extern Priests in Diocese	90
Ordinations:	
Diocesan Priests	3
Religious Priests	2
Transitional Deacons	7
Permanent Deacons in Diocese	152
Total Brothers	153
Total Sisters	1,326
Parishes	
Parishes	217
With Resident Pastor:	
Resident Diocesan Priests	188
Resident Religious Priests	23
Without Resident Pastor:	
Administered by Priests	6
Pastoral Centers	6
Professional Ministry Personnel:	
Brothers	10
Sisters	121
Lay Ministers	199
Welfare	
Catholic Hospitals	4
Total Assisted	944,645
Health Care Centers	30
Total Assisted	862,413
Homes for the Aged	6
Total Assisted	1,400
Residential Care of Children	6
Total Assisted	8,334
Day Care and Extended Day Care Centers	20
Total Assisted	2,143
Specialized Homes	35
Total Assisted	13,450
Special Centers for Social Services	92
Total Assisted	87,329
Residential Care of Disabled	75
Total Assisted	3,396
Other Institutions	25
Total Assisted	2,980
Educational	
Seminaries, Diocesan	1
Students from This Diocese	16
Students from Other Diocese	4
Diocesan Students in Other Seminaries	19
Seminaries, Religious	2
Total Seminarians	35
Colleges and Universities	3
Total Students	19,080
High Schools, Diocesan and Parish	4
Total Students	1,949
High Schools, Private	16
Total Students	15,300
Elementary Schools, Diocesan and Parish	152
Total Students	54,607
Elementary Schools, Private	2
Total Students	351
Non-residential Schools for the Disabled	1
Total Students	113
Catechesis/Religious Education:	
High School Students	1,150
Elementary Students	52,795
Total Students Under Catholic Instruction	145,380
Teachers in the Diocese:	
Priests	14
Brothers	60
Sisters	271
Lay Teachers	3,830
Vital Statistics	
Receptions into the Church:	
Infant Baptism Totals	21,901
Adult Baptism Totals	927
Received into Full Communion	1,375
First Communions	15,598
Confirmations	11,167
Marriages:	
Catholic	3,594
Interfaith	547
Total Marriages	4,141
Deaths	10,898
Total Catholic Population	1,651,304
Total Population	4,268,939

Former Bishops—Rt. Rev. JOHN LOUGHLIN, D.D., First Bishop of Brooklyn; ord. Oct. 18, 1840; cons. Oct. 30, 1853; died Dec. 28, 1891.—Rt. Rev. CHARLES E. MCDONNELL, D.D., Second Bishop of Brooklyn; ord. May 19, 1878; cons. April 25, 1892; died Aug. 8, 1921.—Most Rev. THOMAS E. MOLLOY, D.D., Third Bishop of Brooklyn; ord. Sept. 19, 1908; cons. Second Auxiliary Bishop of Brooklyn, Oct. 3, 1920; appt. Bishop of Brooklyn, Nov. 21, 1921; installed Feb. 15, 1922; died Nov. 26, 1956.—Most Rev. BRYAN J. MCENTEGART, D.D., LL.D., Fourth Bishop of Brooklyn; ord. Sept. 8, 1917; appt. Bishop of Ogdensburg, June 5, 1943; cons. Aug. 3, 1943; appt. Rector of the Catholic University of America, Washington, DC, June 26, 1953; appt. Titular Bishop of Aradi, Aug. 19, 1953; appt. Bishop of Brooklyn, April 16, 1957; installed June 13, 1957; retired and appt. Titular Archbishop of Gabii, July 17, 1968; died Sept. 30, 1968.—Most Rev. FRANCIS J. MUGAVERO, D.D., Fifth Bishop of Brooklyn; ord. May 18, 1940; Bishop of Brooklyn; appt. July 15, 1968; cons. Sept. 12, 1968; installed Sept. 12, 1968; retired Feb. 20, 1990; died July 12, 1991.

Central Offices—75 Greene Ave., Brooklyn, 11238., Mailing Address: P.O. Box C, Brooklyn, 11202-3604. Tel: 718-399-5900. Office Hours: Mon.-Fri. 9-4:30.

Vicar General and Moderator of the Curia—Rev. Msgr. OTTO L. GARCIA, J.C.D., V.G., *75 Greene Ave., P.O. Box C, Brooklyn, 11202.* Tel: 718-399-5900; Fax: 718-399-5965.

Regional Bishop of Brooklyn West and Episcopal Vicar for Human Services—Most Rev. JOSEPH M. SULLIVAN, M.S.W., M.P.A., V.E., *191 Joralemon St., Brooklyn, 11201.* Tel: 718-722-6000.

Regional Bishop of Queens North and Episcopal Vicar for Elderly and Racial Concerns—Most Rev. RENE A. VALERO, M.S.W., V.E., *7200 Douglaston Pkwy., Douglaston, 11362.* Tel: 718-229-8001, Ext. 710; 700.

Regional Bishop of Queens South and Episcopal Vicar for Evangelization and Spiritual Development—Most Rev. IGNATIUS A. CANTANELLO, Ph.D., V.E., *St. John's University, St. John's Hall, Rm. 103, 8000 Utopia Pkwy., Jamaica, 11439.* Tel: 718-990-6161, Ext. 5490.

Regional Bishop of Brooklyn East—Vacant.

Episcopal Vicars-Territorial—Brooklyn West: Rev. Msgr. MICHAEL J. BRENNAN, V.E., *St. Cecilia, 84 Herbert St., Brooklyn, 11222.* Tel: 718-389-0010. Brooklyn East: Rev. Msgr. JOHN E. MAHONEY, V.E., *St. Thomas Aquinas, 1550 Hendrickson St., Brooklyn, 11234.* Tel: 718-253-4404. Queens South: Rev. Msgr. JAMES SPENGLER, V.E., *St. Catherine of Sienna, 118-22 Riverton St., St. Albans, 11412.* Tel: 718-528-1220. Queens North: Rev. Msgr. EDWARD A. RYAN, V.E., *Mary's Nativity, 46-02 Parson's Blvd., Flushing, 11355.* Tel: 718-359-5996.

Episcopal Vicar for Temporalities—Rev. Msgr. JOHN J. BRACKEN, *310 Prospect Park W., P.O. Box 159013, Brooklyn, 11215-0013.* Tel: 718-965-7300; Fax: 718-965-7311.

Finance Officer—Mr. FRANCIS W. GALLIGAN, CFO. Tel: 718-399-5900; Fax: 718-399-5966.

Parish Services Corp.—Rev. Msgr. AUSTIN P. BENNETT, J.C.D., Dir. FLORENCE C. FLYNN, Mgr., *The Chancery, 75 Greene Ave., Brooklyn, 11202.* Tel: 718-399-5900; Fax: 718-399-5942.

Development Office—Rev. Msgr. JOHN J. BRACKEN, Dir. Tel: 718-965-7300; Fax: 718-965-7341.

Building and Property Administration—Mr. GERARD TANGREDI, Dir. Tel: 718-965-7300; Fax: 718-965-7353.

Institutional Services—Rev. MICHAEL HARDIMAN, Exec. Dir. ROBERT RYMERS, Dir. of Oper., *The Immaculate Conception Center, 7200 Douglaston Pkwy., Douglaston, 11362.* Tel: 718-229-8001, Ext. 8290; Fax: 718-279-3004.

Episcopal Vicar for Education—Rev. Msgr. GUY J. PUGLISI, *310 Prospect Park W., P.O. Box 159013, Brooklyn, 11215-0013.* Tel: 718-965-7300; Fax: 718-965-7323.

Chancery Office—75 Greene Ave., P.O. Box C, Brooklyn, 11202. Tel: 718-399-5990; Fax: 718-399-5934.

Chancellor—Rev. ANDREW J. VACCARI, J.C.L.

Vice-Chancellors—Sr. JANE SCANLON, C.N.D., M.Div.; Rev. STEVEN J. AGUGGIA, J.C.L.

Diocesan Archivist—JOSEPH W. COEN, C.A., Mailing Address: *310 Prospect Park W., P.O. Box 159013, Brooklyn, 11215-0013.* Tel: 718-965-7300, Ext. 1001.

Censors of Books—Revs. PETER I. VACCARI, S.T.L.; FRANK J. CAGGIANO, S.T.D., *75 Greene Ave., P.O. Box C, Brooklyn, 11202.*

Secretary to the Diocesan Bishop—Rev. Msgr. RALPH J. MARESCA, M.Div. Tel: 718-399-5970; Fax: 718-399-5975.

Masters of Ceremonies to Bishops—Bishop Daily—Rev. Msgr. RALPH J. MARESCA, M.Div., *Bishop Sullivan*—Revs. JOSEPH R. GIBINO; MICHAEL A. CARRANO; JOSEPH FONTI; KEVIN MCBRIEN; RICHARD LONG, *Bishop Valero*—Revs. ROBERT POWERS; ROBERT ARMATO; JOSEPH GRIMALDI; STEVEN J. AGUGGIA; THOMAS C. MACHALSKI, *Bishop Catanello*—Revs. THOMAS AHEARN; THOMAS G. CASERTA; FRED MARANO; GREGORY C. WIELUNSKI; EDWARD R. STEWART.

Tribunal—7200 Douglaston Pkwy., Douglaston, 11362. Tel: 718-229-8131; Fax: 718-631-1339.

Officialis-Judicial Vicar—Rev. Msgr. EDWARD B. SCHARFENBERGER, S.T.L., J.C.L., J.D.

Vice Officiales-Associate Judicial Vicars—Revs. HUGO BEDOYA, S.T.L., J.C.D.; THOMAS CHENG, J.C.D., M.A.; JOSEPH R. GRIMALDI, J.C.L.; THOMAS C. MACHALSKI, J.C.L.; GREGORY C. WIELUNSKI, J.C.D.

Defenders of the Marriage Bond—Revs. JOHN J. BROWN, S.T.L., J.C.L.; ROBERT J. YOUNG, J.C.L.; ANDREW J. VACCARI, J.C.L.

Promoter of Justice—Rev. Msgr. WILLIAM A. VARVARO, P.A., S.T.D., J.C.D.

Attorneys and Counselors at Canon Law—Revs. EDWARD G. BROPHY, M.Div.; JOHN D. CAPILLO, M.Div.; Deacon JEROME KREBS; Rev. RUSS MACARANAS, J.C.D.; MARIA CHRISTINA PRINCE, M.A.; Sr. JOSITA WALSH, R.S.M., M.A.

Senior Priests, Episcopal Delegate for—Rev. Msgr. GEORGE ZATARGA, *7200 Douglaston Pkwy., Douglaston, 11362.* Tel: 718-229-8001, Ext. 411.

Religious, Episcopal Delegate for—Sr. MARYANN LOPICCOLO, S.C., *75 Greene Ave., P.O. Box C, Brooklyn, 11202.* Tel: 718-399-5900.

Cemeteries—Rev. MICHAEL J. REID, Dir., *80-01 Metropolitan Ave., Middle Village, 11379.* Tel: 718-894-4888.

Education, Offices—(See Institutions Located in the Diocese for details).

Family Life Office—Mrs. CATHERINE BALA, Dir.; Deacon LEON F. MILLER, Asst. Dir. for Hispanics, *7200 Douglaston Pkwy., Douglaston, 11362.* Tel: 718-229-8001, Ext. 342.

Human Resources Office—MICHAEL MONAHAN, Admin., *310 Prospect Park W., P.O. Box 159013, Brooklyn, 11215-0013.* Tel: 718-965-7300; Fax: 718-965-7363.

Pension Office—MICHAEL MONAHAN, Admin. Tel: 718-965-7300; Fax: 718-965-7363.

Medical Insurance Office—MICHAEL MONAHAN, Admin. Tel: 718-965-7300; Fax: 718-965-7363.

Liturgical Office—Rev. Msgr. JOHN C. TOSI, Exec. Sec., *75 Greene Ave., P.O. Box C, Brooklyn, 11202.* Tel: 718-399-5980; Fax: 718-399-5930.

Mediation and Arbitration, Board of—Rev. Msgr. EDWARD J. BREEN, Exec. Sec., *Mailing Address: P.O. Box C, Brooklyn, 11202.*

Ministerial Development Program—Rev. THOMAS CASERTA. Tel: 718-229-8001.

Newspaper "The Tablet"—Mr. FRANK DEROSA, Assoc. Publisher; ED WILKINSON, Editor, *310 Prospect Park W., P.O. Box 159013, Brooklyn, 11215-0013.* Tel: 718-965-7300; Fax: 718-965-7339.

Permanent Diaconate Program—Rev. Msgr. EDWARD V. WETTERER, Dir.; Deacon SALVATORE V. LICATA, Exec. Sec., *75 Greene Ave., P.O. Box C, Brooklyn, 11202.* Tel: 718-399-5900.

Office of Clergy Personnel—Rev. Msgr. JOHN J. BROWN, S.T.L., J.C.L., Dir., *75 Greene Ave., P.O. Box C, Brooklyn, 11202.* Tel: 718-399-5941; Fax: 718-399-7194.

Assignment Board—Rev. Msgr. JOHN J. BROWN, S.T.L., J.C.L., Chm.; Rev. Msgr. JAMES SPENGLER; Rev. Msgr. MICHAEL BRENNAN; Rev. Msgr. JOHN E. MAHONEY; Rev. Msgr. EDWARD A. RYAN; Rev. Msgr. JOHN MCGUIRL; Rev. KEVIN MCBRIEN.

Personnel Board (Clergy)—Rev. Msgr. JOHN J. BROWN, S.T.L., J.C.L., Chm.; Rev. Msgr. JOHN MAHONEY; Revs. WILLIAM SWEENEY; EDWARD BROPHY; Rev. Msgr. PAUL SANCHEZ.

Propagation of the Faith—Rev. JOHN BROGAN, Office: *191 Joralemon St., P.O. Box 200, Brooklyn, 11202.* Tel: 718-875-4375.

Holy Childhood, Pontifical Association—Rev. JOHN BROGAN, *191 Joralemon St., P.O. Box 200, Brooklyn, 11202.*

Public Information Office—FRANK DEROSA, Dir., *75 Greene Ave., P.O. Box C, Brooklyn, 11202.* Tel: 718-399-5955; Fax: 718-399-5957.

Retirement Board (Priests)—Most Rev. RENE A. VALERO, M.S.W., V.E., Chm., *Mailing Address: 7200 Douglaston Pkwy., Douglaston, 11362.*

Vocations, Office of—Rev. JAMES F. FITZPATRICK, Dir.; Sr. REGINA WILSON, I.H.M., Assoc. Dir., *75 Greene Ave., P.O. Box C, Brooklyn, 11202.* Tel: 718-399-5900.

Consultative Bodies

Presbyteral Council—Rev. Msgr. JOHN C. ANTONCIC, Exec. Sec.; Rev. Msgr. MICHAEL BRENNAN; Rev. Msgr. JOHN O'BRIEN; Rev. Msgr. FAUSTINO CORDERO; Most Rev. JOSEPH M. SULLIVAN, M.S.W., M.P.A., V.E.; Most. Rev. RENE A. VALERO, M.S.W., V.E.; Most Rev. IGNATIUS A. CATANELLO, Ph.D., V.E.; Rev. Msgr. OTTO L. GARCIA, V.G.; Rev. Msgr. HOWARD BASLER; Rev. Msgr. RALPH MARESCA; Rev. Msgr. D. JOSEPH FINNERTY; Revs. THOMAS AHEARN; CALEB BUCHANAN; WILLIAM HOPPE; THADDEUS KAZANECKI; PETER GILLEN; NEIL MAHONEY; ANDREW VACCARI; EDWARD MAURER; JAMES O'BRIEN; ARTHUR PURCELL; PATRICK WEST; EDWARD BROPHY; JAMES KING, *75 Greene Ave., P.O. Box C, Brooklyn, 11202.*

Diocesan Budget Committee—Rev. Msgr. JOHN J. BRACKEN, Chm.

Subcommittee for Assisted Schools and Parishes—Rev. THOMAS V. DOYLE.

Subcommittee for Agencies—Rev. Msgr. JOHN J. BRACKEN.

Subcommittee for Parishes—Rev. Msgr. RAYMOND W. KUTNER.

Subcommittee for Schools—Sr. KAREN LADEMANN, O.P.

Diocesan Consultors—Rev. Msgr. OTTO L. GARCIA, J.C.D., V.G., Sec.; Most Rev. RENE A. VALERO, M.S.W., V.E.; Most Rev. IGNATIUS A. CATANELLO, Ph.D., V.E.; Rev. Msgr. MICHAEL BRENNAN; Rev. Msgr. JOHN O'BRIEN; Rev. Msgr. JOHN STRYNKOWSKI; Revs. ANDREW J. VACCARI; NEIL MAHONEY; PETER GILLEN; WILLIAM HOPPE, *75 Greene Ave., P.O. Box C, Brooklyn, 11202.*

Diocesan Pastoral Council—WILLIAM FARREN, Pres.; Rev. CHARLES P. KEENEY, Bishop's Liaison.

Brothers' Senate—Bro. LAWRENCE SEWARD, S.C., *71-06 31st Ave., East Elmhurst, 11370.* Tel: 718-898-9600.

Commissions and Offices for Pastoral Services

Alcoholism Committee—Rev. Msgr. KIERAN MARTIN, Chm., *1550 Hendrickson St., Brooklyn, 11234.* Tel: 718-951-7302; Fax: 718-951-7233.

Art and Architecture Commission—Rev. Msgr. JOHN C. TOSI, Exec. Sec.; Sr. MARY JANE KELLY, O.P., Chm.; Revs. ROBERT J. ARMATO; VITO BUONANNO; THOMAS V. DOYLE; THOMAS G. PETTEI, Office: *75 Greene Ave., P.O. Box C, Brooklyn, 11202.*

Black Ministry, Office of—MADELINE ANDERSON, Exec. Dir., *Immaculate Conception Center, 7200 Douglaston Pkwy., Douglaston, 11362.* Tel: 718-229-8001.

Hispanic Ministry, Office of—Deacon ARTURO GONZALEZ, *7200 Douglaston Pkwy., Douglaston, 11362.* Tel: 718-229-8001, Ext. 741.

Catholic Charities—Most Rev. JOSEPH M. SULLIVAN, Episcopal Vicar, Human Svcs., *191 Joralemon St., Brooklyn, 11201.* Tel: 718-722-6000; Fax: 718-643-0522. (See Institutions Located in the Diocese for details).

Catholic Migration and Refugee Office—(See Institutions Located in the Diocese for details).

Catholic Migration Services, Inc.—Rev. Msgr. RONALD T. MARINO, Dir. Tel: 718-236-3000.

Diocesan Institute of Languages—Rev. MICHAEL J. HARDIMAN, Dir., *7200 Douglaston Pkwy., Douglaston, 11362.* Tel: 718-229-8001.

Chaplains and Uniformed Services, Official—Police Department: Rev. Msgr. JOHN P. MCCULLAGH; Rev. ROBERT ROMANO,Fire Department: Rev. JOHN DELENDICK, Sanitation Department: Rev. VINCENT J. TERMINE,BMT Holy Name Society: Rev. Msgr. WILLIAM J. FLOOD.

Diocesan Building Commission—Rev. WILLIAM F. KRLIS, Chm., Mailing Address: *7200 Douglaston Pkwy., Douglaston, 11362.*

Diocesan Real Estate Board—Rev. Msgr. RAYMOND W. KUTNER, Chm.; Rev. JOHN DELENDICK. Consultants: Rev. WILLIAM F. KRLIS; Mr. KEVIN KEARNEY; Mr. JOHN TYNAN, Mailing Address: *34-43 93rd St., Jackson Heights, 11372.*

Diocesan Food Service—Mr. JAMES AUSTIN, Dir., *7200 Douglaston Pkwy., Douglaston, 11362.* Tel: 718-229-8001, Ext. 100.

Ecumenical and Interreligious Affairs, Diocesan Commission for—Rev. GUY MASSIE, M.Div., Exec. Sec.

Committee for Eastern Orthodox-Catholic Relations—Prof. THOMAS E. BIRD, Chm.

Committee for Christian Relations—Rev. GUY MASSIE, M.Div., Chm.

Committee for Catholic-Jewish Relations—Rev. GUY MASSIE, M.Div.

Catholic-Muslim Dialogue—Rev. MICHAEL LYNCH, S.T.L., Chm.

Catholic Hindu/Buddhist Dialogue—Rev. JOSEPH GIBINO, Chm.

Evangelization Commission—Most Rev. IGNATIUS CATANELLO, Chm.; Rev. DENNIS MCAULIFFE, Exec. Sec. Office of Religious Education: Rev. MICHAEL CARRANO; Rev. JOSEPH GIBINO; Sr. ALICE MICHAEL; Sr. DOLORES RYAN, C.S.J.; Mrs. JOAN SOKOLL; Sr. EILEEN SWEENEY,Episcopal Liaison: Most Rev. IGNATIUS A. CATANELLO, Auxiliary Bishop of Brooklyn; Rev. DENNIS MCAULIFFE, Ph.D., Exec. Sec. Tel: 718-492-1800.

Home School Association—Rev. Msgr. THOMAS A. GRAHAM. Tel: 718-525-9099.

Liturgical Commission—Rev. Msgr. JOHN C. TOSI, Exec. Sec.; Sr. THERESA AGLIARDI, R.S.M.; Rev. Msgr. EDWARD J. BREEN; Revs. JOHN F. BROGAN; FRANK J. CAGGIANO; JOSEPH R. GIBINO; Mr. GREGORY JACK; Sr. MARY JANE KELLY, O.P.; Rev. Msgr. JOHN E. MAHONEY, V.E.; Sr. MARY ALICE PIIL, C.S.J.; Dr. JULIE UPTON, R.S.M., Office: *75 Greene Ave., P.O. Box C, Brooklyn, 11202.*

Music Commission—TERESA BRYANT; EDWARD BURKARD; Rev. PETER D. GILLEN; STEVEN R. GIUSTO; CHARLES MALLIA; MERRY A. NADDEO, Ed.D.; Rev. SEAN G. OGLE; JOSEPHINE SANGES; JOSEPH B. SMITH; Rev. Msgr. JOHN C. TOSI, Exec. Sec. ROBERT ZAPPULLA, Office: *75 Greene Ave., P.O. Box C, Brooklyn, 11202.*

Pastoral Care of the Sick Office—(See Institutions Located in the Diocese for details).

Pastoral Communications, Office of—Rev. Msgr. MICHAEL J. DEMPSEY, Dir., *1712 10th Ave., Brooklyn, 11215.* Tel: 718-499-9705. Legal Title: *Trans Video Communications, Inc.*

Pastoral Institute—Sr. ANGELA GANNON, C.S.J., *7200 Douglaston Pkwy., Douglaston, 11362.* Tel: 718-631-4267.

Prison Ministries Office—(See Listing Under Catholic Charities).

Religious Education, Office of—Evangelization and Catholic Formation: Rev. Msgr. GUY PUGLISI, Dir.; Sr. EILEEN SWEENEY, O.S.F., Dir. Elementary Rel. Educ. JOAN R. SOKOLL, Dir. Rel. Educ., Elementary; Rev. MICHAEL A. CORRANO, Dir. Youth Min. & Adolescent Catechesis, Dir. College Campus Min.; Sr. ALICE MICHAEL, Dir. Rel. Educ., Cultural & Ethnic Groups, Coord. R.C.I.A.; Rev. JOSEPH R. GIBINO, Dir. Adult Rel. Educ.; Rev. DENNIS MCAULIFFE, Ph.D., Coord. Evangelization; Sr. DOLORES RYAN, C.S.J., Dir. Curriculum & On-Going Professional Devel. for Rel. Educ. Administrators and Principals.

Respect Life Office—Vacant, Dir., *75 Greene Ave., P.O. Box C, Brooklyn, 11202.* Tel: 718-399-5900.

Cluster Planning and Collaboration, Office of—Rev. CORNELIUS H. MAHONEY, Dir., Mailing Address: *7200 Douglaston Pkwy., Douglaston, 11362.* Tel: 718-229-8001, Ext. 736; Fax: 718-428-4574.

Apostolic Organizations

Catholic Youth Organization, Diocesan—MICHAEL ABERNETHY, Dir., *191 Joralemon St., Brooklyn, 11201.* Tel: 718-722-6117.

Charismatic Groups, Catholic—

Charismatic Renewal (English-speaking) of the Diocese of Brooklyn—JOSEPHINE CACHIA, Dir. JOSEPHINE MCNALLY, Sec., *240 Jay St., Brooklyn, 11201.* Tel: 718-260-9111; Fax: 718-260-9121.

Renouveau Charismatique of the Diocese of Brooklyn—(serving the Haitian Charismatics of the Diocese); Rev. Msgr. JOSEPH MALAGRECA, Dir., *218-26 105th Ave., Queens Village, 11429.* Tel: 718-465-0124; Fax: 718-479-3548.

Renovacion Carismatica of the Diocese of Brooklyn—(serving the Hispanic Charismatics of the Diocese); Rev. Msgr. JOSEPH MALAGRECA, Dir., *218-26 105th Ave., Queens Village, 11429.* Tel: 718-465-0124; Fax: 718-479-3548.

Confraternity of the Guard of Honor and Confraternity of the Holy Hour—Rev. Msgr. THOMAS F. CRIBBIN, Dir., *St. Joseph's Residence, 256 Clinton Ave., Brooklyn, 11205.*

Confraternity of the Precious Blood—Rev. Msgr. AUSTIN P. BENNETT, Dir., *5300 Fort Hamilton Pkwy., Brooklyn, 11219.* Tel: 718-436-1120.

Courage Ministry—Rev. Msgr. WALTER C. MURPHY, *Immaculate Conception Center, 7200 Douglaston Pkwy., Douglaston, 11362.* Hotline: 718-229-1748

Guilds—

Accountants—Rev. Msgr. WALTER C. MURPHY, Dir.

Catholic Cemetery Guild—Rev. MICHAEL J. REID, Moderator.

Lawyers—Rev. EDWARD B. SCHARFENBERGER, S.T.L., J.C.L., J.D., Kings Co.; Rev. Msgr. THOMAS F. DONOVAN, Queens Co.

Pharmacist—Vacant, Dir.

Physicians—Rev. Msgr. JOSEPH C. KONRAD, J.C.D., Kings Co. Chapter Moderator.

Teachers—Rev. Msgr. THOMAS F. NOONAN, M.S., Dir.

Holy Name Society—Rev. RAYMOND MCKIERNAN, Moderator.

Marriage Encounter—Coords.: BOB NOBBS; MELINDA NOBBS. Tel: 718-805-7232.

National Council of Catholic Women—CLAIRE DUNNE, Pres.; Rev. Msgr. LAWRENCE J. MCALISTER, Spiritual Dir., *35-60 158th St., Flushing, 11358.*

Legion of Mary—Rev. Msgr. VINCENT F. FULLAM, Dir.; Rev. Msgr. JOSEPH ROSA, Spanish Curia; Deacon JEAN BAPTISTE BOURSIQUOT, Haitian Curia; Revs. JOSEPH AMN, Korean Curia; ALFRED WEINLICH, Flushing Curia; CHARLES REPOLE, O.F.M.Cap., N.W. Queens Curia; JOSEPH MARRIN, C.SS.R., Bay Ridge Curia, *82-00 35th Ave., Jackson Heights, 11372.* Tel: 718-429-2333.

Nocturnal Adoration Society—Rev. Msgr. JOHN F. WILSON, *245 Prospect Park W., Brooklyn, 11215.*

Priests' Eucharistic League—Rev. Msgr. JOHN F. WILSON, *245 Prospect Park W., Brooklyn, 11215.*

Sodality Union—Vacant.

St. John's Priests Relief Society—Rev. Msgr. GEORGE M. SCHUSTER, Pres.

CLERGY, PARISHES, MISSIONS AND PAROCHIAL SCHOOLS

CITY OF NEW YORK
BOROUGH OF BROOKLYN

1—THE CATHEDRAL-BASILICA OF ST. JAMES (Jay St. at Tillary), Rev. Msgr. John C. Tosi. In res., Rev. Msgr. Otto L. Garcia, J.C.D., V.G.; Rev. Joseph R. Gibino, Ph.D.
Res., 250 Cathedral Pl., 11201. Tel: 718-852-4002; Fax: 718-852-9452.

2—ST. AGATHA'S, Rev. Msgr. Paul R. Sanchez; Rev. Lewis H. Maynard; Sr. Anne Burke, C.S.J., Pastoral Assoc.; Deacons George M. Tokarcsik; Juan R. Vargas.
Res., 702 48th St., 11220. Tel: 718-436-1080; Fax: 718-436-8870.
School—736 48th St., 11220. Tel: 718-435-3137; Fax: 718-437-7505. Sr. Mary Davies, O.P., Prin.
Sisters of Mercy 1; Sisters of St. Joseph 1; Lay Teachers 13; Students 288.
Catechesis/Religious Programs—Tel: 718-438-4512. Debra Wang, D.R.E.
Students 470.

3—ST. AGNES, Rev. William A. McLaughlin; Deacon Aurelio Pagan.
Res., 417 Sackett St., 11231. Tel: 718-625-1717; Fax: 718-625-1929.

4—ALL SAINTS, Rev. Donald J. Kenna.
Res., 115 Throop Ave., 11206. Tel: 718-388-1951; Fax: 718-388-7712.
School—113 Throop Ave., 11206. Tel: 718-782-0569. Mrs. Martha Targes McNulty, Prin.
Lay Teachers 9; Students 192.

5—ST. ALPHONSUS. Merged 1976. Records at St. Anthony of Padua-St. Alphonsus.

6—ST. AMBROSE. Merged 1978. Records at Our Lady of Monserrate-St. Ambrose.

7—ST. ANDREW THE APOSTLE, Rev. Guy Massie; Deacons Gregory Dixon; William Wander.
Res., 6713 Ridge Blvd., 11220. Tel: 718-680-1010; Fax: 718-680-3160.

8—ST. ANN-ST. GEORGE,
Res., 207 York St., 11201. Tel: 718-625-0794; Fax: 718-625-4986.

9—ANNUNCIATION OF THE BLESSED VIRGIN MARY, Rev. Msgr. David L. Cassato, Admin.
Res., 259 N. Fifth St., 11211. Tel: 718-387-2111; Fax: 718-782-4459.
Catechesis/Religious Programs—D.R.E.: Margariete Ocasio; John Fruner.
Students 15.

10—ST. ANSELM'S, Rev. Msgr. Michael J. Phillips; Revs. Charles McLaughlin; Martin R. Kull; Joseph Vu; Deacon Thomas Davis. In res., Rev. Herbert A. Travis.
Res., 356 82nd St., 11209. Tel: 718-238-2900; Fax: 718-238-2902.
School—357 83rd St., 11209. Tel: 718-745-7643. Sr. Eileen Mary McMahon, S.S.N.D., Prin.
Sisters of Notre Dame 3; Lay Teachers 28; Students 636.
Catechesis/Religious Programs—Sr. Anne Bernadette, M.S.B.T., D.R.E.; Sr. Regina Corde, O.P., Pastoral Ministry, Tel: 718-836-0780; Sr. Mary Gilmore, O.P., Dir. of Spirituality, Tel: 718-238-2900.
Students 151.
Missionary Cenacle—351 83rd St., 11209. Tel: 718-836-0957.
Missionary Servants of the Most Blessed Trinity 2.

11—ST. ANTHONY OF PADUA-ST. ALPHONSUS, Revs. Robert W. Czok; William A. McLaughlin; Bro. Richard O'Brien, C.S.C. In res., Rev. Patrick J. Diffley; Rev. Msgr. Anthony F. Passarella, Pastor Emeritus.
Res., 862 Manhattan Ave., 11222. Tel: 718-383-3339; Fax: 718-383-6958.
School—725 Leonard St., 11222. Tel: 718-383-5860; Fax: 718-389-5953. Sr. Ann Franklin, C.S.J., Prin.
Lay Teachers 18; Students 292.
Catechesis/Religious Programs—Tel: 718-389-5953. Rose Accetta, Prin.
Students 300.

12—ASSUMPTION OF THE BLESSED VIRGIN MARY, Revs. Michael A. Carrano; Peter Mahoney; Sr. Maria Klosterman, S.F.F., Pastoral Assoc. In res., Rev. Msgr. Thomas F. Cribbin.
Res., 64 Middagh St., 11201. Tel: 718-625-1161; Fax: 718-625-7223.

13—ST. ATHANASIUS, Rev. Msgr. Fernando A. Ferrarese, M.Div.; Revs. Richard E. Long, M.D.V., M.B.A.; Bryan Patterson.
Res., 2154 61st St., 11204. Tel: 718-236-0124; Fax: 718-236-4960.
School—6120 Bay Pkwy., 11204. Tel: 718-236-4791; Fax: 718-621-1423. Mrs. Lorraine Garone-Tesoro, M.A., M.S., Prin.
Lay Teachers 12; Students 243.
Catechesis/Religious Programs—Tel: 718-331-8811; Fax: 718-331-2582. Mrs. Nicoletta Milo, D.R.E.
Students 340.
Convent—2201 62nd St., 11204. Tel: 718-236-2680.

14—ST. AUGUSTINE, Rev. Robert J. Whelan; Deacon Joseph Bichotte. In res., Revs. Robert Freuh; Anthony Minielli (NY); Angelo Pinto, (St. Boniface, Winnipeg, Canada); Peter A. Suvakeen (India); Terrence W. Klein (COL).
Res., 116 Sixth Ave., 11217. Tel: 718-783-3132; Fax: 718-638-4669.

15—ST. BARBARA, Rev. Msgr. John J. Powis. In res., Rev. Adrian Alicea.
Res., 138 Bleecker St., 11221. Tel: 718-452-3660; Fax: 718-452-1279.

16—ST. BENEDICT'S. Closed. For inquiries for parish records contact the Chancery.

17—ST. BERNARD. Closed. For inquiries for parish records contact the Chancery.

18—ST. BERNADETTE, Revs. Robert J. Romano, M.Div.; Robert J. Armaio; Kaleem Umrahn. In res., Rev. Msgr. Cosmo G. Saporito, Pastor Emeritus; Revs. David J. Dettmer; Joseph K. Dolan.
Res., 8201 13th Ave., 11228. Tel: 718-837-3400; Fax: 718-236-5883.
School—1313 83rd St., 11228. Tel: 718-236-1560.
Religious Teachers Filippini 4; Lay Teachers 14; Students 295.

19—ST. BERNARD'S, Revs. Ralph Caputo; James W. King; Deacon Frank J. D'Accordo. In res., Rev. James P. Collins.
Res., 2055 E. 69th St., 11234. Tel: 718-763-5533; Fax: 718-763-0224.
School—2030 E. 69th St., 11234. Tel: 718-241-6040; Fax: 718-241-7258. Linda Mele, Prin.
Lay Teachers 15; Students 362.
Catechesis/Religious Programs—Tel: 718-444-4674.
Students 398.

20—ST. BLAISE. Merged with St. Francis of Assisi in 1980. Records at St. Francis of Assisi-St. Blaise.

21—BLESSED SACRAMENT, Revs. Thomas F. Brosnan; Robert M. Powers; Sr. Catherine Thornton, O.P., Pastoral Assoc. In res., Rev. Anselm E. Onuoha (Nigeria); Deacon Humberto Alvia.
Res., 198 Euclid Ave., 11208. Tel: 718-827-1200; Fax: 718-827-2422.
School—187 Euclid Ave., 11208. Tel: 718-235-4863; Fax: 718-235-1132. Catherine Marlowe, Prin.
Lay Teachers 14; Students 339.
Catechesis/Religious Programs—Tel: 718-277-3231.
Students 670.

22—ST. BONIFACE, Very Rev. Dennis M. Corrado, C.O., Pastor & Provost, Brooklyn Oratory; Rev. Mark J. Lane, C.O., Vicar. In res., Bro. James Simon, C.O., Dir. Devel.; Rev. Joel M. Warden, C.O.
Res., 109 Willoughby St., 11201. Tel: 718-875-2096; Fax: 718-875-4678.

23—ST. BRENDAN'S, Revs. Arthur D. Purcell; Joseph D. Pasciuto; Deacon Joseph P. McGuire. In res., Rev. Msgr. Thomas C. Clancy.
Res., 1525 E. 12th St., 11230. Tel: 718-339-2828; Fax: 718-339-5951.

24—ST. BRIGID, Rev. Msgr. James J. Kelly; Rev. Mauricio Sanango; Deacon Philip J. Ehresmann. In res., Rev. John H. Wilkinson.
Res., 409 Linden St., 11237. Tel: 718-821-1690; Fax: 718-386-4302.
School—438 Grove St. E., 11237. Tel: 718-821-1477; Fax: 718-821-1079. Jean Flynn, Prin.
Sisters 1; Lay Teachers 10; Students 312.
Catechesis/Religious Programs—Tel: 718-821-6401. Sr. Patricia Neary, O.P., D.R.E.
Students 1,039.

25—ST. CASIMIR (Polish). Merged with Our Lady of Czestochowa in 1980. Records at Our Lady of Czestochowa-St. Casimir.

26—ST. CATHARINE OF ALEXANDRIA, Revs. John S. Wtulich; Adnel Burgos.
Res., 1119 41st St., 11218. Tel: 718-436-5917; Fax: 718-871-5140.
School—1053 41st St., 11219. Tel: 718-436-9721; Fax: 718-853-3347. Anna Marie Bartone, Prin.
Sisters, Religious Sisters of the Sacred Heart of Mary 1; Lay Teachers 10; Students 188.
Catechesis/Religious Programs—Tel: 718-438-2613. Sr. Rosalind Picciano, C.S.J., D.R.E.
Students 400.

27—ST. CATHERINE OF GENOA, Revs. Gerald Dumont; Anthony Iroh (Nigeria).
Res., 520 Linden Blvd., 11203. Tel: 718-282-7162; Fax: 718-282-5568.
School—870 Albany Ave., 11203. Tel: 718-284-1050; Fax: 718-284-3461.
Lay Teachers 16; Students 360. Co-Principals: Patricia Maio; Mary Blanchard.

28—ST. CECILIA, Rev. Kevin J. O'Donoghue; Deacon Carlos Valderama. In res., Rev. Msgr. Michael J. Brennan, Vicar of Brooklyn West.
Res., 84 Herbert St., 11222. Tel: 718-389-0010; Fax: 718-389-5090.
School—Tel: 718-389-3161; Fax: 718-389-4333. Sr. Miriam Daniels, C.S.J., Prin.
Sisters 3; Lay Teachers 21; Students 475.
Catechesis/Religious Programs—1-15 Monitor St., 11222. Tel: 718-389-2546. Sr. Paul Maria, D.R.E.
Students 142.

29—ST. CHARLES BORROMEO, Revs. Charles A. Kraus; Thaddeus A. Grzelak; Bro. Becket Ryan, O.S.F.; Deacon John Flannery.
Res., 21 Sidney Pl., 11201. Tel: 718-625-1177; Fax: 718-624-1627.
School—23 Sidney Pl., 11201. Tel: 718-596-1362; Fax: 718-875-9471. Sr. Eileen McGuire, C.S.J., Prin.
Sisters of St. Joseph 1; Lay Teachers 14; Students 215.
Catechesis/Religious Programs—Students 75.

30—ST. COLUMBA, Revs. Edward J. Kiernan; Charles J. Matonti; Sr. Emily Masse, O.P., Pastoral Assoc.; Deacon Lawrence Coyle.
Res., 2245 Kimball St., 11234. Tel: 718-338-6265; Fax: 718-377-6440.
Catechesis/Religious Programs—Tel: 718-253-8840. Nancy Azzaro, D.R.E.
Students 229.

31—ST. COLUMBKILLE. Closed. Parochial records are located at SS. Cyril and Methodius. Became a mission in 1939.

32—SS. CYRIL AND METHODIUS (Polish), Revs. Joseph Mietelski, C.M.; Stephen J. Minkiel, C.M.; Rafael Kopystynski, C.M.
Res., 150 Dupont St., 11222. Tel: 718-389-4424; Fax: 718-389-4191.

33—ST. DOMINIC, Revs. Frank Caggiano; Marc Swartvagher; Jose Lopez; Sr. Margaret Cavanagh, O.P., Pastoral Min.; Deacons Carlo V. Mellace; Dante Colandrea.
Res., 2001 Bay Ridge Pkwy., 11204. Tel: 718-259-4636; 4637; 4638; Fax: 718-259-3066.
Catechesis/Religious Programs—Tel: 718-259-3066.
Students 425.

34—ST. EDMUND'S, Revs. Joseph A. Cestaro; Edward Brophy. In res., Rev. Msgr. Thomas F. Noonan; Rev. Francis Mann.
Res., 2460 Ocean Ave., 11229. Tel: 718-743-0102; Fax: 718-891-7834.
School—1902 Avenue T, 11229. Tel: 718-648-9229. Patricia O'Connor, Prin.
Lay Teachers 19; Students 325.
High School—Denis Maloney Institute/St. Edmund Preparatory High School, 2474 Ocean Ave., 11229. Tel: 718-743-0102; Fax: 718-743-5243. Mr. John Lorenzetti, Prin.; Mr. James Benson, Asst. Prin.; Sr. Barbara Doyle, Campus Min.
Sisters 2; Lay Teachers 35; Students 615.
Catechesis/Religious Programs—Tel: 718-743-8107. Mr. James Sullivan, D.R.E.
Students 156.

35—ST. EDWARD. Merged with St. Michael Archangel in 1942. Parochial records are at St. Michael-St. Edward, 108 St. Edwards St., 11205.

36—ST. EPHREM'S, Rev. Msgr. Peter V. Kain; Revs. Edward R. Stewart; Robert A. Moore, (Retired); Andrew Moon Soo Kim; Deacons William Malone; Wilfred N. Horne.
Res., 929 Bay Ridge Pkwy., 11228. Tel: 718-833-1010; Fax: 718-921-5232.
School—Tel: 718-833-1440; Fax: 718-745-5301. Sr. Nora Ashe, C.S.J., Prin.
Sisters of St. Joseph and Servants of the Immaculate Heart of Mary 4; Lay Teachers 22; Students 427.
Catechesis/Religious Programs—Tel: 718-745-7486. Diane Mosconi, D.R.E.
Students 269.
Convent—935 Bay Ridge Pkwy., 11228. Tel: 718-833-1555.

37—EPIPHANY, Rev. Msgr. Matthew F. Foley; Deacon Angel Baez.
Res., 96 S. Ninth St., 11211. Tel: 718-387-6328; Fax: 718-387-2449.
Catechesis/Religious Programs—Students 90.
Arriba Juntos—Forward Together, Inc. Center—96 S. Ninth St., 11211. Tel: 718-384-2121.

38—ST. FINBAR'S, Revs. Joseph T. Holcomb; Luke Wei; Deacon Giovanni Rizzo.
Res., 138 Bay 20th St., 11214. Tel: 718-236-3312; Fax: 718-236-3750.
School—1825 Bath Ave., 11214. Tel: 718-256-0818. Sr. Mary Hyacinth, C.S.A.C., Prin.
Sisters of the Catholic Apostolate 4; Lay Teachers 13; Students 190.
Catechesis/Religious Programs—Tel: 718-837-3935. Sr. Ann Joachim, C.S.A.C., D.R.E.
Students 325.

39—ST. FORTUNATA, Rev. Freddy Cintron; Deacon Edward Aigbojie. In res., Rev. Msgr. James W. Ryan, Pastor Emeritus.
Res., 2609 Linden Blvd., 11208. Tel: 718-647-2632; Fax: 718-647-1321.
School—2635 Linden Blvd., 11208. Tel: 718-647-6440; Fax: 718-647-2166. Miss Marian J. Siconolfi, Prin.
Lay Teachers 15; Students 341.
Catechesis/Religious Programs—Rev. Freddy Cintron, D.R.E.
Students 111.

40—FOURTEEN HOLY MARTYRS. Merged with St. Martin of Tours in 1976. Records at St. Martin of Tours-Fourteen Holy Martyrs.

41—ST. FRANCES CABRINI, Rev. Msgr. Richard E. Marchese; Rev. Gaetano J. Sbordone.
Res., 35 Bay 11th St., 11228. Tel: 718-236-9165; Fax: 718-331-8139.
School—21 Bay 11th St., 11228. Tel: 718-232-6700; Fax: 718-234-5651. Sr. Martin Marie Doran, O.P., Prin.
Sisters of St. Dominic 2; Lay Teachers 9; Students 296.
Catechesis/Religious Programs—Tel: 718-232-4228.
Students 265.

42—ST. FRANCES CABRINI CHAPEL. Closed. For inquiries for parish records contact the Chancery.

43—ST. FRANCES DE CHANTAL, Revs. Andrzej Kurowski, S.A.C.; Slawomir Siok, S.A.C.; Piotr Karaszewski, S.A.C.; Leszek Wiecaszek, S.A.C. In res., Rev. Michael J. Hunt, Pastor Emeritus.
Res., 1273 58th St., 11219. Tel: 718-436-6407; Fax: 718-854-2761.
Catechesis/Religious Programs—Lay Teachers 18; Students 320.

44—ST. FRANCIS IN THE FIELDS. Closed. For inquiries for parish records contact the Chancery.

45—ST. FRANCIS OF ASSISI-ST. BLAISE, Revs. John Boldyc, S.M.; Gerard G. Pelletier, S.M.; Roger Bourgea, S.M.
Res., Tel: 718-756-2015; Fax: 718-756-1773.
Church—319 Maple St., 11225.
School—Tel: 718-778-1300. Sr. Theresa Scanlon, C.S.J., Prin.
Lay Teachers 15; Students 371.
Catechesis/Religious Programs—Tel: 718-778-1302. Mrs. Gilbert Verna, D.R.E.
Students 261.

46—ST. FRANCIS OF PAOLA (Italian), Rev. Andrew R. Varano.
Res., 219 Conselyea St., 11211. Tel: 718-387-0256; Fax: 718-387-6344.
Catechesis/Religious Programs—Tel: 718-387-0256; Fax: 718-387-6344.
Students 85.

47—ST. FRANCIS XAVIER, Revs. Gregory A. Stankus; Joseph Koilparampil; Deacons John Franca; James Ramos. In res., Rev. Paul W. Farin.
Res., 225 Sixth Ave., 11215. Tel: 718-638-1880; Fax: 718-638-2839.
School—763 President St., 11215. Tel: 718-857-2903. Sr. Kathleen Sullivan, C.S.J., Prin.
Sisters of St. Joseph 3; Lay Teachers 19; Students 475.
Catechesis/Religious Programs—Tel: 718-857-2903. Sr. Helene Conway, D.R.E.
Students 100.

48—ST. GABRIEL THE ARCHANGEL, Revs. Carlos Walker, I.V.E. (Argentina); Marcelo Navarro, I.V.E. (Argentina).
Res., 749 Linwood St., 11208. Tel: 718-257-0612; Fax: 718-257-5258.
Catechesis/Religious Programs—666 Essex St., 11208. Tel: 718-649-0450; Fax: 718-649-0450.
Students 228.

49—ST. GEORGE. Merged with St. Ann in 1986. Records at St. Ann-St. George.

50—GOOD SHEPHERD, Rev. Msgr. Thomas F. Brady; Revs. Timothy J. Teahan; James J. Krische.
Res., 1950 Batchelder St., 11229. Tel: 718-998-2800; Fax: 718-382-5428.
School—1943 Brown St., 11229. Tel: 718-339-2745; Fax: 718-645-4513. Mr. Anthony Paparelli, Prin.
Lay Teachers 24; Students 580.
Catechesis/Religious Programs—Tel: 718-375-0899; Fax: 718-645-4513.
Students 500.

51—ST. GREGORY THE GREAT, Rev. Gary P. Rogers; Deacons Roy N. George; Andres De Leon, Jr.
Res., 224 Brooklyn Ave., 11213-2505. Tel: 718-773-0100; Fax: 718-773-4198.
School—991 St. Johns Pl., 11213-2532. Tel: 718-774-3330; Fax: 718-774-3332. Cynthia O. Tege, Prin.
Lay Teachers 15; Students 325.
Catechesis/Religious Programs—Tel: 718-773-0100; Fax: 718-773-4198. Julia Bramwell, D.R.E.
Students 140.

52—GUARDIAN ANGEL, Rev. Msgr. Perfecto Vazquez; Rev. Andrzej Lukianiuk; Deacon Anthony J. Russo.
Res., 2978 Ocean Pkwy., 11235. Tel: 718-266-1561; Fax: 718-372-1603.
Catechesis/Religious Programs—Tel: 718-372-1967. Ariene Ambert, D.R.E.
Students 225.

53—HOLY CROSS, Revs. Thomas Nohilly; John E. Vesey.
Res., 2530 Church Ave., 11226. Tel: 718-469-5900; Fax: 718-469-5901.
School—Tel: 718-282-1710. Sr. Angela Patrice Murray, C.S.J., Prin.
Lay Teachers 11; Students 221.
Catechesis/Religious Programs—Tel: 718-941-5066.
Students 600.

54—HOLY FAMILY, Rev. Thomas E. Fox; Deacon Hector Montalvo. In res., Revs. Bartholomew Chidili, O.S.A.; John Prakasam.
Res., 205 14th St., 11215. Tel: 718-768-0736; Fax: 718-832-2879.

55—HOLY FAMILY, Revs. John A. McShane; Edward R. Kane. In res., Rev. Msgr. Raymond Rau, (Retired).
Res., 9719 Flatlands Ave., 11236. Tel: 718-257-4423; Fax: 718-257-4806.
School—216 Conklin Ave., 11236. Tel: 718-257-2954. Mary Lou Reitz, Prin.
Lay Teachers 15; Students 300.
Catechesis/Religious Programs—Tel: 718-257-8016; Fax: 718-257-4806. Elizabeth Mathew, D.R.E.
Students 500.

56—HOLY FAMILY (Slovak), Rev. John Menonkari, C.M.I. (India).
Res., 21 Nassau Ave., 11222. Tel: 718-388-5145; Fax: 718-387-1877.

57—HOLY INNOCENTS, Revs. Joseph J. Weber; Luis Carlos Pisfil; Jean-Miguel Auguste; Deacon Antoine Felix; Rev. Robert B. Hume, Pastor Emeritus.
Res., 279 E. 17th St., 11226. Tel: 718-469-9500; Fax: 718-941-4931.
School—249 E. 17th St., 11226. Tel: 718-282-5294. Sr. Mary Immaculate, R.S.M., Prin.
Sisters of Mercy 2; Lay Teachers 17; Students 329.
Catechesis/Religious Programs—Tel: 718-469-8159.
Students 392.

58—HOLY NAME, Revs. Dennis J. Farrell; Raymond McKiernan; Benedict Gomes; Gary Sommermeyer; Deacon Abel Torres. In res., Rev. Msgr. John F. Wilson, Pastor Emeritus.
Res., 245 Prospect Park W., 11215. Tel: 718-768-3071; Fax: 718-369-2039.
School—241 Prospect Park W., 11215. Tel: 718-768-7629; Fax: 718-768-3007. Robert Hughes, Prin. & D.R.E.
Sisters of St. Joseph 1; Lay Teachers 16; Students 225.
Catechesis/Religious Programs—241 Prospect Park W., 11215. Tel: 718-768-7629; Fax: 718-768-3007.
Students 214.

59—HOLY ROSARY, Rev. William Smith.
Res., 141 Chauncey St., 11233. Tel: 718-493-8001; Fax: 718-493-8002.

60—HOLY SPIRIT, Rev. Jerome T. Jecewiz; Deacons Wilfredo Hernandez; Louis Gonzalez. In res., Rev. Bartholomew Okagbue.
Res., 1712 45th St., 11204. Tel: 718-436-5565; Fax: 718-436-5586.
School—1668 46th St., 11204. Tel: 718-633-3959; Fax: 718-633-2830.
Sisters of St. Joseph 2; Lay Teachers 10; Students 187.
Convent—1679 47th St., 11204.

61—MOST HOLY TRINITY, Revs. Russell Governale, O.F.M.Conv.; Michael Sokalski, O.F.M.Conv.; Bro. Vincent Vivian, O.F.M.Conv.; Rev. Pedro de Oliverira, O.F.M. Conv.
Res., 138 Montrose Ave., 11206. Tel: 718-384-0215; Fax: 718-384-3030.
School—140 Montrose Ave., 11206. Tel: 718-384-1101; Fax: 718-384-6567. Sr. Karen Lademann, O.P., Prin.

62—ST. IGNATIUS, Revs. John R. Hyatt, S.J.; Alfredo S. Quevedo, S.J.; Rocco C. Danzi, S.J.; Deacons Berthal Beaubrun; Jean-Baptiste Boursiquot.
Res., 1101 Carroll St., 11225. Tel: 718-774-2102; Fax: 718-774-5821.
Catechesis/Religious Programs—Tel: 718-774-2102; Fax: 718-774-5821.
Students 180.

63—IMMACULATE CONCEPTION OF THE BLESSED VIRGIN MARY, Revs. Robert P. Morales, Admin.; Gonzalo Betancur (Colombia).
Res., 72 Maujer St., 11206. Tel: 718-384-0765; Fax: 718-384-2898.
Catechesis/Religious Programs—Students 99.

64—IMMACULATE HEART OF MARY, Revs. John J. Costello; John E. Capillo; Matthew W. Sheridan. In res., Rev. Edward T. O'Connor, Pastor Emeritus.
Res., 2805 Ft. Hamilton Pkwy., 11218. Tel: 718-871-1310; Fax: 718-633-1866.
School—3002 Ft. Hamilton Pkwy., 11218. Tel: 718-438-7373. Sr. Theresa Sweeney, Prin.
Sisters 2; Lay Teachers 12; Students 250.
Catechesis/Religious Programs—Tel: 718-854-7326. Joyce Checkett, D.R.E., Tel: 718-854-7326.
Students 265.

65—ST. JEROME'S, Revs. Guy Sansaricq; Antonius P. Gopaul; Deacons Anthony Arthur; Magloire Marcel.
Res., 2900 Newkirk Ave., 11226. Tel: 718-462-0223; Fax: 718-462-7753.
School—465 E. 29th St., 11226. Tel: 718-462-0211; Fax: 718-462-1828. Mrs. Satti Marchan, Prin.
Lay Teachers 9; Students 225.
Catechesis/Religious Programs—Paul Norman, D.R.E.
Students 230.

66—ST. JOHN THE BAPTIST, Revs. Joseph V. Agostino, C.M.; Eugene F. Sheridan, C.M.; Charles T. Pluck, C.M. In res., Rev. Thomas S. Krafinski, C.M.

Res., 75 Lewis Ave., 11206. Tel: 718-455-6864; Fax: 718-452-3738.
School—82 Lewis Ave., 11206. Tel: 718-453-1000; Fax: 718-453-1000. Sr. Mary Jane Raeihle, C.S.J., Prin.
Lay Teachers 29; Students 669.
Catechesis/Religious Programs—Sr. Patricia Evanick, D.C., D.R.E.
Students 225.

67—ST. JOHN CANTIUS, Rev. John A. Gurrieri; Deacon Rafael Marte; Sr. Mary Alice MacKenzie, S.C., Pastoral Assoc.
Res., 479 New Jersey Ave., 11207. Tel: 718-342-2679; Fax: 718-342-4878.
School—Tel: 718-385-7494; Fax: 718-566-1928. Mrs. Margaret Otunba, Prin.
Lay Teachers 12; Students 308.
Catechesis/Religious Programs—Students 225.

68—ST. JOHN THE EVANGELIST, Rev. Msgr. Joseph Nugent.
Res., 250 21st St., 11215. Tel: 718-768-3751; Fax: 718-768-4689.

69—ST. JOHN'S CHAPEL. Closed. For inquiries for parish records contact the Chancery.

70—ST. JOSEPH'S, Rev. Robert Vitaglione; Sr. Mirian Therese, D.D.L., Pastoral Assoc.
Res., 856 Pacific St., 11238. Tel: 718-783-4500; Fax: 718-398-2410.
Catechesis/Religious Programs—Students 100.

71—ST. JOSEPH PATRON OF THE UNIVERSAL CHURCH. (Scalabrini Fathers). Revs. Gianni Agostinelli, C.S.; Luis Antonio Diaz Lamus.
Res., 185 Suydam St., 11221. Tel: 718-386-0175; Fax: 718-821-1726.
School—St. Frances Cabrini, 181 Suydam St., 11221. Tel: 718-386-9277. Miss Maria Crifasi, Prin.
Lay Teachers 11; Students 250.

72—SHRINE CHURCH OF ST. JUDE, Revs. Mateo J. Rizzo; Michael Tedone; Deacon Arthur J. Cuccia.
Res., 1677 Canarsie Rd., 11236. Tel: 718-763-6300; Fax: 718-531-9655.
School—1696 Canarsie Rd., 11236. Tel: 718-241-6633.
Lay Teachers 15; Students 300.
Catechesis/Religious Programs—Tel: 718-241-4030. Mr. Ronald Rizzuto, D.R.E.
Students 200.
Convent—(Amityville) 2195 Canarsie Rd., 11236. Tel: 718-763-5087. Sisters of St. Dominic

73—ST. LAURENCE, Rev. Frank A. Black; Sr. Theresa Agliardi, R.S.M., Pastoral Assoc.
Res., 1020 Van Siclen Ave., 11207. Tel: 718-649-0545; Fax: 718-649-1606.
Catechesis/Religious Programs—Tel: 718-927-3310. Sr. Mary Jareth, D.R.E.
Students 200.
Convent—990 Van Siclen Ave., 11207. Tel: 718-272-2875.
Sisters of Mercy, Brooklyn 3.

74—ST. LEONARD OF PORT MAURICE. Closed 1978. Records at St. Joseph, Patron of the Universal Church.

75—ST. LOUIS. Closed. Became a Mission of St. Lucy in 1939. Parochial records are at St. Lucy-St. Patrick's, 285 Willoughby Ave., 11205. Tel: 718-622-8748; Fax: 718-622-6330.

76—ST. LUCY-ST. PATRICK, Revs. Francis Shannon; James O'Shea, C.P.; Cristiana Perez, Pastoral Assoc.; Deacon Jose Ramos.
Res., 285 Willoughby Ave., 11205. Tel: 718-622-8748; Fax: 718-622-6330.
Catechesis/Religious Programs—Students 210.

77—ST. MALACHY'S, Revs. Raymond J. Kelly; Francisco Ares; Remedios Guerrero, M.A., Pastoral Assoc. In res., Rev. Joseph W. Denzer.
Res., 207 Hendrix St., 11207. Tel: 718-647-5900; Fax: 718-348-4744.
Catechesis/Religious Programs—Tel: 718-235-3562. Remedios Guerrero, M.A., D.R.E.
Students 283.

78—ST. MARGARET MARY, Rev. Walter A. Mitchell; Deacon Charles J. Smith. In res., Rev. Francis J. Passenant.
Res., 215 Exeter St., Manhattan Beach, 11235. Tel: 718-743-1824; Fax: 718-743-0232.

79—ST. MARK'S, Rev. Joseph R. Grimaldi, J.C.L., Pastor Emeritus; Rev. Msgr. Gerard J. Arella; Revs. Cyril J. Doody; Edward M. Kachurka; Sr. Gloria Lepere, O.P., Pastoral Assoc. In res., Rev. Joseph P. Quigley.
Res., 2609 E. 19th St., 11235. Tel: 718-891-3100; Fax: 718-891-9677.
Church—Ocean Ave. & Ave. Z, 11235.
School—2602 E. 19th St., 11235. Tel: 718-332-9604; Fax: 718-891-9677. Sr. Catherine Roche, O.P., Prin.
Sisters of St. Dominic 1; Lay Teachers 15; Students 254.
Catechesis/Religious Programs—Tel: 718-769-6311; Fax: 718-891-9677. Mr. Kevin McCutchan, D.R.E.
Students 210.

80—ST. MARTIN OF TOURS-FOURTEEN HOLY MARTYRS, Rev. Patrick G. Burns. In res., Rev. John F. Brogan.
Res., 1288 Hancock St., 11221. Tel: 718-443-8484; Fax: 718-443-2968.
School—See St. Elizabeth Seton under Consolidated Elementary Schools in the Institutions located in the Diocese. Tel: 718-386-4050; Fax: 718-386-1565.
Catechesis/Religious Programs—Sr. Judy Fay, C.S.J., D.R.E.
Students 358.

81—ST. MARY MOTHER OF JESUS, Rev. Msgr. Rocco D. Villani; Rev. Angelo A. Venuti. In res., Rev. Steven J. Aguggia.
Res., 2326 84th St., 11214. Tel: 718-372-4000; Fax: 718-372-4002.
School—8401 23rd Ave., 11214. Tel: 718-372-0025. Sr. Thomasine Stagnitta, C.S.J., Prin.
Sisters of St. Joseph 5; Lay Teachers 16; Students 530.
Catechesis/Religious Programs—Tel: 718-449-8263; Fax: 718-265-6209. Sr. Patricia Conroy, R.S.M., D.R.E.
Students 530.

82—ST. MARY OF THE ANGELS (Lithuanian). Closed 1981. Records at Annunciation Parish, Brooklyn.

83—MARY QUEEN OF HEAVEN, Revs. William R. Dulaney; John A. Burns, Pastor Emeritus; Jamie J. Gigantiello; Deacon John Joseph Murphy.
Res., 1395 E. 56th St., 11234. Tel: 718-763-2330; Fax: 718-763-6592.
School—1326 E. 57th St., 11234. Tel: 718-763-2360. Sisters 1; Lay Teachers 15; Students 250.
Catechesis/Religious Programs—Tel: 718-763-2590.
Students 330.

84—ST. MARY, STAR OF THE SEA, Revs. Thomas Doyle; Gerald Akata; Francis X. Nelson. In res., Stephen Shin; Rev. Raymond Roden.
Res., 467 Court St., 11231. Tel: 718-625-2270; Fax: 718-624-9017.

85—ST. MATTHEW'S, Revs. Andrew L. Struzzieri, D.Min.; Hilaire Ruiz Belizaire; Pat Nolan; Deacons Florencio Cruz; Dennis A. DaCosta; Herve Desdunes.
Res., 1123 Eastern Pkwy., 11213. Tel: 718-774-6747; Fax: 718-953-4895.
Catechesis/Religious Programs—Sr. Christine Scherer, D.W., D.R.E.
Students 517.
Social Action Coord.—Sr. Dolores Augustine, P.V.M.I.

86—ST. MICHAEL'S, Revs. John Delendick; Ricardo Raveneau. In res., Rev. Youssef Bochra Nasri.
Res., 352 42nd St., 11232. Tel: 718-768-6065; Fax: 718-768-3336.
School—4222 Fourth Ave., 11232. Tel: 718-768-3582. Sr. Margaret M. Ford, C.S.J., Prin.
Sisters of St. Joseph 2; Lay Teachers 8; Students 212.
Catechesis/Religious Programs—Tel: 718-788-3442. Sr. Helene Jakubowski, R.S.M., D.R.E.
Students 240.

87—ST. MICHAEL'S, Rev. Philip F. Bohan, O.F.M.Cap.; Deacon Leon F. Miller; Sr. Rita Rompre, C.N.D.
Parish Address—284 Warwick St., 11207. Tel: 718-647-1818; Fax: 718-647-2384.
Res., St. Michael Friary, 225 Jerome St., 11207. Tel: 718-827-6990; Fax: 718-827-5789. Revs. Raphael Iannone, O.F.M.Cap., Guardian; William Hugo, O.F.M.Cap.; Knute Kenlon, O.F.M. Cap.
School—Tel: 718-277-6766; Fax: 718-348-0533.
Catechesis/Religious Programs—Tel: 718-647-1818; Fax: 718-647-2384.
Students 254.

88—ST. MICHAEL ARCHANGEL AND ST. EDWARD, Rev. James A. Hughes.
Res., 108 St. Edward's St., 11205. Tel: 718-625-3017; Fax: 718-625-2536.

89—NATIVITY OF OUR BLESSED LORD. Merged with St. Peter Claver in 1973. Records at St. Peter Claver Church.

90—ST. NICHOLAS, In res., Rev. Fidelis Ekemgba (Nigeria).
Res., 26 Olive St., 11211. Tel: 718-388-1420; Fax: 718-388-9516.
School—287 Powers St., 11211. Tel: 718-388-7992. Sr. Joan Losson, O.P., Prin.
Lay Teachers 15; Students 252.
Convent—312 De Voe St., 11211.

91—OUR LADY OF ANGELS, Revs. James E. Devlin, Pastor; Kenneth J. Calder; Richard Lewkiewicz; Deacon Michael J. Troy. In res., Rev. Msgr. Guy Puglio; Rev. Thomas F. Kelly.
Res., 7320 Fourth Ave., 11209. Tel: 718-836-7200; Fax: 718-238-2466.
School—Tel: 718-238-5045. Sr. Elizabeth Schroeder, C.S.J., Prin.
Lay Teachers 17; Students 291.
Catechesis/Religious Programs—Tel: 718-748-6553. Sr. Lucille Aliperti, C.S.J., D.R.E.
Students 300.

92—OUR LADY OF CHARITY, Rev. Dennis McAuliffe.
Res., 1669 Dean St., 11213. Tel: 718-774-5100; Fax: 718-778-3335.
Catechesis/Religious Programs—Tel: 718-774-5100; Fax: 718-778-3338. Ethel Ando-Menson, D.R.E.
Students 60.

93—OUR LADY OF CONSOLATION (Polish), Revs. Wlodzimierz R. Las, S.D.S. (Poland); Grzegorz Szewczyk, S.D.S. (Poland); Wieslaw P. Strzadala, S.D.S. (Poland).
Res., 184 Metropolitan Ave., 11211. Tel: 718-388-1942; Fax: 718-388-8993.

94—OUR LADY OF CZESTOCHOWA-ST. CASIMIR (Polish), Revs. Witold Mroziewski; Andrzej Gorczyca. In res., Rev. Msgr. Antoni Boszko.
Res., 183 25th St., 11232. Tel: 718-768-5724; Fax: 718-768-4996.
Catechesis/Religious Programs—Students 186.

95—OUR LADY OF GOOD COUNSEL, Rev. James Bukofsky; Deacons Isaac Duncan; John Gigglio.
Res., 915 Putnam Ave., 11221. Tel: 718-443-7211; Fax: 718-443-0121.
Catechesis/Religious Programs—Mrs. Sonia Andrews, D.R.E.
Students 160.

96—OUR LADY OF GRACE, Revs. Dominick F. Cutrone; Thomas Murtagh; Deacon Philip Siani; Sr. Jane Talbot, Pastoral Min.
Res., 430 Avenue W, 11223. Tel: 718-627-2020; Fax: 718-336-8033.
School—385 Avenue W, 11223. Tel: 718-375-2081; Fax: 718-376-7685. Mrs. Joan McMaster, Prin.
Lay Teachers 16; Students 280.
Catechesis/Religious Programs—Tel: 718-375-0404; Fax: 718-376-7685. Linda Nacinovich, D.R.E.
Students 275.

97—OUR LADY OF GUADALUPE, Rev. Msgr. Kevin B. Noone; Revs. John C. Miller; Joseph G. Fonti; Sr. Ann Elizabeth, O.P, Pastoral Assoc.
Res., 7201 Fifteenth Ave., 11228. Tel: 718-236-8300; Fax: 718-236-8119.
School—1514 72nd St., 11228. Tel: 718-331-2070; Fax: 718-331-2070. Sr. Lora Bannon, O.P., Prin.; Sr. Jean Asst. Prin.; Albert Fry, O.P., Asst. Prin.
Sisters of St. Dominic 3; Sisters of St. Joseph 1; Lay Teachers 23; Students 643.
Catechesis/Religious Programs—Tel: 718-331-4003. Mrs. Suzanne O'Connor, D.R.E.
Students 307.

98—OUR LADY HELP OF CHRISTIANS, Revs. Anthony M. Rucando; William A. With.
Res., 1315 E. 28th St., 11210. Tel: 718-338-5242; Fax: 718-258-5341.
School—1340 E. 29th St., 11210. Tel: 718-377-1800; Fax: 718-377-6374. Ms. Joanne Aldorisio, Prin.
Lay Teachers 13; Students 208.
Catechesis/Religious Programs—Tel: 718-377-6932; Fax: 718-258-5341. Stephen Rzonca, D.R.E.
Students 101.

99—OUR LADY OF LORETO, Revs. Michael J. Lynch; Fredi A. Rosales.
Res., 124 Sackman St., 11233. Tel: 718-385-3740; Fax: 718-385-3446.

100—OUR LADY OF LOURDES, Rev. Willaim A. Smith.
Res., 11 DeSales Pl., 11207. Tel: 718-452-2260; Fax: 718-452-6828.
School—2-12 Aberdeen St., 11207. Tel: 718-455-0037.
Lay Teachers 14; Students 230.

101—OUR LADY OF MERCY, Rev. James H. Sweeney.
Res., 680 Mother Gaston Blvd., 11212. Tel: 718-346-3166; Fax: 718-346-5776.
Catechesis/Religious Programs—Sr. Bernadette Sassone, D.W., D.R.E.
Students 400.

102—OUR LADY OF MERCY. Closed 1908. Second church at Schermerhorn & Bond closed April, Debevoise Place & DeKalb Ave. For inquiries for parish records contact the chancery.

103—OUR LADY OF MIRACLES, Revs. Thomas F. Leach; James G. Hannan; Giovanna Piccioli, Pastoral Outreach; Deacon Ernst Paul.
Res., 757 E. 86th St., 11236. Tel: 718-257-2400; Fax: 718-257-4634.
School—Tel: 718-649-0271; Fax: 718-649-3113. Bruno Marchan, Prin.
Sisters 1; Lay Teachers 12; Students 292.
Catechesis/Religious Programs—Carmel Ann Sperti DeArmas, D.R.E., Tel: 718-649-1006.
Students 300.

104—OUR LADY OF MONSERRATE-ST. AMBROSE, Revs. Francis Shannon; James O'Shea, C.P.; Sr. Maryellen Kane, C.S.J., Pastoral Assoc.
Res., 134 Vernon Ave., 11206. Tel: 718-388-5196; Fax: 718-388-5153.
Catechesis/Religious Programs—Mrs. Justina Velqzquez, D.R.E.
Students 180.

105—SHRINE OF OUR LADY OF MOUNT CARMEL (Italian), Rev. Msgr. David L. Cassato; Revs. Carmelo Gagliardi, O.F.M.Cap.; Anthony S. Aracich, S.J. Pastoral Assocs.: Giuditta Coccia, O.A., Italian Apostolate; John S. Fruner.
Res., 275 N. Eighth St., 11211. Tel: 718-384-0223; Fax: 718-384-5838.
School—Northside Catholic Academy at Mt. Carmel, 10 Withers St., 11211. Tel: 718-782-1110; Fax: 718-782-3344. Sr. Helen Gulczynski, C.S.J., Prin.
Catechesis/Religious Programs—Students 160.

106—OUR LADY OF PEACE (Italian), Rev. Roderick A. Crispo, O.F.M. In res., Revs. Bruno Ciardiello, O.F.M.; Samuel Karimi.
Res., 522 Carroll St., 11215. Tel: 718-624-5122; Fax: 718-852-6149.
Catechesis/Religious Programs—Students 102.
Convent—209 First St., 11215. Tel: 718-624-6720; Fax: 718-852-6149. Hermanas Franciscanas de la Immaculada

107—OUR LADY OF PERPETUAL HELP BASILICA, Very Rev. Kevin Moley, C.SS.R., Pastor & Rector; Revs. Norman S. Bennett, C.SS.R.; Joseph Buono, C.SS.R.; Edward Byrne, C.SS.R.; Martin Crowe, C.SS.R.; Edward Dunne, C.SS.R.; Sylvester E. Feeley, C.SS.R.; Thomas F. Hickey, C.SS.R.; Joseph A. Keenan, C.SS.R.; John McGuire, C.SS.R.; Thomas Maceda, C.SS.R.; Ruskin Piedra, C.SS.R.; John Hamrogue, C.SS.R.; Pierce Kenny, C.SS.R.; Joseph Marron, C.SS.R.; John J. Travers, C.SS.R.; John Murray, C.SS.R. Pastoral Assocs.: Sr. Bernard Loretto, C.S.J.; Sr. Noraleen Murphy, C.S.J.; Deacons Abdon Mejia (Peru); Eduviges Lopez; Jesus Soto. In res., Most Rev. Ronald Connors, C.SS.R., (Retired).
Res., 526-59th St., 11220. Tel: 718-492-9200; Fax: 718-439-8528.
School—Tel: 718-492-8067; Fax: 718-439-8081. Sr. Madeline Therese DiCarlo, C.S.J., Prin.
Sisters 6; Lay Teachers 14; Students 278.
Catechesis/Religious Programs—584 60th St., 11220. Tel: 718-492-4019; Fax: 718-439-8528.
Students 434.

108—OUR LADY OF THE PRESENTATION, Revs. Michael J. Lynch; Fredi A. Rosales; Deacon Jaime Landron.
Res., 1661 St. Marks Ave., 11233. Tel: 718-345-2604; Fax: 718-345-4639.

109—OUR LADY OF REFUGE, Rev. Michael Perry; Rev. Msgr. Rollin Darbouze; Revs. Augustin Almy; Benedict Verghese, C.M.I.
Res., 2020 Foster Ave., 11210. Tel: 718-434-2090; Fax: 718-859-7411.
School—1087 Ocean Ave., 11230. Tel: 718-434-4117. Joyce Dul Jacufki, Prin.
Sisters of St. Dominic 1; Lay Teachers 19; Students 427.

110—OUR LADY OF THE ROSARY OF POMPEII, Rev. Frank Amato, S.A.C.
Res., 225 Seigel St., 11206. Tel: 718-497-0614; Fax: 718-366-3236.

111—OUR LADY OF SOLACE (1900), Rev. Albert Bellantonio; Deacon Dan J. Marley.
Res., 2866 W. 17th St., 11224. Tel: 718-266-1612; Fax: 718-946-3651.
School—2865 W. 19th St., 11224. Mr. Robert P. Thomas, Prin.
Lay Teachers 10; Students 165.
Catechesis/Religious Programs—Mr. Augusto Lucero, D.R.E.
Students 200.

112—OUR LADY OF SORROWS. Merged with St. Leonard in 1942. Parochial records are at St. Joseph Patron of the Universal Church.

113—OUR LADY OF VICTORY, Revs. Martin J. Carter, S.A.; Martin Madison, S.A.
Res., 583 Throop Ave., 11216-2496. Tel: 718-574-5772; Fax: 718-919-2265.
Catechesis/Religious Programs—Tel: 718-574-5772; Fax: 718-919-2265.
Students 100.

114—ST. PATRICK'S. Merged with St. Lucy's in 1974. Records at St. Lucy-St. Patrick's.

115—ST. PATRICK, Rev. Msgr. Fursey O'Toole; Rev. Msgr. Martin Bannan, B.A., M.S.W.; Revs. Thomas Anastasio; James J. Reynolds (STL); Cletus Forson; Sr. Jeanne Elaine, Pastoral Assoc. In res., Rev. Msgr. Joseph K. Parks, Pastor Emeritus; Deacon Charles Postler.
Res., 9511 Fourth Ave., 11209. Tel: 718-238-2600; Fax: 718-238-1508.
School—401 97th St., 11209. Tel: 718-833-0124; Fax: 718-238-6840. Mrs. Mary T. Biers, Prin.
Lay Teachers 20; Students 255.
Catechesis/Religious Programs—Tel: 718-238-2600. Mrs. Michele Twomey, D.R.E., Tel: 718-238-2600.
Students 223.

116—ST. PETER-ST. PAUL-OUR LADY OF PILAR, Revs. Astor L. Rodriguez; Jaime Pico, C.M.; Robin E. Rodriguez, C.M. In res., Revs. Javier Serra, C.M.; Pedro Gomez, C.M.
Res., 234 Congress St., 11201. Tel: 718-624-3425; Fax: 718-834-0380.
Catechesis/Religious Programs—Tel: 718-797-9262.
Students 123.

117—ST. PETER CLAVER, Rev. Patrick J. West.
Res., 29 Claver Pl., 11238. Tel: 718-622-4647; Fax: 718-622-3304.
Catechesis/Religious Programs—Mr. Peter Altman, D.R.E.
Students 64.

118—SS. PETER AND PAUL'S, Rev. Msgr. Agustin Ruiz.
Res., 71 S. Third St., 11211. Tel: 718-388-9576; Fax: 718-388-0714.
School—Tel: 718-388-1041. Mr. Robert Russo, Prin.
Lay Teachers 10; Students 224.
Catechesis/Religious Programs—Sr. Maria Monserrat.
Students 181.

119—MOST PRECIOUS BLOOD, Rev. Msgr. Joseph Rosa; Revs. Joseph Attard; Michael Salamone.
Res., 70 Bay 47th St., 11214. Tel: 718-372-8022; Fax: 718-996-6575.
School—133-157 27th Ave., 11214. Tel: 718-373-7343; Fax: 718-373-5887. Sr. Doloretta Silanos, S.O.L.M., Prin.
Sisters 4; Lay Teachers 6; Students 246.
Catechesis/Religious Programs—Natalie Coangelo, D.R.E.
Students 138.

120—QUEEN OF ALL SAINTS, Rev. Casper J. Furnari. In res., Revs. John J. Brown; Patrick J. West.
Res., 300 Vanderbilt Ave., 11205. Tel: 718-638-7625; 7626; Fax: 718-638-7393.
School—300 Vanderbilt Ave., 11205. Tel: 718-857-3114; Fax: 718-857-0632. Theresa Attianese, Prin.
Sisters 1; Lay Teachers 14; Students 252.
Catechesis/Religious Programs—Students 70.

121—REGINA PACIS VOTIVE SHRINE. Attended by St. Rosalia, 65 St. & 12th Ave.
1230 65th St., 11219. Tel: 718-236-0909; Fax: 718-236-5357.

122—RESURRECTION, Rev. Msgr. Francis J. Fahy; Rev. Msgr. Raymond R. Shevlin, Pastor Emeritus; Rev. James T. O'Brien.
Res., 2331 Gerritsen Ave., 11229. Tel: 718-743-7234; 7235; Fax: 718-743-0152.
School—2335 Gerritsen Ave., 11229. Tel: 718-332-9806; Fax: 718-743-0152. Ms. Diana C. Meringolo, Prin.
Lay Teachers 10; Students 252.
Catechesis/Religious Programs—Tel: 718-891-0888; Fax: 718-743-0152. Mrs. Angela Parente, D.R.E.
Students 325.

123—RESURRECTION CATHOLIC COPTIC CHAPEL, Rev. Youssef Bochra Nasri, (Coptic Catholic Patriarchate).
Mailing Address: 352 42nd St., 11232. Tel: 718-965-0422.
Church—328 14th St., 11215. Tel: 718-499-6946.

124—ST. RITA'S, Rev. Msgr. John T. Peyton; Deacon Ronald Ronacher.
Res., 275 Shepherd Ave., 11208. Tel: 718-647-4910; Fax: 718-827-2767.
School—280 Shepherd Ave., 11208. Tel: 718-647-6040. William Geasor, Prin.
Sisters 3; Lay Teachers 20; Students 620.
Catechesis/Religious Programs—Mrs. Annemarie Ronacher, D.R.E.
Students 345.

125—ST. ROCCO'S, Rev. Faustino Cordero. In res., Rev. George Ebejer.
Res., 216 27th St., 11232. Tel: 718-768-9798; Fax: 718-768-7748.
Catechesis/Religious Programs—Karen Salinas, D.R.E.
Students 144.

126—ST. ROSALIA-REGINA PACIS, Rev. Msgr. Dino M. Zeni; Revs. Anthony J. Sansone; Edward A. Cassar; Deacon Joseph Cafiero. In res., Rev. Msgr. Ronald T. Marino.
Res., 1230 65th St., 11219. Tel: 718-236-0909; Fax: 718-236-5357.
Center Regina Center, Inc.—1258 65th St., 11219. Tel: 718-232-4340.
School—1201 66th St., 11219. Tel: 718-236-8150; Fax: 718-236-3846. Mr. Vincent Tannacore, Prin.
Lay Teachers 12; Students 175.
Catechesis/Religious Programs—Tel: 718-331-5465. Mr. Vincent Tannacore, D.R.E.
Students 475.
Mission—Brooklyn, Regina Pacis Votive Shrine.

127—ST. ROSE OF LIMA, Rev. Joseph P. Byrns. In res., Rev. Njoroge Ngugi.
Res., 269 Parkville Ave., 11230. Tel: 718-434-8040; Fax: 718-421-4223.
School—259 Parkville Ave., 11230. Tel: 718-434-1739.
Sisters of St. Joseph 3; Lay Teachers 11; Students 178.
Catechesis/Religious Programs—Students 176.

128—SACRED HEART, Revs. Pedro Nel Ossa; Richard Bretone; Sr. Eileen Neary, R.S.M., Pastoral Assoc. & D.R.E. In res., Rev. Msgr. Walter Murphy, Pastor Emeritus.
Res., 41 Adelphi St., 11205. Tel: 718-625-5115; Fax: 718-625-2918.

129—SACRED HEART CHAPEL. Closed. 1996. For inquiries for parish records contact the Chancery.

130—SACRED HEART MISSION. Closed. 1942. For inquiries for parish records contact the Chancery.

131—SACRED HEARTS OF JESUS AND MARY AND ST. STEPHEN, Revs. Anthony J. Acciarito; Simon Joseph; Paul Tunacao; Sr. Mary Alphonsina, M.F.S. In res., Revs. Vincent La Rocca; Charles P. Nichols.
Res., 108 Carroll St., 11231. Tel: 718-596-7750; Fax: 718-260-9233.
School—Tel: 718-625-2267; Fax: 718-625-0916.
Lay Teachers 10; Students 200.

132—ST. SAVIOUR, Rev. Msgr. Joseph P. Nagle; Revs. Darrell A. Da Costa; Robert Lawsine; Deacon William Williamsen; Sr. Patricia Hanvey, O.P., Pastoral Assoc. In res., Rev. Joseph F. Mali (Nigeria).
Res., 611 Eighth Ave., 11215. Tel: 718-768-4055; 768-7983; Fax: 718-768-4872.
School—701 Eighth Ave., 11215. Tel: 718-768-8000. Mr. James Flanagan, Prin.
Lay Teachers 23; Students 455.
High School—588 Sixth St., 11215. Tel: 718-768-4406; Fax: 718-369-2688. Sr. Valeria Belanger, S.S.N.D., Prin.
Students 298.
Catechesis/Religious Programs—Tel: 718-768-4055; Fax: 718-768-4872.
Students 65.

133—SS. SIMON AND JUDE, Revs. Edward A. Floretta; Paul Vazhapilly.
Res., 185 Van Sicklen St., 11223. Tel: 718-375-9600; Fax: 718-375-6642.
School—Tel: 718-449-1857; Fax: 718-449-0212.
Lay Teachers 14; Students 150.
Catechesis/Religious Programs—Tel: 718-372-0733.
Students 380.

134—ST. STANISLAUS KOSTKA, Revs. Roman Gorowski, C.M.; Stanislaw Miekina, C.M.; Joseph Lachowski, C.M.; Edmund Gutowski, C.M.; Joseph Wisniewski, C.M.; Tadeusz Maciejewski, C.M.; Jan Urbaniak, C.M.
Res., 607 Humboldt St., 11222. Tel: 718-388-0170; Fax: 718-384-5290.
School—10 Newel St., 11222. Tel: 718-383-1970; Fax: 718-383-1711. Sr. Dorothea Jurkowski, Prin.
Priests 7; Sisters of the Holy Family of Nazareth 7; Lay Teachers 18; Students 420.
Catechesis/Religious Programs—Tel: 718-388-0170.
Students 432.

135—ST. STANISLAUS MARTYR. Merged with Holy Family (14th St.) in 1979. Records at Holy Family, 14th St., between Sixth and Seventh Aves.

136—ST. STEPHEN. Merged with Sacred Hearts in 1941. Parochial records are at Sacred Hearts-St. Stephen Church, Carroll St.

137—ST. SYLVESTER, Revs. Thomas M. Haggerty; Raymond C. Gruhn. In res., Rev. Charles P. Vogel.
Res., 416 Grant Ave., 11208. Tel: 718-647-1995; Fax: 718-348-4035.
School—396 Grant Ave., 11208. Tel: 718-235-4729; Fax: 718-235-4729. Carmen Padin, Prin.
Lay Teachers 12; Students 300.
Catechesis/Religious Programs—Sr. Elizabeth Folles, D.R.E.
Students 317.

138—ST. TERESA OF AVILA, Revs. Philip Pizzo, Pastor; James Yaro (Nigeria).
Res., 563 Sterling Pl., 11238. Tel: 718-622-6500; Fax: 718-622-2234.
School—Tel: 718-638-5884; Fax: 718-638-0893. Dr. Kenneth J. Cottrell, Ed.D., Prin.
Lay Teachers 22; Students 400.
Catechesis/Religious Programs—Students 110.

139—ST. THERESE OF LISIEUX. (The Little Flower). Revs. Alfred P. LoPinto; Godfred Bonnet (Nigeria); Francois Augustin (Haiti); Deacons Mauclair Simon; Ronald Agnant; Gordon Daniel.

Res., 1281 Troy Ave., 11203. Tel: 718-451-1500; Fax: 718-451-1502.
School—4410 Avenue D, 11203. Tel: 718-629-9330; Fax: 718-629-6854. Sr. Paulette Pollina, R.S.M., Prin.
Sisters of Mercy 3; Lay Teachers 23; Students 400.
Catechesis/Religious Programs—Tel: 718-451-1671. Frances McCormick, D.R.E.
Students 202.

140—ST. THOMAS AQUINAS, Revs. Sean Harlow, O. Carm., Pastor; Robert Owens, O.Carm.
Res., 249 Ninth St., 11215. Tel: 718-768-9471; Fax: 718-965-4022.
School—211 Eighth St., 11215. Tel: 718-768-9007; Fax: 718-768-9007.
Lay Teachers 10; Students 243.
Catechesis/Religious Programs—Tel: 718-768-9471. Ms. Lynda Larsen, D.R.E.
Students 165.

141—ST. THOMAS AQUINAS, Rev. Msgr. Brian F. Callahan; Revs. Thomas J. Lyons; Thomas Basquel, C.S.Sp. In res., Rev. Msgr. John E. Mahoney, V.E.; Rev. Msgr. Kieran J. Martin; Sr. Carole Fitzpatrick, C.S.J.
Res., 1550 Hendrickson St., 11234. Tel: 718-253-4404; Fax: 718-951-7573.
School—1501 Hendrickson St., 11234. Tel: 718-377-0442; Fax: 718-677-4138. Sr. M. Alice Traynor, O.S.U., Prin.
Lay Teachers 15; Students 315.
Catechesis/Religious Programs—Tel: 718-338-3542. Rev. Thomas Basquel, C.S.Sp., D.R.E.
Students 451.

142—TRANSFIGURATION, Rev. Msgr. Bryan J. Karvelis; Deacon German Martinez.
Res., 263 Marcy Ave., 11211. Tel: 718-388-8773; Fax: 718-388-8774.
School—Tel: 718-388-1120; Fax: 718-388-2822. Sr. Mary Anne Ricioppo, Prin.
Lay Teachers 8; Students 178.
Catechesis/Religious Programs—Students 258.
Southside Mission for Social Services—280 Marcy Ave., 11211. Tel: 718-388-3784. Sr. Kathryn Walsh, Dir.

143—ST. VINCENT DE PAUL, Rev. Richard J. McCormack. In res., Rev. Msgr. John P. McCullagh; Rev. Justo Beltran (Philippines).
Res., 167 N. Sixth St., 11211. Tel: 718-388-4218; Fax: 718-486-0615.
School—Northside Catholic Academy, 180 N. 7th St., 11211. Fax: 718-384-6937. Sr. Helen Gulczynski, C.S.J., Prin.
Lay Teachers 7; Students 156.
Catechesis/Religious Programs—Students 5.

144—ST. VINCENT FERRER, Revs. Coman V. Brady; George R. Cowan; Mrs. Mary Anne Muller, Pastoral Assoc.
Res., 1603 Brooklyn Ave., 11210-3495. Tel: 718-859-0041; 859-9009; Fax: 718-859-9032.
Church—E. 37th St. & Glenwood Rd., 11210.
School—Tel: 718-859-3505; Fax: 718-859-9545. Ms. Jean Guy, Prin.
Lay Teachers 20; Students 425.
Catechesis/Religious Programs—Tel: 718-859-9000. Mary Anne Muller, D.R.E.
Students 250.

145—VISITATION OF THE BLESSED VIRGIN MARY, Rev. Neil Tiedemann, C.P.
Res., 98 Richards St., 11231. Tel: 718-624-1572; Fax: 718-722-7748.
Catechesis/Religious Programs—Sr. Marjorie McHugh, R.S.M., D.R.E.
Students 148.

BOROUGH AND COUNTY OF QUEENS

146—ST. ADALBERT, Revs. Timothy Pasek, O.F.M.Conv., Guardian; Paul Miskiewicz, O.F.M.Conv.; Rev. Paul Marut, O.F.M. Conv.; Bro. Hugh Dymski, O.F.M.Conv. In res., Rev. Michael Panful.
Res., 52-29 83rd St., Elmhurst, 11373. Tel: 718-639-0212; Fax: 718-651-1705.
School—52-17 83rd St., Elmhurst, 11373. Tel: 718-424-2376.
Sisters 5; Lay Teachers 24; Students 432.
Catechesis/Religious Programs—Tel: 718-446-8622. Mary Hellman, D.R.E.
Students 182.
Office for Pastoral Care of the Sick—Tel: 718-429-2005.

147—ST. ALOYSIUS, Revs. Christopher T. Cashman; Anthony V. Dell'Anno; Deacon Fabio Flaim; Sr. Noemi Valdes, S.M.R., Min. to Homebound.
Res., 382 Onderdonk Ave., Ridgewood, 11385. Tel: 718-821-0231; Fax: 718-628-7304.
School—360 Seneca Ave., Ridgewood, 11385. Tel: 718-821-7384. Sr. Naomi Varrone, O.P., Prin.
Sisters of St. Dominic 1; Lay Teachers 12; Students 320.
Catechesis/Religious Programs—Tel: 718-417-6327; Fax: 718-464-6411. Blanche Ciangiulli, D.R.E.
Students 115.
Pastoral Care Office—Tel: 718-963-7689.

148—AMERICAN MARTYRS, Rev. Msgr. John F. Keppler; Rev. John J. Murray; Deacon Stanley J. Galazin. In res., Rev. Anthony S. Ercolano.
Res., 79-43 Bell Blvd., Bayside, 11364. Tel: 718-464-4582; Fax: 718-464-5488.
School—216-15 Peck Ave., Bayside, 11364. Tel: 718-776-3779. Sr. Maureen Coyne, O.P., Prin.
Religious 1; Lay Teachers 12; Students 270.
Catechesis/Religious Programs—Tel: 718-464-6411. Ms. Christine Rahner, D.R.E.
Students 250.

149—ST. ANASTASIA, Rev. Msgr. Michael J. Cantley; Revs. John J. Gribbon; George J. Lutjen.
Res., 45-14 245th St., Douglaston, 11362. Tel: 718-631-4454; Fax: 718-631-1774.
School—45-11 245th St., Douglaston, 11362. Tel: 718-631-3153. Mrs. JoAnn Dolan, Prin.
Lay Teachers 18; Students 298.
Catechesis/Religious Programs—Tel: 718-225-5191. Janine Kramer, D.R.E.
Students 400.

150—ST. ANDREW AVELLINO, Rev. Msgr. James P. Grace, S.T.L.; Revs. Matthew J. Diamond; Michael J. McGee; Wilfred Dewan, C.S.P. In res., Rev. Msgr. Lawrence J. McAlister, Pastor Emeritus.
Res., 35-60 158th St., Flushing, 11358. Tel: 718-359-0417; Fax: 718-539-2830.
School—35-50 158th St., Flushing, 11358. Tel: 718-359-7887; Fax: 718-359-2295.
Lay Teachers 25; Students 394.
Catechesis/Religious Programs—Tel: 718-445-7012; Fax: 718-539-2830.
Students 282.

151—ST. ANN'S, Revs. George A. Pfundstein, Pastor; Joseph N. Grisaitis; Anthony Sikandar (Pakistan).
Res., 142-30 58th Ave., Flushing, 11355. Tel: 718-886-3890; Fax: 718-358-4964.
School—142-25 58th Rd., Flushing, 11355. Tel: 718-463-1238; Fax: 718-539-6618. Mr. Frank E. Sauro, Prin.
Sisters 2; Lay Teachers 16; Students 336.
Catechesis/Religious Programs—Tel: 718-359-8019; Fax: 718-358-4964. Sr. Patricia A. Anglin, O.P., D.R.E.
Students 110.

152—ST. ANTHONY OF PADUA, Revs. James J. Mueller; Thomas Muthukattil (India); Joseph Hadgkiss; Deacon J. Edward Joesten.
Res., 133-25 128th St., South Ozone Park, 11420. Tel: 718-843-7410; 843-3356; Fax: 718-659-1478.
School—125-18 Rockaway Blvd., South Ozone Park, 11420. Tel: 718-641-0212; Fax: 718-641-8079. Sr. Julia Mary, S.S.N.D., Prin.
School Sisters of Notre Dame 2; Sisters of Mercy 1; Lay Teachers 19; Students 447.
Catechesis/Religious Programs—Tel: 718-848-1127. Marcella Slobodzian, D.R.E.
Students 96.

153—ASCENSION, Rev. Vito Buonanno. In res., Rev. Msgr. Charles A. Bleilevens, Pastor Emeritus; Revs. Peter Chidi Osuagwu; Francisco J. Walker.
Res., 86-13 55th Ave., Elmhurst, 11373. Tel: 718-335-2626; Fax: 718-335-4181.
School—86-37 53rd Ave., Elmhurst, 11373. Tel: 718-335-9755; Fax: 718-335-2234.
Sisters 1; Lay Teachers 9; Students 230.
Catechesis/Religious Programs—Students 80.

154—ST. BARTHOLOMEW'S, Revs. Joseph M. Hoffman; James Cunningham; Francisco Walker (Argentina); Eugene Soriano (Philippines). In res., Rev. Msgr. James E. Gotimer.
Res., 43-22 Ithaca St., Elmhurst, 11373. Tel: 718-424-5400; Fax: 718-899-5257.
School—44-15 Judge St., Elmhurst, 11373. Tel: 718-446-7575.
Sisters of St. Dominic 4; Sisters of St. Frances 2; Lay Teachers 32; Students 725.
Catechesis/Religious Programs—Tel: 718-898-0096. James Thompson, D.R.E.
Students 650.

155—ST. BENEDICT JOSEPH LABRE, Rev. Msgr. John H. O'Brien; Rev. Christopher O'Connor; Deacon Angel R. Rivera. In res., Rev. John W. Jurgensen.
Res., 94-40 118th St., Richmond Hill, 11419. Tel: 718-849-4048; Fax: 718-856-0732.
School—94-25 117th St., Richmond Hill, 11419. Tel: 718-441-6674; Fax: 718-441-4367.
Sisters 3; Lay Teachers 20; Students 533.
Convent—94-24 118th St., Richmond Hill, 11419. Tel: 718-849-5571.

156—ST. BENEDICT, THE MOOR, Rev. Paul C. Palmiotto.
Res., 171-17 110th Ave., Jamaica, 11433. Tel: 718-526-4018; Fax: 718-526-4825.
Catechesis/Religious Programs—Students 20.

157—BLESSED SACRAMENT, Rev. Edward J. Smith; Rev. Msgr. Raymond W. Kutner; Revs. Jesus Cuadros; Richard Conlon; Deacon Roberto J. Pouso. In res., Most Rev. Rene A. Valero.
Res., 34-43 93rd St., Jackson Heights, 11372. Tel: 718-639-3888; Fax: 718-478-5536.
School—34-20 94th St., Jackson Heights, 11372. Tel: 718-446-4449; Fax: 718-446-5366.
Grey Nuns of the Sacred Heart 5; Lay Teachers 20; Students 482.

158—BLESSED VIRGIN MARY, HELP OF CHRISTIANS, Revs. Donald M. Berran; Christopher Lee Coleman; Sr. Mary Conroy, C.S.J., Pastoral Assoc.; Deacon Kevin Ryan. In res., Revs. Thomas M. Catania; James Moyna, O.P.
Res., 70-31 48th Ave., Woodside, 11377. Tel: 718-672-4848; Fax: 718-457-4055.
School—70-20 47th Ave., Woodside, 11377. Tel: 718-639-8042. Mary Basiles, Prin.
Lay Teachers 14; Students 204.
Catechesis/Religious Programs—Tel: 718-672-4784. Patricia Wise, D.R.E.
Students 200.

159—ST. BONAVENTURE'S, Rev. Paul C. Palmiotto; Deacons Harry Coleman; Pascual Olivas.
Res., 114-58 170th St., Jamaica, 11434. Tel: 718-526-0040; Fax: 718-526-4825.
Catechesis/Religious Programs—Mrs. Angela Lewis, D.R.E.
Students 85.

160—ST. CAMILLUS, Revs. James M. Dunne; Mathew Maniampra, C.M.I.
Res., 99-15 Rockaway Beach Blvd., Rockaway Beach, 11694. Tel: 718-634-8229; Fax: 718-634-8193.
School—185 Beach & 99th St., Rockaway Beach, 11694. Tel: 718-634-5260; 634-8353; Fax: 718-634-8353. Sr. Agnes White, C.S.J., Prin.
Sisters of St. Joseph 3; Lay Teachers 9; Students 220.
Catechesis/Religious Programs—Tel: 718-474-3101. Sr. St. Claude, D.R.E.
Students 135.

161—ST. CATHERINE OF SIENNA, Rev. John J. Amann; Deacons James Burrell; Luis Taylor. In res., Rev. Msgr. James F. Spengler, Vicar for Vicariate.
Res., 118-22 Riverton St., St. Albans, 11412. Tel: 718-528-1220; Fax: 718-528-7907.
School—Tel: 718-528-1857; Fax: 718-949-8739. Sr. Barbara Kradick, O.P., Prin.
Lay Teachers 19; Religious 2; Students 470.
Catechesis/Religious Programs—Mary Harris, D.R.E.
Students 150.

162—CHRIST THE KING, Rev. Jeffry T. Dillon; Deacon Winston M. Mayers.
Res., 145-39 Farmers Blvd., Springfield Gardens, 11434. Tel: 718-528-6010; Fax: 718-949-3255.
Catechesis/Religious Programs—Tel: 718-528-6010; Fax: 718-949-3255.
Students 143.

163—ST. CLARE, Rev. Msgr. James Cooney; Revs. Joseph Diele; Louis Uzoh. In res., Rev. William F. Sweeney.
Res., 137-35 Brookville Blvd., Rosedale, 11422. Tel: 718-341-1018; Fax: 718-276-2001.
School—137-25 Brookville Blvd., Rosedale, 11422. Tel: 718-528-7174; 276-2001; Fax: 718-528-4389. Mrs. Mary Jane Finley, Prin.
Lay Teachers 20; Students 510.
Catechesis/Religious Programs—Tel: 718-527-6153. Richard Pipchinski, D.R.E.
Students 204.

164—ST. CLEMENT POPE, Rev. Edward J. Brenkert; Deacon Nathaniel J. Smith.
Res., 141-11 123rd Ave., Jamaica, 11436. Tel: 718-529-0273; Fax: 718-529-3089.
School—Tel: 718-659-9011. Bro. Ronald J. Travers, S.C., Prin.
Religious 2; Lay Teachers 15; Students 340.
Catechesis/Religious Programs—Students 127.

165—CORPUS CHRISTI, Rev. Msgr. Richard F. Dunn; Revs. Jose Herrera; John O'Neill; Deacon Carlos Trochez. In res., Rev. James Frost.
Res., 31-30 61st St., Woodside, 11377. Tel: 718-278-8114; Fax: 718-278-3619.
School—31-29 60th St., Woodside, 11377. Tel: 718-721-2484; Fax: 718-278-3619. Lucetta Daragh, Prin.
Lay Teachers 16; Students 274.
Catechesis/Religious Programs—Tel: 718-721-2484.
Students 150.

166—ST. ELIZABETH'S, Revs. John A. Thompson; Joseph C. Vella; Sr. Charlene Kay, O.P., Parish Min. In res., Rev. Thomas D. Dolan.
Res., 94-20 85th St., Ozone Park, 11416. Tel: 718-296-4900; Fax: 718-296-1140.
School—Tel: 718-641-6990; Fax: 718-323-5010. Barbara Samide, Prin.

Lay Teachers 11; Students 330.
Catechesis/Religious Programs—Tel: 718-738-3294. Ruth Arrao, D.R.E.
Students 150.

167—St. Fidelis, Revs. Arthur G. Minichello; Ronald M. D'Antonio; Nazareno C. Javier; Sr. Helen Muhlbauer, O.P., Pastoral Min.; Deacon John Reichert; Angela DiPaola, Pastoral Assoc.
Res., 123-06 14th Ave., College Point, 11356. Tel: 718-445-6164; Fax: 718-445-1623.
School—124-06 14th Ave., College Point, 11356. Tel: 718-539-2628. Bro. Robert Russo, C.S.C., Prin.
Sisters of St. Dominic 1; Lay Teachers 23; Students 459.
Catechesis/Religious Programs—Tel: 718-359-1249. Joan Colombo, D.R.E.
Students 436.

168—St. Francis of Assisi, Rev. Emilio J. Salerno; Deacons John Sucich; Savior Hili. In res., Rev. Msgr. Thomas P. Campbell, Pastor Emeritus; Rev. Charles P. Keensy.
Res., 21-17 45 St., Long Island City, 11105. Tel: 718-728-7801; Fax: 718-728-7853.
School—21-18 46th St., Astoria, 11105. Tel: 718-726-9405; Fax: 718-721-2577. Barbara McArdle, Prin.
Lay Teachers 20; Students 410.
Catechesis/Religious Programs—Tel: 718-278-0259. Gerry Catoggio, D.R.E.
Students 200.

169—St. Francis de Sales, Rev. Msgr. Martin T. Geraghty; Rev. Louis J. DeGaetano. In res., Rev. Msgr. Howard B. Basler.
Res., 129-16 Rockaway Beach Blvd., Belle Harbor, 11694. Tel: 718-634-6464; Fax: 718-634-0716.
School—216 Beach & 130th St., Belle Harbor, 11694. Tel: 718-634-2775; Fax: 718-634-6673. Sr. Patricia Chelius, C.S.J., Prin.
Sisters of St. Joseph 3; Lay Teachers 29; Students 770.
Catechesis/Religious Programs—Tel: 718-945-6911. Dr. Virginia Clark, D.R.E.
Students 440.

170—St. Gabriel, Rev. Robert F. Barclay. In res., Revs. Celestine Anyanwu (Nigeria); Robert Titone; James Fitzpatrick; John J. Tobin Arago; John J. Arango (Colombia); Deacon Eulogio S. Dupuy.
Res., 26-26 98th St., East Elmhurst, 11369. Tel: 718-639-0474; Fax: 718-639-2810.
School—26-25 97th St., East Elmhurst, 11369. Tel: 718-426-7170; Fax: 718-426-1741. Bro. Edward Shields, F.S.C., Prin.
Sisters 3; Brothers 3; Lay Teachers 16; Students 415.
Catechesis/Religious Programs—Tel: 718-426-9577.
Students 206.

171—St. Genevieve, Rev. John Cullinane.
Res., 6 Beach 178 St., Rockaway Point, 11697. Tel: 718-634-7276; Fax: 718-318-7905.
Catechesis/Religious Programs—Students 20.

172—St. Gerard Majella, Revs. Edward P. Doran, Ph.D.; John Mendonca; Deacons Guillermo Gomez; Luis Roman. In res., Rev. Msgr. Eugene A. Feldhaus, Senior Priest.
Res., 188-16 91st Ave., Hollis, 11423. Tel: 718-468-6565; Fax: 718-468-3136.
School—Tel: 718-468-1166.
Sisters 1; Lay Teachers 11; Students 120.

173—St. Gertrude, Rev. Brendan W. Downing; Deacon Alfred L. Whelan.
Res., 336 Beach 38th St., Far Rockaway, 11691. Tel: 718-327-5673; Fax: 718-471-6405.
Catechesis/Religious Programs—Students 85.

174—St. Gregory the Great, Revs. Joseph L. Cunningham, S.T.L.; Kevin F. McBrien, S.T.L.; Stephen Placa; Deacon Arthur Cutter.
Res., 242-20 88th Ave., Bellerose, 11426. Tel: 718-347-3707; Fax: 718-347-0583.
School—244-44 87th Ave., Bellerose, 11426. Tel: 718-343-5053; Fax: 718-347-1142. Mrs. Teresa Gerstner, Prin.
Lay Teachers 25; Students 507.
Catechesis/Religious Programs—Tel: 718-347-0525. Regina Joyce, D.R.E.
Students 355.
Convent—88-19 Cross Island Pkwy., Bellerose, 11426.

175—St. Helen, Rev. Msgr. Joseph C. Pfeiffer; Revs. Francis J. Hughes; John P. Cush; Sr. Hannah Marie Cox, P.B.V.M., Pastoral Assoc.; Deacon Armand D'Accordo.
Res., 157-10 83 St., Howard Beach, 11414. Tel: 718-738-1616; Fax: 718-835-5144.
School—83-09 157th Ave., Howard Beach, 11414. Tel: 718-835-4155; Fax: 718-848-8728.
Religious 2; Lay Teachers 16; Students 425.
Catechesis/Religious Programs—Tel: 718-835-6216.
Students 560.

176—Holy Child Jesus, Revs. Daniel S. Murphy; John J. Boylan. In res., Rev. Msgr. Lawrence E. Hinch; Deacons Sal Licata; Dean Tully.
Res., 111-11 86th Ave., Richmond Hill, 11418. Tel: 718-847-1860; Fax: 718-847-2696.
School—112-02 86th Ave., Richmond Hill, 11418. Tel: 718-849-3988.
Sisters of St. Joseph 2; Lay Teachers 23; Students 400.
Catechesis/Religious Programs—Tel: 718-849-8560. Sr. Catherine Bernadette, M.S.B.T., D.R.E.
Students 165.
Missionary Cenacle—86-22 112th St., Richmond Hill, 11418. Tel: 718-849-8560. Missionary Servants of the Most Blessed Trinity.

177—Holy Cross (Polish), Revs. Peter Zendzian; Ryszard Koper (Poland).
Res., 61-21 56th Rd., Maspeth, 11378-2498. Tel: 718-894-1387; Fax: 718-416-9245.
School—56-01 61st St., Maspeth, 11378-2499. Tel: 718-894-2356; Fax: 718-326-5194. Ms. Susanne Dziepak, Prin.
Sisters 1; Lay Teachers 9; Students 259.

178—Holy Family, Rev. Msgr. Joseph L. Stafford; Revs. Thaddeus Abraham (India) Pastoral Assoc.; Bartholomew Egan, C.S.Sp. In res., Rev. Edward M. Keane; Most Rev. Ignatius Catanello, D.D.
Res., 175-20 74th Ave., Flushing, 11366. Tel: 718-969-2448.
School—75th Ave. & 175th St., Flushing, 11366. Tel: 718-969-2124; Fax: 718-380-2183. Sr. Matthew Mary Gay, C.S.J., Prin.
Sisters of St. Joseph 5; Lay Teachers 21; Students 480.
Catechesis/Religious Programs—Tel: 718-591-6438. D.R.E.: Barbara Makolin; Jane Lawson.
Students 250.

179—Holy Trinity, Revs. Marcello J. Latona; James F. Fraser; Joseph A. Pfaff, D.R.E. In res., Rev. James E. Sullivan, Senior Priest.
Res., 14-51 143rd St., Whitestone, 11357. Tel: 718-746-7730; Fax: 718-767-1368.
School—Tel: 718-746-1479; Fax: 718-746-4793. Eleanor Menna, Prin.
Lay Teachers 12; Students 265.
Catechesis/Religious Programs—Students 125.

180—Immaculate Conception, Revs. Thomas Joyce, C.P.; Theophane Cooney, C.P.; Edward Buchheit; Leo O'Boyle, C.P.
Res., 86-45 Edgerton Blvd., Jamaica, 11432. Tel: 718-739-0880; Fax: 718-657-0543.
School—179-14 Dalny Rd., Jamaica, 11432. Tel: 718-739-5933; Fax: 718523-7436. Dr. Charlene Jaffie, Prin.
Sisters of St. Joseph 6; Lay Teachers 18; Students 462.
Catechesis/Religious Programs—86-16 Midland Pkwy., Jamaica, 11432. Tel: 718-291-3080. Sr. Elizabeth Gildea, C.S.J., D.R.E.
Students 280.

181—Immaculate Conception, Rev. Msgr. Charles P. Boccio. In res., Revs. Vitalis D. Dzokapor (Nigeria); Evaristus Osuagwu (Nigeria); Leo V. Rosero (Philippines).
Res., 21-47 29th St., Long Island City, 11105. Tel: 718-728-1613; Fax: 718-956-9229.
School—21-63 29th St., Long Island City, 11105. Tel: 718-728-1969. Sr. Jeanne Stegmann, S.U.S.C., Prin.
Sisters 2; Lay Teachers 19; Students 415.
Catechesis/Religious Programs—Tel: 718-956-4494. Marylyn Crum, D.R.E.
Students 345.
Convent—21-60 31st St., Long Island City, 11105. Fax: 718-959-9229.

182—Incarnation, Rev. Msgr. John F. Casey; Rev. Dagoberto Noguera; Deacon Francois Innocent. In res., Rev. Msgr. Edward J. Nolan, Pastor Emeritus.
Res., 89-43 Francis Lewis Blvd., Queens Village, 11427. Tel: 718-465-8534; Fax: 718-465-3834.
School—89-15 Francis Lewis Blvd., Queens Village, 11427. Tel: 718-465-5066; Fax: 718-464-4128. Sr. Ellen Patrice, Prin.
Sisters of St. Dominic (Amityville) 5; Lay Teachers 20; Students 500.
Catechesis/Religious Programs—Tel: 718-776-8956. Elizabeth Bennett, D.R.E.
Students 200.

183—SS. Joachim and Anne, Rev. Msgr. Joseph P. Malagreca; Rev. John W. Byrnes.
Res., 218-26 105 Ave., Queens Village, 11429. Tel: 718-465-0124; Fax: 718-479-3548.
School—218-19 105th Ave., Queens Village, 11429. Tel: 718-465-2230. Linda Freebes, Prin.
Sisters of Notre Dame de Namur 1; Lay Teachers 20; Students 606.
Catechesis/Religious Programs—Teresa Rosero, D.R.E.
Students 351.

184—St. Joan of Arc, Rev. Msgr. John A. McGuirl; Rev. Msgr. James F. Donegan, Pastor Emeritus; Revs. Jose M. Perez; Stephen Valdazo; Barry Frazzita.
Res., 82-00 35th Ave., Jackson Heights, 11372. Tel: 718-429-2333; Fax: 718-672-5881.
School—35-27 82nd St., Jackson Heights, 11372. Tel: 718-639-9020; Fax: 718-639-5428. Linda C. Kelly, Prin.
Lay Teachers 26; Students 580.
Catechesis/Religious Programs—Tel: 718-478-5593.
Students 605.

185—St. John Vianney, Rev. Brian P. Dowd; Deacon John McGreevey.
Res., 140-10 34th Ave., Flushing, 11354. Tel: 718-762-7920; Fax: 718-460-8032.
Catechesis/Religious Programs—Tel: 718-961-5092; Fax: 718-460-8032. Eileen Nesi, D.R.E.
Students 220.

186—St. Josaphat (Polish), Rev. Francis P. Bien. In res., Rev. Thomas Machalski.
Res., 34-32 210th St., Bayside, 11361. Tel: 718-229-1663; Fax: 718-229-8018.

187—St. Joseph (Polish), Rev. Andrzej Kielkowski, S.D.S. (Poland).
Res., 108-43 Sutphin Blvd., Jamaica, 11435. Tel: 718-739-4781; Fax: 718-658-5447.

188—St. Joseph, Revs. George J. Ryan; Edward L. Maurer; Deacon Felipe J. Alvarez.
Res., 43-19 30th Ave., Long Island City, 11103. Tel: 718-278-1611; Fax: 718-956-3589.
School—28-46 44th St., Long Island City, 11103. Tel: 718-728-0724; Fax: 718-728-8372.
Sisters of St. Dominic 2; Lay Teachers 29; Students 560.
Catechesis/Religious Programs—Tel: 718-545-7338.
Students 425.

189—St. Kevin, Rev. James T. Smith; Rev. Msgr. George V. Fogarty, Pastor Emeritus; Revs. John P. Maloney; Charles B. Kehoe. In res., Revs. Michael Parisi; Paul A. Wood.
Res., 45-21 194 St., Flushing, 11358. Tel: 718-357-8888; Fax: 718-357-3671.
School—45-50 195th St., Flushing, 11358. Tel: 718-357-8110; Fax: 718-357-2519.
Sisters of Mercy (Dallas, PA) 3; Lay Teachers 21; Students 468.
Catechesis/Religious Programs—Tel: 718-357-5317. Mrs. Laura Stroligo, D.R.E.
Students 270.

190—St. Leo, Revs. William Krlis; Joaquin Suran; Deacon Rafael Diaz.
Res., 104-05 49th Ave., Corona, 11368. Tel: 718-592-7569; Fax: 718-271-6726.
School—104-19 49th Ave., Corona, 11368. Tel: 718-592-7050; Fax: 718-592-0787. Mrs. Maureen Blaine, Prin.
Lay Teachers 21; Students 456.
Catechesis/Religious Programs—Tel: 718-699-8565.
Students 171.
Mission—Brooklyn, Queens Co., Our Lady of Mount Carmel, 103-56 52nd Ave., Corona, 11368. Tel: 718-592-7569.

191—St. Luke, Rev. Msgr. Nicholas J. Capua; Revs. Joaquin S. Longres; Joseph F. Wilson; Deacon Harry A. Svebel. In res., Rev. Msgr. James W. Asip.
Res., 16-34 Clintonville St., Whitestone, 11357. Tel: 718-746-8102; Fax: 718-746-3589.
School—16-01 150th Pl., Whitestone, 11357. Tel: 718-746-3833; Fax: 718-747-2101. Mrs. Barbara Reiter, Prin.
Sisters of St. Dominic 2; Lay Teachers 22; Students 335.
Catechesis/Religious Programs—Tel: 718-746-3409. Theresa Mulgrew Agrusa, D.R.E.
Students 520.

192—St. Margaret, Rev. Msgr. William A. Varvaro; Revs. Leonard F. Badia, Ph.D., P.A.; Ralph Barile. In res., Revs. Gregory Wielunski; Nicholas Iwuagwu.
Res., 66-05 79th Pl., Middle Village, 11379. Tel: 718-326-1911; Fax: 718-326-1883.
School—66-10 80th St., Middle Village, 11379. Tel: 718-326-0922. Sr. Bridget Olwell, O.S.U., Prin.
Sisters of St. Dominic 2; Lay Teachers 22; Students 540.
Catechesis/Religious Programs—Margaret Walter, D.R.E.
Students 249.

193—St. Margaret Mary, Rev. Edmund P. Brady; Sr. Maryann McHugh, C.S.J., Pastoral Assoc.
Res., 9-18 27th Ave., Long Island City, 11102. Tel: 718-721-9020; Fax: 718-721-3729.
Catechesis/Religious Programs—Amelia Heiskell, D.R.E.
Students 125.

194—ST. MARY, Rev. Christopher J. Turczany. In res., Rev. Hugo Bedoya, C.M.
Res., 10-08 49th Ave., Long Island City, 11101. Tel: 718-786-0705; Fax: 718-482-7115.
Catechesis/Religious Programs—Students 33.

195—ST. MARY GATE OF HEAVEN, Revs. Matthew J. Considine, S.M.M.; Bernard Brault, S.M.M.; James Brady, S.M.M.; Bros. Paul Llorens, S.M.M.; Richard Polite, S.M.M.; Deacons Thomas Heaphy; Richard Gilligan.
Res., 101-25 104th St., Ozone Park, 11416. Tel: 718-847-5957; Fax: 718-846-6489.
School—104-06 101st Ave., Ozone Park, 11416. Tel: 718-846-0689; Fax: 718-846-1059. Patrick Scannell, Prin.
Sisters 2; Lay Teachers 23; Students 650.
Catechesis/Religious Programs—Tel: 718-849-9329. Sr. Kathy Hickey, C.S.J., D.R.E.
Students 228.

196—ST. MARY MAGDALENE, Rev. John Maloney; Deacon Lee C. Williams; Sr. Ave Regina Gould, C.S.J.
Res., 218-12 136th Ave., Springfield Gardens, 11413. Tel: 718-949-4311; Fax: 718-528-7208.

197—MARY'S NATIVITY, Rev. Msgr. Edward J. Bottino; Rev. Thaddeus J. Kazanecki. In res., Rev. Msgr. Edward A. Ryan; Rev. Joseph F. Wiseman.
Res., 46-02 Parsons Blvd., Flushing, 11355. Tel: 718-359-5996; Fax: 718-939-6737.
School—146-28 Jasmine Ave., Flushing, 11355. Tel: 718-359-1800. Mrs. Eileen Burke Ogoff, Prin.
Lay Teachers 13; Students 240.
Catechesis/Religious Programs—Tel: 718-353-5961. Donna Marie Sticco, D.R.E.
Students 290.

198—ST. MARY STAR OF THE SEA, Revs. Sean G. Ogle; Fulgencio Gutierrez; Rev. Msgr. James J. McKenna, Pastor Emeritus.
Res., 1920 New Haven Ave., Far Rockaway, 11691. Tel: 718-327-1133; Fax: 718-327-3276.
School—595 Beach 19th St., Far Rockaway, 11691. Tel: 718-327-2242. Miss Angela Brucia, Prin.
Priests 2; Lay Teachers 18; Students 355.
Catechesis/Religious Programs—1920 New Haven Ave., Far Rockaway, 11691.
Students 200.

199—ST. MATTHIAS, Rev. Msgr. Anthony F. Sherman; Revs. Richard J. Beuther; Lukasz Pawel Trocha; Deacons John Sands; Lawrence Mule. In res., Rev. Msgr. Joseph G. Konrad.
Res., 58-15 Catalpa Ave., Ridgewood, 11385. Tel: 718-821-6447; 6448; 6449; Fax: 718-821-6876.
School—58-25 Catalpa Ave., Ridgewood, 11385. Tel: 718-381-8003; Fax: 718-381-5319. Miss Barbara Wehnes.
Sisters of Notre Dame 6; Lay Teachers 10; Students 340.
Catechesis/Religious Programs—Tel: 718-386-1077; Fax: 718-821-6876. Mrs. Carol E. Powell, D.R.E.
Students 502.

200—ST. MEL, Rev. Msgr. John J. Antoncic; Revs. Victor Mbanisi; James S. Musumeci.
Res., 28-20 154th St., Flushing, 11354. Tel: 718-886-0201; 886-0881; Fax: 718-886-0882.
School—154-24 26th Ave., Flushing, 11354. Tel: 718-539-8211. Sr. Mary Spencer, O.P., Prin.
Sisters 6; Lay Teachers 22; Students 544.
Catechesis/Religious Programs—Tel: 718-461-9840; Fax: 718-886-0882. Marie Hayes, D.R.E.
Students 262.

201—ST. MICHAEL, Rev. Msgr. Edward V. Wetterer; Revs. Jose R. Aldegunde; Michael Melendez; Edwin Mania (Philippines); Sr. Joan S. Dawber, S.C., Pastoral Asst.; Deacon Elias Yepes.
Res., 136-76 41st Ave., Flushing, 11355. Tel: 718-961-0295; 961-0182; Fax: 718-961-1403.
School—136-58 41st Ave., Flushing, 11355. Tel: 718-961-0246. Mrs. Maureen Rogone, Prin.
Sisters of St. Joseph 1; Lay Teachers 19; Students 357.
Catechesis/Religious Programs—Tel: 718-961-0312. Mrs. Zilia V. Hirsch, Admin.
Students 350.

202—ST. MONICA (Jamaican). Closed. For inquiries for parish records contact the Chancery.

203—MOST PRECIOUS BLOOD, Rev. Msgr. Raymond W. Stafford; Rev. Msgr. George T. Voiland, (Retired); Revs. Michael J. McHugh; Robert Zubovic (Croatia); Vincent F. Miceli; Deacon Giacomo Panessa.
Res., 32-23 36th St., Long Island City, 11106. Tel: 718-278-3337; Fax: 718-278-4354.
School—32-52 37th St., Long Island City, 11103. Tel: 718-278-4081; Fax: 718-278-3089. Mr. Anthony Biscione, Prin.
Sisters of St. Joseph 3; Lay Teachers 32; Students 691.
Catechesis/Religious Programs—Tel: 718-721-9850.
Students 265.
Convent—32-16 36th St., Long Island City, 11106. Tel: 718-278-4706.

204—NATIVITY OF THE BLESSED VIRGIN MARY, Rev. Msgr. Robert J. Thelen; Revs. Angelo B. Pezzullo; Frank W. Spacek; Deacon Andrew A. Marchello. In res., Rev. Michael Barimah-Apay.
Res., 101-41 91st St., Ozone Park, 11416. Tel: 718-845-3691; Fax: 718-845-8978.
School—101-60 92nd St., Ozone Park, 11416. Tel: 718-845-3074; Fax: 718-845-5068. Sr. Marguerite Torre, O.S.U., Prin.
Sisters 3; Lay Teachers 18; Students 428.
Catechesis/Religious Programs—101-38 92nd St., Ozone Park, 11416. Tel: 718-845-1524. Michael Rosa, D.R.E.
Students 250.

205—ST. NICHOLAS OF TOLENTINE, Revs. Robert J. McConnin; Kevin J. Sweeney; Deacon Lionel Knight. In res., Rev. Msgr. Thomas M. O'Brien, Pastor Emeritus.
Res., 150-75 Goethals Ave., Jamaica, 11432. Tel: 718-969-3226; Fax: 718-380-0345.
School—80-22 Parsons Blvd., Jamaica, 11432. Tel: 718-380-1900; Fax: 718-591-6977. Sr. Elizabeth McNeela, S.C., Prin.
Sisters of Charity (Halifax) 4; Lay Teachers 23; Students 510.
Catechesis/Religious Programs—Tel: 718-591-6536.
Students 150.

206—OUR LADY OF THE ANGELUS, Rev. Msgr. John R. Dwyer; Rev. Alexander Abugel; Deacon Edwin Cancel. In res., Rev. Msgr. William T. Hickey, Pastor Emeritus; Rev. Rafael R. Macaranas (Philippines).
Res., 63-63 98th St., Rego Park, 11374. Tel: 718-897-4444; Fax: 718-897-1453.
School—Tel: 718-896-7220; Fax: 718-896-5723. Ms. Mary Ann Rys, Prin.
Sisters 2; Lay Teachers 12; Students 250.
Catechesis/Religious Programs—Tel: 718-896-4388; Fax: 718-897-1453. Sr. Jo Ann Schwarz, D.R.E.
Students 300.

207—OUR LADY OF THE BLESSED SACRAMENT, Rev. Msgr. Vincent A. Keane; Revs. William J. Rueger; Peter DeSanctis; Roy Mejias, D.C.D. (Philippines).
Res., 34-24 203rd St., Bayside, 11361. Tel: 718-229-5929; Fax: 718-229-3354.
School—34-45 202nd St., Bayside, 11361. Tel: 718-229-4434; Fax: 718-229-5820.
Sisters 1; Lay Teachers 28; Students 469.
Catechesis/Religious Programs—Tel: 718-225-6179. Mary Mullaney, D.R.E.
Students 260.

208—OUR LADY OF THE CENACLE, Rev. Msgr. Cornelius T. Kneafsey; Rev. David Espinoza. In res., Revs. Pablo Sans, Hospital Chap., (Retired); Hyacinth Alia; Deacon Eduardo Sencion.
Res., 136-06 87th Ave., Richmond Hill, 11418. Tel: 718-291-2540; Fax: 718-291-6211.
School—Tel: 718-657-6690. Mrs. Rosemarie McGoldrick Prin.
Sisters of Charity (Halifax) 2; Lay Teachers 11; Students 312.
Catechesis/Religious Programs—Sr. Florence Symes, C.S.J., D.R.E.
Students 273.

209—OUR LADY OF CHINA CHAPEL, Rev. Thomas Sung, C.S.J.B. (Taiwan).
Res., 54-09 92nd St., Elmhurst, 11373. Tel: 718-699-1929; Fax: 718-592-5981.
School—
Catechesis/Religious Programs—Fax: 718-371-3215.
Students 870.
Chinese School—Ming Yuan Chinese School, Tel: 718-271-3944. See Monasteries and Residences for Priests and Brothers for the Religious Community.

210—OUR LADY OF FATIMA, Rev. Msgr. Edward J. Breen; Revs. Eugene F. Donnelly; Jose Jimenez; John J. Gildea. In res., Rev. Patrick J. Frawley.
Res., 25-02 80th St., Jackson Heights, 11370. Tel: 718-899-2801; Fax: 718-429-6404.
School—25-38 80th St., Jackson Heights, 11370. Tel: 718-429-7031; Fax: 718-899-2811. Mrs. Cassie Zelic, Prin.
Lay Teachers 30; Students 746.
Catechesis/Religious Programs—Tel: 718-457-3457; Fax: 718-429-6404.
Students 300.
Convent—25-56 80th St., Jackson Heights, 11370. Tel: 718-446-7097.

211—OUR LADY OF GRACE, Rev. Msgr. William Flood; Rev. John Maduri; Deacon Joseph Campisi. In res., Rev. Francis J. Labita.
Res., 100-05 159th Ave., Howard Beach, 11414. Tel: 718-843-6218; Fax: 718-738-8208.
School—158-12 101st St., Howard Beach, 11414. Tel: 718-848-7440; Fax: 718-641-3464. Elvira Anselmo, Prin.
Lay Teachers 24; Students 420.
Catechesis/Religious Programs—Tel: 718-835-2765. Sr. Ann Martha, O.P., D.R.E.
Students 280.

212—OUR LADY OF HOPE, Rev. Msgr. Nicholas W. Sivillo; Rev. Arthur A. Candreva, I.V.Dei. In res., Rev. Msgr. Anthony J. Barretta; Deacons Robert F. Lavanco; Robert McGee.
Res., 61-27 71st St., Middle Village, 11379. Tel: 718-429-5438; Fax: 718-429-2764.
School—Tel: 718-458-3535; Fax: 718-458-9031.
Sisters 3; Lay Teachers 30; Students 674.
Catechesis/Religious Programs—Tel: 718-335-8394.
Students 218.

213—OUR LADY OF LOURDES, Rev. Msgr. Robert J. Pawson; Rev. Donald Kavanagh; Deacon Warren Winkler. In res., Rev. John A. McNeill.
Res., 92-96 220th St., Queens Village, 11428. Tel: 718-479-5111; Fax: 718-479-0826.
School—92-80 220th St., Queens Village, 11428. Tel: 718-464-1480; Fax: 718-740-4091. Sr. Josephine Barbiere, C.S.J., Prin.
Religious 1; Lay Teachers 26; Students 503.
Catechesis/Religious Programs—Tel: 718-740-4090. Joanne Russo, D.R.E.
Students 304.

214—OUR LADY OF MERCY, Rev. Msgr. Gerald J. Langelier; Rev. John Cremins; Deacon Edward Smolinski. In res., Rev. Msgr. Edward B. Scharfenberger; Rev. August J. Iantosca.
Res., 70-01 Kessel St., Forest Hills, 11375. Tel: 718-268-6143; Fax: 718-544-3764.
School—70-25 Kessel St., Forest Hills, 11375. Tel: 718-793-2086.
Sisters Servants of the Immaculate Heart of Mary 4; Lay Teachers 14; Students 302.

215—OUR LADY OF THE MIRACULOUS MEDAL, Rev. Msgr. George M. Schuster; Rev. Msgr. Anthony Danna; Revs. Al Barozzi; Marc Caliwan; Deacon Jerome Krebs. In res., Rev. Andrew J. Vaccari.
Res., 62-81 60th Pl., Ridgewood, 11385. Tel: 718-366-3360; Fax: 718-456-0564.
School—Bleecker & 61st St., Ridgewood, 11385. Tel: 718-821-2221. Ms. Margaret A. Baxter, Prin.
Lay Teachers 14; Students 289.
Catechesis/Religious Programs—Tel: 718-456-3275. Mary Macchiaroli, D.R.E.
Students 385.

216—OUR LADY OF MOUNT CARMEL, Revs. Frank Lynch; Joseph Pham; Anthony Raso. In res., Rev. Edmund P. Brady.
Res., 23-25 Newtown Ave., Long Island City, 11102. Tel: 718-278-1834; Fax: 718-278-0998.
School—25-15 Newtown Ave., Long Island City, 11102. Tel: 718-728-8376. Ms. Angela Fazio, Prin.
Lay Teachers 11; Students 324.
Catechesis/Religious Programs—Tel: 718-545-7987; Fax: 718-278-0998.
Students 285.

217—OUR LADY OF PERPETUAL HELP, Revs. Edward W. Richards; John G. Garkowski; John Ugochukwu; Deacon Juan Carattini. In res., Rev. James T. Devine.
Res., 111-50 115th St., South Ozone Park, 11420. Tel: 718-843-1212; Fax: 718-843-3554.
School—111-10 115th St., South Ozone Park, 11420. Tel: 718-843-4184; Fax: 718-323-2333. Mrs. Frances DeLuca, Prin.
Lay Teachers 21; Students 543.
Catechesis/Religious Programs—Tel: 718-641-6165. Thomas Columbia, D.R.E.
Students 200.

218—OUR LADY, QUEEN OF MARTYRS, Rev. Msgr. Joseph A. Funaro; Revs. Daniel Weiscopf; Robert W. Blauvelt; Deacon Thomas McCarthy, (Retired). In res., Rev. Msgr. Michael J. Dempsey.
Res., 110-06 Queens Blvd., Forest Hills, 11375. Tel: 718-268-6251; Fax: 718-793-2584.
School—Sisters 1; Lay Teachers 16; Students 328.
Convent—109-04 72 Rd., Forest Hills, 11375.

219—OUR LADY OF THE SKIES CHAPEL, Rev. James T. Devine, Admin.
Church—Kennedy International Airport, International Arrivals Bldg., Second Floor, Jamaica, 11430. Tel: 718-656-5348; Fax: 718-656-8162.

220—OUR LADY OF THE SNOWS, Rev. Msgr. Raymond F. Chappetto; Revs. Michael Ittykunju (India); Kenneth J. Grande; George J. Stack; Deacons Henry J. Smith; Matthew Oellinger.
Res., 258-15 80th Ave., Floral Park, 11004. Tel: 718-347-6070; Fax: 718-343-3221.
School—79-33 258th St., Floral Park, 11004. Tel: 718-343-1346; Fax: 718-343-7303. Sr. Roberta Oberle, Prin.
Sisters of St. Joseph 1; Lay Teachers 20; Students 530.

Catechesis/Religious Programs—Tel: 718-347-3511.
Students 350.

221—OUR LADY OF SORROWS, Revs. Thomas J. Healy; Lawrence Gellel, S.J.; Raul O. Gelvez; Deacon Orlando Pascal.
Res., 104-11 37th Ave., Corona, 11368. Tel: 718-424-7554; Fax: 718-424-4910.
School—35-34 105th St., Corona, 11368. Tel: 718-426-5517. Sr. Katherine Hanrahan, C.S.J., Prin.
Sisters of St. Joseph 1; Lay Teachers 22; Students 375.
Catechesis/Religious Programs—Tel: 718-651-5682. Deacon Elias Yepes, D.R.E.
Students 1,000.

222—ST. PANCRAS, Revs. Vincent Gallo; Brian M. Keller. In res., Rev. Henry Williams.
Res., 72-22 68th St., Glendale, 11385. Tel: 718-821-2323; Fax: 718-417-8021.
School—Myrtle Ave. & 68th St., Glendale, 11385. Tel: 718-821-6721. Sr. Jane Creighton, O.P., Prin.
Lay Teachers 17; Students 359.
Catechesis/Religious Programs—Tel: 718-479-0590. Mary E. McIntyre, D.R.E.
Students 400.

223—ST. PASCAL BAYLON, Rev. Msgr. Robert R. McCourt. Pastoral Assocs.: Sr. Mary Jane Rolston, O.P.; Sr. Susan Smolinsky, S.C. In res., Rev. John W. Maloney.
Res., 112-43 198th St., St. Albans, 11412. Tel: 718-468-3511; Fax: 718-479-2303.
Catechesis/Religious Programs—Tel: 718-468-3511; Fax: 718-479-2403.
Students 90.

224—ST. PATRICK, Rev. Robert M. Robinson, S.T.B., M.A., Pastor. In res., Very Rev. Jean-Pierre Ruiz, S.T.D.
Res., 39-38 29th St., Long Island City, 11101. Tel: 718-729-6060; Fax: 718-729-1276.
Catechesis/Religious Programs—Tel: 718-937-1239. Sr. Flora Marinelli, C.S.J., D.R.E.
Students 125.

225—ST. PAUL THE APOSTLE, Rev. Paul W. Jervis. In res., Rev. Jose Sanchez (Philippines).
Res., 98-16 55 Ave., Corona, 11368. Tel: 718-271-1100; Fax: 718-760-3496.
Catechesis/Religious Programs—Students 300.

226—ST. PAUL CHONG HA-SANG ROMAN CATHOLIC CHAPEL (Korean Apostolate), Revs. Insung (John Vianney) Kim; Il Yung (Peter) Kim; Heebong Nam; Deacon Paul M. Chin.
Office: 32-15 Parsons Blvd., Flushing, 11354. Tel: 718-321-7676; Fax: 718-321-7005.
Catechesis/Religious Programs—D.R.E.: Sr. Marie Jona Yoo, O.S.B.; Sr. Mos Park, O.S.B.
Students 461.
Convent—32-15 Parsons Blvd., Flushing, 11354. Olivetan Benedictine Sisters
St. Augustine Yu Chin-gil Chapel: 2115 61st St., Brooklyn, 11204. Tel: 718-729-0132; Fax: 718-729-0132.

227—ST. PIUS V, Revs. Richard J. Ahlemeyer; Luiz Antonio DeAguiar (Brazil).
Res., 106-12 Liverpool St., Jamaica, 11435. Tel: 718-739-3731; Fax: 718-739-7086.
Catechesis/Religious Programs—Students 200.

228—ST. PIUS X, Rev. Msgr. Thomas A. Graham; Revs. James F. Marron; Joachim Fernando (Sri Lanka). In res., Rev. Denis M. Dore, (Retired).
Res., 148-10 249th St., Rosedale, 11422. Tel: 718-525-9099; Fax: 718-276-2467.
School—147-65 249th St., Rosedale, 11422. Tel: 718-525-7171. John Toomey, Prin.
Lay Teachers 10; Students 263.
Catechesis/Religious Programs—Marianne Gratto, D.R.E.
Students 125.

229—PRESENTATION OF THE BLESSED VIRGIN MARY, Revs. Michael M. Greene, Pastor; Stephen Lynch; Luiz Antonio DeAguire; Deacon Ukafor Uzoigiue. In res., Rev. Richard J. Ahlemeyer.
Res., 88-19 Parsons Blvd., Jamaica, 11432. Tel: 718-739-0241; Fax: 718-739-2753.
Providence House III—159-23 89th Ave., Jamaica, 11432. Tel: 718-739-1348.
School—Tel: 718-739-2003; Fax: 718-526-8153. Ms. Dori Breen, Prin.
Lay Teachers 12; Students 291.
Catechesis/Religious Programs—Tel: 718-526-4152.
Students 325.

230—QUEEN OF ANGELS, Revs. Vincent M. Daly; George M. Hernandez; Deacon Juan Calvo.
Res., 44-04 Skillman Ave., Long Island City, 11104. Tel: 718-392-0011; 0012; Fax: 718-472-2625.
School—41-12 44th St., Long Island City, 11104. Tel: 718-786-2990; Fax: 718-472-4862. Sr. Adrienne Ryniewicz, R.S.M., Prin.
Sisters of Mercy 1; Lay Teachers 14; Students 235.
Catechesis/Religious Programs—Tel: 718-937-5174.
Students 40.

231—QUEEN OF PEACE, Rev. James Tighe; Deacon Michael Vicinanza. In res., Rev. Msgr. Celsus O. Collini, Pastor Emeritus; Rev. John C. Reilly, Pastor Emeritus.
Res., 141-36 77th Ave., Flushing, 11367. Tel: 718-380-5031; Fax: 718-969-2025.
School—141-25 77th Rd., Flushing, 11367. Tel: 718-969-3640; Fax: 718-969-5640. Mrs. Louise McNamara, Prin.
Lay Teachers 11; Students 340.
Convent—Tel: 718-380-4293. Sisters of St. Dominic

232—ST. RAPHAEL, Revs. Thomas G. Pettei; Gabriel Lee.
Res., 35-20 Greenpoint Ave., Long Island City, 11101. Tel: 718-729-8957; Fax: 718-729-5238.
School—48-25 37th St., Long Island City, 11101. Tel: 718-784-0482. Sr. Maureen Ahlemeyer, P.B.V.M., Prin.
Sisters of the Presentation 1; Lay Teachers 13; Students 283.
Catechesis/Religious Programs—Students 120.

233—RESURRECTION-ASCENSION, Rev. Msgr. Joseph P. Bynon; Revs. Salvatore Amato; Kevin P. Cavallyzz.
Res., 61-11 85th St., Rego Park, 11374. Tel: 718-424-5212; Fax: 718-639-8679.
School—85-25 61st Rd., Rego Park, 11374. Tel: 718-426-4963; Fax: 718-426-0940. Sr. Margaret Sweeney, C.S.J., Prin.
Sisters 1; Lay Teachers 21; Students 340.
Catechesis/Religious Programs—Tel: 718-533-7898.
Students 195.

234—ST. RITA, Rev. John P. Harrington; Deacon Vincent Parisi.
Res., 36-25 11th St., Long Island City, 11106. Tel: 718-361-1884; Fax: 718-786-4573.
School—36-14 12th St., Long Island City, 11106. Tel: 718-729-1594. Mrs. Mary Sandoz, Prin.
Lay Teachers 11; Students 120.
Catechesis/Religious Programs—Tel: 718-361-1884; Fax: 718-786-4573.
Students 120.

235—ST. ROBERT BELLARMINE, Rev. Msgr. John B. Lavin; Rev. Msgr. Joseph C. Mulqueen; Revs. Abraham P. Mathew; Daniel Suh, S.J. In res., Rev. Henry A. Lang.
Res., 56-15 213th St., Bayside, 11364. Tel: 718-229-6465; Fax: 718-229-8126.
School—56-10 214th St., Bayside, 11364. Tel: 718-225-8795; Fax: 718-423-5612. Sr. Mary Ann Carotenuto, C.S.J., Prin.
Sisters of St. Joseph 4; Lay Teachers 18; Students 435.
Catechesis/Religious Programs—Students 210.

236—ST. ROSE OF LIMA, Revs. Peter D. Gillen; Francis J. McGee; Anthony C. Casey.
Res., 130 Beach 84th St., Rockaway Beach, 11693. Tel: 718-634-7394; Fax: 718-634-6591.
School—154 Beach 84th St., Rockaway Beach, 11693. Tel: 718-474-7079; Fax: 718-634-0524. Mrs. Theresa Andersen, Prin.
Sisters 2; Lay Teachers 15; Students 345.
Catechesis/Religious Programs—Tel: 718-945-4850. Ms. Antoinette Camarda, D.R.E.
Students 125.

237—SACRED HEART OF JESUS, Rev. Msgr. Thomas F. Donovan; Revs. Kenneth J. Hand; Timothy Hirten; Sr. Kathleen Masterson, Pastoral Min. In res., Rev. Coleman Costello.
Res., 215-35 38th Ave., Bayside, 11361. Tel: 718-428-2200; Fax: 718-428-5840.
School—216-33 38th Ave., Bayside, 11361. Tel: 718-631-4804. Dennis J. Farrell, Prin.
Lay Teachers 25; Students 525.
Catechesis/Religious Programs—Tel: 718-631-1307. Mrs. Georgette Lyons, D.R.E.
Students 1,080.

238—SACRED HEART, Revs. Michael C. Gribbon; Calonge Lemaine; Felix Akpabio (Nigeria); Caleb A. Buchanan; Deacons Paul Dorsinville; Roy Dudley. Pastoral Assocs.: Sr. Margaret Mary Igoe, O.P.; Sr. Carmele Nerette, F.D.M. In res., Rev. Joseph M. Nolan.
Res., 115-58 222 St., Cambria Heights, 11411. Tel: 718-528-0577; Fax: 718-341-0253.
School—115-50 221st St., Cambria Heights, 11411. Tel: 718-527-0123; Fax: 718-527-1204.
Lay Teachers 24; Students 390.
Catechesis/Religious Programs—Elizabeth Wright, D.R.E.
Students 90.

239—SACRED HEART, Revs. John J. Fullum; James Stapleton, C.S.P. In res., Rev. Romano Zanon.
Res., 83-17 78th Ave., East Glendale, 11385. Tel: 718-821-6434; Fax: 718-497-2881.
School—84-05 78th Ave., East Glendale, 11385. Tel: 718-456-6636.
Sisters of St. Dominic 1; Lay Teachers 18; Students 322.
Catechesis/Religious Programs—Tel: 718-386-5616.
Students 375.

240—ST. SEBASTIAN, Rev. Msgr. D. Joseph Finnerty; Revs. John Francis; Frank C. Tumino; Sabino Estrada; Deacons Stephen Damato; Julio K. Park.
Res., 39-63 57th St., Woodside, 11377. Tel: 718-429-4442; Fax: 718-429-7581.
School—39-68 58th St., Woodside, 11377. Sr. Kathleen Michael, S.C.H., Prin.
Sisters of Charity (Halifax) 2; Lay Teachers 22; Students 442.
Catechesis/Religious Programs—39-66 58th St., Woodside, 11377. Tel: 718-899-3341. Mr. Jorge Diez, Admin.; Miss Virginia de la Rosa, Coord.
Students 657.

241—ST. STANISLAUS BISHOP AND MARTYR, Revs. James J. Meszaros; Dariusz Andrzej Kiewicz.
Res., 88-10 102nd Ave., Ozone Park, 11416. Tel: 718-845-6206; Fax: 718-843-6408.
School—90-01 101st Ave., Ozone Park, 11416. Tel: 718-845-3188; Fax: 718-835-9447. Sr. Francis Marie, C.S.F.N., Prin.
Lay Teachers 9; Students 225.
Catechesis/Religious Programs—Students 70.

242—ST. STANISLAUS KOSTKA, Revs. Michael J. Walsh, S.T.D.; Robert B. Adamo; Joseph Palackal, C.M.I (India).
Res., 57-15 61st St., Maspeth, 11378. Tel: 718-326-2185; Fax: 718-416-2108.
School—61-17 Grand Ave., Maspeth, 11378. Tel: 718-326-1815; Fax: 718-326-1745.
Lay Teachers 18; Students 300.
Catechesis/Religious Programs—Students 148.

243—ST. TERESA, Rev. Msgr. Denis M. Herron; Rev. Noel Moynihan, C.S.S.P. (Ireland); Deacon Martin Soraire.
Res., 50-20 45th St., Woodside, 11377. Tel: 718-784-2123; Fax: 718-706-6797.
School—50-15 44th St., Woodside, 11377. Tel: 718-784-0178; Fax: 718-784-3288. Martin C. Abruzzo, Prin.
Lay Teachers 11; Students 250.
Catechesis/Religious Programs—Tel: 718-937-4819.
Students 350.

244—ST. TERESA OF AVILA, Revs. Richard Hoare, Pastor; Carmel Borg; Deacons Ramon Smith; Louis Panico; John Dennehy.
Res., 109-26 130th St., South Ozone Park, 11420. Tel: 718-529-3587; Fax: 718-529-0324.
School—Tel: 718-641-1316; Fax: 718-843-0769. Ms. Loretta Rybacki, Prin.
Lay Teachers 12; Students 304.
Catechesis/Religious Programs—Tel: 718-641-5710. Elaine L'Etoile, D.R.E.
Students 225.

245—ST. THOMAS APOSTLE, Revs. William M. Hoppe; Felice J. De Laura; Eugene Stucklie.
Res., 87-19 88th Ave., Woodhaven, 11421. Tel: 718-847-1353; Fax: 718-849-3776.
School—87-49 87th St., Woodhaven, 11421. Tel: 718-847-3904.
Sisters 1; Lay Teachers 22; Students 408.
Catechesis/Religious Programs—Tel: 718-441-8409. Jean Tuohy, D.R.E.
Students 486.

246—ST. THOMAS MORE-ST. EDMUND, Rev. Msgr. Michael J. Connelly; Rev. Hugh A. Byrne; Deacons Bernard M. Deschier; Richard G. Lee.
Res., 204-25 Rockaway Point Blvd., Rockaway Point, 11697. Tel: 718-634-6357; Fax: 718-634-7900.

247—TRANSFIGURATION (Lithuanian), Revs. James T. Rooney, Pastor; Vytautas Volertas; Deacon William Oggeri.
Res., 64-14 Clinton Ave., Maspeth, 11378. Tel: 718-326-2236; Fax: 718-326-2249.

248—ST. VIRGILIUS, Rev. Charles H. White.
Res., 210 Noel Rd., Broad Channel, 11693-1091. Tel: 718-634-5680; Fax: 718-474-1538.
School—Tel: 718-634-6237; Fax: 718-634-2325. Diane M. Pizzo, Prin.
Lay Teachers 9; Students 150.
Catechesis/Religious Programs—Students 106.

Chaplains of Public Institutions

BROOKLYN. *Bernard Fineson Development Center*. Rev. Gordon Kugi.
Beth Israel Medical Center/Kings Hgwy. Bro. James Brennan, Metropolitan Detention Center, Rev. Anthony Rigonan.
Brookdale Hospital Medical Center. Michael Moran.
Brooklyn Development Center. Rev. Gordon Kugi.
The Brooklyn Hospital. (Vacant).
Brooklyn House of Detention. Rev. Frank Passenant; Sr. Dorothea Gillen, R.S.M.

Coney Island Hospital. Rev. Joseph P. Quigley.
Downstate Medical Center. Sr. Karen O'Neil, C.S.J.
Kings County Hospital Center. Rev. Lucien Charlot.
Kingsboro Psychiatric Center. Rev. Robert Frueh.
Long Island College Hospital. Has an interfaith Chaplain.
Lutheran Medical Center. Bro. John Cherry, F.M.S.
Maimonides Medical Center of Brooklyn. Sr. Mary Catherine Murphy, R.S.H.M.
Methodist Hospital. Sr. Therese Marie Camardella, C.S.J.
Veterans Administration Medical Center. Revs. Thomas Mullin; Luke Karpil; Vito Tiboni.
Victory Memorial Hospital. (Vacant).
Woodhull Medical & Mental Health Center. Rev. Justo Beltran Regado; Sr. Claudia Paredes.
Wyckoff Heights Hospital. Rev. Jevito Carungay.

QUEENS. *Creedmoor Psychiatric Center*. Revs. Paul Chenot, C.P.; August J. Iantosca.
Elmhurst General Hospital. Revs. Alan Briceland, S.J.; Jose Sanchez.
Flushing Hospital and Medical Center. Sr. Florence Dippold, C.S.J.
Jamaica Hospital - Trump Pavilion. Rev. Hyacinth Alia, C.M.I.
Long Island Jewish Hospital. Sr. Benedicta Dega, F.S.S.J.
N.Y. Hospital Medical Center of Queens. Sr. Rosarine Quinn, C.S.J.
Peninsula Hospital Center. Sr. Catharine Crowley, C.N.D.
Queens Hospital Center—Pastoral Care Office. Rev. Jose Cadusale (Philippines).
Queens House of Detention. Rev. John H. Wilkinson.
Queensboro Correctional Facility. Deacon Frank DeTucci.
Veterans Affairs Extended Care Center, St. Albans, NY. (Vacant).
Western Queens Community Hospital. (Vacant).

Special Assignment:
Reverend Monsignors—
Maresca, Ralph, Sec. Bishop
Reilly, Philip J., Chap., Monastery of the Precious Blood, 5400 Ft. Hamilton Pkwy., Brooklyn, NY 11219
Reverend Fathers—
Pomilio, Matthew

Military Chaplains:
Reverend Monsignors—
Gilhooley, John P., (Retired), 1260 Stevens Ave., Arbutus, MD 21227
Reverend Fathers—
Ceriello, Joseph A., NAB Chapel, Naval Amphibious Base, Little Creek, Norfolk, VA 23521
Dillon, James P., 1834 Tara Dr., Prattville, AL 36060
Leibold, James C., Office of the Base Chap., MCB, Camp 5.D. Butler, Butler, FPO AP 96373-5001
Leone, James M., 126 Laurelton Dr., P.O. Box 426, Mastic Beach, NY 11951
Mulkerin, Terrence J., Chaplain's Office, USCG Reserve Training Center, Yorktown, VA 23690-9761
Vella, Joseph C., 1297B Redwood Dr., Grand Forks AFB, ND 58204

Released from Diocesan Assignment:
Reverend Monsignors—
Ecker, Robert J., 300 Second St., Coronado, CA 92118
LaRocca, Vincent R., 108 Carroll St., Brooklyn, NY 11231
Maksymowicz, John H., Apostolic Nunciature, 3339 Massachusetts Ave., N.W., Washington, DC 20008
Sarno, Robert J., Congregation for the Causes of Saints, Vatican City State 00120
Strykowski, John J., National Conference of Catholic Bishops, 3211 Fourth St., Washington, DC 20017
White, Leo J., St. George's Cathedral House, Westminster Bridge Rd., London SE1 7HY, England
Reverend Fathers—
Bordeleau, Normand G.
Boyd, James A., Chap., Dept. Naval Air Sta., Barbers Point, HI 96862-5050
Catania, Thomas M., B.V.M. Help of Christians, 70-31 48th Ave., Woodside, NY 11377
Curran, Michael J., Casa Santa Maria, Villa Dell' Umilta, '30, 00187 Rome, Italy
D'Albro, Thomas G., 62A Widmer Rd., Wappingers Falls, NY 12590
Finley, James F., Kath. Amerikanische Gemeinde, Huttenweig, 46, 14195 Berlin, Germany
Folchetti, John T., Christian Brothers Academy, 850 Newman Springs Rd., Lincroft, NJ 07738
Heffernan, James F., Chap., Veterans Admin. Medical Center, Northport, NY 11768
Heffernan, Thomas A., Northwest Covenant Medical Center, Denville, NJ 07834
Himes, Michael J., Department of Theology, Boston College, Chestnut Hill, MA 02167-3806
Johnston, John F., Oratory Prep School, One Beverly Rd., Summit, NJ 07901
Lauder, Robert E., Cathedral Residence, 7200 Douglaston Pkwy., Douglaston, NY 11362
Mariano, John M., 1620 S. Ocean Blvd. (9N), Pompano Beach, FL 33062
McNicholas, Edward J., Bishop Mugavero Residence, 7200 Douglaston Pkwy., P.O. Box 630433, Little Neck, NY 11363-0433
McVernon, John J., 16-34 Clintonville St., Whitestone, NY 11357
Nadine, Jerome E., St. Elizabeth Ann Seton Church, 18-11 Pueblo Vista Dr., Las Vegas, NV 89128
Passenant, Francis J., St. Margaret Mary, 215 Exeter ST., Brooklyn, NY 11235
Paterno, Salvatore D., St. Mary, 42 Goshen Ave., Washingtonville, NY 10992
Penta, Leo J., Am Hegewinkel 5B, D-14169 Berlin, Germany
Ruiz, Jean-Pierre, S.T.D., St. Patrick Rectory, 39-38 29th St., Long Island City, NY 11101
Schuck, Joseph J., 1011 State Hwy. 7, Unadilla, NY 13847-9771
Sears, William J., 1745 Padre Ln., Englewood, FL 34223
Smith, LeRoy J., P.O. Box 23, Old Chatham, NY 12136
Steinhauser, Kenneth B., Belmont Abbey College, Belmont, NC 28012
Tivenan, John J., Mercy Medical Center, 1512 12th Ave. Rd., Nampa, ID 83686
Trombetta, Paul N., 219 Old Oak Bucket Rd., Scituate, MA 02066
Upson, Michael G., Immaculate Conception Church, 445 Frederick Douglas St., Rochester, NY 14608
Vaccari, Peter I., Immaculate Conception Seminary, W. Neck Rd.-Lloyd Harbor, Huntington, NY 11743
Vendetti, Michael A., 94-26 Sutter Ave., Ozone Park, NY 11417
Wulinski, Stanley F., 1701 N.E. 42nd St., Beacon Heights, FL 33064

Graduate Studies:
Reverend Fathers—
Caccavale, Charles, Casa Santa Maria, 00187 Rome, Italy
Hernandez, Anthony

Absent on Sick Leave:
Reverend Monsignors—
Demski, Arthur A.
Reverend Fathers—
Denzer, Joseph W.
Early, William F.
Esposito, Joseph J.
Failla, Anthony
Flynn, Francis J.
Grant, Matthew M.
Newell, John J.
O'Brien, David G.
Prochaski, Adam F.

Absent on Leave:
Reverend Monsignors—
Manzo, Francis J.
Reverend Fathers—
Barbetta, Philip
Beliveau, Richard
Boyle, Victor J.
Brown, Charles L.
Ferraro, Romano J.
Ferro, Robert A.
Higuero, Francisco J.
Kozma, Raymond M.
Lazar, John E.
Liona, Kenneth J.
Mason, Edward J.
Miller, Joseph A.
Morris, James J.
Morrow, Thomas O.
Peyton, Thomas
Piro, Gerald J.
Prochaski, Adam F.
Ryan, Barry
Sabatos, Daniel C.
Sexton, Patrick D.
Visich, Eduard C.
Walsh, John F.

Retired:
Reverend Monsignors—
Adessa, Dominick J., 555 Albany Ave., Amityville, NY 11701
Arella, Gerard J., St. Mark, 2609 E. 19th St., Brooklyn, NY 11235
Asip, James W., 16-34 Clintonville St., Whitestone, NY 11357
Barretta, Anthony J., 61-27 71st St., Middle Village, NY 11379
Bednartz, August C., 130 Arcadia Walk, Rockaway Pt., NY 11697
Bennett, Austin P., 75 Greene Ave., P.O. Box C, Brooklyn, NY 11202
Bleilevens, Charles A., 86-13 55th Ave., Elmhurst, NY 11373-4394
Brugli, Angelo F., Msgr. Fitzpatrick Pavilion, 152-11 89th Ave., Jamaica, NY 11421
Burke, William F., Bishop Mugavero Residence, 7200 Douglaston Pkwy., P.O. Box 433, Little Neck, NY 11363-0433
Burns, John A., 1395 E. 56th St., Brooklyn, NY 11234
Campbell, Thomas P., 21-17 45th St., Long Island City, NY 11105
Cavanagh, James M., 7320 4th Ave., Brooklyn, NY 11209
Clancy, Thomas C., 1525 E. 12th St., Brooklyn, NY 11230
Collini, Celsus O., 141-36 77th Ave., Kew Gardens Hills, NY 11367
Cribbin, Thomas F., 64 Middagh St., Brooklyn, NY 11201
D'Anca, Achille, 274 Beachway Dr., Palm Coast, FL 32137
Deas, George T., Bishop Mugavero Residence, 7200 Douglaston Pkwy., P.O. Box 630433, Little Neck, NY 11363-0433
Demski, Arthur A., P.O. Box 55129, Trenton, NJ 08638
Diviney, Charles E., Queen of Peace Residence, 110-30 221 St., Queens Village, NY 11429
Donegan, James F., Redemptoris Mater, 672 Passaic Ave., Kearney, NY 07032
Ecker, Robert J., 300 Second St., Coronado, CA 92118
Fagan, John T., Little Flower Children's Services, N. Wading River Rd., Wading River, NY 11792
Feldhaus, Eugene A., 188-16 91st Ave., Hollis, NY 11423
Fitzpatrick, Franklin E., 91-18 86th Ave., Woodhaven, NY 11421
Flanagan, Thomas J., P.O. Box 804, Beatrice Ct., Hampton Bays, NY 11946
Florido, Raphael A., Ozanam Hall, 42-41 201st. St., Bayside, NY 11361
Fogarty, George V., Bishop Mugavero Residence, 7200 Douglaston Pkwy., Little Neck, NY 11362
Gotimer, James, 43-22 Ithaca St., Elmhurst, NY 11373
Gradilone, Thomas, Bishop Mugavero Residence, 7200 Douglaston Pkwy., Douglaston, NY 11362
Haggarty, James J., St. Pius, 1100 Woodside Rd., Redwood City, CA 94061
Haggerty, James J., Ozanam Hall, 42-41 201st St., Bayside, NY 11361
HartmanN, John F., P.O. Box 1222, Madison, CT 06443
Hendel, Thomas W., 104 Cassata Ct., Kings Park, NY 11754
Jolley, Edward W., Bishop Mugavero Residence, 7200 Douglaston Pkwy., P.O. Box 433, Little Neck, NY 11363-0433
King, James P., Bishop Mugavero Residence, 7200 Douglaston Pkwy., Little Neck, NY 11362
Konrad, Joseph G., 5815 Catalpa Ave., Ridgewood, NY 11385
LaRocca, Vincent, Sacred Hearts of Jesus and Mary and St. Stephen, 108 Carroll St., Brooklyn, NY 11231
Martin, Kieran J., 1550 Hendrickson St., Brooklyn, NY 11234
Martusciello, Joseph A., 7200 Douglaston Pkwy., Douglaston, NY 11362
McAlister, Lawrence J., 1820 Briarwood Terr., S. Belmar, NJ 07719-2906
McKenna, James J., St. Mary Star of the Sea, 1920 New Haven Ave., Far Rockaway, NY 11691
McMahon, James B., 7200 Douglaston Pkwy., Douglaston, NY 11362
Mooney, George A., 194 Withers St., Brooklyn, NY 11211
Mulhall, Francis X., Bishop Mugavero Residence, 7200 Douglaston Pkwy., Little Neck, NY 11362
Nolan, Edward J., 89-43 Francis Lewis Blvd., Queens Village, NY 11427
Noonan, Thomas F., St. Edmund, 2460 Ocean Ave., Brooklyn, NY 11229
Parks, Joseph K., St. Patrick, 9511 Fourth Ave., Brooklyn, NY 11209
Passarella, Anthony F., Filomel - Meadowbrook Ln., Stratsburg, NY 12580
Piombini, Mario G., Ozanam Hall, 42-41 201st St., Bayside, NY 11361
Rau, Raymond F., 1302 Lantana St., Corpus Christi, TX 78407
Rodgers, William J., Queen of Peace Residence, 110-30 221st St., Queens Village, NY 11429

Ryan, James W., 2609 Linden Blvd., Brooklyn, NY 11208
Sapporito, Cosmo G., St. Bernadette, 8201 13th Ave., Brooklyn, NY 11228
Shevlin, Raymond R., 23 Gerritsen Ave., Brooklyn, NY 11229
Voiland, George T., 32-23 36th St., Long Island City, NY 11106
Waldron, John E., 7200 Douglaston Pkwy., Douglaston, NY 11362
Welsh, Robert E., 199 River Rd., Nissequoque, NY 11780
Wilson, John F., 245 Prospect Park W., Brooklyn, NY 11215

Reverend Fathers—
Abrams, John L., Bishop Mugavero Residence, 7200 Douglaston Pkwy., Little Neck, NY 11362
Angles, Sebastian, 2601 Muscatello St., Orlando, FL 32821
Baltrucki, Leon S., 19 Wright St., Gardner, MA 01440
Bartruff, Louis B., Bishop Mugavero Residence, 7200 Douglaston Pkwy., Little Neck, NY 11362
Blaeser, Alfred A., 1088 Lloyd St., Franklin Square, NY 11010
Borzaga, Rinaldo, Manhattan College, Riverdale, NY 10471
Brown, Vincent A., Msgr. Fitzpatrick Pavilion, 152-11 89th Ave., Jamaica, NY 11432
Buckley, Joseph F., 7200 Douglaston Pkwy., Douglaston, NY 11362
Buetow, Harold A., Bishop Mugavero Residence, 7200 Douglaston Pkwy., Little Neck, NY 11362
Byrnes, Francis J., 7200 Douglaston Pkwy., Douglaston, NY 11362
Byrnes, John W., 218-26 105th Ave., Queens Village, NY 11429
Calderwood, Vincent T., McCarrick Care Center, 15 Dellwood Ln., Somerset, NJ 08893
Coyle, Eugene P., 7200 Douglaston Pkwy., Douglaston, NY 11362
Cronin, John F., Bishop Mugavero Residence, 7200 Douglaston Pkwy., Little Neck, NY 11362
Culkin, Harry M., Bishop Mugavero Residence, 7200 Douglaston Pkwy., P.O. Box 630433, Little Neck, NY 11363-0433
Cushing, Charles B., Noreen McKeen Residence, 315 S. Flagler Dr., W. Palm Beach, FL 33401
D'Amato, James J., 1331 East 35th St., Brooklyn, NY 11210
Daly, Joseph F., Ozanam Hall Residence, 42-41 201st St., Bayside, NY 11361
Dolan, Thomas D., 94-20 85th St., Ozone Park, NY 11416
Donnelly, Eugene F., 25-02 80th St., Jackson Heights, NY 11370
Dore, Denis M., Bishop Mugavero Geriatric, 155 Dean St., Brooklyn, NY 11231
Duran, Ernesto, Santa Beatriz 269, Apt. 503, Santiago 9, Chile S.A.
Ebejer, George, 216 27th St., Brooklyn, NY 11232
Esposito, Joseph J., P.O. Box 370772, Las Vegas, NV 89137
Flynn, Francis J., Sts. Joachim & Anne Residence, 2720 Surf Ave., Brooklyn, NY 11224
Forsyth, George W., Holy Family Home, 1740 84th St., Brooklyn, NY 11214
Franco, Salvator, 83 First St., New Hyde Park, NY 11040
Galuszka, Walter, 350 Cuba Hill Rd., Huntington, NY 11743
Giuliano, Louis A., 52-10 NW 53rd. Ave., Cocoanut Creek, FL 33073
Grant, Matthew, 204-13 Marshall Ave., Rockaway Point, NY 11697
Guarracino, Ralph J., 600 Henry St., Brooklyn, NY 11231
Gural, Marion A., 123 Henry Rd., Southampton, NY 11968
Harth, Charles F., Queen of Peace Residence, 110-30 221 St., Queens Village, NY 11429
Heffernan, James F., 146 Swan Lake, Poughkeepsie, NY 12605
Hickey, William T., 63-63 98th St., Rego Park, NY 11374
Hogan, Edward P., St. Thomas More, 204-25 Rockaway Pt. Blvd., Rockaway Point, NY 11697
Hughes, John F., Queen of Peace Residence, 110-30 221st St., Queens Village, NY 11429
Hume, Robert B., Holy Family Home, 1740 84th St., Brooklyn, NY 11214
Jurgensen, John W., 94-40 118th St., Richmond Hill, NY 11419
Keane, Edward M., 175-20 74th Ave., Flushing, NY 11366
Keane, Joseph P., 204 E. Palm Dr., Rte. 10, Fort Myers, FL 33908
Kelly, Thomas F., 7320 Fourth Ave., Brooklyn, NY 11209
Kenny, Albert N., 273 78th St., Brooklyn, NY 11209
Kiernan, John L., 88-25 153rd St., Jamaica, NY 11432
Kirrane, James A., Holy Family, 5 Fordham Ave., Hicksville, NY 11801
Labita, Francis J., 100-05 159th St., Howard Beach, NY 11414
Lang, Henry A., 56-15 213th St., Bayside Hills, NY 11364
Luis, Anthony F., 7200 Douglaston Pkwy., Douglaston, NY 11362
Lyons, Thomas J., 1550 Hendrickson St., Brooklyn, NY 11234
Maceli, Anthony J., 6908 Stonesthrow Cir. N., St. Petersburg, FL 33710
Malleck, Joseph L., 24 Steven St., Plainview, NY 11803
Mankowski, Edmund A., R.R. 2, Box 319 Locust Dr. & Noyack Rd., Sag Harbor, NY 11963
Mannion, Thomas F., St. Charles Church, 49323 Gauntlett St., Gold Beach, OR 97444
McCarren, William J., 8000 Roma N.E., Albuquerque, NM 87108
McElroy, Herbert, Holy Family Home, 1740 84th St., Brooklyn, NY 11214
McGee, Francis J., 130 Beach 84th St., Rockaway Beach, NY 11693
McGovern, Eugene F., St. Aloysius, 383 Onderdonk Ave., Ridgewood, NY 11385
McGuirk, Raymond A., Holy Family Home, 1740 84th St., Brooklyn, NY 11214
McNeill, John A., Our Lady of Lourdes, 92-96 220th St., Queens Village, NY 11428
McNicholas, Edward J., 7200 Douglaston Pkwy., Douglaston, NY 11362
Milde, Robert F., Bishop Mugavero Residence, 7200 Douglaston Pkwy., Little Neck, NY 11362
Moore, Robert A., 929 Bay Ridge Pkwy., Brooklyn, NY 11228
Morgan, Raymond J., Bishop Mugavero Residence, 7200 Douglaston Pkwy., Little Neck, NY 11362
Mueller, Anthony E., Queen of Peace Residence, 110-30 221 St., Queens Village, NY 11429
Mullen, Joseph A., c/o Sr. Grace Bletsch, O.P., 1000 Hempstead Ave., Rockville Centre, NY 11571-5002
Nichols, Charles P., Sacred Hearts of Jesus & Mary - St. Steven, 108 Carroll St., Brooklyn, NY 11231
Nolan, Joseph M., 115-58 222nd St., Cambria Heights, NY 11411
O'Brien, Thomas, 150-75 Goethals Ave., Jamaica, NY 11432
O'Connor, Edward T., 6255 S.E. Charleston Pl., Hobe Sound, FL 33455
O'Sullivan, Martin, 8 Green Hills Rd., East Brunswick, NJ 08816-3876
Palubinskas, Vytautas A., Vilnius Seminary, Kalvariju 225B, LT2021, Vilnius, Lithuania
Parisi, Michael R., St. Kevin, 45-21 194th St., Flushing, NY 11358
Pikturna, Vytautas, Matulaitis Nursing Home, 10 Thurber Rd., Putnam, CT 06267
Powers, Anthony F., 124 Beaver Dr., Mastic Beach, NY 11951
Pupin, Vito A., Mugavero Geriatric Center, 155 Dean St., Brooklyn, NY 11217
Raila, Stanislaus, Bishop Mugavero Residence, 7200 Douglaston Pkwy., Little Neck, NY 11362
Rau, Raymond F., 1302 Lantana St., Corpus Christi, TX 78407
Reilly, John C., 141-36 77 Ave., Kew Gardens Hills, NY 11367
Rizzi, Salvatore, 126 Pond Rd., Woodbury, NY 11797
Sans, Pablo, 136-06 87th St., Richmond Hill, NY 11418
Schmidt, Jerome J., Resurrection, 2331 Gerritsen Ave., Brooklyn, NY 11229
Schuck, Joseph J., 1011 State Hwy. 7, Unadilla, NY 13849
Schwind, Donald F., 182 Monitor St., Brooklyn, NY 11222
Setzer, Frank A., S.M.M., Nonfort Missionaries, 26 South Saxon Ave., Bayshore, NY 11706
Sheridan, Matthew W., 2805 Ft. Hamilton Pkwy., Brooklyn, NY 11218
Sullivan, James E., 14-51 143rd St., Whitestone, NY 11357
Suran, Joachim, 98-16 55th Ave., Corona, NY 11368-3015
Termine, Vincent J., 3736 Bayview Ave., Brooklyn, NY 11224
Travis, Herbert A., St. Anselm, 356 82nd St., Brooklyn, NY 11209
Tully, James J., 24 Brookway Dr., Greensboro, NC 27410
Vivona, Anthony, 922 E. 96th St., Brooklyn, NY 11236-2304
Vogel, Charles P., 416 Grant Ave., Brooklyn, NY 11208
Wang, Barnabas, Bishop Mugavero Residence, 7200 Douglaston Pkwy., Douglaston, NY 11362
Weinlich, Alfred J., Queen of Peace Residence, 110-30 221st St., Queens Village, NY 11429
White, Leo J., St. George Cathedral House, Westminster Bridge Rd., London, SE 1 7HY England
Wiseman, Joseph F., 46-02 Parsons Blvd., Flushing, NY 11355
Young, Robert J., Bishop Mugavero Residence, 7200 Douglaston Pkwy, Little Neck, NY 11362
Zaccagnigno, Raffaele, Rome

Permanent Deacons:
Agnant, Ronald Y., St. Therese of Lisieux, Brooklyn
Aigbojie, Edward A., St. Fortunata, Brooklyn
Almodovar, Ismael, Diocese of Orlando
Alvarez, Felipe J., St. Joseph, Long Island City
Alvia, Humberto R., Blessed Sacrament, Brooklyn
Arcand, Dennis A., Diocese of Savannah
Aris, Anthony J., Inactive
Arthur, Anthony H., St. Jerome, Brooklyn
Baez, Angel, Epiphany, Brooklyn
Beaubrun, Berthal, St. Ignatius, Brooklyn
Bichotte, Joseph, St. Augustine, Brooklyn
Bobadilla, Antonio, St. Mary Star of the Sea, Far Rockaway
Boursiquot, Jean B., St. Ignatius, Brooklyn
Burrell, James, St. Catherine of Siena, St. Alban
Caceres, Ycelso, Inactive
Cafiero, Joseph D., St. Rosalia, Brooklyn
Cajiao, Henry, Diocese of St. Petersburg
Calvo, Juan, Queen of Angels, Long Island City
Campisi, Joseph, Our Lady Grace, Howard Beach
Cancel, Edwin, Our Lady of the Angelus, Rego Park
Carattini, Juan M., Our Lady of Perpetual Help, South Ozone Park
Cardona, Ramon, Diocese of Mayaguez, PR
Casares, Gabriel, Diocese of St. Petersburg
Cederroth, Charles J., Diocese of Trenton
Chin, Paul M., St. Paul Chong Ha-Sang Chapel, Flushing
Coffey, John P., Christ the King, Springfield Gardens
Colandrea, Dante, St. Dominic, Brooklyn
Coleman, Harry J., St. Bonaventure, Jamaica
Colon, Rafael, St. Augustine, Brooklyn
Coyle, Lawrence J., St. Columba, Brooklyn
Cruz, Florencio, St. Matthew, Brooklyn
Cruz, Rafael, Archdiocese of Miami
Cutter, Arthur, St. Gregory the Great, Bellerose
D'Accordo, Armand C., St. Helen, Howard Beach
D'Accordo, Frank J., Saint Bernard, Brooklyn
Da Costa, Dennis A., St. Matthew, Brooklyn
Damato, Stephen T., St. Sebastian, Woodside
Daniel, Gordon V., St. Terese of Lisieux, Brooklyn
Davis, Thomas G., St. Anselm, Brooklyn
De Cola, Joseph P., Diocese of Palm Beach
De Tucci, Frank A., Catholic Charities Office for Prison Ministry
De Tucci, Frank A., Chap., Queensboro Correctional Facility
DeLeon, Andres, St. Gregory the Great, Brooklyn
Deming, Everett A., Our Lady of Mt. Carmel, Brooklyn
Dennehy, John P., St. Teresa of Avila, South Ozone Park
Deschler, Bernard M., St. Thomas More/St. Edmund
Desdunes, Herve, St. Matthew, Brooklyn
Devaney, Thomas J., Immaculate Heart of Mary, Brooklyn
Dixon, Gregory D., St. Andrew the Apostle, Brooklyn
Dorsinville, Paul C., Sacred Heart, Cambria Heights
Dudley, Roy A., Sacred Heart, Cambria Heights
Duncan, Isaac, Our Lady of Good Counsel, Brooklyn
Dupuy, Eulogio S., St. Gabriel, East Elmhurst
Earley, George G., Diocese of Rockville Centre
Ehresmann, Philip J., St. Brigid, Brooklyn
Felix, Antoine, Holy Innocents, Brooklyn
Flaim, Fabio, St. Aloysius, Ridgewood
Flannery, John A., St. Charles Borromeo, Brooklyn
Franca, John J., St. Francis Xavier, Brooklyn
Francis, John J., Unassigned
Galazin, Stanley J., American Martyrs, Bayside
Garamella, Robert, Diocese of Rockville Centre
George, Roy N., St. Gregory the Great, Brooklyn
Giglio, John P., Our Lady of Good Counsel, Brooklyn
Gilligan, Richard J., St. Mary Gate of Heaven, Ozone Park
Gomez, Guillermo D., St. Gerard Majella, Hollis
Gonzalez, Jorge A., St. Michael, Brooklyn
Gonzalez, Louis A., Holy Spirit, Brooklyn
Gonzalez, Rafael, Diocese of Orlando
Heaphy, Thomas F., St. Mary Gate of Heaven, Ozone Park
Heinrich, Joseph, Office of Disabled Persons, Catholic Charities
Hernandez, Rafael, Diocese of Orlando
Hernandez, Wilfredo, Holy Spirit, Brooklyn
Hili, Saviour, St. Francis of Assisi, Long Island City

Horne, Wilfred N., St. Ephrem, Brooklyn
Huckemeyer, Edward J., On Personal Leave
Innocent, Francois, Incarnation, Brooklyn
Joesten, F. Edward, St. Anthony of Padua, South Ozone Park
Kennedy, James F., Diocese of St. Petersburg, FL
Knight, Lionel A., St. Nicholas of Tolentine, Jamaica
Krebs, Jerome H., Our Lady Miraculous Medal, Brooklyn
Landron, Jaime, Our Lady of the Presentation, Brooklyn
Lavanco, Robert F., Our Lady of Hope, Middle Village
Lee, Richard G., St. Thomas More-St. Edmund, Rockaway Point
Licata, Salvatore V., Exec. Sec. Permanent Diaconate Office
Lima, Ramon, St. Raphael, Long Island City
Lonergan, Robert P., St. Andrew Avellino, Flushing
Lopez, Eduvigis, Our Lady of Perpetual Help, Brooklyn
Lopez, Hiram, Archdiocese of New York
Maldonado, Andres, Diocese of Ponce, PR
Malone, William F., St. Ephrem, Brooklyn
Marcel, Magloire, St. Jerome, Brooklyn
Marchello, Andrew A., Nativity of the Blessed Virgin Mary, Queens
Marley, Daniel J., Our Lady of Solace, Brooklyn
Marte, Rafael, St. John Cantius, Brooklyn
Martinez, German, Transfiguration, Brooklyn
Mayers, Winston M., Christ the King, Springfield Gardens
Mazza, Nicholas, St. Cecilia, Brooklyn
McCarthy, Thomas R., (Retired)
McGee, Robert J., Our Lady of Hope, Middle Village
McGreevey, John F., St. John Vianney, Brooklyn
McGuire, Joseph P., St. Brendan, Brooklyn
Mejia, Abdon, Our Lady of Perpetual Help, South Ozone Park
Mellace, Carlo V., St. Dominic, Brooklyn
Miller, Leon F., St. Michael, East New York
Montalvo, Hector, Holy Family, Brooklyn
Morales, Julio A., Diocese of Orlando
Mule, Lawrence C., St. Matthias, Ridgewood
Mulroy, Martin B., Diocese of Metuchen, NJ
Murphy, John J., Mary Queen of Heaven, Brooklyn
Occhiuto, Joseph J., Inactive
Oellinger, Matthew J., Our Lady of the Snows, North Floral Park
Oggeri, William, Transfiguration, Maspeth
Olivas, Pascual B., St. Bonaventure, Jamaica
Orlandello, John P., St. Francis of Paola, Brooklyn
Panessa, Giacomo, Most Precious Blood, Astoria
Panico, Louis J., St. Teresa of Avila, South Ozone Park
Parisi, Vincent, St. Rita, Long Island City
Park, Julio, St. Sebastian, Woodside
Pascal, Orlando, Our Lady of Sorrows, Corona
Paul, Ernst, St. Rita, Brooklyn
Postler, Charles A., St. Patrick, Brooklyn
Pouso, Roberto J., Blessed Sacrament, Jackson Heights
Proce, Horatio A., Inactive
Ramirez, Manuel, Diocese of Scranton
Ramos, James, St. Francis Xavier, Brooklyn
Ramos, Jose A., St. Lucy-St. Patrick, Brooklyn
Ramos, Pedro, Diocese of Caguas, PR
Reichert, John P., St. Fidelis, College Point
Rivera, Angel R., St. Benedict Joseph Labre, Richmond Hill
Rivera, Hector R., Archdiocese of San Juan, PR
Rizzo, Giovanni A., St. Finbar, Brooklyn
Roberts, Lionel V., Diocese of Rockville Centre
Roman, Luis A., St. Gerard Majella, Hollis
Ronacher, Ronald M., St. Rita, Brooklyn
Rosati, Frank J., Chap., Holy Family Home for Aged
Ruiz, Jose D., Diocese of Ponce, PR
Russo, Anthony J., (Retired)
Ryan, Kevin F., Blessed Virgin Mary Help of Christians, Queens
Sands, John E., St. Matthias, Ridgewood
Sawney, Ira, Florida
Sclafani, Leonard A., St. Paul Center, Long Island City
Sencion, Eduardo, Our Lady of the Cenacle, Richmond Hill
Siani, Philip J., Our Lady of Grace, Brooklyn
Simon, Mauclair, St. Therese of Lisieux, Brooklyn
Sinisi, Henry C., On Leave
Smith, Charles J., St. Margaret Mary, Brooklyn
Smith, Henry J., Our Lady of the Snows, North Floral Park
Smith, Nathaniel J., St. Clement Pope, South Ozone Park
Smith, Ramon, St. Teresa of Avila, South Ozone Park
Smolinski, Edward A., Our Lady of Mercy, Forest Hills
Soraire, Martin D., St. Teresa, Woodside
Soto, Jesus, Our Lady of Perpetual Help, Brooklyn
Sucich, John R., St. Francis of Assisi, Long Island City
Svebel, Harry A., St. Luke, Whitestone
Taylor, Luis C., St. Catherine of Sienna, St. Alban
Tierney, John A., Diocese of Albany
Tokarcsik, George M., St. Agatha, Brooklyn
Torres, Abel, Holy Name, Brooklyn
Trochez, Carlos A., Corpus Christi, Woodside
Troy, Michael J., Our Lady of Angels, Brooklyn
Tully, Dean T., Holy Child Jesus, Richmond Hill
Uzoigwe, Okafor C., Presentation of the Blessed Virgin Mary, Jamaica
Valderrana, Carlos, St. Cecilia, Brooklyn
Valle Valle, Esteban, Archdiocese of San Juan, PR
Van Wassenhove, Raymond J., Diocese of Peoria
Vargas, Juan R., St. Agatha, Brooklyn
Vermilyea, Richard, Inactive
Vicinanza, Michael W., Queen of Peace, Kew Garden Hills
Wander, William H., St. Andrew the Apostle, Brooklyn
Whelan, Alfred L., St. Gertrude, Far Rockaway
Williams, Lee C., St. Mary Magdalene, Springfield Gardens
Williamsen, William, St. Saviour, Brooklyn
Winkler, Warren A., Our Lady of Lourdes, Queens Village
Yepes, Elias H., St. Michael, Flushing

INSTITUTIONS LOCATED IN THE DIOCESE

[A] PASTORAL CENTERS

DOUGLASTON. *Immaculate Conception Center*, 7200 Douglaston Pkwy., 11362-1997. Tel: 718-229-8001; Fax: 718-229-2658.
E-mail: director@iccdouglaston.org
Rev. Michael J. Hardiman, Dir.; Mr. Thomas D. Flynn, Asst. Dir., Controller & Site Financial Officer; Mr. Gerard King, Asst. Dir. Bldg. Svcs. & Maintenance; Mr. James Austin, Asst. Dir. Dining Svcs., Diocesan Food Svcs. In res. Rev. Msgr. John E. Waldron; Revs. James Bradley; Cornelius H. Mahoney.
Offices Located at the Center include Cathedral Seminary Residence; Bishop Mugavero Residence; The Tribunal; Institutional Svcs., Inc.; Pastoral Institute; Regl. Bishop of Queens-N.; Hispanic Ministry; Family Life Ministry, Institute of Languages and Cultures, Francis X. McDermott Religious Studies Library; Evangelization Commission; Cluster Planning & Collaboration; Vicar for Senior Priests; Respect Life.

[B] SEMINARIES, DIOCESAN

DOUGLASTON. *Cathedral Seminary Residence of the Immaculate Conception*, 7200 Douglaston Pkwy., 11362. Tel: 718-229-8001. Residence for college level and post college level candidates for Priesthood. Rev. Msgr. Octavio Cisneros, M.Div., Rector; Revs. Conrad R. Dietz, Ph.D., Academic Dean, Philosophy Prof.; Thomas G. Caserta, M.A., M.Div., D.Min., Spiritual Dir.; Dennis D. Klein, Ph.D., Philosophy Prof. In res. Revs. Martin F. Kirby, M.A.; Robert E. Lauder, Ph.D.; Cornelius H. Mahoney, M.Div. Priests 4; Lay Teachers 3; Seminarians 15.

ELMHURST. *Cathedral Preparatory Seminary of the Immaculate Conception*, 56-25 92nd St., 11373. Tel: 718-592-6800; Fax: 718-592-5574.
E-mail: revjpc@aol.com
Revs. Joseph P. Calise, Rector & Prin.; Fred Marano, Spiritual Dir.; Thomas Ahearn. In res. Rev. Sofronio LoFranco. Priests 3; Brothers 1; Sisters 2; Lay Teachers 13; Seminarians 183.

[C] SEMINARIES, RELIGIOUS

WHITESTONE. *St. Alphonsus Formation Residence*, 22-04 Parsons Blvd., 11357-3440. Tel: 718-321-1096; Fax: 718-321-1246.
E-mail: psousacssr@aol.com
Web site: www.baltcssr.com
Very Rev. Peter E. Sousa, C.SS.R., Rector & Dir. of Formation; Revs. Paul J. Borowski, C.SS.R., Asst. Dir.; Philip Dabney, C.SS.R., Vocation Dir.; Robert Cheesman, C.SS.R. Priests 4; Students 7.

[D] COLLEGES AND UNIVERSITIES

BROOKLYN. *St. Francis College*, 180 Remsen St., 11201. Tel: 718-489-5200
For a complete listing, refer to the Colleges and Universities section.

St. Joseph's College, 245 Clinton Ave., 11205. Tel: 718-636-6800; Fax: 718-636-7245.
E-mail: fburns@sjcny.edu
For a complete listing, refer to the Colleges and Universities section.

JAMAICA. *St. John's University*, 8000 Utopia Pkwy., 11439. Tel: 718-990-6161; Fax: 718-990-5723.
Web site: www.stjohns.edu
For a complete listing, refer to the Colleges and Universities section.

STATEN ISLAND. *St. John's University, Staten Island Campus*, 300 Howard Ave., 10301. Tel: 718-390-4545; Fax: 718-816-4520.
Web site: www.stjohns.edu
For a complete listing, refer to the Colleges and Universities section.

[E] CATHOLIC EDUCATION OFFICES

BROOKLYN. *Office of Religious Education: Evangelization and Catholic Formation*, 310 Prospect Part West, 11215-7323.
E-mail: Dirre6025@aol.com
Web site: http:www.bkevanreled.org
Mailing Address: P.O. Box 159013, 11215. Sr. Dolores Ryan, CS.J., Dir. of D.R.E. Personnel; Rev. Michael A. Carrano, Dir. Youth Ministry & Adolescent Catechesis & Dir. College Campus Ministry; Sr. Alice Michael, S.U.S.C., Dir. Rel. Educ. for Cultural and Ethnic Groups & Coord. RCIA, Reg. Dir. Brooklyn East; Deacon John Coffey, Regional Dir., Brooklyn West.; Rev. Joseph R. Gibino, Ph.D., Dir. of Adult Rel. Educ., Regional Dir., Queens North; Deacon Michael W. Vicinanza, Regional Dir., Queens, South. Diocesan Evangelization Commission. Tel: 718-965-7300. Most Rev. Ignatius A. Catanello, Episcopal Liason; Rev. Msgr. Guy J. Puglisi, Ph.D; Rev. Dennis McAuliffe, Exec. Sec.

Campus Ministers and Ministry Centers. Revs. Guy A. Massie, Brooklyn College; Paul Wood, Queens College; Bros. John Reidy, C.F.C., Kingsboro Community College; Thomas Grady, O.S.F., St. Francis College; Sr. Margaret Smith, C.I.J., Long Island University; Sr. Alice Danaher, O.P., Queensboro Community College.
Legal Titles & Corporations: Newman Apostolate, Inc.

Office of the Superintendent of Schools, 310 Prospect Park W., 11215-7323. Tel: 718-965-7300; Fax: 718-965-7323.
E-mail: dobsuptsch@impresso.com
Rev. Msgr. Guy J. Puglisi, Supt. of Schools; Dr. Patricia Kelly-Stiles, Assoc. Supt. Personnel; Mrs. Mary Santos, Assoc. Supt. Prog. Mgmt.; Sr. Jane Ellis, I.H.M., Asst. Supt. Prin. Personnel; Sr. Sheila Conley, S.C., Assoc. Supt. Curriculum; Ms. Joan Sokoll, Assoc. Supt. Religion; Sr. Margaret Schmit, O.P., Asst. Dir. Personnel & Office Mgr.; Miss June Stuart, Admin. Asst. Personnel; Mr. William E. Slow, Assoc. Supt., Special Ed.; Mrs. Dorothy LaMere, Dist. Supt. - Queens North Schools; Mr. Thomas Chadzutko, Dist. Supt. - Brooklyn W. Schools; Sr. Miriam Blake, C.S.J., Dist. Supt. - Brooklyn East Schools; Mr. Anthony Danile, Dist. Supt. - Queens South Schools; Bro. William Clifford, C.S.C., Dir. of Ed. Technology; Eileen King Dwyer, Exec. Dir. Prog. for the Devel. of Human Potential.

Diocese of Brooklyn Education Offices. Legal Titles & Corporations: Department of Education, Diocese of Brooklyn; Henry M. Hald High School Association; Saint John's Preparatory School, Brooklyn.

[F] HIGH SCHOOLS, DIOCESAN

BROOKLYN. *Bishop Loughlin Memorial High School*, 357 Clermont Ave., 11238. Tel: 718-857-2700; Fax: 718-398-4227.
E-mail: rwickman@blmhs.org
Web site: www.bishoploughlin.org
(Coed).
Legal Corp.: Henry M. Hald Assoc. Bro. Robert J. Wickman, F.S.C., Prin.; Rev. Patrick J. West, Chap. Brothers of the Christian Schools 7; Priests 1; Sisters 2; Lay Teachers 52; Students 860.

[G] HIGH SCHOOLS, PRIVATE

BROOKLYN. *Bishop Ford Central Catholic High School*, 500 19th St., 11215. Tel: 718-965-6400; Fax: 718-965-6405.
(Coed). Mr. James G. Mullaney, Pres.; Mr. Frank V. Brancato, Prin.; Mr. Rocco V. Grella, Asst. Prin. Sisters 3; Lay Teachers 45; Students 850.

Bishop Kearney High School, 2202 60th St., 11204-2599. Tel: 718-236-6363; Fax: 718-236-7784.
E-mail: jmcavoy@bishopkearneyhs.org
Web site: www.bishopkearneyhs.org
(Girls). Sr. Joan McAvoy, C.S.J., Prin.; Rev. James P. Collins, M.Div., Chap. Priests 2; Sisters of St. Joseph (Brentwood Community) 28; Sisters 2; Lay Teachers 57; Students 1,120.

Catherine McAuley, 710 E. 37th St., 11203. Tel: 718-462-7282; Fax: 718-462-7284.
(Girls). Sr. Peggy Lake, R.S.M., Prin.; Rev. John W. Maloney, Spiritual Dir. Sisters of Mercy 7; Lay Teachers 21; Students 300.

Fontbonne Hall, 9901 Shore Rd., 11209. Tel: 718-748-2244; Fax: 718-745-3841.
E-mail: clancy@fontbonne.org
(Girls). Sr. Anne P. Clancy, C.S.J., Prin. Sisters of St. Joseph (Brentwood Community) 10; Lay Teachers 40; Students 575.

Nazareth Regional, 475 E. 57th St., 11203. Tel: 718-763-1100.
(Coed). Dr. Robert Muccigrosso, Ph.D., Prin. Sisters 1; Lay Teachers 30; Students 585.

St. Joseph, 80 Willoughby St., 11201. Tel: 718-624-3618; Fax: 718-723-3477.
E-mail: admin@jhsbridge.org
(Girls). Sr. Eugenia Calabrese, C.S.J., Prin. Sisters of St. Joseph (Brentwood Community) 17; Other Religious 3; Lay Teachers 20; Students 300.

Xaverian, 7100 Shore Rd., 11209. Tel: 718-836-7100; Fax: 718-836-7114.
E-mail: jmarino@xaverian.org
Web site: www.xaverian.org
(Boys). Dr. Salvatore Ferrera, Pres.; Dr. Joseph Marino, Prin.; Ms. Sarah Kelly, Dir. Admissions & Devel.; Mr. George Donnelly, Asst. Prin. Academics; Ms. Johanna Motta, Asst. Prin. Staff Devel.; Mr. Thomas Burns, Asst. Prin. Discipline; Domenick Laurendi, Asst. Prin. Discipline; Mr. Sigfried Heiles, Dir. of Alumni Affairs; Rev. David J. Dettmer, Chap. Priests 1; Xaverian Brothers 7; Lay Teachers 83; Students 1,300.

Queens

ASTORIA. *St. John Preparatory School*, 21-21 Crescent St., 11105-3398. Tel: 718-721-7200; Fax: 718-545-3469.
Web site: www.stjohnsprepschool.org
(Coed). Mr. William A. Higgins, Prin.; Rev. Charles P. Keeney, Spiritual Dir. Priests 2; Sisters 6; Lay Teachers 78; Students 1,480.

BRIARWOOD. *Archbishop Molloy*, 83-53 Manton St., 11435. Tel: 718-441-2100; Fax: 718-849-8251.
E-mail: president@molloyhs.org
Web site: www.molloyhs.org
(Coed). Bros. Richard Van Houten, F.M.S., Pres.; Roy George, F.M.S., Prin. Brothers 20; Sisters 2; Lay Teachers 58; Students 1,380.

COLLEGE POINT. *St. Agnes Academic*, 13-20 124 St., 11356-1814. Tel: 718-353-6276; Fax: 718-353-6068.
(Girls). Sr. Joan Martin, O.P., Prin. Sisters of St. Dominic (Amityville) 19; Lay Teachers 20; Students 400.

EAST ELMHURST. *Monsignor McClancy*, 71-06 31st Ave., 11370. Tel: 718-898-3800.
(Boys). Bro. Robert Connolly, S.C., Prin. Brothers 11; Sisters 1; Lay Teachers 27; Boys 530.

FLUSHING. *Holy Cross High School*, 26-20 Francis Lewis Blvd., 11358. Tel: 718-886-7250; Fax: 718-886-7257.
E-mail: info@holycrosshs.org
Web site: www.holycrosshs.org
(Boys). Bro. Stephen LaMendola, C.S.C., Pres.; Mr. Joseph Giannuzzi, Prin. Brothers of Holy Cross 14; Sisters 1; Lay Teachers 46; Students 935.

FRESH MEADOWS. *St. Francis Preparatory School*, 6100 Francis Lewis Blvd., 11365. Tel: 718-423-8810; Fax: 718-224-2108.
E-mail: 21stcentury@stfrancisprep.org
Web site: www.stfrancisprep.org
(Coed). Bro. Leonard Conway, O.S.F., Prin.; Rev. William F. Sweeney, Chap. Priests 1; Franciscan Brothers 12; Sisters 22; Lay Teachers 131; Students 2,750.

JAMAICA ESTATES. *The Mary Louis Academy (College Preparatory)*, 176-21 Wexford Ter., 11432. Tel: 718-297-2120; Fax: 718-739-0037.
(Girls). Sr. Kathleen McKinney, C.S.J., Prin. Priests 1; Sisters of St. Joseph (Brentwood Community) 28; Sisters of St. Dominic (Amityville) 1; Sisters of Mercy (Brooklyn) 1; Lay Teachers 60; Students 973.

MIDDLE VILLAGE. *Christ the King*, 6802 Metropolitan Ave., 11379. Tel: 718-366-7400.
(Coed). Daughters of Wisdom. Mr. Michael J Lynch, Prin.; Rev. Anthony S. Ercolano, Chap. Priests 1; Sisters 5; Lay Teachers 88; Students 1,815.

ROCKAWAY PARK. *Stella Maris*, Beach 112th St., 11694. Tel: 718-634-4994; Fax: 718-634-5267.
E-mail: gmartinez@stellamarishigh.org
Web site: www.stellamarishs.org
(Girls). Miss Geri Martinez, Prin. Sisters of St. Joseph (Brentwood) 2; Franciscan Brothers 1; Lay Teachers 42; Students 482.

Maura Clarke Coed Jr. High Program. (Grades 7-8). Tel: 718-634-4994; Fax: 718-256-5761. Miss Edna Walker.

[H] HIGH SCHOOLS PAROCHIAL

BROOKLYN. (Girls). Sr. Mary Febronia, C.S.J., Prin.; Ms. Patricia Conley, Asst. Prin. Priests 1; Sisters 10; Lay Teachers 16; Students 186.

Denis Maloney Institute/St. Edmund Preparatory High School, 2474 Ocean Ave., 11229. Tel: 718-743-6100; Fax: 718-743-5243.
E-mail: principal@stedmundhs.org
(Coed). Mr. John P. Lorenzetti, Prin.; Mr. Jim Benson, Asst. Prin. Sisters 2; Lay Teachers 35; Students 615.

St. Saviour High School, 588 6th St., 11215. Tel: 718-768-4406; Fax: 718-369-2688.
E-mail: belanger.sv@stsaviour.org
Web site: www.stsaviour.org
(Girls). Sr. Valeria Belanger, S.S.N.D., Prin.; Mrs. Margaret Bernstein, Asst. Prin. School Sisters of Notre Dame 4; Lay Teachers 28; Students 300.

[I] SPECIAL SCHOOLS

BROOKLYN. *Robert F. Kennedy Incentive Program*, 2635 Linden Blvd., 11208-4992. Tel: 718-235-0744; Fax: 718-235-0744.
(Coed). Bro. Adrian Fannon, O.S.F., Prin. Brothers 1; Sisters 1; Lay Teachers 4; Students 70.

St. Catherine Laboure Special Education Program, Dept. of Education, 310 Prospect Park W., 11215. Tel: 718-965-7300, Ext. 1229; Fax: 718-965-7323. Program for mentally challenged students ages 5-21 and learning disabled students grades 6-8. William E. Slow, Assoc. Supt. Lay Teachers and Staff 23; Students 113.

St. Francis de Sales School for the Deaf, 260 Eastern Pkwy., 11225. Tel: 718-636-4573; Fax: 718-636-4577.
E-mail: sfdssd@earthlink.net
Infant through Elementary Grades. Edward McCormack, M.A., Supt. Sisters 4; Lay Teachers 50; Students 160.

St. Francis De Sales School for the Deaf Development Fund, 260 Eastern Pkwy., 11225. Tel: 718-626-4573; Fax: 718-636-4577.

SPRINGFIELD GARDENS. *Martin de Porres School*, 136-25 218th St., 11413-2226. Tel: 718-525-3414; Fax: 718-525-0982.
E-mail: mdpschool @metrocon.com
Web site: www.mdp.org
Specialized day school for emotionally disturbed children, ages 7-21. Brothers 2; Sisters 1; Staff 65; Capacity 200.

[J] ELEMENTARY SCHOOLS PRIVATE

BROOKLYN. *St. Agnes Seminary*, 2221 Avenue R, 11229. Tel: 718-376-2756; Fax: 718-376-8834.
E-mail: dobsc103@impresso.com
Web site: www.saintagnes seminary.org
Sr. Grace Eidt, C.S.J., Prin. Sisters of St. Joseph 2; School Sisters of Notre Dame 1; Lay Teachers 16; Students 182.

St. Angela Hall Academy, 290 Washington Ave., 11205. Tel: 718-622-6919; Fax: 718-622-7005. Sr. Mary Sivillo, C.S.J., Prin.
Under supervision of Sisters of St. Joseph. Sisters 1; Lay Teachers 9; Students 115.

Visitation Academy, 8902 Ridge Blvd., 11209. Tel: 718-680-9452; Fax: 718-680-4441.
E-mail: dobsc261@impresso.com
Sr. Marie de Chantal Mannino, V.H.M., Supr. & Pres.; Mrs. Kathleen O'Sullivan-O'Donnell, Prin. Sisters of the Visitation 7; Lay Teachers 16; Girls 185.

[K] CONSOLIDATED ELEMENTARY SCHOOLS (REGIONAL)

BROOKLYN. *St. Elizabeth Seton*, 751 Knickerbocker Ave., 11221. Tel: 718-386-4050; Fax: 718-386-1565.
E-mail: dobsc137@connectinc.com
Consolidated from Fourteen Holy Martyrs and St. Martin of Tours. Sr. Mary Tully, C.S.J., Prin. Lay Teachers 16; Students 375.

St. Frances Cabrini, 181 Suydam St., 11221. Tel: 718-386-9277.
E-mail: dobsc145@connectinc.com
Maria Crifasi, Prin. Lay Teachers 11; Students 229.

St. Michael, 237 Jerome St., 11207. Tel: 718-277-6766. Sr. Margaret Merritt, O.P., Prin. Sisters 1; Lay Teachers 17; Students 375.

[L] CATHOLIC CHARITIES

BROOKLYN. *Catholic Charities*, Central Office, 191 Joralemon St., 11201. Tel: 718-722-6000; Fax: 718-722-6096.
Web site: www.ccbg.org
Most Revs. Thomas V. Daily, D.D., Corp. Member; Joseph M. Sullivan, D.D., M.S., M.P.A., Exec. Vice Pres. & Episcopal Vicar for Human Svcs.; Mr. Thomas A. DeStefano, M.S.W., Exec. Dir. & CEO; Mr. Antonio M. Blanco, C.S.W., Assoc. Exec. Dir.; Rev. Msgr. Thomas F. Cribbin, Assoc. Exec. Dir.; Carlo de Rege, M.U.P., Assoc. Exec. Dir.; Robert Siebel, M.S.W., Assoc. Exec. Dir. & COO; Emmie Glynn Ryan, Esq., Dir. Legal Affairs; Sr. Frances Picone, R.S.M., Regl. Admin. Brooklyn East; Sr. Ellen Patricia Finn, O.P., Regl. Admin. Brooklyn West; Robert Marquez, Regl. Admin. Queens North; Robert Mundy, Regl. Admin. Queens South; Rev. Msgr. Joseph A. Funaro, Special Asst. to Exec. Dir.; Sr. Lorna Colin, C.S.J., Special Asst. to Exec. Dir.; Sr. Kathleen Newell, B.V.M., Special Asst. to Exec. Dir.; Joan M. Murphy, M.A., C.F.R.E., Dir. Public Affairs; Thaddeus Taberski, M.S.W., M.B.A., Dir. Govt. Rels. & Public Policy; Mary O'Reilly, Assoc. Dir. Family Svcs.; Fran Kommor, Assoc. Dir. Residential Svcs.; Rev. Peter Mahoney, Assoc. Dir. Evaluation; Lisa Rosen, Dir. Quality Assurance; Barbara Conley, M.S.W., Dir. Child Care & Planning; Sr. Bernadette Downes, C.I.J., Research & Devel. & Pastoral Svcs.; John Tynan, M.U.P., Dir. Housing; Gayle DeRienzis, M.S.W., Assoc. Dir. Targeted Svcs.; Rev. Msgr. Howard B. Basler, M.A., Dir. Social Action & Campaign for Human Devel.; Rosalyn Ferguson, M.S.W., Employee Assistance Prog.; Edwin Colon, Human Resources; Marie Meyer, Dir. Financial Affairs; Kenneth Haag, Dir. Financial Svcs., B.F.F.Y.; Frank Paterno, Dir. Computer Svcs.; Margaret Keaveney, Dir. Communications.
Aging Services:

Golden Age Clubs, 191 Joralemon St., 11201. Tel: 718-722-6022; Fax: 718-722-6039.
Human Services:

Center for Pregnant Women, 191 Joralemon St., 11201. Tel: 718-722-6121; Fax: 718-722-6233.
Family Centers:

Brooklyn West, 191 Joralemon St., 11201. Tel: 718-722-6002; Fax: 718-722-6045.

Brooklyn East, 1987 Flatbush Ave., 11234. Tel: 718-677-9848; Fax: 718-677-1869.

Queens North, 23-40 Astoria Blvd., Astoria, 11102. Tel: 718-726-9790; Fax: 718-725-8817.

Queens South, 90-39 189th St., Hollis, 11423. Tel: 718-217-1238; Fax: 718-464-1317.
Services For Disabled Persons:

Deafness Services, 191 Joralemon St., 11201. Tel: 718-722-6214; Fax: 718-722-6233.
Comprehensive Human Services:

Builders for the Family and Youth of the Diocese of Brooklyn, Inc. Tel: 718-722-6000; Fax: 718-722-6096. Most Rev. Joseph M. Sullivan, Pres.; Mr. Thomas A. De Stefano, Vice Pres. Operations; Mr. Antonio M. Blanco, Vice Pres. Svcs.; Mr. Kenneth Haag, Exec. Sec.
B.F.F.Y. - Administration: Regional Office - Brooklyn West, 191 Joralemon St., 11201. Tel: 718-722-6050; Fax: 718-722-6045. Regional Office - Brooklyn East, 1987 Flatbush Ave., 11234. Tel: 718-677-9848; Fax: 718-677-1869. Regional Office - Queens South, 90-39 189th St., Hollis, 11423. Tel: 718-217-1440; Fax: 718-464-1317. Regional Office - Queens North, 23-40 Astoria Blvd., Astoria, 11102. Tel: 718-726-9790; Fax: 718-728-8817.
Aging Services:

Alzheimers Adult Day Care, 157-16 65th Ave., Flushing, 11357. Tel: 718-358-3541; Fax: 718-961-4712.

Bayside Senior Center, 221-15 Horace Harding Expwy., Bayside, 11364. Tel: 718-225-1144; Fax: 718-229-7320.

Bay Ridge Alzheimer Services, 255 Ovington Ave., 11220. Tel: 718-748-2882; Fax: 718-837-1957.

Bayside Senior Services, 45-50 195th St., Flushing, 11358. Tel: 718-357-4903; Fax: 718-357-4903.

Bensonhurst Senior Services Center, 1867 Bath Ave., 11241. Tel: 718-236-3205; Fax: 718-837-1957.

Hillcrest Senior Center, 168-01 B. Hillside Ave., Jamaica, 11432. Tel: 718-297-7171; Fax: 718-657-2247. Pete McGuinnes Senior Center, 842 Manhatten Ave., 11222. Tel: 718-383-1940; Fax: 718-383-1960. Northside Senior Center, 179 N. 6th St., 11211. Tel: 718-387-2316; Fax: 718-387-3235.

Catherine Sheridan Senior Center, 35-24 83rd St., Jackson Heights, 11372. Tel: 718-458-4600; Fax: 718-458-5665.

Narrows Senior Center, 7907 New Utrecht Ave., 11214. Tel: 718-256-1166; Fax: 718-234-6161.

Ozone Park Senior Center, 103-12 101st Ave., Ozone Park, 11420. Tel: 718-847-2100; Fax: 718-847-2166.

Peter J. Della Monica Center for Seniors, 23-56 Broadway, Astoria, 11106. Tel: 718-626-1500; Fax: 718-278-4432.

Richmond Hill Senior Center, 87-25 118th St., Richmond Hill, 11418. Tel: 718-846-2877; Fax: 718-849-9089.

Sheepshead Bay Senior Services, 1215 Avenue O, 11230. Tel: 718-375-3377; Fax: 718-627-8640.

Southwest Queens Senior Services, 87-04 88th Ave., Woodhaven, 11421. Tel: 718-847-9200; Fax: 718-805-9496.

Growing Assets Child Care Development, 231 E. 17th St., 11226. Tel: 718-856-4738; Fax: 718-756-4871.

St. Charles Jubilee Center, 55 Pierrepont St., 11201. Tel: 718-855-0326; Fax: 718-852-5415.

St. Louis Senior Center, 230 Kingston Ave., 11213. Tel: 718-771-7945; Fax: 718-467-2524.

St. Mary's Senior Center, 10-15 49th Ave., Long Island City, 11101. Tel: 718-729-2688; Fax: 718-729-5377.

Steinway Senior Center, 20-43 Steinway St., Astoria, 11105. Tel: 718-728-8472; Fax: 718-278-5301.

Wakefield Senior Center, 135-45 Lefferts Blvd., South Ozone Park, 11420. Tel: 718-641-0454; Fax: 718-641-2418.

Woodhaven Senior Center, 87-04 88th Ave., Woodhaven, 11421. Tel: 718-847-9200; Fax: 718-805-9496.

Woodside Senior Assistance Center, 70-11 48th Ave., Woodside, 11377. Tel: 718-799-1234; Fax: 718-779-7775.

B.F.F.Y. - Child Care & Head Start Programs:

Coney Island Child Care Center, 2757 W. 33rd St., 11224. Tel: 718-946-8759; Fax: 718-266-6879.

Farragut Child Care Center, 32 Navy St., 11201. Tel: 718-875-7555; Fax: 718-596-9649.

J. Di Marco Child Care Center, 36-49 11th St., Long Island City, 11106. Tel: 718-786-1166; Fax: 718-706-7608.

J.F. Kennedy Child Care Center, 103-15 Farragut Rd., 11236. Tel: 718-272-8751; Fax: 718-272-6035.

John Oravecz Child Care Center, 25 Nassau Ave., 11222. Tel: 718-782-2727; Fax: 718-782-5166.

R.F. Kennedy Child Care Center, 741 Flushing Ave., 11206. Tel: 718-782-0766; Fax: 718-782-0767.

Vincent J. Caristo Child Care Center, 5901 13th Ave., 11219. Tel: 718-853-8300; Fax: 718-871-8186.

De Paul Head Start, 71 Lincoln Pl., 11215. Tel: 718-622-2060; Fax: 718-622-1941.

Madeline Jones Head Start, 3415 Neptune Ave., 11224. Tel: 718-266-5962; Fax: 718-266-5891.

Padre Kennedy Head Start, 288 Berry St., 11211. Tel: 718-387-3679; Fax: 718-599-3319.

St. Barbara's Head Start, 139 Menahan St., 11221. Tel: 718-443-9800; Fax: 718-443-1919.

St. Joseph's Head Start, 300 Vernon Ave., 11206. Tel: 718-455-5900; Fax: 718-455-7513.

St. Margaret Mary Head Start, 9-16 27th Ave., Long Island City, 11102. Tel: 718-721-8065; Fax: 718-721-7454.

Therese Cervini Head Start, 35-34 104th St., Corona, 11368. Tel: 718-478-2169; Fax: 718-478-3993.

St. Malachy Child Development Center, 220 Hendricks St., 11207. Tel: 718-647-0966; Fax: 718-647-1042.

St. Malachy Head Start, 220 Hendricks St., 11207. Tel: 718-647-0966; Fax: 718-647-1042.

B.F.F.Y. - Human Services:

Compeer, 165-15 88th Ave., Jamaica, 11432. Tel: 718-291-4848; Fax: 718-291-5485.

F.A.N. Program, 89-56 162nd St., Jamaica, 11432. Tel: 718-523-2220; Fax: 718-523-2333.

B.F.F.Y. - Mental Health Services:

Brooklyn Community Living, 2000 Flatbush Ave., 11234. Tel: 718-253-1366; Fax: 718-253-4893.

Corona - Elmhurst Clinic, 37-22 82 St., Jackson Heights, 11372. Tel: 718-779-1600; Fax: 718-803-0895.

Corona Elmhurst Community Support Systems, 37-22 82nd St. & 37-66 72nd St., Jackson Heights, 11372. Tel: 718-779-2803; Fax: 718-639-0167.

Flatbush Addiction Treatment Center, 1463 Flatbush Ave., 11234. Tel: 718-951-9009; Fax: 718-951-9719.

Flatlands Guidance Clinic, 2000 Flatbush Ave., 11234. Tel: 718-377-5755; Fax: 718-577-0752.

Glendale Guidance Center, 67-29 Myrtle Ave., Glendale, 11385. Tel: 718-456-7001; Fax: 718-456-9470.

Human Outreach Mobile Exc., 200 Gold St., 11201. Tel: 718-875-5015; Fax: 718-875-4367.

Queens Homeless Outreach, 165-15 88th Ave., Jamaica, 11432. Tel: 718-291-4848; Fax: 718-291-1531.

Innovation Club, 80-45 Winchester Blvd., Queens Village, 11427. Tel: 718-468-4700; Fax: 718-464-5640.

Jamaica CSS - King Solomon Manor for Adults, 160-11 89th Ave., Jamaica, 11432. Tel: 718-291-7173; Fax: 718-291-5485.

Jamaica CSS - Cont. Treatment, 165-15 88th Ave., Jamaica, 11432. Tel: 718-291-4848; Fax: 718-291-5485.

Mobile Crisis Psych. Team, 13-29 Beach Channel Dr., Far Rockaway, 11691. Tel: 718-337-6800; Fax: 718-337-0940.

On-Site School Project, 67-29 Myrtle Ave., Glendale, 11385. Tel: 718-456-7001; Fax: 718-456-9470.

Partnership of Hope, 715 Dean St., 11238. Tel: 718-398-0153; Fax: 718-789-5050.

Queen Community Living Program, 35-24 83rd St., Jackson Heights, 11372. Tel: 718-639-0700; Fax: 718-639-7684.

Rockaway CSS - Central Manor, 1509 Central Ave., Far Rockaway, 11691. Tel: 718-471-6334; Fax: 718-868-3782.

Rockaway CSS - Surfside Manor, 95-02 Rockaway Beach Blvd., Rockaway Park, 11693. Tel: 718-945-6161; Fax: 718-945-6735.

Rockaway CSS - Screening Team, 13-29 Beach Channel Dr., Far Rockaway, 11691. Tel: 718-471-7586; Fax: 718-868-3782.

Freedom Village Psychosocial Club, 13-29 Beach Channel Dr., Far Rockaway, 11691. Tel: 718-337-0504; Fax: 718-868-3782.

Rockaway Community Life Skills - Cont. Treatment, 13-29 Beach Channel Dr., Far Rockaway, 11691. Tel: 718-337-6850; Fax: 718-868-3782.

Rockaway Mental Health Clinic, 13-29 Beach Channel Dr., Far Rockaway, 11691. Tel: 718-337-6800; Fax: 718-337-0940.

Rose House (RCCA), 80-45 Winchester Blvd., Queens Village, 11427. Tel: 718-468-4700; Fax: 718-464-5640.

Mercy Gardens SRO, 249 Glasson Ave., 11205. Tel: 718-399-8141; Fax: 718-399-3208.

The Open Door, 2000 Flatbush Ave., 11234. Tel: 718-377-7757; Fax: 718-377-0752.

Woodside Senior Assistance Center, 61-20 Woodside Ave., Woodside, 11377. Tel: 718-799-1234; Fax: 718-779-7775.

Monica House, 161-01 89th Ave., Jamaica, 11432. Tel: 718-262-8190; Fax: 718-739-4331.

B.F.F.Y. - Prevention of Foster Care:

Coney Island Family Resource Center, 2201 Neptune Ave., 11224. Tel: 718-372-6400; Fax: 718-372-8302.

Family Support Center of East New York, 2635 Linden Blvd., 11208. Tel: 718-827-5700; Fax: 718-827-1226.

Jamaica Family & Youth Center, 120-09 141st. St., South Ozone Park, 11432. Tel: 718-738-2500; Fax: 718-529-8522.

B.F.F.Y. - Services for Disabled Persons:

Peter J. Connelly Residence, 15 Willow St., 11201. Tel: 718-625-5590; Fax: 718-625-4856.

Adessa House, 101-38 92 St., Ozone Park, 11416. Tel: 718-848-1940; Fax: 718-323-1250.

Alhambra Day Treatment Center, 11-29 Catherine St., 11211. Tel: 718-388-5900; Fax: 718-388-3927.

Caldwell House, 121-01 116th Ave., South Ozone Park, 11420. Tel: 718-845-1200; Fax: 718-323-1267.

Carmel Residence, 275 N. Eighth St., 11211. Tel: 718-388-6109; Fax: 718-388-6522.

Cribbin House, 218-20 104th Ave., Queens Village, 11429. Tel: 718-776-4190; Fax: 718-464-4849.

Dawson Manor, 94-17 84th St., Ozone Park, 11416. Tel: 718-296-1172; Fax: 718-296-1247.

Donald Savio Residence, 104-22 48th Ave., Corona, 11368. Tel: 718-699-7800; Fax: 718-699-3773.

Fitzpatrick Residence, 240 McKinley Ave., 11208. Tel: 718-647-7070; Fax: 718-647-6458.

Garfield Manor, 305 Garfield Pl., 11215. Tel: 718-622-2100; Fax: 718-857-9308.

Golden Residence, 225 Brooklyn Ave., 11213. Tel: 718-953-4444; Fax: 718-953-0622.

Graci Residence, 132-14 90th St., Ozone Park, 11416. Tel: 718-848-1970; Fax: 718-323-7349.

Helen Owen Carey Residence, 174 Java St., 11222. Tel: 718-383-2451; Fax: 718-383-1488.

McLees House, 112-16 200th St., St. Albans, 11412. Tel: 718-217-0285; Fax: 718-217-9491.

Mugavero Manor, 145-16 Farmers Blvd., Springfield Gardens, 11434. Tel: 718-712-9054; Fax: 718-718-2877.

Mulrooney Manor, 479 E. 29th St., 11226. Tel: 718-287-7553; Fax: 718-826-2519.

Senior F.U.N., 415 Bleeker St., 1121. Tel: 718-417-5316; Fax: 718-381-9407.

Jeanne Noel Hower Residence, 156 Midwood St., 11225. Tel: 718-282-8045; Fax: 718-469-2874.

Mark Wayrick Residence, 90-37 189th St., Hollis, 11423. Tel: 718-464-4090; Fax: 718-468-8919.

Straus Residence, 3730 Shore Pkwy., 11233. Tel: 718-769-8836; Fax: 718-368-0418.

Supportive Living Apartments, 479 E. 29 St., 11226. Tel: 718-287-7553; Fax: 718-826-2519.

The Francis De Falco Dental Clinic, 11-29 Catherine St., 11211. Tel: 718-384-0303; Fax: 718-388-3927.

B.F.F.Y. - Services for Persons Living with AIDS:

Circle of Hope, 2520 Flatbush Ave., Rm 7, 11234. Tel: 718-338-4716; Fax: 718-338-5383.

B.F.F.Y. - Youth Services:

Queens South Young Parents, 90-39 184th St., Hoddis, 11423. Tel: 718-217-1238; Fax: 718-464-1317.

North West Queens. Parenting Partnership, 23-40 Astoria Blvd., Astoria, 11102. Tel: 718-726-9790; Fax: 718-728-8817.

Project Bridge, 144 Bleeker St., 11221. Tel: 718-455-4649; Fax: 718-455-9311.

Rainbow Workshops for Youth - Queens Helping Adolescents Reach Peers (HARP), 144 Bleeker St., 11221. Tel: 718-455-4649. 90-39 189th St., Hoddis, 11423. Tel: 718-740-6733; Fax: 718-464-1317.

Housing Development and Management Services: Tel: 718-722-6000; Fax: 718-722-6045.

Progress of Peoples Development Corporation. John Tynan, M.U.P., Dir.

Progress of Peoples Management Corporation. Tel: 718-722-6155; Fax: 718-722-6134. Maureen McKeown, Dir. Housing Svcs.; Terri Mejillones, Assoc. Dir. Fiscal Svcs.

Housing Corporations:

Bellerose Senior Housing, HDFC, Inc., 191 Joralemon St., 11201. Tel: 718-479-4739; Fax: 718-479-6612.

Bethlehem Community HDFC, Inc., 191 Joralemon St., 11201. Tel: 718-722-6000; Fax: 718-722-6045.

Bishop Boardman Apartments, HDFC, Inc., 191 Joralemon St., 11201. Tel: 718-965-4444; Fax: 718-965-3577.

Bishop Francis J. Mugavero, HDFC, Inc., 191 Joralemon St., 11201. Tel: 718-643-6490; Fax: 718-643-6492.

Sr. Lucian Apartments, HDFC, Inc., 191 Joralemon St., 11201. Tel: 718-417-4102; Fax: 718-381-9407.

Caring Communities Associates, HDFC, Inc., 191 Joralemon St., 11201. Tel: 718-857-2266; Fax: 718-857-5866.

Mary Star of the Sea HFDC, Inc., 191 Joralemon St., 11201. Tel: 718-858-7263; Fax: 718-858-7265.

Mount Carmel Senior HDFC, 191 Joralemon St., 11201. Tel: 718-722-6000; Fax: 718-722-6045.

Pope John Paul II HDFC, Inc., 191 Joralemon St., 11201. Tel: 718-748-2882; Fax: 718-748-4455.

Pierrepont House for the Elderly, Inc., 191 Joralemon St., 11201. Tel: 718-852-3390; Fax: 718-852-3352.

Queens Rehab, 191 Joralemon St., 11201. Tel: 718-722-6000; Fax: 718-722-6045.

St. Brendans, HDFC, Inc., 191 Joralemon St., 11201. Tel: 718-645-7112; Fax: 718-645-7180.

St. Lucy/St.Patrick HDFC, 191 Joralemon St., 11201. Tel: 718-722-6000; Fax: 718-722-6045.

Msgr. John O'Brien, HDFC, Inc., 191 Joralemon St., 11201. Tel: 718-972-4556; Fax: 718-972-9265.

St. Paul the Apostle Senior HDFC, 191 Joralemon St., 11201. Tel: 718-722-6000; Fax: 718-722-6045. Jeanne M. Diulio, Contact Person.

Sunset Park HFDC, Inc., 191 Joralemon St., 11201. Tel: 718-438-1119.

Long Island City Senior House HFDC, Inc., 191 Joralemon St., 11201. Tel: 718-545-0816; Fax: 718-545-0817.

Families Together HDFC, Inc., 191 Joralemon St., 11201. Tel: 718-722-6000; Fax: 718-722-6045.

Parkville Houses Senior HDFC, Inc., 191 Joralemon St., 11201. Tel: 718-859-9248.

Holy Spirit HDFC, Inc., 191 Joralemon St., 11201. Tel: 718-854-0050; Fax: 718-854-8521.

Msgr. Joseph F. Stedman Residence, HDFC, Inc., 191 Joralemon St., 11201. Tel: 718-722-6000; Fax: 718-722-6134.

161-01 89th Avenue Corp., 191 Joralemon St., 11201. Tel: 718-262-8190; Fax: 718-739-4331.

Our Lady of Fatima HDFC, Inc., 191 Joralemon St., 11201. Tel: 718-507-1933; Fax: 718-507-1214.

The David Minkin Residence, HDFC, Inc., 191 Joralemon St., 11201. Tel: 718-438-7998; Fax: 718-438-0052.

Emmaus of the Diocese of Brooklyn, Inc., 191 Joralemon St., 11201. Tel: 718-722-6000; Fax: 718-722-6096.

St. Pius V Senior HDFC, Inc., 191 Joralemon St., 11201. Tel: 718-722-6000; Fax: 718-722-6045.

Youth Development and Recreation:

Catholic Youth Organization of the Diocese of Brooklyn, Inc., 191 Joralemon St., 11201. Tel: 718-722-6074; Fax: 718-722-6233.

Nursing Home:

Ss. Joachim & Anne Residence, 2720 Surf Ave., 11224. Tel: 718-714-4800; Fax: 718-714-0874.

Home Care for the Sick:

Care at Home for the Diocese of Brooklyn, Inc., 241 37th St., 11232-2409. Tel: 718-832-0550; Fax: 718-965-7010.

Residences for Women:

Providence House, Inc., Administrative Office, 703 Lexington Ave., P.O Box 210529, 11221. Tel: 718-455-0197; Fax: 718-455-0692. Sr. Janet Kinney, C.S.J., Exec. Dir., Providence House 1, 2518

Church Ave., 11226. Providence House 2, 172 Bainbridge St., 11233. Providence House 3, 159-23 89th Ave., Jamaica, 11432. Providence House 4, 89 Sickles Ave., New Rochelle, 10801. Providence House 5, 396 Lincoln Rd., 11225. Providence House 6, 2876 W. 17 St., 11224.

Permanent Housing, 85 & 87 Sickles Ave., New Rochelle, 10801.

Community Centers:

Dr. White Community Center, 200 Gold St., 11201. Tel: 718-875-8801; Fax: 718-875-4367.

Other Affiliated Agencies:

Anthonian Hall, Inc. Tel: 718-722-6000; Fax: 718-722-6096. Thomas A. De Stefano, Treas.; Most Rev. Joseph M. Sullivan, Treas.; Rev. Msgr. Thomas F. Cribbin, Sec.

Catholic Guild for the Blind, Diocese of Brooklyn, Inc., 191 Joralemon St., 11201. Rev. Msgr. Thomas F. Cribbin.

Ecclesial Consultants, Inc., 191 Joralemon St., 11201. Tel: 718-722-6000; Fax: 718-722-6096.

A management service for Church agencies and organizations. Directors: Most Rev. Joseph M. Sullivan; Rev. Msgr. Emmet Fagan (RVC); Rev. Msgr. Charles J. Fahey (RVC).

Ferrini Welfare League, 98-21 101 Ave., Ozone Park, 11416. Tel: 718-845-0539.

Flowers With Care, Diocese of Brooklyn, Inc., 23-40 Astoria Blvd., Astoria, 11102. Tel: 718-726-9790; Fax: 718-722-8817.

Italian Board of Guardians, 7808 18 Ave., 11214. Tel: 718-232-4242; Fax: 718-232-6402. Rev. Fernando Ferrarese, Mod.; Maria Patalano, Exec. Dir.; Mrs. Beatrice Rizzo, Exec. Sec.

Mary's Hall, Inc., 191 Joralemon St., 11201. Tel: 718-722-6000; Fax: 718-722-6096. Most Rev. Joseph M. Sullivan, Pres.

Society of St. Vincent de Paul in Diocese of Brooklyn, Central Office, 191 Joralemon St., 11201. Tel: 718-625-1400; Fax: 718-625-1421. Most Rev. Thomas V. Daily, D.D., Spiritual Advisor; Rev. Msgr. James W. Asip, Assoc. Spiritual Advisor; Mr. Joseph Martino, Pres., District Council of Kings, 191 Joralemon St., 11201. Tel: 718-625-1400; Fax: 718-625-1421. Rev. Raymond J. Kelly, S.T.L., Spiritual Advisor; Mr. Carlos Harris, Pres., District Council of Queens, 191 Joralemon St., 11201. Tel: 718-625-1400; Fax: 718-625-1421. Rev. Msgr. James W. Asip, Spiritual Advisor; Mr. Vito Buccaria, Pres.

Bread & Life Soup Kitchen, 75 Lewis Ave., 11206. Tel: 718-574-0058. Rev. James J. Maher, C.M., Pres.

Pierrepont Housing Development Fund Corporation, 55 Pierrepont St., 11201. Tel: 718-722-6084. Emmie Glynn Ryan, Contact Person.

[M] NURSING SERVICES

BROOKLYN. *Nursing Sisters Home Visiting Service, Inc.*, 500 19th St., 11215. Tel: 718-768-7271; Fax: 718-965-2035. Sr. Mary Nadine Casey, C.I.J., Chair, Board of Directors; Keith Kertland, Pres. & CEO, Nursing Service Offices, 500 19th St., 11215. Tel: 718-768-7271; Fax: 718-965-2035. Ms. Lillian Torres, Mgr. Branch Svs.

[N] HOSPITALS

BROOKLYN. *St. Mary's Hospital of Brooklyn*, 70 Buffalo Ave., 11213. Tel: 718-221-3000

For a complete listing, refer to the Hospitals section.

JAMAICA. *Catholic Medical Centers of Brooklyn & Queens*, 88-25 153rd St., 11432. Tel: 718-558-6900; Fax: 718-558-7286

For a complete listing, refer to the Hospitals section.

[O] SPECIAL CARE FACILITIES

BROOKLYN.

Bishop Francis J. Mugavero Center for Geriatric Care, Inc., 155 Dean St., 11217. Tel: 718-694-6700; Fax: 718-694-6710. Paul Rosenfeld, Chairman; Ida Santos, Admin. Affiliated with Catholic Medical Centers. Beds 288.

St. Jerome's Health Services Corp. dba Holy Family Home, 1740 84th St., 11214. Tel: 718-232-3666. John Salandra, Chm.; Mary Ann Rose, Admin. Affiliated with Catholic Medical Centers. Beds 200.

[P] CHILD CARE AGENCIES

BROOKLYN. *Angel Guardian Children and Family Services, Inc.*, 6301 12th Ave., 11219. Tel: 718-232-1500; Fax: 718-232-0331.

E-mail: spelan@erols.com

Ms. Sheila N. Pelan, Exec. Dir. Sisters 6; Children in Care 750.

Foster Boarding Home and Adoption Services, 372 Clinton Ave., 11238. Tel: 718-638-7424; Fax: 718-638-2287. McAuley Residence for Mother & Baby Supervised Independent Living Program.

Preventive Programs, Fort Greene, 186 Montague St., 11201. Tel: 718-624-2100; Fax: 718-624-7740.

Family Support Center, 57 Willoughby St., 11201. Tel: 718-855-7778; Fax: 718-855-9813.

Angel Guardian Foundation, 6301 12th Ave., 11219. Tel: 718-232-1500; Fax: 718-837-9543. Sr. Lois Keller, Pres.; Sr. Patricia Kearney, Sec.

Catholic Child Care Society of the Diocese of Brooklyn, 540 Atlantic Ave., 11217. Tel: 718-797-6094; Fax: 718-797-6092. John J. Bennett, Jr., Pres.; Belinda M. Conway, C.S.W., Exec. Dir.

Good Shepherd Services, 441 Fourth Ave., 11215. Tel: 718-788-0666; Fax: 718-965-0365. Sr. Paulette LoMonaco, R.G.S., Exec. Dir. Provides a comprehensive range of neighborhood family services to individuals & youth from the South Brooklyn community. Services include educational support, employment, counseling & crisis intervention, literacy, skills training & advocacy services to children & families as well as foster care & adoption & residences for teenagers.

HeartShare Human Services of New York, Roman Catholic Diocese of Brooklyn, 191 Joralemon St., 11201. Tel: 718-422-HEART; Fax: 718-522-4506.

E-mail: Heartshare@aol.com

Web site: www.heartshare.com

William R. Guarinello, M.S., Pres. & CEO. Foster Boarding Home Program, Adoption Program, Family Service Centers. Programs for Developmentally Disabled: Group Homes, Supportive Apartments, Preschool Program (Early Childhood Centers), Respite/ Recreation Program, Day Treatment/Day Habilitation Programs, Services for People with HIV/AIDS, School-Based Beacon Programs, Youth Services, Traditional Preschool Program.

HeartShare Human Services - Clinton Residence, 217 Clinton Ave., 11205. Tel: 718-638-2625; Fax: 718-638-3046.

HeartShare Human Services - Clermont Residence, 26 Clermont Ave., 11205. Tel: 718-834-9317; Fax: 718-834-9364.

HeartShare Human Services - Msgr. Thomas G. Hagerty Residence, 128 Montrose Ave., 11206. Tel: 718-387-3595; Fax: 718-387-3597.

HeartShare Human Services - Dr. Catherine White Residence, 175 Metropolitan Ave., 11211. Tel: 718-782-9104; Fax: 718-782-1394.

HeartShare Human Services - Rocco Anthony Torre Residence, 1966 54th St., 11204. Tel: 718-259-4432; Fax: 718-259-1735.

HeartShare Human Services - Antonetta Ferraro Residence, 603 Beach 19 St., Far Rockaway, 11691. Tel: 718-327-9000; Fax: 718-327-9270.

HeartShare Human Services - Thomas J. Cuite Residence, 50-36 45th St., Woodside, 11377. Tel: 718-786-3113; Fax: 718-786-2949.

HeartShare Human Services - 35th Avenue Residence, 172-07 35th Ave., Flushing, 11358. Tel: 718-961-7673; Fax: 718-961-7753.

HeartShare Human Services - Doonan-Drake Residence, 300 E. 18th St., 11226. Tel: 718-469-5000; Fax: 718-469-5002.

HeartShare Human Services - Hart Street Residence, 689 Hart St., 11221. Tel: 718-919-7477; Fax: 718-919-7194.

HeartShare Human Services - James and Kathleen Buckley Residence, 977-979 E. 92nd St., 11236. Tel: 718-272-1441; Fax: 718-272-2668.

HeartShare Human Services - Columbia Street Residence, 296 Columbia St., 11231. Tel: 718-246-9124; Fax: 718-246-9109.

HeartShare Human Services - Frances Aiello Day Treatment Center, 163 MacDonough St., 11206. Tel: 718-443-5071; Fax: 718-443-5741.

HeartShare Human Services - Eileen and William Lavin Day Treatment Center, 545 Broadway, 11206. Tel: 718-388-1665; Fax: 718-388-0149.

HeartShare Human Services - John and Lillian Sharkey, Sr. Residence, 60-12 56th St., Maspeth, 11378. Tel: 718-417-6846; Fax: 718-417-6890.

HeartShare Human Services - Harry Hoffman Day Treatment Center, 62-10 Northern Blvd., Woodside, 11377. Tel: 718-899-2752; Fax: 718-899-9365.

HeartShare Human Services - Matilda Raffa Cuomo First Step Early Childhood Center, 115-15 101st Ave., Richmond Hill, 11419. Tel: 718-441-5333; Fax: 718-805-0657.

HeartShare Human Services - Lefferts/Liberty Kiwanis First Step Early Childhood Center, 82-12 151st Ave., Howard Beach, 11414. Tel: 718-848-0300; Fax: 718-835-2862.

HeartShare Human Services - Dolly and Frank Russo Sr. First Step Early Childhood Center, 118-01/03 101 Ave., Richmond Hill, 11419. Tel: 718-805-7117; Fax: 718-805-7124.

HeartShare Human Services - Red Hook Family Services, 732 Henry St., 11231. Tel: 718-858-8387; Fax: 718-858-7211.

HeartShare Human Services - Residential Housing Program, 221 Smith St., 11201. Tel: 718-596-3391.

HeartShare Human Services - South Brooklyn Family Services, 213 Smith St., 11201. Tel: 718-596-3391; Fax: 718-596-9258.

HeartShare Human Services - East Brooklyn Family Services, 3005 Glenwood Rd., 11210. Tel: 718-434-7900; Fax: 718-434-6715.

HeartShare Human Services - Bensonhurst Family Services, 138 Bay 20th St., 11214. Tel: 718-234-1717; Fax: 718-331-1541.

HeartShare Human Services - Beacon & Family Services Program at P.S. 288, 2950 W. 25 St., 11224. Tel: 718-449-8000; Fax: 718-714-6758.

HeartShare Human Services - Community Follow-up Program, 2882 W. 15 St., 11224. Tel: 718-372-0580; Fax: 718-372-0634.

HeartShare Human Services - Bay Ridge Early Childhood Center, 7002 Fourth Ave., 11209. Tel: 718-238-4637; Fax: 718-238-9584.

HeartShare Human Services - Adult Day Habilitation Program, 61-58 Springfield Blvd., Bayside, 11364. Tel: 718-281-0480; Fax: 718-281-0478. Total Assisted 10,291.

HeartShare Human Services - Family Support Services Program, 186 Joralemon St., 10th Floor, 11201. Tel: 718-422-3271; Fax: 718-422-3324.

HeartShare Human Services - Group Homes Program, 186 Joralemon St., 10th Floor, 11201. Tel: 718-422-3304; Fax: 718-422-3324.

HeartShare Human Services - Supportive Apartment Program, 50 Court St., Rm. 1008, 11201. Tel: 718-797-0891; Fax: 718-797-0890.

HeartShare Human Services - Adult Day Habilitation Program, 50 Court St., 9th Floor, 11201. Tel: 718-330-2202; Fax: 718-330-2209.

HeartShare Human Services - Foster Care / Adoption Services (Brooklyn Office), 191 Joralemon St., 11201. Tel: 718-422-HEART; Fax: 718-625-5014; (Adoption)718-422-4229.

HeartShare Human Services - Youth Services / Summer Camps. Tel: 718-422-HEART; Fax: 718-625-5014.

HeartShare Human Services - Foster Care / Adoption Services (Queens Office), 90-04 161st St., 2nd Floor, Jamaica, 11432. Tel: 718-739-5000; Fax: 718-739-6828.

HeartShare Human Services - First Step Early Childhood Evaluation Center, 162-30 Cross Bay Blvd., Howard Beach, 11414. Tel: 718-323-2877; Fax: 718-323-2897.

HeartShare Human Services - Foster Care / Adoption Services (Manhattan), 1854 Amsterdam Ave., 4th Floor, New York, 10031. Tel: 212-870-1375; Fax: 212-491-4455.

HeartShare Human Services - Beacon Program at I.S. 259, 7301 Fort Hamilton Pkwy., 11228. Tel: 718-422-4218.

Little Flower Children's Services, 186 Remsen St., 11201. Tel: 718-260-8840. Rev. Msgr. John T. Fagan, M.S.W., Exec. Vice Pres.; Mary G. Ryder, Exec. Dir.; Sr. Rita Wasilewski, C.S.F.N., Supr. Foster Care, Adoption & Post Adoption Services, Services for Adult MR/DD clients; Residential Treatment Center, U.F.S.D., & Family Day Care at Wading River, NY; Teen Mothers & Infants in Foster Homes.

Mercy Home for Children, 243 Prospect Park W., 11215. Tel: 718-832-1075; Fax: 718-832-7612. Sr. Catherine Crumlish.

Under the sponsorship of the Sisters of Mercy. Eight Intermediate Care Facilities (Residences) for adolescents & adults who are severely developmentally disabled: Visitation Residence; Harold Warren Residence, de Porres Residence; Littlejohn Residence; Santulli Residence; Kevin Keating Residence, S. Chrys Residence and Gail Addeo Residence. Sisters 6; Staff 188; Residents 83.

St. Francis Home for Boys, 132 Eagle St., 11222. Tel: 718-383-9870.

Web site: www.youth2000ny.com

Rev. Benedict J. Groeschel, C.F.R., Exec. Dir.; Mr. Joseph Campo, Dir. Residents 7.

St. Joseph Services for Children and Families, 540 Atlantic Ave., 11217. Tel: 718-858-8700. Belinda M. Conway, C.S.W., Exec. Dir. Programs: Foster Boarding Homes, Group Homes, 24 Hour Emergency Foster Boarding Homes, Adoption Services, Williamsburgh Family Services, Bushwick Family Services, S.T.A.R.S. (Specialized Treatment & AIDS Related Services), Mother/Child Residential Program.

St. Vincent's Services, Inc. (Formerly St. Vincent's Home for Boys and St. Vincent's Hall, Inc.), 66 Boerum Pl., 11201. Tel: 718-522-3700; Fax: 718-875-8536. Rev. Msgr. Robert M. Harris, M.S.W., M.Phil, M.A., Pres. & CEO. Services include: Foster Boarding Homes, Group Homes, Adoption Services, Pediatric AIDS Program, Refugee Assistance Program, Enhanced Independent Living Program, Mental Health and Physical Health OutPatient Services & Residences for the Developmentally Disabled. Sisters 6; Priests 2; Children 1,300.

ROCKAWAY PARK. *St. John's Residence for Boys, Inc.*, 144-Beach 111 St., 11694. Tel: 718-945-2800; Fax: 718-945-4662. Bro. Thomas N. Trager, S.M., Exec. Dir. Conducted by the Brothers of Society of Mary

(Marianists). Residential care for adolescent boys. Diagnostic Reception Centers, Non-Secure Detention/Independent Living Program. Brothers 6; Residents 85.

SEA CLIFF. *St. Christopher-Ottilie*, Park and Downing Aves., 11579. Tel: 516-671-1253; 718-895-8670; Fax: 516-671-2899. Mr. Robert J. McMahon, Exec. Dir.; Mary Hall, Dir. of Intake and Placement. Residential Treatment Center for the profoundly & severely mentally retarded, Intermediate Care Facilities, Group Homes for Adolescent Teenage Boys and Girls, Teen Mother-Child Residence Program, Homeless Program for Teenage RS, Preventive Programs (3), EFBH Network, Supervised Independent Living Apartments, Therapeutic Foster Boarding Homes, Residential Treatment Facility, Article 81 School. Regular Foster Care Program for Mentally Retarded Individuals, Crisis Respite, Home & Community Based Waiver Services, Madonna Heights Services, Family dynamics, Center for family life. Children 2,650.

[Q] GROUP HOMES FOR RETARDED CHILDREN

SPRINGFIELD GARDENS. *Martin De Porres Group Homes*, 136-25 218th St., 11413. Tel: 718-527-0606; Fax: 718-528-7475
For a complete listing, refer to the Special Care Facilities section.

[R] SUMMER CAMPS AND DAY CAMPS

CENTERPORT. *Camp Alvernia*, Prospect Rd., P.O. Box 301, 11721. Tel: 631-261-5730; Fax: 613-754-4204.
E-mail: alvernia@juno.com
Web site: www.alvernia.org
Under the supervision of the Franciscan Brothers.

COMMACK. *Bishop McDonnell Camp*. Mailing Address: Society of St. Vincent de Paul, 191 Joralmeon St., Brooklyn, 11201. Tel: 718-625-1400. Jack Leonard, Dir. Day Outings for Senior Citizen Groups, Handicapped & Children from poor areas. Sponsored by the Society of St. Vincent de Paul Brooklyn Diocese.

[S] RESIDENCES FOR THE AGED

BROOKLYN. *Holy Family Home*, 1740 84th St., 11214. Tel: 718-232-3666; Fax: 718-259-9180
For a complete listing, refer to the Special Care Facilities section.

SS. Joachim & Anne Residence, Inc., 2720 Surf Ave., 11224. Tel: 718-714-4800
For a complete listing, refer to the Special Care Facilities section.

BAYSIDE. *Ozanam Hall of Queens Nursing Home, Inc.*, 42-41 201st St., 11361. Tel: 718-423-2000; Fax: 718-224-7598.
E-mail: ozanamgen@chcn.org
For a complete listing, refer to the Special Care Facilities section.

JAMAICA. *Msgr. James H. Fitzpatrick Pavilion for Skilled Nursing Care*, 152-11 89th Ave., 11432. Tel: 718-558-2800; Fax: 718-558-2476
For a complete listing, refer to the Special Care Facilities section.

QUEENS VILLAGE. *Queen of Peace Residence*, 110-30 221st St., 11429. Tel: 718-464-1800
For a complete listing, refer to the Special Care Facilities section.

[T] SETTLEMENT ASSOCIATIONS

GLENDALE. *Kolping Center*, 65-04 Myrtle Ave., 11385. Tel: 718-456-7727. Ms. Louise G. Conte, Pres. Legal Title: *Catholic Kolping Society (Katholischer Gesellen Verein) of Brooklyn, Inc.*

[U] CATHOLIC MIGRATION AND REFUGEE OFFICES

BROOKLYN. *Catholic Migration & Refugee Office, Catholic Migration Services, Inc.*, 1258 65th St., 11219. Tel: 718-236-3000; Fax: 718-256-9707.
E-mail: migration@aol.com
Rev. Msgr. Ronald T. Marino, Dir. Apostolate Coordinators.

Brazilian Apostolate. Tel: 718-479-5111; Fax: 718-479-0826. Rev. Amarilho Checon, Coord.

Chinese Apostolate-Queens. Tel: 718-699-1929; Fax: 718-271-3215. Rev. Thomas Sung.

Chinese Apostolate-Brooklyn. Tel: 718-236-3000; Fax: 718-256-9707. Rev. Msgr. Ronald T. Marino, Interim Coord.

Croation Apostolate. Tel: 718-278-3337; Fax: 718-278-4354. Rev. Robert Zubovic, Coord.

Filipino Apostolate. Tel: 718-424-5400; Fax: 718-899-5257. Rev. Eugene Soriano, Coord.

Ghanaian Apostolate. Tel: 718-282-3178; Fax: 718-282-5568.

Haitian Apostolate. Tel: 718-426-0223; Fax: 718-426-7753. Rev. Msgr. Guy Sansaricq, Coord.

Hispanic Ministry Office. Tel: 718-229-8001, Ext. 741; Fax: 718-229-2658. Deacon Jorge A. Gonzalez.

Indian Apostolate. Tel: 718-375-9600; Fax: 718-375-6642. Rev. Paul Vazhapilly, Coord.

Indonesian Apostolate. Tel: 718-236-3000; Fax: 718-256-9707. Rev. Msgr. Ronald T. Marino, Interim Coord.

Irish Apostolate. Tel: 718-969-3226; Fax: 718-380-0345. Rev. Kevin Sweeney, Coord.

Italian Apostolate. Tel: 718-837-8670; Fax: 718-259-3066. Deacon Carlo Mellace.

Korean Apostolate. Tel: 718-236-3000; Fax: 718-256-9707. Rev. Msgr. Ronald T. Marino, Temporary Coord.

Knanaya Indian Apostolate. Tel: 718-347-6070; Fax: 718-343-3221. Rev. Michael Ittykunju.

Nigerian Apostolate. Tel: 718-341-1018; Fax: 718-276-2001. Rev. Louis Uzoh.

Pakistan Apostolate. Tel: 718-886-3890; Fax: 718-358-4964. Rev. Anthony Sikandar.

Polish Apostolate. Tel: 718-899-1387; Fax: 718-416-9245. Rev. Peter W. Zendzian, Coord.

Russian Apostolate. Tel: 212-226-8075. Rev. John Soles.

Vietnamese Apostolate. Tel: 718-238-2900; Fax: 718-238-2902. Rev. Joseph Vu.

West Indian Apostolate. Tel: 718-574-5772; Fax: 718-919-2265. Rev. Martin J. Carter, S.A., Coord.

Resources, Inc., 1258 65th St., 11219. Tel: 718-236-3000; Fax: 718-256-9707. Rev. Msgr. Ronald T. Marino, Dir.; Michael Campo, Mgr. Maint. Dept.; Charles Hendershott, Mgr. Graphics Dept.

Catholic Immigrant Ministries, Inc., 1258 65th St., 11219. Tel: 718-236-3000; Fax: 718-256-9707. Rev. Msgr. Ronald T. Marino, Dir.

Apostleship of the Sea. Stella Maris Center, 45 DeGraw St., 11231. Tel: 718-834-1234; Fax: 718-834-1407. Rev. Alfred Guthrie, Port Chap.; Armando Munoz.

[V] MONASTERIES AND RESIDENCES OF PRIESTS AND BROTHERS

BROOKLYN. *Carmelites of Mary Immaculate, Inc.*, 21 Nassau Ave., 11222. Tel: 718-388-5145. Rev. John Mendnkar, C.M.I. (India), Sup. of Regl. Coord.

Christian Brothers Residence, 367 Clermont Ave., 11238. Tel: 718-857-4311; Fax: 718-783-7576. Bros. Peter Bonventre, F.S.C.; David Carroll, F.S.C.; Robert Ferguson, F.S.C.; Richard Grieco, F.S.C.; John Guascon, F.S.C.; Charles Guglielmo, F.S.C.; Jose Luis Jasso; William Kemmerer, F.S.C.; James Loxham, F.S.C.; John McMahon, F.S.C.; Frederick Del Antonio, F.S.C.; Peter Iorlano, F.S.C.; Ralph Darmento, F.S.C.; Philip Zeller, F.S.C. Brothers 13; Postulants 1.

Curial Residence, 378 Clermont Ave., 11238. Tel: 718-638-0697. Most Rev. Joseph M. Sullivan, M.S.W., D.D.; Rev. Msgr. Austin P. Bennett, J.C.D.

Little Brothers of the Gospel, 554 Hart St., 11221. Bros. Rick Dixon; Jay McGowan; Giorgio Gonella.

Oratory of Saint Philip Neri, Congregation Pontifical Rite, 109 Willoughby St., 11201. Tel: 718-875-2096; Fax: 718-875-4678.
E-mail: philipneri@aol.com
Web site: Brooklyn-oratory.org
Very Rev. Dennis M. Corrado, C.O., Provost; Revs. Mark J. Lane, C.O.; Joel M Warden, C.O.; Bro. James Simon, C.O. Priests 3; Brothers 1.

Our Lady of Good Counsel Residence, 7509 Shore Rd., 11209. Tel: 718-833-1900; Fax: 718-630-5666. Provincial Residence for Redemptorist Fathers and Brothers. Very Rev. George J. Keaveney, C.SS.R., Prov. Supr.; Revs. Patrick F. Woods, C.SS.R., Prov. Vicar; Albert R. Schreiber, C.SS.R., Sec. of Prov.; Lawrence E. Lover, C.SS.R., Curate; Francis P. Nelson, C.SS.R., Procurator; Gerard J. Knapp, C.SS.R., Asst. Procurator; Carl W. Hoegerl, C.SS.R., Prov. Archivist; Lawrence F. Dolan, C.SS.R., Curate. Priests 7; Brothers 1.

St. Casimir's Monastery, Printing Plant and Cultural Center, 361 Highland Blvd., 11207. Tel: 718-235-5962. Franciscan Fathers of the Lithuanian Province of St. Casimir. Most Rev. Paul Baltakis, O.F.M.; Rev. Francis Giedgaudas, O.F.M., Dir. Printery & Supr. Priests 1; Brothers 1.

St. Francis Monastery-Generalate Offices of Franciscan Brothers, 135 Remsen St., 11201-4212. Tel: 718-858-8217; Fax: 718-858-8306. Bros. Kevin Smith, O.S.F., Supr. Gen.; James McVeigh, O.S.F., Vocation Dir.; Joseph Moloney, O.S.F., 1st Councillor; Robert Smith, O.S.F., 2nd Councillor; Campion Lally, O.S.F., 3rd Councillor & Bus. Mgr.; Joshua Di Mauro, O.S.F., 4th Councillor; Edwin Gill, O.S.F., Treas. Gen. Brothers 100.

St. John the Baptist Rectory, 75 Lewis Ave., 11206. Tel: 718-455-6864; Fax: 718-452-3738. Revs. Stephen M. Grozio, C.M., Pastor; Thomas S. Krafinski, C.M.; Joseph V. Agostino, C.M.; Eugene F. Sheridan, C.M., Supr.; Bro. Joseph Taurasо, C.M.

St. Joseph's Priest Residence, 256 Clinton Ave., 11205. Tel: 718-783-4989. Rev. Msgr. Thomas F. Cribbin; Rev. Msgr. Howard B. Basler, S.T.B., M.A.; Rev. Msgr. Martin Bannan, B.A., M.S.W.; Rev. Robert Frueh, M.S.

St. Michael's Friary, 225 Jerome St., 11207. Tel: 718-827-6990; Fax: 718-827-5189. Revs. Raphael Iannone, O.F.M.Cap., Supr. & Co-Dir. of Capuchin Postulancy Prog.; William Hugo, O.F.M.Cap., Friary Vicar & Co-Dir. of Capuchin Postulancy Prog.; Philip F. Bohan, O.F.M.Cap., Pastor. In res. Rev. Knute Joseph Kenlon, O.F.M.Cap. Priests 4.

ASTORIA. *Congregation of St. John the Baptist of China*, 23-15 Newtown Ave., 11102. Tel: 718-278-6797; Fax: 718-278-6889. Revs. Stanislaus Su, C.S.J.B., Vice Supr. & Rector; Thomas Sung, C.S.J.B. (Taiwan), Prior; Dehua Zhang, C.S.J.B.; Stephen Lui, C.S.J.B.; John Tran, C.S.J.B.; Antonius Ho, C.S.J.B. Priests 6; Brothers 9.

DOUGLASTON. *Bishop Mugavero Residence*, 7200 Douglaston Pkwy., 11362. Tel: 718-229-8001; Fax: 718-229-2658. Rev. Msgr. George F. Zartaga, Dir. In res. Rev. Msgr. George T. Deas; Rev. Msgr. George V. Fogarty; Rev. Msgr. Edward W. Jolley; Rev. Msgr. James P. King; Rev. Msgr. Joseph A. Martusciello; Rev. Msgr. James B. McMahon; Rev. Msgr. Francis X. Mulhall; Rev. Msgr. Thomas J. Gradilone; Rev. Msgr. William F. Burke; Revs. John L. Abrams; Louis B. Bartruff; Joseph F. Buckley; Harold A. Buetow; Francis Byrnes; Eugene P. Coyle; John F. Cronin; Harry M. Culkin; Anthony F. Luis; Edward J. McNicholas; Robert F. Milde; Raymond J. Morgan; Stanislaus Raila; Robert J. Young; Barnabas Wang.

Institutional Services Residence, 7200 Douglaston Pkwy., 11362-1997. Tel: 718-229-8290; Fax: 718-279-3004. Rev. Michael J. Hardiman, Exec. Dir.; Mr. Robert Rymers, Dir. Oper.; Mr. Thomas D. Flynn, Controller; Mr. Frederick Puglisi, Dir. Purchasing.

JAMAICA. *Immaculate Conception Monastery*, 86-45 Edgerton Blvd., 11432. Tel: 718-739-6502; Fax: 718-657-0578. Very Rev. Jack Douglas, C.P., Rector; Revs. Lawrence Rywalt, C.P., Vice Rector; Stanislaus Wasek, C.P.; Lawrence Bellew, C.P., Chap.; Jerome Bracken, C.P.; Albert Catanzaro, C.P.; Paul Chenot, C.P., Chap.; Theophane Cooney, C.P., Asst. Pastor; Paul Joseph Fullam, C.P.; Mario Gallipoli, C.P.; Thomas Griffiths, C.P.; Joseph D. Guzinski, C.P.; Colman Haggerty, C.P.; Arnold Horner, C.P.; Ernest Hotz, C.P.; Thomas Joyce, C.P., Pastor; Owen Lally, C.P.; Albert Pellicane, C.P., Chap.; John Chrysostom Ryan, C.P.; Theodore Walsh, C.P.; Nicholas Zitz, C.P.; Neil Davin, C.P., Officialis; John R. Mescall, C.P.; John P. Moore, C.P.; Kenan Peters, C.P.; Claudio Piccinini, C.P.; James Price, C.P., Vocation & Retreat Dir.; Cletus Dawson, C.P.; Angelo Iacovone, C.P.; Henry Kavanagh, C.P.; David Roberts, C.P.; Isaias Powers, C.P.; Leo O'Boyle, C.P.; Edward Buchheit, C.P.; Michael Greene, C.P.; Xavier Hayes, C.P.; Bros. Vincent Basile, C.P.; Philip Maggiulli, C.P.; Kenneth Pughe, C.P.; Paul J. Morgan, C.P.; Anselm Catalucci, C.P.; Louis Mitchell, C.P.; Terence Skorka, C.P., Preaching Office. Priests 36; Brothers 7.

Parsons Manor, 88-25 153rd St., 11432. Tel: 718-558-6900; Fax: 718-558-7286. Revs. Louis D. Aufiero; Jose Cadusale (Philippines); Romano J. Ferraro; John L. Kiernan; James P. Sweeney.

Saint Charles House of Studies, 168-41 84th Ave., 11432. Tel: 718-526-3917; Fax: 718-739-5515.
E-mail: jfugolo@aol.com
Revs. Joseph Fugolo, C.S., Admin. & Dir.; Vincenzo Ronchi, C.S., Asst. Dir.

St. Vincent's House, 84-15 Kendrick Pl., 11432. Tel: 718-262-8265. Vincentian Fathers. Revs. James F. Kiernan, C.M., Supr.; Joseph V. Daly, C.M.; John B. Freund, C.M.; Donald J. Harrington, C.M.; James J. Maher, C.M.; John McKenna, C.M.; Bernard M. Tracey, C.M.; Robert R. Vignola, C.M.; Dennis Holtschneider, C.M.

Vincentian Residence, St. John's University, 8000 Utopia Pkwy., 11439. Tel: 718-990-6744. Revs. Michael J. Carroll, C.M., Supr.; Peter J. Albano, C.M.; Harry Arnone, C.M.; Michael J. Callaghan, C.M.; Thomas A. Casella, C.M.; Thomas V. Concagh, C.M.; Stephen J. Denig, C.M.; James Dorr, C.M.; Peter D. Goldbach, C.M.; Walter F. Graham; James Kelly, C.M.; Kevin G. Creagh; John McDonnell, C.M.; Michael F. Mullen, C.M.; John B. Murray, C.M.; John P. Murray, C.M.; Joseph M. O'Donnell, C.M.; Kenneth F. Slattery, C.M.; James E. Smith, C.M.; Daniel J. Sullivan, C.M.; Robert J. Swain; Michael D. Whalen, C.M.; Bro. Carmen V. Ciardullo, C.M.

JAMAICA ESTATES. *Paulist Fathers - Generalate*, 86-11 Midland Pkwy., 11432. Tel: 718-291-5995; Fax: 718-291-6646.
Web site: www.paulist.org

KEW GARDENS. *St. Columbans Foreign Mission Society*, 118-32 80 Rd., 11415. Tel: 718-847-3700; Fax: 718-847-3702. Revs. Thomas Patrick Parker; James D. Dwyer, S.S.C.; Gerard A. Markey, S.S.C. Priests 3.

LONG ISLAND CITY. *Holy Ghost Fathers of Ireland*, 48-49 37th St., 11101. Tel: 718-729-5273; Fax: 718-729-6949. Revs. Patrick Doody, C.S.Sp., Prov. Delegate; Michael J. McCarthy, C.S.Sp.; Patrick Holohan,

C.S.Sp.; James Delaney, C.S.Sp.; Noel P. O'Meara, C.S.Sp.; Vincent O. O'Connell, C.S.Sp.

OZONE PARK. *Montfort Missionaries Provincialate (Missionaries of the Company of Mary) - Formation Community*, 101-18 104th St., 11416. Tel: 718-849-5885; 849-1684 (Formation); 849-0071 (Vocations); Fax: 718-849-7518.
E-mail: fitzsimmi@aol.com
Web site: montfortmissionaries.com
Revs. Gerald J. Fitzsimmons, S.M.M., Prov. Supr.; Matthew J. Considine, S.M.M., Prov. Treas.; James Brady, S.M.M., Formation Dir.; Roy Tvrdik, S.M.M., Vocation Dir. Priests 4.
Priests of Province Serving Abroad: Revs. Everett Brown, S.M.M., Chontales, Nicaragua; Peter D'Abele, S.M.M., Chontales, Nicaragua; John Breslin, S.M.M., Dominican Republic; William J. Considine, S.M.M., Superior General, Rome, Italy.

QUEENS VILLAGE. *DePaul Residence*, 80-14 217th St., 11427. Tel: 718-468-2900; Fax: 718-468-2903. Revs. Richard J. Devine, C.M.; Stephen C. Bicsko, C.M.; Michael J. Cummins, C.M.

SOUTH OZONE PARK. *Sacred Heart Provincialate*. (NY Province), 141-11 123 Ave., 11436-1426. Tel: 718-322-3309; Fax: 718-529-6004.
E-mail: bro_rocco@prodigy.net
Bro. Joseph Rocco, S.C., Prov. Brothers 3.

SPRINGFIELD GARDENS. *Martin De Porres Brothers Community*, 136-01 219th St., 11413. Tel: 718-978-7155; Fax: 718-525-0982.
E-mail: cbcmdp@nyc.rr.com

[W] CONVENTS AND RESIDENCES FOR SISTERS

BROOKLYN. *Discalced Carmelite Nuns*, The Chancery Office, P.O. Box C, 11202. Tel: 718-399-5900.

Franciscan Sisters of the Poor, Congregational Office, 133 Remsen St., 11201. Tel: 718-643-1919; Fax: 718-643-9710.
E-mail: franciscansrs@cs.com
Web site: www.franciscansisters.org
Sr. Jeanne M. Glisky, S.F.P., Congregational Min.

Missionaries of Charity, Contemplative Our Lady of Lourdes Convent, 34 Aberdeen St., 11207. Tel: 718-443-2868. Sr. Mary Ann, M.C., Supr.; Sr. Mary Lourdes, M.C., Supr. Sisters 7.

Monastery of the Sisters Adorers of the Precious Blood, 54th St. and Ft. Hamilton Pkwy., 11219. Tel: 718-438-6371; Fax: 718-438-6381. Sr. Margaret Mary; Rev. Msgr. Austin P. Bennett, Dir. Confraternity of the Precious Blood; Rev. Msgr. Philip J. Reilly, Chap. Sisters 16.

Monastery of the Visitation, 8902 Ridge Blvd., 11209. Tel: 718-745-5151; Fax: 718-680-4441. Sr. Marie de Chantal Mannino, V.H.M., Supr. Professed Sisters 19.

Motherhouse and Convent of the Sisters of Mercy of the Americas, Brooklyn Regional Community, 273 Willoughby Ave., 11205-1487. Tel: 718-622-5840; Fax: 718-398-7866.
E-mail: brooklynmercy@aol.com
Sr. Camille D'Arienzo, R.S.M., Pres. Sisters 27.

Sisters of the Good Shepherd, 348 Ninth St., 11215. Tel: 718-499-9212; Fax: 718-369-1691. Sisters 2. Provincial Office, 82-31 Doncaster Pl., Jamaica, 11432. Tel: 718-380-3270; Fax: 718-591-9376. Carol Beristo, Prov. Off.

JAMAICA. *Provincialate of the Sisters of the Good Shepherd*, 82-31 Doncaster Pl., 11432. Tel: 718-380-3270; Fax: 718-591-9376.
E-mail: hhayes2085@aol.com
Web site: goodshepherdsistersna.com
Legal Title: *Sisters of the Good Shepherd, Province of New York*. Sr. Helene Hayes, R.G.S.; Zenovia Jackson, Prov. Sec. Sisters 4.

Ursuline Provincial Administration Office, Glengarda, 81-15 Utopia Pkwy., 11432. Tel: 718-591-0681; Fax: 718-969-4275.
Web site: http//tressy.tripod.com
Sr. Catherine Talia, O.S.U., Prov. Supr.

QUEENS VILLAGE. *Little Sisters of the Poor*, Provincial Residence, 110-30 221st St., 11429. Tel: 718-464-1800; Fax: 718-468-5132. Mother Genevieve Regina, L.S.P., Prov. Sisters 165.

St. Ann's Novitiate, Little Sisters of the Poor, 110-39 Springfield Blvd., P.O. Box 280356, 11428. Tel: 718-464-4920; Fax: 718-479-3126. Sr. Mary Richard, L.S.P., Supr. & Mistress of Novices; Rev. James Pereda, C.R.C., Chap. Sisters 6; Novices 5; Postulants 5.

REGO PARK. *Blessed Trinity Missionary Cenacle*, 85-10 61 Rd., 11374. Tel: 718-424-7563; Fax: 718-507-6867. Parish Social Ministry, Ministry to the Handicapped, Elderly, Bereaved and Homebound. Missionary Servants of the Most Blessed Trinity 5.

RIDGEWOOD. *Convent of the Sisters of Mary Reparatrix*, 62-67 60 Pl., 11385. Tel: 718-456-4242: 386-1107 (Altar Bread Department); Fax: 718-386-2254.
E-mail: smmy@worldnet.att.net
Web site: http//smrny.home.att.net
Sr. Patricia Mullen, S.M.R., Supr. Sisters 6.

ROCKAWAY PARK. *Stella Maris Convent, Sisters of St. Joseph*, 11694-2497. Tel: 718-634-1886. Sisters 11.

[X] EVANGELIZATION AND RENEWAL CENTERS

BROOKLYN. *Centro Evangelizacion San Vicente de Paul*, 118 Congress St., 11201. Tel: 718-624-5670; Fax: 718-624-5806.
E-mail: cesvip@aol.com
Revs. Victor Rodriguez, C.M. (Chile), Dir. & Dir. Cursillo Movement; Javier Antonio Serra, C.M. (Spain), Dir. Jornada Movement.

ASTORIA. *St. Paul Center*, 21-35 Crescent St., 11105. Tel: 718-932-0752; Fax: 718-721-9391. Rev. James Fitzpatrick, Dir.
Staff: Mrs. Carolyn Conides; Mr. Phil Crivelli; Mrs. Carmela Crivelli; Deacon Len Sclafani; Ms. Maureen Powers, Sec. Center for Lay Spirituality; American Cursillo in English; Christian Awakening.

FLUSHING. *Cenacle Center for Spiritual Renewal*, 154-27 Horace Harding Expwy., 11367. Tel: 718-463-2073; Fax: 718-353-3514.
E-mail: centflushing @juno.com
Web site: www.cenaclesisters.org
Sr. Mary Guido, p.c., Coord.

JAMAICA. *Bishop Molloy Retreat House for Laymen*, 86-45 Edgerton Blvd., 11432. Tel: 718-739-1229; Fax: 718-739-3421.
Web site: www.bishopmolloy.org
Passionist Fathers. Rev. James Price, C.P., Retreat Dir. Associates: Revs. Michael Greene, C.P.; Xavier Hayes, C.P.; Sr. Maria Regina Loures, I.H.M.

[Y] SECULAR INSTITUTES

BROOKLYN. *The Institute of Apostolic Oblates*, 730 E. 87th St., 11236. Tel: 718-649-0324; Fax: 718-272-5012.
E-mail: apostolicoblates@prodigy.net
Giovanna Piccioli, Local Mod.

FOREST HILLS. *Asociacion Misioneros Contemplativos Laicos*. (Lay Association of Contemplative Missionaries), 72-81 113th St., Apt. 5A, 11375. Antonio Alvarez, Pres.; Isabelle Echverri, Vice Pres.; Amparo Aponte, Sec.; Trinidad Smith, Treas.

[Z] MISCELLANEOUS LISTINGS

BROOKLYN. *Alive in Hope Foundation of the Diocese of Brooklyn*, 310 Prospect Park West, 11215. Tel: 718-965-7300. Rev. Msgr. John J. Bracken, Dir.

Casa Betsaida-Home for people with AIDS, 267 Hewew St., 11211. Tel: 718-218-8262; Fax: 718-218-8264.
E-mail: mreyescb@aol.com
Dr. Francisco Quinteros.

En El, Inc., 75 Greene Ave., 11238.

Franciscan Brothers Charitable Trust, 135 Remsen St., 11201. Tel: 718-858-8217; Fax: 718-858-8306. Trustees: Richard T. Arkwright; Edwin Gill; Robert Schaefer.

Franciscan Sisters of the Poor Charitable Trust, 133 Remsen St., 11201. Tel: 718-643-1919; Fax: 718-643-9710. Sr. Jeanne M. Glisky, S.F.P., Contact Person.

Good Shepherd Volunteers, Saint Germaines Services, 235 Prospect Park W., 11215. Tel: 718-768-8452. Sr. Maureen McGowan, R.G.S., Dir.

HeartShare Human Services of NY - Clermont Residence, 26 Clermont Ave., 11205. Tel: 718-834-9317; Fax: 718-834-9364. Miss Sharon Bewry, Res. Mgr. Residence for Developmentally Disabled Adults.

Jornada Movement, 118 Congress St., 11201. Tel: 718-624-5670; Fax: 718-624-5806.
E-mail: jornadista@aol.com
Web site: www.catholic_church.org/jornada
Rev. Javier Antonio Serra, C.M. (Spain), Dir.

Latvian Roman Catholic Mission. (Our Lady of Aglona Center), 361 Highland Blvd., 11207. Rev. Msgr. Leons Varna, S.T.D., Dir.

Mercy Montessori School, 1397 Brooklyn Ave., 11203. Tel: 718-469-2834. Sr. Mary Harvey, R.S.M., Dir.

National Center of the Haitian Apostolate, 455 E. 29th St., 11226. Tel: 718-856-3323; Fax: 718-703-0980.
E-mail: haitiapost.com
Rev. Guy Sansaricq, Exec. Dir.

Neighbors Together, 160 Thomas S. Boyland St., P.O. Box 330-562, 11233. Tel: 718-498-7256. Anne Kohler, Exec. Dir. Services for the Poor. Soup Kitchen and Social Services Advocacy.

New Horizons Adult Education Program, Inc., St. John's Center, 75 Lewis Ave., 11206. Tel: 718-455-1166; 455-1033; Fax: 718-452-3047.

Pro Sanctity Movement, 730 E. 87th St., 11236. Tel: 718-649-0324; Fax: 718-272-5012.
E-mail: apostolicoblates@prodigy.net
Web site: www.prosanctitate.org
Ms. Rosemary Darmstadt, Dir.; Rev. John J. Costello, Spiritual Advisor.

The Roman Catholic Pontifical Lay Association Memores Domini, 218 76 St., 11209. Tel: 718-833-3992; Fax: 718-833-7374.

Men's House, 218 76 St., 11209. Tel: 718-833-3992; Fax: 718-833-7374. Christopher G. Bacich, Head of the House.

Women's House, 5757 Faraday Ave., Riverdale, 10471. Tel: 718-601-2349. Elvira Parravicini, Head of the House.

St. James Cathedral Foundation, Inc., 250 Cathedral Pl., 11201. Tel: 718-852-4002; Fax: 718-852-9452. Rev. Msgr. John C. Tosi, Sec.

St. John's Bread & Life Program, Inc. (Soup Kitchen, Employment Counseling, HIV/AIDS Support Group/ Food Pantry, Counseling, Referrals and Advocacy), 75 Lewis Ave., 11206. Tel: 718-574-0058. Mr. Hossein Saadat, M.S.A., Exec. Dir.; Sr. Bernadette Szyhczak, D.C., Soup Kitchen Coord.

Society of the Immaculate Conception of Brooklyn. (Missionary Society), 191 Joralemon St., 11201-4306. Tel: 718-875-4375, Ext. 743; Fax: 718-875-2702. Rev. John F. Brogan, Exec. Dir.

The Maura Clarke Ita Ford Center, 138 Bleecker St., 11221. Tel: 718-452-0167; Fax: 718-452-5173.
E-mail: mcifcenter@aol.com
Co-Directors: Sr. Mary Burns, S.C.; Sr. Mary Dowd, O.S.U.; Sr. Judy Fay, C.S.J.

ASTORIA. *Flowers With Care Youth Services, Diocese of Brooklyn, Inc.*, 23-40 Astoria Blvd., 11102. Tel: 718-726-9790. Paula Beltrone, Exec. Dir.

BAYSIDE. *Ozanam Geriatric Foundation*, 42-41 201 St., 11361. Tel: 718-971-2200; Fax: 718-971-2290.
E-mail: gedonova@chcn.org

BRENTWOOD. *Congregation of the Sisters of St. Joseph*, Charitable Trust, Brentwood Rd., 11717-5587. Tel: 516-273-1187; Fax: 516-273-1345.
E-mail: jlarkin33@aol.com
Sr. Joan Larkin, Treas.

DOUGLASTON. *The Futures in Education Foundation, Inc.*, 7200 Douglaston Pkwy., 11362. Tel: 718-229-8001. Ms. Jean O'Shea, Exec. Sec.

FLORAL PARK. *Glencara, Inc.*, 82-15 259th St., 11001. Tel: 718-470-6759. Sr. Sean Foley, R.S.M., Pres.; Sr. Kathleen Quinn, R.S.M., Vice Pres.; Sr. Regina Shelley, R.S.M., Sec.; Sr. Francene Horan, R.S.M., Treas.

FLUSHING.

Women Helping Women, P.O. Box 580086, 11358-0086. Tel: 718-539-9111; Fax: 718-961-3322.
E-mail: whwcol@aol.com

JAMAICA. *Global Women's Exchange*, 82-31 Doncasper Pl., 11432. Tel: 718-380-3270; Fax: 718-591-9376.
E-mail: glbwmex@aol.com

Mary Immaculate, Inc., 88-25 153rd St., 11432. Tel: 718-558-6900.

Vincentian Service Corps.-East Inc., Saint John's University - Annex, 11439. Tel: 718-990-6266; Fax: 718-990-8939.
E-mail: vsceast@stjohns.edu
Web site: vscorps.org
A program for laywomen and men willing to commit to one year of service to the poor. Mr. Paul K. Cavanaugh, M.S.W., Dir.

LONG ISLAND CITY. *Hour Children*, 36-11A 12th St., 11106. Tel: 718-443-4724; Fax: 718-729-6398.
E-mail: hour.children@worldnet.att.net
Sr. Teresa Fitzgerald, C.S.J., Exec. Dir.

World Compassion Link. Mailing Address: P.O. Box 4279, 11104-9808. 48-49 37th St., 11101. Tel: 718-433-2894; Fax: 718-433-2190. Revs. Noel P. O'Meara, C.S.Sp., Pres.; Patrick Doody, C.S.Sp., Vice Pres.; Michael J. McCarthy, C.S.Sp., Treas.; James Delaney, C.S.Sp., Dir. Development.

QUEENS. *Focolare Movement*. Queens Office, 6359 83rd St., Middle Village, 11379. Tel: 718-898-2611.

RELIGIOUS INSTITUTES OF MEN REPRESENTED IN THE DIOCESE

For further details refer to the corresponding bracketed number in the Religious Institutes of Men or Women section.

[0140]—*The Augustinians*.—O.S.A.
[1350]—*Brothers of St. Francis Xavier*. (Sacred Heart Prov.).—C.F.X.
[0330]—*Brothers of the Christian Schools*.—F.S.C.
[0600]—*Brothers of the Congregation of Holy Cross*.—C.S.C.
[1100]—*Brothers of the Sacred Heart*.—S.C.
[0470]—*The Capuchin Friars*. (Prov. of St. Mary).—O.F.M.Cap.
[0270]—*Carmelite Fathers & Brothers*. (St. Elias Prov.).—O.Carm.
[1330]—*Congregation of the Mission*. (Eastern, New England, Spanish Provs.).—C.M.
[1210]—*Congregation of the Missionaries of St. Charles*.—C.S.
[1000]—*Congregation of the Passion*. (Prov. of St. Paul of the Cross).—C.P.
[0480]—*Conventual Franciscans*. (Polish Prov.).—O.F.M.Conv.
[0490]—*Franciscan Brothers of Brooklyn*.—O.S.F.

[0520]—*Franciscan Friars.* (Immaculate Conception Prov.; Lithuanian Vicariate).—O.F.M.
[0650]—*Holy Ghost Fathers.*—C.S.Sp.
[0690]—*Jesuit Fathers and Brothers.* (New York Prov.).—S.J.
[]—*Little Brothers of the Gospel.*—L.B.G.
[0770]—*The Marist Brothers.*—F.M.S.
[0780]—*The Marist Fathers.*—S.M.
[0870]—*Montfort Missionaries (Missionaries of the Company of Mary).*—S.M.M.
[0950]—*Oratorians.* (Brooklyn).—C.O.
[1030]—*Paulist Fathers.*—C.S.P.
[0610]—*Priests of the Congregation of Holy Cross.* (Eastern Prov.).—C.S.C.
[1070]—*The Redemptorists.*—C.SS.R.
[0760]—*Society of Mary (Marianists).* (New York Prov.).—S.M.
[0370]—*Society of St. Columban.*—S.S.C.
[0990]—*Society of the Catholic Apostolate.*—S.A.C.
[1200]—*Society of the Divine Savior.*—S.D.S.

RELIGIOUS INSTITUTES OF WOMEN REPRESENTED IN THE DIOCESE

[]—*Altagracia Sisters.* (Dominican Republic).
[0340]—*Carmelite Sisters of Charity.*—C.Ch.
[0330]—*Carmelite Sisters of the Aged and Infirm.*—O.Carm.
[2980]—*Congregation of Notre Dame.*—C.N.D.
[2950]—*Congregation of Notre Dame de Sion.*—N.D.S.
[]—*Congregation of Olivetan Benedictine Sisters.* (Korea).
[]—*Congregation of Our Lady of Sion.*
[3110]—*Congregation of Our Lady of the Retreat in the Cenacle.*—R.C.
[2230]—*Congregation of the Infant Jesus.*—C.I.J.
[0760]—*Daughters of Charity of St. Vincent de Paul.*—D.C.
[0960]—*Daughters of Wisdom.*—D.W.
[1070-01]—*Dominican Sisters.*—O.P.
[1070-02]—*Dominican Sisters.*—O.P.
[1070-05]—*Dominican Sisters.*—O.P.
[1070-06]—*Dominican Sisters.*—O.P.
[1070-11]—*Dominican Sisters.*—O.P.
[1400]—*Franciscan Missionary Sisters of the Sacred Heart.*—F.M.S.C.
[1180]—*Franciscan Sisters of Allegany, NY.*—O.S.F.
[1425]—*Franciscan Sisters of Peace.*—F.S.P.
[1420]—*Franciscan Sisters of Ringwood.*—F.S.R.
[1470]—*Franciscan Sisters of St. Joseph.*—F.S.S.J.
[1190]—*Franciscan Sisters of the Atonement.*—S.A.
[]—*Franciscan Sisters of the Immaculate (Honduras).*—H.F.I.
[1440]—*Franciscan Sisters of the Poor.*—S.F.P.
[1840]—*Grey Nuns of the Sacred Heart.*—G.N.S.H.
[]—*Little Sisters of the Gospel.* (France).—L.S.G.
[2340]—*Little Sisters of the Poor.*—L.S.P.
[2420]—*Marist Missionary Sisters (Missionary Sisters of the Society of Mary) Inc.*—S.M.S.M.
[2470]—*Maryknoll Sisters of St Dominic.*—M.M.
[2710]—*Missionaries of Charity.*—M.C.
[2860]—*Missionaries of the Sacred Heart.*—M.S.C.
[1360]—*Missionary Franciscan Sisters of the Immaculate Conception.*—O.S.F.
[2790]—*Missionary Servants of the Most Blessed Trinity.*—M.S.B.T.
[3160]—*Parish Visitors of Mary Immaculate.*—P.V.M.I.
[2070]—*Religious of the Holy Union of the Sacred Hearts.*—S.U.S.C.
[3465]—*Religious of the Sacred Heart of Mary.*—R.S.H.M.
[3430]—*Religious Teachers Filippini.*—M.P.F.
[2970]—*School Sisters of Notre Dame.* (Wilton, CT; Baltimore, MD).—S.S.N.D.
[0110]—*Sisters Adorers of the Precious Blood.*—A.P.B.
[0650]—*Sisters of Charity of St. Vincent de Paul of New York.*—S.C.
[0640]—*Sisters of Charity of St. Vincent de Paul, Halifax.*—S.C.
[0430]—*Sisters of Charity of the Blessed Virgin Mary.*—B.V.M.
[1000]—*Sisters of Divine Providence of Kentucky.*—C.D.P.
[2575]—*Sisters of Mercy of the Americas.* (Brooklyn, NY; Dallas, TX).—R.S.M.
[3000]—*Sisters of Notre Dame de Namur.*—S.N.D.deN.
[2670]—*Sisters of Our Lady of Mercy.*—S.O.L.M.
[3820]—*Sisters of St. John the Baptist.*—C.S.J.B.
[3830-05]—*Sisters of St. Joseph.*—C.S.J.
[3140]—*Sisters of the Catholic Apostolate-Pallottine.*—C.S.A.C.
[3180]—*Sisters of the Cross and Passion.*—C.P.
[1830]—*Sisters of the Good Shepherd.*—R.G.S.
[1970]—*Sisters of the Holy Family of Nazareth.* (Immaculate Heart of Mary Prov.).—C.S.F.N.
[3320]—*Sisters of the Presentation of the B.V.M.* (Newburgh).—P.B.V.M.
[2160]—*Sisters, Servants of the Immaculate Heart of Mary.*—I.H.M.
[2460]—*Society of Mary Reparatrix.*—S.M.R.
[4070]—*Society of the Sacred Heart.*—R.S.C.J.
[4130]—*Ursuline Sisters of the Congregation of Tildonk, Belgium.*—O.S.U.
[4190]—*Visitation Nuns.*—V.H.M.

DIOCESAN CEMETERIES

BROOKLYN. *Holy Cross*, Brooklyn & Tilden Ave., 11203. Rev. Msgr. Anthony J. Barretta, Chap.
FARMINGDALE. *Resurrection*, Conklin St., 11735. Tel: 516-249-8700.
St. Charles, Conklin St., 11735. Tel: 516-249-8700. Rev. Msgr. August C. Bednartz, Chap.
FLUSHING. *Mount St. Mary*, 172-00 Booth Memorial Ave., 11365. Tel: 718-353-1560. Rev. Romano Zanon, Chap.
MIDDLE VILLAGE. *St. John's*. Administration Offices for the Diocesan Cemeteries. 80-01 Metropolitan Ave., 11379. Tel: 718-894-4888. Rev. Ralph Guarracino, Chap.

PARISH CEMETERIES

AMITYVILLE. *Most Holy Trinity*. Most Holy Trinity Parish, Brooklyn.
Trinity. Most Holy Trinity Parish, Brooklyn.
ROCKAWAY. *St. Mary Star of the Sea*, Rockaway Blvd., 11691. Tel: 718-894-4888.

NECROLOGY

† Bihler, Joseph J., (Retired). —Died Feb. 28, 2000.
† Brennan, Edward C., Douglaston, NY Immaculate Conception Center. —Died Jan. 19, 2000.
† Cavanagh, Rev. Msgr. James M., Brooklyn, NY Our Lady of Angels. —Died June 21, 2000.
† Colbert, Joseph, Glendale, NY St. Pancras. —Died Oct. 10, 2000.
† Diviney, Rev. Msgr. Charles E., Brooklyn, NY St. Charles Borromeo. —Died June 28, 2000.
† Dore, Dennis W., Rosedale, NY St. Pius X. —Died Dec. 5, 2000.
† Hannon, Michael G., Whitestone, NY St. Luke. —Died Jan.19, 2000.
† Hunt, Michael J., Brooklyn, NY St. Frances de Chantal. —Died Nov. 4, 2000.
† McGuirk, Raymond A., Brooklyn, NY Holy Innocents. —Died Nov. 30, 2000.
† McNelis, Patrick J., Babylon, NY Immaculate Heart of Mary. —Died Oct. 19, 2000.
† O'Sullivan, John J., Babylon, NY St. Joseph. —Died Oct. 29, 2000.
† Oravecz, John, Woodburg, NY Holy Name of Jesus. —Died March 22, 2000.
† Pakalniskis, John L., Brooklyn, NY Annunciation. —Died June 26, 2000.
† Privitera, Rev. Msgr. Santi J., Brooklyn, NY St. Bernadette. —Died Sept. 4, 2000.
† Seeger, Francis J., Flushing, NY Holy Family. —Died Jan. 25, 2000.
† Stonebridge, John H., Glendale, NY Sacred Heart. —Died June 13, 2000.
† Wildgruber, Francis C., Syosset, NY St. Edward the Confessor. —Died April 30, 2000.

Diocese of Brownsville

(Dioecesis Brownsvillensis)

Most Reverend

RAYMUNDO J. PENA, D.D.

Bishop of Brownsville; ordained May 25, 1957; appointed Titular Bishop of Trisipa and Auxiliary of San Antonio October 16, 1976; consecrated December 13, 1976; appointed Bishop of El Paso April 29, 1980; installed June 18, 1980; appointed Bishop of Brownsville May 23, 1995; installed August 6, 1995. *Mailing Address: P.O. Box 2279, Brownsville, TX, 78522-2279.*

Most Reverend

JOHN J. FITZPATRICK, D.D.

Retired Bishop of Brownsville; ordained December 13, 1942; appointed Auxiliary of Miami June 24, 1968; consecrated August 28, 1968; appointed Bishop of Brownsville April 27, 1971; installed May 27, 1971; retired November 30, 1991. *Mailing Address: P.O. Box 2279, Brownsville, TX, 78522-2279.*

ESTABLISHED JULY 10, 1965.

Square Miles 4,226.

Comprises the four Counties of Cameron, Hidalgo, Starr and Willacy in the State of Texas.

For legal titles of parishes and diocesan institutions, consult the Catholic Pastoral Center.

Catholic Pastoral Center: 1910 E. Elizabeth St., P.O. Box 2279, Brownsville, TX, 78522-2279. Tel.: 956-542-2501; Fax: 956-542-6751.

Web site address: www.cdob.org

E-mail address: cdob@cdob.org

STATISTICAL OVERVIEW

Personnel	
Bishop	1
Retired Bishops	1
Priests: Diocesan Active in Diocese	44
Priests: Active Outside Diocese	5
Priests: Retired, Sick or Absent	9
Number of Diocesan Priests	58
Religious Priests in Diocese	38
Extern Priests in Diocese	9
Ordinations:	
Diocesan Priests	3
Transitional Deacons	1
Permanent Deacons in Diocese	81
Total Brothers	14
Total Sisters	127
Parishes	
Parishes	64
With Resident Pastor:	
Resident Diocesan Priests	33
Resident Religious Priests	22
Without Resident Pastor:	
Administered by Priests	9
Missions	43
Pastoral Centers	1
New Parishes Created	1
Professional Ministry Personnel:	
Brothers	5
Sisters	33
Lay Ministers	133
Welfare	
Health Care Centers	1
Total Assisted	111
Homes for the Aged	2
Total Assisted	250
Day Care and Extended Day Care Centers	2
Total Assisted	175
Special Centers for Social Services	4
Total Assisted	33,591
Other Institutions	2
Total Assisted	3,078
Educational	
Diocesan Students in Other Seminaries	22
Total Seminarians	22
High Schools, Private	2
Total Students	721
Elementary Schools, Diocesan and Parish	7
Total Students	2,278
Elementary Schools, Private	2
Total Students	683
Catechesis/Religious Education:	
High School Students	7,836
Elementary Students	28,665
Total Students Under Catholic Instruction	40,205
Teachers in the Diocese:	
Priests	3
Brothers	6
Sisters	15
Lay Teachers	381
Vital Statistics	
Receptions into the Church:	
Infant Baptism Totals	4,393
Adult Baptism Totals	4,095
Received into Full Communion	368
First Communions	6,569
Confirmations	3,023
Marriages:	
Catholic	918
Interfaith	109
Total Marriages	1,027
Deaths	2,321
Total Catholic Population	799,217
Total Population	940,255

Former Prelates—Rt. Rev. DOMINIC MANUCY, Titular Bishop of Delma and Vicar Apostolic of Brownsville; cons. Dec. 8, 1874; transferred to Mobile, March 9, 1884; reappointed to Vicariate Apostolic of Brownsville, Feb. 1, 1885; died Dec. 4, 1885.—Rt. Rev. PETER VERDAGUER, Titular Bishop of Aulon and Vicar Apostolic of Brownsville; cons. Nov. 9, 1890; died Oct. 26, 1911.—Rt. Rev. CLAUDE JAILLET, O.P., Administrator of Vicariate Apostolic of Brownsville, 1911-1913.

Former Bishops—Most Rev. ADOLPH MARX, D.D., J.C.D., First Bishop of Brownsville; ord. May 2, 1940; appt. Titular Bishop of Citrus and Auxiliary Bishop of Corpus Christi, July 6, 1956; cons. Oct. 9, 1956; appt. first Bishop of Brownsville, July 19, 1965; installed Sept. 2, 1965; died in Cologne, Germany Nov. 1, 1965.—His Eminence HUMBERTO CARDINAL MEDEIROS, D.D., second Bishop of Brownsville; appt. April 14, 1966; cons. June 9, 1966; installed Bishop of Brownsville, June 29, 1966; appt. Archbishop of Boston, Sept. 8, 1970; installed Archbishop of Boston, Oct. 7, 1970; created Cardinal, March 5, 1973; died Sept. 17, 1983.—Most Rev. JOHN J. FITZPATRICK, D.D., third Bishop of Brownsville; ord. Dec 13, 1942; appt. Auxiliary Bishop of Miami, June 24, 1968; cons. Aug. 28, 1968; appt. Bishop of Brownsville, April 27, 1971; installed May 27, 1971; retired Nov. 30, 1991.—Most Rev. ENRIQUE SAN PEDRO, S.J., S.T.D., S.S.L., fourth Bishop of Brownsville; ord. March 18, 1957; appt. Auxiliary Bishop of Galveston-Houston April 1, 1986; cons. June 29, 1986; appt. Coadjutor of Brownsville, Aug. 13, 1991; installed Sept. 26, 1991; succeeded to the See, Nov. 30, 1991; died July 17, 1994.

Office of the Bishop—Most Rev. RAYMUNDO J. PENA, *1910 E. Elizabeth St., P.O. Box 2279, Brownsville, 78522-2279.* Tel: 956-550-1510; Fax: 956-550-1565. Rev. RODOLFO FRANCO, Administrative Asst. & Master of Ceremonies. Tel: 956-550-1576. Mrs. INA L. PEREZ, Exec. Sec., Assistant Secretaries: Mrs. ALEJANDRA TREVINO, Miss ANGELA CRUZ, (part-time).

Bishop Emeritus—Most Rev. JOHN J. FITZPATRICK, *St. Mary, Mother of the Church, 1914 Barnard Rd., Brownsville, 78520-8247.* Tel: 956-546-3800.

Vicar General—Rev. GEORGE E. HARRIS, V.G., Office: *1910 E. Elizabeth St., P.O. Box 2279, Brownsville, 78522-2279.* Tel: 956-550-1546; Fax: 956-542-6751., Parish: *121 Garrison, San Benito, 78586.* Tel: 956-399-8929. Vacant, Sec.

Deans—Rev. GUSTAVO BARERRA, Brownsville. Tel: 956-546-3800. Rev. HEBERTO M. DIAZ, JR., Harlingen. Tel: 956-423-4670. Rev. GERARD BARRETT, O.M.I., McAllen. Tel: 956-783-1196. Rev. ROBERT E. MAHER, Mission. Tel: 956-383-3728. Rev. HUGO VAN DE BUSSHE, O.M.I., Rio Grande City. Tel: 956-487-2317. Rev. RUBEN DELGADO, Weslaco. Tel: 956-968-2691.

Development Office—Mr. JESSE SALINAS, Dir.; Vacant, Sec., *1910 E. Elizabeth St., P.O. Box 2279, Brownsville, 78522-2279;* Fax: 956-542-6751.

Stewardship Office—Vacant, Dir.

Tribunal—*1910 E. Elizabeth St., P.O. Box 2279, Brownsville, 78522-2279.* Tel: 956-550-1512; Fax: 956-542-6751.

Judicial Vicar—Rev. LUIS JAVIER GARCIA, J.C.L.

Notary—Mrs. SYLVIA W. GARCIA.

Secretary—Mrs. GRISELDA RAMOS. Tel: 956-550-1512.

Assistant Secretary—Mrs. ARACELI S. RANGEL. Tel: 956-550-1516.

Procurators and Advocates—Sr. MARY DOLORES DOYLE, C.C.V.I. Tel: 956-550-1515. Bro. FRANCIS J. GARZA, F.M.S.; Mr. JAIME GOMEZ; Mrs. ANN WILLIAM CASS.

Court Expert—Ms. LITA ORTIZ.

Judges—Most Rev. JOHN J. FITZPATRICK; Revs. MICHAEL ANUNZIATO, SS.CC.; HERMAN DEFLER, M.S.F.; THOMAS KULLECK.

Defenders of the Bond—Revs. F. ROBERT DAVOLA; GUSTAVO BARRERA.

Office of the Chancellor—*1910 E. Elizabeth St., P.O. Box 2279, Brownsville, 78522-2279.* Tel: 956-550-1528; Fax: 956-542-6751. Rev. IVAN M. ROVIRA, Chancellor, Ms. CLARA M. MARTINEZ, Vice-Chancellor, Rev. THOMAS G. KULLECK, Historical Archivist. Tel: 956-550-1526. Mrs. NATIVIDAD R. HINOJOSA, Sec. Tel: 956-550-1528. Miss CLAUDIA MONTEMAYOR, Office Clerk. Tel: 956-550-1517. Mrs. MELISSA SALINAS, Receptionist. Tel: 956-542-2501.

Moderator of the Curia—Rev. IVAN M. ROVIRA, *1910 E. Elizabeth St., P.O. Box 2279, Brownsville, 78522-2279.* Tel: 956-550-1528; Fax: 956-542-6751. Rev. LUIS JAVIER GARCIA, J.C.L., Assoc. Moderator of the Curia; Mrs. NATIVIDAD R. HINOJOSA, Sec.

Secretariat for the Diocesan Synod—Mr. LUIS ZUNIGA, Gen. Sec., Mrs. IRMA CANTU, Sec.; Rev. CARLOS ZUNIGA, Clergy Liaison, *P.O. Box 116, La Feria, 78559.* Tel: 956-797-2666., *1910 E. Elizabeth St., P.O. Box 2279, Brownsville, 78522-2279.* Tel: 956-550-1519; Fax: 956-542-6751.

Diocesan Relations—*1910 E. Elizabeth St., P.O. Box 2279, Brownsville, 78522-2279.* Tel: 956-550-1541; Fax: 956-542-6751. Mrs. BRENDA NETTLES RIOJAS, Dir., Mrs. JUANITA URBANO, Sec.

Fiscal Office—*1910 E. Elizabeth St., P.O. Box 2279, Brownsville, 78522-2279.* Tel: 956-550-1538; Fax: 956-550-1563. Mr. ROLANDO MARTINEZ.

Accountant—Mr. RUBEN OLIVARES.

Accounting Clerk—Ms. GERTRUDIS "TRUDY" CONTRERAS.

Parish/School Accounting—Auditors: Ms. MARY GUAJARDO. Tel: 956-550-1532. Mrs. SOCORRO PADILLA. Tel: 956-550-1547. Mrs. SARA SALAS, Clerk. Tel: 956-550-1533.

Information Systems—*1910 E. Elizabeth St., P.O. Box 2279, Brownsville, 78522-2279.* Tel: 956-542-2501; Fax: 956-550-1585., *700 N. Virgen de San Juan Blvd., San Juan, 78589.* Tel: 956-784-5011; Fax: 956-784-5097. Mr. JESSE CANDANOZA, Dir., Mr. DAVID KOWALSKI, Asst. Tel: 956-550-1521. Technicians: Mr. OSCAR SALINA. Tel: 956-784-5004. Mr. JUAN C. RODRIGUEZ. Tel: 956-784-5003. Mr. ROBERT SALAZAR. Tel: 956-784-5002.

Human Resources Office—*1910 E. Elizabeth St., P.O. Box 2279, Brownsville, 78522-2279.* Tel: 956-550-1544; Fax: 956-542-6751. Mrs. GENOVEVA TREVINO, Dir., Mr. ABEL OBREGON, Safety Office, Mrs. MINDY GONZALEZ, Sec.

Insurance and Pensions—*1910 E. Elizabeth St., P.O. Box 2279, Brownsville, 78522-2279.* Tel: 956-550-1549; Fax: 956-542-6751. Ms. JUDY PLATA, Dir., Mrs. PATRICIA GOMEZ, Sec./Asst. Tel: 956-550-1549. Mrs. CELIA TORRES, Clerk. Tel: 956-550-1557.

Building/Property/Construction Management—*700 N. Virgen de San Juan Blvd., San Juan, 78589.* Tel: 956-782-1728; Fax: 956-782-0418. Mr. GEORGE MENDOZA, Dir.; Mr. JOSE R. GUERRERO, Asst. Dir.; Mr. GUSTAVO A. MORENO, Asst.; Ms. YESENIA TORRE, Sec.

Episcopal Vicar for the Clergy—Rev. Msgr. PATRICK DOHERTY, *555 W. St. Francis, Brownsville, 78520.* Tel: 956-542-2706; Fax: 956-546-5162. St. John Vianney Retirement Home for Priests.

Office for Vocations—*1910 E. Elizabeth St., P.O. Box 2279, Brownsville, 78522-2279.* Tel: 956-550-1576; Fax: 956-542-6751. Rev. RODOLFO FRANCO, Dir., Sr. NINFA GARZA, M.J., Asst. Tel: 956-533-1812. Miss ANGELA CRUZ, Sec.

Office for Seminarians—*1910 E. Elizabeth St., P.O. Box 2279, Brownsville, 78522-2279.* Tel: 956-544-1528; Fax: 956-542-6751. Rev. IVAN M. ROVIRA, Dir., Mrs. NATIVIDAD HINOJOSA, Sec.

Office for Permanent Deacons—*600 S. Oklahoma Ave., Weslaco, 78596.* Tel: 956-968-7471; Fax: 956-969-3040. Rev. JOSE LUIS GARCIA, Dir.

Episcopal Vicar for Communications—Rev. PEDRO BRISENO, *P.O. Box 2147, Harlingen, 78551.* Tel: 956-421-4111; Fax: 956-421-4150.

Episcopal Vicar for Evangelization—Rev. JUAN NICOLAU, *400 Virgen de San Juan Blvd., San Juan, 78589.* Tel: 956-787-0033; Fax: 956-787-2908. Mr. ENRIQUE DE LA CRUZ, Asst.; Ms. MARY CANALES, Sec.

Episopal Vicar for Religious—Rev. LOUIS BRUM, *P.O. Box 1159, Alamo, 78516.* Tel: 956-787-2963; Fax: 956-787-6788. Sr. NORMA PIMENTEL, M.J. Tel: 956-542-2180.

Division for Youth and Young Adult Ministry—

Episcopal Vicar—Rev. FRANCISCO ACOSTA. Tel: 956-541-9697; Fax: 956-504-2615., *UTB/TSC Campus, 1860 Ridgely Rd., Brownsville, 78520., UTPA Campus, 1615 W. Khun St., Edinburg, 78539.* Mrs. LINDA DE LOS SANTOS, Exec. Sec.; Miss MARIA G. AVILA, Sec. Tel: 956-383-0133. Miss ANABEL CASTILLO, Office Clerk.

Campus Minister - Brownsville—Mrs. HILDA ESCANDON; Ms. ELIZABETH PAREDES, Asst., *UTB/TSC Campus, 1850 Ridgely Rd., Brownsville, Tx, 78520.* Tel: 956-542-3942; Fax: 956-542-3942.

Campus Minister - Edinburg—Mr. HILARIO "LARRY" MOLINA, JR.; Mrs. MARIA G. AVILA, Sec., *UTPA Campus, 1615 Kuhn St., Edinburg, 78539.* Tel: 956-383-0133; Fax: 956-387-0738.

Youth Ministry—*UTB/TSC Campus, 1860 Ridgely Rd., Brownsville, 78520.* Tel: 956-541-9697; Fax: 956-504-2615. Sr. ANGELICA HUERTA, M.J.

Young Adult Ministry—Vacant, Dir.

Division for Catholic Charities—

Moderator—Sr. CECILIA CASAS, R.S.M., *700 N. Virgen de San Juan Blvd., San Juan, 78589.* Tel: 956-702-4088; Fax: 956-784-5099.

Diocesan Campaign for Human Development—Rev. CRAIG CAROLAN, *412 South C St., Harlingen, 78550.* Tel: 956-423-0855.

Diocesan Catholic Relief Services—Rev. BERT DIAZ, *1313 W. Buchanan St., Harlingen, 78550.* Tel: 956-423-4670.

Catholic Social Services—*700 N. Virgen de San Juan Blvd., San Juan, 78589.* Tel: 956-702-4088; Fax: 956-784-5099. Vacant, Dir.; Deacon RICARDO AYALA, JR., Counselor. Tel: 956-702-4088. Mr. EDDIE SANCHEZ, Case Worker. Tel: 956-784-5068. Ms. ABBY TORRE, Sec. Tel: 956-784-5067., *47 W. Elizabeth St., Brownsville, 78520.* Tel: 956-541-0220. Mr. LOUIS GEORGE, Counselor, Ms. IRMA VASQUEZ, Case Worker; Mrs. ENELDA MATA, Sec.

Jail Ministry—*P.O. Box 2282, 47 W. Elizabeth St., Brownsville, 78520.* Tel: 956-541-0220; Fax: 956-544-7580., *700 N. Virgen de San Juan Blvd., San Juan, 78589;* Fax: 956-784-5099. Sr. JULIANA GARCIA, M.J., Dir. Chaplains: Rev. LIONEL LOPEZ, *1108 Hackberry Ave., McAllen, 78501.* Tel: 956-686-0251. Rev. JOSE VILLALON, *2355 E. Tyler, Brownsville, 78520.* Tel: 956-546-6975. Mr. JAIME GOMEZ, *P.O. Box 2282, 47 W. Elizabeth St., Brownsville, 78520.* Tel: 956-541-0220.

Immigration Office—*700 N. Virgen de San Juan Blvd., San Juan, 78589.* Tel: 956-784-5022; Fax: 956-784-5099. Mr. A. MARCO GARCIA, Dir., Mrs. SANTA ACUNA, Sec. Tel: 956-787-8571.

Division for Education and Formation—Tel: 956-787-8571.

Moderator—Sr. MARCELLA EWERS, D.C., *700 N. Virgen de San Juan Blvd., San Juan, 78589-3042.* Sr. CHARLES ANNE SOLOMON, O.P., Asst. Moderator. Tel: 956-784-5052.

Media Resource/Library Coordinator—Sr. MAUREEN CROSBY, S.S.D. Tel: 956-784-5041.

Teacher of Religion for Adults—Ms. GRACE MACKINNON. Tel: 956-784-5042.

Office Manager—Mrs. OFELIA MARTINEZ. Tel: 956-784-5010.

Secretaries—Mrs. OLGA GARZA. Tel: 956-784-5013. Mrs. EDNA GARCIA. Tel: 956-784-5012. Mrs. ANA ESTRADA. Tel: 956-784-5011.

Catholic Schools Office—*700 N. Virgen de San Juan Blvd., San Juan, 78589-3042.* Tel: 956-784-5050. Sr. MARCELLA EWERS, D.C., Supt., Sr. CHARLES ANNE SOLOMON, O.P., Counselor; Ms. CONNIE LEACH, Admin. Asst. Tel: 956-784-5051.

Family Life Office—*700 N. Virgen de San Juan Blvd., San Juan, 78589-3042.* Tel: 956-784-5030. Mrs. LYDIA PESINA, Dir., Vacant, Assoc. Dir.; Mrs. WILLY KOPECKY, Natural Family Planning, *1012 W. Third, Weslaco, 78596.* Tel: 956-969-3079.

Office of Catechesis—*700 N. Virgen de San Juan Blvd., San Juan, 78589-3042.* Tel: 956-784-5040. Sr. MARGUERITE BRODERICK, D.C., Dir., Deacon VICENTE MORENO, Assoc. Tel: 956-784-5054.

Division for Health Care Ministries—

Moderator—Sr. BARBARA ARNESEN, C.N.D., *700 N. Virgen de San Juan Blvd., San Juan, 78589.* Tel: 956-784-4088; Fax: 956-784-5099.

Director for Pro-Life Activities—*P.O. Box 216, Progreso, 78579.* Tel: 956-565-6856. Rev. MATTHEW KREMPLE, O.F.M.

Hospital Chaplains—Sr. BARBARA ARNESEN, C.N.D., Dir., *700 N. Virgen de San Juan Blvd., San Juan, 78589.* Tel: 956-702-4088.

Brownsville Medical Center—Sr. GLORIA MORALES, M.J., *1040 W. Jefferson, Brownsville, 78520.* Tel: 956-544-1426.

Edinburg Regional Medical Center—Sr. EMMA MARIE STILLMAN, I.W.B.S., *P.O. Box 2000, Edinburg, 78589.* Tel: 956-388-6235; Fax: 956-388-6020.

Knapp Medical Center—Rev. GEORGE GONZALEZ, *P.O. Box 1110, Weslaco, 78599.* Tel: 956-968-8567; Fax: 956-968-6290.

McAllen Medical Center—Sr. EBERE ANOSIKE, D.D.L., *301 W. Exwy. 83, McAllen, 78503.* Tel: 956-632-4177; Fax: 956-632-4010.

McAllen Heart Hospital—Sr. THERESE ANNE RIDGE, I.W.B.S., *1900 S. D St., McAllen, 78503.* Tel: 956-994-2107; Fax: 956-994-2052.

Mission Hospital—Ms. JUDY KRESE, *900 S. Bryan Rd., Mission, 78572.* Tel: 956-584-4562; Fax: 956-580-9430.

Rio Grande Regional Hospital—Sr. HELEN ROPER, S.S.N.D., *101 E. Ridge, McAllen, 78503.* Tel: 956-632-6616; Fax: 956-632-6621.

Star Co. Memorial Hospital—Sr. ANNE MIRIAM LANDOLT, S.S.N.D., *P.O. Box 78, Rio Grande City, 78582.* Tel: 956-487-5561, Ext. 2296.

Valley Baptist Medical Center—Chaplains: Rev. FRANK CLANCY, S.C.J.; Sr. ROSALY SAVARIMUTHU, C.I.C.; Deacon IGNACIO R. GONZALES, *2101 Peace, Harlingen, 78550.* Tel: 956-389-1194; Fax: 956-389-1189.

Valley Regional Medical Center—Dr. ETHEL WINCHESTER DIDSBURY, Chap., *P.O. Box 5107, Brownsville, 78520.* Tel: 956-350-7124.

Diocesan Attorney—Mr. DAVID GARZA, *680 E. St. Charles, Brownsville, 78520.* Tel: 956-541-4914; Fax: 956-542-7403.

Presbyteral Council—Revs. AMADOR GARZA, Catholic Charities Commission; GERALD FRANK, Communications Commission; PEDRO BRISENO, O.F.M., Education & Formation Commission; IVAN M. ROVIRA, Evangelization Commission; GEORGE E. HARRIS, V.G., Health Care Commission; SAMUEL ARIZPE, Justice & Peace Commission; JUAN NICOLAU, Marriage & Family Life Commission; RODOLFO FRANCO, Basilica of the National Shrine of Our Lady of San Juan del Valle Commission; PHILIP SOSA, M.S.F., Parish Needs Commission; IGNACIO LUNA, Clergy Life & Ministry; LEE DACOSTA, Vocations & Seminarians; CARLOS GARZA, Liturgy & Worship Commission; CRAIG CAROLAN, Youth & Young Adult Ministry.

Diocesan College of Consultors—Revs. PEDRO BRISENO; GEORGE E. HARRIS, V.G.; IGNACIO LUNA; JUAN NICOLAU; IVAN M. ROVIRA; PHILIP SOSA, M.S.F.

Parish Priests' Consultors & Priest Personnel Board—Revs. GUSTAVO BARRERA; F. ROBERT DAVOLA; HEBERTO M. DIAZ, JR.; GEORGE E. HARRIS, V.G.; IGNACIO LUNA.

Diocesan Finance Council—Most Rev. RAYMUNDO J. PENA; Mr. NOBLE ALLEN; Mr. ALONZO CANTU; Mr. CHARLES ELLARD; Mr. H. HUGH EMERSON; Mr. MATT GORGES; Mr. MICHAEL POWERS; Rev. IVAN M. ROVIRA.

Encuentro Matrimonial—ALFONSO GONZALEZ; MINNIE GONZALEZ, *Rte. 3, Box 6095, Harlingen, 78552.* Tel: 956-428-4625.

Engaged Encounter—JOE AGUILAR; DELIA AGUILAR, *608 W. 7th St., Weslaco, 78596.* Tel: 956-969-3556.

Boy Scouts—Rev. CRAIG G. CAROLAN, *412 S. "C" St., Harlingen, 78550.* Tel: 956-423-0855; Fax: 956-421-1071.

Marriage Encounter—JESSIE ROBLES; TERRY ROBLES, *1642 Hamilton, Harlingen, 78550.* Tel: 956-425-6827.

Movimiento Familiar Cristiano—JOSE HORACIO; REYES FUENTES, *Rt. 6, Box 250, McAllen, 78501.* Tel: 956-968-8330. ABEL CRUZ; TENA CRUZ, *108 Sunset Dr., Brownsville, 78520.* Tel: 956-546-8127; Fax: 956-541-3212.

Catholic Foundation of the Rio Grande Valley—Mr. ROY DE LEON; Mr. RICHARD WALKER; Mr. LUIS CORTINAS; Ms. GRACIELA GUTIERREZ; Rev. IVAN M. ROVIRA, *P.O. Box 2279, Brownsville, 78522-2279.* Tel: 956-542-2501; Fax: 956-542-6751.

Building Committee—Mr. JOSE A. CHANIN; Mr. OSCAR FALCON; Mr. CESAR R. PEREZ.

The Basilica of the National Shrine of Our Lady of San Juan Del Valle—

Board of Directors—Most Rev. RAYMUNDO J. PENA; Mr. RICHARD ALANIZ; Judge ROBERTO GARZA; Mr. JORGE MEDINA; Mr. LOUIE TIJERINA; Mr. BENITO MARTINEZ, Consultant.

Housing Board—Mr. RICARDO HERNANDEZ; Mr. ROBERT VELA; Mrs. ANITA A. RODRIGUEZ; Mrs. ANA ZAMARRIPA, Mgr., *El Rosario Homes, P.O. Box 971, Mission, 78572.* Tel: 956-585-5051., *La Merced Homes, P.O. Box 806, Mercedes, 78570.* Tel: 956-565-2622.

Propagation of the Faith—Rev. IVAN M. ROVIRA, *P.O. Box 2279, Brownsville, 78522-2279.* Tel: 956-550-1528.

Serra Club International—Brownsville: Dr. RUBEN GALLEGOS, *5220 Wilderness Dr., Brownsville, 78520.* Tel: 956-504-3365. Rev. RODOLFO FRANCO, Chap., *1910 E. Elizabeth St., Brownsville, 78522-2279.* Tel: 956-542-2501. McAllen: Mr. ISRAEL SAGREDO, Pres., *P.O. Box 9021, Mission, 78572.* Tel: 956-581-2733; Fax: 956-581-2253. Rev. IVAN ROVIRA, Chap., *1910 E. Elizabeth St., Brownsville, 78520.* Tel: 956-542-2501. Rio Grande City: Dr. ANTONIO E. GARCIA, *District Governor of Serra Clubs, 2016 Heron, McAllen, 78504.* Tel: 956-618-3626. Mrs. SYLVIA HINOJOSA, Pres., *Rio Grande Serra Club, P.O. Box 149, Grulla, 78548-0149.* Tel: 956-487-0026. Sr. NINFA GARZA, M.J., Liaison, *P.O. Box 2279, Brownsville, 78520.* Tel: 956-550-1576. Harlingen: Mr. JESSE GALLEGOS, Pres., *2806 Swiss Pine Court, Harlingen, 78550.* Rev. CRAIG CAROLAN, Chap., *412 South C St., Harlingen, 78550.* Tel: 956-423-0855.

Knights of Columbus—Mr. TOMMY GOMEZ, Diocesan Deputy East, *143 Shoreline Dr., Brownsville, 78521.* Tel: 956-546-3887. Mr. ABEL PORRAS, Diocesan Deputy West, *101 Valle St., Rio Grande City, 78582.* Tel: 956-487-5074.

CLERGY, PARISHES, MISSIONS AND PAROCHIAL SCHOOLS

CITY OF BROWNSVILLE
(Cameron County)

1—IMMACULATE CONCEPTION CATHEDRAL (1849), Revs. Richard Sheehan, O.M.I.; Pasquale Lanese, O.M.I.; Deacons John Kinch; Arturo Rodriguez.
Res., 1218 E. Jefferson St., P.O. Box 311, 78522. Tel: 956-546-3178; Fax: 956-546-1284.
Missions—Brownsville, Cameron Co., St. Thomas, 155 E. Jefferson St., 78520; Brownsville, Cameron Co., Sacred Heart, 602 E. Elizabeth St., 78520.
Chapel—La Muralla, D St., 78520.

2—CHRIST THE KING (1953), Revs. Alfonso M. Guevara; Theo Nlandu, C.I.C.M.; Deacon Felipe Trevino.
2255 Southmost Rd., 78521. Tel: 956-546-1982; Fax: 956-546-7120.
Mission—Brownsville, Cameron Co., Blessed Juan Diego de Guadalupe, Valle Escondido, 78521.

3—CHURCH OF THE GOOD SHEPHERD (1968), Revs. Horacio Chavarria; Carlos Alberto Villareal; Deacon Paul McArdle.
Res., 2645 Tulipan, 78521. Tel: 956-542-5142; Fax: 956-542-5278.

4—HOLY FAMILY (1966), Rev. Jose M. Villalon; Deacon Alejandro Flores.
Res., 2308 E. Tyler, 78520. Tel: 956-546-6975; Fax: 956-550-8884.

5—OUR LADY OF GOOD COUNSEL (1966), Rev. Larry Klein; Deacons Enrique Saldana; Alvino C. Olvera.
1055 Military Hwy., 78520. Tel: 956-541-8341; Fax: 956-548-0229.
Mission—San Pedro, San Pedro.

6—OUR LADY OF GUADALUPE (1928), Rev. Honecimo Figueroa; Deacons Jose Guerra; Ramon Leal.
Res., 1200 E. Lincoln St., 78521. Tel: 956-542-4823; Fax: 956-542-5944.

7—ST. EUGENE DE MAZENOD (1996), Rev. Harry Schuckenbrock, O.M.I.; Deacon Bruno Cedillo.
Res., 5409 Austin Rd., 78251. Tel: 956-831-9923; Fax: 956-831-3110.

8—ST. JOSEPH (1953), Rev. Msgr. Patrick J. Doherty.
Res., 555 W. St. Francis St., 78520. Tel: 956-542-2709; Fax: 956-546-5162.

9—ST. LUKE (1974), Rev. Juan Victor Heredia; Deacon Juan Pablo Navarro.
Res., 2800 Rockwell Dr., 78521. Tel: 956-541-1480; Fax: 956-542-8043.
School—2850 Price Rd., 78521. Tel: 956-544-7982; Fax: 956-544-4874. Dr. Christina Saavedra, Prin.
Lay Teachers 17; Students 248.

10—SAINT MARY, MOTHER OF THE CHURCH (1967), Revs. Gustavo Barrera; Tom Kulleck; Deacons Gilbert Borja; Roberto Cano; Heriberto Solis; Heriberto Trevino. In res., Most Rev. John J. Fitzpatrick, (Retired).
Res., 1914 Barnard Rd., 78520-8247. Tel: 956-546-3800; Fax: 956-546-1589.
School—1300 Los Ebanos Blvd., 78520. Tel: 956-546-1805; Fax: 956-546-0787. Mr. Juan Barreda, Prin.
Religious 3; Lay Teachers 28; Students 612.

11—SAN FELIPE DE JESUS (1996), Rev. Michael Seifert, S.M.; Bro. Albert Phillipp, F.M.S., Pastoral Assoc.
P.O. Box 8093, 78526-8093.
Res., 2215 Avenida Rancho Viejo, 78521. Tel: 956-982-2007; Fax: 956-541-4177.

OUTSIDE THE CITY OF BROWNSVILLE

Alamo, Hidalgo Co., Resurrection (1926). (Formerly St. Joseph/Our Lady of Fatima). Rev. Louis L. Brum; Deacon Jesus P. Galvan.
Res., 834 E. Citrus St., P.O. Box 1159, 78516. Tel: 956-787-2963; Fax: 956-787-6788.

Alton, Hidalgo Co., San Martin de Porres (1967), Rev. Albert Lelo-Luemba, C.I.C.M.
Res., 1111 W. Main St., P.O. Box 9023, Mission, 78572. Tel: 956-585-8001; Fax: 956-585-0715.

Donna, Hidalgo Co., St. Joseph (1928), Revs. Herman J. Defler, M.S.F.; Philip Sosa, M.S.F.; Deacon Eduardo Ovalle, Sr.
Res., 306 S. D Salinas Blvd., 78537. Tel: 956-464-3331; Fax: 956-464-6808.
Mission—Colonia Nueva, Christ the King.

Edcouch, Hidalgo Co., St. Theresa of the Infant Jesus (1948), Rev. Gregory M. Kuczmanski; Deacon Alvin H. Gerbermann.
Res., 200 P. Salazar, P.O. Box 307, 78538. Tel: 956-262-1347; Fax: 956-262-1348.
Mission—La Villa, Our Lady of Guadalupe.

Edinburg, Hidalgo Co., Holy Family (1967), Rev. Esteban Hernandez, M.S.F.; Deacon Ruben Lopez.
Res., 1302 E. Champion, 78539-4864. Tel: 956-383-5472; 383-4593; Fax: 956-383-5034.

Sacred Heart (1927), Revs. Michael Annunziato, SS.CC.; Richard Czerwien, SS.CC.; Deacons Jose Solis; Gilberto Lopez. In res., Rev. Fredrick Meyer, SS.CC.
Res., 215 N. 16th Ave., 78539. Tel: 956-383-3253.
Mission—Lull, Capilla de San Jose.

St. Joseph (1948), Rev. Robert E. Maher; Deacons Silvestre Garcia; Irineo Gonzalez, Jr.
Res., 122 W. Fay St., 78539. Tel: 956-383-3728; Fax: 956-383-8630.
School—119 W. Fay St., 78539. Tel: 956-383-3957. Sr. Kathleen Murray, D.C., Prin.
Religious 1; Lay Teachers 14; Students 193.

Elsa, Hidalgo Co., Sacred Heart (1948), Rev. Emmanuel Bialoncik, O.F.M.
Res., 1100 N. Broadway, P.O. Box 6, 78543. Tel: 956-262-1406; Fax: 956-262-4265.
Mission—Monte Alto, Hidalgo Co., Christ the King, Holy Cross Catechetical Center, Mile 15, Monte Alto, 78538.

Escobares, Starr Co., Sacred Heart (1967), Rev. Alfonso G. Torres.
Res., P.O. Box 1180, Roma, 78584. Tel: 956-849-1741; Fax: 956-849-4589.
Missions—Rosita, Santa Rosa de Lima; El Sauz, Our Lady of Guadalupe.

Grulla, Starr Co., Holy Family (1967), Rev. Isaac Emeka Erondu; Deacons Benito Saenz; Rodolfo Carlos Salinas.
Res., P.O. Box 67, 78548. Tel: 956-487-3365; Fax: 956-487-4727.
Missions—Cristo Rey, La Victoria; La Casita, Our Lady of the Peace.

Harlingen, Cameron Co.,

1—OUR LADY OF THE ASSUMPTION, (1958), Rev. Heberto M. Diaz, Jr.; Deacons Ignacio Gonzales; Jesus Reyes.
1313 W. Buchanan St., 78550. Tel: 956-423-4670; Fax: 956-423-5970.
Mission—San Felipe, Austin Co., Rangerville Rd., San Felipe, 77473.

2—IMMACULATE HEART OF MARY, (1927), Revs. Craig G. Carolan; Jerome Felion, (Retired); Basil Onyia; Deacon Abel Castillo.
Res., 412 S. C St., 78550. Tel: 956-423-0855; Fax: 956-421-1071.

3—QUEEN OF PEACE, (1967), Revs. Matthias Shanley, SS.CC.; Alphonsus McHugh, SS.CC.; Deacon Juan Valenzuela.
Res., 1509 New Combes Hwy., 78550. Tel: 956-423-6341; Fax: 956-423-2864.

4—ST. ANTHONY, (1940), Rev. Thomas L. Pincelli.
Res., 209 S. 10th, 78550. Tel: 956-428-6111; Fax: 956-428-4276.
School—1015 E. Harrison St., 78550. Tel: 956-423-2486; Fax: 956-412-0084. Ms. Johna Hays, Prin.
Lay Teachers 18; Students 261.

Hidalgo, Hidalgo Co., Sacred Heart (1967), Rev. Joseph Bukase, C.I.C.M.
Res., 308 E. Camelia St., P.O. Box 742, 78557. Tel: 956-843-2463; Fax: 956-843-2463.

La Feria, Cameron Co., St. Francis Xavier (1930), Rev. Carlos Zuniga.
Res., 500 S. Canal St., P.O. Box 116, 78559. Tel: 956-797-2666; Fax: 956-797-3387.

La Joya, Hidalgo Co., Our Lady, Queen of Angels (1960), Revs. Plutarco Belanggoy, C.I.C.M.; Charles Phukuta, C.I.C.M.; Donatus Ironuma; Deacons Alberto Chapa; Lucio Flores.
Res., P.O. Drawer D, 78560. Tel: 956-585-5223; Fax: 956-585-4878.
Missions—Abram, St. Mary Magdalene; Penitas, St. Anthony; Los Ebanos, St. Michael; Sullivan City, St. William.

Los Fresnos, Cameron Co., St. Cecilia (1964), Rev. Carlos Garza; Deacon Augusto Chapa, Jr.
Res., 606 W. Ocean Blvd., 78586. Tel: 956-233-5619; Fax: 956-233-5565.
Mission—Olmito, Our Heavenly Father.

Lyford, Willacy Co., Prince of Peace (1967), Revs. David Jackson, S.C.J.; Richard MacDonald, S.C.J.
Res., 1100 Park Ave., P.O. Box 460, 78569. Tel: 956-347-3580; Fax: 956-347-3649.
Missions—Santa Monica, Santa Monica; Sebastian, Willacy Co., St. Martin, Box 247, Sebastian, 78594.

McAllen, Hidalgo Co.,

1—OUR LADY OF PERPETUAL HELP, (1967), Revs. Francisco Acosta; Mario Alberto Castro; Deacon Rene Villalon, Sr., S.F.O.
Res., 2209 Kendlewood Ave., 78501. Tel: 956-682-4238; Fax: 956-682-0289.

2—OUR LADY OF SORROWS, (1941), Rev. Agostinho S. Pacheco; Deacons John Schwarz; Israel Sagredo. In res., Rev. Lionel Lopez.
Res., 1108 Hackberry St., 78501-4304. Tel: 956-686-0251; Fax: 956-686-0322.
School—1100 Gumwood, 78501. Tel: 956-686-3651; Fax: 956-686-0324. Mrs. Jeanne L. Bruton, Prin. & Dir. of Day Care.
Religious 1; Lay Teachers 28; Students 566.
Day Care—.

3—SACRED HEART, (1917), Revs. James Pfeifer, O.M.I.; Henry Janssen, O.M.I.; Deacon Eduardo Reyna.
Res., 306 S. 15th St., P.O. Box 370, 78505-0370. Tel: 956-686-7711; Fax: 956-686-2028.

4—ST. JOSEPH THE WORKER, (1967), Revs. Bart A. Flaat, C.I.C.M.; Ramel Portula, C.I.C.M.; Deacons Alejandro Gamboa; Salvador Rojas.
Res., 2315 Ithaca St., 78501. Tel: 956-682-1351; Fax: 956-618-3317.

5—HOLY SPIRIT, (1981), Rev. Gerald W. Frank; Deacons Lorenzo Contreras, Jr.; Carlos S. Trevino.
Res., 2201 Martin Ave., 78504. Tel: 956-631-5295; Fax: 956-631-5460.
Preschool & Day Care Center—Tel: 956-682-6562. Mrs. Toni F. Espinoza, Dir.

McCook, Hidalgo Co., Immaculate Conception (1950), Rev. Willy Verboomen, C.I.C.M.
Rte. 3, Box 188-E, Edinburg, 78539. Tel: 956-842-3663.

Mercedes, Hidalgo Co., Our Lady of Mercy (1909), Rev. Armando Escobedo; Deacon Juan Trevino.
Res., 322 S. Vermont Ave., 78570. Tel: 956-565-1141; Fax: 956-565-1640.

Sacred Heart Church (1969), Rev. Rafael Hernandez; Deacon Roberto Cantu.
Res., 920 Anacuitas, 78570. Tel: 956-565-0271; Fax: 956-565-0272.

Mission, Hidalgo Co.,

1—OUR LADY OF GUADALUPE, (1899), Revs. Roy Lee Snipes, O.M.I.; Timothy Paulsen, O.M.I.; Deacons Ricardo Ayala, Jr.; Bill Castaneda.
Res., 620 Dunlap St., P.O. Box 1047, 78572-1047. Tel: 956-585-2623; Fax: 956-584-5856. [CEM]
Chapel—La Lomita.

2—OUR LADY OF THE HOLY ROSARY, (1968), Rev. Vicente Azcoiti.
Res., 923 Matamoros St., P.O. Box 1439, 78572. Tel: 956-581-2193; Fax: 956-581-1906.
Missions—Madero, Our Lady of Lourdes; Granjeno, Our Lady of Fatima.

3—OUR LADY OF ST. JOHN OF THE FIELDS, (1967), Rev. Francisco Castillo; Deacons Daniel Zamora; Peter Requenez.
Res., 1052 Washington St., 78572. Tel: 956-585-2325; Fax: 956-585-8179.

4—ST. PAUL, (1915), Rev. F. Robert DaVola; Deacon Ismael Garcia.
Res., 1119 Francisco Ave., 78572. Tel: 956-585-2701; Fax: 956-581-4801.

Pharr, Hidalgo Co.,

1—ST. ANNE, MOTHER OF MARY, (1973), Rev. Gerry Shanley, SS.CC.; Deacon Jose R. Castro.
Res., 710 E. Lucas, 78577. Tel: 956-787-8122; Fax: 956-787-8272.

2—ST. FRANCES XAVIER CABRINI, (1999), Rev. Eduardo Villa.
P.O. Box 8538, Hidalgo, 78557-8538. Tel: 956-787-3554; Fax: 956-787-2686.

3—ST. JUDE THADDEUS, (1951), Very Rev. Leo Francis Daniels, C.O.; Revs. Jose Encarnacion Losoya, C.O.; Mario Alberto Aviles, C.O.
Res., 505 S. Ironwood, P.O. Drawer J, 78577-1210. Tel: 956-781-2489; Fax: 956-783-4614.
School—Oratory Academy, P.O. Drawer ii, 78577. Tel: 956-781-3056; Fax: 956-702-3047. Mrs. G. Yvonne Perez, Dir.
Religious 3; Lay Teachers 24; Students 442.

4—ST. MARGARET MARY, (1927), Rev. James Brown; Deacon Pedro F. Sanchez.
Res., 122 W. Hawk Ave., 78577. Tel: 956-787-8563; Fax: 956-702-4509.

Port Isabel, Cameron Co., Our Lady Star of the Sea (1927), Revs. Joseph J. O'Brien, O.M.I.; Jack Franko, O.M.I.
Res., 705 S. Longoria St., Box 6504, 78578. Tel: 956-943-1297; Fax: 956-943-1422.

Progreso, Hidalgo Co., Holy Spirit (1969), Rev. Matthew Krempel, O.F.M.
Res., P.O. Box 216, 78579. Tel: 956-565-6856; Fax: 956-565-3462.
Missions—Santa Maria, St. Margaret Ann; Bluetown, Cristo Rey.

Ranchito, Cameron Co., St. Ignatius (1967), Rev. Pedro Briseno.
24380 W. U.S. Hwy. 281, San Benito, 78586. Tel: 956-399-2022; Fax: 956-399-1213.
Missions—La Paloma, Our Lady of Lourdes; Las Rucias, Sacred Heart.

Raymondville, Willacy Co., Our Lady of Guadalupe (1927), Revs. Richard J. MacDonald, S.C.J.; Steve Pujdak, S.C.J.; Gregory M. Speck, S.C.J.; Deacon Juan Francisco Gonzalez.
Res., 693 N. Third St., 78580. Tel: 956-689-2408; Fax: 956-689-3151.
Missions—La Sara, St. Patrick; Hargill, St. Frances Xavier Cabrini.

St. Anthony (1907), Rev. Gabriel Ezeh.
Res., 464 S. First St., 78580. Tel: 956-689-3380; Fax: 956-689-3380.
Mission—San Perlita, St. Anne, Mother of Mary.

Rio Grande City, Starr Co., Immaculate Conception (1880), Revs. Amador Garza; Faustin Boleli, C.I.C.M.
Res., P.O. Box 1, 101 E. Third St., 78582. Tel: 956-487-2317; Fax: 956-487-8246. [CEM]
School—305 N. Britton Ave., 78582. Tel: 956-487-2558; Fax: 956-487-6478. Mr. Robert Schmidt, Prin.
Religious 2; Lay Teachers 26; Students 248.
Missions—La Puerta, St. Paul; Los Garcias Ranch, Sacred Heart. Deacon Benito Saenz.

Rio Hondo, Cameron Co., St. Helen (1943), Rev. Terrence Gorski, O.F.M.; Deacon Genaro Ibarra.
Res., 228 Huisache, P.O. Box 451, 78583. Tel: 956-748-2327; Fax: 956-748-0089.
Mission—Lozano, St. Vincent de Paul.

Roma, Starr Co., Our Lady of Refuge (1853), Rev. Hugo Van den Bussche, O.M.I.
Res., P.O. Box 156, 78584. Tel: 956-849-1455; Fax: 956-849-2257.
Missions—Falcon Heights, Holy Trinity; Salineno, St. Joseph; Los Saenz, Holy Family; Fronton, Lamb of God.

San Benito, Cameron Co., Our Lady, Queen of the Universe (1960), Rev. George Harris, V.G.; Deacon Andres Munoz.
Res., 121 Garrison Dr., 78586. Tel: 956-399-2865; Fax: 956-399-2045.
Mission—San Benito, St. Joseph, 1001 W. Hwy. 77, 78586.

St. Benedict (1912), Rev. Ignacio Luna; Deacons Manuel Sanchez; Margarito Briones.
Res., 351 S. Bowie, P.O. Box 950, 78586. Tel: 956-399-2353; Fax: 956-399-5701.

St. Theresa (1954), Rev. Patrick K. Seitz; Deacons Benito Flores; Gilberto Perez.
Res., 1300 Combes St., P.O. Box 1830, 78586. Tel: 956-399-3247; Fax: 956-399-0094.
St. Theresa Child Development—Tel: 956-361-0609; Fax: 956-399-0094. Mrs. Esmeralda Galvan, Dir.

San Carlos, Hidalgo Co., St. Joseph the Worker (1970), Rev. Samuel Arizpe; Deacon Hector Perez.
Res., Rte. 1, Box 202-E, Edinburg, 78539-9801. Tel: 956-383-5880; Fax: 956-383-0420.
Missions—San Manuel, St. Anne; Faysville, St. Theresa.

San Isidro, Starr Co., St. Isidore (1964), Rev. Willy Verboomen, C.I.C.M.
Rte. 1, Box 2, 78588. Tel: 956-481-3392; Fax: 956-481-3869.

San Juan, Hidalgo Co., The Basilica of the National Shrine of Our Lady of San Juan del Valle, Revs. Juan Nicolau, Rector; Genaro Henriquez; Luis J. Garcia, J.C.L.
Res., 400 Virgen de San Juan Blvd., 78589. Tel: 956-787-0033; Fax: 956-787-2908.

St. John the Baptist (1949), Rev. Gerard Barrett, O.M.I.; Deacons Agapito L. Cantu; Julio Castilleja. 216 W. First St., P.O. Box 1196, 78589. Tel: 956-783-1196; Fax: 956-702-7447.
Mission—Lopezville, Immaculate Conception.

Santa Rosa, Cameron Co., St. Mary (1967), Rev. Alfredo Garcia, SS.CC.
Res., 101 San Antonio Ave., P.O. Box 365, 78593. Tel: 956-636-1211.

Weslaco, Hidalgo Co., St. Joan of Arc (1929), Revs. Lee DaCosta; Jose Luis Garcia; Deacons Jesus Aguayo; Francisco Caballero.
Res., 109 S. Illinois Ave., 78596. Tel: 956-968-3670; Fax: 956-968-1872.

San Martin de Porres (1967), Revs. George Gonzales; Ruben Delgado; Deacons Juan Delgado; Jose G. Garza.
Res., 901 N. Texas Blvd., 78596. Tel: 956-969-2691; Fax: 956-968-1473.
School—905 N. Texas Blvd., 78596. Tel: 956-973-8642; Fax: 956-973-0522. Sr. Helen Rottier, C.S.J., Prin.
Missions—Weslaco, St. Jude Chapel; Expressway Heights, Nuestra Senora de Guadalupe.

St. Pius X (1955), Rev. Lee DaCosta.
Res., 600 S. Oklahoma Ave., 78596. Tel: 956-968-7471; Fax: 956-968-3040.

Chaplains of Public Institutions

BROWNSVILLE. *Brownsville Medical Center* 1040 W. Jefferson St., 78520. Tel: 956-544-1426, Ext. 26. Sr. Gloria Morales, M.J., Chap.
Brownsville Valley Regional Medical Center P.O. Box 5107, 78520. Tel: 956-350-7124. Dr. Ethel Winchester-Didsbury, Chap.
Cameron County Jail. Sr. Juliana Garcia, M.J., Chap., Mailing Address:47 W. Elizabeth St., 78521. Tel: 956-541-0220.
Ruben M. Torres I 47 W. Elizabeth St., 78521. Tel: 956-541-0220. Sr. Juliana Garcia, M.J., Dir.
Ruben M. Torres II 47 W. Elizabeth St., 78521. Tel: 956-541-0220. Sr. Juliana Garcia, M.J., Dir.

EDINBURG. *Boot Camp*. Sr. Juliana Garcia, M.J., Dir., 47 W. Elizabeth St., Brownsville, 78521. Tel: 956-541-0220.
Edinburg Regional Medical Center 1102 W. Trenton, 78539. Sr. Emma Marie Stillman, I.W.B.S., Chap. Coord.
Evins Rg. Juvenile Ctr. Sr. Juliana Garcia, M.J., Dir., 47 W. Elizabeth St., Brownsville, 78521. Tel: 956-541-0220.
Hidalgo County Jail. Sr. Juliana Garcia, M.J., Dir., 47 W. Elizabeth St., Brownsville, 78521. Tel: 956-541-0220.
La Villa. Sr. Juliana Garcia, M.J., Dir., 47 W. Elizabeth St., Brownsville, 78521. Tel: 956-541-0220.
Lopez. Sr. Juliana Garcia, M.J., Dir., 47 W. Elizabeth St., Brownsville, 78521. Tel: 956-541-0220.
Segovia Unit (State). Sr. Juliana Garcia, M.J., Dir., 47 W. Elizabeth St., Brownsville, 78521. Tel: 956-541-0220.

HARLINGEN. *Valley Baptist Medical Center* 2101 Pease St., 78550. Tel: 956-389-1194; Fax: 956-389-1189. Chaplains: Rev. Frank Clancy, S.C.J.; Sr. Rosaly Savarimuthu, C.I.C.; Deacon Ignacio R. Gonzalez, Chap. Asst.

LOS FRESNOS. *Bayview Detention Center* Buena Vista Rd., 78577. Tel: 956-541-0220. Sr. Juliana Garcia, M.J., Chap.; Rev. Carlos Garza, Chap.

MCALLEN. *McAllen Heart Hospital* 1900 S. "D" St., 78503. Tel: 956-994-2107; Fax: 956-994-2052. Sr. Therese Ann Ridge, I.W.B.S., Chap.
McAllen Medical Center 301 W. Exwy 83, 78503. Tel: 956-632-4177; Fax: 956-632-4010. Sr. Ebere Anisike, D.D.L.
Rio Grande Regional Hospital 101 E. Ridge Rd., 78501. Tel: 956-632-6616; Fax: 956-632-6621. Sr. Helen Roper, S.S.N.D., Chap.

MISSION. *Mission Hospital* 900 S. Byron Rd., 78572. Tel: 956-584-4562; Fax: 956-580-9430. Mrs. Judy Krese, Chap.

RAYMONDVILLE. *Wackenhut St. Corrections*. Sr. Juliana Garcia, M.J., Dir., 47 W. Elizabeth St., Brownsville, 78521. Tel: 956-541-0220.

RIO GRANDE CITY. *Memorial Hospital* P.O. Box 78, 78582. Tel: 956-487-5561. Sr. Anne Miriam Landolt, S.S.N.D, Chap.
Starr County Jail. Deacon R. C. Salinas, Chap., Mailing Address:304 N. East, 78582. Tel: 956-487-3112.

SAN BENITO. *Boot Camp*. Sr. Juliana Garcia, M.J., Dir., 47 W. Elizabeth St., Brownsville, 78521. Tel: 956-541-0220.
Darrell B. Hester Juvenile. Sr. Juliana Garcia, M.J., Dir., 47 W. Elizabeth St., Brownsville, 78521. Tel: 956-541-0220.

WESLACO. *Youth Village*. Sr. Juliana Garcia, M.J., Dir., 47 W. Elizabeth St., Brownsville, 78521. Tel: 956-541-0220.

On Assignment Outside the Diocese:
Reverend Fathers—
Mestas, Leonard J., St. Joseph the Worker Church, 10816 Mount View Ave., Loma Linda, CA 92354

Graduate Studies:
Reverend Fathers—
Garcia, Ricardo
Ortega, Eduardo

Retired:
Reverend Fathers—
Cabanas, R. Jaime, 2930 Emerald Lake Dr., Harlingen, TX 78550
Diaz, Robert, P.O. Box 2279, Brownsville, TX 78520-2279
Gomez, Frank, 5609 John Stockbauer, 8101, Victoria, TX 77904. Tel: 956-578-2376
Lambert, John C., 400 Virgen de San Juan Blvd., Edinburg, TX 78539. Tel: 956-383-4037
Mateos, Tomas, 400 N. Nebraska, San Juan, TX 78589
O'Malley, John A., P.O. Box 2576, San Juan, TX 78589. Tel: 956-783-1013
Ortiz, Benedicto, 2735 E. 31st St., Brownsville, TX 78521. Tel: 956-546-4510
Smith, Peter J., P.O. Box 570, Rhineback, NY 12572
Sweeney, Robert L., P.O. Box 994, San Juan, TX 78589. Tel: 956-782-4371

Permanent Deacons:
Aguayo, Jesus, St. Joan of Arc, Weslaco
Aiken, Bruce, (Retired)
Ayala, Ricardo, Jr., Catholic Social Services, San Juan
Barrera, Ernesto, (Retired)
Borja, Gilberto, St. Mary, Mother of the Church, Brownsville
Briones, Margarito, St. Benedict, San Benito
Caballero, Francisco, St. Joan of Arc, Weslaco
Cano, Roberto, St. Mary, Mother of the Church, Brownsville
Cantu, Agapito L., St. John the Baptist, San Juan
Cantu, Roberto, (On Leave of Absence)
Cardosa, Abraham, (Retired)
Castaneda, Bill, Our Lady of Guadalupe, Mission
Castilleja, Julio, St. John the Baptist, San Juan
Castillo, Abel, Immaculate Heart of Mary, Harlingen
Castro, Jose R., St. Anne, Mother of Mary, Pharr
Cedillo, Bruno, St. Eugene de Mazenod, Brownsville
Chapa, Alberto X., Our Lady, Queen of Angels, La Joya
Chapa, Augusto, Jr., St. Cecilia, Los Fresnos
Contreras, Lorenzo, Jr., Holy Spirit, McAllen
Crixell, Alfred V., Catholic Social Services, Brownsville
de la Cruz, Hugo, Sacred Heart, Elsa
Delgado, Juan, San Martin de Porres, Weslaco
Diaz, Inocencio, Holy Family, Edinburg
Eklund, Bruce, Albuquerque, NM
Flores, Alejandro, Holy Family, Brownsville
Flores, Benito, St. Theresa, San Benito
Flores, Julio, Jr., St. Anthony, Harlingen
Flores, Lucio, Our Lady, Queen of Angels, La Joya
Galvan, Jesus P., Resurrection, Alamo
Gamboa, Alejandro, St. Joseph the Worker, McAllen
Garcia, Ismael, St. Paul, Mission
Garcia, Silvestre, St. Joseph, Edinburg
Garza, Francisco, St. Luke, Brownsville
Garza, Jose G., San Martin de Porres, Weslaco
Gerbermann, Alvin H., St. Theresa of the Infant Jesus, Edcouch
Gonzales, Ignacio R., Our Lady of Assumption, Harlingen
Gonzalez, Irineo, Jr., St. Joseph, Edinburg
Gonzalez, Juan F., Our Lady of Guadalupe, Raymondville
Gonzalez, Leopoldo, Inactive
Grimaldo, Jose N., Inactive
Guerra, Jose, Our Lady of Guadalupe, Brownsville
Ibarra, Genaro, St. Helen, Rio Hondo
Jurado, Mariano, St. Joseph, Edinburg
Kinch, John, Immaculate Conception Cathedral, Brownsville
Leal, Ramon G., Our Lady of Guadalupe, Brownsville
Ledesma, Robert, St. Paul, Mission
Lopez, Albert C., Inactive
Lopez, Gilberto, Sacred Heart, Edinburg
Lopez, Ruben, Holy Family, Edinburg
McArdle, Paul, Good Shepherd, Brownsville
Munoz, Andres, St. Cecilia, Los Fresnos
Navarro, Juan Pablo, St. Luke, Brownsville
Oden, Luis, Inactive
Olvera, Alvino C., Our Lady of Good Counsel, Brownsville

Ovalle, Eduardo, Sr., St. Joseph, Donna
Perez, Gilberto, St. Theresa, San Benito
Perez, Hector, St. Joseph the Worker, San Carlos
Perez, Jose Oscar, (On Leave of Absence)
Requenez, Peter, Our Lady of St. John of the Fields, Mission
Reyes, Jesus H., Our Lady of Assumption, Harlington
Reyna, Eduardo, Sacred Heart, McAllen
Rodriguez, Arturo, Immaculate Conception Cathedral, Brownsville
Rojas, Salvador, St. Joseph the Worker, McAllen
Rousset, Louis, Inactive
Saenz, Benito, Jr., Holy Family, Grulla
Sagredo, Israel, Our Lady Of Sorrows, McAllen
Saldana, Enrique, Our Lady of Good Counsel, Brownsville
Saldivar, Salvador G., St. Ignatius, Ranchito
Salinas, Rodolfo C., Immaculate Conception, Rio Grande City
Sanchez, Manuel, St. Benedict, San Benito
Sanchez, Pedro F., St. Margaret Mary, Pharr
Schwarz, John, Our Lady of Sorrows, McAllen
Solis, Heriberto, St. Mary, Mother of the Church, Brownsville
Solis, Jose, Sacred Heart, Edinburg
Trevino, Carlos S., Holy Spirit, McAllen
Trevino, Felipe, Christ the King, Brownsville
Trevino, Heriberto, St. Mary, Mother of the Church, Brownsville
Trevino, Juan, Our Lady of Mercy, Mercedes
Valenzuela, Juan, Queen of Peace, Harlingen
Villalon, Rene, Sr., S.F.O., Our Lady of Perpetual Help, McAllen
Villarreal, Arturo, (Retired)
Webre, Alfred L., Jr., (Retired)
Zamora, Daniel, Our Lady of St. John of the Fields, Mission

INSTITUTIONS LOCATED IN THE DIOCESE

[A] HIGH SCHOOLS, PRIVATE

BROWNSVILLE. *St. Joseph Academy.* (Grades 7-12), 101 St. Joseph Dr., 78520. Tel: 956-542-3581. Bro. John Venturella, F.M.S., Prin. Marist Brothers, Esopus Province. Religious 2; Lay Teachers 55; Students 690.

[B] ELEMENTARY SCHOOLS, PRIVATE

BROWNSVILLE. *Guadalupe Academy*, 1200 E. Lincoln St., 78521. Tel: 956-986-0614.

Incarnate Word Academy Elementary and Middle School. (Convent Academy of the Incarnate Word), 244 Resaca Blvd., 78520. Tel: 956-546-4486. Sisters of the Incarnate Word and Blessed Sacrament. Sr. Teresita Rodriguez, I.W.B.S., Prin. (Elementary); Miss Christina Moreno, Prin. (Middle). Religious 3; Lay Teachers 21; Students 231.

PHARR. *Oratory Academy*, P.O. Drawer ii, 78577. Tel: 956-781-3056. Mrs. G. Yvonne Perez, Dir. Clergy 3; Lay Teachers 20; Students 426.

[C] CATHOLIC SOCIAL SERVICES

BROWNSVILLE. *Catholic Charities.* 700 N. Virgen de San Juan Blvd., San Juan, 78589. Tel: 956-702-4088. Legal Title: *Catholic Charities of the Diocese of Brownsville, a Texas Non-Profit Corporation.* Most Rev. Raymundo J. Pena, Chm.; Sr. Cecilia Casas, R.S.M., Mod.

Catholic Social Services, 47 W. Elizabeth St., 78520. Tel: 956-541-0220; 702-4088 (Dir.); Fax: 956-702-4042. Louis George, Counselor.

Jail Ministry, 47 W. Elizabeth St., 78520. Tel: 956-541-0220. Chaplains: Jaime Gomez; Revs. Lionel Lopez; Jose Villalon; Sr. Juliana Garcia, S.J.

SAN JUAN. *Catholic Social Services*, 700 Virgen de San Juan Blvd., P.O. Box 128, 78589. Tel: 956-702-4088; Fax: 956-702-4042. Deacon Ricardo Ayala, Jr., Family Counseling.

Immigration Office, 700 N. Virgen de San Juan Blvd., 78589. Tel: 956-784-5022. Marco Garcia, Dir.

Jail Ministry, 700 N. Virgen de San Juan Blvd., 78589. Tel: 956-784-5022. Sr. Juliana Garcia, M.J., Dir.

[D] HOMES FOR THE AGED

BROWNSVILLE. *Mother of Perpetual Help Nursing Home, Inc.*, 519 A East Madison St., 78520. Tel: 956-546-6745; Fax: 956-546-0711

For a complete listing, refer to the Special Care Facilities section.

SAN JUAN. *San Juan Hospice*, 300 Virgen de San Juan Blvd., P.O. Box 2359, 78589. Tel: 956-782-0333; 800-816-6625; Fax: 956-782-0335

For a complete listing, refer to the Special Care Facilities section.

San Juan Nursing Home, 300 Virgen de San Juan Blvd., P.O. Box 1238, 78589. Tel: 956-787-1771; Fax: 956-787-8091

For a complete listing, refer to the Special Care Facilities section.

[E] RESIDENCES FOR PRIESTS AND BROTHERS

BROWNSVILLE. *Congregation of Christian Brothers.* Our Lady of Guadalupe. 1200 E. Lincoln St., 78521. Tel: 956-540-6532. Brothers 1.

Marist Brothers, St. Joseph Academy, 101 St. Joseph Dr., 78520. Tel: 956-546-2608. Brothers 6.

HARLINGEN. *Priests of the Sacred Heart*, 144 W. Spencer Ct., 78550. Tel: 956-428-8344. Rev. Frank Clancy, S.C.J.

PHARR. *Oratory of St. Philip Neri, of Pontifical Right*, P.O. Box J, 78577-1235. Tel: 956-843-8217; Fax: 956-843-2946. Very Rev. Leo Francis Daniels, C.O., Provost; Revs. Jose Encarnacion Losoya, C.O., Sec. & Treas.; Mario Alberto Aviles, C.O.

RAYMONDVILLE. *Sacred Heart Fathers*, Rte. 2, Box 788, 78580. Tel: 956-689-6428. Priests 4; Brothers 1.

SAN BENITO. *Our Lady of Tenderness Fraternity, Inc.* (El Ranchito), Rte. 1, Box 159, 78586. Tel: 956-399-2552. In res. Bro. David Lopez, O.S.F.

[F] CONVENTS AND RESIDENCES FOR SISTERS

BROWNSVILLE. *Dominican Sisters of Charity of the Presentation*, 934 W. St. Charles St., 78520. Tel: 956-542-7225. Sisters 3.

Missionaries of Jesus, 1501 W. Adams, 78520. Tel: 956-542-2180. Sisters 10.

Sisters of the Incarnate Word and Blessed Sacrament, 535 W. St. Charles St., 78520. Tel: 956-544-2542; 546-8298. Sisters 3.

ALAMO. *Missionary Sisters of the Immaculate Heart of Mary*, Rte. 2, Box 133A, 78516. Tel: 956-702-2141.

EDINBURG. *Sisters of St. Joseph of Carondelet*, 502 W. Kuhn St., 78539. Tel: 956-383-6870. 2.

HARLINGEN. *Franciscan Sisters of Mary*, 3401 Business 83, #85, 78552-3517. Tel: 956-423-9447.

MISSION. *Misioneras Catequistas de los Pobres*, 615 Dunlap, 78572. Tel: 956-585-1376.

Sisters of St. Joseph of Carondelet, 1711 W. Gastel Cir., 78572-3037. Tel: 956-585-4870. Sisters 2.

PORT ISABEL. *Sisters of St. Francis*, 705 Manautau St., P.O. Box 6504, 78578. Tel: 956-943-2136.

RAYMONDVILLE. *Sisters of the Holy Cross*, Casa de la Luz, 317 S. King St., 78580-2307. Tel: 956-689-3059. Sisters 2.

RIO GRANDE CITY. *Benedictine Sisters of the Good Shepherd*, 6 Monastery Ln., 78582. Tel: 956-486-2680. Sisters 3.

[G] RETREAT HOUSES

SAN JUAN. *St. Eugene de Mazenod Christian Renewal Center*, P.O. Box 747, 78589. Tel: 956-787-0033.

[H] CAMPUS MINISTRY

BROWNSVILLE. *Young Adult Ministry / University of Texas at Brownsville-Texas Southmost College*, 1850 Ridgely Rd., 78520. Tel: 956-542-3942. Hilda Escandon, Campus Min.

EDINBURG. *University of Texas Pan American Campus at Edinburg / Young Adult Ministry*, 1615 W. Kuhn St., 78539. Tel: 956-383-0133. Mr. Hilario Molina, Jr., Campus Min.

[I] MISCELLANEOUS

BROWNSVILLE. *Bishop Enrique San Pedro, S.J. Ozanam Center*, 656 N. Minnesota Ave., 78521. Tel: 956-831-6331; Fax: 956-831-8577. Alejandro Fuentes, Dir.

Incarnate Word Project, 200 Resaca Blvd., 78520. Tel: 956-541-9533; Fax: 956-541-9533. E-mail: smlg627@aol.com Sr. Mary Lucy Garcia, I.W.B.S., Dir.

Society of St. Vincent De Paul District Council, 1304 E. Tyler, 78521. Tel: 956-541-1755; Fax: 956-541-2171. Joan Cortinas, District Pres.

Villa Maria Language Institute, 224 Resaca Blvd., 78520. Tel: 956-546-7196; Fax: 956-504-3960. Sr. Mary Lelia Aguilar, I.W.B.S., Dir.

ALAMO. *Women Religious - Arise Inc.*, 806 N. Alamo Rd. (Tabor), P.O. Box 778, 78516. Tel: 956-783-6959; Fax: 956-783-0274. Sr. Gerrie Naughton, R.S.M., Pres. Legal Title: *Women Religious-Arise, Inc.*

HARLINGEN. *KMBH-TV 60 / KHID-FM 88.1 / KMBH-FM 88.9*, P.O. Box 2147, 78551. Tel: 956-421-4111; Fax: 956-421-4150. Rev. Pedro Briseno, Station Dir.

MCALLEN. *Comfort House / Casa del Conseulo*, 617 Dallas Ave., 78501. Tel: 956-687-7367; Fax: 956-630-6423. Sr. Marian Strohmeyer, R.S.M., Admin. & Dir. Bed Capacity 10. AIDS Education & Outreach.

Secular Franciscan Order, Fraternity of Our Lady of Guadalupe, 3600 N. 23rd, Ste. 205, 78501. Tel: 956-687-6816. Virginia Rivas, Vice Min.; Rosemary Hendricks, Councilor; Rev. Tomas Mateos, S.F.O., Asst. Spiritual Dir.; Paula Cortez, Sec. & Treas.; Maria Celia Solis, Min.; Sr. Teresita L. MacLang, S.F.O., Spiritual Animator.

MERCEDES. *La Merced Charitable Trust*, 413 S. Virginia, P.O. Box 806, 78570. Tel: 956-565-2622. Housing Board: Mr. Ricardo Hernandez; Mr. Robert Vela; Mrs. Anita A. Rodriguez; Mrs. Ana Zamarripa, Housing Mgr.

MISSION. *Cursillos* (San Juan), 1100 Elm St., 78572. Tel: 956-585-1337. Rev. Juan Nicolau, Dir. Tel: 956-787-0033, 400 Virgen de San Juan Blvd., San Juan, 78589. Tel: 956-787-0033; Fax: 956-787-2908. Deacon Salvador Rojas, Sr., Asst. Dir. Tel: 956-682-1351.

El Rosario Charitable Trust, 119 Retama, P.O. Box 971, 78572. Tel: 956-585-5051.

SAN JUAN. *The Basilica of the National Shrine of Our Lady of San Juan*, 400 Virgen de San Juan Blvd., 78589. Tel: 956-787-0033; Fax: 956-787-2908. Revs. Juan Nicolau, Rector; Genaro Henriquez; Mr. Pablo H. Villescas, Operations Dir.

San Juan Retreat Center. Tel: 956-787-0033.

San Juan Pilgrim House / Hotel. Tel: 956-787-0033, Ext. 249. Mr. Ruben Martinez, Mgr.

Religious Gift & Book Store. Tel: 956-787-0033, Ext. 332. Ms. Jania Guajardo, Mgr.

San Juan Print Shop. Tel: 956-787-0033, Ext. 350. Mr. Juan Reyes, Mgr.

Human Resources. Tel: 956-787-0033. Mr. Albert Rodriguez, Coord.

Finance. Tel: 956-787-0033. Mr. Manuel Silva, Comptroller.

San Juan Cafeteria. Tel: 956-787-0033.

Worship. Tel: 956-787-0033. Mr. Francisco Morales, Mgr.

RELIGIOUS INSTITUTES OF MEN REPRESENTED IN THE DIOCESE

For further details refer to the corresponding bracketed number in the Religious Institutes of Men or Women section.

[0310]—*Congregation of Christian Brothers.*—C.F.C.
[0630]—*Congregation of the Missionaries of the Holy Family.*—M.S.F.
[1130]—*Congregation of the Priests of the Sacred Heart.*—S.C.J.
[1140]—*Fathers of the Sacred Hearts.*—SS.CC.
[0410]—*Franciscans-Assumption BVM Province.*—O.F.M.
[0770]—*The Marist Brothers.*—F.M.S.
[0780]—*Marist Priests and Brothers of the Society of Mary.*—S.M.
[]—*Missionaries of the Holy Spirit.*—M.S.P.S.
[0860]—*Missionhurst Congregation of the Immaculate Heart of Mary.*—C.I.C.M.
[0910]—*Oblates of Mary Immaculate.*—O.M.I.
[0950]—*Oratorians of St. Philip Neri.*—C.O.

RELIGIOUS INSTITUTES OF WOMEN REPRESENTED IN THE DIOCESE

[]—*Benedictine Sisters of Grand Rapids, Michigan.*—O.S.B.
[]—*Benedictine Sisters of the Good Shepherd (Monastery).*—O.S.B.
[]—*Congregation of Divine Providence (Helotes).*—C.D.P.
[]—*Congregation of Notre Dame.*—C.N.D.
[0470]—*Congregation of the Sisters of Charity of the Incarnate Word, Houston, Texas.*—C.C.V.I.
[1920]—*Congregation of the Sisters of the Holy Cross.*—C.S.C.
[0760]—*Daughters of Charity of St. Vincent de Paul.*—D.C.
[]—*Dominican Sisters of Grand Rapids, Michigan.*—O.P.
[]—*Dominican Sisters of Sinsinawa, WI.*—O.P.
[]—*Dominican Sisters of St. Catherine of Kentucky.*—O.P.
[1070-09]—*Dominican Sisters of St. Dominic.* (Racine, WI).—O.P.
[1070-05]—*Dominican Sisters of the Presentation.*—O.P.
[1200]—*Franciscan Sisters of Baltimore.*—O.S.F.
[1415]—*Franciscan Sisters of Mary.*—F.S.M.
[2470]—*Maryknoll Sisters of St. Dominic, Inc.*—M.M.
[1150]—*Misioneras Eucaristicas Franciscanas.*—M.E.F.
[2690]—*Missionary Catechists of Divine Providence.*—M.C.D.P.
[]—*Missionary Daughters of the Most Pure Virgin Mary.*—M.D.P.V.M.

[]—*Missionary Sisters of Jesus.*—M.J.

[2750]—*Missionary Sisters of the Immaculate Heart of Mary.*—I.C.M.

[]—*Missioneras Catequistas de los Pobres.*—M.C.P.

[]—*Missioneras del Espiritu Santo Y la Sagrada Familia.*—M.E.S.S.F.

[2970]—*School Sisters of Notre Dame.* (Prov. of Dallas).—S.S.N.D.

[0440]—*Sisters of Charity of Cincinnati, Ohio.*—S.C.

[0460]—*Sisters of Charity of the Incarnate Word.* (San Antonio, TX).—C.C.V.I.

[]—*Sisters for a Christian Community.*—S.F.C.C.

[1010]—*Sisters of Divine Providence of St. Louis.*—C.D.P.

[]—*Sisters of Mercy (PA).*—R.S.M.

[2575]—*Sisters of Mercy of the Americas.* (St. Louis, MO; Cincinnati, OH).—R.S.M.

[3790]—*Sisters of St. Dorothy.*—S.S.D.

[1720]—*Sisters of St. Francis of Our Lady of Lourdes.*—O.S.F.

[3840]—*Sisters of St. Joseph of Carondelet.* (St. Paul & St. Louis Provs.).—C.S.J.

[]—*Sisters of St. Joseph of Lyon.*

[2980]—*Sisters of the Congregation of Notre Dame of Montreal.*—C.N.D.

[]—*Sisters of the Franciscan Order.*—S.F.O.

[2050]—*Sisters of the Holy Spirit and Mary Immaculate.*—S.H.Sp.

[2200]—*Sisters of the Incarnate Word and Blessed Sacrament.*—I.W.B.S.

[3320]—*Sisters of the Presentation of the Blessed Virgin Mary.*—P.B.V.M.

[3670]—*Sisters of the Sacred Heart of Jesus.*—S.S.C.J.

[]—*Ursuline Sisters.*—O.S.U.

NECROLOGY

† Day, Edward E, Raymondville, TX St. Anthony. —Died Aug. 19, 2000.

Diocese of Buffalo

(Dioecesis Buffalensis)

Most Reverend

HENRY J. MANSELL, D.D.

Bishop of Buffalo; ordained December 19, 1962; appointed Titular Bishop of Marazane and Auxiliary of New York November 24, 1992; ordained January 6, 1993; appointed to Buffalo April 18, 1995; installed June 12, 1995. *Res., 77 Oakland Pl., Buffalo, NY, 14222-2041.*

Most Reverend

EDWARD D. HEAD, D.D.

Bishop Emeritus of Buffalo; ordained January 27, 1945; appointed Titular Bishop of Ardstratha and Auxiliary of New York January 27, 1970; consecrated March 19, 1970; appointed to Buffalo January 17, 1973; installed March 19, 1973; retired June 12, 1995. *Res., 795 Main St., Buffalo, NY, 14203-1250.*

Most Reverend

BERNARD J. McLAUGHLIN, D.D., V.G.

Retired Auxiliary Bishop of Buffalo; Titular Bishop of Mottola; ordained December 21, 1935; appointed December 28, 1968; consecrated January 6, 1969; retired January 15, 1988. *Res., 204 Knoche Rd., Tonawanda, NY, 14150.*

Most Reverend

EDWARD M. GROSZ, D.D.

Auxiliary Bishop of Buffalo; Titular Bishop of Morosbisdo; ordained May 29, 1971; appointed November 22, 1989; consecrated February 2, 1990. *Res., St. Stanislaus Kostka Rectory, 2437 Niagara St., Niagara Falls, NY, 14303-1925.*

ESTABLISHED APRIL 23, 1847.

Incorporated under the laws of the State of New York October 30th, 1897. Re-incorporated by special act passed April 5, 1951, Chapter 568 of the laws of 1951. Corporate Title: *The Diocese of Buffalo, N.Y.*

Square Miles 6,357.

Comprises the Counties of Erie, Niagara, Genesee, Orleans, Chautauqua, Wyoming, Cattaraugus and Allegany in the State of New York.

For legal titles of parishes and diocesan institutions, consult the Chancery Office.

Chancery Office: 795 Main St., Buffalo, NY, 14203. Tel.: 716-847-5500; Fax: 716-847-5557.

Web site address: www.buffalodiocese.org

E-mail address: dob@buffalodiocese.org

STATISTICAL OVERVIEW

Personnel	
Bishop	1
Auxiliary Bishops	1
Retired Bishops	2
Priests: Diocesan Active in Diocese	285
Priests: Active Outside Diocese	10
Priests: Retired, Sick or Absent	129
Number of Diocesan Priests	424
Religious Priests in Diocese	179
Extern Priests in Diocese	9
Ordinations:	
Diocesan Priests	1
Religious Priests	2
Permanent Deacons	7
Permanent Deacons in Diocese	100
Total Brothers	41
Total Sisters	1,362
Parishes	
Parishes	266
With Resident Pastor:	
Resident Diocesan Priests	209
Resident Religious Priests	19
Without Resident Pastor:	
Administered by Priests	36
Administered by Deacons	1
Administered by Women Religious	1
Missions	10
Pastoral Centers	2
Professional Ministry Personnel:	
Sisters	83
Lay Ministers	172
Welfare	
Catholic Hospitals	6
Total Assisted	1,417,252
Health Care Centers	1
Total Assisted	1,100
Homes for the Aged	15
Total Assisted	1,766
Day Care and Extended Day Care Centers	3
Total Assisted	216
Specialized Homes	2
Total Assisted	740
Special Centers for Social Services	4
Total Assisted	263,920
Residential Care of Disabled	5
Total Assisted	36
Other Institutions	3
Total Assisted	2,925
Educational	
Seminaries, Diocesan	2
Students from This Diocese	29
Students from Other Diocese	8
Diocesan Students in Other Seminaries	7
Seminaries, Religious	1
Total Seminarians	36
Colleges and Universities	7
Total Students	15,251
High Schools, Private	17
Total Students	5,972
Elementary Schools, Diocesan and Parish	89
Total Students	21,561
Elementary Schools, Private	4
Total Students	1,000
Non-residential Schools for the Disabled	1
Total Students	629
Catechesis/Religious Education:	
High School Students	13,148
Elementary Students	39,539
Total Students Under Catholic Instruction	97,136
Teachers in the Diocese:	
Priests	62
Brothers	11
Sisters	129
Lay Teachers	2,554
Vital Statistics	
Receptions into the Church:	
Infant Baptism Totals	6,741
Adult Baptism Totals	485
Received into Full Communion	527
First Communions	7,890
Confirmations	5,842
Marriages:	
Catholic	1,987
Interfaith	701
Total Marriages	2,688
Deaths	7,380
Total Catholic Population	725,452
Total Population	1,553,471

Former Bishops—Rt. Rev. JOHN TIMON, D.D., C.M., cons. Oct. 17, 1847; died April 16, 1867.—Rt. Rev. STEPHEN V. RYAN, D.D., C.M., cons. Nov. 8, 1868; died April 10, 1896.—Rt. Rev. JAMES EDWARD QUIGLEY, D.D., cons. Bishop of Buffalo, Feb. 24, 1897; promoted to the Archdiocese of Chicago, Feb. 19, 1903; died July 10, 1915.—Rt. Rev. CHARLES HENRY COLTON, D.D., cons. Aug. 24, 1903; died May 9, 1915.—His Eminence DENNIS CARDINAL DOUGHERTY, D.D., cons. Bishop of Nueva Segovia, June 14, 1903; transferred to the Diocese of Jaro, April 19, 1908; transferred to the Diocese of Buffalo, Dec. 6, 1915; promoted to Archdiocese of Philadelphia, May 1, 1918; created Cardinal, March 7, 1921; died May 31, 1951.—Most Rev. WILLIAM TURNER, D.D., cons. March 30, 1919; died July 10, 1936.—Most Rev. JOHN A. DUFFY, D.D., cons. Bishop of Syracuse, June 29, 1933; transferred to the Diocese of Buffalo, April 14, 1937; died Sept. 27, 1944.—His Eminence JOHN CARDINAL O'HARA, C.S.C., ord. Sept. 9, 1916; appt. Military Delegate of the Armed Forces and Titular Bishop of Mylasa, Dec. 11, 1939; cons. Jan. 15, 1940; transferred to Buffalo, March 10, 1945; installed May 8, 1945; promoted to the Archdiocese of Philadelphia, Nov. 23, 1951; created Cardinal, Dec. 15, 1958; died Aug. 28, 1960.—Most Rev. JOSEPH A. BURKE, D.D., cons. Titular Bishop of Vita and Auxiliary, June 29, 1943; promoted to the See, Feb. 9, 1952; died Oct. 16, 1962.—Most Rev. JAMES A. McNULTY, D.D., cons. Oct. 7, 1947; Titular Bishop of Methone and Auxiliary Bishop of Newark, NJ; appt. Bishop of Paterson, NJ April 9, 1953; transferred to Buffalo, Feb. 12, 1963; died Sept. 4, 1972.—Most Rev. EDWARD D. HEAD, D.D., ord. Jan. 27, 1945; appt. Titular Bishop of Ardstratha and Auxiliary of New York, Jan. 27, 1970; cons. March 19, 1970; appt. Bishop of Buffalo, Jan. 17, 1973; installed March 19, 1973; retired June 12, 1995.

Vicars General—Most Rev. EDWARD M. GROSZ, D.D.; Rev. Msgr. ROBERT J. CUNNINGHAM, P.A., J.C.L.

Chancery Office—795 Main St., Buffalo, 14203. Tel: 716-847-5500; Fax: 716-847-5557. Office Hours: Mon.-Fri. 9-4:30.

Chancellor—Rev. Msgr. ROBERT J. CUNNINGHAM, P.A., J.C.L., V.G.

Vice Chancellor—Rev. PAUL A. LITWIN, J.C.L.

Secretary to Diocesan Bishop and Vice Chancellor—Rev. DAVID G. LIPUMA.

Diocesan Tribunal—795 Main St., Buffalo, 14203. Tel: 716-847-8769; Fax: 716-847-8772. Send all rogatory commissions to the Tribunal.

Judicial Vicar—Rev. SALVATORE MANGANELLO, S.T.L., J.C.L.

Adjunct Judicial Vicar—Rev. PAUL P. SABO.

Defenders of the Bond—Revs. FRANCIS T. NOWAK; EDWARD R. CZARNECKI; FRANCIS X. MAZUR; GREGORY M. FAULHAUBER; DENNIS A. FRONCZAK; Rev. Msgr. ROBERT CUNNINGHAM, J.C.L.

Advocates—Deacons DANIEL E. BRICK; MICHAEL P. MCKEATING; Revs. RICHARD DIGIULIO; ROBERT W. VOGT; Sr. MARY HARTLEY, S.S.M.N.

Promoter of Justice—Rev. Msgr. W. JEROME SULLIVAN, J.C.D.

Judges—Revs. JAMES M. AUGUSTYN; VINCENT J. BECKER; FRED D. INGALLS; Sr. JOLENE JASINSKI, C.S.S.F., J.C.L.; Revs. DONALD E. LEVAN, J.C.L.; PAUL A. LITWIN, J.C.L.; Sr. SANDRA MAKOWSKI, S.S.M.N., J.C.L.; Revs. SALVATORE MANGANELLO, J.C.L.; HENRY A. ORSZULAK; PAUL P. SABO; Rev. Msgr. GEORGE B. YIENGST.

Notaries—Sr. AGNITA BROWN; LUCILLE BUCZEK; ROBIN COLVIN; DOROTHY MAY.

Consultors, College of—Most Rev. EDWARD M. GROSZ, D.D.; Rev. Msgr. ROBERT J. CUNNINGHAM, P.A., J.C.L., V.G.; Rev. Msgr. ALBERT W. CLODY; Rev. Msgr. HENRY J. GUGINO; Revs. JOHN A. KETTELBERGER, C.M.; ROBERT M. MOCK; RONALD W. SAMS, S.J.; Rev. Msgr. ROBERT C. WURTZ.

Council of Priests—Most Rev. HENRY J. MANSELL, D.D., Pres.; Most Rev. EDWARD M. GROSZ, D.D.; Rev. Msgr. ROBERT J. CUNNINGHAM, P.A., J.C.L., V.G.; Rev. Msgr. LEONARD E. BINISZKIEWICZ; Revs. JOHN A. KETTELBERGER, C.M.; THOMAS J. QUINLIVAN; JOSEPH S. ROGLIANO; ARTHUR J. SMITH; DANIEL A. YOUNG; Rev. Msgr. ALBERT W. CLODY; Rev. Msgr. JOHN J. CONNIFF; Revs. GREGORY J. DOBSON; JOSEPH G. FIFAGROWICZ; Rev. Msgr. HENRY J. GUGINO; Revs. MICHAEL P. MCNICHOLL; ROBERT M. MOCK; DAVID A. BELLITTIERE; JOSEPH F. POWER, O.S.F.; DANIEL F. FIEBELKORN; RICHARD W. SIEPKA; BERNARD C. STASZAK; PAUL W. STELLER; RONALD W. SAMS, S.J.; MICHAEL G. UEBLER; JOSEPH S. SPATORICO; JAMES VACCO, O.F.M.; CARLTON J. WESTFIELD; Rev. Msgr. JAMES E. WALL; Rev. Msgr. ROBERT C. WURTZ; Rev. Msgr. GEORGE B. YIENGST.

Finance Council—Most Rev. HENRY J. MANSELL, D.D.; Most Rev. EDWARD M. GROSZ, D.D.; Rev. Msgr. ROBERT J. CUNNINGHAM, P.A., J.C.L., V.G.; Rev. Msgr. THOMAS J. BEASLEY; Rev. Msgr. PAUL J. BURKARD; Rev. Msgr. ANGELO M. CALIGIURI; Rev. Msgr. JAMES F. CAMPBELL; Rev. Msgr. THOMAS F. MALONEY; Mr. JOHN R. O'BRIEN; Rev. Msgr. RAYMOND F. PAA; Mr. STEVEN D. TIMMEL; Rev. MARK J. WOLSKI; Rev. Msgr. ROBERT C. WURTZ.

Vicariates—

Vicars—Rev. PAUL R. BOSSI, Northwest Buffalo; Rev. RODERICK M. BROWN, O.P., Central Buffalo; Rev. Msgr. MATTHEW S. KOPACZ, Southeast Buffalo; Rev. Msgr. RUPERT A. WRIGHT, Northern Erie; Rev. Msgr. DAVID S. SLUBECKY, Eastern Erie; Rev. Msgr. ROBERT C. WURTZ, Western Erie; Rev. DENNIS G. WOLF, Allegany; Rev. LAWRENCE M. MILBY, Northern Cattaraugus; Rev. GREGORY J. DOBSON, Southern Cattaraugus; Rev. PATRICK H. ELIS, Northern Chautauqua; Rev. Msgr. ANTOINE P. ATTEA, Southern Chautauqua; Rev. Msgr. LEO F. MCCARTHY, Genesee; Rev. Msgr. PAUL J. BELZER, Eastern Niagara; Most Rev. EDWARD M. GROSZ, Western Niagara; Rev. RICHARD A. CSIZMAR, Orleans; Rev. RICHARD W. BLAZEJEWSKI, Wyoming.

The Diocese of Buffalo, N.Y.—A corporation under the laws of the State of New York. Most Rev. HENRY J. MANSELL, D.D., Pres.; Most Rev. EDWARD M. GROSZ, D.D., Vice Pres.; Rev. Msgr. ROBERT J. CUNNINGHAM, J.C.L., Sec.

Diocesan Offices and Directors

All offices are located at: *795 Main St., Buffalo, 14203.* Tel: 716-847-8700; Fax: 716-847-5557. (Unless otherwise noted)

Apostleship of Prayer—Rev. Msgr. WALTER O. KERN, Dir., *5337 Genesee St., Bowmansville, 14026.*

Apostleship of the Sea—Rev. Msgr. JOHN I. DUCETTE, Dir., *Res., 565 E. Park Dr., Tonawanda, 14150.*

Archives—Rev. Msgr. WALTER O. KERN, Dir.; Sr. MARTIN JOSEPH JONES, S.S.M.N., Asst. Dir. Tel: 716-847-5500.

Bishop's Committee for Christian Home and Family—Rev. Msgr. FRED R. VOORHES, Moderator. Tel: 716-847-2210.

Black Ministry Office—Mrs. BRENDA EASLEY WEBB, Dir. Tel: 716-847-8391; Fax: 716-847-2206.

Boy Scouts—Rev. JOHN E. KELLY, Chap. Tel: 716-847-8789. VINCENT J. HARMON, Lay Dir., *99 Clark St., Tonawanda, 14150.* Tel: 716-693-7558.

Buildings and Properties—MICHAEL J. SULLIVAN, Dir. Tel: 716-847-8750; Fax: 716-847-8756.

Camping—Rev. GARY J. BAGLEY. Tel: 716-847-8789.

Catholic Alumni Club—ROBERT A. LIPOME, Pres.; Rev. RICHARD W. BLAZEJEWSKI, Chap., *P.O. Box 87, Kenmore, 14223.*

Catholic Charities—Rev. Msgr. HENRY J. GUGINO, Dir., *525 Washington St., Buffalo, 14203.* Rev. JOSEPH J. SICARI, Assoc. Dir. Tel: 716-856-4494; Fax: 716-856-2005.

Catholic Charities Appeal—Rev. Msgr. HENRY J. GUGINO, Dir., Office: *525 Washington St., Buffalo, 14203.* Tel: 716-856-4494.

Catholic Communications of Western New York, Inc.—CLAIRE RUNG, Senior Producer. Tel: 716-847-8719.

Catholic Relief Services—Rev. Msgr. HENRY J. GUGINO, Dir., *525 Washington St., Buffalo, 14203.* Tel: 716-856-4494.

Church Ministry, Office of—Mrs. KATHLEEN B. HEFFERN, Coord. Tel: 716-847-5531; Fax: 716-847-5593.

Council of Catholic Men—Rev. Msgr. WILLIAM A. SCHWINGER, Moderator, *50 Franklin St., Buffalo, 14202.* Tel: 716-852-6040.

Council of Catholic Women—Rev. Msgr. JAMES E. WALL, Moderator, *6892 Lake Shore, P.O. Box 816, Derby, 14047.*

Cemeteries—CARMEN COLAO, Dir., *Mt. Olivet Cemetery, 4000 Elmwood Ave., Kenmore, 14217.* Tel: 716-873-6500; Fax: 716-873-3247.

Censors—Board of Diocesan Censors of Books and Vigilance for the Faith—Rev. Msgr. SAMUEL J. FAIOLA, S.T.D.; Rev. Msgr. THOMAS E. CRANE, S.S.L.

Charismatic Renewal Program—Rev. RICHARD S. DIGIULIO, Dir.; Deacon JOHN SETERA, Asst. Dir.

Christian Life Communities (Sodalities)—Rev. JOHN D. GARVEY, S.J., Diocesan Dir., *2001 Main St., Buffalo, 14208.* Tel: 716-883-7000.

Central Buffalo Ministries—Rev. RODERICK BROWN, O.P., Vicar. Tel: 716-847-8391; Fax: 716-847-2206.

Clergy Personnel Board—Rev. PAUL W. STELLER, Coord. Tel: 716-847-5537. Rev. Msgr. PAUL R. JUENKER; Rev. Msgr. ANGELO M. CALIGIURI; Rev. Msgr. FRANCIS G. WELDGEN; Revs. CHARLES E. SLISZ; RICHARD E. ZAJAC.

Commission on Women in Church and Society—JANE DRISCOLL, Co-Chm., *210 Smallwood Dr., Snyder, 14226.* MARY REGULA, Co-Chm., *99 Oakhill Dr., Hamburg, 14075.*

Communication—Mr. KEVIN A. KEENAN, Dir. Tel: 716-847-8719; Fax: 716-847-8722.

Diocesan Directory—Mrs. ROMANA REGER.

Public Relations, Assistant Director of Communications—KRISTINA P. CONNELL.

Assistant Director of Communications for Radio—GREGG PRINCE.

Coordinator of Telecommunications—LISA STUTZ.

Computer Services (Diocesan)—JAMES C. KAVANAGH, Dir. Tel: 716-847-5500.

Continuing Education for Clergy—Co-Directors: Rev. Msgr. JAMES E. WALL; Rev. RICHARD W. SIEPKA, *Christ the King Seminary, P.O. Box 607, East Aurora, 14052.* Tel: 716-652-8900; Fax: 716-652-8903.

Cursillo Movement—Deacon JOSEPH BARR, Spiritual Dir. Tel: 716-675-1912.

Deaf—Rev. CONRAD P. STACHOWIAK, Chap., *425 Penora St., Depew, 14043-3721.* Tel: 716-683-3038.

Due Process—Rev. SALVATORE MANGANELLO, J.C.L., Chm., Catholic Center. Tel: 716-847-8769; Fax: 716-847-8772.

Ecumenism—(Ecumenical Liaison Committee): Revs. RICHARD E. ZAJAC; THOMAS D. DOYLE; JAMES C. CROGLIO; A. MARK ILLIG; JACOB C. LEDWON; BRENDA EASLEY WEBB; Sr. DIANE LOUTTIT, D.C.; Rev. FRANCIS X. MAZUR, Chm.

Catholic Education (Superintendent of)—Bro. ROBERT R. BIMONTE, F.S.C., *795 Main St., Buffalo, 14203-1250.* Tel: 716-847-5501; Fax: 716-847-5593. Mrs. JUDITH M. MACDONALD, Diocesan Dir. Schools; Miss DENISE MCKENZIE, Diocesan Dir., Rel. Educ.; Mrs. MARY LOU SCHULZ, Regl. Dir., Rel. Educ. in Eastern Niagara, Orleans, Genesee & Wyoming Counties, *Batavia.* Tel: 716-343-3104. Sr. JULIE UHRICH, O.S.F., Regl. Dir., Rel. Educ. in Allegany, Southern Cattaraugus and Southern Chautauqua Counties. Tel: 716-968-5776. Mrs. SHARON URBANIAK, Regl. Dir., Rel. Educ. in Northern Chautauqua & Northern Cattaraugus Counties, *Fredonia.* Tel: 716-679-4175. Mr. DANIEL J. GRANDE, Dir. Curriculum and Instruction; Sr. MARIA PARES, O.S.F., Dir. Athletics & Physical Education; Mr. THOMAS E. PETERS, Dir. Govt. Programs; Sr. M. EVARISTA GOLEN, F.S.S.J., School Psychologist; Mrs. TINA TABERSKI, Office Mgr.

Evangelization Commission—Rev. DANIEL J. PALYS, Chm., *5271 Clinton St., Elma, 14059.* Tel: 716-668-4017.

Family Life—Rev. Msgr. FRED R. VOORHES, Dir. Tel: 716-847-2210; Fax: 716-847-2206.

Finance Office—JOHN R. O'BRIEN. Tel: 716-847-5500; Fax: 716-847-5557.

Guild for the Blind, Inc.—Rev. Msgr. HENRY J. GUGINO, Chap., Office: *525 Washington St., Buffalo, 14203.* Tel: 716-856-4494.

Health Care Apostolate—Rev. Msgr. HENRY J. GUGINO, Bishop's Rep., *525 Washington St., Buffalo, 14203.* Tel: 716-856-4494.

Hispanic Apostolate—Rev. Msgr. DAVID M. GALLIVAN, Dir. Tel: 716-847-2217; Fax: 716-847-2206.

Holy Childhood (Pontifical) Association—Rev. Msgr. HAROLD WAGNER, Dir. Tel: 716-847-8773.

Holy Name Society—Rev. Msgr. FRANCIS B. JUCHNOWSKI, Moderator. Tel: 716-847-2202.

Hospital Chaplains—Rev. RICHARD H. AUGUSTYN, Dir. Hospital Ministry, *100 High St., Buffalo, 14203.* Tel: 716-859-5600.

Human Resources—PAUL C. EBERHARDT, Dir. Tel: 716-847-8376; Fax: 716-847-5593.

Insurance Services—JOHN SCHOLL, Dir. Tel: 716-847-8394; Fax: 716-847-5538.

Legion of Mary—Rev. FREDERICK M. HINTON, Moderator. Tel: 716-847-5545.

Liturgical Commission—Sr. JUDITH MARIE KUBICKI, C.S.S.F., Pres.; Rev. DAVID R. GLASSMIRE, Vice Pres.

Natural Family Planning—Mrs. BEVERLY MALONA. Tel: 716-847-5533; Fax: 716-847-2206.

Newman Club Chaplains—Rev. EUGENE P. ULRICH, *Vicar Campus Ministry and Newman Club Centers, P.O. Box 1154, Alfred, 14802.* Tel: 607-276-5304.

Newspaper—*"The Western New York Catholic"*, KEVIN A. KEENAN, Editor in Chief. Tel: 716-847-8719. RICK FRANUSIAK, Mng. Editor. Tel: 716-849-8720; Fax: 716-847-8722.

Pamphlet Society (Catholic) of Buffalo, Inc.—Rev. Msgr. WALTER O. KERN, Dir., *120 Old Maryvale Dr., Cheektowaga, 14225.* Tel: 716-833-6617.

Pastoral Council—Rev. Msgr. WILLIAM J. MCDONNELL, Pres., *885 Sweet Home Rd., Buffalo, 14226.* Tel: 716-835-8905.

Peace and Justice (Diocesan Commission)—Rev. Msgr. JAMES G. KELLY, *1395 Hertel Ave., Buffalo, 14216.*

Permanent Diaconate—Deacon PAUL F. WEISENBERGER, Dir.; Deacon THADDEUS V. PIJACKI, Dir. Formation. Tel: 716-847-5543; Fax: 716-847-5593.

Priests, Vicar for—Rev. Msgr. JAMES E. WALL, *6892 Lake Shore Rd., Derby, 14047.* Tel: 716-947-5449.

Pro-Life Activities—JUDITH A. GORMAN, Coord. Tel: 716-847-2205; Fax: 716-847-2206.

Propagation of the Faith—Rev. Msgr. HAROLD WAGNER. Tel: 716-847-8773; Fax: 716-847-2206.

Purchasing (Diocesan)—Mr. PETER M. MCKEE. Tel: 716-847-8711; Fax: 716-847-8702.

Research and Planning—Sr. REGINA MURPHY, S.S.M.N. Tel: 716-847-5539; Fax: 716-847-5593.

St. Peter Claver Youth Program, Inc.—BARBARA PITKIN, Exec. Dir., *185 Lang Ave., Buffalo, 14215.* Tel: 716-893-4651.

St. Vincent de Paul Society—Rev. Msgr. HENRY J. GUGINO, Spiritual Moderator; MARK ZIRNHELD, Exec. Dir., *1298 Main St., Buffalo, 14209.* Tel: 716-882-3360; Fax: 716-882-3556.

Worship and Catechumenate, Office Of—Mrs. JUDITH WAGGONER, Dir. Tel: 716-847-5545; Fax: 716-847-5593.

Vicar for Religious—Sr. M. CHARLENE NOWAK, C.S.S.F.; Rev. JAMES J. RUDDICK, S.J., Assoc. Dir. Tel: 718-847-5529; Fax: 716-847-5593.

Vocations—Rev. LEON J. BIERNAT, Dir. Tel: 716-847-5535; Fax: 716-847-5593.

Diocesan Youth Council—Rev. GARY J. BAGLEY, Dir. Tel: 716-847-8789; Fax: 716-847-8797.

Young Adult Ministry—PATRICIA BUBAR. Tel: 716-847-8788; Fax: 716-847-8797.

Youth Department, Jamestown—KATHY NECASTRO, Prog. Coord., Southern Tier; MILLIE TORRES, Asst. Prog. Coord., Youth and Hispanic Ministries, *10 Prospect St., Jamestown, 14701.* Tel: 716-484-9869.

CLERGY, PARISHES, MISSIONS AND PAROCHIAL SCHOOLS

CITY OF BUFFALO
(Erie County)

1—ST. JOSEPH'S CATHEDRAL (1851), Rev. Msgr. James F. Campbell, Rector. In res., Rev. Msgr. William A. Schwinger; Deacon Thomas A. McDonnell.

Res., 50 Franklin St., 14202. Tel: 716-854-5855; Fax: 716-854-5861.

School—Catholic Academy of West Buffalo Regional School. See separate listing under Regional and Consolidated Elementary Schools in the Institutions located in the Diocese.

Catechesis/Religious Programs—Mary Alice

Hartwell, D.R.E.
Students 14.

2—ST. ADALBERT'S BASILICA (1886) (Polish), Rev. Thaddeus Nicholas Bocianowski.
Res., 212 Stanislaus St., 14212. Tel: 716-895-8091; Fax: 716-895-8773. [CEM]
Catechesis/Religious Programs—130 Kosciuszko St., 14212. Tel: 716-894-8366.
Students 50.

3—ST. AGATHA (1921), Rev. Adolph M. Kowalozyk.
Res., 54 Alamo Pl., 14220. Tel: 716-822-2668; Fax: 716-828-1405.
School—Tel: 716-824-4510. Ms. Dolores Oakes, Prin.
Lay Teachers 13; Students 139.
Catechesis/Religious Programs—Students 87.

4—ST. AGNES (1883), Revs. Guy F. Siracuse; James B. Cunningham, Admin.
Res., 194 Ludington St., 14206. Tel: 716-893-0509; Fax: 716-896-0987.
School—Tel: 716-892-1441; Fax: 716-896-0934. Sr. Ann Helene Koenig, O.S.F., Prin.
Lay Teachers 15; Students 228.
Catechesis/Religious Programs—Mrs. Donna Weber, D.R.E.
Students 126.
Catholic Charities—Tel: 716-893-6418. Sr. Rose Therese Di Gregorio, O.S.F., TLCIM Project Dir.

5—ALL SAINTS (1911), Rev. Msgr. Albert W. Clody; Rev. Joseph F. Moreno.
Res., 127 Chadduck Ave., 14207-1531. Tel: 716-875-8183; Fax: 716-875-6597.
School—Tel: 716-875-4174. Mrs. Cynthia Jacobs, Prin.
Sisters 1; Lay Teachers 20; Students 235.
Catechesis/Religious Programs—Nancy Schorb, D.R.E.
Students 150.

6—ST. AMBROSE (1930), Rev. Msgr. David M. Lee; Sr. Martha Mary Whelan, R.S.M., Pastoral Assoc.
Res., 65 Ridgewood Rd., 14220. Tel: 716-822-5962; Fax: 716-822-0966.
School—Tel: 716-824-6360. June F. Neuner, Prin.
Sisters 2; Lay Teachers 21; Students 399.
Catechesis/Religious Programs—Tel: 716-826-4125. Sr. Pauline Petruzzella, R.S.M., D.R.E.
Students 208.

7—ST. ANN (1858), Rev. James L. Pierce, S.J.; Sr. Marie Davis, O.S.F., Pastoral Assoc. In res., Rev. James F. Joyce, S.J.
Office: 491 Emslie St., 14212. Tel: 716-852-3316; Fax: 716-854-4131.
Res., 501 Emslie St., 14212. Tel: 716-854-3742; Fax: 716-854-4131.
School—Catholic Central Regional School. See separate listing under Regional and Consolidated Elementary Schools in the Institutions located in the Diocese.
Catechesis/Religious Programs—Students 20.

8—ANNUNCIATION (1885), Rev. Bartholomew W. Lipiec.
Res., 18 Greenwood Pl., 14213. Tel: 716-885-2469; Fax: 716-885-3385.
Church—Lafayette Ave. & Grant St., 14213.
School—Catholic Academy of West Buffalo Regional School. See separate listing under Regional and Consolidated Elementary Schools in the Institutions located in the Diocese. Tel: 716-886-5384.
Catechesis/Religious Programs—Tel: 716-881-2914. Darice Destino, D.R.E.
Students 104.
Convent—257 Lafayette Ave., 14213. Tel: 716-885-6252. Sisters of St. Mary of Namur

9—ST. ANTHONY OF PADUA (1891) (Italian), Rev. Secondo Casarotto, C.S.
Res., 160 Court St., 14202. Tel: 716-854-2563; Fax: 716-854-2564.
School—Catholic Academy of West Buffalo Regional School. See separate listing under Regional and Consolidated Elementary Schools in the Institutions located in the Diocese.

10—ASSUMPTION (1888) (Polish). Linked with St. Elizabeth, Buffalo. Rev. Richard Jedrzejewski. In res., Rev. Thomas P. Taton.
Res., 435 Amherst St., 14207. Tel: 716-875-7626; Fax: 716-447-1027.
School—Our Lady of Black Rock Consolidated, 16 Germain St., 14207. Tel: 716-873-7497. Sr. Francianne Zielezinski, C.S.S.F., Principal.
Felician Sisters 1; Students 132.
Catechesis/Religious Programs—Tel: 716-873-7187. Mary Lou Wyrobek, D.R.E.
Students 62.

11—ST. BARTHOLOMEW. Closed 1993. Merged with Blessed Trinity Church. Records at the Catholic Center, 795 Main St., Buffalo, 14203.

12—ST. BENEDICT THE MOOR. Closed. For inquiries for parish records contact the Chancery.

13—ST. BERNARD (1906), Rev. Msgr. Francis B. Juchnowski; Rev. Donald J. Lutz. In res., Rev. Francis J. Chmielewski.
Res., 414 S. Ogden, 14206. Tel: 716-822-8856; Fax: 716-822-8856.
School—Tel: 716-822-8057; Fax: 716-822-0280. Congregation of Sisters of St. Felix 1; Lay Teachers 14; Students 265.

14—BLESSED SACRAMENT (1887), Rev. Paul R. Bossi. In res., Rev. Salvatore Manganello.
Res., 1035 Delaware Ave., 14209-1689. Tel: 716-884-0053; Fax: 716-884-2279.
School—Catholic Academy of West Buffalo Regional School. See separate listing under Regional and Consolidated Elementary Schools in the Institutions located in the Diocese. Tel: 716-885-6111.
Catechesis/Religious Programs—James J. Kennedy, D.R.E.
Students 80.

15—BLESSED TRINITY (1906), Rev. George L. Reger.
Res., 317 Leroy Ave., 14214. Tel: 716-833-0301; Fax: 716-834-4711.
School—Catholic Central Regional School. See separate listing under Regional and Consolidated Elementary Schools in the Institutions located in the Diocese.

16—ST. BONIFACE. Closed. For inquiries for parish records contact the Chancery.

17—ST. BRIGID. Merged with St. Columba. For inquiries for parish records contact SS. Columba & Brigid, Buffalo.

18—ST. CASIMIR (1890) (Polish), Rev. Msgr. Matthew S. Kopacz; Rev. James T. Bartnik.
Res., 160 Cable St., 14206. Tel: 716-824-9589; Fax: 716-824-2004.
Catechesis/Religious Programs—1833 Clinton St., 14206. Tel: 716-826-9338.
Students 101.

19—SS. COLUMBA & BRIGID (1888), Rev. Roy T. Herberger, Admin.
Res., 418 N. Division St., 14204. Tel: 716-852-3331; Fax: 716-852-3331.
Montessori School—Tel: 716-842-6213. Sr. Diane Bernbeck, O.S.F., Prin.
Students 55.
School—Catholic Central Regional School. See separate listing under Regional and Consolidated Elementary Schools in the Institutions located in the Diocese.

20—CORONATION OF THE BLESSED VIRGIN MARY (1950). Attended by Our Lady of Loretto, Buffalo. Rev. Donald J. Blesnuk.
Res., 348 Dewitt St., 14213. Tel: 716-882-2650.
School—Our Lady of Black Rock School. See separate listing under Regional and Consolidated Elementary Schools in the Institutions located in the Diocese. Tel: 716-875-7626.
Catechesis/Religious Programs—Tel: 716-882-6360. Frank Antonucci, D.R.E.
Students 30.

21—CORPUS CHRISTI (Polish). (St. Anthony's Convent). Revs. Karl Kolodziejski, O.F.M.Conv.; Gregory Kwapisz, O.F.M.Conv. In res., Revs. Roman Siola, O.F.M.Conv.; Joseph Trawinski, O.F.M.Conv.; Valentine Rajter, O.F.M.Conv.; Anthony M. Konieczny, O.F.M.Conv., Pastor Emeritus.
Res., 199 Clark St., 14212-1407. Tel: 716-896-1050.
Catechesis/Religious Programs—Students 43.

22—ST. ELIZABETH OF HUNGARY (1906) (Hungarian). Attended by Assumption, Buffalo. Rev. Richard Jedrzejewski, Admin.
Res., 435 Amherst St., 14207. Tel: 716-875-6586; Fax: 716-876-3193.
Catechesis/Religious Programs—Clustered with Assumption, Buffalo.

23—ST. FLORIAN (1917) (Polish), Rev. John Posiewala, S.A.C.
Res., 567 Hertel Ave., 14207. Tel: 716-875-3246; Fax: 716-876-6410.
School—Our Lady of Black Rock Consolidated School. See separate listing under Regional and Consolidated Elementary Schools in the Institutions located in the Diocese.
Catechesis/Religious Programs—Students 42.

24—ST. FRANCIS OF ASSISI (1909), Rev. Richard S. DiGiulio.
Res., 118 Schiller St., 14206. Tel: 716-895-6813; Fax: 716-891-4609.
Catechesis/Religious Programs—Students 81.

25—ST. FRANCIS XAVIER (1849) (German). Attended by St. John the Baptist, Buffalo. Rev. George J. Stephan; Sr. Ann Hughes, R.S.M., Pastoral Assoc.; Deacon Richard W. Parker.
Res., 157 East St., 14207. Tel: 716-873-1911; Fax: 716-871-0623. [CEM]
School—Our Lady of Black Rock Consolidated School. See separate listing under Regional and Consolidated Elementary Schools in the Institutions located in the Diocese. Tel: 716-873-7497.

Catechesis/Religious Programs—Sr. Susan Bowles, S.S.M.N., D.R.E.
Students 10.

26—ST. GERARD (1902), Rev. Francis X. Mazur.
Res., 1190 E. Delavan Ave., 14215. Tel: 716-895-5761; Fax: 716-895-6311.
Catechesis/Religious Programs—Tel: 716-895-3751. Debra Stafford, D.R.E.
Students 58.

27—HOLY ANGELS (1852), Revs. Louis R. Lougen, O.M.I.; Martin J. McMahon, O.M.I. In res., Revs. Eugene Tremblay, O.M.I.; Stephen Vasek, O.M.I.; George Kirwin, O.M.I., Supr.; Daniel F. O'Leary, O.M.I.
Res., 348 Porter Ave., 14201. Tel: 716-885-3767; Fax: 716-882-8211.
School—Catholic Academy of West Buffalo Regional School. See separate listing under Regional and Consolidated Elementary Schools in the Institutions located in the Diocese. Tel: 716-885-6111; Fax: 716-882-8211.
Catechesis/Religious Programs—Students 185.

28—HOLY APOSTLES SS. PETER AND PAUL (1909) (Polish), Rev. Ronald A. Bagienski.
Res., 660 Smith St., 14210. Tel: 716-854-8971; Fax: 716-854-4458.
Catechesis/Religious Programs—Joint program with SS. Rita and Patrick. Tel: 716-856-5790; Fax: 716-856-4019.

29—HOLY CROSS (1914), Rev. Msgr. David M. Gallivan.
Res., 345 Seventh St., 14201. Tel: 716-847-6930; Fax: 716-847-6934.
School—Catholic Academy of West Buffalo Regional School. See separate listing under Regional and Consolidated Elementary Schools in the Institutions located in the Diocese. Tel: 716-885-6111; Fax: 716-885-6452.
Catechesis/Religious Programs—D.R.E.: Marangely Gonzalez; Jodi Miller; Sr. Olivia Ortiz, C.S.S.F.
Students 45.

30—HOLY FAMILY (1902), Rev. William R. Bigelow; Deacon Paul F. Carmody.
Res., 1885 S. Park Ave., 14220. Tel: 716-822-0308; Fax: 716-826-6018.
School—Tel: 716-826-6017. Sr. Patricia Collins, R.S.M., Prin.
Sisters of Mercy 2; Lay Teachers 10; Students 175.

31—HOLY NAME OF JESUS (1887), Rev. Robert J. Hora, Admin.
Res., 1947 Bailey Ave., 14211. Tel: 716-892-8056; Fax: 716-892-0836.
Catechesis/Religious Programs—1190 E. Delavan Ave., 14215. Tel: 716-895-3751.
Students 13.

32—HOLY SPIRIT (1910), Rev. Msgr. Charles T. Griffin; Rev. Robert J. Orlowski; Deacon William J. Hynes, Jr.
Res., 91 Dakota Ave., 14216. Tel: 716-875-8102; Fax: 716-875-4186.
School—85 Dakota Ave., 14216. Tel: 716-875-9478. Miss Karen Adamski, Prin.
Lay Teachers 14; Students 130.
Catechesis/Religious Programs—Tel: 716-875-8103.
Students 58.

33—IMMACULATE CONCEPTION (1849), Rev. Antonio L. Rodriguez.
Res., 144 Edward St., 14201. Tel: 716-886-5627.
School—Catholic Academy of West Buffalo Regional School. See separate listing under Regional and Consolidated Elementary Schools in the Institutions located in the Diocese. Tel: 716-885-6111.
Catechesis/Religious Programs—D.R.E.: Kim Vargas; Giorgio Cappuzzello.
Students 85.

34—IMMACULATE HEART OF MARY (1946), Rev. Richard H. Augustyn, Admin.
Res., 381 Edison St., 14215. Tel: 716-894-6953; Fax: 716-892-1370.

35—ST. JAMES (1916), Rev. Robert L. Gebhard; Sr. Katherine Bogner, S.S.M.N., Pastoral Assoc.; Deacon Peter J. Bedard.
Res., 10 Hastings Ave., 14215. Tel: 716-834-5601; Fax: 716-834-5601.
Convent—36 Davidson St., 14215. Tel: 716-836-7835.

36—ST. JOACHIM. Closed. For inquiries for parish records contact the Chancery.

37—ST. JOHN THE BAPTIST (1867). Linked wtih St. Francis Xavier, Buffalo. Rev. George J. Stephan.
Res., 60 Hertel Ave., 14207-2595. Tel: 716-875-4390.
Parish Center—410 East St., 14207. Tel: 716-873-8660.
School—Our Lady of Black Rock Consolidated School. See separate listing under Regional and

Consolidated Elementary Schools in the Institutions located in the Diocese. Tel: 716-873-7497.
Catechesis/Religious Programs—Students 7.

38—St. John the Evangelist (1906), Rev. Daniel P. Walsh; Sr. Kathleen McDonald, R.S.M., Pastoral Assoc.
Res., 2315 Seneca St., 14210. Tel: 716-822-2315; Fax: 716-822-2295.
Catechesis/Religious Programs—Tel: 716-825-1252.
Students 123.

39—St. John Kanty (1892) (Polish), Rev. Anthony Lutostanski.
Res., 101 Swinburne St., 14212. Tel: 716-893-0412; Fax: 716-893-9864.

40—St. Joseph (1850), Rev. Jacob C. Ledwon; Sr. Jeremy Midura, Pastoral Assoc.; Deacon Thaddeus V. Pijacki.
Res., 3269 Main St., 14214. Tel: 716-833-0298; Fax: 716-833-7339.
School—3275 Main St., 14214. Tel: 716-835-7395; Fax: 716-833-6550.
Sisters of St. Joseph 1; Sisters of St. Mary of Namur 2; Sisters of St. Francis of Penance and Christian Charity 2; Lay Teachers 12; Students 264.
Catechesis/Religious Programs—Tel: 716-837-2971.
Students 243.

41—St. Lawrence (1929), Rev. Paul D. Seil; Deacon Paul Weisenburger. In res., Rev. Norbert F. Orsolits.
Res., 1520 E. Delavan Ave., 14215. Tel: 716-892-2471; Fax: 716-892-1315.
School—Kolbe Catholic Regional School. See St. John Gualbert, Cheektowaga for details. Tel: 716-895-3127.
Catechesis/Religious Programs—Tel: 716-896-0047. Sr. Bernadette Kapfer, C.S.S.F., D.R.E.
Students 92.

42—St. Louis (1829), Rev. Msgr. Robert A. Mack.
Res., 35 Edward St., 14202. Tel: 716-852-6040; Fax: 716-853-9225.
School—Catholic Academy of West Buffalo Regional School. See separate listing under Regional and Consolidated Elementary Schools in the Institutions located in the Diocese.

43—St. Luke (Polish). Closed. For inquiries for parish records contact the Chancery.

44—St. Margaret (1916), Rev. Msgr. James G. Kelly; Rev. Arthur E. Mattulke; Deacon Alex Molnar.
Res., 1395 Hertel Ave., 14216. Tel: 716-876-5318; Fax: 716-875-9068.
School—Tel: 716-876-8885; Fax: 716-876-7553.
Sisters of St. Joseph 1; Lay Teachers 13; Students 202.
Catechesis/Religious Programs—Tel: 716-876-6122.
Students 173.

45—St. Mark (1908), Rev. Msgr. Francis Braun.
Res., 401 Woodward Ave., 14214. Tel: 716-836-1600; Fax: 716-836-1611.
School—Tel: 716-836-1191; Fax: 716-836-0391. Sr. Jeanne Eberle, S.S.J., Prin.
Sisters of St. Joseph 2; Lay Teachers 15; Students 310.
Catechesis/Religious Programs—Students 49.
Convent—223 Summit Ave., 14214. Tel: 716-837-9055.

46—St. Martin (1926), Rev. Vincent J. Becker. In res., Rev. Thomas N. Shepherd.
Res., 1140 Abbott Rd., 14220. Tel: 716-823-7077; Fax: 716-823-4197.
School—Tel: 716-824-0726; 0727; Fax: 716-825-7685. Sr. M. Roberta, R.S.M., Prin.
Lay Teachers 22; Students 366.
Catechesis/Religious Programs—Students 78.

47—St. Mary of Sorrows (1872), Sr. Mary Augusta Kaiser, S.S.J., Parish Life Coord.; Sr. Jean Marie Zirnheld, S.S.J., Pastoral Assoc.
Church & Offices—333 Guilford St., 14211. Tel: 716-892-4115; Fax: 716-892-4116.
School—Catholic Central Regional School. See separate listing under Regional and Consolidated Elementary Schools in the Institutions located in the Diocese.
Catechesis/Religious Programs—Students 41.
Convent—20 Rich St., 14211. Tel: 716-892-4116; Fax: 716-892-4116. Sisters of St. Joseph

48—St. Matthew. Closed. For inquiries for parish records contact St. Martin de Porres, Buffalo.

49—St. Martin de Porres (1993) (African American), Rev. Roderick M. Brown, O.P.; Deacon Ronald Walker; Sr. Philip Marie, S.S.J., Pastoral Assoc.
Office: 555 Northampton St., 14215. Tel: 716-883-7729; Fax: 716-886-4101.
Res., 26 Wyoming Ave., 14215. Tel: 716-893-6079.
School—Catholic Central Regional School. See Regional and Consolidated Elementary Schools under Institutions Located in the Diocese. Tel: 716-852-6854.
Catechesis/Religious Programs—Students 60.

50—St. Michael (1851), Revs. Gerald J. McMahon, S.J.; Cornelius J. Carr, S.J.; Edward L. Guth, S.J.; John G. Sturm, S.J.; Joseph R. Spellerberg, S.J.; Richard J. Hoar, S.J.; H. James Roleke, S.J.; Bro. James Dennehy, S.J. In res., Rev. Richard J. Zanoni, S.J.
Res., 651 Washington St., 14203. Tel: 716-854-6726; Fax: 716-854-4616.
School—Catholic Academy of West Buffalo Regional School. See separate listing under Regional and Consolidated Elementary Schools in the Institutions located in the Diocese. Tel: 716-885-6111; 886-5384.

51—St. Monica. Closed. For inquiries for parish records contact the Chancery.

52—The Nativity of the Blessed Virgin (1898), Rev. Angelo M. Chimera.
Res., 20 Herkimer St., 14213. Tel: 716-885-1344; Fax: 716-885-2385.
School—Catholic Academy of West Buffalo Regional School. See separate listing under Regional and Consolidated Elementary Schools in the Institutions located in the Diocese. Tel: 716-885-6111; Fax: 716-885-6452.
Catechesis/Religious Programs—Tel: 716-882-6360. Frank Antonucci, D.R.E.
Students 45.

53—Our Lady of Loretto (1940). Linked with Coronation, Buffalo. Rev. Donald J. Blesnuk; Deacon Roberto Miranda; Ronald Thaler, Pastoral Assoc.
Res., 172 15th St., 14213. Tel: 716-885-7573; Fax: 716-885-0739.
School—Catholic Academy of West Buffalo Regional School. See separate listing under Regional and Consolidated Elementary Schools in the Institutions located in the Diocese.
Catechesis/Religious Programs—Tel: 716-881-2635. Elise McDowell, D.R.E.
Students 114.

54—Our Lady of Lourdes. Closed. For inquiries for parish records contact the Chancery.

55—Our Lady of Perpetual Help (1897). Linked with St. Valentine, Buffalo. Rev. Dennis G. Riter.
Res., 115 O'Connell Ave., 14204. Tel: 716-852-2671; Fax: 716-852-2672.
Catechesis/Religious Programs—Students 75.

56—Precious Blood (1899) (Polish), Rev. Msgr. Ronald P. Sciera.
Res., 140 Lewis St., 14206. Tel: 716-854-4623; Fax: 716-854-3077.
Catechesis/Religious Programs—Students 42.

57—Queen of the Most Holy Rosary (Polish). Closed. For inquiries for parish records contact the Chancery.

58—Queen of Peace (1920) (Polish), Rev. Richard M. Poblocki, Admin.
Res., 1955 Genesee St., 14211. Tel: 716-892-5646; Fax: 716-897-2411.

59—SS. Rita & Patrick (1854), Revs. John Alderson, O.F.M.; Paul Osborne, O.F.M.; Bro. Maurice V. Swartout, O.F.M., Pastoral Assoc. In res., Revs. David D. Blake, O.F.M.; Robert Struzynski, O.F.M.; Bros. Timothy S. Dauenhauser, O.F.M.; Michael Oberst, O.F.M.
Res., St. Patrick Friary, 102 Seymour St., 14210. Tel: 716-856-5790; Fax: 716-856-4019.
Catechesis/Religious Programs—Students 150.

60—St. Rose of Lima (1925), Revs. Harry E. Winter, O.M.I.; Anthony F. Rigoli, O.M.I.
Res., 500 Parker Ave., 14216. Tel: 716-834-6688; Fax: 716-834-6689.
School—201 Winston Rd., 14216. Tel: 716-833-4100; Fax: 716-834-3617. Joseph Duttweiler, Prin.
Lay Teachers 16; Students 214.
Catechesis/Religious Programs—Tel: 716-833-4130. Mrs. Amy Vossen Vukelic, D.R.E.
Students 115.

61—St. Stanislaus (1873) (Polish), Rev. Msgr. John R. Gabalski, P.A.
Res., 123 Townsend St., 14212. Tel: 716-854-5511; Fax: 716-854-0170. [CEM]
School—Tel: 716-854-1803.
Felician Sisters 2; Lay Teachers 9; Students 89.
Catechesis/Religious Programs—Students 28.

62—St. Stephen (1875), Rev. Robert A. Stolinski.
Res., 193 Elk St., 14210-1499. Tel: 716-823-2358; Fax: 716-826-2168.
Catechesis/Religious Programs—Students 80.

63—St. Teresa (1897), Rev. Msgr. S. Theodore Berg. In res., Rev. Msgr. Richard C. Crumlish.
Res., 1974 Seneca St., 14210. Tel: 716-822-0608.
School—Tel: 716-822-4546. Sr. Angela Marie Mastandrea, R.S.M., Prin.
Sisters 3; Lay Teachers 13; Students 262.
Catechesis/Religious Programs—Students 120.

64—St. Thomas Aquinas (1920), Rev. Arthur J. Smith. In res., Rev. Msgr. Eugene E. O'Loughlin.
Res., 450 Abbott Rd., 14220-1796. Tel: 716-822-1250; Fax: 716-822-2594.
School—20 Athol St., 14220-1796. Tel: 716-824-5046; Fax: 716-824-2539. Bernetta Kelly, Prin.
Lay Teachers 24; Students 385.
Catechesis/Religious Programs—Tel: 716-826-0888.
Students 109.

65—Transfiguration (Polish). Closed. For inquiries for parish records contact the Chancery.

66—St. Valentine (1920) (Polish). Attended by Our Lady of Perpetual Help, Buffalo. Rev. Dennis G. Riter.
Res., 522 S. Park Ave., 14204. Tel: 716-854-7193; Fax: 716-852-2672.
Catechesis/Religious Programs—Tel: 716-852-2671.
Students 14.

67—St. Vincent de Paul. Closed. For inquiries for parish records contact the Chancery.

68—The Visitation of the B.V.M. (1898), Rev. Paul P. Sabo.
Res., 1040 Lovejoy St., 14206. Tel: 716-892-2289; Fax: 716-897-3310.
Catechesis/Religious Programs—Students 27.

OUTSIDE THE CITY OF BUFFALO

Akron, Erie Co., St. Teresa of Avila (1859), Rev. Msgr. Robert J. Williamson.
Res., 5771 Buell St., P.O. Box 168, 14001. Tel: 716-542-9103; Fax: 716-542-2444. [CEM]
Catechesis/Religious Programs—Tel: 716-542-9717; Fax: 716-542-2444. Sr. Mary Ruth Warejko, C.S.S.F., D.R.E.
Students 235.

Albion, Orleans Co., St. Mary Assumption (1891) (Polish). Attended by St. Joseph, Albion. Rev. Richard A. Csizmar; Deacon James L. Collichio.
Res., 47 Brown St., 14411. Tel: 716-589-4243; 589-5162; Fax: 716-589-0734.

St. Joseph (1852). Linked with St. Mary Assumption, Albion. Rev. Richard A. Csizmar; Deacon James L. Collichio.
Res., 106 S. Main St., 14411. Tel: 716-589-4243; Fax: 716-589-0734. [CEM]
Catechesis/Religious Programs—Tel: 716-589-4492. Carol Pilon, D.R.E.
Students 260.

Alden, Erie Co., St. John the Baptist (1850), Revs. Fred D. Ingalls; Ivan Skenderovic; Deacon Richard J. Mahaney.
Res., 2021 Sandridge Rd., 14004. Tel: 716-937-6959; Fax: 716-937-0075. [CEM]
School—Tel: 716-937-9483; Fax: 716-937-9794. Mary Jane Liszewski, Prin.
Lay Teachers 17; Students 160.
Catechesis/Religious Programs—Tel: 716-937-3448. Margaret McCartin Orcutt, D.R.E.
Students 550.

Allegany, Cattaraugus Co., St. Bonaventure (1854), Rev. Kevin Downey, O.F.M.
Res., 95 E. Main St., 14706. Tel: 716-373-1330; Fax: 716-373-4220.
School—Southern Tier Catholic Regional School. See separate listing under Regional and Consolidated Elementary Schools in the Institutions located in the Diocese. Tel: 716-372-2891.
Catechesis/Religious Programs—Tel: 716-373-0430. Peg Reitz, D.R.E.
Students 231.
Mission—Vandalia, Cattaraugus Co., St. John the Baptist, S. Nine Mile Rd., 14706.

Almond, Allegany Co., SS. Brendan and Jude (1992), Rev. Eugene P. Ulrich. Pastoral Assocs.: Susan Fowler; Robert Donius.
Mailing Address: St. Jude Chapel, Lower College Dr., Alfred, 14802. Tel: 607-587-9411; Fax: 607-587-9431.
Church—11 S. Main St., Box G, 14804. Tel: 607-276-5304.
Catechesis/Religious Programs—Students 70.

Amherst, Erie Co., St. Leo the Great (1953), Rev. Msgr. William J. McDonnell; Revs. John J. Cullen; John E. Kelly; Sr. Jean Becker, O.S.F., Pastoral Assoc.
Res., 885 Sweet Home Rd., Buffalo, 14226. Tel: 716-835-8905; Fax: 716-835-8997.
School—Tel: 716-832-6340. Mr. Patrick J. Brady, Prin.
Sisters of Third Order of St. Francis 1; Lay Teachers 19; Students 184; Preschool Students 80.
Catechesis/Religious Programs—Tel: 716-833-8359. Sr. Judith Beiswanger, O.S.F., D.R.E.
Students 372.

Andover, Allegany Co., Blessed Sacrament (1855). Linked with St. John of the Cross, Whitesville. Rev. Fred G. Fingerle.
Res., One Church St., Box 761, 14806-0761. Tel: 607-478-8885. [CEM]
Catechesis/Religious Programs—Students 23.

Angelica, Allegany Co., Sacred Heart (1848), Rev. Joseph E. Vatter.
Res., 5 Milton St., Belmont, 14813-1119. Tel: 716-268-7272; Fax: 716-268-9128.
Church—Park Cir., 14709.
Catechesis/Religious Programs—Combined with St. Mary, Belmont.

Angola, Erie Co., Most Precious Blood (1871), Revs. Bernard U. Nowak; James A. Staebell. In res., Rev. Msgr. Gerald J. Kreuzer.
Res., 22 Prospect St., P.O. Box 153, 14006. Tel: 716-549-0420; Fax: 716-549-0425. [CEM]
School—17 Prospect St., 14006. Tel: 716-549-1818. Franciscan Sisters of St. Joseph 2; Lay Teachers 8; Students 149.
Catechesis/Religious Programs—Students 320.

Arcade, Wyoming Co., SS. Peter and Paul (1907). Linked with St. Mary, East Arcade. Rev. Michael G. Uebler.
Res., 417 Main St., 14009-1195. Tel: 716-492-5330; Fax: 716-492-1047. [CEM]
School—St. Aloysius Regional School. See separate listing under Regional and Consolidated Elementary Schools in the Institutions located in the Diocese.
Catechesis/Religious Programs—Students 160.

Athol Springs, Erie Co., St. Francis of Assisi (1929), Revs. Steven G. Frenier, O.F.M.Conv.; Joseph Dorniak, O.F.M.Conv.
Res., S-4263 St. Francis Dr., 14010. Tel: 716-627-2710; Fax: 716-627-5263.
Catechesis/Religious Programs—Tel: 716-627-3357. Annette Breen, D.R.E.
Students 410.

Attica, Wyoming Co., St. Vincent de Paul (1857), Rev. Stanley R. Chwalinski.
Res., 50 East Ave., 14011. Tel: 716-591-1228; Fax: 716-591-1614. [CEM]
School—Genesee-Wyoming Catholic Central Consolidated School. See separate listing under Regional and Consolidated Elementary Schools in the Institutions located in the Diocese. Tel: 716-591-2515; Fax: 716-591-2516.
Catechesis/Religious Programs—Students 241.

Barker, Niagara Co., St. Patrick (1856). Linked to St. Charles Borromeo, Olcott. Rev. James F. Hassett.
Res., 14012. Tel: 716-795-3331; Fax: 716-795-3919. [CEM]
Catechesis/Religious Programs—Students 152.

Batavia, Genesee Co.,

1—St. Anthony, (1908) (Italian), Rev. Joseph S. Spatorico.
Res., 122 Liberty St., 14020. Tel: 716-343-0914; Fax: 716-344-8376.
School—Tel: 716-343-5561; Fax: 716-343-5653. Sisters of Mercy 1; Lay Teachers 14; Students 120.
Catechesis/Religious Programs—Students 245.

2—St. Joseph, (1849), Rev. Msgr. Leo F. McCarthy; Rev. Marek Gnidzinski; Deacon John Stone. In res., Rev. John P. Mack.
Res., 303 E. Main St., 14020. Tel: 716-343-5800; Fax: 716-345-9525. [CEM]
School—Tel: 716-343-6154; Fax: 716-343-8911. William R. Sabio, Prin.
Lay Teachers 25; Students 343; Preschool Students 45.
Catechesis/Religious Programs—Students 168.

3—St. Mary, (1906), Revs. Donald W. Becker; Ivan R. Trujillo.
Res., 18 Ellicott St., 14020. Tel: 716-343-5400; Fax: 716-344-0213.
School—Tel: 716-343-6866; Fax: 716-344-6603. Miss Nancy J. Sedita, Prin.
Lay Teachers 10; Students 113.
Catechesis/Religious Programs—40 Woodrow Rd., 14020. Tel: 716-343-6866.
Students 173.

4—Sacred Heart, (1904) (Polish), Rev. Eugene S. Slomba.
Res., 15 Sumner St., 14020. Tel: 716-343-1796; Fax: 716-344-3752. [CEM]
Catechesis/Religious Programs—Students 94.

Belfast, Allegany Co., St. Patrick (1859). Attended by St. Patrick, Fillmore. Rev. Michael P. Juran.
Res., 31 E. Hughes St., 14711. Tel: 716-365-2115. [CEM]
Catechesis/Religious Programs—Students 51.

Belmont, Allegany Co., St. Mary (1861). Linked with Sacred Heart, Angelica. Rev. Joseph E. Vatter.
Res., 5 Milton St., 14813. Tel: 716-268-7272; Fax: 716-268-7272.
Catechesis/Religious Programs—Students 92.
Mission—Scio, Allegany Co., St. Joseph, (1844) Rte. 19 at Day Brook Rd., 14880. Tel: 716-268-7272; Fax: 716-268-7272. [CEM]

Bemus Point, Chautauqua Co., Our Lady of Lourdes (1948), Rev. John L. Kuhlmann.
Res., 42 Main St., P.O. Box 500, 14712. Tel: 716-386-2400; Fax: 716-386-5562.
School—Holy Family Catholic School. See listing under Regional Consolidated Elementary Schools in the Institutions located in the Diocese.

Bennington Center, Wyoming Co., Sacred Heart of Jesus (1872). Linked with Our Lady of Good Counsel, Darien Center. Rev. Joseph A. Fiore.
Res., 1230 Clinton St., Attica, 14011. Tel: 716-591-0176; Fax: 716-591-4818. [CEM]
School—Genesee-Wyoming Catholic Central Consolidated School. See separate listing under Regional and Consolidated Elementary Schools in the Institutions located in the Diocese. Tel: 716-591-2515; Fax: 716-591-1614.
Catechesis/Religious Programs—Tel: 716-591-0205. Mrs. Wendy Murray, D.R.E.
Students 125.

Bergen, Genesee Co., St. Brigid (1861), Rev. Richard J. Keppeler.
Res., P.O. Box 219, 14416. Tel: 716-494-1110; Fax: 716-494-1895. [CEM]
Catechesis/Religious Programs—Students 132.
Mission—South Byron, Genesee Co., St. Michael, (1892) Byron-Stafford Rd., South Byron 14557. Tel: 716-494-1110; Fax: 716-494-1895.

Blasdell, Erie Co., Our Mother of Good Counsel (1905), Revs. Lawrence E. Burns; Edward R. Czarnecki; Sr. Marcella Bauerlein, S.S.J., Pastoral Assoc.
Res., 3688 S. Park Ave., 14219. Tel: 716-822-2630; Fax: 716-821-5980.
School—15 Oakwood Ave., 14219. Tel: 716-823-6286; Fax: 716-823-6286. Mrs. Bonnie Ryan, Prin. Sisters of St. Joseph 1; Lay Teachers 14; Students 170.
Catechesis/Religious Programs—Alice Appenheimer, D.R.E.
Students 357.

Bliss, Wyoming Co., St. Joseph (1907). Attended by St. Nicholas, North Java. Rev. Edward E. Muerder.
Res., St. Nicholas Rectory, Rte. 98, North Java, 14113. Tel: 716-535-7457.
Church—P.O. Box 80, 14024. Tel: 716-322-8866.
Catechesis/Religious Programs—Students 44.

Blossom, Erie Co., St. Gabriel (1925), Revs. Daniel J. Palys; Peter J. Karalus. Pastoral Assocs.: Sr. Joseph Marie Marczak, C.S.S.F.; Ann Bauman.
Res., 5271 Clinton St., Elma, 14059-7617. Tel: 716-668-4017; Fax: 716-656-0616.
Catechesis/Religious Programs—Tel: 716-668-2070. Rose Andrews, D.R.E.
Students 1,210.

Bolivar, Allegany Co., St. Mary (1903). Attended by Sacred Heart, Portville. Rev. Robert J. Schober.
Res., Sacred Heart, 43 Maple Ave., Portville, 14770. Tel: 716-933-6394; Fax: 716-933-0275. [CEM]
Church—111 Wellsville St., 14715. Tel: 716-928-1024.

Boston, Erie Co., St. John the Baptist (1869), Rev. Msgr. Paul F. Stengel.
Res., 6895 Boston Cross Rd., 14025-9601. Tel: 716-941-3549; Fax: 716-941-3030. [CEM]
School—St. Aloysius Regional School, Springville. See separate listing under Regional and Consolidated Elementary Schools in the Institutions located in the Diocese.
Catechesis/Religious Programs—Tel: 716-941-6363.
Students 261.

Bowmansville, Erie Co., Sacred Heart (1920), Rev. Msgr. Walter O. Kern; Rev. Msgr. Arnold J. Schneider.
Res., 5337 Genesee St., 14026-1098. Tel: 716-683-2375; Fax: 716-683-0412. [CEM]
School—SS. Peter & Paul Consolidated School. See separate listing under Regional and Consolidated Elementary Schools in the Institutions located in the Diocese. Tel: 716-683-8049.

Brant, Erie Co., Our Lady of Mt. Carmel (1906), Rev. James E. Fitzgerald.
Res., 10708 Brant-Angola Rd., P.O. Box 225, 14027-0225. Tel: 716-549-2418; Fax: 716-549-7740. [CEM]
Catechesis/Religious Programs—Students 68.

Brocton, Chautauqua Co., St. Patrick (1922), Rev. Robert G. Beiter.
Res., 12 Central Ave., P.O. Box P, 14716-0675. Tel: 716-792-4125; Fax: 716-792-4772.
School—Northern Chautauqua Catholic Regional School. See separate listing under Regional and Consolidated Elementary Schools in the Institutions located in the Diocese.
Catechesis/Religious Programs—Diana Giambra, D.R.E.
Students 102.

Canaseraga, Allegany Co., St. Mary (1855). Attended by Assumption B.V.M., Portageville. Rev. Robert M. Mock.
Mailing Address: P.O. Box 404, Portageville, 14536-0404. Tel: 716-468-2643.
Res., 7 North St., Box 234, 14822. Tel: 607-545-8943; Fax: 716-468-2126. [CEM]
Catechesis/Religious Programs—Students 21.

Cassadaga, Chautauqua Co., Immaculate Conception. Linked with St. John the Evangelist, Sinclairville. Rev. Patrick H. Elis.
Res., 14718. Tel: 716-595-3141.

Cattaraugus, Cattaraugus Co., St. Mary (1863), Rev. William E. Frankhauser, S.J., Temp. Admin.
Res., 36 Washington St., 14719. Tel: 716-257-9351.
Catechesis/Religious Programs—Students 58.
Convent—65 South St., 14719. Tel: 716-257-9781. Missionary Sisters of the Divine Child
Mission—Little Valley, Cattaraugus Co., St. Mary.
Oratory—East Otto, Cattaraugus Co., St. Isidore, (1957).

Cheektowaga, Erie Co.,

1—St. Aloysius Gonzaga, (1940), Rev. Msgr. Peter J. Popadick.
Res., 157 Cleveland Dr., Buffalo, 14215. Tel: 716-833-1715; Fax: 716-837-5703.
School—Tel: 716-836-4549; Fax: 716-836-2191. Sr. Marilyn Ann Dudek, C.S.S.F., Prin.
Sisters of St. Felix of Cantalice 2; Lay Teachers 18; Students 151.
Catechesis/Religious Programs—Students 126.

2—Infant of Prague, (1946), Rev. Msgr. Angelo M. Caligiuri; Rev. Richard A. Massar; Deacon Alan A. Meister. In res., Rev. Patrick Zengierski.
Res., 921 Cleveland Dr., 14225. Tel: 716-634-3660; Fax: 716-634-3661.
School—Tel: 716-632-5482; 632-5539. Robert L. Figueroa, Prin.
Lay Teachers 26; Students 280.
Catechesis/Religious Programs—Sr. M. Antonita Sikorski, C.S.S.F., D.R.E.
Students 335.

3—St. John Gualbert, (1917) (Polish), Revs. Daniel A. Pokornowski; David W. Bialkowski; Deacon Franklyn C. Steffen.
Res., 83 Gualbert Ave., 14211. Tel: 716-892-5746; Fax: 716-897-3906.
School—Kolbe Catholic, Tel: 716-895-3127; Fax: 716-895-7347. Rose Mary Buscaglia, Prin.
Lay Teachers 16; Students 213.
Catechesis/Religious Programs—Tel: 716-897-2619. Mrs. Karen Pszczolkowski, D.R.E.
Students 98.

4—St. Josaphat, (1906) (Polish), Rev. Theodore C. Rog; Deacon Robert W. Badaszewski. In res., Rev. Bernard T. Sokolowski.
Res., 20 Peoria Ave., 14206. Tel: 716-893-1086; Fax: 716-893-1099.
School—Tel: 716-893-6448. Sr. Margaret M. Smith, O.S.F., Prin.
Order of St. Francis 1; Lay Teachers 15; Students 194.
Catechesis/Religious Programs—Tel: 716-896-5007. Maryanne Mann, D.R.E.
Students 189.

5—Most Holy Redeemer, (1913), Rev. F. Norman Sullivan. In res., Rev. Francis D. Sullivan, O.F.M.
Res., 25 Avery Pl., 14225. Tel: 716-895-7589; Fax: 716-895-7590.
School—Kolbe Catholic. See St. John Gualbert, Cheektowaga.
Catechesis/Religious Programs—Marie Zimmer, D.R.E.
Students 6.

6—Mother of Divine Grace, (1946), Rev. Msgr. S. Paul Ayoub.
Res., 120 Old Maryvale Dr., 14225. Tel: 716-834-8488; Fax: 716-834-0335.
Catechesis/Religious Programs—Tel: 716-834-8533; Fax: 716-834-0335.
Students 162.

7—Our Lady Help of Christians, (1890). National Historic Society. Rev. Richard A. Jesionowski.
Res., 4125 Union Rd., 14225. Tel: 716-634-3420; 634-3428; Fax: 716-634-3464. [CEM]
School—Tel: 716-632-4199; Fax: 716-632-4298. Lay Teachers 16; Students 151; Preschool 73.
Catechesis/Religious Programs—Tel: 716-632-3532. Denise Seeley, D.R.E.
Students 360.

8—Our Lady of Czestochowa, (1922) (Polish American), Rev. Harry F. Szczesniak.
Res., 23 Willowlawn Pkwy., Buffalo, 14206. Tel: 716-822-5590; Fax: 716-828-9001.
School—Tel: 716-824-2225.
Lay Teachers 11; Students 95.
Catechesis/Religious Programs—Tel: 716-826-3497.
Students 65.

9—St. Philip the Apostle, (1967), Revs. Joseph H. Penkaul; Fabian J. Maryanski; Deacon Walter N. Fudala. In res., Rev. Msgr. Anthony J. Jasinski, Pastor Emeritus.
Res., 950 Losson Rd., 14227. Tel: 716-668-8370; Fax: 716-668-3824.

Catechesis/Religious Programs—Tel: 716-668-3344. Madeline Fuller, D.R.E.
Students 1,010.

10—QUEEN OF MARTYRS, (1946), Rev. Daniel A. Lapinski. In res., Rev. John J. Sardina.
Res., 180 George Urban Blvd., Buffalo, 14225-3095. Tel: 716-892-1746; Fax: 716-892-3005.
School—Tel: 716-895-6280; Fax: 716-895-6359. Sr. Diane Marie, C.S.S.F., Prin.
Felician Sisters 2; Lay Teachers 15; Students 137.
Catechesis/Religious Programs—Tel: 716-895-2162. Kathy Seibold, D.R.E.
Students 240.

11—RESURRECTION, (1944), Rev. Walter L. Matuszak.
Res., 130 Como Park Blvd., 14227. Tel: 716-683-3712; Fax: 716-683-3712.
School—Tel: 716-683-8785; Fax: 716-683-8785. Sr. M. Christinette Lojewski, C.S.S.F., Prin.
Sisters 1; Lay Teachers 11; Students 95.
Catechesis/Religious Programs—Tel: 716-683-3422.
Students 176.

Cherry Creek, Chautauqua Co., St. Elizabeth. Closed. For inquiries for parish records contact the Chancery.

Clarence, Erie Co., Our Lady of Peace (1922), Rev. Msgr. Richard L. Wetter.
Res., 10950 Main St., 14031. Tel: 716-759-8554; Fax: 716-759-8537.
Catechesis/Religious Programs—Students 445.

Clarence Center, Erie Co., St. Augustine (1949), Rev. Edward H. Schroeder; Deacon Norman Foster.
Res., 8700 Goodrich Rd., 14032. Tel: 716-741-2258; Fax: 716-741-5195.
Catechesis/Religious Programs—Rosey Frost, D.R.E.
Students 239.

Colden, Erie Co., Our Lady of the Sacred Heart (1912), Rev. Richard C. Coveny.
Res., 8428 Heath Rd., 14033. Tel: 716-941-5817; Fax: 716-941-5342.
School—St. Aloysius Regional School, Springville. See separate listing under Regional and Consolidated Elementary Schools in the Institutions located in the Diocese.
Catechesis/Religious Programs—Students 100.

Collins Center, Erie Co., St. Frances Cabrini (1955). Linked with St. Martin, Langford and St. Mary, New Oregon. Rev. Lawrence P. Damian.
Res., 13940 Sisson Hwy., P.O. 332, 14035. Tel: 716-532-9431; Fax: 716-532-9431.
School—St. Aloysius Regional School, Springville. See separate listing under Regional and Consolidated Elementary Schools.
Catechesis/Religious Programs—Students 118.

Corfu, Genesee Co., St. Francis of Assisi (1898), Rev. Robert E. Waters.
Res., W. Main St., 14036. Tel: 716-599-4833; Fax: 716-937-9883. [CEM]
Mission—Crittenden, Erie Co., St. Patrick, Alden-Crittenden Rd, Crittenden, 14038. Tel: 716-599-4833; Fax: 716-937-9883.

Crittenden, Erie Co., St. Patrick (1857). Mission of St. Francis of Assisi, Corfu. Rev. Robert E. Waters.
Alden-Crittenden Rd., 14038. Tel: 716-599-4833; Fax: 716-937-9883.; W. Main St., Corfu, 14036.

Cuba, Allegany Co., Our Lady of Angels (1850), Rev. Jerome M. Dissek.
Res., 50 South St., 14727. Tel: 716-968-2885; Fax: 716-968-0123. [CEM]
School—Southern Tier Catholic Regional School. See separate listing under Regional and Consolidated Elementary Schools in the Institutions located in the Diocese.
Catechesis/Religious Programs—Students 65.
Mission—Friendship, Allegany Co., Sacred Heart, 20 W. Main St., Friendship 14739. Tel: 716-968-2885.

Darien Center, Genesee Co., Our Lady of Good Counsel (1911). Attended by Sacred Heart of Jesus, Bennington Center. Rev. Joseph A. Fiore. In res., Rev. Francis P. Kowalewski.
Res., 14040. Tel: 716-547-3547; Fax: 716-547-3547. [CEM]
School—Genesee-Wyoming Catholic Central Consolidated School. See separate listing under Regional and Consolidated Elementary Schools in the Institutions located in the Diocese.
Oratory—Bennington, Wyoming Co., Our Lady Help of Christians, 1670 Church Rd., 14040.

Dayton, Cattaraugus Co., St. Paul of the Cross. Closed. For inquiries for parish records contact St. John Fisher, South Dayton.

Delevan, Cattaraugus Co., Blessed Sacrament (1947). Linked wtih Holy Family, Machias. Rev. Raymond F. Uschold.
Res., 10 N. Main St., P.O. Box 188, 14042. Tel: 716-492-2383; Fax: 716-492-3214.
School—St. Aloysius Regional School, Springville. See separate listing under Regional and Consolidated Elementary Schools in the Institutions Located in the Diocese.
Catechesis/Religious Programs—716-353-4033 Deborah Gambino, D.R.E.
Students 31.

Depew, Erie Co.,

1—ST. AUGUSTINE, (1909) (Polish), Rev. Conrad P. Stachowiak.
Res., 425 Penora St., 14043. Tel: 716-683-3038; Fax: 716-683-9918. [CEM]
Catechesis/Religious Programs—Students 61.

2—ST. BARNABAS, (1960), Rev. Msgr. John W. Madsen; Deacon Thaddeus P. May. In res., Rev. Daniel J. Fawls.
Res., 2049 George Urban Blvd., 14043. Tel: 716-685-2350; Fax: 716-685-8679.
School—Tel: 716-684-1444; Fax: 716-685-2350. Sr. M. Rosa Mystica, O.S.F., Prin.
Sisters 1; Lay Teachers 11; Students 97.
Catechesis/Religious Programs—2099 George Urban Blvd., 14043. Tel: 716-685-2000; Fax: 716-685-2350. Patricia Kern, D.R.E.
Students 600.

3—ST. JAMES, (1897), Rev. David J. Borowiak.
Res., 496 Terrace Blvd., 14043. Tel: 716-683-2746; Fax: 716-683-3121.
School—500 Terrace Blvd., 14043. Tel: 716-683-0050. Sr. Mary Georgette, C.S.S.F., Prin.
Sisters 4; Lay Teachers 16; Students 143.
Catechesis/Religious Programs—Janet Corda, D.R.E.
Students 229.
Convent—55 Westfield Ave., 14043. Tel: 716-683-6653. Felician Nuns

4—SS. PETER AND PAUL, (1896) (Polish), Rev. Stanley F. Nowak.
Res., 86 Burlington Ave., 14043. Tel: 716-683-1645; Fax: 716-685-6754.
School—SS. Peter & Paul Consolidated School. See separate listing under Regional and Consolidated Elementary Schools in the Institutions located in the Diocese. Tel: 716-683-8049; Fax: 716-683-0699.
Catechesis/Religious Programs—Tel: 716-686-9501. Sr. Thaddeus Pogorzala, D.R.E.
Students 166.

5—OUR LADY OF THE BLESSED SACRAMENT, (1965), Rev. Louis S. Dolinic. In res., Rev. Leon J. Biernat.
Res., 10 French Rd., 14043. Tel: 716-684-6342; Fax: 716-684-1853.
School—20 French Rd., 14043. Tel: 716-685-2544; Fax: 716-685-9103.
Felician Sisters 1; Lay Teachers 15; Students 236.
Catechesis/Religious Programs—Tel: 716-685-2546.
Students 502.

Dunkirk, Chautauqua Co.,

1—ST. HEDWIG, (1902) (Polish), Rev. Joseph J. Janaczek.
Res., 324 Townsend St., 14048. Tel: 716-366-1615; 366-2307 (Office); Fax: 716-363-0106. [CEM]
School—Northern Chautauqua Catholic Regional School. See separate listing under Regional and Consolidated Elementary Schools in the Institutions located in the Diocese.

2—HOLY TRINITY, (1908) (Italian), Rev. Martin L. Pavlock; Deacons Donald W. Shultz, Sr.; Jeffrey T. Vogt.
Res., 1032 Central Ave., 14048. Tel: 716-366-2306; Fax: 716-366-4738. [CEM]
School—Northern Chautauqua Catholic Regional School. See separate listing under Regional and Consolidated Elementary Schools in the Institutions located in the Diocese. Tel: 716-366-0630; Fax: 716-366-5101.
Catechesis/Religious Programs—Tel: 716-366-0499. D.R.E.: Roberta Coniglio; Donna Seyedian.
Students 160.

3—ST. HYACINTH, (1875) (Polish American), Rev. Michael Parker; Deacon Daniel Mackowiak.
Res., 295 Lakeshore Dr. E., 14048. Tel: 716-366-7266; Fax: 716-363-0031. [CEM]
School—Tel: 716-366-1950; Fax: 716-366-1192.
Felician Sisters 3; Lay Teachers 11; Students 181.
Catechesis/Religious Programs—Tel: 716-366-5707.
Students 154.

4—ST. ELIZABETH ANN SETON, (1975), Rev. Thomas J. Wopperer; Deacons Thomas Nadeau; Moises N. Cruz; Jose J. Ruiz. In res., Rev. Walter Werbicki.
Res., 328 Washington Ave., 14048. Tel: 716-366-1750; Fax: 716-366-4398. [CEM]
School—Northern Chautauqua Catholic Regional School. See separate listing under Regional and Consolidated Elementary Schools in the Institutions located in the Diocese. Tel: 716-366-0630.
Catechesis/Religious Programs—Tel: 716-366-2827. Samuel Mancuso, D.R.E.
Students 353.

East Arcade, Wyoming Co., St. Mary's (1846). Attended by SS. Peter and Paul, Arcade. Rev. Michael G. Uebler.
Mailing Address: 6785 E. Arcade Rd., Arcade, 14009. Tel: 716-492-2282; Fax: 716-492-2282.
Res., 417 Main St., Arcade, 14009. Tel: 716-492-5330; Fax: 716-492-1047. [CEM]
Catechesis/Religious Programs—Students 68.

East Aurora, Erie Co., Immaculate Conception (1901), Rev. Msgr. Kevin T. O'Neill; Rev. George Poltorak, S.A.C. (Poland); Deacon John Ruh.
Res., 520 Oakwood Ave., 14052. Tel: 716-652-6400; Fax: 716-652-7168. [CEM]
School—510 Oakwood Ave., 14052. Tel: 716-652-5855. Susan K. Gregg, Prin.
Lay Teachers 15; Students 231.
Catechesis/Religious Programs—Tel: 716-655-0067. Cheryl A. Bennett, D.R.E.
Students 683.

East Bethany, Genesee Co., Immaculate Conception, Rev. Thomas L. Kemp.
Res., 5865 Ellicott St., 14054. Tel: 716-343-4537; Fax: 716-343-4537.
Catechesis/Religious Programs—Students 99.

East Eden, Erie Co., St. Mary (1835), Rev. James A. Grimmer.
Res., 8175 E. Eden Rd., 14057. Tel: 716-992-4237; Fax: 716-992-2435. [CEM]
School—Regionalized School of the Immaculate Conception. See separate listing under Regional and Consolidated Elementary Schools under Institutions located in the Diocese.
Catechesis/Religious Programs—Tel: 716-992-3123. Dorothy Zydel, D.R.E.
Students 180.

East Pembroke, Genesee Co., Holy Name of Mary (1868), Rev. David J. Scheider, Admin.
Res., P.O. Box 219, 14056. Tel: 716-762-9006; Fax: 716-762-9036.

Eden, Erie Co., Immaculate Conception (1908), Revs. Walter P. Grabowski; Francis Parella, S.S.P.; Deacon Richard H. Kelsey; Mrs. Patricia Casseri, Pastoral Assoc.
Res., 8791 S. Main St., 14057. Tel: 716-992-3933; Fax: 716-992-2201. [CEM]
School—Regionalized School of the Immaculate Conception. See separate listing under Regional and Consolidated Elementary Schools under Institutions located in the Diocese.
Catechesis/Religious Programs—D.R.E.: Sharon Reed; Theresa S. Hains.
Students 367.

St. Mary of Immaculate Conception (1858). Attended by St. Frances Cabrini, Collins Center. Rev. Lawrence P. Damian.
Res., 5107 Langford Rd. (New Oregon), 14057. Tel: 716-337-2291; Fax: 716-532-9431. [CEM]
School—Regionalized School of the Immaculate Conception. See separate listing under Regional and Consolidated Elementary Schools under Institutions located in the Diocese.
Catechesis/Religious Programs—Students 114.

Eggertsville, Erie Co., St. Benedict (1920), Rev. Msgr. John M. Ryan; Rev. Patrick T. O'Keefe.
Res., 1317 Eggert Rd., 14226. Tel: 716-834-1041; Fax: 716-835-5949.
School—Tel: 716-835-2518; Fax: 716-834-4932. Christine Balcerek, Prin.
Sisters of St. Francis of Penance and Christian Charity 1; Lay Teachers 22; Students 350.
Catechesis/Religious Programs—Tel: 716-836-6444. Sr. Virginia Judge, O.S.F., D.R.E.
Students 422.

Elba, Genesee Co., Our Lady of Fatima (1947), Rev. Robert A. Martin, Admin.
Res., 65 S. Main St., P.O. Box 185, 14058-0185. Tel: 716-757-6891; Fax: 716-757-2472.
Catechesis/Religious Programs—Students 138.

Ellicottville, Cattaraugus Co., Holy Name of Mary (1850), Rev. Ronald B. Mierzwa.
Res., P.O. Box 543, 14731. Tel: 716-699-2592; Fax: 716-699-8439. [CEM]
Catechesis/Religious Programs—Students 176.

Elma, Erie Co., Annunciation of the Blessed Virgin Mary (1906), Revs. Emil P. Swiatek; Robert W. Wood; Deacons Joseph Mercurio; Dennis Kapsiak.
Res., 7580 Clinton St., 14059. Tel: 716-683-5254; Fax: 716-685-2401. [CEM]
School—Tel: 716-681-1327.
Lay Teachers 18; Students 162; Preschool Students 48.
Catechesis/Religious Programs—Tel: 716-683-5515.
Students 670.

Falconer, Chautauqua Co., Our Lady of Loreto (1912). Linked with Our Lady of Victory, Frewsburg. Rev. Joseph A. Gullo.
Res., 309 W. Everett St., 14733. Tel: 716-665-4253; Fax: 716-664-9223.

School—Holy Family Catholic School. See listing under Regional and Consolidated Elementary Schools in the Institutions located in the Diocese.
Catechesis/Religious Programs—Tel: 716-665-3764. Beverly Smeragliuolo, D.R.E.
Students 110.

Farnham, Erie Co., St. Anthony's (1904), Rev. James W. Fliss.
Res., 421 Commercial St., 14061. Tel: 716-549-1159; Fax: 716-549-7722. [CEM]
Catechesis/Religious Programs—Fax: 716-549-7742. Sandra Walch, D.R.E.
Students 154.

Fillmore, Allegany Co., St. Patrick (1881). Linked with St. Patrick, Belfast. Rev. Michael P. Juran.
Res., 14735. Tel: 716-567-2282; Fax: 716-567-4172. [CEM]
Catechesis/Religious Programs—Students 38.

Forestville, Chautauqua Co., St. Rose of Lima (1850). Attended by St. John Bosco, Sheridan. Rev. Gerald P. Sheehan.
Res., 2773 Main Rd., Sheridan, 14135. Tel: 716-679-4951; Fax: 716-679-4952.

Franklinville, Cattaraugus Co., St. Philomena (1906), Rev. Michael D. O'Hara.
Res., 26 N. Plymouth Ave., 14737. Tel: 716-676-3629; Fax: 716-676-2104. [JC]
Catechesis/Religious Programs—Tel: 716-676-2123. Kathy Berry, D.R.E.
Students 64.

Fredonia, Chautauqua Co., St. Anthony (1905), Rev. Carlton J. Westfield; Deacon Moises Cruz.
Res., 42 Orchard St., 14063. Tel: 716-679-4050; 679-4096 (Office); Fax: 716-672-8576 (Office); 679-0326(Rectory).
School—Northern Chautauqua Catholic Regional School. See separate listing under Regional and Consolidated Elementary Schools in the Institutions located in the Diocese. Tel: 716-366-0630.
Catechesis/Religious Programs—Tel: 716-674-1268. Mrs. Barbara O'Connell, D.R.E.
Students 300.

St. Joseph (1899), Rev. Charles J. Zadora; Deacon Matthew A. Podniesinski.
Res., 145 E. Main St., 14063. Tel: 716-679-4116; Fax: 716-679-1352 (1-5 P.M.).
School—Northern Chautauqua Catholic Regional School. See separate listing under Regional and Consolidated Elementary Schools in the Institutions located in the Diocese. Tel: 716-366-0630.
Catechesis/Religious Programs—Tel: 716-672-2647.
Students 194.

French Creek, Chautauqua Co., St. Matthias (1873). Linked with Our Lady of the Snows, Panama. Rev. Bernard C. Staszak.
Res., 1762 French Creek Mina Rd., Clymer, 14724-0660. Tel: 716-355-8891; Fax: 716-355-2576. [CEM]
School—Holy Family Catholic School. See listing under Regional and Consolidated Elementary Schools in the Institutions located in the Diocese.
Catechesis/Religious Programs—Students 68.

Frewsburg, Chautauqua Co., Our Lady of Victory (1950). Attended by Our Lady of Loreto, Falconer. Rev. Joseph A. Gullo.
Res., 14738. Tel: 716-569-4725; Fax: 716-569-2292.
School—Holy Family Catholic School. See listing under Regional and Consolidated Elementary Schools in the Institutions located in the Diocese.
Catechesis/Religious Programs—Beverly Smeragliuolo, D.R.E.
Students 55.

Friendship, Allegany Co., Sacred Heart (1912). Mission of Our Lady of the Angels, Cuba. Rev. Jerome M. Dissek.
Res., 81 W. Main St., 14739. Tel: 716-973-2871; Fax: 716-968-0123. [CEM]

Gasport, Niagara Co., St. Mary (1968). Linked with St. Stephen, Middleport. Rev. Joseph P. Badding; Deacon Nelson Darroch.
Res., 8110 West Ave., 14067. Tel: 716-772-7803; Fax: 716-772-7931.
Catechesis/Religious Programs—Deborah Brown, D.R.E.
Students 100.

Getzville, Erie Co., St. Pius X (1958), Rev. Msgr. George B. Yiengst; Deacons Brian Walkowiak; Donald E. Seyfried.
Res., 1700 N. French Rd., P.O. Box 162, 14068-0162. Tel: 716-688-9143; Fax: 716-688-1203.
Catechesis/Religious Programs—Tel: 716-688-5417.
Students 640.

Gowanda, Erie Co., St. Joseph (1900), Rev. Lawrence M. Milby.
Res., 26 Erie Ave., 14070. Tel: 716-532-5100; Fax: 716-532-4096. [CEM]
School—Tel: 716-532-2520; Fax: 716-532-4172. Mr. Vincent George, Prin.
Lay Teachers 10; Students 110.
Catechesis/Religious Programs—Tel: 716-992-4151.
Students 121.

Grand Island, Erie Co., St. Stephen (1862), Revs. Paul M. Nogaro; Daniel F. Fiebelkorn; Deacon John A. Polizzi.
Res., 2100 Baseline Rd., 14072. Tel: 716-773-7647; Fax: 716-773-5792. [CEM]
School—2080 Baseline Rd., 14072. Tel: 716-773-4347. Sr. Christina Marie Luczynski, C.S.S.F., Prin.
Felician Sisters 1; Lay Teachers 22; Students 265.
Catechesis/Religious Programs—Tel: 716-773-2002. D.R.E.: Angela Diebold; Donna Wilson.
Students 917.

Hamburg, Erie Co., SS. Peter and Paul (1844), Revs. Mark J. Wolski; James D. Ciupek; Paul S. Salemi.
Res., 66 E. Main St., 14075. Tel: 716-649-2765; Fax: 716-649-5218. [CEM]
School—68 E. Main St., 14075. Tel: 716-649-7030. Kathleen Walters, Prin.
Lay Teachers 21; Students 312.
Catechesis/Religious Programs—Tel: 716-649-0231. D.R.E.: Mary Ann Senchyne; Sr. Eileen Steen, R.S.M.
Students 1,011.

St. Mary of the Lake (1948), Rev. Msgr. W. Jerome Sullivan.
Res., S-4737 Lake Shore Rd., 14075. Tel: 716-627-3123; Fax: 716-627-7062.
School—Tel: 716-627-7700. Mrs. Patricia E. Bollenbacher, Prin.
Franciscan Sisters of St. Joseph 2; Lay Teachers 19; Students 156.
Catechesis/Religious Programs—Tel: 716-627-7150. Ms. Mary Margaret Joyce, D.R.E.
Students 462.

Harris Hill, Erie Co., Nativity of the Blessed Virgin Mary (1954), Rev. Msgr. Raymond F. Paa; Rev. Daniel A. Young; Deacons Frank R. Krahling; Peter Bellavance.
Res., 4375 Harris Hill Rd., Williamsville, 14221. Tel: 716-632-8838; Fax: 716-632-7898.
School—Tel: 716-633-7441. Mrs. Cherie M. Ansuini, Prin.
Lay Teachers 16; Students 193.
Catechesis/Religious Programs—8550 Main St., Williamsville, 14221. Tel: 716-634-3130. Mrs. Mary Ann Hoag, D.R.E.
Students 842.

Hinsdale, Cattaraugus Co., St. Helen (1947), Rev. Barry J. Allaire, Admin.
Res., 3826 Main St., P.O. Box 248, 14743-0248. Tel: 716-557-8841; Fax: 716-372-6707.
School—Southern Tier Catholic Regional School. See separate listing under Regional and Consolidated Elementary Schools in the Institutions located in the Diocese.
Catechesis/Religious Programs—Students 25.

Holland, Erie Co., St. Joseph (1890), Rev. Dennis A. Fronczak.
Res., 46 N. Main St., 14080-9509. Tel: 716-537-9434; Fax: 716-537-9988. [CEM 2]
Catechesis/Religious Programs—D.R.E.: Mrs. Theresa Leach Tel: 716-537-9868; Mrs. Joyce Faust Tel: 716-537-9778; Mrs. Diana Claus Tel: 716-537-2111.
Students 270.

Holley, Orleans Co., St. Mary (1866). Linked with St. Mark, Kendall. Rev. Joseph F. Kozlowski.
Res., 11 S. Main St., 14470-1107. Tel: 716-638-6718; Fax: 716-638-3210. [CEM]
Catechesis/Religious Programs—Tel: 716-638-6027. Jean M. Mullins, D.R.E.
Students 151.
Oratory—Hulberton, Orleans Co., St. Rocco, 14470.

Humphrey, Cattaraugus Co., St. Pacificus, Mission of St. Bonaventure University Friary (1855), Rev. J. Gregory Brennan, O.F.M.
Res., St. Bonaventure University, St. Bonaventure, 14778. Tel: 716-375-2545; Fax: 716-375-7620. [CEM]
Catechesis/Religious Programs—Joint program with Holy Name of Mary, Ellicottville.

Jamestown, Chautauqua Co., St. James (1910) (Italian), Rev. Msgr. Antoine Attea; Rev. Patrick O. Fernandes.
Res., 27 Allen St., 14701. Tel: 716-487-0125; Fax: 716-661-3677. [CEM]
School—Holy Family Catholic School. See separate listing under Regional and Consolidated Elementary Schools under Institutions located in the Diocese.
Catechesis/Religious Programs—Tel: 716-664-4237. Julie Rodriguez, D.R.E.
Students 258.

St. John (1939), Rev. Donald S. Fafinski.
Res., 270 Newton Ave., 14701. Tel: 716-664-4556; Fax: 716-483-2108.
Parish Center: Tel: 716-484-1875.
School—Holy Family Catholic School. See separate listing under Regional and Consolidated Elementary Schools under Institutions located in the Diocese.
Catechesis/Religious Programs—Students 80.

St. Peter and Paul (1854), Rev. Dennis W. Mende.
Res., 508 Cherry St., 14701. Tel: 716-664-5703; Fax: 716-664-5288. [CEM 2]
School—Holy Family Catholic School. See separate listing under Regional and Consolidated Elementary Schools under Institutions Located in the Diocese.
Catechesis/Religious Programs—Tel: 716-484-8958.
Students 221.

Java Center, Wyoming Co., St. Patrick (1838). Attended by St. Nicholas, North Java. Rev. Edward E. Muerder.
Res., 14082. Tel: 716-457-9532.
School—Genesee-Wyoming Catholic Central Consolidated School. See separate listing under Regional and Consolidated Elementary Schools in the Institutions located in the Diocese.
Catechesis/Religious Programs—Mary Gentner, D.R.E.
Students 82.

Kendall, Orleans Co., St. Mark (1984). Attended by St. Mary, Holley. Rev. Joseph F. Kozlowski.
Res., 11 S. Main St., Holley, 14470-1107. Tel: 716-638-6718; Fax: 716-638-3210.
Catechesis/Religious Programs—Tel: 716-659-8631. Sr. Mary Anne Rapp, O.S.F., D.R.E.
Students 120.

Kenmore, Erie Co., St. Andrew (1944), Rev. Charles E. Slisz; Deacon David P. McDermott; Sr. Mary Courts, G.N.S.H., Pastoral Assoc. In res., Rev. Vincent J. Ferraro, Chap.
Res., 1525 Sheridan Dr., 14217. Tel: 716-873-6716; Fax: 716-873-2214.
School—Tel: 716-877-0422.
Lay Teachers 40; Students 584.
Catechesis/Religious Programs—Tel: 716-877-3034.
Students 355.

St. John the Baptist (1836), Revs. Richard A. Reina; Michael H. Burzynski; Deacon Bernard M. Thomann.
Res., 1085 Englewood Ave., 14223. Tel: 716-873-1122; Fax: 716-873-3305. [CEM]
School—Englewood & Belmont, 14223. Tel: 716-877-6401; Fax: 716-877-9139. Marilynn Camp, Prin.
Lay Teachers 50; Students 645.
Catechesis/Religious Programs—Tel: 716-877-0474. Catherine Salzman, D.R.E.
Students 385.

St. Paul (1897), Revs. John R. Gaglione; Frederick Hinton; Richard E. Sowinski.
Res., 33 Victoria Blvd., 14217. Tel: 716-875-2730; Fax: 716-874-3475.
School—Tel: 716-877-6308; Fax: 716-877-3874. Louise Lopardi, Prin.
Sisters of St. Mary 1; Lay Teachers 28; Students 420.
Catechesis/Religious Programs—Tel: 716-873-9429.
Students 700.

Knapp Creek, Cattaraugus Co., Sacred Heart, Mission of Allegany. Closed. For sacramental records contact St. Mary of the Angels, Olean.

Lackawanna, Erie Co.,

1—Basilica of Our Lady of Victory, (1854). (National Shrine). Rev. Msgr. Robert C. Wurtz, P.A.; Rev. Msgr. John H. Bugman; Rev. Msgr. Robert E. Murphy; Revs. Edward F. Jost, Jr.; Matthew J. Zirnheld; Deacon Thomas M. Forcucci.
Res., 767 Ridge Rd., 14218. Tel: 716-828-9444; Fax: 716-828-9429.
School—Tel: 716-828-9434; Fax: 716-828-9429. Sr. Ellen O'Keefe, Prin.
Sisters 7; Lay Teachers 19; Students 363.
Catechesis/Religious Programs—Tel: 716-828-9437. Sheila Flynn, D.R.E.
Students 200.

2—St. Anthony, (1917), Rev. Peter J. Drilling; Deacon Michael D. Quinn.
Res., 306 Ingham Ave., 14218. Tel: 716-823-0782; Fax: 716-827-1381.
Catechesis/Religious Programs—Tel: 716-827-8384.
Students 104.

3—Assumption, (1918) (Hungarian), Rev. Kalman Miskolczy, Sch.P., Admin.
Church—80 Steelawanna Ave., 14218. Tel: 716-822-9828.

4—St. Barbara, (1903) (Polish), Rev. Lawrence F. Cobel.
Res., 551 Ridge Rd., 14218. Tel: 716-822-3470; Fax: 716-822-2412.
Catechesis/Religious Programs—Tel: 716-825-8955.
Students 38.

5—St. Hyacinth, (1910) (Polish), Rev. Henry A. Orszulak, Admin.
Res., 253 Ridge Rd., 14218. Tel: 716-823-0845; Fax: 716-826-2292.

6—St. Michael the Archangel, (1921) (Polish), Rev. James M. Augustyn.
Res., 144 Warsaw St., 14218. Tel: 716-826-0880; Fax: 716-828-1867.
Catechesis/Religious Programs—Tel: 716-822-8526. Sr. Mary Thomas Frys, C.S.S.F., D.R.E.
Students 62.

7—Our Lady of Bistrica, (1917) (Croatian), Rev. Christopher Coric, O.F.M.Conv. (Croatia).
Res., 1619 Abbott Rd., 14218. Tel: 716-822-0818; Fax: 716-822-0818.

8—Queen of All Saints, (1949). Merged with St. Anthony, Lackawanna.

Lake View, Erie Co., Our Lady of Perpetual Help (1922), Rev. Msgr. John W. Zeitler; Sr. Sharon Erickson, R.S.M.; Deacon Mark J. Hooper.
Res., 2052 Lake View Ave., 14085. Tel: 716-627-2910; Fax: 716-627-7972.
School—Southtowns Catholic Consolidated School. See separate listing under Regional and Consolidated Elementary Schools in the Institutions located in the Diocese. Tel: 716-627-5011.
Catechesis/Religious Programs—Tel: 716-627-9397. Mrs. Barbara Manley, D.R.E.
Students 450.

Lakewood, Chautauqua Co., Sacred Heart (1912), Rev. Msgr. Joseph M. Dowdell.
Res., 380 E. Fairmount Ave., 14750-2197. Tel: 716-763-2815; Fax: 716-763-5646. [JC]
School—Holy Family Catholic School. See separate listing under Regional and Consolidated Elementary Schools in the Institutions located in the Diocese.
Catechesis/Religious Programs—Marilyn Wozneak, Pastoral Assoc. & D.R.E.
Students 327.

Lancaster, Erie Co., St. Mary of the Assumption (1850), Rev. Msgr. Frederick D. Leising; Revs. Berard Pulikoottil; David R. Glassmire.
Res., 1 St. Mary's Hill, 14086-2094. Tel: 716-683-6445; Fax: 716-684-8446. [CEM]
School—Tel: 716-683-2112; Fax: 716-683-2134. Sr. Barbara Jean Wajda, O.S.F., Prin.
Sisters of Third Order of St. Francis 2; Lay Teachers 20; Students 314.
Catechesis/Religious Programs—Tel: 716-683-8564. Mrs. Elaine Driscoll, D.R.E.
Students 664.

Our Lady of Pompeii (1909), Rev. Jay W. McGinnis. In res., Rev. John P. Mack; Rev. Msgr. Samuel L. Lombardo.
Res., 158 Laverack Ave., 14086. Tel: 716-683-6522; Fax: 716-685-8066.
School—(Grades PreK-8). Tel: 716-684-4664. Mrs. Christine M. Schierer, Prin.
Sisters 1; Lay Teachers 15; Students 215.
Catechesis/Religious Programs—D.R.E.: Antoinette Duran, (Elementary); Joseph Blatz, (High School).
Students 500.

Langford, Erie Co., St. Martin (1851). Attended by St. Frances Cabrini, Collins Center. Rev. Lawrence P. Damian.
Res., 10893 Sisson Hwy. (Langford), North Collins, 14111. Tel: 716-337-2686; Fax: 716-532-9431. [CEM]
School—St. Aloysius Regional School, Springville. See separate listing under Regional and Consolidated Schools in the Institutions located in the Diocese.
Catechesis/Religious Programs—Students 83.

Le Roy, Genesee Co., St. Joseph (1907) (Italian), Rev. Msgr. Emil P. Zupa.
Res., 27 Lake St., 14482. Tel: 716-768-6600; Fax: 716-768-6136. [JC]
Catechesis/Religious Programs—Tel: 716-768-7110.
Students 80.

St. Peter (1849). Linked with St. Anthony, Lime Rock. Rev. Michael R. Rock, O.de.M., Admin.
Res., 44 Lake St., 14482. Tel: 716-768-6543; Fax: 716-768-7093. [CEM]
School—Holy Family School, Tel: 716-768-7390; Fax: 716-768-6680. Mrs. Barbara McVean, Prin.
Lay Teachers 7; Students 130.
Catechesis/Religious Programs—Tel: 716-768-6720.
Students 245.

Lewiston, Niagara Co., St. Peter (1851), Rev. Sebastian C. Pierro.
Res., 620 Center St., 14092. Tel: 716-754-4118; Fax: 716-754-4120.
School—Tel: 716-754-4470; Fax: 716-754-0167. Mr. James M., Allen, Prin.
Franciscan Sisters of St. Joseph 1; Lay Teachers 16; Students 227.
Catechesis/Religious Programs—Tel: 716-754-2812.
Students 327.
Convent—421 Plain St., 14092. Tel: 716-754-4761.

Lime Rock, Genesee Co., St. Anthony (1907). Attended by St. Peter, Le Roy. Rev. Michael R. Rock, O.de.M., Admin.
E. Main Rd. & Church Rd.
Res., 44 Lake St., Le Roy, 14482. Tel: 716-768-6543; Fax: 716-768-7093.

Limestone, Cattaraugus Co., St. Patrick (1875). Attended by St. Bonaventure Friary, Allegany. Rev. Jerome J. Stelmach, Admin. In res., Deacon Don Radlinski.
Res., 16 Church St., 14753. Tel: 716-925-8596. [CEM]
Catechesis/Religious Programs—Students 23.

Little Valley, Cattaraugus Co., St. Mary (1874). Mission of St. Mary's, Cattaraugus. Rev. William E. Frankhauser, S.J., Temp. Admin.
Mailing Address: 36 Washington St., Cattaraugus, 14719. Tel: 716-257-9351.
Catechesis/Religious Programs—Students 20.

Lockport, Niagara Co.,

1—St. Anthony, (1928). Linked with St. Joseph, Lockport. Rev. Joseph S. Rogliano.
Res., 9 Bristol Ave., 14094. Tel: 716-434-5025; Fax: 716-434-6332.
School—DeSales Catholic Consolidated School. See separate listing under Regional and Consolidated Elementary Schools in the Institutions located in the Diocese.
Catechesis/Religious Programs—D.R.E.: Anita Mullane; Kathleen D'Agostino.
Students 130.

2—St. John the Baptist, (1834), Rev. Msgr. Donald L. Wangler; Rev. Joseph C. Dumphrey, O.S.F.S.
Res., 168 Chestnut St., 14094. Tel: 716-433-8118; Fax: 716-433-3562.
School—DeSales Catholic School. See separate listing under Regional and Consolidated Elementary Schools in the Institutions located in the Diocese. Tel: 716-433-6422; Fax: 716-434-4002.
Catechesis/Religious Programs—Tel: 716-438-9029. Sally Sayward, D.R.E.
Students 637.

3—St. Joseph, (1912) (Italian). Attended by St. Anthony, Lockport. Rev. Joseph S. Rogliano.
Res., 391 Market St., 14094. Tel: 716-433-5792; Fax: 716-438-5613.
School—DeSales Catholic School. See separate listing under Regional and Consolidated Elementary Schools in the Institutions located in the Diocese. Tel: 716-433-6422.
Catechesis/Religious Programs—Tel: 716-434-3194. Eleanor N. Xapsos, D.R.E.
Students 142.

4—St. Mary, (1859) (German), Rev. Gary R. Kibler.
Res., 5 Saxton St., 14094. Tel: 716-434-6316; Fax: 716-438-5495. [JC]
School—DeSales Catholic School. See separate listing under Regional and Consolidated Elementary Schools in the Institutions located in the Diocese. Tel: 716-433-6422.
Catechesis/Religious Programs—Tel: 716-433-0340.
Students 53.

5—St. Patrick, (1864), Rev. Francis M. Schimscheiner, O.S.F.S. In res., Revs. Gerald L. Bartko, O.S.F.S.; Joseph C. Dumphrey, O.S.F.S.
Res., 76 Church St., 14094. Tel: 716-433-3707; Fax: 716-438-5608. [CEM]
School—DeSales Catholic School. See separate listing under Regional and Consolidated Elementary Schools in the Institutions located in the Diocese. Tel: 716-433-6422; Fax: 716-434-4002.
Catechesis/Religious Programs—Tel: 716-433-6672. Sr. Rene Ruberto, S.S.M.N., D.R.E.
Students 241.
Convent—138 N. Transit St., 14094. Tel: 716-433-9193.

Lyndonville, Orleans Co., St. Joseph (1962). Attended by Sacred Heart, Medina. Revs. Joseph G. Fifagrowicz; Albert J. Bosack.
Res., 38 Lake Ave., P.O. Box 496, 14098. Tel: 716-765-9722; Fax: 716-798-2833.
Catechesis/Religious Programs—Students 65.

Machias, Cattaraugus Co., Holy Family (1948). Attended by Blessed Sacrament, Delevan. Rev. Raymond F. Uschold.
Res., 10 N. Main St., P.O. Box 188, Delevan, 14042. Tel: 716-492-2383; Fax: 716-492-3214.
School—St. Aloysius Regional School. See separate listing under Regional and Consolidated Elementary Schools in the Institutions located in the Diocese.
Catechesis/Religious Programs—Tel: 716-492-0691.
Students 32.

Mayville, Chautauqua Co., St. Mary (1925). Linked with St. Isaac Jogues, Sherman. Rev. Raymond A.J. Donohue.
Res., 24 E. Chautauqua St., Box 148, 14757. Tel: 716-753-2332; Fax: 716-753-3836.
School—Holy Family Catholic School. See separate listing under Regional and Consolidated Elementary Schools in the Institutions located in the Diocese.
Catechesis/Religious Programs—Students 70.

Medina, Orleans Co., St. Mary (1840), Rev. Msgr. Paul J. Whitney.
Res., 211 Eagle St., 14103. Tel: 716-798-0112; Fax: 716-798-2834. [CEM]
Catechesis/Religious Programs—Tel: 716-798-5399.
Students 281.

Sacred Heart (1910). Linked with St. Joseph, Lyndonville. Rev. Joseph G. Fifagrowicz.
Res., 208 Ann St., 14103. Tel: 716-798-0356; Fax: 716-798-2833. [CEM]
Catechesis/Religious Programs—Students 69.

Middleport, Niagara Co., St. Stephen (1854). Attended by St. Mary, Gasport. Rev. Joseph P. Badding.
Res., 21 Vernon St., 14105-1321. Tel: 716-735-9433; Fax: 716-735-9433. [CEM]
Catechesis/Religious Programs—Students 127.

Newfane, Niagara Co., St. Bridget (1859). Linked with Our Lady of the Rosary, Wilson. Rev. John J. Leising.
Res., 3455 Ewings Rd., Box 87, 14108-0087. Tel: 716-778-9822; Fax: 716-778-8786. [CEM]
Catechesis/Religious Programs—Tel: 716-778-9822. Carol Piech, D.R.E.
Students 225.

Niagara Falls, Niagara Co.,

1—St. Charles Borromeo, (1970), Rev. Robert S. Hughson.
Res., 5604 Lindbergh Ave., 14304-3111. Tel: 716-283-7602; Fax: 716-283-1371.
Catechesis/Religious Programs—Tel: 716-283-1371.
Students 154.

2—St. George, (1915) (Lithuanian), Rev. Seweryn J. Koszyk, S.A.C.
Res., 1910 Falls St., 14303. Tel: 716-282-4587; Fax: 716-282-4587. [JC]

3—Holy Trinity, (1902) (Polish). Linked with St. Stanislaus, Niagra Falls. Most Rev. Edward M. Grosz, D.D., V.G.
Res., 1419 Falls St., 14303. Tel: 716-284-6628; Fax: 716-282-2297. [CEM]
Catechesis/Religious Programs—Tel: 716-284-8944.
Students 9.

4—St. John de La Salle, (1907), Rev. Jerome E. Kopec; Deacon David P. Slish, Pastoral Assoc.
Res., 8027 Buffalo Ave., 14304. Tel: 716-283-2238; Fax: 716-283-7973.
School—Tel: 716-283-3031; Fax: 716-283-4540.
Lay Teachers 14; Students 139.
Catechesis/Religious Programs—Tel: 716-283-8442.
Students 210.

5—St. Joseph, (1903) (Italian), Rev. Msgr. Richard S. Amico; Sr. Francis Marie Vallone, F.M.D.C., Pastoral Assoc.
Res., 1413 Pine Ave., 14301. Tel: 877-864-7131 (Toll Free); 716-282-1379; Fax: 716-285-3704. [CEM]
School—625 Tronolone Pl., 14301. Tel: 716-282-8144.
Franciscan Sisters of Allegany 2; Lay Teachers 14; Students 188.
Catechesis/Religious Programs—Tel: 716-283-8442. Mrs. Rae Pullo, D.R.E.
Students 183.

6—St. Leo, (1957), Rev. David G. Griffin; Deacon Ben Marino, Pastoral Assoc.
Res., 2748 Military Rd., 14304. Tel: 716-297-3690; Fax: 716-297-8314.
Catechesis/Religious Programs—Tel: 716-297-3085.
Students 295.

7—St. Mary of the Cataract, (1847), Rev. Michael H. Burzynski, Admin. In res., Revs. Mark M. Friel, Chap., Memorial Medical Center; Francis Gross, O.S.F.S.; Bro. Francis Murray, O.S.F.S.

Res., 259 Fourth St., 14303. Tel: 716-282-0059; Fax: 716-282-3372.

8—OUR LADY OF LEBANON, (1914) (Lebanese), Rev. Henry M. Bradbury, C.M.
Res., 1120 Niagara St., 14303. Tel: 716-282-0729; Fax: 716-782-4779.
Catechesis/Religious Programs—Students 35.

9—OUR LADY OF MOUNT CARMEL, (1949), Rev. Duane R. Klizek.
Res., 2486 Grand Ave., 14301. Tel: 716-282-5546; Fax: 716-282-6395.
School—2499 Independence Ave., 14301. Tel: 716-282-0645; Fax: 716-282-7681.
Lay Teachers 15; Students 200.
Catechesis/Religious Programs—Students 155.

10—OUR LADY OF THE ROSARY, (1906), Rev. David J. Peter.
Res., 339 22nd St., 14303. Tel: 716-282-0264; Fax: 716-282-0264.
Catechesis/Religious Programs—Tri-Parish Religious Education Program, 335 24th St., 14303. Tel: 716-284-8944.

11—PRINCE OF PEACE, (1943), Revs. William C. McGarry; Francis J. Zmozynski.
Res., 1040 Cayuga Dr., 14304. Tel: 716-283-2715; Fax: 716-236-4157.
School—(Grades PreK-6). Tel: 716-283-1455. Sr. Mary Asarese, S.S.M.N., Prin.
Sisters 3; Students 254.
Catechesis/Religious Programs—Tel: 716-283-0569.
Students 359.

12—SACRED HEART, (1854), Rev. James J. Kasinski.
Res., 1917 11th St., 14305. Tel: 716-282-1749; Fax: 716-282-1665.
School—Tel: 716-282-8484. Miss Jeanne Rougeux, Prin.
Lay Teachers 10; Students 106.
Catechesis/Religious Programs—Patricia McCarthy, D.R.E.
Students 105.

13—ST. STANISLAUS KOSTKA, (1917) (Polish). Linked with Holy Trinity, Niagra Falls. Most Rev. Edward M. Grosz, D.D., V.G. In res., Rev. Msgr. Edward J. Scanlan.
Res., 2437 Niagara St., 14303. Tel: 716-285-3604; Fax: 716-282-2297.
Catechesis/Religious Programs—Tel: 716-284-8944.
Students 58.

14—ST. TERESA OF THE INFANT JESUS, (1930), Rev. Msgr. Leonard E. Biniszkiewicz.
Res., 3840 Macklem Ave., 14305. Tel: 716-282-5583; Fax: 716-282-0453.
Catechesis/Religious Programs—Tel: 716-282-0795; Fax: 716-282-2447. Catherine Halliday, D.R.E.
Students 215.

North Collins, Erie Co., Holy Spirit (1958), Rev. James G. Judge.
Res., 2017 Halley Rd., 14111. Tel: 716-337-2544; Fax: 716-337-3803. [CEM 2]
School—Regional School of the Immaculate Conception, Eden. See separate listing under Regional and Consolidated Elementary Schools.
Catechesis/Religious Programs—Tel: 716-337-3701. Sr. Ellen Bowman, D.R.E.
Students 183.

North Evans, Erie Co., St. Vincent (1914), Revs. William R. Tuyn; Brian M. Hatrick.
Res., 2050 S. Creek Rd., 14112. Tel: 716-627-3382; Fax: 716-627-3176. [CEM]
School—Southtowns Catholic Consolidated School. See separate listing under Regional and Consolidated Elementary Schools in the Institutions located in the Diocese. Tel: 716-627-5011; Fax: 716-627-2455.
Catechesis/Religious Programs—Tel: 716-627-7673. Ann Kirkpatrick, D.R.E.
Students 398.

North Java, Wyoming Co., St. Nicholas (1890). Linked with St. Patrick, Java Center and St. Joseph, Bliss. Rev. Edward E. Muerder.
Res., 14113. Tel: 716-535-7457. [CEM]
School—Genesee-Wyoming Catholic Central Consolidated School. See separate listing under Regional and Consolidated Elementary Schools in the Institutions located in the Diocese.

North Tonawanda, Niagara Co.,

1—ASCENSION, (1887), Rev. Gary Szczepankiewicz.
Res., 168 Robinson St., 14120. Tel: 716-693-1211; Fax: 716-693-1263.
School—North Tonawanda Consolidated Catholic School. See separate listing under Regional and Consolidated Elementary Schools in the Institutions located in the Diocese. Tel: 716-693-2828; Fax: 716-693-0169.
Catechesis/Religious Programs—Tel: 716-694-3754. D.R.E.: Kathleen Kocsis; Suzanne Ruska.
Students 226.

2—ST. ALBERT THE GREAT, (1960), Rev. Msgr. Edward T. Fisher; Deacon Daniel E. Brick, Esq.; Mr. Gary Copeland, Pastoral Assoc. In res., Rev. Duane G. Fimbel.
Res., 1520 Kingston Ave., 14120. Tel: 716-694-0540; Fax: 716-694-8943.
Catechesis/Religious Programs—Tel: 716-694-4540.
Students 653.

3—ST. JOSEPH, (1947), Rev. Msgr. Thomas E. Crane.
Res., 1451 Payne Ave., 14120. Tel: 716-693-2791; Fax: 716-743-1405.
School—North Tonawanda Catholic Consolidated School. See separate listing under Regional and Consolidated Elementary Schools in the Institutions located in the Diocese. Tel: 716-693-4769.
Catechesis/Religious Programs—Tel: 716-693-0421. Mrs. Lorraine Schintzius, D.R.E.
Students 560.

4—OUR LADY OF CZESTOCHOWA, (1903) (Polish), Rev. Dennis F. Fronckowiak; Deacon Michael R. Kopczynski.
Res., 64 Center Ave., 14120. Tel: 716-693-3822; Fax: 716-693-3882.
School—North Tonawanda Catholic Consolidated School. See separate listing under Regional and Consolidated Elementary Schools in the Institutions located in the Diocese. Tel: 716-694-3644; Fax: 716-693-0169.
Catechesis/Religious Programs—Tel: 716-693-3855.
Students 157.
Convent—Tel: 716-692-0276.

Oakfield, Genesee Co., St. Cecilia (1905), Rev. Thomas D. Doyle.
Res., 56 Maple Ave., 14125. Tel: 716-948-5344; Fax: 716-948-8239. [CEM]
Catechesis/Religious Programs—Students 143.
Mission—Wheatville, Genesee Co., St. Patrick, Lewiston Rd at Knowlesville Rd., 14013. Tel: 716-948-5344; Fax: 716-948-8239.

Olcott, Niagara Co., St. Charles Borromeo (1912). Attended by St. Patrick, Barker. Rev. James F. Hassett. In res., Rev. Eugene L. Wagner, Pastor Emeritus.
Res., 5969 Washington St., 14126. Tel: 716-778-7592; 795-3331 (Church). [CEM]
Catechesis/Religious Programs—Students 95.

Olean, Cattaraugus Co., St. John (1896), Rev. Msgr. William O. Wangler.
Res., 931 N. Union St., 14760. Tel: 716-372-5313; Fax: 716-373-0919.
School—Southern Tier Catholic Regional School. See separate listing under Regional and Consolidated Elementary Schools in the Institutions located in the Diocese. Tel: 716-372-2891; Fax: 716-373-1175.
Catechesis/Religious Programs—Tel: 716-372-6633.
Students 210.

St. Mary of the Angels (1876), Rev. Gregory J. Dobson.
Res., 202 S. Union St., 14760. Tel: 716-372-4841; Fax: 716-372-5905.
School—Southern Tier Catholic Regional School. See separate listing under Regional and Consolidated Elementary Schools in the Institutions located in the Diocese. Tel: 716-372-2891; Fax: 716-373-1175.
Catechesis/Religious Programs—205 W. Henley St., 14760. Tel: 716-373-1855.
Students 195.

Transfiguration (1902) (Polish), Rev. Jerome J. Stelmach.
Res., 1102 Walnut St., 14760. Tel: 716-372-5430; Fax: 716-373-4719.
School—Southern Tier Catholic Regional School. See separate listing under Regional and Consolidated Elementary Schools in the Institutions located in the Diocese. Tel: 716-372-2891; Fax: 716-373-1175.
Catechesis/Religious Programs—Tel: 716-373-5446.
Students 17.

Orchard Park, Erie Co.,

1—NATIVITY OF OUR LORD, (1908), Rev. Msgr. Thomas J. Beasley; Revs. Karl E. Loeb; Eric L. Sikora.
Res., 26 Thorn Ave., 14127. Tel: 716-662-9339; Fax: 716-662-2195. [CEM]
School—Tel: 716-662-7572. Ruth Frost, Prin.
Sisters of St. Francis of Penance and Christian Charity 1; Lay Teachers 28; Students 415.
Catechesis/Religious Programs—Tel: 716-662-2169. Mary Ann Pietrzak, D.R.E.
Students 744.

2—ST. BERNADETTE, (1957), Rev. Msgr. Richard T. Nugent; Revs. Raymond J. McNicholas, S.S.C.; Ronald P. Sajdak.
Res., 5930 S. Abbott Rd., 14127-4516. Tel: 716-649-3090; Fax: 716-649-0211.
School—Tel: 716-649-3369. Sr. Diane Swanson, Prin.
Lay Teachers 21; Students 255.
Catechesis/Religious Programs—Tel: 716-648-1720. Joan Ersing, D.R.E.
Students 850.

3—OUR LADY OF THE SACRED HEART, (1920), Rev. Msgr. Paul J.E. Burkard; Revs. Joseph D. Wolf; Mieczyslaw F. Nycz.
Res., 3148 Abbott Rd., 14127. Tel: 716-824-2935; Fax: 716-827-7643.
School—3144 Abbott Rd., 14127. Tel: 716-824-8208; Fax: 716-827-7643. John Sheffield, Prin.
Sisters of Mercy 2; Lay Teachers 37; Students 570.
Catechesis/Religious Programs—Tel: 716-824-8209. Paula White, D.R.E.
Students 689.

4—ST. JOHN VIANNEY, (1958), Rev. Msgr. William J. Gallagher.
Res., 2950 Southwestern Blvd., 14127. Tel: 716-674-9133; Fax: 716-674-9134.
School—Tel: 716-674-9232; Fax: 716-674-9248.
Lay Teachers 17; Students 124.
Catechesis/Religious Programs—Tel: 716-674-9145. Sharon Kirsch, D.R.E.
Students 669.

Panama, Chautauqua Co., Our Lady of the Snows (1946). Attended by St. Matthias, French Creek. Rev. Bernard C. Staszak.
Mailing Address: P.O. Box 236, 14767.
Res., 1762 French Creek Mina Rd., 14767. Tel: 716-355-8891; Fax: 716-355-2576.
School—Holy Family Catholic School. See separate listing under Regional and Consolidated Elementary Schools in the Institutions located in the Diocese.
Catechesis/Religious Programs—Students 63.

Pavilion, Genesee Co., St. Mary (1865), Rev. Joseph C. Carlo.
Res., 14525. Tel: 716-584-3280; Fax: 716-584-8628. [CEM]
Catechesis/Religious Programs—Mary Shaughnessy, D.R.E.
Students 142.

Pendleton, Niagara Co., Good Shepherd (1847), Rev. Msgr. Paul J. Belzer. In res., Rev. Samuel J. Venne.
Res., 5442 Tonawanda Creek Rd., North Tonawanda, 14120-9699. Tel: 716-625-8594; Fax: 716-625-8365. [CEM]
Catechesis/Religious Programs—Tel: 716-625-8817. Elizabeth McDermott, D.R.E.
Students 233.

Perry, Wyoming Co., St. Joseph (1879). Linked with St. Stanislaus Kostka, Perry. Rev. Richard W. Blazejewski; Deacon Daniel J. McGuire.
Res., 8 Park St., 14530. Tel: 716-237-2625; Fax: 716-237-0150. [CEM]
Catechesis/Religious Programs—Students 111.

St. Stanislaus Kostka (1910) (Polish). Attended by St. Joseph, Perry. Rev. Richard J. Blazejewski; Deacon Daniel J. McGuire.
Res., 8 Park St., 14530. Tel: 716-237-3869; Fax: 716-237-0150. [CEM]
Catechesis/Religious Programs—Students 16.

Perrysburg, Cattaraugus Co., St. Joan of Arc (1950). All Records are kept at St. John Fisher, South Dayton. Rev. Stanislaw Dudek, Admin.
Office: St. John Fisher Church, South Dayton, 14138. Tel: 716-988-5568; Fax: 716-988-5568.
Res., P.O. Box 222, 14129-0222. Tel: 716-532-4556.
Catechesis/Religious Programs—At St. John Fisher, S. Dayton.

Portageville, Wyoming Co., Assumption B.V.M. (1849). Linked with St. Mary, Canaseraga. Rev. Robert M. Mock.
Res., P.O. Box 404, 14536. Tel: 716-468-2643; Fax: 716-468-2126. [CEM]
Catechesis/Religious Programs—Students 35.

Portville, Cattaraugus Co., Sacred Heart (1909). Linked with St. Mary, Bolivar. Rev. Robert J. Schober.
Res., 14770. Tel: 716-933-6394; Fax: 716-933-0275.
School—Southern Tier Catholic Regional School. See separate listing under Regional and Consolidated Elementary Schools in the Institutions located in the Diocese.

Randolph, Cattaraugus Co., St. Patrick (1853), Rev. Msgr. Leon M. Neu.
Res., 189 Main St., 14772. Tel: 716-358-2991; Fax: 716-358-2122. [CEM]
School—Holy Family Catholic School. See separate listing under Regional and Consolidated Elementary Schools in the Institutions located in the Diocese.
Catechesis/Religious Programs—Students 112.

Ransomville, Niagara Co., Immaculate Conception (1891), Revs. Herold M. Nuwer; Salvatore J. Piazza, (Retired).
Res., 4671 Townline Rd., Rte. 429, 14131-9740. Tel: 716-731-4822; Fax: 716-731-4911.

Catechesis/Religious Programs—Mrs. Judith A. Kirkpatrick, D.R.E.
Students 351.

Ripley, Chautauqua Co., St. Thomas More (1941). Mission of St. James, Westfield. Rev. Robert A. Wozniak.
66 E. Main St., Rte. 20, 14775. Tel: 716-736-5200; Fax: 716-326-2816.

Rushford, Allegany Co., St. Mark (1948), Rev. Francis J. Jann.
Mailing Address: P.O. Box 37, 14777. Tel: 716-437-5332; Fax: 716-437-5532.
Res., 7693 State Rte. 243, Caneadea, 14717. Tel: 716-365-9977.
Catechesis/Religious Programs—Students 32.

Salamanca, Cattaraugus Co., Holy Cross (1893) (Polish). Attended by St. Patrick, Salamanca. Rev. Joseph D. Porpiglia.
Res., 79 River St., 14779-1414. Tel: 716-945-4966; Fax: 716-945-0676.
Catechesis/Religious Programs—Linked with St. Patrick, Salamanca.

St. Patrick (1868). Linked with Holy Cross, Salamanca. Rev. Joseph D. Porpiglia.
Res., 79 River St., 14779-1414. Tel: 716-945-5522; Fax: 716-945-0676. [CEM]
Catechesis/Religious Programs—Tel: 716-945-2666.
Students 151.

Sardinia, Erie Co., St. Jude (1953), Rev. Alfons M. Osiander, Admin.
Res., 12820 Genesee Rd., 14134-0267. Tel: 716-496-7535; Fax: 716-496-7535. [JC]
School—St. Aloysius Regional School, Springville. See separate listing under Regional and Consolidated Elementary Schools in the Institutions located in the Diocese.
Catechesis/Religious Programs—Students 60.

Scio, Allegany Co., St. Joseph (1844). Mission of St. Mary, Belmont. Rev. Joseph E. Vatter.
Rte. 19 at Day Brook Rd., 14880. Tel: 716-268-7272; Fax: 716-268-7272.
Res., 5 Milton St., P.O. Box 570, Belmont, 14813-1119.
Catechesis/Religious Programs—Students 12.

Sheldon, Wyoming Co., St. Cecilia (1848), Rev. Donald C. Weber.
Res., Strykersville, 14145. Tel: 716-457-9437; Fax: 716-535-0477. [CEM 2]
School—Genesee-Wyoming Catholic Central Consolidated School. See separate listing under Regional and Consolidated Elementary Schools in the Institutions located in the Diocese. Tel: 716-591-2515; Fax: 716-591-2516.

Sheridan, Chautauqua Co., St. John Bosco (1949). Linked with St. Rose of Lima, Forestville. Rev. Gerald P. Sheehan.
Res., Box 3, 14135. Tel: 716-679-4951; Fax: 716-679-4952.
Catechesis/Religious Programs—Linked with St. Joseph, Fredonia. Tel: 716-679-4116.

Sherman, Chautauqua Co., St. Isaac Jogues (1947). Attended by St. Mary, Mayville. Rev. Raymond A.J. Donohue.
Res., 24 E. Chautanqua St., Box 148, Mayville, 14757. Tel: 716-753-2332; Fax: 716-753-3836.
School—Holy Family Catholic School.
See separate listing under Regional and Consolidated Elementary Schools in the Institutions located in the Diocese.

Silver Creek, Chautauqua Co., Our Lady of Mt. Carmel (1882), Rev. John J. Mitka.
Res., 165 Central Ave., 14136. Tel: 716-934-2233; Fax: 716-934-6216. [CEM]
School—Northern Chautauqua Catholic Regional School. See separate listing under Regional and Consolidated Elementary Schools in the Institutions located in the Diocese. Tel: 716-366-0630.
Catechesis/Religious Programs—Tel: 716-934-4891.
Students 230.

Silver Springs, Wyoming Co., St. Mary (1892). Attended by St. Michael, Warsaw. Rev. John J. Heigl, M.Afr.; Deacon John Kelly.
Res., 23 Church St., Box 305, 14550. Tel: 716-493-5265. [CEM]
Catechesis/Religious Programs—Tel: 716-786-2400; Fax: 716-786-3977.
Students 57.

Sinclairville, Chautauqua Co., St. John the Evangelist. Attended by Immaculate Conception, Cassadaga. Rev. Patrick H. Elis.
Res., 14782. Tel: 716-962-3781.

Sloan, Erie Co., St. Andrew (1915) (Polish), Rev. Robert D. Moss.
Res., 34 Francis St., 14212. Tel: 716-892-0425; Fax: 716-892-0425.
School—Tel: 716-896-2566; Fax: 716896-2501.
Felician Sisters 1; Lay Teachers 13; Students 131.
Catechesis/Religious Programs—Students 105.

Snyder, Erie Co., Christ the King (1926), Rev. Msgr. James J. Lichtenthal; Rev. David A. Bellittiere. In res., Rev. Joseph J. Sicari.
Res., 30 Lamarck Dr., 14226. Tel: 716-839-1430; Fax: 716-839-1433.
School—Tel: 716-839-0473; Fax: 716-839-0473.
Franciscan Sisters of Allegany 1; Lay Teachers 17; Students 240.
Catechesis/Religious Programs—Tel: 716-839-0946.
Students 576.

South Byron, Genesee Co., St. Michael (1892). Mission of St. Brigid, Bergen. Rev. Richard J. Keppeler.
Res., P.O. Box 219, Bergen, 14416.
Rte. 237, 14557. Tel: 716-494-1110; Fax: 716-494-1895.

South Dayton, Cattaraugus Co., St. John Fisher (1946). Linked with St. Joan of Arc, Perrysburg. Rev. Stanislaw Dudek, Admin.
Mailing Address: P.O. Box 242, 14138. Tel: 716-988-5568; Fax: 716-988-5568.
Res., Perrysburg, 14129. Tel: 716-532-4556.
Catechesis/Religious Programs—Students 66.

Springbrook, Erie Co., St. Vincent (1850), Rev. James A. Walter.
Res., 14140. Tel: 716-652-3972; Fax: 716-652-3972. [CEM]
School—Tel: 716-652-8697; Fax: 716-652-3972. Ms. Jane Hibschweiler, Prin.
Lay Teachers 9; Students 150.
Catechesis/Religious Programs—Tel: 716-652-7242. Marjory Moretta, D.R.E.
Students 450.

Springville, Erie Co., St. Aloysius (1853), Rev. John S. Kwiecien.
Res., 190 Franklin St., 14141-1199. Tel: 716-592-2701; Fax: 716-592-4347. [CEM]
School—St. Aloysius Regional School. See separate listing under Regional and Consolidated Elementary Schools in the Institutions located in the Diocese.
Catechesis/Religious Programs—Tel: 716-592-4869.
Students 301.

Strykersville, Wyoming Co., St. Mary, Queen of the Rosary (1885), Rev. Michael P. McNicholl.
Res., 3854 Main St., 14145. Tel: 716-457-3021; 457-3222; Fax: 716-457-1310. [CEM]
Catechesis/Religious Programs—Students 152.

Swormville, Erie Co., St. Mary (1849), Rev. Robert M. Yetter; Deacon Howard J. Edbauer, Jr.
Res., 6919 Transit Rd., Box 460, 14146. Tel: 716-688-9380; Fax: 716-688-6173. [CEM]
School—Tel: 716-689-8424.
Sisters of the Third Order of St. Francis 2; Lay Teachers 15; Students 282.
Catechesis/Religious Programs—Tel: 716-688-0599.
Students 1,060.

Tonawanda, Erie Co.,

1—St. Amelia, (1953), Rev. Msgr. Thomas F. Maloney; Revs. A. Mark Illig; Norman P. McTigue. Pastoral Assocs.: Sr. Rita Claire, S.S.M.N.; Sr. Jeanne Thomas, R.S.M.; Sr. Helen Buscarino, F.M.D.C. In res., Rev. Donald L. Measer.
Res., 210 St. Amelia Dr., 14150. Tel: 716-836-0011; Fax: 716-832-5439.
School—Tel: 716-836-2230; Fax: 716-832-9700. James Mule, Prin.
Lay Teachers 39; Students 550.
Catechesis/Religious Programs—Tel: 716-833-8647. Elaine Dankowski, D.R.E.
Students 935.

2—St. Andrew Kim, (1993). Mission for Korean Catholics. Rev. Dominic Jung, C.PP.S., Chap.
Parish Center: 9 O'Hara Rd., 14150. Tel: 716-693-7116; Fax: 716-693-7130; Worship Site: St. Stephen the Protomartyr (PSC).

3—Blessed Sacrament, Rev. Msgr. Robert K. Golombek.
Res., 263 Claremont Ave., 14223. Tel: 716-834-4282; Fax: 716-834-9573.
School—Felician Sisters 2; Lay Teachers 15; Students 150.
Catechesis/Religious Programs—Students 175.

4—St. Christopher, (1928), Rev. Msgr. Francis G. Weldgen; Rev. Jeffrey J. Sturmer; Deacon Francis A. Zwack.
Res., 2660 Niagara Falls Blvd., 14150. Tel: 716-692-2660; Fax: 716-693-5639.
School—Tel: 716-693-5604; Fax: 716-693-5127.
Lay Teachers 35; Students 488.
Catechesis/Religious Programs—Tel: 716-694-4310.
Students 1,150.

5—St. Edmund, (1965), Rev. Msgr. Onofrio R. Smiroldo; Deacon Robert Bauer.
Res., 530 Ellicott Creek Rd., 14150. Tel: 716-694-5656; Fax: 716-694-5902.
School—Tel: 716-694-5900; Fax: 716-695-7248.
Lay Teachers 11; Students 142.
Catechesis/Religious Programs—Students 250.

6—St. Francis of Assisi, (1858), Revs. Albert M. Hansen; James M. Monaco; Deacon Paul Schnettler.
Res., 73 Adam St., 14150. Tel: 716-693-1150; Fax: 716-693-2025. [CEM]
School—Tel: 716-692-7886.
Lay Teachers 15; Students 165.
Catechesis/Religious Programs—Tel: 716-694-5342.
Students 344.

7—St. Timothy, (1960), Rev. Msgr. John I. Ducette; Deacon Gordon J. Steinagle. In res., Rev. Msgr. John Kempczynski.
Res., 565 E. Park Dr., 14150. Tel: 716-875-9430; Fax: 716-874-3483.
Catechesis/Religious Programs—Students 217.

Vandalia, Cattaraugus Co., St. John the Baptist (1900). Mission of St. Bonaventure, Allegany. Rev. Kevin Downey, O.F.M.
Res., St. Bonaventure, 95 E. Main St., Allegany, 14706-1397. Tel: 716-373-1330; Fax: 716-373-1330.
School—Sourthern Tier Catholic Regional School. See separate listing under Regional and Consolidated Elementary Schools in the Institutions located in the Diocese.

Varysburg, Wyoming Co., St. Joseph (1910), Rev. Msgr. Joseph A. Boruszewski.
Res., 14167. Tel: 716-535-7342; Fax: 716-535-7342. [CEM]
School—Genesee-Wyoming Catholic Central Consolidated School. See separate listing under Regional and Consolidated Elementary Schools in the Institutions located in the Diocese. Tel: 716-591-2515; Fax: 716-591-2516.
Catechesis/Religious Programs—Students 61.

Warsaw, Wyoming Co., St. Michael (1858). Linked with St. Mary, Silver Springs. Rev. John J. Heigl, M.Afr.; Deacon John J. Kelly.
Res., 171 N. Main St., 14569. Tel: 716-786-2400; Fax: 716-786-3977. [CEM]
School—(Grades PreK-6) 16 North St., 14569. Tel: 716-786-8561. Mary Ann Moore, Prin.
Lay Teachers 10; Students 81.
Catechesis/Religious Programs—Students 170.

Wellsville, Allegany Co., Immaculate Conception (1850), Rev. Dennis G. Wolf.
Res., 6 Maple Ave., 14895. Tel: 716-593-4834; Fax: 716-593-7167. [CEM]
School—(Grades PreK-8) 24 Maple Ave., 14895. Tel: 716-593-5840; Fax: 716-593-5846. Sr. Alice Roach, Prin.
Sisters of Mercy 2; Lay Teachers 13; Students 174.
Catechesis/Religious Programs—Tel: 716-593-1862. D.R.E.: Mrs. Carol Gardner, (Grades 9-11); Sr. Margaret M. Gleason, (Grades PreK-8).
Students 208.

West Falls, Erie Co., St. George (Jewettville) (1942), Rev. Walter J. Szczesny, Admin.
Res., 74 Old Glenwood Rd., 14170. Tel: 716-652-3153; Fax: 716-687-1336.
Catechesis/Religious Programs—Tel: 716-652-0126.
Students 157.

Westfield, Chautauqua Co., St. James (1860), Rev. Robert A. Wozniak.
Res., 15 Union St., 14787-1494. Tel: 716-326-2816; Fax: 716-326-4863. [CEM 2]
Catechesis/Religious Programs—Tel: 716-326-2338; Fax: 716-326-2732. Dianna Giambra, D.R.E.
Students 90.
Mission—Ripley, Chautauqua Co., St. Thomas More, 66 E. Main St., Rte 20, 14775. Tel: 716-736-5200.

West Seneca, Erie Co.,

1—St. Bonaventure, (1918), Revs. Benoit J. Drapeau, C.J.M., Supr.; Ronald M. Bagley, C.J.M., Dir.; J. Gregory Sampson, C.J.M.
Res., 36 Flohr Ave., 14224. Tel: 716-823-1090; Fax: 716-825-4376.
Preschool—.
Students 15.
School—2784 Seneca St., 14224. Tel: 716-822-7260; Fax: 716-822-7296.
Lay Teachers 16; Students 153.
Catechesis/Religious Programs—Tel: 716-825-5053. Mrs. Lynn Lipczynski, D.R.E.
Students 305.

2—St. Catherine of Siena, (1967), Rev. Pascal D. Ipolito; Deacon Joseph M. Barr; Suzanne M. Buttino, Pastoral Assoc.
Res., 4928 Seneca St., 14224. Tel: 716-675-0531; Fax: 716-675-8323.
Catechesis/Religious Programs—Students 201.

3—FOURTEEN HOLY HELPERS, (1864), Rev. Msgr. David S. Slubecky; Rev. Dennis J. Mancuso.
Res., 1345 Indian Church Rd., 14224. Tel: 716-674-2374; Fax: 716-675-4864. [CEM]
School—Tel: 716-674-1670. Ms. Susan Jagosh, Prin.
Lay Teachers 18; Students 319.
Catechesis/Religious Programs—Tel: 716-674-2180.
Students 353.

4—ST. WILLIAM, (1926), Rev. Robert W. Wardenski; Joan Morreal, Pastoral Assoc.
Res., One Arcade St., 14224. Tel: 716-822-5449; Fax: 716-822-5457.
School—Affiliated with St. Bonaventure and Fourteen Holy Helpers. Tel: 716-822-7260 (St. Bonaventure); 674-1670 (Fourteen Holy Helpers); Fax: 716-822-7296 (St. Bonaventure); 675-4864.
Catechesis/Religious Programs—Tel: 716-822-5449.
Students 167.

5—QUEEN OF HEAVEN, (1955), Rev. Thomas J. Quinlivan. In res., Rev. Msgr. Joseph F. Coughlin.
Res., 4220 Seneca St., 14224. Tel: 716-674-3468; Fax: 716-674-3475.
School—839 Mill Rd., 14224. Tel: 716-674-5206. Mrs. Judith Talbot, Prin.
Lay Teachers 24; Students 331.
Catechesis/Religious Programs—Tel: 716-675-3714. D.R.E.: Sr. Lori High, S.S.M.N.; Dorothy Flynn.
Students 630.

West Valley, Cattaraugus Co., St. John the Baptist (1904), Rev. Thomas J. McCarthy.
Res., 5381 Depot St., P.O. Box 315, 14171-0315. Tel: 716-942-3259; Fax: 716-942-3259. [CEM]
School—St. Aloysius Regional School, Springville. See separate listing under Regional and Consolidated Elementary Schools in the Institutions located in the Diocese.
Catechesis/Religious Programs—Tel: 716-942-6874. Janet Vant, D.R.E.
Students 136.

Wheatville, Genesee Co., St. Patrick (1882). Mission of St. Cecilia, Oakfield. Rev. Thomas D. Doyle.
Res., 56 Maple Ave., Oakfield, 14125.
Lewiston Rd. at Knowlesville Rd., 14013. Tel: 716-948-5344; Fax: 716-948-8239.

Whitesville, Allegany Co., St. John of the Cross (1949). Attended by Blessed Sacrament, Andover. Rev. Fred G. Fingerle.
Res., One Church St., Box 761, Andover, 14806. Tel: 607-478-8885.
Church—540 Main St., Box 137, 14897.
Catechesis/Religious Programs—Students 4.

Williamsville, Erie Co., St. Gregory the Great (1958), Rev. Msgr. Rupert A. Wright; Revs. James R. Bastian; William J. Quinlivan; Deacon Ronald Dains.
Res., 260 St. Gregory Ct., 14221. Tel: 716-688-5678; 5679; Fax: 716-688-2315.
School—250 St. Gregory Ct., 14221. Tel: 716-688-5323; Fax: 716-688-6629. Mrs. Patricia Boyd, Prin.
Sisters 1; Lay Teachers 36; Students 644.
Catechesis/Religious Programs—Tel: 716-688-5760; Fax: 716-639-8251. Mrs. Joan Rischmiller, D.R.E.
Students 1,429.

SS. Peter and Paul (1836), Rev. James C. O'Connor; Deacon George Klein; Mrs. Linda Downey, Pastoral Assoc.
Res., 5480 Main St., 14221. Tel: 716-632-2559; Fax: 716-626-0971. [CEM 2]
School—Tel: 716-632-6146. Mrs. Marianne Maines, Prin.
Lay Teachers 16; Students 357.
Catechesis/Religious Programs—Tel: 716-632-2678. D.R.E.: Ms. Denise Peplowski, (Grades K-6); Susan Cowan, (Grades 7-8).
Students 831.

Wilson, Niagara Co., Our Lady of the Rosary (1920). Attended by St. Bridget, Newfane. Rev. John J. Leising; Deacon Charles Griesbaum.
Res., 359 Lake St., Box 116, 14172-0116. Tel: 716-751-6459.
Catechesis/Religious Programs—Mrs. Kathleen Higgins, D.R.E.
Students 115.

Woodlawn, Erie Co., Our Lady of Grace (1940), Rev. John F. Kasprzak.
Res., S. 3319 Lake Shore Rd., 14219. Tel: 716-822-0607; Fax: 716-822-1366.
Catechesis/Religious Programs—BettyLou Regueira, D.R.E.
Students 140.

Youngstown, Niagara Co., Holy Family (1953). (Tuscarora Indian Nation). Rev. Ubaldo M. Fior, C.R.S.P.
Res., 1023 Swan Rd., 14174-9797. Tel: 716-754-7489; Fax: 716-754-9130. [JC]
Catechesis/Religious Programs—Students 9.

St. Bernard's (1946), Rev. Msgr. J. Thomas Moran.
Res., 218 Hinman St., 14174. Tel: 716-745-7460; Fax: 716-745-1359. [CEM]
Catechesis/Religious Programs—Blanche Sylvester, D.R.E.
Students 260.

Chaplains of Public Institutions

BUFFALO. *Buffalo General Hospital*. Revs. Douglas F. Faraci; Norbert F. Orsolits; Richard H. Augustyn; Deacon Joseph Gill.
Buffalo Psychiatric Center 400 Forest Ave., 14213. Rev. Norman P. McTigue.
Children's Hospital. Sr. Brenda Whelan, R.S.M.
Erie County Holding Center. Rev. Ivan R. Trujillo; Deacon Thomas A. McDonnell.
Erie County Juvenile Detention Center. Deacon Frank Shaughnessy.
Erie County Medical Center. Rev. Robert A. Stolinski; Deacon Peter J. Bedard.
Hospice of Buffalo. Rev. Norbert F. Orsolits.
Millard Fillmore Hospital. Rev. Thomas P. Taton.
Roswell Park Memorial Institute. Rev. Douglas F. Faraci.
Sheehan Memorial Emergency Hospital. Rev. Roy T. Herberger.
Veterans Hospital. Rev. Francis J. Chmielewski, 414 S. Ogden St., 14206. Tel: 716-822-8856.

ALBION. *Albion Correctional Facility*. Rev. Eugene S. Slomba Tel: 716-343-1796; Sr. Dolores Ann O'Dowd, G.N.S.H.
Orleans Correction Facility. Rev. Thomas D. Doyle, 50 Maple Ave., Oakfield, 14125. Tel: 716-386-2400. Deacons Thomas Bringenberg, Jr.; Heinz Friedman.

ALDEN. *Erie County Correctional Facility*. Rev. Robert Moreno (STF), 11580 Walden Ave., 14004. Tel: 716-937-5693.
Wende Correctional Facility. Deacons Gordon Steinagle; Timothy Maloney.

AMHERST. *Millard Fillmore Suburban Hospital*. Rev. Joseph W. Bertha (PSC).

ATTICA. *Attica Correctional Facility*. Revs. John Kilian; Ivan R. Trujillo; Sr. Rosalind Rosolowski, C.S.S.F.
Wyoming Correctional Facility. Deacon Brian Walkowiak.

BATAVIA. *Veterans Hospital*. Rev. John P. Bernard.

COLLINS. *Collins Correctional Facility*. Deacons John H. Burke; Carlos Ramos; Sr. Mary Lou Schnitzer, S.S.J.

DUNKIRK. *Brooks Memorial Hospital*. Deacons Matthew A. Podniesinski, Chap.; Jose Ruiz.

GOWANDA. *Gowanda Correctional Facility*. Deacons Carlos Ramos; John Gainey.

JAMESTOWN. *Jamestown Women's Christian Association Hospital*. Rev. John L. Kuhlmann, Chap., 42 Main St., P.O. Box 500, Bemus Point, 14172-0500. Tel: 716-386-2400.

LAKEVIEW. *Lakeview Shock Incarceration Correctional Facility*. Rev. Walter Werbicki.

LOCKPORT. *Wyndham Lawn Home for Children*. Deacon Norman Foster.

NIAGARA FALLS. *Niagara Falls Memorial Medical Centers*. Rev. Mark M. Friel.

NORTH TONAWANDA. *DeGraff Memorial Hospital* 1520 Kingston Ave., 14120. Tel: 716-694-4500. Rev. Duane G. Fimbel.

OLEAN. *Olean General Hospital*. Deacon Michael Anderson.

WEST SENECA. *Development Center*. Deacon Albert Fox; Carol Ann Corey.

On Duty Outside the Diocese:
Reverend Fathers—
Conoscenti, Frederick M., 605 Grove St., D4, Clifton, NJ 07013
Enright, James C., Auburn Correctional Facility, 135 State St., Auburn, NY 13021
Klos, Joseph, Divine Word College, 1025 Michigan Ave., Washington, DC 20017-1895
Krysa, Czeslaw M., SS. Cyril & Methodius Seminary, Orchard Lake, MI 48033
Nielsen, Kenneth M., Salem State College, 352 Lafayette St., Salem, MA 01970
Sheedy, Edward J., Wadhams Hall Seminary, Ogdensburg, NY 13669
Wild, Robert A., Madonna House, Combermere, Ontario, Canada
Zapfel, Robert E., S.T.D., Congregation for Catholic Education, 00120 Vatican City State

---

Military Chaplains:
Reverend Fathers—
Koester, Timothy J., HQ BTN, HQ USMC, Henderson Hall, Arlington, VA 22214-5001
Zuffoletto, Michael P., U.S. Navy, 3747 Bengal Rd., Gulf Breeze, FL 32561

Absent on Leave:
Reverend Fathers—
Biesinger, Robert J.
Gresock, Thomas G.
Swartz, Michael R.
Zwifka, David A.

Retired:
Reverend Monsignors—
Acquavia, Paschal L., Brothers of Mercy Rehabilitation Center, 10570 Bergtold Rd., Clarence, NY 14031-2198
Brennan, George J., 4 Lockwood Ln., Orchard Park, NY 14127-2713
Bugman, John H., Our Lady of Victory, 767 Ridge Rd., Lackawanna, NY 14218-1697
Cahill, Richard M., 1825 Alberta Dr., Clearwater, FL 33756
Caine, Martin J., 4000 Ridgeline Dr., Austin, TX 78731
Caligiuri, Anthony J., O'Hara Residence, 69 O'Hara Rd., Tonawanda, NY 14150-6227
Connelly, James N., O'Hara Residence, 69 O'Hara Rd., Tonawanda, NY 14150-6227
Conniff, John J., 1088 Delaware Ave., Apt. 15C, Buffalo, NY 14209-1627
Coughlin, Joseph F., Queen of Heaven Rectory, 4220 Seneca St., West Seneca, NY 14224-3199
Cronin, Paul T., Sheehan Residence, 330 Linwood Ave., Buffalo, NY 14209-1689
Crumlish, Richard C., 1974 Seneca St., Buffalo, NY 14210-2368
DelVecchio, Michael E., P.O. Box 22, Orchard Park, NY 14127
Duggan, John M., 127 Keil St., North Tonawanda, NY 14120-6921
Engelhardt, Herbert G., 43 Circle End Dr., West Seneca, NY 14224-3925
Faiola, Samuel J., 72B Lexington Ct., Lockport, NY 14094-5365
Gernatt, David A., 11742 Markham Rd., Gowanda, NY 14070-9680
Gill, Richard, 103 E. 7th St., Dunkirk, NY 14048-2650
Graeber, Richard A., 3020 Elmwood Ave., Apt. #1, Kenmore, NY 14217
Green, Gerard L., 9686 Oak Grove Dr., Angola, NY 14006-8904
Hammerl, Leo E., O'Hara Residence, 69 O'Hara Rd., Tonawanda, NY 14150-6227
Higgins, Grant J., 170 Countryside Ln., Apt. #4, Orchard Park, NY 14127
Jasinski, Anthony J., 950 Losson Rd., South Cheektowaga, NY 14227-2598
Joseph, Joseph D., 10537 Oldro Hill Rd., Steamburg, NY 14783-9998
Juenker, Paul R., O'Hara Residence, 69 O'Hara Rd., Tonawanda, NY 14150-6227
Kazmierczak, Edward L., 172 Laurelton Dr., Buffalo, NY 14224-3914
Kempczynski, John, St. Timothy Rectory, 565 E. Park Dr., Tonawanda, NY 14150-6705
Klein, Stanley H., Chap. Col., 11 Philip Dr., Buffalo, NY 14227-2512
Kozminski, Max M., 150 Brush Creek Rd., Williamsville, NY 14221-2743
Kreuzer, Gerald J., Most Precious Blood Rectory, 22 Prospect St., P.O. Box 153, Angola, NY 14006-0153
Lackovic, Stephen F., Our Lady of Bistrica, 1619 Abbott Rd., Lackawanna, NY 14218-2999
LaRusch, Alton J., 132 E. Main St., Hamburg, NY 14075-5133
Letourneau, Paul R., O'Hara Residence, 69 O'Hara Rd., Tonawanda, NY 14150-6227
Lombardo, Samuel L., Sheehan Residence, 330 Linwood Ave., Buffalo, NY 14209-1689
Lorenzetti, Dino J., O'Hara Residence, 69 O'Hara Rd., Tonawanda, NY 14150-6227
Meloch, Chester A., 1065 Woodville Hwy., Crawfordville, FL 32327-1619
Murphy, Robert E., Our Lady of Victory Basilica, 767 Ridge Rd., Lackawanna, NY 14218-1697
Myszka, Daniel J., 391 Bristol St., Buffalo, NY 14206-3721
O'Loughlin, Eugene E., St. Thomas Aquinas Rectory, 450 Abbott Rd., Buffalo, NY 14220-1796
Radon, Eugene M., Coronation of BVM, 348 Dewitt St., Buffalo, NY 14213-1191
Ronald, Roy K., 200 Boncroft Dr., West Seneca, NY 14224-2851
Scanlan, Edward J., 2437 Niagara St., Niagara Falls, NY 14303-1925
Schneider, Arnold J., 5337 Genesee St., Bowmansville, NY 14026-1034
Schwab, Robert C., 2164 N.E. 36th St., Apt. 49, Lighthouse Point, FL 33064-7555
Schwinger, William A., 50 Franklin St., Buffalo, NY 14202-4098

Skupien, Francis M., P.O. Box 424, Kendall, NY 14476-0424
Skupien, Joseph F., 7546 Chestnut Ridge, Orchard Park, NY 14127-3820
Sobierajski, Edward J., O'Hara Residence, 69 O'Hara Rd., Tonawanda, NY 14150-6299
Sorci, Francis P., 34 Loch Lee, Williamsville, NY 14221-4934
Stachewicz, Henry J., 103 Kokomo, Depew, NY 14043-3705
Stanton, William G., 1124 Indian Church Rd. #49, West Seneca, NY 14224-1346
Stillwell, William J., Sheehan Residence, 330 Linwood Ave., Buffalo, NY 14209-1689
Streng, James E., P.O. Box 167, Crittenden, NY 14038-0167
Sutherland, William J., P.O. Box 106, Cassadaga, NY 14718-0106
Swiatkowski, Francis M., O'Hara Residence, 69 O'Hara Rd., Tonawanda, NY 14150-6227
Szabo, Julius J., O'Hara Residence, 69 O'Hara Rd., Tonawanda, NY 14150-6227
Szostak, Danile J., 975 Church Rd., Angola, NY 14006-9718
Trevett, Cyril I., 16 Lake Ave., Blasdell, NYNY 14219-1704
Ulaszeski, Edward J., St. Jude Center, 760 Ellicott St., Buffalo, NY 14203-1198
Waclawski, Joseph P., 81 Forest View Rd., Depew, NY 14043-1715
Walker, Edward J., 31 Stevenson St., Buffalo, NY 14220
Wendzikowski, Mecislaus S., 142 Phyllis Ave, Buffalo, NY 14215-2826
Yunk, Michael J., 47 Linwood Ave., Williamsville, NY 14221-6501
Zak, Casimir A., O'Hara Residence, 69 O'Hara Rd., Tonawanda, NY 14150-6227

Reverend Fathers—
Aurelio, John R., 5501 Kent Rd., Venice, FL 34293-6439
Bernard, John P., 4327 Lockport Rd., Elba, NY 14058-9723
Bohn, Raymond G., Sheehan Residence, 330 Linwood Ave., Buffalo, NY 14209-1689
Bosack, Albert J., St. Joseph Rectory, 38 Lake Ave., Box 496, Lydonville, NY 14098-9761
Coppola, Paul R., 112 Maverick Trail, Interlachen, FL 32148-9188
Crowley, Thomas J., Sheehan Residence, 330 Linwood Ave., Buffalo, NY 14209-1689
Cusimano, Salvatore J., O'Hara Residence, 69 O'Hara Rd., Tonawanda, NY 14150-6227
Czechowicz, Bernard J., Sheehan Residence, 330 Linwood Ave., Buffalo, NY 41209-1689
Daley, James M., Quaker Towne Apartments, 150 Countryside Ln., Orchard Park, NY 14127-1349
Della Neve, Louis, 6A Lexington Ct., Lockport, NY 14094-5365
Federico, Ralph P., 83 Wilderness Park, Clarendon, PA 16313-9747
Ferens, Boniface D., Suwalki, Noniewicza 95 M8, 16-400, Woj Podlaskie, Poland
Fitzgerald, Donald J., Box 3100, Bonita Springs, FL 34133-3100
Flynn, James P., Sacred Heart Home, 4520 Ransom Rd., Clarence, NY 14031-2108
Fox, John J., P.O. Box 852, Amherst, NY 14226
Gagliardo, Anthony F., 1301 Wynkoop Dr., Colorado Springs, CO 80909
Gimbrone, Richard J., 157 Pennsylvania Ave., Buffalo, NY 14201
Gonter, Louis J., 9980 S.E. 161st Pl., Summerfield, FL 34491-5761
Haran, James E., 81 South St., Cattaraugus, NY 14719-1216
Hennessey, John P., 1955 Eleventh St., S.W., Largo, FL 33778-1118
Hogan, Francis T., 2792 N. Breeze Rd., Melbourne, FL 32935-2010
Hughes, Donald R., McAuley Residence, 1503 Military Rd., Kenmore, NY 14217-1339
Jann, Francis J., P.O. Box 37, Rushford, NY 14777-0037
Kasprzyk, James H., St. George Rectory, 74 Old Glenwood Rd., West Falls, NY 14170-9706
Kaukus, Edwin J., 245 Richmond Ave., Buffalo, NY 14222
Kibuka, Matthias W., 434 Ellmwood Ave., Niagara Falls, NY 14301
Klos, Walter, Albertine Home, 1501 Hoffman St., Hammond, IN 46327-1764
Kowalewski, Francis P., Our Lady of Good Counsel, 10675 Allegany Rd., Darien Center, NY 14040-9701
Kwiatkowski, Constantine, 26 Sanford Dr., Jamestown, NY 14701-7410
Kwolek, Joseph, Sheehan Residence, 330 Linwood Ave., Buffalo, NY 14209-1689
Lex, Henry V., Sheehan Residence, 330 Linwood Ave., Buffalo, NY 14209-1689
Lowry, Joseph K., 124 Division St., Salamanca, NY 14779-1759
Mach, Bernard M., 55012 Kent R., Venice, FL 34293-6439
Martlock, Loville N., P.O. Box 10, Jemez Springs, NM 87025
McGrath, James R., 536 St. Lawrence Ave., Buffalo, NY 14216-1529
Measer, Donald L., St. Amelia, 210 St. Amelia Dr., Tonawanda, NY 14150-7126
Meegan, William H., Father Baker Manor, 6400 Powers Rd., Orchard Park, NY 14127-4841
Mergenhagen, John J., P.O. Box 36, South Wales, NY 14139-0036
Naber, John T., P.O. Box 868, Buffalo, NY 14205-0868
Nowak, Francis T., 25 Euclid Ave., Buffalo, NY 14211
O'Connor, John J., Brothers of Mercy Health Facility, 4520 Ransom Rd., Clarence, NY 14031-2108
O'Shea, John T., 3178 Merchant Rd., Warsaw, NY 14569-9320
Paa, Joseph F., 21 Foxwood Row, Depew, NY 14043-5019
Piazza, Salvatore J., 4671 Townline Rd. (Rte.429), Ransomville, NY 14131-9740
Pulikoottil, Abraham, 297 Collins Ave., West Seneca, NY 14224-1185
Roche, David V., Sheehan Residence, 330 Linwood Ave., Buffalo, NY 14209-1689
Rossello, Nicholas A., 101 East Ave., Westfield, NY 14787
Russell, Raymond R., Sheehan Residende, 330 Linwood Ave., Buffalo, NY 14209-1689
Schreck, Paul, 90 Meyer Rd, Apt. 524, Amherst, NY 14226-1005
Selzler, Norbert E., 5020 Carpenter Rd., Hamburg, NY 14075-6618
Shepherd, Thomas N., 1140 Abbot Rd., Buffalo, NY 14220-2794
Snyder, Clatus E., 101 Century Rd., Buffalo, NY 14215-1309
Sokolowski, Bernard T., St. Josaphat Rectory, 20 Peoria Ave., Cheektowaga, NY 14206-2695
Staebell, James A., 12428 Barone Dr., Silver Creek, NY 14136-1204
Tomiak, Walter L., St. Elizabeth Home, 5539 Broadway, Lancaster, NY 14086-2299
Vallone, Louis A., 17140 S.E. 115 Terrace Rd., Summerfield, FL 34491-7823
Vogt, Robert W., 128 Kinsey Ave., Kenmore, NY 14217
Wagner, Eugene L., St. Charles Borromeo, 5969 Washington St., Olcott, NY 14126-9998
Ward, William G., 10500 Bergtold Rd., Apt. 245, Clarence, NY 14031-2126
Werth, Charles M., 108 Wellington Ct., Buffalo, NY 14221-6750
Wright, Vincent L., 10848 Bowen Rd., Attica, NY 14011-9411
Zancan, Robert D., P.O. Box 3424, Victorville, CA 92323

Permanent Deacons:
Anderson, Michael L.
Badaszewski, Robert W.
Barr, Joseph M.
Bauer, Robert A.
Bedard, Peter J.
Bellavance, Peter G.
Boyd, Jimmie L., Sr.
Brick, Daniel E.
Bringenberg, Thomas B.
Burke, John H.
Burns, Robert E.
Carmody, Paul F.
Carroll, Melvin W.
Casey, Christopher T.
Collichio, James L.
Crimi, Victor
Cruz, Moises C.
Dains, Ronald
Darroch, Nelson
Edbauer, Howard J., Jr.
Eschbach, Lawrence D.
Forcucci, Thomas M.
Fortuna, Chester J., M.D.
Foster, Norman E.
Fox, Albert F.
Friedman, Heinz H.
Fudala, Walter N.
Gainey, John C.
Gill, Joseph J.
Griesbaum, Charles J., Jr.
Hart, Thomas J.
Hooper, Mark J.
Houck, William
Howard, Edward R.
Hynes, William J.
Jerome, David R.
Kapsiak, Dennis W.
Kelly, John J.
Kelsey, Richard H.
Klein, George L.
Kopczynski, Michael R.
Krahling, Francis R.
Lankes, George A.
Licata, Thomas G.
Mackowiak, Daniel H.
Mahaney, Richard J.
Maloney, Timothy
Marino, Benjamin
Markowski, Lawrence
Matthews, Richard F.
May, Thaddeus P.
McDermott, David P.
McDonnell, Thomas A.
McGuire, Daniel G.
McKeating, Michael P.
Meister, Alan A.
Menke, Richard A.
Mercurio, Joseph P.
Miranda, Roberto G.
Molik, Daniel J.
Molnar, Alexander S.
Moses, Robert J.
O'Connell, Edward G.
Parker, Richard W.
Penksa, Daniel M.
Pijacki, Thaddeus V.
Podniesinski, Matthew A.
Polizzi, Frank S.
Polizzi, John A.
Quinn, Michael D.
Radlinski, Donald
Ramos, Carlos W.
Ruh, John M.
Ruiz, Jose J.
Santana, Reinaldo
Schnettler, Paul J.
Schultz, Thomas E.
Setera, John T.
Seyfried, Donald E.
Shaughnessey, Frank J.
Shultz, Donald W., Sr.
Slish, David P.
Stahl, Raymond H.
Steffen, Franklyn C.
Steinagle, Gordon J.
Stone, John G.
Terrana, Gary C.
Thomann, Bernard M.
Vega, Francisco
Vogt, Jeffrey T.
Walders, Peter J.
Walek, Edward S.
Walker, Ronald
Walkowiak, Brian C.
Weisenburger, Paul F.
Wetter, Donald A.
Wick, John G.
Willis, William W.
Zwack, Francis A.
Zymanek, Caesar F.

INSTITUTIONS LOCATED IN THE DIOCESE

[A] SEMINARIES

BUFFALO. *Pope John Paul II Residence*, 217 Winston Rd., 14216. Tel: 716-836-5526; Fax: 716-836-3303. E-mail: jcpgatto@aol.com
Rev. Joseph C. Gatto, Dir. Students 7; Priests 1; Total Staff 1.

EAST AURORA. *Christ the King Seminary*. Graduate School of Theology, 711 Knox Rd., P.O. Box 607, 14052. Tel: 716-652-8900; Fax: 716-652-8903. E-mail: cksacad@pcom.net
Interdiocesan Theologate. Owned and operated by the Diocese of Buffalo. Seminarians are assigned by the Bishop of any diocese for preparation for ordination to Priesthood. Administration and Faculty: Revs. Richard W. Siepka, M.A., S.T.L., Pres. Rector; Gregory M. Faulhaber, Vice Rector & Dir. of Formation; Sr. Judith M. Kubicki, C.S.S.F., Ph.D., Academic Dean; Rev. Lynn Morgan, Asst. to the Academic Dean; Mrs. Nancy Ehlers, Treas.; Mr. J. Patrick Hulsman, Dir. of Institutional Advancement; Mr. Michael Murphy, Dir. of Facilities; Rev. Bonaventure F. Hayes, O.F.M., M.A., S.T.L, M.L.S., Dir. Library. Faculty: Revs. Charles R. Amico, Ph.D., S.T.D.; Joel A. Campbell, O.F.M.; Richard Cassidy, Ph.D.; Charles O'Connor, O.F.M., S.T.D.; Gabriel Scarfia, O.F.M., S.T.D.; Joseph C. Gatto; Joseph F.

Burke, S.J.; Walter Szczesny; Paul L. Varuvel, S.T.D.; Mr. Alan Lukas, B.A., M.A., Dir. of Music; Rev. Thomas Sheehan, O.F.M., M.Div., Dir. of Alumni; Sr. M. Tiburtia, Gorecki, F.S.S.J., M.L.S., Librarian; Rev. Peter J. Drilling, Th.D.; Dr. Susan Roll, Ph.D.; Dr. Dennis Castillo; Kathy Castillo, M.A. Adjunct Faculty: Rev. Msgr. John Weimer; Rev. Paul Litwin, J.C.L.; E. Christine Moll, Ph.D., N.C.C.; Patricia Bubar; Mark Hammer. Priests 15; Sisters 2; Lay Staff 36; Students 102; Total Staff 53.

[B] SEMINARIES, RELIGIOUS

YOUNGSTOWN. *The National Shrine Basilica of Our Lady of Fatima*, 1023 Swan Rd., 14174. Tel: 716-754-7489; Fax: 716-754-9130.
E-mail: FatimaShr@aol.com
Web site: www.catholic-church.org/barnabites
Very Rev. Julio M. Ciavaglia, C.R.S.P., Rector. Assoc. Directors: Revs. Paul M. Keeling, C.R.S.P.; Peter M. Calabrese, C.R.S.P. Priests 3; Total Staff 18.

St. Anthony M. Zaccaria Seminary, The Barbabite Fathers, Inc. 981 Swann Rd., 14174. Tel: 716-754-7489; Fax: 716-754-9130.
E-mail: BarnabitesUSA@aol.com
Web site: www.catholic-church.org/barnabites
Revs. Peter M. Calabrese, C.R.S.P.; Paul M. Keeling, C.R.S.P.; Julio M. Ciavaglia, C.R.S.P., Shrine Dir., Prov. Supr., & Comm. Supr.; Ubaldo M. Fior, C.R.S.P.; Joseph M. Gariolo, C.R.S.P.; Luciano M. Visconti, C.R.S.P. Priests 6; Total Staff 8.

[C] COLLEGES AND UNIVERSITIES

BUFFALO. *Canisius College*, 2001 Main St., 14208-1098. Tel: 716-883-7000; Fax: 716-888-2525.
E-mail: cookev@canisius.edu
Web site: www.canisius.edu
For a complete listing, refer to the Colleges and Universities section.

D'Youville College, 320 Porter Ave., 14201. Tel: 716-881-3200; Fax: 716-881-7780.
E-mail: Brayjd@dyc.edu
Web site: www.dyc.edu
For a complete listing, refer to the Colleges and Universities section.

Trocaire College, 360 Choate Ave., 14220. Tel: 716-827-2423; Fax: 716-828-6109.
E-mail: hurleyp@trocaire.edu
Web site: www.trocaire.edu
For a complete listing, refer to the Colleges and Universities section.

Villa Maria College of Buffalo, 240 Pine Ridge Rd., 14225-3999. Tel: 716-896-0700; Fax: 716-896-0705.
Web site: www.villa.edu
For a complete listing, refer to the Colleges and Universities section.

HAMBURG. *Hilbert College*, 5200 S. Park Ave., 14075. Tel: 716-649-7900; Fax: 716-649-0702.
E-mail: edmunette@hilbert.edu
Web site: www.hilbert.edu/
For a complete listing, refer to the Colleges and Universities section.

NIAGARA UNIVERSITY. *Niagara University*, Lewiston Rd., 14109-2015. Tel: 716-285-1212; Fax: 716-286-8355.
E-mail: jbm@niagara.edu
Web site: www.niagara.edu
For a complete listing, refer to the Colleges and Universities section.

ST. BONAVENTURE. *St. Bonaventure University*, 14778. Tel: 716-375-2000; Fax: 716-375-2055.
E-mail: fstorms@sbu.edu
Web site: www.sbu.edu
For a complete listing, refer to the Colleges and Universities section.

[D] HIGH SCHOOLS, PRIVATE

BUFFALO. *Bishop Timon-St. Jude High School*, 601 McKinley Pkwy., 14220. Tel: 716-826-3610; Fax: 716-824-5833. Owned and operated by Bishop Timon Board of Trustees. Rev. Joel A. Campbell, O.F.M., Pres.; Mr. Thomas J. Sullivan, Prin. Franciscans 4; Lay Teachers 30; Students 330; Total Staff 40.

Canisius High School, 1180 Delaware Ave., 14209. Tel: 716-882-0466; Fax: 716-883-1870.
E-mail: president@canisiushigh.org
Web site: www.canisiushigh.org
Society of Jesus. Revs. James F. Fox, S.J., Pres.; John J. Mattimore, S.J., Prin.; Peter K. Arabia, S.J.; Louis T. Garaventa, S.J.; James P. Higgins, S.J.; Joseph J. Kamiensky, S.J.; Mark G. Kriz, S.J.; James R. Van Dyke, S.J.; Ronald W. Sams, S.J.; Richard J. Zanoni, S.J.; Eugene A. Zimpfer, S.J. Priests 11; Lay Teachers 50; Students 750; Total Staff 80.

Holy Angels Academy, 24 Shoshone Dr., 14214-1097. Tel: 716-834-7120; Fax: 716-834-7121.
E-mail: viceprin@buffnet.net
Web site: www.holyangelsacademy.org
Jo Anne Grippi, Prin. Priests 1; Grey Nuns of the Sacred Heart 5; Lay Teachers 40; Religious 1; Students 315; Total Staff 48.

Mt. Mercy Academy, 88 Red Jacket Pkwy., 14220. Tel: 716-825-8796; Fax: 716-825-0796; 825-0129 (Devel. Fax). Sisters of Mercy. Sr. Barbara Ciarico, R.S.M., Pres.; Mr. Terrence J. Smerka, Prin. Students 490; Total Staff 65.

Nardin Academy High School, 135 Cleveland Ave., 14222. Tel: 716-881-6262; Fax: 716-881-4190. Miss Barbara Rapier, D.H.M., Pres.; Rev. Jeffrey M. Sturmer, Chap. Lay Teachers 53; Girls 457.

St. Joseph's Collegiate Institute, 845 Kenmore Ave., 14223-3195. Tel: 716-874-4024; Fax: 716-874-4956.
E-mail: brotomsjci@msn.com
Web site: www.sjcibuf.org
Brothers of the Christian Schools. (De La Salle Christian Brothers). Rev. James Croglio, Chap. of School and Brothers' Community; Bros. Thomas Lackey, F.S.C., Pres.; Edward Martin, F.S.C., Community Dir. Priests 1; Brothers 5; Lay Teachers 55; Students 825; Total Staff 65.

Turner Carroll High School, 185 Lang Ave., 14215. Tel: 716-896-4911; Fax: 716-896-4947.
E-mail: turnerchs@aol.com
Owned and operated by Turner/Carroll Board of Trustees. Peter A. Hazzan, Prin. Sisters 1; Lay Teachers 23; Students 140; Total Staff 35.

Villa Maria Academy, 600 Doat St., 14211. Tel: 716-894-0398; Fax: 716-894-0468.
E-mail: adm@vmabuffalo.org
Web site: www.vmabuffalo.org
Felician Sisters. Sr. Mary Kevin Szeluga, Prin. Sisters 12; Lay Teachers 18; Students 165; Total Staff 30.

ATHOL SPRINGS. *St. Francis High School*, 4129 Lake Shore Rd., 14010-0185. Tel: 716-627-1200; Fax: 716-627-4610.
E-mail: SFHS4FJB@aol.com
Web site: stfrancishigh.org
St. Anthony Province of the Order of Friars Minor Conventual. Revs. Joseph Benicewicz, Pres. & Prin.; Charles Jagodzinski, OFM Conv.; Michael Lasky, OFM Conv.; Michael Miller, O.F.M.Conv.; Mark David Skura, OFM Conv.; Bro. Lawrence LaFlame, OFM Conv. Priests 6; Deacons 1; Brothers 1; Sisters 1; Lay Teachers 41; Total Staff 62; Students 550.

BATAVIA. *Notre Dame High School of Batavia*, 73 Union St., 14020. Tel: 716-343-2783; Fax: 716-343-7323.
E-mail: ndhs@ndhsbatavia.com
Web site: www.ndhsbatavia.com
Owned and operated by Notre Dame Board of Trustees. Mr. Frank C. Ferrando, Pres. & Prin.; Mr. Mike Rapone, Dean Students; Rev. Robert A. Martin. Priests 2; Lay Teachers 21; Students 261; Total Staff 39.

EGGERTSVILLE. *Buffalo Academy of the Sacred Heart*, 3860 Main St., 14226. Tel: 716-834-2101; Fax: 716-834-2944.
E-mail: shalib@buffnet.net
Web site: www.sacredheartacademy.org
Sisters of St. Francis of Penance and Christian Charity. Sr. Edith Wyss, O.S.F., Prin. Sisters 7; Lay Teachers 39; Students 357; Total Staff 60.

HAMBURG. *Immaculata Academy*, 5138 S. Park Ave., 14075. Tel: 716-649-6161; Fax: 716-646-1782. Franciscan Sisters of St. Joseph. Sr. Lynne Anne Schimminger, F.S.S.J., Pres.; David T. Christian, Prin. Sisters 4; Lay Teachers 18; Students 134; Total Staff 28.

KENMORE. *Mt. St. Mary Academy*, 3756 Delaware Ave., 14217. Tel: 716-877-1358; Fax: 716-877-0548.
E-mail: jmspencer@mtstmaryacademy.kenmore.ny.us
Web site: mtstmaryacademy.kenmore.ny.us
Owned and operated by the Mt. St. Mary Academy Board of Trustees. Mrs. Joan M. Spencer, Prin. Lay Teachers 37; Girls 300; Day Care Center 130.

LANCASTER. *St. Mary's High School*, 142 Laverack Ave., 14086. Tel: 716-683-4824; Fax: 716-683-4996.
E-mail: lancer@smhlancers.org
Web site: www.smhlancers.org
Owned and operated by St. Mary's Board of Trustees. Joseph A. Casimino, Ed.D., Prin. Sisters 1; Lay Teachers 35; Students 351; Total Staff 53.

NIAGARA FALLS. *Niagara Catholic Junior-Senior High School*, 520-66th St., 14304. Tel: 716-504-1192; Fax: 716-283-6574.
E-mail: dkersten@niagaracatholic.org
Web site: www.niagaracatholic.org
Owned and operated by Niagara Catholic Board of Trustees. David J. Kersten, Pres.; Ms. Antonia B. Pellegrino, Prin.; Revs. Stewart Lindsay, O.S.F.S.; Gerald L. Bartko, O.S.F.S. Priests 2; Lay Teachers 22; Students 270.

OLEAN. *Archbishop Walsh High School*, 208 N. 24th St., 14760-1985. Tel: 716-372-8122; Fax: 716-372-6707. Owned and operated by Archbishop Walsh Board of Trustees. Ann Sitter, Prin.; Rev. Barry J. Allaire. Priests 1; Lay Teachers 12; Students 104; Total Staff 25.

TONAWANDA. *Cardinal O'Hara High School*, 39 O'Hara Rd., 14150. Tel: 716-695-2600; Fax: 716-692-8697. Philip J. Marron, Prin. Lay Teachers 27; Students 257. Owned and operated by Cardinal O'Hara Board of Trustees.

[E] ELEMENTARY SCHOOLS, PRIVATE

BUFFALO. *Mount St. Joseph Academy.*
Web site: www.msja.org
Elementary Division: 2064 Main St., 14208. Tel: 716-883-1515; Fax: 716-882-9053. Mr. Matthew Moran, Acting Prin. Sisters 1; Lay Teachers 25; Students 193.

Nardin Academy, 135 Cleveland Ave., 14222. Tel: 716-881-6262; Fax: 716-881-4190. (Montessori-Grade 12). Priests 1; Sisters 1; Lay Teachers 121; Students 898.

LEWISTON. *Sacred Heart Villa School.* (Grades PreK-6), 5269 Lewiston Rd., 14092. Tel: 716-284-8273; 285-9257 (school); Fax: 716-284-8273.
E-mail: shvschool@adelphia.net
Web site: www.dotc.com/shvs
Sr. Elizabeth Domin, S.S.H.J., Prin. Sisters 8; Lay Teachers 3; Students 90; Total Staff 14.

STELLA NIAGARA. *Stella Niagara Education Park*, 4421 Lower River Rd., 14144. Tel: 716-754-4314. Sisters of St. Francis of Penance and Christian Charity. Sr. Nicholas Macoretta, O.S.F., Prin. Sisters 2; Lay Teachers 26; Students 247.

[F] ELEMENTARY SCHOOLS, SPECIAL

BUFFALO. *Cantalician Center for Learning, Inc.*, 3233 Main St., 14214. Tel: 716-833-5353; Fax: 716-833-0108.
E-mail: cc3@wzrd.com
Web site: www.cantalician.org
Program for the disabled: Infant, Toddler and Preschool; Elementary and Secondary. Workshop for adult individuals with disabilities, day treatment-lite program, & day habilitation for retired, disabled adults. Group homes/I.R.A. for adult individuals with disabilities; Daycare. Sr. Patricia Tomasik, C.S.S.F., Exec. Dir.; Rev. Msgr. Harold Wagner, Chap. Priests 1; Sisters 6; Laystaff 287; Students 629; Total Staff 294.

[G] REGIONAL AND CONSOLIDATED ELEMENTARY SCHOOLS

BUFFALO. *Catholic Academy of West Buffalo.*
E-mail: lmyszka@cawb.org
Delaware Campus: (Grades 3-8), 1069 Delaware Ave., 14209. Tel: 716-885-6111; Fax: 716-885-6452.
E-mail: lmyszka@cawb.org
Lafayette Campus: (Grades PreK-2), 279 Lafayette Ave., 14213. Tel: 716-886-5384; Fax: 716-886-5393. Miss Louise M. Myszka, Supervising Prin.; Sr. Gail Glenn, S.S.J., Bldg. Prin. (Delaware Campus); Mrs. Geraldine Kizielewicz, Bldg. Prin., (Lafayette Campus).
Sponsoring parishes: Annunciation, St. Anthony, Blessed Sacrament, Holy Angels, Holy Cross, Immaculate Conception, St. Joseph's Cathedral, St. Louis, St. Michael, Nativity, Our Lady of Loretto. Sisters 1; Lay Teachers 27; Students 383; Total Staff 30.

Catholic Central School. (Grades K-8), 476 Emslie St., 14212. Tel: 716-852-6854; Fax: 716-852-8410.
E-mail: CatholicCentral@catholic.org
Patricia G. Duffy, Prin.
Sponsoring parishes: St. Ann, Blessed Trinity, SS. Columba & Brigid, St. Mary of Sorrows, & St. Martin de Porres. Sisters 5; Lay Teachers 17; Students 220; Total Staff 33.

Our Lady of Black Rock, 16 Germain St., 14207. Tel: 716-873-7497; Fax: 716-447-1027.
E-mail: OLBR@n2education.com
Sr. Mary Francianne Zielezinski, C.S.S.F., Prin.
Sponsoring parishes: Assumption, St. Florian, St. Francis Xavier, Coronation, St. Elizabeth, St. John the Baptist. Sisters 1; Lay Teachers 11; Students 131; Total Staff 12.

ATTICA. *Genesee-Wyoming Catholic Central Consolidated School*, 72 East Ave., 14011. Tel: 716-591-2515; Fax: 716-591-2516. William F. Schofield, Prin. Sponsoring parishes: Attica, St. Vincent; Bennington Center, Sacred Heart; Darien Center, Our Lady of Good Counsel; Java Center, St. Patrick; North Java, St. Nicholas; Sheldon, St. Cecelia; Varysburg, St. Joseph; Warsaw, St. Michael. Lay Teachers 14; Students 143.

CHEEKTOWAGA. *Kolbe Catholic Regional School*, 120 Alexander Ave., 14211. Tel: 716-895-3127; Fax: 716-895-7347.
E-mail: rbuscaglia@juno.com
Rose Mary Buscaglia, Prin.
Sponsoring Parishes: St. Lawrence, Holy Name, St. Gerard, St. John Kanty, St. John Gualbert, Most Holy Redeemer. Lay Teachers 18; Students 213; Total Staff 30.

DEPEW. *SS. Peter & Paul Catholic School*, 52 Burlington Ave., 14043. Tel: 716-683-8049; Fax: 716-683-0699.
E-mail: nwichrowsk@catholicwebs.org
Sr. Mary Nicolette Wichrowski, C.S.S.F., Prin.
Sponsoring parishes: SS. Peter & Paul, Depew; Sacred Heart, Bowmansville. Sisters 3; Lay Teachers 14; Students 162; Total Staff 17.

DUNKIRK. *Northern Chautauqua Catholic*, 336 Washington Ave., 14048. Tel: 716-366-0630; Fax: 716-366-5101. Kathy Y. Moser, Prin.
Sponsoring parishes: Brocton, St. Patrick; Dunkirk: St. Elizabeth Ann Seton, St. Hedwig, Holy Trinity; Fredonia: St. Anthony, St. Joseph; Silver Creek: Our Lady of Mt. Carmel; Cassadaga: Immaculate Conception; Sinclairville: St. John the Evangelist; Westfield: St. James Major; Ripley: St. Thomas More; Sheridan: St. John Bosco; Forestville: St. Rose of Lima. Lay Teachers 15; Students 207; Total Staff 26.

EDEN. *Regionalized School of the Immaculate Conception*, 8783 S. Main St., 14057-1397. Tel: 716-992-3508; Fax: 716-992-2243.
E-mail: iceden@catholic.org
Harold Shepard, Prin.
Sponsoring parishes: Eden, Immaculate Conception; E. Eden, St. Mary; New Oregon, St. Mary of the Immaculate Conception; N. Collins, Holy Spirit. Lay Teachers 13; Students 111.

JAMESTOWN. *Holy Family Catholic School*, 1135 N. Main St., 14701-3199. Tel: 716-483-3245; Fax: 716-483-8492.
E-mail: HFCS@netsync.net
Tina Rosage, Prin.
Sponsoring parishes: Jamestown, St. James, St. John, SS. Peter & Paul; Bemus Point, Our Lady of Lourdes; Falconer, Our Lady of Loreto; Frewsburg, Our Lady of Victory; French Creek, St. Matthias; Lakewood, Sacred Heart; Mayville, St. Mary; Panama, Our Lady of the Snows; Randolph, St. Patrick; Sherman, St. Isaac Jogues. Lay Teachers 21; Students 218; Total Staff 28.

LAKE VIEW. *Southtowns Catholic*, 2052 Lakeview Rd., Box 86, 14085. Tel: 716-627-5011; Fax: 716-627-5335.
E-mail: gbaldelli@catholic.org
Mr. Gerald. R. Baldelli, Prin.
Sponsoring parishes: St. Vincent de Paul, North Evans; Our Lady of Perpetual Help, Lake View. Lay Teachers 19; Students 267; Total Staff 26.

LOCKPORT. *DeSales Catholic School*, 6914 Chestnut School, 14094. Tel: 716-433-6422; Fax: 716-434-4002. Sr. Carol Kleindinst, S.S.M.N.
Sponsoring parishes: Lockport, St. Anthony, St. John the Baptist, St. Joseph, St. Mary, St. Patrick; Gasport, St. Mary; Middleport, St. Stephen; Newfane, St. Bridget, Wilson, Our Lady of the Rosary; Barker, St. Patrick; Olcott, St. Charles Borromeo; Ransomville, Immaculate Conception; N. Tonawanda, Good Shepherd; Clarence Center, St. Augustine. Sisters 2; Lay Teachers 33; Students 557; Total Staff 45.

NORTH TONAWANDA. *North Tonawanda Catholic*. Ascension Campus: (Grades 4-8), 75 Keil St., 14120. Tel: 716-693-2828; Fax: 716-693-0169.
E-mail: RKutsko@catholic.org
Sr. Rosemarie Kutsko, C.S.S.F., Supervising Prin., OLC Campus: (Grades K-3), 57 Center Ave., 14120. Tel: 716-694-3644. St. Joseph Campus: (Grades Preschool), 1469 Payne Ave., 14120. Tel: 716-693-4769.
Sponsoring parishes: Ascension, Our Lady of Czestochowa, St. Albert the Great and St. Joseph. Sisters 3; Lay Teachers 22; Students 272; Total Staff 25.

OLEAN. *Southern Tier Catholic*, 205 W. Henley St., 14760. Tel: 716-372-2891; Fax: 716-373-1175.
E-mail: SOTIERCS@netsynch.net
Mrs. Ann Marie Sitter, Prin.
Sponsoring parishes: Allegany, St. Bonaventure; Cuba, Our Lady of the Angels; Hinsdale, St. Helen; Portville, Sacred Heart; Olean, St. Joseph's & St. Mary of the Angels; St. John; Transfiguration; Vandalia; St. John the Baptist. Lay Teachers 19; Students 248; Total Staff 28.

SPRINGVILLE. *St. Aloysius Regional School*, 186 Franklin St., 14141-1198. Tel: 716-592-7002; Fax: 716-592-4347.
E-mail: brenzi@catholic.org
Bonnie Renzi, Prin. Sisters 1; Lay Teachers 18; Students 162.

[H] CATHOLIC CHARITIES

BUFFALO. *The Catholic Charities of the Diocese of Buffalo*, 525 Washington St., 14203. Tel: 716-856-4494; Fax: 716-856-2005.
Web site: www.ccharitiesbflo.net
Rev. Msgr. Henry J. Gugino, Diocesan Dir.
Central Office: All Offices, Directors, and Supervisors are located at 525 Washington St., Buffalo, NY 14203, unless otherwise indicated.

Finance Dept. Tel: 716-856-4494; Fax: 716-856-2005. Theodore S. Lesinski, Comptroller. Tel: 716-856-4494; James P. Hayes, Dir. Devel. Tel: 716-856-4494; Peggy Penders, Dir. Communications & Public Relations. Tel: 716-856-4494; Mrs. Margaret Connors, Admin. Asst.

Catholic Charities Program Services. Rev. Msgr. Henry J. Gugino, Exec. Dir. Tel: 716-856-4494; Rev. Joseph J. Sicari, Assoc. Dir. Tel: 716-856-4494; Mr. Dennis Walczyk, COO. Tel: 716-856-4494.

Central Intake. Mrs. Kathryn Heavey, Supvr.

Kenfield Office, 188 Oakmont Ave., 14215. Tel: 716-835-6894; Fax: 716-832-8286. Jesselyn Garcia, Supvr.

Black Rock/Riverside Office, 819 Tonawanda St., 14207. Tel: 716-877-4716; Fax: 716-447-1180. Cindy Manne, Supvr.

West Side Family Counseling Center, 412 Niagara St., 14201. Tel: 716-854-3622; Fax: 716-842-1366. Supervisors: Marjorie Quartley; Sandy Taltos.

Lackawanna Family Counseling Center, 33-37 Wilkesbarre Ave., Lackawanna, 14218. Tel: 716-822-6877; Fax: 716-827-1726. Donna Felser, Supvr.

Preventive Services & Batterer's Intervention Program, 1581 Bailey Ave., 14212. Tel: 716-896-6390; Fax: 716-896-4236. Greg White, Supvr. Legal Title: *Preventive Services and Batterer's Intervention Program, and Therapeutic Supervised Visitation Program.*

School Intervention Service, 3370 Delaware Ave., Kenmore, 14217. Tel: 716-877-8822; Fax: 716-874-5245. Cindy Manne, Supvr., 9 E. Union, P.O. Box 94, Hamburg, 14075. Tel: 716-648-6515; Fax: 716-648-7101. Martha Blackstock, Supvr., 3719 Union Rd., Ste. 214, Cheektowaga, 14225. Tel: 716-681-7394; Fax: 716-685-9087. Sara Murphy, Supvr., 4498 Main St., Amherst, 14226. Tel: 716-839-4066; Fax: 716-839-4082. Cindy Sawicki, Supvr.

Department of Workforce Development, 170 Kerns Ave., 14211. Tel: 716-893-3500; Fax: 716-893-0807. Michael Talluto, Dir.

Niagara County Diversion (PINS), 345 Third St., Ste. 505, Niagara Falls, 14303. Tel: 716-282-2351; Fax: 716-282-0146. Maria Picone, Supvr.

Diocesan Resettlement Division, 73 Edward St., 14203. Tel: 716-842-6816; Fax: 716-842-0509. Ann Brittain, Supvr.

Youth Careers Program, 170 Kerns Ave., 14211. Tel: 716-893-3500; Fax: 716-893-0807. Michael Talluto, Dir.

Department of Parish Based Social Services. Tel: 716-856-4494; Fax: 716-856-2005. Sr. Mary Anne Weldon, R.S.M., Dir.

Office of Pastoral Ministry With Handicapped Persons. Tel: 716-856-4494; Fax: 716-856-2005.

Chautauqua Elderly Project, 741 Falconer St., Jamestown, 14701. Tel: 716-665-4374; Fax: 716-488-9233. Claire Trubits, Supvr.

Adoptions, Child Care Division and Young Parents Program. Tel: 716-856-4494; Fax: 716-855-1312. Gail Sunshine-May, Supvr.

Batavia, 113-119 Main St., Batavia, 14020. Tel: 716-343-0614; Fax: 716-344-3868. Margaret Meyer, Supvr.

Dunkirk, 314 Central Ave., Ste. 207, Dunkirk, 14048. Tel: 716-366-3533; Fax: 716-363-1184.

Jamestown, 413 N. Main St., Jamestown, 14701. Tel: 716-484-9188; Fax: 716-484-0766.

Niagara Falls, 345 Third St., Ste. 515, Niagara Falls, 14303. Tel: 716-282-2351; Fax: 716-282-0146. Kathleen Hall, Supvr.

Olean, 520 W. State St., P.O. Box 554, Olean, 14140. Tel: 716-372-0101. Jon Anderson, Supvr.

Women, Infants & Children (W.I.C.) of Niagara County, 237 Fourth St., Niagara Falls, 14303. Tel: 716-285-0975; Fax: 716-282-7015. Joan Ward, Supvr. Catholic Charities Satellite Offices: Blackrock-Riverside, 819 Tonawanda St., 14207. Tel: 716-877-4716. Bailey-Broadway Office, 1581 Bailey Ave., 14212. Tel: 716-896-6390; Fax: 716-896-4236. Grider Street, 359 Grider St., 14215. Tel: 716-895-7715 (DDFSP); 716-895-7718 (GOTT); Fax: 716-895-1544 (DDFSP); 716-893-1692 (GOTT, Ext.). Oakmont Avenue, 188 Oakmont Ave., 14215. Tel: 716-835-6894; Fax: 716-832-8286. Perry Street, 488 Perry St., 14204. Tel: 716-856-4456; Fax: 716-852-2343. South Buffalo, 2315 Seneca St., 14210. Tel: 716-821-1929; Fax: 716-825-2199. Albion, 243 S. Main St., Albion, 14411. Tel: 716-589-7477; Fax: 716-344-3868. Amherst, 4498 Main St., Amherst, 14226. Tel: 716-839-4066; Fax: 716-839-4082. Cheektowaga, 3719 Union Rd., Cheektowaga, 14225. Tel: 716-681-7394; Fax: 716-685-9087. Hamburg, 9 E. Union St., 14075. Tel: 716-648-6515; Fax: 716-648-7101. Kenmore, 3370 Delaware Ave., Kenmore, 14217. Tel: 716-877-8822; Fax: 716-874-5245. Lockport, 39 East Ave., Lockport, 14094. Tel: 716-433-0246; Fax: 716-433-0246. North Tonawanda, 1089 Kinkead Ave., Ste. 203, North Tonawanda, 14120. Tel: 716-692-1440. Southtowns Office, 34 Barnstead Dr., Springville, 14141. Tel: 716-592-3420. Warsaw, 4 W. Buffalo St., Ste. B, Warsaw, 14569. Tel: 716-786-3440; Fax: 716-344-3868. Wellsville, 25 E. Pearl St., Box 106, Wellsville, 14895. Tel: 716-593-2015. West Seneca, 4105 Seneca St., P.O. Box 244, West Seneca, 14224. Tel: 716-675-3785; Fax: 716-677-0289.

Catholic Charities Appeal. Tel: 716-856-4494; Fax: 716-856-2005. Rev. Msgr. Henry J. Gugino, Diocesan Dir.; Rev. Joseph J. Sicari, Assoc. Dir.

Department of Clinical Services-Msgr. Carr Clinic, 76 W. Humboldt Pkwy. Tel: 716-835-9745; Fax: 716-835-6785. Brian O'Herron, Dir.

Marriage Counseling Center, 4498 Main St., 14226. Tel: 716-839-4406; Fax: 716-839-4082. David Catalano, Supvr.

St. Joseph's Day Training Center, 930 Fillmore Ave., 14211. Tel: 716-896-6038; Fax: 716-896-4355. Marsha Sladeski, Ph.D., Supvr.

Developmental Disabilities/Family Support Program, 359 Grider St., 14215. Tel: 716-895-7715; Fax: 716-895-1544. Arry Green, Supvr.

Diocesan Counseling Service for Clergy and Religious, 16 Columbus St., Cheektowaga, 14227. Tel: 716-894-2743; Fax: 716-896-6394. Sr. Anne Marie Jablonicky, C.S.S.F., Dir.

Chemical Dependency Program, Substance Abuse Prevention & Counseling Program, 76 W. Humboldt Pkwy., 14214. Tel: 716-835-9745; Fax: 716-835-6785. Judith Vogtli, Ph.D., Dir.

Geriatrics Outreach Treatment Team, 359 Grider St., 14218. Tel: 716-895-7715; Fax: 716-893-1692. Arry Green, Supvr.

Department of Services to the Aging. Tel: 716-856-4494; Fax: 716-856-2005. Ms. Mary Jo Giambelluca, Dir.

Home Care Services. Tel: 716-856-4494; Fax: 716-856-2005. Deborah Alberth, R.N., Supvr.

Family Focus Program, 30 Rich St., 14211. Tel: 716-896-8262; Fax: 716-894-3088. Kathleen Pharris, Supvr.

Senior Day Center, 30 Rich St., 14211. Tel: 716-896-6388; Fax: 716-894-3088. Kathleen Pharris, Dir.

Guardian Angel Day Care, 1193 Delaware Ave., 14209. Tel: 716-882-9146; Fax: 716-881-7051. Dana Cassiano, Supvr.

Holy Innocents Day Care, 30 Rich St., 14211. Tel: 716-896-6386; Fax: 716-894-3088. Debbie Coyne, Supvr.

Housing and Supportive Services. Tel: 716-856-4494; Fax: 716-856-2005. Marie Bakowski, Supvr.

Foster Grandparents Program. Tel: 716-856-4494; Fax: 716-856-2005. Dorothy Turchiarelli, Supvr.

Friendly Phones. Tel: 716-856-4494; Fax: 716-856-2005. Dorothy Turchiarelli, Supvr.

Volunteer Agencies:

Catholic Guild for the Blind. Tel: 716-856-4494; Fax: 716-856-2005. Sr. Michael Jordan, Prog. Dir.

Guild of St. Apollonia. Tel: 716-856-4494; Fax: 716-856-2005. Rev. Msgr. Henry J. Gugino, Spiritual Dir.

Ladies of Charity, 1122 Broadway, 14212. Tel: 716-895-4001. Rev. Msgr. Henry J. Gugino; Mrs. Eileen Nowak, Prog. Dir.

Society of St. Vincent de Paul, 1298 Main St., 14209. Tel: 716-852-7415. Rev. Msgr. Henry J. Gugino, Spiritual Dir.; Mr. Mark S. Zirnheld, Dir.

Delta Development Low Income Housing Development & Management. Tel: 716-856-4494; Fax: 716-856-2005. Total Assisted 210; Total Staff 39.

St. Clare Apartments Housing Development, c/o Catholic Charities, 525 Washington St., 14203. Tel: 716-856-4494; Fax: 716-856-2005. Rev. Msgr. Henry J. Gugino.

[I] ORPHANAGES AND INFANT HOMES

BUFFALO. *German Roman Catholic Orphan Home*, 795 Main St., 14203
For a complete listing, refer to the Special Care Facilities section.

[J] PROTECTIVE INSTITUTES

BUFFALO. *The Franciscan Center, Inc.*, 1910 Seneca St., 14210-1842. Tel: 716-822-8017; Fax: 716-822-8537
For a complete listing, refer to the Special Care Facilities section.

LACKAWANNA. *Baker Victory Services*, 780 Ridge Rd., 14218. Tel: 716-828-9500; 888-287-9986; Fax: 716-828-9526.
E-mail: baker@buffnet.net
Web site: www.bakervictoryservices.org
For a complete listing, refer to the Special Care Facilities section.

[K] GENERAL HOSPITALS

BUFFALO. *Catholic Health System, Inc.* Marian Professional Center, 515 Abbott Rd., Ste. 508, 14220. Tel: 716-828-2750; Fax: 716-828-2703.
For a complete listing, refer to the Hospitals section.

McAuley Mercy Corporation, 515 Abbott Rd., 14220. Tel: 716-828-2750
For a complete listing, refer to the Hospitals section.

Mercy Hospital, 565 Abbott Rd., 14220. Tel: 716-826-7000; Fax: 716-828-2700.
E-mail: JPD@whychs.org
For a complete listing, refer to the Hospitals section.
Sisters Hospital Foundation, Inc., 2130 Main St., 14214. Tel: 716-862-2533; Fax: 716-835-8643.
E-mail: jhazzan@wnychs.org
For a complete listing, refer to the Hospitals section.
Sisters of Charity Hospital of Buffalo, NY, 2157 Main St., 14214. Tel: 716-862-1000; Fax: 716-862-1899.
E-mail: mdougherty@wnychs.org
Web site: http://www.sisters-buffalo.org81
For a complete listing, refer to the Hospitals section.

CHEEKTOWAGA. *McAuley-Seton Home Care*, 14 Appletree Business Park, 14227. Tel: 716-685-4870; Fax: 716-651-9613
For a complete listing, refer to the Hospitals section.
St. Joseph Hospital, 2605 Harlem Rd., 14225-4097. Tel: 716-891-2400; Fax: 716-891-2616
For a complete listing, refer to the Hospitals section.

KENMORE. *Kenmore Mercy Foundation Inc.*, 2950 Elmwood Ave., 14217. Tel: 716-447-6204; Fax: 716-447-6052.
E-mail: swierskikaren@netscape.net
For a complete listing, refer to the Hospitals section.
Kenmore Mercy Hospital, 2950 Elmwood Ave., 14217. Tel: 716-447-6100; Fax: 716-447-6090
For a complete listing, refer to the Hospitals section.

LACKAWANNA. *Our Lady of Victory Hospital*, 55 Melroy at Ridge Rd., 14218. Tel: 716-825-8000; Fax: 716-825-4681
For a complete listing, refer to the Hospitals section.
Our Lady of Victory Hospital Auxiliary, 55 Melroy at Ridge Rd., 14218. Tel: 716-825-8000
For a complete listing, refer to the Hospitals section.

LEWISTON. *Mount St. Mary's Hospital of Niagara Falls*, 5300 Military Rd., 14092-1997. Tel: 716-297-4800; Fax: 716-298-2333 (Gen.);716-298-2001 (Pres.)
For a complete listing, refer to the Hospitals section.

LOCKPORT. *Niagara Homemaker Services, dba Mercy Home Care of Western New York*, 111 Main St., 14094. Tel: 716-434-2388; Fax: 716-434-2621.
E-mail: bholmesdo@aol.com
For a complete listing, refer to the Hospitals section.

[L] HEALTH CARE FACILITIES

BUFFALO. *St. Francis Geriatric and Healthcare Services, Inc.*, 2787 Main St., 14214. Tel: 716-837-4200; Fax: 716-837-4218
For a complete listing, refer to the Special Care Facilities section.

[M] HOMES FOR AGED

BUFFALO. *Nazareth Nursing Home*, 291 North St., 14201. Tel: 716-881-2323; Fax: 716-881-1578
For a complete listing, refer to the Special Care Facilities section.

BATAVIA. *St. Luke Manor*, 17 Wiard St., 14020. Tel: 716-343-8806; Fax: 716-343-0959
For a complete listing, refer to the Special Care Facilities section.

CLARENCE. *Brothers of Mercy Housing Co., Inc.*, 10500 Bergtold Rd., 14031. Tel: 716-759-2122
For a complete listing, refer to the Special Care Facilities section.
Brothers of Mercy Nursing & Rehabilitation Center, 10570 Bergtold Rd., 14031. Tel: 716-759-6985; Fax: 716-759-6223.
E-mail: BOMNRC@aol.com
Web site: www.BrothersOfMercy.org
For a complete listing, refer to the Special Care Facilities section.
Brothers of Mercy Sacred Heart Home, Inc., 4520 Ransom Rd., 14031. Tel: 716-759-2644; Fax: 716-759-6433.
E-mail: BOMSHH@aol.com
For a complete listing, refer to the Special Care Facilities section.

DUNKIRK. *St. Vincent's Home for the Aged*, 319 Washington Ave., 14048. Tel: 716-366-2066; Fax: 716-366-0545.
E-mail: stvhome@netsync.net
For a complete listing, refer to the Special Care Facilities section.

KENMORE. *Kenmore Mercy Homes, Inc. (dba McAuley Residence)*, Administrative Offices, 2950 Elmwood Ave., 14217. Tel: 716-447-6101; Fax: 716-447-6090
For a complete listing, refer to the Special Care Facilities section.

LANCASTER. *St. Elizabeth's Home*, 5539 Broadway, 14086. Tel: 716-683-5150; Fax: 716-683-4049
For a complete listing, refer to the Special Care Facilities section.

LOCKPORT. *St. Clare Manor*, 543 Locust St., 14094. Tel: 716-434-4718; Fax: 716-434-5900
For a complete listing, refer to the Special Care Facilities section.

NIAGARA FALLS. *Mount St. Mary's LTC Facility, Inc.*, 2600 Main St., 14305. Tel: 716-285-9155; Fax: 716-285-4558.
E-mail: MSMLTCF@aol.com
For a complete listing, refer to the Special Care Facilities section.
St. Mary's Manor, 515 Sixth St., 14301. Tel: 716-285-3236; Fax: 716-285-4199
For a complete listing, refer to the Special Care Facilities section.

OLEAN. *St. Joseph Manor*, 2211 W. State St., 14760. Tel: 716-372-7810; Fax: 716-373-4375.
E-mail: stjmanor@eznet.net
For a complete listing, refer to the Special Care Facilities section.

ORCHARD PARK. *W.N.Y. Catholic LongTerm Care, Inc. dba Father Baker Manor*, 6400 Powers Rd., 14127. Tel: 716-667-0001; Fax: 716-667-0028.
E-mail: bakermanor@aol.com
For a complete listing, refer to the Special Care Facilities section.

SILVER CREEK. *St. Columbans on the Lake, Home for the Aged*, 2546 Lake Rd., 14136. Tel: 716-934-4515; Fax: 716-934-3919
For a complete listing, refer to the Special Care Facilities section.

WILLIAMSVILLE. *Holy Family Home*, 410 Mill St., 14221. Tel: 716-634-5400; Fax: 716-634-5730
For a complete listing, refer to the Special Care Facilities section.
St. Francis Home of Williamsville, 147 Reist St., 14221. Tel: 716-633-5400; Fax: 716-663-6404
For a complete listing, refer to the Special Care Facilities section.

[N] DAY CARE CENTERS

BUFFALO. *Guardian Angel Day Care Center*, 1193 Delaware Ave., 14209. Tel: 716-882-9146; Fax: 716-881-7051. Dana M. Cassiano, Admin. Lay Staff 15; Children 72; Total Staff 15.
Holy Innocents Day Care Center, 30 Rich St., 14211. Tel: 716-896-6386; Fax: 716-894-3088. Mrs. Deborah L. Coyne, Dir. Day care for children age 6 weeks to 12 yrs. Children 113; Total Staff 21.

[O] MONASTERIES AND RESIDENCES OF PRIESTS AND BROTHERS

BUFFALO. *Bishop's Residence*, 77 Oakland Pl., 14222. Most Rev. Henry J. Mansell, D.D.; Rev. Msgr. Robert J. Cunningham; Revs. David G. LiPuma; Paul A. Litwin.
Canisius Jesuit Community, 2001 Main St., 14208. Tel: 716-883-7000; Fax: 716-886-6506.
E-mail: higgins@canisius.edu
Web site: www.canisius.edu
Legal Title: *The Jesuits of Canisius College, Inc.* Revs. James P. Higgins, S.J., Rector; Peter K. Arabia, S.J.; Joseph F. Burke, S.J.; Bro. Thomas J. Casey, S.J.; Revs. J. Peter Conroy, S.J.; Vincent M. Cooke, S.J.; Paul J. Dugan, S.J.; Edward T. Dunn, S.J.; Benjamin Fiore, S.J.; James F. Fox, S.J.; Richard H. Galligan, S.J.; Louis T. Garaventa, S.J.; John J. Garvey, S.J.; Robert A. Haus, S.J.; Richard D. Hunt, S.J.; Daniel P. Jamros, S.J.; Ladislaus F. Juhasz, S.J. (Hungary); Joseph J. Kamiensky, S.J.; Mark G. Kriz, S.J.; Daniel P. Liderbach, S.J.; Patrick J. Lynch, S.J., Min.; Edward C. Lynch, S.J.; John J. Mattimore, S.J.; Paul J. McCarthy, S.J.; Vincent M. McNally, S.J.; Martin X. Moleski, S.J.; Paul W. Nochelski, S.J.; Thomas A. O'Connor, S.J.; Michael H. Pastizzo, S.J.; Frederick J. Reisert, S.J.; James J. Ruddick, S.J.; John J. Ryan, S.J.; Ronald W. Sams, S.J.; Brendan T. Scott, S.J.; Edward P. Sullivan, S.J.; Michael F. Tunney, S.J.; James R. Van Dyke, S.J.; Eugene A. Zimpfer, S.J.; Daniel J. Lusch, S.J., Elmwood 4, 4845 Transit Rd., 14043. Tel: 716-668-3251. Total in Residence 39; Total Staff 15.
Maryknoll House, 71 Jewett Pkwy., 14214-2396. Tel: 716-834-6065; Fax: 716-834-3478.
E-mail: mklbuffalo@aol.com
Web site: www.maryknoll.com
Rev. Joseph Turowski, M.M., Dir. Total in Residence 1; Total Staff 3.
Sheehan Residence for Priests, 330 Linwood Ave., 14209-1689. Tel: 716-884-9679; Fax: 716-881-5268. Residence for retired priests. Revs. Robert J. Biesinger; Raymond G. Bohn; Rev. Msgr. Paul T. Cronin; Rev. Msgr. Samuel F. Lombardo; Revs. Thomas J. Crowley; Henry V. Lex; Joseph Kwolek; David V. Roche; Raymond R. Russell.

ATHOL SPRINGS. *Father Justin Rosary Hour Radio Apostolate*, St. Anthony of Padua Friary, 4190 St. Francis Dr., 14010. Tel: 716-627-3861; Fax: 716-627-4059.
E-mail: office@rosaryhour.net
Web site: www.rosaryhour.net
Revs. Marion M. Tolczyk, O.F.M.Conv., Guardian & Dir.; Piotr R. Miodek, O.F.M.Conv. (Poland); Eligius Kozak, O.F.M.Conv. (Poland); Wladek Mezyk, O.F.M.Conv. (Poland). Staff to the Rosary Hour Apostolate: Sr. Mary Angelica Bielski, C.S.S.F., Executive Secretary; Sr. Mary Rosette Kubisty, C.S.S.F. Total Staff 4; Total in Residence 4.
St. Francis of Assisi Friary, 4129 Lake Shore Rd., 14010-0185. Tel: 716-627-5762; Fax: 716-627-4610. Faculty Residence for St. Francis High School. Revs. Aurelian W. Brzezniak, O.F.M.Conv.; Bernard Olszewski, O.F.M.Conv.; Charles Jagodzinski, O.F.M.Conv., Vicar; Felix Bracikowski, O.F.M.Conv.; Mark David Skura, O.F.M.Conv., Guardian; Joseph Benicewicz, O.F.M.Conv., Pres. & Prin.; Michael Lasky, O.F.M.Conv.; Michael Miller, O.F.M.Conv.; Bro. Lawrence LaFlame, O.F.M.Conv. Priests 8; Brothers 1; Total in Residence 9.

CLARENCE. *Provincial Motherhouse of Brothers of Mercy*, 4520 Ransom Rd., 14031. Tel: 716-759-8341; Fax: 716-759-8341. Legal Title: *Brothers of Mercy, Inc.* Bro. Jude Holzfoerster, F.M.M., Prov.; Rev. John J. Sardina, Chap. Brothers 16; In Formation 2.

DERBY. *Society of St. Paul.* Mailing Address: Box 757, 14047. Tel: 716-947-5407; Fax: 716-947-5407.
E-mail: ssp-usprovince@msn.com
Web site: www.albahouse.org
Very Rev. Matthew Roehrig, S.S.P., Prov. Supr.

LACKAWANNA. *Piarist Fathers.* Assumption of the Blessed Virgin Mary, 80 Steelawanna Ave., 14218-0343. Tel: 716-822-9828; Fax: 716-822-9828.
E-mail: maurice1921@yahoo.com
Revs. Alphonse Vercek, Sch.P., (Nursing Home); Kalman Miskolczy, Sch.P., Treas.; Nicholas Vitez Fodor, Sch.P., Supr. Total in Residence 3; Total Staff 2.

LEROY. *Order of the BVM of Mercy/Mercedarian Friars*, Mercygrove, 7758 E. Main Rd., 14482-9701. Tel: 716-768-7110; Fax: 716-768-4803.
E-mail: mercygrove@aol.com
Web site: www.orderofmercy.org
United States headquarters for the community. Pre-novitiate and Novitiate formation community. Revs. Arcangelo Manzi, O.de.M., Supr. & Master of Postulants; Eugene Costa, O.de.M., Novice Master; Michael Rock, O.de.M., Devel. Officer; Wayne C. Genereux, O.de.M., Vocation Dir. & Master of Postulants. Total in Community: Professed Religious 3; Postulants 4.
St. Raymond Nonnatus Novitiate. Order of the BVM of Mercy. Mercygrove, 7758 E. Main Rd., 14482-9701. Tel: 716-768-7110; Fax: 716-768-4803.
E-mail: mercygrove@aol.com
Web site: www.orderofmercy.org
Rev. Eugene Costa, O.de.M., Novice Master. Novices 1.

NIAGARA FALLS. *Catholic Worker Center*, 931 Niagara Ave., P.O. Box 297, 14305. Tel: 716-282-8683; Fax: 716-282-3545. Patricia J. Merino, Managing Dir.

NIAGARA UNIVERSITY. *Vincentian Community at Niagara University*, Meade Hall, 14109-2209. Tel: 716-286-8110; Fax: 716-286-8766.
E-mail: meade@niagara.edu
Revs. John A. Kettelberger, C.M., Supr.; Joseph G. Hubbert, C.M., Asst.; Bro. Augustine D. Towey, C.M., Sub-Asst.; Revs. William M. Allegretto, C.M.; William L. Green, C.M.; Dennis Holtschneider, C.M.; Joseph L. Levesque, C.M.; Thomas P. Mallaghan, C.M.; Thomas P. McGourty, C.M.; Daniel F. O'Leary, O.M.I.; Vincent J. O'Malley, C.M.; Francis X. Prior, C.M.; Martin J. Sleasman, C.M.; Louis P. Trotta, C.M.; Michael J. Tumulty, C.M.; Bros. Stephen J. Kennedy, C.M.; Martin J. Schneider, C.M. Total in Residence 17.

NORTH TONAWANDA. *Society of the Catholic Apostolate.* Infant Jesus Delegature, 3452 Niagara Falls Blvd., P.O. Box 563, 14120-0563. Tel: 716-694-4313; Fax: 716-743-5430. Revs. John Posiewala, S.A.C., Supr. & Prov. Delegate; Francis A. Cegielka, S.A.C.; George C. Maj, S.A.C.; Andrzej Kurowski, S.A.C.; Seweryn J. Koszyk, S.A.C.; Ryszard Lukomski, S.A.C.; George Poltorak, S.A.C.; Ignatius Curzydlo, S.A.C., Chap, VA Hospital.

ST. BONAVENTURE. *St. Bonaventure Friary*, 14778. Tel: 716-375-2000; Fax: 716-375-2424.
Web site: http://www.sbu.edu
Revs. Thomas D. Blow, O.F.M., Guardian; Michael Blastic, O.F.M.Conv.; David D. Blake, O.F.M.; J. Gregory Brennan, O.F.M.; Michael Cusato, O.F.M.; Regis A. Duffy, O.F.M.; Richard C. Flaherty, O.F.M.; David Flood, O.F.M.; Robert Karris, O.F.M.; Xavier J. Seubert, O.F.M., Vicar; Francis Storms, O.F.M., Treas.; Peter Schneible, O.F.M.; Robert Stewart, O.F.M.; Alphonsus A. Trabold, O.F.M.; James Vacco, O.F.M.; Allen Weber, O.F.M.; William J. Weiksnar, O.F.M.; Gervase F. White, O.F.M.; Robert H. White, O.F.M.; Allan Wolter, O.F.M.; Bros. Zachary Elliot, O.F.M.; David Haack, O.F.M.; Anthony J. LoGalbo, O.F.M.; Salvador Miranda, O.F.M.; Michael W. Montgomery, O.F.M.; James V. Pisto, O.F.M.; Adrian A. Riester, O.F.M.; Julian Riester, O.F.M.; Basil J. Valente, O.F.M. Fathers 20; Brothers 9.

TONAWANDA. *O'Hara Residence*, 69 O'Hara Rd., 14150-6227. Tel: 716-743-0037; Fax: 716-743-8772. Rev. Msgr. Anthony J. Caligiuri, P.A.; Rev. Msgr. James N. Connelly; Rev. Salvatore J. Cusimano; Rev. Msgr.

Leo E. Hammerl; Rev. Msgr. Paul R. Juenker, P.A.; Rev. Msgr. Paul R. Letourneau; Rev. Msgr. Dino J. Lorenzetti; Rev. Msgr. Edward J. Sobierajski; Rev. Msgr. Francis M. Swiatkowski; Rev. Msgr. Julius J. Szabo; Rev. Msgr. Casimir A. Zak. Total in Residence 12; Total Staff 4.

WEST SENECA. *Eudist Fathers, St. John Eudes Center*, 36 Flohr Ave., 14224-1818. Tel: 716-823-1090; Fax: 716-825-4376. Revs. Benoit J. Drapeau, C.J.M., Pastor, Supr.; Ronald M. Bagley, C.J.M., Dir. St. John Eudes Center; J. Gregory Sampson, C.J.M. Total in Residence 3; Total Staff 5.

[P] CONVENTS AND RESIDENCES FOR SISTERS

BUFFALO. *Congregation of the Sisters of St. Joseph Generalate.*
E-mail: Buffssj@aol.com
Web site: www.ssjbuffalo.org
Administrative Offices, 23 Agassiz Cir., 14214-2611. Tel: 716-838-4400; Fax: 716-838-4102. Professed Sisters 145.

Discalced Carmelite Monastery of St. Teresa of the Child Jesus (1920), 75 Carmel Rd., 14214. Tel: 716-837-6499; Fax: 716-837-3517. Mother Miriam of Jesus, O.C.D., Prioress. Cloistered Professed Sisters 16; Extern Professed Sisters 2; Novices 2; Postulants 2.

Holy Name Province - Provincial Motherhouse.

Sisters of St. Francis of Holy Name Province, Inc., 4421 Lower River Rd., Stella Niagara, 14144. Tel: 716-754-4312; Fax: 716-754-7657.
E-mail: hnprov@frontiernet.net
Sr. Mary McCarrick, O.S.F., Prov. Min.

Center of Renewal, Inc., 4421 Lower River Rd., Stella Niagara, 14144. Tel: 716-754-7376; Fax: 716-754-1223. Sr. Mary McCarrick, O.S.F., Prov. Min.

Francis Center, 1301 Ferry Ave., Niagara Falls, 14301. Tel: 716-282-3783. Sr. Mary McCarrick, O.S.F., Prov. Min.

Stella Niagara Education Park, Inc., 4421 Lower River Rd., Stella Niagara, 14144. Tel: 716-754-4311; Fax: 716-754-1223. Sr. Mary McCarrick, O.S.F., Prov. Min.

The Stella Niagara Education Park Endowment Foundation, 4421 Lower River Rd., Stella Niagara, 14144. Tel: 716-754-4311; Fax: 716-754-1223. Sr. Mary McCarrick, O.S.F., Prov. Min.

The Sisters of St. Francis Retirement Fund, 4421 Lower River Rd., Stella Niagara, 14144. Tel: 716-754-4312; Fax: 716-754-7657. Sr. Mary McCarrick, O.S.F., Prov. Min.

The Providence Fund, 4421 Lower River Rd., Stella Niagara, 14144. Tel: 716-754-4312; Fax: 716-754-7657. Sr. Mary McCarrick, O.S.F., Prov. Min.

Buffalo Academy of the Sacred Heart, Inc., 3860 Main St., Eggertsville, 14226. Tel: 716-834-2101; Fax: 716-834-2944.
E-mail: shalib@buffnet.net
Web site: www.sacredheartacademy.org
Sr. Mary Ambrose Wozniak, C.S.S.F., Prov. Vicar.

Immaculate Heart of Mary Provincial House and Convent. Villa Maria, 600 Doat St., 14211. Tel: 716-892-4141; Fax: 716-892-4177.
E-mail: felbflo@buffnet.net
Sr. Mary Ambrose Wozniak, C.S.S.F., Prov. Vicar; Rev. Donald E. Levan, Chap. Felician Sisters 285.

Mercy Center, 625 Abbott Rd., 14220. Tel: 716-825-5531; Fax: 716-826-1518.
E-mail: mercybuf@buffnet.net
Total in Residence 75.

Monastery of Our Lady of the Rosary, 335 Doat St., 14211-2199. Tel: 716-892-0066; Fax: 716-892-8846.
E-mail: MTNOP3@aol.com
Mother Rose of St. Mary, O.P., Prioress. Legal Title: *Dominican Nuns of the Perpetual Rosary, Buffalo, NY.* Professed Nuns 29; Postulants 5; Sisters in Temporary Vows 2; Novices 2.

Sisters of Mercy of the Buffalo Diocese Retirement Corp., 625 Abbott Rd., 14220. Tel: 716-825-5531; 826-6248; Fax: 716-826-1518.
E-mail: mercybuf@buffnet.net
Sr. Nancy Hoff, R.S.M., Pres.

Sisters of Mercy-Regional Community Offices, 625 Abbott Rd., 14220. Tel: 716-825-5051; 826-6248; Fax: 716-826-1518.
E-mail: mercybuf@buffnet.net
Sisters of Mercy. Sr. Nancy Hoff, R.S.M., Pres. Sisters Professed 180; Candidates 1.

Sisters of Social Service District Residence & Novitiate, 296 Summit Ave., 14214. Tel: 716-834-0197; Fax: 716-834-0197.
E-mail: sss@pcom.net
Sr. Agnes Pataki, S.S.S., District Moderator. Sisters 3.
Other Convents: Generalate, Bathori Laszlo u 10, Budapest, Hungary, H-1029. Tel: 011-361-275-7057; Fax: 011-361-275-7057. Sr. Anne Lehner, S.S.S., Gen. Moderator, St. Scholastica House, 210 Winston Rd., 14216. Tel: 716-833-7412.
E-mail: Scholastica@pcom.net
Sisters 2; Sisters Living Alone 3 (Buffalo Dio.) 2 (Other Dio.); Sisters in Other Religious Retirement Homes 3; Sisters in Nursing Home 1. Sara House, 42 Linden Ave., 14214. Tel: 716-836-0685. Sisters 3. Bethany House, 152 Kinsey Ave., Kenmore, 14217. Tel: 716-873-6179. Sisters 2.

Sisters of St. Mary of Namur, 250 Bryant St., 14222. Tel: 716-884-8221; Fax: 716-884-2950.
E-mail: eprovmq@juno.com
Web site: www.ssmn.org
Provincial House of the Sisters of St. Mary of Namur. Sr. Maureen Quinn, S.S.M.N., Prov. Supr.; Sr. Barbara Riter, S.S.M.N., Prov. Councillor. Professed Sisters 109.

ALLEGANY. *St. Elizabeth's Motherhouse*, 14706. Tel: 716-373-0200; Fax: 716-372-5774.
E-mail: fsaalleg@eznet.net
Web site: www.fsalleg.org
Motherhouse of the Franciscan Sisters of Allegany. Sr. Margaret Mary Kimmins, O.S.F., Gen. Min.; Sr. Noella Lachat, O.S.F., Local Min. Sisters 96; Total Staff 28.

BELMONT. *Immaculate Conception Convent*, 5173 State Rte. 244, 14813. Tel: 716-268-5524. Franciscan Missionary Sisters of the Divine Child. Conducts catechetical centers in 7 villages. Sr. Rosemary Benson, Supr.

CLARENCE. *Sisters of St. Joseph.* Clarence Residence, 4975 Strickler Rd., 14031. Tel: 716-759-6893; Fax: 716-759-2488.
E-mail: Clarencessj@yahoo.com
Coordinators: Sr. Marian Schwenk, S.S.J.; Sr. Marie Denise Heineman, S.S.J. Total in Residence 58; Total Staff 20.

DELEVAN. *Franciscan Sisters of Allegany, New York-Blessed Sacrament Mission Center*, 8 N. Main St., P.O. Box188, 14042. Tel: 716-492-2266. Conducted by Franciscan Sisters of Allegany. Services Region 21. Sr. Mary Richard Burke, O.S.F., Chaplaincy Svc.; Sr. Ellen Michael Schafer, O.S.F.

HAMBURG. *Immaculate Conception Convent*, 5286 S. Park Ave., 14075. Tel: 716-649-1205; Fax: 716-649-5958.
E-mail: genadmin@fssj.org
Motherhouse of the Franciscan Sisters of St. Joseph. Sr. M. Paulette Tirone, F.S.S.J., Gen. Min.; Rev. Ronald Sermak, O.F.M.Conv., Chap. Sisters 107.

North American Union of the Sisters of Our Lady of Charity, 3800 Howard Rd., 14075. Tel: 716-648-4988; Fax: 716-648-3062. Legal Title: *Sisters of Our Lady of Charity of the Refuge, Inc.* Sr. Bernard Clement, Local Supr. Sisters 18.

LACKAWANNA. *Sisters of Charity of St. Vincent de Paul of Zagreb, Croatia*, 211 W. Elmview Ave., 14218. Tel: 716-825-1461. Sr. Bernadette Copak, Supr. Sisters 2.

LEWISTON. *Sisters of the Sacred Heart of Jesus (S.S.H.J.)*, Sacred Heart School & Convent, 5269 Lewiston Rd., 14092. Tel: 716-284-8273; Fax: 716-284-8273.
E-mail: shvschool@adelphia.net
Sr. M. Ambrogia Alderuccio, S.S.H.J., Supr. Sisters 8.

SILVER CREEK. *Missionary Sisters of St. Columban, St. Columban's on the Lake*, 2546 Lake Rd., 14136. Tel: 716-934-4515; Fax: 716-934-3919. Rev. Peter Cronin, S.S.C., Chap. Professed Sisters 10.

WEST SENECA. *Sisters of Charity of St. Vincent de Paul of Zagreb, Croatia*, 171 Knox Ave., 14224. Tel: 716-825-5859; 822-6841; Fax: 716-822-2841. Sr. Stella Simetich, V.Z., Supr. Professed Sisters 14. Legal Title: *Sisters of Charity of St. Vincent de Paul of Zagreb, Croatia - U.S.A. Delegacy Headquarters.*

WILLIAMSVILLE. *Franciscan Missionary Sisters of the Divine Child, Inc.*, 6380 Main St., 14221. Tel: 716-632-3144; Fax: 716-626-1332.
E-mail: fmdcwilliamsville@altavista.com
Sr. Concetta DeFelice, Min. Gen.; Sr. Christine Winterhalter, Asst. Supr. Sisters 28.

Sisters of St. Francis of the Third Order Regular, St. Mary of the Angels, P.O. Box 275, 14231-0275. Tel: 716-632-2155; Fax: 716-632-0339.
E-mail: mnachreiner@osfwmsv.org
Motherhouse of the Sisters of St. Francis of the Third Order Regular. Sr. Patricia Burkard, Gen. Min.; Rev. Msgr. Fred R. Voorhes, Chap. Sisters 128.

[Q] RETREAT HOUSES

BUFFALO. *Blessed Sacrament Center of Eucharist Worship*, 15 University Ave., 14214. Tel: 716-834-6290; Fax: 716-834-6290.
E-mail: sacramentines.buffalony@worldnet.att.net
Directors: Sr. Mary of the Rosary, O.S.S.; Sr. Maria Christi, O.S.S. Total Staff 2; Total in Residence 2.

DERBY. *St. Columban's Center*, 6892 Lake Shore Rd., P.O. Box 816, 14047-0816. Tel: 716-947-4708; Fax: 716-947-5759.
E-mail: columban@buffnet.net
Web site: www.stcolumbancenter.org/
Rev. Msgr. James E. Wall, Dir.; Sr. Mary Leah Krauth, O.S.F., Assoc. Dir.; Sr. Mary Catherine Cummins, O.S.U., Assoc. Dir. Total in Residence 3; Total Staff 20.

LEROY. *St. Peter Nolasco Spiritual Center*, Mercygrove, 7770 E. Main Rd., 14482-9701. Tel: 716-768-7110; 768-6408; Fax: 716-768-4803.
E-mail: mercygrove@aol.com
Web site: www.orderofmercy.org
Offering directed or private retreats. Facility available for overnight programs. Rev. Arcangelo Manzi, O.de.M., Dir.

WEST CLARKSVILLE. *Mount Irenaeus, Franciscan Mountain Retreat & Holy Peace Friary*, P.O. Box 100, 14786. Tel: 716-973-2470; Fax: 716-973-2400.
E-mail: mmarc@sbu.edu
Order of Friars Minor Holy Name Province. Revs. Daniel P. Riley, O.F.M., Pres. & Guardian; Daniel A. Hurley, O.F.M.; Bro. Joseph Kotula, O.F.M.; Rev. Louis M. McCormick, O.F.M. Total in Residence 4.

[R] CAMPUS MINISTRY AND NEWMAN CENTERS

ALFRED. *Campus Ministry*, P.O. Box 1154, 14802. Tel: 607-587-9411. Rev. Eugene P. Ulrich, Vicar of Campus Ministry.

Canisius College. Campus Ministry Office, 2001 Main St., Buffalo, 14208. Tel: 716-888-2420; Fax: 716-888-3144. Rev. Richard R. Galligan, S.J., Dir. Assoc. Campus Ministers: Revs. Vincent M. McNally, S.J.; Thomas A. O'Connor, S.J.; John J. Ryan, S.J.; Sr. Patricia Brady, S.S.M.N.; Ms. Joy N. Africano; Ms. Susan Fischer; Mr. Joseph VanVolkenburg.

Daemen College. Campus Ministry Office, 4380 Main St., Buffalo, 14226. Tel: 716-839-3600, Ext. 237. Revs. A. Mark Illig, Dir.; Cassandra Salter-Smith.

D'Youville College. 320 Porter Ave., Buffalo, 14201. Tel: 716-881-7693; Fax: 716-881-7760. Sr. Patricia Eileen McKeon, G.N.S.H.; Revs. Anthony F. Rigoli, O.M.I., Dir.; Jan Mahle.

Erie Community College. City Campus, 121 Ellicott St., Buffalo, 14203. Tel: 716-851-1016; Fax: 716-881-7634. Sr. Ruth Marie Penksa, G.N.S.H., Dir. Campus Ministry, North Campus, Newman Center, 6325 Main St., Williamsville, 14221. Tel: 716-632-8898. Rev. Paul W. Steller, Dir.; Carol Kwadrans, Sec., South Campus, Newman Center, 3800 Howard Rd., Bldg. 5, Hamburg, 14075. Tel: 716-649-6186. Sr. Francis Gangloff, O.S.F., Dir.; Rev. Msgr. David M. Lee, Chap.

Medaille College. Campus Ministry, 18 Agassiz Cir., Buffalo, 14214. Tel: 716-884-3281.

Niagara University, Lewiston Rd., Niagara University, 14109. Tel: 716-286-8400; Fax: 716-286-8477. Revs. John A. Kettelberger, C.M.; William M. Allegretto, C.M.; Ms. Mary Beth Coates, Dir.; Ms. Monica Saltarelli; Mr. Thomas Hughes.

State University College at Buffalo. Newman Center, 1219 Elmwood Ave., Buffalo, 14222. Tel: 716-882-1080; Fax: 716-882-6914. Rev. Msgr. John C. Weimer, Dir. Assoc. Directors: Sr. Charlene Fontana, S.S.J.; Ms. Laura Heyden; Jonathan Neureuther, Sec.

State University of New York at Buffalo (Main St. South Campus), St. Joseph's University Parish, 3269 Main St., Buffalo, 14214. Tel: 716-833-0298; Fax: 716-833-7339. Rev. Jacob C. Ledwon, Dir.; Ms. Rebecca Calvo.

Trocaire College, 110 Red Jacket Pkwy., Buffalo, 14220. Tel: 716-827-2428; Fax: 716-828-6107. Sr. Marie Andre Main, R.S.M., Dir.

Villa Maria College, 240 Pine Ridge Rd., Buffalo, 14225. Tel: 716-896-0700; Fax: 716-896-0705. Mr. Frank Antonnucci, Dir.

St. Jude's Chapel at Alfred University & Alfred State College, Box 1154, Lower College Dr., 14802. Tel: 607-587-9411; Fax: 607-587-9431. Rev. Eugene P. Ulrich, Dir.; Robert Donius; Sue Fowler.

State University of New York at Buffalo (North Campus) Newman Center, UB Commons-Ste. 209, Amherst, 14228. Tel: 716-636-7495; Fax: 716-636-7496. Rev. Msgr. J. Patrick Keleher, Dir.; Anne Tupper; Maria Clare.

State University College at Fredonia, 222 Temple St., Fredonia, 14063. Tel: 716-679-4686; Fax: 716-679-3486. Robert Reisch, Dir.

Hilbert College. Campus Ministry Office, 5200 S. Park Ave., Hamburg, 14075. Tel: 716-649-7900; Fax: 716-649-0702. Rev. Bernard Olszewski, O.F.M.Conv.; Sr. Jacqueline Benbenek, C.S.S.F., Dir.

St. Bonaventure University, St. Bonaventure, 14778. Tel: 716-375-2600; Fax: 716-375-2618. Revs. Daniel A. Hurley, O.F.M.; James Vacco, O.F.M.; Daniel P.

Riley, O.F.M.; Sr. M. Kathryn Dougherty, O.S.F., Dir.; Ms. Tina Denena; Ms. Holly Schubert.

[S] CAMPS AND COMMUNITY CENTERS

ALLEGANY STATE PARK. *Camp Turner.* (Coed)Office, 795 Main St., Buffalo, 14203. Tel: 716-847-8789; Fax: 716-847-8789.
E-mail: Director@CampTurner.com
Web site: www.campturner.com
Rev. Gary J. Bagley.

ANGOLA. *St. Vincent de Paul Camp.* Tel: 716-549-2950; Fax: 716-882-3556.
Web site: www.SVDPWNY.org
Office, 1298 Main St., Buffalo, 14209. Tel: 716-882-3360. (Camp for needy boys and girls). Rev. Msgr. Henry J. Gugino, Spiritual Dir.

[T] MISCELLANEOUS

BUFFALO. *158 Chenango Street Housing Development Fund Company, Inc.*, 525 Washington St., 14203.
50-60 Kosciuzko Street Housing Development Fund Company, Inc., 525 Washington St., 14203.
Catholic Charities of Buffalo, NY, Foundation, Inc., 525 Washington St., 14203. Tel: 716-856-4494; Fax: 716-856-2005.
Catholic Communications of Western New York, Inc., 795 Main St., 14203. Tel: 716-847-8719; Fax: 716-847-8722. Catholic Communications of Western New York produces and distributes Catholic print and electronic programs.
Catholic Union Store, 795 Main St., 14203. Tel: 716-847-8715; Fax: 716-847-8702.
E-mail: cus@buffalodiocese.org
Peter M. McKee, Dir.
Federation of Catholic School Parents, Diocese of Buffalo, NY, 795 Main St., 14203. Tel: 716-847-5501; Fax: 716-847-5593.
Web site: www.buffalodce.org
Barbara B. Ashcroft, Pres.
The Foundation of the Roman Catholic Diocese of Buffalo, NY, Inc., 795 Main St., 14203-1250. Tel: 716-847-5500; Fax: 716-842-5557.
Franciscan Mystery Players, Inc., 102 Seymour St., 14210.
Gerard Place Housing Development Fund Company, Inc., 625 Abbott Rd., 14220. Tel: 716-827-2480; Fax: 716-828-6107.
E-mail: gormanm@trocaire.edu.
Sr. Margaret Mary Gorman, R.S.M., Pres. & Contact Person.
Good Counsel Apartments, 525 Washington St., 14203. Housing for handicapped & elderly of low income. Rev. Msgr. Henry J. Gugino, Pres. Total in Residence 39; Total Staff 4.
Hope of Buffalo, Inc., 335 Grider St., 14215. Tel: 716-892-8224; Fax: 716-894-2317.
E-mail: KarenKhope@hotmail.com
Sr. Karen Klimczak, Dir. Total in Residence 10; Total Staff 1.
Immaculate Heart of Mary Home for Children, Inc., 600 Doat St., 14211. Tel: 716-892-4141; Fax: 716-892-4177.
E-mail: felbflo@buffnet.net
Kolping Catholic Young Men's Association of Buffalo, NY dba Kolping Society of Buffalo, 25 Delphi Dr., 14227-3605. Tel: 716-668-0077. Norman Kuerzdoerfer, Pres.; Rev. Msgr. Paul R. Letourneau, Mod.
La Casa Del Tainos Housing Development Fund Company, Inc., 525 Washington St., 14203. Rev. Msgr. Henry J. Gugino, Dir.
Monsignor Adamski Village Housing Development Fund Company, Inc., 123 Townsend St., 14212. Tel: 716-854-5510; Fax: 716-854-0170.
Monsignor Adamski Village, Inc., 123 Townsend St., 14212. Tel: 716-854-5510; Fax: 716-854-0170. Rev. Msgr. John R. Gabalski. Facility for elderly and handicapped persons of low income.
Monsignor Carr Institute, 76 W. Humboldt Pkwy., 14214. Tel: 716-835-9745; Fax: 716-835-6785. Field Agency of Catholic Charities for Psychiatric and Psychological, Substance Abuse Treatment and Developmental Disabilities, and Community Outreach Treatment Team. Brian T. O'Herron, M.Ed., M.B.A., Dir. Total Assisted 12,405; Total Staff 38.
Monsignor Kirby Apartments Housing Development Fund Company, Inc., 525 Washington St., 14203. Tel: 716-853-4424, Ext. 3095. Rev. Msgr. Henry J. Gugino, Contact Person. Total in Residence 39; Total Staff 2.
Mother of Divine Grace Housing Development Fund Company, Inc., 3233 Main St., 14214. Tel: 716-833-5353; Fax: 716-833-0108.
E-mail: cc3@wzrd.com
Web site: www.cantalician.org
Purpose: To provide housing for persons of low income, particularly handicapped mentally retarded and developmentally disabled adults. Sr. Mary Patricia Tomasik, Exec. Dir. Total in Residence 10; Total Staff 10.
Nativity Housing Development Fund Company, Inc., 3233 Main St., 14214. Tel: 716-833-5353; Fax: 716-833-0108.
E-mail: cc3@wzrd.com
Web site: www.cantalician.org
Purpose: To provide housing for persons of low income, particularly handicapped mentally retarded and developmentally disabled adults. Sr. Mary Patricia Tomasik, Exec. Dir. Total in Residence 11; Total Staff 10.
Our Lady of Peace Housing Development Fund Company, Inc., 3323 Main St., 14214. Tel: 716-833-5353; Fax: 716-833-0108.
E-mail: cc3@wzrd.com
Web site: www.cantalician.org
Purpose: To provide housing for persons of low income, particularly handicapped mentally retarded and developmentally disabled adults. Total Residents 5; Total Staff 11.
St. Rita's Home for Children, Inc., 600 Doat St., 14211. Tel: 716-892-4141; Fax: 716-892-4141.
E-mail: felbflo@buffnet.net
St. Timothy's Park Villa Housing Development Fund Company, Inc., 525 Washington St., 14203. Tel: 716-853-4424, Ext. 3095. Rev. Msgr. Henry J. Gugino, Contact Person. Total in Residence 49; Total Staff 3.
Salesian Studios, 152 Plymouth Ave., 14201-1214. Tel: 716-886-6597. Rev. Thomas Ribits, O.S.F.S.
Santa Maria Towers, Office, 525 Washington St., 14203. Housing for handicapped and elderly of low income.
Monsignor Gambino Tower, Ltd. Most Rev. Henry J. Mansell, Pres.
Timon Towers Housing Development Fund Company, Inc., 525 Washington St., 14203. Rev. Msgr. Henry J. Gugino, Pres. Low income housing for the handicapped and elderly. Total Staff 5.
Wheatfield Housing Development Fund Company, Inc., 525 Washington St., 14203. Tel: 716-856-4494. Rev. Msgr. Henry J. Gugino, Sec. & Treas.

ALLEGANY. *St. Francis Respite Program, Inc.*, 115 E. Main St., 14706. Tel: 716-373-5663.
E-mail: arothmeier@aol.com
Web site: www.FSalleg.com
Sr. Anne Rothmeier, O.S.F., Dir. Total assisted 25.

LACKAWANNA. *Our Lady of Victory Homes of Charity*, 780 Ridge Rd., 14218. Tel: 716-828-9648; Fax: 716-828-9643.
E-mail: olv@buffnet.net
Web site: www.OurLadyofVictory.org
Rev. Msgr. Robert C. Wurtz, Exec. Vice Pres. & Treas.
(Formerly Association of Our Lady of Victory). Legal Titles: *Our Lady of Victory Homes of Charity.; Society for the Protection of Destitute Roman Catholic Children at Buffalo, NY.; Father Baker's.* Includes the following Institutions: Baker Victory Services 716-828-9500 or 1-888-287-9986 (Formerly Baker Hall, Our Lady of Victory Infant Home, St. Joseph Orphanage and St. John's Protectory). Total Assisted 3,000; Total Staff 100.
Western New York Catholic Healthcare Corporation, Our Lady of Victory Hospital, 55 Melroy Ave., 14218.

NEW YORK. *St. Bonaventure Lake House West Bank Perimeter Road at Kinzua South Valley, N.Y.*, 126 W. 32nd St., 10001-3202. Tel: 212-967-6300; Fax: 212-967-6344.
E-mail: hnp@hnp.com
Web site: www.ofm.org

NIAGARA UNIVERSITY. *Our Lady of Angels Association.* Marian House, 14109-1918. Tel: 716-286-8150; Fax: 716-286-8155.
E-mail: wobrien@niagara.edu
Web site: www.niagara.edu/olaa/
Rev. William J. O'Brien, C.M., Exec. Dir. Development Office for the Congregation of the Mission, Eastern Province. Total Staff 8.

NORTH TONAWANDA. *Shrine of the Infant Jesus.* Administered by the Pallottine Fathers. 3452 Niagara Falls Blvd., P.O. Box 563, 14120-0563. Tel: 716-694-4313; Fax: 716-743-5430.

STELLA NIAGARA. *DeSales Resource Center*, 4421 Lower River Rd., 14144-1001. Tel: 716-754-4948; Fax: 716-754-4948.
E-mail: desales@desalesresource.org
Web site: www.desalesresource.org
Rev. Joseph Power, O.S.F.S., Dir.; Joanne Kinney, Administrative Asst.; Andrea DiNieri, Business Mgr. Total Staff 3.

WEST SENECA. *Victorious Missionaries*, 791 Seneca Creek Rd., 14224. Tel: 716-675-5891. Deacon William W. Willis, Spiritual Dir. A spiritual and social movement for the handicapped and chronically ill.

WILLIAMSVILLE. *400 Mill Street, Inc.* (Formerly Mount St. Mary's Hospital of Niagara Falls), P.O. Box 275, 14231-0275. Tel: 716-632-2155; Fax: 716-632-0339.
E-mail: mnachreiner@osfwmsv.org
Annabachmann, Inc. (Formerly St. Francis Geriatric & Healthcare Services, Inc.), P.O. Box 275, 14231-0275. Tel: 716-632-2155; Fax: 716-632-0339.
E-mail: mnachreiner@osfwmsv.org

RELIGIOUS INSTITUTES OF MEN REPRESENTED IN THE DIOCESE

For further details refer to the corresponding bracketed number in the Religious Institutes of Men or Women section.

[0810]—*Brothers of Mercy.*—F.M.M.
[0330]—*Brothers of the Christian Schools.* (New York Prov.).—F.S.C.
[0160]—*Clerics Regular of St. Paul.*—C.R.S.P.
[0450]—*Congregation of Jesus and Mary.*—C.J.M.
[1330]—*Congregation of the Mission.* (Eastern Prov.).—C.M.
[0390]—*Consolata Missionaries.*—I.M.C.
[0480]—*Conventual Franciscans.* (St. Anthony of Padua).—O.F.M.Conv.
[0520]—*Franciscan Friars.* (Holy Name Prov.).—O.F.M.
[0690]—*Jesuit Fathers and Brothers.* (New York Prov.).—S.J.
[0800]—*Maryknoll.* (Buffalo).—M.M.
[0850]—*Missionaries of Africa.*—M.Afr.
[1210]—*Missionaries of St. Charles-Scalabrinians.*—C.S.
[0910]—*Oblates of Mary Immaculate.* (Eastern Prov.).—O.M.I.
[0920]—*Oblates of St. Francis De Sales.*—O.S.F.S.
[0270]—*Order of Carmelites.*—O.Carm.
[0970]—*Order of Our Lady of Mercy.* (Le Roy).—O.deM.
[0430]—*Order of Preachers-Dominicans.* (Provs. of St. Joseph; St. Albert the Great).—O.P.
[1020]—*Pauline Fathers and Brothers.* (Derby).—S.S.P.
[1040]—*Piarist Fathers.*—Sch.P.
[0370]—*Society of St. Columban.*—S.S.C.
[0990]—*Society of the Catholic Apostolate.* (Christ the King Prov.).—S.A.C.
[1060]—*Society of the Precious Blood.*—C.P.P.S.
[0560]—*Third Order Regular of St. Francis.*—T.O.R.

RELIGIOUS INSTITUTES OF WOMEN REPRESENTED IN THE DIOCESE

[0760]—*Daughters of Charity of St. Vincent de Paul.*—D.C.
[0810]—*Daughters of the Heart of Mary.*—D.H.M.
[0420]—*Discalced Carmelite Nuns.*—O.C.D.
[1060]—*Dominican Contemplative Sisters.*—O.P.
[1170]—*Felician Sisters.*—C.S.S.F.
[1330]—*Franciscan Missionaries of Assisi.*—S.F.M.A.
[1340]—*Franciscan Missionary Sisters of the Divine Child.*—F.M.D.C.
[1180]—*Franciscan Sisters of Allegany, New York.*—O.S.F.
[1310]—*Franciscan Sisters of Little Falls, MN.*—O.S.F.
[1470]—*Franciscan Sisters of St. Joseph.*—F.S.S.J.
[1280]—*Franciscan Sisters of the Immaculate Conception.*—O.S.F.
[1840]—*Grey Nuns of the Sacred Heart.*—G.N.S.H.
[2575]—*Institute of the Sisters of Mercy of the Americas.*—R.S.M.
[2830]—*Missionary Sisters of Our Lady of Mercy.*—M.O.M.
[2880]—*Missionary Sisters of St. Columban.*—S.S.C.
[3040]—*Oblate Sisters of Providence.*—O.S.P.
[3490]—*Religious of the Order of the Blessed Sacrament and of Our Lady (Sacramentines).*—O.S.S.
[1680]—*School Sisters of St. Francis.*—O.S.F.
[0630]—*Sisters of Charity of St. Vincent de Paul of Zagreb.*—S.V.Z.
[3000]—*Sisters of Notre Dame de Namur.* (Ohio Province).—S.N.D.deN.
[3070]—*Sisters of Our Lady of Charity.*—N.A.U.-O.L.C.
[3950]—*Sisters of Saint Mary of Namur.*—S.S.M.N.
[4090]—*Sisters of Social Service.*—S.S.S.
[1620]—*Sisters of St. Francis of Millvale, PA.*—O.S.F.
[1630]—*Sisters of St. Francis of Penance and Christian Charity.*—O.S.F.
[1650]—*Sisters of St. Francis of Philadelphia.*—O.S.F.
[1660]—*Sisters of St. Francis of the Providence of God.*—O.S.F.
[1800]—*Sisters of St. Francis of the Third Order Regular.* (Williamsville, NY).—O.S.F.
[3830]—*Sisters of St. Joseph.*—S.S.J.
[3658]—*Sisters of the Sacred Heart of Jesus.*—S.S.H.J.
[4120]—*Ursuline Sisters of Cleveland.*—O.S.U.

DIOCESAN CEMETERIES

CHEEKTOWAGA. *Holy Sepulchre.*

GRAND ISLAND. *Assumption.*

KENMORE. *Mount Olivet*, 4000 Elmwood Ave., 14217. Tel: 716-873-6500; Fax: 716-873-3247.
E-mail: ccolas@buffalodiocese.org
Web site: www.cathcemsbflo.com
Carmen A. Colao, Dir.

LACKAWANNA. *Holy Cross.*

LOCKPORT. *Queen of Heaven.*

NIAGARA FALLS. *Gate of Heaven.*

NECROLOGY

† Borowiak, Henry M., (Retired). —Died July 27, 2000.

† Borucki, Wallace T., Cattaraugus, NY St. Mary. —Died Sept. 9, 2000.

† Engler, Rev. Msgr. Francis V., (Retired). —Died Oct. 24, 2000.

† Hogan, Rev. Msgr. Robert J., (Retired). —Died April 17, 2000.

† Kuntz, Aloysius G., (Retired). —Died Oct. 30, 2000.

† Miller, Francis N., (Retired). —Died Feb. 21, 2000.

† Priester, Robert E., (Retired). —Died Sept. 3, 2000.

† Skrapits, John, Buffalo, NY St. Elizabeth. —Died March 29, 2000.

† Synowiak, Rev. Msgr. Edward F., Buffalo, NY St. Florian. —Died Oct. 23, 2000.

Diocese of Burlington

(Dioecesis Burlingtonensis)

Most Reverend

KENNETH A. ANGELL, D.D.

Bishop of Burlington; ordained May 26, 1956; appointed Auxiliary Bishop of Providence August 9, 1974; consecrated October 7, 1974; transferred to Bishop of Burlington October 6, 1992; installed November 9, 1992. *Mailing Address: 351 North Ave., P.O. Box 489, Burlington, VT, 05402-0489; Fax: 802-658-0436.*

ESTABLISHED JULY 29, 1853.

Square Miles 9,135.

Comprises the State of Vermont.

For legal titles of parishes and diocesan institutions, consult the Chancery Office.

Chancery Office: 351 North Ave., P.O. Box 489, Burlington, VT, 05402-0489. Tel.: 802-658-6110; Fax: 802-658-0436.

Web site address: www.vermontcatholic.org

E-mail address: kangell@together.net

STATISTICAL OVERVIEW

Personnel	
Bishop	1
Priests: Diocesan Active in Diocese	83
Priests: Active Outside Diocese	2
Priests: Retired, Sick or Absent	46
Number of Diocesan Priests	131
Religious Priests in Diocese	51
Extern Priests in Diocese	5
Ordinations:	
Transitional Deacons	1
Permanent Deacons	4
Permanent Deacons in Diocese	45
Total Brothers	18
Total Sisters	219
Parishes	
Parishes	87
With Resident Pastor:	
Resident Diocesan Priests	68
Resident Religious Priests	12
Without Resident Pastor:	
Administered by Priests	8
Missions	43
Pastoral Centers	1
Professional Ministry Personnel:	
Sisters	23
Welfare	
Homes for the Aged	4
Total Assisted	129
Special Centers for Social Services	1
Total Assisted	6,377
Other Institutions	1
Total Assisted	12,072
Educational	
Diocesan Students in Other Seminaries	11
Total Seminarians	11
Colleges and Universities	3
Total Students	4,685
High Schools, Diocesan and Parish	2
Total Students	738
Elementary Schools, Diocesan and Parish	12
Total Students	2,037
Elementary Schools, Private	3
Total Students	719
Catechesis/Religious Education:	
High School Students	2,856
Elementary Students	9,688
Total Students Under Catholic Instruction	20,734
Teachers in the Diocese:	
Priests	2
Sisters	9
Lay Teachers	412
Vital Statistics	
Receptions into the Church:	
Infant Baptism Totals	1,679
Adult Baptism Totals	138
Received into Full Communion	160
First Communions	1,830
Confirmations	1,196
Marriages:	
Catholic	480
Interfaith	248
Total Marriages	728
Deaths	1,581
Total Catholic Population	148,712
Total Population	590,883

Former Bishops—Rt. Rev. LOUIS DE GOESBRIAND, D.D., cons. Oct. 30, 1853; died Nov. 3, 1899.—Rt. Rev. JOHN S. MICHAUD, D.D., cons. Coadjutor Bishop with right of succession June 29, 1892; succeeded to Nov. 3, 1899; died Dec. 22, 1908.—Most Rev. JOSEPH J. RICE, D.D., cons. April 14, 1910; died April 1, 1938.—Most Rev. MATTHEW F. BRADY, D.D., cons. Oct. 26, 1938; transferred to Manchester, NH, Nov. 11, 1944; died Sept. 20, 1959.—Most Rev. EDWARD F. RYAN, D.D., cons. Jan. 3, 1945; died Nov. 3, 1956.—Most Rev. ROBERT F. JOYCE, D.D., cons. Auxiliary Bishop Oct. 28, 1954; installed Diocesan Bishop Feb. 26, 1957; retired Jan. 24, 1972; died Sept. 2, 1990.—Most Rev. JOHN A. MARSHALL, D.D., cons. and installed January 25, 1972; transferred to Springfield, MA, Dec. 27, 1991; died July 3, 1994.

Vicar General—Rev. WENDELL H. SEARLES, V.G.

Vicar for Ministries—Rev. MICHAEL W. DEFORGE.

Chancery Office—Rev. WALTER D. MILLER, J.C.D., Chancellor, *351 North Ave., P.O. Box 489, Burlington, 05402-0489.* Tel: 802-658-6110; Fax: 802-658-0436. Office Hours: Mon.-Fri. 9-12 & 1-5.

Finance Office—Mr. KEVIN J. HEFFERNAN, C.P.A., Chief Financial Officer, *351 North Ave., P.O. Box 489, Burlington, 05402-0489.* Tel: 802-658-6110; Fax: 802-658-0436.

Episcopal Vicar for Administration and Secretary to the Most Rev. Bishop—Rev. WALTER D. MILLER, J.C.D., *351 North Ave., P.O. Box 489, Burlington, 05402-0489.* Tel: 802-658-6110.

Office of the Tribunal—351 North Ave., P.O. Box 489, Burlington, 05402-0489. Tel: 802-658-6110; Fax: 802-658-4118.

Judicial Vicar—Rev. WALTER D. MILLER, J.C.D.

Judges—Rev. Msgr. JOHN R. MCSWEENEY, J.C.L.; Revs. THOMAS V. MATTISON, M.Div., J.C.L., M.C.L.; WILLIAM D. CORCORAN, J.C.L.

Promoter of Justice—Rev. BERNARD F. DEPEAUX, J.C.L.

Defender of the Bond—Rev. MICHEL J. ST. PIERRE.

Advocates—Revs. JOHN G. FELTZ; RAYMOND A. GIROUX; PETER A. ROUTHIER.

Notaries—Mr. TODD THIBAULT; Mrs. JANE B. KELLNER; Mrs. ANNE AICHER.

Diocesan Administrative Board—Most Rev. KENNETH A. ANGELL, D.D., Chm.; Revs. WENDELL H. SEARLES, V.G.; MICHAEL W. DEFORGE; Sr. SHIRLEY DAVIS, S.S.J.; Mrs. MARY MCCLINTOCK.

Diocesan Consultors—Rev. Msgr. JOHN R. MCSWEENEY, J.C.L.; Revs. BERNARD E. GAUDREAU; DENIS R. BRETON; WENDELL H. SEARLES, V.G.; WALTER D. MILLER, J.C.D.; MAURICE J. ROY; MICHAEL W. DEFORGE; FRANCIS M. HOLLAND; MARCEL R. RAINVILLE, S.S.E.

Deans—Revs. JOHN W. HAMILTON; JULIEN J. LAFLAMME; RICHARD G. LAVALLEY; JOSEPH A. LIVELY; PETER A. ROUTHIER; MAURICE J. ROY; RICHARD W. TINNEY; DONAL WARD; JAMES MATTISON; LAURENCE OLSZEWSKI, C.S.E.; FREDERICK MCLACHLAN, S.S.E.

Diocesan Offices and Directors

Apostolate for the Deaf—Rev. PETER Y. WILLIAMS, *St. Patrick Rectory, P.O. Box 18, Fairfield, 05455.* Tel: 802-827-3203.

Apostolate for the Handicapped—Vacant, *Office of Catholic Formation, Special Needs Ministry, 351 North Ave., P.O. Box 489, Burlington, 05402-0489.* Tel: 802-658-6110.

Bishop's Commission on Women—Mrs. CONNIE COONEY, Chm., *351 North Ave., P.O. Box 489, Burlington, 05402-0489.* Tel: 802-658-6110.

Bishop's Fund Office—Mr. KEVIN J. HEFFERNAN, C.P.A., Exec. Dir.; Vacant, Dir., *351 North Ave., P.O. Box 489, Burlington, 05402-0489.* Tel: 802-658-6110.

Boy Scouts—Rev. YVON J. ROYER, *St. Edward Rectory, 250 Main St., P.O. Box 397, Derby Line, 05830.*

Building Commission—Mr. RICHARD WIEMANN, Chm., *Chancery Office, 351 North Ave., P.O. Box 489, Burlington, 05402-0489.* Tel: 802-658-6110.

Vermont Catholic Charities Inc.—Mrs. MARY M. MCNAMARA, Dir., *Central Office, 351 North Ave., P.O. Box 489, Burlington, 05402-0489.* Tel: 802-658-6110; Fax: 802-860-0451., Rutland Office: *24 1/2 Center St., Rutland, 05701.* Tel: 802-773-3379.

Campaign for Human Development—Mrs. MARY M. MCNAMARA, Dir., *351 North Ave., P.O. Box 489, Burlington, 05402-0489.* Tel: 802-658-6110; Fax: 802-860-0451.

Catholic Daughters of The Americas—Rev. PATRICK J. FORMAN, *St. Paul Rectory, Eastern Ave., Barton, 05822.* Tel: 802-525-3711.

Catholic Relief Services—Mrs. MARY M. MCNAMARA, *351 North Ave., P.O. Box 489, Burlington, 05402-0489.* Tel: 802-658-6110; Fax: 802-860-0451.

Catholic Women, Vermont Council of—Rev. GEORGE H. DUPUIS, Diocesan Moderator, *St. Margaret Mary Rectory, Main St., Arlington, 05250.* Tel: 802-375-2849.

Censor Librorum—Rev. MICHEL J. ST-PIERRE, *351 North Ave., P.O. Box 489, Burlington, 05402-0489.* Tel: 802-658-6110.

Charismatic Renewal—Rev. GERALD R. RAGIS, *Our Lady of Mt. Carmel Rectory, P.O. Box 158, Charlotte, 05445.* Tel: 802-425-2637.

Chief Administrator for Catholic Formation—Sr. MARIANNE REED, R.S.M., M.Ed., C.A.E.S., *Office of Catholic Formation, 351 North Ave., P.O. Box 489, Burlington, 05402-0489.* Tel: 802-658-6110.

Diocesan Archives—Mr. DAVID BLOW, *351 North Ave., P.O. Box 489, Burlington, 05402-0489.* Tel: 802-658-6110.

Diocesan Coordinator of the Vietnamese Ministry—Rev. FRANCIS M. HOLLAND, *8 Cedar Glen N., Burlington, 05403.* Tel: 802-899-3114.

Office of Communications—GLORIA J. GIBSON, Dir., *351 North Ave., P.O. Box 489, Burlington, 05402-0489.* Tel: 802-658-6110.

Daughters of Isabella—Rev. JOHN M. MILANESE, Chap., *Sts. Donatian & Rogatian Rectory, 25 S. Pleasant St., Randolph, 05060.* Tel: 802-728-3227.

Diocesan Board of Vicars—
Vicar General—Rev. WENDELL H. SEARLES, V.G.
Vicar for Administration—Rev. WALTER D. MILLER, J.C.D.
Vicar for Ministries—Rev. MICHAEL W. DEFORGE.
Chief Administrator for Catholic Formation—Sr. MARIANNE REED, R.S.M., M.Ed., C.A.E.S.
Chief Financial Officer—Mr. KEVIN J. HEFFERNAN, C.P.A.
Judicial Vicar—Rev. WALTER D. MILLER, J.C.D.

Diocesan Cemeteries—Mr. PETER WELLS, *Chancery Office, 351 North Ave., P.O. Box 489, Burlington, 05402-0489.* Tel: 802-658-6110. Mr. PATRICK JENNINGS, Chm., *45 Morrill Dr., Burlington, 05401.* Tel: 802-864-5071., *Resurrection Park, South Burlington, 05403.* Tel: 802-862-1530., *St. Joseph's Cemetery, Burlington, 05401.*

Diocesan Finance Council—Ex Officio Members: Most Rev. KENNETH A. ANGELL, D.D.; KEVIN J. HEFFERNAN, C.P.A., CFO & Chm. Board Members: JAMES STROUSE; JOHN KELLY; RICHARD COUTURE; DAVID LAMARCHE; JOYCE ENGELKEN.

Diocesan Insurance Office—PETER WELLS, Dir., *351 North Ave., P.O. Box 489, Burlington, 05402-0489.* Tel: 802-658-6110.

Ecumenical Commission—JAMES G. CASE, *R.F.D., Box 80, Richmond, 05477.* Tel: 802-482-2420.

Education, Board of—Ms. MEGHAN FOLEY, Chm., *351 North Ave., P.O. Box 489, Burlington, 05402-0489.*

Evangelization—Rev. JOSEPH T. SULLIVAN, Dir., *351 North Ave., P.O. Box 489, Burlington, 05402-0489.* Tel: 802-658-6110.

Office of Family Life/Respect Life Office—Mrs. JUDY KANYA, *P.O. Box 225, Bennington, 05201-0225.* Tel: 802-447-5718.

Engaged Encounter—Rev. RICHARD M. MYHALYK, S.S.E. Coordinating Couple: LAURIE QUEOR; PATRICK QUEOR, *P.O. Box 489, Burlington, 05402-0489.*

Finance Office—KEVIN J. HEFFERNAN, C.P.A., Chief Financial Officer, *351 North Ave., P.O. Box 489, Burlington, 05402-0489.* Tel: 802-658-6110.

Liturgical Commission—Rev. PETER A. ROUTHIER, *St. Monica, 79 Summer St., Barre, 05641.* Tel: 802-479-3253.

Holy Childhood Association—Rev. FRANCIS M. HOLLAND, *8 Cedar Glen N., South Burlington, 05403.* Tel: 802-865-8082.

House of Discernment—Rev. MICHAEL W. DEFORGE, Dir., *The Catholic Center at UVM, 390 S. Prospect St., Redstone Campus, Burlington, 05401.* Tel: 802-862-8403; Fax: 802-865-9480.

Knights of Columbus—Rev. FRANCIS PRIVE, State Chap., *St. Thomas, P.O. Box 3, Underhill Center, 05490.* Tel: 802-899-4632.
State Friar—Rev. JOHN M. MILANESE, *25 S. Pheasant St., Randolph, 05060.* Tel: 802-728-3227.

Leap—Rev. MARCEL R. RAINVILLE, S.S.E., *St. Michael's College, Winooski Park, Colchester, 05439.* Tel: 802-654-2332.

Marriage Encounter, Vermont—JOHN FORCIER; DIANE FORCIER, *156 Lost Nation Rd., Essex Junction, 05452.* Tel: 802-878-1274.

Diocesan Master of Ceremonies—Rev. WALTER D. MILLER, J.C.D., *351 North Ave., P.O. Box 489, Burlington, 05402-0489.* Tel: 802-658-6110; Fax: 802-658-0436.

Office of Ministerial Formation and Continuing Education for Clergy—Rev. BERNARD E. GAUDREAU, Dir., *Blessed Sacrament Rectory, Mountain Rd., P.O. Box 27, Stowe, 05672.* Tel: 802-253-7536; Fax: 802-253-4445.

National Catholic Conference for Interracial Justice—Rev. WALTER D. MILLER, J.C.D., Diocesan Coord., *351 North Ave., P.O. Box 489, Burlington, 05402-0489.* Tel: 802-658-6110; Fax: 802-658-0436.

National Shrine of the Immaculate Conception, Washington—Rev. ROGER L. CHARBONNEAU, *Holy Cross Rectory, 416 Church Rd., Colchester, 05446.* Tel: 802-863-3002.

Office of Catholic Formation—Deacon IVAN HAWK, III, Dir., *351 North Ave., P.O. Box 489, Burlington, 05402-0489.*
Youth Ministry—Vacant.

Office of Diocesan Pastoral Planning—Rev. WENDELL H. SEARLES, V.G., Dir., *351 North Ave., P.O. Box 489, Burlington, 05402-0489.* Tel: 802-658-6110; Fax: 802-658-0436.

Permanent Diaconate—Rev. BERNARD E. GAUDREAU, Dir., *Blessed Sacrament Rectory, Mountain Rd., P.O. Box 27, Stowe, 05672.* Tel: 802-253-7536; Fax: 802-253-4445.

Diocesan Presbyteral Council—Members Ex Officio: Most Rev. KENNETH A. ANGELL, D.D.; Revs. WENDELL H. SEARLES, V.G.; WALTER D. MILLER, J.C.D.; MICHAEL W. DEFORGE; BERNARD E. GAUDREAU. Elected Members: Revs. GEORGE H. DUPUIS; DENIS R. BRETON; MAURICE J. ROY; BRIAN E. MEAD; JAMES J. MCSHANE; DONALD RAVEY; JOHN J. MCDERMOTT; JEROME MERCURE; JAMES A. LAWRENCE; MARCEL R. RAINVILLE, S.S.E.; FRANCIS M. HOLLAND; DANIEL RUPP.

Newspaper—*"The Vermont Catholic Tribune"*; Most Rev. KENNETH A. ANGELL, D.D., Publisher; Mrs. PATRICIA GORE, Editor, Editorial & Business Office: *351 North Ave., P.O. Box 489, Burlington, 05402-0489.* Tel: 802-658-6110; Fax: 802-658-0436.

Priests' Benefit Fund—Rev. FRANCIS R. PRIVE, Chm., *351 North Ave., P.O. Box 489, Burlington, 05402-0489.* Tel: 802-658-6110.

Prison Ministry—Deacon STEPHEN RATTE, *351 North Ave., P.O. Box 489, Burlington, 05402-0489.* Tel: 802-658-6110.

Propagation of the Faith—Rev. FRANCIS M. HOLLAND, *351 North Ave., P.O. Box 489, Burlington, 05402-0489.* Tel: 802-658-6110.

Rural Life—Deacon JEAN LOUIS RAINVILLE, *Box 122G, R.F.D., Gore Rd., Highgate Center, 05459.*

Office of Catholic Schools—Sr. MARIANNE REED, R.S.M., M.Ed., C.A.E.S., Supt. of Schools; Sr. SHIRLEY DAVIS, S.S.J., Asst. Supt., *351 North Ave., P.O. Box 489, Burlington, 05402-0489.* Tel: 802-658-6110; Fax: 802-658-0436.

Senate of Sisters—Sr. MARY POLWORTH, S.S.J., *Sisters of St. Joseph Convent, 131 Convent Ave., Rutland, 05701.* Tel: 802-775-5133.

Vermont Cursillo Secretariat—Rev. FRANCIS EKSTEROWICZ, *All Saints, 152 Main St., Richford, 05476.* Tel: 802-848-7741.

Vocations and Seminarians—Rev. MICHAEL W. DEFORGE, Dir., *The Catholic Center at UVM, 390 South Prospect St., Redstone Campus, Burlington, 05401.* Tel: 802-862-8403; Fax: 802-865-9480.

CLERGY, PARISHES, MISSIONS AND PAROCHIAL SCHOOLS

CITY OF BURLINGTON
(Chittenden County)

1—CATHEDRAL OF THE IMMACULATE CONCEPTION (1830), Rev. Thomas J. Ball, Rector.
Res., 20 Pine St., 05401. Tel: 802-658-4333.

2—ST. ANTHONY'S (1903), Rev. Roland J. Rivard; Deacon Louis Meunier. In res., Rev. Michel J. St-Pierre.
Res., 305 Flynn Ave., 05401. Tel: 802-864-0478.

3—CHRIST THE KING (1940), Rev. Roland J. Rivard.
Res., 136 Locust St., 05401-4849. Tel: 802-862-5784; Fax: 802-651-3021.
School—Tel: 802-862-6696.
Lay Teachers 23; Students 233.

4—ST. JOSEPH'S (1850), Revs. Stephen W. Hornat, S.S.E.; Raymond J. Doherty, S.S.E.; Howard J. Muehlberger, S.S.E.
Res., 85 Elmwood Ave., 05401. Tel: 802-863-2388; Fax: 802-863-2380. [CEM]
School—Tel: 802-864-5623; Fax: 802-860-2627.
Lay Teachers 14; Students 209.

5—ST. MARK'S (1940), Revs. John G. Feltz, D. Min.; Joseph H. Blahner.
Res., 1251 North Ave., 05401. Tel: 802-864-7686; Fax: 802-651-9391.

OUTSIDE THE CITY OF BURLINGTON

Alburg, Grand Isle Co., St. Amadeus (1886), Rev. Maurice U. Boucher, S.S.E.
Res., 05440. Tel: 802-796-3481; Fax: 802-796-3481. [CEM 2]
Mission—Isle La motte, Grand Isle Co., St. Joseph, P.O. Box 49, Alburg, 05440. [CEM]
Chapel—Isle La motte, St. Anne's Shrine.

Arlington, Bennington Co., St. Margaret Mary (1946), Rev. George H. Dupuis; Deacon Peter Putis.
Res., 3938 Route 7A, Box 39, 05250-0039. Tel: 802-375-2849; Fax: 802-375-2849. [CEM]

Barre, Washington Co., St. Monica (1892), Revs. Peter A. Routhier; Daniel James Rupp; Deacons Fernand R. Rivard; David Bisson; Daniel Pudvah.
Res., 79 Summer St., 05641. Tel: 802-479-3253; Fax: 802-479-3154.
School—Tel: 802-476-5015; Fax: 802-476-0861.
Lay Teachers 15; Students 176.
Convent—73 Summer St., 05641. Tel: 802-476-6514.

Barton, Orleans Co., Conversion of St. Paul (1893), Rev. Patrick J. Forman, Admin.
Res., 85 St. Paul Lane, 05822. Tel: 802-525-3711; Fax: 802-525-1292. [CEM]
School—Tel: 802-525-6578.
Lay Teachers 5; Students 50.

Bellows Falls, Windham Co., St. Charles (1871), Rev. Brian E. Mead.
Res., 31 Cherry Hill, 05101. Tel: 802-463-3128; Fax: 802-463-8179. [CEM]
Sacred Heart (1909), Rev. Felix J. Reczek, O.F.M., Admin.; Deacon John Blicharz.
Res., 39 Green St., 05101. Tel: 802-463-4110. [CEM]

Bennington, Bennington Co., Sacred Heart St. Francis de Sales (1995), Revs. Laurence M. Olszewski, C.S.C.; William H. Kelley, C.S.C. In res., Rev. Douglas W. Hawkins, C.S.C.
Parish Office: 238 W. Main St., 05201. Tel: 802-442-3141; Fax: 802-442-3142.
School—Sacred Heart School, 307 School St., 05201. Tel: 802-442-2446; Fax: 802-442-3584. Mr. David B. Estes, Prin.
Lay Teachers 15; Students 212.
Mission—North Pownal, Our Lady of Lourdes.
Station—Vermont Veterans Home, Tel: 802-442-6353.

Bethel, Windsor Co., St. Anthony (1950), Rev. John J. Whalen (Om) Admin.
Res., P.O. Box 63, Church St., 05032. Tel: 802-234-9916.
Missions—Rochester, Windsor Co., St. Elizabeth; South Royalton, Windsor Co., St. Matthew.

Bradford, Orange Co., Our Lady of Perpetual Help (1945), Revs. Omer St. Onge, S.M.; Philip Parent, S.M.; Deacon Kelly Fitzpatrick.
Res., Box 314, 05033. Tel: 802-222-5268; Fax: 802-222-5268.
Missions—Norwich, Windsor Co., St. Francis of Assisi; Wells River, Orange Co., St. Eugene; South Strafford, Orange Co., Our Lady of Light.

Brandon, Rutland Co., St. Mary's (1867), Rev. Albert G. Baltz.
Res., 38 Carver St., 05733. Tel: 802-247-6351; Fax: 802-247-6396. [CEM]
Mission—Leicester, Addison Co., St. Agnes.

Brattleboro, Windham Co., St. Michael (1855), Revs. Stanley Deresienski, S.S.E., Admin.; Charles R. Danielson.
Res., 47 Walnut St., 05301. Tel: 802-257-5101; 254-5229; Fax: 802-257-5102. [CEM]
School—Tel: 802-254-5666; Fax: 802-254-5229. Mr. Frank J. Vara, Prin.
Lay Teachers 14; Students 299.
Convent—77 Grove St., 05301. Tel: 802-254-9431.

Bristol, Addison Co., St. Ambrose (1893), Rev. Pierre A. LaVallee.
Res., 11 School St., 05443. Tel: 802-453-2488; Fax: 802-453-7712. [CEM]

Cambridge, Lamoille Co., St. Mary (1964), Rev. Francis R. Prive.
P.O. Box 129, 05444. Tel: 802-644-5073; Fax: 802-644-2546.

Canaan, Essex Co., Assumption of the Blessed Virgin Mary (1950), Rev. John B. Loughnane, Jr (MAN).
Res., P.O. Box 176, Beecher Falls, 05902. Tel: 603-246-8829; Fax: 603-246-7169. [CEM]

Castleton, Rutland Co., St. John the Baptist (1899), Rev. J. Charles Durham.
Res., P.O. Box 128, 05735. Tel: 802-468-5706; Fax: 802-468-5299.

Charlotte, Chittenden Co., Our Lady of Mount Carmel (1858), Rev. Gerald R. Ragis.
Res., P.O. Box 158, 2894 Spear St., 05445. Tel: 802-425-2637. [CEM]

Chester, Windsor Co., St. Joseph (1946), Rev. Paul E. Sackevich; Deacon Eugene Allen, Jr.
Res., 96 Main St., P.O. Box 1129, 05143. Tel: 802-875-2610; Fax: 802-875-1113.

Mission—Proctorsville, Windsor Co., Holy Name of Mary.
Station—Londonderry, St. Joseph Chapel.

Chittenden, Rutland Co., St. Robert (1965), Rev. James A. Lawrence.
Res., Immaculate Heart of Mary, 18 Lincoln Ave., P.O. Box 266, Rutland, 05743. Tel: 802-775-0846; Fax: 802-775-9640.
Mission—Killington, Rutland Co., Our Lady of the Mountains, Killington.

Colchester, Chittenden Co., Holy Cross (1950), Rev. Roger L. Charbonneau; Deacon Ivan Hawk, III.
Res., 416 Church Rd., 05446. Tel: 802-863-3002; Fax: 802-862-5687. [CEM]
Our Lady of Grace (1966), Rev. Jay C. Haskin; Deacon William Glinka.
Res., 800 Main St., 05446. Tel: 802-878-5987; Fax: 802-878-9308.

Derby Line, Orleans Co., St. Edward (1946), Rev. Yvon J. Royer, Admin.; Deacon John P.E. Gratton.
Res., 250 Main St., P.O. Box 397, 05830. Tel: 802-873-3522; Fax: 802-873-3299. [CEM]
Mission—West Charleston, Orleans Co., St. Benedict Labre.

East Dorset, Bennington Co., St. Jerome (1868), Rev. Julien J. LaFlamme.
Res., c/o St. Paul Rectory, 398 Bonnet St., Manchester Center, 05255-9502. Tel: 802-362-1380. [CEM]
Mission—Danby, Rutland Co., Holy Trinity.

Enosburg Falls, Franklin Co., St. John the Baptist (1874), Rev. Gerard P. Leclerc.
Res., P.O. Box 563, 05450. Tel: 802-933-4464; Fax: 802-933-4225. [CEM]

Essex Center, Chittenden Co., St. Pius X (1957), Rev. William P. Giroux.
Res., 20 Jericho Rd., Essex Junction, 05452-2707. Tel: 802-878-5997; Fax: 802-878-7793.

Essex Junction, Chittenden Co., Holy Family (1893), Rev. Thomas L. Mosher. In res., Rev. Lance W. Harlow.
Res., 4 Prospect St., 05452. Tel: 802-878-5331; Fax: 802-878-5332. [CEM]
St. Lawrence, Martyr (1968), Rev. Paul F. St. James.
Res., 158 West St., 05452. Tel: 802-878-8271; Fax: 802-879-8687.

Fairfax, Franklin Co., St. Luke (1943), Rev. Francis E. Connors; Deacon Stephen Ratte.
Res., 17 Huntsville Rd., P.O. Box 7, 05454. Tel: 802-849-6205; Fax: 802-849-6078. [CEM]
Mission—Georgia, Franklin Co., Ascension.

Fairfield, Franklin Co., St. Patrick (1858), Rev. Peter Y. Williams.
Res., P.O. Box 18, 05455. Tel: 802-827-3203; Fax: 802-827-9940. [CEM]
Mission—East Fairfield, Franklin Co., St. Anthony-St. George.

Fair Haven, Rutland Co., Our Lady of Seven Dolors (1866), Rev. Richard W. Tinney.
Res., 10 Washington St., 05743. Tel: 802-265-3135. [CEM]
Mission—West Castleton, Rutland Co., St. Matthew of Avalon.

Graniteville, Washington Co., St. Sylvester (1899), Rev. Donald J. Roy.
Res., 217 Church Hill Rd., 05654. Tel: 802-476-3913; Fax: 802-476-1332. [CEM]
Mission—East Barre, Washington Co., St.Cecilia & St. Frances Cabrini.

Hardwick, Caledonia Co., St. Norbert (1911), Rev. Michael E. Augustinowitz.
Mailing Address: 193 S. Main St., P.O. Box 496, 05843.
Res., 15 S. Main St., 05843. Tel: 802-472-5544; Fax: 802-472-5543. [CEM 2]
Missions—Greensboro Bend, Orleans Co., St. Michael; Craftsbury, Orleans Co., Our Lady of Fatima.

Highgate Center, Franklin Co., St. Louis (1886), Rev. Charles H. Ranges, S.S.E.; Deacon Jean-Louis Rainville.
Mailing Address: P.O. Box 78, 05459. Tel: 802-868-4517; Fax: 802-868-4262.
Res., 65 Canada St., Swanton, 05488. Tel: 802-862-4502. [CEM 2]

Hinesburg, Chittenden Co., St. Jude the Apostle (1946), Rev. Gerald R. Ragis.
Res., P.O. Box 69, 05461-0069. Tel: 802-482-2290; Fax: 802-482-5263.

Island Pond, Essex Co., St. James the Greater (1871), Rev. James H. Mattison.
Res., P.O. Box 407, 05846. Tel: 802-723-4312. [CEM]
Mission—Norton, Essex Co., St. Bernard.

Ludlow, Windsor Co., Annunciation (1885), Rev. Robert C. Richardson.
Res., 7 Depot St., 05149. Tel: 802-228-3451; Fax: 802-228-7012.

Lyndonville, Caledonia Co., St. Elizabeth (1891), Rev. Stephen J. Nichols; Deacon Alfred Toborg.
Res., 630 Hill St., P.O. Box 141, 05851-0141. Tel: 802-626-5267; Fax: 802-626-3324. [CEM]
Mission—Danville, Caledonia Co., Our Lady Queen of Peace, P.O. Box 141, Lyndonville 05851-0141. Tel: 802-684-3944.

Manchester Center, Bennington Co., Conversion of St. Paul (1896), Rev. Julien J. LaFlamme.
Res., 398 Bonnet St., 05255. Tel: 802-362-1380.
Missions—East Dorset, Bennington Co., St. Jerome; Danby, Rutland Co., Holy Trinity.

Middlebury, Addison Co., Assumption of the Blessed Virgin Mary (1855), Rev. John J. McDermott.
Res., 326 College St., 05753. Tel: 802-388-2943; Fax: 802-388-2943. [CEM]
School—St. Mary's, 86 Shannon St., 05753. Tel: 802-388-8392.
Lay Teachers 7; Students 67.
Mission—Bridport, Addison Co., St. Bernadette.

Middletown Springs, Rutland Co., St. Anne (1963), Rev. Adam J. Krempa; Deacon Richard Perkins.
St. Raphael Rectory: Main St., Poultney, 05764. Tel: 802-235-2156.
Missions—West Pawlet, Rutland Co., St. Frances Cabrini; Wells, Rutland Co., St. Paul.

Milton, Chittenden Co., St. Ann (1866), Rev. Ronald A. Soutiere; Deacon Roger Lauziere.
Res., P.O. Box 1, 05468. Tel: 802-893-2487. [CEM]

Montpelier, Washington Co., St. Augustine (1850), Revs. William R. Beaudin; Paul C. Houde; Deacons Regis Cummings; Walter Brenneman, Jr.
Res., 16 Barre St., 05602. Tel: 802-223-5285; Fax: 802-223-3621. [CEM]
School—St. Michael School, 46 Barre St., 05602. Tel: 802-223-6430; Fax: 802-229-4827.
Sisters 1; Lay Teachers 15; Students 159.
Mission—Marshfield, Washington Co., North American Martyrs, (1963).

Morrisville, Lamoille Co., Holy Cross (1913), Revs. Denis R. Breton; Daniel J. Jordan; Deacon Thomas Cooney.
Res., P.O. Box 339, 05661. Tel: 802-888-3318; Fax: 802-888-6177.
Missions—Johnson, Lamoille Co., St. John the Apostle; Eden, Lamoille Co., St. Gabriel; Hyde Park, Lamoille Co., St. Teresa.

Newport, Orleans Co., St. Mary Star of the Sea (1873), Revs. Leopold J. Bilodeau; Jim Beauregard.
Res., 191 Clermont Ter., 05855. Tel: 802-334-5066; Fax: 802-334-8067. [CEM]

North Bennington, Bennington Co., St. John the Baptist (1885), Rev. Robert J. Baffa.
Res., 7 Houghton St., P.O. Box 219, 05257. Tel: 802-447-7504; Fax: 802-442-6620. [CEM]

Northfield, Washington Co., St. John the Evangelist (1865), Rev. Kevin E. Rooney.
Res., 206 Vine St., 05663. Tel: 802-485-8313; Fax: 802-485-3043. [CEM]
Mission—Williamstown, Orange Co., St. Edward.

North Troy, Orleans Co., St. Vincent de Paul (1939), Rev. George A. Paulin.
Res., Pleasant St., 05859. Tel: 802-988-2608; Fax: 802-988-9920. [CEM]

Orleans, Orleans Co., St. Theresa of Child Jesus (1942), Rev. Thomas A. Bransfield.
Res., 5 Willoughby Ave., 05860. Tel: 802-754-6049. [CEM 2]
Mission—Irasburg, Orleans Co., St. John Vianney.

Orwell, Addison Co., St. Paul (1886), Rev. Robert J. McKnight.
Res., P.O. Box 41, 05760. Tel: 802-948-2951. [CEM]
Mission—Shoreham, Addison Co., St. Genevieve.

Pittsford, Rutland Co., St. Alphonsus Liguori (1893), Rev. Joseph E. Romano.
Res., 2918 U.S. Rte. 7, 05763-9499. Tel: 802-483-2301; Fax: 802-483-2136. [CEM]

Poultney, Rutland Co., St. Raphael (1884), Rev. Adam J. Krempa.
Res., 21 E. Main St., 05764-1107. Tel: 802-287-5703. [CEM]

Proctor, Rutland Co., St. Dominic (1888), Rev. Msgr. Paul M. Bresnehan.
Res., 45 South St., 05765. Tel: 802-459-2221. [CEM]

Putney, Windham Co., Our Lady of Mercy (1931), Revs. John T. Scully, S.S.E.; Frederick E. McLachlan, S.S.E.; Deacon Robert Degnon. In res., Rev. James R. Coombs, S.S.E., (Retired).
Res., 52 Old Depot Rd., P.O. Box 246, 05346. Tel: 802-387-5861.
Missions—Saxtons River, Windham Co., St. Edmund of Canterbury; Stratton Mountain, Windham Co., Chapel of the Snows; Townshend, Windham Co., Our Lady of the Valley; Wardsboro, Windham Co., Our Lady of Hope.

Randolph, Orange Co., SS. Donatian and Rogatian (1903), Rev. John M. Milanese; Deacon Paul Lissandrello.
Res., 25 S. Pleasant St., P.O. Box 428, 05060. Tel: 802-728-3227; Fax: 802-728-3570. [CEM]

Readsboro, Bennington Co., St. Joachim (1895), Rev. Joseph H. Tate, C.S.C.
Res., 342 Tunnel St., 05350-9738. Tel: 802-423-5267; 423-9961; Fax: 802-423-5267.
Mission—Stamford, Bennington Co., St. John Bosco.

Richford, Franklin Co., All Saints (1899), Rev. Frank C. Eksterowicz; Deacons Clifford Chagnon; Jon Ramey.
Res., 152 Main St., 05476. Tel: 802-848-7741; Fax: 802-848-3150. [CEM]
Missions—East Berkshire, Franklin Co., Our Lady of Lourdes; Montgomery Center, Franklin Co., St. Isidore.

Richmond, Chittenden Co., Our Lady of the Holy Rosary (1860), Rev. Ronald H. Benoit.
Res., 64 W. Main St., P.O. Box 243, 05477. Tel: 802-434-2521. [CEM 2]

Rutland, Rutland Co., Christ the King (1907), Revs. Reid C. Mayo; Thomas V. Mattison.
Res., 66 S. Main St., 05701. Tel: 802-773-6820; Fax: 802-773-6820, Ext. 136.
School—Sisters 3; Lay Teachers 22; Students 310.
Immaculate Heart of Mary (1869), Rev. James J. McShane. In res., Rev. James A. Lawrence.
Res., 18 Lincoln Ave., 05701. Tel: 802-775-0846; Fax: 802-775-9640. [CEM]
St. Peter (1855), Revs. Wilfred Andre Houle; John J. Herbert.
Res., 134 Convent Ave., 05701. Tel: 802-775-1994; Fax: 802-775-0178. [CEM]

St. Albans, Franklin Co., Holy Angels (1872), Rev. Maurice J. Roy.
Res., 246 Lake St., 05478. Tel: 802-524-2585; Fax: 802-524-2585. [CEM]
Immaculate Conception (1847), Rev. Leonidas B. Laroche; Deacon John Rixon.
Res., 45 Fairfield St., 05478. Tel: 802-527-7775. [CEM]

St. Albans Bay, Our Lady of the Lake. Closed. For inquiries for parish records contact Holy Angels 246 Lake St., St. Albans, VT 05478. Tel.: 802-524-2585.

St. Johnsbury, Caledonia Co., St. John the Evangelist (1896), Revs. Joseph A. Lively; Justin J. Baker; Deacons Bruce Burk; Raymond Desilets; Bernier Mayo.
Res., 49 Winter St., 05819. Tel: 802-748-8129; Fax: 802-748-7863. [CEM]
Missions—Gilman, Essex Co., St. Theresa; Lunenburg, Essex Co., St. Leo.

Shelburne, Chittenden Co., St. Catherine of Siena (1906), Rev. Philip R. LaMothe.
Res., 72 Church St., P.O. Box 70, 05482. Tel: 802-985-2373; Fax: 802-985-9181. [CEM]

Sheldon Springs, Franklin Co., St. Anthony (1906), Rev. Bernard J. Bechard, S.S.E.
Res., P.O. Box 97, 05485-0097. Tel: 802-933-8921; Fax: 802-933-8921. [CEM 2]
Mission—Franklin, Franklin Co., St. Mary.

South Burlington, Chittenden Co., St. John Vianney (1940), Rev. John W. Hamilton; Deacons Joseph Lane; Anthony Previti.
Res., 160 Hinesburg Rd., 05403. Tel: 802-864-4166; Fax: 802-863-6065.

South Hero, Grand Isle Co., St. Rose of Lima (1895), Rev. Philip J. Branon.
Res., 501 Rte. 2, 05486. Tel: 802-372-4092; Fax: 802-372-4770.
Missions—Grand Isle, Grand Isle Co., St. Joseph; North Hero, Grand Isle Co., St. Benedict Joseph Labre.

Springfield, Windsor Co., Maternity of the Blessed Virgin Mary (1900), Rev. Douglas W. Hawkins, C.S.C., Admin.
Res., 40 Summer St., 05156. Tel: 802-885-3400; Fax: 802-885-2250. [CEM]

Stowe, Lamoille Co., Blessed Sacrament (1954), Rev. Bernard E. Gaudreau.
Res., 728 Mountain Rd., P.O. Box 27, 05672. Tel: 802-253-7536; Fax: 802-253-4445.

Swanton, Franklin Co., Nativity of the Blessed Virgin Mary (1854), Rev. Charles H. Ranges, S.S.E.
Res., 65 Canada St., 05488. Tel: 802-868-4517; Fax: 802-868-4262. [CEM]

Troy, Orleans Co., Sacred Heart of Jesus (1931), Rev. Jerome Mercure, Admin.
Res., P.O. Box 109, 05868. Tel: 802-744-2239. [CEM]
Mission—Lowell, Orleans Co., St. Ignatius Loyola.

Underhill Center, Chittenden Co., St. Thomas (1856), Rev. Francis R. Prive.
Res., P.O. Box 3, 05490-0003. Tel: 802-899-4632; Fax: 802-899-5120. [CEM 3]

Vergennes, Addison Co., St. Peter (1881), Rev. Donal Ward.
Res., 85 S. Maple St., P.O. Box 324, 05491. Tel: 802-877-2367; Fax: 802-877-1063. [CEM]

Waitsfield, Washington Co., Our Lady of the Snows (1964), Rev. Donald E. Ritchie.
Mailing Address: c/o 109 S. Main St., Waterbury, 05676. Tel: 802-244-7734.
Mission—Moretown, Washington Co., St. Patrick.

Wallingford, Rutland Co., St. Patrick (1910), Rev. Joseph M. Quinn, C.S.C.
Res., 218 N. Main St., P.O. Box 99, 05773-0099. Tel: 802-446-2161; Fax: 802-446-2161. [CEM]
Mission—Mount Holly, Rutland Co., St. Mary.

Waterbury, Washington Co., St. Andrew (1869), Rev. Bernard W. Bourgeois, Admin.
Res., 109 S. Main St., 05676. Tel: 802-244-7734; Fax: 802-244-7934. [CEM]
Missions—Waitsfield, Washington Co., Our Lady of the Snows; Moretown, Washington Co., St. Patrick.

West Rutland, Rutland Co., St. Bridget (1857), Rev. Raymond A. Giroux.
Res., 28 Church St., 05777-0087. Tel: 802-438-2490. [CEM 2]
St. Stanislaus Kostka (1904), Rev. Frank S. Warzocha.
Res., 23 Barnes St., 05777. Tel: 802-438-5671. [CEM]

White River Junction, Windsor Co., St. Anthony (1869), Revs. Ronald Saunders, S.M.; Adrien O. Pelletier, S.M.; Deacon John P. Guarino.
Res., 15 Church St., 05001. Tel: 802-295-2225; Fax: 802-296-6008. [CEM 2]
Religious Education Center: 53 Church St., 05001. Tel: 802-295-6607.
Station—White River Junction, Veterans Administration Hospital, Tel: 802-295-9363.

Williston, Chittenden Co., Immaculate Heart of Mary (1951), Rev. Donald J. Ravey.
Res., P.O. Box 1047, 05495. Tel: 802-878-4513.

Wilmington, Windham Co., Our Lady of Fatima (1959), Rev. Charles L. Wallen, C.S.C., Admin.; Deacon Paul Mello.
Res., P.O. Box 188, 05363. Tel: 802-464-7329.

Windsor, Windsor Co., St. Francis of Assisi (1886), Rev. Paul Belhumeur, M.S.
Res., 30 Union St., P.O. Box 46, 05089. Tel: 802-674-2157; Fax: 802-674-9416. [CEM]

Winooski, Chittenden Co., St. Francis Xavier (1868), Rev. Richard G. Lavalley; Deacons Norman Langlois; John F. Place.
Res., 3 St. Peter St., 05404. Tel: 802-655-2290; Fax: 802-655-3036. [CEM]
School—Tel: 802-655-2600; 655-3096.
Sisters 1; Lay Teachers 12; Students 200.
Convent—Tel: 802-655-2395; Fax: 802-655-3888.
St. Vincent de Paul Center—Tel: 802-655-3006.
Daycare—Tel: 802-655-4660.
St. Stephen (1882), Revs. Richard G. Lavalley, Admin.; Benedict Kiely, O.F.M.
Res., 115 Barlow St., 05404. Tel: 802-655-0318. [CEM]

Woodstock, Windsor Co., Our Lady of the Snows (1894), Rev. William P. Gallagher.
Res., 7 South St., P.O. Box 397, 05091-0397. Tel: 802-457-2322; Fax: 802-457-5805.

Chaplains of Public Institutions

BURLINGTON. *Fletcher Allen Health Care* 05401. Tel: 802-656-2770. Revs. Lance W. Harlow; John Nuagbaracha, D.S.; Simon P. Gallagher, O.S.B.; Sr. Monica Rock, R.H.S.J., Pastoral Assoc.

WATERBURY. *State Hospital*. Rev. Bernard Bourgeois.

WHITE RIVER JUNCTION. *Veterans Administration Hospital*. Rev. Adrien O. Pelletier, S.M.

On Duty Outside the Diocese:
Reverend Fathers—
Corcoran, William D., Congregation for the Oriental Churches, Vatican City, Res., Casa Giovanni XXIII, Via Torre Rossa 68, Rome 00165 Italy. Tel: 39-06-660-48337
Dowd, Barry G., Mary Queen of the Universe Shrine, 8300 Vineland Ave., Orlando, FL 32821

On Special or Other Diocesan Assignment:
Reverend Fathers—
Gallagher, Simon P., O.S.B., Fletcher Allen Health Care
Harlow, Lance, Fletcher Allen Health Care
Miller, Walter D., Chancery Office
Nuagbaracha, John, Fletcher Allen Health Care

Other Residence:
Reverend Fathers—
Bruder, John W., O.C.S.O., 800 Waldon Hill Rd., Danville, VT 05828

Retired:
Reverend Monsignors—
Adams, Raymond A., 9 Cascadnac Ave., Essex Junction, VT 05452. Tel: 802-878-5914
Flanagan, Francis B., 59 Meadow St., Rutland, VT 05701
Gelineau, Edward J., St. Joseph's Home, 243 N. Prospect St., Burlington, VT 05401. Tel: 802-865-9240
McSweeney, John R., 125 Kennedy Dr., Unit #36, South Burlington, VT 05403. Tel: 802-863-6017
Powers, Robert J., Allerton House, 43 School House Rd., #162, Weymouth, MA 02188
Reverend Fathers—
Bean, Donald A., Michaud Manor, 47 Herrick Rd., Derby Line, VT 05830
Beary, Thomas J., St. Joseph's Home, 243 N. Prospect St., Burlington, VT 05401
Brackett, Anthony H., 9854 Wildginger Dr., S.W., Fort Myers, FL 33919. Tel: 941-482-5749
Brochu, Gerard H., P.O. Box 7223, Statesville, NC 28687. Tel: 704-872-3178
Chant, William S., 20 Gray Meadow Dr., Burlington, VT 05401. Tel: 518-561-9608
Couture, Bernard G., c/o Mrs. Gisele Fournier, Box 202, East Barre, VT 05639
Davignon, Charles P., Holy Cross Rectory, 416 Church Rd., Colchester, VT 05446-6552
Demasi, Michael A., Autumn Acres, R.R. #2, Box S 887, Bennington, VT 05201
Dennigan, Patrick J., P.O. Box 931, North Adams, MA 01247
Depeaux, Bernard F., 351 North Ave., P.O. Box 489, Burlington, VT 05402-0489. Tel: 802-658-6110
Duquette, Lucien G., 6 Roland Ct., Winooski, VT 05404. Tel: 407-664-8442
Falvella, Richard J., Crystal Haven Rd., Bomoseen, VT 05732. Tel: 802-273-2104
Foley, James F., Burlington Health & Rehab Center, 300 Pearl St., Burlington, VT 05401
Fowler, Richard A., St. George Catholic Community, 300 E. 16th St., Apache Jct., AZ 85219. Tel: 480-982-2929
Guischard, John A., The Kervick Home, 131 Convent Ave., Rutland, VT 05701
Hackett, John P., P.O. Box 1474, St. Albans, VT 05478. Tel: 802-527-2374
Hart, Edward J., St. Joseph's Home, 243 N. Prospect St., Burlington, VT 05401
Hawkins, Douglas W., C.S.C., Sacred Heart St. Francis de Sales, 238 W. Main St., Bennington, VT 05201. Tel: 802-442-3141
Holland, Francis M., 8 Cedar Glen N., South Burlington, VT 05403. Tel: 802-865-8082
Kennedy, David G., P.O. Box 846, Dewey, AZ 86327-0846
Kenney, John B., 8 Hullcrest Ln., Shelburne, VT 05482. Tel: 802-985-2333
Lagor, Joseph J., P.O. Box 4696, White River Jct., VT 05001. Tel: 802-296-3010
Laliberte, William F., 113 Robbins St., Rutland, VT 05701. Tel: 802-773-2982
Lapan, Robert, Mt. Marie Health Ctr., 34 Lower Holyoke Rd, Holyoke, MA 01040
Laplante, Jean-Paul, 64 N. Elm St., St. Albans, VT 05478. Tel: 802-527-1498
Lawlor, Brendan W., 1735 Peachtree Ln., Crofton, MD 21114-2646
Ledoux, John C., 119 Grice Brook Rd., St. Albans, VT 05478. Tel: 802-527-3986
McCarthy, Joseph, 130 Curtis Ave., Burlington, VT 05401. Tel: 802-862-3183
Moore, Edward F., 86 Westview Heights Dr., Stowe, VT 05672-4361. Tel: 802-253-5085
Morgan, William P., P.O. Box 292, Lyndon Center, VT 05850. Tel: 802-633-2870
Mulligan, William R., 20 N. 28th Ave., Longport, NJ 08403. Tel: 609-823-1901
Murtagh, George O., 2640 N.E. 52nd Ct., #42, Silver Springs, FL 34488-9402. Tel: 352-236-3202
Pagliuca, Joseph P., 142 Via Serafino Rinaldi, 67057 Pescino (AQ), Italy
Pray, Joseph N., P.O. Box 85, Castleton, VT 05735. Tel: 802-273-2621
Ritchie, Donald E., 8213 Cagel Rd., Ft. Washington, MD 20744. Tel: 301-567-6116
Rousseau, Peter A., 16 Clover Dr., B1, Essex Jct., VT 05452. Tel: 802-879-6934
Sullivan, Joseph T., P.O. Box 421, St. Albans Bay, VT 05481. Tel: 802-527-0272
Vignoe, Joseph M., 109 Preston Ln., P.O. Box 532, Bomoseen, VT 05732. Tel: 802-468-5349
von Fauer, Stephen C., Mary Theotokos Center, P.O. Box 88, West Burke, VT 05871. Tel: 802-467-1132
Walsh, Raymond D., The Loretto Home, 59 Meadow St., Rutland, VT 05701. Tel: 802-773-8840
Whalen, Robert B., Holy Name, P.O. Box 774198, Steamboat Springs, CO 80477. Tel: 970-879-0671

Permanent Deacons:
Allen, Eugene, Jr., St. Joseph, Chester
Bisson, David A., St. Monica, Barre
Blicharz, John F., Sacred Heart, Bellow Falls
Brennehan, Walter, St. Augustine, Montpelier
Brown, William, III, St. Theresa, Gilman
Burk, Bruce, St. John, St. Johnsbury
Chagnon, Clifford, All Saints, Richford
Cooney, Thomas, Holy Cross, Morrisville
Cummings, Regis E., St. Augustine, Montpelier
Degnon, Robert F., Our Lady of Hope, West Wardsboro
Desilets, Raymond J., St. John, St. Johnsbury
Fitzpatrick, Kelly, Our Lady of Perpetual Help, Bradford
Glinka, William, Our Lady of Grace, Colchester
Graden, William, St. James, Island Pond
Gratton, John, St. Benedict, West Charleston
Griffin, Gary, St. Mary, Brandon
Guarino, John P., St. Anthony, White River Junction
Hawk, Ivan, Holy Cross, Colchester
Krawczyk, Eugene, On Duty Outside of the Diocese
Lane, Joseph W., Sr., St. John Vianney, South Burlington
Langlois, Norman S., St. Francis Xavier, Winooski
Lauziere, Roger J., St. Ann, Milton
Lissandrello, Paul, Sts. Donatian and Rogatian, Randolph
Mayo, Bernier L., St. John, St. Johnsbury
Mello, Paul, Our Lady of Fatima, Wilmington
Meunier, Louis A., St. Anthony and Christ the King, Burlington
Nadeau, Thomas, On Duty Outside the Diocese
Perkins, Richard, St. Frances Cabrini, West Pawlet
Place, John F., St. Francis Xavier, Winooski
Previti, Anthony, St. John Vianney, South Burlington
Pudvah, Daniel, St. Monica, Barre
Putis, Peter, St. Paul, Manchester Center
Rainville, John L., St. Louis, Highgate Center
Ramey, Jon, St. Isidore, Montgomery Center
Ratte, Stephen J., St. Luke, Fairfax
Rivard, Fernand R., St. Monica, Barre
Rixon, John, St. Mary, St. Albans
Rock, James E., On Duty Outside of the Diocese
Toborg, Alfred, St. Elizabeth, Lyndonville
Vincelette, Alan, St. Amadeus, Alburg

INSTITUTIONS LOCATED IN THE DIOCESE

[A] COLLEGES AND UNIVERSITIES

BURLINGTON. *Trinity College of Vermont*, President's Office, 208 Colchester Ave., 05401. Tel: 802-658-0337; Fax: 802-846-7003.
E-mail: kieslich@trinityvt.edu
Web site: www.trinityvt.edu
For a complete listing, refer to the Colleges and Universities section.

COLCHESTER. *St. Michael's College*, Winooski Park, 05439. Tel: 802-654-2000; 654-2386; Fax: 802-654-2701.
E-mail: mcormier@smcvt.edu
Web site: www.smcvt.edu
For a complete listing, refer to the Colleges and Universities section.

RUTLAND. *College of St. Joseph in Vermont*, 71 Clement Rd., 05701-3899. Tel: 802-773-5900; Fax: 802-773-5900, Ext. 3.
E-mail: fmiglorie@csj.edu
Web site: www.csj.edu
For a complete listing, refer to the Colleges and Universities section.

[B] CENTRAL HIGH SCHOOLS, DIOCESAN AND PAROCHIAL

RUTLAND. *Mt. St. Joseph Academy*, 127 Convent Ave., 05701. Tel: 802-775-0151; Fax: 802-775-0424.
E-mail: principal@msjvt.org
Web site: www.msjvermont.org
Sisters of St. Joseph. Mr. Robert P. Lukaskiewicz, Prin.; Mr. Anthony J. Cirelli, Asst. Prin.; Elizabeth Hughes, Guidance Dir. Priests 1; Lay Teachers 25; Students 211.

SOUTH BURLINGTON. *Rice Memorial High School*, 99 Proctor Ave., 05403. Tel: 802-862-6521; Fax: 802-864-9931.
E-mail: rice@ricehs.k12.vt.us
Web site: www.together.net/~ricemhs/ricemhs.htm
Mr. John McCarthy, Prin.; Mr. Lloyd Hulburt, Asst. Prin. Priests 1; Sisters 1; Lay Teachers 42; Students 527.

[C] ELEMENTARY SCHOOLS, PAROCHIAL

BURLINGTON. *Christ The King.* (Grades PreK-8), 136 Locust St., 05401. Tel: 802-862-6696; Fax: 802-658-6553.
E-mail: cksburl@aol.com
Dr. Jay L. Morris, Ph.D., Prin. Lay Teachers 15; Students 233.

Mater Christi School, 50 Mansfield Ave., 05401. Tel: 802-658-3992; Fax: 802-863-1196.
Web site: www.mcschool.org
Barbara Gaida, Prin. Sisters 3; Lay Teachers 30; Students 396.

St. Joseph. (Grades PreK-8), 20 Allen St., 05401. Tel: 802-864-5623; Fax: 802-860-2627. Evelyn Rogerson, Prin. Sisters 1; Lay Teachers 14; Students 209.

BARRE. *St. Monica's.* (Grades PreK-8), 73 Summer St., 05641. Tel: 802-476-5015; Fax: 802-476-0861. Mrs. Betty Foley, Prin. Lay Teachers 15; Students 176.

BARTON. *St. Paul's.* (Grades K-8), 54 Eastern Ave., 05822. Tel: 802-525-6578; Fax: 802-525-6578.
E-mail: stpaul@together.net
Maureen Fountain, Prin. Lay Teachers 5; Students 55.

BENNINGTON. *Sacred Heart.* (Grades K-6), 307 School St., 05201. Tel: 802-442-2446; Fax: 802-442-3584.
E-mail: destes@sover.net
Web site: www.rc.net/burlington/
Mr. David Estes, Prin. Lay Teachers 11; Students 207.

BRATTLEBORO. *St. Michael's.* (Grades PreK-6), 23 Walnut St., 05301. Tel: 802-254-5666; Fax: 802-254-5229.
E-mail: stmikesb@together.net
Web site: together.net/~stmikesb/
Mr. Frank J. Vara, Prin. Lay Teachers 21; Students 299.

MIDDLEBURY. *St. Mary School.* (Grades PreK-6), 86 Shannon St., 05753. Tel: 802-388-2943. Robert Baroz, Prin. Lay Teachers 6; Students 67.

MONTPELIER. *St. Michael's School.* (Grades K-8), 46 Barre St., 05602. Tel: 802-223-6430; Fax: 802-229-4827.
E-mail: stmikes@plainfield.bypass.com
Deacon Paul Lissandrello, Prin. Sisters 1; Lay Teachers 8; Students 157.

MORRISVILLE. *Bishop John A. Marshall School.* (Grades K-8), P.O. Box 387, 05661. Tel: 802-888-4758; Fax: 802-888-6177.
Web site: bishopmarshallschool.com
Mr. Bruce A. Batchelder, Prin. Lay Teachers 10; Students 116.

NEWPORT. *Sacred Heart Schools, Inc.* (Grades K-8), 47 Clermont Ter., 05855-2194. Tel: 802-334-8185; Fax: 802-334-7803. Mrs. Janet Schmidt, Interim Prin. Lay Teachers 15; Students 101.

RUTLAND. *Christ the King.* (Grades PreK-8), 60 S. Main St., 05701. Tel: 802-773-6820, Ext. 117. Mrs. Rose-Maria Doren, Prin. Sisters 3; Lay Teachers 22; Students 305.

ST. JOHNSBURY. *Good Shepherd School.* (Grades PreK-8), P.O. Box 384, 05819. Tel: 802-751-8223; Fax: 802-751-8223. Mr. Robert Gessner, Prin. Lay Teachers 14; Students 147.

SPRINGFIELD. *Holy Family Catholic School*, 38 Pleasant St., 05156. Tel: 802-885-4733; Fax: 802-885-3699.
E-mail: kkiniry@sover.net
Web site: www.springfield.k12.vt.us/schools/hfs/holyfamilyschool.htm
Kim E. Kiniry, Prin. Lay Teachers 9; Students 58.

WINOOSKI. *St. Francis Xavier.* (Grades PreK-8), St. Peter St., 05404. Tel: 802-655-2600; Fax: 802-655-3096.
E-mail: st.fxi@together.net
Gail F. Tisseur, Prin. Sisters 1; Lay Teachers 12; Students 205.

[D] HOMES FOR AGED

BURLINGTON. *St. Joseph's Home*, 243 N. Prospect St., 05401. Tel: 802-864-0264; Fax: 802-864-5640
For a complete listing, refer to the Special Care Facilities section.

DERBY LINE. *Michaud Memorial Manor*, 05830. Tel: 802-873-3152; Fax: 802-873-9206.
E-mail: manor@together.net
Web site: www.vermontcatholic.org
For a complete listing, refer to the Special Care Facilities section.

RUTLAND. *Loretto Home for Aged*, 05701. Tel: 802-773-8840; Fax: 802-773-9638.
E-mail: lhometc@sover.net
For a complete listing, refer to the Special Care Facilities section.

St. Joseph Residence/Kervick Home, 131 Convent Ave., 05701. Tel: 802-775-5133
For a complete listing, refer to the Special Care Facilities section.

[E] MONASTERIES AND RESIDENCES OF PRIESTS AND BROTHERS

ARLINGTON. *Carthusian Foundation, Charterhouse of the Transfiguration*, 1800 Beartown Rd., 05250. Tel: 802-362-2550; Fax: 802-362-3584. Revs. Johan de Bruijn, O.Cart. (Holland); Lorenzo Maria Tolentino de la Rosa, Jr., O.Cart. (Philippines), Prior, Novice Master of Brothers; Mary Joseph Kim, O.Cart (Korea), Novice Master of Cloister Monks, Antiquior; Mary Paul Chapeau, O.Cart. (France), Vicar.
Carthusian Foundation, Association Fraternelle Romande. Choir Monks: Solemn Professed 4; Converse Brothers: Solemn Professed 5; Perpetual Donates 2; Postulants 1.

COLCHESTER. *Society of St. Edmund.* (Edmundite Generalate), 270 Winooski Park, 05439. Tel: 802-654-3400; Fax: 802-654-3409.
E-mail: generalate@aol.com
Web site: www.sse.org
Central Offices, Society of Saint Edmund. Revs. Richard M. Myhalyk, S.S.E., Supr. Gen.; James R. Coombs, S.S.E.; Eymard Galligan, S.S.E.; Edward J. Dubriske, S.S.E. (Venezuela); Philippe Simonnet, S.S.E. (France).

Society of St. Edmund. (Edmundite Community at St. Michael's College), 05439. Tel: 802-654-2000. Revs. Michael P. Cronogue, S.S.E., Supr.; Marcel R. Rainville, S.S.E.; Richard N. Berube, S.S.E.; Paul E. Couture, S.S.E.; Brian J. Cummings, S.S.E.; Raymond J. Doherty, S.S.E.; Joseph M. McLaughlin, S.S.E.; Romeo A. Trahan, S.S.E.; Richard L. VanderWeel, S.S.E.; Bro. Anthony Krutch, S.S.E.

WESTON. *Priory of Benedictine Monks*, 58 Priory Hill Rd., 05161-6400. Tel: 802-824-5409; Fax: 802-824-3573. Very Rev. Richard Iaquinto, O.S.B., Prior; Revs. Peter Claude Anctil, O.S.B.; Robert J. Kiernan, O.S.B.; Mark Ronald Nicolosi, O.S.B.; John Hammond, O.S.B. Priests 5; Brothers 10.

[F] CONVENTS AND RESIDENCES OF SISTERS

BURLINGTON. *Mount St. Mary Convent*, 100 Mansfield Ave., 05401. Tel: 802-863-6835; Fax: 802-863-1486.
E-mail: rsmvermont@hotmail.com
Motherhouse and Novitiate of Sisters of Mercy. Sr. Jeannine Mercure, R.S.M., Pres. In res. Rev. Wendell H. Searles, V.G., Chap.

Institute for Spiritual Development, 208 Colchester Ave., 05401. Tel: 802-846-7084. Sisters 79.

COLCHESTER. *Religious Hospitallers of St. Joseph*, 786 College Pkwy., 05446. Tel: 802-655-1160; Fax: 802-847-2690.
E-mail: rhfa@juno.com
Sr. Rita Vallee, R.H.S.J., Supr. Sisters 19.

NEWPORT. *Sacred Heart Convent.* (Daughters of Charity of the Sacred Heart), 119 Clermont Ter., 05855. Tel: 802-334-7058. Sisters 6.

RUTLAND. *Sisters of St. Joseph Society, Inc.*, 7 Clement Rd., 05701. Tel: 802-775-0665.
E-mail: vermontssj@aol.com
Administrative Offices, 7 Clement Rd., 05701. Tel: 802-775-0665; Fax: 802-775-0105.
Other Residences: St. Francis Residence, 11 Clement Rd., 05701. Tel: 802-775-0693. Business Office, Avila Hall, 7 Clement Rd., 05701. Tel: 802-775-0665; Fax: 802-775-0105. Marion Hall, 9 Clement Rd., 05701. Tel: 802-775-0665. Fontbonne Hall (Residence), 13 Clement Rd., 05701. Tel: 802-775-4231. St. Joseph Assisted Living Residence - Kervick Home, 131 Convent Ave., 05701. Tel: 802-775-5133. Sisters 39.

WESTFIELD. *Monastery of the Immaculate Heart of Mary*, 4103 Rte. 100, 05874. Tel: 802-744-6525; Fax: 802-744-6236. Benedictine Cloistered Nuns, Congregation of Solesmes. Rev. Mother Marguerite Derome, O.S.B., Prioress; Sr. Laurence A. M. Couture, O.S.B., Sub-Prioress; Rev. Dom Lawrence Brown, O.S.B., Res. Chap., Monk of Clear Creek, OK. Professed Nuns 14; Postulants 1; Novices 1.

WINOOSKI. *Missionary Sisters of Our Lady of Africa (M.S.O.L.A.)*, 47 W. Spring St., 05404. Tel: 802-655-4003; Fax: 802-655-3888. Sr. Nora Indelicato, Supr. Sisters 4.

Our Lady of Providence Convent, 47 W. Spring St., 05404. Tel: 802-655-2395; Fax: 802-655-3888.
E-mail: olopr@aol.com
Sr. Lorraine Boyer, S.P., Coord. Sisters 28; Missionary Sisters of Africa 4.

[G] SUMMER CAMPS

BURLINGTON. *Camp Holy Cross, Inc.*, 351 North Ave., 05401. Tel: 802-827-3203 (Winter); 863-5986 (Summer). Rev. Peter Y. Williams, Exec. Dir., St. Patrick's, P.O. Box 18, Fairfield, 05455. Summer Camp for Boys. Day Camp for Boys and Girls. Diocesan institution under direction of Board of Trustees. Capacity 100.

Camp Tara, Catholic Charities Central Office, 351 North Ave., P.O. Box 489, 05402-0489. Tel: 802-658-6110; Fax: 802-860-0451.
E-mail: vccbrlngton@aol.com
Web site: www.vermontcatholic.org
Summer camp for needy Vermont children. Diocesan program under direction of Vermont Catholic Charities. Capacity 220.

[H] NEWMAN CENTERS

BURLINGTON. *University of Vermont-The Catholic Center at UVM*, 390 S. Prospect St., Redstone Campus, 05401. Tel: 802-862-8403; Fax: 802-865-9480.
E-mail: cathuvm@together.net
Web site: www.uvm.edu/~catholic/
Chaplains: Revs. Michael W. DeForge; Benedict Kiely, O.F.M.

Castleton State College, St. John Rectory, P.O. Box 128, Castleton, 05735. Tel: 802-468-5706; Fax: 802-468-5299. Rev. J. Charles Durham, Chap.

Goddard College, Plainfield, 05667. Tel: 802-223-5285; Fax: 802-223-3621. Rev. William R. Beaudin.

Green Mountain College, St. Raphael Rectory, Main St., Poultney, 05764. Tel: 802-287-5703. Rev. Adam J. Krempa.

Johnson State College (Johnson). Attended by St. Mary, Cambridge. P.O. Box 129, Cambridge, 05444. Tel: 802-644-5073; Fax: 802-644-2546. Rev. Francis R. Prive.

Lyndon State College, Lyndon Center, 05850. Tel: 802-656-5267; Fax: 802-656-3324. Rev. Stephen J. Nichols, St. Elizabeth Church, P.O. Box 141, Lyndonville, 05851.

Middlebury College, St. Mary Rectory, 326 College St., Middlebury, 05753. Tel: 802-388-2943; Fax: 802-388-2943. Rev. John McDermott, Chap.

Norwich Newman Apostolate, Norwich University, Northfield, 05663. Tel: 802-862-8403; Fax: 802-865-9480. Chaplains: Rev. Michael W. DeForge, The Catholic Center at UVM, 390 S. Prospect St., Redstone Campus, 05401. Tel: 802-862-8403; Fax: 802-865-9480. Rev. Richard G. LaValley, St. Francis Xavier Rectory, 3 St. Peter St., Winooski, 05404. Tel: 802-655-2290; Fax: 802-655-3036.

Vermont Technical College, Sts. Donatian and Rogatian Rectory, 25 S. Pleasant St., Randolph, 05060. Tel: 802-728-3227; Fax: 802-728-3570. Rev. John M. Milanese.

[I] MISCELLANEOUS

BURLINGTON. *Institute for Spiritual Development*, 208 Colchester Ave., 05401. Tel: 802-846-7084, Ext. 410; Fax: 802-846-7001. Sr. Claire Boissy, R.S.M., Admin. Dir.

Mercy Consolidated Asset Management Program (MCAMP), Sisters of Mercy of the Americas, Regional Community of Vermont, 100 Mansfield A, 05401. Tel: 802-863-6835.
MCAMP Members & Regional Communities. Sr. Patricia McDermott, R.S.M., (Silver Spring, MD); Sr. Catherine McGrarty, R.S.M., (Dallas, TX); Sr. Margaret Beatty, R.S.M., (Baltimore, MD); Sr. Jeannine Mercure, R.S.M., (Burlington, VT); Sr. JoAnne Courneen, R.S.M., (Erie, PA); Sr. Barbara Riley, R.S.M., (Cumberland, RI); Sr. Patricia Forret, R.S.M., (Omaha, NE); Sr. Patricia Wolf, R.S.M., (Hartsdale, NY).

BENSON. *Lumen Christi Retreat House*, 56 Howard Hill Rd., 05743. Tel: 802-537-4531. Sr. Judy Fortune, R.S.M., Spiritual Dir. Reservations for retreat call Tel: 802-846-7084.

BRATTLEBORO. *Neringa, Inc.*, 147 Neringa Rd., 05301. Tel: 802-254-8090.
E-mail: neringai@yahoo.com

COLCHESTER. *Fanny Allen Hospital*, 101 College Pkwy., 05446. Tel: 802-847-6448; Fax: 802-847-6535.
E-mail: irene.duchesneau@vtmed.net.org
Sr. Irene Duchesneau, R.H.S.J., Corporate Sponsor Liaison. Fanny Allen Hospital has the oversight responsibility to assure that the Fletcher Allen Health Care Corporation does not conduct actions on the Fanny Allen Campus that conflicts with the teachings, traditions, Canons or other laws of the Roman Catholic Church or the Constitutions and Directives of the Religious Hospitallers of St. Joseph.

ISLE LA MOTTE. *St. Anne's Shrine*, 05463. Tel: 802-928-3362; Fax: 802-928-3305.
E-mail: fstanne@aol.com
Web site: www.sse.org
Conducted by Fathers of Society of St. Edmund. Rev. Maurice U. Boucher, S.S.E., Spiritual Dir. Open May 15-Oct. 15.

RANDOLPH. *Prelature of the Holy Cross and Opus Dei*, Wynnview Center, R.D. 1, 05060. Tel: 802-728-5414; Fax: 802-728-3334.
Web site: www.opusdei.org
Legal Names: Opus Dei; The Work of God.

RELIGIOUS INSTITUTES OF MEN REPRESENTED IN THE DIOCESE

For further details refer to the corresponding bracketed number in the Religious Institutes of Men or Women section.

[0200]—*Benedictine Monks.*—O.S.B.

[0300]—*Cistercian Order of the Strict Observance (Trappists).*—O.C.S.O.

[0520]—*Franciscan Friars.*—O.F.M.

[0780]—*Marist Fathers.*—S.M.

[0720]—*The Missionaries of Our Lady of La Salette.* (Prov. of the Immaculate Heart of Mary).—M.S.

[0280]—*Order of Carthusians.*—O.Cart.

[0610]—*Priests of the Congregation of Holy Cross.* (Eastern Prov.).—C.S.C.

[0440]—*Society of Saint Edmund.*—S.S.E.

RELIGIOUS INSTITUTES OF WOMEN REPRESENTED IN THE DIOCESE

[0170]—*Benedictine Cloistered Nuns of the Congregation of Solesmes.*—O.S.B.

[0750]—*Daughters of the Charity of the Sacred Heart of Jesus.*—F.C.S.C.J.

[0820]—*Daughters of the Holy Spirit.*—D.H.S.

[0960]—*Daughters of Wisdom.*—D.W.

[1070]—*Dominican Sisters.*—O.P.

[1190]—*Franciscan Sisters of the Atonement.*—S.A.

[]—*Missionary Sisters of Our Lady of Africa.*—M.S.O.L.A.

[3440]—*Religious Hospitallers of Saint Joseph.*—R.H.S.J.

[1930]—*Sisters of Holy Cross.*—C.S.C.

[2550]—*Sisters of Mercy.*—R.S.M.

[3000]—*Sisters of Notre Dame de Namur.*—S.N.D.deN.

[3340]—*Sisters of Providence.*—S.P.

[3830-01]—*Sisters of St. Joseph (Boston, MA).*—C.S.J.

[3830-07]—*Sisters of St. Joseph (Burlington, VT).*—S.S.J.

[4130]—*Ursuline Sisters of the Congregation of Tildonk, Belgium.*—O.S.U.

DIOCESAN CEMETERIES

BURLINGTON. *St. Joseph's Cemetery,* 05401.

SOUTH BURLINGTON. *Resurrection Park Cemetery,* 05403.

NECROLOGY

† Bombardier, Gerald, Winooski, VT St. Stephen. —Died Sept. 3, 2000.

† Foster, Edward C., (Retired). —Died April 14, 2000.

† Logue, Louis, (Retired). —Died Dec. 28, 1999.

† Maloney, Raymond G., (Retired). —Died Nov. 12, 1999.

† Nadeau, J.H. Normand, Brattleboro, VT St. Michael. —Died Aug. 3, 2000.

Diocese of Camden

(Dioecesis Camdensis)

Most Reverend

NICHOLAS A. DIMARZIO D.D., PH.D

Bishop of Camden; ordained May 30, 1970; appointed Titular Bishop of Mauriana and Auxiliary Bishop of Newark September 10, 1996; consecrated October 31, 1996; appointed June 8, 1999; installed July 22, 1999. *Res., Marywood, 1600 Peter Cheeseman Rd., Blackwood, NJ, 08012. Office: Camden Diocesan Center, 631 Market St., Camden, NJ, 08102.*

Most Reverend

JAMES L. SCHAD, D.D.

Retired Auxiliary Bishop of Camden; appointed Titular Bishop of Panatoria October 18, 1966; consecrated December 8, 1966; retired January 26, 1993. *Res., Neumann House, St. Mary's Home, Ste. 102, 250 St. Mary's Dr., Cherry Hill, NJ, 08003.*

Legal Corporate Title: "The Diocese of Camden, New Jersey."

ESTABLISHED DECEMBER 9, 1937.

Square Miles 2,691.

Comprises six Counties in the State of New Jersey—viz., Atlantic, Camden, Cape May, Cumberland, Gloucester and Salem.

For legal titles of parishes and diocesan institutions, consult the Chancery Office.

Chancery Offices: Camden Diocesan Center, 631 Market St., P.O. Box 708, Camden, NJ, 08101 or 1845 Haddon Ave., P.O. Box 709, Camden, NJ, 08101-0709. Tel.: 856-756-7900; Fax: 856-963-2655.

STATISTICAL OVERVIEW

Personnel	
Bishop	1
Retired Bishops	1
Priests: Diocesan Active in Diocese	221
Priests: Active Outside Diocese	16
Priests: Diocesan in Foreign Missions	2
Priests: Retired, Sick or Absent	75
Number of Diocesan Priests	314
Religious Priests in Diocese	46
Extern Priests in Diocese	11
Ordinations:	
Diocesan Priests	4
Transitional Deacons	6
Permanent Deacons in Diocese	122
Total Brothers	17
Total Sisters	328
Parishes	
Parishes	127
With Resident Pastor:	
Resident Diocesan Priests	121
Resident Religious Priests	6
Missions	5
Pastoral Centers	24
New Parishes Created	1
Professional Ministry Personnel:	
Brothers	2
Sisters	38
Lay Ministers	20
Welfare	
Catholic Hospitals	1
Total Assisted	247,886
Health Care Centers	2
Total Assisted	11,216
Homes for the Aged	5
Total Assisted	1,094
Residential Care of Children	1
Total Assisted	11
Day Care and Extended Day Care Centers	2
Total Assisted	192
Specialized Homes	1
Total Assisted	994
Special Centers for Social Services	12
Total Assisted	9,113
Residential Care of Disabled	1
Total Assisted	720
Other Institutions	1
Total Assisted	2,300
Educational	
Diocesan Students in Other Seminaries	31
Total Seminarians	31
High Schools, Diocesan and Parish	8
Total Students	4,861
High Schools, Private	3
Total Students	1,317
Elementary Schools, Diocesan and Parish	59
Total Students	16,276
Elementary Schools, Private	1
Total Students	42
Non-residential Schools for the Disabled	2
Total Students	844
Catechesis/Religious Education:	
High School Students	672
Elementary Students	35,784
Total Students Under Catholic Instruction	59,155
Teachers in the Diocese:	
Priests	20
Brothers	12
Sisters	90
Lay Teachers	998
Vital Statistics	
Receptions into the Church:	
Infant Baptism Totals	6,894
Adult Baptism Totals	666
Received into Full Communion	721
First Communions	6,932
Confirmations	5,367
Marriages:	
Catholic	1,351
Interfaith	562
Total Marriages	1,913
Deaths	4,351
Total Catholic Population	430,867
Total Population	1,294,470

Former Bishops—Most Rev. BARTHOLOMEW J. EUSTACE, S.T.D., First Bishop of Camden; cons. March 25, 1938; died Dec. 11, 1956.—Most Rev. JUSTIN J. MCCARTHY, S.T.D., LL.D., Second Bishop of Camden; cons. June 17, 1954; appt. to Camden, Jan. 27, 1957; died Dec. 26, 1959.—Most Rev. CELESTINE J. DAMIANO, D.D., Third Bishop of Camden; cons. Feb. 11, 1953; transferred to Camden, Jan. 24, 1960, with the personal title of Archbishop; died Oct. 2, 1967.—Most Rev. GEORGE H. GUILFOYLE, D.D., J.D., ord. March 25, 1944; appt. Titular Bishop of Marazanae and Auxiliary Bishop of New York, Oct. 17, 1964; cons. Fourth Bishop of Camden, Nov. 30, 1964; appt. Jan. 2, 1968; installed March 4, 1968; retired May 22, 1989; died June 11, 1991.—Most Rev. JAMES T. MCHUGH, S.T.D., ord. May 25, 1957; appt. Titular Bishop of Morosbisdo and Auxiliary Bishop of Newark, Nov. 20, 1987; cons. Jan. 25 1988; appt. Fifth Bishop of Camden, May 13, 1989; installed June 20, 1989; appt. Coadjutor Bishop of Rockville Centre, Dec. 6, 1998.

Diocesan Offices

The Chancery, Camden Diocesan Center—631 Market St., Camden, 08102. Tel: 856-756-7900.

Camden Diocesan Center—1845 Haddon Ave., Camden, 08103. Tel: 856-756-7900. Some offices are listed at separate locations.

The Diocese of Camden—A corporation under the laws of the State of New Jersey.

Officers—Rev. Msgr. DAVID F. BUDNEY, V.G., Vice Pres.; Rev. Msgr. JOSEPH W. POKUSA, J.C.D., Sec.

Diocesan Bishop—Most Rev. NICHOLAS A. DIMARZIO, Ph.D. D.D., *631 Market St., Camden, 08102,* Ext. 5213.

Retired Auxiliary Bishop—Most Rev. JAMES L. SCHAD, D.D. Tel: 856-489-0133.

Vicar General—(Administration)—Rev. Msgr. DAVID F. BUDNEY, V.G., *631 Market St., Camden, 08102,* Ext. 5206.

Vicar General—(Pastoral Life); Rev. Msgr. JAMES R. TRACY, Ph.D., *1845 Haddon Ave., Camden, 08103,* Ext. 6208.

Moderator of the Curia & Vice Chancellor—Rev. Msgr. JAMES F. CHECCHIO, J.C.D., *631 Market St., Camden, 08102,* Ext. 5207.

Assistant Chancellor—Deacon ROBERT WILLSON, *631 Market St., Camden, 08102,* Ext. 5263.

Chancellor and Episcopal Vicar for Canonical Affairs—Rev. Msgr. JOSEPH W. POKUSA, J.C.D., *631 Market St., Camden, 08102,* Ext. 5216.

Judicial Vicar—Rev. Msgr. LEONARD G. SCOTT, J.C.D., *1845 Haddon Ave., Camden, 08103,* Ext. 6201.

Episcopal Vicars

Episcopal Vicar for Camden City—Rev. Msgr. ROBERT T. MCDERMOTT, V.E., *St. Joseph Pro-Cathedral, 2907 Federal St., Camden, 08105.* Tel: 856-964-2776.

Episcopal Vicar for Clergy Health Care—Rev. Msgr. JAMES P. MCINTYRE, V.E., *Holy Family, 226 Hurfville Rd., Sewell, 08080.* Tel: 856-228-1616.

Episcopal Vicar for Catholic Schools—Rev. Msgr. THOMAS J. MCINTYRE, V.E., *St. Jude, 402 S. Black Horse Pike, Blackwood, 08012.* Tel: 856-227-0572.

Episcopal Vicar for Hispanics—Rev. Msgr. VICTOR S. MURO, *Spanish Catholic Center, 410 S. 8th St., Vineland, 08360.* Tel: 856-692-8992.

Episcopal Vicar for Human Services—Rev. Msgr. HARRY J. JORDAN, *631 Market St., Camden, 08102,* Ext. 5217.

Episcopal Vicar for Pastoral Planning and Budgeting—Rev. Msgr. CHARLES J. GIGLIO, Ph.D., *631 Market St., Camden, 08102,* Ext. 5264.

Episcopal Vicar for Priests—Rev. Msgr. JOHN T. FREY, *St. Isidore, 1655 Magnolia Rd., Vineland, 08361.* Tel: 856-691-9077.

Deaneries and Vicars Forane—

Atlantic Deanery—Rev. Msgr. DONALD D. VELOZO, V.F., *St. Bernadette, 1421 New Rd., Northfield, 08225.* Tel: 609-646-3499.

Cape May Deanery—Rev. Msgr. WILLIAM QUINN, V.F., *St. Ann, 2900 Pacific Ave., Wildwood, 08260.* Tel: 609-522-5583.

Camden City Deanery—Rev. Msgr. ROBERT T. MCDERMOTT, V.E., *St. Joseph Pro-Cathedral, 2907 Federal St., Camden, 08105.* Tel: 856-964-2776.

Camden North Deanery—Rev. Msgr. WILLIAM P. BRENNAN, V.F., *St. Pius X, 344 Kresson Rd., Cherry Hill, 08034.* Tel: 856-429-1330.

Camden South Deanery—Rev. WILLIAM P. GRAHAM, V.F., *St. Lawrence, 100 South Ave., Lindenwold, 08021.* Tel: 856-627-2222.

Camden West Deanery—Rev. Msgr. THOMAS M. FLYNN, V.F., *St. Aloysius, 37 W. Haddon Ave., Oaklyn, 08107.* Tel: 856-854-2352.

Central Deanery—Rev. JOHN F. BOURKE, V.F., *Our Lady of Mount Carmel, 178 W. White Horse Pike, Berlin, 08009.* Tel: 856-767-2563.

Cumberland Deanery—Rev. VINCENT G. CARPINELLI, *St. Mary, Morton Ave., Rosenhayn, 08352.* Tel: 856-451-8763.

Gloucester Deanery—Rev. JAMES P. CURRAN, V.F., *Our Lady of Lourdes, 500 Greentree Rd., Glassboro, 08028.* Tel: 856-881-0909.

Southwest Deanery—Rev. Msgr. ROCCO A. CONTINILLO, V.F., *Corpus Christi, 369 Georgetown Rd., Carneys Point, 08069.* Tel: 856-299-3833.

Diocesan Tribunal. Tel: 856-756-7900

Judicial Vicar—Rev. Msgr. LEONARD G. SCOTT, J.C.D., Ext. 6251; Fax: 856-756-0113.

Adjutant Judicial Vicars—Rev. EDWARD J. LIPINSKI.

Judicial Vicar for Second Instance Cases—Rev. Msgr. EUGENE J. FITZSIMMONS, J.C.D.

Assistant Judicial Vicar—Mr. GLENN CARROZZA.

Judges—Rev. Msgr. EDWARD D. ALLEYNE; Rev. Msgr. BERNARD P. HEWITT, V.F.; Rev. Msgr. JOHN R. LUBICKY; Rev. Msgr. EDWARD F. MULLEN; Rev. Msgr. THOMAS H. SHARKEY, J.C.D.; Revs. FRANCIS P. GAFFNEY, J.C.L.; JOSEPH A. SALERNO, J.C.L.

Notaries—CATHERINE FIOLKOWSKI; CATHERINE GOLDY; RANDEE HAYDEN; LEILA MONSERRATE.

Presbyteral Council—

President Delegate—Most Rev. JAMES L. SCHAD, D.D. Officers: Most Rev. NICHOLAS DIMARZIO, Pres.; Rev. Msgr. JOHN T. FREY, Exec. Sec.; Rev. JOSEPH D. WALLACE, Recording Sec.

Membership—Representatives by Seniority: Rev. Msgr. JOSEPH F. O'CONNELL; Rev. Msgr. JOSEPH P. JOYNES; Revs. JOHN T. FREY; KENNETH P. HALLAHAN; THOMAS J. BARCELLONA.

Retired Priest—Rev. Msgr. JAMES A. CARR.

Religious Priest—Vacant. Representatives by County: Rev. Msgr. DONALD D. VELOZO; Rev. Msgr. ROCCO A. CONTINILLO; Revs. WILLIAM P. BRENNAN; MARK R. CAVAGNARO; PATSY C. AMABILE; JOSEPH D. WALLACE. Appointed Members: Rev. Msgr. JOSEPH V. DIMAURO; Rev. Msgr. ROBERT T. MCDERMOTT, V.E.; Rev. Msgr. THOMAS J. MCINTYRE; Rev. Msgr. VICTOR S. MURO; Rev. Msgr. WILLIAM QUINN; Rev. Msgr. PATRICK M. TIERNEY; Revs. JAMES F. CHECCHIO; RONALD S. FALOTICO; HARRY J. JORDAN; RUSSELL L. ROCK. Ex Officio Members: Rev. Msgr. DAVID F. BUDNEY, V.G.; Rev. Msgr. JAMES R. TRACY, V.G.; Rev. Msgr. JOSEPH W. POKUSA, J.C.D. Consultants: Rev. JAMES F. BARRY; Rev. Msgr. CHARLES J. GIGLIO; Rev. Msgr. JAMES P. MCINTYRE; Rev. Msgr. LEONARD G. SCOTT, J.C.D.

College of Consultors—

President Delegate—Most Rev. JAMES L. SCHAD, D.D.

Executive Secretary—Rev. Msgr. CHARLES P. BARTH.

Members of the College—Rev. Msgr. DAVID F. BUDNEY, V.G.; Rev. Msgr. JOSEPH V. DIMAURO; Rev. Msgr. THOMAS J. MCINTYRE; Rev. Msgr. JOSEPH W. POKUSA, J.C.D.; Rev. Msgr. WILLIAM QUINN, V.F.; Rev. Msgr. PATRICK M. TIERNEY; Rev. Msgr. JAMES R. TRACY, V.G.; Rev. Msgr. DONALD D. VELOZO; Rev. Msgr. WILLIAM P. BRENNAN; Rev. Msgr. JAMES F. CHECCHIO; Rev. Msgr. HARRY J. JORDAN; Rev. Msgr. RUSSELL L. ROCK.

Diocesan Pastoral Council—

Ex Officio Members—Most Rev. NICHOLAS DIMARZIO; Rev. Msgr. DAVID F. BUDNEY; Rev. Msgr. JAMES R. TRACY.

Executive Committee—Sr. ALBERTINE CONWAY, S.S.J.; Mr. EDWARD C. BARRY; Ms. GERTRUDE EVANS; Ms. ANNE MARIE GAVIN; Ms. JEANNE LORGE; Mr. VINCENT PREMONE; Mr. JAMES SCHWARZWALDER; Ms. CAROLE SMITH; Ms. KATHI TERRY; Ms. HELEN YECCO.

Lay Representatives—Ms. ALICE K. BAKLEY; Mr. VINCENT J. BRUNO; Ms. GERALDINE BUSBY; Ms. BARBARA CHICANO; Mr. JEFFREY CORDNER; Mr. WILLIAM F. EZEKIEL, JR.; Ms. ROSE FORCINITO; Ms. CONSTANCE J. GLEDHILL; Mr. MARTIN IDLER; Mr. GERARD JABLONOWSKI; Ms. BERNADETTE LOVELAND; Mr. ROBERT NOTO; Mr. JAMES O'DONNELL, JR.; Ms. ELIZABETH PHELAN; Ms. VERA T. PIERCE; Ms. JUDITH POLISTINA; Mr. JON RANIA; Mr. EMIL VAN HOOK; Ms. RUTH L. WILKERSON.

Deacon Representatives—Deacons WILLIAM CARLUCCI; WILLIAM JOHNSON; PAUL LEE; JOSEPH W. LOUNGO; ROCCO A. MANGINO; WILLIAM V. NORQUIST; MIGUEL A. RIVERA.

Priest Representatives—Revs. A. ROBERT CAIRONE; EDWARD J. LIPINSKI; JAMES M. MAGGART; CADMUS D. MAZZARELLA; Rev. Msgr. VICTOR S. MURO; Revs. JOSEPH AN NGUYEN; LUONG T. PHAM.

Women Religious Representatives—Sr. RITA DEFLAVIA, F.M.I.H.M.; Sr. ANTOINE LAWLOR, I.H.M.; Sr. PHILOMMENA NOWICKA, L.S.I.C.; Sr. MARIE ST. JAMES, I.H.M.

Sisters' Council—Sr. MARIANNE MCCANN, M.P.F., Pres., *Paul VI Convent, Hopkins Rd., Haddon Twp., 08033.* Tel: 856-854-3678.

Diocesan Finance Council—Rev. Msgr. DAVID F. BUDNEY, V.G.; Rev. Msgr. JOSEPH V. DIMAURO; Rev. Msgr. JOSEPH P. HERRON; Rev. Msgr. RUSSELL L. ROCK; Rev. Msgr. PATRICK M. TIERNEY, V.F.; Mr. WILLIAM CONWAY; Mr. FRANCIS KARDOS; Mr. WILLIAM LEAHY; Mr. WILLIAM RENNIE.

Offices Reporting to Bishop

Office of Priest Personnel—Rev. GEORGE C. SEITER, Dir., Ext. 5261; Fax: 856-338-0826. Ms. MARCIA FIAMINGO, Coord., Ext. 5215.

Priest Personnel Board—Rev. Msgr. THOMAS J. MORGAN, Chm.; Revs. JOSEPH J. ADAMSON; JAMES P. CURRAN; WILLIAM H. HART; PAUL D. HARTE; ROBERT E. HUGHES; CADMUS D. MAZZARELLA; BRIAN E. O'NEILL; CARLTON C. STOEGBAUER.

Advanced Studies for Priests—Rev. Msgr. CHARLES J. GIGLIO, Ext. 5264.

Liaison with Retired Priests—Rev. Msgr. THOMAS A. GUENTHER, Ext. 6222.

Vicariate for Clergy Health Care—Rev. Msgr. JAMES P. MCINTYRE, V.E.

Clergy Health Panel—Rev. Msgr. JAMES P. MCINTYRE, V.E., Chm. Members: Rev. Msgr. JAMES A. CARR; Rev. Msgr. ROBERT T. MCDERMOTT, V.E.; Rev. LEWIS A. BATTISTI; Rev. Msgr. ANDREW MARTIN; Revs. THOMAS A. NEWTON; MARCEL TABONE; FRED VOLTAGGIO; Dr. JOSEPH W. SOKOLOWSKI.

Vocations Apostolate—Rev. JOSEPH T. SZOLACK, Dir., Ext. 5259. Sr. DOROTHY ALOISIO, Assoc. Dir., Ext. 5267.

Vocation Advisory Board—Rev. JOSEPH T. SZOLACK; Sr. DOROTHY ALOISIO; Rev. Msgr. ROBERT T. MCDERMOTT, V.E.; Rev. Msgr. THOMAS FITZSIMMONS; Revs. WILLIAM A. HODGE; KENNETH JOHNSTON; CADMUS D. MAZZARELLA; JOSEPH NGUYEN.

Assistant Vocation Directors for Recruitment—Revs. CHRISTOPHER BAKEY; CADMUS D. MAZZARELLA; RONAN B. MURPHY; ROBERT C. PASLEY; THOMAS M. ZITO.

Amicus—Rev. JOHN T. FREY, Chap.

Nazareth House—Rev. ROGER MCGRATH, Dir. Tel: 856-910-4900.

Friends of the Sacred Heart—Rev. Msgr. CHARLES P. BARTH, J.C.D., Chap. Tel: 856-663-1371.

Serra Clubs International—District 35: Mr. THOMAS HALPIN, Governor, Ext. 5425. Atlantic County East: Mr. JAMES STECHER, Pres.; Rev. BRENDAN V. SULLIVAN, Chap.; Cape May County: Mr. JOHN DWYER, Pres.; Rev. MARK CAVAGNARO, Chap.; Cumberland County: Mr. PHILIP BORGESE, Pres.; Rev. RAYMOND GORMLEY, Chap.

Office of the Vicar General for Administration—

Vicar General—Rev. Msgr. DAVID F. BUDNEY, P.A., V.G., *631 Market St., Camden, 08102,* Ext. 5206.

Agencies Reporting to the Vicar General for Administration

Department of Lay Personnel & Insurance Program; College of Consultors; Bishop's Representative to Labor Unions.—Rev. Msgr. THOMAS A. GUENTHER, Ext. 6222.

Office of Mission Awareness—Rev. Msgr. THOMAS A. GUENTHER, Dir., Ext. 6222. Rev. JOHN C. MUSCAT, Asst. Propagation of the Faith; Holy Childhood Association; Brazilian Missions. Rev. EDWARD WALSH, Ext. 6220. Catholic Relief Services; Operation Rice Bowl.

Department of Health Benefits—Meeker-Sharkey. Tel: 856-387-8000.

Special Collections—Rev. Msgr. JAMES F. CHECCHIO, Ext. 5207.

Special Committees—Deposit and Loan Fund; Parish Finance Councils; New Parish Development Committee.

Secretariat for Diocesan Parish Finances—

Secretary—Mr. WILLIAM J. MURRAY, Ext. 5234; Fax: 856-063-2655.

Accounting Services Comptroller—Mrs. LISA M. CILIBERTO, C.P.A., Ext. 5274.

Accounting—Mr. PAUL J. WORTHINGTON, Ext. 5280.

Management Information Services—Mrs. MARIANNE LINKA, Ext. 5232.

Director of Buildings—Mr. ARTHUR BASCIANO, A.I.A., Ext. 5277.

Diocesan Engineer—Mr. THOMAS BECHARD, Ext. 5289.

Director of Plant Facilities—Mr. ROBERT SPEAKMAN, Ext. 5235.

Department of Cemeteries—Mr. ARTHUR HEINTZ, Dir., Ext. 5411.

Department of Real Estate—Mr. KENNETH MCILVAINE, Ext. 5237.

Vicariate for Human Services

Vicar—Rev. Msgr. HARRY J. JORDAN, V.E., Dir., Ext. 5217; Fax: 856-338-0826.

Chief Financial Officer—Mr. FRANCIS J. KARDOS, *250 St. Mary's Dr., Cherry Hill, 08003.*

Executive Director, Health Affairs—Mr. MARTIN IDLER, *250 St. Mary's Dr., Cherry Hill, 08003.* Tel: 856-489-9536; Fax: 856-424-2896.

Executive Director—SUZANNE HEMP, A.C.S.W., L.C.S.W., *Catholic Charities, 2830 Marlton Pike, Pennsauken, 08105.* Tel: 856-663-9800; Fax: 856-663-0253.

Sacred Heart Residence for Priests—Rev. Msgr. CHARLES P. BARTH, Dir., *200 St. Mary's Dr., Cherry Hill, 08003.* Tel: 856-751-2010; Fax: 856-489-8999.

Vianney Villa Residence for Priests—Rev. WILLIAM D. TITMAS, Dir., *230 St. Mary's Dr., Cherry Hill, 08003.* Tel: 856-424-2035.

Hospital Ministry—Mr. MARTIN IDLER, Exec. Dir., *250 St. Mary's Dr., Cherry Hill, 08003.* Tel: 856-489-9536.

Prison Ministry—Ms. SUZANNE HEMP, A.C.S.W., L.C.S.W. Tel: 856-663-9800.

Health Affairs—Mr. MARTIN IDLER, Exec. Dir., *250 St. Mary's Dr., Cherry Hill, 08003.* Tel: 856-489-9536; Fax: 856-424-2896.

Long Term Care Facilities—

St. Mary's Catholic Home—Sr. BEATRIX WIECZOREK, L.S.I.C., L.N.H.A., Admin., *220 St. Mary Dr., Cherry Hill, 08003.* Tel: 856-424-9521.

Mater Dei Nursing Home—Sr. ANNE EBERSOLD, M.S.C., L.N.H.A., Admin., *176 Rte. 40, Newfield, 08344.* Tel: 856-358-2061.

Our Lady's Residence—ANNA TOSTI, L.N.H.A., Acting Admin., *1100 Clematis Ave., Pleasantville, 08232.* Tel: 609-646-2450.

Bishop McCarthy Residence—Sr. LUCY MAROOR, H.S.M., L.N.H.A., Admin., *1045 E. Chestnut Ave., Vineland, 08360.* Tel: 856-692-2850.

Manor at St. Mary's—Sr. FRANCIS M. SZYMANSKA, L.S.I.C., C.A.L.A., Admin., *220 St. Mary's Dr., Cherry Hill, 08003.* Tel: 856-424-3817.

Department of Housing—Ms. THERESA MOSTEIG, Acting Dir., *250 St. Mary's Dr., Cherry Hill, 08003.* Tel: 856-424-8429.

Victorian Towers—Ms. MAUREEL FARRELL, Office Mgr., *608 Washington St., Cape May, 08204.* Tel: 609-884-5883.

Village Apartments of St. Mary's—Ms. THERESA MOSTEIG, Office Mgr., *212 Lourdes Ct., Cherry Hill, 08003.* Tel: 856-424-7913.

Clinics—

St. Luke Catholic Medical Services—LESLY D'AMBOLA, M.D., Dir., *511 State St., Camden, 08102.* Tel: 856-365-4642.

Guadalupe Family Services—Sr. HELEN COLE, S.S.J., Dir., *511 State St., Camden, 08102.* Tel: 856-365-8081.

St. John Prenatal Clinic—Ms. PATRICIA A. CHICO, L.P.N., Coord., *6th and Erie Sts., Camden, 08102.* Tel: 856-757-7928.

Offices Reporting Jointly to the Executive Director for Catholic Charities & Executive Director for Health Affairs

Special Education—Ms. KATHLEEN FLYNN, Dir., *P.O. Box 709, Camden, 08101.* Tel: 856-756-7900, Ext. 6293.

Charter Schools—Rev. Msgr. HARRY J. JORDAN, Coord., Ext. 5217.

Catholic Charities—SUZANNE HEMP, A.C.S.W., L.C.S.W., Exec. Dir. Tel: 856-663-9800; Fax: 856-663-0253.

Offices Reporting to Catholic Charities

Executive Director—SUZANNE HEMP, A.C.S.W., L.C.S.W. Tel: 856-663-9800; Fax: 856-663-0253.

Camden County—SUZANNE HEMP, A.C.S.W., L.C.S.W., Exec. Dir., *2830 Marlton Pike, Pennsauken, 08105.* Tel: 856-663-9800. CEREIDA MEDINA, Coord., *1484-86 Mt. Ephraim Ave., Camden, 08104.* Tel: 856-964-2133. LAURA CARABALLO, Case Mgr. Aide, *St. Joseph Pro-Cathedral, 2907 Federal St., Camden, 08105.* Tel: 856-964-2776. LAURA CARABALLO, Case Mgr. Aide, *St. Anthony of Padua, 2814 River Rd., Camden, 08105.* Tel: 856-963-5884., *Stratford Office (Camden County Outreach), 39 Hunt Ave., Stratford, 08104.* Tel: 856-627-1226.

Atlantic County—Sr. GRACE NOLAN, R.S.M., B.A., Coord., *9 N. Georgia Ave., Atlantic City, 08401.* Tel: 609-345-3448.

Cape May County—DAWN THOMPSON, B.S.W., Coord., *1304 Hwy. 47 S., Rio Grande, 08242.* Tel: 609-886-2662.

Cumberland County—JOHN DESPARROIS, B.A., C.S.W., Coord., *810 Montrose Ave., Vineland, 08360.* Tel: 856-691-1841.

Gloucester County—ROBERT SKRZOT, B.A., Coord., *1200 Delsea Dr., Ste. One, Westville, 08093.* Tel: 856-845-9200.

Salem County—CLARENCE WILKINS, B.A., Coord., *14-16 W. Main St., Penns Grove, 08069.* Tel: 856-299-1296.

Counseling Services—

Counseling Center Cape/Atlantic—MICHAEL MURPHY, L.C.S.W., B.D.C., Dir., *21 W. Verona Ave., Pleasantville, 08232.* Tel: 609-383-0909.

Counseling Center Camden/Gloucester—PATRICIA PEACH, M.A., L.M.F.T., Dir., *320 Memorial Ave., Gibbstown, 08027.* Tel: 856-224-0945.

Counseling Center at Newfield/Salem—SYLVIA LOUMEAU, L.C.S.W., Dir., *951 Main Rd., Vineland, 08360.* Tel: 856-697-0744.

Family Treatment of Addiction Center—Rev. FRANK X. HUDSON, L.C.S.W., C.A.D.C., Dir., *141 S. Black Horse Pike, Ste. 7, Blackwood, 08012.* Tel: 856-227-9002.

Crisis Pregnancy and Adoption Services—ANN GALLAGHER, L.C.S.W., Supvr., *810 Montrose Ave., Vineland, 08360.* Tel: 856-691-1841.

Project Rachel—(Post-Abortion Counseling and Support)—SYLVIA LOUMEAU, L.C.S.W., Coord., *St. Anne Rectory, 213 Woodbine Ave., Westville, 08093.* Tel: 856-697-1159. Rev. ANDREW J. BOLCAR, Moderator. Tel: 856-456-4136.

AIDS Ministry—Sr. RUTH HARKINS, I.H.M., M.A., Coord., *2830 Marlton Pike, Pennsauken, 08105.* Tel: 856-663-0085.

Migration and Refugee Services—Mr. TUAN "TIMMY" NGUYEN, Dir., *1845 Haddon Ave., Camden, 08103.* Tel: 856-756-0070.

Legal Assistance to the Poor & Immigration Services—VINCENT G. GUEST, J.D., *Camden Center for Law and Social Justice, 511 State St., Camden, 08102.* Tel: 856-966-8896.

Ladies of Charity—Mrs. KATALINA UYEHARA, *167 N. Mansfield Blvd., Cherry Hill, 08034.* Tel: 856-795-4340. Rev. JAMES J. DURKIN, Spiritual Dir. Tel: 856-783-5555.

St. Vincent De Paul Society—Mrs. THELMA REPASS, Pres., *1230 Old Black Horse Pike, Blackwood, 08012.* Tel: 856-227-4684. Rev. FRANK GRAMIGNA, Spiritual Dir. Tel: 856-547-2313.

Representative to Archbishop Damiano School and St. John of God—Rev. Msgr. HARRY J. JORDAN, Ext. 5217.

Chaplaincy Apostolates—

Office of the Vicar General of Pastoral Life

Vicar General—Rev. Msgr. JAMES R. TRACY, Ph.D., V.G., *1845 Haddon Ave., Camden, 08103,* Ext. 6208; Fax: 856-225-0096.

Offices Reporting to the Vicar General for Pastoral Life—

Vicar for Religious—Very Rev. STEPHEN LAROSA, O.S.A. Tel: 856-697-9660.

Diocesan Delegate for Women Religious—Sr. JUDY MERTZ, S.C., Ext. 6289.

Vicariate for Catholic Schools—Rev. Msgr. THOMAS J. MCINTYRE, V.E., Vicar. Tel: 856-667-2440.

Assistant Vicar—Rev. Msgr. RUSSELL L. ROCK. Tel: 856-858-4900.

Superintendent of Schools—DAVID T. COGHLAN, Ph.D., Ext. 6288; Fax: 856-756-0225.

Assistant Superintendent of Schools—Sr. STELLA LOTZ, S.S.J, Ext. 6256.

Assistant Superintendent for Religious Education—Sr. ANTOINE THERESE LAWLOR, I.H.M, Ext. 6264.

Assistant Superintendent for Educational Services—Sr. ST. EUGENE FIORINO, O.S.F., Ext. 6271.

Assistant Superintendent for Educational Programs—Sr. ROSE DIFLURI, I.H.M., Ext. 6288.

Board of Education—Mrs. HELEN NOTO, Pres.

Parent-Teacher Association—Rev. JAMES P. CURRAN, Moderator. Tel: 856-881-0909. Mrs. RAE O'NEAL, Pres., *702 N. New St., Clayton, 08312.* Tel: 856-881-7185.

Secretariate for Evangelization and Catechetical Formation

Secretary—MICHAEL E. STEIER, D.Min., Ext. 6287; Fax: 856-756-0225.

Continuing Education & Spiritual Formation of Priests (CESF)—Rev. ROGER E. MCGRATH, Dir. Tel: 856-910-4900.

Permanent Diaconate—(Preparation)—Rev. FREDERICK G. LINK, Dir., Ext. 5252.

Office of Lay Leadership Development—MICHAEL E. STEIER, D.Min., Dir., Ext. 6287.

Office of Evangelization and Adult Faith Formation—Dr. FRANCIS BLEE, Ph.D., Dir., Ext. 6227.

R.C.I.A. Office—Rev. JOSEPH ADAMSON, Dir., Ext. 6247.

R.C.I.A. Commission—Rev. JOSEPH ADAMSON, Chm., Ext. 6247.

Campus Ministry—Rev. MICHAEL MANNION, S.T.L., M.A., Coord. Tel: 856-225-1077.

Office of Youth Ministry and Young Adult Catechesis—Rev. THOMAS J. BARCELLONA, Moderator, Ext. 6219; Fax: 856-756-0297.

Scouting—Rev. ALBERT E. HARSHAW, Chap.; Mr. ANSON WAGER, Chm. Tel: 856-547-3197.

Catholic Family Health and Recreation Center—Mr. JOHN MILLER, Dir., *P.O. Box 250, Blackwood, 08012.* Tel: 856-227-1359.

Office of Children's Catechesis—Sr. MARY BETH COYLE, I.H.M., Dir., Ext. 6284.

Media Center—Ms. CONNIE TEESDALE, Dir., Ext. 6346.

Secretariat for Parish Life and Worship

Secretary—Deacon LEO MCBLAIN, Ext. 6257.

Permanent Diaconate—(Post Ordination)—Rev. FREDERICK LINK, Dir., Ext. 5252.

Office of Family Life—Deacon LEO MCBLAIN, Exec. Dir., Ext. 6257; Fax: 856-964-3401.

Family Life Ministries—Mr. STEVEN BOZZA, Dir., Ext. 6464.

Marriage and Family Enrichment—Mr. STEVEN BOZZA, Ext. 6464.

Natural Family Planning—CECILIA LECHEVALLIER, Ext. 6315.

Chastity Education—MARY ANN CHEZIK, Ph.D., Ext. 6314.

Singles Never Married—TERRI GILLESPIE, Ext. 6242.

Fertility—Mr. STEVEN BOZZA, Ext. 6464.

L.I.F.E. Training—MARY KOENKE, Ext. 6297.

Marriage Preparation—Rev. PAUL D. HARTE, Coord., Ext. 6202.

Office of Social Concerns—

Pro Life—JOYCE LIVELY, Dir., Ext. 6292.

Rachel's Vineyard—

Justice and Peace—

Legislative Issues—

Community Affairs—Rev. EDWARD J. WALSH, Ext. 6220.

Office of Worship—Rev. ROBERT E. HUGHES, Dir., Ext. 5248.

School of Liturgy—Mrs. TRUDY CRANSTON, Coord., Ext. 5248.

Diocesan Music Office—Mr. JON RANIA, Dir., Ext. 5355.

Liturgical Commission—Revs. JOHN H. BURTON, Chm. THOMAS S. DONIO; ROBERT E. HUGHES; THOMAS A. NEWTON; ROBERT C. PASLEY; PAUL A. OLSZEWSKI; Ms. PATRICIA INNOCENZO; Dr. THEODORE KIEFER; Mr. JON RANIA; Ms. JOAN SANDEL.

Office of Ecumenical and Interreligious Affairs—Rev. JOSEPH D. WALLACE, Coord., Ext. 6370.

Commission on Ecumenical and Interreligious Affairs—Rev. Msgr. EUGENE J. FITZSIMMONS, J.C.D., Chm. Tel: 856-858-1313.

St. Pius X Spiritual Life Center—Rev. Msgr. LOUIS A. MARUCCI, Exec. Dir.; Rev. CADMUS D. MAZZARELLA, Spiritual Dir.; Mr. JOHN SANDERS, Mgmt. Dir., *P.O. Box 216, 1840 Peter Cheeseman Rd., Blackwood, 08012.* Tel: 856-227-1436; Fax: 856-227-2907.

Secretariate for Special Ministries

Secretary—Sr. JUDY MERTZ, S.C., Ext. 6289.

Office of Black Ministry—Deacon WILLIAM JOHNSON, Dir., Ext. 6363.

Office of Ethnic Ministries—Rev. RONALD S. FALOTICO. Tel: 609-641-0285.

Office of Spanish Apostolate—Rev. Msgr. VICTOR S. MURO, Dir., *414 S. 8th St., Vineland, 08360.* Tel: 856-691-5992; Fax: 856-691-5522.

Office of Deaf Ministry—Rev. BRIAN E. O'NEILL. Tel: 856-429-1330.

Office of Men's Ministry—Rev. THOMAS A. NEWTON. Tel: 856-228-3311.

Office of Women's Ministry—

Charismatic Renewal—Rev. Msgr. JAMES P. MCINTYRE, Moderator; Deacon JOSEPH COSTELLO, Diocesan Liaison. Tel: 609-522-6586.

Marian Commission—Rev. WILLIAM A. HODGE, Chm., *St. Nicholas of Tolentine, 1409 Pacific Ave., Atlantic City, 08401.* Tel: 609-344-1040.

Legion of Mary—Rev. WILLIAM A. HODGE, Spiritual Dir. Tel: 609-344-1040.

Holy Name Society—Rev. JEROME C. ROMANOWSKI, Dir., *St. Mary, 256 Dutch Mill Rd., P.O. Box M, Malaga, 08328.* Tel: 856-694-2576.

Cursillo/Spanish Cursillo—Rev. ALVERO DIAZ, Spiritual Dir. Tel: 856-691-9077.

Offices Reporting to the Moderator of the Curia

Moderator of the Curia—Rev. Msgr. JAMES F. CHECCHIO, J.C.D., Ext. 5207.

Vicariate for Pastoral Planning and Budgeting—Rev. Msgr. CHARLES J. GIGLIO, Ph.D., V.E., Ext. 5264.

Pastoral Planning—SHARON A. TUMULTY, Ph.D., Dir., Ext. 5275.

Budgeting—EDWARD J. LOCASALE, C.P.A., Ext. 5278.

Pastoral Statistics and Data—Rev. JAMES F. BARRY, Coord., Ext. 5265.

Office of Development—Rev. Msgr. LOUIS A. MARUCCI, Dir., Ext. 5244.

House of Charity/Bishop's Annual Appeal—

Fund for Educational Development—

Inter-Parochial Fund—

Jubilate Deo Chorale and Orchestra—Rev. Msgr. LOUIS A. MARUCCI, Exec. Dir., Ext. 5256. Rev. Msgr. CARL J. MARUCCI, Conductor.

Stewardship—Rev. JAMES J. DURKIN. Tel: 856-691-7526.

Office of Communications—Rev. Msgr. JAMES F. CHECCHIO, Ext. 5207.

Office of Public Relations—Mr. ANDREW WALTON, Ext. 5282.

Offices Reporting to the Chancellor and Episcopal Vicar for Canonical Affairs

Chancellor and Episcopal Vicar for Canonical Affairs—Rev. Msgr. JOSEPH W. POKUSA, J.C.D., Ext. 5216.

Human Resources—Mr. JOHN J. RAFTERY, Dir., Ext. 5203.

Consultative Councils—

Censor Liborum—

Diocesan Historian—Rev. JAMES BETZ. Tel: 856-467-0037.

Diocesan Newspaper—*"The Catholic Star Herald", P.O. Box 709, Camden, 08103.* Tel: 856-756-7900; Fax: 856-756-7938.

Executive Editor—Rev. JOSEPH D. WALLACE, Ext. 6220.

Managing Editor—Mr. CARL D. PETERS, Ext. 6218.

CLERGY, PARISHES, MISSIONS AND PAROCHIAL SCHOOLS

CITY OF CAMDEN

(Camden County)

1—IMMACULATE CONCEPTION CATHEDRAL (1864), Rev. Msgr. Charles J. Giglio; Rev. Michael T. Mannion. In res., Rev. Albert E. Harshaw.

Res., 642 Market St., 08102. Tel: 856-964-1580; Fax: 856-757-0438. [CEM]

2—ST. ANTHONY OF PADUA (1945), Revs. Paul Breslin, O.F.M.; Todd Carpenter, O.F.M.; Deacon Felix Miranda.

Res., 2818 River Ave., 08105. Tel: 856-963-5884; Fax: 856-635-1286.

School—Tel: 856-966-6791; Fax: 856-966-1616. Mrs. Linda Meehan, Prin.

Lay Teachers 9; Students 206.

Catechesis/Religious Programs—Students 153.

3—ST. BARTHOLOMEW'S (1940) (African-American), Rev. Wayne Patrick Lavin.

Res., 751 Kaighns Ave., 08103. Tel: 856-365-0573; Fax: 856-365-0744.
Catechesis/Religious Programs—Students 38.

4—HOLY NAME (1913), Revs. Gerald J. Fitzpatrick, S.J.; Jeffery P. Puthoff, S.J.; Sr. Linda Stilling, S.S.N.D., Pastoral Assoc. In res., Revs. Charles G. Gonzalez, S.J.; Richard G. Malloy, S.J.; Francis X. Moan, S.J.
Res., 522 State St., 08102-1919. Tel: 856-963-1621; Fax: 856-338-0793.
School—Tel: 856-365-7930; Fax: 856-365-8041. Mrs. Patricia Munyan, Prin.
Sisters 1; Lay Teachers 12; Students 223.
Catechesis/Religious Programs—Students 335.
Convent—517 State St., Tel: 856-964-1233. Sisters of St. Joseph (Chestnut Hill) School Sisters of Notre Dame (Baltimore), Tel: 856-488-3540.

5—ST. JOAN OF ARC (1920), Revs. Kenneth P. Hallahan, S.T.D.; Gerald C. Marable; Deacon Emil Ralbusky.
Res., 3107 Alabama Rd., 08104. Tel: 856-962-8642; Fax: 856-962-7123.

6—ST. JOSEPH'S (1892) (Polish), Rev. Msgr. Edward H. Bucia; Rev. Piotr Szamocki.
Res., 1010 Liberty St., 08104. Tel: 856-963-1285; Fax: 856-963-2466. [CEM]

7—ST. JOSEPH'S PRO-CATHEDRAL (1893), Rev. Msgr. Robert T. McDermott; Sr. Margaret Mary Schmicker, O.S.F., Pastoral Min.; Sr. Connie Trainor, S.S.J., D.R.E.; Sr. Clarissa Vazquez, S.S.T., Hispanic Min., Tel: 856-964-1227; Ms. Patricia Slater, Director, Romero Ctr. In res., Rev. Andrew E. Martin.
Res., 2907 Federal St., 08105. Tel: 856-964-2776; Fax: 856-964-0044.
School—Tel: 856-964-4336; Fax: 856-964-1080. Mrs. Kathleen Shiflet, Prin.
Lay Teachers 18; Students 284.
Nursery School—17 Church St., Tel: 856-963-9502; Fax: 856-963-0103.
Sisters 2; Children 65. Franciscan Sisters of the Infant Jesus. Sr. Angela D'Alessandro, F.M.I.J., Supr.
Catechesis/Religious Programs—Tel: 856-541-4944.
Students 217.

8—OUR LADY OF MOUNT CARMEL/FATIMA (1903) (Hispanic-Italian), Rev. Salvatore A. Scuderi, M.SS.CC.; Deacons Miguel Rivera; Aladino Velez. In res., Bro. David Graber, M.SS.CC.
Res., 832 S. 4th St., 08103. Tel: 856-541-7618; Fax: 856-541-2835.

9—SACRED HEART (1885), Rev. Michael Doyle. In res., Rev. Arthur T. Anderson.
Res., 1739 Ferry Ave., 08104. Tel: 856-966-6700; Fax: 856-756-0102.
School—Fourth & Jaspers Sts., 08104. Tel: 856-963-1341; Fax: 856-963-3551. Mrs. Janet Williams, Prin.
Sisters 1; Lay Teachers 12; Students 262. Records for St. George kept at Sacred Heart, Camden. Records for Sts. Peter and Paul kept at the Cathedral of the Immaculate Conception, Camden. Records for St. John the Baptist kept at St. Joseph Pro-Cathedral, Camden.
Catechesis/Religious Programs—Students 262.

OUTSIDE THE CITY OF CAMDEN

Absecon, Atlantic Co., St. Elizabeth Ann Seton (1975), Rev. Carlton C. Stoegbauer; Deacon Joseph Becker.
Res., 591 New Jersey Ave., 08201. Tel: 609-641-1480; Fax: 609-641-7396.
School—Assumption Regional School, Pomona. See separate listing. Tel: 609-652-7134; Fax: 609-965-4149.
Catechesis/Religious Programs—Tel: 609-641-7043; Fax: 609-641-5709.
Students 660.

Atco, Camden Co., Assumption (1947), Revs. John O'Leary; Thomas Barcellona; Deacons Charles McAleer; Charles Smith.
Parish Office: 318 Carl Hasselhan Dr., 08004. Tel: 856-767-0719; Fax: 856-753-7917.
Res., 2131 Cooper Rd., 08004. Tel: 856-767-0848; Fax: 856-753-7917.
School—Tel: 856-767-0569; Fax: 856-753-7917. Mrs. Paula Angiletta, Prin., Tel: 856-767-0569.
Lay Teachers 10; Students 213.
Catechesis/Religious Programs—Tel: 856-767-3414.
Students 465.

Atlantic City, Atlantic Co.,

1—HOLY SPIRIT, (1908), Rev. J. Overton Jones, Admin.; Deacon Angel Vega.
Res., c/o 108 N. Pennsylvania Ave., 08401. Tel: 609-345-1786.

2—ST. MICHAEL'S, (1904) (Italian), Rev. Michael H. D'Amico; Deacon Raymond Ferrario.
Res., 10 N. Mississippi Ave., 08401. Tel: 609-344-8536; Fax: 609-344-5304.

3—ST. MONICA'S, (1925), Rev. J. Overton Jones.
Res., 108 N. Pennsylvania Ave., 08401. Tel: 609-345-1786; Fax: 609-344-5090.
Catechesis/Religious Programs—Students 52.

4—ST. NICHOLAS OF TOLENTINE, (1855), Revs. William A. Hodge; Joseph V. Jurkowski.
Res., 1409 Pacific Ave., 08401. Tel: 609-344-1040; Fax: 609-344-2471.
Catechesis/Religious Programs—Students 8.

5—OUR LADY STAR OF THE SEA, (1894), Revs. Patrick J. Brady; Paul C. Wise; Joseph Luong Pham; Deacon James Tully.
Res., 2651 Atlantic Ave., 08401. Tel: 609-345-1878; Fax: 609-348-0248.
School—Tel: 609-345-0648. Sr. Mary Shamus, R.S.M., Prin. & Supr.
Sisters 6; Lay Teachers 9; Students 332.
Catechesis/Religious Programs—Students 304.
Convent—15 N. California Ave., Tel: 609-347-0434. Sisters of Mercy

Audubon, Camden Co., Church of the Holy Maternity (1957), Rev. Michael J. McGilley.
Res., 431 W. Nicholson Rd., 08106. Tel: 856-547-0444; Fax: 856-547-0045.
School—Annunication Regional School, Bellmawr, Tel: 609-931-0122; Fax: 609-931-0155.
Catechesis/Religious Programs—Students 181.

Avalon, Cape May Co., Maris Stella (1961), Rev. Msgr. Patrick M. Tierney.
Res., 5012 Dune Dr., 08202. Tel: 609-967-3746; Fax: 609-967-8172.
School—St. Joseph Regional School, Sea Isle City. See separate listing. Tel: 609-263-4296.

Barrington, Camden Co., St. Francis de Sales (1955), Rev. Francis J. Gramigna; Deacon Michael Harkins. In res., Rev. Msgr. William F. Poyatt.
Res., 199 Willmont Ave., 08007. Tel: 856-547-2313; Fax: 856-547-8225.
School—St. Francis de Sales Regional School. See separate listing. Tel: 856-547-7958; Fax: 856-547-0472.
Catechesis/Religious Programs—Students 209.
Convent—424 Browning Rd., Bellmawr, 08031. Tel: 856-931-8973.

Bellmawr, Camden Co., Annunciation (1951), Rev. William F. Ryan; Deacon Michael J. DiGirolamo.
Res., 601 W. Browning Rd., 08031. Tel: 609-931-6307; Fax: 609-931-0155.
School—Tel: 856-931-0122; Fax: 856-931-4390. Sr. Marie St. James, I.H.M., Prin.
Sisters 3; Lay Teachers 11; Students 370.
Catechesis/Religious Programs—Tel: 856-931-8590.
Students 225.
Convent—603 W. Browning Rd., Tel: 856-931-7192. Sisters Servants of Immaculate Heart of Mary

Mary, Mother of the Church (1965), Rev. Msgr. Joseph C. Downing. In res., Rev. Robert E. Hughes; Deacon Ron Olesiewicz.
Res., 20 Braisington Ave., 08031. Tel: 856-931-0204; Fax: 856-933-5120.
School—St. Francis de Sales Regional, Barrington. See separate listing. Tel: 856-547-7958.
Catechesis/Religious Programs—Students 85.

Berlin, Camden Co., Our Lady of Mt. Carmel (1903), Revs. Fred Voltaggio; Laserian I. Nwoga; Deacon Joseph Beebe.
Res., 178 W. White Horse Pike, 08009. Tel: 856-767-2563; Fax: 856-767-8791.
School—Our Lady of Mt. Carmel Regional School. See separate listing. Tel: 856-767-1751; Fax: 856-767-1293.
Catechesis/Religious Programs—Tel: 856-767-1537; Fax: 856-767-3304.
Students 520.

Blackwood, Camden Co., St. Agnes (1946), Rev. Msgr. Joseph V. DiMauro; Revs. Thomas A. Newton; Michael G. Spagnolo; Deacons Henry S. Custodio; Joseph Buccilli; John Werner. In res., Rev. Msgr. John R. Lubicky, (Retired).
Res., 701 Little Gloucester Rd., 08012. Tel: 856-228-4331; Fax: 856-227-0743.
School—St. Agnes Regional School, Blackwood. See separate listing. Tel: 856-228-7076; Fax: 856-228-7527.
Catechesis/Religious Programs—200 Coles Rd., 08012. Tel: 856-227-0555; Fax: 856-228-4920.
Students 1,054.

St. Jude's (1961), Rev. Msgr. Patrick S. Chiarilli; Rev. John C. Muscat; Deacons William J. Drum; Michael McDonaugh.
Res., 402 S. Black Horse Pike, 08012. Tel: 856-227-0572; Fax: 856-227-1276.
School—St. Jude Regional School, Blackwood. See separate listing. Tel: 856-227-4442; Fax: 856-401-1622.
Catechesis/Religious Programs—Tel: 856-227-8558.
Students 425.

Blue Anchor, Camden Co., St. Lucy's (1925), Rev. Robert J. Gregorio, S.T.D.
Res., 250 S. Rte. 73, 08037-9805. Tel: 609-561-6116; Fax: 609-561-9305. [CEM]
School—St. Joseph Regional School, Hammonton. See separate listing.
Catechesis/Religious Programs—Students 228.
Mission—Cedar Brook, Camden Co., Sacred Heart, (1904).

Bridgeton, Cumberland Co., Immaculate Conception (1874), Revs. James P. Rush; John D. Wasilewski; Deacons C. J. Achee; Carmen Bischer. In res., Revs. John P. Connor; Robert P. Weber.
Res., 312 N. Pearl St., 08302. Tel: 856-451-0254; Fax: 856-451-7842. [CEM]
School—Immaculate Conception Regional School, Bridgeton. See separate listing. Tel: 856-451-2134.

St. Teresa of Avila, Cumberland, (1961), Rev. Msgr. Stanley E. Kloskowski; Deacon William Johnson. In res., Rev. Daniel A. DiNardo.
Res., 46 Central Ave., 08302. Tel: 856-455-2323; Fax: 856-455-7291.
School—Immaculate Conception Regional School, Bridgeton. See separate listing. Tel: 856-451-2134.

Brigantine, Atlantic Co., St. Thomas (1958), Rev. Msgr. Joseph P. Joynes; Rev. James Dabrowski. In res., Rev. Joseph A. Perreault.
Res., 331 8th St. S., 08203. Tel: 609-266-2123; Fax: 609-266-6416.
School—Tel: 609-266-3154.
Lay Teachers 10; Students 165.
Catechesis/Religious Programs—Students 280.

Brooklawn, Camden Co., St. Maurice's (1955), Rev. Thomas E. Ploude.
Res., 401 Community Rd., 08030. Tel: 856-456-9039; Fax: 856-456-0161.
Catechesis/Religious Programs—Students 46.

Cape May, Cape May Co., Our Lady Star of the Sea (1878), Rev. Msgr. Timothy A. Ryan; Rev. Glenn Hartman.
Res., 525 Washington St., 08204. Tel: 609-884-5311; Fax: 609-884-0162. [CEM]
School—Our Lady Star of the Sea School, Cape May. See separate listing. Tel: 609-884-4437; Fax: 609-884-4788.
Catechesis/Religious Programs—Students 235.
Chapel—Cape May Point, St. Agnes.

Cape May Court House, Cape May Co., Our Lady of the Angels (1956), Rev. Edward D. Lyons. In res., Rev. Max S. Fasciglione.
Res., 106 Mechanic St., P.O. Box 324, 08210. Tel: 609-465-5245; Fax: 609-465-7822.
School—Bishop McHugh Regional Catholic School, Dennis Township.

Carneys Point, Salem Co., Corpus Christi (1966), Rev. Msgr. Rocco A. Continillo, V.F.
Res., 369 Georgetown Rd., 08069. Tel: 856-299-3833; Fax: 856-299-3834.
School—Bishop Guilfoyle Regional Catholic School, Carney's Point.
Catechesis/Religious Programs—Students 144.

Cedarville, Cumberland Co., St. Michael's (1942), Rev. William James Bleiler.
Res., 367 Main St., P.O. Box 327, 08311. Tel: 856-447-3480; Fax: 856-447-3480.
School—Immaculate Conception Regional School, Bridgeton. See separate listing.
Catechesis/Religious Programs—Students 44.
Mission—Port Norris, Cumberland Co., St. Anthony, 1560 Main St., 08349.
Stations—NJ State Medium Security Prison, Bayside Prison, Rte. 47, Leesburg, 08327. Tel: 856-785-0040, Ext. 242; Laurel Lake, Our Lady of the Lake Chapel, Battle Ln., Laurel Lake, 08332.; Delmont, Southern State Correctional Facility.

Cherry Hill, Camden Co.,

1—ST. MARY'S, (1961), Revs. John C. Killeen; Joseph Wallace.
Res., 2001 Springdale Rd., 08003. Tel: 856-424-1454; Fax: 856-424-8270.
School—Holy Rosary Regional School, Cherry Hill. See separate listing. Tel: 856-428-4855; Fax: 856-428-9152.
Catechesis/Religious Programs—Tel: 856-424-2679.
Students 550.

2—HOLY ROSARY, (1958), Rev. Michael M. Signiski; Deacon Raymond Radziak. In res., Rev. Msgr. Leonard G. Scott.
Res., 99 Burnt Mill Rd., 08003. Tel: 856-428-2382 (Res.); 856-428-9456 (Office); Fax: 856-428-9152.
School—Tel: 856-428-4855; Fax: 856-428-0249. Mrs. Patricia Connell, Prin.
Lay Teachers 9; Students 185.
Catechesis/Religious Programs—Mrs. Anita D'Imperio, D.R.E.
Students 250.
Convent—Tel: 856-429-1364. Sisters of Saint Joseph

3—St. Peter Celestine, (1961), Rev. Msgr. Thomas J. McIntyre; Revs. Michael J. Field; Donald F. Trinkle; Deacons W. Leo McBlain; William Watts; William Iannuzzi; Paul Lee.
Res., 402 N. Kings Hwy., 08034. Tel: 856-667-2440; Fax: 856-482-0332.
School—Tel: 856-667-3034; Fax: 856-667-9160. Mrs. Camille Forrest, Prin.
Sisters of St. Joseph (Chestnut Hill, PA) 2; Lay Teachers 25; Students 333; Special Educ. Students 24.
Catechesis/Religious Programs—Tel: 856-667-4250.
Students 486.

4—St. Pius X, (1961), Revs. William P. Brennan; Brian E. O'Neill; Deacon Peter J. Powell. In res., Rev. Msgr. James R. Tracy.
Res., 344 Kresson Rd., 08034. Tel: 856-429-1330; Fax: 856-429-8679.
School—Christ the King Regional School, Haddonfield. See separate listing.
Catechesis/Religious Programs—Tel: 856-428-9207.
Students 750.

5—St. Thomas More, (1968), Rev. Msgr. David F. Budney; Rev. Joseph Adamson.
Res., 1439 Springdale Rd., 08003. Tel: 856-424-3212; Fax: 856-424-2411.
School—Holy Rosary Regional School, Cherry Hill. See separate listing. Tel: 856-428-4855.
Catechesis/Religious Programs—Students 270.

6—Queen of Heaven, (1955), Rev. Msgr. Edward D. Alleyne; Rev. Raymond P. Gormley; Deacons Charles C. Reiss; James H. Rocks. In res., Revs. Thomas H. Jarka; David E. Beebe.
Res., 700 W. Marlton Pike, 08002. Tel: 856-429-3334; Fax: 856-795-3318.
School—Tel: 856-428-2890; Fax: 856-428-4640. Sr. Rita Marotta, I.H.M., Prin.
Sisters 6; Lay Teachers 9; Students 204.
Catechesis/Religious Programs—Students 230.
Convent—Queen of Heaven Convent, 10 Massachusetts Ave., 08002. Tel: 856-428-8818.

Clayton, Gloucester Co., St. Catherine's (1943), Rev. Edward F. Heintzelman; Deacon Matthew J. Hanrahan.
Res., 49 W. North St., 08312. Tel: 856-881-9155; Fax: 856-881-9166.
Preschool—(Children ages 2 1/2-5). Tel: 856-881-8707; Fax: 856-881-9820. Mrs. Lynne Holscher, Dir. Students 45.
School—51 W. North St., 08312. Tel: 856-881-0067; Fax: 856-863-0850. Miss Janice Bruni, Prin.
Lay Teachers 9; Students 220.

Collings Lakes, Atlantic Co., Our Lady of the Lakes (1976), Rev. Marjan L. Bober; Deacon Edward Freed.
Res., 19 Malaga Rd., 08094. Tel: 609-561-8313; Fax: 609-561-8374.
School—Notre Dame Regional School, Landisville. See separate listing.
Catechesis/Religious Programs—Tel: 609-561-3999.
Students 125.

Collingswood, Camden Co., St. John's (1903), Rev. Msgr. Martin J. Mannion; Rev. John Connors; Deacon Frank P. Gargin.
Res., 809 Park Ave., 08108. Tel: 856-858-0298; Fax: 856-858-2796.
School—Tel: 856-858-1562; Fax: 856-858-2943. Miss Joan Simpson, Prin.
Lay Teachers 16; Students 269.
Catechesis/Religious Programs—Students 305.

Delair, Camden Co., St. Veronica's (1961), Rev. James T. McCall.
Res., 8329 Holman Ave., 08110. Tel: 856-662-8050; Fax: 856-662-9477.
Catechesis/Religious Programs—Students 95.

Deptford, Gloucester Co., St. John Vianney (1971), Rev. Msgr. James J. Rynne; Deacon John Berstecher. In res., Rev. Frank Hudson.
Res., 2901 Good Intent Rd., 08096. Tel: 856-227-2623; Fax: 856-228-1823.
School—St. Agnes Regional School, Blackwood. See separate listing. Tel: 856-228-7076; Fax: 856-228-7527.
Catechesis/Religious Programs—Students 250.

Egg Harbor City, Atlantic Co., St. Nicholas (1864), Revs. Daniel M. Sherman; John Polentarutti, I.M.C.; Deacon Michael H. Guerrieri.
Res., 525 St. Louis Ave., 08215-2224. Tel: 609-965-0350; Fax: 609-804-1313.
School—526 Chicago Ave., Tel: 609-965-2398; Fax: 609-804-1658. Joan Dollinger, Prin.
Sisters 1; Lay Teachers 15; Students 171.
Catechesis/Religious Programs—Tel: 609-965-0720.
Students 260.

Egg Harbor Township, Atlantic Co., St. Katharine Drexel, Rev. Joseph R. Ferrara.
c/o St. Bernadette Rectory: 1421 New Rd., Northfield, 08225. Tel: 609-646-3499; Fax: 609-484-8345.

Elmer, Salem Co., St. Ann's (1961), Rev. Francis Gaffney, Admin.; Deacons Edward J. Harkins; Robert Fanelli.
Res., 115 Broad St., 08318. Tel: 856-358-3106; Fax: 856-358-3117.
School—St. Rose Regional School, Newfield. See separate listing.
Catechesis/Religious Programs—Students 90.

Franklinville, Gloucester Co., Nativity (1961), Rev. William F. Collins.
Res., P.O. Box 249, 08322. Tel: 856-694-2349; Fax: 856-694-4131.
School—St. Rose Regional School, Newfield. See separate listing.
Catechesis/Religious Programs—Students 231.

Gibbsboro, Camden Co., St. Andrew the Apostle (1963), Rev. Msgr. Ciaran P. O'Mearain; Rev. Robert W. Kunze; Deacon Paul Johnson. In res., Rev. Paul H. Trinh.
Res., 120 United States Ave., 08026. Tel: 856-784-3878; Fax: 856-435-7508.
School—Our Lady of Mt. Carmel Regional School, Berlin. See separate listing. Tel: 609-767-2563; Fax: 609-767-8791.
Catechesis/Religious Programs—Tel: 856-783-0550; Fax: 856-783-7935.
Students 923.

Gibbstown, Gloucester Co., St. Michael's (1940), Rev. John E. Bruni; Deacons James Kiley; Robert Willson.
Res., 313 Memorial Ave., 08027. Tel: 856-423-0007; Fax: 856-423-1445.
Catechesis/Religious Programs—Students 312.

Glassboro, Gloucester Co., St. Bridget's (1887) (Italian), Revs. Robert V. Smith; Peter A. McLaughlin; Sr. Dianne M. Durak, C.S.S.F., Pastoral Assoc.; Deacon Joseph W. Loungo.
Res., 125 Church St., 08028. Tel: 856-881-2753; Fax: 856-881-9697. [CEM]
School—St. Bridget's Regional School, Glassboro. See separate listing. Tel: 856-881-2578; Fax: 856-881-8771.
Catechesis/Religious Programs—Students 258.

Our Lady of Lourdes (1966), Revs. James P. Curran; Eldridge T. Evans; Deacons Nicholas Mortelliti; Michael J. Carter. In res., Rev. Msgr. James J. Gaffney, (Retired).
Res., 500 Greentree Rd., 08028. Tel: 856-881-0909; Fax: 856-881-5457.
School—St. Bridget Regional School, Glassboro. See separate listing.
Catechesis/Religious Programs—Tel: 856-881-1552.
Students 738.

Gloucester, Camden Co., St. Mary's (1848), Rev. Msgr. Harry J. Jordan; Revs. Bernard Gannon; Ronan B. Murphy; Deacon Frank Crosson.
Res., 426 Monmouth St., 08030. Tel: 856-456-0052; Fax: 856-456-1837. [CEM]
School—Tel: 856-456-0913; Fax: 856-456-7382. Sr. Nora Foley, O.P., Prin.
Dominican Sisters of Hope 3; Lay Teachers 13; Students 375.
Catechesis/Religious Programs—Students 254.

Haddonfield, Camden Co., Christ the King (1927), Rev. Msgr. Thomas J. Morgan; Rev. Daniel Rocco. In res., Rev. James Barry.
Res., 200 Windsor Ave., 08033. Tel: 856-429-1600; Fax: 856-429-2734.
School—Christ the King Regional School, Haddonfield. See separate listing. Tel: 856-429-2084; Fax: 856-429-4959.
Lay Teachers 28; Students 388.
Catechesis/Religious Programs—Tel: 856-354-5030.
Students 450.
Convent—134 Kings Hwy. W., 08033. Tel: 856-428-0824. St. Mary of the Angels Convent

Haddon Heights, Camden Co., St. Rose's (1896), Rev. Msgr. Richard J. Callahan; Revs. Edward M. Friel; Michael P. Hegarty; Deacons Frank A. Iula, M.D.; Gerald DeMuro.
Res., 300 Kings Hwy, 08035-1397. Tel: 856-547-0564; Fax: 856-547-7311.
School—Tel: 856-546-6166. Mrs. Kathryn Lange, Prin.
Sisters of St. Dominic (Newburgh, NY) 1; Lay Teachers 17; Students 399.
Catechesis/Religious Programs—Tel: 856-546-9326.
Students 540.

Haddon Township, Camden Co., St. Vincent Pallotti (1963), Rev. Msgr. John H. Casey. In res., Rev. Msgr. Russell L. Rock; Rev. Msgr. Eugene J. Fitzsimmons.
Res., 901 Hopkins Rd., Haddonfield, 08033. Tel: 856-858-1313; 1314; Fax: 856-869-9010.
Catechesis/Religious Programs—Students 200.

Hammonton, Atlantic Co., St. Anthony of Padua (1964), Rev. Joseph H. Burns; Deacon Rocco A. Mangino. In res., Rev. John M. Fleming.
Res., P.O. Box 1087, 285 Rte. 206, 08037. Tel: 609-561-3313; Fax: 609-567-7764.
School—St. Joseph Regional School, Hammonton. See separate listing. Tel: 908-704-2400.

St. Joseph's (1886), Revs. Louis Micca, S.A.C.; Michael Parente, S.A.C.; Robert Nolan, S.A.C.; Deacon Ismael Perez Tavarez.
Res., 226 French St., 08037. Tel: 609-561-0180; Fax: 609-561-6808. [CEM]
School—St. Joseph Regional School, Hammonton. See separate listing.

St. Martin de Porres (1962), Rev. John A. DelDuca. In res., Rev. Timothy L. Hubbs.
Res., 129 Park Ave., 08037. Tel: 609-561-4322; Fax: 609-561-4433.
School—St. Joseph Regional School, Hammonton. See separate listing. Tel: 609-704-2400.
Catechesis/Religious Programs—Students 320.

Landisville, Atlantic Co., Our Lady of Victories (1952), Rev. John J. Vignone; Deacon Joseph Perella.
Res., 202 N.W. Blvd., 08326. Tel: 856-697-1450; Fax: 856-697-3874.
School—Notre Dame Regional School, Landisville. See separate listing. Tel: 856-697-3456; Fax: 856-697-5114.
Catechesis/Religious Programs—Tel: 856-697-6320.
Students 126.

Lindenwold, Camden Co., St. Lawrence's (1896), Revs. William P. Graham; Stephen J. Ropposelli. In res., Rev. Zbigniew J. Jezierski.
Res., 100 South Ave., 08021. Tel: 856-627-2222; 627-7522; Fax: 856-627-8210.
School—Tel: 856-783-0710. Mrs. Lynn Domenico, Prin.
Lay Teachers 13; Students 240.
Catechesis/Religious Programs—Tel: 856-346-0902.
Students 305.

Linwood, Atlantic Co., Our Lady of Sorrows (1965), Revs. Malcolm C. McLeod, M.SS.CC.; John Perdue, M.SS.CC.
Res., 724 Maple, 08221. Tel: 609-927-1154; Fax: 609-927-0398.
Catechesis/Religious Programs—Tel: 609-927-0121.
Students 602.

Longport, Atlantic Co., Epiphany (1954), Rev. Msgr. Joseph P. Herron.
Res., 2801 Ventnor Ave., 08403. Tel: 609-822-8940; Fax: 609-822-1050.
School—Blessed Sacrament Regional School, Margate. See separate listing. Tel: 609-822-7105.

Magnolia, Camden Co., St. Gregory's (1955), Rev. Msgr. Joseph W. Pokusa; Rev. Msgr. Edward L. Korda; Rev. A. Robert Cairone; Deacon Leonard P. Carlucci.
Res., 340 E. Evesham Ave., 08049. Tel: 856-784-4090; Fax: 856-784-6371.
School—Our Lady of Grace Regional School, Somerdale. See separate listing. Tel: 856-784-0372.
Catechesis/Religious Programs—230 E. Evesham Ave., Tel: 856-784-1440.
Students 180.
Convent—230 E. Evesham Ave., 08049. Tel: 856-784-1576.

Malaga, Gloucester Co., St. Mary's (1961), Rev. Jerome C. Romanowski.
Res., Dutch Mill Rd., P.O. Box M, 08328. Tel: 856-694-2576; Fax: 856-694-4636.
School—Notre Dame Regional School, Newfield. See separate listing.
Catechesis/Religious Programs—Students 132.

Mantua, Gloucester Co., Incarnation (1956), Revs. Joseph A. Salerno; Paul A. Olszewski; Deacon Thomas F. O'Brien.
Res., 234 Shadow Pl., P.O. Box 295, 08051. Tel: 609-468-1314; Fax: 609-468-4886.
School—School St. Margaret Regional School, Woodbury Heights. See separate listing. Tel: 609-845-5200.
Catechesis/Religious Programs—Tel: 609-468-7566.
Students 830.

Margate, Atlantic Co., Blessed Sacrament (1945), Rev. Lewis A. Battisti. In res., Rev. Perry A. Cherubini.
Res., 11 N. Kenyon Ave., 08402. Tel: 609-822-7105; Fax: 609-822-3817.
School—Blessed Sacrament Regional School, Margate. See separate listing. Tel: 609-822-9243; Fax: 609-822-2036.
Catechesis/Religious Programs—Tel: 609-822-8810.
Students 241.

Convent—14 N. Jerome Ave., 08402. Tel: 609-822-5543. Sr. Kathryn Rush, O.S.F., Local Supr.

Marmora, Cape May Co., The Church of the Resurrection (1975), Revs. Mark R. Cavagnaro; Michael J. Matveenko.
Res., 200 W. Tuckahoe Rd., 08223. Tel: 609-390-0664; Fax: 609-390-8717.
School—Bishop McHugh Regional School, Cape May Court House, Tel: 609-624-1900.
Catechesis/Religious Programs—Tel: 609-390-2203.
Students 593.

Mays Landing, Atlantic Co., St. Vincent de Paul (1906), Revs. John F. Sugrue; Edward J. Maher; Deacon Richard Wigglesworth.
Res., 114 Rte. 50, 08330. Tel: 609-625-2124; Fax: 609-625-8718. [CEM]
School—Tel: 609-625-1565; Fax: 609-625-4703. Miss Linda Pirolli, Prin.
Lay Teachers 10; Students 224.
Catechesis/Religious Programs—5809 Main St., 08330. Tel: 609-625-1567.
Students 355.
Convent—5807 Main St., 08330. Tel: 609-625-1566. Sisters of St. Joseph of Chestnut Hill
Mission—Dorothy, Atlantic Co., St. Bernard. [CEM]

Merchantville, Camden Co., St. Peter's (1903), Revs. Anthony J. Manuppella; John A. Cauagnaro; Thomas Zito; John J. Byrnes; Deacons Peter J. Gilmartin; Ray Ellis. In res., Rev. George C. Seiter.
Res., 43 W. Maple Ave., 08109. Tel: 856-663-1373; Fax: 856-488-0647.
School—Tel: 856-665-5789; Fax: 856-665-4943. Sr. Alice Ivanyo, M.P.F., Prin.
Lay Teachers 18; Students 440.
Catechesis/Religious Programs—Sheila O'Boyle, C.R.E.
Students 369.

Millville, Cumberland Co., St. Mary Magdalen's (1864), Revs. Frederick G. Link; David V. Minniti; Deacon Hipolito Lagares.
Res., 621 Dock St., 08332. Tel: 856-825-0021; Fax: 856-825-4338. [CEM]
School—7 W. Powell St., 08332. Tel: 856-825-3600; Fax: 856-825-9119. Sr. Armida Fabela, M.D.P.V.M., Prin.
Sisters 9; Lay Teachers 9; Students 307.
Catechesis/Religious Programs—Students 212.
Convent—3 W. Powell St., 08332. Tel: 856-327-2235. Missionary Daughters of the Most Pure Virgin Mary Sr. Armida Fabela, M.D.P.V.M., Supr.

St. John Bosco (1966), In res., Rev. William C. Pierce; Deacon Francis Duffy.
Res., 2 Hillcrest Ave., 08332. Tel: 856-825-1513; Fax: 856-765-9489.
Catechesis/Religious Programs—Students 175.

Minotola, Atlantic Co., St. Michael's (1902), Rev. John J. Vignone.
Mailing Address: 504 S.W. Ave., P.O. Box 587, 08341-0587. Tel: 856-697-0942; Fax: 856-697-3874.
School—Notre Dame Regional School, Newfield. See separate listing. Tel: 856-697-0155; Fax: 856-697-8540.
Catechesis/Religious Programs—Notre Dame Regional School, Central Ave., Landisville, 08326. Tel: 856-697-6320.
Students 126.

Mount Ephraim, Camden Co., Sacred Heart (1939), Rev. Robert J. Dunphy; Deacon William Norquist.
Res., 11 N. Black Horse Pike, 08059. Tel: 856-931-1441; Fax: 856-931-9433.
Catechesis/Religious Programs—Students 195.

Mullica Hill, Gloucester Co., Holy Name of Jesus (1901), Revs. Michael P. Rush; Joseph Ganiel; Deacons Sam Nastasi; Phillip Giordano.
Res., 17 Earlington Ave., 08062. Tel: 856-478-2294; Fax: 856-478-0222. [CEM]
Catechesis/Religious Programs—Tel: 856-478-9694.
Students 895.

National Park, Gloucester Co., St. Matthew's (1915), Revs. Edward F. Sobolewski; Charles Conaty; Deacon William J. Rumaker.
Res., 307 Wesley Ave., 08063. Tel: 856-845-2523; Fax: 856-251-0822.
School—St. Matthew Regional School. See separate listing. Verga, 08093. Tel: 856-845-7203; Fax: 856-853-7711.
Catechesis/Religious Programs—Tel: 856-845-3891.
Students 235.
Convent—Hessian Ave., Verga, 08093. Tel: 856-845-7204; Fax: 856-853-7771.

Newfield, Gloucester Co., St. Rose of Lima (1922), Rev. John Joseph Tumosa.
Res., 104 Catawba Ave., 08344. Tel: 856-697-3232; Fax: 856-697-1455.
School—Notre Dame Regional School, Newfield. See separate listing. Tel: 856-697-0155; Fax: 856-697-8540.
Catechesis/Religious Programs—108 Church St., 08344.
Students 102.

North Cape May, Cape May Co., St. John of God (1966), Rev. Richard L. Forbes. In res., Rev. Stanley Witcoski.
Res., 680 Town Bank Rd., 08204. Tel: 609-884-1656; Fax: 609-898-0673.
School—St. Raymond Regional School, Villas. See separate listing.

Northfield, Atlantic Co., St. Bernadette (1966), Rev. Msgr. Donald D. Velozo.
Res., 1421 New Rd., 08225. Tel: 609-646-3499; 646-5611; Fax: 609-484-8345.
School—Blessed Sacrament Regional School, Margate. See separate listing. Tel: 609-822-9243; Fax: 609-822-3817.
Catechesis/Religious Programs—Tel: 609-484-0249.
Students 450.

Oaklyn, Camden Co., St. Aloysius (1935), Rev. Msgr. Thomas M. Flynn.
Res., 37 W. Haddon Ave., 08107. Tel: 856-854-2352; Fax: 856-854-4189.
School—St. John Regional School, Collingswood. See separate listing.
Catechesis/Religious Programs—Students 150.

Ocean City, Cape May Co., St. Augustine's (1894), Rev. Msgr. Edward F. Mullen.
Res., 1310 Ocean Ave., 08226. Tel: 609-399-0648; Fax: 609-399-0063.
School—St. Augustine Regional School, Ocean City. See separate listing. Tel: 609-399-1435; Fax: 609-399-8675.
Catechesis/Religious Programs—Tel: 609-399-2316.
Students 185.

St. Frances Cabrini (1966), Rev. Msgr. Patrick A. McCabe.
Res., 114 Atlantic Ave., 08226. Tel: 609-399-4776; Fax: 609-391-9412.
School—St. Augustine Regional School, Ocean City. See separate listing. Tel: 609-399-1435; Fax: 609-399-0063.
Catechesis/Religious Programs—Tel: 609-391-9412.
Students 150.

Our Lady of Good Counsel (1961), Rev. Msgr. Andrew Duignan; Rev. Msgr. Thomas A. Guenther, Admin.
Res., 3948 Central Ave., 08226. Tel: 609-399-2085; 398-3654 (Office); Fax: 609-399-3761.
School—St. Augustine Regional School, Ocean City. See separate listing. Tel: 609-399-1435; Fax: 609-399-8675.

Paulsboro, Gloucester Co., St. John's (1904) (Italian-Irish), Revs. William J. Fallon; Anthony L. Minniti, Admin.
Res., 647 Beacon Ave., 08066. Tel: 856-423-0086; Fax: 856-423-0123.
Catechesis/Religious Programs—712 Mantua Ave., 08066. Tel: 856-423-0099.
Students 108.
Convent—700 Seventh St., 08066. Tel: 856-423-0723. Sr. Ann Byrnes, R.S.M., Supr.

Pennsauken, Camden Co., St. Cecilia's (1939), Rev. Anthony DiBardino, Admin.; Deacon D. Eugene Burns.
Res., 4824 Camden Ave., 08110. Tel: 856-662-2721; Fax: 856-486-2089.
School—Tel: 856-662-0149. Mrs. Theresa Pietrowski, Prin.
Lay Teachers 8; Students 225.
Catechesis/Religious Programs—49th & Camden Ave., 08110. Tel: 856-661-9489.
Students 210.

St. Stephen (1952), Rev. Msgr. Dominic J. Bottino.
Res., 6306 Browning Rd., 08109. Tel: 856-662-9338; Fax: 856-662-4679.
School—Tel: 856-662-5935; Fax: 856-662-6128. Sr. Kathleen M. Boyle, S.S.J., Prin.
Sisters of St. Joseph 2; Lay Teachers 18; Students 230.
Catechesis/Religious Programs—Students 113.

Penns Grove, Salem Co., St. James (1901), Rev. William S. Vandegrift; Deacon Joseph A. Ganci.
Res., 114 State St., 08069. Tel: 856-299-0399; Fax: 856-299-3728.
Catechesis/Religious Programs—Students 80.

Pennsville, Salem Co., Queen of the Apostles (1955), Rev. William F. Moore.
Res., 391 S. Broadway, 08070. Tel: 856-678-5400; Fax: 856-678-4153.
School—Bishop Guilfoyle Regional School, Carney's Point, Tel: 856-299-0400.
Catechesis/Religious Programs—Students 229.

Pine Hill, Camden Co., St. Edward's (1953), Revs. John P. Ward; Dennis W. Bajkowski. In res., Rev. E. Joseph Byerley.
Res., 500 Erial Rd., 08021. Tel: 856-783-2670; Fax: 856-627-9373.
School—Tel: 856-784-4853; Fax: 856-435-2191. Sr. Bridget Gedji, S.O.L.M., Prin. & Supr.
Sisters of Mercy (Rome) 5; Lay Teachers 8; Students 173.
Catechesis/Religious Programs—Tel: 856-783-0293; Fax: 856-627-9393.
Students 625.

Pitman, Gloucester Co., Our Lady Queen of Peace (1949), Rev. Msgr. John F. Cooke.
Res., 161 Pitman Ave., 08071. Tel: 856-589-5673; Fax: 856-589-0102.
School—St. Bridget Regional School, Glassboro. See separate listing.

Pleasantville, Atlantic Co., St. Peter's (1896), Revs. Ronald S. Falotico; Robert F. Walker; Clemens Lee. In res., Rev. Felipe Moyano.
Res., 25 W. Verona Ave., 08232. Tel: 609-641-0285; Fax: 609-641-0385.
School—Tel: 609-646-3057; Fax: 609-646-3467. Mrs. Aida Montalvo, Prin.
Lay Teachers 9; Students 179.
Catechesis/Religious Programs—Students 167.

Pomona, Atlantic Co., Assumption (1938), Revs. Joseph P. Rush; Robert J. Fritz; Deacon James Teeney. In res., Rev. Peter F. Finnerty.
Res., 276 W. White Horse Pike, 08240. Tel: 609-965-4021; Fax: 609-965-4149.
School—Assumption Regional School, Pomona. See separate listing. Tel: 609-652-7134; Fax: 609-652-2544.
Catechesis/Religious Programs—Tel: 609-965-7368.
Students 850.

Rosenhayn, Cumberland Co., St. Mary's (1914), Rev. Vincent G. Carpinelli. In res., Rev. Sebastian V. Annino.
Res., Morton Ave., P.O. Box 376, 08352-0376. Tel: 856-451-8763; Fax: 856-453-8831. [CEM]
School—Immaculate Conception Regional School, Bridgeton. See separate listing. Tel: 856-451-2134; Fax: 856-451-8268.
Catechesis/Religious Programs—Students 206.

Runnemede, Camden Co., St. Maria Goretti (1965), Rev. Edward J. Lipinski.
Res., 321 Orchard Ave., 08078. Tel: 856-933-0037; Fax: 856-933-0036.
School—St. Teresa Regional School, Runnemede. See separate listing.
Catechesis/Religious Programs—Students 187.

St. Teresa of the Infant Jesus (1929), Revs. Kenneth J. Johnston; Krzysztof Wtorek.
Res., 13 E. Evesham Rd., 08078. Tel: 856-939-1681; Fax: 856-939-3878.
School—St. Teresa Regional School, Runnemede. See separate listing. Tel: 856-939-0333; Fax: 856-939-1204.
Catechesis/Religious Programs—Tel: 856-939-0592.
Students 355.

Salem, Salem Co., St. Mary's (1864), Rev. Richard J. Hadyka; Sr. Carol Adams, C.S.J.P., Pastoral Assoc.
Res., 25 Oak St., 08079. Tel: 856-935-0288. [CEM]

Sea Isle City, Cape May Co., St. Joseph's (1884), Revs. Stephen Carey; Marcel M. Tabone; Deacons Liam C. O'Clisham; Norbert Klimaszewski.
Res., 4308 Landis Ave., 08243. Tel: 609-263-8696; Fax: 609-263-7884.
Catechesis/Religious Programs—Tel: 609-263-2087.
Students 275.

Sicklerville, Camden Co., St. John Neumann (1977), Rev. Edward B. Rosinski; Deacons John Schiavo; Anthony Kijonka.
Res., 234 Sicklerville Rd., Box G, 08081-0438. Tel: 856-728-1060; Fax: 856-728-1060.
Catechesis/Religious Programs—Students 362.

Somerdale, Camden Co., Our Lady of Grace (1954), Rev. Msgr. Carl J. Marucci; Revs. Henry McBride; Timothy Byerley.
Res., 35 N. White Horse Pike, 08083. Tel: 856-783-2256; Fax: 856-435-1722.
School—Our Lady of Grace Regional School, Somerdale. See separate listing. Tel: 856-784-0372; Fax: 856-784-5496.
Catechesis/Religious Programs—Tel: 856-627-3036.
Students 398.

Somers Point, Atlantic Co., St. Joseph's (1946), Revs. Josef A. Wagenhoffer; Hugh J. Bradley. In res., Rev. Robert T. Matysik.
Res., 606 Shore Rd., 08244. Tel: 609-927-3568; Fax: 609-653-8707.
School—St. Joseph Regional School. Regionalized with Our Lady of Sorrows Parish, Linwood. Tel: 609-927-2228. Sr. Grace Christi Costello, Prin.
Sisters 6; Lay Teachers 11; Students 340.

Catechesis/Religious Programs—Tel: 609-927-3302.
Students 750.
Convent—580 Shore Rd., 08244. Tel: 609-926-9127. Sisters of St. Joseph

Stone Harbor, Cape May Co., St. Paul's (1911), Rev. Msgr. William Quinn.
Res., 9910 Third Ave., 08247. Tel: 609-368-3091; Fax: 609-368-2775.
School—Bishop McHugh Regional School, Cape May Court House. See separate listing. Tel: 609-624-1900; Fax: 609-624-9696.

Stratford, Camden Co., St. Luke (1961), Revs. James J. Durkin; Michael J. Coffey; Deacon George R. Liss.
Res., 55 Warwick Rd., 08084. Tel: 856-783-5555; Fax: 856-782-8336.
School—Tel: 856-783-3088; Fax: 856-783-8889. Mrs. Cathleen Sheridan, Prin.
Lay Teachers 13; Students 323.
Special Education—.
Lay Teachers 2; Students 14.
Catechesis/Religious Programs—Students 330.

Swedesboro, Gloucester Co., St. Joseph's (1854), Revs. James F. Betz; John A. Cavagnaro; Deacons Joseph S. Lopes; Pablo Berrios.
Res., 140 N. Broad St., 08085. Tel: 856-467-0037; Fax: 856-467-0038. [CEM 2]
School—Bishop Guilfoyle Regional School, 350 Georgetown Rd., Carney's Point, 08069. Mr. Dennis Reitano, Prin.
Catechesis/Religious Programs—Tel: 856-467-3123.
Students 497.

Ventnor, Atlantic Co., St. James (1922), Revs. Brendan V. Sullivan; James R. Ryan; Deacon Agatino Garufi. In res., Rev. C. Jeffries Burton, S.J.
Res., 6415 Atlantic Ave., 08406. Tel: 609-822-2176; Fax: 609-487-8137.
School—Tel: 609-822-2234. Sr. Joan Mary Baldridge, O.P., Prin.
Sisters 4; Lay Teachers 8; Students 258.
Convent—Portland & Atlantic Ave., 08406. Tel: 609-487-8110. Dominican Sisters (Sinsinawa, WI)

Villas, Cape May Co., St. Raymond (1937), Revs. John H. Burton; Christopher T. Bakey; Deacon George Del Rossi.
Res., 25 E. Hudson Ave., 08251. Tel: 609-886-5366; Fax: 609-886-9415.
School—St. Raymond Regional School, Villas. See separate listing. Tel: 609-886-2893; Fax: 609-889-8335.
Catechesis/Religious Programs—Tel: 609-886-7640.
Students 154.

Vineland, Cumberland Co.,

1—Our Lady of Pompeii, (1909), Rev. Peter M. Saparito.
Res., 4680 Dante Ave., 08361. Tel: 856-691-7526; Fax: 856-692-2686. [CEM]
School—St. Mary Regional School, Vineland. See separate listing. Tel: 856-692-8537; Fax: 856-692-5034.

2—Sacred Heart, (1874) (Italian), Revs. Patsy C. Amabile; David J. Klein; Raymond P. Gormley. In res., Rev. Carmel F. Polidano.
Res., 1010 Landis Ave., 08360. Tel: 856-691-0420; Fax: 856-691-1516. [CEM]
School—Sacred Heart Regional School, Vineland. See separate listing. Tel: 856-691-4490; Fax: 856-691-5579.
Catechesis/Religious Programs—922 E. Landis Ave., Tel: 856-696-0325.
Students 706.

3—St. Francis of Assisi, (1961), Revs. Ernest R. Soprano; Sergio Bicomong. In res., Rev. Msgr. Victor S. Muro.
Res., 23 W. Chestnut Ave., 08360. Tel: 856-691-9181; Fax: 856-794-9029.
School—Tel: 856-691-9184; Fax: 856-691-2043. Mrs. Kathryn Chesnut, Prin.
Lay Teachers 10; Students 230.
Catechesis/Religious Programs—Students 160.
Convent—W. Chestnut Ave., 08360. Tel: 856-691-8129. Daughters of Mercy

4—St. Isidore, (1962), Rev. Msgr. John T. Frey; Rev. Cornelius Lambert. In res., Revs. Edward P. Sommers; Alvaro Diaz, O.F.M.
Res., 1655 Magnolia Ave., 08361-6598. Tel: 856-691-9077; Fax: 856-692-3305.
School—Sacred Heart Regional School, Vineland. See separate listing. Tel: 856-691-4490; Fax: 856-691-1516.
Catechesis/Religious Programs—Tel: 856-563-0482; Fax: 856-692-3305. Sr. Catherine Kane, O.S.F., D.R.E.
Students 278.

5—St. Mary's, (1887), Rev. Paul P. Onufer. In res., Rev. Edward F. Namiotka.
Res., 736 Union Rd., 08360. Tel: 856-691-9721; Fax: 856-696-8872. [CEM]
School—St. Mary Regional School. See separate listing. Tel: 856-692-8537; Fax: 856-692-5034.
Catechesis/Religious Programs—741 Union Rd., Tel: 856-692-5097. Sr. Mary Grace, D.M., D.R.E.
Students 331.
Mission—Richland, Atlantic Co., St. Joseph.

Washington Township, Gloucester Co., St. Charles Borromeo (1965), Rev. Msgr. Joseph F. O'Connell; Rev. Albert J. McLaverty; Deacons John R. Gallimore; Joseph B. Chandler.
Res., 176 Stagecoach Rd., Sicklerville, 08081. Tel: 856-629-0411; Fax: 856-629-9109.
School—St. Jude Regional School, Blackwood. See separate listing.
Catechesis/Religious Programs—Tel: 609-228-5694. Mrs. Mary Ann Exler, D.R.E.
Students 900.

SS. Peter and Paul (1973), Revs. John A. Clarke; Brendan J. Meaney; Deacon Edward X. Guidotti. In res., Rev. Howard E. Muhlbaier.
Res., Ganttown Rd., P.O. Box 1022, Turnersville, 08012. Tel: 856-589-3366; Fax: 856-256-1964.
School—St. Jude Regional School, Blackwood. See separate listing.
Catechesis/Religious Programs—Tel: 856-589-6451.
Students 975.

Holy Family (1974), Rev. Msgr. James P. McIntyre; Rev. John M. Stabeno; Deacons Vincent Fausto; George M. Ferland; Frank Pepe.
Res., 226 Hurffville Rd., Sewell, 08080. Tel: 856-228-1616; Fax: 856-228-6332.
School—St. Jude Regional School, Blackwood. See separate listing. Tel: 856-227-4442; Fax: 856-227-1276.
Catechesis/Religious Programs—Tel: 856-228-2215; Fax: 856-401-1817.
Students 1,550.

Waterford, Camden Co., St. Anthony (1966), Rev. John F. Bourke.
Res., 436 Pennington Ave., 08089. Tel: 856-767-7535; Fax: 856-767-7372.
School—St. Joseph Regional School, Hammonton. See separate listing.

West Collingswood, Camden Co., Transfiguration (1950), Rev. Richard J. Lodge; Deacon William C. Robinson. In res., Rev. James F. Barry.
Res., 445 White Horse Pike, 08107. Tel: 856-854-0364; Fax: 856-869-5129.
Catechesis/Religious Programs—Students 142.

Westmont, Camden Co., Holy Saviour (1928), Rev. Terry M. Odien.
Res., 50 Emerald Ave., 08108. Tel: 856-854-0022; Fax: 856-854-5741.
School—30 Emerald Ave., 08108. Tel: 856-858-1966. Sr. Janice Novak, Prin.; Sr. Rita DeFlavia, Supr.
Sisters, Franciscan Missionaries of the Immaculate Heart of Mary 3; Lay Teachers 8; Students 239.
Catechesis/Religious Programs—Students 373.

Westville, Gloucester Co., St. Anne's (1921), Rev. Andrew J. Bolcar; Deacon Anthony C. Como.
Res., 213 Woodbine Ave., 08093. Tel: 856-456-4136; Fax: 856-456-7502.
School—St. Matthew Regional School, National Park. See separate listing. Tel: 856-845-7203; Fax: 856-853-7711.
Catechesis/Religious Programs—Tel: 856-456-4136.
Students 165.

Westville Grove, Gloucester Co., Most Holy Redeemer (1958), Revs. Neal F. Dante; Julian Karczewski.
Res., 1219 Delsea Dr., 08093. Tel: 856-848-6779; Fax: 856-848-6208.
School—Tel: 856-848-6826; Fax: 856-251-0344. Mrs. Patricia Mancuso, Prin.; Sr. Hugh Marie Tyndall, S.S.J., Supr.
Sisters of St. Joseph (Chestnut Hill) 1; Lay Teachers 10; Students 248.
Catechesis/Religious Programs—Tel: 856-384-6070. Ms. Kathleen G. Rando, D.R.E.
Students 215.

Wildwood, Cape May Co., St. Ann's (1895), Rev. Msgr. William Quinn, V.F.; Revs. Jaromir Michalak; Thomas B. Fitzsimmons; Deacon Joseph Pierce.
Res., 2900 Pacific Ave., 08260. Tel: 609-522-2709; Fax: 609-522-9375.
School—St. Ann Regional School Regionalized with Assumption Parish, Wildwood Crest, 2901 New Jersey Ave., 08260. Tel: 609-522-2704; Fax: 609-522-5329. Sr. Sheila Murphy, S.S.J., Prin.
Sisters of St. Joseph 3
Catechesis/Religious Programs—Students 125.
Convent—119 E. Glenwood Ave., 08260. Tel: 609-522-5721.

Wildwood Crest, Cape May Co., Assumption B.V.M. (1961), Revs. Thomas S. Tracey; James Creedon, H.S.A.; Deacons Joseph A. Costello; Ralph M. Catanese; Thomas J. Hafner.
Res., 7110 Seaview Ave., 08260. Tel: 609-522-4114; 522-6071; Fax: 609-523-9069.
School—St. Ann Regional School, Wildwood. See separate listing under St. Ann's Parish. Tel: 609-522-2704.
Catechesis/Religious Programs—Students 134.

Williamstown, Gloucester Co., St. Mary's (1906), Revs. Carmen A. Carlone; Thomas S. Donio; Deacons John J. Leyden; John Kirk; John Kacy.
Res., 32 Carrol Ave., 08094. Tel: 856-629-6142; Fax: 856-875-2097.
School—Tel: 856-629-6190; Fax: 856-728-1437. Miss Judith McBride, Prin.
Lay Teachers 33; Students 596.
Catechesis/Religious Programs—Tel: 856-629-0614.
Students 980.
Convent—640 S. Main St., 08094. Tel: 856-262-1358. St. Joseph Sisters

Woodbine, Cape May Co., St. Casimir's (1939), Rev. Albert E. Harshaw.
Res., 304 Clay St., P.O. Box 533, 08270. Tel: 609-861-3771; Fax: 609-861-7112. [CEM]
School—St. Joseph Regional School, Sea Isle City. See separate listing.
Catechesis/Religious Programs—Tel: 609-861-1601.
Students 105.
Mission—Goshen, Cape May Co., St. Elizabeth, Rte. 47, Goshen, 08218. Tel: 609-861-5218. [CEM]

Woodbury, Gloucester Co., St. Patrick's (1877), Revs. J. Gerald Gallagher; Peter M. Idler; Walter N. Smith; Deacon David Murnane.
Res., 64 Cooper St., 08096. Tel: 856-845-0123; Fax: 856-845-7409.
School—Tel: 856-845-1660. Mrs. Dorice Palumbo, Prin.
Lay Teachers 11; Students 247.
Catechesis/Religious Programs—Tel: 856-853-6681.
Students 245.

Woodbury Heights, Gloucester Co., St. Margaret's (1961), Revs. Calogero N. LaVerde; David A. Grover; Deacons Robert M. Kenney; Nicholas A. Danze.
Res., 334 Beech Ave., 08097. Tel: 856-848-0047; Fax: 856-384-8123.
School—St. Margaret Regional School, Woodbury Heights. See separate listing. Tel: 856-845-5200; Fax: 856-845-2405.
Catechesis/Religious Programs—Tel: 856-845-5251; Fax: 856-845-5251.
Students 600.

Woodlynne, Camden Co., Immaculate Heart of Mary (1949) (Korean), Rev. Joseph An Nguyen.
Res., 201 Cooper Ave., 08107. Tel: 856-962-8610; Fax: 856-962-7123.

Woodstown, Salem Co., St. Joseph's (1895), Rev. Stephen F. Cervoni.
Res., 51 Broad St., 08098. Tel: 856-769-0004; Fax: 856-769-0004. [CEM]
Catechesis/Religious Programs—Students 223.

Chaplains of Public Institutions

Camden. *Camden County Jail* 08104. Rev. Charles S. Gonzalez, S.J., Chap., Sacred Heart, Tel: 856-966-6700.
Riverfront Prison 08102. Chaplains: Revs. Frank Kaminski, S.J.; Jeffrey Putthoff, S.J., Holy Name, Tel: 856-963-1621.

Ancora. *New Jersey State Mental Hospital*. 2239 Carolyn Ave., Atco, 08004. Tel: 856-768-8630. Deacon Charles Smith.

Bridgeton. *Southwoods State Prison* 08302. Rev. Robert P. Weber, Chap., Immaculate Conception, 08302. Tel: 856-451-0254.

Delmont. *Southern State Correctional Facility* Tel: 856-451-0254. Rev. Robert P. Weber.

Fairton. *Federal Correctional Institution* P.O. Box 280, 08320. Tel: 856-227-1436. Rev. Sergio Bicomong, Chap.

Lakeland. *Camden County Hospital at Lakeland* St. Joseph's Chapel, Blackwood Post Office, 08012. Tel: 856-227-1436. Sr. Mary de Sales Vesey, S.S.J., Chap.

Leesburg. *New Jersey State Medium Security Prison* 08327. Tel: 856-447-3480. Rev. William James Bleiler.

Vineland. *Vineland State School*. Attended by Sacred Heart Church, Vineland. 1010 E. Landis Ave., 08360. Tel: 856-691-0420.

Woodbine. *State Colony*. St. Casimir's Church, 304 Clay St., 08270. Tel: 609-861-3771.

On Duty Outside the Diocese:
Reverend Monsignors—
Daiber, Sean J., Brazilian Missions, Central Mailing Address, Paroguia de Sao Jose Rua 107, Setor Sul, Caiza Postal 716, 74,000 Goiania Goias, Brazil S.A.

Reverend Fathers—
Gomes, Robert, St. Joan of Arc, 13485 Spring Hill Dr., Spring Hill, FL 34609. Tel: 352-688-0663
Kocik, Franc W., St. Patrick, Pincourt, Ile Perrot, Province of Quebec, Canada
Kunzman, Richard T., 36 Peaceful Rd., Pine City, NY 14871
Norton, Daniel J., Brazilian Missions
Stout, O. Hugh, Holy Ghost, 2015 Louisiana Ave., New Orleans, LA 70015
Wade, Edward C., Queen of Peace, 3011 Telephone Rd., Houston, TX 77023

On Sick Leave:
Reverend Fathers—
Bean, Charles S.
Gerbino, A. Richard
Hardin, Roy
Pisik, Timothy E.
Shannon, Joseph E.
Sommers, Edward P.

On Leave of Absence:
Reverend Fathers—
Weaver, Patrick

Retired:
Reverend Monsignors—
Adamo, Salvatore J., 114 James St., Burlington, NJ 08016
Boyle, Lawrence P., 1023 Church St., P.O. Box 1391, Millville, NJ 08332
Cannon, Thomas, St. Peter, 359 W. New York Ave., P.O. Box 3700, Deland, FL 32723
Carr, James A., 918 Society Hill, Cherry Hill, NJ 08003
Clark, John J., 644 Pleasure Ave., Ocean City, NJ 08226
Coyne, Michael J., P.O. Box 95, Leeds Point, NJ 08220
Davis, Charles J., (Military), RR 1, Box 20-1, Woodsville, NH 03785
Flaherty, J. Francis, St. Stephen, 6306 Browning Rd., Pennsauken, NJ 08109
Gaffney, James J., J.C.D., Our Lady of Lourdes, 500 Green Tree Rd., Glassboro, NJ 08028-1427
Hewitt, Bernard P., Garden Lakes Trailer Park, 1402 Rte. 9 South Unit 114, Cape May Court House, NJ 08210
Kennedy, Edward J., Sacred Heart Residence for Priests, 210 St. Mary's Dr., Cherry Hill, NJ 08003
Kernan, Eugene J., 91 Geneva Ave., Westmont, NJ 08108
Korda, Edward L., St. Gregory, 340 Evesham Ave., Magnolia, NJ 08049
Lubicky, John R., St. Agnes, 701 Little Gloucester Rd., Blackwood, NJ 08012-7309
McDaid, Edward J., Sacred Heart Priests Residence, 200 St. Mary's Dr., Cherry Hill, NJ 08003-2517
O'Connor, Edward J., 921 Park Pl., Apt. 1009, Ocean City, NJ 08226
O'Connor, Paul, 23 N. Wissahickan Ave, Ventnor, NJ 08406
Rigney, Philip, 5480 N. Ocean Dr., Singer Island, FL 33404
Robertson, Glendon E., 4800 Harper Beach Blvd., #4106, Brigantine, NJ 08203
Seidenburg, Augustine J., 150 W. Cedar Ave., Somers Point, NJ 08244
Sharkey, Thomas H., 3 Catherine Pl., Northfield, NJ 08225
Sprecace, Francis A., 856 Palermo Rd., St. Augustine, FL 32086
Stoerlein, Joseph G., 97 Hobart Ave., Absecon, NJ 08201
Welsh, James F., Sacred Heart Residence for Priests, 200 St. Mary's Dr., Cherry Hill, NJ 08003
Wieckowski, John F., Sacred Heart Residence for Priests, 210 St. Mary's Dr., Cherry Hill, NJ 08003
Reverend Fathers—
Barr, Stanley J., 3 South Wissahickon Ave., Ventnor, NJ 08406
Bernard, John P., 4327 Lockport Rd., Elba, NY 14058
Bloh, John F., 805 Abbey Ct., Sicklerville, NJ 08081
Burns, Thomas E., 6713A Monmounth Ave., Ventnor, NJ 08406-2128. Tel: 609-822-7102
Campuzano, J. Eduardo, Puerto del Carmen 4-A, Maspalomas 35100 (Las Palmas), Spain
Darby, Bernard M., 6548 165th St., Flushing, NY 11365
Davis, Charles J., RR 1, Box 20-1, Woodsville, NH 03785
Delelse, Salvatore, 618 W. Glenside Ave., Glenside, PA 19038
Eckert, William F., 9 Lori Ct., Pittsfield, MA 01201-7145
Hart, William H., 504-A Mulberry Cove, Mt. Laurel, NJ 08054
Hayden, Joseph M., 4747 N. Road 33 N., Lot 354, Lakeland, FL 33805
Hewett, Alfred J., St. Rose of Lima, 300 Kings Hwy., Haddon Heights, NJ 08035-1397
Hope, Abbott J., Sacred Heart Residence for Priests, 200 St. Mary's Dr., Cherry Hill, NJ 08003
Kolton, Stanislaus J., P.O. Box 72, Spring Lake, NJ 07762
Kuhl, Charles E., 8 Oakview Dr., RD 4, Berlin, NJ 08009
Maguire, Paul J., St. Ann, 2900 Pacific Ave., Wildwood, NJ 08260-4943
McGarvey, Joseph F., 32 Central Ave., Audubon, NJ 08106-1904
Melvin, James M., Sacred Heart Priests Residence, 200 St. Mary's Dr., Cherry Hill, NJ 08003-2517
Mroczkowski, Leonard A., 1981 Washington Ave., Seaside Heights, NJ 08751
Newton, John G., 579 Keolu Dr., Kailua, HI 96734
Orsini, Joseph E., 42 W. 50th St., Bayonne, NJ 07002
Pastore, Peter J., 1211 Eucalyptus St., San Antonio, TX 78245-3309
Plummer, James, 216 N. Jerome Ave., Margate, NJ 08402
Reese, Donald B., (Military), P.O. Box 8173, Asheville, NC 28814
Selleck, John P., St. Dominic, 5012 Whitaker St., Panama City, FL 32404
Tovar, Ireneo Lopez, 121 Country Club Dr., Tower II, Apt. 403, Lake Placid, FL 33852
Walsh, Edward J., 216 Bartram Ln., Ocean City, NJ 08226
Weber, George A., Box 272114, Tampa, FL 33688-2114
Yori, Robert O., 13 W. 4th St., Hazleton, PA 18201

Permanent Deacons:
Achee, C. J.
Andreaccho, Robert A.
Becker, Joseph F.
Beebe, Joseph F.
Berrios, Pablo
Berstecher, John L.
Bischer, Carmen M.
Bradley, Patrick T.
Buccilli, Joseph C.
Burns, D. Eugene
Carlucci, Leonard P.
Carson, Robert L., S.J.
Carter, Michael J.
Catanese, Ralph A.
Chandler, Joseph B.
Como, Anthony C.
Costello, Joseph A.
Crosson, Francis W.
Custodio, Henry S.
Danze, Nicholas A.
Del Rossi, George C.
Demarest, Kenneth H., (Retired)
DeMuro, Gerard V.
DiGirolamo, Michael V.
Drum, William J.
Duffy, Francis A.
Dushney, Thomas M.
Ellis, Raymond V.
Fanelli, Robert M.
Fausto, Vincent J.
Ferland, George M.
Ferrario, Raymond C.
Freed, Edward E.
Gallimore, John R.
Ganci, Joseph A.
Gargin, Frank P.
Garufi, Agatino A.
Gilmartin, Peter J.
Giordano, Philip
Gonzalez, Angel A.
Gonzalez, Carmelo
Guerrieri, Michael H.
Guidotti, Edward R.
Hafner, Thomas J.
Hanrahan, Matthew J.
Hardy, Robert
Harkins, Edward J., (Retired)
Harkins, Michael J.
Harris, Philip G.
Iannuzzi, William P.
Iula, Frank A., M.D.
Johnson, Paul F.
Johnson, William G.
Kacy, John J.
Kearney, Brian J., (Retired)
Kenney, Robert M.
Kijonka, Anthony V.
Kiley, James W.
Kirk, John T.
Klimaszewski, Norbert J.
Lagares, Hipolito
Lauth, William
Lee, Paul K.
Leone, John A.
Leyden, John J.
Liss, George R.
Long, Joseph D.
Lopes, Joseph S.
Lorenzo, Robert G.
Loungo, Joseph W.
Ludovich, Nicholas P.
Lytle, George V.
Majewski, Walter
Mangino, Rocco A.
Mauro, John M.
McAleer, Charles L.
McBlain, W. Leo
McCarthy, Richard F., (Retired)
McDonaugh, Michael L.
McLeer, Eugene L.
Mija, Theodore, (Retired)
Miranda, Felix T.
Mortelliti, Nicholas V.
Murnane, David W.
Nastasi, Santo A.
Norquist, William V.
O'Brien, Thomas F.
O'Clisham, Liam C.
Olesiewicz, Ronald J.
Pepe, Frank J.
Perella, Joseph A.
Picknally, Ernest F.
Pierce, Joseph R.
Porowicz, Alfred T.
Powell, Peter J.
Quiles, Bernardino S.
Radziak, Raymond R.
Ralbusky, Emil A.
Reiss, Charles C.
Rios, Jose R.
Rivera, Miguel A.
Riviello, Albert J.
Robinson, William C.
Rocks, James H.
Rumaker, William J.
Schiavo, John A.
Seppanen, Henry R., Ph.D.
Smith, Charles L.
Tavarez, Ismael P.
Teeney, James J.
Traxler, Harold G.
Tully, James M.
Valle, Wilfredo
Vargo, Frank T., (Retired)
Vega, Angel Ramos
Velez, Aladino
Watts, William L.
Werner, John F.
Wigglesworth, Richard J.
Willson, Robert F.

INSTITUTIONS LOCATED IN THE DIOCESE

[A] HIGH SCHOOLS, DIOCESAN

ABSECON. *Holy Spirit High School*, New Rd., 08201. Tel: 609-646-3000; Fax: 609-646-1770. Rev. Joseph A. Perreault, Prin. Sisters of Mercy 1; Priests 2; Lay Teachers 40; Students 867.

CHERRY HILL. *Camden Catholic High School*, Rte. 38 and Cuthbert Rd., 08002. Tel: 856-663-2247; Fax: 856-661-0632.
E-mail: framcchs@aol.com
Web site: www.camdencatholic.org
Rev. Msgr. Andrew E. Martin, Prin.; Rev. William C. Hart. Priests 2; Sisters of Mercy 1; Lay Teachers 43; Students 925.

HADDONFIELD. *Paul VI High School*, 901 Hopkins Rd., Ste. B, 08033. Tel: 856-858-4900; Fax: 856-858-6832. Rev. Msgr. Russell L. Rock, Prin.; Sr. Marianne McCann, M.P.F., Asst. Prin.; Revs. E. Joseph Byerley; Robert Pasley. Priests 3; Religious Teachers Filippini 3; Lay Teachers 50; Students 1,200.

HAMMONTON. *St. Joseph Regional*, 133 N. 3rd St., 08037. Tel: 609-704-2400; Fax: 609-561-4940. James J. Cavalieri, Prin. Priests 1; Religious Sisters Filippini 2; Lay Teachers 25; Students 383.

[B] HIGH SCHOOLS, PAROCHIAL

GLOUCESTER. *Gloucester Catholic High School*, 333 Ridgeway St., 08030. Tel: 856-456-4400; Fax: 856-456-3599.
E-mail: gchsalum@aol.com
Mr. John T. Colman, Prin. Priests 2; Deacons 1;

Dominican Sisters 1; Lay Teachers 43; Students 813.

NORTH WILDWOOD. *Wildwood Catholic High School*, 1500 Central Ave., 08260. Tel: 609-522-7257; Fax: 609-522-2453. Mr. Richard J. Turco, Prin.; Mr. Frank Smith, Vice Prin.; Bro. Robert Carson, Assistant Prin. Priests 1; Brothers 1; Sisters of St. Joseph 3; Lay Teachers 19; Students 360.

VINELAND. *Sacred Heart High School*, 15 N. East Ave., 08360. Tel: 856-691-4491; Fax: 856-563-1644.
Web site: www.sacredhearthighvineland.org
Rev. Edward F. Namiotka, Prin. Priests 1; Lay Teachers 22; Students 314.

[C] HIGH SCHOOLS, PRIVATE

NEWFIELD. *Our Lady of Mercy Academy*, 1001 Main Rd., 08344. Tel: 856-697-2008; Fax: 856-697-2887.
E-mail: srgrace@aol.com
Web site: www.olmanj.org
Daughters of Our Lady of Mercy. Sr. Grace Marie, D.M., Prin. Sisters 4; Lay Teachers 10; Students 180.

PENNSAUKEN. *Bishop Eustace Prep School*, 5552 Rte. 70, 08109-4798. Tel: 856-662-2160, ext. 214; 662-0865 (Res.); Fax: 856-662-0802.
Web site: www.eustace.org
Society of the Catholic Apostolate, Province of the Immaculate Conception. Revs. Joseph Capella, S.A.C., Rector; James MacDonald, S.A.C., Province Vocation Dir.; Bro. James Beamesderfer, S.A.C. Priests 3; Brothers 1; Lay Teachers 72; Students 800.

RICHLAND. *St. Augustine Preparatory School*, 611 N. Cedar Ave., P.O. Box 279, 08350. Tel: 856-697-2600; 697-2612 (Monastery); Fax: 856-697-8389.
E-mail: admin@hermits.com
Web site: www.hermits.com
Order of St. Augustine, Province of St. Thomas of Villanova. Revs. Paul W. Galetto, O.S.A., Pres.; Stephen J. La Rosa, O.S.A.; Cherubin Kerr, O.S.A.; Ronald A. Hamaday, O.S.A.; Martin L. Smith, O.S.A.; Bros. Frank Cucinotta, O.S.A.; David Graber, M.SS.CC. Priests 4; Brothers 1; Deacons 1; Lay Teachers 25; Students 415.

[D] ELEMENTARY SCHOOLS, PRIVATE

CAMDEN. *San Miguel School, Inc.* (Grades 6-8), 836 S. 4th St., 08103. Tel: 856-342-6707; Fax: 856-342-6708.
E-mail: sanmiguel3@juno.com
Web site: www.delasallebrothers.org/smiguel
Bro. William Johnson, F.S.C., Prin. De La Salle Christian Brothers 3; Lay Teachers 6; Students 50.

[E] REGIONAL SCHOOLS, ELEMENTARY

BARRINGTON. *St. Francis de Sales*, West Gloucester Pike, 08007. Tel: 856-547-7958; Fax: 856-547-0472.
E-mail: sistercatherine@hotmail.com
Web site: www.erols.com/sfdsale
Sr. Rita Butler, Supr.; Sr. Catherine Mulcahy, F.D.N.S.C., Supr. & Prin. Daughters of Our Lady of the Sacred Heart 9; Lay Teachers 10; Students 334. Serving St. Francis de Sales, Barrington and Mary, Mother of the Church, Bellmawr.

BERLIN. *Our Lady of Mt. Carmel*, One Maple Ave., 08009. Tel: 856-767-2115; Fax: 856-767-1293.
E-mail: SMinnockO@aol.com
Web site: www.olmcparish.net
Sr. M. Agnes, R.S.M., Prin.; Sr. Carmel Minnock. Sisters of Mercy (American Province) 5; Lay Teachers 12; Students 277. Serving Our Lady of Mt. Carmel, Berlin and St. Andrew, Gibbsboro.

BLACKWOOD. *St. Agnes School*, 117 W. Church St., 08012. Tel: 856-228-7076.
E-mail: stagnesnj@home.com
Mr. John T. Cafagna, Prin. Lay Teachers 10; Students 243. Serving St. Agnes, Blackwood; St. John Vianney, Deptford.

St. Jude, 420 S. Black Horse Pike, 08012. Tel: 856-227-4442; 401-1622. Sr. Paula Marie Randow, O.S.F., Prin. Franciscan Sisters 2; Lay Teachers 19; Students 496. Serving St. Jude, Blackwood; SS. Peter & Paul, St. Charles Borromeo, & Holy Family, Washington Township.

BRIDGETON. *Immaculate Conception Regional School*, 398 N. Pearl St., 08302. Tel: 856-451-2134; Fax: 856-451-8268. Mrs. Kathleen Bischer, Prin. Lay Teachers 9; Students 154. Serving Immaculate Conception, St. Teresa of Avila, Bridgeton; St. Michael, Cedarville; St. Mary, Rosenhayn.

CAPE MAY. *Our Lady, Star of the Sea School*, 520 Lafayette St., 08204. Tel: 609-884-4437; Fax: 609-884-4788. Ms. Barbara Byrne, Prin. Sisters of St. Joseph 1; Lay Teachers 15; Students 236. Serving Our Lady, Star of the Sea, Cape May.

CAPE MAY COURT HOUSE. *Bishop McHugh Regional School*, 2221 NJSH Rte. 9, 08210. Tel: 609-624-1900; Fax: 609-624-9696. Sr. Rosalie Pronsati, R.S.M., Prin.

CARNEY'S POINT. *Bishop Guilfoyle Regional School*, 350 Georgetown Rd., 08069. Tel: 856-299-0400; Fax: 856-299-6556. Claire Whittaker, Prin.

COLLINGSWOOD. *St. John School*, 100 Lees Ave., 08108. Tel: 856-858-1562; Fax: 856-858-2943. Miss Joan Simpson, Prin. Lay Teachers 11; Students 269. Serving St. John, Collingswood; St. Aloysius, Oaklyn.

GLASSBORO. *St. Bridget Regional School*, 25 W. High St., 08028. Tel: 856-881-2578; Fax: 856-881-8771.
E-mail: tgregal@stbridget.net
Jane Dickerman, Prin. Felician Sisters 2; Lay Teachers 15; Students 305. Serving St. Bridget, Our Lady of Lourdes, Glassboro; Our Lady, Queen of Peace, Pitman.

HADDONFIELD. *Christ the King Regional School*, 164 Hopkins Ave., 08033. Tel: 856-429-2084. Mrs. Gail Corey, Prin. Franciscan Sisters of Allegany 1; Lay Teachers 25; Students 333. Serving Christ the King, Haddonfield; St. Pius X, Cherry Hill.

HAMMONTON. *St. Joseph School*, 133 N. 3rd St., 08037. Tel: 609-561-5980. Sr. Barbara Ranere, M.P.F., Prin. Religious Teachers Filippini 5; Lay Teachers 12; Students 300. Serving St. Joseph, St. Martin de Porres, St. Anthony of Padua, Hammonton; St. Anthony, Waterford; St. Lucy, Blue Anchor; Sacred Heart Mission, Cedar Brook.

MARGATE. *Blessed Sacrament School*, 14 N. Jerome Ave., 08402. Tel: 609-822-9243; Fax: 609-822-2036. Sr. Rosaline Walters, O.S.F., Prin. Sisters of St. Francis of Syracuse, NY 3; Lay Teachers 8; Students 262. Serving Blessed Sacrament, Margate; St. Bernadette, Northfield; Epiphany, Longport.

NEWFIELD. *Notre Dame Regional School*, 108 Church St., 08344. Tel: 856-697-0155, (Newfield) (Grades K-4); 856-697-3456, (Grades K5-8); (Landisville; Fax: 856-697-5114.
E-mail: ndrsnj@aol.com
Web site: www.asd.com
Mrs. Mary Brogan, Prin. Lay Teachers 16; Students 280. Serving Our Lady of Victories, Landisville; St. Michael, Minotola; Our Lady of the Lakes, Collings Lakes; St. Rose, Newfield; St. Mary, Malaga; Nativity, Franklinville; St. Ann, Elmer.

OCEAN CITY. *St. Augustine Regional School*, 1337 Asbury Ave., 08226-3299. Tel: 609-399-1435; Fax: 609-399-8675. Sr. de Paul Juliano, O.S.F. Sisters of St. Francis 1; Lay Teachers 9; Students 235. Serving St. Augustine, St. Frances Cabrini, Our Lady of Good Counsel, Ocean City.

POMONA. *Assumption Regional School*, White Horse Pike, 08240. Tel: 609-652-7134; Fax: 609-652-2544. Mary Jude Filep, Prin. Lay Teachers 16; Students 276. Serving Assumption, Pomona; St. Elizabeth Ann Seton, Absecon.

RUNNEMEDE. *St. Teresa School*, 18 Ardmore Rd., 08078. Tel: 856-939-0333; Fax: 856-939-1204.
E-mail: #12strsofficePassword000000@snip.net
Sr. Regina Marion Copple, I.H.M., Supr. & Prin. Sisters Servants of the Immaculate Heart of Mary 7; Lay Teachers 9; Students 258. Serving St. Teresa, St. Maria Goretti, Runnemede.

SOMERDALE. *Our Lady of Grace School*, 105 N. White Horse Pike, 08083. Tel: 856-784-0372; Fax: 856-784-5496. Joan M. Ciccone, Ph.D., Prin. Lay Teachers 14; Students 280. Serving Our Lady of Grace, Somerdale; St. Gregory, Magnolia.

VERGA. *St. Matthew School*, 08093. Tel: 856-845-7203; Fax: 856-853-7711.
E-mail: stmatthewschool@juno.com
Sr. Maria Liber, Prin. Little Servant Sisters of the Immaculate Conception 4; Lay Teachers 8; Students 231. Serving St. Matthew, National Park; St. Anne, Westville.

VILLAS. *St. Raymond School*, 25 E. Ocean Ave., 08251. Tel: 609-886-2893; Fax: 609-889-8335.
E-mail: straytprincipal@saintraymondschool.capemayschools.com
Sr. Kathleen Nuckols, I.H.M., Supr. & Prin. Servants of the Immaculate Heart of Mary 7; Lay Teachers 8; Students 190. Serving St. Raymond, Villas; St. John of God, North Cape May.

VINELAND. *Sacred Heart School*, 922 E. Landis Ave., 08360. Tel: 856-691-4490; Fax: 856-691-5579.
E-mail: mainoffice@sacredheart.pvt.k12.nj.us
Web site: school.nj.com/school/sacredheart
Michael D. Healy, M.Ed., Prin. Lay Teachers 20; Students 400. Serving Sacred Heart, St. Isidore, Spanish Catholic Center, Vineland.

St. Mary Regional School, 735 Union Rd., 08360. Tel: 856-692-8537; Fax: 856-692-5034.
E-mail: smrschool@aol.com
Web site: www.cambel.com/stmarys
Sr. M. Bernardine, D.M., Prin. Daughters of Our Lady of Mercy 3; Lay Teachers 16; Students 359. Serving St. Mary; St. Joseph Mission, Richland; Our Lady of Pompeii, East Vineland.

WOODBURY HEIGHTS. *St. Margaret School*, 773 Third St., 08097. Tel: 856-845-5200; Fax: 856-845-2405.
Web site: www.stmargarets-rs.org
Sr. Lorraine Klein, F.M.I.J., Prin. & Supr. Sisters 4; Lay Teachers 15; Students 655. Serving St. Margaret, Woodbury Heights; Incarnation, Mantua.

[F] SCHOOLS FOR SPECIAL CHILDREN

WESTVILLE GROVE. *Archbishop Damiano School / St. John of God Community Services*, 1145 Delsea Dr., 08903. Tel: 856-848-4700; Fax: 856-848-3965.
E-mail: ads@jersey.net
Ms. Muncie Buckalew, Exec. Dir. Brothers 4; Sisters 2; Lay Teachers 76; Students 600; Total Staff 178.

[G] CATHOLIC FOUNDATIONS

CAMDEN. *Francis, Elizabeth and Edward Roger Welsh Scholarship Trust*, 631 Market St., 08102. Rev. Msgr. Joseph W. Pokusa, Advisory Committee Chair.

The Frank J. and Rosina W. Suttill Catholic Foundation, 631 Market St., 08102. Rev. Msgr. Joseph P. Herron, Sec.

The Tuition Assistance Fund, Inc., 631 Market St., 08102. Rev. Msgr. Thomas J. McIntyre, Sec.

NORTHFIELD. *The Sharkey Family Charitable Trust*, Three Catherine Pl., 08225-2503. Rev. Msgr. Thomas H. Sharkey, Trustee.

[H] GENERAL HOSPITALS

CAMDEN. *Our Lady of Lourdes Medical Center, Inc.* 1600 Haddon Ave., 08103. Tel: 856-757-3500; Fax: 856-757-3611.
For a complete listing, refer to the Hospitals section.

[I] NURSING HOMES

CHERRY HILL. *St. Mary's Nursing Home*, 210 St. Mary's Dr., 08003. Tel: 856-424-9521; Fax: 856-424-5143
For a complete listing, refer to the Special Care Facilities section.

NEWFIELD. *Mater Dei Nursing Home*, 176 Rte. 40, 08344. Tel: 856-358-2061; Fax: 856-358-0403
For a complete listing, refer to the Special Care Facilities section.

PLEASANTVILLE. *Our Lady's Residence*, 1100 Clematis Ave., 08232. Tel: 609-646-2450; Fax: 609-646-7569
For a complete listing, refer to the Special Care Facilities section.

VINELAND. *Bishop McCarthy Residence*, 1045 E. Chestnut Ave., 08360. Tel: 856-692-2850; Fax: 856-696-5770.
E-mail: bmr02@aol.com
For a complete listing, refer to the Special Care Facilities section.

[J] VISITING NURSES

CAPE MAY COURT HOUSE. *Holy Redeemer Rehabilitation Center*, 1261 Rte. 9 S., Ste. 1, 08210. Tel: 609-465-3866. Barbara O'Shea, P.T., Chief Therapist.

MAYS LANDING. *Atlantic Co. Office*, 701 Rte. 50, 08330. Tel: 609-625-2200; 800-788-3029; Fax: 609-625-2992.

SWAINTON. *Holy Redeemer Visiting Nurse Agency, Inc.* Subsidiary of Holy Redeemer Health System, Inc. 1801 Rte. 9 N., 08210. Tel: 609-465-2082; 800-745-4693; Fax: 609-463-6121. Sponsored by Sisters of the Holy Redeemer, C.S.R. Sr. Mary Anne McDonagh, Agency Admin.

[K] HOUSING FOR AGED

CAPE MAY. *Victorian Towers Associates*, 608 Washington St., 08204. Tel: 609-884-5883; Fax: 609-884-5625.
E-mail: victoriantowers@snip.net
For a complete listing, refer to the Special Care Facilities section.

CHERRY HILL. *The Manor at St. Mary's*, 220 St. Mary's Dr., 08003. Tel: 856-424-3817; Fax: 856-424-5128
For a complete listing, refer to the Special Care Facilities section.

Marian Residence, 1000 Cropwell Rd., 08003. Tel: 856-424-1131; Fax: 856-424-5333
For a complete listing, refer to the Special Care Facilities section.

Village Apartments of Cherry Hill, NJ, Inc., 212 Lourdes Ct., 08003. Tel: 856-424-7913; Fax: 856-424-9211
For a complete listing, refer to the Special Care Facilities section.

[L] CHILD CARE CENTERS

CAMDEN. *St. Joseph's Nursery School*, 17 Church St., P.O. Box 1443, 08105. Tel: 856-963-9202; 365-0604 (Convent); Fax: 856-963-0103 (Convent). Sr. Maria DiRosa, Prin.; Sr. Angela D'Alessandro, Supr. Franciscan Missionary Sisters of the Infant Jesus 4.

[M] MONASTERIES AND RESIDENCES OF PRIESTS AND BROTHERS

CAMDEN. *Dominican Sisters of the Perpetual Rosary Chaplain's Residence*, 1500 Haddon Ave., 08103. Tel: 856-365-4427. Rev. Raymond M. McCabe, O.P. In res. Rev. Anthony I. Cataudo, O.P.

BLACKWOOD. *Bishop's Residence*. Marywood, 1600 Peter Cheeseman Rd., 08012. In res. Most Rev. Nicholas DiMarzio, D.D., Ph.D; Rev. Msgr. James Checchio.

CHERRY HILL. *Neumann House*, 250 St. Mary's Dr., 08003. Tel: 856-424-1741; Fax: 856-424-2896.

Vianney Villa, 230 St. Mary Dr., 08003. Tel: 856-424-2035. Rev. William D. Titmas, Dir. In res. Rev. Msgr. Joseph W. Devlin; Revs. A. Richard Gerbino; Gerald Clements; Roy Hardin; Thomas Harkins.

LINWOOD. *Villa Pieta*. Missionaries of the Sacred Hearts of Jesus & Mary. 2249 Shore Rd., 08221. Tel: 609-927-5600; 927-5262.
E-mail: frpatrizio@aol.com
Web site: www.missionofsacredhearts.org
Revs. Anthony Patrizio, M.SS.CC., Rector & Delegate; Leonard Carrieri, M.SS.CC.; Robert McDade, M.SS.CC.

MARGATE. *Franciscan Friary*. Holy Name Province. 118 S. Mansfield Ave., 08402. Tel: 609-822-9552; Fax: 609-822-0601. Rev. Alvin Faddish, O.F.M., Curator. Total Staff 1.

OCEAN CITY. *Augustinian Friars Summer Home*. St. Rita of Cascia Cottage, 823 5th St., 08226. Tel: 609-398-1299.

Ocean Rest Summer School and Retreat House, 3045 Central Ave., 08226. Tel: 609-399-6480; Fax: 609-398-7520. Brothers of Christian Schools Summer Home and Retreat House. Mailing Address: Brother Provincial, P.O. Box 29, Adamstown, MD, 21710-0029. Tel: 301-874-5188.

PITTSGROVE. *Villa St. Joseph*, 9 Harding Hwy., 08318. Tel: 856-358-2841; Fax: 856-358-2099.
E-mail: VILLASJ@conectiv.net
Oblates of St. Francis de Sales. Revs. Joseph A. Connolly, O.S.F.S.; Nicholas C. DiIenno, O.S.F.S.; J. Stuart Dooling, O.S.F.S.; Francis J. Hanlon, O.S.F.S., Supr.; James Patrick Kelly; Thomas W. Kelley, O.S.F.S.; John Gavin; John Muzdakis; Edmund F. O'Rourke, O.S.F.S.; Joseph A. Travers, O.S.F.S.; R. Douglas Smith, O.S.F.S.; Bro. Eugene J. Rehrman, O.S.F.S. Total in Residence 12.

VENTNOR. *St. Benilde Community*, 107 S. Derby Ave., 08406. Tel: 609-487-6995; Fax: 609-487-6882.
Web site: www.delasallebrothers.org
Brothers of the Christian Schools & De La Salle Christian Brothers. Provincialate, P.O. Box 29, Adamstown, MD, 21710. Tel: 301-874-5188; Fax: 301-874-5674. Bro. Andrew Bartley, F.S.C., Dir.

WESTVILLE GROVE. *Hospitaller Order of St. John of God*, 1145 Delsea Dr., 08093. Tel: 856-848-4700; Fax: 856-848-7305.
E-mail: stogvocationsnj@aol.com
Bro. Bernard Farrell, O.H., Supr. & Dir. Vocations. Brothers 3.

[N] CONVENTS AND RESIDENCES FOR SISTERS

CAMDEN. *Monastery of the Dominican Nuns of the Perpetual Rosary*, 1500 Haddon Ave., 08103. Tel: 856-342-8340. Mother Mary of the Immaculate Heart, O.P., Prioress; Rev. Raymond M. McCabe, O.P., Chap. Sisters 7.

ATLANTIC CITY. *St. John's Retreat House and Rest Home*, 128 S. Dover Ave., 08401. Tel: 609-345-7361. Little Servant Sisters of the Immaculate Conception. Sr. Xavier Czachor, L.S.I.C., Supvr. Sisters 3.

CHERRY HILL. *Franciscan Missionary Sisters of the Infant Jesus*. U.S. Province and Novitiate, 1215 Kresson Rd., 08003. Tel: 856-428-8834; Fax: 856-428-7930.
E-mail: fmijusdelcatt@att.net
Sr. Chiara Lilia Ferrario, F.M.I.J., Delegate Supr. Sisters 4.

Little Servant Sisters of the Immaculate Conception. Provincialate and Novitiate. 1000 Cropwell Rd., 08003. Tel: 856-424-1962; Fax: 856-424-5333.
E-mail: LSICProv@aol.com
Mother M. Leonarda, L.S.I.C., Prov.; Rev. Eugene Mixtacki, O.F.M.Cap., Chap. Professed Sisters 23.

ELMER, 856-358-4030. *The Sisters of Mary Immaculate of Nyeri, Inc.* 08318, 400 State St. Sr. Mary Jennifer Wandia, S.M.I., Pres. & Contact Person.

HADDONFIELD. *St. Mary of the Angels Convent*, 134 Kings Hwy. W., 08033. Tel: 856-428-0824. Franciscan Sisters of Allegany. Sr. Anne Henry Wusteney, Treas. Sisters 6.

NEWFIELD. *Villa Rossello*. Provincial House and Novitiate of Daughters of Our Lady of Mercy. 1009 Main Rd., 08344. Tel: 856-697-2983; Fax: 856-697-8595.
E-mail: dmnewfield@juno.com
Sr. Grace Marie, D.M., Prov. Sisters 26.

PLEASANTVILLE. *Hospitaler Sisters of Mercy Novitiate*, 915 S. Main St., 08232. Tel: 609-272-7659.

Hospitaler Sisters of Mercy Convent, 909 S. Main St., 08232. Tel: 609-272-7659. Sisters 8.

Villa Raffaella, 917 S. Main St., 08232. Tel: 609-645-9300; Fax: 609-645-9600. Total Staff 10; Beds 40. Senior Assisted Living Community, Hospitaler Sisters of Mercy. Total in Residence 2.

SEA ISLE CITY. *The Sisters of St. Francis of Philadelphia*, 55th & Landis Ave., 08243. Tel: 610-558-7676; Fax: 610-558-6122.
E-mail: kparisi@osfphila.org
Web site: www.osfphila.org
Mailing Address: Our Lady of Angels Convent, 609 S. Convent Rd., Aston, PA, 19014.

STONE HARBOR. *Villa Maria by the Sea*, 08247. Tel: 609-368-3621. Summer retreat house for Sisters Servants of the Immaculate Heart of Mary. (Immaculata, PA).

SWAINTON. *Sisters of the Holy Redeemer*. Our Lady of Peace Convent, 8 Brooks Ave., 08210. Tel: 609-465-3549; Fax: 609-463-6121.
Web site: www.sistersholyredeemer.org
Total in Residence 2.

VENTNOR. *The Benedictine Sisters of Elizabeth, NJ*, 114 S. Troy Ave., 08406. Tel: 609-823-9843.
E-mail: bensisnj@aol.com

Convent of Mary the Ocean Star, 112 S. Dorset Ave., 08406. Tel: 609-823-3977. Sisters of Charity of St. Vincent De Paul (Mt. St. Vincent, NY).

Holy Family, Seaside Convent, 110 S. Dorset Ave., 08406. Tel: 609-822-5127. Sisters of St. Dominic (Blauvelt, NY).

McAuley House, 102 S. Derby Ave., 08406. Tel: 609-822-7944. Sisters of Mercy (Baltimore Regl. Community).

Mercy By-the-Sea, 114 S. Portland Ave., 08406. Sisters of Mercy (Plainfield - Watchung).

Mercy Villa, 104 S. Derby Pl., 08406. Sisters of Mercy (Prov. of New York).

VINELAND. *Bishop McCarthy Residence Convent*, 1045 E. Chestnut Ave., 08360. Tel: 856-692-2850; Fax: 856-696-5770.
E-mail: bmro2@aol.com
Sr. Eletta Felli, Supr. Hospitaler Sisters of Mercy 5.

WILDWOOD CREST, 317 Charleston E., 08260. Tel: 609-523-1167.

[O] RETREAT HOUSES

BLACKWOOD. *St. Pius X Retreat House*, 1840 Peter Cheeseman Rd., Box 216, 08012. Tel: 856-227-1436; Fax: 856-227-2907.
E-mail: jsanders@stpius10th.org
Rev. Cadmus D. Mazzarello, Spiritual Dir.; Mr. John Sanders, Dir. of Oper.; Bro. Nicholas Crosby, S.D.S. In res. Revs. Louis A. Marucci; Joseph M. Messina; Sam Vaccarella, T.O.R.

VINELAND. *Pope John Paul II Retreat Center*, 414 S. 8th St., 08360. Tel: 856-691-2299; Fax: 856-691-5522.
E-mail: sccpjIIrc@aol.com
Rev. Msgr. Victor Muro, Dir.

[P] APOSTOLIC CENTERS

CAPE MAY POINT. *Marianist Family Retreat Center*, 417 Yale Ave., Box 488, 08212-0456. Tel: 609-884-3829; Fax: 609-884-0545.
E-mail: capemaymarianists@jersey.com
Rev. Theodore Cassidy, S.M., Local Community Dir.; Mr. Anthony Fucci, Center Dir.; Bros. Albert Koch, S.M.; Edward Underdorfer, S.M.

VINELAND. *Spanish Catholic Center*, 410 S. 8th St., 08360. Tel: 856-692-8992. Rev. Msgr. Victor S. Muro, Dir., 23 W. Chestnut Ave., 08360. Rev. Alvaro Diaz, St. Isidore, 1655 Magnolia Rd., 08360. Deacon Bernardino Quiles.

[Q] LOCAL OFFICES OF CATHOLIC CHARITIES

CAMDEN. *Catholic Charities*, 1484-86 Mt. Ephraim Ave., 08104. Tel: 856-964-2133; Fax: 856-225-1384. Cereida Medina, Coord.

St. John the Baptist Pre-Natal Clinic, 6th St. & Erie St., 08102. Tel: 856-757-9540; Fax: 856-757-9541. Patricia A. Chico, L.P.N., Admin.

ATLANTIC CITY. *Catholic Charities - Atlantic County*, 9 N. Georgia Ave., 08401. Tel: 609-345-3448; Fax: 609-345-7180. Sr. Grace Nolan, R.S.M., Coord.

BLACKWOOD. *Family Treatment of Addiction Center*, 141 S. Black Horse Pike, Ste. 7, 08012. Tel: 856-227-9002; Fax: 856-227-9005.
E-mail: ftoac@aol.com
Rev. Frank X. Hudson.

GIBBSTOWN. *Catholic Charities, Camden/Gloucester Counseling Center*, 320 Memorial Ave., 08027. Tel: 856-224-0945; Fax: 856-224-0487. Patricia Peach, M.A., L.M.F.T., Dir. Total Staff 12.

PENNS GROVE. *Catholic Charities - Salem County*, 14-16 W. Main St., 08069. Tel: 609-299-1296; Fax: 609-299-4010. Clarence Wilkins, B.A., Coord.

PENNSAUKEN. *Catholic Charities*. Administrative Office, AIDS Ministry, Camden County Emergency Service Center, 2830 Marlton Pike, 08105. Tel: 856-663-9800; Fax: 856-663-0253.
E-mail: css4@snip.net
Suzanne M. Hemp, ACSW, LCSW, Exec. Dir.; Sr. Ruth Harkins, I.H.M., M.A. Tel: 856-663-0085; 856-663-0253 (Fax). Aids Ministry.

PLEASANTVILLE. *Catholic Charities*. Cape/Atlantic Counseling Center, 21 W. Verona Ave., 08232. Tel: 609-383-0909; Fax: 609-383-2084. Mr. Michael Murphy, L.C.S.W., BCD, Dir.

RIO GRANDE. *Catholic Charities*. Cape May County Office. Village Shoppes, 1304 Rte. 47 S., 08242. Tel: 609-886-2662; Fax: 609-886-3583. Dawn Thompson, BSW, Coord.

VINELAND. *Catholic Charities Counseling Center in Newfield*, 951 Main Rd., 08360. Tel: 856-697-0744; Fax: 856-697-0742.

Catholic Charities of Vineland. Crisis Pregnancy and Adoption Services, 810 Montrose St., 08360. Tel: 609-691-1909; Fax: 609-692-6575. Ann Gallagher, LCSW, Supvr.

WESTVILLE. *Catholic Charities of Gloucester County*, 1200 N. Delsea Dr., Ste. One, 08093. Tel: 856-845-9200; Fax: 856-845-8905. Mr. Robert S. Skrzot, Coord.

[R] CAMPUS MINISTRIES

CAMDEN. *Rutgers University - Camden Campus*, 642 Market St., 08102. Tel: 856-255-1077; Fax: 856-255-1730. Rev. Michael T. Mannion, Diocesan Campus Ministry Coord.

GLASSBORO. *Rowan University*, Newman Center, Rte. 322 and Bowe Blvd., 08028. Tel: 856-881-5642; Fax: 856-881-4183.
E-mail: frmazz@erols.com
Rev. Cadmus D. Mazzarella, Dir.

MAYS LANDING. *Atlantic Community College*, 08330. Rev. C. Jeffries Burton, S.J., St. James Rectory, 6407 Atlantic Ave., Ventor, 08406. Tel: 609-487-7540.

POMONA. *Richard Stockton College of New Jersey*, Jim Leeds Rd., 08240. Tel: 609-487-7540; Fax: 609-487-8137.
E-mail: frjeffsj@bellatlantic.net
Rev. C. Jeffries Burton, S.J.

[S] MEDICAL CLINICS

CAMDEN. *Saint Luke's Catholic Medical Services, Inc.*, 511 State St., 08102. Tel: 856-365-4642; Fax: 856-365-0539
For a complete listing, refer to the Hospitals section.

[T] LEGAL SERVICES

CAMDEN. *Camden Center for Law and Social Justice, Inc.*, 509 State St., 08102. Tel: 856-966-8896; Fax: 856-541-8826.
E-mail: jjgrogan@superlink.net
John J. Grogan, Esq. Total Assisted 1,200; Total Staff 4.

[U] FOOD CENTERS

CAMDEN. *The Cathedral Soup Kitchen, Inc.*, 642 Market St., 08102. Tel: 856-964-6771 (Office) 856-338-1529 (Kitchen). Total Assisted 56,000; Total Staff 4.

[V] MISCELLANEOUS

CAMDEN. *Guadalupe Family Services*, 509 State St., 08102. Tel: 856-365-8081; Fax: 856-365-8247.

NORTH CAPE MAY. *Christ Child Society, Cape May County Chapter*, P.O. Box 882, 08204. Tel: 609-884-1486.

RELIGIOUS INSTITUTES OF MEN REPRESENTED IN THE DIOCESE

For further details refer to the corresponding bracketed number in the Religious Institutes of Men or Women section.

[0140]—*The Augustinians*. (Vice Prov. of Our Lady of Good Counsel, Villanova, PA).—O.S.A.
[0330]—*Brothers of the Christian Schools*.—F.S.C.
[0480]—*Conventual Franciscans*. (Syracuse, NY).—O.F.M.Conv.
[0520]—*Franciscan Friars*. (Prov. of the Most Holy Name of Jesus).—O.F.M.
[0670]—*Hospitaller Brothers of St. John of God*.—O.H.
[0690]—*Jesuit Fathers and Brothers*.—S.J.
[1120]—*Missionaries of the Sacred Hearts of Jesus and Mary*.—M.SS.CC.
[0920]—*Oblates of St. Francis De Sales*. (Wilmington-Philadelphia).—O.S.F.S.
[0430]—*Order of Preachers-Dominicans*. (St. Joseph Prov., New York).—O.P.
[0760]—*Society of Mary*.—S.M.
[0990]—*Society of the Catholic Apostolate*.—S.A.C.
[1200]—*Society of the Divine Savior*.—S.D.S.
[0560]—*Third Order Regular of Saint Francis*.—T.O.R.

RELIGIOUS INSTITUTES OF WOMEN REPRESENTED IN THE DIOCESE

[0230]—*Benedictine Sisters of Pontifical Jurisdiction*. (Newark, NJ).—O.S.B.
[2410]—*Congregation of the Marianites of Holy Cross*.—M.S.C.
[0900]—*Daughters of Our Lady of the Sacred Heart*.—F.D.N.S.C.

[1050]—*Dominican Contemplative Nuns.*—O.P.
[1070-03]—*Dominican Sisters.*—O.P.
[1170]—*Felician Sisters.* (Immaculate Conception Prov., Lodi, NJ).—C.S.S.F.
[1365]—*Franciscan Missionary Sisters of the Infant Jesus.*
[1180]—*Franciscan Sisters of Allegany, New York.*—O.S.F.
[]—*Hospitaler Sisters of Mercy.* (Pleasantville, NJ).—H.S.M.
[2575]—*Institute of the Sisters of Mercy of the Americas.* (Merion, PA; Baltimore, MD).—R.S.M.
[2300]—*Little Servant Sisters of the Immaculate Conception.*—L.S.I.C.
[]—*Missionary Daughters of the Most Pure Virgin Mary.*—M.D.P.V.M.
[2790]—*Missionary Servants of the Most Blessed Trinity.*—M.S.B.T.
[3430]—*Religious Teachers Filippini.* (Morristown, NJ).—M.P.F.
[0650]—*Sisters of Charity of St. Vincent de Paul, of New York.*—S.C.
[0660]—*Sisters of Christian Charity.*
[]—*Sisters of Mary Immaculate.* (Pleasantville, NJ).—S.M.I.
[2517]—*Sisters of Mercy.*
[2670]—*Sisters of Our Lady of Mercy.*—S.O.L.M.
[3893]—*Sisters of Saint Joseph of Chestnut Hill, Philadelphia.*—S.S.J.
[1650]—*Sisters of St. Francis of Philadelphia.*—O.S.F.
[3890]—*Sisters of St. Joseph of Peace.*—C.S.J.P.
[2000]—*Sisters of the Holy Redeemer.*—C.S.R.
[1490]—*Sisters of the Third Franciscan Order.*—O.S.F.
[2170]—*Sisters, Servants of the Immaculate Heart of Mary.*—I.H.M.

NECROLOGY

† Beausang, Rev. Msgr. Charles C., (Retired). —Died Aug. 24, 2000.

† Carta, Umberto, (Retired). —Died March 6, 2000.

† Leary, Rev. Msgr. Joseph W., (Retired). —Died July 30, 2000.

† McCormick, George C., (Retired). —Died March 16, 2000.

† McDonnell, Cyril, (Retired). —Died May 17, 2000.

Diocese of Charleston

(Dioecesis Carolopolitana)

Most Reverend

ROBERT J. BAKER, S.T.D

Bishop of Charleston; ordained March 21, 1970; appointed July 13, 1999; consecrated September 29, 1999. *Res., 114 Broad St., Charleston, SC, 29401. Office: 119 Broad St., Charleston, SC, 29401. Mailing Address: P.O. Box 818, Charleston, SC, 29402.* Tel.: 843-853-2130; Fax: 843-724-6387.

Most Reverend

DAVID B. THOMPSON, D.D., J.C.L.

Retired Bishop of Charleston; ordained May 27, 1950; appointed Coadjutor Bishop of Charleston April 22, 1989; ordained May 24, 1989; succeeded to Bishop of Charleston February 22, 1990; retired July 13, 1999. *Res., 4479 Downing Pl., Mount Pleasant, SC, 29466.* Tel.: 843-971-2810.

ESTABLISHED JULY 11, 1820.

Square Miles 31,055.

Comprises the State of South Carolina.

For legal titles of parishes and diocesan institutions, consult the Chancery Office.

Chancery Office: 119 Broad St., P.O. Box 818, Charleston, SC, 29402. Tel.: 843-723-3488; Fax: 843-724-6387.

Web site address: www.catholic-doc.org

E-mail address: jim@catholic-doc.org

STATISTICAL OVERVIEW

Personnel	
Bishop	1
Retired Bishops	1
Abbots	1
Retired Abbots	1
Priests: Diocesan Active in Diocese	56
Priests: Active Outside Diocese	7
Priests: Diocesan in Foreign Missions	1
Priests: Retired, Sick or Absent	23
Number of Diocesan Priests	87
Religious Priests in Diocese	34
Extern Priests in Diocese	14
Ordinations:	
Diocesan Priests	2
Transitional Deacons	1
Permanent Deacons in Diocese	70
Total Brothers	29
Total Sisters	151
Parishes	
Parishes	85
With Resident Pastor:	
Resident Diocesan Priests	59
Resident Religious Priests	15
Without Resident Pastor:	
Administered by Priests	7
Administered by Deacons	7
Administered by Professed Men Religious	1
Administered by Women Religious	2
Administered by Pastoral Teams, etc.	1
Missions	30
Pastoral Centers	10
Professional Ministry Personnel:	
Brothers	4
Sisters	29
Lay Ministers	66
Welfare	
Catholic Hospitals	2
Total Assisted	381,625
Homes for the Aged	1
Total Assisted	18
Special Centers for Social Services	7
Total Assisted	127,294
Educational	
Diocesan Students in Other Seminaries	13
Total Seminarians	13
High Schools, Diocesan and Parish	2
Total Students	1,145
High Schools, Private	2
Total Students	213
Elementary Schools, Diocesan and Parish	25
Total Students	6,782
Catechesis/Religious Education:	
High School Students	2,066
Elementary Students	9,248
Total Students Under Catholic Instruction	19,467
Teachers in the Diocese:	
Priests	2
Brothers	1
Sisters	16
Lay Teachers	652
Vital Statistics	
Receptions into the Church:	
Infant Baptism Totals	2,290
Adult Baptism Totals	262
Received into Full Communion	512
First Communions	2,225
Confirmations	1,752
Marriages:	
Catholic	347
Interfaith	378
Total Marriages	725
Deaths	1,019
Total Catholic Population	130,255
Total Population	4,012,012

Former Bishops—Rt. Rev. JOHN ENGLAND, D.D., first Bishop; cons. Sept. 21, 1820; died April 11, 1842.—Rt. Rev. WILLIAM CLANCY, D.D., cons. Dec. 21, 1834, Coadjutor made Vicar-Apostolic of British Guiana, April 12, 1837; died June 19, 1847.—Rt. Rev. IGNATIUS A. REYNOLDS, D.D., second Bishop; cons. March 19, 1844; died March 6, 1855.—Rt. Rev. PATRICK N. LYNCH, D.D., third Bishop; cons. March 14, 1858; died Feb. 26, 1882.—Rt. Rev. HENRY P. NORTHROP, D.D., fourth Bishop; cons. Titular-Bishop of Rosalia and Vicar-Apostolic of North Carolina, Jan. 8, 1882; transferred to Charleston, by brief dated Jan. 27, 1883; died June 7, 1916.—Rt. Rev. WILLIAM T. RUSSELL, D.D., fifth Bishop; cons. March 15, 1917; died March 18, 1927.—Most Rev. EMMET M. WALSH D.D., sixth Bishop; cons. Sept. 8, 1927; transferred to Youngstown, Ohio, as Coadjutor Bishop, Sept. 8, 1949.—Most Rev. JOHN J. RUSSELL, D.D., seventh Bishop; cons. March 14, 1950; transferred to Bishop of Richmond, July 10, 1958.—Most Rev. PAUL J. HALLINAN, D.D., eighth Bishop; cons. Oct. 28, 1958; transferred to Archbishop of Atlanta, Feb. 21, 1962.—Most Rev. FRANCIS F. REH, S.T.L., J.C.D., ninth Bishop; cons. June 29, 1962; appt. Titular Bishop of Macriana in Mauretania and Rector of North American College, Rome, Italy, Sept. 5, 1964; transferred to Saginaw, Dec. 18, 1968; installed Feb. 26, 1969; retired April 29, 1980.—Most Rev. ERNEST L. UNTERKOEFLER, D.D., J.C.D., S.T.L., tenth Bishop; ord. May 18, 1944; appt. Titular Bishop of Latopolis and Auxiliary Bishop of Richmond, Dec. 13, 1961; cons. Feb. 22, 1962; appt. Bishop of Charleston, Dec. 12, 1964; resigned Feb. 22, 1990; died Jan. 4, 1993.—Most Rev. DAVID B. THOMPSON, D.D., J.C.L., eleventh Bishop; ord. May 27, 1950; appt. Coadjutor Bishop of Charleston April 22, 1989; ord. May 24, 1989; succeeded to Bishop of Charleston Feb. 22, 1990; retired July 13, 1999.

Vicar General—Rev. Msgr. JAMES A. CARTER, P.A., V.G.; Rev. Msgr. JOSEPH R. ROTH, V.G.; Sr. SUSAN SCHORSTEN, H.M., Asst. to V.G.

Chancery Office—119 Broad St., P.O. Box 818, Charleston, 29402. Tel: 843-853-2130, Ext. 0; Fax: 843-724-6387.

Chancellor—CLEO E. CANTEY.

Archivist—MARY M. GILES. Tel: 843-724-8372.

Office of Finance—DENNIS F. ATWOOD, Chief Financial Officer; BERNADETTE M. FARETRA, Controller, *1662 Ingram Rd., Charleston, 29407.* Tel: 843-402-9115, Ext. 12; Fax: 843-402-9071.

Diocesan Curia—Rev. Msgr. JAMES A. CARTER, P.A., V.G., Moderator; Rev. Msgr. JOSEPH R. ROTH, V.G.; Rev. Msgr. LEIGH A. LEHOCKY, V.F., Vicar for Ecumenical Affairs & Pastoral Organizations; Rev. Msgr. CHARLES H. ROWLAND, Vicar for Judicial Affairs; Rev. Msgr. E. CHRISTOPHER LATHEM, V.F., Dir. Priest Personnel; Rev. Msgr. LAWRENCE B. MCINERNY; Sr. SUSAN SCHORSTEN, H.M., Asst. to V.G. DOROTHY GRILLO, Dir. Catholic Charities & Diocesan Social Ministry; Rev. MARTIN T. LAUGHLIN, Vicar Pro Tem,

Christian Formation/Education; DENNIS F. ATWOOD, Chief Financial Officer; DEIRDRE C. MAYS, Dir., Office of Communications & Information; LISA M. RAWLONS, Dir. Planning.

Diocesan Tribunal—114 Rear Broad St., P.O. Box 818, Charleston, 29402. Tel: 843-724-8363.

Vicar Judicial—Rev. Msgr. CHARLES H. ROWLAND, J.C.L.

Adjutant Vicar Judicial—Rev. Msgr. THOMAS X. HOFMANN, J.C.L.

Director of the Tribunal—MARY E. MCKENZIE.

Judges—Most Rev. DAVID B. THOMPSON, J.C.L.; Rev. Msgr. ROBERT J. KELLY; Rev. Msgr. JOSEPH R. ROTH, V.G.; Rev. H. GREGORY WEST, J.C.L.

Defenders of the Bond—Rev. Msgr. THOMAS R. DUFFY, V.F.; Revs. EDWARD W. FITZGERALD; JAMES L. LE BLANC; DENNIS B. WILLEY; Sr. CHRISTINA MURPHY; MARY E. MCKENZIE.

Promoter of Justice—Rev. DENNIS B. WILLEY.

Notaries—LUCINDA BRYAN; CLEO E. CANTEY.

College of Consultors—Rev. Msgr. JAMES A. CARTER, P.A., V.G.; Rev. Msgr. THOMAS R. DUFFY, V.F.; Rev. Msgr. ROBERT J. KELLY; Rev. Msgr. E. CHRISTOPHER LATHEM, V.F.; Rev. Msgr. LEIGH A. LEHOCKY, V.F.; Rev. Msgr. CHARLES H. ROWLAND; Very Revs. MICHAEL R. DEANTONIO, V.F.; JOSEPH A. WAHL, C.O.; Revs. PETER CLARKE; THOMAS A. EVATT; MICHAEL F. MCCAFFERTY; PAUL M. WILLIAMS, O.F.M.

Deans—Rev. Msgr. E. CHRISTOPHER LATHEM, V.F., Coastal Deanery; Rev. Msgr. LEIGH A. LEHOCKY, V.F., Midlands Deanery; Rev. Msgr. THOMAS R. DUFFY, V.F., Pee Dee Deanery; Very Rev. MICHAEL R. DE ANTONIO, V.F., Piedmont Deanery.

Diocesan Finance Committee—Rev. Msgr. JAMES A. CARTER, P.A., V.G., Chm., *P.O. Box 818, Charleston, 29402.* Tel: 843-853-2130, Ext. 6.

Presbyteral Council—Most Rev. ROBERT J. BAKER; Rev. Msgr. JAMES A. CARTER, P.A., V.G., Facilitator; Rev. Msgr. JOSEPH R. ROTH, V.G.; Rev. Msgr. THOMAS R. DUFFY, V.F.; Rev. Msgr. ROBERT J. KELLY; Rev. Msgr. E. CHRISTOPHER LATHEM, V.F.; Rev. Msgr. LEIGH A. LEHOCKY, V.F.; Rev. Msgr. CHARLES H. ROWLAND; Very Rev. MICHAEL R. DE ANTONIO, V.F.; Very Rev. JOSEPH A. WAHL, C.O.; Revs. PETER CLARKE; THOMAS A. EVATT; RICHARD D. HARRIS; JOSEPH F. HANLEY, JR.; TIMOTHY M. LIJEWSKI; PAUL M. WILLIAMS, O.F.M.; Sr. BRIDGET SULLIVAN, O.L.M., Sec.; Sr. SUSAN SCHORSTEN, H.M., Asst. to Vicar Gen.

Bishop's Missionary Support Committee—Rev. Msgr. ROBERT J. KELLY, *P.O. Box 1257, Folly Beach, 29439.* Tel: 843-588-2336.

Building Committee—Rev. Msgr. JAMES A. CARTER, P.A., V.G., Chm., *P.O. Box 724, Mt. Pleasant, 29465.* Tel: 843-884-5587.

Catholic Charities—DOROTHY GRILLO, Dir., *1662 Ingram Rd., Charleston, 29407.* Tel: 843-402-9115, Ext. 15.

Catholic Women, Council of—Rev. WILLIAM F. PENTIS, C.O., Moderator, *P.O. Box 11586, Rock Hill, 29731.* Tel: 803-327-2097.

Cemeteries—WARREN R. STUCKEY, JR., Dir., *604 Fort Johnson Rd., Charleston, 29412.* Tel: 843-795-2111.

Charismatic Renewals and Prayer Groups—JOSEPH BALAZS, Diocesan Liaison, *114 Horseshoe Cove, Sumter, 29150.* Tel: 803-773-1160.

Commission for Divine Worship and Sacraments—Rev. STEVEN L. BROVEY, Chm., *1209 Brushy Creek Rd., Taylors, 29687.* Tel: 864-268-4352.

Christian Formation/Education—Rev. MARTIN T. LAUGHLIN, Vicar Pro Tem, Education & Evangelization; GARY GELO, Supt. Catholic Schools; PAUL D. SCHROEDER, M.T.S., Dir., Catechesis, Initiation & Evangelization; GERALD C. WHITE, M.A., Dir., Youth & Young Adult Ministry; Vacant, Dir. Campus Ministry, *1662 Ingram Rd., Charleston, 29407.* Tel: 843-402-9115, Ext. 19.

Holy Childhood Association—Rev. Msgr. ROBERT J. KELLY, Dir., *P.O. Box 1257, Folly Beach, 49439.* Tel: 843-588-2336.

Marian Programs—Rev. D. ANTHONY DROZE, Moderator, *111 Hampton Ave., Greenville, 29601.* Tel: 864-271-8422.

Master of Episcopal Ceremonies—Rev. H. GREGORY WEST, J.C.L., Diocesan.

Office of Prayer & Worship—Rev. STEVEN L. BROVEY, *1209 Brushy Creek Rd., Taylors, 29687.* Tel: 864-268-4352.

Newspaper—*"The New Catholic Miscellany"*, JORDAN B. MCMORROUGH, Editor, *P.O. Box 818, Charleston, 29402.* Tel: 843-724-8375; Fax: 843-724-8368.

Propagation of the Faith—Rev. Msgr. ROBERT J. KELLY, Dir., *P.O. Box 1257, Folly Beach, 29439.* Tel: 843-588-2336.

Office of Communications & Information—DEIRDRE C. MAYS, Dir., *P.O. Box 818, Charleston, 29402.* Tel: 843-724-8375; Fax: 843-724-8368.

Vocations—Rev. DENNIS B. WILLEY, *1662 Ingram Rd., Charleston, 29407.* Tel: 843-402-9115, Ext. 22; 795-3821.

Bishop's Missionary League—*P.O. Box 818, Charleston, 29402.* Tel: 843-853-2130, Ext. 0.

Cursillo Movement—Vacant, Dir.

Permanent Diaconate—Rev. Msgr. JOSEPH R. ROTH, V.G., Dir., *503 37th Ave. N., Myrtle Beach, 29577.* Tel: 843-448-5930.

Campaign for Human Development—DOROTHY GRILLO, Chm., *1662 Ingram Rd., Charleston, 29407.* Tel: 843-402-9115, Ext. 15.

Office of Stewardship & Mission Advancement—MICHAEL J. GOCSIK, Sec., *P.O. Box 818, Charleston, 29402.* Tel: 843-853-2130, Ext. 211.

Personnel Committee—Rev. Msgr. E. CHRISTOPHER LATHEM, V.F., Chm.; Rev. Msgr. JAMES A. CARTER, P.A., V.G.; Rev. Msgr. THOMAS R. DUFFY, V.F.; Rev. Msgr. LEIGH A. LEHOCKY, V.F.; Rev. Msgr. CHESTER M. MOCZYDLOWSKI; Rev. Msgr. JOSEPH R. ROTH, V.G.; Very Rev. MICHAEL R. DE ANTONIO, V.F.; Rev. DENNIS B. WILLEY; Sr. MARY LAURA LESNIAK, S.S.M.N.; Sr. GUADALUPE STUMP, R.S.M.; Mr. JOHN CARROLL.

Priests' Retirement—*P.O. Box 818, Charleston, 29402.* Tel: 843-853-2130, Ext. 206.

Scouting Program—SAM E. HANVEY, *P.O. Box 639, Charleston, 29402.* Tel: 843-577-2600.

Office of Planning—LISA M. RAWLINS, Dir., *P.O. Box 818, Charleston, 29402.* Tel: 843-835-2130, Ext. 215.

Vietnamese Ministry—Sr. SUSAN SCHORSTEN, H.M., *P.O. Box 818, Charleston, 29402.* Tel: 843-853-2130, Ext. 206.

Vicar for African American Catholics—Rev. PAUL M. WILLIAMS, O.F.M., *307 Gower St., Greenville, 29611.* Tel: 803-233-7717.

Vicar for Ecumenism—Rev. Msgr. LEIGH A. LEHOCKY, V.F., *P.O. Box 1896, Columbia, 29202.* Tel: 803-779-0036.

Office for Hispanics—Sr. GUADALUPE STUMP, R.S.M., *P.O. Box 483, Hardeeville, 29927.* Tel: 843-784-6500.

Society of St. Vincent de Paul—DOROTHY GRILLO, Dir., *1662 Ingram Rd., Charleston, 29407.* Tel: 843-402-9115, Ext. 15.

Office of Black Catholic Ministry—Sr. SUSAN SCHORSTEN, H.M., Interim Coord., *P.O. Box 818, Charleston, 29402.* Tel: 843-853-2130, Ext. 206.

CLERGY, PARISHES, MISSIONS AND PAROCHIAL SCHOOLS

GREATER CHARLESTON
(Charleston County)

1—CATHEDRAL OF ST. JOHN THE BAPTIST, Rev. Msgr. Chester M. Moczydlowski.
Mailing Address: Cathedral Center, 120 Broad St., 29401. Tel: 843-724-8395; Fax: 843-724-6386.
Res., 105 Queen St., 29401.
School—Charleston Catholic School. See Sacred Heart for details.

2—ST. MARY'S, Rev. Msgr. Chester M. Moczydlowski.
Res., 89 Hasell St., 29401. Tel: 843-722-7696; Fax: 843-577-5036. [CEM]

3—ST. PATRICK'S, Rev. Basil P. Congro.
Res., 125 St. Philip St., P.O. Box 20726, 29413. Tel: 843-723-6066; Fax: 843-853-8114. [CEM]
School—Charleston Catholic School. See Sacred Heart for details.

4—SACRED HEART, Rev. Jeffrey A. Kendall.
Res., 888 King St., 29403-4139. Tel: 843-722-7018; Fax: 843-579-9604.
School—Charleston Catholic School, Tel: 843-577-4495; Fax: 843-577-6662. Yvonne T. Orr, Prin.
Lay Teachers 14; Students 218.

5—OUR LADY OF MERCY, Rev. Basil P. Congro.
Res., 77 America St., 29403. Tel: 843-723-6066; Fax: 843-853-8114.

6—ST. JOHN'S, Bros. Edward E. Bergeron, C.F.C., Parish Life Facilitator; Daniel P. McDonough, C.F.C.; Leonard A. Quinn, C.F.C.
Res., 3921 St. John's Ave., North Charleston, 29405-7158. Tel: 843-744-6201; Fax: 843-744-6493.
School—Tel: 843-744-3901; Fax: 843-744-3689. Ms. Carol Anne White, Prin.
Lay Teachers 10; Students 87.

7—BLESSED SACRAMENT, Rev. Joseph F. Hanley.
Res., 5 St. Teresa Dr., 29407. Tel: 843-556-0801; Fax: 843-556-2851.
School—7 St. Teresa Dr., 27407. Tel: 843-766-2128. Sr. Linda Marie Bolinski, SS.C.M., Prin.
Lay Teachers 26; Students 482.
Convent—O Moore Dr., 29407. Tel: 843-766-5120.

8—ST. PETER'S. Closed. For inquiries for parish records contact St. Patrick, P.O. Box 20726, Charleston, SC 29413.

9—DIVINE REDEEMER, Berkeley Co., Rev. James L. LeBlanc.
Office: 1106 Fort Dr., Hanahan, 29406. Tel: 843-553-0340; Fax: 843-553-0346.
Res., 1022 Recess Rd., Hanahan, 29406. Tel: 843-572-3532.
School—1104 Fort Dr., Hanahan, 29406. Tel: 843-553-1521; Fax: 843-553-7109. Jean Steinoff, Prin.
Lay Teachers 11; Students 260.

10—STELLA MARIS, Rev. Msgr. Lawrence B. McInerny.
Res., 1204 Middle St., P.O. Box 280, Sullivan's Island, 29482. Tel: 843-883-3108 (Office); 883-9158 (Rectory); Fax: 843-883-3160.

11—CHURCH OF THE NATIVITY, Rev. Dennis B. Willey. In res., Rev. Nicholas R. Bayard, (Retired).
Office & Mailing Address: 1061 Folly Rd., 29412. Tel: 843-795-3821; Fax: 843-795-2714.
Res., 1129 Pittsford Cir., 29412. Tel: 843-795-5525; Fax: 843-795-2714.
School—Tel: 843-795-3975. Dr. David Knab, Prin.
Lay Teachers 28; Students 310.
Mission—Folly Beach, Charleston Co., Our Lady of Good Counsel, 56 Center St., P.O. Box 1257, Folly Beach, 29439. Tel: 843-588-6384; Fax: 843-588-3478. Rev. Msgr. Robert J. Kelly.

12—ST. JOSEPH, Rev. Gabriel J. Smith.
Office & Mailing Address: 1695 Wallenberg Blvd., 29407. Tel: 843-556-4611; Fax: 843-556-4612.
Res., 1549 Montclair St., 29407.

13—ST. JOSEPH'S. Closed. For inquiries for parish records contact St. Joseph, 1695 Wallenberg Blvd., Charleston, SC 29407.

14—ST. THOMAS THE APOSTLE, Rev. William F. Leonard (MET).
Res., 6650 Dorchester Rd., Charleston Heights, 29418. Tel: 843-552-9045; 552-2223; Fax: 843-552-9077.

15—CHURCH OF THE HOLY SPIRIT, Rev. James Parker.
Res., 2545 Bohicket Rd., Johns Island, 29455. Tel: 843-559-0353; Fax: 842-559-4364. [CEM]

16—CHRIST THE DIVINE TEACHER, Rev. Jeffrey A. Kendall.
Mailing Address: MSC 58, The Citadel, 171 Moultrie St., 29409-0058. Tel: 843-953-7692; 722-7018 (Res.); Fax: 843-953-4811 (Res.).

17—CHRIST OUR KING, Rev. Msgr. James A. Carter, V.G.; Rev. Robert A. Spencer.
Res., 1122 Russell Dr., P.O. Box 724, Mount Pleasant, 29465. Tel: 843-884-5587; Fax: 843-884-7086.
Station—Mt. Pleasant, East Cooper Catholic Community, 1280 15 Miles Landing Rd., Awendaw, 29429-5915. Tel: 843-928-3437; Fax: 843-928-3447. Rev. Paul A. Brenninkmeijer, O.S.B.
School—Christ Our King-Stella Maris School, 1183 Russell Dr., Mount Pleasant, 29464. Tel: 843-884-4721; Fax: 843-971-9666. Sr. Stella Maris Craven, O.L.M., Prin.
Sisters 1; Lay Teachers 35; Students 708.

OUTSIDE OF THE CITY OF CHARLESTON

Abbeville, Abbeville Co., Sacred Heart, Sr. Joan Kobe, D.W., Parish Life Faciliatator.
Res., 230 N. Main St. at Pinckney St., P.O. Box 812, 29620. Tel: 864-459-5150; 465-3615 (Office); Fax: 864-465-3615 (Office).
Mission—McCormick, McCormick Co., Good Shepherd, P.O. Box 1468, McCormick, 29835. Tel: 864-465-3615. Sr. Joan Kobe, D.W., Parish Life Facilitator.
Station—Abbeville, McCormick Correction Institution.

Aiken, Aiken Co., St. Mary, Help of Christians, Rev. Msgr. Thomas A. Evatt; Rev. Gade Show Reddy (Warangal).
Res., 219 York St. S.E., P.O. Box 438, 29802. Tel: 803-649-4777; Fax: 803-642-6421. [CEM]
School—Tel: 803-649-2071; Fax: 803-643-0092. Mr. D. Keith Darr, Prin.
Sisters of Charity of Our Lady of Mercy 1; Lay Teachers 30; Students 320.
St. Gerard's, Rev. Thomas M. Gillin, S.J.
Res., 640 Edrie St., N.E., 29801. Tel: 803-649-3030; Fax: 803-649-3030.
School—Merged with St. Mary's School.

Anderson, Anderson Co., St. Joseph's, Rev. James N. Dubrouillet.
Office: 1303 McLees Rd., 29621. Tel: 864-225-5341; Fax: 864-224-0538.
Res., 1107 McLees Rd., P.O. Box 1013, 29622. Tel: 864-224-4415.
Church—1200 Cornelia Rd., 29621.

School—1200 Cornelia Rd., 29621. Tel: 864-225-2143; Fax: 864-224-0538. Mrs. Jacqueline Hogberg, Interim Prin.
Lay Teachers 7; Students 164.

St. Mary of the Angels, Rev. David L. Hyman, O.F.M. In res., Rev. Thomas F. Vigliotta, O.F.M.
Res., 1821 White St., P.O. Box 3, 29622. Tel: 864-226-8621; Fax: 864-226-2536.

Batesburg, Lexington Co., St. John of the Cross, Rev. Robert J. Sayer.
Res., 320 W. Columbia Ave., P.O. Box 2279, Batesburg-Leesville, 29070-2279. Tel: 803-532-1208.

Beaufort, Beaufort Co., St. Peter's, Rev. Ronald R. Cellini (PIT).
Res., 70 Lady's Island Dr., 29902. Tel: 843-522-9555; Fax: 843-522-0667. [CEM]
School—Tel: 843-522-2163. Mr. William Gabrielson, Prin.
Lay Teachers 12; Students 193.
Mission—Saint Helena Island, Beaufort Co., Holy Cross.

Bluffton, Beaufort Co., St. Gregory the Great, Rev. H. Gregory West, J.C.L.
Office & Mailing address: 338 Fording Island Rd., 29910. [CEM]
Res., 232 Pinckney Colony Rd., 29910. Tel: 843-815-3100; Fax: 843-815-3150.
Chapel—St. Andrew, 220 Pinckney Rd., 29910.
Mission—Hardeeville, Jasper Co., St. Anthony, P.O. Box 487, Hardeeville, 29927. Tel: 843-784-2943; Fax: 843-784-5338. Sr. Mary Gallagher, R.S.M., Parish Life Facilitator.

Camden, Kershaw Co., Our Lady of Perpetual Help, Rev. James M. Crowley, O.M.I.
Res., 1709 Lyttleton St., 29020. Tel: 803-432-6131; Fax: 803-432-3440.

Chapin, Lexington Co., Our Lady of the Lake, Rev. Andrew J. Vollkommer.
Mailing Address: 195 Amicks Ferry Rd., P.O. Box 549, 29036. Tel: 803-345-3962; Fax: 803-345-8933.
Res., 2 Oak Stand Ct., Irmo, 29063. Tel: 803-781-8767.

Cheraw, Chesterfield Co., St. Peter's, Revs. Patrick E. Cooper; Bernardino S. Yebra (Manila).
Res., 602 Market St., P.O. Box 905, 29520. Tel: 843-537-7351.
Missions—Bennettsville, Marlboro Co., St. Denis; Pageland, Chesterfield Co., St. Ernest.

Chester, Chester Co., St. Joseph's, Rev. Thomas F. Morrison; Deacon James P. Hyland, Parish Life Facilitator.
Res., 110 West End, P.O. Box 869, 29706. Tel: 803-377-4695; Fax: 803-581-7848.

Clemson, Pickens Co., St. Andrew, Revs. Bernard J. Campbell, C.S.P.; Gerard J. Aylward, C.S.P.; Augustus S. McGuire, C.S.P.; James M. Brucz, C.S.P.
Res., 123 Folger St., P.O. Box 112, 29633. Tel: 864-654-2711; 654-1757; Fax: 864-654-2950.
Missions—Seneca, Oconee Co., St. Paul the Apostle; Walhalla, Oconee Co., St. Francis of Assisi.
Station—Clemson, Clemson University.

Columbia, Richland Co.,

1—ST. PETER'S, Rev. Msgr. Leigh A. Lehocky.
Mailing Address: P.O. Box 1896, 29202.
Res., 2125 Raven Tr., West Columbia, 29169.
Church—1529 Assembly St., 29201. Tel: 803-779-0036; Fax: 803-799-2438. [CEM 3]
School—Tel: 803-252-8285. Mrs. Madeline McMillion, Prin.
Lay Teachers 20; Students 192.
Station—Columbia, South Carolina State Hospital.

2—ST. JOSEPH, Rev. Msgr. Charles H. Rowland; Rev. Craig Thomas Miles.
Office: 3512 Devine St., 29205. Tel: 803-254-7646; Fax: 803-799-7607.
Res., 3451 Blossom St., 29205. Tel: 803-540-1910.
Church—3600 Devine St., 29205.
School—3700 Devine St., 29205. Tel: 803-254-6736; Fax: 803-540-1913. Sr. Christina Murphy, S.N.D., Prin.
Ursuline Nuns of the Congregation of Paris 2; Lay Teachers 32; Students 354.
Mission—Winnboro, Fairfield Co., St. Theresa, c/o 9720 Wilson Blvd., Blythewood, 29016. Tel: 803-735-0512; Fax: 803-735-1742. Rev. R. Inna Reddy; Sr. Clare Reinert, S.S.N.D., Parish Life Facilitator.

3—SAINT MARTIN DE PORRES, Rev. Steven J. Pavignano, O.F.M.
Res., 2229 Hampton St., 29204. Tel: 803-254-6862; Fax: 803-799-4720.
School—Mrs. Sandra Leatherwood, Prin. Lay Teachers 10; Students 125.
Station—Columbia, Correctional Institutions in the Greater Columbia Area.

4—OUR LADY OF THE HILLS, Rev. Robert H. Fix.
Mailing Address: & Religious Education Center: 2700 Ashland Rd., 29210. Tel: 803-772-7400; Fax: 803-798-8030.
Res., 120 Marydale Ln., 29210. Tel: 803-772-6692.

5—ST. JOHN NEUMANN, Rev. Frederick F. Masad.
Res., 2816 Bancroff Rd., P.O. Box 23689, 29224. Tel: 803-788-1274; 788-0811 (Office); Fax: 803-788-1501 (Office).
Church—100 Polo Rd., 29223. Tel: 803-788-1478.
School—721 Polo Rd., 29223. Tel: 803-788-1367; Fax: 803-788-7330. Dr. Margaret Adams, Prin.
Lay Teachers 35; Students 404.
Mission—Blythewood, Transfiguration Catholic Community, 9720 Wilson Blvd., Blythewood, 29016. Tel: 803-735-0512; Fax: 803-735-1742. Rev. R. Inna Reddy; Sr. Clare Reinert, S.S.N.D., Parish Life Facilitator.

6—GOOD SHEPHERD, Rev. William D. Ladkau.
Mailing Address: P.O. Box 1298, 29202.
Res., 1625 Granby Rd., Cayce, 29033. Tel: 803-791-4596; 765-1334 (Office); Fax: 803-765-2208.

Conway, Horry Co., St. James, Rev. Frederick LaBrecque.
Church & Office: 1071 Academy Dr., 29526. Tel: 843-347-5168; Fax: 843-347-1212.
Res., 181 Long Ave., 29526. Tel: 843-248-7148.
Mission—Loris, Horry Co., Church of the Resurrection, 1929 Business Hwy. 9E, Loris, 29569. Tel: 843-756-6168.

Dillon, Dillon Co., St. Louis, Deacon John S. Larkin (PAT) Parish Life Facilitator.
Res., 607 N. Fourth Ave., 29536. Tel: 843-774-1582; 774-0255 (Office); Fax: 843-774-0257.
Mission—Marion, Marion Co., Infant Jesus.

Edgefield, Edgefield Co., St. Mary's, Rev. Robert W. Ninedorf.
Res., 302 Jeter St., 29824. Tel: 803-637-6248; Fax: 803-637-6248. [CEM]
Church—305 Buncombe St., 29824.

Florence, Florence Co., St. Anthony's All Souls Memorial, Rev. Arturo O. Dalupang.
Res., 2536 W. Hoffmeyer Rd., P.O. Box 5327, 29502. Tel: 843-665-5853; 662-5674; Fax: 843-662-4800.
School—Tel: 843-662-1910; Fax: 843-662-5335. Mrs. Barbara A. Cole, Prin.
Priests 2; Lay Teachers 17; Students 276.

St. Ann, Rev. Michael T. Corrigan (GAL).
Res., 113 S. Kemp St., 29501. Tel: 843-662-1736; Fax: 843-676-9001.

Gaffney, Cherokee Co., Sacred Heart, Rev. Raymond J. Carlo (STA).
Res., 407 Grace St., 29340. Tel: 864-489-9453; Fax: 864-488-2302.

Garden City, Horry Co., St. Michael, Rev. Msgr. Thomas R. Duffy; Revs. Anthony Pasala (Warangal); Robert James Sayer.
Mailing Address: P.O. Box 2659, Murrells Inlet, 29576.
Res., 572 Cypress Ave., 29576. Tel: 843-651-3737; Fax: 843-651-6316.
School—(Grades K-5). Tel: 843-651-6795; Fax: 843-651-6803. Sr. Roberta Thoen, S.S.M.N., Prin.
Lay Teachers 5; Students 65.

Georgetown, Georgetown Co., St. Mary's, (Our Lady of Ransom). Rev. Gerald J. Ryfinski.
Office: 317 Broad St., P.O. Box 766, 29442. Tel: 843-546-7416; Fax: 843-546-7003.
Res., 810 Highmark St., 29442.
Missions—Andrews, Georgetown Co., St. Leo the Great; McClellanville, Charleston Co., McClellanville Mission.

St. Cyprian, Rev. Gerald J. Ryfinski; Sr. Kathleen Driscoll, D.C., Parish Life Facilitator.
Center & Mailing Address: 1905 Front St., P.O. Box 2037, 29442. Tel: 843-546-1470; Fax: 843-527-2139.

Gloverville, Aiken Co., Our Lady of the Valley, Rev. John L. Lawlor, C.M.; Deacon Robert J. Waters, Parish Life Facilitator.
Mailing Address: P.O. Box 419, 29828. Tel: 803-593-2241; Fax: 803-593-2241.
Res., 2429 Augusta Rd., 29828. Tel: 803-593-2241.
Parish Community Center—Tel: 803-593-2241.
Convent—Horsecreek Valley Convent, P.O. Box 358, 29828. Tel: 803-593-9862.
Daughters of Charity 4.

Goose Creek, Berkeley Co., Immaculate Conception, Revs. Frank Palmieri, C.R.M.; Nicholas Capetola, C.R.M.
Res., 510 St. James Ave., 29445. Tel: 843-553-1386; 572-1270; Fax: 843-572-3128.

Greenville, Greenville Co., St. Mary's, Revs. D. Anthony Droze; Justin S. Ukpong (UYO). In res., Rev. Louis J.P. Kennedy (RK).
Mailing Address: 111 Hampton Ave., 29601. Tel: 864-271-8422; Fax: 864-370-9880.
Res., 338 W. Washington St., 29601. Tel: 864-235-2868.
School—101 Hampton Ave., 29601. Tel: 864-271-3870. Sr. Veronica Janas, O.L.M., Prin.
Sisters of Charity of Our Lady of Mercy 1; Lay Teachers 23; Students 347.

Our Lady of the Rosary, Rev. Charles J. Day.
Res., 3710 Augusta Rd., P.O. Box 8396, 29604. Tel: 864-422-1648; Fax: 864-277-5969.
School—Tel: 864-277-5350; Fax: 864-277-7745. Mrs. Therese Gallivan, Acting Prin.
Lay Teachers 17; Students 234.

St. Anthony of Padua, Rev. Paul M. Williams, O.F.M. In res., Rev. Francis A. Gorman, O.F.M., (Retired).
Res., 307 Gower St., 29611. Tel: 864-233-7717; Fax: 864-233-2852.
School—309 Gower St., 29611. Tel: 864-271-0167; Fax: 864-271-2936. Sr. Catherine Noecker, O.S.F., Prin.
Sisters of St. Francis of Williamsville 4; Lay Teachers 8; Students 125.

Greenwood, Greenwood Co., Our Lady of Lourdes, Rev. Richard D. Harris.
Office: 110 E. Laurel Ave., 29649. Tel: 864-223-8410; Fax: 864-223-5555.
Res., 120 Colonial Dr., 29649. Tel: 864-223-3003.

Greer, Greenville Co., Blessed Trinity, Rev. Louis J.P Kennedy (BRK).
Res., 904 River Rd., 29651. Tel: 864-801-4101; Fax: 864-879-4225.
Church—901 River Rd., P.O. Box 1371, 29652. Tel: 864-879-4225.

Hartsville, Darlington Co., St. Mary the Virgin Mother, Rev. Karl Roesch, O.S.B.
Res., 115 Church St., 29550. Tel: 843-332-7773; 332-3136; Fax: 843-332-2812.
Mission—Darlington, Darlington Co., St. Joseph the Worker.

St. Joseph's. Closed. For inquiries for parish records contact St. Mary's, 115 Church St., Hartsville, SC 29550.

Hilton Head Island, Beaufort Co., Holy Family, Rev. Edmund M. McCaffrey.
Res., 24 Pope Ave., P.O. Box 5397, 29938. Tel: 843-785-2895; 785-2876; Fax: 843-842-7494.

St. Francis By the Sea, Rev. Michael F. McCafferty.
Res., 45 Beach City Rd., 29926-2423. Tel: 843-681-6350; Fax: 843-689-5502.
School—29926. Tel: 843-681-6501; Fax: 843-689-3725. Mrs. Mary Fallon, Prin.
Lay Teachers 12; Students 227.

Joanna, Laurens Co., St. Boniface, Rev. Alexei Choquet (CHL); Sr. Mary Laura Lesniak, S.S.M.N., Parish Life Facilitator.
Office: 403 Main St., P.O. Box 188, 29351. Tel: 864-697-6745.
Mission—Laurens, Laurens Co., Holy Spirit, P.O. Box 864, Laurens, 29360. Tel: 864-984-2880; Fax: 864-984-2880. Sr. Mary Laura Lesniak, S.S.M.N., Parish Life Facilitator.
Station—Clinton, Laurens Co., Whitten Center.

Kingstree, Williamsburg Co., St. Ann's, Rev. Jerome A. Ward, O.M.I.; Deacon John D. Kiely, Parish Life Facilitator.
Res., 300 Ashton Ave., 29556. Tel: 843-394-8343; Fax: 843-394-8343.
Center—906 Thorne Ave., 29556. Tel: 843-354-9415.
Convent—908 Thorne Ave., 29556. Tel: 843-354-9415.
Felician Sisters 2.

Lake City, Florence Co., St. Philip's, Rev. John A. Ward, O.M.I.; Deacon John D. Kiely, Parish Life Facilitator.
Res., 146 Anderson St., P.O. Box 399, 29560. Tel: 843-394-8343; Fax: 843-394-8343.
Mission—Johnsonville, Florence Co., St. Patrick.

Lancaster, Lancaster Co., St. Catherine's, Rev. Thomas F. Morrison.
Res., 720 W. Meeting St., 29720. Tel: 803-283-3362; Fax: 803-283-3363.
Mission—Great Falls, Chester Co., St. Michael.

Lexington, Lexington Co., Corpus Christi, Rev. Robert J. Sayer.
Res., 2350 Augusta Hwy., 29072. Tel: 803-359-4391; Fax: 803-359-8885.

Mauldin, Greenville Co., St. Elizabeth Ann Seton, Rev. Howard L. Coughlin.
Mailing & Office Address: P.O. Box 672, 29662-0672. Tel: 864-963-3959; 963-8428; Fax: 864-967-9726.
Res., 115 Ivy Dr., Simpsonville, 29680-6124. Tel: 864-967-3125.

Moncks Corner, Berkeley Co., St. Philip Benizi, Rev. Hayden J. Vaverek.
Res., 1404 Old Hwy. 52 S., 29461. Tel: 843-761-3777; Fax: 843-761-0905.
Mission—Bonneau, Berkeley Co., Our Lady of Peace, 224 Murry Ferry Rd., Bonneau, 29431.

Murphy Village, Edgefield Co., St. Edward, Rev. Peter Clarke.
Res., 1370 Edgefield Rd., P.O. Box 6340, North Augusta, 29861. Tel: 803-279-1837; Fax: 803-279-9655.

Myrtle Beach, Horry Co., St. Andrew's, Rev. Msgr. Joseph R. Roth, V.G.; Revs. Ronald J. Farrell; John C. McGinnity (WH).
Parish Center—512 36th Ave. N., 29577. Tel: 843-448-5930; Fax: 843-448-3947.
Res., 503 37th Ave. N., 29577. Tel: 843-448-5930; Fax: 843-448-3947.
School—3601 N. Kings Hwy., 29577. Tel: 843-448-0315; Fax: 843-626-8644. Mrs. Mary H. Halasz, Prin.
Sisters 1; Lay Teachers 13; Students 255.

Newberry, Newberry Co., St. Mark, Rev. Alexei R. Choquet (CHL).
Res., 928 Boundary St., 29108. Tel: 803-276-6446; Fax: 803-276-0856.

North Augusta, Alken Co., Our Lady of Peace, Rev. C. Alexander McDonald.
Res., 856 Old Edgefield Rd., P.O. Box 6605, 29861-6605. Tel: 803-279-0315; Fax: 803-279-5247.
School—Mr. Michael Orsin, Prin. Lay Teachers 16; Students 181.

North Myrtle Beach, Horry Co., Our Lady Star of the Sea, Rev. George F. Moynihan.
Office: 1100 Eighth Ave. N., 29582. Tel: 843-249-2356; Fax: 843-249-8514.
Res., 1105 Golf View Dr., 29582. Tel: 843-249-8049.

Orangeburg, Orangeburg Co., Holy Trinity, Rev. Michael J. Polewczak (ALB).
Office & Mailing Address: 2202 Riverbank Dr., 29118-4044. Tel: 803-534-8177; Fax: 802-535-0012.
Res., 2161 Griffith Dr., N.W., 29116.
Brothers Residence—1710 Amelia St., N.E., 29115. Tel: 803-534-2302.
Xaverian Brothers (St. Joseph Prov.) 4.
Missions—Allendale, Barnwell Co., St. Mary; Barnwell, Barnwell Co., St. Andrew the Apostle, c/o Rev. Michael J. Oenbrink, 168 Madison St., Barnwell, 29812. Tel: 803-259-7593; Blackville, Barnwell Co., Sacred Heart; Springfield, Orangeburg Co., St. Theresa.
Christ the King. Closed. For inquiries for parish records contact Holy Trinity, 2202 Riverbank Dr., N.W. 29118-4044. Tel: 803-534-8177.

Pawleys Island, Georgetown Co., Precious Blood of Christ, Rev. Patrick J. Stenson, M.S.C.
Res., 100 Arcadia Rd., 29585.
Office: 1633 Waverly Rd., 29585. Tel: 843-237-3428; Fax: 843-237-2293.

Pickens, Pickens Co., Holy Cross, Rev. Francis J. Travis.
Res., 416 John St., P.O. Box 855, 29671. Tel: 864-878-0574.
Church—558-560 Hampton St., 29671. Tel: 864-878-3820; Fax: 864-878-0028.
Mission—Easley, Anderson Co., St. Luke, Tel: 864-269-6891.

Ridgeland, Jasper Co., St. Anthony's, Rev. Michael J. Hussey, O.M.I.
Res., U.S. Hwy. 17, P.O. Box 548, 29936. Tel: 843-726-3606; Fax: 843-726-3606.
Mission—Hampton, Hampton Co., St. Mary.

Rock Hill, York Co., St. Anne's, Rev. William F. Pentis, C.O.
Office & Mailing Address: 1694 Bird St., 29730. Tel: 803-329-2662; Fax: 803-329-2190.
Res., 434 Charlotte Ave., 29731. Tel: 803-327-3236.
School—Tel: 803-324-4814; Fax: 803-324-4281. Mr. Frederick J. McKay, Jr., Prin.
Lay Teachers 22; Students 366.
Mission—Fort Mill, York Co., St. Philip Neri, 292 Munn Rd., Fort Mill, 29715. Tel: 803-548-7282; Fax: 803-547-2999. Rev. John P. Giuliani, C.O., Admin.
St. Mary's, Bro. David Boone, C.O., Parish Life Facilitator; Sr. Francis K. Saring, M.S.B.T., Parish Life Facilitator.
Office—Bannon Hall, 902 Crawford Rd., P.O. Box 11982, 29731. Tel: 803-329-1008; Fax: 803-329-3799.
Convent—Missionary Servants of the Most Blessed Trinity. 915 Crawford Rd., 29730. Tel: 803-327-7450. St. Mary's Missionary Cenacle
Saint Martin de Porres Recreation Center—911 Crawford Rd., 29730.

Simpsonville, Greenville Co., St. Mary Magdalene, Revs. Herbert K. Conner, S.J.; John T. O'Holohan, S.J.
Res., 107 Wickersham Dr., 29681. Tel: 864-234-5323.
Church & Office: 2252 Woodruff Rd., 29681. Tel: 864-288-4884; Fax: 864-297-5804.

Spartanburg, Spartanburg Co., St. Paul the Apostle, Very Rev. Michael R. DeAntonio, V.F.; Rev. Santiago A. Mora, T.O.R.
Res., 161 N. Dean St., 29302. Tel: 864-582-0674; Fax: 864-582-0716.
School—Tel: 864-582-6645; Fax: 864-582-1225. Mrs. Marsha Calvert, Prin.
Lay Teachers 18; Students 181.
St. Joseph's. Closed. For inquiries for parish records contact St. Paul the Apostle, Spartanburg.
Jesus Our Risen Savior, Rev. Eugene A. Leonard.
Res., 2575 Reidville Rd., P.O. Box 17059, 29301. Tel: 864-576-1164; 576-0726; Fax: 864-576-0860.

Summerton, Clarendon Co., St. Mary's, Deacon Charles M. Walsh, Parish Life Facilitator.
Res., 10 N. Cantey St., P.O. Box 960, 29148. Tel: 803-485-2925; Fax: 803-473-5111.
Mission—Holly Hill, Orangeburg Co., St. Ann, 8309 Old State Rd., P.O. Box 1520, Holly Hill, 29059. Tel: 803-496-7636. Rev. Scott J. A. Buchanan.
Station—Santee, Orangeburg Co., Santee Catholic Community.

Summerville, Dorchester Co., St. John the Beloved, Rev. Msgr. E. Christopher Lathem.
Res., 28 Sumter Ave., 29483. Tel: 843-873-0631; Fax: 843-873-1431.
School—Summerville Regional Catholic School, (Grades K-8) 226 Black Oak Blvd., 29483. Tel: 843-873-9310; Fax: 843-873-5709. Dr. Dianne Kochamba, Prin.
Sisters 1; Lay Teachers 21; Students 369.
St. Theresa the Little Flower, Rev. Msgr. Edward D. Lofton.
Res., 11001 Dorchester Rd., 29485. Tel: 843-875-5002; 875-3609; Fax: 843-875-4884.
Station—Summerville, MacDougall Correction Center.

Sumter, Sumter Co., St. Anne's, Revs. Daniel J. Carboy, C.SS.R.; Alistair J. McKay, C.SS.R.
Res., 216 E. Liberty St., 29150. Tel: 803-773-3524; Fax: 803-778-1644. [CEM]
School—Tel: 803-775-3692. Mr. John Fer, Prin.
Lay Teachers 13; Students 210.
St. Jude, Rev. Michael Varady, C.SS.R.
Res., 611 W. Oakland Ave., P.O. Box 1589, 29150. Tel: 803-773-9244; Fax: 803-775-6913.
Preschool & Tutorial Program—114 S. Purdy St., 29150. Tel: 803-775-4895.

Taylors, Greenville Co., Prince of Peace, Rev. Steven L. Brovey.
Mailing Address: 1209 Brushy Creek Rd., 29687. Tel: 864-268-4352; Fax: 864-322-2239.
Res., 1201 Brushy Creek Rd., 29687. Tel: 864-244-7799.

Union, Union Co., St. Augustine's, Rev. Raymond J. Carlo, (STA).
Res., 103 E. South St., P.O. Box 507, 29379. Tel: 864-427-7240.

Walterboro, Colleton Co., St. Anthony's, Rev. Paul F.X. Seitz.
Res., 925 S. Jefferies Blvd., P.O. Box 933, 29488. Tel: 843-549-5230; Fax: 843-549-9176.
Mission—Ritter, Colleton Co., St. James. [CEM]
St. Joseph's. Closed. For inquiries for parish records contact St. Anthony's, P.O. Box 933, Walterboro, SC 29488.

Ward, Saluda Co., St. William's, Rev. Robert W. Ninedorf; Deacon John P. Klein, Parish Life Facilitator.
Res., Saluda Hwy. No. 39, 29166. Tel: 864-445-7215; Fax: 864-445-7215. [CEM]

Yonges Island, Charleston Co., St. Mary, Rev. William G. Kinney.
Res., 4255 State Hwy. 165, 29449. Tel: 843-889-8549; Fax: 843-869-0124.
Mission—Edisto Island, Charleston Co., SS. Frederick & Stephen, P.O. Box 602, Edisto Island, 29438.

York, York Co., Divine Saviour, Rev. Edward P. McDevitt, C.O.
Res., 232 Herndon Ave., P.O. Box 341, 29745. Tel: 803-684-3431; 327-2097; Fax: 803-684-3431.
Mission—Lake Wylie, York Co., All Saints.

Chaplains of Public Institutions

LEXINGTON. *Correctional Institutions in the Greater Columbia Area* 4214 Grand St., 29203. Tel: 803-786-7177. Mr. Roland L. Thomas.

Special Assignment:
Reverend Monsignors—
Hofmann, Thomas X., P.O. Box 818, Charleston, SC 29402
Reverend Fathers—
Juya, Filemon (Colombia), 1000 Windsor Dr., Apt. 26 B, Columbia, SC 29223
Kennedy, Ernest E., 105 Driftwood, Bonneau, SC 29431

On Duty Outside the Diocese:
Reverend Monsignors—
Gorski, J. Donald, Casa Parroquial, Zorritos-Tumbes, Peru
Reverend Fathers—
Abbott, Donald S., St. Dorothy's Church, 11 Harnden St., Wilmington, MA 01887-3519
Danel, Christopher M., North American Pontifical College, Pontificial University of St. Thomas Aquinas, Rome, Italy
Fitzgerald, Edward W., Pontifical North American College, Vatican State, 00120
McDuffie, Paul A., Aloysius Gonzaga Church, 2025 Stuart Ave., Baton Rouge, LA 70808-3998
Newman, J. Scott, Pontifical College Josephinum, 7625 N. High St., Columbus, OH 43235
White, Leland J., Theology Dept., St. John's Univ., c/o P.O Box 757, Charleston, SC 29402

Military Chaplains:
Reverend Fathers—
Linsky, Gary S., U.S. Air Force
Torm, Agustin, U.S. Army

Absent On Leave:
Reverend Fathers—
Bench, John F.
Bleiler, William C.
Condon, Eugene L.
Davino, Michael J.
Dilley, Gary D.
Mintegui, Marc A.
Sorce, John J.
Watters, Timothy J.

Retired:
Reverend Monsignors—
Aiken, Roy F., P.O. Box 1728, Columbia, SC 29202
Hamburger, Donald C., P.O. Box 1051, Columbia, SC 29202
Hopwood, Frederick J.
McManus, J. Fleming, 1809 Mepkin Dr., Charleston, SC 29407
Simonin, John A., 826 N. Shem Dr., Mt. Pleasant, SC 29464-4009
Reverend Fathers—
Bayard, Nicholas R., 1129 Pittsford Cir., Charleston, SC 29412
Burke, Henry J., 720 Garden Lake St., Murrells Inlet, SC 29576
Burn, William C., 2107 Westchase Dr., Charleston, SC 29407-8829
Cilwick, Theodore T., 2225 Ashley River Rd., Apt. 182, Charleston, SC 29414
Mullen, Edward F., 1175 Haywood Rd., Apt. 11A, Greenville, SC 20615-2275
Owens-Howard, Robert J.
Patat, St. John E., 1333 Ashley River Rd., Charleston, SC 29407-5315
Powers, Jerome C., 606 Muller Ave., Columbia, SC 29203
Riplog, Duane T., 298 Summerset Ln., Summerville, SC 29483-8338
Snopek, Charles J., 2200 Kirkland Dr., Conway, SC 29529

Permanent Deacons:
Anonie, Joseph A., Immaculate Conception Church, Goose Creek
Biviano, Joseph P., Our Lady of the Lake Church, Chapin
Brown, John H., St. Joseph's Church, Charleston
Cahill, Joseph F., Christ Our King Church, Mount Pleasant
Carmody, Joseph E., St. John the Beloved Church, Summerville
Cassandra, Anthony J., Our Lady of the Rosary Church, Greenville
Cole, Stephen D., (Retired)
Crocker, Dr. Jack L., Our Lady of the Hills Church, Columbia
Cuomo, Nicholas G., (Retired)
Dashnaw, Donald R. (OG), Divine Redeemer Church, Hanahan
Davis, Thomas E., St. Theresa the Little Flower Church, Summerville
DeBlasio, Anthony A. (MET), St. Andrew's Church, Myrtle Beach
Delmonte, Richard (HRT), St. John the Beloved Church, Summerville
Dillard, Henry, St. Anthony's Church, Greenville
DiRusso, Charles R., Our Lady of the Hills Church, Columbia
Dotson, Robert (CHL), St. Andrew, Bluffton
Dwyer, Jon, St. Joseph, Chester
Easterling, Charles M., St. Peter's Church, Columbia
Efken, Donald C. (STL), St. Michael's Church, Garden City
Elliott, Thomas B. (WDC), St. Theresa the Little Flower Church, Summerville
Ellis, Billy, Maj. Gen. (Retired), St. Jude's Church, Sumter
Farina, Frank J., St. Mary's Church, Greenville
Fiore, Charles (MIA), St. Michael's Church, Garden City
Gorman, Chester E., St. Andrew's Church, Myrtle Beach

Grismore, Gerald, Prince of Peace Church, Taylors
Hanvey, Samuel E., Cathedral of St. John the Baptist, Charleston
High, Raymond, Corpus Christi Church, Lexington
Hyland, James P., St. Anne's Church, Rock Hill
Johnson, James H., St. Ann's Church, Florence
Jones, Dennis N., On Duty Outside the Diocese
Jones, Robert L., On Duty Outside the Diocese
Karandisevsky, John F., St. Mary's Church, Greenville
Kemper, Joseph C., (Retired)
Kiely, John D. (TR), St. Philip the Apostle Church, Lake City
Klein, John P. (NY), St. William's Church, Ward
Kronyak, Robert C. (Pat), St. Ann's Church, Holly Hill
Larkin, John S. Jr. (PAT), St. Louis Church, Dillon
Lenny, William P. (DET), St. Elizabeth Ann Seton Church, Mauldin
Lorenzo, Anthony J. (RVC), (Retired)
Lozada, Mariano L. (PH), Jesus Our Risen Savior Church, Spartanburg
Mahaffey, Robert L., Jr., St. Paul the Apostle Church, Spartanburg
McDonald, Thomas F., Divine Redeemer Church, Hanahan
Meyer, John P. (PAT), St. James Church, Conway
Meyer, Philip M., Stella Maris Church, Sullivan Island
Mirande, August J., Our Lady Star of the Sea Church, North Myrtle Beach
Murtaugh, Richard J., Jr., St. Elizabeth Ann Seton Church, Mauldin
Nazzaro, Joseph J. (NEW), St. Francis by the Sea Church, Hilton Head
Nunez, Guillermo (NEW), The Oratory, Rock Hill
O'Donnell, John D., St. Anthony's Church, Florence
O'Grady, Lowell A. (VEN), Blessed Trinity Church, Greer
Osbourne, R. Michael, Stella Maris Church, Sullivan's Island
Pecko, Harry C., St. Augustine's Church, Union
Petrusak, Frank T., St. Thomas the Apostle Church, Charleston
Pezanowski, Walter S., Stella Maris Church, Sullivan's Island
Poole, Charles P., Jr., St. Joseph's Church, Columbia
Ramirez, Jorge V., (CHI), St. Thomas the Apostle Church; St. Peter's Church, Beaufort
Richardson, David W. (NEW), Holy Spirit Church, Johns Island
Rock, Paul J., On Duty Outside the Diocese
Shook, Paul F., St. Jesus Our Risen Savior Church, Spartanburg
Sturm, Robert M., Our Risen Savior Church, Spartanburg
Thomas, Roland L., St. Martin de Porres Church, Columbia
Tierney, George, St. Mary's Magdalene Church, Simpsonville
Traxler, Harold Gr. Jr. (CAM), St. Andrew's Church, Clemson
Tyson, Robert J. (ALN), Our Lady Star of the Sea Church, North Myrtle Beach
Walsh, Charles Michael (CHI), St. Mary's Church, Summerton
Waters, Robert J., St. Mary Help of Christians Church, Aiken
West, James L., On duty outside of the diocese.
Whitford, James E. Sr. (ROC), Immaculate Conception Church, Goose Creek
Wright, Winston C., St. Anthony's Church, Greenville
Young, James R., St. Mary's Church, Georgetown

INSTITUTIONS LOCATED IN THE DIOCESE

[A] HIGH SCHOOLS, DIOCESAN

CHARLESTON. *Bishop England High School*, 363 Seven Farms Dr., 29492-7534. Tel: 843-849-9599; Fax: 843-849-9221.
E-mail: dheld@behs.com
Web site: www.behs.com
Rev. Msgr. Robert J. Kelly; Mr. David F. Held, Prin..Priests 1; Lay Teachers 68; Students 895.

COLUMBIA. *Cardinal Newman High School.* (Grades 7-12), 4701 Forest Dr., 29206. Tel: 803-782-2814; Fax: 803-782-9314.
E-mail: jimmcintyrecns@hotmail.com
Mr. Jim McIntyre, Prin..Sisters 1; Lay Teachers 37; Students 400.

[B] HIGH SCHOOLS, PRIVATE

GREENVILLE. *St. Joseph's High School*, 4810 Frontage Rd., 29607. Tel: 864-234-9009. Keith F. Kiser, Prin. Lay Teachers 22; Students 165.

SUMTER. *St. Xavier High School*, 15 School St., 29150. Tel: 803-773-0210; Fax: 803-775-0119.
E-mail: sfxhs@ftc-1.net
Frank J. Cottone, Prin..Lay Teachers 6.

[C] GENERAL HOSPITALS

CHARLESTON. *Bon Secours St. Francis Hospital*, 2095 Henry Tecklenburg Dr., 29414. Tel: 843-402-1000
For a complete listing, refer to the Hospitals section.

GREENVILLE. *Bon Scours St. Francis Health System, Inc.*, One St. Francis Dr., 29601. Tel: 864-255-1000; Fax: 864-255-1034
For a complete listing, refer to the Hospitals section.

[D] HOMES FOR AGED

CHARLESTON. *Carter-May Home*, 1660 Ingram Rd., 29407. Tel: 843-556-8314; Fax: 843-402-9071
For a complete listing, refer to the Special Care Facilities section.

[E] MONASTERIES AND RESIDENCES OF PRIESTS AND BROTHERS

MONCKS CORNER. *Mepkin Abbey.* (Trappist Monks), 1098 Mepkin Abbey Rd., 29461-4796. Tel: 843-761-8509; Fax: 843-761-6719.
E-mail: mepkin@infoave.net
Web site: www.mepkinabbey.org
Rt. Revs. Francis Kline, O.C.S.O.; Christian Aidan Carr, O.C.S.O., (Retired); Revs. James Brennan (PH); Benjamin Clark, O.C.S.O.; Leonard A. Cunningham, O.C.S.O.; Aelred Hagan, O.C.S.O., Novice Dir.; Guerric Frederick A. Heckel; Feliciano Manalili, O.C.S.O.; Richard G. McGuire, O.C.S.O.; Bros. Stephen Petronek, O.C.S.O., Prior; Stan Gumula, O.S.C.O., Bus. Mgr. Professed Monks 24; Priests 9; Postulants 1; Novices 2; Number in Community 26.

ROCK HILL. *Oratory of St. Philip Neri, Congregation of the Oratory of Pontifical Rite*, 434 Charlotte Ave., Box 11586, 29730. Tel: 803-327-2097; Fax: 803-327-6264. Mailing Address: P.O. Box 11586, 29731-1586. Very Rev. Joseph A. Wahl, C.O., S.T.D., Provost; Revs. David D. Valtierra, C.O., First Deputy, Vicar; Edward P. McDevitt, C.O., Sec.; Bros. David Boone, C.O., Treas.; Joseph Guyon, C.O., Sec.; Revs. Robert S. Dell, C.O.; John P. Giuliani, C.O.; Edward P. McDevitt, C.O.; James Moran, C.O.; William F. Pentis, C.O.; Halbert Weidner, C.O., Ph.D.; Clarence Edward Jones, C.O.; Joseph Francis Pearce, C.O. Fathers 10; Brothers 5; Scholastics 2.

[F] CONVENTS AND RESIDENCES FOR SISTERS

CHARLESTON. *Convent of the Franciscan Sister*, 5 Riverside Dr., 29403. Tel: 843-722-2335.

Daughters of St. Paul Convent, 243 King St., 29401. Tel: 843-577-0175; Fax: 843-577-9833.
E-mail: charleston@pauline.org
Web site: www.pauline.org
Sr. Michelle Jane Black, F.S.P., Local Supr..Sisters 4.

May Forest, Generalate and Motherhouse of the Sisters of Charity of Our Lady of Mercy, 424 Ft. Johnson Rd., 29412. Tel: 843-795-6083; Fax: 843-795-6083, Ext. 15. Mailing Address: P.O. Box 12410, 29422. Sr. Anne Francis Campbell, O.L.M., Gen. Supr. Tel: 843-795-2866. Professed Sisters in Community 29.

GREENVILLE. *Monastery of St. Clare*, 1916 N. Pleasantburg Dr., 29609-4080. Tel: 864-244-4514; Fax: 864-268-9379. Franciscan Poor Clare Nuns. Sr. Rucia Rauton, O.S.C., Abbess. Cloistered Nuns in Solemn Vows 15; Novices 2; Extern in Perpetual Vows 1.

ST. HELENA ISLAND. *Franciscan Center*, 85 Mattis Rd., U.S. Hwy. 21, P.O. Box 682, 29920. Tel: 843-838-3924; Fax: 843-838-2152.
E-mail: franctr@islc.net
Web site: www.islc.net/~franctr
Sisters of St. Francis of Philadelphia, Glen Riddle-Aston, PA 2.

[G] CATHOLIC CHARITIES

CHARLESTON. *Catholic Charities of the Diocese of Charleston*, 1662 Ingram Rd., 29407. Tel: 843-402-9115, Ext. 15; Fax: 843-402-9071.
E-mail: dorothy@catholic-doc.org
Dorothy Grillo, Dir., Coastal Regional Office, 3921 St. John's Ave, North Charleston, 29405-7158. Tel: 843-402-9115, Ext. 16; Fax: 843-402-9071. Sr. Pat Keating, O.P., Regl. Coord., Midlands Regional Office, 1012 Taylor St., P.O. Box 7245, Columbia, 29202-7245. Tel: 803-254-9776; Fax: 803-252-7605. Mrs. Tracy Kroll, Regl. Coord., Pee Dee Regional Office, 1071 Academy Dr., Conway, 29526. Tel: 843-347-5157; Fax: 843-347-9546. Mrs. Diane Bullard, Regl. Coord., Piedmont Regional Office, 111 Hampton Ave., P.O. Box 216, Greenville, 29602-0216. Tel: 864-242-2233; Fax: 864-370-9880. Sr. Margie Hosch, O.S.F., Regl. Coord.

Echo House-Inner City Apostolate, 1911 Hackemann Ave., 29405. Tel: 843-554-7319; Fax: 843-554-1244.

Neighborhood House-Inner City Apostolate, 77 America St., 29403. Tel: 843-723-5129.

[H] CAMPUS MINISTRIES

CHARLESTON. *The Catholic Campus Ministry of the College of Charleston; Medical University of South Carolina*, c/o 119 Broad St., 29401.

Charleston Southern University. Mailing Address: c/o 6650 Dorchester Rd., Charleston Heights, 29418. Tel: 843-552-2223. Rev. William F. Leonard (MET).

The Citadel, MSC 58, The Citadel, 171 Moultrie St., 29409-0058. Tel: 843-953-7692; 722-7018; Fax: 843-953-4811. Rev. Jeffrey A. Kendall.

AIKEN. *University of South Carolina, Aiken Extension*, P.O. Box 438, 29802. Tel: 803-649-4777. Rev. Gade Show Reddy (Warangal).

ANDERSON. *Anderson College*, 1303 McLees Rd., 29621. Tel: 864-225-5341; Fax: 864-224-0538. Rev. James N. Dubrouillet.

BEAUFORT. *University of South Carolina, Beaufort Extension*, 70 Lady's Island Dr., 29902. Tel: 843-522-9555. Rev. Ronald R. Cellini (PIT).

CLEMSON. *Clemson University, Southern Wesleyan University*, 209 Sloan St., P.O. Box 112, 29633. Tel: 864-654-7804; 654-1757; 654-9670. Rev. James M. Brucz, C.S.P.; Mr. Daniel Johnson, Campus Min. Legal Title: *Clemson University - Catholic Campus Ministry at St. Andrew's Church and the Catholic Student Association.*

CLINTON. *Presbyterian College.* c/o 928 Boundry St., Newberry, 29108. Tel: 803-276-6446. Rev. Alexei R. Choquet (CHL).

COLUMBIA. *Allen University, Benedict College*, c/o St. Martin de Porres Church, 2229 Hampton St., P.O. Box 4187, 29240. Tel: 803-254-6862; Fax: 803-799-4720. Deacon Roland L. Thomas.

University of South Carolina, St. Thomas More Center, 1610 Greene St., 29201. Tel: 803-799-5870; Fax: 803-765-0800.
E-mail: tlijewski@aol.com
Rev. Timothy M. Lijewski.

CONWAY. *Coastal Carolina University*, P.O. Box 1754, 29526. Tel: 843-349-2026; Fax: 843-349-2127. Timothy McCormick, Prof.

DUE WEST. *Erskine College.* P.O. Box 812, Abbeville, 29620. Tel: 864-459-5150; Fax: 864-465-3615. Sr. Joan Kobe, D.W.

FLORENCE. *Francis Marion University*, 113 S. Kemp St., 29501. Tel: 843-662-1736; Fax: 843-676-9001. Rev. Michael T. Corrigan (GAL).

GAFFNEY. *Limestone College*, 407 Grace St., 29340. Tel: 864-489-9453. Rev. Raymond J. Carlo (STA).

GREENVILLE. *Furman University*, 307 Gower St., 29611. Tel: 864-233-7717; Fax: 864-233-2852. Rev. Paul M. Williams.

GREENWOOD. *Lander College*, Office, 110 E. Laurel Ave., 29649. Tel: 864-223-8410. Rev. Richard D. Harris.

HARTSVILLE. *Coker College*, 115 Church St., P.O. Box 1378, 29550. Tel: 843-332-6664; 332-3136. Rev. Karl Roesch, O.S.B.

NEWBERRY. *Newberry College*, 928 Boundry St., 29108. Tel: 803-276-6446. Rev. Alexei R. Choquet (CHL).

ORANGEBURG. *South Carolina State University & Claflin College*, 1710 Amelia St., N.E., 29115. Tel: 803-534-2302; Fax: 803-539-0974.
E-mail: xbrothers@oburg.net
Served by Xaverian Brothers.

ROCK HILL. *Winthrop University, York Co. Tech Center*, 434 Charlotte Ave., Box 11586, 29731. Tel: 803-327-6450. Rev. David D. Valtierra, C.O.

SPARTANBURG. *Converse College, Spartanburg Methodist College*, 161 N. Dean St., 29302. Tel: 864-582-0674. Very Rev. Michael R. DeAntonio, V.F.; Deacon Robert L. Mahaffey, Jr.

Wofford College, 429 N. Church St., 29303-3668. Tel: 864-597-4180. Mr. Doyle Boggs, Advisor.

SUMTER. *Morris College*, P.O. Box 1589, 29151. Tel: 803-773-9244. Rev. Michael Varady, C.SS.R.

[I] RETREAT CENTERS

EDISTO ISLAND. *Sea of Peace House of Prayer*, 59 Palmetto Pointe Rd., 29438. Tel: 843-869-0513; Fax: 843-869-0513.
E-mail: econdon@awod.com

KINGSTREE. *Springbank Christian Center-Dominican Retreat House*, Rte. 2, Box 180, 29556. Tel: 843-382-3426; 1-800-671-0361; Fax: 843-382-5340.

[J] MISCELLANEOUS

CHARLESTON. *Ladies of Charity of Sacred Heart Church*, 888 King St., 29403-4138. Tel: 843-722-7018.

Pauline Books & Media, 243 King St., 29401. Tel: 843-577-0175; Fax: 843-577-9833.
E-mail: charleston@pauline.org
Web site: www.pauline.org
Daughters of St. Paul.

The Sisters of Charity of Our Lady of Mercy Charitable Trust, 424 Ft. Johnson Rd., P.O. Box 12410, 29422. Tel: 843-795-2866; Fax: 843-795-6083, Ext. 15.

COLUMBIA. *CSA Providence Ministries*, 1441 Main St., Ste. 1500, 29201. Tel: 1-888-223-1886; Fax: 216-696-2204.

Sisters of Charity Foundation of South Carolina, 2601 Laurel St., Ste. 250, 29204. Tel: 803-254-0230; Fax: 803-748-0444.
E-mail: scfsc@usit.net
Web site: www.sistersofcharitysc.com

GREENVILLE. *SFH, Inc.*, One St. Francis Dr., 29601. Tel: 964-255-1000.

JOHNS ISLAND. *Our Lady of Mercy Community Outreach Services, Inc.*, 1684 Brownswood Rd., 29455. Tel: 843-559-4109; Fax: 843-559-8819. P.O. Box 607, 29457.
Sponsored by Sisters of Charity of Our Lady of Mercy.

RELIGIOUS INSTITUTES OF MEN REPRESENTED IN THE DIOCESE

For further details refer to the corresponding bracketed number in the Religious Institutes of Men or Women section.

[0100]—*Adorno Fathers.*—C.R.M.
[0200]—*Benedictines.*—O.S.B.
[1350]—*Brothers of St. Francis Xavier.* (St. Joseph Prov.).—C.F.X.
[0350]—*Cistercians Order of the Strict Observance-Trappist.*—O.C.S.O.
[0310]—*Congregation of Christian Brothers.*—C.F.C.
[1330]—*Congregation of the Mission.* (Eastern Prov.).—C.M.
[0520]—*Franciscan Friars.* (Prov. of the Most Holy Name).—O.F.M.
[0690]—*Jesuit Fathers and Brothers.* (New Orleans; New England Provs.).—S.J.
[1110]—*Missionaries of the Sacred Heart.*—M.S.C.
[0910]—*Oblates of Mary Immaculate.* (Eastern American Prov.).—O.M.I.
[0950]—*Oratorians.*—C.O.
[1030]—*Paulist Fathers.*—C.S.P.
[1070]—*Redemptorist Fathers.* (Richmond Vice Prov.).—C.SS.R.

RELIGIOUS INSTITUTES OF WOMEN REPRESENTED IN THE DIOCESE

[0270]—*Congregation of Bon Secours.*—C.B.S.
[1000]—*Congregation of Divine Providence.* (KY).—C.D.P.
[1730]—*Congregation of the Sisters of the Third Order of St. Francis.* (Oldenburg, IN).—O.S.F.
[0760]—*Daughters of Charity of St. Vincent de Paul.*—D.C.
[0960]—*Daughters of Wisdom.* (American Prov.).—D.W.
[1070-03]—*Dominican Sisters.* (Sinsinawa, WI).—O.P.
[1070-11]—*Dominican Sisters.* (Sparkill, NY).—O.P.
[1070-13]—*Dominican Sisters.* (Adrian, MI).—O.P.
[1070-04]—*Dominican Sisters.* (San Rafael, CA).—O.P.
[1170]—*Felician Sisters.*—C.S.S.F.
[1415]—*Franciscan Sisters of Mary.*—F.S.M.
[1425]—*Franciscan Sisters of Peace.*—F.S.P.
[1440]—*Franciscan Sisters of the Poor.*—S.F.P.
[1360]—*Missionary Franciscan Sisters of the Immaculate Conception.*—M.F.I.C.
[2790]—*Missionary Servants of the Most Blessed Trinity.*—M.S.B.T.
[3760]—*Order of St. Clare.*—O.S.C.
[0950]—*Pious Daughters of St. Paul.*—F.S.P.
[2970]—*School Sisters of Notre Dame.*—S.S.N.D.
[0500]—*Sisters of Charity of Nazareth.*—S.C.N.
[0510]—*Sisters of Charity of Our Lady of Mercy.*—O.L.M.
[0580]—*Sisters of Charity of St. Augustine.*—C.S.A.
[2575]—*Sisters of Mercy of the Americas.* (Chicago, IL; Pittsburgh, PA;).—R.S.M.
[3000]—*Sisters of Notre Dame.* (Baltimore, MD).—S.N.D.deN.
[3950]—*Sisters of Saint Mary of Namur.*—S.S.M.N.
[3780]—*Sisters of Saints Cyril and Methodius.*—SS.C.M.
[1540]—*Sisters of St. Francis.* (Clinton, IA).—O.S.F.
[1620]—*Sisters of St. Francis of Millvale, Pennsylvania.*—O.S.F.
[1650]—*Sisters of St. Francis of Philadelphia.*—O.S.F.
[1570]—*Sisters of St. Francis of the Holy Family.*—O.S.F.
[1800]—*Sisters of St. Francis of the Third Order Regular.* (Williamsville, New York).—O.S.F.
[3840]—*Sisters of St. Joseph of Carondelet.* (Prov. of St. Louis).—C.S.J.
[2110]—*Sisters of the Humility of Mary.*—H.M.
[]—*Sisters of the Sacred Heart of Jesus.* (Mexico).—H.C.J.S.
[1720]—*Sisters of the Third Order of St. Francis of the Congregation of Our Lady of Lourdes.* (Rochester).—O.S.F.
[1890]—*Society of Helpers.*—H.H.S.
[4048]—*Society of Sisters Faithful Companions of Jesus.*—F.C.J.
[4120-03]—*Ursuline Nuns, of the Congregation of Paris.*—O.S.U.

DIOCESAN CEMETERIES

CHARLESTON. *St. Lawrence and Holy Cross*, 604 Ft. Johnson Rd., 29412. Tel: 843-795-2111. Mr. Warren R. Stuckey, Jr., Dir.

NECROLOGY

† Baum, Rev. Msgr. Charles James, (Retired). —Died Dec. 19, 2000.
† Buchanan, Scott James Allen, Holly Hill, SC St. Ann. —Died Jan. 8, 2001.
† Eyckmans, A. John, (Retired). —Died Aug. 24, 2000.
† Maley, William Austin, Hartsville, SC St. Mary. —Died Sept. 22, 2000.
† Schiller, David Joseph, (Retired). —Died June 10, 2000.
† Schwab, Jerome Frederick, Lexington, SC Corpus Christi. —Died Nov. 15, 2000.

Diocese of Charlotte

(Dioecesis Carolinana)

Most Reverend

WILLIAM G. CURLIN, D.D.

Bishop of Charlotte; ordained May 25, 1957; appointed Auxiliary Bishop of Washington November 2, 1988; consecrated December 20, 1988; appointed Bishop of Charlotte February 22, 1994; installed April 13, 1994. *Res., 1521 Dilworth Rd., Charlotte, NC, 28203.* Tel.: 704-376-4337; Fax: 704-375-7359.

Most Reverend

MICHAEL J. BEGLEY, D.D.

Retired Bishop of Charlotte; ordained May 26, 1934; appointed November 30, 1971; consecrated First Bishop of Charlotte January 12, 1972; retired 1984. *Mailing Address: 1315 Greensboro Rd., High Point, NC, 27260.*

ESTABLISHED JANUARY 12, 1972.

Square Miles 20,470.

Comprises the Counties of Alexander, Alleghany, Anson, Ashe, Avery, Buncombe, Burke, Cabarrus, Caldwell, Catawba, Cherokee, Clay, Cleveland, Davidson, Davie, Forsyth, Gaston, Graham, Guilford, Haywood, Henderson, Iredell, Jackson, Lincoln, Macon, Madison, McDowell, Mecklenburg, Mitchell, Montgomery, Polk, Randolph, Richmond, Rockingham, Rowan, Rutherford, Stanley, Stokes, Surry, Swain, Transylvania, Union, Watauga, Wilkes, Yadkin and Yancey in the State of North Carolina.

For legal titles of parishes and diocesan institutions, consult the Chancery.

Chancery: P.O. Box 36776, Charlotte, NC, 28236. Tel.: 704-370-6299; Fax: 704-370-3378.

Web site address: charlottediocese.org

E-mail address: chancery@charlottediocese.org

STATISTICAL OVERVIEW

Personnel	
Bishop	1
Retired Bishops	1
Abbots	1
Priests: Diocesan Active in Diocese	59
Priests: Active Outside Diocese	7
Priests: Retired, Sick or Absent	27
Number of Diocesan Priests	93
Religious Priests in Diocese	96
Extern Priests in Diocese	11
Ordinations:	
Diocesan Priests	7
Transitional Deacons	4
Permanent Deacons in Diocese	63
Total Brothers	3
Total Sisters	134
Parishes	
Parishes	68
With Resident Pastor:	
Resident Diocesan Priests	44
Resident Religious Priests	23
Without Resident Pastor:	
Administered by Women Religious	1
Missions	23
Pastoral Centers	4
Professional Ministry Personnel:	
Brothers	3
Sisters	28
Lay Ministers	64
Welfare	
Health Care Centers	5
Total Assisted	238,600
Homes for the Aged	1
Total Assisted	125
Day Care and Extended Day Care Centers	5
Total Assisted	502
Specialized Homes	3
Total Assisted	156
Residential Care of Disabled	1
Total Assisted	174
Educational	
Diocesan Students in Other Seminaries	20
Total Seminarians	20
Colleges and Universities	2
Total Students	925
High Schools, Diocesan and Parish	2
Total Students	1,228
Elementary Schools, Diocesan and Parish	15
Total Students	6,075
Catechesis/Religious Education:	
High School Students	2,480
Elementary Students	13,706
Total Students Under Catholic Instruction	24,434
Teachers in the Diocese:	
Priests	4
Brothers	1
Sisters	7
Lay Teachers	479
Vital Statistics	
Receptions into the Church:	
Infant Baptism Totals	3,733
Adult Baptism Totals	209
Received into Full Communion	638
First Communions	3,305
Confirmations	2,322
Marriages:	
Catholic	444
Interfaith	395
Total Marriages	839
Deaths	673
Total Catholic Population	129,385
Total Population	3,984,578

Former Bishops—Most Rev. MICHAEL J. BEGLEY, ord. May 26, 1934; appt. Nov. 30, 1971; cons. first Bishop of Charlotte Jan. 12, 1972; retired 1984.—Most Rev. JOHN F. DONOGHUE, ord. June 4, 1955; appt. Nov. 6, 1984; cons. Dec. 18, 1984; appt. Archbishop of Atlanta June 22, 1993; cons. Aug. 19, 1993.

Vicar General In Curia—Very Rev. MAURICIO W. WEST, *P.O. Box 36776, Charlotte, 28236.* Tel: 704-370-6299.

Chancery—*P.O. Box 36776, Charlotte, 28236.* Tel: 704-370-6299; Fax: 704-370-3379.

Chancellor—Very Rev. MAURICIO W. WEST, *P.O. Box 36776, Charlotte, 28236.* Tel: 704-370-6299; 370-3326.

Vice Chancellor—Deacon CURTISS P. TODD, *1123 S. Church St., Charlotte, 28203.* Tel: 704-370-3339.

Chief Financial Officer—WILLIAM G. WELDON, C.P.A., *1123 S. Church St., Charlotte, 28203.* Tel: 704-370-3313.

Controller—TRACY HILDRETH, *1123 S. Church St., Charlotte, 28203.* Tel: 704-370-3312.

Diocesan Properties—Deacon GUY A. PICHE, Dir., *1123 S. Church St., Charlotte, 28203.* Tel: 704-370-3304.

Employee Benefits—TERRI WILHELM, *1123 S. Church St., Charlotte, 28203.* Tel: 704-370-3338.

Diocesan Tribunal—*1123 S. Church St., Charlotte, 28203.* Tel: 704-370-3343.

Judicial Vicar—Rev. PETER J. JUGIS, J.C.D.; MARY L. HILDRETH, Dir., *1123 S. Church St., Charlotte, 28203.*

Diocesan Consultors—Very. Rev. MAURICIO W. WEST, V.G.; Rev. Msgr. JOSEPH SHOWFETY; Very Rev. RICHARD BELLOW; Very Rev. MICHAEL BUTTNER; Very Rev. PAUL GARY; Very Rev. PETER JUGIS; Rev. IGNATIUS ZAMPINO, O.F.M.Cap.

Vicar for Education—Rev. JAMES HAWKER (BO), *1123 S. Church St., Charlotte, 28203.* Tel: 704-370-3210; Fax: 704-370-3291.

Vicars—Rev. Msgr. WILLIAM N. PHARR, V.F., Charlotte; Rt. Rev. PATRICK SHELTON, O.S.B., V.F., Albemarle; Very Rev. JOHN AURELIA, O.F.M.Cap., V.F., Asheville; Very Rev. JOHN SCHNEIDER, V.F., Boone; Very Rev. ERIC HOUSEKNECHT, V.F., Gastonia; Very Rev. JAMES O'NEILL, O.S.F.S., V.F., Greensboro; Very Rev. MICHAEL BUTTNER, V.F., Hickory; Very Rev. JOHN SMYTHE, C.SS.R., V.F., Salisbury; Very Rev. GEORGE KLOSTER, V.F., Smoky Mountains; Very Rev. FRANCIS J. O'ROURKE, V.F., Winston-Salem.

Vicar for Priests—Rev. WILBUR N. THOMAS, *P.O. Box 18253, Asheville, 28814-0253.* Tel: 828-250-9023.

Diocesan Offices and Directors

Apostleship of Prayer—Rev. EUGENE MCCREESH, S.J., *St. Peter Church, 507 S. Tryon St., Charlotte, 28202.* Tel: 704-332-2901.

Archives—JOHANNA B. MIMS, Dir., *1123 S. Church St., Charlotte, 28203.* Tel: 704-370-3215; Fax: 704-370-3378.

Boy Scouts—Deacon JAMES R. JOHNSON, *St. Charles Borromeo Church, 714 W. Union St., Morganton, 28655.* Tel: 704-437-3221; 437-3461.

Campus Ministry—Ms. COLLEEN MCDERMOTT, Dir., *1123 S. Church St., Charlotte, 28203.* Tel: 704-370-3212; Fax: 704-370-3378.

Office of Faith Formation—Dr. CRIS VILLAPANDO, Program Dir., *1123 S. Church St., Charlotte, 28203.* Tel: 704-370-3246; Fax: 704-370-3378.

Youth Ministry—PAUL KOTLOWSKI, *1123 S. Church St., Charlotte, 28203.* Tel: 704-370-3211.

Development—JAMES K. KELLEY, Dir. BARBARA ROHRMAN, Assoc. Dir., *1123 S. Church St., Charlotte, 28203.* Tel: 704-370-3301; 3302; Fax: 704-370-3378.

Evangelization—Vacant, *1123 S. Church St., Charlotte, 28203.* Tel: 704-370-6299; Fax: 704-370-3378.

Foundation of the Roman Catholic Diocese of Charlotte, Inc., The—JAMES KELLEY, Exec. Dir., *1123 S. Church St., Charlotte, 28203.* Tel: 704-370-3301.

Hispanic Ministry—Rev. VINCENT H. FINNERTY, C.M., Diocesan Dir., *Centro Catolico Hispano, 2117 Shenandoah Ave., Charlotte, 28205-6021.* Tel: 704-335-1281; 527-6745.

Holy Childhood Association—Rev. Msgr. ANTHONY KOVACIC, Dir., *1123 S. Church St., Charlotte, 28203.* Tel: 704-370-6299; Fax: 704-370-3378.

Home Missions—Rev. Msgr. ANTHONY KOVACIC, *1123 S. Church St., Charlotte, 28203.* Tel: 704-370-6299; Fax: 704-370-3378.

Human Resources—CURTISS P. TODD, Dir. TERRI WILHELM, Assoc., *1123 S. Church St., Charlotte, 28203.* Tel: 704-370-3338; 3339; Fax: 704-370-3378.

Korean Catholic Cultural Center—Rev. THADDEUS SEONG-EOK LEE, (Korea), Dir., *7109 Robinson Church Rd., Charlotte, 28215.* Tel: 704-531-8417.

Lay Ministry—Sr. M. TIMOTHY WARREN, R.S.M., Dir., *1123 S. Church St., Charlotte, 28203.* Tel: 704-370-3213; Fax: 704-370-3378.

African-American Ministry—Deacon CURTISS P. TODD, Coord., *1123 S. Church St., Charlotte, 28203.* Tel: 704-370-3339.

Media Resource Center—Sr. PATRICIA DURBIN, R.S.M., *1123 S. Church St., Charlotte, 28203.* Tel: 704-370-3242.

Cathedral Publishing Corporation—Mailing Address: P.O. Box 37267, Charlotte, 28237. Tel: 704-370-6299. *1123 S. Church St., Charlotte, 28203.* Tel: 704-370-3336.

Newspaper: "Catholic News & Herald"—JOANN KEANE, Editor; JAMES T. ROSTAR, Assoc. Editor, *P.O. Box 37267, Charlotte, 28237.* Tel: 704-370-3336; 370-3334; Fax: 704-370-3382.

Permanent Diaconate—Very Rev. MAURICIO W. WEST, V.G.; Deacon BERNARD W. WENNING, JR., Assoc., *P.O. Box 36776, Charlotte, 28236.* Tel: 704-370-6299; Fax: 704-370-3379.

Planning—GEORGE COBB, Dir., *1123 S. Church St., Charlotte, 28203.* Tel: 704-370-3328; Fax: 704-370-3378.

Propagation of the Faith—Rev. Msgr. ANTHONY KOVACIC, *1123 S. Church St., Charlotte, 28203.* Tel: 704-370-6299; Fax: 704-370-3378.

St. Vincent de Paul—ELIZABETH THURBEE, A.C.S.W., *1123 S. Church St., Charlotte, 28203.* Tel: 704-370-3227; Fax: 704-370-3377.

School—MICHAEL F. SKUBE, Ed.D., Supt. of Schools, *1123 S. Church St., Charlotte, 28203.* Tel: 704-370-3271; Fax: 704-370-3291.

Mecklenburg Area Catholic Schools—1123 S. Church St., Charlotte, 28203. Tel: 704-370-3270; Fax: 704-370-3291.

Presbyteral Council—Most Rev. WILLIAM G. CURLIN, D.D.; Very Rev. MAURICIO W. WEST, V.G.; Revs. RICHARD BELLOW; VINCENT H. FINNERTY, C.M.; PAUL Q. GARY; PETER J. JUGIS; ERIC HOUSEKNECHT; M. JOSEPH KELLEHER; GEORGE M. KLOSTER; MARK LAWLOR; ANTHONY MARCACCIO; EUGENE MCCREESH, S.J.; FIDEL MELO; JAMES W. O'NEILL, O.S.F.S.; JOHN T. PUTNAM; WILBUR N. THOMAS; RAY WILLIAMS; IGNATIUS ZAMPINO, O.F.M.Cap.; JOSEPH C. ZUSCHMIDT, O.S.F.S., *1123 S. Church St., Charlotte, 28203.*

Social Services—ELIZABETH THURBEE, A.C.S.W., Diocesan Dir., *1123 S. Church St., Charlotte, 28203.* Tel: 704-370-3228.

Campaign for Human Development—Dr. BARNEY OFFERMAN, Dir., *1123 S. Church St., Charlotte, 28203.* Tel: 704-370-3234; Fax: 704-370-3288.

Justice and Peace—JOSEPH PURELLO, Dir., *1123 S. Church St., Charlotte, 28203.* Tel: 704-370-3225; Fax: 704-370-3288.

Vietnamese Apostolate—4929 Sandy Porter Rd., Charlotte, 28273. Tel: 704-504-0907. Rev. TAN VAN LE, Chap.

Vocations—Most Rev. WILLIAM G. CURLIN, D.D., Dir., *1123 S. Church St., Charlotte, 28203.* Tel: 704-370-3353; Fax: 704-370-3378.

Worship—Rev. ANTHONY MARCACCIO, *St. Pius Tenth Church, 2210 N. Elm St., Greensboro, 27408.*

CLERGY, PARISHES, MISSIONS AND PAROCHIAL SCHOOLS

CITY OF CHARLOTTE
(Mecklenburg County)

1—ST. PATRICK CATHEDRAL. (Phelan Memorial). Very Rev. Paul Q. Gary; Rev. Dean E. Cesa; Deacon Nicholas Fadero.
Res., 1621 Dilworth Rd., E., 28203. Tel: 704-334-2283; Fax: 704-377-6403.
Catechesis/Religious Programs—Tel: 704-334-2283, Ext. 27.
Students 240.

2—OUR LADY OF THE ASSUMPTION, Rev. Francis J. Gillespie, S.J.; Deacons Stephen J. Horai; Peter Duca.
Res., 4207 Shamrock Dr., 28215. Tel: 704-535-9965; 535-9970; Fax: 704-535-3621.
Catechesis/Religious Programs—Martha Roman, D.R.E., Tel: 704-535-3310.
Students 155.

3—OUR LADY OF CONSOLATION, Revs. Jude Duffy, O.F.M. Cap; Martin Schratz, O.F.M. Cap.; Deacon Curtiss P. Todd. In res., Rev. Stephen Hoyt, O.F.M.Cap.
Res., 1224 Dearborn Ave., 28206-2491. Tel: 704-375-4339; Fax: 704-375-8039.
Catechesis/Religious Programs—Students 74.
Mission—Spencer Mountain, Gaston Co., St. Helen.

4—ST. ANN, Revs. Conrad Hoover; Thomas Selvaras (India). In res., Rev. James Hawker (BO).
Church—3635 Park Rd., 28209. Tel: 704-523-4641; Fax: 704-527-8671.
Res., 632 Hillside Ave., 28209.
Catechesis/Religious Programs—Tel: 704-527-0122; Fax: 704-527-8671.
Students 132.
Convent—3430 Willow Oak Rd., 28209. Tel: 704-523-0331.

5—ST. GABRIEL, Revs. Richard Bellow; Matthew Leonard; John D. Hanic; Deacons Bernard Wenning; Robert Gettlefinger; Louis A. Pais.
Res., 3016 Providence Rd., 28211. Tel: 704-364-5431; Fax: 704-362-5049.
Catechesis/Religious Programs—Tel: 704-366-2738. Susan Krasniewski, D.R.E., Tel: 704-362-5047, Ext. 271.
Students 815.

6—ST. JOHN NEUMANN, Revs. Thomas J. Meehan, O.S.A.; Patrick F. Leonard, O.S.A.; Bro. Joseph Spindler, O.S.A.; Deacon Joseph Mack. In res., Rev. James Cassidy, O.S.A.
Res., 8451 Idlewild Rd., 28227. Tel: 704-536-6520; Fax: 704-536-3147.
Catechesis/Religious Programs—Tel: 704-535-4197.
Students 747.

7—ST LUKE, Rev. Joseph V. Mulligan.
Res., 13700 Lawyers Rd., 28227. Tel: 704-545-1224; Fax: 704-545-7288.
Catechesis/Religious Programs—Tel: 704-545-0065.
Students 364.

8—ST. MATTHEW, Rev. Msgr. John J. McSweeney; Rev. Matthew Kauth; Sr. Jeanne Marie Kienast, R.S.M., Pastoral Assoc.; Deacons James Hamrlik; Jeffrey Evers.
Office: 8015 Ballantyne Commons Pkwy., 28277. Tel: 704-543-7677; Fax: 704-542-7244.
Res., 5726 Ballantyne Commons Pkwy., 28277. Tel: 704-846-6311; Fax: 704-846-6311.
Catechesis/Religious Programs—Tel: 704-541-8362; Fax: 704-542-7244. Patricia Tomilson, D.R.E.
Students 1,975.

9—ST. PETER, Revs. Joseph A. Sobierajski, S.J.; Lucian C. Martinez, S.J. In res., Revs. Robert J. Paquet, S.J.; Eugene P. McCreesh, S.J.
Res., 507 S. Tryon St., 28202. Tel: 704-372-6808; Fax: 704-358-0050.
Catechesis/Religious Programs—Tel: 704-332-2901; Fax: 704-358-0050.
Students 120.

10—ST. THOMAS AQUINAS, Revs. Ignatius Zampino, O.F.M.Cap.; Martin Schratz, O.F.M.Cap; Stanley Kobel, O.F.M.Cap.; Deacon Carl Macero; Sr. Anastacia Pagulan, O.P., D.R.E.; Miriam Picconi, Pastoral Assoc.
Res., 1400 Suther Rd., 28213. Tel: 704-549-1607; Fax: 704-549-1614.
Catechesis/Religious Programs—Tel: 704-549-0199.
Students 798.

11—ST. VINCENT DE PAUL, Rev. Msgr. William N. Pharr; Revs. Richard N. Hanson; Peter Thang Quoc Pham; Deacons Gerald P. Hickey; Neil F. Chirico.
Res., 6828 Old Reid Rd., 28210. Tel: 704-554-7088; Fax: 704-554-0490.
Catechesis/Religious Programs—Tel: 704-554-1622; Fax: 704-554-0490. Joan Mahony, D.R.E.
Students 173.

OUTSIDE THE CITY OF CHARLOTTE

Albemarle, Stanly Co., Our Lady of the Annunciation, Rev. Lawrence W. Heiney.
Res., 416 N. Second St., 28001. Tel: 704-982-2910; Fax: 704-982-0881.
Catechesis/Religious Programs—Tel: 704-982-1048. Jane Snyder, D.R.E.
Students 98.
Mission—Biscoe, Montgomery Co., Our Lady of the Americas, 105 Hyde St., P.O. Box 1187, Biscoe, 27209. Tel: 910-428-3051; Fax: 910-428-1136. Rev. Fidel Melo, Admin.

Andrews, Cherokee Co., Holy Redeemer, Rev. Robert Bond.
Res., 214 Aquone Rd., 28901. Tel: 828-321-4463.
Mission—Robbinsville, Graham Co., Prince of Peace, 704 Talluah Rd., Rte. #129, Robbinsville, 28771.
Catechesis/Religious Programs—Students 6.

Arden, Buncombe Co., St. Barnabas, Rev. Roger Arnsparger; Deacon Arthur J. Kingsley.
Mailing Address: P.O. Box 38, 28704. Tel: 828-684-6098; Fax: 828-684-6152.
Res., 4 Pointview Ct., 28704. Tel: 828-684-5343.
Catechesis/Religious Programs—Miss Sheryl Peyton, D.R.E.
Students 305.

Asheboro, Randolph Co., St. Joseph, Rev. Joseph W. Mack.
Res., 512 W. Wainman Ave., 27203. Tel: 336-629-0221; Fax: 336-629-6968.
Catechesis/Religious Programs—Students 245.

Asheville, Buncombe Co., Basilica of St. Lawrence, Revs. Wilbur N. Thomas; Frank Seabo.
Res., 97 Haywood St., 28801. Tel: 828-252-6042; Fax: 828-254-0414.
Catechesis/Religious Programs—Tel: 828-252-8816; Fax: 828-254-0414. Mrs. Elizabeth Girton, D.R.E.
Students 185.

St. Eugene, Rev. Francis T. Cancro.
Office: One Culvern St., 28804.
Mailing Address: P.O. Box 8160, 28814. Tel: 704-254-5193; Fax: 704-254-5797.
Catechesis/Religious Programs—Students 358.

St. Joan of Arc, Rev. John M. Pagel.
Res., 919 Haywood Rd., 28806. Tel: 828-252-3151; Fax: 828-252-4154.
Catechesis/Religious Programs—Students 80.

Belmont, Gaston Co., Queen of the Apostles, Rev. Richard P. Hokanson. Pastoral Assocs.: Sr. John Madden; Sr. Josephine Thomas.
Church—503 N. Main St., 28012. Tel: 704-825-9600; Fax: 704-825-1413.
Res., 2121 Ferncliff Ln., 28012. Tel: 704-825-9907.
Catechesis/Religious Programs—Students 208.

Boone, Watauga Co., St. Elizabeth, Revs. John Schneider; Shawn O'Neal.
Mailing Address: P.O. Box 1052, 28607.
Office: 259 Pilgrim's Way, 28607. Tel: 828-264-8338; 264-6347; Fax: 828-262-3721.
Res., 333 Poplar Hill Dr., 28607. Tel: 828-963-2560.
Catechesis/Religious Programs—Carol Brown, D.R.E.
Students 200.
Mission—Blowing Rock, Epiphany, 163 Galax Ln., 28607.

Brevard, Transylvania Co., Sacred Heart, Rev. Carl Del Giudice.
Res., 4 Brian Berg Ln., 28712. Tel: 828-883-9572; Fax: 828-883-9587.
Catechesis/Religious Programs—Students 89.
Mission—Sapphire Valley, Transylvania Co., St. Jude, P.O. Box 543, Highlands, 28741. Tel: 828-526-2418. Rev. William Morris Evans.

Bryson City, Swain Co., St. Joseph, Rev. Ray Williams, Admin.
Res., P.O. Box 727, 28713. Tel: 828-488-6766; Fax: 828-488-4390.
Catechesis/Religious Programs—Tel: 828-479-8014; Fax: 828-488-4390.
Students 35.
Mission—Cherokee, Swain Co., Our Lady of Guadalupe, P.O. Box 202, Cherokee, 28719. Tel: 828-497-9755.

Clemmons, Forsyth Co., Holy Family, Very Rev. Francis J. O'Rourke, V.F.; Rev. Ricardo F. Sanchez; Deacons Gerard Schumacher; Michael Langsdorf.
Office Address: P.O. Box 130, 27012.
Res., 2890 Knobb Hill Dr., 27012. Tel: 336-766-1882.
Church—4820 Kinnamon Rd., Winston-Salem, 27103. Fax: 336-766-2918.
Catechesis/Religious Programs—Tel: 336-766-0600. Mrs. Mary Langsdorf, D.R.E.
Students 466.
Mission—Yadkinville, Yadkin Co., Cristo Rey Catholic Hispanic Center of Yadkin Valley, U.S. Hwy. 601 & Hoot Rd., P.O. Box 788, Yadkinville, 27055. Tel: 336-463-5533.

Concord, Cabarrus Co., St. James, Very Rev. John Smyth, C.SS.R., V.F.; Revs. Joseph Gorney, C.SS.R.; Karl Aschmann, C.SS.R.; Bro. Darrell Cevasco, C.SS.R.; Deacon J. Daniel Carl.
Mailing Address: P.O. Box 123, 28026. Tel: 704-720-0600; Fax: 704-720-0610.
Res., 251 Union St. N., 28025. Tel: 704-786-9132.
Catechesis/Religious Programs—D.R.E.: Cecelia Rouse; Reggie Mattingly, (St. Joseph Mission).
Students 610.
Mission—Kannapolis, Cabarrus Co., St. Joseph, 108 St. Joseph St., P.O. Box 220, Kannapolis, 28082. Tel: 704-932-4607.

Denver, Lincoln Co., Holy Spirit, Rev. Joseph Ayathupadam; Deacon Richard Kauth.
Church—537 N. Hwy. 16, 28037-9235. Tel: 704-483-6448; Fax: 704-483-6898.
Res., 6789 Hawks Nest Ln., Stanley, 28164. Tel: 704-820-0153.
Catechesis/Religious Programs—Students 123.

Eden, Rockingham Co., St. Joseph of the Hills, Sr. Bernadette McNamara, R.S.M., Parochial Admin.; Deacon Gerald W. Potkay.
Res., 316 Boone Rd., 27288. Tel: 336-623-2661.
Catechesis/Religious Programs—Tel: 336-623-1538.
Students 56.

Forest City, Rutherford Co., Immaculate Conception, Rev. Gabriel Meehan; Deacon Andrew Cilone.
Res., 1024 W. Main St., 28043. Tel: 828-245-4017.
Catechesis/Religious Programs—Students 98.

Franklin, Macon Co., St. Francis of Assisi, Rev. C. Morris Boyd, D.Min.
Res., 299 Maple St., 28734. Tel: 828-524-2289; Fax: 828-369-0809.
Catechesis/Religious Programs—Tel: 828-369-8131. D.R.E.: Sharon Edwards; Ron Brahmer.
Students 108.
Mission—Highlands, Macon Co., Our Lady of the Mountains, P.O. Box 2729, Highlands, 28741. Tel: 828-526-2418; Fax: 828-526-1705. Rev. William Morris Evans.

Gastonia, Gaston County, St. Michael, Revs. John Andrew Allen; Christopher Gober.
Res., 708 St. Michael's Ln., 28052. Tel: 704-853-8808.
Church—Tel: 704-867-6212; Fax: 704-867-6379.
School—Tel: 704-865-4382.
Lay Teachers 17; Students 238.
Catechesis/Religious Programs—Tel: 704-865-5537.
Students 227.

Greensboro, Guilford Co.,

1—Our Lady of Grace. (Ethel Clay Price Memorial). Revs. Mark Lamprich, M.I.C.; Eric Kowalski; Deacons Timothy Rohan; Paul Teich.
Mailing Address: P.O. Box 10498, 27404-0498.
Res., 2205 W. Market St., 27403. Tel: 336-274-6520 (Office); 275-5376 (Rectory); Fax: 336-274-7326.
School—Tel: 336-275-1522. Roberta Hutchcraft, Prin.
Lay Teachers 25; Students 457.
Catechesis/Religious Programs—Tel: 336-274-0415. James D. McCullough, D.R.E.
Students 329.

2—St. Benedict, Rev. Msgr. Joseph S. Showfety; Deacon Philip Killian.
Res., 109 W. Smith St., 27401. Tel: 336-272-0303.
Catechesis/Religious Programs—Students 20.

3—St. Mary, Revs. Robert J. Prior, C.M.; Michael M. Nguyen, C.M.; Deacon Vincent Shaw. In res., Revs. Joseph A. Elzi, C.M.; Vincent H. Finnerty, C.M.
Mailing Address: P.O. Box 21012, 27420.
Res., 812 Duke St., 27401. Tel: 336-272-8650; Fax: 336-274-5396.
Social Ministry Office—Tel: 336-275-8377.
St. Vincent de Paul Office—Tel: 336-272-0336.
Catechesis/Religious Programs—Students 115.

4—St. Paul the Apostle, Very Rev. James W. O'Neill, O.S.F.S.; Revs. Tony Gilborges; Anthony J. Larry, O.S.F.S.; Deacons Gordon L. Forester; William Shaw.
Res., 2715 Horsepen Creek Rd., 27410. Tel: 336-294-6160; 294-4696 (Office); Fax: 336-294-6149.
Catechesis/Religious Programs—Students 857.

5—St. Pius X, Rev. Anthony J. Marcaccio. Pastoral Assocs.: Sr. Phyllis Tierney, S.S.J., M.S.W.; Tracy Earl Welliver, M.T.S.
Office: 2210 N. Elm St., 27408. Tel: 336-272-4681; 272-8598; Fax: 336-274-8112.
School—Tel: 336-273-9865; Fax: 336-273-0199. Mrs. Celeste Usischon, Prin.
Lay Teachers 32; Students 495.
Catechesis/Religious Programs—Tel: 336-273-9860.
Students 210.
Franciscan Center—233 N. Greene St., 27401. Tel: 336-273-2554.
Catholic Campus Connection (Thea House)—1009 Bluford St., 27401. Tel: 336-272-5868.

Hamlet, Richmond Co., St. James, Rt. Rev. Patrick Shelton, O.S.B., V.F.; Rev. David Draim, O.S.B.
Mailing Address: P.O. Box 1208, 28345. Tel: 910-582-0207; 582-8776 (Rectory).
Catechesis/Religious Programs—Ann Peters, D.R.E.
Students 89.
Mission—Wadesboro, Anson Co., Sacred Heart, 205 Rutherford St., P.O. Box 1123, Wadesboro, 28710. Tel: 704-674-5183.

Hendersonville, Henderson Co., Immaculate Conception, Very Rev. John C. Aurilia, O.F.M.Cap., V.F.; Rev. John Salvas, O.F.M.Cap.
Parish Office: 208 7th Ave., W., 28791-3602. Tel: 828-693-6901; Fax: 828-697-1656.
Res., 717 Buncombe St., 28791-3609. Tel: 828-692-0550.
School—Immaculata, 711 Buncombe St., 28791-3609. Tel: 828-693-3277; Fax: 828-696-3677. Mr. William Meehan, Prin.
Lay Teachers 18; Students 206.
Catechesis/Religious Programs—Tel: 828-697-7420. Sandy Donecho, D.R.E.
Students 92.

Hickory, Catawba Co., St. Aloysius, Rev. Edward J. Sheridan; Deacons Joseph E. Garavaglia; Hugo L. May; Thomas A. Rasmussen. In res., Rev. William H. Tanguay (RI) (Oct.-May).
Res., 921 Second St., N.E., 28601. Tel: 828-327-2341; Fax: 828-327-3376.
Catechesis/Religious Programs—Students 715.

High Point, Guilford Co., Immaculate Heart of Mary, Revs. Joseph C. Zuschmidt, O.S.F.S.; John J. Kelly, O.S.F.S.; Deacons Thomas Kak; Joseph T. Smith.
Res., 512 Montlieu Ave., 27262. Tel: 336-884-5212; Fax: 336-884-1849.
School—Tel: 336-887-2613; Fax: 336-884-1849. Margene Wilkins, Prin.
Lay Teachers 24; Students 240.
Catechesis/Religious Programs—Tel: 336-885-5210. Betsy Strauss, D.F.F.
Students 354.

Christ the King, Rev. Philip Kollithanath.
Res., 1505 Kivett Dr., 27260. Tel: 336-884-0244; Fax: 336-887-1200.
Catechesis/Religious Programs—Students 80.

Huntersville, Mecklenburg Co., St. Mark, Rev. Msgr. Joseph A. Kerin; Rev. David Brzoska.
Res., 14740 Stumptown Rd., 28078. Tel: 704-948-0231; Fax: 704-948-8018.
Catechesis/Religious Programs—Tel: 704-948-1306.
Students 1,118.

Jefferson, Ashe Co., St. Francis of Assisi, Rev. Mark Lawlor.
Mailing Address: P.O. Box 1, 28640. Tel: 336-246-9151; Fax: 336-246-5925.
Catechesis/Religious Programs—Students 53.
Mission—Sparta, Alleghany Co., St. Frances of Rome, P.O. Box 367, Sparta, 28675. Tel: 336-372-8846.

Kernersville, Forsyth Co., Holy Cross, Rev. Joseph E. Tustin, O.S.F.S.
Res., 616 S. Cherry St., 27284. Tel: 336-996-5109; Fax: 336-996-5115.
Child Developmental Center—Tel: 336-996-5144; Fax: 336-996-5115. Vivian Harris, Dir.
Catechesis/Religious Programs—Tel: 336-996-5109; Fax: 336-996-5115. Marie Kinney, D.R.E.
Students 376.

Lenoir, Caldwell Co., St. Francis of Assisi, Very Rev. Michael Buttner, V.F.; Deacon Ronald Caplette.
Res., 328-B Woodsway Ln., N.W., 28645-4356. Tel: 828-754-5281; Fax: 828-754-5281.
Catechesis/Religious Programs—Students 189.
Mission—Taylorsville, Alexander Co., Holy Trinity, Hwy. 90 W., 655 W. Main Ave., Taylorsville, 28681. Tel: 828-632-8009. In res., Rev. Joseph Waters.

Lexington, Davidson Co., Our Lady of the Rosary, Rev. Albert J. Gondek, O.S.F.S.
Res., 619 S. Main St., 27292. Tel: 336-248-2463; Fax: 336-238-3241.
Catechesis/Religious Programs—Students 71.

Lincolnton, Lincoln Co., St. Dorothy, Rev. Thomas J. Kessler (ALN); Deacon Carlos Medina.
Res., 148 St. Dorothy Ln., 28092. Tel: 704-735-5575; Fax: 704-735-5890.
Catechesis/Religious Programs—Students 130.

Maggie Valley, Haywood Co., St. Margaret, Rev. Francis J. Doyle, O.S.A. In res., Rev. Terrance W. Hyland, O.S.A.; Bro. William C. Harkin, O.S.A.
Mailing Address: P.O. Box 1359, 28751. Tel: 828-926-0106; Fax: 828-926-0855.
Res., 37 Murphy Dr., 28751. Tel: 828-926-0855.

Mars Hill, Madison Co., St. Andrew the Apostle, Rev. Edward M. Ifkovits, S.J.
Mailing Address: P.O. Box 1406, 28754-1406. Tel: 828-689-3719.
Res. & Church—149 Brook St., 28754.
Missions—Burnsville, Yancey Co., Sacred Heart, P.O. Box 1406, Mars Hill, 28754-1406.; Hot Springs, Madison Co., Chapel of the Redeemer. Jesuit House of Prayer. P.O. Box 7, Hot Springs, 28743. Tel: 828-622-7366. Revs. George R. Hohman, S.J.; Joseph J. McGovern, S.J.; Francis X. Reese, S.J.
Catechesis/Religious Programs—Fax: 828-689-3719.
Students 56.

Mocksville, Davie Co., St. Francis of Assisi, Rev. Andrew Draper, T.O.R.
Mailing Address: P.O. Box 642, 27028. Tel: 336-751-2973; Fax: 336-751-2973.
Church—862 Yadkinville Rd., 27028.
Catechesis/Religious Programs—Students 81.

Monroe, Union Co., Our Lady of Lourdes, Revs. Carlo DiNatale Tarasi; Luis Osorio.
Res., 725 Deese St., 28112. Tel: 704-289-2773; Fax: 704-283-7210.
Catechesis/Religious Programs—Tel: 704-289-2773; Fax: 704-283-7210.
Students 300.

Mooresville, Iredell Co., St. Therese, Revs. James F. McAndrews, S.J.; William J. Kelley, S.J. In res., Revs. James Keogh, S.J.; William J. Lynch, S.J.; Deacon John Sims.
Res., 217 Brawley School Rd., 28117. Tel: 704-664-3992; Fax: 704-660-6321.
Catechesis/Religious Programs—Tel: 704-664-7762.
Students 495.

Morganton, Burke Co., St. Charles Borromeo, Rev. Kenneth L. Whittington; Deacon James R. Johnson.
Res., 714 W. Union St., 28655. Tel: 828-437-3108; Fax: 828-437-6262.
Catechesis/Religious Programs—Terri Martino, D.R.E.
Students 183.
Mission—Marion, McDowell Co., Our Lady of the Angels, P.O. Box 1006, 28752. Tel: 828-652-8690. Rev. John Tuller, (Retired).

Mount Airy, Surry Co., Holy Angels, Rev. Thomas D. Stott.
Res., 1208 N. Main St., Mt. Airy, 27030. Tel: 336-786-8147; Fax: 336-786-8147.
Catechesis/Religious Programs—Linda Gallasetti-Simmons, D.R.E.
Students 110.
Mission—Dobson, Surry Co., Sacred Heart, Rt. 601, 27017.

Murphy, Cherokee Co., St. William, Very Rev. George M. Kloster, V.F.; Deacon Carl Hubbel.
Res., 763 Andrews Rd., P.O. Box 546, 28906. Tel: 828-837-2000; Fax: 828-835-9889.
Catechesis/Religious Programs—Students 43.
Mission—Hayesville, Clay Co., Immaculate Heart of Mary, U.S.Hwy 64 W., Hayesville, 28906.

Newton, Catawba Co., St. Joseph, Rev. James M. Collins.
Church—720 W. 13th St., 28658-3899. Tel: 828-464-9207; Fax: 828-466-3896.
Holy Family Parish Center—Tel: 828-465-2878.
Catechesis/Religious Programs—Tel: 828-465-2878.
Students 250.

North Wilkesboro, Wilkes Co., St. John Baptist de LaSalle, Rev. Michael T. Kottar (MET) Admin.; Deacons Frank Aversa; Harold Markle.
Res., 275 C.C. Wright School Rd., 28659. Tel: 336-838-5562.
Catechesis/Religious Programs—Students 105.
Mission—Elkin, Surry Co., St. Stephen, 101 Hawthorne, Elkin, 28621. Tel: 336-835-3007.

Reidsville, Rockingham Co., Holy Infant, Rev. Christopher Davis, Admin.
Res., 1042 Freeway Dr., P.O. Box 1197, 27323. Tel: 336-342-1448; Fax: 336-616-1877.
Catechesis/Religious Programs—Students 79.

Salisbury, Rowan Co., Sacred Heart, Revs. John T. Putnam; Joseph Long Dinh; Deacon Patrick Vallandingham.
Res., 128 N. Fulton St., 28144. Tel: 704-633-0591; Fax: 704-647-0126.
School—Tel: 704-633-2841; Fax: 704-633-6033. Mrs. Kathleen Miller, Prin.
Lay Teachers 21; Students 251.
Catechesis/Religious Programs—Tel: 704-638-0172.
Students 215.
Convent—425 W. Council St., 28144. Tel: 704-636-4070; Fax: 704-636-2564. Sisters of Mercy

Shelby, Cleveland Co., St. Mary's, Very Rev. Eric Houseknecht, V.F.
Res., 818 McGowan Rd., 28150. Tel: 704-484-3241; Fax: 704-487-0187.
Catechesis/Religious Programs—D.R.E.: John Hess; Ann Marie Bridges.
Students 155.
Mission—Kings Mountain, Cleveland Co., Christ the King, 714 Stone St., Kings Mountain, 28086. Tel: 704-739-3214.

Spruce Pine, Mitchell Co., St. Lucien, Rev. Aloysius J. D'Silva.
Res., 695 Summit Ave., P.O. Box 688, 28777. Tel: 828-765-2224; Fax: 828-765-0086.
Mission—Linville, Avery Co., St. Bernadette, P.O. Box 1252, Linville, 28646. Tel: 828-898-6900.
Catechesis/Religious Programs—Students 24.

Statesville, Iredell Co., St. Philip the Apostle, Rev. Peter L. Fitzgibbons; Deacon Charles Brantley. In res., Rev. James M. Byer.
Mailing Address: P.O. Box 882, 28687-0882.
Office: Tel: 704-872-2579; Fax: 704-872-2579.
Res., 525 Camden Dr., 28677. Tel: 704-873-8641.
Catechesis/Religious Programs—Tel: 704-872-2579; Fax: 704-872-2579.
Students 213.

Swannanoa, Buncombe Co., St. Margaret Mary, Rev. Andrew J. Latsko.
Office: Tel: 828-686-8833; Fax: 828-686-8833.
Res., 102 Andrews Pl., Box 99, 28778.
Catechesis/Religious Programs—Tel: 828-299-3069. Jo Gibbs, D.R.E.
Students 46.

Sylva, Jackson Co., St. Mary, Rev. James P. Cahill.
Res., 22 Bartlett St., 28779. Tel: 828-586-9496; Fax: 828-631-3586.
Catechesis/Religious Programs—Tel: 828-586-9496.
Students 75.

Thomasville, Davidson Co., Our Lady of the Highways, Rev. Thomas J. Fitzpatrick, O.S.F.S.; Deacon Wayne Adams.
Res., 943 Ball Park Rd., 27360. Tel: 336-475-2732; 475-2667; Fax: 336-476-3337.
Catechesis/Religious Programs—Tel: 336-475-2732; Fax: 336-476-3337.
Students 86.

Tryon, Polk Co., St. John the Baptist, Rev. Gregory J. Littleton (MET).
Mailing Address: P.O. Box 1597, 28782.
Res., 600 Laurel Ave., 28782. Tel: 828-859-9574; Fax: 828-859-5932.
Catechesis/Religious Programs—Tel: 828-859-9574, Ext. 7; Fax: 828-859-3732.
Students 86.

Waynesville, Haywood Co., St. John the Evangelist, Revs. Dennis M. McGowan, O.S.A.; Christopher W. Nowak, O.S.A.
Res., 234 Church St., 28786. Tel: 828-456-6707; Fax: 828-453-4329.
Catechesis/Religious Programs—Tel: 828-456-7450.
Students 81.
Mission—Canton, Haywood Co., Immaculate Conception.

Winston-Salem, Forsyth Co., Our Lady of Mercy, Revs. Joseph Barry Angelini, O.F.M. Conv.; Joseph Madden, O.F.M.Conv. In res., Revs. George Sullivan, O.F.M.Conv.; Jude T. DeAngelo, O.F.M.Conv.; Friar Gregory Spuhler, O.F.M.Conv.; Deacons Joseph Schumacher; John Hubbarth.
Res., 1910 S. Main St., 27127. Tel: 336-724-6806; Fax: 336-768-8292.
Church—1919 S. Main St., 27127. Tel: 336-722-7001; Fax: 336-722-0465.
School—Tel: 336-722-7204; Fax: 336-725-2294. Sandra McMonagle, Prin.
Sisters of St. Joseph 2; Lay Teachers 16; Students 267.
Catechesis/Religious Programs—Tel: 336-722-7001; Fax: 336-722-0465.
Students 138.
Convent—1922 S. Main St., 27127. Tel: 336-727-0925.
Mission—Winston-Salem, Forsyth Co., Our Lady of Fatima, 211 W. 3rd St., Winston-Salem, 27101. Tel: 336-723-8238.

St. Benedict the Moor, Rev. Lawrence J. Hunt, S.J.
Res., 1625 E. Twelfth St., 27101. Tel: 336-725-9200; Fax: 336-777-1062.
Mission—King, Stokes Co., Good Shepherd, P.O. Box 1149, King, 27021. Tel: 336-983-2680.
Catechesis/Religious Programs—Students 123.

St. Leo's, Revs. Cecil W. Tice; Herbert Burke (WDC); Deacons Dennis O'Madigan; Robert DeSautels.
Res., 334 Springdale Ave., 27104. Tel: 336-724-5314.
Church—335 Springdale Ave., 27104. Tel: 336-724-0561; Fax: 336-724-7036.
School—333 Springdale Ave., 27104. Tel: 336-748-8252; Fax: 336-748-9005.
Sisters of St. Joseph 2; Lay Teachers 11; Students 278.
Catechesis/Religious Programs—Tel: 336-724-0561; Fax: 336-724-7036.
Students 387.
Convent—1975 Georgia Ave., 27104. Tel: 336-723-3639.

Special Assignment:
Reverend Fathers—
Hoover, John P.
Thomas, Wilbur N., Vicar for Priests
West, Mauricio W., Vicar Gen. & Chancellor

On Duty Outside the Diocese:
Reverend Fathers—
Choquet, Alexei H.
Farrell, William, Diocese of Ogdensburg, NY
Farwell, Richard B.
Valentine, Joseph R., F.S.S.P., Fraternity of St. Peter
Wilderotter, Paul C.

Military Chaplains:
Reverend Fathers—
Fitzgibbons, Peter L., U.S. Army
Klepacki, Michael S., U.S. Navy

Absent On Leave:
Reverend Fathers—
Baker, Donald P.
Bradley, John Paul
DeAguilar, Arturo
Kaltreider, Carl E.
Kuhn, Dennis R.
Lynch, Damion
Orlando, Samuel
Williamson, Thomas

Retired:
Reverend Monsignors—
Allen, Richard F.
Burke, Thomas P., c/o Sacred Heart Convent-Marian Center, Belmont, NC 28012
Duncan, Arthur L., Maryfield Nursing Home, 1315 Greensboro Rd., High Point, NC 27260
Kovacic, Anthony, 411 Dogwood Ln., Belmont, NC 28012
Reverend Fathers—
Berg, Ramon A., 2500 Morgan Mill Rd., Brevard, NC 28712
Cintula, Francis M.
Clements, Thomas P.
Connolly, Francis T.
Erb, Vincent I., 1001 Easton Rd., Apt. 615, Willow Grove, PA 19090
Gavigan, P. Patrick, Maryfield Nursing Home, 1315 Greensboro Rd., High Point, NC 27270
Hourihan, Raymond B., 507 Fulton St., Elmira, NY 14904
Kelleher, Joseph, 1525 Woods Rd., #101, Winston-Salem, NC 27106
Kimbrough, Conrad, 620 S. Ellis St., Salisbury, NC 28144
Kirsch, Edmund D., 3515 Golf Haven Ter., Sebring, FL 33872
Manley, Bernard A., 420 Lakeshore Dr., Asheville, NC 28804
McCarthy, Joseph L., Maryfield Nursing Home, 1315 Greensboro Rd., High Point, NC 27270
McCue, Richard T., P.O. Box 153, Hampton, NH 03842
Reese, Charles T., 800 Bay Dr., No. 25, Niceville, FL 32578
Solari, James K.
Sullivan, D. Edward
Tuller, John
Walsh, Thomas R., 12 N. 6th St., Allegany, NY 14706

Permanent Deacons:
Adams, Wayne, Our Lady of the Highways, Thomasville
Aversa, Frank, St. John, North Wilkesboro
Brantley, Charles, St. Philip the Apostle, Statesville
Burke, John, Sacred Heart, Brevard
Caplette, Ronald, St. Francis of Assisi, Lenoir
Carl, Daniel, St. James, Concord
Chirico, Neil, St. Vincent de Paul, Charlotte
Cilone, Andrew, Immaculate Conception, Forest City
Crosby, James, Immaculate Conception, Hendersonville
DeSautels, Charles, St. Leo, Winston-Salem
Duca, Peter, Our Lady of the Assumption, Charlotte
Evers, Jeffrey, St. Matthew, Charlotte
Fadero, Nick, St. Patrick, Charlotte
Fohn, Kurt, Pope John XXIII Seminary
Forester, Gordon L., St. Paul the Apostle, Greensboro
Garavaglia, Joseph E., St. Aloysius, Hickory
Gettlefinger, Robert, St. Gabriel, Charlotte
Hamrlik, James, St. Matthew, Charlotte
Harkin, William, St. Margaret, Maggie Valley
Heine, Charles, (Unassigned)
Herbers, Jerome, St. Mary, Sylva
Hickey, Gerald P., St. Vincent, Charlotte
Horai, Stephen J., Our Lady of the Assumption, Charlotte
Hubbarth, John, Our Lady of Mercy, Winston-Salem
Hubbell, Carl, St. William, Murphy
Johnson, James R., St. Charles, Morganton
Kak, Thomas, Immaculate Heart of Mary, High Point
Kauth, Richard, Holy Spirit, Denver
Killian, Philip, Jr., St. Benedict, Greensboro
Kingsley, Arthur, St. Barnabas, Arden
Langsdorf, Michael, Holy Family, Clemmons
Macero, Carl, St. Thomas Aquinas, Charlotte
Mack, Joseph H., Jr., St. John Neumann, Charlotte
Manning, Franklin L., Sr., (Retired)
Marini, Anthony, Immaculate Conception, Hendersonville
Markle, Harold, St.John Baptist de la Salle, No. Wilkesboro
May, Hugo L., (Retired)
McGuirk, Eugene, (Unassigned)
McMahon, George, St. Charles Borromeo, Morganton
Medina, Carlos A., Sr., Hispanic Center, Charlotte
Moss, Charles, Out of Diocese
O'Madigan, Dennis T., St. Leo, Winston-Salem
Pais, Louis, St. Gabriel, Charlotte
Piche, Guy, Catholic Conference Center, Hickory
Potkay, Gerald, St. Joseph of the Hills, Eden
Rasmussen, Thomas, St. Aloysius, Hickory
Renuart, Albert, Immaculate Conception, Hendersonville
Rinkus, Louis, (Retired)
Rodriguez, Edwin, Hispanic Center, Charlotte
Rohan, Timothy, Our Lady of Grace, Greensboro
Schumacher, Gerard, Holy Family, Clemmons
Schumacher, Joseph N., Our Lady of Mercy, Winston-Salem
Shaw, Vincent H., Jr., St. Mary, Greensboro
Shaw, William S., St. Paul the Apostle, Greensboro
Sims, John E., St. Therese, Mooresville
Smith, Joseph T., Immaculate Heart of Mary, High Point
Steinkamp, Ronald F., St. Pius Tenth, Greensboro
Szalony, George, St. Luke, Charlotte
Teich, Paul, Our Lady of Grace, Greensboro
Todd, Curtiss, Our Lady of Consolation, Charlotte
Torres, Rafael, Hispanic Center, Charlotte
Triana, Rudolph J., (Unassigned)
Vallandingham, Patrick, Sacred Heart, Salisbury
Weisenhorn, John P., St. Michael, Gastonia
Wenning, Bernard W., Jr., St. Gabriel, Charlotte

INSTITUTIONS LOCATED IN THE DIOCESE

[A] COLLEGES AND UNIVERSITIES

BELMONT. *Belmont Abbey College*, 100 Belmont-Mount Holly Rd., 28012-1802. Tel: 704-825-6700; Fax: 704-825-6670.
E-mail: schup@crusader.bac.edu
Web site: belmontabbeycollege.edu
For a complete listing, refer to the Colleges and Universities section.

Sacred Heart College, 100 Mercy Dr., 28012-4805. Tel: 704-829-5100; Fax: 704-829-5137
For a complete listing, refer to the Colleges and Universities section.

[B] HIGH SCHOOLS

WINSTON-SALEM. *Bishop McGuinness Memorial High School*, 1730 Link Rd., 27103. Tel: 336-725-4247; Fax: 336-725-6669.
E-mail: georgerepass@bishopmcguinness.com
Web site: www.bishopmcguinness.com
George L. Repass, M.Ed., Prin..Sisters of St. Joseph 1; Lay Teachers 29; Students 286.

[C] ELEMENTARY SCHOOLS, INTER-PAROCHIAL

ASHEVILLE. *Asheville Catholic School*, 12 Culvern St., 28804. Tel: 828-252-7896; Fax: 828-252-5708. Veronica C. Berreen, Ph.D., Prin. Lay Teachers 20; Students 240.

[D] REGIONAL SCHOOLS

CHARLOTTE. *Mecklenburg Area Catholic Schools (M.A.C.S.).* Education Foundation, Inc., 1123 S. Church St., 28203. Tel: 704-370-3303; Fax: 704-370-3378. Janet Atherton, Business Mgr.

Charlotte Catholic High School (Bishop Hafey Memorial), 7702 Matthews-Mint Hill Rd., 28226. Tel: 704-543-1127; Fax: 704-543-1217. Rev. James W. Cassidy, O.S.A., Prin.; Mary Jane Dawson, Campus Min. Clergy 2; Lay Teachers 71; Students 939.

Charlotte Catholic High School Athletic Association. Tel: 704-543-1127; Fax: 704-543-1217.

Charlotte Catholic High School Alumni Association. Tel: 704-543-9118; Fax: 704-543-1217.

Charlotte Catholic High School Home School Association. Tel: 704-543-1127; Fax: 704-543-1217.

Holy Trinity Middle School, 3100 Park Rd., 28209. Tel: 704-527-7822; Fax: 704-525-7288. Gerald A. Healy, Prin. Lay Teachers 65; Students 1,000.

All Saints Catholic School, 7100 Endhaven Ln., 28277. Tel: 704-544-2070; Fax: 704-544-2184. Mrs. Betsy DesNoyer, Prin. Lay Teachers 38; Students 653.

Our Lady of the Assumption School, 4225 Shamrock Dr., 28215. Tel: 704-531-0067; Fax: 704-531-7633. Mrs. Patricia Murphy, Prin. Lay Teachers 25; Students 331.

St. Ann School, 600 Hillside Ave., 28209. Tel: 704-525-4938; Fax: 704-525-2640. Sr. Helene Nagle, S.S.J., Prin. Lay Teachers 26; Students 402.

St. Gabriel School, 3028 Providence Rd., 28211. Tel: 704-366-2409; Fax: 704-362-5063. Sharon Broxterman, Prin. Lay Teachers 34; Students 577.

St. Patrick School, 1125 Buchanan St., 28203. Tel: 704-333-3174; Fax: 704-333-3178. Angela Montague, Prin. Lay Teachers 27; Students 417.

[E] GENERAL HOSPITALS

ASHEVILLE. *ARP/Phoenix*, 129 Biltmore Ave., 28801. Tel: 828-254-2700
For a complete listing, refer to the Hospitals section.

Sisters of Mercy Services Corporation, 345 Biltmore Ave., 28801. Tel: 828-281-1268; Fax: 828-254-4102
For a complete listing, refer to the Hospitals section.

Sisters of Mercy Urgent Care, Inc., 345 Biltmore Ave., 28801. Tel: 828-281-2598; Fax: 828-254-4102.
E-mail: bill@somse.org
For a complete listing, refer to the Hospitals section.

[F] SPECIAL CARE FACILITIES

BELMONT. *Holy Angels, Inc.*, 6600 Wilkinson Blvd., P.O. Box 710, 28012. Tel: 704-825-4161; Fax: 704-825-0553.
E-mail: info@holyangelsnc.org
Web site: www.holyangelsnc.org
For a complete listing, refer to the Special Care Facilities section.

[G] CATHOLIC SOCIAL SERVICES

CHARLOTTE. *Catholic Social Services of the Diocese of Charlotte, Inc.*

The Catholic Center, 1123 S. Church St., 28203. Tel: 704-370-3228; Fax: 704-370-3377.
E-mail: EKTHURBEE@Charlottediocese.org
Web site: www.cssnc.org
Elizabeth K. Thurbee, A.C.S.W., Diocesan Dir.
Area Offices:

Asheville-Smoky Mountain Vicariates, 50 Orange St., Asheville, 28801. Tel: 828-255-0146; Fax: 828-253-7339. Sr. Marie Frechette, M.S.B.T., A.C.S.W., Dir.

Albemarle-Charlotte-Gastonia Vicariates, 1123 S. Church St., 28203. Tel: 704-370-3232; Fax: 704-370-3377. Geri King, M.S.W., Dir.

Boone-Greensboro-Hickory-Winston-Salem Vicariates. P.O. Box 10962, Winston-Salem, 27108. Tel: 336-714-3201; Fax: 336-714-3232. 621 W. Second St., Winston-Salem, 27101. Tel: 336-714-3201; Fax: 336-714-3232. David W. Harold, A.C.S.W., Dir.

Catholic Social Services Refugee Office, 1123 S. Church St., 28203. Tel: 704-370-3260; 370-3290, Ext. 29. Cira Ponce, Dir.

Special Ministries:

Adoption. Contact the Domestic Adoption Unit at CSS offices. Tel: 828-255-0146, Asheville; Tel: 336-714-3201, Winston-Salem; Tel: 704-370-3232, Fax: 704-370-3377, Charlotte.

Adoption International, Asheville. Tel: 828-255-0146; 888-990-4199; Fax: 828-253-7339. Carol Meyerriecks, M.S.W.

Elder Services. Contact Diocesan Office. Tel: 704-370-3220; 3228; Fax: 704-370-3377. Sandra Breakfield, Contact Person.

Disaster. Contact the Office of Special Ministries, Diocesan Office. Tel: 704-370-3250; Fax: 704-370-3377. Gerard Carter, Contact Person.

Marriage Preparation. Contact Diocesan Office. Tel: 704-370-3228; Fax: 704-370-3377. Marlo Wallace, Contact Person.

Family Life. Contact the Office of Special Ministries, Diocesan Office. Tel: 704-370-3250; Fax: 704-370-3377. Gerard Carter, Dir.

Hand to Hand. Contact Winston-Salem Office., Winston-Salem. Tel: 336-725-4263; Fax: 336-714-3232. Connie McVey, Contact Person.

Project Hope, 1505 E. Kivett Dr., High Point, 27260. Tel: 336-884-5858; Fax: 336-887-1200. Sr. Maria Celine, Contact Person.

Hispanic/Migrant Outreach. Contact Asheville, Winston-Salem, or Charlotte Offices. Tel: 828-255-0146 (Asheville); 336-727-0705 (Winston-Salem); 704-370-3235 (Charlotte); Fax: 704-370-3377 (Charlotte).

Host Homes. Contact Winston-Salem Office., Winston-Salem. Tel: 336-725-4678; Fax: 336-727-9333. Mable Stevenson, Contact Person.

Natural Family Planning. Contact the Diocesan Office. Tel: 704-370-3250; Fax: 704-370-3377. Cathy Tepper, Contact Person.

Office of Justice and Peace, 1123 S. Church St., 28203. Tel: 704-370-3225; Fax: 704-370-3377. Joseph Purello, Dir.

Catholic Campaign for Human Development. Contact Office of Justice and Peace. Tel: 704-370-3234; Fax: 704-370-3377. Dr. Bernard Offerman, Contact Person.

Catholic Relief Services. Contact Office of Justice and Peace. Tel: 704-370-3225; Fax: 704-370-3377. Joseph Purello, Contact Person.

Operation Rice Bowl. Contact Office of Justice and Peace. Tel: 704-370-3231; Fax: 704-370-3377. Terri Jarina, Contact Person.

Prison Ministry. Contact Diocesan Office. Tel: 704-370-3228; Fax: 704-370-3377. Mr. Bill Matevie, Contact Person.

Problem Pregnancy. Contact the pregnancy support worker at any of the CSS offices. Tel: 704-370-3232 (Charlotte); 828-255-0146 (Asheville); 336-727-0705 (Winston-Sal; Fax: 704-370-3377 (Charlotte).

Respect Life. Contact the Diocesan Office. Tel: 704-370-3229; Fax: 704-370-3377. Maggi Nadol, Contact Person.

Widowed-Separated-Divorced. Contact the Diocesan Office. Tel: 704-370-3228; Fax: 704-370-3377. Gerard Carter, Contact Person.

HAMPTONVILLE. *Well of Mercy Inc.*, 181 Mercy Ln., 27020. Tel: 704-539-5449; Fax: 704-539-4487.
E-mail: mercy@yadtel.net
Co-Directors: Sr. Brigid McCarthy, R.S.M.; Sr. Donna Marie Vaillancourt, R.S.M. Retreats and psycho-spiritual development programs.

[H] HOME HEALTH CARE

ROSMAN. *Frances Warde Health Service*, Star Rte. 1, Box 581, 28772. Tel: 828-884-7990; Fax: 828-966-9609.
E-mail: jdewarrsm@juno.com
For a complete listing, refer to the Special Care Facilities section.

[I] NURSING HOMES

HIGH POINT. *Maryfield Nursing Home*, 1315 Greensboro Rd., 27260. Tel: 336-886-2444; Fax: 336-886-4036.
E-mail: srlucy@hpe_infi.net
Web site: www.greensboro.com/mnh
For a complete listing, refer to the Special Care Facilities section.

[J] MONASTERIES AND RESIDENCES OF PRIESTS AND BROTHERS

CHARLOTTE. *Jesuit Community*, 507 S. Tryon St., 28202. Tel: 704-372-6808; Fax: 704-358-0050. Legal Title: *Jesuit Community in Western North Carolina.* Revs. Vincent P. Alagia, S.J.; Raymond J. Donaldson, S.J., (Scholastic); Francis J. Gillespie, S.J.; George R. Hohman, S.J.; Lawrence J. Hunt, S.J.; Edward M. Ifkovits, S.J.; William J. Kelley, S.J.; James Keogh, S.J.; William J. Lynch, S.J.; Lucian C. Martinez, S.J.; James F. McAndrew, S.J.; Eugene P. McCreesh, S.J., Supr.; Joseph J. McGovern, S.J.; Robert J. Paquet, S.J.; Francis X. Reese, S.J.; Joseph A. Sobierajski, S.J.; Robert D. Weisenbaugh, S.J.

BELMONT. *Belmont Abbey*, 100 Belmont-Mount Holly Rd., 28012-1802. Tel: 704-825-6675; Fax: 704-825-6680.
E-mail: placid@crusader.bac.edu
Web site: www.bac.edu/monastery
Legal Title: *Southern Benedictine Society of North Carolina, Inc.* Rt. Revs. Oscar C. Burnett, O.S.B., (Retired); Placid D. Solari, O.S.B., S.Th.D.; Very Revs. Arthur J. Pendleton, O.S.B., Prior; David G. Brown, O.S.B., Sub-Prior; Revs. Anselm G. Biggs, O.S.B., Ph.D.; Bede C. Lightner, O.S.B.; Raymond J. Geyer, O.S.B.; Matthew T. McSorley, O.S.B.; John A. Oetgen, O.S.B.; Kenneth A. Geyer, O.S.B.; David R. Kessinger, O.S.B.; Kieran A. Neilson, O.S.B.; Francis P. Forster, O.S.B.; Lawrence R. Willis, O.S.B.; Paschal M. Baumstein, O.S.B., Custos Archivorum Emeritus; Christopher A. Kirchgessner, O.S.B. Abbots 2; Monk Priests of Abbey 14; Priests in Residence 13; Brothers 2.

GREENSBORO. *Franciscan Friary*, 613 Kimberly Dr., 27408-5198. Tel: 336-379-7568. Rev. Louis Canino, O.F.M., Dir.

The Franciscan Center, 233 N. Greene St., 27401. Tel: 336-273-2554.

[K] CONVENTS AND RESIDENCES FOR SISTERS

CHARLOTTE. *Blessed Trinity Missionary Cenacle*, 801 Bromley Rd., 28207. Tel: 704-377-3254. Social work.

Coolock House, 2328 Red Barn Ln., 28210. Tel: 704-554-1967; Fax: 704-554-1967.
E-mail: therese-galligan@yahoo.com
Parish and bereavement care. Sisters of Mercy of the Americas 2.

Missionaries of Charity, 236 S. Torrence St., 28204. Tel: 704-334-8685. Ministry for poor. Sisters 4.

Sisters of St. Francis Convent, 4516 Randolph Rd., Apt. 87, 28211. Tel: 704-364-1361.
E-mail: CSOCHARLOTTE@impresso.com
Sisters 2.

Sisters' Residence, Carmel House, 3035 Carmel Rd., 28226. Tel: 704-552-2899; Fax: 704-552-2899. Administration; Caregiver Assisted Living and Shut-ins. Sisters 2.

ASHEVILLE. *Sisters of Mercy Convent*, 428 Biltmore Ave., 28801. Tel: 828-232-1160; Fax: 828-232-0084. Sisters 4; Health Care 3; Parish.

BELMONT. *Sisters of Mercy of North Carolina, Inc.*, Sacred Heart Convent, 100 Mercy Dr., 28012-4805. Tel: 704-829-5100; Fax: 704-829-5137.
Web site: www.AsaSystems.com/mercy
Motherhouse of Sisters of Mercy of the Americas, Regional Community of North Carolina. Sr. Mary Rosalind Picot, R.S.M., Pres.; Sr. Mary Andrew Ray, R.S.M., Motherhouse Coord. Sisters in Motherhouse 37; Professed Sisters in Community 124. Connected with the Motherhouse are Holy Angels, Inc., The McAuley Center, House of Mercy, Inc., and Catherine's House, Inc.

HIGH POINT. *Congregation of the Sisters of Charity of St. Vincent De Paul*, St. Vincent Convent, 1507 E. Kivett Dr., 27260. Tel: 336-884-0244; Fax: 336-887-1200. Sr. Maria Celine, S.C.V., Supr.; Sr. Philo, Asst. Supr.; Sr. Pushpa, Treas.; Sr. Molly Jose, Sec.; Sr. Primosa, Supr. Gen.; Sr. Stella, Gen. Councillor & Asst. Supr. Gen.; Sr. Liliosa, Gen. Councillor; Sr. Ancitta, Gen. Councillor; Sr. Lucyantony, Gen. Councillor & Gen. Sec.; Sr. Jositta, Treas. Gen.

ROSMAN. *Sisters Residence*, Star Rte. 1, Box 581, 28772. Tel: 828-884-7990; 884-9528; 883-2789; Fax: 828-966-9609.
E-mail: jdewarrsm@juno.com
Sisters 4. Health service.

VALE. *Maryvale Motherhouse*, 2522 June Bug Rd., 28168. Tel: 704-276-2626; Fax: 704-276-2626. Mother Mary Louis, Foundress and Supr. Congregation of Our Lady Help of the Clergy, (Maryvale Sisters). Sisters 5. Parish ministry, day-care center, spiritual/retreat center, religious education and pastoral ministry.

[L] CAMPUS MINISTRY CENTERS

CHARLOTTE. *Diocesan Office of Campus Ministry.* Colleen McDermott, Dir., Res., 1123 S. Church St., 28203. Tel: 704-370-3212; Fax: 704-370-3291.
E-mail: cmmcdermott@charlottediocese.org
University of North Carolina-Charlotte, ORA, 9201 University City Blvd., UNC-Charlotte, 28223-0001. Tel: 704-547-4069. Mary Wright, Catholic Campus Min.
University of North Carolina-Asheville, c/o St. Eugene Church, 1 Culvern St., Asheville, 28804. Tel: 828-254-5193. Rev. Frank Cancro.
Belmont Abbey College, 100 Belmont-Mount Holly Rd., Belmont, 28012. Tel: 704-829-7196; 825-6697.
E-mail: Kponitale@juno.com
Dr. Katy Volponi, Dir. Campus Ministry; Rev. Kieran A. Neilson, O.S.B., Chap. Tel: 704-825-6836.
Appalachian State University, 232 Faculty St., Boone, 28607. Tel: 828-264-7087; Fax: 828-262-0970.
E-mail: Ingleses@Boone.net
Dr. Sal Inglese, Catholic Campus Min.
Western Carolina University, Catholic Student Center, P.O. Box 364, Cullowhee, 28723-0364. Tel: 828-293-9374; 586-8068.
E-mail: wcu.catholic@wcu.edu
Gloria Schweizer, Catholic Campus Min.
Davidson College. (Davidson), P.O. Box 314, Davidson, 28036. Tel: 704-894-2917.
E-mail: BB195@aol.com
Barbara Bagnall, Catholic Campus Min.
NC Agricultural and Technical State University & Bennett College, 1009 Bluford St., Greensboro, 27401. Tel: 336-272-5868; 545-1468.
E-mail: theahouse1@juno.com
Alberta Hairston.
University of North Carolina-Greensboro, Greensboro College & Guilford College, 1331 W. Friendly Ave., Greensboro, 27403. Tel: 336-334-5548.
E-mail: dougcampbell66@aol.com
Mr. Douglas Campbell.
Catawba College and Livingston AME, 128 N. Fulton St., Salisbury, 28144. Tel: 704-633-0591; Fax: 704-647-0126. Lynda Cody, Parish Contact.
Wake Forest University and Winston-Salem University, P.O. Box 7204, Reynolda Station, Winston-Salem, 27109. Tel: 336-758-5018.
Salem College and N.C. School of the Arts, P.O. Box 10548, Chaplain's Office, Salem College, Winston-Salem, 27108. Tel: 336-758-5018; Fax: 336-758-4462.
E-mail: Deangeit@wfu.edu
Rev. Jude T. DeAngelo, O.F.M.Conv., Catholic Campus Min.; Friar Gregory Spuhler, O.F.M.Conv., Intern; Julianne Ostergaard, Intern.
Johnson C. Smith University/Barber Scotia College, 6517 Wickville Dr., 28215. Tel: 704-536-2340. Mrs. Nannette Lide, Parish Contact.
Brevard College, 4 Brian Berg Ln., Brevard, 28712. Tel: 828-883-9572.
E-mail: gallivant@citcom.net

[M] RETREAT CENTERS

HOT SPRINGS.
Jesuit House of Prayer, P.O. Box 7, 28743. Tel: 828-622-7366; Fax: 828-622-3586.
E-mail: vpaul@madison.main.nc.us
Web site: www.geocities.com/~jesuit_housenc
Sr. Margaret Verstege, R.S.M., Dir.; Revs. Joseph J. McGovern, S.J.; George R. Hohman, S.J.; Francis X. Reese, S.J. Directed, private individual retreats and small group retreats for men and women, as well as ecumenical.

[N] REFLECTION CENTERS

BELMONT. *The McAuley Center.* Center for Adult Religious Education. 100 Mercy Dr., 28012. Tel: 704-829-5113; Fax: 704-829-5137. Sr. Mary Hugh Mauldin, Dir.

MAGGIE VALLEY. *Living Waters Catholic Reflection Center*, 103 Living Waters Ln., 28751. Tel: 828-926-3833; Fax: 828-926-1997.
E-mail: lwcrc@main.nc.us
Web site: www.catholicretreat.org
Rev. Terrance W. Hyland, O.S.A., Dir. Retreats, days of recollection, and continuing education.

[O] HISPANIC MINISTRY

CHARLOTTE. *Centro Catolico Hispano*, 2117 Shenandoah Ave., 28205-6021. Tel: 704-335-1281; Fax: 704-334-5475. Rev. Vincent H. Finnerty, C.M., Diocesan Dir. Hispanic Ministry; Deacons Rafael Torres; Edwin Rodriguez.

[P] CONFERENCE CENTERS

HICKORY. *Catholic Conference Center*, 1551 Trinity Lane, 28602-9247. Tel: 828-327-7441; 888-536-7441 (Toll Free); Fax: 828-327-0872.
E-mail: ccc@twave.net
Web site: www.catholicconference.org
Deacon Guy A. Piche, Dir. & Chap.

[Q] MISCELLANEOUS

CHARLOTTE.
Room at the Inn, Inc., P.O. Box 30544, 28230-0544. Tel: 704-521-2774; Fax: 704-521-2751. Cindy Brown, Exec. Dir. Room at the Inn-Charlotte, 3737 Weona Ave., Charlotte, NC 28209. Tel: 704-525-4673. Long-term residence for single, pregnant women, with or without previous children.
Seton Media House, Inc., 7421 Carmel Executive Park, Ste. 214, 28226. Tel: 704-544-2077; Fax: 704-542-0867.
E-mail: setonhouse@aol.com
Robert M. Gallagher, Pres. & CEO; Stephen M. Wilfong, Exec. Dir. Pupose: Distribution of printed materials reflective of Catholic teaching to Catholic schools, and religious education programs at no cost to students, family or school.
Sisters of Mercy of North Carolina Foundation, Inc., 2115 Rexford Rd., Ste. 401, 28211. Tel: 704-366-0087; Fax: 704-366-8850. Sr. Mary Jerome Spradley, R.S.M., Pres.
ASHEVILLE. *McAuley Foundation, Inc.*, 345 Biltmore Ave., 28801. Tel: 828-281-1268; Fax: 828-254-4102.
BELMONT.
Catherine's House, 400 Mercy Dr., P.O. Box 1633, 28012. Tel: 704-825-9599; Fax: 704-825-2734.
E-mail: catherineshouse@email.com
Web site: www.geocities.com/catherineshouse/index.html
Laura Flaccus, Pres. & CEO. Transitional housing for women and women with children who are homeless.
House of Mercy, Inc., 701 Mercy Dr., 28012. Tel: 704-825-4711; Fax: 704-825-9976.
E-mail: hse4mercy@aol.com
Mailing Address: P.O. Box 808, 28012. Provides a home for persons living with AIDS in the advanced stages who have no other housing alternative in an 11 county region. Stan Patterson, Pres. & CEO. Beds 6.
Mercy Community Housing North Carolina (MCHNC), 101 Mercy Dr., 28012-2898. Tel: 704-829-5264, Ext. 1230.
E-mail: michelle@mercync.org
Web site: www.mercyhousing.org
Kathleen Brownlee, Pres.; Patricia O'Roark, Vice Pres.; Dolan Hyde, Treas.
Sisters of Mercy of North Carolina, Inc., 101 Mercy Dr., 28012-2898. Tel: 704-829-5260; Fax: 704-829-5267.
E-mail: ncreg@mercync.org
Web site: www.mercync.org
Sr. M. Rosalind Picot, R.S.M., Pres.
BELTMONT. *Mercy Housing, South East, Inc.*, 101 Mercy Dr., 28012-2898. Tel: 704-829-5260, Ext. 123; Fax: 704-829-5267.
E-mail: michelle@mercync.org
Michelle Allen, Project Developer. Purpose: provide housing and supportive services to low income, homeless and seniors.
GREENSBORO. *Society of St. Vincent De Paul*, 1414 Gorrell St., 27401. Tel: 336-272-0336. Financial assistance, food and clothing.

RELIGIOUS INSTITUTES OF MEN REPRESENTED IN THE DIOCESE

For further details refer to the corresponding bracketed number in the Religious Institutes of Men or Women section.

[0140]—*Augustinians.* (Villanova, PA).—O.S.A.
[0200]—*Benedictine Monks.* (Belmont, NC).—O.S.B.
[0470]—*The Capuchin Friars Province of the Stigmata.*—O.F.M.Cap.
[]—*Carmelites of Mary Immaculate.*—C.M.I.
[0740]—*Congregation of Marians of the Immaculate Conception.*—M.I.C.
[1330]—*Congregation of the Mission.* (Eastern Prov.).—C.M.
[0480]—*Conventual Franciscans.* (Union City, NJ).—O.F.M.Conv.
[0520]—*Franciscan Friars.* (New York, NY).—O.F.M.
[0570]—*Glenmary Home Missioners.*—Glmy.
[0690]—*Jesuit Fathers and Brothers.* (Maryland Prov.).—S.J.
[0920]—*Oblates of St. Francis De Sales.* (Wilmington-Philadelphia).—O.S.F.S.
[1070]—*Redemptorist Fathers.* (Baltimore Prov.).—C.SS.R.
[0560]—*Third Order Regular of St. Francis.* (Pittsburg, PA).—T.O.R.

RELIGIOUS INSTITUTES OF WOMEN REPRESENTED IN THE DIOCESE

[2980]—*Congregation de Notre Dame.*—C.N.D.
[3080]—*Congregation of Our Lady, Help of the Clergy.*—C.L.H.C.
[]—*Congregation of the Sisters of St. Vincent DePaul.* (India).—S.C.V.
[1070]—*Dominican Sisters.*—O.P.
[1110]—*Dominican Sisters of St. Catherine of Sienna.*—O.P.
[]—*Glenmary Lay Missioners.*—G.L.M.
[2470]—*Maryknoll Sisters.*—M.M.
[2710]—*Missionaries of Charity.*—M.C.
[2790]—*Missionary Servants of the Most Blessed Trinity.*—M.S.B.T.
[3640]—*Poor Servants of the Mother of God.*—S.M.G.
[]—*School Sisters of St. Francis.* (Milwaukee, WI).—O.S.F.
[0590]—*Sisters of Charity of Saint Elizabeth, Convent Station.*—S.C.
[0650]—*Sisters of Charity of St. Vincent de Paul, of New York.*—S.C.
[0990]—*Sisters of Divine Providence.*—C.D.P.
[2575]—*Sisters of Mercy of the Americas.* (Belmont, NC; Dallas, PA; Detroit, MI; Watchung, NJ; Cincinatti, OH).—R.S.M.
[3000]—*Sisters of Notre Dame de Namur.*—S.N.D.deN.
[]—*Sisters of St. Francis.* (Tiffin, OH).—O.S.F.
[]—*Sisters of St. Francis.* (Rochester, MN).—O.S.F.
[1570]—*Sisters of St. Francis of the Holy Family.*—O.S.F.
[3893]—*Sisters of St. Joseph .* (Chestnut Hill, PA).—S.S.J.
[3830-14]—*Sisters of St. Joseph.* (Rochester, NY).—S.S.J.
[4060]—*Society of the Holy Child Jesus.* (Drexel Hill).—S.H.C.J.

NECROLOGY

† Morse, Guy E., (Retired). —Died June 6, 2000.
† Roueche, Rev. Msgr. John F., (Retired). —Died June 1, 2000.

Diocese of Cheyenne

(Dioecesis Cheyennensis)

Most Reverend

JOSEPH HART, D.D.

Bishop of Cheyenne; ordained May 1, 1956; appointed July 1, 1976; appointed Titular Bishop of Timida Regia; episcopal ordination August 31, 1976; installed June 12, 1978. *Res., P.O. Box 1468, Cheyenne, WY, 82003.*

Most Reverend

DAVID LAURIN RICKEN, D.D., J.C.L.

Coadjutor Bishop of Cheyenne; ordained September 12, 1980; consecrated January 6, 2000.

ESTABLISHED AUGUST 2, 1887.

Square Miles 97,548.

Comprises the State of Wyoming and Yellowstone National Park.

For legal titles of parishes and diocesan institutions, consult the Chancery Office.

Chancery Office: 2121 Capitol Ave., P.O. Box 1468, Cheyenne, WY, 82003-0426. Tel.: 307-638-1530; Fax: 307-637-7936.

Web site address: www.cheycathdiocese.org

E-mail address: bishop@dioceseofcheyenne.org

STATISTICAL OVERVIEW

Personnel	
Bishop	2
Priests: Diocesan Active in Diocese	36
Priests: Active Outside Diocese	1
Priests: Retired, Sick or Absent	15
Number of Diocesan Priests	52
Religious Priests in Diocese	9
Extern Priests in Diocese	3
Ordinations:	
Diocesan Priests	1
Permanent Deacons	4
Permanent Deacons in Diocese	14
Total Brothers	1
Total Sisters	24
Parishes	
Parishes	36
With Resident Pastor:	
Resident Diocesan Priests	29
Resident Religious Priests	5
Without Resident Pastor:	
Administered by Priests	2
Missions	42
Professional Ministry Personnel:	
Brothers	1
Sisters	11
Lay Ministers	31
Welfare	
Homes for the Aged	2
Total Assisted	105
Day Care and Extended Day Care Centers	7
Total Assisted	325
Specialized Homes	1
Total Assisted	181
Special Centers for Social Services	10
Total Assisted	11,000
Educational	
Diocesan Students in Other Seminaries	12
Total Seminarians	12
High Schools, Private	1
Total Students	53
Elementary Schools, Diocesan and Parish	6
Total Students	998
Catechesis/Religious Education:	
High School Students	1,900
Elementary Students	6,050
Total Students Under Catholic Instruction	9,013
Teachers in the Diocese:	
Sisters	2
Lay Teachers	100
Vital Statistics	
Receptions into the Church:	
Infant Baptism Totals	932
Adult Baptism Totals	173
Received into Full Communion	162
First Communions	976
Confirmations	898
Marriages:	
Catholic	156
Interfaith	182
Total Marriages	338
Deaths	616
Total Catholic Population	48,781
Total Population	480,000

Former Bishops—Rt. Rev. MAURICE F. BURKE, D.D., cons. Oct. 28, 1887; transferred to the See of St. Joseph, MO, June 19, 1893; died March 17, 1923.—Rt. Rev. THOMAS M. LENIHAN, D.D., cons. Feb. 24, 1897; died Dec. 15, 1901.—Most Rev. JAMES J. KEANE, D.D., cons. Bishop of Cheyenne Oct. 28, 1902 raised to the archiepiscopal dignity and transferred to Archdiocese of Dubuque, Aug. 11, 1911; died Aug. 2, 1929.—Most Rev. PATRICK A. MCGOVERN, D.D., LL.D., ord. Aug. 18, 1895 assistant at the Pontifical Throne; appt. Jan. 19, 1912; cons. April 11, 1912; died Nov. 8, 1951.—Most Rev. HUBERT M. NEWELL, D.D., LL.D., ord. June 15, 1930; appt. Coadjutor Aug. 2, 1947; cons. Sept. 24, 1947; succeeded to the See Nov. 8, 1951; retired Jan. 3, 1978; died Sept. 8, 1987.

Chancery Office—2121 Capitol Ave., P.O. Box 1468, Cheyenne, 82003-1468. Tel: 307-638-1530; Fax: 307-637-7936.

Catholic Ministries Office—623 S. Wolcott, Casper, 82601. Tel: 307-237-2723; Fax: 307-235-9157.

Vicar General—Most Rev. DAVID L. RICKEN, V.G., *P.O. Box 1468, Cheyenne, 82003.* Tel: 307-638-1530; Fax: 307-637-7936.

Vicar-General/Moderator of the Curia—Very Rev. EUGENE SULLIVAN, V.G., *P.O. Box 2024, Sheridan, 82801.* Tel: 307-674-7441; 672-2848; Fax: 307-674-9187.

Chancellor—CAROL DELOIS, *P.O. Box 1468, Cheyenne, 82003-1468.* Tel: 307-638-1530; Fax: 307-637-7936.

Vice-Chancellors—Revs. VERNON CLARK, M.C.L., J.C.L.; MICHAEL CARR; CHARLES F. TAYLOR, J.C.D.

College of Consultors—Very Rev. Msgr. EUGENE SULLIVAN, V.G.; Revs. THOMAS E. CRONKLETON, JR., J.C.L.; AUGUST KOEUNE; GARY RUZICKA; JOHN SAVIO; Very Rev. Msgr. GERALD A. SULLIVAN.

Council of Priests—Most Rev. JOSEPH HART, D.D.; Most Rev. DAVID L. RICKEN, D.D., J.C.L.; Very Rev. EUGENE SULLIVAN, V.G., Ex Officio; Revs. MICHAEL CARR, Chm. MICHAEL HELLMAN, Vice Chm. AUGUST KOEUNE; THOMAS E. CRONKLETON, JR., J.C.L.; RORY SCHIFFBAUER; PETER JOHNSON; Rev. Msgr. LAWRENCE ETCHINGHAM; Revs. GARY RUZICKA; JOHN SAVIO; Very Rev. Msgr. GERALD A. SULLIVAN; Rev. RAY MOSS; Very Rev. JOHN MURRAY; Rev. RON STOLCIS.

Episcopal Vicar for Priestly Life and Ministry—Rev. GARY RUZICKA, *P.O. Box 1269, Cheyenne, 82003-1269.* Tel: 307-635-9261; Fax: 307-635-5723.

Vicars Forane—Very Rev. PHILIP COLIBRARO, Casper Deanery; Very Rev. Msgr. GERALD SULLIVAN, Cheyenne Deanery; Very Rev. JOHN MURRAY, Rock Springs Deanery; Very Rev. Msgr. EUGENE SULLIVAN, V.G., Sheridan Deanery; Very Rev. WILLIAM ESPENSHADE, Thermopolis Deanery.

Director of Diocesan Programs—FINN MCCARTHY, *623 S. Wolcott, Casper, 82601.* Tel: 307-237-2723; Fax: 307-235-9157.

Finance Officer—JAMES S. VANCE, *P.O. Box 1468, Cheyenne, 82003-1468.* Tel: 307-638-1530; Fax: 307-637-7936.

Finance Council—Most Rev. JOSEPH HART, D.D.; Most Rev. DAVID L. RICKEN, D.D., J.C.L. Ex Officios: Very Rev. Msgr. EUGENE SULLIVAN, V.G.; Rev. GARY RUZICKA; Mr. HOWARD BAKER. Ex Officios, Non-Voting: Revs. THOMAS E. CRONKLETON, JR.; THOMAS OGG; Mr. JAMES S. VANCE; Mr. FINN MCCARTHY; Mr. JAMES FAULKNER. Appointed Members, Voting: JANE

SCHNAUBER; JAMES T. DINNEEN; WILLIAM DOWNES; ORION LORENZI; FRANK ROTELLINI, Chm.; Rev. JOHN SAVIO; CHUCK HARKINS; DEBBIE ROBBINS; JOSEPH STANBURY; PAUL VAN MAREN.

Tribunal Office—All marriage correspondence is to be directed to: *The Tribunal Office, P.O. Box 1468, Cheyenne, 82003-1468.* Tel: 307-638-1530; 800-788-4606; Fax: 307-637-7936.

Judicial Vicar—Rev. THOMAS E. CRONKLETON, JR., J.C.L., J.C.D. (Cand.).

Director of the Tribunal—DARLENE FLYNN.

Auditors—DARLENE FLYNN; CONNIE KASSAHN.

Administrative Assistant/Ecclesiastical Notary—CONNIE KASSAHN.

Bookkeeper/Clerk/Ecclesiastical Notary—LESLIE CONNAGHAN.

Promoter of Justice—Rev. CHARLES F. TAYLOR, J.C.D.

Judges—Revs. MICHAEL CARR; GERALD F. CHLEBORAD, J.C.L.; THOMAS E. CRONKLETON, JR., J.C.L.; DARLENE FLYNN.

Defenders of the Bond—Rev. VERNON F. CLARK, M.C.L., J.C.L.; Very Rev. WILLIAM T. ESPENSHADE; Revs. THOMAS G. OGG; SAMUEL HAYES; Very Rev. Msgr. GERALD A. SULLIVAN; Revs. RICHARD R. RYAN, J.C.D.; CHARLES F. TAYLOR, J.C.D.; CARL GALLINGER.

Advocates—SUSAN SIMON; BONNIE BAUMBERGER; Revs. THOMAS KADERA; AUGUST KOEUNE; RORY SCHIFFBAUER; Deacon EDWARD MCCARTHY; PAT MCCARTHY; DORENE MCINTYRE.

Diocesan Administrative Offices and Boards

Catholic Social Services of Wyoming, Inc.—BETSY GROOM, M.S.W., Dir., *P.O. Box 1468, Cheyenne, 82003-1468.* Tel: 307-638-1530; Fax: 307-637-7936. Board of Directors: Most Rev. JOSEPH HART, D.D.; Most Rev. DAVID L. RICKEN, D.D., J.C.L.; Very Rev. Msgr. EUGENE SULLIVAN, V.G.; BOBBIE CLONINGER, Chm. Board of Trustees: Very Rev. Msgr. GERALD A. SULLIVAN; BOBBIE CLONINGER, Chm. PAT NOVAK, Vice Chm. ELIZABETH GROOM, M.S.W., Dir. NANCY SNIFFEN, Sec. GEORGE BURNS; LES CLONINGER; DICK DESOMBER; JO DESOMBER; MIKE CHADEY; LYNN CHADEY; MARY GUENZEL.

Education Office—Deacon ED MCCARTHY, Dir. MARY SUTTON, Media Consultant, *623 S. Wolcott, Casper, 82601.* Tel: 307-237-2723; Fax: 307-235-9157.

Education Office Board—Most Rev. JOSEPH HART, D.D.; Most Rev. DAVID L. RICKEN, D.D., J.C.L.; Deacon ED MCCARTHY, Supt. Educ.; Revs. ANDREW DUNCAN; ROBERT G. LYNCH, S.J.; MARY SUTTON, Media Consultant; ANDREA CHOJNACKY, (Glenrock); MARY ANN CUMMINS, (Buffalo); DONNA DUNCAN, (Torrington); JANE JOHNSON, (Gillette); PAT MCCARTHY, Family Life Dir. JIM ZIERDEN, Youth Dir.

Catholic Family and Respect Life Ministries—PAT MCCARTHY, Dir., *623 S. Wolcott, Casper, 82601.* Tel: 307-237-2723; Fax: 307-235-9157.

Catholic Family and Respect Life Ministries Board—Most Rev. JOSEPH HART, D.D.; Most Rev. DAVID L. RICKEN, D.D., J.C.L.; Very Rev. Msgr. EUGENE SULLIVAN, V.G.; Rev. RAY ROGRIGUEZ; MARY ANN DURAN; RUTHIE HALVORSEN; LINDA HURLESS; CHARLIE LUX; FRANK MCGINTY; DICK MILLS; PAT MILLS; RALPH SPECHT; CAROL SPECHT; BETSY VIGNERI; BRAD ZETTL; JENNIFER ZETTL; BYRON ZUEHLSDORFF; TRACY ZUEHLSDORFF.

Lay Ministry Office—Deacon ED MCCARTHY, Dir., *623 S. Wolcott, Casper, 82601.* Tel: 307-237-2723; Fax: 307-235-9157.

Lay Ministry Formation Board—Most Rev. JOSEPH HART, D.D.; Most Rev. DAVID L. RICKEN, D.D., J.C.L.; Deacon ED MCCARTHY, Dir.; Revs. AUGUST KOEUNE; THOMAS OGG; Dr. MARY BURKE; Dr. TOM BURKE; ALISON MCNULTY; DAVID MCNULTY.

Newspaper "Wyoming Catholic Register"—published by the Catholic Press Society of Wyoming. ROSS DOMAN, Editor, *P.O. Box 1468, Cheyenne, 82003-1468.* Street Address: *2121 Capitol Ave., Cheyenne, 82001.* Tel: 307-638-1530; Fax: 307-637-7936.

Newspaper, Wyoming Catholic Register Board—Most Rev. JOSEPH HART, D.D.; Most Rev. DAVID L. RICKEN, D.D., J.C.L.; ROSS DOMAN, Editor; Very Rev. WILLIAM ESPENSHADE.

Planned Giving Office—FINN MCCARTHY, Dir., *623 S. Wolcott, Casper, 82601.* Tel: 307-237-2723; Fax: 307-235-9157.

Vocation Office—Rev. CARL GALLINGER, Dir., *1800 E. Grand Ave., Laramie, 82070.* Tel: 307-745-5461; Fax: 307-742-0521.

Youth Office—JIM ZIERDEN, Dir. MARY O'CONNOR, Asst. Dir., *623 S. Wolcott, Casper, 82601.* Tel: 307-237-2723; Fax: 307-235-9257.

Youth Ministry Board—Revs. CARL GALLINGER; DREW DUNCAN; CLIFF JACOBSON; RAY RODRIGUEZ; Mr. BEN CAROTTA; KYLE ELLIOTT; MARY O'CONNOR; MARK HORAN; LORRAINE LEAVITT; JIM SCALIA; DEAN MENARDI; JIM ZIERDEN.

Other Diocesan Boards, Councils and Programs

Diocesan Trustees, Board of Directors—Most Rev. JOSEPH HART, D.D.; Most Rev. DAVID L. RICKEN, D.D., J.C.L.; Very Rev. Msgr. EUGENE SULLIVAN, V.G.; Rev. GARY RUZICKA; Mr. HOWARD BAKER.

Apostolate for Evangelization—Rev. RAY MOSS, *617 S. 4th St., Laramie, 82070.* Tel: 307-745-3115.

Bishop's Annual Campaign, "Bishop's Appeal"—JAMES S. VANCE, *P.O. Box 1468, Cheyenne, 82003-1468.* Tel: 307-638-1530; Fax: 307-637-7936. FINN MCCARTHY, *623 S. Wolcott, Casper, 82601.* Tel: 307-237-2723; Fax: 307-235-9157.

Boy and Girl Scouts—THOMAS RYDER, *29 Meandering Way, Lander, 82520.* Tel: 307-332-9816.

Building Commission—Most Rev. JOSEPH HART, D.D.; Most Rev. DAVID L. RICKEN, D.D., J.C.L.; ROGER BAALMAN, A.I.A., Chm.; Very Rev. Msgr. EUGENE SULLIVAN, V.G.; Rev. GERALD F. CHLEBORAD; Very Rev. PHILIP COLIBRARO; Revs. MICHAEL HELLMAN; JOHN SAVIO; CAROL DELOIS; Mr. JOHN STEIL; Mr. VIRGIL SLOUGH; JAMES S. VANCE, Sec.

Catholic Relief Services—BETSY GROOM, M.S.W., *P.O. Box 1468, Cheyenne, 82003-1468.* Tel: 307-638-1530.

Catholic Telecommunications—Deacon JOHN ALOISIO, *St. Margaret's School, 220 N. 7th E., Riverton, 82501.* Tel: 307-856-5922; Fax: 307-857-5892.

Catholic University, Friends of—Very Rev. CHARLES F. TAYLOR, *532 N. Lobban, Buffalo, 82834.* Tel: 307-684-7268.

Confraternity of Christian Doctrine—Deacon ED MCCARTHY, Dir., *623 S. Wolcott, Casper, 82601.* Tel: 307-237-2723.

Council of Religious—Sr. RUTH ANN HEHN, S.C.L.; Sr. GLADYS NOREEN, O.S.B.

Cursillo Board—Very Rev. WILLIAM ESPENSHADE; VICTOR VILLALVA, Pres. LLOYD HEARNS; VIRGINIA SPINDLER; TERRI TREVINO.

Diaconate Program, Permanent—Rev. CARL GALLINGER, *1800 E. Grand Ave., Laramie, 82070.* Tel: 307-745-5461; Fax: 307-742-0521.

Diaconate Board—Most Rev. JOSEPH HART, D.D.; Most Rev. DAVID L. RICKEN, D.D., J.C.L.; Revs. CARL GALLINGER, Bishop's Delegate and Dir. Deacons; CLIFF JACOBSON; KARL MILLIS; Deacons JOHN ALOISIO; JOSEPH KRISTUFEK.

Ecumenism Commission—Revs. PETER JOHNSON; GERALD F. CHLEBORAD; Ms. PAT MCCARTHY.

Endowment Funds and Trusts—

Catholic Schools Endowment Fund, Seminarian Education Endowment—JAMES S. VANCE, *P.O. Box 1468, Cheyenne, 82003-1468.* Tel: 307-638-1530.

Knights of Columbus Charitable Trust for Seminarian Education and Priests' Retirement—FINN MCCARTHY, *623 S. Wolcott, Casper, 82601.* Tel: 307-237-2723.

St. Mary's School Foundation—Rev. GARY RUZICKA, *P.O. Box 1268, Cheyenne, 82003-1268.* Tel: 307-635-9261.

Catholic Family and Respect Life Divisions—PAT MCCARTHY, Dir.

Beginning Experience for Divorced or Widowed—VIKKI EPPERSON; JESS THIEL; LAVERNE LESTER, *P.O. Box 9953, Casper, 82609.* Tel: 307-234-2551; 237-6013.

Bereavement Ministry—TERRY CASSIDY. Tel: 307-635-4965.

Divorced/Separated/Widowed Ministry—LINDA HURLESS. Tel: 307-265-3509.

Engaged Encounter—JAN MARTIN; STEVE MARTIN, *1340 Nottingham Dr., Casper, 82609.* Tel: 307-577-3009.

Marriage Encounter—RANDY COX; KATHI COX, *P.O. Box 1082, Douglas, 82633.* Tel: 307-358-6548.

Marriage Preparation—PAT MCCARTHY.

Natural Family Planning—PAT MCCARTHY.

Rainbows for All God's Children—AMY ROJO; LINDA HURLESS, *121 S. Connor, Sheridan, 82801.* Tel: 307-674-7301.

Respect Life Catholic Pro-Life Ministry—PAT MCCARTHY.

Retrouvaille, Ministry for Hurting Marriages—PAT MCCARTHY.

Holy Child Pontifical Association—Deacon ED MCCARTHY, Dir., *623 S. Wolcott, Casper, 82601.* Tel: 307-237-2723.

Housing—Very Rev. Msgr. GERALD SULLIVAN, *P.O. Box 5720, Cheyenne, 82003-5720.* Tel: 307-632-5872. JUDY GRIFFIN, Admin., *St. Anthony Manor, 211 E. Sixth, Casper, 82601.* Tel: 307-237-0843. Sr. RUTH ANN HEHN, S.C.L., Admin., *Holy Trinity Manor, 2516 E. 18th St., Cheyenne, 82001.* Tel: 307-778-8850.

Information Office—ROSS DOMAN, *P.O. Box 1468, Cheyenne, 82003-1468.* Tel: 307-638-1530; Fax: 307-637-7936.

Liturgical Commission—Most Rev. JOSEPH HART, D.D.; Most Rev. DAVID L. RICKEN, D.D., J.C.L.; Revs. GARY RUZICKA, Exec. Sec. GERALD F. CHLEBORAD; THOMAS CRONKLETON, JR.; MICHAEL HELLMAN; Ms. BETTY MCCARTHY; BRENDA WILKING.

Pastoral Council—Most Rev. JOSEPH HART, D.D., Chm.; Most Rev. DAVID L. RICKEN, D.D., J.C.L.; CYNTHIA JOHNSON, Vice-Chm.; Very Rev. Msgr. EUGENE SULLIVAN, V.G., Ex Officio; FINN MCCARTHY, Ex Officio; PAULA EPPERSON, Exec. Sec., *623 S. Wolcott, Casper, 82601.* Tel: 307-237-2723. Casper Deanery: Rev. ANDREW DUNCAN; CATHY STRONG; WYOMA GROENENBERG; EVIE HANKINS. Cheyenne Deanery: Rev. JAMES SCHUMACHER; SANDY GADDIS; LARRY STOLZ; ROB SPAULDING. Rock Springs Deanery: Rev. JOHN SAVIO; KATHY BETTAS; PAUL FOVEL; DON CYWINSKI. Sheridan Deanery: Rev. BRUCE CLAPHAM; CARL HINZ; JOE GREGSON; JOHN BLACK. Thermopolis Deanery: Deacon JOHN ALOISIO; CLEO MEDINA; KELLY SPIERING; APRIL PENDLETON. Religious: Sr. M. LUCIA DALUZ, O.S.F.; Sr. FRANCES SCHAF, O.S.U.; Sr. THERESE STEINER, S.C.L.; MADELINE SPOONHUNTER, Native American Rep.

Priests' Personnel Board—Most Rev. JOSEPH HART, D.D., Chm.; Most Rev. DAVID L. RICKEN, D.D., J.C.L.; Revs. GERALD F. CHLEBORAD; CARL GALLINGER; JOHN SAVIO; Very Rev. Msgr. GERALD SULLIVAN.

Propagation of the Faith—Deacon JOHN ALOISIO, *220 N. 7th E., Riverton, 82501.* Tel: 307-856-5922.

Rural Life Conference—Rev. PETER JOHNSON, *P.O. Box 231, Greybull, 82426.*

St. Joseph's Society for Priests (Clergy Mutual Benefit Society)—Most Rev. JOSEPH HART, D.D.; Most Rev. DAVID L. RICKEN, D.D., J.C.L.; Revs. THOMAS OGG, Pres. DANIEL COLIBRARO; RONALD STOLCIS; CHARLES F. TAYLOR, J.C.D.; THOMAS E. CRONKLETON, JR., J.C.L.; KEVIN KOCH; Very Rev. Msgr. GERALD A. SULLIVAN; Mr. LEO RILEY, Admin.

Spanish-Speaking Apostolate Board—Most Rev. JOSEPH HART, D.D.; Most Rev. DAVID L. RICKEN, D.D., J.C.L.

CLERGY, PARISHES, MISSIONS AND PAROCHIAL SCHOOLS

CITY OF CHEYENNE
(Laramie County)

1—ST. MARY'S CATHEDRAL (1868), Revs. Gary J. Ruzicka; James Schumacher; Deacon Lee Pico. In res., Rev. Joseph E. Moroney.
Mailing Address: P.O. Box 1268, 82003-1268. Tel: 307-635-9261; Fax: 307-637-5723. [CEM]
School—Tel: 307-638-9268; Fax: 307-635-2847. Kristina Giger, Prin.
Lay Teachers 28; Students 299.
Catechesis/Religious Programs—Tel: 307-637-4009; 635-9261. D.R.E.: Roserita Du Fresne, (Grades PreK-6); Janelle Wingert, (Grades 7-8); Rob Zlomke, (Grades 9-12).
Students 495.
Convent—716 E. 21st St., 82001. Tel: 307-638-6005.

2—HOLY TRINITY (1957), Rev. Gerald A. Sullivan; Deacon David Zelenka. In res., Rev. Msgr. William Delaney, (Retired); Rev. Msgr. Lawrence Etchingham, (Retired); Rev. James Doudican, (Retired).
Res., 1836 Hot Springs Ave., P.O. Box 5720, 82003-5720. Tel: 307-632-5872; 637-7150; Fax: 307-632-1810.
Catechesis/Religious Programs—Tel: 307-632-4482. D.R.E.: Martha Thein; Terri Mercer.
Sisters of Charity of Leavenworth 1; Students 262.

3—ST. JOSEPH'S (1929) (Hispanic), Rev. Vernon F. Clark.
Mailing Address: P.O. Box 1141, 82003-1141. Tel: 307-634-4625; Fax: 307-635-4700.
Office: 314 E. Sixth St., 82007.
Res., 515 House, 82007. Tel: 307-634-4625; Fax: 307-635-4700. [CEM]
Church—300 E. 6th St., 82007.
Catechesis/Religious Programs—Tel: 307-778-7107. Eva Estorga, D.R.E.
Students 178.

OUTSIDE CITY OF CHEYENNE

Buffalo, Johnson Co., St. John the Baptist (1885) (Basque), Rev. Charles F. Taylor.
Res., 532 N. Lobban, 82834. Tel: 307-684-7268; Fax: 307-684-5490. [JC]
Catechesis/Religious Programs—Tel: 307-684-7217. Mary Ann Cummins, D.R.E.
Students 150.
Missions—Clearmont, Johnson Co., St. Mary, 82834.; Kaycee, Johnson Co., St. Hubert, 82834.

Casper, Natrona Co., St. Anthony of Padua (1903), Revs. Michael Carr; Robert Cook; Deacon Don Stewart.
Office: 604 S. Center, 82601. Tel: 307-266-2666; Fax: 307-266-4127.
School—218 E. Seventh, 82601. Tel: 307-234-2873; Fax: 307-235-4946. Mary Kozola, Prin.
Lay Teachers 17; Students 219.
Catechesis/Religious Programs—Students 167.
Mission—Midwest, Natrona Co., St. Francis Mission, 17 Navy Row, Midwest, 82643. Tel: 307-266-2666.

Our Lady of Fatima (1954), Revs. Philip Colibraro; Daniel Colibraro, (Retired); Deacon Ed McCarthy.
Res., 1401 CY Ave., 82604. Tel: 307-265-5586; Fax: 307-266-2958.
Catechesis/Religious Programs—Tel: 307-473-2076; Fax: 307-266-2958. Teresa Sears, D.R.E.
Students 107.

Saint Patrick's (1963), Rev. Sam W. Hayes; Rev. Msgr. James O'Neill, (Retired); Deacon Russ Humphreys.
Res., 425 S. Illinois, Box 50397, 82605-0397. Tel: 307-235-5535; 266-2495; Fax: 307-237-7244.
Catechesis/Religious Programs—D.R.E.: Marilyn Crull; Sam Carrick.
Students 205.

Cody, Park Co., St. Anthony (1942), Rev. Joseph A. Daley.
Res., 1333 Monument Dr., 82414-3406. Tel: 307-587-3388; Fax: 307-587-3383.
Catechesis/Religious Programs—Tel: 307-587-2567; Fax: 307-587-3383. Judy Philpot, D.R.E.
Students 167.
Missions—Yellowstone National Park, Park Co. Sunday Masses at Old Faithful, Lake Lodge, Canyon Junction, and Grant Village in summer only. 1333 Monument, 82414. Tel: 307-587-3388; Meeteetse, Park Co., St. Therese.

Douglas, Converse Co., St. James (1907), Rev. Andrew Duncan.
Res., 243 S. Fifth St., P.O. Box 1500, 82633-1500. Tel: 307-358-2338; Fax: 307-358-5540. [JC]
Catechesis/Religious Programs—Ruthie Halvorsen, D.R.E.
Students 155.
Mission—Glendo, Platte Co., Our Lady of Lourdes, 423 A St., Glendo, 82213. Tel: 307-358-2338.

Evanston, Uinta Co., St. Mary Magdalen (1878), Rev. Rory D. Schiffbauer.
Mailing Address: Box 163, 82931-0163. Tel: 307-789-2189; Fax: 307-789-2788.
Catechesis/Religious Programs—Tel: 307-789-3757.
Students 135.
Mission—Fort Bridger, Uinta Co., St. Helen, P.O. Box 183, Fort Bridger, 82933. Tel: 307-782-6190.
Catechesis/Religious Programs—Tel: 307-787-6590.
Students 50.

Gillette, Campbell Co., St. Matthew's (1926), Revs. Thomas Kadera; Karl Millis.
Res., 900 Butler Spaeth Rd., 82716. Tel: 307-682-3319; Fax: 307-682-6386. [JC]
Catechesis/Religious Programs—Tel: 307-682-5321.
Students 643.
Missions—Wright, Campbell Co., Blessed Sacrament, 624 Wright Blvd., Wright, 82732. Tel: 307-464-0809; Moorcroft, Crook Co., St. Patrick, 216 N. Belle Fourche, Moorcroft, 82721. Tel: 307-756-9478.

Glenrock, Converse Co., St. Louis (1920), Rev. Ralph H. Talkin, S.J.
Mailing Address: P.O. Box 27, 82637-0027. Tel: 307-436-9529. [JC]
Catechesis/Religious Programs—Tel: 307-436-5769. Andrea Chojnacky, D.R.E.
Students 73.

Green River, Sweetwater Co., Immaculate Conception (1884), Rev. Michael P. Hellman.
Mailing Address: P.O. Box 70, 82935-0070. Tel: 307-875-2441; Fax: 307-875-2184 (Office hours only).
Catechesis/Religious Programs—Tel: 307-875-2184. Peggy Hyslope, D.R.E.
Students 262.

Greybull, Big Horn Co., Sacred Heart (1919), Rev. Peter Johnson.
Mailing Address: P.O. Box 231, 82426-0231. Tel: 307-765-2438.
Catechesis/Religious Programs—Esther Lindsey, D.R.E.
Students 52.
Mission—Basin, Big Horn Co., St. Philip, Ave. D, 82410. Tel: 307-765-2938.

Guernsey, Platte Co., St. Anthony's (1969), Rev. Robert H. Cousineau, S.J.
Res., P.O. Box 430, 82214-0430. Tel: 307-836-2586.
Catechesis/Religious Programs—Tel: 307-836-2051. Kari Gerhold, D.R.E.
Students 33.

Jackson, Teton Co., Our Lady of the Mountains (1955), Rev. Carl A. Beavers; Deacon Robert Miller.
Mailing Address: P.O. Box 992, 83001-0992. Tel: 307-733-2516; Fax: 307-739-1478. [JC]
Catechesis/Religious Programs—Tel: 307-733-6391. D.R.E.: Susie Palmer, (Elementary); Stephen Grieco, (High School).
Students 125.
Mission—Afton, Lincoln Co., Holy Family, P.O. Box 231, Afton, 83110.
Chapel—Moran, Sacred Heart.

Kemmerer, Lincoln Co., St. Patrick's (1901), Rev. John E. Murray.
Mailing Address: Box 311, 83101-0311. Tel: 307-877-4573; Fax: 307-877-3354. [JC]
Catechesis/Religious Programs—Students 114.
Missions—Cokeville, Lincoln Co., St. Dominic, P.O. Box 296, 83114. Tel: 307-279-3426; La Barge, Lincoln Co., La Barge Catholic Community Center, P.O. Box 42, 83123. Tel: 307-386-9257.

Lander, Fremont Co., Holy Rosary (1882), Rev. Ray Rodriguez. In res., Rev. Robert K.C. Siu (HON).
Res., 163 Leedy Rd., P.O. Box 1047, 82520-1047. Tel: 307-332-4952; Fax: 307-332-6141.
Catechesis/Religious Programs—Tel: 307-332-4803. Sr. Delores Herbeck, D.R.E.
Students 148.
Missions—Hudson, Fremont Co., Ascension, P.O. Box 72, Hudson, 82515.; Jeffrey City, Freemont Co., St. Brendan.

Laramie, Albany Co., St. Laurence O'Toole (1872), Rev. Ray Moss.
Mailing Address: 617 S. Fourth St., 82070-1045. Tel: 307-745-3115; Fax: 307-745-3131. [CEM][JC]
School—(Grades K-6). Tel: 307-742-6363; Fax: 307-745-3131. Mr. Thomas Wilhelm, Prin.
Lay Teachers 7; Students 85.
Catechesis/Religious Programs—Trisha Sparks, D.R.E.
Students 120.

St. Paul's Newman Center (1957), Rev. Roger W. Schmit, O.S.B.; Lincoln A. Wood, Pastoral Assoc.; Joseph A. Zenk, Campus Min. In res., Rev. Carl J. Gallinger.
Mailing Address: Parish, 1800 E. Grand Ave., 82070-4316. Tel: 307-745-5461; Fax: 307-742-0521.
Catechesis/Religious Programs—Students 82.

Lovell, Big Horn Co., St. Joseph's (1979), Rev. Peter Johnson.
Res., P.O. Box 185, 82431-0185. Tel: 307-548-2282.
Church—1141 Shoshone Ave., 82431. Tel: 307-765-2438.
Catechesis/Religious Programs—Josephino Rodriguez, D.R.E.
Students 50.

Lusk, Niobrara Co., St. Leo's (1911), Rev. Evan P. Shea.
Res., 900 W. Fifth St., Box 959, 82225-0959. Tel: 307-334-2702; Fax: 307-334-3161. [JC]
Catechesis/Religious Programs—Tel: 307-334-3096. Connie Sampers, D.R.E.
Students 30.

Newcastle, Weston Co., Corpus Christi (1890), Rev. Bruce R. Clapham; Deacon Kenneth Pitlick, Pastoral Assoc.
Res., 19 W. Winthrop, 82701. Tel: 307-746-4219; Fax: 307-746-9909.
Catechesis/Religious Programs—Students 46.
Mission—Sundance, Crook Co., St. Paul, P.O. Box 28, Sundance, 82729. Tel: 307-283-2382.
Catechesis/Religious Programs—Students 31.
Mission—Upton, Weston Co., St. Anthony, P.O. Box 177, Upton, 82730. Tel: 307-468-2236.
Catechesis/Religious Programs—Students 30.
Mission—Hulett, Crook Co., St. Matthew's, 26 Hunter, Hulett, 82720.
Catechesis/Religious Programs—Students 25.

Pine Bluffs, Laramie Co., St. Paul's (1913), Rev. Thomas E. Cronkleton, Jr.
Res., P.O. Box 97, 82082-0097. Tel: 307-245-3761;245-3519.
Catechesis/Religious Programs—Tel: 307-246-3255. D.R.E.: Carleen Graves; Cindy Rohde.
Students 40.
Missions—Albin, Laramie Co., St. Joseph; Carpenter, Laramie Co., St. Peter.

Pinedale, Sublette Co., Our Lady of Peace (1940), Rev. Robert G. Lynch, S.J.
Mailing Address: P.O. Box 70, 82941-0070. Tel: 307-367-2359; Fax: 307-367-3553.
Catechesis/Religious Programs—Tel: 307-367-2802. Sue Shenefelt, D.R.E.
Students 65.
Missions—Big Piney, Sublette Co., St. Anne, Box 742, Big Piney, 83113. Tel: 307-276-3227; Eden, Sweetwater Co., St. Christopher, Eden, 82926.

Powell, Park Co., St. Barbara (1910), Rev. Thomas Ogg.
Res., 115 E. Third, P.O. Box 818, 82435-0818. Tel: 307-754-2480; Fax: 307-754-5018.
Catechesis/Religious Programs—Tel: 307-754-3361. Pokey Heny, D.R.E.
Students 147.
Mission—Clark, Park Co., Our Lady of the Valley, P.O. Box 818, 82435. Tel: 307-754-2480.

Rawlins, Carbon Co., St. Joseph's (1867), Rev. Malcolm Reid; Deacon Jesus P. Juarez.
Mailing Address: P.O. Box 68, 82301-0068. Tel: 307-324-4631; Fax: 307-324-3288. [JC]
Catechesis/Religious Programs—Tel: 307-324-4033. Catherine Faber, D.R.E.
Students 210.
Mission—Baggs, Carbon Co., Our Lady of the Sage, P.O. Box 26, Baggs, 82321. Tel: 307-383-2695.

Riverton, Fremont Co., St. Margaret's (1908), Revs. William T. Espenshade; Lawrence Fedor, O.S.B.
Res., 622 E. Park, 82501. Tel: 307-856-3757; Fax: 307-856-8533.
School—(Grades PreK-5). Tel: 307-856-5922; Fax: 307-857-5892. Deacon John Aloisio, Prin.
Lay Teachers 10; Students 80.
Catechesis/Religious Programs—Tel: 307-856-3724; Fax: 307-857-5892. Marlene Aloisio, D.R.E.
Students 143.
Missions—Shoshoni, Fremont Co., St. Joseph, 211 Wyoming St., Shoshoni, 82649. Tel: 307-876-2760; Dubois, Fremont Co., Our Lady of the Woods, 4 S. Riverton St., P.O. Box 1134, Dubois, 82513. Tel: 307-455-2533; Kinnear, Fremont Co., St. Edward, Kinnear Rectory, 11350 US Hwy. 26, P.O. Box 34, Kinnear, 82516. Tel: 307-856-5502.

Rock Springs, Sweetwater Co., Holy Spirit Catholic Community (1887), Revs. John Savio; Thomas Sheridan; Deacon Randal Hruska.
Mailing Address: P.O. Box 6038, 82901. Tel: 307-362-2611; Fax: 307-382-4911.
Office: 116 Broadway, 82901.
Res., 633 Bridger Ave., 82901. Tel: 307-362-3493.
School—Holy Spirit Catholic School, Tel: 307-362-6077; Fax: 307-362-2177. Sr. Lucia Daluz, Prin.
Religious 1; Lay Teachers 11; Students 96.
Catechesis/Religious Programs—Fax: 307-382-4911. Dean and Elaine Menardi, D.R.E.
Students 225.
Missions—Superior, Sweetwater Co., St. Vivian; Wamsutter, Sweetwater Co., Catholic Community.

SS. Cyril and Methodius (1910). Consolidated with Our Lady of Sorrows Church, Rock Springs to form Holy Spirit Catholic Community.

Our Lady of Sorrows. Consolidated with SS. Cyril and Methodius to form Holy Spirit Catholic Community.

Saratoga, Carbon Co., St. Ann's (1957), Rev. Gerald Chleborad.
Mailing Address: P.O. Box 667, 82331-0667. Tel: 307-326-5461; Fax: 307-326-5461.
Catechesis/Religious Programs—Tel: 307-326-8190. D.R.E.: Marilyn Verplancke; Janet Young.
Students 49.
Missions—Hanna, Carbon Co., St. Joseph, P.O. Box 782, Hanna, 82327. Tel: 307-325-9712; Medicine Bow, Carbon Co., St. Malachy, P.O. Box 223, Medicine Bow, 82329.

St. Stephens, Fremont Co., St. Stephen's (1884) (Native American). Indian Mission for the Shoshone and Arapahoe Indians. St. Stephen's Indian Mission, Inc. Revs. David G. Matzko, S.J.; J. Robert Hilbert, S.J.; Daniel J. Gannon, S.J.
Mailing Address: Box 250, 82524-0250. Tel: 307-856-5937; Fax: 307-857-1802. [CEM]
Catechesis/Religious Programs—Tel: 307-856-7806.
Students 86.
Missions—Ethete, Fremont Co., St. Joseph, Box 8358, Ethete, 82520. Tel: 307-332-4415; Fort Washakie, Fremont Co., Blessed Sacrament, Box 307, Fort Washakie, 82514-0307. Tel: 307-332-2252.

Sheridan, Sheridan Co., Holy Name (1885) (European), Very Rev. Eugene P. Sullivan; Revs. Cliff Jacobson; Ronald Stolcis; Deacon Joe Kristufek.
Mailing Address: Box 2024, 82801-2024. Tel: 307-674-7441; Fax: 307-674-9187. [JC]
School—121 S. Connor, 82801. Tel: 307-672-2021; Fax: 307-672-2021. Dr. M. V. Morton, Prin.
Sisters of Charity (Leavenworth) 1; Lay Teachers 14; Students 132.
Catechesis/Religious Programs—Tel: 307-672-7455. Cel Hope, D.R.E.
Students 227.
Missions—Story, Sheridan Co., Our Lady of the Pines, P.O. Box 2024, 82801. Tel: 307-674-7441; Ranchester, Sheridan Co., St. Edmund, P.O. Box 197, Ranchester, 82839. Tel: 307-655-2357.

Thermopolis, Hot Springs Co., St. Francis (1906), Revs. Michael O. Ehiemere; William A. Caspers, (Retired).
Mailing Address: P.O. Box 272, 82443-0272. Tel: 307-864-2674.

Catechesis/Religious Programs—Tel: 307-864-9408. Andrew Stropko, D.R.E. Students 40.

Torrington, Goshen Co., St. Rose (1906), Rev. Kevin A. Koch; Deacon Rolland Raboin.
Res., 605 E. 22nd Ave., 82240. Tel: 307-532-5556; Fax: 307-534-2329.
Catechesis/Religious Programs—Tel: 307-532-3125. D.R.E.: Darci Haraldson; Lynette Saucedo. Students 225.

Wheatland, Platte Co., St. Patrick's (1891), Rev. Jan Joseph Santich, Admin.
Res., 1009 Ninth St., 82201. Tel: 307-322-2070; Fax: 307-322-2386.
Catechesis/Religious Programs—Tel: 307-322-4213.
Students 150.
Mission—Chugwater, Platte Co., Mary Queen of Heaven, 401 5th St., Chugwater 82201. Tel: 307-322-2070.

Worland, Washakie Co., St. Mary Magdalen (1949), Rev. August Koeune.
Mailing Address: Box 901, 82401-0901. Tel: 307-347-2820; Fax: 307-347-2450. [JC]
Shipping Address: 1099 Charles Ave., 82401.
Catechesis/Religious Programs—Tel: 307-347-6441.
Students 135.
Mission—Ten Sleep, Washakie Co., St. Brigid's.

Chaplains of Public Institutions

CHEYENNE. *U.S. Veterans Administration Hospital 1* 90 MW/HC, F.E. Warren AFB, 82005. Rev. John Cusack Tel: 307-773-3434.

EVANSTON. *Wyoming State Hospital*. Vacant.

RAWLINS. *Wyoming State Penitentiary*. Mailing Address: P.O. Box 468, 82301-0068. Tel: 307-324-4631. Rev. Malcolm Reid.

SHERIDAN. *U.S. Veterans Administration Hospital*. Mailing Address: Box 4013, 82801-4013. Tel: 307-672-3473, Ext. 263. Rev. John Norton, O.P.

In Residence:
Reverend Fathers—
Siu, Robert K.C., Holy Rosary Church, P.O. Box 1047, Lander, WY 82520-1047

On Duty Outside the Diocese:
Reverend Fathers—
Wendel, Alfred W., Immaculate Heart of Mary, 2855 Briarcliff Rd., N.E., Atlanta, GA 30329

On Leave of Absence:
Reverend Fathers—
Velasquez, Charles

Retired:
Reverend Monsignors—
Carroll, Daniel, 639 Ave. H, #157, Powell, WY 82435. Tel: 307-754-9746
Delaney, William, P.O. Box 5720, Cheyenne, WY 82003-5720
Etchingham, Lawrence, P.O. Box 5720, Cheyenne, WY 82003
Godley, James, Ballyheige, Kerry Ireland
O'Neill, James, P.O. Box 50397, Casper, WY 82605-0397. Tel: 307-235-5535

Reverend Fathers—
Caspers, William A., #1 Easy St., 3990 S. 136 W., Mountain Home, ID 83647
Colibraro, Daniel, 1401 CY Ave., Casper, WY 82604-3511
Doudican, James, P.O. Box 5720, Cheyenne, WY 82003
Fahey, Thomas C., O.F.M., Chap., Victory Noll Sisters, 1900 W. Park Dr., Box 109, Huntington, IN 46750
Fraher, Joseph P., 412 Kearney St., Laramie, WY 82070
Gianola, William, 23 Lemans Dr., Naples, FL 34112
Moroney, Joseph E., P.O. Box 1268, Cheyenne, WY 82003
Prado, Cletus, 802 N. 29th St., Phoenix, AZ 85008
Wright, John A., 35 Rd. 1 AFW, Powell, WY 82435

Permanent Deacons:
Aloisio, John, St. Margaret's Catholic School, Riverton
Bradley, Patrick, UMC Chap.; St. Joseph, Cheyenne
Hruska, Randy, Holy Spirit, Rock Springs
Humphreys, Russ, St. Patrick's Church, Casper
Juarez, Jesus, St. Joseph, Rawlins
Kristufek, Joseph, Holy Name Church, Sheridan
Lux, Charles, Holy Spirit, Rock Springs
McCarthy, Ed, Our Lady of Fatima, Casper
Miller, Robert, Our Lady of the Mountains, Jackson
Pico, Lee, St. Mary's Cathedral, Cheyenne
Pitlick, Ken, Corpus Christi, New Castle
Stewart, Don, St. Anthony's Church, Casper
Zelenka, David, Holy Trinity, Cheyenne

INSTITUTIONS LOCATED IN THE DIOCESE

[A] PROTECTIVE INSTITUTIONS

TORRINGTON. *St. Joseph's Children's Home*, Box 1117, 82240-1117. Tel: 307-532-4197; Fax: 307-532-8405.
E-mail: stjch@prairieweb.com
For a complete listing, refer to the Special Care Facilities section.

[B] HOUSING FOR THE ELDERLY (LOW INCOME)

CHEYENNE. *Holy Trinity Manor*, 2516 E. 18th St., 82001. Tel: 307-778-8850; Fax: 307-778-8850.
E-mail: htscl@cheyenneweb.com
For a complete listing, refer to the Special Care Facilities section.

CASPER. *St. Anthony Manor*, 211 E. Sixth St., 82601. Tel: 307-237-0843; Fax: 307-237-3516
For a complete listing, refer to the Special Care Facilities section.

[C] MONASTERIES AND RESIDENCES FOR PRIESTS AND BROTHERS

ST. STEPHENS. *St. Stephens Mission - Jesuit Community*, Box 250, 82524. Tel: 307-866-5937; Fax: 307-857-1802.
E-mail: dmatzko@wyoming.com
Revs. J. Robert Hilbert, S.J.; Daniel J. Gannon, S.J.; David G. Matzko, S.J.

[D] CONVENTS AND RESIDENCES FOR SISTERS

DAYTON. *Benedictine Sisters of Perpetual Adoration*, San Benito Monastery, P.O. Box 510, 82836-0520. Tel: 307-655-9013; Fax: 307-655-9052.
E-mail: sanbenit@cyberhighway.net
Web site: www.icon-stl.net/~congbspa/index/html
Sr. M. Hope Rodenborn, Supr. Sisters 4.

[E] CAMPUS MINISTRY

CASPER. *Casper Community College*, St. Francis Newman Center, 1732 S. Elm St., 82601. Tel: 307-577-1421.
E-mail: bzettl@coffey.com
Brad Zettl, Dir. Total Staff 1.
Attended by St. Anthony of Padua, Casper.

LARAMIE. *University of Wyoming*, St. Paul's Newman Center, University Catholic Parish, 1800 E. Grand Ave., 82070-4316. Tel: 307-745-5461; Fax: 307-742-0521.
E-mail: newman@newmancenter.org
Web site: www.newmancenter.org
Rev. Roger W. Schmit, O.S.B. Total Staff 9.

POWELL. *NorthWest College*, John Henry Newman Center, 674 N. Absaroka, 82435. Tel: 307-754-9220. Rev. Thomas Ogg, Chap. & Dir.
Attended by St. Barbara, Powell.

[F] MISCELLANEOUS LISTINGS

CHEYENNE. *Mall at St. Vincent DePaul*, 2112 Snyder Ave., 82001. Tel: 307-432-0253. Mary Genereux, Mgr. Total Staff 5; Total Assisted 885.
St. Mary's Goods Bookstore, 2417 Central Ave., 82001. Tel: 307-635-4228. Zula Samuelson, Mgr. Total Staff 2; Total Assisted 150.
The Wyoming Catholic Ministries Foundation, P.O. Box 1468, 82003. Tel: 307-638-1530; Fax: 307-637-7936.

CASPER.
Holy Cross Food Center, Inc., 1030 N. Lincoln, 82601. Tel: 307-577-1041. Operated by Holy Cross Center, Inc. Bro. Francis Kjeldgaard, C.S.C., Dir. Total Staff 33; Total Assisted 12,086.
Mother Seton Housing, Inc., 906 N. Beach St., 82601. Tel: 307-577-8026; Fax: 307-577-8026.
E-mail: setonhouse@caspers.net
Emergency/Transitional Housing for Homeless Women and Children/Homeless Men and Children. Pam Kozola, Exec. Dir., Shelter, 324 E. H St., 82601. Tel: 307-234-1119. Total Assisted 60-65 families per year; Individuals 417.

ROCK SPRINGS. *Rock Springs Catholic School Foundation*, P.O. Box 6038, 82901-0038. Tel: 307-362-2611; Fax: 307-382-4911.
E-mail: holyspirit@wyoming.com
Rev. John Savio.

ST. STEPHENS. *St. Stephens Indian Mission Foundation* (1974), P.O. Box 278, 82524-0278. Tel: 307-856-6797; Fax: 307-857-1802.
E-mail: dmatzko@wyoming.com
Rev. David G. Matzko, S.J., Dir.

RELIGIOUS INSTITUTES OF MEN REPRESENTED IN THE DIOCESE

For further details refer to the corresponding bracketed number in the Religious Institutes of Men or Women section.

[0200]—*Benedictine Monks.*—O.S.B.

[0600]—*Brothers of the Congregation of Holy Cross.* (South-West Prov.).—C.S.C.

[0690]—*Jesuit Fathers and Brothers Jesus.*—S.J.

[0430]—*Order of Preachers (Dominicans).*—O.P.

RELIGIOUS INSTITUTES OF WOMEN REPRESENTED IN THE DIOCESE

[0230]—*Benedictine Sisters of Pontifical Jurisdiction.*—O.S.B.

[1070-03]—*Dominican Sisters.* (Sinsinawa).—O.P.

[]—*Dominican Sisters of Hope.*—O.P.

[1430]—*Franciscan Sisters of Our Lady of Perpetual Help.*—O.S.F.

[3130]—*Our Lady of Victory Missionary Sisters.*—O.L.V.M.

[1680]—*School Sisters of St. Francis.* (Milwaukee, WI).—O.S.F.

[0480]—*Sisters of Charity of Leavenworth, Kansas.*—S.C.L.

[1650]—*Sisters of St. Francis of Philadelphia.*—O.S.F.

[3830]—*Sisters of St. Joseph.*—C.S.J.

[4120-03]—*Ursuline Nuns, of the Congregation of Paris.*—O.S.U.

DIOCESAN CEMETERIES

CHEYENNE. *Olivet Cemetery.*

NECROLOGY

(No Deaths)

Perfect for Any Parish or Fu

Special Events

A-64
Crystal Angel

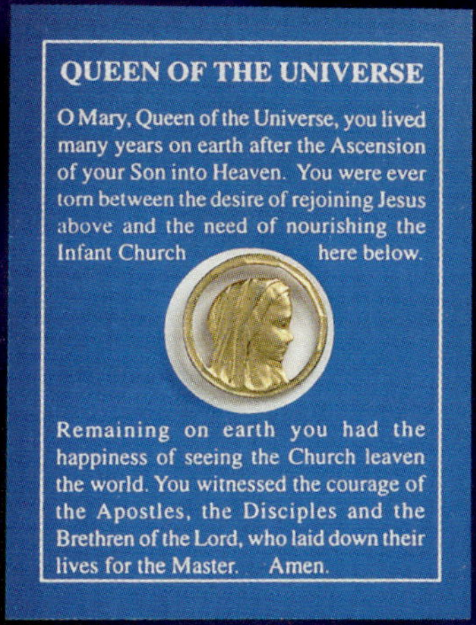

D-110
Halo Madonna

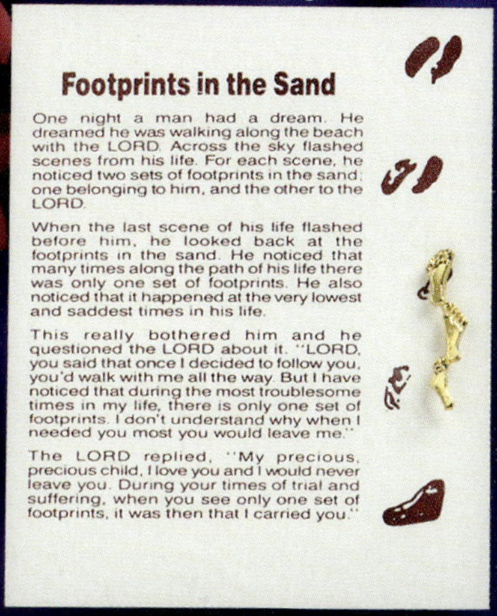

A-25
Footprints

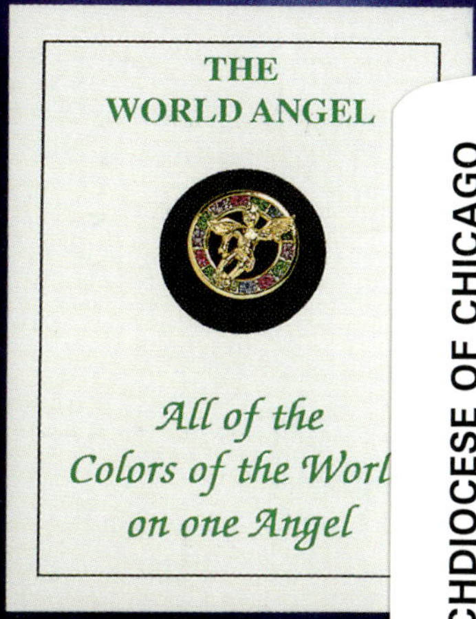

D-115
World Angel

ARCHDIOCESE OF CHICAGO

CHRISTMAS

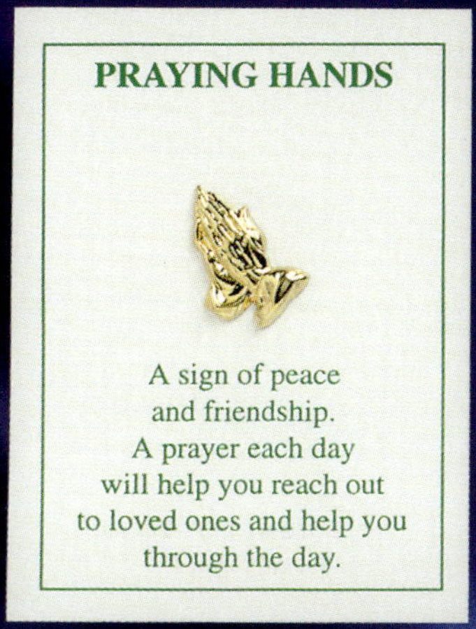

A-42
Praying Hands

A-54
Christmas Angel

— PIN SALE PRICES —

	100	500	1000
Crystal Angel (A-64)	1.75	1.65	1.59
Halo Madonna (D-110)	.89	.79	.69
Starburst Cross (D-111)	1.00	.95	.89
Footprints (A-25)	.75	.69	.64

World Angel (
Crystal Heart
Praying Hand
Christmas An
Gold Crucifix

TO PLACE ORDER — 800-243-5305 • I

BEAUT

Lent & Easter

Cro

Mother's Day

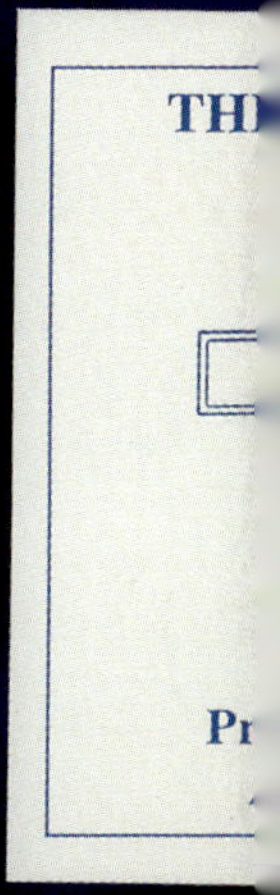

Go

Pins 80% Actual Size

Angel

Cross & Robe (D-
Cross & Crown (D
Claddagh (D-103)
Gold Cross (D-10

Jame

IFUL ALL OCCASION PINS W/GIFT CARD

— Select a Pin for Special Event —

50% OFF SALE

D-101
ss & Robe

D-102
Cross & Crown

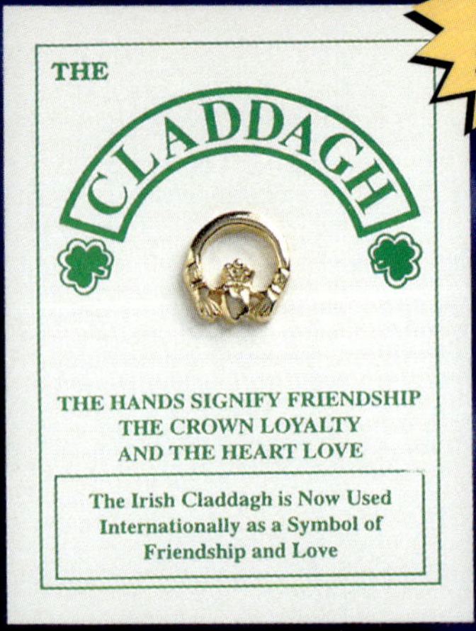

D-103
Claddagh

St. Patrick's Day

D-104
ld Cross

D-105
Angel w/Rose Crystal

D-106
Cross-Flag

Father's Day

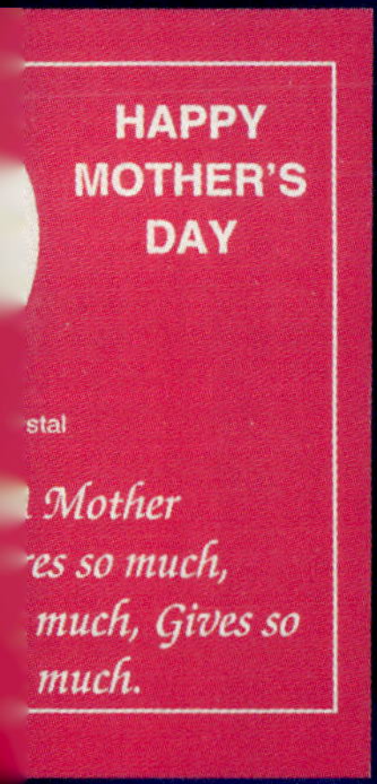

D-107
w/Pink Rose

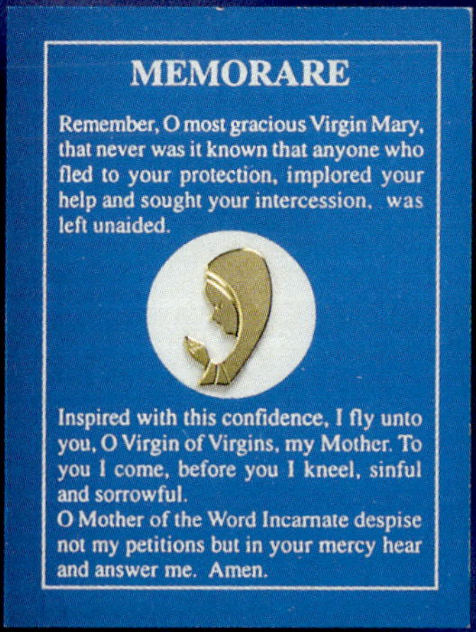

D-108
Praying Madonna

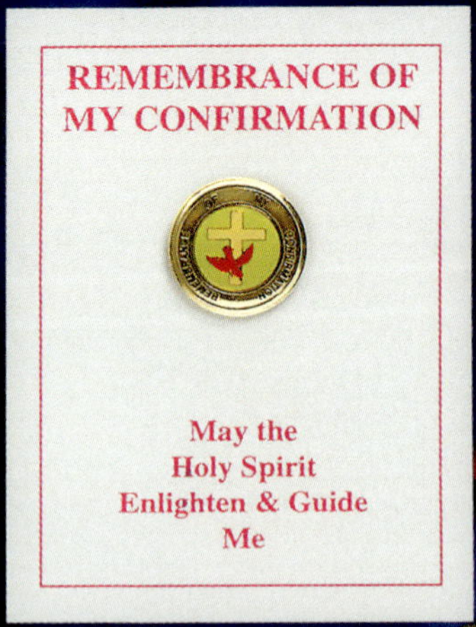

D-109
Confirmation

CONFIRMATION

— PIN SALE PRICES —

	100	500	1000
01)	.69	.63	.59
-102)	.69	.63	.59
	.69	.63	.59
)	.69	.63	.59

	100	500	1000
Angel w/Rose Crystal (D-105)	1.39	1.29	1.09
Cross-Flag (D-106)	1.00	.95	.85
Angel w/Pink Rose (D-107)	.95	.85	.75
Praying Madonna (D-108)	.69	.63	.59
Confirmation (D-109)	.69	.63	.59

s Doherty Inc. • 1-800-243-5305 • Fax: 570-346-2851

Archdiocese of Chicago

(Archidioecesis Chicagiensis)

Most Reverend

TIMOTHY J. LYNE

Retired Auxiliary Bishop of Chicago; ordained May 1, 1943; appointed Auxiliary Bishop of Chicago and Titular Bishop of Vamalla October 31, 1983; consecrated December 13, 1983; retired January 24, 1995. *Res., 730 N. Wabash, Chicago, IL, 60611.*

Most Reverend

THAD J. JAKUBOWSKI

Auxiliary Bishop of Chicago; ordained May 3, 1950; appointed Auxiliary Bishop of Chicago and Titular Bishop of Plestia February 16, 1988; consecrated April 11, 1988. *Res., 6002 W. Berteau Ave., Chicago, IL, 60634-1630.* Tel.: 773-202-7720; Fax: 773-202-7725.

Most Reverend

JOHN R. GORMAN

Auxiliary Bishop of Chicago and Titular Bishop of Catula; ordained May 1, 1952; appointed February 16, 1988; consecrated April 11, 1988. *Res., 2330 W. 118th St., Chicago, IL, 60643.* Tel.: 773-779-8440; Fax: 773-779-8469.

Most Reverend

RAYMOND E. GOEDERT

Auxiliary Bishop of Chicago; ordained May 1, 1952; appointed Auxiliary Bishop of Chicago and Titular Bishop of Tamazeni July 8, 1991; consecrated August 29, 1991. *Res., 1555 N. State Pkwy., Chicago, IL, 60610.*

Most Reverend

EDWIN M. CONWAY

Auxiliary Bishop of Chicago; ordained May 3, 1960; appointed Auxiliary Bishop of Chicago and Titular Bishop of Auguro January 24, 1995; consecrated March 20, 1995. *Mailing Address: 1651 W. Diversey Pkwy., Chicago, IL, 60614.* Tel.: 773-388-8670; Fax: 773-388-8676.

His Eminence

FRANCIS CARDINAL GEORGE, O.M.I., PH.D., S.T.D.

Archbishop of Chicago; Profession of Perpetual Vows September 8, 1961; ordained December 21, 1963; appointed Bishop of Yakima July 10, 1990; Episcopal Ordination and Installation September 21, 1990; appointed Archbishop of Portland in Oregon April 30, 1996; installed May 27, 1996; appointed Archbishop of Chicago April 8, 1997; installed May 7, 1997; created Cardinal Priest February 21, 1998. *Res., 1555 N. State Pkwy., Chicago, IL, 60610.*

The Pastoral Center: P.O. Box 1979, Chicago, IL, 60690. Tel.: 312-751-7999 ext. 8200.

Web site address: www.archdiocese-chgo.org

Most Reverend

GERALD F. KICANAS

Auxiliary Bishop of Chicago; ordained April 27, 1967; appointed Auxiliary Bishop of Chicago and Titular Bishop of Bela January 24, 1995; consecrated March 20, 1995. *Mailing Address: 200 N. Milwaukee Ave., Libertyville, IL, 60048.* Tel.: 847-549-0160; Fax: 847-549-0163.

Most Reverend

JOHN R. MANZ

Auxiliary Bishop of Chicago; ordained May 12, 1971; appointed Auxiliary Bishop of Chicago and Titular Bishop of Mulia January 23, 1996; consecrated March 5, 1996. *Mailing Address: 1820 S. Leavitt St., Chicago, IL, 60608.* Tel.: 312-243-4655; Fax: 312-243-4970.

Most Reverend

JOSEPH N. PERRY

Auxiliary Bishop of Chicago; ordained May 24, 1975; appointed Auxiliary Bishop of Chicago and Titular Bishop of Lead May 5, 1998; consecrated June 29, 1998. *Mailing Address: P.O. Box 733, South Holland, Chicago, IL, 60473-0733.* Tel.: 708-339-2474; Fax: 708-339-2477.

Most Reverend

JEROME E. LISTECKI

Auxiliary Bishop of Chicago; ordained May 14, 1975; appointed Auxiliary Bishop of Chicago and Titular Bishop of Nara November 7, 2000; consecrated January 8, 2001. *Res., 6559 N. Glenwood, Chicago, IL, 60626.* Tel.: 773-764-5936; Fax: 773-764-4360.

ESTABLISHED NOVEMBER 28, 1843; CREATED 1880.

Square Miles 1,411.

Comprises the Counties of Cook and Lake in the State of Illinois.

Legal Title: The Catholic Bishop of Chicago, a Corporation Sole.

For legal titles of institutions, consult The Pastoral Center.

STATISTICAL OVERVIEW

Personnel	
Cardinal	1
Auxiliary Bishops	8
Retired Bishops	2
Retired Abbots	1
Priests: Diocesan Active in Diocese	579
Priests: Active Outside Diocese	24
Priests: Diocesan in Foreign Missions	3
Priests: Retired, Sick or Absent	291
Number of Diocesan Priests	897
Religious Priests in Diocese	817
Extern Priests in Diocese	80
Ordinations:	
Diocesan Priests	9
Religious Priests	15
Transitional Deacons	10
Permanent Deacons	19
Permanent Deacons in Diocese	618
Total Brothers	361
Total Sisters	3,340
Parishes	
Parishes	378
With Resident Pastor:	
Resident Diocesan Priests	302
Resident Religious Priests	50
Without Resident Pastor:	
Administered by Priests	23
Administered by Women Religious	3

Missions	12
Pastoral Centers	7
Professional Ministry Personnel:	
Brothers	15
Sisters	169
Lay Ministers	595
Welfare	
Catholic Hospitals	22
Total Assisted	2,965,798
Health Care Centers	1
Total Assisted	5,000
Homes for the Aged	43
Total Assisted	5,383
Residential Care of Children	3
Total Assisted	3,682
Day Care and Extended Day Care Centers	34
Total Assisted	3,726
Specialized Homes	4
Total Assisted	431
Special Centers for Social Services	99
Total Assisted	369,116
Residential Care of Disabled	6
Total Assisted	1,264
Other Institutions	9
Total Assisted	176,042
Educational	
Seminaries, Diocesan	3
Students from This Diocese	304

Students from Other Diocese	153
Diocesan Students in Other Seminaries	6
Seminaries, Religious	1
Students Religious	155
Total Seminarians	465
Colleges and Universities	6
Total Students	43,032
High Schools, Diocesan and Parish	7
Total Students	2,194
High Schools, Private	37
Total Students	29,055
Elementary Schools, Diocesan and Parish	264
Total Students	95,604
Elementary Schools, Private	2
Total Students	529
Non-residential Schools for the Disabled	6
Total Students	516
Catechesis/Religious Education:	
High School Students	10,655
Elementary Students	105,300
Total Students Under Catholic Instruction	287,350
Teachers in the Diocese:	
Priests	58
Brothers	43
Sisters	281
Lay Teachers	5,782

Vital Statistics

Receptions into the Church:	
Infant Baptism Totals	41,083
Adult Baptism Totals	2,008
Received into Full Communion	1,756
First Communions	30,237
Confirmations	21,516
Marriages:	
Catholic	8,591
Interfaith	1,776
Total Marriages	10,367
Deaths	18,252
Total Catholic Population	2,394,000
Total Population	5,803,000

Former Bishops—Rt. Rev. WILLIAM QUARTER, D.D., cons. March 10, 1844; died April 10, 1848.—Rt. Rev. JAMES O. VAN DE VELDE, D.D., cons. Feb. 11, 1849; transferred to Natchez, July 29, 1853; died Nov. 13, 1855.—Rt. Rev. ANTHONY O'REGAN, D.D., cons. July 25, 1854; resigned 1858; died Nov., 1866.—Rt. Rev. JAMES DUGGAN, D.D., cons. Bishop of Antigone, and Coadjutor to the Archbishop of St. Louis, May 1, 1857; transferred to Chicago, Jan. 21, 1859; hospitalized, 1869; died March 27, 1899.—Rt. Rev. THOMAS FOLEY, D.D., Coadjutor-Bishop and Administrator of the diocese; cons. Bishop of Pergamus, Feb. 27, 1870; died Feb. 19, 1879.—Most Rev. PATRICK A. FEEHAN, D.D., First Archbishop of Chicago; cons. Bishop of Nashville, Nov. 1, 1865; promoted to Chicago, Sept. 10, 1880; died July 12, 1902.—Most Rev. JAMES EDWARD QUIGLEY, D.D., Archbishop of Chicago; ord. April 12, 1879; cons. Bishop of Buffalo, Feb. 24, 1897; promoted to Archbishop of Chicago, Jan. 8, 1903; died July 10, 1915.—His Eminence GEORGE CARDINAL MUNDELEIN, Archbishop of Chicago; ord. June 8, 1895; cons. Titular Bishop of Loryma and Auxiliary Bishop of Brooklyn, Sept. 21, 1909; promoted to the See of Chicago, Dec. 9, 1915; created Cardinal Priest, March 24, 1924; died Oct. 2, 1939.—His Eminence SAMUEL CARDINAL STRITCH, Archbishop of Chicago; ord. May 21, 1910; appt. Bishop of Toledo, Aug. 10, 1921; promoted to Archbishop of Milwaukee, Aug. 26, 1930; transferred to Archbishop of Chicago, Dec. 27, 1939; created Cardinal Priest Feb. 18, 1946; elevated to the Roman Curia, Sacred Congregation for the Propagation of the Faith, March 1, 1958; died in Rome, May 27, 1958.—His Eminence ALBERT CARDINAL MEYER, Archbishop of Chicago; ord. July 11, 1926; appt. Bishop of Superior, Feb. 18, 1946; promoted to Archbishop of Milwaukee, July 21, 1953; transferred to Archbishop of Chicago, Sept. 19, 1958; created Cardinal Priest, Dec. 14, 1959; died April 9, 1965.—His Eminence JOHN CARDINAL CODY, Archbishop of Chicago; ord. Dec. 8, 1931; appt. Auxiliary Bishop of St. Louis, May 14, 1947; cons. July 2, 1947; promoted to Coadjutor of St. Joseph, Jan. 27, 1954; transferred to Kansas City-St. Joseph, Aug. 29, 1956; promoted to Coadjutor Archbishop of New Orleans, Aug. 14, 1961; acceded the See of New Orleans, Nov. 8, 1964; transferred to the Archdiocese of Chicago, June 16, 1965; created Cardinal Priest in the Consistory, June 26, 1967; died April 25, 1982.—His Eminence JOSEPH CARDINAL BERNARDIN, Archbishop of Chicago; ord. April 26, 1952; appt. Auxiliary Bishop of Atlanta, March 9, 1966; cons. April 26, 1966; appt. Archbishop of Cincinnati, Nov. 21, 1972; appt. Archbishop of Chicago, July 10, 1982; installed Aug. 25, 1982; created Cardinal Priest, Feb. 2, 1983; died Nov. 14, 1996.

Vicar General—Most Rev. RAYMOND E. GOEDERT.

Episcopal Vicars—Most Rev. GERALD KICANAS, Vicariate I (Deaneries A, B); Most Rev. EDWIN M. CONWAY, Vicariate II (Deaneries A, B, C, D, E, F); Most Rev. JOHN R. MANZ, Vicariate III (Deaneries A, B, D, E); Most Rev. THAD J. JAKUBOWSKI, Vicariate IV (Deaneries A, B, C); Most Rev. JOHN R. GORMAN, Vicariate V (Deaneries A, B, C, D, E); Most Rev. JOSEPH N. PERRY, Vicariate VI (Deaneries A, B, C, D).

Deans—Revs. FARRELL KANE, Deanery I-A; WILLIAM J. ZAVASKI, Deanery I-B; FRANCIS J. KANE, Deanery II-A; LAWRENCE F. MADDOCK, Deanery II-B; ROBERT J. HEIDENREICH, Deanery II-C; JOHN R. HOFFMAN, Deanery II-D; RONALD N. KALAS, Deanery II-E; MICHAEL A. WULSCH, Deanery II-F; THOMAS A. TIVY, Deanery III-A; MICHAEL DANEK, C.R., Deanery III-B; KENNETH M. BRIGHAM, Deanery III-D; JAMES W. MILLER, Deanery III-E; DANIEL G. MAYALL, Deanery IV-A; FRANCIS C. JENKS, Deanery IV-B; MAURICE J. KISSANE, Deanery IV-C; ROBERT J. ROLL, Deanery V-A; STANLEY G. RATAJ, Deanery V-B Midway-East-California Corridor; MARCEL J. PASCIAK, Deanery V-B Midway-West; LAWRENCE R. DOWLING, Deanery V-C; GERALD F. MULCAHY, Deanery V-D; EDWARD F. UPTON, Deanery V-E; DAVID A. JONES, Deanery VI-A; LAWRENCE M. DURIS, Deanery VI-B; THOMAS FRANZMAN, Deanery VI-C; THOMAS E. CIMA, Deanery VI-D.

College of Consultors—Revs. JEREMIAH M. BOLAND; GINO DALPIAZ, C.S.; LAWRENCE R. DOWLING; EDWARD R. FIALKOWSKI; JOHN L. HARVEY; PATRICK R. LAGGES; PETER B. MCQUINN; PATRICK J. POLLARD; GEORGE J. RASSAS; FRANCIS ROG, C.R.; DONALD SENIOR, O.P.; THOMAS J. PAPROCKI, Sec.

Presbyteral Council—Revs. GEORGE J. RASSAS, Chm.; PATRICK R. LAGGES, Vice Chm.; JOSEPH W. ALTMAN, Sec.; MICHAEL S. MICHELINI, Treas.; Mrs. ANN SUPPLITT, Exec. Sec.

Finance Council—Vice Chairmen: Rev. R. PETER BOWMAN; Mr. FRANK W. CONSIDINE; Mr. JAMES M. DENNY; Rev. KEVIN J. SPIESS. Members: Mr. JOHN A. BUCK; Miss EILEEN T. CORCORAN; Mr. JOHN W. CROGHAN; Most Rev. RAYMOND E. GOEDERT; Mr. WILLIAM M. GOODYEAR; Mr. DONALD GOSS; Sr. LOIS GRAVER, R.S.M.; Mr. RICHARD J. GUZIOR; Revs. RICHARD M. HOMA; RICHARD HYNES; DAVID JONES; Hon. GEORGE N. LEIGHTON; Mr. WILLIAM A. MCINTOSH; Mr. ANDREW J. MCKENNA, SR.; Mr. KENNETH MEYER; Mr. R. MICHAEL MURRAY, JR.; Mr. OLIVER NICKLIN; Mr. THOMAS H. QUINN; Mr. PHILIP P. ROONEY; Rev. GEORGE L. SCHOPP; Mr. FIDELIS N. UMEH; Mr. ARTHUR R. VELASQUEZ; Rev. RUFUS WICKLAND, O.M.I.

Pastoral Council—NORMAN BOWERS, Chm.; JAMES MANIKA, Vice Chm.; Mrs. ANN SUPPLITT, Exec. Sec. Tel: 312-751-5357.

Consejo Pastoral Hispano Arquidiocesano—Rev. ESEQUIEL SANCHEZ, Exec. Dir. Tel: 312-751-8308. Most Rev. JOHN R. MANZ, Archbishop's Delegate. Tel: 312-243-4655.

Provincial Offices

The Catholic Conference of Illinois—Mr. DOUGLAS DELANEY, Exec. Dir., *65 E. Wacker Pl., Ste. 1620, Chicago, 60601.* Tel: 312-368-1066; Fax: 312-368-1090.

Provincial Court of Appeals—Revs. ROBERT L. KEALY, S.T.L., J.D., J.C.D., Judicial Vicar; JOHN P. LUCAS, Adjutant Judicial Vicar; JOHN E. MULVIHILL, J.C.L., S.T.D.; Ms. MARI HANS, Chief Notary, *20 N. Wacker Dr., Ste. 3420, Chicago, 60606.* Tel: 312-553-4080; 800-572-7835 (In Illinois); Fax: 312-553-4085.

Archdiocesan Offices

All Archdiocesan Departments can be contacted through *The Pastoral Center, 155 E. Superior St., Chicago, IL 60611.* (Street & Package Delivery Address). Address all mail to: *P.O. Box 1979, Chicago, IL 60690.* Tel: 312-751-7999, Ext. 8200. unless otherwise indicated

Office of the Archbishop—Sr. ANN MCCAHILL, S.P., Admin. Asst. to the Archbishop. Tel: 312-751-7999, Ext. 8217. Rev. JOHN J. MCDONNELL, Personal Asst. for Scheduling, Travel & Correspondence. Tel: 312-751-7999, Ext. 8219. Rev. RAYMOND C. BAUMHART, S.J., Personal Consultant to the Cardinal. Tel: 312-751-7999, Ext. 8346. Special Assistants: Mr. EDWARD BARRETT; Ms. MARIE KNOLL. Tel: 773-751-7999, Ext. 8299.

The Chancery—See Office of the Chancellor.

The Metropolitan Tribunal—See Office for Canonical Services.

Vicar General

Vicar General—Most Rev. RAYMOND E. GOEDERT. Tel: 312-751-7999, Ext. 8271.

Vicar for Priests—Revs. LAWRENCE P. MCBRADY; JAMES T. KACZOROWSKI, *645 N. Michigan Ave., Ste. 543, Chicago, 60611.* Tel: 312-642-1837. Rev. ANDREW J. MCDONAGH, Asst. to Vicar for Priests, *6939 N. Hiawatha, Chicago, 60646.* Tel: 312-642-1837.

Commission on the Mission and Life of the Diocesan Priest—*645 N. Michigan Ave., Ste. 543, Chicago, 60611.* Tel: 312-642-1837.

Priests' Placement Board—Revs. JEREMIAH BOLAND, Exec. Sec. JOHN W. CLEMENS. Tel: 312-751-5270; Fax: 312-751-5281.

Office for International Priests—Rev. MICHAEL G. MCGOVERN, Archbishop's Delegate. Tel: 312-751-8211.

Mundelein Seminary—Revs. JOHN F. CANARY, Rector; JOHN G. LODGE, Academic Dean; KEVIN J. FEENEY, Dean of Formation, *Mundelein, 60060.* Tel: 847-566-6401.

St. Joseph Seminary at Loyola University—Rev. JAMES PRESTA, Rector, *6551 N. Sheridan Rd., Chicago, 60626.* Tel: 773-973-9700.

Archbishop Quigley Preparatory Seminary—Rev. DAVID A. JONES, Pres., *103 E. Chestnut, Chicago, 60611.* Tel: 312-787-9343.

Bishop Abramowicz House—Rev. RICHARD MILEK, Dir., *1447 W. Superior, Chicago, 60622.* Tel: 312-455-0598; Fax: 312-666-0714.

Casa Jesus—Rev. ROBERT G. CASEY, Dir.; Ms. KAREN HERMAN DEMURO, Dir. Devel., *1335 W. Harrison St., Chicago, 60607.* Tel: 773-243-7400.

Office of the Chancellor

Chancellor—Mr. JIMMY M. LAGO. Tel: 312-751-7999, Ext. 8220.

Department Directors—Revs. JOHN E. POLLARD, Evangelization & Catechesis; R. PETER BOWMAN, Specialized Ministries; Mr. RAYMOND P. COUGHLIN, Stewardship and Development; Rev. MICHAEL M. BOLAND, Human Svcs.; Mr. THOMAS M. BRENNAN, Financial Svcs.; Mr. JAMES W. VODAK, Communication & Public Rels.; Dr. CAROL L. FOWLER, Personnel Svcs.; Vacant, Catholic Schools.

Racial Justice—Sr. ANITA P. BAIRD, D.H.M., Dir. Tel: 312-751-7999, Ext. 8236.

Legal Services—Mr. JOHN C. O'MALLEY, Dir. Tel: 312-751-7999, Ext. 5379.

Information Technology—Ms. ELLEN M. ANDERSON, Dir. Tel: 312-751-7999, Ext. 5330; Fax: 312-751-3879. Mr. GANG CHEN, Mgr. Tel: 312-751-7999, Ext. 5331; Fax: 312-751-5346. Mr. HUGH O'NEILL, Mgr. Technical Svcs. Tel: 312-751-5227.

Research & Planning—Ms. JEAN WELTER, Dir. Tel: 312-751-7999, Ext. 8345; Fax: 312-751-8766. Mr. DAVID F. SCHWARTZ, Assoc. Dir. Tel: 312-751-7999, Ext. 8344.

Vice Chancellor—Ms. MARY A. HALLAN FIORITO. Tel: 312-751-7999, Ext. 8211.

Archives and Records—Mr. JOHN J. TREANOR, *711 W. Monroe St., Chicago, 60606.* Tel: 312-831-0711.

Office of Canonical Services

Canonical Services—Rev. PATRICK R. LAGGES, J.C.D., Vicar. Tel: 312-751-7999, Ext. 8250. Associate Vicars: Rev. RICHARD B. SAUDIS. Tel: 312-751-7999, Ext. 8382. Rev. WILLIAM H. WOESTMAN, O.M.I. Tel: 312-751-7999, Ext. 8362.

Metropolitan Tribunal—

Judicial Vicar—Rev. PATRICK R. LAGGES, J.C.D. Tel: 312-751-7999, Ext. 8250; Fax: 312-751-8314.

Adjutant Judicial Vicar—Rev. DANIEL A. SMILANIC, J.C.D. Tel: 312-751-7999, Ext. 8206.

Applications Coordinator—GLENDA MCFADDEN. Tel: 312-751-7999, Ext. 8523.

Promoter of Justice—Rev. WILLIAM WOESTMAN, O.M.I.

Judges—Rev. MICHAEL A. HACK, J.C.D.; Sr. JOYCE HOBEN, S.N.D.; Revs. STANLEY DREWNIAK; JOHN GRIFFITHS, J.C.D.; JOHN C. HERGENROTHER; PATRICK R. LAGGES, J.C.D.; DANIEL SMILANIC, J.C.D.; Sr. CARMEN GONZALEZ, C.D.P., J.C.L.; Revs. DAVID M. HYNOUS, O.P.; MARK SIMPSON, J.C.L.; MICHAEL BRADLEY, J.C.L.

Defenders of the Bond—Rev. JOHN A. ROLEK, B.A.; Sr. THERESE GUERIN SULLIVAN, S.P.; Rev. MICHAEL KURZ, J.C.L.; Mr. OLEGARIO CASTILLO, J.C.L.

Delegate of the Archbishop for Privilege Cases—Rev. JOHN A. ROLEK, B.A.

Advocates—Revs. STEFAN FILIPOWICZ, S.J.; JOSEPH MOL.

Auditors—Rev. ALEC WOLFF; Ms. MONICA MAVRIC; Ms. SUSAN MILLER; Sr. NATALIA COMPOS-SOLIS, R.S.C.J.

Office of Conciliation—RALPH BONACCORSI, Exec. Dir. Tel: 312-751-8291.

Department of Evangelization and Catechesis

Evangelization and Catechesis—Rev. JOHN E. POLLARD, Dir. Tel: 312-751-8388. Sr. MARILYN KOFLER, S.P., Admin. Asst. Tel: 312-751-8385.

Office for Catechesis—Dr. CAROL EIPERS, Dir. Associate Directors: Dr. JACQUELYNNE POKORNY; Sr. JUDITH DIETERLE, S.S.L., *1025 W. Fry St., Chicago, 60622.* Tel: 312-243-3700; Fax: 312-243-3801.

Special Religious Education (SPRED)—Rev. JAMES H. MCCARTHY, Dir., *2956 S. Lowe, Chicago, 60616.* Tel: 312-842-1039; Fax: 312-842-4449. Sr. MARY THERESE HARRINGTON, S.H.; Sr. SUSANNE GALLAGHER, S.P.

Ministry in Higher Education—JAN SLATTERY, Dir., *700 S. Morgan, Chicago, 60607.* Tel: 312-829-0670.

Office for Evangelization—Rev. JOSEPH KRUSZYNSKI, O.F.M., Dir. Tel: 312-751-5353.

Family Ministries—Mr. FRANCIS P. HANNIGAN, Dir. Tel: 312-751-8351.

Cana Conference—Mr. FRANCIS P. HANNIGAN, Contact. Tel: 312-751-8340. Mr. ANDREW LYKE. Tel: 312-751-8264.

Chicago Marriage Encounter—Tel: 312-455-1930.

World Wide Marriage Encounter—Contacts: KEN RUSSELL; PAT RUSSELL. Tel: 847-838-1924.

Beginning Experience—PAULINE CORDELL, Contact. Tel: 847-724-5434.

Retrouvaille—Tel: 630-985-0363.

Naim (Widowers & Widows)—PAT WEIMER, Contact. Tel: 773-743-6605.

Hispanic Family Ministries—VALENTIN ARAYA, Contact. Tel: 312-751-8240.

Natural Family Planning in Spanish—MARIA GARCIA, Contact. Tel: 312-751-8240.

Elizabeth Ministry—MARIA GARCIA, Contact. Tel: 312-751-8240.

Bereavement Ministry—MARTHA BURKE TRESSLER, Contact. Tel: 312-751-5389.

Ecumenical and Interreligious Affairs, Office for—Sr. JOAN MCGUIRE, O.P., Dir. Tel: 312-751-7999, Ext. 5325. Assoc Directors: Sr. MARY ELLEN COOMBE, N.D.S.; Ms. RITA GEORGE. Tel: 312-751-5325.

Institute for Catholic Jewish Education—Sr. MARY ELLEN COOMBE, N.D.S., Dir. Tel: 312-251-8800, Ext. 316.

Catholic Youth Office—Revs. JOHN P. SMYTH, Dir. DAVID RYAN, Asst. Exec. Dir., *1658 W. Grand Ave., Chicago, 60622.* Tel: 312-733-7405.

Divine Worship, Office for—Vacant, Dir.; Mr. TODD WILLIAMSON, Assoc. Dir.; Ms. JENNIFER KERR-BREEDLOVE, Dir. Liturgical Music; Ms. KATHLEEN SULLIVAN-STEWART, L.I.C. Dir.; Mr. JOSE CASTILLO, Coord. Hispanic Programs; Ms. COURTNEY MURTAUGH, Prog. Coord.; Art & Environment; Rev. PHILIP HORRIGAN, Dir. Liturgy Training Publications (LTP); Mr. GABE HUCK, Dir., *1800 N. Hermitage Ave., Chicago, 60622.* Tel: 773-486-5153 (ODW); 486-8970 (LTP); Fax: 773-486-7094.

Young Adult Ministry/Singles—Rev. JOHN C. CUSICK, Dir.; Ms. KATHERINE F. DEVRIES, Assoc. Dir., *711 W. Monroe St., Chicago, 60661.* Tel: 312-466-9473.

Department of Specialized Ministries

Specialized Ministries—Rev. R. PETER BOWMAN, Interim Dir. Tel: 312-751-5250.

Vocation Office—Tel: 312-751-5240.

Insearch Program—Rev. PATRICK HENRY, *11005 S. Homan Ave., Chicago, 60661.* Tel: 773-779-7181.

Christian Family Movement—Rev. R. PETER BOWMAN, Chap., *155 E. Superior St., Chicago, 60611.* Chicago Federation Chaircouple: MARK REYNOLDS; PAT REYNOLDS, *436 S. Yale, Arlington Heights, 60005.* Tel: 847-255-4909. Area Chaircouple: MARY LOU GORMAN; PHIL GORMAN, *900 E. Wilmette Rd. (#122), Palatine, 60067.* Tel: 847-202-1032.

Respect Life/Pro-Life Activities—Ms. NORA O'CALLAGHAN, Dir. Tel: 312-751-5355; Fax: 312-787-1554.

Project Rachel—*155 E. Superior St., Chicago, 60611.* Tel: 312-337-1962.

Prison Ministry/Kolbe House—Rev. LAWRENCE J. CRAIG, Dir., *2434 S. California, Chicago, 60608.* Tel: 773-247-0700.

Parish Pastoral Councils—Ms. RITA KATTNER, Dir. Tel: 312-751-8364.

Christ Renews His Parish—Ms. RITA KATTNER, Dir. Tel: 312-751-8364.

Catholic Missions Office—

Propagation of the Faith—Co-Dirs.: Rev. JOHN J. GRACE; Sr. MARIA BURKE, S.Sp.S., *721 N. LaSalle St., Chicago, 60610.* Tel: 312-382-3322; Fax: 312-642-1599.

Holy Childhood Association—Co-Dirs.: Rev. JOHN J. GRACE; Sr. MARIA BURKE, S.Sp.S., *721 N. LaSalle St., Chicago, 60610.* Tel: 312-382-3322.

Chicago Bolivia Medical Mission Partnership—*230 N. Old Rand Rd., Lake Zurich, 60047.* Tel: 847-762-0172.

Ethnic Ministries, Office for—Rev. JOHN P. BOIVIN, Dir.; Mrs. SHEILA ADAMS, African-American Dir.; Mrs. TERESITA L. NUVAL, Asian-American Dir.; Mrs. KRYSTYNA ZAMBRZYCKI, European-American Dir.; Rev. ESEQUIEL SANCHEZ, Hispanic-American Dir. Tel: 312-751-8301; Fax: 312-751-5313.

Vicariate Hispanic Coordinators—

Vicariate I—GRACIELA CONTRERAS, *200 N. Milwaukee Ave., Ste. 212, Libertyville, 60048.* Tel: 847-549-0164.

Vicariate II—JORGE RIVERA, *1651 W. Diversey, Chicago, 60614.* Tel: 773-388-8675.

Vicariate III—ROBERTO RIVAS, *1840 S. Leavitt, Chicago, 60608.* Tel: 312-432-9804; 432-9805.

Vicariate IV—Ms. MODESTA MARTINEZ, *1115 N. 23rd Ave., Melrose Park, 60160.* Tel: 708-345-3683.

Vicariate V—JUAN RAMIREZ, *2330 W. 118th St., Chicago, 60643.* Tel: 773-779-9324.

Vicariate VI—Ms. CLEMENCIA PADILLA, *16160 Seton Rd., South Holland, 60473.* Tel: 708-339-5044.

Ministry Missions or Centers—

Native American Apostolate—Sr. DOMINGA ZAPATA, S.H., Acting Dir., *Anawin Center, 4545 N. Broadway, Ste. 258, Chicago, 60640.* Tel: 773-561-6155.

Blessed Alojzije Cardinal Stepanic Mission—Rev. NICHOLAS DUGANDZIC, O.P., Dir., *6346 N. Ridge Ave., Chicago, 60660.* Tel: 773-262-0535.

Czech Catholic Mission—Rev. DUSAN HLADIK, *2340 S. 61st Ave., Cicero, 60804.*

Chinese Catholic Mission (St. Therese Chinese Catholic Church)—Rev. MICHAEL DAVITTI, S.X., Dir., *218 W. Alexander, Chicago, 60616.* Tel: 312-842-6777.

Haitian Catholic Center—Rev. JOSEPH ERNEST, Dir., *7851 S. Jeffery Blvd., Chicago, 60649.* Tel: 773-768-0105.

Holy Trinity Polish Mission—Rev. WLADYSLAW GOWIN, S.Ch., Dir., *1118 N. Noble, Chicago, 60622.* Tel: 773-489-4140.

Indochinese Catholic Center—Rev. PETER HUNG, Dir., *4827 N. Kenmore, Chicago, 60640.* Tel: 773-784-1932.

Irish Catholic Apostolate—Rev. THOMAS O'HALLORAN, Chicago Chap. to the Young Irish, *7142 N. Osceola Ave., Chicago, 60631.* Tel: 773-631-4127; Fax: 773-631-4150.

Italian Catholic Apostolate—Rev. GINO DALPIAZ, C.S., *1621 N. 39th Ave., Stone Park, 60165.* Tel: 708-345-3842.

Knanya Catholic Mission—Rev. PHILIP JOSEPH THODU KAYIL, Dir., *3834 N. Spaulding, Chicago, 60618.* Tel: 773-509-9147.

Korean Catholic Mission of Chicago—Rev. JOHN SMITH, S.S.C., Dir., *4115 N. Kedvale, Chicago, 60641.* Tel: 773-283-3979.

Blessed George Matulaitis Lithuanian Catholic Mission—Rev. ALGIRDAS PALIOKAS, S.J., Dir., *14915 127th St., Unit 101, Lemont, 60439.* Tel: 630-257-5613.

St. Paul Chong Hasang Korean Catholic Mission—Rev. PIUS LEE, Dir., *675 Dursey Ln., Des Plaines, 60016.* Tel: 847-699-6334; Fax: 847-966-1029.

Sacred Heart Mission House (Polish Jesuits)—Rev. PAWEL KOSINSKI, S.J., Supr., *4105 N. Avers Ave., Chicago, 60618.* Tel: 773-588-7476.

BL. A.M. Slomsek Slovenian Catholic Mission—Rev. DAVID SRUMPF, Dir., *14246 Main St., P.O. Box 608, Lemont, 60439.* Tel: 630-257-2068.

Slovak Catholic Mission—Rev. EDWARD SLOSARCIK, Dir. Emeritus; Sr. JOHN VIANNEY, Exec. Dir., *5157 S. California, Chicago, 60632.* Tel: 773-436-1045.

Syro-Malabar Catholic Mission—Rev. JOCOB ANGADIATH, Dir., *Mar Thoma Shleeha Center, 5000 St. Charles Rd., Bellwood, 60104.* Tel: 708-544-7250.

Syro-Malankara Catholic Center—Rev. THOMAS VARUGHESE, Dir., *1634 W. Gregory St., Chicago, 60640.*

Catholic Charismatic Renewal Center of Chicago (CCRCC)—Revs. PATRICK J. HENRY, Archbishop's Liaison; RICHARD T. SIMON, Liaison for Hispanics, *12905 S. Division St., Blue Island, 60406.* Tel: 708-371-2727.

Cursillo Movement—English Liaison, Rev. MICHAEL FURLAN, Spiritual Dir. Tel: 773-846-6146. Spanish Liaison: Rev. MICHAEL MICHELINI, Spiritual Dir. Tel: 312-226-0340.

Office for Peace & Justice—Mr. BILL PURCELL, Dir. Tel: 312-751-8390; Fax: 312-787-1554.

Catholic Campaign for Human Development—Ms. ELENA SEGURA. Tel: 312-751-5333.

Catholic Relief Services—Ms. ELENA SEGURA, Dir. Tel: 312-751-5333.

Housing Coordinator—Mr. JONATHAN NJUS. Tel: 312-751-8367.

Parish Sharing Program—Ms. TERRY ANGELOTTI. Tel: 312-751-8390.

Chaplaincies—

The Catholic Ministry at Chicago O'Hare International Airport—Rev. JOHN A. JAMNICKY, Chap., *P.O. Box 66353, Chicago, 60666-0353.* Tel: 773-686-2636.

Airport, Midway—Rev. GEORGE P. MCKENNA, Chap. Tel: 773-767-0500.

Firefighters/Paramedics—Rev. THOMAS A. MULCRONE, Chap., *1140 W. Jackson Blvd., Chicago, 60607.* Tel: 312-738-9246.

Police—Revs. THOMAS R. NANGLE, Chap. MICHAEL P. KNOTEK, Assoc. Chap., *1140 W. Jackson Blvd., Chicago, 60607.* Tel: 312-738-7588; Fax: 312-738-2825.

Seafarers—Rev. JAMES P. KEATING, Chap., *10201 S. Ewing, Chicago, 60617.* Tel: 773-734-1383.

Archdiocesan Council of Catholic Women (ACCW)—GERI SORIANO, Pres.; Rev. STAN JANKOWSKI, O.F.M., Dir. Tel: 312-751-8325.

Lay Groups and Organizations—

Archdiocesan Council of Catholic Men—Rev. JOHN C. CUSICK, *711 W. Monroe St., Chicago, 60661.* Tel: 312-466-9473.

Amate House/Young Adult Volunteer Program—Vacant, Dir., *2601 N. Sayre Ave., Chicago, 60635.* Tel: 773-745-0002; 800-383-2038.

Semilla—Rev. WILLIAM SPINE, S.J., Cardinal's Liaison. Tel: 773-508-8558.

Knights of Columbus—Tel: 312-751-5250.

Legion of Mary—Tel: 312-751-5250.

Department of Stewardship and Development

Stewardship and Development—RAYMOND P. COUGHLIN, Dir. Tel: 312-655-7911.

Parish Services—RAYMOND P. COUGHLIN, Dir. Tel: 312-655-7911.

Vicariate Stewardship Coordinators—MICHAEL J. GLEASON; JANE O'BRIEN. Tel: 312-655-7911.

Development Services—Mr. TIMOTHY DOCKERY. Tel: 312-655-7911.

Planned Giving/Annuities—Mr. RICHARD S. GOODE, Devel. Assoc. MABLE MCKNUCKLES, Admin. Asst. Tel: 312-655-7911.

Parish Development Consultant—DAN CHORNEY, Dir., *312-655-7911.*

Seminary Development-Archbishop Quigley Preparatory—PATRICIA HERMAN. Tel: 312-655-7911.

St. Joseph Seminary—MARIE COMPOSTO. Tel: 773-973-9721.

St. Mary of the Lake, Mundelein—Vacant. Tel: 847-566-6401.

Big Shoulders Fund—JUDITH SILEKIS. Tel: 312-655-7911.

Department of Human Services

Director—Rev. MICHAEL M. BOLAND, *126 N. Desplaines St., Chicago, 60661.* Tel: 312-655-7031.

Catholic Charities of Chicago—Revs. MICHAEL M. BOLAND, Admin.; CHARLES T. RUBEY, Dir. Programs; Mr. WALTER OUSLEY, Dir. Operations; CYNTHIA D. SNETANA, Dir. Admin. Assoc. Admins.: Revs. RICHARD E. BULWITH; FRANCIS A. CIMARRUSTI; ROGER J. COUGHLIN; DANIEL M. HOLIHAN; JAMES M. RAY, *126 N. Desplaines St., Chicago, 60661-2357.* Tel: 312-655-7000. (Refer to Catholic Charities section under the Institutions located in the Archdiocese for further listings.).

Catholic Office of the Deaf—Rev. JOSEPH A. MULCRONE, Dir.; Ms. NANCY HUBER, Rel. Educ. Dir., *721 N. LaSalle, Chicago, 60610.* Tel: 312-655-7899.

Apostolate of the Handicapped—Rev. CHARLES F. KELLY, Moderator, *5330 S. Nashville, Chicago, 60638.* Tel: 312-583-1223; Fax: 773-973-5214.

Health/Hospital Affairs—Most Rev. EDWIN M. CONWAY, Liaison; Most Rev. JEROME LISTECKI, Assoc. Liaison; Rev. JAMES RAY, Asst. Liaison. Tel: 773-388-8670.

Mercy Home for Boys and Girls—Rev. JAMES J. CLOSE, Pres.; Rev. SCOTT DONAHUE, Assoc. Pres., *1140 W. Jackson, Chicago, 60607.* Tel: 312-738-7560; Fax: 312-738-0484.

Office for Persons with Disabilities—Rev. CHARLES T. RUBEY, *6300 N. Ridge, Chicago, 60660.* Tel: 773-973-6300.

Department of Financial Services

Director—THOMAS M. BRENNAN. Tel: 312-751-8218.

Facilities and Construction—C. GREGORY VEITH, Mgr. Tel: 312-751-8342.

Treasurer's Office—ERIC WAGNER, Interim Treas. Tel: 312-751-5277.

Controller's Operations—MARK COSENTINO, Mgr. Tel: 312-751-5266.

Office Services—PHIL WAGNER, Mgr. Tel: 312-751-8246.

Insurance—MATTHEW KAMINSKI, Mgr. Tel: 312-751-8295.

Real Estate—Ms. MAUREEN O'BRIEN, Mgr. Tel: 312-751-8221.

Vicariate Administrative Consultants (VACS)—

Vicariate Administrative Manager—TAFFIE IWANICKI. Tel: 312-751-5312. JASON BERTRAND, Vicariate Coord. for Vicariates III and VI. Tel: 312-751-5399.

Vicariate I—MICHAEL GIBBS. Tel: 312-751-5322, Vicariate Office: Tel: 847-549-0165.

Vicariate II—GENE MYERS. Tel: 312-751-5321, Vicariate Office: Tel: 773-763-1661.

Vicariate III—Vacant. Tel: 312-751-5323, Vicariate Office: Tel: 312-243-1135.

Vicariate IV—PATRICIA POMYKALSKI. Tel: 312-751-5312, Vicariate Office: Tel: 773-202-7722.

Vicariate V—TOM BARTHOLOMEW. Tel: 312-751-5318, Vicariate Office: Tel: 773-779-9165.

Vicariate VI—JASON BERTRAND. Tel: 312-751-5342, Vicariate Office: Tel: 708-333-6132.

Catholic Cemeteries—Rev. PATRICK J. POLLARD, Dir. DONALD MASSARO, Exec. Dir., *1400 S. Wolf Rd., Hillside, 60162.* Tel: 708-449-6100; Fax: 708-449-3419.

Department of Communications and Public Relations

Department of Communications and Public Relations—JAMES W. VODAK. Tel: 312-751-8289; Fax: 312-751-5306.

Communications, Office of—JAMES DWYER, Dir. Communication; MARY MCDONOUGH, Communications Svc. Mgr. Tel: 312-751-8277; Fax: 312-751-5306.

Marketing—MIKE KRIVICH, Dir. Tel: 312-751-8268. AGNES MLECZEK, Web Designer. Tel: 312-751-5239; Fax: 312-751-5307.

Catholic Information Service—BECKY SUTTON, Dir. Tel: 312-751-7999, Ext. 8204.

New World Publications—THOMAS H. SHERIDAN, Editor & Gen. Mgr. MARY CLAIRE GART, Asst. Editor,

721 N. LaSalle St., Chicago, 60610. Tel: 312-655-7777; Fax: 312-642-7310.
Media Chaplain—Rev. JOHN J. WALL, Dir., *718 W. Adams, Chicago, 60606.* Tel: 312-782-6171.

Department of Personnel Services

Director—Dr. CAROL FOWLER. Tel: 312-751-8349.
Human Resources—FRED VAN DEN HENDE, Mgr. Tel: 312-751-5352.
Lay Ecclesial Ministry, Office for—Mrs. LUCILLE M. MERLIHAN, Dir. ALICE ALTIVEROS-LADAO, Ministry Openings. Tel: 312-751-5262; 751-7999 (Hotline), Ext. 3; Fax: 312-751-5281.
Office of Ministerial Evaluation—MARY YUNGER, Dir. Tel: 312-751-5265; Fax: 312-751-5281.
Religious, Office for—Sr. JOAN MCGLINCHEY, M.S.C., Dir.; Sr. MARGARET COLEMAN, Retirement Collection. Tel: 312-751-8333.
Priests' Retirement and Mutual Aid Association (PRMAA)—Mr. ALEX BECKER, Admin., *4951 Harrison St., Hillside, 60162.*
Vicar for Senior Priests—Most Rev. TIMOTHY J. LYNE, Vicar. Asst. Vicars: Revs. DONALD J. AHEARN; JOHN A. KUZINSKAS. Tel: 312-787-8040.
Vicar for Diaconate Community—Rev. EDWARD P. SALMON, *816 Marengo, Forest Park, 60130.* Tel: 708-366-8900. THOMAS MCGOREY, Assoc. Dir. Personnel; CHARLES O'DONNELL, Assoc. Dir. Ministerial Devel.
Diaconate Formation Program—Mundelein Seminary, 1000 E. Maple, Mundelein, 60060-1174. Tel: 847-837-4563; Fax: 847-837-4565. Deacon JOHN PISTONE, Dir.; JUSTINE SPINA, Assoc. Dir.; Rev. DAVID DOWDLE, Dir. Spiritual Formation.
Office of Professional Responsibility—KATHLEEN LEGGDAS, Dir., *676 N. St. Clair, Ste. 1910, Chicago, 60611.* Tel: 312-751-8256.
Office of Professional Fitness Review—KATHLEEN LEGGDAS, Admin., *676 N. St. Clair, Ste. 1910, Chicago, 60611.* Tel: 312-751-5205; 800-994-6200; Fax: 312-751-5279.
Cardinal Stritch Retreat House—Revs. LOUIS J. CAMELI, Dir.; EDMUND J. SIEDLECKI, Admin.; JOHN M. MICHET, Assoc. Admin., *P.O. Box 455, Mundelein, 60060.* Tel: 847-566-6060; Fax: 847-566-6082.
Lay Ministry Programs—GRAZIANO MARCHESCHI, Dir.; CATHERINE SIMS, Assoc. Dir., *1000 E. Maple Ave., Mundelein, 60060-1174.* Tel: 847-837-4556; Fax: 847-837-4565.
Instituto De Liderazgo Pastoral (Hispanic Programs for Lay Ministry and Permanent Diaconate)—Mr. ENRIQUE ALONSO, Dir. Assoc. Directors: Mrs. ANA M. RIVAS; Sr. NATALIA E. CAMPOS-SOLIS, R.S.C.J. Tel: 847-837-4556.
Center for Development in Ministry (CDM)—Rev. JOSEPH C. GEDERS, C.M., Dir., *University of St. Mary of the Lake, 1000 E. Maple Ave., Mundelein, 60060-1174.* Tel: 847-970-4925.

Department of Catholic Schools

Department of Catholic Schools—Superintendents: Sr. JUDITH A. CAULEY, C.S.J.; Ms. JANET SISLER. Tel: 312-751-5200.
Food Service Professionals, Archdiocese—Mr. RON HUNTER, Dir., *5150 Northwest Hwy., Chicago, 60638.* Tel: 773-385-5100.

Miscellaneous Archdiocesan Agencies

Apostleship of Prayer—Rev. Msgr. JAMES C. HARDIMAN, Dir., *4126 W. 99th St., Oak Lawn, 60453.* Tel: 312-751-8346.
Apostleship of the Sea—Rev. JAMES P. KEATING, *10201 S. Ewing, Chicago, 60617.* Tel: 773-734-1383.

CLERGY, PARISHES, MISSIONS AND PAROCHIAL SCHOOLS

CITY OF CHICAGO
(Cook County)

1—CATHEDRAL OF THE HOLY NAME, Revs. Robert E. McLaughlin, Rector and Pastor of Parish; William J. Sheridan; John Boivin; John A. Farry. Pastoral Associates: Ms. Kristin Sadie; Mrs. Ann Klocke; Ms. Cathleen Mika, Pastoral Min.; Deacon Michael McCloskey; Mary Ann Hoban, D.Min., Coord. of Ministry of Care; Mr. Matthew Walsh, Dir. Music; Mrs. Rosalie V. Clifford, Business Mgr.; Ms. Cynthia A. Carter, Parish Sec.; Sr. Michaeleen Gibbons, B.V.M., Financial Admin.; Dr. Mary Ann Clemens, D.R.E. In res., Most Rev. Timothy J. Lyne, Pastor Emeritus & Auxiliary Bishop of Chicago (Retired); Rev. Msgr. John J. Egan; Revs. Michael M. Boland; William J. Moriarity; James P. Roache; Eugene F. Durkin, (Retired); Eugene F. Durkin, (Retired). Rectory: 730 N. Wabash Ave., 60611. Tel: 312-787-8040; Fax: 312-787-9113.
Cardinal's Residence—1555 N. State Pkwy., 60610. Most Rev. Raymond E. Goedert, Auxiliary Bishop & Vicar General; Rev. John J. McDonnell, Sec. to the Archbishop.
School—Frances Xavier Warde School, 751 N. State St., 60611. Tel: 312-466-0700; Fax: 312-337-7180. Sr. Mary Ellen Caron, R.S.M., Prin.
Religious 1; Lay Teachers 70; Students 605.
Convents—750 N. Wabash Ave., 60611. Tel: 312-664-1462. Sisters of Charity of the Blessed Virgin Mary; 740 N. Wabash Ave., 60611. Tel: 312-787-8040; Fax: 312-787-9113. Little Sisters of the Holy Family

2—ST. ADALBERT, Revs. Michael S. Michelini; Alejandro Garrido; Deacon Joseph Mally.
Res., 1650 W. 17th St., 60608. Tel: 312-226-0340; Fax: 312-266-0194.
Catechesis/Religious Programs—Students 265.

3—ST. ADRIAN, Rev. Theodore L. Ostrowski.
Res., 7000 S. Fairfield Ave., 60629. Tel: 773-434-3223.
Church—70th and S. Washtenaw Ave., 60619.

4—ST. AGATHA, Rev. Daniel J. McCormack; Deacon Gregory Shumpert.
Res., 3147 W. Douglas Blvd., 60623. Tel: 773-522-3050; Fax: 773-522-3842.
School—Campus No. One—Our Lady of the Westside Catholic School. Serving the following parishes: St. Agatha and Presentation. Totals represent all two campuses. Tel: 773-762-1809.
Sisters 6; Lay Teachers 23; Students 609.
Convent—3143 W. Douglas Blvd., 60623. Tel: 773-762-7969.

5—ST. AGNES OF BOHEMIA, Revs. Matthew E. Foley; Francis T. Pribyl, Pastor Emeritus; Mark Bartosic; Timothy J. O'Malley; Felipe Vaglienty. Pastoral Assocs.: Sr. Maria De Los Angeles Ramos; Sr. Blanca Esthela Salido; Deacon Angel Favila.
Res., 2651 S. Central Park Ave., 60623. Tel: 773-522-0142; Fax: 773-522-0172.
School—2643 S. Central Park Ave., 60623. Tel: 773-522-0143; Fax: 773-522-0132.
Lay Teachers 20; Students 600.
Catechesis/Religious Programs—Tel: 773-277-5446.
Students 903.
Convent—2658 S. Central Park Ave., 60623. Tel: 773-762-3229. Misioneras de San Pio X

6—ST. AILBE, Rev. John S. Breslin; Deacon Bruce T. McElrath; Mrs. Marie C. Davis, Pastoral Assoc.
Res., 9015 S. Harper Ave., 60619. Tel: 773-374-2345; Fax: 773-374-7096.
School—9137 S. Harper Ave., 60619. Tel: 773-734-1386; Fax: 773-734-1440. Sr. Kathryn Hartnett, Prin.
Sisters of St. Dominic (Adrian, MI) 2; Lay Teachers 15; Students 320.
Catechesis/Religious Programs—Students 130.

7—ALL SAINTS-ST. ANTHONY, Rev. Raymond P. Devereux; Deacons Peter Liberti; Martin Mackert, (Ret.); Duke Vemich.
Res., 518 W. 28th Pl., 60616. Tel: 312-842-2744; Fax: 312-842-2791.
School—Participant in Bridgeport Catholic Academy. See separate listing for Consolidated Elementary Schools.
Catechesis/Religious Programs—Students 160.

8—ST. ALOYSIUS, Rev. Nicholas R. Desmond; Deacons Adolph Lopez; Dennis Ramos.
Res., 2300 W. Le Moyne St., 60622. Tel: 773-278-4808; Fax: 773-278-4898.
Catechesis/Religious Programs—1526 N. Claremont, 60622. Tel: 773-489-1343.
Students 115.

9—ST. ALPHONSUS (German), Revs. James F. Hurlbert; John Blazek; John Gomes (Sri Lanka); Deacon Joseph Riffner.
Res., 1429 W. Wellington Ave., 60657. Tel: 773-525-0709; Fax: 773-525-3238.
School—Tel: 773-348-4629; Fax: 773-348-4829.
Lay Teachers 12; Students 199.
Catechesis/Religious Programs—Students 35.

10—ST. AMBROSE, Rev. David A. Jones.
Res., 1012 E. 47th St., 60653. Tel: 773-624-3695; Fax: 773-624-3697.
School—1014 E. 47th St., 60653-3698. Tel: 773-373-7311; Fax: 773-451-2684.
Lay Teachers 10; Students 210.

11—ST. ANDREW, Rev. John W. Parker. In res., Rev. Joseph J. Wojcik.
Res., 3546 N. Paulina St., 60657. Tel: 773-525-3016; Fax: 773-525-4124.
School—1710 W. Addison, 60613. Tel: 773-248-2500; Fax: 773-248-2709.
Lay Teachers 16; Students 360.
Catechesis/Religious Programs—Students 80.

12—ST. ANGELA, Revs. Kenneth M. Brigham, Admin.; Dennis S. Riley; Sr. Joseph Ellen Keitzer, S.P., Pastoral Assoc.; Deacon Jose Uroza.
Res., 5758 W. Potomac Ave., 60651. Tel: 773-379-7700; Fax: 773-379-7701.
School—Tel: 773-626-2655.
Sisters 4; Lay Teachers 29; Students 350.
Catechesis/Religious Programs—1332 N. Massasoit Ave., 60651. Tel: 773-626-2656.
Students 37.

13—ST. ANN, Rev. John J. Keehan; Deacon Rodrigo Silva. In res., Rev. Louis J. Zake.
Res., 1840 S. Leavitt St., 60608. Tel: 312-733-7486.
School—2211 W. 18th Pl., 60608. Tel: 312-829-4153. Sr. Michael Marie Franzak, Prin.
Lay Teachers 8; Students 300.

14—ANNUNCIATA, Revs. George Luznicky, O.S.M.; Mark M. Dennehy, O.S.M., Pastor Emeritus; Paul M. Cullen, O.S.M.; Bro. Brian Fitzpatrick, O.S.M., Pastoral Assoc.; Mr. Mike Schnabel, Business Mgr. In res., Rev. Conrad M. Borntrager, O.S.M.
Res., 11128 S. Avenue G, 60617. Tel: 773-221-1040; Fax: 773-221-1556.
School—Lay Teachers 12; Students 300.

15—ST. ANSELM, Rev. William Hegarty. Pastoral Assocs.: Bros. Rogers Hannah, S.V.D.; Vinh Trinh, S.V.D. In res., Revs. Donald J. Ehr, S.V.D.; Mark Weber, S.V.D.
Res., 6045 S. Michigan Ave., 60637. Tel: 773-493-5959; Fax: 773-363-1887.
Catechesis/Religious Programs—Students 75.

16—ST. ANTHONY (Italian), Revs. Charles LaVerde, C.S.; Guillermo Garcia, C.S.; Deacons Edward Ryan; Juan Morales.
Res., 11530 S. Prairie Ave., 60628. Tel: 773-468-1200; Fax: 773-468-3570.
School—Lay Teachers 11; Students 155.

17—ASSUMPTION OF THE BLESSED VIRGIN MARY, Revs. John M. Dowd, O.S.M.; Peregrine M. Grassius, O.S.M. In res., Revs. Anthony M. O'Connell, O.S.M.; John M. Pawlikowski, O.S.M., Ph.D.; David M. Brown, O.S.M.; Paul M. Novak, O.S.M.
Res., 323 W. Illinois St., 60610. Tel: 312-644-0036; Fax: 312-644-1838.

18—ASSUMPTION OF THE B.V.M./ST. CATHERINE OF GENOA, Rev. Edward D. Gleeson, Admin.; Deacon Tommy West.
Res., 640 W. 118th St., 60628. Tel: 773-785-6600; Fax: 773-785-6602.
Catechesis/Religious Programs—Students 16.

19—ASSUMPTION, Revs. Lawrence J. Craig; David A. Kelly, C.P.P.S.; Deacons Ronald DeRose; John W. Harrington.
Res., 2434 S. California Ave., 60608. Tel: 773-247-6644; Fax: 773-247-0569.
Convent—2831 W. 24th St. Blvd., 60623. Tel: 773-247-3560.
Kolbe House—Catholic Prison Ministry. Tel: 773-247-0070. Rev. Lawrence J. Craig, Dir.
Catechesis/Religious Programs—Students 230.

20—ST. BARBARA, Rev. Michael T. Yakaitis; Deacon Andrew Brongiel; Sr. Kathy Brazda, Pastoral Assoc. In res., Revs. Edward B. Panek; Charles T. Durkin; Samuel Citero, O.Carm.
Res., 2859 S. Throop St., 60608. Tel: 312-842-7979; Fax: 312-842-7978.
School—2867 S. Throop St., 60608. Tel: 312-326-6243.
Sisters of St. Joseph of the Third Order of St. Francis (Chicago, IL) 1; Lay Teachers 11; Students 240.
High School—Tel: 312-842-0042.
Sisters of St. Joseph of the Third Order of St. Francis (Chicago, IL) 1; Lay Teachers 12; Students 170.

21—ST. BARNABAS, Revs. Raymond J. Tillrock; Kenneth J. Fleck; Ms. Keiren O'Kelly, Pastoral Assoc.; Deacons James Temple; William Sullivan; James L. Conway.
Res., 10134 S. Longwood Dr., 60643. Tel: 773-779-1166; Fax: 773-445-9671.
School—10121 S. Longwood Dr., 60643. Tel: 773-445-7711; Fax: 773-445-9815.
Dominican Sisters (Sinsinawa, WI) 1; Lay Teachers 37; Students 659.
Catechesis/Religious Programs—Students 257.

22—ST. BARTHOLOMEW, Rev. George F. Cerny; Sr. Geraldine Moorman, B.V.M., Pastoral Assoc.; Deacons Robert Puhala; Jose Gonzales; Mrs. Nancy Kleiber, Lay Min. In res., Revs. Casimir J. Kozien, (Retired); J. Edward Duggan, (Retired); J. Lester Mollohan, (Retired); Eduardo Pinzon, S.J.
Res., 4949 W. Patterson Ave., 60641. Tel: 773-286-7871; Fax: 773-286-4808.
School—4941 W. Patterson Ave., 60641. Tel: 773-282-9373; Fax: 773-282-4757.
Sisters 2; Lay Teachers 27; Students 453.
Catechesis/Religious Programs—Students 130.
Convent—Tel: 773-545-2119.

23—ST. BASIL/VISITATION, Rev. Brian G. Walker, O.P. In res., Rev. Robert M. Kelly, O.P.
Res., 843 W. Garfield Blvd., 60621. Tel: 773-846-3570; Fax: 773-783-3348.
School—Visitation School, 900 W. Garfield Blvd., 60609. Tel: 733-373-5200; Fax: 733-373-5201.
Sisters 8; Lay Teachers 19; Students 353.
Catechesis/Religious Programs—Students 287.

24—ST. BEDE THE VENERABLE, Revs. Brian Lisowski; Marion Soprych; Neil Van Dyke; Deacon James F. Delaney.
Res., 8200 S. Kostner Ave., 60652. Tel: 773-582-9100; Fax: 773-582-0026.
School—4420 W. 83rd St., 60652. Tel: 773-582-8800; Fax: 773-582-3366.
Lay Teachers 39; Students 807.
Catechesis/Religious Programs—Tel: 773-767-2186; Fax: 773-767-9254.
Students 106.

25—ST. BENEDICT, Revs. Robert A. Heidenreich; Dennis B. O'Neill; Jason A. Malave; Deacon Robert Jacob.
Res., 2215 W. Irving Park Rd., 60618. Tel: 773-588-6484; Fax: 773-588-4927.
School—3920 N. Leavitt St., 60618. Tel: 773-463-6797; Fax: 773-463-0782.
Lay Teachers 21; Students 357.
High School—3900 N. Leavitt St., 60618. Tel: 773-539-0066; Fax: 773-539-3397.
Sisters 5; Lay Teachers 36; Students 517.
Catechesis/Religious Programs—Students 135.

26—ST. BENEDICT THE AFRICAN (EAST), Rev. David E. Baldwin. Pastoral Assocs.: Sr. Mary Pokorny; Sr. Joanne Delehanty; Sr. Eileen Hauswald.
Res., 340 W. 66th St., 60621. Tel: 773-873-4464; Fax: 773-873-2354.
School—Academy of St. Benedict the African.
Total Students for 3 Sites: 960.
Stewart Site—6547 S. Stewart, 60636. Tel: 773-944-6100.
Catechesis/Religious Programs—Students 24.

27—ST. BENEDICT THE AFRICAN (WEST), Revs. David R. Straub; Daniel C. Jankowski; Sr. Joann Sambs, Pastoral Assoc.; Deacon Louis Constanopolis.
Worship Site—7033 S. Honore, 60636.
Office—6012 S. Laflin St., 60636. Tel: 773-476-4831; Fax: 773-925-1010.
Rectory: 1818 W. 71st St., 60636. Tel: 773-925-2535.
School—Academy of St. Benedict the African.
Total Students for 3 Sites: 960.
Honore Site—7033 S. Honore St., 60636. Tel: 773-476-2258; Fax: 773-476-0753.
Laflin Site—6020 S. Laflin St., 60636. Tel: 773-776-3316; Fax: 773-776-3715.
Stewart Site—6547 S. Stewart St., 60636. Tel: 773-994-6100; Fax: 773-994-1433.
Catechesis/Religious Programs—Students 138.

28—BLESSED ALOJZIJE CARDINAL STEPANIC MISSION. (Independent Mission). Rev. Nicholas Dugandzic, O.P., Admin.
Res., 6346 N. Ridge, 60660. Tel: 773-262-0535; Fax: 773-262-4603.

29—BLESSED SACRAMENT, Rev. William Bueche, C.Ss.R.; Bro. Eugene Patin, C.Ss.R.; Deacon Juan Sierra. In res., Rev. John Phelps, C.Ss.R.
Res., 2153 S. Millard Ave., 60623. Tel: 773-521-5595; Fax: 773-521-6076.
School—2130 S. Central Park Ave., 60623.
Lay Teachers 11; Students 265.
Convent—2135 S. Central Park Ave., 60623. Sisters of Charity of the Blessed Virgin

30—ST. BONAVENTURE, Rev. James A. Heneghan; Sr. Patricia Doody, O.S.F., Pastoral Assoc.; Deacons Emiliano Rodriguez; Tito Roman. In res., Revs. Richard E. Bulwith; Louis J. Cameli.
Res., 1641 W. Diversey Pkwy., 60614. Tel: 773-281-6588; Fax: 773-281-1051.
School—Cardinal Bernardin Early Childhood Center, 1651 W. Diversey Pkwy., 60614. Tel: 773-975-6330; Fax: 773-975-6339. Sr. Barbara Jean Ciszek, C.S.J., Prin.

31—ST. BRIDE, Rev. Robert J. Kyfes.
Res., 7811 S. Coles Ave., 60649. Tel: 773-731-8822.
School—7760 South Shore Dr., 60649. Tel: 773-721-5459; Fax: 773-721-0673.
Lay Teachers 10; Students 229.

32—ST. BRONISLAVA, Revs. Michael J. Bonner, S.V.D., Admin.; Jesus Puentes (Colombia).
Res., 8708 S. Colfax Ave., 60617. Tel: 773-734-0776; Fax: 773-734-1426.

33—ST. BRUNO, Revs. Joseph P. Grembla; Edmund S. Szlanga, Pastor Emeritus; Idzi Stacherczak; Antonio Bury (Ext-Poland); Deacons Sal Villa; Lawrence Chyba. In res., Rev. Ernest D. Ciemiega, (Retired); Mr. Brad Danna Mulick, Pastoral Assoc.
Res., 4751 S. Harding Ave., 60632. Tel: 773-523-3467; Fax: 773-523-4253.
School—Tel: 773-847-0697; Fax: 773-847-1620.
Lay Teachers 11; Students 320.
Catechesis/Religious Programs—Students 285.

34—ST. CAJETAN, Rev. John H. Barkemeyer. Pastoral Assocs.: Sr. Annette Kelley, O.P.; Deacon Don Newhall. In res., Rev. John Kilcrann, C.S.Sp.
Parish Center Office: 2445 W. 112th St., 60655.
Res., 11234 S. Artesian Ave., 60655. Tel: 773-238-4100; Fax: 773-238-4955.
School—2447 W. 112th St., 60655. Tel: 773-233-8844; Fax: 773-239-5322.
Lay Teachers 27; Students 528.
Catechesis/Religious Programs—Students 159.

35—ST. CAMILLUS, Revs. Peter Galek; Jan Henk. In res., Rev. Norman M. Czajka, Pastor Emeritus.
Res., 5426 S. Lockwood Ave., 60638. Tel: 773-767-8183; Fax: 773-284-3812.
School—5432 S. Lockwood Ave., 60638. Tel: 773-767-6977; Fax: 773-767-2633.
Sisters of the Holy Family of Nazareth 4; Lay Teachers 9; Students 214.
Catechesis/Religious Programs—Students 420.

36—CHRIST THE KING, Revs. Patrick J. Pollard; William Wilkosz; Deacons Larry Antonsen; William Hurley; Terry Childers. In res., Rev. Thomas J. Raftery, (Retired).
Res., 9235 S. Hamilton Ave., 60620. Tel: 773-238-4877; Fax: 773-238-4963.
School—9240 S. Hoyne Ave., 60620. Tel: 773-779-3329.
Lay Teachers 23; Students 303.

37—CHRIST THE REDEEMER BYZANTINE BIELARUSIAN, Rev. John J. McDonnell, Admin.
Res., 3107 W. Fullerton Ave., 60647. Tel: 773-342-7373.

38—ST. CHRISTINA, Revs. Martin E. O'Donovan; Patrick J. Henry; Stanley S. Drewniak (Poland); Deacon Thomas Ryan.
Res., 11005 S. Homan Ave., 60655. Tel: 773-779-7181; Fax: 773-238-2942.
School—Tel: 773-445-2969; Fax: 773-445-0444.
Lay Teachers 28; Students 800.
Catechesis/Religious Programs—3333 W. 10th St., 60655. Tel: 773-445-2969; Fax: 773-238-2942.
Students 800.

39—ST. CLARE OF MONTEFALCO, Rev. Anthony B. Pizzo, O.S.A.; Deacon Gregorio Bustos. In res., Revs. Daniel J. Hartigan, O.S.A.; Gerrardo M. Garcia, O.S.A., (Retired); Bro. Mark Thedens, O.S.A.
Res., 5443 S. Washtenaw Ave., 60632. Tel: 773-436-4422; Fax: 773-476-1888.
School—5450 S. Talman Ave., 60632. Tel: 773-434-2427. Iris Foley, Prin.
Religious 2; Lay Teachers 9; Students 192.

40—ST. CLEMENT, Revs. Thomas E. Hickey; Michael P. Knotek; Sr. Mary Frost, Pastoral Assoc. In res., Rev. Michael McGovern.
Res., 642 W. Deming Pl., 60614. Tel: 773-281-0371; Fax: 773-281-2509.
School—2524 N. Orchard St., 60614. Tel: 773-348-8212; Fax: 773-348-4712.
Lay Teachers 22; Students 236.
Catechesis/Religious Programs—Students 143.

41—ST. CLOTILDE, Rev. John B. Atoyebi. In res., Rev. John Adewoye (Nigeria).
Res., 8430 Calumet Ave., 60619. Tel: 773-874-1022; Fax: 773-874-1736.
School—321 E. 84th St., 60619. Tel: 773-488-4214. Mr. Joseph Cailles, Prin.
Lay Teachers 10; Students 202.

42—ST. COLUMBA, Revs. Kilian M. Knittel; Henry A. Olejniczak, Pastor Emeritus.
Res., 13323 S. Greenbay Ave., 60633. Tel: 773-646-2660; Fax: 773-646-6821.
School—Tel: 773-646-0751; Fax: 773-646-0640.
School Sisters of Notre Dame 1; Lay Teachers 6; Students 80.

43—ST. COLUMBANUS, Rev. Matthew S. Eyerman; Deacons William McKinnis; George Borka.
Res., 331 E. 71st St., 60619. Tel: 773-224-1022.
School—7120 S. Calumet, 60619. Tel: 773-224-3811; Fax: 773-224-3810.
Lay Teachers 25; Students 376.
Catechesis/Religious Programs—Students 35.

44—ST. CONSTANCE, Revs. Thomas R. Rzepiela; Martin R. Borowczyk, Pastor Emeritus; Andrew Izyk; Jason Torba (Poland); Sr. Marie Ellen Sullivan, Pastoral Assoc.; Deacons Ted Lisowski; George Gniech; James Schiltz.
Res., 5843 W. Strong St., 60630. Tel: 773-545-8581; Fax: 773-545-0227.
School—5841 W. Strong St., 60630. Tel: 773-283-2311.
Lay Teachers 17; Students 269.

45—ST. CORNELIUS, Revs. Edwin D. Pacocha; Thomas Refermat; Deacons Carl D. Olson; Edward Condon. In res., Rev. Robert S. Brodfuehrer, (Retired).
Res., 5205 N. Lieb Ave., 60630. Tel: 773-283-5222; Fax: 773-283-8484.
School—Tel: 773-283-2192; Fax: 773-283-1377.
Lay Teachers 21; Students 350.
Catechesis/Religious Programs—Students 100.

46—CORPUS CHRISTI, Rev. Christian Reuter, O.F.M.
Res., Corpus Christi Friary, 4920 King Dr., 60615-2306. Tel: 773-285-7720; Fax: 773-285-2572.
Catechesis/Religious Programs—Students 20.

47—ST. DANIEL THE PROPHET, Revs. Lawrence J. Malcolm; John M. Cassidy; Peter Gacki, O.F.M.Cap.; Charles F. Kelly, Pastor Emeritus; Sr. Eileen Tierney, C.N.D., Pastoral Assoc.; Deacons Albert Malec; Chester Golab.
Res., 5330 S. Nashville Ave., 60638. Tel: 773-586-1223; Fax: 773-586-1238.
School—5337 S. Natoma Ave., 60638.
Lay Teachers 32; Students 681.

48—ST. DENIS, Revs. Lawrence R. Dowling; Natale Ezama; Sr. Norine Burns, O.P., Pastoral Assoc.; Deacons Thomas Ewers; Thomas Solon; Mr. Richard Conrad, D.R.E.
Res., 8301 S. St. Louis Ave., 60652. Tel: 773-434-3313; Fax: 773-776-3922.
School—8332 S. St. Louis Ave., 60652. Tel: 773-925-8515. Sr. Elizabeth Lynch, O.P., Prin.
Sisters 2; Lay Teachers 14; Students 270.
Catechesis/Religious Programs—Students 160.

49—ST. DOROTHY, Rev. James J. Martin.
Res., 450 E. 78th St., 60619. Tel: 773-651-7000; Fax: 773-651-0969.
School—7740 S. Eberhart Ave., 60619. Tel: 773-783-0555; Fax: 773-783-3736.
Sisters of the Presentation of the Blessed Virgin Mary 1; Lay Teachers 15; Students 308.
Catechesis/Religious Programs—Students 46.

50—ST. EDWARD, Revs. John M. Murphy; John J. Donohue, Pastor Emeritus; Edward A. Carlson. In res., Rev. Joseph C. Taylor, (Retired).
Res., 4350 W. Sunnyside Ave., 60630-4147. Tel: 773-545-6496; Fax: 773-545-1136.
School—4343 W. Sunnyside Ave., 60630-4147. Tel: 773-736-9133; Fax: 773-736-9280.
Dominican Sisters (Springfield, IL) 7; Lay Teachers 22; Students 404.
Catechesis/Religious Programs—Students 162.

51—ST. ELIZABETH, Revs. Richard Andrus, S.V.D.; George Kintiba, S.V.D.; Bros. Thomas Joseph, S.V.D.; Gary Burr, S.V.D.
Res., 50 E. 41st St., 60653. Tel: 773-268-1518; Fax: 773-373-8632.
School—4052 S. Wabash, 60653. Tel: 773-548-4100; Fax: 773-548-8641.
Sisters 7; Lay Teachers 18; Students 435.

52—EPIPHANY, Revs. Peter B. McQuinn; John P. Enright, Pastor Emeritus. In res., Rev. Msgr. John M. Hayes, Pastor Emeritus.
Res., 2524 S. Keeler Ave., 60623. Tel: 773-521-1112; Fax: 773-521-4394.
School—4225 W. 25th St., 60623. Tel: 773-762-1542. Mrs. Francesca McDonald, Prin.
Sisters 3; Lay Teachers 13; Students 170.
Catechesis/Religious Programs—Sr. Berta Lopez, M.H.S.P.X., D.R.E.
Students 720.

53—ST. ETHELREDA, Rev. James F. Nallen.
Res., 8754 S. Paulina St., 60620. Tel: 773-238-6118; Fax: 773-238-6059.
School—8734 S. Paulina St., 60620. Tel: 773-238-1757; Fax: 773-238-6059.
Lay Teachers 15; Students 263.

54—ST. EUGENE, Revs. James J. O'Brien; Francis W. Shaunessy, Pastor Emeritus; Philip J. Grib, S.J.; William J. Costello; Deacons Gerard Kwasegroch; Edward O'Leary.
Res., 7958 W. Foster Ave., 60656-1698. Tel: 773-775-6659; Fax: 773-775-2832.
School—7930 W. Foster Ave., 60656. Tel: 773-763-2235; Fax: 773-763-2775.
Sisters of Charity B.V.M. 1; Lay Teachers 26; Students 597.

55—ST. FELICITAS, Revs. John T. Boyle; Thomas S. Boyle, Pastor Emeritus; Deacon James Hubbard. In res., Rev. Casimir Eke, C.S.Sp.
Res., 1526 E. 84th St., 60619. Tel: 773-734-2300; Fax: 773-731-5381.
School—1501 E. 83rd Pl., 60652. Tel: 773-721-0858; Fax: 773-731-0142.
Lay Teachers 13; Students 200.
Catechesis/Religious Programs—Students 40.

56—ST. FERDINAND, Revs. David J. Cortesi; Maxim Lasrado, O.C.D.; Walter Juszczak, C.Ss.R.; Walter J. Takuski; William M. Holbrook; Mr. Daniel P. Costigan, Pastoral Assoc.; Deacons Irwin Hotcaveg; Ron Weiner. In res., Revs. Joseph Kromenaker; Joseph Varkey.
Res., 5900 W. Barry Ave., 60634. Tel: 773-622-5900; Fax: 773-622-5903.
School—3131 N. Mason Ave., 60634. Tel: 773-622-3022; Fax: 773-622-2807. Mr. Paul T. Busceni, Prin.
Lay Teachers 33; Students 540.
Catechesis/Religious Programs—Students 123.

57—ST. FIDELIS, Sr. Leonette Kaluzny, S.Sp.S., Pastoral Coord.; Rev. Francis A. Cimarrusti; Deacon Jose Alvarez.
Res., 1406 N. Washtenaw Ave., 60622. Tel: 773-486-8700; Fax: 773-486-8944.

58—Five Holy Martyrs, Revs. Thomas J. Paprocki, Admin.; Edmund J. Siedlecki, Pastor Emeritus; Deacon Richard Wieczorek.
Res., 2905 W. Pope John Paul II Dr., 60632. Tel: 773-254-3636; Fax: 773-254-3609.
School—Pope John Paul II School, Five Holy Martyrs Campus, 4325 S. Richmond St., 60632. Tel: 773-523-6161; Fax: 773-254-9194.
Sisters 4; Lay Teachers 26; Students 605.
Catechesis/Religious Programs—Students 199.

59—St. Florian, Rev. James A. Mezydlo.
Res., 13145 S. Houston Ave., 60633. Tel: 773-646-4877; Fax: 773-646-5965.
School—Tel: 773-646-2868; Fax: 773-646-2891.
Lay Teachers 12; Students 144.

60—St. Francis of Assisi (Hispanic), Rev. Donald J. Nevins; Deacons Zeferino Ochoa; Manuel Rodriguez; Arturo Velasco.
Res., 813 W. Roosevelt Rd., 60608. Tel: 312-226-7575; Fax: 312-226-6283.
Catechesis/Religious Programs—Students 340.

61—St. Francis of Assisi/Our Lady of the Angels, Rev. Lawrence Choate, O.S.M., Admin.; Deacons Salvador Sanchez; Sabino Sanchez.
Res., 932 N. Kostner, 60651. Tel: 773-235-3132; Fax: 773-486-7726.
School—3814 W. Iowa St., 60651.
Catechesis/Religious Programs—4418 W. Walton, 60651.
Students 150.

62—St. Francis Borgia, Revs. Daniel G. Mayall; Robert S. Brodfuehrer, Pastor Emeritus; Joseph T. Noonan; Deacons Robert Cnota; Casimir Fronczek; Ralph Hinch; Charles Huber; Emil L. Melkovitz. In res., Revs. Joseph A. Mulcrone; Martin R. Borowczyk, (Retired).
Res., 8033 W. Addison St., 60634. Tel: 773-625-1118; Fax: 773-625-1110.
School—Tel: 773-589-1000.
Lay Teachers 22; Students 520.
Catechesis/Religious Programs—Students 200.
Convent—3521 N. Panama St., 60634. Tel: 773-625-1705.

63—St. Francis de Sales, Revs. Arturo Perez Rodriguez, Admin.; Alberto Piedrahita; Jozef Timmers, O.F.M.Capuchin; Deacon Joseph Pastirik, (Retired). In res., Revs. James P. Keating, Pastor Emeritus; Ildephonse Skorup, O.F.M.
Res., 10201 S. Ewing Ave., 60617. Tel: 773-734-1383; Fax: 773-734-3022.
Catechesis/Religious Programs—Students 350.

64—St. Gabriel, Rev. John P. McNalis.
Res., 4522 S. Wallace St., 60609. Tel: 773-268-9595.
Church—45th St. and Lowe Ave., 60609.
School—4500 S. Wallace St., 60609. Tel: 773-268-6636; Fax: 773-268-2501.
Lay Teachers 14; Students 263.
Catechesis/Religious Programs—Students 80.

65—St. Gall, Revs. John W. Dearhammer; Raul Martinez (Mexico); Deacons Michael Slajchert; Albert Herrera; John Bumbul.
Res., 5511 S. Sawyer Ave., 60629. Tel: 773-737-3113; Fax: 773-737-0272.
School—5515 S. Sawyer Ave., 60629. Tel: 773-737-3454.
Lay Teachers 15; Students 281.
Catechesis/Religious Programs—Students 504.

66—St. Gelasius, Rev. Michael Mulhall, O.Carm.; Deacon James Morgan. In res., Revs. Martin Curtis, O.Carm.; John Benedict, O.Carm.
Res., 6415 S. Woodlawn Ave., 60637. Tel: 773-363-6500; Fax: 773-363-3279.
School—Lay Teachers 10; Students 237.

67—St. Genevieve, Revs. Leoncio S. Santiago; Thomas F. Maher, Pastor Emeritus; Rev. Msgr. Thomas J. Mohan, Pastor Emeritus; Rev. Flavio V. Gonzalez; Sr. Jean Michael Rafferty, S.P., Pastoral Assoc.; Deacon Benito Centeno.
Res., 4835 W. Altgeld St., 60639. Tel: 773-237-3011; Fax: 773-237-3043.
School—4854 W. Montana St., 60639. Tel: 773-237-7131; Fax: 773-237-7265.
Lay Teachers 17; Students 297.
Catechesis/Religious Programs—Tel: 773-637-6086; Fax: 773-237-3043.
Students 326.

68—St. George (Slovenian), Revs. David Zywiec, O.F.M.Cap., Admin.; Jozef Timmers, O.F.M.Capuchin; Alberto Piedrahita. In res., Rev. Kenneth Stewart, O.F.M.Cap.
Res., 9546 S. Ewing Ave., 60617. Tel: 773-734-0554.

69—St. Gertrude, Revs. William G. Kenneally; John R. Lynch; Mr. Peter Buttitta, Pastoral Assoc.
Res., 1420 W. Granville Ave., 60660. Tel: 773-764-3621; Fax: 773-761-4164.
School—Northside Catholic Academy, 6216 N. Glenwood Ave., 60660. Tel: 773-743-6277; Fax: 773-743-6174.
Sisters 1; Lay Teachers 17; Students 300.
Catechesis/Religious Programs—Students 65.

70—Good Shepherd, Rev. Donald J. Lund.
Res., 2719 S. Kolin Ave., 60623. Tel: 773-762-2322.
School—2733 S. Kolin Ave., 60623.
Lay Teachers 11; Students 200.

71—St. Gregory, Revs. Bartholomew S. Winters; Thomas Varughese Vattaparambil (India); Donatus Chukwu; Sr. Barbara Quinn, S.N.D.deN., Pastoral Assoc.
Res., 1634 W. Gregory St., 60640. Tel: 773-561-3546; Fax: 773-728-3827.
School—Northside Catholic Academy, Tel: 773-907-2094; Fax: 773-907-2121.
Lay Teachers 10; Students 107.
High School—1677 W. Bryn Mawr Ave., 60660. Tel: 773-907-2100; Fax: 773-907-2120.
Lay Teachers 19; Students 288.
Catechesis/Religious Programs—Students 100.

72—St. Hedwig, Revs. Gary Hogan, C.R.; Casimir V. Polinski, C.R.; In res., Revs. Walter Wilczek, C.R.; Eugene Szarek, C.R.; Deacons Gilberto Cintron; Salomon Villegas; Agapito Lopez.
Res., 2226 N. Hoyne Ave., 60647. Tel: 773-486-1660; Fax: 773-486-1684.
Catechesis/Religious Programs—Students 80.

73—St. Helen, Rev. Bronislaus Chmiel; Deacon Daniel Sutton.
Res., 2315 W. Augusta Blvd., 60622. Tel: 773-235-3575; Fax: 773-235-3810.
School—2347 W. Augusta Blvd., 60622. Tel: 773-486-1055; Fax: 773-486-837.
Lay Teachers 16; Students 304.
Catechesis/Religious Programs—Fax: 773-235-3810.
Students 301.

74—St. Helena, Revs. Thomas J. Kaminski; Augustine Ogumere, C.S.S.P.; Deacon Daniel Sutton.
Res., 10121 S. Parnell Ave., 60628. Tel: 773-779-2243; Fax: 773-779-2749.
School—10115 S. Parnell Ave., 60628. Tel: 773-238-5432; Fax: 773-238-6026.
Lay Teachers 11; Students 242.

75—St. Henry, Revs. Edward A. Harasim; Simon Braganza (India); Deacon Frank G. Duffy.
Res., 6335 N. Hoyne Ave., 60659. Tel: 773-764-7413; Fax: 773-764-5994.
School—Northside Catholic Academy, 6325 N. Hoyne, 60659. Tel: 773-274-5227; Fax: 773-274-2157.
Convent—1956 W. Devon, 60660.

76—St. Hilary, Revs. Robert G. Darow; Matt A. Bednarz, Pastor Emeritus; Deacons Edmund Tryba; Donald Wehling. In res., Rev. Daniel J. Cassidy.
Res., 5600 N. Fairfield Ave., 60659. Tel: 773-561-3474; Fax: 773-561-1129.
School—5614 N. Fairfield Ave., 60659. Tel: 773-561-5885; Fax: 773-561-6409.
Lay Teachers 17; Students 405.
Catechesis/Religious Programs—Students 100.

77—Holy Angels, Revs. John W. Calicott; Robert J. Miller; Deacons Jasper Roy; Dexter Watson. In res., Rev. David Kusi.
Res., 607 E. Oakwood Blvd., 60653. Tel: 773-624-5375.
School—545 E. Oakwood Blvd., 60653.
Priests 1; Sisters 18; Lay Teachers 30; Students 1,000.

78—Holy Cross/Immaculate Heart of Mary, Revs. Bruce Wellems, C.M.F.; Thomas Joyce, C.M.F.; George Ruffolo, C.M.F. In res., Revs. Miguel Estrada, C.M.F.; Wayne Schimmelman, C.M.F.; Theodore Cirone, C.M.F.
Res., 4557 S. Wood St., 60609. Tel: 773-376-3900; Fax: 773-376-8929.
Catechesis/Religious Programs—Students 800.

79—Holy Family, Sr. Marion Murphy, B.V.M., Pastoral Coord.; Rev. Ronald Stua, C.M.F.; Deacon Rudolph Kotleba.
Res., 1019 S. May St., 60607. Tel: 312-492-8442; Fax: 312-492-8430.
Catechesis/Religious Programs—Students 20.

80—Holy Innocents, Revs. Richard J. Klajbor; Antoni Bradlo, C.Ss.R.; Sr. Lauren Lapinski, C.S.S.F., Pastoral Assoc.
Res., 743 N. Armour St., 60622. Tel: 312-666-3675; Fax: 312-666-0714.
School—1444-56 W. Superior St., 60622. Tel: 312-243-9887; Fax: 312-243-4524.
Felician Sisters (Chicago, IL) 3; Lay Teachers 11; Students 200.
Catechesis/Religious Programs—Students 115.

81—Holy Name of Mary, Revs. James F. Flynn; Anthony J. Vader, Pastor Emeritus; Deacon Richard Boyd.
Res., 11159 S. Loomis St., 60643. Tel: 773-238-6800; Fax: 773-445-1248.
School—1421 W. 112th St., 60643. Tel: 773-445-3277.
Oblate Sisters of Providence 4; Lay Teachers 9; Students 217.
Mission—Chicago, Cook Co., Sacred Heart, 11652 S. Church St., 60643. Tel: 773-233-3955.
Catechesis/Religious Programs—Students 55.

82—Holy Rosary, Rev. Richard C. Creagh. In res., Rev. Ronald L. Kondziolka.
Res., 351 E. 113th St., 60628. Tel: 773-568-4455; Fax: 773-568-4456.
Catechesis/Religious Programs—Students 60.

83—Holy Rosary, Most Rev. Lawrence Sabatini, C.S.; Deacon Jorge Roso. In res., Rev. William Woestman, O.M.I.
Res., 612 N. Western Ave., 60612. Tel: 773-278-4820; Fax: 773-278-3770.
Catechesis/Religious Programs—Students 5.

84—Holy Trinity (Croatian), Revs. Charles W. Dahm, O.P., Admin.; Harvey Blaschko, O.P.
Res., 1850 S. Throop St., 60608. Tel: 312-226-2736.
Catechesis/Religious Programs—1840 S. Throop St., 60608. Sr. Maria del Rayo Cuaya-Castillo, S.H., D.R.E.
Priests 1.

85—Holy Trinity Mission (Polish), Revs. Wladyslaw Gowin, S.Ch.; Piotr Nowacki, S.Chr.; Andrzej Salapata, S.Ch. In res., Rev. Jozef Furman, S.Ch.
Res., 1118 N. Noble St., 60622-4015. Tel: 773-489-4140; Fax: 773-489-5918.
Catechesis/Religious Programs—Students 758.

86—St. Hyacinth, Revs. Michael Osuch, C.R.; Francis Rog, C.R.; Andrzej Lewandowski, C.R.; Chester Mitoraj, C.R.; Stanislaw Suwala, C.R.; Deacons Fred Girjatowicz; Stefan Stanczak. In res., Rev. Wieslaw Janowski, C.R.; Bro. Thomas Iwicki, C.R.
Res., 3636 W. Wolfram St., 60618. Tel: 773-342-3636; Fax: 773-342-3638.
School—3640 W. Wolfram St., 60618.
Sisters of the Holy Family of Nazareth (Des Plaines) 3; Lay Teachers 15; Students 269.
Catechesis/Religious Programs—Students 12.

87—St. Ignatius, Most Rev. Jerome E. Listecki, Auxiliary Bishop of Chicago; Rev. John Ross Sima, S.J.
Res., 6559 N. Glenwood Ave., 60626. Tel: 773-764-5936; Fax: 773-764-4360.

88—Immaculate Conception, Revs. Michael J. Hoolahan, C.P.; Eric Meyer, C.P.; Peter Berendt, C.P.
Res., 7211 W. Talcott Ave., 60631. Tel: 773-775-3833; Fax: 773-631-1024.
School—7263 W. Talcott Ave., 60631. Tel: 773-775-0545; Fax: 773-775-3822.
Lay Teachers 37; Students 615.
Catechesis/Religious Programs—Students 94.

89—Immaculate Conception (Lithuanian), Revs. Thomas R. Koys; Edward J. Maza; Deacon Vincente Estrada. In res., Rev. Jaunius Kelpsas (Lithuania).
Res., 2745 W. 44th St., 60632-1999. Tel: 773-523-1402; Fax: 773-523-8465.
School—Consolidated with Five Holy Martyrs to form Pope John Paul II School. See Five Holy Martyrs, Chicago for details.
Catechesis/Religious Programs—Students 150.

90—Immaculate Conception of the Blessed Virgin Mary, Rev. Patrick J. Lee. In res., Rev. Lawrence J. McBrady.
Res., 1431 N. North Park Ave., 60610. Tel: 312-944-1230; Fax: 312-944-0673.
Catechesis/Religious Programs—Students 91.

91—Immaculate Conception of the Blessed Virgin Mary, Rev. Michael P. Enright. In res., Rev. Anthony O. Adebusuyui.
Parish Office and Rectory: 2944 E. 88th St., 60627. Tel: 773-768-2100; Fax: 773-221-9121.
Church—88th & Commercial Ave., 60617.
Catechesis/Religious Programs—Tel: 773-221-1423.
Students 330.

92—Immaculate Heart of Mary, Revs. James F. Blazek; Norbert J. Zawistanowicz, Pastor Emeritus; Joji Thanugundla; Deacons John Kearney; Kenneth Jenney, Jr.; David Reyes. In res., Revs. Robert Onofrey, C.PP.S.; Phillip Thodukayil.
Res., 3817 N. Christiana Ave., 60618. Tel: 773-478-1157; Fax: 773-478-6044.
School—3820 N. Spaulding Ave., 60618. Tel: 773-478-6554.
Lay Teachers 15; Students 350.
Catechesis/Religious Programs—Students 100.

93—Immaculate Heart of Mary Vicariate. Closed. See Holy Cross, Wood St.

94—Saint Ita, Revs. Laurence F. Maddock; Alberto Rojas.
Res., 1220 West Catalpa Ave., 60640. Tel: 773-561-5343; Fax: 773-561-5609.
School—Northside Catholic Academy, 5525 N. Magnolia Ave., 60640. Tel: 773-271-2008; Fax: 773-271-3101.
Sisters 2; Lay Teachers 11; Students 230.

95—St. James, Rev. Thomas M. Frayne. In res., Rev. Jamels James (India).
Res., 2942 S. Wabash Ave., 60616. Tel: 312-842-1919; Fax: 312-842-3612.
School—2920 S. Wabash Ave., 60616.
Sisters 2; Lay Teachers 12; Students 270.

96—St. James, Revs. Wojciech Kwiecien; John L. Wodniak, Pastor Emeritus; Piotr Wasek (Extern-Poland). In res., Rev. Joseph Lee.
Res., 5730 W. Fullerton Ave., 60639. Tel: 773-237-1474; Fax: 773-237-1546.
School—2456 N. Mango Ave., 60639. Tel: 773-237-0549; Fax: 773-237-0563.
Lay Teachers 12; Students 204.
Catechesis/Religious Programs—Students 385.

97—St. Jane de Chantal, Rev. Thomas E. Srenn; Sr. Jan Brynda, O.P., Pastoral Assoc.; Deacon Ron Morowczynski.
Res., 5252 S. Austin Ave., 60638. Tel: 773-767-2411; Fax: 773-767-2769.
School—5201 S. McVicker Ave., 60638.
Lay Teachers 13; Students 276.

98—St. Jerome, Revs. Thomas J. Bradley; Lys Floval, C.S.Sp.; Deacons Fritz Jean-Pierre; Sigifredo Hernandez; Victor LaCoursiere; Robert Murphy; Raymond Ward. In res., Revs. William P. Grogan; Harold A. Bonin.
Res., 1709 W. Lunt Ave., 60626. Tel: 773-262-3170; Fax: 773-262-2834.

99—St. Jerome (Croatian), Revs. Jozo Grubisic, O.F.M.; Jozo Grbes, O.F.M.
Res., 2823 S. Princeton Ave., 60616. Tel: 312-842-1871; Fax: 312-842-6427.
School—2813 S. Princeton Ave., 60616.
Sisters Adorers of the Blood of Christ 2; Lay Teachers 10; Students 157.

100—St. Joachim, Rev. John M. Collins.
Res., 700 E. 91st St., 60619. Tel: 773-488-4488; Fax: 773-994-8945.

101—St. John de la Salle, Revs. Oliver Jennings; Bernard E. Okafor (Nigeria).
Res., 10205 King Dr., 60628. Tel: 773-785-2022.
School—Tel: 773-785-2331. Sharon Dale, Prin.
Lay Teachers 10; Students 150.

102—St. John Berchmans, Revs. Eugene W. Gratkowski; William B. Gubbins, Pastor Emeritus; Sergio Romo; Deacons Virgilio Bonifazi; Jorge Cabrera; Guillermo Mendizabal; Marcial Herrera.
Res., 2517 W. Logan Blvd., 60647. Tel: 773-486-4300.
School—2509 W. Logan Blvd., 60647. Tel: 773-486-1334; Fax: 773-486-1782.
Dominican Sisters (St. Catherine, KY) 1; Lay Teachers 34; Students 598.

103—St. John Bosco, Revs. William Bucciferro, S.D.B.; Serges Lamaute, S.D.B.; Gonzalo Tejedor, S.D.B.; Juan Bosco Jiminez, S.D.B.; Deacons Pedro Soto; Ronald Swiatek; Ron Weiner. In res., Rev. Richard Sadowski, S.D.B.; Bro. Alvaro Guerrero, S.D.B.
Res., 2250 N. McVicker Ave., 60639. Tel: 773-622-4620; Fax: 773-622-5040.

104—St. John Cantius (Polish), Revs. C. Frank Phillips, C.R.; Edwin Karlowicz, C.R.; Burns K. Seeley (Puerto Rico); Edmund Jastrzebski (Poland).
Res., 825 N. Carpenter St., 60622. Tel: 312-243-7373; Fax: 312-666-4653.
Catechesis/Religious Programs—Students 40.

105—St. John Fisher, Revs. Thomas J. Purtell; Frank Latzko; Daniel F. Costello; Gerald J. Van Overbeck, O.S.A.; Deacons Sidney Mench; Raymond Reilly; Clayton Kort; Martin Mongan.
Res., 10234 S. Washtenaw Ave., 60655. Tel: 773-445-6565; Fax: 773-445-1644.
School—10200 S. Washtenaw Ave., 60642. Tel: 773-445-4737.
Sisters of St. Joseph (LaGrange, IL) 2; Lay Teachers 47; Students 800.
Catechesis/Religious Programs—Students 130.

106—St. Josaphat, Rev. Dominic J. Grassi.
Res., 2311 N. Southport Ave., 60614. Tel: 773-327-8955; Fax: 773-327-2047.
School—2245 N. Southport Ave., 60614. Tel: 773-549-0909; Fax: 773-327-2047.
Lay Teachers 15; Students 245.
Catechesis/Religious Programs—Students 50.

107—St. Joseph, Rev. Sebastian C. Lewis, O.S.B.
Res., 1107 N. Orleans St., 60610. Tel: 312-787-7174; Fax: 312-787-9825.
School—Tel: 312-573-3940.
Lay Teachers 9; Students 114.
Catechesis/Religious Programs—Students 15.

108—St. Joseph, Rev. Eugene Michel, O.F.M.
Res., 4821 S. Hermitage Ave., 60609. Tel: 773-254-2366; Fax: 773-254-2640.
School—4831 S. Hermitage, 60609. Tel: 773-927-8312; Fax: 773-523-7340.
Lay Teachers 11; Students 180.
Convent—4818 S. Paulina St., 60609. Tel: 773-927-5792; Fax: 773-523-7718.
Shrine—Shrine of St. Joseph, Tel: 773-254-2366; Fax: 773-254-2640.
Catechesis/Religious Programs—Students 500.

109—St. Juliana, Revs. Philip J. Dressler; Donald J. Ahearn, Pastor Emeritus; Roger J. Caplis; Ms. Pam Francisco, Pastoral Assoc.; Deacons Michael Finnegan; Robert Ryan; Edward Dolan; Louis Wojtowicz. In res., Rev. Thomas O'Halloran.
Res., 7142 N. Osceola Ave., 60631. Tel: 773-631-4127; Fax: 773-631-4150.
School—7400 W. Touhy, 60648. Tel: 773-631-2256.
Lay Teachers 35; Religious 2; Students 714.
Catechesis/Religious Programs—Students 160.

110—St. Kevin, Rev. Alfredo Gundrum, O.F.M.Cap. In res., Rev. David Zywiec, O.F.M.Cap.
Res., 10509 S. Torrence Ave., 60617. Tel: 773-721-2563; Fax: 773-721-2208.

111—St. Kilian, Revs. William E. Vanecko; John W. Shirey, (Retired).
Res., 8725 S. May St., 60620. Tel: 773-651-4000; Fax: 773-651-5876.

112—St. Ladislaus, Revs. Stephen F. Kanonik; William J. Lisowski, Pastor Emeritus; Peter Kreis (Poland); Andrezej Bartos (Poland); Kazimierz Rzonca (Poland). In res., Rev. John Hergenrother.
Res., 5345 W. Roscoe St., 60641. Tel: 773-725-2300; Fax: 773-725-6042.
School—3330 N. Lockwood Ave., 60641. Tel: 773-545-5600; Fax: 773-545-5676.
Sisters of the Holy Family of Nazareth (Des Plaines, IL) 3; Lay Teachers 12; Students 250.
Catechesis/Religious Programs—Tel: 773-545-1811; Fax: 773-545-4340.
Students 165.

113—St. Laurence, Rev. Gerald K. O'Reilly; Deacons Willie Cooper; Roy Lilly.
Res., 7140 S. Dorchester Ave., 60619. Tel: 773-493-1118.

114—St. Leo the Great, Rev. Michael J. Furlan; Deacons Dorsey Chappell; Mervin O. Johnson. In res., Rev. Paschal Atomori (Nigeria).
Res., 7747 S. Emerald Ave., 60620. Tel: 773-846-6146; Fax: 773-846-0049.
School—7746 S. Emerald Ave., 60620. Tel: 773-483-2335; Fax: 773-483-7599.
Lay Teachers 11; Students 230.

115—Santa Lucia-Santa Maria Incoronata, Rev. Nicholas A. Marro, C.S.
Res., 3022 S. Wells St., 60616. Tel: 312-842-6115; Fax: 312-842-0103.
School—3017 S. Wells St., 60616. Geraldine Maratea, Prin.
Lay Teachers 11; Students 200.

116—St. Malachy, Rev. Patrick T. Casey, O.M.I., Admin.
Res., 2248 W. Washington Blvd., 60612. Tel: 312-733-1068.
School—2252 W. Washington Blvd., 60612.
Sisters 6; Brothers 2; Lay Teachers 10; Students 200.

117—St. Margaret of Scotland, Rev. Daniel J. Mallette.
Res., 9837 S. Throop St., 60643. Tel: 773-779-5151; Fax: 773-779-6198.
School—9833 S. Throop St., 60643. Tel: 773-238-1088; Fax: 773-238-1033.
School Sisters of Notre Dame 3; Lay Teachers 15; Students 320.
Shelter—Maryville/St. Margaret of Scotland.
Students 35.

118—St. Margaret Mary, Revs. Mark B. Sorvillo; William T. Corcoran; Ha Nam Thanh Dao. In res., Rev. Oliver Nwachukwu.
Res., 2324 W. Chase Ave., 60645. Tel: 773-764-0615; Fax: 773-764-0641.
School—Tel: 773-764-0641; Fax: 773-764-1095.
Lay Teachers 27; Students 300.
Catechesis/Religious Programs—Students 65.

119—Santa Maria Addolorata, Revs. Louis Gandolfi, C.S.; Alex Peloso, C.S., Pastor Emeritus; Deacons Arthur DeLuna; Luis Perez.
Res., 528 N. Ada St., 60622. Tel: 312-421-3122.
School—1337 W. Ohio St., 60622. Tel: 312-421-5482.
Joliet Franciscan 1; Sisters of the Holy Family of Nazareth 1; Lay Teachers 10; Students 219.

120—St. Mark, Rev. Michael J. Shanahan; Deacons Jorge Gutierrez; Ignacio Ortega; Antonio Villalobos; Mel Maldonado; Antonio Navarro. In res., Most Rev. Enrique Hernandez (Puerto Rico).
Res., 1048 N. Campbell Ave., 60622. Tel: 773-342-1516; Fax: 773-342-1372.
School—2510 W. Cortez St., 60622. Tel: 773-486-0430.
Sisters of Providence 3; Lay Teachers 9; Students 270.

121—St. Martin De Porres, Revs. Julien Cormier, M.Afr.; George Salles, M.Afr.; Deacon Anthony Llorens.
Res., 5112 W. Washington Blvd., 60644. Tel: 773-287-0206; Fax: 773-261-2344.
School—5072 W. Jackson Blvd., 60661. Tel: 773-261-6061; Fax: 773-626-0780.
Lay Teachers 18; Students 320.

122—Old St. Mary, Revs. James W. Donovan, C.S.P.; Charles J. Brunick, C.S.P.; Robert J. O'Donnell, C.S.P. In res., Revs. James O'Gara, C.S.P.; Joseph J. Ciccone, C.S.P.; Deacon Timothy Donovan.
Res., 21 E. Van Buren St., 60605. Tel: 312-922-3444; Fax: 312-922-3447.
Catechesis/Religious Programs—Students 23.

123—St. Mary of the Angels, Revs. Hilary F. Mahaney; John P. Debicki. In res., Rev. Charles M. Ferrer.
Res., 1850 N. Hermitage Ave., 60622. Tel: 773-278-2644; Fax: 773-278-8904.
School—1810 N. Hermitage Ave., 60622. Tel: 773-486-0119.
Sisters of the Resurrection (Chicago, IL) 1; Lay Teachers 12; Students 211.
Catechesis/Religious Programs—Students 225.

124—St. Mary of the Assumption, Rev. John L. Harvey, Admin.; Deacon John Amberg.
Res., 310 E. 137th St., 60827. Tel: 773-568-1611; Fax: 773-568-6268.
School—Our Lady of the Gardens, 13300 S. Langley Ave., 60627. Tel: 773-568-4099; Fax: 773-568-4718.
Daughters of Charity 311.

125—St. Mary of the Lake, Most Rev. Edwin M. Conway, Episcopal Vicar & Resident; Rev. James A. Colleran; Deacons Paul Spalla; John Navolio; Ubaldo Munoz, Pastoral Assoc. In res., Revs. Daniel J. Collins; Robert Grodnicki, O.S.A.
Res., 4200 N. Sheridan Rd., 60613. Tel: 773-472-3711; Fax: 773-327-2899.
School—1026 W. Buena Ave., 60613. Tel: 773-281-0018; Fax: 773-281-0112.
Lay Teachers 11; Students 248.
Catechesis/Religious Programs—Students 140.

126—St. Mary Magdalene, Rev. John L. Marini, C.S.Sp.
Res., 8426 S. Marquette Ave., 60617. Tel: 773-768-1700; Fax: 773-734-8518.
Catechesis/Religious Programs—Students 24.

127—St. Mary of Perpetual Help, Rev. Donald R. Craig.
Res., 1039 W. 32nd St., 60608. Tel: 773-927-6646; Fax: 773-523-4565.
School—Participant in Bridgeport Catholic Academy. See separate listing under Consolidated Elementary Schools in the Institutions section.
Catechesis/Religious Programs—Students 110.

128—St. Mary, Star of the Sea, Revs. Michael J. Adams; Antony Aravindassery (India); Daniel Jarosewic; Deacons Jesse Navarro; Gregory Serratore.
Res., 6435 S. Kilbourn Ave., 60629. Tel: 773-767-1246.
School—6424 S. Kenneth Ave., 60629. Tel: 773-767-6160.
Lay Teachers 30; Students 830.
Catechesis/Religious Programs—Tel: 773-767-7078.
Students 130.

129—St. Mary of the Woods, Revs. Gregory Sakowicz; Leo T. Mahon, Pastor Emeritus; Andrew J. McDonagh, Pastor Emeritus; Deacons William Mages; George Henning. In res., Rev. Thomas F. Maher; Marcia Mahoney, Pastoral Assoc.
Res., 7033 N. Moselle Ave., 60646. Tel: 773-763-0206; Fax: 773-763-4968.
School—Tel: 773-763-7577; Fax: 773-763-4293.
Religious 1; Lay Teachers 34; Students 492.
Catechesis/Religious Programs—Students 154.

130—Maternity of the Blessed Virgin Mary, Revs. Thomas Pelton; Manuel G. Padilla. In res., Rev. Antonio Jorge Tchingui (Africa).
Res., 3647 W. North Ave., 60647. Tel: 773-772-9401; Fax: 773-772-7454.
School—1537 N. Lawndale Ave., 60651. Tel: 773-227-1140; Fax: 773-227-2939.
Sisters of Providence of Saint Mary-of-the-Woods, IN 2; Lay Teachers 17; Students 310.
Catechesis/Religious Programs—Students 390.

131—St. Matthias, Revs. Terence M. Keehan; Thomas J. McHugh, Pastor Emeritus; Deacons John Fay; Andres Pecson; D.J. Shinkle. In res., Rev. Francis A. Cimarrusti.
Res., 2310 W. Ainslie St., 60625. Tel: 773-561-6020; Fax: 773-561-6915.
School—4910 N. Claremont Ave., 60625. Tel: 773-784-0999; Fax: 773-784-3601.
Sisters 7; Lay Teachers 11; Students 290.

132—St. Maurice, Sr. Marie Paryse, S.S.S.F., Pastoral Coord.; Deacon Dismas Fernandez.
Res., 3615 S. Hoyne Ave., 60609. Tel: 773-847-3357; Fax: 773-847-3804.
School—McKinley Park Catholic, 3625 S. Hoyne

Ave., 60609. Tel: 773-847-1244; Fax: 773-847-5399. Students 240.
Catechesis/Religious Programs—Students 90.

133—ST. MICHAEL, Revs. John Schmidt, C.Ss.R.; Kenneth Sedlak, C.Ss.R.; Michael Quinn, C.Ss.R. In res., Revs. Edward Wilhelm, C.Ss.R.; John Paul Andree, C.Ss.R.; John Dowd, C.Ss.R.; Stephen Benden, C.Ss.R.; Walter George, C.Ss.R.; James Nugent, C.Ss.R.; Peter Schavitz, C.Ss.R.; Matthew Kessler, C.Ss.R.; Gregory May, C.Ss.R.
Res., 1633 N. Cleveland Ave., 60614. Tel: 312-642-2498; Fax: 312-642-9283.
Perpetual Help Confraternity Office—Tel: 312-642-9399; Fax: 312-642-9283. Bro. Patrick Considine, C.Ss.R.
Catechesis/Religious Programs—Students 80.

134—ST. MICHAEL ARCHANGEL (Italian), Rev. Vincent Gennardo, C.S.
Res., 2325 W. 24th Pl., 60608. Tel: 773-847-2727; Fax: 773-847-7618.
School—2315 W. 24th Pl., 60608. Tel: 773-847-9070; Fax: 773-847-7618.
Missionary Sisters of St. Charles 3; Lay Teachers 7; Students 173.
Catechesis/Religious Programs—Students 173.

135—ST. MICHAEL, Revs. Thomas R. Franzman; Joseph G. Nowak, Pastor Emeritus; Paul J. Kalchik; Deacon Albin J. Wegner, Jr.
Res., 8237 South Shore Dr., 60617. Tel: 773-734-4921; Fax: 773-734-8723.
School—8231 South Shore Dr., 60617. Tel: 773-221-0212. Sr. Judine Hilbing, O.P., Prin.
Lay Teachers 12; Students 325.
Catechesis/Religious Programs—Students 147.

136—ST. MICHAEL THE ARCHANGEL (Slovak), Revs. John E. Tilford; Alfredo del Toro, M.C.C.J.; Sr. Rosemary Bell, D.S.M.P., Pastoral Assoc.
Res., 4821 S. Damen Ave., 60609. Tel: 773-523-1248; Fax: 773-523-0955.
Catechesis/Religious Programs—Students 380.

137—ST. MONICA, Revs. Michael A. Wulsch; Christopher Ciomek; Prasad Policetti (India); Sr. Kathleen Maloney, O.S.B., Pastoral Assoc.
Office—5136 N. Nottingham Ave., 60656. Tel: 773-763-1661; Fax: 773-763-4917.
Res., 5135 N. Mont Clare Ave., 60656.
School—Tel: 773-631-7880; Fax: 773-631-3266.
Sisters 1; Lay Teachers 22; Students 425.
Catechesis/Religious Programs—Tel: 773-631-7810; Fax: 773-763-4917.
Students 98.

138—NATIVITY OF THE BLESSED VIRGIN MARY, Revs. Michael T. Yakaitis, S.T.D.; Rimantas Gudelis (LIT); John A. Kuzinskas, Pastor Emeritus; Anthony J. Zakarauskas, Pastor Emeritus. In res., Rev. Vito E. Mikolaitis, (Retired).
Res., 6812 S. Washtenaw Ave., 60629. Tel: 773-776-4600; Fax: 773-776-0677.
School—6820 S. Washtenaw Ave., 60629. Tel: 773-476-0571; Fax: 773-476-0065.
Sisters of St. Casimir 2; Lay Teachers 9; Students 230.
Convent—6804 S. Washtenaw Ave., 60629. Tel: 773-476-5135.

139—NATIVITY OF OUR LORD, Rev. James P. Kehoe; Deacon Francis Henry. In res., Rev. Michael Flynn, O.Carm.
Res., 653 W. 37th St., 60609. Tel: 773-927-6263.
School—Participant in Bridgeport Catholic Academy. See separate listing under Consolidated Elementary Schools in the Institutions section.

140—ST. NICHOLAS OF TOLENTINE, Revs. Stanley G. Rataj; Edward J. Brzozowski, Pastor Emeritus; Francis P. Cassidy; Deacons Edwin Hill; Joaquin Verela.
Res., 3721 W. 62nd St., 60629. Tel: 773-735-1121; Fax: 773-735-1135.
School—3743 W. 62nd St., 60629. Tel: 773-735-0772; Fax: 773-735-5414.
Lay Teachers 17; Students 365.
Catechesis/Religious Programs—Tel: 773-284-2635.
Students 170.

141—NOTRE DAME, Rev. Steven M. Lanza. In res., Rev. Robert G. Casey; Deacons Candelario Rodriguez; Joseph Siranovic.
Res., 1335 W. Harrison St., 60607-3318. Tel: 312-243-7400; Fax: 312-243-7614.
Catechesis/Religious Programs—Students 45.

142—OUR LADY OF AGLONA (Latvian), (Independent Mission), Revs. Boleslaus Baginskis, M.I.C.; Victor Civzelis, M.I.C.
Res., 2541 W. Wabansia, 60647. Tel: 773-276-9566.

143—OUR LADY OF FATIMA, Revs. Anthony A. Englert; Pierre J. Barr, Pastor Emeritus; Raymond J. Gerrity, Pastor Emeritus; Deacon Candido Torres.
Res., 2751 W. 38th Pl., 60632. Tel: 773-927-2421.
School—Pope John Paul II School, Our Lady of Fatima Campus, 2744 W. Pershing Rd., 60632.
Lay Teachers 12; Students 200.

144—OUR LADY GATE OF HEAVEN, Rev. Mel Hermanns, O.F.M.Cap.
Res., 2338 E. 99th St., 60617. Tel: 773-375-3059; Fax: 773-375-3091.
School—2330 E. 99th St., 60617. Tel: 773-375-7350. Mr. Charles Carroll, Prin.
Religious 1; Lay Teachers 7; Students 174; Preschool 44.
Catechesis/Religious Programs—Students 40.

145—OUR LADY OF GOOD COUNSEL, Revs. James M. Hyland; Richard J. O'Donnell, Pastor Emeritus; Jaime Sepulchre, O.S.A.
Res., 3528 S. Hermitage Ave., 60609. Tel: 773-523-3917; Fax: 773-247-9285.
School—McKinley Park Catholic. (Merged with St. Maurice & SS. Peter & Paul). 3540 S. Hermitage Ave., 60609. Tel: 773-376-2622; Fax: 773-376-0614.
Lay Teachers 6; Students 136.

146—OUR LADY OF GRACE, Revs. Thomas A. Tivy; Jose Leonardo Gomez; Sr. Florence Norton, S.P., Pastoral Assoc.; Deacons James Kwasigroch; Enrique Alonso; Gregorio Lugo; Carlos Nazario; Ernesto Robles. In res., Rev. Lawrence E. Gorski.
Res., 2455 N. Hamlin Ave., 60647. Tel: 773-772-5900; Fax: 773-276-4469.
School—2446 N. Ridgeway Ave., 60647. Tel: 773-341-0170.
Dominican Sisters (Springfield, IL) 6; Lay Teachers 12; Students 268.
Catechesis/Religious Programs—Students 345.

147—OUR LADY OF GUADALUPE, Revs. James F. Maloney, C.M.F.; Michael Fernandez, C.M.F.; Thomas McGann, C.M.F.; Thomas Moran, C.M.F.; Deacons Margarito Alvarez; Raul Nunez; Juan Valdivia.
Res., 3200 E. 91st, 60617. Tel: 773-768-0793; Fax: 773-768-3245.
School—Tel: 773-768-0999; Fax: 773-768-0529.
Lay Teachers 12; Students 297.
Shrine—National Shrine of St. Jude. (Claretian Missionaries). Tel: 312-236-7782.

148—OUR LADY HELP OF CHRISTIANS, Rev. Kenneth M. Brigham.
Res., 832 N. Leclaire Ave., 60651. Tel: 773-287-0244; Fax: 773-287-1258.
Catechesis/Religious Programs—Students 74.

149—OUR LADY OF LOURDES, Rev. Curtis Lambert; Deacons Roy Henry; John Klemanovic; Miguel Valle. In res., Revs. Carlos Liagas, S.J.; Matei Alex Mung'aho (East Africa); James T. Kaczorowski.
Res., 4640 N. Ashland Ave., 60640. Tel: 773-561-2141; Fax: 773-561-9853.
School—4641 N. Ashland Ave., 60640. Tel: 773-561-9348. Ms. Noel Ferrera, Prin.
Lay Teachers 15; Students 225.
Catechesis/Religious Programs—Students 300.

150—OUR LADY OF LOURDES, Rev. Ramon Dompke, C.SS.R.; Sr. Caritas Wehrman, S.S.N.D., Pastoral Assoc.
Res., 1444 S. Keeler Ave., 60623. Tel: 773-762-5700; Fax: 773-762-5960.
School—Blessed Sacrament/Our Lady of Lourdes, Central Park and Cermak, 60623. Tel: 773-277-8575.
Students 250.
Catechesis/Religious Programs—Students 22.

151—OUR LADY OF MERCY, Rev. Donald J. Headley. Pastoral Assocs.: Ms. Theresita Perez; Mr. Walter Fircowycz; Deacons Manuel R. Del Llano; Roberto Rivas. In res., Revs. Patrick R. Lagges; Patrick Rugen.
Res., 4432 N. Troy St., 60625. Tel: 773-588-2620; Fax: 773-866-1838.
School—4416 N. Troy, 60625. Tel: 773-588-1637; Fax: 773-588-1690. Debbie Sullivan, Prin.
Lay Teachers 21; Students 232.
Catechesis/Religious Programs—Students 580.

152—OUR LADY, MOTHER OF THE CHURCH, Revs. Daniel R. Fallon; Joseph F. Ognibene, Pastor Emeritus; Peter F. Hayes, Pastor Emeritus.
Res., 8747 W. Lawrence Ave., 60656. Tel: 773-625-3369; Fax: 773-625-0226.

153—OUR LADY OF MOUNT CARMEL, Revs. Thomas I. Healy; Joseph Thai Nguyen; Deacon Edmund Gronkiewicz. In res., Rev. Peter Snieg.
Res., 690 W. Belmont Ave., 60657. Tel: 773-525-0453; Fax: 773-525-9438.
School—708 W. Belmont Ave., 60657. Tel: 773-525-8779; Fax: 773-525-7810.
Lay Teachers 19; Students 268.
Catechesis/Religious Programs—Students 83.

154—OUR LADY OF PEACE, Rev. Lawrence M. Duris; Deacon John Hill.
Res., 7851 S. Jeffrey Ave., 60649. Tel: 773-768-0105; Fax: 773-721-3835.
School—Lay Teachers 8; Students 138.

155—OUR LADY OF POMPEII. Closed. For inquiries for parish records contact the Chancery.

156—OUR LADY OF THE SNOWS, Revs. Robert J. Wielosinski; Waclaw Jamroz, S.D.S. In res., Rev. Dennis A. Ziomek.
Res., 4858 S. Leamington Ave., 60638. Tel: 773-582-2266; Fax: 773-582-3363.
School—4810 S. Leamington Ave., 60638. Tel: 773-735-4810; Fax: 773-884-4430.
Lay Teachers 11; Students 200.
Catechesis/Religious Programs—Tel: 773-767-7860.
Students 140.

157—OUR LADY OF SORROWS, BASILICA OF, Rev. Donald M. Siple, O.S.M.; Deacon Joseph Lewis.
Res., 3121 W. Jackson Blvd., 60612. Tel: 773-638-0159; Fax: 773-638-3036.
Catechesis/Religious Programs—Students 17.

158—OUR LADY OF TEPEYAC, Revs. James W. Miller; Mark J. Krylowicz; Deacons Ramon Echeverria; Vincente Limon; Maria Brito-Ramos, Pastoral Assoc.
Res., 2226 S. Whipple St., 60623. Tel: 773-521-8400; Fax: 773-521-4890.
School—2235 S. Albany, 60623. Tel: 773-522-0024; Fax: 773-522-4577.
Lay Teachers 9; Students 180.
High School—2228 S. Whipple St., 60623. Tel: 773-522-0023; Fax: 773-522-0508.
Sisters 5; Lay Teachers 13; Students 290.
Catechesis/Religious Programs—Tel: 773-277-0320.
Students 490.

159—OUR LADY OF VICTORY, Revs. Philip E. Cyscon; Gary J. Lewanski; Eugene R. Winkowski; Deacons Robert Leck; Rudolph Schoewe; Dennis Ranke; Michael Ahern; Mrs. Mary Catherine Meek, D.R.E. In res., Rev. Norbert J. Zawistanowicz, (Retired).
Res., 5212 W. Agatite Ave., 60630. Tel: 773-286-2950; Fax: 773-286-8579.
School—4434 N. Laramie, 60630. Tel: 773-283-2229; Fax: 773-283-0842. Sr. Mary Sarah, O.P., Prin.
Dominican Sisters of St. Celicia 3.
Convent—5244 W. Cullom St., 60641.
Dominican Sisters of St. Cecilia 4.

160—ST. PANCRATIUS, Revs. Andrew P. Wypych; Jose Sequeira Mora.
Res., 4025 S. Sacramento Ave., 60632. Tel: 773-523-5666; Fax: 773-523-5666.
School—2940 W. 40th Pl., 60632.
Franciscan Sisters of Chicago 1; Lay Teachers 8; Students 206.

161—ST. PASCAL, Revs. Gary M. Miller; Thomas S. Campana; Deacons Eugene Dorgan; Thomas Stubstad.
Res., 3935 N. Melvina Ave., 60634. Tel: 773-725-7641; Fax: 773-725-9368.
School—6143 W. Irving Park Rd., 60634. Tel: 773-736-8806; Fax: 773-725-3461.
Lay Teachers 21; Students 409.
Ciezadlo Center—3954 N. Meade Ave., 60634. Tel: 773-545-9453.
Catechesis/Religious Programs—Students 148.

162—ST. PATRICK, Revs. John J. Wall; John C. Cusick. In res., Rev. William B. Gubbins, (Retired).
Res., 700 W. Adams St., 60606. Tel: 312-782-6171.

163—ST. PAUL, Revs. Peter Rodriguez, C.M.F.; Marino Novoa, C.M.F.; Richard J. Todd, C.M.F. In res., Rev. Richard Bartlett, C.M.F.
Res., 2127 W. 22nd Pl., 60608. Tel: 773-847-7622; Fax: 773-847-8687.
School—2114 W. 22nd Pl., 60608. Tel: 773-847-6078.
Sisters 3; Lay Teachers 8; Students 275.
Catechesis/Religious Programs—Students 87.

164—ST. PETER'S, Revs. Thomas Aldworth, O.F.M.; Mario DiCicco, O.F.M. In res., Revs. Barnabas Diekemper, O.F.M.; Andre Schludecker, O.F.M.
Res., St. Peter's Friary, 110 W. Madison St., 60602. Tel: 312-372-5111; Fax: 312-853-2361.
Priests 16; Brothers 6. (For complete listing of residents see Section N - Residences of Priests and Brothers.).

165—ST. PETER CANISIUS, Rev. Robert E. Bridge; Deacon Leopoldo Cervantes. In res., Rev. John T. Hillenbrand.
Res., 5057 W. North Ave., 60639-4565. Tel: 773-637-2075; Fax: 773-889-3929.
Catechesis/Religious Programs—Students 94.

166—SS. PETER AND PAUL, Revs. Edward D. Gleeson, Admin.; Bruno B. Grinis, Pastor Emeritus.
Res., 12433 S. Halsted St., 60628. Tel: 773-785-1200.

167—SS. PETER AND PAUL, Revs. Robert J. Roll; Stephen F. Lesniewski; Michael O'Connor (Extern-England).
Res., 3745 S. Paulina St., 60609. Tel: 773-523-3410; Fax: 773-523-0540.

Convent—1640 W. 38th St., 60608. Tel: 773-523-0916.
Felician Sisters 3; Poor Handmaids of Jesus Christ 2.
Catechesis/Religious Programs—Students 70.

168—ST. PHILIP NERI, Revs. Lawrence M. Duris; Robert J. Gilbert; Deacons Wilmer Hatch; Aaron Pressie. In res., Most Rev. Joseph N. Perry; Rev. William H. Sheridan.
Res., 2132 E. 72nd St., 60649. Tel: 773-363-1700.
School—2110 E. 72nd St., 60649.
Lay Teachers 13; Students 200.

169—ST. PHILOMENA, Revs. Thomas A. Tivy, Admin.; Scott Hebden; Deacons Francisco Ramos; Israel Valentin; Edwin Martinez; Benjamin Diaz.
Res., 1921 N. Kedvale Ave., 60639. Tel: 773-489-1100; Fax: 773-489-1088.
School—4131 W. Cortland Ave., 60639. Tel: 773-235-0120.
Lay Teachers 10; Students 350.
Catechesis/Religious Programs—Tel: 773-342-3462.
Students 351.

170—ST. PIUS V, Revs. Charles W. Dahm, O.P.; Matthias R. Mueller, O.P.
Res., 1914 S. Ashland Ave., 60608. Tel: 312-829-1931; Fax: 312-226-6119.
School—1919 S. Ashland Ave., 60608. Mrs. Nancy Nasko, Prin.
Dominican Sisters 1; Lay Teachers 9; Students 268.
Shrine—Shrine of St. Jude Thaddeus, Tel: 312-226-0020.

171—PRECIOUS BLOOD, Revs. Patrick T. Casey, O.M.I.; Gerald T. McGovern, O.M.I.; Deacon Mario Avila.
Res., 2411 W. Congress Pkwy., 60612. Tel: 312-733-5331; Fax: 312-733-1285.
Catechesis/Religious Programs—Students 210.

172—PRESENTATION, Rev. Thomas P. Walsh.
Res., 734 S. Springfield Ave., 60624. Tel: 773-533-2820; Fax: 773-638-2803.
School—Campus No. Two—Our Lady of the Westside School, Tel: 773-638-6555.
Catechesis/Religious Programs—Students 375.

173—ST. PRISCILLA, Revs. John J. Cunningham; Darrio L. Boscutti; Deacons Robert Odegard; Fred Spitzerri. In res., Rev. Albert P. Judy, O.P.
Res., 6949 W. Addison St., 60634. Tel: 773-545-8840; Fax: 773-545-8919.
School—7011 W. Addison St., 60634. Tel: 773-685-3581.
Lay Teachers 22; Students 409.
Catechesis/Religious Programs—Students 150.

174—ST. PROCOPIUS, Revs. Timothy A. Howe, S.J.; Charles W. Niehaus. In res., Rev. John P. Foley, S.J.
Res., 1641 S. Allport St., 60608. Tel: 312-226-7887; Fax: 312-226-0812.
School—Tel: 312-421-5135; Fax: 312-492-8368.
Lay Teachers 10; Students 243.
Catechesis/Religious Programs—Students 250.

175—PROVIDENCE OF GOD, Rev. Robert R. Perez; Deacon Max Carrizales.
Res., 717 W. 18th St., 60616. Tel: 312-226-2929; Fax: 312-226-3694.
Catechesis/Religious Programs—1814 S. Union, 60616.
Students 75.

176—QUEEN OF ALL SAINTS BASILICA, Revs. Wayne F. Prist; Kenneth J. Baker; George Koeune; Deacons Michael Monnelly; Raymond Ward; William Malloy; Mrs. Charlene Keane, Pastoral Assoc. In res., Revs. Wayne F. Watts; Rodel Peji (Philippines).
Res., 6280 N. Sauganash Ave., 60646. Tel: 773-736-6060; Fax: 773-736-6099.
School—Sisters 3; Lay Teachers 33; Students 792.

177—QUEEN OF ANGELS, Revs. William J. O'Brien; Thomas E. Lamping; Deacons Richard Hankett; Bienvenido Nieves; Donald O'Grady, (Retired). In res., Rev. John M. Griffiths.
Parish Office: 4412 N. Western Ave., 60625. Tel: 773-539-7510; Fax: 773-539-3408.
Res., 2330 W. Sunnyside Ave., 60625.
School—4520 N. Western Ave., 60625. Tel: 773-769-4211; Fax: 773-769-4289.
Lay Teachers 23; Students 363.
Catechesis/Religious Programs—Students 141.

178—QUEEN OF THE UNIVERSE, Rev. Lawrence R. McNally; Sr. Helen Glynn, O.P., Pastoral Assoc.; Deacon Juan Rodgriguez.
Res., 7114 S. Hamlin Ave., 60629. Tel: 773-582-4662; Fax: 773-581-3313.
School—7130 S. Hamlin Ave., 60629. Tel: 773-582-4266; Fax: 773-585-7254.
Lay Teachers 16; Students 282.
Catechesis/Religious Programs—Students 200.

179—ST. RENE GOUPIL, Revs. Thomas R. Kasputis; Peter P. Paurazas, Pastor Emeritus; Deacon Owen Boehm.
Res., 6949 W. 63rd Pl., 60638. Tel: 773-229-8523; Fax: 773-229-1252.
School—6340 S. New England Ave., 60638. Tel: 773-586-4414; Fax: 773-586-3747. Valerio Bellucci, Prin.
Sisters 1; Lay Teachers 13; Students 300.

180—RESURRECTION, Revs. Juan Sanchez-Espinoza; Phillip C. Kiley; Deacons Paul Bovyn; Feliciano Crespo; George Fuller, (Retired); Uriol Rodriguez. In res., Rev. Esquiel Sanchez.
Business Office: 3043 N. Francisco Ave., 60618. Tel: 773-478-9705; Fax: 773-478-1387.
Res., 2840 W. Nelson St., 60618. Tel: 773-478-1441.
School—2845 W. Barry, 60618. Tel: 773-478-9191; Fax: 773-478-9920.
Lay Teachers 9; Students 195.
Catechesis/Religious Programs—Tel: 773-478-8399.
Students 277.

181—ST. RICHARD, Revs. Thomas A. Bernas; Jerome S. Siwek, Pastor Emeritus; Andrzej Bartosz (Poland); Deacon Albert Schroetlin.
Res., 5032 S. Kostner Ave., 60632. Tel: 773-585-1221; Fax: 773-585-4959.
School—5025 S. Kenneth Ave., 60632. Tel: 773-582-8083.
Lay Teachers 14; Students 309.
Catechesis/Religious Programs—Students 122.

182—ST. RITA OF CASCIA, Revs. William E. Lego, O.S.A.; Edward J. Kersten, O.S.A.; Deacon Juan Rodriguez. In res., Rev. Robert F. Dueweke, O.S.A.; Bro. William Wiegel, O.S.A.
Res., 6243 S. Fairfield Ave., 60629. Tel: 773-434-9600; Fax: 773-434-9668.
Catechesis/Religious Programs—Students 271.

183—ST. ROBERT BELLARMINE, Rev. Michael A. Goergen; Deacon Ben Aurelio. In res., Rev. L. Scott Donahue.
Res., 4646 N. Austin Ave., 60630. Tel: 773-777-2666; Fax: 773-777-2770.
School—6036 W. Eastwood Ave., 60630. Tel: 773-725-5133; Fax: 773-777-2770.
Sisters 6; Lay Teachers 20; Students 415.
Catechesis/Religious Programs—Tel: 773-286-0456.
Students 162.

184—ST. ROMAN, Revs. David P. Pavlik; Javier De La Fuente, M.C.M.; Deacon Jose Marrero.
Res., 2311 S. Washtenaw Ave., 60608. Tel: 773-247-6645; Fax: 773-927-1610.
Catechesis/Religious Programs—Students 430.

185—ST. SABINA, Rev. Michael L. Pfleger.
Res., 1210 W. 78th Pl., 60620. Tel: 773-483-4300; Fax: 773-483-7583.
School—7801 S. Throop St., 60620. Tel: 773-483-5000; Fax: 773-483-7583.
Dominican Sisters (Sinsinawa, WI) 2; Congregation of Mother of Carmel 3; Lay Teachers 18; Students 535.
Catechesis/Religious Programs—Students 160.

186—SACRED HEART (Croatian), Revs. Steven Bedenikovic, O.F.M.; Mark Kozina, O.F.M.; Nikola Pasalic, O.F.M.
Res., 2864 E. 96th St., 60617. Tel: 773-768-1423; Fax: 773-768-3750.
School—2906 E. 96th St., 60617. Tel: 773-773-3728; Fax: 773-768-5034.
School Sisters of St. Francis 3; Lay Teachers 8; Students 190.

187—SACRED HEART MISSION OF HOLY NAME OF MARY, Rev. Anthony J. Vader.
Res., 11652 S. Church St., 60643. Tel: 773-233-3955.

188—ST. SIMON THE APOSTLE, Rev. Francis Q. Kub; Laura L. Zbella, Pastoral Assoc. In res., Rev. Charles J. Kouba, (Retired).
Res., 5157 S. California Ave., 60632. Tel: 773-436-1045; Fax: 773-436-4684.
School—5135 S. California Ave., 60632. Tel: 773-434-5036; Fax: 773-436-4667.
Sisters of Ss. Cyril & Methodius 3; Lay Teachers 9; Students 238.
Catechesis/Religious Programs—Students 202.

189—ST. STANISLAUS, BISHOP AND MARTYR, Revs. Anthony Dziorek, C.R.; Richard Balazs, C.R.; Marion Wroblewski, C.R.; Jacek Praski; Deacons Zygfryd Oborski; Mitchell Szady. In res., Revs. Jerome Andracki, C.R.; Francis Grzechowiak, C.R.
Res., 5352 W. Belden Ave., 60639. Tel: 773-237-5800; Fax: 773-237-7029.
School—2318 N. Lorel Ave., 60639. Tel: 773-622-3342; Fax: 773-622-9160.
Lay Teachers 15; Students 270.
Catechesis/Religious Programs—Students 200.

190—ST. STANISLAUS KOSTKA (Polish, Spanish, English), Revs. Anthony Bus, C.R.; Emil Stec, C.R.; Deacons Nicolas Flores; Miguel Garcia; Juan Ibarra; Faustino Villasenor.
Res., 1351 W. Evergreen Ave., 60622. Tel: 773-278-2470; Fax: 773-278-2471.
School—1255 N. Noble St., 60622.
Sisters 1; Lay Teachers 11; Students 215.

191—ST. STEPHEN. Closed. See Cristo Rey High School under High Schools, Private in the Institution Section.

192—ST. STEPHEN, KING OF HUNGARY, Rev. Michael E. Danek, C.R., Admin.
Res., 2015 W. Augusta Blvd., 60622. Tel: 773-486-1896; Fax: 773-486-1902.

193—ST. SYLVESTER, Revs. Michael T. Herman; Joseph Tito; Deacons Confessor DeJesus; Sigifredo Ortiz; Santos Soto; Hipolito Crespo; Carlos Soria.
Res., 2157 N. Humboldt Blvd., 60647. Tel: 773-235-3646; Fax: 773-489-0974.
School—Tel: 773-772-5222; Fax: 773-722-0352.
Lay Teachers 14; Students 325.
Catechesis/Religious Programs—Tel: 773-772-9082.
Students 652.

194—ST. SYMPHOROSA AND SEVEN SONS, Revs. Marcel J. Pasciak; Francis N. Maniola, Pastor Emeritus; Norman J. Trela. In res., Rev. Edmund S. Szlanga, (Retired).
Res., 6135 S. Austin Ave., 60638. Tel: 773-767-1523; Fax: 773-767-6135.
School—6125 S. Austin Ave., 60638.
Lay Teachers 28; Students 546.

195—ST. TARCISSUS, Revs. Daniel P. McCarthy; John J. Grace, Pastor Emeritus; Leonard J. Felczak, Pastor Emeritus; Thomas F. Baldonieri; Sleeva R. Policetti (India); Deacon Gregory M. Bzdon. In res., Rev. Bruno Switalski (Poland).
Res., 6020 W. Ardmore Ave., 60646. Tel: 773-763-8228; Fax: 773-774-8461.
School—6040 W. Ardmore Ave., 60646. Tel: 773-763-7080.
Lay Teachers 30; Students 706.
Catechesis/Religious Programs—Students 70.

196—ST. TERESA, Rev. John R. Hoffman; Deacon Hector Rivera. In res., Rev. R. Peter Bowman.
Res., 1037 W. Armitage Ave., 60614. Tel: 773-528-6650; Fax: 773-871-6766.
School—Cardinal Bernardin Early Childhood Center, 1651 W. Diversey Pkwy., 60614. Tel: 773-975-6330; Fax: 773-975-6339. Sr. Barbara Jean Ciszek, C.S.J., Prin.

197—ST. THADDEUS, Rev. Frank M. Sasso; Deacon Jimmie Flewellen.
Res., 9540 S. Harvard Ave., 60628. Tel: 773-568-7077; Fax: 773-928-5447.
School—Tel: 773-568-8115. Sr. Barbara Bowers, S.S.N.D., Prin.
Lay Teachers 10; Students 165.

198—ST. THECLA, Revs. Gerard E. Rogala; Matt A. Bednarz, Pastor Emeritus; Kenneth A. Budzikowski; Slawek M. Mankowski (Poland); Deacon Eugene Bates.
Res., 6725 W. Devon Ave., 60631. Tel: 773-792-3077; Fax: 773-792-3820.
School—6323 N. Newcastle Ave., 60631. Tel: 773-763-3380; Fax: 773-763-6151.
Lay Teachers 10; Students 255.
Catechesis/Religious Programs—Students 115.

199—ST. THERESE CATHOLIC CHINESE CHURCH, Rev. Michael Davitti, S.X. In res., Rev. Fernandes Herondi, S.X.
Res., 218 W. Alexander St., 60616. Tel: 312-842-6777; Fax: 312-567-1389.
School—247 W. 23rd St., 60616. Tel: 312-326-2837; Fax: 312-326-6068.
Sisters 1; Lay Teachers 14; Students 240.
Catechesis/Religious Programs—Students 21.

200—ST. THOMAS APOSTLE, Revs. Michael G. Foley; Thomas J. Fitzgerald, Pastor Emeritus; Thomas R. Seitz, (Retired); Deacon Robert Monica.
Res., 5472 S. Kimbark Ave., 60615. Tel: 773-324-2626; Fax: 773-753-7415.
School—5467 S. Woodlawn Ave., 60615. Tel: 773-667-1142; Fax: 773-753-7434.
Dominican Sisters (Sinsinawa, WI) 3; Lay Teachers 20; Students 405.
Catechesis/Religious Programs—Students 132.

201—ST. THOMAS OF CANTERBURY, Revs. Richard T. Simon; Trinh Peter Hung, (Vietnamese Apostolate); Deacons Orlando Perez; Duc Nguyen.
Res., 4827 N. Kenmore Ave., 60640. Tel: 773-878-5507.
School—Tel: 773-271-8655.
Lay Teachers 15; Students 282.
Catechesis/Religious Programs—Students 285.

202—ST. THOMAS MORE, Revs. Anthony J. Brankin; Theodore McNulty; Robert C. Behnke. In res., Revs. John P. Frawley, (Retired); Thomas J. Curley, (Retired); J. Austin Graff, (Retired); John McGrath, (Retired).
Res., 2825 W. 81st St., 60652. Tel: 773-436-4444; Fax: 773-778-9087.

School—8130 S. California Ave., 60652. Tel: 773-434-4575; Fax: 773-434-2026.
Dominican Sisters (Sinsinawa, WI) 4; Lay Teachers 19; Students 360.

203—ST. TIMOTHY, Revs. Harold B. Murphy; Gilbert A. Carroll, Pastor Emeritus. In res., Rev. Maximus Ssekiwala (Uganda).
Res., 6326 N. Washtenaw Ave., 60659. Tel: 773-262-6600; Fax: 773-262-9214.
Catechesis/Religious Programs—Students 50.

204—TRANSFIGURATION OF OUR LORD, Rev. John J. Rudnik. In res., Revs. Robert A. Florido (Philippines); Rene L. Pareja (Philippines).
Res., 2609 W. Carmen Ave., 60625. Tel: 773-561-7953; Fax: 773-561-7635.
School—5044 N. Rockwell, 60625. Tel: 773-334-0239; Fax: 773-334-0107.
Lay Teachers 10; Students 252.
Catechesis/Religious Programs—Students 93.

205—ST. TURIBIUS, Rev. Ralph H. Zwirn; Rev. Msgr. Joseph Mroczkowski, Pastor Emeritus; Revs. Michael Bowler; Waldemar Dynak.
Res., 5646 S. Karlov Ave., 60629. Tel: 773-581-2730.
School—4120 W. 57th St., 60629. Tel: 773-585-5150; Fax: 773-585-5328.
Felician Sisters 4; Lay Teachers 19; Students 470.

206—ST. VIATOR, Revs. Lawrence D. Lentz, C.S.V.; John E. Eck, C.S.V.; Deacons Camillo Vera; Carlos Perez; Joseph Cascino. In res., Rev. Robert Lachaine, C.S.V. (Canada); Bro. Corey Brost, C.S.V.
Res., 4170 W. Addison St., 60641. Tel: 773-286-4040; Fax: 773-286-4122.
School—4140 W. Addison St., 60641. Tel: 773-545-2173; Fax: 773-794-1697.
Lay Teachers 28; Students 457.
Catechesis/Religious Programs—Students 180.

207—ST. VINCENT DE PAUL, Rev. Donald Ours, C.M.
Res., 1010 W. Webster Ave., 60614. Tel: 773-327-1113; Fax: 773-327-2326.

208—ST. WALTER, Rev. Peter J. Heidenrich; Deacon Thomas O'Connell; Mr. Richard A. Conrad, Pastoral Assoc. In res., Rev. P. T. Thomas (India).
Res., 11722 S. Oakley Ave., 60643. Tel: 773-779-1515; Fax: 773-779-0381.
School—11741 S. Western Ave., 60643. Tel: 773-445-8850.
Lay Teachers 9; Students 240.
Catechesis/Religious Programs—Students 50.

209—ST. WENCESLAUS, Rev. Michael E. Danek, C.R.
Res., 3400 N. Monticello Ave., 60618. Tel: 773-588-1135; Fax: 773-588-3735.
Catechesis/Religious Programs—Students 24.

210—ST. WILLIAM, Revs. William J. Hastings; Henry J. Michalek, Pastor Emeritus; Thomas Hoffman; Daniel J. Brandt; Deacon Dennis Colgan.
Res., 2600 N. Sayre Ave., 60707. Tel: 773-637-6565; Fax: 773-745-4200.
School—2559 N. Sayre Ave., 60707. Tel: 773-637-5130; Fax: 773-745-4208.
Lay Teachers 16; Students 302.
Catechesis/Religious Programs—Students 90.

OUTSIDE THE CITY OF CHICAGO

Alsip, Cook Co., St. Terrence, Revs. William J. Lyons; Patrick J. O'Neill.
Res., 4300 W. 119th Pl., 60803. Tel: 708-597-0970; Fax: 708-597-9118.
Catechesis/Religious Programs—Students 943.

Antioch, Lake Co., St. Peter, Revs. Ronald H. Anglim; Roland H. Folger; Deacons Robert A. Gagnon; Frank M. Colette, (Retired); Paul M. Neurauter; Jeffery Barton.
Res., 557 W. Lake St., 60002. Tel: 847-395-0274; Fax: 847-395-4553.
School—Tel: 847-395-0037; Fax: 847-395-2532.
Lay Teachers 20; Students 243.
Catechesis/Religious Programs—559 Elizabeth, 60002. Tel: 847-395-0246; Fax: 847-395-2532.
Students 569.

Argo, Cook Co., St. Blase, Rev. Michael L. Zoufal; Deacon Raymundo Diaz DeLeon. In res., Revs. Norbert J. Waszak, Pastor Emeritus; Franciszek Florczyk (Poland).
Res., 6101 S. 75th Ave., 60501. Tel: 708-458-0007; Fax: 708-458-0276.
Catechesis/Religious Programs—Tel: 708-458-0246.
Students 356.

Arlington Heights, Cook Co., St. Edna, Revs. John J. Hurley; Daniel F. Sullivan; Victor Miranda; Deacons Raymond Graffia, Jr.; Robert Manthie. In res., Rev. Eugene J. Faucher.
Res., 2525 N. Arlington Heights Rd., 60004. Tel: 847-398-3362; Fax: 847-394-5226.
Catechesis/Religious Programs—Students 906.

St. James, Revs. William J. Zavaski; Timothy J. Fairman; William A. Burke; Kenneth G. Kiepura; Sr. Kathleen A. Donohoe, O.S.F., Pastoral Assoc.; Deacons Robert Plantz, (Retired); Louis Lekan; Armand Ferrini; Matt Hennessy.
Office: 820 N. Arlington Heights Rd., 60004. Tel: 847-253-6305; Fax: 847-253-0269.
School—821 Arlington Heights Rd., 60004. Tel: 847-255-6746; Fax: 847-259-4223.
Lay Teachers 57; Students 910.

Our Lady of the Wayside, Revs. Vincent F. Costello; Justin G. Kusibab, O.F.M.Conv.; John J. Mackin, Pastor Emeritus; Deacons Robert Duffy; Donald Grossnickle; Brendan Foley; Donna Cunningham, Pastoral Assoc.
Res., 432 W. Park St., 60005. Tel: 847-253-5353; Fax: 847-253-7175.
School—Lay Teachers 42; Students 725.
Catechesis/Religious Programs—423 S.Mitchell, 60005. Tel: 847-398-5011.
Students 684.

Barrington, Lake Co., St. Anne, Revs. John W. Dewes; Arthur J. Dillon, Pastor Emeritus; Ronald C. Lewandowski; Britto Berchmans, S.D.B.; Deacons Richard Baum; Robert C. Brauch; James Condill; Richard Seveska.
Res., 120 N. Ela St., 60010. Tel: 847-382-5300; Fax: 847-382-5363.
School—312 E. Chestnut St., 60010. Tel: 847-381-0311; Fax: 847-381-0384.
School Sisters of St. Francis 6; Lay Teachers 30; Students 600.

Bartlett, Cook Co., St. Peter Damian, Revs. William L. Lupo; Jerome G. Klug, Pastor Emeritus; Deacons David Sattler; Robert Newton; Gregory Stevens.
Res., 109 S. Crest Ave., 60103. Tel: 630-837-5411; Fax: 630-837-9424.
Catechesis/Religious Programs—Tel: 630-830-2295.
Students 778.

Bellwood, Cook Co., St. Simeon, Revs. John J. McCarville; Mariano L. Vita, Pastor Emeritus. In res., Revs. Joseph Ekpo; George Joseph Nangachiveettil (India).
Res., 430 Bohland Ave., 60104. Tel: 708-547-6868.
School—501 Bellwood Ave., 60104. Tel: 708-547-7350.
Lay Teachers 8; Students 140.
Catechesis/Religious Programs—Students 60.

Berwyn, Cook Co., St. Leonard, Rev. William J. Curran; Rev. Msgr. John J. Farrell, Pastor Emeritus; Revs. William J. Martin, Pastor Emeritus; Kenneth S. Laske; Deacon Joel Chrastka. In res., Rev. John A. Rolek.
Res., 3318 S. Clarence Ave., 60402. Tel: 708-484-0015; Fax: 708-484-6982.
School—3322 S. Clarence Ave., 60402. Tel: 708-749-3666; Fax: 708-788-2681.
Lay Teachers 22; Students 415.
Convent—6634 W. 34th St., 60402. Tel: 708-788-2681. Sisters of St. Joseph (La Grange, IL)
Catechesis/Religious Programs—Tel: 708-795-5919.
Students 307.

St. Mary of Celle, Revs. Richard J. Prendergast; Phien T. Nguyen; William J. Clavey.
Res., 1428 Wesley Ave., 60402. Tel: 708-788-0876; Fax: 708-788-0242.
School—1448 S. Wesley Ave., 60402. Tel: 708-749-1989; Fax: 708-749-2120.
Lay Teachers 12; Students 207.
Catechesis/Religious Programs—Tel: 708-795-6460.
Students 180.

St. Odilo, Revs. Peter J. Cyscon; Gregory W. Warmuz, O.Cist. In res., Revs. Richard B. Saudis; Thomas J. Kaveney, (Retired).
Res., 2244 S. East Ave., 60402. Tel: 708-484-2161; Fax: 708-788-0565.
School—2301 S. Clarence Ave., 60402. Tel: 708-484-0755. William Donegan, Prin.
Sisters of Charity B.V.M. 2; Lay Teachers 14; Students 300.
Catechesis/Religious Programs—Students 180.
National Shrine—Poor Souls. Tel: 708-484-2161; Fax: 708-788-0565.

Blue Island, Cook Co., St. Benedict, Revs. George L. Schopp; Kevin M. Birmingham; Deacons Juan Limon; Abundio Valadez.
Res., 2339 York St., 60406. Tel: 708-385-8510; Fax: 708-371-2631.
School—2324 New St., 60406. Tel: 708-385-2016; Fax: 708-385-4490.
Lay Teachers 9; Students 295.
Catechesis/Religious Programs—Students 200.
Mission—Robbins, Cook Co., St. Peter Claver, 14125 Claire Blvd., Robbins, 60472. Tel: 708-389-2434; Fax: 708-389-2434.

St. Donatus, Revs. Robert Kleiner, M.C.C.J.; Hugo Riva, M.C.C.J. In res., Rev. Archimede Fornasari, M.C.C.J.
Res., 1939 Union St., 60406. Tel: 708-385-2890; Fax: 708-385-4708.
Catechesis/Religious Programs—Tel: 708-388-7886.
Students 285.

St. Isidore, Revs. Gregory A. Rom; Ernest D. Ciemiega, Pastoral Emeritus; Sr. Patricia Walsh, O.P., Pastoral Assoc.
Res., 1811 W. Burr Oak Ave., 60406. Tel: 708-388-0807; Fax: 708-388-5077.
School—12731 S. Wood St., 60406. Tel: 708-388-6914.
Sisters 1; Lay Teachers 8; Students 157.
Catechesis/Religious Programs—Students 10.

Bridgeview, Cook Co., St. Fabian, Revs. Walter J. Turlo; Jan Krutewicz; Meiczyslaw Wilk, O.F.M. Conv.; Deacons Kenneth Schoenfeld; Charles Tipperreiter.
Res., 8300 S. Thomas Ave., 60455. Tel: 708-599-1110; Fax: 708-599-0673.
Catechesis/Religious Programs—7450 83rd St., 60455. Tel: 708-458-6150; Fax: 708-458-2398.
Students 1,225.

Brookfield, Cook Co., St. Barbara, Revs. Maurice J. Kissane; Robert Bacchi; Sr. Margaret Halligan, C.S.J., Pastoral Assoc.; Deacons John Debnar; Dave Brencic.
Res., 4008 Prairie Ave., 60513. Tel: 708-485-0589; Fax: 708-485-2343.
School—8900 Windemere Ave., 60513. Tel: 708-485-0806; Fax: 708-485-2343.
Lay Teachers 16; Students 219.
Catechesis/Religious Programs—Students 416.

Buffalo Grove, Lake Co., St. Mary, Revs. Marc W. Reszel; Donald J. Duffy, Pastor Emeritus; John S. Plotkowski; Harold Bonin; Deacons I. James Young, M.D.; Eugene Kukla; Bruce Peters; Kevin Kanter; Gary Long.
Res., 75 N. Buffalo Grove Rd., 60089. Tel: 847-541-1450; Fax: 847-541-2443. [CEM]
School—50 N. Buffalo Grove Rd., 60089. Tel: 847-459-6270; Fax: 847-537-2810.
Lay Teachers 46; Students 700.
Catechesis/Religious Programs—Tel: 847-537-9423.
Students 1,200.

Burbank, Cook Co., St. Albert the Great, Revs. Robert A. Stepek; Joseph P. Lynch, Pastor Emeritus; Bruno Janik; Marek B. Grzela; Deacon Irvin Bryce.
Res., 5555 W. State Rd., 60459. Tel: 708-423-0321; Fax: 708-425-4329.
School—5535 W. State Rd., 60459. Tel: 708-424-7757.
Dominican Sisters (Adrian, MI) 2; Lay Teachers 22; Students 400.
Catechesis/Religious Programs—Tel: 708-636-0406.
Students 680.

Burnham, Cook Co., Mother of God, Rev. Edmund F. Guz.
Res., 14207 S. Green Bay Ave., 60633. Tel: 708-862-8777; Fax: 708-891-1349.

Calumet City, Cook Co., St. Andrew the Apostle, Revs. Martin E. Michniewicz; Michael G. Zaniolo; Deacon Robert Banet.
Res., 768 Lincoln Ave., 60409. Tel: 708-862-4165; Fax: 708-862-4124.
School—331-155th Pl., 60409. Tel: 708-862-4143; Fax: 708-862-4148.
Sisters of the Holy Family of Nazareth (Des Plaines, IL) 2; Lay Teachers 15; Students 262.
Catechesis/Religious Programs—Students 85.

Our Lady of Knock, Revs. Donald J. Fenske; Patrick M. Lyons; Sr. Alban Hermes, O.P., Pastoral Assoc.; Deacons Albert Lundy; Edward Ryan.
Res., 501 163rd St., 60409. Tel: 708-862-3011; Fax: 708-862-9618.
School—497 163rd St., 60409. Tel: 708-862-0275.
Lay Teachers 13; Students 235.
Catechesis/Religious Programs—Tel: 708-868-1711.
Students 385.

St. Victor, Revs. Thomas E. Cima; Ignatius I. Anaele; Sr. Clara Chandler, H.M., D.R.E.; Deacon Daniel Ragonese.
Res., 553 Hirsch Ave., 60409. Tel: 708-891-8920; Fax: 708-891-8943.
School—Tel: 708-891-8930; Fax: 708-891-8943.
Lay Teachers 17; Students 369.
Catechesis/Religious Programs—Tel: 708-891-8931.
Students 105.

Calumet Park, Cook Co., Seven Holy Founders, Rev. Aldo Pozza, M.C.C.J.
Res., 12400 S. Ada St., 60827. Tel: 708-385-8459; Fax: 708-385-2143.
Catechesis/Religious Programs—Students 75.

Chicago Heights, Cook Co., St. Agnes, Revs. John S. Siemanowski; Claudio Diaz; Deacon Thomas Nowack.
Res., 1501 Chicago Rd., 60411. Tel: 708-709-2694; Fax: 708-709-2693.

School—1501 Chicago Rd., 60411.
Lay Teachers 16; Students 250.
Catechesis/Religious Programs—Students 105.

St. Kieran, Revs. William A. Eddy; Daniel A. Flens; Deacons Eugene La Belle; William Jablonski; Bernard Halper, (Retired).
Res., 724 W. 195th St., 60411. Tel: 708-755-0074; Fax: 708-754-2246.
School—700 W. 195th St., 60411. Tel: 708-754-8999.
Lay Teachers 15; Students 236.
Catechesis/Religious Programs—Tel: 708-754-0484.
Students 239.

St. Paul, Rev. William T. O'Connor; Deacon Juan L. Garza.
Res., 206 E. 25th St., 60411. Tel: 708-754-3120; Fax: 708-754-0076.
Catechesis/Religious Programs—Students 397.

Chicago Ridge, Cook Co., Our Lady of the Ridge, Rev. Paul Burak; Rev. Msgr. M. Edward Roche, Pastor Emeritus; Rev. Kenneth F. Carlson; Deacons Michael Krapez; Terris Albano.
Res., 10811 S. Ridgeland Ave., 60415. Tel: 708-425-3800; Fax: 708-425-2792.
School—10859 S. Ridgeland Ave., 60415. Tel: 708-424-4409.
Lay Teachers 12; Students 299.
Catechesis/Religious Programs—Students 471.

Cicero, Cook Co.,

1—St. Anthony, Revs. James J. Kastigar; Marco A. Mercado; William E. Zimmer; Deacons Alfonso Salgado; Claude Hensley.
Res., 1515 S. 50th Ave., 60804. Tel: 708-652-0231; Fax: 708-652-0228.
St. Anthony Center—1510 S. 49th Ct., 60804. Tel: 708-652-0231; Fax: 708-652-0228.
Catechesis/Religious Programs—Students 725.

2—St. Frances of Rome, Revs. James D. Beath; Daniel P. Buck.
Res., 1428 S. 59th Ct., 60804. Tel: 708-652-2140; Fax: 708-652-6513.
School—1400 S. Austin Blvd., 60804. Tel: 708-652-2277.
Lay Teachers 10; Students 200.

3—St. Mary of Czestochowa, (Polish/Spanish), Revs. Thaddeus Dzieszko; Harris J. D'Souza (Argentina).
Res., 3010 S. 48th Ct., 60804. Tel: 708-652-0948; Fax: 708-652-0646.
School—3009 S. 49th Ave., 60804. Tel: 708-656-5010; Fax: 708-656-4043.
Sisters of St. Joseph of the Third Order of St. Francis 3; Lay Teachers 13; Students 230.
Catechesis/Religious Programs—Students 130.

4—Mary, Queen of Heaven, Revs. John W. Hurley, Admin.; Francis J. Spellman, Pastor Emeritus; Deacons Julio Rosado; Armando Herrera.
Res., 5300 W. 24th St., 60804. Tel: 708-863-6608; Fax: 708-863-2349.
School—5314 W. 24th Pl., 60804. Tel: 708-652-6312.
Lay Teachers 10; Students 260.

5—Our Lady of Charity, Revs. Leonard M. Kruzel; Frank Drzaic, S.V.D.; Deacon Antonio Ponce.
Res., 3600 57th Ct., 60804. Tel: 708-863-1207; Fax: 708-863-1209.
School—3620 57th Ct., 60804. Tel: 708-652-0262; Fax: 708-652-0601.
Lay Teachers 11; Students 211.
Convent—Tel: 708-656-3220.
School Sisters of St. Francis 4.
Catechesis/Religious Programs—Students 150.

6—Our Lady of the Mount, Revs. Lawrence E. Collins; Michael V. Kalck; Ramiro M. Trejo, O.F.M.Cap.; Joseph T. LeVoy, (Retired); Deacons Robert E. Devereux; Antonio Llano. In res., Rev. Dusan Hladik (Extern-Czech.).
Res., 2414 S. 61st Ave., 60804. Tel: 708-652-2791; Fax: 708-863-6014.
School—2400 S. 61st Ave., 60804.
Lay Teachers 10; Students 306.

Country Club Hills, Cook Co., St. Emeric, Revs. Paul G. Seaman; John J. Rochford, Pastor Emeritus; Deacons James Detloff; Thomas O'Brien, (Retired); Philip DuBrownik.
Res., 4330 W. 180th St., 60478. Tel: 708-798-0757; Fax: 708-798-0799.
School—4300 W. 180th St., 60478.
Lay Teachers 12; Students 73.
Catechesis/Religious Programs—Students 60.

Deerfield, Lake Co., Holy Cross, Rev. Harold B. Stanger. Pastoral Assocs.: Sr. Dee Peppard, B.V.M.; Anne Schank; Deacons Jerome Kasimatis; Robert Smith. In res., Rev. Jeremiah M. Boland.
Res., 724 Elder Ln., 60015. Tel: 847-945-0430; Fax: 847-945-7651.
School—720 Elder Ln., 60015. Tel: 847-945-0135; Fax: 847-945-0805. Ms. Lorraine Gawlik, Prin.
Lay Teachers 25; Students 436.
Catechesis/Religious Programs—Tel: 847-945-0581; Fax: 847-945-0582. Mrs. Marilyn Peters Krawczyk, D.R.E.
Students 645.

Des Plaines, Cook Co.,

1—St. Mary, Revs. Gene J. Dyer; Paul F. Rosemeyer, Pastor Emeritus; Charles H. Schlax; David R. Ford.
Res., 794 Pearson St., 60016. Tel: 847-824-8144; Fax: 847-824-3906.
School—Our Lady of Destiny (North Campus), 795 Center St., 60016. Tel: 847-824-2762; Fax: 847-824-3465.
Lay Teachers 7; Students 114.
Catechesis/Religious Programs—Tel: 847-298-1435; Fax: 847-824-3906.
Students 567.

2—St. Paul Chong Hasang, Cook, Rev. Pius Lee (Korea).
Res., 675 Dursey Ln., 60016. Tel: 847-699-6334; Fax: 847-699-1281.
Catechesis/Religious Programs—Students 150.

3—St. Stephen Protomartyr, Revs. Michael A. Olivero; Leonard T. Mezydlo, Pastor Emeritus; Deacon Donald J. Telposky. In res., Rev. Haldane Mysliwiec.
1267 Everett Ave., 60018-2398. Tel: 847-824-2026; Fax: 847-824-3842.
School—Our Lady of Destiny (South Campus), 1880 Ash St., 60018-2343. Tel: 847-827-2900; Fax: 847-827-0475.
Lay Teachers 6; Students 100.
Catechesis/Religious Programs—1253 Everett Ave., 60018. Tel: 847-297-3844; Fax: 847-824-3842.
Students 175.

4—St. Zachary, Revs. Joseph P. McGinnity; Lawrence F. Springer, Admin.; Deacons Peter N. Lagges; John J. Smith; Robert Jablonski. In res., Rev. Thomas P. Conley, (Retired).
Res., 567 W. Algonquin Rd., 60016. Tel: 847-956-7020; Fax: 847-981-1148.
School—Tel: 847-437-4022.
Sisters 1; Lay Teachers 18; Students 320.
Catechesis/Religious Programs—Tel: 847-956-1175.
Students 320.

Elk Grove Village, Cook Co., St. Julian Eymard, Revs. Leon J. Rezula; John F. Dedek, Pastor Emeritus.
Res., 601 Biesterfield Rd., 60007. Tel: 847-956-0130; Fax: 847-956-0189.

Queen of the Rosary, Revs. Arthur J. Fagan; Francis J. Cerniglia, Pastor Emeritus; John A. Robinson; Deacon Ted Czarnecki. In res., Rev. Robert L. Ebrom.
Res., 750 Elk Grove Blvd., 60007. Tel: 847-437-0403; Fax: 847-437-0336.
School—690 Elk Grove Blvd., 60007.
Lay Teachers 22; Students 398.

Elmwood Park, Cook Co., St. Celestine, Revs. Lawrence J. Sullivan; Donald J. Mulsoff. Pastoral Assocs.: Sr. Jean Schulte, R.S.M.; Deacons James Devine; Michael DeLarco. In res., Rev. Bernard C. White.
Res., 3020 N. 76th Ct., 60707. Tel: 708-453-2555; Fax: 708-462-0560.
School—Tel: 708-453-8234; Fax: 708-452-0237.
Lay Teachers 22; Students 591.
Catechesis/Religious Programs—3017 N. 77th Ave., 60707.
Students 290.

Evanston, Cook Co., St. Athanasius, Revs. Thomas A. Libera; James Heyd; Sr. Mary Crimmin, B.V.M., Pastoral Assoc.; Deacon Richard S. Jay. In res., Rev. Vincent Chembakassery (India).
Res., 1615 Lincoln St., 60201. Tel: 847-328-1430; Fax: 847-328-1809.
School—2510 Ashland, 60201. Tel: 847-864-2650; Fax: 847-475-7385.
Lay Teachers 25; Students 340.
Catechesis/Religious Programs—Students 210.

St. Mary, Revs. Michael J. Solazzo; Valerian Laini (Africa); Deacon John Arndt.
Res., 1012 Lake St., 60201. Tel: 847-864-0333; Fax: 847-864-0354.
Parish Center—Tel: 847-864-0333; Fax: 847-864-0354.
School—Consolidated with St. Nicholas Parish to form Pope John XXIII School. See St. Nicholas for further details. Tel: 847-475-5678; Fax: 847-475-5683.
Catechesis/Religious Programs—Students 125.

St. Nicholas, Rev. Robert H. Oldershaw. In res., Rev. James R. Halstead, O.S.A.
Res., 806 Ridge Ave., 60202. Tel: 847-864-1185; Fax: 847-864-7810.
School—Consolidated with St. Mary Parish to form Pope John XXIII School. 1120 Washington, 60202. Tel: 847-475-5678. Mrs. Rosalie Musiala, Prin.
Lay Teachers 22; Students 336.
Catechesis/Religious Programs—Students 210.

Evergreen Park, Cook Co., St. Bernadette, Rev. Kurt D. Boras.
Res., 9343 Francisco Ave., 60805. Tel: 708-422-8995; Fax: 708-422-8699.
School—9311 S. Francisco Ave., 60805. Tel: 708-422-6429.
Dominican Sisters (Springfield, IL) 5; Lay Teachers 18; Students 354.
Catechesis/Religious Programs—Students 341.

Most Holy Redeemer, Revs. Richard J. Dempsey; Richard J. Martin; Anthony L. Markus. In res., Rev. Albert R. Adamich, (Retired).
Res., 9525 S. Lawndale Ave., 60805. Tel: 708-425-5354; Fax: 708-346-8182.
School—9535 S. Millard Ave., 60805. Tel: 708-422-8280; Fax: 708-422-4193.
Dominican Sisters of Sinsinewa 2; Lay Teachers 23; Students 480.
Catechesis/Religious Programs—Tel: 708-346-8185.
Students 480.

Queen of Martyrs, Revs. Edward M. Mikolajczyk; William P. Murphy, Pastor Emeritus; John J. Doyle.
Res., 10233 S. Central Park, 60805-3799. Tel: 708-423-8110; Fax: 708-423-7372.
School—3550 W. 103rd St., 60805.
Lay Teachers 29; Students 635.

Flossmoor, Cook Co., Infant Jesus of Prague, Revs. Michael A. Hack; William J. Flaherty, Pastor Emeritus; Richard L. Hills, Pastor Emeritus; Andrew J. Santos; Deacon George Brooks. In res., Revs. Matthias H. Hoffman; William J. Finnegan.
Res., 1131 Douglas Ave., 60422. Tel: 708-799-5400.
School—1101 Douglas Ave., 60422.
Lay Teachers 22; Students 500.

Forest Park, Cook Co., St. Bernardine, Revs. Patrick M. Tucker; William J. Quinlan, Pastor Emeritus; Phillip F. Cioffi; Deacons Timothy Rehor; John Walters. In res., Rev. Francis J. Grady, S.S.C.
Res., 7246 Harrison St., 60130. Tel: 708-366-0839; Fax: 708-366-3136.
School—815 Elgin Ave., 60130. Tel: 708-366-6890; Fax: 708-366-8015.
Lay Teachers 16; Students 265.
Catechesis/Religious Programs—Tel: 708-366-3553.
Students 173.

Franklin Park, Cook Co., St. Gertrude, Rev. Alfred P. Corbo; Deacons Robert Murphy; Lorenzo Chaidez. In res., Rev. Edmund J. Schreiber.
Res., 9613 Schiller Blvd., 60131. Tel: 847-455-1100; Fax: 847-455-1209.
Catechesis/Religious Programs—9617 Schiller Blvd, 60131. Tel: 847-455-5810.

Glenview, Cook Co., St. Catherine Laboure, Revs. James P. Murphy; Robert G. Mair; Deacons Ray Gavin; Michael Bretz; Frank Beil; Tom Lambert.
Res., 3535 Thornwood Ln., 60025. Tel: 847-729-1414; Fax: 847-729-5184.
School—3425 Thornwood Ln., 60025. Tel: 847-724-2240; Fax: 847-724-5805.
Sisters 1; Lay Teachers 24; Students 312.
Catechesis/Religious Programs—Students 274.

Our Lady of Perpetual Help, Revs. John E. Flavin; Thomas Bishop; John M. Thinnes; Patrick Tyrell, S.J. (Ext.-Ireland); Deacons James Revord; Alan Sedivy.
Res., 1775 Grove St., 60025. Tel: 847-729-1525; Fax: 847-724-7025.
School—1123 Church St., 60025.
School Sisters of St. Francis 4; Lay Teachers 74; Students 1,060.
Catechesis/Religious Programs—Students 1000.

Glenwood, Cook Co., St. John, Rev. John J. Sullivan.
Res., 301 S. Cottage Grove Ave., 60425. Tel: 708-758-5098; Fax: 708-758-0408.
Catechesis/Religious Programs—Students 225.

Grayslake, Lake Co., St. Gilbert, Revs. Robert W. Beaven; Dean F. Semmer; Deacons Chester Kozuchowski; Henry Iwan; Jeffrey Newman; Chris Mondello; Richard Globis.
Res., 301 E. Belvidere Rd., 60030. Tel: 847-223-4731; Fax: 847-223-5840.
School—251 E. Belvidere Rd., 60030. Tel: 847-223-8600.
Sisters of the Holy Family of Nazareth 1; Lay Teachers 27; Students 680.
Catechesis/Religious Programs—Students 700.

Gurnee, Lake Co., St. Paul the Apostle, Revs. Farrell J. Kane, O.Carm.; Raymond Clennon, O.Carm.; Deacon Michael Penich.
Res., 6401 Gages Lake Rd., 60031. Tel: 847-918-0600; Fax: 847-918-0640.
Catechesis/Religious Programs—Tel: 847-816-8677; Fax: 847-918-0640.
Students 1,610.

Hanover Park, Cook Co., St. Ansgar, Rev. John W. Tapper; Deacons Louis Barone; Nick Tereza; Robert Ziomek; Clement Petricca; Oscar Monterroso; Jose Garcia; Ronald Weber.
Res., 2040 Laurel Ave., 60103. Tel: 630-837-5553; Fax: 630-837-9847.
Catechesis/Religious Programs—Students 317.

Harvey, Cook Co., Ascension-St. Susanna, Rev. Joseph W. Altman; Deacons Thomas R. Carvlin; Henry Burke, Jr.
Res., 15234 Myrtle Ave., 60426. Tel: 708-333-0931; Fax: 708-333-3281.
School—Mary of Nazareth, 15727 S. Emerald Ave., 60426. Tel: 708-331-7108.
Sisters of the Holy Family of Nazareth 4; Lay Teachers 5; Students 108.
Catechesis/Religious Programs—Students 30.

St. John the Baptist (Polish), Revs. Edward Romanski (Poland) Admin.; Clarence J. Juchcinski, Pastor Emeritus; Michael Wasiel, (Retired).
Res., 15746 Union Ave., 60426. Tel: 708-333-0184; Fax: 708-333-0861.
School—15727 Emerald Ave., 60426. Tel: 708-331-5076; Fax: 708-331-6870.
Sisters of the Holy Family of Nazareth (Des Plaines, IL) 2; Lay Teachers 8; Students 178.
Catechesis/Religious Programs—Students 38.

Harwood Heights, Norridge, Cook Co., St. Rosalie, Revs. John C. Cain; Richard J. Ehrens; Deacon Joseph E. Bishop, Pastoral Assoc.
Res., 4401 N. Oak Park Ave., Harwood Heights-Norridge, 60656. Tel: 708-867-8817; Fax: 708-867-8615.
Catechesis/Religious Programs—6740 W. Montrose, Harwood Hts., IL 60706. Tel: 708-867-4588; Fax: 708-867-0774.
Students 295.

Hazel Crest, Cook Co., St. Anne, Revs. Leonard A. Dubi; Robert J. Keener; Sr. Joan Klega, S.P., Pastoral Assoc.; Deacons John Leonas, (Retired); Herman Benthey; Steven Moore; William Churilla.
Res., 16802 S. Lincoln St., 60429. Tel: 708-335-3221; Fax: 708-335-1953.
School—16801 Dixie Hwy., 60429. Tel: 708-335-2288.
Lay Teachers 5; Students 128.
Early Learning Center—16777 Dixie Hwy., 60429. Tel: 708-335-4831.
Pre-school-Daycare 96.
Catechesis/Religious Programs—Tel: 708-335-2286.

Hickory Hills, Cook Co., St. Patricia, Revs. Gerald F. Mulcahy; Norbert A. Chapell, Pastor Emeritus; Michael E. Flynn; Deacons Charles Keegan; Norbert Weitendorf. In res., Rev. Joseph C. Mol.
Res., 9050 S. 86th Ave., 60457. Tel: 708-598-5222; Fax: 708-598-5280.
School—9000 S. 86th Ave., 60457.
Sisters of the Holy Family of Nazareth (Des Plaines, IL) 4; Lay Teachers 17; Students 525.

Highland Park, Lake Co., Immaculate Conception, Revs. Robert L. Kealy; John E. O'Brien, Pastor Emeritus; George Velloorattil; Deacons James Fruge; Louis Vignocchi. In res., Rev. Edward J. Norkett.
Res., 770 W. Deerfield Rd., 60035. Tel: 847-433-0130; Fax: 847-433-0669.
Catechesis/Religious Programs—Tel: 847-433-2224.
Students 315.

Highwood, Lake Co., St. James, Revs. James O'Malley; Ronald E. Scarlata, Pastor Emeritus; Deacons Bruno Pagliai; James Gallagher; Ellsworth Cordesman. In res., Rev. John E. Mulvihill.
Res., 134 North Ave., 60040. Tel: 847-433-1494; Fax: 847-433-2011.
School—140 North Ave., 60040.
Lay Teachers 15; Students 205.
Catechesis/Religious Programs—Students 170.

Hillside, Cook Co., St. Domitilla, Revs. Frank M. Falco, O.S.M.; Mark M. Franceschini, O.S.M.; Deacons Angelo Marotto; Kenneth Bell; Larry Spohr. In res., Revs. Christopher M. Krymski, O.S.M.; Walter M. Brennan, O.S.M.
Res., 4940 Washington St., 60162. Tel: 708-449-8430; Fax: 708-449-2009.
School—601 Hillside Ave., 60162. Tel: 708-449-7420.
Sisters 3; Lay Teachers 10; Students 300.
Catechesis/Religious Programs—Tel: 708-449-1558.
Students 130.

Hoffman Estates, Cook Co., St. Hubert, Revs. Eugene J. Nowak; Richard M. Zborowski; Deacon James Knippen.
Res., 729 Grand Canyon St., 60194. Tel: 847-885-7700; Fax: 847-885-4631.
School—Lay Teachers 44; Students 830.

Hometown, Cook Co., Our Lady of Loretto, Rev. James J. Donovan; Sr. Kathryn McDonald, B.V.M., Pastoral Assoc.; Deacon Thomas Meehan. In res., Revs. John J. Mackin, (Retired); Ronald Mahon, C.PP.S.
Res., 8925 S. Kostner Ave., 60456. Tel: 708-424-7471; Fax: 708-424-7588.
School—Tel: 708-636-8668.
Lay Teachers 13; Students 293.
Catechesis/Religious Programs—Students 162.

Homewood, Cook Co., St. Joseph, Revs. James M. Sayers; Richard J. Kozak; Deacons Jack O'Leary; George Maddock.
Res., 17951 Dixie Hwy., 60430. Tel: 708-798-0622; Fax: 708-798-6137.
School—17949 Dixie Hwy., 60430. Tel: 708-798-0467; Fax: 708-957-5659.
Dominican Sisters (Adrian, MI) 1; Lay Teachers 17; Students 284.
Catechesis/Religious Programs—Tel: 708-798-3567.
Students 297.

Indian Creek, Lake Co., St. Mary of Vernon, Revs. Joseph C. Curtis; John P. Finnegan, Pastor Emeritus; Steven W. Patte; Deacons Mark R. Zwolski; Dante D. Virgilio; James Wogan.
Res., 236 U.S. Hwy. 45, 60061. Tel: 847-362-1005; Fax: 847-362-6375.
Catechesis/Religious Programs—Tel: 847-362-0653.
Students 1,200.

Ingleside, Lake Co., St. Bede, Rev. John F. Krebs; Deacons John McMahon; Edward Quackenbush. In res., Revs. Robert J. Fitzpatrick, Pastor Emeritus; John E. Hefferan.
Res., 36455 N. Wilson Rd., 60041. Tel: 847-587-2251; Fax: 847-973-1765.
School—36399 N. Wilson Rd., 60041. Tel: 847-587-5541; Fax: 847-587-2713.
Lay Teachers 16; Students 305.
Catechesis/Religious Programs—Tel: 847-587-2301.
Students 180.

Inverness, Cook Co., Holy Family, Rev. Patrick J. Brennan; Deacons Robert Antiss; James Multeri. In res., Rev. Denis Carneiro (India).
Res., 2515 W. Palatine Rd., 60067. Tel: 847-359-0042; Fax: 847-359-0639.
Catechesis/Religious Programs—Students 1931.

La Grange, Cook Co., St. Cletus, Revs. Raymond F. Klees; Charles Gallagher, Pastor Emeritus.
Res., 600 W. 55th St., 60525. Tel: 708-352-6209; Fax: 708-352-0707.
School—700 W. 55th St., 60525. Tel: 708-352-4820; Fax: 708-352-0707.
Lay Teachers 25; Students 451.
Catechesis/Religious Programs—Tel: 708-352-2383.
Students 646.

St. Francis Xavier, Revs. William J. Stenzel; Lawrence M. Lisowski.
Res., 124 N. Spring Ave., 60525. Tel: 708-352-0168; Fax: 708-352-4904.
School—145 N. Waiola Ave., 60525. Tel: 708-352-2175; Fax: 708-352-2057.
Lay Teachers 48; Students 688.
Catechesis/Religious Programs—Tel: 708-352-4555.
Students 712.

La Grange Park, Cook Co., St. Louise de Marillac, Revs. Fred W. Tomzik; Cletus J. Lynch, Pastor Emeritus; Michael J. Wanda; Deacons Michael McLynn; Dennis Huslig; David Kowalski; James Grevenites.
Res., 1144 Harrison Ave., 60526. Tel: 708-352-7388; Fax: 708-352-0714.
School—Tel: 708-352-2202; Fax: 708-352-6654.
Lay Teachers 20; Students 250.
Youth Ministry—1144 Harrison Ave., 60526. Tel: 708-352-7388; Fax: 708-352-0714.
Catechesis/Religious Programs—1125 Harrison Ave., LaGrange Park, 60526. Tel: 708-482-8814.
Students 450.

Lake Forest, Lake Co., St. Mary, Revs. George J. Rassas; Christopher M. Gustafson; Deacons James L. Kenney; Joseph G. Krakora. Pastoral Assocs.: Joan O'Keefe; Patricia Moran. In res.,
Res., 175 E. Illinois Rd., 60045. Tel: 847-234-0205; Fax: 847-234-9860.
School—185 E. Illinois Rd., 60045. Tel: 847-234-0371; Fax: 847-234-9593.
Lay Teachers 43; Students 710.
Catechesis/Religious Programs—Tel: 847-234-0090; Fax: 847-234-2755.
Students 671.

St. Patrick, Rev. William J. McNulty.
Res., 991 S. Waukegan Rd., 60045. Tel: 847-234-1401; Fax: 847-234-1433.
Catechesis/Religious Programs—Tel: 847-234-2179; Fax: 847-234-1433.
Students 643.

Lake Villa, Lake Co., Prince of Peace, Revs. Richard M. Yanos; Richard W. Fassbinder, Pastor Emeritus; Steven G. Dombrowski; Deacons Timothy Leonard; Leonard Milender.
Res., 135 S. Milwaukee Ave., 60046. Tel: 847-356-7915; Fax: 847-265-1678.
School—Tel: 847-356-6111; Fax: 847-356-6121.
Lay Teachers 12; Students 241.
Catechesis/Religious Programs—Tel: 847-356-5850; Fax: 847-265-1678.
Students 600.

Lake Zurich, Lake Co., St. Francis de Sales, Revs. Ronald J. Gollatz; James E. Schmaus.
Res., 277 E. Main St., 60047. Tel: 847-438-6622; Fax: 847-438-6638.
School—11 S. Buesching Rd., 60047. Tel: 847-438-7921; Fax: 847-438-7114.
Lay Teachers 27; Students 570.
Catechesis/Religious Programs—Tel: 847-438-3233; Fax: 847-438-7114.
Students 1,796.

Lansing, Cook Co., St. Ann, Revs. Michael A. Gabriel; John R. Price; Sr. Julie Flynn, O.P., Pastoral Assoc.
Parish Office: 3010 Ridge Rd., 60438. Tel: 708-895-6700; Fax: 708-895-6877.
Res., 3026 Ridge Rd., 60438. Tel: 708-895-6700; Fax: 708-895-6877.
School—3014 Ridge Rd., 60438. Tel: 708-895-1661.
Lay Teachers 36; Students 657.
Catechesis/Religious Programs—Tel: 708-895-5970.
Students 473.

Lemont, Cook Co.,

1—St. Alphonsus, Revs. Kevin J. Spiess; Julian G. Grinis, Pastor Emeritus.
Res., 210 E. Logan, 60439. Tel: 630-257-2414; Fax: 630-257-2476.
School—St. Alphonsus-St. Patrick Consolidated, (Grades K-8) Admin. Office: 205 Cass St., 60439. Tel: 708-257-2380.
Sisters 3; Lay Teachers 15; Students 300.
Catechesis/Religious Programs—Students 430.

2—Blessed Jurgis Matulaitis, Rev. Algirdas Paliokas, S.J. In res., Rev. Msgr. Ignatius L. Urbonas (GRY).
Res., Lithuanian Catholic Mission, 14915-127th St., Unit 101, 60439. Tel: 630-257-5613.

3—SS. Cyril and Methodius, Revs. Victor J. Sivore; Richard M. Jozwiak, Pastor Emeritus; Jan F. Kaplan (Poland); Deacon Norbert Lesnieski.
Res., 608 Sobieski St., 60439. Tel: 630-257-2776; Fax: 630-257-9372.
School—607 Sobieski St., 60439. Tel: 630-257-6488; Fax: 630-257-6465.
Lay Teachers 17; Students 583.
Catechesis/Religious Programs—Tel: 630-257-9314.
Students 400.

4—St. James at Sag Bridge, Revs. Edwin V. Bohula; James P. Davitt, Pastor Emeritus.
Res., 10600 Archer Rd., 60439. Tel: 630-257-7000; Fax: 630-257-7912. [CEM]
Catechesis/Religious Programs—Students 124.

5—St. Patrick, Revs. Richard J. Shannon; John J. McCaig, Pastor Emeritus.
Res., 200 Illinois St., 60439. Tel: 630-257-6134; Fax: 630-257-0401.
School—St. Alphonsus-St. Patrick Consolidated, (Grades PreK-8) Admin. Office: 205 Cass St., 60439. Tel: 630-257-2380.
Lay Teachers 14; Students 278.

6—Blessed A.M. Slomsek Slovenian Catholic Mission, Rev. David Srumpf, O.F.M.; Deacon John Vidmar.
Res., 14246 Main St., P.O. Box 608, 60439-0608. Tel: 630-257-2068; Fax: 630-257-2359.

Libertyville, Lake Co., St. Joseph, Revs. John E. Hennessey; John T. Noga; Deacons Dennis I. Mudd; Dennis J. Dunn; Robert E. Matthews; William Sands. In res., Rev. Victor J. Ivers.
Res., 121 E. Maple Ave., 60048. Tel: 847-362-2073; Fax: 847-362-6821.
School—221 Park Pl., 60048. Tel: 847-362-0730; Fax: 847-362-8130.
Lay Teachers 32; Students 581.
Catechesis/Religious Programs—116 Hurlburt Ct., 60048. Tel: 847-362-5797; Fax: 847-362-6821.
Students 1,301.

Lyons, Cook Co., St. Hugh, Revs. Thomas A. Moran; James W. Keating, Pastor Emeritus; Rev. Msgr. Devadas Sagili (India); Deacon Willaim Rueth.
Res., 7939 W. 43rd St., 60534. Tel: 708-447-3108; Fax: 708-447-9870.
School—4315 Joliet Ave., 60534. Tel: 708-447-3125; Fax: 708-447-9870.
Lay Teachers 11; Students 143.
Catechesis/Religious Programs—Tel: 708-447-5711.
Students 70.

Markham, Cook Co., St. Gerard Majella, Rev. Michael J. Nallen, Admin.
Res., 3536 W. 161st St., 60426. Tel: 708-331-8400.

Matteson, Cook Co., St. Lawrence O'Toole, Revs. Michael A. Nacius; Joseph T. Cook; Deacons Timothy Keating; Wayne Morton; Gerald Savercool; Ronald Zanardo; Thomas Dehler.
Res., 4101 St. Lawrence Ave., 60443. Tel: 708-748-6090; Fax: 708-748-4055.
School—Tel: 708-747-3322.
Lay Teachers 21; Students 520.
Catechesis/Religious Programs—Tel: 708-747-2050.
Students 325.

Maywood, Cook Co., St. Eulalia, Rev. James V. Quinlan; Rev. Msgr. William J. Quinn, Pastor Emeritus; Deacons Ben Bacchi; Giulio Camerini; George Lambert. In res., Rev. Michael Adaickalam, S.S.S.
Res., 1851 S. 9th Ave., 60153. Tel: 708-343-6120.
School—815 Lexington St., 60153. Tel: 708-343-5652.
Sisters 4; Lay Teachers 10; Students 225.

St. James, Rev. Herbert J. Meyr; Deacons Antonio Maney; Roman Revering; Norberto Ojeda.
Res., 305 S. 6th Ave., 60153. Tel: 708-343-5210; Fax: 708-343-9317.
Catechesis/Religious Programs—611 Maple, 60153.
Students 192.

Melrose Park, Cook Co., St. Charles Borromeo, Rev. Claire Antonio Orso, C.S.; Deacon Dominic Marella.
Res., 1637 N. 37th Ave., 60160. Tel: 708-343-7646; Fax: 708-343-3527.

Our Lady of Mount Carmel (Italian), Rev. Richard Zanotti, C.S.; Richard Zanetti, Pastoral Assoc.
Res., 1101 N. 23rd Ave., 60160. Tel: 708-344-4140; Fax: 708-344-0902.
School—1102 N. 22nd Ave., 60160. Tel: 708-343-7030; Fax: 708-344-0902.
Lay Teachers 10; Students 170.
Catechesis/Religious Programs—Nereida Pareda, D.R.E.
Students 350.

Sacred Heart, Revs. Cosmo F. Militello; Erwin J. Friedl; Deacons Raymond Behrendt; Victor Colucci. In res., Rev. Peter Kunnalakatt (India).
Res., 819 N. 16th Ave., 60160. Tel: 708-344-0757; Fax: 708-344-5906.
School—1503 W. Rice St., 60160. Tel: 708-344-4960.
Sisters of the Third Order of St. Francis of the Holy Family 1; Lay Teachers 20; Students 201.
Catechesis/Religious Programs—Students 100.

Midlothian, Cook Co., St. Christopher, Revs. William E. Killeen; Ralph E. Starus; Deacons Joseph Brady; Michael Smith.
Res., 14641 S. Keeler Ave., 60445. Tel: 708-388-8190; Fax: 708-388-0072.
School—14611 S. Keeler Ave., 60445. Tel: 708-385-8776; Fax: 708-385-8102.
Sisters 3; Lay Teachers 21; Students 444.
Catechesis/Religious Programs—Tel: 708-388-4040.
Students 479.

Morton Grove, Cook Co., St. Martha, Revs. Robert J. Burnell; Eugene J. Faucher, Pastor Emeritus; Deacons Bernard Berquist; Peter Meehan.
Res., 8523 Georgiana Ave., 60053. Tel: 847-965-0262; Fax: 847-965-2535.
Catechesis/Religious Programs—Tel: 847-965-8062. Sr. M. Constance Kuczwara, C.S.F., D.R.E.
Students 220.

Mt. Prospect, Cook Co.,

1—St. Cecilia, Revs. Daniel J. Brady; Elzear Gehlen, S.V.D.
Res., 700 S. Meier Rd., 60056. Tel: 847-437-6208; Fax: 847-437-2520.
Catechesis/Religious Programs—Students 286.

2—St. Emily, Revs. Dennis Stafford; Mark P. Canavan; Deacons Bill DiCanio; James R. Sanford; Sr. Joanne Marie Schutz, S.S.C.M., Pastoral Assoc.
Res., 101 N. Horner Ln., 60056. Tel: 847-824-5049; Fax: 847-297-0358.
School—1400 E. Central Rd., 60056. Tel: 847-296-3490; Fax: 847-296-1155.
Sisters of the Holy Family of Nazareth 4; Lay Teachers 30; Students 620.
Catechesis/Religious Programs—Students 600.

3—St. Raymond de Penafort, Revs. Bernard J. Pietrzak; William J. Buhrfeind, Pastor Emeritus; Jerome Jacob; Edwin Henseler, Jr.; Deacons Thomas Corcoran; John Lorbach. In res., Rev. Charles J. Skach, (Retired).
Res., 311 S. Ioka St., 60056. Tel: 847-253-2444; Fax: 847-253-0023.
School—300 S. Elmhurst Rd., 60056. Tel: 847-253-8555; Fax: 847-253-8939.
Lay Teachers 46; Students 591.
Catechesis/Religious Programs—847-253-8600
Students 820.

4—St. Thomas a Becket, Revs. John W. Roller; Ralph R. Mollan, Pastor Emeritus; Sr. Marylyn Welter, S.S.F., Pastoral Assoc.
Res., 1321 Burning Bush Ln., 60056. Tel: 847-827-9220; Fax: 847-827-0370.
Catechesis/Religious Programs—Tel: 847-296-9051.
Students 280.

Mundelein, Lake Co., Santa Maria Del Popolo, Revs. James W. Kinn; Jackson Colomb; M. David Arcilia, O.D.C. (Colombia); Deacons John Simmons; Bill Dunn; Dave Auld. In res., Rev. William J. Shields, (Retired).
Res., 116 N. Lake St., 60060. Tel: 847-949-8300; Fax: 847-949-2339.
School—126 N. Lake St., 60060. Tel: 847-949-2335; Fax: 847-949-9721.
Lay Teachers 24; Students 405.
Catechesis/Religious Programs—Tel: 847-949-2327.
Students 580.
Convent—133 N. Lincoln Ave., 60060. Tel: 847-566-7343.

St. Mary (Fremont Center), Revs. Ronald J. Lewinski; Kenneth Kiepura; Deacon Robert A. Poletto.
Res., 22333 W. Erhart Rd., 60060. Tel: 847-223-0010; Fax: 847-223-5960.
School—Tel: 847-223-4021; Fax: 847-223-3489.
Franciscan Sisters of the Sacred Heart 1; Lay Teachers 9; Students 220.
Catechesis/Religious Programs—Tel: 847-223-0011.
Students 415.

Niles, Cook Co., St. Isaac Jogues, Revs. Edward Fialkowski; Tirso S. Villaverde; Deacons Frederick W. Ray, (Retired); Robert C. O'Keefe; Paul Stanton.
Res., 8149 Golf Rd., 60714. Tel: 847-967-1060; Fax: 847-967-1070.
Catechesis/Religious Programs—Tel: 847-966-1180; Fax: 847-966-0159.
Students 340.

St. John Brebeuf, Revs. Thomas P. May; Arthur J. Olsen; Adams S. Galek (Poland); Deacons John Perkowitz; Thomas Paluch; Lawrence Skaja.
Res., 8307 N. Harlem Ave., 60714. Tel: 847-966-8145; Fax: 847-966-0014.
School—8301 Harlem Ave., 60714. Tel: 847-966-3266; Fax: 847-966-5351.
Sisters 2; Lay Teachers 16; Students 433.
Catechesis/Religious Programs—Tel: 847-966-3269.
Students 486.

Our Lady of Ransom, Revs. John R. Hall; Xamie M. Reyes; Deacons Robert Crandall; Charles O'Donnell.
Ministry Center: 8624 W. Normal, 60714. Tel: 847-823-2550; Fax: 847-823-4291.
School—8350 N. Greenwood, 60714. Tel: 847-696-4413; Fax: 847-696-0031.
Felician Sisters 3; Lay Teachers 23; Students 376.
Catechesis/Religious Programs—Tel: 847-696-2994.
Students 350.

Norridge, Cook Co., Divine Savior, Rev. Stephen J. Tebes; Deacons Gus Jeffery; William Lehman; Ronald Gronek.
Res., 7740 W. Montrose, 60706. Tel: 708-456-9000; Fax: 708-456-7838.
School—7750 W. Montrose, 60706. Tel: 708-456-9074; Fax: 708-456-7856.
Sisters 5; Lay Teachers 9; Students 180.
Catechesis/Religious Programs—Students 260.

Northbrook, Cook Co., St. Norbert, Revs. Richard J. Mueller; Robert J. Lutz, Pastor Emeritus; Richard J. Valker; Susan Martin, Pastoral Assoc.
Res., 1809 Walters Ave., 60062. Tel: 847-272-7090; Fax: 847-272-7771.
School—1817 Walters Ave., 60062. Tel: 847-272-0051; Fax: 847-272-5274. Sr. Ann Busch, S.S.S.F., Prin.
Sisters of St. Casimir 2; School Sisters of St. Francis 2; Lay Teachers 29; Students 444.
Catechesis/Religious Programs—Tel: 847-272-3086; Fax: 847-272-7771.
Students 525.

Our Lady of the Brook, Revs. Richard E. Sztorc; Robert G. Herne, Pastor Emeritus; Robert Grib, S.J.
Res., 3700 W. Dundee Rd., 60062. Tel: 847-272-5686; Fax: 847-498-0899.
Catechesis/Religious Programs—Tel: 847-272-5131; Fax: 847-498-0899.
Students 347.

North Chicago, Lake Co., Queen of Peace, Rev. James E. Merold; Sr. Lucy Giachetti, S.S.N.D., Pastoral Assoc.; Deacons Gary Munda; Dean Hermann; Irvin Boppart; Pedro Martinez.
Res., 910 14th St., 60064. Tel: 847-473-4079; Fax: 847-473-4143.
Catechesis/Religious Programs—Tel: 847-473-1238.
Students 190.

Northfield, Cook Co., St. Philip the Apostle, Rev. Laurence J. Dunn.
Res., 1962 Old Willow Rd., 60093. Tel: 847-446-8383; Fax: 847-446-8338.
School—1980 Old Willow Rd., 60093. Tel: 847-446-5744.
Lay Teachers 15; Students 121.
Catechesis/Religious Programs—1962 Old Willow Rd., 60093. Tel: 847-446-9390.
Students 170.

Northlake, Cook Co., St. John Vianney, Cure of Ars, Revs. Charles V. Fanelli; Andrew Godlewski (Poland); Deacon John Zurawski. In res., Revs. Joseph S. Thomas, (Retired); Salvador Simoni; Jerome Twarog, C.R.
Res., 46 N. Wolf Rd., 60164. Tel: 708-562-0500; Fax: 708-562-1824.
School—Tel: 708-562-1466; Fax: 708-562-1958.
Lay Teachers 20; Students 252.
Catechesis/Religious Programs—Tel: 708-562-2580.
Students 393.

North Riverside, Cook Co., Mater Christi, Rev. M. Cyril Nemecek; Deacon Richard Gordus.
Res., 2431 S. 10th Ave., 60546. Tel: 708-442-5611; Fax: 708-442-1306.
School—2400 S. 10th Ave., 60546. Tel: 708-442-7115; Fax: 708-447-1062.
Lay Teachers 9; Students 146.
Catechesis/Religious Programs—Students 117.

Oak Forest, Cook Co., St. Damian, Rev. Michael G. Meany; Rev. Msgr. Martin J. O'Day, Pastor Emeritus; Revs. Francis G. Scanlan; Francis Kaucky; Deacons Patrick O'Donnell, (Retired); Len Steinbeigle; Thomas Hipelius; William Stearns.
Res., 5220 W. 155th St., 60452. Tel: 708-687-1370; Fax: 708-687-1377.
School—5300 W. 155th St., 60452. Tel: 708-687-4230. Barbara Wesolowski, Prin.
Lay Teachers 32; Students 804.
Catechesis/Religious Programs—Tel: 708-687-7788.
Students 1000.

Oak Lawn, Cook Co.,

1—St. Catherine of Alexandria, Revs. William J. Lion; John R. Dolehide, O.P.; George P. McKenna, Pastor Emeritus; Edward S. Stockus; Sr. Mary Cullen, O.P., Pastoral Assoc.; Deacon Richard Feltes.
Res., 4100 W. 107th St., 60453. Tel: 708-425-2850; Fax: 708-425-2313.
School—10621 S. Kedvale Ave., 60453. Tel: 708-425-5547; Fax: 708-425-3701.
Lay Teachers 19; Students 520.
Catechesis/Religious Programs—Tel: 708-425-5747; Fax: 708-425-3701.
Students 208.

2—St. Gerald, Revs. Richard J. LoBianco; William J. White, Pastor Emeritus; Martin T. Marren; Sr. Mary Fearon, Ministry of Care. In res., Revs. William J. Buhrfeind, (Retired); Robert E. Dovick, (Retired); John L. White, S.M., (Retired).
Parish Office: 9310 S. 55th Ct., 60453. Tel: 708-422-0234; Fax: 708-422-0822.
Res., 9349 S. Central Ave., 60453. Tel: 708-422-0234; Fax: 708-422-0822.
School—9320 S. 55th Ct., 60453. Tel: 708-422-0121; Fax: 708-422-9216.
Sisters of St. Francis (Clinton, IA) 2; Adrian Dominicans 1; Lay Teachers 23; Students 430.
Catechesis/Religious Programs—Tel: 708-423-0458.
Students 500.

3—St. Germaine, Revs. William E. Malloy; William O. Goedert, Pastor Emeritus; Mark J. Walter; Deacons John Flanagan; Donald Daum; John L. Malone; Everett Helmer.
Res., 4240 W. 98th St., 60453. Tel: 708-636-5060; Fax: 708-636-8007.
School—9735 S. Kolin, 60453. Tel: 708-425-6063.
Sisters of the Presentation of the B.V.M. 1; Lay Teachers 18; Students 390.

4—St. Linus, Rev. Joseph E. Auer; Rev. Msgr. John I. Cardiff, Pastor Emeritus; Rev. Charles Balskus; Deacons Edward Gadomski; James Reinhart.
Res., 10300 S. Lawler Ave., 60453. Tel: 708-422-2400; Fax: 708-422-2707.
School—10331 Linus Ln., 60453. Tel: 708-425-1656.
Felician Sisters 2; Lay Teachers 25; Students 560.
Catechesis/Religious Programs—Tel: 708-636-4373.
Students 360.

5—St. Louis de Montfort, Revs. William J. Quinn; Frank J. Burek; Deacons Michael Karnoski; Michael Sharwarko; William Sullivan.
Res., 8808 S. Ridgeland, 60453. Tel: 708-599-5300; Fax: 708-599-2678.
School—Tel: 708-599-5781; Fax: 708-599-5782.
Lay Teachers 11; Students 226.

Catechesis/Religious Programs—8840 S. Ridgeland, 60453. Tel: 708-598-1092.
Students 135.

Oak Park, Cook Co.,

1—ASCENSION, Revs. Francis C. Jenks; John Moulder.
Res., 815 S. East Ave., 60304. Tel: 708-848-2703; Fax: 708-848-2773.
School—601 Van Buren, 60304. Tel: 708-386-7282.
Lay Teachers 25; Students 450.
Catechesis/Religious Programs—Tel: 708-848-3099.
Students 300.

2—ST. CATHERINE OF SIENA-ST. LUCY, Revs. Daniel Whiteside; John W. Murray; John J. Carolan, Pastor Emeritus; Sr. Patricia Lucas, D.H.M., Pastoral Assoc.; Deacon Bruce Bardford.
Res., 38 N. Austin Blvd., 60302. Tel: 708-386-8077; Fax: 708-386-7755.
School—27 Washington Blvd., 60302. Tel: 708-386-5286; Fax: 708-386-7328.
Sisters of Mercy 2; Lay Teachers 12; Students 200.

3—ST. EDMUND, Rev. Joseph B. Ruiz; Sr. Madeleva Deegan, R.S.M., Pastoral Assoc.; Deacons James Przepasniak; Edward P. DeLorenzo. In res., Revs. John P. Lucas; Edward C. Dufficy.
Res., 188 S. Oak Park Ave., 60302. Tel: 708-848-4417; Fax: 708-848-0049.
School—200 S. Oak Park Ave., 60302. Tel: 708-386-5131; Fax: 708-386-5616.
Lay Teachers 14; Students 250.
Catechesis/Religious Programs—Tel: 708-848-7220.
Students 260.

4—ST. GILES, Revs. Thomas M. Dore; Leroy A. Wickowski; Deacons Loretto J. Madonia; John A. Henricks. In res., Rev. Edward P. Salmon.
Res., 1045 Columbian Ave., 60302. Tel: 708-383-3430; Fax: 708-383-8644.
School—1030 Linden Ave., 60302. Tel: 708-383-6279; Fax: 708-383-9952.
Lay Teachers 26; Students 507.
Catechesis/Religious Programs—Tel: 708-383-4185; Fax: 708-383-8669.
Students 232.

Orland Hills, Cook Co., St. Elizabeth Seton, Revs. William T. O'Mara; Brian Ardagh; Deacon Frank Gildea.
Res., 9300 W. 167th St., 60477. Tel: 708-403-0101; Fax: 708-403-0105.
School—Cardinal Joseph Bernardin. Inter-Parish School serving St. Elizabeth Seton, St. Francis of Assisi, St. Julie Billiart and St. Stephen, Deacon and Martyr. 9250 W. 167th St., 60477. Tel: 708-403-6525; Fax: 708-403-8621.
Catechesis/Religious Programs—16699 S.94th Ave., 60477. Tel: 708-403-0101; Fax: 708-403-9810.
Students 2,407.

Orland Park, Cook Co., St. Francis of Assisi, Revs. Edward F. Upton; Michael J. Weidman.
Res., 15050 S. Wolf Rd., 60467. Tel: 708-460-0042; Fax: 708-460-0136.
Catechesis/Religious Programs—Tel: 708-460-0155.
Students 1,398.

St. Michael, Revs. Edward J. McLaughlin; Louis J. Tylka; Robert J. Clark; Sr. Marietta Umlor, C.S.C., Pastoral Assoc.; Deacons Michael McDonough; Thomas Bartholomew; Tony Cocco.
Res., 14327 Highland Ave., 60462. Tel: 708-349-0903; Fax: 708-349-6015.
School—14355 Highland Ave., 60462. Tel: 708-349-0068; Fax: 708-349-2658.
Sisters 1; Lay Teachers 30; Students 893.
Catechesis/Religious Programs—14345 Highland Ave., 60462. Tel: 708-349-0769.
Students 925.

Our Lady of the Woods, Revs. Michael W. O'Connell; William J. Finnegan, Pastor Emeritus; Deacon Daniel Welter.
Res., 10731 W. 131st St., 60462. Tel: 708-361-4754; Fax: 708-361-5965.
Catechesis/Religious Programs—Tel: 708-361-9435.
Students 975.

Palatine, Cook Co., St. Theresa, Revs. John P. McNamara; Edward J. Barrett; Vinh Van Ha; Deacons Stephen Norys; John Conick; Francis P. Gildea; Richard Pizzato; Lou Riccio; Jeffrey Shaw. In res., Rev. Paul F. Rosemeyer, (Retired).
Res., 455 N. Benton, 60067. Tel: 847-705-2080; Fax: 847-202-8941.
Church—465 N. Benton, 60067. Tel: 847-358-7760.
Ministry Center: 455 N. Benton, 60067. Tel: 847-359-2846.
School—445 N. Benton, 60067. Tel: 847-359-1820; Fax: 847-705-2084.
Lay Teachers 40; Students 780.
Catechesis/Religious Programs—Tel: 847-358-2846.

Mission Juan Diego, Revs. Moises Marin, Admin.; Edward J. Maloney, Pastor Emeritus; Raphael Orozco, Pastor Emeritus.
Res., 36 W. Wilson St., 60067. Tel: 847-202-1028; Fax: 847-202-4603.

St. Thomas of Villanova, Revs. Raymond A. Yadron; Joseph M. Jackson, Admin.; Deacons Edward Kaczmarek; Kevin Leo; Thomas Maloney; Thomas Dunne; James Zdeb; Richard Willer; Eugene O'Hern; Mark Duffey.
Office: 1152 E. Anderson Dr., 60067. Tel: 847-358-6999; Fax: 847-934-4919.
School—1141 E. Anderson Dr., 60067. Tel: 847-358-2110.
Lay Teachers 14; Students 310.

Palos Heights, Cook Co., Incarnation, Revs. Ronald J. Mass; Robert E. Dovick, Pastor Emeritus; David J. Byrne; Deacons John Seitz; James Langwell.
Res., 5757 W. 127th St., 60463. Tel: 708-597-3180; Fax: 708-597-2452.
School—Tel: 708-385-6250; Fax: 708-597-0588.
Lay Teachers 15; Students 313.
Catechesis/Religious Programs—Tel: 708-388-4004; Fax: 708-597-0588.
Students 400.

St. Alexander, Revs. Edward J. Cronin; Frank A. Kurucz; Mr. Harry Leddy, Pastoral Assoc.
Res., 7025 W. 126th St., 60463. Tel: 708-448-4861; Fax: 708-448-0039.
School—126th St. at 71st Ave., 60463. Tel: 708-448-0408; Fax: 708-448-5947.
Sisters of Providence of Saint Mary-of-the-Woods, IN 2; Lay Teachers 30; Students 483.
Catechesis/Religious Programs—Tel: 708-448-6624.
Students 499.

Palos Hills, Cook Co., Sacred Heart, Revs. Richard M. Homa; Robert F. McGinnity, Pastor Emeritus; Deacon William Barker. In res., Rev. Robert G. Herne, (Retired).
Res., 8245 W. 111th St., 60465. Tel: 708-974-3336; Fax: 708-974-3556.

Park Forest, Cook Co., St. Irenaeus, Rev. Daniel J. O'Sullivan.
Res., 78 Cherry St., 60466. Tel: 708-748-6891.

Park Ridge, Cook Co., Mary, Seat of Wisdom, Revs. Ronald N. Kalas; Michael F. Conroy, S.P.S.; Theodore Stone; Deacon Michael Ruffner.
Res., 920 Granville Ave., 60068. Tel: 847-825-3153; Fax: 847-825-3484.
School—1352 S. Cumberland, 60068. Tel: 847-825-2500; Fax: 847-825-1943.
Lay Teachers 36; Students 650.
Catechesis/Religious Programs—Tel: 847-825-8763; Fax: 847-825-3484.
Students 668.

St. Paul of the Cross, Revs. Carl Morello; Joseph J. Kinane, Pastor Emeritus; Robert C. Rizzo; Neil E. Fackler; Deacon Aloysius J. Memmel. In res., Rev. Daniel A. Smilanic.
Res., 320 S. Washington St., 60068. Tel: 847-825-7605; Fax: 847-825-5186.
School—Sisters 2; Lay Teachers 27; Students 604.
Catechesis/Religious Programs—Tel: 847-692-2758.
Students 1,030.

Posen, Cook Co., St. Stanislaus Bishop and Martyr, Rev. David B. Krolczyk; Deacons Joseph Wilczynski; Daniel Dutkiewicz.
Res., 14414 McKinley Ave., 60469. Tel: 708-597-4910; Fax: 708-597-4841.
School—14418 McKinley Ave., 60469. Tel: 708-388-9211; Fax: 708-388-8755.
Lay Teachers 10; Students 250.

Prospect Heights, Cook Co., St. Alphonsus Liguori, Revs. Robert P. Heinz; Richard J. Maginot, Pastor Emeritus; Raymond A. Dunne, S.J.; Deacon Norbert Ciesil.
Res., 411 N. Wheeling Rd., 60070. Tel: 847-255-7452; Fax: 847-255-7520.
School—Tel: 847-255-5538.
Sisters 1; Lay Teachers 20; Students 341.
Catechesis/Religious Programs—Tel: 847-255-9490.
Students 325.

Riverdale, Cook Co., Queen of Apostles, Rev. Daniel M. Tomich; Deacon Gerald Hahn.
Res., 207 W. 145th St., 60827. Tel: 708-849-4901; Fax: 708-849-5903.
School—14419 S. Atlantic, 60827. Tel: 708-849-3848; Fax: 708-849-5903.
Lay Teachers 10; Students 240.
Catechesis/Religious Programs—Tel: 708-841-0252.
Students 7.

River Forest, Cook Co., St. Luke, Revs. Kenneth J. Fischer; Michael F. McMahon; Deacons Terry Norton; John O'Neill; Thomas Coffey; Paul Faherty; Robert Zima.
Res., 528 Lathrop Ave., 60305. Tel: 708-771-8250; Fax: 708-771-8809.
School—519 Ashland Ave., 60305. Tel: 708-366-8587; Fax: 708-366-3831.
Lay Teachers 25; Students 400.
Catechesis/Religious Programs—Tel: 708-771-5959; Fax: 708-771-5960.
Students 320.

St. Vincent Ferrer, Revs. Robert J. Botthof, O.P.; Robert Kilbridge, O.P.; Kevin R. Fane, O.P. In res., Revs. Brian Chrzastek, O.P.; David Delich, O.P.; Vincent I. Zarlenga, O.P.; John J. O'Malley, O.P.; Harold D. Ostidek, O.P.; Louis S. Morrone, O.P.; Richard De Ranitz, O.P.; Kevin O'Rourke, O.P.; Paul Whittington, O.P.; Deacons Robert C. Sassetti; Jerome Trakszelis.
Res., 1530 Jackson Ave., 60305. Tel: 708-366-7090; Fax: 708-366-7092.
Church—1530 Jackson Ave., 60305.
School—1515 Lathrop Ave., 60305. Tel: 708-771-5907; Fax: 708-771-7114.
Dominican Sisters 1; Sisters of St. Joseph 1; Lay Teachers 24; Students 415.
Catechesis/Religious Programs—Tel: 708-366-0322.
Students 240.

River Grove, Cook Co., St. Cyprian, Revs. Ronald E. Navoy; Michael B. Alcantara; Thomas M. Powers, Pastor Emeritus; Waldemar Kilian; Deacons James Platt; Greg Stevens.
Res., 2601 Clinton St., 60171. Tel: 708-453-4800; Fax: 708-453-6141.
School—2565 Clinton St., 60171. Tel: 708-453-6300; Fax: 708-453-6141.
Religious 3; Lay Teachers 10; Students 181.
Catechesis/Religious Programs—Tel: 708-453-5719; Fax: 708-453-6141.
Students 251.

Riverside, Cook Co., St. Mary, Revs. Gerald T. Gunderson; Leon R. Wagner, Pastor Emeritus; Robert S. Banzin; Sr. Margaret Sannasardo, B.V.M., Pastoral Assoc.
Res., 126 Herrick Rd., 60546. Tel: 708-447-1020; Fax: 708-447-3309.
School—97 Herrick Rd., 60546. Tel: 708-442-5747; Fax: 708-442-0125.
Sisters 6; Lay Teachers 25; Students 466.
Catechesis/Religious Programs—Tel: 708-447-6812.
Students 355.

Rolling Meadows, Cook Co., St. Colette, Revs. Michael P. Ahlstrom; Robert L. Tuzik; Deacons John Connor; Al Gaspari. In res., Rev. Joseph F. Ognibene, (Retired).
Res., 3900 S. Meadow Dr., 60008. Tel: 847-394-8100; Fax: 847-394-8102.
School—Lay Teachers 16; Students 288.

Rosemont-Des Plaines, Cook Co., Our Lady of Hope, Revs. William D. Mannion; Thomas E. Schwab, Pastor Emeritus; Deacon James J. Ernst. In res., Rev. Kenneth J. Velo.
Res., 9711 W. Devon Ave., Rosemont, 60018. Tel: 847-825-HOPE (4673).

Round Lake, Lake Co., St. Joseph, Revs. Raymond F. Skriba; Alfredo J. Salera; Deacons John Brooks; David Kamka.
Res., 114 N. Lincoln Ave., 60073. Tel: 847-546-3610; Fax: 847-546-3449.
School—Lay Teachers 21; Students 430.
Catechesis/Religious Programs—Tel: 847-546-3554.
Students 450.

Sauk Village, Cook Co., St. James, Rev. Thomas P. Conde; Deacons Thomas McCarthy; Thomas Schroeder. In res., Rev. Paul E. Schwartz, (Retired).
Res., 22400 S. Torrence Ave., 60411-5144. Tel: 708-757-2170; Fax: 708-757-2176.
School—22410 S. Torrence Ave., 60411-5144. Tel: 708-757-2175.
Sisters of Providence (Terre Haute, IN) 2; Lay Teachers 10; Students 180.
Catechesis/Religious Programs—Tel: 708-757-2174; Fax: 708-757-2176.
Students 215.
Convent—21903 Orion St., 60411. Tel: 708-758-5431.

Schaumburg, Cook Co., St. Marcelline, Revs. Denis Condon; Warren J. McCarthy, Pastor Emeritus; Peter M. Yangas; Deacons Edward Boggio; Joe Garcia; Richard Flam; John Zeller; Phil Ontiveros.
Res., 822 Springinsguth, 60193. Tel: 847-524-4429; Fax: 847-524-4597.
Catechesis/Religious Programs—Tel: 847-524-3960.
Students 617.

Church of the Holy Spirit, Revs. William Tkachuk; George J. Kane, Pastor Emeritus; Deacons Raymond Doud; Lowell Taylor, (Retired); Timothy Kryszak, Sr.; Luis Trevino; Wayne Beyer; Mario Contreras; Mike Enger; Sung Han.

Res., 1451 W. Bode Rd., 60194. Tel: 847-882-7580; Fax: 847-882-1845.
Catechesis/Religious Programs—Tel: 847-882-7584.
Students 1,188.

St. Matthew, Revs. Joseph M. Wilk; Kenneth R. Bratko, C.R.; Deacons William Reisen; Thomas Duszynski.
Res., 1001 E. Schaumburg Rd., 60194. Tel: 847-891-1220; Fax: 847-891-3140.
Catechesis/Religious Programs—1005 Schaumberg Rd., Schaumberg, 60194. Tel: 847-891-8408; Fax: 847-891-4291.
Students 850.

Schiller Park, Cook Co., St. Beatrice, Rev. John J. Bresnahan.
Res., 4157 Atlantic Ave., 60176. Tel: 847-678-0138; Fax: 847-678-3974.
School—Tel: 847-678-1752.
Lay Teachers 13; Students 280.

St. Maria Goretti, Rev. Thomas C. McNeff.
Res., 3929 N. Wehrman Ave., 60176. Tel: 847-678-3988.
School—Lay Teachers 12; Students 150.

Skokie, Cook Co., St. Joan of Arc, Revs. James L. Barrett; James F. Moriarty, Pastor Emeritus; John J. McMahon, Pastor Emeritus.
Res., 9248 N. Lawndale Ave., Evanston, 60203. Tel: 847-673-0409; Fax: 847-673-9626.
School—Tel: 847-679-0660; Fax: 847-673-0689.
Lay Teachers 18; Students 249.

St. Lambert, Revs. Andrew E. Luczak; William P. Welsh; Deacon John O'Leary.
Res., 8148 Karlov Ave., 60076. Tel: 847-673-5090; Fax: 847-677-5135.
School—Tel: 847-675-3060; Fax: 847-675-0280.
Sisters 1; Lay Teachers 14; Students 152.
Catechesis/Religious Programs—Tel: 847-329-1201.
Students 158.

St. Peter, Revs. Edward D. Grace; Henry C. Kricek; Deacon James Wills.
Res., 8116 Niles Center Rd., 60077. Tel: 847-673-1492; Fax: 847-673-6979.
School—8140 Niles Center Rd., 60077. Tel: 847-673-0918; Fax: 847-673-6469.
Lay Teachers 20; Students 320.
Catechesis/Religious Programs—Tel: 847-679-1202; Fax: 847-673-6469.
Students 370.

South Holland, Cook Co., St. Jude the Apostle, Revs. Thomas S. Cabala; John J. Powers, Pastor Emeritus; Deacons Herbert Drazba; Arthur Nylen.
Res., 880 E. 154th St., 60473. Tel: 708-333-3550; Fax: 708-339-3336.
School—900 E. 154th St., 60473. Tel: 708-333-8173.
Sisters 4; Lay Teachers 21; Students 405.
Catechesis/Religious Programs—Tel: 708-225-1180.
Students 50.

Holy Ghost, Revs. Joseph R. Bennett; Richard J. Feller, Pastor Emeritus.
Res., 700 E. 170th St., 60473. Tel: 708-333-7011; Fax: 708-333-1996.
School—Tel: 708-333-7010; Fax: 708-333-1693.
Lay Teachers 13; Students 250.
Catechesis/Religious Programs—Tel: 708-333-7011.
Students 59.

Stickney, Cook Co., St. Pius X, Revs. Thomas E. Unz; Thomas P. Conley, Pastor Emeritus; Deacon Marvin Kocar. In res., Rev. James F. Moriarty, (Retired).
Res., 4314 S. Oak Park Ave., 60402. Tel: 708-484-7951; Fax: 708-749-8515.
Catechesis/Religious Programs—Tel: 708-788-6090; Fax: 708-749-8518.
Students 270.

Streamwood, Cook Co., St. John the Evangelist, Revs. Robert F. Tonelli; Fred C. Pesek; John M. Kyle, Pastor Emeritus; Deacons Earl Dahl; Louis Farinella; James Furey; Robert DeFiore; Ronald Lino; Michael Nugent; Larry Rybicki.
Res., 427 Cedarcrest Dr., 60107. Tel: 630-837-6500; Fax: 630-483-3153.
School—Tel: 630-289-3040; Fax: 630289-3026.
Lay Teachers 9; Students 206.
Catechesis/Religious Programs—Tel: 630-837-1060.
Students 635.

Summit, Cook Co., St. Joseph, Revs. Thaddeus J. Bojczuk; Henry Pozdol, Pastor Emeritus; Gerald C. Kroeger, O.P.; Deacons Ben Michalowski; Peter Manning.
Res., 7240 W. 57th St., 60501. Tel: 708-458-0501.
School—5641 S. 73rd Ave., 60501. Tel: 708-458-2927.
Sisters 1; Lay Teachers 9; Students 200.

Tinley Park, Cook Co., St. George, Revs. Donald C. Cahill; Gerald Walsh; Christopher E. Doering; Deacons Richard Kristinat; Paul Gilbert; Dominick Dattoli; John Ficker; Joseph Panek. In res., Rev. Blaise Coelho.
Res., 6707 W. 175th St., 60477. Tel: 708-532-2243; Fax: 708-532-2055.
School—6700 W. 176th St., 60477. Tel: 708-522-2626; Fax: 708-532-2025.
Mantellate Sisters 2; Felician Sisters 1; Lay Teachers 22; Students 584.
Catechesis/Religious Programs—Tel: 708-532-8211.
Students 825.

Saint Julie Billiart, Revs. Anthony C. Puchenski, Admin.; James Curry; Deacons Richard Miska; Michael Kiley. In res., Rev. Robert M. Duffy, (Retired).
Res., 7399 W. 159th St., 60477. Tel: 708-429-6767; Fax: 708-429-6788.
Catechesis/Religious Programs—Students 1,419.

St. Stephen, Deacon and Martyr, Rev. James Finno; Deacons Joseph Stalcup, Sr.; Kenneth Zawadzki.
Res., 8019 Mallow Dr., 60477. Tel: 708-342-2400; Fax: 708-342-1545.
Catechesis/Religious Programs—Students 160.

Volo, Lake Co., St. Peter, Rev. Donald Dietz, O.M.I., Admin.
Res., 27551 Volo Village Rd., 60073. Tel: 815-385-5496; Fax: 516-514-4647.

Wadsworth, Lake Co., St. Patrick, Revs. Patrick G. Cecil; George J. Dyer, Pastor Emeritus; Deacons Dennis Brown, Pastoral Assoc.; John Richardson; Louis Abboud; Phillip Fragassi; Edward Tomkowiak; David Egan; Daniel Simmet.
Res., 15000 Wadsworth Rd., 60083. Tel: 847-244-4161; Fax: 847-336-0630.
School—Tel: 847-623-8446; Fax: 847-623-3119. Marcella Bosnak, Prin.
Lay Teachers 24; Students 555.
Catechesis/Religious Programs—Tel: 847-244-4161; Fax: 847-336-0630.
Students 522.

Wauconda, Lake Co., Transfiguration, Revs. Thomas M. Enright; Robert G. Aguirre; Byron G. Maher, Pastor Emeritus; Deacons Stephen Cenek; Marion Omiatek; John Zimmerman. Pastoral Ministers: Marilyn Omiatek; Dee Zimmerman.
Res., 318 Bangs St., 60084. Tel: 847-526-2400; Fax: 847-526-2961.
School—Tel: 847-526-6311; Fax: 847-526-4637.
Lay Teachers 26; Students 345.
Catechesis/Religious Programs—Tel: 847-526-6400.
Students 526.

Waukegan, Lake Co.,

1—St. Anastasia, Revs. Terrence A. McCarthy; Edward S. Maraczewski, Pastor Emeritus; Aloysius Funtila.
Res., 624 Douglas Ave., 60085. Tel: 847-623-2875; Fax: 847-623-4882.
School—Lay Teachers 18; Students 439.

2—St. Bartholomew. Merged with St. Joseph. See Holy Family for details.

3—St. Dismas, Revs. John M. Ryan; Paul J. Cull, Pastor Emeritus; Deacons Anthony Sacramento; Paul Telle.
Res., 2600 Sunset Ave., 60087. Tel: 847-623-5050; Fax: 847-623-5292.
Catechesis/Religious Programs—2226 McAree Rd., 60087. Tel: 847-244-9510; Fax: 847-623-5092.
Students 135.

4—Holy Family, Revs. Gary M. Graf; Sergio Solis; Deacons Ralph Bufano; Julio A. Negron; Edward Scarbalis; Angel Velazquez. In res., Rev. Michael Boehm.
Res., 501 S. Utica St., P.O. Box 440, 60085. Tel: 847-623-2655; Fax: 847-623-9479.
School—Participant in Lake Shore Catholic Academy. 515 S. Utica St., 60085.

5—St. Joseph. Merged with St. Bartholomew. See Holy Family listing for details.

6—Immaculate Conception B.V.M., Revs. Frank W. Plotka; Antoni Kretowicz (Extern-Poland). In res., Rev. James P. Shields.
Res., 508 Grand Ave., 60085. Tel: 847-336-3684; Fax: 847-336-9040.
School—Lay Teachers 16; Students 200.

Westchester, Cook Co., Divine Infant, Revs. Gerald P. Joyce; William M. Henkel, Pastor Emeritus; Thomas Winikates.
Res., 1601 Newcastle Ave., 60154. Tel: 708-865-8071.
School—Tel: 708-865-0122.
Lay Teachers 21; Students 270.
Catechesis/Religious Programs—Students 275.
Convent— Institute of the Blessed Virgin Mary (I.B.V.M.)

Divine Providence, Revs. John C. Rosemeyer; Timothy R. Fiala; Sr. Kay Buechele, O.P., Pastoral Assoc.; Deacon Frank DeVita, (Retired).
Res., 2550 S. Mayfair Ave., 60154. Tel: 708-562-3364; Fax: 708-562-3134.
School—2500 S. Mayfair Ave., 60154. Tel: 708-562-2258.
Lay Teachers 13; Students 217.
Catechesis/Religious Programs—Tel: 708-562-3422; Fax: 708-562-3134.
Students 114.

Western Springs, Cook Co., St. John of the Cross, Revs. Richard P. Hynes; Joseph F. McDonnell, Pastor Emeritus; John W. McGivern; Sr. Jeanne Bonneau, C.N.D., Pastoral Assoc.; Deacons William Engler; Thomas McGorey; Joseph Pepitone. In res., Rev. Michael J. Cronin.
Res., 5005 Wolf Rd., 60558. Tel: 708-246-4404; Fax: 708-246-4566.
School—705 51st St., 60558. Tel: 708-246-4454; Fax: 708-246-9010.
Sisters 1; Lay Teachers 39; Students 805.
Catechesis/Religious Programs—51st St. & Wolf Rd., 60558. Tel: 708-246-6760; Fax: 708-246-9010.
Students 990.

Wheeling, Cook Co., St. Joseph the Worker, Rev. Frederick L. Brandstrader; Deacons Perry Duderstadt; Steve Stecker.
Res., 181 W. Dundee Rd., 60090. Tel: 847-537-2740; Fax: 847-537-7914.
Catechesis/Religious Programs—Tel: 847-537-4182.
Students 800.

Wilmette, Cook Co., St. Francis Xavier, Revs. Edward F. Harnett; George W. Klein. Pastoral Assocs.: Sr. Joyce Shanabarger, O.S.F.; Dr. Patty Jane Pelton; Deacons Michael Cavanaugh; William Thesing. In res., Rev. Richard Jakubik.
Office: 524 Ninth St., 60091. Tel: 847-256-4250; Fax: 847-256-4254.
School—808 Linden Ave., 60091. Tel: 847-256-0644. Sr. Mary K. O'Brien, B.V.M., Prin.
Sisters 1; Lay Teachers 28; Students 437.
Catechesis/Religious Programs—Tel: 847-251-6730; Fax: 847-256-4254.
Students 660.

St. Joseph, Revs. Francis J. Kane; John Szmyd; Ms. Dana McKenna, Pastoral Assoc. In res., Revs. John E. Pollard; Thomas M. Powers.
Res., 1747 Lake Ave., 60091. Tel: 847-251-0771; Fax: 847-251-5715.
School—1757 Lake Ave., 60091. Tel: 847-256-7870. Marlene A. Bowne, Prin.
Lay Teachers 17; Students 260.
Catechesis/Religious Programs—Tel: 847-251-3254.
Students 385.

Winnetka, Cook Co., SS. Faith, Hope and Charity, Rev. Thomas F. Ventura; Rev. Msgr. Eugene F. Lyons, Pastor Emeritus; Rev. Gene F. Smith; Deacons Terrence Levins; Roger Mullaney. In res., Rev. William J. Flaherty.
Res., 191 Linden St., 60093. Tel: 847-446-7646; Fax: 847-446-7630.
School—180 Ridge Ave., 60093. Tel: 847-446-0031; Fax: 847-446-9064.
Sisters 1; Lay Teachers 35; Students 452.
Catechesis/Religious Programs—Students 658.

Sacred Heart, Revs. Robert E. Ferrigan; Thomas J. Raftery, Pastor Emeritus; Mark Simpson; Jacque Beltran (Philippines); Deacons D. J. Shinkle; Michael McNulty; John Fay.
Res., 905 Burr Ave., 60093. Tel: 847-446-0856; Fax: 847-501-5311.
Parish Center—1077 Tower Rd., 60093. Tel: 847-446-0856.
School—1095 Gage St., 60093. Tel: 847-446-0005.
Lay Teachers 24; Students 255.
Catechesis/Religious Programs—Students 396.

Zion-Beach Park, Lake Co., Our Lady of Humility, Rev. David J. Mulvihill; Deacons James Askew; Philip Horne; Max Jinkens; Michael Mercure.
Res., 10655 Wadsworth Rd., 60099. Tel: 847-872-8778; Fax: 847-872-8780.
School—10601 Wadsworth Rd., 60099. Tel: 847-746-3722; Fax: 847-731-2870. Ms. Deborah Poturalski, Prin.
Lay Teachers 13; Students 245.
Catechesis/Religious Programs—Tel: 847-746-3744; Fax: 847-872-8780.
Students 415.

Syro-Malabar Rite

Bellwood, Cook Co., Syro-Malabar Catholic Mission of the Archdiocese of Chicago, Rev. Jacob Angadiath, Dir.
Center Mar Thoma Shleeba Church: 5000 St. Charles Rd., 60104. Tel: 708-544-7250; Fax: 708-544-5890.
Catechesis/Religious Programs—Students 395.

Chicago, Cook Co., Knanite Syro-Malabar Catholic Mission of the Archdiocese of Chicago, Rev. Philip Joseph Thodukayil, Dir.
Res., Immaculate Heart of Mary, 3834 N. Spaulding, 60618. Tel: 773-509-9147; Fax: 773-478-1844.

Malankara Rite

Chicago, Cook Co., Syro-Malankara Catholic Mission of the Archdiocese of Chicago,
Divine Liturgy at: 1208 Ashland St., Evanston, 60202. Tel: 847-475-4093. Rev. Msgr. Geevarchese Mannikarott, Dir.

Chaplains of Public Institutions

CHICAGO. *Chicago O'Hare International Airport* P.O. Box 66353, 60666. Rev. John A. Jamnicky.
Cook County Hospital. Revs. Jacek Walkiewicz, S.Ch.; William O. Madden, S.J.; John F. Pennington, S.J.; Sr. Marie Louise Jilk, S.Sp.S.
Hines V.A. Hospital. Rev. James E. Burnett (DAV).
V.A. Lakeside Medical Center. Rev. Robert J. Borre (MAD).

NORTH CHICAGO. *Veterans Affairs Medical Center*. Revs. William F. Vander Heyden (GB); Edward E. Lisowski (MIL).

OAK FOREST. *Oak Forest Hospital* 4700 W. 159th St., 60452. Tel: 708-687-2035. Revs. Adam Wolf, O.F.M.; Wayne H. Wurst.

On Duty Outside the Archdiocese:
Reverend Monsignors—
Sarauskas, R. George, Office to Aid Central/Eastern Europe Catholic, 3211 4th St. N.E., Washington, DC 20017-1194
Trisco, Robert F., Curley Hall, Catholic University of America, Washington, DC 20064
Reverend Fathers—
Barnum, Martin, Sacred Heart School of Theology, 7335 S. Hwy. 100, P.O. Box 429, Hales Corners, WI 53130-0429
Brankin, Patrick M., St. Theresa, P.O. Box 297, Collinsville, OK 74021-0297
Broccolo, Gerard T., 1011 S. Valentia St., #135, Denver, CO 80231
Clements, George H., 1000 16th St. N.W., #702, Washington, DC 20026
Coughlin, Daniel P., Office of the Chaplain, U.S. House of Representatives, H B 25 The Capitol, Washington, DC 20004
Dempsey, Robert J., Editor, L'Osservatore Romano, Villa Stritch, Via della Nocetta, 63, 00164 Rome, Italy
Hotchkin, John F., Bishops' Commission for Ecumenical Affairs, 4001 14th St., N.E., Washington, DC 20017-1194
Keusal, Eugene L., Our Lady of Mt. Carmel, 48-422 Kamehameha Hwy., Waikane, HI 96744
Kiley, J. Cletus, NCCB-USCC Staff House, 4001 14th St., N.E., Washington, DC 20017
Lorenz, Matthais E., 5531 E. Lake Dr., Lisle, IL 60532
Place, Michael D., S.T.D., The Catholic Health Association of the United States, 4455 Woodson Rd., P.O. Box 5889A, St. Louis, MO 63134-9916

Military Chaplains:
Reverend Monsignors—
Dobes, George E., Archdiocese for the Military Services U.S.A., P.O. Box 4469, Washington, DC 20017-0469
Reverend Fathers—
Falkenthal, Thomas W., P.O. Box 55001, MCAS, Beaufort, SC 29904-5001
Joslyn, James W., PSC 451, Box 914, FPO, AE 09834-2800
Kloak, David G., Chap. Dept., USS Constellation (CV-64), 96635-2780 Japan
Simpson, Brian L., Marine Memorial Chapel, Box 555024, Camp Pendelton, CA 92055-5024
Stake, Ronald P., PSC 556 Box 315, FPO AP, 96386-0315

Graduate Studies:
Reverend Fathers—
Bradley, Michael J., The American College, Naamsestraat 100, 3000 Leuven, Belgium
Grob, Jeffrey S., 1300 Richmond Rd., #411, K2B 8L2 Canada
Huitrado, Juan, Calle Seminario No. 26, Col Santa Ursula Xitla, 1400 Mexico DF
Kunkel, Ronald T., Pontifical North American College, 00120 Rome, Italy
Wolff, Alec J., Casa Santa Maria, Via dell' Umilta 30, 00187 Rome, Italy

Missionary Work:
Reverend Fathers—
Cleary, Philip C., Nuestros Pequenos Hermanos, Apartado Postal, 333, 62000 Cuernavaca, Morelos, Mexico
Cowell, Raymond, Parroquia Nuestra Senoria de Fatima, El Pari Casilla 919, Santa Cruz, Bolivia
Hays, Kevin W., Society of St. James the Apostle, 24 Clark St., Boston, MA 02109

Other Assignments:
Reverend Fathers—
Allen, Joseph P., St. John the Baptist, 205 S. Locus St., Box 133, Arcola, IL 61910
Barzyk, Andrew A., 2905 W. Pope John Paul II Dr., Chicago, IL 60632
Becker, Charles P., Handmaids of Precious Blood Convent, 24140 W. Petite Lake Rd., Lake Villa, IL 60046
Clair, John J., Misericordia-North, 6300 N. Ridge Ave., Chicago, IL 60660
Clemens, John W., 1634 W. Gregory St., Chicago, IL 60640
Coleman, Robert P., c/o Rev. Pablo Straub, C.Ss.R., 1605 B Pacific Rim Ct., PMB 009/439015, San Diego, CA 92143-9015
DeRoeck, Walter G., 645 N. Michigan Ave., #543, Chicago, IL 60611
Egan, Gerard P., Loyola University, 820 N. Michigan, Chicago, IL 60611
Ezerskis, Charles E., 15234 Myrtle Ave., Harvey, IL 60626-3194
Galivan, James F., 14641 S. Keeler Ave., Midlothian, IL 60445
Garza, Jesse P., 11044 E. Creek Rd., Clinton, WI 53525
Gilligan, Michael J., American Catholic Press, 16565 S. State St., South Holland, IL 60473
Grzela, Andrew S., 5032 S. Kostner, Chicago, IL 60632
Hannigan, John T., St. Maurice, P.O. Box 45, 706 E. Fourth St., Morrisonville, IL 62546-0045
Hurtado-Badillo, Domingo, 916 N. Noble, P.O. Box 220351, Chicago, IL 60622
Ivers, Michael T., c/o James Cox, 1008 Paseo Del Pueblo Sur #307, Taos, NM 87571
LaChance, Charles P., 810 W. Montrose Ave., Chicago, IL 60613
Laz, Medard P., P.O. Box 300415, Chicago, IL 60630
Lefebure, Leo D., Christ the King, 740 N. Broadway, Yonkers, NY 10701
Maday, Norbert J., P.O. Box 455, Mundelein, IL 60060
Maloney, William P., 3646 W. 125th St., Alsip, IL 60803
McCarthy, James H., Special Religious Ed. Div., 2953 S. Lowe, Chicago, IL 60616
McGlinn, Robert J., Cristo Rey Parish, 800 Wisconsin Ave., Racine, WI 53403
McKenna, Edward J., 645 N. Michigan Ave., Ste. 543, Chicago, IL 60611
Milek, Richard, Bishop Abramowicz House, 1147 W. Superior, Chicago, IL 60622
Nangle, Thomas R., Police Chaplaincy, 1140 W. Jackson, Chicago, IL 60607
O'Keefe, Millard, 2525 59th St., Wood Ridge, IL 60517-1114
Ray, James M., P.O. Box 167233, Chicago, IL 60616-7233
Ruge, Kenneth C., P.O. Box 455, Mundelein, IL 60060
Sevick, John M., 75-246 Malulani Dr., Kailuna-Kona, HI 96740
Sheahan, Kevin, 124 N. Spring Ave., LaGrange, IL 60525
Steiner, Daniel R., Bonaventure House, 825 W. Wellinton, Chicago, IL 60657
Strand, Ralph S., P.O. Box 455, Mundelein, IL 60060
Strus, Walter A., 2905 W. Pope John Paul II Dr., Chicago, IL 60632
Swade, Thomas J., 2058 N. Clark St., Chicago, IL 60614
Szabelski, Joseph R., Queen of Peace Retirement Center, 24955 N. Hwy. 12, Lake Zurich, IL 60047
Tabor, Kenneth F., St. Benedict Home, 6930 W. Touhy, Niles, IL 60714
Talarico, Anthony, 645 N. Michigan #543, Chicago, IL 60611
Tanghal, Alberto R., 6949 W. Addison St., Chicago, IL 60634
Vitro, Thomas J., P.O. Box 932, Lake Geneva, WI 53147

Retired:
Reverend Monsignors—
Bergin, Clifford E., 5912 Cleveland, Morton Grove, IL 60053
Cardiff, John I., St. Linus, 10300 S. Lawler Ave., Oak Lawn, IL 60453
Carroll, Donald M., 7260 W. Peterson, Chicago, IL 60631
Egan, John J., 730 N. Wabash, Chicago, IL 60611
Farrell, John J., St. Andrew Home, 7000 N. Newark, Niles, IL 60714
Hardiman, James C., 4126 W. 99th St., Oak Lawn, IL 60453
Hayes, John M., 2524 S. Keeler Chicago, IL 60623
Higgins, George C., Curley Hall 220, Catholic University of America, Washington, DC 20064
Koenig, Harry C., Addolorata Villa, 555 McHenry Rd., Wheeling, IL 60090
Lyons, Eugene F., c/o Eugene Flynn, 21770 W. Hidden Valley, Kildeer, IL 60047
McDermott, Ignatius D., The McDermott Foundation, 932 W. Washington St., Chicago, IL 60607
Mohan, Thomas J., Addolorata Villa, 559 McHenry Rd., Wheeling, IL 60090
Mozeris, Damasus A., Resurrection Life Center, 7370 W. Talcott, Chicago, IL 60631
Mroczkowski, Joseph J., 1501 Hoffman St., Hammond, IN 46327
O'Day, Martin J., 13240 W. Circle Dr., No. 305, Crestwood, IL 60445
Quinn, William J., St. Eulalia, 1851 S. 9th Ave., Maywood, IL 60153
Roche, M. Edward, St. Benedict Home, 6930 W. Touhy Ave., Niles, IL 60714-4522
Reverend Fathers—
Adamich, Albert R., Most Holy Redeemer, 9525 S. Lawndale Ave., Evergreen Park, IL 60042
Ahearn, Donald J., St. Juliana, 7142 N. Osceola, Chicago, IL 60631
Ahern, John J., 6804 Joliet Rd., Indian Head Park, IL 60525
Ahern, John J., St. Benedict Home, 6930 W. Touhy, Niles, IL 60714
Baldwin, John F., CHC,USN (Retired), 5100 Marine Dr., #27-M, Chicago, IL 60640
Ballweber, Eugene L., 2302 Julie S.W., Albuquerque, NM 87105
Barr, Pierre J., 3825 S. California Ave., Chicago, IL 60633
Barron, Edward M., 1515 E. 154th St., #130, Dolton, IL 60419
Bednarz, Matt A., 5600 N. Fairfield, Chicago, IL 60659-4817
Borowczyk, Martin R., St. Francis Borgia, 8033 W. Addison, Chicago, IL 60634
Boyle, Thomas S., One Cambridge Ct., Michigan City, IN 46360
Brett, James D., c/o Michelle Schlesser, 380 N. Oaklawn Ave., Elmhurst, IL 60126-2120
Brodfuehrer, Robert S., 5205 N. Lieb, Chicago, IL 60630-1433
Brzozowski, Edward J., 13356 Buffalo Ave., Chicago, IL 60633
Buhrfeind, William J., St. Gerald, 9349 S. Central, Oak Lawn, IL 60453
Bull, Albert D., 13047 W. Ballad Dr., Sun City West, AZ 85375-1812
Burns, Eugene P., 797 Waverly Rd., LaPorte, IN 46350
Bykowski, Norbert H., 1318 Millstream Dr., McHenry, IL 60050
Carolan, John J., St. Juliana, 7142 N. Osceola Ave., Chicago, IL 60631
Carroll, Gilbert A., St. Timothy, 6326 N. Washtenaw, Chicago, IL 60659
Cerniglia, Francis J., Queen of the Rosary, 750 Elk Grove Blvd., Elk Grove, IL 60007-4298
Chapell, Norbert A., 7737 Golf View Dr., Palos Heights, IL 60463
Chen, Anthony K., Chung-jen, School of Nursing, 217 Hung Mao PI, Taiwan
Chisek, Anthony S., 1 Thornwood Mall, Apt. 1002, University Park, IL 60466
Ciemiega, Ernest D., St. Bruno, 4751 S. Harding, Chicago, IL 60632
Coffey, Edward N., St. Andrew Home, 7000 N. Newark, Niles, IL 60714
Conley, Thomas P., St. Zachary, 567 N. Algonquin Rd., Des Plaines, IL 60016
Corcoran, Edward G., 17530 S. 70th Ave., Tinley Park, IL 60477
Coughlin, Roger J., 721 N. LaSalle St., Chicago, IL 60610
Crosby, John M., 7933 Golf Dr., Apt. #1B, Palos Heights, IL 60463
Cross, Robert A., 700 Ashland, River Forest, IL 60305
Cull, Paul J., 920 Vost Dr., Apt. #212, Gurnee, IL 60031
Cullen, George H., St. Benedict Home, 6930 W. Touhy, Niles, IL 60714
Curley, Thomas J., 2825 W. 81st St., Chicago, IL 60652
Czajka, Norman M., 5426 S. Lockwood, Chicago, IL 60638
Davitt, James P., St. Benedict Home, 6030 W. Touhy, Room #3, Nilest, IL 60714
Dedek, John F., 1130 S. Michigan Ave., #3811, Chicago, IL 60605
Devine, William J., P.O. Box 53, Worth, IL 60482
Dilla, Francis E., P.O. Box 88, New Carlisle, IN 46552

Dillon, Arthur J., P.O. Box 125, Powers Lake, WI 53159
Dolciamore, John V., Mundelein Seminary of the University of St. Mary of the Lake, Mundelein, IL 60060
Donohue, John J., 2400 Archbury Ln., Park Ridge, IL 60068
Dovick, Robert E., St. Gerald, 9349 S. Central Ave., Oak Lawn, IL 60453
Downes, Thomas J., 2630 Sierra Dr., Colorado Springs, CO 80917
Doyle, James P., 2 Beechwood Ln., Largo, FL 33770
Dufficy, Edward C., St. Edmund, 188 S. Oak Park Ave., Oak Park, IL 60302
Duffy, Donald J., Resurrection Life Center, 7370 W. Talcott, Chicago, IL 60631
Duffy, Robert M., 7399 W. 159th St., Tinley Park, IL 60477
Duggan, J. Edward, St. Bartholomew, 4949 W. Patterson Ave., Chicago, IL 60641
Durkin, Eugene F., Holy Name Cathedral, 730 N. Wabash Ave., Chicago, IL 60611
Dyer, George J., St. Patrick, 15000 Wadsworth Rd., Wadsworth, IL 60083
Enright, John P., 1801 W. 35th St., #1217, Oakbrook, IL 60521
Fassbinder, Richard W., 135 S. Milwaukee Ave., Lake Villa, IL 60046
Faucher, Eugene J., St. Edna, 2525 N. Arlington Heights Rd., Arlington Heights, IL 60004
Felczak, Leonard J., 4325 S. Spaulding, Chicago, IL 60632
Feller, Richard J., 1201 Bonita Dr., Park Ridge, IL 60068-5017
Festle, Robert H., 5046 N. Ashland Ave., Chicago, IL 60640
Finnegan, John P., St. Mary of Vernon, 236A U.S. Hwy. 45, Indian Creek, IL 60061
Finnegan, William J., Infant Jesus of Prague, 1131 Douglas Ave., Flossmoor, IL 60422
Fisher, Frederick J., Our Lady of Holy Cross Care Center, San Pierre, IN 46374
Fitzgerald, Edward P., Mercy Hospital and Medical Center, Stevenson Expwy. at King Dr., Chicago, IL 60616
Fitzgerald, Thomas J., 5472 S. Kimbark, Chicago, IL 60615
Fitzpatrick, Edmund J., 444 Fullerton, #1604, Chicago, IL 60614
Fitzpatrick, Robert J., St. Bede Parish, 36455 N. Wilson Rd., Ingleside, IL 60041-9609
Flaherty, William J., 191 Linden St., Winnetka, IL 60093-3832
Fraser, Gerald D., 23 Asheford Ct., Lincolnshire, IL 60069-2121
Frawley, John P., 2825 W. 81st St., Chicago, IL 60652-2722
Gallagher, Charles G., St. Cletus, 600 W. 55th St., La Grange, IL 60525
Gerrity, Raymond J., 917 S. 8th Ave., #2, LaGrange, IL 60525
Giese, Vincent J., Cardinal Stritch Retreat House, 1000 E. Maple Ave., P.O. Box 455, Mundelein, IL 60060
Goedert, William O., St. Germaine, 4240 W. 98th St., Oak Lawn, IL 60453
Grace, James N., 1833 E. Wildberry Dr., Glenview, IL 60025
Grace, John J., St. Tarcissus, 6020 W. Ardmore Ave., Chicago, IL 60646
Graff, J. Austin, St. Thomas More, 2825 W. 81st St., Chicago, IL 60652
Greeley, Andrew M., N.O.R.C., 1155 E. 60th St., Chicago, IL 60637
Grinis, Bruno B., 12433 S. Halsted St., Chicago, IL 60628
Grinis, Julian G., Mother Theresa Home, 1270 Franciscan Dr., Lemont, IL 60439
Gruchot, Stanley J., 7000 Newark, Chicago, IL 60643
Gubbins, William B., 718 W. Adams St., Chicago, IL 60661
Gunia, Edward S., 904 Joliet Rd., Room #2, Countryside, IL 60525
Hanley, Lawrence F., 7112 Concord Cir., Fox Lake, IL 60020
Hayes, Peter F., St. Benedict Home, 6930 W. Touhy Ave., Niles, IL 60714
Hefferan, John E., St. Bede, 36455 N. Wilson Rd., Ingleside, IL 60041-9609
Helfrich, George J., 7958 W. Foster Ave., Chicago, IL 60656
Henkel, William A., Mother Theresa Home, 1270 Franciscan Dr., Lemont, IL 60439
Herne, Robert G., Sacred Heart Parish, 8245 W. 111th St., Palos Hills, IL 60465
Hills, Richard L., St. Benedict Home, 6930 W. Touhy Ave., Niles, IL 60714
Hock, William T., St. Benedict Home, 6930 W. Touhy Ave., Niles, IL 60714
Hoffman, Matthias H., 1131 Douglas Ave., Flossmoor, IL 60422
Hosty, Thomas J., 8419 Bailey Rd., Darien, IL 60561
Hughes, Edward J., 6930 W. Touhy, E-5, Niles, IL 60714
Huske, Leonard G., 347 Daffodil Ln., Matteson, IL 60443
Ivers, Victor J., St. Joseph, 121 E. Maple Ave., Libertyville, IL 60048-2283
Jarzynski, Edward M., Resurrection Life Center, 7370 W. Talcott, Chicago, IL 60631
Jasinski, Raymond J., Handmaids of the Precious Blood, 724 Petite Lake Rd., Lake Villa, IL 60046
Jozwiak, Richard M., 385 N. Edinburgh, Frankfort, IL 60423
Juchcinski, Clarence J., 16001 Lowe Ave., Harvey, IL 60426
Kane, George J., 1700 Cambourne, Schaumburg, IL 60194
Kash, Robert J., 21 S. Spring Ave., Unit A, LeGrange, IL 50525-2272
Kastigar, John J., 1774 Lexington Dr., Sierra Vista, AZ 85635
Kauzlarich, John, 9997 Cambridge Ct. D, Mokena, IL 60448-7095
Kaveney, Thomas J., St. Odilo, 2244 S. East Ave., Berwyn, IL 60402
Keating, James W., St. Andrew Home, 7000 N. Newark, Niles, IL 60714
Keating, James P., 10201 S. Ewing Ave., Chicago, IL 60617
Kelly, Charles F., Box 455, Powers Lake, WI 53155-0455
Kelly, William J., c/o Jones, 3332 S. 59th Ave., Cicero, IL 60650
Kinane, Joseph J., St. Paul of the Cross, 320 S. Washington St., Park Ridge, IL 60068
Kireilis, Fabian P., 9838 S. 81st Ave., Palos Hills, IL 60465
Kirkilas, Michael, 6666 20th Ave., N.E., St. Petersburg, FL 33710
Kleiber, Kenneth R., 15202 N. 40th St., #223-2, Phoenix, AZ 85032-4652
Klug, Jerome G., 26166 W. Mattalina Ct., Ingleside, IL 60041
Kouba, Charles J., 5157 S. California, Chicago, IL 60632
Kozien, Casimir J., 4949 W. Patterson Ave., Chicago, IL 60641
Kuzinskas, John A., 12375 McCarthy Rd., Lemont, IL 60438
Kyle, John M., 7000 N. Newark, No. 516, Niles, IL 60648
Lambert, Rollins E., 4924 Arroyo Chamisa, Alburquerque, NM 87111
Lee, Joseph, 5730 W. Fullerton, Chicago, IL 60639
LeVoy, Joseph T., St. Benedict Home, 6930 W. Touhy Ave., W4, Niles, IL 60714
Limanowski, Stanley C., 100 Mutiny Ln., Apt. #104, Merritt Island, FL 32952-2521
Lisowski, William J., 15714 Old Orchard Ct., Orland Park, IL 60462
Lutz, Robert J., St. Norbert, 1809 Walters Ave., Northbrook, IL 60062
Lynch, Cletus J., 1010 American Eagle Blvd., #609, Sun City Center, FL 33573
Lynch, Joseph P., 14130 Green Valley Dr., Orland Park, IL 60462
Lyons, James W., 410 N. 1st St., Cary, IL 60013
Lyons, Leo J., 14226-84th Ave., Orland Park, IL 60462
Mackin, John J., 8925 S. Kostner, Hometown, IL 60456
Maginot, Richard J., St. Alphonsus Liguori, 411 N. Wheeling Rd., Prospect Heights, IL 60070
Maher, Byron G., 416 E. Jefferson, Burlington, WI 53105
Maher, Thomas F., St. Mary-of-the-Woods, 7033 N. Moselle Ave., Chicago, IL 60646
Mahon, Leo T., St. Mary of the Woods, 7033 N. Moselle Ave., Chicago, IL 60646
Makuch, Thaddeus J., St. Mary Czestochowa, 3010 S. 48th Ct., Cicero, IL 60804
Maloney, Edward J., 7417 Channahon Ct., Fox Lake, IL 60020
Maniola, Francis N., 6135 S. Austin, Chicago, IL 60638
Maraczewski, Edward S., 1516 E. Lowden, Mt. Prospect, IL 60056
Marszalek, Paul B., 15103 Quail Hollow Dr., Unit #601, Orland Park, IL 60462
Martin, William J., Bethlehem Woods, 1571 W. Ogden Ave., LeGrange Park, IL 60525
McCaig, John J., (Sept.-April), Vilas de Golf, #1206, 12300 Vonn Rd., Largo, Fl 345644
McCarthy, Warren J., 1080 W. Irving Park Rd., Schaumburg, IL 60172
McDonagh, Andrew J., 6939 N. Hiawatha, Chicago, IL 60646
McDonald, Matthew D., Resurrection Retirement Community, 7260 W. Peterson, Chicago, IL 60631
McDonnell, Joseph F., 17 W. 706 Butterfield Rd., Oakbrook Terrace, IL 60181
McGinnity, Joseph P., St. Zachary, 567 W. Algonquin Rd., Des Plaines, IL 60016
McGinnity, Robert F., Sacred Heart, 8245 W. 111th St., Palos Hills, IL 60465
McGrath, John F., 10726 S. Sacramento, Chicago, IL 60655
McHugh, Thomas J., St. Matthias Parish, 2310 W. Ainslie, Chicago, IL 60625
McKenna, George P., Chaplain Midway Airport, 9720 S. Kedzie, Evergreen Park, IL 60805
McKiernan, Thomas M., 7939 Lakeview Ct., Palos Heights, IL 60463
McLaughlin, Charles J., Alden-Long Grove Nursing Home, 2308 Old Hicks Rd., Long Grove, IL 60047
McMahon, John J., 2535 Lake Ave., Wilmette, IL 60092
Meyer, Charles R., Mundelein Seminary, University of St. Mary-of-the-Lake, Mundelein, IL 60060
Mezydlo, Leonard T., St. Stephen Protomartyr Parish, 1267 Everett St., Des Plaines, IL 60018
Michalek, Henry J., 7264 W. Peterson Ave., C-605, Chicago, IL 60631
Mikolaitis, Vito E., 6812 S. Washtenaw, Chicago, IL 60629
Millea, Thomas V., 4342 N. Lieb, Chicago, IL 60630
Mollan, Ralph R., 1321 Burning Bush Ln., Mt. Prospect, IL 60056
Mollohan, James L., 4949 W. Patterson, Chicago, IL 60641
Morgan, Edward J., 119 Evergreen Dr., Frankfort, IL 60423
Moriarty, James F., St. Pius X, 4314 S. Oak Park, Stickney, IL 60402
Morris, John J., 2214 S.W. 29th Ter. No. 33, Topeka, KS 66611-1956
Murphy, William P., Queen of Martyrs, 10233 S. Central Pk., Evergreen Park, IL 60642
Nicola, John J., P.O. Box 1505, Pinehurst, NC 28370
Norkett, Edward J., Immaculate Conception Parish, 1590 Green Bay Rd., Highland Park, IL 60035
Novak, Robert J., 2960 N. Lake Shore Dr., Apt. 1209, Chicago, IL 60657
Nowak, Joseph G., 8237 S. Shore Dr., Chicago, IL 60617
O'Brien, John E., 12365 First Ct., Pleasant Prairie, WI 53158-5308
O'Brien, Joseph J., 300 N. State St., Chicago, IL 60610
O'Connor, James T., St. Emily, 101 N. Horner Ln., Mt. Prospect, IL 60056
O'Donnell, Richard J., 3528 S. Hermitage, Chicago, IL 60609
Ognibene, Joseph F., St. Colette, 3900 S. Meadow Dr., Rolling Meadows, IL 60008
Olejniczak, Henry A., 15704 Lake Hills Ct., Orland Park, IL 60462
Orozco, Raphael R., 200 W. Wood St., Palatine, IL 60067-5346
Ouletta, James F., 141 S. Lake Shore, EG, Racine, WI 53403
Pastick, Joseph A., 4939 Floramar Ter., #608, New Port Richey, FL 34652-3310
Paurazas, Peter P., Maria H.S. Convent, 6727 S. California Ave., Chicago, IL 60629
Peng, John B., 3420 N. Kolmar, Chicago, IL 60641
Powers, John J., St. Jude the Apostle, 880 E. 154th St., South Holland, IL 60473
Powers, Thomas M., St. Joseph, 1747 Lake Ave., Wilmette, IL 60091
Pozdol, Henry, 7240 W. 57th St., Summit, IL 60501
Pribyl, Francis T., 2651 S. Central Park, Chicago, IL 60623
Quinlan, William J., June-Nov., Our Lady of the Wayside, 432 W. Park St., Arlington Heights, IL 60005
Raftery, Thomas J., Christ the King, 9235 S. Hamilton, Chicago, IL 60620
Rochford, John J., 18102 S. 66th Ct., #401, Tinley Park, IL 60477
Rodell, Jeremiah J., 7330 Galeview Ln., Frankfort, IL 60423
Rosemeyer, Paul F., St. Theresa, 467 Benton, Palatine, IL 60067
Rudcki, Stanley R., 7712 W. Oak Ridge Ct., #2B, Palos Heights, IL 60463
Scarlata, Ronald E., 1662 Willow Circle Dr., Cresthill, IL 60435
Schouten, Francis L., 5242 Opal Ln., T203, New Port Richey, FL 34652
Schreiber, Edmund J., 9613 Schiller Blvd., Franklin Park, IL 60131
Schroeder, Richard F., 7216 Oxford Cir., Fox Lake, IL 60020
Schwab, Thomas E., 9711 W. Devon Ave., Rosemont, IL 60018

Schwartz, Paul E., St. James, 22244 S. Torrence Ave., Sauk Village, IL 60411-5144
Seitz, Joseph W., 9131 S. Sacramento, Evergreen Park, IL 60805
Seitz, Thomas R., St. Thomas the Apostle, 5472 S. Kimbark, Chicago, IL 60615
Shaunessy, Francis W., St. Benedict Home, 6930 W. Touhy Ave., Niles, IL 60714
Sheridan, William H., 2132 E. 72nd St., Chicago, IL 60649
Shields, James P., Immaculate Conception, 509 Julian St., Waukegan, IL 60085
Shields, William J., 116 N. Lake St., Mundelein, IL 60060
Shirey, John W., 8725 S. May, Chicago, IL 60620
Siedlecki, Edmund J., Cardinal Stritch House, 1000 E. Maple, P.O. Box 455, Mundelein, IL 60060
Siwek, Jerome S., St. Benedict Home, 6930 W. Touhy Ave., Niles, IL 60714
Skach, Charles J., P.O. Box 509, Mt. Prospect, IL 60056
Skupien, Edward D., St. Andrew Home, 7000 N. Newark, Niles, IL 60714
Slominski, George A., Resurrection Life Center, 7370 W. Talcott, Chicago, IL 60631
Slosarcik, Edward A., 13950 Main St., Lemont, IL 60439
Somerville, Walter F., 7574 E. Camine de Querabi, Tuscon, AZ 85715
Spellman, Francis J., St. Benedict Home, 6930 W. Touhy, Niles, IL 60714
Stefanski, Walter, 29 E. McEldowney St., Chicago Heights, IL 60411
Sullivan, C. Otis, St. Benedict Home, 6930 W. Touhy Ave., Niles, IL 60714
Sullivan, Daniel J., 3217 W. 184th St., Homewood, IL 60430
Szatkowski, Casimir M., 8030 S. Pulaski, Chicago, IL 60652
Szlanga, Edmund S., St. Symphorosa, 6135 S. Austin Ave., Chicago, IL 60638
Taylor, Joseph C., 4350 W. Sunnyside Ave., Chicago, IL 60630
Tessmer, Richard A., 800 W. Biesterfield Rd., Elk Grove Village, IL 60007
Thomas, Joseph S., St. John Vianney, 42 N. Wolf Rd., Northlake, IL 60164
Tlapa, Richard J., 6350 S. Taft Ave., Merrillville, IN 46410
Troy, Henry A., c/o Mr. Edward L. Troy, 9727 Lindgren Ave., Sun City, AZ 85373
Tuite, Howard A., 700 S. Paulina, #922, Chicago, IL 60612
Vader, Anthony J., 11652 S. Church St., Chicago, IL 60643
Velutis, John, 11129 S. Homan, Chicago, IL 60655
Vita, Mariano L., 1809 E. 31st St., La Grange Park, IL 60525
Wagner, Leon R., 2435 Seabrook Island Rd., John Island, SC 29455
Walsh, Michael J., Sacred Heart, 8245 W. 111th St., Palos Hills, IL 60465
Wasiel, Michael J., 546 E. 155th St., Harvey, IL 60426
Waszak, Norbert J., 6101 S. 75 Ave., Argo, IL 60501
Weber, Gerard P., 4316 Lanai Rd., Encino, CA 91436
White, Bernard C., 3020 N. 76th Ct., Elmwood Park, IL 60707
White, William J., 10418 S. Keating Ave., #3D, Oak Lawn, IL 60453
Windle, John J., 459 Homestead, La Grange Park, IL 60525
Winters, Martin N., Benedictine Monastery of Our Lady of Sorrows, 5800 W. 147th St., Oak Forest, IL 60452
Wodniak, John L., 5730 W. Fullerton, Chicago, IL 60639
Wojcik, Richard J., Mundelein Seminary of the Univerisity of St. Mary-of-the-Lake, Mundelein, 60060
Zakarauskas, Anthony J., P.O. Box 42915, Evergreen Park, IL 60805
Zawistanowicz, Norbert J., Our Lady of Victory Parish, 5212 W. Agatite Ave., Chicago, IL 60630

Permanent Deacons:
Abboud, Louis, St. Patrick, Wadsworth
Ahern, Michael, Our Lady of Victory
Albano, Terris, Our Lady of the Ridge, Chicago Ridge
Allen, Leslie, Jr., St. Sabina, Chicago
Allen, Warren, St. Kilian, Chicago
Alonso, Enrique, Our Lady of Grace, Chicago
Alvarez, Ignacio, St. Rita
Alvarez, Jose, St. Fidelis, Chicago
Alvarez, Margarito, Our Lady of Guadalupe, Chicago
Amberg, John, St. Mary of the Assumption, Chicago
Antiss, Robert S., Holy Family, Inverness
Antonsen, Larry, Christ the King, Chicago
Askew, James, Our Lady of Humility, Beach Park/Zion
Auld, David D., Santa Maria del Popolo, Mundelein
Aurelio, Benjamin, Jr., St. Robert Bellarine, Chicago
Avila, Mario, Precious Blood, Chicago
Bacchi, Benedict, St. Eulalia, Maywood
Banet, Robert, St. Andrew the Apostle, Calumet City
Barker, William, Sacred Heart, Palos Hills
Barone, Louis, St. Ansgar, Hanover Park
Bartholomew, Thomas, St. Michael, Orland Park
Barton, Jeffrey, St. Peter, Antioch
Bates, Eugene, (Retired), St. Thecla, Chicago
Baum, Richard, St. Anne, Barrington
Behrendt, Raymond J., Sacred Heart, Melrose Park
Beil, Frank, St. Catherine Laboure, Glenview
Belanger, James, (Retired)
Bell, Kenneth, St. Domitilla, Hillside
Benthey, Herman, St. Anne, Hazel Crest
Bergquist, Bernard, (Retired), St. Tarcissus, Chicago
Beyer, Wayne, Church of Holy Spirit, Schaumburg
Bishop, Joseph, St. Rosalie, Harwood Heights
Blais, Emile, St. Mary of the Angels
Blanco, Jesus, St. Ann
Boehm, Owen, St. Rene, Chicago
Boggio, Edward, St. Marcelline, Schaumburg
Bohannon, Morris E., (Retired), St. Clotilde, Chicago
Boharic, Robert, St. Mary, Riverside
Bonifazi, Virgilio, St. John Berchmans, Chicago
Borha, George, St. Columbanus, Chicago
Bovyn, Paul, Resurrection, Chicago
Bradford, Bruce, St. Catherine of Siena/St. Lucy, Oak Park
Brady, Joseph, St. Christopher, Midlothian
Brauch, Robert, St. Anne, Barrington
Brencic, David, St. Barbara, Brookfield
Bretz, Michael, St. Catherine Laboure, Glenview
Brongiel, Andrew, St. Barbara, Chicago
Brooks, George, Infant Jesus of Prague, Flossmoor
Brooks, John, (Retired), St. Joseph, Round Lake
Brown, Dennis G., St. Patrick, Wadsworth
Bryce, Irvin, St. Albert the Great, Burbank
Bumbel, John, St. Gall, Chicago
Burke, Henry, Ascension/St. Susanna, Harvey
Burns, James, St. Donatus, Blue Island
Bustos, Gregorio, St. Clare of Montefalco, Chicago
Bzdon, Gregory M., St. Tarcissus, Chicago
Cabrera, Jorge, St. John Berchmans, Chicago
Camerini, Guilio, St. Eulalia, Maywood
Carrizales, Maximiliano, Providence of God, Chicago
Carroll, Daniel, St. Walter, Chicago
Carvlin, Thomas, Ascension/St. Susanna, Harvey
Cascino, Joseph, Jr., St. Viator, Chicago
Castanon, Toribio, Holy Cross-Immaculate Heart of Mary, Chicago
Cavanaugh, Michael, St. Francis Xavier, Wilmette
Cenek, Stephen, Transfiguration, Wauconda
Centeno, Benito, St. Genevieve, Chicago
Cervantes, Leopoldo, St. Peter Canisius, Chicago
Cesario, Carmen, (Retired), Our Lady, Mother of the Church
Chaidez, Lorenzo, St. Gertrude, Franklin Park
Chappel, Dorsey, (Retired), St. Leo the Great, Chicago
Chausse, Joseph, (Retired), St. George, Tinley Park
Chavez, Abraham, St. Simeon, Bellwood
Childers, Terry D., Christ the King, Chicago
Chrastka, Joel, St. Leonard, Berwyn
Churilla, William, St. Anne, Hazelcrest
Chyba, Lawrence J., St. Bruno
Ciesil, Norbert, St. Alphonsus, Prospect Heights
Cintron, Gilberto, St. Hedwig, Chicago
Cnota, Robert F., St. Francis Borgia, Chicago
Cocco, Anthony, St. Michael, Orland Park
Coffey, Thomas W., St. Luke, River Forest
Colgan, Dennis L., St. William, Chicago
Colucci, Victor, Sacred Heart, Melrose Park
Condill, James, St. Anne, Barrington
Condon, Edward, St. Cornelius, Chicago
Connor, John, St. Colette, Rolling Meadows
Constanopolis, Louis, St. Benedict the African (West), Chicago
Contreras, Mario, Church of the Holy Spirit, Schaumburg
Conway, James, St. Barnabas, Chicago
Cooper, Willie, (Retired), St. Laurence, Chicago
Corcoran, Thomas, St. Raymond de Penafort, Mount Prospect
Cordesman, Ellsworth, (Retired), St. James, Highwood
Cordoba, Angelo, St. Joseph (Hermitage Ave.), Chicago
Crandall, Robert, (Retired), Our Lady of Ransom, Niles
Crane, Walter James, St. Ann, Barrington
Crespo, Feliciano
Crespo, Hipolito, St. Sylvester
Czarnecki, Thaddeus, Queen of the Rosary, Elk Grove Village
Dahl, Earl, St. John the Evangelist, Streamwood
Dattoli, Dominick, St. George, Tinley Park
Daum, Donald, St. Germaine, Oak Lawn
Davis, James, (Retired), St. Martin de Porres, Chicago
Deabel, Raymond, St. James Hospital, Chicago Heights
Debnar, John, St. Barbara, Brookfield
DeFiore, Robert, St. John the Evangelist, Streamwood
Dehler, Thomas, St. Lawrence O'Toole, Matteson
DeJesus, Confesor, St. Sylvester, Chicago
Del Llano, Manuel, Our Lady of Mercy, Chicago
Delaney, James, St. Bede the Venerable, Chicago
DeLarco, Michael, St. Celestine, Elmwood Park
DeLorenzo, Edward, St. Edmund, Oak Park
DeLuna, Arthur, Sta. Maria Addolorata, Chicago
DeRose, Ronald, Kolbe House, Chicago
Detloff, James, St. Emeric, Country Club Hills
Devereux, Robert, Our Lady of the Mount, Cicero
Devine, James, St. Celestine, Elmwood Park
DeVita, Frank, (Retired), Divine Providence, Westchester
Diaz, Benjamin, St. Philomena, Chicago
Diaz De Leon, Raymundo, St. Blase, Argo
DiCanio, Vito W., St. Emily, Mt. Prospect
Dienberg, Clifford
Disparte, Philip, St. Matthew, Schaumburg
DiVirgilio, Dante, St. Mary of Vernon, Indian Creek
Dixon, Roscoe B., St. Dorothy
Dolan, Edward, St. Juliana, Chicago
Donovan, Timothy, Old St. Mary's, Chicago
Dorgan, Eugene J., St. Pascal, Chicago
Doud, Raymond, Church of the Holy Spirit, Schaumburg
Drazba, Herbert, St. Jude the Apostle, South Holland
Dubrownik, Phillip, St. Emeric, Country Club Hills
Duderstadt, Peery, St. Joseph the Worker, Wheeling
Duffy, Frank, St. Henry, Chicago
Duffy, Mark, St. Thomas of Villanova, Palatine
Duffy, Robert, Our Lady of the Wayside, Arlington Heights
Dulen, John, (Retired), St. John Brebeuf, Niles
Dunn, Dennis, St. Joseph, Libertyville
Dunn, William F., Jr., Santa Maria del Popolo, Mundelein
Dunne, Thomas, St. Thomas of Villanova, Palatine
Duszynski, Thomas, St. Matthew, Schaumburg
Dutkiewicz, Daniel, St. Stanislaus, Bishop & Martyr, Posen
Dwyer, James T., (Retired), Church of the Holy Spirit, Schaumburg
Echevarria, Ramon, Our Lady of Tepeyac, Chicago
Egan, David, St. Patrick, Wadsworth
Ende, Gilbert, Special Ministry
Enger, Michael, Church of the Holy Spirit, Schaumburg
Engler, William, St. John of the Cross, Western Springs
Ernst, James, Our Lady of Hope, Rosemont
Estrada, Vincente, Immaculate Conception, Chicago
Ewers, Thomas, St. Denis, Chicago
Faherty, Paul, St. Luke, River Forest
Farinella, Louis A., St. John the Evangelist, Streamwood
Favila, Angel, St. Agnes of Bohemia, Chicago
Fay, John, Sacred Heart, Winnetka
Feltes, Richard, St. Catherine of Alexandria, Oak Lawn
Fernandez, Dismas, St. Maurice, Chicago
Ferrini, Armand, St. James, Arlington Heights
Ficker, John, St. George, Tinley Park
Figueroa, Roberto, St. Gregory, Chicago
Finnegan, Michael, St. Juliana, Chicago
Flam, Richard, St. Marcelline, Schaumburg
Flanagan, John, St. Germaine, Oak Lawn
Flewellen, James, St. Thaddeus, Chicago
Flores, Nicolas, St. Stanislaus Kostka, Chicago
Foley, Brendan, Our Lady of the Wayside, Arlington Heights
Fox, Gerald, (Retired), St. Barbara, Brookfield
Fragassi, Phillip, St. Patrick, Wadsworth
Fronczek, Casimir, St. Francis Borgia Deaf Center, Chicago
Fruge, James, Immaculate Conception, Highland Park
Fuller, George, (Retired), Resurrection, Chicago
Furey, James P., St. John the Evangelist, Streamwood
Gadomski, Edward, St. Linus, Oak Lawn
Gagnon, Robert, St. Peter, Antioch
Gallagher, James, St. James, Highwood
Gallagher, John, (Retired)
Garcia, Jose, St. Marcelline, Schaumburg
Garcia, Miguel, St. Stanislaus Kostka, Chicago

Garza, Juan L., St. Paul, Chicago Heights
Gaspari, Alfred V., St. Colette, Rolling Meadows
Gavin, Raymond, St. Catherine Laboure, Glenview
Gembara, Emil, (Retired), St. Alexander, Palos Heights
Gilbert, Paul, St. George, Tinley Park
Gildea, Francis, St. Elizabeth Seton, Orland Park
Girjatowicz, Frank, St. Hyacinth
Glatz, John, St. Cajetan, Chicago
Globis, Richard J., St. Gilbert, Grayslake
Gniech, George, St. Constance, Chicago
Golab, Chester J., St. Daniel the Prophet, Chicago
Gonzales, Jose M., St. Bartholomew
Gordus, Richard, Mater Christi, North Riverside
Graffia, Raymond, St. Edna, Arlington Heights
Green, Richard, St. Turibius, Chicago
Grevenites, James, St. Louise de Marillace, LaGrange Park
Gronek, Ronald, Divine Savior, Norridge
Gronkiewicz, Edmund, Our Lady of Mount Carmel, Chicago
Grossnickle, Donald R., Our Lady of the Wayside, Arlington Heights
Gutierrez, Jorge, St. Mark, Chicago
Hahn, Gerald E., Queen of Apostles, Riverdale
Halper, Bernard, (Retired), St. Kieran, Chicago Heights
Han, Sung, Church of the Holy Spirit, Schaumburg
Hankett, Richard G., Queen of Angels, Chicago
Hare, Martin, (Retired), Holy Rosary, Chicago
Harrington, John, Kolbe House
Harris, Wallace, St. Dorothy, Chicago
Hart, Vernon, Seven Holy Founders, Calumet Park
Hatch, Wilmer, (Retired), St. Philip Neri, Chicago
Hayden, Thomas L., St. Hubert, Hoffman Estates
Helmer, Everett, (Retired), St. Germaine, Oak Lawn
Hempen, Harold, St. Irenaeus, Park Forest
Hennessy, Matthew, St. James, Arlington Heights
Henning, George J., St. Mary of the Woods
Henricks, John, St. Giles, Oak Park
Henry, Francis, Nativity of Our Lord, Chicago
Henry, Roy, Our Lady of Lourdes, Chicago
Hensley, Claude, St. Anthony, Cicero
Hermann, Dean, Queen of Peace, North Chicago
Hernandez, Sigifredo, St. Jerome, Chicago
Herrera, Albert, St. Gall, Chicago
Herrera, Armando, Mary Queen of Heaven, Chicago
Herrera, Marcial, St. John Berchmans, Chicago
Hess, Rudolf, Our Lady of Good Counsel
Hill, Edwin, St. Nicholas of Tolentine, Chicago
Hill, John, (Retired), Our Lady of Peace, Chicago
Hinch, Ralph, St. Francis Borgia Deaf Center, Chicago
Hipelius, Thomas, St. Damian, Oak Forest
Horne, Philip G., Our Lady of Humility, Zion
Hotcaveg, Irwin E., St. Ferdinand, Chicago
Howard, Samuel E., Infant Jesus of Prague, Flossmoor
Hubbard, James, St. Felicitas, Chicago
Huber, Charles, St. Francis Borgia, Chicago
Hudzik, Richard, St. Maria Goretti, Schiller Park
Hurley, William, Christ the King, Chicago
Huslig, Dennis, St. Louise de Marillac, La Grange Park
Hyde, Thomas, St. Joseph, Summitt
Ibarra, Juan, St. Stanislaus Kostka, Chicago
Iwan, Henry, St. Gilbert, Grayslake
Jablonski, Robert, St. Zachary, Des Plaines
Jablonski, William, St. Kieran, Chicago Heights
Jacob, Robert, St. Benedict, Chicago
Jay, Richard, (Retired), St. Athanasius, Evanston
Jean-Pierre, Fritz, St. Jerome, Chicago
Jeffrey, August, Divine Savior, Norridge
Jenney, Kenneth, Jr., Immaculate Heart of Mary, Chicago
Jinkens, Max R., Our Lady of Humility, Zion
Johnson, Mervin, St. Leo the Great, Chicago
Kaczmarek, Edward, St. Thomas of Villanova, Palatine
Kalivoda, Bill, Addolorata Villa, Wheeling
Kamka, David, St. Joseph, Round Lakes
Kancler, Lawrence, Special Ministry
Karnoski, Michael, St. Louis de Montfort, Oak Lawn
Kasimatis, Jerome, Holy Cross, Deerfield
Kearney, John, Immaculate Heart of Mary, Chicago
Keating, Timothy, St. Lawrence O'Toole, Matteson
Keegan, Charles, St. Patricia, Hickory Hills
Kenney, James, St. Mary, Lake Forest
Kiley, Michael E., St. Julie Billart, Tinley Park
Klemanovic, John, Our Lady of Lourdes, Chicago
Klonicke, Ronald, St. Helen, Chicago
Knippen, James, (Retired), St. Hubert, Hoffman Esttes
Kocar, Marvin, St. Pius X, Stickney
Kort, Clayton, St. John Fisher, Chicago
Kotleba, Rudolf, Holy Family/St. Francis Assisi, Chicago
Kotwas, Donald, (Retired), St. Bede the Venerable, Chicago
Kowalski, David J., St. Louise de Marillac, LaGrange Park
Kozuchowski, Chester, St. Gilbert, Grayslake
Krakora, Joseph, St. Mary, Lake Forest
Krapez, Michael, Our Lady of the Ridge, Chicago Ridge
Kristinat, Richard L., St. George, Tinley Park
Kryszak, Timothy, Holy Spirit, Schaumburg
Kukla, Eugene, St. Mary, Buffalo Grove
Kwasegroch, Gerald, St. Eugene, Chicago
Kwasigroch, James, Our Lady of Grace, Chicago
La Belle, Eugene, St. Kieran, Chicago Heights
LaCoursiere, Victor, St. Jerome, Chicago
Lagges, Peter, St. Zachary, Des Plaines
Lambert, George, (Retired), St. Eulalia, Maywood
Lambert, Thomas, St. Catherine Laboure, Glenview
Langwell, James E., Incarnation, Palos Heights
Lara, Luis, Immaculate Conception, Highland Park
Lawson, Richard, St. Hubert, Hoffman Estates
Leck, Robert, Our Lady of Victory, Chicago
Lehman, William B., Divine Savior, Norridge
Lekan, Louis, St. James, Arlington Heights
Leo, Kevin, St. Thomas of Villanova, Palatine
Leonard, Timothy, Prince of Peace, Lake Villa
Leonas, John, (Retired), St. Anne, Hazel Crest
Lesnieski, Norbert, SS. Cyril & Methodius, Lemont
Levins, Terrence, SS. Faith, Hope & Charity, Winnetka
Lewis, Joseph, Our Lady of Sorrows, Chicago
Liberti, Peter, All Saints-St. Anthony, Chicago
Lilly, Leroy, (Retired), St. Laurence, Chicago
Limon, Juan, St. Benedict, Blue Island
Limon, Vincente, Our Lady of Tepeyac, Chicago
Lino, Ronald, St. John the Evangelist, Streamwood
Lisowski, Thaddeus, St. Constance, Chicago
Llano, Antonio, Our Lady of the Mount, Cicero
Llorens, Anthony, St. Martin de Porres, Chicago
Long, Gary, St. Mary, Buffalo Grove
Lopez, Adolf, St. Aloysius, Chicago
Lopez, Agapito, St. Hedwig, Chicago
Lopez, Bricio, University of Illinois Hospitals
Lorbach, John, St. Raymond de Penafort, Mt. Prospect
Lugo, Gregorio, Our Lady of Grace, Chicago
Lundy, Albert, Our Lady of Knock, Calumet City
Mackert, Martin, (Retired), All Saints-St. Anthony, Chicago
Maddock, George, St. Joseph, Homewood
Madonia, Loretto, St. Giles, Oak Park
Mages, William, St. Mary of the Woods, Chicago
Maldonado, Meliquides, (Retired), St. Mark, Chicago
Malec, Albert, St. Daniel the Prophet, Chicago
Malloy, William, Queen of All Saints Basilica
Mally, Joseph, St. Adalbert, Chicago
Malone, Jack, St. Germaine, Oak Lawn
Maloney, Thomas J., St. Thomas of Villanova, Palatine
Maney, Antonio, St. James, Maywood
Manning, Peter, St. Joseph, Summit
Manthie, Robert, St. Edna, Arlington Heights
Marella, Dominic, St. Charles Borromeo, Melrose Park
Marotto, Angelo, St. Domitilla, Hillside
Marquez, J. Frank, (Retired), St. Pascal, Chicago
Marrero, Jose, St. Roman, Chicago
Martinez, Francisco, St. Philomena, Chicago
Martinez, Pedro, Queen of Peace, North Chicago
Mason, Frederick
Matthews, Robert, St. Joseph, Libertyville
Mauch, Richard, (Retired), St. Ann, Lansing
Maune, William, St. Irenaeus, Park Forest
Maurer, William, Infant Jesus of Prague, Flossmoor
McAllister, Dennis F., Our Lady of the Brook, Northbrook
McCarthy, Thomas, St. James, Sauk Village
McCloskey, Michael, Holy Name Cathedral, Chicago
McDonough, Michael, St. Michael, Orland Park
McElrath, Bruce, St. Ailbe, Chicago
McGorey, Thomas, St. John of the Cross, Western Springs
McKinnis, William, St. Columbanus, Chicago
McLynn, Michael, St. Louis de Marillac, La Grange Park
McMahon, John, St. Bede, Ingleside
McNulty, Michael, Sacred Heart, Winnetka
Meehan, Peter, St. Martha, Morton Grove
Meehan, Thomas, (Retired), Our Lady of Loretto, Hometown
Mele, John, Special Ministry
Melkovitz, Emil, (Retired), St. Francis Borgia, Chicago
Memmel, Aloysius, St. Paul of the Cross, Park Ridge
Mench, Sidney, (Retired), St. John Fisher, Chicago
Mendez, Genaro, Special Ministry
Mendizabal, Guillermo, St. John Berchmans, Chicago
Mercure, Michael, Our Lady of Humility, Zion-Beach Park
Metallo, Arthur, St. Francis Hospital, Evanston
Michalowski, Benedict, St. Joseph, Summit
Milender, Leonard, Prince of Peace, Lake Villa
Miska, Richard, St. Julie Billiart, Tinley Park
Mondello, Christopher, St. Gilbert, Grayslake
Mongan, Martin, St. John Fisher, Chicago
Monica, Robert, St. Thomas the Apostle, Chicago
Monnelly, Michael, Queen of All Saints, Chicago
Monterroso, Oscar, St. Ansgar, Hanover Park
Moore, Steven, St. Anne, Hazel Crest
Morales, Juan, St. Anthony, Cicero
Moran, Charles, (Retired), St. John the Evangelist, Streamwood
Moreno, Eusebio, Holy Family, Waukegan
Morgan, James, St. Gelasius, Chicago
Moritz, Richard H., Immaculate Conception (Talcott Rd.)
Morowczynski, Romuald, St. Jane de Chantal, Chicago
Morton, Wayne, St. Lawrence O'Toole, Matteson
Mudd, Dennis, St. Joseph, Libertyville
Mujica, Ines, (Retired)
Mullaney, Roger, SS. Faith, Hope & Charity, Winnetka
Multeri, James R., Holy Family, Inverness
Munda, Gary, Sr., Queen of Peace, North Chicago
Munoz, Romeo, St. Jude the Apostle, South Holland
Munoz, Ubaldo, St. Mary of the Lake
Murphy, Robert, St. Gertrude, Franklin Park
Murphy, Robert, St. Jerome, Chicago
Murray, Michael, (Retired), Our Lady of the Brook, Northbrook
Navarro, Anthonio, St. Mark, Chicago
Navarro, Jesse, St. Mary, Star of the Sea, Chicago
Navolio, John, St. Mary of the Lake
Nazario, Carlos, Our Lady of Grace, Chicago
Negron, Julio A., Queen of Peace, North Chicago
Neurauter, Paul, St. Peter, Antioch
Newhall, Redondo, St. Cajetan, Chicago
Newman, Jeffrey, St. Gilbert, Grayslake
Newton, Robert, St. Peter Damian, Bartlett
Nguyen, Duc Van, St. Thomas of Canterbury, Chicago
Nieves, Bienvenido, Queen of Angels, Chicago
Nimietz, James, (Retired), St. John the Evangelist, Streamwood
Nolan, John, St. Julian Eymard, Elk Grove Park
Norton, Terrence, St. Luke, River Forest
Norys, Stephen, St. Theresa, Palatine
Nowak, Thomas, St. Agnes, Chicago Heights
Nugent, J Michael, St. John the Evangelist, Streamwood
Nunez, Raul, Our Lady of Guadalupe, Chicago
Nylen, Arthur A., St. Jude the Apostle, South Holland
O'Brien, Thomas, (Retired), St. Emeric, Country Club Hills
O'Connell, Thomas, St. Walter, Chicago
O'Donnell, Charles, Our Lady of Ransom, Niles
O'Donnell, Patrick, (Retired), St. Damian, Oak Forest
O'Grady, Donald A., (Retired), Queen of Angels, Chicago
O'Hern, Eugene, St. Thomas of Villanova, Palatine
O'Keefe, Robert C., St. Isaac Jogues, Niles
O'Leary, Edward, St. Eugene, Chicago
O'Leary, John A., St. Joseph, Homewood
O'Leary, John, St. Lambert, Skokie
O'Malley, James, (Retired)
O'Neill, John, St. Luke, River Forest
Oborski, Zygfryd, St. Stanislaus Bishop & Martyr, Chicago
Ochoa, Jesus, St. Rita, Chicago
Ochoa, Zeferino, Holy Family/St. Francis of Assisi, Chicago
Odegard, Robert, St. Priscilla, Chicago
Ojeda, Norberto, St. James, Maywood
Olson, Carl, St. Cornelius, Chicago
Omiatek, Marion, Transfiguration, Wauconda
Ontiveros, Philip, St. Marcelline, Schaumburg
Ortega, Ignacio, St. Mark, Chicago
Ortiz, Sigifredo, St. Sylvester, Chicago
Pagliai, Bruno, St. James, Highwood
Palmer, Donald, St. Joseph (Orleans St.), Chicago
Palmer, Lawrence, St. Benedict, Blue Island
Paluch, Thomas M., St. John Brebeuf, Niles
Pane, Peter, St. John the Evangelist, Streamwood
Panek, Joseph, St. George, Tinley Park
Paskauskas, Vitas, Nativity, B.V.M.
Pastirik, Joseph, (Retired), St. Francis de Sales, Chicago
Pecson, Andres, Our Lady, Mother of the Church
Pena, Leonardo, Area Hispanic Ministry
Penich, Michael, Jr., St. Paul the Apostle, Gurnee
Pepitone, Joe, St. John of the Cross, Western Springs

Perez, Alphonse M., (Retired), Assumption, Chicago
Perez, Carlos, (Retired)
Perez, Luis, Santa Maria Addolorata, Chicago
Perez, Miguel, St. Pius V., Chicago
Perez, Orlando, St. Thomas of Canterbury, Chicago
Perkowitz, John, St. John Brebeuf, Niles
Peters, Bruce, St. Mary, Buffalo Grove
Peterson, George A., (Retired)
Petricca, Clemente, St. Ansgar, Hanover Park
Phillippi, Joseph, St. James, Arlington Heights
Pineda, Javier, St. Adrian, Chicago
Pistone, John, St. Thomas of Villanova, Palatine
Pizzato, Richard, St. Theresa, Palatine
Plantz, Robert, (Retired), St. James, Arlington Heights
Platt, James, St. Cyprian, River Grove
Poletto, Robert, St. Mary, Fremont Center, Mundelein
Ponce, Antonio, Our Lady of Charity, Cicero
Price, Gregory, St. Symphorosa, Chicago
Przepasniak, James, St. Edmund, Oak Park
Puhala, Robert, St. Bartholomew, Chicago
Quackenbush, Edward, St. Bede, Ingleside
Quinn, Eugene, Holy Ghost, South Holland
Ragonese, Dan, St. Victor, Calumet City
Ramirez, Juan, St. Pancratius, Chicago
Ramos, Dennis, St. Aloysius, Chicago
Ramos, Eliseo, St. Jerome
Ramos, Francisco, St. Philomena, Chicago
Ranke, Dennis, Our Lady of Victory, Chicago
Ray, Frederick W., (Retired), St. Isaac Jogues, Niles
Rehor, Timothy, St. Bernardine, Forest Park
Reinert, William, St. James, Arlington Heights
Reinhart, James, St. Linus, Oak Lawn
Reisen, William, St. Matthew, Schaumburg
Renk, Dennis, Special Ministry
Revering, Roman, St. James, Maywood
Revord, James, Our Lady of Perpetual Help, Glenview
Reyes, David, Immaculate Heart of Mary
Riccio, Louis, Charismatic Renewal Office; St. Theresa, Palatine
Richardson, John, St. Patrick, Wadsworth
Richardson, Leonard M., St. Sabina, Chicago
Riffner, Joseph, St. Alphonsus, Chicago
Riner, Edwin, (Retired)
Rios, Jamie, St. Wenselaus, Chicago
Rivas, Roberto, Our Lady of Mercy, Chicago
Rivera, Hector, St. Teresa of Avila, Chicago
Robles, Ernesto, Our Lady of Grace, Chicago
Rodriguez, Candelario, Notre Dame, Chicago
Rodriguez, Emiliano, St. Bonaventure, Chicago
Rodriguez, Juan, Queen of the Universe, Chicago
Rodriguez, Manuel, St. Francis of Assisi, Chicago
Rodriguez, Milton, Maternity of B.V.M., Chicago
Rodriguez, Uriol, Resurrection, Chicago
Roman, Francisco, St. Sylvester, Chicago
Roman, Tito, St. Bonaventure, Chicago
Romano, Michael, St. Joseph Hospital, Chicago
Rosado, Julio, St. Francis of Rome, Cicero
Roy, Jasper, Holy Angels, Chicago
Rozo, Jorge, Holy Rosary, Chicago
Rueth, William, St. Hugh, Lyons
Ruffner, R. Michael, Mary, Seat of Wisdom, Park Ridge
Ryan, Edward, St. Anthony, Chicago
Ryan, Robert E., Sr., St. Juliana, Chicago
Ryan, Thomas, St. Christina, Chicago
Rybicki, Lawrence, St. John the Evangelist, Streamwood
Sacramento, Anthony, St. Dismas, Waukegan
Salgado, Alfonso, St. Anthony, Cicero
Sanchez, Sabino, St. Francis and Our Lady of the Angels, Chicago
Sanchez, Salvador, St. Francis of Assisi/Our Lady of the Angels, Chicago
Sandoval, Jose M., Immaculate Conception
Sands, William, St. Joseph, Libertyville
Sanford, James, St. Emily, Mount Prospect
Sanzone, Michael, Special Ministry
Sassetti, Robert C., St. Vincent Ferrer, River Forest
Sattler, David, St. Peter Damien, Bartlett
Savercool, Gerald, St. Lawrence O'Toole, Matteson
Scarbalis, Edward, Holy Family, Waukegan
Schiltz, James, St. Constance, Chicago
Schoenfeld, Kenneth, St. Fabian, Bridgeview
Schoewe, Rudolph, Our Lady of Victory, Chicago
Schroeder, Thomas, St. James, Sauk Village
Schultz, Ronald, (Retired), St. Victor, Calumet City
Sedivy, Alan, Our Lady of Perpetual Help, Glenview
Seitz, John, Incarnation, Palos Heights
Serna, Francisco, St. Helen
Serratore, Gregory, St. Mary Star of Sea, Chicago
Seveska, Richard, St. Anne, Barrington
Sharwarko, Michael, St. Louis de Monfort, Oak Lawn
Shaw, Jeffrey L., St. Theresa, Palatine
Shaw, Ralph, St. Ambrose
Sheehan, Patrick P., St. James, Arlington Heights
Shinkle, Derald, Sacred Heart, Winnetka
Shumpert, Gregory, St. Agatha
Silva, Rodrigo, St. Ann, Chicago
Simmet, Daniel, St. Patrick, Wadsworth
Simmons, John, Santa Maria del Popolo, Mundelein
Sinacore, James M., Divine Infant, Westchester
Siranovic, Joseph, Notre Dame de Chicago, Chicago
Skaja, Lawrence, St. John Brebeuf, Niles
Slajchert, Michael, St. Gall, Chicago
Smith, John J., St. Zachary, Des Plaines
Smith, Michael E., St. Christopher, Midlothian
Smith, Robert S., Jr., Holy Cross, Deerfield
Solon, Thomas, St. Denis, Chicago
Soria, Carlos, St. Sylvester
Soto, Pedro, St. John Bosco, Chicago
Soto, Santos, St. Sylvester, Chicago
Spalla, Paul, St. Mary-of-the-Lake, Chicago
Spitizzeri, Fred, St. Priscilla, Chicago
Spohr, Lawrence, St. Domitilla, Hillside
Staddler, Ted, Queen of the Rosary, Elk Grove Village
Stalcup, Joseph, Sr., St. George, Tinley Park
Stanczak, Stefan, (Retired), St. Hyacinth, Chicago
Stanton, Paul, St. Isaac Jogues, Niles
Stasinski, Melvin, St. Jude the Apostle, South Holland
Stearns, William, St. Damian, Oak Forest
Stecker, Stephen, St. Joseph the Worker, Wheeling
Steinbeigle, Francis, St. Damian, Oak Forest
Stevens, Gregory, St. Peter Damian, Bartlett
Stubstad, Thomas, St. Pascal, Chicago
Sullivan, William, St. Barnabas, Chicago
Sullivan, William, St. Louis de Montfort, Oak Lawn
Sutton, Daniel, St. Helena of the Cross, Chicago
Swiatek, Ronald, St. John Bosco, Chicago
Swiech, Edward, (Retired), St. Robert Bellarmine, Chicago
Szady, Mitchell, St. Stanislaus B & M, Chicago
Taylor, Lowell, (Retired), Church of the Holy Spirit, Schaumburg
Telle, Paul, St. Dismas, Waukegan
Telposky, Donald, St. Stephen, Des Plaines
Temple, James, St. Barnabas, Chicago
Tereza, Nick, St. Ansgar, Hanover Park
Thesing, William, St. Francis Xavier, Wilmette
Tipperreiter, Charles, St. Fabian, Bridgeview
Tomkowiak, Edward, St. Patrick, Wadsworth
Torres, Candido, Our Lady of Fatima, Chicago
Trakszelis, Jerome, St. Vincent Ferror, River Forest
Trevino, Luis, Chicago-O'Hare International Airport
Troy, Daniel J., Holy Ghost, South Holland
Tryba, Edmund, (Retired), St. Hilary, Chicago
Uroza, Jose, St. Angela, Chicago
Valadez, Abundio, St. Benedict, Chicago
Valdivia, Juan, Our Lady of Guadalupe, Chicago
Valentin, Israel, St. Philomena, Chicago
Valle, Miguel Angel, Our Lady of Lourdes, Chicago
Varela, Joaqium, St. Nicholas of Tolentine
Vargas, Miguel, Mision Juan Diego, Palatine
Vazquez, Jose, Maternity B.V.M., Chicago
Velasco, Arturo, St. Francis of Assisi, Chicago
Velasco, Benito, Maternity B.V.M., Chicago
Velazquez, Angel, Holy Family, Waukegan
Vellurattil, Matthew, St. Ladislaus
Vemich, Duke, All Saints-St. Anthony, Chicago
Vera, Camilo, St. Viator, Chicago
Vidmar, John, Bl. A.M. Slomsek Slovenian Catholic Mission, Lemont
Vignocchi, Louis, Immaculate Conception, Highland Park
Villa, Salvatore, St. Bruno, Chicago
Villalobos, Antonio, St. Mark, Chicago
Villasenor, Faustino, St. Mary, Des Plaines
Villegas, Salomon, St. Hedwig, Chicago
Virruso, Christopher, Our Lady, Mother of the Church, Chicago
Walters, John, St. Bernardine, Forest Park
Ward, Raymond, (Retired), Queen of All Saints, Chicago
Ward, Raymond E., St. Jerome, Chicago
Warfield, Richard, Chap. Police Dept., Chicago
Watson, Dexter, Holy Angels, Chicago
Weber, Ronald J., St. Ansgar, Hanover Park
Wegner, Albin J., Jr., St. Michael, Chicago
Wehling, Donald, St. Hilary, Chicago
Weiner, Ronald, St. Ferdinand, Chicago
Weitendorf, Norbert, St. Patricia, Hickory Hills
Welter, Daniel, Our Lady of the Woods, Orland Park
West, Tommy, Assumption/St. Catherine of Genoa, Chicago
White, Philip, Mercy Mission, Chicago
Wieczorek, Richard, Five Holy Martyrs, Chicago
Wilczynski, Joseph, St. Stanislaus B & M, Posen
Willer, Richard, St. Thomas of Villanova, Palatine
Wills, James, St. Peter, Skokie
Winblad, Joseph, St. Patrick, Lemont
Wogan, James, St. Mary of Vernon, Indian Creek
Young, Irving, St. Mary, Buffalo Grove
Zadruzny, Wieslaw, St. Helen
Zanardo, Ronald, St. Lawrence O'Toole, Matteson
Zavala, Eduardo, Notre Dame
Zawadzki, Kenneth, St. Stephen, Deacon & Martyr, Tinley Park
Zdeb, James, St. Thomas of Villanova, Palatine
Zeller, John, St. Marcelline, Schaumburg
Zima, Robert, St. Luke, River Forest
Zimmerman, Edward, (Retired)
Zimmermann, John, Transfiguration, Wauconda
Ziomek, Robert, St. Ansgar, Hanover Park
Zurawski, John, St. John Vianney, Northlake
Zwolski, Mark, St. Mary of Vernon, Mundelein
Zych, Gerald, St. Cyprian, River Grove

INSTITUTIONS LOCATED IN THE ARCHDIOCESE

[A] SEMINARIES, ARCHDIOCESAN

CHICAGO. *Archbishop Quigley Preparatory Seminary*, 103 E. Chestnut St., 60611. Tel: 312-787-9343; Fax: 312-787-9167.
E-mail: info@quigley.org
Web site: http://www.quigley.org
Revs. David A. Jones, Pres.; Wayne F. Watts; Peter Snieg, Rector; Richard Jakubik; Paul Sims, C.R.; Joseph J. Wojcik; Louis J. Zake; Dennis A. Ziomek. Priests 8; Lay Teachers 23; Students 200.

St. Joseph Seminary, The Seminary College at Loyola University, 6551 N. Sheridan Rd., 60626. Tel: 773-973-9700; Fax: 773-973-9718.
E-mail: jpresta@orion.it.luc.edu
Web site: www.stjoseph.luc.edu
Seminary Administration: Revs. James Presta, M.Div., S.T.B., S.T.L., S.T.D. (Cand.), Rector-Pres.; William M. Frigo, O.F.M.Cap., M.S.W., Instructor; Ronald A. Hicks, B.A., M.Div. Administrative Faculty: Rev. Thomas J. Hurley, B.A., M.Div., M.A. (Cand.), Dir. Vocations; Dr. Dennis M. Composoto, M.A., M.Ed., Ph.D., Ed.D. (Cand.), Comptroller, Dir. of Financial Aid, Political Science & Education Asst. Prof.; Mr. Michael D. Martino, M.A., Dir. of Pre-College Prog. Administrative Staff: Mr. Patrick McCarthy, B.S., Assoc. Dir. of Vocations; Mrs. Marie Composto, Dir. Office Inst. Advancement; Mrs. Yuvanka Juarez, B.A., Financial Aid Admin.; Mr. John A. Houlihan, M.A., M.S., J.D., Computer Science Dir.; Ms. Denise LaGrassa, Dir. of Grant Writing; Mrs. Maria Rivera, Admin. Asst. to the Dir. of Institutional Advancement; Ms. Theresa Rooney, Dir. of Community Relations; Mrs. Sally Walsh, Sec. to the Rector. Faculty: Dr. Dennis M. Composto, M.P.A., M.Ed., Ph.D.; Mr. Charles Gerace, M.A., Communication & Theatre; Mr. Thomas Kleeman, M.A., Athletic Dir.; Rev. James J. Kastigar, M.Div., M.A., Spanish.

MUNDELEIN. *University of St. Mary of the Lake-Mundelein Seminary*, 60060. Tel: 847-566-6401; Fax: 847-566-7330.
E-mail: rectorusml@vocations.org
Web site: http://www.vocations.org
Resident Faculty: Very Rev. John F. Canary, Rector, Pres.; Revs. John G. Lodge, M.Div., M.A., S.T.L., S.S.L., S.T.D., Academic Dean; Lawrence R. Hennessey, Ph.D., Dean of Canonically Recognized Faculty; Kevin J. Feeney, M.A.S., M.Div., Dean of Formation; Sr. Linda Sevcik, S.M., S.T.L., Dir. Field Ed.; Sr. Karen Klaffenback, O.S.U., M.A.; Rev. Raymond J. Webb, Ph.D., Dir. Newly Ordained Program; Thomas W. McQuaid, Vocation Dir.; Revs. August J. Belauskas, Ph.D. (Cand.), Admissions Dir.; Patrick J. Boyle, S.J., Ph.D.; Dennis J. Lyle, S.T.L.; Sr. Sara Butler, M.S.B.T., Ph.D.; Rev. Msgr. Francis Mannion, Dip.Th. (B.D.), M.A., Ph.D., D.D., Dir., The Liturgical Institute; Revs. Victor Alvarez, S.S.P., B.A.; Robert E. Barron, S.T.D. (Cand.); John V. Dolciamore, J.C.L.; Brian J. Fischer, S.L.D. (Cand.); Stephen Giorno, S.T., B.A., M.A.; Charles R. Meyer, S.T.D., Prof. Emeritus; James P. McIlhone, Ph.D.; Patrick O'Malley, M.A., S.T.L.; Martin Zielinski, Ph.D.; Joseph C. Mol, Canonical Recorder; Arlene Michna, Mus. B., Mus. M.; Dr. C. Colt Anderson, M.A., Ph.D.; Dr. Denis McNamara, B.A., M.Arch. H., Ph.D.; Bro. Henry Baldwin, F.S.C., M.A., M.L.S., M.Ed., Dir. Inculturation Research; Revs. Peter Damian Akpunonu, S.S.L., S.T.D.; Thomas A. Baima, A/SC., A.B., M.Div., M.B.A., S.T.D., (Cand.); Peter J. Iorio, B.A., M.Div.; Terrance M. Johnson, B.A., M.A., M.Div.; Paul Murray, O.P., S.T.L., Ph.D.; Phong Pham, B.A., S.T.B.; Robert L. Schoenstene, S.S.L. (JOL); Daniel S. Siwek, S.T.L.;

Paul H. Wachdorf, M.C.Sp.; Richard J. Wojcik, M.C.G., Prof. Emeritus; Dennis M. Zalecki; Mr. Herman Peterson, M.S., M.T.S., Librarian; Rev. Anthony M. O'Connell, O.S.M., Psy.D., Non-Resident. In res. Rev. Stephen E. Grunow. Priests 30; Sisters 3; Lay Teachers 4; Students 209.

Convent. Tel: 847-566-6401; Fax: 847-566-7330. Sr. Margarita Ramirez, Supr. Oblate Sisters of Jesus the Priest 9.

[B] SEMINARIES, RELIGIOUS OR SCHOLASTICATES

CHICAGO. *The Catholic Theological Union at Chicago,* 5401 S. Cornell Ave., 60615. Tel: 773-324-8000; Fax: 773-324-8490.
E-mail: bernicef@ctu.edu
Web site: www.ctu.edu
Major Seminary. Serving the following: Franciscans, Servites, Passionists, Augustinians, Norbertines, Society of the Divine Word, Missionaries of the Precious Blood, Claretians, Crosier Fathers, Holy Ghost Fathers, Sacred Heart Missionaries, Viatorians, Comboni Missionaries, Franciscans Capuchins, Sacred Heart Fathers and Brothers, Ukrainian Catholic Diocese, Congregation of the Blessed Sacrament, Columban Missionaries, Redemptorist Fathers, Oblates of Mary Immaculate, Xaverian Missionaries, Maryknoll Missionaries, Conventual Franciscans, Oratorians, Scalabrinians, Discalced Carmelites, Vincentians. Revs. Donald Senior, C.P., S.T.D., Pres.; Gary L. Riebe-Estrella, S.V.D., S.T.D., Vice Pres. & Academic Dean; Kenneth O'Malley, C.P., Ph.D., Dir. Library; Ms. Bernice Frederick, Vice Pres. Finance; Mr. William Booth, Dir. Institutional Advancement; Ms. Priscilla Sporrong, M.B.A., Dir. Marketing/Communications; Mr. Milton Kobus, M.A., Dir. Admissions & Recruitment; Ms. Vanessa White, M.T.S., Dir. Augustus Tolton Prog.; Rev. Alphonse Spilly, C.PP.S., Ph.D., Dir. Bernardin Center; Sr. Barbara Dohery, S.P., Ph.D., Dir. Institute for Rel. Formation; Rev. Eugene Lauer, Dir. Hesburgh Center, Cont. Formation in Ministry; Sr. Joris Binder, Assoc. Dir. Hesburgh Center; Sr. Stephanie Pilchowski, S.S.N.D., Registrar; Mr. Jaime Bascunan, M.S., Dir. Romero Prog.; Ms. Mary Jo Curtsinger, M. Div., Dir. Israel Study Prog.; Ms. Opal Easter, Ed.D., Dir. Continuing Educ.& Ministeral Formation; Rev. Vaughn Fayle, O.F.M., D.Phil, Dir. Philosophy Prog.; Bro. Steven J. Herro, O. Praem, M.S., Dir. Educ. Technology; Rev. Francis Landry, C.P., M.A., Assoc. Dir. Institute for Religious Studies; Ms. Judy Logue, M.A., Dir. Emmaus Prog.; Rev. John J. Neville, O.S.C., Ed.D., Dir. Lilly Technology Grant; Mr. Michal Ryan, Dir. Admin. Svcs.; Ms. Pat Shevlin, Assoc. Dir. Devel. Faculty: Mr. Michel Andraos, Ph.D., Prof. Cross Cultural Studies; Mr. Scott C. Alexander, Ph.D., Prof. & Dir. Catholic-Muslim Studies; Rev. Claude-Marie Barbour, S.T.D.; Sr. Dianne Bergant, C.S.A., Ph.D., Dir. D.Min. Prog.; Rev. Stephen B. Bevans, S.V.D., Ph.D., Dir. CCGM Prog.; Sr. Barbara Bowe, R.S.C.J., Th.D.; Sr. Jeanette Lucinio, S.P., Dir. M.A.P.S. Prog. & Dir. Field Educ.; Sr. Eleanor Doidge, L.O.B., D.Min.; Mr. Richard E. McCarron, Ph.D., Prof. Liturgy; Dr. Kevin Madigan, Ph.D., Dir. M.A. Prog.; Revs. Richard Fragomeni, Ph.D.; Edward Foley, O.F.M.Cap., Ph.D., M.Mus.; Archimede Fornasari, M.C.C.J., Ph.D.; Ms. Mary Frohlich, Ph.D.; Sr. Marianne Race, C.S.J., M.A., Dir. Israel Study Programs; Ms. Linda Strozdas, Psy.D., Prof. Pastoral Care; Revs. James J. Gill, S.J., M.D.; Anthony Gittins, C.S.Sp., Ph.D.; Zachary Hayes, O.F.M., Dr.Th.; Leslie J. Hoppe, O.F.M., Ph.D.; John E. Linnan, C.S.V., S.T.D.; Thomas Nairn, O.F.M., Ph.D.; James C. Okoye, C.S.Sp.; Sr. Carolyn Osiek, R.S.C.J., Th.D.; Revs. Gilbert Ostdiek, O.F.M., S.T.D.; John M. Pawlikowski, O.S.M., Ph.D.; Rabbi Hayim Goren Perelmuter, D.H.L.; Sr. Barbara Reid, O.P., Ph.D.; Sr. Dawn Nothwehr, O.S.F., Ph.D.; Revs. Gary l. Riebe-Estrella, S.V.D., Ph.D., S.T.D.; Robert Schreiter, C.PP.S., Th.D.; Roger P. Schroeder, S.V.D., D.Miss., Dir. M.Div. Prog.; Donald Senior, C.P., S.T.D.; Gilberto Cavazos-Gonzales, O.F.M., S.L.T. Priests 23; Brothers 1; Sisters 11; Lay Teachers 5; Lay Administrators 11; Non-Catholic Clergy 2; Students 386.

TECHNY. *Divine Word Residence.* (Formerly Divine Word Seminary-St. Mary's Mission House), P.O. Box 6000, 60082-6000. Tel: 847-272-2700; Fax: 847-272-2873.
E-mail: uscsvd1@aol.com
Web site: www.divineword.org
Legal Title: *Divine Word Techny Community Corporation.* Revs. Kazimierz Garbacz, S.V.D., Rector; John Beemster, S.V.D.; James Bergin, S.V.D.; Michael J. Bonner, S.V.D.; Edward Borkowski, S.V.D.; James Braband, S.V.D.; Walter Bracken, S.V.D.; John Cannuli, S.V.D.; Thomas Commons, S.V.D.; Joseph Connors, S.V.D.; John Donaghey, S.V.D.; Francis Drzaic, S.V.D.; Charles Erb, S.V.D.; Joaquin Ferrer, S.V.D.; John Fu, S.V.D.; Dariusz Garbaciak, S.V.D.; Gerald Garry, S.V.D.; Gilbert Gawlik, S.V.D.; Elzear Gehlen, S.V.D.; Thomas Griffith, S.V.D.; Walter Hafner, S.V.D.; Thomas Halleran, S.V.D.; Leo Hotze, S.V.D.; Francis Hughes, S.V.D.; Francis J. Kamp, S.V.D.; John Koster, S.V.D.; Anthony Krajci, S.V.D.; Albert Kretschmer, S.V.D.; Thomas A. Krosnicki, S.V.D.; Joseph LeBeau, S.V.D.; Paschal LoBianco, S.V.D.; Louis Luzbetak, S.V.D.; Andrew Masters, S.V.D.; Wilbert Morman, S.V.D.; Robert Myers, S.V.D.; Edward Norton, S.V.D.; Chester Nowicki, S.V.D.; Lawrence Poetz, S.V.D.; Raymond Quetchenbach, S.V.D.; Frederick Rudolph, S.V.D.; Charles Schoderbek, S.V.D.; Eugene Stoll, S.V.D.; John Swift, S.V.D.; John Szukalski, S.V.D.; Lawrence Thornton, S.V.D.; Stanley Uroda, S.V.D.; Bros. Leonard Bauer, S.V.D.; Rene Gawlik, S.V.D.; George Haegele, S.V.D.; Rudolph Heckel, S.V.D.; Patrick Hogan, S.V.D.; James Hunt, S.V.D.; Clement Meyer, S.V.D.; Dennis Newton, S.V.D.; Henry Oeser, S.V.D.; Joachim Oros, S.V.D.; Stephen Pardy, S.V.D.; Gerard Pashia, S.V.D.; Pius Resch, S.V.D.; Cyril Schroeder, S.V.D.; Joseph Urban, S.V.D.; Kenneth Valois, S.V.D.; Vincent Webb, S.V.D.; Mathew Zemel, S.V.D.

Divine Word Theologate. Major Seminary of the Chicago Province. 5342 S. University Ave., Chicago, 60615. Tel: 773-288-2777; Fax: 773-288-6307. Rev. Edward Peklo, S.V.D., Rector. Staff: Revs. Roger S. Arnold, S.V.D.; Stephen B. Bevans, S.V.D.; Lloyd Cunningham, S.V.D.; Emil Kralik, S.V.D.; Gary L. Riebe-Estrella, S.V.D.; Roger P. Schroeder, S.V.D.; Derek Simons, S.V.D.; Mark Schramm, S.V.D.; Mark E. Weber, S.V.D. Priests 10. Edward McGuinn, S.V.D. Residence, 5712 S. Kenwood, Unit 3, Chicago, 60657. Tel: 773-643-1518. Revs. Stephen B. Bevans, S.V.D.; Gary L. Riebe-Estrella, S.V.D.

[C] COLLEGES AND UNIVERSITIES

CHICAGO. *De Paul University,* One E. Jackson Blvd., 60604. Tel: 312-362-8000.
Web site: www.depaul.edu
For a complete listing, refer to the Colleges and Universities section.

Jesuit Community at Loyola University of Chicago, Jesuit Residence, 6525 N. Sheridan Rd., 60626. Tel: 773-508-8800; Fax: 773-508-2098.
E-mail: jocalla@luc.edu
Web site: www.luc.edu
For a complete listing, refer to the Colleges and Universities section.

Loyola University-Chicago. Tel: 312-915-6000; 773-274-3000.
Web site: www.luc.edu
President's Office, 820 N. Michigan Ave., 60611. Tel: 312-915-6400; Fax: 312-915-6414.
For a complete listing, refer to the Colleges and Universities section.

Saint Xavier University, 3700 West 103rd St., 60655. Tel: 773-298-3000
For a complete listing, refer to the Colleges and Universities section.

LAKE FOREST. *Barat College,* 700 E. Westleigh Rd., 60045. Tel: 847-234-3000; Fax: 847-615-5000.
E-mail: dimengo@barat.edu
Web site: www.barat.edu
For a complete listing, refer to the Colleges and Universities section.

RIVER FOREST. *Dominican University (Formerly Rosary College),* 7900 W. Division St., 60305. Tel: 708-366-2490; Fax: 708-524-5990.
E-mail: webmaster@email.dom.edu
Web site: www.dom.edu
For a complete listing, refer to the Colleges and Universities section.

[D] HIGH SCHOOLS, PRIVATE

CHICAGO. *Brother Rice High School,* 10001 S. Pulaski Rd., 60655-3356. Tel: 773-779-3410; Fax: 773-779-5239.
E-mail: kwalczak@brrice.chi.il.us
Web site: http://www.brrice.chi.il.us
Congregation of Christian Brothers. Bro. Karl J. Walczek, Pres.; Mr. James P. Antos, Prin. Priests 2; Brothers 10; Lay Teachers 64; Students 1,210.

Cristo Rey Jesuit High School, Inc., 1852 W. 22nd Pl., 60608. Tel: 773-890-6800; Fax: 773-254-4901. Rev. John P. Foley, S.J., Pres.; Sr. Judith Murphy, O.S.B., Prin. Priests 3; Sisters 2; Brothers 1; Lay Teachers 21; Students 400.

Shrine of St. Stephen. Tel: 773-376-4334. Rev. Stanley Wisniewski, S.J., Rector.

Cristo Rey Work/Study Program, Inc., 1852 W. 22nd Pl., 60608. Tel: 773-523-6800; Fax: 773-843-7148. Preston Kendall, Dir.

De La Salle Institute, 3455 S. Wabash Ave., 60616. Tel: 312-842-7355; Fax: 312-842-4142.
E-mail: webmaster@dls.org
Web site: www.dls.org
Legal Title: *De La Salle Institute.* Brothers of the Christian Schools. Bros. Michael Quirk, F.S.C., Pres.; Michael Flaherty, F.S.C. Brothers 8; Lay Teachers 55; Students 912.

Good Counsel High School, Inc., 3900 Peterson Ave., 60659. Tel: 773-478-3655; Fax: 773-478-6029.
E-mail: mquailegc@aol.com
Web site: goodcounselhs.org
Legal Title: *Good Counsel High School, Inc.* Day School. Sisters 8; Lay Teachers 44; Students 447.

Gordon Tech High School, 3633 N. California Ave., 60618-4602. Tel: 773-539-3600; Fax: 773-539-9158.
Web site: www.gordontech.org
Rev. Joseph Glab, C.R., Pres.; Mr. Fred Kane, Prin.; Revs. Ken Bratko, C.R.; Fred Ciesla, C.R.; Adolph Istok, C.R.; Edward J. Jaskula, C.R.; Stephen Juda, C.R.; Joseph Korabik, C.R.; Thomas Kubik, C.R.; Joseph Malczyk, C.R.; Frank Majewicz, C.R.; Charles Mrowinski, C.R.; Paul Sims, C.R., Supr.; John Stephen, C.R.; Donald Zinn, C.R.; Bro. Ed Jaszkowski, C.R. Priests 7; Brothers 2; Lay Teachers 49; Students 740.

Hales Franciscan High School, Inc., 4930 Cottage Grove Ave., 60615. Tel: 773-285-8400; Fax: 773-285-7025. Mr. Robert Anderson, Pres.; Mr. Thomas Calhoun, Prin.; Revs. John Paul Cafiero, O.F.M., D.Min., Dir. Campus Ministry; Phil D. Hogan, O.F.M., Coord. Student Activities & Spec. Prog.; David Rodriguez, O.F.M., M.F.A., Fine Arts & Theology Chair; Bro. Fred Smith, O.F.M., Mgr. Bookstore. Priests 3; Brothers 1; Lay Teachers 28; Students 400.

Holy Spirit Friary. Tel: 773-285-8402, Ext. 257. Revs. Charles E. Payne, O.F.M., Ph.D.; Thomas Nairn, O.F.M., Ph.D.; Gilberto Canazos, O.F.M., Ph.D.; Frank Folinio, O.F.M., M.A.; Michael Ward, O.F.M., B.A.

Holy Trinity High School, 1443 W. Division St., 60622. Tel: 773-278-4212; Fax: 773-278-0144.
E-mail: psmith1792@aol.com
Brothers of Holy Cross. Bro. Philip R. Smith, C.S.C. Priests 3; Brothers 6; Sisters 5; Lay Teachers 30; Students 400.

Josephinum High School, 1501 N. Oakley Blvd., 60622. Tel: 773-276-1261; Fax: 773-292-3963.
Web site: www.josephinum.org
Legal Title: *Josephinum High School, Inc.* Fully accredited high school. Sisters 3; Lay Teachers 21; Girls 200.

Leo High School, 7901 S. Sangamon, 60620. Tel: 773-224-9600; Fax: 773-224-3856.
E-mail: leo@inil.com
Mr. Robert W. Foster, Pres.; Mr. Peter W. Doyle, Prin. Boys 348.

Lourdes High School, 4034 W. 56th St., 60629. Tel: 773-581-2555; Fax: 773-581-9358; 581-7104.
E-mail: lourdian@mcs.net
Sisters of St. Joseph, Third Order of St. Francis. Sr. Josita Krzeminski, Prin. Sisters 8; Lay Teachers 23; Students 410.

Madonna High School, 4055 W. Belmont, 60641. Tel: 773-282-2552; Fax: 773-282-2403.
E-mail: madonnahs@worldnet.att.net
Franciscan Sisters of Chicago. Sr. Carol Marie Schommer, O.S.F., Prin. Priests 1; Sisters 3; Lay Teachers 20; Students 250.

Maria High School. (Formerly St. Casimir Academy), 6727 S. California Ave., 60629. Tel: 773-925-8686; Fax: 773-925-8885.
E-mail: maria8686@hotmail.com
Web site: catholic-church.org/mariahighschool
Sisters of St. Casimir. Sr. Margaret Zalot, S.S.C., Pres.; Ms. Kathleen B. King, Prin. Sisters 7; Lay Teachers 55; Students 750.

Marist High School, 4200 W. 115th St., 60655-4306. Tel: 773-881-6360; Fax: 773-881-0595.
E-mail: vicki@marist.net
Web site: marist.net
Marist Brothers. Tel: 773-881-5300; Fax: 773-881-0595. Larry F. Tucker, Prin. Brothers 13; Lay Teachers 63; Students 1,246.

Mother McAuley Liberal Arts High School, 3737 W. 99th St., 60655. Tel: 773-881-6500; Fax: 773-881-6562.
Web site: www.mothermcauley.k12.il.us
Sisters of Mercy. Sr. Rose Wiorek, R.S.M. Sisters 10; Lay Teachers 110; Students 1,899.

Mt. Carmel High School, 6410 S. Dante Ave., 60637. Tel: 773-324-1020; Fax: 773-324-9235.
E-mail: principal@mchs.org
Web site: http://www.mchs.org
Res., 6401 S. Harper Ave., 60638. Carmelites: Revs. Benjamin Aguilar, O.Carm.; Carl J. Markelz, O.Carm., Prin.; Daniel Carroll, O.Carm.; Glen Snow, O.Carm.; Leander Troy, O.Carm.; George L. O'Keefe, O.Carm.; William Wert, O.Carm., Vocation Dir., Prior. Carmelites in Residence 7; Lay Teachers 50; Students 815.

Notre Dame High School, 3000 N. Mango Ave., 60634. Tel: 773-622-9494; Fax: 773-622-8511.
E-mail: bmurphy@ndhs4girls.org
Web site: www.ndhs4girls.org
Sisters of Notre Dame de Namur. Sr. Mary Bridget Murphy, Pres.; Mr. Robert E. Keeley, Jr., Prin. Sisters 4; Lay Teachers 43; Girls 525.

Resurrection High School, 7500 W. Talcott Ave., 60631. Tel: 773-775-6616; Fax: 773-775-0611.
Web site: resurrectionhs.pvt.k12.il.us
Sisters of the Resurrection. Mrs. Jo Marie Yonkus, Prin.; Sr. Stephanie Blaszczynski, C.R., Pres. Sisters 3; Lay Teachers 54; Girls 905.

St. Francis de Sales High School, 10155 S. Ewing Ave., 60617. Tel: 773-731-7272; Fax: 773-731-7888. Mr. Walter Schultz, Pres.; Rev. Bernard Danber, O.S.A., Prin. Priests 2; Lay Teachers 30; Students 400.

St. Ignatius College Prep, 1076 W. Roosevelt Rd., 60608-1594. Tel: 312-421-5900; Fax: 312-829-5846.
E-mail: brian.paulson@ignatius.org
Web site: ignatiuschicago.com
Revs. Brian G. Paulson, S.J., Pres.; James C.L. Arimond, S.J., Rector; Dr. William Watts, Ph.D., Prin.; Revs. John Belmonte, S.J.; Joseph T. Brennan, S.J.; Patrick Fairbanks, S.J.; James S. Vorwoldt, S.J.; Robert C. Thul, S.J. Priests 7; Sisters 2; Lay Teachers 80; Students 1,321.

St. Ignatius Jesuit Community, 1025 W. Taylor, 60607. Tel: 312-829-2297; Fax: 312-829-9552. Revs. James C.L. Arimond, S.J., Rector; John M. Belmonte, S.J.; Joseph T. Brennan, S.J.; Louis E. Busemeyer, S.J.; James E. Chambers, S.J.; John P. Coakley, S.J.; James J. Creighton, S.J.; Patrick A. Fairbanks, S.J.; Philip J. Grib, S.J.; William O. Madden, S.J.; Brian G. Paulson, S.J.; Robert C. Thul, S.J.; James F. Vorwoldt, S.J.; Stanley Wisniewski, S.J.; Bro. Anthony R. Kreutzjans, S.J. Priests 7; Sisters 2; Lay Teachers 75.

St. Patrick High School, 5900 W. Belmont Ave., 60634. Tel: 773-282-8844; Fax: 773-282-2361. Legal Title: *St. Patrick High School*. Brothers of the Christian Schools. Bro. Konrad Diebold, F.S.C., Pres.; Dr. Joseph Schmidt, Prin.; Mr. Charles Schmidt, Asst. Prin. Brothers 4; Lay Teachers 60; Students 985.

St. Rita High School. (See Monasteries and Residences of Priests and Brothers), 7740 S. Western Ave., 60620. Tel: 773-925-6600. Rev. Michael J. O'Connor, O.S.A., Pres.; Mr. Joseph F. Bamberger, Prin.; Rev. Edward Andrews, O.S.A., Prior. Priests 6; Sisters 1; Lay Teachers 40; Students 764.

St. Scholastica Academy, 7416 N. Ridge Blvd., 60645. Tel: 773-764-5715; Fax: 773-764-0304.
E-mail: benedict@ais.net
Web site: www.scholastica.chicago.il.us
Sr. Judith Zonsius, O.S.B., Prin. Sisters 5; Lay Teachers 24; Students 315.

Convent, 7430 N. Ridge Blvd., 60645. Tel: 773-764-2413; Fax: 773-761-5131.

ARLINGTON HEIGHTS. *St. Viator High School*, 1213 E. Oakton St., 60004. Tel: 847-392-4050; Fax: 847-392-4101.
E-mail: tvblv@aol.com
Web site: www.viator.k12.il.us
Clerics of St. Viator. Revs. Thomas R. von Behren, C.S.V., Pres.; George G. Harris, C.S.V.; Arnold E. Perham, C.S.V.; John E. VanWiel, C.S.V.; Bros. Doug Hudson, C.S.V.; Robert Ruhl, C.S.V.; Michael Gosch, C.S.V.; Rob Robertson, C.S.V. Priests 4; Brothers 4; Lay Teachers 66; Students 970.

BURBANK. *Queen of Peace High School*. (Girls). 7659 S. Linder Ave., 60459. Tel: 708-458-7600; Fax: 708-458-5734.
E-mail: qnpeacehs@aol.com
Ms. Patricia Nolan Fitzgerald, Prin. Sisters 5; Lay Teachers 69; Students 1,035.

St. Laurence High School, Inc., 5556 W. 77th St., 60459. Tel: 708-458-6900; Fax: 708-458-6908.
Web site: www.stlaurence.com
Congregation of Christian Brothers. Mr. Thomas J. Ondrla, Prin. Priests 1; Brothers 8; Lay Teachers 49; Students 851.

CHICAGO HEIGHTS. *Marian Catholic High School*, 700 Ashland Ave., 60411. Tel: 708-755-7565; Fax: 708-756-9758.
E-mail: mchsinfo@marianchs.com
Web site: http://www.marianchs.com
Dominican Sisters (Springfield, IL). Sr. M. Paul McCaughey, O.P., Pres., Prin. Sisters 16; Lay Teachers 77; Students 1,661.

LAGRANGE PARK. *Nazareth Academy*, 1209 W. Ogden Ave., 60526. Tel: 708-354-0061; Fax: 708-354-0109.
E-mail: jkschmitz1@aol.com
Web site: www.nazacad.com
Sisters of St. Joseph. Sr. Jacqueline Schmitz, C.S.J., Prin. Sisters 8; Lay Teachers 50; Students 760.

LAKE FOREST. *Woodlands Academy of the Sacred Heart*, 760 E. Westleigh Rd., 60045-3298. Tel: 847-234-4300; Fax: 847-234-4348.
E-mail: info@woodlands.lfc.edu
Web site: www.woodlands.lfc.edu
Religious of Sacred Heart. Sr. Carol Campbell, R.S.C.J., Head of School. Sisters 3; Lay Teachers 35; Students 186.

LEMONT. *Mt. Assisi Academy*, 13860 Main St., 60439. Tel: 630-257-7844; Fax: 630-257-6362. Sisters of St. Francis of Christ the King. Sr. Mary Francis Werner, O.S.F. Sisters 8; Lay Teachers 25; Students 383.

MUNDELEIN. *Carmel High School*, One Carmel Pkwy., 60060. Tel: 847-566-3000; Fax: 847-566-8465.
Web site: http://www.carmel.k12.il.us
Sr. Mary Frances McLaughlin, B.V.M., Pres.; Rev. Robert Carroll, O.Carm., Prin. Priests 4; Sisters 4; Brothers 2; Lay Teachers 68; Students 1,344.

NILES. *Notre Dame High School*. (Boys), 7655 Dempster St., 60648. Tel: 847-965-2900; Fax: 847-965-2975.
Web site: ndhs4boys.niles.il.us
Rev. Kenneth Molinaro, C.S.C., Pres.; Mr. Paul Maloney, Prin.; Rev. Jerome Esper, C.S.C.; Mr. George Rattin, Dir. Devel.; Mr. Steven Zeier, Asst. Prin. Academics; Mr. Michael Hennessey, Asst. Prin. Student Life; Mr. James Boylan, Dean of Men; Bro. Patrick Lynch, C.S.C., Finance Officer, Rel. Supr.; Mrs. Donna Cassidy, Dir. Guidance; Mr. Michael Hennessey, Dir. Athletics; Revs. William Brinker, C.S.C., (Retired); Richard Conyers, C.S.C.; Michael Couhig, C.S.C.; Jerome Esper, C.S.C.; Christopher A. Kuhn, C.S.C.; W. Patrick Hannon, C.S.C.; Bro. Patrick Lynch, C.S.C., Finance Officer, Religious Supr. Priests 6; Retired Priests 1; Brothers 1; Deacons 1; Sisters 1; Lay Teachers 41; Students 685.

OAK PARK. *Fenwick High School*, 505 Washington Blvd., 60302. Tel: 708-386-0127; Fax: 708-386-3052.
Web site: www.fenwick.pvt.k12.il.us
Dominican Order. Revs. Richard C. LaPata, O.P., Pres.; William J. Bernacki, O.P.; Malachy R. Dooley, O.P.; Joseph Ekpo; John M. Gambro, O.P.; Harold Ostdiek, O.P.; Thomas Saucier, O.P.; Michael A. Winkels, O.P.; Joseph I. Hren, O.P.; Robert M. Kelly, O.P.; Paul Whittington, O.P.; Bro. Gabriel J. Dault, O.P.; Sr. Barbara Kwiatkowski, O.S.F. Priests 10; Brothers 1; Sisters 1; Lay Teachers 57; Students 1,147.

RIVER FOREST. *Trinity High School*, 7574 W. Division St., 60305. Tel: 708-771-8383. Dominican Sisters (Sinsinawa, WI). Sr. Michelle Germanson, O.P., Pres.; Sr. Jeanne Bessette, O.S.F., Prin. Sisters 5; Lay Teachers 40; Students 522.

RIVER GROVE. *Holy Cross High School*, 3000-80th, 60171-1202. Tel: 708-456-5110; Fax: 708-456-9637.
E-mail: dougroach@juno.com
Web site: www.holycross-hs.org
Brothers of Holy Cross. Bro. Douglas Roach, C.S.C., Pres.; Mr. Doug Demeter, Dir. Campus Ministry. Priests 3; Brothers 3; Sisters 1; Lay Teachers 31; Students 503. (See Monasteries and Residences of Priests and Brothers).

Mother Theodore Guerin High School, 8001 Belmont Ave., 60171. Tel: 312-625-3278; Fax: 708-453-6296. Sisters of Providence. Sr. Cathy Campbell, S.P., Pres.; Sr. Ann Welch, R.S.M. Sisters 6; Lay Teachers 44; Students 718.

SOUTH HOLLAND. *Seton Academy*, 16100 Seton Rd., 60473-1899. Tel: 708-333-6300; Fax: 708-333-1534.
E-mail: seton@setonacademy.com
Web site: www.setonacademy.com
Lay Teachers 24; Students 287.

WESTCHESTER. *Immaculate Heart of Mary High School*, 10900 W. Cermak Rd., 60154. Tel: 708-562-3115. Sisters, Servants of the Immaculate Heart of Mary. Catherine A. Karl, Ph.D., Prin. Sisters 1; Lay Teachers 36; Students 545.

St. Joseph High School, 1840 Mayfair, 60154-4299. Tel: 708-562-4433; Fax: 708-562-4459.
E-mail: stjoehs@mediaone.net
Web site: stjoeshs.org
Brothers of the Christian Schools. Mr. David McCreery, Pres.; Mr. David L. Hotek, Prin.; Mr. Thomas Reif, Asst. Prin. Brothers 3; Lay Teachers 44; Students 530.

WILMETTE. *Loyola Academy*, 1100 N. Laramie Ave., 60091. Tel: 847-256-1100; Fax: 847-853-4512.
Web site: www.goramblers.org
Revs. Theodore G. Munz, S.J., Pres.; Norman E. Harland, S.J., Rector; Terrence A. Baum, S.J., Headmaster; Mr. William A. Graf, Assoc. Athletic Dir.; Mr. John E. Hoerster, Athletic Dir.; Dr. Lorraine Ozar, Academic Dean; Mr. Kenneth Maziarka, Dean of Students; Sr. Sheila Carney, D.C., Business Mgr.; Revs. Peter W. Breslin, S.J.; Steven F. Hurd, S.J.; Paul J. Faulstich, S.J.; Bros. James W. Small, S.J.; Eric J. Knapp, S.J.; Rev. Robert A. Ytsen, S.J. Priests 6; Sisters 2; Brothers 2; Lay Teachers 150; Students 2,010.

Regina Dominican High School, 701 Locust Rd., 60091. Tel: 847-256-7660; Fax: 847-256-3726.
Web site: www.reginadominican.pvt.k12.il.us
Sisters of St. Dominic (Adrian, MI). Sr. Ann Fallon, O.P., Pres.; Nancy McCabe, Ph.D., Prin. Sisters 11; Lay Teachers 38; Students 450.

[E] ELEMENTARY SCHOOLS, PRIVATE

CHICAGO. *Sacred Heart Schools (Academy of the Sacred Heart for Girls, Hardey Prep. for Boys)*. (Grades K-8), 6250 N. Sheridan Rd., 60660-1799. Tel: 773-262-4446; Fax: 773-262-6178.
E-mail: nsh13ad@aol.com
Web site: www.shschicago.org
Religious of the Sacred Heart. Sr. Susan Maxwell, R.S.C.J., Dir. Schools; Mrs. Janet Underwood, Head of Lower School; Mr. Daniel Flaherty, Head of Middle School. Sisters 3; Lay Teachers 40; Students 450.

[F] CONSOLIDATED ELEMENTARY SCHOOLS

CHICAGO. *Bridgeport Catholic Academy*, Admin. Office, 1040 W. 32nd Pl., 60608. Tel: 773-376-0142. Nona Barrientos, Prin.
Serving the following parishes: All Saints-St. Anthony (518 W. 28th Pl.); St. Mary of Perpetual Help (1039 W. 32nd St.); Nativity of Our Lord (653 W. 37th St.). Lay Teachers 10; Students 200.

[G] CATHOLIC CHARITIES

CHICAGO. *Catholic Charities of the Archdiocese of Chicago-Archdiocesan Offices*, 126 N. Desplaines St., 60661. Tel: 312-655-7000; Fax: 312-655-0219.
Web site: catholiccharities.net
Administers charitable activities of the Archdiocese. Rev. Michael M. Boland, Admin.; Mr. Walter H. Ousley, Dir. Oper.; Rev. Charles T. Rubey, Dir.-Programs. Assoc. Administrators.: Revs. Roger J. Coughlin; Richard E. Bulwith; Daniel M. Holihan; Gerard P. Kelly, C.M., Staff Chap.; James M. Ray; Francis A. Cimarrusti; Charles T. Rubey; Most Rev. Edwin M. Conway, Consultant.

Dept. of Development. Tel: 312-655-7289; Fax: 312-655-0605.

Dept. of Communications. Tel: 312-655-7024; Fax: 312-441-0529. William J. Sullivan, Jr., Dir.

Office of Board Relations. Tel: 312-655-7171; Fax: 312-930-0425. Ms. Laina Lurito.

Financial Services, 126 N. Desplaines, 60661. Tel: 312-655-7864; Fax: 312-655-0219. Ms. Cynthia Smetana, Dir. Admin. Svcs.

Division of Family and Parish Support Services. Tel: 312-655-7136; Fax: 312-427-3130. Ms. Ellen E. Gorney, Div. Mgr.

Central Information and Referral Services. Tel: 312-655-7700; Fax: 312-655-0678. Ms. Kathleen Donahue, Dept. Dir.

Emergency Assistance Program, 121 W. Superior St., 60610. Tel: 312-655-7500; Fax: 312-654-9861. Ms. Christene Dykes-Sorrells, Prog. Dir., Legal Services, 721 N. LaSalle, 60610. Tel: 312-655-7538. Michele Bianchi, Dir.

Dept. of Family and Aging Services. Tel: 312-655-7153; Fax: 312-879-0208. Ms. Veronica Glodowski, Dept. Dir.

Archdiocesan AIDS Ministry Office. Tel: 312-655-7294; Fax: 312-263-4290.

Specialized Mental Health Services Network. Tel: 312-655-7298.

Holbrook Center for Counseling and Psychotherapy, 721 N. LaSalle, 60610. Tel: 312-655-7550; Fax: 312-664-5490. Ms. Dorothy Auw, Dept. Dir.

Community Family Service Center, Cordi-Marian Center, 1100 S. May, 60607. Tel: 312-733-5661. Ms. Sigrid Brooks, Prog. Dir.

Immigration & Naturalization Services and Refuge Resettlement Program, 126 N. Desplaines St., 60661. Tel: 312-655-7359; Fax: 312-427-3130. Mr. J. Zeferino Ochoa, Dept. Dir.

LOSS (Loving Outreach to Survivors of Suicide), 126 N. Desplaines St., 60661. Tel: 312-655-7285; Fax: 312-655-0219. Jill Scott, Prog. Dir.

Joseph Cardinal Bernardin Family Shelter Program, 126 N. Desplaines St., 60661. Tel: 312-655-7268; Fax: 312-655-1002. Ms. Mildred Lincoln, Dept. Dir.

St. Francis de Paula Hospitality House, 7811 S. Ellis, 60619. Tel: 773-487-8615; Fax: 773-651-0857.

St. Sylvester Family Shelter, 2915 W. Palmer St., 60647. Tel: 773-278-8253; Fax: 773-862-9388.

St. Susanna Family Shelter, 14926 S. Honore, Harvey, 60426. Tel: 708-331-8211; Fax: 708-339-4398.

Sousa Transitional Shelter, 7000 S. Aberdeen, 60621. Tel: 773-874-4000. Ms. Darlene Rivers, Supr. Tel: 312-874-4400.

Cooke's Manor Transitional Housing For Men, 124 N. Sangamon, 60607. Tel: 312-655-8686; Fax: 312-733-0759. Rev. Richard E. Bulwith, Dept. Dir.

Forever Free -Transitional Housing For Women, 8235 S. Shore Dr., 60621. Tel: 773-374-8165; Fax: 312-374-2177. Ms. Josephine Abi-Rached, Prog. Dir.

Society of St. Vincent De Paul of Chicago, 645 W. Randolph St., 60661. Tel: 312-655-7181; Fax: 312-454-0101. Mrs. Claudia Pieske, Pres.; Rev. Thomas A. Grace, C.M., Exec. Dir.; Mr. Robert Kill, Dir.; Rev. Michael M. Boland, Spiritual Advisor; Ms. Bonnie McVey, Pres. District Council I; Mr. Thomas Van Wazer, Pres. District Council III; Mr. William Stein, Pres. District Council IV; Mr. Ben Gallardo, Pres. District Council VII; Mr. John Hovorka, Pres. District Council VIII; Mr. Richard Kress, Pres. District Council IX; Mrs. Carole Stauder, Pres. District Council X; Ms. Rose Reynaud, Pres. District Council XI; Mr. Larry Brandon, Pres. District Council XII; Mr. Richard Kress,

Regional Coord.; Ms. Janet Deckenbach, Regl. Coord.; Joseph O'Shea, Youth Coord.; Mr. Thomas Van Wazer, Disaster Chm. & Regl. Coord.; Mrs. Mary Van Wazer, Elder Care Coord.; Mr. Edward Bara, Sr., Ozanam Cause Coord.; Deacon John Perkowitz, Funding & Twinning Coord. & Asst. to Pres.; Mr. Karl Gawlas, Treas.; Mr. Ed Stachon, Vice Pres.; Mrs. Margaret O'Brien, ADC Sec.

St. Stanislaus Kostka Soup Kitchen, 1351 W. Evergreen, 60622. Tel: 773-278-2470; Fax: 773-278-2471. Sr. Ann Schaffer, Dir.

Transition to the Workplace Program, 126 N. DesPlaines, 60610. Tel: 312-655-2007; Fax: 312-879-0208. Kimberly Piccin, Dept. Dir.

Lake County Services. Joseph Cardinal Bernardin Center for Lake County Services, 671 S. Lewis Ave., Waukegan, 60085. Tel: 847-782-4000; Fax: 847-782-1040. Ms. Mary Clare Jakes, Assoc. Div. Mgr., Community Casework Services, 671 S. Lewis Ave., Waukegan, 60085. Tel: 847-782-4131; Fax: 847-782-1030. Ms. Maureen Murphy, Prog. Dir.

Samaritan House, 671 S. Lewis Ave., Waukegan, 60085. Tel: 847-782-4000; Fax: 847-782-1030.

North/Northwest Suburban Services, 1717 Rand Rd., Des Plaines, 60016. Tel: 847-376-2100; Fax: 847-390-8214. Mary Beth Hartmann, N. Sub. Reg. Rep.; Cheryle Margiewicz, N.W. Sub. Reg. Rep., Cicero: West Suburban Services, 1400 S. Austin Blvd., Cicero, 60804. Tel: 708-222-1491; Fax: 708-222-1495. Susanne A. Dillon, Regl. Svcs. Representative, South Suburban Services, 16100 Seton Dr., South Holland, 60473. Tel: 708-333-8379; Fax: 708-333-9514. Karen Bacon, Regl. Svcs. Representative, Chicago Services Regional Offices, 126 N. Desplaines, 60621. Tel: 312-655-7298; Fax: 312-263-4290. Arlene Jackson-Ervin, Chicago Regl. Svcs. Representative, Southwest Suburban Services, 10661 Roberts Rd., Palos Hills, 60465. Tel: 708-430-0428; Fax: 708-430-0502. Cosima Dean, Regl. Svcs. Representative, Physician Referral Service, 3265 N. Arlington Hts. Rd., Ste. 310, Arlington Heights, 60004. Tel: 847-870-0202; Fax: 847-870-0170. Ms. Karen Kordisch, Prog. Dir.

Division of Non-Residential Services for Children and Youth for Cook and Lake Counties, 641 W. Lake St., Ste. 306, 60661. Tel: 312-655-7097; Fax: 312-879-0293. Mr. Everett T. Petlicki, Div. Mgr.

Child Protective Services, 901 W. Jackson, 60607. Tel: 312-382-2526; Fax: 312-432-0498. 671 S. Lewis Ave., Waukegan, 60085. Tel: 847-782-4000; Fax: 847-782-1040.

Family Based Services, 916 N. Western Ave., 60622. Tel: 312-655-7601; Fax: 773-292-5713. Patricia Green, Dept. Dir.

Maternity/Adoption Services, 651 W. Lake St., 60661. Tel: 312-655-7071; Fax: 312-236-5384. Noreen Chesebro, Dept. Dir.

Jadonal E. Ford Center for Adolescent Parenting, 11255 S. Michigan Ave., 60628. Tel: 773-995-1737; Fax: 773-995-0125. Velma Brown-Walker, Dir.

Children & Adolescent Parent Program, 721 N. La Salle, 60610. Tel: 312-655-7848; Fax: 312-879-0293. Sandra Braine, Dept. Dir.

Arts of Living Institute, 916 N. Western Ave., 60622. Tel: 312-655-7388; Fax: 312-642-2078. Ms. Patricia Canessa, Dept. Dir.

Relative Family Care Services, 901 W. Jackson, 60607. Tel: 312-655-7646; Fax: 312-432-0497. Ms. Sylvia Flory, Assoc. Div. Mgr.

Traditional and Specialized Foster Care Services, 651 W. Lake St., 60661. Tel: 312-655-7250; Fax: 312-236-5384. Mr. George Thibeault, Assoc. Div. Mgr.

Div. of Residential Child-Adult Care Services. Tel: 312-655-7289; Fax: 312-655-0605.

Division of Community Development and Outreach Services, 721 N. La Salle, 60610. Tel: 312-655-7474; Fax: 312-655-0219. Mr. Dennis E. McSwain, Div. Mgr.

Addiction Consultation and Educational Services, 721 N. La Salle, 60610. Tel: 312-655-7450; Fax: 312-335-9853. Ms. Mary Ellen Flynn, Prog. Dir.

Central States Institute for Addiction, 721 N. LaSalle, 60610. Tel: 312-655-7540; Fax: 312-654-0849. Mr. Anthony Rizzato, Dept. Dir. Tel: 312-266-9027.

Disruptive Behavior Intervention. Tel: 312-655-7000. Bro. William Tomes, Consultant.

Division of Economic Development and Self Sufficiency, 721 N. LaSalle St., 60610. Tel: 312-655-8345; Fax: 312-335-9853. Mr. Joseph Antolin, Div. Mgr.

El Centro De La Causa, 731 W. 17th St., 60616. Tel: 312-243-8508; Fax: 312-243-8414. Mr. Felip (Phil) Ayala, Dept. Dir.

Respond Now, 1439 Emerald Ave., P.O. Box 215, 60411. Tel: 708-755-4357; Fax: 708-755-4381. Mr. Dennis Condon, Prog. Dir.

Keen Ager News, 126 N. Desplaines, 60610. Tel: 312-655-7425; Fax: 312-441-0529. Ms. Alejandra Torres, Editor.

Mother and Child Food and Nurtition Program (MAC), 721 N. La Salle, 60610. Tel: 312-655-7484; Fax: 312-943-8295. Mr. Aldo Pedrosa, Dir.

WIC Food Centers Program, 721 N. La Salle St., 60610. Tel: 312-655-7480; Fax: 312-943-8295. Mr. Phil Parson, Dir.

WIC Food Centers: 907 N. Larrabee, Chicago, IL 60610; 2907 S. Wabash Ave., Chicago, IL 60616; 416 E. 43rd St., Chicago, IL 60653; 5060 S. State St., Chicago, IL 60609; 6202 S. Halsted St., Chicago, IL 60621; 2310 W. Roosevelt Rd., Chicago, IL 60608; 5332 S. Western, Chicago, IL 60609; 3110 W. Armitage, Chicago, IL 60647; 4500 W. Chicago Ave., Chicago, IL 60651; 1643 W. Cermak Rd., Chicago, IL 60608; 1734 W. Chicago Ave., Chicago, IL 60622; 3932 W. Madison St., Chicago, IL 60624; and at 5125 W. Chicago, Chicago, IL 60651; 1802 E. 71st St., Chicago IL 60649; 11255 S. Michigan Ave., Chicago, IL 60628; 4620 W. Diversey Ave., Chicago, IL 60639; 8959 S. Commercial Ave., Chicago, IL 60617.

Garfield Alternative High School, 220 W. 45th Pl., 60609. Tel: 773-924-0543; Fax: 773-924-0546. Mr. Oyemola Kale, Prog. Dir.

Employment and Training Program, 721 N. LaSalle, 60610. Tel: 312-655-8490.

Early/Childhood Development, Day Care/Head Start, 721 N. LaSalle St., 60610. Tel: 312-655-7700. Ethel Barnes, Dept. Dir. Tel: 312-655-7875.

Division of Senior Social Services, 721 N. La Salle Dr., 60610. Tel: 312-655-7572. Wendy S. Seifent, Div. Mgr.

Northeast/Northwest Chicago Case Management Services, 5801 N. Pulaski, Bldg. A, 60646. Tel: 773-583-9224; Fax: 773-583-2373. Sarah Cohen, Dept. Dir.

South Suburban Senior Services and Senior Activity Center, 15300 S. Lexington, Harvey, 60426. Tel: 708-596-2222; Fax: 708-596-9567. Gwen Westley, Dept. Dir.

Lake County Senior Case Management Services, 116 N. Lincoln, Round Lake, 60073. Tel: 847-546-5733; Fax: 847-546-7114. Jan Ahlgrin, Dept. Dir.

Congregate Senior Housing, Maplehurst, 2312 Elisha, Zion, 60099. Tel: 847-872-7527; Fax: 847-782-4296. Frank Phillps, Dept. Dir.

Lake County Senior Community Services & Nutrition Program Site, 414 S. Lewis Ave., Waukegan, 60085. Tel: 847-662-0085; Fax: 847-662-0747. Frank Phillips, Dept. Dir., Antioch Area Center, 817 Holbeck St., Antioch, 60002. Tel: 847-395-7120; Fax: 847-395-7647. Mr. Paul Howard, Ctr. Dir., Ela Township Area Center, 95 E. Main St., Lake Zurich, 60047. Tel: 847-438-0303. Ms. Rusty Miller, Ctr. Dir., Libertyville Civic Center, 135 W. Church St., Libertyville, 60048. Tel: 847-367-8210; Fax: 847-367-8216. Mary Matzi, Ctr. Dir.

Lake County Nutrition Programs for Seniors. Round Lake Senior Center, 814 Hart Rd., Round Lake, 60073. Tel: 847-546-0056. Fox Lake Community Senior Center, 79 E. Keystone, Fox Lake, 60020. Tel: 847-587-3335.

Northwest Suburban Senior Services, 306 W. Park St., Arlington Heights, 60005. Tel: 847-253-5500; Fax: 847-253-9597. Ms. Cindy Gunderson, Prog. Dir.

Cook County Senior Community Services, 6414 S. Halsted, 60621. Tel: 773-994-8923; Fax: 773-488-5878. Ms. Barbara Carlo, Dept. Dir.

Ada S. Niles Senior Center and Adult Day Care Services, 6412-14 S. Halsted St., 60621. Tel: 773-874-2400; Fax: 773-488-5878. Ms. Denise King, Senior Ctr. Dir.; Ms. Norma Nalls, Day Care Senior Center Supvr.

Senior Aides Employment Program. Tel: 773-874-2400; Fax: 773-488-5878. Mr. Victor Dodd, Supr.

St. Joseph Center, 7240 W. 57th St., Summit, 60501. Tel: 708-458-0501; Fax: 708-458-7635. Mr. Henry Lambke, Ctr. Dir.

Catholic Home Care, Inc., 721 N. La Salle St., 60610. Tel: 312-655-7415; Fax: 312-337-2705.

Division of Residential Housing and Catholic Charities Housing Development Corp., 721 N. LaSalle St., 5th Floor, 60610. Tel: 312-655-7490; Fax: 312-944-1550. William G. D'Arcy, Div. Mgr. Assoc. Div. Mgrs.: Lawrence Brozek; Isabella Eckardt. Under Development: Ozanam Village, St. Ailbe Assisted Housing, St. Ailbe Apts. Phase 2, St. Emeric Senior Housing, Bishop T.J. Lyne Residence for Retired Priests, Holy Family Villa Skilled Nursing Facility.

St. Ailbe Faith Apartments, 1244 E. 93rd St., 60619. Tel: 773-721-0903.

Senior Residences:

Cortland Manor Retirement Home, 1900 N. Karlov, 60639. Tel: 773-235-3670; Fax: 773-235-0709. Maureen Scholle, Admin.

Hayes Manor, 1211 W. Marquette Rd., 60636. Tel: 773-873-7400; Fax: 773-873-1709. Delores Davis, Admin.

Matthew Manor, 271 N. Albany Ave., 60612. Tel: 773-533-0001; Fax: 773-533-0622. Margaret Bridgmon, Admin.

Roseland Manor, 11717 S. State St., 60628. Tel: 773-995-9000; Fax: 773-995-1310. Shirley Caldwell, Admin.

St. Brendan Apts., 6717 S. Elizabeth St., 60636. Tel: 773-846-8600; Fax: 773-846-0531. Sylvia Moore, Admin.

St. Sabina Elders Village, 1222 W. 79th St., 60620. Tel: 773-994-7850; Fax: 773-994-7945. Yvonne Plummer, Admin.

St. Theodore Apts., 6209 S. Paulina St., 60636. Tel: 773-776-0200; Fax: 773-846-8600. Sylvia Moore, Admin.

Tolton Manor, 6345 S. Stewart, 60621. Tel: 773-783-7800; Fax: 773-783-6362. Lee Cole, Admin.

Frances Manor, 1270 E. Golf Rd., DesPlaines, 60016. Tel: 847-390-1270; Fax: 847-390-9331. Dottie Fursek, Admin.

Lawrence Manor, 21425 Southwick, Matteson, 60443. Tel: 708-481-1200; Fax: 708-481-3168. Ron Zanardo, Admin.

Bernardin Manor, 1700 Memorial Dr., Calumet City, 60409. Tel: 708-832-1700; Fax: 708-832-9160. Elaine Layden, Admin.

Maryhaven, Inc., 1700 E. Lake Ave., Glenview, 60025. Tel: 847-729-1300; Fax: 847-729-9620. Judy Pitzele, Admin.

Bethlehem Woods Retirement and Assisted Living Center, 1571 Ogden Ave., LaGrange Park, 60526. Tel: 708-579-3663; Fax: 708-579-7159. Deborah Anderson, Admin.

Holy Family Villa, 12375 McCarthy Rd., Lemont, 60439. Tel: 630-257-2291; Fax: 630-257-2334. Roberta Magurany, Admin.

St. Andrew Home, 7000 N. Newark Ave., Niles, 60714. Tel: 847-647-8332; Fax: 847-647-7073. Jim Kouzios, Admin.

St. Benedict Home, 6930 W. Touhy Ave., Niles, 60714. Tel: 847-647-0003; Fax: 847-647-1936. Peter Coschy, Admin.

Casa San Carlo, 420 N. Wolf Rd., Northlake, 60164. Tel: 708-562-4300; Fax: 708-562-5677. Barbara Paccione, Admin.

Villa Scalabrini, 480 N. Wolf Rd., Northlake, 60164. Tel: 708-562-0040; Fax: 708-562-5180.

Human Resources. Tel: 312-655-7115; Fax: 312-831-1321. Ed Guerrero, Dir.

Facilities Operations. Tel: 312-655-7104; Fax: 312-879-0289. Arlene Norton-White.

Governmental Relations, 721 N. La Salle, 60610. Tel: 312-655-7314; Fax: 312-751-2350. Ms. Laurie Barretto, Dept. Dir.

Research and Planning Services, 721 N. La Salle, 60610. Tel: 312-655-7492; Fax: 312-266-2142. Ms. Jean Mirrabella-Beck, Dept. Dir.

Mission of the Holy Cross, 126 N. Deplaines St., 60606. Tel: 312-655-7460; Fax: 312-655-0219. Rev. Michael M. Boland.

[H] RESIDENTIAL CHILD-YOUTH CARE

CHICAGO. *Mission of Our Lady of Mercy-Mercy Home for Boys and Girls*, 1140 W. Jackson Blvd., 60607. Tel: 312-738-7560.

Web site: www.mercyhome.org

Revs. James J. Close, Pres. & CEO; L. Scott Donahue, Assoc. Pres.; Cheryl Murphy, Chief Fin. Officer; Tita Yutuc, Exec. Vice Pres. Youth Prog.; Mark Mroz, Exec. Vice Pres. Communications & CQI Planning; Mimi LeClair, Exec. Vice Pres. Devel.; Sr. Mary Hrovat, O.P., Asst. to Pres.; Rob Gaskill, The Mission Press. Staff 110; Full Time Religious 5; Youths 221.

DES PLAINES. *Maryville Academy*, 1150 N. River Rd., 60016. Tel: 708-824-6126. Legal Title: *Maryville Academy.* Rev. John P. Smyth, Exec. Dir. Students 273.

[I] DAY NURSERIES, SETTLEMENTS AND SOCIAL CENTERS

CHICAGO. *Cordi-Marian Center*, 1100 S. May St., 60607. Tel: 312-666-3787. Cordi-Marian Missionary Sisters. Sr. M. Theressa Cruz, M.C.M., Supr. Sisters 4; People under care 500; Day Care capacity 200.

Marillac Social Center, 2822 W. Jackson Blvd., 60612. Tel: 773-722-7440. Sr. Yvonne Thranow, D.C., Exec. Dir. Day care for children ages 2 1/2 to 12 years; Recreation programs for ages 6 to 25 years; emergency assistance food and clothing for poor families; day shelter for the homeless; child abuse and neglect treatment; counselling services; programs for pregnant & parenting teens and their babies; home bound elderly; services for teenage mothers. Day Care capacity 422.

Port Ministries. A Franciscan outreach of the Assumption of the Blessed Virgin Mary Province, Pulaski, WI. Soup Kitchen, food pantry, overnight shelters (men, women & family), GED, ESL, family services, mobile soup kitchen, neighborhood gym. 5013

S. Hermitage Ave., 60609. Tel: 773-778-5955; Fax: 773-778-2451.
E-mail: port532857@aol.com
Web site: portministries.org
Rev. Augustin Milon, O.F.M., Founder & Pres. Total Staff 30; Total Assisted 7,000.

Resurrection Day Care Center, 1849 N. Hermitage Ave., 60622. Tel: 773-384-7142. Sisters of the Resurrection. Sr. Kathleen Ann Skrocki, C.R., Supr.; Sr. M. Paulette Pieta, C.R., Admin. Sisters 4; Daily Attendance 28 Children.

St. Rose Center, 4911 S. Hoyne, 60609. Tel: 773-436-1433; Fax: 773-436-2280.
E-mail: strosecenter@aol.com
Sr. Theresa Tamburo, D.S.M.P., Admin. Day training program for mentally impaired adults. Sisters 2; Developmental Instructors 1; Developmental Trainers 5; Work Activity Director 1; Capacity 50.

St. Vincent de Paul Center, 2145 N. Halsted St., 60614. Tel: 312-943-6776. Sr. Catherine Mary Norris, D.C., Admin. Day care for children 4 mos. to 11 yrs.; family social services. Daughters of Charity 4; Capacity 421. Provides youth and adult recreational and athletic programs for ages 18 years through adult. Individual registration 468. Provides case management, counseling and emergency relief for senior citizens. Provides intergenerational living quarters for 15 seniors (low income) and 5 young adults. Individual registration 175. Provides outreach to the homeless in the form of case management and other concrete services. Individuals served 60.

San Miguel Febres Cordero School, Inc. Operated by DeLaSalle Christian Brothers. Gratuitous Catholic Middle School for at risk youth; Adult education (ESL); after school and evening youth programs, ages 11-18; parenting skills classes. Mentoring and scholarship assistance to graduates who study in Catholic high schools. 1949 W. 48th St., 60609-4145. Tel: 773-890-1481; Fax: 773-254-3382.
E-mail: sanmiguelchgo@hotmail.com
Web site: www.san-miguel.org
Bros. Edwin Dupre, F.S.C.; Gordon Hannon, F.S.C.; Ed Siderewicz, F.S.C. Total Staff 19; Total Assisted 200.

[J] HOSPITALS

CHICAGO. *Columbus Hospital*, 2520 N. Lakeview Ave., 60614
For a complete listing, refer to the Hospitals section.

Holy Cross Hospital, 2701 W. 68th St., 60629. Tel: 312-471-8000
For a complete listing, refer to the Hospitals section.

Mercy Hospital and Medical Center, 2525 S. Michigan Ave., 60616. Tel: 312-567-5544; Fax: 312-567-6575.
Web site: www.mercy-chicago.org
For a complete listing, refer to the Hospitals section.

Our Lady of the Resurrection Medical Center, 5645 W. Addison, 60634. Tel: 773-282-7000; Fax: 773-794-7671.
Web site: www.reshealth.org
For a complete listing, refer to the Hospitals section.

Resurrection Medical Center, 7435 Talcott Ave., 60631. Tel: 773-774-8000; Fax: 773-792-9926.
Web site: www.reshealth.org
For a complete listing, refer to the Hospitals section.

St. Anthony Hospital, 2875 W. 19th St., 60623. Tel: 773-521-1710
For a complete listing, refer to the Hospitals section.

St. Bernard Hospital & Health Care Center, 326 W. 64th St., 60621. Tel: 773-962-3900
For a complete listing, refer to the Hospitals section.

St. Elizabeth's Hospital, 1431 N. Claremont Ave., 60622. Tel: 773-278-2000
For a complete listing, refer to the Hospitals section.

St. Joseph Hospital, 2900 N. Lake Shore Dr., 60657. Tel: 773-665-3000
For a complete listing, refer to the Hospitals section.

St. Mary of Nazareth Hospital Center, 2233 W. Division, 60622. Tel: 312-770-2000; Fax: 312-770-3391.
Web site: stmaryofnazareth.org
For a complete listing, refer to the Hospitals section.

BLUE ISLAND. *St. Francis Hospital and Health Center*, 12935 S. Gregory St., 60406. Tel: 708-597-2000; Fax: 708-389-9489.
Web site: www.stfrancisblueisland.com
For a complete listing, refer to the Hospitals section.

CHICAGO HEIGHTS. *Alverno Lakeside Corporation*, 1423 Chicago Rd., 60411
For a complete listing, refer to the Hospitals section.

St. James Hospital and Health Centers, 1423 Chicago Rd., 60411. Tel: 708-756-1000; Fax: 708-756-6863.
Web site: www.stjameshhc.org
For a complete listing, refer to the Hospitals section.

DES PLAINES. *Holy Family Medical Center*, 100 N. River Rd., 60016. Tel: 847-297-1800; Fax: 847-297-1863.
Web site: chicagotribune.com/link/holyfamily
For a complete listing, refer to the Hospitals section.

ELK GROVE VILLAGE. *Alexian Brothers Medical Center*, 800 Biesterfield Rd., 60007-3397. Tel: 847-437-5500.
E-mail: SchwartM@HBEG.HBOCWIN.COM
Web site: http://www.wswwalexian.org
For a complete listing, refer to the Hospitals section.

EVANSTON. *Saint Francis Hospital*, 355 Ridge Ave., 60202. Tel: 847-316-4000; Fax: 847-316-7733
For a complete listing, refer to the Hospitals section.

EVERGREEN PARK. *Little Company of Mary Hospital and Health Care Centers*, 2800 W. 95th St., 60805. Tel: 708-422-6200; Fax: 708-425-9756.
Web site: www.lcmh.org
For a complete listing, refer to the Hospitals section.

HOFFMAN ESTATES. *Alexian Brothers Behavioral Health Hospital*, 1650 Moon Lake Rd., 60194. Tel: 847-882-1600; Fax: 847-755-8060.
Web site: abbhh.org
For a complete listing, refer to the Hospitals section.

St. Alexius Medical Center, 1555 N. Barrington Rd., 60194. Tel: 847-843-2000.
E-mail: dmcaneiro@yahoo.com
For a complete listing, refer to the Hospitals section.

MAYWOOD. *Foster G. McGaw Hospital of Loyola University of Chicago*, 2160 S. First Ave., 60153. Tel: 708-216-9056; Fax: 708-216-1121
For a complete listing, refer to the Hospitals section.

OAK PARK. *Oak Park Hospital*, 520 S. Maple Ave., 60304. Tel: 708-383-9300; Fax: 708-660-6658
For a complete listing, refer to the Hospitals section.

WAUKEGAN. *Provena Saint Therese Medical Center*, 2615 Washington St., 60085. Tel: 847-249-3900; Fax: 847-249-5897
For a complete listing, refer to the Hospitals section.

[K] HEALTH CARE CENTERS

CHICAGO. *St. Basil Health Service - Free People's Clinic*, 1850 W. Garfield, 60609. Tel: 773-436-4758; Fax: 773-436-2749
For a complete listing, refer to the Hospitals section.

[L] PROTECTIVE INSTITUTIONS

CHICAGO. *Big Sisters*, 721 N. LaSalle St., Room 434, 60610. Tel: 312-751-0111; Fax: 312-751-1085
For a complete listing, refer to the Special Care Facilities section.

House of the Good Shepherd, 1114 W. Grace St., 60613. Tel: 773-935-3434; Fax: 773-935-3523
For a complete listing, refer to the Special Care Facilities section.

L'Arche Chicago, 1049 S. Austin Blvd., 60644. Tel: 773-287-8249.
E-mail: larchechicago@juno.com
For a complete listing, refer to the Special Care Facilities section.

Misericordia Home South, 2916 W. 47th St., 60632. Tel: 773-254-9595; Fax: 773-254-6856
For a complete listing, refer to the Special Care Facilities section.

Misericordia/Heart of Mercy Center, 6300 N. Ridge, 60660. Tel: 773-973-6300; Fax: 773-973-5214
For a complete listing, refer to the Special Care Facilities section.

St. Joseph's Carondelet Child Center, 739 E. 35th St., 60616. Tel: 773-624-7443; Fax: 773-624-7676.
E-mail: jbmc@stjccc.org
For a complete listing, refer to the Special Care Facilities section.

St. Mary of Providence, 4200 N. Austin Ave., 60634. Tel: 773-545-8300; Fax: 773-545-8035.
E-mail: srpatmc@aol.com
For a complete listing, refer to the Special Care Facilities section.

BARTLETT. *Bartlett Learning Center*, 801 W. Bartlett Rd., 60103. Tel: 630-289-4221; Fax: 630-289-4390
For a complete listing, refer to the Special Care Facilities section.

LAKE ZURICH. *Mt. St. Joseph Home*, 24955 North Hwy. 12, 60047. Tel: 847-438-5050; Fax: 847-438-1561
For a complete listing, refer to the Special Care Facilities section.

OAK PARK. *Ephpheta Center and Hearing Conservation Service*, 119 S. Harvey Ave., 60302
For a complete listing, refer to the Special Care Facilities section.

PALOS PARK. *St. Coletta's of Illinois*, 123rd and Wolf Rd., 60464. Tel: 708-448-6520; Fax: 708-923-3532
For a complete listing, refer to the Special Care Facilities section.

[M] SENIOR CARE INSTITUTIONS

CHICAGO. *Cortland Manor Retirement Home*, 1900 N. Karlov, 60639. Tel: 773-235-3670
For a complete listing, refer to the Special Care Facilities section.

Jugan Terrace, 2300 N. Racine, 60614. Tel: 773-935-9600; Fax: 773-935-4291
For a complete listing, refer to the Special Care Facilities section.

Little Sisters of the Poor Center for the Aging, 2325 N. Lakewood Ave., 60614. Tel: 773-935-9600; Fax: 773-935-9614
For a complete listing, refer to the Special Care Facilities section.

Resurrection Retirement Community, 7262 W. Peterson Ave., 60631. Tel: 773-792-7930; Fax: 773-792-8316
For a complete listing, refer to the Special Care Facilities section.

St. Joseph Home of Chicago, Inc., 2650 N. Ridgeway Ave., 60647. Tel: 773-235-8600; Fax: 773-235-2933
For a complete listing, refer to the Special Care Facilities section.

DES PLAINES. *Holy Family Health Center*, 2380 Dempster, 60016. Tel: 847-296-3335
For a complete listing, refer to the Special Care Facilities section.

Nazarethville, 300 N. River Rd., 60016. Tel: 847-297-5900; Fax: 847-297-0504
For a complete listing, refer to the Special Care Facilities section.

GLENVIEW. *Maryhaven Inc.*, 1700 East Lake Ave., 60025. Tel: 847-729-1300; Fax: 847-729-9202
For a complete listing, refer to the Special Care Facilities section.

HOMEWOOD. *Mercy Health Care and Rehabilitation Center*, 19000 S. Halsted St., 60430. Tel: 708-957-9200; Fax: 708-799-4787
For a complete listing, refer to the Special Care Facilities section.

JUSTICE. *Rosary Hill Home*, 9000 W. 81st St., 60458. Tel: 708-458-3040; Fax: 708-458-7230.
E-mail: rosaryhill@cometlink.com
For a complete listing, refer to the Special Care Facilities section.

LEMONT. *Alvernia Manor*, 13950 Main St., 60439. Tel: 630-257-7721; Fax: 630-257-0338.
E-mail: am13950@aol.com
For a complete listing, refer to the Special Care Facilities section.

Holy Family Villa, 12375 McCarthy Rd., 60439
For a complete listing, refer to the Special Care Facilities section.

Mother Theresa Home, 1270 Franciscan Dr., 60439. Tel: 630-257-5801; Fax: 630-257-1328.
E-mail: tkolaz@fv.fsoc.com
For a complete listing, refer to the Special Care Facilities section.

NILES. *St. Andrew Home for the Aged*, 7000 N. Newark Ave., 60714-4497. Tel: 847-647-8332
For a complete listing, refer to the Special Care Facilities section.

St. Benedict Home for the Aged, 6930 W. Touhy Ave., 60714. Tel: 847-647-0003; Fax: 847-647-1936
For a complete listing, refer to the Special Care Facilities section.

NORTHLAKE. *Villa Scalabrini*, 480 N. Wolf Rd., 60164-1667. Tel: 708-562-0040
For a complete listing, refer to the Special Care Facilities section.

OLYMPIA FIELDS. *Mercy Residence at Tolentine Center*, 20300 Governors Hwy., 60461. Tel: 708-748-9500; Fax: 708-481-2090
For a complete listing, refer to the Special Care Facilities section.

PALATINE. *St. Joseph's Home for the Elderly*, 80 W. Northwest Hwy., 60067. Tel: 847-358-5700; Fax: 847-358-5763
For a complete listing, refer to the Special Care Facilities section.

PARK RIDGE. *Resurrection Nursing and Rehabilitation Center*, 1001 N. Greenwood, 60068. Tel: 847-692-5600; Fax: 847-692-2305
For a complete listing, refer to the Special Care Facilities section.

WHEELING. *Addolorata Villa*, 555 McHenry Rd., 60090-3899. Tel: 847-537-2900; Fax: 847-215-5805
For a complete listing, refer to the Special Care Facilities section.

[N] MONASTERIES AND RESIDENCES OF PRIESTS AND BROTHERS

CHICAGO. *Brandsma House*, 1036 W. Loyola Ave., #3, 60626-5233. Tel: 773-761-5139; Fax: 773-761-8599. Revs. Eamon R. Carroll, O.Carm.; Aloysius A. Sieracki, O.Carm.

Carmelite Priory of St. Cyril, 6401 S. Harper Ave., 60637. Tel: 312-684-0112; Fax: 312-684-0113. Bro. Timothy Sklopan, O.Carm., Prior & Prin.; Revs. Jerry Williams, O.Carm.; Leander Troy, O.Carm., (Retired); Daniel Carroll, O.Carm.; George L. O'Keefe, O.Carm., (Retired); Glen Snow, O.Carm. Residing here are all the priests who teach at Mt. Carmel High School. Revs. Carl Markelz, O.Carm., Prin.; John Knoerschild, O.Carm.

Chaplains: Revs. Melchior Toczek, O.F.M., Vicar; Victorian Haladus, O.F.M., Supr. In res. Rev. Michael Windolph, O.F.M.; Bro. Crispin Koeppl, O.F.M. Priests 3; Brothers 1.

Chicago Province of the Society of Jesus-Provincial Office, 2050 N. Clark St., 60614. Tel: 773-975-6363; Fax: 773-975-0230.
E-mail: clarkst@luc.edu
Very Rev. Richard J. Bauman, S.J., Prov.; Revs. Richard H. McGurn, S.J., Exec. Asst. & Asst. Formation; George E. Von Kaenel, S.J., Asst. Intl. Apostolates, Jesuit Intl. Missions, & Social Ministries; James A. Stoeger, S.J., Asst. Secondary Education & Pastoral Ministries; James P. Gschwend, S.J., Asst. for Continuing Ed. & Asst. for Jesuits in Diaspora; John F. Costello, S.J., Asst. for Devel. & Communications; Paul V. Robb, S.J., Asst. Treas.; Daniel L. Flaherty, S.J., Asst. for Business & Finance; William O. Madden, S.J., Asst. Records & Res.; David A. Godleski, S.J., Asst. for Vocation Promotion.
Jesuits Serving Abroad: Rev. Kevin E. Gallagher, S.J., Interprovince Liaison, Apdo 18-0853, Lima 18, Peru. Tel: 5114-275-1000; Fax: 5114-275-0948. Revs. Robert E. Beckman, S.J. (Peru); Kevin H. Flaherty, S.J. (Peru); Jeffrey L. Klaiber, S.J. (Peru); Lewis C. Murtaugh, S.J. (Peru); James M. O'Leary, S.J. (Peru).
Residing elsewhere in the U.S.: Revs. Paul V. Mankowski, S.J. (Rome); John R. Crocker, S.J. (Rome); Joseph H. Boel, S.J. (Africa); Mark W. Andrews, S.J. (DET); James M. Dixon, S.J. (LR); Robert J. Ochs, S.J. (OAK); Charles A. Hofmann, S.J. (SFR); Denis A. Dirscherl, S.J. (BAL); Bradley M. Schaeffer, S.J. (WDC); Thomas W. Florek, S.J. (DET); Henry T Chamberlain, S.J. (Rome); Walter C. Deye, S.J. (WDC); Robert J. Geisinger, S.J. (Rome); Michael W. Cooper, S.J. (SP); Lester E. Love, S.J. (OAK); Joseph F. Wagner, S.J. (OAK); Thomas C. Widner, S.J. (WDC).

Clark Street Jesuit Residence, 2050 N. Clark St., 60614. Tel: 773-975-6900; Fax: 773-975-0230. Revs. James F. Bresnahan, S.J.; John F. Costello, S.J.; Michael E. Dorrler, S.J.; James P. Gschwend, S.J.; George A. Lane, S.J.; Patrick J. McAteer, S.J.; Richard H. McGurn, S.J.; Francis P. O'Donnell, S.J. (CHI); John F. Pennington, S.J.; Edward W. Schmidt, S.J.; Gerald C. Walling, S.J. Priests 12.

Woodlawn Jesuit Community, 5810 S. Harper, 60637. Tel: 773-955-3738; Fax: 773-955-0247. Revs. Philip J. Chmielewski, S.J., Supr.; Robert E. Finn, S.J.; James J. Gill, S.J.; Michael N. Madubuko, S.J.; Paul J. Nienaber, S.J.; F.N. Gamini Perera, S.J.; Robert J. Scullin, S.J.

Claretian Missionaries, St. Jude League, Inc., 205 W. Monroe, 60606. Tel: 312-236-7782; Fax: 312-236-7230.
Web site: claret.org
Editorial Offices: "U.S. Catholic" and other Claretian newsletters. Directors: Revs. Leonard J. Brown, C.M.F.; Mark J. Brummel, C.M.F.

Columban Fathers Mission Center, 6449 N. Magnolia Ave., 60626. Tel: 773-274-9111; Fax: 773-274-9053. Revs. Thomas P. Reynolds, S.S.C.; Thomas G. Glennon, S.S.C.; Sean Conneely, S.S.C.

Columban Fathers Theologate, 5103 S. Ellis Ave., 60615. Tel: 773-955-0660; Fax: 773-955-0805. Rev. Mark Mengel, S.S.C., Rector. Priests 3; Columban Seminarians 10.

Comboni Missionaries Theologate (M.C.C.J.), Verona Fathers, 5512 Hyde Park Blvd., 60637. Tel: 773-667-8920; Fax: 773-667-6414.
E-mail: chicombtheo@msn.com
Revs. Ramon Vargas, M.C.C.J. (Equador); Mussie Abraham, M.C.C.J. (Eritrea). Theology students 20.

Congregation of Alexian Brothers-Alexian Brothers Novitiate, 6007 N. Kenmore Ave., 60660-2953. Tel: 773-275-9300; Fax: 773-275-9373.
E-mail: abkenmore@juno.com
Bro. Dan Pisano, C.F.A., Dir. Novices. Professed Brothers 2; Novices 1.

Congregation of Christian Brothers, Brother Rice Community, 10001 S. Pulaski Rd., 60642. Tel: 773-445-5048. Bros. Eugene O. Carty, C.F.C.; Thomas J. Collins, C.F.C., Community Leader; Edmund V. Corrigan, C.F.C.; George G. Gremley, C.F.C.; David J. Haas, C.F.C.; Charles E. Joyce, C.F.C.; James A. Houlihan, C.F.C.; John B. Moore, C.F.C.; Patrick B. Martin, C.F.C.; John Toole, C.F.C.; James B. Sloan, C.F.C.; Patrick T. Varilla, C.F.C.; Frank S. Verre, C.F.C.; John S. O'Keefe, C.F.C.; Francis R. Finch, C.F.C.; William L. McInerney, C.F.C. Brothers 16.

Congregation of Marian Fathers of the Immaculate Conception, 6336 S. Kilbourn Ave., 60629-5588. Tel: 773-582-8191 (Provincial Office); 767-1687 (Religious House); Fax: 773-582-8961 (Provincial Office).
E-mail: promic@aol.com
Web site: www.marians.org
Very Rev. Donald S. Petraitis, M.I.C., Prov.; Revs. Timothy Roth, M.I.C., Councillor I; Jerome A. Zalonis, M.I.C., Councillor II; Daniel Cambra, M.I.C., Councillor III; Bros. Donald Schaefer, M.I.C., Prov. Treas.; Brian Manian, M.I.C., Councillor IV; Revs. Vytautas Bagdanavicius, M.I.C.; Jonas Duoba, M.I.C., Local Supr.; John Jancius, M.I.C.; Victor Rimselis, M.I.C.; Jonas Sakevicius, M.I.C. Priests 6.

Conventual Franciscans of St. Bonaventure Province, 6107 N. Kenmore Ave., 60660. Tel: 773-274-7681; Fax: 773-274-9751. Very Rev. Anthony Labedis, O.F.M.Conv., Prov.; Bro. Thomas Surmann, O.F.M.Conv., Treas.; Rev. Joseph Kruszynski, O.F.M.Conv., Guardian. In res. Bros. George Searles, O.F.M.Conv.; Joseph Graff, O.F.M. Conv.; Rev. James Giaramitaro, O.F.M. Conv.
Assigned but serving elsewhere: Rev. Francis Kiley, O.F.M.Conv., Vianney Renewal Center, Eime Rd., P.O. Box 130, Dittmer, MO, 63023. Rev. Aloysius Romanowski, O.F.M.Conv., Mount St. Joseph Institute - Chaplaincy, 24955 N. Highway 12, Lake Zurich, 60047-9752. Rev. Bernard Geiger, O.F.M.Conv., Apostolate for Family Consecration, 3375 County Rd. 36, Bloomingdale, OH, 43910-7903.
Friars of the Province Serving Abroad: Revs. John Calgaro, O.F.M.Conv. (Mexico); Abraham Crisostomo, O.F.M.Conv. (Mexico); Bro. Paschal Metzger, O.F.M.Conv. (Mexico).

The Conventual Franciscans of Saint Bonaventure Province Corporation. Legal Title: *The Conventual Franciscans of Saint Bonaventure Province Charitable Continuing Care Trust Fund.*

Franciscan Friars Educational Corporation.

St. Hedwig Cemetery and Mausoleum Corporation. Legal Title: *Franciscan Friars Retirement Corporation.*

Croatian Dominican Fathers, 6346 N. Ridge, 60660. Tel: 773-262-0535; Fax: 773-262-4603. Revs. Nicholas Dugandzic, O.P., Asst. Chap., Croatian Catholic Mission Blessed Alojzije; Zvonko Dzankic, O.P., Asst. Chap.

Croatian Franciscan Custody of the Holy Family, 4851 S. Drexel Blvd., 60615. Tel: 773-536-0552; Fax: 773-536-2094.
E-mail: pajdo@aol.com
Rev. Slavko Soldo, O.F.M., Custos, Croatia Franciscan Custody of the Holy Family.

St. Anthony's Friary, 4848 S. Ellis Ave., 60615. Tel: 773-373-3463. Revs. Jerome Kucan, O.F.M., Guardian; Vjekoslav Bambir, O.F.M.; Timothy Majic, O.F.M.; Doiminik Coric, O.F.M.; Miron Lasic, O.F.M.; Kvirin Vasilj, O.F.M.; Theodore Benkovic, O.F.M.; Bruno Raspudic, O.F.M.; Stephen Raich, O.F.M.; Ljubo Krasic, O.F.M., Vicar; Vincent Cvitkovic, O.F.M.; Mark Kozina, O.F.M.

Crosier Community of Chicago, 5401 S. Cornell Ave., 60615. Tel: 773-684-6975; Fax: 773-684-8357. Revs. Thomas Enneking, O.S.C.; John Neville, O.S.C.; Bro. David Donnay, O.S.C.

Daneo Hall. (Passionist Retirement Wing), 5700 N. Harlem, 60631. Tel: 312-631-5179.
E-mail: chundcp@visioni.com
Revs. Leo Brady, C.P.; William Browning, C.P.; Brian Mahedy, C.P.; John B. Pechulis, C.P.; Thaddeus Tamm, C.P.; Cyprian Towey, C.P.; Kenny Lynch, C.P.; Bros. Patrick Keeney, C.P.; Joachim Saunders, C.P.; John Gebauer, C.P.; Carl Hund, C.P., Dir. Priests 7; Brothers 4.

DePaul Vincentian Residence, 2233 N. Kenmore Ave., 60614-3594. Tel: 773-880-2968. Legal Title: *Society of Priests of the Congregation of the Mission of Chicago.* Rev. Paul Sisul, C.M.; Mr. Michael Walsh, Treas.
Members of the Vincentian Community (Congregation of the MIssion): Bros. Paul P. Joseph, C.M.; Leo Keigher, C.M.; Revs. Patrick Flanagan, C.M.; Thomas J. Meik, C.M.; John P. Minogue, C.M.; Thomas P. Munster, C.M.; Andres Rey, C.M.; Manuel J. Pelleteri, C.M.; Mark Pranaitis, C.M.; Donald Ours, C.M.; Anthony Dosen, C.M.; John F. Cawley, C.M.; Tesfamariam Texlemariam, C.M.; Edward J. Tomasiewicz, C.M.; Charles J. Welter, C.M.; Raymond F. White, C.M.; Jose Nazhianpara, C.M.; Robertus Wijanarko, C.M.

Discalced Carmelite Friars; Edith Stein House of Studies, 5345 S. University Ave., 60615. Tel: 773-752-6943; 493-6066; Fax: 773-752-6594. Revs. Kevin Culligan, O.C.D.; Marc Foley, O.C.D., Rector; Michael Dodd, O.C.D. Friars: Charles Gamen, O.C.D.; Frank Salamone, O.C.D. Priests 3; Students 2.

Divine Word Theologate, 5342 S. University, 60615. Tel: 773-288-2777; Fax: 773-288-6307.
E-mail: theologate@aol.com
Web site: http://www.svd.org
Revs. Edward Peklo, S.V.D., Rector; Mark Schramm, S.V.D., Vice-Rector; Roger S. Arnold, S.V.D., Dir. Formation; Gary L. Riebe-Estrella, S.V.D.; Peter De Ta Vo, S.V.D.; Stephen B. Bevans, S.V.D.; Lloyd Cunningham, S.V.D.; Emil Kralik, S.V.D.; Roger P. Schroeder, S.V.D.; Derek Simons, S.V.D. Priests 10; Students 49.

Dominican Community, 1914 S. Ashland Ave., 60608. Tel: 312-829-0074. Revs. Charles W. Dahm, O.P.; Matthias R. Mueller, O.P.

Dominicans (Provincial Office), St. Pius V. Priory, 1909 S. Ashland Ave., 60608. Tel: 312-226-0074. Provincial Office. Tel: 312-666-3244; Fax: 312-829-8471.
E-mail: domcenprov@mac.domcentral.org
Legal Title: *Dominicans, Province of St. Albert the Great, U.S.A. (Central Dominican Province).* Provincial Staff: Very Rev. Edward M. Ruane, O.P., Prior Prov.; Revs. Benjamin J. Russell, O.P., Dir. Vocational Support; Frank C. Quinn, O.P., Regent Studies; John J. Meany, O.P., Syndic; David F. Wright, O.P., Socius & Vicar Prov., Prov. Archivist; Louis S. Morrone, O.P., Dir. Vocations; Bede R. Jagoe, O.P., Dir. St. Dominic Mission & Shrine of St. Jude Thaddeus; John J. Meany, O.P., Dir. Dominican Conference Center; Dennis C. Woerter, O.P., Promoter of Social Justice; Steven F. Kuhlmann, O.P., Dir. Dominican Social Action Fund; Thomas J. Johnston, O.P., Promoter of Dominican Laity; Vincent I. Zarlenga, O.P., Dir., Fra Angelico Art Foundation; Bro. William E. Carroll, O.P., Vicar Prov.

St. Pius V Priory. Tel: 312-226-0074. Very Revs. Edward M. Ruane, O.P., Prior Prov.; David F. Wright, O.P., Socius & Vicar Prov.; Revs. Robert L. Barry, O.P.; Patrick M.J. Clancy, O.P.; Michael A. Garcia, O.P.; Robert A. Goedert, O.P.; Thomas A. Morrison, O.P.; Benjamin J. Russell, O.P.; Deacon J. Reid Perkins-Buzo, O.P.; Bros. William E. Carroll, O.P., Vicar Prov.; Jordan D. Coonen, O.P.; Paul T. Leahy, O.P.; Gerald Pidcock, O.P.
Assigned but Serving Elsewhere: Revs. Roderick M. Brown, O.P.; Vincent W. Bryce, O.P.; John R. Dolehide, O.P.; Francis X. Dyer, O.P.; John C. Fabian, O.P.; Rapael A. Fabish, O.P.; James M. Karepin, O.P.; Gerald C. Kroeger, O.P.; Daniel W. Morrissey, O.P.; Frank M. Nouza, O.P.; Richard J. Woods, O.P.; Bro. Benedict G. Baer, O.P.
Priests of the Province Serving Abroad: Revs. Gerard B. Cleator, O.P. (Mexico); Eric deWasseige, O.P., Bolivia; Thomas P. Lynch, O.P., Bolivia; Joseph P. Kenny, O.P., Nigeria; Thomas K. McDermott, O.P., Nigeria; Peter Otillio, O.P., Nigeria; Mark R. Paraday, O.P., Bolivia; Justus M. Pokrzewinski, O.P., Nigeria; Patrick R. Rearden, O.P., Bolivia; Edward H. Riley, O.P., Nigeria; Lewis M. Shea, O.P., Kenya; James A. Spahn, O.P., Bolivia; Gerald L. Stookey, O.P., Italy; Gilbert J. Thesing, O.P., Nigeria; Benedict T. Viviano, O.P., Switzerland; Benedict T. Viviano, O.P., Switzerland; Ambrose P. Windbacher, O.P., Nigeria; Bro. Stephen D. Lucas, O.P., Nigeria. Legal Titles: *Spirituality Today Journal, Inc.*; *Shrine of St. Jude Thaddeus.*; *Society for Vocational Support, Inc.*; *St. Dominic Mission Society.*; *Dominican Social Action Fund.*; *Dominican Laity.*; *Fra Angelico Art Foundation.*; *The Bolivian Trust of the Dominicans.*; *Office for Mission Advancement.*

Franciscan House of Studies, 6107 N. Kenmore Ave., 60660. Tel: 773-764-8811; Fax: 773-274-9751. A Formation House of Conventual Franciscan Friars.

Holy Evangelists Friary. Order of Friars Minor. 4513 N. Ashland Blvd., 60650-5401. Tel: 773-878-3723.
E-mail: rfpawell@aol.com
Revs. Fred Radtke; Robert Pawell; Eulogio Roselada. Priests 3.

Holy Name Friary, Assumption BVM Province, 4930 S. Woodlawn Ave., 60615-2812. Tel: 773-285-1636; Fax: 773-285-1637. Revs. Leslie J. Hoppe, O.F.M., Prof. Catholic Theological Union; Lawrence Janowski, O.F.M., Faculty, Wright College, Harper College; Bros. David Dodge, O.F.M., Vicar & Student Xavier; David Kobak, O.F.M., M.Div. (Cand.), CTU; William Stout, O.F.M., M.Div. (Cand.), CTU; Jose Rodriguez, O.F.M., M.Div. (Cand.), CTU.

Korean Catholic Center, 4115 N. Kedvale, 60641. Tel: 773-283-3979. Rev. John Smith, S.S.C., Dir.

Lithuanian American Jesuits. (Della Strada Residence and Lithuanian Youth Center), 2345 W. 56th St., 60636. Tel: 773-737-8400; Fax: 773-737-0486. Legal Title: *Jesuit Fathers of Della Strada.* Rev. Juozas Vaisnys, S.J., Vice Supr., Editor of Letters to Lithuanians.
Members of the Community: Revs. Vaclovas Gutauskas, S.J.; Algirdas Paliokas, S.J., Chap. Dir.

Blessed Jurgis Matulaitis Mission, 14911 E. 127th St., Lemont, 60439. Tel: 630-257-5613. Bro. Petras Kleinotas, S.J. Priests 3; Brothers 1.

Lithuanian Youth Center, 5620 S. Claremont Ave., 60636. Tel: 773-778-7500.

Marist Brothers, 1016 W. Polk St., 60607. Tel: 312-491-9301. Bro. John Murray, F.M.S.

Marist Brothers, Monastery Community, 4200 W. 115th St., 60655. Tel: 773-881-6380; Fax: 773-881-0595.
E-mail: jm5816@aol.com
Web site: www.marist.net
Bros. Gerard Brown, Dir.; M. Oswald Ouellette; Clement Legare; Philip McEnaney; Patrick Magee; Kevin Moran; Julian Roy; Paul Forgues; Richard Grenier; Sumner Herrick; Christopher Shannon.

Marist Brothers, St. Ann Residence, 10114 S. Leavitt, 60643. Tel: 773-239-4116. Bros. Timothy Brady, Dir.; Vito Aresto, Dir.; Louis Richard; Hugh Turley; Henry Hammer.

Maryknoll Fathers & Brothers, 3600 S. Seeley Ave., 60609. Tel: 773-927-9257; Fax: 774-927-7305.
E-mail: mklchicago@aol.com
Web site: http://www.maryknoll.org
Legal Title: *The Catholic Foreign Mission Society of America*. Revs. Clyde Phillips, M.M., Dir.; Carl P. Meulemans, M.M.; John C. Moynihan, M.M.; Bro. Adrian R. Mazuchowski, M.M.

Miguel Pro Jesuit Community, 1611 S. Allport St., 60608. Tel: 312-226-6496; Fax: 312-226-2915. Revs. Richard J. Baumann, S.J.; Joao Ramon Eidt, S.J.; John P. Foley, S.J., Local Supr.; Charles W. Niehaus, S.J.; James G. Gartland, S.J.; Timothy A. Howe, S.J.; Paul R. Mueller, S.J.; Stephen W. Planning, S.J.; Bro. David L. Henderson, S.J.

Missionaries of Africa, St. Martin de Porres, 5112 W. Washington, 60644. Tel: 773-287-0206; Fax: 773-261-2344.
E-mail: africago@aol.com
Revs. Georges Salles, M.Afr., (France); Julien Cormier, M.Afr. (Canada). Priests 2.

Monastery of the Holy Cross, 3111 S. Aberdeen St., 60608-6503. Tel: 773-927-7424; Fax: 773-927-5734.
E-mail: porter@chicagomonk.org
Web site: http://www.chicagomonk.org
Benedictine Monks (Subiaco Congregation). Revs. Thomas-Benedict Baxter, O.S.B., Prior; Brendan D. Creeden, O.S.B., Novice Master; Edward J. Gianzmann, O.S.B., Guest Master; Bro. Peter Funk, O.S.B. Postulants 2.

The Oblate House of Theology, 5535 S. Kenwood Ave., 60637. Tel: 773-493-3590; Fax: 773-493-6239.
E-mail: omichicago@aol.com
Revs. William Sheehan, O.M.I., Supr.; Philip Singarayar, O.M.I., Assoc.; Vaugn Fayle, O.M.I.; Stanley Zowada, O.M.I. Scholastics 5.

Order of Friar Servants of Mary (Servites) United States of America Province, Inc., Servite Provincial Center, 3121 W. Jackson Blvd., 60612-2729. Tel: 773-533-0360; Fax: 773-533-8307. Very Rev. Michael M. Guimon, O.S.M., Prior Prov.; Rev. Peregrine M. Graffius, O.S.M., Asst. Prov.; Bro. Brian M. Fitzpatrick, O.S.M., Prov. Councilor; Revs. Gerald M. Horan, O.S.M., Prov. Councilor; Christopher M. Krymski, O.S.M., Prov. Councilor; Bro. Joel A. Lechner, O.S.M., Prov. Councilor; Rev. Eugene M. Smith, O.S.M., Prov. Councilor; Bros. Edmund Baran, O.S.M., Prov. Treas.; Michael M. Callary, O.S.M., Prov. & Corp. Sec. Mission Procurator; Revs. Conrad M. Borntrager, O.S.M., Prov. Archivist & Historian; Walter M. Brennan, O.S.M., Prov. Marian Center Co-Dir.; Joseph M. Cheah, O.S.M., Prov. Marian Center Co-Dir.; Paul M. Gins, O.S.M., Prov. Vocation Dir.; Gerald M. Horan, O.S.M., Pres., Servite High School, Anaheim, CA; Christopher M. Krymski, O.S.M., Province St. Peregrine Ministry; Vidal Matinez, O.S.M., Natl. Asst. for Servite Secular Order; Philip M. McGlynn, O.S.M., Prov. Devel. Dir.; John Topper, O.S.M., Dir., The Sanctuary of Our Sorrowful Mother "The Grotto", Portland, OR; Robert M. Warsey, O.S.M., Prov. Formation Dir.; Bro. Martin M. Doherty, O.S.M., Prov. Sacristan.

Servite Marian Center, 3121 W. Jackson Blvd., 60612-2729. Tel: 773-638-5800, Ext. 19; Fax: 773-533-8307. Rev. Walter M. Brennan, O.S.M.

Monastery of Our Lady of Sorrows, 3121 W. Jackson Blvd., 60612-2729. Tel: 773-638-5800; Fax: 773-533-8307. Bros. Edmund M. Baran, O.S.M.; Robert M. Fandel, O.S.M.; Joseph Fundak, O.S.M.; Bonfilius M. McGovern, O.S.M.; Revs. Charles M. Brennan, O.S.M.; Lawrence M. Choate, O.S.M.; Donald M. Gantley, O.S.M.; Donald M. Siple, O.S.M.; Robert M. Warsey, O.S.M.

Annunciata Priory, 11128 S. Avenue G, 60617. Tel: 773-221-1043; Fax: 773-221-1556. Bro. Brian M. Fitzpatrick, O.S.M.; Revs. Conrad M. Borntrager, O.S.M.; Mark M. Dennehy, O.S.M.; George M. Luznicky, O.S.M.; Paul M. Cullen, O.S.M.

Assumption Priory, 323 W. Illinois St., 60610. Tel: 312-644-0392; Fax: 312-644-1838. Revs. David M. Brown, O.S.M.; John M. Dowd, O.S.M.; Paul M. Novak, O.S.M.; Anthony M. O'Connell, O.S.M.; John M. Pawlikowski, O.S.M., Ph.D.; Peregrine M. Graffius, O.S.M.

St. Bonfilius Priory, 3401 S. Home Ave., Berwyn, 60402-3327. Tel: 708-484-2595; Fax: 708-484-0064. Very Rev. Michael M. Guimon, O.S.M.; Bros. Michael Callary, O.S.M.; Martin Doherty, O.S.M.; Revs. Thomas M. Heskin, O.S.M.; Peter M. Rookey, O.S.M.

Servants of Mary (Servite) Development Office, 1439 S. Harlem Ave., Berwyn, 60402. Tel: 708-795-8885; Fax: 708-795-8892. Rev. Philip M. McGlynn, O.S.M.

St. Domitilla Priory, 4940 Washington, Hillside, 60162-1297. Tel: 708-449-8430; Fax: 708-449-2009. Revs. Walter M. Brennan, O.S.M.; Frank M. Falco, O.S.M.; Mark M. Franceschini, O.S.M.; Christopher M. Krymski, O.S.M.; Philip M. McGlynn, O.S.M.

Members of the Province Located Elsewhere in the Archdiocese of Chicago and Other Locations in the U.S.: Revs. Bernard M. Barnes, O.S.M., Resurrection Retirement Center, Chicago, IL; Richard Boyle, O.S.M., Seven Holy Founders Priory, Anaheim, CA; Louis M. Breton, O.S.M., Sanctuary of Our Sorrowful Mother, Portland, OR; Joseph M. Carbone, O.S.M., Our Lady of Mount Carmel Priory, Denver, CO; Joseph M. Chamblain, O.S.M., Seven Holy Founders Priory, Afton, MO; Damian M. Charbonneau, O.S.M., St. Peregrine Priory, Kissimmee, FL; Joseph M. Cheah, O.S.M., St. Mary's College High School, Berkeley, CA; Louis M. Cortney, O.S.M., Addolorata Villa, Wheeling, IL; Thomas M. Crotty, O.S.M., St. Peregrine Priory, Kissimmee, FL; Patrick M. Donovan, O.S.M., St. Juliana Falconieri Priory, Fullerton, CA; Lawrence Michael Doyle, O.S.M., Seven Holy Founders Proiry, Affton, MO; Thomas M. Duff, O.S.M., Resurrection Life Center, Chicago, IL; Donald M. Duplessis, O.S.M., St. Juliana Falconieri Priory, Fullerton, CA; Edward M. Edwards, O.S.M., Diocese of Metuchen, NJ; Carl M. Feil, O.S.M., Our Lady of Belen Priory, Belen, NM.; John M. Fontana, O.S.M., Seven Holy Founders Priory, Affton, MO; Albert M. Gallegos, O.S.M., Our Lady of Guadalupe Parish, Peralta, NM; David M. Gallegos, O.S.M., Our Lady of Belen Priory, Belen, NW; Anthony M. Gaydos, O.S.M., St. Marie du Lac Parish, Ironton, MO; Paul M. Gins, O.S.M., Seven Holy Founders Priory, Anaheim, CA; Loren M. Gonzales, O.S.M., Seton Catholic High School, Chandler, AZ; Thomas M. Greaney, O.S.M., Our Lady of Belen Priory, Belen, NM.; Hugh Guentner, O.S.M., Assumption Priory, Benever, CO; Jude M. Herlihy, O.S.M., St. Juliana Falconieri Priory, Fullerton, CA; Gerald M. Horan, O.S.M., Seven Holy Founders Priory, Anaheim, CA; Jerome M. Hurley, O.S.M., Resurrection Life Center, Chicago, IL; Ignatius M. Kissel, O.S.M., St. Philip Benizi Priory, Fullerton, CA; Bruce M. Klikunas, O.S.M., Paolo Sarpi Priory, Berkeley, CA; Damian M. Kobus, O.S.M., Sanctuary of Our Sorrowful Mother Priory, Portland, OR; David M. Kondik, O.S.M., St. Juliana Falconieri Priory, Fullerton, CA; Timothy M. Kremen, O.S.M., St. Philip Benizi, Fullerton, CA; Dennis Kriz, O.S.M., St. Peregrine Priory, Kissimmee, FL; Augustine M. Kulbis, O.S.M., Our Lady of Mount Carmel Priory, Denver, CO; Roger M. Manning, O.S.M., Little Sisters of the Poor, Denver, CO; Vidal Martinez, O.S.M., St. Peregrine Priory, Kissimmee, FL; Manuel Maya-Chavez, O.S.M., St. Philip Benizi Priory, Fullerton, CA; Perry M. McCoy, O.S.M., Sanctuary of Our Sorrowful Mother, Portland, OR; Patrick M. McNamara, O.S.M., Sanctuary of Our Sorrowful Mother, Portland, OR; Nicholas M. Norusis, O.S.M., Resurrection Life Center, Chicago, IL; George M. O'Connell, O.S.M., Little Sisters of the Poor, Chicago, IL; Vincent M. O'Shea, O.S.M., Little Sisters of the Poor, Chicago, IL; Edward M. Penonzek, O.S.M., Seven Holy Founders Priory, Anaheim, CA; Justin M. Pisciotta, O.S.M., St. Philip Benizi Priory, Fullerton, CA; Michael M. Pontarelli, O.S.M., Seven Holy Founders Priory, Anaheim, CA; Gabriel M. Ramacciotti, O.S.M., Assumption Priory, Denver, CO; Stephen M. Ryan, O.S.M., Queen of Angels Community, Los Angeles, CA; Michael M. Scanlon, O.S.M., Addolorata Villa, Wheeling, IL; Philip M. Scherer, O.S.M., Mother of Sorrows Convent, Blue Island, IL; Eugene M. Smith, O.S.M., Seven Holy Founders Priory, Anaheim, CA; Luke M. Stano, O.S.M., St. John Berchmans-St. Juliana, Detroit, MI; John M. Topper, O.S.M., The Sanctuary of Our Sorrowful Mother, Portland, OR; Lawrence M. Walling, O.S.M., Our Lady of Mount Carmel Priory, Denver, CO; Gabriel M. Weber, O.S.M., Our Lady of Mount Carmel Priory, Denver, CO; Bros. Gregory M. Atherton, O.S.M., The Sanctuary of Our Sorrowful Mother, Portland, OR; Philip M. Eikmeyer, O.S.M., Assumption Priory, Denver, CO; Joel A. Lechner, O.S.M., Seven Holy Founders Priory, Anaheim, CA; Robert M. Lee, O.S.M., The Sanctuary of Our Sorrowful Mother, Portland, OR; Christopher Moran, O.S.M., Our Lady of Belen Priory, Belen, NM.

Members of the Province Serving Abroad: Revs. Robert M. Anderson, O.S.M., Kwazulu-Natal, Republic of South Africa; Patrick M. Boyle, O.S.M., Wanneroo, Australia; Thomas M. Carroll, O.S.M., Kwazulu-Natal, Republic of South Africa; Frank M. Christie, O.S.M., Booragoon, Australia; Declan M. Doherty, O.S.M., Kwazulu-Natal, Republic of South Africa; James M. Dore, O.S.M., Kwazulu-Natal, Republic of South Africa; Matthew M. Ford, O.S.M., Benburb, Northern Ireland; John M. Huels, O.S.M., Ottawa, Canada; Edwin M. Kinch, O.S.B., Kwazulu-Natal, Republic of South Africa; Robert M. Kucera, O.S.M., Kwazulu-Natal, Republic of South Africa; John M. LeMay, O.S.M., Kwazulu-Natal, Republic of South Africa; Mel M. Loftus, O.S.M., Kwazulu-Natal, Republic of South Africa; Myles M. Lynch, O.S.M., Tuart Hill, Australia; Liam M. Mackle, O.S.M., Parkville, Australia; Carlo M. Marchetti, O.S.M., Tuart Hill, Australia; Camillus M. McGrane, O.S.M., Kwazulu-Natal, Republic of South Africa; Sibusiso Mngomezulu, O.S.M., Kwazulu-Natal, Republic of South Africa; Alphonse M. Mooney, O.S.M., Kwazulu-Natal, Republic of South Africa; Mafanisa Mthembu, O.S.M., Kwazulu-Natal, Republic of South Africa; Thulani Ntsele, O.S.M., Kwazulu-Natal, Republic of South Africa; Most Rev. Michael M. O'Shea, O.S.M., Kwazulu-Natal, Republic of South Africa; Revs. Christopher M. Ross, O.S.M., Tuart Hill, Australia; Leo M. Spicer, O.S.M., Parkville, Australia; Charles M. Toland, O.S.M., Kwazulu-Natal, Republic of South Africa; Amideus M. Wickers, O.S.M., Dusseldorf-Nord, Germany; Robert M. Zivkovic, O.S.M., Wanneroo, Australia; Bros. Oscar M. Aguilera Acosta, O.S.M., Rome, Italy; Philip M. Allebone, O.S.M., Kwazulu-Natal, Republic of South Africa; Stephen M. Barker, O.S.M., Wanneroo, Australia; Emelio M. Kasaba, O.S.M., Kwazulu-Natal, Republic of South Africa (Novice); Andrew M. Motsko, O.S.M., Kwazulu-Natal, Republic of South Africa; Arnaldo Sanchez, O.S.M., Rome, Italy (Novice). Priests 102; Brothers 14; Temporary Professed 2; Novices 2.

Passionist Community-CTU, 5401 S. Cornell Ave., 60615-5698. Tel: 773-324-2704; Fax: 773-324-2557.
E-mail: omalleyK@ctu.lib.il.us
Revs. Kenneth O'Malley, C.P., Supr.; Francis Landry, C.P., Dir.-Students; James Barry, C.P.; Robert Carbonneau, C.P.; David Monaco, C.P.; Donald Senior, C.P. Scholastics: William Maguire, C.P.; Patrick Daugherty, C.P.; Isaac Murphy, O.S.B.; Lee Harvey, C.P. Priests 6; Scholastics 4. Legal Title: *Congregation of the Passion: St. Vincent Strambi Community.*

Passionist Community-Immaculate Conception Monastery, 5700 N. Harlem Ave., 60631-2342. Tel: 773-631-1686; Fax: 773-631-8059.
E-mail: mste339153@aol.com
Legal Title: *Congregation of the Passion: Immaculate Conception Province*. Revs. Michael Joseph Stengel, C.P., Supr.; Myron Gohmann, C.P.; Luke Connolly, Dir., Passionist Missions Appeals; Peter Kumle, C.P.; Frederick Sucher, C.P.; Warren Womack, C.P., Asst. Supr.; Donald Webber, C.P., Prov. Consultor; Louis Doherty, C.P.; Michael J. Hoolahan, C.P., Pastor, Immaculate Conception Parish; Paul I. Bechtold, C.P.; Roger Mercurio, C.P., Prov. Archivist; Rian Clancy, C.P.; John T. Render, C.P., Dir. Passionist Resource Center; Leon Grantz, C.P., Chap., Our Lady of the Resurrection Hospital; Francis X. Keenan, C.P., Chap., Lutheran General Hospital; John F. Kobler, C.P.; Eric Meyer, C.P.; Michael Higgins, C.P., Prov. Supr.; Peter Berendt, C.P.; Philip Schaefer, C.P.; Bros. Peter Fitzpatrick, C.F.X.; Raymond Sanchez, C.P., Chap. Cook Co. Jail; Joseph Stadtfeld, C.P.; John Monzyk, C.P. Priests 20; Brothers 4.

Passionist Provincial Office, 5700 N. Harlem Ave., 60631-2342. Tel: 773-631-6336; Fax: 773-631-8059.
E-mail: mail@passionist.org
Web site: passionist.org
Legal Title: *Congregation of the Passion (Holy Cross Province)*. Very Rev. Michael Higgins, C.P., Prov.; Revs. Donald Webber, C.P., Asst. Prov.; James G. Strommer, C.P., Consultor; Alexander Steinmiller, C.P., Consultor; Richard Parks, C.P., Consultor.
Special Assignment: Most Rev. Paul M. Boyle, C.P., Diocesan Bishop of Mandeville, P.O. Box 8, Mandeville, Jamaica, West Indies. Tel: 876-962-1269; Fax: 876-962-1297. Rev. Richard Johnson, C.P., 2412 Linda Ave., Key West, FL, 33040-5100. Tel: 305-293-0490. Rev. John Gabriel R. Mulnix, C.P., Ch. Col., 204-A E. Losey St., Scott AFB, 62225. Tel: 618-256-3303. Rev. Robert Coward, C.P., Curia Generalizia Dei Passionist, Piazza SS. Giovanni e Paolo 13, Rome, Italy, 00184. Tel: 011-39-06-772-711; Fax: 001-39-06-700-8454. Rev. Arhtur Carrillo, C.P., Curia Generalizia Dei Passionisti, Piazza SS. Giovanni e Paolo 13, Rome, Italy, 00184. Tel: 011-39-06-772-711; Fax: 011-39-06-700-8454. Rev. John P. Day, C.P., St. Robert Bellarmine, 1414 First Capitol Dr., S., St. Charles, MO, 63303-3702. Tel: 636-946-6799; Fax: 636-946-0380. Rev. Louis Doherty, C.P., RR #2, Box 36, Pierce City, MO, 65723. Tel: 417-476-2281. Rev. Joseph Van Leeuwen, C.P., Ashram J.X.P., Pallichal Rd. - Palluruthy, Kochi 682-006, Kerela, South India. Tel: 011-91-484-231-309; Fax: 011-91-484-223-652. Rev. Thomas M. Newbold, C.P., Sisters of Mercy Motherhouse, 535 Sacramento St., Auburn, CA, 95603. Tel: 530-823-3841. Bro. Kevin O'Malley, C.P., 530 N. Noble Ave., #3R, 60622. Tel: 312-666-6679; Fax: 312-666-7112. Rev. Paul Wadell, C.P., 1975 Ridgeway Dr., #31,

DePere, WI, 54115. Tel: 920-983-8326. Rev. Faustinus Moran, C.P., 5900 Delhi Rd., Mount St. Joseph, OH, 45051. Tel: 513-347-5311; Fax: 513-451-1793. Rev. Joseph Moons, C.P., Regl. Vicar, Passionist Jyotir Bhavan, Carmelaram P.O., Bangalore, India, 560-035. Tel: 011-91-80-843-9527; Fax: 011-91-80-553-3358.

Stauros U.S.A. Tel: 773-752-5732; Fax: 773-752-5741. Laurence Huiras, Exec. Dir., Catholic Theological Union, 5401 S. Cornell Ave., 60615-5698. Tel: 773-324-8000; Fax: 773-324-8490.

Passionist Missions of India, 5700 N. Harlem Ave., 60631. Tel: 773-631-6336; Fax: 773-631-8059. Rev. Walter Kaelin, C.P., Procurator.

Congregation of the Passion. Mother of Good Counsel Community, 5700 N. Harlem Ave., 60631. Tel: 773-631-1686; Fax: 773-631-8059.

Passionist Missions, Inc., 5700 N. Harlem Ave., 60631. Tel: 773-631-1686; Fax: 773-631-8059. Mr. Edward Scholl, Dir.; Rev. Luke Connolly, C.P., Mission Appeals.

Passionist Lay Missioners, 5700 N. Harlem Ave., 60631. Tel: 773-631-6336; Fax: 773-631-8059. Co-Directors: Loretta Pequeno; Soyun Kim.

Premonstratensian Fathers and Brothers (Norbertines), 4841 S. Woodlawn Ave., 60615. Tel: 773-548-8020; Fax: 773-548-8023.
Web site: www.norbertines.org
Holy Spirit House of Studies. Revs. Andrew G. Gribben, O.Praem., Supr.; Brian Prunty, O.Praem.; Bro. Terrence Lauerman, O.Praem.; Rev. James Stein, O.Praem.; Bro. Steven Herro, O.Praem.; Frater Michael Doyle, O.Praem.; Frater Onwuham Akpa, O.Praem.; Frater Robert Campbell, O.Praem. Priests 3; Students 3; Simply Professed 2; Novices 1.

Priests of the Sacred Heart. (House of Studies), 4840 S. Woodlawn Ave., 60615-1920. Tel: 773-373-2793; Fax: 773-373-8704.
E-mail: rdileo@juno.com
Revs. Mark Fortner, S.C.J., Dir.; Richard DiLeo, S.C.J., Coord.; Guy Blair, S.C.J., Asst. Dir.; Timothy Grat, S.C.J., Dir. Justice & Peace. Priests 4; Scholastics 3. Robert W. Bossie, S.C.J., 4946 N. Sheridan, Apt. 222, 60640. Tel: 773-275-9516. Rev. Michael McMillen, S.C.J., 6227 N. Magnolia, #2, 60660. Tel: 773-743-7247.

Provincial Office of the Congregation of the Resurrection, 7050 N. Oakley Ave., 60645. Tel: 773-465-8320; Fax: 773-465-8314. Very Rev. John H. Nowak, C.R., Prov.; Rev. Gary Hogan, C.R., Vocation Dir. Tel: 773-486-1660.
Priests serving abroad: Very Rev. Norbert W. Raszeja, C.R., Via San Sebastianello 11, 00187 Rome, Italy. Tel: 011-39-06-679-5908; Fax: 011-39-06-678-4397. Rev. Glen Baptiste, C.R., St. Theresa Cathedral, P.O. Box HM1191, Hamilton, Bermuda HM EX. Tel: 441-292-0607; 292-5383; Fax: 441-292-2477. Revs. Stephen Glab, C.R.; Richard Grek, C.R.; Eugene Majewski, C.R., Resurrection Center Retreat House, 2710 S. Country Club Rd., Woodstock, 60098. Tel: 815-338-1032; Fax: 815-338-1017. Resurrection Parish, 2918 S. Country Club Rd., Woodstock, 60098. Tel: 815-338-7330; Fax: 815-338-7365. Revs. Jerzy Zieba, C.R.; Dennis Sanders, C.R., Archbishop Joseph Weber House, 7050 N. Oakley Ave., 60645-3426. Tel: 847-297-5900; Fax: 847-297-0504. Legal Titles: *Weber High School, Inc., Tel: 773-465-8320.*; *Weber Endowment Fund. Tel: 773-465-8320.*

Redemptorist Theology Residence, 1027 E. Hyde Park Blvd., 60615-2807. Tel: 773-363-2094; Fax: 773-363-2095.
E-mail: bcarlin114@aol.com
Revs. Charles C. Beierwaltes, C.SS.R., Formation Dir.; Bernard L. Carlin, C.SS.R., Formation Dir. & Supr.; Bro. Timothy Doody, C.SS.R.; Revs. Matthew Bonk, C.SS.R.; Nghia Cao, C.SS.R.; Bros. Brian Gilles, C.SS.R.; John Kuehner, C.SS.R.; Larry Lujan, C.SS.R.; Chuong Van Cao, C.SS.R.; Steven J. Nyl, C.SS.R.; Charles A. Wehrley, Jr., C.SS.R.; Steven N. Wilson, C.SS.R. In res. Rev. Stephen Rehrauer, C.SS.R. (DEN). Priests 3; Students 10.

Sacred Heart Mission House, 4105 N. Avers Ave., 60618. Tel: 773-588-7476; Fax: 773-588-6517.
E-mail: polmes@jezuicichicago.org
Web site: jezuicichicago.org
Legal Title: *The Polish Messenger of The Sacred Heart, Inc.* Revs. Pawel Kosinski, S.J., Supr.; Stefan Filipowicz, S.J., Editor, The Messenger of The Sacred Heart in Polish language; Leslaw Balczewski, S.J.; Stanislaw Jurus, S.J.; Bro. Jerzy Piskorek, S.J. Priests 4; Brothers 1.

Jan Beyzym Society, Inc. (Polish Jesuit Foreign Missions), 4105 N. Avers Ave., 60618. Tel: 773-588-7476; Fax: 773-588-6517. Rev. Stefan Filipowicz, S.J.

St. Clare Friary, 3407 S. Archer Ave., 60608-6817. Tel: 773-890-1238; Fax: 773-847-7409. Rev. Mark Joseph Costello, O.F.M.Cap., Local Min.; Friars David Heffron, O.F.M.Cap.; William Frigo, O.F.M.Cap.; Jerome Johnson, O.F.M.Cap.; Steven Kropp, O.F.M.Cap.; Robert Roemer, O.F.M.Cap.; Jack Talbot, O.F.M.Cap.; Rev. Lawrence Webber, O.F.M.Cap.

St. John Stone Friary, 1165 E. 54th Pl., 60615-5109. Tel: 773-684-6510; Fax: 773-684-9830. Rev. James Thompson, O.S.A., Dir. Formation, Prior; Bro. Fred Kaiser, O.S.A., Treas.; Revs. David Petraitis, O.S.A.; John Szura, O.S.A.; Luis Vera, O.S.A.; Bro. Santiago Cortes-Sjorberg, O.S.A.

St. Joseph Interprovincial Post-Novitiate Formation House. (A Franciscan House of the Sacred Heart Province), 5495 S. Hyde Park Blvd., 60615. Tel: 773-363-0072; Fax: 773-363-0076. Revs. Robert Sprott, O.F.M., Formation Staff; Neal Kaminski, O.F.M., Guardian & Formation Staff; Arthur Anderson, O.F.M., Formation Staff; Zachary Hayes, O.F.M., Professor CTU; Gil Ostdiek, O.F.M., Professor CTU. Professed 15.

St. Joseph's Priory, 4747 S. Dorchester Ave., 60615. Tel: 773-268-9745. Revs. Daniel O'Neill, O.Carm.; David Murphy, O.Carm.; Bro. Timothy Sklopan, O.Carm.

St. Patrick's Missionary Society, 1347 W. Granville Ave., 60660. Tel: 773-973-3737; Fax: 773-973-6049.
E-mail: st@ameritech.net
Revs. Karl Langsdorf, Supr.; Frank Conlisk; Patrick Feeney; Brian Maguire.

St. Peter's Friary, 110 W. Madison St., 60602-4196. Tel: 312-372-5111. Order of Friars Minor. Revs. Thomas Aldworth; Elric Sampson; Boniface Baum, O.F.M.; Eugene Michel, O.F.M.; Lawrence Janezic, O.F.M.; Andre Schludecker, O.F.M.; Bro. John Bush; Revs. Vincent Callahan; Wenceslaus Church; Michael Clarahan; Bro. Sammy Danna; Revs. Barnabas DieKemper; Kenan Dulzer; Thomas Ess; Charles Faso; Bro. James Finn; Revs. Thomas Fratus; Francis Jerome Gray; Bro. Patrick Hanrahan; Revs. Robert Hutmacher; Robert Karris, O.F.M.; Bros. Clarence Klingert; Thomas Krull; William Lanning; Revs. Clement Leahy; George Musial; Fred Radtke; Bros. Terrence Santiapillai, O.F.M.; Raymond Shuhert; Rev. Joseph Windolph.

St. Rita Monastery, 7740 S. Western Ave., 60620-5867. Tel: 773-476-3879; Fax: 773-925-2451. (See High Schools, Private). Revs. Christopher Howe, O.S.A.; Thomas McCarthy, O.S.A.; Bros. John M. Hibbard, O.S.A.; Gary L. Hresil, O.S.A.; Santiago Cork's-Sjoberg, O.S.A.

Scalabrini House of Theology, 5121 S. University Ave., 60615. Tel: 773-684-5230; 684-4340; Fax: 773-684-5240.
E-mail: totohily@juno.com
Revs. Gerardo Garcia, C.S., Rector; Hily Gonzales, C.S., Animator; Luigi Gandolfi, C.S., Spiritual Dir. Priests 3; Students 15.

Viatorian Residence, 1201 W. Belden, 60614. Tel: 773-871-3613; Fax: 773-871-3628. Revs. William L. Carpenter, C.S.V.; John E. Linnan, C.S.V.; Robert M. Egan; Bro. Donald P. Houde, C.S.V. Priests 3; Brothers 1.

Vincentian Community, Congregation of the Mission, Midwest Province, 2210-12 N. Racine Ave., 60614. Tel: 773-880-2968; Fax: 773-348-4802.
E-mail: tcroak@wppost.depaul.edu
Revs. Thomas Croak, C.M., Supr.; Joseph C. Geders, C.M.; Robert Lucas, C.M.; Edward R. Udovic, C.M.; Thomas A. Grace, C.M.; J. Patrick Murphy, C.M.; David Nygren, C.M.; Daniel Theiss, C.M.; Gerard P. Kelly, C.M.; Bros. Mark Elder, C.M.; Timothy Opferman, C.M.

Xaverian Missionaries (S.X.), 1347 E. Hyde Park Blvd., 60615-2924. Tel: 773-643-5745; Fax: 773-643-6907.
E-mail: xaverchi@megsinet.net
Revs. Rocco N. Puopolo, S.X., Rector; Lino Sgarbossa, S.X.

ARLINGTON HEIGHTS. *Clerics of St. Viator-Provincial Residence*, 1212 E. Euclid St., 60004. Tel: 847-398-1354; Fax: 847-394-4507. Rev. Robert M. Egan, C.S.V., Prov.; Bros. Corey Brost, C.S.V.; Michael Gosch, C.S.V.; Doug Hudson, C.S.V.; Rob Robertson, C.S.V. Priests 3; Brothers 4.

Viatorian Mission House, 1212 E. Euclid St., 60004. Tel: 847-255-9292; Fax: 847-398-6247. Clerics of St. Viator. Rev. Robert M. Egan, C.S.V., Mission Procurator, Dir. of Viatorian Seminary Aid Assn. & Dir. of Pious A.

Viatorian Province Center-Clerics of St. Viator, 1212 E. Euclid St., 60004. Tel: 847-398-1350; Fax: 847-394-4507. Revs. George Auger, C.S.V.; Thomas G. O'Brien, C.S.V.; William C. Mayer, C.S.V.; Charles L. Maranto, C.S.V.; Thomas P. McCarthy, C.S.V.; Casimir C. Kicmal, C.S.V.; Arthur A. Lemrise, C.S.V.; Michael J. O'Brien, C.S.V.; John C. Puisis, C.S.V.; James E. Michaletz, C.S.V.; Thomas F. McMahon, C.S.V.; Robert E. Erickson, C.S.V.; Donald J. Fitzsimmons, C.S.V.; Patrick J. Hayes, C.S.V.; Thomas R. von Behren, C.S.V.; John A. Toolan, C.S.V.; Bro. Leo V. Ryan, C.S.V.
Priests of the Province Serving Abroad: Revs. Carlos L. Claro, C.S.V.; Pedro E. Herrera, C.S.V.; Luis E. Lopez, C.S.V.; John A. Pisors, C.S.V.; Albeyro Vanegas, C.S.V., Colegio San Viator, Kilmetro 14, Autopista del Norte, Bogota 2, D.E., Columbia, 54-11-62. Tel: 011-57-1-676-0997; Fax: 011-57-1-676-0208. Mailing Address: Apartado Aereo 102413, Bogota 10, D.E., Columbia. Bros. Alejandro Adame, C.S.V.; Fredy Santos, C.S.V.; Carlos Florez, C.S.V.; Felipe Montes, C.S.V.; Rev. Roger C. Drolet, C.S.V., 38 Takan-Tsuen, Pali Hsiang, Taipei, Hsien (249), Taiwan, R.O.C. Revs. Christopher Glancy, C.S.V.; Daniel Hall, C.S.V., Catholic Mission Corozal, P.O. Box 34, Corozal Town, Belize, Central America. Tel: 011-501-422-018.
Priests Serving Elsewhere In U.S.A.: Rev. Victor E. Bertrand, North Little Rock, AR. Tel: 501-791-0078. Rev. Joseph B. Tremonti, 428 S. Indians Ave., Kankakee, 60901. Tel: 815-932-6716. Revs. Donald W. Huntimer, C.S.V., Tucson, AZ; Thomas G. Kass, C.S.V., Manchester, NH; Alan M. Syslo, C.S.V., Monterey, CA; Robert H. Carey, C.S.V., Las Vegas, NV.

BLUE ISLAND. *Marist Brothers*, 12212 Irving Ave., 60406. Tel: 708-385-1488.
E-mail: fmsbi@aol.com
Bros. John Kachinstry, Dir.; Richard Carey, F.M.S.

COUNTRYSIDE. *St. Gratian Friary, Franciscan Friars*, 5536 S. Edgewood Ave., 60525-3426. Tel: 708-482-4546; Fax: 708-481-8676.
E-mail: stgratian@aol.com
Revs. James Walton, O.F.M.; Dennis Koopman, O.F.M.; James A. Hoffman, O.F.M.; Ildephonse Skorup, O.F.M.; Kieran Kemner, O.F.M.; Don Blaeser, O.F.M.; Bro. Leon Beranek, O.F.M. Priests 6; Brothers 1.

ELK GROVE VILLAGE. *Congregation of Alexian Brothers Immaculate Conception Province, Inc.*, 600 Alexian Way, 60007. Tel: 847-640-7550; Fax: 847-981-5561.
E-mail: krueger@abeg.hbocvan.com
Bro. Lawrence Krueger, C.F.A., Prov. Supr. Provincial Councilors: Bros. Thomas Keusenkothen, C.F.A.; Eugene Gizzi, C.F.A.; James Classon, C.F.A.; John Howard, C.F.A.; Richard Lowe, C.F.A., Vocations Dir.; Valentino Bianco, C.F.A., Community Dir., Res., 801 Gloucester Dr., 60007. Tel: 847-439-5845.

Brothers of St. Alexius Health and Welfare Fund, Inc.

EVANSTON. *Canisius House*, 201 Dempster St., 60201-4704. Tel: 847-475-1825; Fax: 847-475-1869. Revs. F. Michael Perko, S.J., Supr.; Joseph F. Downey, S.J.; Daniel L. Flaherty, S.J.; Thomas L. Kenealy, S.J.; Donald J. McGuire, S.J.

GLENVIEW. *The Redemptorists of Glenview, Illinois.* North American Redemptorist Novitiate, Redemptorist Foreign Mission Office and Villa Redeemer Retreat Center, 1111 N. Milwaukee Ave., P.O. Box 6, 60025. Tel: 847-724-0425; Fax: 847-724-8953. Revs. Raymond Maiser, C.Ss.R., Local Supr.; Joseph T. Hurley, C.Ss.R., Novice Dir.; Henry Novak, C.Ss.R., Treas.; Kevin Fraher, C.Ss.R., Asst. Novice Dir.; Bro. Thomas Sanhuber, C.Ss.R.

Redemptorist Denver Province Foreign Mission Office. Rev. Charles C. Beierwaltes, C.Ss.R., Dir., 1111 N. Milwaukee Ave., P.O. Box 6, 60025. Tel: 847-724-0425; Fax: 847-724-8953.

LA GRANGE PARK. *Comboni Mission Center*, 1615 E. 31st St., 60526-1377. Tel: 708-354-1999; Fax: 708-354-2006.
E-mail: combonilmp@igc.org
Revs. Tom Vermiglio, M.C.C.J., Supr.; Valentino Saoncella, M.C.C.J., Mission Promotor; Sixtus Agostini, M.C.C.J., Lay Miss. Prog.; Charles Walter, M.C.C.J., CTU Prof.; Paul Longo, M.C.C.J., Prof. Priests 5.

LEMONT. *Legion of Christ*, 89 W. Logan, 60439. Tel: 630-243-6389; Fax: 630-243-6388. Revs. James Larson, L.C., Supr.; Daniel Long, L.C.; Bro. Scott S. Herrera, L.C.

The Slovene Franciscan Fathers, Order of Friars Minor, Commissariat of the Holy Cross, 14246 Main St., P.O. Box 608, 60439. Tel: 630-257-2494; Fax: 630-257-8559. Revs. Blase Chemazar, O.F.M., Pres. & Guardian; Vendelin Spendov, O.F.M.; Callistus Langerholz, O.F.M.; Leonard Bogolin, O.F.M.; Benno Korbic, O.F.M.; Bernardin Susnik, O.F.M.; Martin Stepanich, O.F.M.; Athanasius Lovrencic, O.F.M.; David Srumpf, O.F.M. Priests 9.

LIBERTYVILLE. *Marytown, Our Lady of Fatima Friary*, 1600 W. Park Ave., 60048-2593. Tel: 847-367-7800; Fax: 847-367-7831. Community of Conventual Franciscan Friars administering the U.S. National Center of the Militia of the Immaculata Movement (M.I.). Bro. Juniper Kriss, O.F.M.Conv., Vicar; Revs. Patrick Greenough, O.F.M.Conv., Guardian & Prov. Asst., J.I. Editorial Office for Immaculata Magazine & Prow Books; Gabriel Ignaszek, O.F.M.Conv.; John Grigus, O.F.M.Conv.; Anthony J. Jelinek; Philip Wozniak.

Conventual Franciscan Friars of Marytown.

Shrine of St. Maximilian Kolbe. Conventual Franciscan Friars 18.

MUNDELEIN. *Carmelite Monastery*, 999 E. McKinley Ave., 60060. Tel: 847-566-4070. Bro. Dominic Saganich, O.Carm., Prior; Revs. Murray Phelan, O.Carm.; Bernhard Bauerle, O.Carm.; John J. Comerford, O.Carm.; Robert Carroll, O.Carm.; Bro. Thomas Murphy, O.Carm.

OAK PARK. *Claretian Fathers Headquarters of U.S.A. Eastern Province*, 400 N. Euclid, 60302. Tel: 708-848-2076; Fax: 708-848-2069.
E-mail: usaeastprov@claret.org
Web site: www.claret.org
Very Rev. Leonard J. Brown, C.M.F., Prov. Supr.; Revs. Robert Fath, C.M.F.; Thomas Paramo, C.M.F.; John Lemrise, C.M.F.; Ronald Luka, C.M.F.; Walter Mischke, C.M.F.; Bros. Richard Wilga; James Santmiquel Oriols.
Priests serving outside Province: Rev. Donald Lavelle, C.M.F., Dominguez Retreat Renewal Center, 18127 S. Alameda St., Rancho Dominguez, CA, 90220. Tel: 213-636-6030; Fax: 319-631-3518. Rev. Richard Farrell, C.M.F., Sacred Heart Parish Center, 150 Fleury Ave., Prescott, AZ, 83601. Tel: 520-445-3141; Fax: 520-717-1074. Priests 41; Scholastics 10; Brothers 4.

Claretian Missionaries Community Support Trust, 400 N. Euclid Ave., 60302. Tel: 708-848-2076; Fax: 708-848-2069. Rev. Leonard J. Brown, C.M.F., Pres. Vice Presidents: Revs. Mark J. Brummel, C.M.F.; Carl Quebedeaux, C.M.F.; Bruce Wellems, C.M.F.; James F. Maloney, C.M.F.

Dominican Community of St. Martin de Porres, 204 S. Humphrey, 60302. Tel: 708-848-4271; Fax: 708-445-0581.
E-mail: stmartin@dominicans.org
Web site: www.dominicans.org
Revs. Michael Winkels, O.P.; James Marchionda, O.P.; Thomas Saucier, O.P.; Bro. Gabriel Dault, O.P.

Missionaries of Saint Charles, Provincial Residence, 546 N. East Ave., 60302. Tel: 708-386-4430; Fax: 708-386-4457.
E-mail: provoff@ix.netcom.com
Legal Title: *Fathers of St. Charles.* Rev. Patrick Murphy, C.S., Prov., Scalabrini Development Office, 546 N.East Ave., 60302. Tel: 708-848-1616; Fax: 708-848-2525. Rev. Aldo Vendramin, C.S.

Scalabrinians Community Support Corporation, Oak Park. Tel: 708-386-4430.

Scalabrinians Community Formation Corporation, Oak Park. Tel: 708-386-4430.

OLYMPIA FIELDS. *The Augustinians-Provincialate*, Tolentine College & Center, 20300 Governors Hwy., 60461. Tel: 708-748-9500; Fax: 708-481-2090.
Web site: www.midwestaugustinians.org
Very Rev. Robert F. Prevost, O.S.A., Prior Prov.; Bros. Kenneth D. Mehn, O.S.A., Prov. Sec.; Bruce A. Jendraszak, O.S.A., Prov. Treas. & Dir. Tolentine Ctr.; Revs. G. Jerome Knies, O.S.A., Asst. Prov. & Personnel Dir.; John D. Merkelis, O.S.A., Vocation Dir.; John W. Beretta, O.S.A.; James V. Corrigan, O.S.A.; Robert J. Dodaro, O.S.A.; Edward G. Grace, O.S.A.; Thomas F. Martin, O.S.A.; Patrick E. Murphy, O.S.A.; Karl A. Gersbach, O.S.A.; Donald W. Harkabus, O.S.A.; Richard M. Jacobs, O.S.A.; Martin S. Laird, O.S.A.; Wes E. Benak, O.S.A.; James R. Halstead, O.S.A.; Gerard J. Theis, O.S.A.
Members working elsewhere: Revs. John L. Burkhart, O.S.A.; Carmen J. Coletta, O.S.A.; W. Timothy Cuny, O.S.A.; Erwin J. Dodge, O.S.A.; Robert Dueweke, O.S.A.; John Fitzgerald, O.S.A.; William A. Hamill, O.S.A.; Bro. Christopher McCartney, O.S.A.
Foreign Missionaries assigned to the Provincialate: Revs. Alfred M. Burke, O.S.A.; Charles J. Bodden, O.S.A.; John J. Dowling, O.S.A.; Most Rev. John J. McNabb, O.S.A.; Revs. Richard D. Palmer, O.S.A.; Christopher C. Steinle, O.S.A.; Most Rev. Daniel T. Turley, O.S.A.; Revs. John P. Tasto, O.S.A.; John A. Tyma, O.S.A.

Austin Friary, 20300 Governors Hwy., 60461-1081. Tel: 708-748-9500; Fax: 708-481-2090. Revs. G. Jerome Kines, O.S.A.; John A. Kret, O.S.A.; Donald J. Bates, O.S.A.; Terry A. Deffenbaugh, O.S.A.; Very Rev. Robert F. Prevost, O.S.A., Prov.; Bros. David W. Adelsbach, O.S.A.; Bruce A. Jendraszak, O.S.A., Prior. Priests 5; Brothers 2.

Tolentine Monastery at Tolentine Center, 20300 Governors Hwy., 60461. Tel: 708-748-9500; Fax: 708-481-2090; 748-0018. Very Rev. Robert F. Provost, O.S.A., Prior Prov.; Revs. James Friedel, O.S.A., Prior; Edward L. Hamel, O.S.A.; John R. Mabarak, O.S.A.; John J. Flaherty, O.S.A.; Edwin R. Kuczynski, O.S.A.; LaVern S. Flach, O.S.A.; Bros. David Sharp, O.S.A.; Anthony Schander, O.S.A.; John Stobba, O.S.A., Sacristan; Angelo Sturn, O.S.A.; Kenneth Mehn, O.S.A., Treas. & Prov. Sec.; Mark Thedens, O.S.A.

RIVER FOREST. *St. Thomas Aquinas Priory*, 7200 Division St., 60305. Tel: 708-771-3030; Fax: 708-771-4510. Very Revs. Peter J. Hereley, O.P., Prior; William J. Bernacki, O.P., Subprior; Revs. Jordan Aumann, O.P.; Richard R. Farmer, O.P., Business Mgr.; Robert Campbell, O.P.; Francis R. Crowe, O.P.; Malachy R. Dooley, O.P.; John M. Gambro, O.P.; Joseph I. Hren, O.P.; David M. Hynous, O.P.; Bede R. Jagoe, O.P.; Thomas J. Johnston, O.P.; Richard C. LaPata, O.P., Vicar; Jordan A. McGrath, O.P.; John J. Meany, O.P.; Robert J. Miller, O.P.; Quentin E. Moriarty, O.P.; Walter T. O'Connell, O.P.; Jerome A. O'Leary, O.P.; Michael Ruthenberg, O.P.; Hugh Wreisner, O.P. Assigned, but not living at the Priory: Revs. Robert I. Campbell, O.P.; Gilbert J. Graham, O.P.; Albert G. Judy, O.P.; Thomas Aquinas O'Meara, O.P.; Robert F. O'Riley, O.P.; David J. Santoro, O.P.; Very Rev. Timothy H. Sparks, O.P.; Bros. Terence G. Bullock, O.P., (Assigned, but living elsewhere); Carlos Griego, O.P.; Regis R. Hovald, O.P.; Joseph Kilikevich, O.P.; Michael McGovern, O.P.; Reginald W. Neu, O.P. Priests 28; Brothers 6.
Legal Subsidiaries and holdings: The Priory Press, theology texts for high schools; "Listening", journal of Religion and Culture; Vestments and Vessels; Dominican Conference Center; Carpentier Art Collection.
American Friends of the Ecole Biblique: Rev. Peter J. Hereley, O.P., Pres.

RIVER GROVE. *Brothers of Holy Cross*, 3000 N. 80th Ave., 60171. Tel: 708-452-5535. Bros. Sigismund Danielski, C.S.C.; Walter Duda, C.S.C.; Joseph Dudek, C.S.C.; Donald Fleischacker, C.S.C.; Thaddeus Gottemoller, C.S.C.; Anthony Jorae, C.S.C.; Joseph Walter Olszowka, C.S.C.; Julian Przybla, C.S.C.; James Reddy, C.S.C.; John Schuszler, C.S.C.; Richard Shea, C.S.C.; James Van Dyke, C.S.C.; Ralph Heppe, F.S.C.
(See High Schools, Private).

TECHNY. *Society of the Divine Word, Provincial Headquarter-Chicago Prov.* (Province of Blessed Joseph Freinademetz, S.V.D.), 1985 Waukegan Rd., P.O. Box 6038, 60082-6038. Tel: 847-272-2700; Fax: 847-272-2517.
E-mail: uscsvd1@aol.com
Web site: www.divineword.org
Very Rev. Stanley Uroda, S.V.D., Prov.; Bro. Dennis Newton, S.V.D., Vice Prov.; Revs. Thomas Griffith, S.V.D., Treas.; Chester Nowicki, S.V.D., Asst. Treas.; John Donaghey, S.V.D., Prov. Admin.; James Braband, S.V.D., Sec. of Educ./Formation/Recruitment; Augustine Wall, S.V.D., Vocation Dir., Divine Word Missionaries, Inc.; Divine Word Funds, Inc.; Catholic Universities, Inc. Revs. Thomas A. Krosnicki, S.V.D., Mission Center Dir.; Francis J. Kamp, S.V.D., Mission Treas.; Walter Bracken, S.V.D., Delegated Supr. For Missionaries on Leave.

Blessed Arnold Charitable Trust. Tel: 847-272-2700; Fax: 847-272-2517. Rev. Thomas Griffith, S.V.D., Pres.

S.V.D. Funds, Inc. Tel: 847-272-2700; Fax: 847-272-2517. Revs. Stanley Uroda, S.V.D., Pres.; Thomas Griffith, S.V.D., Treas.; Chester Nowicki, S.V.D., Asst. Treas.; Raymond Quetchenbach, S.V.D., Dir., Charitable Gift Annuities.

Divine Word International, 2001 Waukegan Rd., P.O. Box 176, 60082-0176. Tel: 847-272-1100; Fax: 847-272-9363. Bro. Patrick Hogan, S.V.D., Dir.

House of Religious Men: Divine Word Theologate, 5342 University Ave., Chicago, 60615. Tel: 773-288-2777; Fax: 773-288-6307. Revs. Edward Peklo, S.V.D., Rector; Roger S. Arnold, S.V.D.; Lloyd Cunningham, S.V.D.; Mark Schramm, S.V.D.; Roger P. Schroeder, S.V.D., Rector; Derek Simons, S.V.D.; Mark E. Weber, S.V.D.

Edward McGuinn House of Studies, 5487 S. Hyde Park, #1N, Chicago, 60615. Tel: 773-643-1518; Fax: 773-288-6307. Revs. Stephen B. Bevans, S.V.D.; Gary L. Riebe-Estrella, S.V.D.

Divine Word Novitiate, 1940 Waukegan Rd., 60082-6000. Tel: 847-272-0299; Fax: 847-272-2873. Rev. James Bergin, S.V.D., Novice Dir.

Divine Word Residence, 1901 Waukegan Rd., P.O. Box 6000, 60082-6000. Tel: 847-272-2700; Fax: 847-272-2873. Rev. Kazimerz Garbacz, S.V.D., Rector.

Mision Verbita, 1002 Jeanette Ave., DesPlaines, 60016. Tel: 847-759-0439. Revs. Crescente de Rivera, S.V.D.; John Szukalski, S.V.D. Fathers 57; Brothers 19.

WILLOW SPRINGS. *Cistercian Fathers, Our Lady Mother of the Church*, 8121 Archer Rd., 60480. Tel: 708-839-6808; Fax: 708-839-6808. Mailing Address: Box 334, Argo, 60501. Rt. Rev. Hubert Kostrzanski, O.Cist., (Retired), Abbot of Szczyrzyc (Poland); Revs. Michael Blicharski, O.Cist.; Gregory Szydlowski, O.Cist., Prior; Alberic Lipinski, O.Cist.; John Muc, O.Cist. Cistercian Priory dependant monastery of the Abbey in Szczyrzyc, Poland (Polish Congregation) est. 1982. Legal Title: *Cistercian Fathers, Our Lady Mother of the Church.* Priests 5.

[O] CONVENTS AND RESIDENCES FOR SISTERS

CHICAGO. *Academy of Our Lady Convent*, 9535 S. Loomis St., 60643. Tel: 773-445-0403. School Sisters of Notre Dame (Chicago Prov.). Sisters 39.

Administrative Center of the Sisters of Mercy of the Americas, Regional Community of Chicago, 10024 S. Central Park, 60655-3132. Tel: 773-779-6011; Fax: 773-779-6094.
E-mail: rsm@mercychicago.com
Sr. Joy Clough, R.S.M., Pres. Sisters 4.

Sisters of Mercy of the Americas, Regional Community of Chicago Charitable Trust. Tel: 773-779-6011; Fax: 773-779-6094.

Benedictine Sisters of Chicago, St. Scholastica Monastery, 7430 N. Ridge Blvd., 60645. Tel: 773-764-2413; Fax: 773-761-5131.
E-mail: bensrscgo@aol.com
Web site: www.benedictine-sisters.org
Sr. Jane Smith, O.S.B., Prioress. Sisters 79.

Daughters of St. Mary of Providence, Provincialate: 4200 N. Austin Ave., 60634-1615. Tel: 773-545-8300; Fax: 773-545-8673.
E-mail: napsrbk@ameritech.net
Sr. Bernardine Kauffmann, Prov.

Daughters of St. Paul, 172 N. Michigan, 60601. Tel: 312-346-4228; 346-3240; Fax: 312-346-5415.
E-mail: fspchicago@aol.com
Web site: www.pauline.org
Sr. Frances Aurelia Obrovac, F.S.P., Supr. Sisters 4.

Little Sisters of Jesus, 1529 S. Sawyer St., 60623. Tel: 773-277-5061.
E-mail: littlesrs.chg@juno.com
Sisters 3.

Little Sisters of the Poor, The, 2325 N. Lakewood Ave., 60614. Tel: 773-935-9600; Fax: 773-935-9614. Sr. Patricia Friel, L.S.P., Supr. Legal Title: *Little Sisters of the Poor of Chicago, Inc.* Sisters 12.

Medical Missionaries of Mary, 3410 W. 60th Pl., 60629. Tel: 773-737-3458; Fax: 773-737-4582.
E-mail: mmmchi@aol.com
Web site: www.medical-missionaries.com
Sisters 5.

Mercy Convent, 10044 S. Central Park, 60655. Tel: 773-238-4887; Fax: 773-238-0024. Sr. Ann Sullivan, R.S.M., Coord. Sisters 55.

Missionaries of Charity, 2234 W. Washington Blvd., 60612. Tel: 312-421-0038. Sr. M. Marilyn, M.C.

Missionary Sisters of Christ the King, 1118 N. Noble St., 60622. Tel: 773-489-0714. Sr. Dorota Galewska, Supr., 5936 W. Barry Ave., 60634-5130. Tel: 773-889-7979. Sr. Kamila Wojtyla, Supr., 2441 N. Menard Ave., 60639-2334. Tel: 773-637-9187. Sr. Weronika Ilnicka, Supr. Sisters 13.

Missionary Sisters of the Sacred Heart of Jesus, Cabrini Hall, 428 St. James Pl., 60614. Tel: 773-388-7314; Fax: 773-281-3148.
Our Lady of Peace Community.
Other Addresses:
Cabrini Retreat Center. 9430 Golf Rd., Des Plaines, 60016. Tel: 773-694-4240; Fax: 847-297-6544.
Guadalupe Community. 2826 W. Cermak Rd., 60623. Tel: 773-843-1954; Fax: 773-843-1955. Holy Spirit Community, 2520 N. Lakeview Ave., 60614. Tel: 773-388-7313; Fax: 773-327-0355. Francisca Community, 2157 W. Cermak Rd., 60608. Sisters 13.

Mother of Good Counsel Provincialate, 3800 Peterson Ave., 60659. Tel: 773-463-3020; Fax: 773-463-3567.
E-mail: cssf@felicianschicago.org
Provincialate of the Felician Sisters, Good Counsel High School, Novitiate, Our Lady of the Angels, St. Ann, Bl. Angela, St. Colette, St. Elizabeth of Hungary, Felician Services, Inc. Sr. Mary Barbara Ann Bosch, C.S.S.F., Prov. Min.; Revs. Stanley Janowski, O.F.M.; Hugh Zurat, O.F.M. Professed Sisters 243.

Queen of the Resurrection House of Prayer, 7430 W. Talcott Ave., 60631. Sr. M. Laurette Winiarski, C.R., Supr. Sisters 20.

Sisters of St. Casimir, Motherhouse and Novitiate, 2601 W. Marquette Rd., 60629-1817. Tel: 773-776-1324; Fax: 773-776-8755. Sr. M. Immacula Wendt, S.S.C., Gen. Supr. Sisters 164.

Sisters of the Good Shepherd, 1114 W. Grace St., 60613. Tel: 773-935-3434; Fax: 773-935-3523. Sr. Kathleen Moore, R.G.S., Supr. Sisters 6.

Sisters of the Holy Cross, 7422 N. Harlem, 60631-4409. Tel: 773-774-5449. Sr. Karen Anne Jackson, C.S.C.
Other Residences: 5140 S. Hyde Park Blvd., 60615. Tel: 773-684-2995. 9964 W. 153rd St., Orland Park, 60462. Tel: 708-403-5134. Sisters of the Holy Cross 6.

Sisters of the Resurrection Provincial House and Novitiate, 7432 Talcott Ave., 60631. Tel: 773-792-6363; Fax: 773-792-9590. Sr. Mary Barbara Sniegowski,

C.R., Prov. Supr. Sisters 25. Congregation of the Sisters of the Resurrection, Chicago Province. Legal Title: *Sisters of the Resurrection.*
Attended by Passionist Fathers.

Society of Helpers. Provincial Office, 3206 S. Aberdeen, 60608. Tel: 773-523-8638; Fax: 773-523-8715. Sr. Margaret Nimbley, S.H., Prov. Professed Sisters 42.
Other residences: 1536 W. Wellington, 60657. 2043 N. Humboldt Blvd., 60647. 1446 W. Chicago Ave., #3, 60622. 1930 N. Kenmore, 60614. 1950 S. Throop St., 60608. 3130 N. Lake Shore Dr., 60657. 303 W. Barry, 60657. Tel: 773-248-8646.

Wright Hall-Sisters of Charity B.V.M., 6364 Sheridan Rd., 60660. Tel: 773-761-7550; Fax: 773-761-4341.
E-mail: wh6364@aol.com
Professed Sisters B.V.M. 65.

ARLINGTON HEIGHTS. *Missionaries of the Sacred Heart of Jesus and Our Lady of Guadalupe M.S.C.Gpe.*, 1212 E. Euclid Ave., 60004. Tel: 847-255-5616.

Sisters of the Living Word, 800 N. Fernandez Ave. B, 60004-5316. Tel: 847-577-5972; Fax: 847-577-5980.
E-mail: slw@slw.org
Web site: http://www.slw.org
Sr. Lea Woll, S.L.W., Supr. Gen. & Coord. of Spiritual Life. Sisters 77.

BARTLETT. *Immaculata Congregational Home*, 801 W. Bartlett Rd., 60103-4401. Tel: 630-837-3502; Fax: 630-837-0052; 837-4061. Congregational Home of the Sisters of St. Joseph, T.O.S.F. Management Team: Sr. Lydia Bilecki, S.S.J.-T.O.S.F.; Sr. Elaine Haiduk, S.S.J.-T.O.S.F.; Sr. Patricia Schafke, S.S.J.-T.O.S.F. Sisters in Residence 58.

BERWYN. *Poor Handmaids of Jesus Christ*, 1916 S. Clarence Ave., 60402. Tel: 708-749-0125.
E-mail: berwyn1@juno.com
Sisters 3.

School Sisters of Notre Dame. (Chicago Province), 1431 Euclid Ave., 60402. Tel: 708-749-1380; 749-1381; Fax: 708-749-9446.
E-mail: kitsssnd@aol.com
Web site: ww.ssnd.org
Sr. Catherine Sarther, S.S.N.D., Prov. Leader. Professed Sisters 134.

BLUE ISLAND. *Franciscan Sisters of Mary*, 12101 Artesian Ave., 60406-1047. Tel: 708-597-2720. Sisters 3.

Mother of Sorrows Convent, 13811 S. Western Ave., 60406. Tel: 708-385-2103; Fax: 708-385-4051. Legal Title: *Mantellate Sisters Servants of Mary.*
Motherhouse of the Servants of Mary. Sr. M. Eleanor Carella, O.S.M., Regl. Supr. Sisters 16.

BURBANK. *Adrian Dominican Sisters, Upper Midwest Mission Chapter*, 8000 Linder Ave., 60459-2099. Tel: 708-636-8178; Fax: 708-636-0031.
E-mail: mmannard@aol.com
Web site: http://www.op.org/adrian
Sr. Mary Margaret Mannard, O.P., Chapter Prioress.

Adrian Dominican Sisters, Midwest Dominican Mission Chapter, 8000 Linder Ave., 60459-2099. Tel: 708-636-7566; Fax: 708-636-0031.
E-mail: sallyfop@aol.com
Web site: www.op.org/adrian
Sr. Sarah Ann Fergus, O.P., Chapter Prioress.

DES PLAINES. *Monastery of Discalced Carmelities*, River Rd. and Central, 60016. Tel: 847-298-4241. Mother Marie Andre of the Holy Spirit, Prioress.
Attended by Holy Cross Fathers.

Provincial House of the Sisters of the Holy Family of Nazareth, 310 N. River Rd., 60016-1211. Tel: 847-298-6760; Fax: 847-803-1941. Sr. Marie Kielanowicz, C.S.F.N., Prov. Supr. Professed Sisters 38.

EVERGREEN PARK. *American Province of Little Company of Mary Sisters.* (Little Company of Mary Sisters), 9350 S. California, 60805. Tel: 708-422-0130; Fax: 708-422-2212.
E-mail: cpacini@cmh.org
Sr. Carol Pacini, Prov. Leader. Total in Community 28.
Charitable Trust: American Province of Little Company of Mary Sisters Charitable Trust.

HOFFMAN ESTATES. *Poor Handmaids of Jesus Christ, Annunciation Convent*, 1480 Ashley Rd., 60195. Tel: 847-519-1384; Fax: 847-885-2757.
E-mail: phjcashley@aol.com
Web site: poorhandmaids.org

JUSTICE. *Immaculate Conception Prov. House and Novitiate of the Dominican Sisters*, 9000 W. 81st St., 60458. Tel: 708-458-3040; Fax: 708-458-7230.
E-mail: rosaryhill@cometlink.com
Sr. Natalie, O.P., Prov. Sisters 39.

LA GRANGE PARK. *Sisters of St. Joseph of La Grange*, 1515 W. Ogden Ave., 60526. Tel: 708-354-9200; Fax: 708-354-9573.
E-mail: mrace3@juno.com
Legal Title: *Nazareth Academy, Sisters of St. Joseph Charitable Trust.* Sr. Marianne Race, C.S.J., Pres. Sponsored ministries include secondary education and School on Wheels, an adult literacy program. Total in Community 106.

LAKE VILLA. *Handmaids of the Precious Blood-Priory of the Heart of Mary*, 24140 W. Petite Lake Rd., 60046. Tel: 847-356-7729. Sr. Mel Pierre, H.P.B., Prioress. Sisters 3.

LAKE ZURICH. *Daughters of St. Mary of Providence*, Novitiate: 24955 N. Hwy. 12, 60047. Tel: 847-438-5050. Sr. Caryn Haas, Formation Dir.

LEMONT. *Mount Assisi Convent, Sisters of St. Francis of Christ the King*, 13900 Main St., 60439-9736. Tel: 630-257-7495; Fax: 630-257-8959.
E-mail: pnasenbeny@hotmail.com
Sr. M. Paula Nasenbeny, O.S.F., Prov. Supr. Sisters 72.

Our Lady of Victory Convent, 14700 Main St., 60439-0956. Tel: 630-257-7776; Fax: 630-257-7887.
E-mail: fradke@chicagofranciscans.com
General Motherhouse and Novitiate of the Franciscan Sisters of Chicago. Legal Title: *Franciscan Sisters of Chicago.* Sr. M. Francis Clare Radke, Gen. Min. Professed Sisters 72.

MELROSE PARK. *Sisters of St. Charles Borromeo.* Provincialate. 1414 N. 37th Ave., 60160. Tel: 708-343-2162; Fax: 708-343-6452.
E-mail: mdaltoe@core.com
Missionary Sisters of St. Charles Borromeo (Scalabrinians). Sr. Marissonia Daltoe, M.S.C.S., Prov. Supr. Sisters 69; Residents 17.

Charitable Trust: Sisters of St. Charles Borromeo, Province of Our Lady of Fatima Charitable Trust. Tel: 708-343-2162; Fax: 708-343-6452.

NORTHLAKE. *Daughters of Divine Love Congregation*, 100 N. Lavergne, 60164. Tel: 708-836-0557. Sr. Mary Paul Asoegwu, D.D.L., Supr.

OAK FOREST. *Our Lady of Sorrows Priory, Benedictine Sisters of Pontifical Jurisdiction*, 5900 W. 147th St., 60452. Tel: 708-687-2877. Sr. Irene Sebo, O.S.B., Prioress. In res. Rev. Martin N. Winters. Professed 6.

TECHNY. *Provincial House of the Missionary Sisters Servants of the Holy Spirit*, 319 Waukegan Rd., P.O. Box 6026, 60082-6026. Tel: 847-441-0126; Fax: 847-441-5587.
E-mail: manorris@claret.orgt
Sr. Margaret Anne Norris, Prov. Supr.; Sr. Mary Pardy. Professed Sisters 94.
Arnold Janssen Foundation.
Helena Stollenwerk Foundation.

WAUKEGAN. *Franciscan Missionaries of Mary*, 726 S. Lincoln St., 60085. Tel: 847-662-8439. Sr. Noreen Murray, F.M.M., Coord. Sisters 4.

WILMETTE. *Maria Immaculata Convent-The Province Center.* Corporation of the Sisters of Christian Charity, Corporation of Mallinckrodt College of the North Shore, 2041 Elmwood Ave., 60091-1431. Tel: 847-920-9341; Fax: 847-920-9346.
E-mail: srjudith@sccwilmette.org
Sr. M. Judith Moran, S.C.C., Prov. Supr. Sisters 5.

Sacred Heart Convent, 2221 Elmwood Ave., 60091-1435. Tel: 847-251-3770; Fax: 847-251-8040. A home for aged and infirm Sisters of Christian Charity. Motherhouse in Wilmette, Illinois. Sr. Harriette Stieber, S.C.C., Supr. Sisters in Residence 70.

[P] SECULAR INSTITUTES

RIVER FOREST. *Caritas Christi*, P.O. Box 5162, 60305. Legal Title: *Cultural Crossroads, Inc.* An International Secular Institute of Pontifical Rite, which forms and gives to the Church laywomen who according to their callings, talents, and professional skills seek to respond to the love of Christ in their providential environment by following the demands of the Gospel.

[Q] PIOUS UNIONS AND OTHER SOCIETIES

LIBERTYVILLE. *Marytown, U.S. National Center of the Militia of the Immaculata Movement*, Shrine of St. Maximilian Kolbe, 1600 W. Park Ave., 60048-2593. Tel: 847-367-7800.
International Latin name: Militia Immaculatae (M.I.). An association of clergy, religious and laity dedicated to Catholic evangelization, founded 1917 in Rome by St. Maximilian Kolbe. Rev. Patrick Greenough, O.F.M.Conv., Prov. Asst. for M.I.

[R] VISITING AND NURSING OF THE SICK IN THEIR HOMES

CHICAGO. *Catholic Home Care*, 721 N. LaSalle St., 60610. Tel: 312-655-7415
For a complete listing, refer to the Special Care Facilities section.

Catholic Home Care Home Services, 721 N. LaSalle St., 60610. Tel: 312-655-7415
For a complete listing, refer to the Special Care Facilities section.

[S] SOCIETIES, CLUBS AND RESIDENCES

CHICAGO. *Kolping Center*, 5826 N. Elston, 60646. Tel: 773-792-2190. Rev. Anthony A. Englert.
The Catholic Kolping Society of Chicago.

WILMETTE. *Equestrian Order of the Holy Sepulchre of Jerusalem.* (North Central Lieutenancy), 2350 Schiller, 60091. Tel: 847-853-0996; Fax: 847-853-0997.
E-mail: nclhs@aol.com
Web site: holysepulchre.net
Sir Thomas J. McCabe, K.G.C.H.S., Lieutenant; Sir Paul Stinneford, K.C.H.S., Sec.

[T] RETREAT HOUSES

CHICAGO. *Congregation of Our Lady of the Retreat in the Cenacle*, 513 Fullerton Pkwy., 60614. Tel: 773-549-0554; Fax: 773-528-6300. Sr. Marguerite Gautreau, Prov. Professed Sisters 34.

Focolare Movement-Mariapolis Center, 5001 S. Greenwood Ave., 60615. Tel: 773-285-2746. Daytime Capacity 60; Overnight Capacity 30.

BARRINGTON. *Bellarmine Hall*, 175 W. County Line Rd., 60011. Tel: 847-381-1261; Fax: 847-381-4695.
E-mail: bellarmine-jesuits@hotmail.com
Jesuit Retreat House serving laity (High School, College & Adults), priests and religious. Rev. John T. Dillon, S.J., Dir.; Bro. William R. Haas, S.J. Overnight Capacity 70.
The Jesuit Retreat League of Chicago. Tel: 847-381-1261; Fax: 847-381-4695. Revs. George W. Steenken, S.J.; Robert C. Dressman, S.J.; Robert I. Grib, S.J.

DES PLAINES. *Cabrini Retreat Center.* (Formerly St. Frances Cabrini Retreat House), 9430 Golf Rd., 60016. Tel: 847-297-6530; Fax: 847-297-6544.
E-mail: bridgetzanin@aol.com
Sr. Bridget Zanin, M.S.C.; Sr. Catherine Garry, M.S.C., Dir. Sisters 2. Retreats for priests, religious, laity & youth. Staffed by Missionary Sisters of the Sacred Heart of Jesus.

GLENVIEW. *Villa Redeemer*, 1111 N. Milwaukee Ave., Box 6, 60025. Tel: 847-724-7804; Fax: 847-724-7816. Retreats for men, women, married and engaged couples and special groups. Conducted by the Redemptorists. Rev. Raymond Maiser, C.SS.R., Dir. Legal Title: *The Redemptorists of Glenview, IL.*

LEMONT. *St. Mary's Retreat House*, 14230 Main St., P.O. Box 608, 60439. Tel: 630-257-5102; Fax: 630-257-6432. Rev. Blase Chemazar, O.F.M., Dir.

MUNDELEIN. *Cardinal Stritch Retreat House*, 1000 E. Maple, P.O. Box 455, 60060. Tel: 847-566-6060; Fax: 847-566-6082.
E-mail: csrhouse@aol.com
Revs. Edmund J. Siedlecki, Admin.; John M. Michet, Assoc. Admin.
Serves the clergy of Chicago and Region VII. Retreatants during year 1,600.

[U] NATIONAL INSTITUTIONS

CHICAGO. *Catholic Church Extension Society, aka Catholic Extension*, 150 S. Wacker Dr., 20th Fl., 60606-4200. Tel: 312-236-7240; Fax: 312-236-5276.
E-mail: mail@catholic-extension.org
Web site: www.catholic-extension.org
aka Catholic Extension. Legal Title: *The Catholic Church Extension Society of the United States of America.* His Eminence Francis E. George, O.M.I., Chancellor; Rev. Msgr. Kenneth Velo, Pres.; Mr. Richard A. Ritter, Vice Pres./Treas.; Paul E. Flaherty, Gen. Sec.

Catholic Guild for the Blind. Provides devotional services including large print Mass, free tape-lending library, spiritual magazine available in Braille, large print and on audio cassette; programs for Catholic schools; the liturgy of the Hours in large print or audio cassette; the sacramental rites in large print; and large print Bibles. 180 N. Michigan Ave., Ste. 1700, 60601-7463. Tel: 312-236-8569; Fax: 312-236-8128.
E-mail: guild@guildfortheblind.org
Web site: www.guildfortheblind.org
Ms. Denise M. Butera, Exec. Dir.

Catholic League for Religious Assistance to Poland, Headquarters, 984 N. Milwaukee Ave., 60622-4199. Tel: 773-276-2334. Legal Title: *Catholic League.* Most Rev. Thad J. Jakubowski, D.D., Exec. Dir.; Revs. Thaddeus Dzieszko, Asst. Dir.; Thomas A. Bernas, Treas.

Center for the Study of Religious Life, 5401 S. Cornell Ave., 60615-5698. Tel: 773-752-2720; Fax: 773-752-2723.
E-mail: csrl@visioni.com
Sr. Barbara Kraemer, O.S.F., Dir. Sponsored by the Conference of Major Superiors of Men, the Leadership Conference of Women Religious and Catholic Theological Union at Chicago to promote reflection and action on the life of religious women and men in the United States and serve as a resource to religious leadership.

Jan Beyzym Society, Inc., 4105 N. Avers Ave., 60618. Tel: 773-588-7476; Fax: 773-588-6517.
E-mail: polmes@jezuicichicago.org
Web site: jezuicichicago.org
Polish Jesuits Foreign Missions.

Jesuit Educational Center for Human Development, 5401 S. Cornell Ave., 60615-5698. Tel: 773-684-8146; Fax: 773-684-8154.
E-mail: cishs@aol.com
Ministries include The Christian Institute for the Study of Human Sexuality and publication of the journal Human Development.

National Coalition for Church Vocations, 5420 S. Cornell, #105, 60615. Tel: 773-955-5453; Fax: 773-363-5530.
E-mail: NCCV400@aol.com
Web site: www.nccv-vocations.org
Sr. Diane Poplawski, O.P., Exec. Dir.

National Organization for Continuing Education of Roman Catholic Clergy, Inc., 1337 W. Ohio, 60622. Tel: 312-226-1890; Fax: 312-829-8915.
E-mail: nocercc@nocercc.org
Web site: www.nocercc.org
Revs. Francis S. Tebbe, O.F.M., Pres.; Michael J. Cronin, Exec. Dir. Description: A professional organization of those involved in the continuing education-formation of clergy in the Catholic Church. Dioceses and religious communities in the U.S. are full members. Institutions and organizations which are concerned with continuing education-formation of clergy are associate members. Dioceses and provinces outside the U.S. may also be associate members. NOCERCC was founded in 1973 through the efforts of the National Federation of Priests Councils. It is governed by a Board of Directors which involves a president selected by the membership, elected representatives from the 13 NCCB Regions and 2 elected religious representatives. Its services include bi-monthly NewsNotes, Resource publications, an Annual Convention, training for new and experienced directors, regional meetings, consultations and service to regional and interdiocesan programs.

National Religious Vocation Conference, 5420 S. Cornell, #105, 60615. Tel: 773-363-5454; Fax: 773-363-5530.
E-mail: NRVC@aol.com
Web site: nrvc.net
Sr. Catherine Bertrand, S.S.N.D., Exec. Dir.

Radio Maryja, P.O. Box 39565, 60639-0595. Tel: 773-385-8472; Fax: 773-385-5631.
E-mail: siostmyloretanki@kaol.com
6965 W. Belmont Ave., 60634. Redemptorist religious radio.

The National Center for the Laity, P.O. Box 291102, 60629. Tel: 773-776-9036; Fax: 773-776-9036.
E-mail: wdroel@cs.com
Web site: www.laity-initiatives.org
Mr. Vaile Scott, Pres. Founded in 1977, the NCL is dedicated to advancing a key insight of Vatican II: that the church is the people of God in service to the modern world. NCL publishes a newsletter, INITIATIVES, furnishes a weekly e-mail message, gfapierce@aol.com, hosts conferences and retreats and maintains a speakers' bureau.

Trinity House. Treatment Center for Clergy and Religious. 3230 S. Lituanica Ave., 60608. Tel: 773-247-7707; Fax: 773-247-1588.
E-mail: ssspsyd@enteract.com
Rev. John Keenan, S.S.S., Psy.D., Ph.D., Dir.

Zambian Rehabilitation Institute. Organized to raise funds and recruit volunteers in the U.S. to assist in the establishment of an addictions treatment center for clergy, religious and laity. Initial location of center in Zambia will also serve Eastern and South Africa. 5414 N. Luna Ave., 60630-1310. Tel: 773-792-2380; Fax: 773-792-9093.
E-mail: zamrehab@aol.com
Mr. Thomas F. Healy, Contact Person.

MOUNT PROSPECT. *Catholic Kolping Society of America-National Endowment Fund*. 1804 Aspen Dr., 60056. Tel: 847-824-8768. William B. Mahrenholz, Treas.

RIVER FOREST.

American Friends of the Ecole Biblique, 7200 W. Division St., 60305-1294. Tel: 708-771-3030; Fax: 708-771-4510.
E-mail: ecolebibli@aol.com
Web site: http://www.op.org/op/ebaf/index-eng.htm
Rev. Peter J. Hereley, O.P., Pres.; Judy Valentine Gerth, Managing Dir. Tel: 847-475-4114. Organized to raise funds in the U.S. to support the work of the Ecole Biblique et Archeologique Francaise de Jerusalem and promote the dissemination of biblical scholarship and archeological research through newsletters, receptions, and seminars with biblical scholars.

Dominican Leadership Conference, 7200 W. Division St., 60305-1294. Tel: 708-771-0909; Fax: 708-771-4510.
E-mail: op7200@theramp.net
Web site: http://www.op.org/dlc/
Sr. Mary Ellen O'Grady, O.P., Exec. Dir. Legal Title: *Dominican Leadership Conference of Dominican Men and Women Religious in the United States of America*.
Conferences:
Parable Conference for Dominican Life and Mission. Tel: 708-771-0088; Fax: 708-771-4510.
Opus: A History of the Order of Preachers in the United States. Tel: 708-921-2538; Fax: 708-921-2207.

STICKNEY.

Ministry Potential Discerner, Inc., St. Pius X Campus, 4314 S. Oak Park Ave., 60402. Tel: 708-795-1221; Fax: 708-795-1226.
E-mail: gil@mpdinc.org
Web site: www.mpdinc.org
Dr. Gil Demange, M.D., M.B.A., Exec. Vice Pres. A self-assessment evangelizing vocational tool designed to aid vocation recruitment in discerning individuals for service to the church as priest or religious.

TECHNY. *Divine Word Missionaries, Inc., Divine Word Funds, Inc.*, 1835 Waukegan Rd., Box 6099, 60082-6099. Tel: 847-272-7600; Fax: 847-272-8572.
E-mail: dwm6099@aol.com
Web site: divineword.org
Revs. Thomas A. Krosnicki, S.V.D., Pres.; David Gallagher, Asst. Treas.

S.V.D., Catholic Universities, Inc., 1835 Waukegan Rd., Box 6099, 60082-6099. Tel: 847-272-7600; Fax: 847-272-8572.
E-mail: dwm6099@aol.com
Revs. Thomas A. Krosnicki, S.V.D., Pres.; David Gallagher, Asst. Treas.

[V] MINISTRY IN HIGHER EDUCATION

CHICAGO. *Ministry in Higher Education*, 700 S. Morgan St., 60607. Tel: 312-829-0670; Fax: 312-326-2631.
E-mail: jslatte@hotmail.com
Ms. Jan Slattery, Dir.
Non-Catholic Institutions:
Chicago State University, 95th & Martin Luther King Dr., 60628. Tel: 773-995-3869; Fax: 312-226-2361. Ms. Corrine Grant, Campus Min.
College of Lake County, 19351 W. Washington, Grayslake, 60030. Tel: 847-543-2740, Ext. 740; Fax: 847-543-2362. Ms. Sarah Hinojosa, Camp. Min.
Moraine Valley Community College, P.O. Box 311, Worth, 60482. Tel: 708-974-5221; Fax: 708-974-1043. Mr. William Droel, Camp. Min.
Northeastern Illinois University, 700 S. Morgan St., 60607. Tel: 312-829-0670; Fax: 312-226-2361. Ms. Karen Rushen, Camp. Min.
Northwestern University / Kendall College, Sheil Center, 2110 N. Sheridan Rd., Evanston, 60201. Tel: 847-328-4648; Fax: 847-328-4660. Rev. Kenneth C. Simpson, B.S., M.Div., D.Min., Dir.
University of Chicago Calvert House, 5735 S. University Ave., 60637. Tel: 312-288-2311; Fax: 773-288-1124. Rev. Willard F. Jabusch, Ph.D., Dir.
University of Illinois at Chicago - John Paul II Newman Center, 700 S. Morgan St., 60607-3429. Tel: 312-226-1880; Fax: 312-226-2361. Rev. Patrick M. Marshall, Dir.
University of Illinois at the Medical Center, 916 S. Wolcott Ave., 60612. Tel: 312-666-9215; Fax: 312-226-2361. Mr. David Kozichek, Camp. Min., Dir. Integritas Institute.
Triton College, P.O. Box 803, Maywood, 60153. Tel: 708-456-0300, Ext. 3752; Fax: 708-583-3162. Sr. Christine Myskow, O.S.F., Camp. Min.
Illinois Institute of Technology, c/o St. James, 2942 S. Wabash Ave., 60616. Tel: 312-567-3160; Fax: 312-567-8917. Mr. Eric Schwister, Camp. Min.
Truman City College, c/o 4827 N. Kenmore Ave., 60640. Tel: 773-784-1932. Rev. Trinh Peter Hung.
Wilbur Wright College, 4300 N. Narragansett Ave., 60634-1591. Tel: 773-481-8874; Fax: 773-481-8892. Karen Rushen, Camp. Min.
Columbia College / Art Institute / John Marshall Law School, c/o Old St. Mary's, 21 E. Van Buren St., 60605. Tel: 312-922-3444. Rev. Robert O'Donnell, C.S.P.
Roosevelt University, 430 S. Michigan, 60605. Tel: 312-341-2015; Fax: 312-341-3539.
Lake Forest College, c/o St. Mary, 175 E. Illinois St., Lake Forest, 60045. Tel: 847-864-0333.
Catholic Institutions:
Barat College, 700 E. Westleigh Rd., Lake Forest, 60045. Tel: 847-604-6224; Fax: 847-615-5659. Sr. Sally Duffy, R.S.C.J.; Sr. Patricia Reiss, R.S.C.J.
De Paul University, Campus Ministry-Stewart Center, 2320 N. Kenmore, 60614. Tel: 773-325-7902; Fax: 773-325-7901. Ms. Cathy Flaherty, Admin. Asst.
De Paul University, Campus Ministry Department, 25 E. Jackson Blvd., 60604. Tel: 312-362-6910; Fax: 312-362-5671. Dr. Robert Ludwig, Dir.
Loyola University of Chicago, University Ministry Dept., 6525 N. Sheridan Rd., 60626. Tel: 773-508-2200; Fax: 773-508-8509. Mr. Lucien Roy, Dir.; Rev. Lawrence Reuter, S.J., Vice Pres. of University Ministry. Tel: 773-508-2089.
Loyola University of Chicago, 820 N. Michigan Ave., 60611. Tel: 312-915-7255; Fax: 312-915-6251. Mr. Lucien Roy, Dir.
Loyola University Medical Center, 2160 S. First Ave., Maywood, 60153. Tel: 708-216-3245; Fax: 708-216-8773. Ms. Maureen Fuechtmann, Dir. & Assoc. VP.
Dominican University, 7900 W. Division St., River Forest, 60305. Tel: 708-366-2490; Fax: 708-266-5360.
St. Xavier University, 3700 W. 103rd St., 60655. Tel: 773-298-3140; Fax: 773-298-3147. Ms. Eileen Doherty, Dir. Camp. Min.

[W] PERSONAL PRELATURE

CHICAGO. *Midtown Center*. Prelature of the Holy Cross and Opus Dei, 1825 N. Wood St., 60622. Tel: 773-292-5450; 292-0660; Fax: 773-292-0996.

Northview University Center. Prelature of the Holy Cross and Opus Dei, 7225 N. Greenview Ave., 60626. Tel: 773-465-3468; Fax: 773-465-1195. Rev. James Socias.

Prelature of the Holy Cross and Opus Dei, Office of the Vicar for the Midwest, 5800 N. Keating Ave., 60646. Tel: 773-283-5800; Fax: 773-202-8179. Very Rev. Peter V. Armenio, Vicar for the Midwest; Revs. John Agnew; Frank Hoffman; Edward G. Maristany.

OAK PARK. *Oak Park Study Center*. Prelature of the Holy Cross and Opus Dei, 831 S. Euclid Ave., 60304. Tel: 708-383-0928; Fax: 708-386-2612. Revs. Richard L. Schendt; Barry Cole; Fred Piegl.

[X] MISCELLANEOUS LISTINGS

CHICAGO. *Mundelein College*. Tel: 312-915-6195; Fax: 312-915-6208. Mailing Address: Office of the General Counsel of Loyola University-Chicago, 820 N. Michigan Ave., 60611. Tel: 312-915-6195. 6525 N. Sheridan Rd., 60626. Tel: 773-508-3029. Dr. Larry A. Braskamp, Pres.; Ms. Ellen Kane Munro, Sec.; Ms. Patricia M. Furgat, Vice Pres. & Treas.

Aid for Women. Dedicated to upholding the principles of Humanae Vitae and Evangelium Vitae, the organization maintains a crisis center where any pregnant woman will find help and encouragement to choose life for her unborn child through pregnancy testing, confidential counseling and referral to community resources. 8 S. Michigan Ave., Ste. 1100, 60603. Tel: 312-621-1100; Fax: 312-621-1972.
E-mail: info@aidforwomen.org
Web site: http://www.aidforwomen.org
Elaine M. Kindler, Dir.

Angel Guardian German Catholic Orphan Society of Chicago, 126 N. Des Plaines St., 60661. Tel: 312-655-7040.

Apostolate of the Handicapped, 721 N. LaSalle, 60610. Tel: 312-655-7188. Robert Roeder, Pres.; Rev. Charles F. Kelly, St. Daniel the Prophet, 5330 S. Nashville, 60638. Active membership 750.

The Aquin Guild, 1025 W. Fry St., 60622. Tel: 312-280-9199. Rev. John W. Clemens, Dir. Provides spiritual direction to Catholics engaged in public and parochial education.

Aquinas Literacy Center (ESL), 3525 S. Hermitage Ave., 60609. Tel: 773-927-0512; Fax: 773-927-8980. Sr. Kathy McNulty, O.S.F., Dir.

The Bolivian Trust of the Dominicans, 1909 S. Ashland Ave., 60608. Tel: 312-666-3244; Fax: 312-829-8471.

Bonaventure House, Inc., 825 W. Wellington Ave., 60657. Tel: 773-327-9921; Fax: 773-327-9113.
E-mail: dsavaiano@bonaventurehouse.org
Web site: www.bonaventurehouse.org
Mr. Robert N. Pfeiffer, CEO. Congregation of Alexian Brothers, Immaculate Conception Province. Residences for persons with AIDS.

Catholic Chaplaincy at O'Hare. Mailing Address: Chicago O'Hare International Airport, P.O. Box 66353, 60666-0353. Tel: 773-686-2636; Fax: 773-686-0130.
E-mail: ORDchapel@aol.com
Web site: ohareairportchapel.org
Rev. John A. Jamnicky, Chap.; Deacon James O'Malley, Assoc. Chap.

Catholic Conference of Illinois, 65 E. Wacker Pl., Ste. 1620, 60601. Tel: 312-368-1066; Fax: 312-368-1090.
E-mail: delaneyCCI@aol.com
Mr. Doug Delaney, Exec. Dir.

Catholic Health Alliance for Metropolitan Chicago, 203 N. Wabash Ave., Ste. 1404, 60601. Sr. Tommasina Lanski, M.S.C.

Catholic Health Partners Services. Sponsored by Ascension Health and the Missionary Sisters of the Sacred Heart of Jesus to operate St. Anthony, Columbus and St. Joseph hospitals. 2913 N. Commonwealth Ave., 60657. Tel: 773-665-3451.
Web site: www.cath-health.org

Catholic Health Partners Development Corporation. Tel: 773-388-5731; Fax: 773-348-3542.

Catholic Health Partners Medical Network. Tel: 773-665-3451; Fax: 773-665-3733.

Partners Occupational Health. Tel: 773-655-3451; Fax: 773-665-3733.

Partners Support Services. Tel: 773-655-3451; Fax: 773-665-3733.

The Catholic New World, 721 N. LaSalle St., 60610. Tel: 312-655-7777; Fax: 312-642-7350.
E-mail: neworld201@aol.com
Web site: www.catholicnewworld.com
Publishers of The Catholic New World; Chicago Catolico; and the Archdiocesan Directory. Thomas H. Sherdian, Editor & Gen. Mgr.; Mary Claire Gart, Asst. Editor; Dawn Vidmar, Adv. & Mktg. Mgr.

Catholic Office of the Deaf, 721 N. LaSalle, 60610. Tel: 312-655-7899 (Voice); 751-8368 (TDD); Fax: 312-751-0394.
E-mail: cathdeafch@aol.com
Rev. Joseph A. Mulcrone, Dir.

Catholic Youth, Archdiocese of Chicago, 1658 W. Grand Ave., 60622. Tel: 312-733-7405. Revs. John P. Smyth, Dir.; David Ryan, Dir., Oper. Mgmt.; Joanne Walczynski, Youth Ministry Coord. of Vicariate I; Patrick Pacer, Youth Ministry Coord. of Vicariate II; Michael Molitor, Youth Ministry Coord. of Vicariate IV; Maria Perez Eraci, Youth Ministry Coord. of Vicariate V; Ms. Kimberly Williams, Coord. Athletics; Irene Friend, Coord. of Training & Faith Formation; Arlene Nash, Sec. & Admin. Asst. to TEC, Day of the Spirit, Boy Scouts, Girl Scouts, Campfire.

Central American Martyrs Center (Su Casa Catholic Worker Community), 5045 S. Laflin, 60609. Tel: 773-376-9263; Fax: 773-376-9241.
E-mail: ucasacw@juno.com
Sr. Mary Davis, I.H.M.; Claudia Thomas; Daniel DelaPava; Karen Schulte-Coman; J. Michael Coman.

The Chicago Marian Center, 7262 W. Foster Ave., 60656. Tel: 773-774-7700; Fax: 773-774-1630.
E-mail: chicagomarian@aol.com
Web site: chicagomarian.com/org
Kathleen Long, Contact Person.

Claret Center, 5536 S. Everett, 60637. Tel: 773-643-6259; Fax: 773-643-6929.
E-mail: claret-center@claret.org
Resources for Counseling and Spiritual Direction. Susan C. Rosenbach, S.S.S.F., Exec. Dir.

Claretian Associates, Inc. Organization to provide affordable housing and encourage neighborhood improvement in South Chicago. 9108 S. Brandon Ave., 60617. Tel: 773-734-9181; Fax: 773-734-9221.
E-mail: lreyes@www.claret.org
Ms. Elizah A. Reyes, Exec. Dir.

Claretian Volunteers and Lay Missionaries, 205 W. Monroe St., 60606. Tel: 312-236-7782; Fax: 312-236-7230.
E-mail: comovol@claret.org
Web site: www.claret.org
Directors: Ms. Becky Morrill; Ms. Joyce Platfoot.

Co-Redemptorist Association Office, 3700 N. Ashland Ave., 60613-3602. Tel: 773-472-8509; Fax: 773-472-8515.
E-mail: cocssr@aol.com
Rev. John Paul Andree, Dir.

Court of Appeals-Province of Chicago, 20 N. Wacker Dr., Ste. 3420, 60606. Tel: 312-553-4080; Fax: 312-553-4085. The Court of Second Instance in matrimonial cases for the Tribunals of the Province of Chicago. Revs. Robert L. Kealy, S.T.L., J.D., J.C.D., Judicial Vicar; John P. Lucas, S.T.L., J.C.L., Adjutant Judicial Vicar; John E. Mulvihill, J.C.L., S.T.D.; Ms. Mari Hans, Chief Notary.

Felician Services, Inc., 3800 W. Peterson Ave., 60659-3197. Tel: 773-463-3806; Fax: 773-463-2059.
E-mail: fsichgo@fs-inc.net
Sr. Mary Clarette Stryzewski, C.S.S.F., Pres. & C.E.O.

Focolare Movement, P.O. Box 53426, 60653. Tel: 773-285-2746; Fax: 773-536-5054. Women, 5017 S. Greenwood Ave., 60615. Tel: 773-536-7873; Fax: 773-536-5054. Ms. Paola Santostefano, Contact Person, Men, 1112 S. Oak Park Ave., Oak Park, 60304. Tel: 708-848-6576; Fax: 708-848-6950. Mr. William Neu, Contact Person.
Work of Mary founded in Trent, Italy in 1943. International headquarters are in Rome, Italy; national formation center in New York.

Foundation for Adult Catechetical Teaching Aids, 6007 N. Sheridan Rd., Ste. 22A, 60660. Tel: 773-334-6774; Fax: 773-334-6806. Rev. Gerard P. Weber, Pres.; M. E. Buckley, Contact Person.

Franciscan Friars Retirement Corporation, 6107 Kenmore Ave., 60660-2797. Tel: 773-274-7681; Fax: 773-274-9751.

Franciscan Outreach Association, 1645 W. LeMoyne St., 60622. Tel: 773-278-6724; Fax: 773-278-7120.
E-mail: outreach@enteract.com
Rev. Larry Janezic, O.F.M., Exec. Dir.
Owns & operates: Marquard Center, Franciscan House of Mary & Joseph and a Case Management Program for the homeless in Chicago.

Friends of the Metropolitan Andrew Sheptysky Hospital, 1651 W. Diversey Pkwy., 60614. Tel: 773-388-8670; Fax: 773-388-8676. Most Rev. Edwin Conway, Pres.

Holy Family Church Inc., 2050 N. Clark St., 60614. Tel: 773-975-6363; Fax: 773-975-0230.

Ignatius Productions, Inc, 2050 N. Clark St., 60614. Tel: 773-975-6363; Fax: 773-975-0230.

Illinois Catholic Health Association, 65 E. Wacker Pl., Ste. 1620, 60601. Tel: 312-368-0011; Fax: 312-368-1701.
E-mail: pkarst4074@aol.com
Web site: il-cha.org
Philip J. Karst, Exec. Dir.

The Illinois Patrons of the Arts in the Vatican Museums, 221 N. LaSalle St., Ste. 1000, 60601. Tel: 312-782-5681; Fax: 312-782-6904. His Eminence Francis E. George, O.M.I.; Mr. Edmund M. Burke, Pres.

Institute for Spiritual Leadership, 5498 S. Kimbark Ave., P.O. Box 53147, 60653-0147. Tel: 773-752-5962; Fax: 773-752-5964.
E-mail: islusa@aol.com
Education Center for Spiritual Direction and Renewal. Sr. Patricia M. Bombard, B.V.M., Exec. Dir.; Mr. Michael Skelley, Pres.

Intercommunity Housing Corporation, 2900 N. Lakeshore Dr., 60657. Tel: 773-665-3129. Janet Bilandic, Exec. Dir.

Jesuit International Missions, Inc., 2050 N. Clark St., 60614. Tel: 773-975-6881; Fax: 773-975-0230.
E-mail: vonkaenel@chicagoprovincejesuits.org
Rev. George E. Von Kaenel, S.J.

Jesuit Seminary Association, 2050 N. Clark St., 60614. Tel: 773-975-6363; Fax: 773-975-0230.

Kolbe House, 2434 S. California Ave., 60608. Tel: 773-247-0070; Fax: 773-247-0569.
E-mail: khjailmin@aol.com
Catholic prison ministry. Revs. Lawrence J. Craig, Exec. Dir.; David A. Kelly, C.PP.S.; Deacons James Morgan; Ronald DeRose; George Brooks; John Harrington; Charles Huber; John Richardson; Jasper Roy; Jack Malone.

Loyola Press, 3441 N. Ashland Ave., 60657. Tel: 773-281-1818; Fax: 773-281-0555.
E-mail: lane@loyolapress.com
Rev. George A. Lane, S.J., Dir.

Lumen Christi Institute, 5735 S. University Ave., 60637-1507. Tel: 773-955-5887; Fax: 773-955-5233.
E-mail: lumenchristi@catholic.org
Web site: lumenchristi.net
The Lumen Christi Institute is a sister institution of Calvert House, the Catholic Center at the University of Chicago. The Institute promotes Catholic faith and culture through formation programs, lectures, courses and conferences both in Chicago and in collaboration with others throughout the Great Lakes region.

Marist Volunteer Program, 4200 W. 115th St., 60655. Tel: 773-881-6360, Ext. 5367; Fax: 773-881-0595.
E-mail: sumnerh@marist.net
Web site: www.marist.net/~mvp
Bro. Sumner Herrick, F.M.S., Exec. Dir.

Martin de Porres House, 3322 Washington Blvd., 60624. Tel: 773-826-9336. Margaret Brooks, Pres.; Cathryn Peters, Vice Pres.; Claire Cummings, Sec.

Mercy Health System of Chicago Liability Self-Insurance Trust, 2525 S. Michigan Ave., 60616. Tel: 312-567-2618; Fax: 312-567-7941.
E-mail: acarlisle@mercy-chicago.org
Ms. Arby Likens Carlisle, Gen. Counsel.

Mercy Housing Corporation, 10024 S. Central Park, 60655-3132. Tel: 773-779-6011; Fax: 773-779-6094.
E-mail: rsm@mercychicago.com
Sisters of Mercy of the Americas, Regional Community of Chicago. Sr. Lois Graver, R.S.M., Contact Person.

Miles Jesu. Tel: 773-262-0861; Fax: 773-267-1093.
E-mail: milesjesu@compuserve.com
Web site: milesjesu.com

Men's Formation Center, 1128 W. Morse Ave., 60636. Tel: 773-262-0861; Fax: 773-262-1093. Mr. David Rey, Vocation Dir.; Rev. Christopher Foeckler, M.J., Formation Dir.

Women's Formation Center, 1126 W. Morse Ave., 60636. Tel: 773-262-0806; Fax: 773-262-1093. Mary Pat Cross, Vocation Dir.

Mother Cabrini League, 434 W. Deming Pl., 60614. Tel: 773-388-7329. The purpose of the League is to spread devotion to St. Frances Xavier Cabrini. Sr. Philippa Provenzano, M.S.C., Editor; Anna Grenvich, Office Supvr.; Sr. Antonia Lanzone, M.S.C., Bus. Mgr.

Nowe Zycie Association, 7015 W. Diversey Ave., 60707. Tel: 773-637-7312; Fax: 773-637-7430.
E-mail: redakcja@nowezycie.com
Web site: www.nowezycie.com
Mr. Roman Harmata, Contact Person.

Oblates for International Pastoral. aka Oblate International Pastoral Investment Trust, 5535 S. Kenwood Ave., 60637-1755.
E-mail: rufusw@omisusa.org
Trustees: Revs. Alfons Keuter, O.M.I.; Thomas Singer, O.M.I.; Rufus J. Whitley, O.M.I.; David Ulrich, O.M.I.; Robert Moosbrugger, O.M.I.

Office for Mission Advancement. Dominicans: Province of St. Albert the Great. 1909 S. Ashland Ave., 60608. Tel: 312-226-0020; Fax: 312-226-6440.
E-mail: dominicans@preachers.org
Web site: www.op.org

Order of Friar Servants of Mary United States of America Province, Inc. The Order of Friar Servants of Mary-U.S.A. Province, Inc. Chicago, IL Retirement Plan of the Order of Frair Servants of Mary-U.S.A. Province, Inc. Chicago, ILCharitable Trust of the Order of Friar Servants of Mary-U.S.A. Province, Inc., Chicago, ILThe Servite Fathers, A California CorporationSanctuary of Our Sorrowful Mother, Inc., Portland, ORCharitable Trust of the Order of Frair Servants of Mary-U.S.A. Province, Inc. Chicago, ILThe Servite Fathers, A California CorporationSanctuary of Our Sorrowful Mother, Inc., Portland, OR, 3121 W. Jackson Blvd., 60612. Tel: 773-533-0360; Fax: 773-533-8307. The Order of Friar Servants of Mary-U.S.A. Province, Inc., Chicago, IL. Retirement Plan of the Order of Friar Servants of Mary-U.S.A. Prov., Inc., Chicago, IL. Charitable Trust of the Order of Friar Servants of Mary-U.S.A. Prov., Inc., Chicago, IL. The Servite Fathers, A California Corporation. Sanctuary of Our Sorrowful Mother, Inc., Portland, OR.

Polish Manual Training School for Boys, 126 N. Des Plaines St., 60661. Tel: 312-655-7040.

Retirement Plan of the Order of Friar Servants of Mary-U.S.A. Province, Inc., 3121 W. Jackson Blvd., 60612. Tel: 773-533-0360; Fax: 773-533-8307.

S.F.V., Inc., 1645 W. LeMoyne St., 60622. Tel: 773-278-6724. Sponsor corporation of St. Francis Village (a retirement village) in Crowley, TX. Rev. J. Michael Ewert, O.F.M., Pres.

St. Hedwig's Industrial School for Girls, 126 N. Des Plaines St., 60661. Tel: 312-655-7040.

St. Joseph Bohemian Orphanage, 126 N. Des Plaines St., 60661. Tel: 312-655-7040.

St. Thomas Aquinas Foundation. (STAF) (St. Albert the Great Prov.), 1909 S. Ashland Ave., 60608-2994. Tel: 312-666-3244; Fax: 312-829-8471. Very Rev. Edward M. Ruane, O.P., Sec. & Treas.

Serra International. U.S./Canada Council, 65 E. Wacker Pl., Ste. 1210, 60601-7203. Tel: 312-782-2163; Fax: 312-782-2358.
E-mail: serraus@aol.com
Web site: http://www.serraus.org
Mr. Robert Raccuglia, Exec. Dir., Serra International; Mr. E. V. Verbeke, Exec. Admin., U.S./ Canada Council; Mr. Walter Drakis, Dir. of Devel., Serra International Foundation.

Shelters for the Homeless, Inc., 126 N. Desplaines St., 60606. Tel: 312-655-7666.

Society of Jesus Worldwide, 2050 N. Clark St., 60614.

The Institute on Religious Life, 3051 N. Christiana, 60618. Tel: 773-267-1195; Fax: 773-267-2044.
E-mail: mail@religiouslife.com.
Web site: www.religiouslife.com
Mailing Address: P.O. Box 41007, 60641. Rev. Thomas Nelson, O.Praem., Exec. Dir.; Michael D. Wick, Dir. of Opers.

United Stand Family Center, 3731 W. 62nd St., 60629. Tel: 773-585-4499. Dr. Kim Mis, C.S.S.F., Exec. Dir. Staff 45. Education, Prevention, Problem Identification, Consultation, and Intervention with Children and Families.

Villa Guadalupe Senior Services Corporation, 3201 E. 91st St., 60617. Tel: 773-933-0344; Fax: 773-933-0822. Organization to provide affordable housing and related services for Senior Citizens in South Chicago. Barbara Kilbourne, Chairwoman; Rev. Mark Brummel, C.M.F., Treas.

ARLINGTON HEIGHTS. *Living Word Charitable Trust*, 800 N. Fernandez Ave.-B, 60004-5316. Tel: 847-577-5972; Fax: 847-577-5980.
E-mail: slw@slw.org
Web site: slw.org

BERWYN. *Academy of Our Lady, Chicago, Inc.*, 1431 Euclid Ave., 60402. Tel: 708-749-1380; Fax: 708-749-9446.

BLUE ISLAND. *St. Francis Health Care Foundation*, 12935 S. Gregory St., 60406. Tel: 708-824-4810; Fax: 708-824-4813.
E-mail: Susan_O'Donovan@ssmhc.com
Member of the SSM Health Care.

ELK GROVE VILLAGE. *Alexian Brothers Community Services*, 600 Alexian Way, 60007. Tel: 847-640-7550; Fax: 847-981-5561.

Alexian Brothers Community Services of St. Louis, 600 Alexian Way, 60007. Tel: 847-640-7550; Fax: 847-981-5561.

Alexian Brothers Health Management, Inc., (ABHM), 600 Alexian Way, 60007. Tel: 847-640-7550; Fax:

847-981-5561. Congregation of Alexian Brothers, Immaculate Conception Province.
Alexian Brothers Health System, 600 Alexian Way, 60007. Tel: 847-640-7550; Fax: 847-981-5561. Congregation of Alexian Brothers, Immaculate Conception Province.
Alexian Brothers Health System Investment Trust, 600 Alexian Way, 60007. Tel: 847-640-7500; Fax: 847-981-5561.
Alexian Brothers of America, Inc., 600 Alexian Way, 60007. Tel: 847-640-7550; Fax: 847-981-5561. Congregation of Alexian Brothers, Immaculate Conception Province.
Chicago Catholic Healthcare System, Inc., 600 Alexian Way, 60007. Tel: 847-640-7550; Fax: 847-981-5561. Congregation of Alexian Brothers, Immaculate Conception Province.
EVANSTON.
Mission FIDES, P.O. Box 5250, 60204-5250. Tel: 773-262-6370; Fax: 773-262-6370.
EVERGREEN PARK. *American Province of Little Company of Mary Sisters Charitable Trust*, 9350 S. California, 60805. Tel: 708-422-0130; Fax: 708-422-2212. E-mail: cpacini@lcmh.org
Little Company of Mary Hospital and Health Care Centers, 2800 W. 95th St., 60642.
INVERNESS.
Alexian Brothers Northwest Mental Health Association, 1606 Colonial Pkwy., 60067. Tel: 847-952-7460; Fax: 847-991-3065.
Web site: alexian-northwest.org
1616 N. Arlington Heights Rd., Arlington Heights, 60004. 224 W. Northwest Hwy., Arlington Heights, 60004. Congregation of Alexian Brothers, Immaculate Conception Province.
Alexian Brothers Northwest Mental Health Center, 1606 Colonial Pkwy., 60067. Tel: 847-952-7460; Fax: 847-991-3065.
Web site: alexian-northwest.org
1616 N. Arlington Heights Rd., Arlington Heights, 60004. 224 W. Northwest Hwy., Arlington Heights, 60004. Congregation of Alexian Brothers, Immaculate Conception Province.
LAGRANGE PARK.
Joyful Again. Support program for widowed men and women. P.O. Box 1365, 60526. Tel: 708-354-7211; Fax: 708-354-7519.
E-mail: joyful@megsinet.net
Rev. Medard P Laz, Exec. Dir.; Charlotte Hrubes, Dir.
Sisters of St. Joseph of LaGrange Charitable Trust, 1515 W. Ogden Ave., 60525. Tel: 708-354-9200; Fax: 708-354-9573.
LEMONT. *Franciscan ElderCare Services/Illinois, Inc.*, 14700 Main St., 60439. Tel: 708-647-6500; Fax: 708-647-6500.
MUNDELEIN. *Civitas Dei Foundation*, P.O. Box 665, 60060. Tel: 847-382-5853. The Journal is named Chicago Studies. Rev. George J. Dyer.
NORTHLAKE. *Italian Catholic Federation*, 46 N. Wolf Rd., 60164. Tel: 708-562-0500; Fax: 708-562-1824.
E-mail: sjvianney1@juno.com
Web site: www.vianney.homepage.com
Rev. Charles V. Fanelli, Chap.
Scalabrini Village, 444 N. Wolf Rd., 60164. Tel: 708-562-4402.
ROLLING MEADOWS. *Rainbows for All God's Children, Inc.*, 2100 Golf Rd., 60008. Tel: 800-266-3206. Mrs. Suzy Yehl Marta, Founder & Pres.
TECHNY. *Blessed Arnold Religious Charitable Trust*, 1985 Waukegan Rd., P.O. Box 6067, 60082-6067. Tel: 847-272-2700; Fax: 847-753-7464.
E-mail: tgriffithsvd@yahoo.com
Society of the Divine Word. Rev. Thomas Griffith, S.V.D., Contact Person.
WAUKEGAN. *The Harbor*, 826 W. North Ave., 60085. Tel: 847-782-8015; Fax: 847-782-0822.
E-mail: ksmith@theharborwaukegan.org
Web site: www.theharborwaukegan.org
Congregation of Alexian Brothers, Immaculate Conception Province. Mr. Robert N. Pfeiffer, CEO. Operated by Bonaventure House, Inc. Residences for persons with AIDS.
Lake Shore Catholic Academy, 510 Tenth St., 60085. Tel: 847-623-4070; Fax: 847-623-5169. Sr. Miriam Patrick Cummings, S.S.N.D., Admin.
WILMETTE. *Musica Pacis*, Office of the Treasurer, P.O. Box 969, 60091-0969. Tel: 708-624-2559.
E-mail: musiczpzcis@ibm.net
Revs. Willard F. Jabusch, Pres.; Robert H. Festle, Sec.; Alec J. Wolff, Treas.

[Y] CLOSED INSTITUTIONS

CHICAGO. *Archdiocese of Chicago's Joseph Cardinal Bernardin Archives and Records Center*, 711 W. Monroe St., 60661. Tel: 312-831-0711; Fax: 312-831-0610.
E-mail: info@chgocatholicarchives.org
Web site: www.archdiocese-chgo.org/archives/home.htm

The following parish, school or institution records may be found at the above address unless otherwise indicated. Notations to sacramental records of closed parishes held by the Archives and Records Center should be directed to the Archives and Records Center and should specify the name of the parish. The location of records periodically changes. Inquiries for records of parishes, schools or institutions not on this list should be directed to the above address.
Academy of St. Benedict the African (May St.).
Academy of the Sacred Heart. Sacred Heart Schools, 6250 N. Sheridan Rd., 60660. Tel: 773-262-4446.
Academy of Our Lady.
St. Adalbert School and Commercial High School, St. Adalbert Parish, 1650 W. 17th St., 60608. Tel: 312-226-0340.
St. Adrian School.
St. Agatha School.
Blessed Agnes Commercial High School and School, St. Agnes of Bohemia School, 2643 S. Central Park, 60623. Tel: 773-522-0143.
Blessed Agnes of Bohemia Church & School, St. Agnes of Bohemia, 2643 S. Central Park, 60623. Tel: 773-522-0143.
St. Agnes (39th St.) (Pershing Rd.).
St. Agnes School (39th St.).
Alexine Learning Center School.
All Saints (State St.).
All Saints School (State St.).
All Saints (Wallace St.).
All Saints School (Wallace St.).
All Saints/St. Anthony School (Wallace).
St. Aloysius School.
St. Aloysius Commercial High School, St. Aloysius Parish.
St. Alphonsus School (Lemont), St. Alphonsus/St. Patrick, 205 Cass St., Lemont, 60439. Tel: 630-257-2380.
St. Alphonsus Commercial High School (Chicago).
Alvernia Conservatory of Music. Unknown.
Alvernia High School.
St. Andrew High School.
St. Andrew Misson (Wadsworth), St. Patrick Parish, 15000 Wadsworth Rd., Wadsworth, 60083. Tel: 847-244-4161.
Angel Guardian Croatian Catholic Mission. at Blessed Alojzije Cardinal Stetinac Mission, 6346 N. Ridge Ave., 60660. Tel: 773-262-0535; Fax: 773-262-4603.
Angel Guardian Orphanage.
St. Ann (Chicago Heights).
St. Ann School (Chicago Heights).
St. Ann High School (Leavitt St.), St. Ann, 2211 W. 18th Pl., 60608. Tel: 312-829-4153.
St. Ann Hospital, St. Elizabeth Hospital, 1431 N. Claremont Ave., 60622. Tel: 773-278-2000.
St. Anne (Garfield Blvd.).
St. Anne School (Garfield Blvd.).
St. Anne (Waukegan), Immaculate Conception, 508 Grand Ave., Waukegan, 60085. Tel: 847-336-3684.
St. Anne Mission Chapel (Richton), St. Liborius, 71 W. 35th St., Steger, 60475. Tel: 708-754-1363.
Annunciation (Wabansia).
Annunciation School (Wabansia).
St. Anselm School.
St. Anthony of Padua (24th Pl.). (Parish), All Saints-St. Anthony, 518 W. 28th Pl., 60616. Tel: 312-842-2744.
St. Anthony of Padua (24th Pl.).
St. Anthony School (Cicero).
St. Anthony High School & Commercial High School (24th Pl.).
St. Anthony School (Prairie).
Aquinas Catholic High School.
Aquinas Dominican High School.
Aquinas High School.
Ascension (Harvey).
Ascension School (Harvey).
Ascension-St. Susanna School (Harvey).
Ascension of Our Lord (Evanston).
Ascension of Our Lord School (Evanston).
Assumption School (24th St.).
Assumption (Marshfield Ave.).
Assumption School (Marshfield Ave.).
Assumption BVM (123rd St.).
Assumption BVM School (123rd St.).
Assumption School (Illinois St.). Unknown.
Assumption/St. Catherine of Genoa School.
St. Attracta (Cicero).
St. Attracta School (Cicero).
St. Attracta-St. Valentine Church (Cicero).
St. Augustine (S. Laflin).
St. Augustine School & High School.
St. Bartholomew. (Waukegan), Holy Family, 501 S. Utica, Waukegan, 60079-0440. Tel: 847-623-2655.
St. Bartholomew School (Waukegan).
St. Basil, St. Basil/Visitation 5443 S. Honore, 60609.
St. Basil School.
Bellarmine School of Theology-Loyola University of Chicago, Dean of Students of Arts and Sciences, 820 N. Michigan Ave., 60611.
St. Bernard (65th St.).
St. Bernard School.
Bishop Quarter Boarding School for Motherless Boys.
Bishop Quarter Junior Military School. aka Bishop Quarter School for Little Boys.
St. Blase School, St. Joseph School, 5641 S. 73rd St., Summit, 60501. Tel: 708-458-2927.
Blessed Sacrament School.
St. Bonaventure School (Diversey).
St. Boniface (N. Noble).
St. Boniface School (N. Noble).
St. Boniface High School. (unknown).
St. Brendan (Racine).
St. Brendan School (Racine).
St. Bridget.
St. Bridget School & High School.
St. Bronislava School.
Brother Candidates High School (Techny), Divine Word Missionaries, Box 107, East Troy, WI, 53120. Tel: 414-642-3300.
Cabrini Green Alternate High School. Garfield Alternative High School (45th Pl.).
St. Callistus Church-Norte Dame Parish, 1335 W. Harrison, 60607.
St. Callistus School.
Cardinal Stritch High School.
Carmel High School. (Boys and Girls), Carmel High School, One Carmel Pkwy., Mundelein, 60060-2499. Tel: 847-566-3000.
St. Carthage (73rd St.).
St. Carthage School.
St. Casimir Academy, Maria High School, 6727 S. California Ave., 60629-1887. Tel: 773-925-8686.
St. Casimir (Chicago Heights).
St. Casimir School (Chicago Heights).
St. Casimir (Whipple St.), Our Lady of Tepeyac, 2226 S. Whipple St., 60623. Tel: 773-521-8400.
St. Casimir School (Whipple St.).
St. Casimir High School. (Whipple St.), Our Lady of Tepeyac High School, 2228 S. Whipple St., 60623. Tel: 773-522-0023.
St. Catherine Academy. see Siena High School.
St. Catherine High School. see Siena High School.
Cathedral College.
Cathedral High School.
Chrysalis Program.
Corpus Christi School.
St. Catherine of Genoa.
St. Catherine of Genoa School.
St. Catherine of Siena (Oak Park).
Sacramental Records: St. Catherine/St. Lucy Parish, 38 N. Austin Blvd., Oak Park, 60302. Tel: 708-386-8077.
School Records: St. Catherine/St. Lucy School, 27 W. Washington Blvd., Oak Park, 60302. Tel: 708-386-5286.
St. Cecelia (Wells St.).
St. Cecelia School (Wells St.).
St. Charles Borromeo (Hoyne Ave.).
St. Charles Borromeo School (Hoyne Ave.).
St. Charles Borromeo School (Melrose Park).
St. Charles Lwanga (W. Garfield).
St. Charles Lwanga School (W. Garfield).
St. Clara (Woodlawn Ave.).
St. Clara School (Woodlawn), St. Gelasius School, 6358 S. Blackstone, 60637. Tel: 773-324-8430.
St. Clara-St. Cyril (S. Woodlawn).
St. Clara-St. Cyril School.
St. Clement High School.
St. Columbkille (Paulina).
St. Columbkille School & Commercial High School.
St. Columbkille High School, Mother Guerin High School, 8001 Belmont Ave., River Grove, 60171. Tel: 708-453-6233.
St. Constance High School.
Convent of the Sacred Heart (Chicago). Sacred Heart Schools, 6250 N. Sheridan Rd., 60660. Tel: 773-262-4446.
Convent of the Sacred Heart (Lake Forest), Woodlands Academy of the Sacred Heart, 760 E. Westleigh Rd., Lake Forest, 60045-3298. Tel: 847-234-4300.
Corpus Christi High School, Hales Franciscan High School, 4930 S. Cottage Grove, 60615. Tel: 773-285-8400.
St. Cyril (Dante Ave.). (Dante Ave.).
St. Cyril College, Mt. Carmel High School.
St. Cyril School.
Ss. Cyril & Methodius Church & School (Hermitage Ave.).
Ss. Cyril & Methodius Church & School (Walton St.).
St. David School.
St. David Church, All Saints-St. Anthony, 518 W. 28th Pl., 60616. Tel: 312-842-2744.
De Lourdes College (Des Plaines), Holy Family College, Registrar's Office, Grant Ave. & Frankford Ave., Philadelphia, PA, 19114. Tel: 215-637-4851.

DePaul Academy, DePaul University, Registrar's Office, 243 S. Wabash, 60604. Tel: 312-341-8610.
DePaul High School. (Unknown).
DePaul University Loop High School. (Unknown).
St. Dionysius (Cicero).
St. Dionysius School (Cicero).
St. Dominic (Locust).
St. Dominic School & High School.
St. Donatus School (Blue Island).
St. Elizabeth High School (41st St.).
St. Emeric Church, St. Stephen King of Hungary, 2015 W. Augusta Blvd., 60622-4947. Tel: 773-486-1896.
Englewood Catholic Academy (Honore St.).
Englewood Catholic Academy (Laflin St.).
Englewood Catholic Academy (May St.).
Englewood Catholic Academy (Princeton St.).
Ephpheta School for the Deaf.
Felician College.
St. Fidelis School (N. Washtenaw).
St. Finbarr Church (14th St.).
St. Finbarr High School and School. Unknown.
St. Florian Mission (52nd & Archer), St. Camillus, 5426 S. Lockwood Ave., 60638. Tel: 773-767-8183.
Ford City Catholic Center.
Fornier Institute, DePaul University, Registrar's Office, 243 S. Wabash, 60604. Tel: 312-341-8610.
Fornier Institute Viatorian Preparatory (Lemont), Viatorian Archives, Arlington Heights.
St. Frances Xavier Cabrini (Lexinton St.).
St. Frances Xavier Cabrini School (Lexinton St.).
St. Francis de Paula.
St. Frances de Paula School (S. Ellis).
St. Francis de Sales School.
St. Francis of Assisi Church (Kostner Ave.), St. Francis of Assisi/Our Lady of the Angels, 3808 W. Iowa St., 60651. Tel: 773-235-3132.
St. Francis of Assisi School (Kostner Ave.).
St. Francis of Assisi School (Roosevelt Ave.).
St. Francis Xavier (Nelson), Resurrection, 2840 W. Nelson, 60618-7012. Tel: 773-478-9705.
St. Francis Xavier School (Nelson).
St. Gabriel Commercial High School.
St. George (Wentworth Ave.).
St. George School & Commercial High School (Lituanica Ave.).
St. George School (Wentworth Ave.).
St. George (Lituanica).
St. George School (Ewing St.).
St. George High School (Evanston), Christian Brothers Center, 200 De La Salle Dr., Romeoville, 60441. Tel: 630-242-1240.
St. Gerard Majella School (Markham).
St. Gertrude School (Chicago).
St. Gertrude School (Franklin Park).
Good Shepherd Chapel. (Illinois Technical School for Colored Girls).
St. Gregory the Great School.
Hardey Preparatory, Sacred Heart Schools, 6250 N. Sheridan Rd., 60660. Tel: 773-262-4446.
Heart of Mary High School.
St. Hedwig Mission. (Washtenaw Ave.), St. John Berchmans, 2517 W. Logan Blvd., 60647. Tel: 773-486-4300.
St. Hedwig Orphanage (Niles).
St. Hedwig School.
St. Henry School.
Holy Child High School (Waukegan), St. Anastasia School, 629 Glen Flora, Waukegan, 60685. Tel: 847-623-8320.
Holy Cross (65th St.).
Holy Cross School (65th St.).
Holy Cross School (Wood St.).
Holy Cross. (46th St.), Holy Cross/Immaculate Heart of Mary, 4541 S. Wood St., 60609. Tel: 773-376-3900; Fax: 773-376-8929.
Holy Family (North Chicago).
Holy Family School (North Chicago).
Holy Family School (May St.).
Holy Family Academy (Division St.).
Holy Family Extension High School (Des Plaines), Sisters of Holy Family of Nazareth, Provincial Archives, 310 N. River Rd., Des Plaines, 60016. Tel: 847-298-6760.
Holy Family Orphanage (unknown).
Holy Ghost Church & School.
Holy Ghost Academy. (Techny), Convent of the Holy Spirit (Techny).
Holy Guardian Angel (Arthington/Cabrini).
Holy Guardian Angel School.
Holy Name Cathedral School.
Holy Rosary Slovak (108th St.).
Holy Rosary Slovak School (108th St.).
Holy Rosary School (113th St.).
Holy Rosary (North Chicago).
Holy Rosary School (North Chicago).
Holy Rosary School (Western Ave.).
Holy Trinity Church, Holy Trinity Polish Mission, 1118 N. Noble St., 60622-4015. Tel: 773-489-4140.
Holy Trinity School (Noble St.).
Holy Trinity (Wolcott).
Holy Trinity School (Wolcott).
Holy Trinity School (Throop).
Holy Trinity School (Taylor, Deaf Children). House of the Good Shepherd.
St. Hyacinth Mission (Spaulding), St. Hyacinth Parish, 3636 N. Wolfram, 60618. Tel: 773-342-3636.
St. Ignatius College, St. Ignatius College Prep., 1073 W. Roosevelt Rd., 60608. Tel: 312-421-5900.
St. Ignatius School.
Illinois Technical School for Colored Girls.
Immaculata High School.
Immaculate Conception School (Exchange Ave.).
Immaculate Conception Commercial High School (Aberdeen St.).
Immaculate Conception-St. Bridget School.
Immaculate Conception (Aberdeen St.).
Immaculate Conception School (Aberdeen St.).
Immaculate Conception School (44th St.).
Immaculate Conception School (Highland Park).
Immaculate Conception School (North Park Ave.).
Immaculate Heart of Mary Vicariate (Ashland Ave.), Holy Cross-Immaculate Heart of Mary Parish, 4541 S. Wood St., 60609. Tel: 773-376-3900.
St. Irenaeus School (Park Forest).
St. Isaac Jogues School (Niles).
St. Ita School.
St. James School (Maywood).
St. James (Mundelein), St. Mary, 22333 W. Erhart Rd., Mundelein, 60060. Tel: 847-223-0010.
St. Jarlath (Jackson).
St. Jarlath School (Jackson).
St. Jean Baptiste Church (33rd Pl.).
St. Jerome School.
Jesuit School of Theology. Loyola University of Chicago, Office of the Dean of Graduate School, 820 N. Michigan Ave, 60611.
Jesus, Our Brother School.
St. Joachim School.
St. John Bosco School.
Old St. John (18th St.).
Old St. John School, Christian Brothers University, 2455 Avery Ave., Memphis, TN, 38112.
St. John Cantius School.
St. John Chrysostom (Bellwood).
St. John Chrysostom School (Bellwood).
St. John Nepmucene Church & School.
St. John of God Church & School (S. Throop).
St. John the Baptist (50th Pl.).
St. John the Baptist Church (Burley Ave.).
St. John the Baptist School (50th Pl.).
St. John the Baptist School (Harvey), Mary of Nazareth School, 15727 S. Emerald, Harvey, 60426. Tel: 708-331-5076.
St. Josaphat Parish Orphanage (unknown).
St. Joseph Bohemian Orphanage. Maryville Academy, 1150 N. River Rd., Des Plaines, 60016. Tel: 708-824-6126.
St. Joseph Commercial Business College (Waukegan).
St. Joseph the Worker School.
St. Joseph High School (Hermitage).
St. Joseph's Institute.
St. Joseph (17th Pl.).
St. Joseph School (17th Pl.).
St. Joseph (Chicago Heights).
St. Joseph School (Chicago Hts.).
St. Joseph (Saginaw St.).
St. Joseph School (Saginaw St.). Res. St. Joseph's Orphan Asylum (unknown).
St. Joseph Orphanage for Boys. (destroyed by fire).
St. Joseph Parish Orphanage (unknown).
St. Joseph Provident Orphanage (unknown).
St. Joseph Military Academy. (See St. Joseph's Institute).
St. Joseph Academy (LaGrange Park). (See St. Joseph's Institute).
St. Joseph & SS. Joseph & Bartholomew (Waukegan), Holy Family, 501 S. Utica, Waukegan, 60079-0440. Tel: 847-623-2655.
St. Joseph School (Waukegan).
St. Joseph & St. Anne Church, Our Lady of Fatima, 2751 W. 38th Pl., 60632-1686. Tel: 773-927-2421.
St. Joseph Mission (13th St.).
St. Joseph Mission School (13th St.).
St. Joseph Servite Seminary (Elgin-St. Charles), Provincial Archives, Servite Provincial Center, 3121 W. Jackson Blvd., 60612. Tel: 773-533-0360.
St. Joseph's Home for the Friendless, St. Joseph's Corondelet Child Center, 739 E. 35th St., 60616. Tel: 773-624-7443.
St. Joseph Technical High School (Techny), Divine Word Missionaries, East Troy, WI.
St. Josaphat Commercial High School.
Josephinum Academy, Josephinum High School.
St. Justin Martyr (71st St.).
St. Justin Martyr School.
St. Kevin School. St. Kevin Parish, 10509 S. Torrence, 60617. Tel: 773-721-2563.
St. Kilian School.
St. Laurence School.
St. Leonard Commercial High School (Berwyn), St. Leonard School, 3322 S. Clarence, Berwyn, 60402. Tel: 708-749-1989.
Lewis Memorial Maternity Hospital.
Little Flower School.
Little Flower High School.
Longwood Academy. see Academy of Our Lady.
Loretto Academy (Woodlawn).
Loretto Academy (Englewood).
Loretto Adult Center (Englewood)- Benjamin Mays Middle College, Kennedy King College, 6800 S. Wentworth, 60621.
Loretto Extension Service (unknown).
St. Louis de France (117th St.).
St. Louis de France School (117th St.).
St. Louis (Polk St.). (school unknown).
St. Louis Academy (117th Ave.), St. Jude the Apostle Convent, 890 E. 154th St., South Holland, 60473. Tel: 708-333-7595.
Loyola Academy. (Chicago) at Loyola Academy (Wilmette), 1100 N. Laramie Ave., Wilmette, 60091. Tel: 847-256-1100.
St. Lucy. Sacramental Records: St. Catherine-St. Lucy, 38 N. Austin Blvd., Oak Park, 60302. Tel: 708-386-8077.
St. Lucy School Records.
St. Ludmilla, Our Lady of Tepeyac, 2226 S. Whipple St., 60623. Tel: 773-521-8400.
St. Ludmilla School.
St. Louise Marillac High School.
St. Malachy High School, St. Malachy School, 2252 W. Washington, 60612. Tel: 312-733-2252.
Mallinckrodt High School.
Mallinckrodt College (Wilmette). (unknown).
St. Margaret's Home & Hospital (unknown).
Marian School for Deaf. Catholic Charities, Division of Services for Children & Youth, 126 N. Des Plaines, 60606. Tel: 312-236-5172, Ext. 429.
Maria Immaculata Academy (Wilmette).
St. Mark the Evangelist School.
Marquette Institute (Clark St.).
St. Martha School (Morton Grove).
St. Martin (Princeton St.).
St. Martin de Porres Academy.
St. Martin School & Commerical High School (Princeton).
St. Mary School (Des Plaines).
St. Mary School (Evanston).
St. Mary (Lemont), St Patrick, 200 Illinois St., Lemont, 60439. Tel: 708-257-6134.
St. Mary (Waukegan), Immaculate Conception, 508 Grand Ave., Waukegan, 60085. Tel: 847-336-3684.
St. Mary Center for Learning (Grenshaw).
St. Mary High School (Grenshaw).
St. Mary Alternative High School (Grenshaw). (to 1976), Collections University of Illinois at Chicago, University Library, Special Collections, Dawson Technical School and University of Chicago Library, P.O. 8198, 60680. Tel: 312-996-2742. St. Mary (Seely St.), Eparchy of Parma (Ruthenian Byzantine Rite), Parma, OH.
St. Mary's Mission (90th St.), Eparch of Parma (Ruthenian Byzantine Rite), Parma, OH.
St. Mary Alternative High School (Grenshaw). (1976-1979) Harold Washington School, 3901 S. State St., 60609. Tel: 312-533-6075.
St. Mary Magdalen School.
St. Mary of the Assumption School (137th St.).
St. Mary of the Lake Mission (Ingleside), St. Bede, 36455 N. Wilson Rd., Ingleside, 60041-9609. Tel: 847-587-2251; Fax: 847-973-1765.
St. Mary of Mt. Carmel (Hermitage St.).
St. Mary of Mt. Carmel School (Hermitage).
St. Mary of Perpetual Help School, Bridgeport Catholic Academy West Campus, 1040 W. 32nd Pl., 60608. Tel: 773-927-1041.
St. Mary of Perpetual Help High School.
St. Mary of the Woods (Highland Park), Immaculate Conception, 700 W. Deerfield Rd., Highland Park, 60035. Tel: 847-433-0130; Fax: 847-433-0669.
St. Mary Mission Seminary (Techny), Catholic Theological Union, 5401 S. Cornell, 60615-5698. Tel: 773-324-8000.
St. Mary Orphanage for Girls. (destroyed in fire).
St. Mary Training School, Maryville Academy, 1150 N. River Rd., Des Plaines, 60016. Tel: 847-824-6126.
St. Mary School of Nursing (Des Plaines), Holy Family College, Registrar's Office, Grant Ave. & Frankford Ave., Philadelphia, PA, 19114. Tel: 215-637-4851.
Marywood High School (Evanston), Mother Guerin High School, 8001 Belmont Ave., River Grove, 60171. Tel: 773-625-3278; 708-453-6233.
Mater Dolorosa Seminary (Hillside). See Servite Seminary, Servite Provincial Archives. 3121 W. Jackson Blvd., 60612.
St. Matthew (Walnut St.).
St. Matthew School (Walnut St.).
St. Maurice School.
St. Mel & St. Mel-Holy Ghost.
St. Mel & St. Mel-Holy Ghost School.

St. Mel High School. (up to 1969), Christian Brothers Center, 200 De La Salle Dr., Romeoville, 60441. Tel: 630-242-1240.
Mendel High School.
Mercy High School.
Mercy Mission High School.
St. Michael School (Cleveland).
St. Michael Central High School (Cleveland & Hudson).
St. Michael (Wabansia St.).
St. Michael School (Wabansia St.).
St. Michael the Archangel School.
St. Michael Commercial High School (South Shore Dr.).
Misericordia Hospital. Sacramental Records in registers of St. Agnes, 39th St. Client Records & Adoption Placements: Catholic Charities, 126 N. Des Plaines, 60606. Tel: 312-876-2288; 236-5172, Ext. 330.
Mission of the Holy Ghost (Northbrook), St. Norbert, 1809 Walters Ave., Northbrook, 60062. Tel: 847-272-7090.
St. Monica (36th St.). (school unknown).
Monastery of Mt. St. Phillip Servite Novitiate. (Granville, WI), Provincial Archives, Servite Provincial Center, 3121 W. Jackson Blvd., 60612. Tel: 773-533-0360.
Montay College.
Mother of God (Waukegan).
Mother of God School & High School (Waukegan).
Mother of Sorrows Grade and High School (Blue Island).
Mount Carmel School (Chicago Heights). (served St. Rocco).
Mundelein College, Loyola University, Office of Registration & Records, 820 N. Michigan Ave., Room 504, 60611. Tel: 312-915-7221.
Mundelein High School.
Municipal Tuberculosis Sanitarium. (Sacred Heart Chapel).
Nativity of Our Lord School & Commercial High School, Bridgeport Catholic Academy South Campus, 3700 S. Lowe, 60609. Tel: 773-376-6223.
St. Nicholas School (Evanston).
St. Nicholas (State St.).
St. Nicholas School (State St.).
Niles College.
Notre Dame de Chicago School.
Our Lady of Bethlehem Academy.
Our Lady of Fatima Mission (Christina Ave.), St. Hyacinth Parish, 3636 N. Wolfram, 60618. Tel: 773-342-3636.
Our Lady of Fatima (39th/Pershing Rd.).
Our Lady of the Garden, St. Mary of the Assumption, 310 E. 137th St., 60627-1896. Tel: 773-568-1611.
Our Lady of Good Counsel (Western Ave.).
Our Lady of Good Counsel School (Western Ave.).
Our Lady of Good Counsel School (Hermitage Ave.).
Our Lady of Guadalupe Chapel, Holy Cross-Immaculate Heart of Mary, 4541 S. Wood St., 60609. Tel: 773-376-3900.
Our Lady Help of Christians School.
Our Lady of Hope School (Des Plaines).
Our Lady of Hungary (93rd St.).
Our Lady of Hungary School (93rd St.).
Our Lady of Lourdes Commercial High School (Keeler St.).
Our Lady of Lourdes School (Keeler St.).
Our Lady of Peace School.
Our Lady of Perpetual Help Vicariate (13th St.).
Our Lady of Perpetual Help Vicariate School (13th St.).
Our Lady of Providence Academy. (records destroyed in flood.)
Our Lady of Solace (Sangamon).
Our Lady of Solace School (Sangamon).
Our Lady of Sorrows School.
Our Lady of Sorrows Seminary, Mater Dolorosa Seminary, Hillside.
Our Lady of the Angels, St. Francis of Assisi/Our Lady of the Angels, 3808 W. Iowa St., 60651. Tel: 773-235-3132.
Our Lady of Angels School.
Our Lady of the Cross Mission Chapel, St. Margaret Mary, 2324 W. Chase, 60645. Tel: 773-764-0615.
Our Lady of Pompeii School.
Our Lady of Pompeii Church, Our Lady of Pompeii Shrine, 1224 W. Lexington, 60607. Tel: 312-421-3757.
Our Lady of Vilna (23rd St.).
Our Lady of Vilna School (23rd St.), St. Paul/Our Lady of Vilna School, 2114 W. 22nd Pl., 60608. Tel: 773-847-6078.
St. Pancratius School.
St. Patrick Academy (Chicago), McAuley High School, 3737 W. 99th St., 60642. Tel: 773-881-6522.
St. Patrick School (Adams St.). (pre-1967).
St. Patrick School (Lemont), St. Alphonsus-St. Patrick School, 205 Cass St., Lemont, 60439. Tel: 630-257-2380.
St. Patrick (Commercial Ave.).
St. Patrick School (Commercial Ave.).
St. Patrick Academy (Des Plaines), McAuley High School, 3737 W. 99th St., 60642. Tel: 773-881-6522.
St. Patrick High School (Adams St.). (Boys), 5900 W. Belmont, 60634. Tel: 773-282-8844.
St. Patrick High School (Adams St.). (Girls).
St. Patrick High School (Commercial) (unknown).
St. Paul School (Chicago Heights).
St. Paul School (22nd St.), St. Paul/Our Lady of Vilna School (22nd St.).
St. Paul High School, Christian Brother Center, 200 De La Salle Dr., Romeoville, 60441. Tel: 630-242-1240.
St. Paul (12th St.). (records destroyed in 1871 fire).
St. Peter School (Volo), St. Peter, 27551 W. Hwy. 120, Round Lake, 60073. Tel: 815-385-5496.
St. Peter School (only) (Madison). Unknown.
St. Peter Canisius School.
SS. Peter and Paul (Exchange St.).
SS. Peter and Paul School (Exchange St.).
St. Peter & Paul School (Halsted St.).
Ss. Peter & Paul School (Paulina St.).
SS. Peter & Paul (Libertyville), St. Joseph, 121 E. Maple, Libertyville, 60048. Tel: 847-362-2073.
SS. Peter & Paul High School (Exchange Ave.), St. Francis de Sales High School, 10155 S. Ewing, 60617. Tel: 773-731-7272.
St. Peter & Paul Church (Central Park Ave.), St. Nicholas (Byzantine Rite), 8103 Columbia Ave., Munster, IN, 46321-1802. Tel: 219-838-9380.
St. Philip Benizi (Maypole St.). (later named St. Mel).
St. Philip Benizi (Oak St.).
St. Philip Benizi School (Oak St.).
St. Philip Evening School. (unknown).
St. Philip High School.
St. Philomena Commercial High School, St. Philomena School, 4131 W. Cortland, 60639. Tel: 773-235-0120.
St. Pius V Commercial High School, St. Pius V School, 1919 S. Ashland, 60608. Tel: 312-226-1590.
St. Pius X School (Stickney).
Precious Blood School.
Presentation School.
Presentation-Precious Blood Unit School. Our Lady of the West Side Catholic, Precious Blood Campus, 2401 W. Congress, 60612. Tel: 773-421-6157.
St. Procopius School. (pre 1983).
St. Procopius High School.
Providence Academy & High School, Mother Guerin High School, 8001 Belmont Ave., River Grove, 60171. Tel: 312-625-3278.
Providence of God School and Commercial High School.
Providence-St. Mel High School, 119 S. Central Park Blvd., 60624. Tel: 773-722-4600.
Quigley Preparatory Seminary North.
Quigley Preparatory Seminary South, Archbishop Quigley Preparatory Seminary, 103 E. Chesnut St., 60611. Tel: 321-787-9343.
Quigley Preparatory Seminary. (pre-1961).
St. Raphael (60th St.).
St. Raphael School (60th St.).
Resurrection (Jackson Blvd.). (Church and School).
St. Rita College. St. Rita High School, St. Rita High School, 7740 S. Western Ave., 60620. Tel: 773-925-6600.
St. Rita of Cascia School.
St. Rocco (Chicago Heights). School Records: see Mt. Carmel School.
St. Roman School.
St. Rosalie School (Harwood Heights).
Rosary House High School (River Forest). Trinity High School, 7574 W. Division St., River Forest, 60305. Tel: 708-771-8383.
Rosary College, Dominican University, 7900 W. Division St., River Forest, 60305. Tel: 708-366-2490.
St. Rose of Lima (W. 48th St.).
St. Rose of Lima School.
Sacred Heart (19th St.).
Sacred Heart School & High School (19th St.).
Sacred Heart (70th St.).
Sacred Heart School & High School (70th St.).
Sacred Heart (Oakley Blvd.).
Sacred Heart School (Oakley Blvd.).
Sacred Heart (Church St.), Sacred Heart Mission, 11652 S. Church St., 60643. Tel: 773-233-3955.
Sacred Heart of Jesus (46th St.).
Sacred Heart of Jesus School (46th St.).
Sacred Heart of Jesus High School (46th St.).
Sacred Heart of Mary High School (Arlington Heights), St. Viator High School, 1213 E. Oakton St., Arlington Heights, 60004. Tel: 847-392-4050.
Sacred Heart Seminary (Melrose Park) (Stone Park), Scalabrini Mission Center, 3800 W. Division St., Stone Park, 60165. Tel: 708-345-8270.
St. Salomea (S. Indiana).
St. Salomea School (S. Indiana).
San Callisto Mission.
San Marcello Mission (Evergreen), Immaculate Conception, 1415 N. North Park, 60610. Tel: 312-944-1230.
Santa Lucia Mission. Sacramental Records: Santa Lucia-Santa Maria Incoranata, 3022 S. Wells, 60616. Tel: 312-842-6115. School Records: Santa Lucia School, 3017 S. Wells, 60616. Tel: 312-326-1839.
Santa Maria Incoranata. Sacramental Records: Santa Lucia-Santa Maria Incoranata, 3022 S. Wells, 60616. Tel: 312-842-6115. School Records: Santa Lucia School, 3017 S. Wells, 60616. Tel: 312-326-1839.
Santa Teresita Vicariate (Palatine), Mision Juan Diego, 35 W. Wood St., Palatine, 60067. Tel: 847-358-6337.
St. Sebastian (W. Wellington).
St. Sebastian School & High School.
Servite Seminary (Hillside), Provincial Archives, Servite Provincial Center, 3121 W. Jackson Blvd., 60612. Tel: 773-533-0360.
Seven Holy Founders School (Calumet Park).
Sheil Institute.
Siena High School, McAuley High School, 3737 W. 99th St., 60642. Tel: 773-881-6522.
St. Stanislaus College, Gordon Technical High School, 3633 N. California, 60618. Tel: 773-539-3600.
St. Stanislaus Kostka High School, St. Stanislaus Kostka Elementary, 1255 N. Noble, 60622. Tel: 773-278-4560.
St. Stephen School (22nd Pl.).
St. Stephen Protomartyr School (Des Plaines).
St. Stephen Church (22nd Pl.), St. Stephen Shrine, 2242 S. Wolcott Ave., 60608. Tel: 773-376-4334.
Old St. Stephen (Ohio St.).
Old St. Stephen School (Ohio St.).
St. Susanna (Harvey), Ascension-St. Susanna, 15234 Myrtle, Harvey, 60426-3194. Tel: 708-333-0931.
St. Susanna School (Harvey).
St. Sylvester Commercial High School, St. Sylvester School, 3027 W. Palmer, 60647. Tel: 773-772-5222.
St. Theodore (S. Paulina).
St. Theodore School.
St. Teresa of Avila School.
St. Therese of the Infant Jesus Church (Wood St.).
St. Therese of the Infant Jesus School. See Little Flower School.
St. Thomas Aquinas (Washington Blvd.). (Church and School).
St. Thomas Mission (River Forest), St. Luke, 528 Lathrop, River Forest, 60305. Tel: 708-771-8250.
St. Thomas the Apostle High School, St. Thomas the Apostle School, 5467 S. Woodlawn, 60615. Tel: 773-667-1142.
St. Timothy School.
Unity Catholic High School.
St. Valentine (Cicero).
St. Valentine School (Cicero).
St. Veronica, Resurrection, 2840 W. Nelson, 60618. Tel: 773-478-9705.
St. Veronica School (Whipple St.).
St. Viator High School (Addison). (unknown).
St. Victor High School (Calumet City). (unknown).
Villa Nazareth High School (Des Plaines).
St. Vincent de Paul School.
St. Vincent de Paul Academy. (Girls) (Depaul High School & St. Vincent Academy, location of records unknown).
St. Vincent de Paul High School Seminary (Lemont). St. Mary Seminary, Perryville, MO, 63775. Tel: 314-547-6533.
St. Vincent Orphanage. Client & School Records: Catholic Charities, Division of Services for Children and Youth, 126 N. Des Plaines, 60606. Tel: 312-876-2288; 236-5172, Ext. 330. Sacramental Records: Holy Name Cathedral, 730 N. Wabash, 60611. Tel: 312-787-8040.
St. Vincent Infant Hospital School of Child Care, St. Vincent de Paul Center, 2145 N. Halsted, 60614. Tel: 312-943-6776.
St. Vincent Ferrer Orphanage. (unknown).
Visitation Church (Garfield Blvd.).
St. Basil-Visitation, 5443 S. Honore, 60609. Tel: 773-625-6311.
Visitation Academy (Evanston). see Marywood High School. Records destroyed in flood.
Visitation High School.
St. Vitus at St. Adalbert Parish, 1650 W. 17th St., 60608. Tel: 312-226-0340.
St. Vitus School.
Weber High School, Gordon Technical High School, 3633 N. California Ave., 60618. Tel: 773-539-3600.
St. Wenceslaus School (Monticello St.).
St. Wenceslaus Church (DeKoven St.).
St. Wenceslaus School (DeKoven St.). Unknown.
St. Willibrord (114th St.).
St. Willibrord School (114th St.).
Willibrord Catholic High School.
St. Willibrord High School.
St. Xavier Academy, Mother McAuley High School, 3737 W. 99th St., 60655. Tel: 773-881-6500.

RELIGIOUS INSTITUTES OF MEN REPRESENTED IN THE ARCHDIOCESE

For further details refer to the corresponding bracketed number in the Religious Institutes of Men or Women section.

[0120]—*Alexian Brothers.*—C.F.A.
[0140]—*The Augustinians (Mother of Good Counsel).* Chicago.—O.S.A.
[0200]—*Benedictine Monks.*—O.S.B.
[0330]—*Brothers of the Christian Schools.*—F.S.C.
[0600]—*Brothers of the Congregation of Holy Cross.*—C.S.C.
[0900]—*Canons Regular of Premontre.* (U.S. Circary).—O.Praem.
[0400]—*Canons Regular of the Order of the Holy Cross.* (Prov. of St. Odilia, Minneapolis, MN).—O.S.C.
[0470]—*The Capuchin Friars.*—O.F.M.Cap.
[0270]—*Carmelite Fathers & Brothers.* (Most Pure Heart of Mary).—O.Carm.
[0340]—*Cistercian Fathers.* (Polish Congr.).—O.Cist.
[0360]—*Claretian Missionaries.*—C.M.F.
[1320]—*Clerics of St. Viator.* (Chicago, IL).—C.S.V.
[0380]—*Comboni Missionaries of the Heart of Jesus-Verona.*—M.C.C.J.
[0310]—*Congregation of Christian Brothers.*—C.F.C.
[0750]—*Congregation of Marianhill Missionaries.*—C.M.M.
[0220]—*Congregation of the Blessed Sacrament.* (Rome, Italy).—S.S.S.
[1330]—*Congregation of the Mission.* (Western Prov.).—C.M.
[1210]—*Congregation of the Missionaries of St. Charles.* (Western Prov.).—C.S.
[1000]—*Congregation of the Passion.* (Western Prov.).—C.P.
[1130]—*Congregation of the Priests of the Sacred Heart.*—S.C.J.
[1080]—*Congregation of the Resurrection.* (Chicago Prov.).—C.R.
[0480]—*Conventual Franciscans.* (St. Bonaventure, Our Lady of Consolation Provs.).—O.F.M.Conv.
[0260]—*Discalced Carmelite Friars.*—O.C.D.
[0520]—*Franciscan Friars.* (Sacred Heart, Assumption of B.V.M. Provs.; Commissariats of the Holy Cross, Holy Family).—O.F.M.
[0650]—*Holy Ghost Fathers.* (Eastern Prov.).—C.SS.P.
[0690]—*Jesuit Fathers and Brothers.* (Chicago, Polish, Lithuanian Provs.).—S.J.
[0730]—*Legionnaires of Christ.*—L.C.
[0740]—*Marian Fathers.*—M.I.C.
[0770]—*The Marist Brothers.*—F.M.S.
[0780]—*Marist Fathers.*—S.M.
[0800]—*Maryknoll.*—M.M.
[0830]—*Mill Hill Missionaries.*—M.H.M.
[0860]—*Missionhurst Congregation of the Immaculate Heart of Mary.*—C.I.C.M.
[0910]—*Oblates of Mary Immaculate.*—O.M.I.
[0430]—*Order of Preachers-Dominicans.*—O.P.
[1030]—*Paulist Fathers.* (New York Prov.).—C.S.P.
[0610]—*Priests of the Congregation of Holy Cross.* (Notre Dame, IN).—C.S.C.
[1070]—*Redemptorist Fathers.* (Denver).—C.SS.R.
[1170]—*St. Patrick Missionary Society.*—S.P.S.
[1190]—*Salesians of Don Bosco.*—S.D.B.
[1220]—*Servants of Charity.*—S.C.
[1240]—*Servites.* (Chicago, IL).—O.S.M.
[1260]—*Society of Christ.*—S.Ch.
[0760]—*Society of Mary.*—S.M.
[0850]—*Society of Missionaries of Africa.*—M.Afr.
[0370]—*Society of St. Columban.*—S.S.C.
[1200]—*Society of the Divine Savior.*—S.D.S.
[0420]—*Society of the Divine Word.*—S.V.D.
[1060]—*Society of the Precious Blood.* (Kansas City Prov.).—C.PP.S.
[1360]—*Xaverian Missionary Fathers.*—S.X.

RELIGIOUS INSTITUTES OF WOMEN REPRESENTED IN THE ARCHDIOCESE

[0100]—*Adorers of the Blood of Christ.*—A.S.C.
[0230]—*Benedictine Sisters of Pontifical Jurisdiction.* (Chicago, IL; Duluth, MN).—O.S.B.
[0690]—*Comboni Missionary Sisters.*—C.M.S.
[3110]—*Congregation of Our Lady of the Retreat in the Cenacle.*—R.C.
[1860]—*Congregation of the Handmaids of the Precious Blood.*—H.P.B.
[2100]—*Congregation of the Humility of Mary.*—C.H.M.
[0460]—*Congregation of the Sisters of Charity of the Incarnate Word.*—C.C.V.I.
[3710]—*Congregation of the Sisters of Saint Agnes.*—C.S.A.
[1920]—*Congregation of the Sisters of the Holy Cross.*—C.S.C.
[1780]—*Congregation of the Sisters of the Third Order of St. Francis of Perpetual Adoration.*—F.S.P.A.
[1710]—*Congregation of the Third Order of St. Francis of Mary Immaculate, Joliet, IL.*—O.S.F.
[1730]—*Congregation of the Third Order of St. Francis, Oldenburg, IN.*—O.S.F.
[0760]—*Daughters of Charity of St. Vincent de Paul.*—D.C.
[0793]—*Daughters of Divine Love.*—D.D.L.
[0940]—*Daughters of St. Mary of Providence.*—D.S.M.P.
[0810]—*Daughters of the Heart of Mary.*—D.H.M.
[0420]—*Discalced Carmelite Nuns.*—O.C.D.
[1070-01]—*Dominican Sisters.*—O.P.
[1070-03]—*Dominican Sisters.*—O.P.
[1070-10]—*Dominican Sisters.*—O.P.
[1070-13]—*Dominican Sisters.*—O.P.
[1070-27]—*Dominican Sisters.*—O.P.
[1070-07]—*Dominican Sisters.*—O.P.
[1170]—*Felician Sisters.*—C.S.S.F.
[1370]—*Franciscan Missionaries of Mary.*—F.M.M.
[1210]—*Franciscan Sisters of Chicago.*—O.S.F.
[1230]—*Franciscan Sisters of Christian Charity.*—O.S.F.
[1310]—*Franciscan Sisters of Little Falls, Minnesota.*—O.S.F.
[1415]—*Franciscan Sisters of Mary.*—F.S.M.
[1430]—*Franciscan Sisters of Our Lady of Perpetual Help.*—O.S.F.
[1450]—*Franciscan Sisters of the Sacred Heart.*—O.S.F.
[1240]—*Franciscan Sisters, Daughters of the Sacred Hearts of Jesus and Mary.*—O.S.F.
[2370]—*Institute of the Blessed Virgin Mary (Loretto Sisters).*—I.B.V.M.
[2330]—*Little Sisters of Jesus.*—L.S.J.
[2320]—*Little Sisters of the Holy Family.*—P.S.S.F.
[2340]—*Little Sisters of the Poor.*—L.S.P.
[3570]—*Mantellate Sisters, Servants of Mary of Blue Island.*—O.S.M.
[2420]—*Marist Missionary Sisters.*—S.M.S.M.
[2430]—*Marist Sisters Congregation of Mary.*—S.M.
[2470]—*Maryknoll Sisters of St. Dominic.*—M.M.
[2480]—*Medical Missionaries of Mary.*—M.M.M.
[2680]—*Misericordia Sisters.*—S.M.
[2710]—*Missionaries of Charity.*—M.C.
[2865]—*Missionaries of the Sacred Heart of Jesus and Our Lady of Guadalupe.*—M.S.C.Gpe.
[2790]—*Missionary Servants of the Most Blessed Trinity.*—M.S.B.T.
[2715]—*Missionary Sisters of Christ the King for Polonia.*—M.S.C.K.
[2900]—*Missionary Sisters of St. Charles Borromeo.*—M.S.C.S.
[3990]—*Missionary Sisters of St. Peter Claver.*—S.S.P.C.
[2860]—*Missionary Sisters of the Sacred Heart.*—M.S.C.
[3530]—*Missionary Sisters Servants of the Holy Spirit.*—S.Sp.S.
[3040]—*Oblate Sisters of Providence.*—O.S.P.
[3130]—*Our Lady of Victory Missionary Sisters.*—O.L.V.M.
[0950]—*Pious Society Daughters of St. Paul.*—F.S.P.
[3230]—*Poor Handmaids of Jesus Christ.*—P.H.J.C.
[3440]—*Religious Hospitallers of Saint Joseph.*—R.H.S.J.
[2970]—*School Sisters of Notre Dame.*—S.S.N.D.
[1680]—*School Sisters of St. Francis.*—O.S.F.
[3590]—*Servants of Mary (Servite Sisters).*—O.S.M.
[3520]—*Servants of the Holy Heart of Mary.*—S.S.C.M.
[0440]—*Sisters of Charity of Cincinnati, Ohio.*—S.C.
[0570]—*Sisters of Charity of Seton Hill, Greensburg, Pennsylvania.*—S.C.
[0630]—*Sisters of Charity of St. Vincent de Paul.*—S.V.Z.
[0430]—*Sisters of Charity of the Blessed Virgin Mary.*—B.V.M.
[0660]—*Sisters of Christian Charity.*—S.C.C.
[0990]—*Sisters of Divine Providence.*—C.D.P.
[2360]—*Sisters of Loretto at the Foot of the Cross.*—S.L.
[2575]—*Sisters of Mercy of the Americas.* (Chicago, IL).—R.S.M.
[3000]—*Sisters of Notre Dame de Namur.*—S.N.D.deN.
[3080]—*Sisters of Our Lady Christian Doctrine.*—R.C.D.
[3350]—*Sisters of Providence.*—S.P.
[3360]—*Sisters of Providence of Saint Mary-of-the-Woods, IN.*—S.P.
[1620]—*Sisters of Saint Francis of Millvale, Pennsylvania.*—O.S.F.
[1540]—*Sisters of Saint Francis, Clinton, Iowa.*—O.S.F.
[3780]—*Sisters of Saints Cyril and Methodius.*—SS.C.M.
[3740]—*Sisters of St. Casimir.*—S.S.C.
[1520]—*Sisters of St. Francis of Christ the King.*—O.S.F.
[1640]—*Sisters of St. Francis of Perpetual Adoration.*—O.S.F.
[1570]—*Sisters of St. Francis of the Holy Family.*—O.S.F.
[1800]—*Sisters of St. Francis of the Third Order Regular (Williamsville, New York).*—O.S.F.
[3830-02]—*Sisters of St. Joseph.*—C.S.J.
[3830-15]—*Sisters of St. Joseph.*—C.S.J.
[3840]—*Sisters of St. Joseph of Carondelet.*—C.S.J.
[3930]—*Sisters of St. Joseph of the Third Order of St. Francis.*—S.S.J.-T.O.S.F.
[0260]—*Sisters of the Blessed Sacrament for Indians and Colored People.*—S.B.S.
[2980]—*Sisters of the Congregation de Notre Dame.*—C.N.D.
[1030]—*Sisters of the Divine Savior.*—S.D.S.
[1830]—*Sisters of the Good Shepherd.*—R.G.S.
[1970]—*Sisters of the Holy Family of Nazareth.*—C.S.F.N.
[2110]—*Sisters of the Humility of Mary.*—H.M.
[2140]—*Sisters of the Immaculate Conception of the Blessed Virgin Mary.* (Lithuanian).
[2270]—*Sisters of the Little Company of Mary.*—L.C.M.
[2350]—*Sisters of the Living Word.*—S.L.W.
[3320]—*Sisters of the Presentation of the B.V.M.*—P.B.V.M.
[3480]—*Sisters of the Resurrection.*—C.R.
[1705]—*Sisters of the Third Order of St. Francis of Assisi.*—O.S.F.
[1720]—*Sisters of the Third Order of St. Francis of the Congregation of Our Lady of Lourdes.*—O.S.F.
[2150]—*Sisters, Servants of the Immaculate Heart of Mary.*—I.H.M.
[1890]—*Society of Helpers.*—H.H.S.
[4060]—*Society of the Holy Child Jesus.*—S.H.C.J.
[4070]—*Society of the Sacred Heart.*—R.S.C.J.

ARCHDIOCESAN CEMETERIES

CHICAGO. *Central Office.* Catholic Cemeteries, 1400 S. Wolf Rd., Hillside, 60162-2197. Tel: 708-449-6100; Fax: 708-449-3419.
Web site: www.cathcemchgo.org
Rev. Patrick J. Pollard, Archdiocesan Dir.; Mr. Donald A. Massaro, Exec. Dir.
Mt. Olivet.
St. Boniface.
St. Casimir.
St. Henry.
CALUMET CITY. *Holy Cross.*
CRESTWOOD. *St. Benedict.*
DES PLAINES. *All Saints.*
EVANSTON. *Calvary.*
EVERGREEN PARK. *St. Mary.*
FOX LAKE. *St. Bede.*
FREMONT CENTER. *St. Mary.*
GLENWOOD. *Assumption.*
HIGHLAND PARK. *St. Mary.*
HILLSIDE. *Mt. Carmel.*
Our Lady of Sorrows.
Queen of Heaven.
JUSTICE. *Resurrection.*
LAKE FOREST. *St. Mary.*
LEMONT. *St. Alphonsus.*
St. James, Sag Bridge.
St. Patrick.
SS. Cyril & Methodius.
LIBERTYVILLE. *Ascension.*
NILES. *Maryhill.*
St. Adalbert.
NORTHBROOK. *Sacred Heart.*
OAK FOREST. *St. Gabriel.*
ORLAND PARK. *St. Michael.*
PALATINE. *St. Michael the Archangel.*
PARK FOREST. *St. Anne.*
RIVER GROVE. *St. Joseph.*
ROSENCRANS. *St. Patrick.*
ROUND LAKE. *St. Joseph.*
SAUK VILLAGE. *St. James.*
SKOKIE. *St. Peter.*
STEGER. *Calvary.*
VOLO. *St. Peter.*
WAUCONDA. *Transfiguration.*
WAUKEGAN. *St. Mary.*
WEST LAKE FOREST. *St. Patrick.*
WILMETTE. *St. Joseph.*
WORTH. *Holy Sepulchre.*

NECROLOGY

† Aschenbrenner, George F., (Retired). —Died Dec. 15, 1999.

† Ball, David F., Chap., US Navy. —Died Nov. 26, 1999.
† Barlog, Raymond M., (Retired). —Died Jan. 17, 2000.
† Boreczky, John V., (Retired). —Died Aug. 23, 2000.
† Carton, Leo F., (Retired). —Died Nov. 26, 1999.
† Chess, Rev. Msgr. Edwin R., (Retired). —Died June 13, 2000.
† Connors, Edward P., (Retired). —Died Oct. 25, 2000.
† Curran, John W., (Retired). —Died March 28, 2000.
† Diemer, Charles J., (Retired). —Died Jan. 24, 2000.
† Fealey, Edward J, Orland Park, IL St. Michael. —Died May 26, 2000.
† Garrity, Francis A., (Retired). —Died May 8, 2000.
† Guirsch, Bernard G., (Retired). —Died Dec. 16, 1999.
† Hanlon, Thomas C., (Retired). —Died Dec. 1, 1999.
† Hayes, John E., (Retired). —Died Dec. 25, 1999.
† Janiak, Anthony J., (Retired). —Died Nov. 21, 2000.
† Joyce, Pierce J., (Retired). —Died March 1, 2000.
† Pellicore, Rev. Msgr. Edward M., (Retired). —Died Dec. 28, 1999.
† Schackmuth, William A., (Retired). —Died April 17, 2000.
† Shannon, Robert J., (Retired). —Died July 25, 2000.
† Stanek, Rev. Msgr. Wenceslaus, (Retired). —Died June 24, 2000.
† Sullivan, Cornelius O., (Retired). —Died Oct. 26, 2000.
† Wozny, William J., (Retired). —Died Jan. 31, 2000.

Archdiocese of Cincinnati

(Archidioecesis Cincinnatensis)

Most Reverend

DANIEL E. PILARCZYK, S.T.D., PH.D.

Archbishop of Cincinnati; ordained December 20, 1959; appointed Titular Bishop of Hodelm and Auxiliary Bishop of Cincinnati November 12, 1974; consecrated December 20, 1974; appointed Archbishop of Cincinnati November 2, 1982; installed December 20, 1982. *Res., 100 E. Eighth St., Cincinnati, OH, 45202-2129.*

Most Reverend

CARL K. MOEDDEL, M.A., M.DIV., D.D.

Auxiliary Bishop of Cincinnati; ordained August 15, 1962; appointed Titular Bishop of Bistue and Auxiliary Bishop of Cincinnati August 24, 1993. *Res., 100 E. Eighth St., Cincinnati, OH, 45202-2129.*

ERECTED DIOCESE JUNE 19, 1821; ARCHDIOCESE JULY 19, 1850.

Square Miles 8,543.

Comprises that part of the State of Ohio lying south of 40 degrees, 41 minutes, being the 19 Counties south of the northern line of Mercer, Auglaize, and Logan, all west of the eastern line of Logan, Champaign, Clark, Greene, Clinton, Highland and Adams Counties .

For legal titles of parishes and archdiocesan institutions, consult the Chancery Office.

Archdiocesan Offices: 100 E. Eighth St., Cincinnati, OH, 45202-2129. Tel.: 513-421-3131; Fax: 513-421-6225.

Web site address: www.archdiocese-cinti.org

STATISTICAL OVERVIEW

Personnel	
Archbishop	1
Auxiliary Bishops	1
Priests: Diocesan Active in Diocese	223
Priests: Active Outside Diocese	8
Priests: Diocesan in Foreign Missions	2
Priests: Retired, Sick or Absent	91
Number of Diocesan Priests	324
Religious Priests in Diocese	242
Extern Priests in Diocese	6
Ordinations:	
Diocesan Priests	4
Transitional Deacons	2
Permanent Deacons in Diocese	137
Total Brothers	164
Total Sisters	1,150
Parishes	
Parishes	231
With Resident Pastor:	
Resident Diocesan Priests	167
Resident Religious Priests	28
Without Resident Pastor:	
Administered by Priests	31
Administered by Deacons	1
Administered by Women Religious	3
Administered by Lay People	1
Closed Parishes	1
Professional Ministry Personnel:	
Brothers	6
Sisters	57
Lay Ministers	284
Welfare	
Catholic Hospitals	10
Total Assisted	1,223,000
Health Care Centers	2
Total Assisted	349
Homes for the Aged	13
Total Assisted	2,570
Residential Care of Children	1
Total Assisted	24
Special Centers for Social Services	6
Total Assisted	45,480
Residential Care of Disabled	3
Total Assisted	40
Other Institutions	6
Total Assisted	1,230
Educational	
Seminaries, Diocesan	1
Students from This Diocese	33
Students from Other Diocese	7
Diocesan Students in Other Seminaries	8
Total Seminarians	41
Colleges and Universities	4
Total Students	22,939
High Schools, Diocesan and Parish	10
Total Students	12,934
High Schools, Private	4
Total Students	2,960
Elementary Schools, Diocesan and Parish	109
Total Students	40,356
Elementary Schools, Private	4
Total Students	1,375
Catechesis/Religious Education:	
High School Students	6,689
Elementary Students	34,219
Total Students Under Catholic Instruction	121,513
Teachers in the Diocese:	
Priests	11
Brothers	22
Sisters	96
Lay Teachers	2,975
Vital Statistics	
Receptions into the Church:	
Infant Baptism Totals	8,182
Adult Baptism Totals	982
Received into Full Communion	1,087
First Communions	9,039
Confirmations	8,554
Marriages:	
Catholic	1,769
Interfaith	1,228
Total Marriages	2,997
Deaths	4,712
Total Catholic Population	513,469
Total Population	2,805,557

Former Bishops—Rt. Rev. EDWARD D. FENWICK, O.P., D.D., cons. Jan. 13, 1822; died Sept. 26, 1832.—Most Rev. JOHN BAPTIST PURCELL, D.D., cons. Oct. 13, 1833; appt. Archbishop, July 19, 1850; died July 4, 1883.—Most Rev. WILLIAM HENRY ELDER, D.D., cons. Bishop of Natchez May 3, 1857; appt. Titular Bishop of Avar, and Coadjutor to the Archbishop of Cincinnati *cum jure successionis,* Jan. 30, 1880; succeeded to the See of Cincinnati, July 4, 1883; died Oct. 31, 1904.—Most Rev. HENRY K. MOELLER, D.D., cons. Bishop of Columbus, Aug. 25, 1900; promoted to Archiepiscopal See of Areopolis and made Coadjutor to the Most Rev. WILLIAM HENRY ELDER *cum jure successionis,* April 27, 1903; succeeded to the See of Cincinnati, Oct. 31, 1904; died Jan. 5, 1925.—Most Rev. JOHN T. MCNICHOLAS, O.P., S.T.M., cons. Bishop of Duluth, MN Sept. 8, 1918; promoted to Archiepiscopal See of Cincinnati, July 8, 1925; appt. Assistant at the Pontifical Throne, Feb. 18, 1923; died April 22, 1950.—Most Rev. KARL J. ALTER, D.D., cons. Bishop of Toledo, June 17, 1931; appt. Assistant to the Pontifical Throne, May 30, 1950; elevated to Archbishop of Cincinnati, June 21, 1950; retired July 23, 1969; died Aug. 23, 1977.—Most Rev. PAUL F. LEIBOLD, D.D., J.C.D., appt. Titular Bishop of Trebenna and Auxiliary of Cincinnati, April 10, 1958; cons. June 17, 1958; installed as Bishop of Evansville, June 15, 1966; transferred to Archdiocese of Cincinnati, July 23, 1969; installed Oct. 2, 1969; died June 1, 1972.—His Eminence JOSEPH CARDINAL BERNARDIN, D.D., appt. Titular Bishop of Lugura and Auxiliary Bishop of Atlanta, March 9, 1966; cons. April 26, 1966; appt. Archbishop of Cincinnati, Nov. 21, 1972; installed Dec. 19, 1972; appt. Archbishop of Chicago, July 10, 1982; installed Aug. 25, 1982; created Cardinal Priest, Feb. 2, 1983; died Nov. 14, 1996.

Vicar General—Most Rev. CARL K. MOEDDEL.

Archdiocesan Department Directors—ROBERT DAVIS, Dir., Community Svcs.; Sr. KATHRYN ANN CONNELLY, S.C., Dir., Educational Svcs.; Revs. CHRISTOPHER R. ARMSTRONG, Dir., Exec. Svcs. HOWARD P. PECQUET, Dir., Financial Svcs.; Most Rev. CARL K. MOEDDEL, Dir., Pastoral Svcs.; VINCENT FRASHER, Dir., Personnel Svcs.

Presbyteral Council—Ex Officio Members: Most Rev. DANIEL E. PILARCZYK; Most Rev. CARL K. MOEDDEL. Priest Councilors: Revs. ERWIN J. BERTKE; THOMAS BRENBERGER, C.PP.S.; THOMAS DIEHL, S.J.; MARK J. BURGER; JOHN R. CIVILLE; R. DANIEL CONLON; ALAN HIRT, O.F.M.; THOMAS F. FELDHAUS; JOSEPH W. GOETZ; STANLEY H. NEIHEISEL; JAMES E. SHAPPELLE; THOMAS M. SHEARER; TERRANCE W. SMITH;

PAUL VIESON, S.M.; RICHARD W. WALLING, Seminary Representative.

Vicarri Foranei (Deans)—Rev. JAMES A. BRAMLAGE, Cathedral Deanery; Rev. MICHAEL PUCKE, St. Andrew Deanery; Rev. GILES PATER, St. Francis de Sales Deanery; Rev. EDWARD L. RUDEMILLER, St. Lawrence Deanery; Rev. RAYMOND E. LARGER, St. Margaret Mary Deanery; Rev. JEFFREY P. SILVER, Hamilton Deanery; Rev. JOHN P. FISCHER, St. Martin Deanery; Rev. DAVID E. BRINKMOELLER, Dayton Deanery; Rev. RICHARD M. WALLING, Springfield Deanery; Rev. EUGENE F. VONDERHAAR, Sidney Deanery; Rev. RONALD H. WILKER, St. Mary's Deanery.

Consultors—Most Rev. CARL K. MOEDDEL, Aux. Bishop; Revs. ERWIN J. BERTKE; MARK J. BURGER; JOHN R. CIVILLE; R. DANIEL CONLON; THOMAS F. FELDHAUS; JOSEPH W. GOETZ; STANLEY H. NEIHEISEL; JAMES E. SHAPPELLE; THOMAS M. SHEARER.

Archdiocesan Offices

All Archdiocesan Offices and Directors are located at 100 E. Eighth St., Cincinnati, OH 45202. Tel: 513-421-3131; Fax: 513-421-6225, unless otherwise indicated

Office of the Archbishop—Rev. MALCOLM S. GRAD, Admin. Asst. LINDA CHOUTEAU, Exec. Sec. to the Archbishop; GAYLE SCOTTI, Sec.

Office of Mediation—JOSEPH B. CROWE, Admin. Tel: 513-421-3131, Ext. 408.

Department Of Executive Services

Director—Rev. CHRISTOPHER R. ARMSTRONG.

Chancery—

Chancellor—Rev. CHRISTOPHER R. ARMSTRONG.

Vice Chancellor—Rev. MALCOLM S. GRAD.

Archivist—DON H. BUSKE,(Special Address & Phone No. for Historical Archives Only), *6616 Beechmont Ave., Cincinnati, 45230.* Tel: 513-231-0810.

Censors—Revs. RICHARD L. KLUG; RALPH J. LAWRENCE; ROBERT L. HAGEDORN; CHRISTOPHER R. ARMSTRONG, J.C.L.; TIMOTHY P. SCHEHR; GILES H. PATER; ROBERT A. STRICKER; RICHARD W. WALLING; DAVID L. ZINK; LORENZO RUIZ, Spanish.

Communications Office—DAN ANDRIACCO, Dir.

Newspaper—"The Catholic Telegraph"—Most Rev. DANIEL E. PILARCZYK, Publisher.

Tribunal-Archdiocese of Cincinnati—Tel: 513-421-3131; Fax: 513-723-1035.

Director—Sr. VICTORIA VONDENBERGER, R.S.M., J.C.L.

Judicial Vicar—Rev. EDWIN F. GEARHART, J.C.L.

Adjutant Judicial Vicars—Revs. JOSEPH R. BINZER, J.C.L.; RAYMOND C. KELLERMAN, J.C.L.; BARRY M. WINDHOLTZ.

Judges—Deacon MICHAEL A. ASCOLESE; Rev. Msgr. LAWRENCE K. BRESLIN; Revs. CHRISTOPHER R. ARMSTRONG, J.C.L.; MICHAEL D. BEATTY; JAMES A. BRAMLAGE; JOHN L. CAVANAUGH, J.C.D.; DENNIS J. CAYLOR, J.C.L.; R. DANIEL CONLON, J.C.D.; J. RAYMOND FAVRET; DAVID E. FAY; JOHN P. FISCHER; MICHAEL T. FLAHERTY; GERALD R. HAEMMERLE; TIMOTHY S. KALLAHER; RICHARD L. KLUG; EMIL J. LABBE, J.C.D.; FRANCIS G. LAMMEIER; NORMAN W. LANGENBRUNNER; RALPH J. LAWRENCE; WALTER J. MACPHERSON; THOMAS C. NOLKER; ROBERT A. OBERMEYER; EDWARD L. RUDEMILLER; OSCAR H. SEGER; R. MARC SHERLOCK; TERRENCE W. SMITH; THOMAS A. SNODGRASS, J.C.L.; LAWRENCE R. STRITTMATTER; LARRY P. THARP; FRANCIS W. VOELLMECKE; EUGENE F. VONDERHAAR; JOHN R. WHITE, J.C.L.

Defenders of the Bond—Revs. HERMAN H. KENNING; WILLIAM H. WYSONG, J.C.L.; Sr. VICTORIA VONDENBERGER, R.S.M., J.C.L.

Promoter of Justice—Sr. VICTORIA VONDENBERGER, R.S.M., J.C.L.

Assessors—Mrs. ELVA E. BRUNNER; Mrs. KELLY M. TERRY.

Auditors—Ms. CHRISTINE M. GATELY; Mrs. CANDY L. ENGELKE; Mrs. BETTY L. MEDER; Mrs. AMI R. TENNER.

Secretary / Auditor—Mrs. PAMELA J. JASPERS.

Department Of Community Services

Director—ROBERT DAVIS.

Archdiocesan Office of Catholic Charities—RAYMOND F. EGAN, Dir.

Association of Ladies of Charity—LENORA WRIGHT, Pres. Tel: 513-421-3131.

Catholic Federation for the Mentally Retarded—DONALD MINK, Pres. Tel: 513-741-9689.

Catholic Residential Services of the Archdiocese of Cincinnati with People with Mental Retardation—Legal Title: Catholic Residential Services of Archdiocese of Cincinnati with People with Mental Retardation. Ms. CHRISTINE HOEKZEMA, Dir., *100 E. Eighth St., Cincinnati, 45202.* Tel: 513-241-7745; Fax: 513-241-4333.

Catholic Social Services of Hamilton—JUDITH FULCHER, Exec. Dir., *140 N. Fifth St., Hamilton, 45011.* Tel: 513-863-6129.

Catholic Social Services of Miami Valley—RONALD A. ECKERLE, Exec. Dir., *922 W. Riverview Dr., Dayton, 45407.* Tel: 513-223-7217.

Catholic Social Services of Southwest Ohio—RAYMOND F. EGAN, Exec. Dir. Tel: 513-241-7745.

Catholic Social Services of Springfield—VINCENT CHASE, Exec. Dir., *641 High St., Springfield, 45505.* Tel: 513-325-8715.

Cemeteries—ROBERT DAVIS, Dir. IRWIN BENKIN, Asst. Dir., *11000 Montgomery Rd., Cincinnati, 45242.* Tel: 513-489-0300.

Ecumenical and Interfaith Relations—LOUISE VERA, Program Coord.

St. Vincent de Paul Society—MARK CASELLA, Pres.; Rev. HERMAN KENNING, Spiritual Dir.; (See Special Listing: St. Vincent de Paul Society).

Health Affairs—ROBERT DAVIS. Tel: 513-241-7745.

Rural Life Conference—BRIAN HENTIES, *266 Bainbridge St., Dayton, 45402.* Tel: 513-224-3026.

Social Action and World Peace—BRIAN HENTIES, Exec. Dir. *Dayton Office*, Vacant, Assoc. Dir., *266 Bainbridge St., Dayton, 45402.* Tel: 513-224-3026.

Department Of Educational Services

Director—Sr. KATHRYN ANN CONNELLY, S.C.

School Office—Sr. KATHRYN ANN CONNELLY, S.C., Supt., Schools, Dayton North, *100 E. Eighth St., Cincinnati, 45202.* Tel: 513-421-3131. Ms. ANNE BATTES KIRBY, Deputy Supt., *Dayton Catholic Schools Office, 266 Bainbridge St., Dayton, 45402.* Tel: 937-223-5151.

Religious Education Office—KENNETH GLEASON, Archdiocesan Dir. DAVID RILEY, Regl. Dir., *226 Bainbridge St., Dayton, 45402.* Tel: 513-223-4075. *Sidney*, JANE PIERRON, Regl. Dir., *401-A S. Main St., Sidney, 45365.* Tel: 513-498-1192.

Department Of Financial Services

Treasurer & Director—HOWARD P. PECQUET.

Office of Property Management-Central Services—GARY RAFFEL, Dir.

Office for Financial Development—JOAN SCHROEDER, Dir.

Department Of Pastoral Services

Director—Most Rev. CARL K. MOEDDEL.

Campus Ministry—Dr. JANE STEINHAUSER, Dir., *444 W. Third St., Dayton, 45402.* (See Special Listing: Campus Ministry).

African American Catholic Ministries—GEORGE C. FINDLEY, Dir.

Family Life—MARGARET BLACK, Dir. *Dayton:* MARY EHRET, Assoc. Dir., *266 Bainbridge St., Dayton, 45402.* Tel: 513-222-0227. *Northern Area:* VELMA JEAN BORGERT, *401-A S. Main St., Sidney, 45365.* Tel: 513-492-4449.

Missions—

Pontifical Mission Aid Societies—Most Rev. CARL K. MOEDDEL.

Missions Office—ARCHIE BRUUN, Dir., *100 E. Eighth St., Cincinnati, 45202.*

Pastoral Council Secretariat—Rev. MALCOLM S. GRAD, Exec. Sec.

Hispanic Catholic Ministry, Dayton—Rev. WILLIAM JANSEN, M.C.C.J., Regl. Dir., *266 Bainbridge St., Dayton, 45402.* Tel: 513-222-1340.

Archdiocesan Office of Hispanic Ministry—Rev. JOSEPH NELSON, O.F.M., Dir., *115 W. Seymour Ave., Cincinnati, 45216.* Tel: 513-761-1588.

Planning and Research—Vacant.

Worship—Rev. LAWRENCE R. TENSI, Dir.

Youth—Mr. SEAN REYNOLDS, Dir., *100 East Eighth St., Cincinnati, 45202.* Tel: 513-421-3131. TIMOTHY E. COLBERT, Regl. Dir.; *Dayton & Northern Area: 266 Bainbridge St., Dayton, 45402.* Tel: 513-223-1001.

Department of Personnel Services

Director—VINCENT FRASHER.

Office of Religious—Sr. MARY GARKE, C.PP.S., Dir.

Permanent Diaconate Office—BERNARD J. MERSMANN.

Personnel Office for Archdiocesan Administrative Offices—VINCE FRASHER, Dir.

Priestly Formation—Rev. THOMAS P. DI FOLCO, Dir.

Priests' Personnel Director—Most Rev. CARL K. MOEDDEL, Dir.

Vocations Office—Rev. MARK T. WATKINS, Dir.

CLERGY, PARISHES, MISSIONS AND PAROCHIAL SCHOOLS

GREATER CINCINNATI (HAMILTON COUNTY)

1—ST. PETER IN CHAINS CATHEDRAL (1822), Revs. James A. Bramlage; Thomas A. Snodgrass. In res., Rev. Mark T. Watkins.
Res., 325 W. Eighth St., 45202. Tel: 513-421-5354; Fax: 513-241-9517.
Church—Eighth & Plum St., 45202.

2—ST. AGNES (Bond Hill) (1892) (African American), Rev. Thomas P. DiFolco; Sr. M. Jerome Buchert, O.S.U., Pastoral Admin.
Res., 1619 California Ave., 45237. Tel: 513-242-4747; Fax: 513-242-4748.
Catechesis / Religious Programs—Students 26.

3—ALL SAINTS (Kenwood) (1948), Rev. J. Dennis Jaspers; Mrs. Jennifer Cmar, Pastoral Assoc.; Hector Rios, Business Mgr.
Res., 8939 Montgomery Rd., 45236. Tel: 513-791-6351; Fax: 513-792-4730.
School—Tel: 513-792-4732; Fax: 513-792-7990. Mrs. Mary E. Stratford, Prin.
Sisters of Charity 1; Lay Teachers 25; Students 492.
Catechesis / Religious Programs—Tel: 513-791-6351, Ext. 103; Fax: 513-792-4730. Mrs. Wilma McGlasson, D.R.E.
Students 210.

4—ST. ALOYSIUS GONZAGA (Bridgetown) (1866), Rev. Paul Rehling; Sr. Josetta Boeing, S.C., Pastoral Assoc.; Deacon Jerry Schneider. In res., Revs. Godfred Boachie-Yiadom (Ghana); George Schmitz.
Res., 4366 Bridgetown Rd., 45211. Tel: 513-574-4840; Fax: 513-574-4402.
School—4390 Bridgetown Rd., 45211. Tel: 513-574-4035; Fax: 513-574-4402. Mrs. Bernadine Stone, Prin.
Lay Teachers 19; Students 340.
Catechesis / Religious Programs—Tel: 513-574-4840; Fax: 513-574-4402. Ms. Kathy Robinson, D.R.E.
Students 125.

5—ST. ALOYSIUS-ON-THE-OHIO (1873), Rev. Donald R. Rettig.
Res., 134 Whipple St., 45233. Tel: 513-941-3445; Fax: 513-941-2257.
School—6207 Portage, 45233. Tel: 513-941-7831; Fax: 513-941-2257.
Lay Teachers 12; Students 184.
Catechesis / Religious Programs—Tel: 513-941-3445; Fax: 513-941-2257.
Students 45.

6—ST. ANDREW (1874), Rev. Terence A. Meehan.
3401 Reading Rd., P.O. Box 29064, 45229. Tel: 513-281-7504; Fax: 513-281-7504.

7—ST. ANN (Groesbeck) (1953), Revs. Thomas J. Dennemann; William Jansen, M.C.C.J.
Res., 2900 Galbraith Rd., 45239. Tel: 513-521-8440; Fax: 513-521-7221.
School—2940 W. Galbraith Rd., 45239. Tel: 513-931-3070; Fax: 513-931-3071. Marriane Rosemond, Prin.
Lay Teachers 22; Students 400.
Catechesis / Religious Programs—Tel: 513-729-2180. Diane C. Ferrier, D.R.E.
Students 200.

8—ANNUNCIATION OF THE BLESSED VIRGIN MARY (1910), Rev. Richard L. Klug. In res., Rev. Edward G. Trippel.
Res., 3547 Clifton Ave., 45220. Tel: 513-861-1295; Fax: 513-281-8009.
School—3545 Clifton Ave., 45220. Tel: 513-221-1230; Fax: 513-281-8009. Sr. Lawrence Sickman, O.S.U., Prin.
Lay Teachers 11; Students 190.
Catechesis / Religious Programs—Tel: 513-861-1295.
Students 48.

9—ST. ANTHONY (Madisonville) (1858), Rev. Leonard C. Wenke; Sr. Jean Masterson, C.S.J., Pastoral Assoc.
Res., 6104 Desmond St., 45227. Tel: 513-271-0920; Fax: 513-271-6630. [CEM]
School—See St. John Vianney Cure of Ars. Tel: 513-271-5510.
Catechesis / Religious Programs—Tel: 513-271-0920. Rita Balcom, D.R.E.
Students 133.

10—ST. ANTONINUS (1944), Revs. Donald G. McCarthy; Lawrence Mick; Deacon William Petrie.
Res., 1500 Linneman Rd., 45238. Tel: 513-922-5400; Fax: 513-451-5871.
School—5425 Julmar Dr., 45238. Tel: 513-922-2500; Fax: 513-922-5519. Mr. James Leisring, Prin.
Lay Teachers 28; Students 559.
Catechesis / Religious Programs—Tel: 513-922-4759. Deacon Robert Schroeder, D.R.E.
Students 48.

11—ASSUMPTION OF THE BLESSED VIRGIN MARY (Walnut Hills) (1872), Rev. Thomas Bokenkotter.
Res., 2622 Gilbert Ave., 45206. Tel: 513-961-3242; 271-0016.

12—ASSUMPTION (Mount Healthy) (1854), Revs. William M. Kennedy; John R. Kummer.
Res., 7711 Joseph St., 45231. Tel: 513-521-7274; Fax: 513-521-3728. [CEM]
School—1500 McMakin Ave., Mt. Healthy, 45231. Tel: 513-522-0071; Fax: 513-728-4946. William J. Walborn, Prin.
Lay Teachers 18; Students 345.
Catechesis/Religious Programs—Tel: 513-728-4953. Sr. Marietta Sharkey, O.S.F., D.R.E.
Students 77.

13—ST. BARTHOLOMEW (1961), Rev. Robert J. Farrell; Lawrence Ungerer, Pastoral Assoc.; Skip Borgman, Business Mgr. In res., Deacon Conrad Kolis.
Res., 9375 Winton Rd., 45231. Tel: 513-522-3680; Fax: 513-728-3141.
School—St. Bartholomew Consolidated School. See separate listing. Tel: 513-521-0860; Fax: 513-728-3110.
Catechesis/Religious Programs—Jenny Luchsinger, D.R.E.
Students 105.

14—ST. BERNARD (1919), Revs. James Shappelle; Michael Paraniuk.
Res., 740 Circle Ave., 45232. Tel: 513-541-3732; Fax: 513-541-0362.
Catechesis/Religious Programs—Students 49.

15—ST. BERNARD (Taylor's Creek) (1867), Rev. Stanley D. Doerger.
Res., 7130 Harrison Rd., 45247. Tel: 513-353-4207; Fax: 513-353-9600.
School—Tel: 513-353-4224; Fax: 513-353-3958.
Lay Teachers 13; Students 264.
Catechesis/Religious Programs—Students 101.

16—ST. BONAVENTURE (1869), Rev. Edwin F. Gearhart; Sr. Joseph Marion Shappelle, S.C., Pastoral Assoc.
Res., 1798 Queen City Ave., 45214. Tel: 513-921-2547; Fax: 513-921-2548.
Chapel—Cincinnati, San Antonio di Padova. (Italian). Tel: 513-921-6411.

17—ST. BONIFACE (1863), Rev. Joseph A. Robinson; Deacon Ted Schmidt.
Res., 1750 Chase Ave., 45223. Tel: 513-541-1563; Fax: 513-541-3939.
School—St. Boniface Consolidated. See separate listing. Tel: 513-541-5122.
Catechesis/Religious Programs—Students 10.

18—ST. CATHARINE (1903), Rev. Robert E. Schmitz; Deacon Thomas Gargan; Therese Bower Hibdon, Pastoral Min.
Res., 2848 Fischer Pl., P.O. Box 111115, 45211. Tel: 513-661-0651; Fax: 513-661-0652.
School—3324 Wunder Ave., 45211. Tel: 513-481-7683; Fax: 513-661-0652. Harry Meyer, Prin.
Lay Teachers 21; Students 428.
Catechesis/Religious Programs—Tel: 513-661-0651.
Students 50.

19—ST. CECILIA (Oakley) (1908), Rev. Elmer W. Smith; Deacon John Slattery.
Res., 3105 Madison Rd., 45209. Tel: 513-871-5757; Fax: 513-533-6066.
School—4115 Taylor Ave., 45209. Tel: 513-533-6060; Fax: 513-533-6068. Ms. Lori Heffner, Prin.
Lay Teachers 12; Students 208.
Catechesis/Religious Programs—Billie Jean Schimian, D.R.E.
Students 35.
Parish Center—4030 Gilmore Ave., 45209. Tel: 513-553-6067.

20—ST. CLARE (College Hill) (1908), Rev. George Jacquemin. In res., Rev. Robert J. Hater.
Res., 1443 Cedar Ave., 45224. Tel: 513-541-2100; Fax: 513-541-2101.
School—5800 Salvia Ave., 45224. Tel: 513-541-5751. Mrs. Michael Kirry, Prin.
Catechesis/Religious Programs—Tel: 513-541-2100.
Students 120.

21—ST. CLEMENT (St. Bernard) (1850), Revs. E. John Stein, O.F.M.; Carl J. Langenderfer, O.F.M.; Bro. Joel Soldenski, O.F.M., Pastoral Assoc.
Res., St. Clement Friary, 4536 Vine St., 45217. Tel: 513-641-3176; 641-2257 (Friary); Fax: 513-641-2262.
School—4534 Vine St., 45217. Tel: 513-641-2137; Fax: 513-242-6036. Mrs. Cathy Stovex, Prin., Tel: 513-641-2137, Ext. 802.
Sisters 2; Lay Teachers 15; Students 250.
Catechesis/Religious Programs—Fax: 513-641-0149. Colleen Gerke, D.R.E., Tel: 513-641-2137, Ext. 808.
Students 51.

22—CORPUS CHRISTI (1958), Revs. Don Holtgrewe, O.F.M.; Bruno Kremp, O.F.M. In res., Revs. Jeremy Harrington, O.F.M.; Thomas Speier, O.F.M.; Connie Leyendecker, Business Mgr.
Res., 2014 Springdale Rd., 45231. Tel: 513-825-0618; Fax: 513-825-0182.
School—St. Bartholomew Consolidated. See separate listing. Tel: 513-521-0860; Fax: 513-728-3110.
Catechesis/Religious Programs—Tel: 513-825-0182. Barbara Conway, D.R.E.
Students 195.

23—ST. DOMINIC (Delhi Hills) (1933), Revs. James J. Walsh; Gregory J. Konerman; Donald A. Behler, (Retired).
Res., 4551 Delhi Pike, 45238. Tel: 513-471-7741; Fax: 513-471-0363.
School—371 Pedretti Ave., 45238. Tel: 513-251-1276; Fax: 513-251-6428. Sr. Patrick Ann O'Connor, S.C., Prin.
Sisters 2; Lay Teachers 31; Students 711.
Catechesis/Religious Programs—Students 186.

24—ST. FRANCIS SERAPH (1859), Rev. Edward Slater, O.F.M.; Bros. Josef Anderlohr, O.F.M.; Ronald Bolfeta, O.F.M.
Res., St. Francis Friary, 1615 Vine St., 45210. Tel: 513-721-4700; Fax: 513-421-9672.
School—14 E. Liberty St., 45210. Tel: 513-721-7778; Fax: 513-721-5445. Ms. Wanda W. Hill, Prin.
Sisters 2; Lay Teachers 11; Students 155.

25—ST. FRANCIS DE SALES (1849), Rev. Edward M. Jach, S.M.; Bro. David Betz, S.M.
Res., 1600 Madison Rd., 45206. Tel: 513-961-1945; Fax: 513-221-4907. [CEM]
School—Tel: 513-961-1953; Fax: 513-221-4907. Sr. Carol Ann Wenning, R.S.M., Prin.
Brothers 1; Sisters 1; Lay Teachers 10; Students 211.

26—ST. FRANCIS XAVIER (1819), Revs. Robert J. Thesing, S.J.; Paul A. Huber, S.J.; Donald O. Nastold, S.J.; Carl J. Moell, S.J.; Robert C. O'Connor, S.J.; Mr. Thomas Choquette, Pastoral Assoc.
Res., 607 Sycamore St., 45202. Tel: 513-721-4045; Fax: 513-723-0451.

27—ST. GABRIEL (Glendale) (1857), Rev. David E. Fay; Sr. Mary Doeker, O.S.U., Pastoral Assoc.; Deacons Herman H. Bryant; James Sonnenberg.
Res., 48 W. Sharon Ave., 45246. Tel: 513-771-4700; Fax: 513-612-4545.
School—St. Gabriel Consolidated School. See separate listing. Tel: 513-771-5220; Fax: 513-771-5133.
Catechesis/Religious Programs—Sr. Charlotte Foppe, R.S.M., D.R.E.
Students 65.

28—ST. GERTRUDE (Madeira) (1923), Revs. Kenneth R. Letoile, O.P.; Walter Wagner, O.P., Novice Master; R. Emmanuel Betrand, O.P.; J. Benedict Croell, O.P.; Brendan Murphy, O.P. In res., Rev. J. Vincent Watson, O.P.
Res., 7630 Shawnee Run Rd., 45243. Tel: 513-561-5954; Fax: 513-527-3971.
School—6551 Miami Ave., 45243. Tel: 513-561-8020; Fax: 513-561-7184. Sr. Maria Christi, O.P., Prin.
Dominican Sisters (Nashville, TN) 3; Lay Teachers 18; Students 445.
Catechesis/Religious Programs—Tel: 513-561-8369.
Students 521.

29—GOOD SHEPHERD (1973), Revs. Thomas R. Axe; Michael F. Leshney; Deacon Raymond Grismer. Pastoral Assocs.: Sr. Terry Maher, C.PP.S.; Donald S. Kruse; Stephen P. Lindner; Patricia Lindner; Elmer H. Fischesser; Scott Mussari; Mary Lee Rossbach; Jeanie Wolf.
Res., 8815 East Kemper Rd., 45249. Tel: 513-489-8815; Fax: 513-489-8521.
Catechesis/Religious Programs—Students 1,088.

30—GUARDIAN ANGELS (Mt. Washington) (1892), Revs. Thomas C. Nolker; Patrick J. Welsh; Deacon Rick Novick. In res., Rev. Carl J. Wollering.
Res., 6531 Beechmont Ave., 45230. Tel: 513-231-7440; Fax: 513-624-3145.
School—6539 Beechmont Ave., 45230. Tel: 513-624-3141; Fax: 513-624-3145. Mr. David A. Reker, Prin.
Lay Teachers 45; Students 853.
Catechesis/Religious Programs—Tel: 513-624-3146.
Students 350.

31—HOLY ANGELS (1859). Merged with St. Francis de Sales, Cincinnati.

32—HOLY CROSS-IMMACULATA (Mount Adams) (1859), Rev. Stanley H. Neiheisel.
Res., 30 Guido St., 45202. Tel: 513-721-6544; Fax: 513-721-6177.

33—HOLY FAMILY (Price Hill) (1883). Includes the consolidation of Our Lady of Grace, Our Lady of Perpetual Help Parishes, Blessed Sacrament and St. Michael. Rev. Mark J. Burger.
Res., 814 Hawthorne Ave., 45205. Tel: 513-921-7527; Fax: 513-921-6033.
School—(Grades K-8) 3001 Price Ave., 45205. Tel: 513-921-8483; Fax: 513-921-2460. Sr. Brenda Busch, S.C., Prin.
Sisters 5; Lay Teachers 5; Students 165.
Catechesis/Religious Programs—Students 214.

34—HOLY NAME (1904), Rev. Terence A. Meehan; Sr. Mary Gallagher, S.C., Pastoral Admin.
Res., 2448 Auburn Ave., 45219. Tel: 513-721-5608.

35—HOLY TRINITY CHURCH (Norwood) (1994), Revs. Raymond C. Kellerman; Edward F. Haskamp.
Res., 2420 Drex Ave., 45212. Tel: 513-366-4400; Fax: 513-366-4404.
School—Holy Trinity School, Tel: 513-366-4406; Fax: 513-366-4420.
Lay Teachers 19; Students 317.
Catechesis/Religious Programs—Tel: 513-366-4400; Fax: 513-366-4404.
Students 20.

36—ST. IGNATIUS LOYOLA (Monfort Heights) (1946), Rev. Thomas L. Bolte; Barb Campbell, Business Mgr. In res., Rev. Thomas A. Nevels.
Res., 5222 N. Bend Rd., 45247. Tel: 513-661-6565; Fax: 513-389-3241.
School—Tel: 513-389-3242; Fax: 513-389-3255. Timothy Reilly, Prin.
Lay Teachers 33; Students 801.
Catechesis/Religious Programs—Tel: 513-389-3247. Kris Schoettmer, D.R.E.
Students 155.

37—IMMACULATE HEART OF MARY (Forestville) (1944), Revs. Jan Kevin Schmidt; Patrick L. Sheridan; Deacons Jerry Etienne; Gene Miller; Bill Mullaney; Dave Shea.
Res., 7820 Beechmont Ave., 45255. Tel: 513-474-5570; Fax: 513-388-4097.
School—Tel: 513-388-4086; Fax: 513-388-4097. Mr. Jay McNitt, Prin.
Brothers 1; Lay Teachers 23; Students 673.
Catechesis/Religious Programs—Tel: 513-388-4093; Fax: 513-388-4097. D.R.E.: Leisa Anslinger; Nancy McCafferty, (Youth Formation).
Students 811.

38—ST. JAMES THE GREATER (White Oak) (1843), Revs. Raymond E. Larger; James A. Simons; Sr. Joan Roach, O.S.U., Pastoral Assoc.; Deacon Paul J. Kluener.
Res., 3565 Hubble Rd., 45247. Tel: 513-741-5300; Fax: 513-741-5302. [CEM]
School—6111 Cheviot Rd., 45247. Tel: 513-741-5333; Fax: 513-741-5312. Aloysius H. Grote, Prin.
Lay Teachers 50; Students 1,151.
Catechesis/Religious Programs—Tel: 513-741-5335; Fax: 513-741-5302.
Students 105.

39—ST. JAMES OF THE VALLEY (Wyoming) (1886), Revs. James R. Collins; James E. Ulrich.
Res., 411 Springfield Pk., 45215. Tel: 513-948-1218; Fax: 513-948-1225.
School—Tel: 513-821-9054. Mrs. Angela Siddall, Prin.
Lay Teachers 12; Students 208.
Catechesis/Religious Programs—Mrs. Jeanne Hunt, D.R.E.
Students 231.

40—ST. JEROME (1853), Rev. Carl J. Wollering.
Church—131 Rohde St., 45228.
Res., 5858 Kellogg Ave., 45228. Tel: 513-231-7042; Fax: 513-231-7042.
Catechesis/Religious Programs—Guardian Angels, 6531 Beechmont Ave., 45230. Tel: 513-624-3146; Fax: 513-624-3145.
Students 32.

41—ST. JOHN THE BAPTIST (Dry Ridge) (1860), Rev. Timothy S. Kallaher.
Res., 5361 Dry Ridge Rd., 45252. Tel: 513-385-8010; Fax: 513-385-8080. [CEM]
School—5375 Dry Ridge Rd., 45252. Tel: 513-385-7970; Fax: 513-385-5554. Mr. Thomas Bailey, Prin.
Sisters 2; Lay Teachers 22; Students 505.
Catechesis/Religious Programs—Tel: 513-385-6239.
Students 125.

42—ST. JOHN THE BAPTIST (Harrison) (1851), Rev. Edward J. Shine.
Res., 110 N. Hill St., Harrison, 45030. Tel: 513-367-9086; Fax: 513-367-6864. [CEM]
School—Tel: 513-367-6826.
Sisters 1; Lay Teachers 26; Students 422.
Catechesis/Religious Programs—Tel: 513-367-9878.
Students 340.

43—ST. JOHN THE EVANGELIST (1891), Rev. Thomas Espelage; Jerry Jones, Business Mgr.
Res., 7121 Plainfield Rd., 45236. Tel: 513-791-3238; Fax: 513-791-3520.
School—7131 Plainfield Rd., 45236. Tel: 513-791-6283; Fax: 513-791-6345. Patricia Sand, Prin.

Lay Teachers 17; Students 220.
Catechesis/Religious Programs—Chris Schell, D.R.E.
Students 65.

44—ST. JOHN FISHER (Newtown) (1947), Rev. Giles H. Pater.
Office: 3227 Church St., 45244. Tel: 513-561-9431; Fax: 513-561-7513.
Res., 3211 Church St., 45244. Tel: 513-271-4904.

45—ST. JOHN VIANNEY (Madison Pl.) (1949), Revs. Paul J. Edrich; William H. Cross.
Res., 4448 Berwick, 45227. Tel: 513-271-5490; Fax: 513-271-5490.
School—Cure of Ars, Tel: 513-271-5510; Fax: 513-271-0205.
Lay Teachers 9; Students 130.
Catechesis/Religious Programs—Tel: 513-272-6347.
Students 24.

46—ST. JOHN NEUMANN (Springfield Township) (1978), Rev. Robert C. Waller. Pastoral Assocs.: Sr. Adria Connors, C.S.C.; Deacon John R. Gobbi.
Res., 12191 Mill Rd., 45240. Tel: 513-742-0953; Fax: 513-742-5875.
School—St. Bartholomew Consolidated. See separate listing. Tel: 513-521-0860.
Catechesis/Religious Programs—Tel: 513-742-0953.
Students 283.

47—ST. JOSEPH (1846) (African American), Rev. Philip O. Seher; Deacon Raphael Simmons.
Res., 745 Ezzard Charles Dr., 45203. Tel: 513-381-4526; Fax: 513-381-5244.
School—Tel: 513-381-2126; Fax: 513-381-6513. Sr. Carol Ann Mause, O.S.F., Prin.
Lay Teachers 15; Students 200.
Catechesis/Religious Programs—Bro. Rey Taylor, C.F.P., D.R.E.
Students 80.

48—ST. JOSEPH (North Bend) (1860), Rev. Harry J. Gerdes.
Mailing Address: P.O. Box 219, 45052.
Res., 25 E. Harrison Ave., 45052. Tel: 513-941-3661; Fax: 513-941-8559.
Catechesis/Religious Programs—Susan K. Rensing, D.R.E.
Students 162.

49—ST. JUDE THE APOSTLE (1956), Revs. Richard E. Dressman; W. Michael Hay; Deacon James Sunderman.
Res., 5924 Bridgetown Rd., 45248. Tel: 513-574-1230; Fax: 513-598-2109.
School—5940 Bridgetown Rd., 45248. Tel: 513-598-2100; Fax: 513-598-2118. Joan Axt, Prin.
Lay Teachers 26; Students 486.
Catechesis/Religious Programs—Tel: 513-598-2100, Ext. 30; Fax: 513-598-2109.
Students 230.

50—ST. LAWRENCE (Price Hill) (1868), Rev. Ralph A. Westerhoff; Sr. Helen Julia Hahn, S.C., Pastoral Assoc. In res., Rev. Erwin J. Bertke.
Res., 3680 Warsaw Ave., 45205. Tel: 513-921-0328; Fax: 513-921-5108.
School—1020 Carson Ave., 45205. Tel: 513-921-4996. Mrs. Alma Lee Joesting, Prin.
Lay Teachers 20; Students 306.
Catechesis/Religious Programs—Students 388.

51—ST. LEO THE GREAT (1886), Rev. Edwin F. Gearhart.
Res., 2573 St. Leo Pl., 45225. Tel: 513-921-0025; Fax: 513-921-8048.
School—St. Boniface Consolidated. See separate listing. Tel: 513-541-5122; Fax: 513-541-3939.
Catechesis/Religious Programs—Students 36.

52—ST. LOUIS (1870), Rev. Christopher R. Armstrong; Sr. Mary William Luxford, O.S.U., Pastoral Assoc.
Res., 29 E. Eighth St., 45202-2086. Tel: 513-263-6621; Fax: 513-333-0579.

53—ST. MARGARET OF CORTONA (Madisonville) (1921), Rev. Leonard Fecko; Deacon William Aufderheide.
Res., 4100 Watterson St., 45227. Tel: 513-271-0856; Fax: 513-271-1513.
School—4100 Simpson Ave., 45227. Tel: 513-271-8288; Fax: 513-272-1740. Mrs. Judy Szilagyi, Prin.
Sisters 1; Lay Teachers 10; Students 143.
Catechesis/Religious Programs—Students 18.
Convent—Tel: 513-271-1956. Sisters of Mercy

54—ST. MARGARET MARY (North College Hill) (1920), Revs. John E. Wall; David Lucas; Deacon Raymond S. Burger.
Res., 1830 W. Galbraith Rd., 45239. Tel: 513-521-7387; Fax: 513-521-7388.
School—1820 W. Galbraith Rd., 45239. Tel: 513-521-8619; Fax: 513-521-8620. Kathy Sparks, Prin.
Lay Teachers 24; Students 341.
Catechesis/Religious Programs—Tel: 513-729-1551. Al Cuchetti, D.R.E.
Students 437.

55—ST. MARK (1904), Rev. Jerry Steinbrunner, C.PP.S.; Bro. Hugh Henderson, C.PP.S., Pastoral Assoc.
Res., 3500 Montgomery Rd., 45207. Tel: 513-961-0472; Fax: 513-961-0492.
School—1712 Duck Creek Rd., 45207. Tel: 513-751-3257; Fax: 513-751-6652. Mr. Michael Murdock, Prin.
Lay Teachers 7; Students 130.

56—ST. MARTIN OF TOURS (Cheviot) (1911), Revs. George C. Kunkel; Ronald J. Piepmeyer; Robert Mick; Deacon Howard R. Wiehe.
Res., 3720 St. Martin Pl., 45211. Tel: 513-661-2000; Fax: 513-661-1432.
School—3729 Harding Ave., 45211. Tel: 513-661-7609; Fax: 513-661-8102. Mrs. Kathryn Lawrence, Prin.
Sisters 1; Lay Teachers 21; Students 461.
Catechesis/Religious Programs—Students 60.

57—ST. MARTIN DE PORRES (Lincoln Heights) (1935) (African American), Rev. Thomas P. DiFolco.
Res., 9927 Wayne Ave., 45215. Tel: 513-554-4010; Fax: 513-554-4191.
School—St. Gabriel Consolidated School. See separate listing. Tel: 513-771-5220.
Catechesis/Religious Programs—Students 15.

58—OLD ST. MARY (1842), Rev. Albert Lauer.
Res., 123 E. 13th St., 45210. Tel: 513-721-2988; Fax: 513-721-2988.

59—ST. MARY (Hyde Park) (1898), Rev. David C. Robisch; Deacon John Thamann. Pastoral Assocs.: Mr. Michael Kleshock; Mrs. Judy Wickert; Mrs. Emily Besl Henry.
Res., 2853 Erie Ave., 45208. Tel: 513-321-1207; Fax: 513-533-5518.
School—2845 Erie Ave., 45208. Tel: 513-321-0703; Fax: 513-533-5517. Jane Welling, Prin.
Lay Teachers 22; Students 539.
Catechesis/Religious Programs—Tel: 513-321-0703; Fax: 513-533-5518.
Students 92.

60—ST. MATTHIAS (Forest Park) (1967), Revs. Robert Goebel, Admin.; Gerard A. Evers; Deacons Raymond George; Michael Metz.
Res., 1050 W. Kemper Rd., 45240. Tel: 513-851-1930; Fax: 513-589-3850.
Catechesis/Religious Programs—Tel: 513-589-3845; Fax: 513-589-3850.
Students 56.

61—ST. MICHAEL (1919), Rev. Michael U. Pucke; Vicki Muhlenkamp, Pastoral Assoc.; Brian Bisig, Dir. Music.
Res., 11144 Spinner Ave., 45241. Tel: 513-563-6377; Fax: 513-554-3543.
School—Tel: 513-554-3555; Fax: 513-554-3551. Jody Farrell, Prin.
Lay Teachers 21; Students 483.
Catechesis/Religious Programs—Tel: 513-554-3547. Sr. Carol Gaeke, O.P., D.R.E.
Students 257.

62—ST. MONICA-ST. GEORGE PARISH NEWMAN CENTER (1993), Revs. Dennet Jung, O.F.M.; Alan Hirt, O.F.M.; Sr. Lucy Zientek, C.D.P., Pastoral Assoc.
Res., 328 W. McMillan St., 45219. Tel: 513-381-6400; Fax: 513-381-2540.
Church—Tel: 513-381-6400.
Catechesis/Religious Programs—Students 20.

63—MOTHER OF CHRIST (1946) (African American), Rev. James Shappelle; Sr. Mary Macke, O.S.U., Pastoral Admin.
Church and Res.: 5301 Winneste Ave., 45232. Tel: 513-242-0164 (Church); 541-3732 (Res); Fax: 513-242-0164 (Church); 541-0362 (Res).
Catechesis/Religious Programs—Students 20.

64—NATIVITY OF OUR LORD (Pleasant Ridge) (1917), Rev. R. Marc Sherlock.
Res., 5935 Pandora Ave., 45213. Tel: 513-531-3164; Fax: 513-531-6368.
School—5936 Ridge Ave., 45213. Tel: 513-531-5138; Fax: 513-531-6368. Robert C. Herring, Prin.
Lay Teachers 21; Students 450.
Catechesis/Religious Programs—Students 100.

65—OUR LADY OF LOURDES (Westwood) (1927), Revs. Edward L. Rudemiller; Steven J. Kolde; Deacon Thomas E. Westerfield; Sr. Ann Mary Lay, Pastoral Min.; Catherine Lucas, Business Mgr. In res., Revs. Robert R. Wolfer; Paul J. Wolfer.
Res., 2832 Rosebud Dr., 45238. Tel: 513-922-0715; 347-2641 (Res.); Fax: 513-347-2644.
School—5835 Glenway Ave., 45238. Tel: 513-347-2660; Fax: 513-347-2663. Ms. Karen A. Rusche, Prin.
Lay Teachers 29; Students 625.
Catechesis/Religious Programs—Tel: 513-347-2646. Carol Grevlich, D.R.E.
Students 131.

66—OUR LADY OF THE ROSARY (Greenhills) (1938), Rev. Charles J. Bowes; Deacon Harry S. Walker.
Res., 17 Farragut Rd., 45218. Tel: 513-825-8626; Fax: 513-825-2783.
School—Tel: 513-825-2336; Fax: 513-825-3410. Mrs. Judith Hoferkamp, Prin.
Lay Teachers 15; Students 209.
Catechesis/Religious Programs—19 Farragut Rd., 45218. Tel: 513-825-2338. Sr. Mary Laura Miceli, S.C., D.R.E.
Students 409.

67—OUR LADY OF THE SACRED HEART (Reading) (1874), Rev. Jack W. Wehman; Deacons James Geraci; Robert Glassmeyer.
Res., 177 Siebenthaler Ave., 45215. Tel: 513-733-4950; Fax: 513-733-4951.
School—Tel: 513-733-5225; Fax: 513-733-0973. Ms. Barbara Adelmann, Prin.
Lay Teachers 18; Students 325.
Catechesis/Religious Programs—Students 79.

68—OUR LADY OF VICTORY (Delhi Hills) (1842), Rev. George Schmitz, Admin.; Deacons Charles Jenkins; Joseph Schultheis; Ms. Donna Watts, Pastoral Assoc.
Res., 810 Neeb Rd., 45233. Tel: 513-922-4460; Fax: 513-922-5476. [CEM]
School—808 Neeb Rd., 45233. Tel: 513-347-2072; Fax: 513-922-5476. Mrs. Sally Hicks, Prin.
Lay Teachers 33; Students 739.
Catechesis/Religious Programs—Tel: 513-347-2071; Fax: 513-922-5476. Mrs. Doris Steidle, D.R.E.
Students 172.

69—OUR LADY OF VISITATION (Mack) (1947), Revs. John E. Wessling; Bernard Weldishofer; Deacon William A. Dehmer; Sr. Gertrude Ann Knipper, C.D.P., Pastoral Assoc.
Res., 3172 South Rd., 45248. Tel: 513-922-2056; Fax: 513-347-2238.
School—3180 South Rd., 45248. Tel: 513-347-2222; Fax: 513-347-2225. Mr. Terry P. Chapman, Prin.
Sisters 1; Lay Teachers 39; Students 852.
Catechesis/Religious Programs—Tel: 513-347-2228; Fax: 513-347-2225. Sr. Mary Tewes, O.S.B., D.R.E.
Students 100.

70—OUR LORD, CHRIST THE KING (Mt. Lookout) (1926), Revs. Robert A. Obermeyer, Pastor; Anthony Muller.
Res., 3223 Linwood Rd., 45226. Tel: 513-321-4121; Fax: 513-871-3978.
School—Cardinal Pacelli, 927 Ellison, 45226. Tel: 513-321-1048; Fax: 513-533-6118. Mary Lottinville, Prin.
Lay Teachers 21; Students 455.
Catechesis/Religious Programs—Students 50.

71—OUR MOTHER OF SORROWS (Roselawn) (1941), Rev. Steven P. Walter; Deacon Michael A. Ascolese.
Res., 7243 Eastlawn Dr., 45237. Tel: 513-731-6480; Fax: 513-731-4640.
School—Tel: 513-731-8838; Fax: 513-731-4640. Kim Roy, Prin.
Lay Teachers 12; Students 142.
Catechesis/Religious Programs—Combined with St. Robert Bellarmine, Cincinnati.

72—STS. PETER AND PAUL (Reading) (1850), Rev. James M. Willig.
Res., 417 W. Vine St., Reading, 45215. Tel: 513-554-1010; Fax: 513-554-0190. [CEM]
School—Tel: 513-554-1311; Fax: 513-554-4667. Mr. Philip Belmont, Prin.
Lay Teachers 11; Students 229.
Catechesis/Religious Programs—Tel: 513-351-2468. Tim Cronin, D.R.E.
Students 217.

73—RESURRECTION OF OUR LORD (1919), Rev. Robert L. Keller.
Res., 1744 Iliff Ave., 45205. Tel: 513-471-2700; Fax: 513-471-2703.
School—1740 Iliff Ave., 45205. Tel: 513-471-6600; Fax: 513-471-6600. Thomas F. Miller, Prin.
Sisters 3; Lay Teachers 10; Students 164.
Catechesis/Religious Programs—Tel: 513-471-2431.
Students 5.

74—ST. ROBERT BELLARMINE (1927), Revs. Richard W. Bollman, S.J.; Albert J. Bischoff, S.J.; Lauren McDonough Renneker, Dir. Social Mission, Tel: 513-745-3008; Guy M. Vanasse, Dir. Music Min., Tel: 513-745-3270; Marcia L. Kersher, Dir. Youth Min., Tel: 513-745-4224.
Res., Xavier University, 3844 Victory Pkwy., 45207. Tel: 513-745-3398; Fax: 513-745-2031.
Catechesis/Religious Programs—Tel: 513-745-3317. Rosemary G. Conrad, D.R.E.
Students 98.

75—ST. ROSE OF LIMA (1867), Rev. Barry Windholtz.
Res., 2501 Eastern Ave., 45202. Tel: 513-871-1162; Fax: 513-871-2851.

76—SACRED HEART (1870) (Italian), Rev. Mario Rauzi, C.S.
Res., 2733 Massachusetts Ave., 45225. Tel: 513-541-4654; Fax: 513-541-4662.
School—Corryville Catholic Elementary School. See separate listing.

77—ST. SAVIOUR (Rossmoyne) (1947), Rev. Patrick H. Crone; Deacon Jerry Cain.
Res., 4136 Myrtle Ave., 45236. Tel: 513-791-9004; Fax: 513-791-6530.
School—4122 Myrtle Ave., 45236. Tel: 513-791-2734; Fax: 513-791-6530. Mary C. DeBrunner, Prin.
Lay Teachers 12; Students 102.
Catechesis/Religious Programs—Tel: 513-791-0119.
Students 62.

78—ST. SIMON THE APOSTLE (1966), Rev. Michael D. Beatty.
Res., 825 Pontius Rd., 45233. Tel: 513-941-3656; Fax: 513-941-1562.
Catechesis/Religious Programs—Tel: 513-941-6173. Carolyn Meyers, D.R.E.
Students 277.

79—ST. STEPHEN (1867), Rev. Ronald J. Averbeck. In res., Rev. Mark C. Schmieder.
Res., 320 Donham Ave., 45226. Tel: 513-871-3373.

80—ST. TERESA (1916), Rev. Larry R. Tharp; Deacon Michael Davenport.
Res., 1175 Overlook Ave., 45238. Tel: 513-921-9200; Fax: 513-921-0307.
School—1194 Rulison Ave., 45238. Tel: 513-471-4530. Barbara A. Cooke, Prin.
Lay Teachers 22; Students 428.
Catechesis/Religious Programs—Tel: 513-471-4530. David L. Donovan, D.R.E.
Students 59.

81—ST. THERESE, THE LITTLE FLOWER (Mt. Airy) (1926), Revs. Thomas M. King; Robert A. Stricker.
Res., 5560 Kirby Ave., 45239. Tel: 513-541-5560; Fax: 513-681-2631.
School—5555 Little Flower Ave., 45239. Tel: 513-542-6787; Fax: 513-542-3658. Mrs. Patricia Kennedy, Prin.
Lay Teachers 24; Students 486.
Catechesis/Religious Programs—Sr. Francis Margaret Maag, C.D.P., D.R.E.
Students 10.

82—ST. VINCENT FERRER (Kenwood) (1946), Rev. Terence J. Hamilton; Judith Verny, Pastoral Assoc.
Res., 7754 Montgomery Rd., 45236. Tel: 513-791-9030; Fax: 513-791-7405.
School—Tel: 513-791-6320; Fax: 513-791-7405. Blane Collison, Prin.
Lay Teachers 15; Students 260.
Catechesis/Religious Programs—Tel: 513-791-6321; Fax: 513-791-7405. Sr. Kaye Lednik, C.S.J., D.R.E.
Students 217.

83—ST. VINCENT DE PAUL (1861), Rev. Gregory J. Lockwood.
Res., 4044 River Rd., 45204. Tel: 513-451-5714; Fax: 513-451-5749.
School—Tel: 513-451-5656. Mrs. Diane Reder, Prin.
Lay Teachers 5; Students 55.

84—ST. VIVIAN (1943), Rev. John E. Filippine; Deacons William R. Michael; Gerald Coomes; Christine Siciliano, Pastoral Assoc.; Kathleen Rothchild, Business Mgr. In res., Rev. Paul L. Gebhardt.
Res., 7600 Winton Rd., 45224. Tel: 513-728-4331; Fax: 513-728-4335.
School—885 Denier Pl., 45224. Tel: 513-522-6858; Fax: 513-728-4336. Kevin Vance, Prin.
Lay Teachers 22; Students 412.
Catechesis/Religious Programs—Tel: 513-728-4333; Fax: 513-728-4335.
Students 53.

85—ST. WILLIAM (1909), Rev. Paul A. Bader; Deacons George Bruce; Thomas Faeth; Mr. Jerry DiCristoforo, Pastoral Min. In res., Rev. Msgr. Francis B. Kennedy.
Res., 4108 W. Eighth St., 45205. Tel: 513-921-0247; Fax: 513-921-2810.
School—4125 St. William Ave., 45205. Tel: 513-471-2989; Fax: 513-471-8226. Ms. Linda Westendorf, Prin.
Sisters 1; Lay Teachers 22; Students 393.

OUTSIDE THE CITY OF CINCINNATI

Amelia, Clermont Co., St. Bernadette's (1944), Rev. Hans H. Gruenbauer.
Res., 1479 Locust Lake Rd., 45102. Tel: 513-753-5566; Fax: 513-753-5566.
School—1453 Locust Lake Rd., 45102. Tel: 513-753-4744. Mr. Chet Augenstein, Prin.
Lay Teachers 15; Students 267.
Catechesis/Religious Programs—Tel: 513-753-5566. Kelly Lafferty, D.R.E.
Students 150.

Arnheim, Brown Co., St. Mary (1837), Rev. Dohrman W. Byers.
Res., 6647 Van Buren St., Georgetown, 45121. Tel: 937-446-2555.
Catechesis/Religious Programs—Combined with St. Elizabeth, Sardinia, OH. Tel: 937-446-3810.
Students 55.

Batavia, Clermont Co., Holy Trinity (1906), Rev. William R. Stockelman; Deacon James Hennessey.
Res., 140 N. 6th St., 45103. Tel: 513-732-2024; Fax: 513-732-0049.
Catechesis/Religious Programs—Tel: 513-732-2024. Patricia Bruce, D.R.E.
Students 102.

Beavercreek, Greene Co., St. Luke (1955), Rev. William J. Kramer. In res., Rev. Felix T. Molumeli, O.M.I. (Lesotho, South Africia).
Res., 1440 N. Fairfield Rd., 45432. Tel: 937-426-1733; Fax: 937-426-3965.
School—(Grades K-8) 1442 N. Fairfield Rd., 45432. Tel: 937-426-8551; Fax: 937-426-6435. Mrs. Leslie Vondrell, Prin.
Lay Teachers 20; Students 473.
Catechesis/Religious Programs—1444 N. Fairfield Rd., 45432. Tel: 937-426-5656.
Students 391.

Bellefontaine, Logan Co., St. Patrick's (1852), Rev. Henry F. Albietz; Deacon Harold Dipple.
Res., 328 E. Patterson Ave., 43311. Tel: 937-592-1656; Fax: 907-592-0971. [CEM]
Catechesis/Religious Programs—320 E. Patterson Rd., 43311. Tel: 937-592-6621. Mrs. Barbara Daly, D.R.E.
Students 240.

Bethel, Clermont Co., St. Mary (1941), Rev. Donald J. West.
Res., 3398 S.R. 125, 45106. Tel: 513-734-4041; Fax: 513-734-3588.
Catechesis/Religious Programs—Tel: 513-734-3676; Fax: 513-734-3588. Joan St. Clair, D.R.E.
Students 205.

Blanchester, Clinton Co., Holy Name (1853), Rev. Michael A. Savino.
Res. & Church: 746 S. S.R. 133, 45107. Tel: 937-783-3956; Fax: 937-783-8905.
Catechesis/Religious Programs—Combined with St. Martin and St. Patrick. Tel: 937-783-2275. Kathy Baxter, D.R.E.

Botkins, Shelby Co., Immaculate Conception (1865) (German), Rev. James F. Trick.
Res., 116 N. Mill St., P.O. Box 519, 45306. Tel: 937-693-2561. [CEM]
Catechesis/Religious Programs—Students 307.

Bradford, Miami Co., Immaculate Conception (1875), Rev. James S. Duell.
Res., 5874 N. Buckneck Rd., R.R. 2, 45308. Tel: 937-448-6220; Fax: 937-473-2476.
Catechesis/Religious Programs—Tel: 937-448-6220.
Students 55.

Burkettsville, Mercer Co., St. Bernard (1874), Rev. Matthew W. Jozefiak, C.PP.S.
Res., 71 W. Main St., P.O. Box 146, 45310. Tel: 419-375-2333.
St. Henry Catechetical Center—See St. Henry, St. Henry for details. Tel: 419-678-3811.
Catechesis/Religious Programs—Students 110.

Camden, Preble Co., St. Mary's (1942), Rev. Francis R. Monnig.
Res., 5304 Jacksonburg Rd., Trenton, 45067. Tel: 513-726-6294.
Church—7721 N. Main St., 45311. Tel: 937-452-3352.
Catechesis/Religious Programs—Students 37.

Carthagena, Mercer Co., St. Aloysius (1865), Rev. David A. Hoying, C.PP.S.
Res., 1509 Cranberry Rd., St. Henry, 45883. Tel: 419-925-4776.
Church—6036 State Rte. 274, Celina, 45822. [CEM]
St. Henry Catechetical Center—For details call Tel: 419-678-3811.

Cassella, Mercer Co., Nativity of the Blessed Virgin Mary (1847), Rev. Frederick Ryder, C.PP.S.
Res., 6524 State Rte. 119, Maria Stein, 45860. Tel: 419-925-4775. [CEM]
Catechesis/Religious Programs—Tel: 419-925-4812. Kathy Broering, D.R.E.
Students 106.

Celina, Mercer Co., Immaculate Conception of the Blessed Virgin Mary (1864), Revs. Thomas Brenberger, C.PP.S.; Richard R. Riedel, C.PP.S.; Deacon Thomas Huff.
Res., 229 W. Anthony St., 45822. Tel: 419-586-6648; Fax: 419-586-6649. [CEM]
School—Tel: 419-586-2379; Fax: 419-586-6649. Ms. Kathryn Mescher, Prin.
Sisters of the Precious Blood 1; Lay Teachers 15; Students 209.
Catechesis/Religious Programs—Wayne & Walnut Sts., Tel: 419-586-2370; Fax: 419-586-6649.
Students 493.

Centerville, Montgomery Co., Incarnation (1945), Revs. Thomas A. Kuhn; Daniel J. Meyer; Charles E. Mentrup. Pastoral Assocs.: Deacon Robert Zinck; Mary Fogler; Tim Niesel; Marilyn Porcino.
Res., 55 Williamsburg Ln., 45459. Tel: 937-433-1188; Fax: 937-433-3263.
School—45 Williamsburg Ln., 45459. Tel: 937-433-1051; Fax: 937-433-9796. Cheryl Reichel, Prin.
Lay Teachers 29; Students 788.
Catechesis/Religious Programs—Tel: 937-433-3377; Fax: 937-433-3263. Paula Weckesser, D.R.E.
Students 722.

St. Francis of Assisi (1969), Rev. John B. Turnbull, O.F.M.; Marilyn Hutter, Parish Sec.; Frances Obringer, Sec. of Rel. Ed.
Res., 6245 Wilmington Pike, 45459. Tel: 937-433-1013; Fax: 937-433-1699.
Catechesis/Religious Programs—Tel: 937-433-0128; Fax: 937-433-1699. Mary Ellen Singer, D.R.E.
Students 491.

Chickasaw, Mercer Co., Most Precious Blood (1903), Rev. John L. Bensman.
Res., Box 26, 35 S. Maple St., 45826-0026. Tel: 419-925-4391. [CEM]
Catechesis/Religious Programs—Tel: 419-935-4391. Margie Ronnebaum, D.R.E.
Students 199.

Coldwater, Mercer Co., Holy Trinity (1867), Revs. Ronald H. Wilker; Thomas M. Mannebach; Deacon Virgil Lochtefeld.
Res., 116 E. Main St., 45828. Tel: 419-678-4802; Fax: 419-678-4803. [CEM]
Catechesis/Religious Programs—110 N. Second St., 45828. Tel: 419-678-3328. D.R.E.: Helen Vagedes; Catherine Wenning.
Students 1,151.

Covington, Miami Co., St. Teresa (1950), Rev. James S. Duell.
Res., 6925 W. U.S. 36, 45318. Tel: 937-473-2970; Fax: 937-473-2476. [JC]
Catechesis/Religious Programs—Tel: 937-473-2970. Ms. Linda Poast, D.R.E.
Students 65.

Cranberry Prairie, Mercer Co., St. Francis (1858), Rev. David A. Hoying, C.PP.S.
Res., 1509 Cranberry Rd., St. Henry, 45883. Tel: 419-925-4776. [CEM]
St. Henry Catechetical Center—See St. Henry, St. Henry for details. Tel: 419-678-3811.

Dayton, Montgomery Co.,

1—ST. ADALBERT, (1903) (Polish), Rev. Michael J. Holloran. Office 1511 Valley St., 45404. Tel: 937-228-8782.
Catechesis/Religious Programs—1509 Valley St., 45404. Arlene Bottenfield, D.R.E.
Students 33.

2—ST. AGNES, (1915), Rev. James R. Schutte; Mary Reaman, Pastoral Admin.
Res., 811 N. Paul L. Dunbar St., 45407. Tel: 937-274-2212; Fax: 937-274-0976.
School—Dayton Catholic Elementary Consolidated. See separate listing. Tel: 937-275-8114.
Catechesis/Religious Programs—Students 20.

3—ST. ALBERT THE GREAT, (1939), Revs. James J. Manning; Lawrence R. Strittmatter; Patrick Adejoh (Nigeria); Sr. Patrice Vales, S.C., Pastoral Assoc. In res., Rev. Thomas Beischel, C.PP.S.
Res., 3033 Far Hills Ave., 45429. Tel: 937-293-1191; Fax: 937-293-1848.
School—Tel: 937-293-9452; Fax: 937-293-1848. Mr. Walt Klimaski, Prin.
Lay Teachers 31; Students 583.
Catechesis/Religious Programs—104 Dorothy Ln., Kettering, 45429. Tel: 937-298-2402; Fax: 937-293-1848. Barbara Leibold, D.R.E.
Students 398.

4—ST. ANTHONY OF PADUA, (1913), Rev. Thomas M. Shearer. In res., Rev. Thomas J. Ballman. Pastoral Assocs.: Janet Gaier; Karen Emmerich.
Res., 820 Bowen St., 45410. Tel: 937-253-9132; Fax: 937-253-6658.
School—Tel: 937-253-6251; Fax: 937-253-1541.
Lay Teachers 21; Students 400.

5—ASCENSION, (1955), Revs. David E. Brinkmoeller; Mark Meyer. Pastoral Assocs.: Sr. Florence Seifert, C.PP.S.; Sr. Marie Langhals, C.PP.S.
Res., 2025 Woodman Dr., Kettering, 45420. Tel: 937-253-5171; Fax: 937-253-0886.
School—Tel: 937-245-5411; Fax: 937-254-1105. Brent Devitt, Prin.
Sisters 1; Lay Teachers 19; Students 417.
Catechesis/Religious Programs—Tel: 937-254-0622. Maryellen Fargey, D.R.E.
Students 296.

6—ASSUMPTION, (1949). Merged with Our Lady of Mercy, Dayton.

7—ST. CHARLES BORROMEO, (1962), Rev. Msgr. Lawrence K. Breslin; Rev. Thomas W. Schmidt; Deacon Leonard Baltes; Mary Schulz, Business Mgr.
Res., 4500 Ackerman Rd., 45429. Tel: 937-434-6081; Fax: 937-434-6251.

School—Tel: 937-434-4933; Fax: 937-434-6692. Miss Judy Ellerbrock, Prin.
Sisters 3; Lay Teachers 30; Students 676.
Catechesis/Religious Programs—Tel: 937-434-9272. Anne Trick, D.R.E.
Students 241.

8—CORPUS CHRISTI, (1911), Rev. James R. Schutte.
Res., 224 Squirrel Rd., 45405. Tel: 937-228-6672; Fax: 937-461-0611.
School—200 Homewood Ave., 45405. Tel: 937-228-3091; Fax: 937-449-2440.
Lay Teachers 13; Students 210.
Catechesis/Religious Programs—Students 34.

9—EMMANUEL, (1837), Revs. Lee L. Sciarrotta, S.M.; Charles T. Bergedick, S.M.
Res., 149 Franklin St., 45402. Tel: 937-228-2013; Fax: 937-228-5354. In res., Rev. Francis J. Kenney, S.M.
Catechesis/Religious Programs—Tel: 937-228-5354.
Students 124.

10—ST. HELEN, (1953), Rev. Paul F. DeLuca; Deacons John J. Jachimowicz; Susano Mascorro; Roy Deardorff.
Res., 605 Granville Pl., 45431. Tel: 937-254-6233; Fax: 937-256-6117.
School—Tel: 937-256-1761; Fax: 937-254-4614. Sr. Annette Paveglio, S.C., Prin.
Sisters 1; Lay Teachers 21; Students 439.
Catechesis/Religious Programs—Tel: 937-256-8815. Joan Torres, D.R.E.
Students 126.
Convent—5098 Burkhardt Rd., 45431. Tel: 937-252-7972. Sisters of Notre Dame

11—ST. HENRY, (1960), Revs. Lawrence E. Mierenfeld; Frank Amberger; Sr. Judy Kroeger, C.PP.S., Pastoral Assoc.; Deacon Alan W. Arber.
Res., 6696 Springboro Rd., 45449. Tel: 937-434-9231; Fax: 937-434-6798.
School—Bishop Leibold Consolidated. See separate listing. Tel: 937-434-9343.
Catechesis/Religious Programs—Tel: 937-433-8220.
Students 415.

12—HOLY ANGELS, (1902), Rev. Thomas E. Meyer; Sr. Ann C. Joseph, S.C., Pastoral Assoc.
Parish Office: 218 K St., 45409. Tel: 937-222-7807; Fax: 937-222-8167.
Church—Brown & L Sts., 45409.
School—Tel: 937-222-0365; Fax: 937-222-1580. Louise P. Moore, Prin.
Lay Teachers 21; Students 300.
Catechesis/Religious Programs—Tel: 937-222-2641. Karen D. Davis, D.R.E.
Students 310.

13—HOLY CROSS, (1914) (Lithuanian), Rev. Michael J. Holloran.
Res., 1924 Leo St., 45404-1997. Tel: 937-228-8902.
Catechesis/Religious Programs—1511 Valley St., 45404. Tel: 937-228-8782.
Students 5.

14—HOLY FAMILY, (1905), Rev. John E. Krumm; Deacon William Stevenson, Jr. In res., Revs. Edward Haggerty; Charles Kanai (Kenya).
Res., 140 S. Findlay St., 45403. Tel: 937-253-1109; Fax: 937-253-2172.
School—121 S. Monmouth St., 45403. Tel: 937-253-4859; Fax: 937-253-8534. G. Janell Klippel, Prin.
Lay Teachers 10; Students 218.
Catechesis/Religious Programs—St. Mary Church, 310 Allen St., 45410. Tel: 937-256-5633; Fax: 937-256-7138.
Students 7.

15—HOLY TRINITY, (1860), Rev. Walter J. Macpherson; Deacon George Zvonar; Mary C. Wlodarski, Christian Formation Min.; Judith L. Trick, Business Mgr.
Res., 272 Bainbridge St., 45402. Tel: 937-228-1223; Fax: 937-445-0232.

16—ST. JAMES, (1919). Merged with Resurrection of Our Lord, Dayton to form St. James/Resurrection of Our Lord, Dayton.

17—ST. JOSEPH, (1847), Rev. Louis Osterhage, C.PP.S.
Res., 411 E. Second St., 45402. Tel: 937-228-9272; 228-9522; Fax: 937-228-6144.

18—ST. MARY'S, (1859), Rev. John E. Krumm; Deacon William Saluke.
Res., 310 Allen St., 45410. Tel: 937-256-5633; Fax: 937-256-7138.
Catechesis/Religious Programs—Tel: 937-256-5633; Fax: 937-256-7138. Dr. Robert Obach, D.R.E.
Students 30.

19—OUR LADY OF THE IMMACULATE CONCEPTION, (1938), Rev. Anthony J. Geraci. Pastoral Assocs.: Deacons Dan Kraus; Vince Orlando; Art Kronenberger.
Res., 2300 S. Smithville Rd., 45420. Tel: 937-252-9919; Fax: 937-252-0890.
School—Tel: 937-253-8831; Fax: 937-252-8832. Sr. Mary Ann Bredice, I.H.M., Prin.
Sisters 1; Lay Teachers 21; Students 400.
Catechesis/Religious Programs—Students 400.

20—OUR LADY OF MERCY, (1928), Rev. P. Del Staigers. Pastoral Assocs.: Sr. Ann Clark, C.PP.S.; Deacon Thomas Platfoot; Mr. Bill Painter; Mrs. Kathy Shirley; Mrs. Avalon Matczynski; Ms. Mary Lauterbach.
Res., 220 W. Siebenthaler Ave., 45405. Tel: 937-274-2107; Fax: 937-274-4363.
School—Tel: 937-278-5483. Ann Vogel, Prin.
Lay Teachers 11; Students 200.
Catechesis/Religious Programs—Students 30.

21—OUR LADY OF THE ROSARY, (1887), Rev. Anthony M. Dattilo; Deacon Henry B. Beck.
Res., 22 Notre Dame Ave., 45404. Tel: 937-228-8802; Fax: 937-228-7021.
School—40 Notre Dame Ave., 45404. Tel: 937-222-7231; Fax: 937-222-7393. Genevieve S. Ritzel, Prin.
Lay Teachers 10; Students 235.

22—ST. PETER, (Huber Heights) (1959), Revs. Earl Francis Simone; Francis B. Pilliod; Anthony E. Cutcher; Victor Ries; Deacons Allen K. Miller; Robert Borgerding; John E. Gould; Timothy J. Harris; Robert M. Correale.
Res., 6161 Chambersburg Rd., 45424. Tel: 937-233-1503; Fax: 937-237-3523.
School—Tel: 937-233-8710; Fax: 937-237-3974. Feliza Poling, Prin.
Lay Teachers 47; Students 936.
Catechesis/Religious Programs—Tel: 937-237-3516; Fax: 937-233-5717. Ms. Joy Blaul, D.R.E.
Students 464.

23—PRECIOUS BLOOD, (1948), Revs. William O'Donnell, C.PP.S.; Richard Friebel, C.PP.S.; Deacon Richard Janowiecki. In res., Rev. Dennis Chriszt, C.PP.S.; Bro. Jerome Schulte, C.PP.S.
4961 Salem Ave., 45416. Tel: 937-276-5954; Fax: 937-276-5955.
Res., Gaspar House, 4880 Denlinger Rd., 45426.
School—4870 Denlinger Rd., 45426. Tel: 937-277-2291; Fax: 937-277-2217. William Cavanaugh, Prin.
Lay Teachers 19; Students 350.
Catechesis/Religious Programs—Tel: 937-277-2454.
Students 270.

24—QUEEN OF APOSTLES, Greene Co., (1973), Rev. H. James Bartlett, S.M., Priest Coord.; Deacon Greg Cecere.
Church—4400 Shakertown Rd., 45430-1075. Tel: 937-429-0510; Fax: 937-429-0881.
Catechesis/Religious Programs—Tel: 937-426-0881; Fax: 937-429-0881. D.R.E.: Mary Clark; Terri Nordmeyer; Patti Gehred.
Students 90.

25—QUEEN OF MARTYRS, (Northridge) (1948), Rev. Thomas R. Hopp; Deacon Skip Royer; Jane Bensman, Pastoral Assoc.
Res., 4144 Cedar Ridge Rd., 45414. Tel: 937-277-2092; Fax: 937-277-2773.
School—Tel: 937-274-5592; Fax: 937-274-4852. Lucianne Lilienthal, Prin.
Sisters 2; Lay Teachers 7; Students 200.
Catechesis/Religious Programs—Tel: 937-277-2092.
Students 35.

26—ST. JAMES/RESURRECTION OF OUR LORD, (1919) (African American), Rev. Francis Tandoh, C.S.Sp.; Deacon Jacob Jerigan. Office: 130 Gramont Ave., P.O. Box 17219, 45417. Tel: 937-228-7023; Fax: 937-228-7181.
Res., 719 Edgemont Ave., 45408.
School—Tel: 937-268-6391; Fax: 937-268-9775. Ms. Debra Johnson, Prin.
Lay Teachers 13; Students 220.
Catechesis/Religious Programs—Tel: 937-268-6697.
Students 67.

27—ST. RITA, (1922), Rev. Kenneth R. Baker; Deacon James C. Olinger.
Res., 5401 N. Main St., 45415. Tel: 937-278-5815; Fax: 937-275-3302.
School—Tel: 937-277-8978; Fax: 937-277-8979. Mary Ann Eismann, Prin.
Lay Teachers 17; Students 340.
Catechesis/Religious Programs—Patricia Cruise, D.R.E.
Students 85.

28—ST. STEPHEN, (North Dayton) (1906) (Hungarian), Rev. Anthony M. Dattilo.
Res., 1114 Troy St., 45404. Tel: 937-223-8306.

Eaton, Preble Co., Visitation of the Blessed Virgin Mary (1853), Rev. J. Thomas Fitzsimmons; Deacon Joseph James.
Res., 407 E. Main St., 45320. Tel: 937-456-3380.
Catechesis/Religious Programs—Tel: 937-456-3395. Sharon Stump, D.R.E.
Students 145.

Egypt, Auglaize Co., St. Joseph (1852), Rev. Thomas R. Brenberger, C.PP.S. In res., Rev. Oscar H. Seger.
Res., 02441 SR 364, 45865. Tel: 419-628-2614; Fax: 419-628-2958. [CEM]
Catechesis/Religious Programs—Students 32.

Englewood, Montgomery Co., St. Paul's (1972), Rev. Todd Grogan; Deacon Joseph Subler.
Res., 1000 W. Wenger Rd., 45322. Tel: 937-836-7535; Fax: 937-836-1130.
Catechesis/Religious Programs—Tel: 937-836-2337. Dr. Sandra Chakeres, D.R.E.
Students 550.

Fairborn, Greene Co., Mary Help of Christians (1862), Rev. Charles Lang; Pat Scanlon, Pastoral Assoc.; Deacon Max Roadruck.
Res., 954 N. Maple Ave., 45324-5498. Tel: 937-878-8353; Fax: 937-879-8800. [CEM]
School—934 N. Maple Ave., 45324-5499. Tel: 937-878-9152; Fax: 937-879-8804. Rob Fortener, Prin.
Lay Teachers 12; Students 187.
Catechesis/Religious Programs—1030 N. Maple Ave., 45324. Tel: 937-878-7325; Fax: 937-878-8800. Gloria L. Leigh, D.R.E.
Students 244.

Fairfield, Butler Co., Sacred Heart of Jesus (1957), Rev. Norman Langenbrunner.
Church—400 Nilles Rd., 45014. Tel: 513-829-4383; Fax: 513-858-4211.
Res., 5202 Mississippi Dr., 45014. Tel: 513-863-5318; Fax: 513-863-5318, Ext. 51.
School—Tel: 513-858-4215; Fax: 513-858-4218. Joseph Nagle, Prin.
Lay Teachers 21; Students 470.
Catechesis/Religious Programs—Tel: 513-858-4213; Fax: 513-858-4211.
Students 275.

Fayetteville, Brown Co., St. Patrick (1837), Rev. Jerome J. Gardner.
Mailing Address: P.O. Box 279, 45118.
Res., 130 Stone Alley, 45118. Tel: 513-875-2082.
Catechesis/Religious Programs—Tel: 513-875-2161. Debbie Rosselot, D.R.E.
Students 125.

Felicity, Clermont Co., Our Mother of Good Counsel. Closed. For inquiries for parish records contact St. Mary Church, Bethel.

Fort Loramie, Shelby Co., St. Michael's (1838), Rev. Steven L. Shoup; Deacon Werner Bensman.
Res., 33 Elm St., P.O. Box 7, 45845. Tel: 937-295-2891; Fax: 937-295-3349. [CEM]
Catechesis/Religious Programs—Tel: 937-295-2179; Fax: 937-295-3349. D.R.E.: Madeline Maurer; Frank Turner.
Students 611.

Fort Recovery, Mercer Co., Mary Help of Christians (1881), Revs. Paul W. Wohlwend, C.PP.S.; Norbert Loshe, C.PP.S.; Deacon John Parker.
Res., 403 Sharpsburg Rd., 45846. Tel: 419-375-4153. [CEM]
Catechesis/Religious Programs—Tel: 419-375-4153; Fax: 419-375-4154.
Students 377.

St. Peter (1860) (German), Rev. Kenneth G. Alt, C.PP.S.
Res., 1477 Philothea Rd., St. Peter, 45846. Tel: 419-375-4344; Fax: 419-375-4030. [CEM]
Catechesis/Religious Programs—Tel: 419-375-4344. Ginny Gehret, D.R.E.
Students 125.

Franklin, Warren Co., St. Mary (1867), Rev. Joseph B. Bruening.
Res., 115 S. Main St., 45005. Tel: 513-746-5404.
Catechesis/Religious Programs—Tel: 513-746-1404; Fax: 513-746-5470.
Students 245.

Frenchtown, Darke Co., Holy Family (1846), Rev. Leo A. Hoying.
Res., 14 E. Wood St., Versailles, 45380. Tel: 937-526-4945. [CEM]
Catechesis/Religious Programs—Tel: 419-336-7875. D.R.E.: Betty Hess; Mary Hartke.
Students 78.

Fryburg, Auglaize Co., St. John (1850) (German), Rev. Oscar H Seger.
Res., 11319 Van Buren St., Wapakoneta, 45895-8467. Tel: 419-738-6043; Fax: 419-738-4364. [CEM]
Catechesis/Religious Programs—D.R.E.: Ann Limbert; Linda Lamarr.
Students 71.

Georgetown, Brown Co., St. George (1902), Rev. Earl O. Metz.
Res., 501 E. State St., 45121. Tel: 937-378-6829.
Church—507 E. State St., 45121-1420. Tel: 937-378-9616.
Catechesis/Religious Programs—Tel: 937-444-3944. Mary Gaskin, D.R.E.
Students 58.

Germantown, Montgomery Co., St. Augustine (1941), Rev. Paul F. Hurst.
Res., 6891 Weaver Rd., 45327. Tel: 937-855-2289.

Catechesis/Religious Programs—Tel: 937-855-2289.
Students 96.

Glynwood, Auglaize Co., St. Patrick (1857) (Irish), Rev. Oscar H. Seger.
Res., 06959 Glynwood Rd., St. Marys, 45885. Tel: 419-738-6308; Fax: 419-738-7113. [CEM]
Catechesis/Religious Programs—Tel: 419-394-8458. Irene Heilers, D.R.E.
Students 45.

Greenfield, Highland Co., St. Benignus (1856), Rev. Ronald C. Cooper.
Res., 218 S. Second St., 45123. Tel: 937-981-2785; Fax: 937-981-4483. [CEM]
Catechesis/Religious Programs—Jessie Spangler, D.R.E.
Students 69.

Greenville, Darke Co., St. Mary (1853), Rev. John R. White.
Res., 233 W. 3rd St., 45331. Tel: 937-548-1616. [CEM]
School—238 W. Third St., 45331. Tel: 937-548-2345; Fax: 937-548-0878.
Lay Teachers 10; Students 108.
Catechesis/Religious Programs—Tel: 937-548-1616.
Students 275.

Hamilton, Butler Co.,

1—St. Ann's, (1909), Rev. Dennis Dettenwanger; Pat Miller, Pastoral Assoc.; Deacon Mark E. Brunner.
Res., 646 Clinton Ave., 45015. Tel: 513-863-4963; Fax: 513-863-2017.
School—3064 Pleasant Ave., 45015. Tel: 513-863-0604. Mrs. Donna L. Weber, Prin.
Sisters 1; Lay Teachers 11; Students 226.
Catechesis/Religious Programs—Tel: 513-863-4963.
Students 40.
Convent—(Oldenburg, IN) 646 Clinton Ave., 45015. Tel: 513-863-1701. Sisters of the Third Order Regular of St. Francis

2—St. Joseph, (1867) (German), Rev. Dennis Dettenwanger; Deacon James Kowalski, Pastoral Admin.
Res., 171 Washington St., 45011. Tel: 513-863-1424; Fax: 513-863-1451.
School—Tel: 513-863-8758; Fax: 513-863-5253. Joseph Pyfrin, Prin.
Lay Teachers 12; Students 220.
Catechesis/Religious Programs—Students 248.

3—St. Julie Billiart, (1989). (This parish is the successor in interest to St. Mary, St. Stephen and St. Veronica parishes, formerly located in Hamilton, OH.). Rev. Jeffrey P. Silver; Deacons James S. McCormick; William B. Renneker, Pastoral Assoc.; Thomas Strodtbeck; Mrs. Betty Meiner, Business Mgr.
Church—224 Dayton St., 45011. Tel: 513-863-1040; Fax: 513-863-1132.
School—(Grades K-8) 1206 Shuler Ave., 45011. Tel: 513-867-8477; Fax: 513-867-0139. Mrs. Margaret Hunsberger, Prin.
Lay Teachers 12; Students 234.
Catechesis/Religious Programs—Mrs. Georgia E. Pate, D.R.E.
Students 84.

4—St. Peter in Chains, (1894) (German), Rev. Timothy S. Bunch.
Res., 382 Liberty Ave., 45013. Tel: 513-863-3938; Fax: 513-863-1257.
School—451 Ridgelawn Ave., 45013. Tel: 513-863-0685; Fax: 513-863-1859.
Lay Teachers 20; Students 411.
Catechesis/Religious Programs—Tel: 513-863-3344.
Students 80.

Hillsboro, Highland Co., St. Mary (1853), Rev. Stanley E. Luehrmann; Leonard Parker, Pastoral Assoc.
Res., 212 S. High St., 45133-1445. Tel: 937-393-1742; Fax: 937-393-1742. [CEM]
Catechesis/Religious Programs—Tel: 937-365-1334. Ellen Parker, D.R.E.
Students 143.

Jamestown, Greene Co., St. Augustine (1870), Rev. William V. Thomas.
Res., 31 S. Chillicothe St., P.O. Box F, South Charleston, 45368-0806. Tel: 937-462-8971; Fax: 937-462-9184.
Catechesis/Religious Programs—Rita Canty, D.R.E., Tel: 937-675-3219.
Students 29.

Lebanon, Warren Co., St. Francis de Sales (1883), Rev. Louis R. Hohlmayer; Deacons Herschel Steward; John Taylor; Ned Ostendorf.
Res., 15 DeSales Ave., 45036. Tel: 513-932-2601.
School—20 DeSales Ave., 45036. Tel: 513-932-6501; Fax: 513-932-9919. Jo Anne Fischesser, Prin.
Lay Teachers 9; Students 251.
Catechesis/Religious Programs—Tel: 513-897-6498.
Students 215.

Liberty Township, Butler Co., St. Maximilian Kolbe (1989), Revs. John Porter; Vincent Tuan Anh Do.
Church & Mailing: 5720 Hamilton-Mason Rd., 45011. Tel: 513-779-3433.
Res., 7168 St. Albans Way, Hamilton, 45011. Tel: 513-777-4322; Fax: 513-777-7264.
School—St. Gabriel Consolidated School. See separate listing.
Catechesis/Religious Programs—Tel: 513-779-3433.
Students 1,000.

Loveland, Clermont Co., St. Columban (1859), Rev. Terrance W. Smith; Deacons Joseph Coll; James Miller; Edward Reising.
Office & Mailing: 894 Oakland Rd., 45140. Tel: 513-683-7903; Fax: 513-683-1389.
Res., 855 Oakland Rd., 45140. Tel: 513-677-8084.
School—896 Oakland Rd., 45140. Fax: 513-683-7904. Sr. Mary Suzanne Rose, S.N.D., Prin.
Sisters 2; Lay Teachers 24; Students 615.
Catechesis/Religious Programs—Tel: 513-683-0105; Fax: 513-683-1389.
Students 195.
Convent—(Covington, KY) 896 Oakland Rd., 45140. Tel: 513-683-0255. Sisters of Notre Dame

Manchester, Adams Co., St. Mary of the Assumption (1878). Closed. For inquiries for parish records please contact Holy Trinity, West Union.

Maria Stein, Mercer Co., St. John the Baptist (1836), Rev. Emil J. Labbe, C.PP.S.; Deacons Carl Franzer; Omer Bertke.
Res., 8533 State Rte. 119, 45860. Tel: 419-925-4522; Fax: 419-925-7522. [CEM]
Catechesis/Religious Programs—Tel: 419-925-4235.
Students 329.

Mason, Warren Co., St. Susanna (1938), Revs. Harry J. Meyer; James A. Hoffbauer; Deacons James A. Merritt; Daniel L. Rader; Gerald L. Barney. Pastoral Assocs.: Sr. Angela Jarboe, O.S.B.; Karen Gottschall; Chris Kreger; Rosie Leugers; Ralph W. Popp, Bus. Mgr.
Office: 305 Fourth Ave., 45040. Tel: 513-398-3821; Fax: 513-398-2254.
School—500 Reading Rd., 45040. Tel: 513-398-3821; Fax: 513-398-1657. Kenneth L. Beiser, Prin.
Lay Teachers 20; Students 433.
Catechesis/Religious Programs—Tel: 513-398-3821.
Students 1,400.

McCartyville, Shelby Co., Sacred Heart of Jesus (1881), Rev. Patrick Duffy.
Res., 9333 State Rte. 119 W., Anna, 45302-9520. Tel: 937-394-3823; 419-628-2502; Fax: (Call for fax number).
Catechesis/Religious Programs—Tel: 937-394-3823. Barbara Riethman, D.R.E.
Students 456.

Mechanicsburg, Champaign Co., St. Michael's (1865), Rev. Clarence G. Heis.
Res., 40 Walnut St., 43044. Tel: 513-834-2413.

Miamisburg, Montgomery Co., Our Lady of Good Hope (1852), Rev. Bernard H. Bruening.
Res., 6 S. Third St., 45342. Tel: 937-866-1432; Fax: 937-859-5035. [CEM]
School—Bishop Leibold Consolidated, Dayton. See separate listing. Tel: 937-866-3021.
Catechesis/Religious Programs—Tel: 937-866-1492.
Students 210.

Middletown, Butler Co., Holy Family (1991). (This parish is the successor in interest to Holy Trinity, St. John the Baptist and St. Mary parishes, formerly located in Middletown, OH). Rev. John R. Civille; Sr. Jean Sora, O.S.F., Pastoral Assoc. In res., Deacons Thomas Coyle; William Krumm.
Office: 201 Clark St., 45042. Tel: 513-422-0602; Fax: 513-424-7416. [JC]
School—John XXIII Consolidated, Middletown. See separate listing. Tel: 513-424-0838; Fax: 513-424-8568.
Catechesis/Religious Programs—Tel: 513-422-0602; Fax: 513-424-7416.
Students 210.

Milford, Clermont Co., St. Andrew (1854), Revs. William C. Wagner; Edward P. Smith.
Res., 552 Main St., 45150. Tel: 513-831-3353; Fax: 513-831-6597. [CEM]
School—St. Andrew-St. Elizabeth Seton, (Grades K-8). Consolidated. 555 Main St., 45150. Tel: 513-831-5277; Fax: 513-831-8436. Donna J. Beebe, Prin.
Lay Teachers 24; Students 628.
Catechesis/Religious Programs—Tel: 513-831-3812; Fax: 513-831-6597. Barbara Aluotto, D.R.E.
Students 171.

Millville, Butler Co., Queen of Peace (1941), Rev. Kenneth J. Schoettmer; Deacon Bill Brunsman.
Res., 2550 Millville Ave., Hamilton, 45013. Tel: 513-863-4344; Fax: 513-863-4364.
School—Tel: 513-863-8705; Fax: 513-863-4310. Cheryl A. Kordes, Prin.
Lay Teachers 14; Students 297.
Catechesis/Religious Programs—Students 168.

Minster, Auglaize Co., St. Augustine (1832), Rev. William Hoyng, C.PP.S.; Deacon John J. Schmiesing.
Res., 48 N. Hanover St., P.O. Box 93, 45865. Tel: 419-628-2614; Fax: 419-628-1078. [CEM]
Catechesis/Religious Programs—47 N. Lincoln St., P.O. Box 93, 45865. Tel: 419-628-3434; Fax: 419-628-1078. D.R.E.: Jane Boeke; Kathy Sommer.
Students 750.

Monroe, Butler Co., Our Lady of Sorrows (1883), Rev. John Kroeger.
Res., 416 Lebanon St., 45050. Tel: 513-539-8383.
Catechesis/Religious Programs—330 Lebanon St., 45050. Tel: 513-539-8061. Sr. Bridget Cottle, S.C.N., D.R.E.
Students 112.

Montezuma, Mercer Co., Our Lady of Guadalupe (1903), Rev. James H. Dugal, C.PP.S.
Res., P.O. Box 69, 45866. Tel: 419-268-2312; Fax: 419-268-1602. [CEM]
Catechesis/Religious Programs—Tel: 419-268-2312. Carol Niekamp, D.R.E.
Students 164.

Morrow, Warren Co., St. Philip the Apostle (1965), Rev. Edward B. Stolze.
Res., 944 East U.S. 22-3, 45152. Tel: 513-899-3601; Fax: 513-899-3601.
Catechesis/Religious Programs—Tel: 513-899-3785; Fax: 513-899-2079. Sr. Jane Roberts, S.N.D-.deN., D.R.E.
Students 169.

Mount Carmel, Clermont Co., St. Veronica (1949), Revs. Michael T. Flaherty; Benedict O'Cinnsealaigh; Deacon Walter Srode.
Res., 4473 Mt. Carmel-Tobasco Rd., Cincinnati, 45244. Tel: 513-528-1622; Fax: 513-528-1622.
School—Tel: 513-528-0442; Fax: 513-528-0513. Mr. Paul McLaughlin, Prin.
Sisters 2; Lay Teachers 17; Students 476.
Catechesis/Religious Programs—Tel: 513-528-8723.
Students 275.

Mount Orab, Brown Co., St. Michael (1944), Rev. Earl O. Metz.
Res., St. George Church, 501 E. State St., Georgetown, 45121-1420. Tel: 937-378-6829.
Church—220 S. High St., 45154. Tel: 937-444-3944.
Catechesis/Religious Programs—Tel: 397-444-3770. Connie Carroll, D.R.E.
Students 16.

Mount Repose, Clermont Co., St. Elizabeth Ann Seton (1976), Rev. David A. Sunberg.
Res., 5890 Buckwheat Rd., Milford, 45150. Tel: 513-575-0119; Fax: 513-575-0957.
School—5900 Buckwheat Rd., Milford, 45150. Tel: 513-575-0093; Fax: 513-575-1078. Ms. Donna Beebe, Prin.
Lay Teachers 24; Students 451.
Preschool—Tel: 513-575-9900. Mrs. Terri Imming, Dir.
Lay Teachers 10; Students 150.
Catechesis/Religious Programs—Ed Alten, D.R.E., Tel: 513-831-8318.
Students 290.

New Bremen, Auglaize Co., Holy Redeemer (1948), Rev. R. Daniel Conlon; Deacon Gregory Bornhorst.
Res., 120 S. Eastmoor Dr., 45869. Tel: 419-629-2543; Fax: 419-629-2543.
Catechesis/Religious Programs—Students 493.

New Carlisle, Clark Co., Sacred Heart (1950), Deacon Robert Kozlowski.
Res., 476 N. Scott St., 45344. Tel: 937-845-3121; Fax: 937-846-1223.
Catechesis/Religious Programs—Tel: 937-845-1373; Fax: 937-846-1223. Joan Steinlage, D.R.E.
Students 246.

New Paris, Preble Co., St. John the Evangelist (1870), Rev. J. Thomas Fitzsimmons.
Res., Visitation, 407 E. Main St., Eaton, 45320. Tel: 937-456-3380.

Newport, Shelby Co., SS. Peter and Paul (1856), Rev. Donald E. Shelander.
Res., 6788 State Rte. 66, Ft. Loramie, 45845. Tel: 937-295-3001; Fax: 937-295-2536. [CEM]
Catechesis/Religious Programs—Tel: 937-295-2536. Jan Stockman, D.R.E.
Students 218.

New Richmond, Clermont Co., St. Peter (1850), Rev. Gary J. Witsken.
Res., 1192 Bethel-New Richmond Rd., 45157. Tel: 513-553-3267; Fax: 513-553-4321. [CEM]

Catechesis/Religious Programs—Tel: 513-553-4321. Linda Rientjes, D.R.E.
Students 130.

New Vienna, Clinton Co., St. Michael (1874), Rev. Ronald C. Cooper.
Res., St. Benignus, 218 S. Second St., Greenfield, 45123. Tel: 937-981-2785; Fax: 937-981-4483.
Catechesis/Religious Programs—Students 32.

North Lewisburg, Champaign Co., Immaculate Conception (1869), Rev. Clarence G. Heis.
Res., 40 Walnut St., Mechanicsburg, 43044. Tel: 937-834-2413.
Catechesis/Religious Programs—Students 19.

North Star, Darke Co., St. Louis (1891), Rev. James M. Schmitmeyer.
Parish Office: P.O. Box 9, Osgood, 45351. Tel: 419-582-2531; Fax: 419-582-2015. [CEM]
Catechesis/Religious Programs—Linda Wehrkamp, D.R.E.
Students 191.

Osgood, Darke Co., St. Nicholas (1909), Rev. James M. Schmitmeyer.
Office: 128 Church St., P.O. Box 9, 45351. Tel: 419-582-2531; Fax: 419-582-2015. [CEM]
Catechesis/Religious Programs—Donna Grieshop, D.R.E.
Students 174.

Owensville, Clermont Co., St. Louis (1856), Rev. Gerard P. Hiland.
Res., 210 N. Broadway, 45160. Tel: 513-732-2218; Fax: 513-732-1748. [CEM]
School—250 N. Broadway, 45160. Tel: 513-732-0636; Fax: 513-732-2368. Ms. Katherine Prosperi, Prin.
Ursuline Sisters 2; Lay Teachers 12; Students 206.
Catechesis/Religious Programs—Tel: 513-732-2580.
Students 52.

Oxford, Butler Co., St. Mary Church and Catholic Campus Ministry (Miami U.) (1853), Rev. Terrance L. Schneider. Pastoral Assocs.: Roberta L. Kinne; Jennifer L. Boyle.
Res., 111 E. High St., 45056. Tel: 513-523-2153; Fax: 513-523-0559. [CEM]

Peebles, Adams Co., St. Mary Queen of Heaven (1952). (Vicariate). Rev. Theodore C. Kosse.
Res., Holy Trinity, 612 E. Mulberry St., West Union, 45693. Tel: 937-544-2757.
Catechesis/Religious Programs—Students 29.

Philothea, Mercer Co., St. Mary (1851) (German), Rev. Louis J. Barga, C.PP.S.
Res., 3821 Philothea Rd., Coldwater, 45828. Tel: 419-678-2795. [CEM]
Catechesis/Religious Programs—Cathy Bruns, D.R.E.
Students 95.

Piqua, Miami Co., St. Boniface (1855), Rev. Rick Unwin.
Res., 310 S. Downing St., 45356. Tel: 937-773-1656; Fax: 937-773-2665. Rev. Angelo C. Caserta Tel: 513-778-9526.
School—Piqua Catholic School, Piqua. (Consolidated) See separate listing. Tel: 937-773-3876.
Catechesis/Religious Programs—Students 150.

St. Mary (1843), Rev. Thomas J. Grilliot; Joan Dunn, Pastoral Assoc. In res., Rev. Anselm F. Boeke (Retired).
Res., 528 Broadway, 45356. Tel: 937-773-1327; Fax: 937-773-2313.
School—Piqua Catholic School, Piqua. See separate listing. Tel: 937-773-1564; Fax: 937-773-0380.
Catechesis/Religious Programs—Tel: 937-778-8770. Michael Worland, D.R.E.
Students 50.

Rhine, Shelby Co., St. Lawrence (1856) (German), Rev. James F. Trick.
Res., 16053 Botkins Rd., P.O. Box 519, Botkins, 45306. Tel: 937-693-2561. [CEM]
Catechesis/Religious Programs—Tel: 937-693-2571.
Students 133.

Ripley, Brown Co., St. Michael (1840), Rev. Thomas F. Feldhaus; Jean M. Stephens, Pastoral Assoc.
Res., 16 N. Fourth St., 45167. Tel: 937-392-1116; Fax: 937-392-1699.
School—Tel: 937-392-4202; Fax: 937-392-4248. Mrs. Ann Boley, Prin.
Lay Teachers 4; Students 45.
Catechesis/Religious Programs—Tel: 937-392-1335.
Students 115.

Rockford, Mercer Co., St. Teresa (1936), Rev. Thomas Brenberger, C.PP.S.
Res., 213 S. Franklin St., P.O. Box 445, 45882. Tel: 419-363-2633; Fax: 419-363-2633.
Catechesis/Religious Programs—Tel: 419-363-2327. Denise Myers, D.R.E.
Students 58.

Russells Point, Logan Co., St. Mary of the Woods (1927), Rev. Harold W. Kist, Pastor; Deacon Steve Brown.
Res., 464 Madison Ave., P.O. Box 329, 43348. Tel: 937-843-3127; Fax: 937-843-3866.
Catechesis/Religious Programs—Madison Ave., 43348. Tel: 937-843-4227. Barbara Daly, D.R.E., Tel: 937-592-6621.
Students 160.
Mission—E. Huntsville, Logan Co., St. George Chapel Marianists of Ohio, 9636 Lake Shore Dr., E. Huntsville, 43324.

Russia, Shelby Co., St. Remy (1846), Rev. Eugene F. Vonderhaar.
Res., 108 E. Main St., 45363. Tel: 937-526-3437; Fax: 937-526-5326.
Catechesis/Religious Programs—Tel: 937-526-3437. Dee Monnin, D.R.E.
Students 279.

St. Anthony, Mercer Co., St. Anthony (1852) (German), Rev. Kenneth G. Alt, C.PP.S.; Deacon Cletus H. Homan.
Res., 471 St. Anthony Rd., Fort Recovery, 45846. Tel: 419-942-1795. [CEM]
Catechesis/Religious Programs—Tel: 419-942-1795.
Students 102.

St. Henry, Mercer Co., St. Henry (1839), Rev. Larry Wyen, C.PP.S.; Bro. Thomas Bohman, C.PP.S., Pastoral Assoc.; Deacon Jerry Buschur.
Res., Box 301, 272 E. Main St., 45883. Tel: 419-678-4118; Fax: 419-678-8285.
Inter-parish Center—162 S. Walnut, 45883. Tel: 419-678-3811.
Catechesis/Religious Programs—Tel: 419-678-3811. Connie Bargdill, D.R.E.
Students 757.

St. Joseph, Mercer Co., St. Joseph 1839 (German), Rev. George Kuzara, C.PP.S.
Res., 1477 Philothea Rd., St. Peter, 45846. Tel: 419-375-4344; Fax: 419-375-4030. [CEM]
Church—1689 St. Joe Rd., Fort Recovery, 45846.
Catechesis/Religious Programs—Students 175.

Saint Martin, Brown Co., Saint Martin (1830), Rev. Michael A. Savino.
Res., 746 S. State Rte. 133, Blanchester, 45107. Tel: 937-783-3956; Fax: 937-783-9035. [CEM]
Church—20864 State Rte. 251, 45118. Tel: 513-875-2790; Fax: 937-783-8905.
Catechesis/Religious Programs—Combined with Holy Name, Blanchester. Tel: 937-364-6107. Terry Brinkman, D.R.E.
Students 89.

St. Marys, Auglaize Co., Holy Rosary (1852), Rev. David A. Heinl. In res., Rev. James O. Byrne.
Res., 511 E. Spring St., 45885. Tel: 419-394-5050.
School—Tel: 419-394-5291. Anna Mae Saum, Prin.
Lay Teachers 12; Students 202.
Catechesis/Religious Programs—Tel: 419-394-5291. Sandi Rammel, D.R.E.
Students 220.

St. Paris, Champaign Co., Sacred Heart (1868), Rev. David L. Zink.
Res., 231 Washington Ave., Urbana, 43078-1728. Tel: 937-653-1375; Fax: 937-653-1376.
Catechesis/Religious Programs—Tel: 937-663-5877; Fax: 937-653-1375.
Students 35.

St. Rose, Mercer Co., St. Rose (1839), Rev. Frederick Ryder.
Res., 7428 State Rte. 119, Maria Stein, 45860. Tel: 419-925-4775. [CEM]
Catechesis/Religious Programs—Tel: 419-925-4542. Joyce Hartings, D.R.E.
Students 96.

St. Sebastian, Mercer Co., St. Sebastian (1852) (German), Rev. John L. Bensman.
Res., Precious Blood Church, 35 S. Maple St., Box 26, Chickasaw, 45826-0026. Tel: 419-925-4391. [CEM]
Church—3280 Co. Rd. 716-A, Celina, 45822.
Catechesis/Religious Programs—Nancy Broering, D.R.E.
Students 74.

St. Wendelin, Mercer Co., St. Wendelin (1856), Rev. Matthew Jozefiak, C.PP.S.
Res., 517 Meiring Rd., Fort Recovery, 45846. Tel: 419-375-2603. [CEM]
Catechesis/Religious Programs—Students 61.

Sardinia, Brown Co., St. Elizabeth Parish (1955), Rev. Dohrman W. Byers.
Res., 6647 Van Buren St., Georgetown, 45121. Tel: 937-446-1996.
Church—122 N. Main St., 45171.
Catechesis/Religious Programs—Combined with St. Mary, Arnheim, OH. Tel: 937-446-3810.
Students 42.

Shandon, Butler Co., St. Aloysius (1867), Rev. David F. Reilly; Deacon Lawrence A. Maag.
Res., P.O. Box 95, 45063. Tel: 513-738-1014; Fax: 513-738-2084. [CEM]
Catechesis/Religious Programs—Tel: 513-738-4641. Joan Mills, D.R.E.
Students 200.

Sharpsburg, Mercer Co., St. Paul (1868), Rev. Matthew Jozefiak, C.PP.S.
Res., 517 Meiring Rd., Fort Recovery, 45846. Tel: 419-375-2603. [CEM]
Catechesis/Religious Programs—Tel: 419-375-2308. Helen Lefevre, D.R.E.
Students 175.

Sidney, Shelby Co., Holy Angels (1848), Revs. Gerald E. Bensman; Patrick L. Sloneker; Deacons Philip Myers; John Holthaus.
Res., 324 S. Ohio Ave., 45365. Tel: 937-498-2307; Fax: (Call for number).
School—Tel: 937-492-9293; Fax: 937-492-8578. Harold Schmiesing, Prin.
Lay Teachers 21; Students 452.
Catechesis/Religious Programs—Tel: 937-498-0433. Marianne Dunson, D.R.E.
Students 446.

South Charleston, Clark Co., St. Charles Borromeo (1866), Rev. William V. Thomas.
Res., 31 S. Chillicothe St., P.O. Box F, 45368-0806. Tel: 937-462-8971; Fax: 907-462-9184. [CEM]
Catechesis/Religious Programs—Tel: 937-883-2168. Arlene Coil, D.R.E., Tel: 937-883-2168.
Students 38.

Springfield, Clark Co.,

1—St. Bernard, (1860), Rev. Donald C. Huebner, Pastor.
Res., 910 Lagonda Ave., 45503. Tel: 937-322-5243; Fax: 937-322-3788. [CEM]
School—800 Lagonda Ave, 45503. Tel: 937-324-4551; Fax: 937-324-4070.
Lay Teachers 10; Students 207.
Catechesis/Religious Programs—Tel: 937-324-2870; Fax: 937-322-3788. Sr. Teresa Noser, O.S.F., D.R.E.
Students 122.

2—St. Joseph, (1882), Rev. Dennis J. Caylor; Deacon Norman G. Horstman.
Res., 802 Kenton St., 45505. Tel: 937-323-7523; Fax: 937-324-1512.
Church—225 E. High St., 45505.
School—Holy Trinity Catholic School, Springfield. See separate listing. Tel: 937-322-8781; Fax: 937-323-2790.
Catechesis/Religious Programs—Students 72.

3—St. Mary, (1921), Rev. David P. Vincent.
Res., 1027 W. High St., 45506-1398. Tel: 937-322-7272; Fax: 937-325-8626.
School—Holy Trinity Catholic School, Springfield. See separate listing. Tel: 937-322-8781; Fax: 937-323-2790.
Catechesis/Religious Programs—Patricia Evans, D.R.E.
Students 32.

4—St. Raphael, (1849), Rev. Dennis J. Caylor; Deacon Norman G. Horstmann.
Res., 225 E. High St., 45505. Tel: 937-323-7523; Fax: 937-324-1512.
School—Holy Trinity Catholic School, Springfield. See separate listing.
Catechesis/Religious Programs—Tel: 937-323-7523.
Students 143.

5—St. Teresa of the Child Jesus, (1931), Rev. Richard W. Walling.
Res., 1827 N. Limestone St., 45503. Tel: 937-342-8861; Fax: 937-399-6971.
School—Tel: 937-399-5451; Fax: 937-342-0042. Mrs. Martha Szczesny, Prin.
Lay Teachers 11; Students 220.
Catechesis/Religious Programs—Tel: 937-399-5451; Fax: 937-399-6971.
Students 100.

Stonelick, Clermont Co., St. Philomena (1837), Rev. Gerard P. Hiland.
Res., 255 N. Broadway, Box 85, Owensville, 45160. Tel: 513-732-2218; Fax: 513-732-1748. [CEM]

Tipp City, Miami Co., St. John the Baptist (1858), Rev. Thomas A. Dorenbusch.
Res., 218 S. Third St., 45371. Tel: 937-667-3419; Fax: 937-667-9267. [CEM]
Catechesis/Religious Programs—Tel: 937-667-6092. Nelda Schwab, D.R.E.
Students 397.

Trenton, Butler Co., Holy Name (1871), Rev. George W. Klein; Deacon William Martin.
Res., 222 Hamilton Ave., 45067. Tel: 513-988-6335; Fax: 513-998-9900. [CEM]
Catechesis/Religious Programs—Tel: 513-988-9348.
Students 108.

Troy, Miami Co., St. Patrick (1857), Revs. Thomas J. Brunner; Charles B. Rohrkemper; Deacons Michael Knight; John Carlin; Mark Chaplin.
Res., 409 E. Main St., 45373. Tel: 937-335-2833; Fax: 937-335-1453.
School—Tel: 937-339-3705; Fax: 937-339-1158. James O'Leary, Prin.
Lay Teachers 7; Students 171.
Catechesis/Religious Programs—409 E. Main St., 45373. Tel: 937-339-5517.
Students 360.

Twenty Mile Stand, Warren Co., St. Margaret of York (1984), Rev. Thomas W. Kreidler; Deacon Raymond Kroger; Ms. Toni Rogers, Pastoral Assoc.
Res., 9483 Columbia Rd., Loveland, 45140. Tel: 513-683-7100; Fax: 513-683-7101.
School—Tel: 513-683-9793. Education Administrative Team: Sr. Mary Ann Trotta, R.S.M.; Mrs. Nancy Shula; Sr. Daria Mitchell, O.S.F.
Lay Teachers 28; Students 706.
Catechesis/Religious Programs—Mark Spanyer, D.R.E.
Students 170.

Urbana, Champaign Co., St. Mary, Rev. David L. Zink.
Res., 231 Washington Ave., OH 43078. Tel: 937-653-1375; Fax: 937-653-1375.
School—Tel: 937-653-1370; Fax: 937-653-1376. Mrs. Karen Berkhofer, Prin.
Lay Teachers 12; Students 115.
Catechesis/Religious Programs—Tel: 937-788-2251.
Students 104.

Vandalia, Montgomery Co., St. Christopher (1957), Rev. Francis J. Keferl; Deacon Stephen Bermick.
Res., 435 E. National Rd., 45377. Tel: 937-898-3542; Fax: 937-898-1017.
School—(Grades K-8). Tel: 937-898-5104.
Lay Teachers 18; Students 367.
Catechesis/Religious Programs—Tel: 937-898-2155.
Students 367.

Versailles, Darke Co., St. Denis (1839), Rev. Leo A. Hoying.
Res., 14 E. Wood St., 45380. Tel: 937-526-4945. [CEM]
Catechesis/Religious Programs—Tel: 937-526-3957. D.R.E.: Arlene Niekamp; Linda Meyer.
Students 538.

Wapakoneta, Auglaize Co., St. Joseph (1839), Revs. William Eilerman, C.PP.S., Admin.; Peter Chiodo, C.PP.S.
Res., 309 S. Perry St., 45895. Tel: 419-738-2115; Fax: 419-738-4525. [CEM]
School—1101 Lincoln Hwy., 45895. Tel: 419-738-3311; Fax: 419-738-7706.
Lay Teachers 12; Students 246.
Catechesis/Religious Programs—Tel: 419-738-2115; Fax: 419-738-4525.
Students 307.

Waynesville, Warren Co., St. Augustine (1876), Rev. Raymond Kammerer.
Res., 5715 Lytle Rd., 45068. Tel: 513-897-2821; Fax: 513-897-2821 (star) 51.
Catechesis/Religious Programs—Tel: 937-433-7114. Pat Ebright, D.R.E.
Students 164.

West Chester, Butler Co., St. John (1880), Rev. James W. Meade. In res., Revs. J. Raymond Favret; Robert B. Buening.
Res., 9080 Cincinnati-Dayton Rd., 45069. Tel: 513-777-6433; Fax: 513-777-9741.
School—Consolidated. See St. Gabriel.
Catechesis/Religious Programs—Tel: 513-755-4974.
Students 580.

West Milton, Miami Co., Transfiguration (1950), Rev. John D. MacQuarrie; Deacon Robert Huffman.
Res., 972 S. Miami St., 45383. Tel: 937-698-4520; Fax: 937-698-4500.
Catechesis/Religious Programs—Students 187.

West Union, Adams Co., Holy Trinity (1950), Rev. Theodore C. Kosse.
Res., 612 E. Mulberry St., 45693. Tel: 937-544-2757; Fax: 937-544-1430.
Catechesis/Religious Programs—Students 50.

Williamsburg, Clermont Co., St. Ann (1947), Rev. William R. Stockelman.
Res., 140 N. Sixth St., Batavia, 45103. Tel: 513-732-2024; Fax: 513-732-0049.
Catechesis/Religious Programs—Carla Simpson, D.R.E.
Students 49.

Wilmington, Clinton Co., St. Columbkille (1866), Rev. James M. Wedig; Deacons Robert G. Baker; Robert E. Meyer.
Res., 73 N. Mulberry St., 45177-2277. Tel: 937-382-2236; Fax: 937-382-0676 (star) 2.
Catechesis/Religious Programs—Tel: 937-382-1596. Daniel L. Thomas, D.R.E.
Students 246.

Withamsville, Clermont Co., St. Thomas More (1940), Revs. John P. Fischer; Joseph A. Bruemmer, (Retired); Deacon Michael E. Metz. Pastoral Assocs.: Sr. Margene Koester, S.N.D.; Mr. Michael Thomas.
Res., 800 Ohio Pike, Cincinnati, 45245-2219. Tel: 513-752-2080, Ext. 10 (Office), Ext. 15 (Pastor); Fax: 513-753-2542.
School—788 Ohio Pike, Cincinnati, 45245. Tel: 513-752-2080, Ext. 22; Fax: 513-753-2554. Mrs. Peggy Fischer, Prin.
Lay Teachers 13; Students 278.
Catechesis/Religious Programs—Tel: 513-752-2080, Ext. 25; Fax: 513-753-2542. Mrs. Becky Ready, D.R.E.
Students 233.

Xenia, Greene Co., St. Brigid (1849), Rev. Kenneth Schartz.
Res., 258 Purcell Ave., 45385. Tel: 937-372-3193; Fax: 937-374-3622. [CEM]
School—Tel: 937-372-3222. Sr. Lois Jean Goettke, S.C., Prin.
Sisters 1; Lay Teachers 10; Students 238.
Convent—216 Purcell Ave., 45385. Tel: 937-372-0994. Sisters of Charity of Cincinnati, OH
Catechesis/Religious Programs—Tel: 937-372-3222.
Students 98.

Yellow Springs, Greene Co., St. Paul (1856), Rev. Joseph R. Raudabaugh; Deacon Paul E. Richardson.
Res., 308 Phillips St., 45387. Tel: 937-767-7450; Fax: 937-767-7465. [CEM]
Catechesis/Religious Programs—Students 120.

Closed and Merged Parishes

Greater Cincinnati

1—COMMUNITY OF HOPE. Consolidated with Holy Family Parish. Records at the Chancery.

2—ST. ALOYSIUS CHURCH (Elmwood Place). Closed. For inquiries for parish records, contact St. Clement, (St. Bernard).

3—ST. CHARLES BORROMEO CHURCH (Carthage). Closed. For inquiries for parish records, contact St. James of the Valley, (Wyoming).

4—ST. ELIZABETH CHURCH (Norwood). Merged with Holy Trinity Church (Norwood).

5—ST. GEORGE PARISH & NEWMAN CENTER. Closed. For inquiries for parish records contact St. Monica-St. George Newman Center.

6—ST. MATTHEW CHURCH (Norwood). Merged with Holy Trinity Church (Norwood).

7—ST. MICHAEL CHURCH. Closed. For inquiries for parish records, contact Holy Family Parish.

8—OUR LADY OF GRACE (Price Hill). Consolidated with Holy Family Parish.

9—OUR LADY OF LORETTO. Merged with St. Margaret of Cortona.

10—OUR LADY OF PERPETUAL HELP (Sedamsville). Consolidated with Holy Family Parish.

11—OUR LADY OF PRESENTATION. Closed. For inquiries for parish records contact St. Leo the Great, Cincinnati.

12—ST. PATRICK (Northside). Merged with St. Boniface, Cincinnati. See listing for details.

13—STS. PETER AND PAUL CHURCH (Norwood). Merged Now known as Holy Trinity Church.

14—ST. PIUS CHURCH. Closed. For inquiries for parish records, contact St. Joseph Parish, Ezzard Charles Dr.

15—ST. RICHARD OF CHICHESTER (College Hill). Merged with St. Therese, the Little Flower, Cincinnati. See listing for details.

16—ST. THOMAS AQUINAS. Closed. For inquiries for parish records, contact St. Clement, (St. Bernard).

17—SAN ANTONIO DI PADOVA (Italian). Refer to St. Bonaventure for records.

Blue Creek, Adams Co., St. Joseph. Closed. For inquiries for parish records contact Holy Trinity, West Union.

Dayton, Montgomery Co., Sacred Heart. Closed. For inquiries for parish records contact Emmanuel, Dayton.

Felicity, Clermont Co., Our Mother of Good Counsel. Closed. For inquiries for parish records, contact St. Mary, (Bethel).

Hamilton, Butler Co., St. Mary. Merged. Now known as St. Julie Billiart.
St. Stephen. Merged. Now known as St. Julie Billiart.
St. Veronica. Merged. Now known as St. Julie Billiart.

Middletown, Butler Co., Holy Trinity. Merged. Now known as Holy Family.
St. John the Baptist. Merged. Now known as Holy Family.
St. Mary. Merged. Now known as Holy Family.

New Miami, St. Lawrence. Merged. Now known as St. Julie Billiart, Hamilton.

St. Patrick, Shelby Co., St. Patrick. Closed. For inquiries for parish records contact St. Michael, Fort Loramie.

Vera Cruz, Brown Co., Holy Ghost (Vicariate). Closed. For inquiries for parish records contact St. Patrick, Fayetteville. [CEM]

On Special and Archdiocesan Assignment:
Reverend Fathers—
Breaker, Donald J., P.O. Box 627, Ft. Leonard Wood, MO 65473
DeVore, David G., c/o Priests' Personnel Office, 100 E. Eighth St., Cincinnati, OH 45202
Elsbernd, James H., 6700 Dawson Rd., Cincinnati, OH 45243
Friedrichs, Paul L., 2426 Grandview, Cincinnati, OH 45206
Goebel, Robert W., 7775 Montgomery Rd., Cincinnati, OH 45236
Grad, Malcolm S., Admin. Asst., Archbishop's Office, 100 E. 8th St., Cincinnati, OH 45202
Guntzelman, Louis J., 10709 Adventure Lane, Cincinnati, OH 45242
Mahoney, Michael T., 4644 Burkhardt Rd., Dayton, OH 45431
Mick, Lawrence E., 3103 Observation Trail, Dayton, OH 45449
Nguyen, Huan Tien, 314 Township Ave., Cincinnati, OH 45216
Peterka, Dale C., 7121 Plainfield Rd., Cincinnati, OH 45236
Rivers, Clarence J., 17 Erkenbrecher Ave., Cincinnati, OH 45220
Tensi, Lawrence R., Dir. Worship Office, 100 E. Eighth St., Cincinnati, OH 45202

On Duty Outside the Archdiocese:
Reverend Fathers—
Angi, Steven J., c/o Priests' Personnel Office, 100 E. Eighth St., Cincinnati, OH 45202
Kelly, William T., 6114 Rena St., Houston, TX 77092
Lemkuhl, David A., P.O. Box 43058, Nairobi, Kenya
McGuire, Frederick J., Blessed Trinity, 1600 54th Ave., St. Petersburg, FL 33712
Pater, Daniel R., Apostolic, 50-C Nitimarg Chanakyapuri, New Delhi, India, 110021
Umberg, Andrew J., North American College, Vatican City, Italy 00120

Military Chaplains:
Reverend Fathers—
Janning, Timothy J., USS Kearsarge (LHD-3), Rel. Min. Dept. APO AE, 09534-1662
Leurck, Raymond J., CH LTC, Chief of Chap., 855 Sunset Blvd., Knob Noster, MO 65336-1700
Niemeier, Dennis, CH LTC, 17th ASG CM-Unit 45013, Box 2272, APO AP, 96338
St. George, Peter T., LTJG, P.O. Box 8528, Camp LeJeunes, NC 28547-8528
Whalen, Frank J., CH COL, 18 HHC HQ Abn Corps, Fort Bragg, NC 28307

Medical Leave of Absence:
Reverend Fathers—
Gaeke, Thomas M., Ste. 129-257, 3225 S. MacDill Ave., Tampa, FL 33619-8171

Leave of Absence:
Reverend Fathers—
Albrecht, G.R. Keith
Lack, Christopher

Retired:
Reverend Monsignors—
Amann, Robert A., 6210 Cleves Warsaw Ave., Cincinnati, OH 45233. Tel: 513-467-2705
Kennedy, Francis B., 4108 W. 8th St., Cincinnati, OH 45205. Tel: 513-921-5767
Klocker, Henry, 5440 Moeller Ave., Cincinnati, OH 45212. Tel: 513-631-2913
Vogelpohl, Henry J., 977 Bayley Place Dr., Cincinnati, OH 45233. Tel: 513-347-5566
Whalen, Earl L., 972 Bayley Place Dr., Cincinnati, OH 45233. Tel: 513-347-5638
Reverend Fathers—
Aichele, Raymond P., 2472 Picnic Woods, Bright, IN 47025. Tel: 812-637-2490
Allison, Joseph C., 6019 Woodford Ct., #3, Cincinnati, OH 45213. Tel: 513-731-5273
Andres, Joseph P., P.O. Box 54458, Cincinnati, OH 45254. Tel: 513-231-0508

Ballman, Thomas J., 820 Bowen St., Dayton, OH 45410. Tel: 513-253-9132
Bastian, Robert J., 1585 N.W. Washington Blvd., Hamilton, OH 45013. Tel: 513-894-1250
Beckman, Joseph F., 6616 Beechmont Ave., Cincinnati, OH 45230. Tel: 513-624-0554
Behler, Donald A., St. Dominic Church, 4551 Delhi Rd., Cincinnati, OH 45238. Tel: 513-471-7741
Berning, John B., P.O. Box 4023, St. Petersburg, FL 33731
Bertke, Erwin J., 3680 Warsaw Ave., Cincinnati, OH 45205. Tel: 513-921-0328
Birarelli, Carl A., 3970 DeFoe Sq., Sarasota, FL 34241. Tel: 941-371-9270
Boeke, Aloysius B., St. Charles Seminary, 2860 St., Rte. 127, Carthegena, OH 45822-9591
Boeke, Anselm F., 528 Broadway, Piqua, OH 45356. Tel: 937-773-1327
Brennan, Elmer F., 7283 Kingswood Dr., West Chester, OH 45069. Tel: 513-777-7372
Broering, Victor F., 9568 Dry Fork Rd., Harrison, OH 45030. Tel: 513-367-0091
Bruemmer, Joseph A., 5 Arbors Cir., Cincinnati, OH 45255. Tel: 513-688-7933
Buening, Robert B., St. John, 9080 Cincinnati-Dayton Rd., West Chester, OH 45069. Tel: 513-777-6433
Buerger, Francis J., Schroder Manor Retirement Community, 1302 Millville Ave., Hamilton, OH 45103. Tel: 513-844-6486
Byrne, James O., 511 Spring St., St. Marys, OH 45885. Tel: 513-394-5050
Caserta, Angelo C., P.O. Box 1636, Piqua, OH 45356. Tel: 937-778-9526
Caserta, Charles W., 133 Douglas, Lewisburg, OH 45338. Tel: 937-962-2500
Cavanaugh, John L., 100 Compton Rd., Cincinnati, OH 45215
Dorrmann, William J., 110 N. Hill St., Harrison, OH 45030. Tel: 513-367-9086
Evers, Gerard A., 1044 W. Kemper Rd., Cincinnati, OH 45240. Tel: 513-851-1930
Favret, Raymond J., St. John, 9080 Cincinnati-Dayton Rd., West Chester, OH 45069. Tel: 513-777-6433
Francis, A. Edwin, Dorothy Love Center, 3003 Cisco Rd., Sidney, OH 45365
Fritz, Francis E., 150 Gateway Dr., Milford, OH 45150. Tel: 513-831-2542
Goetz, Joseph W., 1528 Turnberry Village Dr., Dayton, OH 45458. Tel: 937-432-6589
Gruber, J. Paul, Bayley Place, 952 Bayley Place Dr., Cincinnati, OH 46233. Tel: 513-347-5573
Hagedorn, Robert L., 808 Schiff Ave. #1, Cincinnati, OH 45205. Tel: 513-921-0379
Haskamp, Edward F., 11080 Montgomery, Cincinnati, OH 45249. Tel: 513-469-9157
Hasselhoff, Robert W., 9375 Winton Rd., Cincinnati, OH 45231
Hater, Robert J., 1443 Cedar Ave., Cincinnati, OH 45224. Tel: 513-541-4611
Henz, Kenneth W., 1805 John Glenn Rd., Dayton, OH 45420. Tel: 937-253-2829
Hussey, Edmund M., 3714 Falls Circle Dr., Hilliard, OH 43026. Tel: 614-771-2736
Jaekle, Lawrence E., 24 Catalpa, Versailles, OH 45380. Tel: 937-526-5862
Jennings, John P., 1227 Ebenezer Rd., Cincinnati, OH 45238. Tel: 513-941-0932
Keller, Neil J., 836 N. Hill Ln., Cincinnati, OH 45224. Tel: 513-522-5578
Kenning, Herman H., 60 Compton Rd., Cincinnati, OH 45215. Tel: 513-821-1886
Kesting, Philip A., 2497 Eastern Ave., Cincinnati, OH 45202. Tel: 513-221-7011
Kneipp, August J., Leibold Home, 476 Riddle Rd., Cincinnati, OH 45220. Tel: 513-281-2648
Lammeier, Francis G., 12120 Regency Run #7, Cincinnati, OH 45240. Tel: 513-742-9982
Lawrence, Ralph J., 140 Ewing Dr., #C, Fairfield, OH 45014. Tel: 513-939-2363
Lutmer, Joseph H., 4688 Largo Dr., Cincinnati, OH 45236. Tel: 513-793-9937
Massarella, Francis A., 235 W. Orchard Springs Dr., Dayton, OH 45415. Tel: 937-275-4377
Mattscheck, John J., 3468 Robb Ave., Cincinnati, OH 45211. Tel: 513-389-9366
Mauntel, Robert J., 19 Mohave Dr., Sardinia, OH 45171. Tel: 513-446-3491
McWilliam, James J., St. Margaret Hall, 1960 Madison Rd., Cincinnati, OH 45206
Mick, Lawrence, 1500 Linneman Rd., Cincinnati, OH 45238. Tel: 513-922-5400
Mick, Robert, 3720 St. Martin Pl., Cincinnati, OH 45211. Tel: 513-661-2000
Miller, Francis J., 4988 Lord Alfred Ct., Cincinnati, OH 45241-2196. Tel: 513-247-0966
Minic, John F., 968 Sharewood Ct., Kettering, OH 45429. Tel: 937-299-2747
Monnin, Robert J., 223 Ranchview Dr., Vandalia, OH 45377. Tel: 937-898-3746
Mueller, Eugene J., 3055 Inwood Dr., Cincinnati, OH 45241. Tel: 513-769-4908
Niehaus, Francis H., P.O. Box 727, Florence, KY 41022
O'Connor, James J., 319 Mulberry Pl., Sidney, OH 45365. Tel: 937-492-9577
Pater, Thomas G., Catholic University of America, Curley Hall, Washington, DC 20064. Tel: 202-238-1663
Perin, Glen W., 233 W. Third St., Greenville, OH 45331. Tel: 937-548-1616
Perryman, John E., 138 Heritage Dr., Urbana, OH 43078. Tel: 937-878-3621
Pilliod, Francis B., 8100 Clyo Rd., Centerville, OH 45458. Tel: 937-435-1460
Plagge, Robert J., 6210 Cleves-Warsaw Pike, Cincinnati, OH 45233. Tel: 513-467-2724
Powers, Alfred J., 2344 N. Limestone #1, Springfield, OH 45503. Tel: 937-399-7757
Poynter, Gail A., 6509 Azure Way, West Carrollton, OH 45449. Tel: 513-438-9001
Ries, Victor F., 6161 Chambersburg Rd., Dayton, OH 45424. Tel: 937-233-1503
Rohrkemper, Charles B., 109 Freedom Ct., Sidney, OH 45365. Tel: 937-492-3010
Sahlfeld, Francis J., 8 Muirfield Ln., Cincinnati, OH 45241-3257. Tel: 513-891-6852
Schetter, Albert E., 11124 Circle Dr., St. Mary's, OH 45885. Tel: 419-394-8672
Schutte, Robert W., 2426 Home Orchard Dr., Springfield, OH 45503
Schwartz, William H., 350 Thomas Blvd., Hamilton, OH 45013. Tel: 513-894-5747
Steinbicker, Carl R., Leibold House, 476 Riddle Rd., Cincinnati, OH 45220
Stolz, Paul L., 100 Compton Rd., Cincinnati, OH 45215
Stricker, Robert A., 5560 Kirby Rd., Cincinnati, OH 45239. Tel: 513-541-5560
Suver, Robert J., 8100 Clyo Rd., Centerville, OH 45458. Tel: 937-434-1312
Thorsen, Robert J., 5002 Lord Alfred Ct., Cincinnati, OH 45241. Tel: 513-469-0921
Trippel, Edward G., 3547 Clifton Ave., Cincinnati, OH 45220. Tel: 513-861-1295
Urbain, Joseph V., 2692 Enterprise Rd., E. #1303, Clearwater, FL 34619. Tel: 727-799-2546
Wiemeyer, Raymond G., 5367 Julmar Dr., Cincinnati, OH 45238. Tel: 513-922-2791
Will, Carl G., Bethany Lutheran Village, 6451 Far Hills, Centerville, OH 45459
Williams, Edward T., 2732 E. Towers Dr., #417, Cincinnati, OH 45238. Tel: 513-661-2861
Wolfer, Paul J., 2832 Rosebud Dr., Cincinnati, OH 45238. Tel: 513-922-0715
Wolfer, Robert R., 2832 Rosebud Dr., Cincinnati, OH 45238. Tel: 513-922-0715
Zugelter, Alvin T., 135 Garfield Pl. #420, Cincinnati, OH 45202. Tel: 513-684-9492

Permanent Deacons:
Arber, Alan W., St. Henry, Dayton
Ascolese, Michael A., Our Mother of Sorrows, Cincinnati
Aufderheide, William, St. Margaret of Cortona, Cincinnati
Baker, Robert, St. Columbkille, Wilmington
Baltes, Leonard W., St. Charles, Kettering
Barney, Gerald L., St. Susanna, Mason
Beck, Henry B., Our Lady of the Rosary, Dayton
Bensman, Werner, SS. Peter & Paul, Newport; St. Michael, Ft. Laramie
Bermick, Stephen C., III, St. Christopher, Vandalia
Bertke, Omer H., St. John the Baptist, Maria Stein
Blum, Raymond, (Retired)
Borgerding, Robert H., St. Peter, Dayton
Bornhorst, Gregory A., Holy Redeemer, New Bremen
Brodeur, Wilfred J., St. Cecilia, Ft. Meyers, FL
Brown, Steven R., St. Mary of the Woods, Russells Point
Bruce, George A., St. William, Cincinnati
Brunner, Mark E., St. Ann, Hamilton
Brunsman, Willard, Queen of Peace, Millville
Bryant, Herman, St. Gabriel, Cincinnati
Burger, Raymond S., St. Margaret Mary, Cincinnati
Buschur, Jerome L., St. Henry, St. Henry
Cain, Jerome J., St. Saviour, Cincinnati
Camele, David G., (Retired)
Carlin, John K., St. Patrick, Troy
Cecere, Gregory, Queen of Apostles, Dayton
Chaplin, Mark, St. Patrick, Troy
Coll, Joseph J., St. Columban, Loveland
Coomes, Gerald L., St. Vivian, Cincinnati
Correale, Robert M., St. Peter, Huber Heights
Couzins, Jerome, Unassigned
Coyle, Thomas J., Holy Family, Middletown
Davenport, Michael D., St. Teresa of Avila, Cincinnati
Dawson, David A., Unassigned
Deardorff, Roy L., St. Helen, Dayton
Dehmer, William A., Our Lady of Visitation, Cincinnati
Dipple, Harold I., St. Patrick, Bellefontaine
Etienne, Jerald F., Immaculate Heart of Mary, Cincinnati
Faeth, Thomas J., St. William, Cincinnati
Fischesser, Elmer, New Jerusalem Community, Cincinnati
Franzer, Carl C., St. John the Baptist, Maria Stein
Gargan, Thomas, St. Catharine, Cincinnati
George, Raymond W., St. Matthias, Cincinnati
Geraci, James L., Our Lady of the Sacred Heart, Reading
Glassmeyer, Robert A., Our Lady of the Sacred Heart, Reading
Gobbi, John R., St. John Neumann, Cincinnati
Gould, John E., St. Peter, Huber Heights
Grismer, Raymond L., Good Shepherd, Cincinnati
Haas, Frederick J., St. Leo, Cincinnati
Harris, Timothy J., St. Peter, Huber Heights
Hennessey, James F., Holy Trinity, Batavia
Holthaus, John G., Holy Angels, Sidney
Homan, Cletus H., St. Anthony, Fort Recovery
Horstman, Norman G., St. Raphael, Springfield
Huff, Thomas, Immaculate Conception, Celina
Huffman, Robert J., Transfiguration, West Milton
Jachimowicz, John J., St. Helen, Dayton
James, Joseph, Visitation, Eaton
Janowiecki, Richard J., Precious Blood, Dayton
Jenkins, Charles J., Our Lady of Victory, Cincinnati
Jernigan, Jacob, Resurrection, Dayton
Keller, David R., St. Clement, Cincinnati
Kluener, Paul J., St. James, White Oak
Knight, Michael R., St. Patrick, Troy
Kolis, Conrad C., St. Bartholomew, Cincinnati
Kostic, Nicholas V., Jr., St. Brigid, Xenia
Kowalski, James, St. Joseph, Hamilton
Kozlowski, Robert R., Sacred Heart, New Carlisle
Kraus, Daniel E., Immaculate Conception, Dayton
Kroger, Raymond, St. Margaret of York, Twenty Mile Stand
Kronenberger, Arthur, Immaculate Conception, Dayton
Krumm, William T., Holy Family, Middletown
Lochtefeld, Virgil V., Holy Trinity, Coldwater
Maag, Lawrence A., St. Aloysius, Shandon
Martin, William, Holy Name, Trenton
Mascorro, Susano, St. Helen, Dayton
McCormick, James S., St. Julie Billiart, Hamilton
Merritt, James A., St. Susanna, Mason
Metz, Michael, St. Thomas More, Withamsville
Meyer, Robert E., St. Columbkille, Wilmington
Michael, William R., St. Vivian, Cincinnati
Miller, Allen K., St. Peter, Dayton
Miller, Eugene M., Immaculate Heart of Mary, Cincinnati
Miller, James A., St. Columban, Loveland
Montgomery, Michael, O.F.M., Unassigned
Mullaney, William M., Immaculate Heart of Mary, Cincinnati
Myers, Philip B., Holy Angels, Sidney
Novick, Rick, Guardian Angels, Cincinnati
Olinger, James C., St. Rita, Dayton
Orlando, Vincent, Immaculate Conception, Dayton
Ostendorf, Edward B., St. Francis de Sales, Lebanon
Parker, John G., Mary, Help of Christians, Fort Recovery
Perry, Robert, Our Lady, Queen of Peace, Wright Patterson Air Force Base
Perryman, Clifton, St. James, Mequon, WI
Petrie, William J., St. Antoninus, Cincinnati
Platfoot, Thomas F., Our Lady of Mercy, Dayton
Rader, Daniel L., St. Susanna, Mason
Reeves, Paul S., (Retired)
Reising, Edward B., St. Columban, Loveland
Renneker, William B., St. Julie Billiart, Hamilton
Richardson, Paul E., St. Paul, Yellow Springs
Riva-Saleta, Luis O., St. Ignatius, Cincinnati
Roadruck, Max, Mary Help of Christians, Fairborn
Royer, Milton W., Queen of Martyrs, Dayton
Runnels, Arthur, Holy Cross-Immaculata, Cincinnati
Saluke, William M., St. Mary, Dayton
Schmidt, Joseph Ted, St. Boniface, Cincinnati
Schmiesing, John J., St. Augustine, Minster
Schneider, Jerry R., St. Aloysious Gonzaga, Cincinnati
Schroeder, Robert J., St. Antoninus, Cincinnati
Schultheis, Joseph R., Our Lady of Victory, Cincinnati
Schumann, K. Michael, St. John, West Chester
Shea, David J., Immaculate Heart of Mary, Cincinnati
Simmons, Raphael, St. Joseph, Cincinnati
Slattery, John M., St. Cecilia, Cincinnati
Sonnenberg, James J., St. Gabriel, Cincinnati
Sprinkle, Joseph, (Retired)
Srode, Walter, St. Veronica, Mt. Carmel

Stevenson, William, Holy Family, Dayton
Steward, Herschel R., St. Francis De Sales, Lebanon
Strodtbeck, Thomas M., St. Julie Billiart, Hamilton
Subler, Joseph, St. Paul, Englewood
Sunderman, James P., St. Jude the Apostle, Cincinnati
Taylor, John, St. Francis de Sales, Lebanon
Thamann, John D., St. Mary, Cincinnati
Vilaboy, Manuel D., Spanish Community, Cincinnati
Waldbillig, Urban J., Unassigned
Walker, Harry S., Our Lady of the Rosary, Cincinnati
Wallace, Forrest, St. Antoninus, Cincinnati
Weitzel, Paul J., (Retired)
Wersching, J. Phillip, St. Francis de Sales, Cincinnati
Westbay, Richard L., St. Joseph, Wapakoneta
Westerfield, Thomas E., Our Lady of Lourdes, Cincinnati
Wiehe, Howard R., St. Martin of Tours, Cincinnati
Winters, Royce E., St. Agnes, Cincinnati
Woeste, James H., Unassigned
Zinck, Robert C., Jr., Incarnation, Centerville
Zvonar, George J., Holy Trinity, Dayton

INSTITUTIONS LOCATED IN THE ARCHDIOCESE

[A] THE ATHENAEUM OF OHIO

CINCINNATI. *The Athenaeum of Ohio*, Mt. St. Mary's Seminary, 6616 Beechmont Ave., 45230. Tel: 513-231-2223; Fax: 513-231-3254.
E-mail: ath@mtsm.org
Most Rev. Daniel E. Pilarczyk, D.D., Archbishop of Cincinnati, Chancellor, Chm. of Bd. of Trustees; Rev. Gerald R. Haemmerle, M.A.; Dr. Terrance D. Callan, Ph.D., Dean, Athenaeum of Ohio; Mr. Dennis K. Eagan, B.B.A., Bus. Mgr. Incorporated March 24, 1928 by the State of Ohio and presently has three divisions: Mt. St. Mary's Seminary of the West; the Lay Pastoral Ministry Program and the Special Studies Division.

Lay Pastoral Ministry Program, 6616 Beechmont Ave., 45230. Tel: 513-231-1200; Fax: 513-231-3254. Ms. Mary Sue O'Donnell, M.A.R., Dir.; Ms. Susan McGurgan, M.A.R., Assoc. Dir.; Sr. Nancy McMullen, C.PP.S., Prog. Coord.; John Gutting, Ph.D., Assoc. Dir.

The St. Gregory Seminary Trust, 100 E. Eighth St., 45202.

[B] SEMINARIES

CINCINNATI. *Mt. St. Mary's Seminary of the West.* (Diocesan), 6616 Beechmont Ave., 45230. Tel: 513-231-2223; Fax: 513-231-3254.
E-mail: ath@mtsm.org
Major seminary for students in Theology. Rev. Gerald R. Haemmerle, M.A., Rector; Dr. Terrance D. Callan, Ph.D., Athenaeum Academic and Seminary Dean; Rev. Charles Singer, M.A. (TOL), Dir. of Pastoral Internship and Dir. of Field Educ. Prog.; Edward Smith, M.A., Dir. of Formation; Mr. Michael E. Sweeney, M.A., Registrar; Dennis K. Eagan, B.B.A., Business Mgr.; William Wester, Ed.D., Dir. Pastoral Counseling Degree. In res. Most Rev. Carl K. Moeddel; Revs. Gerald R. Haemmerle, M.A.; J. Robert Jack, M.A.; Jeffrey M. Kemper, Ph.D.; Theodore Ross, S.J.; Timothy P. Schehr, Ph.D.; Michael Seger, S.T.D.; Edward Smith, M.A.; Francis W. Voellmecke, Ph.D. Non-Resident Faculty: Mr. Terrance Callan, Ph.D.; Mr. Anthony Dicello, M.M.; John Gutting, Ph.D.; Sr. Deborah Harmeling, M.S.L.; Sr. Betty Jane Lillie, Ph.D. In res. Rev. Joseph F. Beckman.

CARTHAGENA. *St. Charles*, Society of the Precious Blood, 45822. Tel: 419-925-4516; Fax: 419-925-4800.
Web site: ma.noacsc.org/stcharl/
Revs. James C. Seibert, C.PP.S., Dir.; George Albers, C.PP.S.; Clement Alt, C.PP.S.; Joseph Anhamatten, C.PP.S.; Milton Ballor, C.PP.S.; Aloysius B. Boeke; Robert Contant (FTW); Robert Conway, C.PP.S.; Rocco Cosentino, C.PP.S.; Raymond Cera, C.PP.S.; Robert Gaertner, C.PP.S.; Harold Diller, C.PP.S.; William Donohoe, C.PP.S.; William Dougherty, C.PP.S.; Richard Elo, C.PP.S.; Cornelius Fenton, C.PP.S.; Aloys Friedrich, C.PP.S.; Anthony Gamble, C.PP.S.; Leo Gaulrapp, C.PP.S.; Raymond Grevencamp, C.PP.S.; Joseph Hajduch, C.PP.S.; Augustine Hanchak, C.PP.S.; Alphonse Jungwirth, C.PP.S.; Gerold Koller, C.PP.S.; William Kramer, C.PP.S.; Clement Kuhns, C.PP.S.; Paul Link, C.PP.S.; Henry Langhals, C.PP.S.; John Lefko, C.PP.S.; Joseph Lima, C.PP.S.; Arnold Meiring, C.PP.S.; James Miller, C.PP.S.; Alfred Naseman, C.PP.S.; Daniel Raible, C.PP.S.; Albert Reed, C.PP.S.; Louis Schmit, C.PP.S.; Kenneth Schroeder, C.PP.S.; Raymond Seifert, C.PP.S.; John Spatt, C.PP.S.; Leonard Sudhoff, C.PP.S.; Anthony Traser, C.PP.S.; Werner Verhoff, C.PP.S.; Anthony Vollmer, C.PP.S.; Carl Wise, C.PP.S.; Bro. Gerald Hall, C.PP.S., Treas. Priests 44; Brothers 16; Sisters 4.

[C] NOVITIATES AND HOUSES OF STUDY

CINCINNATI. *Dominican Novitiate*, 7630 Shawnee Run Rd., 45243. Tel: 513-527-3972; Fax: 513-527-3973.
E-mail: wcw93@juno.com
Web site: www.op-stjoseph.org/
Rev. Walter C. Wagner, O.P., Novice Master. Novices 6.

St. Anthony Shrine, Francisan Candidacy, St. John the Baptist Province, 5000 Colerain Ave., 45223. Tel: 513-541-2146; Fax: 513-541-9347. Revs. Clyde Young, O.F.M., Vicar; Dennis Bosse, O.F.M., Instructor; Aquinas Schneider, O.F.M., Hospital Chap.; Stephen Schneider, O.F.M., (Retired); Kenan Freson, O.F.M., Prov. Treas.; Frank Geers, O.F.M., Dir. of Candidates; Bros. Gabriel Balassone, O.F.M.; Vincent Delorenzo, O.F.M., Guardian; Scott Obrecht, O.F.M.; Donald Rewers, O.F.M. Priests 6; Brothers 4; Candidates 1.

DAYTON. *Marianist Novitiate*, 4435 E. Patterson Rd., 45430-1095. Tel: 937-426-5721; Fax: 937-429-4686.
E-mail: tedesco@flyernet.udayton.edu
Rev. Joseph P. Tedesco, S.M., Dir. Priests 2; Brothers 7; Novices 2.

[D] COLLEGES AND UNIVERSITIES

CINCINNATI. *College of Mount St. Joseph*, 5701 Delhi Rd., 45233-1670. Tel: 513-244-4200; Fax: 513-244-4601.
E-mail: greg_grady@mail.msj.edu
Web site: www.msj.edu
For a complete listing, refer to the Colleges and Universities section.

Xavier University, 3800 Victory Pkwy. at Dana Ave., 45207. Tel: 513-745-3000; Fax: 513-745-4223.
Web site: www.xu.edu
For a complete listing, refer to the Colleges and Universities section.

DAYTON. *The University of Dayton*, (1850) 300 College Park Ave., 45469-1624. Tel: 937-229-1000.
Web site: www.udayton.edu
For a complete listing, refer to the Colleges and Universities section.

SAINT MARTIN. *Chatfield College*, Brown County Ursulines, 20918 State Rte. 251, 45118. Tel: 937-875-3344; Fax: 937-875-3912.
E-mail: margaret@chatfield.edu
Web site: www.chatfield.edu
For a complete listing, refer to the Colleges and Universities section.

[E] HIGH SCHOOLS, INTER-PAROCHIAL

CINCINNATI. *Elder High School*, 3900 Vincent Ave., 45205-1699. Tel: 513-921-3744; Fax: 513-921-8123.
Web site: www.elderhs.org
Revs. James G. Kiffmeyer; Donald R. Rettig. Priests 2; Lay Teachers 63; Students 1,007.

LaSalle High School, 3091 N. Bend Rd., 45239-7696. Tel: 513-741-3000; Fax: 513-741-2666.
Web site: www.cincinnatilasalle.net/
Mr. Thomas Luebbe, Prin. Lay Teachers 54; Students 889.

McAuley High School, 6000 Oakwood Ave., 45224. Tel: 513-681-1800; Fax: 513-681-1802.
E-mail: sucher_c@hccanet.org
Web site: www.mcauleyhs.net
Mrs. Cheryl A. Sucher, Prin.; Mrs. Connie Kampschmidt, Asst. Prin.; Mr. Al Early, Asst. Prin. Sisters of Mercy 2; Lay Teachers 59; Girls 891. Convents, 1768 Cedar Ave. 5925 Oakwood Ave. 5764 Belmont Ave., 45224.

McNicholas High School, 6536 Beechmont Ave., 45230. Tel: 513-231-3500; Fax: 513-231-1351. Mr. Thomas R. Bill, Prin. Lay Teachers 64; Students 919.

Moeller High School, 9001 Montgomery Rd., 45242. Tel: 513-791-1680; Fax: 513-792-3343.
E-mail: bbalbach@moeller.org
Web site: www.moeller.org
Mr. Daniel J. Ledford, Prin.; Rev. Jeffrey Fulmer. Sisters of Mercy 1; Diocesan Priest 1; Brothers 5; Lay Teachers 55; Students 930.

Mother of Mercy High School, 3036 Werk Rd., 45211. Tel: 513-661-2740; Fax: 513-661-1842.
E-mail: merkle_n@hccanet.org
Web site: www.hccanet.org/motherofmercy
Sr. Nancy Merkle, R.S.M., Prin. Sisters of Mercy 4; Lay Teachers 52; Girls 663.

Mt. Notre Dame High School, 711 E. Columbia Ave., 45215. Tel: 513-821-3044; Fax: 513-821-6068.
E-mail: cmtnd@connectinc.com
Web site: www.mndhs.org
Mrs. Maureen Baldock, Prin. Sisters 4; Lay Teachers 65; Girls 750.

Purcell Marian High School. (Walnut Hills), 2935 Hackberry St., 45206. Tel: 513-751-1230; Fax: 513-751-1395.
E-mail: janismkennedy@aol.com
Web site: purcellmarian.com
Janis M. Kennedy, Prin.; Terry Meinking, Business Mgr.; Mr. David Campbell, Dir. Ministry. Priests 1; Brothers 3; Sisters 3; Lay Teachers 55; Students 725.

Roger Bacon High School, 4320 Vine St., 45217. Tel: 513-641-1300; Fax: 513-641-0498.
E-mail: bosse_r@hcca.ohio.gov
Web site: www.w3.one.net/~sputnik/spartans
Franciscan Friars of the Cincinnati Province of St. John the Baptist. Revs. Roger T. Bosse, O.F.M., Prin.; Patrick McCloskey, O.F.M., Teacher; Dennis Bosse, O.F.M., Teacher & Chap.; Bro. Christopher Cahill, O.F.M., Computer Network Coord. Teacher; Rev. Mark Hudak, O.F.M., Teacher. Priests 4; Brothers 1; Sisters 1; Lay Teachers 53; Students 810.

Seton High School. (Price Hill), 3901 Glenway Ave., 45205. Tel: 513-471-2600; Fax: 513-471-0529.
E-mail: gibbons_s@hccanet.org
Ms. Susan M. Gibbons, Prin.; Mr. Gordon MacIntosh, Assoc. Prin. Academics; Mr. Thomas McKiernan, Foundation Chair.; Mrs. Janice Linz, Campus Min. Sisters of Charity of Cincinnati 10; Lay Teachers 41; Students 703.

DAYTON. *Archbishop Alter High School*, 940 E. David Rd., 45429. Tel: 937-434-4434; Fax: 937-434-0507.
E-mail: npalter@mdeca.org
Web site: www.alterhighschool.com
Ms. Katherine Beimesche, Prin. Sisters 2; Lay Teachers 55; Students 725.

Carroll High School, 4524 Linden Ave., 45432. Tel: 937-253-8188; Fax: 937-258-7001.
E-mail: npcajsens@mdeca.org
Web site: carrollhs.org
Mr. Joseph R. Sens, Prin. Sisters 1; Lay Teachers 66; Students 1,140.

Chaminade-Julienne High School, 505 S. Ludlow St., 45402. Tel: 937-461-3740; Fax: 937-461-0356.
E-mail: gocjeagles@aol.com
Web site: www.udayton.cdu/cj/
Conducted by the Society of Mary (Marianists) and Sisters of Notre Dame de Namur. Mr. Lorcan Barnes, Pres.; Mr. Mike Trainor, Prin.; Ms. Joyce Detzel, Asst. Prin., Academics; Mrs. Patsy Puterbaugh, Asst. Prin. Student Svcs.; Mr. Matt Ernst, Dir. Admin. Svcs.; Rev. Christopher Wittman, S.M., Dir. Pastoral Svcs.; Sr. Damienne Grismer, S.N.D.deN. Priests 1; Brothers 1; Sisters 3; Lay Teachers 70; Students 962.

HAMILTON. *Stephen T. Badin High School*, 571 New London Rd., 45013. Tel: 513-863-3993; Fax: 513-785-2844.
E-mail: fmargello@stephen-t-badin.cnd.pvt.k12.oh.us
Web site: stephen-t-badin.cnd.pvt.k12.oh.us
Ms. Margaret R. Winkeljohn, Prin. Lay Teachers 51; Students 721.

MIDDLETOWN. *Bishop Fenwick High School*, 3800 Manchester Rd., 45042. Tel: 513-423-0723; Fax: 513-420-8690.
E-mail: c1_birck@swoca.ohio.gov
Web site: bishop-fenwickcnd.pvt.k12.oh.us
Rev. Charles E. Mentrup, Prin. Priests 1; Deacons 1; Lay Teachers 30; Students 424.

SIDNEY. *Lehman High School*, 2400 St. Mary's Ave., 45365. Tel: 937-498-1161; Fax: 937-492-3911.
E-mail: 1c_le_mbarhors@woca-k12.org
Mr. Michael Barhorst, Prin. Sisters 1; Lay Teachers 25; Students 394.

SPRINGFIELD. *Catholic Central High School*, 1200 E. High St., 45505-1124. Tel: 937-325-9204; Fax: 937-328-7426.
E-mail: tlaengle@yahoo.com
Web site: www.catholiccentral.cnd.pvt.k12.oh.us
Sr. Teresa Marie Laengle, S.C., Prin. Sisters 2; Lay Teachers 21; Students 325.

[F] HIGH SCHOOLS, PRIVATE

CINCINNATI. *St. Ursula Academy High School*, 1339 E. McMillan St., 45206. Tel: 513-961-3410; Fax: 513-961-3856.
E-mail: fromweber@saintursula.org
Web site: www.saintursula.org
Frances Romweber, Prin.; Judith A. Wimberg, Pres. Lay Teachers 49; Girls 650.

St. Xavier High School, 600 N. Bend Rd., 45224. Tel: 513-761-7600; Fax: 513-761-3811.
Web site: www.stxavier-cincy.org
Mr. David B. Mueller, Prin.; Rev. William L. Verbryke, S.J., Pres.; Mr. William Sandquist, Jr., Asst. Prin.; Revs. John J. Beckman, S.J.; R. Michael Brophy, S.J.; Edward L. Pigott, S.J.; Francis J. Daly, S.J., Rector. Priests 4; Sisters 1; Lay Teachers 100; Students 1,440.

Ursuline Academy of Cincinnati. Senior High School. 5535 Pfeiffer Rd., 45242. Tel: 513-791-5791; Fax: 513-791-3170.
E-mail: drdi@ursuline-cinci.com
Web site: www.ursulineacademy.org
Ursuline Sisters of Brown Co. Saint Martin, OH. Rev. John E. Wessling; Dr. Diane Castelli, Pres. Priests 1; Sisters 3; Lay Teachers 68; Girls 627.

[G] CONSOLIDATED ELEMENTARY SCHOOLS

CINCINNATI. *Corryville Catholic Elementary School*, 108 Calhoun St., 45219. Tel: 513-281-4856.
E-mail: smith-ma@haccanet.org
Sr. Marie Smith, S.N.D., Prin. Sisters 6; Lay Teachers 10; Students 200.
Consolidated school serving the parishes of St. George, St. Monica, Holy Name, St. Andrew, Assumption and Sacred Heart.

St. Bartholomew. (Grades K-8), 9375 Winton Rd., 45231. Tel: 513-521-0860; Fax: 513-728-3110.
E-mail: carver_m@hccanet.org
Ms. Mary R. Carver, Prin.; Mrs. Mary Hedger, Asst. Prin. Lay Teachers 28; Students 714.
Consolidated school serving the parishes of St. Bartholomew, Corpus Christi and St. John Neumann, Cincinnati.

St. Boniface School, 4305 Pitts Ave., 45223. Tel: 513-541-5122; Fax: 513-541-3939.
E-mail: sessman_t@hccanet.org
Mr. Thomas Sessman, Prin. Sisters 2; Lay Teachers 9; Students 183.
Serving the parishes of St. Boniface and St. Leo, Cincinnati.

St. Gabriel Consolidated School. (Grades K-8), 18 W. Sharon Ave., 45246. Tel: 513-771-5220; Fax: 513-771-5133.
Joseph Epplen, Prin. Lay Teachers 19; Students 416.
Consolidated school serving the parishes of St. Gabriel, Glendale; St. John, West Chester; St. Martin de Porres, Lincoln Heights; St. Matthias, Forest Park; St. Maximilian Kolbe, West Chester.

DAYTON. *Bishop Leibold School.* West Campus: (Grades K-2), 24 S. Third St., Miamisburg, 45342. Tel: 937-866-3021. East Campus: (Grades 3-8), 6666 Springboro Rd., 45449. Tel: 937-434-9343; Fax: 937-436-3048. Mr. Charles Lanasa, Prin. Lay Teachers 30; Students 590.
Serving the Parishes of St. Henry, Dayton and Our Lady of Good Hope, Miamisburg.

Dayton Catholic Elementary School. (Grades K-8), 3805 King's Hwy., 45406. Tel: 937-275-8114; Fax: 937-275-5737.
E-mail: kjhecker@aol.com
Web site: www.daycath.cnd.pvt.k12.oh.us
Mrs. Karyn J. Hecker, Prin. Lay Teachers 11; Students 235.
Serving the parishes of St. Agnes, and St. James, Dayton.

HAMILTON. *St. Joseph Consolidated School.* (Grades K-8), 925 S. Second St., 45011. Tel: 513-863-8758; Fax: 513-863-5253.
E-mail: 08_stenger@swocai.swoca.net
Joseph Pyfrin, Prin. Lay Teachers 13; Students 220.
Serving the parishes of St. Aloysius, Shandon and St. Joseph, Hamilton.

MIDDLETOWN. *John XIII Catholic Elementary School.* East Campus: (Grades K-5), 3907 Central Ave., 45044. Tel: 513-424-0838; Fax: 513-424-8568. North Campus: (Grades 6-8), 3806 Manchester Rd., 45042. Tel: 513-424-1196; Fax: 513-420-8480.
E-mail: c2_krista@swocai.swoca.net
Sr. Nancy Krista, S.N.D., Prin. Sisters 3; Lay Teachers 24; Students 494.
Serving the parishes of Holy Family, Middletown and St. Mary, Franklin.

PIQUA. *Piqua Catholic School.* North St. Campus: (Grades 4-8), 503 W. North St., 45356. Tel: 937-773-1564; Fax: 937-773-0380. Downing St. Campus: (Grades K-3), 218 S. Downing St., 45356. Tel: 937-773-3876; Fax: 937-773-5875. Mr. David Skelton, Prin. Sisters 2; Lay Teachers 18; Students 420.
Serving the parishes of St. Boniface and St. Mary.

SPRINGFIELD. *Holy Trinity Catholic School.* (Grades K-8), 1035 W. High St., 45506. Tel: 937-322-8781; Fax: 937-323-2790.
E-mail: hlty_sblank@k12server.mveca.org
Web site: www.holytrinity.cnd.pvt.k12.oh.us
Sr. Sharon Blank, Prin. Lay Teachers 10; Students 191.
Serving the parishes of St. Joseph, St. Mary and St. Raphael.

[H] ELEMENTARY SCHOOLS, PRIVATE

CINCINNATI. *St. Ursula Villa.* (Grades PreK-8), 3660 Vineyard Pl., 45226. Tel: 513-871-7218; Fax: 513-871-0082.
E-mail: loechle_p@hccanet.org
Paul Loechle, Prin. Lay Teachers 37; Students 507.

Summit Country Day School. (Grades PreK-12), 2161 Grandin Rd., 45208-3300. Tel: 513-871-4700; Fax: 513-533-5373.
E-mail: summitinfo@summitcds.org
Web site: www.summitcds.org
Edward C. Tyrrell, Headmaster and Pres. Lay Teachers 142; Students 1,187.

MONROE. *Mother Teresa Catholic Elementary School*, 330-B Lebanon St., 45050-1409. Tel: 513-539-2273; Fax: 513-539-8213.
Web site: www.catholic-church.org/mtces
Mr. Christopher Roll, School Board Chm.; Sr. Anne Mary Schulz, C.PP.S., Prin. Sisters 1; Lay Teachers 2; Students 59.

[I] CHILD CARE INSTITUTIONS

CINCINNATI. *St. Aloysius Orphanage*, 4721 Reading Rd., 45237. Tel: 513-242-7600; Fax: 513-242-2845.
E-mail: bclevenger@staloysiuscincinnati.org
Web site: www.staloysiuscincinnati.org
For a complete listing, refer to the Special Care Facilities section.

St. Joseph Infant and Maternity Home dba St. Joseph Home, 10722 Wyscarver Rd., 45241. Tel: 513-563-2520; Fax: 513-563-1958.
E-mail: smvanvurst@sjh-cincy.com
Web site: www.sjh-cincy.com
For a complete listing, refer to the Special Care Facilities section.

St. Joseph Orphanage, 5400 Edalbert Dr., 45239-7695. Tel: 513-741-3100; Fax: 513-741-5656.
E-mail: sjoe@one.net
Web site: www.stjosephorphanage.org
For a complete listing, refer to the Special Care Facilities section.

[J] SPECIAL SCHOOLS

CINCINNATI. *St. Rita School for the Deaf*, 1720 Glendale-Milford Rd., 45215. Tel: 513-771-7600; Fax: 513-326-8264.
E-mail: ernst_g@hccanet.org
Web site: www.srsdeaf.org
Mr. Gregroy R. Ernst, Exec. Dir.; Ms. Mary Ann Stansfield, Dir. Special Svcs.; Rev. William H. Wysong. Sisters of Charity 2; Lay Teachers 35; High School Students 38; Elementary Students 56; Pre-School 38. Residential and day school for deaf and hard of hearing children.

[K] GENERAL HOSPITALS

CINCINNATI. *Good Samaritan Hospital*, 375 Dixmyth Ave., 45220. Tel: 513-872-1400; Fax: 513-872-3435.
Web site: trihealth.com
For a complete listing, refer to the Hospitals section.

Mercy Health Plaza dba Mercy Franciscan Hospital-Western Hills, 3131 Queen City Ave., 45238. Tel: 513-389-5000; Fax: 513-389-9207
For a complete listing, refer to the Hospitals section.

Mercy Health Plaza dba Mercy Franciscan Hospital-Mt. Airy, 4340 Glendale-Milford Rd., 45242. Tel: 513-853-5000; Fax: 513-853-5910
For a complete listing, refer to the Hospitals section.

Mercy Hospital Anderson, 7500 State Rd., 45255. Tel: 513-624-4500
For a complete listing, refer to the Hospitals section.

BATAVIA. *The Sisters of Mercy Of Clermont County, Ohio dba Mercy Hospital Clermont*, 3000 Hospital Dr., 45103. Tel: 513-732-8200; Fax: 513-732-8537
For a complete listing, refer to the Hospitals section.

DAYTON. *Franciscan Medical Center - Dayton Campus*, One Franciscan Way, 45408. Tel: 937-229-6000
For a complete listing, refer to the Hospitals section.

Good Samaritan Hospital, 2222 Philadelphia Dr., 45406. Tel: 937-278-2612
For a complete listing, refer to the Hospitals section.

FAIRFIELD. *Mercy Health Plaza*, 2990 Mack Rd., 45242. Tel: 513-874-6440
For a complete listing, refer to the Hospitals section.

HAMILTON. *The Sisters of Mercy of Hamilton, Ohio dba Mercy Hospital of Hamilton-Fairfield*, 100 Riverfront Plaza, P.O. Box 418, 45011. Tel: 513-867-6400; Fax: 513-867-9043
For a complete listing, refer to the Hospitals section.

SPRINGFIELD. *Mercy Health System - Western Ohio*, 1343 N. Fountain Blvd., 45501-1380. Tel: 937-390-5000; Fax: 937-890-5507.
E-mail: sdarch@health-partners.org
For a complete listing, refer to the Hospitals section.

URBANA. *Mercy Memorial Hospital*, 904 Scioto St., 43078. Tel: 937-653-5231; Fax: 937-652-1866.
E-mail: kzalar@health-partners.org
For a complete listing, refer to the Hospitals section.

[L] SENIOR RESIDENCES

CINCINNATI. *Archbishop Leibold Home for the Aged*, 476 Riddle Rd., 45220-2493. Tel: 513-281-8001; Fax: 513-281-4943
For a complete listing, refer to the Special Care Facilities section.

Mercy Franciscan Senior Health and Housing Services Inc. dba Mercy St. Theresa Center, 7010 Rowan Hill Dr., 45227. Tel: 513-271-7010; Fax: 513-527-0143
For a complete listing, refer to the Special Care Facilities section.

Mercy Franciscan Senior Health and Housing Services, Inc. dba Mercy Franciscan Terrace, 100 Compton Rd., 45215. Tel: 513-761-9036; Fax: 513-761-5199
For a complete listing, refer to the Special Care Facilities section.

Mercy Franciscan Senior Health and Housing Services, Inc. dba Mercy Franciscan at West Park, 2950 West Park Dr., 45238. Tel: 513-451-8900; Fax: 513-451-3728
For a complete listing, refer to the Special Care Facilities section.

St. Margaret Hall, 1960 Madison Rd., 45206-1896. Tel: 513-751-5880; Fax: 513-751-9813
For a complete listing, refer to the Special Care Facilities section.

Sisters of Charity Senior Care Corp., dba Bayley Place, 990 Bayley Place Dr., 45233. Tel: 513-347-5500; Fax: 513-347-5553.
E-mail: bayleyplace@srcharitycinti.org
Web site: www.bayleyplace.org
For a complete listing, refer to the Special Care Facilities section.

CENTERVILLE. *The Franciscan at St. Leonard*, 8100 Clyo Rd., 45458. Tel: 937-433-0480; Fax: 937-439-7165
For a complete listing, refer to the Special Care Facilities section.

DAYTON. *The Maria Joseph Living Care Center*, 4830 Salem Ave., 45416. Tel: 937-278-2692; Fax: 937-278-9016.
E-mail: mariajoseph@mariajoseph.org
Web site: www.mariajoseph.org
For a complete listing, refer to the Special Care Facilities section.

Mercy Siena Springs, 6215 N. Main St., 45415. Tel: 937-274-4790; Fax: 937-274-9812
For a complete listing, refer to the Special Care Facilities section.

Mercy Siena Woods, 235 W. Orchard Springs Dr., 45415. Tel: 937-278-8211; Fax: 937-278-8046.
E-mail: shayes@health-partners.org
For a complete listing, refer to the Special Care Facilities section.

HAMILTON. *Mercy Franciscan Senior Health and Housing Services, Inc. dba Mercy Franciscan at Schroder*, 1302 Millville Ave., 45013. Tel: 513-867-1300; Fax: 513-867-1415.
E-mail: m/morgan@health-partners.org
For a complete listing, refer to the Special Care Facilities section.

SPRINGFIELD. *Oakwood Village Retirement Community*, 1500 Villa Rd., 45503. Tel: 937-390-9000; Fax: 937-390-9333.
E-mail: razechiel@health-partners.org
For a complete listing, refer to the Special Care Facilities section.

URBANA. *Mercy McAuley Center-Mercy Health Systems*, 906 Scioto St., 43078. Tel: 937-653-5432; Fax: 937-652-2072.
E-mail: kzalar@health-partners.org
For a complete listing, refer to the Special Care Facilities section.

[M] MONASTERIES AND RESIDENCES OF PRIESTS AND BROTHERS

CINCINNATI. *The Catholic Foreign Mission Society of America, Inc.*, 6930 Greenfield Dr., 45224-1626. Tel: 513-681-7888; Fax: 513-681-7893 (Call first).
E-mail: mklcin@aol.com
Web site: www.maryknoll.org
Maryknoll Fathers. Revs. Leslie F. Blowers, M.M., Dir.; Peter L. Chabot, M.M.

Comboni Missionaries (Verona Fathers)-Comboni Mission Center. Houses Comboni Missionaries of the Heart of Jesus, Inc., The Offices of the Province of North America, including the Office of the Provincial. 8108 Beechmont Ave., 45255-3194. Tel: 513-474-4997; Fax: 513-474-0382.
E-mail: klcomoni@juno.com
Web site: www.combonimissionaries.org
Revs. Dennis Conway, M.C.C.J., Prov. Tel: 513-474-3818; Joseph Bragotti, M.C.C.J., Dir. of Mission Office; Brian Quigley, M.C.C.J., Prov. Treas.; Sr. Roseanne White, O.S.U., Finance Dir.; Revs. Mario Ongaro, M.C.C.J., Personnel Dir.; Paul Donohue, M.C.C.J., Editor Comboni Missions Newsletter & Comboni Press Feature Service; Jose Luis Cuevas, M.C.C.J., Editor "Mundo Joven"; Cindy Browne, Mgr. & Editor, CPN Newsletter; Tim McDowell, Devel. Dir.; Revs. Kenneth Gerth, M.C.C.J.; William Jansen, M.C.C.J.; Bro. Giovanni (John) Soster. Priests 8; Brothers 1.

De Sales Crossings Marianist Community, 1600 Madison Rd., 45206-1815. Tel: 513-961-1945. Bros. Lawrence W. Corbin, S.M., Dir.; David K. Betz, S.M.; Giancarlo Bonutti, S.M.; Robert A. Politi,

S.M.; Daniel R. Stupka, S.M.; Robert N. Wiethorn, S.M.; William I. Grundish, S.M.; Rev. Edward M. Jack, S.M. Priests 1; Brothers 7.

Faber Jesuit Community, 790 Clinton Springs Ave., 45229. Tel: 513-961-7700; Fax: 513-569-4582. Revs. Edward W. Carter, S.J.; John N. Felten, S.J.; John M. Ferone, S.J.; Robert J. Hagee, S.J.; John P. Heim, S.J., Supr.; Donald O'Shaughnessy, S.J.; Herbert J Raterman, S.J.; Harold Sommer, S.J.; Peter Sharkey, S.J.; John Beckman, S.J. Tel: 513-791-4735; James Brichetto, S.J.

4105 Hoffman Ave., 45236. Rev. Robert J. Ross, S.J.

2028 Mackoy Ave., 41014. Bros. Donald H. Bengert, S.J.; John P. Martin, S.J. Priests 12; Brothers 2.

Headquarters of Glenmary Home Missioners, P.O. Box 465618, 45246-5618. Tel: 513-874-8900; Fax: 513-874-1690.

E-mail: infor@glenmary.org

Web site: www.glenmary.org

4119 Glenmary Trace, Fairfield, 45014. Tel: 513-874-8900; Fax: 513-874-1690. Also known as The Home Missioners of America. Revs. Jerry Dorn, Glmy., Pres.; Dan Dorsey, Glmy., 1st Vice Pres. & Dir. of Education Dept.; Bro. Jack Henn, Glmy., 2nd Vice Pres. Senior Members: Revs. Robert C. Berson, Glmy.; Joseph Dean, Glmy.; Joseph Gartner, Glmy.; John Garvey, Glmy.; Edward Haggerty, Glmy.; Robert Healy, Glmy.; Del Holmes, Glmy.; Charles Hughes, Glmy.; James Kelly, Glmy.; George Mathis, Glmy.; John McNearney, Glmy.; Joseph O'Donnell, Glmy.; Patrick O'Donnell, Glmy.; Raymond Orlett, Glmy.; John Otterbacher, Glmy.; Robert Rademacher, Glmy.; Francisco Schenk, Glmy.; Leo Schloemer, Glmy.; William Smith, Glmy.; James Willmes, Glmy.; Bros. Robert Hoffman; Thomas Kelly; Charles Kennedy; George Sauer; Bernie Stern; Vincent Wilmes. In res. Revs. Dominic Duggins, Glmy., Development Dir.; August Guppenberger, Glmy.; Richard Kreimer, Glmy., Mission OFC; Bro. Dennis Craig, Glmy., Senior Member Coordinator.

On Special Assignment: Revs. Donald Levernier, Glmy., On Loan to Lithuania; John Rausch, Human Economics Ministry, Berea, KY.

Jesuit Community at Xavier University, Jesuit Community Residence, 3844 Victory Pkwy., 45207. Tel: 513-745-3591; Fax: 513-745-3858. Members of the Jesuit Community (Society of Jesus, S.J.). Revs. Joseph A. Bracken, S.J.; Albert J. Bischoff, S.J.; Robert C. Baumiller, S.J.; Richard W. Bollman, S.J., Rector; Eugene J. Carmichael, S.J.; Michael J. Graham, S.J.; James E. Hoff, S.J.; Thomas P. Kennealy, S.J.; William F. King, S.J.; J. Leo Klein, S.J.; John J. LaRocca, S.J.; Timothy J. Meier, S.J.; Robert W. Schmidt, S.J.; Edward T. O'Donnell, S.J.; Theodore C. Thepe, S.J.; Benjamin J. Urmston, S.J.; George B. Wilson, S.J.; Bro. Jerome J. Pryor, S.J. Priests 17; Brothers 1.

Jesuit Community at St. Xavier High School, Jesuit Community7361 View Pl., 45224. Tel: 513-761-5522; Fax: 513-761-0514. Revs. Francis J. Daly, S.J., Rector; Michael Brophy, S.J.; Gil Martinez, S.J., Scholastic; Eugene J. Nevins, S.J.; Edward L. Pigott, S.J.; Robert J. Thesing, S.J.; William L. Verbryke, S.J.

Marianist Community, 2708 Johnstone Pl., 45206-1822. Tel: 513-961-6244. Brothers 3.

Marianist Community, 9025 Montgomery Rd., 45242-7711. Tel: 513-793-4777; Fax: 513-792-3343.

E-mail: rflaherty@moeller.org

Web site: www.moeller.org

Bro. Robert M. Flaherty, S.M., Dir.; Rev. Lawrence L. Schoettelkotte, S.M. Priests 1; Brothers 6.

Marianist Community, 118 Findlay St., Apt. #1, 45210-2402. Tel: 513-369-0388; Fax: 513-369-0408.

Web site: www.geocities.com/heartland/prairie/9125index.htm/

Rev. Michael L. Lisbeth, S.M.; Bros. Robert P. Donovan, S.M., Dir.; J. Mitchell Schweickart, S.M.; Paul Hoffman, S.M. Brothers 3; Priests 1.

Pleasant Street Friary, 1723 Pleasant St., 45210. Tel: 513-621-0599; Fax: 513-621-0519.

E-mail: dja@franciscan.org

Friars Daniel J. Anderson, O.F.M.; Jack R. Wintz, O.F.M.; Murray L. Bodo, O.F.M.

St. Ann Friary, 2936 W. Galbraith Rd., 45239. Tel: 513-522-7420; Fax: 513-522-1752.

E-mail: schreckj@aol.com

Revs. Dennet Jung, O.F.M.; Joseph Rayes, O.F.M.; Joseph Ricchini, O.F.M.; Bros. John Schreck, O.F.M.; Kevin Schroeder, O.F.M.

St. Clare Friary, 5831 Saranac Ave., 45224. Tel: 513-541-5742; Fax: 513-541-5774. Revs. Patrick McCloskey, O.F.M.; James M. Bok, O.F.M.; Bros. Gene Mayer, O.F.M.; Francisco Meyer, O.F.M.

St. Clement Friary. St. John the Baptist Province. Residence for Retired Friars, Pastors of St. Clement Parish and other Friars. 4536 Vine St., 45217. Tel: 513-641-2257; Fax: 513-641-2262.

E-mail: langender@aol.com

Revs. E. John Stein, O.F.M., Pastor; Carl J. Langenderfer, O.F.M., Local Min. & Assoc. Pastor; Stanley Bir, O.F.M., Prov. Personnel Advisor; Joel Byrne, O.F.M., (Retired); Alan Heet, O.F.M., (Retired); Howard Hudepohl, O.F.M., Chap., Mercy Franciscan Terrrace; Marcan Hetteberg, O.F.M., Asst. Archivist & Prov. Librarian; Chris Schneider, O.F.M., (Retired); Roger T. Bosse, O.F.M., Prin., Roger Bacon High School; Valens J. Waldschmidt, O.F.M., (Retired); Juvenal Pfalzer, O.F.M., (Retired); Roman Pfalzer, O.F.M., (Retired); Adrian Schneider, O.F.M., (Retired); Paul Wild, O.F.M., (Retired); Bros. Conrad F. Rebmann, O.F.M., (Retired); Louis Lamping, O.F.M., Treas. & Fraternal Svc.; Linus Border, O.F.M., Fraternal Svs.; Bernard Jennings, O.F.M., (Retired); Kenneth Beetz, O.F.M., Maintenance; Joel Soldenski, O.F.M., Sacristan; Jerry Jackson, O.F.M., Fraternal Svc.; Joseph Haley, O.F.M., Purchaser, Notre Dame Sisters; Francis Williams, O.F.M., (Retired). Priests 14; Brothers 9.

St. Francis Seraph Friary. Provincial Headquarters of the Province of St. John the Baptist of the Order of Friars Minor. 1615 Vine St., 45210. Tel: 513-721-4700; Fax: 513-421-9672.

E-mail: secsjb@franciscan.com

Revs. Edward Slater, O.F.M., Pastor; Fred Link, O.F.M., Prov. Min.; Jeffrey Scheeler, O.F.M., Vicar Prov.; Kenan Freson, O.F.M., Prov. Treas.; James M. Bok, O.F.M., Dir. Devel.; Francis S. Tebbe, O.F.M., Dir. Ongoing Formation; Rock Travnikar, O.F.M., Vocation Dir.; Ms. Toni Cashnelli, Dir. Communications; Revs. Henry Beck, O.F.M., Office of Justice, Peace and Integrity of Creation; Peter Paul James, O.F.M., (Retired); Simeon Cleves, O.F.M., Chap., Christ Hospital; Bros. Scott Obrecht, O.F.M., Dir. Franciscan Mission Office & Missionary Union; Gene Mayer, O.F.M., Prov. Sec.; Josef Anderlohr, O.F.M., Assoc. Pastor, Liturgical Design Consultant, & Guardian; John Carey, O.F.M., Assoc., Mission Office; David Crank, O.F.M., Office for Senior Friars; Dominic Lococo, O.F.M., SAM Sales Rep.; Robert Lucero, O.F.M., SAM Production Mgr. & Vicar; Bill Spond, O.F.M., Porter; Ronald Bolfeta, O.F.M., Parish Admin., Prov. Councilor, Exec. Dir., O.F.M. English-Speaking Conference. Priests 3; Brothers 7.

Friars of the Province Serving Abroad: Rev. Lawrence Landini, O.F.M., Santa Sophia Friary, P.O. Box 17004, Groenkloof, Pretoria, 0027 South Africa. Tel: 011-27-12-346-1778; Fax: 011-27-12-346-1438. Rev. Malachy Brogan, O.F.M., St. Anthony Church, 51 Yafet St., P.O. Box 8423, 61083 Jaffa, Israel, 00165. Tel: 011-972-3-822667. Rev. Carl Kemphues, O.F.M., Franciscan Renewal Center, Tungkop, Minglanilla, 6046 Cebu, Philippines. Bro. Cletus Riederer, O.F.M., Our Lady of the Angels Seminary, P.O. Box 191 Bagbag, Novaliches, 117 Quezon City, Philippines. Tel: 011-63-02-939-5545; Fax: 011-63-02-937-9321. Rev. Daniel Kroger, O.F.M., 69 San Pedro Bautista St., San Francisco del Monte, 1104 Quezon City, Philippines. Tel: 011-63-02-373-2973; Fax: 011-63-02-373-2972. Rev. Harold Geers, O.F.M., Mt. Laverna, 6501 Palo Leyte, Philippines. Bro. Philip Wilhelm, O.F.M., Sanctuario de San Antonio, P.O. Box 2215 MCC, Forbes Park, Makati, Metro Manila, Philippines, 1299. Tel: 011-63-02-843-8830; Fax: 011-63-02-843-9223. Bro. Roger Covero, O.F.M., San Vincente Ferrer Parish, Tambis Circle, Sambag, 6000 Cebu City, Philippines. Tel: 011-63-32-71106; Fax: 011-63-32-254-0107. Rev. John Quigley, O.F.M., Franciscans International, P.O. Box 97, 1211 Geneva 25, Switzerland. Tel: 011-41-22-346-5169; Fax: 011-41-22-346-4103. Rev. James Fehrenbach, O.F.M., Ainmillerstr. 5 Whg. 608, Munich, Germany, 80801. Tel: 011-49-89-399081; Fax: 011-49-33-019087. Rev. Robert Bruno, O.F.M., Ramstein Air Base, PSC 2, Box 9994, APO AE, Germany, 09012. Tel: 011-49-637195-3775; Fax: 011-49-6371-7010. Rev. Henry Beck, O.F.M., Mary, Gate of Heaven Friary, P.O. Box 2654, Negril, Westmorland, Jamaica, WI. Tel: 876-957-4900; Fax: 876-957-4625. Bro. Mark Gehret, O.F.M., Mary, Gate of Heaven Friary, P.O. Box 2654, Negril, Westmorland, Jamaica, WI. Tel: 876-957-4900; Fax: 876-957-4625. Rev. Humbert Moster, O.F.M., St. Joseph Friary, P.O. Box 66, Savanna-la-mar, Westmorland, Jamaica, WI. Tel: 876-955-2648. Bro. Louis Zant, O.F.M., St. Joseph Friary, P.O. Box 66, Savanna-la-mar, Westmorland, Jamaica, WI. Tel: 876-955-2648.

St. Gertrude Priory, 7630 Shawnee Run Rd., 45243. Tel: 513-561-5954; Fax: 513-527-3971.

Web site: www.stgertrude.org

Revs. Walter Wagner, O.P., Novice Master; William Garrott, O.P., Asst. Novice Master and Assoc.; Kenneth R. Letoile, O.P., Prior; J. Benedict Croell, O.P., Assoc.; Brendan Murphy, O.P., Assoc. In res. Rev. J. Vincent Watson, O.P.

St. John the Baptist Friary, 10722 Wyscarver Rd., 45241-3803. Tel: 513-733-4849; Fax: 513-733-4967. Bro. Edward Demyanovich, O.F.M.; Revs. Loren Connell, O.F.M.; Bill Reichel, O.F.M.; Ernest Porsch, O.F.M.; Matthias Crehan, O.F.M.; Varin Slacke, O.F.M.; Fridolin Voegele, O.F.M.; Michael Lenz, O.F.M.

DAYTON. *Marianist Provincialate*. Cincinnati Province of the Society of Mary (Brothers of Mary, Marianists), 4435 E. Patterson Rd., 45430-1095. Tel: 937-429-0794; Fax: 937-429-3195.

E-mail: kamis@flyernet.udayton.edu

Web site: marianists.org or marianists.udayton.edu

Revs. Joseph H. Lackner, S.M., Asst. Prov. & Asst. for Educ.; Joseph P. Tedesco, S.M., Asst. for Religious Life; Bros. Joseph H. Kamis, S.M., Prov.; Robert J. Metzger, S.M., Asst. for Temporalities & Prov. Treas.; Bernard J. Ploeger, S.M., Councilor; Joseph T. Markel, S.M., Asst. Treas.; Ms. Geraldine V. Maschinot, Sec.

Priests of the Province on Special Assignment: Rev. Robert E. Hogan, S.M., Casa San Juan, 1701 Alametos, San Antonio, TX, 78201. Tel: 210-734-6727. Rev. Thomas A. Stanley, S.M., Marianist Community, 5000 Monroe St., Hollywood, FL, 33021-7270. Tel: 954-961-2362. Rev. Dennis J. Gatto, S.M., 7787 S.W. 86th St., Apt E-311, Miami, FL, 33143. Tel: 305-275-7383. Rev. James A. Russell, S.M., Holy Rosary Church, 159 Camino Santa Maria, San Antonio, TX, 78228-4901. Tel: 210-433-3241; Fax: 210-433-2133. Rev. John L. Bakle, S.M., St. Agatha Rectory, 1860 Northam Rd., Columbus, 43221-3299. Tel: 614-488-6149. Rev. Norbert C. Brockman, S.M., 3303 W. Woodlawn Ave., San Antonio, TX, 78228-4852. Tel: 210-436-0182; Fax: 210-436-0188. Rev. Robert J. Bouffier, S.M., St. Anthony Parish, 43 Holton St., Allston, MA, 02134. Tel: 617-738-2448. Rev. Raymond J. Kacirk, S.M., 25149 Hanover St., Dearborn Heights, MI, 48125-1831. Tel: 313-292-0629. Rev. Kenneth J. Sommer, S.M., 5440 Moeller Ave., Cincinnati, 45212. Tel: 513-351-3204. Rev. James F. Kunes, S.M., 4649 Country Ln., Apt. D, St. Louis, MO, 63074-1254. Tel: 314-428-7990. Rev. John J. Klobuka, S.M., Our Lady of Guadalupe Church, 13715 Riggs Rd., Helotes, TX, 78023-3971. Tel: 210-695-8791; Fax: 210-695-9957.

Priests of the Province Serving Overseas: Rev. Michael R. Reaume, S.M., St. Columba, Church Ave., Ballybrack, Ireland. Tel: 011-353-1285-8301 (Cmty); Fax: 011-353-1235-2789 (Cmty).

Priests of the Province Serving in the Missions: Rev. Martin A. Solma, S.M., Bro. Vincent House, P.O. Box 25156, Nairobi, Kenya. Tel: (011-254-2) 566644. Rev. Charles J. Stander, S.M., Marianist Regional House, P.O. Box 50504, Nairobi, Kenya. Tel: (011-254-2) 559625. Rev. Richard A. Loehrlein, S.M., Chaminade Marianist Community, P.O. Box 100, Karonga, Malawi. Tel: 011-873-762-095059 (Cmty). Rev. Michael F. Nartker, S.M., Marianist Noritiate, P.O. Box 210, Limuru, Kenya. Tel: (011-254-0154) 73158.

Marianist Community, 100 Chambers St., 45409-2817. Tel: 937-627-8998. Bro. Thomas E. Oldenski, Acting Dir.; Revs. Bertrand A. Buby, S.M; J. Eugene Contadino, S.M.; Joseph H. Lackner, S.M. Priests 2; Brothers 5.

Marianist Community, 149 Franklin St., 45402-2598. Tel: 937-228-2013. Revs. Lee L. Sciarrotta, S.M., Dir.; Francis J. Kenney, S.M. Priests 2; Brothers 2.

Marianist Community, Meyer Hall, 4435 East Patterson Rd., 45430-1095. Tel: 937-426-7852; 426-7858. Revs. Richard K. Knuge, S.M., Dir.; John D. Mulligan, S.M. (NY). Priests 2; Brothers 6.

Marianist Community, Novitiate, 4435 E. Patterson Rd., 45430-1095. Tel: 937-426-5721; Fax: 937-429-4686. Revs. Joseph P. Tedesco, S.M., Dir. & Master of Novices; H. James Bartlett, S.M. Priests 2; Brothers 7.

Marianist Community, 141 Washington St., 45402-2530. Tel: 937-224-9978. Revs. John A. McGrath, S.M. (NY), Dir.; Charles T. Bergedick, S.M.; Thomas A. Schroer, S.M.; Robert W. Hertweck, S.M.; Paul M. Marshall, S.M. Priests 5; Brothers 10.

Marianist Community, 62 Indiana Ave, 45410-2308. Tel: 937-258-3212. Bro. John J. Jansen, S.M., Dir.; Revs. Norbert C. Burns, S.M.; Cyril G. Middendorf, S.M. Tel: 937-258-3250. Priests 2; Brothers 3.

Marianist Community, 340 Stonemill Rd., 45409-2543. Tel: 937-627-8611. Revs. Gerald T. Chinchar, S.M.; Christopher W. Conlon, S.M. (NY). Priests 2; Brothers 1.

Marianist Community, 121 Sawmill Rd., 45409-2524. Tel: 937-222-4928. Bro. Alex J. Tuss, S.M., Dir.; Revs. Matthew F. Kohmescher, S.M.; Thomas A. Schoen, S.M. Priests 2; Brothers 3.

Marianist Community, 1903 Trinity Ave., 45409-2445. Tel: 937-293-9744. Bro. Daniel L. Klco, S.M., Acting Dir.; Revs. James F. Fitz, S.M.; James L. Heft, S.M.; Christopher T. Wittmann, S.M. Priests 3; Brothers 5.

The Marianist Mission, 119 Franklin St., 45402-2599. Tel: 937-222-4641; 1-800-348-4732; Fax: 937-222-3038. Bro. Ronald L. Overman, S.M., Dir., Marianist Community, Alumni Hall, University of

Dayton, 45469-0300. Tel: 937-229-4695; 229-4703 (Office). Revs. Paul F. Vieson, S.M., Dir.; Robert E. Hughes, S.M. (Pacific); John J. Kelley, S.M.; Theodore A. Koehler, S.M. (France); Joseph F. Kozar, S.M.; Rev. Yukinori F.X. Matsumoto, S.M. (Japan); Revs. James R. McKay, S.M.; John S. Putka, S.M.; Johann B.G. Roten, S.M. (Suisse); Thomas A. Thompson, S.M.; Adolf M. Windisch, S.M. (STL). Priests 11; Brothers 17.

The Franciscan at St. Leonard, Assisted Living & Health and Rehab, 8100 Clyo Rd., 45458. Tel: 937-439-7188. Bro. James R. Vorndran, S.M., Dir. Priests 7; Brothers 12.
Assisted Living: Revs. Donald F. Bracht, S.M. (Pacific); Joseph S. McDonald, S.M.; Edmund L. Rhodes, S.M.; Bernard C. Stueve, S.M.; Louis J. Wiesner, S.M.
Health & Rehab. Revs. John D. Pawlos, S.M. (NY); Bernard L. Horst, S.M.

Marianist Community, 1234 Duckview Ct., 45458. Tel: 937-439-5941. Bro. James R. Vorndran, S.M., Dir.; Rev. Philip C. Hoelle, S.M. Brothers 3; Priests 1.

Marianist Community, 301 Kiefaber St., 45409. Tel: 937-627-8091. Bro. Thomas J. Pieper, S.M., Dir.; Revs. Kenneth A. Templin, S.M.; Joseph H. Lackner, S.M. Priests 2; Brothers 1.

Marianist Network for the Arts. Tel: 937-320-5450; Fax: 937-429-3195. Religious 3; Total Staff 3.

North American Center for Marianist Studies. Tel: 937-429-2521; Fax: 937-429-3195. Religious 2; Total Staff 8.

Marianist Mission. Tel: 937-222-4641; 800-348-4732; Fax: 937-222-3038. Religious 6; Total Staff 65.

Marianist Environmental Education Center. Tel: 937-429-3582; Fax: 937-429-3195. Religious 2; Total Staff 6.

Provincial Office of the Cincinnati Province of the Society of the Precious Blood, 431 East Second St., 45402-1764. Tel: 937-228-9263; Fax: 937-228-6878.
E-mail: cincicpps@aol.com
Web site: www.swiftsite.com/preciousblood
Very Rev. Angelo Anthony, C.PP.S., Prov. Dir.; Bro. Joseph J. Fisher, C.PP.S., Treas.; Revs. Dennis Chriszt, C.PP.S., Dir. of Vocations. Tel: 937-228-6224; Larry J. Hemmelgarn, C.PP.S., Prov. Sec.; William A. Nordenbrock, C.PP.S., Dir. of Devel./Mission Coord. Members of the Provincial Council: Rev. William A. O'Donnell, C.PP.S., Vice Prov., Precious Blood Church, 4961 Salem Ave., 45416-1717. Tel: 937-276-5954; Fax: 937-276-5955. Rev. James C. Seibert, C.PP.S., 1st Councilor, St. Charles Center, 2860 U.S. Rte. 127, Carthegena, 45822-9591. Tel: 419-925-4516; Fax: 419-925-4800. Rev. Thomas Hemm, C.PP.S., 2nd Councilor, St. Peter and Paul Church, 307 N. Locust St., Ottawa, 45875-1495. Tel: 419-523-5216; Fax: 419-523-4048. Rev. Alfred Naseman, C.PP.S., 3rd Councilor, St. Charles Center, 2860 U.S. Rte.127, Carthegena, 45822 -9591. Tel: 419-925-4516, Ext. 353; Fax: 419-925-4800. Bro. Joseph J. Fisher, C.PP.S., 4th Councilor, 431 E. Second St., 45402-1764. Tel: 937-228-9263; Fax: 937-228-6878. Rev. James Dugal, C.PP.S., 5th Councilor, Our Lady of Guadalupe, 6701 St. Rte. 219, P.O. Box 69, Montezuma, 45866- 0069. Tel: 419-268-2312; Fax: 419-268-1602.
Military: Rev. Eugene H. Schnipke, C.PP.S., PSC7 Box 42, APO AE, 09104-0042. Tel: 011-49-2451-63-229. Rev. John S. Srode, C.PP.S., 12 FTW/HC, 2 Washington Cir., Randolph AFB, TX, 78150-4568. Tel: 210-652-2546.
Priests of the Province Serving Abroad: Rev. Frederick T. Licciardi, C.PP.S., Bergstrasse 3, 8044, Zurich, Switzerland. Tel: 011-41-1-382-0206. Very Rev. Barry J. Fischer, C.PP.S., Mod. Gen., Viale di Porta Ardeatina, 66, I-00154 Rome, Italy. Tel: 011-39-06-574-1656; Fax: 011-39-06-574-2874.
Foreign Mission: Rev. Richard L. Beischel, C.PP.S., Casilla 619, Valdivia, Chile. Tel: 011-56-63-214200; Fax: 011-56-63-224528. Rev. William J. Beuth, C.PP.S., Apartado 2483, 01901 Guatemala City, Guatemala. Tel: 011-502-364-1135. Rev. Paul A. Buehler, C.PP.S., San Francisco de Boria, Apartado 1983, Lima 100, Peru. Tel: 011-51-1-476-5181; Fax: 011-51-1-475-6266. Rev. Joseph F. Deardorff, C.PP.S., Nuestra Senora de la Luz, Apartado 2348, Lima, 100, Peru. Tel: 011-51-1-536-9592. Rev. Gerald G. Dreiling, C.PP.S., Apartado 07-0148, Lima 07, Peru. Tel: 011-51-1-546-0285; Fax: 011-51-1-546-0285. Rev. John F. Falter, C.PP.S., Casilla 619, Valdivia, Chile. Tel: 011-56-63-222124. Rev. James E. Gaynor, C.PP.S., Casa Gasper, Apartado 17-0026 Magdalena Del Mar, Lima, Peru, S.A. Tel: 011-51-1-461-2981. Rev. James W. Bender, C.PP.S., Parroquia Cristo Rey, Apartado 36, La Oroya, Peru. Tel: 011-51-64-39-1675; Fax: 011-51-64-39-1675. Rev. Daniel J. Mangen, C.PP.S., Parroquia San Sebastian, Casilla 194, Purranque, Chile. Tel: 011-56-64-351340; Fax: 011-56-64-353534. Rev. Ernest W. Ranly, C.PP.S., Casa San Francisco Javier, Apartado 1983, Lima, 100, Peru. Tel: 011-51-1-476-5181; Fax: 011-51-1-475-6266. Rev. Donald J. Thieman, C.PP.S., N.S. de la P. Sangre, Casilla 176 Correa 2, Santiago, Chile. Tel: 011-56-2-643-7042.
Returned to U.S.A.:
In Residences Not Listed Elsewhere: Rev. Paul Aumen, C.PP.S., 315 Brick Ln., New Oxford, PA, 17350-9050. Tel: 717-624-2562. Rev. Benjamin Basile, C.PP.S., Calumet College, 2400 New York Ave., Whiting, IN, 46394-2146. Tel: 219-922-1794; Fax: 219-473-4259. Rev. John Behen, C.PP.S., 421 W. 3rd St., Sedalia, MO, 65301-4303. Tel: 660-827-2311. Rev. Thomas Beischel, C.PP.S., St. Albert the Great Church, 3033 Far Hills Ave., Kettering, 45429-2509. Tel: 937-294-5624. Rev. John Bolan, C.PP.S., 16359 Emerald Pt., Middleburg Hts, 44130-2574. Tel: 216-526-3030, Ext. 6265. Rev. James Grothjan, C.PP.S., 1135 Bayshore Dr., Valparaiso, FL, 32580-1342. Tel: 850-678-4853. Bro. Joseph Mary Hrezo, C.PP.S., Precious Blood Center, 2140 Hughes Rd., Liberty, MO, 64068-9376. Tel: 816-792-2637. Rev. Robert Hunt, C.PP.S., 14037 Fairway Island Dr., Apt. 226, Orlando, FL, 32837-5250. Tel: 407-251-0909. Rev. Edward Joyce, C.PP.S., 22866 Montalvo Rd., Laguna Niguel, CA, 92677-2740. Tel: 714-493-2800. Rev. Frederick Lang, C.PP.S., 10315 Burgess Rd., Colorado Springs, CO, 80908-4149. Rev. Howard Lesch, C.PP.S., 1115 Coral Dr., Niceville, FL, 32578-3538. Tel: 850-678-7297. Rev. Francis McCarthy, C.PP.S., 52411 County Rd. 425, Fresno, 43824-9779. Rev. William O'Neill, C.PP.S., University of St. Thomas Mail 4046, 2115 Summit Ave., St. Paul, MN, 55105-1048. Tel: 651-962-7482. Rev. Robert Onofrey, C.PP.S., 15700 Orlan Brook Dr., Apt. #169, Orland Park, IL, 60462-4829. Tel: 708-873-1078. Rev. Joseph Pax, C.PP.S., 4830 Salem Ave., 45416-1716. Tel: 937-278-8018. Rev. Joseph Rodak, C.PP.S., 5311 Stateline Ave., Hammond, IN, 46320-1822. Tel: 219-933-2590. Rev. Paul Schaaf, C.PP.S., 100 Bluff View Dr., #106C, Belleair Bluffs, FL, 33770-1322. Rev. Louis Schmit, C.PP.S., St. Charles Center, 2860 U.S. Rte. 127, Carthagena, 45822-9591. Tel: 419-925-4516. Rev. Kenneth Schroeder, C.PP.S., St. Charles Center, 2860 U.S. Rte. 127, Carthagena, 45822-9591. Tel: 419-925-4516. Rev. Raymond Schultheis, C.PP.S., 4197 W. 20th St., Apt.207, Cleveland, 44109-3462. Tel: 216-485-9244. Rev. Emil Schuwey, C.PP.S., 1108 Fenley Ave., Louisville, KY, 40222-6726. Tel: 502-423-0050. Rev. Alphonse Spilly, C.PP.S., 652 Stewart Ct., Whiting, IN, 46394-1464. Tel: 312-751-8299. Rev. David Van Horn, C.PP.S., P.O. Box 12, Manitou Beach, MI, 49253. Tel: 517-547-3212.

HAMILTON. *St. Francis Friary*, 723 Main St., 45013-2548. Tel: 513-896-5326.
E-mail: tau723@fuse.net
Brothers of the Poor of St. Francis. Bros. Eric Lauer, C.F.P.; Howard Parent, C.F.P.; Julian Lane, C.F.P.

HUNTSVILLE. *St. George Chapel of Marianist Community*, 9636 Lakeshore Dr., E., 43324-9633. Tel: 513-842-4902.
E-mail: govisl@bright.net
Bros. Donald L. Smith, S.M., Dir.; William A. Deanhoffer, S.M.; Alva J.M. Gillis, S.M.; Robert V. Kelly, S.M.; Revs. John F. Mueller, S.M.; Robert J. Hoeper, S.M. Priests 2; Brothers 4.

[N] CONVENTS AND RESIDENCES FOR SISTERS

CINCINNATI. *Central Office of Sisters of St. Joseph of Medaille*, 1821 Summit Rd., Ste. 210, 45237-2819. Tel: 513-761-2888; Fax: 513-761-9957.
E-mail: patti@sistersofstjoseph.org
Web site: csjmedaille.org
Sr. Lucy Silvio, C.S.J., Pres.; Sr. Maria Hill, C.S.J., Vice Pres. General Councilors: Sr. Caroline Benken, C.S.J.; Sr. Mary Ann Farris, C.S.J. Sisters in Archdiocese 22; Total Congregation 181.

Convent of St. Dominic, 916 York St., 45214. Tel: 513-621-5899.
E-mail: gaia916@juno.com
Dominican Sisters of Hope 4.

Franciscan Monastery of St. Clare (Poor Clares), 1505 Miles Rd., 45231-2427. Tel: 513-825-7177; Fax: 513-825-4071.
E-mail: pccinti@juno.com
Web site: www.poorclare.org/cincinnati
Sr. Dianne Short, O.S.C., Abbess. Sisters 6.

McAuley Convent, 1768 Cedar Ave., 45224. Tel: 513-681-2100; Fax: 513-681-9265. Sr. Kathleen Marie Noonan, R.S.M., Dir. Sisters of Mercy 42.

Mercy Center Convent, 2335 Grandview Ave., 45206. Tel: 513-221-1800; Fax: 513-221-0207.
E-mail: mercycin@aol.com
Sr. Eileen Veeley, R.S.M., Local Coord. Professed Sisters 6.

Mercy Hall, 2317 Grandview Ave., 45206. Tel: 513-475-6726; Fax: 513-221-0207.
E-mail: memattsrsm@aol.com
Professed Sisters 5.

Provincial House, Health Center of Sisters of Notre Dame de Namur, 701 E. Columbia Ave., 45215. Tel: 513-821-7448; Fax: 513-761-6159.
E-mail: ohprovoff@aol.com
Web site: www.sndohio.org
Sr. Elizabeth Marie Bowyer, S.N.D.deN., Prov.; Sr. Joan Krimm, S.N.D.deN., Local Mod.; Sr. Donna Wisowaty, S.N.D.deN., Admin. Sisters 103.

St. Clare Convent, Franciscan Sisters of the Poor. Regional offices for the Franciscan Sisters of the Poor in the U.S.A. 60 Compton Rd., 45215. Tel: 513-761-9040; Fax: 513-948-9116.
E-mail: stclareconvent@fuse.net
Sr. Therese Martin Hessler, S.F.P., Community Min.; Sr. Marilyn Trowbridge, S.F.P., Regl. Min.; Rev. Herman H. Kenning, Res. Chap. Sisters 16.

Sisters of Charity of Cincinnati, Ohio, 5900 Delhi Rd., 45051. Tel: 513-347-5201; Fax: 513-347-5228.
E-mail: spm@scexec.org
Web site: www.srcharitycinti.org
Sr. Mary Ellen Murphy, S.C., Pres. Sisters in Congregation 597; Sisters in Archdiocese 435.

Sisters of Mercy, Administrative Offices, 2335 Grandview Ave, 45206. Tel: 513-221-1800; Fax: 513-221-0207.
E-mail: mercycin@aol.com
Represented in: Archdioceses of Cincinnati, Detroit, Louisville, St. Louis, Washington; Dioceses of Amarillo, Brooklyn, Brownville, Charlotte, Cleveland, Knoxville, Lansing, Las Cruces, Lexington, Memphis, Nashville, Newark, Oakland, Orlando, Owensboro, Portland (ME), Richmond, Saginaw, Toledo and Youngstown. Institute of the Sisters of Mercy of the Americas 3.

Sisters of Mercy of the Americas Regional Community of Cincinnati, 2335 Grandview Ave., 45306. Tel: 513-221-1800; Fax: 513-221-0207.
E-mail: mercycin@aol.com
Sr. Marjorie Rudemiller, R.S.M., Pres. Regl. Community of Cincinnati; Sr. Mary Ellen Matts, R.S.M., Vocation Dir. Professed Sisters 363; Novice 1.

Sisters of the Good Shepherd. (Cincinnati Prov.), 125 E. Court St., Ste. 350, 45202. Tel: 513-241-4110. Sr. Marilyn Atwell, Sec.

Sisters of the Good Shepherd, 2351 Beechmont Ave., 45230. Tel: 513-232-2969.

Ursulines of Cincinnati, 1339 E. McMillan St., 45206. Tel: 513-961-3410; Fax: 513-872-7177.
E-mail: selang@juno.com
Ursuline Sisters. Sisters 26.
Sisters of this community sponsor one high school, sponsor one elementary school, serve in pastoral ministry, counseling, and adult education.

BATAVIA. *Sisters of Mercy*, Clermont, 4315 Elizabeth Dr., 45103. Tel: 513-732-6335.

DAYTON. *Sisters of the Precious Blood Generalate*, 4000 Denlinger Rd., 45426. Tel: 937-837-3302; Fax: 937-837-8825.
E-mail: srs.cpps@spbdo.com
Web site: www.bright.net/~cppsnews
Sr. Maryann Bremke, C.PP.S., Pres.; Sr. Nancy Raley, C.PP.S., Vice Pres. & Councilor; Sr. M. Elise Calmus, C.PP.S., Councilor & Sec.; Sr. Nadine Kaschalk, C.PP.S., Councilor; Sr. Benita Volk, C.PP.S., Councilor; Sr. Barbara Brown, C.PP.S., Treas.; Sr. Noreen Jutte, C.PP.S., Archivist.

Sisters of the Precious Blood, Salem Heights Convent, 4960 Salem Ave., 45416-1797. Tel: 937-278-0871; Fax: 937-278-8722.
E-mail: bettew@fuse.net
Web site: www.bright.net/~cppsnews
Bette Wismann, Admin.; Sr. Mary Ellen Andrisin, C.PP.S., Dir. Resident Life; Rev. Joseph Pax, C.PP.S., Chap. Sisters 93.

HAMILTON. *The Sisters of Mercy of Hamilton, Ohio dba Mercy Franciscan at St. Raphael, Inc.*, 233 Dayton St., 45011. Tel: 513-863-3184; Fax: 513-887-6163. David Ferrell, Pres.; Sauni Lerner-Bolin, Exec. Dir. Assist Social Service. Provides food and other emergency services and self-sufficiency programs to over 10,000 clients annually.

SAINT MARTIN. *Ursuline Convent of the Immaculate Heart of Mary*. (Also known as Ursulines of Brown County), Ursuline Center, 20860 State Rte. 251, 45118-9705. Tel: 513-875-2020, Ext. 27; Fax: 513-875-2311.
E-mail: nvollman@tds.net
Ursuline Order, Congregation of Paris. Sr. Nacy Vollman, O.S.U., Supr. Sisters 39.

[O] RESIDENCES FOR ADULTS AND YOUTHS

CINCINNATI. *Friars Club*, 65 W. McMillan St., 45219. Tel: 513-381-5432; Fax: 513-381-7909.
E-mail: hn7029@earthlink.com
Beth Bowsky, Exec. Dir.; George Blake, Pres. Bd. of Trustees. Residential programs for male teens, residency for men, transitional living for mentally ill, counseling, education for teen school dropouts, youth sports, and community outreach for high risk youth, family resource center, housing & support for homeless families.

[P] RETREAT HOUSES, CONFERENCE AND RENEWAL CENTERS

CINCINNATI. *Friarhurst Retreat Center*, 8136 Wooster Pike, 45227. Tel: 513-561-2270; Fax: 513-561-0367. Revs. Lambert R. Dannenfelser, O.F.M.; Hilarion H. Kistner, O.F.M.; Warren Zeisler, O.F.M.; Bro. Norbert Bertram, O.F.M.

DAYTON. *Bergamo*, 4400 Shakertown Rd., 45430-1075. Tel: 937-426-2363; Fax: 937-426-1090.
E-mail: info@bergamocenter.org
Web site: www.bergamocenter.org
Mr. Dick Flack, Exec. Dir.; Bro. Joseph Markel, S.M., Chief Financial Officer; Karen Ander Francis, Dir. Adult Programs; Barbara Kozlowski, Dir. Youth Programs; Patricia O'Grady, Dir. Reservations.

MILFORD. *Milford Spiritual Center*, 5361 S. Milford Rd., 45150-9746. Tel: 513-248-3500; Fax: 513-248-3503.
E-mail: milfordspiritualcenter@zoomtown.com
Web site: milfordspiritualcenter.org
Revs. Richard W. Anderson, S.J., Supr.; Frank M. Oppenheim, S.J.; George W. Traub, S.J.; Thomas J. Diehl, S.J.; Bro. Paul F. Mattingly, S.J.; Daniel O. Roche, Exec. Dir. Officers: Rev. Thomas Gannon, S.J., Chm.

[Q] CAMPUS MINISTRY AND NEWMAN CENTERS

CINCINNATI. *College of Mt. St. Joseph Campus Ministry*, 5701 Delhi Rd., 45233-1670. Tel: 513-244-4844; Fax: 513-244-4594.
E-mail: monica_gundler@mail.msj.edu
Web site: www.msj.edu
Sr. Monica Gundler, S.C., Coor. Spiritual Dev. Tel: 513-244-4844.

University of Cincinnati Newman Center, 328 W. McMillan St., 45219-1224. Tel: 513-381-6400; Fax: 513-381-2540.
E-mail: stmonica.stgeorge@fuse.net
Web site: home.fuse.net/stmonica-stgeorge
Revs. Alan Hirt, O.F.M., Pastor; Dennet Jung, O.F.M.; Sr. Lucy Zientek, C.D.P.; Ms. Mickey Buchanan; Mrs. Jill Kreinbrink; Ms. Linda Martin.

Xavier University Campus Ministry, 3800 Victory Pkwy., 45207-2411. Tel: 513-745-3567; Fax: 513-745-1959.
E-mail: goetzi1@admin.xu.edu
Web site: www.xu.edu/spiritual
Ms. Chris Potter, Dir.; Mr. Tom Sheibley, Assoc. Dir.; Mr. Guy Vanasse, Coord. Liturgical Music; Sr. Myra James Bradley, S.C. Campus Ministers: Rev. Albert J. Bischoff, S.J.; Ms. Megan Halverson.

DAYTON. *Sinclair Community College Campus Ministry*, 444 W. Third St., 45402. Tel: 937-512-2768.
E-mail: jsteinha@sinclair.edu
Dr. V. Jane Steinhauser, Archdiocesan Dir. of Campus Ministry.

University of Dayton Campus Ministry, 45469-0408. Tel: 937-229-3339; Fax: 937-229-2035.
E-mail: campus-ministry@udayton.edu
Web site: www.udayton.edu/~campmin/
Revs. James F. Fitz, S.M., Dir. Tel: 937-229-3339; Gerald T. Chinchar, S.M. Tel: 937-229-2725; Christopher W. Conlon, S.M. Tel: 937-229-4767; Kenneth A. Templin, S.M. Tel: 937-229-3570; Sr. Nancy Bramlage, S.C. Tel: 937-229-2576; Sr. Mary Louise Foley, F.M.I. Tel: 937-229-2093; Sr. Jody O'Neil, S.P. Tel: 937-229-2574; Sr. Kathleen Rossman, O.S.F. Tel: 937-229-4587; Bros. Philip Aaron, S.M. Tel: 937-229-2575; Thomas Pieper, S.M. Tel: 937-229-2211; Nick Cardilino, Assoc. Dir./Center of Social Concern & Coord. of Community Outreach and Service Clubs. Tel: 937-229-2524; Yolanda Copeland, Sec./Center of Social Concern. Tel: 937-229-2524; Bridget Ebbert, Campus Min./Marycrest Hall & Campus S. Tel: 937-229-1754; Terri Lauer, Office Mgr. & Sec./ Campus Min. Tel: 937-229-3339; Peggy Matley, Chapel & Wedding Coord. Tel: 937-229-2019; Conor McIntyre, Coord. for Retreats & Faith Devel. Tel: 937-229-4813; Victor Perez, Coord. of Latin American Studies. Tel: 937-229-3635; Allen Stock, Dir. of Music Min. Tel: 937-229-2019; Patti Stock, Asst. Dir. of Music Min. Tel: 937-229-2019; Jen Violi, Asst. Retreats Coord. Tel: 937-229-2010.

FAIRBORN. *Catholic Campus Ministry*, 3650 Colonel Glenn Hwy., 45324-2096. Tel: 937-426-1836; Fax: 937-426-3490.
E-mail: christian.rohmiller@wright.edu
Web site: www.wright.edu/studentorgs/ministry/newman
Rev. Christian A. Rohmiller, Campus Min.; Ms. Joan Marquis, Asst. Campus Min.; Mr. Steven McDermott, Sec.

OXFORD. *Miami University Catholic Campus Ministry*, 111 E. High St., 45056. Tel: 513-523-2153; Fax: 513-523-0559.
E-mail: stmary1@fuse.net
Rev. Terrance L. Schneider; Roberta L. Kinne, Pastoral Assoc.; Michael Puglielli, D.R.E.; Jennifer L. Boyle, Interim Dir.

SPRINGFIELD. *Mercy Medical Center*, 1343 N. Fountain Blvd., 45501. Tel: 937-390-5000. Rev. Marvin R. Hackman, Regl. Priest Chap.

URBANA. *Urbana University Campus Ministry*, 231 Washington Ave., 43078. Tel: 937-653-1375. Rev. David L. Zink.
Pastoral care available through St. Mary Parish.

WILMINGTON. *Wilmington College Campus Ministry*, 73 N. Mulberry St., 45177. Tel: 937-382-2236; Fax: 937-382-0672[*]2.
E-mail: stcolumbille@erinet.com
Web site: www.stcolumbkille.org
Rev. James M. Wedig.
Pastoral care available through St. Columbkille Parish.

YELLOW SPRINGS. *Antioch College Campus Ministry*, St. Paul Catholic Church, 308 Phillips St., 45387. Tel: 937-767-7450; Fax: 937-767-7465. Rev. Joseph R. Raudabaugh.
Pastoral care available through St. Paul Parish.

[R] COMMUNITY CENTERS

CINCINNATI. *Mercy Connections*, 2540 Woodburn Ave., 45206. Tel: 513-221-7331; Fax: 513-221-5498.
E-mail: mercycon@queencity.com
Sr. Sarah Marie Sherman, R.S.M., Exec. Dir.; Bro. Lawrence Corbin, S.M., Pres.; Ms. Carolyn Turner, R.S.M., Vice Pres.; Mr. Raymond Normile, Sec.; Sr. Mary Jo McGowan, Treas.

Mercy Franciscan at St. John, P.O. Box 14368, 45250. Tel: 513-241-2186; Fax: 513-651-6476.
Web site: www.franciscan-stjohn.com
A member of Mercy Health Partners. 1212 Sycamore St., 45210. Tel: 513-241-2186; Fax: 513-651-6476. Ms. Marylyn Middendorf, Exec. Dir.; Julie Hanser, Pres. Provides emergency assistance, temporary shelter for families, job training classes, shared housing for seniors, a senior center and program for male responsibility.

Program for the Medically Underserved of Cincinnati, 3131 Queen City Ave., 45238. Tel: 513-389-5295; Fax: 513-389-5548. Kathleen Brogle, M.S.W., Exec. Dir. Annual Participants 4,000.

SPRINGFIELD. *Mercy-St. John's Center*, 100 W. McCreight Ave., 45504. Tel: 937-399-9910; Fax: 937-399-9449.
E-mail: mgiles@health-partners.org
Richard M. Giles, II, Admin.
Day care center for adults, skilled & intermediate long term care facility for all ages, Alzheimer's unit, ventilator unit. Total Assisted 242; Total Staff 210.

[S] ST. VINCENT DE PAUL SOCIETY

CINCINNATI. *Archdiocesan Central Council of Cincinnati*, 1125 Bank St., 45214. Tel: 513-562-8841; 8842; Fax: 513-562-8843. Rev. Louis R. Hohlmayer, Spiritual Advisor.
Central Council: Mr. Mark A. Casella, Pres.; Mr. Robert Young, Vice Pres.; Mr. Marvin E. Doane, Sec.; Mr. Richard J. Powell, Treas.

District Council of Cincinnati and Subordinate Parish Conferences. 1125 Bank St., 45214. Tel: 513-562-8841; Fax: 513-562-8843. Mr. Richard J. Powell, Pres.; Deacon George Bruce, Spiritual Advisor.

District Council of Dayton and Subordinate Parish Conferences. 1133 Edwin C. Moses Blvd., Ste. 400, Dayton, 45408. Tel: 937-222-7349; Fax: 937-222-7944. Deacon Robert Zinck, Spiritual Advisor; Mr. Robert Young, Pres. & Contact; Robert Young, Treas.

District Council of Hamilton and Subordinate Parish Conferences, 401 N. Washington Blvd., Hamilton, 45013. Tel: 513-863-5091. Mr. Howard Hetterich, Pres.

District Council of Springfield and Subordinate Parish Conferences, 2425 E. High St., Springfield, 45505. Tel: 937-323-8707. Deacon Norman G. Horstman, Spiritual Advisor; Ms. Audrey Farland, Pres.

District Council of Saint Martin and Subordinate Parish Conferences, 6336 Trailridge Ct., Milford, 45140. Tel: 513-683-4166; Fax: 513-791-4294. Patrick White, Pres.

St. Vincent de Paul Stores, Inc., 1125 Bank St., 45214. Tel: 513-621-3265; Fax: 513-562-8843. Ms. Elizabeth Carter, Exec. Dir.

St. Vincent de Paul Stores of Dayton, Ohio, Inc. Tel: 937-222-5555. 945 S. Edwin C. Moses Blvd., Dayton, 45408. Mr. James H. Butler, Exec. Dir.

St. Vincent de Paul Store of Springfield, OH, 2425 E. High St., Springfield, 45505. Tel: 937-325-9111; 325-8880.

St. Vincent Hotel, Inc., 1133 Edwin C. Moses Blvd., Ste.400, Dayton, 45408. Tel: 937-222-7349; Fax: 937-222-7944. James H. Butler, Exec. Dir.

DePaul Center, 1133 Edwin C. Moses Blvd., Ste. 400, Dayton, 45408. Tel: 937-222-7349; Fax: 937-222-7944. Mr. James H. Butler, Dir.

[T] HEALTH CARE SYSTEMS

CINCINNATI. *Catholic Healthcare Partners*, 615 Elsinore Pl., 45202. Tel: 513-639-2800; Fax: 513-639-2700.
Web site: www.health-partners.org
Michael Connelly, Pres. & CEO. 27 acute care hospitals, 14 long-term care facilities, 9 elderly housing projects. Catholic Healthcare Partners is co-sponsored by the Sisters of Mercy, Cincinnati Regional Community; Sisters of Mercy, Dallas (PA) Regional Community; Covenant Health System, Sisters of the Humility of Mary, Franciscan Sisters of the Poor. Patients assisted annually 4.3 Million; Residence for Senior Citizens 384.

Mercy Health Partners of Southwest Ohio dba Mercy Health Partners, 4340 Glendale-Milford Rd., 45242. Tel: 513-483-5200; Fax: 513-769-3420. M. Julia Hanser, Pres. & CEO.

Mercy Medical Associates, 4340 Glendale-Milford Rd., 45242. Tel: 513-956-5961; Fax: 513-956-5350.
E-mail: pchiltz@health-partners.org

DAYTON. *Franciscan Health System of the Ohio Valley (FHSOV)*, One Franciscan Way, 45408. Tel: 937-229-6000; Fax: 937-229-7093. James E. Grobmeyer, Acting Pres. & C.E.O.

Franciscan Health System of the Ohio Valley operations in Dayton, OH, One Franciscan Way, 45408. Tel: 937-229-6000. James E. Grobmeyer, Acting Pres. & CEO. Includes Franciscan Medical Center-Dayton Campus; The Franciscan at St. Leonard; Franciscan Medicenters; St. Elizabeth Hopeland Family Practice Center; St. Elizabeth Family Practice Residency Program; Franciscan Home Health Services; Franciscan Rehabilitation Centers; Franciscan Sports Medicine Centers; Franciscan Senior Network; Franciscan Workplace Health; Franciscan Medical Management Services.

Franciscan Health System of the Ohio Valley, Inc., One Franciscan Way, 45408. Tel: 937-229-6000; Fax: 937-229-7093. James E. Grobmyer, Acting Pres. & C.E.O. Includes Franciscan Hospital-Mt. Airy Campus, The Franciscan Hospital- Western Hills Campus; Franciscan at St. Clare; The Franciscan at West Park; The Franciscan at St. John; The Franciscan at St. Leonard; The Franciscan at Schroder; Franciscan at St. Raphael; Franciscan Home Health Services; Franciscan Rehabilitation Centers; Franciscan Sports Medicine Centers; Franciscan Holistic Health Center; Franciscan Workplace Health; Franciscan Senior Network.

Samaritan Health Partners, 2222 Philadelphia Dr., 45406. Tel: 937-278-2612.
Web site: www.goodsamdayton.org
Affiliate of Catholic Health Initiative.

SPRINGFIELD. *Mercy Health Partners, Sisters of Mercy*, One S. Limestone St., P.O. Box 688, 45501-0688. Tel: 973-328-7013; Fax: 937-328-8006.
E-mail: armcc@health-partners.org
Web site: www.mercy-allyour care.org
Andrew R. McCulloch, Pres. & CEO; Sr. Betty Anne Darch, Senior Vice Pres. Mission Svcs.

[U] FOUNDATIONS AND ENDOWMENTS

CINCINNATI. *Community Support Charitable Trust*, 1615 Vine St., 45210. Tel: 513-721-4700; Fax: 513-421-9672. Trustees: Revs. Kenan Freson, O.F.M.; Jeremy Harrington, O.F.M.; Bart Pax, O.F.M. Legal Title: *Community Support Charitable Trust for the Province of St. John the Baptist of the Order of Friars Minor*.

The Congregation of Our Lady of Charity of the Good Shepherd, Community Support Trust, c/o David W. Burleigh, Deters, Bencinger and LaVelle, 125 E. Court St, Ste.350, 45402. Tel: 513-241-4100.
E-mail: rgscincy@worldnet.att.net

Friars Club Foundation, Inc., 1615 Vine St., 45210. Tel: 513-721-4700; Fax: 513-287-8488. Trustees: Mr. Thomas Klinedinst, Jr., Trustee & Pres.; Rev. Kenan Freson, O.F.M., Trustee & Treas.; Mr. John O'Connor, Vice Pres. & Sec.

Good Samaritan Hospital Foundation of Cincinnati, Inc., 375 Dixmyth Ave., 45220-2489. Tel: 513-872-3786; Fax: 513-872-3788.
E-mail: Jane_Tenhover@trihealth.com

Mercy Health Partners of Southwest Ohio Foundation, 4340 Glendale-Milford Rd., 45242. Tel: 513-956-5808; Fax: 513-769-3420.
E-mail: bmdrenik@health-partners.org
Robert Wiwi, Pres. A Subsidiary of Mercy Health Partners of Southwest Ohio.

Roger Bacon High School Endowment, 4320 Vine St., 45217. Tel: 513-641-1300; Fax: 513-641-0498.
E-mail: bosse-r@hcca.ohio.gov
Web site: www.rogerbacon.org
Rev. Roger T. Bosse, O.F.M.

SC Ministry Foundation, Inc., 345 Neeb Rd., 45233. Tel: 513-347-1122; Fax: 513-347-1017.
E-mail: jwasser@scministryfdn.org
Web site: www.scministryfdn.org
Sr. Maryanna Coyle, S.C., Exec. Dir.

Seton High School Foundation, 3901 Glenway Ave., 45205. Tel: 513-471-2600; Fax: 513-471-0529. Mr. Thomas E. McKiernan, Chm.; Mrs. Mary Sullivan Schultz, Sec./Treas.

Sisters of Charity of Cincinnati-Charitable Trust, 5900 Delhi Rd., 45051. Tel: 513-347-5201; Fax: 513-347-5228. A designated trust fund to primarily support older and infirmed members of the congregation. Sr. Mary Ellen Murphy, S.C., Pres.

Sisters of Notre Dame De Namur, Ohio Province, Charitable Trust, 701 E. Columbia Ave., 45215. Tel: 513-761-7636; Fax: 513-761-6159.
E-mail: ohprovoff@aol.com
Web site: www.sndohio.org
Sr. Elizabeth Marie Bowyer, S.N.D. deN., Prov.

The Summit Country Day School Foundation, 2161 Grandin Rd., 45208. Tel: 513-272-1932; Fax: 513-272-3299. Edward C. Tyrrell, Pres.; Raymond E. Schilderink, Chm.; Thomas D. Grote, Jr., Sec. & Treas.

Ursulines of Cincinnati, Ohio Charitable Trust, 1339 E. McMillan St., 45206. Tel: 513-961-3410; Fax: 513-872-7177.
E-mail: selang@juno.com
Sr. Elizabeth Lang, O.S.U.

DAYTON. *Community Support Charitable Trust*, 431 E. Second St., 45402. Tel: 937-228-9263; Fax: 937-228-6878. Trustees: Revs. Albert A. Reed, C.PP.S.; Thomas R. Brenberger, C.PP.S.; Scott T. Kramer, C.PP.S.; Thomas J. Beischel, C.PP.S.; Bros. Joseph J. Fisher, C.PP.S.; Thomas R. Bohman, C.PP.S.

Samaritan Health Foundation, 2222 Philadelphia Dr., 45406. Tel: 937-278-5770; Fax: 937-278-5140.
E-mail: ktormey@shp-dayton.org
J. Kay Tormey, Pres. Affiliate of Catholic Health Initiatives and Samaritan Health Partners.

FAIRFIELD. *Glenmary Home Missioners Charitable Trust*, 4119 Glenmary Trace, 45014. Tel: 513-874-8900. Rev. Robert C. Berson, Trustee.

[V] MISCELLANEOUS LISTINGS

CINCINNATI. *Apostleship of Prayer*, 607 Sycamore St., 45202. Tel: 513-721-4045; Fax: 513-723-0451. Rev. Paul A. Huber, S.J.

Apostolate to Aid the Dying, Markam Prayer Card, 80 Compton Rd., 45215. Tel: 513-761-9036. Sr. M. Cornelia Evans, S.F.P.

Catholic Alumni Club (Cincinnati Chapter), 100 E. 8th St., 45202. Tel: 513-421-3131.

Catholic Charismatic Renewal Liaison, 5924 Bridgetown Rd., 45248. Tel: 513-574-1230; Fax: 513-598-2109.
E-mail: fredress@aol.com
Rev. Richard E. Dressman.

Catholic Cursillo of Cincinnati, P.O. Box 317655, 45231.
E-mail: idcronin@voyager.net
Web site: www.cincinnati-cursillo.org
Cooky Cronin, Dir. Tel: 937-323-5409.

Cincinnati Catholic Women's Association, 958 Marion Ave., 45229. Tel: 513-961-3566. Judy Fey, Pres.; Bette DiSalvo, Vice Pres.

The Comboni Lay Missionaries Association, 8108 Beechmont Ave., 45255-3194. Tel: 513-474-4997; Fax: 513-474-0382.
E-mail: combonilmp@igc.org
Web site: www.combonimissionaries.org
Rev. Sixtus Agostini, M.C.C.J., Pres.; Ms. Mary Ellen O'Donnell, Vice Pres.; Sr. Jeanne Oursler, C.S.J., Sec. & Treas.

The Comboni Missionaries Auxiliary, Inc., 8108 Beechmont Ave., 45255-3194. Tel: 513-474-4997; Fax: 513-474-0382.
E-mail: klcomboni@juno.com
Web site: www.combonimissionaries.org
Bernice Sutter, Pres.; Mary Myer, Vice Pres.; Kate Salotto, Treas.; Sue Langguth, Sec.; Mario Ongaro, M.C.C.J., Spiritual Advisor.

Concerned Catholics for Gay/Lesbian Inclusion - Within Archdiocese of Cincinnati, P.O. Box 19890, 45219-0890. Tel: 513-381-6400. Rev. Alan Hirt, O.F.M., Contact Person.

Franciscan Central Purchasing, St. Clement Friary, 4536 Vine St., 45217. Tel: 513-641-2257; Fax: 513-641-2262. Rev. Maynard Tetreault, O.F.M., Dir.

Franciscan Home Development, Inc. A member of Mercy Health Partners. 1300 Main St., 45210. Tel: 513-651-6457; Fax: 513-651-6472. Thomas S. Urban, Pres.; Ms. Stephanie Sweeney, Exec. Dir. Provides housing to over 200 persons in over 171 residential units.

Franciscan Ministry Services, 2446 Kipling Ave., 45239. Tel: 937-229-6021. Rev. Mark Zoellner, C.F.O.

Franciscan Missionary Union, 1615 Vine St., 45210-1297. Tel: 513-721-4700, Ext. 3222; Fax: 513-421-9672.
E-mail: sjbfmu@franciscan.org
Web site: www.franciscan.org
Bro. Scott Obrecht, O.F.M., Exec. Dir.

Franciscans Network, 4820 Glenway Ave., 48238. Tel: 513-251-6200.
E-mail: dhlmercy9aol.com
Ms. Diane H. Laake, Contact Person. Board of Trustees: Revs. John Quigley, O.F.M.; Murray Bodo, O.F.M.; Alan Hartman, S.F.O.

Hispanic Ministries at St. Charles, Archdiocese of Cincinnati, 115 W. Seymour Ave., 45216. Tel: 513-761-1588; Fax: 513-761-9538.
E-mail: joenels@juno.com
Web site: www.archdiocese-cinti.org
Rev. Joseph Nelson, O.F.M., Dir.

HIV/AIDS Ministry Team, Archdiocese of Cincinnati, 100 E. Eighth St., 45202. Tel: 513-357-6187. Ms. Kathy Cox, Coord.

Jesuit Development Office, 2245 Gilbert Ave., 45206. Tel: 513-751-6688; Fax: 513-751-2340.
E-mail: mark@chicagoprovincejesuits.org
Mark J. McLaughlin, Dir.

Legion of Mary, 3105 Madison Rd., 45209. Tel: 513-871-5757; Fax: 513-533-6066. Rev. Elmer W. Smith, Spiritual Dir.

Living Monuments of Reparation, P.O. Box 29372, 45229. Tel: 513-569-4587; Fax: 513-569-4582. Rev. Herbert J. Raterman, S.J., Dir.

Marian Center of Cincinnati, 5365 Cleves Warsaw, 45238. Tel: 513-922-1250. Mr. Robert E. Hater, Lay Dir.; Rev. Robert J. Plagge, Spiritual Dir.

Mater Ecclesia Institute, 3020 Erie Ave., 45208-2406. Tel: 513-871-5430; Fax: 513-871-5430.
E-mail: materecclesia@juno.com
Web site: www.materecclesia.org
Jack Helbling, Contact Person. Tel: 513-983-5461.

Ministers of Service, 745 Ezzard Charles, 45203. Tel: 513-381-0630; Fax: 513-742-9096. Mr. Jack D. McWilliams, Dir. The Ministers of Service Program, which began in 1979, provides training in urban ministry, primarily but not exclusively for African American laypersons. The Ministers of Service Program focuses on parish/community ministry to prepare laypersons to take active roles in church ministry.

New Jerusalem Community, 745 Derby Ave., 45232. Tel: 513-541-4748; Fax: 513-541-4811. Leadership Council: Jeanne Kortekamp; Maggie Jones-Prendergast; Roger Aver; Carol Metz, Coord. Community Life; Teresa Coleman, Admin; William A. Zins, Bookkeeper.

North American Ursuline Education Services, 5535 Pfeiffer Rd., 45242. Tel: 513-791-5791; Fax: 513-791-3170.
E-mail: lcastillon@ursulinest1.org
Web site: ursulinestl.org/naves
Sr. Lois Castillon, O.S.U., Exec. Dir.; Sr. Patricia Homan, O.S.U., Representative. N.A.U.E.S. is a service to all Ursuline Schools.

Notre Dame Collaborative - U.S.A., 701 East Columbia Ave., 45215. Tel: 513-662-9729; Fax: 513-662-9742.
E-mail: annrene@aol.com
Sr. Ann Rene McConn, S.N.D.deN., Pres.
Sponsored by the Sisters of Notre Dame de Namur. Purpose: to provide education and training services for poor women and children.

Priests Eucharistic League, 100 E. Eighth St., 45202. Tel: 513-421-3131; Fax: 513-421-6225.
Web site: www.catholiccincinnati.org
Rev. Christopher R. Armstrong, Dir.

St. Andrew Kim Korean Catholic Community, 3171 Struble Rd., 45251. Tel: 513-851-3065; Fax: 513-851-8233. Revs. John E. Porter; Leslie F. Blowers, M.M.; Joon Shik Ok, Pastoral Min.

St. Anthony Messenger, St. Anthony Messenger Press and Franciscan Communications, 1615 Republic St., 45210. Tel: 513-241-5615; Fax: 513-241-0399.
E-mail: st.anthony@americancatholic.org
Web site: www.americancatholic.org
Operated by the St. John the Baptist Province of the Franciscan Friars.

St. Dymphna Ministry, The Lewis Center, State Mental Hospital, P.O. Box 16061, 45216. Tel: 513-641-2257. Rev. Valens J. Waldschmidt, O.F.M.

St. Francis Bookshop. Conducted by the St. John the Baptist Province of the Franciscan Friars. 1618 Vine St., 45210. Tel: 513-241-7304; Fax: 513-241-7654.
E-mail: stfrancis@isoc.net
Web site: www.isoc.net/stfrancis

St. Francis Center, 1615 Vine St., 45210. Tel: 513-721-4700, Ext. 3204; Fax: 513-421-9672.
E-mail: sjbsec@franciscan.org
Bro. Gene Mayer, O.S.F., Prov. Sec.

St. Xavier Church Property Corporation, 607 Sycamore St., 45202. Tel: 513-721-4045; Fax: 513-723-0451. Revs. Robert J. Thesing, S.J., Contact Person & Trustee; Richard J. Baumann, S.J.

Secular Franciscan Order. Holy Trinity Regional Fraternity, Inc. 8497 Pringle Dr., 45231. Founded by St. Francis of Assisi before A.D. 1215. Anita Bidleman, Min., (Cincinnati, OH); Don Lipps, Sec., (Cincinnati, OH); Rosemary Menetrey, (Ft. Thomas, KY); Ralph Schluetter, Formation Dir., (Cincinnati, OH).

Seton Family Center, 712 Purcell Ave., 45205. Tel: 513-471-9169; Fax: 513-251-7922.
E-mail: setonfam@aol.com
Web site: members.aol.com/setonfam
Sr. Jacqueline Kowalski, S.C., Pres. & Contact Person; Sr. Rose Marie Hewitt, S.C., Board Chair; Sr. Barbara Jean Krekeler, S.C., Vice Chair. Sponsored by: Sisters of Charity of Mt. St. Joseph. Purpose: to provide services that enable families to relate in a more wholesome fashion.

Sisters of Mercy H.O.M.E. Program, 2900 Woodburn Ave., 45206. Tel: 513-221-1080. Sr. Mary Ann Fuerst, R.S.M., Contact Person.

Stimuli, Inc., 17 Erkenbrecher Ave., 45220-2202. Tel: 513-221-5538; 221-3889.
E-mail: stimuli@eos.net
The inculturation of African American culture with Catholic worship. Rev. Clarence Rufus J. Rivers, Ph.D., Pres.

The Couple to Couple League International. Mailing Address: P.O. Box 111184, 45211. 4290 Delhi Pk., 45238. Tel: 513-471-2000; Fax: 513-557-2449.
E-mail: ccli@ccli.org
Web site: www.ccli.org
Mark E. Hayden, Exec. Dir.

Vietnamese Catholic Community of Our Lady of Lavang, 314 Township Ave., 45216. Tel: 513-242-2933. Rev. Huan Tien Nguyen, Chap.

CENTERVILLE. *Catholic Alumni Club (Dayton Chapter)*, 55 Williamsburg Ln., 45459. Tel: 937-433-1188; Fax: 937-433-3263. Rev. Daniel J. Meyer, Chap.

St. Leonard Faith Community, 8100 Clyo Rd., 45458. Tel: 937-435-3626; 433-7224 (Friary); Fax: 937-435-3626.
E-mail: faithcom@bright.net
Rev. Msgr. Anthony J. Giannamore, Moderator & Chap.

MARIA STEIN. *Maria Stein Center Shrine of the Holy Relics*, 2291 St. John Rd., 45860. Tel: 419-925-4532; Fax: 513-925-5044.
E-mail: ekammererer@bright.net
Sr. Barbara Ann Hoying, C.PP.S., Dir. Includes The National Marian Shrine of the Holy Relics, The Heritage Museum, and The Pilgrim Gift Shop.

RELIGIOUS INSTITUTES OF MEN REPRESENTED IN THE ARCHDIOCESE

For further details refer to the corresponding bracketed number in the Religious Institutes of Men or Women section.

[0460]—*Brothers of the Poor of St. Francis.*—C.F.P.
[0380]—*Comboni Missionaries of the Heart of Jesus (Verona).*—M.C.C.J.
[0520]—*Franciscan Friars.* (Province of St. John the Baptist).—O.F.M.
[0570]—*Glenmary Home Missioners.*—Glmy.
[0650]—*Holy Ghost Fathers.* (Eastern Province).—C.S.Sp.
[0690]—*Jesuit Fathers and Brothers.* (Chicago Province).—S.J.
[0800]—*Maryknoll.*—M.M.
[1210]—*Missionaries of St. Charles (Scalabrinians).*—C.S.
[0430]—*Order of Preachers (Dominicans).* (St. Joseph Province).—O.P.
[0760]—*Society of Mary (Marianists).* (Cincinnati Province).—S.M.
[1060]—*Society of the Precious Blood.* (Cincinnati Province).—C.PP.S.

RELIGIOUS INSTITUTES OF WOMEN REPRESENTED IN THE ARCHDIOCESE

[0230]—*Benedictine Sisters of Pontifical Jurisdiction.* (Beech Grove, IN; Covington, KY).—O.S.B.
[0330]—*Carmelite Sisters for the Aged and Infirm.*—O.Carm.
[0870]—*Congregation of the Daughters of Mary Immaculate (Marianist Sisters).*—F.M.I.
[1920]—*Congregation of the Sisters of the Holy Cross.*—C.S.C.
[1730]—*Congregation of the Sisters of the Third Order of St. Francis, Oldenburg, IN.*—O.S.F.
[1710]—*Congregation of the Third Order of St. Francis of Mary Immaculate, Joliet, IL.*—O.S.F.
[1050]—*Dominican Contemplative Sisters.* (Washington, D.C.; Los Angeles, CA) O.P.
[1070-07]—*Dominican Sisters.* (Adrian, MI).—O.P.
[1070-13]—*Dominican Sisters.* (St. Mary of the Springs, Columbus, OH).—O.P.
[1070-16]—*Dominican Sisters.* (Nashville, TN).—O.P.
[1070-17]—*Dominican Sisters.* (St. Catherine de Ricci)—O.P.
[1070-15]—*Dominican Sisters of Hope.*—O.P.
[1415]—*Franciscan Sisters of Mary.*—F.S.M.
[1440]—*Franciscan Sisters of the Poor.*—S.F.P.
[2340]—*Little Sisters of the Poor.*—L.S.P.
[2470]—*Maryknoll Sisters of St. Dominic.*—M.M.
[2490]—*Medical Mission Sisters.*—M.M.S.
[2790]—*Mission Helpers of the Sacred Heart*M.H.S.H.
[3760]—*Order of St. Clare-Poor Clares.*—O.S.C.
[3130]—*Our Lady of Victory Missionary Sisters.*—O.L.V.M.

[3230]—*Poor Handmaids of Jesus Christ.*—P.H.J.C.
[0440]—*Sisters of Charity of Cincinnati, Ohio.*—S.C.
[0500]—*Sisters of Charity of Nazareth.*—S.C.N.
[0570]—*Sisters of Charity of Seton Hill, Greensburg, Pennsylvania.*—S.C.
[1000]—*The Sisters of Divine Providence of Kentucky.*—C.D.P.
[2575]—*Sisters of Mercy of the Americas.* (Cincinnati, OH).—R.S.M.
[2630]—*Sisters of Mercy of the Holy Cross.*—S.C.S.C.
[2580]—*Sisters of Mercy of the Union of the United States of America.*—R.S.M.
[2990]—*Sisters of Notre Dame.* (Covington Prov.).—S.N.D.
[2990]—*Sisters of Notre Dame.* (Toledo Prov.)—S.N.D.
[3000]—*Sisters of Notre Dame de Namur.*—S.N.D.deN.
[3360]—*Sisters of Providence of Saint Mary-of-the-Woods, Indiana.*—S.P.
[1630]—*Sisters of St. Francis of Penance and Christian Charity, Stella Niagara, NY.*—O.S.F.
[3840]—*Sisters of St. Joseph of Carondolet.* (Latham, NY)C.S.J.
[3880]—*Sisters of St. Joseph of Medaille.* (Cincinnati Prov.).—C.S.J.
[1830]—*The Sisters of the Good Shepherd.*—R.G.S.
[2110]—*Sisters of the Humility of Mary.*—H.M.
[3260]—*Sisters of the Precious Blood.* (Dayton, OH).—C.PP.S.
[1760]—*Sisters of the Third Order of St. Francis of Penance and Charity.*—O.S.F.
[2150]—*Sisters, Servants of the Immaculate Heart of Mary.*—I.H.M.
[4110]—*Ursuline Nuns (Roman Union).*—O.S.U.
[4120]—*Ursuline Nuns of the Congregation of Paris.* (Saint Martin).—O.S.U.
[4120-01]—*Ursuline Nuns of the Congregation of Paris (Cincinnati, OH).*—O.S.U.

CEMETERIES

CINCINNATI. *Calvary*, 1721 Duck Creek Rd., 45207. Tel: 513-961-2179; Fax: 513-961-8006.
Gate of Heaven, 11000 Montgomery Rd., 45242. Tel: 513-489-0300; Fax: 513-489-1817.
St. John, 701 Ross Ave., 45217. Tel: 513-242-4191.
St. Joseph, Eighth St. & Seton Ave., 45205. Tel: 513-921-3050.
St. Joseph New, 4500 Foley Ave., 45238. Tel: 513-251-3110; Fax: 513-251-1075.
St. Mary, 701 Ross Ave., 45217. Tel: 513-242-4191.

DAYTON. *Calvary*, Calvary & Dixie Ave., 45409. Tel: 513-293-1221.

SPRINGFIELD. *Calvary*, 3155 E. Possum Rd., 45502. Tel: 513-513-7474.

NECROLOGY

† Brinkman, Norbert C., (Retired). —Died April 3, 2000.
† Buschmiller, Robert J., Cincinnati, OH St. Cecilia Parish. —Died May 27, 2000.
† Calme, Stephen J., (Retired). —Died Feb. 10, 2000.
† DeFrancesco, Albert J., (Retired). —Died March 8, 2000.
† Drain, William A., Cincinnati, OH St. Matthias. —Died June 29, 2000.
† Gratsch, Edward J., Cincinnati, OH Mt. St. Mary Seminary. —Died July 21, 2000.
† Kesting, Philip A., (Retired). —Died Sept. 19, 2000.
† Koegel, Victor C., (Retired). —Died March 8, 2000.
† Krumpe, William F., Cincinnati, OH Our Lady of Victory. —Died Aug. 29, 2000.
† Krusling, Lawrence R., Cincinnati, OH St. Rose. —Died Feb. 22, 2000.
† Marheuser, Richard A., Cincinnati, OH Mt. St. Mary Seminary. —Died March 30, 2000.
† Steinbicker, Carl L., (Retired). —Died Nov. 27, 2000.

Diocese of Cleveland

(Dioecesis Clevelandensis)

Most Reverend

ANTHONY M. PILLA, D.D., M.A.

Bishop of Cleveland; ordained May 23, 1959; appointed Auxiliary and Titular Bishop of Scardona June 30, 1979; consecrated August 1, 1979; named Apostolic Administrator of Cleveland July 29, 1980; appointed Bishop of Cleveland November 18, 1980; installed January 6, 1981. *Office: 1027 Superior Ave., Cleveland, OH, 44114.* Tel.: 216-696-6525; 800-869-6525 (Ohio only); Fax: 216-696-6547.

Most Reverend

A. EDWARD PEVEC, PH.D.

Auxiliary Bishop of Cleveland; ordained April 29, 1950; appointed Auxiliary and Titular Bishop of Mercia April 13, 1982; consecrated July 2, 1982. *Office: Center for Pastoral Leadership, 28700 Euclid Ave., Wickliffe, OH, 44092.* Tel.: 216-944-1400; Fax: 216-943-7577.

Most Reverend

A. JAMES QUINN, J.C.D., J.D.

Auxiliary Bishop of Cleveland; ordained May 24, 1958; appointed Auxiliary and Titular Bishop of Socia October 14, 1983; consecrated December 5, 1983. *Office: 2500 Elyria Ave., Lorain, OH, 44055.* Tel.: 216-244-2120; 579-0326 (Cleveland Line); Fax: 216-899-1122.

ESTABLISHED APRIL 23, 1847.

Square Miles 3,414.

Comprises since July 22, 1943, eight Counties in the north-central part of the State of Ohio, namely Ashland, Cuyahoga, Geauga, Lake, Lorain, Medina, Summit and Wayne Counties.

For legal titles of parishes and diocesan institutions, consult the Chancery Office.

Chancery Building: 1027 Superior Ave., Cleveland, OH, 44114. Tel.: 216-696-6525; 800-869-6525 (Ohio only); Fax: 216-621-7332.

Web site address: www.cle-dioc.org

E-mail address: Wiatrowski@CCD.CLE-DIOC.ORG

STATISTICAL OVERVIEW

Personnel	
Bishop	1
Auxiliary Bishops	2
Abbots	1
Priests: Diocesan Active in Diocese	348
Priests: Active Outside Diocese	14
Priests: Diocesan in Foreign Missions	5
Priests: Retired, Sick or Absent	113
Number of Diocesan Priests	480
Religious Priests in Diocese	142
Extern Priests in Diocese	40
Ordinations:	
Diocesan Priests	6
Religious Priests	4
Transitional Deacons	3
Permanent Deacons	7
Permanent Deacons in Diocese	174
Total Brothers	71
Total Sisters	1,479
Parishes	
Parishes	235
With Resident Pastor:	
Resident Diocesan Priests	214
Resident Religious Priests	15
Without Resident Pastor:	
Administered by Priests	2
Administered by Deacons	2
Administered by Professed Men Religious	1
Administered by Women Religious	1
Missions	1
Pastoral Centers	2
Professional Ministry Personnel:	
Brothers	2
Sisters	111
Lay Ministers	218
Welfare	
Catholic Hospitals	3
Total Assisted	475,971
Homes for the Aged	25
Total Assisted	3,778
Residential Care of Children	1
Total Assisted	197
Day Care and Extended Day Care Centers	6
Total Assisted	950
Specialized Homes	6
Total Assisted	1,180
Special Centers for Social Services	23
Total Assisted	516,318
Residential Care of Disabled	2
Total Assisted	316
Other Institutions	3
Total Assisted	30,524
Educational	
Seminaries, Diocesan	2
Students from This Diocese	45
Students Religious	4
Total Seminarians	49
Colleges and Universities	3
Total Students	6,483
High Schools, Diocesan and Parish	7
Total Students	4,130
High Schools, Private	16
Total Students	10,294
Elementary Schools, Diocesan and Parish	132
Total Students	47,289
Elementary Schools, Private	8
Total Students	2,639
Non-residential Schools for the Disabled	2
Total Students	183
Catechesis/Religious Education:	
High School Students	6,317
Elementary Students	43,723
Total Students Under Catholic Instruction	121,107
Teachers in the Diocese:	
Priests	28
Brothers	30
Sisters	225
Lay Teachers	3,637
Vital Statistics	
Receptions into the Church:	
Infant Baptism Totals	9,228
Adult Baptism Totals	2,455
Received into Full Communion	957
First Communions	12,162
Confirmations	9,971
Marriages:	
Catholic	2,642
Interfaith	1,510
Total Marriages	4,152
Deaths	8,685
Total Catholic Population	816,912
Total Population	2,818,711

Former Bishops—Rt. Rev. AMADEUS RAPPE, D.D., cons. Oct. 10, 1847; resigned Aug. 22, 1870; died Sept 8, 1877.—Rt. Rev. RICHARD GILMOUR, D.D., cons. April 14, 1872; died April 13, 1891.—Rt. Rev. IGNATIUS F. HORSTMANN, D.D., cons. Feb. 25, 1892; died May 13, 1908.—Rt. Rev. JOHN P. FARRELLY, D.D., cons. May 1, 1909; died Feb. 12, 1921.—Most Rev. JOSEPH SCHREMBS, S.T.D., Archbishop-Bishop of Cleveland; cons. Feb. 22, 1911; transferred to the See of Cleveland, June 16, 1921; installed Sept. 8, 1921; appt. Archbishop, March 25, 1939; died November 2, 1945.—Most Rev. EDWARD F. HOBAN, S.T.D., Ph.D., L.L.D., Archbishop-Bishop of Cleveland; cons. Dec. 21, 1921; transferred to Cleveland as Coadjutor Bishop "cum jure successionis" Nov. 14, 1942; succeeded to See of Cleveland, Nov. 2, 1945; appt. Archbishop, July 23, 1951; died Sept. 22, 1966.—Most Rev. CLARENCE G. ISSENMANN, S.T.D., cons. May 25, 1954; transferred to Cleveland as Coadjutor Bishop "cum jure successionis" and Titular Bishop of Filaca. Ap-Adm. Oct. 7, 1964; succeeded to See of Cleveland, Sept. 22, 1966; retired June 5, 1974; died July 27, 1982.—Most Rev. JAMES A. HICKEY, S.T.D., J.C.D., cons. April 14, 1967; appt.

Bishop of Cleveland, June 5, 1974; installed July 16, 1974; appt. Archbishop of Washington, DC June 18, 1980; created Cardinal by Pope John Paul II in the consistory on June 28, 1988.

Vicars General—Most Rev. A. EDWARD PEVEC, Ph.D., *Center For Pastoral Leadership, 28700 Euclid Ave., Wickliffe, 44092.* Tel: 440-944-1400. Most Rev. A. JAMES QUINN, J.C.D., J.D., *2500 Elyria Ave., Lorain, 44055.* Tel: 440-244-2120; 216-579-0326 (Cleveland Line). Rev. RALPH E. WIATROWSKI, J.C.D., S.T.L., Chancellor, *1027 Superior Ave., Cleveland, 44114.* Tel: 216-696-6525.

College of Consultors—Rev. CHARLES T. DIEDRICK; Rt. Rev. ROGER GRIES, O.S.B.; Revs. JOHN R. HENGLE; LAWRENCE N. MARTELLO; THOMAS V. O'DONNELL; DOUGLAS M. PROEHL; PAUL ROSING; R. STEPHEN VELLENGA; RALPH E. WIATROWSKI, Sec.

Presbyteral Council—Most Rev. ANTHONY M. PILLA, Pres.; Rev. LAWRENCE N. MARTELLO, Moderator; Rt. Rev. ROGER GRIES, O.S.B.; Revs. CHARLES T. DIEDRICK; PAUL HRITZ; LAWRENCE JURCAK; MARK LATCOVICH; BRENDAN MCNULTY; THOMAS MONTAVAN; STEPHEN MORAN; PATRICK O'CONNOR; PAUL ROSING; DANIEL SCHLEGEL; THOMAS WOOST,Presbyteral Conveners: Revs. RALPH COLETTA; MARK DINARDO; THOMAS J. HAREN; JOHN R. HENGLE; ERNEST HEPNER; STEPHEN KAMINSKI; DENNIS J. KLEINWEBER; LAWRENCE N. MARTELLO; JAMES MCGONEGAL; THOMAS V. O'DONNELL; DOUGLAS PROEHL; EDWARD SCHWET; STEPHEN VELLENGA.

Diocesan Finance Advisory Committee—Most Rev. ANTHONY M. PILLA, Pres. Rev. JOSEPH H. SMITH, Financial & Legal Sec./CFO; Sr. MARGARET HESS, S.N.D.; PETER CARFAGNA; ANTHONY LANG; JOHN P. MCGINTY; KEVIN O'DONNELL; NORMAN T. PATTON; WILLIAM J. REIDY.

Diocesan Pastoral Council—Most Rev. ANTHONY M. PILLA; JUDITH DRAZBA, Chm.; STAN KOCI, Vice Chm. JEAN S. CLEARY, Exec. Sec.

Conference of Religious Leadership—Sr. REGINA KUSNIR, V.S.C., *1160 Broadway Ave., Bedford, 44146-4593.* Tel: 440-232-4755. Rev. ANTHONY SCHUELLER, S.S.S., Sec. & Treas., *5384 Wilson Mills Rd., Highland Heights, 44143-3092.* Tel: 440-442-6311.

Diocese of Cleveland—

Chancery Building—1027 Superior Ave., Cleveland, 44114.

Catholic Center—1031 Superior Ave., Cleveland, 44114.

All Diocesan Offices in the Chancery Building or in the Catholic Center may be reached at:Tel: 216-696-6525 or 800-869-6525 (Ohio only); Fax: 216-781-8243.

Address dispensations and all business communication to the Chancery Office.

Chancellor—Rev. RALPH E. WIATROWSKI, J.C.D., S.T.L., Office: *Chancery Building.* Fax: 216-621-7332.

Vice-Chancellor—Rev. DAVID J. WALKOWIAK, J.C.D., Office: *Chancery Building.*

Assistant Chancellors—Revs. EDWARD T. ESTOK, JR., M.A., M.Div., Office: *Catholic Center,* PAUL J. ROSING, Office: *795 Russell Ave., Akron, 44307.* Tel: 330-434-4114. Sr. LAURA BOUHALL, O.S.U., Office: *Chancery Building.*

Secretary to Bishop Pilla—Rev. EDWARD T. ESTOK, JR., M.A., M.Div., Office: *Catholic Center.*

Judicial Offices—

Office of Mediation—Sr. DONNA MIKULA, O.S.U., *Chancery Building.* Tel: 216-696-6525; 800-869-6525.

Tribunal—Office: *1027 Superior Ave., Ste. 500, Cleveland, 44114.* Tel: 216-696-6525, Ext. 4000; 800-869-6525 (Ohio only); 800-676-4431 (Outside Ohio); Fax: 216-696-3226.

Judicial Vicar—Rev. DONALD P. BRICKMAN, J.C.L.

Adjutant Judicial Vicars—Revs. MARK Q. FEDOR, J.C.D.; WILLIAM M. JERSE, J.C.L.; LAWRENCE JURCAK, J.C.L.; GARY D. YANUS, J.C.D.; PETER D. WASLO, J.C.L.

Judges—Deacon LOUIS G. PECEK, Ph.D.; Sr. MARY ANN ANDREWS, C.S.A., J.C.L.

Defenders of the Bond—Rev. JOSEPH A. BACEVICE, M.Div.; Sr. CHRISTINE M. RODY, V.S.C., J.C.L.; Sr. JEAN C. IFFARTH, O.S.U., J.C.L.; Rev. MICHAEL J. TROHA, M.A., M.Div.

Associate Judicial Vicars—Revs. MIRKO HLADNI, J.C.L.; EDWARD J. LUCA, J.C.D.; JOHN R. OLSAVSKY, J.C.L.; WILLIAM P. O'NEILL, J.C.L.; ROBERT F. PFEIFFER, J.C.L.; ROBERT J. SANSON, J.C.D.; DAVID J. WALKOWIAK, J.C.D.; EDWARD F. WEIST, J.C.D.; ROBERT M. WENDELKEN, M.Div.; RALPH E. WIATROWSKI, J.C.D.

Associate Judges—Deacon JAMES L. AGRIPPE; Revs. MARTIN J. AMOS; NELSON J. CALLAHAN, M.Div.; GARY D. CHMURA, M.Div.; CHARLES T. DIEDRICK, M.A.; JEROME J. DUKE; JOHN R. HENGLE; EDWARD J. KORDAS; ALAN R. LAUBENTHAL, S.T.D.; JOHN E. MANNING, M.Div.; LAWRENCE N. MARTELLO, M.Div.; THOMAS W. MCCANN; JOHN J. MUELLER; PAUL J. ROSING, M.Div.; THOMAS R. SMITH, M.Div.; DONALD E. SNYDER, M.Div.; CHARLES J. STOLLENWERK, M.Div.; ALBERT J. TESEK; ANTHONY W. ZEPP, M.Div.

Auditor/Assessor—Revs. ALLEN F. CORRIGAN, M.Div.; DONALD P. OLEKSIAK, M.Div.; Ms. LYNETTE TAIT, M.A.; CHARLES F. STREBLER, M.A.; Rev. DAVID R. TRASK, M.Div.

Advocates—Revs. JOSEPH HILINSKI, M.Div.; THEODORE MARSZAL, S.T.D.; DAVID C. WEBER, M.Div.

Promoter of Justice—Sr. CHRISTINE RODY, V.S.C., J.C.L.

Ecclesiastical Notaries—Ms. MARY M. BRYAN, Notary Public; Miss CYNTHIA M. QUINLAN, Notary Public; AMANDA L. JOHNS.

Translators—Revs. RICHARD R. BOBER, Ph.D.; EDWARD ESTOK, M.A., M.Div.; BEDE KOTLINSKI, O.S.B.; AUGUSTINE PHAM VAN LAN, Ph.D.; JOHN F. WESSEL.

Administrator of Buildings—MICHAEL E. SUHY, *Chancery Building.*

Archivist—Rev. RALPH E. WIATROWSKI; CHRISTINE L. KROSEL, Archival Research Dir. PHILIP HAAS, Archives Admin., *Chancery Building.*

Catholic Cemeteries Association—Rev. JOHN J. WRIGHT, CEO & Dir. ANDREJ LAH, COO, *10000 Miles Ave., Box 05310, Cleveland, 44105.* Tel: 216-641-7575.

Callistian Guild—P.O. Box 605044, Cleveland, 44105. Tel: 216-641-7575.

Central Purchasing—EDWARD J. ZAMISKA, Dir., *3020 Superior Ave., Cleveland, 44114.* Tel: 216-696-4811; 800-362-9016.

Communications Department—ROBERT D. TAYEK, Dir., Media & Pub. Rel., *Chancery Building.* Tel: 216-696-6525, Ext. 4460.

"Catholic Universe Bulletin"—Most Rev. ANTHONY M. PILLA, Publisher; JOSEPH M. POLITO, Assoc. Publisher & CEO, *Chancery Building.* Tel: 216-696-6525, Ext. 5870; 696-6525, Ext. 2770 (after 5 p.m.).

Catholic Universe Bulletin Publishing Company, Inc.—Chancery Building.

Diocesan Pastoral Planning Office—RICHARD S. KRIVANKA, Dir. DAVID DE LAMBO, Consultant for Planning, Research & Parish Pastoral Councils; V. GAIL ROUSSEY, Consultant for Pastoral Planning & Stewardship; JEAN S. CLEARY, Office Coord., Office: *Chancery Building.*

Mission Office, Society for the Propagation of the Faith—Rev. DENIS L. ST. MARIE, Dir., Office: *The Catholic Center,* Ext. 4240.

Pontifical Programs—Society for the Propagation of the Faith; Society of St. Peter the Apostle; Missionary Union of the Clergy; Holy Childhood Assoc.

National Programs—Latin-American Program; Lay Mission Volunteers.

Diocesan Programs—Missionary Cooperation Plan; St. Francis Xavier Mission Assoc.; Cleveland Diocesan Mission, C.A.

National Shrine of Immaculate Conception—Washington, DC. Rev. RALPH E. WIATROWSKI, Chancellor, *Chancery Building.*

Financial & Legal

Financial & Legal—JOSEPH H. SMITH, J.D., C.P.A., Sec. & CFO, *Ninth St. Plaza, 1404 E. 9th St.*

Legal—SANTIAGO FELICIANO, *Ninth St. Plaza.*

Catholic Lawyers' Guild of Cleveland—Chancery Building.

Catholic Lawyers' Guild of Cleveland Endowment Trust—Chancery Building.

Diocesan Budget Committee—Co-Chm.: MICHELLE CREGER; RICHARD KLINGSHIRN, *Ninth St. Plaza, 1404 E. 9th St.*

Diocesan Building Commission—Coordinators: JOSEPH H. SMITH; KEVIN T. BURKE.

Department of Diocesan Fund Development—AUGUST A. NAPOLI, Jr., Coord.

Diocesan Insurance Service Committee—(DISC). Members: J. THOMAS HANNON; THOMAS MCGOWAN, III.

Diocesan Financial Advisory Committee—Most Rev. ANTHONY M. PILLA, Chm.; JOSEPH H. SMITH, Financial & Legal Sec./CFO.

Health Benefits—PALMIRA JUREVICIUS, *Ninth St. C.D.C.*

Property/Casualty Insurance—PALMIRA JUREVICIUS, *Ninth St. C.D.C.*

Group Life and Pension Plans—ANTHONY GIELTY, *Ninth St. Plaza.*

Workers' Compensation Office—ANTHONY GIELTY, *Ninth St. Plaza.*

Secretariat for Education

Secretary—Sr. CAROL ANNE SMITH, H.M., *The Catholic Center.* Tel: 216-696-6525, Ext. 3280; Fax: 216-696-6217.

Departments—

School Food Services/Summer Food Service Program—EDWARD MOREL, Dir., *Catholic Center.*

Buildings and Grounds/Technology—DANIEL BRODNIK, Dir., *Catholic Center.*

Department of Fund Development—Mrs. KENDRA GEVRY, Dir., *Catholic Center.*

Catholic Education Endowment Trust—Catholic Center—

Inner-City School Fund—Catholic Center—

Office of Catechetical Services—JOYCE M. KELLEHER, Dir., *Catholic Center,* Ext. 2880.

Newman Campus Ministry—MAUREEN MASTERSON, Assoc. Dir., *Catholic Center,* Ext. 8920.

Ministers—TIMOTHY BARRON, *Akron University.* Tel: 330-376-3585. HEATHER KINNEY, *Case Western Reserve University, Hallinan Center.* Tel: 216-421-1522. Rev. KEVIN M. CONROY, M.Div., *Ashland University.* Tel: 419-994-4396. MAUREEN MASTERSON, *College of Wooster.* Tel: 216-263-2096. EMILY HOLTEL-HOAG, *Baldwin-Wallace College.* Tel: 216-243-4955. Rev. EDWARD KORDAS, *Oberlin College.* Tel: 216-775-8103. WILLIAM FLYNN, *Newman Commuter Faith Community for Cleveland State, Lorain Community, Lakeland Community and Cuyahoga Community, Hallinan Center.* Tel: 216-421-1522.

Religious Education Office—JOYCE M. KELLEHER, Dir., *Catholic Center,* Ext. 2880.

Catechetical Consultants—BRIAN HALDERMAN, *Western Area Office, 2500 Elyria Ave., Lorain, 44055.* Tel: 440-233-1612; 440-871-5246 (Cleveland line). DENISE SMITHBERGER; PATRICIA FLAHERTY, *Southern Area, 1025 Clay St., Akron, 44301.* Tel: 330-773-7621. MARY LOU NECKEL, *Eastern Area Office, Hallinan Center, 11303 Euclid Ave., Cleveland, 44106.* Tel: 216-421-1522.

Media Library—WILLIAM MILLER, *Catholic Center.* Tel: 216-696-6525, Ext. 4330.

Office of Catholic Education—Sr. CAROL ANNE SMITH, H.M., Sec. for Educ. & Supt.; Sr. KATHLEEN SKUTA C.S.F.N., Sec. Asst., *Catholic Center.* Tel: 216-696-6525, Ext. 3280.

Administrative Support Services—JANET POLEVACIK, Dir., *Catholic Center,* Ext. 4150.

Curriculum—Sr. MARY ELLEN RYAN, S.I.W., Dir. Catholic Ctr., , Ext. 3330.

Assistant Superintendents—JEAN TAKACS, *Eastern Area Office, Hallinan Center, 11303 Euclid Ave., Cleveland, 44106.* Tel: 216-421-1522. Sr. LUCIA BUCHOLTZ, S.S.J.-T.O.S.F., *Western Area Office, 2500 Elyria Ave., Lorain, 44055.* Tel: 440-244-1612; 871-5246 (Cleveland line).

Associate Superintendent—Sr. PATRICIA KIDDER, I.H.M., *Southern Area Office, 1025 Clay St., Akron, 44301.* Tel: 330-773-7621.

Education Consultant—MARY LOU TOLER, *Catholic Center,* Ext. 3250.

School Planning Process—Sr. ANNE GLASER, S.N.D., Dir., *Catholic Center,* Ext. 3780.

Catholic Parent Teacher League—DEBORAH OSYSKO, Pres., *7641 Hidden Valley Lane, Parma, 44129.* Tel: 440-884-7701. JENNIFER KRACH, Corresponding Sec. Tel: 440-842-8024.

Finance, Policy and Planning—ZRINA JUKIC, Dir., *Catholic Center,* Ext. 6300.

Secondary Education—MARGARET LYONS, Assoc. Supt., *Catholic Center,* Ext. 2450.

Government Programs—MICHAEL VOINOVICH, Dir., *Catholic Center,* Ext. 3350.

Mandated Services—Consultants: MICHELE SCHREFLER; JENNIFER MUSGRAVE; PAMELA OUTZ, *Catholic Center.*

Secretariat for Parish Life and Development

Secretary—Sr. RITA MARY HARWOOD, S.N.D., *Catholic Center,* Ext. 3500.

Blue Army of Our Lady of Fatima—Marian Center, 6626 Pearl Rd., Parma Heights, 44130-3808. Tel: 440-888-8553.

Catholic Renewal Ministries—Rev. ROBERT FRANCO, *367 E. 260, Euclid, 44132-1495.* Tel: 216-731-1515., *Bishop's Delegate, Presentation House, 28706 Euclid Ave., #4, Wickliffe, 44092.* Tel: 440-944-9445.

Central City Ministry with Poor—Rev. JAMES P. O'DONNELL, *2186 E. 35th St., Cleveland, 44115.* Tel: 216-566-0531.

Cleveland Diocesan Council, NCCW—ELSIE MAJ, Pres., *Catholic Center;* Rev. RALPH HUDAK, Moderator, *4427 Rocky River Dr., Cleveland, 44135.* Tel: 216-251-8286.

Diocesan Interfaith Commission—Rev. JOSEPH J. HILINSKI, Delegate, *Catholic Center,* Ext. 5110.

Enthronement of the Sacred Heart—Diocesan Center, St. John Cathedral Rectory, 1007 Superior Ave., Cleveland, 44114. Tel: 216-267-4713. MARGARET OLLE, Sec.

Ethnic Ministries—

Diocesan Hispanic Office—Sr. ALICIA ALVARADO, O.P., Dir., *Catholic Center,* Ext. 4300.

Korean Catholic Apostolate—Rev. PETER KIL-OU KWAK, *St. Andrew Kim (Korean Pastoral Center), 2310 West 14th St., Cleveland, 44113.* Tel: 216-861-4630.

Native American Ministry—Sr. JOAN LANG, C.S.J., Dir., *Catholic Center,* Ext. 3500.

Office of Ministry to African American Catholics—VANESSA GRIFFIN CAMPBELL, Dir., *Catholic Center,* Ext. 3020.

Philippine-American Ministry—Rev. JOSELITO DE LOS REYES, Dir., *12021 Mayfield Rd., Cleveland, 44106.* Tel: 216-421-2995; 721-5476.

Vietnamese-American Apostolate—Rev. AUGUSTINE PHAM VAN LAN, Dir., *3545 W. 54th St., Cleveland, 44102.* Tel: 216-961-2713.

Office of Evangelization—Sr. MARGARET MACH, V.S.C., Dir., *Catholic Center,* Ext. 2540.

Holy Name Societies, Cleveland Diocesan Union—Rev. THOMAS HAREN, Spiritual Dir., *15000 Lake Shore Blvd., Cleveland, 44110-1298.* Tel: 216-481-8200.

Pastoral Ministry Office—KATHLEEN HAASE-FALBO, Dir., *Center for Pastoral Leadership, 28700 Euclid Ave., Wickliffe, 44092.* Tel: 440-943-7670.

Legion of Mary—Rev. HERMAN B. PETERS, Spiritual Dir., Office: *1007 Superior Ave., Cleveland, 44114.*

Office for Pastoral Liturgy—Rev. J-GLENN MURRAY, S.J., Dir., *Catholic Center,* Ext. 4120.

Office for Women in Church and Society—DEBRA MARSEY, Dir., *Catholic Center,* Ext. 3030.

St. Joseph Christian Life Center—Rev. WALTER J. HYCLAK, Exec. Dir., *18485 Lake Shore Blvd., Cleveland, 44119.* Tel: 216-531-7370.

Secretariat for Clergy and Religious

Secretary—Rev. JOHN F. MURPHY, Ph.D., Vicar for Clergy and Religious, *The Catholic Center.*

Borromeo Seminary—See Seminaries.

Clergy Personnel Board—Rev. LAWRENCE JURCAK, J.C.L., M.Div., Dir., *The Catholic Center.*

Continuing Education and Formation of Ministers—Revs. EDWARD T. ESTOK, Dir. THOMAS DRAGGA, Assoc. Dir.; Deacon JEROME ZIEMKIEWICZ, Assoc. Dir.; Mrs. KAREN ROMAN, Assoc. Dir., *The Center for Pastoral Leadership, 28700 Euclid Ave., Wickliffe, 44092.*

Office for Religious—Sr. MARIETTA STARRIE, C.S.J., Delegate, *The Catholic Center.*

Diaconate Office—Deacon KENNETH PIECHOWSKI, Dir., *The Center for Pastoral Leadership, 28700 Euclid Ave., Wickliffe, 44092.*

Retirement Board—Revs. THOMAS H. WEBER, Chm., *Center for Pastoral Leadership, 28700 Euclid Ave., Wickliffe, 44092.* Tel: 440-943-7600. Rev. JAMES STENGER, Recording Sec., *St. Columbkille, 6740 Broadview Rd., Parma, 44134.* Tel: 216-524-1987.

St. Mary Seminary—See Seminaries.

Senior Priests—Rev. LAWRENCE JURCAK, Delegate, *The Catholic Center.*

Vocations Office—Rev. ROBERT STEC, Dir., *The Catholic Center.*

Avilas of the Diocese of Cleveland—CAROL BARANOWSKI, Pres., *The Catholic Center.*

Parents of Priests—DONALD TRASK, Pres., *The Catholic Center.*

Secretariat for Catholic Charities Health and Human Services

Catholic Charities Health and Human Services—J. THOMAS MULLEN, M.S.W., C.S.W., Pres. & CEO, Ext. 4160. Executive Vice Presidents: JOHN KLEE, Ext. 4170. PATRICIA HOLIAN, Ext. 4410., *1027 Superior Ave., Cleveland, 44114.* Tel: 216-696-6525; Fax: 216-861-9795.

Catholic Charities Parish Services—TERRENCE FLANAGAN, Senior Dir., *1031 Superior Ave., Cleveland, 44114.* Tel: 216-696-6525, Ext. 5030; Fax: 216-566-0963.

Pastoral Care Services—Rev. FRANK GODIC, *1027 Superior Ave., Cleveland, 44114.* Tel: 216-696-6525, Ext. 2380.

Office of Ministry for Persons with Disabilities—Rev. JOSEPH MCNULTY, M.Div., M.Th., Exec. Dir., *St. Augustine Church, 2486 W. 14th St., Cleveland, 44113.* Tel: 216-781-5530; Fax: 216-781-1124.

Marriage and Family Office—Rev. STEPHEN J. DOHNER, Dir., *1031 Superior Ave., Cleveland, 44114.* Tel: 216-696-6525, Ext. 3570.

Catholic Information and Referral Service (CIRS)—CHRISTINE SHEARIN, Dir., *1031 Superior Ave., Cleveland, 44114.* Tel: 216-696-HELP (4357); 800-869-6525, Ext. 2460; Fax: 216-566-0963.

Youth and Young Adult Ministry and CYO Office—GREG MOSER, Dir., *1031 Superior Ave., Cleveland, 44114.* Tel: 216-696-6525, Ext. 1070.

Migration and Refugee Services—MARJEAN PERHOT, Dir., *7800 Detroit Ave., Cleveland, 44102.* Tel: 216-287-7005.

Pro Life Office—MARY E. COLLINGWOOD, Dir., *1031 Superior Ave., Cleveland, 44114.* Tel: 216-696-6525, Ext. 5230; Fax: 216-781-8243. Satellite Office: *795 Russell, Akron, 44037.* Tel: 330-535-5767.

Catholic Charities Services Corporation—THOMAS W. WOLL, Pres. & CEO; MICHAEL HAGGERTY, Exec. Vice Pres. & COO, *1111 Superior Ave., Cleveland, 44114.* Tel: 216-696-6525, Ext. 8020; Fax: 216-344-9962.

Children and Family Services—MICHAEL HAGGERTY.

Disabilities Services—DENNIS MCNULTY, Senior Dir., Ext. 2490.

Emergency Assistance Services—KAREN GILLOOLY, Dir., Ext. 3730.

Other Adult Services—DAVE MODARSKY, Senior Dir. Tel: 216-631-3499; Fax: 216-631-3654.

Catholic Charities Facilities Corp.—LAWRENCE E. MURTAUGH, Pres. & CEO, Ext. 5540. CAROLYN SCHUEMANN, Exec. Vice Pres. & CFO, Ext. 8970., *1111 Superior Ave., Cleveland, 44114.* Tel: 216-696-6525; Fax: 216-861-1176.

Catholic Charities Corporation—JOHN P. KLEE, Pres., *1027 Superior Ave., Cleveland, 44114.* Tel: 216-696-6525, Ext. 4170; Fax: 216-861-9795.

Diocesan Social Action Office—THOMAS J. ALLIO, Dir., *1031 Superior Ave., Cleveland, 44114.* Tel: 216-696-6525, Ext. 3740; Fax: 216-781-8243.

Catholic Action Commission of Lorain County—SHARON KLEPPEL, Dir., *2500 Elyria Ave., Lorain, 44055.* Tel: 216-244-6037; Fax: 216-899-1122.

Catholic Commission of Lake and Geauga Counties—*Schrembs Hall, 28706 Euclid Ave., Wickliffe, 44092.* Tel: 216-585-7745; Fax: 216-585-7747.

Catholic Commission (Summit County)—THOMAS J. ALLIO, Dir., *729 Russell Ave., Akron, 44307.* Tel: 330-535-2787; Fax: 330-535-9040.

Catholic Commission of Wayne, Ashland and Medina Counties—PATRICK O'BRIEN, Exec. Dir., *521 Beall Ave., P.O. Box 15, Wooster, 44691.* Tel: 330-263-6176; Fax: 330-262-4633.

Campaign for Human Development—ROCKY ORTIZ, Coord., *1031 Superior Ave., Cleveland, 44114.* Tel: 216-696-6525, Ext. 2280; Fax: 216-781-8243.

Catholic Relief Services—ROCKY ORTIZ, Dir., *1031 Superior Ave., Cleveland, 44114.* Tel: 216-696-6525, Ext. 2280.

The Catholic Diocese of Cleveland Foundation—AUGUST A. NAPOLI, JR., Pres. & CEO, *1111 Superior Ave., Cleveland, 44114.* Tel: 216-696-6525, Ext. 6100; Fax: 216-861-1176.

CLERGY, PARISHES, MISSIONS AND PAROCHIAL SCHOOLS

CITY OF CLEVELAND
(Cuyahoga County)

1—CATHEDRAL OF ST. JOHN THE EVANGELIST (1848), Rev. David C. Weber, Rector; Sr. Margaret Ann Kelley, O.S.U., Pastoral Assoc. In res., Revs. Edward T. Estok; Lawrence Jurcak; John F. Murphy; James J. Grandillo; Donald P. Brickman; Peter Young- Keu Sin.
Res., 1007 Superior Ave., N.E., 44114-2582. Tel: 216-771-6666; Fax: 216-781-5646.
Church—E. 9th St. & Superior Ave., N.E., 44114.

2—ST. ADALBERT (1883), Rev. Kenneth F. Pleiman, C.PP.S.
Res., 2347 E. 83rd St., 44104-2198. Tel: 216-881-7647; Fax: 216-881-7670.
School—2345 E. 83rd St., 44104. Tel: 216-881-6250; Fax: 216-881-9030. Mrs. Kathryn Harris, Prin.
Lay Teachers 14; Students 345.

3—ST. AGNES - OUR LADY OF FATIMA (1980), Rev. Michael K. Barth, S.T.
Res., 6800 Lexington Ave., 44103-3297. Tel: 216-391-3947; 391-1655 (Office); Fax: 216-391-7919.
Church—6800 Lexington Ave., 44103. Tel: 216-391-1655.

4—ST. ALOYSIUS - ST. AGATHA (1975), Revs. William Behringer, S.M.; Eldon Reichert, S.M.; Bro. Michael O'Grady, Admin.
Res., 10932 St. Clair Ave., 44108-1939. Tel: 216-451-3262; 3263; Fax: 216-268-3830.
Schools—640 Lakeview Rd., N.E., 44108. Tel: 216-451-2050; Fax: 216-541-1601. Sr. Sandra Sabo, S.S.J.-T.O.S.F., Prin.
Sisters 2; Lay Teachers 8; Students 242; St. Joseph School, Tel: 216-451-2143; Fax: 216-451-8832.
Sisters 1; Lay Teachers 10; Students 251.
Catechesis/Religious Programs—Students 31.

5—ST. ANDREW (1906) (Slovak), Rev. Raphael Zbin, O.S.B.
Res., 5135 Superior Ave., 44103-1239. Tel: 216-431-2057.

6—ST. ANDREW KIM (1988) (Korean), Rev. Peter Kilou Kwak.
Res., 2310 West 14th St., 44113-3613. Tel: 216-861-4630; Fax: 216-241-6366.
Catechesis/Religious Programs—Students 90.
Convent—2496 W. 14th St., 44113. Tel: 216-861-4408.

7—ANNUNCIATION (1924), Rev. Russell J. Banner. Pastoral Assocs.: Sr. Janet Bednar, C.S.J.; Sr. Marilyn Nickol, C.S.J.
Res., 4697 W. 130th St., 44135-3798. Tel: 216-671-2015; Fax: 216-941-1014.
Catechesis/Religious Programs—Students 7.

8—ASCENSION (1946), Rev. Joseph J. Fortuna. Pastoral Assocs.: Ms. Laurel A. Jurecki; Ms. Lori Ashyk; Deacon John Koch.
Res., 14040 Puritas Ave., 44135-2822. Tel: 216-671-5890; 5891; Fax: 216-671-2320.
School—4400 W. 140th St., 44135. Tel: 216-941-3715; Fax: 216-941-6051. Sr. Laura Bregar, O.S.U., Prin.
Sisters 2; Lay Teachers 16; Students 370.
Catechesis/Religious Programs—Students 18.
Convent—4370 W. 140th St., 44135.

9—ST. AUGUSTINE (1860), Rev. Joseph D. McNulty. Pastoral Assocs.: Sr. Corita Ambro, C.S.J.; Mary Ellen Czelusniak; Sr. Audrey Koch, C.S.J.; Mary Ortiz; Sr. Miriam Fidelis Pinchot, O.S.U.; Deacons John M. Rivera; Edmund J. Karecki; Louis Woyton.
Res., 2486 W. 14th St., 44113-4498. Tel: 216-781-5530; Fax: 216-781-1124.
Catechesis/Religious Programs—Mrs. Sheila Gelzinis, D.R.E.
Students 352.
Convent—2432 W. 14th St., 44113. Tel: 216-579-1306.

10—ST. BARBARA (1905) (Polish), Revs. Michael S. Dyrcz, Admin.; Chester C. Cudnik, Pastor Emeritus.
Res., 1505 Denison Ave., 44109. Tel: 216-741-2067.
Catechesis/Religious Programs—Students 22.
Convent—3855 W. 16th St., 44109. Tel: 216-661-0547.

11—ST. BENEDICT. Closed. For inquiries for parish records contact the Chancery.

12—BLESSED SACRAMENT (1903), Rev. Matthew A. Ischay.
Res., 3381 Fulton Rd., 44109. Tel: 216-741-8338; Fax: 216-741-9397.
School—3389 Fulton Rd., 44109. Tel: 216-741-0172; Fax: 216-741-0172. Ms. Jane Bouman, Prin.
Lay Teachers 9; Students 142.
Catechesis/Religious Programs—Students 16.

13—ST. BONIFACE (1903), Rev. Augustine Pham Van Lan; Sr. Dianne Skubby, C.PP.S., Pastoral Assoc.
Res., 3545 W. 54th St., 44102. Tel: 216-961-2713; 961-2714; Fax: 216-961-1859.
School—Metro Catholic Parish School. See Separate Listing Under Elementary Schools, Parochial and Private Diocesan. Tel: 216-631-5733; Fax: 216-634-2844.
Convent—3588 W. 52nd St., 44102. Tel: 961-0669.

14—ST. CASIMIR (1891) (Polish), Rev. Msgr. Leo Telesz. In res., Rev. John M. Wachala.
Res., 8223 Sowinski Ave., 44103. Tel: 216-361-4322.
Convent—1116 East 82nd St., 44103. Tel: 216-361-5008.

15—ST. CATHERINE (1898), Rev. William Dickinson, Admin. Pastoral Assocs.: Sr. M. Kathleen McCafferty, S.N.D.; Sr. Mary Janeta Stamper, S.N.D.
Res., 9412 Heath Ave., 44104-5512. Tel: 216-341-3353; 341-5542; Fax: 216-341-5542.
Church—E. 93rd & St. Catherine Ave., 44104.
School—See Archbishop Lyke School. Tel: 216-341-7212; Fax: 216-641-8184.
Catechesis/Religious Programs—Students 38.

16—ST. CECILIA (1915), Revs. Daniel L. Begin; Herman B. Peters, Pastor Emeritus; Sr. Rosella Holloman, C.S.A., Pastoral Assoc.; Deacon William Ansley Love.
Res., 3476 E. 152nd St., 44120-4272. Tel: 216-921-3310; 921-3311; Fax: 216-921-2932.
Church—Kinsman Rd. & E. 152nd St., 44120.
Catechesis/Religious Programs—Students 75.

17—ST. COLMAN (1880), Rev. Robert T. Begin; Deacon William H. Corrigan. Administrators: Sr. Ann Kilbane, C.S.J.; Sr. Carol English, C.S.J., Pastoral Assoc.; Sr. Lucy Dragonette, C.S.J., Pastoral Assoc.; Linda Dlugo, Pastoral Assoc.
Res., 2027 W. 65th St., 44102-4394. Tel: 216-651-0550; Fax: 216-651-1663.
Catechesis/Religious Programs—Students 38.
Convent—2007 W. 65th St., 44102. Tel: 216-961-1550.

18—CONVERSION OF ST. PAUL (1931), Rev. Robert Marva, O.F.M.Cap. In res., Revs. Andrew Hohman, O.F.M.Cap.; Eric Gauchet, O.F.M.Cap.; Michael Joyce, O.F.M.Cap.
Res., Connected with the monastery of the Poor Clares of Perpetual Adoration. 4120 Euclid Ave., 44103-3728. Tel: 216-431-8854; 8855; Fax: 216-361-1951.

Convent—4108 Euclid Ave., 44103-3728. Tel: 216-361-0783.

19—CORPUS CHRISTI (1935), Rev. Ronald J. Szudarek; Deacons David J. Lundeen; Charles Zawadzki.
Res., 5204 Northcliff Ave., 44144-4065. Tel: 216-351-8738; 8739; Fax: 216-741-5620.
School—4850 Pearl Rd., 44109. Tel: 216-351-2974; Fax: 216-661-9188. Mrs. Rose Witmer, Prin.
Lay Teachers 10; Students 146.
Convent—.

20—CRISTO REY, CAPILLA DE (1983) (Hispanic). Closed. For inquiries for parish records contact La Sagrada Familia.

21—ST. ELIZABETH (1892) (Hungarian), Rev. Andras Antal, Admin.
Mailing Address: P.O. Box 20175, 44120-0175. Tel: 216-231-0325; Fax: 216-421-0461.
Church—9016 Buckeye Rd., 44104.

22—ST. EMERIC (1904 & Territorial 1964) (Magyar), Rev. Sandor Siklodi, Admin.
Res., 1860 W. 22nd St., 44113. Tel: 216-861-1937.

23—EPIPHANY (1944), Rev. Daniel L. Begin; Sr. Sheila Marie Tobbe, O.S.U., Pastoral Assoc.
Res., 11901 Oakfield Ave., 44105. Tel: 216-561-3975; Fax: 216-561-2794.
School—See Mount Pleasant Catholic Elementary Education Center, 3845 E. 131st St., 44105. Tel: 216-991-1615.

24—ST. FRANCIS (1887), Rev. Thomas F. Martin; Sr. Geraldine M. Tengler, S.N.D., Pastoral Assoc.; Deacon Frank Lozada.
Office: 7206 Myron Ave., 44103. Tel: 216-361-4133; Fax: 216-361-1673.
School—Tel: 216-361-4858. Sr. Karen Somerville, S.N.D., Prin.
Sisters of Notre Dame 4; Lay Teachers 7; Students 268.
Catechesis/Religious Programs—Students 39.
Convent—7119 Superior Ave., 44103. Tel: 216-361-5094.

25—ST. GEORGE (1901) (Lithuanian), Rev. Joseph A. Bacevice.
Res., 6527 Superior Ave., 44103-2698. Tel: 216-431-5794; Fax: 216-391-8233.
Hunger Center—Tel: 216-391-9160.

26—ST. HENRY (1946), Rev. Robert J. Kropac. Pastoral Assocs.: Gerry Kynkor; Ms. Barbara Price. In res., Rev. J. Glenn Murray, S.J.; Deacon Shelby M. Friend.
Res., 18200 Harvard Ave., 44128-1726. Tel: 216-921-0725; 0726; 921-7030; Fax: 216-767-0454.
School—Archbishop James P. Lyke Elementary School. See Elementary Schools, Parochial and Diocesan under Institutions Located in the Diocese. Tel: 216-991-9644; Fax: 216-991-9470.
Catechesis/Religious Programs—Students 41.

27—HOLY FAMILY (1911). Closed. For inquiries for parish records contact the Chancery.

28—HOLY NAME (1854), Rev. Thomas V. O'Donnell; Deacon Martin J. Wendzicki. In res., Rev. John C. Dalton, Pastor Emeritus.
Res., 8328 Broadway Ave. S.E., 44105-3931. Tel: 216-271-4242; 4243; 271-6995; Fax: 216-271-0886.
School—Tel: 216-341-0084; Fax: 216-341-1122. Sr. Marie Patrice Joyce, S.C., Prin.
Sisters 2; Lay Teachers 7; Students 179.
Catechesis/Religious Programs—Students 60.

29—HOLY REDEEMER (1924) (Italian), Revs. Martin F. Polito; James J. Grandillo, Pastor Emeritus; Sr. Beth Rancourt, S.N.D., Pastoral Assoc.; Deacon Charles Doerpers.
Res., 15712 Kipling Ave., 44110-3104. Tel: 216-531-3313; Fax: 216-531-4717.
School—15720 Kipling Ave., 44110. Tel: 216-486-0935; Fax: 216-486-1064. Jennifer DiPietro, Prin.
Sisters of Notre Dame 1; Lay Teachers 8; Students 150.
Catechesis/Religious Programs—Students 18.
Convent—924 Ruple Rd., 44110. Tel: 216-481-2740.

30—HOLY ROSARY (1892) (Italian), Rev. Philip G. Racco; Sr. Mary Ann Isabella, S.N.D., Pastoral Assoc. In res., Rev. Joselito de las Reyes.
Res., 12021 Mayfield Rd., 44106. Tel: 216-421-2995; 2996.

31—HOLY TRINITY - ST. EDWARD (1975), Revs. Robert Marva, O.F.M.Cap.; Peter J. Woll, Pastor Emeritus.
Res., 7211 Woodland Ave., 44104. Tel: 216-431-1134; 431-8854; Fax: 216-361-1951.

32—ST. HYACINTH (1906) (Polish), Rev. John S. Deka; Deacon Kenneth J. Piechowski.
Res., 6114 Francis Ave., 44127. Tel: 216-641-3944.
Convent—2971 E. 61st St., 44127. Tel: 216-641-1508.

33—ST. IGNATIUS OF ANTIOCH (1902), Rev. James R. McGonegal; Rev. Msgr. James P. McIntyre, Pastor Emeritus; Rev. Timothy M. Daw; Sr. Dianne Piunno, S.N.D., Pastoral Assoc.; Deacon Billy Malcolm. In res., Rev. Gary D. Yanus.
Res., 10205 Lorain Ave., 44111-5470. Tel: 216-251-0300; 0301; 0302; Fax: 216-251-0302.
School—Tel: 216-671-0535; Fax: 216-671-0536. Joyce M. Needham, Prin.
Religious 1; Lay Teachers 19; Students 418.
Catechesis/Religious Programs—Students 40.
Convent—10212 Bernard Ave., 44111. Tel: 216-251-3446.

34—IMMACULATE CONCEPTION (1865), Revs. Frank G. Godic; Albert J. Mackert, Pastor Emeritus. In res., Rev. John J. Hayes.
Res., 4129 Superior Ave., 44103-1179. Tel: 216-431-5900; Fax: 216-431-0463.
School—Tel: 216-361-1883; Fax: 216-881-4274. Dr. Marlene M. Matis, Prin.
Lay Teachers 10; Students 185.

35—IMMACULATE HEART OF MARY (1894) (Polish), Revs. Ralph Hudak; Andrew Knapik.
Res., 6700 Lansing Ave., 44105-3797. Tel: 216-341-2734; 2735; Fax: 216-341-7200. [CEM]
School—Jesus and Mary Consolidated, (Grades 4-8). (See Sacred Heart of Jesus listing). 6804 Lansing Ave., 44105-3797. Tel: 216-441-0886; Fax: 216-441-1515. Mr. Frank W. Przybojewski, Prin.
Lay Teachers 14; Students 293.
Convent—6804 Lansing Ave., 44105. Tel: 216-641-7121.

36—ST. JEROME (1919), Revs. Thomas A. Haren; Anthony Cassese; Deacon Peter Travalik. In res., Rev. Joseph A. Goebel.
Res., 15000 Lake Shore Blvd., 44110-1298. Tel: 216-481-8200; Fax: 216-481-8201.
School—15100 Lake Shore Blvd., 44110. Tel: 216-486-3587; Fax: 216-486-4288. Margaret Cosgriff, Prin.
Ursuline Nuns of Cleveland 1; Lay Teachers 11; Students 242.
Convent—15025 Ridpath Ave., 44110. Tel: 216-531-6118.

37—ST. JOHN CANTIUS (1898) (Polish), Revs. Lucjan Stokowski; Ralph A. Bodziony, Pastor Emeritus. In res., Rev. Msgr. Casimir S. Ciolek, A.C.S.W.
Res., 906 College Ave., S.W., 44113-4494. Tel: 216-781-9095; Fax: 216-696-6065.
Catechesis/Religious Programs—Students 9.
Convent—2265 W. 10th St., 44113. Tel: 216-861-1349.

38—ST. JOHN NEPOMUCENE (1902) (Bohemian), Revs. Robert J. Jasany; William F. Tezie, Pastor Emeritus.
Res., 3785 Independence Rd., 44105-3357. Tel: 216-641-8444; 8445; Fax: 216-341-4466.
Church—Fleet Ave. & E. 50th St., 44105. Tel: 216-641-8444.
School—3777 Independence Rd., 44105. Tel: 216-341-1347; Fax: 216-341-4466. Mrs. Roswitha Wunker, Prin.
Lay Teachers 11; Students 209.
Catechesis/Religious Programs—Students 58.
Convent—Tel: 216-341-6393.

39—ST. JOSAPHAT (1908). Closed. For inquiries for parish records contact the Chancery.

40—ST. JOSEPH (Woodland). Closed. For inquiries for parish records contact the Chancery.

41—ST. JOSEPH (Collinwood) (1877). Closed. For inquiries for parish records contact St. Aloysius, Cleveland.

42—ST. LAWRENCE (1901) (Slovenian), Revs. Anthony Rebol, Pastor Emeritus; Dominic Mondzelewski, O.S.B., Admin.
Res., 3547 E. 80th St., 44105. Tel: 216-341-3880; Fax: 216-341-0496.
Church—3532 E. 81st St., 44105.
Catechesis/Religious Programs—Students 2.
Convent—3551 E. 80th St., 44105. Tel: 216-341-1235.

43—ST. LEO THE GREAT (1948), Revs. Robert M. Bielek; Thomas L. Weber; Michael K. Gurnick; Deacon Thomas J. Waken. Pastoral Assocs.: Sr. Kathleen Lyons, S.N.D.; Ms. Kathleen Burke.
Res., 4940 Broadview Rd., 44109. Tel: 216-661-1006; 1007; 1008; Fax: 216-661-0887.
School—4900 Broadview Rd., 44109. Tel: 216-661-2120; Fax: 216-661-7125. Michael Fasciano, Prin.
Lay Teachers 24; Students 588.
Catechesis/Religious Programs—Students 216.

44—COMMUNITY OF ST. MALACHI (1975). (Personal Parish). Revs. Anthony J. Schuerger; Paul J. Hritz, Pastor Emeritus.
Res., 2459 Washington Ave., 44113-2380. Tel: 216-781-3110; Fax: 216-861-5340.
Church—W. 25th & Detroit Ave., 44113.
Catechesis/Religious Programs—Students 107.

45—ST. MALACHI (1865), Revs. Anthony J. Schuerger; Paul J. Hritz, Pastor Emeritus.
Res., 2459 Washington Ave., 44113-2380. Tel: 216-861-5343; 5344; Fax: 216-861-5340.
School—Urban Community School. (Intermediate Level) (See St. Wendelin listing for Primary Level) 2401 Washington Ave., 44113. Tel: 216-771-8014; Fax: 216-771-7888. Sr. Maureen Doyle, O.S.U., Prin.
Sisters 3; Lay Teachers 21; Students 370.
Convent—2456 Vermont Ave., 44113. Tel: 216-781-3481.

46—ST. MARK (1945), Revs. Douglas H. Koesel; Anthony J. Muzic, Pastor Emeritus; Joseph F. Wagner, Pastor Emeritus; Deacon Joseph McGraw; Donna M. Wimbiscus, Pastoral Assoc.
Res., 15800 Montrose Ave., 44111. Tel: 216-226-7577; 7578; Fax: 216-221-8664.
School—15724 Montrose Ave., 44111. Tel: 216-521-4115; Fax: 216-221-8664. Dr. Marilyn Kurnath, Prin.
Sisters of Immaculate Heart of Mary 2; Lay Teachers 19; Students 469.
Catechesis/Religious Programs—Students 123.

47—ST. MARY (1905) (Slovenian), Revs. John M. Kumse; Victor N. Tomc, Pastor Emeritus.
Res., 15519 Holmes Ave., 44110-2497. Tel: 216-761-7740; 761-1837; 761-5524 (Ministry House); Fax: 216-761-6673.
School—716 E. 156th St., 44110. Tel: 216-451-1717; Fax: 216-451-7911. Sr. Mary Ellen Brinovec, O.S.U., Prin.
Religious 3; Lay Teachers 8; Students 167.
Convent—717 E. 155th St., 44110. Tel: 216-851-3234.
Catechesis/Religious Programs—Students 12.

48—ST. MARY OF CZESTOCHOWA (1913) (Polish). Closed. For inquiries for parish records contact the Chancery.

49—ST. MEL (1945), Revs. Mark Q. Fedor; Edwin J. Schenkelberg, Pastor Emeritus; Ray J. Horley.
Res., 14436 Triskett Rd., 44111. Tel: 216-941-4313; 4314; 941-6589; Fax: 216-941-1093.
School—14440 Triskett Rd., 44111. Tel: 216-941-6879; Fax: 216-941-1005. Patricia Kelly, Prin.
Lay Teachers 19; Students 391.
Catechesis/Religious Programs—Students 4.
Convent—14538 Grapeland Ave., 44111. Tel: 216-941-6589.

50—ST. MICHAEL (1882), Revs. Dennis R. O'Grady; James H. McCreight; Sr. Mary Reean Coyne, S.N.D., Pastoral Assoc.; Deacons Miquel Figueroa; Jose Ramos.
Res., 3114 Scranton Rd., 44109-1689. Tel: 216-861-6297; 6298; 621-3847 (Spanish); Fax: 216-696-9351.
School—Metro Catholic Parish School. See Separate Listing Under Elementary Schools, Parochial and Diocesan. Tel: 216-281-4044; Fax: 216-634-2853.
Catechesis/Religious Programs—Students 88.

51—NATIVITY OF THE BLESSED VIRGIN MARY. Closed. For inquiries for parish records contact the Chancery.

52—OUR LADY OF ANGELS (1922), Revs. John J. Cregan; Ronald Turek; Deacon Thomas J. Senn.
Res., 3644 Rocky River Dr., 44111. Tel: 216-252-2332; Fax: 216-252-2383.
School—Tel: 216-251-6841; Fax: 216-251-7831. Miss Kathleen A. Lynch, Prin.
Lay Teachers 27; Students 579.
Catechesis/Religious Programs—Students 14.
Convent—3550 Rocky River Dr., 44111.

53—OUR LADY OF GOOD COUNSEL (1873), Revs. Leroy Moreeuw, C.PP.S.; John Zvijak, C.PP.S.; Deacon Patrick F. Berigan.
Res., 4423 Pearl Rd., S.W., 44109-4266. Tel: 216-749-2323; 2324; Fax: 216-741-7183.
School—4419 Pearl Rd., 44109. Tel: 216-741-3685; Fax: 216-741-7183. Sr. Margaret O'Brien, O.S.U., Prin.
Religious 2; Lay Teachers 18; Students 362.
Catechesis/Religious Programs—Students 58.

54—OUR LADY OF LOURDES (1883) (Bohemian), Rev. James J. Masek.
Res., 3395 E. 53rd St., 44127-1692. Tel: 216-641-2829; 2830; Fax: 216-641-0043.
Church—E. 53rd St. & Hamm Ave., 44127-1692.
Convent—3401 E. 53rd St., 44127.

55—OUR LADY OF MERCY (1922) (Slovak), Revs. Joseph T. Hilinski; Andrew P. Laheta, Pastor Emeritus.
Res., 2425 W. 11th St., 44113-4496. Tel: 216-781-8277 (Parish House); 216-781-7928 (Laheta Hall).
Catechesis/Religious Programs—Students 4.

56—OUR LADY OF MOUNT CARMEL (East) (1936) (Italian). Officially closed as a parish on July 29, 1990, however, still in existence as an Oratory. Mrs. Rose Marie Criniti, Admin.
Res., 2615 Martin Luther King Blvd., 44104-2553. Tel: 216-421-0140.
Oratory—Cleveland, 11501 Mount Carmel Rd., 44104.

57—OUR LADY OF MOUNT CARMEL (West) (1926) (Italian), Revs. Richard Rasch, O.de.M.; Marino Frascati, O.de.M.; Michael J. Donovan, O.de.M. In res.,

Rev. Vincent Caruso, O.de.M.; Bro. John M. Zyckowski, O.de.M.
Res., 6928 Detroit Ave., 44102-3093. Tel: 216-651-5043; 651-2547; 651-1611; Fax: 216-651-6641.
School—1355 W. 70th St., 44102. Tel: 216-281-7146; Fax: 216-281-6651. Sr. Rosario Vega, H.M.S.S., Prin.
Sisters of Most Holy Trinity 4; Lay Teachers 8; Students 272.
Catechesis/Religious Programs—Students 12.
Convent—1355 W. 70th St., 44102.

58—OUR LADY OF PEACE (1919), Rev. Gary D. Chmura; Deacon William E. Dirk; Mrs. Nancy McIntosh, Pastoral Assoc. In res., Rev. Chinoye Bede Aboh.
Res., 12503 Buckingham Ave., 44120-1498. Tel: 216-421-4211; 4212; Fax: 216-421-1612.
Church—Shaker Blvd. & E. 126th St., 44120.
School—12406 Buckingham Ave., 44120-1419. Tel: 216-795-7161; Fax: 216-795-7370. Mrs. Sheila Bolek, Prin.
Lay Teachers 10; Students 206.
Catechesis/Religious Programs—Students 47.

59—OUR LADY OF PERPETUAL HELP (1929) (Lithuanian), Rev. Gediminas Kijauskas, S.J. Pastoral Assocs.: Nijole Kersnauskas; Stasys Ignatavicius.
Res., 18022 Neff Rd., 44119-2644. Tel: 216-531-4263; Fax: 216-531-8441.
Convent—18021 Marcella Rd., 44119.

60—SAGRADA FAMILIA (1997) (HISPANIC), Revs. David F. Fallon; James H. McCreight; Deacons Ceferino Medina; Epifanio Torres; Victor Colon; Ignacio Miranda; Frederick Simon; Marilyn Hernandez, Pastoral Assoc.
Church—7719 Detroit Ave., 44102. Tel: 216-631-6817; 631-2888; 2889; Fax: 216-631-3305.
Catechesis/Religious Programs—Sr. Ann Dorenbusch, S.C., D.R.E.
Students 220.

61—ST. PATRICK (1853), Rev. Mark A. DiNardo; Mary Jane Treichel, Pastoral Assoc.; Deacon William Merriman.
Res., 3602 Bridge Ave., 44113-3314. Tel: 216-631-6872; 6873; 6874; Fax: 216-631-0267.
School—Urban Community School. See St. Malachi listing. Tel: 216-771-8014.
Catechesis/Religious Programs—Students 72.

62—ST. PATRICK (West Park) (1848), Revs. Thomas J. Hagedorn; Thomas D. Mahoney; Deacons Richard C. Beercheck; William Staab. In res., Revs. Joseph C. Pednekar, M.S.F.S.; Eugene Katoski, O.F.M.
Res., 4427 Rocky River Dr., 44135-2551. Tel: 216-251-8286; 8287; Fax: 216-251-8555. [CEM]
School—17720 Puritas Ave., 44135. Tel: 216-671-4314; Fax: 216-671-5277. Catherine White, Prin.
Ursuline Nuns of Cleveland 1; Lay Teachers 27; Students 583.
Catechesis/Religious Programs—Students 18.
Convent—17712 Puritas Ave., 44135. Tel: 216-941-1088.

63—ST. PAUL (1902) (Croatian), Rev. Mirko Hladni.
Res., 1369 E. 40th St., 44103-1194. Tel: 216-431-1895; Fax: 216-431-1128.
Catechesis/Religious Programs—Students 61.

64—ST. PETER (1853) (German), Rev. Robert J. Marrone.
Res., 1533 E. 17th St., 44114. Tel: 216-861-1798; Fax: 216-861-1799.
Catechesis/Religious Programs—Students 32.

65—SS. PHILIP AND JAMES (1950), Revs. J. Brendan McNulty; Robert F. Brennan, Pastor Emeritus, (Retired).
Res., 10812 Adeline Rd., 44111-4806. Tel: 216-941-6808; 6809; Fax: 216-941-3808.
Church—3727 Bosworth Rd., 44111.

66—ST. PHILIP NERI (1914), Rev. Norman N. Smith; Deacon Carl Varga; Sr. Wilma Apack, C.S.J., Pastoral Assoc.
Res., 8215 St. Clair Ave., 44103-3728. Tel: 216-431-2583.
School—St. Thomas Aquinas-St. Philip Neri, 9101 Superior Ave., 44106. Tel: 216-421-4668; Fax: 216-721-8444. Althea Cheatham, Prin.
Lay Teachers 20; Students 313.
Convent—799 E. 82nd St., 44103. Tel: 216-431-0224.

67—ST. PROCOP (1872) (Bohemian), Rev. Mark J. Peyton.
Res., 3181 W. 41st St., 44109-1275. Tel: 216-631-0365; 631-0367.
Catechesis/Religious Programs—Students 15.

68—ST. ROCCO (1922) (Italian), Revs. Michael Contardi, O.de.M.; Paschal Rosca, O.de.M. In res., Bro. Martin J. Jarocinski, O.de.M.
Res., 3205 Fulton Rd., 44109-1495. Tel: 216-961-8331; 961-7384; Fax: 216-961-1845.
School—Tel: 216-961-8557; Fax: 216-961-1112. Sr. Judith Wulk, O.SS.T., Prin.
Sisters of Most Holy Trinity 3; Lay Teachers 8; Students 215.
Catechesis/Religious Programs—Students 30.
Convent—Tel: 216-961-2378.

69—ST. ROSE OF LIMA (1899), Rev. James A. Viall; Sr. Ruth Donnelly, O.S.U., Pastoral Assoc.
Res., 11411 Detroit Ave., 44102-2399. Tel: 216-521-0133; Fax: 216-521-1306.
Church—Detroit Ave. & W. 114th St., 44102.
School—1441 W. 116th St., 44102. Tel: 216-226-4525; Fax: 216-226-0413. Miss Julie Onacila, M.A., Prin.
Lay Teachers 12; Students 163.
Catechesis/Religious Programs—Students 40.
Convent—1418 W. 114th St., 44102.

70—SACRED HEART OF JESUS (1888) (Polish), Rev. Joseph S. Mecir.
Res., 6916 Krakow Ave., 44105. Tel: 216-341-2828; 271-1889; Fax: 216-271-1889.
Church—E. 71st & Kazimier Ave., 44105.
School—Jesus and Mary Consolidated, (Grades K-3). See Immaculate Heart of Mary listing. 6804 Lansing Ave., 44105.

71—SAN JUAN BAUTISTA (1975) (Spanish-Non Territorial). Closed. For inquiries for Parish Records contact La Sagrada Familia.

72—ST. STANISLAUS (1873) (Polish), Revs. William E. Gulas, O.F.M.; Michael Surafka, O.F.M.; George Kusy; Sr. Celeste Hupeart, C.S.F.N., Pastoral Assoc.
Res., 3649 E. 65th St., 44105-1293. Tel: 216-341-9091; 9092; Fax: 216-341-2688.
Church—Forman Ave. & E. 65th St., 44105.
School—6615 Forman Ave., 44105. Tel: 216-883-3307; Fax: 216-883-0514. Mrs. Alice Torrence, Prin.
Sisters 2; Lay Teachers 17; Students 336.
Convent—6615 Forman Ave., 44105. Tel: 216-341-0934.

73—ST. STEPHEN (1869) (German), Rev. S. Michael Franz.
Res., 1930 W. 54th St., 44102-3298. Tel: 216-631-5633; Fax: 216-631-5634.
School—Metro Catholic Parish School. See Separate Listing under Elementary Schools, Parochial and Diocesan. Tel: 216-281-4044; Fax: 216-634-2853. Sr. Anne Mary Maline, S.N.D., Prin.
Catechesis/Religious Programs—Students 8.
Convent—1891 W. 57th St., 44102. Tel: 216-631-0754.

74—ST. THOMAS AQUINAS. Closed. For inquiries for parish records contact the Chancery.

75—TRANSFIGURATION (1943). Closed. For inquiries for parish records contact the Chancery.

76—ST. VINCENT DE PAUL (1922), Revs. John E. Manning; Urban A. Reichlin, Pastor Emeritus; Daniel P. Redmond; Deacons Kenneth J. Hill; Billy Malcolm.
Res., 13400 Lorain Ave., 44111-3470. Tel: 216-252-2626; Fax: 216-251-0455.
Church—Lorain Ave. & Berea Rd., 44111.
School—13442 Lorain Ave., 44111. Tel: 216-251-3932. Sr. Caroline Kocur, O.S.U., Prin.
Sisters 1; Lay Teachers 19; Students 467.
Catechesis/Religious Programs—Students 65.

77—ST. VITUS (1893) (Slovenian), Rev. Joseph P. Boznar; Sr. Mary Avsec, S.N.D., Pastoral Assoc. In res., Rev. Vincent J. Moraghan.
Res., 6019 Glass Ave., 44103. Tel: 216-361-1444; 1445; Fax: 216-361-1445.
School—6111 Glass Ave., 44103. Tel: 216-881-1689; Fax: 216-881-8303. Mrs. Jeanette Polomsky, Prin.
Sisters of Notre Dame 1; Lay Teachers 11; Students 238.
Catechesis/Religious Programs—Students 231.
Convent—6104 Glass Ave., 44103. Tel: 216-361-7330.

78—ST. WENDELIN (1903) (Slovak), Rev. Jerome M. Lajack.
Res., 2281 Columbus Rd., 44113. Tel: 216-861-1141; Fax: 216-861-1141.
School—Urban Community School. (Primary and Junior High) (See St. Malachi listing for Intermediate Level) 2281 Columbus Rd., 44113. Tel: 216-861-4706; Fax: 216-781-0034. Joy Smith, Prin.
Catechesis/Religious Programs—Students 1.
Convent—2259 Columbus Rd., 44113. Tel: 216-241-1773.

OUTSIDE THE CITY OF CLEVELAND

Akron, Summit Co.,

1—ANNUNCIATION, (1907), Rev. Paul J. Rosing. Pastoral Ministers: Jean J. Jordan; Diana Herhold. In res., Rev. James J. Berardi.
Res., 87 Broad St., 44305. Tel: 330-535-4141; Fax: 330-762-8456.
Church—Broad St. & Kent St., 44305.
School—Annunciation-St. John the Baptist, 88 Kent St., 44305. Tel: 330-253-5311; Fax: 330-762-8456. Barbara Mesko, Prin.
Lay Teachers 13; Students 225.
Catechesis/Religious Programs—Students 115.

2—ST. ANTHONY OF PADUA, (1933) (Italian), Revs. James V. Ragnoni; Robert Labella.
Res., 83 Mosser Pl., 44310. Tel: 330-762-7277; Fax: 330-762-2229.
School—80 E. York St., 44310. Tel: 330-253-6918. Sr. Elizabeth Szilvasi, M.P.F., Prin.
Religious Teachers Filippini 1; Lay Teachers 9; Students 201.
Catechesis/Religious Programs—Students 39.
Convent—93 Mosser Pl., 44310. Tel: 216-376-1735.

3—ST. BERNARD, (1861), Rev. Paul E. Schindler; Sr. Catherine Walsh, Pastoral Assoc.; Deacon Daniel J. Matusicky. In res., Revs. Norman K. Douglas; Frances Ejimofor; Albert I. Reymann, M.M.
Res., 44 University Ave., 44308-1609. Tel: 330-253-5161; 5162; 253-5265; 253-5364; Fax: 330-253-6949. [CEM]
Catechesis/Religious Programs—Students 115.

4—CHRIST THE KING, (1935), Revs. Francis J. Basa; Victor J. Cimperman, Pastor Emeritus.
Res., 1584 Creighton Ave., 44310-2699. Tel: 330-633-8418.
School—1558 Creighton Ave., 44310. Tel: 330-633-1383; Fax: 330-633-4512. Sr. Paula Krizancic, F.D.C., Prin.
Daughters of Divine Charity 1; Lay Teachers 7; Students 122.
Convent—Tel: 330-633-8217.

5—ST. FRANCIS DE SALES, (1948), Revs. James R. Schleicher; Sean Donnelly; Deacon Richard C. Butz.
Res., 4019 Manchester Rd., 44319-2193. Tel: 330-644-2225; 644-2226.
School—4009 Manchester Rd., 44319. Tel: 330-644-0638. Carol Trifonoff, Prin.
Sisters Servants of Immaculate Heart of Mary 1; Lay Teachers 17; Students 419.
Catechesis/Religious Programs—Students 264.

6—ST. HEDWIG, (1912) (Polish), Rev. Thaddeus M. Swirski.
Res., 215 E. Glenwood Ave., 44310-3837. Tel: 330-376-6979.
Catechesis/Religious Programs—Students 8.

7—ST. HILARY, (1958), Revs. Gordon A. Yahner; Salvatore M. Ruggeri; Deacon Lee F. Hindersheid. Pastoral Assocs.: Sr. Marlene LoGrasso; Mrs. Mary Lou Grossman; Mrs. Patricia Schnee. In res., Rev. Patrick Nicanda Allala.
Mailing Address: 2750 W. Market St., Fairlawn, 44333.
Res., 615 Moorfield Rd., Fairlawn, 44333. Tel: 330-867-1055; 1056; Fax: 330-869-2312.
Church—2750 W. Market St., Fairlawn, 44333.
School—645 Moorfield Rd., Fairlawn, 44333. Tel: 330-867-8720; Fax: 330-867-5081. Dr. Patricia Nugent, Prin.
Lay Teachers 32; Students 646.
Catechesis/Religious Programs—Students 514.

8—IMMACULATE CONCEPTION, (1923), Rev. Michael B. Smith; Melissa Keegan, Pastoral Assoc.; Deacon Dennis L. Smith. In res., Rev. Samuel R. Ciccolini.
Res., 2101 17th St. S.W., 44314-2315. Tel: 330-753-8429; Fax: 330-753-7440.
Church—2100 16th St. S.W., 44314. Tel: 800-311-8429.
School—2128 16th St. S.W., 44314. Tel: 330-745-3544; Fax: 330-745-2051. Elaine Faessel, Prin.
Congregation of St. Joseph 2; Lay Teachers 8; Students 149.
Catechesis/Religious Programs—Students 72.

9—ST. JOHN THE BAPTIST, (1907) (Slovak), Rev. Ralph V. Coletta. In res., Rev. Emmanuel K. Amedzi.
Res., 1034 Brown St., 44301. Tel: 330-773-9114; Fax: 330-773-3613.
School—Annunciation-St. John the Baptist School, 88 Kent St., 44305. Tel: 330-253-5311; Fax: 330-762-8456. Barbara Mesko, Prin.
Lay Teachers 13; Students 225.
Catechesis/Religious Programs—Students 19.

10—ST. MARTHA, (1919), Rev. Michael A. Matusz. Pastoral Assocs.: Sr. Eileen Keating, C.S.A.; Mrs. Kathleen Lux.
Res., 300 E. Tallmadge Ave., 44310-2399. Tel: 330-376-5144; 5145; 374-6909; Fax: 330-376-5311.
School—Tel: 330-535-8817; Fax: 330-374-6903. Christine Lackney, Prin.
Lay Teachers 11; Students 239.
Catechesis/Religious Programs—Students 117.

11—ST. MARY, (1887), Revs. Edward A. Burba; Raymond J. Smith.
Res., 750 S. Main St., 44311-1094. Tel: 330-762-9247; Fax: 330-252-1768.
School—Tel: 330-253-1233; Fax: 330-253-1472. Kathleen Allio, Prin.
Lay Teachers 10; Students 214.
Catechesis/Religious Programs—Students 33.

12—ST. MATTHEW, (1943), Rev. Thomas A. McGovern; Deacon James A. White. In res., Rev. William P. Lyons.

Res., 2603 Benton St., 44312-1694. Tel: 330-733-9944; Fax: 330-733-9424.
Church—Berne & Woolf St., 44312.
School—2580 Benton St., 44312. Tel: 330-784-1711. Mr. Thomas S. Maroon, Prin.
Dominican Sisters 1; Lay Teachers 20; Students 398.
Catechesis/Religious Programs—Students 126.
Convent—2578 Benton St., 44312. Tel: 330-733-1001.

13—NATIVITY OF THE LORD JESUS, (1977), Rev. David J. Halaiko; Rosemary Frey, Pastoral Assoc.
Res., 2425 Myersville Rd., 44312-4951. Tel: 330-699-5086; Fax: 330-699-4299.
Catechesis/Religious Programs—Students 259.

14—ST. PAUL, (1919), Revs. John M. Jenkins; Robert E. Stein; Therese Nesline, Pastoral Assoc.; Deacon Francis R. Lonteen.
Res., 433 Mission Dr., 44301-2798. Tel: 330-724-1263; Fax: 330-724-7680.
School—1580 Brown St., 44301-2798. Tel: 330-724-1253; Fax: 330-724-1127. Mrs. Rosemary Capotosto, Prin.
Lay Teachers 25; Students 428.
Catechesis/Religious Programs—Students 79.

15—ST. PETER, (1917). Closed. For inquiries for parish records contact St. Mary Parish, Akron.

16—SACRED HEART OF JESUS, (1915) (Hungarian), Rev. Robert E. Clancy, Admin.; Deacon Geza Balassy.
Res., 212 E. Voris St., 44311. Tel: 330-434-4348.
Church—734 Grant St., 44311.

17—ST. SEBASTIAN, (1928), Revs. William D. Karg; John T. McDonough, Pastor Emeritus; Robert H. Jackson; Chima Nwamadi; Deacon Terry W. Peacock.
Res., 476 Mull Ave., 44320-1299. Tel: 330-836-2233; 2234; 2235; Fax: 330-836-2235.
School—500 Mull Ave., 44320. Tel: 330-836-9107; Fax: 330-836-7690. Mr. Howard J. Sheetz, Prin.
Lay Teachers 19; Students 426.
Catechesis/Religious Programs—Students 90.
Convent—352 Elmdale Ave., 44320. Tel: 330-864-2902.

18—ST. VINCENT, (1837), Rev. Joseph H. Kraker; Sr. Joan Radar, O.P., Pastoral Assoc.
Res., 164 W. Market St., 44303-2395. Tel: 330-535-3135; Fax: 330-535-4160. [CEM]
Church—W. Market St. & Maple St., 44303.
School—17 S. Maple St., 44303. Tel: 330-762-5912; Fax: 330-535-2515. William D. Hackman, Prin.
Lay Teachers 14; Students 251.
Catechesis/Religious Programs—Students 88.

Amherst, Lorain Co., St. Joseph (1864), Revs. Lawrence N. Martello; Anthony L. Kreps, Pastor Emeritus; James P. Schmitz; Sr. Mary Ann Burke, S.N.D., Pastoral Assoc.; Deacon Donald Hancock. In res., Rev. Thomas V. Rath.
Res., 200 St. Joseph Dr., 44001-1663. Tel: 216-988-2848; 2849; 871-4415 (Cleveland); Fax: 216-984-2301. [CEM]
School—175 St. Joseph Dr., 44001. Tel: 216-988-4244. John Gregory, Prin.
Lay Teachers 16; Students 345.
Catechesis/Religious Programs—Students 504.
Convent—151 St. Joseph Dr., 44001. Tel: 216-988-2621.

Ashland, Ashland Co., St. Edward (1853), Rev. James M. Cassidy; Deacon James A. Kaniecki.
Res., 501 Cottage St., 44805-2167. Tel: 419-289-7224; 289-8333; Fax: 419-289-0515. [JC]
Administration Center—149 Pleasant St., 44805.
School—433 Cottage St., 44805. Tel: 419-289-7456; Fax: 419-289-9474. Suellen Valentine, Prin.
Lay Teachers 9; Students 204.
Catechesis/Religious Programs—Students 234.
Convent—Tel: 419-289-8333.

Avon, Lorain Co., Holy Trinity (1833), Revs. John A. Misenko; John J. Gorski, Pastor Emeritus.
Res., 33601 Detroit Rd., 44011-1999. Tel: 440-937-5363; Fax: 440-937-5128. [CEM]
School—2610 Nagel Rd., 44011. Tel: 440-937-6420; Fax: 440-937-6420. Sr. Sean Groh, S.N.D., Prin.
Notre Dame Sisters 1; Lay Teachers 12; Students 262.
Catechesis/Religious Programs—Students 415.
Convent—2620 Nagel Rd., 44011. Tel: 440-937-5005.

St. Mary of the Immaculate Conception (1841), Revs. C. Thomas Cleaton; Arthur B. Egan, Pastor Emeritus.
Res., 2640 Stoney Ridge Rd., 44011-1899. Tel: 440-934-4212; Fax: 440-934-0507. [CEM]
School—2680 Stoney Ridge Rd., 44011. Tel: 440-934-6246; Fax: 440-934-6250. Miss Linda A. Kenzik, Prin.
Sisters of Notre Dame 1; Lay Teachers 9; Students 197.
Catechesis/Religious Programs—Students 207.
Convent—Tel: 440-934-5173.

Avon Lake, Lorain Co., Holy Spirit (1965), Rev. James H. Beatty; Sr. Maureen Grady, O.S.U., Pastoral Assoc.
Res., 410 Lear Rd., 44012-2004. Tel: 440-933-3777; 871-8157; Fax: 440-871-8157.
Catechesis/Religious Programs—Students 393.

St. Joseph's (1949), Rev. Timothy J. O'Connor; Sr. Thomasine Antenucci, S.S.J.-T.O.S.F., Pastoral Assoc.
Res., 32929 Lake Rd., 44012. Tel: 440-933-3152; Fax: 440-933-8919.
School—Tel: 440-933-6233; Fax: 440-933-2463. Mrs. Patricia Vaccaro, Prin.
Lay Teachers 12; Students 323.
Catechesis/Religious Programs—Students 377.
Convent—32911 Lake Rd., 44012. Tel: 216-933-5769.

Barberton, Summit Co.,

1—ST. AUGUSTINE, (1898), Revs. Richard Burchell; Robert W. Wisniewski; Paul J. Clines, Pastor Emeritus; Deacon Robin Adair.
Res., 204 Sixth St., N.W., 44203-2198. Tel: 330-745-0011; 0012; Fax: 330-745-0012.
Church—Sixth St. & Lake St., 44203.
School—195 Seventh St., N.W., 44203. Tel: 330-753-6435; Fax: 330-753-4095. Michael Ziegelhofer, Prin.
Lay Teachers 20; Students 425.
Catechesis/Religious Programs—Students 251.

2—SS. CYRIL AND METHODIUS, (1906), Rev. Edward F. Lajack.
Res., 189 15th St. N.W., 44203-7052. Tel: 330-825-7089; 825-7081; Fax: 330-825-7181.
Church—183 15 St. N.W., 44203.

3—HOLY TRINITY, (1911) (Hungarian), Rev. Carl A. Ciprian.
Res., 398 Van St., 44203-2329. Tel: 330-745-4735.
Church—380 Wooster Rd. N., 44203-2329.

4—ST. MARY'S, (1912) (Polish), Revs. Richard Arko, Admin.; Claude J. Gaebelein, Pastor Emeritus.
Res., 122 21st St. N.W., 44203. Tel: 330-825-6231.

5—SACRED HEART, (1916) (Slovenian), Rev. Albert A. Kunkel.
Res., 1263 Shannon Ave., N.W., 44203-6792. Tel: 330-825-9543.

Bay Village, Cuyahoga Co., St. Raphael (1946), Revs. Nelson J. Callahan; Timothy W. Gareau; Sr. Ardath Blake, H.M., Pastoral Assoc.
Res., 525 Dover Center Rd., 44140-2366. Tel: 440-871-1100; Fax: 440-899-2911.
School—Tel: 440-871-6760; Fax: 440-871-1358. Beverly Nemec, Prin.
Lay Teachers 33; Students 775.
Catechesis/Religious Programs—Students 598.

Bedford, Cuyahoga Co., St. Mary (1910), Rev. Thomas J. Winkel; Rev. Msgr. Francis E. Gasbarre, Pastor Emeritus.
Res., 300 Union St., 44146-4594. Tel: 440-232-9393; 9394; Fax: 440-232-7752.
Church—340 Union St., 44146.
School—270 Union St., 44146. Tel: 440-232-2303; Fax: 440-439-4419. Michelle Nowakowski, Prin.
Lay Teachers 11; Students 240.
Catechesis/Religious Programs—Students 55.
Convent—36 Paul St., 44146. Tel: 216-439-1667.

St. Pius X (1952), Rev. Robert Wenz; Sr. Irene Mraz, V.S.C., Pastoral Assoc. In res., Rev. Benson C. Okpara.
Res., 400 Center Rd., 44146-2296. Tel: 440-232-8166; 8167; Fax: 440-786-9929.
School—370 Center Rd., 44146-2297. Tel: 440-232-1531; Fax: 440-232-1534. Mrs. Mary Ann Murnyack, Prin.
Lay Teachers 10; Students 211.
Catechesis/Religious Programs—Students 115.

Bedford Heights, Cuyahoga Co., Holy Trinity (1965), Rev. Ernest C. Hepner; Joan McGinty, Pastoral Assoc.
Res., 24821 Columbus Rd., 44146-2599. Tel: 440-232-2044; 2045; Fax: 440-232-3720.
Catechesis/Religious Programs—Students 23.

Berea, Cuyahoga Co., St. Adalbert (1873) (Polish), Rev. Gerald J. Keller; Deacon Donald P. Butkovic.
Res., 66 Adelbert St., 44017-1799. Tel: 440-234-6830; Fax: 440-234-2588. [CEM]
School—56 Adelbert St., 44017. Tel: 440-234-5529. Mrs. Stephanie West, Prin.
Lay Teachers 11; Students 239.
Catechesis/Religious Programs—Students 139.
Convent—56 Adelbert St., Tel: 440-234-1096.

St. Mary's (1852), Rev. John M. Garrity; Mrs. Anne Chadwoski, Pastoral Assoc.
Res., 250 Kraft St., 44017-1449. Tel: 440-243-3877; 3878; Fax: 440-891-9417. [CEM]
School—265 Baker St., 44017-1515. Tel: 440-243-4555; Fax: 440-243-6214.
Lay Teachers 12; Students 336.
Catechesis/Religious Programs—Students 608.

Brecksville, Cuyahoga Co., St. Basil the Great (1960), Revs. Walter H. Jenne; Edward J. Camille, Pastor Emeritus; William R. Dickinson; Deacon David Pecot. Pastoral Assocs.: Sr. Susan Imburgia, C.S.J.; Mrs. Carol Gaby. In res., Revs. Lloyd J. Boymer; Anthony Rebol.
Res., 8700 Brecksville Rd., 44141-1999. Tel: 216-526-1686; 1687; Fax: 216-526-2373.
Catechesis/Religious Programs—Tel: 440-526-3520; 526-3587.
Students 1,237.
Convent—6901 Mill Rd., 44141. Tel: 440-526-2850; 2851.

Broadview Heights, Cuyahoga Co., Assumption (1857), Revs. Christopher Schwartz, O.S.B.; Clement Zeleznik, O.S.B.; Deacon Robert C. Bubnick, Sr.; Sr. Therese Horan, Pastoral Assoc.
Res., 9183 Broadview Rd., 44147-2596. Tel: 440-526-1177; 1178; Fax: 440-526-2838.
School—Tel: 440-526-4877; Fax: 440-526-3752. Sr. Carol Tobler, S.I.W., Prin.
Sisters of Incarnate Word 1; Lay Teachers 9; Students 251.
Catechesis/Religious Programs—Students 429.
Convent—9139 Broadview Rd., 44147. Tel: 216-526-4069.

Brooklyn, Cuyahoga Co., St. Thomas More (1946), Revs. James J. Vesely; John S. Juhas; Thomas G. Fanta; Sr. Elaine Theresa Burrows, S.I.W., Pastoral Assoc.; Deacons Rudolph Jarosh, Jr.; Martin A. Thiel.
Res., 4170 N. Amber Dr., 44144-1399. Tel: 216-749-0414; Fax: 216-749-1001.
School—4180 N. Amber Dr., 44144. Tel: 216-749-1660; Fax: 216-398-4265. Nancy D. Brewer, Prin.
Sisters 1; Lay Teachers 22; Students 467.
Catechesis/Religious Programs—Students 379.

Brook Park, Cuyahoga Co., Assumption of Mary (1860), Rev. Thomas A. Boone; Deacon Francis B. Wilson. In res., Rev. Adelbert J. Gassert.
Res., 5445 Smith Rd., 44142-2077. Tel: 216-267-0630; Fax: 216-267-3064. [CEM]
Church—5555 Smith Rd., 44142. Tel: 216-267-1775.
Catechesis/Religious Programs—Students 100.

St. Peter the Apostle (1968), Rev. Robert A. Burge; Deacons Robert G. Sabol; James Vincent. In res., Rev. Dismas Boeff, O.S.B.
Res., 6455 Engle Rd., 44142-3503. Tel: 216-433-1440; 1441; Fax: 216-433-1434.
Catechesis/Religious Programs—Students 425.

Brunswick, Medina Co., St. Ambrose (1957), Revs. Robert C. Hilkert; Allen F. Corrigan; John A. Valencheck; Deacons Clement J. Belter; John Miklosovic; Thomas J. Sheridan; Frank Weglicki.
Res., 929 Pearl Rd., 44212-2597. Tel: 330-225-3116; Fax: 330-225-5425.
School—923 Pearl Rd., 44212. Tel: 330-225-2116. Sr. Mary Ann Senia, H.M., Prin.
Sisters of Humility of Mary 2; Lay Teachers 16; Students 453.
Catechesis/Religious Programs—Students 1,308.

St. Colette (1977), Rev. Thomas G. Montavon. In res., Rev. Joseph F. Wagner.
Res., 330 W. 130th St., 44212-2309. Tel: 330-273-5500; Fax: 330-225-7909.
Catechesis/Religious Programs—Students 293.

Chagrin Falls, Holy Angels (1977), Rev. Joseph P. Labbe; Sr. Susan Javorek, S.N.D., Pastoral Assoc.
Mailing Address: 18205 Chillicothe Rd., 44023-4879.
Res., 8390 Stoney Brook Dr., 44023-4879. Tel: 440-543-2636 (Rectory); Fax: 440-708-0787.
Church—18046 Chillicothe Rd., 44023-4879. Tel: 440-708-0000.
Catechesis/Religious Programs—Tel: 440-708-0808.
Students 768.

St. Joan of Arc, Cuyahoga Co., (1948), Revs. John R. Olsavsky; John J. Kinkopf, Pastor Emeritus; David J. Majikas; Sr. Joanne Laurienzo, S.N.D., Pastoral Min.; Deacons Louis J. Capek; Jeffrey Dunlop.
Res., 496 E. Washington St., 44022-2999. Tel: 440-247-7183; 247-3606; Fax: 440-247-2327.
School—498 E. Washington St., 44022-2998. Tel: 440-247-6530; Fax: 440-247-2045. Mrs. Shelley Wither, Prin.
Lay Teachers 13; Students 240.
Catechesis/Religious Programs—Students 513.
Convent—456 E. Washington St., 44022. Tel: 440-247-4419.

Chardon, Geauga Co., St. Mary (1909), Revs. Thomas C. Gilles; Gregory F. Schaut; Deacons Edward J. McCarthy, Jr.; Lawrence Boehnlein.
Res., 400 North St., 44024-1087. Tel: 440-285-7051; Fax: 440-285-2818.
School—401 North St., 44024. Tel: 440-286-3590. Sr. Mary Sandra Nativio, S.N.D., Prin.
Sisters of Notre Dame 2; Lay Teachers 20; Students 378.
Catechesis/Religious Programs—Students 487.

Convent—315 North St., 44024. Tel: 440-286-5641.

Chesterland, Geauga Co., St. Anselm (1961), Revs. Thomas M. Sweany; John F. Anderson, Pastor Emeritus; Barry T. Gearing; Deacons Dale A. Bacik; Donald E. Sill.
Res., 12969 Chillicothe Rd., 44026-3199. Tel: 440-729-9575; Fax: 440-729-9103.
Church—13013 Chillicothe Rd., 44026.
School—Tel: 440-729-7806; Fax: 440-729-3524. Sr. Gretchen Rodenfels, O.S.U., Prin.
Sisters of Notre Dame 2; Lay Teachers 20; Students 400.
Catechesis/Religious Programs—Students 575.
Convent—13055 Chillicothe Rd., 44026. Tel: 440-729-0292.

Chippewa Lake, Medina Co., Jesus Divine Redeemer (1976). Attended by Our Lady Help of Christians, Litchfield.

Cleveland Heights, Cuyahoga Co., St. Ann (1915), Rev. James E. Singler; Ms. Renee Barber, Pastoral Assoc.
Res., 2175 Coventry Rd., 44118-2898. Tel: 216-321-0024; Fax: 216-321-7702.
School—2160 Stillman Rd., 44118. Tel: 216-932-4177; Fax: 216-932-7439. Sr. Anne McGreevey, O.S.B., Prin.
Sisters 1; Lay Teachers 22; Students 309.
Catechesis/Religious Programs—Students 83.

St. Louis (1947), Rev. Leonard J. Zamborsky; Deacon Richard E. Woods; Sr. Marie Manning, S.N.D., Pastoral Assoc. In res., Rev. Stephen J. Dohner.
Res., 2475 N. Taylor Rd., 44118-1397. Tel: 216-382-0440; 0441; 382-1071; Fax: 216-382-1605.
Church—2463 N. Taylor Rd., 44118.
School—2463 N. Taylor Rd., 44118. Tel: 216-382-0033; Fax: 216-382-5933. Julie Dougherty, Prin.
Lay Teachers 12; Students 168.
Catechesis/Religious Programs—Students 151.
Convent—2425 N. Taylor Rd., 44118. Tel: 216-381-3034.

Clinton, Summit Co., St. George (1908), Rev. Msgr. Robert E. Bacher.
Res., 7615 Second Ave. N., 44216. Tel: 330-882-3353; Fax: 330-882-3353.
Church—7609 Second Ave. N., 44216.
Catechesis/Religious Programs—Students 27.

Columbia Station, Lorain Co., St. Elizabeth Ann Seton (1976), Rev. Charles J. Ryba.
Mailing Address: P.O. Box 968, 44028-0968.
Res., 25777 Royalton Rd., 44028-0968.
Church—25801 Royalton Rd., 44028. Tel: 440-236-5095; Fax: 440-236-5804.
Catechesis/Religious Programs—Tel: 440-236-3711.
Students 204.

Concord Twp., Lake Co., St. Gabriel (1966), Revs. Frederick F. Pausche; John G. Vrana; Deacons Norman H. Davis; Ronald Adkins; Carolyn Jablonski, Pastoral Assoc. In res., Rev. David G. Woost.
Res., 9925 Johnnycake Ridge Rd., 44060-6294. Tel: 440-352-8282; 953-3867 (Cleveland); Fax: 440-354-7558.
School—9935 Johnnycake Ridge Rd., 44060. Tel: 440-352-6169; Fax: 440-639-0143. Sr. Josephmarie Bunosky, S.N.D., Prin.
Sisters of Notre Dame 3; Lay Teachers 28; Students 775.
Catechesis/Religious Programs—Students 849.
Convent—9918 Johnnycake Ridge Rd., 44060. Tel: 440-354-7553.

Copley, Summit Co., Guardian Angels (1964), Rev. J. Norman Riley; Rev. Msgr. Robert C. Wolff, Pastor Emeritus.
Res., 1676 Cleveland-Massillon Rd., 44321-1976. Tel: 330-666-1373.
Church—1686 Cleveland-Massillon Rd., 44321-1976.
Catechesis/Religious Programs—Students 241.

Cuyahoga Falls, Summit Co., Immaculate Heart of Mary (1952), Revs. Thomas W. McCann; John R. Rathfon, Pastor Emeritus; Thomas G. Woost; Robert E. Pahler, (Retired); Deacon J. David Seal.
Res., 1905 Portage Trail, 44223-1792. Tel: 330-929-8361; 8362; 929-8399; Fax: 330-929-8496.
School—2859 Lillis Dr., 44223. Tel: 330-923-1220; Fax: 330-929-4373. Barbara Kimberly Greene, Prin.
Lay Teachers 23; Students 538.
Catechesis/Religious Programs—Students 277.

St. Eugene (1963), Rev. B. Thomas Zeisig.
Res., 1821 Munroe Falls Ave., 44221-3699. Tel: 330-923-5244; Fax: 330-923-8436.
Catechesis/Religious Programs—Students 156.

St. Joseph (1831), Rev. James J. Marsick; Deacon Robert Kochanski, Pastoral Assoc.
Res., 215 Falls Ave., 44221. Tel: 330-928-2173; Fax: 330-928-3082.
Church—1761 Second St., 44221.
School—1909 Third St., 44221-3894. Tel: 330-928-2151; Fax: 330-928-3139. Robert Kochanski, Prin.
Deacons 1; Lay Teachers 18; Students 398.
Catechesis/Religious Programs—Students 111.

Doylestown, Wayne Co., SS. Peter and Paul (1827), Rev. David J. McCarthy.
Res., 161 W. Clinton St., 44230-1297. Tel: 330-658-2145. [CEM][JC]
School—169 W. Clinton St., 44230. Tel: 330-658-2804; Fax: 330-658-2287. Marian Gillen, Prin.
Lay Teachers 10; Students 181.
Catechesis/Religious Programs—Students 164.

East Cleveland, Cuyahoga Co., Christ the King (1928), Rev. Michael A. Wittman; Deacon Raymond Daull. Pastoral Assocs.: Sr. Marietta Rohr, C.S.A.; Warrennette Reed; Mary Ann Toth, Admin.
Res., 1862 Noble Rd., 44112-1636. Tel: 216-851-4388; 4389; Fax: 216-851-4040.
School—Noble & Terrace Rd., 44112. Tel: 216-451-4756; Fax: 216-451-0831. Mr. Kevin James, Prin.
Lay Teachers 10; Students 152.
Catechesis/Religious Programs—Students 14.
Convent—16005 Terrace Rd., 44112.

St. Philomena (1902), Rev. Dennis J. Kleinweber; Delores Breckenridge, Pastoral Assoc. In res., Rev. John R. McCarthy (STU).
Res., 13824 Euclid Ave., 44112-4299. Tel: 216-541-3540; Fax: 216-541-3545.

Eastlake, Lake Co., St. Justin Martyr (1962), Revs. Kevin M. Liebhardt; David R. Ireland; Deacon Jerry J. Bals, (On Leave); Joanne E. Novak, Pastoral Assoc.
Mailing Address: 35781 Stevens Blvd., 44095-5095. Tel: 440-946-1177; Fax: 440-946-9126.
Administration Center—Tel: 440-946-1177.
Res., 35701 Stevens Blvd., 44095.
School—35741 Stevens Blvd., 44095. Tel: 440-946-5414; Fax: 440-946-2074. Sr. Mary Quinlan, Prin.
Sisters of Notre Dame 2; Lay Teachers 13; Students 341.
Catechesis/Religious Programs—Students 423.
Convent—35711 Stevens Blvd., 44095. Tel: 440-946-1013.

Elyria, Lorain Co.,

1—St. Agnes, (1914), Rev. Michael D. Ausperk; Bro. Leonard Siwierka, C.S.C., Pastoral Assoc.
Res. & Church: 611 Lake Ave., 44035-3541. Tel: 440-322-5622; Fax: 440-322-0231.
Catechesis/Religious Programs—Students 97.

2—Holy Cross, (1922) (Polish), Rev. James D. Schorr, Admin.
Church & Res.: 1417 West Ave., 44035-7637. Tel: 440-323-1022; Fax: 440-323-8277.
Catechesis/Religious Programs—Students 25.

3—St. Jude, (1943), Revs. Frank P. Kosem; Patrick J. O'Connor; Deacon Patrick J. Humphrey. Pastoral Assocs.: Sr. Marie Gillich, C.S.J.; Sr. Angela Nihill, O.S.U.
Res., 590 Poplar St., 44035-3999. Tel: 440-366-5711; 366-6052; Fax: 440-366-1916.
School—594 Poplar St., 44035. Tel: 440-366-1681; Fax: 440-366-5238. Sr. Mary Berigan, S.N.D., Prin.
Sisters of Notre Dame 1; Lay Teachers 22; Students 511.
Catechesis/Religious Programs—Students 348.
Convent—342 Longford, 44035. Tel: 440-366-1551.

4—St. Mary, (1845), Revs. Joseph C. Weigand; Gary J. Malin; Deacon Frank A. Humphrey, III.
Res., 320 Middle Ave., 44035-5796. Tel: 440-323-5530; 323-5539; Fax: 440-322-2329. [CEM]
School—237 Fourth St., 44035. Tel: 440-322-2808; Fax: 440-323-0886. Mr. Fred A. Visci, Prin.
Lay Teachers 18; Students 406.
Catechesis/Religious Programs—Tel: 440-322-3054.
Students 170.
Convent—235 Fourth St., 44035-5796. Tel: 440-322-1423.

5—Sacred Heart of Jesus, (1922) (Magyar), Rev. George M. Guschwan; Sr. Cheryl Saucier, S.S.J., T.O.S.F., Pastoral Assoc.; Deacon Edward R. Dillon.
Res., P.O. Box 417, 44036-0417. Tel: 440-323-3382; Fax: 440-323-1434.
Church—162 Irondale St., 44036.
Catechesis/Religious Programs—Students 39.

Elyria Township, Lorain Co., St. Vincent de Paul (1949), Revs. James R. Ols; Liam J. Kitt, Pastor Emeritus; Deacon John K. Slatcoff.
Res., 41295 N. Ridge Rd., 44035-1098. Tel: 440-324-4212; 277-5285; Fax: 440-324-2892.
School—41315 N. Ridge Rd., 44035-1098. Tel: 440-277-6208; Fax: 440-324-9552. Mrs. Margaret Malenich, Prin.
Lay Teachers 10; Students 257.
Catechesis/Religious Programs—Students 230.

Euclid, Cuyahoga Co.,

1—St. Christine, (1925), Revs. Francis R. Sterk; Francis M. Paik, Pastor Emeritus.
Res., 840 E. 222nd St., 44123-3317. Tel: 216-261-1410; 261-6210; 261-6144; 261-6383; Fax: 216-261-9039.
School—860 E. 222nd St., 44123. Tel: 216-731-6244; Fax: 216-261-6003. Mrs. Mary Benns, Prin.
Lay Teachers 12; Students 247.
Catechesis/Religious Programs—Students 47.

2—St. Felicitas, (1950), Pastoral Team Members: Revs. Richard J. Bober, Coord.; Neil G. Walters; Deacon Thomas B. DeHaas, Jr.; MaryBeth Muehle.
Res., 140 Richmond Rd., 44143-1299. Tel: 216-289-0770; Fax: 216-289-0740.
School—Tel: 216-261-1240; Fax: 216-261-5843. Anne Marie Woyma, Prin.
Lay Teachers 22; Students 535.
Catechesis/Religious Programs—Students 275.

3—Holy Cross, (1924), Revs. John P. McNulty; William Bouhall. Pastoral Assocs.: Sr. Kathleen Flannery, O.S.U.; Deacons Jerome B. Vrabel; Robert Payne; James Croniger.
Res., 19951 Lake Shore Blvd., 44119. Tel: 216-486-0850; 0851; 486-0853; Fax: 216-486-0851.
Church—Lake Shore Blvd. & E. 200th St., 44119.
School—Tel: 216-481-6824; Fax: 216-481-9841. Patricia Patterson, Prin.
Ursuline Nuns of Cleveland 1; Lay Teachers 19; Students 445.
Catechesis/Religious Programs—Students 157.
Convent—19951 Lake Shore Blvd., 44119. Tel: 216-486-0088.

4—St. Paul, (1860), Rev. Francis C. Mulvanity; Deacon Louis G. Pecek; Barbara Pallo, Pastoral Assoc. In res., Rev. William M. Jerse.
Res., 1231 Chardon Rd., 44117-1192. Tel: 216-531-0900; 0901; Fax: 216-531-5117. [CEM]
School—1200 E. 200th St., 44117. Tel: 216-481-6060; Fax: 216-481-0919. Sr. Donna Galetovich, S.N.D., Prin.
Ursuline Nuns of Cleveland 1; Lay Teachers 9; Students 194.
Catechesis/Religious Programs—Students 31.
Convent—1050 E. 200th St., 44117. Tel: 216-531-9178.

5—St. Robert Bellarmine, (1950), Rev. Dennis M. McNeil. In res., Rev. Peter J. Woll.
Res., 23802 Lake Shore Blvd., 44123-1200. Tel: 216-731-2606; 2607; Fax: 216-731-2607.
School—Tel: 216-731-2108; Fax: 216-731-2109. Mary A. Pittinger, Prin.
Lay Teachers 10; Students 251.
Catechesis/Religious Programs—Students 42.

6—St. William, (1946), Revs. David G. Baugh; Robert J. Franco. In res., Sr. Irene Charette, O.S.U., Pastoral Assoc.
Res., 367 E. 260th St., 44132-1495. Tel: 216-731-1515; Fax: 216-731-7611.
School—351 E. 260th St., 44132. Tel: 216-731-3060; Fax: 216-731-0300. Mary Heramb, Prin.
Lay Teachers 19; Students 401.
Catechesis/Religious Programs—Students 118.
Convent—321 E. 260th St., 44132. Tel: 216-731-5645.

Fairport Harbor, Lake Co., St. Anthony of Padua (1887), Revs. Peter M. Mihalec; William J. Englert, Pastor Emeritus; Deacon John T. Wenzel; Dorothy M. Trepal, Pastoral Assoc.
Res., 316 Fifth St., 44077. Tel: 440-354-4525; Fax: 440-354-8313.
Catechesis/Religious Programs—Students 96.

Fairview Park, Cuyahoga Co., St. Angela Merici (1923), Revs. Douglas M. Proehl; Curtis L. Kondik; Neil P. Kookoothe; Curtis L. Kondik; Anthony Iezzi, Ph.D., Pastoral Assoc.; Deacon James L. Agrippe.
Res., 20970 Lorain Rd., 44126-2096. Tel: 440-333-2133; Fax: 440-333-8061.
School—20830 Lorain Rd., 44126. Tel: 440-333-2126; Fax: 440-333-8480. Mrs. Harriet Davis, Prin.
Lay Teachers 32; Students 674.
Catechesis/Religious Programs—Tel: 216-333-2133.
Students 426.

Garfield Heights, Cuyahoga Co.,

1—St. Monica, (1952), Rev. John P. Seabold, Coord. of Pastoral Team. Pastoral Team: Rev. Donald P. Oleksiak; Deacon Ralph W. Netzband; Sr. Helen Weis, S.J.S.M.; Rev. Michael A. Matusz.
Res., 13623 Rockside Rd., 44125-5197. Tel: 216-662-8685; 8686; 8687; 662-8625; Fax: 216-662-1245.
School—13633 Rockside Rd., 44125. Tel: 216-662-9380; Fax: 216-662-3137. Sr. Helen Weis, S.J.S.M., Prin.
Sisters of St. Joseph Third Order of St. Francis 3; Lay Teachers 19; Students 515.
Catechesis/Religious Programs—Students 267.
Convent—Tel: 216-581-0810.

2—SS. Peter and Paul, (1927) (Polish), Revs. Theodore Marszal; Anthony W. Zepp, Pastor Emeritus; Rev. Msgr. Casimir S. Ciolek, A.C.S.W., Pastor Emeritus; Rev. Marian Bendyk.
Res., 4750 Turney Rd., 44125-1448. Tel: 216-429-1515; 1516; Fax: 216-429-1889.

School—4740 Turney Rd., 44125. Tel: 216-271-6564; Fax: 216-271-0504. Mrs. Mary Tetlak, Prin.
Religious 1; Lay Teachers 17; Students 332.
Catechesis/Religious Programs—Students 73.
Convent—Tel: 216-429-2666.

3—ST. THERESE, (1927), Revs. Norman A. Gajdzinski; Mark R. Blinn, Pastor Emeritus; Albert Veigas; Deacon Lawrence Cermak.
Res., 5276 E. 105th St., 44125-2628. Tel: 216-581-2852; 2853; Fax: 216-581-5091.
School—10608 Penfield Ave., 44125. Tel: 216-581-3080; Fax: 216-581-3031. Sr. Jane Morgan, O.S.U., Prin.
Ursuline Nuns of Cleveland 2; Lay Teachers 18; Students 369.
Catechesis/Religious Programs—Students 201.
Convent—10430 Granger Rd., 44125. Tel: 216-581-2864.

4—ST. TIMOTHY, (1923), Rev. John J. Wright; Deacon Joseph H. Newman.
Res., 4341 E. 131st St., 44105. Tel: 216-581-0981; 0982; Fax: 216-581-8222.
School—Archbishop James P. Lyke Elementary School. See Elementary Schools, Parochial and Diocesan under Institutions Located in the Diocese. Tel: 216-581-3517; Fax: 216-581-6204.

Gates Mills, Cuyahoga Co., St. Francis of Assisi (1943), Revs. James L. Caddy; Sylvester W. Fridrich, Pastor Emeritus; Ralph W. Thomas; Leonard G. Obloy; Sr. Beverly Bodnar, C.PP.S., Pastoral Assoc.; Deacons Leo F. McNulty; William T. Elwood.
Res., 6850 Mayfield Rd., 44040-9635. Tel: 216-461-0066; Fax: 216-461-9053.
School—Tel: 216-442-7450; Fax: 216-446-1132. Mr. Mark W. Talarico, Prin.
Lay Teachers 23; Students 309.
Catechesis/Religious Programs—Students 284.
Convent—Tel: 216-449-1352.

Grafton, Lorain Co., Assumption (1894) (Polish), Rev. Ralph A. Bodziony, Admin.
Res., 1033 Elm St., 44044. Tel: 440-926-2364.
Catechesis/Religious Programs—Students 94.
Immaculate Conception (1835), Rev. Robert R. Vieweg.
Res., 708 Erie St., 44044. Tel: 216-926-2268. [CEM]
Catechesis/Religious Programs—Students 238.

Green, Summit Co., Queen of Heaven (1964), Revs. David R. Durkee; Robert E. Pahler, Pastor Emeritus; Deacon Francis R. Lonteen.
Res., P.O. Box 296, 44232. Tel: 330-896-2345; 896-3332; Fax: 330-896-8882.
Church—1800 Steese Rd., 44232.
Catechesis/Religious Programs—Students 468.

Highland Heights, Cuyahoga Co., St. Paschal Baylon (1953), Revs. Michael J. Arkins, S.S.S.; Donald J. Jette, S.S.S.; Roger Bourgeois, S.S.S.; Mrs. Annette Cicatelli; Deacons Robert J. Bowers; Joseph Bourgeois. In res., Rev. Scott Haig, S.S.S.
Res., 5384 Wilson Mills Rd., 44143-3092. Tel: 440-442-3410; 449-7532; 449-7758; Fax: 440-442-2001.
School—5360 Wilson Mills Rd., 44143. Tel: 440-442-6766; Fax: 440-446-9037. Mr. John V. Bednar, Prin.
Lay Teachers 28; Students 509.
Catechesis/Religious Programs—Students 491.
Convent—Tel: 440-442-2380.

Hinckley, Medina Co., Our Lady of Grace (1965), Rev. William P. O'Neill. In res., Rev. John T. McDonough.
Res., 1088 Ridge Rd., 44233-9602. Tel: 330-278-2834; 278-4121; Fax: 330-278-2834.
Catechesis/Religious Programs—Students 271.

Hudson, Summit Co., St. Mary (1860), Revs. Joseph J. Costello; Vincent P. O'Dea, Pastor Emeritus; Stephen K. Brunovsky; Kathee Sterbenz, Pastoral Assoc.
Res., 340 N. Main St, 44236-2242. Tel: 216-653-8118; 656-2558 (Cleveland); 463-5753 (Cleveland); 650-0722 (Akron); Fax: 216-463-5759. [CEM]
Church—340 N. Main St., 44236.
Catechesis/Religious Programs—Students 1,353.

Independence, Cuyahoga Co., St. Michael (1851), Revs. Carl L. D'Agostino; Denis L. St. Marie; Adelbert J. Gassert, Pastor Emeritus; Deacon Robert Weniger. In res., Rev. William F. Gibbons.
Res., 6912 Chestnut Rd., 44131-3399. Tel: 216-524-1394; 1395; Fax: 216-328-8537. [CEM]
Church—Brecksville Rd., 44131.
School—6906 Chestnut Rd., 44131. Tel: 216-524-6405; Fax: 216-524-7538. Sr. Carol Marek, S.N.D., Prin.
Sisters of Notre Dame 2; Lay Teachers 16; Students 415.
Catechesis/Religious Programs—Tel: 216-447-4406.
Students 345.
Convent—6800 Chestnut Rd., 44131-3399. Tel: 216-447-4406.

Kirtland, Lake Co., Divine Word (1977), Rev. Norman N. Smith; Deacons Carl M. Varga, Pastoral Assoc.; Lawrence Somrack. In res., Revs. John J. Kinkopf; Joseph McMahon.
Res., 8100 Eagle Rd., 44094-9714. Tel: 440-256-1412; 1413; 256-1417; Fax: 440-256-4929.
School—Peaceful Children Montessori, Tel: 440-256-1976. Mary Potosky, Prin.
Catechesis/Religious Programs—Students 251.

Lakewood, Cuyahoga Co.,

1—ST. CLEMENT, (1922), Revs. Alfred H. Winters; Joseph R. Spolny; Sr. Mary Jame Masterson, C.S.J., Pastoral Assoc.
Res., 2022 Lincoln Ave., 44107-6099. Tel: 216-226-5116; Fax: 216-226-5117.
Church—Madison & Lincoln Aves., 44107.
School—14505 Madison Ave., 44107. Tel: 216-226-1942; Fax: 216-226-9459. Mrs. Arlene Polen, Prin.
Lay Teachers 10; Students 222.
Catechesis/Religious Programs—Students 144.
Convent—14505 Madison Ave., 44107.

2—SS. CYRIL AND METHODIUS, (1902) (Slovak), Revs. Richard J. Ondreyka, M.S., Pastor Emeritus; Jerome J. Duke.
Res., 12608 Madison Ave., 44107-4997. Tel: 216-521-7288; 521-9091; Fax: 216-521-7005.
Church—Madison Ave. & Lakewood Ave., 44107.
School—1639 Alameda Ave., 44107. Tel: 216-221-9409. Rosemary Hannibal, Prin.
Lay Teachers 11; Students 159.
Catechesis/Religious Programs—Tel: 216-221-9402.
Students 103.
Convent—1635 Alameda Ave., 44107. Tel: 216-221-3164.

3—ST. HEDWIG, (1905) (Polish), Rev. John J. Bryk.
Res., 12903 Madison Ave., 44107-4939. Tel: 216-521-5086; 521-4463.
Church—12905 Madison Ave., 44107-4939.

4—ST. JAMES, (1908), Revs. John J. Weigand; Thomas J. Behrend; Deacon James R. Stewart; Miss Kathryn Haag, Pastoral Assoc. In res., Rev. Thomas P. Kowatch.
Res., 17514 Detroit Ave., 44107. Tel: 216-221-0233; Fax: 216-221-2431.
Church—Detroit & Granger Ave., 44107.
School—17415 Northwood Ave., 44107. Tel: 216-221-1225; Fax: 216-529-7950. Miss Sheila Mannix, Prin.
Lay Teachers 18; Students 289.
Catechesis/Religious Programs—Students 278.

5—ST. LUKE, (1922), Revs. Francis P. Walsh; Kenneth J. Jakubowski; Sr. Miriam Erb, C.S.A., Pastoral Assoc.; Deacon David A. Streeter. In res., Rev. Ralph E. Wiatrowski.
Res., 1212 Bunts Rd., 44107-2699. Tel: 216-521-0184; 0185; 0186; Fax: 216-521-9360.
School—13889 Clifton Blvd., 44107. Tel: 216-521-7033; Fax: 216-521-9127. Mr. Mark Dudek, Prin.
Ursuline Nuns of Cleveland 1; Lay Teachers 18; Students 309.
Catechesis/Religious Programs—Students 187.
Convent—1221 Chase Ave., 44107.

Litchfield, Medina Co., Our Lady Help of Christians Parish (1976), Rev. Ronald J. Bryda, Coord. Pastoral Team. Pastoral Team: Rev. Edward F. Weist; Sr. Margaret Duffy, O.S.U.; Sr. Mary Lou Misciasci, C.S.J.; Deacon John M. Buda; Sandra J. Lynn.
Administration Center—9608 Norwalk Rd., 44253-9598. Tel: 330-722-1180; 273-1500 (Cleveland); Fax: 330-723-5891.
Catechesis/Religious Programs—Students 390.
Convent—9608 Norwalk Rd., 44253.
Missions—Litchfield, Medina Co., Jesus the Christ Child; Chippewa Lake, Medina Co., Jesus Divine Redeemer; Nova-Savannah, Medina Co., Jesus the Good Shepherd 356 N. Main St.,; Seville-Creston, Medina Co., Jesus Emmanuel 60 High St.,; Spencer, Medina Co., Jesus Our Savior; Lodi, Medina Co., Jesus Our Teacher.

Lodi, Medina Co., Jesus Our Teacher (1976). Attended by Our Lady Help of Christians, Litchfield.

Lorain, Lorain Co.,

1—ST. ANTHONY OF PADUA, (1923), Revs. Christian Moore, O.F.M.Conv.; Regis T. Schlagheck, O.F.M.Conv. In res., Rev. Charles Henkle, O.F.M. Conv.; Bro. Campion Erdei, O.F.M.Cap.
Res., 1305 E. Erie Ave., 44052. Tel: 440-288-0106; 0107; Fax: 440-288-0143.
School—1339 E. Erie Ave., 44052. Tel: 440-288-2155; Fax: 440-288-2159. Robert Halloway, Prin.
Lay Teachers 11; Students 286.
Catechesis/Religious Programs—Students 99.

2—SS. CYRIL AND METHODIUS, (1905) (Slovenian), Rev. Paul Krajnik.
Res., 1709 E. 31st St., 44055. Tel: 440-277-8286.
Church—1705 E. 31st St., 44055.
Catechesis/Religious Programs—Students 7.

3—HOLY TRINITY, (1906) (Slovak), Rev. David A. Novak.
Res., 2428 Elyria Ave., 44055-1366. Tel: 440-244-1253; 244-2418.
Catechesis/Religious Programs—Students 13.

4—SACRED HEART CHAPEL, (1952) (Hispanic), Rev. William A. Thaden; Sr. Theresa Stegman, C.D.P., Pastoral Assoc.; Deacons Tomas Badillo; Jose A. Flores; Carlos Rivera; Jose A. DeGracia; Jose Luis Piniero.
Mailing Address: 4301 Pearl Ave., 44055-2634.
Res., 3921 Seneca Ave., 44055. Tel: 440-277-7231; 7232; 277-7379 (Rectory); Fax: 440-277-4886.
Church—4301 Pearl Ave., 44055.
Catechesis/Religious Programs—Students 324.

5—ST. JOHN, (1900), Revs. Thomas V. Rath, Pastor Emeritus; Thomas R. Smith.
Res., 2143 Homewood Dr., 44055-2799. Tel: 440-277-7266.
School—2140 E. 36th St., 44055-2798. Tel: 440-277-6285. Mrs. Penelope Lins, Prin.
Lay Teachers 9; Students 156.
Catechesis/Religious Programs—Students 55.

6—ST. JOSEPH, (1896) (German), Revs. Robert J. Reidy; William F. Gibbons, Pastor Emeritus; Deacon Luis Maldonado.
Res., 317 W. 15th St., 44052-3488. Tel: 440-244-2179.
Church—Reid Ave. & 15th St., 44052.

7—ST. LADISLAUS, (1890) (Hungarian), Revs. Patrick J. Shields, Admin. Pro Tem; Alex D. Demetzky, Pastor Emeritus.
Res., 1412 E. 29th St., 44055. Tel: 440-277-8187.
Catechesis/Religious Programs—Students 25.

8—ST. MARY, (1873), Revs. Daniel O. Divis; John J. Kline, Pastor Emeritus; Mrs. Patricia Shullick, Pastoral Assoc.
Res., 309 Eighth St., 44052-1879. Tel: 440-245-5283; Fax: 440-246-0804.
School—307 Seventh St., 44052. Tel: 440-244-1697; Fax: 440-244-3423. Mr. Hobart Johnson, Prin.
Lay Teachers 13; Students 214.
Administration Center—309 Seventh St., 44052.
Catechesis/Religious Programs—Students 75.

9—NATIVITY OF THE BLESSED VIRGIN MARY, (1898) (Polish), Rev. Robert J. Glepko; Deacon Robert J. Dybo.
Res., 418 W. 15th St., 44052. Tel: 440-244-9090; 621-6445 (Cleveland); Fax: 440-244-0421.
Church—1454 Lexington Ave., 44052.

10—ST. PETER, (1909), Revs. Kenneth J. Wolnowski; G. Michael Williamson; Deacon Ralph Krupp.
Res., 3501 Oberlin Ave., 44053-2759. Tel: 440-282-9103; 9104; 282-8104; 892-8641 (Cleveland); Fax: 440-282-9490.
School—3601 Oberlin Ave., 44053. Tel: 440-282-9909; Fax: 440-892-1693. Sr. Annamae Murphy, S.N.D., Prin.
Sisters of Notre Dame 1; Lay Teachers 27; Students 578.
Catechesis/Religious Programs—Students 253.
Convent—3651 Oberlin Ave., 44053. Tel: 440-282-2378.

11—ST. STANISLAUS, (1908) (Polish), Rev. Kevin L. Shemuga; Deacon William E. Schill.
Res., 2702 Elyria Ave., 44055-1337. Tel: 440-244-4185; Fax: 440-244-4212.
Catechesis/Religious Programs—Students 32.

12—ST. VITUS, (1922) (Croatian), Rev. Simon J. Nekic.
Res., 1785 E. 32nd St., 44055. Tel: 440-277-8210.
Catechesis/Religious Programs—Students 13.

Loudonville, Ashland Co., St. Peter (1870), Rev. Kevin M. Conroy.
Res., 132 N. Wood St., 44842. Tel: 419-994-4396; Fax: 419-994-5263. [CEM]
Catechesis/Religious Programs—Tel: 419-994-3329.
Students 122.

Lyndhurst, Cuyahoga Co., St. Clare (1944), Revs. Stanley J. Klasinski; G. David Bline; Edward J. Janoch; Deacons Ross C. DeJohn, Sr.; Robert J. Matoney, Jr.
Res., 5659 Mayfield Rd., 44124. Tel: 440-449-4242; Fax: 440-646-9648.
School—5655 Mayfield Rd., 44124. Tel: 440-449-1554; Fax: 440-449-1497. Miss Ruth Downey, Prin.
Ursuline Nuns of Cleveland 2; Lay Teachers 21; Students 456.
Catechesis/Religious Programs—Students 398.

Macedonia, Summit Co., Our Lady of Guadalupe (1967), Revs. David R. Trask; Lloyd J. Boymer, Pastor Emeritus; Deacon Mario Vinciguerra; Mrs. Nancy Freibott, Pastoral Assoc.
Res., 9080 Shepard Rd., 44056-1450. Tel: 330-468-2194; Fax: 330-468-2196.
Catechesis/Religious Programs—Students 344.

Madison, Lake Co., Immaculate Conception (1863), Rev. Luigi C. Miola; Deacons Thomas G. Hupertz; Richard F. Kuhlman.

Res., 2846 Hubbard Rd., 44057-2998. Tel: 440-428-5164; 5165; 428-3988; 975-0729 (Cleveland); Fax: 440-428-3075.
Catechesis/Religious Programs—Students 422.

Maple Heights, Cuyahoga Co., St. Martin of Tours (1960), Revs. James F. Mazanec; John J. Gerrity, Pastor Emeritus; Matthew J. Glaros; Deacon John R. Bender.
Res., 14600 Turney Rd., 44137-4788. Tel: 216-475-4300; 4301; Fax: 216-475-8242. [CEM]
School—Tel: 216-475-3633; Fax: 216-475-2484. Rozann Swanson, Prin.
Lay Teachers 11; Students 251.
Catechesis/Religious Programs—Students 143.

St. Wenceslas (1923), Rev. Clyde K. Foster; Rev. Msgr. Joseph C. Heruday, Pastor Emeritus; Deacon Daniel C. Terrion. In res., Rev. Stephen J. Walick.
Res., 17825 Libby Rd., 44137-1598. Tel: 216-475-2477; 2478; 475-3304; Fax: 216-475-3304.
Church—Libby Rd. & Cato St., 44137.
School—5254 Arch St., 44137. Tel: 216-662-0180; Fax: 216-662-8101. Mrs. Sharon Vejdovec, Prin.
Sisters 2; Lay Teachers 9; Students 251.
Catechesis/Religious Programs—Students 37.

Medina, Medina Co., St. Francis Xavier (1860), Revs. Mark L. Hollis; Stephen Kaminski; Russell G. Rauscher; Deacons Joseph E. Loutzenhiser; James T. Schlund; Daniel E. Norris.
Res., 606 E. Washington St., 44256-2183. Tel: 330-725-4968; 225-3940 (Cleveland); Fax: 330-723-6234. [CEM]
Church—600 E. Washington St., 44256.
School—612 E. Washington St., 44256. Tel: 330-725-3345; Fax: 330-721-8626. Sandra Bevec, Prin.
St. Felix of Cantalice 1; Lay Teachers 24; Students 575.
Catechesis/Religious Programs—Tel: 330-722-7700.
Students 885.

Holy Martyrs (1980), Rev. Robert F. Pfeiffer. Pastoral Assocs.: Mary Frances Ehlinger; Suzanne Kozub.
Res., 3100 S. Weymouth Rd., 44256-9207. Tel: 330-722-6633; 722-8951; 273-1188 (Cleveland); Fax: 330-722-6633.
Catechesis/Religious Programs—Students 704.

Mentor, Lake Co., St. Bede the Venerable (1964), Revs. John J. Sullivan; Michael Woost. Pastoral Assocs.: Mrs. Judith A. Cox; Mrs. Lottie A. Sroczynski; Mrs. Karen J. Roman; Deacons Robert P. Ulman; John Burke, Jr.; Kenneth Knight.
Res., 9114 Lake Shore Blvd., 44060-1697. Tel: 440-257-5544; 5545; Fax: 440-257-2318.
Catechesis/Religious Programs—Tel: 216-257-6988.
Students 586.

St. John Vianney (1969), Revs. Robert W. Kline, Pastor Emeritus; Thomas W. Johns; Dennis J. Kristancic; Anthony F. Sejba; Deacons Wayne W. Snyder; James J. Duffy; Mary Kovach, Pastoral Assoc.
7575 Bellflower Rd., 44060-3997. Tel: 440-943-3445 (Cleveland); 255-0600; Fax: 440-255-6482.
School—All Saints of St. John Vianney, Wickliffe. See separate listing under Institutions Located in the Diocese. Tel: 440-943-1395; Fax: 440-944-3341.
Catechesis/Religious Programs—Tel: 440-255-7266.
Students 1,001.

St. Mary of the Assumption (1857), Revs. Wilfred T. Smith; Robert J. Lamby; Deacons Raymond C. Beebe; James T. Martin; Joseph R. Kovitch.
Res., 8560 Mentor Ave., 44060-5853. Tel: 440-255-3404; 3405; 942-1774 (Cleveland); Fax: 440-974-8107.
School—8540 Mentor Ave., 44060. Tel: 440-255-9781; Fax: 440-974-8107. Mrs. Judy A. Tucci, Prin.
Ursuline Nuns of Cleveland 1; Lay Teachers 23; Students 518.
Catechesis/Religious Programs—Students 358.
Convent—Tel: 440-255-8550.

Middleburg Heights, Cuyahoga Co., St. Bartholomew (1956), Revs. John A. Leahy, Pastor Emeritus; Leonard M. Bacik; Thomas G. Elsasser.
Res., 14865 E. Bagley Rd., 44130-5502. Tel: 440-842-5400; 5401; Fax: 440-842-2691.
School—Academy of St. Bartholomew, 14875 E. Bagley Rd., 44130-5502. Tel: 440-845-6660; Fax: 440-845-6672. Mrs. Donna Hujarski, Prin.
Sisters 1; Lay Teachers 18; Students 495.
Catechesis/Religious Programs—Students 292.

Middlefield, Geauga Co., St. Lucy (1958), Rev. Harry S. Winca.
Mailing & Church Address: 16280 Kinsman Rd., 44062-9405. Tel: 440-632-5824; 548-8091.
Catechesis/Religious Programs—Students 113.

Newbury, Geauga Co., St. Helen (1949), Rev. James G. McPhillips; Deacon Willard Payne; Mary Weber, Pastoral Assoc. In res., Rev. William J. Johnson.
Res., 12060 Kinsman Rd., 44065. Tel: 440-564-5805; 338-3358 (Cleveland); Fax: 440-338-1734.
School—Tel: 440-564-7125. Sr. Christin Alfieri, S.N.D., Prin.
Sisters of Notre Dame 2; Lay Teachers 7; Students 215.
Catechesis/Religious Programs—Students 268.

Northfield, Summit Co., St. Barnabas (1956), Revs. Charles T. Diedrick; Robert A. Lorkowski; Daniel McBride; Marie Mikovsky, Pastoral Assoc.; Deacon Gerald Butler.
Res., 9451 Brandywine Rd., 44067. Tel: 330-467-7959; 467-7941; 467-6424; Fax: 330-467-6424.
School—9200 Olde Eight Rd., 44067. Tel: 330-467-7921; Fax: 330-468-1926. Miss Beverly Tabacco, Prin.
Lay Teachers 30; Students 723.
Catechesis/Religious Programs—Students 634.

North Olmsted, Cuyahoga Co., St. Brendan (1964), Revs. Cornelius J. Murray; Stephen M. Spisak. Pastoral Assocs.: Sr. Mary Ann Phillip, O.P.; Deborah Patton.
Church & Mailing Address: 4242 Brendan Ln., 44070.
Res., 3920 Brendan Ln., No. 615H, 44070-2999. Tel: 440-777-7222; 7223; Fax: 440-779-7997.
School—Tel: 440-777-8433. Mary Mackin, Prin.
Lay Teachers 16; Students 319.
Catechesis/Religious Programs—Students 315.

St. Clarence (1978), Revs. Thomas A. Flynn; Allan R. Laubenthal; Sr. Sonna M. Bradesca, O.S.U., D.Min., Pastoral Assoc.; Deacons Wayne A. Bosau; Homer L. Sherman.
Res., 30106 Lorain Rd., 44070-3986. Tel: 440-734-2414; Fax: 440-734-4255.
Catechesis/Religious Programs—Students 619.
Convent—30072 Lorain Rd., 44070. Tel: 440-777-5258.

St. Richard (1950), Revs. Charles J. Stollenwerk; George A. Vrabel; Deacon John Zdolshek; Sr. M. Jerome Fitzgerald, S.I.W., Pastoral Assoc.; Mrs. Janet O'Donnell. In res., Rev. Elmer E. Marquard.
Res., 26855 Lorain Rd., 44070-3260. Tel: 440-777-5050; 5051; 5052; Fax: 440-777-3577.
School—Tel: 440-777-2922; Fax: 440-777-7374. Mr. Michael Cappabianca, Prin.
Sisters 3; Lay Teachers 22; Students 567.
Catechesis/Religious Programs—Students 204.
Convent—5053 Whitethorn Ave., 44070. Tel: 216-777-2168.

North Ridgeville, Lorain Co., St. Julie Billiart (1978), Rev. Richard A. Gonser; Sr. Nancy North, S.N.D., Pastoral Assoc.; Deacon John M. Rivera.
Res., 5545 Opal Dr., 44039-2025. Tel: 440-327-1978; 1979; Fax: 440-327-1994. [JC]
Church—5500 Lear Nagle Rd., 44039.
Catechesis/Religious Programs—Students 189.

St. Peter (1875), Revs. Thomas J. Hyland; Thomas J. Pajk.
Res., 35777 Center Ridge Rd., 44039-3097. Tel: 440-327-2201; 327-2204; Fax: 440-327-2204. [CEM]
School—35749 Center Ridge Rd., 44039. Tel: 440-327-3212; Fax: 440-327-6843. Sr. Mary Patricia Vovk, S.N.D., Prin.
Sisters of Notre Dame 2; Lay Teachers 17; Students 417.
Catechesis/Religious Programs—Students 393.
Convent—7209 Wil-Lou Ln., Tel: 440-327-8713.

North Royalton, Cuyahoga Co., St. Albert the Great (1959), Revs. John L. Viall; Jeffrey M. Weaver; Charles F. Strebler. In res., Rev. Albert J. Tesek.
Res., 6667 Wallings Rd., 44133-3067. Tel: 440-237-6760; 6761; Fax: 440-237-5945.
School—Tel: 440-237-1032; Fax: 440-237-3308. Mr. Thomas Brownfield, Prin.
Lay Teachers 31; Students 792.
Catechesis/Religious Programs—Students 1,031.

Norton, Summit Co., St. Andrew the Apostle (1951), Revs. James G. Maloney; John A. Wittreich, Pastor Emeritus.
Res., 4022 Johnson Rd., 44203-5998. Tel: 330-825-2617; Fax: 330-825-5309.
Church—Johnson & Hametown Rd., 44203.
Catechesis/Religious Programs—Tel: 330-825-8264.
Students 158.

Oberlin, Lorain Co., Sacred Heart (1880), Revs. William B. Padavick; Robert A. Bonnell, Pastor Emeritus.
Res., 410 W. Lorain St., 44074-1002. Tel: 440-774-6791; 774-1337; Fax: 440-775-1306.
Catechesis/Religious Programs—Students 113.

Olmsted Falls, Cuyahoga Co., St. Mary of the Falls (1854), Revs. Robert J. Cole; Daniel R. Fickes; Deacons Richard Mueller; Thomas Daw.
Res., 25615 Bagley Rd., 44138-1915. Tel: 440-235-2222; 2223; Fax: 440-235-2937. [CEM]
School—8262 Columbia Rd., 44138-2242. Tel: 440-235-4580; Fax: 440-235-6833. Mrs. Priscilla Shields, Prin.
Lay Teachers 11; Students 252.
Catechesis/Religious Programs—Tel: 216-235-2808.
Students 650.

Orange Village, Cuyahoga Co., St. Margaret of Hungary (1921) (Hungarian), Rev. Ladislaus Rosko.
Res., 4680 Lander Rd., 44022-1704. Tel: 440-248-2618; 248-8148; Fax: 440-248-8706.
Catechesis/Religious Programs—Students 12.

Orrville, Wayne Co., St. Agnes (1879), Rev. Paul J. Wysocki.
Res., 541 Spring St., 44667-2414. Tel: 330-682-3606; 682-2611.
Church—E. Oak St. & Lake St., 44667.
Catechesis/Religious Programs—Students 264.

Painesville, Lake Co., St. Mary (1848), Revs. R. Stephen Vellenga; Patrick Henry; Robert G. Hanzo, Pastor Emeritus; John T. Ostrowski; Deacon Paul Hlabse.
Res., 242 N. State St., 44077-4095. Tel: 440-354-4381; 4382; 358-9741; Fax: 440-354-9174. [CEM]
School—268 N. State St., 44077. Tel: 440-352-9414; Fax: 440-352-8712. Kathleen H. Cherney, Prin.
Vincentian Sisters of Charity 2; Lay Teachers 16; Students 289.
Catechesis/Religious Programs—Students 247.
Convent—339 Erie St., 44077-4095. Tel: 440-354-3762.

Parkman, Geauga Co., St. Edward (1928), Rev. Harry S. Winca.
Res., P.O. Box 709, 44080-0709. Tel: 440-548-8091; 548-3812.
Church—16150 Center St., 44080.
Catechesis/Religious Programs—Students 83.

Parma, Cuyahoga Co.,

1—St. Anthony of Padua, (1959), Revs. Dale W. Staysniak; Don Rooney; Deacon Robert J. Jasany. Pastoral Assocs.: Sr. Karen Kellereski, C.S.F.N.; Sr. Roberta Goebel, O.S.U.
Res., 6750 State Rd., 44134-4518. Tel: 440-842-2666; 2667; 2668; Fax: 440-845-9549.
School—6800 State Rd., 44134. Tel: 440-845-3444; Fax: 440-884-4548. Mr. Frank M. Kuhar, Prin.
Lay Teachers 19; Students 502.
Catechesis/Religious Programs—Students 347.
Convent—6834 State Rd., 44134. Tel: 440-842-2211.

2—St. Bridget, (1956), Revs. Lawrence J. Bayer; Jerome A. Lukachinsky. In res., Rev. William R. Krizner.
Res., 5620 Hauserman Rd., 44130-1698. Tel: 440-886-4434; 4435; Fax: 440-886-4431.
School—Tel: 440-886-1468; Fax: 440-886-5121. Sr. Alice Rooney, C.S.J., Prin.
Sisters of St. Joseph 2; Lay Teachers 11; Students 315.
Catechesis/Religious Programs—Students 130.
Convent—Tel: 440-886-2555.

3—St. Charles Borromeo, (1923), Revs. John T. Carlin; Dwayne Bednar; Richard A. Evans, M.Div.; Stephen P. Moran; Sr. Denise Marie Vlna, O.S.U., Pastoral Assoc.; Deacon John A. Talerico. In res., Rev. James A. Conry.
Res., 5891 Ridge Rd., 44129-3642. Tel: 440-884-3030; 3031; 884-3232; Fax: 440-884-5326.
School—7107 Wilber Ave., 44129. Tel: 440-886-5546; Fax: 440-886-1163. Mr. James E. Flynn, Prin.
Ursuline Nuns of Cleveland 2; Lay Teachers 32; Students 787.
Catechesis/Religious Programs—Students 474.
Convent—6818 Charles Ave., 44129. Tel: 440-886-0390.

4—St. Columbkille, (1956), Revs. Neil D. O'Connor; Stephen F. Radecky, Pastor Emeritus; Eric S. Orzech; James R. Stenger; Michael J. Lanning; Deacon Edward A. Telepak.
Res., 6740 Broadview Rd., 44134. Tel: 216-524-1987; 1988; 524-1516; Fax: 216-524-9146.
School—Tel: 216-524-4816; Fax: 216-524-4153. Miss Rita Klement, Prin.
Lay Teachers 22; Students 580.
Catechesis/Religious Programs—Students 357.
Convent—.

5—St. Francis de Sales, (1931), Revs. Donald J. Balogh, Pastor Emeritus; Robert L. Hoban; Douglas T Makowski; Deacon Robert J. Piskach.
Res., 3434 George Ave., 44134-2904. Tel: 440-884-2319; 2320; 2321; Fax: 440-884-1661.
Church—State & Snow Rd., 44134.
School—3421 Snow Rd., 44134-2596. Tel: 440-884-2340; Fax: 440-884-8211. Anne Sweeney, Prin.
Ursuline Nuns of Cleveland 1; Lay Teachers 18; Students 354.
Catechesis/Religious Programs—Students 278.
Convent—3425 Snow Rd., 44134. Tel: 440-884-7242.

6—Holy Family, (1872), Revs. James P. Costello; Edward Holland; James McManamon, O.F.M.; Edwin M. Leonard; Kenneth F Wallace; Kenneth F. Wallace; Sr. Mary Petronella, V.S.C., Pastoral

Assoc.; Deacons Russell J. Glorioso; Joseph P. Litke.
Res., 7367 York Rd., 44130-5162. Tel: 440-842-5533; Fax: 440-842-3090. [CEM]
School—Tel: 440-842-7785; Fax: 440-842-3634. Kathleen Hrutkay, Prin.
Lay Teachers 33; Students 656.
Catechesis/Religious Programs—Students 297.
Convent—.

7—St. Matthias, (1980), Rev. Raymond A. Sutter.
Res., 1200 W. Sprague Rd., 44134-6801. Tel: 440-888-8220; 8221; Fax: 440-888-8146.
Catechesis/Religious Programs—Students 304.

Parma Heights, Cuyahoga Co., St. John Bosco (1963), Revs. David D. Liberatore; Edward M. Tulley, Pastor Emeritus; John A. Ocilka; Deacon Roger Polefko.
Res., 6480 Pearl Rd., 44130. Tel: 440-886-3500; 3501; 3502; Fax: 440-886-0966.
School—6460 Pearl Rd., 44130. Tel: 440-886-0061; Fax: 440-884-4115. Mrs. Martha K. Jacobs, Prin.
Lay Teachers 22; Students 485.
Catechesis/Religious Programs—Students 292.
Convent—12213 Denver Dr., Parma, 44130. Tel: 216-267-0133.

Peninsula, Summit Co., Mother of Sorrows (1882), Revs. John D. Terzano; Robert W. Donohoe, Pastor Emeritus.
Res., 6034 S. Locust St., 44264-9726. Tel: 330-657-2631; 657-2075; 467-5549 (Cleveland Line); Fax: 330-657-2631.
Catechesis/Religious Programs—Students 101.

Perry, Lake Co., St. Cyprian (1968), Revs. James J. Patton; Anthony F. Alexander, Pastor Emeritus; Deacons Andrew Novak; Paul Hlabse; James F. Daley, Jr.
Res., 4223 Middle Ridge Rd., 44081-9794. Tel: 440-259-2344; Fax: 440-259-2255.
Catechesis/Religious Programs—Students 383.

Richfield, Summit Co., St. Victor (1964), Revs. Raymond Bartnikowski, Pastor Emeritus; Arthur A. Bacher.
Church & Res.: 3435 Everett Rd., 44286-0461. Tel: 330-659-6591; 659-6321; 659-3398; Fax: 330-659-3618.
Catechesis/Religious Programs—Students 219.

Rittman, Wayne Co., St. Anne (1855), Revs. Phillip P. Pritt; Frank J. Kuta, Pastor Emeritus.
Res., 139 S. First St., 44270-1492. Tel: 330-927-2941; Fax: 330-927-3002. [CEM]
Church—E. Ohio & S. First St., 44270.
Catechesis/Religious Programs—Students 37.

Rocky River, Cuyahoga Co., St. Christopher (1922), Revs. John C. Chlebo; Edward F. Prendergast, Pastor Emeritus; Daniel F. Schlegel; Ms. Gayle Cilimburg, Pastoral Assoc. In res., Rev. Msgr. James P. McIntyre.
Res., 20141 Detroit Rd., 44116-2420. Tel: 440-331-4255; 4256; Fax: 440-331-3885.
School—1610 Lakeview Ave., 44116-2409. Tel: 440-331-3075; Fax: 440-331-0674. Sr. Patricia Twohig, C.S.J., Prin.
Sisters of Humility of Mary 3; Lay Teachers 23; Students 504.
Catechesis/Religious Programs—Tel: 440-331-6226.
Students 491.

Seville-Creston, Medina-Wooster Counties, Jesus Emmanuel (1976). Attended by Our Lady Help of Christians, Litchfield.

Shaker Heights, Cuyahoga Co., St. Dominic (1945), Revs. Martin J. Amos; Joseph Cappalletti; Sr. Mary Ann Mehling, I.H.M., Pastoral Assoc.
Res., 3450 Norwood Rd., 44122-4967. Tel: 216-991-1444; 991-1445; Fax: 216-491-0190.
Church—19000 Van Aken Blvd., 44122.
School—3455 Norwood Rd., 44122-4901. Tel: 216-561-4400; Fax: 216-561-1573. Joan Agresta, Prin.
Sisters of the Precious Blood 1; Lay Teachers 11; Students 253.
Catechesis/Religious Programs—Students 307.

Sheffield, Lorain Co., St. Teresa of Avila (1845), Revs. Edward J. Luca; Raymond J. Grismer, Pastor Emeritus; Sr. Mary Floranne, S.N.D., Pastoral Assoc.
Church—1878 Abbe Rd., 44054-2322. Tel: 440-934-4227; Fax: 440-934-4500. [CEM]
Catechesis/Religious Programs—Students 18.

Sheffield Lake, Lorain Co., St. Thomas the Apostle (1962), Rev. Stephen L. Shields.
Res., 521 Harris Rd., 44054-1409. Tel: 440-949-7744; Fax: 440-949-8611.
School—719 Harris Rd., 44054. Tel: 440-949-6275; Fax: 440-949-5183. Sr. Helene F. Minut, S.N.D., Prin.
Sisters of Notre Dame; Sisters 1; Lay Teachers 9; Students 175.
Catechesis/Religious Programs—Students 189.
Convent—37954 French Creek Rd., 44054. Tel: 440-934-6964.

Solon, Cuyahoga Co., St. Rita (1929), Revs. Robert M. Wendelken; Robert J. Jasany; Mark R. Riley; Deacons William Donlin; Gerard Ziemkiewicz; Robert Anderson; Mr. Albert E. Leko, Pastoral Assoc.
Res., 32820 Baldwin Rd., 44139-4098. Tel: 440-248-1350; Fax: 440-248-2094.
School—33200 Baldwin Rd., 44139. Fax: 440-248-9442. Ms. Beverly Moore, Prin.
Lay Teachers 25; Students 504.
Catechesis/Religious Programs—Students 798.

Resurrection of Our Lord (1971), Revs. J. Mark Hobson, Coord., Pastoral Team; Louis J. Trivison, Pastor Emeritus. Pastoral Team: Sr. Mary Jeanette Brown, S.N.D.; Ms. Elisabeth Frey.
Res. & Church: 32001 Cannon Rd., 44139-1699. Tel: 440-248-0980; 0981; Fax: 440-248-0992.
Catechesis/Religious Programs—Students 392.
Convent—5710 Janet Blvd., 44139. Tel: 216-248-4364.

South Amherst, Lorain Co., Nativity of Blessed Virgin Mary (1933), Revs. Edward J. Kordas; Wallace F. Roth, Pastor Emeritus.
Res., 333 S. Lake St., 44001-2013. Tel: 440-986-7011; Fax: 440-986-7012.
Catechesis/Religious Programs—Students 128.

South Euclid, Cuyahoga Co., St. Gregory the Great (1922), Rev. Msgr. William N. Novicky; Revs. Francis G. Van Bergen; John G. Crawford; Deacon John P. Sferry. Pastoral Assocs.: Sr. Monica Schmitt, S.N.D.; Sr. Mary Callista Antolik, S.N.D.; Sr. Lucille Myers, S.I.W.
Res., 1545 S. Green Rd., 44121-4085. Tel: 216-382-7601; 7602; 7603; Fax: 216-382-4992.
School—4478 Rushton Rd., 44121-4084. Tel: 216-381-0363; Fax: 216-382-7561. Miss Lucy Iemmolo, Prin.
Sisters of Notre Dame 1; Lay Teachers 38; Students 817.
Catechesis/Religious Programs—Students 265.

St. Margaret Mary (1948), Revs. Richard E. Hudak; Thomas J. Lusoski, Pastor Emeritus; Loius A. Pizmoht. In res., Rev. Anselm Nzekwe.
Res., 4217 Bluestone Rd., 44121-3427. Tel: 216-382-4114; 4115.
School—4205 Bluestone Rd., 44121. Tel: 216-382-4272; Fax: 216-382-4559. Sr. Mary Ann Murphy, O.S.U., Prin.
Sisters of Notre Dame 2; Lay Teachers 8; Students 185.
Catechesis/Religious Programs—Students 106.
Convent—4215 Bluestone Rd., 44121. Tel: 216-381-8787.

Spencer, Medina Co., Jesus Our Savior (1976). Attended by Our Lady Help of Christians, Litchfield.

Stow, Summit Co., Holy Family (1946), Revs. Joseph J. Lieberth; Neil A. Crosby; Deacon Philip P. Kamlowsky; Joan Skalak, Pastoral Assoc.
Res., 3450 Sycamore Dr., 44224-3999. Tel: 330-688-6411; 6412; 6413; Fax: 330-689-0186.
Church—3179 Kent Rd., 44224.
School—3163 Kent Rd., 44224. Tel: 330-688-3816; Fax: 330-688-3474. Miss Susan Jelenic, Prin.
Lay Teachers 33; Students 737.
Catechesis/Religious Programs—Students 562.

Strongsville, Cuyahoga Co., St. John Neumann (1977), Revs. Robert J. Kraig; Steven H. Breck; Edward N. Schwet; Steven H. Breck; Deacon Thomas Grasson. Pastoral Assocs.: Sr. Mary Popoczy S.N.D.; Sr. Patricia Sylvester, S.N.D.
Res., 16271 Pearl Rd., 44136-6095. Tel: 440-238-1770; 1771; Fax: 440-238-2030.
School—SS. Joseph & John Interparochial. See St. Joseph, Strongsville. Tel: 440-238-4877; Fax: 440-238-8745.
Catechesis/Religious Programs—Students 1,386.

St. Joseph (1946), Revs. Robert J. Sanson; John P. Miceli; Deacons Pete Moore; Howard J. Masony; Sr. Betty Gulick, S.S.J.-T.O.S.F., Pastoral Assoc.
Res., 12700 Pearl Rd., 44136-3484. Tel: 440-238-5555; 5556; 238-1038; Fax: 440-238-1059.
School—SS. Joseph and John Interparochial, 12580 Pearl Rd., 44136-3422. Tel: 440-238-4877; Fax: 440-238-8745. Mrs. Darlene Thomas, Prin.
Sisters of St. Joseph 1; Lay Teachers 31; Students 791.
Catechesis/Religious Programs—Tel: 216-238-5231.
Students 741.
Convent—12600 Pearl Rd., 44136. Tel: 440-238-6352.

Tallmadge, Summit Co., Our Lady of Victory (1944), Rev. John R. Hengle; Diane Hardick, Pastoral Assoc.
Mailing Address: Administration Center, 73 North Ave., 44278-1996. Tel: 330-633-3637; 633-3672; Fax: 330-633-6978.
Church—105 North Ave., 44278.
Rectory: 55 North Ave., 44278.
Catechesis/Religious Programs—Students 513.

Thompson, Geauga Co., St. Patrick (1854), Rev. Paul F. Smith.
Res., 16550 Rock Creek Rd., Rte. 166, 44086-8753. Tel: 440-298-1327; Fax: 440-298-1846. [CEM]
Catechesis/Religious Programs—Students 114.

Twinsburg, Summit Co., SS. Cosmas and Damian (1963), Rev. Robert E. Friedel; Deacon Vincent L. Belsito.
Res., 10419 Ravenna Rd., 44087-1726. Tel: 330-425-8141; 8142; Fax: 330-963-6597.
Church—10439 Ravenna Rd., 44087-1726. Tel: 216-425-8141.
School—10429 Ravenna Rd., 44087. Tel: 330-425-4279; Fax: 330-405-2947. Mrs. Patricia Zaranec, Prin.
Lay Teachers 9; Students 130.
Catechesis/Religious Programs—Students 516.

University Heights, Cuyahoga Co., Gesu (1926), Revs. James E. Von Tobel, S.J.; Edward M. Nemeth, S.J.; Lorn Snow, S.J.; Deacon James K. O'Donnell.
Res., 2470 Miramar Blvd., 44118-3896. Tel: 216-932-0616; 0618; 0618; Fax: 216-932-0731.
Church—2490 Miramar Blvd., 44118.
School—2450 Miramar Blvd., 44118. Tel: 216-932-0620; Fax: 216-932-8326. Sr. Linda Martin, O.S.U., Prin.
Sisters of Notre Dame 2; Lay Teachers 36; Students 817.
Catechesis/Religious Programs—Students 288.
Convent—4070 Meadowbrook Blvd., 44118. Tel: 216-932-1660.

Valley City, Medina Co., St. Martin of Tours (1840), Rev. Thomas R. Dunphy.
Res., 1824 Station Rd., 44280-9522. Tel: 330-483-3808; Fax: 330-483-3848. [CEM]
Catechesis/Religious Programs—Tel: 330-483-5925.
Students 355.

Wadsworth, Medina Co., Sacred Heart of Jesus (1866), Revs. Joseph L. Labak; James A. Conry, Pastor Emeritus; Deacon Roger N. Klaas.
Res., 260 Broad St., 44281-2113. Tel: 330-336-3049; Fax: 330-336-0143. [JC]
School—110 Humbolt Ave., 44281. Tel: 330-334-6272; Fax: 330-334-3236. Michelle Noack, Prin.
Vincentian Sisters of Charity 1; Lay Teachers 18; Students 379.
Catechesis/Religious Programs—Students 465.
Convent—268 Broad St., 44281. Tel: 330-336-0143.

Warrensville Heights, Cuyahoga Co., St. Jude (1945), Revs. Thomas Carolan, O.F.M.; Melchior Toczex, O.F.M.; Susan Horvath, Pastoral Assoc. In res., Rev. Emmanuel Beunen, O.F.M.; Bro. Joseph DiSanto, O.F.M.
Res., 4761 Richmond Rd., 44128-5986. Tel: 216-292-6600; 6601; 6602; Fax: 216-292-0454.
Catechesis/Religious Programs—Students 38.

Wellington, Lorain Co., St. Patrick (1851), Rev. James J. Reymann.
Res., 512 N. Main St., 44090-1198. Tel: 440-647-4375; Fax: 440-647-4675.
Catechesis/Religious Programs—Students 293.

Westlake, Cuyahoga, Co., St. Bernadette (1950), Revs. James F. Kramer; John W. Krasen; James T. Klein; Deacon Stanley J. Fulton. Pastoral Assocs.: Sr. Theresa Sullivan, C.S.J.; Mrs. Catherine Vaughan; Mrs. Diane Portorreal; Mrs. Marianne Betters; Mrs. Judy Head; Mrs. Christine Krysiak.
Res., 2256 Clague Rd., 44145-4328. Tel: 440-734-1300; 1301; 1302; 734-3220; Fax: 440-734-1584.
School—2300 Clague Rd., 44145. Tel: 440-734-7717; Fax: 440-734-9198. Mrs. Denise King, Prin.
Religious 1; Lay Teachers 19; Students 534.
Catechesis/Religious Programs—Students 485.

St. Ladislas (1973), Revs. Donald E. Snyder; Thomas F. Cullen, Pastor Emeritus. Pastoral Assocs.: Sr. Mary Joan Grisez, O.S.U.; Deacons David L. Kinzel; William Gorman; Robert C. Hertl; Coletta Fratus. In res., Most Rev. A. James Quinn.
Res. & Church Address: 2345 Bassett Rd., 44145-2999. Tel: 216-835-2300; Fax: 216-835-5895.
Catechesis/Religious Programs—Students 399.

West Salem, Wayne Co., St. Stephen (1952), Rev. Carl A. Uhler.
Res., 44 Britton St., 44287-9318. Tel: 419-853-4946; Fax: 419-853-7037.
Catechesis/Religious Programs—Students 122.

Wickliffe, Lake Co., Our Lady of Mount Carmel (1921), Revs. David L. McCafferty; Thomas E. Stock; Nnamdi Nwankwo; Sr. Rosemary Diba, V.S.C., Pastoral Assoc.; Deacon John W. Strmac. In res., Rev. John M. Richards.
Res., 1730 Mount Carmel Dr., 44092-1896. Tel: 440-585-0700; Fax: 440-585-0870.
Church—29850 Euclid Ave., 44092.
School—29840 Euclid Ave., 44092. Tel: 440-585-0800; Fax: 440-585-9391. Susan Pohly, Prin.
Lay Teachers 21; Students 407.

Catechesis/Religious Programs—Students 172.

Willoughby, Lake Co., Immaculate Conception (1866), Revs. Francis D. Curran; Eric B. Leissa; Deacon Edward J. Feldkamp.
Res., 37935 Wright St., 44094-5899. Tel: 440-942-4500; Fax: 440-942-1540.
School—37940 Euclid Ave., 44094. Tel: 440-942-2121; Fax: 440-942-6766. Mrs. Rosalie A. Lewis, Prin.
Ursuline Nuns of Cleveland 1; Lay Teachers 21; Students 418.
Catechesis/Religious Programs—Students 279.

Willoughby Hills, Lake Co., St. Noel (1980), Rev. George Smiga. Pastoral Assocs.: Alice M. Hinkel; Anthony Camino.
Res., 35200 Chardon Rd., 44094-9193. Tel: 440-946-0887; Fax: 440-946-4331.
Catechesis/Religious Programs—Mrs. Marianne Slattery, D.R.E.
Students 379.

Willowick, Lake Co., St. Mary Magdalene (1949), Pastoral Team: Revs. John P. Singler, Coord. Pastoral Team; Ronald Wearsch; Theodore Lucas; Sr. Joan Franklin, O.P.; Sr. Mercia Madigan, O.S.U.; Deacon Carl Toomey.
Res., 460 East 321 St., 44095-3663. Tel: 440-943-2133; Fax: 440-943-3780.
Church—32114 Vine St., 44095.
School—Tel: 440-944-7222; Fax: 440-944-8416. Ms. Judy Nakasian, Prin.
Lay Teachers 16; Students 306.
Catechesis/Religious Programs—Tel: 216-944-2523.
Students 528.
Convent—32010 Vine St., 44095. Tel: 440-944-1134.

Wooster, Wayne Co., St. Mary of the Immaculate Conception (1846), Rev. John J. Mueller; Deacon Bernard E. Hosfeld. Pastoral Assocs.: Mrs. Jacquelynn Lee.
Res., 527 Beall Ave., P.O. Box 109, 44691-0109. Tel: 330-264-8824; 264-8822; Fax: 330-262-4633. [CEM]
Church—527 Beall Ave., 44691.
School—535 E. Bowman St., P.O. Box 109, 44691. Tel: 330-262-8671; Fax: 330-262-0990. Cathleen Mark, Prin.
Lay Teachers 15; Students 212.
Catechesis/Religious Programs—Students 165.
Convent—.

Cleveland Diocesan Mission

El Salvador, C.A. *Casa Parroquial San Pedro Teotepeque*. La Libertad dept La Libertad El Salvador, Central America. Rev. John D. King.
The Catholic Center. Rev. Denis L. St. Marie, Dir. Society for the Propagation of the Faith.
Parroquial de Nuestra Senora de Guadalupe. Chirilagua Depto San Miguel, El Salvador. Revs. Joseph H. Callahan; Richard C. Antall; Sr. Lisa Marie Belz, O.S.U.; Sr. Mary Lou Tadsen, O.S.U.
Parroquial Inmaculada Concepcion. Puerto de La Libertad, El Salvador. Revs. Robert J. Reidy; William A. Thaden.

Chaplains of Public Institutions

Cleveland. *Airport, Cleveland Hopkins International*. Rev. Msgr. Casimir S. Ciolek, A.C.S.W. Tel: 216-781-9095.
Cleveland Clinic Foundation. Revs. Vincent Moraghan Tel: 216-881-7089; Joseph P. Owens, S.J. Tel: 216-397-4689.
Cleveland House of Correction. Rev. Emmanuel Beunen, O.F.M. Tel: 216-292-6602.
Cleveland Psychiatric. (CPI). Rev. Thomas Gallagher Tel: 216-791-3800.
Cuyahoga County Detention Home. Rev. James P. O'Donnell Tel: 216-566-9953.
Cuyahoga County Jail. Deacon Thomas J. Senn Tel: 440-962-3858.
Cuyahoga Hills Boys School. Pastoral Care Services, Tel: 216-696-6525, Ext. 2380.
Deaconess Hospital. Rev. Raymond Schultheis, C.PP.S. Tel: 216-749-2323.
Euclid General Hospital Tel: 216-481-8200. Rev. Joseph A. Goebel Tel: 216-486-0850.
Fairview General Hospital. Attended from Our Lady of Angels.
Grace Hospital. Attended from St. Augustine. Tel: 216-781-5530.
Health Hill Hospital for Children. Attended from St. Andrew Abbey. Tel: 216-721-5300.
Hillcrest Hospital. Attended from St. Francis of Assisi. Tel: 216-461-0066.
Huron Road Hospital. Attended from St. Philomena. Tel: 216-541-3540.
Kaiser Foundation Hospital. Attended from St. Bridget. Snow Rd., 44129. Tel: 216-886-4434.
Lakewood Hospital Tel: 216-226-5116. Rev. Thomas P. Kowatch.
Lutheran Medical Center. Rev. Michael Donovon, O. de M., Tel: 216-651-5043.
Metro Health Medical Center & Rehabilitation Center. (Hospital). Rev. Arthur Snedeker, Chap., Tel: 216-781-8277.
Metzenbaum Children's Center. Attended from St. Augustine. Tel: 216-781-5330.
Northeast Pre Release Center. Rev. James O'Donnell Tel: 216-566-9953.
Parma Community Hospital. Rev. James R. Semonin Tel: 216-843-8781.
Rainbow Hospital. (See University Hospitals).
Richmond Heights Hospital. Attended from St. Felicitas. Tel: 216-289-0770.
St. Michael Hospital Tel: 216-429-8000. Rev. John Tezie.
South Pointe Hospital. Rev. Stephen J. Walick Tel: 216-475-1766.
SouthWest General Hospital. Rev. Dismas Boeff Tel: 216-433-0696.
University Hospitals. Rev. William Severt Tel: 216-941-6808.
University Hospitals Bedford Medical Center. Rev. Stephen J. Walick Tel: 215-475-1766.
Veterans Administration Hospitals, Brecksville V.A 1000 Brecksville Rd., 44141. Tel: 216-526-3030. Rev. John E. Bolan, C.PP.S., Chap., Cleveland V.A., 10701 East Blvd., 44106. Tel: 216-791-3800, Ext. 305.

Akron. *Akron City Hospital*. Rev. James J. Berardi Tel: 330-535-4141.
Akron General Hospital. Rev. Robert E. Clancy Tel: 330-434-4348.
Edwin C. Shaw Hospital. Attended from Nativity of the Lord Jesus. Tel: 440-669-5086.
Summit County Jail Tel: 330-724-8043. Deacon Daniel Matusicky.

Amherst. *Amherst Hospital*. Attended from St. Joseph. Tel: 440-988-2848.

Apple Creek. *Apple Creek State Institute*. Apostolate for Persons with Developmental Disabilities. Tel: 216-696-6525, Ext. 2700.

Ashland. *Ashland County Jail*. Attended from St. Edward. Tel: 419-289-7224.
Samaritan Hospital. Attended from St. Edward. Tel: 419-289-0491.

Avon. *Our Lady of the Wayside* Tel: 216-651-0550. Rev. Robert T. Begin.

Barberton. *Barberton Citizens Hospitals*. Attended from St. Augustine. Tel: 330-745-0011.

Chagrin Falls. *Windsor Hospital*. Attended from St. Joan of Arc. Tel: 440-247-7183.

Chardon. *Geauga Community Hospital*. Attended from St. Helen, Newbury. Tel: 440-564-5805; 338-3358 (Cleveland).
Geauga County Jail Tel: 440-834-8055. Deacon Frederick Giel.

Cuyahoga Falls. *Fallsview Mental Health Center*. Attended from St. Eugene. Tel: 330-923-5244.
General Hospital. Attended from St. Joseph. Tel: 330-928-2173.

Elyria. *Elyria Memorial Hospital*. Sacred Heart, Elyria. Tel: 440-323-3221. Sr. Joan Tomchey, O.S.U., Chap., Pastoral Care, Tel: 216-933-5769.

Grafton. *Grafton Correctional Institution*. Rev. Charles J. Ryba Tel: 440-236-5095; Deacons Jose DeGracia Tel: 440-244-1725; John Rivera Tel: 440-327-4426.

Hudson. *Youth Development Center*. Attended from St. Andrew Abbey. Tel: 216-721-5300.

Lodi. *Lodi Hospital*. Attended from Our Lady Help of Christians. Tel: 216-722-1180; 273-1500 (Cleveland).

Lorain. *Lorain Correctional Institution* Tel: 440-236-5095. Rev. Charles J. Ryba.

Loudonville. *Kettering Hospital*. Attended from St. Peter. Tel: 419-994-4396.

Medina. *Medina Community Hospital*. Attended from St. Francis Xavier. Tel: 330-725-4968.
Medina County Jail Tel: 330-725-4968. Deacon Daniel Norris.

Northfield. *Western Reserve Psychiatric Habilitation Center* 44067. Tel: 216-467-7131. Rev. Adelbert J. Gassert.

Oberlin. *Allen Memorial Hospital*. Attended from Sacred Heart. Tel: 330-774-6791.

Orrville. *Dunlap Memorial Hospital*. Attended from St. Agnes. Tel: 330-682-3606.

Painesville. *Lake County Jail* Tel: 440-953-3867. Deacon Norman Davis.
Lake County Memorial Hospital-East Tel: 330-585-0700. Rev. John M. Richards.

Smithville. *Boys Village of Ohio*. Attended from St. Mary, Wooster. Tel: 330-264-8824.

Wadsworth. *Wadsworth Health Care Center*. Attended from Sacred Heart of Jesus. Tel: 330-336-3049.
Wadsworth-Rittman Hospital. Attended from Sacred Heart of Jesus. Tel: 330-336-3049.

Willoughby. *Lake County Memorial Hospital-West*. Rev. John M. Richards Tel: 440-585-0700.

Wooster. *Wayne County Jail*. Attended from St. Mary of the Immaculate Conception. Tel: 330-264-8824.
Wooster Community Hospital. Attended from St. Mary. Tel: 330-264-8824.

Released from Diocesan Assignment:
Reverend Monsignors—
Broglio, Timothy, Secretariat of State, Vatican City State, 00120
Reverend Fathers—
Berthiaume, Gary D.
Klamet, Francis X., 1050 Glenn Ave., Washington Courthouse, OH 43160-2603
Lang, Joseph J., Church of the Resurrection, 9504 100th Ave., Fort St. John, BC V1J 1X7 Canada
Lyons, John F., 3175 W. 165th St., Cleveland, OH 44115
Myers, Kenneth C., VIP SAL #1813, P.O. Box 025364, Miami, FL 33102-5364. Tel: 011-503-228-0979
Papes, Louis M., c/o Clergy Personnel, 1031 Superior Ave., Cleveland, OH 44114
Patrick, William J., St. Jude Hospital & Rehabilitation Center, 3733 N. Harbor #15, Fullerton, CA 92835
Valley, John, 37825 Lake Shore Blvd., Eastlake, OH 44095
Zingales, Jonathan A., St. Leo Abbey, P.O. Box 2364, St. Leo, FL 33574. Tel: 352-588-8626

Military Chaplains:
Reverend Fathers—
Buckon, Neal
Czech, Edward M.
McCausland, Joseph E.
Sheil, James

Absent on Leave:
Reverend Fathers—
Alberts, Keith
Ausperk, Michael
Baranek, Raymond
Brodnick, Joseph
Burg, Thomas R.
Burkley, John
Colletti, Peter
Dimengo, Michael
Enzman, David
Hamlin, Raymond
Lehane, Joseph
Lonteen, Daniel
Lowe, Russell
Rupp, Edward F.

Retired:
Reverend Monsignors—
Ciolek, Casimir S., A.C.S.W., 906 College Ave., Cleveland, OH 44113
Gasbarre, Francis E., Holy Trinity, c/o Ray Gasbarre, 924 Pittsburg Ave., Wooster, OH 44691
Goldikovskis, Alexander I., 1 Gateway Dr., Cleveland, OH 44119
Heruday, Joseph C., 6765 State Rd., Parma, OH 44134
McIntyre, James P., 20141 Detroit Rd., Rocky River, OH 44116
Spitzig, Joseph, 1264 Tupelo Ln., West Salem, OH 44287
Wolff, Robert C., 4516 Rex Lake Dr., Akron, OH 44319
Reverend Fathers—
Alexander, Anthony F., 344 Sanford St., Painesville, OH 44077
Anderson, John F., 12969 Chillicothe Rd., Chesterland, OH 44026
Bacher, Arthur, 5269 Mill Creek Blvd., Brunswick Hills, OH 44212
Balogh, Donald J., 785 W. Perimeter Rd., Frewsburg, NY 14738
Becherer, James R., 4963 E. Lake Rd., Sheffield Lake, OH 44054
Blinn, Mark R., Harbor Side Manor, 27601 Westchester Pkwy., Westlake, OH 44145
Bonnell, Robert A., 143 E. College St., Apt. 313, Oberlin, OH 44074
Boymer, Lloyd J., St. Basil the Great, 8700 Brecksville Rd., Brecksville, OH 44141
Brennan, Robert F., 1076 Sylvan Ave., Lakewood, OH 44107
Bruening, Allen
Camille, Edward J., St. Basil, 8700 Brecksville Rd., Brecksville, OH 44141
Cauley, Robert W., Eliza Jennings, 10603 Detroit Ave., Rm 1409, Lakewood, OH 44107
Cimperman, Victor J., 1240 E. 61st St., Cleveland, OH 44103
Clines, Paul J., St. Augustine Parish, 965 Norton Ave., Barberton, OH 44203
Conroy, James A., 5891 Ridge Rd., Parma, OH 44129
Conway, Neil, 4045 Wetmore Rd., Cuyahoga Falls, OH 44223

Cudnik, Chester C., 886 Eastlawn Dr., Highland Hts., OH 44143
Cullen, Thomas F., 2284 Winward Dr., Westlake, OH 44145
Dalton, John, Holy Name, 8328 Broadway, Cleveland, OH 44105
Demetzky, Alex D., 7611 Eve Ave., Cleveland, OH 44102
Donohue, Robert W., St. Augustine Manor, 7801 Detroit Rd., Cleveland, OH 44102
Egan, Arthur, 800 Brick Mill Run #519, Westlake, OH 44145
Englert, William J., 534 W. Bullard Ave., Fresno, CA 93704
Fridrich, Sylevester W., 4070 W. 212 St., Fairview Pk., OH 44126
Gaebelein, Claude J., 4291 Richmond Rd., Warrenville Heights, OH 44122
Gallagher, Thomas J., 1664 W. Market St., Akron, OH 44303
Gassert, Adelbert J., 5445 Smith Rd., Brook Park, OH 44142
Gerrity, John J., 4291 Richmond Rd., Warrensville Heights, OH 44122
Gibbons, William F., 6912 Chestnut Rd., Independence, OH 44131
Goebel, Joseph A., 1500 Lakeshore Blvd., Cleveland, OH 44110-1298
Gorski, John J., 2935 N. Bay Dr., Apt. H-14, Westlake, OH 44145
Grandillo, James J., 1007 Superior Ave., Cleveland, OH 44144
Grismer, Raymond J., Issenmann Place, 4185 Brookway Ln., Brooklyn, OH 44144
Hanzo, Robert G., 5406 Pebble Creek Ln., Painesville, OH 44077
Hayes, John, 4129 Superior Ave., Cleveland, OH 44103
Hritz, Paul J., 28700 Euclid Ave., Wickliffe, OH 44092
Jezeski, Henry, 7551 Pleasant Run Rd., Seven Hills, OH 44131-5906
Johnson, William J., 12060 Kinsman Rd., Newbury, OH 44065
Kilcoyne, John, Issenmann Place, 4185 Brookway Ln., Brooklyn, OH 44144
Kinkopf, John J., Divine Word, 8100 Eagle Rd., Kirtland, OH 44094
Kitt, William J., Castleblakeney, Ballinasloe, Co. Galway, Ireland
Kline, John J., 33803 Electric Blvd., #E-6, Avon Lake, OH 44012
Kline, Robert W., 28700 Euclid Ave., Wickliffe, OH 44092
Kreps, Anthony L., 7821 Lake Ave., Cleveland, OH 44102
Kuta, Frank J., 8795 N. Kane Rd., Warrensville, OH 44281
Laheta, Andrew P., 5232 Broadview Rd., Richfield, OH 44286
Leahy, John A., 1200 Lake Ave., Unit 213, Lakewood, OH 44107
Lusoski, Thomas J., 21108 Franklin Rd., Maple Hts., OH 44137
Lyons, William P., 2603 Benton St., Akron, OH 44312
Mackert, Albert J., 13719 Tartan Dr., Sun City West, AZ 85375
McDonough, John T., 1088 Ridge Rd., Hinckley, OH 44233
McMahon, John F., 4185 Brookway Ln., Brooklyn, OH 44144
McMahon, Joseph W., 8100 Eagle Rd., Kirtland, OH 44095
McShane, Patrick E., 180 Shawmut Ave, Apt. 707, Boston, MA 02118
Michalski, Thaddeus C., Issenmann Place, 4185 Brookway Ln., Brooklyn, OH 44144
Minnoggio, Ferrando, North American College, Vatican City State, 00120
Mulica, James
Muzic, Anthony J., 1160 Broadway Ave., Bedford, OH 44146
Myers, Albert J., 10515 E. River Rd., Rm. 109, Columbia Station, OH 44028
O'Dea, Vincent P., Issenmann Place, 4185 Brookway Ln., Brooklyn, OH 44144
Ondreyka, Richard J., P.O. Box 1132, Norton, OH 44203
Pahler, Robert E., 1905 Portage Tr., Cuyahoga Falls, OH 44223-1792
Paik, Francis M., 12340 Bass Lake Rd., #B27, Chardon, OH 44024
Peters, Herman B., Regina Healthcare, 5232 Broadview Ln., Richfield, OH 44286
Piskura, Joseph, 29050 Detroit Rd., Ste. 129, Westlake, OH 44145
Prendergast, Edward F., 29591 Detroit Rd., Ste. 1, Westlake, OH 44145
Radecky, Stephen F., 8392 Waters Rd., Macedonia, OH 44056
Rath, Thomas V., 200 St. Joseph Dr., Amherst, OH 44001
Rathfon, John R., 273 Robinhood Circle #102, Naples, FL 34104-9404
Rebol, Anthony, St. Basil the Great, 8700 Brecksville Rd., Brecksville, OH 44141-1999
Reichlin, Urban A., 76 Westshore Dr., Avon Lake, OH 44012
Roth, Wallace F., Issenmann Place, 4185 Brookway Lane, Brooklyn, OH 44144
Schenkelberg, Edwin J., 33050 Cedar Branch Cr., North Ridgeville, OH 44039
Sheehan, Thomas W., c/o Holy Family, 7367 York Rd., Parma, OH 44130-5196
Silva, David E., 2899 E. Ridgewood Dr., Seven Hills, OH 44131
Smith, James A., 12783 Cedar Rd., Cleveland Heights, OH 44106
Storey, John R., 5232 Broadview Rd., Richfield, OH 44286
Sullivan, Thomas F., 39 N. Portage Path, Akron, OH 44303
Tesek, Albert J., 6667 Wallings Rd., North Royalton, OH 44133-3099
Tezie, William F., 4242 Brendan Ln., North Olmsted, OH 44070
Tomc, Victor N., 20654 Centuryway Rd., Maple Heights, OH 44137
Tomicky, Ronald, 6164 Westminster Dr., Parma, OH 44129-4924
Trivison, Louis J., 283 Union St., Bedford, OH 44146
Tulley, Edward M., 6765 State Rd., Parma, OH 44134. Tel: 440-843-7800
Valentini, Francis M., 2749 Orchid Oaks Dr., #302-A, Sarasota, FL 34239
Wagner, Joseph F., St. Colette, 330 W. 130th St., Brunswick, OH 44212
Weber, Thomas H., 28700 Euclid Ave., Wickliffe, OH 44092
Wessel, John F., 2451 Crimson Dr., Westlake, OH 44145
Wittreich, John A., 3131 Smith Rd., Fairlawn, OH 44333
Woll, Peter J., St. Robert Parish, 23802 Lake Shore Blvd., Euclid, OH 44123
Yavorsky, James A., 5232 Broadview Rd., Richfield, OH 44286
Zepp, Anthony, 6705 Lansing Ave., Cleveland, OH 44105

Permanent Deacons:
Adair, Robin, St. Augustine, Barberton
Adkins, Ronald M., St. Gabriel, Concord Township
Agrippe, James L., St. Angela Merici, Fairview Park
Anderson, Robert C., St. Rita, Solon
Bacik, Dale A., St. Anselm, Chesterland
Badillo, Tomas, Sacred Heart Chapel, Lorain
Balassy, Geza J., Sacred Heart, Akron
Bals, Jerry J., Leave of Absence
Beebe, Raymond C., St. Mary, Mentor
Beercheck, Richard C., St. Patrick, (Rocky River), Cleveland
Belsito, Vincent L., Sts. Cosmas and Damian, Twinsburg
Belter, Clement J., St. Ambrose, Brunswick
Bender, John R., St. Martin of Tours, Maple Heights
Berigan, Patrick F., Our Lady of Good Counsel, Cleveland
Boehnlein, Lawrence A., St. Mary, Chardon, Diaconate Staff
Bosau, Wayne A., St. Clarence, North Olmsted
Bowers, Robert J., St. Paschal Baylon, Highland Heights
Broering, J. Harry, Jr., Washington, N. Carolina
Bubnick, Robert C., Sr., Apostolate for the Mentally Retarded, Assumption, Broadview Heights
Buda, John M., Our Lady Help of Christians, Litchfield
Burke, John Jr., St. Bede the Venerable, Mentor
Butkovic, Donald P., St. Adalbert, Berea
Butz, Richard C., St. Francis de Sales, Akron
Capek, Louis J., Rep. Diocesan Vocation Council, St. Joan of Arc, Chagrin Falls
Cermak, Lawrence, St. Therese, Garfield Heights
Colon, Victor R., Sagrada Familia, Cleveland
Corrigan, William H., St. Colman, Cleveland
Cowell, Bruce R., (Unassigned)
Croniger, James D., Holy Cross, Euclid
Daley, James F., St. Cyprian, Perry
Damukaitis, Joseph B., Leave of Absence
Daull, Raymond L., Christ the King, Cleveland
Davis, Norman H., St. Gabriel, Mentor
Davison, John H., Leave of Absence
Daw, Thomas B., St. Mary of the Falls, Olmsted Falls
DeGracia, Jose A., Sacred Heart Chapel, Lorain
DeHaas, Thomas B., Jr., St. Felicitas, Euclid
DeJohn, Ross C., Sr., St. Clare, Lyndhurst
Diaz, Juan A., Unassigned
Dietrich, Harold R.
Dillon, Edward R., Sacred Heart of Jesus, Elyria
Dirk, William E., Our Lady of Peace, Cleveland; Mount Sinai Hospital; St. Luke Hospital
Doerpers, Charles B., Holy Redeemer, Cleveland
Donlin, William A., St. Rita, Solon
Duffy, James J., (Retired)
Duhlop, Jeffrey F., St. Joan of Arc, Chagrin Falls
Dybo, Robert J., Nativity of the Blessed Virgin Mary, Lorain
Elwood, William T., St. Francis of Assisi, Gates Mills; Youth & Family Ministry, Eastern Region
Feldkamp, Edward J., Immaculate Conception, Willoughby
Figueroa, Miguel A., St. Michael, Cleveland
Flores, Jose A., Sacred Heart Chapel, Lorain
Friend, Shelby M., St. Henry, Cleveland
Fulton, Stanley J., St. Bernadette, Westlake
Giel, Frederick F., (On Duty Outside the Diocese)
Girard, Charles C., Tuscon, AZ
Glorioso, Russell J., Holy Family, Parma
Grasson, Thomas J., St. John Neumann, Strongsville
Hancock, Daniel J., Region VI Rep., St. Joseph, Amherst
Hill, Kenneth J., St. Vincent de Paul, Cleveland
Hinderscheid, Lee F., St. Hilary, Fairlawn
Hlabse, Paul J., St. Cyprian, Perry; St. Mary, Painesville
Hosfeld, Bernard E., St. Mary of the Immaculate Conception, Wooster
Humphrey, Frank A., III, St. Mary, Elyria
Humphrey, Patrick J., St. Jude, Elyria
Hupertz, Thomas G., Immaculate Conception, Madison
Jarosh, Rudolph, Jr., St. Thomas More, Brooklyn
Jasany, Robert J., St. Anthony of Padua, Parma
Johnson, Charles O., (Retired)
Johnson, Joseph W., Jacksonville, FL
Kamlowsky, Philip P., Holy Family, Stow
Kaniecki, James A., St. Edward, Ashland
Karecki, Edmund J., St. Augustine, Cleveland
Kinzel, David L., St. Ladislas, Westlake
Klaas, Roger N., Sacred Heart, Wadsworth
Knight, Kenneth, St. Bede the Venerable, Mentor
Koch, Alfred J., Holy Martyrs, Medina
Koch, John A., Ascension, Cleveland
Kochanski, Robert M., St. Joseph, Cuyahoga Falls
Kovitch, Joseph R., St. Mary, Mentor
Krupp, Ralph J., St. Peter, Lorain
Kuhlman, Richard F., Immaculate Conception, Madison
Litke, Joseph P., Holy Family, Parma
Lobdell, Donald W., Waupaca, Wisconsin
LoCascio, Phillip A., Phoenix, AZ
Lonteen, Francis R., St. Paul, Akron; Queen of Heaven, Greensburg
Loutzenhiser, Joseph E., St. Francis Xavier, Medina
Love, Wm. Ansley, (Retired)
Lozada, Frank, St. Francis, Cleveland
Lundeen, David J., Corpus Christi, Cleveland
Malcolm, Billy J., St. Ignatius of Antioch & St. Vincent De Paul, Cleveland
Maldonado, Louis, St. Joseph Lorain
Martin, James T., St. Mary of the Assumption, Mentor
Masony, Howard J., Diaconate Staff, St. Joseph the Worker, Strongsville
Matoney, Robert, Jr., St. Clare, Lyndhurst
Matusicky, Daniel J., St. Bernard, Akron
McCarthy, Edward J., Jr., Diaconate Staff, St. Mary, Chardon
McGraw, Joseph E., St. Mark, Cleveland
McNulty, Leo F., St. Francis of Assisi, Gates Mills, St. Joseph Christian Life Center
Medina, Ceferino, Sagrada Familia, Cleveland
Merriman, William C., St. Patrick, Cleveland
Miklosovic, John, St. Ambrose, Brunswick
Miranda, Ignacio, Sagrada Familia, Cleveland
Mueller, Richard A., St. Mary of the Falls, Olmstead Falls
Netzband, Ralph W., St. Monica, Garfield Heights
Newman, Joseph H., St. Timothy, Garfield Heights
Norris, Daniel F., St. Francis Xavier, Medina.
Novak, Andrew J., St. Cyprian, Perry; St. Patrick, Thompson
O'Connell, Frank J., (On Duty Outside the Diocese)
O'Donnell, James K., Interfaith Commission, Diaconate Staff, Gesu, University Heights
Paul, James, St. Aloysius-St. Agatha, Cleveland
Payne, Robert H., Holy Cross, Euclid
Payne, Willard C., St. Helen, Newbury
Peacock, Terry W., St. Sebastian, Akron
Pecek, Louis G., Diocesan Tribunal, St. Paul, Euclid
Pecot, David E., DPC Representative, St. Basil the Great, Brecksville
Piechowski, Kenneth J., Dir. Diaconate & St. Hyacinth, Cleveland

Pineiro, Jose L., Sacred Heart Chapel, Lorain
Piskach, Robert J., St. Francis de Sales, Parma
Polefko, Roger F., St. John Bosco, Parma Heights
Quiles, Rafael, (Retired)
Ramos, Jose L., St. Michael, Cleveland
Rapp, Robert, Garrettsville, OH
Reiland, George J., Jr., (Retired)
Rivera, Carlos, Sacred Heart Chapel, Lorain
Rivera, John M., St. Augustine, Cleveland; St. Julie Billiart, North Ridgeville
Rodriguez, Alfonso, Palm Bay, FL
Sabol, Robert G., St. Peter the Apostle, Brook Park
Savage, Joseph J., Plymouth, MI
Schad, Kenneth E., On Leave
Schill, William E., St. Stanislaus, Lorain
Seal, J. David, Immaculate Heart of Mary, Cuyahoga Falls
Senn, Thomas J., Our Lady of Angels, Cleveland; Cuyahoga County Jail
Sferry, John P., Diaconate Staff, St. Gregory, South Euclid
Sheridan, Thomas, St. Ambrose, Brunswick
Sherman, Homer L., St. Clarence, North Olmsted
Shin, Charles C., St. Andrew Kim Pastoral Center, Cleveland
Sill, Donald E., St. Anselm, Chesterland
Simon, Frederick F., Diaconate Staff, Sagrada Familia, Cleveland
Skrha, Joseph W., M.D., Dir., Pastoral Care Dept., St. Michael Hospital, Cleveland
Slatcoff, John K., St. Vincent De Paul, Elyria Township
Smith, Dennis L., Immaculate Conception, Akron
Snyder, Wayne W., St. John Vianney, Mentor
Somrack, Lawrence A., St. Augustine Hunger Center, Cleveland; Divine Word, Kirtland
Staab, William M., St. Patrick, Cleveland
Stewart, James R., St. James, Lakewood
Stokes, Troy F., Epiphany, Cleveland
Streeter, David A., St. Luke, Lakewood
Strmac, John W., Diaconate Staff, Our Lady of Mount Carmel, Wickliffe
Talerico, John A., St. Charles Borromeo, Parma
Telepak, Edward A., St. Columbkille, Parma
Terrion, Daniel C., St. Wenceslas, Maple Heights
Thiel, Martin A., St. Thomas More, Brooklyn
Toomey, Carl M., St. Mary Magdalene, Willowick
Torres, Epifanio, Sagrada Familia, Cleveland
Travalik, Peter M., St. Jerome, Cleveland
Ulman, Robert P., St. Bede the Venerable, Mentor
Varga, Carl M., Divine Word, Kirtland; St. Philip Neri, Cleveland
Vicens, Prudo, (Retired)
Vincent, James C., St. Peter the Apostle, Brook Park
Vinciguerra, Mario J., Our Lady of Guadelupe, Macedonia
Volek, Ronald J., St. George, Clinton
Vrabel, Jerome B., Holy Cross, Euclid
Waken, Thomas J., Pastoral Care Coord., St. Joseph Hospital; St. Leo, Cleveland
Walsh, John J. (Y), Pittsburgh, Pennsylvania
Weglicki, Frank L., Jr., St. Ambrose, Brunswick
Wendzicki, Martin J., Holy Name, Cleveland
Weniger, Robert L., St. Michael, Independence
Wenzel, John T., St. Anthony of Padua, Fairport Harbor
Wilson, Francis B., Assumption of Mary, Brook Park
Woods, Richard E., St. Louis, Cleveland Heights
Woyton, Louis M., St. Augustine, Cleveland
Zawadzki, Charles W., Corpus Christi, Cleveland
Zdolshek, John R., St. Richard, North Olmstead
Ziemkiewicz, Gerard J., NADO Representative, Diaconate Staff, St. Rita, Solon

INSTITUTIONS LOCATED IN THE DIOCESE

[A] SEMINARIES, DIOCESAN

WICKLIFFE. *Borromeo Seminary*, 28700 Euclid Ave., 44092-2585. Tel: 440-943-7600; Fax: 440-943-7577.
E-mail: borromeo@dioceseofcleveland.org
Web site: www.a-full-life.com
Very Rev. Thomas M. Dragga, D.Min., Pres. & Rector; Rev. Robert Stec, M.A., M.Div., Vocation Dir.; Kathryn C. Simmons, Registrar; Revs. Donald Lippert, O.F.M.Cap., M.A., Philosophy; John F. Loya, M.Div., M.A., Spiritual Dir.; Bro. Charles McElroy, O.F.M.Cap., Religious Studies; Mr. Brian F. Houlahan, Treas.; Rev. Timothy Plavac, M.Div., M.A., Religious Studies; Sr. Rosemarie Carfagna, O.S.U., Ph.D., Academic Dean; Rev. Donald Dunson, Formation Advisor. Lay Teachers: Ed Kaczuk, M.M.; Ray Leopold, M.Lit.; William Tighe, B.S. In res. Rev. Robert W. Kline. Priests 6; Brothers 1; Sisters 1; Lay Teachers 3; Seminarians 21.

St. Mary Seminary and Graduate School of Theology. (Our Lady of the Lake), 28700 Euclid Ave., 44092-2585. Tel: 440-943-7600; Fax: 440-943-7577. Revs. Donald B. Cozzens, Ph.D., Pres. & Rector; Thomas W. Tifft, Ph.D., Vice Rector; Mark A. Latcovich, Ph.D., Academic Dean; Revs. David J. Walkowiak, J.C.D., Dean of Students; John F. Loya, M.A., M.Div., Spiritual Dir.; Ms. Kathryn C. Simmons, Registrar; Sr. Maribeth Howell, O.P., S.T.D., Ph.D.; Sr. Mary McCormick, O.S.U., Ph.D., Candidate; Revs. Gerald J. Bednar, Ph.D.; Donald Dunson, Ph.D.; Thomas M. Dragga, D.Min.; Michael G. Woost, S.T.L.; Lorenzo Tosco, C.S.J., S.S.L.; Paul Hritz, Ph.D.; Mr. Edward J. Kaczuk, M.M.; Mr. Alan K. Rome, M.L.S., Librarian; Mr. Brian F. Houlahan, Treas. Priests 11; Sisters 2; Adjunct Faculty 10; Students for Priesthood, Diocesan 28; Permanent Diaconate 32; Other 80.

[B] COLLEGES AND UNIVERSITIES

CLEVELAND. *John Carroll Jesuit Community.*
E-mail: jesuits@jcu.edu John Carroll University, University Heights, 44118. Tel: 216-397-1886; Fax: 216-397-4228.
For a complete listing, refer to the Colleges and Universities section.

John Carroll University, 20700 N. Park Blvd., 44118. Tel: 216-397-1886; Fax: 216-397-4256.
Web site: www.jcu.edu
For a complete listing, refer to the Colleges and Universities section.

Notre Dame College of Ohio 4545 College Rd. South Euclid, 44121. Tel: 216-381-1680; Fax: 216-381-3802.
For a complete listing, refer to the Colleges and Universities section.

Ursuline College 2550 Lander Rd. Pepper Pike, 44124. Tel: 440-449-4200; Fax: 440-646-8102.
For a complete listing, refer to the Colleges and Universities section.

[C] HIGH SCHOOLS, DIOCESAN

CLEVELAND. *Cleveland Central Catholic High School*, Administration: Forman Campus, 6550 Baxter Ave., 44105. Tel: 216-441-4700; Fax: 216-441-8353.
E-mail: cccjanice@aol.com
Scranton Campus, 3146 Scranton Rd., 44109. Tel: 216-441-8354; Fax: 216-441-8356. Janice T. Roccosalva, Prin. Sisters 2; Lay Teachers 37; Total Staff 60; Students 465.

Villa Angela-St. Joseph High School, 18491 Lake Shore Blvd., 44119. Tel: 216-481-8414; Fax: 216-486-1035.
E-mail: vikingVASJ@aol.com
Web site: www.VASJ.com
Margaret T. Lynch, Prin. Marianists 5; Ursuline Nuns 1; Lay Teachers 40; Students 515.

BEDFORD. *St. Peter Chanel High School*, 480 Northfield Rd., 44146. Tel: 440-232-5900; Fax: 440-232-9283.
E-mail: chanelhs@aol.com
Web site: www.stpeterchanel.com
Mr. Roger R. Abood, Prin. Sisters 1; Lay Teachers 30; Students 401.

ELYRIA. *Elyria Catholic High School.* (Coed), 725 Gulf Rd., 44035. Tel: 216-365-1821; Fax: 216-365-7536. Mr. Wayne Uehlein, M.A., Prin.
Serving Elyria, Avon, Sheffield, North Ridgeville, Grafton, Oberlin, and Amherst. Lay Teachers 41; Students 546.

LORAIN. *Lorain Catholic High School.* (Grades 7-12), 760 Tower Blvd., 44052. Tel: 440-282-8216; Fax: 440-282-8123.
Web site: www.loraincatholic.org
Mrs. Chris Paul, Prin.; Mr. James W. Lawhead, Asst. Prin.; Rev. Giampietro Gasparin, C.S.J., M.Div., Chap. Priests 1; Sisters of Notre Dame 1; Lay Teachers 27; Students 386.

MENTOR. *Lake Catholic High*, 6733 Reynolds Rd., 44060. Tel: 440-951-0077; Fax: 440-974-9087. Sr. St. Ann Waldron, O.S.U., Prin.; Rev. David G. Woost, Chap. Priests 1; Ursuline Nuns of Cleveland (O.S.U.) 3; Lay Teachers 53; Students 910.

PARMA HEIGHTS. *Holy Name High School.* (Coed), 6000 Queens Hwy., 44130. Tel: 440-886-0300; Fax: 440-886-1267.
E-mail: rram@zapmail.net
Raymond R. Ramicone, Prin.; Rev. William R. Krinzner, Chap. Priests 1; Sisters 3; Lay Teachers 61; Administration 4; Students 1,000.

[D] HIGH SCHOOLS, PRIVATE

CLEVELAND. *Beaumont School.* 3301 N. Park Blvd., Cleveland Heights, 44118. Tel: 216-321-2954; Fax: 216-321-3947.
E-mail: Info@beaumontschool.org
Web site: www.beaumontschool.org
Beaumont Convent, 3240 Fairmount Blvd., 44118. Tel: 216-321-2157; Fax: 216-321-3947. Ursuline Sisters. Sr. Ritamary Welsh, O.S.U., Pres.; Sr. Susan Mary Rathbun, O.S.U., Prin. Sisters 13; Lay Teachers 40; Students 448.

Benedictine High School, 2900 Martin Luther King Dr., 44104-4898. Tel: 216-421-2080; Fax: 216-421-1100.
E-mail: benedictine@mail-now.com
Web site: www.cbhs.net
Rt. Rev. Roger W. Gries, O.S.B., Pres.; Dereck Slesh, Treas. & Bus. Mgr.; Rev. Gerard Gonda, O.S.B., Prin.; Mr. August Pisa, Asst. Prin. and Academic Dean; Mr. Larry Becker, Dir. of Development; Mr. Anthony Russ, Dean Student Affairs; Revs. Paschal Petcavage, O.S.B.; Michael Brunovsky, O.S.B.; Timothy Buyansky, O.S.B.; Gary Hoover, O.S.B., School Chap.; Bede Kotlinski, O.S.B.; Joachim Pastirik, O.S.B.; Anselm Zupka, O.S.B.; Dominic Mondzelewski; Justin Dyrwal, O.S.B.; Bros. Peter Ancell, O.S.B.; Patrick Ryan, O.S.B.; Mario Parisi, O.S.B. Priests 10; Brothers 3; Lay Teachers 26; Students 380.

Magnificat High School. (Girls), 20770 Hilliard Blvd., 44116. Tel: 440-331-1572; Fax: 440-331-7257.
E-mail: smpcook@magnificaths.org
Web site: magnificaths.org
Sr. Carolyn Marshall, H.M., Pres.; Sr. Mary Pat Cook, H.M., Prin. Sisters 4; Lay Teachers 73; Students 874.

Regina High School. (Girls), 1857 S. Green Rd., 44121. Tel: 216-382-2110; Fax: 216-382-3555.
E-mail: rhs@stratos.net
Web site: reginahigh.com
Sisters of Notre Dame. Sr. Maureen Burke, S.N.D., Prin. Sisters 10; Lay Teachers 21; Students 260.

St. Edward High School. (Boys). 13500 Detroit Ave., Lakewood, 44107. Tel: 216-221-3776; Fax: 216-221-4609.
Web site: sehs.net
Bro. James Spooner, C.S.C., Pres. Brothers 9; Lay Teachers 52; Total Staff 93; Students 905.

St. Ignatius High School, 1911 W. 30th St., 44113. Tel: 216-651-0222; Fax: 216-651-6313.
Web site: ignatius.edu
Revs. Timothy Kesicki, S.J., Pres.; Bernard J. Streicher, S.J., Rector; Richard F. Clark, Prin.; Revs. Steven J. Agostino, S.J.; Thomas J. Bain, S.J.; Robert J. Dietrich, S.J.; James E. Farrell, S.J.; Raymond Guiao, S.J.; John H. Kleinhenz, S.J.; James V. Lewis, S.J.; Lawrence M. Ober, S.J.; Kenneth A. Styles, S.J.; Glenn F. Williams, S.J.; John White, S.J.; Dennis T. Dillon, S.J.; Michael A. Vincent, S.J. Priests 15; Lay Teachers 89; Students 1,361.

St. Joseph Academy, 3430 Rocky River Dr., 44111. Tel: 216-251-6788; Fax: 216-251-5809.
E-mail: kasper2@apk.net
Web site: www.stjoeacademy.org
Jacqualine Kasprowski, Pres./Prin. Sisters 11; Lay Teachers 53; Students 585.

Trinity High School, 12425 Granger, 44125. Tel: 216-581-1644; Fax: 216-581-9348.
E-mail: tmaher@ths.org
Web site: www.ths.org
Sisters of St. Joseph of the Third Order of St. Francis. Sr. Shawn Lee, S.S.J.-T.O.S.F., Pres.; Patrick J. Riley, D.Min., Asst. to the Pres.; Thomas M. Maher, Ph.D., Prin.; Mr. Daniel J. Thomeier, Business Mgr.; Mr. Joseph A. Waler, M.A., M.Ed., Assoc. Prin. Sisters of St. Joseph 5; Lay Teachers 49; Students 661.

AKRON. *Archbishop Hoban High School.* (Coed), 400 Elbon Ave., 44306. Tel: 330-773-6658; Fax: 330-773-9100.
E-mail: beitingm@hoban.org
Web site: hoban.org
Brothers of Holy Cross. Bro. Kenneth Haders, C.S.C., Pres.; Mrs. Mary Anne Beiting, Prin. Brothers 7; Sisters 1; Lay Teachers 40; Students 736.

Our Lady of the Elms School. (Grades 7-12), 1220 W. Market St., 44313-7108. Tel: 330-836-9384; Fax: 330-836-9351.
E-mail: admissions@elms.k12.oh.us
Web site: www.elms.k12.oh.us
Sr. Dorothy Sarachene, O.P., Dir. Education; Connie Hardy, Prin. Please see complete listing under Elementary Schools. 2; Lay Teachers 29; Students 280.

St. Vincent-St. Mary High School, 15 North Maple, 44303. Tel: 330-253-9113; Fax: 330-996-0020.
E-mail: webmaster@stum.com
Web site: www.stvm.com
David V. Rathz, Headmaster; Phyllis Griffith, Dir. of Devel.; Patricia Burdon, Dir. of Admissions; Ranoi Bostick, Bus. Mgr.; Dan Nichols, Dean of Students; Joanne Zaratsian, Dir. Fiscal Resources; Lorene Haddox, Campus Min. Chaplains: Revs. Robert H. Jackson; Salvatore Ruggerio. Priests 2; Lay Teachers 35; Students 530.

CHARDON. *Notre Dame-Cathedral Latin School*, 13000 Auburn Rd., 44024. Tel: 440-286-6226; 888-214-8108 (toll free); Fax: 440-286-7199.
E-mail: ndclschool@excite.com
Web site: www.ndcl.cld.pvt.k12.oh.us
Sisters of Notre Dame. Sr. Allison Marie Gusdanovic, S.N.D., Prin. Sisters 11; Lay Teachers 55; Students 825.

CUYAHOGA FALLS. *Walsh Jesuit High School*, 4550 Wyoga Lake Rd., 44224. Tel: 330-929-4205; 800-686-4694 (Cleveland); Fax: 330-929-9749.
E-mail: peppardp@walshjesuit.org
Web site: www.walshjesuit.org
Revs. Patrick F. Peppard, S.J., Religious Supr.; Vincent A. Hagarman, S.J.; Donald J. Hayes, S.J.; Emmett P. Holmes, S.J.; James J. King, S.J.; Paul D. Panaretos, S.J.; Donald J. Petkash, S.J., Pres.; James S. Prehn, S.J.; Richard M. Rosenfelder, S.J.; Priests 6; Lay Teachers 51; Students 855.

GATES MILLS. *Gilmour Academy*. (Grades PreK-12). Private. 34001 Cedar Rd., 44040-9356. Tel: 440-473-8000; Fax: 440-473-8010.
E-mail: laveller@gilmour.org
Web site: www.gilmour.org
Day and Resident College Preparatory School. Congregation of Holy Cross. Mr. Murlan J. Murphy, Jr., Chm., Board of Trustees; Bro. Robert Lavelle, C.S.C., Headmaster; Dr. Elizabeth Fesler, Ph.D., Dir. of Upper School; Todd R. Sweda, Dir. Middle School; Dr. Monica Veto, Dir. of Lower School; Rev. John Blazek, C.S.C., Campus Minister. Priests 1; Brothers 2; Sisters 1; Students 685; Residents 43; Lay Teachers 63.

LAKEWOOD. *St. Augustine Academy*, 14808 Lake Ave., 44107. Tel: 216-221-4227; Fax: 216-221-7453.
E-mail: splen@aol.com
Web site: www.st-aug-academy.org
Sr. Patricia Lenard, C.S.F.N., Dir. Sisters of the Holy Family of Nazareth 4; Lay Teachers 25; Total Staff 32; Girls 238.

PARMA. *Padua Franciscan High School*, 6740 State Rd., 44134. Tel: 440-845-2444; Fax: 440-845-5710.
E-mail: padua@paduafranciscan.com
Web site: www.paduafranciscan.com
Rev. Walter Dolan, O.F.M., Pres.; Gerald R. Jindra, Vice Pres. for Institutional Advancement; Timothy Giulivo, Prin.; David Stec, Campus Ministry; Bro. Tom Carroll, O.F.M., Academic Dean. Priests 2; Sisters 1; Brothers 2; Lay Teachers 63; Students 1,112.

[E] ELEMENTARY SCHOOLS

CLEVELAND. *Incarnate Word Academy*, 6618 Pearl Rd., 44130. Tel: 440-842-6818; Fax: 440-888-1377. Sr. Eileen Fitzgerald, S.I.W., Prin.; Rev. Kenneth Katricak, O.S.B. Sisters 8; Lay Teachers 21; Students 563.

AKRON. *Our Lady of the Elms School*. (Grades 1-6), 1220 W. Market St., 44313-7108. Tel: 330-836-9384; Fax: 330-836-9351.
E-mail: admissions@elms.k12.oh.us
Web site: www.elms.k12.oh.us
Sr. Dorothy Sarachene, O.P., Dir. Education. Sisters 1; Lay Teachers 15; Students 186.

CHARDON. *Notre Dame Elementary School*, 13000 Auburn Rd., 44024. Tel: 440-286-3672; Fax: 440-286-1235.
E-mail: mtgrady@ndec.org
Sr. Mary Therese Grady, S.N.D., Prin. Sisters of Notre Dame 10; Lay Teachers 18; Students 451.
Notre Dame PreSchool, 13000 Auburn Rd., 44024. Tel: 440-286-7101, Ext. 592; Fax: 440-286-9364. Sr. Margaret McGovern, S.N.D., Dir. Sisters of Notre Dame 1; Lay Teachers 2; Aides 2; Students 48.

HUDSON. *Seton Catholic School*, 6923 Stow Rd., 44236. Tel: 330-342-4200; Fax: 330-342-4276.
Web site: www.setoncatholicschool.org
Sr. Marie Damicone, Prin.; Patrick Kirk, Treas. Sisters 1; Lay Teachers 9; Students 173.

[F] ELEMENTARY SCHOOLS, PAROCHIAL AND DIOCESAN

CLEVELAND. *Archbishop James P. Lyke Elementary School*. St. Henry, St. Timothy and St. Catherine Schools consolidated to form Archbishop James P. Lyke Elementary School. 18230 Harvard Ave., 44128. Tel: 216-991-9644; Fax: 216-991-9470. Sr. Brigetta Waldron, O.S.U., Dir. Lay Teachers 30; Students 658.
St. Catherine Campus. (Grades K-1), 3443 E. 93rd St., 44104. Tel: 216-341-7212; Fax: 216-641-8184. Sr. Mary Beth Daly, S.N.D., Prin. Students 145.
St. Henry Campus. (Grades 2-4), 18230 Harvard Ave., 44128. Tel: 216-991-9644; Fax: 216-991-9470. Ms. Mary Pat Hable, Prin. Students 250.
St. Timothy Campus. (Grades 5-8), 4351 E. 131st St., Garfield Heights, 44105. Tel: 216-581-3517; Fax: 216-641-8184. Mrs. Margarete W. Smith, Prin. Students 263.
Metro Catholic School. Tel: 216-281-4044; Fax: 216-634-2853. St. Stephen Bldg. (Grade 5-8), 1910 W. 54th St., 44102. Tel: 216-281-4044; Fax: 216-234-2853. St. Michael Bldg. (Grades 2-4), 1903 W. 57th St., 44102. Tel: 216-634-2847; Fax: 216-634-2853. St. Boniface Bldg. (PreK-1), 3555 W. 54th St., 44102. Tel: 216-631-5733; Fax: 216-634-2853. Sr. Anne Mary Maline, S.N.D., Prin. Sisters of Notre Dame 9; Ursuline Nun 2; Lay Teachers 24; Students 570.
Urban Community School, 2401 Washington Ave., 44113. Tel: 216-771-8014; Fax: 216-771-7888.
E-mail: mdoyle2401@aol.com
Sr. Maureen Doyle, O.S.U., Dir. Ursuline Nuns 3; Lay Teachers 24; Students 413.

WICKLIFFE. *All Saints of St. John Vianney School*. (Grades PreK-8), 28702 Euclid Ave., 44092. Tel: 216-943-1395; Fax: 216-943-4468. Mrs. Rosemary Wilson, Prin. Sisters 1; Lay Teachers 20; Students 388.

[G] SPECIAL SCHOOLS AND CENTERS

For Exceptional Children

CLEVELAND. *Julie Billiart*. Tel: 216-381-1191; Fax: 216-381-2216. 4982 Clubside Rd., Lyndhurst, 44124-2596. Tel: 216-381-1191; Fax: 216-381-2216. Non-graded school for children having learning problems. Sr. Agnesmarie, S.N.D., Prin. Sisters 10; Lay Teachers 7; Students 115.
OLA-St. Joseph Center, 2346 W. 14th St., 44113. Tel: 216-621-3451; Fax: 216-621-6104.
E-mail: olasjc@mail.cle-dioc.org
Non-graded school for developmentally handicapped children, ages 6-16. Mrs. Pamela Delly, Prin. Lay Teachers 10; Students 80.

[H] PRESCHOOL AND DAY CARE CENTERS

CLEVELAND. *Catholic Charities Services/Head Start*, 1031 Superior Ave., 6th Floor, 44114. Tel: 216-696-6525, Ext. 2870; Fax: 216-696-3631.
E-mail: ctwalker@ccd.cle-dioc.org
Lay Teachers 57; Children 1,417.
Villa Montessori Center, 5620 Broadway Ave., 44127. Tel: 216-641-4770; Fax: 216-641-4771.
E-mail: villageecc@ad.com
Web site: school.cleveland.com/school/villa
Sr. Marie Veres, H.M., Dir./Prin.

GARFIELD HEIGHTS. *Marymount Child Care Center*, 12215 Granger Rd., 44125. Tel: 216-581-3540; Fax: 216-581-4264.
E-mail: felmann@aol.com
Sr. Felicia Mann, S.S.J.-T.O.S.F., Dir. Total Assisted 230; Total Staff 20.

[I] GENERAL HOSPITALS

(For information on other Catholic related hospitals please contact the Chancery Office.)

CLEVELAND. *Marymount Hospital, Inc.*, 12300 McCracken Rd., 44125. Tel: 216-581-0500; Fax: 216-587-8212.
E-mail: ttrudell@marymount.org
Web site: www.marymount.org
For a complete listing, refer to the Hospitals section.
St. John Hospital, 2351 E. 22nd St., 44115. Tel: 216-696-5560; Fax: 216-696-2204.
Web site: www.csahealthsystem.org
For a complete listing, refer to the Hospitals section.

LORAIN. *Community Health Partners Health System*. Tel: 440-233-1053; Fax: 440-246-5390.
E-mail: karen_yacobucci@hmis.org 3700 Kolbe Rd., 44053-1697. Tel: 440-960-4000; Fax: 440-960-4630.
For a complete listing, refer to the Hospitals section.

[J] TRAINING SCHOOLS FOR NURSES

CLEVELAND. *Marymount School of Practical Nursing*. Tel: 216-587-8160; Fax: 216-587-8632.
E-mail: sleonard@marymount.org
12300 McCracken Rd., Garfield Heights, 44125. Tel: 216-587-8160; Fax: 216-587-8632.
E-mail: sleonard@marymount.org
Suzan Leonard, R.N., B.S.N., M.Ed., Dir. Students 36.

[K] SPECIAL HOSPITALS

CLEVELAND. *Holy Family Home*, 6707 State Rd., 44134. Tel: 440-885-3100; Fax: 440-885-0644.
E-mail: www.holyfamilyhome.com
For a complete listing, refer to the Special Care Facilities section.
Rose Mary, The Johanna Grasselli Rehabilitation and Education Center, 19350 Euclid Ave., 44117. Tel: 216-481-4823; Fax: 216-481-4154
For a complete listing, refer to the Special Care Facilities section.

[L] PROTECTIVE INSTITUTIONS

CLEVELAND. *Christ Child - DePaul Day Care Center*, 2320 E. 24th St., 44115. Tel: 216-687-0007; Fax: 216-687-0403
For a complete listing, refer to the Special Care Facilities section.

INDEPENDENCE. *Marycrest*, 8010 Brookside Rd., 44131. Tel: 216-524-5280; Fax: 216-524-2127
For a complete listing, refer to the Special Care Facilities section.

PARMA. *CCSC/Parmadale*, 6753 State Rd., 44134. Tel: 440-845-7700; Fax: 440-845-5910.
E-mail: pdale@mail.cle-dioc.org
Web site: www.cle-dioc.org
For a complete listing, refer to the Special Care Facilities section.

[M] HOMES FOR AGED

CLEVELAND. *Jennings Hall Center for Older Adults*, 10204 Granger Rd., 44125. Tel: 216-581-2900; Fax: 216-581-4505; 216-581-1517.
E-mail: jenninghal@aol.com
For a complete listing, refer to the Special Care Facilities section.
Mount St. Joseph, 21800 Chardon Rd., 44117. Tel: 216-531-7426; Fax: 216-531-4033.
E-mail: mountstjoe@aol.com
For a complete listing, refer to the Special Care Facilities section.
St. Augustine Manor, 7801 Detroit Ave., 44102. Tel: 216-634-7400; Fax: 216-634-7483.
E-mail: p.gareau@worldnet.att.net
Web site: www.staugustinemanor.org
For a complete listing, refer to the Special Care Facilities section.
Sts. Mary and Joseph Home for the Aged, 4291 Richmond Rd., 44122-6199. Tel: 216-464-1222; Fax: 216-591-9255
For a complete listing, refer to the Special Care Facilities section.

AKRON. *Francesca Residence*, 39 N. Portage Path, 44303. Tel: 330-867-6334; Fax: 330-867-6334
For a complete listing, refer to the Special Care Facilities section.

BEACHWOOD. *Villa Sancta Anna Home for the Aged, Inc.*, 25000 Chagrin Blvd., 44122-5665. Tel: 216-464-9250; Fax: 216-464-9274
For a complete listing, refer to the Special Care Facilities section.

BEDFORD. *Light of Hearts Villa, Inc.*, 283 Union St., 44146. Tel: 216-232-1991; Fax: 440-232-1782.
E-mail: lightofhearts@worldnet.att.net
Web site: home.att.net/lightofhearts/
For a complete listing, refer to the Special Care Facilities section.

FAIRLAWN. *St. Edward Home dba The Village at St. Edward Nursing Care and Assisted Living*, 3131 Smith Rd., 44333. Tel: 330-666-1183; Fax: 330-666-2721
For a complete listing, refer to the Special Care Facilities section.

PARMA. *Franciscan Communities - Mount Alverna Home* 6765 State Rd., 44134. Tel: 440-843-7800; Fax: 440-843-7107.
For a complete listing, refer to the Special Care Facilities section.

RICHFIELD. *Regina Health Center*, 5232 Broadview Rd., 44286-9608. Tel: 216-659-4161; Fax: 216-659-5113.
E-mail: bflannery@reginahealthcenter.org
For a complete listing, refer to the Special Care Facilities section.

[N] RESIDENCE FOR RETIRED PRIESTS

BROOKLYN. *Issenmann Place*, 4185 Brookway Ln., 44144. Tel: 216-661-1470. William Brady, Asst. Admin. Total in Residence 7; Total Staff 3.

[O] MONASTERIES AND RESIDENCES OF PRIESTS AND BROTHERS

CLEVELAND. *Benedictine Order of Cleveland*, St. Andrew Abbey, 10510 Buckeye Rd., 44104. Tel: 216-721-5300; Fax: 216-721-1253.
E-mail: rogerabbot@aol.com
Web site: www.en.com/users/brother
Rt. Rev. Roger W. Gries, O.S.B.; Revs. Joachim Pastirik, O.S.B.; Clement Zeleznik, O.S.B., Assumption Church, 9183 Broadview Rd., Broadview Heights, 44147. Tel: 440-526-1177; Fax: 440-526-2838. Revs. Timothy Buyansky, O.S.B.; Dominic Mondzelewski, O.S.B.; Placid Pientek, O.S.B.; Dismas Boeff, O.S.B., Chap., Southwest General Hospital, St. Peter, 6455 Engle Rd., 44142. Tel: 216-433-1440; Fax: 216-433-1434. Revs. Gerard Gonda, O.S.B.; Armand E. Gress, O.S.B.; Gary Hoover, O.S.B.; Kenneth J. Katricak, O.S.B., Chap., Incarnate Word, 6618 Pearl Rd., Parma Heights, 44130. Tel: 440-886-6996; Fax: 440-888-1377. Revs. Albert Marflak, O.S.B., Vocation Dir. & Abbey Procurator; Paschal Petcavage; Andrew Pier, O.S.B.; Benedict Sellers, O.S.B.; Lawrence Sevcik, O.S.B.; Anselm Zupka, O.S.B., Prior. Priests 2; Brothers 1.
Other Assignments: Revs. Bede Kotlinski, O.S.B.; William T. Matyas, O.S.B.; Ronald Mahnke, O.S.B.; Anthony J. Ozimek, O.S.B., St. Vincent Hospital, Billings, MT, 59107-5200. Tel: 406-657-7000. Rev. Christopher Schwartz, O.S.B., Assumption Church,

9183 Broadview Rd., 44147. Tel: 440-526-1177; Fax: 440-526-2838. Rev. Raphael Zbin, O.S.B., St. Andrew, 5135 Superior Ave., 44103. Tel: 216-431-2057. Rev. Michael Brunovsky, Novice Master.

Blessed Sacrament Community, 5384 Wilson Mills Rd., 44143-3092. Tel: 440-442-3411.
Web site: blessedsacrament.com
Very Rev. Anthony L. Schueller, S.S.S., Prov. Supr.; Revs. Michael Arkins, S.S.S.; Roger Bourgeois, S.S.S.; Donald J. Jette, S.S.S., Supr.; Raymond J. Dubois, S.S.S.; Roger Pageot, S.S.S.; Edward J. Stapleton, S.S.S., Prov. Treas.; Edmund Slattery, S.S.S.; William F. Fickel, S.S.S.; William T. Young, S.S.S.; Frederick Roberge, S.S.S.; Deacon Joseph Bourgeois; Bros. Eugene Blee, S.S.S.; Edmund Hardy, S.S.S.; Gerard Hickey, S.S.S.; Thomas F. Flanagan, S.S.S.; Gary L. Laverdiere, S.S.S.; Michael J. O'Leary, S.S.S.; Anthony Ornelas, S.S.S.; Ignatius J. Montgomery, S.S.S. Novices: Gerard Delaney; Arthur DaLamba; Joseph Patrick. Priests 10; Deacons 1; Brothers 8. Regina Health Center, 5232 Broadview Rd., Richfield, 44286-9608. Rev. George Evans, S.S.S. Priests 1.

Congregation of the Blessed Sacrament Provincial House. 5384 Wilson Mills Rd., Highland Heights, 44143-3092. Tel: 440-442-6311; Fax: 440-442-8175.
E-mail: aschueller@aol.com
Web site: blessedsacrament.com
Province of St. Ann. Very Rev. Anthony L. Schueller, S.S.S., Prov. Supr.; Rev. Edward J. Stapleton, S.S.S., Prov. Treas.
Priests Serving Outside Country: Rev. Ralph Roberts, S.S.S., Blessed Sacrament, Parrocchia S. Marko Evangelista, Via Del Modiano 1/1, Trieste, Italia, 34148.
Priests attached to Provincialate: Rev. Andrew Beaudoin, S.S.S., 11487 Kerridale Ave., Spring Hill, FL, 34608-3111. Tel: 352-686-8078. Rev. Rene A. Belanger, S.S.S., 58 Dudley St., New Bedford, MA, 02744-1503. Tel: 508-993-3717. Rev. Peter Cops, S.S.S., Retreat House, Rte. 1, Box 110, Waverly, NE, 68462-9646. Tel: 402-786-2705. Rev. Edward Roberts, S.S.S., 36 Monument Sq., Apt. 4, Charlestown, MA, 02129-3429. Tel: 617-241-9121. Rev. John Keenan, S.S.S., Hampton House, 5300 S. Shore Dr., Apt. 95, Chicago, IL, 60615-5708. Tel: 773-684-5770; Fax: 773-955-2990. Rev. Robert S. Pittman, S.S.S., P.O. Box 410, Waldorf, MD, 20604. Tel: 301-888-2566. Rev. Joachim Viet-Chau, S.S.S., Vietnamese Apostolate, P.O. Box 1419, Gretna, LA, 70054-1419. Tel: 504-392-1630; Fax: 504-392-5440. Rev. Nicholas Zohnerowicz, S.S.S., 32 W. Franklin Ave., Pequannock, NJ, 07440-1502. Tel: 973-684-6727. Rev. George Evans, S.S.S., Regina Health Center, 5232 Broadview Rd., Richfield, 44286-9608. Tel: 330-659-4161.

Marianist Community, 18340 Marcella Rd., 44119-2622. Tel: 216-481-1007. Priests 2; Brothers 7.

Maryknoll Fathers, 10309 Edgewater Dr., 44102. Tel: 216-651-2121; Fax: 216-651-8242.
E-mail: mklcleve@aol.com
Web site: www.maryknoll.org
Revs. James H. Huvane, M.M., Dir.; Richard S. Kardian, M.M. Total in Residence 2; Total Staff 1.

Mercedarians, 6928 Detroit Ave., 44102-3093. Tel: 216-651-5043; Fax: 216-651-6641.
E-mail: OLMC1@en.com
Web site: www.massintransit.com
Order of the BVM of Mercy. Rev. Richard Rasch, O.de.M., Supr. In res. Revs. Michael Donovan, O.de.M.; Marino Frascati, O.de.M.; Bro. John Michael Zyckowski, O.de.M. Priests 3; Brothers 1.

Missionary Servants of the Most Holy Trinity. Tel: 216-391-3947; Fax: 216-391-7919.
E-mail: FRmikeb@cs.com
Web site: www.cleveland.catholicnet.com
St. Agnes-Our Lady of Fatima, 6800 Lexington Ave., 44103. Tel: 216-391-1655; Fax: 216-391-7919. Rev. Michael K. Barth, S.T.

Padua Franciscan Friary. 7022 State Rd., Parma, 44134. Tel: 440-888-7742. Revs. Walter Dolan, O.F.M.; Theodore Haag, O.F.M.; James McManamon; Bros. Thomas Carroll, O.F.M., Guardian; Richard Baranski, O.F.M.; Joseph Manning, O.F.M. Priests 3; Brothers 3.

St. Jude Friary, 4760 Richmond Rd., 44128. Tel: 216-292-6602; Fax: 216-292-0454. Revs. Emmanuel Beunen, O.F.M.; Thomas Carolan, O.F.M., Supr.; Melchoir Toczek, O.F.M.; Bro. Joseph Di Santo, O.F.M. Priests 3; Brothers 1; Total Assisted 60.

St. Paul Friary, 4120 Euclid Ave., 44103. Tel: 216-431-8854; Fax: 216-361-1951.
E-mail: Stpaulshrine@aol.com
Revs. Robert Marva, O.F.M.Cap.; Michael Joyce, O.F.M.Cap.; Andrew Hohman, O.F.M.Cap.; Eric Gauchat, O.F.M.Cap. Priests 4.

St. Stanislaus Friary, 3649 E. 65th St., 44105-1293. Tel: 216-341-9091; Fax: 216-341-2688.
E-mail: ststan@en.com
Web site: ststanislaus.org
Revs. William E. Gulas, O.F.M.; Michael Surufka, O.F.M.; George Jaskulski, O.F.M. (Pulaski, WI), Chap., Marymount Convent, Garfield Heights, 44125. Tel: 516-581-2225. Rev. Lazarus Macior, O.F.M. (Pulaski, WI), Prof., University of Akron, Akron, 44325-3908. Tel: 330-972-7163; Fax: 330-972-8445. The Franciscan Friars, Province of the Assumption of the Blessed Virgin. Priests 4.

AVON. *Congregation of St. Joseph*, 4076 Case Rd., 44011. Tel: 440-934-6270; Fax: 440-934-6270.
E-mail: lato@aol.com
Web site: www.murialdo.org
Revs. Lawrence Tosco, C.S.J.; Leo Dechant, C.S.J.; Libero Ballestrazzi, C.S.J.; Gaetano Menegatto, C.S.J.; Giampietro Gasparin, C.S.J. Priests 5.

[P] CONVENTS AND RESIDENCES FOR SISTERS

CLEVELAND. *Carmel of the Holy Family*, 3176 Fairmount Blvd., 44118-4199. Tel: 216-321-6568. Discalced Carmelite Nuns. Sr. Mary Lavin, O.C.D., Prioress. Professed Nuns 15; Vowed Religious Transfer Sisters in Formation 1.

Marymount Congregational Home. Tel: 216-581-3535; Fax: 216-581-3564.
E-mail: MCH125@aol.com
12215 Granger Rd., Garfield Heights, 44125. Tel: 216-581-3535; Fax: 216-581-3564.
Residence of the Sisters of St. Joseph, Third Order of St. Francis. Contact Persons: Sr. Esther Romalke; Sr. Dominica Fick; Rev. George Jaskulski, O.F.M., Chap. Sisters 65.

Monastery of the Poor Clares. Poor Clare Nuns (Colettine), 3501 Rocky River Dr., 44111-2998. Tel: 216-941-2820. Observing the Primitive Rule of St. Clare (strictly cloistered solemn vows). Perpetual exposition of the Blessed Sacrament. Rev. Eugene Katoski, O.F.M., Chap. Cloistered Nuns 25; Extern Sisters 3.

Motherhouse and Novitiate of the Sisters of the Holy Spirit, 10102 Granger Rd., 44125. Tel: 216-581-2941; Fax: 216-581-4505.
E-mail: JenningHal@aol.com
Sr. Assumpta Zabas, C.S.Sp., Supr. Gen. Professed Sisters 8.

Motherhouse and Novitiate of the Ursuline Sisters, 2600 Lander Rd., 44124. Tel: 440-449-1200; Fax: 440-449-3588.
Web site: www.ursuline.edu/ursulines
Sr. Virginia DeVinne, O.S.U., Gen. Supr. Legal Title: *The Ursuline Academy of Cleveland*. Professed Nuns 256.

Motherhouse of the Sisters of St. Joseph, 3430 Rocky River Dr., 44111. Tel: 216-252-0440; Fax: 216-941-3430.
E-mail: info@sistersofstjoseph.com
Web site: www.sistersofstjoseph.com
Exec. Team: Sr. Mary Brinkman, C.S.J.; Sr. Patricia Kozak, C.S.J.; Sr. Mary Schrader, C.S.J. Sisters 145.

St. Joseph Wellness Center. Tel: 216-251-7062; Fax: 216-251-2886. Sisters 6; Co-members 3.

Seeds of Literacy. Tel: 216-651-4302; Fax: 216-651-4305. Total Staff 2.

Wellspring Bookstore & Gift Shop. Tel: 440-323-4466; Fax: 440-323-1761. Total Staff 2.

St. Joseph Conference & Learning Center. Tel: 216-688-1111; Fax: 216-688-1116. Total Staff 2.

Poor Clares of Perpetual Adoration, 4108 Euclid Ave., 44103. Tel: 216-361-0783; Fax: 216-361-0979. Mother Mary James, P.C.P.A., Supr. Cloistered Sisters 17. Monastery adjoins Conversion of St. Paul Church, where they maintain Perpetual Adoration.

Provincialhouse of Sisters of the Most Holy Trinity, 21281 Chardon Rd., 44117. Tel: 216-481-8232; Fax: 216-481-6577.
E-mail: trinity@acclink.com
Web site: www.srstrinity.org
Sr. Phyllis Ann Lavalle, O.SS.T., Regl. Delegate. Attended from Borromeo Seminary. Sisters 24; Total in Residence 13.

Sisters of St. Joseph of St. Mark. General Motherhouse and Novitiate of Sisters of St. Joseph of St. Mark-Generalate, Diocese of Cleveland. 21800 Chardon Rd., 44117. Tel: 216-531-7426; Fax: 216-531-4033.
E-mail: mountstjoe@aol.com
Mother M. Therese Trunk, Gen. Supr. Sisters 17.

Sisters of the Incarnate Word and Blessed Sacrament, 6618 Pearl Rd., 44130. Tel: 440-886-6440; Fax: 440-842-6391.
E-mail: sctobler@yahoo.com
Sr. Carol Tobler, S.I.W., Congregational Leader. Legal Title: *Motherhouse and Novitiate of the Sisters of the Incarnate Word and Blessed Sacrament*. Final Professed Sisters 37. In res. Rev. Kenneth Katricak, O.S.B., 6634 Pearl Rd., Parma Heights, 44130. Tel: 440-886-6996.

AKRON. *Motherhouse of the Sisters of St. Dominic of the Immaculate Heart of Mary*, Our Lady of the Elms Convent, 1230 W. Market St., 44313-7108. Tel: 330-836-4908; Fax: 330-836-5913.
E-mail: ssd1230@akronop.org
Web site: www.elms.k12.oh.us
Sisters 98.

Provincial Motherhouse and Novitiate of the Daughters of Divine Charity, 39 N. Portage Path, 44303-1183. Tel: 330-867-4960; Fax: 330-867-6334.
E-mail: smpakron@aol.com
Sr. Christine Cochenet, F.D.C., Prov. Supr.; Rev. Thomas F. Sullivan, Chap. Tel: 330-864-6700. Sisters 21.

BEDFORD. *Motherhouse and Novitiate of the Vincentian Sisters of Charity*, Villa San Bernardo, 1160 Broadway, 44146-4523. Tel: 440-232-4755; Fax: 440-232-7832.
E-mail: a.vscoffice@att.net
Sr. Christine Rody, Gen. Supr.; Sr. Regina Kusnir, Formation; Sr. Anita Maroun, Vocation-Contact Person. Sisters 67.

CHARDON. *Provincial House of the Sisters of Notre Dame, Juniorate, Novitiate*, Notre Dame Educational Center, 13000 Auburn Rd., 44024. Tel: 440-286-7101; Fax: 440-286-3377.
E-mail: msvoboda@ndec.org
Web site: www.snd1.org
Rev. Paul J. Sciarrotta, Chap. Sisters 430.

INDEPENDENCE. *Contemplative Sisters of the Good Shepherd*. (Infirmary), 7800 Brookside Rd., 44131. Tel: 216-524-8692; Fax: 216-524-5699. Sisters 24.

Sisters of the Good Shepherd, dba Marycrest of the City of Cleveland, 7800 Brookside Rd., 44131. Tel: 216-524-4578; Fax: 216-524-6669. Sr. Monica Nowak, Exec. Dir., Marycrest Community Services, 1862 Noble Rd., East Cleveland, 44112. Tel: 216-687-0313.

RICHFIELD. *Mount Augustine, Motherhouse of the Sisters of Charity of St. Augustine*, 5232 Broadview Rd., 44286-9608. Tel: 330-659-5100; Fax: 330-659-3899.
E-mail: snh@srsofcharity.org
Web site: www.srsofcharity.org
Sr. Nancy Hendershot, C.S.A., Congregational Leader.

Regina Health Center. Tel: 330-659-4161; Fax: 330-659-5113. Religious Congregations 22; Total Assisted Care 74; Skilled Nursing Beds 81.

Sisters of Charity of St. Augustine Foundation of Cleveland. Tel: 216-241-9300; Fax: 216-241-9345.

Saint Ann Foundation. Tel: 216-241-9300; Fax: 216-241-9345. Finally Professed Sisters 88.

[Q] SECULAR INSTITUTES

CLEVELAND HEIGHTS. *Society of Our Lady of the Way*, c/o Mary Ann Tady, 1064 Oxford Rd., 44121. Tel: 216-381-5502; Fax: 920-468-5280.
E-mail: margaret817@earthlink.net
Web site: www.coffey.com/~bryan/main.html
Secular Institute for Single Women.

[R] HOMES FOR WOMEN

AKRON. *Leonora Hall*, 39 N. Portage Path, 44303. Tel: 330-867-1752; Fax: 330-867-6334, Ext. 330.
E-mail: smpakron@aol.com
For a complete listing, refer to the Special Care Facilities section.

[S] LAY ASSOCIATIONS

CLEVELAND. *Community of Little Brothers and Sisters of the Eucharist, Inc.*, 2186 East 35th St., 44115-3039. Tel: 216-566-0531; Fax: 216-566-9370. Maggie Conrad, Dir.

[T] RETREAT HOUSES

CLEVELAND. *Jesuit Retreat House*, 5629 State Rd., 44134. Tel: 440-884-9300; Fax: 440-885-1055.
E-mail: jrhcleve@worldnet.att.net
Rev. Clem Metzger, S.J., Dir. Spirituality Team: Revs. James Farrell, S.J.; Joseph Scharf, S.J.; Thomas W. Gedeon, S.J.

St. Joseph Christian Life Center, 18485 Lake Shore Blvd., 44119-1299. Tel: 216-531-7370; Fax: 216-531-0629.
E-mail: frontdesk@stjosephchristianlife.com
Web site: stjosephchristianlife.com
Rev. Walter J. Hyclak, Exec. Dir.; Jackie Cherep, Oper. Mgr. & Finance Coord.; Pat Kassay, Program Dir.; Pat Meyer, Devel. Dir.; Carol Jauch, Facility Coord.; Deacon Leo McNulty. Total Staff 32.

AKRON. *Loyola of the Lakes Jesuit Retreat House, Inc.* Tel: 800-827-1416; Fax: 330-896-0858.
E-mail: lotljrh@acorn.net
Web site: community.ohio.com/realcities/lotlretreat
700 Killinger Rd., Clinton, 44216-9628. Tel: 330-896-2315; 800-827-1416; Fax: 330-896-0858. Mrs. Elizabeth R. Flynt, Exec. Dir. In res. Revs. Vincent A. Hagarman, S.J.; Paul D. Panaretos, S.J., Retreat Master.

AVON. *St. Leonard Youth Retreat Center*, 4076 Case Rd., 44011. Tel: 440-934-6735.
E-mail: FrLeoDechant@aol.com
Web site: www.murialdo.it/youthretreat
Rev. Leo Dechant, C.S.J., Dir.; Tammie Frank, Youth Min.

BEDFORD. *Poustinia*, 1160 Broadway, 44146-4523. Tel: 440-232-4755; Fax: 440-232-7832.
E-mail: a.vscoffice@att.net
Vincentian Sisters of Charity.

Tabor Center, 1160 Broadway, 44146-4523. Tel: 440-232-4755; Fax: 440-232-7832.
E-mail: a.vscoffice@att.net
Vincentian Sisters of Charity. Judy Kendrick, Contact Person. Maximum Capacity 5.

[U] SOCIAL SERVICE AGENCIES AND INSTITUTIONS

For information call Catholic Information and Referral Services (CIRS) Tel: 216-696-HELP (4357).

CLEVELAND. *Bishop William M. Cosgrove Family Center*, 1736 Superior Ave., 44114. Tel: 216-781-8262; Fax: 216-566-9161.
E-mail: SFFIELDS@aol.com
Total Assisted 20,000; Total Staff 11.

Catholic Charities Corporation, 1027 Superior Ave., 44114. Tel: 216-696-6525, Ext. 4170; 696-6525, Ext. 5950 (Catholic Charities Appeal), Ext. 4170; Fax: 216-861-9795.
E-mail: JPKlee@ccd.cle-dioc.org
John P. Klee, Pres.

Catholic Charities Facilities Corporation, 1111 Superior Ave., #420, 44114. Tel: 216-696-6525, Ext. 5540; Fax: 216-861-1176.
E-mail: lemurtau@ccd.cle-dioc.org
Lawrence E. Murtaugh, Pres.

Catholic Charities Services Corporation, Eaton Center, 1111 Superior Ave., 44114. Tel: 216-696-6525; Fax: 216-344-9962.
E-mail: txwoll@ccd-cledioc.org
Web site: www.cle-dioc.org
Catholic Charities Services Corporation is part of the health and human services delivery system of the Diocese. Utilizing a holistic approach to healing, the system focuses on four service groups: children and families, persons with disabilities, older adults and persons with emergency and transitional needs. Thomas Woll, Pres.; Michael Haggerty, Vice Pres. & COO.

Catholic Charities Services Corporation, 1111 Superior Ave., 44114. Tel: 216-696-6525; Fax: 216-344-9962.
E-mail: txwoll@ccd.cle-dioc.org

Bishop William M. Cosgrove Family Center, 1736 Superior Ave., 44114. Tel: 216-781-8262; Fax: 216-566-9161. Sharon Fields, Dir.

Catholic Charities Services of Ashland, Medina, and Wayne Counties, 246 Northland Dr., Medina, 44256. Tel: 330-723-9615 (Medina); Fax: 330-764-8795 (Medina).
Tel: 419-289-1903 (Ashland); Fax: 419-281-8342 (Ashland).
Tel: 330-262-7386 (Wayne); Fax: 330-262-2867 (Wayne). Timothy Putka, Dir.

Catholic Charities Services of Cuyahoga County, 7800 Detroit Ave., 44102. Tel: 216-631-3499; Fax: 216-631-3654.
E-mail: towers@mail.cle-dioc.org
Web site: www.cle-dioc.org
Mike Haggerty, Exec. Vice Pres.

Catholic Charities Services of Geauga County, 1077 Mayfield Rd., 44024-9323. Tel: 800-242-9755; Fax: 440-285-4909. Anthony J. Marjenin, Dir.

Catholic Charities Services of Lake County, 8 N. State St., Suite 455, Painesville, 44077-3954. Tel: 440-946-7264; Fax: 440-953-1608. Anthony Marjenin, Dir.

Catholic Charities Services of Lorain County, 628 Poplar St., Elyria, 44035. Tel: 440-366-1106; 877-566-1106, Ext. 440; Fax: 440-366-5645. Barbara Alflen, Dir.

Chemical Dependency Services - Midtown Professional Center, 3135 Euclid Ave., Room 202, 44115-2507. Tel: 216-391-2064; Fax: 216-391-8946.

Employment & Training Services - Midtown Professional Center, 3135 Euclid Ave., Room 203, 44115-2507. Tel: 216-426-9870; Fax: 216-426-9932.

Fatima Family Center, 6600 Lexington Ave., 44103. Tel: 216-391-0505; Fax: 216-391-1118. LaJean Ray, Dir.

Head Start, 1031 Superior Ave., 44114. Tel: 216-696-6525; Fax: 216-696-3631. Constance Walker, Dir.

Hispanic Senior Center, 7800 Detroit Ave., 44102. Tel: 216-631-3599; Fax: 216-631-3654. Teo Feliciano, Program Dir.

Matt Talbot Inn, 2270 Professor Ave., 44113-4489. Tel: 216-781-0288; Fax: 216-781-6270. Terry Morris, Program Dir.

Matt Talbot For Women at St. Vincent Charity Hospital, 2351 E. 22nd St., 44115. Tel: 216-592-2800; Fax: 216-592-2854. Colleen McKenna, Dir.

OLA/St. Joseph Center, 2346 W. 14th St., 44113-3697. Tel: 216-621-3451; Fax: 216-621-6104. Pamela Delly, Prin.

Parmdale, 6753 State Rd., Parma, 44134-4596. Tel: 440-845-7700; Fax: 440-845-5910. Anne Mengerink, Dir.

St. Martin de Porres Family Center, 1264 E. 123rd St., 44108-4042. Tel: 216-268-3909; Fax: 216-268-0207. Marsha Blanks, Dir.

Special Ministry to the Aged, 6804 Lansing Ave., 44105-1521. Tel: 216-441-5402; Fax: 216-441-4510. Sr. Anna Kaszuba, Dir.

Matt Talbot For Women, a St. Vincent Charity Hospital, 2351 E. 22nd St., 44115. Tel: 216-592-2800; Fax: 216-592-2854.

CATHOLIC CHARITIES PARISH SERVICES: Camps:

Camp Corde, 2901 Ridgewood Ave., Parma, 44134. Tel: 440-884-3950; Fax: 440-884-3950, Ext. 51.

Camp Christopher, Ira & Hametown Rd., Bath, 44210. Tel: 800-CYO-CAMP; Fax: 330-762-2001.

Affiliated Corporations within the Secretariat for Catholic Charities Health & Human Services (Under membership structure of Bishop, Secretary for Health & Human Services & Chairperson of Board of Trustees): Catholic Community Care, 7801 Detroit Ave., 44102. Tel: 216-939-7720; Fax: 216-634-7483.
E-mail: amhorne@worldnet.att.net

Catholic Social Services of Summit County, 640 N. Main St., Akron, 44310. Tel: 330-762-7481; Fax: 330-762-7484.

CYO & Community Services of Summit County, 812 Birutha St., Akron, 44307. Tel: 330-762-2961; Fax: 330-762-2001.

Rose-Mary, The Johanna Grasselli Rehabilitation and Education Center, 19350 Euclid Ave., 44117. Tel: 216-481-4823; Fax: 216-481-4158.

St. Augustine Corporation, 7801 Detroit Ave., 44102. Tel: 216-634-7400; Fax: 216-634-7483.

The Society of St. Vincent de Paul (not under membership structure), 1027 Superior Ave., 44114. Tel: 216-696-6525; Fax: 216-589-4772. Total Staff 3; Total Assisted 20,000.

Catholic Charities Services of Ashland, Medina, and Wayne Counties. 246 Northland Dr., Medina, 44256-1598.
E-mail: medina@mailcle-dioc.org
Medina. Tel: 330-723-9615; Fax: 330-764-8795. Ashland. Tel: 419-289-1903; Fax: 419-281-8342. Brunswick-Cleveland. Tel: 330-225-7100. Wadsworth-Akron. Tel: 330-336-6657. Wooster. Tel: 330-262-7836; Fax: 330-262-2867. Timothy J. Putka, M.S., Dir. Provides counseling, casework, and family life education in Ashland, Wayne, and Medina Counties.

Catholic Charities Services of Cuyahoga County, St. Augustine Towers, 7800 Detroit Ave., 44102-2895. Tel: 216-631-3499; Fax: 216-631-3654.
E-mail: towers@mail.cle-dioc.org
Web site: www.cle-dioc.org
Maureen Dee, L.I.S.W., C.C.D.C. III, Dir. Chemical Dependency Svcs.; David J. Mordarski, A.C.S.W., L.I.S.W., Dir. Older Adult Svcs.; Robert Math, L.I.S.W., Dir. Employment & Training Svcs.; Elbert Clark, Jr., L.S.W., Dir. Early Childhood Prog.; Kenneth E. Trivison, M.A., L.P.C.C., Dir. Outpatient Mental Health Svcs. A multi-function social service agency which offers social service programs. Individual, family, and group counseling; marital counseling, psychiatric consultations; and outpatient psychiatric services for children, youth, and adults. Chemical dependency assessments and outpatient counseling for youth and families having alcohol and other drug-related problems. Bilingual services for Hispanic youth and families. Child day care; school for pregnant teens; pregnancy counseling and planning; adoption; older adult programs, senior citizens counseling and respite care; employment services. Midtown Center. Chemical Dependency Svcs. 3135 Euclid Ave., Ste. 202, 44115-2507. Tel: 216-391-2067; Fax: 216-391-8946. Employment & Training Svcs. 3135 Euclid Ave., Ste. 203, 44115-2507. Tel: 216-426-9870; Fax: 216-426-9932. Parmadale, 6753 State Rd., Parma, 44134. Tel: 440-845-7700; Fax: 440-845-5610. Hispanic Services, 2012 W. 25th St., Rm. 517, 44113. Tel: 216-696-2089; Fax: 216-696-2088.

Catholic Charities Services of Geauga County.
E-mail: geauga@mail.cle-dioc.org
10771 Mayfield Rd., Chardon, 44024-9323. Tel: TDD: 440-285-3537; 800-242-9755 (Ohio); Fax: 440-285-4909. Anthony J. Marjenin, M.S.S.A., L.I.S.W., Dir. Outpatient counseling for families and individuals. Substance abuse counseling. Parenting programs. Services for the elderly. Services to strengthen and enrich the valued relationships of families and individuals for effective and healthy living.

Malachi House, Inc., 2810 Clinton Ave., 44113. Tel: 216-621-8831; Fax: 216-621-8841.
E-mail: malachihouse@malachihouse.org
Web site: www.malachihouse.org
Malachi House provides unskilled, family-like care to the dying poor without cost. Serves individuals who need an available caregiver, who have limited or no financial resources and are in need of special home care in the final stages of life. A trained staff and volunteers provide spiritual, emotional and physical support with the assistance of a hospice team. Acceptable only if care is manageable in a home setting. Handicapped access. Total assisted annually 60; Total Staff 18.

St. Malachi Center, Inc., 2461 Superior Viaduct, 44113. Tel: 216-771-3036; Fax: 216-771-3659. Total Assisted 120 per day (Neighborhood Center); 30 per Monday (Health Services); Total Staff 6.

Society of St. Vincent de Paul, Diocesan Central Council, Chancery Bldg., 1027 Superior Ave., 44114. Tel: 216-696-6525, Ext. 3580; Fax: 216-589-4772.
E-mail: lglauter@ccd.dioc-cle.org
Web site: www.sudpcle.org
Rev. Msgr. Casimir S. Ciolek, A.C.S.W., Spiritual Dir.; Frank J. Fearon, Diocesan Pres.; Lawrence Lauter, A.C.S.W., L.I.S.W., M.Div, Exec. Dir.; Rev. James R. Schleicher, Spiritual Dir.

Akron District Council, 4533 Pineridge Dr., Stow, 44224. Tel: 330-929-9230. Leonard Sikora, Pres.

Cleveland District Council, Chancery Building, 1027 Superior Ave., 44114. Tel: 216-696-6525, Ext. 3580; Fax: 216-589-4772. Lawrence Lauter, Exec. Dir.

Lorain District Council, 6587 Lake Ave., Elyria, 44035. Tel: 440-3224-4589. Carl Snezek, Pres.

St. Vincent de Paul Thrift Stores, 875 E. 70th, 44103. Tel: 216-391-9655; Fax: 216-391-8910. 16730 Lorain Ave., 44111. Tel: 216-252-8764. 5700 Broadway Ave., 44127. Tel: 216-341-3445. 700 E. 185th St., 44119. Tel: 216-486-9122.

Recycle For Re-Use, 6984 Machinery Ave., 44103. Tel: 216-391-9655; Fax: 216-881-7448.

AKRON. *Catholic Social Services of Summit County, Inc.*, 640 N. Main St., 44310-3098. Tel: 330-762-7481; Fax: 330-762-7484.
E-mail: csocialser@stratus.net
Patrick A. McGrath, M.S.S.W., Exec. Dir. Service sites throughout Summit County. Total Assisted 17,000; Total Staff 30.

CYO & Community Services, 812 Biruta St., 44307. Tel: 330-762-2961; Fax: 330-762-2001.
E-mail: DFinn@akroncyo.org
Web site: www.akroncyo.org
CYO Adult Day Services:
812 Biruta St., 44307. Tel: 330-762-2000; Fax: 330-762-2001. Donald P. Finn, Exec. Dir. Total Assisted 191; Total Staff 22.
1945 Portage Tr., Cuyahoga Falls, 44223-1742. Tel: 330-923-0641; Fax: 330-923-0662.
Recreation (camping and athletics), programs for youths & persons with disabilities. Total Assisted 22,612; Total Staff 166.

Interval Brotherhood Home Alcohol-Drug Rehabilitation Center, 3445 S. Main St., 44319. Tel: 330-644-4095; Fax: 330-645-2031.
E-mail: sam@ibh.org
Web site: www.ibh.org
Rev. Samuel R. Ciccolini, Dir. Total in residential treatment 385; Total Staff 84.

Leonora Hall. (Refer to Homes for Women).

St. Patrick Manor, Inc. c/o Humility of Mary Housing, Inc., 733 W. Market St., P.O. Box 22250, 44302-0250. Tel: 330-384-1555; Fax: 330-384-2144.
E-mail: dmhmhi@juno.com
Web site: www.humilityofmaryhousing.com
Sr. Denise Maher, H.M., Pres.; Patricia Lindley, Sec.

ELYRIA. *Catholic Charities Services of Lorain County*, 628 Poplar St., 44035. Tel: 440-366-1106; Fax: 440-324-2985. Barbara Alflen, Dir.

Senior Achievement Center, 3114 Pearl Ave., Lorain, 44055. Tel: 440-277-4860; Fax: 440-277-4860. Nancy Carrell, Prog. Admin.

Catholic Charities Family Center, 203 Eighth St., Lorain, 44052. Tel: 440-244-9915; Fax: 440-245-1057. James Gepperth, Prog. Admin. Total Staff 26.

GARFIELD HEIGHTS. *Brendan Manor, Inc.*, 13401 Cranwood Dr., 44105. Tel: 216-475-5230; Fax: 216-475-5852. Diane Kalchert, Admin. Licensed nonprofit, nondenominational shared living home for low to moderate income older adults. Total in Residence 16; Total Staff 7.

NORTHFIELD. *St. Barnabas Villa, Inc.*, 9234 Olde Eight Rd., 44067. Tel: 330-467-3758; 467-4044; Fax: 330-467-4044. A shared living facility for nine people over 60 years of age. Sr. M. Germaine Maximovich, V.S.C., Mgr.; Mrs. Jo Ann Smith, Asst. Mgr. Total in Residence 9; Total Staff 2.

PAINESVILLE. *Catholic Charities Services of Lake County*, 8 N. State St., No. 455, 44077-3954. Tel: 440-352-6191:946-7264; Fax: 440-953-1608. Anthony J. Marjenin, M.S.S.A., L.I.S.W., Dir.

Satellite Offices-Adoption/Foster Care/Maternity Services to Birthparents. 28706 Euclid Ave., Wickliffe, 44092. Tel: 440-943-5552; 800-394-4598; Fax: 440-585-8469.

St. Anthony Center. (Adult Day Care), 28700 Euclid Ave., Wickliffe, 44092. Tel: 440-943-7800; Fax: 440-943-7893.

[V] SHRINES

CLEVELAND. *Our Lady of Lourdes.* Euclid, (U.S. Rtes. 20 & 6). Administered by the Sisters of the Most Holy Trinity. 21281 Chardon Rd., 44117. Tel: 216-481-8232; Fax: 216-481-6577.
E-mail: Trinity@acclink.com
Web site: www.srstrinity.org
Sr. Phyllis Ann Lavalle, O.SS.T., Regnl. Supr. Total in Residence 13.

BEDFORD. *Our Lady of Levocha Shrine.* (Ohio Rte. 14). Administered by the Vincentian Sisters of Charity (V.S.C.). 1160 Broadway, 44146-4523. Tel: 440-232-4755; Fax: 440-232-7832.
E-mail: a.vscoffice@att.net
Sr. Christine Rody, V.S.C., Contact Person.

GARFIELD HEIGHTS. *Our Lady of Czestochowa Shrine.* (Ohio Rte. 17). Administered by the Sisters of St. Joseph Third Order of St. Francis (S.S.J.-T.O.S.F.), 12215 Granger Rd., 44125. Tel: 216-581-3535; Fax: 216-581-3564.
E-mail: MCH125@com
Sr. Dominica, Shrine Contact.

PARMA. *Our Lady, Queen of the Holy Rosary.* (U.S. Rte. 42). Administered by the Sisters of the Incarnate Word and Blessed Sacrament (S.I.W.). 6618 Pearl Rd., 44130. Tel: 440-886-6440; Fax: 440-842-6391.
E-mail: sctabler@yahoo.com

[W] MINISTRY TO THE SPANISH SPEAKING

CLEVELAND. *Office of Hispanic Ministry*, Diocese of Cleveland, 1031 Superior Ave., 44114-2519. Tel: 216-696-6525, Ext. 2530; Fax: 216-781-8243.
E-mail: aalvarado@dioceseofcleveland.org
Web site: mail-now.com/~ohm/
Sr. Alicia Alvarado, O.P., Dir.

Hispanic Parishes: Iglesia La Sagrada Familia, 7719 Detroit Ave., 44102. Tel: 216-631-6817; Fax: 216-631-3305. Rev. David F. Fallon.

Sacred Heart Chapel, 4301 Pearl Ave., Lorain, 44055. Tel: 440-277-7231; 277-7379; Fax: 440-277-7232. Rev. William A. Thaden, Admin.

Parishes with Ministry to Spanish Speaking: St. Bernard, 47 University Ave., Akron, 44308. Tel: 330-253-5161; Fax: 330-253-6949. Rev. Paul E. Schindler.

St. Francis, 7119 Superior Ave., 44103. Tel: 216-361-4133; Fax: 216-361-1673. Rev. Thomas F. Martin; Deacon Frank Lozada.

St. Michael, 3114 Scranton Rd., 44109. Tel: 216-861-6297; Fax: 216-696-9351. Rev. Dennis R. O'Grady.

St. Mary's - Painesville, 242 N. State St., Painesville, 44077. Tel: 440-354-4381; Fax: 440-354-9174. Rev. R. Stephen Vellenga.

[X] NEWMAN CENTERS

CLEVELAND. *Office of Newman Campus Ministry*, 1031 Superior Ave., 44114. Tel: 440-243-4955; Fax: 440-243-4955. Joyce M. Kelleher, Dir.

170 E. Center St., Berea, 44017. Tel: 440-243-4955; Fax: 440-243-4955.
E-mail: mmasterson@dioceseofcleveland.org
Web site: www.nccm.org
Ms. Maureen Masterson, Assoc. Dir. Campus Ministers: Mr. Timothy Barron; Mr. William Flynn; Ms. Emily Holtel-Hoag; Ms. Heather Kinney.

Case-Western Reserve University. Tel: 216-421-1522; Fax: 216-421-2925. Heather Kinney, Campus Min.

Cleveland State University, Hallinan Center, 11303 Euclid Ave., 44106. Tel: 216-421-1522; Fax: 216-421-2925.

University of Akron. (Akron), Newman Center, 44 University Ave., Akron, 44308. Tel: 330-376-3585. Mr. Timothy Barron, Campus Min.

Ashland College, Lower Chapel, 401 College Ave., Ashland, 44842. Tel: 419-994-4396; Fax: 419-289-5209. Rev. Kevin M. Conroy, B.A., M.Div., Campus Min.

Baldwin-Wallace College Newman Center. (Berea), 170 E. Center St., Berea, 44017. Tel: 216-243-4955; Fax: 216-243-0354. Mrs. Emily Holtel, Hoag. Campus Min.

Oberlin College. (Oberlin), Office of Chaplains, 217 Wilder Hall, Oberlin, 44074. Tel: 440-775-8103. Rev. Edward J. Kordas, D.Min.

The College of Wooster. (Wooster), Box C-3135, Wooster, 44691. Tel: 330-263-2096; Fax: 440-243-4955. Total Staff for 6 Newman Centers 6.

[Y] ENDOWMENT TRUSTS

CLEVELAND. *Good Shepherd-Marycrest Endowment Fund.* Tel: 216-524-4578; Fax: 216-524-6669.
E-mail: sgscleveland@buckeyeweb.com
8010 Brookside Dr., Independence, 44131. Tel: 216-524-5280; Fax: 216-524-2127.

St. John Cathedral Endowment Trust, 1007 Superior Ave., 44114. Tel: 216-771-6666; Fax: 216-781-5646. Rev. David C. Weber.

Sisters of St. Joseph Community Support Charitable Trust, 3430 Rocky River Dr., 44111-2997. Tel: 216-252-0440; Fax: 216-941-3430.
E-mail: info@sistersofstjoseph.com
Web site: www.sisterofsjoseph.com
Sr. Jeanne Cmolik, C.S.J., Contact Person.

Villa Angela - St. Joseph High School Education Endowment Foundation, 18491 Lake Shore Blvd., 44119. Tel: 216-481-8414; Fax: 216-486-1035.
E-mail: vikingnasj@aol.com
Web site: www.vasj.com

AKRON. *The Daughters of Divine Charity, St. Mary Province, Charitable Trust*, 39 N. Portage Path, 44303-1183. Tel: 330-867-4960; Fax: 330-867-6334.

Our Lady of the Elms-Sisters of St. Dominic Foundation, 1230 W. Market St., 44313. Tel: 330-836-4908; Fax: 330-836-5913.
E-mail: ssd1230@akronop.org
Web site: www.elms.k12.oh.us

St. Vincent-St. Mary High School Endowment Trust (1983), 15 N. Maple St., 44303. Tel: 330-253-9113; Fax: 330-996-0020.
E-mail: Development@stvm.com
Web site: www.stvm.com
Phyllis Griffith, Dir. Devel.

CHARDON. *The Sisters of Notre Dame Charitable Trust*, 13000 Auburn Rd., 44024. Tel: 440-942-6716; Fax: 440-286-3377.
E-mail: msvoboda@ndec.org
Web site: www.snd1.org
Sr. Melannie Svoboda, S.N.D., Chm.

FAIRLAWN.

St. Hilary Parish Foundation, 2750 W. Market St., 44333. Tel: 330-867-1055; Fax: 330-869-2312. Mr. Edward F. Carter, Pres.

MENTOR. *St. Mary of the Assumption Parish Endowment Trust*, 8560 Mentor Ave., 44060-5853. Tel: 440-255-3404.

PARMA HEIGHTS. *Incarnate Word Endowment Trust*, 6618 Pearl Rd., 44130. Tel: 440-886-6440; Fax: 440-842-6391.
E-mail: sctobler@yahoo.com
Sr. Carol Tobler, S.I.W., Chm.

SEVEN HILLS. *Sisters Servants of Mary Immaculate Endowment Fund in Memory of Sr. Amelia Kuska*, 285 Panorama Dr., 44131. Tel: 216-441-5402; Fax: 216-441-4510. Sr. Anna Kaszuba, S.S.M.I., Pres.

WELLINGTON. *St. Patrick Church Endowment Trust*, 512 N. Main St., 44090. Tel: 440-647-4375; Fax: 440-647-4675.

WOOSTER. *St. Mary of the Immaculate Conception Elementary Day School Endowment Trust*, 527 Beall Ave., P.O. Box 109, 44691. Tel: 330-264-8824; Fax: 330-262-4633.
E-mail: stmwoost@bright.net

[Z] MISCELLANEOUS

CLEVELAND. *Cleveland Slovenian Community Center*, 15519 Holmes Ave., 44110-2497. Tel: 216-761-7740. Rev. John M. Kumse.

COAR Peace Mission, Inc., 4395 Rocky River Dr., 44135-2569. Tel: 216-252-5572; Fax: 216-252-5573.
E-mail: COAR@compuserve.com
Astrid Martinez-Jones, Exec. Dir. COAR Staff: Melissa Acierno, Executive Asst.; Patty Eggers, Bookkeeper.

COAR Children's Village. (Zaragoza, El Salvador, C.A.). Sr. Ermitania Hernandez, C.C.V.I., Dir.; Rev. Kenneth C. Myers, Founder. COAR Children's Village is in Zaragoza, El Salvador, providing a refuge for orphaned, abandoned and street children for over 900 children attend the COAR school. This includes children from the surrounding area. The COAR Clinic serves the medical and dental needs of the resident children from the surrounding communities and assists 80 people on a weekly basis. COAR was begun in August 1980 by Rev. Kenneth C. Myers.

CSA Health Network, 2351 East 22nd St., 44115. Tel: 216-659-5560; Fax: 216-696-2204.
Web site: www.csahealthsystem.org
Sr. Judith Ann Karam, C.S.A., Pres. & CEO. Serves as the general partner to the joint venture ownership of Catholic healthcare providers.

CSA St. John Ministries fka St. John West Shore Hospital, 2351 E. 22nd St., 44115. Tel: 888-223-1816; Fax: 216-696-2204.
Web site: www.csahealthsystem.org
Sr. Judith Ann Karam, C.S.A. Pres. & CEO.

CSA St. Vincent Charity Ministries fka St. Vincent Charity Hospital, 2351 E. 22nd St., 44115. Tel: 888-223-1816; Fax: 216-696-2204.
Web site: www.csahealthsystem.org
Sr. Judith Ann Karam, C.S.A. Pres. & CEO.

The Greater Cleveland/Akron Corporation United for Education, 1404 E. Ninth St., 8th Fl., 44114-1722. Tel: 216-696-6525, Ext. 436; Fax: 216-696-8084. Rev. John J. Wright, Exec. Dir.; Andrej N. Lah, Attorney; Joseph Smith, Treas.

L'Arche, Cleveland, P.O. Box 20450, 44120. Tel: 216-721-2614; Fax: 216-229-2311.
E-mail: rebecca_larchecleveland@juno.com
An ecumenical community providing homes for adults with mental retardation and developmental disabilities. Residents 14; Total Staff 20.

National Catholic Ministry to the Bereaved, Inc., 28700 Euclid Ave., 44092-2527. Tel: 440-943-3480; Fax: 440-943-3500.
E-mail: NCMBereave@aol.com
Web site: www.griefwork.org
Jerry Bowers, N.C.M.B. Admin., Natl. Office; Rev. Terence P. Curley, Pres. N.C.M.B. offers pastoral and spiritual support to the bereaved, caregivers, agencies, dioceses, congregations, and parishes through education and resources toward the development of grief support groups. Total Staff 1; Total Assisted 3,000.

Ninth Street CDC, 1404 E. Ninth St., 8th Fl., 44114-1722. Tel: 216-696-6525; Fax: 216-696-8084. Rev. John J. Wright, Pres.

St. Philip Neri/Divine Word Church in the City Partnership Inc., 8215 St. Clair Ave., 44103. Tel: 216-431-2583; Fax: 216-431-2583. Deacon Carl Carga, Contact Person.

Sisters of Charity Foundation of Cleveland, The Hanna Building, #425, 1422 Euclid Ave., 44115-1901. Tel: 216-241-9300; Fax: 216-241-9345.
E-mail: SOCF@multiverse.com
Sr. Catherine Lee, C.S.J., Exec. Dir.

Sisters of Charity of St. Augustine Health System, 2351 E. 22nd St., 44115. Tel: 216-696-5560; Fax: 216-696-2204.
Web site: www.csahealthsystem.org
Sr. Judith Ann Karam, C.S.A., Pres. & CEO.
Serves as the Member of foundations and health and human service corporations sponsored by the Sisters of Charity of St. Augustine, Richfield, OH. Serves as one of two members of the joint venture corporation operating St. John West Shore Hospital, St. Luke Medical Center and St. Vincent Charity Hospital, Ohio Health Choice, and Professional Medical Equipment.

St. Augustine Services Corporation, 7801 Detroit Ave., 44102. Tel: 216-634-7400; Fax: 216-634-7483.
E-mail: p.gareau@worldnet.att.net
Mr. Patrick Gareau, Pres. Total Staff 15.

AKRON. *First Friday Club of Greater Akron*, 795 Russell Ave., 44307. Tel: 330-762-2961; Fax: 330-535-9040. Frank Comunale, Pres.

H.M. Housing Development Corporation, 733 W. Market St., Ste. 105, 44303. Tel: 330-384-1555; Fax: 330-384-2144.
E-mail: dmhmhi@juno.com
Web site: www.humilityofmaryhousing.com
Sr. Denise Maher, H.M., Pres. & CEO.

H.M. Life Opportunity Services, Box 8174, 44320. Tel: 330-376-5600; Fax: 330-376-2277. Central Office, 733 W. Market St., Suite 101, 44313. Tel: 330-376-5600; Fax: 330-376-2277. Sr. Loretta Rafter, H.M., Exec. Dir.

Humility of Mary Housing, Inc., P.O. Box 22250, 44302-0250. Tel: 330-384-1555; Fax: 330-384-2144.
E-mail: dmhmhi@juno.com
Web site: www.humilityofmaryhousing.com
Sr. Denise Maher, H.M., Pres. & CEO. Affordable housing and housing related services for low and moderate income individuals. Total Assisted 1,800; Total Staff 6.

BEDFORD. *Emmaus Conference Center*, Vincentian Sisters of Broadway, 1160 Broadway, 44146-4523. Tel: 440-232-4755; Fax: 440-232-7832.
E-mail: a.vscoffice@att.net

CHARDON. *Christ Child Society-Geauga Chapter*, P.O. Box 1133, 44024. Cathy Rubal, Pres.

EUCLID. *Faith and Light U.S.A., Inc.*, 26351 Drakefield Ave., 44132. Pearl Cahoon.

St. Robert's Holy Name Society Boosters, 23802 Lakeshore Blvd., 44123. Tel: 216-731-2606; Fax: 216-731-2607. Rev. Dennis McNeil, Pastor.

GARFIELD HEIGHTS. *Jennings Manor Housing Corporation*, 10200 Granger Rd., 44125. Tel: 216-587-0842; Fax: 216-587-0875.
E-mail: jenninghal@aol.com
Martha M. Kutik, Pres.; Allison Salopeck, Admin.; Jane Carbeck, Housing Mgr. 60 unit apartment building - HUD 202 Supportive Housing for Older Adults.

Marymount Health Care Systems. Provides comprehensive health and human services in response to the needs of the local community by owning, leasing, and operating health care facilities and services, including Marymount Place, a 104-unit Senior Living Community for the Well-Elderly/ Assisted Living and Clare Hall, a 28 bed Medicaid Licensed Nursing Home, within the philosophy and objectives of the Sisters of St. Joseph of the Third Order of St. Francis and is the Special Member of Marymount Hospital, Inc. 12200 McCracken Rd., 44125. Tel: 216-581-0500; Fax: 216-587-8212.
E-mail: ttrudell@marymount.org
Web site: www.marymount.org

MHCS Real Estate Holding Company. To assist in the provision of comprehensive health care services by acquiring, holding, owning and leasing real estate (and interests therein) and health care facilities, including but not limited to leasing such real estate and facilities to Marymount Hospital, consistent with the philosophy and objectives of the Roman Catholic religious congregation known as the Sisters of St. Joseph of the Third Order of St. Francis and the values and principles inherent in the medical-moral teachings of the Roman Catholic Church as promulgated by the National Conference of Catholic Bishops and the local Ordinary.Holds the Title to Marymount Hospital as a part of the Marymount Health Care Systems Special Member responsibility. 12300 McCracken Rd., 44125-2975. Tel: 216-587-8080; Fax: 216-587-8212. Mr. Thomas J. Trudell, Pres.

HUDSON.
Laurel Lake Retirement Community, Inc., 200 Laurel Lake Dr., 44236. Tel: 330-656-3651; Fax: 330-650-0576.
E-mail: Kathy_Chadwick@hmis.org
Web site: www.laurellake.com
Paul Younger, Pres. & CEO. Independent Living Residents 336; Assisted Living Residents 26; Skilled Nursing Residents 75; Total Staff 287.

INDEPENDENCE. *UHHS / CSAHS - Cuyahoga, Inc.*, 2 Summit Park Dr., Summit Two Office Building, Ste. 425, 44131. Tel: 216-436-4640; Fax: 216-436-4646. Michael Rutherford, Interim Pres.

LORAIN. *Community Health Partners*, 3700 Kolbe Rd., 44053. Tel: 440-233-1053; Fax: 440-246-5390.
E-mail: karen_yacobucci@hmis.org
Web site: eHealthConnection.com

LOUDONVILLE. *Lay Apostolate for Immigrant Catholic Indians of America, Inc.*, P.O. Box 349, 44842. Tel: 419-994-3983; Fax: 419-994-3982.
E-mail: LAICIA@yahoo.com
Web site: layapostolate.org
Dr. Abraham C. Kuttothara, M.D., Dir.

OBERLIN. *Common Ground Center for Community Renewal*, 14240 Baird Rd., 44074. Tel: 440-965-5551; Fax: 440-965-5570.
E-mail: rbator1625@aol.com
Sr. Rose Bator, H.M., Dir.

PARMA. *Society of St. Joseph the Worker*, 7033 State Rd., 44134-4952. Tel: 440-888-4872; Fax: 440-888-6825.
E-mail: bsjw@msn.com
Web site: www.bsjw.org
Lawrence R. Verbiar, Dir.

PEPPER PIKE. *New Ventures Network*, 2600 Lander Rd., 44124. Tel: 440-442-4160, Ext. 226; Fax: 440-442-4587.
E-mail: SOPHIADC@juno.com
Sr. Donna Capuano, O.S.U.

The O'Neill Brothers Foundation, 3550 Lander Rd. #140, 44124. Tel: 216-464-2121; Fax: 216-464-1517.
E-mail: lstopar@aol.com
Mr. Robert K. Healey, Pres.

Ursuline Sophia Center, 2600 Lander Rd., 44124. Tel: 440-442-4160; Fax: 440-442-4587.
E-mail: SOPHICRT@apk.net
Web site: www.ursuline.edu/ursulines
Sr. Donna Capuano, O.S.U., Dir. Total Staff 15; Total Assisted 4,000.

ROCKY RIVER. *The Center for Learning*, 21590 Center Ridge Rd., 44116. Tel: 440-331-1404; Fax: 440-331-5414.
E-mail: cfl@stratos.net
Web site: www.centerforlearning.org
Sr. Rose Schaffer, H.M., M.A., Pres. & CEO; Sr. Bernadette Vetter, H.M., M.A., Vice Pres.
Educational Publisher of values-based curriculum: Religion for Catholic schools and parishes; English/ Language Arts, Social Studies, and Novel/Drama Curriculum Units for all schools. Owned and operated by the Sisters of the Humility of Mary. Directed by an ecumenical lay board.
Administrative-Editorial Office in Rocky River. Shipping-Business Office, Evergreen Rd., P.O. Box 910, Villa Maria, PA, 16155. Tel: 800-767-9090; 724-964-8083; Fax: 888-767-8080.

Heartbeats, 20015 Detroit Rd., 44116. Tel: 440-356-8601; Fax: 440-356-8078.
E-mail: heartbt@en.com
Web site: www.en.com/users/heartbt
Sr. Margaret Cessna, H.M., Dir., 20015 Detroit Rd., 44116. Tel: 440-356-8601.

WICKLIFFE. *Center for Pastoral Leadership Services, Inc.*, 28700 Euclid Ave., 44092-2585. Tel: 440-943-7600; Fax: 440-943-7577. Mrs. Kathleen Haase-Falbo, Pres.; Mr. Brian F. Houlahan, COO.

RELIGIOUS INSTITUTES OF MEN REPRESENTED IN THE DIOCESE

For further details refer to the corresponding bracketed number in the Religious Institutes of Men or Women section.

[0200]—*Benedictine Monks.* (St. Andrew Abbey).—O.S.B.
[0600]—*Brothers of the Congregation of Holy Cross.* (Midwest Prov.).—C.S.C.
[0470]—*The Capuchin Friars.*—O.F.M.Cap.
[0910]—*Oblates of Mary Immaculate.*—O.M.I.
[0065]—*Congregation of the Holy Ghost and of the Immaculate Heart of Mary.*—C.S.S.P.
[]—*Apostles of Jesus.* (Karen, Kenya).—A.J.
[1150]—*Congregation of St. Joseph.*—C.S.J.
[0220]—*Congregation of the Blessed Sacrament.*—S.S.S.
[0520]—*Franciscan Friars.* (Provs. of Our Lady of Consolation & Assumption).—O.F.M.
[0480]—*Franciscan Friars (Conv.).*—O.F.M.Conv.
[0690]—*Jesuit Fathers and Brothers.* (Maryland Prov.).
[0690]—*Jesuit Fathers and Brothers.* (Detroit Prov.).
[0780]—*Marist Fathers.* (Washington Prov.).—S.M.
[0800]—*Maryknoll.*—M.M.
[0840]—*Missionary Servants of the Most Holy Trinity.*—S.T.
[0970]—*Order of Our Lady of Mercy.*—O.de.M.
[0610]—*Priests of the Congregation of the Holy Cross.* (Indiana Prov.).—C.S.C.
[0760]—*Society of Mary-Marianists.* (Dayton, OH).—S.M.
[1060]—*Society of the Precious Blood.* (Cincinnati Prov.).—C.PP.S.

RELIGIOUS INSTITUTES OF WOMEN REPRESENTED IN THE DIOCESE

[0790]—*Daughters of Divine Charity*— F.D.C.
[2590]— *Sisters of Mercy of the Blessed Sacrament*—H.M.S.S.
[0230]—*Benedictine Sisters of Pontifical Jurisdiction.* (Erie, PA).—O.S.B.
[]—*Byzantine Nuns of St. Clare.*—B.N.S.C.
[1730]—*Congregation of the Sisters of the Third Order of St. Francis.* (Oldenburg).—O.S.F.
[1710]—*Congregation of the Third Order of St. Francis of Mary Immaculate, Joliet, IL.*—O.S.F.
[1830]—*Contemplative Sisters of the Good Shepherd.*—C.G.S.
[0420]—*Discalced Carmelite Nuns.*—O.C.D.
[1070-14]—*Dominican Sisters.*—O.P.
[1070-23]—*Dominican Sisters.*—O.P.
[1070-28]—*Dominican Sisters.*—O.P.
[1170]—*Felician Sisters.*—C.S.S.F.
[1210]—*Franciscan Sisters of Chicago.*—O.S.F.
[2340]—*Little Sisters of the Poor.*—P.S.D.P.
[3760]—*Order of St. Clare-Poor Clare Colettine Nuns.*—P.C.C.
[3130]—*Our Lady of Victory Missionary Sisters.*—O.L.V.M.
[0950]—*Pious Society Daughters of St. Paul.*—F.S.P.
[3210]—*Poor Clares of Perpetual Adoration.*—P.C.P.A.
[3420]—*Religious of the Eucharist.*—R.E.
[1830]—*Religious of the Good Shepherd.*—R.G.S.
[3430]—*Religious Teachers Filippini.*—M.P.F.
[0440]—*Sisters of Charity of Cincinnati, Ohio.*—S.C.
[0580]—*Sisters of Charity of St. Augustine.*—C.S.A.
[0990]—*Sisters of Divine Providence.*—C.D.P.
[2580]—*Sisters of Mercy of the Americas.* (Cincinnati).—R.S.M.
[2990]—*Sisters of Notre Dame.*—S.N.D.
[3830-08]—*Sisters of St. Joseph.*—C.S.J.
[3910]—*Sisters of St. Joseph of St. Mark.*—S.J.S.M.
[3930]—*Sisters of St. Joseph of the Third Order of St. Francis.*—S.S.J.-T.O.S.F.
[1970]—*Sisters of the Holy Family of Nazareth.*—C.S.F.N.
[2030]—*Sisters of the Holy Spirit.*—C.S.Sp.
[2110]—*Sisters of the Humility of Mary.*—H.M.
[2210]—*Sisters of the Incarnate Word and Blessed Sacrament.*—S.I.W.
[2350]—*Sisters of the Living Word.*—S.L.W.
[2060]—*Sisters of the Most Holy Trinity.*—O.SS.T.
[3730]—*Sisters of the Order of St. Basil the Great.*—O.S.B.M.
[3260]—*Sisters of the Precious Blood.* (Dayton, Ohio).—C.PP.S.
[1710]—*Sisters of the Third Franciscan Order.*—O.S.F.
[3620]—*Sisters, Servants of Mary Immaculate.*—S.S.M.I.
[2150]—*Sisters, Servants of the Immaculate Heart of Mary.*—I.H.M.
[4120-04]—*Ursuline Nuns of the Congregation of Paris.*—O.S.U.
[4120-07]—*Ursuline Nuns of the Congregation of Paris.*—O.S.U. []—Sisters of Divine Providence. Korea.
[4170]—*Vincentian Sisters of Charity.* (Bedford, OH).—V.S.C.

DIOCESAN CEMETERIES

CLEVELAND. *Assumption of Mary*, 14900 Brookpark Rd., 44135.
Calvary, 10000 Miles Ave., P.O. Box 605310, 44105.
St. John, 7000 Woodland Ave., 44104.
St. Joseph, 7916 Woodland Ave, 44104.
St. Mary, 2677 W. 41st St., 44113.

AKRON. *Holy Cross*, 100 E. Waterloo Rd., 44319.

AVON. *Holy Trinity*, 33601 Detroit Rd., P.O. Box 326, 44011.
Holy Trinity, Jaycox Rd.
St. Joseph, 32787 Detroit Rd., P.O. Box 326, 44011.

BEREA. *St. Mary of the Falls*, 1260 Bagley Rd., 44017.

BROOK PARK. *Holy Cross*, 14609 Brookpark Rd., 44142.

CHARDON. *All Souls*, 10366 Chardon Rd., P.O. Box 11, 44024.

CUYAHOGA HEIGHTS. *St. Mary*, 4720 E. 71st St., 44125.

ELYRIA. *St. Mary*, 7284 Lake Ave., 44035.

LORAIN. *Calvary*, 555 N. Ridge Rd. W., 44053.

NORTHFIELD. *All Saints*, 480 Highland Rd., 44067.

VALLEY CITY. *Resurrection*, 6303 Center Rd., 44280.

NECROLOGY

† Balogh, Donald J., Parma, OH St. Francis de Sales. —Died Nov. 19, 2000.
† Cooper, R. John, (Released from Diocesan Assignment). —Died Dec. 28, 1999.
† Kraker, John J., Euclid, OH St. Felicitas. —Died Feb. 20, 2000.
† Lyons, William P., Akron, OH St. Matthew. —Died Nov. 10, 2000.
† Moriarty, Joseph T., Parma Heights, OH Incarnate Word Academy. —Died July 27, 2000.
† Mosovsky, James J., Avon Lake, OH Holy Spirit. —Died Jan. 25, 2000.
† O'Boyle, Andrew F., Newbury, OH St. Helen. —Died Dec. 31, 1999.
† Teknipp, Robert J., Green, OH Queen of Heaven. —Died Feb. 28, 2000.
† Towell, Stephen A., South Euclid, OH St. Gregory the Great. —Died June 9, 2000.
† Walker, John H., Sheffield, OH St. Teresa of Avila. —Died June 11, 2000.
† Yavorsky, James A., Barberton, OH SS. Cyril and Methodius. —Died May 31, 2000.

Diocese of Colorado Springs

Most Reverend

RICHARD C. HANIFEN, D.D., J.C.L.

Bishop of Colorado Springs; ordained June 6, 1959; appointed Titular Bishop of Abercorn and Auxiliary of Denver July 6, 1974; consecrated September 20, 1974; appointed First Bishop of Colorado Springs November 10, 1983; installed January 30, 1984. *Office: 29 West Kiowa, Colorado Springs, CO, 80903-1498.* Tel.: 719-636-2345; Fax: 719-636-1216.

Legal Title: Diocese of Colorado Springs.

ESTABLISHED AND CREATED A DIOCESE JANUARY 30, 1984.

Square Miles Approximately 15,500.

Comprising the Counties of Chaffee, Cheyenne, Douglas, Elbert, El Paso, Kit Carson, Lake, Lincoln, Park and Teller.

For legal title of parishes and diocesan institutions, consult the Diocesan Offices.

Diocesan Offices: 29 West Kiowa, Colorado Springs, CO, 80903-1498. Tel.: 719-636-2345; Fax: 719-636-1216.

STATISTICAL OVERVIEW

Personnel	
Bishop	1
Priests: Diocesan Active in Diocese	23
Priests: Active Outside Diocese	2
Priests: Retired, Sick or Absent	11
Number of Diocesan Priests	36
Religious Priests in Diocese	22
Extern Priests in Diocese	6
Ordinations:	
Permanent Deacons	3
Permanent Deacons in Diocese	25
Total Brothers	2
Total Sisters	127
Parishes	
Parishes	32
With Resident Pastor:	
Resident Diocesan Priests	15
Resident Religious Priests	10
Without Resident Pastor:	
Administered by Priests	3
Administered by Deacons	1
Administered by Lay People	2
Completely Vacant	1
Missions	9
New Parishes Created	1
Professional Ministry Personnel:	
Sisters	2
Lay Ministers	69
Welfare	
Catholic Hospitals	2
Total Assisted	265,232
Health Care Centers	2
Total Assisted	109
Homes for the Aged	2
Total Assisted	103
Educational	
Diocesan Students in Other Seminaries	4
Total Seminarians	4
High Schools, Diocesan and Parish	1
Total Students	374
Elementary Schools, Diocesan and Parish	5
Total Students	1,459
Catechesis/Religious Education:	
High School Students	2,780
Elementary Students	7,252
Total Students Under Catholic Instruction	11,869
Teachers in the Diocese:	
Sisters	1
Lay Teachers	114
Vital Statistics	
Receptions into the Church:	
Infant Baptism Totals	1,543
Adult Baptism Totals	184
Received into Full Communion	207
First Communions	1,504
Confirmations	943
Marriages:	
Catholic	223
Interfaith	124
Total Marriages	347
Deaths	390
Total Catholic Population	86,951
Total Population	749,355

Diocesan Offices—29 W. Kiowa St., Colorado Springs, 80903-1498. Tel: 719-636-2345; Fax: 719-636-1216. Office Hours: Mon.-Fri. 8:30-4:30.

Vicar General and Moderator of the Curia—Very Rev. DONALD F. DUNN.

Executive Assistant to the Bishop—Sr. PEG MALONEY, R.S.M.

Director of Planning & Accountability—EDWARD GAFFNEY.

Chancellor—Rev. GEORGE V. FAGAN, J.C.L., *29 W. Kiowa St., Colorado Springs, 80903.* Tel: 719-636-2345.

Diocesan Consultors—Very Rev. DONALD F. DUNN, V.G.; Rev. ERNEST W. BOND; Rt. Rev. WARREN S. HEIDGEN, O.S.B.; Revs. JAY JUNG, C.M.; PAUL WICKER; JOHN AUER; EDWARD GAFFNEY.

Finance Officer—ROBERT G. DOERFLER, JR.

Archivist—Sr. JOSEPH MARIE JACOBSEN, O.S.B.

Judicial Vicar—Rev. GEORGE V. FAGAN, J.C.L.

Associate Judges—Revs. JAMES I. DONLON, J.C.D.; JOSEPH KOURY, S.J., J.C.D.

Defender of the Bond—Rev. MARK PLEWKA, J.C.L.

Procurator-Advocates—Revs. KARL USELDINGER; ERNEST W. BOND; Sr. JOSEPH MARIE JACOBSEN, O.S.B.; Deacons GEORGE D. LINEHAN, JR.; JOHN H. KUNSEMILLER.

Ecclesiastical Notary—SHIRLEY WELLS.

Catholic Charities of Colorado Springs, Inc.—KRZYS MYSZKOWSKI, Exec. Dir.

Office of Pastoral Administration—ROBERT G. DOERFLER, JR., Dir.

Human Resource Manager—TERRI SORTOR.

Office of Stewardship and Development—BILL LYONS, Dir.

Office of Total Catholic Education—Sr. EVELINA BELFIORE, O.P., Dir.; Sr. ANN GOGGIN, Dir. Aquinas Ministry; DONNA GAFFNEY, Resource Ctr. Coord.

Propagation of the Faith—Very Rev. DONALD F. DUNN, Diocesan Dir.

Vocations Office—Very Rev. DONALD DUNN, V.G., Dir. Seminarians & Vocations.

Regionalization—Metro-Central Region (Colorado Springs): Very Rev. DONALD F. DUNN, Vicar; Metro-North Region (Colorado Springs): Rev. PAUL WICKER, Vicar; Metro-South Region (Colorado Springs): Rev. JOHN AUER, Vicar; Eastern Region: Rev. JAY JUNG, C.M., Vicar; Northern Region: Rev. ERNEST W. BOND, Vicar; Western Region: Rt. Rev. WARREN HEIDGEN, O.S.B., Vicar.

CLERGY, PARISHES, MISSIONS AND PAROCHIAL SCHOOLS

CITY OF COLORADO SPRINGS

(County of El Paso)

1—ST. MARY'S CATHEDRAL (1887), Very Revs. Donald F. Dunn, V.G., Rector; Theodore A. Haas, Rector Emeritus; Rev. Sylvian Cibangu (Africa).

Office: 22 W. Kiowa St., 80903. Tel: 719-473-4633; Fax: 719-473-5248.

Catechesis/Religious Programs—Kerry Susser, D.R.E.

Students 225.

Mission—Wheat Ridge, Jefferson Co., Immaculate Conception Community, P.O. Box 1063, Colorado Springs, CO 80034-1063. Chaplains: Revs. Jose Salgado, F.S.S.P.; Thomas Fritschen, F.S.S.P.

2—CORPUS CHRISTI (1916), Rev. Stephen J. Parlet; Deacon Benedict Cruise.

Res., 2318 N. Cascade Ave., 80907. Tel: 719-633-1457; Fax: 719-473-7567.

School—2410 N. Cascade Ave., 80907. Tel: 719-632-5092; Fax: 719-578-9124. Rosanne Malek, Prin.

Lay Teachers 35; Students 445.

Catechesis/Religious Programs—Tel: 719-473-8363; Fax: 719-473-7567. Laurie Steffes, D.R.E. Students 445.

3—DIVINE REDEEMER (1950), Revs. William Jarema, S.M.M.; Dan Ayers; Deacon David Van Matre.

Res., 1520 E. Yampa St., 80909. Tel: 719-633-5559; Fax: 719-575-9180. [JC]

School—901 N. Logan, 80909. Tel: 719-471-7771; Fax: 719-575-9180. Sarah Miller, Prin.

Lay Teachers 24; Students 467.

Catechesis/Religious Programs—Bernadette Tittle, D.R.E.

Students 160.

4—HOLY APOSTLES (1973), Revs. Paul F. Wicker; Brad Noonan; Deacons Michael Leverington; Charles Matzker; Raymond Milberg.

Res., 4925 N. Carefree Cir., 80917. Tel: 719-597-4249; Fax: 719-591-1816.

Preschool—4925 N. Carefree, 80917. Tel: 719-591-1566; Fax: 719-591-1816. Mary Parsons, Dir.

Lay Teachers 11; Students 145.

Catechesis/Religious Programs—Tel: 719-597-4249. Mary Margaret Melanson, D.R.E.

Students 673.

5—HOLY TRINITY (1968), CoCo Soper, Parish Dir.

Office: 3122 Poinsettia Dr., 80907. Tel: 719-633-2132; Fax: 719-633-0975.

School—3115 Larkspur Dr., 80907. John McGee, Prin.; Norm Hale, Asst. Prin.

Lay Teachers 13; Students 209.

Catechesis/Religious Programs—D.R.E: Mary Ellen White; Andrea Simpleman.

Students 200.

6—OUR LADY OF GUADALUPE (1948) (Hispanic), Rev. Robert Sullivan, S.J.

Res., 2715 E. Pikes Peak, 80909. Tel: 719-633-7204; Fax: 719-630-3184.

Catechesis/Religious Programs—Tel: 719-527-5221; Fax: 719-630-3184.

Students 420.

7—OUR LADY OF THE PINES-BLACK FOREST (1965), Rev. Gerard J. Borer, S.J.; Deacons Gene Eastham; Lynn Sherman.

Res., 11020 Teachout Rd., 80908. Tel: 719-495-2351; Fax: 719-495-9062.

Catechesis/Religious Programs—Vickie Welsh, D.R.E.

Students 247.

8—SACRED HEART (1891), Revs. Duane Balcerski, C.S.C.; Donald Dilg, C.S.C., Admin.

Office: 2021 W. Pikes Peak Ave., 80904. Tel: 719-633-8711; Fax: 719-633-1859.

Catechesis/Religious Programs—D.R.E.: Kathleen Moriarty; Tena Jelinek.

Students 280.

Missions—Manitou Springs, El Paso Co., Our Lady of Perpetual Help, 218 Ruxton Ave., Manitou Springs, 80829.; Cascade, El Paso Co., Holy Rosary, 4435 Holiday Tr., Cascade, 80809.

9—ST. ANDREW KIM QUASI PARISH (1981) (Korean), Rev. Berchmans Yong-Woo Lee, S.J. (Korea).

Office: 2910 N. Powers Blvd. PMB 159, 80922. Tel: 719-638-0100; 638-0105 (Rectory); Fax: 719-638-0101.

10—ST. FRANCIS OF ASSISI (1981), Dr. Marie Gatza, Parish Dir.; Deacon Michael Ciletti.

Office: 2650 Parish View, 80919. Tel: 719-599-5031; Fax: 719-599-3360.

Catechesis/Religious Programs—Terri Kowalczyk, D.R.E.

Students 565.

11—ST. GABRIEL THE ARCHANGEL (1998), Rev. August Stewart, Admin.; Deacon Robert Hunter.

Office: 3470 Briargate Blvd., 80920. Tel: 719-528-8407; Fax: 719-598-1696.

Catechesis/Religious Programs—Students 332.

12—ST. JOSEPH'S (Southgate) (1968), Rev. Khanh San Hoang; Deacon Albert E. Kimminau; Donald Broeker, Admin.; Randall Brungardt, Pastoral Assoc.

Res., 1830 S. Corona Ave., 80906. Tel: 719-632-9903; Fax: 719-632-9170.

Catechesis/Religious Programs—Tel: 719-635-3166.

Students 352.

13—ST. PATRICK'S (1981), Rev. Donald Brownstein; Deacons Chuck Specht; Richard Brown.

Office: 6455 Brookpark Dr., 80918. Tel: 719-598-3595; Fax: 719-599-5741.

Res., 6602 Snowbird Dr., 80918.

Catechesis/Religious Programs—Angelita M. Dykes, D.R.E.

Students 605.

14—SAINT PAUL (1925), Rev. John Auer; Deacons Patrick Bidon; Richard Bowles.

Office: 9 El Pomar Rd., 80906. Tel: 719-471-9700; Fax: 719-471-3009.

School—Pauline Memorial Catholic School, Tel: 719-632-1846; Fax: 719-632-0495. Sr. Marilyn Beyers, Prin.

Lay Teachers 15; Students 216.

Catechesis/Religious Programs—Students 270.

15—THE VIETNAMESE HOLY MARTYRS QUASI-PARISH (1993) (Vietnamese), Rev. Matthew Minh Thanh Tran.

Res. & Mailing Address: 2902 Airport Rd. #214, 80910. Tel: 719-635-6892. [CEM]

Parish Center—29 W. Kiowa (lower level), 80903. Tel: 719-633-2274.

OUTSIDE THE CITY OF COLORADO SPRINGS

Bailey, Park Co., St. Mary of the Rockies (1990), Rev. Ernest W. Bond.

Res., P.O. Box 319, 80421-8319. Tel: 303-838-2375; Fax: 303-816-2399.

Buena Vista, Chaffee Co., St. Rose of Lima (1880), Rt. Rev. Warren J. Heidgen, O.S.B.; Deacon Richard Willburn.

Res., 114 S. Gunnison, P.O. Box 458, 81211. Tel: 719-395-8424; Fax: 719-395-8424.

Catechesis/Religious Programs—Students 118.

Mission—Fairplay, Park Co., St. Joseph. (Send all correspondence to Buena Vista address.) 5th & Castello, Fairplay, 80440. Tel: 719-395-8424.

Burlington, Kit Carson Co., St. Catherine of Siena (1916), Rev. R. William Rhinehart, C.M.

Res., P.O. Box 57, Stratton, 80836. Tel: 719-348-5336; Fax: 719-348-5336.

Church—P.O. Box 38, 80836. Tel: 719-346-7156.

Catechesis/Religious Programs—Students 90.

Calhan, El Paso Co., St. Michael's (1920). Unassigned.

Res., Box 199, 80808. Tel: 719-347-2290; Fax: 719-347-2848.

Catechesis/Religious Programs—Students 50.

Castle Rock, Douglas Co., St. Francis of Assisi (1888), Rev. Herbert Hayek, O.P., Admin.; Deacon John Kunsemiller.

Res., 2746 E Hwy. 86, 80104. Tel: 303-688-3025; Fax: 303-688-4016.

Catechesis/Religious Programs—Tel: 303-688-9522. Lynne K. Lane, D.R.E.

Students 700.

Cheyenne Wells, Cheyenne Co., Sacred Heart (1918), Rev. Thomas Kloppenborg, C.M.

Res., P.O. Box 819, 80810. Tel: 719-767-5272.

Mission—Kit Carson, Cheyenne Co., St. Augustine, P.O. Box 82, Kit Carson, 80825. Tel: 719-962-3552.

Catechesis/Religious Programs—D.R.E.: Dianne Smith; Sharon Baker; Eleanor Dechant.

Students 76.

Fountain, El Paso Co., St. Joseph (1970), Deacon Roger K. Eberwein, Parish Dir.

101 N. Main St., P.O. Box 277, 80817. Tel: 719-382-7086.

Catechesis/Religious Programs—Students 67.

Highlands Ranch, Douglas Co., Pax Christi Catholic Church (1988), Rev. Kenneth Przybyla.

Office: 5761 McArthur Ranch Rd., Littleton, 80124. Tel: 303-799-1036; Fax: 303-799-1072.

Catechesis/Religious Programs—Debbie Vasicek, D.R.E.

Students 692.

St. Mark, Rev. Lawrence T. Solan.

c/o 9961 S. Silver Maple Rd., 80129. Tel: 720-348-9700; Fax: 720-344-6847.

Leadville, Lake Co., Catholic Community of Leadville, Annunciation (1879) & St. Joseph (1899), Rev. Thomas M. Killeen, O.M.I., Admin.

Res., 609 Poplar St., 80461. Tel: 719-486-1382; Fax: 719-486-3930. [CEM][JC]

Catechesis/Religious Programs—Students 112.

Limon, Lincoln Co., Our Lady of Victory(1925), Rev. Jay Jung, C.M.

Res., 489 H Ave., P.O. Box 790, 80828. Tel: 719-775-2118; Fax: 719-775-9230.

Catechesis/Religious Programs—Limon & Missions.

Students 103.

Missions—Hugo, Lincoln Co., St. Anthony of Padua. (Send all correspondence to Limon address.) 133 Fifth St., P.O. Box 275, Hugo, 80821. Tel: 719-743-2373; Flagler, Kit Carson Co., St. Mary. (Send all correspondence to Limon address.) Flagler, 80815. [CEM]

Monument, El Paso Co., St. Peter (1911), Rev. Robert E. Jaeger.

Res., 55 N. Jefferson, Box 827, 80132. Tel: 719-481-2554; Fax: 719-481-9606.

Catechesis/Religious Programs—Tel: 719-481-3511. Kathy Campbell, D.R.E.

Students 725.

Parker, Douglas Co., Ave Maria (1983), Revs. Dennis E. Dwyer; Khanh Pham Nguyen; Deacons George D. Linehan, Jr.; Robert Huber.

Res., 9056 E. Parker Rd., 80138-7209. Tel: 303-841-3750; Fax: 303-841-2412.

School—(2000). James F. Profirio, Prin.

Lay Teachers 6; Students 140.

Catechesis/Religious Programs—Lynne K. Lane, D.R.E.

Students 1,350.

Mission—Elizabeth, Elbert Co., Our Lady of the Visitation, 34201 County Rd. 33, P.O. Box 1689, Elizabeth, 80107. Tel: 303-646-4964; Fax: 303-646-4964.

Salida, Chaffee Co., St. Joseph (1907), Rev. Jim Williams. In res., Rev. Anthony C. Uhl, Chap. Colorado Dept. of Corrections.

Res., P.O. Box 847, 81201. Tel: 719-539-6419; Fax: 719-539-7127.

Catechesis/Religious Programs—Students 145.

Security, El Paso Co., Holy Family (1957), Rev. Lawrence W. Carmody.

Res., 331 Main St., 80911. Tel: 719-392-7653; Fax: 719-392-1651.

Catechesis/Religious Programs—Cathy Jane King, D.R.E.

Students 583.

Stratton, Kit Carson Co., St. Charles Borromeo (1910), Rev. R. William Rhinehart, C.M.

Res., P.O. Box 57, 80836. Tel: 719-348-5336; Fax: 719-348-5336.

Catechesis/Religious Programs—Students 88.

Woodland Park, Teller Co., Our Lady of the Woods (1954). Unassigned.

Res., P.O. Box 416, 80866. Tel: 719-687-9345; Fax: 719-687-0893.

Catechesis/Religious Programs—Students 181.

Missions—Cripple Creek, Teller Co., St. Peter's. (Send all correspondence to Woodland Park address.); Victor, Teller Co., St. Victor's. (Send all correspondence to Woodland Park address.).

On Duty Outside Diocese:

Reverend Fathers—

Grabrian, Dennis, P.O. Box 347, Safford, AZ 85546

Useldinger, Karl, Divine Word College, 1025 Michigan Ave., N.E., Washington, DC 20017

Retired:

Reverend Fathers—

Bruggeman, Gerald H., Chap., Penrose Hospital, 2215 N. Cascade Ave., Colorado Springs, CO 80907

Dresen, Arthur G., 4559 Sunnyhill Dr., Colorado Springs, CO 80916

Halloran, James, Castle West Apartments, 3770 E. Uintah A23, Colorado Springs, CO 80909

Halloran, Joseph H., Fountain Terrace Apartments, 3211 E. Fountains Blvd., #103, Colorado Springs, CO 80910

Krenzke, John, c/o Christ the King, 845 Fairfax St., Denver, CO 80220

Leonard, Edward, 15 Hewlett Ave., New Castle, DE 19720

McHugh, Owen, 7161 White Buffalo Rd., Colorado Springs, CO 80919

Myers, Rawley, St. Mary's Cathedral, 22 W. Kiowa, Colorado Springs, CO 80903

Slattery, John

Vollmer, William C., 35 Tilly Ln., Castle Rock, CO 80104

Permanent Deacons:

Bidon, Patrick, Dir., Deacon Personnel, St. Paul's, Colorado Springs

Bowles, Richard, St. Paul & Fort Carson, Colorado Springs

Breaux, Allen, (Retired)

Brown, Richard, St. Patrick, Colorado Springs

Ciletti, Michael, Service to mentally and physically challenged communities, St. Francis of Assisi, Colorado Springs

Cruise, Ben, (On Sabbatical)

Eastham, Eugene S., Our Lady of the Pines, Colorado Springs

Eberwein, Roger, Parish Dir., St. Joseph, Fountain

Huber, Robert A., Douglas/Elbert Counties Prison Ministry; Northern Region Ministry; Ave Maria, Parker

Hunter, Robert, St. Gabriel the Archangel, Colorado Springs

Kimminau, Albert E., St. Joseph's, Southgate, Colorado Springs; Holy Family, Security

Kunsemiller, John H., St. Francis of Assisi, Castle Rock

Leverington, Michael, Holy Apostles, Colorado Springs

Linehan, George D., Jr., Ave Maria, Parker

Matzker, Charles, Holy Apostles, Colorado Springs and Catholic Charismatic Renewal Services

McLean, Arthur J., (Retired)

Milberg, Raymond, Holy Apostles

Moss, Charles J., Catholic Community of Leadville, Leadville

Parrish, Thomas E., Jail Ministry

Romero, Ernest, Our Lady of Guadalupe, Colorado Springs

Sherman, Lynn, Our Lady of the Pines, Colorado Springs

Sherpa, Lee, (Retired)

Specht, Charles W., Dir., Deacon Formation, St. Patrick, Colorado Springs

Van Matre, Dave, Divine Redeemer, Colorado Springs

Willburn, Richard, St. Rose of Lima, Buena Vista

INSTITUTIONS LOCATED IN THE DIOCESE

[A] HIGH SCHOOLS

COLORADO SPRINGS.
St. Mary's High School, 2501 E. Yampa, 80909. Tel: 719-635-7540.
E-mail: stmarys@stmarys-hs.com
Web site: www.stmarys-hs.com
Ms. Karen Levi, Contact Person; Patty Beckert, Prin. Students 381.

[B] EDUCATIONAL INSTITUTIONS

COLORADO SPRINGS.
The Center at Benet Hill Monastery, 2577 N. Chelton Rd., 80909. Tel: 719-473-6184.
E-mail: benet@clsp.uswest.net
Web site: www.geocities.com/Wellesley/2815
Sr. Diane Liston, O.S.B., Contact Person. Sisters 2; Lay Staff 4.

[C] GENERAL HOSPITALS

COLORADO SPRINGS. *Penrose-St. Francis Health Services*, 2215 N. Cascade Ave., P.O. Box 7021, 80907. Tel: 719-776-5000; Fax: 719-776-2770.
E-mail: LucilleKrippel@centura.org
Web site: www.centura.org
For a complete listing, refer to the Hospitals section.
Penrose-St. Francis Healthcare Foundation, 961 E. Colorado at Centerpoint, 80903. Tel: 719-634-2046; Fax: 719-630-0832.
Web site: www.JerryBogg@Centura.com
For a complete listing, refer to the Hospitals section.

[D] NURSING HOMES

COLORADO SPRINGS. *St. Francis Nursing Center*, 7550 Assisi Heights, 80919. Tel: 719-598-1336; Fax: 719-598-6472
For a complete listing, refer to the Special Care Facilities section.

[E] SPECIAL CARE FACILITIES

COLORADO SPRINGS. *Centura Health-Namaste Alzheimer Center*, 2 Penrose Blvd., 80906. Tel: 719-776-8500; Fax: 719-520-9709
For a complete listing, refer to the Special Care Facilities section.
The Medalion (East), 1719 E. Bijou St., 80909. Tel: 719-471-4800; Fax: 719-471-4807
For a complete listing, refer to the Special Care Facilities section.
The Medalion (West), 417 E. Kiowa St., 80903. Tel: 719-471-2578; Fax: 719-471-4807
For a complete listing, refer to the Special Care Facilities section.

[F] RESIDENCES FOR MEN RELIGIOUS

CASCADE. *Holy Cross Novitiate*, 7872 W. Hwy. 24, Box 749, 80809. Tel: 719-684-9277; Fax: 719-684-2485.
E-mail: dlguffey@aol.com
Congregation of Holy Cross. Rev. David L. Guffey, Dir. Novices & Supr. Staff: Rev. Jeffrey A. Cooper, C.S.C.; Bro. Thomas Moser, C.S.C., Asst. Supr. In res. Revs. Wilred A. Menard, C.S.C.; Thomas A. Stella, C.S.C. Priests 4; Brothers 1; Novices 15.

SEDALIA. *Sacred Heart Jesuit Community*, Box 185, 80135-0185. Tel: 303-688-5198; Fax: 303-688-9633.
E-mail: shjesrh@aol.com
Web site: www.gabrielmedia.org/shjrh
Revs. Louis J. McCabe, S.J., Supr.; Vincent E. Hovley, S.J.; William W. Williams, S.J.; Stephen E. Baird, S.J.; E. Eugene Arthur, S.J.; Bro. Richard P. May, S.J.

[G] RESIDENCES FOR WOMEN RELIGIOUS

COLORADO SPRINGS.
Benet Hill Monastery, 2555 N. Chelton Rd., 80909. Tel: 719-633-0655.
E-mail: benet@clsp.uswest.net
Web site: www.geocities.com/wellesley/2815
Motherhouse of the Sisters of St. Benedict (1963). Sr. Rose Ann Barmann, O.S.B., Prioress; Sr. Diane Liston, O.S.B., Community Archivist.
Properties owned: The Center at Benet Hill Monastery and Benet Pines. Professed Sisters 42; Temporary Professed 2; Novices 1.
Mount St. Francis, 7665 Assisi Hts., 80919-3836. Tel: 719-598-5486; Fax: 719-598-1518.
Web site: www.stfrancis.org
Provincial and Formation House. Sisters of St. Francis of Perpetual Adoration, Province of St. Joseph (The Sisters of St. Francis of Colorado Springs). Sr. Clarice Gentrup, O.S.F., Prov.; Rev. George V. Fagan, Jr., Chap. Professed Sisters 103.
Spirit of Life Monastery, 2430 N. Murray Blvd., 80915. Tel: 719-550-3716. Sr. Katherine Wawersich, O.S.B., Prioress.

[H] RETREAT CENTERS

COLORADO SPRINGS.
Benet Pines, 15780 Hwy. 83, 80921. Tel: 719-495-2574. Sr. Marian Belotti, O.S.B., Dir.; Sr. Jan Ginzkey, O.S.B. Total in Residence 2; Total Staff 3.
Franciscan Retreat Center at Mount St. Francis, 7740 Deer Hill Grove, 80919-3836. Tel: 719-598-5486; Fax: 719-260-8044.
E-mail: srchris@franciscanretreatcenter.org
Web site: www.franciscanretreatcenter.org
Sr. Christine Hayes, O.S.F., Dir. Total Guests 13,000; Total Staff 7.

SEDALIA. *Sacred Heart Jesuit Retreat House*, Box 185, 80135-0185. Tel: 303-688-4198; Fax: 303-688-9633.
E-mail: shjesrh@aol.com
Web site: www.gabrielmedia.org/shjrh
Revs. Louis J. McCabe, S.J.; Stephen E. Baird, S.J.; E. Eugene Arthur, S.J.; Vincent E. Hovley, S.J.; Bro. Richard P. May, S.J.; Sr. Eleanor Sheehan, C.S.J.; Rev. William W. Williams, S.J. Total in Residence 5.

[I] MISCELLANEOUS LISTINGS

COLORADO SPRINGS. *Catholic Charismatic Renewal Services c/o Holy Apostles Church.* (CCRS), 4925 N. Carefree Cir., 80917. Tel: 719-597-4249; Fax: 719-591-1816. Deacon Chuck Matzker, Liaison to Bishop Hanifen for Charismatic Renewal.
Catholic Charities of Colorado Springs, Inc., 29 W. Kiowa St., 80903.
The Catholic Foundation of the Diocese of Colorado Springs, Inc., 29 W. Kiowa, 80903-1498. Tel: 719-636-2345; Fax: 719-636-1216.
Web site: www.re.net/coloradosprings/foundation
Bill Lyons, Pres. & Exec. Dir.
Colorado Springs Council of Black Catholics, 29 W. Kiowa St., 80903.
Colorado Springs Diocesan Council of Catholic Women, 29 W. Kiowa, 80903.
Franciscan Family Wellness Program, Inc., 7665 Assisi Hts., 80919. Tel: 719-598-5486, Ext. 7720; Fax: 719-598-0346.
E-mail: ffwpinc@juno.com
Web site: www.ffwpinc.com
Sr. Judith Ann Schaeffer, Ph.D., Exec. Dir. Total Assisted 2,100; Total Staff 7.
The Franciscan Foundation of Colorado Springs, 7665 Assisi Hts., 80919-3836. Tel: 719-598-5486; Fax: 719-598-1578. Sr. Clarice Gentrup, O.S.F., Contact Person.
Jail Ministries, c/o Diocese of Colorado Springs, 29 W. Kiowa St., 80903. Tel: 719-636-2345. Deacon Thomas E. Parrish, Coord.
Mercy Center, Inc., 520 W. Buena Ventura St., 80907. Tel: 719-633-2302; Fax: 719-633-1031.
Web site: www.mercycenter.com
Mr. Timothy J. Fogle, Exec. Dir.
Partners in Housing, Inc., 7 E. Bijou St., Ste. 211, 80903. Staff 10; Annually Assisted 558.
S.E.T. of Colorado Springs, 2316 N. Nevada, 80909. Tel: 719-328-0908; Fax: 719-328-0910. Maureen McGrain, Pres. & CEO.
Society of Missionaries of Mary, 520 W. Buena Ventura St., 80907. Tel: 719-633-2302; Fax: 719-633-1031. Rev. William Jarema, S.M.M., Founder.
St. Mary's Catholic Education Foundation, 2501 Yampa St., 80809. Thomas Kelly, Contact person.
Villa San Jose, Inc., 1810 S. Corona, 80906. Tel: 719-632-7444; Fax: 719-520-9345.
E-mail: villas@cex.com
Web site: www.freeservers.villasinsouthgate.com
Jason Dea Bueno, Admin. Total in Residence 50; Total Staff 12.
Villa Santa Maria, Inc., 405 E. St. Elmo Ave., 80906. Tel: 719-520-9344. Jason Dea Bueno, Admin. Staff 6; Total in Residence 50.

NECROLOGY

(No Deaths)

Diocese of Columbus

(Dioecesis Columbensis)

Most Reverend

JAMES A. GRIFFIN, J.D., J.C.L.

Bishop of Columbus; ordained May 28, 1960; consecrated Titular Bishop of Holar and Auxiliary to the Bishop of Cleveland August 1, 1979; appointed Tenth Bishop of Columbus February 7, 1983; installed April 25, 1983. *Res., 198 E. Broad St., Columbus, OH, 43215.* Tel.: 614-224-2251.

ESTABLISHED 1868.

Square Miles 11,310.

Comprises the following 23 Counties in the State of Ohio: Hardin, Marion, Morrow, Knox, Holmes, Tuscarawas, Union, Delaware, Licking, Coshocton, Madison, Franklin, Muskingum, Fayette, Pickaway, Fairfield, Perry, Ross, Hocking, Pike, Jackson, Vinton and Scioto.

For legal titles of parishes and diocesan institutions, consult the Chancery Office.

Chancery Office: 198 E. Broad St., Columbus, OH, 43215. Tel.: 614-224-2251; 224-8718 (Sat.-Sun. and other times); Fax: 614-224-6306.

STATISTICAL OVERVIEW

Personnel	
Bishop	1
Priests: Diocesan Active in Diocese	129
Priests: Active Outside Diocese	5
Priests: Retired, Sick or Absent	59
Number of Diocesan Priests	193
Religious Priests in Diocese	38
Extern Priests in Diocese	16
Ordinations:	
Diocesan Priests	2
Transitional Deacons	2
Permanent Deacons in Diocese	59
Total Brothers	3
Total Sisters	376
Parishes	
Parishes	107
With Resident Pastor:	
Resident Diocesan Priests	91
Resident Religious Priests	7
Without Resident Pastor:	
Administered by Priests	8
Administered by Women Religious	1
Missions	5
New Parishes Created	1
Professional Ministry Personnel:	
Sisters	30
Lay Ministers	87
Welfare	
Catholic Hospitals	4
Total Assisted	1,274,425
Homes for the Aged	17
Total Assisted	1,955
Day Care and Extended Day Care Centers	1
Total Assisted	126
Special Centers for Social Services	8
Total Assisted	291,400
Residential Care of Disabled	1
Total Assisted	98
Educational	
Seminaries, Diocesan	1
Students from This Diocese	13
Students from Other Diocese	89
Diocesan Students in Other Seminaries	4
Total Seminarians	17
Colleges and Universities	1
Total Students	2,191
High Schools, Diocesan and Parish	11
Total Students	4,912
Elementary Schools, Diocesan and Parish	45
Total Students	13,874
Elementary Schools, Private	2
Total Students	337
Catechesis/Religious Education:	
High School Students	941
Elementary Students	24,678
Total Students Under Catholic Instruction	46,950
Teachers in the Diocese:	
Priests	1
Brothers	1
Sisters	20
Lay Teachers	953
Vital Statistics	
Receptions into the Church:	
Infant Baptism Totals	4,083
Adult Baptism Totals	522
Received into Full Communion	711
First Communions	4,214
Confirmations	3,506
Marriages:	
Catholic	638
Interfaith	625
Total Marriages	1,263
Deaths	1,634
Total Catholic Population	198,116
Total Population	2,283,842

Former Bishops—Rt. Rev. SYLVESTER HORTON ROSECRANS, D.D., cons. Titular Bishop of Pompeiopolis and Auxiliary to the Bishop of Cincinnati, March 25, 1862; transferred to Columbus, March 3, 1868; died Oct. 21, 1878.—Rt. Rev. JOHN AMBROSE WATTERSON, D.D., cons. Aug. 8, 1880; died April 17, 1899.—Most Rev. HENRY MOELLER, D.D., cons. Bishop of Columbus, Aug. 25, 1900; promoted to the Archiepiscopal See of Areopolis and made Coadjutor to the Archbishop of Cincinnati, with the right of succession, April 27, 1903; succeeded to the See of Cincinnati, Oct. 31, 1904; died Jan. 5, 1925.—Most Rev. JAMES JOSEPH HARTLEY, D.D., cons. Feb. 25, 1904; died Jan. 12, 1944.—Most Rev. MICHAEL JOSEPH READY, D.D., cons. Dec. 14, 1944; died May 2, 1957.—Most Rev. CLARENCE GEORGE ISSENMANN, S.T.D., cons. Titular Bishop of Phytea and Auxiliary Bishop of Cincinnati May 25, 1954; appt. Bishop of Columbus Dec. 5, 1957; transferred to Cleveland as Apostolic Administrator. "cum jure successionis," Oct. 7, 1964; died July 27, 1982.—His Eminence JOHN CARDINAL CARBERRY, D.D., appt. Titular Bishop of Elis and Coadjutor of Lafayette in Indiana "cum jure successionis," May 3, 1956; cons. July 25, 1956; succeeded to See Nov. 20, 1957; transferred to Columbus Jan. 20, 1965; transferred to the Archdiocese of St. Louis, March 24, 1968; created Cardinal April 28, 1969.—Most Rev. CLARENCE E. ELWELL, D.D., cons. Dec. 21, 1962; appt. to Columbus May 29, 1968; died Feb. 16, 1973.—Most Rev. EDWARD J. HERRMANN, D.D., appt. Auxiliary Bishop of Washington and Titular Bishop of Lamzella, March 4, 1966; cons. April 26, 1966; appt. Ninth Bishop of Columbus, June 26, 1973; installed Aug. 21, 1973; retired Sept. 18, 1982; named Apostolic Administrator Sept. 1982 to April 1983; died Dec. 22, 1999.

Vicar General/Chancellor—Rev. Msgr. STEPHAN J. MOLONEY, M.A., M.Div., J.C.L.

Episcopal Vicar for Charities and Social Concerns—MARK H. HUDDY, J.D.

Episcopal Vicar for Education—LUCIA D. MCQUAIDE, M.S.Ed.

Episcopal Vicar for Church Ministry—Sr. JOAN M. HARPER, C.D.P.

Episcopal Vicar for Spiritual Life—Rev. ROBERT E. WILLMANN, S.T.B., J.C.L., J.C.D. (Cand.).

Chancery Office—198 E. Broad St., Columbus, 43215. Office Hours: Mon.-Fri. 8-4:30. Tel: 614-224-2251 (Sat.-Sun.); 224-8718 (other times); Fax: 614-224-6306.

Chancellor—Rev. Msgr. STEPHAN J. MOLONEY, M.A., M.Div., J.C.L.

Vice Chancellor—Rev. ROBERT E. WILLMANN, S.T.B., J.C.L., J.C.D. (Cand.).

Diocesan Consultors—Most Rev. JAMES A. GRIFFIN, J.D., J.C.L.; Rev. Msgr. STEPHAN J. MOLONEY; Revs. RODNEY M. DAMICO; WILLIAM A. DUNN; JAMES A. GEIGER; MARK V. GHILONI; STEPHEN L. KRILE; ROBERT E. WILLMANN.

Parochial Examiners—Revs. G. MICHAEL GRIBBLE; STEPHEN B. HAWKINS; PAUL A. NOBLE; JEROME P. RODENFELS.

Vicars Forane—Vicariate 1: Center City: Deacon ROGER F. PRY, *Sts. Augustine & Gabriel Parish, 1567 Loretta Ave., Ste. 111, Columbus, 43211.* Vicariate 2: Northwest: Rev. THOMAS SHONEBARGER, *St. Timothy Church, 1088 Thomas Lane, Columbus, 43220-7401.* Vicariate 3: North High: Rev. Msgr. WILLIAM A. DUNN, *St. Michael Church, 5750 N. High St., Worthington, 43085-3986.* Vicariate 4: Northland: Rev. RODRIC J. DIPIETRO, *St. Elizabeth Church, 1682 Lynnhurst Rd., Columbus, 43229.* Vicariate 5: West: Rev. JOHN L. BAKLE, S.M., *St. Agatha Church, 1860 Northam Rd., Columbus, 43221.* Vicariate 6: South:; Vacant; Vicariate 7: East: Rev. LEO L. CONNOLLY, *St. Philip Church, 1573 Elaine Rd., Columbus, 43227.* Vicariate 8: Marion: Rev. KEVIN J. KAVANAGH, *St. Mary Church, 82 E. Willliam St., Delaware, 43015.* Vicariate 9: Zanesville: Rev. CHARLES F. KLINGER, *St. Nicholas Church, 925 E. Main St., Zanesville, 43701.* Vicariate 10: Knox-Licking: Rev. RICHARD L. METZGER, *Church of the Ascension, 276 S. Main St., Johnstown, 43031-1231.* Vicariate 11: Tusc.-Holmes: Rev. Msgr. GEORGE J. SCHLEGEL, *Sacred Heart Church, 139 3rd St., N.E., New Philadelphia, 44663.* Vicariate 12: Lancaster: Rev. JUSTIN J. REIS, *St. Bernadette Church, 1343 Wheeling Rd., Lancaster, 43130.* Vicariate 13: Chillicothe: Rev. JAMES P. BLACK, *St. Peter Church, 122 Church St., Chillicothe, 45601.* Vicariate 14: Scioto County: Rev. MARK V. GHILONI, *Holy Redeemer Church, 1325 Gallia St., Portsmouth, 45662.* Vicariate 15: Perry County: Rev. ADRIAN L. DIONNE, O.P., *Holy Trinity-St. Joseph Parish, P.O. Box 190, Somerset, 43783-0190.*

Priests' Senate—Revs. STANLEY BENECKI, Chm. JOHN E. STATTMILLER, Vice Chm. JEFFREY J. CONING, Sec.

JAN C.P. SULLIVAN; PAUL A. NOBLE; DANIEL J. MILLISOR; MICHAEL DETEMPLE, O.P.; PATRICK A. TONER; MICHAEL F. NIMOCKS; RICHARD J. PENDOLPHI; PETER M. GIDEON; TIMOTHY M. HAYES; JAMES A. WALTER; Rev. Msgr. JAMES L. RUEF. Ex Officio Members: Rev. Msgr. STEPHAN J. MOLONEY; Rev. ROBERT E. WILLMANN.

Diocesan Pastoral Council—JOAN BUEMEL, Chm.; Sr. PHYLLIS DUGAN, S.N.D.deN., Exec. Sec., *197 E. Gay St., Columbus, 43215.* Tel: 614-228-1646.

Tribunal—197 E. Gay St., Ste. 500, Columbus, 43215-3290. Tel: 614-241-2500. Commissions should be addressed to the Diocese of Columbus, Tribunal.

Judicial Vicar—Rev. MARK J. HAMMOND, S.T.L., J.C.L.

Adjutant Vicar Judicial—Rev. Msgr. JOHN G. JOHNSON, J.C.D.

Diocesan Judges—Rev. Msgr. JOHN K. CODY, M.Div.; Rev. Msgr. F. THOMAS GALLEN, C.G.M.; Rev. Msgr. ANTHONY BORRELLI, J.C.L.; Rev. Msgr. JOHN J. DREESE, S.S.L.; Rev. Msgr. DAVID V. SOROHAN, M.A., S.T.L. Ph.D.; Rev. Msgr. EDWARD F. TRENOR, J.C.L.; Rev. Msgr. JOHN V. WOLF, S.T.D.; Rev. Msgr. JOSEPH N. FETE, M.S.T.; Rev. Msgr. FRANK P. LANE, Ph.D.; Rev. Msgr. JOHN T. DITTOE, S.T.L.; Revs. THOMAS J. CADDEN, M.A.; JAMES A. GEIGER, A.B., Ph.D.; LEO L. CONNOLLY, M.Div.; CHARLES F. KLINGER, M.Div.; ROBERT E. WILLMANN, J.C.L.; G. MICHAEL GRIBBLE, M.Div.; WILLIAM L. ARNOLD, M.Ed.; DANIEL J. MILLISOR, M.Div.; MARTIN V. WEITHMAN, M.S.T., M.R.E.; TIMOTHY M. HAYES, S.T.L.; RICHARD C. WEYLS, S.T.L.; PAUL A. NOBLE, M.A.; WILLIAM A. METZGER, B.A.; CHARLES T. THOMAS, M.A., M.Div.; DENNIS E. STEVENSON, J.C.L.; KEVIN J. KAVANAGH, S.S.L.

Priest/Psychological Expert—Rev. STEPHEN G. VIRGINIA, Ph.D.

Defenders of the Bond—Rev. JOSEPH N. BAY, J.C.L.; Sr. WANDA SCHERER, O.S.F., M.A.

Auditors/Notaries—Sr. MARY LINDA LORENZ, O.P., M.A.; HELEN THOMAS; SAUNDRA BURNS; BEVERLY WADDELL.

Notaries—Sr. RAYMUNDA BROOKS, O.P., M.A.; ANGELA NESMITH.

Promoter of Justice—Rev. Msgr. STEPHAN J. MOLONEY, J.C.L.

Presiding Judge in Second Instance—Rev. Msgr. JAMES L.T. RUEF, M.A., J.D., J.C.L.

Building Commission—Rev. Msgr. EDWARD F. TRENOR, Chm. & Contact Person, *Christ the King, 2770 Dover Rd., Columbus, 43209.*

Catholic Center—Diocesan Office Building, 197 E. Gay St., Columbus, 43215. Tel: 614-228-2453.

Catholic Charities and Social Concerns—MARK H. HUDDY, J.D., Vicar, *197 E. Gay St., Columbus, 43215.* Tel: 614-241-2540.

Catholic Conference of Ohio—TIMOTHY V. LUCKHAUPT, Dir., *9 E. Long St., Ste. 201, Columbus, 43215.* Tel: 614-224-7147; Fax: 614-224-7150.

Catholic Record Society—DONALD SCHLEGEL, Sec., *197 E. Gay St., Columbus, 43215.* Tel: 614-241-2571.

Catholic Relief Services—MARK H. HUDDY, J.D., Diocesan Admin., *Dept. of Social Concerns, 197 E. Gay St., Columbus, 43215.* Tel: 614-241-2540.

Catholic Social Services—SARA K. MURPHY, Pres., *197 E. Gay St., Columbus, 43215.* Tel: 614-221-5891.

Cemeteries—RICHARD FINN, Dir., *6440 S. High St., Lockbourne, 43137.* Tel: 614-491-2751.

Censor of Books—Rev. Msgr. JOHN V. WOLF, S.T.D.

Central Purchasing Service, Inc.—Deacon JOHN VELLANI, Dir., *1567 Loretta Ave., Ste. 212, Columbus, 43211.* Tel: 1-800-842-8319; 614-262-0010.

Catholic Charismatic Renewal, Inc.—Rev. JUSTIN J. REIS, Bishop's Liaison, *St. Bernadette, 1343 Wheeling Rd., Lancaster, 43130-8701.* Tel: 740-654-1893. MAXINE POWERS, Dir., *Catholic Charismatic Center, 4207 E. Broad St., Ste. C, Columbus, 43213.* Tel: 614-237-7080; Fax: 614-237-6847.

St. Vincent Family Centers—W. JOSEPH HAMBOR, Pres. & C.E.O., *1490 E. Main St., Columbus, 43205.* Tel: 614-252-0731.

Main Campus—1490 E. Main St., Columbus, 43205. Tel: 614-252-0731.

Franklinton Office—840 W. State St., Columbus, 43222. Tel: 614-221-7855.

Communication Office—THOMAS M. BERG, JR., Dir., *197 E. Gay St., Columbus, 43215.* Tel: 614-241-2555.

Council of Religious—Sr. ROSITA SCHILLER, R.S.M., *1385 Bluff Ave., Apt. A, Columbus, 43212-3771.*

Deaf Apostolate—Rev. STANLEY BENECKI, *Sts. Augustine and Gabriel, 1567 Loretta Ave., Ste. 111, Columbus, 43211.* Tel: 614-261-0339 (TDD); 268-3123 (Voice); Fax: 614-268-8130.

Department of Education—LUCIA D. MCQUAIDE, M.S.Ed., Vicar-Supt., *197 E. Gay St., Columbus, 43215.* Tel: 614-221-5829.

Diocesan Council of Catholic Women—JEAN HOWLEY, Pres., *197 E. Gay St., Columbus, 43215.* Tel: 614-228-8601.

Development Office—HELMUT J. NAUNHEIMER, Dir., *197 E. Gay St., Columbus, 43215.* Tel: 614-241-2550.

Diocesan Finance Committee—FRANK BETTENDORF, Chm.; Most Rev. JAMES A. GRIFFIN; Rev. Msgr. STEPHAN J. MOLONEY; Rev. Msgr. JOSEPH M. HENDRICKS; Rev. Msgr. EDWARD F. TRENOR; Rev. ROBERT E. WILLMANN; ANN O'ROURKE; DONALD BORROR; HUGH DORRIAN; WILLIAM HEROLD; THOMAS MCAULIFFE; LUCIA D. MCQUAIDE; JAMES J. CSASZAR; W. MATTHEW BROWN, *198 E. Broad St., Columbus, 43215.* Tel: 614-224-1221.

Diocesan Finance Council—Most Rev. JAMES A. GRIFFIN; Rev. Msgr. STEPHAN J. MOLONEY; Rev. ROBERT E. WILLMANN; W. MATTHEW BROWN, *198 E. Broad St., Columbus, 43215.* Tel: 614-224-1221.

Priests Personnel Board—Rev. Msgr. A. ANTHONY FRECKER, Chm., *7820 White Ash Court, Canal Winchester, 43110.* Tel: 614-920-1563.

Diocesan Retirement Plans for Priests, Lay Employees and Lay Teachers—Rev. Msgr. EDWARD F. TRENOR, Chm. Admin. Board for Plans. Tel: 614-237-0401.

Family Life Office—STEPHANIE JENEMANN, Dir., *197 E. Gay St., Columbus, 43215.* Tel: 614-241-2560.

Finance Office—W. MATTHEW BROWN, Dir., *198 E. Broad St., Columbus, 43215.* Tel: 614-224-1221; 224-1235.

Foundation of the Catholic Diocese of Columbus—KATHLEEN SPENCER, Exec. Dir., *197 E. Gay St., Columbus, 43215.* Tel: 614-241-2566.

Health Affairs Department (Hospitals)—Rev. MARK J. HAMMOND, Coord., *197 E. Gay St., Columbus, 43215.* Tel: 614-445-9668.

Holy Childhood, Pontifical Association—Sr. M. PAULETTE BOLL, O.P., Dir., *197 E. Gay St., Columbus, 43215.* Tel: 614-228-8603.

House of Retreats—MARY E. MURPHY, Dir., *St. Therese Retreat Center, 5277 E. Broad St., Columbus, 43213.* Tel: 614-866-1611.

Insurance—Diocesan Finance Office, 198 E. Broad St., Columbus, 43215. Tel: 614-224-1221.

J.O.I.N. (Joint Organization for Inner-City Needs)—Mrs. RUTH BECKMAN, Dir., *197 E. Gay St., Columbus, 43215.* Tel: 614-241-2530.

Legion of Mary—Rev. Msgr. CHARLES J. FOELLER, Dir., *Sacred Hearts Church, 4680 U.S. Rt. 42, Cardington, 43315.* Tel: 419-946-3611.

Liturgical Commission—Rev. KENNETH J. ANDERSON, *1899 McCoy Rd., Columbus, 43220.* Tel: 614-451-4290.

Liturgy Office—Sr. RENE SIMONELIC, O.S.F., Dir., *197 E. Gay St., Columbus, 43215.* Tel: 614-221-4640.

Ministry Formation Office—LESLIE J. YOUNG, Ph.D., Dir. JAMES HATFIELD, Prog. Coord., *197 E. Gay St., Columbus, 43215.* Tel: 614-241-2544.

Newspaper—"The Catholic Times", MARK MORETTI, Editor, *197 E. Gay St., Columbus, 43215.* Tel: 614-224-5195.

Missions Office—Sr. M. PAULETTE BOLL, O.P., Dir., *197 E. Gay St., Columbus, 43215.* Tel: 614-228-8603.

Pastoral Services, Office of—Sr. PHYLLIS DUGAN, S.N.D-.deN., Dir., *197 E. Gay St., 4th Floor, Columbus, 43215.* Tel: 614-228-1646.

Permanent Diaconate Program—Deacons FRANK A. IANNARINO, Dir. THOMAS V. JOHNSTON, Assoc. Dir. Formation, Office: *197 E. Gay St., Columbus, 43215.* Tel: 614-241-2545., School: *Pontifical College Josephinum, 7625 N. High St., Columbus, 43235.* Tel: 614-885-5585.

Personnel Services—JOAN THORNTON PALKUTI, Sec., *197 E. Gay St., Columbus, 43215.* Tel: 614-241-2590.

Priests Continuing Education—Rev. G. MICHAEL GRIBBLE, *St. Joseph Cathedral, 212 E. Broad St., Columbus, 43215.* Tel: 614-224-1295.

Propagation of the Faith and Opus Sancti Petri—Sr. M. PAULETTE BOLL, O.P., Dir., *197 E. Gay St., Columbus, 43215.* Tel: 614-228-8603.

Printing Services—NANCY EYERMAN, Mgr., *197 E. Gay St., Columbus, 43215.* Tel: 614-224-0261.

Real Estate—DONALD A. BORROR, Consultant, *5501 Frantz Rd., P.O. Box 7166, Dublin, 43017.* Tel: 614-761-6000.

Religious Education Office—BARBARA ROMANELLO-WICHTMAN, Dir., *197 E. Gay St., Columbus, 43215.* Tel: 614-221-4633.

Retreats—MARY E. MURPHY, Dir., *St. Therese Retreat Center, 5227 E. Broad St., Columbus, 43213.* Tel: 614-866-1611.

Rural Life Apostolate—JERALD FREEWALT, Dir., *197 E. Gay St., Columbus, 43215.* Tel: 614-241-2540.

St. Stephen's Community House—JUDITH STATTMILLER, Dir., *1500 E. 17th Ave., Columbus, 43219.* Tel: 614-294-6347; Fax: 614-294-0258.

St. Vincent de Paul Society—BILL HAMMOND, Pres., *197 E. Gay St., Columbus, 43215.* Tel: 614-221-3554.

St. Vincent de Paul Shop—424 E. Locust St., Lancaster, 43130. Tel: 740-653-6037.

Scout Chaplain—Deacon GILBERT L. PLUMMER, Dir., *St. Brendan Church, 4475 Dublin Rd., Hilliard, 43026.*

Department of Social Concerns—MARK H. HUDDY, Dir., *197 E. Gay St., Columbus, 43215.* Tel: 614-241-2540.

Spanish Speaking Apostolate—Rev. JOSE PEREZ, *Santa Cruz Parish, 256 E. Rich St., Columbus, 43215-5232.* Tel: 614-469-9178.

Vocations Office—Rev. MATTHEW N. HOOVER, Dir., *197 E. Gay St., Columbus, 43215.* Tel: 614-221-5565.

Youth and Young Adult Ministry—MARK BUTLER, Dir., *197 E. Gay St., Columbus, 43215.* Tel: 614-241-2565.

CLERGY, PARISHES, MISSIONS AND PAROCHIAL SCHOOLS

CITY OF COLUMBUS
(Franklin County)

1—ST. JOSEPH CATHEDRAL (1878), Revs. G. Michael Gribble, Rector; David A. Poliafico; Deacon Thomas Johnston. In res., Rev. David W. Sizemore.

Res., 212 E. Broad St., 43215. Tel: 614-224-1295; Fax: 614-224-1176.

Church—E. Broad St. & N. Fifth St., 43215.

2—ST. AGATHA (Upper Arlington) (1940), Rev. Msgr. David R. Funk; Sr. Mary Catherine Kaeppner, Pastoral Min. In res., Revs. Robert J. Schuer; Robert E. Willmann; John L. Bakle, S.M.

Res., 1860 Northam Rd., 43221. Tel: 614-488-6149; Fax: 614-488-6596.

School—1880 Northam Rd., 43221. Tel: 614-488-9000; Fax: 614-488-5783. Mrs. Joan Mastell, Prin. Lay Teachers 25; Students 419.

Catechesis/Religious Programs—Tel: 614-488-4975. Mrs. Jeanne Altiero, D.R.E. Students 374.

3—ST. AGNES (1954), Rev. Msgr. Mario A. Serraglio.

Res., 2364 W. Mound St., 43204-2997. Tel: 614-276-5413; Fax: 614-276-5608.

Catechesis/Religious Programs—Students 22.

4—ST. ALOYSIUS (1906), Rev. Dennis E. Stevenson, J.C.L., Admin. In res., Rev. Msgr. Donald C. Schulz. Res., 32 Clarendon Ave., 43223. Tel: 614-276-6587.

Catechesis/Religious Programs—2350 W. Mound St., 43204. Tel: 614-276-5413; Fax: 614-276-5608. Students 23.

5—ST. ANDREW (1955), Revs. Michael B. Watson; Kenneth Joseph Anderson.

Res., 1899 McCoy Rd., 43220. Tel: 614-451-4290; Fax: 614-451-8300.

School—McCoy Rd. & Reed Rd., 43220. Tel: 614-451-1626. Raenita Kownacki, Prin. Lay Teachers 25; Students 534.

Catechesis/Religious Programs—Tel: 614-451-2855. Ann Brown, D.R.E. Students 276.

6—SAINT ANTHONY (1963), Rev. John L. Swickard; Mrs. Colleen Buzenski, Pastoral Asst.

Res., 4913 Atwater Dr., 43229. Tel: 614-885-4857.

School—(Grades K-8) 1300 Urban Dr., 43229. Tel: 614-888-4268; Fax: 614-888-4435. Chris Iaconis, Prin. Lay Teachers 9; Students 240.

Catechesis/Religious Programs—(Grades 1-8). Tel: 614-888-8190. Judy McElwee, D.R.E. Students 92.

7—STS. AUGUSTINE AND GABRIEL (1984), Rev. Stanley Benecki; Deacon Roger Pry.

Office: 1567 Loretta Ave., Ste. 111, 43211-1677. Tel: 614-268-3123;261-0339(TDD); Fax: 614-268-8130.

Church—1550 E. Hudson St., 43211.

Catechesis/Religious Programs—Students 24.

8—ST. CATHARINE (1931), Rev. Msgr. David V. Sorohan; Sr. Christella Ritchey, O.S.F., Pastoral Assoc.; James Kebe, Chap., Pastoral Care, Tel: 614-231-4509. In res., Revs. Joseph E. Murphy; Joseph N. Bay.

Res., 500 S. Gould Rd., 43209. Tel: 614-231-4509; Fax: 614-231-8366.

School—2865 Fair Ave., 43209. Tel: 614-235-1396; Fax: 614-235-9708. Mrs. Janet Weisner, Prin. Lay Teachers 17; Students 286.

Catechesis/Religious Programs—Tel: 614-231-4500. D.R.E.: Sr. Christella Ritchey, O.S.F.; Mrs. Chris Schleicher. Students 243.

9—ST. CECILIA (1882), Revs. Craig R. Eilerman; Shawn D. Corcoran.

Res., 434 Norton Rd., 43228. Tel: 614-878-5353; Fax: 614-878-0459.

School—440 Norton Rd., 43228. Tel: 614-878-3555; Fax: 614-878-6852. Sr. Regina Snyder, O.S.F., Prin. Lay Teachers 14; Students 290.

Catechesis/Religious Programs—Tel: 614-878-0133. Richard Keyes, D.R.E.
Students 264.

10—CHRIST THE KING (1946), Rev. Msgr. Edward F. Trenor; Deacon Peter C. Labita. In res., Rev. Msgr. Clement F. Faistl; Rev. James W. Jones.
Res., 2770 Dover Rd., 43209. Tel: 614-237-0401; Fax: 614-237-4689.
School—2855 E. Livingston Ave., 43209. Tel: 614-231-3391; Fax: 614-338-2170. Ms. Barb Davis, Prin.
Lay Teachers 10; Students 235.
Catechesis/Religious Programs—Tel: 614-231-8374. Karen Laihr, D.R.E.
Students 65.

11—ST. CHRISTOPHER (1947), Rev. Arthur W. Wiles; John J. Dawson, Business Mgr. In res., Rev. Paul O. Smith.
Res., 1420 Grandview Ave., 43212. Tel: 614-486-0457; Fax: 614-486-0433.
School—Trinity, 1381 Ida Ave., 43212. Tel: 614-488-7650; Fax: 614-488-4687. Mrs. Diane Hayhurst, Prin.
Sisters 1; Lay Teachers 12; Students 285.
Catechesis/Religious Programs—Susan Bellotti, D.R.E.
Students 127.

12—CORPUS CHRISTI (1925), Rev. John E. Stattmiller; Deacon J. Jerry Butts.
Res., 1111 E. Stewart Ave., 43206. Tel: 614-444-9871; Fax: 614-444-1018.
Catechesis/Religious Programs—Clustered with St. Ladislas, Columbus.

13—SANTA CRUZ PARISH (1993) (Spanish), Rev. Jose Perez (Venezuela).
Church—256 E. Rich St., 43215. Tel: 614-469-9178; Fax: 614-469-9178.

14—ST. DOMINIC (1889) (African American), Rev. James L. Colopy; Deacon Robert A. Neely.
Mailing Address: and Res.: 453 N. 20th St., P.O. Box 83572, 43203-0572. Tel: 614-252-4913; Fax: 614-252-1655.
Catechesis/Religious Programs—Students 42.

15—ST. FRANCIS OF ASSISI (1892), Rev. Richard C. Weyls.
Res., 386 Buttles Ave., 43215. Tel: 614-299-5781; Fax: 614-299-1987.

16—ST. ELIZABETH (1967), Rev. Rodric J. DiPietro; Deacons Frank X. Ball; John J. Rericha; Frank X. McDevitt.
Res., 1682 Lynnhurst Rd., 43229. Tel: 614-882-1782; Fax: 614-882-1782.
Church—6077 Sharon Woods Blvd., 43229. Tel: 614-891-0150; Fax: 614-891-3243.
Catechesis/Religious Programs—Students 131.

17—ST. GABRIEL. Merged with St. Augustine. See separate listing.

18—HOLY CROSS (1833) (German), Rev. Jerome D. Stluka. In res., Rev. Msgr. Lawrence J. Corcoran, P.A.
Res., 204 S. Fifth St., 43215. Tel: 614-224-3416; Fax: 614-224-9916.

19—HOLY FAMILY (1877), Rev. Kevin F. Lutz; Deacon W. Earl McCurry. In res., Rev. Msgr. John K. Cody.
Res., 584 W. Broad St., 43215-2710. Tel: 614-221-4323; Fax: 614-221-4323.
Catechesis/Religious Programs—Students 52.

20—HOLY NAME (1905), Rev. Msgr. James L.T. Ruef.
Res., 154 E. Patterson Ave., 43202. Tel: 614-262-0390.
Catechesis/Religious Programs—Students 9.

21—HOLY SPIRIT (Whitehall) (1947), Rev. Raymond Larussa.
Res., 4383 E. Broad St., 43213. Tel: 614-861-1521; Fax: 614-861-3746.
School—4382 Duchene Ln., 43213. Tel: 614-861-0475; Fax: 614-861-3746. Sr. Shawn Fitzpatrick, O.P., Prin.
Lay Teachers 10; Students 294.
Catechesis/Religious Programs—Tel: 614-861-4559. Michael T. Millisor, D.R.E.
Students 65.

22—IMMACULATE CONCEPTION (1917), Rev. Msgr. Anthony N. Missimi; Rev. Msgr. Thomas M. Bennett.
Res., 414 E. North Broadway, 43214. Tel: 614-267-9241; Fax: 614-267-7720.
School—366 E. North Broadway, 43214. Tel: 614-267-6579. John Grossman, Prin.
Lay Teachers 20; Students 480.
Catechesis/Religious Programs—440 E. North Broadway, 43214. Tel: 614-267-0279. John Hoffman, D.R.E.
Students 720.

23—ST. JAMES-THE-LESS (1947), Revs. Richard Nieberding, C.PP.S.; Patrick Patterson, C.PP.S.; Deacon Joseph P. Checca; Mr. Art Bischoff, Business Mgr.
Res., 1652 Oakland Park Ave., 43224. Tel: 614-262-1179; 262-1170; Fax: 614-262-6798.
School—1628 Oakland Park Ave., 43224. Tel: 614-268-3311; Fax: 614-262-6798. Kathleen O'Reilly, Prin.
Lay Teachers 20; Students 419.
Catechesis/Religious Programs—Bev Cremeans, D.R.E.
Students 80.

24—ST. JOHN THE BAPTIST (1896) (Italian), Rev. William A. Metzger.
Res., 720 Hamlet St., 43215. Tel: 614-294-5319; Fax: 614-294-4303.
Catechesis/Religious Programs—Students 8.

25—COMMUNITY OF HOLY ROSARY AND ST. JOHN (1979), Revs. Frederick J. Benda, S.J.; Edward A. Flint, S.J.; John E. Beez, S.J.; Bro. James F. Gates, S.J.; Deacon James R. Davis.
Res., 648 S. Ohio Ave., 43205. Tel: 614-252-5926; Fax: 614-252-5933.
Catechesis/Religious Programs—Sr. Diane Kozlowski, O.P., D.R.E.
Students 61.

26—ST. LADISLAS (1908) (Hungarian), Rev. John E. Stattmiller.
Res., 1111 E. Stewart Ave., 43206. Tel: 614-444-9871; Fax: 614-444-1018.

27—ST. LEO (1903) (German). Closed. For inquiries for parish records please see St. Mary, Columbus.

28—ST. MARGARET OF CORTONA (1921), Rev. Msgr. Anthony Borrelli; Sr. Juliana D'Amato, O.P., Pastoral Assoc.
Res., 1600 Hague Ave., 43204-1606. Tel: 614-279-1690; Fax: 614-279-2386.
Catechesis/Religious Programs—Sharon Curtin, D.R.E.
Students 331.

29—ST. MARY (1865) (German), Rev. Mark J. Hammond; Mary Koors, Pastoral Assoc. In res., Revs. Arthur J. Dimond; Joseph E. Stanton.
Res., 684 S. Third St., 43206. Tel: 614-445-9668; Fax: 614-444-1688.
School—700 S. Third St., 43206. Tel: 614-444-8994; Fax: 614-445-2853. Kathleen McClernon, Prin.
Lay Teachers 15; Students 271.

30—ST. MARY MAGDALENE (1928), Revs. Charles E. Cotton; Carmen J. Arcuri.
Res., 473 S. Roys Ave., 43204. Tel: 614-274-1121; Fax: 614-274-1122.
School—2940 Parkside Rd., 43204. Tel: 614-279-9935; Fax: 614-279-9575. Carol Flanagan, Prin.
Lay Teachers 26; Students 420.
Catechesis/Religious Programs—Tel: 614-875-0346.
Students 100.

31—ST. MATTHIAS (1956), Rev. James T. Smith; Sr. Marie Shields, S.N.D.deN., Pastoral Assoc.
Res., 1582 Ferris Rd., 43224. Tel: 614-267-3406.
School—1566 Ferris Rd., 43224. Tel: 614-268-3030; Fax: 614-268-4681. Mr. Daniel Kinley, Prin.
Sisters 1; Lay Teachers 11; Students 300.
Catechesis/Religious Programs—Nancy Mead, D.R.E.
Students 90.

32—ST. MICHAEL (1946), Rev. Msgr. William A. Dunn; Rev. Thomas J. Brosmer; Deacons John R. Crerand; John Vellani.
Res., 5750 N. High St., Worthington, 43085. Tel: 614-885-7814; Fax: 614-885-3446.
School—64 E. Selby Blvd., Worthington, 43085-3986. Tel: 614-885-3149; Fax: 614-885-1249. Miss Christine Armbrust, Prin.
Religious 1; Lay Teachers 24; Students 618.
Catechesis/Religious Programs—Tel: 614-888-5384. Mrs. Carol O'Connor, D.R.E.
Students 320.

33—OUR LADY OF THE MIRACULOUS MEDAL (1967), Revs. William H. DeVille; Frederick A. Loyd; Deacon Joseph D. Poland. Pastoral Assocs.: Mrs. Anita Remy; Deacon Stephen A. Venturini.
Res., 5225 Refugee Rd., 43232. Tel: 614-861-1242; Fax: 614-861-1499.
Catechesis/Religious Programs—Tel: 614-868-1414. Mr. Steve Mustard, D.R.E.
Students 94.

34—OUR LADY OF PEACE (1946), Rev. Msgr. Kenneth F. Grimes; Deacon John D. Rankin; Sr. Mary Agnes Jones, O.P., Pastoral Min.
Res., 20 E. Dominion Blvd., 43214. Tel: 614-263-8824; Fax: 614-263-3383.
School—40 Dominion Blvd., 43214. Tel: 614-267-4535; Fax: 614-267-2333. Carol Folian, Prin.
Lay Teachers 13; Students 269.
Catechesis/Religious Programs—Andrea McAuliffe, D.R.E.
Students 30.

35—OUR LADY OF VICTORY (1922), Rev. Msgr. Romano Ciotola; Deacon Richard L. Baumann. In res., Rev. Stephen G. Virginia.
Res., 1559 Roxbury Rd., 43212. Tel: 614-488-2428; Fax: 614-488-0507.
School—Trinity. See St. Christopher, Columbus for details. Tel: 614-486-7650; Fax: 614-486-0433.
Catechesis/Religious Programs—Tel: 614-486-7678. Sr. Patricia Rooks, S.N.D.deN., D.R.E.
Students 221.

36—ST. PATRICK (1852) (Irish), Revs. Ambrose Eckinger, O.P.; Stephen D. Hayes, O.P.; Andre Joseph LaCasse, O.P. In res., Rev. Luke Tancrell, O.P.
Res., 376 E. Naghten St., 43215. Tel: 614-224-9522; Fax: 614-240-5928.
Catechesis/Religious Programs—Tel: 614-240-5925; Fax: 614-240-5928.
Students 206.

37—ST. PETER (1970), Rev. Msgr. John G. Johnson; Rev. Robert Penhallurick (United Kingdom); Deacons Joseph E. Schermer; Philip M. Paulucci.
Res., 6899 Smoky Row Rd., 43235-1998. Tel: 614-889-2221; Fax: 614-889-6612.
Catechesis/Religious Programs—Tel: 614-889-1407; Fax: 614-889-0543.
Students 542.

38—ST. PHILIP THE APOSTLE (1956), Rev. Leo L. Connolly; Deacon Joseph W. Farry; Katie Seipel, Pastoral Assoc. In res., Rev. Patrick W. Rogers.
Res., 1573 Elaine Rd., 43227. Tel: 614-237-1671; Fax: 614-231-8416.
School—1555 Elaine Rd., 43227. Tel: 614-237-5278; Fax: 614-231-8416. Jeffrey I. Kanowsky, Prin.
Sisters of St. Francis 1; Lay Teachers 11; Students 235.
Catechesis/Religious Programs—Tel: 614-237-6500. Brad Walters, D.R.E.
Students 45.

39—SAINT STEPHEN THE MARTYR (1963), Sr. Anne McCarrick, S.N.D.deN., Pastoral Admin.; Rev. John L. Bakle, S.M.; Rev. Msgr. Stephan J. Moloney.
Res., 4031 Clime Rd., 43228. Tel: 614-272-5206; Fax: 614-272-5200.
Catechesis/Religious Programs—Students 37.

40—ST. TIMOTHY (1961), Rev. Thomas Shonebarger. In res., Rev. Robert Michael Ellifritz.
Res., 1088 Thomas Ln., 43220. Tel: 614-451-2671; Fax: 614-451-4181.
School—1070 Thomas Ln., 43220. Tel: 614-451-0739; Fax: 614-451-3108. Norma A. Horan, Prin.
Lay Teachers 12; Students 260.
Catechesis/Religious Programs—Tel: 614-451-3867; Fax: 614-451-3108. Paul Saelzier, D.R.E.
Students 90.

41—SACRED HEART (1875), Rev. Samuel E. Ritchey.
Res., 893 Hamlet St., 43201. Tel: 614-299-4191; Fax: 614-299-4192.

42—SHRINE OF BLESSED MARGARET OF CASTELLO (1957), c/o St. Patrick: (Entrance to Shrine is through St. Patrick.) 376 E. Naghten St., 43215.

43—ST. THOMAS THE APOSTLE (1900), Rev. Ronald J. Atwood.
Res., 2692 E. Fifth Ave., 43219. Tel: 614-252-0976; Fax: 614-252-0977.
School—767 N. Cassady Ave., 43219. Tel: 614-252-7136. Sr. Pat Russi, O.P., Prin.
Lay Teachers 9; Students 202.

44—KOREAN CATHOLIC COMMUNITY (1978) (Asian), Rev. Jong-Hyun Lee (Korea).
Mailing Address: 5500 Broadview Rd., Gahanna, 43230. Tel: 614-476-9974; Fax: 614-476-9974. [CEM]
Catechesis/Religious Programs—Students 55.

OUTSIDE THE CITY OF COLUMBUS

Ada, Hardin Co., Our Lady of Lourdes (1874), Rev. Daniel J. Millisor; Deacon John P. Stahl.
Res., 222 E. Highland Ave., 45810. Tel: 419-634-2626.
Catechesis/Religious Programs—Tel: 419-634-2445. Mr. David Savino, D.R.E.
Students 152.

Bremen, Fairfield Co., St. Mary (1917), Rev. Msgr. Thomas G. Bender.
Res., 602 Marietta St., 43107. Tel: 740-569-4272. [CEM]
Catechesis/Religious Programs—Tel: 740-569-7724. Patricia Davis, D.R.E.
Students 55.

Bolivar, Tuscarawas Co., Holy Trinity (1995), Rev. Michael F. Nimocks.
Res., 141 Water St., S.W., 44612. Tel: 330-874-4716; Fax: 330-874-4461. [CEM 4]

Buckeye Lake, Licking Co., Our Lady of Mt. Carmel (1929), Rev. Msgr. Frank J. Meagher. Pastoral Assocs.: Deacon Joe Farmer, (Retired); Betty Friend.
Res., 5133 Walnut Rd., S.E., P.O. Box 45, 43008. Tel: 740-928-3266; Fax: 740-928-3266.
Catechesis/Religious Programs—Tel: 740-928-3264. Silvia Zaboroski, D.R.E.
Students 84.

Canal Winchester, Fairfield Co., Pope John XXIII, Rev. Msgr. A. Anthony Frecker.
Res., 7820 White Ash Ct., 43110. Tel: 614-920-1563; Fax: 614-920-1564.

Cardington, Morrow Co., Sacred Hearts (1868), Rev. Msgr. Charles J. Foeller.
Res., 4680 U.S. Rte. 42, 43315. Tel: 419-946-3611.
Catechesis/Religious Programs—D.R.E.: Kevin Tebbe; Sharon Tebbe.
Students 80.

Chillicothe, Ross Co., St. Mary (1837), Rev. Lawrence L. Hummer; Deacon George L. Lovensheimer.
Res., 61 S. Paint St., 45601. Tel: 614-772-2061; Fax: 614-772-2061. [CEM][JC]
School—Tel: 614-774-2970; Fax: 614-774-2998. Dr. James Bonnell, Prin.
Sisters 1; Lay Teachers 22.
Catechesis/Religious Programs—570 Parsons Ave., 45601.
Students 88.

St. Peter (1845) (German), Rev. James P. Black; Deacon Richard T. Krick. In res., Rev. Charles R. Griffin.
Res., 122 Church St., 45601. Tel: 740-774-1407. [CEM][JC]
School—Bishop Flaget Consolidated, (Grades PreK-8) 570 Parsons Ave., 45601. Tel: 740-774-2970; Fax: 740-774-2889. Mr. James Bonnell, Ph.D., Prin.
Lay Teachers 17; Students 283.
Catechesis/Religious Programs—Tel: 740-773-3455.
Students 84.

Circleville, Pickaway Co., St. Joseph's (1840), Rev. Stephen L. Krile; Mary Kay Wood, Pastoral Assoc.
Res., 134 W. Mound St., P.O. Box 659, 43113. Tel: 740-477-2549. [CEM]
Catechesis/Religious Programs—Theresa Jenkins, D.R.E.
Students 285.

Corning, Perry Co., St. Bernard (1882), Rev. Msgr. John J. Dreese. In res., Rev. Msgr. F. Thomas Gallen.
Res., 425 Adams St., 43730. Tel: 614-347-4700.
Catechesis/Religious Programs—Students 26.

Coshocton, Coshocton Co., Sacred Heart (1897), Rev. Msgr. Robert E. Schneider; Sr. Mary Emma Muckensturm, Pastoral Assoc.; Deacon Frank A. Duda.
Res., 805 Main St., 43812. Tel: 740-622-8817; Fax: 740-622-8818. [CEM]
School—39 Burt Ave., 43812. Tel: 740-622-3728; Fax: 740-622-9151. Deacon Frank A. Duda, Prin.
Lay Teachers 8; Students(K-6) 127; Students (PreK) 35.
Catechesis/Religious Programs—(Grades PreK-6) 128 Burt Ave., 43812. Tel: 740-623-0882. Ms. Amy McNichols, D.R.E.
Students 91.

Crooksville, Perry Co., Church of the Atonement (1896), Rev. Francis M. Stanton.
Res., 320 Winter St., 43731. Tel: 740-982-3816. [CEM]
Catechesis/Religious Programs—Patricia Musick, D.R.E.
Students 60.

Danville, Knox Co., St. Luke (1820), Rev. F. Richard Snoke.
Res., 307 S. Market St., P.O. Box P, 43014. Tel: 740-599-6362. [CEM]
Catechesis/Religious Programs—St. Luke Community Center, 7 W. Rambo, P.O. Box P, 43014-0616. Tel: 740-599-7367. Thomas Harrmann, D.R.E.
Students 130.

Delaware, Delaware Co., St. Mary (1835), Rev. Kevin J. Kavanagh; Sr. Cecilia Taphorn, C.PP.S., Pastoral Assoc.; Deacon Felix Azzola.
Res., 82 E. William St., 43015. Tel: 740-363-4641; 369-9644; Fax: 740-363-9915. [CEM]
School—66 E. William St., 43015. Tel: 740-362-8961. Becky Piela, Prin. (Grades PreK-8).
Lay Teachers 18; Students 301.
Catechesis/Religious Programs—Tel: 740-369-8228. Sandy Murray, D.R.E.
Students 330.

Dennison, Tuscarawas Co., Immaculate Conception (1871), Rev. Martin J. Ralko. In res., Rev. Kenneth F. Wise.
Res., 206 N. First St., 44621. Tel: 614-922-3533; Fax: 614-922-2486. [CEM]
School—100 Sherman St., 44621. Tel: 614-922-3539; Fax: 614-922-2486. John Zucal, Prin.
Lay Teachers 10; Students 147.
Catechesis/Religious Programs—Richard Passio, D.R.E.
Students 30.

Dover, Tuscarawas Co., St. Joseph (1849) (German-Italian), Rev. William L. Arnold; Sr. Barbara Sir, C.S.J., Pastoral Assoc.; Deacons Ronald H. Fondriest; Mark D. Allison.
Res., 613 N. Tuscarawas Ave., 44622. Tel: 330-364-6661; Fax: 330-602-7488. [CEM 2]
School—600 N. Tuscarawas Ave., 44622. Tel: 330-343-9134; Fax: 330-343-3704. Sr. Valerie Shaul, O.P., Prin.
Lay Teachers 14; Students 258.
Catechesis/Religious Programs—Tel: 330-364-8257. Ms. Cindy Teynor, D.R.E.
Students 213.

Dresden, Muskingum Co., St. Ann's (1889), Rev. William J. Metzger.
Res., 405 Chestnut St., Box 107, 43821. Tel: 740-754-2221.
Catechesis/Religious Programs—Tel: 740-754-3018.
Students 9.
Mission—Mattingly Settlement, Muskingum Co., St. Mary, 6280 St. Mary's Rd., Nashport, 43830. [CEM]

Dublin, Franklin Co., St. Brigid of Kildare (1987), Rev. Msgr. Joseph M. Hendricks; Rev. Jeffrey Coning; Deacon Frank A. Iannarino; Sr. Patricia McMahon, O.S.F., Pastoral Assoc.; Jean Bonk, Dir. Liturgy/Music.
Res., 7179 Avery Rd., P.O. Box 3130, 43016-0062. Tel: 614-761-3734; Fax: 614-889-6638.
School—7175 Avery Rd., 43017. Tel: 614-718-5825; Fax: 614-718-5831. Mr. Kevan Hartman, Prin.
Lay Teachers 29; Students 661.
Catechesis/Religious Programs—Tel: 614-761-1176; Fax: 614-718-5831. Mary Fran Cassidy, D.R.E.
Students 1,290.

Gahanna, Franklin Co., St. Matthew (1959), Rev. Paul A. Noble. In res., Rev. Msgr. Stephan J. Moloney; Rev. Matthew N. Hoover.
Res., 807 Havens Corners Rd., 43230. Tel: 614-471-0212; Fax: 614-471-0247.
School—795 Havens Corners Rd., 43230. Tel: 614-471-4930; Fax: 614-471-1673. Carole G. Marsh, Prin.
Lay Teachers 25; Students 610.
Catechesis/Religious Programs—Tel: 614-471-2067; Fax: 614-471-1693. Julie Zarichny, D.R.E.
Students 582.

Granville, Licking Co., St. Edward the Confessor (1946), Rev. Msgr. Paul P. Enke; Deacon Paul C. Belhorn; Sr. Mary Caryl Perkinson, O.S.F., Pastoral Assoc.
Res., 785 Newark Rd., 43023. Tel: 740-587-3254; Fax: 740-587-0149.
Catechesis/Religious Programs—Tel: 740-587-4160.
Students 350.

Grove City, Franklin Co., Our Lady of Perpetual Help (1954), Rev. Msgr. Stephen B. Hawkins; Rev. Deogratias Biabandi (Rwanda).
Church & Mailing Address: 3730 Broadway, 43123. Tel: 614-875-3322; Fax: 614-875-6033.
School—3752 N. Broadway, 43123. Tel: 614-875-6779. Mr. William R. Groce, Prin.
Lay Teachers 21; Students 493.
Catechesis/Religious Programs—Tel: 614-875-9345. Mrs. Martha J. Hurd, D.R.E.
Students 376.

Groveport, Franklin Co., St. Mary's (1871), Rev. J. Lawrence Reichert; Deacon Frederick J. Schmitt.
Res., 5684 Groveport Rd., 43125. Tel: 614-497-1324; Fax: 614-497-2706.
Catechesis/Religious Programs—Tel: 614-497-1437. Alice Doran, D.R.E.
Students 233.

Heath, Licking Co., St. Leonard (1962), Revs. Michael J. Reis; Jack G. Maynard; Deacon Albert E. Cain.
Res., 57 Dorsey Mill Rd., 43056. Tel: 740-522-5270; Fax: 740-522-5261.
Catechesis/Religious Programs—Tel: 740-323-0400. Marge Moretti, D.R.E.
Students 70.

Hilliard, St. Brendan (1957), Rev. Msgr. William J. Maroon; Rev. Joseph J. Trapp, II; Deacons Patrick J. Wiggins; Gilbert L. Plummer.
Res., 4475 Dublin Rd., 43026. Tel: 614-876-1272; Fax: 614-876-1482.
School—(Grades 1-8). Tel: 614-876-6132; Fax: 614-529-8929. Mary Lang, Prin.
Lay Teachers 20; Students 435.
Catechesis/Religious Programs—Tel: 614-876-9533.
Students 1,350.

Jackson, Jackson Co., Holy Trinity (1875), Rev. Msgr. Robert E. Metzger.
Res., 215 Columbia St., 45640. Tel: 740-286-1428. [CEM]
Catechesis/Religious Programs—Karen Ochsenbein, D.R.E.
Students 67.

Johnstown, Licking Co., Church of the Ascension (1912), Rev. Richard L. Metzger.
Res., 276 S. Main St., 43031. Tel: 740-967-7871. [CEM]
Catechesis/Religious Programs—Tel: 740-967-1203. Kathy Wahlenmaier, D.R.E.
Students 130.

Junction City, Perry Co., St. Patrick (1820), Rev. Msgr. John J. Dreese; Mr. Al Kunkler, Pastoral Assoc.
Res., 1170 S.R. 668S, 43748. Tel: 740-987-2691. [CEM]
Catechesis/Religious Programs—Sr. Marie Tessmer, S.C., D.R.E.
Students 35.

Kenton, Hardin Co., Immaculate Conception (1836), Rev. William J. Faustner.
Res., 215 E. North St., 43326. Tel: 419-675-1162. [CEM]
Parish Center—220 E. North St., 44326. Tel: 419-675-9461.
Catechesis/Religious Programs—Tel: 419-675-1162. Jean M. Bruner, D.R.E.
Students 25.

Lancaster, Fairfield Co., St. Bernadette (1963), Rev. Justin J. Reis; Deacon Mark A. Scarpitti.
Res., 1343 Wheeling Rd., 43130-8701. Tel: 740-654-1893.
School—1325 Wheeling Rd., 43130. Tel: 740-654-3137; Fax: 740-653-9819. Pam Eltringham, Prin.
Lay Teachers 9; Students 213.
Catechesis/Religious Programs—Tel: 740-468-2268. Mary Good, D.R.E.
Students 258.

St. Mark (1960), Rev. Ronald L. Arter. In res., Rev. Msgr. Robert L. Noon.
Res., 324 Gay St., 43130. Tel: 740-654-2874; Fax: 740-653-8329. [JC]
Catechesis/Religious Programs—331 Gay St., 43130. Tel: 740-653-1229. Cheryl Oelker, D.R.E.
Students 182.

St. Mary (1818), Revs. Donald E. Franks; Denis S. Kigozi; Sr. Mary Cecil Grandpre, O.P., Pastoral Assoc.
Res., 132 S. High St., 43130. Tel: 740-653-0997; Fax: 740-653-0337. [CEM]
School—309 E. Chestnut St., 43130. Tel: 740-654-1632; Fax: 740-654-0877. Carlton B. Rider, Prin.
Lay Teachers 23; Students 443.
Catechesis/Religious Programs—Tel: 740-653-5054; Fax: 740-653-0337. Sr. Louis Mary Passeri, O.P., D.R.E.
Students 184.

La Rue, Marion Co., St. Joseph's (1864), Rev. Joseph F. Losh.
Res., 285 N. High St., P.O. Box 347, 43332-0347. Tel: 740-499-3614.

Logan, Hocking Co., St. John (1841) (German), Rev. Richard J. Pendolphi; Deacon Frank A. Paniccia.
Res., 351 N. Market St., 43138. Tel: 740-385-2549; Fax: 740-380-2837. [CEM]
School—321 N. Market St., 43138. Tel: 740-385-2767; Fax: 740-385-9727. Joan M. Miller, Prin.
Lay Teachers 5; Students 90.
Catechesis/Religious Programs—Tel: 740-385-8608. Cathy Kerns, D.R.E.
Students 63.

London, Madison Co., St. Patrick (1865) (German-Irish), Rev. Theodore K. Sill; Deacon Daniel W. Hann.
Res., 61 S. Union St., 43140. Tel: 740-852-0942; Fax: 740-852-5008. [CEM]
School—(Grades K-8) 226 Elm St., 43140. Tel: 740-852-0161; Fax: 740-852-0602. Dr. Jacob Froning, Prin.
Lay Teachers 12; Students 143.
Catechesis/Religious Programs—Students 196.

Marion, Marion Co., St. Mary (1864), Revs. James A. Klima; Rodney M. Damico.
Res., 251 N. Main St., 43302. Tel: 740-382-2118; Fax: 740-382-2110. [CEM]
School—274 North Prospect St., 44302. Tel: 740-382-1607. Bob Rush, Prin.
Lay Teachers 11; Students 148.
High School—(Grades 7-12). Tel: 740-389-2381; Fax: 740-389-5243.
Lay Teachers 17; Students 143.
Catechesis/Religious Programs—Tel: 740-382-2262.
Students 237.

Marysville, Union Co., Our Lady of Lourdes (1869), Rev. John B. Bentz; Deacon Gordon T. Kunkler.
Res., 1033 W. Fifth St., 43040. Tel: 937-644-6020; Fax: 937-644-6020. [CEM]
Catechesis/Religious Programs—Tel: 937-644-6030. Diane Campbell, D.R.E.
Students 286.
Mission—St. Thomas d'Aquin.

Millersburg, Holmes Co., St. Peter (1877), Rev. Ronald J. Aubry.
Res., 379 S. Crawford St., 44654-1463. Tel: 330-674-1671. [CEM][JC]
Catechesis/Religious Programs—Tel: 330-674-0333. Patricia A. Huebner, D.R.E.
Students 66.

Mission—Glenmont, Holmes Co., SS. Peter and Paul, SR 520, Glenmont, 44628.

Mineral City, Tuscarawas Co., Saint Patrick. Closed. For sacramental records contact Holy Trinity, Bolivar.

Mt. Vernon, Knox Co., St. Vincent de Paul (1842), Rev. Charles Theodore Thomas; Sr. Jean Welling, S.C., Pastoral Assoc.
Res., 303 E. High St., 43050. Tel: 740-392-4711; Fax: 740-392-4714. [CEM]
School—206 E. Chestnut St., 43050. Tel: 740-393-3611; Fax: 740-393-0236. Deborah Leibold, Prin.
Lay Teachers 12; Students 168.
Catechesis/Religious Programs—Tel: 740-393-0826. Shirley Lower, D.R.E.
Students 295.

Murray City, St. Philip Neri. Closed. For inquiries for sacramental records contact St. John, Logan.

New Albany, Franklin Co., Church of the Resurrection (1983), Rev. Msgr. J. Colby Grimes; Sr. Sarah Gass, S.C., Pastoral Assoc.
Res., 6300 E. Dublin-Granville Rd., 43054. Tel: 614-855-1400; Fax: 614-855-0779.
Catechesis/Religious Programs—(Grades K-6). Tel: 614-939-1794; Fax: 614-855-0779. Ms. Joan Lucius, D.R.E.
Students 764.

Newark, Licking Co., St. Francis de Sales (1842), Revs. Dean Mathewson; William Anthony Hritsko; Sr. Barbara Catalano, O.P., Pastoral Assoc.
Res., 66 Granville St., 43055. Tel: 740-345-9874; Fax: 740-345-1585. [CEM 2]
School—38 Granville St., 43055. Tel: 740-345-4049; Fax: 740-345-9768. Gretchen O'Neil, Prin.
Sisters of St. Dominico 1; Lay Teachers 28; Students 515.
Catechesis/Religious Programs—Tel: 740-349-7978. D.R.E.: Michael Barone; Eddie Cotter, (Junior High School).
Students 342.

Church of the Blessed Sacrament (1904), Rev. Timothy M. Hayes; Deacons Charles F. Stevens, (Retired); Jack W. Elam; Robert W. Ghiloni.
Res., 378 E. Main St., 43055. Tel: 740-345-4290; Fax: 740-345-3890. [JC]
School—15 Penny Ave., 43055. Tel: 740-345-4125; Fax: 740-345-6168. Robert Heigle, Prin.
Lay Teachers 10; Students 175.
Catechesis/Religious Programs—Tel: 740-763-4304. Debbie Wills, D.R.E.
Students 50.

New Boston, Scioto Co., St. Monica (1915), Rev. Peter M. Gideon; Sr. Theresa Kehres, O.S.F., Pastoral Assoc.
Res., 4252 Pine St., 45662. Tel: 740-456-5154; Fax: 740-456-5154. [CEM]
Catechesis/Religious Programs—Students 56.

Newcomerstown, Tuscarawas Co., St. Francis de Sales (1918), Rev. Edward L. Keck.
Res., 440 River St., 43832. Tel: 740-498-7368. [JC]
Catechesis/Religious Programs—Tel: 740-498-5497. Jane Morris, D.R.E.
Students 59.

New Lexington, Perry Co., St. Rose of Lima (1867), Rev. Msgr. John J. Dreese; Sr. Diana Durling, S.C., Pastoral Min.
Res., 309 N. Main St., 43764. Tel: 740-342-1348. [JC]
School—119 W. Water St., 43764. Tel: 740-342-3043; Fax: 740-342-1082. Mr. Charles Robinson, Prin.
Lay Teachers 9; Students 149.
Catechesis/Religious Programs—Tel: 740-987-2691; 342-3043. Sr. Marie Tessmer, S.C., D.R.E.
Students 71.

New Philadelphia, Tuscarawas Co., Sacred Heart (1895), Rev. Msgr. George J. Schlegel.
Res., 139 3rd St., N.E., 44663-3900. Tel: 330-343-6976; Fax: 330-343-1406. [CEM 2]
School—320 Fair Ave., N.E., 44663-3914. Tel: 330-343-1721; Fax: 330-364-4334. Scott Power, Prin.
Lay Teachers 12; Students 204.
Catechesis/Religious Programs—Tel: 330-364-2527.
Students 100.

Otway, Scioto Co., Our Lady of Lourdes (1917), Rev. David E. Young.
Res., 2215 Galena Pike, West Portsmouth, 45663. Tel: 740-858-4600; Fax: 740-858-4600. [CEM]
Catechesis/Religious Programs—Students 21.
Otway Community Service Center—P.O. Box 8, 45657. Tel: 740-372-2202.

Pickerington, Fairfield Co., Seton Parish (1978), Revs. Martin V. Weithman; Dwayne A. McNew; Deacons David J. Kruse; Martin Davies.
Res., 600 Hill Rd., 43147. Tel: 614-833-0482; Fax: 614-833-4154.
Catechesis/Religious Programs—Tel: 614-833-0485. Mrs. Mary Houze, D.R.E.
Students 965.

Plain City, Madison Co., St. Joseph (1864), Rev. Patrick A. Toner.
Res., 6604 Perry Pk., 43064. Tel: 614-873-8850; Fax: 614-873-8850.
Catechesis/Religious Programs—Tel: 614-873-8551. Heidi Kellett, D.R.E.
Students 132.
Mission—Milford Center, Union Co., Sacred Heart, P.O. Box 166, 43064.

Portsmouth, Scioto Co., St. Mary (1841) (German), Rev. Theodore F. Machnik; Deacon George E. Horsley.
Res., 524 Sixth St., 45662. Tel: 740-354-4551; Fax: 740-354-5799. [CEM]
Catechesis/Religious Programs—Students 49.

Holy Redeemer (1852) (Irish), Rev. Mark V. Ghiloni; Sr. Rita Hawk, S.C., Pastoral Assoc., Tel: 740-353-4425.
Office: 805 Offnere St., 45662. Tel: 740-353-4425. [CEM][JC]
Res., 1325 Gallia St., 45662. Tel: 740-354-8691; Fax: 740-354-4586.
School—Notre Dame Elementary, (Grades PreK-6). Serving all 7 parishes in Scioto County. 1401 Gallia St., 45662. Tel: 740-353-8610; Fax: 740-353-6769. Kay Kern, Prin.
Lay Teachers 25; Students 327.

Powell, Delaware Co., St. Joan of Arc (1987), Revs. Jeffrey J. Rimelspach; Jeffrey E. Tigyer; Deacons Thomas M. Berg; James A. Rouse.
Res., 10700 Liberty Rd. S., 43065-9303. Tel: 614-761-0905; Fax: 614-761-0850.
Catechesis/Religious Programs—Tel: 614-761-0903. Natalie Hutchison, D.R.E.
Students 969.

Reynoldsburg, Franklin Co., St. Pius X (1958), Revs. Daniel L. Ochs; Joseph A. Ehwald. Pastoral Assocs.: Ms. Christin Jungers; Ms. Regina Courey.
Res., 1051 Waggoner Rd., 43068. Tel: 614-866-2859; Fax: 614-866-1499.
School—1061 Waggoner Rd., 43068. Tel: 614-866-6050; Fax: 614-866-6187. Shirley Poirier, Prin.
Lay Teachers 31; Students 619.
Catechesis/Religious Programs—Tel: 614-864-3505. Richard LaBrake, D.R.E.
Students 298.

Roswell, Tuscarawas Co., St. Elizabeth. Closed. For sacramental records contact Sacred Heart Parish, New Philadelphia.

Shawnee, Perry Co., St. Mary & St. Augustine. Closed. For sacramental records contact St. Rose of Lima Parish, New Lexington.

Somerset, Perry Co., St. Joseph's (1818), Rev. Adrian L. Dionne, O.P.; Deacon Eugene O. Dawson.
Res., 5757 State Rte. 383 N.E., P.O. Box 190, 43783. Tel: 740-743-1317. [CEM]

Holy Trinity (1827), Rev. Adrian L. Dionne, O.P.; Deacon Eugene O. Dawson.
Res., 5757 State Rte. 383 N.E., P.O. Box 190, 43783. Tel: 740-743-1317. [CEM]
School—S. Columbus St., 43783. Tel: 740-743-1324; Fax: 740-743-1324. Mrs. Catherine Fields, Prin.
Sisters of St. Dominic 1; Lay Teachers 7; Students 146.
Catechesis/Religious Programs—Tel: 740-743-1855.
Students 42.

Strasburg, Tuscarawas Co., St. Aloysius (1911). Closed. For sacramental records contact Holy Trinity, Bolivar.

Sugar Grove, Fairfield Co., St. Joseph (1892), Rev. Msgr. James A. Geiger.
Res., 306 Elm St., 43155. Tel: 740-746-8302. [CEM][JC]
Catechesis/Religious Programs—Tel: 740-746-8302. Lisa Spires, D.R.E.
Students 69.

Sunbury, Delaware Co., St. John Neumann (1983), Rev. James A. Walter.
Res., 275 Carters Corner Rd., 43074-9536. Tel: 614-965-1358; Fax: 614-965-1377.
Church—9633 E. State Rte. 37, 43074-9593. Tel: 614-965-1358.
Catechesis/Religious Programs—Tel: 614-965-4877. Robert M. Steinbauer, D.R.E.
Students 233.

Utica, Licking Co., Church of the Nativity (1909), Rev. Stephen A. Metzger, Admin.
Res., 271 Jefferson St., P.O. Box 506, 43080. Tel: 740-892-2321.
Catechesis/Religious Programs—Rose Gorius, D.R.E.
Students 74.

Wainwright, Tuscarawas Co., Parish Community of St. Therese and St. Paul. Closed. For St. Therese's sacramental records contact Immaculate Conception, Dennison. For St. Paul's sacramental records contact Sacred Heart, New Philadelphia.

Washington Court House, Fayette Co., St. Colman (1885), Rev. Jan C. Sullivan.
Office: 219 S. North St., 43160. Tel: 740-335-5000.
Res., 223 E. East St., 43160. Tel: 740-335-3457. [CEM]
Catechesis/Religious Programs—Tel: 740-335-5005. Tracie Rush, D.R.E. (Grades PreK-12).
Students 126.

Waverly, Pike Co., St. Mary, Queen of the Missions (1878), Rev. James P. Black.
Res., 407 S. Market St., 45690. Tel: 740-947-2436. [JC]
Catechesis/Religious Programs—Students 30.

Wellston, Jackson Co., SS. Peter and Paul (1881), Rev. Donald M. Maroon.
Res., 227 S. New York Ave., 45692. Tel: 740-384-2359; Fax: 740-384-2945. [CEM]
School—229 S. New York Ave., 45692. Tel: 740-384-6354. Sr. Joellen Kohlmann, Prin.
Franciscan Sisters of Christian Charity 4; Lay Teachers 5; Students 113.
Catechesis/Religious Programs—Students 120.

Westerville, Delaware Co., St. Paul the Apostle (1913), Rev. Msgr. Edward J. Fairchild; Revs. Homer D. Blubaugh; Raymond E. Lavelle; Deacons Thomas Barford; William J.F. Davis; Mickey B. Hawkins. In res., Rev. Alan M. Sprenger.
Res., 313 N. State St., 43082. Tel: 614-882-2109; Fax: 614-891-7476.
School—61 Moss Rd., 43082. Tel: 614-882-2710; Fax: 614-882-5998. Anne O'Flynn, Prin.; Sharon Gillivan, Asst. Prin.
Lay Teachers 34; Students 901.
Catechesis/Religious Programs—Tel: 614-882-5045. Janet Brewer, D.R.E.
Students 975.

West Jefferson, Madison Co., SS. Simon and Jude (1866) (German-Irish), Revs. Michael J. Devaney, O.M.I.; Ralph J. Karl, O.M.I., (Retired); Deacon Ralph L. Parsons.
Res., 95 W. Main St., 43162-1295. Tel: 614-879-8562; Fax: 614-879-7605. [CEM]
Catechesis/Religious Programs—Tel: 614-878-0611; Fax: 614-853-3553. Kathleen Maggied, D.R.E.
Students 117.

West Portsmouth, Scioto Co., Our Lady of Sorrows (1944), Rev. David E. Young.
Res., 2215 Galena Pike, 45663. Tel: 740-858-4600; Fax: 740-858-4600. [CEM]
New To You Service Center—Mary Horn, Dir.
Catechesis/Religious Programs—P.O. Box 31, Otway, 45657. Tel: 740-372-7115; Fax: 740-372-7115.
Students 16.
Mission—Pond Creek, Scioto Co., Holy Trinity, 2215 Galena Pike, West Portsmouth, 45663.

Wheelersburg, Scioto Co., St. Peter (1855), Rev. Peter M. Gideon.
Res., 2167 Lick Run Lyra Rd., 45694. Tel: 740-574-5486. [CEM]
Catechesis/Religious Programs—Nancy Stegman, D.R.E.
Students 120.

Wills Creek, Our Lady of Lourdes. Closed. For sacramental records contact Sacred Heart, Coshocton.

Zaleski, Vinton Co., St. Sylvester (1862), Rev. David E. Gwinner.
Res., 22 N. Second St., P.O. Box 264, 45698-0264. Tel: 740-596-5474. [CEM]
Catechesis/Religious Programs—Students 26.

Zanesville, Muskingum Co., St. Nicholas (1842) (German), Revs. Charles F. Klinger; James C. Csaszar. Pastoral Assocs.: Sr. Anne Marie Selinsky, O.S.F.; Sr. Ruth Flynn, C.D.P.; Deacons B. N. Peterson, Jr.; James P. Feerick; Robert E. Staker.
Res., 925 E. Main St., 43701. Tel: 740-453-0597; Fax: 740-453-0590. [CEM]
School—1030 E. Main St., 43701. Tel: 740-453-2637; Fax: 740-454-0653. Mrs. Karen Robinson, Prin.
Franciscan Sisters of Christian Charity 2; Lay Teachers 15; Students 305.
Catechesis/Religious Programs—Tel: 740-450-7461. Judy Schiele, D.R.E.
Students 97.

St. Thomas Aquinas (1820), Revs. Michael DeTemple, O.P.; Thomas V. DiFede, O.P.; Sr. Maureen Mahon, O.S.F., Pastoral Assoc.
Res., 130 N. Fifth St., 43701. Tel: 740-453-3301; Fax: 740-453-0333. [CEM 2]
School—139 N. Fifth St., 43701. Tel: 740-454-9731; Fax: 740-454-9732. Ms. Erin Feerick, Prin.
Lay Teachers 14; Students 251.
Catechesis/Religious Programs—Tel: 740-453-3301, Ext. 15. Melanie Von Gunten, D.R.E.
Students 205.
Mission—Philo, Muskingum Co., St. Ann, 79 Main St., Philo, 43771. Tel: 740-674-6448.

Chaplains of Public Institutions

COLUMBUS. *Children's Hospital.* Vacant.
Regency Manor. Rev. Msgr. Edward F. Trenor.

CHILLICOTHE. *Chillicothe Correctional Institution.* Rev. Charles R. Griffin, Mailing Address: P.O. Box 5500, 45601. Tel: 740-773-2616, Ext. 248. Res., 122 Church St., 45601. Tel: 740-773-4391.
Ross Correctional Institution and Honor Camp. Rev. Charles R. Griffin, Mailing Address: P.O. Box 7010, 45601. Tel: 740-774-4182, Ext. 2519. Res., 122 Church St., 45601. Tel: 740-773-4391.
Veteran's Affairs Medical Center 17273 S.R. 104, 45601. Tel: 740-773-1141, Ext. 7203. Rev. Jose C. Bengco (Philippines), Res., 109 South Shore, 45601.

LANCASTER. *Southeastern Correctional Institution* Tel: 740-653-4324. Rev. Edward L. Kessler, Chap., Res., P.O. Box 264, Sugar Grove, 43155. Tel: 740-746-8007.

LONDON. *London Correctional Institution.* Rev. Patrick A. Toner Tel: 740-852-2454 Ext. 451.

LUCASVILLE. *Southern Ohio Correctional Facility.* Vacant. Tel: 740-259-5544.

MARION. *Marion Correctional Institution.* Deacon Robert A. Neely Tel: 740-382-5781, Ext. 2346.

MARYSVILLE. *Ohio Reformatory for Women.* Rev. John B. Bentz Tel: 937-642-1065; Deacon Gregory L. Eiden, 305 Acton Rd., Columbus, 43214. Tel: 614-267-7500.

MOUNT VERNON. *Mount Vernon State Institute* St. Vincent de Paul Parish, 303 E. High St., 43050. Tel: 740-392-4711. Rev. P. Wayne Meyer Tel: 740-397-5094.

ORIENT. *Orient Correctional Institution.* Vacant.

Special Assignment:
Reverend Fathers—
Petry, Thomas G.

On Duty Outside the Diocese:
Reverend Monsignors—
Fete, Joseph N., (Sabbatical)
Reverend Fathers—
Ascencio, Joseph A., Chap., Federal Prison System, CO
Kessler, Thomas Peter, O.S.B., Abbey of St. Mary & St. Louis, St. Louis, MO
Klein, Terrance W., St. John University, Jamaica, NY
Naughton, Patrick J., St. David, Davie, FL
Schilder, David M., Chap., Elkton Federal Correctional Institution, Elkton, KY

Military Chaplains:

Graduate Studies:
Reverend Monsignors—
Cody, John K.
Reverend Fathers—
Buffer, Thomas J.
Petry, Thomas G.

Leave of Absence:
Reverend Fathers—
Getreu, David E.
Rodenfels, Jerome P.

Retired:
Reverend Monsignors—
Berendt, James M., Villa at St. Therese, 5253 E. Broad St., Columbus, OH 43213
Carroll, James J., 12915 Galaxy Dr., Sun City W., AZ
Clagett, Carl P., 2601 Aspen Rd., Frazeysburg, OH 43822
Corcoran, Lawrence J., Holy Cross, 204 S. 5th St., Columbus, OH 43215
Dittoe, John T., 3547 Chowning Ct., Columbus, OH 43220
Faistl, Clement F., Christ the King Church, 2770 Dover Rd., Columbus, OH 43209
Gallen, F. Thomas, 425 Adams St., Box 416, Corning, OH 43730
Griffin, Patrick J., 3881 Monterey Dr., Grove City, OH 43123
Hanley, James P., 2492 Timberside Dr., Columbus, OH 43235
Healey, Edward F., Villas at St. Therese, 5253 E.Broad St., # 108, Columbus, OH 43213
Huntzinger, Ralph J., 8797 State Rte. 273 W., Belle Center, OH 43310-9580
McFarland, Edward J., 6818 Albany Woods Blvd., New Albany, OH 43054
Noon, Robert L., St. Mark Church, 324 Gay St., Lancaster, OH 43130
Nugent, Michael A., 300 E. Rich St. Rm. 1010, Columbus, OH 43215
Schmidt, Robert R., Seton Square E., 1235 Briarcliff Rd, #126, Reynoldsburg, OH 43068
Schulz, Donald C., St. Aloysius Church, 32 Clarendon Ave., Columbus, OH 43223
Schweitzer, Francis X., Nazareth Towers, 300 E. Rich St., #410, Columbus, OH 43215
Spiers, Edward F., Villas at St. Theresa, 5253 E. Broad St. #119, Columbus, OH 43313
Winel, Roland T., P.A., Nazareth Towers, 300 E. Rich St., Apt. 1306, Columbus, OH 43215
Wolf, John V., 104 N. Mulberry St., Fredericktown, OH 43019-1051. Tel: 614-694-2505
Reverend Fathers—
Bernans, Arvids, 4970 Deer Run Pl., Westville, OH 43081
Byrne, Patrick J., 4468 Beachwood Lake Dr., Naples, FL 34112
Carter, Raymond J., Villas at St. Therese, 5253 E. Broad St., #204, Columbus, OH 43213
Connor, William J., 10248 W. Snead Cir. N., Sun City, AZ 85351
Dimond, Arthur J., St. Mary, 684 S. 3rd St., Columbus, OH 43206
Durbin, Clement B., Sharon Brook Inn, 920 Sharon Vally Rd., #219, Newark, OH 43055
Engle, Richard F., 192 Grand Ave., Chillicothe, OH 45601
Essman, Charles P., Thurber Towers, 645 Neil Ave. #409, Columbus, OH 43215
Fulcher, John M., 619 W. Market St., # B, Baltimore, OH 43105
Gamba, John J., P.O. Box 184, Doylestown, OH 44230
Gately, Robert E., 5815 5th Ave. N., St. Petersburg, FL 33710
Griffin, Charles R., 122 Church St., Chillicothe, OH 45601
Haluska, Charles A., 37950 TR 344, Rte. 3, Warsaw, OH 43844
Jerabeck, Joseph F., Villas at St. Therese, 25 Noe Bixby Rd., Columbus, OH 43213
Jones, James W., 2770 Dover Rd., Columbus, OH 43209
Kessler, Edward L., 107 W. 4th St., P.O. Box 264, Sugar Grove, OH 43155
Klee, Robert A., St. Charles Preparatory School, 2010 E. Broad St., Columbus, OH 43209
Laurinaitis, Saulius P., P.O. Box 1417, Hilliard, OH 43026
Lavelle, Raymond E., 6415 Pinehurst Pointe, Westerville, OH 43082
Manning, Robert T., Box 177, Uhrichsville, OH 44683
Marzluf, George J., 7807 Rockville Rd. S.W., Navarre, OH 44662
McClory, Bernard J., 1288 S. 4th St., Columbus, OH 43206
McNulty, Edwin J., St. Rita Home, 880 Greenlawn Ave., Columbus, OH 43223
Metzger, John L., P.O. Box 55, New Lexington, OH 43764
Meyer, Paul Wayne, 406 E. High St., Mount Vernon, OH 43050
Miller, Frank P., 521 Fuhr St., #2, Dennison, OH 44621
Raiser, Jerome K., Corpus Christi Church, 1111 E. Stewart Ave., Columbus, OH 43206
Reilly, Robert F., Nazareth Towers, 300 E. Rich St. #1203, Columbus, OH 43215
Schaefer, Francis R., 11438 E. Huffman Rd. #4, Cleveland, OH 44130
Schneider, Harold E., 913 Hartney Dr., Gahanna, OH 43230
Schuer, Robert J., St. Agatha, 1860 Northam Rd., Columbus, OH 43221
Sprenger, Alan H., St. Paul Church, 313 N. State St., Westerville, OH 43082
Stanton, Joseph E., St. Mary, 684 S. 3rd St., Columbus, OH 43206
Totten, Raymond F., 329 Carnegie Pl., Pittsburgh, PA 15208
Wise, Kenneth F., Immaculate Conception Church, 206 N. First St., Dennison, OH 44621

Permanent Deacons:
Allison, Mark D., St. Joseph, Dover
Azzola, Feliz F., St. Mary, Delaware
Ball, Frank X., St. Elizabeth, Columbus
Barford, Thomas M., St. Paul, Westerville
Baumann, Richard L., Our Lady of Victory, Columbus
Belhorn, Paul C., St. Edward, Granville
Berg, Thomas M., St. Joan of Arc, Powell
Bonacci, Anthony C., St. Joseph, Plain City
Butts, Jerome J., Corpus Christi, Columbus
Cain, Albert E., St. Leonard, Heath
Checca, Joseph P., St. James the Less, Columbus
Crerand, John R., St. Michael, Worthington
Davis, James R., Holy Rosary-St. John Community, Columbus
Davis, William J.F., St. Paul, Westerville
Dawson, Eugene O., St. Joseph, Somerset
Duda, Frank A., Sacred Heart, Coshocton
DuPrey, John L., Leave of Absence
Eiden, Gregory L., St. Francis of Assisi, Columbus
Elam, Jack W., Blessed Sacrament, Newark
Farmer, Joseph A., (Retired)
Farry, Joseph W., St. Philip, Columbus
Feerick, James P., (Retired)
Fondriest, Ronald H., St. Joseph, Dover
Franks, Michael J., Sr., St. Francis, Newark
Ghiloni, Robert W., Blessed Sacrament, Newark
Gorman, William J., Leave of Absence
Gornick, Thomas W., Leave of Absence
Hann, Daniel W., Chap., Madison Correctional Institution
Horsley, George E., St. Mary, Portsmouth
Iannarino, Francis A., St. Brigid of Kildare, Dublin; Bishop Watterson High School, Columbus
Johnston, Thomas V., St. Joseph Cathedral, Columbus
Koebel, Lawrence F., Chap., Pickaway Correctional Institute
Krick, Richard T., St. Peter, Chillicothe
Kruse, David J., St. Elizabeth Ann Seton, Pickerington
Kunkler, Gordon T., Our Lady of Lourdes, Marysville
Labita, Peter C., Christ the King, Columbus
Lampe, Elmer L., Unassigned
Larcomb, Dwight T., Leave of Absence
Lovensheimer, George L., St. Mary, Chillicothe
McCurry, William E., County Sheriff's Office, Marion; Holy Family, Columbus
McDevitt, Francis X., St. Elizabeth, Columbus
Neely, Robert A., St. Dominic, Columbus; Chap., Marion Correctional Institute
Paniccia, Frank A., St. John, Logan
Parsons, Ralph L., Sts. Simon & Jude, West Jefferson
Paulucci, Philip M., St. Peter, Columbus
Peterson, Burdette N., St. Nicholas, Zanesville
Plummer, Gilbert L., Sr., St. Brendan, Hilliard
Poland, Joseph D., Our Lady of Miraculous Medal, Columbus
Pry, Roger F., Sts. Augustine & Gabriel, Columbus
Rankin, John, Our Lady of Peace, Columbus
Rericha, John J., St. Elizabeth, Columbus
Rouse, James A., St. Joan of Arc, Powell
Rzewnicki, Phil E., Unassigned
Scarpitti, Mark A., St. Joseph, Circleville
Schermer, Joseph E., St. Peter, Columbus
Schmitt, Frederick J., St. Mary, Groveport
Spina, Philip V., Jr., Leave of Absence
Stahl, John P., Our Lady of Lourdes, Ada
Staker, Eugene R., St. Nicholas, Zanesville
Stevens, Charles F., (Retired)
Turner, Harry
Vellani, Albert J., St. Michael, Worthington
Venturini, Stephen A., Our Lady of the Miraculous Medal, Columbus
Wiggins, Patrick J., St. Brendan, Hilliard

INSTITUTIONS LOCATED IN THE DIOCESE

[A] SEMINARIES, PONTIFICAL COLLEGES

COLUMBUS. *Pontifical College Josephinum*, 7625 N. High St., 43235-1498. Tel: 614-885-5585; Fax: 614-885-2307.
Web site: www.pcj.edu
General Administrative Offices: Most Revs. Gabriel Montalvo, Nuncio, Chancellor; James A. Griffin, J.D., J.C.L., Bishop of Columbus & Vice Chancellor; Rev. Msgr. Earl Boyea, Ph.D. (DET), Rector&Pres.; Rev. Brian R. Moore, Ph.D (DOD), Vice Rector, School of Theology; Rev. Msgr. Frank P. Lane, Ph.D., Vice Rector, College of Liberal Arts; Rev. Joseph A. Murphy, S.J., S.T.L., S.T.D., Academic Dean; Mr. Patrick J. O'Reilly, Treas.; Dr. Byron W. Thorsen, Registrar; Mr. Peter Veracka, Dir. of the Library; Mr. Christopher Norman, Chief Dev. Officer; Mary Patricia Mulligan, M.A., Dir. Field Education School Theology & Dir. M.Div. Program.
Theology Administrative Offices: Revs. William M. Fitzgerald, O.Praem. (STL), Dir. Liturgy; Richard J. Tomasek, S.J., S.T.L., Dir. Spiritual Formation; Kevin C. Louis (LC), Dean Personal Formation & Acting Dean Men. Priests on Theology Teaching Staff: Revs. Robert J. Bauer, S.D.B., S.S.L.; William Dettling, O.P., S.T.D.; James Garneau, Ph.D.;

William D. Lynn, S.J., S.T.D.; John Michael McDermott, S.J., S.T.D. Theology Teaching Staff: Sr. Carolyn Thomas, S.C.N., Ph.D.; James Keating, Ph.D.; James A. Yeager, D.M.A.
College Administrative Offices: Revs. Michael Hickin (FAR), Dir. of Pastoral Formation; Brian Van Hove, S.J., M.Th., S.T.L., Dir. Spiritual Formation; Jay Scott Newman, S.J., S.T.L. (CHR), Dean of Men. Priests in College Teaching Staff: Revs. Robert A. Gonzales, Ph.D. (TUC); Charles A. Jackson, S.T.L.; Laurence C. Landini, O.S.M., Personal Formation Dir.
College Teaching Staff: Alma Amell, Ph.D.; Caren Calendine, Ph.D.; David J. DeLeonardis, Ph.D.; Carolyn Scott, Ph.D. Total Staff 29; Total Enrollment 106.

[B] COLLEGES AND UNIVERSITIES

COLUMBUS. *Ohio Dominican College*, 1216 Sunbury Rd., 43219. Tel: 614-253-2741; Fax: 614-252-0776.
E-mail: admissions@odc.edu
Web site: www.odc.edu
For a complete listing, refer to the Colleges and Universities section.

[C] HIGH SCHOOLS, DIOCESAN OR INTERPAROCHIAL

COLUMBUS. *Bishop Hartley High School*, 1285 Zettler Rd., 43227. Tel: 614-237-5421; Fax: 614-237-3809.
E-mail: mwinters@cd.pvt.k12.oh.us
Mike Winters, Prin.; Randy Kortokrax, Dean of Students; Dave Thompson, Athletic Dir. Religious 1; Lay Teachers 42; Students 606.

Bishop Ready High School, 707 Salisbury Rd., 43204. Tel: 614-276-5263; Fax: 614-276-5116.
E-mail: cseamen@cdeducation.org
Web site: www.brhs.org
Celene A. Seamen, Prin. Lay Teachers 34; Students 485.

Bishop Watterson High School, 99 E. Cooke Rd., 43214. Tel: 614-268-8671; Fax: 614-268-0551.
E-mail: www.cdeducation.org/schools/bw
Web site: http://www.cd.pvt.kiz.oh.us/schools/bw/
Mrs. Marian Hutson, Prin.; Deacon Frank A. Iannarino, Chap. Deacons 1; Sisters 1; Lay Teachers 62; Students 1,068. Development Office, 100 Indian Springs Dr., 43214. Tel: 614-268-3041; Fax: 614-268-4309.

St. Charles Preparatory School, 2010 E. Broad St., 43209. Tel: 614-252-6714; Fax: 614-251-6800.
E-mail: dcavello@cd.pvt.k12.oh.us
Web site: www.cd.pvt.kiz.oh.us/schools/sc/index.html
Dominic J. Cavello, Prin.; Scott M. Pharion, Asst. Prin.; James Lower, Asst. Prin.; Rev. Msgr. Thomas M. Bennett; Sr. Margaret Hoffman. Priests 1; Sisters 1; Lay Teachers 32; Students 527.

St. Francis de Sales High School, 4212 Karl Rd., 43224. Tel: 614-267-7808; Fax: 614-265-3375.
Web site: http://www.cd.pvt.kiz.oh.us
Mr. Patrick D. Rossetti, Prin.; Mr. Dan Garrick, Asst. Prin.; Jackie Messerschmitt, Asst. Prin. Convent, 4212 Karl Rd., 43224. Lay Teachers 57; Students 995.

LANCASTER. *William V. Fisher Catholic High School*, 1803 Granville Pike, 43130. Tel: 740-654-1231; Fax: 740-654-1233. Mr. James P. Condron, Prin.; Al Kovacic, Campus Min. Lay Teachers 22; Students 322.

MARION. *Marion Catholic High School*, 1001 Mt. Vernon Ave., 43302. Tel: 740-389-2381; Fax: 740-389-5243.
E-mail: mchs@cd.pvt.k12.oh.us
David Hartline, Prin. Lay Teachers 16; Students 139.

NEW PHILADELPHIA. *Central Catholic High School*, 777 Third St., N.E., 44663. Tel: 330-343-3302; Fax: 330-343-6388.
E-mail: jbrannon@cd.pvt.k12.oh.us
Web site: http://webl.tusco.net/tcc/
Joseph A. Brannon, Ph.D., Prin. Lay Teachers 12; Students 142.

NEWARK. *Newark Catholic High School*, 1 Green Wave Dr., 43055. Tel: 740-344-3594; Fax: 740-344-0421.
E-mail: bhill@cdeducation.edu
Al Hoffman, Campus Min. Lay Teachers 26; Students 297.

PORTSMOUTH. *Notre Dame High School*. (Grades 7-12), 2220 Sunrise Ave., 45662. Tel: 614-353-0719; Fax: 740-353-2526.
E-mail: kmilliga@zoomnet.net
Kathleen Milligan, Prin. Sisters 1; Lay Teachers 18; Students 184.

ZANESVILLE. *Bishop Rosecrans High School*, 1040 E. Main St., 43701. Tel: 740-452-7504; Fax: 740-455-5080.
E-mail: dmorland@cd.pvt.k12.oh.us
David E. Morland, Prin.; Rev. James C. Csaszar. Priests 1; Lay Teachers 17; Students 238.

[D] MONTESSORI SCHOOLS

COLUMBUS. *St. Joseph Montessori School*, 933 Hamlet St., 43201-3595. Tel: 614-291-8601; Fax: 614-291-7411.
E-mail: dbarton@cd.pvt.k12.oh.us
Web site: http://www.sjms.net
Donna Barton, Admin. Lay Teachers 25; Students 279.

[E] PRIVATE SCHOOLS

COLUMBUS. *Our Lady of Bethlehem and Childcare*, 4567 Olentangy River Rd., 43214. Tel: 614-451-6631; Fax: 614-451-3706. Preschool - 3rd grade childcare and latchkey program. Marilyn P. Dono, Prin. Total Staff 32; Children 292.

[F] GENERAL HOSPITALS

COLUMBUS. *Mohun Health Care Center*, 2320 Airport Dr., 43219. Tel: 614-253-8517; Fax: 614-251-0338.
E-mail: jacquelinebaum@usa.net
Web site: columbusdominicans.org
For a complete listing, refer to the Hospitals section.

Mount Carmel Health System, 793 W. State St., 43222. Tel: 614-234-5423; Fax: 614-234-5985.
Web site: mountcarmelhealth.com
For a complete listing, refer to the Hospitals section.

Trinity Continuing Care, dba Saint Angela Nursing and Rehabilitation Center, 5700 Karl Rd., 43229. Tel: 614-846-5420; Fax: 614-846-3247
For a complete listing, refer to the Hospitals section.

ZANESVILLE. *Genesis Healthcare System*, 800 Forest Ave. & 2951 Maple Ave, 43701. Tel: 740-454-4638; Fax: 740-455-4914
For a complete listing, refer to the Hospitals section.

[G] HOMES FOR AGED AND HOUSING FOR ELDERLY

COLUMBUS. *Nazareth Towers*, 300 E. Rich St., 43215. Tel: 614-464-4780; Fax: 614-464-1733
For a complete listing, refer to the Special Care Facilities section.

St. Raphael Home for the Aged, Inc., 1550 Roxbury Rd., 43212. Tel: 614-486-0436; Fax: 614-486-1640.
E-mail: st50raph@aol.com
For a complete listing, refer to the Special Care Facilities section.

St. Rita Home, 880 Greenlawn Ave., 43223. Tel: 614-443-9433; Fax: 614-443-1196
For a complete listing, refer to the Special Care Facilities section.

Seton South Columbus, Inc., 155 Highview Blvd., 43207. Tel: 614-492-9944; Fax: 614-861-8022
For a complete listing, refer to the Special Care Facilities section.

Seton Square North, 1776 Drew Ave., 43235. Tel: 614-451-1995; Fax: 614-451-1995
For a complete listing, refer to the Special Care Facilities section.

Seton Square, West, 3939 Clime Rd., 43228. Tel: 614-451-8750
For a complete listing, refer to the Special Care Facilities section.

COSHOCTON. *Seton Coshocton, Inc.*, 377 Clow Ln., 43812. Tel: 330-343-3611; Fax: 330-343-4473.
E-mail: setondover@juno.com
For a complete listing, refer to the Special Care Facilities section.

DOVER. *Seton Square Dover, I, Inc.*, 501 James St., 44622. Tel: 330-343-3611; Fax: 330-343-4473.
E-mail: setondover@juno.com
For a complete listing, refer to the Special Care Facilities section.

Seton Square Dover, II, Inc., 139 Fillmore St., 44622. Tel: 330-343-3611; Fax: 330-343-4473.
E-mail: setondover@juno.com
For a complete listing, refer to the Special Care Facilities section.

KENTON. *Seton Kenton, Inc.*, 699 Morningside Dr., 43326. Tel: 419-673-7202; Fax: 419-673-7202
For a complete listing, refer to the Special Care Facilities section.

LANCASTER. *Seton Lancaster, Inc.*, 232 Gay St., 43130. Tel: 740-681-1403; Fax: 740-681-9178
For a complete listing, refer to the Special Care Facilities section.

LONDON. *Seton London, Inc.*, 350 Cambridge Dr., 43140. Tel: 740-852-4233
For a complete listing, refer to the Special Care Facilities section.

MARION. *Seton Square Marion, Inc.*, 255 Richland Rd., 43302. Tel: 740-389-4746; Fax: 740-389-9780
For a complete listing, refer to the Special Care Facilities section.

REYNOLDSBURG. *Seton Square East, Inc.*, 12235 Briarcliff Rd., 43068. Tel: 614-861-4860; Fax: 614-861-8022
For a complete listing, refer to the Special Care Facilities section.

WASHINGTON COURT HOUSE. *Seton Washington Court House, Inc.*, 400 N. Glenn Ave., 43160. Tel: 740-335-2292; Fax: 740-335-2291
For a complete listing, refer to the Special Care Facilities section.

WELLSTON. *Seton Square Wellston, Inc.*, 570 W. First St., 45692. Tel: 740-384-6174
For a complete listing, refer to the Special Care Facilities section.

ZANESVILLE. *Seton Housing, Inc.*, 516 Sheridan St., 43701. Tel: 740-453-4422
For a complete listing, refer to the Special Care Facilities section.

[H] MONASTERIES AND RESIDENCES OF PRIESTS AND BROTHERS

COLUMBUS. *Salesian Center*, 80 S. 6th St., 43215. Tel: 614-224-8000; Fax: 614-224-8000, Ext. 7.
E-mail: sdbcol1@aol.com
Web site: www.sbgcc.org
Revs. William A. Ferruzzi, S.D.B., Dir.; Robert J. Bauer, S.D.B.; Dennis Donovan, S.D.B., Vice Dir. & Exec. Dir. Boys & Girls Club; Richard Cressman, S.D.B.; Francis Anthony Kombarakaran, S.D.B.; Bros. Salvatore Sammarco, S.D.B., Coord. Youth Ministry; Michael Brinkman, S.D.B. Brothers 2; Total Staff 7.

NEWARK. *P.I.M.E. Mission & Retreat Center*, 2734 Seminary Rd., S.E., 43056-9339. Tel: 740-928-4246; Fax: 740-928-1512.
E-mail: pimenewark@prodigy.net
Revs. Ronald Boccali, P.I.M.E., Rector; Dino S. Vanin, P.I.M.E.; Casto Marrapese, P.I.M.E.; Adriano Cadei, P.I.M.E. Total in Residence 4.

SOMERSET. *St. Joseph's Rectory*, 5757 State Rte. 383 N.E., P.O. Box 190, 43783. Tel: 740-743-1317. Rev. Adrian L. Dionne, O.P. Total Staff 2; Total in Residence 1.

WEST JEFFERSON. *SS. Simon and Jude*, 95 W. Main St., 43162-1225. Tel: 614-879-8562; Fax: 614-879-7605.
E-mail: fathermike@juno.com
Revs. Michael J. Devaney, O.M.I.; Ralph J. Karl, O.M.I., (Retired); Deacon Ralph L. Parsons.

[I] CONVENTS AND RESIDENCES FOR SISTERS

COLUMBUS. *Carmelite Sisters for Aged and Infirm*, Queen of Hope Residence, 5749 Willow Creek Cir., 43213. Tel: 614-501-8038; Fax: 614-501-8035. Carmelite Sisters operate the Villas of St. Therese.

St. Mary of the Springs, 2320 Airport Dr., 43219-2098. Tel: 614-252-2137; Fax: 614-252-7435.
E-mail: sheila.mcintyre@juno.com
Web site: www.columbusdominicans.org
Leadership Team: Sr. Mary Faith Geelan, O.P., Prioress; Sr. Anne Kilbride, O.P., Vicaress; Sr. Sheila Marie McIntyre, O.P., Councilor, Secretary-General; Sr. Ellen Dunn, O.P., Councilor; Sr. Arleen Kisiel, O.P., Councilor.
Sisters' Residence: Sr. Virginia King, Coordinator.

Mohun Health Care Center. Tel: 614-253-8517; Fax: 614-251-0338. Sr. Jacqueline Baum, O.P., Admin.; Sr. Mary Patricia Gallagher, O.P., Dir. of Resident Life; Rev. Benedict Joseph, O.P., Chap. Sisters 129; Novices 1; Total inCongregation 315.

Sisters of the Good Shepherd, 2440 Dawnlight Ave., 43211. Tel: 614-471-2626; Fax: 614-475-2264.
E-mail: srelise @juno.com
Sr. Elise Kramer, R.G.S., Supr. Sisters of Our Lady of Charity of the Good Shepherd 5. Good Shepherd International Missions.

PORTSMOUTH. Oratory. *St. Joseph Adoration Monastery, Poor Clares of Perpetual Adoration*. (Public Chapel), 2311 Stockham Ln., 45662-3049. Tel: 740-353-4713. Mother Mary Agnes, P.C.P.A., Abbess; Rev. William C. Patterson, Chap. Professed Cloistered Nuns 5; Postulants 1.

[J] NEWMAN CENTERS

COLUMBUS. *Campus Ministry*. Ohio State University, 64 W. Lane Ave., 43201. Tel: 614-291-4674; Fax: 614-291-2065.
E-mail: newmanosu@aol.com
Web site: www.thenewmancenter.com
Revs. David W. O'Brien, C.S.P., Dir.; Vincent W. McKiernan, C.S.P.; Mark D. Janus, C.S.P.; Mark A. Villano, C.S.P.; Deacon Phil E. Rzewnicki; Rev. Charles Theodore Thomas, Diocesan Dir. Campus Min., 303 E. High St., Mt. Vernon, 43050. Tel: 740-392-4711.

[K] FOUNDATIONS

COLUMBUS.

The Foundation of the Catholic Diocese of Columbus, 197 E. Gay St., 43215. Tel: 614-241-2566; Fax: 614-241-2567. Kathy Spencer, Exec. Dir.

Legacy of Catholic Learning Endowment Program, 198 E. Broad St., 43215. Tel: 614-224-1221.

LANCASTER.

William V. Fisher Catholic High School Endowment Fund, 1803 Granville Pike, 43130. Tel: 740-654-1231; Fax: 740-654-1233.

MARION. *Marion Catholic High School Endowment Fund*, 1001 Mount Vernon Ave., 43302. Tel: 740-389-2381; Fax: 740-389-5243.
E-mail: mchs@cd.pvt.k12.oh.us

NEW PHILADELPHIA. *Tuscarawas Central Catholic High School Endowment Fund*, 777 Third St. N.E., 44663. Tel: 330-343-3302; Fax: 330-343-6388.
E-mail: jbrannon@cd.pvt.k12.oh.us

NEWARK.
Newark Catholic High School Endowment Fund, One Green Wave Dr., 43055. Tel: 740-344-5671; Fax: 740-344-0412.

ZANESVILLE. *Bishop Rosecrans High School Foundation*, 1040 E. Main St., 43701. Tel: 740-450-7993; Fax: 740-450-7994.
E-mail: gpellegr@cdeducation.org
Web site: www.cdeducation.org/schools/bro

[L] MISCELLANEOUS

COLUMBUS. *Blessed Margaret Guild, Inc. c/o St. Patrick Church*, 376 E. Naghten St., 43215. Tel: 614-240-5910; Fax: 614-240-5928. Total Staff 1.

Catholic Alumni Club, P.O. Box 695, 43216.
E-mail: peggyschano@email.msn.com
Web site: www.angelfire.com/oh/CatholicAlumniClub
Peggy Schano, Contact Person. Tel: 614-263-7686; Dan Doell, Contact Person. Tel: 614-846-7489.

The Christ Child Society of Columbus, Inc., P.O. Box 340091, 43234-0091. Tel: 614-279-9660; 614-451-2863.
E-mail: njohanni@aol.com
Norma Johanni, Pres.

Diocesan Retirement Community Corp., 198 E. Broad St., 43215. Tel: 614-224-2251; Fax: 614-224-6306. Rev. Joseph M. Hendricks, Pres. & C.E.O.; Mrs. Carol L. Oravec, Project Coord.

St. Stephen's Community House, 1500 E. 17th Ave., 43219. Tel: 614-294-6347; Fax: 614-294-0258.
E-mail: sschjs@aol.com
Ms. Judith Stattmiller, Exec. Dir. Total Assisted 34,000; Total Staff 101.

The Villas at St. Therese Assisted Living, Inc., 25 Noe-Bixby Rd., 43213-1461. Tel: 614-864-3576; Fax: 614-864-3577. Sr. Ann Brown, O.Carm., Admin.; Rev. Msgr. Joseph M. Hendricks, Contact Person.

The Villas at St. Therese Independent Living, Inc., 5253 E. Broad St., 43213. Tel: 614-864-3576; Fax: 614-864-3577. Rev. Msgr. Joseph M. Hendricks, Contact Person.

LANCASTER.
St. Mary of the Assumption Foundation, 132 S. High St., 43130. Tel: 740-653-0997; Fax: 740-653-0337. Rev. Donald E. Franks, Contact Person.

ZANESVILLE. *St. Nicholas Foundation*, 925 E. Main St., 43701. Tel: 740-453-0597; Fax: 740-453-0590.
E-mail: charlieatnick@prodigy.net

RELIGIOUS INSTITUTES OF MEN REPRESENTED IN THE DIOCESE

For further details refer to the corresponding bracketed number in the Religious Institutes of Men or Women section.

[0900]—*Canons Regular of Premontre*.—O.Praem.
[0350]—*Cistercians Order of the Strict Observance-Trappists*.—O.C.S.O.
[0690]—*Jesuit Fathers and Brothers*. (Detroit and Maryland Provs.).—S.J.
[0910]—*Oblates of Mary Immaculate*.—O.M.I.
[0430]—*Order of Preachers-Dominicans*. (Prov. of St. Joseph).—O.P.
[1030]—*Paulist Fathers*.—C.S.P.
[1050]—*Pontifical Institute for Foreign Missions*.—P.I.M.E.
[1190]—*Salesians of St. John Bosco*.—S.D.B.
[0760]—*Society of Mary*.—S.M.
[1060]—*Society of the Precious Blood*. (Cincinnati Prov.).—C.PP.S.

RELIGIOUS INSTITUTES OF WOMEN REPRESENTED IN THE DIOCESE

[0330]—*Carmelite Sisters for the Aged and Infirm*.—O.Carm.
Congregation of Divine Providence, KY.—C.D.P.
[3710]—*Congregation of the Sisters of St. Agnes*.—C.S.A.
[1920]—*Congregation of the Sisters of the Holy Cross*.—C.S.C.
[1730]—*Congregation of the Sisters of the Third Order of St. Francis, Oldenburg, IN*.—O.S.F.
[1710]—*Congregation of the Third Order of St. Francis of Mary Immaculate, Joliet, IL*.—O.S.F.
[1070-02]—*Dominican Sisters*. (Columbus, OH).—O.P.
[1070-13]—*Dominican Sisters*. (Adrian, MI).—O.P.
[1070-25]—*Dominican Sisters*. (Kenosha, WI).—O.P.
[1230]—*Franciscan Sisters of Christian Charity*. (Manitowoc, WI).—O.S.F.
[1440]—*Franciscan Sisters of the Poor*.—S.F.P.
[3790]—*Institute of the Sisters of St. Dorothy*.—S.S.D.
[3210]—*Poor Clares of Perpetual Adoration*.—P.C.P.A.
[1070-03]—*Sinsinawa Dominican Congregation of the Most Holy Rosary*.—O.P.
[0440]—*Sisters of Charity of Cincinnati, Ohio*.—S.C.
[0500]—*Sisters of Charity of Nazareth, Kentucky*.—S.C.N.
[0990]—*Sisters of Divine Providence*.—C.D.P.
[2575]—*Sisters of Mercy of the Americas*. (Detroit Prov.).—R.S.M.
[3000]—*Sisters of Notre Dame de Namur*.—S.N.D.deN.
[1630]—*Sisters of St. Francis of Penance and Christian Charity*. (Stella Niagara, NY).—O.S.F.
[1530]—*Sisters of St. Francis of the Congregation of Our Lady of Lourdes, Sylvania, OH*.—O.S.F.
[3830-05]—*Sisters of St. Joseph*. (Brentwood, NY).—C.S.J.
[3830-08]—*Sisters of St. Joseph*. (Cleveland, OH).—C.S.J.
[3830-13]—*Sisters of St. Joseph*. (Baden, PA).—C.S.J.
[1830]—*Sisters of the Good Sheperd*.—R.G.S.
[3220]—*Sisters of the Poor Child Jesus*.—P.C.J.
[3260]—*Sisters of the Precious Blood*. (Dayton, OH).—C.PP.S.
[3320]—*Sisters of the Presentation of the B.V.M.*—P.B.V.M.
[1760]—*Sisters of the Third Order of St. Francis of Penance and of Charity*.—O.S.F.
[1720]—*Sisters of the Third Order Regular of St. Francis of the Congregation of Our Lady of Lourdes*.—O.S.F.
[4120-04]—*The Ursuline Nuns of Cleveland*.—O.S.U.

DIOCESAN CEMETERIES

COLUMBUS. *Mount Calvary*, 518 Mt. Calvary Ave., 43223-2217. Tel: 614-491-2751. Rich Finn, Dir. & Gen. Mgr.

LEWIS CENTER. *Resurrection*, 9571 N. High St., 43035-9413. Tel: 614-888-1805; Fax: 614-888-1810. Rich Finn, Dir. & Gen. Mgr.

LOCKBOURNE. *St. Joseph*, 6440 S. High St., 43137-9208. Tel: 614-491-2751; Fax: 614-491-4264. Rich Finn, Dir. & Gen. Mgr.

PATASKALA. *Holy Cross*, 11539 National Rd. S.W., 43062-8304. Tel: 740-927-4442; Fax: 740-927-4645. Rich Finn, Dir. & Gen. Mgr.

NECROLOGY

✠ Herrmann, Most Rev. Edward J., (Retired). —Died Dec. 22, 1999.

† Applegate, Rev. Msgr. Bennett, (Retired). —Died March 22, 2000.

† Dodd, Rev. Msgr. Richard F., (Retired). —Died Feb. 26, 2000.

Diocese of Corpus Christi

(Dioecesis Corporis Christi)

Most Reverend

EDMOND CARMODY, D.D.

Seventh Bishop of Corpus Christi; ordained June 8, 1957; appointed Auxiliary Bishop of the Archdiocese of San Antonio November 8, 1988; consecrated December 15, 1988; appointed Bishop of the Diocese of Tyler March 24, 1992; installed May 25, 1992; appointed Bishop of the Diocese of Corpus Christi February 3, 2000; installed March 17, 2000. *Mailing Address: P.O. Box 2620, Corpus Christi, TX, 78403-2620.* Tel.: 361-882-6191; Fax: 361-654-1270.

Most Reverend

RENE H. GRACIDA, D.D.

Bishop Emeritus of Corpus Christi; ordained May 23, 1959; appointed Titular Bishop of Masuccaba and Auxiliary of Miami December 6, 1971; consecrated January 25, 1972; appointed Bishop of Pensacola-Tallahassee October 1, 1975; transferred to Corpus Christi May 19, 1983; installed July 11, 1983; retired April 1, 1997. *Res., 4126 Ocean Dr., Corpus Christi, TX, 78411-1224. Office: 620 Lipan St., P.O. Box 2620, Corpus Christi, TX, 78403-2620.* Tel.: 361-882-6191.

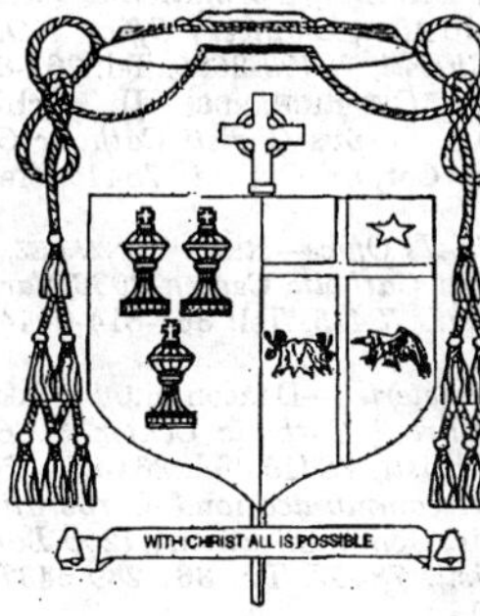

ERECTED A VICARIATE APOSTOLIC IN 1874; ELEVATED TO A DIOCESE MARCH 23, 1912.

Square Miles 17,294.

The territory embraced by the Diocese of Corpus Christi comprises the Counties of Aransas, Bee, Brooks, Duval, Jim Wells, Kleberg, Kenedy, Live Oak, Nueces, Refugio, San Patricio, and parts of McMullen in the State of Texas.

For legal titles of parishes and diocesan institutions, consult the Chancery Office.

The Chancery Office: 620 Lipan St., P.O. Box 2620, Corpus Christi, TX, 78403-2620. Tel.: 361-882-6191; Fax: 361-882-1018; 883-8850.

Web site address: www.diocesecc.org

E-mail address: chancery@diocesecc.org

STATISTICAL OVERVIEW

Personnel	
Bishop	1
Retired Bishops	1
Abbots	1
Retired Abbots	1
Priests: Diocesan Active in Diocese	68
Priests: Active Outside Diocese	8
Priests: Diocesan in Foreign Missions	1
Priests: Retired, Sick or Absent	23
Number of Diocesan Priests	100
Religious Priests in Diocese	46
Extern Priests in Diocese	7
Ordinations:	
Diocesan Priests	2
Permanent Deacons in Diocese	63
Total Brothers	24
Total Sisters	193
Parishes	
Parishes	66
With Resident Pastor:	
Resident Diocesan Priests	51
Resident Religious Priests	15
Missions	33
Pastoral Centers	1
Professional Ministry Personnel:	
Brothers	16
Sisters	19
Lay Ministers	17
Welfare	
Catholic Hospitals	6
Total Assisted	559,931
Homes for the Aged	2
Total Assisted	137
Day Care and Extended Day Care Centers	3
Total Assisted	251
Specialized Homes	1
Total Assisted	100
Special Centers for Social Services	2
Total Assisted	11,490
Other Institutions	1
Total Assisted	2,150
Educational	
Diocesan Students in Other Seminaries	18
Total Seminarians	18
Colleges and Universities	1
Total Students	29
High Schools, Private	1
Total Students	349
Elementary Schools, Diocesan and Parish	15
Total Students	2,406
Elementary Schools, Private	2
Total Students	478
Catechesis/Religious Education:	
High School Students	3,255
Elementary Students	10,271
Total Students Under Catholic Instruction	16,806
Teachers in the Diocese:	
Priests	1
Sisters	40
Lay Teachers	200
Vital Statistics	
Receptions into the Church:	
Infant Baptism Totals	3,426
Adult Baptism Totals	163
Received into Full Communion	598
First Communions	2,903
Confirmations	885
Marriages:	
Catholic	682
Interfaith	138
Total Marriages	820
Deaths	1,803
Total Catholic Population	165,921
Total Population	548,198

Former Bishops—Rt. Rev. DOMINIC MANUCY, cons. Dec. 8, 1874; transferred to Mobile March 9, 1884; reappointed to Vicariate Apostolic of Brownsville Feb. 1, 1885; died Dec. 4, 1885, before taking possession.—Rt. Rev. PETER VERDAGUER, cons. Nov. 9, 1890; died Oct. 26, 1911.—Rt. Rev. PAUL JOSEPH NUSSBAUM, C.P., D.D., cons. May 20, 1913; resigned March 26, 1920; Bishop of Marquette; appt. Nov. 14, 1922; died June 24, 1935.—Most Rev. EMMANUEL B. LEDVINA, D.D., LL.D., appt. April 30, 1921; cons. June 14, 1921; Assistant at Pontifical Throne May 30, 1931; resigned March 15, 1949; died Dec. 15, 1952.—Most Rev. MARIANO S. GARRIGA, D.D., LL.D., Coadjutor *cum jure successionis,* appt. June 20, 1936; cons. Sept. 21, 1936; succeeded to See March 15, 1949; assistant at Pontifical Throne April 14, 1951; died Feb. 21, 1965.—Most Rev. THOMAS J. DRURY, D.D., Fourth Bishop of Corpus Christi; Bishop of San Angelo; appt. Oct. 16, 1961; cons. Jan. 24, 1962; fourth Bishop of Corpus Christi; appt. July 19, 1965; installed Sept. 1, 1965; retired Bishop of Corpus Christi; appt. May 19, 1983; died July 22, 1992.—Most Rev. RENE H. GRACIDA, D.D., Bishop Emeritus; Fifth Bishop of Corpus Christi; appt. Titular Bishop of Masuccaba and Auxiliary of Miami Dec. 6, 1971; cons. Jan. 25, 1972; appt. Bishop of Pensacola-Tallahassee Oct. 1, 1975; transferred to Corpus Christi May 19, 1983; installed July 11, 1983; retired April 1, 1997.—Most Rev. ROBERTO O. GONZALEZ, O.F.M., Sixth Bishop of Corpus Christi; appt. Titular Bishop of Ursona and Auxiliary Bishop of Boston July 19, 1988; ord. Oct. 3, 1988; appt. Coadjutor Bishop of Corpus Christi May 16, 1995; transferred to Corpus Christi June 26, 1995; succeeded to See April 1, 1997; appt. Apostolic Administrator to Corpus Christi March 26, 1999; installed Archbishop of San Juan, Puerto Rico May 8, 1999.—Most Rev. EDMOND CARMODY, D.D., Seventh Bishop of Corpus Christi; cons. Dec. 15, 1988; appt. Bishop of Tyler March 24, 1992; installed May 25, 1992; appt. Bishop of Corpus Christi Feb. 3, 2000; installed March 17, 2000.

Diocesan Curia—620 Lipan St., P.O. Box 2620, Corpus Christi, 78403-2620.

Office of the Bishop—Most Rev. EDMOND CARMODY, D.D.;

Rev. Msgr. RICHARD SHIRLEY, V.G., Vicar General; Rev. Msgr. DANIEL E. FLORES, Chancellor; Rev. Msgr. THOMAS L. MEANY, P.A., Judicial Vicar; Rev. THOMAS P. FEENEY, A.J.V., J.C.L. (Cand.), Adjutant Judicial Vicar.

Bishop's Office—620 Lipan St., P.O. Box 2620, Corpus Christi, 78403-2620. Tel: 361-882-6191; Fax: 361-654-1270. Mr. MARTY WIND, Dir. Communications; Sr. KATHLEEN MCDONAGH, I.W.B.S., Dir. Consecrated Life; Deacon STANLEY MILLSAP, Dir. Deacons & Personnel Svcs.; Dr. FRANK LUCIDO, Diocesan Catechetical Rel. Educ.; Rev. Msgr. LEONARD D. PIVONKA, J.C.D., Health Care; Rev. Msgr. THOMAS MCGETTRICK, Vicar for Priests; Revs. FRANCISCO MARTINEX, S.L.T., Dir. Pastoral Ministries; GLENN MULLAN, Dir. Seminary Formation & Vocations.

Consultative Bodies—620 Lipan St., P.O. Box 2620, Corpus Christi, 78403-2620.

Council Of Religious—Sr. KATHLEEN MCDONAGH, I.W.B.S.

Deans—Rev. Msgr. LEONARD PIVONKA, Alice Deanery; Rev. Msgr. JOHN KILEEN, Beeville; Rev. MARK CHAMBERLIN, Corpus Christi Central Deanery; Rev. Msgr. LAWRENCE WHITE, Corpus Christi Westside Deanery; Rev. MATTHEW J. LYNG, Fivepoints Deanery; Rev. Msgr. THOMAS P. MCGETTRICK, Southside Deanery; Rev. PAUL A. HESSE, Kingsville Deanery; Rev. CELESTINE MURRAY, Refugio.

Diaconal Screening Committee—Dr. FRANK LUCIDO; Sr. ANNETTE WAGNER; Rev. MARK CHAMBERLIN; Dr. MARSHALL VORIS; Dr. SHIRLEY GOOD; Mrs. SANDRA CARLISLE; Deacons JAMES CARLISLE; RICARDO COSTLEY; MICHAEL MANTZ, Assoc. Dir. STANLEY MILLSAP, Dir. for Deacons.

Finance Council—Most Rev. EDMOND CARMODY, D.D.; Rev. Msgr. RICHARD SHIRLEY; Rev. Msgr. THOMAS MEANY; Rev. GREGORY DEAN; Sr. AGNES MARIE TENGLER, I.W.B.S.; Mrs. ROBIN PERRONE, C.P.A.; Mr. CECILE CARLISLE; Mr. THOMAS DURAN; Ms. NELDA MARTINEZ. Consultants: Mr. GREGOR SEAGRAVE; Mr. GARY A. RAMIREZ.

Personnel Board - Priests—Rev. Msgr. RICHARD SHIRLEY, V.G., Chm.; Rev. MATTHEW LYNG; Rev. Msgr. JOHN P. KILLEEN; Rev. MARK CHAMBERLIN; Rev. Msgr. THOMAS P. MCGETTRICK; Revs. CELESTINE MURRAY; PAUL A. HESSE; LEONARD PIVONKA, J.C.D.; Rev. Msgr. LAWRENCE WHITE.

Presbyteral Council—Revs. ROGER SMITH, Chm. MARK CHAMBERLIN, Vice Chm. LOWERY ROSS, Sec.

Telecommunications Corporation—MARTY WIND, Exec. Vice Pres. & Gen. Mgr.

Tribunal—Rev. Msgr. THOMAS L. MEANY, P.A., Judicial Vicar, *620 Lipan St., P.O. Box 2620, Corpus Christi, 78403-2620.* Tel: 361-882-6191; Fax: 361-882-1018.

Judges—Rev. Msgr. THOMAS L. MEANEY, P.A., J.V.; Rev. THOMAS P. FEENEY, A.J.V., J.C.L. (Cand.); Rev. Msgr. LEONARD PIVONKA, J.C.D.; Revs. JAMES HAMILTON; DONALD DOWNEY, J.C.L.; Rev. Msgr. MICHAEL HOWELL; Revs. ROGER SMITH; MARK CHAMBERLIN; Deacon ROY M. GRASSEDONIO.

Defenders of the Bond—Rev. Msgr. RICHARD SHIRLEY, V.G.; Rev. ANGEL MONTANO, J.C.L.

Notaries-Secretaries—MELISSA JASSO; BELINDA HARRIS.

Instructor—Rev. ANTONIO HERRERA FLOVER, J.C.L.

Villa Maria, Inc., Board—EDMUND ROTTER, Pres.; Rev. Msgr. ROBERT FREEMAN, P.A., Vice Pres. VERNON SMITH, Treas.; Sr. AGNES MARIE TENGLER, Sec.

Administrative Offices

The Chancery Office—620 Lipan St., P.O. Box 2620, Corpus Christi, 78403-2620. Tel: 361-882-6191; Fax: 361-882-1018 (Admin.); 883-8850 (Fiscal Office); 654-1270 (Bishop's Office). Office Hours: Mon.-Fri., 8:30-5. Closed holy days and holidays.

Office of the Bishop—Most Rev. EDMOND CARMODY, D.D.

Office of the Bishop Emeritus—Most Rev. RENE H. GRACIDA, D.D.

Canonical Affairs—Rev. Msgr. THOMAS L. MEANY, P.A., J.V.

Master of Ceremonies to the Bishop Emeritus—Deacon ROY M. GRASSEDONIO.

Secretary to Bishops for Appointments—OLGA CARRIRON.

Vicar General—Rev. Msgr. RICHARD SHIRLEY, V.G.

Judicial Vicar—Rev. Msgr. THOMAS L. MEANY, P.A., J.V.

Director for Pastoral Ministries—Rev. FRANCISCO MARTINEZ, S.L.T.

Director for Deacons & Personnel Services—Deacon STANLEY MILLSAP.

Vicar for Priests—Rev. Msgr. THOMAS P. MCGETTRICK.

Chancellor—Rev. Msgr. DANIEL E. FLORES, S.T.L.

Family Life Office—Rev. FRANCISCO MARTINEZ, S.L.T.

Fiscal Officer—GREGOR SEAGRAVE.

Controller—PAUL A. DAMEROW, C.P.A.

Bishop's Annual Appeal—Mr. DALE BAIRD, Devel. Consultant.

Data Processing Office—CATHY LOPEZ, MIS Technical Dir.

Real Property Office—CY RICHARDS, Mgr.

Human Life Office—Rev. FRANCISCO MARTINEZ, S.L.T.

Personnel Office—Deacon STANLEY MILLSAP.

Propagation of the Faith Office—Rev. RAYMOND YRLAS.

Secretary for Seminary Formation & Vocations—Rev. GLENN MULLAN, *Chancery Office, P.O. Box 2620, Corpus Christi, 78403-2620.* Tel: 361-882-6191.

Archives—Mr. CY RICHARDS, III, Archivist Mon.-Thurs. 9-2. *Corpus Christi Catholic Center, 3036 Saratoga, Corpus Christi, 78415.* Tel: 361-855-2345.

Catholic Schools Office—RENE GONZALEZ, Supt., *Corpus Christi Catholic Center, 3036 Saratoga, Corpus Christi, 78415.* Tel: 361-814-0444; Fax: 361-814-1831.

Catholic Cemeteries—Deacon LUIS TREVINO, Dir., *Corpus Christi Catholic Center, 3036 Saratoga, Corpus Christi, 78415.* Tel: 361-851-1534.

Diocesan Telecommunications Corporation—MARTY WIND, Dir. Communications, *1200 Lantana, Corpus Christi, 78407.* Tel: 361-289-6437; Fax: 361-289-1420.

Education—RENE GONZALEZ, Supt., *Corpus Christi Catholic Center, 3036 Saratoga, Corpus Christi, 78415.* Tel: 361-814-0475; Fax: 361-814-1831.

Corpus Christi Catholic Center—Rev. BRADLEY BARBER, Dir., *3036 Saratoga, Corpus Christi, 78415.* Tel: 361-851-1443; Fax: 361-851-1552. Office Hours: Mon.-Fri. 8:30-5. Closed holy days and holidays.

Bishop Rene H. Gracida Retreat House—Rev. BRADLEY BARBER, Dir. Tel: 361-851-1443.

Natural Family Planning - Understanding Sexuality—JANE TISDALE, Dir., *4639 Corona, Ste. 13B, Corpus Christi, 78411.* Tel: 361-852-0222; 852-2067.

Newspaper "The South Texas Catholic"—Most Rev. EDMOND CARMODY, D.D., Publisher; PAULA ESPITIA, Editor, *P.O. Box 2620, Corpus Christi, 78403-2620.* Tel: 361-882-6191; Fax: 361-883-2556.

Pastoral Institute for Ministry and Christian Service—Rev. BRADLEY A. BARBER, Dir., *Corpus Christi Catholic Center, 3036 Saratoga, Corpus Christi, 78415.* Tel: 361-814-5030; Fax: 361-814-1831.

Office for Persons with Disabilities—Rev. DAVID WALSH, C.Ss.R., Dir., *1322 Comanche, Corpus Christi, 78401.* Tel: 361-814-2181; Fax: 361-814-1831.

Religious Education—Dr. FRANK LUCIDO, Dir. Catechetical Religious Education, *Corpus Christi Catholic Center, 3036 Saratoga, Corpus Christi, 78415.* Tel: 361-814-5689; Fax: 361-814-1831.

Office of Youth And Young Adult Ministry—TONI CHAPA, Dir., *Chancery Office, P.O. Box 2620, Corpus Christi, 78403-2620.* Tel: 361-882-6191; Fax: 361-882-1157.

Eastern Vicariate Perpetual Benefit Endowment Fund, Inc.—P.O. Box 2620, Corpus Christi, 78403-2620. Tel: 361-882-6191.

Eastern Vicariate Deposit and Loan Fund, Inc.—P.O. Box 2620, Corpus Christi, 78403-2620. Tel: 361-882-6191.

Other Offices and Organizations

Alhambra—Mr. DELBERT HOOPER, Grand Commander, *1610 Candelwood, Corpus Christi, 78412.* Mrs. JACKIE BRANNIGAN, *11109 Stonewall, Corpus Christi, 78410.* Tel: 361-241-8297.

Apostleship of the Sea—Rev. VINCENT PATRIZI, Dir., *Our Lady Star of the Sea, P.O. Box 1899, Corpus Christi, 78403.* Tel: 361-883-4507.

Birthright Counseling—MILDRED HOFFER, Pres., *1422 Baldwin, Corpus Christi, 78404.* Tel: 361-884-2662.

Blue Army (World Apostolate of Fatima)—Mrs. MARTHA MAJEK, Pres., *4918 Brandesky, Corpus Christi, 78415.* Tel: 361-853-1066.

Campus Ministries—Texas A&M University-Kingsville, St. Thomas Aquinas University Catholic Center, *1120 S. 8th St., Kingsville, 78363.* Tel: 361-592-5781. *Del Mar College, Collegiate Parish of St. Thomas More, 2045 18th St., Corpus Christi, 78404.* Tel: 361-883-9308. *The Cardinal John Henry Newman Catholic Student Center, at Texas A&M University-Corpus Christi, 6300 Ocean Dr., Corpus Christi, 78412.* Tel: 361-993-5898.

Catholic Daughters of the Americas—THERESE NEWCHURCH, Dist. 16: Corpus Christi. Tel: 361-850-8544. ROSALINDA GUTIERREZ, Dist. 23: Kingsville. Tel: 361-952-2580. CORINA GUERRERO, Dist. 36: Corpus Christi. Tel: 361-241-1028. JOSEFINA GONZALES, Dist. 41: Corpus Christi. Tel: 361-883-0688. ISAURA OLIVEIRA, Dist. 43: Benavides. Tel: 361-256-3212. DALIA SANCHEZ, Dist. 47: Portland. Tel: 361-643-3244.

Catholic Charities—Rev. Msgr. ROBERT E. FREEMAN, P.A.; Sr. PATRICK BRUEN, O.L.C., Admin., *1322 Comanche, Corpus Christi, 78401.* Tel: 361-884-0651; Fax: 361-884-3956.

Center for Spiritual Direction—Sr. JOAN MICHELE RAKE, C.D.P., Spiritual Dir., *4103 Ocean Dr., Corpus Christi, 78411.* Tel: 361-853-0170.

Charismatic Movement—Spiritual Directors: Deacons WALTER N. BRELAND; RAUL HINOJOSA; EDWARD NARTOWICZ; Deacons MARIO RIVERA, Area Coord. ANTONIO LARA, Diocesan Dir. Charismatic Renewal.

Cursillo Movement Eastern Vicariate—Dr. MICHAEL MEANEY, Pres. Secretariat; Rev. JAMES JANECEK, Spiritual Dir., *3360 San Antonio, Corpus Christi, 78411.* Tel: 361-855-3534; Fax: 361-855-3534.

Diocesan Council Of Catholic Women—BRENDA KALENIC, Pres. Tel: 361-664-6109.

Disaster Relief—Rev. Msgr. ROBERT E. FREEMAN, P.A., Dir., *1322 Comanche St., Corpus Christi, 78401.* Tel: 361-884-0651.

Emergency Aid—Sr. PATRICK BRUEN, O.L.C., Admin., *1322 Comanche, Corpus Christi, 78401.* Tel: 361-884-0651.

Family Counseling—CSS-Corpus Christi Catholic Social Services: Sr. PATRICK BRUEN, O.L.C., Admin., *1322 Comanche St., Corpus Christi, 78401.* Tel: 361-884-0651.

Catholic Engaged Encounter—Rev. FRANCISCO MARTINEZ, S.L.T., Dir., *P.O. Box 2620, Corpus Christi, 78403.* Tel: 361-882-6191, Ext. 356.

Immigration Services—Sr. PATRICK BRUEN, O.L.C., Admin., *1322 Comanche, Corpus Christi, 78401.* Tel: 361-884-0651.

Jail Ministries—Rev. FRANCISCO MARTINEZ, S.L.T., Dir., *P.O. Box 2620, Corpus Christi, 78403-2620.* Tel: 361-882-6191.

Lay Maryans—MANUEL GARCIA, Dir., *5310 Hitching Post Ln., Corpus Christi, 78415.* Tel: 361-855-9288.

Legion of Mary—MILLIE GARNER, Pres., *1110 Bunice, Corpus Christi, 78412.* Tel: 361-992-5234. MANUEL GARCIA, Laredo Area Contact. Tel: 956-723-4333.

Marriage Encounter—Coordinators: BOB TABONE; HULI TABONE, *304 Estes Dr., Rockport, 78382.* Tel: 361-729-9481.

Radio Stations - KLUX FM—RUSSEL WAYNE MARTIN, Dir. Broadcast Oper., *1200 Lantana St., Corpus Christi, 78407.* Tel: 361-289-2487.

Serra International—AL HESSE, Pres., *930 Egyptian Circle, Corpus Christi, 78412.* Tel: 361-991-4063.

Theresians—Dr. MARY MCCASKEY, Pres., *250 Cape Henry, Corpus Christi, 78412.* Tel: 361-991-6200.

Villa Maria, Inc.—BARBARA A. MERLIN, Dir., *Box 4, 3146 Saratoga Blvd., Corpus Christi, 78415.* Tel: 361-857-6171.

CLERGY, PARISHES, MISSIONS AND PAROCHIAL SCHOOLS

CITY OF CORPUS CHRISTI

(Nueces County)

1—CORPUS CHRISTI CATHEDRAL (1853), Rev. Msgr. Michael Howell, Rector; Rev. Msgr. Daniel E. Flores; Deacon Michael Mantz.

Res., 505 N. Upper Broadway, 78401. Tel: 361-883-4213; Fax: 361-883-1918. [CEM]

Catechesis/Religious Programs—Tel: 361-883-4213; Fax: 361-883-1918.

Students 164.

Chapels—Emmanuel.; Blessed Sacrament.; Perpetual Eucharistic Adoration.

2—CHRIST THE KING (1946) (Mexican), Rev. Juan Antonio Perez, O.SS.T.; Deacons Antonio Castillo; Israel Blanco.

Res., 3423 Rojo, 78415. Tel: 361-883-2821; Fax: 361-883-3448.

Catechesis/Religious Programs—Tel: 361-883-1404. Carol A. Enloe, D.R.E.

Students 206.

Convent—1625 Arlington, 78415. Tel: 512-883-0212.

3—HOLY CROSS (1914) (African American), Rev. Msgr. Patrick Higgins.

Res., 1109 N. Staples St., 78401. Tel: 361-888-4012; Fax: 361-888-5338.

Catechesis/Religious Programs—Tel: 361-888-8485.

Students 43.

4—HOLY FAMILY (1946), Revs. Francisco Xavier Martinez, S.T.L., Pastor; Jose Angel Ortiz; Isaias Estepa.

Res., 2509 Nogales St., 78416. Tel: 512-882-3245; Fax: 512-882-4968.

Catechesis/Religious Programs—Tel: 361-882-3245.

Students 220.

Convent—1723 Frio St., 78417. Tel: 512-884-9142. Sisters of Mercy of the Blessed Sacrament 8.

Mission—Corpus Christi, Nueces Co., Mary, Mother

of the Church, 1755 Frio St., 78417. Tel: 361-852-0249.

5—Most Precious Blood (1966), Rev. Bob Dunn.
Res., 3502 Saratoga Blvd., 78415. Tel: 361-854-3800; Fax: 361-854-9253.
Catechesis/Religious Programs—Tel: 361-854-9219.
Students 509.

6—Our Lady of Guadalupe (1969) (Hispanic), Rev. Manuel Hernandez, Jr.; Deacon Armando Cavada.
Res., 540 Hiawatha, 78405. Tel: 361-882-1951; Fax: 361-888-5813.
Catechesis/Religious Programs—Tel: 361-882-8801. Mary Cabriales, D.R.E.
Students 168.

7—Our Lady of the Rosary (1967) (Hispanic), Deacon Homer T. Martinez, Jr., Admin. In res., Rev. Mahendra Anandappa, S.S.S (FTW).
Res., 1123 Main Dr., 78409. Tel: 361-241-2004; Fax: 361-242-1099.
Catechesis/Religious Programs—Students 18.
Missions—Petronila, Nueces Co., St. Vivian, FM 665, Petronila, 78415.; Corpus Christi, Nueces Co., Our Lady of Mount Carmel, 1080 S. Clarkwood, Corpus Christi, 78406.

8—Our Lady of Perpetual Help (1954), Rev. Msgr. Michael Heras, Pastor; Revs. Ernesto Perez; Angel Baldonado (Phillippines). In res., Rev. David Walsh, C.SS.R.
Res., 5830 Williams Dr., 78412-4415. Tel: 361-991-7891; Fax: 361-993-1211.
Catechesis/Religious Programs—Tel: 361-991-3261.
Students 310.

9—Our Lady of the Pillar (1964) (Hispanic), Rev. Marcos Martinez; Deacon Armando Bolanos.
Res., 1101 Bloomington St., 78416. Tel: 512-852-6327; Fax: 512-852-2614.
Catechesis/Religious Programs—Tel: 512-852-6843.
Students 231.

10—Our Lady Star of the Sea (1950), Rev. Vincent M. Patrizi, Pastor Emeritus; Deacon M.M. Peter Horseman.
Res., 3110 E. Causeway Blvd., P.O. Box 1899, 78403. Tel: 361-883-4507; Fax: 361-888-6411. [CEM]
Catechesis/Religious Programs—Students 50.

11—Sacred Heart (1916) (Hispanic), Rev. Jose M. Gutierrez; Sr. Paulina Ramirez, O.P., Pastoral Assoc.
Res., 422 N. Alameda St., 78401-2604. Tel: 361-883-6082; Fax: 361-883-6248. [CEM]
Catechesis/Religious Programs—Students 125.
Stations—Nueces County Jail.; Navarro Place.

12—Saint Andrew By the Sea Parish (1986), Rev. Richard Filice.
Res., 14238 Encantada Ave., Padre Island, 78418-6432. Tel: 361-949-7193; Fax: 361-949-0717.
Catechesis/Religious Programs—Tel: 361-949-8834.
Students 79.

13—St. Anselm Anglican Use Community (1992). Unassigned.
Res., 3036 Saratoga Blvd., 78415-5715. Tel: 361-854-3688; Fax: 361-852-8965.

14—SS. Cyril and Methodius (1947) (Hispanic), Rev. Msgr. Lawrence E. White, Pastor; Rev. Ramiro Trejo, Vicar; Deacons Ron Dubuque; Rudy Ramirez.
Res., 3210 S. Padre Island Dr., 78415. Tel: 512-853-7371; Fax: 512-851-1438.
Catechesis/Religious Programs—Tel: 512-852-1651. Mona Lucido, D.R.E.
Students 520.

15—St. Joseph (1952) (Hispanic), Revs. David Tonary, M.S.F.; Joseph Lawless, M.S.F.; Deacon Armando Botello; Bro. Rolland Kapsner, M.S.F.
Res., 710 S. 19th St., P.O. Box 5196, 78465-5196. Tel: 361-882-7912; Fax: 361-882-6853.
Catechesis/Religious Programs—Elizabeth Contreras, D.R.E.
Students 98.
Convent—2100 Morris St., 78405. Tel: 361-888-4027.
Sisters 3.

16—St. Michael the Archangel Latin Mass Community (1995), Rev. Paul L. Roman, F.S.S.P.
Res., 3036 Saratoga Blvd., 78415. Tel: 361-855-8244.

17—St. Patrick (1944), Revs. Roger R. Smith; Edmund Benedetti, S.J.; Prince Kuruvila, S.J. (India); Deacon W. Oliver.
Res., 3350 S. Alameda St., 78411. Tel: 361-855-7391; Fax: 361-853-4790.
Catechesis/Religious Programs—Tel: 361-855-7567.
Students 290.

18—St. Paul the Apostle (1967), Revs. Bruno Mikolajczyk; James G. Stembler.
Res., 2233 Waldron Rd., 78418. Tel: 361-937-3864; Fax: 361-939-7774.
Catechesis/Religious Programs—Tel: 361-937-6908. Sr. M. Purificacion Palis, O.P., D.R.E.
Students 205.

19—St. Peter Prince of Apostles (1967), Rev. Morgan Rowsome.
Res. & Mailing Address: 3901 Violet Rd., 78410. Tel: 361-241-3249; Fax: 361-241-0533.
Catechesis/Religious Programs—Tel: 361-241-3372. Marian Tajchman, D.R.E.
Students 575.
Mission—Corpus Christi, Nueces Co., St. Mary, 4849 Cynthia, 78410. Tel: 361-241-3432.

20—St. Philip The Apostle (1982), Rev. Msgr. Thomas P. McGettrick; Deacon Stacy Millsap.
Res., 6333 N. Washam St., 78414. Tel: 361-993-9474.
Church—3513 Cimarron Rd., 78414. Tel: 361-991-5146; Fax: 361-991-9135.
Catechesis/Religious Programs—Tel: 361-993-1710; Fax: 361-993-1710.
Students 524.

21—St. Pius X (1963), Rev. Msgr. Richard Shirley; Revs. Bradley A. Barber; Richard Libby; Tomasz Kozub, S.C.; Deacons Salvador Alvarado; George Phillips.
Res., 5620 Gollihar Rd., 78412. Tel: 361-993-4053; Fax: 361-992-0352.
Catechesis/Religious Programs—Tel: 512-993-9024.
Students 199.

22—St. Theresa (1947), Rev. Eckley Macklin, S.O.L.T. In res., Rev. Msgr. Raymond F. Rau (BRK).
Res., 1302 Lantana St., 78407. Tel: 361-289-2759; Fax: 361-299-2018.
Catechesis/Religious Programs—Tel: 361-289-2238; Fax: 361-299-2018. Mrs. Josie Martinez, D.R.E.
Students 90.
Convent—1253 Lantana St., 78407. Tel: 361-289-5534.

23—Collegiate Parish of St. Thomas More (1990), Rev. Hanh Van Pham.
Church—2045 18th St., 78404-3862. Tel: 512-888-9308; Fax: 512-888-6119.
Catechesis/Religious Programs—Students 45.

OUTSIDE THE CITY OF CORPUS CHRISTI

Agua Dulce, Nueces Co., St. Frances of Rome (1934), Rev. James A. Hayes, M.S.C.
Mailing Address: P.O. Box 598, 78330. Tel: 512-998-2216.
Catechesis/Religious Programs—Mrs. Doretta McDonough, D.R.E.
Students 115.
Mission—Banquete, Nueces Co., St. Michael, Tel: 512-998-2216.
Catechesis/Religious Programs—Rebecca Cisneros, D.R.E.
Students 150.

Alice, Jim Wells Co., Our Lady of Guadalupe (1969) (Hispanic), Rev. Raynaldo Yrlas, Jr.
Res., 1318 Guerra St., P.O. Box 411, 78332. Tel: 512-664-2953; Fax: 512-664-4001.
Catechesis/Religious Programs—Tel: 512-664-2957. Dora Rosales, D.R.E.
Students 269.
Mission—Alice, Jim Wells Co., Santo Nino De Atocha, Rte. 3 Box 273, 78332. Tel: 512-664-2953.

St. Elizabeth (1918), Rev. Leonard Pivonka, J.C.D.; Deacons James A. Carlisle; Alan K. Borse.
603 E. 5th St., 78333.
Res., 518 N. Almond St., P.O. Box 1009, 78333. Tel: 361-664-6481; Fax: 361-664-7243.
Catechesis/Religious Programs—Tel: 361-664-7719.
Students 230.
Mission—Ben Bolt, Jim Wells Co., St. Peter's Church, P.O. Box 1009, 78333. Tel: 361-664-1688.

St. Joseph (1911) (Hispanic), Revs. Emilio B. Jimenez, Admin.; Angel Montano; Deacon Mario Rivera.
Res., 801 S. Reynolds St., 78332. Tel: 361-664-7551; Fax: 361-664-2388.
Catechesis/Religious Programs—311 Dewey St., 78332. Tel: 361-664-4642; Fax: 361-664-4642.
Students 120.
Convent—808 S. Wright, P.O. Box 868, 78332. Tel: 361-664-6283.
Sisters 5.
Mission—Alice, Jim Wells Co., Sacred Heart.
Chapel—Perpetual Eucharistic Adoration.

Aransas Pass, San Patricio Co., St. Mary, Star of the Sea (1948), Rev. Michael Lenihan.
Res., 342 S. Rife St., 78336. Tel: 361-758-2662; Fax: 361-758-3964.
Catechesis/Religious Programs—Ginny Vega, D.R.E.
Students 278.

Beeville, Bee Co.,

1—Our Lady of Victory, (1908) (Hispanic), Rev. Richard Gonzales.
Mailing Address: 707 North Ave. E, 78102.
Res., 403 W. Carter St., 78102. Tel: 361-358-3761; Fax: 361-358-2028. [CEM 2]
Catechesis/Religious Programs—Tel: 361-358-9442. Sr. Encarnacion D.R.E. (Elem.); Iantha Richardson, D.R.E. (Jr.High/H.S.).
Students 139.

2—Sacred Heart Mission, (1966). (Independent). Rev. Patrick K. Donohoe; Deacon Manuel G. Carranco, Admin.
Mailing Address: St. Joseph Church, 609 E. Gramman St., 78102. Tel: 361-358-3239 (Office); 361-375-2512 (Church); Fax: 361-358-4270.
Catechesis/Religious Programs—Guadalupe Aguirre, D.R.E.
Students 30.

3—St. James, (Alta Vista) (1966) (Hispanic), Rev. Tom P. O'Donovan; Deacon Juan Vasquez.
Res., 605 Alta Vista, 78102. Tel: 361-358-4825; Fax: 361-358-5150.
Catechesis/Religious Programs—Miss Mary Elizabeth Garcia, D.R.E.
Students 96.

4—St. Joseph, (Alta Vista) (1891), Rev. Patrick K. Donohoe; Deacons Luis Trevino; Rolando Salazar.
Res., 609 E. Gramman St., 78102. Tel: 361-358-3239; Fax: 361-358-4270. [CEM]
Catechesis/Religious Programs—Tel: 361-358-6935. Debra Olivares, D.R.E.
Students 340.
Convent—610 E. Gramman St., 78102. Tel: 361-358-9405; Fax: 361-362-0973.
Sisters 6.

Benavides, Duval Co., St. Rose of Lima (1941) (Hispanic), Rev. Epifanio Rodriguez, O.P.
Res., Hackberry St., P.O. Drawer W, 78341. Tel: 361-256-3427.
Catechesis/Religious Programs—Tel: 361-256-3319. Gracie Garcia, D.R.E.
Students 149.
Mission—San Jose Ranch, Duval Co., St. Joseph, P.O. Box W, San Jose Ranch, 78341.

Bishop, Nueces Co., St. James (1938), Rev. Patrick O'Connor, M.S.C.
Res., 601 W. 3rd St., P.O. Box 843, 78343. Tel: 361-584-3250; Fax: 361-584-1046. [CEM]
Catechesis/Religious Programs—Students 57.
Mission—Driscoll, Nueces Co., St. James, Driscoll, 78351.

Falfurrias, Brooks Co., Sacred Heart (1914), Rev. Matthew J. Stephan.
Res., 304 S. Caldwell St., 78355. Tel: 361-325-3455; Fax: 361-325-2486. [CEM]
Catechesis/Religious Programs—Tel: 361-325-5067.
Students 474.
Mission—Encino, Brooks Co., St. Ann, c/o Sacred Heart Parish, Falfurrias, 78355.

Freer, Duval Co., St. Mary (1968), Rev. Peter J. McNamara; Deacon Eluterio Bitoni.
Res., 1500 Duval St., Box B, 78357. Tel: 361-394-6832.
Catechesis/Religious Programs—Tel: 361-394-7188. Mrs. A. Bitoni, D.R.E.
Students 241.

George West, Live Oak Co., St. George (1924), Rev. John P. Killeen.
Oratory—George West, Live Oak Co., Crockett St., P.O. Box 580, 78022. Tel: 361-449-1893; Fax: 361-449-1886. [CEM][JC]
Catechesis/Religious Programs—Tel: 361-449-1336. D.R.E.: Rev. John P. Killeen; Debbie Brown; Noreen Brown.
Students 200.
Mission—Gussetville, Live Oak Co., St. Joseph, Tel: 361-449-1893. [CEM][JC]

Gregory, San Patricio Co., Immaculate Conception (1926) (Hispanic), Rev. Jose A. Almazan, C.M. (Spain); Deacons Juan Gomez; Rey Rojas.
Res., 107 Church St., P.O. Box 108, 78359-0108. Tel: 361-643-4505; Fax: 361-643-1509.
Catechesis/Religious Programs—Tel: 361-643-4505, Ext. 108. Sr. Isabel Torres, C.M.S.T., D.R.E.
Students 379.

Ingleside, San Patricio Co., Our Lady of the Assumption (1970), Rev. Thomas Wellar.
Res., 2414 Main, 78362. Tel: 361-776-2644; 776-2446; Fax: 361-776-3963.
Catechesis/Religious Programs—Faith Repka, D.R.E.
Students 170.
Our Lady of the Assumption Early Learning Center—Tel: 361-776-3643.

Kingsville, Kleberg Co.,

1—Our Lady of Good Counsel, (1967) (Mexican), Rev. Piotr A. Koziel.
Res., 1102 E. Kleberg, 78363. Tel: 361-592-3489;

Fax: 361-592-3489. [JC]
Catechesis/Religious Programs—Tel: 361-592-9546. Norma Hinojosa, D.R.E.
Students 71.

2—St. Gertrude, (1908), Revs. Paul A. Hesse; Raju D. Thottankara (India).
Res., 1120 S. 8th St., 78363. Tel: 361-592-7351; Fax: 361-592-0028.
School—(Grades K &4-6). Tel: 361-592-6522; Fax: 361-592-0100.
Students 135.
Catechesis/Religious Programs—Tel: 361-592-2443. Sr. Margaret Gerken, C.C.V.I., D.R.E.
Students 171.
Convent—400 E. Caesar Ave., 78363. Tel: 361-592-2443.
Mission—Kingsville, Kleberg Co., St. Thomas Aquinas Catholic Campus Center - Texas A & M, P.O. Box 2193, Kingsville, 78363. Tel: 361-592-5781.

3—St. Joseph, (1973) (Hispanic), Rev. Richard Philion, O.M.I.
Res., 1400 Brookshire, P.O. Box 1602, 78364-1602. Tel: 361-592-5689.
Catechesis/Religious Programs—Tel: 361-592-5689. Belinda Carmona, D.R.E.
Students 202.

4—St. Martin, (1914) (Hispanic), Rev. James Foelker, O.M.I.; Deacons Tiburcio Garcia; Raul G. Rosales. In res., Rev. Angel Villalba, O.M.I.
Res., 715 N. Eighth St., 78363. Tel: 361-592-4602; Fax: 361-592-4602.
Catechesis/Religious Programs—Tel: 361-592-0881. Gloria DeLeon, D.R.E.
Students 186.
Convent—919 N. Ninth St., 78363. Tel: 361-595-1087.
Sisters 7.
Mission—King Ranch, Kleberg Co., Christ the King.

5—St. Thomas Aquinas, University Catholic Center, (1990), Rev. Piotr A. Koziel.
Res. & Mailing Address: 1120 S. 8th, 78363. Tel: 361-592-5781; Fax: 361-592-0028.
Church—1119 W. Santa Gertrudis, 78363.

Mathis, San Patricio Co., Sacred Heart (1942), Revs. Jose Angel Salazar; Romeo Salinas.
Res., 114 S. Aransas, P.O. Box 608, 78368-0608. Tel: 361-547-9181; Fax: 361-547-6111. [JC]
Catechesis/Religious Programs—Rosie Aguilar, D.R.E.
Students 291.
Mission—San Patricio, San Patricio Co., St. Patrick, Tel: 512-547-5748.

Odem, San Patricio Co., Sacred Heart (1919) (Hispanic), Rev. Paul A Hesse.
Res., 401 Willis St., P.O. Box 276, 78370. Tel: 361-368-9156.
Catechesis/Religious Programs—Tel: 361-368-2746. Sr. Elsa Miranda, C.M.S.T., D.R.E.
Students 352.
Convent—402 Borden, 78370. Tel: 512-368-2560.
Sisters 2.
Mission—Edroy, San Patricio Co., Our Lady of Guadalupe, County Rd. 50B, Edroy, 78352. Tel: 512-368-9156.

Orange Grove, Jim Wells Co., St. John of the Cross (1925), Rev. Lowery A. Ross, Admin.
Mailing Address: P.O. Box 329, 78372. Tel: 361-384-2795; Fax: 361-384-0056. [CEM]
Catechesis/Religious Programs—Tel: 361-384-2246.
Students 293.
Station—Sandia, St. Pius X.

Port Aransas, Nueces Co., St. Joseph (1860), Rev. Msgr. Gregory S. Deane.
Mailing Address: 412 Lantana St., 78373. Tel: 512-749-5825; Fax: 512-749-5509. [JC]
Catechesis/Religious Programs—Students 47.

Portland, San Patricio Co., Our Lady of Mount Carmel (1961), Rev. Mark Chamberlin.
Res., 1008 Austin St., 78374. Tel: 361-643-7533; Fax: 361-643-5544.
Catechesis/Religious Programs—Tel: 361-643-3548. Mrs. Melanee Warner, D.R.E.
Students 336.

Premont, Jim Wells Co., St. Theresa of the Infant Jesus (1958), Deacon Raul Hinojosa.
Res., 235 S.W. 4th St., P.O. Box 569, 78375. Tel: 361-348-2202; Fax: 361-348-3533. [JC]
Catechesis/Religious Programs—Students 255.
Missions—Concepcion, Duval Co., Immaculate Conception; Rios, Duval Co., St. Francis of Assisi; Ramirez, Duval Co., Our Lady of Guadalupe.

Refugio, Refugio Co., Our Lady of Refuge (1795), Rev. Msgr. Robert E. Freeman, P.A.; Rev. Gnana Prakasham Chinnabathini (India).
Res., 1008 S. Alamo St., 78377. Tel: 361-526-2083; Fax: 361-526-5653. [CEM][JC]
Catechesis/Religious Programs—106 W. Roca, 78377. Tel: 361-526-2053.
Students 183.

St. James the Apostle (1886) (Hispanic), Rev. Msgr. Robert E. Freeman, P.A.; Rev. Ghana Prakasham Chinnabathini (India).
Res., 1008 S. Alamo St., 78377. Tel: 361-526-2083; Fax: 361-526-5653. [CEM][JC]
Catechesis/Religious Programs—(Clustered with Our Lady of Refuge, Refugio.). Tel: 361-526-2714.

Robstown, Nueces Co., St. Anthony (1914) (Hispanic), Revs. Vincent Albano, S.O.L.T.; James Flanagan, S.O.L.T.; John McHugh, S.O.L.T.; Edward C. Roche, S.O.L.T.; Isidore Usit Nyein, S.O.L.T.; Robert Shaldone, S.O.L.T.; Peter Pham, S.O.L.T.; James Blount, S.O.L.T.; John Mary Perez, S.O.L.T.; Deacon Francis Hohenadel.
Res., 204 Dunne St., P.O. Box 792, 78380. Tel: 361-387-2774; Fax: 512361. [CEM]
Catechesis/Religious Programs—Tel: 361-387-9874. Eva Hernandez, D.R.E.
Students 310.
Convent—612 Indiana, 78380. Tel: 512-387-3810.
Mission—Robstown, Nueces Co., St. Mary.

St. John Nepomucene (1924) (Czech), Rev. Gerard J. Sheehan, S.O.L.T.
Res., 603 N. First St., 78380. Tel: 361-387-3705; Fax: 361-387-3681.
Catechesis/Religious Programs—Tel: 361-387-3011. Rachael Saenz, D.R.E.
Students 65.

St. Thomas the Apostle (1980), Rev. Matthew Lyng; Deacon Bill Cleavelin.
Office: 16602 F.M. 624, 78380. Tel: 512-387-1312; Fax: 512-387-9311.
Catechesis/Religious Programs—Shirley Syamken, D.R.E.
Students 300.

Rockport, Aransas Co., Sacred Heart (1838), Rev. Msgr. Louis F. Kihneman; Deacons Jerre Ledbetter; George Wiest.
Res., 704 Cornwall St., 78382. Tel: 361-729-2174; Fax: 361-729-1989.
Catechesis/Religious Programs—Tel: 361-729-8283.
Students 282.
Convent—114 N. Church St., 78382. Tel: 361-729-5311.

St. Peter Indo-Chinese Parish (1989) (Vietnamese), Rev. Peter Phan Van Nguyen, C.S.S.R. In res., Rev. Quang Dang Nguyen, (Retired).
Mailing Address: P.O. Box 1060, 78382. Tel: 361-729-3008; Fax: 361-729-3008. [JC]
Catechesis/Religious Programs—1011 Farm Rd. 1781, 78382-1060.
Students 30.

San Diego, Duval Co., St. Francis de Paula (1866), Rev. Benito Retortillo, O.P.
Res., 401 S. Victoria St., P.O. Box 279, 78384. Tel: 361-279-3596; Fax: 361-279-8288.
Catechesis/Religious Programs—411 S. Victoria St., 78384. Tel: 361-279-3586.
Students 403.
Mission—Palito Blanco, Jim Wells Co., St. Joseph, San Diego, 78384.

Sarita, Kenedy Co., Our Lady of Guadalupe (1935), Rev. Edward W. Couch, O.M.I.
Mailing Address: P.O. Box 6, 78385. Tel: 361-294-5350; Fax: 361-294-5350.
Catechesis/Religious Programs—Students 33.
Mission—Norias Ranch, Kenedy Co., Santa Elena.

Sinton, San Patricio Co., Our Lady of Guadalupe (1954) (Hispanic), Rev. David Taurasi, Pastor.
Res., 725 Sodville Ave., 78387. Tel: 361-364-2210; Fax: 361-364-5818. [CEM][JC]
Catechesis/Religious Programs—Tel: 361-364-4542.
Students 361.

Sacred Heart (1918), Rev. Thomas P. Feeney.
Res., 906 E. Sinton St., P.O. Box 266, 78387. Tel: 361-364-1768; Fax: 361-364-5325.
Catechesis/Religious Programs—Tel: 361-364-1772. D.R.E.: Mary Connors; Solomon T. Willis, III.
Students 271.
Mission—St. Paul, San Patricio Co., St. Paul, P.O. Box 266, Sinton, 78387.

Skidmore, Bee Co., Immaculate Conception (1915), Rev. John Ayang, S.O.L.T., Admin.
Res., 600 First St., P.O. Box 189, 78389. Tel: 361-287-3256; Fax: 361-287-3696. [JC]
Catechesis/Religious Programs—Students 95.
Mission—Tynan, Bee Co., St. Francis Xavier, Frio St., Tynan, 78384.

Taft, San Patricio Co., Holy Family (1957), Rev. George Kunnath, M.C.B.S.
Mailing Address: P.O. Box 868, 78390-0868. Tel: 361-528-3132; Fax: 361-528-3907.
Res., 646 McIntyre, 78390. Tel: 361-528-2584. [JC]
Catechesis/Religious Programs—Students 84.

Immaculate Conception (1928), Rev. Jesus Francisco Lopez; Deacon Alonzo T. Rodriguez.
Res. & Mailing Address: 120 E. Escobedo, P.O. Box 868, 78390. Tel: 361-528-2626; Fax: 361-528-3907.
Catechesis/Religious Programs—Tel: 361-528-5300.
Students 574.

Three Rivers, Live Oak Co., Sacred Heart (1948), Rev. Zenon Konowalek.
303 E. Alexandra, P.O. Box 729, 78071-0729. Tel: 361-786-3398; 786-1010.
Catechesis/Religious Programs—Students 133.
Mission—Pawnee, Bee Co., Our Lady of Guadalupe, P.O. Box 729, Pawnee, 78071.

Tivoli, Refugio Co., Our Lady of Guadalupe (1936), Rev. Timothy J. Kinast.
Mailing Address: P.O. Drawer I, 77990-0001. Tel: 361-286-3349; Fax: 361-286-3665.
Catechesis/Religious Programs—Maria T. Carabajal, D.R.E.
Students 85.
Missions—Austwell, Refugio Co., St. Anthony of Padua; O'Connor Ranch, Refugio Co., St. Dennis.

Vattman, Kleberg Co., Our Lady of Consolation (1914), Rev. Brendan Michael Ashe.
Res., Rte. 1, Box 21, 78379. Tel: 361-297-5255; Fax: 361-297-5155. [CEM]
Catechesis/Religious Programs—Students 52.
Missions—Riviera, Kleberg Co., Our Lady of Guadalupe; Ricardo, Kleberg Co., Sacred Heart.

Violet, Nueces Co., St. Anthony (1910), Rev. Donald David Downey.
Res., 3918 County Rd. 61, Robstown, 78380. Tel: 361-387-4434; Fax: 361-767-3881. [CEM]
Catechesis/Religious Programs—Students 23.

Woodsboro, Refugio Co., St. Therese, The Little Flower (1915), Rev. Celestine Murray; Deacon Reynaldo Rodriguez Tel: 361-543-4611.
Res., 315 Pugh St., Drawer 1076, 78393-1140. Tel: 361-543-4166; Fax: 361-543-5922. [CEM]
Catechesis/Religious Programs—Students 173.
Mission—Bayside, Refugio Co., St. Mary.

On Special Assignment:
Reverend Fathers—
Spencer, Robert
Walsh, David, C.SS.R., Dir., Office of Persons with Disabilities

---

On Duty Outside the Diocese:
Reverend Fathers—
Bauta, Krzysztof T., 1802 Wagon Wheel, Arlington, Tx 76013
Bergin, Paschal, Our Lady of Peace Parish, 1 Notre Dame Pl., Kenedy, TX 78119
Masin, Richard H., P.P., Catholic Church & Parish/ Transfiguration, ul. Sovietskaya 61, Tver (Kalinin), Russia 170 000
Masterson, Clyde, 245 Waterman Ave., No. Providence, RI 02911
McGerity, Francis X., 45 Holyoke Rd., Westfield, MA 01035-1608
Walsh, Arthur, Church of Our Savior, Fifty Nine Park Ave., New York, NY 10016

Military Chaplains:
Reverend Monsignors—
Chilen, Michael D., 17th ASG CM UNIT 45013, Box 2207, APO AP, 96338-5013
Reverend Fathers—
Shuley, Keith, C.C., U.S. Coast Guard Training Center, Petaluma, CA

Retired:
Most Rev.—
Garcida, Rene H., P.O. Box 2620, Corpus Christi, TX 78403-2620
Reverend Monsignors—
Adams, Michael, Mount Carmel Home, 4130 S. Alameda, Corpus Christi, TX 78411
Clarke, Hugh, 3146 Saratoga Blvd., Box 18, Corpus Christi, TX 78415
Rau, Raymond, 1302 Lantana St., Corpus Christi, TX 78407
Tengler, Alvin, 1011 7th St., Corpus Christi, TX 78404
Thompson, William P.A., 4809 Fern Forest, Corpus Christi, TX 78413
Reverend Fathers—
Anders, Arnold, Mt. Carmel Home, 4130 S. Alameda, Corpus Christi, TX 78411
Bradley, Robert, Villa Maria Apartments, 3146 Saratoga Blvd., Box 45, Corpus Christi, TX 78415. Tel: 512-855-3767
Brown, W.T. St. John, 1177 E. Mesquite Ave., Palm Springs, CA 92264-8416. Tel: 760-325-0354
Burke, Michael, C/O Immaculate Conception Rectory, P.O. Box 1670, Waterbury, CT 06721-1670
Critchlow, Donald E., Mount Carmel Home, 4130 S. Alameda, Corpus Christi, TX 78411

De Llano, Domingo, 6106 Vance Jackson #5, San Antonio, TX 78230

Doherty, Charles, 127 Lakeview Rd., Rockport, TX 78382

Feminelli, John, Villa Maria, 3146 Saratoga, Corpus Christi, TX 78415

Fidalgo, Federico, 8326 N. Vandiver, #508, San Antonio, TX 78209

Hamilton, James, c/o St. Mary Star of the Sea, 342 S. Rife St., Aransas Pass, TX 78336

Iglesias, Luis Fernando, Villa Maria Apartments, 3146 Saratoga Blvd., Box 39, Corpus Christi, TX 78415

Joseph, Louis, Homewood Retirement Ctr., 6410 Meadow Vista, Corpus Christi, TX 78414

Kircher, Edward, 310 East Ward St., Refugio, TX 78377

McGowan, Seamus, 132 Sabine, Portland, TX 78374

Noone, Sean, Villa Maria Apartments, 3146 Saratoga Blvd., Box 12, Corpus Christi, TX 78415. Tel: 512-853-4814

Vidiella, Felix, 5702 Santa Clara, Santa Clara Estates, Robstown, TX 78380

Permanent Deacons:

Ahlers, Ray, Most Precious Blood, Corpus Christi

Alvarado, Salvador, St. Pius X, Corpus Christi

Alvardo, Carlos, Our Lady of Perpetual Help, Corpus Christi

Barbour, Tony R., St. Thomas Aquinas Collegiate Parish, Kingsville

Beyns, Victor, Our Lady of Perpetual Help, Corpus Christi

Bitoni, Eluterio, St. Mary Parish, Freer

Blanco, Israel, Christ the King, Corpus Christi

Bolanos, Armando M., Our Lady of Pillar, Corpus Christi

Borse, Alan T., St. Elizabeth, Alice

Botello, Armando, St. Joseph, Corpus Christi

Breland, Walter N., Spiritual Dir., Cursillo Movement, St. John of the Cross, Orange Grove

Carlisle, James A., Dir., Diaconate Formation, St. Elizabeth, Alice

Carranco, Manuel G., Chap. & Deanery Rep., Sacred Heart Mission; Bee County Jail, Beeville.

Carrizales, Alejandro, Admin., Holy Family, Corpus Christi

Castillo, Antonio M., Christ the King, Corpus Christi

Cavada, Armando, Chap., Our Lady of Guadalupe, Corpus Christi

Cleavelin, William, St. Thomas the Apostle, Robstown

Costley, Ricardo E., Assoc. Dir. of Formation & Deanery Rep., Sacred Heart, Falfurrias

de Anda, Candido, St. Francis of Rome, Agua Dulce

Dubuque, Roland, SS. Cyril & Methodius Parish, Corpus Christi

Flores, Arturo, St. Gertrude, Kingsville

Frazier, Garland, Deanery Rep., Most Precious Blood, Corpus Christi

Garcia, Tiburcio, St. Martin, Kingsville

Gomez, Gaspar, Collegiate Parish of St. Thomas More, Corpus Christi

Gomez, Juan, Deanery Representative, Immaculate Conception, Taft

Grassedonio, Roy M., St. Andrew by the Sea, Corpus Christi

Hinojosa, Raul, Spiritual Dir. Cursillo Movement, Mission of St. Theresa of the Infant Jesus, Premont

Horseman, M. M. (Pete), Our Lady Star of the Sea, Corpus Christi

Kaizen, Joseph, (Retired), Our Lady of Guadalupe Chapel, N.A.S., Corpus Christi

Lara, Antonio S., Diocesan Dir. Charismatic Renewal, Immaculate Conception, Skidmore

Ledbetter, Jerre H., Deanery Rep., Sacred Heart, Rockport

Lickteig, Wayne, S.O.L.T., Dir., Lay Council of Society, St. Anthony, Robstown

Maldonado, Manny, Holy Family, Corpus Christi

Mantz, Michael, Assoc. Dir. Eastern Vicariate, Corpus Christi Cathedral, Corpus Christi

Martinez, Ciprian, (Retired), Sacred Heart, Rockport

Martinez, Homer, Jr., Our Lady of the Rosary, Corpus Christi

Millsap, Stacy, St. Phillip the Apostle, Corpus Christi

Millsap, Stanley, Dir. for Deacons & Personnel Svcs.

Moore, Paul, Cathedral, Corpus Christi

Nartowicz, Edward, Catholic Social Services, Assoc. Spiritual Dir. Cursillo Movement, St. Paul the Apostle, Our Lady of Guadalupe Chapel, N.A.S., Corpus Christi

Nowicki, Edward, (Retired)

Oliver, Willard F., St. Patrick, Corpus Christi

Ouellette, Roland, Sacred Heart, Three Rivers

Panas, George, (Retired)

Phillips, George, St. Pius X, Corpus Christi

Ramirez, Rudy, St. Cyril & Methodius, Corpus Christi

Rauen, Mike, Our Lady of Guadalupe N.A.S. & St. Paul the Apostle, Corpus Christi

Rivera, Gonzalo, Chap., Sacred Heart, Rockport; Brooks County Jail, Falfurrias

Rivera, Mario, Area Coord. Cursillo Movement & Deanery Representative, St. Joseph, Alice

Rodriguez, Alonzo, Immaculate Conception, Taft

Rodriguez, Fernando G., Most Precious Blood, Corpus Christi

Rodriguez, Reynaldo, Jr., Diocesan Chap., St. Therese, Woodsboro

Rojas, Rey, Immaculate Conception, Gregory

Rosales, Raul G., Consultant for Mission 2000 Regional Dept. of Schools, St. Martin, Kingsville

Salazar, Rolando R., St. Joseph, Beeville

Susik, Frank, St. Theresa, Corpus Christi

Sutherland, John W., Our Lady of Mount Carmel, Portland

Tamayo, Carlos, St. Francis de Paula, San Diego

Trevino, Luis, Dir. Diocesan Cemeteries, St. Joseph, Beeville

Vasquez, Juan, St. James, Beeville

Vasquez, Guadalupe C.

Wiest, George Joe, Outreach Coord. for St. Vincent de Paul Society & Chap., Shoreline Treatment Facility, Taft, Sacred Heart, Rockport

Ybarra, Pedro M., (Retired), St. Joseph, Corpus Christi

INSTITUTIONS LOCATED IN THE DIOCESE

[A] HIGH SCHOOLS

CORPUS CHRISTI. *Incarnate Word Academy High School.* (Private), 2910 S. Alameda, 78404. Tel: 361-883-0857; Fax: 361-883-2185.
E-mail: iwaccsl@intcomm.net; scolemaniwa@hotmail.com
Web site: www.iwacc.org
Suzanne Coleman, Prin. Sisters 7; Lay Teachers 20; Students 349.

LAREDO. *St. Augustine High School.* (Diocesan), 1300 Galveston St., 78040. Tel: 956-724-8131; Fax: 956-725-9241.
E-mail: almarose@st-augustine.org
Sr. Alma Rose Booty, C.D.P., Prin. Lay Teachers 35; Students 612.

[B] JUNIOR HIGH AND ELEMENTARY SCHOOLS

CORPUS CHRISTI. *Bishop Garriga Middle School.* (Diocesan), 3114 Saratoga Blvd., 78415. Tel: 512-851-0853; Fax: 512-853-5145.
E-mail: mmcg@caller.infi.net
Web site: mmcg@bgms.org
Mrs. Margaret McGettrick, Prin.; Rev. Glen Mullan, Chap. Lay Teachers 11; Students 150.

Central Catholic Elementary. (Parochial), 1218 Comanche St., 78401. Tel: 512-883-3873; Fax: 361-883-5879.
E-mail: centralcatelem@Hotmail.com
Sr. Denise Cassidy, I.W.B.S., Prin. Sisters 2; Lay Teachers 5; Students 105.

Christ the King School. (Parochial), 1625 Arlington Dr., 78415. Tel: 361-883-5391; Fax: 361-888-9207. Priests 1; Sisters 2; Lay Teachers 6; Students 120.

Holy Family School. (Parochial), 2526 Soledad St., 78416. Tel: 361-884-9142; Fax: 361-884-1750. Sr. Patricia Rodriguez, H.M.S.S., Prin.; Rev. Francisco Xavier Martinez, S.T.L., Pastor. Sisters 3; Lay Teachers 12; Students 232.

Incarnate Word Elementary. (Private), 450 Chamberlain, 78404. Tel: 361-883-0857; Fax: 361-883-2185.
E-mail: mclerran@intercomm.net
Web site: www.iwacc.org
Sr. Camelia Herlihy, Prin. Sisters 5; Lay Teachers 10; Students 264.

Incarnate Word Middle School. (Private), 2917 Austin St., 78404. Tel: 361-883-0857; Fax: 361-882-9193.
E-mail: mclerran@intercomm.net
Web site: www.iwacc.org
Ms. Jean McLerran, Prin. Sisters 2; Lay Teachers 13; Students 214.

Most Precious Blood School. (Parochial), 3502 Saratoga Blvd., 78415. Tel: 361-852-4800; Fax: 361-855-8707. Mrs. Jolene Murray, Prin. Religious Teachers 1; Lay Teachers 11; Students 220.

Our Lady of Perpetual Help School. (Parochial), 5814 Williams Dr., 78412. Tel: 361-991-3305; Fax: 361-994-1806.
Web site: www.olphcctex.org
Ms. Linda Cantu, Prin. Lay Teachers 11; Students 179.

St. Patrick School. (Parochial), 3340 S. Alameda St., 78411. Tel: 361-852-1211; Fax: 361-852-4855.
E-mail: sps@trip.net
Julia Strubhart, Prin. Lay Teachers 17; Students 300.

St. Pius X School. (Parochial), 737 St. Pius Dr., 78412. Tel: 361-992-1343; Fax: 361-992-0329.
E-mail: dcccsspxscc@connectinc.com
Web site: www.stpiusxcc.org
Dr. Patricia Stegall, Prin. Lay Teachers 11; Students 189.

SS. Cyril and Methodius School. (Parochial), 5002 Kostoryz Rd., 78415. Tel: 361-853-9392; Fax: 361-853-0282.
E-mail: princhatch@aol.com
Web site: www.mahpro.com/sscm.html
Mrs. Nannette Hatch, Prin. Lay Teachers 12; Students 160.

ALICE. *St. Elizabeth School.* (Parochial), 615 E. Fifth, 78332. Tel: 361-664-6271; Fax: 361-668-4250.
E-mail: seschool@ccbcnet.com
Selina M. Rodriguez, Prin. Lay Teachers 9; Students 99.

St. Joseph School. (Parochial), P.O. Box 157, 78333. Tel: 361-664-4642; Fax: 361-664-2388. Mrs. Patricia C. Flores, Prin. Sisters 3; Lay Teachers 7; Students 115.

BEEVILLE. *St. Mary's Academy School.* (Grades PreK-8). (Diocesan), 410 N. Tyler, 78102. Tel: 316-358-5089; Fax: 316-358-7672. Miss Elida Ramirez, Prin. St. Dominic Sisters 5; Lay Teachers 6; Students 150.

KINGSVILLE. *St. Gertrude School.* (Parochial), 400 E. Caesar St., 78363. Tel: 361-592-6522; Fax: 361-592-0100.
E-mail: stgertrude@interconnect.net
Web site: www.stgertrudeparish.com
Mrs. Jean Claire Turcotte, Prin. Lay Teachers 10; Students 135.

LAREDO. *Blessed Sacrament School*, 1501 N. Bartlett St., 78043. Tel: 210-722-1222; Fax: 956-722-5635.
E-mail: DCCCSBSSL@impresso.com
Sr. Patrice Floyd, I.W.B.S., Prin. Lay Teachers 8; Students 110.

Mary Help of Christians School. (Private), 10 E. Del Mar Blvd., 78045. Tel: 210-722-3966. Sr. Barbara Campbell, F.M.A., Prin. Sisters 13; Lay Teachers 60; Students 745.

Our Lady of Guadalupe School. (Parochial), 400 Callaghan St., 78040-3834. Tel: 210-722-3915; Fax: 210-727-2840. Sr. Veronica Mitchell, S.H.Sp., Prin. Sisters 2; Lay Teachers 9; Students 116.

St. Augustine Elementary School. (Diocesan), 1300 Galveston, 78040. Tel: 210-724-1176; Fax: 210-725-9891. Sr. Marie Elise van Dijk, Prin. Sisters 1; Lay Teachers 11; Students 223.

St. Peter's Memorial School. (Diocesan), 1519 Houston St., P.O. Box 520, 78040. Tel: 210-723-6302. Mr. Alfonso H. Ornelas, Prin. Sisters 1; Lay Teachers 9; Students 116.

ROBSTOWN. *St. Anthony School.* (Parochial), 203 Dunne St., 78380. Tel: 361-387-3814; Fax: 361-387-3814.
E-mail: jnpcolunga@altavista.com
Rev. John Colunga, Prin. Sisters 2; Lay Teachers 9; Students 118.

ROCKPORT. *Sacred Heart School.* (Parochial), 111 N. Church St., 78382. Tel: 361-729-2672; Fax: 361-729-9382.
E-mail: shsoff1@pyramid3.net
Katherine K. Barnes, Prin. Sisters 1; Lay Teachers 7; Students 139.

[C] DAY NURSERY, PRE-KINDER, KINDER

CORPUS CHRISTI. *Carmelite Learning Center of Corpus Christi.* (Private), 4015 MacArthur St., 78416-1907. Tel: 512-853-6970; Fax: 512-853-6670.
E-mail: sr.m.m.m@worldnet.att.net
Sr. M. Michelle, Carmel D.C.J., Dir. Day Care and Kindergarten. Carmelite Sisters of the Divine Heart of Jesus 4; Lay Teachers 10; Students 60.

Our Lady of the Rosary Learning Center, 2237 Waldron Rd., 78418. Tel: 512-939-9847; Fax: 361-937-0890.
E-mail: rosary7@swbell.net
Sr. Maria Paz Aribon, O.P., Dir. Sisters 9; Lay missionary 1; Students 133.

[D] ORPHANAGES AND INFANT HOMES

LAREDO. *Sacred Heart Children's Home*, 3310 S. Zapata Hwy., 78046. Tel: 956-723-3343; Fax: 956-723-3409
For a complete listing, refer to the Special Care Facilities section.

[E] GENERAL HOSPITALS

CORPUS CHRISTI. *CHRISTUS Spohn Health System*, 1702 Santa Fe, 78404. Tel: 361-881-3400; Fax: 361-885-0566.
E-mail: jake_henry@iwhs.org
For a complete listing, refer to the Hospitals section.
CHRISTUS Spohn Hospital Shoreline Mailing Address: 1702 Santa Fe, 78404.
For a complete listing, refer to the Hospitals section.
CHRISTUS Spohn Hospital Memorial Mailing Address: 1702 Santa Fe, 78404.
For a complete listing, refer to the Hospitals section.
CHRISTUS Spohn Hospital South Mailing Address: 1702 Santa Fe, 78404.
For a complete listing, refer to the Hospitals section.

ALICE. *CHRISTUS Spohn Hospital Alice* Mailing Address: 1702 Santa Fe Corpus Christi, 78404.
For a complete listing, refer to the Hospitals section.

BEEVILLE. *CHRISTUS Spohn Hospital Beeville* Mailing Address: 1702 Santa Fe Corpus Christi, 78404.
For a complete listing, refer to the Hospitals section.

KINGSVILLE. *CHRISTUS Spohn Hospital Kleberg* Mailing Address: 1702 Santa Fe Corpus Christi, 78404.
For a complete listing, refer to the Hospitals section.

LAREDO. *Mercy Regional Medical Center*, 1515 Logan, P.O. Box 2068, 78044. Tel: 210-718-6222; Fax: 210-718-6904.
Web site: www.mhst.smhs.com
For a complete listing, refer to the Hospitals section.

[F] HOMES FOR THE AGED

CORPUS CHRISTI. *Casa San Lucas*, 222 Ocean View, 78411. Tel: 512-857-5758
For a complete listing, refer to the Special Care Facilities section.
Mount Carmel Home, 4130 S. Alameda St., 78411. Tel: 512-855-6243; Fax: 512-854-8513
For a complete listing, refer to the Special Care Facilities section.
Villa Maria, Inc., 3146 Saratoga Blvd., 78415. Tel: 361-857-6171; Fax: 361-857-6173
For a complete listing, refer to the Special Care Facilities section.

[G] RETREAT HOUSE

CORPUS CHRISTI. *Bishop Rene H. Gracida Retreat House*, 3036 Saratoga Blvd., 78415. Tel: 361-851-1443; Fax: 361-851-1552.
E-mail: CatholicCenter@interconnect.net
Rev. Bradley A. Barber, Dir.

LAREDO. *Holy Spirit Retreat and Conference Center*, 501 S. Century Dr., 78046. Tel: 956-726-4352; Fax: 956-726-4363.
E-mail: stjohn@border.net
Web site: www.stjean.com/laredo/hsrc/holy.htm
Rev. Dominique F. Peridans, F.J., Prior; Bro. John Mary Ignaatius Crawley, F.J., Guestmaster. Total Staff 4; Total in Residence 2; Postulants 6.

SANDIA. *Benedictine Retreat Center*, HC #2, Box 6300, 78383-9989. Tel: 512-547-9797; Fax: 512-547-9599.
E-mail: ccabbeyretreat@juno.com
Bro. Aelred Guerra, O.S.B., Dir. Total Staff 1.

SARITA. *Lebh Shomea House of Prayer*, La Parra Ranch, P.O. Box 9, 78385-0009. Tel: 361-294-5369; Fax: 361-294-5791.
E-mail: admin@lebhshomea.org
Web site: www.lebhshomea.org
Rev. Francis Kelly Nemeck, O.M.I. Total in Residence 7; Total Staff 4.

[H] MONASTERIES AND RESIDENCES OF PRIESTS AND BROTHERS

HEBBRONVILLE. *Catholic Solitudes*, Rancho Maria, P.O. Box 748, 78361. Tel: 361-527-4636; Fax: 361-527-4482.
E-mail: cathsol@aol.com
Rev. Patrick Meaney, Dir.; John-Mary Foster, Dir. Special Apostolate: A fraternal community stressing eremitical contemplative prayer, welcoming eremitical vocations and spiritual formational retreats for young people under directives of Diocesan Bishop. Total Staff 7; Total in Residence 11.
Franciscan Friars - O.F.M., 504 E. Santa Clara St., 78361. Tel: 512-527-3865; Fax: 512-527-5548. Rev. Adalberto Ramirez, O.F.M., Pastor. Total Staff 7; Total Assisted 31.

LAREDO. *Marist Brothers*, 1511 E. Cherry Hill Dr., 78041. Tel: 956-724-2651; Fax: 956-724-1963.
E-mail: fmslaredo@prodigy.net
Bros. Philip R. Degagne, F.M.S., Dir.; Joseph E. Herrera, F.M.S.; Thomas W. Coyne, F.M.S.; John A. Allen, F.M.S.; Robert Warren, F.M.S. Marist Brothers 5.
St. John's Priory, (F.J.), 505 Century Dr. S., 78046. Tel: 956-722-3399; Fax: 956-722-3299. Congregation of St. John. Revs. Dominique F. Peridans, F.J., Prior; Didier-Marie Dugas Viallis (France); Juan de Dios Saavedra (Spain); Marianus Hough (Canada); Bros. Louis-Mary Ketterhagen; John Victor Shoemaker; John Mary Ignatius Crawley; Deacon John Therese Crews (Philippines). Priests 3; Brothers in Formation (Postulants) 12; Total in Residence 20.

ROBSTOWN. *Society of Our Lady of the Most Holy Trinity*, P.O. Box 152, 78380-0792. Tel: 512-387-2754; Fax: 512-387-8090. Deacon Roy M. Grassedonio, Chancellor; Revs. Vincent Albano, S.O.L.T.; Anthony Anderson, S.O.L.T., Voc. Dir.; Peter J. Auer, S.O.L.T. (GF); James H.T. Brady, S.O.L.T. (WH); Alberto A. Brancaccio, S.O.L.T. (ALB); Scott Brossart, S.O.L.T.; George Carlin, S.O.L.T.; Phillip Chavez, S.O.L.T.; Robert Copsey, S.O.L.T.; John Corapi, S.O.L.T. (SAC); Robert Cronin, S.O.L.T. (GLP); Jacques Dolbec, S.O.L.T. (FAR); James Flanagan, S.O.L.T.; Peter Fremont-Smith, S.O.L.T.; Alfredo Gaytan, S.O.L.T.; Thomas P. Gier, S.O.L.T.; Kevin Gillen, S.O.L.T.; Paul E. Grala, S.O.L.T.; Joseph Hadgkiss, S.O.L.T.; Gene Hart, S.O.L.T.; Edward Horan, S.O.L.T.; Jeffrey Johnson, S.O.L.T. (BO); Michael Jordan, S.O.L.T.; James R. Kelleher, S.O.L.T.; Eckley Macklin, S.O.L.T. (KC); J. Guilbert Mariani, S.O.L.T.; John McHugh, S.O.L.T.; Joseph McManus, S.O.L.T.; Glenn Meaux, S.O.L.T.; Christopher Myers, S.O.L.T.; Thien Chi Nguyen, S.O.L.T.; Vincent A. Nicosia, S.O.L.T. (SFE); Joseph O'Connell, S.O.L.T.; Frank Papa, S.O.L.T. (HRT); John Mary Perez, S.O.L.T.; Tan Pham, S.O.L.T.; Santan Pinto, S.O.L.T. (SFE); John Purtell, S.O.L.T. (BO); Edward C. Roche, S.O.L.T.; Robert Shaldone, S.O.L.T.; Gerald Sheehan, S.O.L.T.; Maurice Shepherd, S.O.L.T.; Thomas Showalter, S.O.L.T.; James Tamborino, S.O.L.T. (MIL); Lawrence E. Tucker, S.O.L.T.; Deacon Wayne Lickteig, S.O.L.T. In res. Rev. Robert Rank, S.O.L.T.; Deacon Francis Hohenadel, S.O.L.T.

SAN DIEGO. *Vicariate of Holy Rosary*, St. Francis de Paul Church, P.O. Box 279, 78384. Tel: 512-279-3596; Fax: 512-279-8288.
E-mail: berem@vsta.com
Order of Preachers, U.S. Foundation of the Province of Spain. Revs. Benito Retortillo, O.P., Local Supr.; Epifanio Rodriguez, O.P.

SANDIA. *Corpus Christi Abbey*. (Benedictine Monastery), HC #2, Box 6300, 78383. Tel: 512-547-3257; Fax: 512-547-5184.
E-mail: ccabbey@yahoo.com
Web site: www.geocities.com/athens/styx/8125/ccabbey.html
Order Saint Benedict-Swiss-American Congregation. Rt. Revs. Louis Hacker, O.S.B.; Luke Buergler, O.S.B., (Retired), (Live Oak Nursing Center); Revs. Sylvester Schad, O.S.B., (Live Oak Nursing Center); Maryon Jordan, O.S.B. (LC); Bartholomew Leon, O.S.B., (Maronite Rite); John Harold McKenzie, O.S.B., Navy Chap.; Gregory Yockey, O.S.B.; Michael DeLeon, O.S.B.; Deacon Dominic Mazoch; Bros. Simon Huggins, O.S.B., Prior; James Orta, O.S.B.; Francis Delgadillo, O.S.B.; Rafiel Lukasik, O.S.B.; David Cobos, O.S.B.; George Strohmeyer, O.S.B.; Benedict Brom, O.S.B.; Matthew O'Meara, O.S.B.; Andrew Suarez, O.S.B.; Gabriel Babin, O.S.B. Brothers 12; Priests 8; Novices 1.

[I] CONVENTS AND RESIDENCES FOR SISTERS

CORPUS CHRISTI. *Bethany Convent*, 2962 Austin St., 78404. Tel: 512-888-7537.
E-mail: mkuntscher@netscape.net
Sisters of the Incarnate Word and Blessed Sacrament 3.
Blessed Sacrament Chapel, 4105 Ocean Dr., 78411-1223. Tel: 361-852-6212; Fax: 361-853-3811.
E-mail: bscccm@cs.com
Sr. Mary Margaret Friedl, S.Sp.S. de A.P., Supr. Sister-Servants of the Holy Spirit of Perpetual Adoration (Motherhouse, Steyl, Holland) 10.
Congregation of the Sisters of the Holy Cross, Holy Cross Convent, 1109 N. Staples, 78401-1836. Tel: 512-888-7753; 888-4012.
Dominican Daughters of Santo Tomas de Aquino, 12201 Hearn Rd., 78410.
Incarnate Word Convent, 2930 S. Alameda, 78404. Tel: 361-882-5413; Fax: 361-880-4152.
E-mail: smigonzalez@hotmail.com
Sisters of the Incarnate Word and Blessed Sacrament. Legal Title: *Convent Academy of the Incarnate Word*. Sr. Maria Irma Gonzalez, I.W.B.S., Supr. Tel: 361-882-6560; Rev. Robert McGrath, O.M.I. Sisters 41; Total Staff 21; Total in Residence 41.
Mount Carmel Home Convent, 4130 S. Alameda St., 78411. Tel: 361-855-6243; Fax: 361-854-8513. Carmelite Sisters of the Divine Heart of Jesus 7.
Mount Tabor Convent, 12940 Leopard St., 78410. Tel: 361-241-1955; Fax: 361-241-5279.
E-mail: rocmjmj@yahoo.com
Novitiate and Central Regional House of the Missionary Sisters of Jesus, Mary, and Joseph. Sr. Raquel D. Gomez, M.J.M.J., Delegation Supr.; Sr. Angeles Berrozpe, M.J.M.J., Supr. Sisters 6; Total Staff 6; Total Assisted 6.
Pax Christi Residence, 4601 Calallen Dr., 78410. Tel: 361-241-2833; Fax: 361-241-5479.
Pax Christi Institute. Mother Teresa Santoyo, P.C.I., Supr. Gen. Sisters 12; Total Staff 8; Total Assisted 3,700.
Religious Missionaries of St. Dominic, Inc. (Congregacion de Religiosas Misioneras de Santo Domingo), 2237 Waldron Rd., 78418. Tel: 361-939-8102; Fax: 361-939-8203.
Our Lady of the Rosary Learning Center. Tel: 361-939-8102; Fax: 361-939-8203. Sr. Esperanza Manas, O.P., Delegate of the Supr. Gen.; Sr. Maria Paz Aribon, Dir.
St. Joseph Home Convent, 4015 MacArthur St., 78416-1907. Tel: 512-853-6970; Fax: 512-853-6670.
E-mail: sr.m.m.m@worldnet.att.net
Carmelite Sisters of the Divine Heart of Jesus. Sr. M. Michelle Miranda, Carmel D.C.J., Supr. Total Staff 10; Sisters 4; Total Assisted 60.
Sisters of Our Lady of Charity Convent, 1201 Lantana St., 78407. Tel: 361-289-2611; Fax: 361-289-5162. Sisters of Our Lady of Charity. Sisters 2.
Spohn Hospital Convent, 1725 2nd St., 78404. Tel: 361-881-3000; 884-0702; Fax: 361-881-3149.
E-mail: margaret_mannion@iwhs.org
Congregation of Sisters of Charity of the Incarnate Word - San Antonio. Sisters 3.
Stella Maris Convent, 1739 Second St., 78404. Tel: 512-887-7920; 887-0587. Congregation of Sisters of Charity of the Incarnate Word - San Antonio. Sr. Julia Delaney, C.C.V.I., Coord.

KINGSVILLE. *Missionary Daughters of the Most Pure Virgin Mary*, 919 N. Ninth St., 78363. Sr. Consuelo Ramirez, M.D.P.V.M., Supr. Sisters 11.

LAREDO. *Mary, Help of Christians Convent*, 10 E. Del Mar Blvd., 78045. Tel: 956-722-3966; Fax: 956-722-1413.
E-mail: fmasuolr@icsi.net
Daughters of Mary Help of Christians Salesian Sisters. Sr. Martina Ponce, F.M.A., Prin. & Supr.; Sr. Aida Flores, F.M.A.; Sr. Rosalba Garcia, F.M.A.; Sr. Esther Lopez, F.M.A.; Sr. Ofelia Lozano, F.M.A.; Sr. Margaret Natal, F.M.A.; Sr. Sylvia Castillo, F.M.A.; Sr. Trinidad Reyes, F.M.A.; Sr. Esperanza Rodriguez, F.M.A.; Sr. Assunta Sanchez, F.M.A.; Sr. Josephine Sanchez, F.M.A.; Sr. Irene Tapia, F.M.A.; Sr. Nguyen Thanh Virgine Thuy, F.M.A. Sisters 13; Total Staff 67.
Sacred Heart Children's Home Convent, 3310 S. Zapata Hwy., 78046. Tel: 956-723-3343; Fax: 956-723-3409. Servants of the Sacred Heart of Jesus and of the Poor. Sr. Maria Teresa Grajeda, S.S.H.J.P., Supr. Sisters 22.
Sisters of Mercy of the St. Louis Regional Community, Inc., 1414 Hendricks Ave., 78040. Tel: 956-723-1364.
E-mail: oobregon@lare.smhs.com
Religious Sisters of Mercy. Sr. Olivia M. Obregon, Local Coord. Sisters 8; Total Staff 4.
Mercy Hospital Convent. Tel: 956-723-1364.
Su Casa, 3906 Monterrey, 78043-6648. Tel: 210-718-8762.
Sisters of St. John, 504 Century Dr. S., 78046. Tel: 956-727-1028; Fax: 956-727-1028. Sr. Marie-Abel Buisset, Local Supr. Total in Residence 6.
Ursuline Convent, 2302 Corpus Christi St., 78043. Tel: 956-723-9185.
E-mail: mvitt2302@aol.com
1415 Jarvis St., 78043. Tel: 956-723-8968. Roman Union Central Province of the U.S. Sr. Margaret Mary Vitt, O.S.U., Prioress. Sisters 8.

ROCKPORT. *Schoenstatt Sisters of Mary*, 130 Front St., Lamar, HC 04, Box 100, 78382-9606. Tel: 361-729-1868; Fax: 361-729-1685. Secular Institute of the Schoenstatt Sisters of Mary. Sr. M. Antoinette Buffler, I.S.S.M., Prov. Supr. Sisters 37; Total in Residence 20.

SARITA. *Lebh Shomea, House of Prayer*, La Parra Ranch, P.O. Box 9, 78385-0009. Tel: 361-294-5369; Fax: 361-294-5791.
E-mail: admin@lebhshomea.org
Web site: www.lebhshomea.org
Total Staff 4; Total in Residence 7.

SKIDMORE. *Our Lady of the Most Holy Trinity Convent*, General Motherhouse, P.O. Box 189, 78389. Tel: 361-287-3570; 287-0062; Fax: 361-287-0063.
E-mail: srmarytrinity@yahoo.com
Sr. Mary of the Redemption, S.O.L.T., Gen. Sister Servant; Sr. Sister Mary of the Trinity Vaughan, S.O.L.T., Gen. Sister Servant; Sr. Mary Carmen Sandoval, S.O.L.T., Regional Sister Servant. Sisters 67.

[J] MISCELLANEOUS

CORPUS CHRISTI. *The Catholic Campaign of America, Inc.*, P.O. Box 2620, 78403-2620. Tel: 361-882-6191; Fax: 361-882-1018.

The Counseling Center, 1322 Comanche, 78401. Tel: 361-884-0651; Fax: 361-884-3956. Ms. Gloria Garcia, Lead Counselor. Total Staff 2; Patients assisted annually 500.

Cursillo Movement Eastern Vicariate, 3360 San Antonio, 78411. Tel: 361-855-3534; Fax: 361-855-3534. Dr. Michael Meaney, Pres.; Rev. James Janecek, Spiritual Dir.

Father Magsam Center for Spiritual Direction, 4103 Ocean Dr., 78411. Tel: 512-853-0170. Sr. Joan Michele Rake, C.D.P., Spiritual Dir. Total Assisted 2,120.

Hope, Faith & Love, Inc., P.O. Box 2620, 78403. Tel: 361-882-6191; Fax: 361-882-1018.

Incarnate Word Academy Foundation, 2930 S. Alameda, 78404. Tel: 361-882-5413; Fax: 361-883-2185.
Web site: www.iwacc.org
Sr. Maria Irma Gonzalez, I.W.B.S., Pres.

Our Lady of Corpus Christi Catholic Undergraduate Liberal Arts.
Web site: www.colcc.com
Mailing Address: P.O.Box 9785, 78469. 1200 Lantana, 78407. Tel: 361-289-9095; Fax: 361-289-0087.
E-mail: colcc@juno.com
Web site: colcc.com
Revs. James R. Kelleher, S.O.L.T., S.T.D., Pres.; Anthony Anderson, S.O.L.T., Vice Pres.; Paul Hu. Total Staff 20; Students 29.

Pope John Paul, II Library, The Corpus Christi Catholic Center, 3036 Saratoga Blvd., 78415.

Search Retreats, 3502 Saratoga Blvd., 78415. Tel: 361-851-0908.
E-mail: searchretreats@yahoo.com
Web site: searchretreats.org
Mr. Donald Harris, Contact Person & Prog. Dir.; Rev. Glen Mullen, Spiritual Dir.

Secular Institute of the Schoenstatt Fathers aka Schoenstatt Fathers, 4343 Gaines St., 78412-2541. Tel: 361-992-9841; Fax: 361-992-9842.
E-mail: frgerold@hotmail.com
Revs. Gerold Langsch, I.Sch., Supr. & Contact Person; Robert DeCock, I.Sch.; Christian Christensen, I.Sch.

INGLESIDE. *Our Lady of the Assumption Early Learning Center*, 2414 Main St., 78362. Tel: 361-776-2644.

LAREDO. *Bethany House*, 819 Hidalgo St., 78040. Tel: 956-722-4152; Fax: 956-726-2349;728-7471. Ms. Barbara Kazen, Pres.; Ms. Nanette Dion, Devel. Svcs.

St. Augustine School Endowment Fund, Inc., 1300 Galveston, 78040. Tel: 956-724-8131; Fax: 956-725-9241.
E-mail: almarose@st.augustine.org
Sr. Antoinette Billeaud, Contact Person.

San Augustin Historical Preservation & Restoration Society, Inc., 200 San Augustin Ave., 78040. Tel: 956-722-1382; Fax: 956-722-0441. Rev. Msgr. James E. Harris, Contact Person.

RELIGIOUS INSTITUTES OF MEN REPRESENTED IN THE DIOCESE

For further details refer to the corresponding bracketed number in the Religious Institutes of Men or Women section.

[0150]—*Augustinian Recollects.*—O.A.R.
[0200]—*Benedictine Monks.*—O.S.B.
[0470]—*The Capuchin Friars.*—O.F.M.CAP.
[]—*Catholic Solitudes (Hermits).*
[0220]—*Congregation of the Blessed Sacrament.*—S.S.S.
[1330]—*Congregation of the Mission (Vincentians).*—C.M.
[0630]—*Congregation of the Missionaries of the Holy Family.*—M.S.F.
[0430]—*Dominican, Order of Preachers.* (Spain).—O.P.
[]—*Faternity Missionary of Mary.* (El Salvador).
[1110]—*Missionaries of the Sacred Heart.*—M.S.C.
[]—*Missionary Congregation of the Blessed Sacrament.* (India).
[0910]—*Oblates of Mary Immaculate.* (Southwest Prov.).—O.M.I.
[1310]—*Order of the Holy Trinity.* (Province of Baltimore).—O.SS.T.
[1065]—*Priestly Fraternity of St. Peter, Society of Apostolic Life.*—F.S.S.P.
[1070]—*Redemptorists.*—C.Ss.R.
[1190]—*Salesians of St. John Bosco.*—S.D.B.
[]—*Schoenstatt Fathers.*—I.Sch.
[1260]—*Society of Christ.* (Poland)—S.Ch.
[0690]—*Society of Jesus.*—S.J.
[0975]—*Society of Our Lady of the Most Holy Trinity, Society of Apostolic Life.*—S.O.L.T.

RELIGIOUS INSTITUTES OF WOMEN REPRESENTED IN THE DIOCESE

[0360]—*Carmelite Sisters of the Divine Heart of Jesus.*—Carmel.D.C.J.
[]—*Catholic Solitudes (Women's Household).*
[0460]—*Congregation of the Sisters of Charity of the Incarnate Word.* (San Antonio, TX).—C.C.V.I.
[1920]—*Congregation of the Sisters of the Holy Cross.*—C.S.C.
[1070-19]—*Dominican Sisters.* (Houston, TX).—O.P.
[]—*Dominican Sisters of St. Thomas Aquinas.*—O.P.
[2590]—*Mercedarian Sisters of the Blessed Sacrament.*—H.M.S.S.
[0390]—*Missionary Carmelites of St. Teresa.*—C.M.S.T.
[2690]—*Missionary Catechists of Divine Providence.* (San Antonio, TX).—M.C.D.P.
[]—*Missionary Daughters of the Most Pure Virgin Mary.* (U.S. Foundation-Mexico).—M.D.P.V.M.
[2770]—*Missionary Sisters of Jesus, Mary, and Joseph.*—M.J.M.J.
[]—*Missionary Sisters of the Rosary of Fatima.*—H.M.R.F.
[]—*Pax Christi Institute.*—P.C.I.
[]—*Religious Missionaries of St. Dominic.* (Spanish Prov.).—O.P.
[]—*Schoenstatt Sisters of Mary (Secular Institute).*—I.S.S.M.
[3540]—*Sister Servants of the Holy Spirit of Perpetual Adoration.*—S.Sp.S.deA.P.
[]—*Sisters of Adoration of the Blessed Sacrament.* (India).
[1010]—*Sisters of Divine Providence of San Antonio, Texas.*—C.D.P.
[3070]—*Sisters of Our Lady of Charity.* (Dallas, TX).—O.L.C.
[3360]—*Sisters of Providence of Saint Mary-of-the-Woods, IN.*—S.P.
[3718]—*Sisters of St. Anne.*—S.S.A.
[]—*Sisters of St. Joseph.* (Pittsburgh).—S.S.J.
[2040]—*Sisters of the Holy Spirit.*—S.H.Sp.
[2205]—*Sisters of the Incarnate Word and Blessed Sacrament.*—I.W.B.S.
[]—*Sisters of the Society of Our Lady of the Most Holy Trinity (Society of Apostolic Life).*—S.O.L.T.

NECROLOGY

† Brasley, Rev. Msgr. Lucean R., (Retired). —Died Dec. 16, 1999.
† Kinlough, Rev. Msgr. William C., (Retired). —Died Sept. 29, 2000.

Diocese of Covington

(Dioecesis Covingtonensis)

Most Reverend

ROBERT W. MUENCH, D.D.

Bishop of Covington; ordained May 18, 1968; appointed Titular Bishop of Mactaris and Auxiliary of New Orleans May 8, 1990; consecrated June 29, 1990; appointed January 5, 1996; installed March 19, 1996. *Mailing Address: P.O. Box 18548, Erlanger, KY, 41018-0548.* Tel.: 859-283-6212.

Most Reverend

WILLIAM A. HUGHES, D.D.

Retired Bishop of Covington; ordained April 6, 1946; appointed Titular Bishop of Inis Cathaig and Auxiliary of Youngstown July 23, 1974; consecrated September 12, 1974; appointed Bishop of Covington April 13, 1979; transferred to Covington May 8, 1979; retired July 4, 1995. *Res., Cathedral Basilica of the Assumption, 1140 Madison Ave., Covington, KY, 41011-3116.*

ESTABLISHED JULY 29, 1853.

Square Miles 3,359.

Comprises 14 Counties of the Commonwealth of Kentucky in the north and east of the Commonwealth, including Bracken, Boone, Campbell, Carroll, Fleming, Gallatin, Grant, Harrison, Kenton, Lewis, Mason, Owen, Pendleton and Robertson Counties.

For legal titles of parishes and diocesan institutions, consult the Chancery Office.

The Catholic Center: P.O. Box 18548, Erlanger, KY, 41018-0548. Tel.: 859-283-6200; Fax: 859-283-6334.

Web site address: www.dioofcovky.org

E-mail address: ddaugh@dioofcovky.org

As of October 1, 2000 the mandatory area code change for the Diocese of Covington is 606 to 859. The option to make this change begins April 2000.

STATISTICAL OVERVIEW

Personnel	
Bishop	1
Retired Bishops	1
Priests: Diocesan Active in Diocese	54
Priests: Active Outside Diocese	2
Priests: Retired, Sick or Absent	55
Number of Diocesan Priests	111
Religious Priests in Diocese	2
Ordinations:	
Diocesan Priests	1
Permanent Deacons in Diocese	25
Total Brothers	6
Total Sisters	418
Parishes	
Parishes	47
With Resident Pastor:	
Resident Diocesan Priests	41
Without Resident Pastor:	
Administered by Priests	2
Administered by Women Religious	4
Missions	10
Professional Ministry Personnel:	
Sisters	14
Lay Ministers	38
Welfare	
Catholic Hospitals	3
Total Assisted	369,025
Homes for the Aged	3
Total Assisted	734
Residential Care of Children	2
Total Assisted	112
Day Care and Extended Day Care Centers	1
Total Assisted	113
Special Centers for Social Services	4
Total Assisted	70,833
Other Institutions	1
Total Assisted	8,180
Educational	
Diocesan Students in Other Seminaries	4
Total Seminarians	4
Colleges and Universities	1
Total Students	1,325
High Schools, Diocesan and Parish	7
Total Students	2,555
High Schools, Private	2
Total Students	718
Elementary Schools, Diocesan and Parish	28
Total Students	8,596
Elementary Schools, Private	2
Total Students	573
Non-residential Schools for the Disabled	1
Total Students	28
Catechesis/Religious Education:	
High School Students	356
Elementary Students	4,375
Total Students Under Catholic Instruction	18,530
Teachers in the Diocese:	
Brothers	1
Sisters	53
Lay Teachers	667
Vital Statistics	
Receptions into the Church:	
Infant Baptism Totals	1,306
Adult Baptism Totals	445
Received into Full Communion	169
First Communions	1,791
Confirmations	1,492
Marriages:	
Catholic	354
Interfaith	198
Total Marriages	552
Deaths	905
Total Catholic Population	86,031
Total Population	452,484

Former Bishops—Rt. Rev. GEORGE ALOYSIUS CARRELL, S.J., D.D., cons. Nov. 1, 1853; died Sept. 25, 1868.—Rt. Rev. AUGUSTUS MARIA TOEBBE, D.D., cons. Jan. 9, 1870; died May 2, 1884.—Rt. Rev. CAMILLUS PAUL MAES, D.D., cons. Jan. 25, 1885; died May 11, 1915.—Rt. Rev. FERDINAND BROSSART, D.D., cons. Jan. 25, 1916; resigned March 14, 1923; died Aug. 6, 1930.—Most Rev. FRANCIS WILLIAM HOWARD, D.D., cons. July 15, 1923; died Jan. 18, 1944.—Most Rev. WILLIAM THEODORE MULLOY, D.D., LL.D., cons. Jan. 10, 1945; died June 1, 1959.—Most Rev. RICHARD HENRY ACKERMAN, C.S.Sp., D.D., cons. May 26, 1956; transferred to Covington April 6, 1960; retired Nov. 28, 1978; died Nov. 18, 1992.—Most Rev. WILLIAM ANTHONY HUGHES, D.D., cons. Sept. 12, 1974; appt. April 13, 1979; retired July 4, 1995.

Vicar General and Chancellor—Very Rev. GERALD L. REINERSMAN, V.G.

Assistant Chancellor—Ms. MARGARET M. SCHACK.

Diocesan Tribunal—Very Rev. JOHN R. SCHULTE, J.C.L., Judicial Vicar; JOHN M. MEECE, Case Promoter; MARY JOAN MEECE, Sec. & Notary.

Judges—Revs. JAMES M. RYAN; ROBERT C. WEHAGE; WILLIAM B. NEUHAUS; BARRY M. WINDHOLTZ; Sr. MARY CATHERINE WENSTRUP, J.C.L.

Defenders of the Bond—Rev. Msgr. ROGER P. COONEY; Revs. GREGORY E. OSBURG, M.A., J.C.L.; GERALD E. TWADELL, Ph.D.; PAUL L. BERSCHIED; GILBERT J. RUTZ; GARY A. MILLER.

Diocesan Consultors—Very Rev. GERALD L. REINERSMAN, V.G.; Very Rev. WILLIAM B. NEUHAUS, V.F.; Revs. EDWARD J. BRODNICK; ROBERT J. HENDERSON; JOHN H. KROGER; JOSEPH N. BOSCHERT; JEROME C. BRITT.

Deans—Very Rev. JOHN W. CAHILL, V.F., Covington; Very Rev. GERALD E. TWADDELL, V.F., Northern Kenton County; Very Rev. EDWARD J. BRODNICK, V.F., Southwest; Very Rev. RICHARD G. BOLTE, V.F., Newport, Bellevue, Dayton; Very Rev. WILLIAM B. NEUHAUS, V.F., Campbell County; Very Rev. WILLIAM H. HINDS, V.F., Southeast.

Diocesan Pastoral Council—Mr. EDWARD P. RAWE, Chm.

Presbyteral Council—Very Rev. WILLIAM B. NEUHAUS, V.F., Chm.; Rev. MARK G. WITTE, Vice-Chm.; Rev. JEROME C. BRITT, Sec.

Due Process Board of Administrative Review—Mr. MICHAEL HAMMONS, J.D., Chm.; Mr. STEPHEN KOPLYAY, Sec.

Diocesan Offices and Directors

The Catholic Center—947 Donaldson Hwy., P.O. Box 18548, Erlanger, 41018-0548. Tel: 859-283-6200; Fax: 859-283-6334. Office Hours: Mon.-Fri. 8:30-4:30.

Archives—Vacant.

Board of Total Catholic Education—Dr. LAWRENCE W. BOWMAN, Ed.D.; Mr. ROGER F. KELLER, Chm.

Campus Ministry-Newman Center—Mr. AL CUCCHETTI, Pastoral Admin., *Northern Kentucky Univ., 512 Johns Hill Rd., P.O. Box 76174, Highland Heights, 41076-1449.* Tel: 859-781-3775.

Cathedral Foundation, Inc.—1140 Madison Ave., Covington, 41011-3116. Tel: 859-431-2060; Fax: 859-431-8444.

Catholic Charities—Sr. JOAN MARIE BOBERG, C.D.P., Dir., *3629 Church St., Covington, 41015-1499.* Tel: 859-581-8974; Fax: 859-581-9595.

Catholic Scouting—Rev. JEROME C. BRITT, Chap.; Mrs. BETH WORLAND, Chm.

Cemeteries—Mr. JOHN NIENABER, Dir.

Censor Librorum—Rev. JAMES E. QUILL, S.T.D.

Charismatic Renewal—Contact Persons: Mr. HARRY HUMPERT; Mr. JOSEPH BESSLER.

Communication—Mr. TIMOTHY L. FITZGERALD, Acting Dir.

Continuing Education of Priests—Rev. RONALD M. KETTELER, Dir.

Corpus Central Purchasing—Ms. SANDRA NARE, Gen. Mgr. Buyers: MIKE FREUDENBERG; BOB MOELLMAN, *845 Isabella St., Newport, 41071-1338.* Tel: 859-491-8100; 800-955-2541; Fax: 859-491-6587.

Cursillo Movement—Rev. GARY A. MILLER, Spiritual Dir.; Mr. DAVID ZERHUSEN, Lay Dir.

Disabilities Commission—Mr. J. DAVID MILLER, Chm.

Ecumenism—Rev. RONALD M. KETTELER, *Thomas More College, 333 Thomas More Pkwy., Crestview Hills, 41017-3428.* Tel: 859-344-3393.

Evangelization and Initiation Commission—MADONNA MARIE KLING, C.D.P., Chm.

Family Ministry—Mrs. SUSAN VOGT, Dir.

Finance—Mr. ANTHONY G. DEPENBROCK, Dir.

Hispanic Ministry—Mr. FERNANDO POPPE, Dir.

Justice and Peace Office—Sr. RUTH KETTMAN, C.S.J., Dir.

Lay Retreat Movement—Deacon EDWARD STIERITZ, Dir., *945 Donaldson Hwy., Erlanger, 41018-1093.* Tel: 859-371-4224.

Legion of Mary—Rev. JOSEPH J. RUETER, Spiritual Dir.

Liaison for Retired Priests—Rev. ROBERT L. VATER.

Ministry Development Program—Assoc. Directors: Sr. MONICA STUHLREYER, I.H.M., Lay Ministry Development; Mrs. ANNE RUSEN, Living Church Program; Rev. GILBERT J. RUTZ, Deacon Formation.

Mission Services—See Stewardship and Missions.

Missions Among Black and Native Americans—Sr. JANET BUCHER, C.D.P.

Mustard Seed Community—Contact Persons: Mr. JOSEPH BESSLER; Mr. HARRY HUMPERT.

Newspaper "Messenger"—Mr. TIMOTHY L. FITZGERALD, Editor-in-Chief.

Pastoral Ministry Formation—Rev. GILBERT J. RUTZ, Dir.

Pastoral Office for the Deaf—Sr. RITA ANN WIGGINTON, O.S.U.

Pastoral Planning and Research—Mrs. JAN VON HANDORF, Dir.

Permanent Diaconate Formation—Rev. GILBERT J. RUTZ, Dir.

Priest Personnel—Rev. Msgr. DONALD F. HELLMANN, Dir.

Priests' Eucharistic League—Rev. LOUIS B. BRINKER, Dir.

Priests' Retirement Committee—Rev. JOSEPH C. BRINK, Vice-Chm.

Religious—Sr. M. CATHERINE HUNT, C.D.P., Dir.

Serra Club of Diocese of Covington—Rev. JOHN J. STERLING, Chap.

St. Vincent de Paul Society—Rev. ROBERT J. REINKE, Spiritual Dir.; Mr. VINCENT BESSLER, Pres.

Stewardship and Missions—Mrs. SUE GRETHEL, Dir. Includes Pontifical Aid Societies, Campaign for Human Development, Catholic Relief Fund, Holy Childhood Assoc., Inner City Missions.

Total Catholic Education—Dr. LAWRENCE M. BOWMAN, Ed.D., Dir. Catholic Education & Supt.; Mr. EUGENE A. KUEHNE, Dir. Business Svcs.; Sr. STELLA MARIE GOUGH, O.S.B., Dir. Catechetical Svcs.

Vocation Council—Rev. JOHN J. STERLING, Dir.

Worship Commission—MADONNA MARIE KLING, C.D.P., Chm.

Office of Worship, Evangelization & Initiation—MADONNA MARIE KLING, C.D.P., Dir.

Office of Youth and Young Adult Ministry—Mrs. BETH WORLAND, Dir.

CLERGY, PARISHES, MISSIONS AND PAROCHIAL SCHOOLS

CITY OF COVINGTON (Kenton County)

1—CATHEDRAL, BASILICA OF THE ASSUMPTION (1837), Very Rev. John W. Cahill; Deacon Edward E. Stieritz. In res., Most Rev. William A. Hughes, (Retired); Rev. William F. Cleves.
Res., 1140 Madison Ave., 41011-3116. Tel: 859-431-2060; Fax: 859-431-8444.

2—ST. AGNES (1930), Revs. Mark A. Keene; James E. Quill, (Retired); Deacons Joseph Cleves; David Flynn; Robert Stoeckle.
Res., 1680 Dixie Hwy., Fort Wright, 41011-2779. Tel: 859-431-1802; Fax: 859-291-7017.
School—Tel: 859-261-0543; Fax: 859-261-9778.
Lay Teachers 36; Students 519.
Catechesis/Religious Programs—Students 158.

3—ST. AUGUSTINE (1870), Rev. Leo C. Schmidt. In res., Rev. Robert J. Reinke, (Retired).
Res., 1839 Euclid Ave., 41014-1162. Tel: 859-431-3943; Fax: 859-431-4036.
School—Tel: 859-261-5564; Fax: 859-261-5402.
Sisters of Notre Dame 2; Lay Teachers 8; Students 173.
Catechesis/Religious Programs—Students 9.

4—ST. BENEDICT (1885), Rev. Douglas J. Lauer; Deacon Philip Racine.
Res., 338 E. 17th St., 41014-1315. Tel: 859-431-5607; Fax: 859-431-5847.
Catechesis/Religious Programs—Students 155.

5—HOLY CROSS (1890), Rev. Thomas C. Barnes; Ms. Marg Wilburs, Pastoral Assoc. In res., Rev. Charles J. Hoffer, (Retired); Deacon Ralph Colatrella.
Res., 3612 Church St., 41015-1431. Tel: 859-431-0636; Fax: 859-431-6917.
School—Tel: 859-581-6599; Fax: 859-581-3462.
Lay Teachers 12; Students 231.
Catechesis/Religious Programs—Students 70.

6—ST. JOHN (1854), Rev. Douglas F. Fortner; Deacon Robert J. Hermann.
Res., 627 Pike St., 41011-2148. Tel: 859-431-5314; Fax: 859-431-8397.
Mission—Covington, Kenton Co., St. Ann, (1860) 1274 Parkway, 41011.

7—MOTHER OF GOD (1841), Rev. Raymond C. Holtz; Deacon Steven I. Durkee.
Res., 119 W. 6th St., 41011-1409. Tel: 859-291-2288; Fax: 859-291-2065.

8—CHURCH OF OUR SAVIOR (1943), Sr. Janet Marie Bucher, C.D.P., Pastoral Admin.; Rev. Robert C. Rosing.
Res., 246 E. 10th St., 41011-3026. Tel: 859-491-5872; Fax: 859-431-8444.
Catechesis/Religious Programs—Students 120.

OUTSIDE THE CITY OF COVINGTON

Alexandria, Campbell Co., St. Mary of the Assumption (1860), Rev. Joseph C. Brink; Deacon Dennis Lehmkuhl.
Res., 121 W. Main St., 41001-1217. Tel: 859-635-4188; Fax: 859-635-4189. [CEM]
School—9 S. Jefferson St., 41001-1398. Tel: 859-635-9539; Fax: 859-448-4824.
Brothers 1; Sisters of Notre Dame 2; Lay Teachers 29; Students 563.
Catechesis/Religious Programs—Students 154.

Augusta, Bracken Co., St. Augustine (1860), Rev. Daniel J. Saner; Deacon Frank Estill.
Res., 215 E. Fourth St., 41002-1117. Tel: 606-756-2377; Fax: 606-756-2377. [JC]
School—Tel: 606-756-3229; Fax: 606-756-2377.
Sisters of Notre Dame 3; Lay Teachers 5; Students 102.
Catechesis/Religious Programs—Students 12.

Bellevue, Campbell Co., Sacred Heart (1874), Rev. Lawrence R. Robotnik.
Res., 318 Division St., 41073-1198. Tel: 859-261-6172; Fax: 859-261-0016.
Catechesis/Religious Programs—Students 22.

St. Anthony (1889), Rev. John H. Kroger.
Res., 320 Poplar St., 41073-1109. Tel: 859-431-7143; Fax: 859-491-4735.
Catechesis/Religious Programs—Students 20.

Brooksville, Bracken Co., St. James (1868), Rev. Daniel J. Saner; Deacon Ernest B. Hillenmeyer, Pastoral Assoc.
Res., P.O. Box 27, 41004-0027. Tel: 606-735-2271; Fax: 606-735-2271. [CEM]
Catechesis/Religious Programs—Students 35.
Mission—Minerva, Mason Co., St. James, Kentucky Rd., Minerva, 41062. Tel: 606-435-1235.

Burlington, Boone Co., Immaculate Heart of Mary (1954), Rev. Jerome C. Britt; Deacon Richard J. O'Donnell.
Church—5876 Veterans Way, 41005-8824. Tel: 859-689-4488; Fax: 859-689-5636.
School—Tel: 859-689-4303; Fax: 859-689-5636.
Sisters of Divine Providence of Kentucky 2; Lay Teachers 25; Students 576.
Catechesis/Religious Programs—Students 615.

California, Campbell Co., Sts. Peter and Paul (1854), Rev. Joseph N. Boschert.
Res., Rte. 2, Box 134, 41007-9713. Tel: 859-635-2924; Fax: 859-635-9184. [CEM 2]
School—Tel: 859-635-4382; Fax: 859-635-9184.
Lay Teachers 8; Students 160.
Catechesis/Religious Programs—Students 51.
Mission—Stepstone, Pendleton Co., Immaculate Conception.

Camp Springs, Campbell Co., St. Joseph (1845), Very Rev. Gerald E. Twaddell, V.F.; Sr. Mary Kevan Seibert, S.N.D., Pastoral Admin.
Mailing Address: Box 225, 41059-9746. Tel: 859-635-2491; Fax: 859-635-7336. [CEM]
School—Tel: 859-635-5652; Fax: 859-635-5652.
Religious 1; Lay Teachers 4; Students 60.
Catechesis/Religious Programs—Students 30.

Carrollton, Carroll Co., St. John the Evangelist (1853), Rev. Michael D. Barth.
Res., 507 Fifth St., 41008-1203. Tel: 502-732-5776; Fax: 502-732-9062. [CEM]
Catechesis/Religious Programs—Students 97.
Mission—Perry Park, Owen Co., Transfiguration.

Cold Spring, Campbell Co., St. Joseph (1870), Revs. Robert J. Henderson; Richard W. Frazier. In res., Rev. Joseph J. Rueter, (Retired).
Res., 4011 Alexandria Pk., 41076-1895. Tel: 859-441-1604; Fax: 859-441-7681. [CEM]
School—Tel: 859-441-2025; Fax: 859-441-2057.
Sisters of Notre Dame 3; Lay Teachers 40; Students 675.
Catechesis/Religious Programs—Students 73.

Crescent Springs, Kenton Co., St. Joseph (1916), Revs. Raymond S. Hartman; John J. Sterling; Deacons Marvin Holstein; Joseph Baker. In res., Rev. Ronald M. Ketteler.
Res., 2470 Lorraine Ct., 41017-1406. Tel: 859-341-6609; Fax: 859-578-2741.
School—Tel: 859-578-2742; Fax: 859-578-2754.
Lay Teachers 32; Students 562.
Catechesis/Religious Programs—Students 125.

Cynthiana, Harrison Co., St. Edward (1872), Rev. Louis B. Brinker.
Res., 123 N. Walnut St., 41031-1225. Tel: 859-234-5444; Fax: 859-234-9823. [CEM]
School—Tel: 859-234-2731; Fax: 859-234-9597.
Lay Teachers 4; Students 77.

Dayton, Campbell Co., St. Bernard (1853), Rev. Michael E. Comer; Deacon Charles Dietz. In res., Rev. Paul J. Brinker, (Retired).
Res., 701 Fifth St., 41074-1139. Tel: 859-261-8506; Fax: 859-581-7260.
School—Tel: 859-581-6759; Fax: 859-581-7260.
Sisters of Divine Providence of Kentucky 3; Lay Teachers 3; Students 112.
Catechesis/Religious Programs—Students 24.

Edgewood, Kenton Co., St. Pius X (1958), Revs. Robert C. Wehage; Richard W. Wurth; Deacon David J. Meyer. In res., Rev. John J. Riesenberg, (Retired).
Res., 340 Dudley Rd., 41017-2609. Tel: 859-341-4900, Ext. 2; Fax: 859-578-8597. [CEM]
School—Tel: 859-341-3435; Fax: 859-341-3440.
Priests 3; Lay Teachers 36; Students 685.
Catechesis/Religious Programs—Students 175.

Elsmere, Kenton Co., St. Henry (1890), Revs. James J. Ryan; Gregory J. Bach; Charlotte Berling, Pastoral Assoc.
Res., 3813 Dixie Hwy., 41018-1809. Tel: 859-342-2540; Fax: 859-342-2542.
School—Tel: 859-342-2551; Fax: 859-342-2554.
Religious 1; Lay Teachers 28; Students 567.
Catechesis/Religious Programs—Students 164.

Erlanger, Kenton Co., St. Barbara (1967), Rev. G. Michael Greer; Deacon Bernard J. Kaiser.
Res., 4042 Turkeyfoot Rd., 41018-2921. Tel: 859-371-3100; Fax: 859-371-3101.
Catechesis/Religious Programs—Students 230.

Mary, Queen of Heaven, Boone Co., (1955), Rev. David B. Gamm; Deacon Thomas Dushney.
Res., 1150 Donaldson Hwy., 41018-1048. Tel: 859-525-6909; Fax: 859-525-7067.
School—Tel: 859-371-8100; Fax: 859-371-8100.
Sisters 1; Lay Teachers 12; Students 272.
Catechesis/Religious Programs—Students 94.

Falmouth, Pendleton Co., St. Francis Xavier (1880), Rev. Louis H. Dickmann.
Res., 202 Second St., 41040-1118. Tel: 859-654-8241; Fax: 859-654-5203. [CEM]
Catechesis/Religious Programs—Students 138.

Flemingsburg, Fleming Co., St. Charles (1859), Rev. Verne F. Hogan.
Res., 211 Mt. Carmel Ave., 41041-1315. Tel: 859-845-4601.

Florence, Boone Co., St. Paul (1832), Revs. Thomas B. Sacksteder; J. Michael Due; Deacons Gerald R. Franzen; Nicholas J. Schwartz. In res., Rev. Msgr. Donald F. Hellmann.
Res., 7301 Dixie Hwy., 41042-2126. Tel: 859-371-8051; Fax: 859-647-4073.
School—Tel: 859-647-4070; Fax: 859-647-0644.
Lay Teachers 30; Students 629.
Catechesis/Religious Programs—Students 357.

Fort Mitchell, Kenton Co., Blessed Sacrament (1920), Revs. Daniel J. Vogelpohl; Mark G. Witte; Sr. Ann Middendorf, O.S.B., Pastoral Assoc. In res., Rev. Paul F. Tenhundfeld, (Retired).
Res., 2415 Dixie Hwy., 41017-2936. Tel: 859-331-4302; Fax: 859-578-4752.
School—Tel: 859-331-3062; Fax: 859-344-7323.
Lay Teachers 33; Students 593.
Catechesis/Religious Programs—Students 190.

Fort Thomas, Campbell Co., St. Catherine of Siena (1930), Rev. James B. Egbers. In res., Rev. Robert L. Vater, (Retired).
Mailing Address: 1803 N. Ft. Thomas Ave., 41075-1170. Tel: 859-441-1352; Fax: 859-572-2686.
School—Tel: 859-572-2680; Fax: 859-572-2686.
Lay Teachers 18; Students 220.
Catechesis/Religious Programs—Students 190.

St. Thomas (1902), Rev. William B. Neuhaus. In res., Rev. Albert E. Ruschman, (Retired).
Mailing Address: 26 E. Villa Pl., 41075-2223. Tel: 859-441-1282; Fax: 859-572-4640.
School—Tel: 859-572-4641; Fax: 859-572-4644.
Lay Teachers 27; Students 242.
Catechesis/Religious Programs—Students 134.

Independence, Kenton Co., St. Cecilia (1880), Rev. Paul L. Berschied; Deacon James C. Auton.
Res., 5313 Madison Pk., P.O. Box 186, 41051-0186. Tel: 859-363-4311; Fax: 859-363-4312. [CEM]
School—Tel: 859-363-4314; Fax: 859-363-4315.
Lay Teachers 15; Students 313.
Catechesis/Religious Programs—Students 215.

Kenton, Kenton Co., St. Matthew (1909), Rev. Gregory E. Osburg.
Res., 13816 Decoursey Pk., P.O. Box 82, 41053-0082. Tel: 859-356-6530; Fax: 859-356-6530[*]51. [CEM]
Catechesis/Religious Programs—Students 60.
Mission—Morning View, Kenton Co., Assumption of the Blessed Virgin, 3711 St. Mary Rd., Morning View, 41063.

Ludlow, Kenton Co., Sts. Boniface and James (1872), Rev. Allan W. Bradley.
Res., 304 Oak St., 41016-1417. Tel: 859-261-5340; Fax: 859-261-5340.
Catechesis/Religious Programs—Students 14.

May's Lick, Mason Co., St. Rose of Lima (1864), Rev. Verne F. Hogan.
Church—P.O. Box 100, 41055-0100. Tel: 859-763-6304.

Maysville, Mason Co., St. Patrick (1847), Rev. William H. Hinds.
Res., 110 E. Third St., P.O. Box 248, 41056-0248. Tel: 859-564-9015; Fax: 859-564-6108. [CEM]
School—Tel: 859-564-5949; Fax: 859-564-8795.
Lay Teachers 12; Students 221.
High School—Lay Teachers 12; Students 100.
Catechesis/Religious Programs—Students 38.

Melbourne, Campbell Co., St. Philip (1908), Rev. Msgr. Roger P. Cooney.
Res., 1402 Mary Ingles Hwy., 41059-9701. Tel: 859-441-8949; Fax: 859-442-0290.
School—Tel: 859-441-3423; Fax: 859-441-2611.
Sisters of Divine Providence of Kentucky 4; Lay Teachers 6; Students 103.
Catechesis/Religious Programs—Students 11.

Newport, Campbell Co.,

1—HOLY SPIRIT, (1997), Rev. Richard G. Bolte.
Res., 825 Washington Ave., 41071-1999. Tel: 859-431-2533; Fax: 859-431-3247.
School—840 Washington Ave., 41071-2485. Tel: 859-431-8745; Fax: 859-431-8745.
Religious Teachers 2; Lay Teachers 7; Students 96.
Junior High School—Grand & Chesapeake, 41071-2485. Tel: 859-292-0487; Fax: 859-292-0487.
Religious Teachers 2; Lay Teachers 4; Students 61.
Catechesis/Religious Programs—Students 28.
Missions—Newport, Campbell Co., Corpus Christi, (1844); Newport, Campbell Co., St. Francis de Sales, (1911); Newport, Campbell Co., St. Stephen, (1854); Newport, Campbell Co., St. Vincent de Paul, (1916).

2—ST. FRANCIS DE SALES. Closed. For sacramental records contact Holy Spirit, Newport.

3—ST. STEPHEN. Closed. For sacramental records contact Holy Spirit, Newport.

4—ST. VINCENT DE PAUL. Closed. For sacramental records contact Holy Spirit, Newport.

Southgate, Campbell Co., St. Therese of the Infant Jesus (1927), Rev. Clarence J. Heitzman. In res., Rev. Msgr. Elmer J. Grosser, (Retired).
Res., 11 Temple Pl., 41071-3133. Tel: 859-441-1654; Fax: 859-441-2395.
School—Tel: 859-441-0449; Fax: 859-441-7988.
Sisters of Notre Dame 2; Lay Teachers 15; Students 357.
Catechesis/Religious Programs—Students 65.

Taylor Mill, Kenton Co., St. Anthony (1878), Rev. Thomas P. Robbins.
Res., 485 Grand Ave., P.O. Box 15219, Covington, 41015-0219. Tel: 859-431-1773; Fax: 859-431-1773.
School—Tel: 859-431-5987; Fax: 859-431-7353.
Lay Teachers 10; Students 200.
Catechesis/Religious Programs—Students 60.

St. Patrick (1968), Rev. Jeffrey D. Von Lehmen.
Mailing Address: 3285 Mills Rd., Covington, 41015-2480. Tel: 859-356-2171; Fax: 859-356-2171.
Catechesis/Religious Programs—Students 170.

Union, Boone Co., St. Timothy (1989), Rev. Edward J. Brodnick; Deacons Thomas Nolan; Frank Eberle.
Res., 10272 Hwy. 42, P.O. Box 120, 41091-0120. Tel: 859-384-1100; Fax: 859-384-1709.
Catechesis/Religious Programs—Students 550.

Vanceburg, Lewis Co., Holy Redeemer (1965), Sr. Joseph Fillenwarth, S.P., Pastoral Admin.; Rev. Bruce C. Brylinski, Glmy.
Mailing Address: P.O. Box 8, 41179-0008. Tel: 606-796-3052; Fax: 606-796-2606.
Catechesis/Religious Programs—Students 7.

Walton, Boone Co., All Saints (1951), Very Rev. John R. Schulte.
Mailing Address: 62 Needmore St., 41094-1029.
Res., 46 Needmore St., 41094-1029. Tel: 859-485-4476; Fax: 859-485-6476. [CEM 2]
Catechesis/Religious Programs—Students 97.

Warsaw, Gallatin Co., St. Joseph (1864), Rev. George J. Schuhmacher.
Mailing Address: P.O. Box 495, 41095-0495.
Res., 602 Sparta Pike, 41095-0495. Tel: 859-567-2425; Fax: 859-567-6941. [CEM]
Catechesis/Religious Programs—Students 70.
Mission—Owenton, Owen Co., St. Edward, (1958) 1335 Hwy. 22 E., R.R. 4, Owenton, 40359-9003.

Wilder, Campbell Co., St. John (1847), Rev. Richard H. McGrath; Ms. Margaret Quirk, Pastoral Assoc.
Res., 1307 John's Hill Rd., 41076-9762. Tel: 859-781-2117; Fax: 859-781-4889.

Williamstown, Grant Co., St. William (1912), Sr. Carol Leveque, S.C., Pastoral Admin.; Rev. Msgr. Donald F. Hellmann.
Res., 6 Church Dr., 41097-9454. Tel: 859-824-5381; Fax: 859-824-0509. [CEM 2]
Catechesis/Religious Programs—Students 93.
Mission—Dividing Ridge, Pendleton Co., St. John's, (1956).

Chaplains of Public Institutions

FORT THOMAS. *St. Luke Hospital East*. Rev. John A. Seiler.
Veterans Hospital. Attended by the Franciscan Fathers (O.F.M.), Cincinnati, Ohio.

On Duty Outside the Diocese:
Reverend Fathers—
Enzweiler, Donald A., Holy Redeemer, 44 Rothesay Dr., Ontario K2L 2X1 Canada

Leave of Absence:
Reverend Fathers—
Bierman, Earl C.
DeLange, Maurice
Gallenstein, Joseph A.
Goeke, John W.
Steidle, Mark A.

Military Chaplains:
Reverend Fathers—
Leslie, Larry B., (LCDR) NWS Charleston, SC (Code C1), 2316 Red Bank Rd., Ste. 100, Goose Creek, SC 29445-8601

Retired:
Most Rev.—
Hughes, William A., 1140 Madison Ave., Covington, KY 41011-3116
Reverend Monsignors—
Fleming, W. Stanley, Regina Cleri Home, 100 Carmel Manor Rd., Fort Thomas, KY 41075-2300
Grosser, Elmer J., St. Therese Rectory, 11 Temple Pl., Southgate, KY 41071-3133
Hellmann, Donald F., St. Paul Rectory
Hickey, Edward T., Carmel Manor, 100 Carmel Manor Rd., Fort Thomas, KY 41075-2300
Meier, Allen J., Notre Dame Academy, 1699 Hilton Dr., Covington, KY 41011-2705
Murphy, John F., 2727 Leatherwood Ct., Crestview Hills, KY 41017-2274
Welp, Harry J., 726 Meadowood, Apt. 1, Villa Hills, KY 41017-4607
Reverend Fathers—
Bierman, Earl C., The Catholic Center, P.O. Box 18548, Erlanger, KY 41018-0548
Brinker, Paul J., P.O. Box 17321, Fort Mitchell, KY 41017-0321
Broering, Joseph H., Regina Cleri, 100 Carmel Manor Rd., Fort Thomas, KY 41075-2300
Broering, Raymond L., 2 Cypress Run, Apt. 21B, Homosassa, FL 34446-4228
Garvey, Charles J., Carmel Manor, 100 Carmel Manor Rd., Fort Thomas, KY 41075-2300
Gerrety, James P., 626 Laurel St., Ludlow, KY 41016
Gruber, Robert L., 1398 Sleepy Hollow Rd., Fort Wright, KY 41016
Hartman, Ralph C., 422 Wallace Ave., Covington, KY 41014-1556
Hoffer, Charles J., Holy Cross Rectory, 3612 Church St., Covington, KY 41015-1431
Holtz, Louis J., 119 W. Sixth St., Covington, KY 41011-1409
Jasper, Louis H., 1400 Sleepy Hollow, Apt. 4, Covington, KY 41011-2757
Kamlage, Herman, Hathaway Court, #416, 1200 Highway Ave., Covington, KY 41011-1095
Keller, Lawrence W., The Franciscan of West Park, 2950 W. Park Dr., Cincinnati, OH 45238
Klein, Robert P., 3516 Misty Creek Dr., Erlanger, KY 41018-2627
Krebs, Paul F., 14 Orchard St., Southgate, KY 41071-3126
McGrath, Richard H., 18 Woodland Hills, Apt. 5, Southgate, KY 41071-2969
McGuire, John J., St. Charles Lodge, 600 Farrell Dr., #123, Fort Wright, KY 41011-5177
McHugh, James L., 209 E. Second St., Maysville, KY 41056-1307
Mertes, William H., 228 Covington Ave., Covington, KY 41011-1414
Modica, John B., Holy Family Home, 2000 St. Anne Dr., Melbourne, KY 41059-9602
Mulhern, Raymond F., 18100 S. 66th Ct., #314, Tinley Park, IL 60477-3554
Nieman, Raymond L., 204 Estelle Ct., Naples, FL 34112-7149
Quill, James E., St. Agnes Rectory, 1680 Dixie Hwy., Covington, KY 41011-2779
Reifsnyder, John A., Sacred Heart Rectory, 310 Shady Ave., Pittsburgh, PA 15206-4306
Reinke, Robert J., St. Augustine Rectory, 1839 Euclid Ave., Covington, KY 41014-1162
Riesenberg, John J., St. Pius X Rectory, 340 Dudley Rd., Edgewood, KY 41017-2609
Rooks, Charles W., 1601 Dixie Hwy., Covington, KY 41011-2798
Rosing, Robert C., Marydale Retreat Center, 945 Donaldson Rd., Erlanger, KY 41018-1093
Rueter, Joseph J., St. Joseph Rectory, 4011 Alexandria Pike, Cold Spring, KY 41076-1817
Ruschman, Albert E., St. Thomas Rectory, 26 E. Villa Pl., Fort Thomas, KY 41075-2223
Shockey, David P., St. Joseph Convent, 13 Mulberry St., Walton, KY 41094-1036
Smith, R. Leroy, 5440 Moeller Ave., Norwood, OH 45212-1211
Tenhundfeld, Paul F., Blessed Sacrament Rectory, 2415 Dixie Hwy., Fort Mitchell, KY 4107-2936
Toner, Edward R., 5614 Long Commons Cir., Sarasota, FL 34235-2401
Trimbur, Edwin H., P.O. Box 452, El Paso, TX 79943-0452
Urlage, Robert J., P.O. Box 75254, Fort Thomas, KY 41075-0254
Vater, Robert L., St. Catherine of Siena Rectory, 10 Wesley Hills Dr., Fort Thomas, KY 41075-1213
Weber, Charles E., St. Charles Lodge, 600 Farrell Dr., #306, Covington, KY 41011-5165
Werner, John P., 104 Highland Ave., Apt. 1, Fort Mitchell, KY 41017-2920
Witt, Robert G., P.O. Box 210455, Royal Palm Beach, FL 33414-0455
Witzemann, Gerald B., 1230 Bracht Rd., Corinth, KY 41010-3465

Permanent Deacons:
Auton, James C., St. Cecilia, Independence
Baker, Joseph, St. Joseph, Crescent Springs
Cleves, Joseph A., St. Agnes, Covington
Colatrella, Ralph, Holy Cross, Latonia
Dietz, Charles, St. Bernard, Dayton
Durkee, Steven I., Mother of God, Covington
Dushney, Thomas M., Mary, Queen of Heaven, Erlanger
Eberle, Frank J., St. Timothy, Union
Estill, Andrew (Frank), St. Augustine, Augusta
Flynn, David J., St. Agnes, Covington
Franzen, Gerald R., St. Paul, Florence
Hermann, Robert J., St. John, Covington

Hillenmeyer, Ernest B., St. James, Brooksville
Holstein, Marvin, St. Joseph, Crescent Springs
Kaiser, Bernard, St. Barbara, Erlanger
Lehmkuhl, Dennis N., St. Mary, Alexandria
Meyer, David J., St. Pius X, Edgewood
Nolan, Thomas L., St. Timothy, Union
Norris, Eugene F., (Retired)
O'Donnell, Richard, Immaculate Heart of Mary, Burlington & Airport Chap.
Racine, Phillip J., St. Benedict, Covington
Schwartz, Nicholas J., St. Paul, Florence
Stieritz, Edward E., Cathedral, Covington
Stoeckle, Robert A., St. Agnes, Fort Wright
Sweigart, James H., (Retired), Airport Chap.

PILGRIMAGE SHRINES

COVINGTON. *Shrine of St. Ann.* Attached to St. Ann Church.

SOUTHGATE. *Shrine of the Little Flower.* Attached to St. Therese Church.

INSTITUTIONS LOCATED IN THE DIOCESE

[A] COLLEGES AND UNIVERSITIES

COVINGTON. *Thomas More College*, 333 Thomas More Pkwy. Crestview Hills, 41017-3495. Tel: 859-341-5800; Fax: 859-344-3649.
E-mail: william.cleves@thomasmore.edu
Web site: www.thomasmore.edu
For a complete listing, refer to the Colleges and Universities section.

[B] HIGH SCHOOLS, DIOCESAN

COVINGTON. *Covington Catholic High School*, 1600 Dixie Hwy., 41011-2797. Tel: 859-431-5351; Fax: 859-655-4325.
E-mail: jkennevan@covcath.org
Web site: www.covcath.org
Mr. Jack Kennevan, Prin.; Rev. Richard W. Wurth, Chap. Lay Teachers 34; Boys 499.

Covington Latin School, 21 E. 11th St., 41011-3196. Tel: 859-291-7044; Fax: 859-291-1939.
E-mail: cls@fuse.net
Web site: www.covingtonlatin.org
Mr. Richard Stewart, Dean; Dr. Frank Little, Headmaster; Rev. J. Michael Due, Chap. Lay Teachers 17; Boys 110; Girls 71.

Holy Cross High School, 3617 Church St., 41015-1498. Tel: 859-431-1335; Fax: 859-655-2184.
E-mail: hchs@fuse.net
Mr. William Goller, Prin.; Rev. Thomas P. Robbins, Chap. Religious 2; Lay Teachers 35; Students 403.

ALEXANDRIA. *Bishop Brossart High School*, Jefferson St. & Grove St., 41001-1295. Tel: 859-635-2108; Fax: 859-635-2135.
E-mail: brossart@juno.com
Web site: www.bishopbrossart.org
Mr. Thomas H. Seither, Prin.; Rev. Richard W. Frazier, Chap. Sisters of Notre Dame 2; Lay Teachers 26; Students 435.

ERLANGER. *St. Henry District High School*, 3755 Scheben Dr., 41018. Tel: 859-525-0255; Fax: 859-525-5855.
E-mail: dmotte@SHDHS.org
Web site: www.SHDHS.org
Mr. David M. Otte, Prin.; Rev. Gregory J. Bach, Chap. Lay Teachers 40; Religious 2; Priests 1; Students 532.

MAYSVILLE. *St. Patrick High School*, 318 Limestone St., 41056-1248. Tel: 859-564-5949; Fax: 859-564-8795.
E-mail: stpats318@hotmail.com
Mr. Jay Jacobs, Prin.; Rev. William H. Hinds, Chap. Lay Teachers 13; Students 100.

NEWPORT. *Newport Central Catholic High School*, 13 Carothers Rd., 41071-2497. Tel: 859-292-0001; Fax: 859-292-0656.
E-mail: ncchs@ix.netcom.com
Web site: www.Jungle.org/public/ncc.htm
Mr. Robert Noll, Prin.; Rev. Richard W. Wurth, Chap.
Administrative Team: Mr. Greg Burwinkel; Mr. Robert Schneider. Lay Teachers 30; Students 454.

[C] HIGH SCHOOLS, PRIVATE

COVINGTON. *Academy of Notre Dame*, 1699 Hilton Dr., 41011-2769. Tel: 859-261-4300; Fax: 859-292-7722.
E-mail: NDA@NDA-cvg.org
Web site: www.NDA-cvg.org
Sisters of Notre Dame. Sr. Mary Rita, S.N.D., Prin. Chaplains: Rev. Msgr. Allen J. Meier; Rev. Mark G. Witte. Sisters 11; Lay Teachers 34; Girls 568.

Villa Madonna High School. 2500 Amsterdam Rd., Villa Hills, 41017-3798. Tel: 859-331-6333; Fax: 859-331-8615.
E-mail: vill@VMA.pvt.K12.US
Web site: www.igloo.com/vma
Sr. Victoria Eisenman, O.S.B., Dir.; Ms. Pamela McQueen, Prin.; Rev. Jeffrey D. Von Lehmen, Chap. Sisters 6; Lay Teachers 13; Students 152.

[D] ELEMENTARY SCHOOLS, INTERPAROCHIAL

COVINGTON. *Holy Family Catholic School*, 338 E. 16th St., 41014-1398. Tel: 859-581-0290; Fax: 859-581-0624.
E-mail: holyfamilycath@aol.com
Lay Teachers 7; Students 98.

Prince of Peace School, 625 Pike St., 41011-2798. Tel: 859-431-5153; Fax: 859-431-5153.
E-mail: dcprince@one.net
Sr. Mary Sharron Goller, S.N.D., Prin. Sisters of Notre Dame 2; Lay Teachers 8; Students 138.

BELLEVUE. *St. Michael School*, 235 Division St., 41073-1101. Tel: 859-291-6937; Fax: 859-291-6970.
E-mail: DCMICHAEL@impresso.com
Sr. M. Norene McCormack, S.N.D., Prin. Sisters of Notre Dame 2; Lay Teachers 8; Students 118.

NEWPORT. *Holy Spirit Elementary School*, 840 Washington Ave., 41071-1946. Tel: 859-431-8745; Fax: 859-431-8745.
E-mail: dcholyspir@impresso.com
Sr. Mary Ruth Lubbers, S.N.D., Prin. Sisters 1; Lay Teachers 4; Students 95.

Holy Spirit Junior High School, Chesapeake Ave. & Grand Ave., 41071-2485. Tel: 859-292-0487; Fax: 859-292-0487.
E-mail: dcholyspir@impresso.com
Sr. Mary Ruth Lubbers, S.N.D., Prin. Sisters 1; Lay Teachers 3; Students 60.

[E] ELEMENTARY SCHOOLS, DIOCESAN

FORT MITCHELL. *Guardian Angel*, P.O. Box 17007, Orphanage Rd., 41017-0007. Tel: 859-331-2040; Fax: 859-344-5022.
E-mail: smac_ga@yahoo.com
Sr. M. Ann Christine Kathman, S.N.D., Prin. School for the Emotional Behavioral Disabled. Sisters 3; Lay Teachers 4; Students 30.

[F] ELEMENTARY SCHOOLS, PRIVATE

COVINGTON. *Villa Madonna Elementary School*. 2500 Amsterdam Rd., Villa Hills, 41017-3798. Tel: 859-331-6333; Fax: 859-331-8615.
E-mail: bmoeller@villamadonna.net
Web site: www.igloo.com/vma
Sr. Victoria Eisenman, O.S.B., Dir.; Mrs. Becky Moeller, Prin. Sisters 1; Lay Teachers 23; Students 289.

WALTON. *St. Joseph Academy*, 48 Needmore St., 41094-1028. Tel: 859-485-6444; Fax: 859-485-9302.
E-mail: SJASISTERPATRICIAJ@juno.com
Sisters of St. Joseph the Worker. Sr. Patricia Jean, S.J.W., Prin. Sisters 6; Lay Teachers 12; Students 283.

[G] MONTESSORI SCHOOLS (PRESCHOOL)

VILLA HILLS. *Villa Madonna Montessori*, 2402 Amsterdam Rd., 41017-5316. Tel: 859-341-5145. Sr. Mary Peter Youtsey, O.S.B., Admin. Sisters of St. Benedict 2; Lay Teachers 7; Students 52.

[H] PRESCHOOLS

COVINGTON. *Julie Learning Center*, 1601 Dixie Hwy., 41011-2798. Tel: 859-291-8555; Fax: 859-291-1774.
E-mail: smpatrycia@aol.com
Sr. M. Patrycia Sweeney, S.N.D., Dir. Daycare with educational emphasis for ages 4-6. Sisters of Notre Dame 1; Lay Teachers 3; Students 50.

[I]GENERAL HOSPITALS

COVINGTON. *St. Elizabeth Medical Center, North*, 401 E. 20th St., 41014-1585. Tel: 859-292-4000; Fax: 859-292-4487.
Web site: www.stelizabeth.com
For a complete listing, refer to the Hospitals section.

EDGEWOOD. *St. Elizabeth Medical Center, South*, One Medical Village Dr., 41017-3441. Tel: 859-344-2000; Fax: 859-344-3968.
Web site: www.stelizabeth.com
For a complete listing, refer to the Hospitals section.

WILLIAMSTOWN. *St. Elizabeth Medical Center, Grant County*, 238 Barnes Rd., 41097-9482. Tel: 859-824-2400; Fax: 859-824-2418
For a complete listing, refer to the Hospitals section.

[J] NURSING HOMES

COVINGTON. *Madonna Manor, Inc.* 2344 Amsterdam Rd. Villa Hills, 41017-3712. Tel: 859-341-3981; Fax: 859-578-7475.
For a complete listing, refer to the Special Care Facilities section.

St. Charles Care Center, Inc., 500 Farrell Dr., 41011-3798. Tel: 859-331-3224; Fax: 859-578-2065.
E-mail: smluann@msn.com
Web site: www.stcharlescare.org
For a complete listing, refer to the Special Care Facilities section.

[K] PROTECTIVE INSTITUTIONS

COVINGTON. *Diocesan Catholic Children's Home* Orphanage Rd., P.O. Box 17007 Fort Mitchell, 41017-2730. Tel: 859-331-2040; Fax: 859-344-5021.
For a complete listing, refer to the Special Care Facilities section.

COLD SPRING. *Campbell Lodge Boys Home*, 150 Skyline Dr., 41076-2099. Tel: 859-781-1214; Fax: 859-442-3473.
E-mail: Mschroth@execs.com
Web site: www.CampbellLodgeboyshome.org
For a complete listing, refer to the Special Care Facilities section.

[L] HOMES FOR AGED

FORT THOMAS. *Carmel Manor*, 100 Carmel Manor Rd., 41075-2395. Tel: 859-781-5111; Fax: 859-781-2337
For a complete listing, refer to the Special Care Facilities section.

Regina Cleri Home for Retired Priests, 100 Carmel Manor Rd., 41075-2395. Tel: 859-781-5111; Fax: 859-781-2337
For a complete listing, refer to the Special Care Facilities section.

[M] MONASTERIES AND RESIDENCES OF PRIESTS AND BROTHERS

COVINGTON. *Brothers of the Poor of St. Francis*, Holy Family Friary, 239 W. Robbins St., 41011-3078. Tel: 859-291-2938; Fax: 859-581-5796.
E-mail: bjcphelan@aol.com
International Office. Bro. Mark Gastel, C.F.P., Res. Minister Gen. In res. Bros. James Phelan, C.F.P.; John Walsh, C.F.P.; Rock Larsen, C.F.P.; Boniface Hracek, C.F.P.; Philip Fitzgerald, C.F.P.; Joseph LaPlante, C.F.P.; Blaise Betley, C.F.P.; Robert Desmond, C.F.P.

[N] CONVENTS AND RESIDENCES FOR SISTERS

COVINGTON. *St. Joseph Heights Provincialate and Novitiate of the Sisters of Notre Dame*, 1601 Dixie Hwy., 41011-2798. Tel: 859-291-2040; Fax: 859-291-1774.
E-mail: smshauna@sndky.org
Sr. Mary Shauna Bankemper, S.N.D., Prov. Supr.; Rev. Charles W. Rooks, Chap. Sisters in Community 170; Sisters in Prov. House 78.

St. Walburg Monastery, 2500 Amsterdam Rd., 41017-5316. Tel: 859-331-6324; Fax: 859-331-2136.
E-mail: walburg@iglou.com
Web site: www.rc.net/covington/walburg
Benedictine Sisters. Sr. Rita Brink, O.S.B., Prioress; Rev. Gerald L. Reinersman, Chap. Professed Sisters 93.

ERLANGER. *Monastery of the Sacred Passion*, 1151 Donaldson Hwy., 41018-1000. Tel: 859-371-8568; Fax: 859-371-8568. Passionist Nuns. Sr. Margaret Mary, C.P., Supr.; Rev. Gary A. Miller. Professed 9.

FORT THOMAS. *Sisters of the Good Shepherd*, Pelletier Hall, 930 Highland Ave., 41075-1707. Tel: 859-441-5531; Fax: 859-441-7340. Sr. Mary Lawrence Crisler, Admin.; Rev. Richard H. McGrath, Chap., Business Office for Cincinnati Province, Sisters of the Good Shepherd, 811 Highland Ave., 41075. Tel: 859-781-8145; Fax: 859-441-7340. Sr. Marilyn Atwell, Admin. Asst. Sisters of the Good Shepherd 22.

KENTON HILLS. *St. Vincent's Convent*, 630 Jerol Ave., 41011. Tel: 859-431-5388. Intercongregational Residence. Sisters 4.

MELBOURNE. *Holy Family Home*, Rte. 8, 2000 St. Anne Dr., 41059-9604. Tel: 859-781-0712; Fax: 859-781-8854. Sr. Claire Osburg, C.D.P., Admin.; Rev. B. John Modica, Chap. Sisters in Residence 58.

St. Anne Convent, 1000 St. Anne Dr., 41059-9603. Tel: 859-441-0679; Fax: 859-441-1510.
E-mail: sbaumann@cdpkentucky.org
Web site: www.cdpkentucky.org
Provincial House and Novitiate of the Sisters of Divine Providence of Kentucky. Sr. Lynn Stenken, C.D.P., Prov. Supr. Sisters in Community 170; Sisters in Provincial House 17; Sisters in Residence 57.

WALTON. *St. William Convent*, One St. Joseph Ln., 41094-1036. Tel: 859-485-4914; 485-4256; Fax: 859-485-9302. Sisters of St. Joseph the Worker. Sr. Celeste Marie Downes, S.J.W., Supr.; Rev. David P. Shockey, Chap., 13 Mulberry St., 41094-1036. Tel: 859-485-7053. Sisters in Community 19; Sisters in Motherhouse 10.

[O] SECULAR INSTITUTES

COVINGTON. *Society of St. Vincent de Paul*, 2655 Crescent Springs Rd., 41017-1504. Tel: 859-341-6995; Fax: 859-341-1610. Vincent J. Bessler, Pres.; Cathy Klug, General Mgr. District Council of Northern Kentucky. Executive Offices and Thrift Stores. 27 Parish Conferences in Northern Kentucky Thrift Stores, including Dayton, Newport, Crescent Springs, Ludlow, and Falmouth. Total stores 5. A Catholic lay organization of over 875,000 members worldwide whose members meet in parish and district groups in order to help in a personal way those in need.

[P] SOCIAL SERVICES

COVINGTON. *Catholic Social Services*, 3629 Church St., 41015-1499. Tel: 859-581-8974; Fax: 859-581-9595.
E-mail: catholiccharities@email.msn.com
Web site: www.catholicsocialservices.com
Sr. Joan Marie Boberg, C.D.P., Dir. Total Assisted 10,000; Staff 43.

Parish Kitchen, Pike St. & Russell St., P.O. Box 1234, 41011-1234. Tel: 859-581-7745; Fax: 859-581-7749.
E-mail: parishkitc@aol.com
Ms. Molly Navin, Dir. Total Assisted 60,000.

Welcome House of Northern Kentucky, Inc., 205 Pike St., 41011-2521. Tel: 859-431-8717; Fax: 859-431-6297.
E-mail: welcome@one.net
Shelter for homeless women and their children, 24 hours a day. Emergency Assistance Center and Representative Payee Program, Family Case Management and Self-Suffiency Housing Programs. Total Assisted 12,269; Staff 45.

[Q] DIOCESAN RETREAT HOUSES

ERLANGER. *Marydale Retreat Center*, 945 Donaldson Hwy., 41018-1093. Tel: 859-371-4224; Fax: 859-647-5682.
E-mail: Marydaleretreat@earthlink.net
Deacon Edward Stieritz, Dir.; Rev. Robert C. Rosing, Chap. Total Assisted 8,180; Staff 20.

[R] NEWMAN CENTERS

HIGHLAND HEIGHTS. *Catholic Newman Center - Northern Kentucky University*, 512 Johns Hill Rd., P.O. Box 76174, 41076-1449. Tel: 859-781-3775. Mr. Al Cucchetti, Pastoral Admin.

[S] INTERFAITH CENTERS

COVINGTON. *Interfaith Commission of Northern Kentucky*. P.O. Box 72296, Newport, 41072-0296. Tel: 859-581-2237; Fax: 859-261-6041. Rev. William C. Neuroth, Exec. Dir. Purpose: A religious organization committed to understanding the various faith traditions of our member bodies, while working together in response to the spiritual and human needs of all people of the Northern Kentucky area.

[T] MISCELLANEOUS

FORT MITCHELL. *Mission Share*, P.O. Box 176356, 41017-6356. Tel: 513-351-6707; Fax: 513-351-6707. Revs. John J. McGuire; William H. Hinds, Pres. Purpose: A mission society whose principle activity is to carry out and advance the function, practices, and liturgy of the Catholic Church in Cali, Colombia, Latin America, and worldwide for medical and dental programs, educational programs, the construction of parish and archdiocesan buildings, and the advancement of the Catholic faith and various other civic and social programs.

RELIGIOUS INSTITUTES OF MEN REPRESENTED IN THE DIOCESE

For further details refer to the corresponding bracketed number in the Religious Institutes of Men or Women section.

[0460]—*Brothers of the Poor of St. Francis*. (Aachen, Germany).—C.F.P.

[0570]—*Glenmary Home Missioners*.—Glmy.

[0690]—*Jesuit Fathers and Brothers*. (Chicago Prov.).—S.J.

RELIGIOUS INSTITUTES OF WOMEN REPRESENTED IN THE DIOCESE

[0230]—*Benedictine Sisters of Pontifical Jurisdiction*.—O.S.B.

[0330]—*Carmelite Sisters for the Aged and Infirm*. (Germantown, NY).—O.Carm.

[3180]—*Congregation of the Passion of Jesus Christ*.—C.P.

[0440]—*Sisters of Charity of Cincinnati, Ohio*.—S.C.

[1000]—*Sisters of Divine Providence of Kentucky*.—C.D.P.

[2990]—*Sisters of Notre Dame*.—S.N.D.

[3360]—*Sisters of Providence of Saint Mary-of-the-Woods, IN*.—S.P.

[1640]—*Sisters of St. Francis of Perpetual Adoration*. (Colorado Springs, CO).—O.S.F.

[3880]—*Sisters of St. Joseph of Medaille*. (Cincinnati, OH).—C.S.J.

[3920]—*Sisters of St. Joseph the Worker*.—S.J.W.

[1830]—*Sisters of the Good Shepherd*.—R.G.S.

[1730]—*Sisters of the Third Order of St. Francis*. (Oldenburg, IN).—O.S.F.

[2150]—*Sisters, Servants of the Immaculate Heart of Mary*. (Monroe, MI).—I.H.M.

[4120]—*Ursuline Nuns, of the Congregation of Paris*. (Brown County, OH).—O.S.U.

[4120-03]—*Ursuline Nuns, of the Congregation of Paris*. (Louisville, KY).—O.S.U.

DIOCESAN CEMETERIES

COLD SPRING. *St. Joseph*.
FORT MITCHELL. *St. John*.
St. Mary.
FORT THOMAS. *St. Stephen*.
WILDER. *St. Joseph*.

NECROLOGY

† Heile, Edwin B., Elsmere, KY St. Henry. —Died Oct. 24, 2000.

† Kriege, Roger L., Vicar Gen. & Chancellor, Erlanger, KY The Catholic Center. —Died Feb. 13, 2000.

† Schneider, George E., Newport, KY Holy Spirit. —Died Jan. 16, 2000.

Diocese of Crookston

(Dioecesis Crookstoniensis)

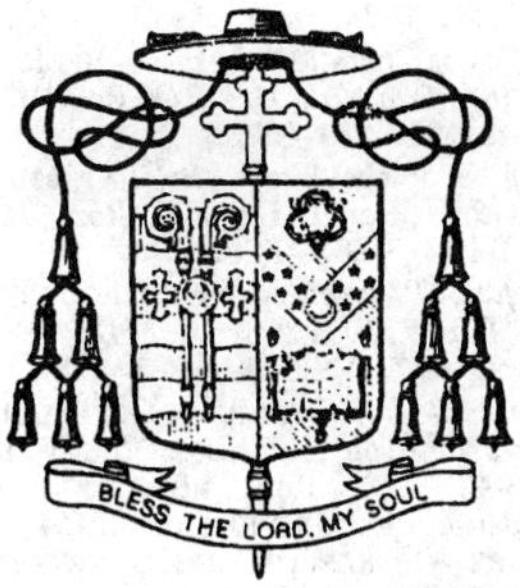

Most Reverend

VICTOR H. BALKE, D.D., PH.D.

Bishop of Crookston; ordained May 24, 1958; appointed July 7, 1976; Episcopal ordination September 2, 1976. *Res., 1200 Memorial Dr., Crookston, MN, 56716.* Tel.: 218-281-4533.

Chancery Office: 1200 Memorial Dr., P.O. Box 610, Crookston, MN, 56716. Tel.: 218-281-4533; Fax: 218-281-3328.

Web site address: www.crookston.org

E-mail address: rgrundhaus@crookston.org

ESTABLISHED BY HIS HOLINESS PIUS X, DECEMBER 31, 1909.

Square Miles 17,210.

Comprises the Counties of Becker, Beltrami, Clay, Clearwater, Hubbard, Kittson, Lake of the Woods, Marshall, Mahnomen, Norman, Pennington, Polk, Red Lake and Roseau in the State of Minnesota.

PATRONESS OF THE DIOCESE: The Immaculate Conception.

Legal Title: Diocese of Crookston.

For legal titles of parishes and diocesan institutions, consult the Chancery Office.

STATISTICAL OVERVIEW

Personnel	
Bishop	1
Priests: Diocesan Active in Diocese	30
Priests: Active Outside Diocese	5
Priests: Retired, Sick or Absent	15
Number of Diocesan Priests	50
Religious Priests in Diocese	2
Extern Priests in Diocese	1
Ordinations:	
Diocesan Priests	1
Transitional Deacons	1
Permanent Deacons	4
Permanent Deacons in Diocese	12
Total Brothers	1
Total Sisters	171
Parishes	
Parishes	69
With Resident Pastor:	
Resident Diocesan Priests	24
Resident Religious Priests	2
Without Resident Pastor:	
Administered by Priests	34
Administered by Deacons	6
Administered by Women Religious	3
Closed Parishes	2
Professional Ministry Personnel:	
Brothers	1
Sisters	13
Lay Ministers	46
Welfare	
Catholic Hospitals	3
Total Assisted	61,584
Homes for the Aged	3
Total Assisted	284
Day Care and Extended Day Care Centers	1
Total Assisted	70
Educational	
Diocesan Students in Other Seminaries	7
Total Seminarians	7
High Schools, Diocesan and Parish	1
Total Students	166
Elementary Schools, Diocesan and Parish	8
Total Students	1,175
Elementary Schools, Private	1
Total Students	68
Catechesis/Religious Education:	
High School Students	2,825
Elementary Students	3,701
Total Students Under Catholic Instruction	7,942
Teachers in the Diocese:	
Sisters	7
Lay Teachers	119
Vital Statistics	
Receptions into the Church:	
Infant Baptism Totals	704
Adult Baptism Totals	23
Received into Full Communion	106
First Communions	637
Confirmations	698
Marriages:	
Catholic	154
Interfaith	152
Total Marriages	306
Deaths	496
Total Catholic Population	40,646
Total Population	235,145

Former Bishops—Most Rev. TIMOTHY CORBETT, D.D., ord. June 12, 1886; cons. May 19, 1910; resigned See Aug. 6, 1938; appt. Titular Bishop of Vita; died July 20, 1939.—Most Rev. JOHN H. PESCHGES, D.D., ord. April 15, 1905; cons. Nov. 9, 1938; died Oct. 30, 1944.—Most Rev. FRANCIS J. SCHENK, D.D., ord. June 13, 1926; cons. May 24, 1945; transferred to Duluth Jan. 27, 1960; died Oct. 28, 1969.—Most Rev. LAURENCE A. GLENN, D.D., ord. June 11, 1927; cons. Sept. 12, 1956; retired July 28, 1970; died Jan. 26, 1985.—Most Rev. KENNETH J. POVISH, D.D., ord. June 3, 1950; appt. Bishop of Crookston July 28, 1970; cons. Sept. 29, 1970; transferred to Lansing Oct. 21, 1975.

Vicar General—Rev. Msgr. ROGER L. GRUNDHAUS, J.C.L., V.G., *1200 Memorial Dr., P.O. Box 610, Crookston, 56716.*

Chancery Office—1200 Memorial Dr., P.O. Box 610, Crookston, 56716. Tel: 218-281-4533; Fax: 218-281-3328.

Chancellor—Rev. DAVID J. SUPER.

Moderator of the Curia—Rev. Msgr. ROGER L. GRUNDHAUS, J.C.L., V.G.

Information Officer—Rev. Msgr. ROGER L. GRUNDHAUS, J.C.L., V.G.

Finance Manager—GEORGE NOEL.

Diocesan Tribunal—1200 Memorial Dr., P.O. Box 610, Crookston, 56716. Tel: 218-281-4533.

Judicial Vicar—Rev. MICHAEL SULLIVAN, J.C.L.

Defenders of the Bond—Revs. RICHARD BOYD; VIRGIL HELMIN, J.C.L.

Advocate—JOANNE TOLLEFSON.

Notary—KATHY MORVIG.

Psychological Consultant—ELIZABETH BARAGA SUPER, Ph.D.

Diocesan Offices And Directors

Diocesan Consultors—Rev. Msgr. ROGER L. GRUNDHAUS, J.C.L., V.G.; Revs. ROBERT SCHREINER; LAWRENCE WIESELER; JOHN KLEINWACHTER; TIMOTHY NOAH; AUGUST GOTHMAN.

Finance Council—Most Rev. VICTOR H. BALKE, D.D.; Rev. Msgr. ROGER L. GRUNDHAUS, J.C.L., V.G.; Rev. DAVID J. SUPER; Rev. Msgr. MICHAEL PATNODE; Revs. MICHAEL FOLTZ; DONALD BRAUKMANN; KAY MACK; ELAINE WHITE; DAN RUST; DEAN MITZEL.

Adoption Referral / Post Adoption Search—BERNADETTE DUNN, *P.O. Box 610, Crookston, 56716.* Tel: 218-281-4533.

Beginning Experience—MARLYS SMITH, Pres. BERNADETTE DUNN, Bishop's Liaison, *P.O. Box 610, Crookston, 56716.* Tel: 218-281-4533.

Boy Scouts—DON VOTAVA, *Rte. 2, Box 172A, Warren, 56762.* Tel: 218-745-5423. Rev. MICHAEL SULLIVAN, Chap.

Catholic Campaign for Human Development—BERNADETTE DUNN, *P.O. Box 610, Crookston, 56716.* Tel: 218-281-4533.

Catholic Relief Services—BERNADETTE DUNN, Dir., *P.O. Box 610, Crookston, 56716.* Tel: 218-281-4533.

Commission on Building and Planning—Rev. RICHARD LAMBERT; Sr. MARGUERITE STREIFEL, O.S.B.; RICHARD RUDE; JIM SHULIND; ROGER WINTER.

Commission on Catholic-Lutheran Rural Life—Rev. TIM LUNDEEN, Chm., *P.O. Box 278, Lancaster, 56735.* Tel: 218-762-1691.

Commission on Ecumenism—ROY DUFAULT, Chm.; Deacon RANDY BAUER; JOAN HARRINGTON; MIKE KASOWSKI; AARON RONGEN; RAY LAGASSE, Bishop's Liaison, *1200 Memorial Dr., P.O. Box 610, Crookston, 56716.* Tel: 218-281-4533.

Commission on Liturgy, Sacred Music and Art—Sr. MARGUERITE STREIFEL, O.S.B., Dir.; Sr. MARDELLE MOHS, O.S.B.; Sr. PATRICE EBLEN, O.S.B.; JULIE MAREK; BONNIE LEE; JIM DOTTENWHY; VIRGINIA MORGAN; MICHELLE DUFFY; Rev. JIM LYONS.

Commission on Respect Life—BERNADETTE DUNN, *P.O. Box 610, Crookston, 56716.* Tel: 218-281-4533.

Commission on Social Justice—BERNADETTE DUNN, *P.O. Box 610, Crookston, 56716.* Tel: 218-281-4533.

Commission on Women—Sr. LORRAINE KRAFT, O.S.B., *Mt. Saint Benedict, 620 Summit Ave., Crookston, 56716.* Tel: 218-281-3441.

Crookston Council of Women Religious—Sr. EVELYN STREI, O.S.B., Pres.; Sr. MARY JEAN GUST, O.S.B., Sec.

Cursillo—ROSE WEBER, Chm. of the Secretariat, *Rte. 3, P.O. Box 116, Crookston, 56716.*

Deans—Rev. LAWRENCE WIESELER, Northwest; Rev. DUANE PRIBULA, Northeast; Rev. DAVID BAUMGARTNER, Western; Rev. GARY LAMOINE, Eastern; Rev. BERNARD FRIEDL, O.S.B., Southwest; Rev. JERRY ROGERS, Southeast; Rev. DENNIS WIELAND, Central.

Diaconate Office—Rev. DAVID BAUMGARTNER, Acting Dir., *405 Thorpe Ave., Ada, 56510.* Tel: 218-784-4131.

Diocesan Board of Conciliation and Arbitration—Rev. Msgr. WILLIAM MEHRKENS, *Red Lake, 56671.* Sr. DOREEN CHAREST, C.S.J., *Moorhead, 56560.* Judge MICHAEL KRAKER, *Mahnomen, 56557.*

School Board, Diocesan—Ex Officio Members: Most Rev. VICTOR H. BALKE, D.D.; Sr. PAT MURPHY, C.S.J.,Members: Rev. Msgr. MICHAEL PATNODE; Rev. DENNIS WIELAND; JOYCE KRAMER; BRAD BREKKEN; JON TIBBETTS; GREG KAISER; DAN MCNAMEE; KEITH BOSEK; MICHAEL CONN; MARK THUNE.

Hispanic Ministry—Sr. LEONA ULEWICZ, C.D.P., Coord., *P.O. Box 610, Crookston, 56716.* Tel: 218-281-4533.

Holy Childhood Association—Rev. Msgr. ROGER L. GRUNDHAUS, J.C.L., V.G., Dir., *P.O. Box 610, Crookston, 56716.*

Native American Task Force—Rev. Msgr. WILLIAM MEHRKENS, Chm., *St. Mary's Mission Church, P.O. Box 189, Red Lake, 56671.* Tel: 218-679-3614.

Natural Family Planning—SUE MODICH; STEVE MODICH, *2750 Ivy Ln., N.E., Bemidji, 56601.* Tel: 218-751-6250.

Newspaper, "Our Northland Diocese"—CAROL EVENSON, Editor & Business Mgr., *Diocese of Crookston, 1200 Memorial Dr., P.O. Box 610, Crookston, 56716-0610.* Tel: 218-281-4533.

Pastoral Council—Most Rev. VICTOR H. BALKE, D.D.; Sr. ROSALIA FINK, O.S.B.; Sr. DOREEN CHAREST, C.S.J.; KAREN LJUNDGREN; BEN KLEINWACHTER; Deacon JOHN BRUGGEMAN; BARBARA KOTTA; MICHAEL MONSRUD; VERNON LINDFORS; TINA REIN; JOE NOEL; RICH VEIT; JOANN KERSTING; JEAN DEMARTELAERE; JIM DULKA; SARA RASMUSSEN, *P.O. Box 610, Crookston, 56716.* Tel: 218-281-4533.

Pastoral Office of Administration—GEORGE NOEL, Dir., *1200 Memorial Dr., P.O. Box 610, Crookston, 56716.* Tel: 218-281-4533.

Pastoral Office of Christian Service—BERNADETTE DUNN, Dir., *1200 Memorial Dr., P.O. Box 610, Crookston, 56716.* Tel: 218-281-4533.

Pastoral Office of the Word—Sr. PAT MURPHY, C.S.J., Dir., *1200 Memorial Dr., P.O. Box 610, Crookston, 56716.* Tel: 218-281-4533.

Pastoral Office of Worship—Sr. MARGUERITE STREIFEL, O.S.B., Dir., *1200 Memorial Dr., P.O. Box 610, Crookston, 56716.* Tel: 218-281-4533.

Priests' Council—Rev. AUGUST GOTHMAN, Chm., *St. Stephen's Church, P.O. Box 507, Stephen, 56757.* Tel: 218-478-2231. Rev. THOMAS FRIEDL, Sec.; Rev. Msgr. ROGER L. GRUNDHAUS, J.C.L., V.G.; Revs. LAWRENCE WIESELER; JOHN KLEINWACHTER; ROBERT SCHREINER; TIMOTHY NOAH.

Priests' Personnel Board—Rev. Msgr. ROGER L. GRUNDHAUS, J.C.L., V.G., Ex Officio Member; Revs. JOE KIESELBACH; DAVID SUPER; DENNIS WIELAND; JOE RICHARDS.

Priests Retirement Board of Trustees—Rev. Msgr. MICHAEL PATNODE; Revs. GARY LAMOINE; LARRY DELANEY.

Propagation of the Faith—Rev. Msgr. ROGER L. GRUNDHAUS, J.C.L., V.G., Dir., *P.O. Box 610, Crookston, 56716.*

Religious Education & Adult Faith Formation—RAY LAGASSE, Dir., *1200 Memorial Dr., P.O. Box 610, Crookston, 56716.* Tel: 218-281-4533.

Schools—Sr. PAT MURPHY, C.S.J., Dir. Office of the Word, *1200 Memorial Dr., P.O. Box 610, Crookston, 56716.* Tel: 218-281-4533.

TEC (Teens Encounter Christ)—NANCY BOUCHER, Mgr., *P.O. Box 610, Crookston, 56716.* Tel: 218-281-4533.

Vocations—Rev. JOSEPH RICHARDS, Dir. RAY HOLLCRAFT, Assoc. Dir., *P.O. Box 610, Crookston, 56716.* Tel: 218-281-4533.

Youth Ministry—RAY HOLLCRAFT, Dir., *P.O. Box 610, Crookston, 56716.* Tel: 218-281-4533.

CLERGY, PARISHES, MISSIONS AND PAROCHIAL SCHOOLS

CITY OF CROOKSTON (Polk County)

1—CATHEDRAL OF THE IMMACULATE CONCEPTION, Revs. David J. Super; Luis S. Buitron; Sr. Mardelle Mohs, O.S.B., Pastoral Assoc.; Deacon Dennis Bivens.
Parish Office—702 Summit Ave., 56716. Tel: 218-281-1735; Fax: 218-281-1747.
Res., 319 S. Ash St., 56716. Tel: 218-281-2638. [JC]
School—The Cathedral School, (Grades K-6). Tel: 218-281-1835; Fax: 218-281-1747. Raymond Dusek, Prin.
Lay Teachers 10; Students 106.
Missions—Euclid, Polk Co., St. Mary; Gentilly, Polk Co., St. Peter.

2—ST. ANNE'S. Closed. For inquiries for parish records contact the Cathedral of the Immaculate Conception, Crookston, for details.

OUTSIDE THE CITY OF CROOKSTON

Ada, Norman Co., St. Joseph's, Rev. David Baumgartner.
Res., 405 E. Thorpe Ave., 56510. Tel: 218-784-4131. [JC]
Missions—Halstad, Norman Co., Holy Family; Twin Valley, Norman Co., St. William.

Akeley, Hubbard Co., St. John's, Rev. John Kleinwachter.
Res., P.O. Box 219, 56433. Tel: 218-652-2785; Fax: 218-652-2785.
Mission—Nevis, Hubbard Co., Immaculate Conception.

Alma, Marshall Co., St. John the Baptist. Served by St. Stephen, Stephen. Tel: 218-478-2231.

Argyle, Marshall Co., St. Rose. (Co-Parish with St. Stephen's, Stephen). Rev. August L. Gothman; Sr. Joanne Johnson, C.S.J., Pastoral Admin. P.O. Box 277, 56713. Tel: 218-437-6341. [CEM]

Badger, Roseau Co., St. Mary's. Served by Sacred Heart, Roseau. Tel: 218-463-2441.

Bagley, Clearwater Co., St. Joseph. Served by St. Mary's, Fosston. Sr. Janice Miller, C.S.J., Pastoral Admin.; Deacon Daniel Hannig.
Res., P.O. Box 67, 56621. Tel: 218-694-6416. [CEM]

Barnesville, Clay Co., Assumption, Rev. Joseph Kieselbach.
Res., 307 Front St. N., P.O. Box 339, 56514. Tel: 218-354-7320. [CEM]
Mission—Sabin, Clay Co., St. Cecilia.

Baudette, Lake of the Woods Co., Sacred Heart. Served by St. Mary's, Warroad. Deacon James Lukenbill, Pastoral Admin.
Res., P.O. Box 738, 56623. Tel: 218-634-2689.
Mission—Williams, Lake of the Woods Co., St. Joseph. [CEM]

Beaulieu, Mahnomen Co., St. Joseph. Served by St. Michael, Mahnomen. Tel: 218-935-2503.

Bejou, Mahnomen Co., Immaculate Conception. Closed. For inquiries for parish records contact St. Michael's, Mahnomen.

Bemidji, Beltrami Co., St. Philip's, Rev. Msgr. Michael Patnode; Rev. James H.C. Lyons; Deacons John Schuiling; Mike Tolin. In res., Revs. William F. Lemen; Edward Nistler.
Res., 710 Beltrami Ave., 56601. Tel: 218-444-4262; Fax: 218-444-4262. [CEM]
School—Mrs. Carol Rettinger, Prin. Lay Teachers 18; Students 291.
Missions—Wilton, Beltrami Co., Sacred Heart; Pennington, Beltrami Co., St. Charles; Bemidji, Beltrami Co., Holy Spirit Newman Center.

Benwood, Roseau Co., St. Joseph The Worker. Served by Sacred Heart, Roseau. Tel: 218-463-2441.

Big Elbow Lake, Becker Co., St. Francis Cabrini. Served by St. Ann, Waubun. Tel: 218-473-2101.

Blackduck, Beltrami Co., St. Ann's. Served by St. Patrick's, Kelliher. Tel: 218-647-8392.

Brooks, Red Lake Co., St. Joseph. Served by St. Joseph's, Red Lake Falls. Tel: 218-253-2685.

Callaway, Becker Co., Assumption. Served by St. Mary of the Lakes, Lake Eunice Township. Deacon Randy Bauer, Pastoral Admin.
Res., P.O. Box 67, 56521. Tel: 218-375-3571; Fax: 218-847-6367. [CEM]

Detroit Lakes, Becker Co., Holy Rosary, Rev. Jerry Rogers; Deacons Randall J. Bauer; James Thomas.
Res., 1016 Washington Ave., 56501. Tel: 218-847-1393; Fax: 218-847-6367. [CEM]
School—Tel: 218-847-5306; Fax: 218-847-6367. Kathleen Klindt, Prin.
Lay Teachers 15; Students 111.

Dilworth, Clay Co., St. Elizabeth. Served by St. Francis Xavier's, Lake Park. Tel: 218-238-6639.

Dorothy, Red Lake Co., St. Dorothy. Closed. For inquiries for parish records contact St. Joseph's, Red Lake Falls.

East Grand Forks, Polk Co., Sacred Heart, Revs. Timothy H. McGee; Larry Delaney.
Res., 200 Third St. N.W., 56721. Tel: 218-773-0877; Fax: 218-773-8312. [CEM]
School—Tel: 218-773-1579; Fax: 218-773-7042. Mr. David Andrys, Prin.
Lay Teachers 14; Students 201.
High School—Tel: 218-773-0230; Fax: 218-773-0318. Mr. Phillip E. Meyer, Prin.
Sisters 1; Lay Teachers 19; Students 166.
Convent—Tel: 218-773-0563. Sr. Marguerite Streifel, O.S.B., Coord.
Missions—Fisher, Polk Co., St. Francis; Tabor, Polk Co., Holy Trinity.

Euclid, Polk Co., St. Mary. Served by the Cathedral of the Immaculate Conception, Crookston. Tel: 218-281-1735.

Falun, Roseau Co., St. Philip. Served by St. Mary's, Warroad. Tel: 218-386-1178.

Felton, Clay Co., St. Lawrence. Closed. For inquiries for parish records contact St. Joseph's, Ada.

Fertile, Polk Co., St. Joseph, Rev. Msgr. Roger L. Grundhaus, V.G.; Sr. Mary Jean Gust, O.S.B., Pastoral Assoc.
Mailing Address: 205 S.E. Elm St., 56540. Tel: 218-945-6649.
Res., 1200 Memorial Dr., Crookston, 56716. Tel: 218-281-4533; Fax: 218-281-3328. [CEM]

Fisher, Polk Co., St. Francis. Served by Sacred Heart, East Grand Forks. Tel: 218-773-0877. [CEM].

Florian, Marshall Co., Assumption. Served by SS. Peter and Paul, Warren. Deacon Courtney Abel.
Mailing Address: Rte. 2, Box 110, Strandquist, 56758. Tel: 218-478-3578. [CEM]

Fosston, Polk Co., St. Mary's, Rev. Gary W. LaMoine; Deacon Jarvis Zitzow.
Res., Rte. 3, Box 19A, 56542. Tel: 218-435-6484. [CEM]
Missions—Bagley, Clearwater Co., St. Joseph; Oklee, Red Lake Co., St. Francis Xavier.

Frazee, Becker Co., Sacred Heart, Rev. Joseph DeCrans.
Res., 202 W. Maple Ave., 56544. Tel: 218-334-4221. [CEM]

Gentilly, Polk Co., St. Peter's. Served by Cathedral of the Immaculate Conception, Crookston. Tel: 218-281-1735.
Mailing Address: Rte. 2, Box 80, Crookston, 56716. Tel: 218-281-1688. [CEM]

Georgetown, Clay Co., St. John. Served by St. Francis de Sales, Moorhead. Tel: 218-233-4780.

Goodridge, Pennington Co., St. Anne. Served by St. Bernard's, Thief River Falls. Tel: 218-681-3571.

Greenbush, Roseau Co., Blessed Sacrament, Rev. Donald Braukman.
Res., P.O. Box A, 56726. Tel: 218-782-2467. [CEM]
Missions—Middle River, Marshall Co., St. Joseph; Karlstad, Marshall Co., St. Edward.

Grygla, Marshall Co., St. Clement. Served by St. Bernard's, Thief River Falls. Tel: 218-681-3571.

Hallock, Kittson Co., St. Patrick's, Rev. Timothy T. Noah.
Res., P.O. Box 519, 56728. Tel: 218-843-2323.
Mission—Lancaster, Kittson Co., Holy Rosary.

Halstad, Norman Co., Holy Family. Served by St. Joseph, Ada. Tel: 218-784-4131. [JC]

Hawley, Clay Co., St. Andrew. Served by St. Francis Xavier, Lake Park. Tel: 218-238-6639; Fax: 218-238-6028.
Mailing Address: 1419 Main St., P.O. Box 129, 56549. Tel: 218-483-4264.

Karlstad, Kittson Co., St. Edward the Confessor. Served by Blessed Sacrament, Greenbush. Tel: 218-782-2467.

Kelliher, Beltrami Co., St. Patrick, Rev. Msgr. William Mehrkens, (Retired); Deacon John Eisbrener, Pastoral Admin.
Res., P.O. Box 187, 56650. Tel: 218-647-8392. [JC]
Missions—Blackduck, Beltrami Co., St. Patrick; Northome, Koochiching Co., St. Michael.

Lake Eunice Township, Becker Co., St. Mary of the Lakes, Rev. Eugene L. Wesely.
Mailing Address: 20996 County Rd. #20, Detroit Lakes, 56501. Tel: 218-439-3938.
Mission—Callaway, Becker Co., Assumption.

Lake Itasca, Clearwater Co., St. Catherine. Closed. For inquiries for parish records contact St. Peter's, Park Rapids.

Lake Park, Becker Co., St. Francis Xavier's, Rev. Thomas Friedl.
Res., 2066 Second St., 56554-4402. Tel: 218-238-6639; Fax: 218-238-6028. [CEM]
Missions—Hawley, Clay Co., St. Andrew; Dilworth, Clay Co., St. Elizabeth.

Lancaster, Kittson Co., Holy Rosary. Served by St. Patrick, Hallock. Tel: 218-843-2323.

Laporte, Hubbard Co., St. Theodore. (Under the jurisdiction of the Diocese of Crookston; administered by the Diocese of Duluth.). Rev. Eugene Lyttle.
P.O. Box 368, Cass Lake, 56633-0368. Tel: 218-335-2359; Fax: 218-335-2618.

Leo, Roseau Co., St. Aloysius. Closed. For inquiries for parish records contact Blessed Sacrament, Greenbush.

Mahnomen, Mahnomen Co., St. Michael's, Rev. Richard D. Lambert.
Res., Rte. 1, Box 22, 56557. Tel: 218-935-2503; Fax: 218-935-2503. [CEM]

School—Tel: 218-935-5222; Fax: 218-935-5222. Sr. Yvonne Schafer, O.S.B., Prin.
Sisters of St. Benedict 2; Lay Teachers 6; Students 70.
Catechesis/Religious Programs—D.R.E.: Sr. Yvonne Schafer, (PreK-6); Jane Erickson, (7-12).
Students 288.
Mission—Beaulieu, Mahnomen Co., St. Joseph. [CEM]

Mentor, Polk Co., St. Lawrence, Rev. Msgr. Roger L. Grundhaus, V.G.; Deacon John A. Bruggeman.
Mailing Address: Box 51, 56736. Tel: 218-637-8178.
Res., 1200 Memorial Dr., Crookston, 56716. Tel: 218-281-4533; Fax: 218-281-3328.

Middle River, Marshall Co., St. Joseph, Husband of Mary. Served by Blessed Sacrament, Greenbush. Mitch & Lee Walski, Pastoral Ministers.
Res., Rte. 2, Box 9, 56737. Tel: 218-222-3392. [CEM]

Moorhead, Clay Co., St. Francis de Sales, Rev. Joseph D. Richards.
601 15th Ave. N., 56560. Tel: 218-233-4780.
Res., 988 18th Ave. Cir. N., 56560. Tel: 218-236-1505. [JC]

St. Joseph's, Revs. Michael H. Foltz, J.C.L.; Vincent P. Miller.
Office: 218 10th St. S., 56560. Tel: 218-236-5066; 236-9503 (Res.); Fax: 218-233-0717. [JC]
School—Tel: 218-233-0553; Fax: 218-233-0717. Valerie Ritland, Prin.
Sisters 1; Lay Teachers 17; Students 193.
Catechesis/Religious Programs—Tel: 218-236-1979. Barbara Schmidt, D.R.E.
Students 381.
Mission—Moorhead, Clay Co., St. Thomas Newman Center, 707-11th St. S., Tel: 218-236-9596; Fax: 218-233-0717.

Naytahwaush, Mahnomen Co., St. Anne. Served by St. Ann's, Waubun. Tel: 218-473-2101. Sr. Jean Schwartz, O.S.B., Pastoral Assoc.
Mailing Address: P.O. Box 157, 56566. Tel: 218-935-5676.

Nebish, Beltrami Co., St. John. Served by St. Mary's Mission, Red Lake. Tel: 218-679-3614.

Nevis, Hubbard Co., Immaculate Conception. Served by St. John's, Akeley. Tel: 218-652-2785.

Ogema, Becker Co., Most Holy Redeemer, Rev. Mietek Bajek, O.M.I.
Res., P.O. Box 57, 56569. Tel: 218-983-3261. [CEM]
Missions—White Earth, Becker Co., St. Benedict; Ponsford, Becker Co., St. Theodore.

Oklee, Red Lake Co., St. Francis Xavier's. Served by St. Mary's, Fosston. Tel: 218-435-6484.
Mailing Address: P.O. Box 160, 56742. Tel: 218-796-5844. [CEM]

Oslo, Marshall Co., St. Joseph. Served by SS. Peter and Paul, Warren. Tel: 218-745-4511. Sr. Lucille Adelman, O.S.B., Pastoral Admin.
Res., P.O. Box 97, 56744. Tel: 218-695-2641. [CEM]

Park Rapids, Hubbard Co., St. Peter's, Rev. Richard Boyd.
Res., P.O. Box 353, 56470. Tel: 218-732-5142 (Office); 732-8852 (Res.); Fax: 218-732-2971. [JC]
Mission—Two Inlets, Becker Co., St. Mary.

Pennington, Beltrami Co., St. Charles. Served by St. Philip's, Bemidji. Tel: 218-444-4262.

Plummer, Red Lake Co., St. Vincent de Paul. Closed. For inquiries for parish records contact St. Francis Xavier, Oklee.

Ponsford, Becker Co., St. Theodore. Served by Most Holy Redeemer, Ogema. Tel: 218-936-3261.

Red Lake, Beltrami Co., St. Mary's Mission Church, Rev. Patrick A. Sullivan. In res., Rev. Msgr. William Mehrkens.
Res., P.O. Box 189, 56671. Tel: 218-679-3614; Fax: 218-679-2212. [CEM]
School—Tel: 218-679-3388. Deacon Dan Hannig, Prin.
Sisters 3; Lay Teachers 6; Students 68.
Mission—Nebish, Beltrami Co., St. John.

Red Lake Falls, Red Lake Co., St. Joseph's, Rev. Timothy F. Bushy; Sr. Lucille Schafer, O.S.B., Pastoral Assoc.
Office & Res.: P.O. Box 400, 56750. Tel: 218-253-2004 (Res.); 253-2685 (Office); Fax: 218-253-2188 (Office). [CEM]
School—112 Edward Ave. N.W., Box 215, 56750. Tel: 218-253-2188; Fax: 218-253-2188. Sr. Richarde Wolf, S.S.N.D., Prin.
Lay Teachers 6; Students 64.
Mission—Brooks, Red Lake Co., St. Joseph. [CEM]

Roseau, Roseau Co., Sacred Heart, Rev. Robert J. LaPlante.
Res., P.O. Box 118, 403 Main Ave. N., 56751. Tel: 218-463-2441; Fax: 218-463-2443. [CEM]
Missions—Badger, Roseau Co., St. Mary's. [CEM]
Benwood, Roseau Co., St. Joseph, The Worker. [CEM]

Sabin, Clay Co., St. Cecilia. Served by Assumption, Barnesville. Tel: 218-354-7320.

Shevlin, Clearwater Co., Our Lady of Victory. Closed. For inquiries for parish records contact St. Joseph's, Bagley.

Stephen, Marshall Co., St. Stephen's. (Co-Parish with St. Rose, Argyle.). Rev. August L. Gothman. In res., Rev. Luis P. Silva.
Res., 515 Fifth St., P.O. Box 507, 56757. Tel: 218-478-2231; Fax: 218-478-2231. [CEM]

Tabor, Polk Co., Holy Trinity Catholic. Served by Sacred Heart, East Grand Forks. Tel: 218-773-0877.

Terrebonne, Red Lake Co., St. Anthony. Closed. For inquiries for parish records contact St. Joseph's, Red Lake Falls.

Thief River Falls, Pennington Co., St. Bernards, Rev. Dennis J. Wieland.
Res., 105 Knight Ave. N., 56701. Tel: 218-681-3571; Fax: 218-681-2261. [CEM]
School—Tel: 218-681-1539. Sr. Kathy Kuchar, O.S.B., Prin.
Lay Teachers 8; Students 139.
Missions—Goodridge, Pennington Co., St. Ann; Grygla, Marshall Co., St. Clement.

Twin Valley, Norman Co., St. William. Served by St. Joseph, Ada. Tel: 218-784-4131.

Two Inlets, Becker Co., St. Mary's. Served by St. Peter's, Park Rapids. Tel: 218-732-5142. Rev. Rick Boyd.
Mailing Address: P.O. Box 287, Park Rapids, 56470. Tel: 218-732-4046. [CEM]

Warren, Marshall Co., SS. Peter and Paul, Rev. Lawrence A. Wieseler.
Res., 208 N. Seventh St., 56762. Tel: 218-745-4511. [CEM]
Missions—Oslo, Marshall Co., St. Joseph, P.O. Box 97, 56744. Tel: 218-695-2641. Sr. Lucille Adelman, O.S.B., Pastoral Admin.; Florian, Marshall Co., Assumption.

Warroad, Roseau Co., St. Mary's, Rev. Duane L. Pribula; Deacon Robert Marvel.
Res., P.O. Box 33, 56763. Tel: 218-386-1178; Fax: 218-386-3054. [CEM]

Mission—Falun, Roseau Co., St. Philip.

Waubun, Mahnomen Co., St. Ann, Rev. Ronald J. Meyer, O.M.I.
Res., Rte. 2, Box 6, 56589. Tel: 218-473-2101; Fax: 218-473-2101. [CEM]
Missions—Naytahwaush, Mahnomen Co., St. Anne; Big Elbow Lake, Becker Co., St. Francis Cabrini.

White Earth, Becker Co., St. Benedict. Served by Most Holy Redeemer, Ogema. Tel: 218-936-3261. Bro. Craig Bonham, O.M.I., Pastoral Assoc.
Res., P.O. Box 417, 56591-0417. Tel: 218-983-3519. [CEM]

Williams, Lake of the Woods Co., St. Joseph. Served by Sacred Heart, Baudette. Tel: 218-634-2689.

Wilton, Beltrami Co., Sacred Heart. Served by St. Philip, Bemidji. Tel: 218-751-4262.

On Duty Outside the Diocese:
Reverend Fathers—
Bester, Robert
Foley, Gerald K.
Schreiner, Robert
Skoczylas, Walter
Sullivan, Michael

Leave of Absence:
Reverend Fathers—
Troska, Llewelyn J.

Retired:
Reverend Monsignors—
Bourassa, Stanley, Rte. 1, Box 80-C, Mentor, MN 56736. Tel: 218-637-2033
Krebs, Donald H., Rte. 1, Box 246, Mentor, MN 56736. Tel: 218-574-2954
Mehrkens, William, P.O. Box 189, Red Lake, MN 56671. Tel: 218-679-3614
Reverend Fathers—
Archer, W. Donald, 444 S. Higley Rd., #213, Mesa, AZ 85206. Tel: 480-807-3497
Bernauer, James, P.O. Box 7, Dent, MN 56528. Tel: 218-758-3377
Carriere, Henry G., Villa St. Vincent, 516 Walsh St., #307, Crookston, MN 56716
Felion, Jerome, 1514 Bamboo Cir., Harlingen, TX 78552. Tel: 956-412-8037
Kulhawik, Frank, P.O. Box 306, Twin Valley, MN 56584. Tel: 218-584-5200
Lemen, William F., 710 Beltrami Ave., Bemidji, MN 56601. Tel: 218-444-4262
Nistler, Edward, 710 Beltrami Ave., Bemidji, MN 56601. Tel: 218-444-4262
Noah, Daniel, Rte. 2, Box 291, Crookston, MN 56716
Noesen, Gerald, Rte. 1, Box 561, Mentor, MN 56736. Tel: 218-574-2424
Palcisko, Raymond, 2769-28th St., N.W., Baudette, MN 56623
Pryor, G. Robert, U.S.A.F, 286 Grantwood Dr., Henderson, NV 89014
Reid, Francis R., HCO5, Box 243a, Park Rapids, MN 56470. Tel: 218-732-9521

Permanent Deacons:
Abel, Courtney, Assumption, Florian
Bauer, Randall, Holy Rosary, Detroit Lakes
Bivens, Dennis, Cathedral of the Immaculate Conception, Crookston
Bruggeman, John, St. Lawrence, Mentor
Eisbrener, John, St. Ann, Blackduck
Hannig, Daniel, St. Joseph, Bagley
Lukenbill, James, Sacred Heart, Baudette
Marvel, Robert, St. Mary's, Warroad
Schuiling, John, St. Philip, Bemidji
Thomas, James, Holy Rosary, Detroit Lakes
Tolin, Mike, St. Philip, Bemidji
Zitzow, Jarvis, St. Mary, Fosston

INSTITUTIONS LOCATED IN THE DIOCESE

[A] ELEMENTARY SCHOOLS, PRIVATE

RED LAKE. *St. Mary's Mission School*, 56671. Tel: 218-679-3388; Fax: 218-679-2212. Benedictine Sisters (St. Joseph, MN). Deacon Daniel P. Hannig, Prin.; Rev. Patrick A. Sullivan. Sisters 3; Lay Teachers 4; Students 68.

[B] CONFRATERNITY OF CHRISTIAN DOCTRINE

CROOKSTON. *Cathedral - Religious Education/Faith Formation*, 702 Summit Ave., 56716. Tel: 218-281-1735; Fax: 218-281-1747. Ray Dusek, R.E. Dir., (Grades PreK-6); Sr. Mardelle Mohs, Junior High Coord.; Nancy Boucher, Senior High Coord. Students (Grades K-8) 250; High School Students (Grades 9-11) 123.

ADA. *St. Joseph Parish, R.E. Program*, 56510. Tel: 218-784-4131. Students 125.

ARGYLE. *St. Rose Parish, R.E. Program*, Box 277, 56713. Tel: 218-437-6341. Marilyn Kuznia, Dir. Students 127.

BEMIDJI. *St. Philips Parish, Religious Formation Program*, 620 Beltrami Ave., 56601. Tel: 218-444-5849. D.R.E.: Kris Jensen, (Grades PreK-8); Mary Hoody, (Grades 9-12). Students (Grades PreK-5) 200; Students (Grades 6-12) 287.

DETROIT LAKES. *Holy Rosary Parish, R.E. Program*, 1032 Washington Ave., 56501. Tel: 218-847-8970; Fax: 218-847-6367. JoAnne Knuttila, Coord. Students 300.

EAST GRAND FORKS. *Sacred Heart Parish, R.E. Program*, 200 Third St., N.W., 56721. Tel: 218-773-0531; Fax: 218-773-8312. D.R.E.: Ginny Osowski, (Grades PreK-6); Valerie Reuter, (Grades 7-11); Sheryl Guzek, (Confirmation Prog.). Students 592.

GREENBUSH. *Religious Education Program*, P.O. Box A, 56726. Tel: 218-782-2263. Gerry Nubson, Coord. Students 125.

THIEF RIVER FALLS. *Religious Education Program*, 105 Knight Ave. N., 56701. Tel: 218-681-6268; 6269. Margaret Rasmussen, Coord. Students 238; High School Students 166.

[C] GENERAL HOSPITALS

BAUDETTE. *Lakewood Health Center*, 600 South Main, 56623. Tel: 218-634-2120; Fax: 218-634-1307
For a complete listing, refer to the Hospitals section.

DETROIT LAKES. *St. Mary's Regional Health Center*, 1027 Washington Ave., 56501. Tel: 218-847-5611; Fax: 218-847-7674
For a complete listing, refer to the Hospitals section.

PARK RAPIDS. *St. Joseph Area Health Services*, 600 Pleasant Ave., 56470. Tel: 218-732-3311; Fax: 218-732-1368
For a complete listing, refer to the Hospitals section.

[D] HOMES FOR THE AGED

CROOKSTON. *Villa St. Vincent*, 516 Walsh St., 56716. Tel: 218-281-3424; Fax: 218-281-4755
For a complete listing, refer to the Special Care Facilities section.

DETROIT LAKES. *St. Mary's Nursing Center,* 56501
For a complete listing, refer to the Special Care Facilities section.

[E] CONVENTS AND RESIDENCES FOR SISTERS

CROOKSTON. *Marywood Residential Community.* (Retirement Residence). Community, R.R. 2, Box 16, 56716-9603. Tel: 218-281-3093; Fax: 218-281-6123. Congregation of the Sisters of St. Joseph of Medaille (Pontifical Jurisdiction). Sr. Vivian Miron, C.S.J., Interim Admin.; Rev. David J. Super, Chap.; Sr. Christine Johnson, C.S.J., Archivist. Marywood Residential Community 16; Crookston Regional Community 30.

Mount St. Benedict Monastery, 620 Summit Ave. E., 56716-2799. Tel: 218-281-3441; Fax: 218-281-6966. Motherhouse of the Order of the Sisters of St. Benedict of Pontifical Jurisdiction-The Federation of St. Gertrude. Sr. Catherine Merck, O.S.B., Prioress; Sr. Kathleen McGeary, Subprioress. Sisters in Community 134.

Sisters of St. Benedict Initial Formation. Tel: 218-281-3441; Fax: 218-281-6966. Sr. Lois Spors, O.S.B.

Sunrise Center for Children and Families. Tel: 218-281-6540; Fax: 218-281-6966. Sr. Judith Moen, O.S.B., Dir.

[F] NEWMAN CENTERS

CROOKSTON. *University of Minnesota Cooperative Campus Ministry,* 56716. Tel: 218-281-8516; Fax: 218-281-8504. Collette M. Conati, Dir. Coop. Campus Ministry.

BEMIDJI. *Holy Spirit Newman Center,* 1701 Birch Ln. N.E., 56601-2607. Tel: 218-444-4762; Fax: 218-751-7244. Rev. Msgr. Michael Patnode; Rev. James H.C. Lyons; Lois Jenkins, Pastoral Assoc.

MOORHEAD. *St. Thomas Aquinas Newman Center,* 707 11th St. S., 56560. Tel: 218-236-9596. Rev. Vincent P. Miller, Dir.; Chris Yarnal, Campus Minister.

[G] MISCELLANEOUS

CROOKSTON.

Mount Saint Benedict Foundation, 620 Summit Ave., 56716. Tel: 218-281-3441; Fax: 218-281-6966.

The Diocese of Crookston Catholic Community Foundation, 1200 Memorial Dr., 56716. Tel: 218-281-4533; Fax: 218-281-3328.

RELIGIOUS INSTITUTES OF MEN REPRESENTED IN THE DIOCESE

For further details refer to the corresponding bracketed number in the Religious Institutes of Men or Women section.

[0910]—*Oblates of Mary Immaculate.*—O.M.I.

RELIGIOUS INSTITUTES OF WOMEN REPRESENTED IN THE DIOCESE

[0230]—*Benedictine Sisters of Pontifical Jurisdiction.* (Congregation of St. Gertrude).—O.S.B.

[0230]—*Benedictine Sisters of Pontifical Jurisdiction (Federation of St. Benedict).*—O.S.B.

[2970]—*School Sisters of Notre Dame.* (Mankato Province).—S.S.N.D.

[1070-03]—*Sinsinawa Dominican Congregation of the Most Holy Rosary.*

[0990]—*Sisters of Divine Providence.*—C.D.P.

[3880]—*Sisters of St. Joseph of Medaille.*—C.S.J.

[0260]—*Sisters of the Blessed Sacrament for Indians and Colored People.*—S.B.S.

NECROLOGY

† Stearns, Rev. Msgr. John D. —Died Dec. 1, 1999.

Diocese of Dallas

(Dioecesis Dallasensis)

Most Reverend

CHARLES V. GRAHMANN, D.D.

Bishop of Dallas; ordained March 17, 1956; appointed Titular Bishop of Equilio and Auxiliary of San Antonio June 30, 1981; consecrated August 29, 1981; appointed First Bishop of Victoria April 14, 1982; installed May 29, 1982; appointed Coadjutor of Dallas December 18, 1989; Reception as Coadjutor of Dallas February 21, 1990; appointed Bishop of Dallas July 14, 1990.

Most Reverend

JOSEPH A. GALANTE, D.D, J.C.D.

Coadjutor Bishop of Dallas; ordained May 16, 1964; appointed Titular Bishop of Equilum and Auxiliary Bishop of San Antonio October 13, 1992; consecrated December 11, 1992; appointed Bishop of Beaumont April 5, 1994; installed Bishop of Beaumont May 9, 1994.

Most Reverend

THOMAS TSCHOEPE

Retired Bishop of Dallas; ordained May 30, 1943; appointed Bishop of San Angelo January 12, 1966; consecrated March 9, 1966; transferred to Dallas August 27, 1969; resigned July 14, 1990. *Res., St. Joseph, P.O. Box 190, Waxahachie, TX, 75165.*

ESTABLISHED DIOCESE OF DALLAS ON JULY 15, 1890.

REDESIGNATED DIOCESE OF DALLAS-FORT WORTH ON OCTOBER 20, 1953.

REDESIGNATED DIOCESE OF DALLAS ON AUGUST 27, 1969.

Square Miles 7,523.

Comprises the following nine Counties in the State of Texas: Collin, Dallas, Ellis, Fannin, Grayson, Hunt, Kaufman, Navarro and Rockwall.

For legal titles of parishes and diocesan institutions, consult the Chancery Office.

Chancery Office: 3725 Blackburn, P.O. Box 190507, Dallas, TX, 75219. Tel.: 214-528-2240; Fax: 214-526-1743.

Web site address: www.cathdal.org

E-mail address: ccfcdal@cathdal.org

STATISTICAL OVERVIEW

Personnel	
Bishop	1
Retired Bishops	1
Abbots	1
Priests: Diocesan Active in Diocese	76
Priests: Active Outside Diocese	9
Priests: Retired, Sick or Absent	19
Number of Diocesan Priests	104
Religious Priests in Diocese	72
Extern Priests in Diocese	28
Ordinations:	
Diocesan Priests	3
Transitional Deacons	2
Permanent Deacons	1
Permanent Deacons in Diocese	147
Total Brothers	4
Total Sisters	153
Parishes	
Parishes	65
With Resident Pastor:	
Resident Diocesan Priests	41
Resident Religious Priests	13
Without Resident Pastor:	
Administered by Priests	10
Administered by Deacons	1
Missions	7
Professional Ministry Personnel:	
Brothers	1
Sisters	42
Lay Ministers	164
Welfare	
Catholic Hospitals	1
Total Assisted	18,800
Homes for the Aged	1
Total Assisted	44
Day Care and Extended Day Care Centers	3
Total Assisted	447
Special Centers for Social Services	15
Total Assisted	62,720
Educational	
Seminaries, Diocesan	1
Students from This Diocese	7
Students from Other Diocese	38
Diocesan Students in Other Seminaries	10
Total Seminarians	17
Colleges and Universities	1
Total Students	3,100
High Schools, Diocesan and Parish	4
Total Students	1,689
High Schools, Private	4
Total Students	1,996
Elementary Schools, Diocesan and Parish	30
Total Students	14,186
Elementary Schools, Private	2
Total Students	584
Non-residential Schools for the Disabled	1
Total Students	125
Catechesis/Religious Education:	
High School Students	4,779
Elementary Students	33,887
Total Students Under Catholic Instruction	60,363
Teachers in the Diocese:	
Priests	29
Brothers	2
Sisters	28
Lay Teachers	996
Vital Statistics	
Receptions into the Church:	
Infant Baptism Totals	13,838
Adult Baptism Totals	658
Received into Full Communion	778
First Communions	8,662
Confirmations	5,201
Marriages:	
Catholic	1,805
Interfaith	653
Total Marriages	2,458
Deaths	1,451
Total Catholic Population	630,156
Total Population	2,979,840

Former Bishops—Rt. Rev. THOMAS F. BRENNAN, D.D., cons. April 5, 1891; resigned Nov. 17, 1892; died March 21, 1916.—Rt. Rev. EDWARD JOSEPH DUNNE, D.D., cons. Nov. 30. 1893; died Aug. 5, 1910.—Most Rev. JOSEPH PATRICK LYNCH, D.D., LL.D., appt. June 8, 1911; cons. July 12, 1911; Assistant at Pontifical Throne, May 13, 1936; died Aug. 19, 1954.—Most Rev. THOMAS K. GORMAN, D.D., D.Sc.Hist., ord. June 23, 1917; Bishop of Reno; appt. April 24, 1931; cons. July 22, 1931; Assistant at the Pontifical Throne, May 4, 1942; appt. Titular Bishop of Rhasus and Coadjutor to the Bishop of Dallas, Feb. 8, 1952; succeeded to Aug. 19, 1954; resigned and appointed Titular Bishop of Pinhel, Aug. 27, 1969. (Title rescinded); died Aug. 16, 1980.

Vicar General—Rev. Msgr. GLENN D. GARDNER, J.C.D.

Chancery Office—3725 Blackburn, P.O. Box 190507, Dallas, 75219. Tel: 214-528-2240; Fax: 214-526-1743. Office Hours: 9-5.

Chancellor—MARY EDLUND.

Diocesan Tribunal—P.O. Box 190507, Dallas, 75219. Tel: 214-528-9970.

Judicial Vicar—Rev. Msgr. JOHN P. BELL, J.C.L.

Assistant Judicial Vicar—Rev. JACK HOPKA, S.F.O., J.C.L.

Director of the Tribunal—WILLIAM C. HARE, III, J.C.L.

Secretary to the Tribunal—MARGARET GILLETT.

Defensores Vinculi—JOHN P. GARGAN, J.C.D.; Rev. MICHAEL G. DUCA, J.C.L.

Diocesan Judges—Rev. Msgr. GLENN D. GARDNER, J.C.D.; Revs. DAVID L. COLELLA, O.SS.T, J.C.D.; JOHN LIBONE, J.C.L.

Notaries—MARGARET GILLETT; JANE HOFMEISTER; ALICE DAHL.

Procurator-Advocates—Deacon LOUIS ADELMANN; LARRIE W. ARNOLD, M.D.; Sr. KATHLEEN BARNES, O.S.U.; Mrs. SUSAN C. BOYD; Mrs. BEBE CANTU; Mrs. JUDY CLARK; Mrs. TRUDY COSTA; Mrs. DIANE DANIELS; Rev. JOHN F. DEEVES, S.J.; Deacon DON FORBRICH; Mrs. DEBBIE FOWLER; Ms. JEANNE MARIE GIRSCH; Ms. SANDRA WARNE GIST; Rev. MICHAEL GUADAGNOLI; Mrs. MARY CATHERINE HARE; Ms. LANAY N. HARTMAN; Mr. RICH HERROD; Deacon JUAN IBARRA; Mrs. MARY L. IZAK; Rev. GREG KELLY; Deacon JOHN PAUL KELLY; Rev. JOSEPH A. MEHAN, JR.; Mrs. LINDA MOSES; Ms. YOLANDA ORTIZ; Mrs. DENISE G. PHILLIPS; Mrs.

MARY A. RASINS; Deacons MICHAEL RASINS; KENNETH REISOR; Mrs. MARY KAY RITCHIE; MARY ROBINSON; Deacons JOSEPH V. SALVO; ROBERT SANCHEZ; Revs. MARK SEITZ; LUIS SERNA; CLIFFORD SMITH; Mr. FRANCIS XAVIER VUONG ANH THUONG; Deacon GARY M. VOGEL.

Consultors of Pastors—Rev. Msgr. RICHARD JOHNSON, V.F.; Rev. Msgr. JOHN MEYERS, V.F.; Revs. HENRY PETTER, V.F.; TIM GOLLOB, V.F.

Diocesan Consultors—Rev. RAMON ALVAREZ, V.F.; Rev. Msgr. JOHN BELL; Revs. TOM CLOHERTY; MICHAEL DUCA; Rev. Msgr. G. DUFF GARDNER, V.G.; Rev. Msgr. LAWRENCE PICHARD; Rev. MARK SEITZ.

Presbyteral Council—Rev. Msgr. GLENN D. GARDNER, V.G., Ex Officio; Rev. RAMON ALVAREZ, V.F.; Rev. Msgr. JOHN BELL; Revs. THOMAS CLOHERTY; J. DOUGLAS DESHOTEL, V.F.; Rev. Msgr. LEON DUESMAN, V.F.; Rev. MIKE DUCA; Rev. Msgr. DONALD FISCHER; Revs. TIM GOLLOB, V.F.; EDUARDO GONZALES, S.D.B.; Rev. Msgr. RICHARD JOHNSON, V.F.; Revs. GREGORY KELLY; ANDREW KOLZOW, O.P.; Rev. Msgr. JOHN MEYERS, V.F.; Revs. HENRY PETTER; WILLIAM RICHARD, V.F.; Rev. Msgr. LAWRENCE PICHARD; Rev. MARK J. SEITZ; Rev. Msgr. DONALD ZIMMERMAN; Rev. ERNESTO TORRES, V.F.

Censor Librorum—Rev. Msgr. GLENN D. GARDNER; Rev. ROBERT M. COERVER.

Diocesan Offices and Directors

Finance Council—Rev. DAVID FLORI, C.P.A.; EUGENE VILFORDI; LOUIS G. MUNIN; J. OLIVER MCGONIGLE; MICHAEL T. WEIS; TOM DORAN.

Building Commission—Rev. Msgr. JEROME P. DUESMAN; Rev. Msgr. LAWRENCE PICHARD; AL SALEM; DAVID FURLOW; MICHAEL T. WEIS.

Pastoral Concerns Board—Rev. Msgr. GLENN D. GARDNER, V.G.; Rev. Msgr. JOHN F. MEYERS; Mrs. MARY EDLUND, Chancellor & Chm.; Mr. BRONSON HAVARD; Mr. WILLIAM KEFFLER; Mrs. KAY ELLIOTT.

Personnel Board—Rev. Msgr. GLENN GARDNER, V.G.; Rev. Msgr. DONALD ZIMMERMAN; Revs. RAMON ALVAREZ; HENRY PETTER; Deacon GEORGE ZACEK; Ms. BEVERLY J. BRADSHAW; Ms. BOZENA CLOUTIER; Mrs. MARY EDLUND; Mr. SHERBIE MATTHEWS.

Ordination & Accreditation Board—Rev. Msgr. JOHN P. BELL; Rev. THOMAS CLOHERTY; Sr. MARIA ELENA FERRER, S.S.N.D.; Deacon JOHN CATSORIS; MARY EDLUND.

Teaching Division

I. Catholic Education—Dr. CHARLES LEBLANC, Dir. Catholic Schools, *P.O. Box 190507, Dallas, 75219.* Tel: 214-528-2360.

Catechetical Services—LILY SALVATO, Dir., *P.O. Box 190507, Dallas, 75219.* Tel: 214-528-2360.

Youth Ministry—SUSAN DORFMEISTER, Dir., *P.O. Box 190507, Dallas, 75219.* Tel: 214-528-2360.

II. Media—

Media Division Head—Rev. Msgr. JOHN BELL, *P.O. Box 190507, Dallas, 75219.* Tel: 214-528-2240.

Newspaper—"The Texas Catholic", Official Catholic Newspaper for the Diocese of Dallas; Most Rev. CHARLES V. GRAHMANN, D.D., Publisher; BRONSON HAVARD, Exec. Editor; ANTONIO RAMIREZ, JR., Business Mgr. Tel: 214-528-8792; Fax: 214-528-3411.

"El Catolico de Texas"—Spanish Language Paper.

Communications Office—MICHAEL MCGEE, Dir. Tel: 214-528-2240.

Sanctifying Division

Worship Office—Rev. T. MICHAEL DUGAN, Dir. Tel: 214-528-2360.

Sacred Places—

Cemeteries—JAMES FOUCH, Exec. Dir., *3235 Lombardy Ln., Dallas, 75220.* Tel: 214-357-5754.

Cathedral Santuario de Guadalupe—Rev. RAMON ALVAREZ, Rector. Tel: 214-871-1362.

Catholic Conference and Formation Center—BARBARA LANDREGAN, Dir., *901 S. Madison Ave., Dallas, 75208., Mailing Address: P.O. Box 190507, Dallas, 75219.* Tel: 214-943-6585; Fax: 214-943-6587.

Sacramental Life Office—Rev. ROBERT COERVER, Dir. Tel: 214-582-2360.

Sacraments of Initiation & Healing—MARTY NOEL, *St. Patrick, 9643 Ferndale, Dallas, 75238.* Tel: 214-348-7380.

Sacrament of Orders—

Seminary—Very Rev. MICHAEL DUCA, Rector, *Holy Trinity Seminary, P.O. Box 140309, Irving, 75014-0309.* Tel: 972-438-2212.

Vocations—Rev. MICHAEL FORGE, Dir.

Diaconal Ministry—Deacon ARNOLD PICON, *901 S. Madison Ave., Dallas, 75208., Mailing Address: P.O. Box 190507, Dallas, 75219.* Tel: 214-943-6585.

Sacrament of Marriage—DIANE DANIELS. Tel: 214-528-2360.

Governing Division

Division Head—MICHAEL T. WEIS, *P.O. Box 190507, Dallas, 75219.* Tel: 214-528-2240.

Business Office—MICHAEL T. WEIS, Dir. Tel: 214-528-2240.

Catholic Community Appeal—PAUL VITANZA, Dir. Tel: 214-528-2240.

Pastoral Planning and Research—LYNN ROSSOL, Dir. Tel: 214-528-2240.

Tribunal—WILLIAM C. HARE, III, J.C.L., Dir. Tel: 214-528-2240.

Archives—STEVE LANDREGAN, Archivist. Tel: 214-528-2240.

Mission Division

Division Head—Sr. MARY ANNE OWENS, S.S.N.D.

Catholic Charities—Sr. MARY ANNE OWENS, S.S.N.D., Dir. Tel: 214-520-6590.

Mission Awareness/Justice and Peace—Sr. NANCY SULLIVAN, D.C., Dir. Tel: 214-528-2240.

CHD Coordinator—Sr. NANCY SULLIVAN, D.C., Dir. Tel: 214-528-2240.

Propagation of Faith and Holy Childhood—Sr. NANCY SULLIVAN, D.C., Dir. Tel: 214-528-2240.

Pastoral Care Ministries—Deacon CHARLIE STUMP, Dir. Tel: 214-528-2240.

Addictions Ministry—PHIL PASCHKE. Tel: 972-960-2166.

Ministries to People with Disabilities—Rev. AUSTIN GREEN, O.P. Tel: 214-528-2240.

Hospital Ministry—Deacon CHARLIE STUMP. Tel: 214-528-2240.

Prison Ministry—Rev. PAUL GRAY, *All Saints Parish, 5231 Meadowcreek, Dallas, 75248.* Tel: 972-778-0307.

Networks

Networks—LYNN ROSSOL, Chm., *P.O. Box 190507, Dallas, 75219.* Tel: 214-528-2240.

Family Life Network—ANN PRAKOPE, Chm.

Asian Network—VIVIEN RIVERA, Chm.

Black Network—Chairmen: EARL OLIVER; LOUIS JENKINS.

Hispanic Network—MARGARET HERNANDEZ, Chm.

Youth Network—JIM GELLER, Chm. Tel: 214-528-2360.

CLERGY, PARISHES, MISSIONS AND PAROCHIAL SCHOOLS

CITY OF DALLAS
(Dallas County)

1—CATHEDRAL-SANTUARIO DE GUADALUPE (1869), Revs. Ramon Alvarez; Salvador Guzman; Deacons Juan Ibarra; Charles Stump; Benito Garcia.
Res., 2215 Ross Ave., 75201. Tel: 214-871-1362; Fax: 214-954-1557.
Catechesis/Religious Programs—Sr. Esther Guerrero, M.C.D.P., D.R.E.
Students 1,550.

2—ALL SAINTS (1976), Revs. Thomas Cloherty; Paul Gray; Richard Weaver; Deacons Denis Simon; Vincent Bathea; John Costello.
Res., 5231 Meadowcreek, 75248. Tel: 972-661-9282; Fax: 972-233-5401.
Catechesis/Religious Programs—Students 458.

3—BLESSED SACRAMENT (1901), Rev. Paul L. Weinberger; Deacons Joe Vollmer-Konig; Jose R. Robles; Ismael A. Guerra.
Res., 231 N. Marsalis Ave., 75203. Tel: 214-948-6535; Fax: 214-948-1660.
Catechesis/Religious Programs—Mr. Francisco Manzo, D.R.E.
Students 2,075.

4—CHRIST THE KING (1941), Rev. Msgr. Donald F. Zimmerman. Pastoral Assocs.: Mary Catherine Hare; William Hare; Deacons Sam Franklin; John de la Garza. In res., Rev. Sean Charles Martin.
Res., 8017 Preston Rd., 75225. Tel: 214-365-1200; Fax: 214-365-1205.
School—4100 Colgate St., 75225. Tel: 214-365-1264; Fax: 214-365-1236.
Lay Teachers 45; Students 418.
Catechesis/Religious Programs—Students 319.

5—HOLY CROSS (1956), Rev. Timothy A. Gollob; Deacons Antonio Trevino; Henry Vault; Armando Murillo; Eliseo Granado. In res., Rev. James George McKenna.
Res., 2926 E. Ledbetter Dr., 75216. Tel: 214-374-7952; Fax: 214-375-7457.
Catechesis/Religious Programs—Students 350.

6—HOLY TRINITY (1907), Revs. Paul W. Sauerbier, C.M.; Thomas Stehlik, C.M.; Deacon Don Forbrich.
Mailing Address: 3826 Gilbert Ave., 75219.
Res., 3811 Oak Lawn Ave., 75219. Tel: 214-526-8555; Fax: 214-526-3477.
School—3815 Oak Lawn Ave., 75219.
Lay Teachers 17; Students 220.
Catechesis/Religious Programs—Students 467.

7—MARY IMMACULATE (1956), Revs. Bruce Bradley; Luis Serna; Deacons Gerard L. Bauwens; Patrick Hayes; William Friedman.
Res., 14032 Dennis Ln., 75234. Tel: 972-243-7104; Fax: 972-406-1254.
School—Tel: 972-243-7105.
Lay Teachers 30; Students 544.
Catechesis/Religious Programs—Judy Grimmett, D.R.E.
Students 1,468.

8—OUR LADY OF LOURDES (1954), Revs. Jesse Torre, O.F.M.Cap. (Spain); Mario Garcia, O.F.M.Cap. (Spain). In res., Very Rev. Ignacio Cizur, O.F.M.Cap. (Spain); Rev. Luis Gerardo Arraiza, O.F.M.Cap. (Spain).
Res., 5605 Bernal Dr., 75212. Tel: 214-637-6673.
Catechesis/Religious Programs—Amy Rodriguez, D.R.E.
Students 880.

9—OUR LADY OF PERPETUAL HELP (1942), Revs. Juan Cruz Gaston, O.F.M.Cap. (Spain); Sabino Erro, O.F.M. (Spain); Deacons Albert Montes; Adolph Orozco, Jr. In res., Rev. Alfonso Casteig, O.F.M.Cap. (Spain).
Res., 7617 Cortland Ave., 75235. Tel: 214-352-6012; Fax: 214-351-9883.
School—7625 Cortland Ave., 75235. Tel: 214-351-3396; Fax: 214-351-9889.
Lay Teachers 13; Students 226.
Catechesis/Religious Programs—Olivia Valenzuela, D.R.E.
Students 607.

10—OUR LADY OF SAN JUAN DE LOS LAGOS AND ST. THERESA (1928), Rev. Alfonso Casteig, O.F.M.Cap. (Spain).
Res., 2601 Singleton Blvd., 75212. Tel: 214-631-9627; Fax: 214-631-6267.
Catechesis/Religious Programs—Tel: 214-688-0942.
Students 163.

11—ST. ANDREW KIM (1977), Rev. Joseph C. Lee.
Res., 2712 Swiss Ave., 75204. Tel: 214-651-9150; Fax: 214-826-9099.
Catechesis/Religious Programs—Ambrose Kim, D.R.E.
Students 109.

12—ST. ANTHONY (1938), Rev. Godwin Oluoha, Admin.
Res., 2711 Romine St., 75215. Tel: 214-428-6926.
School—3732 Myrtle St., 75215. Tel: 214-421-3645; Fax: 214-421-7416.
Lay Teachers 18; Students 215.

13—ST. AUGUSTINE CATHOLIC CHURCH (1937), Revs. Ernesto Torres; Dindo Cuario; Deacon Robert Sanchez. In res., Rev. Solh Saez.
Res., 1047 N. St. Augustine Dr., 75217. Tel: 214-398-1513; Fax: 214-398-2580.
School—1064 N. St. Augustine Dr., 75217. Tel: 214-391-1381; Fax: 214-391-8781.
Sisters 2; Lay Teachers 12; Students 173.
Catechesis/Religious Programs—Sr. Catherine Killoran, S.H.Sp., D.R.E.
Students 1,354.

14—ST. BERNARD OF CLAIRVAUX (1947), Rev. August A. Melito; Deacon John Kelly.
Res., 1404 Old Gate Ln., 75218. Tel: 214-321-0454; Fax: 214-320-0119.
School—1420 Old Gate Ln., 75218. Tel: 214-321-2897; Fax: 214-321-4060.
Lay Teachers 22; Students 332.
Catechesis/Religious Programs—Juanita Mitchell, D.R.E.
Students 498.

15—ST. CECILIA (1933), Rev. Edmundo Paredes; Deacons Gonzalo Gonzales; Onesimo Martinez. In res., Rev. Msgr. Mario Magbanua.
Res., 1809 W. Davis St., 75208. Tel: 214-941-5821; Fax: 214-946-4466.
School—635 Marycliff Rd., 75208. Tel: 214-948-8628.
Sisters of St. Mary of Namur 1; Lay Teachers 11; Students 220.
Catechesis/Religious Programs—Students 1,077.

16—ST. EDWARD (1903), Revs. Eduardo Gonzalez, S.D.B.; Rodolfo Garcia; Deacons Juan G. Gonzalez; Guadalupe Carreon.
Res., 4014 Simpson St., 75246. Tel: 214-823-1291; Fax: 214-823-7535.
Catechesis/Religious Programs—Claudia Mora, D.R.E.
Students 925.

17—ST. ELIZABETH (1956), Revs. T. Michael Dugan; Fred Sidler; Alex Buitrago; Deacons Edward Jones; Denis Simon.
Res., 4015 S. Hampton Rd., 75224. Tel: 214-331-4328; Fax: 214-331-2464.

School—4019 S. Hampton Rd., 75224. Tel: 214-331-5139; Fax: 214-467-4346.
Lay Teachers 21; Students 394.
Catechesis/Religious Programs—Mrs. Thelma Cooper, D.R.E.
Students 106.

18—ST. JAMES (1934), Rev. Efren Ortega; Deacons Vincent F. Jimenez; Jose Lincon.
Mailing Address: P.O. Box 763338, 75376.
Res., 1002 E. Saner Ave., 75216. Tel: 214-371-9209; Fax: 214-371-0226.
Catechesis/Religious Programs—Students 685.

19—ST. JUDE CHAPEL AND INFORMATION CENTER (Downtown Dallas) (1968), Rev. Gilbert J. Graham, O.P., Admin.
Res., 1521 Main St., 75201. Tel: 214-742-2508; Fax: 214-748-5282.

20—ST. MARY OF CARMEL (1944), Rev. Jesus Sancho, O.C.D.
Res., 2900 Vilbig Rd., 75212. Tel: 214-747-1433; Fax: 214-748-7481.
School—1716 Singleton Blvd., 75212. Tel: 214-748-2934; Fax: 214-760-9052.
Sisters of the Holy Spirit 4; Lay Teachers 11; Students 168.
Catechesis/Religious Programs—Students 255.

21—ST. MONICA (1954), Revs. John F. Meyers; Brindley Mills; Jonathan G. Austin; Anibal Adorno; Deacons Larry Lucido; Bob Marrinan; Brian Mitchell; Abel Cortes.
Res., 9933 Midway Rd., 75220. Tel: 214-358-1453; Fax: 214-351-1887.
School—4140 Walnut Hill Ln., 75229. Tel: 214-351-5688; Fax: 214-352-2608.
Lay Teachers 56; Students 894.
Catechesis/Religious Programs—Ms. Patricia Foley, D.R.E.
Students 1,037.

22—ST. PATRICK (1963), Rev. Msgr. Richard E. Johnson; Rev. John Libone; Deacon John C. Nordick.
Res., 9643 Ferndale Rd., 75238. Tel: 214-348-7380; Fax: 214-340-5956.
School—9635 Ferndale Rd., 75238. Tel: 214-348-8070; Fax: 214-503-7230.
Sisters of the Incarnate Word and Blessed Sacrament 2; Lay Teachers 31; Students 534.
Catechesis/Religious Programs—Mrs. Martha Noel, D.R.E.
Students 569.

23—ST. PETER (1905), Rev. Stanislaw Michalek, S.Ch.
Res., 2907 Woodall Rodgers Fwy., 75204. Tel: 214-855-1384; Fax: 214-855-1309.
Catechesis/Religious Programs—Students 95. D.R.E.: Mercy Hamilton; Sr. Teresa Mika.

24—ST. PETER VIETNAMESE CATHOLIC MISSION (1996), Rev. Jospeh Bau Chau, C.S.S.R.
10123 Garland Rd., 75218. Tel: 214-320-2219.

25—ST. PHILIP (1954), Rev. Stephen J. Mocio.
Res., 8131 Military Pkwy., 75227. Tel: 214-388-5464; Fax: 214-388-2839.
School—8151 Military Pkwy., 75227. Tel: 214-381-4973; Fax: 214-381-0466.
Sisters of the Holy Spirit 3; Lay Teachers 15; Students 233.
Catechesis/Religious Programs—Jeannine McClellan, D.R.E.
Students 256.

26—ST. PIUS X (1954), Rev. Msgr. Larry Pichard; Revs. Cliff Garner; Denis O'Brien, M.M.; Deacons David Leerssen; Michael Shaw; John Schell.
Res., 3030 Gus Thomasson Rd., 75228. Tel: 972-279-6155; Fax: 972-686-7510.
School—Tel: 972-279-2339; Fax: 972-613-2059.
Lay Teachers 33; Students 601.
Catechesis/Religious Programs—Tel: 972-279-2558. Kassie Andries, D.R.E.
Students 910.

27—ST. RITA (1961), Revs. Gerald Hughes, S.J.; John J. Heaney, S.J.; Patrick H. Koch, S.J.; Wayne Herpin, S.J.; Deacons William Schuster; Charles Sylvester; Michael McLean.
Office: 12521 Inwood Rd., 75244. Tel: 972-934-8388; Fax: 972-934-8965.
Res., 12626 Planters Glen, 75244. Tel: 972-239-5205.
School—12525 Inwood Rd., 75244. Tel: 972-239-3203; Fax: 972-934-3657.
Lay Teachers 42; Students 633.
Catechesis/Religious Programs—Deacon William Schuster, D.R.E.
Students 453.

28—ST. THOMAS AQUINAS (1952), Rev. Stephen W. Bierschenk.
Res., 6306 Kenwood Ave., 75214. Tel: 214-821-3360; Fax: 214-821-5395.
School—3741 Abrams Rd., 75214. Tel: 214-826-0566; Fax: 214-826-0251.
Lay Teachers 51; Students 563.
Catechesis/Religious Programs—Mrs. Mary Xuereb, D.R.E.
Students 228.

29—SANTA CLARA (1993), Revs. David L. Colella, O.SS.T.; Antonio Liberman Ormaza, S.C.S. (Ecuador); Deacon Alberto Villarreal.
Res., 321 Calumet St., 75211. Tel: 214-337-3936; Fax: 214-333-9148.
School—Santa Clara of Assisi Catholic Academy, Tel: 214-333-9423. Ms. Elizabeth Lopez, Prin.
Catechesis/Religious Programs—Students 800.

OUTSIDE THE CITY OF DALLAS

Allen, Collin Co., St. Jude (1981), Revs. Timothy A. Church, Admin.; George Monaghan; Deacons Ronald Fejeran; Shawn French; George Polcer.
Mailing Address: P.O. Box 869, 75013.
Res., 1515 N. Greenville, 75002. Tel: 972-727-1177; Fax: 972-727-1401.
Catechesis/Religious Programs—Tel: 972-727-9998. Carole Anne Horstman, D.R.E.
Students 1,300.

Bonham, Fannin Co., St. Elizabeth, Rev. Felix Vistal, Jr.; Deacons Joe Culling; William Beste.
Res., 409 W. 10th St., 75418. Tel: 903-583-7734; Fax: 903-583-7359.

Carrollton, Dallas Co., Sacred Heart of Jesus Christ (1999), Rev. Joseph Son Nguyen.
2121 N. Denton, 75006. Tel: 972-446-3461; Fax: 972-446-9551.

Commerce, Hunt Co., St. Joseph (1895), Rev. D. Stanley Corcoran.
Res., 2904 Melmar Pk., 75428. Tel: 903-886-7135.
Catechesis/Religious Programs—Students 125.

Coppell, Dallas Co., St. Ann (1985), Rev. Msgr. Kilian J. Broderick; Rev. John Dick; Deacons Ed Scarbrough; Joe Salvo; Pedro Herran.
Church—180 Samuel Blvd., 75019. Tel: 972-393-5544; 393-7951 (Res.); Fax: 972-462-1617.
Catechesis/Religious Programs—Tel: 972-393-2725. Sr. Ruth Ellen Dean, D.R.E.
Students 2,160.

Corsicana, Navarro Co., Immaculate Conception (1871), Rev. Robert Williams; Deacon Lewis Palos.
Res., 3000 Hwy. 22 W., P.O. Box 798, 75151. Tel: 903-874-4473; Fax: 903-874-2619.
School—James L. Collins Catholic School, Tel: 903-872-1751.
Lay Teachers 13; Students 185.
Catechesis/Religious Programs—Charles Bonin, D.R.E.
Students 171.

Denison, Grayson Co., St. Patrick (1872), Deacon Gary Vogel, Pastoral Admin.
Res., 314 N. Rusk Ave., 75020. Tel: 903-463-3275; Fax: 903-463-3447.
Catechesis/Religious Programs—D.R.E.: Catherine L. Haraldsen; Philip W. Melton.
Students 150.

Duncanville, Dallas Co., Holy Spirit (1974), Revs. Timothy Heines; Michael Guadagnoli, P.V.; Deacons Eugene Schlebach; Les Alt.
Res., 1111 W. Danieldale Rd., 75137-3719. Tel: 972-298-4971; Fax: 972-709-1443.
Catechesis/Religious Programs—D.R.E.: Aggie Gladbach; Nanette Corbitt.
Students 795.

Ennis, Ellis Co., St. John Nepomucene (1902), Rev. Fred Caldwell; Deacons Dean Darnall; Don Griffith; Frutos Vega.
Res., 401 E. Lampasas St., 75119. Tel: 972-878-2834; Fax: 972-875-2452. [CEM]
School—701 S. Paris St., 75119. Tel: 972-878-5411; Fax: 972-878-2226.
Sisters of Divine Providence 4; Lay Teachers 10; Students 144.
High School—Lay Teachers 11; Students 89.
Catechesis/Religious Programs—Students 438.

Ferris, Ellis Co., Corpus Christi (1977), Rev. Raul Garza, C.M.
Res., 117 N. Wood, 75125. Tel: 972-842-2288; Fax: 972-842-2288.
Catechesis/Religious Programs—Students 127.

Forney, Kaufman Co., St. Martin (1891), Rev. Joseph A. Mehan, Jr.; Deacon Craig McAlister.
Res., 806 N. Washington St., Kaufman, 75142. Tel: 972-962-3247; Fax: 972-962-3247.
Catechesis/Religious Programs—Students 146.

Frisco, Collin Co., St. Francis of Assisi (1966), Rev. Msgr. Leon Duesman; Rev. John Heugh; Deacons Frank Reyna; Joe McQuade.
Res., 8760 Third St., 75034. Tel: 972-712-2645; Fax: 972-712-1087.
Catechesis/Religious Programs—Students 544.

Garland, Dallas Co.,

1—GOOD SHEPHERD, (1944), Revs. Robert R. Crisp; Ernesto Villarroya (Philippines); Deacon Leroy Berens. In res., Rev. Abraham Chacko (India).
Res., 201 S. 13th St., 75040. Tel: 972-276-8587; Fax: 972-494-3653.
School—214 S. Garland Ave., 75040. Tel: 972-272-6533; Fax: 972-272-0512.
Brothers 1; Lay Teachers 27; Students 305.
Catechesis/Religious Programs—Alex Sandoval, D.R.E.
Students 524.

2—MOTHER OF PERPETUAL HELP, (Vietnamese), Revs. Dominic Hai Dinh, C.SS.R.; Thong Nguyen, C.SS.R.
Res., 2121 Apollo Rd., 75044. Tel: 972-414-7073.
Catechesis/Religious Programs—Bro. Nghia Ho, D.R.E.
Students 300.

3—ST. MARY MALANKARA, (1996), Rev. Abraham Chacko.
116 E. Ave. D, 75040. Tel: 972-494-5356.
Res., c/o Good Shepherd Church, 201 S. 13th St., 75040. Tel: 972-272-4641; Fax: 972-494-3653.
Catechesis/Religious Programs—Students 36.

4—ST. MICHAEL THE ARCHANGEL, (1980), Rev. James R. Sharp, Ph.D., Admin.; Deacon Joe Perez. In res., Rev. Marcus Chidozie.
Res., 950 Trails Pkwy., 75043. Tel: 972-279-6581; 681-8026 (Rectory); Fax: 972-279-6647.
Catechesis/Religious Programs—Adela Miller, D.R.E.
Students 1,172.

5—ST. THOMAS THE APOSTLE, (1992), Rev. John Melepuram.
Res., 4922 Rose Hill Rd., 75043. Tel: 972-303-5404.
Catechesis/Religious Programs—Students 154.

Grand Prairie, Dallas Co.,

1—IMMACULATE CONCEPTION (1916), REVS. MATTHEW BAGERT; ALBERT CUSCHIERI; DEACONS FERNANDO L. ARGUMANIZ; MANUEL VEYNA; MICHAEL S. RASINS; JESSE GONZALES; DAVID MAIDA.
Res., 610 N.E. 17th St., 75050. Tel: 972-262-5137; Fax: 972-264-7657.
School—400 N.E. 17th St., 75050. Tel: 972-264-8777; Fax: 972-264-7742.
Sisters of the Holy Family of Nazareth 3; Lay Teachers 17; Students 307.
Catechesis/Religious Programs—Diane Gutierrez, D.R.E.
Students 820.

2—ST. JOSEPH VIETNAMESE CATHOLIC COMMUNITY (1993), REV. PETER PHONG NGUYEN.
Res., 802 E. Coral Way, 75051. Tel: 972-264-9441.
Catechesis/Religious Programs—Students 248.

3—ST. MICHAEL THE ARCHANGEL (1985), REV. CLIFFORD G. SMITH, ADMIN.; DEACON DENNIS BRYANT.
2910 Corn Valley, 75052.
Res., 2925 Lake Park Dr., 75051. Tel: 972-262-0552; Fax: 972-642-5429.
Catechesis/Religious Programs—Tel: 972-262-6590.
Students 296.

Greenville, Hunt Co., St. William (1892), Rev. Antonio Oscar Diez, Admin.; Deacon Lee Davis.
Res., 4300 Stuart St., 75401. Tel: 903-450-1177; Fax: 903-455-7134.
Catechesis/Religious Programs—Tel: 903-455-8201. Carolyn Dorman, D.R.E.
Students 246.
Mission—Quinlan, Hunt Co., Our Lady of Fatima, 1979 E. Quinlan Pkwy., 57474.

Irving, Dallas Co., Chapel of the Incarnation (1973), Denise Phillips, Admin.
Res., University of Dallas, 1845 E. Northgate Dr., 75062. Tel: 972-721-5375; Fax: 972-721-5351.

Holy Family of Nazareth (1964), Rev. Msgr. Jerome P. Duesman; Rev. Aidan O'Donovan, M.S.C.; Deacons Lee Stieber; Kenneth Hale; Robert Miller; Fred Bourland.
Res., 2330 Cheyenne St., 75062. Tel: 972-252-5521; Fax: 972-252-5523.
School—2323 Cheyenne St., 75062. Tel: 972-255-0205; Fax: 972-252-4167.
Sisters of the Holy Family of Nazareth 2; Lay Teachers 27; Students 377.
Catechesis/Religious Programs—Kay Lehrberger, D.R.E.
Students 314.

St. Luke (1902), Rev. J. Douglas Deshotel, V.F.; Deacons Louis F. Adelmann; Jose Trevino; Daniel Segovia. In res., Rev. Jose Luis Azcona, O.C.D.
Res., 1015 Schulze Dr., 75060. Tel: 972-259-3222; Fax: 972-259-3339.
School—1023 Schulze Dr., 75060. Tel: 972-253-8285; Fax: 972-259-3339.
Lay Teachers 20; Students 301.
Catechesis/Religious Programs—Jo Ann Dreyer, D.R.E.
Students 1,052.

Kaufman, Kaufman Co., St. Ann (1935), Rev. Joseph A. Mehan, Jr.; Deacons James Burkel; Hector Pena; Sergio Morales; Craig McAlister.
Res., 806 N. Washington St., 75142. Tel: 972-962-3247.

Catechesis/Religious Programs—Nick Gigneaux, D.R.E.
Students 173.

Lancaster, Dallas Co., St. Francis of Assisi (1973), Rev. Arthur D. Mallinson; Deacons Jose F. Hernandez; Ed Armsted.
Res., 1001 Alicia, 75134. Tel: 972-227-4124; Fax: 972-227-2882.
Catechesis/Religious Programs—Tel: 972-227-0770. Sherry Granello, D.R.E.
Students 340.

McKinney, Collin Co., St. Gabriel the Archangel (1996), Rev. Gregory Kelly; Deacon Vic Machiano.
Mailing Address: 2110 Rockhill Rd., 75070. Tel: 972-562-0638; Fax: 214-544-1488.
Catechesis/Religious Programs—Students 495.
St. Michael (1892), Rev. J. Carl Vogel.
Res., 411 Paula Rd., 75069. Tel: 972-562-4444; Fax: 972-562-0752.
Catechesis/Religious Programs—Barbara Woodroof, D.R.E.
Students 403.
Mission—Van Alstyne, Grayson Co., Holy Family, P.O. Box 482, Van Alstyne 75495.

Plano, Collin Co., Prince of Peace (1991), Revs. R. James Balint; Lawrence A. Beyer; Deacons Robert Staib; Louis L. Munoz; David E. Tompsett.
Res., 5100 W. Plano Pkwy., 75093. Tel: 972-380-2100; Fax: 972-380-5162.
School—Tel: 972-380-5505; Fax: 972-380-2570.
Lay Teachers 42; Students 589.
Catechesis/Religious Programs—Students 878.
St. Elizabeth Ann Seton (1976), Revs. Henry V. Petter; Robert Shortall (DAV); Andrew V. Semler; Deacons Ted Perez; Thomas Roche; Bill Flynn; Harry Pusateri; Roger David; Mike Picard.
Res., 2800 Piedra Ln., 75023. Tel: 972-596-5505; Fax: 972-985-7573.
Catechesis/Religious Programs—Tel: 972-596-1923; Fax: 972-985-0431. D.R.E.: Mary Frazier; Jim Gelller.
Students 3,025.
St. Mark the Evangelist (1966), Rev. Msgr. Glenn D. Gardner; Revs. Thomas M. Speiser; Godwin Oluoha (Nigeria); Deacons Bob Scoggins; Michael A. Carrell; Ed Putonti; Arnold Picon. In res., Rev. Mark Link, S.J.
Res., 1201 Alma Dr., 75075. Tel: 972-423-5600; Fax: 972-423-5024.
School—Tel: 972-578-0610; Fax: 972-423-3299.
Lay Teachers 37; Students 621.
Catechesis/Religious Programs—Deacon Mike Carrell, D.R.E.
Students 1,558.

Richardson, Dallas Co., Mission of the Sacred Heart of Jesus (1993) (Chinese), Rev. Peter Chen.
Res., 14277 Preston Rd. #1027, Dallas, 75240. Tel: 972-716-0077; Fax: 972-789-9537.
Church—812 S. Sherman, 75081. Tel: 972-480-8472.
Catechesis/Religious Programs—Bernadette Wang, D.R.E.
Students 53.
St. Joseph (1976), Rev. Msgr. Don L. Fischer; Rev. William Hebekeuser; Deacon Jim Daniels.
Res., 600 S. Jupiter Rd., 75081. Tel: 972-231-2951; Fax: 972-231-2875.
Catechesis/Religious Programs—Tel: 972-690-5588.
Students 872.
St. Paul the Apostle (1956), Rev. David J. Flori; Deacons Carl Thelin; Paul Reittinger; Jesse Olivarez.
Res., 709 James Dr., 75080. Tel: 972-235-6105; Fax: 972-480-8528.
School—720 S. Floyd Rd., 75080. Tel: 972-235-3263; Fax: 972-690-1542.
Lay Teachers 28; Students 476.
Catechesis/Religious Programs—Tel: 972-235-2598; Fax: 972-664-9993. Jeremy (Jerri) Brandenburg, D.R.E.
Students 761.

Rockwall, Rockwall Co., Our Lady of the Lake (1978), Rev. William Richard; Deacons Jesus Cerrato; Clifford Kopinski; Bronson Havard.
Res., P.O. Box 191, 75087. Tel: 972-771-6671 (Office); Fax: 972-771-7283.
Catechesis/Religious Programs—Tel: 972-771-4253. Aline Kindle, D.R.E.
Students 475.

Rowlett, Dallas Co., Sacred Heart (1899), Rev. Daniel J. Clayton; Deacons Frank Dunlop, Sr.; James Welsh; Paul Husting; Ken Melston.
Res., 3905 Hickox Rd., 75088. Tel: 972-475-4405; Fax: 972-475-6658.
Catechesis/Religious Programs—Sandy Guancial, D.R.E.
Students 367.

Sherman, Grayson Co., St. Mary (1872), Revs. Jeremy Myers; Antonio Aureus; Deacons John Le Blanc; Tomas Avila.
Res., 727 S. Travis, 75090. Tel: 903-893-5148; Fax: 903-813-5489.
School—713 Travis St., 75090. Tel: 903-893-2127.
Lay Teachers 15; Students 165.
Catechesis/Religious Programs—Annie Kremer, D.R.E.
Students 242.
Mission—Whitesboro, Grayson Co., St. Francis of Assisi.

Terrell, Kaufman Co., St. John (1876), Rev. George J. Weber, C.M.; Deacons Leo Rener; Fermin Rodriquez.
Res., 701 N. Frances St., 75160. Tel: 972-563-3643; Fax: 972-563-9718.
Catechesis/Religious Programs—Susan Warner, D.R.E.
Students 316.

Waxahachie, Ellis Co., St. Joseph (1875), Rev. Mark Joseph Seitz; Most Rev. Thomas Tschoepe; Rev. Jerome Jayasuriya; Deacons Denver Crawley; Hugo Monsanto; Larry Hatch; Denis Corbin.
Office: 512 E. Marvin St., Waxahachi, 75165.
Res., 504 E. Marvin St., 75165. Tel: 972-938-1953; Fax: 972-938-1956.
School—St. Joseph Catholic School, 506 E. Marvin St., 75165. Tel: 972-938-2652. Erin Finn, Prin.
Lay Teachers 9; Students 117.
Catechesis/Religious Programs—Tel: 972-938-2858. Cheryl Bain, D.R.E.
Students 525.
Mission—Italy, Ellis Co., Epiphany, 434 S. Ward, Italy, 76651.

Wylie, Collin Co., St. Anthony (1900), Rev. Loyd Morris, Admin.; Deacons Peter Martinez; Warner Washington; Walter Gove.
Res., 404 N. Ballard, 75098. Tel: 972-442-2765; Fax: 972-429-9215. [CEM]
Catechesis/Religious Programs—Students 422.

Chaplains of Public Institutions

DALLAS. *Veterans Administration Hospital* 2926 E. Ledbetter Dr., 75216. Tel: 214-374-7952. Rev. Timothy A. Gollob.

BONHAM. *Veterans Administration Hospital* 404 W. 10th St., 75418. Tel: 903-583-4942. Rev. Felix Vistal, Jr.

GRAND PRAIRIE. *Hensley Field Naval Base*. Vacant.

SEAGOVILLE. *Federal Correctional Institution*. Vacant.

TERRELL. *State Hospital* 702 N. Frances St., 75160. Tel: 972-563-3643. Rev. George J. Weber, C.M.

Special Assignment:
Reverend Fathers—
Lucio, Justin, 5904 Ross Ave., Dallas, TX 75206
Pratt, Dean, Hospital Ministry, 906 Lake Point Cir., McKinney, TX 75070

On Duty Outside the Diocese:
Reverend Fathers—
Drozd, Henry J., P.O. Box 42063, Savannah, GA 31409-0001
Hopka, John, P.O. Box 07912, Milwaukee, WI 53207
McKenna, James George, P.O. Box 190507, Dallas, TX 75219
Phan, Cho Dink Peter, Catholic University

Absent on Leave:
Reverend Fathers—
Brown, Richard
Cox, Robert
Honea, Lonnie
Saldana, Jose
Tullius, Richard

Retired:
Reverend Monsignors—
Gulczynski, John T., 3700 Abrams Rd., Dallas, TX 75214
Johnson, Edwin, 213 Goodford Rd., Philadelphia, PA 19154
Johnson, Robert, 14 Greccio Ct., Crowley, TX 76036
McCallum, John V., 3406 Tipps Dr., Greenville, TX 75401
Rehkemper, Robert C., Our Lady of Good Hope, P.O. Box 517, Hope, AR 71801
Weinzapfel, Thomas, 321 Crooked Creek, Garland, TX 75043
Reverend Fathers—
Eades, B. G., 1503 Cedar Hill Ave., Dallas, TX 75208
Fernandez, Edward P., 5392 Bramble Ln., Las Vegas, NV 89120
Flanagan, Michael, 2061 Province Ln., Dallas, TX 75228
Fowler, John W., 1444 Rodando, Garland, TX 75042. Tel: 972-205-9307
Haberman, Lawrence R., 620 Blanton Dr. #125, Sherman, TX 75092
Haugh, John, St. Francis, Frisco, TX
Lynch, Patrick
O'Rourke, John G., V
Roberts, Kenneth
Schumacher, William
Scott, Raymond, 6011 Melody Ln. #403, Dallas, TX 75231
Slovacek, Emil C., 1815 Hamlet, Dallas, TX 75203
White, Gale, 4306 Walnut Hill Ln., Dallas, TX 75229. Tel: 214-357-4312

Permanent Deacons:
Adelman, Louis
Alt, Les
Argumaniz, Fernando L.
Armstead, Edward
Arredondo, Pastor G., (Retired)
Avila, Tomas
Bathea, Val Vincent
Bauwens, Gerald
Berens, LeRoy J.
Beste, William B.
Bourland, Fred
Bryant, Dennis Phillip
Burkel, James
Carrell, Michael A.
Carreon, Guadalupe A.
Catsoris, John A., On Duty Outside the Diocese
Cerrato, Jesus, Jr.
Chung, Hoan Moses
Coffey, Thomas, On Duty Outside the Diocese
Corbin, Denis D.
Cortes, Abel
Costello, John R.
Crawley, Denver
Culling, Joseph
Daniels, James
Darnall, Dean
Davis, Lee B.
Davis, Roger
De La Garza, John
Delin, Fred O.
Dorsey, Timothy, On Duty Outside the Diocese
Dunlop, Frank W., Sr.
Elsberg, Alick, On Duty Outside the Diocese
Fejeran, Ronald
Flynn, Bill
Forbrich, Donald
Franklin, Sam
Freeman, Mike, On Duty Outside the Diocese
French, Shawn Patrick
Friedman, William L.
Gaines, Stanley
Garcia, Benito
Gonzales, Gonzalo
Gonzales, Jesse
Gonzales, Juan G.
Gonzalez, Ronald, On Duty Outside the Diocese
Gordon, Ralph R., (Retired)
Gove, Walter
Granado, Eliseo
Griffith, Don
Guerra, Ismael A.
Hale, Kenneth, Inactive
Hancock, John, On Duty Outside the Diocese
Harvard, Bronson
Hatch, Larry G.
Hayes, Pat
Henvey, Thomas, On Duty Outside the Diocese
Hernandez, Jose F.
Herran, Pedro
Husting, Paul
Ibarra, Juan
Jimenez, Roberto, On Duty Outside the Diocese
Jimenez, Vincent
Jones, Edward S.
Kelly, John Paul
Kopinski, Clifford H.
Kozarevich, Frank
LeBlanc, John D.
Leerssen, David
Leicht, Robert R., Jr., On Duty Outside the Diocese
Lincon, Jose
Lucido, Larry
Lugo, Lonie
Macero, Carl, On Duty Outside the Diocese
Machiano, Vic
Maida, David
Marrinan, Robert, Sr.
Martinez, Onesimo
Martinez, Pete A., (Retired)
McAlister, Craig
McLean, Michael J.
McQuade, Joseph
Melston, Kenneth
Miller, Carl V., On Duty Outside the Diocese
Miller, J. Robert
Milliken, Frank M.
Mitchell, Brian

Monsanto, Hugo
Montes, Alberto
Morales, Sergio
Muldoon, Tim
Munoz, Louis L.
Murillo, Armando
Nordick, John C.
Noriega, Ramon, On Duty Outside the Diocese
Olivarez, Jesse
Olvera, Isidro
Orozco, Adolph, Jr.
Palos, Lewis J.
Pena, Hector B.
Perez, Joe R.
Perez, Ted, Jr., (Retired)
Picard, Michael
Picon, Arnold
Polcer, George
Pusateri, Harry, (Retired)
Putonti, Edward
Rasins, Michael
Reisor, Kenneth
Rener, Bonnie Leo
Rettinger, Paul
Reyna, Frank
Ricard, Robert A., (Retired)
Robles, Jose R.
Roche, Thomas
Rodriguez, Fermin
Rodriguez, Pedro P.
Salerno, John, On Duty Outside the Diocese
Salinas, Hugo A.
Salvo, Joseph
Sanchez, Robert
Scarbrough, Ed
Schell, John A.
Schlebach, Eugene M.
Schnurr, Don, (Retired)
Schuster, William J.
Scoggins, Robert C., Jr.
Segovia, Daniel D.
Shaw, Michael, Jr.
Simon, Denis
Slovacek, Emil
Staib, Bob
Stieber, Lee
Stump, Charles, Jr.
Sykora, Richard
Sylvester, Charles T.
Thelin, Carl
Thompoett, David
Trevino, Antonio D.
Trevino, Jose
Van Scoy, Donald G.
Vara, Rudolph R., (Retired)
Vault, Henry, Jr.
Vega, Frutos
Veyna, Manuel
Villarreal, Albert
Vogel, Gary M.
Vollmer-Konig, Josef
Washington, Warner
Webb, Philip E., On Duty Outside the Diocese
Weithman, James C., (Retired)
Welsh, James L.
Wong, Peter
Zacek, George E., On Duty Outside the Diocese
Zoeller, William C., On Duty Outside the Diocese

INSTITUTIONS LOCATED IN THE DIOCESE

[A] SEMINARIES, DIOCESAN

IRVING. *Holy Trinity Seminary*, P.O. Box 140309, 75014-0309. Tel: 972-438-2212; Fax: 972-438-6530.
E-mail: htsirv@cathdal.org
Diocesan College and Pre-Theology Seminary. Very Rev. Michael Duca, Rector; Revs. James Orosco, Vice Rector; Jose Luis Ortega, Formation; John Collet, Spiritual Dir. & Coord. Liturgy; Sr. St. John Begnaud, S.S.M.N., Academic Dean; Mr. Henry McDowell, Dir. Music; Mr. Eric Hendry, Formation. Priests 4; Seminarians 45. In res. Joseph Galante.

[B] COLLEGES AND UNIVERSITIES

IRVING. *University of Dallas*, President's Office, 1845 E. Northgate, 75062. Tel: 972-721-5000; Fax: 972-721-5017
For a complete listing, refer to the Colleges and Universities section.

[C] HIGH SCHOOLS, DIOCESAN

DALLAS. *Bishop Dunne Catholic School, Inc.* (Grades 7-12). (Coed), 3900 Rugged Dr., 75224. Tel: 214-339-6561; Fax: 214-339-1438.
E-mail: kdailey@bdhs.org
Web site: www.bdhs.org
Kate C. Collins Dailey, Prin. Lay Teachers 45; Administrators 6; Students 538.

Bishop Lynch High School, Inc., 9750 Ferguson Rd., 75228. Tel: 214-324-3607; Fax: 214-324-3600.
E-mail: leyde@mail.bishoplynch.org
Web site: www.bishoplynch.org
Mr. Edward E. Leyden, Pres.; Carol Olsen, Prin.; Rev. Victor Bartolotta. Lay Teachers 75; Students 1,088.

[D] HIGH SCHOOLS, PRIVATE

DALLAS. *Jesuit College Preparatory School.* (Boys), 12345 Inwood Rd., 75244. Tel: 972-387-8700; Fax: 972-661-9349.
Web site: http://www.jesuitcp.org
Society of Jesus. Mr. Michael A. Earsing, Prin.; Revs. Michael D. Dooley, S.J., Rector; Philip S. Postell, S.J., Pres.; Eugene Sessa, S.J.; John F. Deeves, S.J.; Charles A. Leininger, S.J.; John G. Stack, S.J.; Mitchell Pacwa, S.J.; Arthur Demkowicz, S.J.; Bro. Gerald J. Landry, S.J. Priests 7; Lay Teachers 76; Students 930; Scholastics 1.

Ursuline Academy. (Girls), 4900 Walnut Hill Ln., 75229. Tel: 214-363-6551; Fax: 214-363-5524.
E-mail: dwilson@ursuline.pvt.kiz.tx.us
Web site: www.ursuline.pvt.kiz.tx.us
Sr. Margaret Ann Moser, O.S.U., Pres.; Elizabeth C. Bourgeois, Prin. Faculty 85; Students 783.

IRVING. *Cistercian Preparatory School.* (Boys), One Cistercian Rd., 75039-4599. Tel: 972-273-2022; Fax: 972-554-2294.
E-mail: pverhalen@cistercian.org
Web site: www.cistercian.org
Cistercian Fathers of Our Lady of Dallas Abbey. Rev. Peter Verhalen, O.Cist., Headmaster. Priests 9; Lay Teachers 24; Students 347.

The Highlands School, 1451 E. Northgate Dr., 75062. Tel: 972-554-1980; Fax: 972-721-1691.
E-mail: highlands@thehighlandsschool.org
Web site: www.TheHighlandsSchool.org
Rev. Steven Reilly, L.C., Pres.; Mr. Mark Salisbury, Prin.; Revs. Eugene Gormley, L.C., Chap.; Edward Hopkins, L.C. Lay Teachers 36; High School Students 72; Elementary 411.

[E] ELEMENTARY SCHOOLS, PRIVATE

DALLAS. *Prince of Peace - Dallas*, 4500 W. Davis St., 75211. Tel: 214-337-0244; Fax: 214-339-1702. Gretchen Montgomery, Prin. Lay Teachers 10; Students 141.

IRVING. *Cistercian Preparatory School.* (Boys), One Cistercian Rd., 75039. Tel: 214-438-4956; Fax: 214-554-0736. Cistercian Fathers of Our Lady of Dallas Abbey. Rev. Peter Verhalen, O.Cist., Headmaster. Priests 9; Lay Teachers 24; Students 337.

The Highland School, 1451 E. Northgate Drive, 75062. Tel: 972-554-1980; Fax: 972-721-1691. Rev. Steven Reilly, L.C., Pres.; Dr. Michael Pennell, Prin. & Dean of Studies; Mark Salisbury, Prin.; Rev. Eugene Gormley, L.C., Chap.

[F] SPECIAL SCHOOLS, PRIVATE

DALLAS. *Notre Dame of Dallas Schools, Inc.*, 2018 Allen St., 75204. Tel: 214-720-3911; Fax: 214-720-3913.
E-mail: notredm@swbell.net
Day School: Provides instructional education for mentally retarded children, ages 5-15. Ms. Theresa Francis, Prin. Students 125. Vocational Center: Provides vocational training for young adults, ages 15-21. Sisters 2; Lay Staff 30.

[G] GENERAL HOSPITALS

DALLAS. *St. Paul Medical Center*, 5909 Harry Hines Blvd., 75235. Tel: 214-879-1000
For a complete listing, refer to the Hospitals section.

St. Paul Medical Center, 5909 Harry Hines Blvd., 75235
For a complete listing, refer to the Hospitals section.

St. Paul Medical Center Foundation Inc., 5909 Harry Hines Blvd., 75235. Tel: 214-879-2000; Fax: 214-879-2019
For a complete listing, refer to the Hospitals section.

IRVING. *CHRISTUS Health Irving System Office*, 6363 N. Hwy. 161, Ste. 450, 75038. Tel: 877-980-0100; Fax: 214-492-8550.
Web site: www.Christushealth.org
For a complete listing, refer to the Hospitals section.

[H] CATHOLIC CHARITIES

DALLAS. *Catholic Charities*, 3725 Blackburn St., P.O. Box 190507, 75219. Tel: 214-520-6590; Fax: 214-520-6595.
E-mail: mowens@cathdal.org
Sr. Mary Ann Owens, S.S.N.D.

Catholic Counseling Services, 3725 Blackburn St., P.O. Box 190507, 75219. Tel: 214-526-2772; Fax: 214-526-2941.
E-mail: sparker@cathdal.org
Susan K. Parker, M.Ed., L.P.C., Admin.

Immigration Counseling Services, 5415 Maple Ave., Ste. 400, 75235. Tel: 214-634-7182; Fax: 214-634-2531. Ms. Vanna Slaughter, M.S.W., Admin.

Marillac Social Center, 2827 Lapsley, 75212. Tel: 214-638-4997. Sr. Rose Ann Aguilar, D.C., Admin. Sisters 2; Lay Staff 58.

Migration Refugee Services; Refugee Resettlement; Refugee Job Placement, 9850 Kingsley Rd., Ste. 228, 75238. Tel: 214-553-9909; Fax: 214-553-8116. Mr. Art Granzeier, Admin.

Monsignor John P. Brady Center, 4009 Elm St., 75226. Tel: 214-826-8330; Fax: 214-826-8579. Mary N. Brown, Admin. Conducted by Catholic Charities. Lay Staff 23.

St. Joseph Adolescent & Family Counseling Center, 5415 Maple Ave., Ste. 320, 75235. Tel: 214-631-8336; Fax: 214-631-1506. Barbara Lucente, Program & Clinical Dir. Treatment Center for adolescent boys and girls ages 13-17. Lay Staff 4; Capacity 20.

St. Martin Family Service Center, Inc., 3725 Blackburn St., 75219. Tel: 214-520-6590; Fax: 214-520-6595.
Purpose: To provide social services to assist the poor and indigent families of Oak Cliff to become self-reliant.

COPPELL. *St. Martin de Porres, Inc.* 1820 Preston Park Blvd., Ste. 1500, Plano, 75093. Tel: 972-727-7341; Fax: 972-747-9950.
E-mail: tcday@hsad.com; wellington@hsad.com
Purpose: To obtain housing for low-income families.

PLANO. *St. Jude, Inc.*, 1820 Preston Park Blvd., Ste. 1500, 75093. Tel: 972-727-7341; Fax: 972-747-9950.
E-mail: tcday@hsad.com
Purpose: To obtain housing for the elderly and needy in Dallas.

Villa Santa Maria, Inc., 1820 Preston Park Blvd., 75093. Tel: 972-727-7341; Fax: 972-747-9950.
E-mail: tcday@hsad.com
Purpose: To obtain housing for the elderly and needy in Dallas.

[I] EDUCATION CENTERS

DALLAS. *Mount Carmel Center*, 4600 W. Davis St., 75211-3498. Tel: 214-331-6224; Fax: 214-330-0844.
Web site: www.professionalwebs.net/mtcarmel/
Discalced Carmelite Fathers of the Southwestern Province. Revs. John M. Svenram, O.C.D., Dir.; Sam Anthony Morello, O.C.D., Asst. Dir.; Marion Bui, O.C.D. In res. Rev. Joseph Neilson, O.C.D.; Bros. Bernard Joseph O'Neill, O.C.D.; Francis Majors, O.C.D.

Mount St. Michael Spiritual Life Center, 4500 W. Davis St., 75211. Tel: 214-331-1754; Fax: 214-333-1659.
E-mail: mmc4500@airmail.net
Sr. Margaret McCaffrey, Major Supr. Sisters of Our Lady of Charity of Refuge 11.

[J] PERSONAL PRELATURES

IRVING. *Opus Dei.* Prelature of the Holy Cross and Opus Dei, 3610 Wingren, 75062. Tel: 972-650-0064; Fax: 972-717-3580.
E-mail: info@opusdei.org
Web site: http://www.opusdei.org
Rev. Jack Solarski.

[K] MONASTERIES AND RESIDENCES OF PRIESTS

DALLAS. *Capuchin Franciscan Friars, Vice Province of Texas*, 2601 Singleton Blvd., 75212. Tel: 214-630-7933. Rev. Juan Cruz Gaston, O.F.M.Cap. Priests 16; Brothers 2.

Congregation of the Mission, Southern Province, 3826 Gilbert Ave., 75219. Tel: 214-526-2421; 526-0234; Fax: 214-526-3477.
E-mail: CongMissSP@aol.com
Rev. George J. Weber, C.M. Priests 28; Brothers 1.

IRVING. *Cistercian Abbey of Our Lady of Dallas*, One Cistercian Rd., 75039. Tel: 214-438-2044; Fax: 972-554-7637.
E-mail: DMFDenis@aol.com
Web site: www.cisterian.org
Rt. Rev. Denis M. Farkasfalvy, O.Cist., S.S.L., M.S., S.T.D., Abbot, Vicar of the Abbot Pres. of Zirc; Revs. Peter Verhalen, O.Cist., M.A., Prior; Bernard Marton, O.Cist., S.T.D., Subprior; Benedict Monostori, O.Cist., Ph.D.; Bede Lackner, O.Cist., Ph.D.; Pascal Kis-Horvath, O.Cist.; Aloysius Kimecz, O.Cist., M.A.; David Balas, O.Cist., Ph.D., S.T.D.; Matthew Kovacs, O.Cist., M.A.; Melchior Chladek, O.Cist., M.A.; Rochus Kereszty, O.Cist., S.T.D.; Julius Leloczky, O.Cist., S.T.D.; Henry Marton, O.Cist., S.T.D.; James Lehrberger, O.Cist., Ph.D.; Robert Maguire, O.Cist., Ph.D.; Gregory Schweers, O.Cist., M.A.; Mark Ripperger, O.Cist., M.A.; Paul McCormick, O.Cist., M.A. (SLT); Bros. Patrick Griffin, O.Cist., M.S.; Gabriel Wagner, O.Cist., B.A.; Lucas Rocha, O.Cist; Francis Nicholson, O.Cist. Priests 19; Scholastics 3. Priests of the Abbey Serving Abroad: Rev. Ralph March, O.Cist., Ph.D., Germany.

Dominican Priory of St. Albert the Great, Prior of Dominican Community, University of Dallas, 1845 E. Northgate Dr., 75062-4799. Tel: 972-438-1626; Fax: 972-554-7664. Very Rev. Thomas M. Cumiskey, O.P., Prior; Revs. John B. Balsam, O.P., Subprior; Edward M. Robinson, O.P.; Austin E. Green, O.P.; Paul G. Hinnebusch, O.P.; Daniel A. Shanahan, O.P.; Andrew K. Kolzow, O.P.; James Burke, O.P.; Angel Vizcarra.
Assigned to this Priory but residing elsewhere due to Ministry: Rev. Daniel P. Brady, O.P., (St. Louis, MO).

Legionaries of Christ, 1451 E. Northgate Dr., 75062. Tel: 972-554-1980; Fax: 972-554-8729. Revs. Steven Reilly, L.C., Supr.; Eugene Gormley, L.C.; Edward Hopkins, L.C.; Bros. Todd Belardi, L.C.; Thanh Nguyen, L.C.; Donald Schabel, L.C.

[L] CONVENTS AND RESIDENCES FOR SISTERS

DALLAS. *Bethany House*, 3017 Mallory, 75216. Tel: 214-371-4867.
E-mail: mkdallas@aol.com
Web site: www.web2.airmail.net/ssmn
Sisters of St. Mary of Namur. Sr. Patricia Ann Ridgley, S.S.M., Contact Person.

The Institute of Divine Mercy Convent, 8351 San Fernando Way, 75218. Tel: 214-324-2607; Fax: 214-319-9996.
E-mail: divmercy@onramp.net
Web site: www.divinemercy.org
Sr. Maria Goretti of Jesus Crucified.

Marillac Daughters of Charity Residence, 2911 Lapsley St., 75212. Tel: 214-631-6757. Sr. Marta Goski, D.C., Supr. Daughters of Charity of St. Vincent de Paul 7.

Missionaries of Charity, 2704 Harlandale, 75216. Tel: 214-374-3351. Sr. Mary Justus, M.C., Supr.; Sr. Mary Imeldina, M.C.; Sr. M. Stellinda, M.C.; Sr. M. Denise, M.C. Sisters 4.

Missionary Catechist of the Poor, 950 N. Montclair Ave., 75208. Tel: 214-942-6243. Sr. Norma E. Munoz, M.C.P., Supr. Sisters 8.

Monastery of Discalced Carmelites, 600 Flowers Ave., 75211. Tel: 214-330-7440. Mother Celine, O.C.D., Prioress. Professed Sisters 9.

School Sisters of Notre Dame, P.O. Box 227275, 75222. Tel: 214-330-9152; Fax: 214-330-9197.
E-mail: daiglejuli@aol.com
Web site: www.ssnd.org
Sr. Juliette Daigle, S.S.N.D.

Provincial House of the Dallas Province, 4500 W. Davis, 75211. Tel: 214-330-9152; Fax: 214-330-9197. Sr. Elizabeth Newman, S.S.N.D. Prov. Sisters 177.
Other Convents: 2930 Storey Ln., Apt. 101, 75220. Tel: 214-904-9547. 2810 Storey Ln., Apt. 101, 75220. Tel: 214-350-2863; Fax: 214-357-1589. 7625 Cortland, 75235. Tel: 214-352-5635. 4401 Highview, 75211. Tel: 214-330-6623. 2826 Storey Ln., Apts. 100 & 101, 75220. Tel: 214-351-0798; Fax: 214-357-1589. 2910 Storey Ln., Apt. 104, 75220. Tel: 214-902-8997; Fax: 214-357-1589. 7550 S. Westmoreland, #118, 75234. Tel: 972-709-8374.

Ursuline Convent, 9905 Inwood Rd., 75220. Tel: 214-369-8159; Fax: 214-369-4004.
E-mail: convent@ursuline.pvt.k12.tx.us
Web site: www.osucentral.org

Ursuline Academy. (Grades 9-12), 4900 Walnut Hill Ln., 75229. Tel: 214-363-6551; Fax: 214-369-4034. Sr. Karen Schwane, O.S.U., Prioress; Sr. Margaret Ann Moser, O.S.U., Pres. Nuns 13.

GRAND PRAIRIE. *Sisters of the Holy Family of Nazareth*. (Blessed Frances Siedliska Province), 1814 Egyptian Way, P.O. Box 530959, 75053. Tel: 972-641-4496; Fax: 972-641-1668. Sr. M. Janice Kobierowski, C.S.F.N., Prov. Supr. Sisters 42.

[M] CAMPUS MINISTRY

IRVING. *Diocese of Dallas Campus Ministry*, University of Dallas, 75062. Tel: 972-721-5375; Fax: 972-721-5351. Denise Phillips, Dir. of Campus Ministry (Liturgy & Catechesis); Diane Pohlmeier, Campus Min.
Southern Methodist University, P.O. Box 282, Dallas, 75275. Tel: 214-692-4504. Rev. Jeremiah J. Cullinane; Michelle Freeman, Campus Min.
East Texas State University, St. Joseph Church, 2904 Melmar Pk., Commerce, 75428. Tel: 903-886-7135. Rev. D. Stanley Corcoran.

[N] MISCELLANEOUS LISTINGS

DALLAS. *Bishop Charles V. Grahmann Seminary Burse Fund*, P.O. Box 190507, 75219. Tel: 214-528-2240; Fax: 214-523-2422. Most Rev. Charles V. Grahmann, Trustee. Trust Fund for education of seminaries for Diocese of Dallas.

Bishop Lynch High School Building and Endowment Trust, 9750 Ferguson Rd., 75228. Tel: 214-324-3607.
E-mail: leyde@mail.bishoplynch.org
Ed Leyden, Pres.

Bishop's Education Endowment Fund, P.O. Box 190507, 75219. Tel: 214-528-2240; Fax: 214-523-2422. Most Rev. Charles V. Grahmann, Trustee. Trust Fund for financial aid to inner city school.

Cathedral Preservation Fund, Inc., 2215 Rose Ave., 75201. Tel: 214-361-8941; Fax: 214-954-1557. Rev. Ramon Alvarez, Contact.

Catholic Charities Endowment Trust, 3725 Blackburn St., 75219. Tel: 214-520-6590. Sr. Mary Anne Owens, S.S.N.D.

Catholic Community Appeal, Inc., 3725 Blackburn St., P.O. Box 190507, 75219. Tel: 214-528-2240; Fax: 214-526-1743. Michael T. Weis, Treas.

The Catholic Pro-Life Committee of North Texas, Inc., P.O. Box 740965, 75374. Tel: 972-612-3630.
E-mail: kegarnett1@juno.com
Karen Garnett, Contact Person.

Christian Community of God's Delight, 4500 W. Davis-Keating Hall, P.O. Box 225008, 75211. Tel: 214-333-2337; Fax: 214-333-2595.
E-mail: bjcavnar@lumen2000.com
Web site: www.TWH@Lumen2000.com

Commission on Ecumenism, P.O. Box 190507, 75219. Tel: 214-528-2240. Revs. Robert R. Crisp, Chm.; Robert Williams, Member; Margie Medlund, Member; Frank Plumlee, Member; Lynn Rossol, Member.

Dallas Vocation Guild, P.O. Box 12153, 75225. Tel: 214-750-1166.
E-mail: JoAnn.stone@juno.com
Jo Ann Stone, Pres.

Dave Fox Inner City School Fund, P.O. Box 190507, 75219. Tel: 214-528-2240; Fax: 214-526-1743. Most Rev. Charles V. Grahmann, Trustee.

Diocesan Charitable Trust, 3725 Blackburn, P.O. Box 190507, 75219. Tel: 214-528-2240; Fax: 214-526-1743. Sponsor of Rent Subsidizing Housing, Colonia Tepeyeac Apartments.

The Institute of Divine Mercy, Inc., 9306 Forest Hill Blvd., 75218-3633. Tel: 214-324-2607; Fax: 214-319-9996.
E-mail: idm@divinemercy.org
Nonprofit corporation formed under the supervision of the diocese of Dallas for the purpose of starting a new order of cloistered nuns. Sr. Maria Goretti of Jesus Crucified, I.D.M.; Rev. Fabian Maria Rosetti, O.Carm, Spiritual Dir.

International Catholic Network, 419 Cockrell Hill Rd., 75211.
E-mail: icn@lumen2000.com
Bobbie Cavnar, Pres.

John Paul II Building and Endowment Trust Fund, P.O. Box 190507, 75219. Tel: 214-528-2240.
E-mail: mweis@cathdal.org
Michael Weis, Contact Person.

John Paul II High School, Inc., 3725 Blackburn St., P.O. Box 190507, 75219. Tel: 214-528-2240; Fax: 214-526-1743. Michael T. Weis, Treas. New Diocesan high school in developmental stage.

Ladies of Charity of Dallas, P.O. Box 595666, 75359-0666. Tel: 214-821-5713.

Mary Benevides Trust, P.O. Box 190507, 75219. Tel: 214-528-2240; Fax: 214-526-1743. Most Rev. Charles V. Grahmann, Trustee. Trust Fund for the education of Hispanics.

The National Cursillo Center and Office of the National Secretariat, 4500 W. Davis, 75211. Tel: 214-339-6321; Fax: 214-339-6322.
E-mail: NATLOFF@natl-cursillo.org
Web site: www.natl-cursillo.org
Mailing Address: P.O. Box 210226, 75211. Tel: 214-339-6321; Fax: 214-339-6322.
E-mail: tomsarg@natl-cursillo.org
Thomas E. Sarg, Exec. Dir.; Joachim Thong Le, Vietnamese Coord., 9362 Asbery Cir., Westminster, CA, 92683. Tel: 714-891-6216; Fax: 714-891-7302. Jorge Barcelo, Hispanic Coord., 441 Columbus Blvd., New Britian, CT, 06051. Tel: 860-224-2542; Fax: 860-224-0116. Louis Robbio, English Coord., 100 Empress Dr., East Greenwich, RI, 02818. Tel: 401-884-2424; Fax: 401-884-7888.

Dallas Cursillo Center, 5605 Bernal Dr., 75212. Tel: 214-631-7775. Rev. Fray Luis Arraiza, O.F.M.Cap., Spiritual Dir.

Nuestra Senora del Pilar Land & Development Trust, 1809 W. Davis, 75208. Tel: 214-941-5821; Fax: 214-946-4466. Rev. Edmundo Parades.

St. Joseph Residence, Inc., 330 W. Pembroke, 75208. Tel: 214-948-3597; Fax: 214-948-1209.
E-mail: sradelaida@juno.com
Sr. Adelaide Bocanegra, Bethl., Admin. For elderly ladies, gentlemen, and couples. Conducted by Daughters of the Sacred Heart of Jesus (Bethlemitas). Sisters 7; Residents 49.

Santa Clara Endowment Fund, P.O. Box 190507, 75219. Tel: 214-528-2240; Fax: 214-526-1743. Most Rev. Charles V. Grahmann, Trustee. Trust Fund to support Santa Clara School.

School Sisters of Notre Dame of Dallas Charitable Trust, 4500 W. Davis, 75211. Tel: 214-330-9152; Fax: 214-330-9197.
E-mail: daiglejuli@aol.com
Web site: www.ssnd.org
Mailing Address: P.O. Box 227275, 75222-7275.

Society of St. Vincent de Paul, 3826 Gilbert St., 75219. Tel: 214-528-7837. Central Office for all society activities in the Diocese of Dallas. Mr. Phillip Young, Pres.

Southwestern Lieutenancy, Equestrian Order of the Holy Sepulchre of Jerusalem, 9716 Trailhill Dr., 75238. Tel: 214-341-4457; 349-6196; Fax: 214-341-6262. Albin J. Brezna, Lieutenant.

Ursuline Academy of Dallas Foundation, Inc., 9905 Inwood Rd., 75220. Tel: 214-369-8159. Sr. Karen Schwane, O.S.U., Prioress.

GARLAND. *Dallas Deanery Council of Catholic Women*, 5110 Presidio Dr., 75043. Tel: 972-681-4868.
E-mail: swgist@aol.com
Sandra Gist, Pres.

GRAND PRAIRIE. *Sisters of the Holy Family of Nazareth - Blessed Frances Siedliska Province Charitable Trust*, 1814 Egyptian Way, P.O. Box 530959, 75053-0959. Tel: 972-641-4496; Fax: 972-641-1668.
Web site: www.TX-CSFN.org
Sr. M. Janice Kobierowski, C.S.F.N., Prov. Supr.

ROCKWALL. *Dallas Diocesan Council of Catholic Women*, 314 Stonebridge Dr., 75087. Tel: 972-771-1592. Ellen Stelmar, Treas.

RELIGIOUS INSTITUTES OF MEN REPRESENTED IN THE DIOCESE

For further details refer to the corresponding bracketed number in the Religious Institutes of Men or Women section.

[0470]—*The Capuchin Friars.*—O.F.M.Cap.
[0340]—*Cistercian Fathers.*—O.Cist.
[0260]—*Discalced Carmelite Friars.* (Oklahoma Prov.).—O.C.D.
[0690]—*Jesuit Fathers and Brothers.* (New Orleans Prov.).—S.J.
[0730]—*Legionaries of Christ.*—L.C.
[]—*Marian Servants of the Holy Spirit.*—M.S.H.S.
[1110]—*Missionaries of Sacred Heart.*—M.S.C.
[0430]—*Order of Preachers (Dominicans).* (Southern Dominican Prov.).—O.P.
[]—*Redemptorists, Congregation of Most Holy Redeemer.*—C.S.S.P.
[1260]—*Society of Christ.*—S.Ch.
[0370]—*Society of St. Columba.*—S.S.C.
[1330]—*Vincentian Fathers.* (Southern Prov.).—C.M.

RELIGIOUS INSTITUTES OF WOMEN REPRESENTED IN THE DIOCESE

[1810]—*Bernardine Sisters of the Third Order of St. Francis.*—O.S.F.
[1920]—*Congregation of the Sisters of the Holy Cross.*—C.S.C.
[0760]—*Daughters of Charity of St. Vincent de Paul.* (St. Louis Prov.).—D.C.
[]—*Daughters of the Sacred Heart of Jesus.*—S.C.I.F.
[0420]—*Discalced Carmelite Nuns.*—O.C.D.
[1070-03]—*Dominican Sisters.*—O.P.
[2710]—*Missionaries of Charity.*—M.C.
[]—*Missionary Catechists of the Poor.* (Mexico).
[3070]—*North American Union Sisters of Our Lady of Charity.*—N.A.U.-O.L.C.
[2970]—*School Sisters of Notre Dame.*—S.S.N.D.
[1010]—*Sisters of Divine Providence of San Antonio, Texas.*—C.D.P.
[3950]—*Sisters of Saint Mary of Namur.* (Western Prov.).—S.S.M.N.
[1970]—*Sisters of the Holy Family of Nazareth.* (Sacred Heart Vice Prov.).—C.S.F.N.
[2050]—*Sisters of the Holy Spirit and Mary Immaculate.*—S.H.Sp.
[4110]—*Ursuline Nuns (Roman Union).* (Central Prov.).—O.S.U.

DIOCESAN CEMETERIES

DALLAS. *Calvary Hill Cemetery & Mausoleum.*
DESOTO. *Holy Redeemer Cemetery & Mausoleum.*
ROWLETT. *Sacred Heart Cemetery & Mausoleum.*
WYLIE. *St. Paul.*

NECROLOGY

† Barrus, Paul W., Plano, TX St. Elizabeth Seton. —Died Jan. 3, 2000.
† Doran, William, Meyersville, TX St. Peter & Paul. —Died May 25, 2000.

Diocese of Davenport

(Dioecesis Davenportensis)

Most Reverend

WILLIAM E. FRANKLIN, D.D.

Bishop of Davenport; ordained February 4, 1956; appointed Titular Bishop of Surista and Auxiliary Bishop of Dubuque January 29, 1987; ordained Bishop April 1, 1987; transferred to Davenport November 12, 1993; installed January 20, 1994. *Res., 2761 Scott St., Davenport, IA, 52803.* Tel.: 319-324-4774. *Office: St. Vincent Center, 2706 N. Gaines St., Davenport, IA, 52804-1998.* Tel.: 319-324-1911.

Chancery: St. Vincent Center, 2706 N. Gaines St., Davenport, IA, 52804-1998. Tel.: 319-324-1911; Fax: 319-324-5842.

Web site address: davenportdiocese.org

ERECTED MAY 8, 1881.

Square Miles 11,438.

Comprises that part of the State of Iowa bounded on the east by the Mississippi River; on the west by the western boundaries of the counties of Jasper, Marion, Monroe and Appanoose; on the south by the State of Missouri; on the north by the northern boundaries of the Counties of Jasper, Poweshiek, Iowa, Johnson, Cedar and Clinton.

For legal titles of parishes and diocesan institutions, consult the Chancery.

STATISTICAL OVERVIEW

Personnel	
Bishop	1
Priests: Diocesan Active in Diocese	87
Priests: Active Outside Diocese	11
Priests: Diocesan in Foreign Missions	1
Priests: Retired, Sick or Absent	47
Number of Diocesan Priests	146
Religious Priests in Diocese	3
Extern Priests in Diocese	5
Ordinations:	
Diocesan Priests	2
Transitional Deacons	1
Permanent Deacons in Diocese	42
Total Brothers	1
Total Sisters	228
Parishes	
Parishes	85
With Resident Pastor:	
Resident Diocesan Priests	51
Resident Religious Priests	3
Without Resident Pastor:	
Administered by Priests	31
Administered by Lay People	1
Missions	1
Pastoral Centers	1
Closed Parishes	1
Professional Ministry Personnel:	
Sisters	14
Lay Ministers	32
Welfare	
Catholic Hospitals	2
Total Assisted	794,135
Homes for the Aged	3
Total Assisted	441
Educational	
Seminaries, Diocesan	1
Students from This Diocese	4
Diocesan Students in Other Seminaries	7
Total Seminarians	11
Colleges and Universities	2
Total Students	3,629
High Schools, Diocesan and Parish	7
Total Students	1,206
Elementary Schools, Diocesan and Parish	21
Total Students	4,604
Catechesis/Religious Education:	
High School Students	3,628
Elementary Students	11,137
Total Students Under Catholic Instruction	24,215
Teachers in the Diocese:	
Priests	6
Sisters	9
Lay Teachers	525
Vital Statistics	
Receptions into the Church:	
Infant Baptism Totals	1,782
Adult Baptism Totals	269
Received into Full Communion	206
First Communions	2,177
Confirmations	2,028
Marriages:	
Catholic	356
Interfaith	350
Total Marriages	706
Deaths	1,172
Total Catholic Population	113,535
Total Population	730,544

Former Bishops—Rt. Rev. JOHN MCMULLEN, D.D., cons. July 25, 1881; died July 4, 1883.—Rt. Rev. HENRY COSGROVE, D.D., cons. Sept. 14, 1884; died Dec. 22, 1906.—Rt. Rev. JAMES DAVIS, D.D., cons. Nov. 30, 1904; died Dec. 2, 1926.—Most Rev. HENRY P. ROHLMAN, D.D., cons. July 25, 1927; appt. Coadjutor-Archbishop of Dubuque and Titular Archbishop of Macra in Rhodope, June 15, 1944; Archbishop of Dubuque, Nov. 18, 1946; appt. Titular Archbishop of Cotrada, Dec. 2, 1954; died Sept. 13, 1957.—Most Rev. RALPH LEO HAYES, D.D., ord. Sept. 19, 1909; appt. Bishop of Helena June 23, 1933; cons. Sept. 21, 1933; appt. Rector of North American College in Rome in Sept. 1935; transferred to Titular See of Hierapolis Oct. 26, 1935; transferred to Davenport Nov. 16, 1944; appt. Assistant at the Pontifical Throne April 30, 1958; transferred to Titular See of Naraggara; retired Oct. 20, 1966; died July 4, 1970.—Most Rev. GERALD FRANCIS O'KEEFE, D.D., ord. Jan. 29, 1944; appt. Auxiliary Bishop of St. Paul and Titular Bishop of Candyba May 5, 1961; cons. July 2, 1961; transferred to Davenport Oct. 20, 1966; installed Jan 4, 1967; retired Nov. 12, 1993; died April 12, 2000.

Chancery—St. Vincent Center, 2706 N. Gaines St., Davenport, 52804-1998. Tel: 319-324-1911; Fax: 319-324-5842.

Vicar General and Moderator of the Curia—Very Rev. DRAKE R. SHAFER, V.G.

Chancellor—IRENE PRIOR LOFTUS, J.D.

Vice-Chancellors—Rev. Msgr. JAMES F. PARIZEK, J.C.L.; CHARLENE MAASKE, C.P.A.; Rev. JOSEPH M. WOLF, J.C.L.

Diocesan Tribunal—St. Vincent Center, 2706 N. Gaines St., Davenport, 52804-1998. Tel: 319-324-1911.

Judicial Vicar—Rev. Msgr. JAMES F. PARIZEK, J.C.L.

Adjutant Judicial Vicar—Rev. Msgr. MICHAEL J. MORRISSEY, J.C.L.

Tribunal Auditor—THERESA M. DORAN.

Promoter of Justice—Very Rev. FRANCIS C. HENRICKSEN, E.V.

Defenders of the Bond—Rev. Msgr. LEO J. FEENEY; Revs. JOHN P. GALLAGHER, J.C.L.; WILLIAM E. REYNOLDS, J.C.L.

Notaries—THERESA M. DORAN; JOANN KAKERT; JUDITH JOHNSON; MARY FRICK.

Judges—Revs. JOSEPH M. WOLF, J.C.L.; JOHN P. BOYLE; ROBERT J. BUSHER; JOSEPH B. DENNING; Very Revs. EDWARD J. FITZPATRICK, V.F.; RUDOLPH T. JUAREZ, J.C.L., E.V.; Revs. ROBERT T. MCALEER; GEORGE W. MCDANIEL.

Diocesan Consultors—Very Rev. DRAKE R. SHAFER, V.G.; Rev. Msgr. MICHAEL J. MORRISSEY, J.C.L., V.F.; Very Rev. JOHN M. HYLAND, V.F.; Revs. MARVIN A. MOTTET; JOSEPH B. DENNING; Very Rev. FRANCIS C. HENRICKSEN, E.V.; Rev. JOSEPH R. SPARKS.

Deans—Rev. Msgr. MICHAEL J. MORRISSEY, J.C.L., V.F., Davenport; Very Rev. H. ROBERT HARNESS, Clinton; Very Rev. EDWARD J. FITZPATRICK, V.F., Iowa City; Very Rev. JOHN M. HYLAND, V.F., Keokuk; Very Rev. JOSEPH MILLER, C.PP.S., Ottumwa; Very Rev. ERNEST E. BRAIDA, Grinnell.

Diocesan Corporate Board—Most Rev. WILLIAM E. FRANKLIN; Very Rev. DRAKE R. SHAFER, V.G.; IRENE PRIOR LOFTUS, J.D.; ROBERT VAN VOOREN, J.D.; KATHY BUSH, C.P.A. Tel: 319-324-1911.

Finance Officer—CHARLENE MAASKE, C.P.A.

Finance Council—Most Rev. WILLIAM E. FRANKLIN; CHARLENE MAASKE, C.P.A.; Rev. Msgr. MICHAEL J. MORRISSEY, J.C.L., V.F.; TERRY KILBURG, C.P.A.; MICHAEL BAUER; ROBERT VAN VOOREN, J.D.; RITA BAWDEN; KATHY BUSH, C.P.A.; JEFF HYLAND, C.P.A.

Vicar for Hispanics—Very Rev. RUDOLPH T. JUAREZ, J.C.L., E.V., *516 Fillmore St., Davenport, 52802.*

Diocesan Offices

Pastoral Center—St. Vincent Center, 2706 N. Gaines St., Davenport, 52804-1998. Tel: 319-324-1911.

Finance and Administration—CHARLENE MAASKE, C.P.A.

Coordinating Director of Stewardship & Development—Vacant.

Database Coordinator—CHERYL CAREY.

Controller—STACEY L. CARY.

Accounting Coordinator—MICHELE TRAVER.

Planning, Publications and Communications—IRENE PRIOR LOFTUS, J.D.

Associate Director of Communication—DAVID MONTGOMERY.

Associate Director of Technology—ROBERT BUTTERWORTH.

Archivist—ARNOLD WIESER.

Pastoral Services—Very Rev. DRAKE R. SHAFER, V.G.

Director of Adult Faith Formation—Vacant.

Adult/Family Formation Coordinator—ILAMAE HANISCH.

Youth Ministry Coordinator—JOE DVORAK.

Religion Formation Coordinator—Vacant.

Curriculum/Media Coordinator—Dr. BOB PILCHER.

Director of Social Action—DAN R. EBENER.

Coordinator of Intercultural Ministry—Vacant.

Immigration Program Coordinator—LAURA RAYA.

Director of Faith Formation and Education/ Superintendent of Schools—MARY M. WIESER.
Director of Clergy Formation & Support—Rev. CHARLES A. ADAM.
Director of Liturgy—Rev. RICHARD J. POSTER.
Scouting—JOE DVORAK, *St. Vincent Center, 2706 N. Gaines St., Davenport, 52804-1998.* Tel: 319-324-1911.
Catholic Relief Services—DAN R. EBENER, Dir., *St. Vincent Center, 2706 N. Gaines St., Davenport, 52804-1998.* Tel: 319-324-1911.
Cemetery Committee—ROBERT MCCABE, Sec., *614 Main St., Davenport, 52801.* Tel: 319-322-4438.
Campaign for Human Development—DAN R. EBENER, *St. Vincent Center, 2706 N. Gaines St., Davenport, 52804-1998.* Tel: 319-324-1911.
Continuing Education of the Clergy—Rev. CHARLES A. ADAM, *St. Ambrose University, 518 W. Locust, Davenport, 52803.* Tel: 319-333-6151.
Liturgical Commission—Rev. RICHARD J. POSTER, *Sacred Heart Rectory, P.O. Box 127, Lost Nation, 52254-0127.* Tel: 319-678-2200.
D.C.C.W.—Rev. TIMOTHY J. REGAN, Dir., *109 N. Lincoln St., Keota, 52248-9757.* Tel: 515-636-3883.
Holy Childhood, Pontifical Association—Rev. Msgr. W. ROBERT SCHMIDT, Dir., *St. Vincent Center, 2706 N. Gaines St., Davenport, 52804-1998.* Tel: 319-324-1911.
Newspaper—"The Catholic Messenger"; Rev. FRANCIS C. HENRICKSEN, E.V., Mng. Editor, *P.O. Box 460, Davenport, 52805.* Tel: 319-323-9959; Fax: 319-323-6612.
Pastoral Council—Most Rev. WILLIAM E. FRANKLIN, D.D., Chm., *St. Vincent Center, 2706 N. Gaines St., Davenport, 52804-1998.* Tel: 319-324-1911.
Permanent Diaconate—Deacon ROBERT MCCOY, *St. Vincent Center, 2706 N. Gaines St., Davenport, 52804-1998.* Tel: 319-324-1911.
Personnel Board—St. Vincent Center, 2706 N. Gaines St., Davenport, 52804-1998. Tel: 319-324-1911.
Presbyteral Council—Rev. ROBERT T. MCALEER, *St. John Vianney Rectory, 4097 18th St., Bettendorf, 52722-2120.* Tel: 319-332-7910.
Priests' Aid Society—Rev. WILLIAM E. REYNOLDS, J.C.L., *St. Mary Rectory, P.O. Box 623, Grinnell, 50112.* Tel: 641-236-5289.
Priests Eucharistic League—Rev. MICHAEL T. PHILLIPS, Dir., *St. Wenceslaus, 623 Fairchild St., Iowa City, 52245-2829.* Tel: 319-337-4975; Fax: 319-337-5822.
Propagation of the Faith—IRENE PRIOR LOFTUS, Dir., *St. Vincent Center, 2706 N. Gaines St., Davenport, 52804-1998.* Tel: 319-324-1911.
Social Action Commission—DAN R. EBENER, *St. Vincent Center, 2706 N. Gaines St., Davenport, 52804-1998.* Tel: 319-324-1911.
Serra Club—JOHN P. MILLER, *2127 Vine St., Davenport, 52804.* Tel: 319-326-2772.
Sisters' Council—Sr. JANET KREBER, O.S.F., *Box 71, Richland, 52585.* Tel: 319-694-3209.
Vicar for Religious—Very Rev. FRANCIS C. HENRICKSEN, E.V., *P.O. Box 460, Davenport, 52805.* Tel: 319-323-9959.
Vocations—Rev. CHARLES ADAM, Dir., *St. Ambrose University, 518 W. Locust, Davenport, 52803.* Tel: 319-333-6151.
Davenport Deanery—Very Rev. DRAKE R. SHAFER, V.G.; Rev. Msgr. MICHAEL J. MORRISSEY, J.C.L., V.F., *2706 N. Gaines St., Davenport, 52804.* Tel: 319-324-1911; 324-0902.

CLERGY, PARISHES, MISSIONS AND PAROCHIAL SCHOOLS

CITY OF DAVENPORT
(Scott County)

1—SACRED HEART CATHEDRAL (1856), Rev. Marvin A. Mottet; Sr. Charla Bulko, S.S.S.F., Pastoral Assoc. In res., Rev. Thomas F. Stratman.
Res., 422 E. 10th St., 52803-5499. Tel: 319-324-3257; Fax: 319-326-6014. [JC]
School—Tel: 319-326-6278. Denise Tatoian, Prin.
Sisters 1; Lay Teachers 14; Students 125.
Catechesis/Religious Programs—Sr. Mary Schmidt, O.S.B., D.R.E.
Students 155.

2—OUR LADY OF VICTORY (1962), Revs. E. William Kaska; Appolinaire 'Apo' Tshipamba MPanda, C.J.; Deacons Paul Hittner; Marcel Mosse; William Ditewig. In res., Rev. Daniel C. Mannhardt.
Res., 4105 N. Division St., 52806. Tel: 319-391-4245; Fax: 319-445-1003. [JC]
School—John F. Kennedy Catholic, Tel: 319-391-3030; Fax: 319-388-5206. Dennis Albertson, Prin.
Lay Teachers 22; Students 307.
Catechesis/Religious Programs—Tel: 319-391-8384. Kay Carruthers, D.R.E.
Students 303.

3—HOLY FAMILY (1897), Rev. Msgr. Michael Morrissey; Rev. Msgr. Leo Feeney; Rev. Jason K. Crossen; Deacons Gerald Timmerman, Pastoral Assoc.; Joseph Rosenthal.
Res., 1923 Fillmore St., 52804. Tel: 319-322-0902 (Rectory); 322-0901; 326-3836 (Office); Fax: 319-884-4965.
School—1926 Marquette St., 52804. Tel: 319-324-3205; Fax: 319-324-9331.
Lay Teachers 27; Students 399.
Catechesis/Religious Programs—D.R.E.: Sharon Weiland, (Grades K-8); Devin Schadt.
Students 173.

4—ST. ALPHONSUS (1903), Rev. David G. Steinle.
Res., 2618 Boies Ave., 52802. Tel: 319-322-0987; Fax: 319-323-1458.
School—Tel: 319-323-3204. Mr. Barry Lahann, Prin.
Lay Teachers 11; Students 158.
Catechesis/Religious Programs—Mary Ann Hagemann, D.R.E.
Students 62.

5—ST. ANTHONY'S (1837) (Irish), Rev. Msgr. W. Robert Schmidt.
Res., 417 N. Main St., 52801. Tel: 319-322-3303; Fax: 319-326-5136.
Catechesis/Religious Programs—Students 310.

6—ST. JOSEPH'S (1855). Closed. For inquiries for parish records contact the Chancery.

7—ST. MARY'S (1867) (Irish), Very Rev. Rudolph T. Juarez; Deacons George D. Strader; Julian Gutierrez.
Res., 516 Fillmore St., 52802. Tel: 319-322-3383; Fax: 319-322-3383.
Catechesis/Religious Programs—Students 125.

8—ST. PAUL THE APOSTLE (1909), Revs. Michael Spiekermeier; William C. Kneemiller; Deacon Robert McCoy.
Res., 916 E. Rusholme St., 52803. Tel: 319-322-7994; Fax: 319-322-7995.
School—Tel: 319-322-2923; Fax: 319-322-9359.
Sisters of Charity of the Blessed Virgin Mary 2; Lay Teachers 26; Students 486.
Catechesis/Religious Programs—Tel: 319-322-3768. Rosie Megraw, D.R.E.
Students 195.

9—VIETNAMESE CATHOLIC COMMUNITY OF THE QUAD CITIES, Rev. Joseph Khan V. Nguyen.
Res., 2706 N. Gaines St., 52804. Tel: 319-324-1911; Fax: 319-324-5842.

OUTSIDE THE CITY OF DAVENPORT

Albia, Monroe Co., St. Mary's (1874) (Irish), Rev. William P. Walter, C.PP.S.
Res., P.O. Box 365, 52531. Tel: 641-932-5130. [CEM]
Catechesis/Religious Programs—Tel: 641-932-5589. Jackie Maddy, D.R.E.
Students 324.

Ardon, Muscatine Co., St. Malachy. Closed. For sacramental records, inquiries should be addressed to St. Joseph Parish, 815 2nd St., Columbus Junction, IA, 52738.

Augusta, Des Moines Co., St. Mary's (1881). Closed. For inquiries for parish records contact the Chancery.

Bauer, Marion Co., St. Joseph. Closed. For inquiries for parish records contact the Chancery.

Bettendorf, Scott Co., Our Lady of Lourdes (1903), Rev. Thomas J. Spiegel; Sr. Rita Lenaghan, C.H.M., Pastoral Assoc.; Deacons Dennis Duff; Terry Starns.
Res., 1506 Brown St., 52722. Tel: 319-359-0345; Fax: 319-344-6017.
School—Tel: 319-359-3466. Mrs. Barbara Herter, Prin.
Lay Teachers 23; Students 412.
Catechesis/Religious Programs—Tel: 319-359-1869.
Students 520.

St. John Vianney (1967), Rev. Robert T. McAleer; Deacons William Donnelly; Daryl Fortin.
Res., 4097 18th St., 52722. Tel: 319-332-7910; Fax: 319-332-0833. [JC]
Catechesis/Religious Programs—Tel: 319-332-7564. Sr. Phyllis Kernz, S.S.N.D., D.R.E. (Elementary) (P-K).
Students 721.

Bloomfield, Davis Co., St. Mary Magdalen (1953). Attended by St. Patrick's, Ottumwa.

Blue Grass, Scott Co., St. Andrew (1976), Rev. Brian J. Shepley; Deacons Randal Bataan; Donald Frericks.
Res., 333 W. Lotte St., 52726. Tel: 319-381-1363; Fax: 319-381-1363.
Catechesis/Religious Programs—Tel: 319-381-1363. Dorothy Spiess, D.R.E.
Students 190.

Brooklyn, Poweshiek Co., St. Patrick, Rev. Richard U. Okumu.
Mailing Address: P.O. Box 512, 52211-0512. Tel: 641-522-7714. [CEM]

Bryant, Clinton Co., St. Mary. Consolidated with St. Joseph, Sugar Creek to form Sts. Mary and Joseph, Sugar Creek.

Buffalo, Scott Co., St. Peter's. Attended by St. Alphonsus, Davenport. Rev. David G. Steinle; Deacon Larry Dankert.
Mailing Address: 406 Fourth St., P.O. Box 488, 52728. Tel: 319-381-2265; 381-2865. [CEM]
Catechesis/Religious Programs—Students 50.

Burlington, Des Moines Co.,
1—ST. JOHN'S (1855). Merged with St. Paul's, Burlington, to form SS. John & Paul, Burlington.

2—ST. PATRICK'S (1870). Merged with St. Mary, West Burlington to form SS. Mary and Patrick, West Burlington.

3—SS. JOHN & PAUL (1855), Very Rev. John M. Hyland; Rev. Patrick Hilgendorf; Deacon Robert Gengenbacher. Pastoral Assocs.: Sr. Nadine Meyer, S.S.N.D.; Sr. Kathy Braun, S.S.N.D.
Res., 700 Division St., 52601-5415. Tel: 319-752-6733; Fax: 319-753-5211. [JC]
Catechesis/Religious Programs—Tel: 319-753-0277. Sr. Mary Assell, D.R.E.
Students 481.

Camanche, Clinton Co., Church of the Visitation (1966), Rev. Joseph B. Denning; Deacon John H. Schmitt.
1032 Middle Rd., 52730-1032. Tel: 319-259-1188; Fax: 319-259-4462.
Catechesis/Religious Programs—Tel: 319-259-8819. Ms. Kay Palmer, D.R.E.
Students 105.

Centerville, Appanoose Co., St. Mary's, Rev. Joseph Miller, C.PP.S. In res., Rev. Joseph Bathke, C.PP.S.
Res., 828 S. 18th St., 52544. Tel: 641-437-1984.
School—Tel: 515-437-1984. Robert Wells, Prin.
Sisters 1; Lay Teachers 6; Students 80.
Catechesis/Religious Programs—Students 150.

Charlotte, Clinton Co.,
1—ASSUMPTION OF THE BLESSED MARY. Consolidated with St. Patrick's, Villa Nova to form Assumption and St. Patrick's, Charlotte.

2—ASSUMPTION AND ST. PATRICK'S, REV. GARY L. BECKMAN.
Res., 147 Broadway St., 52731. Tel: 319-677-2758; Fax: 319-677-2739. [CEM]
Catechesis/Religious Programs—Students 121.

Clear Creek, Keokuk Co., SS. Peter & Paul. See Holy Trinity, Keota.

Clinton, Clinton Co., Jesus Christ, Prince of Peace (1990), Revs. Anthony Herold; Lawrence Smith; Deacons Arthur Donart; Ramon Hilgendorf; Patrick Lennon; David Schnier, Bus. Mgr.; Phil O'Gara, Devel. Dir.
Parish Office: (Maintained for all four churches in Clinton.) 505 Ninth Ave. S., 52732. Tel: 319-242-3311; Fax: 319-242-3323. [CEM]
Churches—St. Mary's, 520 Ninth Ave. S., 52732.; Sacred Heart, 316 S. Fourth Ave., 52732.; St. Boniface, 2500 N. Pershing Blvd., 52732.; St. Irenaeus, 2811 N. Second St., 52732.
School—Nancy Peart, Prin. Students 380.
Catechesis/Religious Programs—Tel: 319-243-8269. Betty Mantsch, D.R.E.
Students 679.

Colfax, Jasper Co., Immaculate Conception (1898), Rev. Philip A. Cardenzana.
Mailing Address: 305 East Howard, 50054-1025. Tel: 515-674-3711; Fax: 515-674-4532.
Catechesis/Religious Programs—Students 92.

Columbus Junction, Louisa Co., St. Joseph, Rev. Patrick L. Lumsden.
Mailing Address: 815 Second St., 52738. Tel: 319-728-8210.

Cosgrove, Johnson Co., St. Peter's. Attended by St. Mary, Oxford.
4022 Cosgrove Rd. S.W., Oxford, 52322. Tel: 319-628-4180; 545-2077.

Delmar, Clinton Co., St. Patrick's (1882), Rev. Edward A. Botkin.
Res., 52037. Tel: 319-674-4240. [CEM]
Catechesis/Religious Programs—Students 87.

DeWitt, Clinton Co., St. Joseph's (1880), Very Rev. H. Robert Harness, V.F.; Sr. Theresa Ann Spitz, R.S.M., Pastoral Assoc.; Deacon Mike Sheil.
Res., 417 Sixth Ave., 52742. Tel: 319-659-3514; Fax:

319-659-2599. [CEM]
School—Tel: 319-659-3812. Patrick Meade, Prin.
Sisters of Mercy 1; Lay Teachers 12; Students 212.
Catechesis/Religious Programs—Ann Donovan, D.R.E.
Students 218.

Dodgeville, Des Moines Co., St. Mary's (1850), Rev. Patrick Lumsden; Deacon Clifford Beckman.
Res., 13204 Dodgeville Rd., Sperry, 52650-9875. Tel: 319-985-2122. [CEM]
Catechesis/Religious Programs—Tel: 319-865-7451. Frieda Vantiger, D.R.E.
Students 91.

East Pleasant Plain, Jefferson Co., St. Joseph's (1902). Attended by St. Francis Xavier Cabrini, Richland. Rev. Charles J. Fladung.
Mailing Address: P.O. Box 130, Richland, 52585. Tel: 319-456-3161; Fax: 319-456-6408. [CEM]
Catechesis/Religious Programs—Students 31.

Eddyville, Mahaska Co., St. Mary's. Closed. For inquiries for parish records contact the Chancery.

Eldon, Wapello Co., St. Aloysius. Closed. For inquiries for parish records contact the Chancery.

Fairfield, Jefferson Co., St. Mary's (1864), Rev. Stephen C. Page.
Res., 402 N. Third, 52556-0903. Tel: 641-472-3179; Fax: 641-472-6137.
Catechesis/Religious Programs—Tel: 641-472-5991. Sr. Ann Marie Dunn, O.S.F., D.R.E.
Students 268.

Farmington, Van Buren Co., St. Boniface (1862), Rev. David F. Wilkening.
Res., 609 Washington St., 52626. Tel: 319-878-3736. [CEM]
Catechesis/Religious Programs—Students 129.

Fort Madison, Lee Co.,

1—St. Joseph's. Consolidated with St. Mary's to form SS. Mary & Joseph Parish.

2—St. Mary's. Consolidated with St. Joseph's to form SS. Mary & Joseph Parish.

3—SS. Mary & Joseph, (1871), Rev. Thomas L. Parlette; Sr. Mary Helen Hotze, S.S.N.D., Pastoral Assoc.
Res., 1013 Ave. E, 52627. Tel: 319-372-3139; Fax: 319-372-7087. [CEM]
Catechesis/Religious Programs—Tel: 319-372-3970.
Students 263.

4—Sacred Heart, (1893), Rev. Timothy J. Sheedy; Deacon Ronald Stein.
Res., 2204 Ave. I, 52627. Tel: 319-372-3179; Fax: 319-372-3321.
Catechesis/Religious Programs—Tel: 319-372-6428; 372-2486.
Students 238.

Georgetown, Monroe Co., St. Patrick's (1851) (Irish). Attended by St. Peter's, Lovilia. Rev. Scott Lemaster.
Mailing Address: P.O. Box 183, Albia, 52531. Tel: 641-726-3529. [CEM]
Catechesis/Religious Programs—Clustered with St. Mary, Albia. Tel: 641-932-5589.

Grand Mound, Clinton Co., Church of St. Philip and James (1876). Unassigned.
Res., 606 Fulton St., P.O. Box 7, 52751-0007. Tel: 319-847-2271. [CEM]
Catechesis/Religious Programs—Students 110.

Grinnell, Poweshiek Co., St. Mary's (1924), Rev. William E. Reynolds; Deacons Stephen J. Witt; William D. Olson.
Res., 1018 Broad St., P.O. Box 623, 50112. Tel: 641-236-5289; Fax: 641-236-7488. [CEM]
Catechesis/Religious Programs—Tel: 641-236-8838.
Students 210.

Harper, Keokuk Co., St. Elizabeth's. See Holy Trinity, Keota.

Hills, Johnson Co., St. Joseph's (1902), Rev. Louis J. Leonhardt.
Res., 208 Iowa St., 52235. Tel: 319-679-2271; Fax: 319-679-2272.
Catechesis/Religious Programs—Students 83.

Holbrook, Iowa Co., St. Michael. Closed. For inquiries for parish records contact the Chancery.

Houghton, Lee Co., St. John's (1895) (German), Rev. Dennis L. Hoffman.
Res., Box 100, 52631. Tel: 319-469-2001. [CEM]
School—(Grades PreK-6). Tel: 319-469-3881. Sr. Pat Siepker, Prin.
Lay Teachers 12; Students 188.
High School—Tel: 319-837-6131. Mr. Dan Kieler, Prin.
Religious 1; Lay Teachers 15; Students 154.
Catechesis/Religious Programs—Tel: 319-469-2000. Dixie Booten, D.R.E.
Students 59.

Iowa City, Johnson Co.,

1—St. Mary, (1840), Revs. Kenneth E. Kuntz; Joseph Van Phung; Sr. Mary Agnes Giblin, B.V.M., Pastoral Assoc.
Res., 220 E. Jefferson St., 52245. Tel: 319-337-4314; Fax: 319-337-8551. [CEM 2][JC]
Catechesis/Religious Programs—Regina Catholic School, (Grades K-9). Tel: 319-351-7638.
Students 391.

2—St. Patrick's, (1872) (Irish), Rev. James J. Vrba.
Res., 228 E. Court St., 52240. Tel: 319-337-2856; Fax: 319-354-5590. [JC]

3—St. Thomas More, Rev. Walter Helms.
Res., 108 McLean St., 52246. Tel: 319-337-2173; Fax: 319-337-2174. [JC]
Catechesis/Religious Programs—Tel: 319-337-4231. Michele Petersen, D.R.E.
Students 533.

4—St. Wenceslaus, (1893) (Bohemian), Rev. Michael T. Phillips.
Res., 623 Fairchild St., 52245. Tel: 319-337-4957; Fax: 319-337-5822. [JC]

Keokuk, Lee Co., All Saints (1982), Revs. Paul E. Connolly; Christopher J. David; Deacon William Cosgrove.
Res., 310 S. Ninth St., 52632. Tel: 319-524-8334.
Catechesis/Religious Programs—Students 154.

Keota, Keokuk Co., Holy Trinity (1992), Rev. Timothy J. Regan.
Res., 109 N. Lincoln St., 52248-9757. Tel: 641-636-3883; Fax: 641-636-3198. [CEM 3]
Churches—St. Mary's, 109 N. Lincoln St., 52248-9757.; St. Elizabeth's, 20486 285th Ave., Harper, 52231.; SS. Peter & Paul, 30832 242nd St., Harper, 52231.
Catechesis/Religious Programs—Tel: 515-636-3731.
Students 148.
St. Mary's. See Holy Trinity, Keota.

Keswick, Keokuk Co., Our Lady of Lourdes (1914) (Irish-German). Attended by St. Mary's, Sigourney. Rev. Philip R. Ryan.
Mailing Address: 415 E. Pleasant Valley St., Sigourney, 52591-1730. Tel: 641-622-3426; Fax: 641-622-2001.
Church—50136. Tel: 319-738-3731.
Catechesis/Religious Programs—Tel: 319-738-3231.
Students 53.

Kinross, Keokuk Co., Sacred Heart. Closed. For inquiries for parish records contact the Chancery.

Knoxville, Marion Co., St. Anthony's (1870), Rev. Mark P. Spring.
Res., 1202 Woodland St., 50138. Tel: 641-828-7050; Fax: 641-828-7915. [CEM]
Catechesis/Religious Programs—Tel: 641-842-3152. Sr. Rachel Beeson, C.H.M., D.R.E.
Students 200.

Le Claire-Princeton, Scott Co., Our Lady of the River (1969), Rev. Stephen P. Ebel.
Res., 28200 226th Pl., P.O. Box 32, LeClaire, 52753. Tel: 319-289-5736.
Catechesis/Religious Programs—Cheryl O'Klock, D.R.E.
Students 131.

Lone Tree, Johnson Co., St. Mary's (1853), Revs. Louis J. Leonhardt; Benedict Okonkwo (Nigeria); Mrs. Carol Kaalberg, Parish Life Coord.
Mailing Address: Box 416, 52755. [CEM][JC]
Res., 214 W. Jayne St., 52755. Tel: 319-629-4225; Fax: 319-629-4944. [CEM][JC]

Long Grove, Scott Co., St. Ann's (1853), Rev. Stephen P. Ebel.
Res., 16550 290th St., 52756. Tel: 319-285-4596; Fax: 319-285-4897. [CEM]
Catechesis/Religious Programs—Tel: 319-285-4020. D.R.E.: Janice Uitenbroek; Fiona Wilson; Margaret Liske; Tammy Zimmer; Betty Zimmer; Ann Mohr.
Students 638.

Lost Nation, Clinton Co., Sacred Heart (1895), Rev. Richard J. Poster; Sr. Kathleen Henneberry, C.H.M., Pastoral Assoc.
Res., P.O. Box 127, 52254. Tel: 319-678-2200; Fax: 319-678-2389. [CEM]

Lovilia, Monroe Co., St. Peter's, Rev. Scott Lemaster.
Mailing Address: P.O. Box 8, 50150. Tel: 641-946-8298. [CEM]
Catechesis/Religious Programs—Clustered with St. Mary, Albia. Tel: 641-932-5589.

Marengo, Iowa Co., St. Patrick's (1878) (Irish), Rev. Joseph F. Roost.
Mailing Address: P.O. Box 183, 52301. Tel: 319-642-5438; Fax: 319-642-5648. [CEM]
Catechesis/Religious Programs—609 E. Randolph, 52301. Tel: 319-642-7680. Jayne Swift, D.R.E.
Students 128.

Mechanicsville, Cedar Co., St. Mary's (1872), Rev. Thomas Doyle.
Res., 52306-0457. Tel: 319-432-6236.
Catechesis/Religious Programs—Tel: 319-432-6678. Tracy Pearson, D.R.E.
Students 70.

Melcher, Marion Co., Sacred Heart (1912), Rev. Mark P. Spring.
315 S. Main, Box 277, 50163. Tel: 641-947-3261. [CEM]
Catechesis/Religious Programs—Tel: 641-947-2902. Jean Bishop, D.R.E.
Students 94.

Melrose, Monroe Co., St. Patrick's (1870) (Irish), Rev. Scott Lemaster.
Res., 200 Trinity Ave., 52569. Tel: 515-726-3457. [CEM]

Montrose, Lee Co., St. Joseph's (1860), Rev. Gerald A. Hoenig.
Res., Box 206, 52639. Tel: 319-463-5443. [JC]
Catechesis/Religious Programs—Tel: 319-463-5571.
Students 30.

Mount Pleasant, Henry Co., St. Alphonsus (1862) (Irish), Rev. Nicholas Adam; Deacon Joe Demeter.
Res., 607 S. Jackson St., 52641. Tel: 319-385-8410; Fax: 319-385-0545. [CEM]
Catechesis/Religious Programs—Tel: 319-385-4937. D.R.E.: Mary Hassenfritz, (Grades PreK-5); Cindy Riley, (Grades 6-8).
Students 316.

Muscatine, Muscatine Co.,

1—St. Mary's, (1876). Merged with St. Mathias to form SS. Mary and Mathias of Muscatine.

2—St. Mathias, (1842). Merged with St. Mary to form SS. Mary and Mathias of Muscatine.

3—SS. Mary and Mathias of Muscatine, Revs. John P. Gallagher, J.C.L.; Bernard E. Weir; Deacons Anton Tometich; James Becker.
Res., 215 W. Eighth St., 52761. Tel: 319-263-1878; 263-1416 (Parish Office); Fax: 319-263-2782.
Catechesis/Religious Programs—Tel: 319-263-3264; 363-3848. Sr. Mary Cheryl Demmer, P.B.V.M., D.R.E.
Students 450.

4—Our Lady of Guadalupe Catholic Mission, (Hispanic), Rev. Bernard E. Weir.
Res., 417 Green St., 52761. Tel: 319-263-7788.

Mystic, Appanoose Co., St. Francis. Closed. For inquiries for parish records contact the Chancery.

Newport, Johnson Co., St. Mary. Closed. For inquiries for parish records contact the Chancery.

Newton, Jasper Co., Sacred Heart (1867), Revs. Ernest E. Braida; Philip A. Cardenzana; Tammy Norcross, Pastoral Min.
Mailing Address: P.O. Box 1478, 50208-1478. Tel: 641-792-4625 (Rectory); Fax: 641-792-5963. [CEM]
McCann Center—(Parish Office and Religious Education Center) 1115 S. Eighth Ave. E., P.O. Box 1478, 50208. Tel: 641-792-2050; Fax: 641-792-5963.
Catechesis/Religious Programs—Marybeth Wagner, D.R.E. (Grades K-12).
Students 335.

Nichols, Muscatine Co., St. Mary's (1874), Revs. Louis J. Leonhardt; Benedict Okonkwo (Nigeria); Mrs. Carol Kaalberg, Parish Life Coord.
201 Short Street, Box B, 52766. Tel: 319-723-4566; Fax: 319-629-4944. [CEM][JC]

Nolan Settlement, Johnson Co., St. Bridget's. Closed. For inquiries for parish records contact the Chancery.

North English, Iowa Co., St. Joseph's (1963), Rev. John J. Whalen.
Res., 52316. Tel: 319-664-3325; Fax: 319-668-2582. [JC]
Catechesis/Religious Programs—Tel: 319-668-2241.
Students 110.

Oskaloosa, Mahaska Co., St. Mary's (1871), Rev. Robert J. Busher.
Res., 311 First Ave. E., 52577. Tel: 641-673-6680; Fax: 641-672-2211. [CEM]
Catechesis/Religious Programs—Tel: 641-673-0659. D.R.E.: Mrs. Richelle Holle; Mrs. Marjie Rinehart.
Students 225.

Ottumwa, Wapello Co., St. Mary of the Visitation (1851) (German), Rev. Robert M. Striegel.
Res., 216 N. Court St., 52501-2586. Tel: 641-682-4559; Fax: 641-682-4433.
Catechesis/Religious Programs—Tel: 641-682-4496.
Students 235.

St. Patrick's (1880), Rev. John D. Spiegel.
Res., 222 N. Ward St., 52501. Tel: 641-682-4212; Fax: 641-682-7915.
Catechesis/Religious Programs—Ottumwa Regional Catholic Religious Education, Tel: 515-682-0320. D.R.E.: Anna Hanson; Gail Bates; Mary Ryan.
Students 348.
Sacred Heart. Merged with St. Mary of the Visitation, Ottumwa.

Oxford, Johnson Co., St. Mary's (1860), Rev. Walter B. Helms.
Box 80, 52322. Tel: 319-828-4180; Fax: 319-828-4059. [CEM]
Catechesis/Religious Programs—Students 219.

Parnell, Iowa Co., St. Joseph's. Attended by St. Joseph, North English. Rev. John J. Whalen.
52325. Tel: 319-668-2366. [CEM]

Pella, Marion Co., St. Mary's (1869), Rev. Robert D. Gruss.
Res., P.O. Box 144, 50219-0144. Tel: 641-628-4262, Ext. '; Fax: 641-628-3165. [CEM]
Catechesis/Religious Programs—Tel: 641-628-3078.
Students 215.

Petersville, Clinton Co., Immaculate Conception (1853), Rev. Edward A. Botkin.
Church—2885 145th St., Charlotte, 52731-9646. Tel: 319-674-4240. [CEM]

Rathbun, Appanoose Co., St. Anthony (1895). Closed. For inquiries for parish records contact the Chancery.

Richland, Keokuk Co., St. Frances Xavier Cabrini (1946), Rev. Charles J. Fladung.
Res., 308 W. Main St., P.O. Box 130, 52585-0130. Tel: 319-456-3161; Fax: 319-456-6408.

Richmond, Washington Co., Holy Trinity, Rev. Mark W. Swanson.
Res., 580 Howard St., Kalona, 52247-9558. Tel: 319-656-2802. [CEM]
Catechesis/Religious Programs—Students 120.

Riverside, Washington Co., St. Mary of the Assumption (1877), Rev. Mark W. Swanson; Deacon David Reha.
Res., 52327. Tel: 319-648-2331; Fax: 319-648-5024. [CEM]
Catechesis/Religious Programs—Tel: 319-656-5144.
Students 108.

St. Paul, Lee Co., St. James (1838) (German). Attended by St. John, Houghton. Rev. Dennis L. Hoffman Tel: 319-469-2001.
Mailing Address: P.O. Box 100, Houghton, 52631-0100. [CEM]
Catechesis/Religious Programs—Dixie Booten, D.R.E.
Students 381.

Sigourney, Keokuk Co., St. Mary's (N. European), Rev. Philip R. Ryan; Deacon James Striegel.
Res., 415 E. Pleasant Valley St., 52591. Tel: 641-622-3426 (Rectory); 622-2316 (Business); Fax: 641-622-2001. [CEM][JC]
Catechesis/Religious Programs—Shirley Shafranck, D.R.E.
Students 117.
Mission—Keswick, Keokuk Co., Our Lady of Lourdes, 107 N. L St., Keswick, 50163. Tel: 319-738-3731.

Solon, Johnson Co., St. Mary's (1858) (Czech), Rev. Joseph R. Sparks.
Res., 1749 Racine Ave., P.O. Box 69, 52333. Tel: 319-624-2228; Fax: 319-624-3564. [CEM]
Catechesis/Religious Programs—Tel: 319-624-3455. Doug Thompson, D.R.E.
Students 343.
SS. Peter & Paul. Closed. For inquiries for parish records contact the Chancery.

String Prairie, Lee Co., St. Mary. Closed. For inquiries for parish records contact the Chancery.

Sugar Creek, Clinton Co., St. Joseph's. Consolidated with St. Mary, Bryant, to form Sts. Mary and Joseph, Sugar Creek.
Ss. Mary and Joseph (1993) (Irish-German), Rev. Gary L. Beckman.
Res., 147 Broadway St., Charlotte, 52731-9686. Tel: 319-689-4355; Fax: 319-677-2739. [CEM 2]
Catechesis/Religious Programs—Tel: 319-689-6122. Barbara Skoff, D.R.E.
Students 102.

Tipton, Cedar Co., St. Mary's (1856), Rev. M. Eugene Benda; Deacons Adrian Panther; Robert Snavely.
Res., 52772. Tel: 319-886-2506. [CEM]
Catechesis/Religious Programs—Tel: 319-886-2506. Mary Wethington, D.R.E.
Students 266.

Toronto, Clinton Co., St. James (1855). Attended by Sacred Heart, Lost Nation. Rev. Richard J. Poster; Sr. Kathleen Henneberry, Pastoral Assoc.
Mailing Address: P.O. Box 127, Lost Nation, 52254. Tel: 319-678-2200; Fax: 319-678-2389. [CEM]
Catechesis/Religious Programs—Mary Stevenson, D.R.E.
Students 62.

Valeria, Jasper Co., Sacred Heart (1892). Closed. For inquiries for parish records contact the Chancery.

Victor, Iowa Co., St. Bridget's (1886) (Belgian), Rev. Richard U. Okumu.
Res., 104 Third St., P.O. Box 266, 52347. Tel: 319-647-2220; Fax: 319-647-3231. [CEM][JC]

Villa Nova, Clinton Co., St. Patrick. Consolidated with Assumption of the Blessed Virgin Mary, Charlotte, to form Assumption and St. Patrick's, Charlotte.

Wapello, Louisa Co., St. Mary's (1867). Attended by St. Joseph, Columbus Junction. Rev. Patrick L. Lumsden.
Mailing Address: 815 Second St., Columbus Junction, 52738. Tel: 319-728-8210.

Washington, Washington Co., St. James (1860), Rev. Dennis C. Martin.
Res., 602 W. Second St., 52353-1994. Tel: 319-653-4504; Fax: 319-653-4504. [JC]
School—Tel: 319-653-3631; Fax: 319-653-3631. Ms. BethAnn McBride, Prin.
Lay Teachers 10; Students 131.
Catechesis/Religious Programs—Tel: 319-653-6213. Sr. Jane McCarthy, O.S.F., D.R.E.
Students 264.

Wellman, Washington Co., St. Joseph (1969) (German), Rev. Mark W. Swanson; Deacon David Reha.
Mailing Address: 580 Howard St., Kalona, 52247-9558. Tel: 319-656-2802. [CEM]
Catechesis/Religious Programs—Tel: 319-646-2807. Donna Reha, D.R.E.
Students 78.

Weller, Monroe Co., St. Mary. Closed. For inquiries for parish records contact the Chancery.

Welton, Clinton Co., St. Anne (1910). Attended by St. Patrick, Delmar. Rev. Edward A. Botkin.
Mailing Address:Delmar, 52037. Tel: 319-674-4240.
Catechesis/Religious Programs—Students 35.

West Branch, Cedar Co., St. Bernadette (1960). Attended by St. Joseph, West Liberty. Rev. Edward A. O'Melia.
507 E. Orange, Box 103, 52358-0103.; Church & Mailing Address: 507 E. Orange, Box 103, 52358-0103. Tel: 319-643-2095; 627-2229 (Pastor Only).
Catechesis/Religious Programs—1720 Madison St., Lipton, 52772. Martha Freeman, D.R.E.
Students 115.

West Burlington, Des Moines Co., SS. Mary and Patrick (1870), Revs. Gerald E. Stouvenel; Patrick Hilgendorf.
Res., 420 W. Mt. Pleasant St., P.O. Box 415, 52655-0415. Tel: 319-752-8771. [CEM]
Catechesis/Religious Programs—700 S. Roosevelt, Burlington, 52601. Tel: 319-753-0277. Sr. Mary Jean Assell, S.S.J., D.R.E.
Students 270.

West Liberty, Muscatine Co., St. Joseph's (1892) (Hispanic), Rev. Edward A. O'Melia.
Res., 107 W. Sixth St., 52776-1246. Tel: 319-627-2229; Fax: 319-627-2552. [CEM]
Catechesis/Religious Programs—Students 260.

West Point, Lee Co., Assumption of the Blessed Virgin Mary, Rev. David F. Wilkening.
Res., 311 Ave. C, 52656. Tel: 319-837-6808. [CEM]

What Cheer, Keokuk Co., St. Joseph's. Closed. For inquiries for parish records contact the Chancery.

Williamsburg, Iowa Co., St. Mary's (1891), Rev. Joseph F. Roost.
Res., 102 E. Penn, Box 119, 52361. Tel: 319-668-1397. [CEM]
Catechesis/Religious Programs—Tel: 319-668-2757.
Students 245.

Wilton, Muscatine Co., St. Mary's (1857), Rev. Brian J. Shepley.
Res., 701 E. 3rd St., 52778. Tel: 319-732-2271. [CEM]
Catechesis/Religious Programs—Tel: 319-732-2269.
Students 110.

Chaplains of Public Institutions

FORT MADISON. *Iowa State Penitentiary*. Rev. Gerald A. Hoenig.

IOWA CITY. *State University of Iowa Hospital*. Revs. Vitolds Valainis; Parker Ogboe (Nigeria).
Veteran's Administration Hospital. Attended from Mercy Hospital, Iowa City. Revs. Andrew E. Kelly; Louis J. Leonhardt.

KNOXVILLE. *Veteran's Administration Hospital*. Rev. Sylvester A. Conrad.

Special Assignment:
Reverend Fathers—
Boyle, John P., 2413 Walden Ct., Iowa City, IA 52246-4118
Hitch, David F., P.O. Box 69, Solon, IA 52333-0069
Martinez, Frank R., 2706 N. Gaines St., Davenport, IA 52804

On Duty Outside the Diocese:
Reverend Fathers—
Bevenour, Richard F., 622 W. Escalon, Fresno, CA 93704
Beyer, Richard J., 1315 Chapelwood Dr., Waco, TX 76712
Cassidy, Dominic J., St. Joseph Hospital, 77 N. Airlite St., Elgin, IL 60120
Colonnese, Louis M., Apartado 109, Sonsonate, Depto. Sonsonate, El Salvador
Deyo, Paul A., Marion Hall, 1122 Grandview Blvd., Apt.5, Sioux City, IA 51103
Farrell, Anthony G., St. Mary of the Lake, 218 Ocklawaha St., Eustis, FL 32726
Otto, John A., 215 11th Ave., Apt. 5, Cold Springs, MN 56320
Shortall, Robert, 916 E. University, No. 147, Dallas, TX 75206
Steckel, Gregory A., 2351 McKinley Ave., Davenport, IA 52802-1769
Sterling, John K., 2665 Woodley Rd, N.W., Washington, D.C. 20008
Young, Ronald E., 420 W. Belmont Ave., #17D, Chicago, IL 52732

Military Chaplains:
Reverend Monsignors—
Spiegel, Robert H., UNC/CFC/USFK/EUSA, CMR 415 Box 4772, APO, AE 09114

Absent on Leave:
Reverend Fathers—
Leu, James E.

Retired:
Reverend Monsignors—
Madsen, Cletus P.
Menke, S. G., St. Vincent Center, 2706 N. Gaines St., Davenport, IA 52804
Walter, Robert J., 3406 Spring St., #3, Davenport, IA 52807-2117
Reverend Fathers—
Albers, Paul C., 611 Bel Aire Dr., West Point, IA 52656
Bass, Francis E., St. Vincent Center, 2706 N. Gaines St., Davenport, IA 52804
Borger, Theodore R., 3265 Landis Ave., San Diego, CA 92104
Brothersen, Maynard J., St. Vincent Center, 2706 N. Gaines St., Davenport, IA 52804
Brownfield, Robert L., O'Keefe Hall, 104 E. Jefferson St., Iowa City, IA 52245
Collins, Edward F., Mercy McMahon Ter., 3856 J St., Sacramento, CA 95816
Conrad, Anthony J., St. Vincent Center, 2706 N. Gaines St., Davenport, IA 52804
Conrad, Sylvester A., 709 4th Ave., E., Albia, IA 52531-2455
Cross, Peter, 2220 10th St., Coralville, IA 52241
Donahue, Paul H., St. Vincent Center, 2706 N. Gaines St., Davenport, IA 52804
Durkin, John R., 8927 Willmon Way, San Antonio, TX 78239
Egert, Clifford A., St. Vincent Center, 2706 N. Gaines St., Davenport, IA 52804
Ferrara, Pasquale L., Kahl Home, 1101 W. Ninth St., Davenport, IA 52804
Gannon, Charles E., St. Vincent Center, 2706 N. Gaines St., Davenport, IA 52804
Graham, John E., The Graham House, Belle Plaine, IA 52208
Grubb, James E., 514 Fahrney Blvd., Ottumwa, IA 52501-3254
Henricksen, Francis C., 1113 First St., Tipton, IA 5277-9289
Hynes, John F., P.O. Box 32, LeClaire, TX 52753
Janssen, James M., St. Vincent Center, 2706 N. Gaines St., Davenport, IA 52804
Kelly, Daniel J., 13263 N. Branch Rd., Sarasota, FL 34231
Kokjohn, Joseph E., 5601 N. 2nd Ave., Apt.224, Boca Raton, FL 33487
Lawrence, James T., St. Vincent Center, 2706 N. Gaines St., Davenport, IA 52804
Lenoch, Francis J., 730 S. Market St, #11, Solon, IA 52333
Linnenbrink, Harry H., Cottage Gove Place, 2115 1st Ave., S.E., Apt. 304, Cedar Rapids, IA 52402
Manning, Martin B., 1900 3rd Ave., Rock Island, IL 61201

Morrissey, John J., St. Vincent Center, 2706 N. Gaines St., Davenport, IA 52804
Mulligan, Louis J., St. Vincent Center, 2706 N. Gaines St., Davenport, IA 52804
Reilman, Thomas J., 2301 Agency St., # 59, Burlington, IA 52601
Rogers, Joseph, Kahl Home, 1101 W. Ninth St., Davenport, IA 52804
Ruppenkamp, Raymond, c/o 374 23rd Pl., Clinton, IA 52732-6901
Shepler, Charles C., 3004 Garfield St., Clinton, IA 52732-1637
Stratman, Thomas F., 422 E. 10th St., Davenport, IA 52803
Stratman, William J., 518 W. Locust St., Davenport, IA 52803
Von Ah, Richard J., Kahl Home, 1101 W. 9th St., Davenport, IA 52804
Waldschmidt, Donald L., St. Vincent Center, 2706 N. Gaines St., Davenport, IA 52804
Weeg, Edmund J., St. Vincent Center, 2706 N. Gaines St., Davenport, IA 52804
Wilson, James E., P.O. Box 778, Camdenton, MO 65020

Permanent Deacons:
Anderson, Arthur, Batavia
Batson, Randol, Blue Grass
Becker, James L., Muscatine
Beckman, Clifford C., Sperry
Carl, Robert L., Muscatine
Clough, John R., West Point
Cosgrove, William T., Keokuk
Dankert, Larry F., Davenport
Demeter, M. Joseph W., Mount Pleasant
Ditewig, William, Davenport
Donart, Arthur C., Thomson, IL
Donnelly, William G., Bettendorf
Duff, Dennis L., Bettendorf
Frericks, Donald E., Blue Grass
Gengenbacher, Robert, Burlington
Gutierrez, Julian, Davenport
Hammer, Richard D., Burlington
Haut, Allen A., Bettendorf
Hilgendorf, Ramon, Clinton
Hittner, Paul F., Davenport
Jones, William, Bettendorf
Larsen, Robert, Algona
Lennon, Patrick, Clinton
Leza, Juan B., Muscatine
McCoy, Robert C., Davenport
Mosse, Marcel G., Davenport
Mueller, Aloysius P., Clinton
O'Connor, Arthur, Olatha, KS
Olson, William D., Grinnell
Panther, Adrian B., Tipton
Rasmussen, Richard J., Bettendorf
Reha, David, Wellman
Rosenthal, Joseph I., Davenport
Schmitt, John H., Low Moor
Schroeder, William E., Carroll
Sheil, Michael D., DeWitt
Sink, Thomas, Cedar Falls
Snavely, Robert E., Tipton
Starns, Terry L., Bettendorf
Stein, Ronald K., Donnellson
Strader, George D., Davenport
Striegel, James L., Delta
Timmerman, Gerald L., Davenport
Tometich, Anton I., Muscatine
Wiegand, William R., Oskaloosa
Witt, Stephen J., Grinnell

INSTITUTIONS LOCATED IN THE DIOCESE

[A] SEMINARIES, DIOCESAN

DAVENPORT. *St. Ambrose University Seminary*, 52803. Tel: 319-333-6151; Fax: 319-333-6243.
E-mail: cadam@saunix.sau.edu
Web site: www.davenportdiocese.org
Revs. Charles A. Adam, Rector; Edmond J. Dunn, Spiritual Dir. Priests 2; Students 5.

[B] COLLEGES AND UNIVERSITIES

DAVENPORT. *St. Ambrose University*, 52803-2898. Tel: 319-333-6300; Fax: 319-333-6243.
E-mail: admit@sau.edu
Web site: www.sau.edu/
For a complete listing, refer to the Colleges and Universities section.

CLINTON. *Mt. St. Clare College*, 400 Bluff Blvd., P.O. Box 2967, 52733-2967. Tel: 319-242-4023.
E-mail: admissns@clare.edu
Web site: www.clare.edu
For a complete listing, refer to the Colleges and Universities section.

[C] SECULAR CAMPUSES

IOWA CITY. *Catholic Chair of Religion*, School of Religion, 314 Gilmore Hall, University of Iowa, 52242-1376. Tel: 319-335-2164.

[D] ADULT RELIGIOUS EDUCATION

DAVENPORT. *New Horizons of Faith, Inc.*, 820 W. Central Park Ave., 52804. Tel: 319-336-8403; Fax: 319-323-5209.
E-mail: joannk@chmiowa
Sr. Joann K. Kuebrich, C.H.M.

[E] HIGH SCHOOLS, INTERPAROCHIAL

DAVENPORT. *Assumption High School*, 1020 W. Central Park Ave., 52804. Tel: 319-326-5313; Fax: 319-326-3510.
E-mail: tasunder@yahoo.com
Dr. Thomas Sunderbruch, Prin.; Ms. Molly Menster, Campus Min. Sisters 1; Lay Teachers 37; Students 525.

BURLINGTON. *Notre Dame High School*, 702 S. Roosevelt Ave., 52601. Tel: 319-754-8431; Fax: 319-752-8690. Clark McFerren, Prin. Sisters 1; Lay Teachers 20; Students 195.

CLINTON. *Prince of Peace Catholic Preparatory*, 312 S. 4th St., 52732. Tel: 319-242-8929; Fax: 319-243-8272. Mrs. Nancy Peart, Prin. Sisters of Charity B.V.M. 1; Lay Teachers 12; Students 70.

FORT MADISON. *Aquinas Junior-Senior High School*, 2600 Ave. A, 52627. Tel: 319-372-2486; Fax: 319-372-6310. Mr. Thomas Walljasper, Prin. Lay Teachers 15; Students 163; Total Staff 21.

WEST POINT. *Marquette School, Inc.* (Marquette School System). See separate listing under Elementary Schools in the Institution section. Tel: 319-837-6131.

[F] EDUCATION CENTERS

CLINTON. *Prince of Peace Early Learning.* (Grades PreK), 2520 Pershing Blvd., 52732. Tel: 319-242-9258. Nancy Peart, Prin. Lay Teachers 1; Students 57.
Prince of Peace Academy. (Grades K-8), 312 S. Fourth St., 52732. Tel: 319-242-8929. Nancy Peart, Prin. Teachers 11; Students 162.

IOWA CITY. *The Regina Catholic Education Center*, 2140 Rochester Ave., 52245. Tel: 319-337-2580; Fax: 319-337-4109.
Web site: www.regina.pvt.k12.ia.us
Mr. Raymond Pechous, Chief Admin. Tel: 319-358-2455; Ms. Sandra Feeney, Business Office.
Regina Junior Senior High School, 2150 Rochester Ave., 52245. Tel: 319-338-5436; Fax: 319-337-4109. Lay Teachers 27; Students 354.
Regina Elementary School, 2120 Rochester Ave., 52245. Tel: 319-337-5739; Fax: 319-337-4109. Ms. Celeste Vincent, Prin. Lay Teachers 31; Students 518.
Regina Religious Education, 2140 Rochester Ave., 52245. Tel: 319-351-7638; Fax: 319-337-4109. Sr. Mary Frances Michalec.
Regina Fundraising Office, 2140 Rochester Ave., 52245. Tel: 319-358-2455; Fax: 319-337-4109.
Regina Preschool-Daycare, 2140 Rochester Ave., 52245. Tel: 319-337-6198; Fax: 319-337-4109. Ms. Mary Pechous.
Regina Development Office. Tel: 319-354-5866; Fax: 319-354-1911.

KEOKUK. *Keokuk Catholic Schools, Inc.*, 2981 Plank Rd., 52632-2399. Tel: 319-524-5450; Fax: 319-524-5450. Jack Turner, Chief Admin.
St. Vincent's Elementary School. (Grades K-6). (Keokuk Catholic Schools, Inc.), 610 Timea St. Tel: 319-524-6375.
St. Vincent's Extended Day Care Program, 610 Timea St., 52632-5452. Tel: 319-524-6375. Jack Turner, Prin. Lay Teachers 8; Students 122.
Cardinal Stritch Junior Senior High School. (Grades 7-12). (Keokuk Catholic Schools, Inc.), 2981 Plank Rd., 52632-5452. Tel: 319-524-5450; Fax: 319-524-5450. Jack Turner, Prin. Lay Teachers 10; Students 104.

[G] ELEMENTARY SCHOOLS, INTERPAROCHIAL

BURLINGTON. *Burlington Area Catholic School System.* (Grades PreK-6), Notre Dame Elementary School, 700 S. Roosevelt Ave., 52601. Tel: 319-752-3776; 754-4417; Fax: 319-752-8690. Ms. Corinne Trautner, Prin. Lay Teachers 23; Students 342.

FORT MADISON. *Aquinas East and West.* (Grades PreK-3). (Primary), Aquinas East, 509 Avenue F, 52627. Tel: 319-372-5013.
E-mail: dukebasset@hotmail.com
Mr. Robert Clifton, Prin. East and West. Lay Teachers 8.
Aquinas West. (Grades 4-6). (Intermediate), 2213 Avenue J, 52627. Tel: 319-372-6428. Sisters 1; Lay Teachers 5.

MUSCATINE. *Hayes Catholic School*, 2407 Cedar St., 52761. Tel: 319-263-3264; Fax: 319-263-6700.
E-mail: mail.mus.hayes.pvt.k12.ia.us
Mrs. Pamela Levine, Prin.; Mrs. Patricia Sheets, Admin. Sisters 1; Lay Teachers 11; Students 188.

OTTUMWA. *Seton Catholic School*, 117 E. Fourth St., 52501. Tel: 515-682-8826; Fax: 515-682-6202.
E-mail: reevesd@aea15.k12.ia.us
Diane Reeves, Prin. Lay Teachers 8; Students 121.

WEST POINT. *Marquette School, Inc.* (Marquette School System), 52656. Tel: 319-837-6131; Fax: 319-837-8112.
Marquette School System: Marquette Primary. (Grades K-3). (Houghton Center), P.O. Box 134, Houghton, 52631. Tel: 319-469-3581. Sr. Pat Siepker, Prin.
Marquette School System: Marquette Intermediate. (Grades PreK & 4-6). (St. Paul Center), Box 71, St. Paul, 52657. Tel: 319-469-3881. Sr. Pat Siepker, Prin.
Marquette School System: Marquette Jr./Sr. High. (Grades 7-12). (West Point), 413 Avenue C, 52656. Tel: 319-837-6131; Fax: 319-837-8112. Mr. Daniel J. Kieler, Prin. Sisters 1; Lay Teachers 28; Students 329.

[H] CATHOLIC STUDENT CENTERS

IOWA CITY. *Newman Catholic Student Center*, 104 E. Jefferson St., 52245. Tel: 319-337-3106; Fax: 319-337-6858.
E-mail: newman-center@uiowa.edu
Web site: www.newman-ic.org
Revs. Edward J. Fitzpatrick, Dir.; John E. Stecher.

[I] RESIDENTIAL ADOLESCENT CARE CENTERS

BURLINGTON. *Young House Family Services, Inc.*, Central Office, 724 N. 3rd St., P.O. Box 845, 52601. Tel: 319-752-4000; Fax: 319-752-6933 or 758-6650.
E-mail: younghse@interl.net
For a complete listing, refer to the Special Care Facilities section.

CLINTON. *Arch, L'Arche in Clinton*, Box 278, 52733-0278. Tel: 319-243-9035; Fax: 319-243-9035.
E-mail: larchia@clinton.net
For a complete listing, refer to the Special Care Facilities section.

[J] GENERAL HOSPITALS

CENTERVILLE. *Mercy Medical Center - Centerville*, One St. Joseph's Dr., 52544. Tel: 641-437-4111; Fax: 641-437-3304.
E-mail: stjocvil@se-iowa.net
For a complete listing, refer to the Hospitals section.

CLINTON. *Mercy Medical Center - Clinton*, 1410 N. Fourth St., 52732. Tel: 319-244-5555; Fax: 319-244-5592.
Web site: www.mercyclinton.com
For a complete listing, refer to the Hospitals section.

IOWA CITY. *Mercy Hospital*, 500 E. Market St., 52245-2689. Tel: 319-339-0300; Fax: 319-339-7800.
E-mail: mercyoncall@mercyic.org
Web site: www.mercyic.org
For a complete listing, refer to the Hospitals section.

[K] SOCIAL ACTION DEPARTMENTS

DAVENPORT. *East Davenport Development Corporation*, 422 East 10th St., 52803-5499. Tel: 319-324-3257. Rev. Marvin A. Mottet, Dir.
Interfaith Housing, Ltd., 422 E. 10th St., 52803-5499. Tel: 319-324-1485; Fax: 319-324-1485.
E-mail: trtheis_interfaithhousing@emailmsn.com
Rev. Marvin A. Mottet, Contact Person.
John Lewis Coffee Shop/Miriam House, 1202 W. 3rd St., P.O. Box 3245, 52808-3245. Tel: 319-322-0518.
E-mail: jlcsiowa@aol.com
Web site: www.jlcs.org
Kate Ridge, Agent. Total Assisted 5,300; Total Staff 35.
Project Renewal of Davenport, Inc., Nazarath House, 906 W. Fifth St., 52802. Tel: 319-324-0800.
E-mail: projectrenewal@revealed.net
Ann Schwickerath.
St. Vincent Center, 2706 N. Gaines St., 52804-1998. Tel: 319-324-1911; Fax: 319-324-5842.
E-mail: shafter@davenportdiocese.org
Web site: www.davenportdiocese.org
Very Rev. Drake R. Shafter, V.G.
Thomas Merton House, Inc., c/o 422 E. 10th St., 52803. Tel: 319-324-3257; Fax: 319-326-6014.
E-mail: shcathedra@aol.com
Rev. Marvin A. Mottet.

[L] HOMES FOR AGED

DAVENPORT. *Kahl Home for the Aged and Infirm*, 1101 W. Ninth St., 52804. Tel: 319-324-1621; Fax: 319-324-1723
For a complete listing, refer to the Special Care Facilities section.

BURLINGTON. *St. Francis Continuation Care and Nursing Home*, 210 S. 5th St., 52601. Tel: 319-752-4564 *For a complete listing, refer to the Special Care Facilities section.*

CLINTON. *The Alverno Health Care Facility*, 52732. Tel: 319-242-1521; Fax: 319-243-3016.
E-mail: ruthcox@sanasys.com
Web site: www.achcamembers.org/alverno
For a complete listing, refer to the Special Care Facilities section.

[M] MONASTERIES AND RESIDENCES FOR PRIESTS AND BROTHERS

DAVENPORT. *St. Vincent Center*, 2706 N. Gaines St., 52804. Tel: 319-324-1911; Fax: 319-324-5842.
E-mail: loftus@davenportdiocese.org
Web site: www.davenportdiocese.org
Rev. Msgr. Leo J. Feeney; Rev. Msgr. Sebastian J. Menke; Rev. Msgr. James F. Parizek; Revs. Maynard J. Brothersen; Anthony J. Conrad; Paul H. Donahue; Clifford A. Egert; Charles E. Gannon; James M. Janssen; James T. Lawrence; Frank R. Martinez; William O. Meyer; John J. Morrissey; Louis J. Mulligan; Joseph Kahn V. Nguyen; Donald L. Waldschmidt; Edmund J. Weeg; Joseph M. Wolf; Francis E. Bass.

IOWA CITY. *O'Keefe Hall*, #104 E. Jefferson St., 52245. Tel: 319-337-3106; Fax: 319-337-6858.
E-mail: newman-center@uiowa.edu
Web site: www.newman-ic.org
Rev. Edward J. Fitzpatrick. In res. Revs. John E. Stecher; Robert L. Brownfield.

WEVER. *Generalate of the Brothers of the Poor of Saint Francis*, 3405 190th St., 52658. Tel: 319-372-9543; Fax: 319-372-9543.
E-mail: markgast@interl.net

[N] CONVENTS AND RESIDENCES FOR SISTERS

DAVENPORT. *Franciscan Sisters of Christ the Divine Teacher*, 2605 Boies Ave., 52802. Tel: 319-323-1502. 4130 Nobis Dr., 52802. Tel: 319-323-7038. Sr. Bernadette Counihan, O.S.F., Supr. Sisters 9.
Humility Convent, 1310 W. Pleasant St., 52804. Tel: 319-326-3257. Sr. Rosalie Riedel.
Humility of Mary Center - Motherhouse of the congregation of the Humility of Mary, 820 W. Central Park Ave., 52804. Tel: 319-323-9466; Fax: 319-323-5209.
E-mail: sisters@chmiowa.org
Web site: chiowa.org
Sr. Jude Fitzpatrick, Pres. Total in Residence 40; Total Staff 14.
Humility of Mary Novitiate, 820 W. Central Park Ave., 52804. Tel: 319-323-8533; Fax: 319-323-5209.
E-mail: sisters@chmiowa.org
Web site: chmiowa.org

CLINTON. *The Canticle*, 841 13th Ave. N., 52732-5162. Tel: 319-242-7903; Fax: 319-242-8024. Residence of the Sisters of St. Francis, Clinton, Iowa. Sr. Marilyn Huegerich, O.S.F., Pres.; Rev. John Stack, Chap.; Anita Vaessen, Admin. Tel: 319-242-7903 Ext. 2343.

ELDRIDGE. *Carmel of the Queen of Heaven Discalced Carmelite Nuns*, 17937 250th St., 52748. Tel: 319-285-8387; Fax: 319-285-7467.
E-mail: solitude@netins.net
Web site: www.netins.net/showcase/solitude
Sr. Catherine Luth, O.C.D., Prioress. Professed Sisters 16; Novices 2.

IOWA CITY. *Dominican Sisters*, 304 Oberlin St., 52245. Tel: 319-339-0993; Fax: 319-338-7475.
E-mail: yahoeh@earthlink.net
Web site: www.op.org/roman
Sisters 3.

[O] RETREAT PROGRAMS-CENTERS

DAVENPORT. *Prayer and Spirituality Center*, 518 W. Locust St., 52803. Tel: 319-333-6189; Fax: 319-333-6234.
E-mail: psc@saunix.sau.edu
Sr. Audrey Cleary, O.S.B., Dir.

BURLINGTON. *Beacon House, House of Prayer*, 915 N. Third, 52601. Tel: 319-752-2121. Bro. Mark Gastel, C.F.P., Dir. Total Staff 1.

WHEATLAND. *Our Lady of the Prairie Retreat*, 2664 145th Ave., 52777. Tel: 319-374-1092; Fax: 319-323-5209.
E-mail: joannk@chmiowa

[P] MISCELLANEOUS

DAVENPORT. *Assumption High School Foundation*, 1020 W. Central Park Ave., 52804. Tel: 319-326-5313; Fax: 319-326-3510. Dr. Thomas A. Sunderbruch.
Catholic Service Board, St. Vincent Center, 2706 N. Gaines St., 52804. Tel: 319-324-1911.
Commitment, St. Vincent Center, 2706 N. Gaines St., 52804. Tel: 319-324-1911. Rev. Louis M. Colonnese, Dir.; Sandy Carlson, Assoc. Dir.
Congregation of the Humility of Mary Charitable Trust, 820 W. Central Park Ave., 52804. Tel: 319-323-9466; Fax: 319-323-5209.
E-mail: sisters@chmiowa.org
Web site: chmiowa.org
Sr. Jude Fitzpatrick, C.H.M., Contact Person, Humility of Mary Housing, INC., 820 W. Central Park Ave., 52804. Tel: 319-323-9466; Fax: 319-323-5209. Sr. Jude Fitzpatrick, C.H.M., Contact Person. Total Assisted 151; Total Staff 11; Total in Residence 151.
Kingdom Co., 2706 N. Gaines St., 52804-1998. Tel: 319-324-1911; Fax: 319-324-5842.
E-mail: maaske@davenportdiocese.org
Web site: www.davenportdiocese.org
Charlene Maaske, C.P.A., Contact Person.
New Horizons of Faith, Inc.: Our Lady of the Prairie Retreat, 820 W. Central Park Ave., 52804. Tel: 319-323-9466; Fax: 319-323-5209. .
Quad Cities Catholic Deaf Ministry, 2706 N. Gaines St., 52804-1998. Tel: 319-324-1918; Fax: 319-324-5842.
E-mail: parizek@davenportdiocese.org
Rev. Msgr. James F. Parizek, Contact Person.
St. Vincent Home Corporation, 2706 N. Gaines St., 52804. Tel: 319-324-1911; Fax: 319-324-5842.
E-mail: ebener@davenportdiocese.org
Web site: www.davenportdiocese.org
Mr. Dan R. Ebener, Contact Person.
Spirit, Inc., 1324 Vine St., 52804. Tel: 319-326-3785. Paul Roe, Contact.

BROOKLYN. *St. Patrick Parish Foundation*, 215 Jackson St., 52211-0512. Tel: 641-522-7714.

BURLINGTON. *Burlington Notre Dame Foundation*, 702 S. Roosevelt Ave., 52601. Tel: 319-752-8690; Fax: 319-752-8690. Debbie Trine, Contact Person.
St. Vincent De Paul Society, St. John the Baptist Church Conference, 700 Division St., 52601. Tel: 319-752-9332. Tom Stevens, Contact Person.
R.E.B.A. (Religious Education Burlington Area) Trust Fund, 700 Division St., 52601. Tel: 319-752-6733; Fax: 319-753-5221.
E-mail: stjohnbu@inter/.net

CENTERVILLE. *St. Mary's Foundation of Centerville*, 828 S. 18th St., 52544.

CLINTON. *Mercy Home Care and Hospice*, 638 S. Bluff, 52732. Tel: 319-244-3766; Fax: 319-244-3719.
E-mail: noej@mercyhealth.com
Joan Noe, Admin.; Tom Hesselmann, CEO.
Mount St. Clare Speech & Hearing Center, 562 N. Bluff Blvd., 52732. Tel: 319-242-4070; Fax: 319-242-2426. Sisters of St. Francis. Sr. Marcella Marie Narlock, Dir.
Sisters of St. Francis, Clinton, Iowa, Charitable Trust, 588 N. Bluff Blvd., 52732. Tel: 319-242-7611; Fax: 319-243-0007.
E-mail: clintonosf@clinton.net
Sr. Marilyn Huegerich, O.S.F., Pres.

IOWA CITY. *Catholic Community Foundation*, 1222 Rochester Ave., P.O. Box 1581, 52245. Tel: 319-354-5866; Fax: 319-354-1911.
E-mail: cff@piano.inav.net
April E. Rouner, Dir.
Mercy Hospital Foundation, 500 E. Market St., 52245-2689. Tel: 319-339-3657; Fax: 319-358-2624. Mary DuCharme, Pres.
Mercy Hospital Guild of Iowa City, Iowa, 500 E. Market St., 52245. Carol Ebinger.
Mercy Outreach Iowa City, Inc., 500 E. Market St., 52245.
Mercy Hospital, Iowa City, Iowa, 500 E. Market St., 52245.

KEOKUK. *Ladies of Charity of Keokuk*, 1524 High St., 52632. Tel: 319-524-7517. Bonnie Pflug, Pres.; Lois Waldron, Welfare Chm.

WEST POINT. *Marquette Foundation*. Tel: 319-837-6749. Mailing Address: Box AA, 52656. Tel: 319-837-6749. Mr. Gene Winnike.

RELIGIOUS INSTITUTES OF MEN REPRESENTED IN THE DIOCESE

For further details refer to the corresponding bracketed number in the Religious Institutes of Men or Women section.

[0460]—*Brothers of the Poor of St. Francis.*—C.F.P.

[1060]—*Society of the Precious Blood.*—C.PP.S.

[0560]—*Third Order Regular of Saint Francis.*—T.O.R.

RELIGIOUS INSTITUTES OF WOMEN REPRESENTED IN THE DIOCESE

[0230]—*Benedictine Sisters of Pontifical Jurisdiction.*—O.S.B.

[0330]—*Carmelite Sisters for the Aged and Infirm.*—O.Carm.

[2100]—*Congregation of the Humility of Mary.*—C.H.M.

[1780]—*Congregation of the Sisters of the Third Order of St. Francis of Perpetual Adoration.*—F.S.P.A.

[1710]—*Congregation of the Third Order of St. Francis of Mary Immaculate, Joliet, IL.*—O.S.F.

[0420]—*Discalced Carmelite Nuns.*—O.C.D.

[1070-03]—*Dominican Sisters.*—O.P.

[1120]—*Dominican Sisters of the Roman Congregation.*—O.P.

[]—*Franciscan Sisters of Christ the Divine Teacher.*—O.S.F.

[2575]—*Institute of the Sisters of Mercy of the Americas.* (Chicago).—R.S.M.

[2420]—*Marist Missionary Sisters.*—S.M.S.M.

[3230]—*Poor Handmaids of Jesus Christ.*—P.H.J.C.

[2970]—*School Sisters of Notre Dame.*—S.S.N.D.

[1680]—*School Sisters of St. Francis.*—O.S.F.

[0430]—*Sisters of Charity of the Blessed Virgin Mary.*—B.V.M.

[1540]—*Sisters of Saint Francis, Clinton, Iowa.*—O.S.F.

[1570]—*Sisters of St. Francis of the Holy Family.*—O.S.F.

[3830]—*Sisters of St. Joseph.*—C.S.J.

[3320]—*Sisters of the Presentation of the B.V.M.*—P.B.V.M.

[1770]—*Sisters of the Third Order of St. Francis.* (Peoria, Illinois).—O.S.F.

[1705]—*Sisters of the Third Order of St. Francis of Assisi.*—O.S.F.

[1760]—*Sisters of the Third Order of St. Francis of Penance and of Charity.* (Tiffin, Ohio).—O.S.F.

NECROLOGY

✠ O'Keefe, Most Rev. Gerald F., Retired Bishop of Davenport. —Died April 12, 2000.

† Hoenig, George B., (Retired). —Died July 19, 2000.

† Kelleher, James P., (Retired). —Died Sept. 20, 2000.

† Strub, Herman A., (Retired). —Died July 10, 2000.

Archdiocese of Denver

Archidioecesis Denveriensis

Most Reverend

CHARLES J. CHAPUT, O.F.M.CAP., D.D.

Archbishop of Denver; ordained August 29, 1970; Episcopal ordination July 26, 1988;; appointed Bishop of Rapid City April 11, 1988; appointed Archbishop of Denver February 18, 1997.

Most Reverend

JOSE H. GOMEZ

Auxiliary Bishop of Denver; ordained August 15, 1978; appointed Auxiliary Bishop of Denver and Titular See of Belali January 23, 2001; ordained March 26, 2001.

ESTABLISHED A VICARIATE-APOSTOLIC IN 1868.

ERECTED A DIOCESE AUGUST 16, 1887; CREATED AN ARCHDIOCESE NOVEMBER 15, 1941.

Square Miles 40,154.

Comprises the northern part of the State of Colorado, including the 24 Counties of Adams, Arapahoe, Boulder, Clear Creek, Denver, Eagle, Garfield, Gilpin, Grand, Jackson, Jefferson, Larimer, Logan, Moffat, Morgan, Phillips, Pitkin, Rio Blanco, Routt, Sedgwick, Summit, Washington, Weld and Yuma.

For legal titles of parishes and archdiocesan institutions, consult the Chancery.

Pastoral Center: 1300 S. Steele St., Denver, CO, 80210. Tel.: 303-715-2000; Fax: 303-715-2041.

Web site address: www.archden.org/archden

E-mail address: dcr@archden.org

STATISTICAL OVERVIEW

Personnel	
Cardinal	1
Archbishop	1
Retired Archbishops	1
Auxiliary Bishops	1
Priests: Diocesan Active in Diocese	114
Priests: Active Outside Diocese	4
Priests: Diocesan in Foreign Missions	1
Priests: Retired, Sick or Absent	44
Number of Diocesan Priests	163
Religious Priests in Diocese	128
Extern Priests in Diocese	28
Ordinations:	
Diocesan Priests	6
Permanent Deacons	147
Permanent Deacons in Diocese	147
Total Brothers	22
Total Sisters	459
Parishes	
Parishes	114
With Resident Pastor:	
Resident Diocesan Priests	94
Resident Religious Priests	11
Without Resident Pastor:	
Administered by Priests	13
Administered by Deacons	2
Missions	37
Professional Ministry Personnel:	
Brothers	2
Sisters	18
Lay Ministers	221
Welfare	
Catholic Hospitals	3
Total Assisted	372,000
Health Care Centers	8
Total Assisted	4,500
Homes for the Aged	11
Total Assisted	1,953
Residential Care of Children	1
Total Assisted	60
Day Care and Extended Day Care Centers	24
Total Assisted	1,305
Specialized Homes	2
Total Assisted	68
Special Centers for Social Services	4
Total Assisted	136,000
Residential Care of Disabled	1
Total Assisted	400
Educational	
Seminaries, Diocesan	1
Students from This Diocese	63
Diocesan Students in Other Seminaries	2
Students Religious	1
Total Seminarians	66
Colleges and Universities	1
Total Students	12,360
High Schools, Diocesan and Parish	2
Total Students	857
High Schools, Private	3
Total Students	2,161
Elementary Schools, Diocesan and Parish	36
Total Students	11,302
Elementary Schools, Private	3
Total Students	504
Catechesis/Religious Education:	
High School Students	3,797
Elementary Students	24,309
Total Students Under Catholic Instruction	55,356
Teachers in the Diocese:	
Priests	6
Brothers	7
Sisters	22
Lay Teachers	712
Vital Statistics	
Receptions into the Church:	
Infant Baptism Totals	9,994
Adult Baptism Totals	925
Received into Full Communion	1,670
First Communions	8,536
Confirmations	4,248
Marriages:	
Catholic	1,483
Interfaith	812
Total Marriages	2,295
Deaths	2,796
Total Catholic Population	373,500
Total Population	2,719,200

Former Bishops—Most Rev. JOSEPH PROJECTUS MACHEBEUF, D.D., cons. Titular Bishop of Epiphania and Vicar Apostolic of Colorado and Utah, Aug. 16, 1868; first Bishop of Denver in 1887; died July 10, 1889.—Most Rev. NICHOLAS CHRYSOSTOM MATZ, D.D., cons. Titular Bishop of Telmessa and Coadjutor of Denver *cum jure successionis,* Oct. 28, 1887; succeeded to the See of Denver, July 10, 1889; died Aug. 9, 1917.—Most Rev. J. HENRY TIHEN, D.D., ord. April 26, 1886; cons. Bishop of Lincoln, July 6, 1911; transferred to the See of Denver, Sept. 21, 1917; resigned Jan. 6, 1931; Apostolic Admin. until July 16, 1931; died Jan. 14, 1940.—Most Rev. URBAN J. VEHR, D.D., ord. May 29, 1915; Bishop of Denver; appt. April 17, 1931; cons. June 10, 1931; installed July 16, 1931; elevated to Archiepiscopal dignity, Nov. 15, 1941; appt. Jan. 6, 1942; installed as Archbishop of Denver; resigned Feb. 22, 1967; died Sept. 19, 1973.—Most Rev. JAMES V. CASEY, D.D., ord. Dec. 8, 1939; Titular Bishop of Citium and Auxiliary of Lincoln; appt. April 5, 1957; cons. April 24, 1957; promoted to Archbishop of Denver, Feb. 22, 1967; died March 14, 1986.—His Eminence J. FRANCIS CARDINAL STAFFORD, D.D., ord. Dec. 15, 1957; cons. Auxiliary Bishop of Baltimore, Feb. 29, 1976; installed Bishop of Memphis; appt. Nov. 16, 1982; installed Archbishop of Denver; appt. June 3, 1986; appt. President of the Pontifical Council for the Laity in Rome, Aug. 1996; elevated to Cardinal Feb. 21, 1998.

The Pastoral Center—1300 S. Steele St., Denver, 80210-2599. Tel: 303-715-2000; Fax: 303-715-2041.

Vicars General—Rev. Msgr. RAYMOND N. JONES; Rev. Msgr. R. WALKER NICKLESS.

Moderator of the Curia—Rev. Msgr. RAYMOND N. JONES, V.G.

Chancellor—FRANCIS X. MAIER.

Vice Chancellor—Mr. TIM J. MCCARTHY, J.C.L.

Executive Assistant to the Archbishop—PATRICIA J. MCDONALD.

Secretary for Permanent Deacons—Deacon ALFONSO M. SANDOVAL.

Secretary Finance Administration and Planning—DENNIS RUSSELL.

Secretary for Development—JAN ZAPAPAS.

Vicar for Clergy—Rev. Msgr. R. WALKER NICKLESS, V.G.

Assistant Secretary for Priests—Rev. THOMAS S. FRYAR.

Secretary for Religious—Sr. SHARON FORD.

Secretary for Social Concerns—DENISE MADDEN.

Secretary for Catholic Education—BETSY H. BOYLE, Ed.D.

Secretary for Evangelization and Catechesis—MARCO ROMAN.

Secretary for Hispanic Ministry—MAR MUNOZ-VISOSO.
Archdiocesan Ecumenical Officer—Vacant.
Archdiocesan Master of Ceremonies—Vacant.
Presbyteral Council—Rev. Msgr. EDWARD HOFFMANN, Chm.; Rev. THOMAS FRYAR, Vice Chm.; Rev. Msgr. R. WALKER NICKLESS, Sec.
Priests' Continuing Education Committee—Rev. Msgr. R. WALKER NICKLESS; Revs. SAMUEL AQUILA; JAMES E. FOX; ROGER LASCELLE; ANDREW KEMBERLING, O.S.B.; SEAN MCGRATH.
Consultors—Rev. Msgr. EDWARD BUELT; Rev. Msgr. EDWARD M. HOFFMANN, V.F.; Rev. Msgr. RAYMOND N. JONES, V.G.; Rev. Msgr. EDWARD T. MADDEN, V.F.; Rev. Msgr. R. WALKER NICKLESS, V.G.; Rev. JOSEPH MONAHAN; Very Rev. DAVID CROAK.
Archdiocesan Finance Council—Most Rev. CHARLES J. CHAPUT, O.F.M.Cap.; Rev. Msgr. RAYMOND N. JONES, V.G.; Rev. Msgr. R. WALKER NICKLESS, V.G.; Mr. DENNIS D. RUSSELL; Mr. JOHN P. BOX; Mr. JEROME R. JUDD; Dr. LAWRENCE F. JOHNSON; Mr. WILLIAM KEEFE; Judge LEONARD P. PLANK; Ms. CAROL THURSTIN; Mr. NICK ZIESER.
Council for Religious—Rev. GEORGE FITZGERALD, C.S.P.; Sr. SHARON FORD, R.S.M., Sec.; Sr. CHRISTINE HOCK, R.G.S.; Sr. MACRINA SCOTT, O.S.F.; Bro. CHARLES MILLER, F.S.C.; Rev. LAWRENCE CHRISTENSEN C.M.; Sr. MARY DEL RAY EKLER, R.S.M.; Sr. LAVONNE GUIDONI, S.C.L.; Rev. CHARLIE MARTINEZ, O.F.M.; Sr. ANN MARTIN KLEE, S.C.; Sr. MARGARET THOMAS, O.P.
Chairman of Deans—Rev. Msgr. R. WALKER NICKLESS, Sec. for Priests & Seminarians. Tel: 303-715-3197.
Deaneries—Very Rev. DARRELL SCHAFFER, V.F., East Denver; Very Rev. ROBERT KINKLE, V.F., North Denver; Very Rev. MELVIN THOMPSON, V.F., West Denver; Rev. Msgr. EDWARD HOFFMANN S.T.D., J.C.L., Southeast Denver; Very Rev. THOMAS FRYAR, V.F., Southwest Denver; Very Rev. DAVID P. CROAK, V.F., Aurora; Rev. Msgr. EDWARD MADDEN, V.F., Boulder; Very Rev. ROBERT AMUNDSEN, V.F., Fort Collins; Very Rev. JAMES R. BAIRD, V.F., Eastern Plains; Very Rev. REINHOLD WEISSBECK, V.F., Greeley; Rev. Msgr. GEORGE SCHROEDER V.F., Western Slope; Very Rev. ROBERT MEZNOR, V.F., West Central Denver; Rev. Msgr. JOHN ANDERSON, V.F., East Central Denver.

Metropolitan Tribunal

Judicial Vicar—Very Rev. JAMES S. MORENO, J.C.D.
Executive Director—Mr. TIMOTHY J. MCCARTHY, J.C.L.
Clerk of Due Process—Mr. TIMOTHY J. MCCARTHY, J.C.L.
Promoter of Justice—Rev. Msgr. EDWARD L. BUELT, J.C.L.
Judges—Very Rev. JAMES S. MORENO, J.C.D.; Rev. Msgr. MICHAEL J. CHAMBERLAIN, J.C.L.; Rev. ROBERT P. HUNDT, J.C.L.; Mr. TIMOTHY J. MCCARTHY, J.C.L.
Defenders of the Bond—Rev. Msgr. EDWARD L. BUELT, J.C.L.; Rev. THOMAS S. FRYAR.
Judicial Auditor—CHRISTOPHER BRUST.
Canonical Advisor—Vacant.
Advocates—Advocates appointed individually for particular cases.
Ecclesiastical Notary—RONDA WHITEHURST.
Coordinator of Second Instance—ELIZABETH O'MALLEY.
The Metropolitan Tribunal—Handles all marriage permissions and dispensations by delegation.
Our Lady of the New Advent Theological Institute—Offers programs of study in philosophy and theology in its three divisions: St. John Vianney Theological Seminary, the Diaconate Formation Program and the Division of Lay Formation.
St. John Vianney Theological Seminary—(See section A, Seminaries, Religious or Scholasticates).
Spirituality Year—Tel: 303-282-3429. Rev. CHRISTOPHER HELLSTROM, Dir. Two-year Philosophy Cycle and Four-year Theology Cycle.
Archbishop Vehr Theological Library—Tel: 303-282-3146. Ms. SYLVIA RAEL, Dir.
Office of Liturgy—Sr. MOIRA DEBONO, Dir.
Diaconate Formation Program—Tel: 303-715-3198. Deacon ALFONSO M. SANDOVAL, Dir. Aspirancy Year, Three Year Study and Continuing Education for Deacons.
Division of Lay Formation—Tel: 303-715-3195. Sr. MACRINA SCOTT, O.S.F., Dir. Tel: 303-715-3101.
Catechetical School—
Catholic Biblical School—Sr. MACRINA SCOTT, O.S.F., Dir. Tel: 303-715-3195.

Archdiocesan Offices and Directors

The Archdiocese of Denver, a corporation sole—Most Rev. CHARLES J. CHAPUT, O.F.M.Cap., Archbishop of Denver, *1300 S. Steele St., Denver, 80210.* Tel: 303-715-3129.
Archdiocesan Campaign for Human Development—DENISE MADDEN, Mission Coord. Tel: 303-715-3165.
Archdiocesan Liaison for Health Care—Sr. SHARON FORD. Tel: 303-715-3198.
Chief Financial Officer—DENNIS D. RUSSELL. Tel: 303-715-3258.
Director of Construction and Engineering—WALTER E. WOSTENBERG.
Director of Property and Real Estate—Vacant.
Director of Cemetery & Mortuary—MICHAEL WRIGHT.
Director of Parish Accounting—ERNEST ARMSTRONG.
Director of Human Resources—BARBARA BUCHANAN.
Director of Information Services—MICHAEL MCKEE.
Director of Insurance & Risk—ROSE MARY NELSON.
Director of Planning—RICHARD SOSA.
Controller—JOYCE TALBURT.
A.C.C.W.—VIE THORGREN, Spiritual Moderator, *3716 S. Forest Way, Denver, 80277.* Tel: 303-757-3722.
AIDS Task Force Members—Deacon JOSEPH BABISH, Chm.
Archdiocese of Denver Mortuary—12801 W. 44th Ave., Wheat Ridge, 80033. Tel: 303-425-9511; Fax: 303-425-0242. MICHAEL WRIGHT, Dir.
Archdiocesan Housing Committee, Inc.—ANNA STROBEL, Exec. Dir., *1544 Pearl St., Denver, 80203.* Tel: 303-830-0215.
Housing Management Services, Inc.—1544 Pearl St., Denver, 80203. Tel: 303-830-0215; Fax: 303-830-2885.
Boy and Girl Scouts—JAY ZOLITOR, *2071 S. Gray Dr., Denver, 80227.* Tel: 303-987-2306.
Building Committee—Very Rev. SAMUEL J. AQUILA; RAYMOND L. CRITES; RICHARD G. DUCEY; PETER J. FURSTENBERG; ALAN D. GILLAN; JAMES M. KLINK; JOHN F. MCGUIRE; GERHARD R. MUELLER; Rev. Msgr. JAMES W. RASBY; MICHAEL D. VANEK; WALTER E. WOSTENBERG.
Secretariat for Catholic Schools—BETSY H. BOYLE, Ed.D., Sec. for Catholic Schools & Supt., Office of Catholic Schools.
Secretariat for Evangelization and Catechesis—MARCO ROMAN, Sec. JEANETTE STACKHOUSE, Dir., Office of Christian Initiation Catholic Schools (RCIA); Rev. ROLAND FREEMAN, Dir., Special Religious Education; Sr. MARY CATHERINE WIDGER, S.L., Assoc. Dir., Education for Developmentally Disabled Persons, *3101 W. Hillside Pl., Denver, 80219.* Tel: 303-934-1999.
Office of Marriage of Family—CHRISTOPHER WEST, Dir. Tel: 303-715-3259; Fax: 303-715-2042.
Regional Catechetical Coordinators—DON SCHNEIDER; Sr. MARY REGIS LEAHY, R.S.M., Northern & East Plains, *336 Emery St., Longmont, 80501.* Tel: 303-678-0900; Fax: 303-772-5636. Sr. MARY ANN FLAX, Western Slope, *P.O. Box 4198, Steamboat Springs, 80477.* Tel: 970-824-4822.
Youth/Young Adult and Campus Ministry—ROBERT SHERWIN, Dir. Tel: 303-715-3203; Fax: 303-715-2042.
Respect Life Office—MIMI ECKSTEIN, Dir. Tel: 303-715-3205; Fax: 303-715-2040.
Office of Young Adult and Hispanic Youth Ministry—JAKE SAMOUR, Coord. Tel: 303-715-3279; Fax: 303-715-2042.
Mt. Olivet Cemetery Association—MICHAEL WRIGHT, Dir., *12801 W. 44th Ave., Wheat Ridge, 80033.* Tel: 303-424-7785.
Catholic Charities and Community Services of the Archdiocese of Denver, Inc.—JAMES H. MAUCK, Pres., *2525 W. Alameda Ave., P.O. Box 19020, Denver, 80219.* Tel: 303-742-0828; Fax: 303-742-0774., *460 Linden Center Dr., Ft. Collins, 80524.* Tel: 303-484-5010. (For further details see Catholic Community Services-Northern, Inc. under Institutions located in the Archdiocese.).
Secretary for Social Concerns—DENISE MADDEN. Tel: 303-715-3171. Missions: Campaign for Human Development; Catholic Relief Services; Society for Propagation of the Faith; Holy Childhood Association; Rural Life Ministry; Archdiocesan Aids Ministry; Liaison for: African American Community; Catholic Deaf Community; Hmong Community; Kateri Catholic Indians; Korean Community; Vietnamese Community.
Colorado Catholic Conference 501(c)(4)—JIM TATTEN. Tel: 303-715-3206.
Secretary for Communications—GREGORY KAIL, *1300 S. Steele St., Denver, 80210.* Tel: 303-715-3123.
Secretary of Development—JAN ZAPAPUS, *1300 S. Steele St., Denver, 80210.* Tel: 303-715-3111; Fax: 303-715-2041.
Holy Childhood Assn.—DENISE MADDEN, Dir., *1300 S. Steele St., Denver, 80210.* Tel: 303-715-3201.
John Paul II Center for the New Evangelization—MICHAEL MCKEE, *1300 S. Steele St., Denver, 80210.* Tel: 303-715-2007.
Legion of Mary—Vacant.
Migrant Ministry Archdiocesan Hispanic Center—3401 Pecos St., Denver, 80211. Tel: 303-433-9013.
Archdiocesan Hispanic Center—MAR MUNOZ-VISOSO, *3401 Pecos St., Denver, 80211.* Tel: 303-433-9013.
Office of Liturgy—Sr. MOIRA DEBONO, Dir. Liturgy. Tel: 303-715-3156.
Diaconate Program—Deacons ALFONSO M. SANDOVAL, Sec. CLARENCE MCDAVID, Assoc. Sec. Tel: 303-715-3198.
Priests' Eucharistic League—Rev. Msgr. JOHN V. ANDERSON, Dir., *1530 Logan St., Denver, 80202.* Tel: 303-831-7010.
Religious—Sr. SHARON FORD, R.S.M., Sec. Tel: 303-715-3239.
Rural Life Conference—RITA MAILANDER, *3990 S. Syracuse Way, Denver, 80237.* Tel: 303-741-2133.
Vocation Office—Sr. SHARON FORD, R.S.M., Assoc. Dir. Tel: 303-715-3239; Fax: 303-715-2048.

CLERGY, PARISHES, MISSIONS AND PAROCHIAL SCHOOLS

CITY OF DENVER
(County of Denver)

1—CATHEDRAL OF THE IMMACULATE CONCEPTION (1860), Rev. Msgr. John V. Anderson, Rector; Deacons Jack Sutton; Joe Babish; Rev. John DiPeentino. In res., Revs. Charlie Martinez, O.F.M.; James Kleiner; David Stahl; Donald Sutton.
Res., 1530 Logan St., 80203. Tel: 303-831-7010; Fax: 303-831-9514.
Catechesis/Religious Programs—Students 109.

2—ALL SAINTS (1950), Rev. James R. Purfield; Deacon Arthur A. Vigil.
Res., 2559 S. Federal Blvd., 80219. Tel: 303-922-3758; Fax: 303-922-3750.
Parish Center—2560 S. Grove St., 80219.
Catechesis/Religious Programs—Tel: 303-922-7690. Students 294.

3—ANNUNCIATION (1883), Rev. Gene J. Emrisek, O.F.M.Cap. In res., Revs. John P. Cousins, O.F.M.Cap.; Edward Judy, O.F.M.Cap.; Cyrus Gallagher, O.F.M.Cap.; Gregory Beyer, O.F.M.Cap.; John Toepfer, O.F.M.Cap.
Office: 3621 Humboldt St., 80205.
Res., 3554 Humboldt St., 80205. Tel: 303-296-5110; Fax: 303-296-1026.
School—3536 Lafayette St., 80205. Tel: 303-296-2515. Sr. Jean Panisko, S.C.L., Prin.
Sisters of Charity of Leavenworth 5; Lay Teachers 9; Students 186.
Catechesis/Religious Programs—Students 148.

4—ASSUMPTION (1912), Revs. Hugh Guentner, O.S.M.; Gabriel M. Ramacciotti, O.S.M.; Bro. Philip Eikmeyer, O.S.M.; Deacon Harold DelReal.
Res., 2361 E. 78th Ave., 80229. Tel: 303-288-2442; Fax: 303-289-2713.
School—2341 E. 78th Ave., 80229. Tel: 303-288-2159. Colleen McManamon, Prin.
Lay Teachers 8; Students 153.
Catechesis/Religious Programs—Tel: 303-289-2713. Students 389.

5—BLESSED SACRAMENT (1912), Rev. Kenneth Liuzzi; Deacon Nathan Coursey.
Mailing Address: & Office: 1912 Eudora St., 80220-1253.
Res., 4930 Montview Blvd., 80207. Tel: 303-355-7361; Fax: 303-355-0894.
School—1973 Elm St., 80220. Tel: 303-377-8835.
Lay Teachers 14; Students 258.
Catechesis/Religious Programs—Students 68.

6—CHRIST THE KING (1947), Rev. J. Darrell Schaffer. In res., Rev. John Krenzke, (Retired).
Res., 845 Fairfax St., 80220. Tel: 303-388-1643; Fax: 303-355-0141.
School—860 Elm St., 80220. Tel: 303-321-2123; Fax: 303-321-2191. Kenneth S. LaRusso, Prin.
Lay Teachers 15; Students 212.
Catechesis/Religious Programs—Students 25.

7—CURE D'ARS (1952), Rev. John P. Cousins, O.F.M.Cap.; Deacon Clarence G. McDavid.
Office: 3050 Dahlia St., 80207. Tel: 303-322-1119; Fax: 303-322-9335.
Church—3201 Dahlia St., 80207. Tel: 303-322-7709.
Catechesis/Religious Programs—Students 108.

8—CHURCH OF THE GOOD SHEPHERD (1981). (Formerly St. John the Evangelist & St. Philomena). Rev. Neal A. Pfister; Deacons Dominic Deprofio; George Marin.
Church and Res.—2626 E. Seventh Ave. Pkwy., 80206-3809. Tel: 303-322-7706; Fax: 303-399-1382.
Business and D.R.E. Offices—2626 E. Seventh Ave. Pkwy., 80206.
Middle School—620 Elizabeth St., 80206.
School—940 Fillmore St., 80206. Tel: 303-377-8018; Fax: 303-377-4034.
Lay Teachers 24; Students 330.

9—GUARDIAN ANGELS (1954), Rev. Sean McGrath; Deacon Richard Borda.
Res., 1843 W. 52nd Ave., 80221. Tel: 303-433-8361; Fax: 303-477-2066.
School—Tel: 303-480-9005. Mary Gold, Prin.
Lay Teachers 13; Students 225.
Catechesis/Religious Programs—Students 175.

10—HOLY CROSS (Thornton) (1957), Rev. Thomas Coyte; Deacons Tim Ritchey; Russell Halpine; Joe Benedetto; Nehemias Ruiz.
Res., 9371 Wigham St., 80229. Tel: 303-289-2258 (Voice TDD); Fax: 303-289-2259.
Catechesis/Religious Programs—Students 375.

11—HOLY FAMILY (1889), Rev. Robert J. Greenslade. In res., Very Rev. James Moreno.
Res., 4377 Utica St., 80212. Tel: 303-455-1664; Fax: 303-455-7732.
Church—W. 44th Ave. & Utica St., 80212.
School—(Grades PreK-8) 4380 Utica St., 80212. Tel: 303-477-4023. Russell Plucinski, Prin.
Lay Teachers 17; Students 179.
Catechesis/Religious Programs—4377 Utica St., 80212. Tel: 303-433-9781.
Students 83.

12—HOLY GHOST (1905), Rev. Msgr. John V. Anderson; Revs. David Stahl; Donald Sutton; Deacon Vernon L. Rompot.
Res., 1900 California St., 80202. Tel: 303-292-1556; Fax: 303-292-5378.
Catechesis/Religious Programs—Students 180.
Mission—Denver, Denver Co., St. Elizabeth of Hungary, 1060 St. Francis Way, Denver, 80204. Tel: 303-534-4014; Fax: 303-534-4140. Deacon James Brown; John Girten, Parish Coord.

13—HOLY PROTECTION OF THE MOTHER OF GOD (Byzantine), Rev. Joseph Hutsko.
Mailing Address: 1074 S. Cook St., 80209. Tel: 303-778-8283.
Church—1201 S. Elizabeth St., 80209.

14—HOLY ROSARY (1918), Rev. Joseph A. Meznar.
Mailing Address: P.O. Box 8685, 80201-8685.
Res., 4695 Pearl St., 80216. Tel: 303-296-3283.
Catechesis/Religious Programs—Students 215.

15—MONTBELLO CATHOLIC PARISH-CHURCH OF THE ASCENSION (1972), Rev. John Gibbons, Admin. In res., Rev. Peter Urban.
Church—14050 Maxwell Pl., 80239. Tel: 303-371-0786; 373-4950 (Church); Fax: 303-373-4954.
Rectory: 13190 E. 48th Ave., 80239.

16—MOST PRECIOUS BLOOD (1952), Rev. Kenneth Koehler; Deacon Lewis Barbato, (Retired).
Res., 2250 S. Harrison, 80210. Tel: 303-756-3083; Fax: 303-756-5628.
School—3959 E. Iliff, 80210. Tel: 303-757-1279. Jerry Ann Walker, Prin.
Lay Teachers 26; Students 340.
Catechesis/Religious Programs—Students 260.

17—MOTHER OF GOD (1949), Rev. Msgr. Raymond N. Jones.
Res., 475 Logan St., 80203. Tel: 303-744-1715; Fax: 303-744-1716.

18—NOTRE DAME (1957), Revs. Leo R. Horrigan; Walter Huber, S.M.B.; Michael J. O'Brien; Deacon Chuck Parker.
Mailing Address: 5100 W. Evans Ave., 80219.
Church—2190 S. Sheridan Blvd., 80227.
Parish Center—Tel: 303-935-3900; Fax: 303-937-6699.
School—2165 S. Zenobia St., 80219. Tel: 303-935-3549; Fax: 303-937-4868. Stephen Furches, Prin.
Lay Teachers 22; Students 758.
Catechesis/Religious Programs—2160 S. Zenobia St., 80219. Tel: 303-922-9875; Fax: 303-937-6699.
Students 542.

19—OUR LADY OF GRACE (1951), Rev. Patrick Kennedy.
Res., 2645 E. 48th Ave., 80216. Tel: 303-297-3440; Fax: 303-297-3430.
Catechesis/Religious Programs—Students 108.

20—OUR LADY OF GUADALUPE (1936) (Hispanic), Rev. Felix Lopez, C.R.
Res., 1209 W. 36th Ave., 80211. Tel: 303-477-1402; 477-8113; Fax: 303-477-4013.

21—OUR LADY OF LOURDES (1947), Rev. Robert D. Fisher; Deacon Philip Harrington.
Res., 2200 S. Logan St., 80210. Tel: 303-722-6861; Fax: 303-722-4810.
School—2256 S. Logan St., 80210. Tel: 303-722-7525. Joan Sheehan, Prin.
Sisters 1; Lay Teachers 12; Students 200.
Catechesis/Religious Programs—Students 102.

22—OUR LADY OF MT. CARMEL (1894) (Italian), Revs. Lawrence E. Kulbis, O.S.M.; Lawrence E. Walling, O.S.M. In res., Revs. Joseph M. Carbone, O.S.M.; Gabriel M. Weber, O.S.M.
Res., 3549 Navajo St., 80211. Tel: 303-455-0447; Fax: 303-455-5487.

23—PRESENTATION OF OUR LADY, Rev. David A. Stahl.
Res., 665 Irving St., 80204. Tel: 303-534-4882; Fax: 303-893-5056.
School—660 Julian St., 80204. Tel: 303-629-6562.
Lay Teachers 12; Students 220.

24—CHURCH OF THE RISEN CHRIST (1967), Very Rev. Edward M. Hoffmann, S.T.D., V.F.; Rev. Grzegorz J. Cioch.
Church—3060 S. Monaco Pkwy., 80222. Tel: 303-758-8826; Fax: 303-782-9667.
Catechesis/Religious Programs—Students 628.

25—SACRED HEART (1879) (Hispanic), Rev. Marcus Medrano.
Res., 2760 Larimer St., 80205. Tel: 303-294-9830; Fax: 303-296-0171.

26—ST. ANTHONY OF PADUA (1947), Revs. Daniel J. Norwick; John H. Karssen, C.M.
Res., 3801 W. Ohio Ave., 80219. Tel: 303-935-2431; Fax: 303-935-8969.
Parish Center—775 S. Newton St., 80219.
Catechesis/Religious Programs—Tel: 303-936-5386; Fax: 303-935-8969.
Students 285.

27—ST. CAJETAN'S (1922) (Hispanic), Revs. James Prohens, C.R.; Tomas Fraile, C.R.; Deacon Filemon F. Gonzales, (Retired).
Res., 299 S. Stuart, 80219. Tel: 303-922-6306; Fax: 303-936-8285.
Church—299 S. Raleigh, 80219. Tel: 303-935-4483.
Catechesis/Religious Programs—4325 W. Alameda, 80219.
Students 334.

28—ST. CATHERINE OF SIENA (1912), Revs. Robert P. Meznar; Manuel Gabel.
Res., 4200 Federal Blvd., 80211. Tel: 303-455-9090; Fax: 303-455-6651.
School—4280 Federal Blvd., 80211. Tel: 303-477-8035. Dilia Mapelli Taylor, Prin.
Lay Teachers 12; Students 203.
Catechesis/Religious Programs—Students 86.

29—ST. DOMINIC'S (1889), Revs. Dennis C. Woerter, O.P.; Brian Bricker, O.P. In res., Revs. Michael G. Kyte, O.P., Novice Master; John Vincent Blake, O.P.; Bro. Henry A. Denier, O.P.
Res., 3005 W. 29th Ave., 80211. Tel: 303-455-3613; Fax: 303-455-3087.
Catechesis/Religious Programs—Students 239.

30—ST. FRANCIS DE SALES (1892), Rev. Msgr. Frank G. Morfeld.
Res., 301 S. Sherman St., 80209. Tel: 303-744-7211; Fax: 303-744-7211.
School—235 S. Sherman St., 80209. Tel: 303-744-7231. Sr. Eleanor O'Hearn, C.S.J., Prin.
Sisters of St. Joseph 3; Lay Teachers 10; Students 225.

31—ST. IGNATIUS LOYOLA (1924), Revs. C. Thomas Jost; John F. Brady, S.J.; Frank J. Schmitt, S.J.; Deacon Guffie Menogan. In res., Revs. J. Patrick Walsh, S.J.; Kevin L. Cullen, S.J.; Patrick Weis, S.J.
Res., 2305 Gaylord St., 80205. Tel: 303-322-8042; Fax: 303-322-2927.
School—2350 Gaylord, 80205. Tel: 303-355-9900.
Sisters of Charity of Cincinnati 4; Lay Teachers 7; Students 140.
Catechesis/Religious Programs—Students 227.

32—ST. JAMES (1909), Rev. David Allen. In res., Rev. Bill Brock.
Res., 1336 Newport St., 80220. Tel: 303-322-7449; Fax: 303-399-2850.
School—Tel: 303-333-8275. Martha Ellis, Prin.
Lay Teachers 14; Students 204.
Catechesis/Religious Programs—Tel: 303-333-5189.
Students 74.

33—ST. JOSEPH'S (1882), Revs. Kyle Fisher, C.SS.R.; Timothy Watson, C.SS.R.; Deacon Alfredo Sanchez. In res., Revs. Michael McAndrew, C.SS.R.; Albert Castellino, C.SS.R.; Robert Simon, C.SS.R.
Res., 605 W. 6th Ave., 80204. Tel: 303-534-4408; Fax: 303-534-4412.
Catechesis/Religious Programs—Tel: 303-534-4412.
Students 155.
Centra Bienstar de San Jose Social Ministry—623 Fox St., 80201. Sr. Alicia Cuaron, O.S.F., Contact Person.

34—ST. JOSEPH'S (1902) (Polish), Rev. Jan Mucha.
Res., 517 E. 46th Ave., 80216. Tel: 303-296-3217.

35—ST. MARY MAGDALENE'S (1907), Rev. Robert J. Greenslade; Deacons Richard Viera, Pastoral Admin.; Mel Corley. In res., Revs. William Brock; Robert Staes, O.P.; Thomas Noeson, O.P.
Res., 2771 Zenobia St., 80212. Tel: 303-477-4533; Fax: 303-477-2049.

36—ST. ROSE OF LIMA (1924), Rev. Patrick Dolan; Deacon Sidney Atencio.
Res., 1320 W. Nevada Pl., 80223. Tel: 303-778-7673; Fax: 303-778-6601.
School—1345 W. Dakota Ave., 80223. Tel: 303-733-5806; Fax: 303-733-0125.
Lay Teachers 11; Students 149.
Catechesis/Religious Programs—Tel: 303-778-1397.
Students 94.

37—ST. VINCENT DE PAUL (1926), Rev. Michael Walsh; Deacons Marvin A. Hegarty; Bob Finan.
Res., 2375 E. Arizona Ave., 80210. Tel: 303-744-6119; Fax: 303-744-6124.
School—1164 S. Josephine St., 80210. Tel: 303-777-3812; Fax: 303-773-9528. Sr. Mary Angela Prin.
Sisters 4; Lay Teachers 35; Students 484.
Catechesis/Religious Programs—Tel: 303-744-0663; Fax: 303-744-0124.
Students 474.

38—TRANSFIGURATION OF OUR LORD (Ukrainian), Rev. Basil Prakaiw.
Res., 4118 Shoshone St., 80211. Tel: 303-433-2347.

SUBURBAN PARISHES OF DENVER

Arvada, Jefferson Co.,

1—SHRINE OF ST. ANNE, (1920), Rev. John D. McCormick; Deacons Michael Ritz, (Retired); Rodger Creel; Ken Hawkins, (Retired).
Res., 7555 Grant Pl., 80002. Tel: 303-420-1280; Fax: 303-420-1341. [CEM]
School—Tel: 303-422-1800; Fax: 303-422-1011. Kathie Kuehl, Prin.
Lay Teachers 22; Students 472.
Catechesis/Religious Programs—Loretta Flom, D.R.E.
Students 488.

2—ST. JOAN OF ARC, (1967), Revs. G. Timothy Gaines; James E. Kleiner; Walter Watson, S.J.; Deacons Gordon Hudec; John Smith.
Res., 12735 W. 58th Ave., 80002. Tel: 303-420-1232; Fax: 303-420-0126.
Catechesis/Religious Programs—Students 407.
Mission—Arvada, Coal Creek Catholic Community.

3—OUR LADY OF MOUNT CARMEL TRIDENTINE LATIN MASS COMMUNITY, Rev. Jose Salgado, F.S.S.P.
Res., 6985 Sheridan Blvd., 80003. Tel: 303-233-5833.
Catechesis/Religious Programs—Students 90.

4—SPIRIT OF CHRIST PARISH, (1974), Revs. Robert J. Kinkel; James J. Cuneo; Deacons Michael Howard; Richard Baker; Hugh Downey; Earl Webster.
Res., 7400 W. 80th Ave., 80003. Tel: 303-422-9173; Fax: 303-422-8251.
Catechesis/Religious Programs—Students 1,711.

Aurora, Arapahoe Co.,

1—QUEEN OF PEACE, (1968), Revs. William E. Breslin; Malachy R. McBride, O.F.M.Cap.; Rocco S. Porter; John Toepfer, O.F.M.Cap.; Deacons John Thunblom; Martin A. Wilhelm.
Res., 13120 E. Kentucky Ave., 80012. Tel: 303-364-1056; Fax: 303-364-3944.
Catechesis/Religious Programs—Students 677.

2—ST. MICHAEL THE ARCHANGEL, (1978), Rev. James E. Fox.
Res., 3320 S. Cathay St., 80013.
Parish Center and Office: 19099 E. Floyd Ave., 80013. Tel: 303-690-6797; Fax: 303-690-6932.
Catechesis/Religious Programs—Tel: 303-690-7697.
Students 849.

3—ST. PIUS X, (1956), Rev. Angelo Ossino; Deacon Gregory Martin.
Res., 13670 E. 13th Pl., 80011. Tel: 303-364-7435; Fax: 303-340-0122.
School—13680 E. 14th Pl., 80011. Tel: 303-364-6515; Fax: 303-364-1822. Mrs. Buss Kuzma, Prin.
Lay Teachers 23; Students 497.
Catechesis/Religious Programs—Students 196.

4—ST. THERESE, (1926), Revs. David P. Croak; Jorge H. Rodriguez; Deacon Richard Brady.
Res., 1243 Kingston St., 80010. Tel: 303-344-0132; Fax: 303-344-0133.
School—Tel: 303-364-7494. Dr. Kelly Kelzenberg, Prin.
Sisters 2; Lay Teachers 21; Students 330.
Catechesis/Religious Programs—Students 118.

5—ST. LAWRENCE KOREAN CATHOLIC CHURCH, (1981), Rev. Costantine K. Bae.
Res., 4310 S. Pitkin St., 80015-1974. Tel: 303-617-7555; Fax: 303-617-8265.
Catechesis/Religious Programs—Students 58.

Broomfield, Boulder, Nativity of Our Lord (1958), Rev. Dennis K. Ryan; Deacons Richard Medenwaldt; Leonard "Buz" Onesky.
Office & Church—900 W. Midway Blvd., P.O. Box 302, 80020. Tel: 303-469-5171; Fax: 303-469-5172.
School—Tel: 303-466-4177. Ms. Mary Win Aiton, Prin.
Lay Teachers 22; Students 409.
Catechesis/Religious Programs—Students 400.

Centennial, Arapahoe Co., St. Thomas More (1971), Revs. Michael Walsh; John J. McGinn; Kent Drotar; James S. Spahn; Deacons Gary Rogge; Lawrence Solan.

Res., 8035 S. Quebec St., 80112. Tel: 303-770-1155; Fax: 303-220-3399.
School—7071 E. Otero Ave., 80112. Tel: 303-770-0441. Sue Roitman, Prin.
Lay Teachers 25; Students 525.
Catechesis/Religious Programs—Students 2,132.

Commerce City, Adams Co., Our Lady Mother of the Church (1946), Rev. Terrence Kissell; Deacon Stephen Blake.
Res., 6690 E. 72nd Ave., 80022. Tel: 303-289-6489; Fax: 303-289-6480.
Catechesis/Religious Programs—Students 400.

Englewood, Arapahoe Co.,

1—ALL SOULS, (1954), Rev. Thomas S. Fryar. In res., Rev. Msgr. Thomas P. Barry; Deacon Sam Lopez.
Res., 4950 S. Logan, 80110. Tel: 303-789-0007; Fax: 303-789-0491.
School—4951 S. Pennsylvania, 80110. Tel: 303-789-2155; Fax: 303-789-0491. William Moore, Prin.
Lay Teachers 22; Students 453.
Catechesis/Religious Programs—Students 210.

2—HOLY NAME, (1894), Rev. William P. Murphy.
Res., 3290 W. Milan Ave., 80110. Tel: 303-781-6093; Fax: 303-781-6398.
Catechesis/Religious Programs—Students 142.

3—ST. LOUIS, (1911), Rev. Robert J. Reycraft; Deacon Marty Wager. In res., Rev. Simon Kalonga (Congo).
Res., 3310 S. Sherman St., 80110. Tel: 303-761-3940; Fax: 303-806-5394.
School—3301 S. Sherman St., 80110. Tel: 303-762-8307; Fax: 303-978-0242.
Lay Teachers 11; Students 168.
Catechesis/Religious Programs—Students 119.

4—OUR LADY OF LORETTO, (1998), Rev. Msgr. Edward Buelt.
Res., 13275 E. Fremont Pl. #205, 80112. Tel: 303-792-9032; Fax: 303-792-3998.
Catechesis/Religious Programs—Students 736.

Golden, Jefferson Co., St. Joseph (1867), Rev. Joseph E. Monahan; Deacon Dennis Kelly.
Res., 969 Ulysses St., 80401. Tel: 303-279-4464; Fax: 303-273-9811.
Catechesis/Religious Programs—Students 399.

Lakewood, Jefferson Co.,

1—ST. BERNADETTE, (1947), Rev. Frank Deml; Deacons L. Kenneth Dreiling; Jim Wall.
Res., 7240 W. 12th Ave., 80215. Tel: 303-233-1523; Fax: 303-233-7285.
Church—W. 12th Ave. & Teller St., 80215.
School—1100 Upham St., 80215. Tel: 303-237-0401. Henrietta Linenbrink, Prin.
Lay Teachers 11; Students 186.
Catechesis/Religious Programs—Deacon Ken Dreiling D.R.E.
Students 64.

2—CHRIST ON THE MOUNTAIN PARISH, (1975), Rev. John Grabrian.
Church—13922 W. Utah Ave., 80228-4110. Tel: 303-988-2222; Fax: 303-986-6956.
Catechesis/Religious Programs—Students 233.

3—OUR LADY OF FATIMA, (1958), Revs. Melvin F. Thompson; Tim I. Evans; Deacon Joseph W. Hawley. In res., Rev. Msgr. R. Walker Nickless, V.G.; Rev. Peter H. Dinh.
Res., 1985 Miller St., 80215. Tel: 303-233-6236; Fax: 303-237-6097.
School—Tel: 303-233-2500; Fax: 303-205-1567. Mrs. Erlene Madsen, Prin.
Lay Teachers 30; Students 430.
Catechesis/Religious Programs—Students 393.

4—ST. JUDE, (1967), Rev. Michael W. Gass; Deacons Joel J. Paulson; Tom Quinlan.
Office: 9405 W. Florida Ave., 80232-5111. Tel: 303-988-6435; Fax: 303-988-6735.
Res., 1666 S. Jellison St., 80226.
Catechesis/Religious Programs—Students 547.

Littleton, Jefferson Co., St. Frances Cabrini Parish (1972), Rev. Kenneth Leone; Deacons Craig Fucci; Paul Grimm.
Res., 6673 W. Chatfield Ave., 80128. Tel: 303-979-7688; Fax: 303-972-8566.
Catechesis/Religious Programs—Students 1,687.

Light of the World Parish (1979), Rev. Jerome M. Rohr; Deacons Charles Lamar; Eugene Mooneyham; Chester Ubowski; Dick Kramb, (Retired).
Mailing Address: 10316 W. Bowles Ave., 80127.
Res., 5903 S. Kline St., 80127. Tel: 303-973-3969; Fax: 303-973-2122.
Catechesis/Religious Programs—Georgia Glover, D.R.E.
Students 909.

St. Mary, Arapahoe Co., (1901), Revs. David Blue Jacket; Joseph T. Cao; Deacon Edward Clements.
Res., 6853 S. Prince, 80120. Tel: 303-798-8506; Fax: 303-347-2270. [JC]
School—(Grades K-8). Tel: 303-794-4757 (Grades K-3); 798-2375 (Grades 4-8). Donald McMaster, Prin.
Lay Teachers 40; Students 659.
Catechesis/Religious Programs—Tel: 720-283-4728.
Students 840.

Northglenn, Adams Co., Immaculate Heart of Mary (1967), Very Rev. Martin Lally, V.F.; Rev. Gregory Beyer, O.F.M.Cap.; Deacons Leo Oehrle; Lynn Waring; James Gollhofer.
Offices & Mailing Address: 11385 Grant Dr., 80233. Tel: 303-452-2041; Fax: 303-452-7546.
Res., 335 E. 112th Dr., 80233. Tel: 303-452-9104.
Catechesis/Religious Programs—Students 650.

Westminster, Adams Co., Holy Trinity (1956), Rev. John L. Hilton; Deacons Rex Pilger; Lloyd Quintana.
Res., 7595 N. Federal, 80030. Tel: 303-428-3594; Fax: 303-427-4125.
School—Tel: 303-427-5632. Sr. Anno La Mere, Prin.
Sisters 2; Lay Teachers 16; Students 274.
Catechesis/Religious Programs—Tel: 303-427-4581.
Students 235.
Mission—Westminster, Adams Co., Our Lady of Visitation, 2531 W. 65th Pl., 80221. Tel: 303-429-7947.

St. Mark (1973), Rev. James R. Fox; Deacons John Pontillo; Darryl Dunn.
Res., 3141 W. 96th Ave., 80031-2714. Tel: 303-466-8720; Fax: 303-466-0998.
3141 W. 96th Ave., 80030.
Catechesis/Religious Programs—Students 311.

Wheat Ridge, Jefferson Co., Queen of Vietnamese Martyrs (1976) (Asian), Revs. Bartholomew Thai Hoa Do, C.M.C.; Martin Tran Van Ban, C.M.C.; Deacons Joseph Van Le Tam; Peter Hung Phi Dang.
Res., 4655 Harlan St., 80033. Tel: 303-431-0382; Fax: 303-431-1876.

SS. Peter and Paul (1949), Rev. James K. Goggins; Deacons Gary E. Miller; Jim Wall.
Res., 3900 Pierce St., 80033. Tel: 303-424-3706; Fax: 303-424-0819.
School—Tel: 303-420-0402. Kathy Byrnes, Prin.
Lay Teachers 21; Students 380.
Catechesis/Religious Programs—Students 462.

OUTSIDE THE CITY OF DENVER

Akron, Washington Co., St. Joseph (1917), Rev. Donald Romero.
Res., 551 W. 6th St., 80720. Tel: 970-345-6996; Fax: 970-345-6504. [CEM]
Catechesis/Religious Programs—Students 114.

Aspen, Pitkin Co., St. Mary (1892), Rev. Michael G. Glen.
Mailing Address: 533 E. Main St., 81611.
Res., 104 S. Galena St., 81611. Tel: 970-925-7339; Fax: 970-925-1889.
Catechesis/Religious Programs—Students 87.
Mission—Aspen, Snowmass in Snowmass Village, Owl Creek Rd., 81615.

Ault, Weld Co., St. Mary. See Our Lady of Peace, Greeley.

Basalt, Eagle Co., St. Vincent (1970), Rev. Thomas Bradtke.
Res., P.O. 518, 81621. Tel: 970-927-0634; Fax: 970-927-0634.
Catechesis/Religious Programs—Students 150.
Mission—Carbondale, Garfield Co., St. Mary of the Crown, P.O. Box 64, 81623. Tel: 970-963-1270.

Boulder, Boulder Co.,

1—SACRED HEART OF JESUS, (1875), Very Revs. Edward T. Madden; Xavier Espinoza; Deacons Robert J. Howard; Richard Pelis.
Res., 2312 14th St., 80302. Tel: 303-442-6158; Fax: 303-442-7905. [JC]
School—(Grades PreK-8). Tel: 303-447-2362; Fax: 303-443-2466. Billie Middleton, Prin.; James J. Feldewerth, II, Asst. Prin.
Lay Teachers 23; Students 455.
Catechesis/Religious Programs—Students 617.
Mission—Nederland, Boulder Co., St. Rita, P.O. Box 901, Nederland, 80466. Tel: 303-642-7348; Fax: 303-642-7348. Deacon Francis Boselli, Admin.

2—SACRED HEART OF MARY, (1874), Rev. Dorino DeLazzer.
Res., 6739 S. Boulder Rd., 80303. Tel: 303-494-7572; Fax: 303-494-7581. [CEM]
Rectory: Tel: 303-494-1266.
Catechesis/Religious Programs—Students 903.

3—ST. MARTIN DE PORRES, (1968), Rev. Hermanagild Jayachandra; Deacon Karl T. Matz.
Res., 3300 Table Mesa Dr., 80303. Tel: 303-499-7744; Fax: 303-494-8754.
Catechesis/Religious Programs—Fax: 303-499-4061.
Students 119.

4—ST. THOMAS AQUINAS UNIVERSITY PARISH, (1950). (Campus Ministry), University of Colorado. Revs. Paul Huesing, C.S.P.; Thomas J. Holahan, C.S.P.
Pastoral Center: 904 14th St., 80302. Tel: 303-443-8383; Fax: 303-443-8399.
Catechesis/Religious Programs—Students 520.

Breckenridge, Summit Co., St. Mary (1875), Rev. Vincent Leo Smith.
Mailing Address: No. 2 W. Miner's Cr. Rd., P.O. Box 2670, Frisco, 80443. Tel: 970-668-8700; Fax: 970-668-3213.
Catechesis/Religious Programs—Students 242.
Mission—Dillon Valley, Summit Co., Our Lady of Peace, Straight Creek Rd. & Little Beaver Trail, Frisco 80443.

Brighton, Adams Co., St. Augustine (1887), Rev. Reinhold B. Weissbeck; Deacon Gilbert Rael.
Res., 675 E. Egbert St., 80601. Tel: 303-659-1410; Fax: 303-659-6449.
Catechesis/Religious Programs—Tel: 303-659-1414.
Students 484.

Brush, Morgan Co., St. Mary (1911), Rev. James R. Baird.
Res., 340 Stanford St., 80723. Tel: 970-842-2216; Fax: 970-842-4461.
Catechesis/Religious Programs—Students 189.
Mission—Stoneham, Morgan Co., St. John, 340 Stanford, Brush 80723.

Byers, Arapahoe Co., Our Lady of the Plains (1978), Rev. Thomas M. Dona.
Res., 186 N. McDonnell, Box 519, 80103. Tel: 303-822-5880; Fax: 303-822-5780.
Catechesis/Religious Programs—Students 137.

Conifer, Our Lady of The Pines (1979), Rev. Reuben Payo; Deacons Douglas Vlchek; Frank W. Kullman, (Retired).
Mailing Address: 9444 Eagle Cliff Rd., 80433. Tel: 303-838-0338; Fax: 303-838-1663.
Catechesis/Religious Programs—Students 263.
Mission—Buffalo Creek, Jefferson Co., St. Elizabeth, 9444 Eagle Cliff, 80433. Deacon Norman Beabout.

Craig, Moffat Co., St. Michael (1920), Rev. Roger L. Lascelle.
Res., 678 School St., 81625. Tel: 970-824-5330; Fax: 970-824-9724.
Catechesis/Religious Programs—Students 110.

Eagle, Eagle Co., St. Mary. See St. Clare of Assisi, Edwards.

Edwards, St. Clare of Assisi (1993), Rev. Edward J. Poehlmann.
Mailing Address: P.O. Box 1390, 81632. Tel: 970-926-2821; Fax: 970-926-5350.
Res., 53 Old County Ln., 81631.
Catechesis/Religious Programs—Students 835.
Missions—Eagle, Eagle Co., St. Mary, 215 Capitol, Eagle, 81631. Tel: 970-328-6396; Beaver Creek, Eagle Co., Beaver Creek Chapel, 33 Elk Track Rd., 81620. Tel: 970-845-9449.

Erie, Weld Co., St. Scholastica (1946). See St. Theresa, Frederick. Rev. Robert Whipkey.
Office: 436 Fifth St., Box 418, Frederick, 80530. Tel: 303-833-2966; Fax: 303-833-3000.
Church—615 Main St., 80516.
Catechesis/Religious Programs—Students 62.

Estes Park, Larimer Co., Our Lady of the Mountains (1947), Rev. James G. Simko.
Res., P.O. Box 1706, 80517. Tel: 970-586-8111; Fax: 970-586-8112.
Catechesis/Religious Programs—Sr. Marie Gerard Peter.
Students 160.

Evergreen, Jefferson Co., Christ the King (1932), Rev. Christopher A. Renner; Deacons George Fitterer (CHI) (Retired); Tom Quinlan; Brian Kerby.
Res., 4291 Evergreen Pkwy., 80439-7723. Tel: 303-674-3155; Fax: 303-674-3285.
Catechesis/Religious Programs—Tel: 303-674-5282.
Students 273.

Fort Collins, Larimer Co.,

1—ST. JOSEPH, (1879), Revs. Philip S. Meredith; Michael V. Delaney, S.J.; Deacons Warren G. Lybarger; Rick Grimler.
Res., 308 W. Mountain Ave., P.O. Box 502, 80522. Tel: 970-482-4148; Fax: 970-221-0635.
School—127 N. Howes St., 80522. Tel: 970-484-1171; Fax: 970-221-0635. Barbara Bullock, Prin.
Lay Teachers 20; Students 267.
Catechesis/Religious Programs—Students 309.
Mission—Red Feather Lakes, Larimer Co., Our Lady of the Lakes, P.O. Box 502, 80522.

2—HOLY FAMILY, (1924) (Hispanic), Rev. Douglas Hunt, C.R.
Res., 326 N. Whitcomb St., 80521. Tel: 970-482-6599; Fax: 970-482-6599.
Catechesis/Religious Programs—Students 104.

3—JOHN XXIII UNIVERSITY PARISH, (1967), Rev. Robert L. Amundsen; Deacons Leonard Benzel; William McClellan. In res., Rev. Marcel Zibognon, O.P. (Ivory Coast).
Res., 1220 University Ave., 80521. Tel: 970-484-3356; Fax: 970-484-3434.

Catechesis/Religious Programs—Students 730.
4—St. Elizabeth Ann Seton, (1981), Rev. Tim J. Evans; Deacon William Trewartha.
Res., 5450 S. Lemay Ave., 80525. Tel: 970-226-1303; Fax: 970-226-5780.
Catechesis/Religious Programs—Tel: 970-226-6549.
Students 675.

Fort Lupton, Weld Co., St. William (1909), Rev. Gregorio L. Mirto.
Res., 1025 Fulton Ave., 80621. Tel: 303-857-6642; 659-3519; 785-6400; Fax: 303-857-6643.
Catechesis/Religious Programs—Tel: 303-857-4754.
Students 310.
Mission—Platteville, Weld Co., St. Nicholas. See Wattenberg, Our Lady of Grace. 514 Marion, 80621. Tel: 970-785-2143; Fax: 970-857-6643.

Fort Morgan, Morgan Co., St. Helena (1910), Revs. Lawrence B. Kaiser; Adalberto DeGante.
Res., 917 W. 7th Ave., 80701. Tel: 970-867-2885.
Catechesis/Religious Programs—923 Pawnee, Ft. Morgan, 80701. Tel: 970-867-5768.
Students 354.
Mission—Weldona, Morgan Co., St. Francis of Assisi, 80701.

Englewood, Arapahoe Co., Our Lady of Loreto (1998), Rev. Msgr. Edward Buelt.
Res., 13275 E. Fremont Pl., #205, 80112. Tel: 303-792-9032; Fax: 303-792-3998.
Catechesis/Religious Programs—Students 736.

Frederick, Weld Co., St. Theresa (1923), Rev. Robert Whipkey.
Res., 436 Fifth St., P.O. Box 418, 80530. Tel: 970-833-2966; 303-654-1106 (Metro); Fax: 303-833-3000.
Catechesis/Religious Programs—Students 210.
Mission—Mead, Weld Co., Guardian Angels, WCR #7 & Welker St., 80530.

Glenwood Springs, Garfield Co., St. Stephen (1885), Revs. Cliff J. McMillan; William L. Smith, C.S.P.; Deacons Victor Kimminau; Charles Sprick.
Res., 1010 Grand Ave., 81601. Tel: 970-945-6673; Fax: 970-945-2089.
School—414 S. Hyland Park Dr., 81601. Tel: 970-945-7746. Connie Sandling.
Sisters 1; Lay Teachers 10; Students 100.
Catechesis/Religious Programs—Tel: 970-945-2580.
Students 130.

Grand Lake, Grand Co., St. Anne (1957), Rev. Francis J. Gerber, Jr.
Res., 219 Hancock St., P.O. Box 510, 80447. Tel: 970-627-3450; Fax: 970-627-3064.
Missions—Granby, Grand Co., Our Lady of the Snow, P.O. Box 510, 80447.; Winter Park, Grand Co., St. Bernard, P.O. Box 510, 80447.

Greeley, Weld Co., St. Mary (1965), Revs. Peter Quang Nguyen; Warren H. Seedorf, C.S.P.; Deacon Joseph H. Meilinger.
Res., 2222 23rd Ave., 80634. Tel: 970-352-1724; Fax: 970-352-1729.
Catechesis/Religious Programs—Students 525.
St. Peter (1903), Rev. Gregory K. Ames; Deacon Frederick Torrez. In res., Rev. Isaac Raney, M.Ss.A.
Office: 915 12th St., 80631. Tel: 970-352-1060; Fax: 970-352-1062.
Catechesis/Religious Programs—Tel: 970-346-9777.
Students 515.
Our Lady of Peace (1948), Rev. Bernard A. Schmitz. In res., Rev. Adalberto DeGante.
Res., 1311 3rd St., 80631. Tel: 970-353-1747; Fax: 970-353-4830.
Catechesis/Religious Programs—1303 13th St., 80631. Tel: 970-351-6473; Fax: 970-353-4830.
Students 450.
Missions—Ault, Weld Co., St. Mary, 267 E. 4th St., 80610. Tel: 970-834-1609; Ault, Weld Co., Sacred Heart, 4th St. & Starbird Rd., 80623.

Holyoke, Phillips Co., St. Patrick (1893), Rev. Daniel Zimmerschied.
Res., 519 S. Interocean, 80734. Tel: 970-854-2762; 859-2866 (Hall); Fax: 970-854-2781.
Catechesis/Religious Programs—Tel: 970-854-2558.
Students 170.
Missions—Haxtun, Phillips Co., Christ the King, 306 N. Iris, Haxtun 80731. Tel: 970-774-7640; Fleming, Logan Co., St. Peter the Apostle, 40027 CR 18, Rt. 1, Fleming 80728. Tel: 970-265-2792. [CEM]

Idaho Springs, Clear Creek Co., St. Paul's (1881), Rev. Michael F. Kerrigan.
Res., P.O. Box 848, 1632 Colorado Blvd., 80452. Tel: 303-567-4662; Fax: 303-567-4662.
Catechesis/Religious Programs—Tel: 303-567-4138.
Students 64.
Missions—Central City, Gilpin Co., St. Mary of the Assumption, P.O. Box 848, 80452.; Georgetown, Clear Creek Co., Our Lady of Lourdes, P.O. Box 848, Idaho Springs 80452. [CEM]

Iliff, Logan Co., St. Catherine of Siena (1927), Very Rev. Robert G. Whipkey, Jr., V.F.
Res., 111 S. Fifth St., P.O. Box 221, 80736. Tel: 970-522-8040; Fax: 970-334-2227.

Johnstown, Weld Co., St. John the Baptist (1937), Rev. Stephen E. Adams.
Res., 809 Charlotte St., 80534. Tel: 970-587-2879.
Catechesis/Religious Programs—Students 132.
Mission—Windsor, Weld Co., Our Lady of the Valley, P.O. Box 1018, 80534. Tel: 970-686-5084.

Julesburg, Sedgwick Co., St. Anthony (1907), Rev. Christopher A. Renner.
Res., 606 W. 3rd St., 80737. Tel: 970-474-2655; Fax: 970-474-2655.
Catechesis/Religious Programs—Students 109.
Mission—Crook, Logan Co., St. Peters, 612 E. 3rd, Crook, 80726.

Kremmling, Grand Co., St. Peter (1944), Rev. John G. Kauffman.
Church and Office: 106 S. 5th St., P.O. Box 428, 80459. Tel: 970-724-3428.
Mission—Walden, Grand Co., St. Ignatius, 80459.

Lafayette, Boulder Co., Immaculate Conception (1954), Rev. John J. Murphy.
Res., 110 W. Simpson, 80026. Tel: 303-665-5103; Fax: 303-604-9077.
Catechesis/Religious Programs—Tel: 303-665-9334.
Students 188.

Longmont, Boulder Co., St. John the Baptist (1882), Revs. Brian Morrow; Gilberto Soto; Deacon William Lee; Mr. David Schreck, Pastoral Assoc.
323 Collyer St., 80501. Tel: 303-776-0737; Fax: 303-772-5636. [JC]
School—350 Emery St., 80501. Tel: 303-776-8760. Ms. Mary Cronley, Prin.
Lay Teachers 24; Students 350.
Catechesis/Religious Programs—Tel: 303-772-5637.
Students 616.
Spirit of Peace Parish (1982), Rev. Donald Willette. Pastoral Team: Mary Franch; Christine Hersey; Julie Lupien; Waldemar Perez.
Church and Office: 1500 Hover Rd., 80501. Tel: 303-772-6322; Fax: 303-772-9415. [JC]
Catechesis/Religious Programs—Students 392.

Louisville, Boulder Co., St. Louis (1884), Revs. Donald Willette; Stanislaw Ligeza; Henri Tshibambe; Daniel Flagherty.
Office: 902 Grant Ave., 80027. Tel: 303-666-6401; Fax: 303-666-0826.
School—925 Grant Ave., 80027. Tel: 303-666-6220.
Lay Teachers 16; Students 271.
Preschool—901 Grant Ave., 80027. Tel: 303-665-0606.
Catechesis/Religious Programs—902 Grant Ave., 80027. Tel: 303-604-6055.
Students 536.

Loveland, Larimer Co., St. John the Evangelist (1902), Rev. Michael G. Palakovich, Admin.; Deacons Warren Lybarger; Robert Haigh, (Retired).
Office: 1515 Hilltop Dr., 80537. Tel: 970-669-2720; Fax: 970-669-5743.
Res., 1523 Hilltop Dr., 80537. Tel: 970-663-3457.
School—1730 W. 12th St., Tel: 970-667-6846.
Sisters 1; Students 292.
Catechesis/Religious Programs—Students 400.

Meeker, Rio Blanco Co., Holy Family (1905), Rev. Roger L. Lascelle.
Res., 889 Park, Box 866, 81641. Tel: 970-878-3300; Fax: 970-878-3300.
Mission—Rangely, Rio Blanco Co., St. Ignatius, 109 S. Stanolind Ave., Rangely, 81648. Tel: 970-675-8935; Fax: 970-675-8935.

Minturn, Eagle Co., St. Patrick's (1913), Rev. Frank Maroney.
Admin. & Mailing Address: 19 Vail Rd., 81657.
Res., 476 Pine St., 81645. Tel: 970-827-5784; Fax: 970-827-9454.
Catechesis/Religious Programs—Students 120.
Missions—Red Cliff, Eagle Co., Our Lady of Mt. Carmel; Vail, Eagle Co., The Interfaith Chapel.

Oak Creek, Routt Co., St. Martin of Tours. See Holy Name, Steamboat Springs.

Peetz, Logan Co., Sacred Heart, Very Rev. Robert G. Whipkey, Jr., V.F.
Res., 621 Logan, P.O. Box D, 80747. Tel: 970-334-2227; Fax: 970-334-2227. [CEM]
Catechesis/Religious Programs—Students 52.

Platteville, Weld Co., St. Nicholas. See St. William, Fort Lupton.
Catechesis/Religious Programs—Students 120.

Rangely, St. Ignatius (1931), Rev. Roger L. Lascelle; Deacon George Fortunato.
Res., 109 S. Stanolind Ave., 81648. Tel: 970-675-8935; Fax: 970-675-8935.
Catechesis/Religious Programs—Students 46.

Red Feathers Lakes, Larimer Co., Our Lady of the Lakes. See St. Joseph, Fort Collins.

Rifle, Garfield Co., St. Mary's (1910), Rev. Robert E. Hehn.
Res., 323 1/2 E. Fifth St., P.O. Box 191, 81650. Tel: 970-625-2547; Fax: 970-625-9025.
Catechesis/Religious Programs—341 E. 5th St., 81650. Tel: 970-625-3914.
Students 160.
Missions—Silt, Garfield Co., Sacred Heart, P.O. Box 191, 81650.; Parachute, Garfield Co., St. Brendan, P.O. Box 191, 81650.

Roggen, Weld Co., Sacred Heart (1924), Rev. Joseph J. Blanco.
Res., 38044 Weld County Rd. 16, 80652. Tel: 303-849-5313; Fax: 303-849-5674.
Catechesis/Religious Programs—Students 133.
Missions—Keenesburg, Weld Co., Holy Family, 38044 Weld County Rd. 16, 80652.; Wiggins, Morgan Co., Our Lady of Lourdes, 38044 Weld County Rd. 16, 80652.

Steamboat Springs, Routt Co., Holy Name (1907), Rev. George M. Schroeder.
Res., 504 Oak St., P.O. Box 774198, 80477-4198. Tel: 970-879-0671; Fax: 970-879-7406.
Catechesis/Religious Programs—Tel: 970-879-1225.
Students 245.
Mission—Oak Creek, Routt Co., St. Martin of Tours, 301 S. Sharp Ave., Oak Creek 80467.

Sterling, Logan Co., St. Anthony (1888), Rev. Michael J. Flaska.
Res., 327 S. 3rd St., 80751. Tel: 970-522-6422; Fax: 970-522-6442.
School—Tel: 970-522-7567.
Lay Teachers 12; Students 128.
Catechesis/Religious Programs—326 S. 3rd St., 80751. Tel: 970-522-7568.
Students 265.

Stoneham, Weld Co., St. John. See St. Mary, Brush.

Vail, Eagle Co., The Interfaith Chapel. See St. Patrick's, Minturn.

Walden, Jackson Co., St. Ignatius. See St. Peter, Kremmling.

Wattenberg, Fort Lupton Co., Our Lady of Grace. See St. William, Fort Lupton.

Weldona, Morgan Co., St. Francis of Assisi. See St. Helena, Fort Morgan.

Wiggins, Morgan Co., Our Lady of Lourdes. See Sacred Heart, Roggen.

Winter Park, Grand Co., St. Bernard of Montjoux. See St. Anne, Grand Lake.

Windsor, Weld Co., Our Lady of the Valley, Rev. Stephen E. Adams; Deacon Harold Kimble.
Office: P.O. Box 1018, 80550. Tel: 970-686-5084; Fax: 970-587-2879.
Res., 809 Charlotte St., Johnstown, 80534. Tel: 303-587-2879.

Wray, Yuma Co., St. Andrew (1891), Rev. Gerald A. Young (LA).
Res., 412 Dexter St., 80758. Tel: 970-332-5858; Fax: 970-332-4604.
Catechesis/Religious Programs—Students 120.

Yuma, Yuma Co., St. John (1888), Rev. Gerald A. Young, Admin.
Res., 508 S. Ash St., 80759. Tel: 970-848-5973; Fax: 970-332-4604.
Catechesis/Religious Programs—Students 125.

Chaplains of Public Institutions

Denver. *Veterans Hospital*. Rev. Thomas J. Woerth.
Aurora. *Fitzsimons Army Medical Center*. Rev. Edward Kucera, O.S.B.

On Duty Outside the Archdiocese:
Reverend Fathers—
Denig, Philip, Chap. (Capt.), P.O. Box 127, HHC 1 SB Unit, 31520, APO AE, Fort Leonardwood, MO 09832
Kelly, Thomas D., 15 ABW / HC, Hickam AFB, HI 96853-5112
Longwill, Cathal, Lisfannon, Buncrana, Eire, Co. Donegal, Ireland
McDaid, J. Anthony, Villa Stritch, Via Della Nocetta 63, Rome, 00164 Italy
Revello, James K.I., Chap. (Lt. Col.), Air Combat USAF, 365 Westview Dr., Hampton, VA 23666

Graduate Studies:
Reverend Fathers—
Wilborn, Jeffrey W., North American College, Vatican City State, 00120

Absent on Leave:
Reverend Fathers—
Dold, John F.
Fuller, Roger J.
McInerney, Maurice
Sczezney, Leonard J.
St. Peter, Lawrence
White, Robert H.

Retired:
Reverend Monsignors—
Barry, Thomas P., 4950 S. Logan St., Englewood, CO 80110-6921
Dentici, Thomas, St. Benedict's Monastery, 1012 Monastery Rd., Snowmass, CO 81654
Jones, William H., 7125 E. 11th Ave., Denver, CO 80220
Rasby, James W., 1011 S. Valencia, Villa 3, Denver, CO 80231
Schmitt, J. Harley, Chap., Mullen Home, 3629 W. 29th Ave., Denver, CO 80211
Reverend Fathers—
Banigan, Herbert, 1670 Sausalita Dr., Colorado Springs, CO 80907
Blach, Leo M., P.O. Box 371, Brighton, CO 80601
Breunig, Robert L., 1901 E. 13th Ave., Denver, CO 80206
Canjar, John A., 6780 E. Cedar Ave., Denver, CO 80204
Durrie, Robert L., 1580 S. Dahlia, Denver, CO 80222
Flaherty, Daniel J., 902 Grant St., Louisville, CO 80027
Gibbons, John, 14050 Maxwell Pl., Denver, CO 80239
Jones, Charles, 1129 Fillmore, Denver, CO 80206. Tel: 303-322-0624
Kane, James E., 2303 S. Vaughn Way, #208, Aurora, CO 80014
Kearney, George W., 3373 W. 36th Ave., Denver, CO 80211
Mihelich, Leopold, 6305 W. 5th Pl., Lakewood, CO 80226
Nevans, Robert V., Villa Madeline, 2771 Zenobia St., Denver, CO 80212
O'Malley, Joseph M., 1542 E. Nicholas Dr., Littleton, CO 80161
Puhl, Albert E., 2771 Zenobia St., Denver, CO 80212
Salmon, Charles P., 2835 W. 32nd, Denver, CO 80211
Sanger, Charles P., 10450 Oakmont Dr., Sun City, AZ 85351
Sullivan, Patrick, Box 274, 8962 E. Hampden Ave., Denver, CO 80231-4996
Weibel, George L., 2312 14th St., Boulder, CO 80304

Permanent Deacons:
Anderson, Ernest J., (Retired)
Ansay, Ronald J., (Retired)
Atencio, Sidney, St. Rose of Lima, Denver
Babish, Joseph T., Immaculate Conception Cathedral
Baker, Richard L., Spirit of Christ, Arvada
Ball, James J., Sr., Immaculate Conception, Lafayette
Barbato, Lewis, M.D., Member of Evaluation Team Class of 2003.
Barrows, Russell, All Souls, Englewood
Beabout, Norman, St. Elizabeth, Buffalo Creek
Benedetto, Joseph, Hearing Impaired Ministry
Benzel, Leonard, John XXIII University, Fort Collins
Blake, Stephen M., Gardens of St. Elizabeth, Denver
Borda, Richard S., Guardian Angels, Arvada
Boselli, Francis "Bud", Admin., St. Rita's Mission, Nederland
Bosovich, Frank J., All Souls, Englewood
Bowles, Richard J., Jr., Ministry in the Diocese of Colorado Springs
Brady, Richard A., St. Therese, Aurora
Brown, James, Queen of Peace, Aurora
Burgess, Lou A., Ministry in Grenada
Clausson, Ronald L., (Leave of absence)
Clements, Edward R., St. Mary, Littleton
Coker, Major Richard, USAF, Ministry in Oklahoma City
Combs, Richard E., Ministry in the Archdiocese of Seattle
Corley, Melvin G., St. Mary Magdalene, White Ridge; Airport Ministry, DIA
Coursey, Nathan D., Blessed Sacrament Parish, Denver
Creel, Rodger L., Shrine of St. Anne, Arvada
Dang, Peter Hung Phi, Queen of Vietnamese Martyrs, Wheat Ridge
Decker, Myles M., Ministry in the Diocese of Palm Beach
Del Real, Harold, Assumption, Denver
DeProfio, Dominic, Church of the Good Shepherd, Denver
DiPentino, John L., Cathedral of the Immaculate Conception, Denver
Dolan, L. Stephen, (Retired)
Donohoe, Joseph H., Light of the World, Littleton
Dorwart, Jason, (Retired)
Downey, Hugh, Spirit of Christ, Arvada
Dreiling, L. Kenneth, St. Bernedette, Lakewood
Dunn, Darryl, St. Mark, Westminster
Elder, R. Taylor, St. Louis, Louisville
Finan, Robert E., St. Vincent de Paul, Denver
Fitterer, George (JOL), (Retired)
Fortunato, George R., (Leave of Absence)
Franklin, John, Holy Name, Steamboat Springs
Frisinger, Howard, (Retired)
Fucci, Craig (LA), St. Francis Cabrini, Littleton
Gallagher, Michael, St. Patrick, Minturn
Gollhofer, James D., Immaculate Heart of Mary, Northglenn
Gonzales, Filemon F., (Retired)
Grimler, Richard, St. Joseph, Fort Collins
Grimm, R. Paul, St. Francis Cabrini, Littleton
Haigh, Robert, (Retired)
Halpine, Russell, Holy Cross, Thronton
Harrington, Philip, Our Lady of Lourdes, Denver
Hawkins, Kenneth I., Jr., (Retired)
Hegarty, Marvin A., St. Vincent de Paul, Denver
Howard, Michael J., (Retired)
Howard, Robert J., Sacred Heart of Jesus & Boulder County Jail, Boulder
Hronek, Dennis R., (Retired)
Hudec, Gordon D., St. Joan of Arc, Arvada
Johnson, Richard, (Retired)
Kelly, Dennis M., St. Joseph, Golden
Kerby, Brian J., Mt. Evans Hospice & Christ the King, Evergreen
Kimble, Harold, Our Lady of the Valley, Windsor
Kimminau, Victor H., St. Stephen, Glenwood Springs
Koch, Kenneth, (Retired)
Kramb, Richard F., (Retired)
Kulinski, Jerome N., (Retired)
Kullman, Frank W., (Retired)
Lamar, Charles (CHI), Light of the World Parish, Littleton
Le, Joseph Tam Ban, (Retired)
Lee, William S., St. John the Baptist, Longmont
Linton, William J., (Retired)
Lopez, Samuel, All Souls, Englewood
Loushine, Albert J., St. Vincent, Basalt
Lujan, Edward, (Retired)
Lybarger, Warren G., St. Joseph, Ft. Collins
Marthe, Daniel M., (Retired)
Martin, Gregory "Dusty", St. Pius X, Aurora
Matz, Karl T., (Retired)
McClellan, William (PEO), St. John XXIII, Ft. Collins
McDavid, Clarence G., Admin., Cure D'Ars, Denver
McKeown, John, (Retired)
Medenwaldt, Richard A., Nativity of Our Lord, Broomfield
Meilinger, Joseph H., St. Mary, Greeley
Menogan, Guffie E., St. Ignatius Loyola, Denver
Mich, Lawrence E., (Retired)
Milhone, Gordon G., Holy Name, Denver
Miller, Gary E., Sts. Peter and Paul Parish, Wheat Ridge
Mooneyham, Eugene, Light of the World, Littleton
Morin, George C., Church of the Good Shepherd, Denver
Neal, John R., Church of Risen Christ, Denver
Oehrle, Leo A., Immaculate Heart of Mary, Northglenn
Onesky, Leonard "Buz", Nativity of Our Lord, Broomfield
Padilla, Carlos L., (Retired)
Parker, Charles J., Jr., Notre Dame, Denver
Paulson, Joel J., St. Jude, Lakewood
Pelis, Richard F., St. Rita, Nederland
Pilger, Rex H., Jr., Holy Trinity Parish, Westminster
Polak, Leonard E., St. Catherine of Siena, Denver
Pontillo, John E., St. Mark, Westminster
Power, Winfield S., (Retired)
Quinlan, Thomas, Christ the King, Evergreen
Quintana, Lloyd, Holy Trinity, Westminster
Rael, Gilbert E., Adams County Jail, St. Augustine, Brighton
Reynolds, Philip J., Diaconal Ministry in the Diocese of Pueblo
Ritchey, Ronald T., Holy Cross, Thornton
Ritz, Michael P., Jr., (Retired)
Rogge, Gary, St. Thomas More, Englewood
Rompot, Vernon L., Holy Ghost Church, Denver
Rouco, Anthony F., Assoc. Sec. for Deacons, St. Mark's, Westminster
Ruiz, Nehemias (SEA), Holy Cross, Thronton; Member Evaluation Team Spanish Formation
Runck, Merle, D.D.S., Diaconal Ministry, Pueblo Diocese
Salvato, Mark, Christ the King, Denver
Sanchez, Alfredo (SFE), Presentation of Our Lady, Denver
Sanchez, Maclovio, (Retired)
Sanchez, Wilfred G., St. Elizabeth, Denver
Sandoval, Alfonso M., Sec. for Deacons
Sandoval, Henry, (Retired)
Scholz, Franz, Ministry in the Diocese of San Diego
Smith, John L., St. Joan of Arc, Arvada
Sorber, William M., (Retired)
Spears, Alan C., Christi on the Mountain, Lakewood
Stemper, Steven, St. Thomas More, Englewood
Stephenson, Billy C., (Retired)
Stow, William J., St. Michael the Archangel, Aurora
Sutton, Jack, (Sabbatical)
Thunblom, John, Queen of Peace, Aurora
Tirgrath, Howard L., Ministry in the Diocese of Reno-Las Vegas
Torrez, Frederick L., St. Peter, Greeley
Trewartha, William D.P.M., (Sabbatical)
Trujillo, Samuel R., (Sabbatical), Member Evaluation Team Spanish Formation
Ubowski, Chester W., Light of the World Parish, Littleton
Vieria, Richard, Jefferson County Jail, St. Mary Magdalene Parish, Denver
Vigil, Arthur A., All Saints Parish, Denver
Vlchek, Douglas, Our Lady of the Pines, Conifer
Wager, Martin A., St. Louis, Englewood, Handicapped Ministry-Carron Center
Wall, James R., St. Bernadette, Lakewood
Ward, William (SLC), Admin., Kateri Indian Community
Waring, Lynn E., Immaculate Heart of Mary, Northglenn
Webster, Earl, Spirit of Christ
Wilhelm, Martin A., Queen of Peace, Aurora
Young, John Joseph, (Retired)

INSTITUTIONS LOCATED IN THE ARCHDIOCESE

[A] SEMINARIES, RELIGIOUS OR SCHOLASTICATES

DENVER. *Redemptoris Mater House of Formation*, 3434 E. Arizona Ave., 80210. Tel: 303-733-2220; Fax: 303-733-2223.
E-mail: remater.den@iname.com
Very Rev. Florian Martin-Calama, Rector; Rev. Angel Molina, Vice Rector. Priests 2; Diocesan Seminarians 32.

St. Andrew's Theatine Religious House, 1050 S. Birch St., 80246. Tel: 303-756-5522; Fax: 303-691-2969. Theatine Fathers. Very Rev. Patrick Valdez, C.R., Prov. Supr.; Rev. Bart Nadal, C.R., Rector. In res. Revs. Angelo Urdiain, C.R.; Franco Placencia; Anthony Homar, C.R.

St. Dominic Priory, 3005 W. 29th Ave., 80211. Tel: 303-455-3614; Fax: 303-455-3087.
E-mail: bspdomin@juno.com
Province of St. Albert the Great. Revs. Michael G. Kyte, O.P.; Dennis R. Zusy, O.P., Contact. Priests 5; Brothers 1.

St. John Vianney Theological Seminary, 1300 S. Steele St., 80210. Tel: 303-282-3427. A division of Our Lady of the New Advent Theological Institute. Rev. Samuel J. Aquila, Rector; Very Rev. Florian Martin-Calama, Rector for Mater Archdiocesan Missionary.

[B] COLLEGES AND UNIVERSITIES

DENVER. *Regis University*, 3333 Regis Blvd., 80221-1099. Tel: 303-458-4100; Fax: 303-458-4921.
Web site: www.regis.edu
For a complete listing, refer to the Colleges and Universities section.

[C] INTER-PAROCHIAL HIGH SCHOOLS

DENVER. *Bishop Machebeuf Catholic High School*, 458 Unita Way, 80230-6934. Tel: 303-344-0082; Fax: 303-344-1582.
Web site: www.machebeuf.org
1958 Elm St., 80220. Bill Giddings, Prin. Sisters 1; Lay Teachers 27; Students 400.

BROOMFIELD. *Holy Family High School*, 5195 W. 144th Ave., 80020. Tel: 303-440-1411; Fax: 303-466-1935. Sr. Mary Rose Lieb, O.S.F., Prin. Priests 1; Sisters 3; Lay Teachers 32; Students 450.

[D] HIGH SCHOOLS, PRIVATE

DENVER. *J.K. Mullen High School, Corp.*, 3601 S. Lowell Blvd., 80236. Tel: 303-761-1764; Fax: 303-761-0502.
E-mail: schwall@mullen.pvt.k.12.co.us
Legal Title: *The Christian Brothers of J.K. Mullen*

High School. Coed Day School. Brothers of the Christian Schools. Vincent J. Greco, Jr., Prin. Brothers 3; Sisters 2; Lay Teachers 55; Students 975.

AURORA. *Regis Jesuit High School*, 16300 E. Weaver Pl., 80016. Tel: 303-699-1598.
Web site: www.regisjesuit.com
Day School for Boys. Revs. Walter T. Sidney, S.J., Pres.; Paul V. Stark, S.J.; James J. Burshek, S.J.; David A. Wayne, S.J., Dir. of Facilities; Thomas Valliquette, S.J., Faculty Chap.; Mr. Rick Sullivan, Prin. Priests 5; Sisters 1; Jesuit Scholastics 2; Sisters 1; Lay Teachers 58; Students 836.

ENGLEWOOD. *St. Mary's Academy High School*, 4545 S. University Blvd., 80110. Tel: 303-762-8300; Fax: 303-783-6201.
Web site: www.smanet.org
Sisters of Loretto at the Foot of the Cross. Judith Baenen, Pres.; Kathryn McNamee, Prin. Lay Teachers 27; Girls 309.

[E] ELEMENTARY SCHOOLS, PRIVATE

DENVER. *Escuela de Guadalupe Elementary School*. (Grades K-5), 3401 Pecos St., 80211. Tel: 303-964-8456; Fax: 303-964-0755. Dr. Anthony Vigil, Prin. Students 60.

St. Mary's Academy Lower School. (Grades PreK-5), 4545 S. University Blvd., 80110. Tel: 303-762-8300; Fax: 303-783-6201.
Web site: www.smanet.org
Sisters of Loretto at the Foot of the Cross. Judith Baenen, Pres.; Sr. Susan Swain, S.L., Prin. Sisters 1; Lay Teachers 17; Students 284.

ENGLEWOOD. *St. Mary's Academy, Middle School*. (Grades 6-8), 4545 S. University Blvd., 80110. Tel: 303-762-8300; Fax: 303-783-6201.
Web site: www.smanet.org
Judith Baenen, Pres.; Mike Radigan, Prin. Lay Teachers 15; Students 218.

[F] SPECIAL EDUCATION

DENVER. *The Bridge Community, Inc.*, 3101 W. Hillside Pl., 80219. Tel: 303-935-4740; Fax: 303-935-7795. Risha Dimas, Contact Person. Sisters 1; Priests 5; Lay Staff 4; Bed Group Home 8.

Mt. St. Vincent's Home, 4159 Lowell Blvd., 80211. Tel: 303-458-7220.
E-mail: kidsfirst@msvhome.org
Web site: www.msvhome.org
Sr. Vickie Perkins, Exec. Dir. Sisters of Charity of Leavenworth 7; Students 65.

LITTLETON. *Havern Center, Inc.*, 4000 S. Wadsworth Blvd., 80123. Tel: 303-986-4587; Fax: 303-986-0590. Sr. Barbara Schulte, S.L., Contact Person.

[G] MINISTRY TO THE HANDICAPPED

DENVER. *The Carron Center*, 1050 S. Birch St., 80222. Tel: 303-759-5150. Mrs. Cary Carron, Supvr.

Special Religious Education-Pastoral Care of Developmentally Disabled Persons, 3101 W. Hillside Pl., 80219. Tel: 303-934-1999. Rev. Roland P. Freeman, Dir.; Sr. Mary Catherine Widger, S.L., Assoc. Dir.; Risha Dimas, Dir. Bridge Community Group Home. Religious education of approximately 400 mentally retarded children and adults; One 8 bed group home.

[H] GENERAL HOSPITALS

DENVER. *Centura Health*, 1601 Lowell Blvd., 80204. Tel: 303-825-2190; Fax: 303-899-5160
For a complete listing, refer to the Hospitals section.

Centura Health St. Anthony Central Hospital, 4231 W. 16th Ave., 80204
For a complete listing, refer to the Hospitals section.

Centura Health St. Anthony Hospital North, 2551 W. 84th Ave., 80030
For a complete listing, refer to the Hospitals section.

Centura Senior Life Center, 1601 Lowell Blvd., 80204
For a complete listing, refer to the Hospitals section.

Provenant Acute Long Stay Hospital, 1601 Lowell Blvd., 80204
For a complete listing, refer to the Hospitals section.

Provenant Home Health and Eldercare Services, 1560 Meade St., 80204
For a complete listing, refer to the Hospitals section.

St. Joseph Hospital, 1835 Franklin St., 80218. Tel: 303-837-7111
For a complete listing, refer to the Hospitals section.

The Villas at Sunny Acres, 2501 E. 104th Ave., 80233. Tel: 303-452-4181; Fax: 303-457-9885.
E-mail: steverigsby@centura.org
For a complete listing, refer to the Hospitals section.

[I] HOMES FOR AGED

DENVER. *Francis Heights, Inc.*, 2626 Osceola St., 80212. Tel: 303-433-6268; Fax: 303-455-5359
For a complete listing, refer to the Special Care Facilities section.

Gardens at St. Elizabeth, 2835 W. 32nd Ave., 80211. Tel: 303-964-2005; Fax: 303-964-2340.
E-mail: jackieleech@centura.org
Web site: www.centura.org
For a complete listing, refer to the Special Care Facilities section.

Little Sisters of the Poor Mullen Home for the Aged, 3629 W. 29th Ave., 80211. Tel: 303-433-7221; Fax: 303-455-9184
For a complete listing, refer to the Special Care Facilities section.

[J] HOMES AND SERVICES FOR AGED AND INFIRMED

DENVER. *Hospice of Peace*, 2420 W. 26th Ave., 200-D, 80211. Tel: 303-561-5000.
E-mail: deemueller@centura.org
For a complete listing, refer to the Special Care Facilities section.

St. Raphael Catholic Center, Inc., 1300 S. Steele St., 80210. Tel: 303-715-2000
For a complete listing, refer to the Special Care Facilities section.

[K] HOUSING FOR THE ELDERLY AND FOR FAMILIES (LOW INCOME)

DENVER. *Archdiocesan Housing Committee*, 1544 Pearl St., 80203. Tel: 303-830-0215; Fax: 303-830-2885.
E-mail: HMSAHCI@aol.com
For a complete listing, refer to the Special Care Facilities section.

Clare Gardens, Inc., 2626 Osceola St., 80212. Tel: 303-433-6268; Fax: 303-455-5359
For a complete listing, refer to the Special Care Facilities section.

Damen House, P.O. Box 11580, 80211. Tel: 303-433-4280; Fax: 303-433-8225
For a complete listing, refer to the Special Care Facilities section.

Dayspring Villa, Inc., 3777 W. 26th Ave., 80211. Tel: 303-455-5066; Fax: 303-455-8966
For a complete listing, refer to the Special Care Facilities section.

Housing Management Services, Inc., 1544 Pearl St., 80203. Tel: 303-830-0215; Fax: 303-830-2885
For a complete listing, refer to the Special Care Facilities section.

WESTMINSTER. *Clare of Assisi Homes - Westminster, Inc.*, 2451 W. 82 Pl., 80003. Tel: 303-427-4406; 462-9271 (Corporate)
For a complete listing, refer to the Special Care Facilities section.

Villa Maria, Inc., 2461 W. 82nd Pl., 80031-4065. Tel: 303-426-1518; Fax: 303-426-4301
For a complete listing, refer to the Special Care Facilities section.

[L] CATHOLIC CHARITIES & COMMUNITY SERVICES

DENVER. *Catholic Charities and Community Services of the Archdiocese of Denver, Inc.*, 2525 W. Alameda Ave., 80219. Tel: 303-742-0828; Fax: 303-742-0774.
E-mail: ccaofd@aol.com
Web site: www.catholiccharitiesdenvr.org
James H. Mauck, Pres., Admin. Day Care Centers 7; Total Assisted 750. Special Centers for Social Services 20; Total Assisted 124,000.

Samaritan House. Shelter for Homeless, 2301 Lawrence St., 80205. Tel: 303-294-0241; Fax: 303-294-9523.

Transitional Housing, Courtyard Commons, 1122 Pearl St., #1-A, 80203. Tel: 303-860-9098; Fax: 303-832-1790.

Lowry Housing, 2525 W. Alameda Ave., 80219. Tel: 303-742-0828; Fax: 303-742-0774.

The Carron Center, 1050 S. Birch St., 80246. Tel: 303-759-5150; Fax: 303-759-5694.
E-mail: carycarron@hotmail.com
Services for Developmentally Disabled Adults and Ministry to deaf persons.
Child Care Centers:

Early Learning Center, 4440 Navajo St., 80211. Tel: 303-477-7610.

Springfield Court Child Care Center, 3851 S. Taft Hill Rd., Bldg. 31-B, Fort Collins, 80525. Tel: 303-206-1564.

Catholic Charities Margery Reed Mayo Day Nursery, 1128 28th St., 80205. Tel: 303-308-1420.

Catholic Charities Child Development Center, 1155 Decatur St., 80204. Tel: 303-629-5466.

Family Services Center, 2525 W. Alameda Ave., 80219. Tel: 303-742-0828. Counseling, Adoption, Foster Care & Senior Services.

Camp Santa Maria, Grant. Tel: 303-742-0828. 2525 W. Alameda Ave., 80219. Tel: 303-742-0828. Camping for Children, Youth & Seniors.

Catholic Charities Head Start Services. (8 locations), 2525 W. Alameda Ave., 80219. Tel: 303-742-0828.

Immigration Services, 2525 W. Alameda Ave., 80219. Tel: 303-742-0828.

Employment Resource Center, 2525 W. Alameda Ave., 80219. Tel: 303-742-0828; Fax: 303-742-4410.

SHARE Colorado, 9360 Federal Blvd., Federal Heights, 80221. Tel: 303-428-0400; Fax: 303-427-4440.

Food Bank Partners, 9360 Federal Blvd., Federal Heights, 80221. Tel: 303-428-1048; Fax: 303-427-4440.

Homeless Prevention Services, 2525 W. Alameda Ave., 80219. Tel: 303-742-0828.

Catholic Charities Northern-Fort Collins, 460 Linden Center Dr., Fort Collins, 80524. Tel: 970-484-5010; Fax: 970-484-0259. Shelter for Homeless, Job Bank, Emergency Assistance, Senior Services & Farm Labor Housing Corp.

Catholic Charities Northern - Greeley, 1311 11th St., Greeley, 80631. Tel: 970-353-6433; Fax: 970-353-3861. Shelter for the Homeless & Senior Services.

Plaza del Milegro, Child Care Center, 2500 1st Ave., #CC, Greeley, 80631. Tel: 970-346-2897.

Garfield Child Care, 872 S. Knox Ct., 80219. Tel: 303-922-9453.

Carino Child Care, 2525 W. Alameda Ave., 80219. Tel: 303-742-0828.

Catholic Charities - Western Slope, 1010 Grand Ave., Glenwood Springs, 81601. Tel: 970-384-2060.

Aurora Family Assistance Center, 1468 Iola St., Aurora, 80010. Tel: 303-363-9543; Fax: 303-363-9544.

North Area Cares Emergency Assistance, 7280-A Irving, #106-A, Westminster, 80030. Tel: 303-427-6256; Fax: 303-650-9551.

Northeast E.A. Center, 6621 E.72nd Ave., Commerce City, 80022. Tel: 303-287-1127; Fax: 303-287-1153.

Central Emergency Assistance Center, 1440 Poplar St., 80220. Tel: 303-399-1558; Fax: 303-393-1560.

Southwest Emergency Assistance Center, 902 S. Sheridan Blvd., 80601. Tel: 303-922-5205; Fax: 303-922-5048.

Brighton Emergency Assistance Center, 178 S. Sixth St., Brighton, 80601. Tel: 303-654-1040; Fax: 303-654-1003.

Plaza del Milegro, Farm Labor Housing, 2500 1st Ave., #CC, Greeley, 80631. Tel: 970-346-2897.

[M] MONASTERIES AND RESIDENCES OF PRIESTS AND BROTHERS

DENVER. *Annunciation Friary*, 3621 Humboldt St., 80205. Tel: 303-296-1024. Capuchin Friars. In res. Revs. Gene J. Emrisek, O.F.M.Cap., Guardian; Edward Judy, O.F.M.Cap., Vicar; Matthew Gross, O.F.M.Cap.; Gregory Beyer, O.F.M.Cap.; Cyrus Gallagher, O.F.M.Cap.; John Toepfer, O.F.M.Cap.; John Cousin, O.F.M.Cap.

Christian Brothers (F.S.C.)- St. Joseph Community, 3601 S. Lowell Blvd., 80236. Tel: 303-295-2515; 761-1764. Bro. Mariano Lopez, Contact.

The Community of the Beatitudes, 2924 W. 43rd Ave., 80211. Tel: 720-855-9412; Fax: 509-275-1658.
E-mail: beatitudes.denver@juno.com
Directors: Christian Meert; Christine Meert.

Congregation of the Mission Midwest Province: De Paul House, 2340 S. University Blvd., 80210. Tel: 303-705-9123; Fax: 303-777-0468. Revs. John H. Karssen, C.M., Supr.; Richard R. Ryan, C.M.; E. Hartrick Sullivan, C.M.; Thomas J. Nelson, C.M.; John Q. O'Connell, C.M.

Fraternidad San Antonio, 3554 Humboldt St., 80205-3940. Tel: 303-292-5110; Fax: 303-292-5148. Christian Meert, Dir.; Christina Meert, Dir.

Loyola Parish - Jesuit Community, 2305 Gaylord St., 80205-5627. Tel: 303-322-8042; Fax: 303-322-2927. Revs. C. Thomas Jost, S.J.; John F. Brady, S.J.; Randall C. Hall, S.J.

Maryknoll Fathers, Catholic Foreign Mission Society of America (Legal Title), 4460 Federal Blvd., 80211. Tel: 303-455-5669; Fax: 303-455-5753.
E-mail: mkldenver@aol.org
Web site: www.maryknoll.org
Revs. Joseph J. McGahren, M.M.; Paul Sykora, M.M.; Bro. Francis Dolphin, M.M., Dir.

The Redemptorists/Denver Province, Provincial Residence, Box 300399, 80203-0399. Tel: 303-370-0035; Fax: 303-370-0036.
Web site: www.redemptorist-denver.org
Res., 2130 E. Fourteenth Ave., 80206. Very Rev. Richard Thibodeau, C.SS.R., Prov. Supr.; Revs. James Keena, C.SS.R., Prov. Vicar; J. Robert Fenili, C.SS.R., Prov. Consultor; Stephen Meyer, C.SS.R., Prov. Consultor; John Steingraeber, C.SS.R., Co-Dir., Financial Svcs.; Bro. Thomas Wright, C.SS.R., Co-Dir., Financial Svcs. Priests 28; Brothers 2.
On Sabbatical: Revs. Richard Schiblin, C.SS.R.; Patrick Keyes, C.SS.R.; Edward Vella, C.SS.R.; Stephen Benden, C.SS.R.
Serving abroad: Most Rev. Alfred Novak, C.SS.R., Residencia do Bispro C.P.531 83203-970, PR, Brasil. Tel: 55-41-422-7717; Fax: 55-41-422-7717. Very Rev. Joseph W. Tobin, C.SS.R., Supr. Gen.; Revs. Anthony Smith, C.SS.R.; Joseph Nolen, C.SS.R., Casa Sant'Alfonso, C.P. 2458, 00100 Rome, Italy.

Tel: 39-06-49490-1; Fax: 39-06-44660-12. Revs. William Cleary, C.SS.R.; Joseph Dorcey, C.SS.R.; William A. Peterson, C.SS.R.; Richard Thiele, C.SS.R.; Very Rev. Joseph W. Tobin, C.Ss.R.; Revs. Robert Wirth, C.SS.R.; John Willett, C.SS.R., P.O. Box 29585 Secretariat, Bodija, Ibadan, Oyo State, Nigeria. Tel: 234-2-810-2870; Fax: 234-2-810-1401. Rev. William Fitzgerald, C.SS.R., C.P. 400, 48900 Juazeiro, Bahia, Brazil. Rev. Harold J. Thiel, C.SS.R., 88 Chotana Rd., T. Chang Phuek A. Muang, Chiang Mai 50300, Thailand. Tel: 66-53-216-598; Fax: 66-53-216-031.

Serving elsewhere, not listed: Rev. John McPhee, C.SS.R., 35637 Cherry Hill Rd., Westland, MI, 48185. Tel: 734-729-2240. Rev. Thomas Fransiscus, C.SS.R., St. Michael Parish, 14075 Mt. Vida St., Reno, NV, 89506. Tel: 702-972-7462. Rev. Pascal Dreici, C.SS.R., 3456 N. Marks, #103, Fresno, CA, 93722. Rev. Ricardo Elford, C.SS.R., P.O. Box 57, Cortaro, AZ, 85652. Tel: 520-744-3400. Rev. Richard Strass, C.SS.R., P.O. Box 207, Seward, AK, 99664. Tel: 907-224-5414; Fax: 907-224-5093. Rev. Roderick J. Garvey, C.SS.R., St. Cecilia's Church, P.O. Box 430, Jal, NM, 88252. Tel: 505-395-2431. Bro. William Green, C.SS.R., 3105 N. 4th, Apt. 17, Coeur d'Alene, ID, 83815. Tel: 288-667-2261. Rev. George Rassley, C.SS.R., Loyalton 205E Anton, Coeur d'Alene, ID, 83815. Tel: 208-667-1366. Rev. Theodore Lawson, C.SS.R., All Saints Church, 22824 Second St., Hayward, CA, 94541. Rev. Vincent Cao dang Minh, C.SS.R., 5404 N.E. Alameda, Portland, OR, 97213.

Regis Jesuit Community (The Jesuits at Regis University), Jesuit House M12, 3333 Regis Blvd., 80221-1099. Tel: 303-458-4100; Fax: 303-964-5525. Revs. Richard W. Dunphy, S.J., Rector; David M. Clarke, S.J.; James B. Guyer, S.J.; Edward L. Maginnis, S.J.; Edward T. Oakes, S.J.; John K. Ridgway, S.J.; Michael J. Sheeran, S.J.; Charles M. Shelton, S.J.; John P. Teeling, S.J.; John J. Vowells, S.J.; Patrick J. Weis, S.J.

St. Francis of Assisi Friary, 3553 Wyandot St., 80211-2948. Tel: 303-477-5542; Fax: 303-477-6925. In res. Rev. Harvey P. Dinkel, O.F.M.Cap., Vicar, Exec. Sec./Treas.; Very Rev. David Gottschalk, O.F.M.Cap., Prov. Min., Guardian; Revs. Thomas More Janeck, O.F.M.Cap., Chap. Poor Clares; John Lager, O.F.M.Cap., Dir. Devel.; Malachy R. McBride, O.F.M. Cap., P.V., Queen of Peace, Aurora; Regis Scanlon, O.F.M.Cap., Prison Ministry; David Songy, O.F.M.Cap., Faculty, St. John Vianney Seminary. Total In Res. 7; Total Staff 1.

Xavier Jesuit Center, 3450 W. 53rd, 80221-6568. Tel: 303-480-3900; Fax: 303-433-6235. Revs. Thomas W. Cummings, S.J., Supr.; Richard F. Bocklage, S.J.; Joseph F. Bona, S.J.; John J. Campbell, S.J.; Robert R. DeRouen, S.J.; Edward F. Flaherty, S.J.; John C. Futrell, S.J.; Harry E. Hoewischer, S.J.; Carl G. Kloster, S.J.; Timothy J. Lawless, S.J.; William T. Miller, S.J.; Anthony J. Short, S.J.; James C. Sunderland, S.J.; William S. Udick, S.J.; James P. Walsh, S.J.; Bros. Herbert A. Bussen, S.J.; John C. Fava, S.J.

AURORA. *Regis Jesuit High School - Jesuit Community*, 16810 E. Caley Ave., 80016. Tel: 303-690-4782; Fax: 303-690-4782. Revs. James J. Burshek, S.J., Supr.; Walter T. Sidney, S.J.; David A. Wayne, S.J.; Thomas M. Valiquette, S.J.

SNOWMASS. *St. Benedict's Monastery*, 1012 Monastery Rd., 81654. Tel: 970-927-3311; Fax: 970-927-3399.
E-mail: retreat@rof.net
Web site: www.snowmass.org
The Order of Cistercians of the Strict Observance (Trappists). Rt. Rev. Joseph Boyle, O.C.S.O.; Revs. Thomas Keating, O.C.S.O.; Theophane Boyd, O.C.S.O.; Daniel Kelliher, O.C.S.O.; William Meninger, O.C.S.O. Professed Monks 12; Novices 1.

[N] CONVENTS AND RESIDENCES FOR SISTERS

DENVER. *Dominican Sisters of Hope*, 2501 Gaylord St., 80205. Tel: 303-322-1413; Fax: 303-322-1608.
Web site: DominicanSisters.org
Sr. Marie Therese McGath, O.P., Contact. Dominican Sisters Home Health Agency of Denver, Inc. Served 105 patients.

Hermanas Josefinas, O.D.C. (Josephine Sisters), Provincial House, 4358 Utica St., 80212. Sr. Maria C. Barba, Prov. Supr.; Sr. Genoveva Romero Martinez, H.J., Contact Person. Sisters 3.

Marycrest Convent Franciscan Sisters, 2851 W. 52nd Ave., 80221. Tel: 303-433-2276; 458-6270; Fax: 303-433-5865. Sr. Gloria Shuffer, O.S.F., Provincial Min. Provincial Motherhouse of Sisters of St. Francis of Penance and Christian Charity, Province of the Sacred Heart #1630. Sr. Alicia Cuaron, Min. Special Center for Social Assistance. Total Assisted 2,500; Total Staff 2. Retreat and Conference Center. Total In Res. 100. Sisters 19; Total in Res. 30.

Missionaries of Charity, 1840 Grant St., 80203. Tel: 303-860-8040. Sr. M. Shantidan, M.C., Supr. & Contact. AIDS Home for 15 People. Total Assisted 37.

Monastery of Our Lady of Light (Capuchin Poor Clares). (Strict Enclosure), 3325 Pecos, 80211. Tel: 303-458-6339. Legal Title: *Capuchin Poor Clares of Denver, Inc.* Mother Maria de Cristo Palafox, O.S-.C.Cap., Abbess; Rev. Thomas More Janeck, O.F.M.Cap., Chap. Sisters 9.

Our Lady of Mercy Convent, Religious Sisters of Mercy, 1330 S. Steele St., P.O. Box 101645, 80250-1645. Tel: 303-765-4592; Fax: 303-765-4595. Religious Sisters of Mercy (Alma, Michigan). Sr. Mary Judith O'Brien, R.S.M., Local Supr. Sisters 5.

Queen of Peace Convent, 5360 Columbine Rd., 80221. Tel: 303-477-9139; Fax: 303-433-9425. Sisters of St. Francis of Penance and Christian Charity. Sr. Marie Therese Archambault, O.S.F.; Sr. Karen McCrory, O.S.F.; Sr. Rita Cammack, O.S.F.; Sr. Sarah Manchester, (Postulant). Sisters 5.

Sisters of the New Covenant, 10620 Livingston Dr., 80234. Tel: 303-451-8677; Fax: 303-438-9556.
Web site: www.catholicevangelizationweb.org
Pious Union. Sr. Angeline Bukowiecki, S.N.C. Sisters 3; Companions 14.

GOLDEN. *Mother Cabrini Shrine*, 20189 Cabrini Blvd., 80401. Tel: 303-526-0758; Fax: 303-526-9795.
E-mail: mcshrine@den-cabrini-shrine.org
Web site: www.den-cabrini-shrine.org
Sr. Bernadette Casciano, M.S.C., Contact; Thomas M. James, Registered Agent. Missionary Sisters of the Sacred Heart of Jesus(M.S.C.) 4.

LAKEWOOD. *Benedictine Sisters of Denver, Inc.*, Spirit of Life Monastery, 10760 W. Glennon Dr., 80226. Tel: 303-986-9234. Sr. Katherine Wawersich, O.S.B., Prioress. Sisters 2; Total Staff 2; Total Assisted in Counselling 60.

LITTLETON. *Carmel of Holy Spirit*, 6138 S. Gallup St., 80120-2702. Tel: 303-798-4176. Discalced Carmelites (O.C.D.). Mother Judith of the Immaculate Heart, D.C., Prioress. Sisters 9.

Loretto Center, 4000 S. Wadsworth, 80123-1309. Tel: 303-986-1541; Fax: 303-795-2378.
E-mail: judiosb@adl.com
Sr. Ann Lucille Ryan, S.L., Coord. Sisters 31.

Sisters of Benedict of Colorado, Inc., 4264 W. Ponds View Dr., 80123. Tel: 303-795-2378.
E-mail: judiosb@aol.com
Sr. Judith Elms, O.S.B., Supr.

VIRGINIA DALE. *Abbey of St. Walburga*, 32109 N. U.S. Hwy. 287, 80536-8942. Tel: 970-472-0612; Fax: 970-484-4342.
E-mail: walburga@ix.netcom.com
Web site: www.walburga.org
Mother Maria-Thomas Beil, O.S.B., Abbess. Benedictine Nuns 20.

[O] RETREAT CENTERS

ALLENSPARK. *Camp St. Malo Religious Retreat and Conference Center*, 10758 Hwy. 7, 80510. Tel: 303-747-2892; 970-586-6061 (Estes Park); 303-444-5177 (Denver); Fax: 303-747-2892.
E-mail: malo@webaccess.net
Blake Fischer, Dir.

LITTLETON. *Jesus Our Hope Hermitage*, 10519 S. Deer Creek Rd., 80127; Fax: 303-697-7539.
E-mail: annd@uswest.net
Contacts: Sr. Marie Joann Rekart, S.L.; Sr. Anndavid Naeger, S.L.

[P] CAMPUS MINISTRY

DENVER. *Auraria Campus.*
Community College of Denver.
Metropolitan State College.
University of Colorado at Denver. Rev. Gary A. Mueller, C.M.
Vincentian Fathers.
St. Francis Center, 1030 St. Francis Center, 80204. Tel: 303-534-4014; 556-3864.

Director of Campus Ministry, 1300 S. Steele St., 80210. Tel: 303-715-3203; Fax: 303-715-2042.
E-mail: onfire@archden.org
Web site: www.archden/archden.org
Mr. Robert Sherwin, Dir. Youth, Young Adult & Campus Ministry.

Regis University (Denver), 3333 Regis Blvd., Ste. 200, 80221. Tel: 303-458-4153; Fax: 303-964-5530.
E-mail: kschaefer@regis.edu
Rev. John J. Vowells, S.J.; Mrs. Kathleen Schaefer, Dir.; Mr. Ken Phillips, Asst. Dir.

University of Denver, Catholic Campus Ministry House, 1795 S. Williams St., 80210. Tel: 303-778-7657. Sr. Maria Regis, S.C.J.

BOULDER. *University of Colorado (Boulder)*, St. Thomas Aquinas Parish, 904 Fourteenth St., 80302. Tel: 303-443-8383; Fax: 303-443-8399.
Web site: www.sttoms.org
Revs. Thomas J. Holahan, C.S.P.; Paul D. Huesing, C.S.P.; David P. Dwyer, C.S.P.; Mr. Gary Kaber; Ms. Kathleen Ahl.

FORT COLLINS. *Colorado State University (Fort Collins)*, John XXIII University Center, 1220 University Ave., 80521-4555. Tel: 303-484-3356; Fax: 303-484-3434.
E-mail: john23@webaccess.net
Web site: www.john23.com
Rev. Robert L. Amundsen; Ms. Rachel Hoch; Ms. Pegge Bernecker; Dr. Joachim Viens, S.T.D.

Resident Catholic Theologian Program, John XXIII University Ctr., 1200 University Ave., 80521. Tel: 970-493-8984; Fax: 970-484-3434.
E-mail: jviens@lamar.colostate.edu
Dr. Joachim Viens, S.T.D., Dir.

GOLDEN. *Colorado School of Mines (Golden)*, 15755 W. 3rd Ave., 80401. Tel: 303-273-3460. Mr. Edward Mantz.

GREELEY. *Fellowship of Catholic University Students (FOCUS)*, 4407 29th St., 80634. Tel: 970-506-0751.
E-mail: jholecek@focusonline.org
Web site: www.focusonline.org
John Holecek, Dir.

University of Northern Colorado (Greeley), St. Peter's Parish, 915 12th St., 80631. Tel: 970-352-1060; Fax: 970-352-1062. Rev. Gregory K. Ames.

LITTLETON. *Arapahoe Community College*, c/o Al Rodriguez, 2500 W. College Ave., P.O. Box 9002, 80160-9002. Tel: 303-797-5910; Fax: 303-797-5935.

RANGELY. *Colorado Northwestern Community College (Rangely)*, 109 S. Stanolind Ave., P.O. Box 370, 81648. Tel: 303-675-8935; Fax: 303-878-5736 (Meeker). Rev. Roger L. Lascelle; Deacon George G. Fortunato.

STEAMBOAT SPRINGS. *Colorado Mountain College*, c/o Holy Name Catholic Church, P.O. Box 774198, 80477-4198. Tel: 970-879-0671; Fax: 970-879-7406.
E-mail: holyname@CMN.net
Web site: www.holynamecathstmbt.org
Rev. George M. Schroeder.

STERLING. *Northeastern Junior College (Sterling)*, St. Anthony Church, 327 S. Third St., 80751. Tel: 303-525-6422. Very Rev. Robert G. Whipkey, Jr., V.F.; Michael Wolsbauer.

WESTMINSTER. *Front Range Community College*, c/o Mr. Frank Sullivan, 3645 W. 112 Ave., 80030. Tel: 303-404-5282; Fax: 303-404-2178.
E-mail: fsulliva@ophir.frcc.cccoes.edu
Web site: frcc.cc.co.us

[Q] MISCELLANEOUS LISTINGS

DENVER. *AOD Management Co.*, 1300 S. Steele St., 80210. Tel: 303-715-3258; Fax: 303-715-2046.

The Archdiocese of Denver Irrevocable Revolving Trust Agreement, 1300 S. Steele St., 80210. Tel: 303-722-4687; Fax: 303-715-2041.

The Archdiocese of Denver Risk Management Property / Casualty Insurance Trust, 1300 S. Steele St., 80210. Tel: 303-722-4687; Fax: 303-715-2041.

The Archdiocese of Denver Welfare Benefits Trust, 1300 S. Steele St., 80210.

Bishop Machebeuf High School, Inc., 1300 S. Steele St., 80210. Tel: 303-715-3263; Fax: 303-715-2043.
E-mail: Vicargen@archden.org
Rev. Msgr. Raymond N. Jones, Vicar General.

Blessed Sacrament Catholic Educational Foundation, 4930 Montview Blvd., 80207. Tel: 303-355-7361; Fax: 303-355-0894. Rev. Kenneth Liuzzi, Exec. Officer & Contact Person.

Camp St. Malo Religious Retreat and Conference Center, Inc., 1300 S. Steele St., 80210.

Catholic Alumni Club of Colorado. P.O. Box 6111, Cherry Creek Station, 80206. Tel: 303-477-3572.
E-mail: cacofco@hotmail.com

The Catholic Foundation of the Archdiocese of Denver, 1300 S. Steele St., 80210.

Catholic Health Initiatives, 1999 Broadway, Ste. 2600, 80202. Tel: 303-298-9100; Fax: 303-298-9690.
E-mail: catholichealthinit.org
Patricia A. Cahill, J.D., Pres. & CEO; Mr. Paul Gustav Neumann, Esq., Contact.

Center for Mission Education, 3550 Marion St., 80205. Tel: 303-296-9480; Fax: 303-286-1196.
E-mail: casakaribu@juno.com

Colorado Vincentian Volunteers, 1732 Pearl St., 80203. Tel: 303-863-8141; Fax: 303-863-8141.
E-mail: cvv@juno.com
Web site: www.covivo.org
Bill Jaster, Exec. Dir.

Denver Catholic Register, Archdiocesan Religious Newspaper, 1300 S. Steele St., 80210. Tel: 303-715-3123. Greg Kail, General Mgr.

Family of Nazareth, Inc., 3434 E. Arizona Ave., 80210. Rev. Florian Martin-Calama, Rector, Redemptorist Mater House of Formation. Tel: 303-758-1280; Donald McCleod, Contact Person.

Franciscan Sisters Charitable Fund of Colorado, Inc., 2626 Osceola St., 80211. Tel: 303-433-6268; Fax: 303-455-5359. Franciscan Sisters, Daughters of the Sacred Heart of Jesus and Mary, (Wheaton, IL). Sr. Theresa Langfield, O.S.F., Pres./Admin.

Hmong Catholic Community, All Saints Parish, 2559 S. Federal Blvd., 80219. Tel: 303-922-3758; 429-6427; Fax: 303-922-3750. Lo Fong Chang, Contact.

Holy Family High School, Inc., 1300 S. Steele St., 80210. Tel: 303-715-3263; Fax: 303-715-2043.
E-mail: Vicargen@archden.org
Rev. Msgr. Raymond N. Jones, Vicar General.

Kateri Catholic Indian Community of Colorado, 2340 S. University Blvd #32, 80210. Tel: 303-778-5966.
E-mail: quentin@priest.com
Rev. John Q. O'Connell, C.M.

Marycrest Health System, 2861 W. 52nd Ave., 80221. Tel: 303-458-6270; Fax: 303-477-4105. Sr. Cecilia Linenbrink, Pres.; Sr. Susan Artone-Fricke, Contact Person.

Mercy Housing, Inc., 601 E. 18th Ave., Ste. 150, 80203. Tel: 303-830-3300; Fax: 303-830-3301.
E-mail: mail@mercyhousing.org
Web site: BHConline.org/mercyhousing
Affordable Housing Properties. Sr. Lillian Murphy, Pres. Units 10,200; Total Served 25,000. Day Care Centers 3; Total Served 200.

Mercy Services Corp., 601 E. 18th Ave., Ste. 150, 80203. Tel: 303-830-3300; Fax: 303-830-3301. Sr. Lillian Murphy, R.S.M., Pres.

Decatur Place, 601 E. 18th Ave., Ste. 150, 80203. Tel: 303-830-3300; Fax: 303-830-3301. Cherie H. Kirschbaum, Pres.

Homes Again Program, 601 E. 18th Ave., Ste. 150, 80203. Tel: 303-830-3300; Fax: 303-830-3301. Cherie H. Kirschbaum, Pres.

Mercy Housing Colorado, 601 E. 18th Ave., Ste. 150, 80203. Tel: 303-830-3300; Fax: 303-830-3301. Cherie H. Kirschbaum, Pres.

Mercy Properties, Inc., 601 E. 18th Ave., Ste. 150, 80203. Tel: 303-830-3397; Fax: 303-830-3301. Lillian Murphy, R.S.M., Pres.

Willow Street Apartments, 601 E. 18th Ave., Ste. 150, 80203. Tel: 303-830-3397. Cherie Kirschbaum, Contact.

Mercy Holly Park East, 601 E. 18th Ave., Ste. 150, 80203. Tel: 303-830-3397; Fax: 303-830-3301. Cherie Kirschbaum, Contact.

Mercy Holly Park West, 601 E. 18th Ave., Ste. 150, 80203. Tel: 303-830-3397; Fax: 303-830-3301. Cherie Kirschbaum, Contact.

Our Lady of the New Advent Theological Institute, 1300 S. Steele St., 80210.

S.E.T. of Colorado, Inc., dba Health S.E.T., Raleigh Bldg., 4200 N. Conejos #436, 80204. Tel: 303-534-8002; Fax: 303-534-8009.
Web site: www.healthset.org
Jim Elfline, Exec. Dir. Total Staff 9; Total Volunteers 130; Total Assisted 4,500.

Sacred Heart House of Denver, 2844 Lawrence St., 80205. Tel: 303-296-6686; Fax: 303-296-2903. Ms. Janet L. Morris, Exec. Dir.

Saint Joseph Hospital Foundation, 1835 Franklin St., 80218. Tel: 303-837-7043; Fax: 303-837-7115.
E-mail: goodwinr@exempla.org
Web site: stjosephhospfdtn.org
Roger A. Goodwin, Exec. Dir.

St. Vincent de Paul Stores, Inc., 2525 W. Alameda Ave., 80219. Tel: 303-742-0828; Fax: 303-742-0774. Mr. James Mauck, C.E.O.

St. Vincent DePaul Society Denver-Metro Council, 2560 S. Grove St., 80219-5814. Tel: 303-922-4430; Fax: 303-922-3750. Robert Concannon, Pres.; Robert S. Huff, Exec. Sec.

Seeds of Hope Charitable Trust, 1300 S. Steele St., 80210. Tel: 303-715-3127; Fax: 303-715-2042.
E-mail: seeds@archden.org
Ms. Therese A. Polakovic, Chief Exec. Dir.; Ms. Mary L. Borda, Contact Person.

Sisters of St. Francis Foundation, 2851 W. 52nd Ave., 80221. Tel: 303-458-6270; Fax: 303-433-5865.
E-mail: Ppmarycrest@aol.com
Sisters of St. Francis. Sr. Kathryn Zochol, Contact.

ARVADA.
Buena Vista, Inc., P.O. Box 745475, 80006-5475. Tel: 303-426-6622; Fax: 303-657-9428.
E-mail: sccbuenavista@compuserve.com
Web site: www.buenavista.org
Amy Sheber Howard, Natl. Coord.

ENGLEWOOD. *Catholic Health Initiatives of Colorado*, 5570 DTC Pkwy., 80111. Tel: 303-290-6500. Mr. Joseph R. Swedish, Pres. & CEO.

Legionaries of Christ, Pastoral Services, Inc., 8077 S. Quince Cir., 80122. Tel: 303-689-9932. Rev. Daniel Polzer, L.C., Dir.

Queen of the Apostles Mission Association, Inc., 8035 S. Quebec St., 80112-3118. Tel: 303-770-3240; Fax: 303-770-0415.
E-mail: qama@aol.com
Matt Werner, Pres.

ESTES PARK.
Our Lady of Tenderness, Poustinia, Box 4311, 80517. Tel: 970-577-1383. Lucille Dupuis, Dir.

GLENDALE.
Havican Insurance Co., 4100 E. Mississippi Ave., Ste. 1500, 80222. Sisters of the Holy Cross.

LITTLETON. *Auxiliary of Mother Cabrini Shrine*, 7295 S. Steele Cir., 80122. Tel: 303-771-4386; Fax: 303-771-4386 (Call first). Zoraide Scordo, Founder.

WHEAT RIDGE.
Christian Life Movement, Inc., 4040 Pierce St., 80033.
E-mail: denverclm@aol.com
Mrs. Rossana Goni, Contact Person.

RELIGIOUS INSTITUTES OF MEN REPRESENTED IN THE ARCHDIOCESE

For further details refer to the corresponding bracketed number in the Religious Institutes of Men or Women section.

[0200]—*Benedictine Monks.* (Canon City, CO).—O.S.B.
[]—*Bethlehem Fathers.*—S.M.B.
[0330]—*Brothers of the Christian Schools.*—F.S.C.
[0460]—*Brothers of the Poor of St. Francis.*—C.F.P.
[0470]—*The Capuchin Friars.* (Denver, CO).—O.F.M.Cap.
[0350]—*Cistercians of the Strict Observance-Trappists.* (St. Benedict Abbey).—O.C.S.O.
[]—*Congregation of Mother Coredemptrix.* (Carthage, MO).—C.M.C.
[1330]—*Congregation of the Mission.* (Western Prov.).—C.M.
[]—*Cor Jesu (Societas Cordis Jesu, Fontis Vitae et Sanctitatis).*
[0520]—*Franciscan Friars.* (Provs. of the Most Holy Name of Jesus & Our Lady of Guadalupe).—O.F.M.
[0690]—*Jesuit Fathers and Brothers.* (Missouri, Milwaukee, Oregon, Maryland Provs.).—S.J.
[0800]—*Maryknoll.* (Denver).—M.M.
[0430]—*Order of Preachers-Dominicans.* (Prov. of St. Albert the Great).—O.P.
[1030]—*Paulist Fathers.*—C.S.P.
[1070]—*Redemptorist Fathers.* (St. Louis Prov.).—C.SS.R.
[1240]—*Servites.* (Western Prov.).—O.S.M.
[1300]—*Theatine Fathers.* (Rome, Italy).—C.R.

RELIGIOUS INSTITUTES OF WOMEN REPRESENTED IN THE ARCHDIOCESE

[0190]—*Benedictine Nuns.*—O.S.B.
[0230]—*Benedictine Sisters of Pontifical Jurisdiction.* (Colorado Springs, CO; Boulder, CO; Denver, CO; Oklahoma City, OK).—O.S.B.
[]—*Capuchin Poor Clares.*—O.S.C.Cap.
[3110]—*Congregation of Our Lady of the Retreat in the Cenacle.*—R.C.
[2100]—*Congregation of the Humility of Mary.* (Davenport, IA).—C.H.M.
[1780]—*Congregation of the Sisters of the Third Order of St. Francis of Perpetual Adoration.* (La Crosse, WI).—F.S.P.A.
[0760]—*Daughters of Charity of St. Vincent de Paul.*—D.C.
[0960]—*Daughters of Wisdom.*—D.W.
[0420]—*Discalced Carmelite Nuns.*—O.C.D.
[1070-14]—*Dominican Sisters.*—O.P.
[1070-16]—*Dominican Sisters.*—O.P.
[1070-18]—*Dominican Sisters.*—O.P.
[1070-24]—*Dominican Sisters.*—O.P.
[1070-28]—*Dominican Sisters.*—O.P.
[1070-03]—*Dominican Sisters.* (Sinsinawa).—O.P.
[]—*Dominican Sisters of the Congregation of St. Cecilia.* (Nashville).
[1240]—*Franciscan Sisters, Daughters of the Sacred Hearts of Jesus and Mary.* (Wheaton, IL).—O.S.F.
[2575]—*Institute of the Sisters of Mercy of the Americas.*—R.S.M.
[2340]—*Little Sisters of the Poor.*—L.S.P.
[2710]—*Missionaries of Charity.*—M.C.
[]—*Missionaries of Charity of Mary Immaculate.*—M.C.M.I.
[2860]—*Missionary Sisters of the Sacred Heart.*—M.S.C.
[3130]—*Our Lady of Victory Missionary Sisters.*—O.L.V.M.
[1680]—*School Sisters of St. Francis.* (Milwaukee, WI).—O.S.F.
[0440]—*Sisters of Charity of Cincinnati, Ohio.*—S.C.
[0480]—*Sisters of Charity of Leavenworth, Kansas.*—S.C.L.
[0430]—*Sisters of Charity of the Blessed Virgin Mary.*—B.V.M.
[2360]—*Sisters of Loretto at the Foot of the Cross.* (Nerinx, KY).—S.L.
[2990]—*Sisters of Notre Dame.*—S.N.D.
[1705]—*Sisters of St. Francis of Assisi.* (Milwaukee, WI).—O.S.F.
[1630]—*Sisters of St. Francis of Penance and Christian Charity.*—O.S.F.
[1640]—*Sisters of St. Francis of Perpetual Adoration.* (Colorado Springs, CO).—O.S.F.
[3830-05]—*Sisters of St. Joseph.*—C.S.J.
[3830-15]—*Sisters of St. Joseph.*—C.S.J.
[3840]—*Sisters of St. Joseph of Carondelet.*—C.S.J.
[3930]—*Sisters of St. Joseph of the Third Order of St. Francis.* (Immaculate Conception Prov.).—S.S.J.-T.O.S.F.
[1830]—*Sisters of the Good Shepherd.*—R.G.S.
[]—*Sisters of the New Covenant.*—S.N.C.
[3260]—*Sisters of the Precious Blood.* (Dayton, OH).—C.PP.S.
[1720]—*Sisters of the Third Order Regular of St. Francis of the Congregation of Our Lady of Lourdes.* (Rochester, MN).—O.S.F.

ARCHDIOCESAN CEMETERIES

DENVER. *St. Simeon Cemetery Association*, 1300 S. Steele St., 80210. Tel: 303-715-3258; Fax: 303-715-2041.

WHEAT RIDGE. *Archdiocese of Denver Mortuary at Mt. Olivet, Inc.*, 12801 W. 44th Ave., 80033. Tel: 303-425-9511; Fax: 303-425-0242.

Mount Olivet Cemetery, 12801 W. 44th Ave., 80033. Tel: 303-424-7785; Fax: 303-424-5263.

NECROLOGY

(No Deaths)

Diocese of Des Moines

(Dioecesis Desmoinensis)

Most Reverend

JOSEPH L. CHARRON, C.PP.S., S.T.D.

Bishop of Des Moines; ordained June 3, 1967; appointed Titular Bishop of Bencenna and Auxiliary Bishop of Saint Paul and Minneapolis November 6, 1989; consecrated January 25, 1990; appointed Bishop of Des Moines November 12, 1993; installed January 21, 1994.

Chancery: 601 Grand Ave., P.O. Box 1816, Des Moines, IA, 50306. Tel.: 515-243-7653; Fax: 515-237-5070.

Web site address: www.dmdiocese.org

E-mail address: bishop@dmdiocese.org

ERECTED BY POPE S. PIUS X, AUGUST 12, 1911.

Square Miles 12,446.

Legal Title: "The Roman Catholic Diocese of Des Moines".

Comprises that part of the State of Iowa which is bounded on the east by the eastern boundaries of the Counties of Polk, Warren, Lucas and Wayne; on the south by the State of Missouri; on the west by the Missouri River; and on the north by the northern boundaries of the Counties of Harrison, Shelby, Audubon, Guthrie, Dallas and Polk.

PATRONS OF THE DIOCESE: I. BLESSED VIRGIN MARY QUEEN; II. POPE SAINT PIUS X.Diocese solemnly consecrated to the Immaculate Heart of Mary on May 16, 1948.

For legal titles of parishes and diocesan institutions, consult the Chancery Office.

STATISTICAL OVERVIEW

Personnel	
Bishop	1
Priests: Diocesan Active in Diocese	79
Priests: Active Outside Diocese	2
Priests: Diocesan in Foreign Missions	1
Priests: Retired, Sick or Absent	25
Number of Diocesan Priests	107
Religious Priests in Diocese	11
Extern Priests in Diocese	3
Ordinations:	
Diocesan Priests	1
Permanent Deacons in Diocese	65
Total Brothers	7
Total Sisters	107
Parishes	
Parishes	85
With Resident Pastor:	
Resident Diocesan Priests	54
Resident Religious Priests	4
Without Resident Pastor:	
Administered by Priests	24
Administered by Deacons	3
Missions	1
Professional Ministry Personnel:	
Sisters	18
Lay Ministers	41
Welfare	
Catholic Hospitals	3
Total Assisted	1,073,775
Homes for the Aged	1
Total Assisted	400
Specialized Homes	1
Total Assisted	1,727
Special Centers for Social Services	4
Total Assisted	65,724
Educational	
Diocesan Students in Other Seminaries	7
Total Seminarians	7
Colleges and Universities	1
Total Students	432
High Schools, Diocesan and Parish	2
Total Students	1,456
Elementary Schools, Diocesan and Parish	17
Total Students	4,839
Catechesis/Religious Education:	
High School Students	2,536
Elementary Students	9,970
Total Students Under Catholic Instruction	19,240
Teachers in the Diocese:	
Priests	3
Sisters	10
Lay Teachers	383
Vital Statistics	
Receptions into the Church:	
Infant Baptism Totals	2,052
Adult Baptism Totals	234
Received into Full Communion	351
First Communions	1,925
Confirmations	1,836
Marriages:	
Catholic	298
Interfaith	311
Total Marriages	609
Deaths	764
Total Catholic Population	96,492
Total Population	671,091

Former Bishops—Most Rev. AUSTIN DOWLING, D.D., first Bishop of Des Moines; ord. June 24, 1891; appt. Bishop Jan. 31, 1912; cons. April 25, 1912; promoted to the See of St. Paul, Jan., 1919.—Most Rev. THOMAS W. DRUMM, D.D., Bishop of Des Moines; ord. Dec. 21, 1901; cons. May 21, 1919; died Oct. 24, 1933.—Most Rev. GERALD T. BERGAN, D.D., ord. Oct. 28, 1915; appt. March 24, 1934; cons. June 13, 1934; Enthroned June 21, 1934; elevated to Archiepiscopal dignity and promoted to Omaha Feb. 9, 1948.—Most Rev. EDWARD C. DALY, O.P., S.T.M., Bishop of Des Moines; ord. June 12, 1921; appt. March 13, 1948; cons. May 13, 1948; named Asst. at Papal Throne, May 23, 1958; died Nov. 23, 1964.—Most Rev. GEORGE J. BISKUP, D.D., ord. March 19, 1937; appt. Auxiliary Bishop of Dubuque, March 9, 1957; cons. April 24, 1957; appt. Bishop of Des Moines, Feb. 3, 1965; appt. Coadjutor Archbishop of Indianapolis, July 26, 1967; succeeded to See Jan. 14, 1970.—Most Rev. MAURICE J. DINGMAN, D.D., Bishop of Des Moines; ord. Dec. 8, 1939; appt. Bishop of Des Moines April 2, 1968; cons. June 19, 1968; installed July 7, 1968; retired Oct. 14, 1986; died Feb. 1, 1992.—Most Rev. WILLIAM H. BULLOCK, ord. June 7, 1952; appt. Auxiliary Bishop of St. Paul and Minneapolis and Titular Bishop of Natchez June 3, 1980; cons. Aug. 12, 1980; appt. Bishop of Des Moines Feb. 10, 1987; installed April 2, 1987; appt. to Diocese of Madison April 13, 1993.

Vicar General and Moderator of the Curia—Rev. Msgr. STEPHEN ORR, *P.O. Box 1816, Des Moines, 50306.* Tel: 515-237-5044; 222-9577(Res.).

Chancery—601 Grand Ave., P.O. Box 1816, Des Moines, 50306. Tel: 515-243-7653; Fax: 515-237-5070. Office Hours: Mon.-Fri. 8:30-4:30.

Chancellor—Rev. DAVID FLEMING,All Matrimonial Correspondence to Tribunal.

Secretary to the Bishop—MARY BARNUM, *P.O. Box 1816, Des Moines, 50306.* Tel: 515-237-5039; Fax: 515-237-5071.

Finance Officer—TAMERA MASON, *P.O. Box 1816, Des Moines, 50306.* Tel: 515-237-5012.

Vicar for Finance—Rev. Msgr. EDWARD HURLEY.

Diocesan Tribunal—601 Grand Ave., P.O. Box 1816, Des Moines, 50306. Tel: 515-237-5030.

Judicial Vicar—Rev. CHRISTOPHER HARTSHORN, J.C.L.

Director of Tribunal—Sr. CAMILLA HUBER, O.S.M.

Defenders of the Bond—Revs. MICHAEL AMADEO; LAWRENCE R. HOFFMANN; SAMUEL PALMER, J.C.L.; DAVID J. POLICH; Deacon ROBERT L. HOWE.

Judges—Rev. Msgr. LAWRENCE A. BEESON, J.C.D.; Revs. DANIEL L. CLARKE; GARRY A. CULVER, J.C.L.; CHRISTOPHER HARTSHORN, J.C.L.; DANIEL F. KRETTEK, J.C.L.; Rev. Msgr. STEPHEN L. ORR; Rev. Msgr. EDWARD B. PFEFFER, J.C.L.; Rev. THOMAS J. PFEFFER, J.C.L.

Notary—DORIS KLANG.

Advocates—Revs. EUGENE R. KOCH; JOHN P. LUDWIG; VINCE G. ROSONKE; JOHN DORTON; Sr. CAMILLA HUBER, O.S.M.; Deacon GREGG ERICKSON; Mr. MICHAEL REILLY; Ms. PHYLLIS CACCIATORE; Ms. SARAH LUFT.

Diocesan Consultors—Rev. Msgr. STEPHEN ORR; Revs. RICHARD BERGMAN; KENNETH GROSS; ROBERT HOEFLER; VINCENT ROSONKE; DANIEL SIEPKER.

Diocesan Corporation Board—Most Rev. JOSEPH L. CHARRON; Rev. Msgr. STEPHEN ORR; Rev. DAVID FLEMING; CYNTHIA EISENHAUER; MICHAEL RILEY; TAMERA MASON.

Diocesan Offices and Directors

Catholic Charities—Rev. Msgr. STEPHEN ORR, Acting Dir., *601 Grand Ave., P.O. Box 723, Des Moines, 50303.* Tel: 515-237-5055.

Social Service Division—Des Moines Office, 601 Grand Ave., P.O. Box 723, Des Moines, 50303. Tel: 515-237-5055.

Council Bluffs Office—411 E. Broadway, Council Bluffs, 51503. Tel: 712-328-3086; Fax: 712-328-1348.

Charismatic Renewal Liaison—Rev. DANIEL KRETTEK, *1521 Center St., Des Moines, 50314.* Tel: 515-282-4839.

Communications, Office of—THOMAS CHAPMAN, Dir., *P.O. Box 1816, Des Moines, 50306.* Tel: 515-237-5041; Fax: 515-237-5071.

Continuing Education for Clergy—Rev. LYLE PETERS, *St. Theresa Church, 1230 Merle Hay Rd., Des Moines, 50311.* Tel: 515-279-4654.

Deaf-Handicapped, Office of—Sr. HELEN SEIVERT, O.S.F., Dir., *315 W. Pierce St., Council Bluffs, 51501.* Tel: 712-328-3086.

Stewardship and Development Office—PATRICIA SHAWD, Dir. Stewardship, *P.O. Box 1816, Des Moines, 50306.* Tel: 515-237-5083.

Diocesan Council of Catholic Women—MARY BRICKER, Pres., *604 N. First St., Greenfield, 50849.* Tel: 641-743-2534.

Diaconate (Permanent)—Deacon GENE JAGER, Dir., *P.O. Box 1816, Des Moines, 50306.* Tel: 515-237-5037.

Evangelization, Office of—JIM BOND, Dir., *P.O. Box 1816, Des Moines, 50306.* Tel: 515-237-5046.

Hispanic Ministry, Office of—Rev. KEVIN CAMERON, *P.O. Box 1816, Des Moines, 50306.* Tel: 515-237-5051.

Holy Childhood, Pontifical Association—Dr. LUVERN GUBBELS, *P.O. Box 1816, Des Moines, 50306.* Tel: 515-237-5013.

Legislative Activities, Office of—PATRICK FINAN, *601 Grand Ave., P.O. Box 723, Des Moines, 50303.* Tel: 515-237-5047.

Newspaper—"The Catholic Mirror", TOM CHAPMAN, Editor, *601 Grand Ave., P.O. Box 10372, Des Moines, 50306.* Tel: 515-237-5060.

Priests' Pension Fund Society—Most Rev. JOSEPH L. CHARRON; Rev. JOHN LUDWIG; Rev. Msgr. EDWARD HURLEY; Rev. ROBERT SCHOEMANN; Rev. Msgr. EDWARD PFEFFER.

Propagation of the Faith—Rev. PAUL BIANCHI, Dir., *Box 1816, Des Moines, 50306-1816.* Tel: 515-237-5029.

Religious Education Office—JOANNE DALHOFF, Dir., *P.O. Box 1816, Des Moines, 50306.* Tel: 515-237-5052.

St. Vincent de Paul Society—Rev. JOHN LUDWIG, Chap., *St. Catherine of Siena Catholic Student Center, 1150 28th St., Des Moines, 50311-4142.* Tel: 515-271-4747.

Schools—Dr. LUVERN GUBBELS, Supt. & Dir. Educ. REBECCA LINDAHL, Curriculum Specialist; JACQUELINE KRESAL, School Prog. Specialist, *P.O. Box 1816, Des Moines, 50306.* Tel: 515-237-5013.

Office of Social Justice—PATRICK FINAN, *P.O. Box 723, Des Moines, 50303.* Tel: 515-237-5047.

Vocations—Rev. JOHN ACREA, Coord., *P.O. Box 1816, Des Moines, 50306.* Tel: 515-237-5014.

Office of Worship (Liturgy, Music, Art and Architecture)—JIM BOND, Dir., *601 Grand Ave., P.O. Box 1816, Des Moines, 50306.* Tel: 515-237-5046.

Youth Ministry, Office of—*St. Thomas More Center, 6177 Panorama Rd., Panora, 50216.* Tel: 515-755-3164.

Office of Ministry Formation—Rev. DAVID FLEMING, Dir., *P.O. Box 1816, Des Moines, 50306.* Tel: 515-237-5014.

Office of Adult Faith Formation—Rev. P. TIMOTHY FITZGERALD, *P.O. Box 1816, Des Moines, 50306.* Tel: 515-237-5026.

Office of Family Ministry—Deacon DENNIS LUFT; SARAH LUFT, *P.O. Box 1816, Des Moines, 50306.* Tel: 515-237-5056.

CLERGY, PARISHES, MISSIONS AND PAROCHIAL SCHOOLS

CITY OF DES MOINES
(Polk County)

1—ST. AMBROSE CATHEDRAL (1856), Revs. James W. Kiernan, Rector; Felix Onuora, C.S.Sp.; Sr. Patricia Scherer, Pastoral Min.; Sr. Virginia Jennings, O.S.F., D.R.E.; Deacons Lee Pao Yang; Dave Garza; Patrick Kirkman.
Res., 607 High St., 50309. Tel: 515-288-7411; Fax: 515-288-3969. [JC]

2—ALL SAINTS (1914), Rev. Anthony Aiello.
650 N.E. 52nd Ave., 50313. Tel: 515-265-5001; Fax: 515-265-5636. [JC]

3—CHRIST THE KING (1939), Rev. Albert G. Sherbo. Pastoral Ministers: Deacon Daniel McGuire.
Res., 5711 S.W. 9th St., 50315. Tel: 515-285-2888; Fax: 515-285-8182.
School—701 Wall St., 50315. Tel: 515-285-3349; Fax: 515-285-0381.
Lay Teachers 16; Students 195.
Catechesis/Religious Programs—Students 330.

4—HOLY TRINITY (1920), Rev. Msgr. Gerald J. Stessman; Rev. Randy Richman; Deacons Robert Howe; Jeff Boehlert; Tom Maly.
Res., 2926 Beaver Ave., 50310. Tel: 515-255-3162; Fax: 515-255-1381.
School—Lay Teachers 33; Students 563.
Catechesis/Religious Programs—Students 120.

5—ST. ANTHONY'S (1905), Revs. Lawrence R. Hoffmann; Gordon Gittins; Deacon William Smith.
Res., 15 Indianola Rd., 50315. Tel: 515-244-4709; Fax: 515-280-6959.
School—16 Columbus Ave., 50315. Tel: 515-243-1874; Fax: 515-243-4467.
Sisters 2; Lay Teachers 23; Students 400.
Catechesis/Religious Programs—Tel: 515-244-1119.
Students 385.

6—ST. AUGUSTIN'S (1923), Revs. James C. Polich; Anthony Adibe, C.S.Sp.; Deacon Fred Pins.
Res., 545 42nd St., 50312. Tel: 515-255-1175; Fax: 515-255-7969.
School—4320 Grand Ave., 50312. Tel: 515-279-5947; Fax: 515-279-8049.
Lay Teachers 21; Students 274.
Catechesis/Religious Programs—Students 254.

7—ST. CATHERINE OF SIENA CATHOLIC STUDENT CENTER (1969). (Non-Territorial University Parish). Rev. John Ludwig.
Church—1150-28th St., 50311-4142. Tel: 515-271-4747; Fax: 515-271-1918.

8—BASILICA OF SAINT JOHN (1905), Rev. Msgr. Frank E. Chiodo; Revs. Richard Wagner; Aquinas Nichols, O.S.B.; Deacons John Jarvis; Patrick Kirkman; Charles Putbrese.
Res., 1915 University Ave., 50314. Tel: 515-244-3101; Fax: 515-244-3165.

9—ST. JOSEPH'S (1924), Rev. Msgr. Robert J. Chamberlain; Rev. Remigius Okere, C.S.Sp.; Deacon Marvin Brewer.
Res., 3300 Easton Blvd., 50317. Tel: 515-266-2226.
School—Tel: 515-266-3433; Fax: 515-266-8348.
Lay Teachers 12; Students 183.
Catechesis/Religious Programs—Students 111.

10—ST. MARY OF NAZARETH (1964), Rev. Msgr. Gerald E. Ryan; Rev. David J. Santoro, O.P.; Deacon George Catanzano.
Res., 4605 N.W. 47th Ct., P.O. Box 13170, 50310. Tel: 515-276-4042; Fax: 515-252-1995.
Catechesis/Religious Programs—Tel: 515-276-7589.
Students 474.

11—ST. PETER'S (1915), Rev. John Dorton; Deacon Eugene Jager.
Res., 607 E. 18th St., 50316. Tel: 515-266-4265; Fax: 515-266-3945.
Catechesis/Religious Programs—Students 24.

12—ST. THERESA OF THE CHILD JESUS (1951), Revs. Robert A. Hoefler; Lyle Peters; Deacon Joe Cortese, II.
Res., 1230 Merle Hay Rd., 50311-2098. Tel: 515-279-4654; Fax: 515-277-0838. [JC]
School—5810 Carpenter, 50311. Tel: 515-277-0178; Fax: 515-255-2415.
Lay Teachers 22; Students 429.
Catechesis/Religious Programs—Students 140.

13—VISITATION (1882), Revs. David Polich; Thomas Pfeffer.
Res., 1271 E. 9th St., 50316. Tel: 515-266-6695; Fax: 515-266-9803.
School—Holy Family, (Grades (PreK-8)). (Consolidated). Tel: 515-262-8025; Fax: 515-280-5482.
Lay Teachers 15; Students 199.
Catechesis/Religious Programs—Tel: 515-266-1027.
Students 421.
Mission—Des Moines, Polk Co., Our Lady of Guadalupe, 601 S.E. 8th St., 50316. Tel: 515-243-9585.

OUTSIDE THE CITY OF DES MOINES

Adair, Adair Co., St. John (1879). Attended by St. Mary, Anita.
Res., P.O. Box 277, Anita, 50020. Tel: 712-762-3484; 762-3773 (Office); Fax: 712-762-3484.
Catechesis/Religious Programs—Students 27.

Adel, Dallas Co., St. John (1917), Rev. Richard E. Gubbels.
Mailing Address: P.O. Box 185, 50003-0185. Tel: 515-993-4482.
Catechesis/Religious Programs—Tel: 515-993-4590.
Students 193.

Afton, Union Co., St. Edward (1878). Attended by Paul VI Pastoral Ministry from Creston.
Mailing Address: 406 W. Clark, Creston, 50801. Tel: 515-782-5278; Fax: 515-782-5924.
Church—104 W. Union, 50830. Tel: 515-347-8452.
Catechesis/Religious Programs—Students 50.

Altoona, Polk Co., SS. John and Paul (1983), Rev. Vince G. Rosonke.
Res., 114 13th St., S.E., 50009. Tel: 515-967-3796; Fax: 515-967-7197.
Catechesis/Religious Programs—Students 490.

Anita, Cass Co., St. Mary (1924), Deacon Fred Cornwell.
Church—P.O. Box 277, 50020. Tel: 712-762-3484; 762-3773 (Office); Fax: 712-762-3484.
Catechesis/Religious Programs—Students 54.

Ankeny, Polk Co., Our Lady's Immaculate Heart (1961), Revs. Gregory Leach; Michael McLaughlin; Deacon Richard Ziller.
Res., 510 E. First St., 50021. Tel: 515-964-3038; Fax: 515-964-5997.
Catechesis/Religious Programs—Tel: 515-964-3545.
Students 1,195.

Atlantic, Cass Co., SS. Peter and Paul (1871), Rev. Msgr. Lawrence A. Beeson.
Res., 106 W. 6th St., 50022. Tel: 712-243-4721.
Catechesis/Religious Programs—Tel: 712-243-2144.
Students 220.

Audubon, Audubon Co., St. Patrick (1918), Revs. Christopher Fontanini; John C. Maier.
Res., 116 E. Division St., 50025. Tel: 712-563-2283; Fax: 712-563-3238. [CEM]
Catechesis/Religious Programs—Students 161.

Avoca, Pottawattamie Co., St. Mary, Mediatrix of All Graces (1882), Rev. John M. Frost; Deacon Clarence Christensen.
Res., 109 N. Maple St., P.O. Box 38, 51521. Tel: 712-343-6948.
Catechesis/Religious Programs—Students 82.

Bayard, Guthrie Co., St. Patrick (1882), Rev. Tan Van Tran.
Res., 214 Prairie St., P.O. Box 274, 50029. Tel: 712-651-2676.

Bedford, Taylor Co., Sacred Heart. Attended by St. Clare, Clarinda. Rev. Thomas Coenen.
Mailing Address: 300 E. Lincoln Blvd., Clarinda, 51632.
Catechesis/Religious Programs—Students 12.

Carlisle, Warren Co., St. Elizabeth Seton (1979), Rev. James M. Laurenzo.
Mailing Address: 256 Scotch Ridge Rd., P.O. Box 35, 50047. Tel: 515-989-0659; Fax: 515-989-4525.
Catechesis/Religious Programs—Students 132.

Carter Lake, Pottawattamie Co., Our Lady of Carter Lake (1970). Attended by Our Lady, Queen of Apostles, Council Bluffs. Rev. Dennis Trausch.
Church—3501 N. 9th St., 51510. Tel: 712-347-6631; Fax: 712-325-2411.

Casey, Guthrie Co., St. Joseph (1898). Closed. For inquiries for parish records contact the Chancery.

Chariton, Lucas Co., Sacred Heart (1869), Rev. William Miller, C.PP.S. Pastoral Ministers: Sr. Jeroma Day, B.V.M.; Sr. Mary Ellen Schulte, B.V.M. Tel: 515-774-5486.
Res., 407 N. Main, 50049. Tel: 515-774-5486; 766-6786.
Catechesis/Religious Programs—Students 90.

Churchville, Warren Co., Assumption of the Blessed Virgin Mary (1855), Rev. Wayne Gubbels.
Res., P.O. Box 88, St. Mary's, 50241. Tel: 515-297-2267.
Catechesis/Religious Programs—Students 16.

Clarinda, Page Co., St. Clare (1942), Rev. Thomas Coenen.
Res., 300 E. Lincoln Blvd., 51632. Tel: 712-542-2030.
Catechesis/Religious Programs—Students 30.

Corning, Adams Co., St. Patrick's (1869), Rev. Daniel E. Siepker.
Res., 504 Grove Ave., 50841. Tel: 515-322-3363; Fax: 515-322-4370. [CEM]
Catechesis/Religious Programs—Students 116.

Corydon, Wayne Co., St. Francis (1969). Attended by Chariton of the South Central Catholic Ministry Team.
Mailing Address: 213 W. Jackson, 50060. Tel: 515-774-4978.
Catechesis/Religious Programs—Students 18.

Council Bluffs, Pottawattamie Co.,

1—HOLY FAMILY, (1908), Rev. Kenneth A. Gross.
Res., 2217 Ave. B, 51501. Tel: 712-328-3869.
Catechesis/Religious Programs—Students 75.

2—OUR LADY, QUEEN OF APOSTLES, (1957), Revs. Thomas Crowley; William Dolan; Deacon Monty Montagne.
Res., 3304 4th Ave., 51501. Tel: 712-323-2916; Fax: 712-323-4716.
Catechesis/Religious Programs—Tel: 712-323-1163.
Students 170.

3—ST. PATRICK, (1924), Revs. John Bertogli; Raphael Masabakhwa; Deacons Charles Hannan; James Webering.
Res., 223 Harmony St., 51503. Tel: 712-323-1484.
Catechesis/Religious Programs—Students 246.

4—ST. PETER, (1887) (German), Rev. Charles Kottas.
Res., One Bluff St., 51503. Tel: 712-322-8889; Fax: 712-323-1442.
Catechesis/Religious Programs—Students 289.
St. Francis Worship Center—238 6th St., 51501. Tel: 712-328-7272.

Creston, Union Co., Holy Spirit (1975), Revs. Leonard A. Kenkel; John Maier.
Res., 406 W. Clark, 50801. Tel: 641-782-5278; Fax: 641-782-5278.
Church—Also serving the parish of St. Edward, Afton. 104 W. Union St., Afton, 50801. Tel: 641-782-5924.
School—St. Malachy, Tel: 641-782-7125; Fax: 641-782-5924.
Lay Teachers 10; Students 138.
Catechesis/Religious Programs—Students 85.

Cumberland, Cass Co., St. Timothy (Reno) (1883), Rev. Paul Mahowald, S.J.
Mailing Address: P.O. Box 605, Griswold, 51535-0605. Tel: 712-778-4540.
Catechesis/Religious Programs—Students 29.

Cumming, Warren Co., St. John (1892), Rev. Robert J. Aubrey.
Res., 204 Cottage Ave., P.O. Box 5, 50061. Tel: 515-981-4855; Fax: 515-981-9188.
Catechesis/Religious Programs—Students 175.

Defiance, Shelby Co., St. Peter (1882). Served from Earling. Rev. Michael Berner.
Res., P.O. Box 127, 51527. Tel: 712-748-3501; Fax: 712-748-3500.
Catechesis/Religious Programs—Students 99.

Dunlap, Harrison Co., St. Patrick, Rev. Paul J. Strittmatter, S.J.
Res., 509 S. 3rd St., 51529. Tel: 712-643-5808.
Catechesis/Religious Programs—Students 168.

Earling, Shelby Co., St. Joseph (1882) (German). Served from St. Peter, Defiance. Rev. Michael Berner.
Res., P.O. Box 225, 51530. Tel: 712-747-2091; Fax: 712-747-9501.
School—See Shelby County Board of Catholic Education under Education Centers in the Institution section. Tel: 712-747-3081.
Catechesis/Religious Programs—Students 47.

Elkhart, Polk Co., St. Mary/Holy Cross (1885), Rev. Michael A. Amadeo.
Res., 214 Washington, P.O. Box 110, 50073. Tel: 515-367-2685; Fax: 515-367-2685.
Catechesis/Religious Programs—Students 164.

Exira, Audubon Co., Holy Trinity. Attended by St. Patrick. Rev. Christopher Fontanini.
116 E. Division St., Audubon, 50025. Tel: 712-563-2283; Fax: 712-268-3238.
Catechesis/Religious Programs—Students 45.

Glenwood, Mills Co., Our Lady of the Holy Rosary (1955), Rev. Paul Monahan; Deacons Joseph Blankenship; Ronald Kohn; Richard Maiers; James Parr.
Res., 24116 Marian Ave., 51534-5291. Tel: 712-527-5211; Fax: 712-527-9115.
Catechesis/Religious Programs—Students 279.

Grand River, Decatur Co., St. Patrick. Unassigned.
Res., 222 E. Pearl, Osceola, 50213. Tel: 515-342-2850.

Granger, Dallas Co., Assumption of the Blessed Virgin Mary (1871), Rev. Eugene R. Koch.
Res., 1906 Sycamore, P.O. Box 177, 50109. Tel: 515-999-2239; Fax: 515-999-2208.
School—Tel: 515-999-2211.
Lay Teachers 9; Students 114.
Catechesis/Religious Programs—Students 145.
Mission—Woodward, Dallas Co., St. Ann.

Greenfield, Adair Co., St. John (1907), Rev. Dean Nimerichter.
Res., 303 N.E. Elm St., 50849. Tel: 515-743-2641; Fax: 515-343-7065.
Catechesis/Religious Programs—Students 115.

Griswold, Cass Co., Our Lady Of Grace (1911), Rev. Paul Mahowald, S.J.
Mailing Address: P.O. Box 605, 51535-0605. Tel: 712-778-4540.
Catechesis/Religious Programs—Students 49.

Guthrie Center, Guthrie Co., St. Mary (1906), Rev. Benedict J. Kenkel.
Res., 603 Main St., 50115. Tel: 515-747-2569.
Catechesis/Religious Programs—Students 89.

Hamburg, Fremont Co., St. Mary (1874). Attended by St. Mary, Shenandoah. Rev. Donald Bruck.
Res., 1306 Washington St., 51640. Tel: 712-382-2871.
Catechesis/Religious Programs—Students 45.

Harlan, Shelby Co., St. Michael (1888), Rev. Howard Fitzgerald; Deacons Patrick Davitt; John Stessman; Leo Gaul.
Res., 1912-18th St., 51537. Tel: 712-755-5244; Fax: 712-755-2604.
School—See Shelby County Board of Catholic Education under Education Centers in the Institution section.
Catechesis/Religious Programs—Tel: 712-755-5366; Fax: 712-755-2604.
Students 325.

Imogene, Fremont Co., St. Patrick (1880), Rev. James Kleffman.
Res., P.O. Box 205, 51645. Tel: 712-386-2123.
Catechesis/Religious Programs—Tel: 712-386-2200.
Students 87.

Indianola, Warren Co., St. Thomas Aquinas (1958), Rev. Frank S. Palmer.
Res., 1202 W. Iowa Ave., 50125. Tel: 515-961-3026; Fax: 515-961-3458.
Catechesis/Religious Programs—Tel: 515-961-0447.
Students 290.

Irish Settlement, Madison Co., St. Patrick (1852), Rev. Wayne Gubbels.
Res., P.O. Box 88, St. Marys, 50241. Tel: 641-297-2267.
Catechesis/Religious Programs—Students 40.

Jamaica, Guthrie Co., St. Joseph (1903). Attended by St. Patrick, Bayard.
214 Prairie, P.O. Box 274, Bayard, 50029. Tel: 712-651-2676.

Lacona, Warren Co., Holy Trinity Church of Southeast Warren County (1978), Rev. Martin G. Chevalier.
Res., 304 N. Washington Ave., P.O. Box 145, 50139-0145. Tel: 641-534-4691; Fax: 641-534-4691.
Worship Centers—St. Mary of the Assumption Church, Lacona (Tel: 641-534-4871); St. Augustine Church, Milo (Tel: 641-942-6395); St. Mary of Perpetual Help Church, Rosemont (Tel: 641-534-3145).
Catechesis/Religious Programs—Students 84.

Lenox, Taylor Co., St. Patrick (1872). Attended by St. Patrick, Corning.
Church—600 W. Michigan, 50851. Tel: 515-336-2893.
Catechesis/Religious Programs—Students 51.

Leon, Decatur Co., St. Brendan (1865) (Irish), Rev. Thomas V. Dooley.
Res., 1001 N.W. Church St., 50144. Tel: 515-446-4789.
Catechesis/Religious Programs—Students 57.

Logan, Harrison Co., St. Anne (1920), Rev. John Harmon.
Res., 112 W. 3rd St., 51546. Tel: 712-644-2535.
Catechesis/Religious Programs—Students 136.

Maloy, Ringgold Co., Immaculate Conception (1874), Rev. Thomas V. Dooley.
Res., 103 Shay St., 50836. Tel: 515-446-4789. [CEM]
Catechesis/Religious Programs—Students 5.

Massena, Cass Co., St. Patrick (1888). Served from Anita. Deacon Fred Cornwell.
P.O. Box 277, Anita, 50020. Tel: 712-762-3484.
Catechesis/Religious Programs—Students 49.

Missouri Valley, Harrison Co., St. Patrick (1877), Rev. Robert Harris.
Res., 215 N. Seventh St., 51555. Tel: 712-642-3124; Fax: 712-642-2518.
School—219 N. Seventh St., 51555. Tel: 712-642-3155; Fax: 712-642-2518.
Lay Teachers 5; Students 61.
Catechesis/Religious Programs—Students 76.

Mondamin, Harrison Co., Holy Family. Attended by St. Anne.
112 W. 3rd St., Logan, 51546. Tel: 712-644-2535.
Catechesis/Religious Programs—Students 8.

Mt. Ayr, Ringgold Co., St. Joseph (1913). Attended by St. Brendan.
Church—100 N. Polk, 50854. Tel: 515-446-4789.
Catechesis/Religious Programs—Students 28.

Neola, Pottawattamie Co., St. Patrick (1882), Rev. Daniel Kirby.
Res., P.O. Box 127, 51559. Tel: 712-485-2124; Fax: 712-485-2124.
Catechesis/Religious Programs—Students 149.

Orient, Adair Co., St. Mark. Closed. For inquiries for parish records contact the Chancery.

Osceola, Clarke Co., St. Bernard (1885). Unassigned.
Res., 222 E. Pearl, 50213. Tel: 342-2850.
Catechesis/Religious Programs—Students 78.

Panama, Shelby Co., St. Mary of the Assumption (1899), Rev. Michael G. Peters.
Res., Box 130, 51562. Tel: 712-489-2030.
School—See Shelby County Board of Catholic Education under Education Centers in the Institution section.

Panora, Guthrie Co., St. Cecilia (1907). Attended by St. Mary, Guthrie Center Tel: 515-747-2569.
Church—220 N. First St., 50216. Tel: 515-755-2658.
Catechesis/Religious Programs—Students 57.

Perry, Dallas Co., St. Patrick (1881), Rev. Raymond Higgins.
Res., 1312 3rd St., 50220. Tel: 515-465-4387; Fax: 515-465-4387.
School—1302 5th St., 50220. Tel: 515-465-4186; Fax: 515-465-9808.
Lay Teachers 11; Students 125.
Catechesis/Religious Programs—Students 80.

Portsmouth, Shelby Co., St. Mary (1885), Rev. Paul Bianchi.
Res., P.O. Box 98, 51565. Tel: 712-743-2625; Fax: 712-743-2010.
Catechesis/Religious Programs—Students 95.

Red Oak, Montgomery Co., St. Mary (1902), Rev. James F. Kleffman.
Res., 1510 Highland Ave., 51566. Tel: 712-623-2744.
Catechesis/Religious Programs—Students 117.

St. Marys, Warren Co., Immaculate Conception (1871), Rev. Wayne Gubbels.
Res., P.O. Box 88, 50241. Tel: 641-297-2267.
Catechesis/Religious Programs—Students 94.

Shenandoah, Page Co., St. Mary, Rev. Donald Bruck; Deacon Ed Miller.
Res., 512 W. Thomas Ave., 51601. Tel: 712-246-1718.
Catechesis/Religious Programs—Students 160.

Stuart, Guthrie Co., All Saints (1876), Rev. Daniel Clarke.
Res., P.O. Box 605, 50250. Tel: 515-523-1497.
Catechesis/Religious Programs—Tel: 515-523-1943.
Students 87.

Urbandale, Polk Co., St. Pius X (1955), Rev. Msgr. Joseph McDonnell; Rev. Samuel Palmer; Deacon Dave Bartemes. Pastoral Ministers: Mary Sue Lone; Barbara Mease; Carol Heim.
3663 66th St., 50322. Tel: 515-276-2059; Fax: 515-276-8351.
School—3601 66th St., 50322. Tel: 515-276-1061; Fax: 515-276-0351. Lawrence Zahm, Prin.
Sisters 1; Lay Teachers 26; Students 387.
Catechesis/Religious Programs—Tel: 515-278-5684. D.R.E.: Mary Heinrich; Cynthia Wells.
Students 470.

Villisca, Montgomery Co., St. Joseph (1947). Attended by St. Clare, Clarinda. Thomas Coenen.
304 E. Lincoln St., Clarinda, 51632. Tel: 712-826-8841.
Catechesis/Religious Programs—Students 9.

Walnut, Pottawattamie Co., St. Patrick (1882). Attended by St. Mary, Mediatrix of All Graces, Avoca. Rev. John M. Frost.
Mailing Address: 109 N. Maple St., P.O. Box 38, Avoca, 51521. Tel: 712-343-6948.
Catechesis/Religious Programs—Students 47.

Waukee, Dallas Co., St. Boniface (1880), Rev. Robert L. Schoemann; Sr. Theresa Engel, S.S.S.F., Pastoral Min.
Res., 250 4th St., 50263-9623. Tel: 515-987-4597; Fax: 515-987-5272.
Catechesis/Religious Programs—Students 300.

West Des Moines, Polk Co., Sacred Heart (1892), Revs. Michael N. Hess; Garry Culver; Jack McClure, C.PP.S.; Deacon Chris Rohwer; Sr. Mary Margaret O'Toole, Pastoral Assoc.
1627 Grand Ave., 50265. Tel: 515-225-6414; Fax: 515-225-0286.
School—1601 Grand Ave., 50265. Tel: 515-223-1284; Fax: 515-223-9413.
Sisters 2; Lay Teachers 27; Students 525.
Catechesis/Religious Programs—Tel: 515-225-1641; Fax: 515-225-0286.
Students 530.

St. Francis of Assisi, Dallas Co., (1991), Rev. Msgr. Edward Hurley; Rev. Raymond McHenry; Deacon David O'Brien.
7075 Ashworth Rd., 50266. Tel: 515-223-4577; Fax: 515-223-4768.
School—Tel: 515-457-7167.
Lay Teachers 13; Students 190.
Catechesis/Religious Programs—Students 500.

Weston, Pottawattamie Co., St. Columbanus (1883). Attended by St. Patrick, Neola. Rev. Daniel Kirby.
Res., St. Patrick's Church, P.O. Box 127, Neola, 51559. Tel: 712-485-2124.
Catechesis/Religious Programs—Students 36.

Westphalia, Shelby Co., St. Boniface (1873), Rev. Michael G. Peters.
Church—207 Duren Strasse, P.O. Box 86, 51578. Tel: 712-627-4255; Fax: 712-627-4257.
Catechesis/Religious Programs—Students 51.

Winterset, Madison Co., St. Joseph (1893), Rev. Christopher Hartshorn.
Res., 607 W. Green St., 50273. Tel: 515-462-1083; Fax: 515-462-2378.
Catechesis/Religious Programs—Students 163.

Woodbine, Harrison Co., Sacred Heart (1902). Attended by St. Patrick's, Dunlap. Rev. Paul J. Strittmatter, S.J.
33 Seventh St., 51579. Tel: 712-647-2871.
Catechesis/Religious Programs—Students 100.

Woodward, Dallas Co., St. Ann (1934). Attended by Assumption of the Blessed Virgin Mary. Rev. Eugene R. Koch.
1906 Sycamore St., P.O. Box 177, Granger, 50109. Tel: 515-999-2239; Fax: 515-999-2208.

Chaplains of Public Institutions

DES MOINES. *City Chaplaincy Program* 1610 60th St., 50322. Rev. Arthur McCann.
United States Veterans Hospital 3019 Pleasant, 50310. Rev. Paul Holt.

CLARINDA. *State Hospital.* Served from St. Clare Church, Clarinda.

COUNCIL BLUFFS. *Iowa School for the Deaf* 411 E. Broadway, 51503. Tel: 712-322-2449. Sr. Helen Seivert, Chap. & D.R.E.

GLENWOOD. *Glenwood State School.* Vacant.

MITCHELLVILLE. *Iowa Correctional Institution for Women.* Kay Kopatich, Chap. & Coord., Svcs. to Catholic Residents.

On Special Assignment:
Reverend Monsignors—
Orr, Stephen, Vicar General
Reverend Fathers—
Amadeo, Michael A., Diocesan Tribunal Office
Cameron, Kevin, Hispanic Ministry
Cordaro, Frank
Fitzgerald, P. Timothy, Office of Adult Faith Formation
Fleming, David, Diocesan Dir. Ministry Formation

On Duty Outside the Diocese:
Reverend Fathers—
Freeman, James, St. Joseph, 215 Craycraft Rd., Tucson, AZ 85711
Grant, Robert, St. Ambrose University, Davenport, IA 52803
Koch, Paul M., Casilla 919, Santa Cruz, Bolivia

On Sabbatical:
Reverend Monsignors—
Bognanno, Frank

Leave of Absence:
Reverend Fathers—
Wilwerding, Jim

Retired:
Reverend Monsignors—
Conley, Raymond J., 1390 Buffalo Rd., West Des Moines, IA 50265
Connelly, Paul J., 615 Park St., #1501, Des Moines, IA 50309
Devine, W. J., Sagamore Towers No. 2, 95 Squantum St., Apt. 609, Quincy, MA 02171
Gorman, John, 1390 Buffalo Rd., West Des Moines, IA 50265
McIlhon, John J., 1390 Buffalo Rd., West Des Moines, IA 50265
Pfeffer, Edward B., 1390 Buffalo Rd., West Des Moines, IA 50265
Ring, Arthur R., 5815 Winwood Dr. #129, Johnston, IA 50131
Ryan, Joseph P., 1390 Buffalo Rd., West Des Moines, IA 50265
Schwarte, Michael W., P.O. Box 43, Portsmouth, IA 51565
Wadsworth, James, 600 Locust, Atlantic, IA 50022
Reverend Fathers—
Bergman, Richard, 1390 Buffalo Rd., West Des Moines, IA 50265
Clarke, John
Cunningham, John E., 1390 Buffalo Rd., West Des Moines, IA 50265
Daleke, Don, 6333 Rancho Mission Rd. #207, San Diego, CA 92108
Elias, Woodrow, 7327 Sawgrass, San Antonio, TX 78244
Fenelon, David, 934 Lincoln St., Waterloo, IA 50703
Gaul, Cornelius, P.O. Box 59, R.R., Earling, IA 51530
Klein, Eugene J., 939 Hwy. 37, Earling, IA 51530
Leto, Nelo A., 710 Davis, Des Moines, IA 50315
Lorenz, John F., 1390 Buffalo Rd., W. Des Moines, IA 50265
Peterson, Cyril P., Longview Home, Inc., Rm. 20, 1010 Longview Dr., Missouri Valley, IA 51555
Reischl, Fred P., 1390 Buffalo Rd., West Des Moines, IA 50265
Reisz, Adam, R.R. 2, Dunlap, IA 51529
Ryan, John R., 1173 20th Pl., West Des Moines, IA 50265

Permanent Deacons:
Ayers, John
Bartemes, David
Blankenship, Joseph
Boehlert, Jeffrey
Bray, Robert
Brewer, Marvin
Catanzano, George
Christensen, Clarence
Coan, Joseph
Cord, Michael
Cornwell, Fred
Cortese, Joseph
Critelli, Anthony, (Retired)
Davitt, Patrick
Doyle, James, (Retired)
Erickson, Gregg
Garza, David
Gaul, Leo, (Retired)
Hannan, Charles
Heitkotter, Jerome, (Retired)
Herman, James
Howe, Robert
Huynh, Joseph, (Retired)
Jacobi, Donald, (Retired)
Jager, Gene
Jarvis, John, (Retired)
Kirkman, Patrick
Kirlin, Dennis
Klein, Marvin
Knotek, Lawrence, (Retired)
Kohn, Ronald
Krawczyk, Gene
Leininger, Jerry, (Retired)
Lovell, David
Lovell, Dennis
Luft, Dennis
Maiers, Richard
Maly, Tom
McCarthy, Michael
McGuire, Dan
Miller, Edward
Montagne, Monty
O'Brien, David
Parr, James
Pins, Fred
Putbrese, Charles
Rallis, Stephen
Richardson, Alan, (Retired)
Rohwer, Chris
Scurlock, Joseph, (Retired)
Smith, William
Stageman, Mark, (Retired)
Starbuck, Tom
Stessman, Gail
Stessman, John
Sullivan, Robert, (Retired)
Vanderckvoorde, Steve
Von Behren, Lyle
Webering, James
Wolford, Charles
Yang, LyPao
Ziller, Richard

INSTITUTIONS LOCATED IN THE DIOCESE

[A] EDUCATION CENTERS

COUNCIL BLUFFS. *Council Bluffs Area Catholic Education Systems, Inc.*, 400 Gleason Ave., 51503. Tel: 712-329-9000; Fax: 712-328-0228.
E-mail: pierip@stalbert.pvt.k12.ia.us
Web site: www.saintalbertschools.org
John James, Pres. Priests 1; Total Lay Teachers 66; Total Staff 121; Total Enrollment (K-12) 929.
St. Albert Junior High School. (Grades 7-8), 400 Gleason Ave., 51503. Tel: 712-328-2316; Fax: 712-328-8316. Rev. Phillip Hobt. Lay Teachers 8; Students 148.
St. Albert Intermediate School. (Grades 4-6), 400 Gleason Ave., 51503. Tel: 712-322-7004; Fax: 712-322-0399. Lay Teachers 10; Students 238.
St. Albert Primary School. (Grades PreK-3), 2912 9th Ave., 51501. Tel: 712-323-3703; Fax: 712-323-6132. Lay Teachers 15; Students 290.
Religious Education Center, 424 Gleason Ave., 51503. Tel: 712-322-4339; Fax: 712-328-0228. Mary B. Fisher, Dir.

PANAMA. *Shelby County Board of Catholic Education*, 208 St. Mary's Ave., 51562-0183. Tel: 712-489-2727; Fax: 712-489-2727.
E-mail: lheese@shelcocath.pvt.k12.ia.us
Web site: www.shelcocath.pvt.k12.ia.us
Elementary Schools: Shelby County Catholic Schools. Tel: 712-489-2727; Fax: 712-489-2727. Sisters 2; Total Lay Teachers 21; Total Staff 23; Total Enrollment 330.
Attendance Centers:
St. Mary's Center. (Grades PreK-3), 208 St. Mary's Ave., 51562-0183. Tel: 712-489-2727; Fax: 712-489-2727. Lay Teachers 5; Students 88.
St. Joseph's Center. (Grades 4-8), 208 Main St., Earling, 51530-0227. Tel: 712-747-3081; Fax: 712-747-3081. Lay Teachers 5; Students 89.
St. Michael's Center. (Grades PreK-6), 205 College Blvd., Harlan, 51537. Tel: 712-755-5634; Fax: 712-755-3332. Lay Teachers 8; Students 153.

WEST DES MOINES. *St. Joseph Educational Center*, 1400 Buffalo Rd., 50265. Tel: 515-225-3000; Fax: 515-222-1056. Dr. Jerry Deegan, Pres.
Religious Education. Tel: 515-222-1044; Fax: 515-222-1056. Rev. James M. Laurenzo, Dir. Adult and Youth Ministries.

[B] COLLEGES AND UNIVERSITIES

DES MOINES. *Mercy College of Health Sciences*, 928-6th Ave., 50309-1239. Tel: 515-643-3180; Fax: 515-643-6698.
E-mail: admissions@mchs.edu
Web site: www.mchs.edu
For a complete listing, refer to the Colleges and Universities section.

[C] HIGH SCHOOLS, INTERPAROCHIAL

COUNCIL BLUFFS. *Saint Albert Catholic Schools*, 400 Gleason Ave., 51503. Tel: 712-328-2316; Fax: 712-328-8316.
E-mail: pierip@stalbert.pvt.k12.ia.us
Web site: www.saintalbertschools.org
John James, Pres., Saint Albert High School (Grades 9-12); Mike Cooper, Prin.; Rev. Phillip Hobt.
Serving all parishes in Council Bluffs; St. Patrick, Missouri Valley; St. Patrick, Neola; Holy Rosary, Glenwood; St. Columbanus, Weston. Priests 1; Lay Teachers 34; Total Staff 62; Students 253 (Gr 9-12).

WEST DES MOINES. *Dowling High School*, 1400 Buffalo Rd., 50265. Tel: 515-225-3000; Fax: 515-222-1056. Dr. Jerry Deegan, Pres.; James Dowdle, Prin.; Mary Bustin, Registrar; Rev. Jim Kirby.
Serving all parishes in Des Moines; Sacred Heart, West Des Moines; St. Francis of Assisi, West Des Moines; St. Boniface, Waukee; Assumption, Granger; St. John, Cumming; St. Mary, Elkhart; Holy Cross, Elkhart; SS. John and Paul, Atoona; Immaculate Heart, Ankeny. Priests 1; Sisters 1; Lay Teachers 80; Students 1,178.

[D] GENERAL HOSPITALS

DES MOINES. *Mercy Medical Center*, 1111 Sixth Ave., 50314. Tel: 515-247-3121; Fax: 515-247-4259.
Web site: www.mercydesmoines.org
For a complete listing, refer to the Hospitals section.

CORNING. *Mercy Midlands: Mercy Hospital*, Rosary Dr., P.O. Box 368, 50841. Tel: 515-322-3121; Fax: 515-322-4872
For a complete listing, refer to the Hospitals section.

COUNCIL BLUFFS. *Bergan Mercy-Alegent Health System: Mercy Hospital*, 800 Mercy Dr., 51502. Tel: 712-328-5306; Fax: 712-325-2432.
Web site: www.alegent.com
For a complete listing, refer to the Hospitals section.

[E] HOMES FOR AGED

JOHNSTON. *Bishop Drumm Retirement Center*, 5837 Winwood Dr., 50131-1651. Tel: 515-270-1100; Fax: 515-276-1714
For a complete listing, refer to the Special Care Facilities section.

[F] SPECIAL CARE FACILITIES

DES MOINES. *House of Mercy*, 1409 Clark St., 50314-1964. Tel: 515-643-6500; Fax: 515-643-6598.
E-mail: tbeveridge@mercydesmoines.org
For a complete listing, refer to the Special Care Facilities section.

[G] SECULAR INSTITUTES

DES MOINES. *Institute of the Heart of Jesus*, P.O. Box 4634, 50306. Tel: 515-222-1089; Fax: 515-222-1056.
E-mail: fatherjfl@aol.com
Web site: www.execpc.com/~uscs/Index.html
Secular Priests and Lay People. Rev. John F. Lorenz.

[H] SPIRITUAL MINISTRY TO THE DIOCESE

DES MOINES. *Emmaus House*, 1521 Center St., 50314. Tel: 515-282-4839. Co-Directors: Rev. Daniel Krettek; Sr. Charlotte Huetteman, O.S.M.

[I] NEWMAN CENTERS

DES MOINES. *St. Catherine of Siena Catholic Student Center.* (Drake Newman Community), 1150-28th St., 50311-4142. Tel: 515-271-4747; Fax: 515-271-1918.
E-mail: John.ludwig@Drake.edu
Rev. John Ludwig. Students 750; Non-Students 250.

[J] MISCELLANEOUS LISTINGS

DES MOINES. *Bishop's Endowment Fund Foundation*, 601 Grand Ave., 50309.

City Hospital Chaplaincy Service, 1610 60th St., 50322-6106. Tel: 515-255-1846. Rev. Arthur McCann.

Serving all non-Catholic hospitals in Des Moines.

Dowling-St. Joseph Alumni Foundation, 1400 Buffalo Rd., 50265. Tel: 515-225-3000; Fax: 515-222-1056. Web site: www.dowlinghighschool.org

Dr. Andy McGuire, Pres.; Dr. Jerry Deegan, Sec.; Bob Ligouri, Vice Pres. Devel.

Holy Family School Inner-City Youth Foundation, P.O. Box 8437, 50301. Tel: 515-262-7466; Fax: 515-266-9803.

E-mail: hfsfoundation@uswest.net

Jean Fitzpatrick, Foundation Admin.

Life in the Spirit Community, Inc., 4601 Ovid Ave., 50310. Tel: 515-255-7534. Michael Freilinger, Co-ord.

Mercy Child Development Center, 6th & University, 50314. Tel: 515-247-4200. Diane Kraemer, Mgr.

Mercy Foundation of Des Moines - Affiliate of Catholic Health Initiatives, 921 Sixth Ave., Ste. A, 50314-1200. Tel: 515-247-3248. Sheila Smith, Ed.D., Pres.

National Catholic Rural Life Conference, 4625 Beaver Ave., 50310. Tel: 515-270-2634; Fax: 515-270-9447.

E-mail: ncrlc@aol.com

Web site: http://www.ncrlc.com

Most Rev. Raymond L. Burke, D.D., J.C.D., Pres., (Bishop of LaCrosse); Bro. David G. Andrews, C.S.C., Exec. Dir.

Roman Catholic Pastoral Center Foundation, 601 Grand Ave., 50309. Tel: 515-237-5044; Fax: 515-237-5070.

E-mail: finance@dmdiocese.org

Web site: www.dmdiocese.org

Rev. Msgr. Stephen Orr, Vicar Gen.

Roman Catholic Priests' Medical Fund Foundation, 601 Grand Ave., 50309.

Roman Catholic Seminary Fund Foundation, 601 Grand Ave., 50309.

St. Gabriel Benedictine Priory, 1913 University Ave., 50314. Tel: 515-283-0341; Fax: 515-244-3165.

E-mail: basilicadm@aol.com

Very Rev. Aquinas Nichols, O.S.B., Prior. Priests 2; Brothers 6.

St. Joseph Emergency Shelter, 1535 - 11th St., 50314.

St. Mary Family Center, 1240 E. 12th, 50316.

Society of Saint Vincent de Paul, 1426 6th Ave., 50314. Tel: 515-282-8327. Larry Schmitz, Pres. Store Operators: Virginia Klemm; Mike Bondura.

COUNCIL BLUFFS. *Mercy Hospital Foundation, Council Bluffs*, 800 Mercy Dr., P.O. Box 1C, 51502. Tel: 712-328-5585; Fax: 712-325-2425. Richard A. Hachten, II, Pres.

St. Albert Educational Foundation, 400 Gleason Ave., 51503. Tel: 712-329-9000; Fax: 712-328-0228.

E-mail: pierip@stalbert.pvt.k12.ia.us

Web site: www.saintalbertschools.org

John James, Pres.

St. Joseph Catholic Cemetery Association, 17510 Sunnydale Rd., 51501. Tel: 712-322-7963. John E. O'Connor, Mgr.

GRISWOLD. *Wakonda Prayer House*, Box 370, 51535. Tel: 712-784-3797.

HARLAN. *Shelby County Catholic Education Foundation*, 711 Court St., 51537. Tel: 712-755-3141; Fax: 712-755-3144.

E-mail: sdslaw@harlannet.com

JOHNSTON. *Bishop Drumm Development Office*. A division of Mercy Foundation - Affiliate of Catholic Health Initiatives and Mercy Health Network. 5837 Winwood Dr., 50131. Tel: 515-270-1100; Fax: 515-276-1714.

E-mail: rhilbert@mercydesmoines.org

PANORA. *St. Thomas More Center*, 6177 Panorama Rd., 50216. Tel: 641-755-3164; Fax: 641-755-4157.

E-mail: stmg@netins.net

Web site: www.netins.net/showcase/stmore

WEST DES MOINES. *Mercy Health Network, Inc.*, 4500 Westown Pkwy., #250, 50266. Tel: 515-224-3260; Fax: 515-224-3546. David H. Vellinga, Chair, Mgmt. Council.

RELIGIOUS INSTITUTES OF MEN REPRESENTED IN THE DIOCESE

For further details refer to the corresponding bracketed number in the Religious Institutes of Men or Women section.

[0600]—*Brothers of the Congregation of the Holy Cross.*—C.S.C.

[]—*Congregation of the Holy Ghost.* (Nigeria).

[0690]—*Jesuit Fathers and Brothers.* (Wisconsin Prov.).—S.J.

[0430]—*Order of Preachers-Dominicans.*—O.P.

[0200]—*Order of St. Benedict.* (Conception, MO).—O.S.B.

RELIGIOUS INSTITUTES OF WOMEN REPRESENTED IN THE DIOCESE

[0230]—*Benedictine Sisters of Pontifical Jurisdiction.*—O.S.B.

[2100]—*Congregation of the Holy Humility of Mary.*—C.H.M.

[1920]—*Congregation of the Sisters of the Holy Cross.*—C.S.C.

[1070-14]—*Dominican Sisters.*—O.P.

[1070-03]—*Dominican Sisters.*—O.P.

[1070-13]—*Dominican Sisters.*—O.P.

[1120]—*Dominican Sisters of the Roman Congregation.*—O.P.

[2575]—*Institute of the Sisters of Mercy of the Americas.* (Cedar Rapids, IA; Omaha, NE; Chicago, IL).—R.S.M.

[1680]—*School Sisters of St. Francis.*—O.S.F.

[3580]—*Servants of Mary.*—O.S.M.

[0480]—*Sisters of Charity of Leavenworth, Kansas.*—S.C.L.

[0430]—*Sisters of Charity of the Blessed Virgin Mary.*—B.V.M.

[2630]—*Sisters of Mercy of the Holy Cross.*—S.C.S.C.

[3000]—*Sisters of Notre Dame de Namur.*—S.N.D.de.N.

[3320]—*Sisters of Presentation of the Blessed Virgin Mary.*—P.B.V.M.

[1540]—*Sisters of Saint Francis, Clinton, Iowa.*—O.S.F.

[1705]—*The Sisters of St. Francis of Assisi.*—O.S.F.

[2960]—Notre Dame Sisters. (Omaha, NE).—N.D.

[1570]—*Sisters of St. Francis of the Holy Family.*—O.S.F.

NECROLOGY

† Kautzky, Jon, Red Oak, IA St. Mary. —Died Jan. 17, 2000.

† Kelly, Rev. Msgr. Edward. —Died June 12, 2000.

† Reece, Frederick, (Retired). —Died Aug. 29, 2000.

† Wingert, LaVern, Griswold, IA Wakonda Prayer House. —Died Dec. 17, 1999.

Archdiocese of Detroit

(Archidioecesis Detroitensis)

His Eminence

ADAM CARDINAL MAIDA, J.C.L., J.D., S.T.L.

Archbishop of Detroit; ordained May 26, 1956; appointed to Green Bay November 8, 1983; consecrated January 25, 1984; installed as Archbishop of Detroit June 12, 1990; created Cardinal on November 26, 1994.

Cardinal's Office: 1234 Washington Blvd., Detroit, MI, 48226; Fax: 313-237-4642.

Most Reverend

THOMAS J. GUMBLETON, D.D.

Auxiliary Bishop of Detroit, Titular Bishop of Ululi; ordained June 2, 1956; appointed March 8, 1968; consecrated May 1, 1968. *Office: 1234 Washington Blvd., Detroit, MI, 48226.*

Most Reverend

WALTER J. SCHOENHERR, D.D.

Retired Auxiliary Bishop of Detroit, Titular Bishop of Timidana; ordained October 27, 1945; appointment March 8, 1968; consecrated May 1, 1968; retired March 7, 1995. *Office: 1234 Washington Blvd., Detroit, MI, 48226.*

Most Reverend

MOSES B. ANDERSON, S.S.E., D.D.

Auxiliary Bishop of Detroit, Titular Bishop of Vatarba; ordained May 30, 1958; appointed December 3, 1982; consecrated January 27, 1983. *Office: Precious Blood Parish, 13305 Grove, Detroit, MI, 48235.*

Most Reverend

LEONARD P. BLAIR, D.D.

Auxiliary Bishop of Detroit, Titular Bishop of Voncariana; ordained June 26, 1976; consecrated August 24, 1999. *Office: 1234 Washington Blvd., Detroit, MI, 48226.*

Most Reverend

KEVIN M. BRITT, D.D.

Auxiliary Bishop of Detroit, Titular Bishop of Esco; ordained June 28, 1970; appointed November 23, 1993; consecrated January 6, 1994. *Office: 1234 Washington Blvd., Detroit, MI, 48226.*

Most Reverend

ALLEN J. VIGNERON, D.D.

Auxiliary Bishop of Detroit, Titular Bishop of Sault Ste. Marie; ordained July 27, 1975; appointed June 12, 1996; consecrated July 9, 1996. *Office: Sacred Heart Seminary, 2701 Chicago Blvd., Detroit, MI, 48206.*

Most Reverend

JOHN C. NIENSTEDT

Auxiliary Bishop of Detroit, Titular Bishop of Alton; ordained July 27, 1974; appointed June 12, 1996; consecrated July 9, 1996. *Office: 1234 Washington Blvd., Detroit, MI, 48226.*

ESTABLISHED MARCH 8, 1833; CREATED AN ARCHBISHOPRIC AUGUST 3, 1937.

Square Miles 3,901.

Comprises the Counties of Lapeer, Macomb, Monroe, Oakland, St. Clair and Wayne.

For legal titles of parishes and archdiocesan institutions, consult the Cardinal's Office.

STATISTICAL OVERVIEW

Personnel	
Cardinal	1
Auxiliary Bishops	6
Retired Bishops	1
Priests: Diocesan Active in Diocese	311
Priests: Active Outside Diocese	18
Priests: Diocesan in Foreign Missions	2
Priests: Retired, Sick or Absent	154
Number of Diocesan Priests	485
Religious Priests in Diocese	294
Extern Priests in Diocese	46
Ordinations:	
Diocesan Priests	5
Transitional Deacons	2
Permanent Deacons	7
Permanent Deacons in Diocese	146
Total Brothers	130
Total Sisters	1,900
Parishes	
Parishes	308
With Resident Pastor:	
Resident Diocesan Priests	261
Resident Religious Priests	32
Without Resident Pastor:	
Administered by Priests	15
Missions	4
New Parishes Created	1
Closed Parishes	2
Professional Ministry Personnel:	
Brothers	130
Sisters	731
Lay Ministers	440
Welfare	
Catholic Hospitals	12
Total Assisted	1,671,343
Health Care Centers	9
Total Assisted	13,128
Homes for the Aged	13
Total Assisted	2,283
Residential Care of Children	8
Total Assisted	1,407
Day Care and Extended Day Care Centers	2
Total Assisted	700
Specialized Homes	8
Total Assisted	2,369
Special Centers for Social Services	12
Total Assisted	21,182
Residential Care of Disabled	1
Total Assisted	104
Educational	
Seminaries, Diocesan	2
Students from This Diocese	30
Students from Other Diocese	54
Diocesan Students in Other Seminaries	1
Seminaries, Religious	2
Students Religious	9
Total Seminarians	40
Colleges and Universities	4
Total Students	19,226
High Schools, Diocesan and Parish	18
Total Students	5,271
High Schools, Private	16
Total Students	8,472
Elementary Schools, Diocesan and Parish	127
Total Students	39,811
Elementary Schools, Private	7
Total Students	1,580
Catechesis/Religious Education:	
High School Students	7,899
Elementary Students	73,963
Total Students Under Catholic Instruction	156,262
Teachers in the Diocese:	
Priests	11
Brothers	14
Sisters	144
Lay Teachers	2,700
Vital Statistics	
Receptions into the Church:	
Infant Baptism Totals	16,763
Adult Baptism Totals	1,535
Received into Full Communion	1,767
First Communions	15,600
Confirmations	11,720
Marriages:	
Catholic	3,662
Interfaith	1,637
Total Marriages	5,299
Deaths	10,286
Total Catholic Population	1,431,565
Total Population	4,266,650

Former Bishops—Rt. Rev. FREDERIC RESE, D.D., cons. Oct. 6, 1833; resigned Aug. 19, 1840; died Dec. 30, 1871.—Rt. Rev. PETER PAUL LEFEVERE, D.D., cons. Nov. 22, 1841; Bishop of Zela, coadjutor and admin. of Detroit; died March 4, 1869.—Rt. Rev. CASPAR HENRY BORGESS, D.D., cons. April 24, 1870; Bishop of Calydon, coadjutor and admin. of Detroit became Bishop of Detroit Dec. 30, 1871; resigned April 16, 1887; died May 3, 1890.—Rt. Rev. JOHN SAMUEL FOLEY, D.D., cons. Nov. 4, 1888; died Jan. 5, 1918.—Most Rev. MICHAEL JAMES GALLAGHER, D.D., cons. Sept. 8, 1915; Bishop of Tipasa, coadjutor of Grand Rapids; became Bishop of Grand Rapids Dec. 26, 1916; transferred to Detroit July 18, 1918; died Jan. 20, 1937.—His Eminence EDWARD CARDINAL MOONEY, D.D., appt. Apostolic Delegate in India Jan. 8, 1926; appt. Titular Archbishop of Irenopolis Jan. 18, 1926; cons. Jan. 31, 1926; appt. Apostolic Delegate in Japan Feb. 25, 1931; transferred to the Diocese of Rochester Aug. 28, 1933; transferred to the Archdiocese of Detroit Aug. 3, 1937; created Cardinal Priest of the title of S. Susanna Feb. 18, 1946; died Oct. 25, 1958.—His Eminence JOHN CARDINAL DEARDEN, D.D., ord. Dec. 8, 1932; cons. Titular Bishop of Sarepta and coadjutor Bishop of Pittsburgh Dec. 22, 1950; installed Archbishop of Detroit Jan. 29, 1959; created Cardinal April 28, 1969; resigned as Archbishop July 15, 1980; died Aug. 1, 1988.—His Eminence EDMUND CARDINAL SZOKA, J.C.L., D.D., Archbishop Emeritus of Detroit; ord. June 5, 1954; appt. Bishop of Gaylord June 15, 1971; cons. July 20, 1971; installed July 20, 1971; promoted to See of Detroit March 28, 1981; installed May 17, 1981; created Cardinal June 28, 1988; appt. Pres., Prefacture for Economic Affairs of the Holy See June 25, 1990.

Archdiocesan Departments and Divisions

Information and Reference—Tel: 313-237-5800.

Cardinal's Office—1234 Washington Blvd., Detroit, 48226; Fax: 313-237-4642. All official mail should be directed to this office. Rev. JEFFREY M. MONFORTON, Cardinal's Appointments Sec. Tel: 313-237-5816. Rev. Msgr. JOHN P. ZENZ, Moderator of the

Curia. Tel: 313-237-5783. Sr. BARBARA CELESKEY, S.J., Chancellor. Tel: 313-237-5847; Fax: 313-237-4643.

Auxiliary Bishops—Most Rev. LEONARD P. BLAIR, D.D., Region 1. Tel: 313-237-5859. Most Rev. ALLEN J. VIGNERON, D.D., Region 2. Tel: 313-883-8501. Most Rev. KEVIN M. BRITT, D.D., Region 3. Tel: 313-237-5848. Most Rev. JOHN C. NIENSTEDT, D.D., Region 4. Tel: 313-237-5788.

College of Consultors—Revs. JEROME A. BRZEZINSKI; FRANCIS BURNS; DONALD HANCHON; Rev. Msgr. JAMES MOLONEY; Revs. KEVIN O'BRIEN; FREDERICK SCHWEIHOFER; Rev. Msgr. ANTHONY TOCCO; Rev. Msgr. JOHN P. ZENZ.

Presbyteral Council—Rev. Msgr. EDWARD BALDWIN; Rev. Msgr. RICK BASS; Revs. ROBERT FISHER; LOUIS GRANDPRE; Rev. Msgr. JOHN P. ZENZ; Sr. BARBARA CELESKEY, S.J.; Revs. JOHN G. BUDDE; MICHAEL COONEY; GEORGE CHARNLEY; JOHN HALL; Rev. Msgr. ROBERT HUMITZ; Revs. TIMOTHY LABOE; GERARD LEBOEUF; Rev. Msgr. JAMES ROBINSON, S.S.E.; Revs. ROBERT SCHUSTER; JAMES WYSOCKI; Rev. Msgr. WILLIAM EASTON; Revs. RONALD JOZWIAK; CHARLES KOSANKE; Rev. Msgr. MICHAEL LEFEVRE; Revs. JOHN WEST; JAMES WIEGING; LAWRENCE ZUREK, O.F.M.; Mr. TODD MISTOR.

Archdiocesan Vicars—Revs. TIMOTHY F. BABCOCK, Pontiac Area (3); RAYMOND H. LEWANDOWSKI, Downriver (4); THOMAS H. CUSICK, Western Wayne (4); JAMES M. PROFOTA, Serf (1); MARK BRAUER, West Detroit (3); JAMES E. COMMYN, Belle River (2); GERARD W. BATTERSBY, Northwest Detroit (3); RENE L. DESMARAIS, Port Huron (2); FRANCIS R. REISS, Southland (4); ANTHONY SULKOWSKI, Monroe (4); JEROME SINGER, East Side (1); MICHAEL SAVICKAS, Vicariate of the Lakes (3); RANDALL R. PHILLIPS, Dearborn (4); TIMOTHY KANE, North Central (2); KENNETH KAUCHECK, Birmingham-Bloomfield-Troy (3); GERALD A. MCENHILL, Farmington-Southfield (3); MARK SOEHNER, O.F.M., The Hub (4); THOMAS JOHNSON, North Macomb (2); GARY SCHULTE, Warren-Centerline (1); DUANE NOVELLY, Detroit-Grosse Pointe (1); ROBERT M. MORAND, West Side Inner City (2); JOSEPH MALLIA, Northwest Wayne (4); GARY T. SMETANKA, East Macomb (1); WAYNE UREEL, Thumb (3); EDWARD F. ZAORSKI, Southwest (4); STEVEN C. KOEHLER, Southeast Oakland (3); RONALD MILLIGAN, Sterling Heights (2).

Archdiocesan Pastoral Council—Ms. PAMELA BEECH; Mr. MICHAEL HARNING.

The Metropolitan Tribunal—305 Michigan Ave., Detroit, 48226. Tel: 313-237-5865; Fax: 313-237-5872. Office Hours: Mon.-Fri. 8:30-4:30.

Judicial Vicar—Very Rev. RONALD T. BROWNE, J.C.L., J.D.

Adjutant Judicial Vicars—Revs. GEORGE P. MILLER, J.C.L.; RONALD J. JOZWIAK, J.C.L.

Diocesan Judges—Rev. Msgr. WALTER A. HURLEY, J.C.L.; Revs. TIMOTHY F. BABCOCK; JAMES BJORUM, J.C.L.; ROBERT BURKE, J.C.L.; Rev. Msgr. MICHAEL LEFEVRE, J.C.L.; Revs. JOACHIM CULOTTA, O.P., J.C.D.; JOHN GAGALA, J.C.L.; JEROME SLOWINSKI, J.C.L.; GARY TIERNEY, J.C.L.; ROBERT H. WILLIAMS, J.C.L.; KENNETH KAUCHECK, J.C.L.

Notaries—GLORIA ANFIELD; PATRICIA BEEDING; ALICE LILEY; ANDREA PINTO; IRENE S. KRAWCZYK; JACQUELINE L. LOVE; PATRICIA MKRTUMIAN; ESTHER SMITH; DARNELL MCQUEEN.

Defenders of Bond—Revs. RICHARD CAVELLIER, J.C.L.; FRANCIS REISS, J.C.L.; Rev. Msgr. RICARDO BASS, J.C.L.; FRANCIS SYLVESTER; Revs. MICHAEL MOLNAR, J.C.L.; NORMAN NAWROCKI, J.C.L.; Sr. DIANE MASSON, C.S.S.F., J.C.L.; Mr. MICHAEL TRUEMAN, J.C.L.

Auditors—Mr. ROBERT CADOTTE.

Court Experts—Mr. FABIAN WEBER; Sr. JUDITH MCMANUS, O.P., L.M.F.T., A.C.S.W.

Department of Christian Service—DANIEL PIEPSZOWSKI, Dir., *305 Michigan Ave., Detroit, 48226.* Tel: 313-237-4685; Fax: 313-237-5866.

Office of Human Services and Pastoral Care—KRISTA BAJOKA. Tel: 313-237-4687.

Office of Institutions and Agencies—CANDY SALAZAR. Tel: 313-237-5903.

Office of Social Ministries—STEVEN SPREITZER. Tel: 313-237-5958.

Department of Communications—NED MCGRATH, Dir., *305 Michigan Ave., Detroit, 48226.* Tel: 313-237-5943; Fax: 313-237-4644.

Office of Public Relations—NED MCGRATH. Tel: 313-237-5943; Fax: 313-237-4644.

Office of Printing and Mailing—DENNIS MILLIGAN, *1501 Sixth St., Detroit, 48226.* Tel: 313-237-5967; Fax: 313-965-8471.

Office of Television—KEN KOLB. Tel: 313-237-5938; Fax: 313-237-5928.

Department of Education—Rev. Msgr. JOHN M. QUINN, Dir., *305 Michigan Ave., Detroit, 48226.* Tel: 313-237-4675; Fax: 313-237-5867.

Catholic Schools—Sr. FRANCES NADOLNY, O.P., Ph.D., Supt. Tel: 313-237-5775.

Office of Catechetics / Religious Education—MAUREEN O'REILLY. Tel: 313-237-4670.

Office of Family Life / Youth Ministry—FRANCIS OZAR. Tel: 313-237-5892.

St. John Center for Family and Youth—Rev. JOHN WEST, Rector, *44011 Five Mile Rd., Plymouth, 48170.* Tel: 734-414-1111; Fax: 734-414-1150.

Cardinal Maida Institute for Leadership Formation—JAMES KIEFER, Dir. Tel: 734-414-1109.

Department of Development—MICHAEL E. MURPHY, Dir., *1234 Washington Blvd., Detroit, 48226.* Tel: 313-883-8657; Fax: 313-883-8681.

Catholic Services Appeal—THERESA J. KACH. Tel: 313-883-8656.

Planned Giving—THOMAS P. SCHOLLER. Tel: 313-883-8657.

Donor Relations—SARAH C. ABATE; JESSICA I. ORZECHOWSKI. Tel: 313-883-8657.

Pathways of Hope—Tel: 313-883-8658.

Stewardship Education—DAVID P. CASNOVSKY. Tel: 313-883-8567.

Department of Finance and Administrative Services—MICHAEL H. GORMAN, Dir., *1234 Washington Blvd., Detroit, 48226.* Tel: 313-237-5834; Fax: 313-237-5868.

Archdiocesan Buildings—DONALD J. SCHEIBLE. Tel: 313-237-5845. JEMAR HARVILLE, Asst. Dir. Bldgs. Tel: 313-237-5806.

Archdiocesan Properties—C. MARY CARLISLE. Tel: 313-237-5820.

Financial Services—ABELARDO B. BUSQUE. Tel: 313-237-5828.

Information Technology—VINCENT CHRISMAN. Tel: 313-237-5797; Fax: 313-237-5979.

Sacred Heart Building Administration—JOHN DUNCAN. Tel: 313-883-8599.

Archdiocese of Detroit Endowment Foundation—1234 Washington Blvd., Detroit, 48226.

Administration—MICHAEL H. GORMAN, Dir. Tel: 313-237-5834; Fax: 313-237-5868.

Development—MICHAEL E. MURPHY, Dir. Tel: 313-883-8657; Fax: 313-883-8681.

Department of Parish Life—CATHERINE WAGNER, Dir. LORY MCGLINNEN, Assoc. Dir., *305 Michigan Ave., Detroit, 48226.* Tel: 313-237-5934; Fax: 313-237-5869.

Evangelization—Rev. DANIEL HAVRON, O.F.M. Tel: 313-237-4686.

Office of Christian Worship—DANIEL MCAFEE. Tel: 313-237-5932.

Council of Catholic Women—THELMA SANBORN, Pres. Tel: 313-237-5896.

Hispanic Catholic Ministries—RAUL FELICIANO. Tel: 313-237-5761.

Black Catholic Ministries—Rev. CLARENCE WILLIAMS, C.PP.S. Tel: 313-237-5934.

Office of Leadership Formation—PAMELA BEECH. Tel: 313-237-5887.

Office of Pastoral Ministers and Permanent Diaconate—Deacon JOHN BALL. Tel: 313-237-5778.

Delegate for Religious—Sr. MARGARET STECHSHULTE, O.P. Tel: 313-237-4682.

Pastoral Resources—Dr. MICHAEL MCCALLION. Tel: 313-237-5760.

"The Michigan Catholic" Newspaper—Rev. THOMAS G. RICE, Editor in Chief, *305 Michigan Ave., Detroit, 48226.* Tel: 313-224-8000.

Archivist—ROMAN P. GODZAK, *1234 Washington Blvd., Detroit, 48226.* Tel: 313-237-5846; Fax: 313-237-4643.

Human Resources—RONALD MCGUIRE. Tel: 313-237-5947; Fax: 313-237-5791.

Propagation of the Faith (Missions)—Rev. Msgr. JAMES A. MOLONEY, *17650 W. Outer Dr., Dearborn Heights, 48127.*

Holy Childhood Association—1230 Washington Blvd., Detroit, 48226. Tel: 313-237-5807.

Catholic Youth Organization—SUZANNE HEATH, Dir.; Detroit: *Gabriel Richard Bldg., 305 Michigan Ave., Detroit, 48226.* Tel: 313-963-7172. Branch office, *22235 Fenkell, Detroit, 48226.* Tel: 313-534-4620. Neighborhood Development, Brightmoor Community.

Archdiocesan Theological Commission—Rev. Msgr. JOHN P. ZENZ. Tel: 313-237-5783.

Vocation Office—Rev. JAMES D. BILOT, Dir. Tel: 313-237-5875. Sr. ANGELA CERNA-PLATA, I.H.M., Asst. Dir., . Fax: 313-237-6070.

Office of Pastoral Services for Clergy—Most Rev. KEVIN M. BRITT, Dir.; Deacon EUGENE KRZEMINSKI, Exec. Asst., *1234 Washington Blvd., Detroit, 48226.* Tel: 313-237-5848; Fax: 313-237-5844.

Office of Parish Support Services—GERALD STEBBINS. Tel: 313-237-6059; Fax: 313-237-4643.

CLERGY, PARISHES, MISSIONS AND PAROCHIAL SCHOOLS

CITY OF DETROIT
(Wayne County)

1—CATHEDRAL, CHURCH OF THE MOST BLESSED SACRAMENT, Rev. Msgr. James P. Robinson, S.S.E., Rector.

Res., 9844 Woodward Ave., 48202. Tel: 313-865-6300; Fax: 313-867-4613.

2—ALL SAINTS, Rev. Edward F. Zaorski.

Res., 7824 W. Fort St., 48209. Tel: 313-841-1428; Fax: 313-841-3009.

3—ST. ALOYSIUS, Revs. Mark Soehner, O.F.M.; Mel P. Brady, O.F.M.; Bro. Dan Nolan, O.F.M.; Sr. Kathleen Gaynor, O.P., Pastoral Assoc.

Res., Chancery Bldg., 1234 Washington Blvd., 48226. Tel: 313-237-5810; Fax: 313-963-9076.

4—ST. ANDREW (Polish), Rev. Julian Chmura.

Res., 7060 McGraw Ave., 48210. Tel: 313-361-1717; Fax: 313-361-9816.

5—SS. ANDREW AND BENEDICT (Slovak), Rev. Edward F. Zaorski.

Res., 2430 S. Beatrice St., 48217. Tel: 313-381-1184; Fax: 313-831-0416.

6—STE. ANNE, Rev. Robert J. Duggan, C.S.B. In res., Revs. L. Leo Reilly, C.S.B.; Marciano Dominguez, C.S.B.

Res., 1000 Ste. Anne St., 48216. Tel: 313-496-1701; Fax: 313-496-0429.

7—ANNUNCIATION, Rev. Michael C. Nkachukwu. Pastoral Assocs. Sr. Virginia Schmitt; Deacon Wyatt Jones.

Res., 1265 Parkview Ave., 48214. Tel: 313-822-1262; Fax: 313-822-8988.

Stapleton Center—9341 Agnes, 48214. Tel: 313-822-0397; Fax: 313-822-3994.

St. Rose Senior Citizen Center—11224 Kercheval, 48214. Tel: 313-824-4242; Fax: 313-824-7300. Sr. Rose Bernadette, Dir.

8—ST. ANTHONY, Rev. Michael C. Nkachukwu.

Office: 5247 Sheridan Ave., 48213. Tel: 313-921-0263; Fax: 313-924-4040.

9—ST. ANTHONY (Lithuanian), Rev. Alphonse Babonas.

Res., 1750 25th St., 48216. Tel: 313-554-1284.

10—ASSUMPTION GROTTO, Rev. Eduard Perrone. In res., Revs. Boleslaus Lipczewski; Felician Houndjame; Aloisius Kocher, O.R.C.

Res., 13770 Gratiot Ave., 48205. Tel: 313-372-0762; Fax: 313-372-2064. [CEM]

11—ST. AUGUSTINE AND ST. MONICA, Rev. Daniel J. Trapp.

Res., 4151 Seminole St., 48214. Tel: 313-921-4107; Fax: 313-921-1115.

12—ST. BARTHOLOMEW, Rev. Boleslaus Krol.

Res., 2291 E. Outer Dr., 48234. Tel: 313-892-1446; Fax: 313-892-1149.

School—Tel: 313-366-3640; Fax: 313-366-0257. Sr. Albina Prin.

Lay Teachers 8; Students 162.

Convent—2251 E. Outer Dr., 48234. Tel: 313-366-0525.

Sisters 4.

13—ST. BRENDAN, Rev. Louis Resma, Admin.

Res., 11433 Beaconsfield, 48224. Tel: 313-372-1644; Fax: 313-372-7195.

14—ST. CECILIA, Rev. Charles G. Kosanke.

Res., Box 04209, 10400 Stoepel Ave., 48204. Tel: 313-933-6788; Fax: 313-933-1439.

Church—Livernois at Stearns, 48204.

School—Tel: 313-933-2400; Fax: 313-933-9332. Sr. Margaret Sweeney, I.H.M., Prin.

Sisters-Servants of the Immaculate Heart of Mary 2; Lay Teachers 10; Students 260.

High School—Tel: 313-864-3330; Fax: 313-864-3648. Sunbeam Hughes, Prin.

Priests 1; Sisters 3; Lay Teachers 24.

15—ST. CHARLES BORROMEO, Revs. David Preuss, O.F.M.Cap.; Augustine Cops, O.F.M.Cap.; Raymond Stadmeyer, O.F.M.Cap.; Sr. Francis W. Schnell, O.P., Pastoral Assoc.

Res., 1491 Baldwin Ave., 48214. Tel: 313-331-0253; Fax: 313-331-4834.

16—ST. CHRISTINE, Rev. Mark S. Brauer.

Office: 15317 Dacosta, 48223. Tel: 313-535-7272; Fax: 313-535-3439.

Res., 23450 W. Davison, 48223. Tel: 313-255-3666; Fax: 313-537-0598.

School—13550 Virgil, 48223. Tel: 313-535-9342;

Fax: 313-455-7355. Sr. M. Laurene Smolinski, C.S.S.F., Prin.
Felician Sisters 2; Lay Teachers 11; Students 128.

17—CHRIST THE KING, Rev. Victor Clore. Pastoral Assocs.: Sr. Fiorentina D'Amore, H.V.M; Ms. C. Sylvia Shorter.
Res., 16805 Pierson, 48219. Tel: 313-532-1211; Fax: 313-532-1216.
Church—20800 Grand River & Burt Rd., 48219.
School—Tel: 313-532-1213. Mrs. Rosanne Jodway, Prin.
Lay Teachers 24; Students 259.

18—ST. CHRISTOPHER, Rev. Richard A. Hartmann; Deacons John Marku; Norbert Motowski.
Res., 7800 Woodmont Ave., 48228. Tel: 313-584-7460; Fax: 313-584-6361.
School—Tel: 313-846-1430; Fax: 313-846-5080. Cynthia Szweda, Prin.
Sisters of the Holy Family of Nazareth 2; Lay Teachers 8; Students 171.
Convent—7800 Woodmont Ave., 48228. Tel: 313-584-7579.

19—ST. CUNEGUNDA, Rev. Zbigniew Grankowski.
Res., 5900 St. Lawrence Ave., 48210. Tel: 313-841-4000; Fax: 313-841-4255.
School—Tel: 313-843-0004; Fax: 313-843-8812. Sr. Mary Alexander, C.S.S.F., Prin.
Lay Teachers 7; Religious 7; Students 160.

20—ST. DOMINIC, Rev. Patrick Casey. In res., Revs. Francis Maguire, O.P.; Jesse Cox, O.P.
Res., 4844 Trumbull Ave., 48208. Tel: 313-831-8790; Fax: 313-831-2965.
Convent—4835 Lincoln Ave., 48208. Tel: 313-831-1028. Missionaries of Charity
Sisters 6.

21—ST. ELIZABETH, Rev. John W. Markham.
Res., 3138 E. Canfield Ave., 48207. Tel: 313-921-9225; Fax: 313-921-9475.

22—ST. FRANCIS D'ASSISI, Rev. Robert J. Wojciechowski.
Res., 4500 Wesson St., 48210. Tel: 313-897-7229; Fax: 313-897-7485.

23—ST. FRANCIS DE SALES, Rev. James E. O'Reilly, S.J. In res., Revs. Justin Kelly, S.J.; David Mastrongelo, S.J.; Bros. Michael Baranek, S.J.; Richard Hittle, S.J.
Res., 10600 Fenkell Ave., 48238. Tel: 313-861-4020; Fax: 313-861-4718.

24—ST. GABRIEL, Revs. Charles P. Farrar, Admin.; Emmanuel Parnis, M.S.S.P. In res., Rev. Anthony F. Bologna, (Retired).
Res., 8118 W. Vernor Hwy., 48209-1524. Tel: 313-841-0753; Fax: 313-841-0916.
Catechesis/Religious Programs—Tel: 313-841-0419.
Students 400.

25—ST. GEMMA GALGANI, Rev. Mark S. Brauer.
Res., 23450 W. Davison, 48223. Tel: 313-255-3666; Fax: 313-537-0598.
School—SS. Christine & Gemma, 13550 Virgil, 48223. Tel: 313-535-9342; Fax: 313-535-9442.
Lay Teachers 9; Students (Grades K-8) 128.

26—ST. GERARD, Revs. Donald Archambault; Gerard Battersby; Deacons Alfons Hogrebe; Hubert Sanders.
Res., 19800 Pembroke, 48219. Tel: 313-537-5770; Fax: 313-537-5773.
School—19900 Evergreen Rd., 48219. Tel: 313-533-4353; Fax: 313-533-2190.
Sisters 1; Lay Teachers 10; Students 220.
Catechesis/Religious Programs—Tel: 313-533-0197. Judith Dantzer, D.R.E.
Students 255.
Convent—19910 Evergreen Rd., 48219.

27—GESU, Revs. Norman Dickson, S.J.; John C. Kehres, S.J. In res., Revs. Kenneth J. Noetzel, S.J.; Jerome K. Odbert, S.J.; Walter L. Farrell, S.J.; Bro. Richard C. Conroy, S.J.
Res., 17204 Oak Dr., 48221. Tel: 313-862-4400; Fax: 313-862-1083.
School—Mr. Richard Seefelt, Prin., Tel: 313-863-4677. Sisters-Servants of the Immaculate Heart of Mary 2; Lay Teachers 29; Students 560.
Convent—17180 Oak Dr., 48221. Tel: 313-861-8877.

28—ST. GREGORY, Rev. Ronald J. DeHondt; Deacon Benjamin Prince.
Res., 15031 Dexter, 48238. Tel: 313-861-0363; Fax: 313-862-6805.

29—GUARDIAN ANGELS, Rev. Louis Resma, Admin.
Res., 12545 Kelly Rd., 48224. Tel: 313-526-0735; Fax: 313-526-7382.

30—ST. HEDWIG, Rev. Christopher P. Maus.
Res., 3245 Junction Ave., 48210. Tel: 313-894-5409; Fax: 313-894-4730.

31—HOLY CROSS (Hungarian), Revs. Barnabas G. Kiss, O.F.M.; Angelus Ligeti, O.F.M.
Res., 8423 South St., 48209. Tel: 313-842-1133; Fax: 313-842-2773.

32—HOLY FAMILY (Italian), Rev. John Stopponi, Admin.
Res., 641 Walter P. Chrysler Expwy., 48226. Tel: 313-963-2046; Fax: 313-961-0065.

33—HOLY REDEEMER, Revs. Donald F. Hanchon; Sean E. Sylvester; Deacon Ronald McIntyre.
Res., 1721 Junction Ave., 48209. Tel: 313-842-3450; Fax: 313-849-0539.
School—Tel: 313-841-5230; Fax: 313-841-3640. Sr. Elizabeth Fleckenstein, I.H.M., Prin.
Sisters Servants of the Immaculate Heart of Mary 4; Lay Teachers 10; Students 253.
High School—Tel: 313-841-4433; Fax: 313-841-2116. Joseph Redican, C.S.B., Prin.; Rev. Dennis Noelke, C.S.B., Asst. Prin.
Sisters 2; Lay Teachers 15; Students 219.
Convent—5678 Eldred Ave., 48209. Tel: 313-841-8420.

34—ST. HYACINTH (Polish), Rev. Francis S. Skalski.
Res., 3151 Farnsworth Ave., 48211. Tel: 313-922-1507; Fax: 313-922-2459.

35—IMMACULATE HEART OF MARY, Revs. Donald Archambault; Gerard Battersby; Mary Caroline Jonah, Pastoral Assoc.
Res., 16000 Pembroke Ave., 48235. Tel: 313-272-0990; Fax: 313-272-9772.
School—19940 Mansfield, 48235. Tel: 313-835-0258. Sr. Stephanie Holub, R.S.M., Prin.
Sisters of Mercy of the Union 3; Lay Teachers 15; Students 127.
Convent—19960 Mansfield Ave., 48235. Tel: 313-272-6810; Fax: 313-272-6811.

36—ST. JEROME. Closed. For inquiries for parish records contact the Chancery.

37—ST. JOHN BERCHMANS-ST. JULIANA, Rev. Luke M. Stano, O.S.M.
Res., 9801 Chalmers, 48213. Tel: 313-526-7254; Fax: 313-526-7553.
School—St. Juliana, 9755 Chalmers, 48213. Tel: 313-526-0062; Fax: 313-526-2988.
Servite Sisters 1; Lay Teachers 10; Students 212.

38—ST. JOHN CANTIUS (Polish), Rev. Edwin A. Szczygiel.
Res., 844 Harbaugh Ave., 48209. Tel: 313-842-2276; Fax: 313-842-2268.

39—ST. JOSAPHAT (Polish), Rev. Ronald J. Jozwiak.
Res., 691 E. Canfield Ave., 48201. Tel: 313-831-1072; Fax: 313-831-1072.

40—ST. JOSEPH, Rev. Msgr. John F. Schweder.
Res., 1828 Jay St., 48207. Tel: 313-393-8212; Fax: 313-393-8294.

41—ST. JUDE, Rev. Raymond J. Sayers; Sr. Judy Lieder, O.P., Pastoral Assoc.
Res., 15889 E. Seven Mile Rd., 48205. Tel: 313-527-0380; Fax: 313-527-3511.
School—15865 E. Seven Mile, 48205. Tel: 313-839-6792; Fax: 313-527-2093.
Sisters 5; Lay Teachers 16; Students 220.
Catechesis/Religious Programs—Students 148.

42—ST. LEO, Most Rev. Thomas J. Gumbleton; Daniel Maxwell, Pastoral Assoc.
Church & Res.: 4860 15th St., 48208. Tel: 313-894-0357; Fax: 313-897-2980.

43—ST. LOUIS THE KING, Revs. Boleslaus Krol; Ron Borg, C.S.B.
Res., 18891 St. Louis Ave., 48234. Tel: 313-891-1766; Fax: 313-891-7959.

44—ST. LUKE, Rev. Robert Kotlarz; Sr. Marie Roy, S.S.J., Pastoral Assoc.
Res., 8017 Ohio Ave., 48204. Tel: 313-935-6161; Fax: 313-935-0788.
School—St. Luke & St. Brigid Elementary School, St. Brigid Montessori Preschool, 8091 Ohio, 48204. Tel: 313-933-9611; Fax: 313-933-9522. Mrs. Clima Fields, Prin.
Lay Teachers 15; Students 161.

45—MADONNA, Rev. Ronald J. DeHondt.
Res., 1125 Oakman Blvd., 48238. Tel: 313-868-4308; Fax: 313-868-9771.

46—MARTYRS OF UGANDA, Rev. Tyrone Robinson; Deacons Douglas Jackson; Peter Schlesser.
Res., 7601 Rosa Parks Blvd., 48206. Tel: 313-896-2335; Fax: 313-896-0925.
School—Martyrs of Uganda Catholic Academy, 4317 Blaine, 48204. Tel: 313-361-1065; Fax: 313-897-2840.
Lay Teachers 8; Students 104.
Catechesis/Religious Programs—Mrs. Mary Brown, D.R.E.
Students 22.

47—ST. MARY, Rev. Martin J. Conroy, C.S.Sp.
Res., 646 Monroe Ave., 48226. Tel: 313-961-8711; Fax: 313-961-4994.

48—ST. MARY'S OF REDFORD, Rev. Ronald R. Williams. Mailing Address: 14750 St. Mary's, 48227. Tel: 313-273-1100; Fax: 313-273-2002.
School—St. Mary of Redford Grade School, 14751 Mansfield, 48227. Tel: 313-835-6834; Fax: 313-836-4184. Sr. Loretta Schroeder, I.H.M., Prin.
Religious 7; Lay Teachers 21; Students 380.
Convent—14601 Mansfield, 48227. Tel: 313-272-2727.
Sisters 4.

49—ST. MATTHEW, Rev. Duane R. Novelly; Sr. Karen Eklund, I.H.M., Pastoral Min.; Deacon William H. Johr.
Res., 6021 Whittier Ave., 48224. Tel: 313-884-4470; Fax: 313-884-4276.
School—Tel: 313-881-9179; Fax: 313-881-2843. Sr. Kathleen DeSmedt, I.H.M, Prin.
Lay Teachers 8; Students 109.

50—MOST HOLY TRINITY, Rev. Russell E. Kohler.
Res., 1050 Porter St., 48226. Tel: 313-965-4450; Fax: 313-965-4453.
Schools—Tel: 313-961-8855. Mrs. Cynthia J. Leaman, Prin.
Lay Teachers 9; Students 114; St. Vincent Middle School, (Grades 5-8) 2020 14th St., 48216. Tel: 313-961-6773; Fax: 313-961-6774. Ms. Kathleen McBride, Prin.
Lay Teachers 4; Students 90.
Convent—1234 Porter St., 48226.

51—NATIVITY OF OUR LORD, Rev. Jerome C. Singer.
Res., 5900 McClellan Ave., 48213. Tel: 313-922-0033; Fax: 313-922-0033.

52—OUR LADY GATE OF HEAVEN, Rev. Dennis D. Duggan, Admin.; Sr. Rosemarie Kieffer, O.P., Pastoral Asoc.
Church—9555 St. Mary's, 48227. Tel: 313-270-5350; Fax: 313-270-5349.

53—OUR LADY OF GOOD COUNSEL, Rev. Andrew J. Tomasko; Deacon Donald Sandstrom, Pastoral Assoc.
Res., 17142 Rowe Ave., 48205. Tel: 313-372-1698; Fax: 313-372-1211.

54—OUR LADY HELP OF CHRISTIANS (Polish), Rev. George A. Rutkowski.
Res., 12635 McDougall Ave., 48212. Tel: 313-892-6116.
Convent—12541 McDougall Ave., 48212. Tel: 313-891-5280.

55—OUR LADY OF MT. CARMEL, Rev. Robert Cini, M.S.S.P.
Res., 555 Oakwood Blvd., 48217. Tel: 313-841-8478; Fax: 313-841-0209.

56—OUR LADY OF THE ROSARY, Rev. Robert Morand.
Res., 5930 Woodward Ave., 48202. Tel: 313-875-6011; Fax: 313-872-0758.

57—OUR LADY OF SORROWS. Closed. For inquiries for parish records contact the Chancery.

58—OUR LADY QUEEN OF ANGELS, Rev. James Henning, O.F.M.Conv.
Res., 4200 Martin Ave., 48210. Tel: 313-897-8160; Fax: 313-897-8126.
School—Tel: 313-894-6266. Mr. Gordon Cameron, Prin.
Franciscan Sisters of St. Joseph 3; Lay Teachers 6; Students 138.
Convent—4108 Martin Ave., 48210. Tel: 313-894-3462.

59—OUR LADY QUEEN OF HEAVEN, Rev. Donald A. Sopiak.
Res., 8200 Rolyat Ave., 48234. Tel: 313-891-4553; Fax: 313-891-5782.

60—ST. PATRICK, Rev. Patrick Casey; Floria Ellison, Pastoral Assoc. In res., Rev. Thomas J. Duffey.
Church—58 Parsons, 48201. Tel: 313-833-0857; Fax: 313-831-1619.
St. Patrick Senior Center, Inc.—Tel: 313-833-7080; Fax: 313-833-0128. Sr. Mary Watson, O.P., Pres.

61—SS. PETER AND PAUL JESUIT, Rev. Carl A. Bonk, S.J. In res., Revs. Francis X. Budovic, S.J.; George R. Follen, S.J.; Thomas W. Florek, S.J.; Javier Saravia Herrera, S.J.; Alberto Vargas Nunez, S.J.; Bro. James Horgan, S.J.
Res., 438 St. Antoine St., 48226. Tel: 313-961-8077; Fax: 313-963-5134.

62—SS. PETER AND PAUL (West Side), Rev. Stanley Tokarski. In res., Revs. John M. Kubik; Mitchell Szarek.
Res., 7685 Grandville Ave., 48228. Tel: 313-846-2222; Fax: 313-584-1484.
School—Tel: 313-336-3600; Fax: 313-336-6220. Wanda Posuniak, Prin.
Sisters 2; Lay Teachers 7; Students 113.

63—ST. PHILOMENA, Rev. Peter S. Lentine.
Res., 4281 Marseilles Ave., 48224. Tel: 313-882-4300; Fax: 313-882-1661.
Catechesis/Religious Programs—Kathleen McKenzie, D.R.E., Tel: 313-884-2422.
Students 205.

64—PRECIOUS BLOOD, Most Rev. Moses B. Anderson, S.S.E.
Res., 13305 Grove Ave., 48235. Tel: 313-342-5292; Fax: 313-342-3513.

65—PRESENTATION-OUR LADY OF VICTORY, Rev. Donald Archambault.
Res., 19760 Meyers Rd., 48235. Tel: 313-342-1333; Fax: 313-342-4182.

66—ST. RAYMOND, Rev. Andrew J. Tomasko.
Res., 20103 Joann Ave., 48205. Tel: 313-527-0525; Fax: 313-527-9776.
Community House—20055 Joann Ave., 48205. Tel: 313-372-0437.

67—ST. RITA, Rev. Timothy Kane.
Res., 1000 E. State Fair, 48203. Tel: 313-366-2340; Fax: 313-891-0677.

68—SACRED HEART-CHALDEAN PARISH, Rev. Jacob O. Yasso.
Res., 310 W. Seven Mile Rd., 48203. Tel: 313-368-6214; Fax: 313-891-0132.

69—SACRED HEART OF JESUS, Rev. Norman P. Thomas.
Res., 1000 Eliot St., 48207. Tel: 313-831-1356; Fax: 313-831-8603.
Catechesis/Religious Programs—Barbara Hunt, D.R.E.
Students 114.

70—ST. SCHOLASTICA, Rev. Livius Paoli, O.S.B.
Res., 17320 Rosemont Rd., 48219. Tel: 313-531-0140; Fax: 313-531-0739.
Church—Southfield Rd. & West Outer Dr., 48219.
School—Tel: 313-532-1916; Fax: 313-532-0140. Faye Vaughn, Elementary Prin.
Sisters of St. Dominic (Adrian) 1; Lay Teachers 22; Students 329.
High School—Benedictine High School, Tel: 313-532-1274; Fax: 313-532-5767. Sam Walker, High School Prin.
Sisters 1; Lay Teachers 19; Students 299.
Convent—17305 Ashton, 48219. Tel: 313-541-4368.

71—ST. STEPHEN-MARY MOTHER OF THE CHURCH, Revs. Marc Gawronski; Rafael Jimenez.
Res., 4311 Central Ave., 48210. Tel: 313-841-0783; Fax: 313-841-4868.
School—Tel: 313-841-2739; Fax: 313-841-3384. Sr. Mary Martinez Rozek, C.S.S.F., Prin.
Religious 1; Lay Teachers 7; Students 158.
Catechesis/Religious Programs—4330 Central Ave., 48210. Tel: 313-841-9103.
Students 180.

72—ST. SUZANNE, Rev. Dennis D. Duggan; Sr. Lucy Abbey, I.H.M., Pastoral Assoc.
Res., 9357 Westwood Ave., 48228. Tel: 313-838-6780; Fax: 313-838-1063.

73—SWEETEST HEART OF MARY (Polish), Revs. Wojciech Baryski, S.Ch.; Darrell Roman, S.Ch.
Res., 4440 Russell St., 48207. Tel: 313-831-6659; Fax: 313-831-8522. [CEM]

74—ST. THOMAS AQUINAS, Rev. William J. Promesso; Deacon John Santeramo. Pastoral Assocs.: Catherine Odom Prowse; Micheleen Troutman.
Parish Center—5780 Evergreen Rd., 48228. Tel: 313-271-3266; Fax: 313-271-8773.
School—Tel: 313-271-8773. Dorian Mantei, Prin.
Sisters of Mercy 1; Lay Teachers 12; Students 205.
Catechesis/Religious Programs—Tel: 313-271-0813. Nikki Zakrzewski, D.R.E.
Students 125.

75—TRANSFIGURATION, Rev. Andrew Wesley.
Res., 5830 Simon K. St., 48212. Tel: 313-892-1310; Fax: 313-893-2478.
School—Tel: 313-366-3810. Sr. Angelica Zajkowski, Prin.
Sisters of the Holy Family of Nazareth 2; Lay Teachers 10; Students 300.
Convent—5821 Rupert, 48212. Tel: 313-891-9273.

OUTSIDE THE CITY OF DETROIT

Algonac, St. Clair Co., St. Catherine, Rev. Douglas J. Bignall.
Res., 1103 Washington, 48001. Tel: 810-794-3301; Fax: 810-794-1849. [CEM]
School—1106 St. Clair Blvd., 48001. Tel: 810-794-4965; Fax: 810-794-4966. Sr. Irene Gumbleton, I.H.M., Prin.
Lay Teachers 9; Students 145.
Catechesis/Religious Programs—Tel: 810-794-3843. Anna Mae Lines, D.R.E.
Students 180.

Allen Park, Wayne Co., St. Frances Cabrini, Revs. Francis Reiss; Mark Borkowski; Dariusz Z. Strzalkowski. In res., Rev. Michael Gormley, S.A.C.
Res., 9000 Laurence Ave., 48101. Tel: 313-381-5601; Fax: 313-381-7837.
School—Tel: 313-928-6610; Fax: 313-928-8502. Joseph Lannen, Prin.
Lay Teachers 28; Students 440.
High School—Tel: 313-388-0110; Fax: 313-388-8515. R. Edward Smith, Prin.
Lay Teachers 22; Students 337.
Catechesis/Religious Programs—Tel: 313-381-7076. Jerome Green, D.R.E.
Students 390.

Allenton, St. Clair Co., St. John the Evangelist, Rev. Gerald Frawley.
Res., 872 Capac Rd., 48002. Tel: 810-395-7074; Fax: 810-395-7718.
Catechesis/Religious Programs—Tel: 810-395-2301.
Students 164.

Anchorville, St. Clair Co., Immaculate Conception, Rev. David G. Burgard.
Mailing Address: P.O. Box 106, 48004. Tel: 810-725-3051; Fax: 810-725-2474. [CEM]
School—7403 Church Rd., 48004. Tel: 810-725-0078; Fax: 810-725-2474. Irene Heidtke, Prin.
Lay Teachers 12; Students 280.
Catechesis/Religious Programs—Jane Petitpren, D.R.E, Tel: 810-725-1762.
Students 275.

Armada, Macomb Co., St. Mary Mystical Rose, Rev. Bradley Forintos.
Res., 24040 Armada Ridge, 48005. Tel: 810-784-5966; Fax: 810-784-9330.
Catechesis/Religious Programs—Students 305.

Auburn Hills, Oakland Co., Sacred Heart, Rev. James A. Mayworm.
Res., 3400 Adams Rd., 48326. Tel: 248-852-4170; Fax: 248-852-5745.
Catechesis/Religious Programs—Tel: 248-852-3620.
Students 320.

St. John Fisher Chapel University Parish, Rev. Jerome A. Brzezinski. Pastoral Assocs.: Sr. Mary Van Gilder; Sr. Mary Ann Dixon; Ms. Lisa Abad; Mr. Eugene Mahon; Mrs. Susan Burrato; Mrs. Nancy Mason Bordley.
Res., 3665 Walton Blvd., 48326. Tel: 248-373-6457; Fax: 248-373-5479.
Catechesis/Religious Programs—Tel: 248-373-3130. Sr. Mary Ann Dixon, O.P., D.R.E.
Students 470.

Belleville, Wayne Co., St. Anthony, Rev. Thomas H. Cusick; Terrence D. Taylor, Pastoral Assoc.; Deacon Peter Cornell.
Res., 409 W. Columbia Ave., 48111. Tel: 734-697-1211; Fax: 734-697-6217.
School—Tel: 734-699-4313; Fax: 734-699-0824. Mrs. Stephanie Tozer, Prin.
Sisters of St. Joseph of the Third Order of St. Francis 1; Lay Teachers 11; Students 153.
Convent—371 W. Columbia Ave., 48111. Tel: 734-697-6661.

Berkley, Oakland Co., Our Lady of La Salette, Rev. Patrick J. Connell; Deacon Daniel Darga, Pastoral Assoc.
Res., 2600 Harvard Rd., 48072. Tel: 248-541-3762; Fax: 248-541-4250.
School—Tel: 248-542-3757; Fax: 248-541-6559. Mrs. Susan Perna, Prin.
Lay Teachers 10; Students 169.
Catechesis/Religious Programs—Students 210.

Beverly Hills, Franklin Co., Our Lady of Albanians, Revs. Primus P. Ndrevashay; Nue Gjergji.
Res., 20855 W. Thirteen Mile Rd., 48025. Tel: 248-642-0816; Fax: 248-642-0251.

Birmingham, Oakland Co., St. Columban, Rev. Sylvester Taube; Patricia Costigan, Pastoral Assoc.; Deacon Robert Ovies.
Res., 2200 Dunstable, 48009. Tel: 248-642-1148; Fax: 248-642-4636.
Church—1775 Melton, 48009. Tel: 248-646-5224; Fax: 248-646-9376.
Catechesis/Religious Programs—Tel: 248-646-5225. Nancy Sullivan, D.R.E.
Students 271.

Holy Name, Rev. Robert E. Burke. Pastoral Assocs.: Sr. Shirlee Hoski, S.S.J.-T.O.S.F.; Deacon Michael J. McKale; Donna M. Hansen; Mary A. Pineau.
Parish Office—630 Harmon St., 48009. Tel: 248-646-2244; Fax: 248-646-2286.
Res., 645 Woodland Ave., 48009.
School—Tel: 248-644-2722; Fax: 248-644-1191. Sr. Annice Mordenski, O.P., Prin.
Sisters 2; Lay Teachers 25; Students 487.
Catechesis/Religious Programs—Tel: 248-642-4130. Mary Morian, D.R.E.
Students 502.

Our Lady Queen of Martyrs, Revs. Robert F. Wyzgoski; Michael J. Heppen, C.S.C.
Res., 32340 Pierce Ave., Beverly Hills, 48025. Tel: 248-644-8620; Fax: 248-644-8623.
School—32460 Pierce Ave., Beverly Hills, 48025. Tel: 248-642-2616; Fax: 248-642-3671. Peter J. Ferguson, Prin.
Lay Teachers 26; Students 500.
Catechesis/Religious Programs—Tel: 248-647-6068. Marie Therese Walbridge, D.R.E.
Students 260.

Bloomfield Hills, Oakland Co., St. Hugo of the Hills, Rev. Msgr. Anthony M. Tocco; Rev. Robert C. Schuster; Deacon Michael T. Smith.
Res., 2215 Opdyke Rd., 48304. Tel: 248-644-5460; Fax: 248-644-1758.
School—380 E. Hickory Grove, 48304. Tel: 248-642-6131; Fax: 248-642-4457. Sr. Margaret Van Velzen, I.H.M., Prin.
Sisters, Servants of the Immaculate Heart of Mary 6; Lay Teachers 34; Students 886.
Catechesis/Religious Programs—Tel: 248-642-6062.
Students 470.

St. Owen, Rev. Msgr. Clifford F. Ruskowski. Pastoral Ministers: Sr. Carolyn Nelson; Sr. Susanne Hofweber, O.P.; Mrs. Laura Broyles; Mrs. Judy Thibodeau.
Res., 6869 Franklin Rd., 48301. Tel: 248-626-0840; Fax: 248-626-0345.
Catechesis/Religious Programs—Tel: 248-626-2300. D.R.E.: Sue Fredenberg; Karen Heuer.
Students 545.

St. Regis, Revs. Norman D. Nawrocki; Michael J. Prince; Deacon Brian Carroll. In res., Rev. Duane Doherty, O.F.M.Conv.
Res., 3695 Lincoln, 48301. Tel: 248-646-2686; Fax: 248-646-4643.
School—Tel: 248-646-2686, Ext. 301; Fax: 248-644-0944. Suzanne M. Pientak, Prin.
Lay Teachers 18; Students 390.
Catechesis/Religious Programs—Tel: 248-644-8668. Robert Metz, D.R.E.
Students 290.

Canton, Wayne Co., Saint John Neumann, Rev. George Charnley; Eugene Kijek, Pastoral Min. In res., Rev. Andrew J. Webster.
Res., 44800 Warren Rd., 48187. Tel: 734-455-5910; Fax: 734-455-6779.
Catechesis/Religious Programs—Ms. Beverly Thompson, D.R.E.
Students 1,220.

Resurrection, Rev. Richard A. Perfetto.
48755 Warren Rd., 48187-1216. Tel: 734-451-0444; Fax: 734-451-0454.
Catechesis/Religious Programs—Students 250.

St. Thomas a Becket, Rev. C. Richard Kelly.
Res., 555 S. Lilley Rd., 48188. Tel: 734-981-1333; Fax: 734-981-1481.
Catechesis/Religious Programs—Tel: 734-981-6680.
Students 1,169.

Capac, St. Clair Co., St. Nicholas, Rev. Gerard Frawley, S.C.A.
Church—4331 Capac Rd., Box 129, Tel: 810-395-7572; Fax: 810-395-7572.

Carleton, Monroe Co., St. Patrick, Rev. Robert A. Bauer.
Res., 2996 Labo Rd., 48117. Tel: 734-654-2500; Fax: 734-654-6594. [CEM]
School—Tel: 734-654-2522; Fax: 734-654-8120. Ms. Ruth Meiring, Prin.
Lay Teachers 11; Students 175.
Catechesis/Religious Programs—Tel: 734-654-6444. Diane Janssens, D.R.E.
Students 250.
Convent—2970 Labo Rd., 48117. Tel: 734-654-2904.

Centerline, Macomb Co., St. Clement, Revs. Ronald J. Victor; Bernard F. Fraser; Sr. Emeline Bash, O.P., Pastoral Assoc. In res., Rev. Carl J. Yagley.
Res., 8075 Ritter Ave., 48015-1499. Tel: 810-757-3306; Fax: 810-757-5390. [CEM]
School—Tel: 810-757-7500; Fax: 810-757-4724. Patricia A. Downey, Prin.
Lay Teachers 24; Students 361.
High School—Tel: 810-757-1739; Fax: 810-757-1797. Deborah A. Michon, Prin.
Lay Teachers 13; Students 148.
Catechesis/Religious Programs—Tel: 810-757-3306; Fax: 810-757-5390. Linda Bauer, D.R.E.
Students 269.

Clarkston, Oakland Co., St. Daniel, Rev. Msgr. Robert S. Humitz; Deacon Alexander Jablonowski.
Res., 7010 Valley Park Dr., 48346. Tel: 248-625-4580; Fax: 248-620-9839.
Catechesis/Religious Programs—Tel: 248-625-1750. D.R.E.: Frieda Arpoika; Betty Haran.
Students 1,000.

Clawson, Oakland Co., Guardian Angels, Revs. Thomas Slowinski; William J. Herman; Deacon Eugene Tombler.
Res., 581 E. 14 Mile Rd., 48017. Tel: 248-588-1222; Fax: 248-588-8767.
School—Tel: 248-588-5545. Mrs. Susan Leslie, Prin.
Dominican Sisters (Adrian) 1; Lay Teachers 24; Students 380.
Catechesis/Religious Programs—Susan Coroci, D.R.E.
Students 266.

Clinton Twp., Macomb Co.,

1—ST. CLAUDE, Revs. Gary T. Smetanka, Admin.; Jack Quinlan; Deacon John Barbera.
Res., 33826 Beaconsfield, 48035. Tel: 810-791-6630; Fax: 810-791-0017.

Catechesis/Religious Programs—Johanna Warren, D.R.E.
Students 60.

2—ST. LOUIS, Rev. Pasquale LoGrasso; Deacon Donald C. Junak, Pastoral Assoc.
Res., 24415 Crocker Blvd., 48036. Tel: 810-468-8734; Fax: 810-468-9647.
Catechesis/Religious Programs—Tel: 810-468-4332. Joyce Appelt, D.R.E.
Students 294.

3—ST. PAUL OF TARSUS, Rev. Louis E. Grandpre; Rev. Msgr. Eugene Edyk; Rev. Arthur Jacobi; Deacon Edward Wilson.
Res., 41300 Romeo Plank Rd., 48038. Tel: 810-228-1210; Fax: 810-228-8935.
Catechesis/Religious Programs—Tel: 810-228-0047. Claudia Dombrowski, D.R.E.
Students 1,237.

4—ST. RONALD, Rev. James Andres, O.F.M.Cap.
Res., 17701 15 Mile Rd., 48035-2401. Tel: 810-792-1190; Fax: 810-792-0765.
Catechesis/Religious Programs—Tel: 810-792-1276.
Students 215.

5—ST. THECLA, Revs. Gary T. Smetanka; Jack Quinlan; Sr. M. Francesca, C.S.S.F., Pastoral Assoc.
Res., 20740 Nunneley Rd., 48035-1628. Tel: 810-791-3930; Fax: 810-791-3890.
School—Tel: 810-791-2170; Fax: 810-791-2356.
Felician Sisters 3; Lay Teachers 23; Students 544.
Catechesis/Religious Programs—Tel: 810-792-0550.
Students 512.

6—ST. VALERIE OF RAVENNA, Rev. Richard Cavellier.
Res., 23300 King Dr., 48035. Tel: 810-791-5450; Fax: 810-791-6876.

7—SAN FRANCESCO COMMUNITY, Rev. Giulio Schiavi, P.I.M.E.
Res., 22870 S. Nunneley Rd., 48035. Tel: 810-792-5346; Fax: 810-792-5119.
Catechesis/Religious Programs—Students 135.

Columbus, St. Clair Co., St. Philip Neri, Rev. Francis A. Zielinski.
Res., 9735 Dolan Rd., 48063. Tel: 810-727-7263; Fax: 810-727-7263. [CEM]
Mission—Smiths Creek, St. Clair Co., Holy Rosary, 7093 Main St., 48074.

Dearborn, Wayne Co.,

1—ST. ALPHONSUS, Rev. Michael W. Quaine; Sr. Margaret Urban, O.P., Pastoral Assoc.
Res., 7455 Calhoun Ave., 48126. Tel: 313-581-5218; Fax: 313-584-9560.
School—Tel: 313-581-1886; Fax: 313-582-5224. Mrs. Michelle Pazur, Grade School Prin.
Lay Teachers 13; Students 229.
High School—Tel: 313-582-4266; Fax: 313-584-9589. Terrence George, High School Prin.
Adrian Dominican Sisters 1; Lay Teachers 10; Students 126.
Catechesis/Religious Programs—Tel: 313-581-5218. Kevin Tishler, D.R.E.
Students 53.
Convent—13541 Gould Ave., 48126. Tel: 313-584-4350.

2—ST. BARBARA, Rev. Zbigniew Grankowski; Deacon Richard B. Hulan, Pastoral Assoc. In res., Rev. Wojciech J. Zolnowski.
Res., 13534 Colson Ave., 48126. Tel: 313-582-8383; Fax: 313-582-1581.

3—ST. BERNADETTE. Closed. For inquiries for parish records contact the Chancery.

4—ST. CLEMENT, Rev. Arnold V. Dachille; Sr. Ann Dineen, S.M., Pastoral Assoc.; Sr. Mary Downey, I.H.M. In res., Rev. Msgr. Vincent J. Horkan; Rev. John Sarosiek.
Res., 5275 Kenilworth Ave., 48126. Tel: 313-581-7495; Fax: 313-581-4233.
Catechesis/Religious Programs—Tel: 313-846-2443. Cristena Flores, D.R.E.
Students 110.

5—DIVINE CHILD, Rev. Msgr. Herman W. Kucyk; Revs. Jeffrey D. Day; Kevin Thomas.
Res., 25001 Hollander, 48128. Tel: 313-277-3110; Fax: 313-277-3211.
School—Tel: 313-562-1090; Fax: 313-562-2045. Sr. Cecilia Bondy, Elementary Prin.
Bernardine Sisters 7; Lay Teachers 28; Students 790.
High School—Tel: 313-562-1990; Fax: 313-562-9361. Sr. Elena Sabalausky, High School Prin.
Bernardine Sisters 6; Lay Teachers 62; Students 892.
Catechesis/Religious Programs—Diana Kinaschuk, D.R.E.
Students 267.
Convent—1045 N. Silvery Ln., 48128. Tel: 313-561-5455.

6—ST. JOSEPH, Rev. Adolph Redwick.
Res., 16101 Rotunda Dr., 48120. Tel: 313-336-3227; Fax: 313-441-6769.

7—ST. MARTHA, Rev. Donald L. Walker; Sr. Joan Blanch, C.S.J., Pastoral Assoc.
Res., 18200 Oakwood Blvd., 48124. Tel: 313-336-4090; Fax: 313-336-3318.

8—SACRED HEART, Rev. Lawrence H. Kaiser; Fran Helner, Pastoral Assoc.
Res., 22430 W. Michigan Ave., 48124. Tel: 313-278-5555; Fax: 313-278-8582. [CEM]
School—22513 Garrison, 48124. Tel: 313-561-9192; Fax: 313-561-1598. Lorelei Darga, Prin.
Sisters 1; Lay Teachers 22; Students 420.
Catechesis/Religious Programs—Judie Schuett, D.R.E.
Students 259.

Dearborn Heights, Wayne Co.,

1—ST. ALBERT THE GREAT, Rev. Daniel Zaleski; Sr. Barbara Ennis, Pastoral Assoc.; Deacon Ray Gabel.
Res., 4855 Parker, 48125. Tel: 313-292-0430; Fax: 313-292-8565.
School—Tel: 313-292-1144.
Sisters, Servants of the Immaculate Heart of Mary 1; Lay Teachers 8; Students 209.
Catechesis/Religious Programs—Tel: 313-292-9370.
Students 209.
Convent—4864 Parker, 48127. Tel: 313-292-0493.

2—ST. ANSELM, Rev. Msgr. James A. Moloney, Pastor and Dir., Society for The Propagation of The Faith; Sr. Mary Ann Thue, R.S.M., Pastoral Assoc. & Prin.
Res., 17650 W. Outer Dr., 48127. Tel: 313-565-4808; Fax: 313-565-7514.
School—Tel: 313-563-3430.
Sisters 2; Lay Teachers 8; Students 263.
Catechesis/Religious Programs—Tel: 313-561-0512. Sr. Mary Ann Thue, R.S.M., D.R.E.
Students 170.
Convent—20495 Brooklawn, 48127. Tel: 313-271-2287.

3—ST. JOHN THE BAPTIST, Rev. Edwin W. Balazy.
Res., 26123 McDonald Ave., 48125. Tel: 313-292-9693; Fax: 313-292-1755.

4—ST. LINUS, Rev. Randall R. Phillips. In res., Rev. George Miller.
Parish Office: 6466 Evangeline, 48127-2086. Tel: 313-274-4500; Fax: 313-562-2821.
School—Tel: 313-274-5320. Sr. Patricia Warbritton, S.S.J., Prin.
Lay Teachers 11; Students 244.
Catechesis/Religious Programs—Tel: 313-274-5778.
Students 182.
Convent—25450 Hass, 48127.

5—ST. MEL, Rev. James G. Livingston; Sr. Carmen Dominguez, O.P., Pastoral Assoc.
Church—7506 Inkster Rd., 48127. Tel: 313-274-0684; Fax: 313-274-4248.
School—Tel: 313-274-6270; Fax: 313-274-9080. Mrs. Georgene Wojciechowski, Prin.
Lay Teachers 12; Students 171.
Catechesis/Religious Programs—Tel: 313-274-3977. Erin DeSante, D.R.E.
Students 135.

6—OUR LADY OF GRACE, Rev. Ronald Cyprys; Deacon Robert DeWitt. In res., Rev. Charles F. O'Neill, (Retired).
Res., 8679 Riverview, 48127. Tel: 313-561-6373; Fax: 313-359-2727.
Church—23700 Joy Rd., 48127.

7—ST. SABINA, Rev. Joseph L. Romano.
Res., 25605 Ann Arbor Tr., 48127. Tel: 313-561-1977; Fax: 313-561-7898.
School—Tel: 313-274-5628.
Sisters 2; Lay Teachers 8; Students 180.
Catechesis/Religious Programs—Tel: 313-274-5635.
Students 80.

8—ST. SEBASTIAN, Revs. William B. Brennan; John Cusmano; Deacon Larry Girard.
Res., 3850 Merrick Ave., Dearborn, 48124. Tel: 313-562-5356; Fax: 313-562-0058.
School—Tel: 313-563-6640.
Franciscan Sisters of St. Joseph 4; Lay Teachers 16; Students 472.
Catechesis/Religious Programs—Tel: 313-563-0960. Susan Campbell, D.R.E.
Students 385.
Convent—20700 Colgate Ave., 48125. Tel: 313-562-7733.

Dryden, Lapeer Co., St. Cornelius, Rev. Wayne G. Ureel.
Res., 3834 Mill St., P.O. Box 208, 48428. Tel: 810-796-2926; Fax: 810-796-9713.

Dundee, Monroe Co., St. Irene, Rev. Ronald J. Alder.
Res., 576 Main St., 48131. Tel: 734-529-2160.

Eastpointe, Macomb Co.,

1—ST. BARNABAS, Rev. George Browne.
Res., 24800 Phlox Ave., 48021. Tel: 810-775-2284; Fax: 810-775-6933.
Catechesis/Religious Programs—James Nowak, D.R.E.
Students 150.

2—ST. BASIL, Rev. James H. Profota.
Parish Center—22851 Lexington Ave., 48021. Tel: 810-777-5610; Fax: 810-779-3341.
Catechesis/Religious Programs—Tel: 810-772-5434.
Students 195.

3—ST. VERONICA, Revs. Stanley L. Pachla, Jr.; Mario Cassar; Kulan-Daisamy Arokiasamy (India).
Res., 21440 Universal Dr., 48021. Tel: 810-777-0331; Fax: 810-777-0615.
School—Tel: 810-775-8333. Sr. Rochelle Holly, C.D.P., Prin.
Sisters of St. Joseph 1; Adrian Dominican 1; Sisters of Divine Providence 1; Lay Teachers 14; Students 240.
Catechesis/Religious Programs—Tel: 810-777-5810. D.R.E.: Sr. Mary Ann Ankoviak, S.S.J.; Sr. Geraldine Arnold, S.S.J.
Students 233.
Convent—21357 Redmond, 48021. Tel: 810-777-0321.

4—OUR LADY OF GRACE VIETNAMESE PARISH, (1999), Rev. Vincent Nguyen An Ninh.
Res., 19300 Stephens, 48021. Tel: 810-447-0504; Fax: 810-447—0508.

Ecorse, Wayne Co., St. Francis Xavier, Rev. Victor Roman.
Res., 4250 W. Jefferson Ave., 48229. Tel: 313-383-8514; Fax: 313-383-7508. [CEM]
Catechesis/Religious Programs—Joan Morrison, D.R.E.
Students 128.

Emmett, St. Clair Co., Our Lady of Mount Carmel, Rev. Jasper F. Sirianni.
Res., 10828 Brandon Rd., 48022. Tel: 810-384-1338; Fax: 810-384-1338.
Catechesis/Religious Programs—10832 Brandon Rd., 48022. Tel: 810-384-6925.
Students 275.

Erie, Monroe Co., St. Joseph, Rev. Joseph Plawecki.
Res., 2214 Manhattan Ave., 48133. Tel: 734-848-6125; Fax: 734-848-2784. [CEM]
School—Tel: 734-848-6985.
Sisters 2; Lay Teachers 10; Students 179.
Convent—2238 Manhattan Ave., 48133. Tel: 734-848-8754.

Farmington, Oakland Co., St. Colman, Rev. Norbert V. Kendzierski; Deacon Frank Chambers; Mrs. Kathleen O. Daray, Pastoral Assoc.
Res., 32500 Middlebelt Rd., Farmington Hills, 48334. Tel: 248-626-0285; Fax: 248-626-5420.
Catechesis/Religious Programs—Tel: 248-626-0287.
Students 58.

St. Gerald, Rev. Gerald A. McEnhill.
Res., 21300 Farmington Rd., 48336. Tel: 248-477-7470; Fax: 248-477-3878.
Catechesis/Religious Programs—Tel: 248-476-7677. Mary Taylor, D.R.E.
Students 262.

Our Lady of Sorrows, Rev. Msgr. Walter A. Hurley; Rev. Scott A. Thibodeau; Sr. Christine Mihelcic, S.J., Dir. Pastoral Svcs. In res., Revs. Arthur W. Fauser; Loren F. O'Dea, (Retired).
Res., 23815 Power Rd., 48336. Tel: 248-474-5720; Fax: 248-474-1340.
School—(Grades K-8). Tel: 248-476-0977. Roberta Clemak, Prin. (Grades K-8).
Lay Teachers 47; Students 952.
Catechesis/Religious Programs—Tel: 248-474-6480. Carol A. Bregand, D.R.E.
Students 584.

Farmington Hills, Oakland Co., St. Alexander, Rev. James B. Wright.
Res., 27835 Shiawassee, 48336. Tel: 248-474-5748; Fax: 248-427-0883.
Catechesis/Religious Programs—Tel: 248-474-8126; Fax: 248-474-8231.
Students 220.

St. Clare of Assisi, Rev. Frederick J. Klettner.
Res., 29200 W. Ten Mile, 48336. Tel: 248-477-9870; Fax: 248-477-4785.

St. Fabian, Rev. Brian J. Chabala.
Church—32200 W. 12 Mile Rd., 48334. Tel: 248-553-4610; Fax: 248-553-6296.
School—Tel: 248-553-2750; Fax: 248-848-3035. Karen Stoller, Prin.
Bernardine Sisters 2; Lay Teachers 24; Students 469.
Catechesis/Religious Programs—Tel: 248-553-4860; Fax: 248-553-6292. D.R.E.: Gina Karl; Nancy Pawlukiewicz.
Students 728.

Convent—32170 Twelve Mile Rd., 48334. Tel: 248-553-4186.

Ferndale, Oakland Co., St. James, Rev. Robert L. Wurm; Sr. Eveleen Forkin, Pastoral Min.; W. Michael O'Neill, Pastoral Assoc.
Res., 241 W. Pearson Ave., 48220-1824. Tel: 248-542-8835; Fax: 248-542-0267.
Catechesis/Religious Programs—W. Michael O'Neill, D.R.E.
Students 303.

Flat Rock, Wayne Co., St. Roch, Rev. Frederick Misiolek; Deacon Harold Goodhue.
Res., 25022 Gibraltar Rd., 48134. Tel: 313-782-4471; Fax: 313-782-5450.

Fraser, Macomb Co., Our Lady Queen of All Saints, Rev. Ronald J. Babich; Sr. Nancy Zajac, O.P., Pastoral Assoc.
Res., 31740 Cyril Dr., 48026. Tel: 810-293-4050; Fax: 810-293-1041.
Catechesis/Religious Programs—Tel: 810-294-6180; Fax: 810-293-1041.
Students 421.

Garden City, Wayne Co., St. Dunstan, Rev. Donald Demmer; Deacon Michael Markulike.
Res., 1646 Belton Ave., 48135. Tel: 734-425-6720; Fax: 734-425-8411.
School—1615 Belton Ave., 48135. Tel: 734-425-4380. Sr. Mariella Chrusciel, Prin.
Sisters 2; Lay Teachers 10; Students 249.
Catechesis/Religious Programs—Tel: 734-425-4396. D.R.E.: Sr. Mary Martin; Trichia O'Keefe.
Students 255.

St. Raphael the Archangel, Rev. Thomas P. Kirwan; Sr. Ritamary Pyzick, Pastoral Min. In res., Rev. Jude Inweregbu (Nigeria).
Parish Center—31530 Beechwood, 48135. Tel: 734-427-1533; Fax: 734-427-8594.
Parish Hall—5875 Merriman, 48135. Tel: 734-422-9617.
School—Tel: 734-425-9771. Judith McBride, Prin.
Lay Teachers 20; Students 438.
Catechesis/Religious Programs—Tel: 734-425-5550. Sr. Diann Cousino, I.H.M., D.R.E.
Students 445.

Gibraltar, Wayne Co., St. Victor, Rev. Roger A. Knapp.
Res., 14100 Navarre, 48173. Tel: 734-675-0100; Fax: 734-675-6952.

Grosse Ile, Wayne Co., Sacred Heart, Rev. James C. Scheick; Deacon Robert Tremmel.
Parish Center: 21599 Parke Ln., 48138. Tel: 734-676-1378; Fax: 734-676-3623. [CEM]
Catechesis/Religious Programs—Students 682.

Grosse Pointe, Wayne Co., Our Lady Star of the Sea, Rev. Msgr. Dennis Harrity; Rev. John M. Currin. In res., Rev. William J. McGoldrick.
Church—467 Fairford, 48236. Tel: 313-884-5554; Fax: 313-885-5591.
School—Tel: 313-884-1070. Patricia Stumb, Prin.
Lay Teachers 28; Students 498.
Catechesis/Religious Programs—Tel: 313-884-7407. Helen L. Goettl, D.R.E.
Students 528.
Convent—19950 Morningside Dr., 48236. Tel: 313-884-4074.

Grosse Pointe Farms, Wayne Co., St. Paul Catholic Church, Most Rev. Leonard P. Blair; Revs. Paul K. Ballien; Robert J. McCabe. Pastoral Assocs.: Deacon Richard Shubik; Sr. Ruthanne Reed, O.P. In res., Rev. Michael G. O'Leary.
Res., 157 Lake Shore Rd., 48236. Tel: 313-885-8855; Fax: 313-886-6467. [CEM]
School—170 Grosse Pointe Blvd., 48236. Tel: 313-885-3430; Fax: 313-885-9357. Elizabeth A. Burns, Prin.
Sisters 2; Lay Teachers 28; Students 538.
Catechesis/Religious Programs—Bernadette Thompson, D.R.E.
Students 573.

Grosse Pointe Park, Wayne Co., St. Ambrose, Rev. Timothy R. Pelc; Mr. Charles J. Dropiewski, Pastoral Assoc.
Res., 15020 Hampton, 48230. Tel: 313-822-2814; Fax: 313-822-9838.
School—Tel: 313-823-0177; Fax: 313-823-6974. Susan Kotyk, Prin.
Lay Teachers 14; Students 200.
Catechesis/Religious Programs—Bernadette Gutowski, D.R.E.
Students 225.

St. Clare of Montefalco, Rev. Joseph E. McCormick, O.S.A.; Bro. Thomas P. Taylor, O.S.A.; Deacon Truman Stevens. In res., Revs. Joseph F. Hartman, O.S.A.; Francis R. McDonnell, O.S.A.; Robert F. Gardella, O.S.A.
Res., 1401 Whittier Rd., 48230. Tel: 313-647-5000; Fax: 313-647-5005.
School—16231 Charlevoix, 48230. Tel: 313-647-5100; Fax: 313-647-5105. Henry Burakowski, Prin.
Catechesis/Religious Programs—Tel: 313-647-5050; Fax: 313-647-5055. Paula Miller, D.R.E.
Students 430.

Hamtramck, Wayne Co., St. Florian, Revs. Wojciech Baryski, S.Ch.; Darrell Roman, S.Ch.
Res., 2626 Poland Ave., 48212. Tel: 313-871-2778; Fax: 313-871-5947.
Church—Florian and Latham Aves., 48212.
School—Tel: 313-875-3040; Fax: 313-872-1242.
Felician Sisters 2; Lay Teachers 10; Students 200.
High School—Tel: 313-875-6347. Patricia Domagala, Prin.
Felician Sisters 2; Lay Teachers 12; Students 120.
Convent—2622 Florian Ave., 48212. Tel: 313-872-5775.

St. Ladislaus (Polish), Rev. Stanley A. Ulman. In res., Rev. Stanislaus Czapiewski, S.J.
Res., 2730 Caniff Ave., 48212. Tel: 313-872-0709; Fax: 313-872-5906.

Our Lady Queen of Apostles (Polish), Rev. Bogdan Milosz.
Res., 3851 Prescott Ave., 48212-3115. Tel: 313-891-1520; 1521; Fax: 313-891-3552.
School—11420 Conant, 48212. Tel: 313-892-8130; Fax: 313-892-1364. Sr. M. Gloria Ertman, C.S.S.F., Prin.
Sisters 3; Lay Teachers 8; Students 161.
Convent—3891 Prescott Ave., 48212-3115. Tel: 313-891-7121.

Harper Woods, Wayne Co., Our Lady Queen of Peace, Rev. David J. Blazek. In res., Revs. John M. Fee, SS.CC.; Eugene F. Fedewa.
Res., 20955 Bournemouth Ave., 48225. Tel: 313-881-5212; Fax: 313-881-7813.
School—Tel: 313-881-3629; Fax: 313-881-4198. Judy Meerschaert, Prin.
Lay Teachers 12; Students 131.
Catechesis/Religious Programs—Tel: 313-884-8744.
Students 131.

St. Peter the Apostle, Rev. Robert J. Keller.
Res., 19851 Anita St., 48225. Tel: 313-886-1771; Fax: 313-886-1489.
School—Tel: 313-885-8062; Fax: 313-885-2961. Mr. Patrick Browne, Prin.
Lay Teachers 18; Students 220.

Harrison Twp., Macomb Co., St. Hubert, Rev. James J. O'Leary.
Res., 38775 Prentiss, 48045. Tel: 810-463-5877; 463-7796; Fax: 810-463-1734.
Catechesis/Religious Programs—Tel: 810-463-5875. Mr. Allan Ranusch, D.R.E.
Students 650.

Harsens Island, St. Clair Co., St. Mark, Rev. James R. Wysocki, Admin.
Res., Church and Rectory, 4190 Green Dr., Harsen's Island, 48028. Tel: 810-748-3828; Fax: 810-748-9148.

Hazel Park, Oakland Co., St. Justin, Rev. Robert Hayes Williams.
Res., 1631 E. Elza St., 48030. Tel: 248-542-2129; Fax: 248-542-2715.

St. Mary Magdalen, Rev. Bede Louzon, O.F.M.Cap.
Res., 50 E. Annabelle, 48030. Tel: 248-542-8060; Fax: 248-542-4563.
School—Tel: 248-547-3363; Fax: 248-547-1610. Suzanne Kisseberth, Prin.
Lay Teachers 10; Students 203.
Catechesis/Religious Programs—Tel: 248-547-0323. Elaine Dulette, D.R.E.
Students 215.

Highland, Oakland Co., Church of the Holy Spirit, Rev. Leo T. Lulko; Deacon Arthur Van Brook.
Church—3700 Harvey Lake Rd., 48356. Tel: 248-887-5364; Fax: 248-889-1374.
Catechesis/Religious Programs—Tel: 248-887-1634. Joann Dalton, D.R.E.
Students 800.

Highland Park, Wayne Co., St. Benedict, Rev. Robert B. McGrath; Deacon Richard Conlin.
Res., 60 Church Ave., 48203. Tel: 313-868-3876; Fax: 313-868-0110.
School—53 Candler, 48203. Tel: 313-868-7502. Kathleen Walker, Prin.
Lay Teachers 15; Students 240.

Holly, Oakland Co., St. Rita, Rev. Joseph P. Killeen.
Res., 309 E. Maple, 48442. Tel: 248-634-4841; Fax: 248-634-4858.
Catechesis/Religious Programs—Tel: 248-634-1658; Fax: 248-634-4863. Dawn M. Sliwa, D.R.E.
Students 270.

Ida, Monroe Co., St. Joseph, Rev. John P. LaCasse, Admin.
Res., 8295 Van Akin St., 48140. Tel: 734-269-3895. [CEM]
Catechesis/Religious Programs—Tel: 734-269-3414. Linda Wilson, D.R.E.
Students 228.

Imlay City, Lapeer Co., Sacred Heart, Rev. Ezequiel Mondragon.
Res., 700 Maple Vista, 48444. Tel: 810-724-1135; Fax: 810-724-0870. [CEM]
Catechesis/Religious Programs—Tel: 810-724-1145.
Students 206.

Inkster, Wayne Co., Holy Family Parish, Rev. John Lehner, O.S.F.S.
Res., 27800 Annapolis Rd., 48141. Tel: 313-563-8242; Fax: 313-563-0696.

SS. Kevin and Norbert, Rev. John Lehner, O.S.F.S.
Office: 27355 Woodsfield, 48141. Tel: 313-563-0993; Fax: 313-563-3148.
Res., 604 Sherbourne Dr., 48141.
Catechesis/Religious Programs—Tel: 313-278-4924; Fax: 313-563-3148.
Students 75.

Lake Orion, Oakland Co., St. Joseph, Revs. John L. Phalen; Bernard J. Mullen; Deacon Joseph A. Hulway. Pastoral Assocs.: Mary Martin; Peggy Bartz-Vieaux.
Res., 715 N. Lapeer Rd., 48362. Tel: 248-693-0440; Fax: 248-693-3724.
School—Tel: 248-693-6215; Fax: 248-693-0958. Sr. Theresa Darga, O.S.F., Prin.
Lay Teachers 12; Students 288.
Catechesis/Religious Programs—Tel: 248-693-9555. Regina Moskal, D.R.E.
Students 1,032.

Lakeport, St. Clair Co., St. Edward's on the Lake, Rev. Joseph M. Esper.
Res., 6945 Lakeshore Rd., 48059. Tel: 810-385-4340; Fax: 810-385-6972. [CEM]
School—(Grades K-5). For grades 6-8 please refer to McCormick Consolidated Academy, Port Huron, under Elementary Schools, Inter-Parochial in the Institutions Located in the Archdiocese section. Tel: 810-385-4461; Fax: 810-385-6070.
Students 142.
Convent—6975 Lakeshore Rd., 48059. Tel: 810-385-9531.

Lapeer, Lapeer Co., Immaculate Conception of the Blessed Virgin Mary, Revs. Douglas J. Terrien; Janusz Iwan; Deacon Gerald Deshaw.
Res., 814 Nepessing, 48446. Tel: 810-664-8594; Fax: 810-664-4564. [CEM]
School—Bishop Kelley School, Tel: 810-664-5011; Fax: 810-664-5606. Miss Barbara Davis, Prin.
Lay Teachers 9; Students 220.
Catechesis/Religious Programs—Tel: 810-664-0808.
Students 408.

Lincoln Park, Wayne Co., Christ the Good Shepherd, Revs. David A. Buersmeyer; Robert A. LaCroix, Jr.; Sr. Marge Zacharias, O.S.F., Pastoral Assoc.
Res., 1540 Riverbank Ave., 48146. Tel: 313-928-1324; Fax: 313-928-1326.
School—Tel: 313-386-0633. Thomas Caruso, Prin.
Lay Teachers 22; Students 450.
Catechesis/Religious Programs—Tel: 313-382-1818. Sr. Rebecca Vonderhaar, D.R.E.
Students 280.

St. Henry, Rev. Gerard J. Cupple.
Res., 1358 Council Ave., 48146. Tel: 313-381-0711; 0712; Fax: 313-381-6746.
Catechesis/Religious Programs—Anne Martus, D.R.E.
Students 85.

Livonia, Wayne Co.,

1—St. Aidan, Rev. Gerald K. Flannery; Dr. Jerard E. Delaney, II, Pastoral Assoc.; Deacon Robert Delbeke.
Res., 17500 Farmington Rd., 48152. Tel: 734-425-5950; Fax: 734-425-3687.
Catechesis/Religious Programs—Tel: 734-425-9333. Mary Ellen Skene, D.R.E.
Students 645.

2—St. Colette, Rev. Henry W. Roodbeen; Deacons Al Morad; Leo D'Argis.
Res., 17600 Newburgh, 48152-2699. Tel: 734-464-4433; Fax: 734-464-1694.
Catechesis/Religious Programs—Tel: 734-464-4435; Fax: 734-464-7817. Joanne Plant, D.R.E.
Students 804.

3—St. Edith, Rev. Timothy J. Murray; Deacons John Kenny; Ric Misiak.
Res., 15089 Newburgh, 48154. Tel: 734-464-1222; Fax: 734-464-7582.
School—Tel: 734-464-1250; Fax: 734-464-6765. Sr. Margaret Kijek, C.S.S.F., Prin.
Felician Sisters 1; Lay Teachers 8; Students 270.
Catechesis/Religious Programs—Tel: 734-464-2020. Elizabeth Nowak, D.R.E.
Students 570.

4—St. Genevieve, Rev. Howard L. Vogan; Deacon R. P. Piro, Pastoral Assoc.
Res., 29015 Jamison, 48154. Tel: 734-427-5220; Fax: 734-422-1763.

School—Tel: 734-425-4420; Fax: 734-458-3915. Sr. M. Juanita Szymanski, C.S.S.F., Prin.
Sisters 1; Lay Teachers 9; Students 192.
Catechesis/Religious Programs—Tel: 734-261-5920. Diana Tarnacki, D.R.E.
Students 377.

5—St. Maurice, Rev. Sidney J. Eckert; Darlene Bellmore, Pastoral Assoc.
Res., 32765 Lyndon Ave., 48154. Tel: 734-522-1616; Fax: 734-522-5092.
Catechesis/Religious Programs—Tel: 734-421-5240. Mrs. Mary Rice, D.R.E.
Students 168.

6—St. Michael, Rev. Alberto P. Bondy.
Res., 11441 Hubbard Ave., 48150. Tel: 734-261-1455; Fax: 734-522-1123.
School—Tel: 734-421-7360; Fax: 734-466-9713. Sr. M. Carolyn Ratkowski, C.S.S.F., Prin.
Felician Sisters 5; Lay Teachers 27; Students 905.
Catechesis/Religious Programs—Tel: 734-261-1790.
Students 165.
Convent—11400 Fairfield, Tel: 734-421-7522.

7—St. Priscilla, Rev. Raymond H. Bucon; Deacon Raymond Kunik.
19120 Purling Brook Rd., 48152. Tel: 248-476-4700; Fax: 248-476-7831.
Catechesis/Religious Programs—Tel: 248-476-4702.
Students 410.

Macomb, Macomb Co., St. Isidore, Revs. Michael Hryoziuszko; Robert McClory; Deacon Tony Kendzierski; Karl DeLisle, Pastoral Assoc.
Res., 18201 Twenty-three Mile Rd., 48042. Tel: 810-286-1700; Fax: 810-286-8753.
Catechesis/Religious Programs—Tel: 810-286-4433. Mary Fedders, D.R.E.
Students 1,300.

St. Maximillian Kolbe, Rev. Robert H. Blondell; Sr. Lois Barror, S.S.J., Pastoral Assoc.
23965 23 Mile Rd., Macomb Township, 48042. Tel: 810-598-3314; Fax: 810-598-3346.

Madison Heights, Oakland Co., St. Vincent Ferrer, Rev. Steven C. Koehler; Sr. Mary Jo Sieg, O.P., Pastoral Assoc.
Res., 1087 E. Gardenia Ave., 48071. Tel: 248-542-8720; Fax: 248-542-8721.
School—1075 E. Gardenia, 48071. Tel: 248-398-4190; Fax: 248-398-4191. Mr. Raymond Dudus, Prin.
Lay Teachers 14; Students 152.
Catechesis/Religious Programs—Michael Novak, D.R.E.
Students 261.

Marine City, St. Clair Co., Holy Cross, Rev. James R. Wysocki; Deacon Gary Krueger. In res., Revs. Alfred Sadler; George Browne; Frederick Bodde.
Res., 610 S. Water St., 48039. Tel: 810-765-3568; Fax: 810-765-2974. [CEM]
School—Holy Cross Elementary, 618 S. Water St., 48039. Tel: 810-765-3591. Mrs. Dianne Lovette, Prin.
Dominican Sisters 1; Lay Teachers 14; Students 185.
High School—Cardinal Mooney Catholic, Tel: 810-765-8825; Fax: 810-765-7164. Sr. Karen Leitz, Prin.
Priests 1; Sisters 4; Lay Teachers 15; Students 189.
Catechesis/Religious Programs—Tel: 810-765-8300. Sr. Kathleen Mulso, O.S.F., D.R.E.
Students 300.

Marysville, St. Clair Co., St. Christopher, Rev. Arthur R. Baranowski; Sr. Lynn Pascoe, O.S.F., Pastoral Min.
Res., 1000 Michigan Ave., 48040. Tel: 810-364-4100; Fax: 810-364-5947.
Catechesis/Religious Programs—Tel: 810-364-7080. Amy Miles, D.R.E.
Students 556.

Maybee, Monroe Co., St. Joseph, Rev. Michael D. Malawy.
Res., 9207 Joseph St., Box 125, 48159. Tel: 313-587-8835; Fax: 313-587-3490. [CEM]
Convent—9147 Joseph St., Box 118, 48159. Tel: 313-587-8785.

Melvindale, Wayne Co., St. Conrad, Rev. Joseph A. Gagnon.
Res., 3320 Melwood, 48122. Tel: 313-383-0303; Fax: 313-383-5704.

St. Mary Magdalen, Rev. Jeffrey Anifer.
Res., 19624 Wood St., 48122. Tel: 313-381-8566; Fax: 313-381-1319.
School—Tel: 313-382-6060. Denise Lokuta, Prin.
Lay Teachers 12; Students 240.
Catechesis/Religious Programs—Tel: 313-382-1099. Mary Whalen, D.R.E.
Students 240.

Memphis, Macomb Co., All Saints, Rev. Dennis Nowinski.
Church—79780 Main St., 48041. Tel: 810-392-2056; 392-3232; Fax: 810-392-3043.
Catechesis/Religious Programs—Toni Zweng, D.R.E.
Students 247.

Milford, Oakland Co., St. Mary, Our Lady of the Snows, Rev. Ronald Anderson; Kathryn Michalik, Pastoral Assoc.; Deacon Archie Noon.
Res., 1955 E. Commerce, 48381. Tel: 248-685-1482; Fax: 248-684-5642. [CEM]
Catechesis/Religious Programs—Tel: 248-685-2702. Michael Maras, D.R.E.
Students 1,090.

Monroe, Monroe Co.,

1—St. Anne, Revs. William F. Fisher, O.S.F.S.; Robert C. Mossett, O.S.F.S.
Res., 2420 N. Dixie Hwy., 48162. Tel: 734-289-2910; Fax: 734-289-1098.
Catechesis/Religious Programs—Students 123.

2—St. John The Baptist, Rev. Terrence D. Kerner.
Res., 511 S. Monroe St. S., 48161. Tel: 734-241-8910; Fax: 734-241-1943.
School—Tel: 734-241-1670. Patricia Cousino, Prin.
Lay Teachers 10; Students 290.
Catechesis/Religious Programs—D.R.E.: Sharon DuVall; Karon Kinsey.
Students 150.

3—St. Joseph's, Rev. William F. Fisher, O.S.F.S.; Sr. Harriet Fitzmaurice, I.H.M., Pastoral Assoc.
Res., 924 E. Second St., 48161. Tel: 734-241-9590; Fax: 734-241-5296. [JC]
Catechesis/Religious Programs—Mrs. Judy Collins, D.R.E.
Students 111.

4—St. Mary's, Rev. Anthony P. Sulkowski; Sr. Jean M. O'Connor, I.H.M., Pastoral Assoc.; Deacon Michael Ingles.
Res., 127 N. Monroe St., 48162. Tel: 734-241-1644; Fax: 734-241-3077. [JC]
School—Tel: 734-241-3377; Fax: 734-241-0497. Mary Ann Lapinski, Prin.
Lay Teachers 14; Students 291.
Catechesis/Religious Programs—Tel: 734-241-6097. Doreen Calvin, D.R.E.
Students 226.

5—St. Michael, Rev. Stephen Rooney. Pastoral Assocs.: Sr. Dorothy Jayne. Krupp, O.S.F.; Mr. Leo Todd Jarret.
Res., 502 W. Front St., 48161. Tel: 734-241-8645; Fax: 734-241-6132. [JC]
School—Tel: 734-241-3923; Fax: 734-241-3924. Karen Pilon, Prin.
Lay Teachers 11; Students 253.
Catechesis/Religious Programs—Sr. Dorothy Jayne Krupp, O.S.F., D.R.E.
Students 172.

Mount Clemens, Macomb Co., St. Peter, Rev. Michael N. Cooney; Sheila Roy, Pastoral Min.; Doris Kallek, Admin.
Admin. Bldg.: 98 New St., 48043. Tel: 810-468-4578; Fax: 810-468-3199. [CEM]
School—St. Mary, Tel: 810-468-4570. Carol Budchuk, Prin.
Lay Teachers 26; Students 598.
Catechesis/Religious Programs—Judy Coll, D.R.E.
Students 455.

New Baltimore, Macomb Co., St. Mary Queen of Creation, Revs. Nicholas Zukowski; Stephen Vileo; Kathryn Carten, Parish Nurse Coord.; Deacons Anthony Lewandoski, (Retired); Richard Damaske.
Res., 51041 Maria St., 48047. Tel: 810-725-2441; Fax: 810-725-3647. [CEM]
Catechesis/Religious Programs—Tel: 810-725-7579; Fax: 810-725-0838. Carolyn Bissett, D.R.E.
Students 928.

New Boston, Wayne Co., St. Stephen, Revs. Alexander J. Wytrwal; Joseph Szewczyk.
Res., 18800 Huron River Dr., 48164-9599. Tel: 734-753-4305; Fax: 734-753-5828. [CEM]
School—Tel: 734-753-4175. Sr. M. Virginia Gola, C.S.S.F., Prin.
Felician Sisters 2; Lay Teachers 13; Students 201.
Catechesis/Religious Programs—Tel: 734-753-4722. Sr. M. Pauline Winowiecki, C.S.S.F., D.R.E.
Students 140.
Convent—Tel: 734-753-9937.

New Haven, Macomb Co., St. Francis of Assisi, Rev. Thomas R. Physician.
Res., 62811 New Haven Rd., Ray Twp., 48096. Tel: 810-749-9584; Fax: 810-749-6021.

Newport, Monroe Co., St. Charles Borromeo, Rev. William H. Tindall; Sr. Pamela J. Nosbusch, O.S.F., Pastoral Assoc.
Res., 8109 Swan Creek Rd., 48166. Tel: 734-586-2531; Fax: 734-586-3900. [CEM]
School—Tel: 734-586-2531, Ext. 3. Charlene Jenkins, Prin.
Lay Teachers 9; Students 197.
Catechesis/Religious Programs—Tel: 734-586-2531, Ext. 4. Mrs. Michaelene Kowalczik, D.R.E.
Students 237.

North Branch, Lapeer Co., St. Mary's Burnside, Rev. Francis Weingartz.
Res., 5622 Summers Rd., 48461. Tel: 810-688-3648; Fax: 810-688-3588. [CEM]
Mission—Brown City, Sanilac Co., Sacred Heart. [CEM]

SS. Peter and Paul, Rev. Jude T. Ellinghausen.
Res., Box 208, 6645 Washington, 48461. Tel: 810-688-3797; Fax: 810-688-2969. [CEM]
Catechesis/Religious Programs—Tel: 810-688-9019. Charlotte Kalbfleisch, D.R.E.
Students 245.
Mission—Clifford, Lapeer Co., St. Patrick's. [CEM]

Northville, Wayne Co., Our Lady of Victory, Revs. Ernest M. Porcari; Steven Wertanen.
Res., 770 Thayer, 48167. Tel: 248-349-2621; Fax: 248-349-7329.
School—Tel: 248-349-3610; Fax: 248-380-7247.
Lay Teachers 19; Students 360.
Catechesis/Religious Programs—Ms. Eileen Moss, D.R.E.
Students 534.
Convent—103 Orchard Dr., 48167. Tel: 248-348-8650.

St. Andrew Kim Korean Catholic Church, Rev. Blase Lee.
Res., 21177 Halsted Rd., 48167. Tel: 248-442-9026; Fax: 248-442-9020.

Novi, Oakland Co., Holy Family, Revs. John G. Budde; Andrew Czarnecki; Deacons William Waldmann; Steven Morello.
Res., 24505 Meadowbrook, 48375. Tel: 248-349-8847; Fax: 248-349-3711.
Catechesis/Religious Programs—Tel: 248-349-8837. Maria Koncius, D.R.E.
Students 970.

St. James, Rev. James F. Cronk.
Church—46325 Ten Mile Road, 48374-3007. Tel: 248-347-7778; Fax: 248-347-9625.
Catechesis/Religious Programs—Paula Brach, D.R.E.
Students 1,250.

Oak Park, Oakland Co., Our Lady of Fatima, Rev. Paul F. Chateau; Sr. Jane Zoltek, S.S.J., Pastoral Assoc. In res., Rev. Nicholas H. Amico (Ecuador).
Res., 13500 Oak Park Blvd., 48237. Tel: 810-545-2310; Fax: 810-545-2312.

Orchard Lake, Oakland Co., Our Lady of Refuge, Rev. William J. Murphy.
Res., 3663 Erie Dr., P.O. Box 240485, 48324. Tel: 248-682-0920; Fax: 248-682-3794.
School—Tel: 248-682-3422; Fax: 248-683-2265. Sr. Mary Ruth Koralewski, C.S.S.F., Prin.
Sisters 2; Lay Teachers 22; Students 488.
Catechesis/Religious Programs—Tel: 248-682-6381. Gloria Boesch, D.R.E.
Students 536.
Convent—3725 Erie Dr., 48324. Tel: 248-682-1876.

Orion Township, Oakland Co., Christ the Redeemer, Rev. Joseph E. Dailey.
Res., 2700 Waldon Rd., Lake Orion, 48360. Tel: 248-391-1621; Fax: 248-391-3412.
Catechesis/Religious Programs—Tel: 248-391-4074. Henry Mucha, D.R.E.
Students 684.

Ortonville, Oakland Co., St. Anne, Rev. C. Michael Vershaeve.
Res., 825 Ortonville Rd., 48462. Tel: 248-627-3965; Fax: 248-627-5153.
Catechesis/Religious Programs—Elaine Young, D.R.E.
Students 381.

Plymouth, Wayne Co., Our Lady of Good Counsel, Revs. John J. Sullivan; Doc Ortman; Elias Salomon, S.S.J.V. (Phillipines); Deacons Don Leach; Tim Sullivan; Charine List, Pastoral Assoc.
Res., 1062 Church St., 48170. Tel: 734-453-0326; Fax: 734-416-9257.
School—Tel: 734-453-3053; Fax: 734-453-3620. Theodore Behn, Prin.
Lay Teachers 21; Students 561.
Catechesis/Religious Programs—Tel: 734-455-0242.
Students 580.

St. Kenneth, Rev. Joseph S. Mallia.
Res., 14951 Haggerty Rd., 48170. Tel: 734-420-0288; Fax: 734-420-2921.
Catechesis/Religious Programs—Tel: 734-420-3031. Mrs. Laurel McGrane, D.R.E.
Students 455.

Pontiac, Oakland Co., St. Joseph, Revs. John P. Wynnycky; Timothy A. Laboe; Sr. M. Patricia Malone, R.S.M., Pastoral Assoc.; Deacon John M. Fleming. Liturgical Presiders: Revs. Fabian B. Slominski; Thomas R. Physician.

400 South Blvd. W., 48341-2465. Tel: 248-332-9872; Fax: 248-334-0528.
Res., 46408 Woodward Ave., 48342. Tel: 248-332-0283.
Mission—Pontiac, Oakland Co., St. Vincent de Paul.

St. Michael, Revs. John P. Wynnycky; Timothy A. Laboe; Deacon Edward Strye.
Res., 120 Lewis, 48342. Tel: 248-332-9167; Fax: 248-332-3901.

St. Vincent de Paul, Revs. John P. Wynnycky; Timothy A. Laboe. Pastoral Assocs.: Sr. Carmen Coccimiglio, S.L.W.; Maria Jimenez; Willie McCray, Minister of Service; Deacons Fernando Valdez; Jesus Vasquez; Brigido Rodriguez; Norman LaLone.
Res., 46408 Woodward Ave., 48342. Tel: 248-332-0283; Fax: 248-332-7041.

Port Huron, St. Clair Co., St. Joseph, Rev. Rene L. Desmarais; Deacon John Connors.
Res., 1317 7th St., 48060. Tel: 810-985-9616; Fax: 810-985-9807. [JC]
School—Tel: 810-982-3201.
Sisters 1; Lay Teachers 7; Students 77.
Catechesis/Religious Programs—Tel: 810-982-2343. Patti Fisher, D.R.E.
Students 120.

St. Mary, Rev. Stanley Wyczawski.
Res., 1505 Ballentine St., 48060. Tel: 810-982-7906; Fax: 810-987-8255.
School—Mrs. Karen Pawlak. Lay Teachers 8; Students 151.
Catechesis/Religious Programs—Patricia Isaacson, D.R.E.
Students 281.

St. Stephen, Rev. David Lesniak.
Res., 325 32nd St., 48060. Tel: 810-984-3220; Fax: 810-984-8559.
Parish Center—2865 Henry, 48060. Tel: 810-984-2689.
Catechesis/Religious Programs—Tel: 810-985-9069. Rose Marie Miller, D.R.E.
Students 127.

Redford, Wayne Co.,

1—St. Agatha, Rev. William Pettit.
Parish Office—19750 Beech Daly Rd., 48240. Tel: 313-531-0371; Fax: 313-531-1805.
Res., 19650 Beech Daly Rd., 48240.
School—Tel: 313-532-6940. Daniel Parent, Prin.
Lay Teachers 11; Students 262.
High School—Tel: 313-532-3317; Fax: 313-532-2277. Timothy Scanlon, Prin.
Sisters 2; Lay Teachers 10; Students 126.
Catechesis/Religious Programs—Students 110.

2—St. John Bosco, Rev. Richard A. Osebold.
Res., 12100 Beech-Daly Rd., 48239. Tel: 313-937-9690; Fax: 313-937-2927.
School—Tel: 313-937-3856. Sr. Rita Sieg, O.P., Prin.
Lay Teachers 7; Students 89.

3—Our Lady of Loretto, Rev. John J. Mech; Sr. Margretta Wojcik, O.S.F., Pastoral Assoc.; Deacon Gary Pardo.
Res., 17116 Olympia Ave., 48240. Tel: 313-534-9000; Fax: 313-534-6744.
School—Tel: 313-532-4764; Fax: 313-794-1506.
Lay Teachers 16; Students 235.
Catechesis/Religious Programs—Tel: 313-532-3707. Christine Laing, D.R.E.
Students 75.

4—St. Valentine, Rev. Thomas A. Belczak.
Res., 25881 Dow, 48239. Tel: 313-532-4394; Fax: 313-537-2237.
School—25875 Hope St., 48239. Tel: 313-533-7149; Fax: 313-533-3060. Laura McClure, Prin.
Lay Teachers 23; Students 324.
Catechesis/Religious Programs—Tel: 313-538-9161. Sharon Larkin, D.R.E.
Students 255.
Convent—25900 Dow St., 48239. Tel: 313-533-7828.

Redford Township, Wayne Co., St. Robert Bellarmine, Rev. Denis B. Theroux.
Res., 27101 W. Chicago, 48239. Tel: 313-937-1500; Fax: 313-937-1185.
School—Tel: 313-937-1655; Fax: 313-937-9755. Nancy Majewski, Prin.
Lay Teachers 23; Students 310.
Catechesis/Religious Programs—Tel: 313-937-1531; Fax: 313-937-5060. Jan Lopata, D.R.E.
Students 265.

St. Hilary, Rev. John T. Nowlan; Sr. Marie Miller, I.H.M.
Res., 23901 Elmira, 48239. Tel: 313-533-1560; Fax: 313-533-1735.

Richmond, Macomb Co., St. Augustine, Rev. James E. Commyn.
Res., 68035 Main St., 48062. Tel: 810-727-5215; Fax: 810-727-3760. [CEM]
School—Tel: 810-727-9365.
Lay Teachers 14; Students 284.
Catechesis/Religious Programs—Tel: 810-727-9290.
Students 190.
Convent—67900 Howard St., 48062. Tel: 810-727-1517.

River Rouge, Wayne Co., Our Lady of Lourdes, Rev. James F. Wieging; Dr. Paul D. Bodrie, Pastoral Assoc.
Res., 1440 Coolidge Highway, 48218. Tel: 313-842-3320; 3321; Fax: 313-842-4507.

Riverview, Wayne Co., St. Cyprian, Revs. Jude Verley, O.S.C.; Francis K. Scheets, O.S.C.; John G. Hawkins, O.S.C. In res., Revs. Dale H. Redwanski, O.S.C.; Richard M. Leliaert, O.S.C.
Res., 13249 Pennsylvania, 48192. Tel: 734-283-0112; Fax: 734-283-2809.
School—Tel: 734-283-9442. William Lindeman, Prin.
Lay Teachers 13; Students 195.
Catechesis/Religious Programs—Tel: 734-283-2239. Mrs. Kathleen Duford, D.R.E.
Students 462.

Rochester, Oakland Co., St. Andrew, Revs. Timothy F. Babcock; Robert J. Shafer; Deacon Charles G. Skubick. Pastoral Assocs.: Sr. Carmela Whitton, O.S.F., Pastoral Assoc.; Sr. Rebecca Hodge, O.P.
Res., 1400 Inglewood, 48307. Tel: 248-651-7486; Fax: 248-651-3950.
Catechesis/Religious Programs—Tel: 248-651-6401; Fax: 248-651-2844. Nancy Clancy, D.R.E.
Students 1,519.

St. Irenaeus, Rev. A. Frank Pollie; Patricia Egan-Myers, Pastoral Assoc. & D.R.E.
Res., 771 Old Perch Rd., Rochester Hills, 48309. Tel: 248-651-9595; Fax: 248-651-1504.
Catechesis/Religious Programs—Tel: 248-651-2443.
Students 603.

Rochester Hills, St. Mary's of the Hills, Rev. Eugene Strain.
Res., 2675 John R, 48307-4652. Tel: 248-853-5390; Fax: 248-853-7989.
Catechesis/Religious Programs—Tel: 248-853-5390. Peggy Casing, D.R.E.
Students 630.

Rockwood, Wayne Co., St. Mary, Rev. Thomas M. Sauter.
Res., P.O. Box 249, 48173. Tel: 734-379-9248; Fax: 734-379-6548. [CEM]
School—Tel: 734-379-9285; Fax: 734-379-9088. Michelle E. Seward, Prin.
Lay Teachers 11; Students 192.
Catechesis/Religious Programs—Tel: 734-379-9406. Ms. Theresa Borawski, D.R.E.
Students 225.
Convent—32477 Church St., 48173.

Romeo, Macomb Co., St. Clement of Rome, Rev. Stephen C. Reckker.
Res., 343 S. Main St., 48065. Tel: 810-752-9611; Fax: 810-752-7795.
Catechesis/Religious Programs—Tel: 810-752-6951; Fax: 810-752-7093. Deborah Knoblock, D.R.E.
Students 800.

Romulus, Wayne Co., St. Aloysius, Rev. Festus Ejimadu.
Res., 11280 Ozga Rd., 48174. Tel: 734-941-5056; Fax: 734-941-6018.
School—Tel: 734-941-3340. Mary Confer, Prin.
Lay Teachers 5; Students 62.

Roseville, Macomb Co.,

1—St. Angela, Revs. Robert J. Fisher; Joy Chakian; Deacon Lee Smith.
Res., 25001 Chippendale, 48066.
Church—Ten Mile Rd. and Chippendale, 48066. Tel: 810-445-6360; Fax: 810-445-6366.
School—Tel: 810-445-6375; Fax: 810-445-6382. Sr. M. LaVerne, C.S.B., Prin.
Sisters 8; Lay Teachers 16; Students 349.
Catechesis/Religious Programs—Tel: 810-445-6377. Elizabeth Hermes, D.R.E.
Students 250.
Convent—25165 Chippendale, 48066. Tel: 810-445-6370.

2—St. Athanasius, Rev. William P. Siebert; Deacon Michael O'Keefe.
Res., 18720 Thirteen Mile Rd., 48066. Tel: 810-772-1170; Fax: 810-776-2945.
Catechesis/Religious Programs—Carol Buboi, D.R.E.
Students 245.

3—St. Donald, Rev. Michael A. Donovan.
Res., 16330 Twelve Mile Rd., 48066. Tel: 313-773-3440; Fax: 810-773-1235.

4—Holy Innocents, Rev. Salvino Briffa.
Res., 26100 Ridgemont Rd., 48066. Tel: 810-777-7543; Fax: 810-777-1536.
School—Tel: 810-777-5266; Fax: 810-777-5231.
Lay Teachers 10; Students 130.
Catechesis/Religious Programs—Robert Dugas, D.R.E.
Students 130.

5—Sacred Heart, Rev. William Bonnici; Sr. Anne Mamienski, Pastoral Assoc.
Res., 18430 Utica Rd., 48066. Tel: 810-777-9116; Fax: 810-777-7958.
Catechesis/Religious Programs—Tel: 810-777-8150; Fax: 810-777-3288. Sr. Theresa Coulter, I.H.M., D.R.E.
Students 113.

Royal Oak, Oakland Co., St. Dennis, Revs. John P. Christ, O.S.C.; Gerald Thaar, O.S.C.
Res., 2200 E. 12 Mile Rd., 48067-1504. Tel: 248-544-2181; Fax: 248-544-9443.
School—1415 N. Stephenson, 48067-1504. Tel: 248-398-6555; Fax: 248-398-2878. Michael Reece, Prin.
Sisters 1; Lay Teachers 16; Students 342.
Catechesis/Religious Programs—Tel: 248-545-1926. Christine Wagberg, D.R.E.
Students 200.

St. Mary, Rev. Michael A. Woroniewicz; Rev. Msgr. Thomas H. Villerot; Sr. Therese Allgeyer, O.P.
Res., 730 Lafayette Ave. S., 48067. Tel: 248-547-1818; Fax: 248-547-4577. [CEM]
School—628 Lafayette Ave. S., 48067. Tel: 248-545-2140; Fax: 248-545-2303. William R. Farrand, Prin.
Lay Teachers 19; Students 290.
Catechesis/Religious Programs—Tel: 248-547-1810. Ms. Bridget Gasior, D.R.E.
Students 119.

Shrine of the Little Flower, Rev. Msgr. William M. Easton; Revs. Joseph R. Horn; Joseph A. Gerardi; Deacon Thomas M. Thomas. In res., Rev. Lambert H. Smits.
Res., 2123 Roseland Ave., 48073. Tel: 248-541-4122 (Office); Fax: 248-541-2838.
Church—2123 Roseland, 48067.
School—1621 Linwood, 48067. Tel: 248-541-4622; Fax: 248-541-6969. Sharon Dixon, Prin.
Lay Teachers 30; Students 639.
Academy—Tel: 248-549-2928; Fax: 248-546-2953. Walter Romano, Prin.
Lay Teachers 8; Students 137.
High School—3500 W. Thirteen Mile Rd., 48073. Tel: 248-549-2925; Fax: 248-549-2953. Thomas Kirkwood, Prin.
Lay Teachers 23; Students 283.
Catechesis/Religious Programs—Tel: 248-541-5133. Judy Maten, D.R.E.
Students 572.

St. Clair, St. Clair Co., St. Mary, Rev. Edward W. Ritter; Sr. Sharon Simon, O.P., Pastoral Assoc.
Res., 415 N. 6th St., 48079. Tel: 810-329-2255; Fax: 810-329-5997. [CEM]
School—Tel: 810-329-4150; Fax: 810-329-5705. Mrs. Marilynn Pavlov, Prin.
Lay Teachers 16; Students 358.
Catechesis/Religious Programs—Tel: 810-329-7801. Mrs. Sue Karas, D.R.E.
Students 553.
Convent—811 Orchard St., 48079. Tel: 810-329-2400.

St. Clair Shores, Macomb Co.,

1—St. Germaine, Rev. James L. Bjorum; Deacon Terrance Downey, Pastoral Assoc.
Office: 28301 Little Mack, 48081. Tel: 810-771-1750; Fax: 810-771-7634.
School—Tel: 810-771-0890. Mr. Gary Gunst, Prin.
Lay Teachers 18; Students 427.
Catechesis/Religious Programs—Edward McLeod, D.R.E.
Students 156.

2—St. Gertrude, Rev. John G. McGreevy, O.P. In res., Revs. Joachim N. Culotta, O.P.; Joseph Fogerty, O.P.
Res., 28839 Jefferson Ave., 48081. Tel: 810-777-9120; Fax: 810-777-8390. [CEM]
Catechesis/Religious Programs—Tel: 810-775-5820; Fax: 810-447-4729. Paul Lippard, D.R.E.
Students 252.

3—St. Isaac Jogues, Rev. Timothy P. Mazur.
Parish Center—21120 Benjamin Dr., 48081. Tel: 810-778-5100; Fax: 810-778-4458.
School—Tel: 810-771-3525; Fax: 810-778-8183.
Lay Teachers 20; Students 380.
Catechesis/Religious Programs—Mrs. Cynthia Branch, D.R.E.
Students 350.

4—St. Joan of Arc, Rev. Msgr. Ricardo E. Bass; Revs. Stanley Obloj; Michael J. Byrnes; Brian K. Cokonougher; Deacons Eugene E. DiCresce; Robert F. Busch.
Parish Center—22412 Overlake, 48080. Tel: 810-777-3670; Fax: 810-774-5528.
School—22415 Overlake, 48080. Tel: 810-777-8370; Fax: 810-447-3574. Mr. Don Ancypa, Prin.
Lay Teachers 35; Students 751.

Catechesis/Religious Programs—Tel: 810-772-1282. Sr. Marie Houle, O.P., D.R.E.
Students 658.

5—ST. LUCY, Rev. John C. Esper; Deacon Robert Herta. In res., Rev. Michael Loyson.
Res., 23401 Jefferson, 48080. Tel: 810-771-8300; Fax: 810-447-4220.
Catechesis/Religious Programs—Tel: 810-447-4222. Ms. Betty Frei, D.R.E.
Students 384.

6—ST. MARGARET OF SCOTLAND, Rev. Ronald W. Kurzawa; Deacon Ronald Channell. In res., Revs. Richard L. Treml; Gary Sylvester.
Res., 21201 Thirteen Mile Rd., 48082. Tel: 810-293-2240; Fax: 810-293-0116.
Catechesis/Religious Programs—Tel: 810-293-3280. Mary Paonessa, D.R.E.
Students 530.

Shelby Twp., St. John Vianney Church, Rev. Jerome J. Machlik.
Res., 54045 Schoenherr Rd., 48315. Tel: 810-781-6525; Fax: 810-781-6527.
Catechesis/Religious Programs—Tel: 810-781-2627. D.R.E.: Fritzi Bohlmann; Mary Lundgaard; Ida Johns.
Students 1,341.

St. Kieran, Rev. H. Thomas Johnson; Deacon James Cron.
Res., 53600 Mound Rd., 48316. Tel: 810-781-4901; Fax: 810-781-6516.
Catechesis/Religious Programs—Tel: 810-781-6515. Patricia Radacsy, D.R.E.
Students 1,205.

St. Therese of Lisieux, Rev. Thomas J. Sutherland.
Church—48115 Schoenherr Rd., 48315-4225. Tel: 810-254-4433; Fax: 810-254-5463.
Catechesis/Religious Programs—Students 774.

Southfield, Oakland Co.,

1—ST. BEATRICE, Rev. John Gagala.
Res., 17235 Mt. Vernon, 48075. Tel: 248-557-3342; Fax: 248-557-3427.

2—ST. BEDE, Rev. Lawrence A. Pettke. In res., Rev. Toma A. Behman.
Res., 18290 Twelve Mile Rd. W, 48076. Tel: 248-559-0577; Fax: 248-559-0752.
Church—Twelve Mile and Southfield Rds., 48076.
School—Tel: 248-559-0572. Beth Fischer, Prin.
Lay Teachers 12; Students 235.
Catechesis/Religious Programs—Tel: 248-559-0578. Pat Metz, D.R.E.
Students 36.

3—DIVINE PROVIDENCE, (Lithuanian), Rev. Aloyzas Volskis.
Res., 25335 W. 9 Mile Rd., 48034. Tel: 248-354-3429; Fax: 248-354-1773.

4—ST. IVES, Rev. William D. Sinatra; Deacon Ronald E. Rohlman.
Res., 29350 Lahser, 48034. Tel: 248-353-3410; Fax: 248-353-5412.
Catechesis/Religious Programs—Tel: 248-353-4550.
Students 99.

5—ST. MICHAEL, Revs. Lawrence W. Zurek, O.F.M.; Alex Kratz, O.F.M.; John C. Market, O.F.M., (Retired); Roch Farland, O.F.M., (Retired); Bro. Michael Schebeci, O.F.M., Pastoral Asoc.
Res., 25225 Code Rd., 48034. Tel: 248-356-8787; Fax: 248-356-1240.
School—Tel: 248-356-6113. Joseph Langs, Prin.
Sisters 2; Lay Teachers 11; Students 197.
Convent—22750 10 Mile Rd., 48034. Tel: 248-356-8785.

Southgate, Wayne Co., St. Pius X, Rev. Peter Petroske.
Office: 14101 Superior Ave., 48195. Tel: 734-285-1100; Fax: 734-285-5310.
Res., 14160 Longtin Ave., 48195.
School—Tel: 734-284-6500. Ann Hall, Elementary Prin.
Lay Teachers 19; Students 345.
Catechesis/Religious Programs—Liela Abass, D.R.E.
Students 196.

St. Hugh, Eugene E. Wojtewicz.
Res., 11300 Reeck Rd., 48195. Tel: 734-287-6990; Fax: 734-287-8109.

South Lyon, Oakland Co., St. Joseph, Rev. Kenneth M. Chase. Pastoral Assocs.: Sr. Eleanor Furman, O.S.F.; Deacon William Otto.
Res., 810 S. Lafayette, 48178. Tel: 248-437-1121; Fax: 248-437-3784.
Catechesis/Religious Programs—Tel: 248-437-3455. Mary Ann Sikorski, D.R.E.
Students 727.

Sterling Heights, Macomb Co.,

1—ST. BLASE, Rev. Msgr. Michael C. LeFevre; Rev. Thomas J. Kramer. Pastoral Assocs.: Sr. Megan McElroy, O.P.; Ms. Patricia DeBruce.
Res., 12151 E. 15 Mile Rd., 48312-5120. Tel: 810-268-2244; Fax: 810-268-1174.
Catechesis/Religious Programs—Tel: 810-268-3050.
Students 747.

2—SS. CYRIL AND METHODIUS, Revs. Elemir Joseph Mikus; Benjamin Kosnac.
Res., 41233 Ryan Rd., 48314. Tel: 810-726-6911; Fax: 810-726-5913.

3—ST. EPHREM, Rev. Ronald Milligan.
Res., 38900 Dodge Rd., 48312. Tel: 810-264-1230; Fax: 810-264-2757.
Catechesis/Religious Programs—Tel: 810-264-2777.
Students 375.

4—ST. JANE FRANCES DE CHANTAL, Rev. Gerard LeBoeuf.
Res., 38750 Ryan Rd., 48310. Tel: 810-977-8080; Fax: 810-977-9305.
Catechesis/Religious Programs—Tel: 810-977-0310.
Students 525.

5—ST. MALACHY, Rev. Joseph J. Gembala; Sr. Alys Currier, I.H.M., Pastoral Assoc.
Res., 14115 14 Mile Rd., 48312-6506. Tel: 810-264-1220; Fax: 810-264-1656.
Catechesis/Religious Programs—Tel: 810-268-4430. Ms. Patricia Whelan, D.R.E.
Students 424.

6—ST. MATTHIAS, Rev. Richard E. Cyr.
Res., 12509 Nineteen Mile Rd., 48313. Tel: 810-731-1300; Fax: 810-731-2576.
Catechesis/Religious Programs—Tel: 810-731-0650. Carol Jadach, D.R.E.
Students 610.

7—ST. MICHAEL, Revs. Lawrence J. Jackson; Francisco Restrepo; Deacon Lawrence Healy; Carrie Orlando, Pastoral Assoc.
Church—40501 Hayes Rd., 48313. Tel: 810-247-0020; Fax: 810-247-4081.
Res., 39443 Heatherheath, Clinton Twp., 48038. Tel: 810-286-3322.
Catechesis/Religious Programs—Tel: 810-247-0098. D.R.E.: Emily Gordon; Catherine McInerney.
Students 884.

8—OUR LADY OF CZESTOCHOWA, Revs. Adam Bobola, S.Ch.; Miroslaw Frankowski; Konrad Urbanowski, S.Ch.
Res., 3100 18 Mile Rd., 48314-3810. Tel: 810-977-7267; Fax: 810-977-2074.
Catechesis/Religious Programs—Sr. Bernadetta Gosciniak, D.R.E.
Students 420.

9—ST. RENE GOUPIL, Rev. Frederick J. Schweihofer; Sr. Mary Schmidlin, O.S.F., Pastoral Assoc.
Res., 35955 Ryan Rd., 48310. Tel: 810-939-7500; Fax: 810-939-7839.
Catechesis/Religious Programs—Mark Mals, D.R.E.
Students 516.

Taylor, Wayne Co.,

1—ST. ALFRED, Rev. Dennis C. Laesch.
Res., 9500 Banner, 48180. Tel: 313-291-6464; Fax: 313-291-2733.
Catechesis/Religious Programs—Tel: 313-291-3210. Beth A. Oley, D.R.E.
Students 250.

2—ST. CONSTANCE, Rev. Leo F. Sabourin; Deacon Joseph Mouro.
Res., 21555 Kinyon Rd., 48180. Tel: 313-291-4050; Fax: 313-291-5655.

3—ST. CYRIL OF JERUSALEM, Rev. Gary Morelli; Deacons Daniel J. Hurley; William A. Thome; Sr. Marion Therese Mackey, O.P., Pastoral Assoc.
Res., 6442 Pelham Rd., 48180. Tel: 313-381-3000; Fax: 313-381-5528.
School—Tel: 313-383-8585. John Champion, Dir.
Catechesis/Religious Programs—Tel: 313-383-5663. Michael Grube, D.R.E.
Students 225.

4—ST. PASCHAL, Rev. Robert Cislo.
Res., 22210 Champaign St., 48180. Tel: 313-291-4880; Fax: 313-291-7514.
School—Tel: 313-291-6650. Marcia Guerra, Prin.
Lay Teachers 9; Students 119.

Temperance, Monroe Co., St. Anthony, Rev. Gregory J. Deters.
Res., 4605 St. Anthony Rd., 48182. Tel: 734-854-1143; Fax: 734-854-4622. [CEM]
School—Tel: 734-854-1160. Sr. M. Joan Furlong, S.N.D., Prin.
Sisters of Notre Dame 4; Dominican Sisters 1; Lay Teachers 6; Students 185.
Catechesis/Religious Programs—Students 152.
Convent—4607 St. Anthony Rd., 48182. Tel: 734-854-2779.

Our Lady of Mt. Carmel, Rev. Alfred J. Miller; Sr. Aloise Paluszak, O.S.F.; Hazel Destatte, Pastoral Assoc.
Res., 810 Donna Dr., 48182. Tel: 734-847-2805; Fax: 734-847-8970.
Catechesis/Religious Programs—Tel: 734-847-1725.
Students 565.

Trenton, Wayne Co., St. Joseph, Rev. James A. Vedro, O.S.C.; Sr. Ellen Baker, I.H.M., Pastoral Assoc.
Parish Center: 2565 Third St., 48183. Tel: 734-676-9082; Fax: 734-676-6255. [JC]
School—Tel: 734-676-2565; Fax: 734-676-9744. Wanda Rovenskie, Prin.
Lay Teachers 10; Students 214.
Catechesis/Religious Programs—Tel: 734-676-7115. Fran Dawson, D.R.E.
Students 340.

St. Timothy, Rev. Charles S. Fontana.
Parish Office: 2901 Manning Dr., 48183. Tel: 734-676-5115; Fax: 734-676-6863.
Catechesis/Religious Programs—Tel: 734-676-5616. D.R.E.: Fritzi Bohlmann; Fran Dawson.
Students 243.

Troy, Oakland Co.,

1—ST. THOMAS MORE, Rev. Edward A. Belczak; Deacon John Vanneste.
Res., 4580 Adams Rd., 48098. Tel: 248-647-2222; Fax: 248-647-8192.
Catechesis/Religious Programs—Tel: 248-647-4680.
Students 1,365.

2—ST. ALAN, Rev. Gary M. Tierney; Sr. Mary Choiniere, S.S.J., Pastoral Assoc. In res., Revs. John A. Blaska; Bernard A. Schroll.
Church—3077 Glouchester, 48084. Tel: 248-649-5510; Fax: 248-649-6729.
Res., 2345 Coolidge Rd., 48084. Tel: 248-649-5511.

3—ST. ANASTASIA, Rev. Kenneth R. Kaucheck. Pastoral Assocs.: Sr. Kay Allberry, O.P.; Deacon Ronald Cook.
Res., 4571 John R. Rd., 48098. Tel: 248-689-8380; Fax: 248-689-7489.
Catechesis/Religious Programs—Tel: 248-689-1431. Elizabeth Murray, D.R.E.
Students 1,073.

4—ST. ELIZABETH ANN SETON, Rev. Ronald J. Essman.
Res., 280 E. Square Lake Rd., 48098. Tel: 248-879-1310; Fax: 248-879-2886.
Catechesis/Religious Programs—Tel: 248-879-1314.
Students 322.

5—ST. LUCY, (Croatian), Rev. Marko Puljic, O.F.M.
Res., 200 E. Wattles Rd., 48098. Tel: 248-619-9910; Fax: 248-619-9912.

Utica, Macomb Co., St. Lawrence, Revs. Timothy J. Szott; Timothy P. Birney; Sr. Janet Sullivan, I.H.M., Pastoral Assoc.
Res., 44633 Utica Rd., 48317. Tel: 810-731-5347; Fax: 810-731-5393.
School—Tel: 810-731-0135. Paul Gielow, Prin.
Lay Teachers 28; Students 737.
Catechesis/Religious Programs—Tel: 810-731-5072. Linda Sheets, D.R.E.
Students 836.

Walled Lake, Oakland Co., St. William, Rev. Michael G. Savickas; Deacons Richard T. Smith; Timothy J. Pilon. In res., Rev. Pascal Igwe.
Res., 531 Common St., 48390. Tel: 248-624-1421; Fax: 248-624-5273.
School—135 O'Flaherty, 48390. Tel: 248-669-4440; Fax: 248-669-2245. Alexandra Leidlein, Prin.
Lay Teachers 12; Students 260.
Catechesis/Religious Programs—Tel: 248-624-1371. Fran Dawson, D.R.E.
Students 630.

Warren, Macomb Co.,

1—ST. ANNE'S, Revs. Michael Kazer; Jerome Slowinski; Sr. Alice Miller, I.H.M., Pastoral Assoc.; Deacon Marvin Strzyzewski.
Res., 32000 Mound Rd., 48092. Tel: 810-268-3434; Fax: 810-268-4142.
School—Tel: 810-264-2911. Dr. Thomas Engel, Prin.
Intercommunity Sisters 1; Lay Teachers 30; Students 876.
Catechesis/Religious Programs—Clare Cooper, D.R.E.
Students 411.

2—ASCENSION, Rev. Norbert Maciejewski.
Res., 21050 Ascension St., 48089. Tel: 810-754-4000; Fax: 810-757-2342.
Catechesis/Religious Programs—Tel: 810-754-6741.
Students 56.

3—ST. CLETUS, Rev. Philip Briffa.
Office: 26256 Ryan Rd., 48091. Tel: 810-755-1313; Fax: 810-756-0724.
Res., 26262 Ryan Rd., 48091.
Catechesis/Religious Programs—Tel: 810-755-1350. Sr. Pauline Starner, S.S.J., D.R.E.
Students 105.

4—ST. DOROTHY, Revs. Richard Welsh; Thomas Puzio; Cathy Gasowski, Pastoral Assoc.
Res., 12255 Frazho, 48089. Tel: 810-754-3232; Fax: 810-754-3152.

Catechesis/Religious Programs—Tel: 810-759-1040.
Students 132.

5—St. Edmund, Revs. Robert J. Witkowski; Wojciech Wojcicki.
Res., 14025 Twelve Mile Rd., 48093. Tel: 810-772-2720; Fax: 810-772-5576.
Catechesis/Religious Programs—Tel: 810-773-9220; Fax: 810-772-5021.
Students 423.

6—St. Leonard of Port Maurice, Rev. Norbert Maciejewski; Sr. Patricia Eeckhout, Pastoral Assoc.; Deacon Edward Swartz.
Res., 14057 E. Nine Mile, 48089. Tel: 810-777-1350; Fax: 810-777-1247.

7—St. Louise, Rev. Thomas G. Rice; Deacons Wilhelm Kessler; Anthony Morici; Gary Meerschaert.
Res., 2500 Twelve Mile Rd., 48092. Tel: 810-751-3340; Fax: 810-751-0603.
Catechesis/Religious Programs—Tel: 810-751-3486. Mrs. Irmgard Kovacs, D.R.E.
Students 225.

8—St. Mark, Rev. Robert A. Ruedisueli; Deacon George R. Posavetz; Joann Loria, Pastoral Assoc.
Res., 4257 Bart, 48091. Tel: 810-759-3020; Fax: 810-759-3024.
Catechesis/Religious Programs—Tel: 810-759-3022.
Students 310.

9—St. Martin de Porres, Revs. Roman Pasieczny; Jacek Brewczynski. Pastoral Assocs.: Sr. Joan Popovits, O.P.; John McGovern.
Res., 31555 Hoover Rd., 48093. Tel: 810-264-7515; Fax: 810-264-4013.
Catechesis/Religious Programs—Tel: 810-264-7970. Dr. Diane Bucko, D.R.E.
Students 371.
Convent—31014 Shaw, 48093. Tel: 810-264-4894.

10—St. Paul Albanian Catholic Community, Rev. Anton Kcira, Admin.
Office: 3411 Twelve Mile Rd., 48092. Tel: 810-573-8110; Fax: 810-573-4107.
Res., 3239 E. Twelve Mile Rd., 48092. Tel: 810-573-8799.

11—St. Sylvester, Revs. Gary Schulte; Artemio Galos. Pastoral Assocs.: Sr. Ann Glombowski, O.P.; Deacon John L. Skladanowski.
Res., 11200 Twelve Mile Rd., 48093. Tel: 810-751-3636; Fax: 810-751-1766.
Catechesis/Religious Programs—Tel: 810-751-3510; Fax: 810-751-2208.
Students 372.

Washington, Macomb Co., SS. John and Paul, Rev. Gary Bueche. Pastoral Assocs.: JoAnne Owens; Lucy Sebastian.
Res., 7777 W. 28 Mile Rd., 48094. Tel: 810-781-9010; Fax: 810-781-7061.
Catechesis/Religious Programs—Tel: 810-781-9488.
Students 390.

Waterford, Oakland Co., Our Lady of the Lakes, Revs. Lawrence Delonnay; James Kean; Deacon Charles F. Johnson.
Res., 5481 Dixie Hwy., 48329. Tel: 248-623-0274; Fax: 248-623-2723.
School—Tel: 248-623-0250; Fax: 248-623-2274. Carl Uberti, Elementary Prin.
Lay Teachers 15; Students 496.
High School—Tel: 248-623-0340. Carl Uberti, Prin.
Sisters 2; Lay Teachers 23; Students 327.
Catechesis/Religious Programs—Tel: 248-623-0291; Fax: 248-623-1280. Patricia Tbla, D.R.E.
Students 460.

St. Benedict, Revs. H. Thomas Kuehnemund; Maria Geryk, Pastoral Assoc.
Parish Office—80 S. Lynn, 48328. Tel: 248-681-1534; Fax: 248-681-4501.
School—Tel: 248-682-5580. Jon Myers, Prin.
Lay Teachers 12; Students 112.
Catechesis/Religious Programs—Tel: 248-681-1536.
Students 152.

St. Perpetua, Rev. Richard S. Rakoczy.
Res., 134 Airport Rd., 48327. Tel: 248-682-6431; Fax: 248-682-7088.
Catechesis/Religious Programs—Bonnie Banaszek, D.R.E.
Students 336.

Wayne, Wayne Co., St. Mary, Rev. Jack H. Baker. Pastoral Assocs.: Sr. Patricia Hergenroether, S.S.J.; Deacon William Meahan.
34530 Michigan Ave., 48184. Tel: 734-721-8745; Fax: 734-721-0260.
School—34516 Michigan Ave., 48184. Tel: 734-721-1240; Fax: 734-467-7381. Ms. Catherine Myszka, Prin.
Lay Teachers 14; Students 297.
Catechesis/Religious Programs—Tel: 734-326-8180.
Students 185.

West Bloomfield, Oakland Co., Prince of Peace, Rev. Arnold J. Kosco; Deacon Edward Hilger.
Res., 4341 Savoie Tr., 48323. Tel: 248-681-9424; Fax: 248-681-5543.
Catechesis/Religious Programs—Tel: 248-681-5070. Carol Wojciak, D.R.E.
Students 479.

Westland, Wayne Co.,

1—St. Bernardine, Rev. Ronald Sayes.
Res., 31463 Ann Arbor Trail, 48185. Tel: 313-427-5150; Fax: 313-427-3319.
Catechesis/Religious Programs—Tel: 313-261-3050. Mary Jane Ayotte, D.R.E.
Students 215.

2—St. Damian, Rev. Lawrence Zurawski.
Res., 30055 Joy Rd., 48185. Tel: 734-421-6130; Fax: 734-513-4916.
School—Tel: 734-427-1680. Sr. M. Eileen, C.S.S.F., Prin.
Felician Sisters 2; Lay Teachers 13; Students 282.
Catechesis/Religious Programs—734-522-5383 Sr. M. Patricia, C.S.S.F., D.R.E.
Students 130.

3—Church of the Divine Savior, Rev. Alexander A. Kuras; Deacon Paul F. Pelchat.
Church—39375 Joy Rd., 48185. Tel: 734-455-3620; Fax: 734-455-7998.
Res., 9249 Caprice, Plymouth, 48170. Tel: 734-455-6964.
Catechesis/Religious Programs—Theresa Biendit, D.R.E.
Students 200.

4—St. Richard, Rev. Terence Treppa.
Res., 35637 Cherry Hill, 48186. Tel: 734-729-2240; Fax: 734-729-3132.
Church Office—35637 Cherry Hill Rd., 48186.
Catechesis/Religious Programs—Tel: 734-729-4411. Jeanne Martin, D.R.E.
Students 247.

5—SS. Simon and Jude, Rev. Gerard V. Bechard.
Office: 32500 Palmer Rd., 48186. Tel: 734-722-1343; Fax: 734-326-5466.
Catechesis/Religious Programs—D.R.E.: Mary Ann Kocsis; Margaret Reyez.
Students 165.

6—St. Theodore of Canterbury, Rev. Gary Michalik; Deacons John Kenny; Joseph Sullivan; James Hensel, (Retired).
Res., 8200 Wayne Rd., 48185. Tel: 734-425-4421; Fax: 734-425-0650.
Catechesis/Religious Programs—Tel: 734-425-7310.
Students 310.

White Lake, Oakland Co., St. Patrick, Revs. Thomas L. Meagher; Eugene Katcher.
Res., 9086 Hutchins Rd., 48386. Tel: 248-698-3100; Fax: 248-698-2350.
School—9040 Hutchins Rd., 48386. Tel: 248-698-2340. Mrs. Linda Meese, Prin.
Lay Teachers 10; Students 299.
Catechesis/Religious Programs—Students 1,198.

Woodhaven, Wayne Co., Our Lady of the Woods, Rev. Richard Macey.
Res., 21892 Gudith Rd., 48183. Tel: 734-671-5102; Fax: 734-671-2901.
Catechesis/Religious Programs—Tel: 734-671-0525. Patricia Butler, D.R.E.
Students 991.

Wyandotte, Wayne Co.,

1—St. Elizabeth, Rev. Charles M. Morris.
Res., 138 Goodell St., 48192. Tel: 734-284-7727; Fax: 734-284-7891.
Native American Ministry—Tel: 734-246-9458; Fax: 734-246-9463. Ms. Rochelle Montour Vaughn, Archdiocesan Coord.

2—St. Helena, Rev. P. Larry Siroskey.
Res., 753 Forest St., 48192. Tel: 734-284-4988; Fax: 734-282-0710.

3—St. Joseph, Rev. Thomas J. Moloney, S.C.A.
Res., 353 Elm St., 48192. Tel: 734-285-9840; Fax: 734-285-9745.
School—Tel: 734-285-2030; Fax: 734-285-0327. Mary Swinkey, Prin.
Lay Teachers 11; Students 173.
Catechesis/Religious Programs—Tel: 734-285-6453. Laurie Spano, D.R.E.
Students 247.

4—Our Lady of Mt. Carmel, (Polish), Rev. Walter J. Ptak.
Res., 976 Superior Blvd., 48192. Tel: 734-284-9135; Fax: 734-284-1367. [CEM]
School—2609 Tenth St., 48192. Tel: 734-285-5520; Fax: 734-285-9245. Miss Millie Bardoni, Elementary Prin.
Felician Sisters 3; Lay Teachers 12; Students 205.
High School—Tel: 734-284-7311; Fax: 734-284-6235. Sr. Mary Cordelia Szynkowski, C.S.S.F., High School Prin.
Felician Sisters 3; Lay Teachers 12; Students 100.
Catechesis/Religious Programs—Tel: 734-284-6145. Sr. Mary Adonia Ockalek, C.S.S.F., D.R.E.
Students 143.
Convent—2609 Tenth St., 48192. Tel: 313-284-7253.

5—St. Patrick, Rev. Raymond H. Lewandowski.
Office: 135 Superior Blvd., 48192. Tel: 734-285-9470; Fax: 734-285-1623.
Res., 105 Superior Blvd., 48192. Tel: 734-285-9472. [JC]
School—Wyandotte Catholic Consolidated School, Tel: 313-285-2030; Fax: 734-285-0327. Mary Swinkey, Elementary Prin.
Lay Teachers 11; Students 173.
High School—Gabriel Richard H.S., Tel: 313-284-1875. John Bres, High School Prin.
Students 520.

6—St. Stanislaus Kostka, (Polish), Rev. John P. Hedges; Deacons Patrick Bruen; Joseph Lennon.
Res., 266 Antoine St., 48192. Tel: 734-285-9509; Fax: 734-285-0124.
School—240 Antoine St., 48192. Tel: 734-282-3105; Fax: 734-282-7425.
Lay Teachers 10; Students 135.

Yale, St. Clair Co., Sacred Heart, Rev. Lawrence E. Dunn.
Res., 310 N. Main St., 48097. Tel: 810-387-2998. [CEM]
Catechesis/Religious Programs—Tel: 810-387-3361. Marian Boike, D.R.E.
Students 158.

Chaplains of Public Institutions

Detroit. *Alexander Blaine Memorial*. Attended from St. Peter and Paul. Tel: 313-961-8077.
Annapolis. Rev. Bernard Pilarski.
Art Centre Hospital. Attended from Lady of the Rosary. Tel: 313-875-6011.
Beaumont Hospital. Revs. Christopher Welch; Lloyd Thiel, O.F.M. Cap.
Bi-County Osteopathic. Rev. Luke Krotkiewicz.
Bon Secours. Sr. Therese Tighe, O.P., Chap.; Rita McEachen Neal, Chap.
Children's Hospital Tel: 313-745-5917. Sr. Janet Ryan, I.H.M., Dir.; Sr. Beverly Hindson, I.H.M., Chap.
Cottage Hospital. Attended from St. Paul's. Tel: 810-785-8855.
Crittendon Hospital. Rev. Walter Lezochowski.
Detroit General Hospital 48226. Tel: 313-224-0541. Sr. Adelaide Eiden, Chap.
Detroit Osteopathic Hospital. Attended from Cathedral of the Most Blessed Sacrament. 48226. Tel: 313-865-6300.
Detroit Psychiatric Institute 48226. Tel: 313-427-1533. Rev. Daniel O'Sullivan.
Detroit Receiving Hospital 48226. Rev. Gabriel Comelo; Sr. Janet Hudspeth, Chap.
Detroit Riverview Hospital. Attended from St. Charles.
Doctor's Hospital. Vacant. St. Peter and Paul, 48226. Tel: 313-961-8077.
Garden City Osteopathic Hospital. Rev. Bernard Pilarski.
Glen Eden Hospital. Attended from the Capuchin Community.
Grace Hospital-Northwest University. Mary Bartnik, Chap.
Harper Hospital and Rehabilitation Center. Revs. Gabriel Cohelo, O.F.M.Cap.; Anthony Abgali.
Henry Ford Hospital. Rev. Emiliano Auwen Diere; Sr. Fran Pokreifka, I.H.M., Chap.; Mrs. Marie Handley, Chap.
Heritage Hospital Tel: 810-295-6700. Sherri Christ.
Hutzel Hospital Tel: 313-831-3139. Rev. Gabriel Comelo, (Emergencies).
Kirkwood Hospital. Attended from St. Gregory. Tel: 313-861-0363.
Lapeer Regional. Attended from Immaculate Conception. Tel: 810-664-8594.
Lincoln Hospital. Attended from Holy Redeemer. Tel: 313-842-3450.
Macomb Hospital Center. (St. John's Health System). Mrs. Katherine Breslin, Chap.
Martin Place East Hospital. Attended from St. Vincent Ferrer. Tel: 810-542-8720.
McNamara Hospital. Attended from the Capuchin Community. Tel: 810-751-0410.
Mercy Hospital Detroit 48226. Sr. Rose Petrozzo, O.P., Chap.
Michigan Health Care Corporation. Vacant.
North Woodward Hospital. Attended from Blessed Sacrament Cathedral. Tel: 313-865-6300.
Northville State Hospital Tel: 810-349-1800. Rev. Stanislaus C. Kukulski.
Oakland General Osteopathic. (St. John's Health System). Sr. Stephanie Thompson, Chap.

Oakwood Hospital. Revs. Michael Gormley, S.A.C.; Richard Lileart; Sr. Ann Foley, Chap.
Palmer Osteopathic Hospital. Attended from St. Benedict. Tel: 313-868-3876.
Palmer Osteopathic Hospital-East. Attended from St. Matthew. Tel: 313-881-4049.
Pontiac Correction Camp. Attended from St. Patrick, Union Lake. Tel: 810-363-2441.
Pontiac General Hospital. Diane Guappone, Chap.
Pontiac Osteopathic Hospital. Diane Guappone, Chap.
Redford Community Hospital. Attended from St. Agatha. Tel: 313-531-0371.
Rehabilitation Institute. Sr. Therese LeBlanc, Dir.; Sr. Leslie Hartway, Chap.
Riverside Osteopathic Hospital. Attended from St. Joseph. Tel: 313-676-9082.
Saratoga General Hospital. Rev. Louis Resma.
Sinai Hospital. Rev. Kenneth J. Noetzel, S.J.
Southwest Detroit Hospital 48226. Tel: 313-963-4539. Rev. Thomas Lumpkin.
Veterans Administration Hospital. Rev. Joseph Duc Vu.
Warren Memorial Hospital. Vacant.
Wayne and Monroe County-Adults 305 Michigan Ave., 48226. Tel: 313-237-4684. John Humphrey, Chap.
Wayne Co 305 Michigan Ave., 48226. Tel: 313-237-4684. Abdulami Osman, Outreach Coord.
Wayne County Juvenile Justice c/o Team for Justice, 1035 St. Antoine, 48226. Tel: 313-965-3242. Bill Kresse, Chap.
Wayne County Youth Home 305 Michigan Ave., 48226. Tel: 313-237-5900. Thomas Carlier, Chap.
Wyandotte General Hospital. Attended from St. Helena. Tel: 313-284-4988.
Yale Community Hospital. Attended from Sacred Heart. Tel: 810-387-2998.
Zieger Osteopathic Hospital. Attended from Our Lady Queen of Angels. Tel: 313-825-4696.

CLINTON TOWNSHIP. *State Prisons* 24415 Crocker Blvd., 48036. Tel: 810-755-9359. Rev. Thomas R. Physician.

FARMINGTON. *Botsford General Hospital* St. Alexander's, 810-474-5748. Rev. Louis Resma.

MOUNT CLEMENS. *Macomb County Adults & Macomb County Jail* c/o Macomb County Jail, 43565 Elizabeth Rd., 48043. Tel: 810-307-9326. Jo Kudela, Chap.
Macomb County Youth Home. Attended from St. Peter's, Mount Clemens. Tel: 313-237-5962.
Monroe County Jail. Vacant. Tel: 313-237-5900.
Mount Clemens General Hospital. Rev. John P. Hedges.

PONTIAC. *Oakland and Lapeer County-Adults* 14 Judson St., 3rd Floor, P.O. Box 431366, 48343-1366. Tel: 810-338-9310. Peggy Devaney, Chap.
Oakland, Lapeer, and St. Clair County 14 Judson St., 3rd Floor, P.O. Box 431366, 48343-1366. Tel: 810-338-9310. Chaplains: Betty Clark; Miguel Rivera.
Oakland, Lapeer, Macomb, and St. Clair Counties-Juveniles 14 Judson St., 3rd Floor, P.O. Box 431366, 48343-1366. Tel: 810-338-9310. Carleen Ward, Chap.

PORT HURON. *Mercy Hospital Port Huron* 48060. Sr. Margaret Weber, R.S.M., Chap.; Sr. M. Frances Villerot, R.S.M., Chap.
Port Huron Hospital. Attended from St. Joseph. 48060. Tel: 810-985-7750.

Special Assignment:
Reverend Monsignors—
Quinn, John M., Dept. of Education
Sable, Robert M., Prelate Auditor of the Roman Rota, Vatican
Zenz, John P., Moderator of the Curia
Reverend Fathers—
Banazak, Gregory, Faculty, Orchard Lake
Bilot, James D., Vocations Office
Browne, Ronald, Judicial Vicar of the Metropolitan Tribunal & Faculty, Sacred Heart Major Seminary
Bugarin, Michael, Catholic Univ., Washington, D.C.
DePorres-Cox, Jesse, O.P., St. Dominic; Evangelization Office at Annunciation Parish
Fabian, John, Companions of Christ the Lamb, Paradise, MI
Farrell, Edward, SHMS Faculty
Halfpenny, Patrick, Vice-Rector, SHMS
Havron, Daniel, O.F.M., Office of Evangelization
Jozwiak, Ronald J., Tribunal & Admin., St. Josaphat, Detroit
Kasza, John, Asst. Chancellor, Faculty SHMS, Office of Christian Worship
Kosanke, Charles, SHMS Faculty
Kreimes, Paul, SHMS Faculty
Lunnon, William, Staff, Bishop Borgess HS
Miller, George, Tribunal
Monforton, Jeffrey M., Sec. Cardinal, 1234 Washington Blvd., Detroit, MI 48226-1808
Slowinski, Jerome, Tribunal, Assoc. Pastor, St. Anne, Warren, MI
West, John H., Rector, St. John's Center for Youth & Families; Spiritual Dir. for Society of St.Vincent de Paul
Williams, Clarence E., C.PP.S., African American Catholic Ministries Office
Williams, Robert Hayes, Tribunal & Pastor, St. Justin, Hazel Park

---

On Duty Outside the Archdiocese:
Reverend Monsignors—
Boyea, Earl, Rector/Pres., Pontifical College Josephinum, Ohio
Reverend Fathers—
Cassidy, Richard, East Aurora, NY
Molnar, Michael, Pastoral Care, Cayman Islands
Reyesmedina, Carlos, Xalatlaro, Edo. de Mexico
Singelyn, Robert K., Recife, Brazil
Trent, James F., Detention Ministry, Diocese of Santa Rosa
Walsh, Jerome, Jackson Heights, NY

Military Chaplains:
Reverend Fathers—
Bjorklund, Brian, U.S. Navy
Borycz, Edmund S., U.S. Army
Hogan, Timothy D., U.S. Navy
Jagielski, James, U.S. Army
Kaul, John, U.S. Naval Reserves

Graduate Studies:
Reverend Fathers—
Byrnes, Michael J., Pontifical Gregorian University, Rome
Jones, Daniel J., Pontifical North American College, Rome
McClory, Robert J., Pontifical North American College, Rome
Ricardo, John C., Pope John Paul II Institute for Family, Washington, DC
Williams, George W., Pontifical Angelicum University, Rome

Absent on Leave:
Reverend Fathers—
Carnago, William J.
Ellis, Matthew
Hogan, Richard
Loyson, Michael
McLaughlin, Andrew
Shirilla, Gerald
Stochmal, Marek

Absent on Sick Leave:
Reverend Fathers—
MacLennan, Donald
Quane, Ralph

Retired:
Reverend Monsignors—
Baldwin, Edward J., Sacred Heart Seminary, 2701 Chicago Blvd., Detroit, MI 48206
DeCneudt, Ferdinand, Father Tallieu Senior Citizen Residence, Apt. B104, 18740 Thirteen Mile Rd., Roseville, MI 48066-1378
Flanigan, Gerald A., 14469-B Levan Rd., Livonia, MI 48154-5094
Horkan, Vincent J., 15181 Ford Rd., Apt. 119, Chapel Ct., Dearborn, MI 48126
Martin, Gerald F., St. Rene Goupil Parish, 35955 Ryan Rd., Sterling Heights, MI 48310
Monticello, Robert V., 14469 Levan Rd., Apt. C, Livonia, MI 48154-5094
Sherzer, William J., St. Priscilla Parish, 19120 Purlingbrook Rd., Livonia, MI 48152-1986
Villerot, Thomas H., 14453 Levan Rd., Apt. A, Livonia, MI 48154-5090
Weier, John A., Maryhaven, 11350 Reeck Rd., Rm. 73, Southgate, MI 48195-2278
Reverend Fathers—
Bartone, Donald E., 1715 River Rd., Apt. 21, St. Clair, MI 480793547
Bauer, Erwin J., 1975 S. Channel, Harsens Island, MI 48028-9797
Berg, Paul, Sacred Heart Major Seminary, 2701 Chicago Blvd., Detroit, MI 48206-1799
Blaska, John A., St. Alan Parish, 2345 Coolidge, Troy, MI 48084-3665
Blaszczyk, Thaddeus J., 2819 Park Dr., Milford, MI 48380-3445
Bodde, Frederick A., 6116 River Rd., East China, MI 48054-4731
Bologna, Anthony F., St. Gabriel Parish, 8118 W. Vernor, Detroit, MI 48209-1524
Borowski, Ladislaus, DeSerrano Res., C-226, 17255 Common Rd., Roseville, MI 48066-1954
Bresnahan, Thomas J., 14453 Levan Rd., Apt. B, Livonia, MI 48154-5090
Britz, Gerald F., 8781 Lakeshore, Lexington, MI 48450-9600
Brock, David F., 41464 Whitetail Ln., Canton, MI 48188-2073
Broderick, Leo P., 407 S. Parkway, Algonae, MI 48001
Browne, George, 165 S. Water St., #204, Marine City, MI 48039
Burke, Walter E., 17582 N. Whitefish Point Rd., Paradise, MI 49768-9615
Burkholder, Robert, 84 - 770 Kili Dr., Apt. 632, Waianae, HI 96792
Burns, Francis H., 810 North Shore, St. Clair Shores, MI 48080-2828
Byrne, Thomas, P.O. Box 375, Flat Rock, MI 48134-0375
Canavan, John D., 11395 Oakwood Dr., Jerome, MI 49249-9516
Child, John F., 18740 W. Outer Dr., Dearborn, MI 48128
Ciesniewski, Richard P., Casa Del Rio Apts., 12751 Plaza Del Rio Blvd., #3107, Peoria, AZ 85381
Complo, Daniel C., 38 E. Willow, Apt. C, Monroe, MI 48162-2644
Curtin, James E., 211 Saratoga, Ferndale, MI 48220
Dacey, Donald, Fairlane Meadows, 5148 Heather Dr., #116, Dearborn, MI 48126-2884
Decker, Maurice C., Rapalo North Condominiums, 306, 1701 S. Flagler, West Palm Beach, FL 33401-7344
Dietz, Francis, 14453 Levan Rd., Apt. C, Livonia, MI 48154-5090
Dorr, Richard J., 38110 John P. St., Clinton Twp., MI 48036-1218
Dowell, William J., 14467 Levan Rd., Apt. A, Livonia, MI 48154-5093
Duffey, Thomas, 665 W. Warren, #115, Detroit, MI 48201
Dunn, John, Casa Maria, 670 Maple Vista, Imlay City, MI 48444-1471
Erpelding, Martin L., 4309 Pratt, Grand Blanc, MI 48439-9114
Esper, Thomas, 164 Shoreline Rd., East Port Sanilac, MI 48469-9769
Fares, Lawrence, 36773 Kelly Rd., Clinton Township, MI 48035-1325
Fauser, Arthur W., Our Lady of Sorrows Parish, 23815 Powers, Farmington, MI 48336-2461
Fedewa, Eugene F., Our Lady Queen of Peace Parish, 20955 Bournemouth, Harper Wds., MI 48225-2301
Femmininеo, Joseph P.
Ferens, Joseph F., 1870 Lakesview Blvd., Oxford, MI 48371-4548
Ferrero, Bartholomew, Instituto Figlie S. Gaetano Casa Boccardo, Via Roma n. 9, 10060 Pancalieri, Torino Italy
Flynn, Thomas P.
Forish, Andrew, 19450 Mayfield, Apt. 104, Livonia, MI 48152-1389
Fortuna, George B., 14467-C Levan Rd., Livonia, MI 48154-5022
Gattari, Valentine A., St. Matthias Parish, 12509 19 Mile Rd., Sterling Heights, MI 48313
Gierut, Joseph A., 9106 Del Prado Dr., Palos Hills, IL 60465-5009
Goentges, Charles J., 14468 Levan Rd., Apt. C, Livonia, MI 48154-5094
Goodrow, Robert A., Chap., USNR, (Retired), 1891 Big Crane Loop, Port Orange, FL 32124
Hadad, Gerard A., 10300 Cypress Cove Dr., #1211, Fort Myers, FL 33908
Haener, Robert W., 14467 Levan Rd., Apt. B, Livonia, MI 48154-5093
Hall, John F., St. Lawrence Parish, 44633 Utica Rd., Utica, MI 48317-5468
Hardy, John J., 2140 Hardy Ln., P.O. Box 488, Ortonville, MI 48462
Hayes, James L., Villa Maria, Apt. 1, 15131 Newburg Rd., Livonia, MI 48154-5035
Heidelberger, Ronald, 555 Brush St., Apt. 2214, Detroit, MI 48226
Herman, Jerome A., 1604 S.E. 9th St., Stuart, FL 34996-3233
Higdon, C. Paul, 3900 Aspen Dr., #345, Port Huron, MI 48060-8622
Hoffmaster, Harry, 2500 River Rd. #41, Marysville, MI 48040-1949
Hubble, Karl D., 1593 River Rd., Apt. 1-D, St. Clair, MI 48079-3543
Immel, William A., 3054 Faye Dr., P.O. Box 166, Port Hope, MI 48468-9364
Janiga, Joseph, 7039 Sarena, Detroit, MI 48210-1549
Jones, Raymond, Sunpoint Senior Living, 5959 Sun Lake Blvd., Sebring, FL 33872
Kaznowski, Valentine J., 7758 Colony Dr., Algonac, MI 48001-4138
Kenna, John A., Maryhaven, 11350 Reeck Rd., Apt. 74, Southgate, MI 48195-2286
Keveney, William

Koltuniak, Michael P., 14464-C Levan Rd., Livonia, MI 48154-5092
Konopka, Edward F., 7950 N. McNab, Apt. 210, Tamarac, FL 33321-8436
Kosicki, Bohdan W., 5630 Klettner, St. Clair, MI 48079-1918
Kosnik, Anthony, 3308 Doremus, Hamtramck, MI 48212
Kowalczyk, Sigismund C., 879 N. Channel Dr., Harsens Island, MI 48028
Kowalski, George, 12765 Walnut St., Southgate, MI 48195-1161
Kowalski, Ralph E., 14467-D Levan Rd., Livonia, MI 48154-5093
Kreft, Henry S., 3621 Port Austin Rd., Port Austin, MI 48467-9624
Krieg, Jerome L., 2300 Watkins Lake Rd., Waterford, MI 48328-1439
Krisciunevicius, Victor, 11427 Irene Ave., Warren, MI 48093-6545
Kubik, John M., SS. Peter & Paul Parish, 7685 Grandville, Detroit, MI 48228-3392
Kukulski, Stanislaus C., 3021 Evaline, Hamtramck, MI 48212
Kundrat, Michael J., 81393 Belle River Rd. #15, Memphis, MI 48041-4441
Kuntz, Donald B., 9245 North River Rd., Algonac, MI 48001-4007
Lipczewski, Boleslaus, Assumption Grotto Parish, 13770 Gratiot, Detroit, MI 48205
Lombardi, Albert U., 14465 Levan Rd., Apt. B, Livonia, MI 48154-5092
Maierle, John P., 15055 Hubbard, #26, Livonia, MI 48154
Maliszewski, Francis S., 986 Wexford Way, Rochester Hills, MI 48307-2973
Maloney, Richard E.
Markham, John W., 3138 E. Canfield St., Detroit, MI 48207-1597
McGoldrick, William J., 467 Fairford Rd., Grosse Pointe, MI 48236-2410
Mikus, Elemir, 90863 Oreske 5, Skalica, Slovakia, Europe
Muir, Edmund D., 443 Cerromar Ln., Apt. 300, Venice, FL 34293-4408
Murphy, Daniel J., 14455 Levan Rd., Apt. A, Livonia, MI 48154
Ndrevashay, Primus P., 3845 E. Greenway, Apt. 215, Phoenix, AZ 85032
Neffy, Arthur, 17825 15 Mile Rd., Apt. #25, Clinton Twp., MI 48035-5035
O'Brien, Kevin, 32090 Grand River Ave., #94, Farmington, MI 48336-4172
O'Callaghan, John F., Marywood Nursing Center, Rm. 209, 36975 Five Mile Rd., Livonia, MI 48154-1871
O'Dea, Loren F., Our Lady of Sorrows Parish, 23815 Power, Farmington, MI 48336-2461
O'Hagan, James P., Fox Manor, 2350 Watkins Lake Rd., Waterford, MI 48328
O'Leary, Michael G., St. Paul Parish, 157 Lake Shore Rd., Grosse Pointe Farms, MI 48236-3760
O'Neill, Charles F., Our Lady of Grace Parish, 8679 Riverview, Dearborn Heights, MI 48127-1482
O'Sullivan, Daniel, 3941 Crooks Rd., Troy, MI 48084
Page, Leon J., 12109 Avondale, Warren, MI 48089-3922
Partensky, Leonard J., 6747 N. Wayne Rd., 440 Bldg. A-3, Westland, MI 48185-2798
Petron, William G., 15745 Charleston Dr., Clinton Township, MI 48038-1016
Pettit, William J., 14469 Levan Rd., Apt. D, Livonia, MI 48154-5094
Prus, Edward J., 48 West Robert St., Hazel Park, MI 48030
Reckinger, Robert A., 14455 Levan Rd., Apt. C, Livonia, MI 48154-5091
Reyesmedina, Carlos, 13909 Deepwood Ct., Sterling Heights, MI 48312
Ryder, Joseph F., 3015 Moonlake Dr., W. Bloomfield, MI 48323-1844
Sadler, Alfred H., 5571 Pointe Dr., E. China, MI 48054-4163
Samonie, Jacob, 34644 Spring Valley Dr., Westland, MI 48185-9457
Scheuerman, Edward L.
Schmidberger, Richard, 4171 Fourth St., Brown City, MI 48416
Schroll, Bernard A., St. Alan Parish, 2345 Coolidge, Troy, MI 48084-3665
Schweihofer, Walter J., Presbyterian Village East, 33875 Kiely Dr., Rm. 414, Chesterfield Township, MI 48047-3604
Sierocki, Paul E., 1723 N. Lafayette, Dearborn, MI 48128-1145
Sirianni, Jasper F., Our Lady of Mt. Carmel Parish, 10828 Brandon Rd., Emmett, MI 48022-4504
Sito, Joseph, 14455 Levan Rd., Apt. B, Livonia, MI 48154-5091
Slominski, Fabian B., 5405 Christi Dr., Warren, MI 48091-4196
Stanievich, J. Walter, 22295 Green Hill, Apt. 29, Farmington Hills, MI 48335-4384
Szarek, Mitchell, SS. Peter & Paul Parish (Westside), 7685 Grandville, Detroit, MI 48228
Trese, John A., P.O. Box 919, Hamburg, MI 48139
Tucci, Italo, Fr. Taillieu Sr. Citizens #107, 18780-13 Mile Rd., Roseville, MI 48066-1382
Ugolik, Richard, 57088 Copper Creek Dr., Washington Township, MI 48094-2822
Van der Linden, Peter J., 1370 Aspen Dr., Apt. 4, Marysville, MI 48040-2047
Villerot, Henry E., De Serrano Residence, 17255 Common Rd. B-200, Roseville, MI 48066-1954
Wallace, Leonard P., 9537 Seaway Dr., Algonac, MI 48001
Weingartz, Francis A., St. Anne Parish, 32000 Mound Rd., Warren, MI 48092-1200
Welch, William F., Marywood Nursing Center, 36975 W. Five Mile Rd., Livonia, MI 48154-1871
Wittstock, John J., 3603 Villa Knolls Dr., Las Vegas, NV 89120-4104
Wolber, Ferdinand A., Woodlore Condominiums, 33399 Fargo, Livonia, MI 48152-1453
Xuereb, Paul, 16900 Paul Revere, Clinton Twp., MI 48035-2379
Yagley, Carl J., St. Clement Parish, 8075 Ritter Ave., Center Line, MI 48015-1499
Zdrodowski, Francis, Marywood Nursing Home, 36975 W. Five Mile Rd., Livonia, MI 48154
Zeeb, Charles, 18569 Manorwood West, Clinton Township, MI 48038-1266
Ziemba, Walter J., St. Mary's College, 3535 Indian Trail, Orchard Lake, MI 48324-1623
Zwers, John B., 14461 Levan Rd., Livonia, MI 48154

Permanent Deacons:
Abler, Donald, Senior Status
Ball, John H., St. Vincent Ferrer, Madison Heights
Barbera, John, St. Valerie/St. Claude, Clinton Twp.
Belleman, Patrick, Ascension, Warren
Berch, James, St. Isaac Joghes, St. Clair Shores
Bloomfield, Richard, Our Lady of Mt. Carmel, Wyandotte
Bovitz, Robert, St. Joseph, Trenton
Bruen, Patrick T., St. Stanislaus Kostka, Wyandotte
Busch, Robert F., St. Joan of Arc, St. Clair Shores
Buyle, Valere, St. Edmund, Warren
Carroll, Brian, St. Regis, Birmingham
Chambers, Frank, St. Colman, Farmington Hills
Channell, Ronald, St. Margaret of Scotland, St. Clair Shores
Cominotto, Anthony, Senior Status
Conlen, Patrick, St. Joan Neumann, Canton
Conlin, Richard R., St. Benedict, Highland Park
Connors, John J., St. Joseph, Port Huron
Cook, Ronald W., St. Anastasia, Troy
Cornell, Peter, St. Anthony, Belleville
Cousino, Wesley, St. Joseph, Erie
Cox, Donald J., St. Blase, Sterling Heights
Cron, James A., St. Kieran, Shelby Twp.
D'Argis, Leo, St. Colette, Livonia
Damaste, Richard, St. Mary Queen of Creation, New Baltimore
Daratony, Joseph J., Resurrection, Canton
Darga, Daniel J., Our Lady of La Salette, Berkley
Delbeke, Robert G., St. Rita, Detroit
Deshaw, Gerald, Immaculate Conception, Lapeer
Desjarlais, Eugene B., Madonna University, Livonia
Desmedt, Frank, St. Lawrence, Utica
DeWitt, Robert N., Our Lady of Grace, Dearborn Heights
DiCresce, Eugene, St. Joan of Arc, St. Clair Shores
Downey, Terrance E., St. Germaine, St. Clair Shores
Dullinger, Aloysius, Senior Status
Feliciano, Raul, St. Anne, Detroit
Fitzgerald, Robert C., St. Patrick, White Lake
Fleming, John Michael, St. Joseph, Pontiac
Fosmire, Charles, St. John Neuman, Canton
Gabel, Raymond, St. Albert the Great, Dearborn Heights
Gergosian, Edward, Senior Status
Girard, Lawrence, St. Sebastian, Dearborn Heights
Gonzalez, Norman, Senior Status
Goodhue, Harold, St. Roch, Flat Rock
Hardwick, Ralph, Senior Status
Healy, Lawrence, St. Michael, Sterling Heights
Hensel, James L., Senior Status
Herta, Robert, St. Lucy, St. Clair Shores
Hulan, Richard, St. Barbara, Dearborn
Hurley, Daniel, St. Cyril, Taylor
Igoe, James, St. Richard, Westland
Ingels, Michael M., St. Mary, Monroe
Iskra, Joseph, St. Raymond, Detroit
Jablonowski, Alexander, St. Daniel, Clarkston
Jackson, Douglas, Jr., Martyrs of Uganda, Detroit
Jamieson, William E., Our Lady Star of the Sea, Grosse Pointe
Jimenez, Rafael, St. Stephen, Mary Mother of the Church
Johnson, Charles, Our Lake of the Lakes, Waterford
Johr, William H., St. Matthew, Detroit
Jones, Wyatt, Annunciation, Detroit
Junak, Donald C., St. Louis, Mount Clemens
Jurewicz, Marion, St. Clemens, Centerline
Kendzierski, Anthony, St. Isidore, Macomb
Kenny, John, St. Edith, Livonia
Kessler, Wilhelm, St. Louise, Warren
Krueger, Gary R., Holy Cross, Marine City
Krzeminski, Eugene, St. Kenneth, Plymouth
Kunik, Raymond L., St. Priscilla, Livonia
LaLone, Norman C., Senior Status
Leach, Donald, Our Lady of Good Counsel, Plymouth
Lewandoski, Anthony, Senior Status
Loafman, Frank, Senior Status
Lubien, Raymond J., St. Bartholomew, Detroit
Machus, Paul H., St. William, Walled Lake
Maiuri, Rocco, St. Isaac Joques, St. Clair Shores
Marks, Stephen, St. Kieran, Shelby Twp.
Marku, John, St. Christopher, Detroit
Markulike, Michael J., Senior Status
McCoy, Elgia, St. Anthony, Detroit
McIntyre, Ronald L., Holy Redeemer, Detroit
McKale, Michael, Holy Name, Birmingham
McLeod, Robert E., St. Mary, St. Clair
Meahan, William, St. Mary, Wayne
Meerschert, Gary, St. Louise, Warren
Mignacca, Egidio, St. Malachy, Sterling Heights
Misiak, Richard, St. Edith, Livonia
Modes, Robert, St. Mel, Dearborn Heights
Morad, Alfred J., Senior Status
Morello, Steven, Holy Family, Novi
Morici, Anthony, St. Louise, Warren
Motowski, Norbert, St. Christopher, Detroit
Mouro, Joseph, St. Constance Parish, Taylor
Murphy, Thomas, Our Lady of the Woods, Woodhaven
Noon, Archie J., St. Mary, Milford
Nowicki, Kenneth, Immaculate Conception, Anchorville
O'Keefe, Michael, St. Athanasius, Roseville
Otto, William, St. Joseph, South Lyon
Ovies, Robert, St. Columban, Birmingham
Pardo, Gary, Our Lady of Loretto, Redford
Pelchat, Paul, Senior Status
Pickett, Brock, St. Irene, Dundee
Piro, Rudolph P., St. Genevieve, Livonia
Posavetz, George, St. Mark, Warren
Prince, Benjamin, St. Gregory the Great, Detroit
Quigley, Donald, Our Lady of Victory, Northville
Renaud, Timothy, St. Mary, Royal Oak
Riopelle, Ernest, St. Conrad, Melvindale
Rivier, Robert, St. Elizabeth, Wyandotte
Rodriguez, Brigido, St. Vincent de Paul, Pontiac
Rohlman, Ronald, St. Ives, Southfield
Sanders, Hubert, St. Gerard, Detroit
Sandstrom, Donald, Our Lady of Good Counsel, Detroit
Santeramo, John, St. Thomas Aquinas, Detroit
Schlesser, Peter, Annunciation, Detroit
Shubik, Richard, St. Paul, Grosse Pointe Farms
Skladanowski, John L., St. Sylvester, Warren
Skubick, Charles G., St. Andrew, Rochester
Smigell, Gerald, St. Thecla, Clinton Twp.
Smith, Lee, St. Angela, Roseville
Smith, Michael T., St. Hugo of the Hills, Bloomfield Hills
Smith, Richard, St. William, Walled Lake
Sobolewski, Don F., St. Ladislaus, Hamtramck
Solomon, James, Redemption, Melkite, Warren
Springer, Mark, St. Alexander, Farmington Hills
Stankiewicz, Clement, St. Christine/St. Gemma, Detroit
Stevens, Truman, St. Clare of Montefalco, Grosse Pointe
Stimpson, Bill, Jr., Precious Blood, Detroit
Strye, Edward, St. Michael, Pontiac
Strzyzewski, Marvin, St. Anne, Warren
Sullivan, Joseph, St. Theodore, Westland
Sullivan, Lawrence
Sullivan, Timothy, Our Lady of Good Counsel, Plymouth
Swartz, Edward, St. Leonard, Warren
Szwarc, John, St. Hugh, Southgate
Thomas, Thomas M., St. Barnabas, Eastpointe; Shrine of the Little Flower, Royal Oak
Thome, William A., St. Cyril of Jerusalem, Taylor
Tombler, Eugene, Guardian Angels, Clawson
Tremmel, Robert, Sacred Heart, Grosse Ile

Valdez, Ferando, St. Vincent de Paul, Pontiac
Van Brook, Arthur, Holy Spirit, Highland
Vanneste, Johnny M., St. Thomas More, Troy
Vasquez, Jesus, St. Vincent de Paul, Pontiac
Vestuto, Richard, St. Michael, St. Joseph & St. Vincent de Paul, Pontiac
Waldmann, William L., Holy Family, Novi
Ward, James, St. Thomas a Becket, Canton
Wilson, Edward C., Jr., St. Paul of Tarsus, Clinton Township
Wright, Richard, St. Michael, Pontiac
Yezak, Thomas, St. Joseph, Lake Orion

INSTITUTIONS LOCATED IN THE ARCHDIOCESE

[A] SEMINARIES, ARCHDIOCESAN

DETROIT. *Sacred Heart Major Seminary, Inc.*, 2701 Chicago Blvd., 48206. Tel: 313-883-8500. Most Rev. Allen H. Vigneron, Rector & Pres.; Revs. Patrick F. Halfpenny, Vice Rector & Dean of Seminarians; Earl Boyea, Dean of Studies; Sr. Mary Ward, O.P., Registrar.

The College of Liberal Arts. Revs. Charles Kosanke, Dir. Undergraduate Seminarians; Richard Macey, Spiritual Dir.; Stephen Vileo; Stanislaw Wszolek; Sr. Mary Finn, H.V.M., Dir. The Apostolic Experience Program; Mrs. Karen Mehaffey, Dir. of Libraries; Dr. Deborah Friauff, Dir. Music; Ms. Jane Schaub, Dir. Learning Center; Dr. John Goyette.

The School of Theology. Revs. Paul Kreimes; Daniel J. Trapp, Spiritual Dir.; Rev. Msgr. Clifford F. Ruskowski; Rev. Ronald Browne, Dir., Graduate Seminarians; Sr. Kathleen Ronan; Revs. Gerard Bolduc, O.F.M.; James Jorgenson, (Orthodox Church in America); Dr. Patricia Cooney-Hathaway; Dr. Mark Latkovic; Sr. Mary Lou Putrow, O.P.; Dr. William Riordan.

The Institute for Pastoral Ministry. Mrs. Patricia A. Rennie, Dean of The Institute for Ministry; Ms. Suzanne Schreiber, Asst. Dean of The Institute for Recruitment & Retention.

Seminary Total: Priests 13; Sisters 4; Lay Faculty 8; Students 280.

ORCHARD LAKE. *SS. Cyril and Methodius Seminary*, 3535 Indian Trail, 48324. Tel: 248-683-0311; 313-963-8075; Fax: 248-738-6735. Rev. Msgr. Stanley E. Milewski, D.H.L. (DET), Emeritus; Rev. Msgr. Francis B. Koper, D.Min. (WIL), Rector; Karen Shirilla, Ph.D., Academic Dean; Mrs. Carol Boulanger, Lay Ministry Formation; Rev. Czeslaw M. Krysa (BUF), Dean of Formation; Gary Lovod, Comptroller; Mrs. Mary Jo Wagener, Registrar; Revs. Stanislaw Flis, S.T.D. (Poland), Dir. Admissions and Recruitment; James K. Mazurek, M.Div. (PIT), Devel. Exec. Sec., Natl. Alumni Assoc.; Roman Nir (Poland), Archivist; Kathleen Castillo, M.A., Dir. Field Ed.; Raymond Myslakowski, Dir. Liturgical Music; Nancy Ward, M.S.L.S., Librarian; Rev. Msgr. Zdzislaw Peszkowski, Ph.D. (Poland), Emeritus; Revs. Gregory Banazak, S.T.D.; Janusz Kukulka, M.A. (Poland); Michael Monshau, O.P., Ph.D.; Vincenty Przepiora, O.Cist., S.T.D. (Poland); Walter J. Ziemba, Ph.D. (DET), Emeritus. Students 95.

[B] SEMINARIES, RELIGIOUS OR SCHOLASTICATES

BERKLEY. *Loyola House.* (Novitiate of the Chicago-Detroit Provinces of the Society of Jesus), 2599 Harvard Rd., 48072. Tel: 248-399-8132; Fax: 248-399-0910. Revs. Timothy J. Shepard, S.J., Dir. Novices; Mark W. Andrews, S.J., Asst. Dir. Novices; Karl Kiser, S.J., House Supr.; Mark George, S.J.; Sr. Theresa Blaquiere, R.S.M., Asst. to Novice Directors. Priests 4; Sisters 1; Novices 9.

OXFORD. *St. Benedict Monastery*, 2711 E. Drahner Rd., 48370. Tel: 248-628-2249; Fax: 248-628-4658. Headquarters Novitiate House of Sylvestrine Benedictine Monks in the United States. Revs. Daniel J. Homan, O.S.B., Conventual Prior & Retreat Dir.; Michael R. Green, O.S.B., Subprior. Priests 3; Brothers 8; Chapels 2.

[C] COLLEGES AND UNIVERSITIES

DETROIT. *Marygrove College*, 8425 W. McNichols Rd., 48221. Tel: 313-927-1200

For a complete listing, refer to the Colleges and Universities section.

University of Detroit Mercy, McNichols Campus, 4001 W. McNichols Rd. at Livernois, 48219-0900. Tel: 313-993-1000; Fax: 313-993-1534

For a complete listing, refer to the Colleges and Universities section.

LIVONIA. *Madonna University*, 36600 Schoolcraft Rd., 48150. Tel: 734-432-5300; Fax: 734-432-5393

For a complete listing, refer to the Colleges and Universities section.

ORCHARD LAKE. *Saint Mary's College*, 3535 Indian Trail, 48324. Tel: 248-683-0521; Fax: 248-683-0433

For a complete listing, refer to the Colleges and Universities section.

[D] HIGH SCHOOLS, INTER-PAROCHIAL

DETROIT. *Bishop Borgess High School*, 11685 Appleton, 48239. Tel: 313-255-1100; Fax: 313-255-1102. Sr. Joan Charnley, I.H.M., Prin.; Ms. Patrice Evans, Youth Minister. Priests 1; Sisters 3; Lay Teachers 18; Lay Admin. & Personnel 2; Students 200.

East Catholic High School, 7320 St. Anthony Pl., 48213. Tel: 313-921-9650; Fax: 313-921-8905. Co-Principals: Ms. Mary Jane Novitsky; Mr. David Soules. Sisters 1; Lay Teachers 12; Students 120.

St. Martin de Porres High, 13436 Grove, 48235. Tel: 313-864-3330; Fax: 313-864-3648. Ms. Sunbeam Hughes, Prin. Priests 1; Sisters 3; Lay Teachers 23; Students 327.

St. Vincent Middle School, 2020 14th St., 48216. Tel: 313-961-6773; Fax: 313-961-6774. Ms. Kathleen McBride, Prin. Lay Teachers 4; Students 95.

HARPER WOODS. *Bishop Gallagher High School*, 19360 Harper, 48225. Tel: 313-886-0855; Fax: 313-886-6398. James J. Wasukawis, Prin. Sisters 2; Lay Teachers 12; Students 190.

MADISON HEIGHTS. *Bishop Foley Catholic High School*, 32000 Campbell Rd., 48071. Tel: 248-585-1210; Fax: 248-585-3667. Alex M. Gajewski, Prin. Priests 1; Sisters 1; Lay Teachers 38; Students 534.

Bishop Foley Venture Fund, 32000 Campbell Rd., 48071. Tel: 248-585-1210; Fax: 248-585-3667. Paul Marzec, Pres.

MARINE CITY. *Cardinal Mooney Catholic College Preparatory School*, 660 S. Water St., 48039. Tel: 810-765-8825; Fax: 810-765-7164. Dr. Elsie L. Ogden, Prin. Priests 1; Sisters 4; Lay Teachers 16; Students 200.

MONROE. *St. Mary Catholic Central High School.* (Coed), 108 W. Elm Ave., 48162. Tel: 734-241-0663; Fax: 734-241-9042. Ms. Beth A. Dusseau, Prin. Sisters 1; Lay Teachers 29; Students 442.

PONTIAC. *Notre Dame Preparatory High School and Marist Academy*, 1300 Giddings Rd., 48340-2108. Tel: 248-373-5300; Fax: 248-373-8024. Revs. Leon M. Olszamowski, S.M., Pres.; David Kennerley, S.M.; Joseph C. Hindelang, S.M.; Deacon Anthony Morici. Priests 3; Brothers 11; Lay Teachers 77; Students 1109.

RIVERVIEW. *Gabriel Richard High School*, 15325 Pennsylvania Rd., 48192. Tel: 313-284-1875; Fax: 313-284-9304. John A. Bres., Prin. Brothers 2; Sisters 2; Lay Teachers 33; Students 530.

ROYAL OAK. *Shrine High School*, 3500 W. 13 Mile Rd., 48073. Tel: 248-549-2925; Fax: 248-549-2953. Mr. Thomas P. Kirkwood, Prin. Priests 1; Lay Teachers 31; Students 290.

[E] HIGH SCHOOLS, PRIVATE

DETROIT. *Dominican High School and Academy*, 9740 McKinney Ave., 48224. Tel: 313-882-8500 (High School & Academy). Adrian Dominican Sisters. Admin. Team: Sr. Tarianne DeYonker, O.P., Pres.; Mrs. Rosalie Cohen, Prin.; Mrs. Janet Demerchant, Business Mgr. Sisters 3; Lay Teachers 19; Students 223.

Loyola High School, 15325 Pinehurst, 48238-1633. Tel: 313-861-2407; Fax: 313-861-4718. Revs. David F. Mastrangelo, S.J., Pres./Prin.; Justin J. Kelly, S.J. Deacons 1; Priests 3; Brothers 2; Sisters 1; Lay Teachers 12; Students 140.

University of Detroit Jesuit High School and Academy, 8400 S. Cambridge, 48221. Tel: 313-862-5400; Fax: 313-862-3299. Revs. Timothy T. Shannon, S.J., Pres.; R. James Kurtz, S.J.; John F. Libens, S.J.; Patrick J. Rice, S.J.; Keith J. Esenther, S.J.; Martin T. Connell, S.J.; Thomas M. Ryan, S.J.; Robert H. Schmidt, S.J.; Ronald F. Torina, S.J.; Bro. James J. Boynton, S.J. Priests 10; Lay Teachers 38; Students 922; Chapels 2.

BLOOMFIELD HILLS. *Academy of the Sacred Heart*, 1250 Kensington Rd., 48304. Tel: 248-646-8900; Fax: 248-646-4143. Religious of the Sacred Heart. Sr. Bridget Bearss, R.S.C.J., Headmistress. Sisters 3; Lay Teachers 60; Students 468.

Brother Rice Endowment Fund. (The "Foundation"), 7101 Lahser Rd., 48301-4045. Tel: 248-647-2526. Bro. William A. Dogan, C.F.C., Prin.; Margie Clugston, Dir. Devel. & Contact Person.

Brother Rice High School, 7101 Lahser Rd., 48301-4045. Tel: 248-647-2526; Fax: 248-647-2532. Congregation of Christian Brothers. Bro. William A. Dogan, C.F.C., Prin. Brothers 4; Sisters 2; Lay Teachers 46; Students 690.

Marian High School for Young Women, 7225 Lahser Rd., 48301. Tel: 248-644-1750; Fax: 248-644-6107. Sr. Lenore Pochelski, I.H.M., Prin. Sisters 2; Lay Teachers 32; Students 460.

FARMINGTON HILLS. *Mercy High School for Girls*, 29300 Eleven Mile Rd., 48336. Tel: 248-476-8020; Fax: 248-476-3691. Sisters of Mercy. Sr. Regina Marie Doelker, R.S.M., Prin. Faculty 68; Students 942.

HARPER WOODS. *Notre Dame High School*, 20254 Kelly Rd., 48225-1287. Tel: 313-371-8965. Marist Fathers. Revs. John Sajdak, S.M., Prin.; John Bryson, S.M.; Raymond Ouellette, S.M.; Normand Martin, S.M.; Juan Gonzales, S.M. Priests 5; Sisters 3; Lay Teachers 28; Students 470.

Regina High School for Girls, 20200 Kelly Rd., 48225-1284. Tel: 313-526-0220; Fax: 313-526-5850. Sr. Mary Leanne, Prin. Sisters of St. Joseph of the Third Order of St. Francis 8; Lay Teachers 42; Students 752.

LIVONIA. *Ladywood High School*, 14680 Newburgh Rd., 48154. Tel: 313-591-1544; Fax: 313-591-4214. (Private School for Girls). Sr. Mary Ann Smith, C.S.S.F., Prin. Students 515.

ORCHARD LAKE. *St. Mary's Preparatory*, 3535 Indian Trail, 48324. Tel: 248-683-0530. Mr. James Glowacki, Headmaster; Rev. Timothy Whalen, Chancellor; Mr. Joseph Whalen, Dir., Admissions; Mr. Leonard Karschnia, Academic Dean. Priests 1; Lay Teachers 42; Students 416.

REDFORD. *The Catholic Central Endowment Trust* 48239-2999, 14200 Breakfast Dr. Tel: 313-534-0660. Gregory Grabowski, Dir.

Catholic Central High School, 14200 Breakfast Dr., 48239. Tel: 313-534-0660; 261-3387 (Res); Fax: 313-534-2683. Basilian Fathers. Revs. Michael A. Buentello, C.S.B.; Richard J. Elmer, C.S.B., Supr.; John J. Ward, C.S.B.; Edward W. Donoher, C.S.B.; Kenneth B. McKernan, C.S.B.; John H. Menner, C.S.B.; Raymond Paramo, C.S.B.; Richard A. Ranalletti, C.S.B., Prin.; Charles C. Smith, C.S.B.; Joseph A. Miller, C.S.B.; John P. Wheeler, C.S.B. Priests 10; Lay Teachers 61; Students 1,123.

WARREN. *De La Salle Collegiate for Boys*, 14600 Common Rd., 48093-3397. Tel: 810-778-2207; Fax: 810-778-5118. High School Brothers of the Christian Schools. Bro. Joseph Jozwiak, F.S.C., Prin. Brothers 5; Sisters 2; Lay Teachers 45; Students 748.

La Salle Warren, Inc., 14600 Common Rd., 48093. Tel: 908-842-7420. Bro. Kevin Gilhooly, F.S.C., Contact Person.

[F] ELEMENTARY SCHOOLS, INTER-PAROCHIAL

DETROIT. *Eastside Vicariate School*, 4230 McDougall, 48207. Tel: 313-921-0023; Fax: 313-921-0009. Ms. Gayle Koyton, Prin.

Genesis Catholic Elementary School, 20045 Joann, 48205. Tel: 313-839-2330. (Combined Parish Schools from Our Lady of Good Counsel and St. Raymond). Ms. Carol A. Smith, Prin. Lay Teachers 15; Total Enrollment 230.

St. Casimir Elementary School, 3361 23rd St., 48208. Tel: 313-894-0880. Sr. M. Leonard Bartkowiak, S.F.C.C., Prin.

CANTON. *All Saints Regional School*, 48735 Warren Rd., 48187-1233. Tel: 734-459-2490; Fax: 734-459-0981. Ms. Jacqueline Brown, Prin. Total Enrollment 455.

PORT HURON. *McCormick Catholic Academy.* (Grades 6-8), 2865 Henry, 48060. Tel: 810-985-9599; Fax: 810-985-9686. Mrs. Deborah A. Krueger, Prin. Lay Teachers 8; Students 70. A consolidation of the following three parish schools in Port Huron: St. Edward (Lakeport), St. Joseph and St. Mary.

ROCHESTER. *Holy Family Regional School*, 1240 Inglewood, 48307. Tel: 248-656-1234; Fax: 248-656-3494. (Regional). Sr. Karen Hawver, S.C., Prin. Students 561.

[G] ELEMENTARY, PRIVATE

BLOOMFIELD HILLS. *Academy of the Sacred Heart*, 1250 Kensington Rd., 48304. Tel: 248-646-8900; Fax: 248-646-4143. Religious of the Sacred Heart. Sr. Margaret Mary Canty, R.S.C.J., Headmistress. Sisters 4; Lay Teachers 54; Students 418.

[H] GENERAL HOSPITALS

DETROIT.

For a complete listing, refer to the Hospitals section.

St. John Hospital and Medical Center, 22101 Moross Rd., 48236. Tel: 313-343-4000

For a complete listing, refer to the Hospitals section.

CLINTON TOWNSHIP. *Mercy Mount Clemens Corporation*, 15855 Nineteen Mile Rd., 48038. Tel: 810-263-2300; Fax: 810-263-2614

For a complete listing, refer to the Hospitals section.

GROSSE POINTE. *Bon Secours Cottage Health Services*, 468 Cadieux Rd., 48230. Tel: 313-343-1900

For a complete listing, refer to the Hospitals section.

Bon Secours Hospital, 468 Cadieux Rd., 48230. Tel: 313-343-1000

For a complete listing, refer to the Hospitals section.

LIVONIA. *Marian Village Corporation*, 36475 Five Mile Rd., 48154. Tel: 734-665-4800, Ext. 2301

For a complete listing, refer to the Hospitals section.

St. Mary Hospital, 36475 W. Five Mile Rd., 48154. Tel: 734-655-4800; Fax: 734-655-1620

For a complete listing, refer to the Hospitals section.

PONTIAC. *St. Joseph Mercy - Oakland*, 900 Woodward Ave., 48341-2985. Tel: 248-858-3000
For a complete listing, refer to the Hospitals section.

PORT HURON. *Mercy Hospital of Port Huron*, 2601 Electric, 48060-6518. Tel: 810-985-1500; Fax: 810-985-1508
For a complete listing, refer to the Hospitals section.

SOUTHFIELD. *Providence Hospital*, 16001 W. Nine Mile Rd., P.O. Box 2043, 48037. Tel: 248-424-3000; Fax: 248-424-3035
For a complete listing, refer to the Hospitals section.

[I] SPECIAL HOSPITALS AND SANATORIA FOR INVALIDS

DETROIT.
For a complete listing, refer to the Special Care Facilities section.

LAKE ORION. *Guest House for Women Religious*, 1840 W. Scripps Rd., Box 68, 48360. Tel: 248-391-3100; Fax: 248-391-1553
For a complete listing, refer to the Special Care Facilities section.

LIVONIA. *Marycrest Manor*, 15475 Middlebelt Rd., 48154. Tel: 734-427-9175; Fax: 734-427-9520
For a complete listing, refer to the Special Care Facilities section.

Marywood Nursing Care Center, 36975 W. Five Mile Rd., 48154. Tel: 734-464-0600; Fax: 734-464-4846
For a complete listing, refer to the Special Care Facilities section.

MOUNT CLEMENS. *St. Joseph Mercy Living Care Center*, 37700 Harper, 48043. Tel: 810-468-0827
For a complete listing, refer to the Special Care Facilities section.

WATERFORD. *Lourdes Nursing Home*, 2300 Watkins Lake Rd., 48328. Tel: 248-674-2241; Fax: 248-674-1211
For a complete listing, refer to the Special Care Facilities section.

[J] HOUSING AND/OR COMMUNITY FACILITIES FOR THE AGING

DETROIT. *St. Catherine's House*, 1641 Webb Ave., 48206. Tel: 313-868-4505
For a complete listing, refer to the Special Care Facilities section.

St. Joseph's Home, 4800 Cadieux Rd., 48224. Tel: 313-882-3800; Fax: 313-882-6944
For a complete listing, refer to the Special Care Facilities section.

ALLEN PARK. *Little Sisters of the Poor*, P.O. Box 610, 48101. Tel: 734-462-2809
For a complete listing, refer to the Special Care Facilities section.

BLOOMFIELD HILLS. *St. Elizabeth's Briarbank*, 39315 Woodward Ave., 48304. Tel: 248-644-1011; Fax: 248-644-1596
For a complete listing, refer to the Special Care Facilities section.

CLINTON TWP. *A Friends House Adult Day Care Center*, 16931 19 Mile Rd., Ste. 140, 48038. Tel: 810-412-8494; Fax: 810-412-8084
For a complete listing, refer to the Special Care Facilities section.

FARMINGTON HILLS. *Trinity Continuing Care Services*, P.O. Box 9185, 48331-9185. Tel: 248-305-7600; Fax: 248-305-7933
For a complete listing, refer to the Special Care Facilities section.

LIVONIA. *Marybrook Manor*, 36975 W. Five Mile Rd., 48154. Tel: 734-464-9667; Fax: 734-464-4846
For a complete listing, refer to the Special Care Facilities section.

Ryan Senior Residences of the Archdiocese of Detroit, Inc., Central Office, 36800 Schdolcraft, 48150. Tel: 313-953-5873
For a complete listing, refer to the Special Care Facilities section.

ST. CLAIR SHORES. *Sisters of Bon Secours Nursing Care Center*, 26001 E. Jefferson, 48081. Tel: 810-779-7000
For a complete listing, refer to the Special Care Facilities section.

SOUTHFIELD. *Sheltering Arms*, 18310 W. 12 Mile, 48076. Tel: 248-557-7373; Fax: 248-559-2309
For a complete listing, refer to the Special Care Facilities section.

WATERFORD. *Fox Manor, Inc.*, 2350 Watkins Lake Rd., 48328. Tel: 248-674-9590
For a complete listing, refer to the Special Care Facilities section.

Lourdes Assisted Living Corporation, 2300 Watkins Lake Rd., 48328. Tel: 248-674-2241; Fax: 248-674-1211
For a complete listing, refer to the Special Care Facilities section.

St. Jude Home, Inc., 2300 Watkins Lake Rd., 48328. Tel: 248-673-5179
For a complete listing, refer to the Special Care Facilities section.

[K] MONASTERIES AND RESIDENCES OF PRIESTS AND BROTHERS

DETROIT. *Jesuit Community at the University of Detroit*, Lansing-Reilly Hall, 4001 W. McNichols Rd., 48221. Tel: 313-993-1000.
(Corporate Title: The Jesuit Community Corporation at the University of Detroit Mercy). Mailing Address: P.O. Box 19900, 48219. Revs. Mark R. Bandsuch, S.J.; Mark G. Henninger, S.J.; Arthur F. McGovern, S.J.; Gary R. Wright, S.J.; Gerald F. Cavanagh, S.J.; Terrence M. Curry, S.J.; Paulinus F. Forsthoefel, S.J.; George F. Lundy, S.J.; Brian P. O'Donnell, S.J.; Oswald A. Mascarenhas, S.J. (India); Norman G. McKendrick, S.J.; Herman J. Muller, S.J.; John D. O'Neill, S.J.; Sushil Sah India; John A. Saliba, S.J. (Malta); D. Clayton Schario, S.J.; Raphael Shen, S.J. (China); John M. Staudenmaier, S.J.; R. Gerard Albright, S.J.; John E. Dister, S.J.; Eugene L. Donahue, S.J.; Bro. Henry C. Kuhn, S.J.

Jesuit Provincial Office-Detroit Province of the Society of Jesus, 7303 W. Seven Mile, 48221-2198. Tel: 313-861-7500; Fax: 313-861-4230. Very Rev. John F. Libens, S.J., Prov.; Revs. Keith J. Esenther, S.J., Exec. Asst. & Asst. for Higher Education; John E. Dister, S.J., Asst. for Pastoral & Dir. of Ignatian Lay Volunteer Corps.; Walter L. Farrell, S.J., Treas.; Jerome K. Odbert, S.J., Bus. Mgr.; Robert J. Scullin, S.J., Asst. for Pastoral Ministries; Dennis T. Dillon, S.J., Asst. for Formation; Richard H. Twohig, S.J., Asst., Secondary Educ.; M. Joseph Casey, S.J., Asst. for Health Care. Priests 156; Brothers 16; Scholastics 12.
Priests assigned outside the U.S.: Rev. Richard M. Mackowski, S.J., Piazza S. Maria Maggiore 7, Rome, Italy, 00185. Tel: 39-6-6701-7140; Fax: 3964465576. Rev. Thomas H. Radloff, S.J., Spiritual Dir. at North American College, 000120 Vatican City State. Tel: 3966869441; Fax: 3966867561. Rev. W. Jared Wicks, S.J., Piazza della Pilotta 4, Rome, Italy, 00187. Tel: 39667015454; Fax: 39667015413. Rev. Michael A. Evans, S.J., Loyola House, P.O. Box 21399, Nairobi, Kenya. Tel: 254-2-569-494. Rev. Theodore W. Walters, S.J., Nyegezi Social Training Institute, P.O. Box 307, Mwanza, Tanzania. Tel: 255-28-50560; Fax: 255-28-50575. Rev. Gregory J. Hyde, S.J., Pedro Arrupe Residence, Ateneo De Manila University, P.O. Box 216, U.P. Campus, 1144, Quezon City, Metro Manilla, Phillipines. Rev. Kevin L. Flannery, S.J., Pontificia Universita Gregoriana, Piazza Della Pilotta 4, 00187 Rome, Italy. Tel: 39-6-6701-5213; Fax: 39-6-6701-5413. Rev. Joseph E. Mulligan, S.J., Colegio Centroamericano, Apdo. 2419, Managua, Nicaragua. Tel: 5052786965.
Members in the U.S. residing outside the Province: Revs. Thomas S. Acker, S.J.; David C. Bayne, S.J.; Peter J. Bernardi, S.J.; Martin J. Calkins, S.J.; Martin L. Chase, S.J.; Joseph P. Daoust, S.J.; J. Peter Deane, S.J., 606 W. Sterns Rd. Apt. F, Temperance, 48182. Tel: 734-847-3738. Revs. Joseph F. Downey, S.J.; Edward A. Flint, S.J.; Francis T. Gignac, S.J.; Dennis T. Glasgow, S.J.; Howard J. Gray, S.J.; Raymond P. Guiao, S.J.; Francis J. Houdek, S.J.; Patrick M. Kelly, S.J.; Timothy J. Kesicki, S.J.; John L. Kieffer, S.J.; William F. King, S.J.; John P. Langan, S.J.; Daniel P. Liderbach, S.J.; John A. Lucal, S.J.; Mark S. Massa, S.J.; Edward J. Mattimoe, S.J.; George C. Maynard, S.J.; J. Thomas McClain, S.J.; John M. McManamon, S.J.; Timothy J. Meier, S.J.; Joseph G. Mueller, S.J.; George B. Murray, S.J.; John W. O'Malley, S.J.; Paul D. Panaretos, S.J.; James S. Prehn, S.J.; James F. Riley, S.J.; Philip C. Rule, S.J.; Robert J. Scullin, S.J.; Donald M. Serva, S.J.; Edward J. Siebert, S.J.; Michael F. Steltenkamp, S.J.; James E. von Tobel, S.J.; Earl A. Weis, S.J.; Robert J. Welsh, S.J.; John V. White, S.J.; Eric A. Zimmer, S.J.; Bro. Jerome J. Pryor, S.J.

Maryknoll Fathers and Brothers, 12709 Pembroke, 48235. Tel: 313-342-0330. Rev. Paul Brien, M.M., Dir.

P.I.M.E. College Community, 17330 Quincy Ave., 48221. Tel: 313-861-2866; Fax: 313-342-6816. Revs. Fernando Milani, P.I.M.E., Rector; Mark Tardiff, P.I.M.E., Spiritual Dir. Seminarians 9. P.I.M.E. Missionaries. (Pontifical Institute for Foreign Missions). P.I.M.E. Mission Center, 17330 Quincy Ave., 48221. Tel: 313-342-4066; Fax: 313-342-6816. Rev. Francis Mosskolder, P.I.M.E., Mission Center Dir. Vocations Office; Foster Parents Mission Club; Leprosy Relief Society; Printing Press; P.I.M.E. World Magazine; Public Relations Office.

P.I.M.E. Missionaries of SS. Peter and Paul. (Pontifical Institute for Foreign Missions). P.I.M.E. Motherhouse in Detroit, 17330 Quincy, 48221. Tel: 313-342-4066; Fax: 313-342-6816. Revs. Bruno Piccolo, P.I.M.E., Prov. Supr.; John B. Boracco, P.I.M.E.; James Coleman, P.I.M.E.; Luciano Ghezzi, P.I.M.E.; George Berendt, P.I.M.E.; Raffaele Magni, P.I.M.E.; Dominic Rossi, P.I.M.E.; Edward Miley, P.I.M.E.; Francis Mosskolder, P.I.M.E.; Giovanni Vecchio, P.I.M.E. Brothers 1; Franciscan Sisters of St. Joseph (Mexico City) 4.

St. Bonaventure Friary, 1740 Mt. Elliott Ave., 48207-3496. Tel: 313-579-2100; Fax: 313-579-2275. Legal Title: *Province of St. Joseph of the Capuchin Order, Inc.* Provincialate: Revs. Daniel Fox, O.F.M.Cap., Prov. Min.; Perry McDonald, O.F.M.Cap., Prov. Vicar; Bro. David Swab, O.F.M.Cap., Sec. Religious Affairs; Rev. Lloyd Thiel, O.F.M.Cap., Public Rels. & Devel.; Mr. John Kook, Sec. & Treas.; Revs. James Zelinski, O.F.M.Cap., Mission Secretariat; James Wolf, O.F.M.Cap., Archivist.
Priests of the Province Assigned Outside the U.S.: Rev. Charles Bantle, O.F.M.Cap., Diocese of Naha - Chancery, # Chome 7-2 Asato (Naha), Okinawa, Japan, 902; Fax: 011-098-863-8474. Rev. Carmel Flora, O.F.M.Cap., St. Lawrence Community, 545 Tingal Rd., Wynnum North, Qld. 4178, Australia; Fax: 011-61-7-3348-5141. Rev. Patrick McSherry, O.F.M.Cap., Capuchin General Curia, Via Piemonte, 70, Rome, Italy, 00187; Fax: 011-3906-482-8267. Rev. John Myers, O.F.M.Cap., 59 Newton Rd., Newton Adelaide SA, 5074 Australia. In Residence in the Archdiocese of Detroit (excluding parishes): Bro. Sam Ciraulo, O.F.M.Cap, Canterbury Woods, 700 Tobin Dr., Apt. 15, Inkster, 48141. Bros. Daniel Vena, O.F.M.Cap; Joseph Monachino, O.F.M.Cap., 28526 Hoover Rd., Apt. #4, Warren, 48093. Assigned to St. Bonaventure Friary: Bro. Larry LaCross, O.F.M.Cap., Local Min.; Revs. Philip Naessuns, O.F.M.Cap., Vicar; Gabriel Prashant Coelho, O.F.M.Cap.; Daniel Fox, O.F.M.Cap.; Charles Hart, O.F.M.; Joseph Maloney, O.F.M.Cap.; Perry McDonald, O.F.M.Cap.; Albert Sandor, O.F.M.Cap.; James Wolf, O.F.M.Cap.; Bros. Mark Carrico, O.F.M.Cap.; Michael Drobnicki, O.F.M.Cap.; Thomas Kroll, O.F.M.Cap.; Daniel Vena, O.F.M.Cap.; Leo Wollenweber, O.F.M.Cap.; Vincent Reyes, O.F.M.Cap.; Richard Merling, O.F.M.Cap.

St. Mary's Friary, 5275 Kensington, 48224. Tel: 313-884-5303; Fax: 313-886-7370. Michael Gaffney, O.F.M.Cap.; Revs. James Zelinski, O.F.M.Cap.; Lawrence Abler, O.F.M.Cap.

St. Paul of the Cross Community, Congregation of the Passion, 23335 Schoolcraft, 48223. Tel: 313-531-0562; Fax: 313-535-9207. A center for the Passionist Fathers & Brothers in mid-western & north central United States. Members of this community conduct parish missions, renewals & retreats for laity, clergy & religious, Forty Hours, Devotion & other ministries. Revs. Sebastian MacDonald, C.P., Supr.; Rene Champagne, C.P.; David Colhour, C.P.; John Devany, C.P.; James Thoman, C.P., Dir. Retreat Center; Randal Joyce, C.P.; Paul Kim, C.P.; Robert Weiss, C.P.; Bros. William Baalman, C.P.; John Gebauer, C.P. Priests 8; Brothers 1.

St. Sylvester Monastery, 17320 Rosemont Rd., 48219. Tel: 313-532-6064; Fax: 313-531-0739. Revs. Livius Paoli, O.S.B., Prior; Bartholomew Kraemer, O.S.B.; John Stopponi, O.S.B.; Leo Cornelli, O.S.B.; John Colautti, O.S.B.; Bernard Schinn, O.S.B., Holy Family Church, 641 Chrysler Express Way. Tel: 313-963-2046; Fax: 313-961-0065.

BLOOMFIELD HILLS. *Congregation of Christian Brothers, Brother Rice Community*, Carroll Hall, 3575 Lincoln Dr., 48301-4001. Tel: 248-647-1547; Fax: 248-647-8170. Bros. Arthur M. Arndt, C.F.C., Supr.; William A. Dogan, C.F.C., Prin. In res. Bros. Robert E. Beckstrom, C.F.C.; Benjamin L. Favero, C.F.C.; Norbert B. Hueller, C.F.C.; David A. MacIntyre, C.F.C.; W. Rudolph Younghans, C.F.C. Brothers 7.

DEARBORN. *Society of St. Paul*, 7050 Pinehurst, 48126. Tel: 313-582-2033; Fax: 313-582-2970. Revs. Anthony Cheveney, S.S.P.; Joseph A. Triano, S.S.P., Supr.; Bros. Gerard T. Roche, S.S.P.; Emmanuel Canas; Peter Lyne, S.S.P.; Patrick Patrky. Priests 1; Brothers 4.

DEARBORN HEIGHTS. *Our Lady of Grace Monastery*, Mariannhill Mission Society, 23715 Ann Arbor Trail, 48127. Tel: 313-561-7140; 561-8888; Fax: 313-561-9486. Vocation Office: Tel: 313-274-2893. Revs. Francis Claerr, C.M.M.; Anthony Kirschner, C.M.M., (Retired); Anthony Gathen, C.M.M., Mission Procurator-Vocation Dir.; Raymond Lucasinsky, C.M.M., Supr. of House; Timothy Mock, C.M.M., Asst. Prov. Treas.; Thomas Szura, C.M.M., Prov. Treas.; Aloysius Blonigen, C.M.M., Retreat Dir.; Reinhold Schmitt, C.M.M.; Thomas Heier, C.M.M., Editor of LEAVES; Vergil Heier, C.M.M.; Lambert Kempkes, C.M.M. In res. Bros. Otto Waldmueller, C.M.M.; Jamie Miller, C.M.M.; Francis Berridge, C.M.M. Priests 11; Brothers 3.

LIVONIA. *Marist Fathers & Brothers Community*, 32509 Scone, 48154-4165. Tel: 734-266-1475; Fax: 734-266-1575. Revs. Ronald DesRosiers, S.M., Local Supr. & Madonna Univ.; Frank Grispino, S.M., Madonna Univ.; John Kiselica, S.M.

RIVERVIEW. *Crosier Community of Riverview*, 13249 Pennsylvania Rd., 48192. Tel: 313-283-0112; Fax: 313-283-2809. Revs. Jude Verley, O.S.C.; John P.

Christ, O.S.C.; Bruce C. Maxwell, O.S.C., U.S. Navy; Neil J. Emon, O.S.C.; Gordon Van Hoof, O.S.C.; Richard M. Leliaert, O.S.C.; Dale H. Redwanski, O.S.C.; Bro. James Scher, O.S.C.; Very Rev. James A. Vedro, O.S.C., Supr.; Revs. Gerald Thaar, O.S.C.; Richard Thompson, O.S.C. Priests 11.

STERLING HEIGHTS. *Society of Christ Provincial Home*, Provincial Home, 3000 18 Mile Rd., 48314. Tel: 810-939-5022; Fax: 810-939-0195. Revs. Andrzej Maslejak, S.Ch., Prov.; Stanislaw Kuczaik, S.Ch., Asst. Prov.; Gerald Grupczynski, S.Ch., Treas.

WYANDOTTE. *Pallottine Fathers*, 3352 Fourth St., 48192. Tel: 313-285-2966. Rev. Stephen Keogh, S.A.C., Rector & Mission Promotions Dir.; Bro. Faustino Paez, S.A.C.

[L] CONVENTS AND RESIDENCES FOR SISTERS

DETROIT. *Adrian Dominican Sisters - Great Lakes Mission Chapter*, 9400 Courville, 48224-2517. Tel: 313-882-8484; Fax: 313-882-0436. Sr. Joan Lawrence Sustersic, O.P., Chapter Prioress.

Adrian Dominican Sisters, Nokomis Mission Chapter, 9400 Courville St., 48224-2517. Tel: 313-343-0573; Fax: 313-882-0436. Sr. Margaret O'Flynn, O.P., Chapter Prioress.

Franciscan Sisters of St. Joseph (Mexico City), 17330 Quincy Ave., 48221. Tel: 313-342-0825; Fax: 313-342-6816. Sr. Magdalena Santiago Cohenete, F.S.S.J., Supr. Sisters 4.

Missionaries of Charity, 4835 Lincoln St., 48208. Tel: 313-831-1028. Sr. M. Christophine, M.C., Supr.

Sisters of Jesus the Savior 1985. (Founded in Elele, Nigeria), St. Scholastica Convent, 17305 Ashton Rd., 48219. Tel: 313-541-4368. Ministry in Education and Social Assistance. Sisters 10.

Sisters, Home Visitors of Mary Convent, 121 E. Boston, 48202. Tel: 313-869-2160; Fax: 313-869-2161. Sr. Barbara Dakoske, H.V.M., Admin.

BLOOMFIELD HILLS. *Daughters of Divine Charity - Holy Trinity Province* (1972), Holy Trinity Provincialate, 39315 N. Woodward Ave., 48304. Tel: 248-644-1011; Fax: 248-644-1596. Sr. M. Paschal Grand, F.D.C., Prov. Supr. Sisters in Community 26.

CLARKSTON. *Servants of Jesus*, 9075 Big Lake Rd., Box 128, 48347. Tel: 313-562-6156; Fax: 313-562-7769. Leadership Team: Sr. Virginia Skurski, S.J., Pres.; Sr. Corinne Weiss, S.J.; Sr. Karen Shirilla, S.J.

S.J. Charitable Trust (Retired & Infirm Sisters), Servants of Jesus Community Support Trust, 9075 Big Lake Rd., Box 128, 48347.

CLINTON TWP. *Monastery of St. Therese of the Child Jesus*, 35750 Moravian Dr., 48035-2138. Tel: 810-790-7255; Fax: 810-790-7271. Discalced Carmelite Nuns. Mother Mary Elizabeth, O.C.D., Prioress. Professed Nuns 8; Extern Sisters 3.

FARMINGTON HILLS. *Adrian Dominican Sisters, South East Adrian Mission Chapter*, 28650 Eleven Mile Rd., 48336-1502. Tel: 248-426-9185; Fax: 248-426-9186. Sr. Lorraine Mordenski, O.P., Chapter Prioress.

Bernardine Franciscan Sisters of Michigan, Our Lady of the Rosary Convent, 27405 W. 10 Mile Rd., 48336-1502. Tel: 810-476-4111. Sisters of the Third Order of St. Francis. Sr. Maria Christine Keller, O.S.F., Province Min. Sisters in Area 55.

Monastery of the Blessed Sacrament, 29575 Middlebelt Rd., 48334-2311. Tel: 248-626-8253; Fax: 248-626-8724. Nuns of the Order of Preachers ((Cloistered Dominican Nuns, Perpetual Adoration). Sr. Mary Rose, O.P., Prioress; Rev. Martin F. McCormick, O.P., Chap. Cloistered Sisters 36; Extern Sister 3.

Sisters of Mercy-Regional Community of Detroit, Inc., 29000 Eleven Mile Rd., 48336. Tel: 248-476-8000; Fax: 248-476-4222. Sr. Linda Werthman, R.S.M., Pres. Sisters 261; U.S.Professed 231; In Argentine-Professed 27; Candidates 1; Novices 2.

Sisters of Mercy of the Americas. Regional Community of Detroit, Charitable Trusts 1 & 2.

IDA. *St. Joseph's Convent*, 2882 Southwick, Box 187, 48140. Tel: 734-269-2505. Missionary Sisters of Our Lady of Victory 2.

LIVONIA. *Provincial House and Novitiate of the Sisters of St. Felix*, 36800 Schoolcraft Rd., 48150. Tel: 734-591-1730; Fax: 734-591-1710. Sr. Mary Renetta Rumpz, C.S.S.F., Prov. Min.; Rev. Michael Daly, Res. Chap.; Rev. Msgr. Vincent J. Horkan, Infirmary Chap. Legal Title: *Provincial House and Novitiate of the Congregation of the Sisters of St. Felix, C.S.S.F., Felician Sisters.* Professed Sisters 226; Novices 1.

MONROE. *Sisters, Servants of the Immaculate Heart of Mary, Leadership Council*, 610 W. Elm Ave., 48162-7909. Tel: 734-240-9700; Fax: 734-240-9784. Sr. Virginia Pfau, I.H.M., Pres.; Sr. Mary Katherine Hamilton, I.H.M., Vice Pres.; Sr. Frances Mlocek, I.H.M., Chief Financial Officer; Leadership Council: Sr. Carolyn Campbell, I.H.M.; Sr. Paula Cooney, I.H.M.; Sr. Anne Crimmins, I.H.M.; Sr. Janet Ryan, I.H.M.; Sr. Barbara Weigand, I.H.M. .

ORTONVILLE. *Our Lady of Mt. Thabor Monastery*, 1295 Bald Eagle Lake Rd., 48462. Tel: 248-627-4355. Dominican Sisters of Mt. Thabor. Sr. Mary Martin, Prioress.

OXFORD. *Dominican Sisters, Congregation of St. Rose of Lima, St. Joseph Convent*, 775 W. Drahner Rd., 48371. Tel: 248-628-2872; Fax: 248-628-1725. Sr. Frances Mary Kernasovich, O.P., Pres.; Sr. Teresita Lipar, O.P., First Vice Pres.; Sr. Sue McMahon, O.P., Second Vice Pres. Professed Sisters 46. General Mother House and Novitiate of the Dominican Sisters; St. Mary Retreat House; Dominican Center; St. Raphael's; Dominican sisters of Oxford Charitable Trust.

RIVERVIEW. *Sisters of Mary Reparatrix*, 17320 Grange Rd., 48192. Tel: 734-285-4510; Fax: 734-285-8147. Sisters 12.

Full Circle House of Prayer.

[M] HOMES FOR MEN AND WOMEN

DETROIT. *St. Mary's Residence*, 2120 Orleans St., 48207. Tel: 313-259-6874; 259-0459

For a complete listing, refer to the Special Care Facilities section.

[N] CATHOLIC SOCIAL SERVICE AGENCIES

DETROIT. *Catholic Social Services of Wayne County*, 9851 Hamilton Ave., 48202. Tel: 313-883-2339; Fax: 313-883-3957. Patrick J. Heron, Pres. & CEO. Family service, marriage counseling, adoption services, services to unwed mothers, planned respite care, substance abuse counseling, foster family care & services to youth & older persons including Foster Grandparent, Senior Companion & Retired Senior Volunteer Programs.

Branches: 20382 Van Born Rd., Dearborn Heights, 48125. Tel: 313-792-9286; Fax: 313-792-0444. 17316 Farmington Rd., Livonia, 48152. Tel: 734-421-3730; Fax: 734-421-3733. 15200 E. Jefferson, Ste. 105, Grosse Pointe Park, 48230. Tel: 313-821-2590; Fax: 313-821-1046. Teen Empowerment Program, 5247 Sheridan, 48213. Tel: 313-922-0094; Fax: 313-922-0514.

CLINTON TOWNSHIP. *Catholic Services of Macomb*, 15980 Nineteen Mile Rd., 48038. Tel: 810-416-2300; Fax: 810-416-2311. Mr. Thomas Reed, Pres. & CEO.

Branch Offices: 12434 Twelve Mile Rd., Ste. 202, Warren, 48093. Tel: 810-558-7551; Fax: 810-573-8016. 18720 Thirteen Mile Rd., Roseville, 48066. Tel: 810-558-7551; Fax: 810-573-8016.

Friend's House Adult Day Care for the Elderly, 16931 Nineteen Mile Rd., Ste. 140, 48038. Tel: 810-412-8054; Fax: 810-412-8084.

LAPEER. *Christian Family Services of Lapeer County, Inc.*, 441 Clay St., 48446. Tel: 810-664-4557; Fax: 810-664-5181.

MONROE. *Catholic Social Services of Monroe County*, 16 E. Fifth St., 48161. Tel: 734-242-3800; Fax: 734-242-6203. Candy S. Salazar, Interim Pres. & CEO, South County Office: 8330 Lewis Ave., P.O. Box 10, Temperance, 48182. Tel: 734-847-1523; Fax: 734-847-1523.

Head Start Office, 502 W. Elm St., 48162. Tel: 734-241-8727; Fax: 734-241-6125.

PONTIAC. *Catholic Social Services of Oakland County*, 50 Wayne St., 3rd Floor, 48342. Tel: 248-333-3700. Margaret A. Huggard, M.S.W., Pres.

Branches: 53 Franklin Blvd., 48341. Tel: 248-334-3595. 6637 Highland Rd., Waterford, 48327. Tel: 248-666-8870. 26105 Orchard Lake Rd., Suite 303, Farmington, 48334. Tel: 248-471-4140. 1424 E. Eleven Mile Rd., Royal Oak, 48067. Tel: 248-548-4044.

Sheltering Arms Adult Day Care, 18310 W. 12 Mile Rd., Southfield, 48076. Tel: 248-557-7373.

PORT HURON. *Catholic Social Services of St. Clair County, Inc.*, 2601 Thirteenth St., 48060. Tel: 810-987-9100; Fax: 810-987-9100. Patrick L. Cogley, M.A., Pres.

[O] SPECIALIZED CHILD CARE FACILITIES AND SCHOOLS

DETROIT. *Christ Child House*, 15751 Joy Rd., 48228. Tel: 313-584-6077; Fax: 313-584-1148

For a complete listing, refer to the Special Care Facilities section.

Don Bosco Hall, Inc., 2340 Calvert, 48206. Tel: 313-869-2200; Fax: 313-869-8220

For a complete listing, refer to the Special Care Facilities section.

DEARBORN HEIGHTS. *Vista Maria*, 20651 W. Warren Ave., 48127. Tel: 313-271-3050; Fax: 313-271-6250

For a complete listing, refer to the Special Care Facilities section.

FARMINGTON HILLS. *Marillac Programs* 22255 Greenfield, Ste. 330 Southfield, 48334. Tel: 248-559-2272; Fax: 248-559-2226.

For a complete listing, refer to the Special Care Facilities section.

St. Vincent and Sarah Fisher Center, 27400 W. Twelve Mile Rd., 48334. Tel: 313-538-6000; 810-626-7527

For a complete listing, refer to the Special Care Facilities section.

Seton Nursery School and Infant-Toddler Child Care Center, 29475 Inkster Rd., 48018. Tel: 810-626-6990

For a complete listing, refer to the Special Care Facilities section.

NORTHVILLE. *Our Lady of Providence Center*, 16115 Beck Rd., 48167. Tel: 734-453-1300; Fax: 734-453-0266

For a complete listing, refer to the Special Care Facilities section.

SOUTHFIELD. *Boysville of Michigan, Inc.*, Community Resource Office, 17117 W. Nine Mile Rd., Ste. 1111, 48075. Tel: 248-569-6630; Fax: 248-569-8171

For a complete listing, refer to the Special Care Facilities section.

St. Francis Family Services, 17500 W. Eight Mile Rd., 48075. Tel: 248-552-0750; Fax: 248-552-9019

For a complete listing, refer to the Special Care Facilities section.

[P] RETREAT HOUSES

DETROIT. *St. Paul of the Cross Retreat Center.* Conducted by the Passionist Community. 23333 Schoolcraft, 48223-2499. Tel: 313-535-9563; Fax: 313-535-9207. Rev. James Thoman, O.P., Retreat Dir. Team Members: Revs. Tu-Jin Paul Kim, C.P.; Peter Cornell; David Colhour, C.P., Asst. Retreat Dir.; Mrs. Cathy Anthony.

BLOOMFIELD HILLS. *Manresa Jesuit Retreat House*, 1390 Quarton Rd., 48304-3554. Tel: 313-564-6455; 248-644-4933; Fax: 248-644-8291. Revs. James K. Serrick, S.J., Dir. Supr.; John A. McGrail, S.J., Retreat Dir.; Bernard J. Owens, S.J., Retreat Dir.; John T. Schuett, S.J., Retreat Dir.; Benno G. Kornely, S.J., Retreat Dir.; Daniel D. Dunnigan, S.J.; Joseph A. Subitowski, S.J., Maintenance. Priests 5; Brothers 1.

CLARKSTON. *Colombiere Center*, 9075 Big Lake Rd., Box 139, 48347. Tel: 248-625-5611; Fax: 248-625-3526. Spirituality Conference Center and Jesuit Health Care Community for the Detroit Province and Chicago Province. Revs. M. Joseph Casey, S.J., Supr./Dir.; Thomas J. Powers, S.J., Asst. Supr.; Thomas F. Ankenbrandt, S.J.; John D. Baggarly, S.J.; Joseph M. Becker; Thomas C. Biecker, S.J.; Henry F. Birkenhauer, S.J.; John L. Blanchard, S.J.; Malcolm Carron, S.J.; Edward E. Cincoski, S.J.; Paul F. Conen; George A. Curran, S.J.; Cornelius L. Curtin, S.J.; Stanislaus Czapiewski, S.J., St. Ladislaus, 2730 Caniff, Hamtramck, 48212. Tel: 313-872-0709. Revs. William A. Dehler, S.J.; Reynaldo A. Garcia, S.J.; Henry C. Gelin, S.J.; Francis X. Grollig, S.J.; John A. Hardon, S.J.; F. Torrens Hecht, S.J.; Fred M. Henley, S.J.; Richard J. Huelsman, S.J.; Robert G. Humbert, S.J.; Lawrence E. Isenecker, S.J.; Kenneth M. Kunert, S.J.; Lester A. Luiz, S.J.; James F. Maguire, S.J.; Oswald J. Marshall, S.J.; Stephen A. Meder, S.J.; Harold R. Meirose, S.J., Pastoral Care, Asst. Dir.; Edmund J. Montville, S.J.; Benjamin R. Morin, S.J.; Edwin A. Mousbrugger, S.J.; William H. Nichols, S.J.; Joseph P. Owens, S.J.; Robert A. Pollauf, S.J.; Francis D. Rabaut, S.J.; John C. Reed, S.J.; Hugh B. Rodman, S.J.; L. Harold Sanford, S.J.; Clayton D. Schario, S.J.; Robert W. Schneider, S.J.; John T. Schuett, S.J.; Joseph F. Small, S.J.; Stanley C. Tillman, S.J.; George T. Tolbert, S.J.; William G. Topmoeller; Jerome F. Treacy; Robert J. Willmes, S.J.; Bros. Robert G. Cardosi, S.J.; Herman F. Elsaesser, S.J.; John E. Foy, S.J.; Bruno W. Karpinski, S.J.; Joseph A. LaMielle, S.J.; Daniel J. McCullough, S.J.; Clayton P. Morell, S.J.; John J. Petrus, S.J.; Bernard L. Polinak, S.J.; George A. Prickril, S.J. Priests 50; Brothers 12.

MONROE. *Visitation Center*, 529 Stewart Rd., 48162. Tel: 313-242-5520; Fax: 313-242-5530. Sponsorship of I.H.M. Congregation. Sisters 3.

PLYMOUTH. *St. John Center for Youth and Family*, 44011 Five Mile Rd., 48170-2555. Tel: 734-414-1111; Fax: 734-414-1150. Rev. John H. West, Dir.

Cardinal Maida Institute for Leadership Formation. James R. Kiefer, Dir.

WASHINGTON. *Capuchin Retreat*, 62460 Mt. Vernon Rd., P.O. Box 188, 48094. Tel: 248-651-4826. Revs. Jogues Constance, O.F.M.Cap.; James R. Andres, O.F.M.Cap.; Gerald Kessel, O.F.M.Cap.; Gerald Pehler, O.F.M.Cap.

[Q] SPECIAL SERVICES

DETROIT. *Capuchin Soup Kitchen*, 1820 Mt. Elliott, 48207. Tel: 313-579-2100; Fax: 313-571-1822. W. DeWayne Wells, Exec. Dir.; Bro. Vincent Reyes, O.F.M.Cap., Pastoral Dir.

Jefferson House, 8311 E. Jefferson, 48214. Tel: 313-331-8900; Fax: 313-331-2322. Transitional alcohol-drug residence. Mr. James Fleming, Site Dir.

Catholic Community Services of the Archdiocese of Detroit, Inc., 1234 Washington Blvd., 48226. Tel: 313-237-5885; Fax: 313-237-4642. His Eminence Adam J. Maida, Pres.; Rev. Msgr. John P. Zenz, Sec.; Mr. Michael Gorman, Treas.

Manna Community Meal. (Soup Kitchen), 1950 Trumbull, 48226. Tel: 313-963-8708.

Pope John XXIII Hospitality House, 3977 2nd Ave., 48201. Tel: 313-832-HELP; Fax: 313-965-4453. Cancer outpatient-residents, Transportation for Area Pediatric Cancer Patients. Rev. Russell E. Kohler.

St. Patrick's Senior Center, Inc., 58 Parsons, 48201. Tel: 313-833-7080; Fax: 313-833-0128. Sr. Mary Watson, O.P., Pres. Lay Staff 10; Patients assisted annually 1,400.

St. Vincent de Paul Society, Archdiocesan Council, 2929 E. Grand Blvd., 48202. Tel: 313-972-3100; Fax: 313-972-3147. James Dumont, Pres.; Roger Playwin, Exec. Dir.; Rev. John H. West, Spiritual Dir.

MEMPHIS. *Sacred Heart Rehabilitation Center, Inc.*, 400 Stoddard Rd., Box 41038, 48041-1038. Tel: 810-392-2167. John Sass, Jr., Pres. Beds 98. Treatment for alcoholism and drug dependency to adult men and women. Detox and residential services.

ONSTED. *St. Patrick's Retreat*, 11528 Killarney Hwy., 49265. Tel: 517-467-7492. Rev. Russell E. Kohler, Dir. Tel: 313-832-4357. Retreats for Family with cancer outpatient; small groups of handicapped-developmentally disabled; small parish team meetings; hospice & chaplain's meetings and offers assistance for patient visits to world shrines.

TROY. *Gabriel Richard Institute*, 3641 Estates Dr., 48084. Tel: 248-643-4039; 800-382-8609; Fax: 248-643-4045. Adult and youth Christopher Leadership training for Catholic laymen, women, clergy & religious. Rev. Thomas J. Bresnahan, Dir.; Dolores Ammar, Exec. Dir.

WARREN. *St. John's Deaf Center*, 8245 Fisher, 48089. Tel: 810-758-0710 (TDD); 758-0714 (Voice). Rev. Richard J. Yost, O.S.F.S., Dir.

WATERFORD. *Lourdes Alzheimers Special Care Center*, 2300 Watkins Lake Rd., 48328. Tel: 248-674-2241. Sr. Sue McMahon, O.P., Contact.

[R] CAMPS AND COMMUNITY CENTERS

DETROIT. *C.Y.O. Boys Camp*, CYO Camps, Catholic Youth Organization, 305 Michigan Ave., 48226. Tel: 313-963-7172. Rev. Brian L. Cokonougher, Camp Dept. Dir.

C.Y.O. Girls Camp, CYO Camps, Catholic Youth Organization, 305 Michigan Ave., 48226. Tel: 313-963-7172. Rev. Brian K. Cokonougher, Camp Svcs. Dir.

Camp Ozanam, Central Office-St. Vincent de Paul Society, 2929 E. Grand Blvd., 48202-0518. Tel: 313-972-3100; Fax: 313-972-3147. A free week long Christian camping experience for boys 8-12. Recruitment through Parish Conferences of the Society of St. Vincent de Paul.

Camp Stapleton-St. Vincent de Paul Society, Central Office, 2929 E. Grand Blvd., 48202. Tel: 313-972-3100; Fax: 313-972-3147. A free week long Christian camping experience for girls 8-12. Recruitment through Parish Conferences of the Society of St. Vincent de Paul.

[S] CAMPUS MINISTRIES

DETROIT. *Marygrove College Campus Ministry*, 8425 West McNichols Rd., 48221. Tel: 313-927-1404, Ext. 275; Fax: 313-927-1345. Sr. Marie Sweeney, I.H.M., Campus Ministry.

University of Detroit Mercy University Ministry. Mailing Address: P.O. Box 19900, 48219-0900.

McNichols Campus. Tel: 313-993-1560. Rev. Gary R. Wright, S.J., Dir.; Sr. Beth Ann Finster, S.S.J., Asst. Dir.

Law School Campus. Tel: 313-596-0220. Andrew F. Moore.

College of Health Professions & School of Dentistry. Tel: 313-993-6216. Bridget Deagan Krause, M.Div.

Wayne State University, Newman Center, 761 Student Center, 48202. Tel: 313-577-3462. Mrs. Fe Desiar Rowland, Chaplain.

AUBURN HILLS. *St. John Fisher Chapel University Parish*, 3665 Walton Blvd., 48326. Tel: 248-373-6457; Fax: 248-373-5479. Campus Ministry for Oakland University. Rev. Jerome A. Brzezinski; Ms. Lisa Abad; Ms. Nancy Mason Bordley; Mrs. Susan Burrato; Sr. Mary Dixon, O.P.; Sr. Mary Van Gilder, I.H.M.; Mr. Eugene Mahon.

DEARBORN. *Univ. of Michigan, Dearborn, Henry Ford Community College Newman Center.* Gabriel Richard Campus Ministry Center, 5001 Evergreen Rd., 48128. Tel: 313-271-6000. Shannon Dyer, B.A., Campus Min.

LIVONIA. *Madonna University Campus Ministry*, 36600 Schoolcraft, 48150. Tel: 734-432-5419; Fax: 734-432-5393. Deacon Eugene Desjarlais, Dir. Campus Min.

Schoolcraft College, Newman House. (Campus Ministry), 17300 Haggerty Rd., 48152. Tel: 734-464-2160; Fax: 734-462-4558.

PORT HURON. *John Courtney Murray Newman Center*, 505 Huron Ave., 48060. Tel: 810-948-5195. Rev. Rene L. Desmarais; Sr. Margaret Dowd, Co-Dir.

WARREN. *Macomb Community College Campus Ministry*, 14500 Twelve Mile Rd., 48093. Tel: 810-445-7378; Fax: 810-445-7172. Sr. Joyce Campbell, I.H.M.; Sr. Kathy Onderbeke, I.H.M.

[T] MISCELLANEOUS LISTINGS

DETROIT. *American Friends of the Vatican Library*, 2701 Chicago Blvd., 48206. Tel: 313-883-8586; Fax: 313-868-6440. Rev. Charles Kosanke, Pres.

The Black Catholic Televangelization Network, P.O. Box 13559, 48213-0559. Tel: 313-521-7777; Fax: 313-521-7766. Rev. Clarence E. Williams, C.PP.S., Ph.D., Pres. Search, Black and Catholic (TV), the Catholic African World Network, and the Institute for Recovery from Racisms.

Cardinal Club, 1234 Washington, 48226. An organization of Catholic laymen in business and professional fields.

Christ Child Society, 15751 Joy Rd., 48228. Tel: 313-584-6077; Fax: 313-584-1148. Rev. Msgr. John P. Zenz, Spiritual Dir.; Mary Woycik, Pres.

Clergy Health Plan, Chancery Building, 1234 Washington Blvd., 48226. Rev. Jack Fabian, Dir.

Co-Chairpersons: Sr. Janet Jeffers, I.H.M.; Rev. David Kelly.

Council of Catholic Women, 305 Michigan Ave., 48226. Tel: 313-237-5896; Fax: 313-237-5869. Thelma J. Sanborn, Pres.

Detroit Federation of Christian Life Communities, 1234 Washington Blvd., 48226. Mrs. Shirley Boots, Pres.

Dominican Literacy Center, 9400 Courville, 48224. Tel: 313-882-4853; Fax: 313-882-0436. Sr. Marie Schoenlein, O.P., Dir.

Foster Parents Mission Club, 17330 Quincy Ave., 48221. Tel: 313-342-4066; Fax: 313-342-6816. Rev. Bruno Piccolo, P.I.M.E., Dir.; Alice Marino, Exec. Sec. An agency of the P.I.M.E. Missionaries.

The Franciscan Project, Inc., 4603 Vinewood, 48208-1879. Tel: 313-896-7103; Fax: 313-896-7103. Mailing Address: P.O. Box 310633, 48231-0633. Sr. Patricia Mary Hackett, S.A., Pres.

Jesuit Seminary Association, 7303 W. Seven Mile Rd., 48221. Tel: 313-861-7500; Fax: 313-861-4230. Rachel M. Brennan, Dir. of Development & of Jesuit Seminary Assoc.

Jesuit International Missions. Rev. Richard H. Twohig.

Jesuit Volunteer Corps. Midwest, Inc., 7333 W. Seven Mile Rd., 48221. Tel: 313-345-3480; Fax: 313-345-5410. Timothy McCabe, Exec. Dir., Mailing Address: P.O. Box 21936, 48221.

Latino Cultural Pastoral Center, 5654 Konkel, 48210. Tel: 313-897-5277; Fax: 313-897-8279. Raul Feliciano, Dir.

Leprosy Relief Society, 17330 Quincy Ave., 48221. Tel: 313-342-4066; Fax: 313-342-6816. Barbara J. Rubaie, Dir. An agency of the P.I.M.E. Missionaries.

Mercy Education Project, 2020 14th St., 48216. Tel: 313-963-5881; Fax: 313-963-0209. Sr. Karen Egri, R.S.M., Exec. Dir.

Midwest Cultural Institute of Leadership, 438 St. Antoine, 48226. Tel: 313-961-7213. Rev. Thomas W. Florek, S.J., Coord.

Pontiac Vision 2000 Schools, Inc., 1234 Washington Blvd., 48226. Tel: 313-237-5803. Michael Gorman, Sec. & Treas.

Pope John Paul II Cultural Foundation, Inc., 1234 Washington Blvd., 48226. Tel: 877-767-3572; Fax: 248-478-4092.
E-mail: info@jp2culturalcenter.org
Web site: www.jp2culturalcenter.org
His Eminence Adam Cardinal Maida, Pres.; Most Rev. Bernard J. Harrington, Episcopal Coord. of Fund Raising; Rev. Msgr. Walter A. Hurley, Treas. & Delegate of Adam Cardinal Maida; Rev. G. Michael Bugarin, Dir. Pope John II Cultural Center.

SS. Peter & Paul Jesuit Church Historical Fund, 438 St. Antoine, 48226. Tel: 313-961-8077; Fax: 313-963-5134.

West Detroit Catholic Schools Alliance, 23450 W. Davison, 48223. Tel: 313-255-3666; Fax: 313-537-0598. Purpose: an alliance of the following Catholic Schools-Bishop Borgess Academy, Bishop Borgess High School, Our Lady of Grace Elementary, Ss. Christine/Gemma Elementary, Ss. Peter and Paul Elementary, St. Thomas Aquinas Elementary, and St. Christopher Elementary. Sr. Diane Odette, O.P., Dir.; Rev. Mark S. Brauer, Vicar.

BLOOMFIELD HILLS. *Amicare Home Health Care - Metro Detroit*, 281 Enterprise Dr., Ste. 200, 48302. Tel: 248-858-7735. Karen Struve, Pres.

Ladies of Charity of St. Vincent de Paul Oakland County Associaton, 1466 Glengarry, 48301. Patricia Hurlbert, Contact Person.

Logos, Inc. (Michigan), 2460 Opdyke Rd., 48304. Tel: 248-922-2084; Fax: 248-642-4668. Rev. Lorenzo Gomez, L.C., Rector; Bro. Santiago Perez, L.C., Vice Rector; Revs. Juan Gabriel Guerra, L.C.; Ned Brown, L.C.; Michael Goodyear, L.C.; Matthew van Smoorenburg, L.C.; Bros. Michael Williams, L.C.; Nathan Knuth, L.C.; Dominic Madrid, L.C.; Christopher Thompson, L.C.; Eric Nielsen, L.C.; Daniel Talkington, L.C.; Jason Clark, L.C.; Michael Sullivan, L.C.

Opdyke, Inc., 2460 Opdyke Rd., 48304. Tel: 248-644-2954; Fax: 248-642-4668. Rev. Lorenzo Gomez, Contact.

WCVA, Inc. - Detroit Catholic Radio, 38500 N. Woodward, Ste. 350, 48304-2964. Tel: 248-642-6226; Fax: 248-642-6027. John F.X. Browne, Contact Person.

CLARKSON. *The Legion of Christ, Inc.*, 5935 Clarkson Rd., 48348. Tel: 248-922-2084; Fax: 248-922-2087. Rev. Lorenzo Gomez, Contact.

CLINTON TOWNSHIP. *St. Mary Magdalen Catholic Community*, Ryan Correctional Facility, 24415 Crocker, 48036. Tel: 810-755-9359. Rev. Thomas R. Physician, Chaplaincy Coord.

DEARBORN. *Archdiocesan Catholic Campus Ministry Association, Gabriel Richards Campus Ministry*, University of Michigan-Dearborn, 5001 Evergreen, 48128. Tel: 313-271-6000. Leadership Team: Shannon Dyer; Michael Laughlin; Silvia Shorter; Kathy Eubanks.

Leo XIII Society, 1840 N. Melborn, 48128. Tel: 313-359-1499; Fax: 313-359-1767. Ernie Scarano, Pres.

DEARBORN HEIGHTS. *Dominican Center for Religious Development*, 7430 N. Inkster Rd., 48127. Tel: 313-730-8759. Sr. Charlotte Hoefer, O.P.

EASTPOINTE. *Detroit Catholic Charismatic Renewal*, Coordinating Center, 22851 Lexington, 48021. Tel: 810-777-7780. Rev. John C. Esper, Liaison. D.C.C.R. Assembly. Arlene Apone, Assoc. Liaison; Ann Bonenfant; Roy Coloma; Clare Cooper; Steve Cooper; Darlene Czop; Jim Lovelock; Jesse Melendez; Tom & Sylvia Murphy; Frank Potter; Judy Siekierski; Ben Stapel.

FARMINGTON HILLS.

Amicare Home Health Services, Inc., P.O. Box 9185, 48333-9185. Tel: 248-305-7921; Fax: 248-305-7632. Karen Struve, Pres.

Amicare Hospice Services, Inc., 34605 Twelve Mile Rd., 48331; Fax: 248-489-6204. Karen Struve, Pres.

Mercy International Health Services, 34605 Twelve Mile Rd., 48331. Tel: 248-489-6100; Fax: 248-489-6102. David Vellinga, Pres.; Patricia Williams, Dir.

Mercy Services for Aging, Non-profit Housing Corporation. Wholly owned subsidiary of Mercy Services for Aging, 34605 Twelve Mile Rd., 48331. Tel: 248-305-7920. Karen Struve, Pres. & CEO.

Trinity Health-Michigan, 34605 Twelve Mile Rd., 48331. Tel: 248-489-6000. Judith C. Pelham, Pres. Organization owns & operates 13 hospital divisions in Michigan & Iowa. Owns & operates 13 nursing home facilities, manages senior housing facilities, alternative health financing activities, home care services, hospice services, rehabilitation services and foundation activities.

GROSSE POINTE. *John Paul II Foundation of Michigan, Inc.*, 35 Warner Rd., 48236. Tel: 313-882-2140; Fax: 313-882-1292. Mrs. Frank A. Germack, Jr., Pres. Conducts religious, cultural, educational, humanitarian and fund raising activities in Michigan in liaison with the John Paul Foundation in Rome. Regular, supporting and life memberships.

HIGHLAND PARK. *Chinese Catholic Society of Michigan, Inc.*, 60 Church St., 48203. Tel: 313-868-3876. Thomas McGuire, Spiritual Dir.

LIVONIA.

Angela Hospice Home Care, Inc., 14100 Newburgh Rd., 48154-5010. Tel: 734-464-7810.

Felician Sisters of Livonia Foundation, 36000 Schoolcraft, 48150. Tel: 734-655-2301. Sr. Mary Renetta Rumpz, C.S.S.F., Pres.

St. Michael Mission, 37677 Professional Center Dr., Ste. 110C, 48154. Tel: 734-464-1282; Fax: 734-464-2936. Katherine Alberts, Contact Person.

MARYSVILLE. *National Alliance of Parishes Restructuring into Communities*, 1000 Michigan Ave., 48040-1466. Tel: 810-364-3500; Fax: 810-364-3555. Rev. Arthur R. Baranowski, Pres.; Margaret Steinhaus, Mgr.; Larry & Judy Berch, Editors. The N.A.P.R.C. networks and supports American & intl. parishes developing small church communities as the primary restructuring of the parish.

MONROE. *SSIHM Charitable Trust (Retired and Infirm Sisters)*, 610 W. Elm Ave., 48162-7909. Tel: 734-241-0092; Fax: 734-241-9114. Sr. Frances Mlocek, I.H.M., Trustee.

NOVI. *Mercy Health Foundation*, P.O. Box 8001, 48376-8001. Tel: 248-489-6784; Fax: 248-489-6180. Judith C. Pelham, Contact Person.

OXFORD. *Queen of the Family Retreat Center*, 751 Drahner Rd., 48371. Tel: 248-625-5560; Fax: 248-628-4898. Rev. Lorenzo Gomez, L.C., Dir.

PARADISE. *Companions of Christ the Lamb*, P.O. Box 12, 49768. Tel: 906-492-3647; Fax: 906-492-3648. Rev. Jack Fabian, Dir.

REDFORD. *Siena Literacy Center*, 11685 Appleton, 48239. Tel: 313-532-8404; Fax: 313-532-8409. Sr. Mary Hemmen, O.P., Dir.

ROMEO.
BVM Foundation, 11070 West Gates, 48065. Tel: 248-656-3890; Fax: 810-752-5077. Brian Palmer, Pres.

ROSEVILLE. *Cursillos in Christianity Movement of the Archdiocese of Detroit*, 18430 Utica Rd., 48066. Tel: 810-776-4533. Rev. Charles M. Morris, Spiritual Advisor; Mr. William Pfannes, Lay Dir. Tel: 810-524-1951.

ST. CLAIR SHORES. *Catholic Kolping Society of America, Detroit Branch, Inc.*, 24409 Jefferson, 48080. Tel: 810-775-9159. Thomas Schultes, Pres. Tel: 248-762-0008; Thekla Abels, Contact Person. Tel: 313-885-1189; Rev. Lawrence Abler, O.F.M.Cap.; Deacon Peter Schlesser, Praese.

Celebrate Life Ministries, 28111 Jefferson, A6, 48081. Tel: 810-778-4446. Ms. Patricia Haas, Coord.

SOUTHFIELD. *Dominican Consultation Center*, 24225 W. Nine Mile Rd., Ste. 114A, 48034-3990. Tel: 248-353-9080. 22811 Greater Mack, Ste. L-9, St. Clair Shores, 48080. Tel: 810-775-5620. Sr. Diane Burgermeister, O.P.

WARREN. *St. John Health System*. Holding Company sponsored by Sisters of St. Joseph and the Daughters of Charity of St. Vincent de Paul which operates: St. John Hospital & Medical Center; St. John Ambulatory Corp.; Affiliated Health Services; St. John Senior Community; Eastwood Community Clinics; St. John Northeast Community Hospital; St. John Oakland Hospital; St. John-North Shores; St. John River District Hospital; St. John Riverview Hospital; St. John Macomb Hospital; Father Murray Nursing Home; St. John Health System Home Services; St. John Health System Foundation; Providence Hospital and Medical Centers; Seiton Health Corporation of Southeast Michigan. 28000 Dequindre Rd., 48092. Tel: 810-753-0911. Dr. Anthony R. Tersigni, Ed.D., Pres. & CEO.

[U] CLOSED INSTITUTIONS

DETROIT. *Archdiocesan Archives*. The following institutional sacramental records can be found at the following address unless otherwise indicated. 1234 Washington Blvd., 48226. Tel: 313-237-5846; Fax: 313-237-4643.

St. Agnes.
St. Albertus.
Anawim Community.
Assumption of the Blessed Virgin Mary.
St. Augustine.
St. Benedict the Moor.
St. Bernadette.
St. Bernadette Chapel.
St. Bernard.
St. Boniface.
St. Brigid.
St. Camillus.
Cardinal Leger Community.
St. Catherine.
St. Casimir.
Corpus Christi.
St. David.
St. Edward.
Emmaus Community.
Epiphany.
St. Eugene.
St. Francis Hospital.
St. George (Lithuanian).
Holy Ghost.
Holy Name of Jesus.
St. Ignatius of Antioch.
Immaculate Conception.
St. Joachim.
St. John the Evangelist.
St. John Nepomucene.
St. John Vianney.
St. Joseph Mercy Hospital.
St. Lawrence.
St. Margaret Mary.
St. Martin.
St. Mary Hospital - Detroit Memorial Hospital.
St. Monica.
Mother of Consolation.
Mother of Our Savior.
Mount Carmel Mercy Hospital.
Our Lady of Guadalupe.
Our Lady of Help.
Our Lady of the Hills.
Our Lady Queen of Hope.
St. Paul Maltese.
Patronage of St. Joseph.
St. Peter (Lithuanian).
St. Philip Neri.
Resurrection.
St. Rose of Lima.
St. Stanislaus Bishop and Martyr.
St. Theresa.
St. Thomas the Apostle.
St. Vincent de Paul.
Santa Maria.
Vida Nueva Community.
Visitation.
St. Wenceslaus.

RELIGIOUS INSTITUTES OF MEN REPRESENTED IN THE ARCHDIOCESE

For further details refer to the corresponding bracketed number in the Religious Institutes of Men or Women section.

[0140]—*The Augustinians.* (Chicago).—O.S.A.
[0170]—*Basilian Fathers.* (Toronto, Ont.).—C.S.B.
[0200]—*Benedictine Monks.* (Detroit Prov.).—O.S.B.
[0330]—*Brothers of the Christian Schools.* (New York Prov., Chicago, IL).—F.S.C.
[0600]—*Brothers of the Congregation of Holy Cross.* (Midwest Prov.).—C.S.C.
[0460]—*Brothers of the Poor of St. Francis.*—C.F.P.
[0400]—*Canons Regular of the Order of the Holy Cross.* (Prov. of St. Odilia).—O.S.C.
[0470]—*The Capuchin Friars.* (St. Joseph Prov.).—O.F.M.Cap.
[0275]—*Carmelites of Mary Immaculate.*—C.M.I.
[0310]—*Congregation of Christian Brothers.* (American Prov.).—C.F.C.
[0750]—*Congregation of Marianhill Missionaries.*—C.M.M.
[0740]—*Congregation of Marians of the Immaculate Conception.* (St. Stanislaus Kostka Prov.).—M.I.C.
[1000]—*Congregation of the Passion.* (Western Prov.).—C.P.
[1140]—*Congregation of the Sacred Hearts of Jesus and Mary.*—SS.CC.
[0480]—*Conventual Franciscans.*—O.F.M.Conv.
[0520]—*Franciscan Friars (Custody of the Holy Family/Croatian; Prov. of St. John the Baptist).*—O.F.M.
[0650]—*Holy Ghost Fathers.* (Eastern Prov.).—C.S.Sp.
[0690]—*Jesuit Fathers and Brothers.* (Detroit Prov.).—S.J.
[0730]—*Legionaries of Christ.*—L.C.
[]—*Little Brothers of Jesus.*
[0780]—*Marist Fathers.* (Northeastern Prov.).—S.M.
[0800]—*Maryknoll.*—M.M.
[0720]—*The Missionaries of Our Lady of La Salette.*—M.S.
[0860]—*Missionhurst Congregation of the Immaculate Heart of Mary.*—C.I.C.M.
[0920]—*Oblates of St. Francis De Sales.*—O.S.F.S.
[0430]—*Order of Preachers-Dominicans.* (Provs. of St. Joseph & St. Albert the Great).—O.P.
[1020]—*Pauline Fathers and Brothers.*—S.S.P.
[1050]—*Pontifical Institute for Foreign Missions.*—P.I.M.E.
[1070]—*Redemptorist Fathers.* (Denver Prov.).—C.SS.R.
[1260]—*Society of Christ.* (American-Canadian Prov.).—S.Ch.
[0440]—*Society of Saint Edmund.*—S.S.E.
[0990]—*Society of the Catholic Apostolate.*—S.A.C.
[1060]—*Society of the Precious Blood.* (Cincinnati Prov.).—C.PP.S.

RELIGIOUS INSTITUTES OF WOMEN REPRESENTED IN THE ARCHDIOCESE

[1810]—*Bernardine Sisters of the Third Order of St. Francis.*—O.S.F.
[0360]—*Carmelite Sisters of the Divine Heart of Jesus Carmel.*—D.C.J.
[3810]—*Catholic Mission Sisters of St. Francis Xavier.*—X.S.
[0270]—*Congregation of Bon Secours.*—C.B.S.
[2410]—*Congregation of the Marianites of Holy Cross.*—M.S.C.
[1730]—*Congregation of the Sisters of the Third Order of St. Francis Oldenburg, IN.*—O.S.F.
[1710]—*Congregation of the Third Order of St. Francis of Mary Immaculate, Joliet, IL.*—O.S.F.
[1830]—*Contemplative Sisters of the Good Shepherd.*—C.G.S.
[0760]—*Daughters of Charity of St. Vincent de Paul.*—D.C.
[0790]—*Daughters of Divine Charity.*—F.D.C.
[]—*Daughters of Mary Immaculate (Chaldean).*—D.M.I.
[0940]—*Daughters of St. Mary of Providence.*—D.S.M.P.
[0810]—*Daughters of the Heart of Mary.*—D.H.M.
[0420]—*Discalced Carmelite Nuns.*—O.C.D.
[1050]—*Dominican Contemplative Nuns.*—O.P.
[1070-13]—*Dominican Sisters (Adrian, MI).*—O.P.
[1070-02]—*Dominican Sisters (Columbus,OH).*—O.P.
[1070-17]—*Dominican Sisters (Elkin Park).*—O.P.
[1070-14]—*Dominican Sisters (Grand Rapids, MI).*—O.P.
[1070-16]—*Dominican Sisters (Hope).*—O.P.
[1070-26]—*Dominican Sisters (Oxford, MI).*—O.P.
[1070-09]—*Dominican Sisters (Racine, WI).*—O.P.
[]—*Dominican Sisters of Mt. Thabor.*—O.P.
[1170]—*Felician Sisters.*—C.S.S.F.
[1470]—*Franciscan Sisters of St. Joseph.*—F.S.S.J.
[1480]—*Franciscan Sisters of St. Joseph.* (Mexico).—F.S.S.J.
[1440]—*Franciscan Sisters of the Poor.*—S.F.P.
[2430]—*Marist Sisters Congregation of Mary.*—S.M.
[2720]—*Mission Helpers of the Sacred Heart.*—M.H.S.H.
[2710]—*Missionaries of Charity.*—M.C.
[]—*Missionaries of the Kingship of Christ.*—S.I.M.
[]—*Missionary Sisters of Christ the King for Polonia.*—M.S.K.C.P.
[3130]—*Our Lady of Victory Missionary Sisters.*—O.L.V.M.
[2970]—*School Sisters of Notre Dame.*—S.S.N.D.
[3560]—*Servants of Jesus.*—S.J.
[3590]—*Servants of Mary (Servite Sisters).*—O.S.M.
[0440]—*Sisters of Charity of Cincinnati, Ohio.*—S.C.
[0520]—*Sisters of Charity of Our Lady, Mother of Mercy.*—S.C.M.M.
[0990]—*Sisters of Divine Providence.*—C.D.P.
[2245]—*Sisters of Jesus the Savior.*—S.J.S.
[2575]—*Sisters of Mercy of the Americas.*—R.S.M.
[2990]—*Sisters of Notre Dame.*—S.N.D.
[1530]—*Sisters of St. Francis of the Congregation of Our Lady of Lourdes, Sylvania, Ohio.*—O.S.F.
[1570]—*Sisters of St. Francis of the Holy Family.*—O.S.F.
[1600]—*Sisters of St. Francis of the Martyr St. George.*—O.S.F.
[3830-11]—*Sisters of St. Joseph.*—S.S.J.
[3930]—*Sisters of St. Joseph of the Third Order of St. Francis.*—S.S.J.-T.O.S.F.
[1830]—*Sisters of the Good Shepherd.*—R.G.S.
[1970]—*Sisters of the Holy Family of Nazareth.*—C.S.F.N.
[1990]—*Sisters of the Holy Names of Jesus and Mary.*—S.N.J.M.
[2350]—*Sisters of the Living Word.*—S.L.W.
[3730]—*Sisters of the Order of St. Basil the Great.*—O.S.B.M.
[3260]—*Sisters of the Precious Blood (Dayton, Ohio).*—C.PP.S.
[2090]—*Sisters, Home Visitors of Mary.*—H.V.M.
[3610]—*Sisters, Servants of Mary Immaculate.*—S.S.M.I.
[2150]—*Sisters, Servants of the Immaculate Heart of Mary.*—I.H.M.
[2460]—*Society of Mary Reparatrix.*—S.M.R.
[4070]—*Society of the Sacred Heart.*—R.S.C.J.
[4120-06]—*Ursuline Nuns of the Congregation of Paris.*—O.S.U.
[]—*Vestiarski Sisters of Jesus.*—V.S.

ARCHDIOCESAN CEMETERIES

DETROIT. *Owned and Operated by the Archdiocese of Detroit.*
Holy Cross.
Holy Sepulchre, Southfield.
Our Lady of Hope, Southgate.
Owned and Operated by the Mt. Elliott Cemetery Association.
Mt. Elliott.
Mt. Olivet.
Resurrection, Clinton Township.
All Saints, Waterford.
Owned and Operated by the Conventual Franciscan Friars.
St. Hedwig, Dearborn Heights.

NECROLOGY

⊕ Krawczak, Most Rev. Arthur H., Retired Bishop of Denver. —Died Jan. 13, 2000.

† Finnigan, Rev. Msgr. Thomas J, Detroit, MI St. Cecilia.

† Haney, Richard M., (Retired). —Died May 18, 2000.

† Hennes, Paul R., (Retired). —Died April 24, 2000.

† Lorenz, Rev. Msgr. Victor O., (Retired). —Died Jan. 29, 2000.

Diocese of Dodge City

(Dioecesis Dodgepolis)

Most Reverend

RONALD M. GILMORE, S.T.L., D.D.

Bishop of Dodge City; ordained June 7, 1969; appointed Bishop of Dodge City May 12, 1998; installed July 16, 1998. *Office: 910 Central Ave., Box 137, Dodge City, KS, 67801.*

Most Reverend

STANLEY G. SCHLARMAN, D.D.

Bishop Emeritus of Dodge City; ordained July 13, 1958; appointed to the Titular See of Capri and Auxiliary Bishop of Belleville, March 13, 1979; consecrated May 14, 1979; appointed Bishop of Dodge City March 1, 1983; installed May 4, 1983. *Res., 16 S. Illinois St., Belleville, IL, 62220-2104.*

Most Reverend

MARION F. FORST, D.D.

Retired Bishop of Dodge City; ordained June 10, 1934; consecrated Bishop of Dodge City March 24, 1960; installed April 5, 1960; resigned from Dodge City; appointed Auxiliary Bishop of Kansas City in Kansas October 16, 1976; retired as Auxiliary Bishop December 23, 1986. *Res., 16600 W. 126 St., Olathe, KS, 66062-1184.*

ESTABLISHED MAY 19, 1951.

Square Miles 23,000.

Comprises the following Counties in the State of Kansas: Barton, Stafford, Pratt, Barber, Rush, Ness, Lane, Scott, Wichita, Greeley, Hamilton, Kearny, Finney, Hodgeman, Pawnee, Edwards, Ford, Gray, Haskell, Grant, Stanton, Morton, Stevens, Seward, Meade, Clark, Kiowa and Comanche.

Principal Patron: Our Lady of Guadalupe.

Secondary Patron: St. John the Baptist.

For legal titles of parishes and diocesan institutions, consult the Chancery Office.

Catholic Church Offices: 910 Central Ave., P.O. Box 137, Dodge City, KS, 67801-0137. Tel.: 316-227-1500; Fax: 316-227-1570.

Web site address: www.dcdiocese.org

E-mail address: dcdiocese@dcdiocese.org

STATISTICAL OVERVIEW

Personnel	
Bishop	1
Retired Bishops	2
Priests: Diocesan Active in Diocese	22
Priests: Active Outside Diocese	2
Priests: Retired, Sick or Absent	18
Number of Diocesan Priests	42
Religious Priests in Diocese	1
Extern Priests in Diocese	8
Ordinations:	
Transitional Deacons	1
Permanent Deacons	4
Permanent Deacons in Diocese	3
Total Sisters	108
Parishes	
Parishes	50
With Resident Pastor:	
Resident Diocesan Priests	25
Resident Religious Priests	1
Without Resident Pastor:	
Administered by Priests	19
Administered by Professed Men Religious	1
Professional Ministry Personnel:	
Sisters	5
Lay Ministers	1
Welfare	
Catholic Hospitals	3
Total Assisted	97,618
Special Centers for Social Services	4
Total Assisted	257,775
Educational	
Diocesan Students in Other Seminaries	3
Seminaries, Religious	2
Total Seminarians	3
Elementary Schools, Diocesan and Parish	10
Total Students	1,114
Catechesis/Religious Education:	
High School Students	2,540
Elementary Students	3,189
Total Students Under Catholic Instruction	6,846
Teachers in the Diocese:	
Sisters	9
Lay Teachers	76
Vital Statistics	
Receptions into the Church:	
Infant Baptism Totals	968
Adult Baptism Totals	364
Received into Full Communion	98
First Communions	740
Confirmations	440
Marriages:	
Catholic	153
Interfaith	100
Total Marriages	253
Deaths	361
Total Catholic Population	42,566
Total Population	212,332

Former Bishops—Most Rev. JOHN BAPTIST FRANZ, D.D., cons. Aug. 29, 1951; transferred to the See of Peoria Aug. 8, 1959.—Most Rev. MARION F. FORST, D.D., cons. March 24, 1960; transferred to See of Kansas City, KS as Auxiliary Oct. 16, 1976; retired as Auxiliary Bishop Dec. 23, 1986.—Most Rev. EUGENE J. GERBER, D.D., cons. Dec. 14, 1976; transferred See of Wichita, KS Nov. 23, 1982.—Most Rev. STANLEY G. SCHLARMAN, D.D., cons. May 14, 1979; appt. Bishop of Dodge City March 1, 1983; installed May 4, 1983; retired May 12, 1998.

Vicar General—Rev. JOHN J. MAES.

Catholic Church Offices—910 Central Ave., P.O. Box 137, Dodge City, 67801-0137. Tel: 316-227-1500; Fax: 316-227-1570. Office Hours: Mon.-Fri. 9-4:30.

Chancellor & Director of the Catholic Chancery—Sr. PATRICIA MCGREEVY, O.S.B., J.C.L.

Diocesan Archivist—Mr. TIMOTHY F. WENZL.

Finance Director—Mr. DANIEL M. STREMEL, C.P.A.

Presbyteral Council & Diocesan Board of Consultors—Most Rev. RONALD M. GILMORE; Revs. GREGORY S. LEBLANC, Sec. & Treas. JAMES E. BAKER, J.C.L.; ANGEL DY; DAVID A. FLAGOR, Vice Chm.; GILBERT HERRMAN; PASCAL L. KLEIN; DAVID H. KRAUS, J.C.L.; JOHN J. MAES, V.G.; CHARLES MAZOUCH; ROBERT A. SCHREMMER, Chm. WARREN L. STECKLEIN.

Deans—Rev. JAMES E. BAKER, V.F., Garden City; Rev. ULTAN P. MURPHY, V.F., Great Bend; Rev. JOHN R. STRASSER, Dodge City.

Matrimonial Tribunal—910 Central Ave., P.O. Box 137, Dodge City, 67801-0137. All matrimonial correspondence is to be sent to the attention of: Secretary of the Tribunal, Sr. Janice Grochowsky, C.S.J.

Judicial Vicar—Rev. JAMES E. BAKER, J.C.L.

Synodal Judge—Rev. JAMES E. BAKER, J.C.L.

Promoter of Justice—Rev. DAVID H. KRAUS, J.C.L.

Defender of the Bond—Rev. DAVID H. KRAUS, J.C.L.

Advocates—Revs. TED A. SKALSKY; ROBERT A. SCHREMMER; WILLIAM A. VOGEL; Deacon ERASMO RODRIGUEZ.

Notary—Sr. JANICE GROCHOWSKY, C.S.J.; PAMELA POLLEY.

Diocesan Offices and Directors

Catholic Education Office and Superintendent of Schools - Elementary School Religious Education—Sr. ROSEMARY HENRICHS, A.S.C.

Catholic Social Service Offices—Rev. TED A. SKALSKY, Exec. Dir., *805 Ave. J, Dodge City, 67801.* Tel: 316-227-3442. DEBBIE SNAPP, Prog. Dir.

Priestly Life and Ministry—Revs. JAMES E. BAKER, J.C.L.; DAVID H. KRAUS, J.C.L.; GREGORY LEBLANC.

Commission for Ministry to Priests—Revs. JOHN J. MAES, V.G.; CHARLES MAZOUCH; TED SKALSKY.

Cursillo—1510 1/2 N. Calhoun, Liberal, 67901.

Diocesan Attorney—Foulston & Siefkin, L.L.P., *810 Frontview, Dodge City, 67801.* Tel: 316-227-8126.

Diocesan Finance Council—Most Rev. RONALD M. GILMORE, Ex Officio; Mr. DANIEL M. STREMEL, C.P.A., Ex Officio, Sec. & Treas. JOHN ACKERMAN, Ex Officio; Sr. PAT MCGREEVY, O.S.B., J.C.L., Ex Officio; CLARINE HEIMAN; EUGENE HEIMAN; CARL HELFRICH, C.P.A.; Rev. WARREN STECKLEIN; RON VRATIL, C.P.A.

Diocesan Fitness Review Board—DAVID H. SNAPP, Admin. Tel: 316-225-5051 (Office); 316-225-2412 (Home).

Diocesan Pastoral Council—Most Rev. RONALD M. GILMORE, Ex Officio; Rev. ULTAN MURPHY, V.F.; Sr. PAT MCGREEVY, O.S.B., J.C.L., Bishop's Representative; DEBBIE HELFRICH; TOM GIESSEL; LEROY THILL; Revs. JAMES E. BAKER, V.F.; JOHN R. STRASSER, V.F.; BECKY HESSMAN; DOROTHY DEVINE; KEITH WIERMAN; GENE JUNO, Chm.; JOHN BROWER; IRENE VELASQUEZ.

Priests' Trust Fund—Revs. ROBERT A. SCHREMMER, Chm.; JOHN R. STRASSER, V.F., Vice Chm.; JAMES P. DIEKER, Sec.; Rev. Msgr. A. F. PREISNER, Treas.; Rev. MARVIN W. REIF.

Diocesan School Council—Most Rev. RONALD M. GILMORE, Ex Officio; Sr. ROSEMARY HENRICHS, A.S.C., Supt. of Schools; Revs. DAVID A. FLAGOR; JAMES P. DIEKER; WILLIAM A. VOGEL; JOHN R. STRASSER, V.F.; Mr. BRUCE KOZLOWSKI; Ms. STEPHANIE BOGNER; Ms. SANDY CHAPPEL; Mr. BRADY GROS; Ms. CAROL BAIN.

Lay Employees' Retirement Plan—Mr. DANIEL M. STREMEL, C.P.A.

Diocesan Newspaper Office—"The Southwest Kansas Register", Diocesan Bimonthly, TIM WENZL, Editor.

Office of Family Ministries—STEVEN POLLEY, Dir.

Office of Liturgy and Worship (R.C.I.A.)—Rev. DAVID A. FLAGOR, Dir., *St. Joseph Church, 214 N. Main, Ellinwood, 67526-1642*. Tel: 316-564-2534. JANE STEIN, Coord., *Immaculate Conception Church, P.O. Box 197, Claflin, 67525-0197*. Tel: 316-587-3628.

Catholic Agency - Migration and Refugee Services—LEVITA ROHLMAN, Exec. Dir., *1510 Taylor Plaza E., Garden City, 67846*. Tel: 316-276-7610; Fax: 316-276-9228.

Diaconate Office—Revs. ROBERT A. SCHREMMER, Co-Dir., Diaconate Office & Formation; ANGEL DY, Co-Dir., Diaconate Office & Formation; TED A. SKALSKY, Dir. Deacon Personnel.

Propagation of the Faith and Pontifical Association of the Holy Childhood—Sr. KAREN ACKERMAN, A.S.C., *St. Lawrence Parish, P.O. Box 278, Jetmore, 67854-0278*. Tel: 316-357-8791.

High School Religious Education, Youth Ministry, Confirmation Retreats—STEVEN D. POLLEY, Dir.

Scouting—Rev. JAMES E. BAKER, *509 St. John St., Garden City, 67846-5294*. Tel: 316-275-4204.

Vocation Office—Revs. MARVIN W. REIF, Dir. Vocations; JOHN J. MAES, V.G., Dir. Seminarians.

CLERGY, PARISHES, MISSIONS AND PAROCHIAL SCHOOLS

CITY OF DODGE CITY
(Ford County)

1—CATHEDRAL OF THE SACRED HEART (1882), Rev. John R. Strasser; Sr. Mary Rose Stein, O.P, Pastoral Min. In res., Rev. Augustine Nguyen.
Office: 903 Central Ave., 67801. Tel: 316-225-4802; Fax: 316-338-8268.
Res., 1000 First Ave., 67801. Tel: 316-227-3772.
School—905 Central Ave., 67801. Tel: 316-227-6532; Fax: 316-227-3221. Mrs. Kathryne Germscheid, Prin.
Lay Teachers 21; Students 362.
Catechesis/Religious Programs—D.R.E.: Samantha Nau, (Elementary); Dave Geist, (High School). Students 120.

2—OUR LADY OF GUADALUPE (1915) (Mexican), Rev. Ted A. Skalsky.
Res., 805 Ave. J, 67801. Tel: 316-227-3442 (Office); Fax: 316-227-9862.
Catechesis/Religious Programs—Students 663.

OUTSIDE THE CITY OF DODGE CITY

Ashland, Comanche Co., Holy Spirit Station (1984) (German). Attended by St. Joseph, Ashland. Rev. Nicanor S. Ferangco, Jr (Philippines).
Mailing Address: c/o St. Joseph Church, 514 Main St., Box 577, 67831. Tel: 316-635-2338; Fax: 316-635-4087. [JC]

St. Joseph, Clark Co., (1886) (German), Rev. Nicanor S. Ferangco, Jr (Philippines).
Res., 514 Main St., P.O. Box 577, 67831-0577. Tel: 316-635-2338; Fax: 316-635-4087. [JC]
Catechesis/Religious Programs—Tel: 316-635-4073. Becky Luerman, D.R.E.
Students 32.

Beaver, Barton Co., St. Joseph. Closed. Sacramental records can be found at St. John, Hoisington.

Belpre, Edwards Co., St. Bernard (1901), Rev. Dennis L. Reed.
Res., 203 Hudson St., P.O. Box 188, 67519-0188. Tel: 316-995-4305.
Catechesis/Religious Programs—Tel: 316-324-5461. Teresa Wetzel, D.R.E.
Students 82.

Bucklin, Ford Co., St. George. Closed. Sacramental records can be found at Our Lady of Guadalupe, Dodge City.

Burdett, Pawnee Co., Holy Rosary. Closed. Sacramental records can be found at Sacred Heart, Larned.

Claflin, Barton Co., Immaculate Conception (1904), Rev. David A. Flagor; Jane Stein, Pastoral Assoc.
Mailing Address: P.O. Box 197, 67525. Tel: 316-587-3628; Fax: 316-587-3204. [JC]
Catechesis/Religious Programs—Students 141.

Coldwater, Holy Spirit. Closed. Sacramental records can be found at St. Joseph, Ashland.

Deerfield, Kearney Co., Christ the King (1937), Rev. James E. Baker, J.C.L.
Mailing Address: P.O. Box 455, 67838. Tel: 316-275-4204.
Catechesis/Religious Programs—Tel: 316-426-6397. Marilyn Danler, D.R.E.
Students 46.

Dighton, Lane Co., St. Theresa (1927). Attended by St. Joseph, Scott City. Rev. David H. Kraus, J.C.L.
Res., 322 S. First St., P.O. Box 787, 67839. Tel: 316-397-5357. [JC]
Catechesis/Religious Programs—Tel: 316-397-5711. Annette Wilson, D.R.E.
Students 57.

Dubuque, Barton Co., St. Catherine. Closed. Sacramental records can be found at St. John the Evangelist, Hoisington.

Elkhart, Morton Co., St. Joan of Arc (1921), Rev. Francis Khoi Nguyen.
Res., 723 S. Baca Ave., P.O. Box 570, 67950-0570. Tel: 316-697-4622. [JC]
Catechesis/Religious Programs—Tel: 316-697-4587. Marita Walls, D.R.E.
Students 55.

Ellinwood, Barton Co., St. Joseph (1876) (German), Rev. David A. Flagor.
Res., 214 N. Main St., 67526. Tel: 316-564-2534; Fax: 316-564-2714.
School—111 W. Third, 67526. Tel: 316-564-2721. Jane A. Dreiling, Prin.
Adorers of the Blood of Christ 2; Lay Teachers 6; Students 66.
Catechesis/Religious Programs—Tel: 316-587-3674. David Tudor, D.R.E.
Students 65.

Fowler, Meade Co., St. Anthony (1910). Attended by St. John the Baptist, Meade. Rev. Zeno Ye Swe (Burma). Pastoral Assocs.: Judy Dewell; Steve Dewell.
Res., 410 Fourth St., P.O. Box 80, 67844. Tel: 316-646-5297; Fax: 316-646-5207. [JC]
Catechesis/Religious Programs—Brenda Harris, D.R.E.
Students 90.

Garden City, Finney Co., St. Dominic (1965), Rev. Joseph E. Bahr; Sr. Catherine Therese Paulie, C.S.J., Pastoral Min.
Office: 615 J. C. St., 67846. Tel: 316-276-2024; Fax: 316-276-2086.
School—617 J. C. St., 67846. Tel: 316-276-8981.
Lay Teachers 9; Students 153.
Catechesis/Religious Programs—Tel: 316-276-3500. Michael Dorsey, D.R.E.
Students 352.

St. Mary (1898), Revs. James E. Baker, J.C.L.; Carlos Garcia-Pena.
Res., 509 St. John St., 67846. Tel: 316-275-4204; Fax: 316-272-9971. [JC 2]
School—503 W. St. John St., 67846. Tel: 316-276-2241; Fax: 316-276-7067. Trina Delgado, Prin.
Lay Teachers 7; Students 93.
Catechesis/Religious Programs—Tel: 316-276-2716. Patricia Nieman, D.R.E.
Students 488.
Mission—Deerfield, Kearny Co., Christ the King, 812 Main St., Deerfield, 67838. Tel: 316-426-6996.

Great Bend, Barton Co., St. Patrick (1960), Rev. Warren L. Stecklein; Sr. Mary Cecilia Lenherr, S.C.L., Pastoral Assoc.
Res., 4100 Broadway, 67530. Tel: 316-792-1396; Fax: 316-792-1397. [JC]
School—4200 Broadway, 67530. Tel: 316-793-3265. Mr. Fred Meyers, Prin.
Lay Teachers 12; Students 142.
Catechesis/Religious Programs—Sr. Malachy Stockemer, D.R.E.
Students 170.

St. Rose of Lima (1878), Revs. Angel Dy; Marvin Reif.
Res., 1423 Holland St., P.O. Box 1007, 67530. Tel: 316-792-3641; Fax: 316-792-3642. [JC]
School—1400 Baker Ave., 67530. Tel: 316-793-5662. Mr. Fred Meyers, Prin.
Lay Teachers 7; Students 96.
Catechesis/Religious Programs—Joyce Haberman, D.R.E.
Students 220.

Greensburg, Kiowa Co., St. Joseph (1952). Attended by Sacred Heart, Pratt. Rev. James P. Dieker.
Res., c/o 332 N. Oak, Pratt, 67124. Tel: 316-672-6352; Fax: 316-672-3748.
Catechesis/Religious Programs—Tel: 316-723-2534; Fax: 316-723-2534.
Students 56.

Hanston, Hodgeman Co., St. Anthony (1908). Attended by St. John the Baptist, Spearville. Rev. Robert A. Schremmer.
Mailing Address: c/o St. Lawrence Church, P.O. Box 278, Jetmore, 67854. Tel: 316-357-8791. [CEM]
Catechesis/Religious Programs—Students 40.

Hoisington, Barton Co., St. John the Evangelist (1892), Rev. Pascal L. Klein; Sr. Alvina Miller, O.P., Pastoral Min.
Office: 122 E. 5th St., 67544. Tel: 316-653-2963; Fax: 316-653-2934.; Rectory: 108 E. 5th St., 67544. Tel: 316-653-2695. [CEM]
Catechesis/Religious Programs—Pam Willis, D.R.E.
Students 181.

Hugoton, Stevens Co., St. Helen (1948), Rev. Francis Khoi Nguyen (Vietnam).
Parish Office: 1011 S. Jefferson St., 67951-2823. Tel: 316-544-2551.
Catechesis/Religious Programs—Tel: 316-544-4644. Phyllis Ackerman, D.R.E.
Students 165.

Ingalls, Gray Co., St. Stanislaus (1909), Revs. Joseph E. Bahr; Francis G. Jordan, (Retired).
Mailing Address: P.O. Box 175, 67853. Tel: 316-335-5202; Fax: 316-335-5865. [JC]
Catechesis/Religious Programs—Kathy Hornung, D.R.E.
Students 151.

Jetmore, Hodgeman Co., St. Lawrence (1923). Attended by St. John the Baptist, Spearville. Rev. Robert A. Schremmer.
Mailing Address: P.O. Box 278, 67854. Tel: 316-357-8791.
Catechesis/Religious Programs—P.O. Box 278, 67854.
Students 58.

Johnson, Stanton Co., St. Bernadette (1949) (Hispanic). Attended by Mary Queen of Peace, Ulysses. Rev. Louis Trung Hoang.
Mailing Address: c/o Mary, Queen of Peace Church, 804 Colorado, Ulysses, 67880. Tel: 316-356-1532; Fax: 316-424-1065.
Catechesis/Religious Programs—Tel: 316-492-1554. Carol Ruth, D.R.E.
Students 75.

Kinsley, Edwards Co., St. Nicholas (1883) (Irish-German), Rev. William Vogel.
Res., 706 E. Sixth St., 67547. Tel: 316-659-2692; Fax: 316-659-2049. [CEM]
School—720 E. Sixth St., 67547. Tel: 316-659-2521. Mrs. Rebecca Burcher, Prin.
Lay Teachers 4; Students 66.
Catechesis/Religious Programs—Students 40.

Kiowa, Barber Co., St. John the Apostle (1885). Attended by Holy Rosary, Medicine Lodge and St. Boniface, Sharon. Rev. Anthony J. Suellentrop.
Res., 920 E. Main St., 67070. Tel: 316-825-4361; 886-1255 (Voice Mail).
Catechesis/Religious Programs—Tel: 316-825-4836. Linda Forester, D.R.E.
Students 41.

LaCrosse, Rush Co., St. Michael (1911), Rev. Benjamin Martin, Admin.
Res., 918 Lincoln St., P.O. Box 309, 67548. Tel: 913-222-2561. [JC]
Catechesis/Religious Programs—Tel: 913-222-3202. Twila Herman, D.R.E.
Students 85.

Lakin, Kearny Co., St. Anthony (1909), Rev. Michael Helms.
Res., 600 Soderberg St., P.O. Box 983, 67860. Tel: 316-355-6405; Fax: 316-355-6406. [JC]
Catechesis/Religious Programs—Tel: 316-355-7119. Delia Stahlecker, D.R.E.
Students 150.

Larned, Pawnee Co., Sacred Heart (1912), Rev. Dennis L. Reed.
Res., 1111 State St., 67550. Tel: 316-285-2035; Fax: 316-285-0097. [JC]
School—527 W. 12th St., 67550. Tel: 316-285-3025.
Lay Teachers 5; Students 56.
Catechesis/Religious Programs—Students 140.

Leoti, Wichita Co., St. Anthony of Padua (1887), Rev. Charles Mazouch.
Res., P.O. Box D, 67861. Tel: 316-779-4431. [CEM][JC]
Catechesis/Religious Programs—Tel: 316-375-2366. Sharon Steinle, D.R.E.
Students 47.

Liberal, Seward Co., St. Anthony (1916), Rev. Henry F. Hildebrandt; Deacon Erasmo L. Rodriguez.
Res., 419 W. First St., 67901. Tel: 316-624-4135; Fax: 316-624-3553.

Catechesis/Religious Programs—Kelly Ramirez, D.R.E.
Students 283.

Liebenthal, Rush Co., St. Joseph (1876) (German). Attended by St. Michael, LaCrosse. Rev. Benjamin Martin, Admin.
Mailing Address: P.O. Box 173, 67553. Tel: 785-222-3160. [CEM]
Catechesis/Religious Programs—Twinned with St. Michaels, LaCrosse. Tel: 785-222-2561.

Loretto, St. Mary, Help of Christians. Closed. Sacramental records can be found at St. Joseph, Liebenthal.

Marienthal, Wichita Co., St. Mary (1886), Rev. Charles Mazouch.
Mailing Address: P.O. Box 7, 67863. Tel: 316-379-4431; Fax: 316-379-4479. [CEM]
Catechesis/Religious Programs—Tel: 316-379-4446. Jolene Berning, D.R.E.
Students 63.

McCracken, Rush Co., St. Mary (1886). Closed. For inquiries for parish records contact the Chancery.

Meade, Meade Co., St. John the Baptist (1889), Rev. Zeno Ye Swe (Burma).
Res., 412 W. Carthage St., P.O. Box 706, 67864. Tel: 316-873-2003. [JC]
Catechesis/Religious Programs—Tel: 316-873-2654. Audrey Flowers, D.R.E.
Students 62.

Medicine Lodge, Barber Co., Holy Rosary (1952). Attended by St. John the Apostle, Kiowa and St. Boniface, Sharon. Rev. Anthony J. Suellentrop.
Mailing Address: 300 Curry Lane, 67104. Tel: 316-886-3596; 886-1255 (Voice Mail).
Catechesis/Religious Programs—Tel: 316-886-3242. Rob Stickney, D.R.E.
Students 57.

Ness City, Ness Co., Sacred Heart (1912), Rev. Gregory S. LeBlanc.
Res., 606 S. School St., P.O. Box 310, 67560. Tel: 913-798-3195. [CEM]
School—510 S. School St., 67560. Tel: 913-798-3530. Connette Eckels, Prin.
Adorers of the Blood of Christ 2; Lay Teachers 6; Students 62.
Catechesis/Religious Programs—Joby Henning, D.R.E.
Students 87.

North Ellinwood, Barton Co., Sts. Peter & Paul. Closed. Sacramental records can be found at St. Joseph, Ellinwood.

North Kinsley, Edwards Co., SS. Peter and Paul. Closed. Sacramental records can be found at St. Nicholas, Kinsley.

Odin, Barton Co., Holy Family (1879), Rev. Pascal L. Klein.
Mailing Address: c/o St. John the Evangelist Parish, 122 E. 5th St., Hoisington, 67544. Tel: 316-653-2963; Fax: 316-653-2934. [CEM]
Catechesis/Religious Programs—Tel: 316-587-2300. Teresa Hickel, D.R.E.
Students 63.

Offerle, Edwards Co., St. Joseph (1876), Rev. William Vogel.
Res., c/o 706 E. Sixth St., Kinsley, 67547. Tel: 316-659-2692. [CEM 2]
Catechesis/Religious Programs—Students 26.

Olmitz, Barton Co., St. Ann (1889), Rev. Ultan P. Murphy.
Res., 115 Cleveland St., P.O. Box 8, 67564. Tel: 316-586-3306. [CEM]
Catechesis/Religious Programs—Tel: 316-586-3282. Terese Frieb, D.R.E.
Students 104.

Plains, Meade Co., St. Patrick (1916). Attended by St. John the Baptist, Meade. Rev. Zeno Ye Swe (Burma).
Res., c/o St. John the Baptist, 412 W. Carthage, P.O. Box 706, Meade, 67864. Tel: 316-873-2003.
Church—601 Superior, P.O. Box 247, 67869. Tel: 316-563-7663. [JC]
Catechesis/Religious Programs—P.O. Box 102, 67869. Tel: 316-563-7874. Kelly Eakes, D.R.E.
Students 81.

Pratt, Pratt Co., Sacred Heart (1887), Rev. James P. Dieker.
Res., 332 N. Oak St., 67124. Tel: 316-672-6352; Fax: 316-672-3748.
School—(Grades PreK-5) 330 N. Oak St., 67124. Tel: 316-672-3687. Shirle Ibeawuchi, Prin.
Lay Teachers 6; Students 111.
Catechesis/Religious Programs—Tel: 316-672-6352. Rita Hitt, D.R.E.
Students 156.

Ransom, Ness Co., St. Aloysius (1903). Attended by Sacred Heart, Ness City. Rev. Gregory S. LeBlanc.
Mailing Address: P.O. Box 96, 67572. Tel: 913-731-2497. [CEM]
Catechesis/Religious Programs—Loretta Flax, D.R.E.
Students 47.

St. John, Stafford Co., St. John the Apostle (1949). Attended by St. Francis Xavier, Steward. Rev. Rene Guesnier, O.S.B.
Res., 609 E. Fourth St., Rte. 2, Box 100, 67576. Tel: 316-549-3538.
Catechesis/Religious Programs—Tel: 316-549-3424; Fax: 316-549-6188. Johnna Stanford, D.R.E.
Students 41.

St. Mary, Hodgeman Co., St. Mary. Closed. Sacramental records can be found at St. John the Baptist, Spearville.

Satanta, Haskell Co., St. Alphonsus (1946) (Hispanic), Rev. Louis Trung Dinh Hoang.
Res., 603 Tecumseh, Box 65, 67870. Tel: 316-649-2692.
Church—601 Tecumseh, 67870.
Catechesis/Religious Programs—Tel: 316-649-2978.
Students 88.

Scott City, Scott Co., St. Joseph (1911), Revs. Francis Khoi Nguyen; David H. Kraus, J.C.L.
Res., 1004 S. Main St., P.O. Box 228, 67871-0228. Tel: 316-872-3644; 872-7388 (Rectory). [JC]
Catechesis/Religious Programs—Tel: 316-872-5405. Don Ruda, D.R.E.
Students 167.

Seward, Stafford Co., St. Francis Xavier (1886), Rev. Rene Guesnier, O.S.B.
Mailing Address: 504 Main St., 67576. Tel: 316-458-5691; Fax: 316-458-3167.

Sharon, Barber Co., St. Boniface (1904). Attended by Holy Rosary, Medicine Lodge and St. John the Apostle, Kiowa. Rev. Anthony J. Suellentrop.
Res., 410 N. Main St., P.O. Box 118, 67138. Tel: 316-294-5526; Fax: 316-886-1255 (Voice Mail). [CEM]
Catechesis/Religious Programs—Tel: 316-294-5401. John Hern, D.R.E.
Students 62.

Spearville, Ford Co., St. John the Baptist (1904), Rev. Robert A. Schremmer.
Res., 100 S. Main St., P.O. Box 187, 67876. Tel: 316-385-2212; Fax: 316-385-2396. [CEM][JC 2]
Catechesis/Religious Programs—Tel: 316-385-2674. Carol Durler, D.R.E.
Students 120.

Syracuse, Hamilton Co., St. Raphael (1906), Revs. Gilbert P. Herrman; Jose Mangulabnan, Jr.
Mailing Address: P.O. Box 731, 67878. Tel: 316-384-7357; Fax: 209-797-4049. [CEM][JC]
Catechesis/Religious Programs—D.R.E.: Mary Ann Fair; Deneen McMillin.
Students 73.

Timken, Rush Co., Holy Trinity (1904) (Czech). Attended by St. Ann, Olmitz. Rev. Ultan P. Murphy.
Mailing Address: c/o St. Ann Church, P.O. Box 8, Olmitz, 67564. Tel: 316-586-3306. [CEM]
Catechesis/Religious Programs—Tel: 913-387-2552. Marie Stremel, D.R.E.
Students 44.

Tribune, Greeley Co., St. Joseph (1950). Attended by St. Raphael, Syracuse. Rev. Jun Mangulabnan.
Mailing Address: Box 67, 67879. Tel: 316-376-2292; Fax: 316-376-2297. [JC]
Catechesis/Religious Programs—Tel: 316-376-2490; Fax: 316-376-2792. Helen Govert, D.R.E.
Students 19.

Ulysses, Grant Co., Mary Queen of Peace (1948) (Hispanic), Rev. Louis Trung Hoang.
Res., 804 N. Colorado, 67880. Tel: 316-356-1532; Fax: 316-424-1065.
Catechesis/Religious Programs—Tel: 316-356-2832. Vikki Mader, D.R.E.
Students 310.

Windthorst, Ford Co., Immaculate Heart of Mary. Closed. Sacramental records can be found at St. John the Baptist, Spearville.

Wright, Ford Co., St. Andrew (1909), Rev. John J. Maes.
Mailing Address: 10893 St. Andrew Rd., P.O. Box 125, 67882. Tel: 316-227-3363; Fax: 316-227-3501. [CEM]
Parish Center—11792 Jewel Rd., 67882. Tel: 316-225-7345.
Catechesis/Religious Programs—Regina Lix, D.R.E.
Students 44.

On Duty Outside the Diocese:
Reverend Fathers—
Fiedler, Donald J.
Moore, Brian R.

Retired:
Reverend Monsignors—
Leahy, Patrick J., 6900 E. 45th St. N., Wichita, KS 67226
Preisner, A. F., 105 Kent, Dodge City, KS 67801
Reverend Fathers—
Birzer, W. L., 1206 S. Patton Rd., Rm. 110, Great Bend, KS 67530
Dreher, Jacob J., 3706 Meadowlark, Great Bend, KS 67530
Kelly, James, 6900 E. 45th St. N., Apt. D-4, Wichita, KS 67226
Kenny, Eugene, 1301 Warner Rd., Great Bend, KS 67530
Kowal, John P., 1918 W. Rd. 10, Ulysses, KS 67880
Lavrih, John, 6900 E. 45th St. N., Apt. D-2, Wichita, KS 67226
O'Neill, Rory, 6900 E. 45th St. N., Wichita, KS 67226
Pottorff, Lisle J., Rte. 2, Box 247, Douglass, KS 67039
Tuzicka, Fred M., 2611 27th St., Apt. 3-38, Great Bend, KS 67530
van Sloun, Eugene G., Rijksweg C.10, 6161EE, Geleen, Netherlands

Permanent Deacons:
Crowley, Norman, (Retired)
Lampe, Dwaine, (Retired), St. Anthony, Fowler
Rodriguez, Erasmo, St. Anthony, Liberal
Rondeau, Richard, (Retired)
Stickney, Harold, (Retired)

INSTITUTIONS LOCATED IN THE DIOCESE

[A] GENERAL HOSPITALS

GARDEN CITY. *St. Catherine Hospital*, 410 E. Walnut, 67846-5672. Tel: 316-272-2222; Fax: 316-272-2566.
Web site: www.stcath-hosp.org
For a complete listing, refer to the Hospitals section.

GREAT BEND. *Central Kansas Medical Center*, 3515 Broadway, 67530. Tel: 316-792-2511; Fax: 316-786-6298.
E-mail: ckmc@greatbend.com
Web site: www.ckmc.org
For a complete listing, refer to the Hospitals section.

LARNED. *Central Kansas Medical Center, St. Joseph Campus*, 923 Carroll St., 67550. Tel: 316-285-3161; Fax: 316-285-8883
For a complete listing, refer to the Hospitals section.

[B] RETREAT CENTERS

GREAT BEND. *Heartland Center for Spirituality*, 3600 Broadway, 67530-3692. Tel: 316-792-1232; Fax: 316-792-1746.
E-mail: hcs@ckan.com
Web site: www.ckan.com/hcs
Retreat Center. Sr. Louise Hageman, O.P., Dir. Total Staff 6.

PAWNEE ROCK. *Heartland Farm*, R.R. 1, Box 37, 67567-9602. Tel: 316-923-4585.
E-mail: hfarm@ruraltel.net
A Ministry of the Dominican Sisters of Great Bend, KS. Organic sustainable agriculture, body massage, retreat opportunities in rural setting. Sr. Mary Terence Wasinger, O.P., Contact Person. Total Staff 7.

[C] EDUCATIONAL ENDOWMENT FUNDS

DODGE CITY. *The Sacred Heart School Endowment*, 903 Central, 67801. Tel: 316-225-4802; Fax: 316-338-8268.

ELLINWOOD. *St. Joseph School Education Endowment Fund*, 214 N. Main St., 67526. Tel: 316-564-2534.

GARDEN CITY. *St. Dominic Grade School Endowment Fund*, 615 J.C. St., 67846. Tel: 316-276-2024; Fax: 316-276-2086.
The St. Mary Catholic Education Endowment Fund, 509 St. John St., 67846.

GREAT BEND. *Catholic Social Service Endowment Fund*, 2546 20th St., 67530. Tel: 316-792-1393; Fax: 316-792-1399.
E-mail: slytle@cpcis.net
The St. Patrick Grade School Education Endowment Fund, 4100 Broadway, 67530.
The St. Rose of Lima Grade School Education Endowment Fund, 1423 Holland St., Box 1007, 67530. Tel: 316-792-3641; Fax: 316-792-3642.

LARNED. *The Sacred Heart Grade School of Larned Education Endowment Fund*, 527 W. 12th St., 67550. Tel: 316-285-3025; Fax: 316-285-0097.
E-mail: heart@larned.net

PRATT. *The Sacred Heart School Education Endowment, Inc.*, 332 N. Oak St., 67124. Tel: 316-672-6352; Fax: 316-672-3748.
E-mail: school@prattusa.com
Web site: www.socencom.net/~ptc/sacred/

[D] CONVENTS AND RESIDENCES FOR SISTERS

GREAT BEND. *Immaculate Conception Convent*, 3600 Broadway, 67530-3692. Tel: 316-792-1232; Fax: 316-792-1746.
E-mail: ksdom@ckan.com
Web site: www.ckan.com/ksdom
Dominican Sisters of Great Bend. Legal Title: *Immaculate Conception Convent, Motherhouse and Novitiate of the Nuns of the Third Order of St. Dominic.* Sr. Gemma Doll, O.P., Prioress; Sr. Francine Schwarzenberger, O.P., Asst. Prioress. Council Members: Sr. LeAnn Probst, O.P.; Sr. Lorena Bolte, O.P.; Sr. Terence Wasinger, O.P. Final Professed Sisters 124; Lay Associates 72.

Great Bend Dominican Sisters Office of Mission and Ministry, 3600 Broadway, 67530-3692. Tel: 316-792-1232; Fax: 316-792-1746. Total in Residence 47. Retreat Center.

[E] SERVICES FOR THE ELDERLY

GREAT BEND. *Cedar Park Place, Inc.*, 3910 Cedar Park Pl., 67530-3692. Tel: 316-793-8115; Fax: 316-792-1746.
E-mail: cedarpark.@ckan.com
Low and Middle Income Housing for Elderly and Handicapped.

[F] MISCELLANEOUS

DODGE CITY. *Manna House*, 1012 First, 67801. Tel: 316-227-6707. Short-term housing and food distribution need. Margaret Witsken, Exec. Dir. Total Staff 2; Total Assisted 2,964.

GARDEN CITY. *Catholic Agency-Migration & Refugee Service*, 1510 Taylor Plaza E., 67846. Tel: 316-276-7610; Fax: 316-276-9228.
E-mail: mrs@gcnet.com
Ms. Levita Rohlman, Exec. Dir. Total Staff 1; Assisted 3,000.

Emmaus House, 802 N. Fifth St., 67846-5638. Tel: 316-275-2008.
E-mail: cmmaus@pld.com
Special Center for Social Services & Assistance. Homeless Shelter, Food Pantry, Soup Kitchen. Robin Marsh, CEO & Exec. Dir. Total Staff 4; Total Assisted 251,000.

GREAT BEND. *Family Crisis Center*, 1806 12th, P.O. Box 1543, 67530. Tel: 316-793-1965; 1966; 792-1885 (Crisis Line); Fax: 316-793-1964.
E-mail: family.crisis@greatbend.com
Patty Linsner-Hansen, Contact Person. Total Staff 8; Total Assisted 711.

Heartland Center for Wholistic Health, 1005 Williams. Tel: 316-793-9067.
E-mail: hcwh@ckan.com
A Ministry of the Dominican Sisters of Great Bend, KS. Reiki, reflexology, body massage, herbals. Sr. Anita Schugart, O.P., Contact Person. Total Staff 4.

St. Rose - Dominican Nurses Alumnae Association, 3600 Broadway, 67530. Tel: 316-792-1232; Fax: 316-792-1746.
E-mail: sisters@ksdom.org
Sr. M. Terence Wasinger, Sec. & Contact Person.

Sommerset Place, 5803 16th Terrace, 67530. Tel: 316-793-8075. 60 Unit Apartment Complex.

RELIGIOUS INSTITUTES OF MEN REPRESENTED IN THE DIOCESE

For further details refer to the corresponding bracketed number in the Religious Institutes of Men or Women section.

[0200]—*Benedictine Monks.*—O.S.B.

RELIGIOUS INSTITUTES OF WOMEN REPRESENTED IN THE DIOCESE

[0100]—*Adorers of the Blood of Christ.*—A.S.C.

[]—*Benedictine Sisters of Erie.* (Mt. St. Benedict Monastery).—O.S.B.

[]—*Incarnate Word.*—C.C.V.I.

[]—*Mexican Passionist Srs.*—C.F.P.

[1070-24]—*Nuns of the Third Order of St. Dominic.*—O.P.

[3830-18]—*Sisters of St. Joseph.*—C.S.J.

NECROLOGY

† Wylie, Stephen, (Retired). —Died Jan. 6, 2000.

Archdiocese of Dubuque

(Archidioecesis Dubuquensis)

Most Reverend

JEROME HANUS, O.S.B., D.D.

Archbishop of Dubuque; ordained July 30, 1966; appointed Bishop of St. Cloud July 6, 1987; ordained and installed August 24, 1987; appointed Coadjutor Archbishop of Dubuque August 23, 1994; welcomed October 27, 1994; succeeded to the See October 16, 1995. *Office: P.O. Box 479, Dubuque, IA, 52004-0479.*

Most Reverend

DANIEL W. KUCERA, O.S.B., PH.D., D.D.

Retired Archbishop of Dubuque; ordained May 26, 1949; appointed Titular Bishop of Natchez and Auxiliary Bishop of Joliet June 6, 1977; ordained Bishop July 21, 1977; appointed Bishop of Salina March 11, 1980; installed May 7, 1980; appointed Archbishop of Dubuque December 20, 1983; installed February 23, 1984; retired October 16, 1995. *13952 E. Marina Dr., #612, Aurora, CO, 80014.*

ESTABLISHED JULY 28, 1837; CREATED AN ARCHDIOCESE JUNE 15, 1893.

Square Miles 17,403.

PATRONS OF THE ARCHDIOCESE: Primary: St. Raphael, the Archangel; Secondary: St. John Mary Vianney, Cure of Ars.

Corporate Title: "The Archdiocese of Dubuque".

Comprises 30 Counties, that part of the State of Iowa north of the Counties of Polk, Jasper, Poweshiek, Iowa, Johnson, Cedar and Clinton and east of the Counties of Kossuth, Humboldt, Webster and Boone.

For legal titles of parishes and archdiocesan institutions, consult the Chancery.

Chancery-Archdiocesan Center: P.O. Box 479, Dubuque, IA, 52004-0479. Tel.: 563-556-2580; Fax: 563-556-5464.

Web site address: www.arch.pvt.k12.ia.us

E-mail address: dbqcco@arch.pvt.k12.ia.us

STATISTICAL OVERVIEW

Personnel	
Archbishop	1
Retired Archbishops	1
Abbots	1
Retired Abbots	2
Priests: Diocesan Active in Diocese	140
Priests: Active Outside Diocese	7
Priests: Retired, Sick or Absent	98
Number of Diocesan Priests	245
Religious Priests in Diocese	33
Extern Priests in Diocese	1
Ordinations:	
Diocesan Priests	5
Transitional Deacons	1
Permanent Deacons in Diocese	59
Total Brothers	25
Total Sisters	889
Parishes	
Parishes	211
With Resident Pastor:	
Resident Diocesan Priests	110
Without Resident Pastor:	
Administered by Priests	91
Administered by Deacons	4
Administered by Professed Men Religious	2
Administered by Women Religious	3
Administered by Lay People	1
Missions	2
Pastoral Centers	1
New Parishes Created	1
Closed Parishes	1
Professional Ministry Personnel:	
Brothers	3
Sisters	50
Lay Ministers	422
Welfare	
Catholic Hospitals	7
Total Assisted	1,195,315
Health Care Centers	4
Total Assisted	306
Homes for the Aged	5
Total Assisted	446
Day Care and Extended Day Care Centers	1
Total Assisted	42
Educational	
Seminaries, Diocesan	1
Students from This Diocese	1
Diocesan Students in Other Seminaries	13
Seminaries, Religious	1
Students Religious	80
Total Seminarians	94
Colleges and Universities	3
Total Students	4,337
High Schools, Diocesan and Parish	7
Total Students	3,133
Elementary Schools, Diocesan and Parish	53
Total Students	13,732
Catechesis/Religious Education:	
High School Students	6,745
Elementary Students	16,836
Total Students Under Catholic Instruction	44,877
Teachers in the Diocese:	
Priests	5
Sisters	31
Lay Teachers	1,027
Vital Statistics	
Receptions into the Church:	
Infant Baptism Totals	3,392
Adult Baptism Totals	138
Received into Full Communion	510
First Communions	3,708
Confirmations	3,355
Marriages:	
Catholic	838
Interfaith	586
Total Marriages	1,424
Deaths	2,189
Total Catholic Population	219,195
Total Population	923,000

Former Bishops—Most Rev. MATHIAS LORAS, D.D., cons. Dec. 10, 1837; died Feb. 19, 1858.—Most Rev. CLEMENT SMYTH, O.C.S.O., D.D., cons. May 3, 1857; died Sept. 22, 1865.—Most Rev. JOHN HENNESSY, D.D.,First Archbishop, cons. Sept. 30, 1866 raised to the Archiepiscopal Dignity, June 16, 1893; died March 4, 1900.—Most Rev. JOHN J. KEANE, D.D., cons. Bishop of Richmond, Aug. 25, 1878; transferred to the Titular See of Jasso, Aug. 12, 1888; elevated to the Archiepiscopal Dignity with the title of Archbishop of Damascus, Jan. 29, 1897; transferred to the See of Dubuque, July 24, 1900; resigned April 3, 1911; appt. Titular Archbishop of Cios, April 28, 1911; died June 22, 1918.—Most Rev. JAMES JOHN KEANE, D.D., ord. Dec. 23, 1882; cons. Bishop of Cheyenne, Oct. 28, 1902; elevated to the Archiepiscopal Dignity and transferred to Dubuque, Aug. 11, 1911; died Aug. 2, 1929.—Most Rev. FRANCIS J. L. BECKMAN, S.T.D., Titular Archbishop of Phulli; ord. June 20, 1902; appt. Bishop of Lincoln, Dec. 23, 1923; cons. Bishop of Lincoln, May 1, 1924 Apostolic Administrator of Omaha, June 1, 1926 to July 4, 1928; elevated to Archiepiscopal Dignity and transferred to Dubuque, Jan. 17, 1930; appt. Assistant at the Pontifical Throne, April 21, 1928; resigned Nov. 11, 1946; died Oct. 17, 1948.—Most Rev. HENRY P. ROHLMAN, D.D., appt. Bishop of Davenport, May 20, 1927; cons. July 25, 1927; appt. Coadjutor Archbishop of Dubuque "cum jure successionis" and Apostolic Administrator, July 15, 1944; installed Sept. 12, 1944; succeeded to Nov. 11, 1946; named Assistant at Pontifical Throne, Sept. 2, 1950; resigned and named Titular Archbishop of Cotrada, Dec. 2, 1954; died Sept. 13, 1957.—Most Rev. LEO BINZ, D.D., ord. March 15, 1924; appt. Titular Bishop of Pinara, Coadjutor Bishop and Apostolic Administrator of Winona, Nov. 21, 1942; cons. Dec. 21, 1942; named Titular Archbishop of Silyum and Coadjutor to the Archbishop of Dubuque "cum jure successionis," Oct. 15, 1949; named Assistant at the Pontifical Throne, June 11, 1954 Archbishop of Dubuque, Dec. 2, 1954; Pallium conferred, June 12, 1958; appt. Archbishop of St. Paul, Dec. 16, 1961; retired July, 1975; died Oct. 9, 1979.—Most Rev. JAMES J. BYRNE, S.T.D., appt. Titular Bishop of Etenna and Auxiliary Bishop of St. Paul, May 10, 1947; ord. Bishop, July 2, 1947; transferred Boise, ID, June 16, 1956; appt. Archbishop of Dubuque, March 19, 1962; retired Aug. 23, 1983; named Apostolic Administrator; died Aug. 2, 1996.—Most Rev. DANIEL KUCERA, O.S.B., Ph.D.,

D.D., ord. May 26, 1949; appt. Titular Bishop of Natchez and Auxiliary Bishop of Joliet, June 6, 1977; ord. Bishop, July 21, 1977; appt. Bishop of Salina, KS, March 11, 1980; installed May 7, 1980; named Archbishop of Dubuque, Dec. 20, 1983; installed Feb. 23, 1984; retired Oct. 16, 1995.

Archbishop—Most Rev. JEROME HANUS, O.S.B., *Archdiocesan Center, 1229 Mt. Loretta Ave., P.O. Box 479, Dubuque, 52004-0479.* Tel: 563-556-2580.

Vicar General and Episcopal Vicar for Dubuque Region—Rev. Msgr. JAMES O. BARTA, Ph.D., *Archdiocesan Center, 1229 Mt. Loretta Ave., P.O. Box 479, Dubuque, 52004-0479.* Tel: 563-556-2580.

Episcopal Vicar for Cedar Rapids Region—Rev. Msgr. RUSSELL M. BLEICH, S.T.L., *P.O. Box 2307, Cedar Rapids, 52406-2307.* Tel: 319-366-1647; Fax: 319-366-0426.

Episcopal Vicar for Waterloo Region—Rev. Msgr. W. DEAN WALZ, J.C.L., *320 Mulberry St., Waterloo, 50703.* Tel: 319-235-5566; Fax: 319-235-5567.

Judicial Vicar—Rev. THOMAS R. ZINKULA, J.D., J.C.L., *Archdiocesan Center, 1229 Mt. Loretta Ave., P.O. Box 479, Dubuque, 52004-0479.* Tel: 563-556-2580.

Chancellor—Sr. LIANA GLYNN, O.P., *Archdiocesan Center, 1229 Mt. Loretta Ave., P.O. Box 479, Dubuque, 52004-0479.* Tel: 563-556-2580.

Finance Officer—RICHARD L. RUNDE, *Archdiocesan Center, 1229 Mt. Loretta Ave., P.O. Box 479, Dubuque, 52004-0479.* Tel: 563-556-2580.

College of Consultors—Most Rev. JEROME HANUS, O.S.B.; Rev. Msgr. W. DEAN WALZ; Rev. Msgr. RUSSELL M. BLEICH; Rev. Msgr. JAMES O. BARTA; Revs. RICHARD J. AMENT; JAMES J. DUSTER; Very Revs. CARL A. RIES; RALPH P. SIMINGTON; Rev. LYLE L. WILGENBUSCH.

Deans—Very Rev. DONALD V. BAKEWELL, Bellevue; Very Rev. CHARLES E. LANG, Cedar Rapids; Very Rev. GARY F. KRAPFL, Decorah; Very Rev. JOSEPH V. O'BRIEN, Dubuque; Very Rev. FLORIAN J. SCHMIDT, Dyersville; Very Rev. FREDERICK C. FANGMANN, Elkader; Very Rev. RALPH P. SIMINGTON, Independence; Very Rev. EVERETT HEMANN, Marshalltown; Very Rev. CARL A. RIES, Mason City; Very Rev. ROGER R. RETHAMEL, New Hampton; Very Rev. DONALD P. SCHMIDT, Waterloo; Very Rev. JAMES L. MILLER, Webster City; Rev. Msgr. ROBERT R. VOGL, Loras College.

Archdiocesan Central Offices

Archdiocesan Pastoral Center—1229 Mt. Loretta Ave., Dubuque, 52003-7800. Tel: 563-556-2580; Fax: 563-556-5464. Office Hours: Mon.-Fri. 8:30-4:30, *Mailing Address: P.O. Box 479, Dubuque, 52004-0479.* Most Rev. JEROME HANUS, O.S.B.; BETTY SCHUELLER, Sec.; Rev. Msgr. JAMES O. BARTA, Vicar Gen. MADONNA WHITAKER, Sec.; Sr. LIANA GLYNN, O.P., Chancellor; BEV RECH, Sec.; Rev. THOMAS E. TOALE, Moderator of the Curia; SHIRLEY ARMSTRONG, Office Mgr.

Adult Catechesis—Archdiocesan Center, 1229 Mt. Loretta Ave, P.O. Box 479, Dubuque, 52004-0479. Tel: 563-556-2580. Sr. MARCI BLUM, O.S.F., Dir. LINDA MATHEWSON, Sec.

Archives—Rev. LORAS C. OTTING, Dir.; Rev. Msgr. EDGAR J. KURT, Archivist Emeritus; LINDA MATHEWSON, Sec.

Boy Scouts—Rev. LYLE L. WILGENBUSCH, Archdiocesan Chap. & Spiritual Dir., *St. Joseph the Worker, 60 S. Algona St., Dubuque, 52001-5605.* Tel: 563-588-1433.

Campaign for Human Development—JAMES L. YEAST, Dir., *1229 Mt. Loretta Ave., P.O. Box 1309, Dubuque, 52004-1309.* Tel: 563-556-2580. ED HABERKORN, Admin. Asst.

Campus Ministry—Rev. JOHN S. HAUGEN, Dir., *St. Stephen the Witness Catholic Student Center, 1019 W. 23rd St., Cedar Falls, 50613-3550.* Tel: 319-266-9863; Fax: 319-266-3706.

Catholic Cemeteries of the Archdiocese of Dubuque—RICHARD L. RUNDE, Dir., Finance Office: *1229 Mt. Loretta Ave., Dubuque, 52003-7800.* Tel: 563-556-2580.

Catholic Charities—

Administrative Offices—JAMES L. YEAST, L.M.S.W., Dir. JOE FEATHERSTON, L.M.S.W., Dir., Professional Svcs. & Assoc. Dir. Catholic Charities; Sr. EILEEN MCGOVERN, B.V.M., Counselor for Hispanic Ministry; ED HABERKORN, Admin. Asst. SUE HIRD, Office Mgr. MARTHA DEVEAUX, Sec. CAROL CALLAHAN, Business Mgr., Business Office: *1229 Mt. Loretta Ave., P.O. Box 1309, Dubuque, 52004-1309.* Tel: 563-556-2580.

Branch Offices—

Ames—MARY JO PFEIFER, *2210 Lincoln Way, Ames, 50014.* Tel: 515-296-2759.

Cedar Rapids—GARY STEJSKAL, Supvr. LYN PIOTROWSKI, Office Mgr. MARIA CAHALAN; MARIA GARLIE, *1430 Second Ave. S.E., Cedar Rapids, 52403.* Tel: 319-364-7121.

Decorah—CHARLES DOPKE, *P.O. Box 1309, Dubuque, 52004-1309.* Tel: 800-772-2758.

Dubuque—JOSEPH FEATHERSTON, Supvr. JOYCE CONNORS; TOM SHEA; ANGELLA LINK, *P.O. Box 1309, Dubuque, 52004-1309.* Tel: 563-556-2580.

Mason City—THOMAS FLAHERTY, *Will F. Muse Center, 600 First St. N.W., Mason City, 50401.* Tel: 515-424-9683.

Waterloo—THOMAS FLAHERTY, Supvr. DENISE MAAS; ORLYN WATHIER; Rev. KENNETH STECHER; MICHELLE SPRIO, Office Mgr., *Kimball Ridge Center, 2101 Kimball Ave., Waterloo, 50702.* Tel: 319-272-2080.

Special Programs—

Adoption—NANCY KINLEY, Dubuque Office.

Refugee Resettlement—JOE FEATHERSTON, Dubuque Office.

Social Concerns/Iowa Catholic Conference—JAMES L. YEAST, Dubuque Office *Catholic Charities may be telephoned toll-free from anyplace in Iowa: 800-772-2758.*

Catholic Charities and St. Mary's Home Boards of Directors—Most Rev. JEROME HANUS, O.S.B., Pres.; Rev. Msgr. JAMES O. BARTA, Vice Pres. JAMES L. YEAST, Treas. ALFRED HUGHES, Sec.

Deanery Representatives—JUDY BOWLING, Bellevue; MARY JO RATER, Cedar Rapids; CLETUS ROONEY, Decorah; FRITZ GANSHIRT, Dubuque; ROBERT BRUNKAN, Dyersville; LARRY MURPHY, Elkader; MARY TWOMEY, Independence; JUDY MCGEE, Marshalltown; SUE FOY, Mason City; WILLIAM FELLER, New Hampton; JEFFREY FITZPATRICK, Waterloo; TERRY ANDERSON, Webster City; ELDON HERRIG, At Large.

Continuing Formation of Clergy and Recently Ordained Program—Rev. DAVID H. O'CONNOR, Dir., *Archdiocesan Center, 1229 Mt. Loretta Ave., Dubuque, 52003-7800.* Tel: 563-556-2580. BEV RECH, Sec.

Council of Catholic Women—Rev. Msgr. W. DEAN WALZ, Moderator; MARGARET KOLASH, Pres., *2853 240th St., Clutier, 52217-9707.* Tel: 319-479-2214. ANNA MEYER, Sec., Office: *Archdiocesan Center, 1229 Mt. Loretta Ave., Dubuque, 52003-7800.* Tel: 563-556-2580. Bellevue Deanery: HELEN ZEIMET, Springbrook. Tel: 563-689-4466. Cedar Rapids Deanery: LILLIAN MCGIVERN, Keystone. Tel: 319-442-3486. Decorah Deanery: JEANETTE BLONG, Waukon. Tel: 563-568-3372. Dubuque Deanery: DORIS M. SLATTERY, Dubuque. Tel: 563-582-2773. Dyersville Deanery: STARLA SCHUSTER, Dyersville. Tel: 563-875-7719. Elkader Deanery: NEVA FISCHER, Strawberry Point. Tel: 563-933-4957. Independence Deanery: PHYLLIS J. HUGHES, Manchester. Tel: 319-927-4510. Marshalltown Deanery: ROSE ANN JERO, Marshalltown. Tel: 641-752-2165. Mason City Deanery: CINDY MARY, Forest City. Tel: 641-585-2082. New Hampton Deanery: FLORENCE SHOOK, Marble Rock. Tel: 641-397-2258. Waterloo Deanery: MARY KIDWELL, Waterloo. Tel: 319-232-1796. Webster City Deanery: MARY ANN SPITLER, Belmond. Tel: 641-444-3174.

Development Office—PAUL FROMMELT, Dir., *P.O. Box 479, Dubuque, 52004-0479.* Tel: 563-556-2580. LOIS THILMANY, Office Mgr. PATRICIA NEISES, Sec. DENISE AIRD, Sec.

Media Services—MARY MESCHER, Dir.; Sr. CAROL HOVERMAN, O.S.F., Media Rels. Coord. LARRY GAUL, Media Technician, *1229 Mt. Loretta Ave., Dubuque, 52003-7800.* Tel: 563-556-2580; 800-876-3546. Media Resource Center Assistants: KIM FELDMAN; CONNIE MCDERMOTT.

Educational System—

Office of Educational Services—Rev. THOMAS E. TOALE, Ph.D., Dir. Educational Svcs. & Supt. of Schools; JAMES OSTERBERGER, Dir., Educational Planning & Technology; CHERIE CASEY, Curriculum Dir. SHIRLEY ARMSTRONG, Office Mgr.

Catholic Schools (in addition to the above)—LYNNE DEVANEY, Dubuque Regl. Dir. Educational Svcs. ANNE MCCLAIN, Sec.; Sr. JEAN MARIE BRADY, B.V.M., Cedar Rapids Regl. Dir. Educational Svcs. JULIE KAPSCH, Sec. ALICE CONLON, Waterloo Regl. Dir. Educational Svcs. MARY WERNER, Sec.

Catechetical Services (in addition to above)—LORETTA RYAN, Dir. Catechetical Svcs. Assoc. Directors Catechetical Services: Sr. MILDRED STREIF, R.S.M., Dubuque; JULIE JOHNSON, Cedar Rapids; BETH DERR, Dyersville; Sr. MARGARET ANNE KRAMER P.B.V.M., Dubuque; PHYLLIS BERTHEL, Sec.

Special Needs—Sr. MARCI BLUM, O.S.F., Dir. LINDA MATHEWSON, Sec.

Family Life Office—COLLEEN PASNIK, Dir. GINNY NEUWOHNER, Office Sec., *Archdiocesan Center, 1229 Mt. Loretta Ave., Dubuque, 52003-7800.* Tel: 563-556-2580.

Engaged Encounter—Coordinators: MARK SCHLATTER; JANET SCHLATTER, *12177 J. Ave., Iowa Falls, 50126.* Tel: 641-648-3159. DOUG LONG; SHEILA LONG, *22997 115th St., Iowa Falls, 50126.* Tel: 641-648-3378. Rev. PHIL SCHMITT, Spiritual Advisor, *3834 E. Ave., N.E., Cedar Rapids, 52402-5627.* Tel: 319-247-0311.

For Registration—Family Life Office, 1229 Mt. Loretta Ave., Dubuque, 52003-7800. Tel: 563-556-2580.

Marriage Encounter—Family Life Office, 1229 Mt. Loretta Ave., Dubuque, 52003-7800. Tel: 563-556-2580.

Worldwide Marriage Encounter—Tel: 800-795-LOVE.

Marriage Retorno—Directors: Deacon MICHAEL OATES; MAUREEN OATES, *127 Kaspend Pl., Cedar Falls, 50613.* Tel: 319-268-0202.

Natural Family Planning—Family Life Office, 1229 Mt. Loretta Ave., Dubuque, 52003-7800. Tel: 563-556-2580.

Pre-Cana—Family Life Office, 1229 Mt. Loretta Ave., Dubuque, 52003-7800. Tel: 563-556-2580. Dubuque Area, SANDY ERNSDORFF, *2085 Hale St., Dubuque, 52001.* Tel: 563-556-2859. Dyersville Area, Directors: JERRY BECKER; KATHY BECKER, *2275 310th Ave., Earlville, 52041.* Tel: 563-875-8656. Decorah, Elkader, New Hampton Areas, For registration contact— *Family Life Office, 1229 Mt. Loretta Ave., Dubuque, 52003-7800.* Tel: 563-556-2580. Independence & Waterloo Areas, JUDY MOODY, *St. Stephen Student Center, 1019 W. 23rd St., Cedar Falls, 50613.* Tel: 319-266-9863. Cedar Rapids Area, Directors: PAT MURPHY; SANDY MURPHY, *1130 33rd St. S.E., Cedar Rapids, 52403.* Tel: 319-365-9839. Marshalltown & Webster City Areas, For registration contact— *Family Life Office, 1229 Mt. Loretta Ave., Dubuque, 52003-7800.* Tel: 563-556-2580. Mason City Area, Directors: CHUCK COOPER; JENNY COOPER, *710 N. Adams, Mason City, 50401.* Tel: 641-424-6251.

Retrouvaille—Contacts: GEORGE CRUM; DEE CRUM, *Box 448, Le Grand, 50142.* Tel: 641-479-2650. DICK SMITH; JOYCE SMITH, *420 10th Ave., S.E., Dyersville, 52040.* Tel: 563-875-8791.

Sponsor Couple—Family Life Office, 1229 Mt. Loretta Ave., Dubuque, 52003-7800. Tel: 563-556-2580.

To Trust Again—Family Life Office, 1229 Mt. Loretta Ave., Dubuque, 52003-7800. Tel: 563-556-2580.

Finance Office—RICHARD L. RUNDE, Finance Officer; PENNY REITTINGER, Auditor; JULIE SANDERS, Accounting; KEN RAHE, Business Mgr. JANICE TUEGEL, Accounting Clerk; MARY FLECKENSTEIN, Bookkeeper/Sec., *P.O. Box 479, Dubuque, 52004-0479.* Tel: 563-556-2580.

Health Care—JANINE MARIE IDZIAK, Ph.D., Consultant, *P.O. Box 479, Dubuque, 52004-0479.* Tel: 563-556-2580. PHYLLIS BERTHEL, Sec.

Hispanic Ministry—Cedar Rapids Office: GABRIELA FINNEGAN; MONICA PAULINA VALLEJO, *866 4th Ave. S.E., Cedar Rapids, 52403.* Tel: 319-362-8689. Dubuque Office: Sr. JEANETTE MCCARTHY, P.B.V.M., *1425 Iowa St., Dubuque, 52001-4890.* Tel: 563-584-0640. Hampton Office: Sr. CAROL BESCH, O.S.F., *1405 N. Federal St., Hampton, 50441.* Tel: 641-456-2797. Iowa Falls Office: Rev. MARK MCGOVERN, *415 Main St., P.O. Box 368, Iowa Falls, 50126-0368.* Tel: 641-648-9547. Marshalltown Office: Sr. CHRISTINE FEAGAN, O.P., *12 W. Linn, Marshalltown, 50158-0642.* Tel: 641-753-7815; Fax: 641-752-6277. Postville Office: Rev. LLOYD P. OUDERKIRK, *St. Bridget Parish, P.O. Box 369, Postville, 52162-0369.* Tel: 563-864-3142. Waterloo Office: Sr. KATHLEEN GRACE, O.S.F., *320 Mulberry St., Waterloo, 50703-3598.* Tel: 319-234-6744.

Priests Assigned to Hispanic Ministry—Revs. LEON L. CONNOLLY; BERNARD C. GRADY; MARK J. MCGOVERN; LLOYD P. OUDERKIRK; Very Rev. JAMES L. MILLER.

Holy Childhood, Pontifical Association—Rev. Msgr. ROBERT L. FERRING, Dir., *Archdiocesan Center, 1229 Mt. Loretta Ave., Dubuque, 52003-7800.* Tel: 563-556-2580. NANCY EISBACH, Sec.

Human Resources—JOAN MANTERNACH, Dir. ITZA HEIM, Sec.

Insurance: Property and Liability (Dubuque Archdiocesan Protection Program)—JEFF KISEL, Field Representative, *Archdiocesan Center, 1229 Mt. Loretta Ave., Dubuque, 52003-7800.* Tel: 563-556-2580. ITZA HEIM, Sec.

Jail and Prison Ministry—Deacon ED WEBER, Coord., *1158 Independence Ave., Waterloo, 50703.* Tel: 319-232-1584.

Lay Ministry Formation—Sr. CARLA POPES, P.B.V.M., Dir. DEB JASPER, Sec., *Archdiocesan Center, 1229 Mt. Loretta Ave., P.O. Box 479, Dubuque, 52004-0479.* Tel: 563-556-2580.

Legion of Mary—Rev. JOHN R. HUSSMANN, *P.O. Box 479, Dubuque, 52004-0479.* Tel: 563-556-2580.

Management Information Services—JEFF WEINBERG, Dir. SARAH DEPOOTER, Email Admin. PEG HENNAGIR, Sec.

Metropolitan Tribunal—P.O. Box 479, Dubuque, 52004-0479. Tel: 563-556-2580. (Please send all dispensation requests to the Tribunal.).

Judicial Vicar—Rev. THOMAS R. ZINKULA, J.D., J.C.L.; CHARLOTTE NEISES, Asst. to the Judicial Vicar & Notary.

Defenders of the Bond—Rev. Msgr. RICHARD P. FUNKE, J.C.L.; Rev. DONALD J. PLAMONDON, J.C.L.; Sr. LIANA GLYNN, O.P., J.C.L.; Rev. Msgr. DAVID A. WHEELER, J.C.D.

Judges—Revs. SCOTT E. BULLOCK, J.C.L.; JOSEPH L. HAUER, J.C.L.; Deacon GERALD JORGENSEN, Ph.D., J.C.L.; Rev. MARK R. NEMMERS; Sr. FRANCINE QUILLEN, P.B.V.M., J.C.L.; Rev. Msgr. ROBERT L. SPAIGHT, J.C.D.; Rev. Msgr. W. DEAN WALZ, J.C.L.; Rev. THOMAS R. ZINKULA, J.D., J.C.L.

Auditor—Rev. DOUGLAS J. LOECKE.

Ecclesiastical Attorneys—Rev. Msgr. RICHARD P. FUNKE, J.C.L.; Rev. Msgr. W. DEAN WALZ, J.C.L.

Promoter of Justice—Rev. Msgr. DAVID A. WHEELER, J.C.D.

Notary and Office Secretary—THERESA HOUSELOG; JOANN KOOPMANN, Sec.

Newspaper "The Witness"—Rev. Msgr. THOMAS J. RALPH, Editor, *Archdiocesan Center, 1229 Mt. Loretta Ave., P.O. Box 917, Dubuque, 52004-0917.* Tel: 563-588-0556. Staff: JUDY BANDY; BRET FEAR; ROSE FLYNN; STEVE MCMAHON.

Pastoral Planning Office—Sr. MARY MONTGOMERY, O.P., Dir. MADONNA WHITAKER, Sec., *P.O. Box 479, Dubuque, 52004-0479.* Tel: 563-556-2580.

Permanent Diaconate Program—Deacon LEN FROYEN, Dir. GAIL FROYER, Sec., *St. Stephen the Witness Student Center, 1019 W. 23rd St., Cedar Falls, 50613.* Tel: 319-266-9863. Asst. Directors: Deacons GERALD JORGENSEN; MICHAEL OATES.

Print Shop—ROBERT GOLDTHORPE, Mgr., *P.O. Box 479, Dubuque, 52004-0479.* Tel: 563-556-2580.

Propagation of the Faith—Rev. Msgr. ROBERT L. FERRING; NANCY EISBACH, Sec., *Archdiocesan Center, 1229 Mt. Loretta Ave., Dubuque, 52003-7800.* Tel: 563-556-2580.

Renew 2000—Sr. MARCIE BLUM, O.S.F., Dir. LINDA MATHEWSON, Sec.

Respect Life Office—JAMES L. YEAST, Dir., Catholic Charities; ED HABERKORN, Admin. Asst., *P.O. Box 1309, Dubuque, 52004-1309.* Tel: 563-556-2580; 800-772-2758.

Rural Life Office—DONALD KLAUKE, Archdiocesan Dir. MARY KLAUKE, Sec., *511 Bear Creek Dr., Dorchester, 52140-7505.* Tel: 800-772-2758.

St. Mary's Home, Inc.—JAMES L. YEAST, L.M.S.W., Dir. DONNA MORRIS, Housing Admin., *1229 Mt. Loretta Ave., P.O. Box 1309, Dubuque, 52003-7800.* Tel: 563-556-2580.

Saint Raphael Priest Fund Society—

Board of Directors/Priest Pension Plan Board of Trustees—Most Rev. JEROME HANUS, O.S.B., Pres.; Rev. Msgr. JAMES O. BARTA, Vice Pres.; Rev. Msgr. JOSEPH P. HERARD, Sec. & Treas. RICHARD L. RUNDE, Plan Admin. Directors: Revs. GERALD A. CONDON; WALTER BRUNKAN; PATRICK GEARY; KARL L. GLOVIK; Rev. Msgr. STANLEY J. HAYEK; Rev. Msgr. ROBERT G. HOGAN; Revs. JERRY F. KOPACEK; EUGENE KUTSCH; Very Rev. RALPH P. SIMINGTON; Rev. Msgr. NEIL W. TOBIN; Rev. THOMAS R. ZINKULA.

Seminarians—Rev. SCOTT E. BULLOCK, Dir. BEV RECH, Sec., *1229 Mt. Loretta Ave., Dubuque, 52003-7800.* Tel: 563-556-2580.

Stewardship Program—Rev. Msgr. ROBERT G. HOGAN, Dir., *1001 9th Ave. S., Clear Lake, 50428.* Tel: 641-357-3214; Fax: 641-357-3210.

Vocation/Awareness—Rev. PHILLIP G. GIBBS, Dir. Vocation Awareness; Rev. DAVID M. BECKMAN, Assoc. Dir., Waterloo Region; Rev. JON M. SEDA, Assoc. Dir., Cedar Rapids Region; Rev. CLAYTON R. LANDHERR, Assoc. Dir., Dubuque Region; BEV RECH, Sec., *Archdiocesan Center, 1229 Mt. Loretta Ave., Dubuque, 52003-7800.* Tel: 563-556-2580.

Worship Office—Vacant, Dir. THERESA HARVEY, Assoc. Dir., *1229 Mt. Loretta Ave., P.O. Box 479, Dubuque, 52004-0479.* Tel: 563-556-2580. DEB JASPER, Sec.

Youth Formation/Young Adult Ministry—DIANE FLAHERTY, Dir. JUDY ARLEN, Sec., *Archdiocesan Center, 1229 Mt. Loretta Ave., Dubuque, 52003.* Tel: 563-556-2580.

Archdiocesan Boards, Commissions and Councils

Archdiocesan Administrative Board—Most Rev. JEROME HANUS, O.S.B.; Rev. Msgr. JAMES O. BARTA; Sr. LIANA GLYNN, O.P.; Sr. MARY MONTGOMERY, O.P.; RICHARD L. RUNDE.

Archdiocesan Adult Formation Committee—SUZANNE BLOUIN; Sr. MARCIE BLUM, O.S.F.; DAVE CUSHING; Sr. LAVERNE DOLPHIN, B.V.M.; Sr. BERNADETTE ENGLEHAUPT, S.S.S.F.; Sr. MADONNA FRIEDMAN, O.S.F.; BARBARA GATCH; Sr. MARY HARGRAFEN, O.S.F.; Sr. MARY LECHTENBERG, O.S.F.; Bro. STEPHEN MARKHAM, F.S.C.; NORMAN SCHAULS; CATHY SCHMITZ.

Advisory Committee of Persons with Disabilities—MITZI BAKER; Sr. MARCI BLUM, O.S.F.; BOB BRUNKAN; FRANCES BRUNKAN; Sr. MARGE BURKLE, O.S.F.; D. J. JAEGER; Rev. JERRY KOPACEK; Deacon STEVE MACDONALD; KIM MAJERUS; CATHY MURPHY; RUTH PALMER; JEAN RIPPLINGER; ANNE SCHMIEDER; KEVIN WILLE; LINDA WOODCOCK; JERRY WOODCOCK.

American Martyrs Retreat House Advisory Board—Sr. M. JEANINE KUHN, P.B.V.M, Dir. JANINE WHIPPS, Chm. JOAN GLAZA, Sec. MARGUERITE BERTELSEN; EDWARD J. GALLAGHER, JR.; ROGER KEUTER; RON LEIBOLD; Rev. Msgr. W. DEAN WALZ, Ex Officio.

Board of Education—PATRICIA MULLEN, Pres., Dubuque Deanery; JIM BOWES, Vice Pres., Appointed by Archbishop; PATRICIA KAYSER, Sec., Independence Deanery; RANDY BENDER, Bellevue Deanery; JULIE BELLENDIER, Cedar Rapids Deanery; MARY HOLTHAUS, Decorah Deanery; BILL BROWN, Dyersville Deanery; T. J. STECKLEIN, Elkader Deanery; PATRICIA GREEN, Marshalltown Deanery; JUDY KRAMER, Mason City Deanery; BERNARD HUEGEL, New Hampton Deanery; RICHARD KLEIN, Waterloo Deanery; EDDA PEED, Webster City Deanery. Appointed by the Archbishop: JAMES COLLINS; ROSA MARIA DE FINDLEY; KAREN VOLZ. Priest Representatives: Revs. JACK R. FLAHERTY; PHILIP E. THOMPSON. Sister Representatives: Sr. BENJAMIN DUSCHNER, P.B.V.M.; Sr. MARIE GEMAR, O.S.F. Ex Officio Members: Most Rev. JEROME HANUS, O.S.B.; Rev. Msgr. JAMES O. BARTA; Rev. Msgr. RUSSELL M. BLEICH; Rev. Msgr. W. DEAN WALZ; Rev. THOMAS E. TOALE; LORETTA RYAN.

Building Commission—Rev. Msgr. RUSSELL M. BLEICH, Chair; RICHARD L. RUNDE, Exec. Sec.; Rev. JOHN R. GALLAGHER; Rev. Msgr. STANLEY J. HAYEK; Rev. Msgr. ROBERT G. HOGAN; JAMES HYNES; Rev. NEIL J. MANTERNACH; WAYNE SNYDER; LEO THEISEN; Rev. Msgr. NEIL W. TOBIN; JAMES YOUNGBLUT; KEN RAHE, Recording Sec.

Church Design/Renovation Commission—Rev. NEIL J. MANTERNACH, Exec. Sec. PAM JOHNSTON; Revs. DENNIS D. JUHL; LYLE L. WILGENBUSCH.

Continuing Formation of Clergy—Revs. DAVID H. O'CONNOR, Chm. RICHARD J. AMENT; JAMES J. GOEDKEN; WALTER J. KLEINFEHN; GARY KRAPFL; MICHAEL J. MESCHER; JAMES SECORA; THOMAS E. TOALE, Ex Officio.

Diaconal Council—Most Rev. JEROME HANUS, O.S.B., Pres.; Deacons TOM LANG, Chm. LEN FROYEN, Ph.D., Exec. Sec.

Ames Region—Deacons STEVE VAN KERCKVOORDE; TOM LANG.

Cedar Rapids Region—Deacons BILL CISLER; AL SCHAROSCH.

Dubuque Region—Deacons BILL MAUSS; JIM STEGER.

Mason City Region—Deacons VIC GROH; NICK SCHMIT.

Waterloo Region—LORI FREET; Deacon DAVE JONES.

Appointed—Deacons MICHAEL BLOUIN, APC Liaison; MICHAEL OATES; LEO SCHMALL.

Due Process Board—ALFRED HUGHES, Chair, Dubuque. Tel: 563-557-7360 (Office); 583-7541 (Home).; Deacon MICHAEL OATES, Cedar Falls; PATRICK BYRNE, Clear Lake; RAY COLEMAN, Tama; Rev. CRAIG STEIMEL, Forest City; Sr. KATHLEEN GRACE, O.S.F., Waterloo; DONNA JORDAN, Cedar Falls; JOYCE MERRITT, Anamosa; Rev. STEVEN ROSONKE, Cedar Rapids; Sr. ELIZABETH PRESSELER, P.B.V.M., Dubuque.

Family Life Advisory Board—KIM VOGEL, Chm.; Rev. PHILLIP G. GIBBS; DICK HENNEBERRY; ARLENE HENNEBERRY; MIKE MCCARVEL; LORI MCCARVEL; TROY MUNDT; GINNY NEUWOHNER; MAGGIE O'CONNOR; COLLEEN PASNIK; Rev. KEN STECHER; DAN WEBER; SAL WEBER.

Finance Commission—Most Rev. JEROME HANUS, O.S.B., Chm. RICHARD L. RUNDE, Exec. Sec. JULIE SANDERS, Recording Sec.; Rev. Msgr. JAMES O. BARTA; DONALD BERGAN; Rev. Msgr. RICHARD P. FUNKE; Rev. Msgr. ROBERT G. HOGAN; Deacon MATTHEW F. BERRY; Sr. MARGARET COSGROVE, B.V.M.; PAUL J. FROMMELT; ANN OSTERHAUS; KAREN STURM; Rev. THOMAS E. TOALE; DAN WELU.

Lay Ministry Advisory Board—Rev. Msgr. JAMES O. BARTA; Revs. JAMES BROKMAN; DENNIS JUHL; MICHAEL BYRNE; DAVID CUSHING; JANET O'MEARA; Sr. CARLA POPES, P.B.V.M.; DENNIS RYAN; CATHY SCHMITZ; MARTHA SIMMONS.

Medical-Moral Commission—JANINE MARIE IDZIAK, Ph.D., Chm.; Sr. JAMES MARIE DONAHUE, R.S.M., Ph.D.; KEVIN HEALY, M.D.; STEPHEN HOY, M.D.; Revs. WILLIAM M. JOENSEN; STEPHEN A. LUNDGREN; CAROL SCHMIDT, R.N.C., M.S.H.; Sr. DOLORES ULLRICH, O.S.F.; RICHARD WHITTY, J.D.

PAMAD (Pastoral Associates/Ministers of the Archdiocese of Dubuque)—KAROL RAE HOTH, Pres. Tel: 319-233-8060. Sr. MARY HARGRAFEN, O.S.F., Vice Pres. Tel: 563-547-3565. Sr. MARLENE MCDONNELL, S.F.C.C., Sec. Tel: 563-852-5104. Sr. BERNADETTE ENGELHAUPT, O.S.F., Treas. Tel: 319-352-2493.

Pastoral Council—Most Rev. JEROME HANUS, O.S.B., Pres. SANDRA SCOTT, Chm. TOM BOCK, Vice Chm. JEANINE MATT, Sec.; Sr. MARY MONTGOMERY O.P., Exec. Sec.; Rev. Msgr. JAMES O. BARTA; Rev. Msgr. RUSSELL M. BLEICH; Deacon MICHAEL BLOUIN; Sr. DONNA BURKE, O.S.F.; PATRICK BYRNE; Sr. MARY HARGRAFEN, O.S.F.; DAVID HEIAR; Sr. MARY CORITA HEID, R.S.M.; MARY HOELSCHER; DONNA JORDAN; LUCILLE KRUSE; PATRICK LENANE; Sr. KAREN LUECK, F.S.P.A.; NORMA MCDONELL; JOYCE MERRITT; CAROL MURGUIA; MARY O'NEILL; Rev. Msgr. W. DEAN WALZ.

Permanent Diaconate Formation Board—Deacon LEN FROYEN, Chm.; Rev. JOHN S. HAUGEN; MARY JENNEY; Deacon GERALD JORGENSEN; MAUREEN OATES; Deacons LEO STATTELMAN; MICHAEL WHITTERS.

Personnel Advisory Board—Revs. WAYNE A. RESSLER, Chm., Age Group II; MARK OSTERHAUS, Sec., Age Group IV; GERALD A. CONDON, Age Group I; MICHAEL J. MESCHER, Chm., Age Group III; Rev. PHILIP E. THOMPSON, At Large.

Priests' Council—Most Rev. JEROME HANUS, O.S.B., Pres.; Rev. SCOTT E. BULLOCK, Chm. Ex Officio Members: Rev. Msgr. JAMES O. BARTA; Rev. Msgr. RUSSELL M. BLEICH; Rev. Msgr. W. DEAN WALZ.

Appointed—Rev. RICHARD J. AMENT; Very Rev. CARL A. RIES; Very Rev. RALPH P. SIMINGTON; Rev. LYLE L. WILGENBUSCH.

Retired Priests' Representatives—Rev. GERALD A. CONDON; Rev. Msgr. DAVID A. WHEELER.

Age Group Representatives—Vacant.

Religious Priests Representative—Rev. MICHAEL HUTCHINS, S.V.D.

Deanery Representatives—Revs. CLAYTON R. LANDHERR, Bellevue Deanery; DAVID J. AMBROSY, Cedar Rapids Deanery; JAMES P. BROKMAN, Cedar Rapids Deanery; LOUIS J. TRZIL, Decorah Deanery; SCOTT E. BULLOCK, Dubuque Deanery; DANIEL J. KNEPPER, Dubuque Deanery; THOMAS R. ZINKULA, Dyersville Deanery; RAYMOND A. BURKLE, Dyersville Deanery; Rev. Msgr. JOHN R. MCCLEAN, Elkader Deanery; Revs. JOHN R. KREMER, Independence Deanery; MARK A. RESSLER, Loras College Deanery; JON M. SEDA, Marshalltown Deanery; CRAIG E. STEIMEL, Mason City Deanery; Rev. Msgr. STANLEY J. HAYEK, New Hampton Deanery; Revs. LEON L. CONNOLLY, Waterloo Deanery; DENNIS J. QUINT, Waterloo Deanery; DAVID M. BECKMAN, Webster City Deanery.

Seminary Board—Rev. SCOTT E. BULLOCK, Chm. ANN M. BECKMAN; Revs. JERRY F. KOPACEK; DENNIS J. QUINT; DONALD P. SCHMITT.

Worship Commission—TERRY SLADE, Chm.; Rev. DAVID M. BECKMAN; BOB BURKE; Sr. SUSAN DUNNWALD, R.S.M., Vice Chm. TODD FLOWERDAY; Rev. EVERETT HEMANN; Deacon JAMES KEAN; Rev. DANIEL J. KNEPPER; Sr. LORRAINE LOECHER, O.S.F.; Rev. DENNIS J. QUINT; Sr. ROSEMARY RIESBERG, F.S.P.A.; BECKY SEARCY.

Young Adult Advisory Board—OLIVERIO COVARRUBIAS; ANN FARMER; DIANE FLAHERTY; KATIE FLAHERTY; Rev. JOHN HAUGEN; JULIE HILL; STEVE HILL; Rev. LOUIS M. JAEGER; KIM KNUTSON; TROY MUNDT; JIM WOLF.

Youth Commission—DIANE FLAHERTY, Exec. Dir. Adult Members: LESLIE BONZER; BETH DERR; BOB GARDNER; Revs. PHIL GIBBS; THOMAS J. MCDERMOTT; FRAN PHELAN. Youth Members: DAN ABBEN; TIFFANY GILBERT; HANNAH GREVE; MARIE HARMS; CHRIS HRUBES; SHEENA JACOBI; MARCUS KNECHT; MEGAN KUHL; JENNY LEHM KUHL; JESSICA MUELLER; MONICA REICKS; KARI ROGERS; LAUREN SCHRAMP; SAM SCHRAMP; JESS STELKEN; KYLE WEBER; LISA WETZEL.

CLERGY, PARISHES, MISSIONS AND PAROCHIAL SCHOOLS

CITY OF DUBUQUE
(Dubuque County)

1—ST. RAPHAEL'S CATHEDRAL (1833), Very Rev. Joseph V. O'Brien, Rector; Barbara Gatch, Pastoral Assoc.; Sr. Ruth Jackson, S.V.M., Music Dir. & Liturgist. In res., Rev. Dwayne J. Thoman.

Res., 231 Bluff St., 52001-6918. Tel: 563-582-7646; Fax: 563-556-6796. [JC]

Catechesis/Religious Programs—Jean Leute, D.R.E. Students 90.

2—ST. ANTHONY'S (1867), Rev. Daniel J. Knepper. Pastoral Assocs.: Sr. Anne Sedgwick, O.S.F.; Sr. Margaret Ann Kramer, P.B.V.M.; Deacon William Mauss.

Res., 1870 St. Ambrose St., 52001-4196. Tel: 563-588-0571; Fax: 563-588-0572. [JC]

Church—1880 St. Ambrose St., 52001.

School—2175 Rosedale, 52001-4147. Tel: 563-556-2820; Fax: 563-556-2131. Lori Apel, Prin.

Lay Teachers 22; Students 409.

Catechesis/Religious Programs—Carol A. Witry, D.R.E.

Students 161.

3—St. Columbkille's (1887), Deacons William Biver; Frank Dunn. In res., Revs. Ardel H. Barta; Philip Kruse.
Res., 1240 Rush St., 52003-7598. Tel: 563-583-9117. [JC]
School—1198 Rush St., 52003-7598. Tel: 563-582-3532. Jean Burgmeier, Prin.
Lay Teachers 19; Students 383.
Catechesis/Religious Programs—Linda Frommelt, D.R.E.
Students 88.

4—St. Mary's (1850), Deacon Timothy LoBianco, Pastoral Admin.; Very Rev. Joseph V. O'Brien, Priest Supvr.; Rev. Ardel H. Barta, Sacramental Priest. In res., Rev. Msgr. David A. Wheeler, (Retired).
Res., 1584 White St., 52001-4905. Tel: 563-582-5469. [JC]
School—St. Mary-St. Patrick Consolidated. See separate listing under Institutions Located in the Archdiocese for details.
Catechesis/Religious Programs—Sr. Mary Kivlahan, O.S.F., D.R.E.
Students 210.

5—St. Patrick's (1862), Deacon Timothy LoBianco, Pastoral Admin.; Very Rev. Joseph V. O'Brien, Priest Supvr.; Rev. Ardel H. Barta, Sacramental Priest.
Parish Office: 1425 Iowa St., 52001-4890. Tel: 563-583-9749. [JC]
School—St. Mary-St. Patrick Consolidated. See separate listing under Institutions Located in the Archdiocese for details.
Catechesis/Religious Programs—Clustered with St. Mary, Dubuque and Holy Trinity, Dubuque. Sr. Mary Kivlahan, O.S.F., D.R.E.

6—Church of the Resurrection (1857), Revs. Donald R. Bruggeman; Mark J. Reasoner; Deacon Gerald Jorgensen.
Res., 4300 Asbury Rd., 52002-0499. Tel: 563-556-7511; Fax: 563-556-7419. [CEM]
School—Steven P. Cornelius, Prin. Sisters of the Presentation 2; Lay Teachers 20; Students 619.
Catechesis/Religious Programs—Peggy Vandal, D.R.E.
Students 292.

7—Sacred Heart (1879), Rev. James T. Chappell. In res., Rev. Harold J. Drexler.
Res., 2215 Windsor Ave., 52001-0698. Tel: 563-583-1709. [JC]
School—Holy Trinity-Sacred Heart Consolidated. See separate listing under Institutions Located in the Archdiocese for details.
Catechesis/Religious Programs—Sr. Mary Kivlahan, O.S.F., D.R.E.
Students 50.

8—Holy Ghost (1896), Revs. Paul J. Otting; David A. Schatz; Sr. Dolores Banowetz, O.S.F., Pastoral Assoc.
Res., 2917 Central Ave., 52001-1999. Tel: 563-582-5443. [JC]
School—Joseph Maloney, Prin. Priests 2; Lay Teachers 21; Students 413.
Catechesis/Religious Programs—Joseph N. White, D.R.E.
Students 103.

9—Holy Trinity (1910), Rev. Mark R. Nemmers.
Res., 1700 Lincoln Ave., 52001-2104. Tel: 563-556-0733. [JC]
School—Holy Trinity-Sacred Heart Consolidated. See separate listing under Institutions Located in the Archdiocese for details.
Catechesis/Religious Programs—Clustered with St. Mary, Dubuque and St. Patrick, Dubuque. Sr. Mary Kivlahan, O.S.F., D.R.E. & Pastoral Assoc.

10—Nativity (1923), Revs. Wayne A. Ressler; James W. Dubert; Deacon David McGhee, Pastoral Assoc.
Office: 1225 Alta Vista St., 52001-4398. Tel: 563-582-1839; Fax: 563-582-1830. [JC]
Res., 1075 University, 52001. Tel: 563-582-1714.
School—Tel: 563-582-7236. Judith Calcari, Prin. Sisters 1; Lay Teachers 24; Students 620.
Catechesis/Religious Programs—Sr. Beth Kress, P.B.V.M., D.R.E.
Students 105.

11—St. Joseph the Worker (1949), Rev. Lyle L. Wilgenbusch; Deacon Stephen MacDonald.
Res., 90 S. Algona St., 52001-5605. Tel: 563-588-2934. [JC]
Office: 60 S. Algona, 52001-5605. Tel: 563-588-1433; Fax: 563-588-4108.
Church—2105 St. Joseph St., 52001. Tel: 563-551-4194.
School—Tel: 563-588-4194. Kimberly Hermsen, Prin. Lay Teachers 23; Students 442.
Catechesis/Religious Programs—Sr. Marilyn Breen, P.B.V.M., D.R.E.
Students 175.

OUTSIDE THE CITY OF DUBUQUE

Ackley, Franklin Co., St. Mary's (1891), Very Rev. James L. Miller; Deacon David Jones.
Mailing Address: 1405 N. Federal, Hampton, 50441-1005. Tel: 641-456-4857. [CEM]
Church—611 Sherman Ave, 50601.
Catechesis/Religious Programs—Shelly Johnson, D.R.E.
Students 96.

Allison, Butler Co., Immaculate Conception. Closed. For inquiries for parish records contact St. Mary's, Greene.

Alta Vista, Chickasaw Co., St. Bernard (1897), Very Rev. Roger R. Rethamel; Betty Boehmer, Pastoral Assoc.
Res., 207 Seventh St., P.O. Box 38, Elma, 50628-0038. Tel: 641-393-2520. [CEM]
Church—114 E. Washington, 50603.
Catechesis/Religious Programs—Irene Huegel, D.R.E.
Students 60.

Ames, Story Co., St. Cecilia (1899), Revs. Terrence Rassmussen, O.F.M.Conv.; Howard Hansen, O.F.M.Conv.; Bro. Bruno Nemcosky, O.F.M.Conv., Pastoral Assoc.; Deacons Gary Aitchison; Tom Lang; John McCully; Richard Tondra.
Res., 2900 Hoover Ave., 50010-4498. Tel: 515-233-3092; Fax: 515-233-6423.
School—(Grades K-6). Tel: 515-232-5290. Joanne Lyons, Prin.
Lay Teachers 9; Students 175.
Catechesis/Religious Programs—Tel: 515-232-3514. William Monosmith, D.R.E.

St. Thomas Aquinas Church (and Catholic Student Center) (1947), Revs. Everett Hemann; James E. Hayes; Robert LeBlanc, Business Mgr. In res., Rev. Msgr. James A. Supple, (Retired). Campus Ministry: Mr. John Donaghy; Crystal Caruana-Sullivan.
Church—2210 Lincoln Ave., 50014-7184. Tel: 515-292-3810; Fax: 515-292-3841.
Res., 129 Ash, 50014. Tel: 515-292-1192.
Catechesis/Religious Programs—Mary Ricke, D.R.E.
Students 241.

Anamosa, Jones Co., St. Patrick's (1861), Very Rev. Charles E. Lang, Priest Supvr.; Rev. Carl J. Manternach, Sacramental Priest; Sr. Susan Dunnwald, R.S.M., Pastoral Admin.
Res., 215 N. Garnavillo St., 52205-1122. Tel: 319-462-2141. [CEM]
School—Tel: 319-462-2688. Marlena Bartlett, Prin. & D.R.E.
Lay Teachers 8; Students 99.
Catechesis/Religious Programs—Students 143.
Oratory—Stone City, St. Joseph. Sacramental Records are located at St Patrick's, Anamosa.

Andrew, Jackson Co., St. John (1914), Rev. Clayton R. Landherr; Rev. Msgr. Thomas J. Ralph, Sacramental Priest; Sr. Virginia Crilly, B.V.M., Pastoral Assoc.
Res. and Mailing Address—St. John Rectory, 507 Elm St., P.O. Box 26, La Motte, 52054-0026. Tel: 563-773-2323.
Church—204 Main St., 52030. [CEM]
Catechesis/Religious Programs—Phyllis Gerlach, D.R.E.
Students 47.

Balltown, Dubuque Co., St. Francis of Assisi (1891), Very Rev. Joseph V. O'Brien, Priest Supvr.; Rev. Thomas R. Zinkula, Sacramental Priest; Sr. Mildred Leuenberger, O.S.F., Pastoral Admin.
Res. and Mailing Address—5131 Sherrill Rd., Sherrill, 52073-9612. Tel: 563-552-2611.
Church—468 Balltown Rd. [CEM]
School—Balltown-Sherrill Consolidated School. See separate listing under Institutions Located in the Archdiocese for details.
Catechesis/Religious Programs—Clustered with SS. Peter and Paul, Sherrill. Mary Anne Manternach, D.R.E.

Bankston, Dubuque Co., St. Clement's (1859), Rev. Paul L. Weis.
Res., 24287 New Vienna Rd., Epworth, 52045-9732. Tel: 563-744-3314. [CEM]
School—Seton Catholic Elementary School, Epworth. See separate listing under Institutions Located in the Archdiocese for details.
Catechesis/Religious Programs—Betty Pins, D.R.E.
Students 31.

Barclay, Blackhawk Co., St. Francis (1862), Very Rev. Donald P. Schmitt.
Res., 7837 E. Airline Hwy., Dunkerton, 50626-9715. Tel: 319-822-7477. [CEM]
Catechesis/Religious Programs—D.R.E.: Arlene Widdel; Julie Rottinghaus.
Students 68.

Belle Plaine, Benton Co., St. Michael (1885), Very Rev. Charles E. Lang, Priest Supvr.; Rev. Steven G. O'Brien, Sacramental Priest; Deacon J.C. Otto, Pastoral Admin.
Mailing Address: 1304 Ninth Ave., 52208-1614. Tel: 319-444-3106; Fax: 319-444-3737.
Catechesis/Religious Programs—Teri Rstom, D.R.E.
Students 123.

Bellevue, Jackson Co., St. Joseph's (1841), Rev. Stephen L. Meyer.
Res., 405 Franklin St., 52031-1596. Tel: 563-872-3234. [CEM]
School—Bellevue Area Catholic Elementary School. See separate listing under Institutions Located in the Archdiocese for details.
Catechesis/Religious Programs—Marc Postiglione, D.R.E.
Students 186.

Belmond, Wright Co., St. Francis Xavier (1870), Rev. David M. Beckman; Regina Lamoureux, Pastoral Assoc.
Parish Office & Mailing Address: 1207 Third St. N.E., 50421-1608. Tel: 641-444-3249. [CEM]
Catechesis/Religious Programs—Mollie Nichols, D.R.E.
Students 101.

Blairstown, Benton Co., St. John (1948), Rev. John J. Walsh; Sr. Nora Rochford, O.S.F., Pastoral Assoc.; Deacon Robert Hurych.
Mailing Address: 105 West St. N.W., P.O. Box 170, 52209-0170. Tel: 319-454-6431.
Res., 405 4th Ave., P.O. Box 250, Van Horne, 52346-0250. Tel: 319-228-8131.
Catechesis/Religious Programs—Patricia Angerman, D.R.E.
Students 65.

Blessing, Blackhawk Co., Immaculate Conception (1875), Rev. Thomas E. Braak; Sr. Lene Rubly, O.S.F., Pastoral Assoc.
Res. and Mailing Address—1435 E. Eagle Rd., Waterloo, 50701-9545. Tel: 319-342-2481.
Church—14004 S. Hudson Rd., Hudson, 50643. [CEM]
Catechesis/Religious Programs—Rita Schmidt, D.R.E.
Students 52.

Bluffton, Winneshiek Co., St. Bridget (1858), Rev. Henry W. Chariper; Sr. Mary Hargrafen, O.S.F., Pastoral Assoc.
Res. and Mailing Address—116 Third St. E., Cresco, 52136. Tel: 563-547-3565.
Church—3094 253rd Ave., Ridgeway, 52165. [CEM]
Catechesis/Religious Programs—Alice Noethe, D.R.E.
Students 48.

Britt, Hancock Co., St. Patrick's (1880), Rev. Marvin J. Bries.
Res., 139 Third St. S.E., 50423-1726. Tel: 515-843-3215. [CEM]
Church—335 First Ave. S.E., 50423.
Catechesis/Religious Programs—Kathryn Smith, D.R.E.
Students 136.

Buffalo Center, Winnebago Co., St. Patrick's (1899), Rev. Craig E. Steimel; Sr. M. Dolores Moes, P.B.V.M., Pastoral Assoc.
Res. and Mailing Address—St. James Rectory, 906 W. O St., Forest City, 50436-0310. Tel: 641-585-4856.
Church—115 5th Ave. N.W., 50424.
Catechesis/Religious Programs—Jody Smith, D.R.E.
Students 46.

Calmar, Winneshiek Co., St. Aloysius (1875), Rev. Donald J. Hawes; Sr. Carol Hemesath, O.S.F., Pastoral Assoc.
Res., 304 S. Maryville, P.O. Box 819, 52132-0819. Tel: 563-562-3603. [CEM]
School—Calmar-Festina-Spillville (CFS) Catholic Elementary School. See separate listing under Institutions Located in the Archdiocese for details.
Catechesis/Religious Programs—Combined with Our Lady of Seven Dolors, Festina and St. Wenceslaus, Spillville. Patty Frana, D.R.E.

Cascade, Dubuque Co., St. Matthias, Rev. Daniel J. Krapfl; Sr. Marlene McDonnell, S.F.C.C., Pastoral Assoc.
Res., 206 Grant St. S.W., P.O. Box 699, 52033-0699. Tel: 563-852-3524. [CEM]
School—Aquin Educational System. See separate listing under Institutions Located in the Archdiocese for details.
Catechesis/Religious Programs—Rebecca Smith, D.R.E.
Students 328.

Castle Grove, Jones Co., Immaculate Conception (1877), Rev. Msgr. Neil W. Tobin; Sr. M. Damian O'Brien, P.B.V.M., Pastoral Assoc.
Mailing Address: 22178 County Rd. D-62, Monticello, 52310-7827. Tel: 319-465-5570.
Res., Sacred Heart, 328 N. Sycamore St., Monticello, 52310-1213. Tel: 319-465-5944. [CEM]

Catechesis/Religious Programs—Sr. M. Damian O'Brien, P.B.V.M., D.R.E.
Students 18.

Cedar Falls, Blackhawk Co., St. Patrick (1855), Revs. James L. Secora; James Starbuck; Deacons Michael Oates; Michael Moetsch; Tom Sciek, Pastoral Assoc. In res., Rev. John S. Haugen.
Mailing Address: 705 Main St., 50613-2950. Tel: 319-266-3523; Fax: 319-266-2179.
Parish Office and Rectory: 115 W. 8th St., 50613-2902.
School—Tel: 319-277-6781. Sr. Marilou Irons, P.B.V.M., Prin.
Sisters 1; Lay Teachers 22; Students 407.
Catechesis/Religious Programs—Amy Hoyer, D.R.E.
Students 346.

Cedar Rapids, Linn Co.,

1—Immaculate Conception, (1858), Rev. Karl L. Glovik. Pastoral Assocs.: Sr. Francesca Oldham, R.S.M.; Deacon Gerald D. Pettit; Mary Ann McEniry. In res., Revs. David J. Ambrosy; Richard J. Hess, (Retired).
Mailing Address: P.O. Box 1247, 52403.
Res., 857 Third Ave. S.E., 52406. Tel: 319-362-7181. [JC]
Catechesis/Religious Programs—Mary Ann McEniry, D.R.E.
Students 120.

2—All Saints, (1947), Very Rev. Charles E. Lang; Rev. James L. Blocklinger; Deacon Mike Blouin.
Parish Office and Mailing Address, 720 29th St. S.E., 52403-3099. Tel: 319-363-6130.
Res., 830 Beaver Ridge Ct. S.E., 52403. Tel: 319-362-1691. [JC]
School—Tel: 319-363-4110. Lora Daily, Prin.
Sisters 1; Lay Teachers 18; Students 396.
Catechesis/Religious Programs—Elaine Collins, D.R.E.
Students 198.

3—John XXIII, Rev. Philip E. Thompson.
3104 80th St. S.W., 52404. Tel: 319-846-3139; Fax: 319-846-3159.

4—St. Jude, (1962), Revs. Richard J. Ament; James P. Brokman; Mark McDermott, Pastoral Assoc.
Res., 3601 First Ave. S.W., 52405. Tel: 319-396-8827. [JC]
Church and Office—50 Edgewood Rd. N.W., 52405-4598. Tel: 319-390-3520.
School—Holy Family Consolidated Catholic School. See separate listing under Institutions Located in the Archdiocese.
Catechesis/Religious Programs—D.R.E.: Mary Beth Siemann; Diann Morse.
Students 353.

5—St. Ludmila's, (1922), Rev. Harry Koelker; Sr. Mary L. Lechtenberg, O.S.F., Pastoral Assoc.; Deacons Richard Manning; James Berger.
Res., 2107 J St. S.W., 52404-3615. Tel: 319-362-7282. [JC]
Church—211 21st Ave. S.W., 52404.
School—Holy Family Consolidated Catholic School.
Catechesis/Religious Programs—Sue Berger, D.R.E.
Students 173.

6—St. Matthew's, (1922), Rev. Mark Osterhaus; Deacon Phil Saunders; Roseann Wiley, Pastoral Assoc. In res., Rev. Steven O'Brien.
Res., 2310 First Ave. N.E., 52402-4999. Tel: 319-363-8269; Fax: 319-363-8260. [JC]
School—Tel: 319-362-3021. Joe Wolf, Prin.
Sisters 1; Lay Teachers 16; Students 350.
Catechesis/Religious Programs—Betsy Schmuck, D.R.E.
Students 283.

7—St. Patrick's, (1886), Rev. Steven J. Rosonke; Sr. Mary Klisart, O.S.F., Pastoral Assoc.; Deacon Daniel Hoeger.
Parish Office: 516 A Ave. N.W., 52405-3935. Tel: 319-362-7966; 366-5369. [JC]
Church—500 First Ave. N.W., 52405.
Catechesis/Religious Programs—Students 123. D.R.E.: Steve Picray; Ann Picray.

8—St. Pius X, (1959), Revs. Donald L. Klein; Andrew F. Lawrence; Deacons Albert Scharosch; Paul Zimmerman. Pastoral Assocs.: Kim Vogel; Liz Pollard.
Church and Office: 4949 Council St. N.E., 52402-2492. Tel: 319-393-4445; Fax: 319-393-9424. [JC]
Rectory: 1500 48th St. N.E., 52402.
School—(Grades K-8). Tel: 319-393-4507. Candace Greene, Prin.
Lay Teachers 21; Students 348.
Catechesis/Religious Programs—D.R.E.: Julie Johnson; Liz Pollard.
Students 912.

9—St. Wenceslaus, (1874), Rev. Karl L. Glovik; Deacon William Cisler.
Mailing Address: 510 16th Ave. S.E., 52401-2612. Tel: 319-362-8061. [JC]
Catechesis/Religious Programs—Mike Schmitz, D.R.E.

Central City, Linn Co., St. Stephen's (1932), Rev. Wayne J. Droessler; Sr. Anne Kisting, O.S.F., Pastoral Assoc.
Res. and Mailing Address—410 Terrace Dr., P.O. Box S, 52214-0420. Tel: 319-438-6625.
Church—307 Commercial St., 52214.
Catechesis/Religious Programs—Joyce Soukup, D.R.E.
Students 122.

Charles City, Floyd Co., Immaculate Conception (1857), Rev. Msgr. Stanley J. Hayek; Sr. M. Jennifer Rausch, P.B.V.M., Pastoral Assoc.
Church and Res.: 106 Chapel Ln., 50616-2810. Tel: 641-228-1071. [CEM]
School—Tel: 641-228-1225. Sr. M. Dianne Michels, P.B.V.M., Prin.
Priests 1; Sisters of the Presentation 2; Lay Teachers 14; Students 225.
Catechesis/Religious Programs—Patricia Rottinghaus, D.R.E.
Students 286.

Chelsea, Tama Co., St. Joseph's (1867), Very Rev. Charles E. Lang, Priest Supvr.; Rev. Steven G. O'Brien, Sacramental Priest; Deacon J.C. Otto, Pastoral Admin.
Mailing Address: 1304 9th Ave., Belle Plaine, 52208-1604. Tel: 319-444-3106.
Church—307 Station St., 52215. [CEM]
Catechesis/Religious Programs—Beth Henning, D.R.E.
Students 57.

Cherry Mound, Allamakee Co., St. Pius (1863), Rev. Louis J. Trzil.
Mailing Address: 1416 Great River Rd., Lansing, 52151. Tel: 563-586-2150. [CEM]
Religious Education Office: 699 State Forest Rd., Harper's Ferry, 52146. Tel: 563-535-7143.
Catechesis/Religious Programs—Lisa Ashbacker, D.R.E.
Students 38.

Chester, Howard Co., St. Stephen's (1916), Rev. Ray E. Atwood.
Res. and Mailing Address—Our Lady of Lourdes Rectory, P.O. Box 146, Riceville, 50466-0146. Tel: 641-985-2028.
Church—408 Main St., 52134.
Catechesis/Religious Programs—Mary Ann Kelly, D.R.E.
Students 34.

Clarion, Wright Co., St. John's (1883), Rev. David M. Beckman; Deacon Michael Whitters; Sr. Mary K. Doughan, R.S.M., Pastoral Assoc.
Church and Mailing Address: 608 Second Ave. N.E., P.O. Box 26, 50525-0026. Tel: 515-532-3586; Fax: 515-532-2478. [CEM]
Catechesis/Religious Programs—Michelle Stitz, D.R.E.
Students 174.

Clear Lake, Cerro Gordo Co., St. Patrick's (1901), Rev. Msgr. Robert G. Hogan.
Res., 1001 Ninth Ave. S., 50428-2615. Tel: 641-357-3214; Fax: 641-357-2091.
Catechesis/Religious Programs—D.R.E.: Christine Carrier; Virginia Copas; Leigh Trembath.
Students 238.

Clermont, Fayette Co., St. Peter's (1855), Rev. Lloyd P. Ouderkirk.
Church and Mailing Address: 608 Larrabee, 52135-0025. Tel: 563-423-7293; Fax: 563-864-3138.
Catechesis/Religious Programs—Mary Olson, D.R.E.
Students 120.

Clutier, Tama Co., Immaculate Conception (1900), Rev. John R. Tilp.
Res. and Mailing Address—1102 Walnut St., Traer, 50675. Tel: 319-478-2222.
Church—501 5th St., 52217. [CEM]
Catechesis/Religious Programs—Barbara Cibula, D.R.E.
Oratory—Carroll Township, St. Wenceslaus. Sacramental Records are located at Immaculate Conception, Clutier.

Coggon, Linn Co., St. John the Evangelist (1912), Rev. Wayne J. Droessler; Sr. Anne Kisting, O.S.F., Pastoral Assoc.
Mailing Address: P.O. Box 47, 52218-0047. Tel: 319-435-2236. [CEM]
Res., 410 Terrace Dr., Central City, 52214-0420. Tel: 319-438-6625.
Church—211 Third St. N., 52218.
Catechesis/Religious Programs—Pamela Klima, D.R.E.
Students 62.

Colesburg, Delaware Co., St. Patrick's (1862), Rev. John J. Friederick.
Res., St. Mark Rectory, 205 S. Locust, P.O. Box 365, Edgewood, 52042-0365. Tel: 563-856-2265. [CEM]
Church—Delaware St.
Catechesis/Religious Programs—D.R.E.: Gene Kruse; Ramona Engelken.
Students 70.

Colo, Story Co., St. Mary's, Rev. Jon M. Seda; Sr. Jeanne Marie Roche, R.S.M., Pastoral Assoc.; Deacon Steven Van Kerckvoorde.
Rectory & Mailing Address: 410 Bailey, P.O. Box 236, 50056-0236. Tel: 641-377-2710. [CEM]
Church—422 Fourth St., 50056.
Catechesis/Religious Programs—Mary Jo McLaughlin, D.R.E.
Students 30.

Corwith, Hancock Co., St. Mary's (1912), Rev. Marvin J. Bries.
Mailing Address: 139 Third St. S.E., Britt, 50423-1726. Tel: 641-843-3215. [CEM]
Church—404 Wayne St., 50430.
Catechesis/Religious Programs—Kate Smith, D.R.E.

Cresco, Howard Co., Assumption of the Blessed Virgin Mary (1858). Merged with St. Joseph's, Cresco to form Notre Dame, Cresco.
St. Joseph's (1870). Merged with Assumption of the Blessed Virgin Mary, Cresco to form Notre Dame, Cresco.
Notre Dame (1999), Rev. Henry W. Chariper; Sr. Mary Hargrafen, O.S.F., Pastoral Assoc.
Mailing Address: & Parish Office:—116 Third St. E., 52136. Tel: 563-547-3565; Fax: 563-547-3835.
Rectory:—221 Third Ave. W., 52136. Tel: 563-547-5826.
Churches—Assumption Worship Center, 229 Third Ave. W., 52136. [JC]
St. Joseph Worship Center, 223 Second Ave. E., 52136. [JC]
School—221 Second Ave. E., 52136. Tel: 563-547-4513. Wendy Schatz, Prin.
Teachers 15; Students 228.
Catechesis/Religious Programs—Tel: 563-547-3760. Alice Noethe, D.R.E.
Students 245.
Convent—221 Second Ave. E., 52136. Tel: 563-547-4023.
Oratory—Plymouth Rock, St. Agnes. Sacramental records are located at Notre Dame, Cresco. [CEM]

Decorah, Winneshiek Co., St. Benedict's (1864), Very Rev. Gary Krapfl.
Church and Res.: 307 W. Main St., 52101-1778. Tel: 563-382-9631; Fax: 563-382-6436. [CEM]
School—Tel: 563-382-4668. Cathy Campbell, Prin.
Lay Teachers 15; Students 196.
Catechesis/Religious Programs—Mary Holthaus, D.R.E.
Students 351.

Delhi, Delaware Co., St. John's (1872), Rev. John R. Kremer.
Res., 307 South St., P.O. Box 187, 52223-0187. Tel: 563-922-2251. [CEM]
Catechesis/Religious Programs—JoLynn Heims, D.R.E.
Students 166.

Dike, Grundy Co., St. Mary (1880), Rev. Dennis J. Quint.
Res. and Mailing Address:—204 G Ave., Grundy Center, 50638-1939. Tel: 319-824-3572; Fax: 319-824-3857.
Church—680 Main St., 50624. [CEM]
Catechesis/Religious Programs—Ann Nicklaus-Schmelzer, D.R.E.
Students 62.

Dorchester, Allamakee Co., St. Mary's (1865), Rev. Allen M. Schmitt; Sr. Erma Rottinghaus, O.S.F., Pastoral Assoc.
Mailing Address: 590 Walnut Creek Dr., P.O. Box 21, 52140-0021. Tel: 563-497-3332. [CEM]
Church—590 Waterloo Creek Rd., Dorcester, 52140.
Catechesis/Religious Programs—Sr. Erma Rottinghaus, D.R.E.
Students 53.

Dougherty, Cerro Gordo Co., St. Patrick's (1870), Rev. Leo P. Riley.
Mailing Address: P.O. Box 208, 50433-0208.
Church—410 Patrick St., 50433.
Res., Sacred Heart Rectory, P.O. Box 30, 305 Elm St. E., Rockwell, 50469-0030. Tel: 641-822-4957. [CEM]
Catechesis/Religious Programs—Dolores Marzen, D.R.E.
Students 64.

Dumont, Butler Co., St. Francis (1890). Closed. For inquiries for parish records please see St. Patrick, Hampton.

Duncan, Hancock Co., St. Wenceslaus (1900), Rev. Michael G. Schueller.
Res. and Mailing Address—St. Boniface Rectory, 660 Bush Ave., Garner, 50438-1513. Tel: 641-923-2329; Fax: 641-923-2480.
Church—2343 Navy Ave., Britt, 50423. [CEM]
Catechesis/Religious Programs—Esther Hadacek, D.R.E.
Students 56.

Dyersville, Dubuque Co., Basilica of St. Francis Xavier (1859), Revs. Edward C. Petty; Jerry W. Blake. Pastoral Assocs.: Sr. Mary Clare Miller, O.S.F.; Sr. Marian Einck, O.S.F.
Res., 104 Third St. S.W., 52040-1696. Tel: 563-875-7325; Fax: 563-875-8716. [CEM]
School—(Grades 1-6). Tel: 563-875-7376; Fax: 563-875-7037. Ralph Pauly, Prin.
Sisters of St. Francis of the Holy Family 2; Lay Teachers 22; Students 334.
Catechesis/Religious Programs—D.R.E.: Nancy Drees; Rose M. Meisch.
Students 170.

Dysart, Tama Co., St. Joseph (1878), Rev. Joseph E. McGuire.
Mailing Address: 2200 S. Second Ave., Vinton, 52349. Tel: 319-472-4448. [CEM]
Church—101 Clark St., 52224.
Catechesis/Religious Programs—Lynn McGivern, D.R.E.
Students 60.

Eagle Center, Blackhawk Co., St. Mary of Mt. Carmel (1859), Rev. Thomas E. Braak; Sr. Lene Rubly, O.S.F., Pastoral Assoc.
Mailing Address: 1435 E. Eagle Rd., Waterloo, 50701-9545. Tel: 319-342-2481. [CEM]
Catechesis/Religious Programs—Nancy Meier, D.R.E.
Students 120.

Eagle Grove, Wright Co., Sacred Heart (1882), Rev. David M. Beckman.
Mailing Address: 221 S. Jackson Ave., 50533-2311. Tel: 515-448-4765; Fax: 515-448-4765. [CEM]
Catechesis/Religious Programs—Alice Harmeyer, D.R.E.
Students 135.

Earlville, Delaware Co., St. Joseph's (1887), Rev. Herbert L. Tegeler; Sr. Lenore Gardner, R.S.M., Pastoral Assoc.; Deacon James Steger.
Res. & Mailing Address: 307 Mary St., P.O. Box 187, 52041-0187. Tel: 563-923-3135; Fax: 563-923-2895. [CEM]
School—(Grades K-6). David Gross, Prin.
Lay Teachers 6; Students 70.
Catechesis/Religious Programs—Joan Steger, D.R.E.
Students 126.

Edgewood, Delaware Co., St. Mark's (1916), Rev. John J. Friederick.
Church and Res.: 205 S. Locust St., P.O. Box 365, 52042-0365. Tel: 563-928-6938; 928-7200. [CEM]
Catechesis/Religious Programs—Jody Kerns, D.R.E.
Students 192.

Eldora, Hardin Co., St. Mary's (1868), Rev. Mark J. McGovern.
Parish Office: 415 Main St., P.O. Box 368, Iowa Falls, 50126-0368. Tel: 641-648-9547.
Church—614 Washington St., 50627-1257. [CEM]
Catechesis/Religious Programs—Mary Reece, D.R.E.
Students 132.

Elkader, Clayton Co., St. Joseph's (1844), Rev. Paul R. Peters; Sr. Carole Freking, O.S.F., Pastoral Assoc.
Res., 330 First St., 52043-0626. Tel: 563-245-2548. [CEM]
Catechesis/Religious Programs—Students 139.
Oratory—Wadena, St. Joseph. Sacramental Records at St. Joseph, Elkader. [CEM]

Elma, Howard Co., Immaculate Conception (1887), Very Rev. Roger R. Rethamel; Betty Boehmer, Pastoral Assoc.
Res., 207 Seventh St., P.O. Box 38, 50628-0038. Tel: 641-393-2520. [CEM]
Catechesis/Religious Programs—Eleanor Burke, D.R.E.
Students 74.

Epworth, Dubuque Co., St. Patrick's (1879), Rev. Raymond A. Burkle; Deacon James Kean.
Res., 104 First St. S.E., P.O. Box 286, 52045-0286. Tel: 563-876-5540. [CEM]
School—Seton Catholic Elementary School, Epworth. See separate listing under Institutions Located in the Archdiocese for details.
Catechesis/Religious Programs—Stephanie Greenwood, D.R.E.
Students 166.

Evansdale, Blackhawk Co., St. Nicholas (1951), Rev. George W. Karnik; Deacon William Jenney. In res., Rev. Patrick G. Geary.
Mailing Address: 443 S. Roosevelt Rd., 50707-1259. Tel: 319-232-9737. [JC]
School—St. John-St. Nicholas Consolidated. See St. John, Waterloo for details.
Catechesis/Religious Programs—Dave Cushing, D.R.E.
Students 46.

Fairbank, Buchanan Co., Immaculate Conception (1858), Rev. Kenneth C. Stecher.
Res., 302 W. Main St., P.O. Box 505, 50629-0505. Tel: 319-635-2211. [CEM]
Catechesis/Religious Programs—Dan Cutsforth, D.R.E.
Students 210.

Fairfax, Linn Co., St. Patrick's (1875), Rev. Thomas J. Schwinn; Sr. Maryann Greenwald, S.S.N.D., Pastoral Assoc.; Deacon John Malone.
Parish Office: 620 Church St., P.O. Box 219, 52228-0219. Tel: 319-846-2025; Fax: 319-846-3472.
Church—324 Church St., 52228. [CEM]
Catechesis/Religious Programs—Shannon Kehoe, D.R.E.
Students 147.

Farley, Dubuque Co., St. Joseph's (1914), Rev. Dennis R. Cain.
Res., 204 Second Ave. S.E., P.O. Box 67, 52046-0067. Tel: 563-744-3865. [CEM]
School—Seton Catholic Elementary School, Epworth. See separate listing under Institutions Located in the Archdiocese for details.
Catechesis/Religious Programs—Monica Lynch, D.R.E.
Students 165.

Fayette, Fayette Co., St. Francis of Assisi (1879), Rev. Dale J. Rausch.
Mailing Address: P.O. Box 276, 52142-0276.
Res., 128 N. Walnut St., West Union, 52175-1347. Tel: 563-422-3184. [CEM]
Church—205 Lovers Lane, 52142.
Catechesis/Religious Programs—Holly Streeter, D.R.E.
Students 85.

Festina, Winneshiek Co., Our Lady of Seven Dolors (1843), Rev. Msgr. Cletus J. Hawes.
Mailing Address: 2348 Co. Rd. B 32, 52144-7701. Tel: 563-532-9366. [CEM]
School—Calmar-Festina-Spillville (CFS) Elementary. See separate listing under Institutions Located in the Archdiocese for details.

Fillmore, Dubuque Co., Sacred Heart (1890), Rev. Dennis J. Colter.
Mailing Address: 19661 Sacred Heart Ln., Bernard, 52032-9722. Tel: 563-879-3103. [CEM]
School—Aquin Elementary School. See separate listing under Institutions Located in the Archdiocese for details.
Catechesis/Religious Programs—Clustered with St. Matthias, Cascade, St. Patrick, Garryowen, and St. Peter, Temple Hill.

Forest City, Winnebago Co., St. James (1870), Rev. Craig E. Steimel; Sr. Mary Dolores Moes, P.B.V.M., Pastoral Assoc.
Res., 906 W. O St., 50436-0310. Tel: 641-585-4856. [CEM]
Catechesis/Religious Programs—Rita Kleemeier, D.R.E.
Students 100.

Fort Atkinson, Winneshiek Co., St. John Nepomucene's (1875), Rev. John A. Moser.
Res., 202 Second St. S.E., 52144-0157. Tel: 563-534-7298. [CEM]
School—Trinity Catholic School, Protivin. See separate listing under Institutions Located in the Archdiocese for details.
Catechesis/Religious Programs—Irene Krivachek, D.R.E.
; Students 106.

Garber, Clayton Co., St. Michael's (1917), Rev. Richard G. Gaul.
Res. and Mailing Address—402 S. Washington, P.O. Box 7, Garnavillo, 52049-0007. Tel: 563-964-2168.
Church—800 Main, 52048. [CEM]
Catechesis/Religious Programs—Nancy Schroeder, D.R.E.
Students 19.

Garnavillo, Clayton Co., St. Joseph's (1846), Rev. Richard G. Gaul.
Res., 402 S. Washington St., P.O. Box 7, 52049-0007. Tel: 563-964-2168. [CEM]
Church—204 W. Oak St., 52049.
Catechesis/Religious Programs—Darlene Wille, D.R.E.
Students 72.

Garner, Hancock Co., St. Boniface (1883), Rev. Michael G. Schueller.
Res., 660 Bush Ave., 50438-1513. Tel: 641-923-2329; Fax: 641-923-2480. [CEM]
Catechesis/Religious Programs—Rebecca Rolling, D.R.E.
Students 205.

Garryowen, Jackson Co., St. Patrick's (1840), Rev. Thomas R. Bisenius.
Res., 28914 46th Ave., Bernard, 52032-9289. Tel: 563-879-3303; Fax: 563-879-3363. [CEM]
School—Aquin Elementary School. See separate listing under Institutions Located in the Archdiocese for details.
Catechesis/Religious Programs—Clustered with St. Matthias, Cascade, Sacred Heart, Fillmore, and St. Peter, Temple Hill. Joann Harry, D.R.E.

Garwin, Tama Co., St. Boniface (1884), Rev. Keith L. Birch.
Office and Mailing Address: 900 Park St., Tama, 52339-1238. Tel: 641-484-3039; Fax: 641-484-8039. [JC]
Catechesis/Religious Programs—Beverly Stanley, D.R.E.
Students 49.

Geneva, Franklin Co., St. Paul. Closed. Sacramental records are located at St. Mary, Ackley.

Gilbert, Story Co., SS. Peter and Paul (1882). Conventual Franciscan Friars. Revs. Terrence Rassmussen, O.F.M.Conv.; Howard Hanson, O.F.M.Conv.
Res., St. Cecilia Rectory, 2900 Hoover, Ames, 50010-4498. Tel: 515-233-3092; Fax: 515-233-6423. [CEM]
Church—14238 500th Ave., 50105.
Catechesis/Religious Programs—D.R.E.: Jean Johnson; Peg Stowell.
Students 92.

Gilbertville, Blackhawk Co., Immaculate Conception (1875), Rev. Rick D. Dagit.
Res., 311 15th Ave., 50634-0136. Tel: 319-296-1092; Fax: 319-296-2087. [CEM]
School—Immaculate Conception-St. Joseph. (Gilbertville-Raymond Consolidated). See separate listing under Institutions Located in the Archdiocese for details.
Catechesis/Religious Programs—Dessie Rottinghaus, D.R.E.

Greeley, Delaware Co., St. Joseph's (1870), Very Rev. Ralph P. Simington; Rev. Kenneth J. Glaser.
Mailing Address: P.O. Box 187, Earlville, 52041-0187. Tel: 563-923-3135. [CEM]
Church—208 E. 2nd Ave., 52050.
Catechesis/Religious Programs—Sr. Charmaine Plotz, O.S.F., D.R.E.
Students 15.

Greene, Butler Co., St. Mary's (1872), Rev. Msgr. Walter L. Brunkan.
Res., 105 N. Main, P.O. Box 480, 50636-0480. Tel: 641-823-4146. [CEM]
Catechesis/Religious Programs—Sherilyn Backer, D.R.E.

Grundy Center, Grundy Co., Sacred Heart (1885), Rev. Dennis J. Quint.
Res., 204 G Ave., 50638-1939. Tel: 319-824-3572; Fax: 319-824-3857. [CEM]
Catechesis/Religious Programs—Ann Nicklaus Schmelzer, D.R.E.
Students 61.

Guttenberg, Clayton Co., St. Mary's (1851), Rev. Msgr. John R. McClean; Deacon James Pfaffly.
Res., 520 S. Second, P.O. Box 847, 52052-0847. Tel: 563-252-1247; Fax: 563-252-4015. [CEM]
School—Guttenberg-North Buena Vista Consolidated. See separate listing under Institutions Located in the Archdiocese for details.
Catechesis/Religious Programs—Julie Rastetter, D.R.E.
Students 150.

Hampton, Franklin Co., St. Patrick's (1870), Very Rev. James L. Miller; Sr. Carol Besch, O.S.F., Deanery Hispanic Min.
Res., 1405 N. Federal, P.O. Box 514, 50441-1005. Tel: 646-456-3406; 456-4857.
Catechesis/Religious Programs—Judy Nelson, D.R.E.
Students 206.

Hanover, Allamakee Co., St. Mary's (1875), Rev. Allen M. Schmitt; Sr. Erma Rottinghaus, O.S.F., Pastoral Assoc.
Mailing Address: 590 Walnut Creek, P.O. Box 21, Dorchester, 52140-0021. Tel: 563-497-3332.
Res., 109 Second St., Waukon, 52172-0146. Tel: 563-568-3671. [CEM]
Church—2096 Hwy. 76, Waukon, 52172.
Catechesis/Religious Programs—Mary Therese Klauke, D.R.E.
Students 27.

Harpers Ferry, Allamakee Co., St. Ann-St. Joseph (1855), Rev. Louis J. Trzil.
Res. and Mailing Address—Immaculate Conception (Wexford) 1416 Great River Rd., Lansing, 52151-7519. Tel: 563-586-2150.
Church—307 W. Orange, Harper's Ferry, 52146. [CEM]
Catechesis/Religious Programs—Brigid Cota, D.R.E.

Haverhill, Marshall Co., Immaculate Conception (1877), Rev. Louis M. Jaeger.
Parish Office and Mailing Address: 221 Olive St., Marshalltown, 50158-4248. Tel: 641-753-7374.
Church—101 Second Ave., 50120-5009. [CEM]
School—Marshalltown Area Consolidated Catholic.

See separate listing under Institutions Located in the Archdiocese for details.
Catechesis/Religious Programs—Students 20.

Hawkeye, Fayette Co., St. Francis Xavier (1891), Rev. John J. Purtell.
Res. and Mailing Address—Immaculate Conception, 413 W. First St., Sumner, 50674-1313. Tel: 563-578-5366.
Church—304 E. Main, 52147.
Catechesis/Religious Programs—Donna Scholbrock, D.R.E.

Hazleton, Buchanan Co., St. Mary's (1881), Rev. John C. Paisley; Deacon Richard Gehrke; Robin Ballard, Pastoral Assoc.
Mailing Address: 207 Benton, P.O. Box 146, 50641-0146. [CEM]
Parish Office: 305 Worth St., P.O. Box 180, Lamont, 50650-0180. Tel: 319-924-2691.
Church—209 Benton, 50641.

Hiawatha, Linn Co., St. Elizabeth Ann Seton Parish (1989), Rev. Neil J. Manternach; Marlene Myers, Pastoral Min.
Res., 1385 Lyndhurst, 52233. Tel: 319-743-3339. [JC]
Church—1350 Lyndhurst Dr., 52233.

Holy Cross, Dubuque Co., Holy Cross (1845), Rev. Donald J. Plamondon.
Res., 875 Church St., P.O. Box 398, 52053-0398. Tel: 563-870-2155. [CEM]
School—Rickardsville-Holy Cross-Luxemburg (RHCL) Catholic. See separate listing under Institutions Located in the Archdiocese for details.

Hopkinton, Delaware Co., St. Luke's (1922), Rev. John R. Kremer; Patricia Hucker, Pastoral Assoc.
Mailing Address: 206 First St., S.E., P.O. Box 159, 52237-0159. Tel: 563-926-2613.
Church—206 First St. S.E., 52237.
Catechesis/Religious Programs—Patricia Hucker, D.R.E.
Students 126.
Oratory—Sand Springs, Immaculate Conception. Sacramental Records at St John's, Delhi.

Independence, Buchanan Co., St. John Evangelist (1856), Rev. Aloysius J. Vorwald; Sharon Bainbridge, Pastoral Min.
Res., 209 Fifth Ave. N.E., 50644-1998. Tel: 319-334-7191; Fax: 319-334-7192. [CEM]
School—Matthew O'Loughlin, Prin. Lay Teachers 11; Students 166.
Catechesis/Religious Programs—Matthew O'Loughlin, D.R.E.
Students 199.

Ionia, Chickashaw Co., St. Boniface's (1899), Rev. John W. Hemann.
Parish Office and Mailing Address: 612 Cedar St., P.O. Box 308, Nashua, 50658-0308. Tel: 641-435-2070. [CEM]
Catechesis/Religious Programs—Bonnie Boggess, D.R.E.
Students 27.

Iowa Falls, Hardin Co., St. Mark's (1855), Rev. Mark J. McGovern.
Res., 415 Main St., P.O. Box 368, 50126-0368. Tel: 641-648-9547. [CEM]
Catechesis/Religious Programs—Judith Connell, D.R.E.
Students 99.

Jesup, Buchanan Co., St. Athanasius (1880), Very Rev. Donald P. Schmitt; Rev. Paul C. Baldwin; Sr. Donna Burke, O.S.F., Pastoral Assoc.
Res., 634 Stevens St., P.O. Box 316, 50648-0316. Tel: 319-827-6682. [CEM]
School—(Grades K-8). Gerald Brown, Prin.
Sisters 1; Lay Teachers 10; Students 148.
Catechesis/Religious Programs—Alice Weber, D.R.E.
Students 87.

Jewell, Hamilton Co., Good Shepherd (1915), Rev. Terrence Rasmussen, O.F.M.Conv.
Mailing Address: Parish Office, 2900 Hoover Ave., Ames, 50010-4498. Tel: 515-233-3092.
Church—503 Edwards St., 50130.
Catechesis/Religious Programs—Students 35.

Key West, Dubuque Co., St. Joseph's (1872), Rev. James J. Goedken.
Res., 10234 Key West Dr., Dubuque, 52003-8936. Tel: 563-582-7392.
Church—10334 Key West Dr., Dubuque, 52003.
School—10244 Key West Dr., Dubuque, 52003. Tel: 563-582-2866. Connie Kessler, Prin.
Lay Teachers 13; Students 249.
Catechesis/Religious Programs—D.R.E.: Laura Glynn; Sharon Foust.
Students 105.

Lake Mills, Winnebago Co., St. Patrick (1870), Rev. Craig E. Steimel; Sr. Mary Dolores Moes, P.V.B.M., Pastoral Assoc.
Res. and Mailing Address: 906 West St., Forest City, 50436-0310. Tel: 641-585-4856. [CEM]
Church—406 S. Grant St., 50450.
Catechesis/Religious Programs—D.R.E.: Linda Reding; Carla Langfald.
Students 66.

Lamont, Buchanan Co., St. Mary's (1894), Rev. John C. Paisley; Robin Ballard, Pastoral Assoc.
Res. and Mailing Address—305 Worth St., P.O. Box 180, 50650-0180. Tel: 563-924-2691.
Church—845 Pearl St., 50650. [CEM]
Catechesis/Religious Programs—D.R.E.: Deb Carpenter; Tina Pech.
Students 71.

La Motte, Jackson Co., Holy Rosary (1893), Rev. Clayton R. Landherr; Rev. Msgr. Thomas J. Ralph, Sacramental Priest; Sr. Virginia Crilly, B.V.M., Pastoral Assoc.
Res., 507 Elm St., P.O. Box 26, 52054-0026. Tel: 563-773-2323. [CEM]
School—Bellevue Area Catholic Elementary. See separate listing under Institutions Located in the Archdiocese for details.
Catechesis/Religious Programs—Marla Kilburg, D.R.E.
Students 22.

Lansing, Allamakee Co., Immaculate Conception (1855), Rev. Daniel J. Knipper.
Res., 648 Main St., 52151-9685. Tel: 563-538-4171. [CEM]
Catechesis/Religious Programs—Karen Weber, D.R.E.
Students 85.

La Porte City, Blackhawk Co., Sacred Heart (1887), Rev. Thomas E. Braak; Sr. Lene Rubly, O.S.F., Pastoral Assoc.
Res., 1021 Poplar St., 50651-1732. Tel: 319-342-2991.
Catechesis/Religious Programs—Margaret Johnson, D.R.E.
Students 139.

Lawler, Chickasaw Co., Our Lady of Mt. Carmel (1869), Rev. Marvin C. Salz.
Mailing Address: 207 E. Main St., P.O. Box 187, St. Lucas, 52166-0187.
Parish Office: 2940 Iowa Hwy. 24, Box 119, 52154. Tel: 563-238-3444. [CEM]
Catechesis/Religious Programs—Leslie Cuvelier, D.R.E.
Students 139.

Little Turkey, Chickasaw Co., Assumption of the B. V. M. (1902), Rev. John A. Moser.
Res. and Mailing Address: 110 Commercial Ave., P.O. Box 205, Protivin, 52163-0205. Tel: 563-569-8259. [CEM]
Church—3303 160th St., Lawler, 52154.
Catechesis/Religious Programs—Kathy Ball, D.R.E.
Students 47.

Lourdes, Howard Co., Our Lady of Lourdes (1875), Very Rev. Roger R. Rethamel; Betty Boehmer, Pastoral Assoc.
Res. & Mailing Address: 207 7th St., P.O. Box 38, Elma, 50628-0038. Tel: 641-393-2520. [CEM]
Church—14068 175th St., Elma, 50628.
Catechesis/Religious Programs—Julie Loftus, D.R.E.
Students 47.

Luxemburg, Dubuque Co., Holy Trinity (1865), Rev. Donald J. Plamondon.
Res. & Mailing Address: 875 Church St., P.O. Box 398, Holy Cross, 52053-0398. Tel: 563-870-2155. [CEM]
Church—103 S. Andres St., 52056.
School—Rickardsville-Holy Cross-Luxemburg (RHCL) Catholic. See separate listing under Institutions Located in the Archdiocese for details.

Lycurgus, Allamakee Co., St. Mary's (1859), Rev. Daniel J. Knipper.
Mailing Address: 648 Main St., Lansing, 52151. Tel: 563-538-4171. [CEM]
Church—1831 Lycurgus Rd., Waukon, 52172-0146.
Catechesis/Religious Programs—Kathy Payne, D.R.E.
Students 33.

Manchester, Delaware Co., St. Mary's (1872), Very Rev. Ralph P. Simington; Rev. Kenneth J. Glaser.
Res., 119 W. Fayette St., 52057-1596. Tel: 563-927-4710; Fax: 563-927-9949. [CEM]
School—(Grades K-6). Joseph Bearns, Prin.
Lay Teachers 14; Students 224.
Catechesis/Religious Programs—Sr. Shiela Geraghty, R.S.M., D.R.E.
Students 587.

Manly, Worth Co., Sacred Heart (1883), Rev. Thomas F. McAndrew; Deacon Robert Mega.
Res., 120 E. North, P.O. Box 160, 50456-0160. Tel: 641-454-2586. [CEM]
Catechesis/Religious Programs—Tammy Nettleton, D.R.E.

Maquoketa, Jackson Co., Sacred Heart (1873), Rev. Thomas J. McDermott; Sr. Romaine Pickart, O.S.F., Pastoral Min.; Deacon Robert Head.
Res., 200 S. Vermont St., P.O. Box 635, 52060-0635. Tel: 563-652-6931; Fax: 563-652-6932. [CEM]
School—Sr. Rita Green, O.S.F., Prin. Sisters 1; Lay Teachers 8; Students 158.
Catechesis/Religious Programs—Toby Kilburg, D.R.E.
Students 139.
Oratory—Baldwin, Jackson Co., Holy Trinity. Closed. Sacramental Records are located at Sacred Heart, Maquoketa. [CEM]

Marion, Linn Co., St. Joseph's (1890), Rev. John A. Gossman; Deacons Leo Schmall; Ed Pantaloni; Rodney Bluml, Pastoral Assoc.
Res., 1790 14th St., 52302-2267. Tel: 319-377-4869; Fax: 319-377-9043. [JC]
School—Sr. Margaret Weigel, R.S.M., Prin. Sisters of Mercy 2; Lay Teachers 20; Students 313.
Catechesis/Religious Programs—D.R.E.: Ruth Ard; Mary Hauschildt.
Students 697.

Marshalltown, Marshall Co., St. Henry's (1959), Rev. Louis M. Jaeger; Deacons Irvin Vaske; Roger Polt; Karen Mroz, Pastoral Assoc.
Parish Office: 221 W. Olive St., 50158-4248. Tel: 641-753-7374; Fax: 641-753-1499. [JC]
Res., 212 Huisman Cir., 50158. Tel: 641-752-2043.
School—Marshalltown Area Consolidated Catholic. See separate listing under Institutions Located in the Archdiocese for details.
Catechesis/Religious Programs—D.R.E.: Karen Koorsen; Mark Dolash.
Students 217.

St. Mary's (1869), Rev. Bernard C. Grady; Sr. Christine Feagan, O.P., Hispanic Min.; Deacon Edward J. Mead.
Res., 9 W. Linn St., P.O. Box 642, 50158-0642. Tel: 641-753-6278; Fax: 641-753-1279. [JC]
School—Marshalltown Area Consolidated Catholic. See separate listing under Institutions Located in the Archdiocese for details.
Catechesis/Religious Programs—Students 186.

Mason City, Cerro Gordo Co., St. Joseph's (1873), Very Rev. Carl A. Ries; Rev. David G. Kucera; Sr. LaVerne Dolphin, B.V.M., Pastoral Assoc.; Deacon Jack Barlow. Parish Office & Res.: 302 Fifth St. S.E., 50401-4005. Tel: 641-423-5001; Fax: 641-423-9553.
School—Newman Catholic. See separate listing under Institutions Located in the Archdiocese for details.
Catechesis/Religious Programs—Ginny Verstegen, D.R.E.
Students 404.

Holy Family (1908), Rev. Dennis H. Cahill; Deacons Matthew Berry; Charles Cooper; Debbie Cahalan, Pastoral Assoc.; Pat Dixon, Pastoral Assoc. In res., Rev. Kenneth B. Gehling.
Res., 714 N. Adams St., 50401-2124. Tel: 641-423-7301; Fax: 641-428-7663. [JC]
School—Newman Catholic. See separate listing under Institutions Located in the Archdiocese for details.
Catechesis/Religious Programs—Clustered with St. Joseph, Mason City. Ginny Verstegen, D.R.E.

Masonville, Delaware Co., Immaculate Conception (1883), Rev. Ivan R. Nienhaus; Sr. Mary Valentine Smith, O.S.F., Pastoral Assoc.
Res. and Mailing Address—555 First St., P.O. Box 236, Winthrop, 50682. Tel: 319-935-3523;927-2740.
Church—Bernhardt St., 50654. [CEM]
Catechesis/Religious Programs—Julie Francois, D.R.E.
Students 31.

McGregor, Clayton Co., St. Mary's (1873), Rev. Ronald G. Friedell.
Res., 311 Seventh St., 52157-9999. Tel: 563-873-2287. [CEM]
Catechesis/Religious Programs—John Kohlstedt, D.R.E.
Students 52.

Meyer, Mitchell Co., Sacred Heart (1900), Rev. Joseph M. Schneider; Sr. Burnita Kaschmitter, O.S.F., Pastoral Assoc.
Parish Office: P.O. Box 396, St. Ansgar, 50472-0396. Tel: 641-737-2262. [CEM]
Church—2695 480th St. W., McIntire, 50455.
School—Visitation (Stacyville-Meyer) Consolidated. See separate listing under Institutions Located in the Archdiocese for details.
Catechesis/Religious Programs—Barbara Brumm, D.R.E.
Students 46.

Monona, Clayton Co., St. Patrick's (1856), Rev. Ronald G. Friedell.
Res., 403 East St. S., P.O. Box U, 52159-0557. Tel: 563-539-4442. [CEM]
Catechesis/Religious Programs—Marilyn Ryan, D.R.E.
Students 211.

Monti, Buchanan Co., St. Patrick's (1855), Rev. Ivan R. Nienhaus; Sr. Mary Valentine Smith, O.S.F., Pastoral Assoc.
Mailing Address: P.O. Box 104, Masonville, 50654-0104. Tel: 319-935-3523.
Church—2856 Washington Ave., 52218. [CEM]
Catechesis/Religious Programs—Linda Dolan, D.R.E.
Students 69.

Monticello, Jones Co., Sacred Heart (1868), Rev. Msgr. Neil W. Tobin.
Office & Res.: 328 N. Sycamore, 52310-1213. Tel: 319-465-5944. [CEM]
Church—302 N. Sycamore, 52310.
School—William Sadler, Prin. Lay Teachers 8; Students 170.
Catechesis/Religious Programs—Linda Becker, D.R.E.
Students 217.

Mount Vernon, Linn Co., St. John's the Baptist (1843), Rev. James J. Duster. In res., Rev. Ernest J. Engler.
Res., 212 7th St. S.E., P.O. Box 169, 52314-0169. Tel: 319-895-6246. [CEM]
Catechesis/Religious Programs—Sue Schettler, D.R.E.
Students 282.

Nashua, Chickasaw Co., St. Michael's (1870), Rev. John W. Hemann.
Res., 612 Cedar St., P.O. Box 308, 50658-0308. Tel: 641-435-2070. [CEM]
Catechesis/Religious Programs—Kendra Gilbert, D.R.E.
Students 121.

Nevada, Story Co., St. Patrick's (1870), Rev. Jon M. Seda; Deacon Steven Vankerckvoorde.
Res. and Mailing Address: 410 Bailey St., P.O. Box 236, Colo, 50056-0236. Tel: 641-377-2710. [CEM]
Catechesis/Religious Programs—Mary Jo McLaughlin, D.R.E.
Students 162.

New Albin, Allamakee Co., St. Joseph's (1910), Rev. Daniel J. Knipper.
Res., 648 Main St., 52160. Tel: 563-538-4171. [CEM]
Catechesis/Religious Programs—Rita Krzebietke, D.R.E.
Students 44.

Newhall, Benton Co., St. Paul's (1914), Rev. John J. Walsh; Sr. Nora Rochford, O.S.F., Pastoral Assoc.; Deacon Robert F. Hurych.
Mailing Address: P.O. Box 447, 52315-0447. Tel: 319-223-5576.
Church—303 Third St. E., 52315.
Catechesis/Religious Programs—Students 202.

New Hampton, Chickasaw Co., St. Joseph's (1870), Rev. Carl L. Schmitt. Pastoral Assocs.: Sr. Lorraine Loecher, O.S.F.; Sr. Phyllis Ann Hackman, F.S.P.A.; Deacon Robert Baltes.
Res., 202 N. Broadway, 50659-1111. Tel: 641-394-2105; Fax: 641-394-5154. [CEM]
School—Kathlee Butler, Prin. Sisters 1; Lay Teachers 15; Students 251.
Catechesis/Religious Programs—D.R.E.: Sr. Lois Erpelding, O.S.F.; Marge Zipse.
Students 188.
St. Mary's (1894), Rev. Carl L. Schmitt; Sr. Lois Erpelding, O.S.F., Pastoral Assoc.
Mailing Address: 239 S. Walnut Ave., P.O. Box 66, 50659-0066. Tel: 641-394-2195. [CEM]
Catechesis/Religious Programs—Clustered with St. Joseph, New Hampton. Marge Zipse, D.R.E.

New Hartford, Butler Co., St. Joseph. Closed. For inquiries for sacramental records please contact St. Patrick, Parkersburg.

New Haven, Mitchell Co., St. Peter's (1876), Rev. Ray E. Atwood.
Church—2985 360th St., Osage, 50461-8517.
Office: 209 E. Main St., P.O. Box 146, Riceville, 50466-0146. Tel: 641-985-2028. [CEM]
Catechesis/Religious Programs—Diane Sullivan, D.R.E.
Students 35.

New Melleray, Dubuque Co., Holy Family (1850), Rev. Richard W. Kuhn.
Res., St. John the Baptist, 241 Peosta Rd., Peosta, 52068-9507. Tel: 563-582-4217.
Church—16500 Holy Family Ln., Peosta, 52068. [CEM]
Catechesis/Religious Programs—Kay Goedken, D.R.E.
Students 96.

New Vienna, Dubuque Co, St. Boniface's (1845), Rev. John J. O'Connor.
Mailing Address: 7401 Columbus St., P.O. Box 215, 52065-0215. Tel: 563-921-2465.
Res., SS. Peter and Paul, 1625-300th Ave., Petersburg, 52040-8736. Tel: 563-875-7992. [CEM]
Church—7401 Columbus St., 52065.
School—Archbishop Hennessy Catholic. See separate listing under Institutions Located in the Archdiocese for details.

North Buena Vista, Clayton Co., Immaculate Conception (1898), Rev. Msgr. John R. McClean.
Mailing Address: 520 Second St., P.O. Box 847, Guttenberg, 52052. Tel: 563-252-1247. [CEM]
Church—218 Main St.N., Buena Vista.

North Washington, Chickasaw Co., Immaculate Conception (1868), Rev. John W. Hemann.
Res., 114 N. Wapsi, 50661. Tel: 641-394-2078. [CEM]
Catechesis/Religious Programs—Mary Roethler, D.R.E.
Students 32.

Norway, Benton Co., St. Michael's (1867), Rev. Walter J. Kleinfehn.
Res., 512 Evergreen, P.O. Box 9, 52318-0009. Tel: 319-227-7169. [CEM]
Catechesis/Religious Programs—Andrea Berger, D.R.E.
Students 135.

Oelwein, Fayette Co., Sacred Heart (1876), Rev. Frederick C. Fangmann; Carol Hamilton, Pastoral Assoc.
Res., 628 S. Frederick Ave., 50662. Tel: 319-283-3743. [CEM]
School—Sr. Benjamin Duschner, P.B.V.M., Prin. Sisters of Mercy 2; Lay Teachers 11; Students 205.
Catechesis/Religious Programs—Michael Meyer, D.R.E.
Students 286.

Osage, Mitchell Co., Sacred Heart (1878), Rev. Philip F. Recker.
Res., 1209 State St., 50461-1844. Tel: 641-732-4342. [CEM]
School—Sr. Lenore Ostdiek, O.S.F., Prin. Sisters 1; Lay Teachers 6; Students 121.
Catechesis/Religious Programs—D.R.E.: Deb Angell; Ann Michels.
Students 208.

Ossian, Winneshiek Co., St. Francis de Sales (1876), Rev. Msgr. Cletus J. Hawes.
Res., 418 E. Main St., 52161-9998. Tel: 563-532-9366. [CEM]
School—Mae Becker, Prin. Lay Teachers 10; Students 171.
Catechesis/Religious Programs—Patricia Frana, D.R.E.

Otter Creek, Jackson Co., St. Lawrence (1854), Rev. Clayton R. Landherr; Sr. Virginia Crilly, B.V.M., Pastoral Assoc. In res., Rev. Msgr. Thomas J. Ralph, Sacramental Priest.
Parish Office: 507 Elm St., P.O. Box 26, La Motte, 52054-0026. Tel: 319-773-2323.
Res., 17486 Bellevue-Cascade Rd., Zwingle, 52079-9688. Tel: 563-686-4228. [CEM]
Catechesis/Religious Programs—Julie Delaney, D.R.E.
Students 35.

Oxford Junction, Jones Co., Sacred Heart (1890), Rev. Richard J. Poster; Sr. Kathleen Henneberry, C.H.M., Pastoral Assoc.
Res. and Mailing Address—301 Hwy. 136, P.O. Box 127, Lost Nation, 52254-0127. Tel: 563-678-2200.
Church—309 Church St., 52323.
Catechesis/Religious Programs—Patti Manuel, D.R.E.
Students 80.

Parkersburg, Butler Co., St. Patrick's (1889), Rev. Dennis J. Quint.
Parish Office: 204 G. Avenue, Grundy Center, 50638-1939. Tel: 319-824-3572. [CEM]
Church—304 Second St., 50665.
Catechesis/Religious Programs—Nancy Brannon, D.R.E.
Students 43.

Peosta, Dubuque Co., St. John the Baptist (1874), Rev. Richard W. Kuhn; Sr. Mary Kent Pearson, O.P., Pastoral Assoc.
Res., 241 Peosta St., 52068-9507. Tel: 563-582-4217. [CEM]
School—Seton Catholic Elementary School, Epworth. See separate listing under Institutions Located in the Archdiocese for details.
Catechesis/Religious Programs—Sr. Mary Kent Pearson, O.P., D.R.E.
Students 111.
Oratory—Lattnerville, Annunciation. Sacramental Records are located at St. John, Peosta.

Petersburg, Delaware Co., SS. Peter and Paul (1867), Rev. John J. O'Connor.
Res. & Mailing Address: 1625 300th Ave., 52040-8736. Tel: 563-875-7992. [CEM]
School—Archbishop Hennessy Catholic, New Vienna. See separate listing under Institutions Located in the Archdiocese for details.

Placid, Dubuque Co., St. John's (1874), Rev. Raymond A. Burkle; Deacon Gerald Koopmann.
Res., 22453 E. Pleasant Grove Rd., Epworth, 52045-9603. Tel: 563-876-5501. [CEM]
School—Seton Catholic Elementary School, Epworth. See separate listing under Institutions Located in the Archdiocese for details.
Catechesis/Religious Programs—Karen Loney.
Students 43.

Plymouth, Cerro Gordo Co., St. Michael (1872), Rev. Thomas F. McAndrew.
Res., Sacred Heart, 120 E. North, P.O. Box 160, Manly, 50456-0160. Tel: 641-454-2586.
Church—901 Rock St., 50464.

Plymouth Rock, Winneshiek Co., St. Agnes (1857). Closed. Sacramental records are located at Notre Dame, Cresco.

Postville, Allamakee Co., St. Bridget's (1872), Rev. Lloyd P. Ouderkirk, Hispanic Min.
Res., 141 W. Williams, P.O. Box 369, 52162-0369. Tel: 563-864-3138.
Catechesis/Religious Programs—Mary Koopmann, D.R.E.
Students 81.

Prairieburg, Linn Co., St. Joseph's (1874), Rev. Wayne J. Droessler; Sr. Anne Kisting, O.S.F., Pastoral Assoc.
Mailing Address: P.O. Box 4248, 52219-4248.
Parish Office: 410 Terrace Dr., P.O. Box S, Central City, 52214-0420. Tel: 319-438-6625. [CEM]
Church—300 West Ave., 52219.

Preston, Jackson Co., St. Joseph's (1881), Very Rev. Donald V. Bakewell.
Res. and Mailing Address: 250 S. Faith St., P.O. Box 309, 52069-0309. Tel: 563-689-5161. [CEM]
Catechesis/Religious Programs—D.R.E.: Irene Entsminger; Rosemary Sievers.
Students 201.

Protivin, Howard Co., Holy Trinity (1878), Rev. John A. Moser.
Res. & Mailing Address: 110 Commercial Ave., P.O. Box 205, 52163-0205. Tel: 563-569-8259. [CEM]
School—Marcia Kruse, Prin. Lay Teachers 10; Students 126.
Catechesis/Religious Programs—D.R.E.: Kay Shindelar; Pat Zajicek.
Students 83.
Oratory—Schley, Holy Cross. Sacramental Records at Holy Trinity, Protivin. [CEM]

Raymond, Blackhawk Co., St. Joseph's (1905), Rev. Rick D. Dagit. In res., Rev. Paul C. Baldwin.
Res. & Mailing Address: 311 15th Ave., P.O. Box 136, Gilbertville, 50634-0136. Tel: 319-296-1092. [CEM]
Church—6916 Lafayette Rd., 50667.
School—Immaculate Conception-St. Joseph (Gilbertville-Raymond Consolidated Elementary). See separate listing under Institutions Located in the Archdiocese for details.

Reinbeck, Grundy Co., Queen of Heaven (1958), Rev. Dennis J. Quint.
Res., Sacred Heart, 204 G Ave., Grundy Center, 50638-1939. Tel: 319-824-3572. [CEM]
Church—1006 Blackhawk St., 50669.
Catechesis/Religious Programs—Ann Nicklaus Schmelzer, D.R.E.
Students 84.

Riceville, Howard Co., Immaculate Conception (1879), Rev. Ray E. Atwood.
Res. and Mailing Address: 209 E. Main St., Box 146, 50466-0146. Tel: 641-985-2028. [CEM]
Catechesis/Religious Programs—Deborah Oulman, D.R.E.
Students 131.

Rickardsville, Dubuque Co., St. Joseph's (1840), Rev. Thomas R. Zinkula.
Res., 20245 St. Joseph Dr., 52039-9757. Tel: 563-552-2233. [CEM]
School—Rickardsville-Holy Cross-Luxemburg (RHCL) Catholic. See separate listing under Institutions Located in the Archdiocese for details.
Catechesis/Religious Programs—Mary Anne Manternach, D.R.E.
Students 52.

Rockford, Floyd Co., Holy Name (1910), Rev. Leo P. Riley.
Parish Office: 507 First Ave. N.W., 50468-1132. Tel: 641-756-3569.
Catechesis/Religious Programs—Brenda Schmitt, D.R.E.
Students 115.

Rockwell, Cerro Gordo Co., Sacred Heart (1878), Rev. Leo P. Riley.
Res. and Mailing Address: 305 Elm St. E., P.O. Box 30, 50469-0030. Tel: 641-822-4957. [CEM]
Catechesis/Religious Programs—Eleanor Nelson, D.R.E.
Students 74.
Oratory—Cartersville, St. John. Closed. Sacramental Records at Sacred Heart, Rockwell.

Roseville, Floyd Co., St. Mary (1867), Rev. Msgr. Walter L. Brunkan.
Res., 105 N. Main, P.O. Box 480, Greene, 50636-0480. Tel: 641-823-4146. [CEM]
Church—2397 Hwy. 14, Marble Rock, 50653.
Catechesis/Religious Programs—Betty Jo Staudt, D.R.E.
Students 75.

Rowley, Buchanan Co., All Saints (1896), Rev. Aloysius J. Vorwald.
Mailing Address: 3103 Michael, 52329-0206.
Res., 209 Fifth Ave. E., Independence, 50644. Tel: 319-334-7191.
Church—219 Park Ave., 52329.
Catechesis/Religious Programs—Brenda Corkery, D.R.E.
Students 26.

Ryan, Delaware Co., St. Patrick's (1882), Very Rev. Ralph P. Simington; Rev. Kenneth J. Glaser.
Mailing Address: 615 Howard St., P.O. Box 219, 52330-0219. Tel: 563-932-2151. [CEM]
Church—606 Franklin St., 52330.
Catechesis/Religious Programs—Students 144.

Sabula, Jackson Co., St. Peter (1840), Joan Head, Pastoral Admin.; Very Rev. Donald V. Bakewell, Priest Supr. & Sacramental Priest.
Parish Office: 504 Elk St., P.O. Box 429, 52070-0429. Tel: 563-687-2525. [CEM]
Catechesis/Religious Programs—Students 29.

St. Ansgar, Mitchell Co., St. Ansgar (1951), Rev. Joseph M. Schneider; Sr. Burnita Kaschmitter, O.S.F., Pastoral Assoc.
Mailing Address: P.O. Box 396, 50472-0396. Tel: 641-737-2262.
Church—704 E. Fourth St., 50472.
Catechesis/Religious Programs—Lisa Heimer, D.R.E.
Students 84.

St. Anthony, Marshall Co., Sacred Heart (1878), Rev. Jon M. Seda; Deacon Steven Van Kerckvoorde.
Parish Office: 1127 Tenth St., Nevada, 50201-1708. Tel: 515-382-2974. [CEM]
Church—416 Main St., 50239.
Catechesis/Religious Programs—Ruth Midler, D.R.E.

St. Catherine, Dubuque Co., St. Catherine's (1887), Bro. Stephen Markham, F.S.C., Pastoral Admin.; Very Rev. Donald V. Bakewell, Priest Supvr.; Rev. Scott E. Bullock, Sacramental Priest.
Res., 5177 St. Catherine Rd., Dubuque, 52003-9566. Tel: 563-583-0092. [CEM]
School—Bellevue Area Catholic Elementary. See separate listing under Institutions Located in the Archdiocese for details.
Catechesis/Religious Programs—Students 55.

St. Cecilia, Howard Co., St. Patrick's. Closed. Sacramental records are located at Immaculate Conception, Elma.

St. Donatus, Jackson Co., St. Donatus (1853), Bro. Stephen Markham, F.S.C., Pastoral Admin.; Very Rev. Donald V. Bakewell, Priest Supvr.; Rev. Scott E. Bullock, Sacramental Priest.
Res. and Mailing Address: 5177 St. Catherine Rd., Dubuque, 52003-9566. Tel: 563-583-0092. [CEM]
Church—E. First St., 52071.
School—Bellevue Area Catholic Elementary. See separate listing under Institutions Located in the Archdiocese for details.

St. Lucas, Fayette Co., St. Luke's (1855), Rev. Marvin C. Salz.
Res., 207 E. Main St., P.O. Box 187, 52166-0187. Tel: 563-778-2370. [CEM]
School—Trinity Catholic School, Protovin. See separate listing under Institutions Located in the Archdiocese for details.
Catechesis/Religious Programs—D.R.E.: Trudy Smith; Deb Dietzenbach.
Students 47.

St. Theresa, Jackson Co., St. Theresa's (1853), Rev. Clayton R. Landherr; Rev. Msgr. Thomas J. Ralph, Sacramental Priest; Sr. Virginia Crilly, B.V.M., Pastoral Assoc.
Res., 34257 230th Ave., LaMotte, 52054-9794. Tel: 563-773-2341. [CEM]
Catechesis/Religious Programs—Helen Maro, D.R.E.
Students 38.

Shell Rock, Butler Co., Holy Name. Closed. Sacramental records are located at St. Mary's, Waverly.

Sherrill, Dubuque Co., SS. Peter and Paul (1852), Sr. Mildred Leuenberger, O.S.F., Pastoral Admin.; Very Rev. Joseph V. O'Brien, Priest Supvr.; Rev. Thomas R. Zinkula, Sacramental Priest.
Res., 5131 Sherrill Rd., 52073-9612. Tel: 563-552-2611. [CEM]
School—Balltown-Sherrill Catholic. See separate listing under Institutions Located in the Archdiocese for details.
Catechesis/Religious Programs—Mary Anne Manternach, D.R.E.
Students 104.

South Garryowen, St. Aloysius. Closed. For inquiries for sacramental records please contact St. Patrick, Garryowen, Bernard.

Spillville, Winneshiek Co., St. Wenceslaus (1860), Rev. Donald J. Hawes; Sr. Carol Hemesath, O.S.F., Pastoral Assoc.
Res., 207 Church St., Box 128, 52168-0128. Tel: 563-562-3637. [CEM]
School—Calmar-Festina-Spillville (CFS) Catholic Elementary. See separate listing under Institutions Located in the Archdiocese for details.
Catechesis/Religious Programs—Combined with St. Aloysius, Calmar, and Our Lady of Seven Dolors, Festina. Helen Pinter, D.R.E.

Springbrook, Jackson Co., SS. Peter and Paul (1864), Very Rev. Donald V. Bakewell; Joan Head, Pastoral Assoc.
Mailing Address: 105 E. Main St., 52075. Tel: 563-872-3875. [CEM]
School—Bellevue Area Catholic Elementary. See separate listing under Institutions Located in the Archdiocese for details.
Catechesis/Religious Programs—Marc Postiglione, D.R.E.

Springville, Linn Co., St. Isidore's (1961), Rev. James J. Duster.
Res. and Mailing Address—212 Seventh St. S.E., P.O. Box 169, Mount Vernon, 52314-0169. Tel: 319-895-6246.
Church—603 6th St. S., 52336.
Catechesis/Religious Programs—Marilyn Andersen, D.R.E.
Students 79.

Stacyville, Mitchell Co., Church of the Visitation (1894), Rev. Joseph M. Schneider; Sr. Burnita Kaschmitter, O.S.F., Pastoral Assoc.
Parish Office: P.O. Box 396, St. Ansgar, 50476-0396. Tel: 641-737-2262. [CEM]
Church—604 N. Broad St., 50476.
School—Visitation (Stacyville-Meyer) Consolidated. See separate listing under Institutions Located in the Archdiocese for details.

State Center, Marshall Co., St. Joseph's (1870), Rev. Jon M. Seda; Deacon Steven Van Kerchvoorde.
Mailing Address: 410 Bailey St., P.O. Box 236, Colo, 50056-0236. Tel: 641-377-2710. [CEM]
Church—610 Third St. S.W., 50247.
Catechesis/Religious Programs—Judy Goodman, D.R.E.
Students 63.

Strawberry Point, Clayton Co., St. Mary's (1876), Rev. John C. Paisley; Robin Ballard, Pastoral Assoc.
Mailing Address: 314 W. Mission St., 52076-9432. Tel: 563-933-6166. [CEM]
Catechesis/Religious Programs—D.R.E.: Patty Hilton, Mary Hamblin.
Students 172.

Sumner, Bremer Co., Immaculate Conception (1894), Rev. John J. Purtell; Eloyce Munk, Pastoral Min.
Res., 413 W. First St., 50674-1313. Tel: 563-578-5366. [CEM]
Catechesis/Religious Programs—Deanna Joebgen, D.R.E.
Students 146.
Oratory—Pinhook, St. Bridget. Sacramental Records at Immaculate Conception, Sumner. [CEM]

Swaledale, Cerro Gordo Co., St. Lawrence. Closed. For inquiries for sacramental records please contact Sacred Heart, Rockwell.

Sylvia, Dubuque Co., Assumption (1896), Rev. Clayton R. Landherr; Rev. Msgr. Thomas J. Ralph, Sacramental Priest; Sr. Virginia Crilly, B.V.M., Pastoral Assoc.
Res., 34257 230th Ave., La Motte, 52054-9794. Tel: 563-773-2341. [CEM]
Church—Washington-Mills Rd., Zwingle, 52079.

Tama-Toledo, Tama Co., St. Patrick's (1864), Rev. Keith L. Birch; Patti Hoffman, Pastoral Assoc.
Res., 900 Park St., Tama, 52339-1238. Tel: 515-484-3039; 484-4242. [CEM]
Church—600 Oswego, Tama, 52339.
Catechesis/Religious Programs—Patricia Green, D.R.E.
Students 202.

Temple Hill, Jones Co., St. Peter's (1852), Rev. Thomas E. Toale.
Res., 20189 Temple Hill Rd., 52033-9802. Tel: 563-852-3448. [CEM]
School—Aquin Elementary School. See separate listing under Institutions Located in the Archdiocese for details.
Catechesis/Religious Programs—Clustered with St. Matthias, Cascade, Sacred Heart, Fillmore, and St. Patrick, Garryowen. Julie Orris, D.R.E.

Traer, Tama Co., St. Paul's (1912), Rev. John R. Tilp.
Res., 1102 Walnut St., 50675-1440. Tel: 319-478-2222. [CEM]

Urbana, Benton Co., St. Mary (1872), Rev. Gabriel C. Anderson.
Res. and Mailing Address—Sacred Heart, 516 Rowley St., P.O. Box 116, Walker, 52352-0116. Tel: 319-448-4316.
Church—401 Ash Ave., 52345. [CEM]
Catechesis/Religious Programs—Students 158.

Van Horne, Benton Co., Immaculate Conception (1869), Rev. John J. Walsh; Sr. Nora Rochford, O.S.F., Pastoral Assoc.; Deacon Robert Hurych.
Res., 405 Fourth Ave., P.O. Box 250, 52346-0250. Tel: 319-228-8131. [CEM]
Catechesis/Religious Programs—Penni Pickering, D.R.E.

Vining, Tama Co., St. Mary's (1874), Rev. John R. Tilp.
Res. and Mailing Address—1102 Walnut St., Traer, 50675-1440. Tel: 319-478-2222.
Church—405 2nd Ave., 52348. [CEM]
Catechesis/Religious Programs—Barbara Cibula, D.R.E.

Vinton, Benton Co., St. Mary's (1878), Rev. Joseph E. McGuire.
Res., 2200 S. Second Ave, 52349. Tel: 319-472-4448. [CEM]
Catechesis/Religious Programs—Diane Watson, D.R.E.
Students 203.

Volga, Clayton Co., Sacred Heart (1889), Rev. Paul R. Peters; Sr. Carole Freking, O.S.F., Pastoral Assoc.
Mailing Address: 330 First St. P.O. Box 135, Elkader, 52043-0626. Tel: 563-245-2548. [CEM]
Church—304 White St., 52077.
Catechesis/Religious Programs—Jennifer Dillon, D.R.E.
Students 44.

Walford, Linn Co., Holy Trinity (1890), Rev. Thomas J. Schwinn; Sr. Maryann Greenwald, S.S.N.D., Pastoral Assoc.; Deacon John Malone.
Mailing Address: 620 Church St., P.O. Box 219, Fairfax, 52228-0219. Tel: 319-846-2025.
Church—110 First St. S., 52351.

Walker, Linn Co., Sacred Heart (1885), Rev. Gabriel C. Anderson; Betty Decker, Parish Min.
Res., 516 Rowley St., P.O. Box 116, 52352-0116. Tel: 319-448-4316. [CEM]
Catechesis/Religious Programs—Students 108.

Waterloo, Blackhawk Co.,

1—ST. JOSEPH'S, (1868), Rev. Leon Connolly; Deacon Larry Gram. In res., Rev. Msgr. W. Dean Walz.
Res., 320 Mulberry St., 50703-3598. Tel: 319-234-4439. [JC]
Catechesis/Religious Programs—Clustered with St. Mary's, Waterloo.

2—ST. MARY'S, (1898), Revs. Paul E. Lippstock; Robert E. Hilmer.
Res., 2127 E. Fourth St., 50703-2699. Tel: 319-232-1326. [JC]
School—Tel: 319-232-2418. Beth Wright, Prin.
Lay Teachers 12; Students 149.
Catechesis/Religious Programs—Bev Byford, D.R.E.
Students 29.

3—SACRED HEART, (1909), Rev. Michael Mescher; Sr. Louann Doerning, P.B.V.M., Pastoral Assoc. In res., Rev. Justin Kane.
Res., 627 W. Fourth St., 50702-1501. Tel: 319-234-4996. [JC]
School—Julie Niemeyer, Prin. Sisters 1; Lay Teachers 18; Students 360.
Catechesis/Religious Programs—Pamela Johnston, D.R.E.
Students 106.

4—ST. EDWARD'S, (1945), Revs. Jerry Kopacek; Robert F. Davies; Karol Rae Hoth, Pastoral Assoc.; Deacon John Baker.
Res., 1423 Kimball Ave., 50702-3837. Tel: 319-233-8060. [JC]
School—Chris Mitchell, Prin. (Elementary). Sisters 1; Lay Teachers 24; Students 597.
Catechesis/Religious Programs—Rose Kodet, D.R.E.
Students 111.

5—ST. JOHN'S, (1923), Rev. George W. Karnik; Sr. JoAnn O'Connell, B.V.M., Pastoral Assoc.; Deacon Edward Weber.
Res., 1701 Mulberry St., 50703-4991. Tel: 319-233-5241. [JC]
School—St. John-St. Nicholas Consolidated. Barbara Emerson, Prin.
Catechesis/Religious Programs—Dave Cushing, D.R.E.
Students 18.

6—Blessed Sacrament, (1947), Rev. Dennis D. Juhl; Sr. Madonna M. Friedman, O.S.F., Pastoral Assoc.; Deacons John Herman; James Freet.
Res., 650 Stephan Ave., 50701-2099. Tel: 319-233-6179. [JC]
School—Tel: 319-233-7863. Bob Burke, Prin. Sisters 1; Lay Teachers 12; Students 248.
Catechesis/Religious Programs—Barbara Duggan, D.R.E.
Students 149.

Watkins, Benton Co., St. Patrick's (1880), Rev. Walter J. Kleinfehn.
Res. and Mailing Address—St. Michael, 512 Evergreen St., P.O. Box 9, Norway, 52318-0009. Tel: 319-227-7169.
Church—2nd St., 52354. [CEM]
Catechesis/Religious Programs—Yvonne Brecht, D.R.E.
Students 39.

Waucoma, Fayette Co., St. Mary's (1898), Rev. Marv C. Salz.
Res. and Mailing Address—207 E. Main, P.O. Box 187, St. Lucas, 52166-0187. Tel: 563-778-2370.
Church—218 3rd St. N.W., 52171. [CEM]
Catechesis/Religious Programs—Maxine Balk, D.R.E.
Students 65.

Waukon, Allamakee Co., St. Patrick's (1851), Rev. Allen M. Schmitt.
Res., 109 Second St. S.W., Box 146, 52172-0146. Tel: 563-568-3671. [CEM]
School—Tel: 563-568-2415. Michael Ward, Prin. Lay Teachers 15; Students 194.
Catechesis/Religious Programs—Kris Ward, D.R.E. Students 216.
Oratory—West Ridge, St. John the Baptist. Sacramental Records at St. Patricks, Waukon. [CEM]

Waverly, Bremer Co., St. Mary's (1856), Rev. James L. Miller; Sr. Bernadette Engelhaupt, S.S.S.F., Pastoral Assoc.
Res., 112 Second Ave. S.E., 50677-3404. Tel: 319-352-2493. [CEM]
Catechesis/Religious Programs—Deacon Guy Beck, D.R.E.
Students 467.

Webster City, Hamilton Co., St. Thomas Aquinas (1870), Rev. John R. Flaherty.
Res., 1010 Des Moines St., 50595-2147. Tel: 515-832-1190. [CEM]
School—Tel: 515-832-1346. Duane Siepker, Prin. Lay Teachers 10; Students 118.
Catechesis/Religious Programs—(Grades K-6). Jennifer Maharry, D.R.E.
Students 150.

West Union, Fayette Co., Holy Name (1870), Rev. Dale J. Rausch.
Res., 128 N. Walnut St., 52175-1347. Tel: 563-422-3184. [CEM]
Catechesis/Religious Programs—D.R.E.: Marion Broghammer; Sue McDonough.
Students 227.

Wexford, Allamakee Co., Immaculate Conception (1851), Rev. Louis J. Trzil.
Res. & Mailing Address: 1416 Great River Rd., Lansing, 52151. Tel: 563-586-2150. [CEM]
Catechesis/Religious Programs—D.R.E.: Patty Manning; Regina Manning.
Students 41.

Williams, Hamilton Co., St. Mary's (1875), Rev. Jack R. Flaherty.
Parish Office: 1010 Des Moines St., Webster City, 50595-2147. Tel: 515-832-1190. [CEM]
Church—404 Fourth St., 50271. Tel: 515-854-2241.
Catechesis/Religious Programs—Students 15.

Winthrop, Buchanan Co., St. Patrick's (1894), Rev. Ivan R. Nienhaus; Sr. Mary Valentine Smith, O.S.F., Pastoral Assoc.
Res., 555 First St., P.O. Box 236, 50682-0236. Tel: 319-935-3523. [CEM]
Catechesis/Religious Programs—Deb Steffen, D.R.E. Students 163.

Woden, Hancock Co., Sacred Heart (1900), Rev. Marvin J. Bries.
Res. and Mailing Address—139 Third St. S.E., Britt, 50423-1726. Tel: 641-843-3215.
Church—147 Howard Ave., 50484.
Catechesis/Religious Programs—Kate Smith, D.R.E. Students 28.

Worthington, Dubuque Co., St. Paul's (1875), Very Rev. Florian J. Schmidt.
Res., 314 Third Ave. S.W., P.O. Box 38, 52078-0038. Tel: 563-855-2405. [CEM]
School—Mary Smock, Prin. Lay Teachers 5; Students 72.
Catechesis/Religious Programs—Julie Bries, D.R.E. Students 59.

Zearing, Story Co., St. Gabriel (1904), Rev. Jon M. Seda; Deacon Steven Van Kerckvoorde.
Mailing Address: 410 Bailey St., P.O. Box 236, Colo, 50056-0236. Tel: 641-377-2710.
Church—302 N. Center, 50278.
Catechesis/Religious Programs—Renee Dreckman. Students 45.

Chaplains of Public Institutions

Anamosa. *Iowa State Men's Reformatory*. Vacant.
Independence. *Mental Health Institute*. 302 W. Main St., P.O. Box 505, Fairbank, 50629. Tel: 319-635-2211. Rev. Kenneth C. Stecher, Part-Time Chap.
Marshalltown. *Veterans' Home*. Sr. Rosemary Vaske, O.S.F., Chap.; Rev. Jon M. Seda.

On Special or Other Archdiocesan Assignment:
Reverend Monsignors—
Barta, James O., Vicar General & Dubuque Region Episcopal Vicar
Bleich, Russell M., Episcopal Vicar, Cedar Rapids Region
Walz, W. Dean, Episcopal Vicar, Waterloo Region

On Duty Outside the Archdiocese:
Reverend Monsignors—
Funke, Richard P., 7974 Sailboat Key Blvd., Box 602, South Pasadena, FL 33707. Tel: 727-363-1754
Reverend Fathers—
Flanagan, James W., Dept. of Religion, Mather House, Case Western Reserve Univ., Cleveland, OH 44106. Tel: 216-791-3030
Zee, Louis C., Ascension Church, 4605 Jetty Ln., Houston, TX 77072-1222. Tel: 281-575-8855

Military Chaplains:
Reverend Fathers—
Remy, David P., PSC 1008, Box 3031, FPO AA, 34051-3031
Schueller, La Verne L., Ch. Col., USSTRATCOM J040, 901 Sac Blvd., Ste. 2D7, Offutt AFB, NE 68113-6040. Tel: 402-294-2281

Graduate Studies:
Reverend Fathers—
Hauer, Joseph L., Casa Santa Maria, Viadell Umilta, 30, 00187 Rome, Italy
Joensen, William, St. Frances de Chantal, 9701 Old Georgetown Rd., Bethesda, MD 20814. Tel: 301-581-3392
Loecke, Douglas J., Casa Santa Maria, Viadell Umilta, 30, 00187 Rome, Italy

Unassigned:
Reverend Fathers—
DeVenney, Timothy
Dolan, Gerald
Goltz, William
Wild, Alexander

On Leave of Absence:
Reverend Fathers—
Fitzgerald, Michael C.
Lynch, Maurice J.
McDermott, John J.

Retired:
Reverend Monsignors—
Blessington, William H., Stonehill Care Center, 3485 Windsor Ave., Dubuque, IA 52001-1312
Chihak, John P., 420 W. Lyon St., Garner, IA 50438
Collins, Bernard G., 3160 E. Main St., Village Grove #8, Mesa, AZ 85213
Dalton, John W., 1301 Rhodes, Naperville, IL 60540
Ferring, Robert L., 3400 Dana Dr., #4, Dubuque, IA 52002
Friedl, Francis P., 3400 Dana Dr., #3, Dubuque, IA 52002
Heineman, Donald P., 108 3rd St., SE, P.O. Box 187, Fort Atkinson, IA 52144-0187
Heles, Frederic G., P.O. Box 1435, Venice, FL 34284-1435
Herard, Joseph P., 705 Heller Dr., E. Dubuque, IL 61025
Heuring, Alvan P., 3458 Edison St., San Mateo, CA 94403-3401
Kurt, Edgar J., Villa Raphael, 1235 Mt. Loretta, Dubuque, IA 52003-8785
Lechtenberg, Edward W., 321 Diagonal St., Lansing, IA 52151
Leonard, William P., 971 Mt. Loretta Ave., Dubuque, IA 52003
Manternach, Albert V., 617 1st Ave., W., Cascade, IA 52033
McAvoy, Ambrose A., Stonehill Care Center, 3485 Windsor Ave., Dubuque, IA 52001-1312
O'Brien, Roger E., Villa Raphael, 1235 Mt. Loretta, Dubuque, IA 52003-8785
Reicks, Leander H., 105 E. Rural St., P.O. Box 223, St. Lucas, IA 52166
Slepicka, Joseph J., 313 N. 13th St., Clear Lake, IA 50428
Spaight, Robert L., Windsor Park, Apt. 109, 801 Davis St., Dubuque, IA 52001
Steimel, Paul T., 3709 W. 9th St., Apt. 8, Waterloo, IA 50702
Supple, James A., 129 Ash St., #2, Ames, IA 50010
Vogl, Robert R., Loras College, 1450 Alta Vista St., P.O. Box 178, Dubuque, IA 52004-0178
Wheeler, David A., St. Mary's Rectory, 1584 White St., Dubuque, IA 52001-4905
Reverend Fathers—
Ament, Robert J., 1375 273rd Ave., Fort Atkinson, IA 52144-7405
Auer, Robert F., 1027 N. Third St., Guttenberg, IA 52052
Axen, Ronald J., St. Francis Village, 105 Trinity Cir., Crowley, TX 76036
Bahning, Frederick C., Stonehill Care Center, 3485 Windsor Ave., Dubuque, IA 52001-1812
Barnes, John G., 114 Sheakley, New Hampton, IA 50659
Benda, Frank M., 1160 Victoria Pl., Dubuque, IA 52003
Bodensteiner, Peter C., 108 W. Spring St., Apt. A-1, Lawler, IA 52154
Burke, Clement J., 2321 Aldrich Ave. S., #315, Minneapolis, MN 55405
Carpender, John W., 720 Duggan Dr., #1, Dubuque, IA 52003-0250
Carpender, Thomas J., Brookwood, Apt. 413, 1320 E. 48th Pl., Tulsa, OK 74105
Condon, Gerald A., 1320 Wenig Rd., N.E. #10, Cedar Rapids, IA 52402
Currier, Thomas F., 925 N. Harrison Ave., Mason City, IA 50401
Devine, William P., 22623 V Ave., Eldora, IA 50627-8012
Drexler, Harold J., Sacred Heart, 2215 Windsor Ave., Dubuque, IA 52001-1698
Einck, Gregory J., Stonehill Care Center, 3485 Windsor Ave., Dubuque, IA 52001
Engler, Ernest J., St. John Rectory, 212 Seventh St. S.E., Mt. Vernon, IA 52314
Evans, Paul J., 400 Blunt St., Charles City, IA 50616
Frana, Clarence L., 3031 Sixth St., S.W., Apt. 9, Cedar Rapids, IA 52404
Friedell, John C., Loras College, 1450 Alta Vista St., P.O. Box 178, Dubuque, IA 52004-0178
Geary, Patrick G., 443 S. Roosevelt Rd., Evansdale, IA 50707-1269
Hamilton, Philip A., 12 Padgett Ct., Bluffton, SC 29910
Heimerman, Francis D., 151 Main St., P.O. Box 623, Nashua, IA 50658
Hemann, Melvin D., 127 Kaspend Pl., Cedar Falls, IA 50613-1683
Herzog, John M., 1004 Mesa Verde Pl., Ames, IA 50014
Hess, Richard J., Immaculate Conception Rectory, 857 3rd Ave. SE, P.O. Box 1247, Cedar Rapids, IA 52406
Hirsch, Robert M., 411 N. Jefferson St., P.O. Box 609, Calmar, IA 52132-0609
Hussmann, John R., Villa Raphael, 1235 Mt. Loretta Ave., Dubuque, IA 52003-8785
Kalb, Bertram J., Stonehill Care Center, 3485 Windsor Ave., Dubuque, IA 52001-1312
Kane, Justin, 627 W. 4th St., Waterloo, IA 50702-1501
Karal, John W., 308 W. Nevada, Marshalltown, IA 50158-2751
Katz, Roger L., 400 17th St. W., Clear Lake, IA 50428
Keppler, Daniel J., 1524 Riverview Dr., Lansing, IA 52151
Kissling, John M., P.O. Box 356, Chetek, WI 54728
Kleve, Arthur W., The Willows, 1000 N. Eisenhower Ave., Mason City, IA 50401
Kruse, Clarence, Villa Raphael, 1235 Mt. Loretta Ave., Dubuque, IA 52003-8785
Kurt, Allan J., P.O. Box 479, Dubuque, IA 52004-0479
Kutsch, Eugene C., 2622 New Haven St., Dubuque, IA 52001
LaBarge, Charles F., 1538 Kehl Ct., Dubuque, IA 52003
Laughlin, Martin T., 38 Huquenin Ln., Bluffton, SC 29910
Levenhagen, Robert J., 283 Harbor Lights Dr., Browerville, MN 55919
Ludwig, Ray A., St. John Nepomucene Rectory, 202 Second St., S.E., Fort Atkinson, IA 52144-0157
Maichen, Richard F., 1009 New St., Manchester, IA 52057
Manternach, Carl J., 420 N. Maple, Monticello, IA 52310

McDonald, Paul F., U.S.A.F., 8915 Willmon Way, San Antonio, TX 78239
Menster, William J., 703 Bluff St., Dubuque, IA 52001
Merfeld, Vincent C., 751 South Windsor Blvd., Los Angeles, CA 90005
Moran, John W., 507 Cherry Dr., P.O. Box 970, Monona, IA 52159
Norton, Claude B., Villa Raphael, 1235 Mt. Loretta Ave., Dubuque, IA 52003-8785
O'Brien, William D., Villa Raphael, 1235 Mt. Loretto Ave., Dubuque, IA 52003
Otting, Loras C., Villa Raphael, 1235 Mt. Loretta Ave., Dubuque, IA 52003-8785
Palen, Robert L., 19 W. 230 Governors Trail, Oak Brook, IL 60521
Pepper, David J., 102 W. Spring, Box 120, Lawler, IA 52154
Perry, Francis J., Villa Raphael, 1235 Mt. Loretto Ave., Dubuque, IA 52003
Pitzen, John J., 215 Vanderbilt St., Fairfax, IA 52228
Ptacek, John P., 206 7th St., S.E., Farley, IA 52046
Purtell, Thomas W., 615 West Prospect St, New Hampton, IA 50659
Raftis, J. Duane, Stonehill Care Center, 3485 Windsor Ave., Dubuque, IA 52001-1312
Rasing, Linus E., 615 West Prospect St., New Hampton, IA 50659
Reuter, Lloyd E., 1905 5th St., P.O. Box 114, Gilbertville, IA 50634
Rhomberg, Thomas W., 1510 Kell Ct., Apt. 6, Dubuque, IA 52003
Rogers, Daniel J., 3839 St. Catherine Rd., Bellevue, IA 52031
Ruhland, Carl J., 3955 Creston St., Dubuque, IA 52002
Saunders, Robert J., 710 Anderson St., Manchester, IA 52057
Schmidt, Wilfred W., Stonehill Care Center, 3485 Windsor Ave., Dubuque, IA 52001-1312
Schmitt, Phillip E., 3834 E Ave, N.E., Cedar Rapids, IA 52402-5627
Schwartz, William T., 6421 S. Oakmont Dr., Chandler, AZ 85249
Simon, Vincent J., 100 South St., P.O. Box 304, Ossian, IA 52161
Smith, John P., Villa Raphael, 1235 Mt. Loretta Ave., Dubuque, IA 52003-8785
Weydert, Donald D., 2249 Del Monaco Dr., Dubuque, IA 52002
Whalen, Charles W., 2245 Chaney Rd., #4, Dubuque, IA 52001-2939
Wilkie, William E., Ph.D., 1920 Cox St., #4, Dubuque, IA, 52001

Permanent Deacons:
Aitchison, Gary, St. Cecilia, Ames
Ayers, John, Clear Lake
Baker, John, St. Edward, Waterloo
Baltes, Robert, St. Joseph, New Hampton
Barlow, Jack, St. Joseph, Mason City
Bassler, Eugene, (Retired), Dubuque
Berger, James, St. Ludmila, Cedar Rapids
Berry, Matthew, Holy Family, Mason City
Biver, William, St. Columbkille, Dubuque
Blouin, Mike, All Saints, Cedar Rapids
Brustkern, Leo J., (Retired), La Porte City
Cashatt, Wayne, (Retired), Eldora
Cisler, William, St. Wenceslaus, Cedar Rapids
Cooper, Charles, Holy Family, Mason City
DiPietre, Dennis, Columbia, MO
Fessler, Ray, (Retired), Dubuque
Fortin, Daryl, Bettendorf
Freet, James, Blessed Sacrament, Waterloo
Frost, Irwin, (Retired), Waterloo
Froyen, Leonard, St. Stephen the Witness Student Center, Cedar Falls
Gehrke, Richard, St. Mary, Hazleton
Gram, Clarence, St. Joseph, Waterloo
Groh, Victor, (Retired), Thornton
Hayes, Joseph, (Retired), Cascade
Head, Robert, Sacred Heart, Maquoketa
Herman, John, Blessed Sacrament, Waterloo
Hoeger, Daniel, St. Patrick, Cedar Rapids
Hurych, Robert F., St. Paul, Newhall; Immaculate Conception, Van Horne; St. John, Blairstown
Jenney, William, St. Nicholas, Evansdale
Jones, David, St. Mary, Ackley
Jorgensen, Gerald, Resurrection, Dubuque
Kean, James, St. Patrick, Epworth
Koopmann, Gerald, St. John, Placid
LoBianco, Timothy, St. Patrick & St. Mary, Dubuque
MacDonald, Stephen, St. Joseph the Worker, Dubuque
Malone, John, St. Patrick, Fairfax; Holy Trinity, Walford
Manning, Richard, St. Ludmila, Cedar Rapids
Mauss, William, St. Anthony, Dubuque
McCully, John, St. Cecilia, Ames
McGhee, David, Nativity, Dubuque
Mead, Edward, St. Mary, Marshalltown
Mega, Robert, Sacred Heart, Manly
Moetsch, Michael, St. Patrick, Cedar Falls
Naso, James, Darien, IL
Oates, Michael, St. Patrick, Cedar Falls
Otto, J. C., St. Michael, Belle Plaine; St. Joseph, Chelsea
Pantaloni, Ed, St. Joseph, Marion
Pettit, Gerald, Immaculate Conception, Cedar Rapids
Pfaffly, James, St. Mary, Guttenberg
Saunders, Phil, St. Matthew, Cedar Rapids
Scharosch, Albert, St. Pius X, Cedar Rapids
Schmall, Leo, St. Joseph, Marion
Schmit, Nick, (Retired), Belmond
Sinnwell, James E., Immaculate Conception, Charles City
Stattelman, Leo W., (Retired), Clear Lake
Steger, James, St. Joseph, Earlville
Tondra, Richard, St. Cecilia, Ames
Vaske, Irvin, St. Henry, Marshalltown
Weber, Edward, St. John, Waterloo
Whitters, Michael, St. John, Clarion
Wilson, James, (Retired), Waterloo
Zimmerman, Paul, St. Pius X, Cedar Rapids

INSTITUTIONS LOCATED IN THE ARCHDIOCESE

[A] SEMINARIES, ARCHDIOCESAN

DUBUQUE. *Seminary of St. Pius X*, Loras College, 1450 Alta Vista St., P.O. Box 178, 52004-0178. Tel: 563-588-7661. Revs. Mark A. Ressler, Rector; David H. O'Connor, Spiritual Dir.; Scott E. Bullock, Dir. Pre-Theology Formation. Students for Archdiocese of Dubuque 1.

[B] SEMINARIES, RELIGIOUS OR SCHOLASTICATES

EPWORTH. *Divine Word College*, 102 Jacoby Dr. S.W., P.O. Box 380, 52045-0380. Tel: 563-876-3353; Fax: 563-876-3407.
E-mail: hutch@dwc:edu
Web site: www.svd.org
Society of the Divine Word (S.V.D.). Very Rev. William Shea, S.V.D., Rector; Revs. Michael Hutchins, S.V.D., Pres.; Kenneth Anich, S.V.D., Vice Pres. for Academic Affairs; Dr. Robert Morrissey, S.V.D., Vice Pres. Devel.; Revs. Quang Duc Dinh, S.V.D., Vice Pres. Formation & Dean of Students; Gus Wall, S.V.D., Vice Pres. Recruitment & Admissions; John-Hue Tran, S.V.D.; Joseph McDermott, S.V.D.; John Tra, S.V.D.; Bros. Rodney Bowers, S.V.D.; Kevin Diederich, S.V.D.; Tony Kreinus, S.V.D.; Wayne Till, S.V.D.; James Zabransky, S.V.D.; Revs. Walter Bunofsky, S.V.D.; Joseph Connors, S.V.D.; James Heiar, S.V.D., Assoc. Devel. Dir.; Francis Kuttikattukunnel, S.V.D.; Dominic Nguyen, S.V.D.; John Szkulaski, S.V.D.; Thanh Van Nguyen, S.V.D. Priests 16; Brothers 5; Sisters 2; Lay Teachers 20; Students 80.

[C] COLLEGES AND UNIVERSITIES

DUBUQUE. *Clarke College*, 1550 Clarke Dr., 52001. Tel: 563-588-6300; Fax: 563-588-6789.
Web site: www.clarke.edu
For a complete listing, refer to the Colleges and Universities section.

Loras College, 1450 Alta Vista St., P.O. Box 178, 52004-0178. Tel: 563-588-7100; Fax: 563-588-7964.
E-mail: jfroehli@loras.edu
For a complete listing, refer to the Colleges and Universities section.

CEDAR RAPIDS. *Mount Mercy College*, 1330 Elmhurst Dr., N.E., 52402-4797. Tel: 319-363-8213; Fax: 319-368-6492.
E-mail: admission@mmc.mtmercy.edu
Web site: www.mtmercy.edu
For a complete listing, refer to the Colleges and Universities section.

[D] HIGH SCHOOLS, INTERPAROCHIAL

DUBUQUE. *Wahlert High School.* (Grades 9-12), 2005 Kane St., 52001. Tel: 563-583-9771; Fax: 563-583-9775. Mr. Donald Miller, Prin.; Rev. Dwayne J. Thoman, Spiritual Dir. Priests 2; Sisters 2; Lay Teachers 62; Students 829.
Serving all Parishes in Dubuque; Holy Family, New Melleray; St. Joseph's, Key West; SS. Peter and Paul, Sherrill.

BELLEVUE. *Marquette High School.* (Grades 9-12), 502 Franklin St., 52031. Tel: 563-872-3356; Fax: 563-872-3285. Very Rev. Donald V. Bakewell, Pastoral Coord.; Kris Egan, Spiritual Dir. Brothers 1; Sisters 1; Lay Teachers 7; Students 126.
Serving St. John's, Andrew; St. Joseph's, Bellevue; St. Catherine's, St. Catherine; St. Donatus, St. Donatus; Holy Rosary, LaMotte; St. Peter's, Sabula; SS. Peter and Paul, Springbrook.

CEDAR RAPIDS. *Metropolitan Office of Catholic Education*, Cedar Rapids Metro Office, 516 A Ave. N.W., P.O. Box 2307, 52406-2307. Tel: 319-366-2517; Fax: 319-366-0426.
E-mail: dbqcrm@arch.put.k12.ia.us
Sr. Jean Brady, B.V.M., Assoc. Dir.

Xavier High School. (Grades 9-12), 6300 42nd St., N.E., 52411. Tel: 319-294-6635; Fax: 319-294-6712. Rev. John A. Grossman, Pastoral Coord.; Jeff Henderson, Prin. & Contact Person; Rev. Steven G. O'Brien, Campus Minister. Priests 1; Lay Teachers 46; Students 701.
Serving Holy Trinity, Walford; St. Patrick's, Fairfax; John XXIII; St. Jude's, St. Ludmila's, St. Patrick's, Immaculate Conception, St. Wenceslaus, St. Matthew, All Saints, St. Pius X,Cedar Rapids; St. Joseph, Marion; St. Elizabeth Ann Seton, Hiawatha.

Xavier High School Foundation, 6300 42nd St., N.E., P.O. Box 1394, 52406. Tel: 319-378-4571; Fax: 319-378-2953. Anne Cunningham, Exec. Dir.; Very Rev. Charles E. Lang, Pastoral Coord.

DYERSVILLE. *Beckman High School.* (Grades 7-12). (Coed), 1325 Ninth St. S.E., 52040. Tel: 563-875-7188; Fax: 563-875-7242. Steve Schute, Prin.; Mr. Wayne Wilgenbusch, Prin.; Rev. Ed Petty, Pastoral Coord. Sisters 1; Lay Teachers 36; Students 351.
Serving the following Parishes: St. Francis Xavier, Dyersville; St. Joseph, Earlville; St. Boniface, New Vienna; Ss. Peter and Paul, Petersburg; St. Paul, Worthington.

GILBERTVILLE. *Don Bosco High School.* (Grades 9-12), 405 16th Ave., 50634. Tel: 319-296-1692; Fax: 319-296-1693.
E-mail: dbqH06@arch.pvt.k12.ia.us
Rev. Donald P. Schmitt, Pastoral Coord.; James Hrabe, Prin.; Rev. Paul C. Baldwin, Spiritual Dir.; Jerry Murray, Guidance Counselor. Lay Teachers 17; Students 201.
Serving St. Francis, Barclay, Dunkerton; Immaculate Conception, Gilbertville; St. Athanasius, Jesup; Sacred Heart, LaPorte City; St. Joseph's, Raymond; St. Mary of Mt. Carmel, Eagle Center.

WATERLOO. *Columbus High School.* (Grades 9-12), 3231 W. Ninth St., 50702. Tel: 319-233-3358; Fax: 319-235-0733.
E-mail: dbqH08@arch.pvt.k12.ia.us
Rev. Mike Mescher, Pastoral Coord.; Mr. Todd Dirth, Prin.; David Sharp, Asst. Admin.; Rev. Paul G. Baldwin, Spiritual Dir. Priests 1; Sisters 1; Lay Teachers 38; Students 474.
Serving all parishes in Waterloo; St. Nicholas, Evansdale; St. Patrick's, Cedar Falls.

[E] SCHOOLS OF RELIGION

CALMAR. *Christian Family School*, P.O. Box 821, 52312. Tel: 563-562-3045; Fax: 563-562-3292.
E-mail: dbqrT1@arch.pvt.k12.ia.us
Rev. Msgr. Cletus J. Hawes, Exec. Coord.; Patty Frana, D.R.E. Priests 1; Lay Teachers 1; Students 218.

CASCADE. *Aquin Religious Education Center*, 608 Third Ave. N.W., 52033. Tel: 563-852-3524; Fax: 563-852-5269.
E-mail: dbq023RE@arch.pvt.k12.ia.us
Rev. Daniel A. Krapfl, Pastoral Coord.; Rebecca Smith, D.R.E. Lay Teachers 2; Students 123.

LANSING. *Lansing School of Religion*, 660 Main St., 52151. Tel: 563-538-3933. Rev. Daniel J. Knipper; Karen Weber, D.R.E. Priests 1; Students 105.

MANCHESTER. *St. Paul's School of Religion*, 408 Clara Ave., 52057. Tel: 563-927-2900.
E-mail: dbqrt3@arch.pvt.k12.ia.us
Very Rev. Ralph P. Simington, Pastoral Coord.; Wilma Billhorn, Dir. Lay Teachers 7; Students 454.

NEW HAMPTON. *St. John's School*, 823 W. Main St., Box 108, 50659. Tel: 515-394-3171.
E-mail: dbqrt@arch.pvt.k12.ia.us
Rev. Carl L. Schmitt, Pastoral Coord.; Marjorie Zipse, Dir. Lay Teachers 3; Students 178.

[F] CONSOLIDATED PARISH SCHOOLS

DUBUQUE. *Holy Trinity-Sacred Heart Consolidation.* (Grades PreK-8), 2222 Queen St., 52001. Tel: 563-588-4657; Fax: 563-584-0115. Todd Wessels, Prin.; Rev. James T. Chappell, Pastoral Coord. Lay Teachers 15; Pre-School 47; Students 234.

St. Mary-St. Patrick Catholic School. (Grades PreK-8), 180 W. 15th St. Martha Wightman, Prin.; Deacon Tim LoBianco, Pastoral Coord., St. Patrick

Attendance Center, 180 W. 15th St., 52001. Tel: 563-582-2127; Fax: 319-585-0082.
E-mail: dbqe25@arch.pvt.k12.ia.us
Sisters 1; Lay Teachers 12; Day Care 106; Pre-School 36; Students 182.

BELLEVUE. *Bellevue Area Catholic Elementary School.* (Grades PreK-8), 403 Park St., 52031. Tel: 563-872-3284; Fax: 563-872-3285. Jim Squires, Prin.; Very Rev. Donald V. Bakewell, Pastoral Coord.
Consolidation of the following parishes: St. Donatus, St. Donatus; SS. Peter & Paul, Springbrook; St. Joseph, Bellevue (School location); Holy Rosary, LaMotte. Lay Teachers 19; Day Care 26; Students 299.

CALMAR. *Calmar-Festina-Spillville (CFS) Catholic Elementary School.* (Grades PreK-8), 300 S. Maryville, Box 815, 52132. Tel: 563-562-3291; Fax: 563-562-3292.
E-mail: dbqe05@arch.pvt.k12.ia.us
Katie Schmitt, Prin.; Rev. Donald J. Hawes, Pastoral Coord.
Consolidation of the following parishes: Our Lady of Seven Dolors (St. Mary's), Festina; St. Wenceslaus, Spillville; St. Aloysius, Calmar; St. Wenceslaus (Grades 1-4); St. Aloysius (Grades K-8). Lay Teachers 13; Pre-School 36; Students 142.

CASCADE. *Aquin Elementary School.* (Grades PreK-8), 608 Third Ave., N.W., P.O. Box 460, 52033-0460. Tel: 563-852-3331; Fax: 563-852-5269.
E-mail: dbqe06@arch.pvtk12.ia.us
Peter Smith, Prin.; Rev. Daniel A. Krapfl, Pastoral Coord.
Consolidation of the following parishes: St. Matthias, Cascade; Sacred Heart, Fillmore; St. Patrick, North Garryowen; St. Peter, Temple Hill. Lay Teachers 19; Pre-School 45; Students 248.

CEDAR RAPIDS. *Holy Family Catholic Consolidated School.*

LaSalle Intermediate. (Grades PreK-8), 3700 First Ave., N.W., 52405. Tel: 319-396-7792; Fax: 319-390-6527.
E-mail: dbe12@arch.pvt.k12.ia.us
Rev. Harry Koelker, Exec. Sec.; David E. Bertling, Chief Admin. Lay Teachers 48; Day Care 75; Pre-School 94; Students 626.

St. Ludmila Center, 215 21st Ave., S.W., 52404. Tel: 319-362-1943; Fax: 319-364-4149.
E-mail: dbqe10@arch.pvt.k12.ia.us
Janet Whitney, Admin. Assoc.

St. Jude Center, 3700 First Ave. N.W., 52405. Tel: 319-396-7818; Fax: 319-390-0952.
E-mail: dbqe09@arch.pvt.k12.ia.us
Jim Clancy, Assoc. Admin.

St. Patrick Center, 509 A Ave., N.W., 52405. Tel: 319-363-1027; Fax: 319-398-0914.
E-mail: dbqmo1@arch.pvt.k12.ia.us
Barbara Stimmel, Prin.

Regis Middle School. (Grades 6-8), 735 Prairie Dr., N.E., 52402. Tel: 319-393-4445; Fax: 319-247-6099.
E-mail: dbqm02@arch.pvt.k12.ia.us
Rev. Donald L. Klein, Pastoral Coord.; Rick Blackwell, Prin.
Mailing Address: 4949 Council St., N.E., 52402.
Sponsored by the Archdiocese of Dubuque.
Purpose: to establish and maintain an accredited educational institution for learning and religious training. Lay Teachers 20; Students 338.

CRESCO. *Notre Dame System of Education.* (Grades PreK-6), 221 Second Ave., E., 52136. Tel: 563-547-4513; Fax: 563-547-3835.
E-mail: dbqe15@arch.pvt.k12.ia.us
Rev. Henry Charipar, Pastoral Coord.; Wendy Schatz, Prin. Lay Teachers 15; Pre-School 53; Students 175.

FARLEY. *Seton Catholic Elementary School.* (Grades PreK-8), 210 Second St., S.E., 52046. Tel: 563-744-3290; Fax: 563-744-3450.
E-mail: dbqe28@arch.pvt.k12.ia.ua
Deb Fleckenstein, Prin.; Rev. Richard Kuhn, Pastoral Sec.
Consolidation of the following parishes: St. Patrick, Epworth; St. John, Peosta; St. John, Placid; St. Joseph, Farley; St. Clement, Bankston. Sisters of the Presentation 1; Lay Teachers 25; Pre-School 100; Students 353.

GILBERTVILLE. *Immaculate Conception-St. Joseph School.* (Grades K-8). (Gilbertville-Raymond Consolidated Elementary School), 311 16th Ave., 50634-0256. Tel: 319-296-1089; Fax: 319-296-3847.
E-mail: dbqe31@arch.pvt.k12.ia.us
Ruth Palmer, Prin.; Rev. Rick A. Dagit, Pastoral Coord.
Consolidation of the following parishes: St. Joseph, Raymond; Immaculate Conception, Gilbertville; St. Joseph (Grades K-2); Immaculate Conception (Grades 3-8). Lay Teachers 22; Infant Care 15; Day Care 45; Pre-School 30; Students 328.

GUTTENBERG. *Guttenberg-North Buena Vista Consolidated School.* (Grades K-8), 510 S. Second St., P.O. Box 100, 52052. Tel: 563-252-1577; Fax: 563-252-4065.
E-mail: dbqe32@arch.pvt.k12.ia.us
Sr. Suzanne Gallagher, P.B.V.M., Prin.; Rev. Msgr. John R. McClean, Pastoral Coord.
Consolidation of the following parishes: St. Mary's, Guttenberg; Immaculate Conception, North Buena Vista. Sisters 1; Lay Teachers 11; Students 139.

HOLY CROSS. *Rickardsville-Holy Cross-Luxemburg (RHCL) Catholic School.* (Grades PreK-8), 835 Church St., P.O. Box 368, 52053-0368. Tel: 563-870-2405; Fax: 563-853-2325.
E-mail: dbqe34@arch.pvt.k12.ia.us
Rev. Donald J. Plamondon, Pastoral Coord.; Mary Smock, Prin.
Consolidation of the following parishes: St. Joseph, Rickardsville; Holy Cross, Holy Cross; Holy Trinity, Luxemburg (Grades K-3); Holy Cross (Grades 4-8). Sisters 1; Lay Teachers 10; Pre-School 26; Students 181.

MARSHALLTOWN. *Marshalltown Area Consolidated Catholic School.* (Grades PreK-6), 10 W. Linn St., 50158. Tel: 641-753-7977; Fax: 641-753-0337.
E-mail: dbqe40@arch.pvt.k12.ia.us
Rebecca Jacobson, Prin.; Rev. Louis M. Jaeger, Pastoral Coord.
Consolidation of the following parishes: St. Mary, Marshalltown; St. Henry, Marshalltown; Immaculate Conception, Haverhill; St. Henry, 310 Columbus (Grades K-2); St. Marys, 10 W. Linn St. (Grades 3-6). Lay Teachers 20; Day Care 25; Pre-School 72; Students 260.

NEW VIENNA. *Archbishop Hennessy Catholic School.* (Grades PreK-6), 7420 Columbus, Box 170, 52065. Tel: 563-921-2635; Fax: 563-921-3003.
E-mail: dbqe33@arch.pvt.k12.ia.us
David Gross, Prin.; Rev. John J. O'Connor, Pastoral Coord.
Consolidation of the following parishes: St. Boniface Center (Grades K-3), New Vienna; SS. Peter & Paul (Grades 4-6), Petersburg. Sisters 1; Lay Teachers 7; Pre-School 15; Students 113.

PROTOVIN. *Trinity Catholic School.* (Grades PreK-6), 116 N. Main St., 52163-0205. Tel: 563-569-8556; Fax: 563-569-8477.
E-mail: dbqe47@arch.pvt.k12.ia.us
Marcia Kruse, Prin.
Consolidation of the following parishes: Holy Trinity, Protovin; St. Luke's, St. Lucas; St. John's, Fort Atkinson. Lay Teachers 10; Pre-School 19; Students 107.

SHERRILL. *Balltown-Sherrill Catholic School.* (Grades PreK-6), 5135 Sherrill Rd., Box 49, 52073. Tel: 563-552-2166.
E-mail: dbqe03@arch.pvt.k12.ia.us
Carol Gebhart, Prin.; Sr. Mildred Leuenberger, O.S.F., Pastoral Coord.
Consolidation of the following parishes: St. Francis, Balltown; SS. Peter & Paul, Sherrill. Sisters 1; Lay Teachers 6; Pre-School 13; Students 52.

STACYVILLE. *Visitation School.* (Grades PreK-8), 603 N. Broad St., 50476. Tel: 641-737-2380; Fax: 641-737-2277.
E-mail: dbqe48@arch.pvt.k12.ia.us
Sr. Lenore Ostdiek, O.S.F., Prin.
Consolidation of the following parishes: Church of the Visitation, Stacyville; Sacred Heart, Meyer. Sisters 2; Lay Teachers 5; Students 42.

[G] CONSOLIDATED K-12 SYSTEMS

MASON CITY. *Newman Catholic.* Newman High and Middle School. (Grades PreK-12), 2245 19th St., S.W., 50401. Tel: 641-423-6939; Fax: 641-423-6653.
E-mail: dbqe41@arch.pvt.k12.ia.us
St. Joseph Center, 320 Fifth St., S.E., 50401-4005. Tel: 641-423-6939. Newman Catholic Child Care, 713 N. Adams, 50401. Tel: 641-423-6653. Revs. Dennis H. Cahill, Pastoral Coord.; Michael G. Schueller; Michael Kavars, Secondary Prin.; Kathy Lloyd, Early Childhood Dir.
Parishes served: Holy Family, St. Joseph, Mason City: St. Patrick, Clear Lake; Sacred Heart, Manly; St. Michael, Plymouth; Sacred Heart, Rockwell; St. Patrick, Dougherty. Priests 1; Sisters 2; Lay Teachers 45; Infant Care 49; Day Care 253; Pre-School 94; Elementary 473; High School 211.

[H] GENERAL HOSPITALS

DUBUQUE. *Mercy Medical Center-Dubuque,* 250 Mercy Dr., 52001. Tel: 563-589-8000; Fax: 563-589-8073
For a complete listing, refer to the Hospitals section.

CEDAR RAPIDS. *Mercy Medical Center, Cedar Rapids, Iowa, Endowment Foundation, Inc.,* 701 Tenth St., S.E., 52403. Tel: 319-398-6278
For a complete listing, refer to the Hospitals section.

Mercy Medical Center-Cedar Rapids, 701 Tenth St., S.E., 52403. Tel: 319-398-6011.
E-mail: mercylib@crpl.cedar-rapids.lib.ia.us
Web site: http.//www.mercycare.org
For a complete listing, refer to the Hospitals section.

Mercycare Service Corporation, 701 10th St., S.E., 52403. Tel: 319-398-6011
For a complete listing, refer to the Hospitals section.

DYERSVILLE. *Mercy Medical Center-Dubuque (Dyersville),* 1111 Third St., S.W., 52040. Tel: 563-875-7101; Fax: 563-875-2957
For a complete listing, refer to the Hospitals section.

MASON CITY. *Mercy Medical Center-North Iowa,* 1000 4th St., S.W., 50401. Tel: 641-422-7000; Fax: 641-422-7827
For a complete listing, refer to the Hospitals section.

NEW HAMPTON. *Mercy Medical Center-New Hampton,* 308 N. Maple Ave., 50659. Tel: 641-394-4121; Fax: 641-394-5628
For a complete listing, refer to the Hospitals section.

OELWEIN. *Mercy Hospital of Franciscan Sisters,* 201 - 8th Ave., S.E., 50662. Tel: 319-283-6000; Fax: 319-283-6004
For a complete listing, refer to the Hospitals section.

WATERLOO. *Covenant Health System, Inc.,* 3421 W. Ninth St., 50702. Tel: 319-272-7302
For a complete listing, refer to the Hospitals section.

Covenant Medical Center, Inc., 3421 W. Ninth St., 50702. Tel: 319-272-8000; Fax: 319-272-7313
For a complete listing, refer to the Hospitals section.

[I] SPECIAL HEALTH CENTERS

DUBUQUE. *Holy Family Hall Infirmary,* 3340 Windsor Ave., 52001-1300. Tel: 563-583-9786; Fax: 563-583-6080.
E-mail: mtstfran@mwci.net
Web site: www.osfdbg.org
For a complete listing, refer to the Special Care Facilities section.

Marian Hall Infirmary, 1050 Carmel Dr., 52003. Tel: 563-556-5474; Fax: 563-588-1975.
E-mail: bvmcong.org
Web site: www.bvmcong.org
For a complete listing, refer to the Special Care Facilities section.

St. Dominic Villa, 600 Mazzuchelli Heights, 52001-7399. Tel: 563-582-7273; Fax: 563-583-1421
For a complete listing, refer to the Special Care Facilities section.

[J] HOMES FOR AGED

DUBUQUE. *Stonehill Franciscan Services, Inc.,* 3485 Windsor Ave., 52001-1312. Tel: 563-557-7180; Fax: 563-557-8934.
E-mail: stonehill@mwci.net
For a complete listing, refer to the Special Care Facilities section.

Villa Raphael, 1235 Mt. Loretta Ave., 52003. Tel: 563-583-4904; Fax: 563-556-5464.
E-mail: dbqvilla@arch.pvt.k12.ia.us
For a complete listing, refer to the Special Care Facilities section.

CEDAR RAPIDS. *Hallmar-Mercy Medical Center,* 701 Tenth St., S.E., 52403
For a complete listing, refer to the Special Care Facilities section.

CRESCO. *Elder Hospitality of Iowa, Inc.,* Franciscan SKEMP Healthcare, 301 First Ave., 52136. Tel: 563-547-3325; 608-791-9505
For a complete listing, refer to the Special Care Facilities section.

DYERSVILLE. *Mercy Medical Center-Dubuque-Dyersville-Oakcrest Manor,* 1111 Third St., S.W., 52040. Tel: 563-875-7101; Fax: 563-875-2957.
Web site: www.mercydubuque.com
For a complete listing, refer to the Special Care Facilities section.

[K] MONASTERIES AND RESIDENCES OF PRIESTS AND BROTHERS

PEOSTA. *New Melleray Abbey, Order of Cistercians of the Strict Observance,* 6500 Melleray Cir., 52068. Tel: 563-588-2319; Fax: 563-588-4117.
E-mail: melleray@mwci.net
Web site: www.osb.org/cist/melleray
Legal Title: *Corporation of New Melleray.* Rt. Revs. Brendan J. Freeman, O.C.S.O., Abbot; David R. Bock, O.C.S.O., Retired Abbot; James J. Kerndt, O.C.S.O., Retired Abbot; David L. Wechter, O.C.S.O., Retired Abbot; Revs. Timothy L. Welsh, O.C.S.O.; Bernard J. Cullen, O.C.S.O.; Daniel F. Lenihan, O.C.S.O.; Kenneth F. Tietjen, O.C.S.O.; Thomas J. McCarty, O.C.S.O.; James E. O'Connor, O.C.S.O.; Thaddeus J. Kennedy, O.C.S.O.; Xavier L. Dieter, O.C.S.O.; Thomas A. MacMaster, O.C.S.O., Prior; Joseph G. Knapp, O.C.S.O.; James B. Henderson, O.C.S.O.; Neil Paquette, O.C.S.O.; Stephen Verbest, O.C.S.O. Total Residents 37; Priests 17; Brothers 19.

[L] CONVENTS AND RESIDENCES FOR SISTERS

DUBUQUE. *Mt. Loretto Convent.* Motherhouse and Novitiate of the Sisters of the Presentation of the B.V.M. 2360 Carter Rd., 52001-2997. Tel: 563-588-2008; Fax: 563-588-4463.
E-mail: joypbum@mwci.net
Sr. Joy Peterson, P.B.V.M., Pres.; Sr. Mary Sharon Kelchen, P.B.V.M., Dir.; Rev. Douglas O. Wathier, Chap. Professed Sisters 68.
International Presentation Association.

Mt. St. Francis, 3390 Windsor Ave., 52001-1311. Tel: 563-583-9786; Fax: 563-583-3250.
E-mail: mtstfran@mwci.net
Web site: www.osfdbq.org
Motherhouse and Novitiate of the Sisters of St. Francis of the Holy Family. Sr. Shirley Kamentz, O.S.F., Contact Person; Sr. Dorothy Heiderscheit, O.S.F., Pres.; Sr. Eileen Miller, O.S.F., Dir. Sister Support Svcs.; Rev. Dennis J. Colter, Chap. Professed Sisters 120. Sisters of St. Francis of the Holy Family Charitable Trust.

Our Lady of the Mississippi Abbey, 8400 Abbey Hill, 52003. Tel: 563-582-2595; Fax: 563-582-5511.
E-mail: misisip@mwci.com
The Cistercian Nuns of the Strict Observance. (Monastery of Trappistine Nuns). Rev. Mother Gail Marie Fitzpatrick, O.C.S.O., Abbess; Rt. Rev. James Kerndt, O.C.S.O., Chap. Professed Nuns 22; Novices 1; Postulants 1.

St. Joseph's Convent, Mount Carmel, 1150 Carmel Dr., 52003. Tel: 563-556-3240; Fax: 563-557-1349.
E-mail: bvmcenter@bvmcong.org
Web site: http://www.bvm.cong.org
Motherhouse of the Sisters of Charity of the Blessed Virgin Mary. Sr. Carol Marie Baum, B.V.M., Admin.; Sr. Eileen Healy, B.V.M., Pastoral Care; Rev. Msgr. James O. Barta, Chap. Professed Sisters 123; Staff 45.

Sisters of Charity of the Blessed Virgin Mary, BVM Center, Mount Carmel, 1100 Carmel Dr., 52003-7991. Tel: 563-588-2351; Fax: 563-588-4832.
E-mail: bvmcenter@bvmcong.org
Web site: http://www.bvmcong.org
Sr. Joellen McCarthy, B.V.M., Pres. Congregation; Sr. Margaret Nolan, B.V.M., 1st Vice Pres.; Sr. Mary Ann Zollman, B.V.M., 2nd Vice Pres.; Sr. Margaret Zimmermann, B.V.M., Admin., B.V.M. Center. Sisters of Charity of the Blessed Virgin Mary: Retirement Trust Plan and Charitable Trust. Total Staff 32.

Sisters of the Visitation, 2950 Kaufmann Ave., 52001-1631. Tel: 563-556-2440.
E-mail: dbqsvm@arch.pvt.k12.ia.us
Sisters of the Visitation of the Congregation of the Immaculate Heart of Mary. Sr. Bernadine Curoe, S.V.M., Pres. Professed Sisters 6.

CEDAR RAPIDS. *Sacred Heart Convent,* 1125 Prairie Dr., N.E., 52402-4737. Tel: 319-364-5196; Fax: 319-364-7383.
E-mail: sacredheartlib@aol.com
Motherhouse of the Sisters of Mercy (Cedar Rapids Regional Community). Sr. Susan O'Connor, R.S.M., Pres.; Sr. Delores Marie Hannon, R.S.M., Vice Pres.; Marianne Arndorfer, Admin. Sacred Heart Convent. Professed Sisters 96; Total Staff 30. Sisters of Mercy, Cedar Rapids.

Sisters of Mercy Charitable Trust. Tel: 319-364-5196; Fax: 319-364-7383.

Catherine McAuley Center for Women, Cedar Rapids. Tel: 319-363-4993; Fax: 319-363-8332.

Mount Mercy College, Cedar Rapids. Tel: 319-363-8213; Fax: 319-363-5270.

Mercy Medical Center, Cedar Rapids. Tel: 319-398-6011.

[M] RETREAT HOUSES

DUBUQUE. *New Melleray Guest House,* 6500 Melleray Cir., 52068. Tel: 563-588-2319; Fax: 563-588-4117.
E-mail: melleray@mwci.net
Web site: www.osb.org/cist/melleray

Shalom Retreat Center, 1001 Davis St., 52001-1398. Tel: 563-582-3592; Fax: 563-582-5872.
E-mail: dbqshalom@arch.pvt.k12.ia.us
Sr. Marie Therese Kalb, O.S.F., Dir. Total Staff 10; Retreatants 8,216.

CEDAR FALLS. *American Martyrs Retreat House,* 2209 North Union Rd., P.O. Box 605, 50613-0605. Tel: 319-266-3543; Fax: 319-266-3543.
E-mail: dbqamrh@arch.pvt.k12.ia.us
Sr. Jeanine Kuhn, P.B.V.M., Dir. Total Staff 21.

HIAWATHA. *Prairiewoods Franciscan Spirituality Center,* 120 E. Boyson Rd., 52233-1277. Tel: 319-395-6700; Fax: 319-395-6703.
E-mail: ecospirit@prairiewoods.org
Web site: www.prairiewoods.org
Sr. Joanne Moeller, F.S.P.A., Contact Person.

[N] NEWMAN CENTERS

AMES. *St. Thomas Aquinas Church and Catholic Student Center (Iowa State University),* 2210 Lincoln Way, 50014-7184. Tel: 515-292-3810; Fax: 515-292-2341.
E-mail: dbq004@arch.pvt.k12.ia.ua
Web site: www.sta.parish.net
Revs. Everett Hemann; James E. Hayes; Rev. Msgr. James A. Supple, (Retired); Sr. Lorraine Schmaltz, Parish Family Life & RCIA Coord.; John Donaghy, Dir. Campus Ministry & Charity, Justice & Peace Coord.; Robert LeBlanc, Church Business Admin.; Nonine Osendorf, Marriage Preparation; Crystal Caruana Sullivan, Campus Min.; Mary Ricke, D.R.E.; Jenifer Fliehler, Devel. Coord. & Youth Min.; Marty Doerning, Liturgist/Music Coord.

CEDAR FALLS. *St. Stephen the Witness Catholic Student Center, University of Northern Iowa,* 1019 W. 23rd St., 50613-3550. Tel: 319-266-9863; Fax: 319-266-3706.
E-mail: frjsh@stephenuni.org
Web site: www.ststephenuni.org
Rev. John S. Haugen, Dir. & Campus Pastor; Deacon Leonard Froyen, Dir. Permanent Diaconate; Sr. Mary Lou Specha, P.B.V.M., Campus Min.; Sr. Julie Marsh, P.B.V.M., Dir. of Liturgy; Judy Moody, Dir Christian Initiation & Pre-Marriage; Regena Huffman, Business Mgr. Staff 13.

WEST UNION. *Upper Iowa University,* 128 N. Walnut, 52175-1347. Tel: 563-422-3184.
E-mail: dbq220@arch.pvt.k12.ia.us
Rev. Dale J. Rausch, Chap., Holy Name Parish, 52175.

[O] MISCELLANEOUS

DUBUQUE. *Archdiocese of Dubuque Deposit and Loan Fund,* 1229 Mt. Loretta, 52003-7800. Tel: 563-556-2580; Fax: 563-556-5464. Richard L. Runde, Finance Officer.

Archdiocese of Dubuque Education Fund, 1229 Mt. Loretta, 52003-7800. Tel: 563-556-2580; Fax: 563-556-5464. Richard L. Runde, Finance Officer.

Archdiocese of Dubuque Perpetual Care Fund, 1229 Mt. Loretta, 52003-7800. Tel: 563-556-2580; Fax: 563-556-5464. Richard L. Runde, Finance Officer.

Archdiocese of Dubuque Seminarian Education Fund, 1229 Mt. Loretta, 52003-7800. Tel: 563-556-2580; Fax: 563-556-5464. Richard L. Runde, Finance Officer.

Cistercian Studies Quarterly, Inc., Mississippi Abbey, 8400 Abbey Hill, 52003. Tel: 563-582-2595; Fax: 563-582-5511.
E-mail: csq@mwci.net
Sr. Sheryl Frances Chen, O.C.S.O., Contact Person. Sponsor: Cistercian Order of the Strict Observance of the USA Region.

Heartland Housing Initiative, 90 Main St., 52001. Tel: 563-583-9653; Fax: 563-583-6490.
E-mail: mmartensen@mercyhousing.org
(A member of the Mercy Housing System, Heartland Housing Initiative.). Sr. Mary Martensen, R.S.M., Regional Vice Pres. Total Staff 3; Total Assisted 282.

Hennessy Charitable Trust, 2360 Carter Rd., 52001-2297. Tel: 563-588-2008; Fax: 563-588-4463.
E-mail: lfang@mwci.net
Web site: www.dubuquepresentations.org
Sr. Mary Joy Peterson, Pres.; Sr. Lynn Fangman, P.B.V.M., Contact Person. Sponsored by the Sisters of the Presentation.

Opening Doors, 1561 Jackson St., 52001. Tel: 563-583-9786; Fax: 563-582-7467.
E-mail: michellebrown5@home.com
Sponsors: Sinsinawa Dominicans, Sisters of the Presentation, Sisters of Charity, B.V.M, Sisters of the Visitation, Dubuque Franciscan Sisters, Sisters of Mercy Regional Community of Detroit. Sr. Janet May, O.S.F., Pres. Purpose: to provide emergency housing, related support services, shelter and temporary transitional housing for women who are alone or with children.

St. Vincent de Paul Society of the Archdiocese of Dubuque.

Dubuque Council, 1351 Iowa St., 52001. Tel: 563-583-8701; Fax: 563-584-2225. Paul Hoppman, Natl. Trustee & Pres.

Waterloo Council, 4114 Heritage Rd., Cedar Falls, 50613. Tel: 319-232-8662. Richard McGrane, Pres.

Cedar Rapids Council, 339 22nd Ave. S.W., Cedar Rapids, 52404. Tel: 319-364-0748. Robert Crawford, Pres.

WATERLOO. *Ridgeway Place, Inc.,* 155 E. Ridgeway Ave., 50702. Tel: 319-272-2622; Fax: 319-272-2633.
Sponsored by the Wheaton Franciscan Sisters, Wheaton, IL and a corporation of Wheaton Franciscan System. Assisted Living Housing Units 96; Patients assisted annually 105.

RELIGIOUS INSTITUTES OF MEN REPRESENTED IN THE ARCHDIOCESE

For further details refer to the corresponding bracketed number in the Religious Institutes of Men or Women section.

[1180]—*Brothers of Saint Pius X.*—C.S.P.X.

[0330]—*Brothers of the Christian Schools.* (Midwest Province).—F.S.C.

[0350]—*Cistercians Order of the Strict Observance-Trappists.* (Our Lady of New Melleray).—O.C.S.O.

[0480]—*Conventual Franciscans.* (Prov. of Our Lady of Consolation).—O.F.M.Conv.

[0420]—*Society of the Divine Word.* (Northern Prov.).—S.V.D.

RELIGIOUS INSTITUTES OF WOMEN REPRESENTED IN THE ARCHDIOCESE

[0670]—*Cistercian Nuns of the Strict Observance.*—O.C.S.O.

[2100]—*Congregation of the Humility of Mary.* (Davenport, IA).—C.H.M.

[1780]—*Congregation of the Sisters of the Third Order of St. Francis of Perpetual Adoration.*—F.S.P.A.

[1070-03]—*Dominican Sisters Congregation of the Most Holy Rosary.* (Sinsinawa).—O.P.

[1820]—*Hospital Sisters of the Third Order of St. Francis.*—O.S.F.

[2960]—*Notre Dame Sisters.* (Omaha).—N.D.

[3130]—*Our Lady of Victory Missionary Sisters.*—O.L.V.M.

[2970]—*School Sisters of Notre Dame.* (Mankato, MN).—S.S.N.D.

[1680]—*School Sisters of St. Francis.* (Milwaukee, WI).—O.S.F.

[]—*Sisters for Christian Communities.* (Cincinnati).

[0430]—*Sisters of Charity of the Blessed Virgin Mary.*—B.V.M.

[2575]—*Sisters of Mercy of the Americas.* (Cedar Rapids).—R.S.M.

[2575.2]—*Sisters of Mercy of the Americas.* (Detroit).—R.S.M.

[1540]—*Sisters of St. Francis.* (Clinton).—O.S.F.

[1570]—*The Sisters of St. Francis of the Holy Family.*—O.S.F.

[3320]—*Sisters of the Presentation of the B.V.M.* (Dubuque; Fargo, SD).—P.B.V.M.

[1720]—*Sisters of the Third Order Regular of St. Francis of the Congregation of Our Lady of Lourdes.*—O.S.F.

[4200]—*Sisters of the Visitation of the Congregation of the Immaculate Heart of Mary.* (Dubuque, IA).—S.V.M.

CEMETERIES

DUBUQUE. *Mount Calvary.*
Mount Olivet.
CEDAR RAPIDS. *Calvary.*
St. John.
St. Joseph.
CRESCO. *Calvary.*
LITTLEPORT. *Sacred Heart.*
MARSHALLTOWN. *St. Mary.*
MCINTIRE. *St. Mel & St. Patrick.*
PRAIRIE. *St. Joseph.*
RHODES. *St. Joseph.*
SOUTH GARRYOWEN. *St. Aloysius.*
SPRUCE CREEK. *St. Nicholas.*
WATERLOO. *Catholic Cemeteries, Inc.*

NECROLOGY

† Arquitt, William, Manly, IA Sacred Heart. —Died March 9, 2000.

† Brosius, Alfred G, Delhi, IA St. John. —Died Feb. 26, 2000.

† Goedken, Nestor B., Castle Grove, IA Immaculate Conception; Prairieburg, IA St. Joseph. —Died May 23, 2000.

† McDonald, J. Robert, Newhall, IA St. Paul. —Died Nov. 18, 1999.

† McTarsney, John F, Fairbank, IA Immaculate Conception. —Died June 6, 2000.

† Roth, Jacob P., Fort Atkinson, IA St. John Nepomucene; Festina, IA Our Lady of Seven Dolors. —Died April 1, 2000.

† Stark, John W, Masonville, IA Immaculate Conception. —Died Dec. 6, 1999.

† Zachar, Rev. Msgr. Albert L, Blairstown, IA St. John. —Died Dec. 30, 1999.

Diocese of Duluth

(Dioecesis Duluthensis)

Most Reverend

DENNIS M. SCHNURR

Bishop of Duluth; ordained July 20, 1974; appointed January 18, 2001; ordained April 2, 2001.

Corporate Title: *Diocese of Duluth.*

ESTABLISHED OCTOBER 3, 1889.

Square Miles 22,354.

Comprises the counties of Aitkin, Carlton, Cass, Cook, Crow Wing, Itasca, Koochiching, Lake, Pine and St. Louis in the State of Minnesota.

For legal titles of parishes and diocesan institutions, consult the Chancery Office.

Pastoral Center: 2830 E. Fourth St., Duluth, MN, 55812. Tel.: 218-724-9111; Fax: 218-724-1056.

Web site address: www.dioceseduluth.org

E-mail address: duluth@dioceseduluth.org

STATISTICAL OVERVIEW

Personnel	
Bishop	1
Priests: Diocesan Active in Diocese	51
Priests: Active Outside Diocese	4
Priests: Retired, Sick or Absent	23
Number of Diocesan Priests	78
Religious Priests in Diocese	12
Extern Priests in Diocese	1
Ordinations:	
Transitional Deacons	1
Permanent Deacons	2
Permanent Deacons in Diocese	27
Total Brothers	2
Total Sisters	165
Parishes	
Parishes	92
With Resident Pastor:	
Resident Diocesan Priests	46
Resident Religious Priests	10
Without Resident Pastor:	
Administered by Priests	34
Administered by Deacons	2
Missions	3
Professional Ministry Personnel:	
Brothers	2
Sisters	4
Lay Ministers	30
Welfare	
Catholic Hospitals	2
Total Assisted	308,067
Homes for the Aged	2
Total Assisted	305
Day Care and Extended Day Care Centers	1
Total Assisted	120
Educational	
Diocesan Students in Other Seminaries	9
Total Seminarians	9
Colleges and Universities	1
Total Students	2,010
Elementary Schools, Diocesan and Parish	12
Total Students	2,033
Catechesis/Religious Education:	
High School Students	3,450
Elementary Students	3,800
Total Students Under Catholic Instruction	11,302
Teachers in the Diocese:	
Sisters	3
Lay Teachers	112
Vital Statistics	
Receptions into the Church:	
Infant Baptism Totals	1,057
Adult Baptism Totals	49
Received into Full Communion	180
First Communions	1,206
Confirmations	977
Marriages:	
Catholic	260
Interfaith	212
Total Marriages	472
Deaths	1,063
Total Catholic Population	78,235
Total Population	475,000

Former Bishops—Rt. Rev. JAMES MCGOLRICK, D.D., cons. Dec. 27, 1889; died Jan. 23, 1918.—Rt. Rev. JOHN T. MCNICHOLAS, O.P., S.T.D., cons. Sept. 8, 1918; appt. Archbishop of Cincinnati July 8, 1925; died April 22, 1950.—Most Rev. THOMAS A. WELCH, D.D., cons. Feb. 3, 1926; died Sept. 9, 1959.—Most Rev. FRANCIS J. SCHENK, D.D., cons. May 24, 1945; appt. to Duluth Jan. 19, 1960; resigned April 30, 1969; died Oct. 28, 1969.—Most Rev. PAUL F. ANDERSON, D.D., appt. Titular Bishop of Polignando and Coadjutor Bishop with right of succession July 19, 1968; cons. Oct. 17, 1968; succeeded to See April 10, 1969; resigned Aug. 7, 1982; appt. Apostolic Administrator Aug. 7, 1982; appt. Auxiliary Bishop of Sioux Falls, SD March 25, 1983; died Jan. 4, 1987.—Most Rev. ROBERT H. BROM, D.D., cons. May 23, 1983; appt. Coadjutor Bishop of San Diego, CA, May 9, 1989.—Most Rev. ROGER SCHWIETZ, O.M.I., cons. Feb. 2, 1990; appt. Coadjutor Archbishop of Anchorage, Jan. 18, 2000.

Vicar General—Vacant.

Chancellor—Rev. DALE NAU, J.C.L.

Pastoral Center—2830 E. Fourth St., Duluth, 55812. Tel: 218-724-9111; Fax: 218-724-1056. Office Hours: Mon.-Fri. 8:30-12 & 1-4:30.

Deans—Revs. PAUL FRUTH, Brainerd; CORNELIUS KELLEHER, Cloquet; JEROME WEISS, Duluth; RONALD GAGNE, Hibbing; JAMES SCHEUER, Virginia.

Diocesan Tribunal—2830 E. Fourth St., Duluth, 55812. Tel: 218-724-9111.

Judicial Vicar—Rev. JAMES BISSONETTE, J.C.L.

Vicar for Canonical Affairs—Rev. DALE NAU, J.C.L.

Defender of the Bond—Rev. DALE NAU, J.C.L.

Advocate—BETTE DAMBERG.

Notary—ROSE MARIE EICHMUELLER.

College of Consultors—Revs. DAVID TUSHAR; RONALD GAGNE; MICHAEL HAYES; ANDREW KNOP, O.M.I; FREDRICK METHOD; KENTON SAILSTAD; JEROME WEISS.

Priests' Pension Board—Revs. WILLIAM FIDER; FREDRICK METHOD; DALE NAU; DAVID TUSHAR; JERRY WEISS; Mr. ROBERT HOWE.

Presbyteral Council—Rev. FREDRICK METHOD, Chm.

Corporate Board—Revs. DALE NAU; DAVID TUSHAR; Mrs. MARILYN GRATTO; Mr. ROBERT MILLER.

Finance Council—Revs. DALE NAU; LAWRENCE O'SHEA; SANDY SONDGEROTH, O.M.I.; DAVID TUSHAR; JAMES BARTKOWSKI; GARY BUBALO; MARILYN GRATTO; DOUG HILDENBRAND; RONALD KARLEN; JIM JAROCKI; Mr. ROBERT MILLER.

Finance Officer—Rev. LAWRENCE O'SHEA.

Diocesan Offices and Directors

Archivist—Mrs. ROSIE KNUDSEN, *2830 E. Fourth St., Duluth, 55812.* Tel: 218-724-9111.

Boy Scouts—Deacon GREGORY HUTAR, *604 E. Boundary St., Ely, 55731.* Tel: 218-365-5906.

Campus Ministry—Rev. DALE NAU, Dir., *421 W. Ste. Marie, Duluth, 55811.* Tel: 218-728-3757.

Cemeteries—Rev. DALE NAU, Dir., *2830 E. Fourth St., Duluth, 55812.* Tel: 218-724-9111.

Censor of Books—Rev. J. W. EVANS, Ph.D., *2830 E. Fourth St., Duluth, 55812.* Tel: 218-724-9111.

Continuing Formation of Priests—Rev. DAVE TUSHAR, *2830 E. Fourth St., Duluth, 55812.* Tel: 218-724-9111.

Director of Catechesis—DENISE MACIEJ, *2830 E. Fourth St., Duluth, 55812.* Tel: 218-724-9111.

Director of Youth Ministry—JANICE KILGORE, *2830 E. Fourth St., Duluth, 55812.* Tel: 218-724-9111.

Council of Catholic Women—Rev. PAUL FRUTH, Moderator, *1108 Willow St., S.E., Brainerd, 56401.* Tel: 218-829-8932.

Cursillo Movement—Rev. ROMAN SPORS, Spiritual Advisor, *Box 266, Emily, 56477.* Tel: 218-763-2101. BRYON HARKER, Lay Dir., *Rte. 1, Box 245, Longville, 56655.* Tel: 218-363-2567.

Ecumenical and Inter-faith Affairs—Rev. DALE NAU, *2830 E. Fourth St., Duluth, 55812.* Tel: 218-724-9111.

Finance Officer—Rev. LAWRENCE O'SHEA, *2830 E. Fourth St., Duluth, 55812.* Tel: 218-724-9111.

Department of Liturgy—Rev. KENT SAILSTAD, S.T.L., Coord., *2830 E. Fourth St., Duluth, 55812.* Tel: 218-724-9111.

Mission Outreach and Propagation of the Faith—Rev. LAWRENCE O'SHEA, Dir., *2830 E. Fourth St., Duluth, 55812.* Tel: 218-724-9111.

Newspaper "Catholic Outlook"—Rev. DALE NAU, Editor, *2830 E. Fourth St., Duluth, 55812.* Tel: 218-724-9111.

Department of Indian Ministry—Sr. MARIE ROSE MESSINGSCHLAGER, C.D.P., Dir., *2830 E. Fourth St., Duluth, 55812.* Tel: 218-724-9111.

Vocations Recruitment—Deacon MIKE KNUTH, Coord., *2830 E. Fourth St., Duluth, 55812.* Tel: 218-724-9111.

Formation—Rev. DAVID TUSHAR, Coord., *2830 E. 4th St., Duluth, 55812.* Tel: 218-724-9111.

Department of Communications—Rev. DALE NAU, Coord., *2830 E. Fourth St., Duluth, 55812.* Tel: 218-724-9111.

Director of Schools—Ms. CYNTHIA ZOOK, *2830 E. Fourth St., Duluth, 55812.* Tel: 218-724-9111.

Department of Development—MIKE BILDEN, Dir., *Pastoral Center, 2830 E. Fourth St., Duluth, 55812.* Tel: 218-724-9111.

Coordinator for the Permanent Diaconate—Deacon DAVID CRAIG, Dir., *2830 E. Fourth St., Duluth, 55812.* Tel: 218-724-9111.

Director of Family Life—Mr. DICK FROST, *2830 E. Fourth St., Duluth, 55812.* Tel: 218-724-9111.

Rural Life—Rev. MICHAEL HAYES, Dir., *112 Cedar, Moose Lake, 55767.* Tel: 218-485-5909.

Director of the Social Apostolate—PATRICE CRITCHLEY-MENOR, *2830 E. Fourth St., Duluth, 55812.* Tel: 218-724-9111.

CLERGY, PARISHES, MISSIONS AND PAROCHIAL SCHOOLS

CITY OF DULUTH
(St. Louis County)

1—CATHEDRAL OF OUR LADY OF THE ROSARY, Revs. David Tushar, Rector; Joel Hastings. In res., Rev. James Crossman.
Res., 2801 E. Fourth St., 55812. Tel: 218-728-3646.
School—Tel: 218-724-8565.
Sisters 3; Lay Teachers 18; Students 336.
Catechesis/Religious Programs—Tel: 218-728-6985. D.R.E.: Mr. Patrick Bliss; Ms. Amy Kane. Students 172.
Convent—443 Lakeview Ave., 55812. Tel: 218-724-4370. Sisters of the Third Order of St. Dominic (Springfield, IL)

2—GOOD SHEPHERD. Closed. For inquiries for parish records contact the Chancery.

3—HOLY FAMILY, Rev. Andrew Knop, O.M.I. In res., Rev. James Datko, O.M.I.
Parish Office: 2430 W. 3rd St., 55806-1801. Tel: 218-722-4445; Fax: 218-722-8979.
Res., 202 N. 25 Ave. W., 55806. Tel: 218-722-0730.
Catechesis/Religious Programs—Desiree Taylor, D.R.E.
Students 116.

4—OUR LADY OF MERCY, Rev. Paul Larson. In res., Rev. Msgr. Patrick McDowell.
Res., 325 E. Third St., 55805. Tel: 218-722-3078.
Church—2002 Minnesota Ave., 55805.

5—ST. ANTHONY. Closed. For inquiries for parish records contact the Chancery.

6—ST. BENEDICT'S, Rev. Jon Wild; Deacon Dennis Anderson.
Office: 1419 St. Benedict St., 55811. Tel: 218-728-4325; Fax: 218-724-4828.
Res., 1419 Arrowhead Rd., 55811. Tel: 218-724-8926.
Catechesis/Religious Programs—Bob Huot, D.R.E. Students 350.
Station—Duluth, Aftenro Home.

7—ST. ELIZABETH'S, Rev. Patrick J. Moran.
Res., 610 99th Ave. W., Duluth, 55808. Tel: 218-626-2283.
Catechesis/Religious Programs—Mrs. Ann Menart, D.R.E.
Students 74.

8—ST. JAMES, Rev. Charles Flynn.
Res., 721 N. 57th Ave. W., Duluth, 55807. Tel: 218-624-0125; Fax: 218-624-3435.
School—Tel: 218-624-1511. Sharon Pristash, Prin. Lay Teachers 8; Students 128.
Catechesis/Religious Programs—Lori Lagergren, D.R.E.
Students 97.

9—ST. JOHN'S (Woodland), Rev. Jerome P. Weiss; Deacon Walt Beier.
Res., 4230 St. John's Ave., 55803. Tel: 218-724-6332.
School—Tel: 218-724-9392; Fax: 218-724-9368. Mr. Daniel Glisczinski, Prin.
Lay Teachers 7; Students 146.
Catechesis/Religious Programs—Students 272.
Mission—Gnesen, St. Joseph. [CEM]

10—ST. JOSEPH'S (Duluth Heights), Rev. Noel Stretton.
Res., 151 W. Linden St., 55811. Tel: 218-722-1021; Fax: 218-727-5579.
Catechesis/Religious Programs—Denise Maciej, D.R.E.
Students 110.

11—ST. LAWRENCE'S, Rev. William Fournier.
Res., 2404 Morris Thomas Rd., 55811. Tel: 218-722-1900; 722-2259; Fax: 218-722-6965.
Catechesis/Religious Programs—Shawna Hansen, D.R.E.
Students 319.

12—ST. MARGARET MARY (Morgan Park), Rev. Patrick J. Moran. In res., Rev. Thomas Foster.
Res., 1467 88th Ave. W., 55808. Tel: 218-626-2379.
Catechesis/Religious Programs—Janet Stanley, D.R.E.
Students 46.

13—ST. MARY STAR OF THE SEA, Rev. Paul Larson; Rev. Msgr. Patrick McDowell.
Res., 325 E. Third St., 55805. Tel: 218-722-3078; Fax: 218-279-5070.
Catechesis/Religious Programs—Shirley Baker, D.R.E.
Students 76.

14—ST. MICHAEL'S, Revs. William P. Fider; Brian Schultz Tel: 218-525-6129.
Office: 4901 E. Superior St., 55804. Tel: 218-525-1902; Fax: 218-525-1904.
Res., 4931 E. Superior, 55804. Tel: 218-525-7513; Fax: 218-525-1904.
School—4628 Pitt St., 55804. Tel: 218-525-1931; Fax: 218-525-0296. Amy Flaig, Prin.
Students 170.
Catechesis/Religious Programs—D.R.E.: Joan Homstad; John Houland; Linda Zimski.
Students 300.

15—ST. PETER'S, Rev. Paul Larson.
Res., 325 E. Third St., 55805. Tel: 218-722-3078.
Church—Third St. & Eighth Ave. W., 55805.

16—SS. PETER AND PAUL. Closed. For inquiries for parish records contact the Chancery.

17—ST. RAPHAEL'S, Rev. Lawrence O'Shea.
Parish Center: 5779 Seville Rd., 55811. Tel: 218-729-7537; Fax: 218-729-8122.
Res., 4458 Midway Rd., 55811. Tel: 218-729-5546.
Catechesis/Religious Programs—Georgiann Kuberra, D.R.E.
Students 234.

18—WEST END CATHOLIC PARISH OF SS. CLEMENT AND JEAN. Closed. For inquiries for parish records contact the Chancery.

OUTSIDE THE CITY OF DULUTH

Aitkin, Aitkin Co., St. James, Rev. Patrick Coyle.
Res., 309 Second St., N.W., 56431. Tel: 218-927-6581. [CEM]
Catechesis/Religious Programs—.
Students 160.

Aurora, St. Louis Co., Holy Rosary, Rev. Joseph Sirba.
Res., 16 W. Fifth Ave. N., 55705. Tel: 218-229-3210; Fax: 218-229-3434.
Catechesis/Religious Programs—Tel: 218-229-3434.
Students 43.

Babbitt, St. Louis Co., St. Pius X, Rev. James Scheuer; Deacon Gregory Hutar, Pastoral Admin. In res., Rev. John Sustarsic.
Res., 15 Ash Blvd., 55706. Tel: 218-827-2291.
Catechesis/Religious Programs—Sherri Scharber, D.R.E.
Students 48.

Ball Club, Itasca Co., St. Joseph's, Rev. Anselm Thevarkunnel.
Res., 51061 Wolf Dr., Deer River, 56636. Tel: 218-246-8105. [CEM]
Missions—Federal Dam, Sacred Heart; Bena, St. Anne's.
Catechesis/Religious Programs—Students 60.

Beroun, Pine Co., St. Joseph's, Rev. Cornelius Kelleher.
Res. and Mailing Address—203 Lawler Ave. S., P.O. Box 490, Hinckley, 55037. Tel: 320-384-6313; Fax: 320-384-6313.
Church—250 Praha Ave., 55063. Tel: 320-629-3442. [CEM]

Bigfork, Itasca Co., Our Lady of the Snows, Rev. Stephen Solors.
Res., P.O. Box 11, 56628. Tel: 218-743-3255.
Chapel—Squaw Lake, St. Catherine's, Tel: 218-659-4353.

Biwabik, St. Louis Co., St. John's, Rev. Frank Perkovich.
Res., Box 569, 55708. Tel: 218-865-6774.
Catechesis/Religious Programs—Tel: 218-744-2454.
Students 56.

Brainerd, Crow Wing Co., St. Andrew's, Rev. Paul Fruth.
1108 Willow St., 56401. Tel: 218-829-8932 (Office); 829-4061 (Rectory); Fax: 218-829-1340.
Catechesis/Religious Programs—D.R.E.: Veronica Besmehn; Cheryl Hawkinson.
Students 400.

St. Francis, Revs. Seamus Walsh; William Skarich; Deacon John Reed.
Office: 412 N. Eighth St., 56401. Tel: 218-829-8753; Fax: 218-829-2514.
Res., 422 N. 3rd St., 56401. Tel: 218-829-3833.; Res., 323 N. 10th St., 56401. Tel: 218-828-0184.
School—817 Juniper St., 56401. Tel: 218-829-2344. Debra Euteneuer, Prin.
Lay Teachers 10; Students 149.
Catechesis/Religious Programs—Kim Koning, D.R.E.
Students 550.

Chapel—Pine Beach, St. Thomas of the Pines. [CEM]

Carlton, Carlton Co., St. Francis, Rev. Kenton Sailstad, Admin.
Res., 509 Sunrise Dr., 55718. Tel: 218-384-4563; Fax: 218-384-4563. [CEM]
Catechesis/Religious Programs—Students 175.

Cass Lake, Cass Co., St. Charles, Rev. Eugene Lyttle.
Res., 308 Central Ave. N., Box 368, 56633. Tel: 218-335-2359.
Catechesis/Religious Programs—Students 37.
Mission—LaPorte, Hubbard Co., St.Theodore.

Chisholm, St. Louis Co., St. Joseph's, Rev. Steven Daigle.
Res., 113 S.W. Fourth St., 55719. Tel: 218-254-5703; Fax: 218-254-3636. [CEM]
Catechesis/Religious Programs—D.R.E.: Deanne Hildenbrand; Kathy Gregorich.
Students 295.
Mission—Buhl, Our Lady of the Sacred Heart, P.O. Box 27, Buhl, 55713. Tel: 218-258-3279.

Cloquet, Carlton Co., Holy Family, Deacon Terry Twomey, Pastoral Admin.
102 4th St., 55720. Tel: 218-879-6793. [CEM][JC 2]
Convent—280 Reservation Rd., 55720. Tel: 218-879-9047. Maryknoll Sisters
Mission—Sawyer, Carlton Co., SS. Mary & Joseph.

Queen of Peace, Rev. Kenton Sailstad; Deacon Terry Twomey.
102 4th St., 55720. Tel: 218-879-6958. [CEM 2]
Office: Tel: 218-879-6793; Fax: 218-879-2654.
School—Tel: 218-879-8516. Mother Colleen Kimbro, F.S.E., Prin.
Sisters 2; Lay Teachers 6; Students 110.
Catechesis/Religious Programs—Irene McKay, D.R.E.
Students 300.
Convent—5613 Lilac Hill Rd., Duluth, 55810. Tel: 218-624-9038. Franciscan Sisters of the Eucharist

Coleraine, Itasca Co., Mary Immaculate, Rev. Lloyd Mudrak.
Res., Box 290, 55722. Tel: 218-245-1684.
Catechesis/Religious Programs—Students 106.

Cook, St. Louis Co., St. Mary's, Rev. Lawrence T. Antus, O.M.I.
Res., Box 609, 55723. Tel: 218-666-5334. [CEM]

Crosby, Crow Wing Co., St. Joseph's, Rev. Howard P. Eisel, S.S.C.
Res., 619 Poplar St., 56441. Tel: 218-546-6559.
Mission—Deerwood, St. Joseph.

Crosslake, Crow Wing Co., Immaculate Heart, Rev. Dennis Hoffman.
Res., Box 155, 56442. Tel: 218-692-3731; Fax: 218-692-3732.
Catechesis/Religious Programs—Students 121.
Chapel—Our Lady of Snows.

Deer River, Itasca Co., St. Mary's, Rev. Bruce Engen.
Res., P.O. Box 98, 56636. Tel: 218-246-8582.
Catechesis/Religious Programs—Students 56.
Mission—Cohasset, St. Augustine.

Ely, St. Louis Co., St. Anthony's, Rev. James Scheuer; Deacon Gregory Hutar.
Res., 231 E. Camp St., 55731. Tel: 218-365-4017; Fax: 218-365-3296.
Catechesis/Religious Programs—Tel: 218-365-4251. D.R.E.: Barbara Condor; Patricia Zupancich. Students 210.

Emily, Crow Wing Co., St. Emily's, Rev. Roman Spors.
Res., Box 25, 56447. Tel: 218-763-2101; Fax: 218-763-2301.
Catechesis/Religious Programs—Students 41.

Eveleth, St. Louis Co., Resurrection, Rev. Eamonn Boland.
Res., Box 586, 55734. Tel: 218-744-3277.
Catechesis/Religious Programs—Tel: 218-744-3305. D.R.E.: Pam Rapacz, (Grades K-6); Janet Eisenbraun, (Grades 7-12).
Students 250.

Floodwood, St. Louis Co., St. Louis, Rev. Richard Kunst.
Res., Box 378, 55736. Tel: 218-476-2367.
Missions—Meadowlands, St. Mary's, Tel: 218-427-2626; Cromwell-Wright, Carlton Co., Immaculate Conception.
Chapel—Elmer, St. Joseph's.

Garrison, Crow Wing Co., Our Lady of Fatima, Rev. Vincent Ott, O.M.I.; Deacon Roger Marks.
9490 Tower Rd., 56450. Tel: 320-692-4466.

Gilbert, St. Louis Co., St. Joseph's, Rev. Frank Perkovich.
Res., Box 788, 55741. Tel: 218-741-9551.
Catechesis/Religious Programs—Tel: 218-741-1624.
Students 114.

Grand Marais, Cook Co., St. John's, Rev. Stephen White.
Res., Box 549, 55604-0549. Tel: 218-387-1409. [CEM]
Catechesis/Religious Programs—Tel: 218-387-1398.
Students 25.
Mission—Grand Portage, Holy Rosary. [CEM]

Grand Rapids, Itasca Co., St. Joseph's, Rev. Thomas Radaich.
Parish Center: 613 First Ave., N.W., 55744. Tel: 218-326-2843; Fax: 218-326-9115.
Res., 726 Second Ave., N.W., 55744.
School—Tel: 218-326-6232. Teresa Matetich, Prin.
Lay Teachers 10; Students 172.
Catechesis/Religious Programs—Tel: 218-326-3720. D.R.E.: Mary Gunderson; Mary Prudhomme; Lori Dowling; Rebecca Adams.
Students 530.

Hibbing, St. Louis Co., Blessed Sacrament, Revs. Peter Muhich; James Hauver.
Office: 218 E. 39th St., 55746. Tel: 218-262-5541.
Res., 2328 Seventh Ave. E., 55746. Tel: 218-263-3681.
School—Assumption.
Lay Teachers 17; Students 246.
Catechesis/Religious Programs—Dan Turnbloom, D.R.E.
Students 520.
Convent—718 E. 23rd St., 55746.
Missions—Hibbing, St.Louis Co., Immaculate Conception, 1928 5th Ave., E., 55746.; Hibbing, St. Louis Co., St. Leo's, 218 E. 39th St., 55746.
Station—Side Lake, Blessed Sacrament Chapel.
Immaculate Conception. Immaculate Conception has become a mission of Blessed Sacrament, Hibbing.
St. Leo's. St. Leo's has become a mission of Blessed Sacrament, Hibbing.

Hill City, Aitkin Co., St. John, Rev. Edward Buczynski.
Res., Box 156, 55748. Tel: 218-697-2465.
Catechesis/Religious Programs—Students 52.
Mission—Warba, St. Paul's.

Hillman, Crow Wing Co., Holy Family, Rev. Vincent Ott, O.M.I.
Res., 1182 County Rd. #8, 56338. Tel: 320-277-3386. [CEM]
Catechesis/Religious Programs—Students 28.

Hinckley, Pine Co., St. Patrick's, Rev. Cornelius Kelleher.
Res., Box 490, 55037-0490. Tel: 320-384-6313; Fax: 320-384-6313.
Catechesis/Religious Programs—Students 66.

Hoyt Lakes, St. Louis Co., Queen of Peace, Rev. Joseph Sirba.
Res., 513 Hampshire Dr., P.O. Box 211, 55750. Tel: 218-225-2867; Fax: 218-225-2867.
Catechesis/Religious Programs—Students 93.

International Falls, Koochiching Co., St. Thomas Aquinas, Revs. Louis Sondgeroth, O.M.I.; Thomas Meyer, O.M.I.
Res., 810 Fifth St., 56649. Tel: 218-283-3293; Fax: 218-283-3553. [CEM]
School—Tel: 218-283-3430. Mrs. Jill Herzig, Prin.
Lay Teachers 11; Students 115.
Catechesis/Religious Programs—Jo McLaughlin, D.R.E.
Students 316.

Keewatin, Itasca Co., St. Mary's, Rev. Ronald Gagne.
Res., Box 219, 55753. Tel: 218-778-6379.

Littlefork, Koochiching Co., St. Columban, Rev. Louis Sondgeroth, O.M.I.
Res., Box 44, 56653. Tel: 218-278-6638; Fax: 218-283-3553.

Longville, Cass Co., St. Edward's, Rev. Roland Antus.
Res., P.O. Box 38, 56655-0038. Tel: 218-363-2799.
Mission—Remer, St. Paul.

McGregor, Aitkin Co., Holy Family, Rev. John J. Fleischhacker, O.S.C.
Res., 55760. Tel: 218-768-2702; Fax: 218-768-2131.
Catechesis/Religious Programs—Students 80.
Chapel—McGrath, Our Lady of Fatima.

Marble, Itasca Co., St. Mary's, Rev. Lloyd Mudrak.
Res., P.O. Box 290, Coleraine, 55722. Tel: 218-247-7368.
Mission—Taconite, St. Joseph's.

Moose Lake, Carlton Co., Holy Angels, Rev. Michael T. Hayes.
Res., P.O. Box 487, 55767. Tel: 218-485-4909.
Catechesis/Religious Programs—Tel: 218-485-4005. D.R.E.: Peggy Rosera; Mary Rose Rosc.
Students 145.

Nashwauk, Itasca Co., St. Cecilia's, Rev. Ronald Gagne.
Res., 326 Second St., 55769. Tel: 218-885-1126; Fax: 218-885-1145.
Catechesis/Religious Programs—Students 134.
Mission—Pengilly, St. Kevin.

Northome, Koochiching Co., St. Michael's. (Under the jurisdiction of the Duluth Diocese; administered by the Crookston Diocese.).
Res., St. Philip's Church, 710 Beltrami Ave., N.W., Bemidji, 56601. Tel: 218-751-4262.

Orr, St. Louis Co., Holy Cross, Rev. Lawrence T. Antus, O.M.I.
Res., Box 218, 55771. Tel: 218-757-3273.
Chapel—Buyck, St. Joseph's.

Pequot Lakes, Crow Wing Co., St. Alice's, Rev. George Zeck; Deacons David Craig; Richard Paine.
Res., Box 159, 56472. Tel: 218-568-4760; Fax: 218-568-6707.
Catechesis/Religious Programs—Students 495.
Mission—Nisswa, St. Christopher's, Tel: 218-563-2766.

Pine City, Pine Co., Immaculate Conception, Rev. Michael J. Lyons; Deacon Eugene Biever.
Res., 535 Eighth St., 55063. Tel: 320-629-2935; Fax: 320-629-7846. [CEM]
School—St. Mary's, 815 W. Sixth Ave., 55063. Tel: 320-629-3953. Sr. Helen Giesen, O.S.B., Prin.
Lay Teachers 5; Students 99.
Catechesis/Religious Programs—Tel: 320-629-3911.
Students 151.

Pine River, Cass Co., Our Lady of Lourdes, Rev. Edward M. Foster.
Res., Box 44, 56474. Tel: 587-4203; Fax: 218-587-3874.
Catechesis/Religious Programs—Students 95.

Proctor, St. Louis Co., St. Rose Catholic Church, Rev. James Bissonette.
Res., 3 Sixth Ave., 55810. Tel: 218-624-0007; Fax: 218-628-1462.
School—Tel: 218-624-0818; Fax: 218-624-0984. Timothy Johnson, Prin.
Lay Teachers 8; Students 95.
Catechesis/Religious Programs—Tel: 218-624-9580. Becky Kubat, D.R.E.
Students 108.
Mission—Saginaw, St. Philip Neri, Saginaw.

St. Mathias, Crow Wing Co., St. Mathias, Rev. Paul Fruth.
Res., 4529 Co. Rd. 121, Fort Ripley, 56449. Tel: 218-829-4061; Fax: 218-829-4061.
Catechesis/Religious Programs—Students 125.
Station—St. Mathias, Crow Wing State Park.

Sandstone, Pine Co., St. Luke's, Rev. Alcuin Henger, O.M.I.
Res., P.O. Box 644, 55072. Tel: 320-245-5175; Fax: 320-245-0411.
Catechesis/Religious Programs—Tel: 320-245-0064.
Students 54.
Missions—Finlayson, St. Joseph's. [CEM]
Bruno, Sacred Heart. [CEM]

Silver Bay, Lake Co., St. Mary's, Rev. Mark Coen; Deacons Fred Wright; Jack Ferris. In res., Rev. Francis Paqueite.
Res., 57 Horn Blvd., 55614. Tel: 218-226-3100; Fax: 218-226-3116.
Catechesis/Religious Programs—Students 71.

Tower, St. Louis Co., St. Martin's, Rev. Rudolph Pakiz.
Res., Box 757, 55790. Tel: 218-753-4310.
Catechesis/Religious Programs—Students 64.

Two Harbors, Lake Co., Holy Spirit, Rev. Mark Coen.
Res., 227 Third St., 55616. Tel: 218-834-4313; Fax: 218-834-7082. [CEM]
Catechesis/Religious Programs—Students 191.

Virginia, St. Louis Co., Holy Spirit, Revs. John O'Donnell; John Doyle.
Res., 306 S. Second St., 55792. Tel: 218-741-6344.
School—Marquette, 311 3rd St. S., 55792. Tel: 218-741-6811.
Catechesis/Religious Programs—Linda Strukel, D.R.E.
Students 250.
Sacred Heart, Revs. John O'Donnell; John Doyle.
Res., 603 12th St. N., 55792. Tel: 218-741-2322.
Catechesis/Religious Programs—Sally Strle, D.R.E.
Students 185.
Mission—Mountain Iron, Sacred Heart.

Walker, Cass Co., St. Agnes, Rev. Frederick Method.
Res., Box 874, 56484. Tel: 218-547-1054; Fax: 218-547-1376.
Catechesis/Religious Programs—Students 130.
Mission—Hackensack, Sacred Heart.
Station—Walker, Ah-Gwah Ching State Nursing Home.

Willow River, Pine Co., St. Mary's, Rev. Norman Pahl, O.M.I.
Res., Box 97, 55795. Tel: 218-372-3446. [CEM]
Catechesis/Religious Programs—Students 72.
Mission—Sturgeon Lake, St. Isidore's. [CEM]
Station—Willow River, Youth Conservation Camp.

INDIAN MISSIONS

Duluth, St. Louis Co., Indian Missions,
c/o Chancery Office: 2830 E. Fourth St., 55812. Tel: 218-724-9111; Fax: 218-724-1056. Sr. Marie Rose Messingschlager, C.D.P.
Missions—Cloquet, Carlton Co., Holy Family Church, 280 Reservation Rd., Cloquet, 55720. Tel: 218-879-6793; Fax: 218-879-2654. [CEM]
Rev. Kenton Sailstad; Deacon Terry Twomey.
Sawyer, Carlton Co., SS. Mary and Joseph, 102 4th St., Cloquet, 55720. Rev. Kenton Sailstad.; Ball Club, Itasca Co., St. Joseph's, 51061 Wolf Dr., Deer River, 56636. Tel: 218-246-8105. [CEM]
Rev. Anselm Thevarkunnel.
Federal Dam, Sacred Heart, HC4 Box 104, Deer River, 56636. Rev. Anselm Thevarkunnel.; Grand Portage, Cook Co., Holy Rosary, P.O. Box 549, Grand Marais, 56604. Tel: 218-387-1409. [CEM]
Rev. Stephen White.
Walker, Ah-Gwah-Ching State Nursing Home, Box 874, Walker, 56484. Tel: 218-547-1054; Fax: 218-547-1376. Rev. Fred Method.; Nett Lake, St. Louis Co., Holy Cross, Box 218, Orr, 55771. Tel: 218-757-3273. Rev. Lawrence T. Antus, O.M.I.

Chaplains of Public Institutions

Hospitals

DULUTH. *Miller Dwan Hospital*. Mrs. Jan Rohweder, Dir of Chap., Tel: 218-727-1089.
St. Luke's Hospital 2002 Minnesota Ave., 55802. Tel: 218-727-1089. Rev. John C. Petrich, Chap.

MOOSE LAKE. *Moose Lake State Hospital* 112 Cedar, 55767. Tel: 218-485-4909. Rev. Michael T. Hayes, Chap., Tel: 218-485-4411.

Correctional Institutions

DULUTH. *Duluth Federal Prison*. Rev. Noel Stretton Tel: 218-722-1021.

SAGINAW. *Northeast Regional Correctional Institution*. Rev. John C. Petrich, Chap., Tel: 218-727-1089.

WILLOW RIVER. *Youth Conservation Camp*. Rev. Norman Pahl, O.M.I., Chap., Tel: 218-372-3446.

On Duty Outside the Diocese:
Reverend Fathers—
Graham, William C., 326 W. 14th St., New York City, NY 10014
Johnson, Lawrence P., 1820 Froude St., San Diego, CA 92107
Kaster, Alfred D., 6716 Woodland Dr., Paradise, CA 95969
Kottiry, Alphonsus, Ramapuran Bazaar, P.O. Box Kattayam Dist., Kerala State S., India

---

Military Chaplains:
Reverend Fathers—
Lambert, Peter, Chap., U.S.A.F., 102 Sirocco Dr., #2, Minot AFB, ND

Absent on Sick Leave:
Reverend Fathers—
Kisting, Thomas

Retired:
Reverend Monsignors—
Popesh, Bernard, 1181 Ring Rock Rd., Ely, MN 55731. Tel: 218-365-6085
Reverend Fathers—
Arimond, Vincent, 330 E. 3rd St., #104, Duluth, MN 55805. Tel: 218-727-4184
Blanchard, Kirby, 727 4th St., S.W., #202, Brainerd, MN 56401. Tel: 218-825-9062
Bouchard, Thomas, 20 6th St., S.W., Chisholm, MN 55712
Cossette, Raymond, 1599 County Rd. 8 SE., Brainerd, MN 56401. Tel: 218-764-2941
Dolsina, Stanley, 2423 Morris Thomas Rd., Duluth, MN 55811
Faith, Rudolph, 330 E. 3rd St., #224, Duluth, MN 55805. Tel: 218-733-0988
Gaber, Francis, 129 E. 6th Ave., Pine City, MN 55063
Golden, James, 204-4th Ave., Keewatin, MN 55753. Tel: 218-778-6949
Golobich, John, 524 N. Oak Bend Drive, #102, Duluth, MN 55811. Tel: 218-723-1566
La Patka, Gerald, 4202 E. Broadway Rd., #75, Mesa, AZ 85206. Tel: 480-325-5103
Marincel, Frank, 8521 Park Villa Drive, #105 W, Mt. Iron, MN 55768. Tel: 218-749-6750
Paquette, Francis, 57 Horn Blvd., Silver Bay, MN 55614. Tel: 218-220-0122
Partika, Richard, 925 Kenwood Ave., #1157, Duluth, MN 55811. Tel: 218-728-3498

Sustarsic, John, 15 Ash Blvd., Babbitt, MN 55706. Tel: 218-827-2291

Zorichak, William, 935 Kenwood Ave., Duluth, MN 55811

Permanent Deacons:

Anderson, Dennis, St. Benedict, Duluth

Anderson, H. L., St. John, Duluth

Baskfield, Jim, Immaculate Conception, Crosslake

Beier, Walter, St. John's, Duluth

Biever, Eugene, Immaculate Conception Church, Pine City

Birkland, Roger, St. Joseph, Gnesen

Christensen, Robert, (Retired)

Craig, David, St. Alice, Pequot Lakes

Ferris, Jack, St. Mary's, Silver Bay

Griffiths, James, Blessed Sacrament Hibbing

Hume, Michael, Central City Parishes, Duluth

Hutar, Gregory, St. Anthony, Ely

Knuth, Michael, St. Alice, Pequot Lakes

Laumeyer, Richard, St. Michael's, Duluth

Marks, Roger, Holy Family, Hillman

Mayer, Philip, St. Joseph's, Crosby

Olson, Barry, Immaculate Heart, Cross Lake

Paine, Richard, St. Alice, Pequot Lakes

Reed, John, St. Francis, Brainerd

Riley, Herbert, St. John, Biwabik

Skala, Mark, Queen of Peace, Hoyt Lakes

Sura, Jerome, Our Lady of the Snows, Bigfork

Szyman, Robert, (Retired)

Twomey, Terence, Queen of Peace, Cloquet

Windus, Theodore, Sr., St. James, Duluth

Wright, Fred, St. Mary's, Silver Bay

INSTITUTIONS LOCATED IN THE DIOCESE

[A] COLLEGES AND UNIVERSITIES

DULUTH. *College of St. Scholastica*, 1200 Kenwood Ave., 55811. Tel: 218-723-6000; Fax: 218-723-6290
For a complete listing, refer to the Colleges and Universities section.

[B] ELEMENTARY SCHOOLS, INTERPAROCHIAL

VIRGINIA. *Marquette Catholic School*, 311 Third St. S., 55792. Tel: 218-741-6811; Fax: 218-741-2158.
E-mail: mcs@the-bridge.net
Serving the parishes of Holy Spirit & Sacred Heart. Marianne Runkle, Prin. Lay Teachers 7; Students 131.

[C] GENERAL HOSPITALS

DULUTH. *St. Mary's Medical Center*, 407 E. Third St., 55805. Tel: 218-786-4000; Fax: 218-786-4383.
E-mail: shofer@smdc.org
Web site: www.smdc.org
For a complete listing, refer to the Hospitals section.

BRAINERD. *St. Joseph's Medical Center*, 523 N. Third St., 56401. Tel: 218-829-2861; Fax: 218-828-3103.
E-mail: care@stjosephsmedicalctr.com
Web site: www.stjosephsmedicalctr.com
For a complete listing, refer to the Hospitals section.

[D] HOMES FOR AGED

DULUTH. *Benedictine Health Center*, 935 Kenwood Ave., 55811. Tel: 218-723-6408; Fax: 218-723-6449
For a complete listing, refer to the Special Care Facilities section.

St. Ann's Senior Residence, 330 E. Third St., 55805. Tel: 218-727-8831; Fax: 218-727-8833.
Web site: www.stanns.com
For a complete listing, refer to the Special Care Facilities section.

[E] CONVENTS AND RESIDENCES FOR SISTERS

DULUTH. *Motherhouse and Novitiate of the Sisters of Saint Benedict*, St. Scholastica Monastery, 1001 Kenwood Ave., 55811. Tel: 218-723-6555; Fax: 218-723-5902.
E-mail: khoferosb@aol.com
Web site: www.peace-duluthmn.org
Sr. Aelred Roehl, O.S.B., Archivist.
In community: Professed Sisters 150.

[F] NEWMAN CENTERS

DULUTH. *University of MN-Duluth*, 421 W. Ste. Marie St., 55811. Tel: 218-728-3757. Rev. Dale Nau, Dir.; Deacon Chico Anderson, Assoc. Dir.

College of St. Scholastica, 1200 Kenwood Ave., 55811. Tel: 218-723-6010. Paul Krenzelok, Campus Ministry Dir.; Molly Weyrens, Asst. Dir.

[G] MISCELLANEOUS LISTINGS

DULUTH. *Benedictine Sisters Benevolent Association.* (Parent Co.), 1001 Kenwood Ave., 55811-2300. Tel: 218-728-1817; Fax: 218-723-5902.
E-mail: khoferosh@aol.com
Web site: www.peace-duluthmn.org
Sr. Kathleen Hofer, O.S.B., Pres.

Benedictine Health System. (Sub. of Benedictine Sisters Benevolent Association), 503 E. Third St., Ste. 400, 55805. Tel: 218-786-2370; Fax: 218-786-2373. Barry J. Halm, Pres. & CEO. Benedictine Health System Subsidiaries Not Located In The Diocese: Benedictine Care Centers; Benedictine Health Dimensions; Good Shepherd Care Center; Madonna Towers of Rochester, Inc.; Mount Carmel Health & Rehabilitation Center; St. Anne Hospice; St. Francis Regional Medical Center; St. Gertrude's Health Center; St. Mary's Care Center; St. Mary's Hospital; St. Mary's Regional Health Center; Tekakwitha Nursing Center, Inc.; Trinity Hospital; Villa St. Benedict; Villa St. Vincent.

St. Mary's Medical Center. (Sub. of Benedictine Health System), 407 E. Third St., 55805. Tel: 218-786-4000; Fax: 218-786-4383. Sr. Kathleen Hofer, O.S.B., Pres. & Chm. Bd.; Peter Person, M.D., CEO. Affiliate: St. Mary's Hospital of Superior.

St. Joseph's Medical Center, Brainerd. (Sub. of Benedictine Health System), 523 N. Third St., Brainerd, 56401. Tel: 218-829-2861; Fax: 218-828-3103. Thomas Prusak, Pres. & CEO.

Benedictine Health System Foundation, Inc. (Sub. of Benedictine Health System), 503 E. Third St., 55805. Tel: 218-786-2370; Fax: 218-786-2373. Tom Bila, Exec. Dir.

Benedictine Health Center. (Sub. of Benedictine Health System), 935 Kenwood Ave., 55811. Tel: 218-723-6408; Fax: 218-723-6449. Mark Broman, Admin. / CEO.

Polinsky Medical Rehabilitation Center, (Sub. of St. Mary's Medical Center), 530 E. Second St., 55805. Tel: 218-786-5360; Fax: 218-786-5340. Ann Bussey, Dir.

St. Mary's/Polinsky Center for Personal Fitness. (Sub. of St. Mary's Medical Center), 5th Ave. E. & 2nd St., 55805. Tel: 218-786-5410; Fax: 218-786-5435.

Benedictine Living Communities. (Sub. of Benedictine Health System), 503 E. Third St., Ste. 400, 55805. Tel: 218-786-2370; Fax: 218-786-2373. Dennis Acrea, Pres. & CEO.

The Blessed Nuno Society, P.O. Box 3484, 55803. Tel: 218-728-0447. Tim Heinan, Dir.

Holy Rosary Parish Endowment Fund, 2801 E. Fourth St., 55812. Tel: 218-728-3646.
E-mail: cathdulth@aol.com

The Human Life and Development Fund of the Diocese of Duluth, 2830 E. Fourth St., 55812. Tel: 218-724-9111; Fax: 218-724-1056. Rev. Dale Nau, Chancellor, Sec. & Treas.

John S. Duss Memorial Music Conservatory, 2211 Greysolon Rd., 55812. Tel: 218-724-2052; Fax: 218-724-3318. Franciscan Sisters of the Eucharist. Part of Franciscan Life Center Network, Inc.

Port Area Catholic Education (PACE), 2830 E. Fourth St., 55812. PACE is a consortium of Catholic parish elementary schools (St. Rose, Proctor; Holy Rosary, St. Michael, St. John, & St. James, Duluth; Queen of Peace, Cloquet).

St. Vincent de Paul Society, 109 W. Fourth St., 55806. Tel: 218-727-9145. Joseph Jodouin, Pres.

HACKENSACK. *S.W. Deanery Chapter of Magnificat of the Diocese of Duluth*, P.O. Box 100, 56452. Betty Garoutte.

RELIGIOUS INSTITUTES OF MEN REPRESENTED IN THE DIOCESE

For further details refer to the corresponding bracketed number in the Religious Institutes of Men or Women section.

[0200]—*Benedictine Monks.*

[0400]—*Canons Regular of the Order of Holy Cross.*—O.S.C.

[0910]—*Oblates of Mary Immaculate.* (Central Prov.).—O.M.I.

[0370]—*Society of St. Columban.*—S.S.C.

RELIGIOUS INSTITUTES OF WOMEN REPRESENTED IN THE DIOCESE

[0230]—*Benedictine Sisters of Pontifical Jurisdiction.* (St. Joseph, MN; Watertown, SD; St. Paul, MN; Duluth, MN).—O.S.B.

[1000]—*Congregation of Divine Providence of Kentucky.*—C.D.P.

[1070-10]—*Dominican Sisters.*—O.P.

[1250]—*The Institute of the Franciscan Sisters of the Eucharist.* (Meriden, CT).—F.S.E.

[2470]—*Maryknoll Sisters of St. Dominic.*—M.M.

[2970]—*School Sisters of Notre Dame.* (Mankato Prov.).—S.S.N.D.

[0430]—*Sisters of Charity of the Blessed Virgin Mary.*—B.V.M.

[1990]—*Sisters of the Holy Names of Jesus and Mary.*—S.N.J.M.

[1720]—*Sisters of the Third Order Regular of St. Francis of the Congregation of Our Lady of the Lourdes.*—O.S.F.

[2150]—*Sisters Servants of the Immaculate Heart of Mary.*—I.H.M.

DIOCESAN CEMETERIES

DULUTH. *Calvary Cemetery*, 1312 Howard Gnesen Rd., 55803. Tel: 218-724-3376. Rev. Dale Nau, Dir.; Mr. Tim Stresow, Supt.

NECROLOGY

† Hughes, Joseph Arthur, Duluth, MN St. John. —Died May 21, 2000.

† Klein, Robert William, (On Leave). —Died Feb. 16, 2000.

Diocese of El Paso

(Dioecesis Elpasensis)

Most Reverend

ARMANDO X. OCHOA, D.D.

Bishop of El Paso; ordained May 23, 1970; appointed Titular Bishop of Sitifi and Auxiliary of the Archdiocese of Los Angeles December 29, 1986; ordained Bishop February 23, 1987; appointed Bishop of El Paso April 1, 1996; installed June 26, 1996.

ERECTED MARCH 3, 1914.

Square Miles 26,686.

Comprises in Texas, the Counties of El Paso, Brewster, Culberson, Hudspeth, Jeff Davis, Loving, Presidio, Reeves, Ward and Winkler.

For legal titles of parishes and diocesan institutions, consult the Chancery Office.

Chancery Office: 499 St. Matthews St., El Paso, TX, 79907. Tel.: 915-595-5000; Fax: 915-595-5095.

Web site address: www.elpasodiocese.org

STATISTICAL OVERVIEW

Personnel	
Bishop	1
Priests: Diocesan Active in Diocese	63
Priests: Active Outside Diocese	2
Priests: Retired, Sick or Absent	27
Number of Diocesan Priests	92
Religious Priests in Diocese	42
Extern Priests in Diocese	2
Ordinations:	
Permanent Deacons	14
Permanent Deacons in Diocese	14
Total Brothers	16
Total Sisters	247
Parishes	
Parishes	58
With Resident Pastor:	
Resident Diocesan Priests	38
Resident Religious Priests	15
Without Resident Pastor:	
Administered by Priests	2
Administered by Women Religious	3
Missions	22
Professional Ministry Personnel:	
Sisters	15
Lay Ministers	26
Welfare	
Health Care Centers	1
Total Assisted	20,319
Homes for the Aged	2
Total Assisted	95
Day Care and Extended Day Care Centers	1
Total Assisted	81
Specialized Homes	1
Total Assisted	78
Special Centers for Social Services	5
Total Assisted	81,411
Educational	
Seminaries, Diocesan	1
Students from This Diocese	3
Diocesan Students in Other Seminaries	4
Seminaries, Religious	2
Students Religious	25
Total Seminarians	32
High Schools, Diocesan and Parish	1
Total Students	673
High Schools, Private	2
Total Students	352
Elementary Schools, Diocesan and Parish	9
Total Students	3,612
Elementary Schools, Private	3
Total Students	867
Catechesis/Religious Education:	
High School Students	5,398
Elementary Students	13,527
Total Students Under Catholic Instruction	24,461
Teachers in the Diocese:	
Priests	6
Brothers	7
Sisters	40
Lay Teachers	299
Vital Statistics	
Receptions into the Church:	
Infant Baptism Totals	9,033
Adult Baptism Totals	136
Received into Full Communion	273
First Communions	5,742
Confirmations	3,842
Marriages:	
Catholic	1,231
Interfaith	113
Total Marriages	1,344
Deaths	1,955
Total Catholic Population	630,573
Total Population	798,763

Former Bishops—Most Rev. JOHN J. BROWN, S.J., preconized Bishop of El Paso, Jan. 22, 1915; resigned June 16, 1915.—Most Rev. ANTHONY J. SCHULER, S.J., D.D., cons. Oct. 28, 1915; died June 3, 1944.—Most Rev. SIDNEY M. METZGER, S.T.D., J.C.D., cons. April 10, 1940; succeeded to See, Nov. 29, 1942; retired May 29, 1978; died April 12, 1986.—Most Rev. PATRICK F. FLORES, D.D., cons. May 5, 1970; installed Bishop of El Paso, May 29, 1978; appt. Archbishop of San Antonio, Aug. 28, 1979.—Most Rev. RAYMUNDO J. PENA, D.D., cons. Dec. 13, 1976; appt. Bishop of El Paso, April 29, 1980; appt. Bishop of Brownsville, May 23, 1995.

Vicars General—Rev. Msgr. FRANCIS J. SMITH; Rev. RICHARD A. MATTY.

Vicar for Clergy—Rev. JUVENTINO CELINO.

Moderator of the Curia—Rev. RICHARD A. MATTY.

Chancellor—Rev. RICHARD A. MATTY.

Vice Chancellor—Sr. HELEN SANTAMARIA, S.L.

Diocesan Pastoral Staff—Rev. RICHARD A. MATTY, Chancellor; Sr. HELEN SANTAMARIA, S.L., Vice Chancellor.

Liaison for Women Religious—Sr. HELEN SANTAMARIA, S.L., *499 St. Matthews St., El Paso, 79907.* Tel: 915-872-8407.

Diocesan Pastoral Center—499 St. Matthews St., El Paso, 79907. Tel: 915-872-8400; Fax: 915-872-8423. Refer all official business to this address.

Diocesan Tribunal—499 St. Matthews St., El Paso, 79907. Tel: 915-872-8402. Rev. RICHARD ZAMORANO, J.C.L., Judicial Vicar. Adjutant Vicars: Revs. STEPHEN PETERS; ROBERT S. KOBE.

Presbyteral Council—Rev. FRANCISCO HERRERA; Rev. Msgr. JOHN PETERS; Revs. THOMAS DEVINE, O.A.R.; FRANK LOPEZ; JOE MOLINA; JOHN RINI; LEONIDES RIVERO; RICARDO RUIZ; RICHARD ZAMORANO. Ex Officio Members: Rev. Msgr. FRANCIS J. SMITH; Revs. RICHARD A. MATTY; JUVENTINO CELINO.

Judges—Revs. RICHARD ZAMORANO, J.C.L.; STEPHEN PETERS; ROBERT S. KOBE; JAMES W. HALL; GILES CARIE, O.F.M.Conv.

Defenders of the Bond—Rev. Msgr. DAVID G. FIERRO; Rev. TRINI FUENTEZ; Deacon GEORGE LEVY.

Advocates—Rev. Msgr. FRANCIS J. SMITH; Revs. JUVENTINO CELINO; FRANCISCO LOPEZ; JOHN LUCIDO.

Lay Advocates—OUISA DAVIS; CARMEN RODRIGUEZ.

Tribunal Ecclesiastical Notary—YOLANDA RUIZ.

Peritus—RICHARD B. PATTERSON, Ph.D.

Vicar for Clergy and Religious—Vacant.

Vicars-Vicariates—St. Peter: Rev. TRINDAD FUENTEZ, *Queen of Peace Parish, 1551 Belvidere, El Paso, 79912.* Tel: 915-584-5817. St. Paul: Rev. RAFAEL GARCIA, S.J., *Sacred Heart Church, 602 S. Oregon, El Paso, 79901.* Tel: 915-532-5447. St. John: Rev. STEPHEN PETERS, *Blessed Sacrament, 9024 Diana Dr., El Paso, 79904.* Tel: 915-755-7658. St. Mark:; Vacant, *St. Thomas - St. Joseph Parish, 838 Bellaire, Kermit, 79745.* Tel: 915-586-4694. St. Luke: Rev. RAUL TRIGUEROS, *Cristo Rey Parish, 8011 Wiliamette, El Paso, 79907.* Tel: 915-591-0688. St. Mark:; Vacant; Our Lady of Guadalupe: Rev. Msgr. FRANCIS J. SMITH, *St. Raphael Parish, 2301 Zanzibar, El Paso, 79925.* Tel: 915-598-3431.

Diocesan Master of Ceremonies—Rev. MARCUS MCFADIN.

Peace & Justice Office—Rev. CARMEN MELE, O.P., Dir., *499 St. Matthews, El Paso, 79907.* Tel: 915-872-8422.

Finance Council—Most Rev. ARMANDO X. OCHOA; Rev. Msgr. FRANCIS J. SMITH; Rev. JOSEPH HERMOSO; E. H. BAEZA; FRANK GORMAN; AL MARTINEZ-FONTS; PHILLIP MULLIN.

Diocesan Building Committee—Most Rev. ARMANDO X. OCHOA; Rev. JUVENTINO CELINO; FRANK ALDERETE; ERNESTO ARMENDARIZ; RICARDO BACA; PEDRO HERRERA; ROSIE TORRES.

Priests' Personnel Advisory Committee—Rev. Msgr. FRANCIS J. SMITH; Revs. RICHARD A. MATTY; TRINI FUENTEZ; RAFAEL GARCIA, S.J.; STEPHEN PETERS; RALPH SOLIS, JR.; RAUL TRIGUEROS.

Catholic Ministry in Hospitals—Mr. EDUARDO CASTORENA. Tel: 915-872-8427.

Laity, Office of the—Rev. Msgr. ARTURO BANUELAS, *Youth Services, 499 St. Matthew St., El Paso, 79907.* Tel: 915-872-8420. Mr. MARCOS MARTINEZ, Youth Office. Tel: 915-872-8410. The following associations are under the direction of the Office of the Laity:

Adoracion Nocturna (Nocturnal Adoration)—Rev. SANTOS PEREZ, O.F.M.

Apostolado de la Cruz (Apostolate of the Cross)—Vacant.

Blue Army—Rev. RICHARD WAIWOOD.

Catholic Daughters of America—Rev. MICHAEL RODRIGUEZ.

Catholic Knights of America—Rev. MICHAEL RODRIGUEZ.
Cursillos de Cristianidad—Rev. Msgr. RAFAEL MIRANDA, *San Judas Tadeo Parish, 4006 Hidden Way, El Paso, 79922.*
Franciscans, Secular Order of Franciscans—Vacant.
Knights of Columbus—Rev. Msgr. FRANCIS J. SMITH.
Knights of the Holy Sepulchre—Rev. Msgr. FRANCIS J. SMITH.
Knights of St. Gregory—Vacant.
Ladies of Charity; Daughters of Charity; Ladies of the Holy Sepulchre—Rev. Msgr. FRANCIS J. SMITH.
Legion of Mary—Vacant.
Serra Club—Rev. RICHARD ZAMORANO.
St. Vincent de Paul Society—Vacant.
Young Adults—Sr. SYLVIA SEDILLO, S.L., *499 St. Matthews, El Paso, 79907.* Tel: 915-872-8438.

Catholic Communications Ministry—Rev. RAUL TRIGUEROS, *499 St. Matthews St., El Paso, 79907.* Tel: 915-872-8414.

Diocesan Newspaper—"Rio Grande Catholic", 499 St. Matthews St., El Paso, 79907. Tel: 915-872-8414.

Persons with Disabilities—Vacant.

Evangelization & Renewal Center—Vacant, *499 St. Matthews St., El Paso, 79907.* Tel: 915-872-8417.

Catholic Emergency Assistance—Sr. MARIAN KLUESNER, F.S.P.A., *1013 E. San Antonio, El Paso, 79901.* Tel: 915-532-9532.

Campaign for Human Development—Rev. CARMEN MELE, O.P. Tel: 915-872-8422. Rev. RICHARD A. MATTY, *499 St. Matthews St., El Paso, 79907.* Tel: 915-595-5007.

Office of Marriage and Family Life—Mr. LUIS ROBLES, *499 St. Matthews St., El Paso, 79907.* Tel: 915-872-8432.

Historical Archives & Diocesan Museum—Rev. RICHARD A. MATTY, *499 St. Matthews St., El Paso, 79907.* Tel: 915-872-8407.

Permanent Diaconate Office—Vacant, *499 St. Matthews St., El Paso, 79907.* Tel: 915-595-5000.

Priests' Retirement and Disability Plan—Rev. Msgr. JOHN PETERS; Rev. Msgr. FRANCIS J. SMITH, Pres.; Rev. Msgr. WILLIAM RYAN; Rev. RICHARD ZAMORANO; Mr. YAZBIK DAW; ROBERT ORTEGA.

Missions Office—Sr. HELEN SANTAMARIA, S.L., *499 St. Matthews St., El Paso, 79907.* Tel: 915-872-8407.

Office of Education—Sr. ELIZABETH SWARTZ, S.S.N.D., Supt., *499 St. Matthews St., El Paso, 79907.* Tel: 915-872-8426.

Tepeyac Institute—Rev. Msgr. ARTURO BANUELAS, S.T.D., Dir.; Sr. ESTHER ORTEGA, O.P., Assoc. Dir.; Sr. DONNA KUSTUSCH, O.P., Teacher, *499 St. Matthews St., El Paso, 79907.* Tel: 915-872-8420.

Retreat House—*499 St. Matthews St., El Paso, 79907.* Tel: 915-872-8406.

Reverence for Life Ministry—Rev. RAFAEL GARCIA, S.J., *499 St. Matthews St., El Paso, 79907.* Tel: 915-872-8400.

Vocations & Seminarians—Rev. RICHARD ZAMORANO, *499 St. Matthews St., El Paso, 79907.* Tel: 915-872-8403.

Jail Ministry—Mr. EDUARDO CASTORENA, *499 St. Matthews St., El Paso, 79907.* Tel: 915-872-8427.

West Texas Ministry—Team Ministry: Sr. MARGIE SILGUERO, M.J.M.J.; Sr. LUZ DONEZ, M.J.M.J., *Box 1118, Marfa, 79843.* Tel: 915-729-3385. Sr. JOSEPHA DWYER, *838 Bellaire, Kermit, 79745.* Tel: 915-586-3922.

Cursillo—Rev. Msgr. JOSE GOMEZ, *104 Fewel, El Paso, 79902.* Tel: 915-532-8462.

Movimiento Familiar Cristiano—Rev. Msgr. JOSE GOMEZ, Dir.

CLERGY, PARISHES, MISSIONS AND PAROCHIAL SCHOOLS

CITY OF EL PASO
(El Paso County)

1—ST. PATRICK'S CATHEDRAL, Revs. Richard A. Matty, Rector; Pablo Matta; Miguel Angel Sanchez; Deacon Ken Flynn.
Res., 1118 N. Mesa St., 79902. Tel: 915-533-4451; Fax: 915-532-8761.
School—(Grades K-8) 1111 N. Stanton St., 79902. Tel: 915-532-4142.
Sisters 1; Lay Teachers 22; Students 451.
Catechesis/Religious Programs—Students 547.

2—ALL SAINTS, Rev. Kennon Y. Ducre, S.T.L.
Res., 1415 Dakota St., 79930. Tel: 915-566-9711.

3—BLESSED JUAN DIEGO PARISH, Rev. Edward G. Roden-Lucero.
Res., 14520 E. Montana, 79938. Tel: 915-855-2217.

4—BLESSED SACRAMENT, Revs. Stephen Peters; Ralph Barranger; Miguel Luna.
Res., 9025 Diana Dr., 79924. Tel: 915-755-7658.
School—(Grades PreK-8). Tel: 915-755-2711. Ms. Guadalupe Varela.
Franciscan Sisters of Our Lady of Perpetual Help 1; Lay Teachers 15; Students 210.
Catechesis/Religious Programs—Teri Valdez, D.R.E. Students 600.

5—CHRIST THE SAVIOR, Rev. Robert S. Kobe; Deacon Paul Andrade.
Res., 5301 Wadsworth Ave., 79924. Tel: 915-821-3766.

6—CORPUS CHRISTI, Rev. Wilson Cuevas.
Res., 9205 N. Loop Dr., 79907. Tel: 915-858-0488; Fax: 915-858-0812.
Catechesis/Religious Programs—Students 789.

7—CRISTO REY CHURCH, Rev. Raul Trigueros.
Res., 8011 Williamette, 79907. Tel: 915-591-0688; Fax: 915-593-0470.

8—GUARDIAN ANGEL, Revs. Jesus Perez Recio, O.A.R.; Jesus Maria P. Arrilucea, O.A.R.
Res., 3021 Frutas Ave., 79905. Tel: 915-533-2077; Fax: 915-533-3649.

9—HOLY FAMILY, Rev. Msgr. Jose A. Gomez.
Res., 104 Fewel St., 79902. Tel: 915-532-8462.

10—IMMACULATE CONCEPTION, Rev. Msgr. William H. Ryan.
Res., 118 N. Campbell St., 79901-2404. Tel: 915-533-3427.

11—LA PURISIMA, Rev. Juan Narez.
Res., 328 S. Nevarez St., 79927. Tel: 915-859-7718.

12—SAINT THERESE OF THE LITTLE FLOWER PARISH, Rev. Francisco Siguenza, O.A.R.
Church—171 Polo Inn, 79915. Tel: 915-772-1285.

13—MOST HOLY TRINITY, Rev. Msgr. Robert S. Calles.
Res., 10000 Pheasant Rd., 79924. Tel: 915-751-6416; Fax: 915-751-3242.
School—(Grades K-8). Tel: 915-751-2566; Fax: 915-751-2596.
Lay Teachers 25; Students 165.

14—OUR LADY OF ASSUMPTION, Revs. Richard Weiss, Admin.; Michael Rodriguez.
Res., 4800 Byron St., 79930. Tel: 915-566-4040; Fax: 915-566-4049.
School—(Grades PreK-8). Tel: 915-565-3411; Fax: 915-565-3411.
Sisters 2; Lay Teachers 10; Students 138.

15—OUR LADY OF GUADALUPE, Revs. Martin Arriaga; Ricardo Rodriguez, O.F.M.; Jorge Frausto, O.F.M.; Bro. Bernardo Alvarado, O.F.M.
Res., 2709 Alabama St., 79930. Tel: 915-562-4304; Fax: 915-562-3509.
Catechesis/Religious Programs—Fax: 915-566-3307. Mrs. Zenaida Servin, D.R.E.
Students 457.

16—OUR LADY OF THE LIGHT, Rev. Msgr. David G. Fierro.
Res., 4700 Delta Dr., 79905. Tel: 915-532-1757.

17—OUR LADY OF MT. CARMEL, Revs. John Stowe, O.F.M.Conv.; Giles Carie, O.F.M.Conv.; John Curran, O.F.M.Conv.
Res., 131 S. Zaragoza, 79907. Tel: 915-859-9848; Fax: 915-860-9340. [CEM]
School—(Grades K-8) 9101 Socorro Rd., 79907. Tel: 915-859-9812.
Sisters 2; Lay Teachers 10; Students 165.

18—OUR LADY OF SORROWS, Revs. Arturo Gonzalez, O.S.M.; Jorge Palacio, O.S.M.; Andres Ponso, O.S.M.
Res., 7712 Rosedale St., 79915. Tel: 915-772-4834; Fax: 915-772-9078.

19—OUR LADY OF THE VALLEY, Rev. John Rini.
Res., 8600 Winchester, 79907. Tel: 915-859-7939.
School—Tel: 915-859-6448; Fax: 915-859-3908. Sr. Caroline Vasquez, O.S.F., Prin.
Lay Teachers 14; Students 225.

20—QUEEN OF PEACE, Rev. Trinidad Fuentez.
Res., 1551 Belvidere, 79912. Tel: 915-584-5817; Fax: 915-584-7761.
Catechesis/Religious Programs—Pat Fowler, D.R.E. Students 586.

21—SACRED HEART, Revs. Rafael Garcia, S.J.; John Paul, S.J.; Bro. Manuel Cabral, S.J. In res., Revs. Edward Schott, S.J.; Michael Gallagher, S.J.; Antonio Concha, S.J.
Res., 602 S. Oregon St., 79901. Tel: 915-532-5447; Fax: 915-533-0013.

22—ST. FRANCES XAVIER CABRINI PARISH, Rev. Frank Lopez.
Res., 12037 Picasso, 79936. Tel: 915-857-1263.
Church—12200 Vista del Sol, 79936.

23—ST. FRANCIS XAVIER, Revs. Esteban Sescon; Roberto Alvarado; Deacon Luis Montes.
Res., 519 S. Latta St., 79905. Tel: 915-532-2761; Fax: 915-544-5103.

24—ST. IGNATIUS OF LOYOLA, Revs. Jeronimo Melendez, O.S.M.; Franco Tentori, O.S.M.; Francisco DiTomasi, O.S.M.
Res., 408 Park St., 79901. Tel: 915-532-9534; Fax: 915-577-0433.

25—ST. JOSEPH'S, Rev. Joseph Hermoso.
Res., 1315 Travis St., 79903. Tel: 915-566-9396; Fax: 915-566-5606.
School—(Grades K-8) 1300 Lamar, 79903. Tel: 915-566-1661; Fax: 915-566-2006. Bro. Edwin Gallagher, Prin.
Brothers 3; Lay Teachers 25; Students 500.

26—ST. LUKE, Rev. Msgr. John Peters.
Res., 930 E. Redd Rd., 79912. Tel: 915-585-0255.

27—ST. MARK, Rev. Leonides Rivero.
Church—11700 Pebble Hills, 79936. Tel: 915-857-2955; Fax: 915-857-2955.

28—ST. MATTHEW, Revs. Juventino Celino; Oscar Alejandro Reyes.
Res., 400 W. Sunset Rd., 79922. Tel: 915-584-3461; Fax: 915-584-2107.
Catechesis/Religious Programs—D.R.E.: Mrs. Alice Teran; Mrs. Allyn Echaniz.
Students 373.

29—ST. PAUL THE APOSTLE, Rev. Emanuel Alcazar; Deacon Vicente Aguirre.
Res., 7424 Mimosa, 79915. Tel: 915-778-5304.

30—ST. PIUS X, Rev. Msgr. Arturo Banuelas; Deacon Jim Szostek.
Res., 1050 N. Clark Rd., 79905. Tel: 915-772-3226; Fax: 915-771-6665.
School—(Grades PreK-8). Tel: 915-772-6598.
Sisters 4; Lay Teachers 33; Students 532.
Catechesis/Religious Programs—Tel: 915-772-0224; Fax: 915-771-6665.
Students 532.

31—ST. RAPHAEL, Rev. Msgr. Francis J. Smith, P.A.; Revs. Vicente Calderon, Jr.; Paul Garcia; Deacons George Levy; Frank Mares; John Paddenburg; Bernard Rulong. In res., Rev. Rodolfo Lacerna.
Res., 2301 Zanzibar Rd., 79925. Tel: 915-598-3431; 3432; Fax: 915-598-0944.
School—(Grades PreK-8) 2310 Woodside, 79925. Tel: 915-598-2241; Fax: 915-598-3002. Elizabeth Wiehe, Prin.
Lay Teachers 50; Students 595.
Catechesis/Religious Programs—Students 1,047.

32—ST. STEPHEN, DEACON AND MARTYR, Revs. Marcus McFadin; Edward C. Carpenter; Deacon Gus Rodriguez, Sr.
Church—1700 George Dieter, 79936. Tel: 915-855-1661; Fax: 915-857-5800.

33—ST. THOMAS AQUINAS, Rev. James W. Hall.
Church—10970 Bywood, 79936. Tel: 915-592-1313.
Catechesis/Religious Programs—Students 591.

34—STS. PETER AND PAUL, Rev. Saul de Jesus Uribe. In res., Rev. Celimo Osorio.
Res., 673 Old Hueco Tanks Rd., 79927. Tel: 915-859-3758; Fax: 915-858-1501.

35—SAN ANTONIO, Revs. Luis Martin; Santiago Alonso.
Res., 503 Hunter, 79915. Tel: 915-598-1457; Fax: 915-590-1312.

36—SAN JOSE, Rev. Jose Alcocer.
Res., 8100 San Jose Rd., 79907. Tel: 915-598-6285.

37—SAN JUAN BAUTISTA, Rev. Msgr. Carlos Frias.
Res., 5649 Dailey Ave., 79905. Tel: 915-779-1583.

38—SAN JUDAS TADEO, Rev. Msgr. Rafael Miranda; Rev. Lorenzo Lucero.
Res., 4006 Hidden Way, 79922. Tel: 915-584-1095.
Mission—El Paso, El Paso Co., Santa Teresita, 3400 Zapal St., 79922.

39—SANTA LUCIA, Rev. Frank Giusta.
Res., 518 Gallagher St., 79915. Tel: 915-592-5245; Fax: 915-592-5336.

40—SANTO NINO DE ATOCHA, Rev. Joe Molina, Admin. Pro-tem.
Res., 210 S. Clark, 79905. Tel: 915-779-3164; Fax: 915-779-1811.

OUTSIDE THE CITY OF EL PASO

Alpine, Brewster Co., Our Lady of Peace, Revs. Ricardo Ruiz; Anthony Celino.
Res., Box 89, 79831. Tel: 915-837-3304; Fax: 915-837-1752. [CEM]
Mission—Terlingua, Brewster Co., St. Mary, P.O. Box 268, Marathon, 79842.

Balmorhea, Reeves Co., Christ the King. Unassigned.
Res., Rte. 1, Box 3, 79718. Tel: 915-375-2347.
Mission—Saragosa, Our Lady of Guadalupe, Tel: 915-375-2636.

Canutillo, El Paso Co., St. Patrick, Rev. Jose Velasquez.
Res., 7065 Second St., P.O. Box 10, 79835. Tel: 915-877-3997.
Mission—Westway, El Paso Co., Immaculate Heart of Mary, 8701 Joplin Rd., 79835. Tel: 915-886-3539. Rev. Miguel Meneses.

Clint, El Paso Co., San Lorenzo, Rev. Edilberto Lopez.
Res., P.O. Box 215, 79836. Tel: 915-851-2255; Fax: 915-851-5251.

Fabens, El Paso Co., Our Lady of Guadalupe, Rev. Antonio Mena.
Res., P.O. Box 356, 127 W. Main St., 79838. Tel: 915-764-3942. [CEM]
Missions—Cuadrilla, San Jose; Tornillo, Santa Rita; La Isla, San Luis.

Fort Davis, Jeff Davis Co., St. Joseph, Sr. Margie Silguero, M.J.M.J., Pastoral Coord.
Res., P.O. Box 787, 79734. Tel: 915-426-3284. [CEM]

Fort Hancock, Hudspeth Co., Santa Teresa, Sr. Regina Burrichter, R.S.M., Pastoral Coord., Tel: 915-769-3711.
Res., P.O. Box 215, 79839.

Horizon City, Holy Spirit. (Independent Mission). Revs. Ralph Solis, Jr.; Lorenzo Lucero.
Res., 1608 McMahon St., El Paso, 79927. Tel: 915-852-3582.

Kermit, Winkler Co., St. Thomas & St. Joseph, Revs. John Lucido, Admin.; Roberto Alvarado.
Res., 838 Bellaire Rd., 79745. Tel: 915-586-3922.
St. Joseph the Worker. Consolidated with St. Thomas in 1990.

Marfa, Presidio Co., St. Mary's, Sr. Margie Silguero, M.J.M.J., Pastoral Coord.
Res., Box 356, 79843. Tel: 915-729-4694. [CEM]

Monahans, Ward Co., St. John the Apostle and Evangelist, Rev. John Lucido.
Res., 5th & S. Ike St., 79756. Tel: 915-943-5114. [JC]
Mission—Grandfalls, Ward Co., St. Gertrude, P.O. Box 181, Grandfalls, 79742. Tel: 915-547-2484.

Pecos, Reeves Co., St. Catherine, Deacon George Vasquez.
Res., P.O. Box 670, 79772. Tel: 915-447-9231.
Mission—Toyah, St. Emily.

Santa Rosa Church, Revs. Benjamin Flores; Miguel Alcuino; Manuel Munoz.
Res., 620 E. 4th St., Box 686, 79772. Tel: 915-445-2309. [CEM]
Mission—Barstow, Our Lady of Refuge.

Presidio, Presidio Co., Santa Teresa de Jesus, Rev. Lazaro Gonzalez, O.F.M.
Res., P.O. Box 2049, 79845. Tel: 915-229-3235. [CEM]
Missions—Shafter, Sgdo. Corazon de Jesus; Redford, San Jose; Candelaria, Our Lady of Peace; Lajitas, Lajitas Mission.

San Elizario, El Paso Co., San Elceario, Rev. Edward C. Carpenter.
Res., P.O. Box 910, 79849. Tel: 915-851-2333. [JC]
San Felipe de Jesus, Rev. Celimo Osorio.
Res., P.O. Box 1070, 79849. Tel: 915-851-3039.

Van Horn, Culberson Co., Our Lady of Fatima, Rev. Alfred Villanueva.
Res., 308 Almond St., P.O. Box 398, 79855. Tel: 915-283-2042.
Missions—Sierra Blanca, Our Lady of Miracles, P.O. Box 15, Sierra Blanca, 79851.; Dell City, San Isidro; Valentine, Sacred Heart, General Delivery, Valentine, 79854.

Chaplains of Public Institutions

El Paso. *El Paso County Jail*. Vacant.
El Paso Juvenile Detention Center. Vacant.

Anthony. *La Tuna Federal*. Vacant. 7045 Second St., P.O. Box 10, Canutillo, 79835.

On Duty Outside of Diocese:
Reverend Fathers—
Aguilera, Salvador, U.S. Navy, U.S. Naval Academy, Annapolis, MD 21402
Rowland, Thomas, Madonna House, Ontario, Combermere K0J 1L0 Canada

Absent on Leave:
Reverend Fathers—
Kleinworth, Robert
Knopp, John
Madrid, Jaime
Maraya, Felipe
Marin, Miguel
Ramirez, Jose Nieves

Retired:
Reverend Fathers—
Acevedo, Luis H.
Ascherl, Vincent
Bertasius, Anthony
Burkus, John
Cervantes, Fidel
Herrera, Francisco
Lafrenz, James
Lucero, Lorenzo
Perera, Paul
Saez, Jose
Stegman, Leonard F.
Waiwood, Richard

Permanent Deacons:
Aguirre, Vicente G., St. Paul, El Paso
Andrade, Paul, Christ the Saviour, El Paso
Flynn, Ken, St. Patrick's Cathedral, El Paso
Grijalua, Pilar, San Elceario, El Paso
Guerrero, Teofilo, Prison Ministry
Levy, George, St. Raphael, El Paso
Mares, Frank J., St. Raphael, El Paso
Montes, Louis A., St. Francis Xavier, El Paso
Paddenburg, John A., St. Raphael, El Paso
Rodriguez, Gus J., St. Stephen, El Paso
Rulong, Bernard, St. Raphael, El Paso
Schuffer, George M., Jr., William Beaumont Army Medical Center, El Paso
Solis, Ralph, Our Lady of Assumption, El Paso
Szostek, James T., St. Pius X, El Paso
Vasquez, George, St. Catherine, Pecos
Wauson, Thomas J., Christ the Saviour, El Paso

INSTITUTIONS LOCATED IN THE DIOCESE

[A] SEMINARIES, DIOCESAN

El Paso. *St. Charles Seminary College Program*, P.O. Box 17548, 79917. Tel: 915-591-9821; Fax: 915-595-0339. Rev. John Telles. Priests 1; Students 4.

[B] SEMINARIES, RELIGIOUS OR SCHOLASTICATES

El Paso. *Roger Bacon College* (1940), 2400 Marr St., 79903. Tel: 915-565-2921. Minor Seminary of the Franciscan Fathers, Province of the Holy Gospel. Revs. Alberto Hernandez, O.F.M.; Guillermo Ordenes, O.F.M.; Aaron Martinez, O.F.M. Priests 3; Brothers 1.

St. Anthony's School of Theology, Hastings St. and Crescent Dr., 79903. Tel: 915-566-2261. Franciscan Fathers of St. Peter and St. Paul Province, Michoacan, Mexico. Revs. Jaime Yanez, O.F.M.; Jorge Rivas, O.F.M.; Joaquin Acevedo, O.F.M.; Fernando Mendoza, O.F.M.; Santos Perez, O.F.M.; Carlos A. Espinoza, O.F.M.; Alejandro Juarez, O.F.M.; Enrique Munoz, O.F.M.; Maximo Rangel, O.F.M. Priests 9; Scholastics 34; Brothers 4.

[C] HIGH SCHOOLS, DIOCESAN

El Paso. *Cathedral High School*. (Boys), 1309 N. Stanton St., 79902. Tel: 915-532-3238; Fax: 915-533-8248.
E-mail: chsirish@elp.rr.com
Mr. Sam Govea, Prin. Sisters 2; Brothers 5; Lay Teachers 35; Students 625.

[D] HIGH SCHOOLS, PRIVATE

El Paso. *Father Yermo High School*, 250 Washington St., 79905. Tel: 915-533-3185; Fax: 915-544-0738. Servants of the Sacred Heart of Jesus and of the Poor. Sisters 3; Lay Teachers 16; Students 168.

Loretto Academy, 1300 Hardaway, 79903. Tel: 915-564-0211. Sisters of Loretto at the Foot of the Cross. Sisters 8; Lay Teachers 60; Students 851; Priests 1.

[E] ELEMENTARY SCHOOLS, PRIVATE

El Paso. *Father Yermo Elementary School*. (Grades K-8), 237 Tobin Pl., 79905. Tel: 915-533-4693. Servants of the Sacred Heart and of the Poor. Sisters 4; Lay Teachers 12; Students 330.

Loretto Academy Middle School, 1300 Hardaway, 79903. Tel: 915-566-8400, Ext. 30; Fax: 915-564-0563. Sisters of Loretto at the Foot of the Cross. Sr. Patricia Williams, S.L., Prin. Sisters 1; Lay Teachers 6; Students 70.

Loretto Elementary School-Loretto Academy. (Grades PreK-5), 4625 Clifton, 79903. Tel: 915-565-2765. Sisters of Loretto at the Foot of the Cross. Mrs. Karla Onick, Prin. Lay Teachers 16; Students 208.

St. Michael School, 616 S. Virginia, 79901. Tel: 915-542-1253; Fax: 915-532-1121. Servants of the Sacred Heart of Jesus and of the Poor: Father Yermo delegation. Sr. Maria Angelica Omana, S.S.H.J.P. Sisters 4; Lay Teachers 5; Students 80.

[F] CLINICS

El Paso. *Centro San Vicente*, 8061 Alameda, 79915. Tel: 915-859-7545
For a complete listing, refer to the Hospitals section.

La Clinica Guadalupana, Inc., 901 Ascencion, 79927. Tel: 915-852-3328; Fax: 915-852-4246.
E-mail: guadalupana@juno.com
For a complete listing, refer to the Hospitals section.

[G] AGENCIES AND INSTITUTIONS OF THE CHARITIES OF THE DIOCESE

El Paso. *Catholic Emergency Assistance*, 1013 E. San Antonio St., 79901. Tel: 915-532-9532. Sr. Marian Kluesner, F.S.P.A., Dir.

[H] DAY CARE CENTERS

El Paso. *St. Joseph of the Valley*, 7681 Barton, 79915. Tel: 915-778-3407. Sisters 3; Lay Teachers 10; Students 150.

[I] HOMES FOR AGED

El Paso. *El Paso Diocese Home for the Aged*, 920 S. Oregon St., 79901. Tel: 915-533-5152
For a complete listing, refer to the Special Care Facilities section.

Nazareth Hall, 4614 Trowbridge, 79903. Tel: 915-565-4677; Fax: 915-566-7530
For a complete listing, refer to the Special Care Facilities section.

[J] MONASTERIES & RESIDENCES FOR PRIESTS & BROTHERS

El Paso. *Christian Brothers*, 1204 N. Mesa, 79902-4012. Tel: 915-532-9314.
E-mail: brothernick@juno.com

[K] CONVENTS AND RESIDENCES FOR WOMEN

El Paso. *Adorers of the Blood of Christ (A.S.C.)*, 2209 Pittsburg, 79930. Tel: 915-566-5855. Sr. Darlene Stoecklein, A.S.C., Contact Person. Sisters 3.

Adrian Dominican Sisters (O.P.), 1011 E. Nevada, 79902. Tel: 915-533-4744. Sr. Donna Kustusch, O.P., Contact Person; Sr. Eleanor Stech, O.P., Contact Person. Sisters 3.

Association of Mary Immaculate (A.I.M.), 3900 La Luz St., 79903. Tel: 915-566-0447. Sr. Sue Castaneda, A.I.M., Contact Person.

Daughters of Charity of St. Vincent De Paul (D.C.), 1020 N. Campbell St., 79902. Tel: 915-533-9013; Fax: 915-859-9862. Sisters 5.

Franciscan Sisters of Our Lady of Perpetual Help (O.S.F.), Blessed Sacrament Convent, 9005 Diana Dr., 79904. Tel: 915-755-4871. Sr. M. Jeanette Danielewicz, O.S.F. Sisters 2.

Hermanas Contemplativas del Buen Pastor (H.B.P.). (Cloistered), Good Shepherd Convent, 8824 Old County Rd., P.O. Box 17254, 79917. Tel: 915-859-3683. Sr. Ernestina Estrada, Supr. Sisters 11.

Hermanas del Servicio Social, 6372 Saint Lo Dr., 79925-1807. Tel: 915-771-0780; Fax: 915-771-0780. Sr. Carmen Aurora Gomez.

Hermanas Dominicas de la Doctrinia Cristiana (O.P.), San Alberto Magno Convent, P.O. Box 17391, 79917. Tel: 915-590-3107; Fax: 915-590-6169. Sr. Celia Gonzalez, Provincial Supr.; Sr. Guadalupe Garcia, O.P., Local Supr. Sisters 22.

Missionary Sisters of Jesus, Mary & Joseph (M.J.M.J.), 7681 Barton Dr., 79915. Tel: 915-778-3407. Sr. Gloria Rodriquez, Supr. Sisters 6.

North American Union Sisters of Our Lady of Charity, 415 N. Glenwood Dr., 79905. Tel: 915-772-0737; Fax: 915-779-2664. Sr. Yolanda Martinez, Supr. Sisters 12.

San Juan Day Care Center, 5636 Frutas St., 79905. Tel: 915-772-1681. Sr. Cruz Celia Gomez, Admin.

School Sisters of St. Francis (O.S.F.), 124 Bauxite, 79932. Tel: 915-581-2776; Fax: 915-581-5662.
E-mail: romel3@juno.com
Sr. Imelda Kaufman, Contact Person; Sr. Bernadette Halbur, Contact Person. Tel: 915-778-7016; Sr. Maureen Jerkowski. Tel: 915-546-4042. Sisters 3.

Servants of the Sacred Heart of Jesus and of the Poor (S.S.H.J.P.), Father Yermo Convent, 237 Tobin Pl., 79905. Tel: 915-533-3338. Sr. Angelica Omana, S.S.H.J.P., Supr. Sisters 12.

Queen of Peace Convent, 3119 Pera Ave., 79905. Tel: 915-533-0590. Sr. Gloria Margarita Rodriguez, Supr. Sisters 10.

Sisters of Loretto at the Foot of the Cross (S.L.), El Convento de Loretto, 1400 Hardaway St., 79903. Tel: 915-566-1628; Fax: 915-566-5127.
E-mail: elconvento@juno.com
M. Judith Flood, Facilities Mgr. Sisters 11.

Sisters of Our Lady of Charity of the Good Shepherd (R.G.S.), Good Shepherd Convent, 8824 Old County Rd., P.O. Box 17635, 79917. Tel: 915-859-6004. Sr. Ma. Emanuel Galvan, Supr. Sisters 10.

Sisters of Perpetual Adoration (A.P.). (Cloistered), Corpus Christi Monastery, 451 Mockingbird Ln., 79907. Tel: 915-591-5662; Fax: 915-598-6203. E-mail: ccmonast@aol.com
Mother Maria Sagrario Perez, A.P., Supr. Sisters 15; Novices 1.

Cristo Rey Monastery of Perpetual Adoration, 145 Cotton St., 79901. Tel: 915-533-5323. Mother Maria de Jesus Armendariz, A.P., Supr. Sisters 17; Novices 2.

Sisters of St. Joseph of Carondelet (C.S.J.), 2200 Hubbert Pl., 79903. Tel: 915-566-7635. Sr. Jacqueline Lawson, C.S.J.; Sr. J. Sue Smith, C.S.J. Sisters 2.

MARFA. *Missionary Sisters of Jesus, Mary & Joseph,* P.O. Box 1118, 79843. Tel: 915-729-3385. Sisters 2.

PRESIDIO. *Sisters of the Most Precious Blood of O'Fallen, Missouri,* P.O. Box 893, 79845. Tel: 915-229-3409 (Residence) 915-229-4246 (Office).
E-mail: calo@brooksdata.net

SIERRA BLANCA. *School Sisters of St. Francis, (S.S.S.F.),* P.O. Box 303, 79851. Tel: 915-369-2062; 369-2651.

[L] RESIDENCES FOR WOMEN

EL PASO. *Queen of Angels Residence for College Girls and Business Women,* 119 W. Nevada Ave., 79902. Tel: 915-533-3173; Fax: 915-541-1123. Sr. Grace I. Vargas, R.J.M., Supr. Residence for Ladies conducted by the Religious of Jesus and Mary. Sisters 13; Residents 21.

[M] NEWMAN CENTERS

EL PASO. *University of Texas at El Paso Catholic Campus Ministry,* Archbishop Oscar Romero Center, 400 E. Robinson, 79902-2619. Tel: 915-544-3883.

ALPINE. *Sul Ross State University Newman Center,* P.O. Box C 78, 79832. Tel: 915-837-2905; Fax: 915-837-8714.
E-mail: plister@sulross.edu
Dr. Paul Lister.

[N] MISCELLANEOUS LISTINGS

EL PASO. *Annunciation House,* 1003 E. San Antonio, 79901. Tel: 915-545-4509. Mr. Ruben Garcia, Dir.

Casa Vides. (Shelter for Refugees), 325 Leon St., 79901. Mr. Ruben Garcia, Dir.

Catholic Counseling Services, Inc., 499 St. Matthews St., 79907. Tel: 915-872-8496. Mr. Jose Castrellon, Exec. Dir.

The Catholic Diocese of El Paso Foundation, 499 St. Matthews, 79907. Mr. Gilber Morales.

Catholic Legal Immigration Network, Inc. (CLINIC). Subsidiary of the NCCB/USCC Southwest Regional Office. 1205 N. Oregon, 79902. Tel: 915-533-3971; Fax: 915-533-3974.
E-mail: clinictx@aol.com
Lily Gutierrez, S.W. Reg. Clinic Coord. Services: National immigration support network to the Catholic Dioceses throughout the U.S. Southwest regional CLINIC office provides technical assistance, basic organizational program services, management assessments, and immigration law training for its diocesan affiliates. CLINIC assists dioceses in applying for agency recognition and staff accreditation before the Immigration Board of Appeals. CLINIC assists dioceses and religious congregations in obtaining legal status for foreign clergy as non-immigrant and legal permanent residents.

Catholic Properties of El Paso, Inc., 499 St. Matthews St., 79907. Mr. Jorge Vergen, Exec. Dir.

Christ Child Society, 432 DeLeon, 79912. Tel: 915-584-0153.

Diocesan Migrant and Refugee Services, 1117 N. Stanton, 79902. Tel: 915-532-3975; 3976; Fax: 915-532-4071.
E-mail: dmrs@whe.net

Diocese of El Paso Catholic Scholarship Trust, 499 St. Matthews St., 79907. Tel: 915-595-5007; Fax: 915-595-5095.

Diocese of El Paso Charity Trust, 499 St. Matthews St., 79907. Tel: 915-595-5007; Fax: 915-595-5095.

Diocese of El Paso Clergy Continuing Education Trust, 499 St. Matthews St., 79907.

Diocese of El Paso Historic Missions Restoration Trust, 499 St. Matthews St., 79907.

Diocese of El Paso Insurance Trust, 499 St. Matthews St., 79907.

Diocese of El Paso Investment Trust, 499 St. Matthews St., 79907.

Diocese of El Paso Seminarian Education Trust, 499 St. Matthews St., 79907.

Historic Missions Restoration, Inc., 499 St. Matthews St., 79907.

La Posada Home, 248 Francis St., 79905-4416. Tel: 915-544-4595. Shelter for Displaced Women. Sisters 3.

Mount Carmel Cemetery Perpetual Care Trust, 499 St. Matthews St., 79907. Tel: 915-595-5007; Fax: 915-595-5095.

Our Lady's Youth Center, 501 E. Paisano, P.O. Box 1422, 79948. Tel: 915-533-5260; 533-9122; Fax: 505-233-3725.
E-mail: ourlady@cs.com
Rev. Richard M. Thomas, S.J., Dir. The Lord's Ranch & The Lord's Food Bank.

Progress for the Diocese of El Paso, 499 St. Matthews St., 79907. Tel: 915-872-8415; Fax: 915-872-8411.
E-mail: gmorales@whc.net
Mr. Gilberto Morales, Exec. Dir.

Zaragosa, Texas Catholic Relief Trust, 499 St. Matthews St., 79907. Tel: 915-595-5007; Fax: 915-595-5095.

RELIGIOUS INSTITUTES OF MEN REPRESENTED IN THE DIOCESE

For further details refer to the bracketed number in the Religious Institutes of Men or Women section.

[0330]—*Brothers of the Christian Schools.* (New Orleans and Santa Fe Provs.).—F.S.C.
[0460]—*Brothers of the Poor of St. Francis.*—C.F.P.
[0480]—*Conventual Franciscan Friars.* (Custody of Our Lady of Guadalupe).—O.F.M.Conv.
[0520]—*Franciscan Friars.* (Holy Gospel Prov. and St. Peter & Paul Prov.).—O.F.M.
[0690]—*Jesuit Fathers and Brothers.* (Prov. of New Orleans).—S.J.
[0150]—*Order of the Augustinian Recollects.* (Prov. of San Nicolas of Tolentino, Italy).—O.A.R.
[1240]—*Servites.* (Province of Mexico).—O.S.M.

RELIGIOUS INSTITUTES OF WOMEN REPRESENTED IN THE DIOCESE

[0100]—*Adorers of the Blood of Christ.*—A.S.C.
[]—*Association of Mary Immaculate.*—A.I.M.
[1010]—*Congregation of Divine Providence of San Antonio, Texas.*—C.D.P.
[1780]—*Congregation of the Sisters of the Third Order of St. Francis of Perpetual Adoration.* (Central Region).—F.S.P.A.
[0760]—*Daughters of Charity of St. Vincent de Paul.*—D.C.
[1070-13]—*Dominican Sisters.*—O.P.
[1070-14]—*Dominican Sisters.*—O.P.
[1430]—*Franciscan Sisters of Our Lady of Perpetual Help.*—O.S.F.
[]—*Franciscan Sisters of the Sorrowful Mother.*—F.S.S.M.
[]—*Hermanas Contemplativas del Buen Pastor.*—H.B.S.
[]—*Hermanas del Buen Pastor.*—S.G.S.
[]—*Hermanas del Servico Social.*—H.S.S.
[]—*Hermanas Dominicanas de la Doctrina Cristiana.*—O.P.
[2770]—*Missionaries of Jesus, Mary and Joseph.*—M.J.M.J.
[3070]—*North American Union of the Sisters of Our Lady of Charity.*—N.A.U.-O.L.C.
[3190]—*Nuns of the Perpetual Adoration of the Blessed Sacrament.*—A.P.
[3450]—*Religious of Jesus and Mary.*—R.J.M.
[1680]—*School Sisters of St. Francis.*—S.S.S.F.
[3660]—*Servants of the Sacred Heart of Jesus and of the Poor.*—S.S.H.J.P.
[2360]—*Sisters of Loretto at the Foot of the Cross.*—S.L.
[4090]—*Sisters of Social Services.*—S.S.S.
[3830-15]—*Sisters of St. Joseph.*—C.S.J.
[3840]—*Sisters of St. Joseph of Carondelet.* (Prov. of St. Paul).—C.S.J.
[1830]—*The Sisters of the Good Shepherd.* (St. Louis Province).—R.G.S.
[3270]—*Sisters of the Most Precious Blood (O'Fallon, MO).*—C.PP.S.
[4100]—*Sisters of the Sorrowful Mother (Third Order of St. Francis).*—S.S.M.

DIOCESAN CEMETERY

EL PASO. *Mount Carmel,* Box 17655, 79917. Tel: 915-860-0605.

NECROLOGY

† Camacho, Gilbert, (Retired). —Died 2000.

Diocese of Erie

(Dioecesis Eriensis)

Most Reverend

DONALD W. TRAUTMAN, S.T.D., S.S.L.

Bishop of Erie; ordained April 7, 1962; appointed Titular Bishop of Sassura and Auxiliary Bishop of Buffalo February 27, 1985; consecrated April 16, 1985; appointed to Erie June 12, 1990; installed July 16, 1990. *Res., 205 West 9th St., Erie, PA, 16501.* Tel.: 814-824-1120; Fax: 814-824-1124.

Most Reverend

MICHAEL J. MURPHY, D.D., S.T.L.

Retired Bishop of Erie; ordained February 28, 1942; appointed Titular Bishop of Arindela and Auxiliary Bishop of Cleveland April 20, 1976; consecrated June 11, 1976; appointed Coadjutor Bishop of Erie November 28, 1978; succeeded to See July 16, 1982; retired July 16, 1990. *Mailing Address: St. Patrick/St. Hedwig Parish Cluster, 130 East 4th St., Erie, PA, 16507.* Tel.: 814-454-8085.

Chancery: St. Mark Catholic Center, P.O. Box 10397, Erie, PA, 16514. Tel.: 814-824-1111; Fax: 814-824-1128.

Web site address: www.eriercd.org

ESTABLISHED 1853.

Square Miles 9,936.

Comprises the following Counties in Northwestern Pennsylvania: Erie, Crawford, Mercer, Venango, Forest, Clarion, Jefferson, Clearfield, Cameron, Elk, McKean, Potter and Warren.

For legal titles of parishes and diocesan institutions, consult the Chancery.

STATISTICAL OVERVIEW

Personnel	
Bishop	1
Retired Bishops	1
Priests: Diocesan Active in Diocese	164
Priests: Active Outside Diocese	10
Priests: Retired, Sick or Absent	64
Number of Diocesan Priests	238
Religious Priests in Diocese	14
Extern Priests in Diocese	5
Ordinations:	
Diocesan Priests	1
Transitional Deacons	3
Permanent Deacons in Diocese	16
Total Brothers	2
Total Sisters	479
Parishes	
Parishes	127
With Resident Pastor:	
Resident Diocesan Priests	103
Resident Religious Priests	7
Without Resident Pastor:	
Administered by Priests	17
Missions	20
Pastoral Centers	1
Professional Ministry Personnel:	
Sisters	12
Lay Ministers	16
Welfare	
Catholic Hospitals	1
Total Assisted	60,000
Homes for the Aged	4
Total Assisted	731
Day Care and Extended Day Care Centers	2
Total Assisted	209
Specialized Homes	2
Total Assisted	329
Special Centers for Social Services	9
Total Assisted	103,204
Other Institutions	1
Total Assisted	1,018
Educational	
Seminaries, Diocesan	1
Students from This Diocese	16
Diocesan Students in Other Seminaries	11
Total Seminarians	27
Colleges and Universities	2
Total Students	6,290
High Schools, Diocesan and Parish	5
Total Students	1,837
High Schools, Private	2
Total Students	1,281
Elementary Schools, Diocesan and Parish	41
Total Students	9,669
Elementary Schools, Private	1
Total Students	393
Catechesis/Religious Education:	
High School Students	6,827
Elementary Students	11,942
Total Students Under Catholic Instruction	38,266
Teachers in the Diocese:	
Priests	24
Sisters	28
Lay Teachers	784
Vital Statistics	
Receptions into the Church:	
Infant Baptism Totals	2,188
Adult Baptism Totals	286
Received into Full Communion	305
First Communions	3,023
Confirmations	2,616
Marriages:	
Catholic	643
Interfaith	468
Total Marriages	1,111
Deaths	2,699
Total Catholic Population	230,016
Total Population	867,197

Former Bishops—Most Rev. MICHAEL O'CONNOR, cons. Bishop of Pittsburgh, Aug. 15, 1843; transferred from Pittsburgh as first Bishop of Erie in 1853; transferred back to Pittsburgh in 1854; died Oct. 18, 1872.—Most Rev. JOSUE M. YOUNG, cons. April 23, 1854; died Sept. 18, 1866.—Most Rev. TOBIAS MULLEN, D.D., cons. Aug. 2, 1868, Bishop of Erie; resigned Aug. 10, 1899, and appt. to Titular See of Germanicopolis; died April 22, 1900.—Most Rev. JOHN E. FITZMAURICE, D.D., cons. Feb. 24, 1898; died June 18, 1920.—Most Rev. EDWARD P. MCMANAMAN, S.T.D., Titular Bishop of Floriana and Auxiliary Bishop of Erie; cons. Oct. 28, 1948; died July 18, 1964.—Most Rev. JOHN MARK GANNON, D.D., Archbishop-Bishop of Erie; ord. Dec. 21, 1901; appt. Titular Bishop of Nilopolis, Nov. 13, 1917; cons. Feb. 6, 1918; transferred to Erie, Aug. 26, 1920; installed Dec. 16, 1920; appt. Assistant at the Pontifical Throne Nov. 4, 1944; appt. Archbishop "ad personam" Nov. 25, 1953; resigned Sept. 21, 1966 and transferred to Titular See of Tacarata, Dec. 14, 1966; died Sept. 5, 1968.—Most Rev. JOHN F. WHEALON, D.D., appt. Titular Bishop of Andrapa and Auxiliary Bishop of Cleveland, June 2, 1961; cons. July 6, 1961; transferred to the See of Erie, Dec. 14, 1966; transferred to the Archdiocese of Hartford; died Aug. 2, 1991.—Most Rev. ALFRED M. WATSON, D.D., Bishop of Erie; ord. May 10, 1934; Titular Bishop of Nationa and Auxiliary Bishop of Erie; appt. May 17, 1965; cons. June 29, 1965; succeeded to See, March 19, 1969; retired July 16, 1982; died Jan. 4, 1990.—Most Rev. MICHAEL J. MURPHY, D.D., S.T.L., Titular Bishop of Arindela and Auxiliary Bishop of Cleveland; appt. April 20, 1976; cons. June 11, 1976; Coadjutor Bishop of Erie; appt. Nov. 28, 1978; succeeded to See, July 16, 1982; retired July 16, 1990.

Vicar General—Rev. Msgr. ROBERT J. SMITH, J.C.L., *St. Mark Catholic Center, P.O. Box 10397, Erie, 16514.* Tel: 814-824-1130.

Office of the Bishop—ROBERTA MUELLER, Sec. to the Bishop, *St. Mark Catholic Center, P.O. Box 10397, Erie, 16514.* Tel: 814-824-1120.

Chancery—*St. Mark Catholic Center, P.O. Box 10397, Erie, 16514.* Tel: 814-824-1135; Fax: 814-824-1124.

Chancellor—Rev. Msgr. LAWRENCE E. BRANDT, J.C.D., Ph.D.

Vice Chancellor—Rev. Msgr. MICHAEL T. GAINES.

Diocesan Archivist and Historian—Rev. ROBERT G. BARCIO, Ph.D.,All Diocesan Offices and Personnel listed in Directory can be reached at: *St. Mark Catholic Center, 429 E. Grandview Blvd., P.O. Box 10397, Erie, 16514-0397.* Tel: 814-824-1111. unless otherwise indicated.

Episcopal Vicars—

Northern Vicariate—Rev. Msgr. ROBERT J. SMITH, J.C.L., *St. Mark Catholic Center, P.O. Box 10397, Erie, 16514.* Tel: 814-824-1130.

Eastern Vicariate—Rev. Msgr. CHARLES A. KAZA, *1100 Hewett St., Brockway, 15824.* Tel: 814-265-1374.

Western Vicariate—Rev. Msgr. MICHAEL T. GAINES, *967 Chancery Ln., Meadville, 16335.* Tel: 814-333-6382.

Vicar for Religious—Sr. MARY RITA KUHN, S.S.J., *St. Mark Catholic Center, P.O. Box 10397, Erie, 16514-0397.* Tel: 814-824-1125.

Director of Planning—WALTER SPILLER, *St. Mark Catholic Center, P.O. Box 10397, Erie, 16514-0397.* Tel: 814-824-1116.

Mission Office and Society for the Propagation of the Faith—Sr. THERESA ZOKY, O.S.B., *St. Mark Catholic Center, P.O. Box 10397, Erie, 16514-0397.* Tel: 814-824-1230.

Advisory To Bishop

Administrative Cabinet—Rev. Msgr. ROBERT J. SMITH, J.C.L., V.G.; Rev. Msgr. CHARLES A. KAZA; Sr. MARY RITA KUHN, S.S.J.; Rev. Msgr. ANDREW H. KARG; Rev. Msgr. LAWRENCE E. BRANDT, J.C.D., Ph.D.; Rev. Msgr. MICHAEL D. MCGRAW, L.S.W., M.Ss.A.; Rev. Msgr. CONRAD KRAUS; DAVID MURPHY; Rev. Msgr. MICHAEL T. GAINES. Special Consultants: WALTER SPILLER; GARY LONCKI.

Consultors—Rev. Msgr. WILLIAM C. KARG; Rev. Msgr. ROBERT L. BRUGGER; Rev. Msgr. HENRY A. KRIEGEL; Rev. Msgr. ROBERT W. COHAN, V.F.; Rev. Msgr. LOUIS J. HEBERLEIN; Rev. Msgr. ROBERT J. SMITH, J.C.L.

Finance Council—Most Rev. DONALD W. TRAUTMAN; Rev. Msgr. RICHARD E. BUTRYN; THOMAS GUELCHER; HAROLD LANZEL; PATRICIA LIEBEL; JAMES F. TOOHEY, Esq.; Sr. CATHERINE MANNING, S.S.J.; PETER J. BUCHEIT; Rev. Msgr. ROBERT L. BRUGGER; Rev. Msgr. CHARLES A. KAZA. Ex Officios: Rev. Msgr. ROBERT J. SMITH, J.C.L.; DAVID MURPHY.

Deans—Rev. Msgr. ROBERT W. COHAN, V.F., Erie East; Rev. Msgr. WILLIAM E. BIEBEL, V.F., Erie West; Very Rev. JOSEPH C. GREGOREK, V.F., Gannon University; Rev. Msgr. EDWARD J. ZEITLER, V.F., Sharon; Very Rev. JOHN W. SWOGER, V.F., Oil City; Very Rev. THEODORE B. MARCONI, V.F., Bradford; Rev. Msgr. H. DESMOND MCGEE, V.F., Clearfield; Rev. Msgr. RICHARD E. BUTRYN, V.F., Meadville; Very Rev. JOSEPH P. STASZEWSKI, Dubois; Rev. Msgr. JOSEPH K. BOBAL, V.F., St. Marys; Rev. Msgr. JOHN J. LUCAS, Warren.

Presbyteral Council—Most Rev. DONALD W. TRAUTMAN, Pres.; Rev. Msgr. RICHARD J. SULLIVAN, Chm.; Rev. PHILLIP A. PINCZEWSKI, Sec.

Priest Personnel Board—Very Rev. MICHAEL GAINES, Chm.; Very Rev. JEFFERY NOBLE, Vice Chm.; Rev. CHRISTOPHER MERRY, Sec.

Priest Retirement Board—Most Rev. DONALD W. TRAUTMAN, Chm. Members: WILLIAM BOLASH; Sr. JEAN BAPTISTE DILUZIO, S.S.J.; JAMES HOLLAND; Rev. Msgr. JOHN J. SLATER; JAMES TOOHEY, Attorney. Ex Officio: Rev. Msgr. LAWRENCE E. BRANDT; Rev. Msgr. RICHARD J. SULLIVAN. Staff: DAVID J. MURPHY; Rev. Msgr. ROBERT L. BRUGGER.

Pennsylvania Catholic Conference—Rev. Msgr. LAWRENCE E. BRANDT, J.C.D., Ph.D., Personal Rep. of the Bishop, *St. Mark Catholic Center, P.O. Box 10397, Erie, 16514.*

The Bishop's Theological Advisory Committee—Rev. Msgr. GERALD L. ORBANEK, M.A., Chm.; Revs. JOHN P. SCHANZ, Ph.D.; EDWARD KRAUSE, Ph.D.; CASIMIR J. WOZNIAK, Ph.D.; RICHARD J. SULLIVAN, M.A.; SCOTT P. DETISCH, Ph.D.; Mr. PATRICK O'CONNELL, Ph.D.; Sr. MICHELLE HEALY, S.S.J., M.A.

Lake Shore Visitor Advisory Board—Most Rev. DONALD W. TRAUTMAN; GINA ADAMS; GARY LONCKI, Editor; Rev. Msgr. WILLIAM E. BIEBEL; Rev. Msgr. GERALD L. ORBANEK; Rev. EDWARD KRAUSE, C.S.C.; PAUL CORBRAN; JAMES BOGNIAK; DAVID SLOMSKI; Rev. Msgr. LAWRENCE BRANDT, Chancellor; Sr. MARY LOUIS EICHENLAUB, O.S.B.; TOM BRENNAN; KEVIN EGAN, Advertising.

Matrimonial Concerns

All requests for marriage dispensations, permissions, and rogatory commissions should be sent to this office

Diocesan Tribunal—*St. Mark Catholic Center, P.O. Box 10397, Erie, 16514.* Tel: 814-824-1140; Fax: 814-824-1128.

Bishop's Delegate for Dispensations—Rev. GEORGE L. GROUCUTT.

Judicial Vicar—Rev. MARK L. BARTCHAK, J.C.D.

Promoter of Justice—Rev. Msgr. LAWRENCE E. BRANDT, J.C.D., Ph.D.

Defenders of the Bond—Rev. Msgr. LAWRENCE E. BRANDT, J.C.D., Ph.D.; Rev. GREGORY A. KIRSCH, J.C.L.

Matrimonial Judges—Rev. Msgr. ROBERT J. SMITH, J.C.L.; Rev. Msgr. RICHARD J. STACK, J.C.L.; Revs. MARK L. BARTCHAK, J.C.D.; JOHN P. BEAL, J.C.D.; Deacon RICHARD D. SHEWMAN, J.C.L.; BARBARA A. BETTWY, J.C.L.

Auditors—Rev. SCOTT E. KATREN; Sr. REBECCA ANN COSTA, S.S.J.; Sr. JEAN BAPTISTE DILUZIO, S.S.J.

Secretary/Notary—CAROL GRYGIER; CINDY MANGIARACINA.

Office of Conciliation & Arbitration—*St. Mark Catholic Center, P.O. Box 10397, Erie, 16514.* Tel: 814-824-1140. Rev. MARK L. BARTCHAK, J.C.D., Dir.

Catholic Education

Episcopal Vicar for Catholic Education—Rev. JOHN M. SCHULTZ, *St. Mark Catholic Center, P.O. Box 10397, Erie, 16514-0397.*

Superintendent for Catholic Schools—Sr. MARY ARNOLD TANN, S.S.J., *St. Mark Catholic Center, P.O. Box 10397, Erie, 16514-0397.*

Secondary Schools—

Directors—CHARLES BANDUCCI, School Finance; JANICE WHITEMAN, Curriculum; ROBERTA BUCCI, Dir. Govt. Programs; Sr. MARY ANN BADER, R.S.M., Teacher Personnel; NED SMITH, Technology & Community Rels. Coord. J. WILLIAM JONES, Coord. Athletic Programs, *St. Mark Catholic Center, P.O. Box 10397, Erie, 16514-0397.*

Youth Athletic Director—J. WILLIAM JONES, *St. Mark's Catholic Center, P.O. Box 10397, Erie, 16514-0397.* Tel: 814-824-1213.

Religious Education—Mr. JOSEPH STREETT, Dir. Religious Education, Curriculum & Catechist Formation; Sr. NANCY FISCHER, S.S.J., Dir. Community Formation & Ministry Training; GREGORY SCHLUETER, Dir. Youth Ministry Heart & Soul Program: JODY DAY, Coord., *St. Mark Catholic Center, P.O. Box 10397, Erie, 16514-0397.* KAREN STREETT, Media Resource Coord. Mktg., *St. Mark Catholic Center, P.O. Box 10397, Erie, 16514-0397.*

Campus Ministry—Sr. LYNETTE PETRUSKA, S.S.J., Campus Ministry Dir., *Gannon University, University Sq., Erie, 16541.* Tel: 814-871-7435. Sr. MARY DREXLER, S.S.J., *Penn State Erie, The Behrend College, Station Rd., Erie, 16563.* Tel: 814-898-6245. See separate listing in the Institution section for details on Campus Ministry and Newman Centers.

Catholic Charities
Affiliated Offices, Agencies and Institutions
Central Administration

Office of Catholic Charities—Rev. Msgr. MICHAEL D. MCGRAW, M.SS.A., L.S.W., Exec. Dir., *St. Mark Catholic Center, P.O. Box 10397, Erie, 16514-0397.*

Catholic Charities of the Diocese of Erie, Inc.—Rev. Msgr. MICHAEL D. MCGRAW, M.SS.A., L.S.W., Exec. Dir., *St. Mark Catholic Center, P.O. Box 10397, Erie, 16514-0397.* Charities program and fiscal development corporation.

Development and Grantwriting—BRADLEY J. FAIRFIELD, Dir., *St. Mark Catholic Center, P.O. Box 10397, Erie, 16514-0397.* Rev. MICHAEL G. BARLETTA, Devel. Assoc., *St. Mark Catholic Center, P.O. Box 10397, Erie, 16514-0397.*

Pastoral Social Services

Family Ministries—MARY MAXWELL, M.A., Dir., *St. Mark Catholic Center, P.O. Box 10397, Erie, 16514-0397.* Office includes Marriage Preparation and Enrichment Programs, Divorced Ministry, Retrouvaille, Parenting and Rainbows.

Respect Life/Justice and Peace—Sr. MARY FROMKNECHT, S.S.J., M.A., *St. Mark Catholic Center, P.O. Box 10397, Erie, 16514-0397.* Office includes advocacy, parish-based social justice education programs and respect life efforts.

Parish Social Ministry—JEAN KECK, M.S., *St. Mark Catholic Center, P.O. Box 10397, Erie, 16514-0397.* Consultant for Parish Care and Concern model and training program for volunteers.

Natural Family Planning—Diocesan Coords.: EDWARD BURKETT; BARBARA BURKETT, *St. Mark Catholic Center, P.O. Box 10397, Erie, 16514-0397.* Natural Family Planning training and education.

Spiritual Ministry to Persons with Disabilites—JACKLYN JOHNSON, R.N., Dir. Ministry is spiritual in natural and focuses on spiritual enrichment and inclusion of persons with disabilities into the life of the parish.

Community Counseling Services

Catholic Charities Counseling and Adoption Services—ROBERT F. MCCRAREY, A.C.S.W., L.S.W., Agency Dir. ROSEMARIE RADOMSKI, M.A., M.S., Clinical Dir.

Northern Vicariate - Erie Office—*329 W. Tenth St., Erie, 16502.* Tel: 814-456-2091., Satellite Office - Warren: *213 W. Third Ave., Office 105, Warren, 16365.* Tel: 814-726-9799.

Western Vicariate - Sharon Office—SUE BURKE, L.S.W., Regl. Supvr., *786 E. State St., Sharon, 16146.* Tel: 412-346-4142., Satellite Office - Meadville: *967 Chancery Ln., Meadville, 16335.* Tel: 814-337-5551.

Eastern Vicariate - DuBois Office—NANCI MATTISON, M.A., Area Supvr., *90 Beaver Dr., DuBois, 15801.*

Residential Services for Older Persons

John XXIII Home—KIRK HAWTHORNE, Admin., *2250 Shenango Fwy., Hermitage, 16148.* Tel: 814-981-3200.

Christ the King Manor—Rev. Msgr. JOHN W. MIGNOT, Admin., *1100 W. Long Ave., Du Bois, 15801.* Tel: 814-371-3180.

Community Social Services

[*] St. Martin Center—CHERYL WEBER, M.A., Dir., *1701 Parade St., Erie, 16503.* Tel: 814-452-6113.

Harborcreek Youth Services—GRACE A. MCCLELLAND, M.A., *5712 Iroquois Ave., Harborcreek, 16421.* Tel: 814-899-7664.

Prince of Peace Center—Sr. CLARE MARIE BEICHNER, S.S.J., L.S.W., Dir., *502 Darr Ave., Box 89, Farrell, 16121.* Tel: 412-346-5777.

Better Housing for Erie, c/o H.A.N.D.S.—CHARLES G. SCALISE, Dir., *139 E. 12th St., Erie, 16501.* Tel: 814-459-1047.

Good Samaritan Center—Rev. JAMES C. MCKEE, S.J., M.A., Dir., *Clearfield.* Tel: 814-236-1896; 768-7229.

Rainbows-Services to Children of Separation/Divorce—ROSE JONES, M.A., Dir., *St. Mark Catholic Center, P.O. Box 10397, Erie, 16514-0397.*

Other Charitable/Social Agencies and Institutions

Gannondale Residential Center for Girls—LOUIS J. GRANDE, A.C.S.W., Exec. Dir., *4635 E. Lake Rd., Erie, 16511.* Tel: 814-899-7659.

St. Mary's Home—Sr. ANASTASIA VALIMONT, S.S.J., Admin., *607 E. 26th St., Erie, 16504.* Tel: 814-459-0621.

Mercy Center For Women—CHRISTINE TOMBAUGH, Dir., *1039 E. 27th St., Erie, 16507.* Tel: 814-455-4577.

Young People Who Care—Sr. THERESE DUSH, C.A., Dir., *Frenchville, 16836.* Tel: 814-263-4177.

Maria House Projects—Rev. Msgr. JAMES PETERSON, Dir., *P.O. Box 10682, Erie, 16514.* Tel: 814-454-0891.

Emmaus Ministries—Sr. MARY MILLER, O.S.B., Dir., *218 E. 11th St., Erie, 16501.* Tel: 814-459-8754.

St. Patrick Haven—Sr. MARY EILEEN MOYER, S.S.J., Dir., *147 E. 12th St., Erie, 16501.* Tel: 814-454-7219.

Parish Services

Liturgy & Worship—Rev. Msgr. CONRAD KRAUS, Dir. MATTHEW CLARK, Assoc. Dir., *St. Mark Catholic Center, P.O. Box 10397, Erie, 16514-0397.*

Community Formation—Sr. NANCY FISCHER, S.S.J., Dir., *St. Mark Catholic Center, P.O. Box 10397, Erie, 16514-0397.*

Lay Ministry Training—Sr. NANCY FISCHER, S.S.J., Dir. JOSEPH STREETT, *St. Mark Catholic Center, P.O. Box 10397, Erie, 16514-0397.*

Rite of Christian Initiation for Adults—Rev. GERARD H. KREBS, *St. Mark Catholic Center, P.O. Box 10397, Erie, 16514-0397.* Tel: 814-824-1272.

Finance and Development

Chief Financial Officer—DAVID J. MURPHY, *St. Mark Catholic Center, P.O. Box 10397, Erie, 16514-0397.*

Finance Office—DAVID J. MURPHY, Dir. JAMES L. BOGNIAK, Mgr., Accounting & Budgeting; THOMAS E. BURIK, C.P.A., Mgr., Parish Financial Services, *St. Mark Catholic Center, P.O. Box 10397, Erie, 16514-0397.* Tel: 814-824-1180.

Development Office—JOSEPH W. HOAG, Dir., *St. Mark Catholic Center, P.O. Box 10397, Erie, 16514-0397.* Rev. Msgr. DANIEL E. MAGRAW, Consultant. Tel: 814-824-1192.

Diocesan Attorney—FRANK L. KROTO, JR., ESQ., *Quinn, Buseck, Leemhuis, Toohey & Kroto, Inc., 2222 W. Grandview Blvd., Erie, 16506.* Tel: 814-833-2222.

Erie Diocesan Cemeteries—Board of Members: Most Rev. DONALD W. TRAUTMAN; Rev. Msgr. ROBERT J. SMITH, J.C.L.; Rev. Msgr. LAWRENCE E. BRANDT, J.C.D., Ph.D.; DAVID J. MURPHY; THOMAS L. COPECK, Dir. JOHN HROMYAK, Operations Mgr., *3325 West Lake Rd., Erie, 16505.* Tel: 814-838-7724.

Clergy Formation

Clergy Personnel—Rev. Msgr. MICHAEL T. GAINES, Dir.

Clergy Continuing Education and Formation—Rev. Msgr. RICHARD R. SIEFER, Dir., *St. Catherine Parish, 116 S. State St., DuBois, 15801.* Tel: 814-371-8556., *St. Mark Catholic Center, P.O. Box 10397, Erie, 16514-0397.* Tel: 814-824-1195.

Seminary Program

Vocation Office—Rev. MARK A. HOFFMAN, Dir., *St. Mark Catholic Center, P.O. Box 10397, Erie, 16514-0397.*

St. Mark Seminary—Rev. MICHAEL T. KESICKI, Rector & Dir. Seminary; Rev. NICHOLAS J. ROUCH, Vice Rector & Assoc. Dir. Seminary; Sr. MARY ANDREW

HIMES, R.S.M., Dir. Liturgical Music, *St. Mark Catholic Center, P.O. Box 10397, Erie, 16514-0397.*

Special Apostolates

Spiritual Apostolates—Rev. JOHN T. CARTER, Dir., *5145 Peach St., Erie, 16509.* Tel: 814-864-0622.

Black Apostolate—Rev. EDWARD C. KRAUSE, C.S.C., *233 E. 16th St., Erie, 16503.* Tel: 814-454-1615.

Hispanic Apostolate—Rev. JORGE VILLEGAS, Dir., *1237 W. 21st St., Erie, 16502.* Tel: 814-459-0543.

Apostleship of the Sea and Chaplain to the Port of Erie—Rev. L. THOMAS SNYDERWINE, Dir., *c/o St. Luke Church, 421 E. 38th St., Erie, 16504-1699.* Tel: 814-825-6920.

Blue Army of Our Lady of Fatima—Rev. OTTO B. PISONI, Dir., *502 Peach St., Erie, 16501-1104.* Tel: 814-454-6494.

Cursillo Movement—Rev. JOHN J. HILBERT, Dir., *1611 Peach St., Ste. 450, Erie, 16501.* Tel: 814-456-2948.

Legion of Mary—Rev. JOHN T. CARTER, Dir., *5145 Peach St., Erie, 16509.* Tel: 814-864-0622.

Charismatic Movement—MICHAEL VEHEC, Diocesan Liaison, *St. Mark Catholic Center, P.O. Box 10397, Erie, 16514-0397.*

Special Ministries—Rev. Msgr. JAMES W. PETERSON, Dir., *P.O. Box 10682, Erie, 16514.* Tel: 814-454-0891.

Bread of Life Community—Rev. LAWRENCE RICHARDS, Moderator, *830 W. 9th St., Erie, 16502.* Tel: 814-456-5698. GENE KOBAL, Pres.

Word of Life Charismatic Renewal—*St. Mark Catholic Center, 429 E. Grandview Blvd., P.O. Box 10397, Erie, 16514-0397.* Tel: 814-824-1286.

Ecumenism

Pennsylvania Conference on Inter-Church Cooperation—Rev. Msgr. LAWRENCE E. BRANDT, J.C.D., Ph.D., Diocesan Rep.

Ecumenical Officers—

Eastern Vicariate—Rev. DENNIS C. HADBERG.

Western Vicariate—Rev. Msgr. WILLIAM C. KARG, *St. Joseph, 79 Case Ave., Sharon, 16146.* Tel: 412-981-3232.

Northern Vicariate—Rev. Msgr. WILLIAM E. BIEBEL, *St. Peter Cathedral, 230 W. 10th St., Erie, 16501.* Tel: 814-453-6677.

Communication

Office of Communications—GARY C. LONCKI, Dir., *P.O. Box 10668, Erie, 16514-0668.* Tel: 814-824-1160; Fax: 814-824-1128.

"Lake Shore Visitor" - Diocesan Newspaper—GARY C. LONCKI, Editor; ANDREA BARAN, Asst. Editor, *P.O. Box 10668, Erie, 16514-0668.* Tel: 814-824-1160; Fax: 814-824-1128.

CLERGY, PARISHES, MISSIONS AND PAROCHIAL SCHOOLS

CITY OF ERIE
(Erie County)

1—ST. PETER CATHEDRAL (1893), Rev. Msgr. William E. Biebel, V.F., Rector; Rev. Joseph P. Reigel; Sr. Mary McCarthy, R.S.M., D.R.E.; Sr. Martha Howick, S.S.J., Pastoral Assoc. In res., Rev. Msgr. Michael T. Gaines; Rev. Robert G. Barcio, Archivist.
Res., 230 W. 10th St., 16501. Tel: 814-453-6677; Fax: 814-456-1351.
Church—10th St. & Sassafras St., 16501.
School—Tel: 814-452-4276; Fax: 814-452-0479.
Lay Teachers 22; Students 344.

2—BLESSED SACRAMENT (1938), Revs. Daniel E. Magraw; Michael P. Ferrick.
Res., 1626 W. 26th St., 16508. Tel: 814-454-0171; Fax: 814-459-6832.
School—Tel: 814-455-1387; Fax: 814-455-1388.
Sisters of St. Joseph 1; Lay Teachers 20; Students 467.

3—HOLY FAMILY/ST. ANN/ST. CASIMIR (1902) (Slovak), Rev. James T. O'Hara. In res., Rev. Msgr. J. Edward Feeney, (Retired).
Office: 913 Fulton St., 16503. Tel: 814-452-4832.
School—Tel: 814-452-4720.
Sisters 1; Lay Teachers 9; Students 126.

4—HOLY ROSARY (1927), Revs. James G. Gutting; Michael P. Allison; Jeffrey J. Lucas.
Res., 2701 East Ave., 16504. Tel: 814-456-4254; Fax: 814-456-4255.
School—Tel: 814-456-7212; Fax: 814-454-5467.
Sisters 1; Lay Teachers 8; Students 197.

5—HOLY TRINITY (1903) (Polish), Rev. David J. Maciukiewicz; Deacon Martin Eisert.
Res., 2220 Reed St., 16503. Tel: 814-456-0671; Fax: 814-461-1150.

6—IMMACULATE CONCEPTION (1946) (African American), Rev. Edward C. Krause, C.S.C., Admin.; Deacon Dalhart Dobbs.
Res., 109 University Square, 16541. Tel: 814-871-7545.
Church—233 E. 16th St., 16503. Tel: 814-454-1615.

7—MOUNT CALVARY (1951), Rev. Thomas M. Aleska.
Res., 2004 East Lake Rd., 16511. Tel: 814-454-0061; Fax: 814-454-7177.
School—Tel: 814-455-1268.
Lay Teachers 10; Students 131.

8—OUR LADY OF MERCY (1946), Rev. Gerald T. Ritchie; Sr. Rosemary O'Brien, S.S.J., Pastoral Min.; Sr. Mary Rose Romeo, S.J., Liturgical Min.
Res., 837 Bartlett Rd., Harborcreek, 16421. Tel: 814-899-5342; Fax: 814-898-3306.

9—OUR LADY OF MT. CARMEL (1960), Rev. Bruce R. Allison; Rev. Msgr. Joseph V. Reszkowski; Deacon Frank Pregler.
Res., 1553 E. Grandview Blvd., 16510. Tel: 814-825-7313; Fax: 814-825-4190.
School—Tel: 814-825-2822; Fax: 814-825-4190.
Lay Teachers 20; Students 358.

10—OUR LADY OF PEACE (1955), Revs. Thomas M. Brooks; Michael G. DeMartinis; Sr. Elizabeth Bauer, O.S.F., Pastoral Assoc.; Deacon Ralph DeCecco. In res., Very Rev. John M. Shultz.
Res., 2401 W. 38th St., 16506. Tel: 814-833-7701; Fax: 814-833-7702.
School—Tel: 814-838-3548. Sr. Claudia Dombrowski, S.S.J., Prin.
Sisters 1; Lay Teachers 29; Students 552.

11—SACRED HEART (1894), Revs. David Findlay; Phillip M. Oriole; Sr. Marian Halligan, R.M.S. In res., Revs. Jerome S. Simmons; Daniel J. Dymski.
Res., 816 W. 26th St., 16508. Tel: 814-456-6256.
School—Tel: 814-459-7247; Fax: 814-459-8838.
Sisters 2; Lay Teachers 18; Students 358.

12—ST. ANDREW (1871), Rev. Msgr. Richard J. Sullivan; Sr. Nancy Sonnenfeld, S.S.J. In res., Rev. Jerry S. Priscaro.
Res., 1116 W. Seventh St., 16502. Tel: 814-454-2486; Fax: 814-456-4443.
School—Tel: 814-454-2454; Fax: 814-456-3737.
Sisters 1; Lay Teachers 10; Students 188.

13—ST. ANN (1887). (See Holy Family for Ministry Team.). Rev. James T. O'Hara. In res., Revs. Chester J. Gawronski; Gerald J. Koos.
Church—921 East Ave., 16503. Tel: 814-453-4681.

14—ST. BONIFACE (1857), Rev. Msgr. Daniel K. Arnold. In res., Rev. Raymond W. Hahn.
Res., 7615 Wattsburg Rd., 16509. Tel: 814-825-4439; Fax: 814-825-4430. [CEM]
School—Tel: 814-825-4238; Fax: 814-825-8101.
Lay Teachers 10; Students 212.

15—ST. CASIMIR (1914) (Polish), Rev. James T. O'Hara.
Church—629 Hess Ave., 16503. Tel: 814-459-7361.

16—ST. GEORGE (1922), Rev. Msgr. Richard G. Mayer; Rev. Msgr. John T. Carter; Rev. Richard J. Allen; Sr. Maria O'Connor, R.M.S., Pastoral Min.; Sr. Regina Przestrzelski, R.M.S., D.R.E.; Deacons Joseph Hodges; Dalhart Dobbs; Norbert Smith.
Res., 5145 Peach St., 16509. Tel: 814-864-0622; Fax: 814-866-7532.
School—Tel: 814-864-4821; Fax: 814-866-7532.
Sisters 2; Lay Teachers 33; Students 645.

17—ST. HEDWIG/ST. PATRICK (1910), Rev. Msgr. William E. Sutherland. In res., Rev. Msgr. Lawrence E. Brandt.
Res., 521 E. 3rd St., 16507. Tel: 814-454-8096.

18—ST. JAMES (1921), Rev. Msgr. Robert W. Cohan, V.F. In res., Rev. James McCormick.
Res., 2635 Buffalo Rd., 16510. Tel: 814-899-6178; Fax: 814-899-7681.
School—Tel: 814-899-3429; Fax: 814-898-8285. Sr. Colette Hilow, C.D.S., D.R.E.
Sisters of the Congregation of the Divine Spirit 4; Lay Teachers 14; Students 297.

19—ST. JOHN THE BAPTIST (1870), Rev. Msgr. Thomas J. McSweeney. In res., Rev. Paschal Kabura.
Res., 509 E. 26th St., 16504. Tel: 814-454-2873; Fax: 814-456-7073.
School—Tel: 814-452-6874; Fax: 814-456-7033.
Lay Teachers 11; Students 241.

20—ST. JOSEPH (1867) (German), Rev. John E. Santor. In res., Rev. Msgr. John M. Gannon, (Retired); Rev. Gerard H. Krebs.
Res., 147 W. 24th St., 16502. Tel: 814-452-2982; Fax: 814-452-4400.

21—ST. JUDE THE APOSTLE (1955), Rev. Msgr. Robert L. Brugger. In res., Rev. Msgr. Ernest J. Daley; Rev. Stephen J. Schreiber.
Res., 2801 W. 6th St., P.O. Box 8408, 16505. Tel: 814-833-0927; Fax: 814-833-9692.
School—Our Lady's Christian, Tel: 814-838-7676; Fax: 814-838-6860.
Lay Teachers 23; Students 455.

22—ST. JULIA (1938), Rev. Msgr. Richard J. McGuire.
Res., 638 Roslyn Ave., 16505. Tel: 814-833-4347; Fax: 814-833-4347.
School—Our Lady's Christian. (See St. Jude the Apostle for details.).

23—ST. LUKE (1954), Revs. L. Thomas Snyderwine; Lawrence Richards; Sr. Margaret Mary Wagner, C.D.P., Pastoral Min.; Deacon Richard Shewman. In res., Rev. Msgr. Robert D. Goodill; Rev. David E. Prenatt.
Res., 421 East 38th St., 16504. Tel: 814-825-6920; Fax: 814-825-6920.
School—Tel: 814-825-7105.
Lay Teachers 20; Students 419.

24—ST. MARK THE EVANGELIST (Lawrence Park) (1938), Revs. Joseph F. Finucane; Scott E. Katren.
Res., 695 Smithson Ave., 16511. Tel: 814-899-3000; Fax: 814-899-5212.

25—ST. MARY (1840) (German), Rev. Msgr. Robert J. Reilly.
Res., 315 E. 9th St., 16503. Tel: 814-452-2410; Fax: 814-455-7992.

26—ST. MATTHEW IN THE WOODS (1966), Rev. Thomas J. Whitman.
Res., 1290 Townhall Rd. West, 16509. Tel: 814-866-6248.

27—ST. PATRICK/ST. HEDWIG (1834), Rev. William E. Sutherland, Admin.; Sr. Mary Pascal Gray, S.S.J., Pastoral Assoc.; Sr. Marie Stephen Kebort, S.S.J., D.R.E. In res., Most Rev. Michael J. Murphy; Rev. Msgr. Joseph V. Wardanski; Revs. Michael G. Barletta; Thomas E. Smith.
Res., 130 E. 4th St., 16507. Tel: 814-454-8085; Fax: 814-459-8685.

28—ST. PAUL (1891) (Italian), Rev. Msgr. Richard J. Stack; Sr. Martha Howick, S.S.J., Pastoral Min. In res., Rev. Ronald E. Gmerek.
Res., 1617 Walnut St., 16502. Tel: 814-459-3173; Fax: 814-459-3173.

29—ST. STANISLAUS (1885) (Polish), Rev. Msgr. Bernard J. Urbaniak; Sr. Elizabeth Oettel, O.S.B., D.R.E.; Sr. Mary Ann White, C.S.F.N., Pastoral Min. In res., Rev. Mark L. Bartchak.
Res., 516 E. 13th St., 16503. Tel: 814-452-6606; Fax: 814-452-6606. [CEM]
School—Tel: 814-452-4825.
Lay Teachers 12; Students 152.

30—ST. STEPHEN (1917), Rev. Jorge C. Villegas; Deacon Miguel Alvarez.
Res., 1237 W. 21 St., 16502. Tel: 814-459-0543.

OUTSIDE THE CITY OF ERIE

Albion, Erie Co., St. Lawrence (1914), Rev. John M. Fischer.
Res., 180 E. State St., 16401. Tel: 814-756-3623; Fax: 814-756-3623.
St. Lawrence Catechetical Center—129 E. Pearl St., 16401. Tel: 814-756-4840.

Anita, Jefferson Co., St. Joseph (1898), Rev. Stephen L. Collins.
Res., Box 24, Walston, 15781. Tel: 814-938-9687. [CEM]

Bradford, McKean Co., St. Bernard (1880), Rev. Leo J. Gallina. In res., Rev. Christopher C. Merry; Rev. Msgr. Jan C. Olowin.
Res., P.O. Box 2394, 16701-5394. Tel: 814-362-6825; Fax: 814-362-1479. [CEM]
School—Tel: 814-368-5891; Fax: 814-368-1464.
Lay Teachers 16; Students 221.

St. Francis of Assisi (1846), Rev. Howard J. King; Bro. Michael W. Hicks, D.R.E.
Res., 574 E. Main St., 16701. Tel: 814-368-6959; Fax: 814-368-6959. [JC]

Brandy Camp, Elk Co., Holy Cross (1908) (Italian), Rev. Msgr. Louis J. Heberlein, Admin.
Mailing Address: P.O. Box 65, 15822. Tel: 814-265-4331.
Res., 287 Treasure Lake, Du Bois, 15821. Tel: 814-371-2899. [CEM]

Brockway, Jefferson Co., St. Tobias (1898), Rev. Msgr. Louis J. Heberlein; Deacons Edward Ward; Robert De Noon. In res., Rev. Msgr. Charles A. Kaza.
Res., 1100 Hewett St., 15824. Tel: 814-268-3655; Fax: 814-268-1147. [CEM]

Brookville, Jefferson Co., Immaculate Conception (1852), Rev. Joseph P. Staszewski.
Res., 129 Graham Ave., 15825. Tel: 814-849-8697. [CEM]
Mission—Sigel, Jefferson Co., St. Dominic. [CEM]

Cambridge Springs, Crawford Co., St. Anthony (1899), Rev. Msgr. Lawrence T. Speice.
Res., 165 Beach Ave., 16403. Tel: 814-398-4234; Fax: 814-734-2868.

Clarion, Clarion Co., Immaculate Conception (1855), Rev. Frank J. Przepierski; Sr. Bernadine Gehinger, S.S.J., Pastoral Assoc.
Res., 720 Liberty St., 16214. Tel: 814-226-8433; Fax: 814-226-1090. [CEM]
School—Tel: 814-226-9690.
Priests 1; Sisters 1; Lay Teachers 10; Students 155.
Catechesis/Religious Programs—Students 395.

Clearfield, Clearfield Co., St. Francis (1830), Rev. Dennis C. Hadberg.
Res., 212 S. Front St., 16830. Tel: 814-765-9671; Fax: 814-765-9489. [CEM]
School—Tel: 814-765-2618; Fax: 814-765-6704.
Lay Teachers 12; Students 170.

Coalport, Clearfield Co., St. Basil the Great (1887), Rev. Alexander D. Amico.
Res., Box 395, 16627. Tel: 814-672-5561; Fax: 814-672-5954. [CEM]

Conneaut Lake, Crawford Co., Our Lady Queen of the Americas (1958), Rev. Stephen A. Anderson.
Res., 9th & Water Sts., Box 110, 16316. Tel: 814-382-7252; Fax: 814-382-9575. [CEM]

Conneautville, Crawford Co., St. Peter (1853) (Irish), In res., Rev. John A. Walsh.
Res., 626 Washington St., P.O. Box F, 16406. Tel: 814-587-3435. [CEM]
Convent—High St., P.O. Box 305, 16406. Tel: 814-587-2011. Sacred Heart

Corry, Erie Co., St. Thomas The Apostle (1856), Rev. Thomas E. Brown.
Res., 203 W. Washington St., 16407. Tel: 814-663-3041; Fax: 814-663-0505. [CEM]
School—Tel: 814-665-7375; Fax: 814-663-0505.
Lay Teachers 11; Students 136.
St. Elizabeth (1876), Rev. Thomas E. Brown.
Res., 26 W. Pleasant St., 16407. Tel: 814-664-7105. [CEM]
Oratory—Spartansburg, Crawford Co., Our Lady of Victory, Spartansburg, 16434. Tel: 814-664-7105.

Coudersport, Potter Co., St. Eulalia (1891), Rev. John F. Weibel; Deacon Leo Flynn.
Res., 16915. Tel: 814-274-8646. [CEM]
Mission—Austin, Potter Co., St. Augustine. [CEM]

Crossingsville, Crawford Co., St. Philip (1840), Rev. Thaddeus T. Kondzielski.
Res., Crossingville, R.D. 2, Edinboro, 16412. Tel: 814-734-7395. [CEM]

Crown, Clarion Co., St. Mary (1848), Rev. Thomas S. Hoderny.
Res., 16220. Tel: 814-744-9919; Fax: 814-744-8624. [CEM 2]
Mission—Marienville, Forest Co., St. Anne.

Curwensville, Clearfield Co., St. Timothy (1915), Rev. Gregory P. Passauer, V.F. In res., Rev. James C. McKee, S.J.
Res., 306 Walnut St., 16833. Tel: 814-236-1845; Fax: 814-236-1845. [CEM]

Daguscahonda, Elk Co., St. Benedict. Closed. Effective April 30, 1995, St. Benedict in Daguscahonda became a Public Oratory (Cannon 1223).

Delancey, Jefferson Co., St. Adrian, Rev. Stephen L. Collins.
Res., Box 24, Walston, 15781. Tel: 814-938-9687.

Du Bois, Clearfield Co., St. Catherine (1877), Revs. Richard R. Siefer; William M. Calabrese; Deacon Robert Kuntz.
Res., 116 S. State St., 15801. Tel: 814-371-8556; Fax: 814-371-0592. [CEM]
School—Tel: 814-371-2570; Fax: 814-371-1551. Joseph Ryan, Prin.
Lay Teachers 14; Students 213.
St. Joseph (1893) (Lithuanian), Rev. Richard R. Siefer.
Res., 15 South Ave., 15801. Tel: 814-371-7956; 371-7604; Fax: 814-371-6687. [CEM]
St. Michael (1912), Rev. Msgr. Henry L. Krebs, V.F. In res., Rev. Mark S. Swoger.
Res., 15 Robinson St., 15801. Tel: 814-371-5773; Fax: 814-371-5794. [CEM]

East Brady, Clarion Co., St. Eusebius (1877), Rev. William M. Kuba.
Res., R.D. 1, Box 747, 16028. Tel: 412-526-3366. [CEM]
Mission—Rimersburg, Clarion Co., St. Richard.

Edinboro, Erie Co., Our Lady of the Lake (1950), Rev. John B. Jacquel.
Res., Box 838, 128 Sunset Dr., 16412. Tel: 814-734-3113; Fax: 814-734-3085.

Eldred, McKean Co., St. Raphael (1847), Rev. Samuel B. Slocum.
Res., 16 First St., Box No. 252, 16731. Tel: 814-225-4231; Fax: 814-225-4298. [CEM 2]
Mission—Sartwell, McKean Co., St. Mary. [CEM]

Emlenton, Venango Co., St. Michael (1867), Rev. Msgr. John W. Swoger, Temporary Admin.
Res., Chestnut St., P.O. Box 177, 16373. Tel: 724-867-2422; Fax: 724-867-6815. [CEM]

Emporium, Cameron Co., St. Mark (1888), Rev. Paul S. Siebert; Sr. Mercedes Muskovish, O.S.B., Parish Min.
Res., 235 E. 4th St., 15834. Tel: 814-486-0569; Fax: 814-486-3298. [CEM]
Mission—Driftwood, Cameron Co., St. James.

Fairview, Erie Co., Holy Cross (1963), Rev. J. Thomas Dugan.
Res., 3627 Shauna Ave., P.O. Box 10, 16415. Tel: 814-474-2605; Fax: 814-474-1256.

Falls Creek, Jefferson Co., St. Bernard (1952), Rev. Stanley J. Swacha.
Res., 205 Taylor Ave., 15840. Tel: 814-371-7419.

Farrell, Mercer Co.,

1—Holy Trinity, (1915) (Hungarian), Rev. John R. Boeckman.
Res., 601 Fruit Ave., 16121. Tel: 412-342-0794; Fax: 412-342-0831. [CEM]

2—Our Lady of Fatima, (1952), Rev. Donald E. Berdis; Deacon Joseph Messina. In res., Rev. Joseph A. Ciaiola.
Res., 601 Roemer Blvd., 16121. Tel: 724-346-3359. [CEM 2]
School—Monsignor Geno Monti School, Tel: 724-347-1440.
Sisters 1; Lay Teachers 8; Students 123.

3—St. Adalbert, (1913), Rev. John R. Boeckman.
Res., 1035 Fruit Ave., 16121. Tel: 724-346-5379; Fax: 724-342-0831. [CEM]

4—St. Ann, (1904) (Slovak), Rev. Richard C. Tomasone.
Res., 1035 Fruit Ave., 16121. Tel: 724-346-5979; Fax: 724-347-5553. [CEM]

Force, Elk Co., St. Joseph (1906), Rev. Donald J. Cooper.
Res., 15841. Tel: 814-787-4151; Fax: 814-787-4151. [CEM]

Franklin, Venango Co., St. Patrick (1867), Revs. John J. Herbein; William J. O'Brien.
Res., 949 Liberty St., 16323. Tel: 814-437-5763; Fax: 814-437-6326. [CEM]
School—Tel: 814-432-8689.
Lay Teachers 9; Students 183.

Frenchtown, Crawford Co., St. Hippolyte (1838), Rev. Monty Sayers.
Res., R.D. 2, Guys Mills, 16327. Tel: 814-789-2022; Fax: 814-789-2025. [CEM]
Mission—Cochranton, Crawford Co., Our Lady of Lourdes.

Frenchville, Clearfield Co., St. Mary of the Assumption (1840), Rev. Samuel Bungo; Sr. Therese Dush, C.A.; Deacon Joseph Lyncha.
Res., P.O. Box 159, 16836. Tel: 814-263-4354; Fax: 814-263-4219. [CEM]
Missions—Grass Flats, Clearfield Co., SS. Peter & Paul. [CEM]
Drifting, Clearfield Co., St. Severin. [CEM]

Fryburg, Clarion Co., St. Michael (1846), Rev. David L. Poulson.
Res., P.O. Box 46, Main St., Rte. 208, 16326. Tel: 814-354-2467. [CEM]
School—Tel: 814-354-2523.
Priests 1; Lay Teachers 7; Students 74.

Galeton, Potter Co., St. Bibiana (1888) (Italian), Rev. Brian E. Vossler.
Res., 111 Germania, 16922. Tel: 814-435-2303. [CEM]
Mission—Genesee, Potter Co., Sacred Heart.

Girard, Erie Co., St. John the Evangelist (1853), Rev. Glenn R. Whitman; Sr. Geraldine Kasper, O.S.F., D.R.E. In res., Rev. Conrad L. Kraus.
Res., 142 E. Main St., Box 336, 16417. Tel: 814-774-4108. [CEM]
School—Tel: 814-774-8865; Fax: 814-774-0604.
Lay Teachers 11; Students 180.

Grampian, Clearfield Co., St. Bonaventure (1833), Rev. Gregory P. Passauer.
Res., P.O. Box 127, 16838. Tel: 814-236-0364. [CEM]

Greenville, Mercer Co., St. Michael (1850), Rev. Msgr. Andrew H. Karg; Rev. Dennis J. Veltri; Sr. Mary Gertrude McElhinny, S.C., Pastoral Min. In res., Rev. Paul A. Schill.
Res., 85 N. High St., 16125. Tel: 412-588-9800; Fax: 412-588-7053. [CEM]
School—Tel: 724-588-7050; Fax: 724-588-7053.
Lay Teachers 17; Students 227.
Mission—Jamestown, Mercer Co., St. Margaret.

Grove City, Mercer Co., Beloved Disciple (1925), Rev. Msgr. Edward J. Zeitler, V.F.; Revs. James A. Wiley; William G. Rice.
Res., 321 N. Broad St., 16127. Tel: 724-458-7145. [CEM]

Hermitage, Mercer Co., Church of Notre Dame (1960), Rev. Msgr. John B. Hagerty; Rev. William G. Rice; Deacon W. Jack Tupper.
Res., 2325 Highland Rd., 16148. Tel: 724-981-5566; Fax: 724-981-3215.
School—Tel: 724-342-2205.
Lay Teachers 14; Students 292.

Houtzdale, Clearfield Co., Christ the King (1970), Rev. Msgr. H. Desmond McGee. In res., Rev. John G. Chaplin, C.S.C.
Res., 123 Good St., 16651. Tel: 814-378-7653. [CEM]
Mission—Madera, Clearfield Co., Immaculate Conception.

Johnsonburg, Elk Co., Holy Rosary (1896), Rev. David J. Wilson.
Res., 606 Penn St., 15845. Tel: 814-965-2819; Fax: 814-965-5528. [CEM]
School—Tel: 814-965-2812.
Sisters 2; Lay Teachers 9; Students 94.

Kane, McKean Co., St. Callistus (1878), Rev. Phillip A. Pinczewski; Sr. Francis Therese Matia, S.S.J., D.R.E.
Res., 342 Chase St., 16735. Tel: 814-837-6694; Fax: 814-837-6694. [CEM]
Convent—116 Haines St., 16735.

Kersey, Elk Co., St. Boniface (1832), Rev. John A. Kuzilla.
Res., 355 Main St., 15846. Tel: 814-885-8941. [CEM]
School—Tel: 814-885-8093; Fax: 814-885-8931. Sr. Laura Vallimont, O.S.B., Prin.
Sisters of St. Benedict 1; Lay Teachers 6; Students 76.

Lewis Run, McKean Co., Our Mother of Perpetual Help (1946), Rev. Howard J. King.
Res., 31 Lafayette, 16738. Tel: 814-368-6355.

Linesville, Crawford Co., St. Philip (1957), Revs. John G. Barwin; William A. Rice.
Res., R.D. 1, Box 1C, 16424. Tel: 814-683-5313. [CEM]

Lucinda, Clarion Co., St. Joseph (1840), Rev. Joseph R. Czarkowski.
Res., 16235. Tel: 814-226-7288; Fax: 814-226-5225. [CEM]
School—Tel: 814-226-8018. Sr. Monica Steiner, O.S.B., Prin., D.R.E.
Sisters 1; Lay Teachers 7; Students 89.

McKean, Erie Co., St. Francis Xavier (1838), Rev. Msgr. A. Joseph Book; Sr. Jane Matheis, S.S.J., Pastoral Min. In res., Rev. Mark A. Nowak.
Res., 16426. Tel: 814-476-7657; Fax: 814-476-7657. [CEM]

Meadville, Crawford Co., St. Agatha (1849), Rev. Msgr. Henry J. Schauerman; Rev. Robert P. Fedor.
Res., 353 Pine St., 16335. Tel: 814-336-1112. [CEM]
School—Seton School. Consolidation of St. Agatha Elementary and St. Brigid Elementary. Tel: 814-336-2320; Fax: 814-336-2328.
Lay Teachers 14; Students 216.
Mission—Saegertown, Crawford Co., St. Bernadette, 222 Renner Ln., Saegertown, 16433. Tel: 814-763-2831. Rev. Mark A. Nowak.
St. Brigid (1865), Rev. Msgr. Richard E. Butryn, V.F.; Rev. Regis J. Meenihan.
Res., 967 Chancery Ln., 16335. Tel: 814-336-4459; Fax: 814-724-2996. [CEM]
St. Mary (1909), Rev. Msgr. Casimir A. Bogniak.
Res., 1085 Water St., 16335. Tel: 814-333-6161.

Mercer, Mercer Co., Immaculate Heart (1838), Rev. James J. Kennelley.
Res., 16137. Tel: 724-662-2999. [CEM]

Morrisdale, Clearfield Co., St. Agnes (1891), Rev. Gregory A. Kirsch; Deacon Robert Hoover.
Res., 16858. Tel: 814-342-2583; Fax: 814-342-6377. [CEM]
Mission—Hawk Run, Clearfield Co., SS. Peter & Paul. [CEM]

Mount Jewett, McKean Co., St. Joseph (1898), Rev. Theodore B. Marconi.
Res., P.O. Box 520, 17 Division St., 16740. Tel: 814-778-5520.

New Bethlehem, Clarion Co., St. Charles (1872), Rev. William M. Laska.
Res., 201 Washington St., 16242. Tel: 814-275-3446. [CEM]
Mission—Crates, Clarion Co., St. Nicholas. [CEM]

North East, Erie Co., St. Gregory Thaumaturgus (1875), Rev. Thomas L. Tyler.
Res., 136 W. Main St., 16428. Tel: 814-725-9691; Fax: 814-725-1225. [CEM]

School—140 W. Main St., 16428. Tel: 814-725-4571.
Sisters of St. Benedict 1; Lay Teachers 11; Students 148.

Oil City, Venango Co.,

1—ASSUMPTION OF THE BLESSED VIRGIN MARY, (1899) (Polish), In res., Rev. John Neff.
Res., 210 Emerald St., 16301. Tel: 814-677-2032.
Mission—Rouseville, Venango Co., St. Venantius.

2—OUR LADY HELP OF CHRISTIANS, (1914), Rev. John P. Mathaner.
Res., 69 Willow St., 16301. Tel: 814-677-3078.

3—ST. JOSEPH, (1865), Rev. John W. Swoger.
Res., 35 Pearl Ave., 16301. Tel: 814-677-4004; Fax: 814-677-5977. [CEM 2]

4—ST. STEPHEN, (1898), Rev. Jeffrey J. Noble.
Res., 210 Reed St., 16301. Tel: 814-677-3020; Fax: 814-678-8841.
School—Tel: 814-677-2053; Fax: 814-677-2053.
Lay Teachers 14; Students 224.

Port Allegany, McKean Co., St. Gabriel the Archangel (1876), Rev. Charles R. Schmitt.
Res., 203 Arnold Ave., 16743. Tel: 814-642-2847. [CEM]
Mission—Roulette, Potter Co., St. Mary.

Punxsutawney, Jefferson Co., SS. Cosmas and Damian (1885), Rev. John F. Bauer.
Res., 616 W. Mahoning St., 15767. Tel: 814-938-6540; Fax: 814-938-7439. [CEM]
School—Tel: 814-938-4224; Fax: 814-939-3759.
Lay Teachers 11; Students 159.

Ramey, Clearfield Co., Holy Trinity (1937), Rev. Killian E. Shuman, T.O.R.
Res., Box 196, 16671. Tel: 814-378-7193. [CEM]

Reynoldsville, Jefferson Co., St. Mary (1872), Rev. Msgr. John W. Mignot.
Res., 607 Main St., 15851. Tel: 814-653-8586. [CEM]

Ridgway, Elk Co., St. Leo the Great (1874), Rev. Msgr. Joseph K. Bobal, V.F.; Revs. Robert Horgas; James G. Faluszak.
Res., 111 Depot St., 15853. Tel: 814-772-3135; Fax: 814-772-3225. [CEM]
School—Tel: 814-772-9775. Sr. Mary Joan Beauseigneur, S.S.J., Prin.
Sisters 1; Lay Teachers 11; Students 153.
Convent—117 Depot St., 15853.

Rouseville, Venango Co., St. Venantius (1870), Rev. Msgr. John W. Swoger, Admin.
Res., 210 Emerald St., Oil City, 16301. Tel: 814-677-2032.
Church—403 Main St., 16344.

St. Marys, Elk Co., St. Mary (1842) (German), Revs. Frank Ziemkiewicz, O.S.B.; Alfred Patterson, O.S.B.; Bro. Edward Alton; Sr. Josephine DePetro, S.S.J., Coord. Inter Parish Svcs.
Res., 144 Church St., St. Mary, 15857. Tel: 814-781-1019; Fax: 814-834-6795. [CEM]
Schools—Tel: 814-834-2665; Fax: 814-834-5339.
Lay Teachers 16; Students 237; St. Mary's Catholic Elementary School System, 303 Church St., St. Mary's, Tel: 814-834-9493. Ms. Mary Agnes Marshall, Prin.

Queen of the World (1954), Revs. Leon Hont, O.S.B.; Matthew T. Laffey, O.S.B.; Sr. Josephine DiPetro, S.S.J., Coord. Inter Parish Svcs.
Res., 134 Queens Rd., 15857. Tel: 814-834-4701; Fax: 814-834-3422.
School—Tel: 814-834-4169.
Lay Teachers 17; Students 291.

Sacred Heart of Jesus (1876), Revs. Daniel L. Wolfel; Ananius G. Buccicone, O.S.B.; Sr. Josephine DePetro, S.S.J., Coord. Inter Parish Svcs.
Res., 323 Center St., 15857. Tel: 814-834-7861; Fax: 814-834-1376. [JC]
School—Tel: 814-834-4017.
Lay Teachers 17; Students 238.

Sharon, Mercer Co.,

1—SACRED HEART, (1864), Rev. Daniel J. Kresinski.
Res., 40 S. Irvine Ave., 16146. Tel: 724-346-3567; Fax: 724-346-3567. [CEM]

2—ST. ANTHONY, (1924) (Croatian), Rev. Matthew Ruyechan, O.F.M.
Res., 804 Idaho St., 16146. Tel: 724-342-7391; Fax: 724-342-7981. [CEM]

3—ST. JOSEPH, (1892), Rev. Msgr. William C. Karg; Revs. Dilworth Davis; James F. Bird; Sr. Sandy Pedone, H.M., D.R.E.
Res., 79 Case Ave., 16146. Tel: 724-981-3232; Fax: 724-981-4174. [CEM][JC]
School—Tel: 412-938-8382.
Lay Teachers 17; Students 311.

4—ST. STANISLAUS KOSTKA, (1931) (Polish), Rev. Victor Maksimovich, O.F.M. In res., Rev. Anthony F. Spilka, O.F.M.Conv.
Res., 370 Spruce Ave., 16146. Tel: 412-347-7526; Fax: 412-347-1760. [CEM]
Catechesis/Religious Programs—Rose DeSantis, D.R.E.
Students 180.

Sharpsville, Mercer Co., St. Bartholomew (1874), Rev. John S. Lynch.
Res., 311 W. Ridge Ave., 16150. Tel: 724-962-7130; Fax: 724-962-1771.

Sheffield, Warren Co., St. Anthony (1878), Rev. Daniel J. Prez; Sr. Kathleen Warner, O.S.B., D.R.E.
Res., P.O. Box 518, Four Mile Rd., 16347. Tel: 814-968-5915.

Shinglehouse, Potter Co., St. Theresa (1901), Rev. Samuel B. Slocum.
Res., P.O. Box 277, 16748. Tel: 814-697-6900. [CEM]

Smethport, McKean Co., St. Elizabeth (1875), Rev. Theodore B. Marconi, Admin.
Res., 307 Franklin St., 16749. Tel: 814-887-9254; Fax: 814-887-1930. [CEM]

Stoneboro, Mercer Co., St. Columbkille (1874), Rev. Henry C. Andrae, Admin.
Res., Franklin St., P.O. Box 206, 16153. Tel: 724-376-3393; Fax: 724-376-3396. [CEM]

Sykesville, Jefferson Co., Assumption of Blessed Virgin Mary (1923), Rev. Mark J. Mastrain.
Res., 20 Shaffer St., 15865. Tel: 814-894-2772; Fax: 814-894-7981. [CEM]

Tidioute, Warren Co., St. John (1866), Rev. V. David Foradori.
Res., 25 First St., 16351. Tel: 814-484-7747; Fax: 814-484-7231. [CEM]
Mission—Tionesta, Forest Co., St. Anthony.

Titusville, Crawford Co., St. Titus (1962), Rev. John J. Detisch; Sr. Edith Hirsch, R.M.S., Pastoral Min.
Res., 513 W. Main St., 16354. Tel: 814-827-4636; Fax: 814-827-4637. [CEM][JC]
School—Tel: 814-827-3312.
Lay Teachers 7; Students 122.
Christian Activities Center—505 W. Walnut St., 16354. Tel: 814-827-7223; Fax: 814-827-8711.
Mission—Mageetown, Crawford Co., Immaculate Conception, Tel: 814-827-2075.

St. Walburga (1872) (German), Rev. Rocco A. Tito.
Res., 120 Brook St., 16354. Tel: 814-827-3958. [CEM]

Union City, Erie Co., St. Teresa of Avila (1906), Rev. F. Thomas Suppa.
Res., 9 Third Ave., 16438. Tel: 814-438-2924. [CEM]
Mission—Canadohta Lake, Crawford Co., Our Lady of Fatima.

Walston, Jefferson Co., St. Anthony (1898), Rev. Stephen L. Collins.
Res., Box 24, 15781. Tel: 814-938-9687.

Warren, Warren Co., Holy Redeemer (1912), Rev. Msgr. John L. Lucas, V.F.; Deacon Joseph Lucia, Jr.
Res., 11 Russell St., 16365. Tel: 814-726-3360; Fax: 814-726-3361.

St. Joseph (1858), Revs. Walter E. Packard; Anthony Attumaly; Sr. Mary Winkelbauer, C.D.P., D.R.E.; Deacon Joseph Lucia, Jr.
Res., 600 Penna. Ave. W., 16365. Tel: 814-723-2090; Fax: 814-723-6042. [CEM][JC]
School—Tel: 814-723-2030.
Lay Teachers 9; Students 195.

Waterford, Erie Co., St. Cyprian (1878), Rev. Thomas J. Whitman.
Church—12775 Donation Rd., Box 535, 16641. Tel: 814-796-4329.

West Middlesex, Mercer Co., Good Shepherd (1955), Rev. Msgr. Joseph J. Riccardo; Deacon William Calabrese.
Res., P.O. Box 226, 16159. Tel: 724-528-3539. [JC]

Wilcox, Elk Co., St. Anne (1890), Rev. Barry M. Hudock.
Res., P.O. Box 65, Clarion St., 15870. Tel: 814-929-5577. [JC]
Mission—Rasselas, Elk Co., Holy Cross. [CEM]

Winburne, Clearfield Co., SS. Cyril and Methodius (1904) (Slovak-Hungarian), Rev. Msgr. Michael E. Tutokie, Admin.
Res., 16879. Tel: 814-345-5674. [CEM][JC]

Youngsville, Warren Co., St. Luke (1958), Rev. William C. Miller.
Res., 420 N. Main St., 16371. Tel: 814-563-4432.

Chaplains of Public Institutions

ERIE. *Erie County Geriatric Center Annex* St. Paul, 1617 Walnut St. Rev. L. Thomas Snyderwine.
Erie County Geriatrics Center. Vacant.
Erie County Prison. Rev. Msgr. John M. Dollinger.
Hamot Medical Center 201 State St., 16550. Rev. Gerald J. Koos.
St. Vincent's Health Center 232 W. 25th St., 16544. Revs. Dennis A. Martin, Chap.; Raymond Gramata, Chap.
Shriners Hospital for Crippled Children. Vacant. 1116 W. 7th St., 16550.
Soldiers and Sailors Home. Rev. J. Daniel Dymski.
Veterans Administration Hospital. Rev. Thomas M. Fialkowski, Chap.

ALBION. *Albion State Correctional Facility*. Vacant.

BRADFORD. *Federal Correction Institution* P.O. Box 5000, 16701-0950. Rev. John G. Barwin.

CAMBRIDGE SPRINGS. *Cambridge Springs Correction Institution*. Rev. Robert G. Craig.

DU BOIS. *Du Bois Regional Hospital* 100 Hospital Ave., 15801. Rev. John R. Neff, Chap.

LEWIS RUN. *Federal Correction Institution*. Vacant. P.O. Box 5000, 16738.

MEADVILLE. *Crawford Country Home* 967 Chancery Ln., 16335. Rev. Richard E. Butryn, Chap.

MERCER. *State Correctional Facility* Box 530, 16137. Rev. Patrick J. Healy, Chap.

POLK. *Polk Center* Box 94, 16342. Rev. Mark J. Mastrian.

WARREN. *Warren State Hospital*. Rev. John F. Bauer.

Special or Diocesan Assignment:
Reverend Fathers—
Fischer, G. William, O.S.F.S., 10018 Seeley St., Lake City, PA 16423-1546

On Duty Outside Diocese:
Reverend Monsignors—
Sanner, James E., Army
Reverend Fathers—
Beal, John P., Washington, DC
Burke, John R., Mexico
Humenay, Robert, WY
Jeselnick, Stephen E., AFB
Kelley, Thomas, TX
Malene, Robert, AZ
Milewski, Robert, Navy

On Leave of Absence:
Reverend Fathers—
Collins, Stephen L., III
Roseto, James
Weiss, James F.

Retired:
Reverend Monsignors—
Barcio, Robert G.
Daniszewski, John D.
Enright, Vincent L.
Gannon, John M.
Goodill, Robert D.
Latimer, Edward H.
Martin, Daniel J.
Meier, Raymond O.
Mitchell, Salvatore P.
Ritchie, G. Carlton
Schriefer, Robert F.
Slater, John J.
Snyder, John R.
Sperry, James E.
Tutokie, Michael E.
Reverend Fathers—
Anderson, Emil
Capozzelli, Anthony M.
Cici, William
Dobosiewicz, Stephen J.
Donovan, Edmund J.
Feeney, J. Edward
Fin, Robert G.
Groucutt, George L.
Jerge, Joseph W.
Kacprowicz, Joseph A.
Kotyuk, Stephen
Kozlowski, Louis
Levis, Robert J.
Lohse, Walter H.
Maloney, William J.
Maryland, Joseph A.
Murray, John L.
Pisoni, Otto B.
Sharpe, Patrick F.
Skinner, Charles D.
Somers, Eldon K.
Stutz, Edward J.
Weber, James H.
Wilson, Edward M.

INSTITUTIONS LOCATED IN THE DIOCESE

[A] SEMINARIES, DIOCESAN

ERIE. *St. Mark's Seminary*. Mailing Address: 429 E. Grandview Blvd., P.O. Box 10397, 16514. Tel: 814-824-1200. Rev. Msgr. Lawrence T. Speice, Rector & Dir. Seminarians; Revs. Michael T. Kesicki, Dir. Spiritual Formation & Continuum Office; Edward M. Lohse, Vocation Dir.

[B] COLLEGES AND UNIVERSITIES

ERIE. *Gannon University*, University Square, 16541. Tel: 814-871-7000.
Web site: www.gannon.edu
For a complete listing, refer to the Colleges and Universities section.

Mercyhurst College, 501 E. 38th St., 16546. Tel: 814-824-2000.
E-mail: igower@mercyhurst.edu
Web site: www.mercyhurst.edu
For a complete listing, refer to the Colleges and Universities section.

[C] HIGH SCHOOLS, DIOCESAN

ERIE. *Cathedral Preparatory School*, 225 W. Ninth St., 16501. Tel: 814-453-7737. Rev. Msgr. Bruce Allison, Headmaster; Mrs. Joann Mullen, Prin.
Faculty: Revs. Raymond W. Hahn; Lawrence Richards; James McCormick; Bruce Allison; William Fischer; Sr. James Francis Mulligan. Priests 6; Sisters 1; Laymen 26; Laywomen 13; Students 668.

BRADFORD. *Bradford Central Christian High School*, 450 W. Washington St., 16701. Tel: 814-362-3815. Miss Linda M. Moshier, Prin. Lay Teachers 12; Students 44.

DU BOIS. *Du Bois Area Catholic Schools*, 204 Hospital Ave., 15801. Tel: 814-371-3060; Fax: 814-371-3215.
E-mail: centralchristian@cch.put.k-12-pa.us
Headmasters: Revs. Mark S. Swoger; Edward J. Walk.
Central Christian High School.
Central Christian Middle School. Priests 2; Sisters 1; Lay Teachers 42; Students 571.

HERMITAGE. *Kennedy Christian High School*, 2120 Fwy., 16148. Tel: 724-346-5531.
E-mail: kch@nauticom.not
Mr. Peter Iacino, Pres.; Rev. Richard C. Tomasone, Asst. Prin.; Mrs. Christine Perry, Prin. Priests 4; Sisters 1; Lay Teachers 24; Students 380.

OIL CITY. *Venango Christian High School*, 1505 W. 1st St., 16301-3298. Tel: 814-677-3098; Fax: 814-676-4453.
E-mail: vchs1@mail.usachoice.net
Rev. John P. Malthaner, Headmaster. Lay Teachers 13; Students 108.

SAINT MARYS. *Elk County Christian High School*, 600 Maurus St., 15857. Tel: 814-834-7800; Fax: 814-781-3441.
E-mail: ecchs@ncentral.com
Mr. John W. Kowach, Headmaster; Rev. James G. Faluszczak, Campus Minister. Priests 2; Lay Teachers 26; Students 394.

[D] HIGH SCHOOLS, PRIVATE

ERIE. *Mercyhurst Preparatory School*, 538 E. Grandview Blvd., 16504. Tel: 814-824-2210; Fax: 814-824-2116.
E-mail: mdste@mpslakers.com
Georgia C. Johnson, Pres.; Margaret Aste, Prin. Sisters 5; Lay Teachers 58; Students 819.

Villa Maria Academy, 2403 W. 8th St., 16505. Tel: 814-838-2061; Fax: 814-838-0376.
E-mail: villa@villamaria.com
Sr. Ann Marie Joint, S.S.J., Prin.; Mrs. Kathleen DiNicola, Asst. Admin.; Mr. John Gardner, Asst. Admin. Sisters 6; Lay Teachers 38; Students 563.

[E] ELEMENTARY SCHOOLS, PRIVATE

ERIE. *Villa Maria Elementary School*, 2551 W. 8th St., 16505. Tel: 814-838-5451. Sr. Margaret Frank, S.S.J., Prin. Sisters of St. Joseph 2; Lay Teachers 21; Students 403.

[F] SPECIAL MINISTRIES

ERIE. *Erie East Coast Migrant Programs*, 345 E. 9th St., 16503. Tel: 814-454-4514. Benedictine Sisters of Erie. Sr. Diane Rabe, O.S.B., Dir. Students 38.

L'Arche Erie, 1101 Peach St., 2nd Fl., 16501. Tel: 814-452-2065; Fax: 814-452-4188.
E-mail: larche@velocity.net

Mercy Center of the Arts, 444 E. Grandview Blvd., 16504. Tel: 814-824-2519.

St. Benedict Child Development Center, 345 E. 9th St., 16503. Tel: 814-454-4515; Fax: 814-452-1905.
E-mail: stbens@erie.net
Sr. Diane Rabe, O.S.B., Admin. Students 120.

St. Benedict Education Center, 330 E. 10th St., 16503. Tel: 814-452-4072; Fax: 814-454-2686.
E-mail: mmashank@stben.org
Sr. Miriam Mashank, O.S.B., Dir. Students 500.

Villa Maria Center, 2551 W. 8th St., 16505. Tel: 814-838-5514; Fax: 814-833-3315.
E-mail: shanley@villamaria.cen.com
Sr. Leonie Shanley, S.S.J., Admin.

Word of Life Catholic Charismatic Renewal, St. Mark Catholic Center, 429 E. Grandview Blvd., P.O. Box 10397, 16514-0397. Tel: 814-824-1286; Fax: 814-824-1128.
E-mail: wolccrc@aol.com

FAIRVIEW. *Camp Notre Dame*, 400 Eaton Rd., P.O. Box 74, 16415. Tel: 814-474-5001; Fax: 814-474-4818.
Web site: www.campnotredame.com
Rev. Mark Novak, Pres.; Rev. Msgr. Lawrence T. Spiece, Vice Pres.

ROULETTE. *Catholic Rural Ministry*, P.O. Box 11, 16746-0011. Tel: 814-544-8017. Sr. Phyllis Schleicher, O.S.B., Contact Person.

[G] GENERAL HOSPITALS

ERIE. *Saint Vincent Health Center*, 232 W. 25th St., 16544. Tel: 814-452-5000; Fax: 814-452-5102
For a complete listing, refer to the Hospitals section.

[H] PROTECTIVE INSTITUTIONS

ERIE. *Gannondale, Inc.*, 4635 E. Lake Rd., 16511. Tel: 814-899-7659; Fax: 814-898-4266.
E-mail: gannondale@aol.com
For a complete listing, refer to the Special Care Facilities section.

HARBORCREEK. *Harborcreek Youth Services*, 5712 Iroquois Ave., 16421. Tel: 814-899-7664; Fax: 814-899-3075.
E-mail: gmcclelland@hys-erie.org
For a complete listing, refer to the Special Care Facilities section.

[I] APARTMENTS FOR SENIOR CITIZENS

ERIE. *Mercy Terrace Apartments*, 430 E. Grandview Blvd., 16504. Tel: 814-825-6791; Fax: 814-824-2127.
E-mail: mta@erie.net
For a complete listing, refer to the Special Care Facilities section.

HARBORCREEK. *Benetwood Apartments for Persons Elderly and Handicapped*, 641 Troupe Rd., 16421-1048. Tel: 814-899-0088
For a complete listing, refer to the Special Care Facilities section.

[J] RESIDENCES FOR RETIRED PRIESTS

ERIE. *Bishop Michael J. Murphy Residence for Retired Priests*, 400 E. Gore Rd., 16509. Tel: 814-825-0680
For a complete listing, refer to the Special Care Facilities section.

[K] NURSING HOMES

ERIE. *St. Mary's Home of Erie*, 607 E. 26th St., 16504. Tel: 814-459-0621; Fax: 814-454-0909
For a complete listing, refer to the Special Care Facilities section.

DU BOIS. *Christ the King Manor, Inc.*, 1100 W. Long Ave., 15801. Tel: 814-371-3180; Fax: 814-371-4101.
E-mail: etkm@penn.com
For a complete listing, refer to the Special Care Facilities section.

HERMITAGE. *John XXIII Home*, 2250 Shenango Fwy., 16148. Tel: 724-981-3200; Fax: 724-981-1677.
E-mail: j23@pathway.net
For a complete listing, refer to the Special Care Facilities section.

[L] SHELTERS FOR MEN AND WOMEN

ERIE. *Mercy Center for Women*, 1039 E. 27th St., 16504. Tel: 814-453-3668
For a complete listing, refer to the Special Care Facilities section.

St. Patrick Haven, Inc., 147 E. 12th St., 16501. Tel: 814-454-7219; 838-5430
For a complete listing, refer to the Special Care Facilities section.

[M] CONVENTS AND RESIDENCES FOR SISTERS

ERIE. *Benet Priory*, 330 E. 10th St., 16503. Tel: 814-459-5103. Benedictine Sisters of Erie 2.

Congregation of the Divine Spirit, 409 W. 6th St., 16507. Tel: 814-455-3590; Fax: 814-454-8899. Mother Patricia O'Connor, C.D.S., Supr. Gen.; Rev. Richard Powers. Members 41.

Holy Family Monastery, 510 E. Gore Rd., 16509-3799. Mother Emmanuel of the Mother of God, O.C.D., Prioress; Rev. Michael G. Barletta, Chap. Discalced Carmelites 6.

Kraus House Priory, 436 E. 9th St., 16503. Tel: 814-454-4846. Benedictine Sisters of Erie. Sisters 4.

Mount Saint Benedict Monastery, 6101 E. Lake Rd., 16511. Tel: 814-899-0614; Fax: 814-898-4004.
E-mail: msbaadmin@erie.net
Sr. Christine Vladimiroff, O.S.B., Prioress. Benedictine Sisters of Erie. Professed Sisters in Community 132; Sisters in Formation 2.

North American Union Sisters of Our Lady of Charity, 4635 E. Lake Rd., 16511. Tel: 814-899-1052; Fax: 814-899-1573. Sr. Rosemary Toth, Local Supr.

Om Shanti, 1239 W. 7th St., 16502. Tel: 814-459-3215.
E-mail: marycook@erie.net
Sr. Diane Cook, O.S.B. Benedictine Sisters of Erie 2.

Sophia House, 1245 W. 10th St., 16502. Tel: 814-454-1212. Benedictine Sisters of Erie 4.

Bethany House, 218 E. 11th St., 16503. Tel: 814-455-4574. Benedictine Sisters of Erie 3.

Peace House, 103 E. 35th St., 16504. Tel: 814-455-6066. Benedictine Sisters of Erie 2.

Benedicta Riepp Priory, 2108 Poplar St., 16502. Tel: 814-455-5699. Benedictine Sisters of Erie 2.

Pax Priory, 345 E. Ninth St., 16503. Tel: 814-452-6318.
E-mail: paxprior@erie.net
Benedictine Sisters of Erie 7.

St. Scholastica Priory, 355 E. 9th St., 16503. Tel: 814-454-4052; Fax: 814-459-8066.
E-mail: schlstca@erie.net
Web site: www.erie.net/~erie-osb
Benedictine Sisters of Erie 4.

St. Walburga Priory, 302 W. 10th St., 16503. Tel: 814-454-3706. Benedictine Sisters of Erie 3.

Sisters of Mercy Motherhouse, 444 E. Grandview Blvd., 16504. Tel: 814-824-2516; Fax: 814-824-2127.
E-mail: rsmpres@mercyerie.org
Sr. Joanne Courneen, R.S.M. Professed Sisters 75.

Villa Maria, 5031 W. Ridge Rd., 16506-1249. Tel: 814-838-4100; Fax: 814-838-5167.
E-mail: ssjrvinc@erie.net
Web site: www.erie.net/~ssjerie
Sr. Ricarda Vincent, S.S.J., Pres.; Rev. Msgr. Gerald L. Orbanek, Chap. The Sisters of St. Joseph of Northwestern PA. Professed Sisters in Community 161.

ST. MARYS. *Benedictine Sisters of Elk County O.S.B. St. Joseph Monastery*, 303 Church St., 15857. Tel: 814-834-2267; Fax: 814-834-3270.
E-mail: Raphael@alltell.net
Sr. M. Raphael Baker, Prioress. Professed Sisters 36.

[N] SOCIOLOGICAL

ERIE. *Emmaus Ministries*, 345 E. 9th St., 16503. Tel: 814-459-8349. Sr. Mary Miller, O.S.B., Dir.

ERIE DAWN, 330 E. Tenth St., 16503. Tel: 814-453-5921; Fax: 814-453-5831.
E-mail: edawn@erie.net
Sr. Phyllis Hilbert, S.S.J., Admin.

Mercy Center for Women, 1039 E. 27th St., 16504. Tel: 814-455-4577; Fax: 814-459-7012.
E-mail: mcw@erie.org
Web site: www.mcwerie.org
Christine Tombaugh, Exec. Dir.

Mercy Center on Aging, 444 E. Grandview Blvd., 16504-2604. Tel: 814-824-2214; Fax: 814-824-2127. Sr. Mary Dolores, R.S.M., Exec. Dir.

Saint Benedict Community Center, 320 E. 10th St., 16503. Tel: 814-459-2406. Sr. Dianne Sabol, O.S.B., Dir.

[O] RETREAT & RENEWAL CENTERS

ERIE. *Ecclesia Center/Renewal Center*, 9101 Ridge Rd., 16417-9625. Tel: 814-774-9691; Fax: 814-774-4893.
E-mail: ecclesia@erie.net
Web site: www.ecclesiacenter.org
Rev. Jerome S. Simmons.

Glinodo Center, 6270 E. Lake Rd., 16511. Tel: 814-899-4584; Fax: 814-899-0253.
E-mail: glindo@glindo.org
Web site: www.glindo.org
Sr. Annette Marshall, O.S.B., Admin. Benedictine Sisters of Erie.

Special Ministries, P.O. Box 10682, 16514. Tel: 814-456-0891. Rev. Msgr. James W. Peterson, Dir.

Theophilus, Theophilus House, 4115 Royal Ave., 16509-1428. Tel: 814-866-6891.
E-mail: theoprayer@aol.com

FRENCHVILLE. *Young People Who Care Center, Caritas Mission*, 16836. Tel: 814-263-4177.
E-mail: caritasm@phoenix.vicon.net
Web site: http://www.vicon.net/~caritasm
Sr. Suzanne Thibault, C.A., Dir.

UNION CITY. *Avila Retreat Center*, 61 E. High St., 16438. Tel: 814-438-7020. Mr. & Mrs. Larry Pline, Dir.

[P] CAMPUS MINISTRY

ERIE. *Newman Centers and Campus Ministry*. c/o Penn State University, The Behrend College, 5091 Station Rd., 16563-0901. Tel: 814-898-6245; Fax: 814-898-6015. Sr. Mary Dexler, S.S.J., Diocesan Dir.-Camp. Ministry.

Allegheny College, P.O. Box 101, Meadville, 16335. Tel: 814-332-2800. Rev. Regis Meenihan.

University of Pittsburgh-Bradford Campus, St. Bernard Parish, 98 E. Corydon St., Bradford, 16701. Tel: 814-362-6825.

Clarion University of Pennsylvania, 720 Liberty St., Clarion, 16214. Tel: 814-226-6869; Fax: 814-226-1090. Rev. David Poulson.

Lockhaven University-Clearfield Campus, St. Francis Parish, 212 S. Front St., 16830. Tel: 814-765-9671; Fax: 814-226-1090.

Penn State University-DuBois Campus, St. Catherine Parish, 116 State St., DuBois, 15801. Tel: 814-371-8556.

Edinboro University of PA, Newman Center, P.O. Box 820, Edinboro, 16412. Tel: 814-734-1651. Rev. Mark A. Nowak, Camp. Min.

Gannon University, University Sq., 16541. Tel: 814-871-7547. Sr. Lynette Petruska, S.S.J., Dir., Camp. Min.; Sr. Marilyn Urine, Assoc.; Andrew Canfield, Graduate Asst.

Grove City College, Beloved Disciple Parish, 321 N. Broad St., Grove City, 16127. Tel: 412-458-7145.

Mercyhurst College, 501 E. 38th St., 16546. Tel: 814-824-2301. Sr. Elisabeth Lintsen, M.S.O.L.A., Camp. Min.; Rev. James Piszker, Chap. & Dir. Tel: 814-824-2467.

Clarion State University of PA-Venango Campus, St. Stephen Parish, 210 Reed St., Oil City, 16301. Tel: 814-677-3020.

Penn State University, The Behrend College, Station Rd., 16563-0901. Tel: 814-898-6245. Rev. John E. Santor, Camp. Min.

Indiana University of PA-Punxsutawney Campus, S.S. Cosmos & Damian Parish, 616 W. Mahoning St., Punxsutawney, 15767. Tel: 814-938-6540.

Penn State University-Shenano Valley Campus, St. Joseph Parish, 74 Case Ave., Sharon, 16146. Tel: 412-981-3232.

Thiel College. Rev. Matthew Ruyechan, O.F.M., Spiritual Dir.; Joanne Schell, Dir. of Career Center. Tel: 724-589-2014.

University of Pittsburgh-Titusville Campus, St. Titus Parish, 513 W. Main St., Titusville, 16354. Tel: 814-827-4636.

[Q] MISCELLANEOUS

ERIE. *Alliance for International Monasticism (AIM)*, 345 E. 9th St., 16503. Tel: 814-453-4724; Fax: 814-459-8066.
E-mail: aim@erie.net
Web site: www.csbsju.edu/osb/intl/aimusa.html
AIM is an organization founded to assist Benedictine and Cistercian monasteries in the Third World. Sr. Mary Lou Kownacki, O.S.B., Exec. Dir.

St. Thomas More Society, 429 E. Grandview Blvd., 16514.

Sisters of St. Joseph Neighborhood Network, Inc., 1611 Peach St., Ste. 135, 16501. Tel: 814-454-7814. Sr. Mary Hermann, S.S.J., Exec. Dir.

FRENCHVILLE. *Anawim Community of Frenchville*, P.O. Box 129, 16836. Tel: 814-263-4518; 263-4177; Fax: 814-263-4855.
E-mail: anawim@uicon.net
Web site: www.ypwc.org

ST. MARYS. *Opportunity for Parochial Education Network (OPEN)*, 575 Charles St., 15857. Tel: 814-834-6181. Richard J. Reuscher, Trustee.

RELIGIOUS INSTITUTES OF MEN REPRESENTED IN THE DIOCESE

For further details refer to the corresponding bracketed number in the Religious Institutes of Men or Women section.

[0200]—*Benedictine Monks*. (St. Vincent's Archabbey).—O.S.B.
[1330]—*Congregation of the Mission*.—C.M.
[0480]—*Conventual Franciscans*. (Anthony of Padua Prov.).—O.F.M.Conv.
[0520]—*Franciscan Friars*.—O.F.M.
[0690]—*Jesuit Fathers and Brothers*.—S.J.
[0610]—*Priests of the Congregation of Holy Cross*.—C.S.C.
[1070]—*Redemptorist Fathers*. (Baltimore Prov.).—C.SS.R.
[1200]—*Society of Divine Savior*.—S.D.S.
[0560]—*Third Order Regular of Saint Francis*. (Most Sacred Heart Prov.).—T.O.R.

RELIGIOUS INSTITUTES OF WOMEN REPRESENTED IN THE DIOCESE

[0230]—*Benedictine Sisters of Elk Co*.—O.S.B.
[0160]—*Benedictine Sisters of Erie*.—O.S.B.
[]—*Congregation of Divine Providence*. (Pittsburgh).—C.D.P.
[]—*Congregation of the Divine Providence*.—C.D.P.
[]—*Congregation of the Divine Spirit*.—C.D.S.
[0420]—*Discalced Carmelite Nuns*.—O.C.D.
[1170]—*Felician Sisters*.—C.S.S.F.
[1840]—*Gray Nuns of the Sacred Heart*.—G.N.S.H.
[2720]—*Mission Helpers of the Sacred Heart*.—M.H.S.H.
[2820]—*Missionary Sisters of Our Lady of Africa*.—M.S.O.L.A.
[3070]—*North American Union of Sisters of Our Lady of Charity*.—N.A.U.-O.L.C.
[1690]—*School Sisters of the Third Order of St. Francis*.—O.S.F.
[0507]—*Sisters of Charity of Seton Hill, Greenburg, PA*.—S.C.
[2570]—*Sisters of Mercy*.—R.S.M.
[1620]—*Sisters of St. Francis of Millvale, PA*.—O.S.F.
[3830]—*Sisters of St. Joseph*.—S.S.J.
[1970]—*Sisters of the Holy Family of Nazareth*.—C.S.F.N.

DIOCESAN CEMETERIES

ERIE. *Queen of Peace*.
Trinity, Calvary & Gate of Heaven.

NECROLOGY

† Capozzelli, Anthony, (Retired). —Died Dec. 23, 2000.
† Dobosiewicz, Stephen J., (Retired). —Died March 9, 2000.
† Kotyuk, Stephen J., (Retired). —Died Nov. 27, 2000.
† Latimer, Rev. Msgr. Edward H., (Retired). —Died Aug. 10, 2000.
† Lynch, Richard D., Erie, PA St. Mark the Evangelist. —Died April 21, 2000.
† Sharpe, Patrick F., (Retired). —Died Jan. 15, 2000.

Diocese of Evansville

(Dioecesis Evansvicensis)

Most Reverend

GERALD ANDREW GETTELFINGER

Bishop of Evansville; born October 20, 1935; ordained May 7, 1961; appointed Fourth Bishop of Evansville March 11, 1989; ordained and installed April 11, 1989. *Res., 3980 Woodcastle, Evansville, IN, 47711. Mailing Address: Catholic Center, 4200 N. Kentucky Ave., P.O. Box 4169, Evansville, IN, 47724-0169.*

Catholic Center: 4200 N. Kentucky Ave., P.O. Box 4169, Evansville, IN, 47724-0169. Tel.: 812-424-5536; Fax: 812-421-1334.

Web site address: www.evansville-diocese.org

ESTABLISHED NOVEMBER 11, 1944.

Square Miles 5,010.

Comprises twelve Counties in the Southwestern part of Indiana: Daviess, Dubois, Gibson, Greene, Knox, Martin, Pike, Posey, Spencer (except township of Harrison), Sullivan, Vanderburgh, Warrick.

The Diocese of Evansville was established by decree of Pope Pius XII, November 11, 1944, and the See was fixed at Evansville.

For legal titles of parishes and diocesan institutions, consult the Chancery.

STATISTICAL OVERVIEW

Personnel	
Bishop	1
Priests: Diocesan Active in Diocese	67
Priests: Active Outside Diocese	3
Priests: Diocesan in Foreign Missions	1
Priests: Retired, Sick or Absent	29
Number of Diocesan Priests	100
Religious Priests in Diocese	8
Ordinations:	
Diocesan Priests	1
Transitional Deacons	2
Permanent Deacons in Diocese	21
Total Brothers	2
Total Sisters	308
Parishes	
Parishes	70
With Resident Pastor:	
Resident Diocesan Priests	51
Resident Religious Priests	3
Without Resident Pastor:	
Administered by Priests	12
Administered by Deacons	1
Administered by Women Religious	3
Pastoral Centers	6
Professional Ministry Personnel:	
Sisters	20
Lay Ministers	42
Welfare	
Catholic Hospitals	2
Total Assisted	390,776
Health Care Centers	1
Total Assisted	60
Homes for the Aged	3
Total Assisted	242
Day Care and Extended Day Care Centers	1
Total Assisted	285
Special Centers for Social Services	9
Total Assisted	130,500
Educational	
Diocesan Students in Other Seminaries	11
Total Seminarians	11
High Schools, Diocesan and Parish	4
Total Students	1,643
Elementary Schools, Diocesan and Parish	24
Total Students	6,044
Non-residential Schools for the Disabled	1
Total Students	22
Catechesis/Religious Education:	
High School Students	2,036
Elementary Students	7,615
Total Students Under Catholic Instruction	17,371
Teachers in the Diocese:	
Priests	2
Brothers	2
Sisters	14
Lay Teachers	468
Vital Statistics	
Receptions into the Church:	
Infant Baptism Totals	1,407
Adult Baptism Totals	173
Received into Full Communion	205
First Communions	1,456
Confirmations	1,628
Marriages:	
Catholic	329
Interfaith	240
Total Marriages	569
Deaths	927
Total Catholic Population	90,812
Total Population	486,500

Former Bishops—Most Rev. HENRY JOSEPH GRIMMELSMAN, D.D., appt. Nov. 11, 1944; cons. Dec. 21, 1944; retired and named Titular Bishop of Tabla Oct. 20, 1965; died June 26, 1972.—Most Rev. PAUL F. LEIBOLD, D.D., appt. Titular Bishop of Trebenna and Auxiliary of Cincinnati April 10, 1958; cons. June 17, 1958; appt. to Evansville April 6, 1966 translated to Archbishop of Cincinnati July 23, 1969; died June 1, 1972.—Most Rev. FRANCIS R. SHEA, appt. Dec. 10, 1969; retired April 11, 1989; died Aug. 18, 1994.

Catholic Center—4200 N. Kentucky Ave., P.O. Box 4169, Evansville, 47724-0169. Tel: 812-424-5536; Fax: 812-421-1334. Office Hours: Mon.-Fri. 8-5.

Vicar General—Rev. Msgr. KENNETH R. KNAPP, A.C.S.W., M.S.

Chancellor—JUDITH A. NEFF.

Executive Director of Diocesan Services—KENNETH W. KRASAVAGE.

Secretary to the Bishop—DEANNA RUSTON.

Treasurer—ROBERT J. COX.

Associate Treasurer—SCOTT BRITT.

Senior Consultant to the Treasurer—Rev. Msgr. OMER MEYER.

Assistant Treasurer—RITA REXING.

Diocesan Tribunal—P.O. Box 4169, Evansville, 47724-0169.

Judicial Vicar—Rev. Msgr. CHARLES J. KOCH, S.T.L., J.C.L.

Adjutant Judicial Vicar—Rev. J. KENNETH WALKER, B.A., M.Div., M.C.L., J.C.L.

Defender of the Bond—Rev Msgr. CLINTON F. HIRSCH, J.C.L.; Rev. JAMES ENDRESS, S.T.L., M.S., M.A.

Judges—Revs. RAYMOND L. KUPER; STEPHEN P. LINTZENICH; WILLIAM M. SCHWENK; MARY GEN BLITTSCHAU, M.A., M.C.L., J.C.L.

Advocates—Revs. JOHN H. SCHIPP; MICHAEL MADDEN.

Secretary and Notary—CHARLEEN HEBERT.

Secretary—JUDY WALLACE.

Archivist—JUDITH A. NEFF.

Diocesan Consultors—Rev. Msgr. KENNETH R. KNAPP; Rev. Msgr. CHARLES KOCH; Revs. DAVID NUNNING; JOSEPH ZILIAK; JAMES ENDRESS; DAVID FLECK; FRANCIS SCHROERING.

Diocesan Council of Priests—Rev. Msgr. KENNETH R. KNAPP; Rev. Msgr. CHARLES J. KOCH; Revs. JACK J. DURCHHOLZ; ROBERT BULTMAN; GREGORY CHAMBERLIN, O.S.B.; DAVID FLECK; EDWARD SCHNUR; JAMES ENDRESS; STEPHEN P. LINTZENICH; LOWELL WILL; JOHN SCHIPP; BERNARD LUTZ.

Personnel Board—Rev. Msgr. KENNETH KNAPP; Revs. FRANCIS SCHROERING; RAYMOND BRENNER; HENRY KUYKENDALL; HILARY VIECK; JAMES BLESSINGER; WILLIAM TRAYLOR.

Deans—Rev. Msgr. KENNETH R. KNAPP, Evansville, East; Rev. DAVID NUNNING, Evansville, West; Rev. DONALD ACKERMAN, Jasper; Rev. JOSEPH ZILIAK, Newburgh; Rev. FRANCIS SCHROERING, Princeton; Rev. WILLIAM TRAYLOR, Vincennes; Rev. LEO KIESEL, Washington.

Censors Of Books—Rev. Msgr. CHARLES J. KOCH, J.C.L., S.T.L.; Rev. JOSEPH ZILIAK, S.T.L.

Diocesan Offices And Directors

Boy Scouts—JACK THOMPSON, Chap.

Campus Ministry—JOSEPH COOK, Coord.

Catholic Charities—JAMES F. COLLINS, Exec. Dir., *Court Building, Ste. 603, 123 N.W. Fourth St., Evansville, 47708.* Tel: 812-423-5456.

Catholic Diocese of Evansville, Inc.—Most Rev. GERALD A. GETTELFINGER.

Catholic Education Endowment, Inc. (Washington)—BRUCE SMITH, Pres.

Catholic Education Foundation, Inc. (Evansville)—MAURICE KELLER, Pres.

The Catholic Foundation of Southwestern Indiana, Inc.—DONNA LEADER, Exec. Dir., *P.O. Box 4169, Evansville, 47724-0169.*

Holy Family Catholic School Foundation, Inc.—WILFRED WEINZAPFEL, Pres., *950 Church Ave., Jasper, 47546.*

Catholic Education, Office of—PHYLLIS BUSSING, Dir. Schools; MARIE BRANDLE, Asst. Dir. RUTH SAALWEACHTER, Sec. MARY GARRETT, Media Clerk & Sec. STEVE BAGBEY, Safety & Security Coord.

Catholic Communication Office—PAUL LEINGANG, Dir., *P.O. Box 4169, Evansville, 47724-0169.*

Catholic Hospitals, Diocesan Representative for—Rev. EARL ROHLEDER, *St. Mary's Medical Center, 3700 Washington Ave., Evansville, 47750.*

Catholic Relief Services—JAMES F. COLLINS, *Court Building, Ste. 603, 123 N.W. Fourth St., Evansville, 47708.* Tel: 812-423-5456.

Cemeteries—Rev. EUGENE SCHROEDER, Dir., *6202 W. St. Joseph Rd., Evansville, 47720.* Tel: 812-963-3273.

Christian Educational Foundation of Vincennes, Inc.—HAROLD TURNER, Pres.

Continuing Education of Clergy—Rev. JAMES SAUER, *P.O. Box 4169, Evansville, 47724-0169.*

Cursillos in Christianity—DAVE GRIES, Lay Dir., *2109 Vogel Rd., Evansville, 47711.* Tel: 812-479-7590.

Deaf Ministry—Rev. HENRY KUYKENDALL, *3635 Pollack, Evansville, 47714.* Tel: 812-476-4646.

Diocesan Finance Council—Ex Officio: Most Rev. GERALD A. GETTELFINGER; Rev. Msgr. KENNETH R. KNAPP; KEN KRASAVAGE; ROBERT COX; GARY BECKMAN; ALAN HOFFMAN; CHRIS MELTON; STEVE WITTING.

Diocese of Evansville Retirement Trust Agreement and Plan for Priests—Office of the Bishop, 4200 N. Kentucky Ave., P.O. Box 4169, Evansville, 47724-0169. Tel: 812-424-5536.

Ecumenism—4200 N. Kentucky Ave., P.O. Box 4169, Evansville, 47724-0169. Tel: 812-424-5536.

Evangelization, Office of—4200 N. Kentucky Ave., P.O. Box 4169, Evansville, 47724-0169. Tel: 812-424-5536.

Girl Scouts—JACK THOMPSON, Chap.

Spanish Speaking Ministry—Rev. EUGENE HEERDINK, Dir.

Propagation of the Faith and Holy Childhood Association—C. JUSTIN CLEMENTS, Dir., *4200 N. Kentucky Ave., P.O. Box 4169, Evansville, 47724-0169.* Tel: 812-424-5536.

Justice and Peace—(Please refer to Catholic Charities for further information).

Legion of Mary—Revs. RAY REISING, Evansville; LOWELL WILL, Washington.

Message, The—Catholic Press of Evansville; Publisher, Most Rev. GERALD A. GETTELFINGER; PAUL LEINGANG, Editor.

Permanent Diaconate Program—Deacon THOMAS HOLSWORTH, *1066 W. Tenth, Jasper, 47546.*

Adult Formation—Sr. GERALDINE HEDINGER, O.S.B., Dir. DONNA GISH, Asst. Dir.

Rural Life Conference—Rev. JOHN BOEGLIN, Dir., *Holy Family Church, 950 E. Church Ave., Jasper, 47546-3797.*

St. Vincent De Paul Society—Deacons ROBERT HAYDEN, Diocesan Chap. CHARLES SEIFERT, Spiritual Dir., Jasper District Council; Revs. WILLIAM TRAYLOR, Spiritual Dir., Vincennes District Council; DAVID MARTIN, Spiritual Dir., Washington District Council.

Sarto Retreat House—GEORGE ANNE RYDER, Dir. CAROLYN SINGER, Sec.

Secretariat for Charismatic Renewal—Rev. WILLIAM TRAYLOR.

Stewardship / Development, Office of—C. JUSTIN CLEMENTS, Dir., *P.O. Box 4169, Evansville, 47724-0169.* Tel: 812-424-5536.

Vocation Office—Rev. BERNARD ETIENNE, Vocation Dir., *P.O. Box 4169, Evansville, 47724-0169.* Tel: 812-424-5536.

Worship / RCIA—Vacant, *4200 N. Kentucky, P.O. Box 4169, Evansville, 47724-0169.* Tel: 812-424-5536.

Youth and Young Adult Ministry—MICHAEL H. EPPLER, Dir., *4200 N. Kentucky, P.O. Box 4169, Evansville, 47724-0169.* Tel: 812-424-5536.

CLERGY, PARISHES, MISSIONS AND PAROCHIAL SCHOOLS

CITY OF EVANSVILLE
(Vanderburgh County)

1—ST. BENEDICT CATHEDRAL, Rev. Gregory D. Chamberlin, O.S.B.; Sr. Mary Agnes Sermersheim, Pastoral Assoc.
Parish Center—1328 Lincoln Ave., 47714-1598. Tel: 812-425-3369; Fax: 812-425-3378.
Res., 1312 Lincoln Ave., 47714.
School—530 S. Harlan Ave., 47714-1598. Tel: 812-425-4596.
Sisters of St. Benedict 1; Lay Teachers 22; Students 327.

2—HOLY TRINITY, Revs. Jean Vogler; Gregory D. Chamberlin, O.S.B., Admin.
219 N.W. Third St., 47708-1233. Tel: 812-422-5150.

3—ASSUMPTION CATHEDRAL. Closed. For inquiries for parish records contact Holy Trinity.

4—CHRIST THE KING, Rev. Msgr. Kenneth R. Knapp.
Res., 3109 Bayard Park Dr., 47714-2602. Tel: 812-476-3061; Fax: 812-476-3062.
School—Lay Teachers 21; Students 269.

5—CORPUS CHRISTI, Rev. James Blessinger.
Res., 5528 Hogue Rd., 47712-3298. Tel: 812-422-2027; Fax: 812-421-8316.
School—Lay Teachers 12; Students 186.

6—GOOD SHEPHERD, Rev. Theodore G. Tempel; Deacons Edward Wilkerson; Cyril Will.
Res., 2301 N. Stockwell, 47715. Tel: 812-477-5405; Fax: 812-469-2907.
School—Lay Teachers 22; Students 359.

7—HOLY REDEEMER, Revs. Ronald Zgunda; Eugene Schmitt; Deacon Robert Hayden.
Res., 918-A W. Mill Rd., 47710. Tel: 812-424-8344; Fax: 812-424-7166.
School—Lay Teachers 22; Students 288.

8—HOLY ROSARY, Revs. Raymond L Kuper; John Breidenbach; Rev. Msgr. Maurilius Bilskie, Pastor Emeritus; Deacon Robert Thurgood.
Res., 1301 S. Green River Rd., 47715. Tel: 812-477-8923; Fax: 812-471-7226.
School—Lay Teachers 24; Students 358.

9—HOLY SPIRIT, Rev. Henry Kuykendall; Sr. Joan Scheller, O.S.B., Pastoral Assoc.
Church—1800 S. Lodge Ave., 47714. Tel: 812-477-1738; Fax: 812-469-6633.
School—Lay Teachers 16; Students 181.
Convent—Sisters of St. Benedict 3.

10—NATIVITY, Rev. Henry Kuykendall; Sr. Rosanna Dorn, O.S.U., Pastoral Assoc.
Res., 3635 Pollack, 47714. Tel: 812-476-7186; Fax: 812-476-7956.
Catholic Ministry of the Deaf Office—Tel: 812-476-4646.

11—RESURRECTION, Rev. Raymond A. Brenner; Sr. Jolinda Naas, O.S.B., Pastoral Assoc.; Deacon Joseph Schapker.
Res., 5301 New Harmony Rd., 47720-1774. Tel: 812-963-3121; Fax: 812-963-1141.
School—Sisters of St.Benedict 2; Lay Teachers 21; Students 366.

12—SACRED HEART, Rev. Eugene Dewig; Rev. Msgr. Omer F. Meyer.
Res., 2701 W. Franklin St., 47712. Tel: 812-425-5505.
School—Westside Catholic Consolidated, (Grades PreK-K).
Lay Teachers 11; Students 129.

13—ST. AGNES, Rev. David H. Nunning; Deacon Richard Grannan.
Res., 1600 Glendale Ave., 47712. Tel: 812-425-9140; Fax: 812-423-4240. [CEM]
School—Westside Catholic Consolidated, (Grades 1-4).
Lay Teachers 10; Students 117.

14—ST. ANTHONY, Rev. John Davidson. Pastoral Assocs.: Sr. Joan Miller, O.S.F.; Sr. Jackie Kissel, O.S.B. In res., Rev. James Lex.
Res., 704 First Ave., 47710. Tel: 812-423-5209; Fax: 812-424-5498.

15—ST. BONIFACE, Rev. Jack Durchholz.
Res., 418 N. Wabash Ave., 47712. Tel: 812-425-8375.
School—Westside Catholic Consolidated, (Grades 5-8). Serves St Agnes, St. Boniface and Sacred Heart Parishes. 2031 W. Michigan St., 47712.
Lay Teachers 10; Students 105.

16—ST. JOHN THE APOSTLE, Sr. Jane Nesmith, S.B.S., Pastoral Life Coord.; Rev. Stephen P. Lintzenich, Pastoral Moderator.
Church—617 Bellemeade Ave., 47713-1707. Tel: 812-424-9261; Fax: 812-424-5933.

17—ST. JOHN THE EVANGELIST, Rev. Robert A. Deig; Robert Vollmer, Pastoral Assoc.
Church—5301 Daylight Dr., 47725-7636. Tel: 812-867-3718.
Res., 4020 E. Boonville-New Harmony Rd., 47725. Tel: 812-867-3987. [CEM]

18—ST. JOSEPH, Revs. Michael Allen; Kenneth Steckler; Sr. Jennifer Miller, O.S.B., Pastoral Assoc.
Res., 600 E. Virginia St., 47711. Tel: 812-422-5668; Fax: 812-425-2730.

19—ST. JOSEPH, Rev. Eugene A. Schroeder.
Res., 6202 W. St. Joseph Rd., 47720. Tel: 812-963-3273; Fax: 812-963-6254. [CEM]
School—Sisters 2; Lay Teachers 11; Students 141.
Convent— Sisters of St. Benedict
Sisters 4.

20—ST. MARY, Rev. Stephen P. Lintzenich. Pastoral Assocs.: Sr. Darlene Boyd, S.F.C.C.; Sr. Marilyn Uline, O.P.; Deacon James Cavera.
Parish Office: 613 Cherry St., 47713.
Res., 609 Cherry St., 47713. Tel: 812-425-1577; Fax: 812-426-1416.

21—ST. THERESA, Rev. Michael Allen; Sr. Annette Langenderfer, O.S.F., Pastoral Assoc.
Mailing Address: 600 Herndon Dr., 47711-3830.
Res., Tel: 812-422-8211; Fax: 812-422-5345, Ext. 238.
School—Lay Teachers 12; Students 245.
Convent—Sisters of St. Benedict 4.

22—ST. WENDEL, Rev. Gordon Mann; Deacon Joseph Blankenberger.
Res., 10542 W. Boonville-New Harmony Rd., 47720-7901. Tel: 812-963-3733; Fax: 812-963-3835. [CEM]
School—Sisters of the Third Order of St. Francis 1; Lay Teachers 9; Students 159.
Convent— Sisters of St. Francis 2.

OUTSIDE CITY OF EVANSVILLE

Bicknell, Knox Co., St. Philip Neri, Rev. Frank G. Renner.
Res., 605 W. Fourth St., 47512. Tel: 812-735-4069.

Bloomfield, Greene Co., Holy Name, Sr. Diane Fischer, O.S.B., Pastoral Life Coord.; Rev. Hilary F. Vieck, Pastoral Moderator.
Res., 700 Lincoln Dr., 47424-0124. Tel: 812-384-8415. [CEM]

Boonville, Warrick Co., St. Clement, Rev. James Koressel; Deacon Tom Lambert.
Res., 422 E. Sycamore, 47601. Tel: 812-897-4653; Fax: 812-897-4653.

Cannelburg, Daviess Co., All Saints. Attended by St. Peter, Montgomery. Rev. Joseph F. Erbacher. Tel: 812-486-3149.

Celestine, Dubois Co., St. Peter Celestine, Rev. Robert S. Bultman.
Res., 6864 E. State Rd. 164, P.O. Box 1, 47521-0001. Tel: 812-634-1875; Fax: 812-634-1875. [CEM]

Chrisney, Spencer Co., St. Martin, Rev. James E. Sauer.
Res., P.O. Box 147, 47611-0147. Tel: 812-362-7313; Fax: 812-362-7390. [CEM]

Dale, Spencer Co., St. Joseph, Rev. William M. Schwenk.
Res., 8 E. Maple St., R.R. 1, Box 308, 47523. Tel: 812-937-2200; Fax: 812-937-4349. [CEM]

Dubois, Dubois Co., St. Raphael, Rev. Wilfred Englert.
Res., 5564 E. St. Raphael St., 47527. Tel: 812-678-2011; Fax: 812-678-2148. [CEM]

Ferdinand, Dubois Co., St. Ferdinand, Rev. William J. Wargel.
Res., 840 Maryland, P.O. Box 156, 47532. Tel: 812-367-1212; Fax: 812-367-1066. [CEM]
Spiritual Life Center—Tel: 812-367-1092.
St. Henry, Rev. Camillus Ellspermann, O.S.B.; Sr. Edith Hohl, O.S.B., Pastoral Assoc.
Res., 1311 W. 1100 S., 47532-9710. Tel: 812-367-2731. [CEM]

Fort Branch, Gibson Co., Holy Cross, Rev. Bernard A. Lutz; Deacon Stephen Hall.
Res., 305 E. Walnut St., 47648. Tel: 812-753-3548. [CEM]
School—Sisters 1; Lay Teachers 9; Students 107.
St. Bernard, Revs. Bernard Lutz; William Deering, Pastor Emeritus; Deacon Stephen Hall, Jr.
Res., R.R. 2, Box 115, 47648. Tel: 812-753-4568. [CEM]

Haubstadt, Gibson Co., St. James, Rev. Kenneth Betz.
Res., R.R. 1, Box 280, 47639. Tel: 812-867-5175; Fax: 812-867-5589. [CEM]
School—Lay Teachers 13; Students 167.
SS. Peter and Paul, Revs. Francis A. Schroering; Mark Kurzendoerfer.
Res., 201 Vine St., 47639. Tel: 812-768-6457; Fax: 812-768-6521. [CEM]
School—(Grades PreK-5).
Lay Teachers 9; Students 184.

Huntingburg, Dubois Co., Visitation of the Blessed Virgin Mary, Rev. Pius Klein, O.S.B.
Res., 313 Washington St., 47542. Tel: 812-683-4903; Fax: 812-683-2747. [CEM]

Ireland, Dubois Co., Annunciation of the Blessed Virgin Mary. (St. Mary's). Rev. Donald K. Ackerman.
Res., P.O. Box 67, 47545. Tel: 812-482-7041; Fax: 812-482-3699. [CEM]

Jasonville, Greene Co., St. Joan of Arc. Attended by St. Mary, Sullivan, Tel: 812-268-4088.

Jasper, Dubois Co., Holy Family, Rev. John Boeglin; Deacon Charles Seifert.
Res., 950 E. Church Ave., 47546-3797. Tel: 812-482-3076; Fax: 812-634-6998. [JC]
School—Sisters of St. Benedict 1; Lay Teachers 26; Students 311.
Convent—Sisters of St. Benedict 5.
Precious Blood, Rev. Joseph E. Kane; Sr. Betty Koressel, S.P., Pastoral Assoc.
Res., 1458 Gregory Ln., 47546.
Church—1385 W. Sixth St., 47546. Tel: 812-482-3589; Fax: 812-482-3589. [JC]
School—(Grades PreK-5).
Lay Teachers 13; Students 217.
Convent—Sisters of Providence 4.

St. Joseph, Revs. Philip Kreilein; Anthony Ernst; Sr. Mary Jane Kiesel, O.S.B., Pastoral Assoc.
Res., 1020 Kundek St., 47546. Tel: 812-482-1805; Fax: 812-482-1814. [JC]

Linton, Greene Co., St. Peter, Rev. Hilary F. Vieck.
Res., 489 E St. N.E., 47441. Tel: 812-847-7821; Fax: 812-847-8892. [CEM]

Loogootee, Martin Co., St. John, Rev. Leo C. Kiesel.
Res., 408 Church St., 47553. Tel: 812-295-2225; Fax: 812-295-2031. [CEM]
St. Martin's, Rev. Thomas Kessler.
Mailing Address: 408 Church St., 47553. Tel: 812-295-2225. [CEM]

Mariah Hill, Spencer Co., Mary, Help of Christians, Rev. Paul Roos.
Church—P.O. Box 176, 47556. Tel: 812-937-4326. [CEM]

Montgomery, Daviess Co., St. Peter, Rev. Joseph F. Erbacher.
Res., P.O. Box 10, 47558. Tel: 812-486-3149. [CEM]
Chapel—Corning, St. Patrick's.

Mount Vernon, Posey Co., St. Matthew, Rev. Michael Madden.
Res., 421 Mulberry St., 47620. Tel: 812-838-2535. [CEM]
School—Sisters 2; Lay Teachers 10; Students 127.
Convent—.Sisters 2.
St. Philip's, Rev. David Fleck.
Res., 3500 St. Philip Rd. S., Mt. Vernon, 47620. Tel: 812-985-2275; Fax: 812-985-2590. [CEM]
School—Lay Teachers 15; Students 299.

New Boston, Spencer Co., St. John Chrysostom, Rev. Paul Roos.
Mailing Address: R.R. 1, Box 156, Evanston, 47531. Tel: 812-357-6531. [CEM]

Newburgh, Warrick Co., St. John the Baptist, Rev. Joseph L. Ziliak. Pastoral Assocs.: Sr. Jeanne Voges, O.S.B.; Lynda Provence; Marty Brown. In res., Rev. J. Kenneth Walker; Deacon Joseph Seibert.
Res., 625 Frame Rd., 47630. Tel: 812-853-6181; Fax: 812-853-6182. [CEM]
School—Lay Teachers 23; Students 389.

New Harmony, Posey Co., Holy Angels, Rev. Earl Rohleder.
Mailing Address: 423 South St., P.O. Box 548, 47631. Tel: 812-682-4224.

Oakland City, Gibson Co., Blessed Sacrament, Rev. Bernard Etienne; Deacon Stephen Hall, Jr.
Res., Rte. 1, Box 72-A, 47660. Tel: 812-749-4474.

Petersburg, Pike Co., SS. Peter and Paul, Rev. Edward Schneider; Deacon Donald Haag.
Res., 711 Walnut St., 47567. Tel: 812-354-6942.

Poseyville, Posey Co., St. Francis Xavier, Rev. William Dietsch; Sr. Leta Zeller, O.S.B., Pastoral Assoc.
Res., 10 N. St. Francis Ave., 47633. Tel: 812-874-2258; Fax: 812-874-2639. [CEM]

Princeton, Gibson Co., St. Joseph, Rev. Bernard Etienne.
Res., 410 S. Race St., P.O. Box 47, 47670. Tel: 812-385-2617; Fax: 812-385-2603. [CEM]
School—Lay Teachers 10; Students 163.

Red Brush, Warrick Co., St. Rupert, Rev. Sylvester Loehrlein.
Church—1244 Red Brush Rd., Newburgh, 47630. Tel: 812-853-3040. [CEM]

Rockport, Spencer Co., St. Bernard, Rev. Edward C. Schnur.
Res., 547 Elm St., 47635. Tel: 812-649-4811; Fax: 812-649-4176. [CEM]
School—Sisters of St. Benedict 1; Lay Teachers 17; Students 153.

St. Anthony, Dubois Co., St. Anthony, Rev. Timothy Tenbarge.
Res., 4444 S. Ohio St., P.O. Box 98, 47575-0098. Tel: 812-326-2777; Fax: 812-326-9028. [CEM]

St. Joseph, Martin Co., St. Joseph's, Rev. Thomas Kessler.
Mailing Address: 408 Church St., Loogootee, 47553. Tel: 812-295-2225. [CEM]
Chapel—Barr Township, St. Mary.

Santa Claus, Spencer Co., St. Nicholas, Rev. James Sauer, Pastoral Moderator; Sr. Mary Terence Knapp, O.S.B., Pastoral Life Coord.
Res., 181 Balthazar, P.O. Box 351, 47579. Tel: 812-937-2380; Fax: 812-937-2385.

Schnellville, Dubois Co., Sacred Heart, Rev. Ralph Schipp.
Res., 2504 Walnut St., 47580. Tel: 812-389-2535. [CEM]

Shoals, Martin Co., St. Mary's. Attended by St. John, Loogootee, Tel: 812-295-2225. @SUBPAR = [CEM]

Sullivan, Sullivan Co., St. Mary, Rev. Kenneth Graehler.
Res., 105 E. Jackson St., P.O. Box 506, 47882. Tel: 812-268-4088.

Vincennes, Knox Co.,

1—Sacred Heart, Rev. Joseph M. Swartz.
Res., 2004 N. Second St., 47591. Tel: 812-882-8382; Fax: 812-886-4676. [JC]
School—Vincennes Schools Consolidated. See St. John the Baptist for details.

2—Basilica of St. Francis Xavier, Rev. John H. Schipp.
Res., 205 Church St., 47591. Tel: 812-882-5638; Fax: 812-882-4042. [JC]
School—Vincennes Schools Consolidated. See St. John the Baptist for details.

3—St. John the Baptist, Rev. William A. Traylor. In res., Rev. Robert S. Nemergut.
Res., 803 Main St., 47591. Tel: 812-882-1762; Fax: 812-886-9151. [JC]
Parish Center—828 Vigo St., 47591.
School—Vincennes Schools Consolidated.
Lay Teachers 18; Students 296.

4—St. Thomas The Apostle, Rev. William A. Traylor, Pastoral Moderator; Deacon Joseph Sturgis, Pastoral Life Coord.
Res., 6268 S. St. Thomas Rd., 47591. Tel: 812-882-2478. [CEM]

5—St. Vincent de Paul, Rev. Albert J. Scheller.
Res., 1837 S. Hart St. Rd., 47591. Tel: 812-882-8968. [CEM]

Washington, Daviess Co., Immaculate Conception, Rev. Lowell C. Will; Yvonne Evans, Pastoral Assoc.
Res., 114 W. Van Trees St., 47501. Tel: 812-254-3187; Fax: 812-257-1133. [JC]
School—Elementary & Middle - Washington Catholic Interparochial Schools. See St. Simon Parish for details.
High School—Washington Catholic Interparochial Schools. See High Schools, Diocesan under Institutions Located in the Diocese for details.
St. Simon, Rev. David A. Martin; Deacon Michael Morris. Pastoral Assocs.: Sr. Cathy Robinson, O.S.B.; Deanna Youngs.
Res., 315 N.E. Third St., 47501. Tel: 812-254-2883; Fax: 812-254-2884. [JC]
Schools—Schools Operated jointly by St. Mary & St. Simon Parishes. Washington Catholic Interparochial Schools Elementary. 310 N.E. Second St., 47501. Dennis Bradley, M.S., Prin.
Lay Teachers 14; Students 280; Washington Catholic Interparochial Schools Middle, (Grades 6-8) 200 W. Main St., 47501.
Sisters 1; Lay Teachers 9; Students 83.
High School—See High Schools, Diocesan under Institutions Located in the Diocese for details.

Special Assignment:
Reverend Monsignors—
Knapp, Kenneth R., Vicar General, 3109 Bayard Pk. Dr., Evansville, IN 47714
Koch, Charles J., Judicial Vicar, P.O. Box 4169, Evansville, IN 47724-0169
Meyer, Omer F., 2701 W. Franklin, Evansville, IN 47712
Reverend Fathers—
Endress, James R., 600 Cullen Ave., Apt. 510, Evansville, IN 47715
Etienne, Bernard, 410 Race St., Princeton, IN 47670
Herr, Kenneth, Faculty Residence, 1500 Lincoln Ave., Evansville, IN 47714
Nemergut, Robert S., 803 Main St., Vincennes, IN 47591
Rohleder, Earl, 856 Lombard Ave., Evansville, IN 47714
Sauer, James, P.O. Box 147, Chrisney, IN 47611
Steckler, Kenneth, 600 E. Virginia St., Evansville, IN 47711
Walker, J. Kenneth, 625 Frame Rd., Newburgh, IN 47630

On Duty Outside the Diocese:
Reverend Monsignors—
Neufelder, Jerome M., St. Meinrad School of Theology, St. Meinrad, IN 47577
Reverend Fathers—
Kissel, Anthony, 14235 21st St., Dade City, FL 33523
Kress, Robert, 2845 Hikes Ln., Apt. 102, Louisville, KY 40218
Wildeman, Richard J., Haiti

On Leave of Absence:
Reverend Fathers—
Verkamp, Bernard J.

Retired:
Reverend Monsignors—
Bilskie, Maurilius, 1301 S. Green River Rd., Evansville, IN 47715
Clarke, Thomas J., St. Augustine Home, 2345 W. 86th St., Indianapolis, IN 46260
Conti, Leo J., P.O. Box 2485, Evansville, IN 47728
Hirsch, Clinton F., Villa Maria, 1640 Lincoln Ave., Apt. 102, Evansville, IN 47714
Kaiser, Charles, Regina Continuing Care, 3900 Washington Ave., Evansville, IN 47714
Kilfoil, Patrick, St. Paul Hermitage, 501 N. 17th Ave., Beech Grove, IN 46107
Lindauer, Clarence, 1236 Lincoln Ave., Evansville, IN 47714
Schoettelkotte, Charles T., Little Sisters of the Poor, 1236 Lincoln Ave., Evansville, IN 47714
Shetler, Carl A., 407 Rumbach Ave., Jasper, IN 47546
Reverend Fathers—
Brune, James, Villa Maria, 1640 Lincoln Ave., Apt. 101, Evansville, IN 47714
Busch, August, 5221 New Harmony Rd., Evansville, IN 47720
Clauss, Joseph, Guadalupe Retreat Center, 39100 Orchard Ave., Cherry Valley, CA 92223
Deering, William, St. Bernard, R.R. 2, Box 115, Fort Branch, IN 47648
Dick, Firmus, 3203 E. 1160S, Ferdinand, IN 47532
Dilger, Donald, 6621 Smith Diamond Rd., Evansville, IN 47712
Egloff, Adolph, 2017 N. Second St., Vincennes, IN 47591
Emge, John P., Regina Continuing Care, 3900 Washington, Evansville, IN 47714
Finis, John, 7363 W. Newton Stewart Rd., Taswell, IN 47175
Foster, Patrick, 962 Forder Crossing Dr., St. Louis, MO 63129
Hoffman, Richard L., 5601 Flagstone Dr., Evansville, IN 47711
Hut, Clemens, 1711 E. Grandview, Mesa, AZ 85203
Lefler, John, 7788 Taylorville Rd., Tennyson, IN 47637
Lex, James, St. Anthony Church, 704 First Ave., Evansville, IN 47710
O'Brien, Christopher, 3904 Park Blvd., Silver Hill, MD 20746
Reising, Raymond, 901-C Erie Ave., Evansville, IN 47715
Rogers, James, 801 N. Shortridge Rd., Apt. F4, Indianapolis, IN 46219
Schroering, Raymond A., Villa Maria, 1640 Lincoln Ave., Apt. 201, Evansville, IN 47714
Spaulding, Donald E., R1, Box 1S, Cannelburg, IN 47519
Wannemuehler, Robert, 3104-B Mt. Vernon Ave., Evansville, IN 47720

Permanent Deacons:
Blankenberger, Joseph V., St. Wendel Parish, Evansville
Cavera, James, St. Mary Parish, Evansville
Dow, Lancaster, Jr., Unassigned
Franklin, David, Unassigned
Grannan, Richard, St. Agnes Parish, Evansville
Haag, Donald, SS. Peter & Paul Parish, Petersburg
Hall, Stephen, St. Bernard Parish & Holy Cross, Fort Branch; Blessed Sacrament, Oakland City
Hayden, Robert, Holy Redeemer, Evansville
Hillenbrand, Francis, Christ the King, Evansville
Holsworth, Thomas, Permanent Deacon Coord.
Lambert, Thomas, St. Clement, Boonville
McFall, Gerald D., Unassigned
Morris, Michael, St. Simon, Washington
Preske, Richard, (Retired)
Schapker, Joseph, Resurrection Parish, Evansville
Seibert, Joseph S., St. John, Newburgh
Seifert, Charles, Holy Family Parish, Jasper
Sturgis, Joseph V., St. Thomas Parish, Vincennes
Thurgood, Robert, (Retired)
Wilkerson, Edward, Good Shepherd, Evansville
Will, Cyril, Good Shepherd, Evansville

INSTITUTIONS LOCATED IN THE DIOCESE

[A] HIGH SCHOOLS, DIOCESAN

Evansville. *Mater Dei High School*, 1300 Harmony Way, 47712. Tel: 812-426-2258; Fax: 812-421-5717. Web site: www.materdeiwildcats.com
Mr. Robert R. Wehde, M.A.Ed., Pres.; Timothy Weaver, M.Ed., Prin.; Rev. Kenneth Steckler, Chap.
Priests 1; Sisters 3; Lay Teachers 49; Students 598.

Reitz Memorial High School, 1500 Lincoln Ave., 47714. Tel: 812-476-4973; Fax: 812-474-2942.

Web site: www.memorial.evansville.net
Robert R. Wehde, M.A.Ed., Pres.; Mr. Gerry Adams, M.A., Ed.S., Prin.; Del Schiavone, Asst. Prin.; Rev. Kenneth Herr, Chap.; Mrs. Lisa Popham, Admin. Asst. Brothers 2; Clergy 2; Sisters 1; Lay Teachers 57; Students 830.

VINCENNES. *Jean Francois Rivet High School.* (Vincennes Area), 210 Barnett St., 47591. Tel: 812-882-6215; Fax: 812-886-1939.
Web site: www.rivet.wvc.net
Richard Kapiszka, Prin. Lay Teachers 19; Students 165.

WASHINGTON. *Washington Catholic Interparochial Schools,* 201 N.E. Second St., 47501. Tel: 812-254-2050; Fax: 812-254-2050.
Web site: www.dmrtc.net/~wchsb/index.html
Gary J. Catalano, M.A., M.A.E., Prin.; Dennis Bradley, M.S., Supt. Sisters 1; Lay Teachers 16; Students 110.

[B] SCHOOLS OF SPECIAL EDUCATION

EVANSVILLE. *Marian Day School,* 700 Herndon Dr., 47711. Tel: 812-422-5346; Fax: 812-422-5345. Bev Williamson, Dir. Lay Teachers 2; Students 22.

[C] DAY CARE CENTERS

EVANSVILLE. *St. Vincent Day Care Center,* 730 W. Delaware, 47710. Tel: 812-424-4780. Sr. Catherine Marie Lowe, D.C., Admin. Sisters of St. Benedict 2; Daughters of Charity of St. Vincent de Paul 2; Children 285.

[D] GENERAL HOSPITALS

EVANSVILLE. *St. Mary's Medical Center of Evansville, Inc.,* 3700 Washington Ave., 47750. Tel: 812-485-4000; Fax: 812-485-4927.
Web site: www.stmarys.org
For a complete listing, refer to the Hospitals section.

JASPER. *Memorial Hospital and Health Care Center, Little Company of Mary of Indiana, Inc.,* 800 W. Ninth St., 47546. Tel: 812-482-2345; Fax: 812-482-0672
For a complete listing, refer to the Hospitals section.
Memorial Hospital Foundation, Inc., 47546. Tel: 812-482-0671; Fax: 812-482-0672
For a complete listing, refer to the Hospitals section.

[E] HOMES FOR AGED

EVANSVILLE. *The Regina Continuing Care Center,* 3900 Washington Ave., 47714. Tel: 812-485-4226; Fax: 812-485-4732
For a complete listing, refer to the Special Care Facilities section.
St. John's Home for the Aged, 1236 Lincoln Ave., 47714. Tel: 812-464-3607; Fax: 812-464-2141
For a complete listing, refer to the Special Care Facilities section.
Seton Residence, 9200 New Harmony Rd., 47720-8918. Tel: 812-963-7600; Fax: 812-963-7654
For a complete listing, refer to the Special Care Facilities section.

JASPER. *Providence Home, Nursing Home for the Needy,* 520 W. Ninth St., 47546. Tel: 812-482-6603; Fax: 812-481-1778
For a complete listing, refer to the Special Care Facilities section.

[F] RETREAT HOUSES

EVANSVILLE. *Sarto Retreat House,* 4200 N. Kentucky Ave., P.O. Box 4169, 47724-0169. Tel: 812-424-5536; Fax: 812-421-1334. Mrs. George-Anne Ryder, Dir.; Mrs. Carolyn Singer, Sec.

FERDINAND. *Kordes Enrichment Center,* 841 E. 14th St., 47532-9216. Tel: 812-367-2777. Sr. Barbara C. Schmitz, O.S.B., Dir.

[G] CONVENTS AND RESIDENCES FOR SISTERS

EVANSVILLE. *Daughters of Charity of St. Vincent de Paul of Indiana, Inc.,* 9400 New Harmony Rd., 47720. Tel: 812-963-3341. Sr. Catherine Madigan, D.C., Visitatrix; Rev. Patrick Harrity, C.M., Prov. Dir. Legal Title: *Daughters of Charity of St. Vincent de Paul of Indiana, Inc., Mater Dei Provincialate, Inc.*
Monastery of St. Clare, 6825 Nurrenbern Rd., 47712. Tel: 812-425-4396. Franciscan Poor Clare Nuns. Sr. Jeanne Maffet, O.S.C., Supr. Solemnly Professed Cloistered Nuns 16.

FERDINAND. *Sisters of St. Benedict of Ferdinand, IN, Inc., Monastery Immaculate Conception,* 802 E. Tenth St., 47532. Tel: 812-367-1411; Fax: 812-367-2313.
Web site: www.thedome.org
Sisters of St. Benedict. Sr. Joella Kidwell, O.S.B., Prioress; Rev. Matthias Neuman, O.S.B., Chap., St. Meinrad Chaplain Team. Professed Sisters in Community 199; Temporary Commitment 21; Novices 4; Postulants 2.

[H] NEWMAN CENTERS & CAMPUS MINISTRY

EVANSVILLE. *Newman Center for the University of Evansville,* 1901 Lincoln Ave., 47714. Tel: 812-477-6446. Joe Cook, Dir.
University of Southern Indiana Newman Center, 8600 University Blvd., 47712. Tel: 812-465-7095. Christine Hoehn, Dir.

OAKLAND CITY. *Oakland City College Newman Center,* Blessed Sacrament Church, R.R. 1, Box 72-A, 47660. Tel: 812-749-4474.

VINCENNES. *Vincennes University-Newman Center,* Vigo Hall, 47591. Tel: 812-888-4572. Ronald Campbell, Dir.

[I] MISCELLANEOUS

EVANSVILLE. *Catholic Education Foundation, Inc.,* P.O. Box 4169, 47724-0169. Linda Montejano, Dir.
East Central Province of Daughters of Charity, Inc., 9400 New Harmony Rd., 47720. Tel: 812-963-3341; Fax: 812-963-7589. Sr. Catherine Madigan, D.C., Board Chm.
Seton Health Corporation of Southern Indiana, 3700 Washington Ave., 47750. Tel: 812-485-8700; Fax: 812-485-8757. Sr. Veronica Ann Brown, D.C., Chm.; Marc Chivcop, Vice Pres.

LOOGOOTEE. *American-Innsbruck Alumni Association,* St. John Parish Church, 408 Church St., 47553. Tel: 812-295-2225. Rev. Leo C. Kiesel, Contact Person.

SANTA CLAUS. *The Outpost,* P.O. Box 64, 47579. Tel: 812-937-2723. Michael H. Eppler; John "Jack" Thompson, Camp Dir.

VINCENNES. *Old Cathedral Library & Museum, Inc.,* 205 Church St., 47591. Tel: 812-882-7016.
Web site: birch.palni.edu/~oldcath/oldcath.htm
Rev. John H. Schipp, Registered Agent.

RELIGIOUS INSTITUTES OF MEN REPRESENTED IN THE DIOCESE

For further details refer to the corresponding bracketed number in the Religious Institutes of Men or Women section.

[0200]—*Benedictine Monks.*—O.S.B.
[0600]—*Brothers of the Congregation of Holy Cross.* (Midwest Prov.).—C.S.C.
[1330]—*Congregation of the Mission.*—C.M.
[0410]—*Sons of Divine Providence.*—F.D.P.

RELIGIOUS INSTITUTES OF WOMEN REPRESENTED IN THE DIOCESE

[0230]—*Benedictine Sisters of Pontifical Jurisdiction.*—O.S.B.
[1070-13]—*Congregation of the Most Holy Rosary.* (Adrian, MI).—O.P.
[1730]—*Congregation of the Third Order of St. Francis.*—O.S.F.
[0760]—*Daughters of Charity of St. Vincent de Paul.*—D.C.
[2340]—*Little Sisters of the Poor.*—L.S.P.
[3760]—*Order of St. Clare.*—O.S.C.
[]—*Sisters for Christian Community.*—S.F.C.C.
[3360]—*Sisters of Providence of Saint Mary-of-the-Woods, Indiana.*—S.P.
[0260]—*Sisters of the Blessed Sacrament.*—S.B.S.
[2270]—*Sisters of the Little Company of Mary.*—L.C.M.
[1760]—*Sisters of the Third Order of St. Francis, of Penance and Charity.*—O.S.F.
[4120]—*Ursuline Nuns of the Congregation of Paris.* (Louisville, KY).—O.S.U.

JOINT CEMETERIES

EVANSVILLE. *St. Joseph,* 2500 Mesker Park Dr., 47712.
JASPER. *Fairview,* 1215 Newton St., 47546.
VINCENNES. *Calvary,* P.O. Box 4, 47591.
WASHINGTON. *St. John,* 101 N. Meridian St., 47501-2931.

NECROLOGY

† Bauer, Francis J., (Retired). —Died Feb. 5, 2000.
† Vollmer, Rev. Msgr. Roman F., (Retired). —Died Jan. 22, 2000.
† Wolf, Rev. Msgr. Michael O.J, Evansville, IN Little Sisters of the Poor. —Died March 26, 2000.

Diocese of Fairbanks

Most Reverend

RICHARD D. CASE, S.J.
Diocesan Administrator

Most Reverend

ROBERT LOUIS WHELAN, S.J., D.D.

Retired Bishop of Fairbanks; ordained June 17, 1944; appointed Titular Bishop of Sicilibba and Coadjutor Bishop of Fairbanks, *"cum jure successionis"* December 6, 1967; consecrated February 22, 1968; succeeded to November 30, 1968; retired July 28, 1985. *Mailing Address: Regis Community, 1107 N. Astor, Spokane, WA, 99202.*

(Vacant See)

Chancery Office: 1316 Peger Rd., Fairbanks, AK, 99709. Tel.: 907-474-0753; Fax: 907-474-8009.

Web site address: www.ptialaska.net/~cbna

E-mail address: chancllr@cbna.org

Corporate Title: "Catholic Bishop of Northern Alaska."

ESTABLISHED AS THE PREFECTURE APOSTOLIC OF ALASKA, JULY 27, 1894.

ERECTED INTO THE VICARIATE OF ALASKA, DEC. 22, 1916.; ELEVATED TO A DIOCESE, AUG. 8, 1962.

Square Miles 409,849.

Comprises all of the State of Alaska, north of the old Territorial Third Judicial Division whose boundary extended in a northwesterly direction from the Canadian Border along the crest of the Alaska range to Mount McKinley, thence southwesterly to Cape Newenham and west along the 58 parallel north of the Pribilof Islands.

For legal titles of parishes and diocesan institutions, consult the Chancery Office.

STATISTICAL OVERVIEW

Personnel	
Retired Bishops	1
Priests: Diocesan Active in Diocese	5
Priests: Active Outside Diocese	1
Priests: Retired, Sick or Absent	1
Number of Diocesan Priests	7
Religious Priests in Diocese	17
Extern Priests in Diocese	5
Ordinations:	
Transitional Deacons	1
Permanent Deacons	4
Permanent Deacons in Diocese	40
Total Brothers	4
Total Sisters	16
Parishes	
Parishes	41
With Resident Pastor:	
Resident Diocesan Priests	6
Resident Religious Priests	4
Without Resident Pastor:	
Administered by Priests	17
Administered by Deacons	1
Administered by Professed Men Religious	4
Administered by Women Religious	4
Administered by Lay People	12
Missions	7
Pastoral Centers	1
Professional Ministry Personnel:	
Brothers	3
Sisters	16
Lay Ministers	3
Welfare	
Special Centers for Social Services	1
Total Assisted	2,020
Educational	
Diocesan Students in Other Seminaries	2
Total Seminarians	2
High Schools, Diocesan and Parish	1
Total Students	216
Elementary Schools, Diocesan and Parish	1
Total Students	268
Catechesis/Religious Education:	
High School Students	607
Elementary Students	1,746
Total Students Under Catholic Instruction	2,839
Teachers in the Diocese:	
Sisters	2
Lay Teachers	43
Vital Statistics	
Receptions into the Church:	
Infant Baptism Totals	405
Adult Baptism Totals	43
Received into Full Communion	38
First Communions	433
Confirmations	299
Marriages:	
Catholic	47
Interfaith	22
Total Marriages	69
Deaths	126
Total Catholic Population	17,132
Total Population	155,224

Former Bishops—Most Rev. JOSEPH RAPHAEL CRIMONT, S.J., D.D., Vicar-Apostolic of Alaska; ord. Aug. 26, 1888; appt. Prefect-Apostolic March 28, 1904; appt. Vicar-Apostolic of Alaska Feb. 15, 1917; preconized Titular Bishop of Ammaedera, March 22, 1917; cons. July 25, 1917; died May 20, 1945.—Most Rev. WALTER J. FITZGERALD, S.J., D.D., Vicar-Apostolic of Alaska; ord. May 16, 1918; appt. Coadjutor Vicar-Apostolic of Alaska *cum jure successionis*, Dec. 14, 1938; cons. Titular Bishop of Tymbrias, Feb. 24, 1939; succeeded to as Vicar-Apostolic of Alaska, May 20, 1945; died July 19, 1947.—Most Rev. GEORGE T. BOILEAU, S.J., D.D., appt. Coadjutor Bishop *cum jure successionis*, April 21, 1964; cons. Titular Bishop of Ausuccura, July 31, 1964; died Feb. 25, 1965.—Most Rev. FRANCIS D. GLEESON, S.J., D.D., ord. July 29, 1926; appt. Titular Bishop of Cotenna and Vicar-Apostolic of Alaska Jan. 8, 1948; cons. April 5, 1948; appt. First Bishop of Fairbanks Aug. 8, 1962; retired Nov. 30, 1968; transferred to Titular See of Cuicul in Numidia and Assistant at the Pontifical Throne by Pope Paul VI, Feb. 3, 1969; died April 30, 1983.—Most Rev. ROBERT LOUIS WHELAN, S.J., D.D., retired Bishop of Fairbanks; ord. June 17, 1944; appt. Titular Bishop of Sicilibba and Coadjutor Bishop of Fairbanks, *cum jure successionis* Dec. 6, 1967; cons. Feb. 22, 1968; succeeded to Nov. 30, 1968; retired July 28, 1985.—Most Rev. MICHAEL J. KANIECKI, S.J., D.D., ord. June 5, 1965; appt. Coadjutor Bishop cumjure successionis, March 8, 1984; cons. May 1, 1984; succeeded to July 28, 1985; died Aug. 6, 2000.

Vicar General—Vacant.

Superior Regular—Rev. MARK A. HOELSKEN, S.J., *Bro. Joe Prince Jesuit Community, St. Mary's Mission Center, P.O. Box 49, St. Marys, 99658.*

Chancery Office—1316 Peger Rd., Fairbanks, 99709. Tel: 907-474-0753; Fax: 907-474-8009.

Chancellor—Sr. MARILYN MARX, S.N.J.M.

Secretary to Bishop—GERALDINE JAUHOLA.

Treasurer—GEORGE W. BOWDER.

Tribunal—Rev. PATRICK TRAVERS, J.C.L., J.D.

Adjutant Judicial Vicar—Rev. PATRICK TRAVERS, J.C.L, J.D.

Defender of the Bond—Rev. JOSEPH E. LAUDWEIN, S.J.

Promoter of Justice—Sr. CAROLYN A. ROEBER, O.P.

Auditor—BARBARA THIEME TOLLIVER.

Notaries—BARBARA THIEME TOLLIVER; Sr. MARILYN MARX, S.N.J.M.; GERALDINE JAUHOLA.

Presbyteral Council—Revs. PATRICK BERGQUIST; WILLIAM E. CARDY, O.F.M.; RICHARD D. CASE, S.J., Diocesan Admin. EDWARD J. HARTMANN; JACK DE VERTEUIL; JOHN A. HINSVARK; AL LEVITRE; JOHN MARTINEK; RICHARD MCCAFFREY, S.J.; GERALD ORNOWSKI, M.I.C.

Diocesan Archivist—Sr. MARILYN MARX, S.N.J.M.; DAVID SCHIENLE, Sec.

Diocesan Offices and Directors

Apostleship of Prayer—Rev. J. ALBERT LEVITRE, JR., Dir.

"Alaskan Shepherd" Office—Rev. LOUIS L. RENNER, S.J., Editor, *1312 Peger Rd., Fairbanks, 99709.* Tel: 907-474-0753.

Catholic Campaign for Human Development—Sr. MARILYN MARX, S.N.J.M.

Campus Ministry—Rev. GERALD ORNOWSKI, M.I.C., *514 Copper Ln. - UAF, P.O. Box 750166, Fairbanks, 99775.* Tel: 907-474-6776.

Catholic Community Resources—Vacant, *1316 Peger Rd., Fairbanks, 99709.* Tel: 907-474-0656.

Fairbanks Counseling and Adoption—MARGARET BROWNE, Dir., *912 Barnette, P.O. Box 1544, Fairbanks, 99707.* Tel: 907-456-4729.

Beginning Experience—Rev. TIMOTHY SANDER, O.S.B., Dir., *Box 74401, Fairbanks, 99707.* Tel: 907-452-1215.

Ecumenical Commission—Rev. AL LEVITRE.

Communications, Radio and TV—THOMAS BUSCH, Dir., KNOM Radio Station, *P.O. Box 988, Nome, 99762.* Tel: 907-443-5221.

Cursillo Movement—PEGGY MANTEI, Lay Dir.; Rev. J. ALBERT LEVITRE, Spiritual Dir.

The Children and Family Life Center—MADELINE NANCE.

Construction Committee—GEORGE W. BOWDER; Deacon PAUL PERREAULT, Chm. GEORGE SUNDBORG, JR.

Engaged Encounter—KELLY HUGHES; CRAIG HUGHES, *Fairbanks.* Tel: 907-479-6402.

Finance Advisory Board—Rev. RICHARD D. CASE, S.J., Chm.; Sr. KATHLEEN RADICH, O.S.F.; DONALD HOOVER; JAMES LYNCH; Sr. MARILYN MARX, S.N.J.M.; MICHAEL KELLIHER; JOSEPH PASKVAN.

Hispanic Ministry—Rev. NORMAND PEPIN, S.J.
Native Alaskan Ministries Coordinator—Sr. KATHLEEN RADICH, O.S.F., *St. Mary's Conf. Ctr., P.O. Box 29, St. Marys, 99658.*
Marriage Encounter—Vacant.
Ministry of Sick, Aged and Imprisoned—Rev. JOSEPH LAUDWEIN, S.J.; Sr. MARITA SOUCY, C.S.J.
Office of Religious Education—GERALD FINKLER, Dir., *1316 Peger Rd., Fairbanks, 99709.* Tel: 907-474-0753.
Office of Native Permanent Diaconate—Rev. THEODORE KESTLER, S.J., Acting Dir., *Jesuit Community, P.O. Box 49, St. Marys, 99658.* Tel: 907-438-2536; Fax: 907-438-2536.
Office of Urban Permanent Diaconate—Vacant, *1316 Peger Rd., Fairbanks, 99709.* Tel: 907-474-0753; Fax: 907-474-8009.
Office of Worship—Vacant.
Personnel—Sr. MARILYN MARX, S.N.J.M.
Pontifical Association of the Holy Childhood—Chancery Office.
Pontifical Society for Propagation of the Faith—Sr. MARILYN MARX, S.N.J.M.,Chancery Office.
Schools—NANCY COOK, Supt., *615 Monroe St., Fairbanks, 99701.* Tel: 907-456-8571.
Vocations—Ordained Ministries Formation Board: Revs. RICHARD D. CASE, S.J.; AL LEVITRE; Sr. MARILYN MARX, S.N.J.M.
Vocation Director—Rev. JOHN HINSVARK.

CLERGY, PARISHES, MISSIONS AND PAROCHIAL SCHOOLS

CITY OF FAIRBANKS NORTH STAR BOROUGH

1—SACRED HEART CATHEDRAL (1966), Rev. Edward J. Hartmann; Deacons Al Mazonna; Bill Dourte.
Res., 1316 Peger Rd., 99709. Tel: 907-474-0836; Fax: 907-479-3327.
Church—2501 Airport Way, 99709. Tel: 907-474-9032.
Catechesis/Religious Programs—Tel: 907-474-9033. Gigi Martinez, D.R.E.
Students 159.

2—IMMACULATE CONCEPTION (1904), Rev. Richard L. McCaffrey, S.J.; Deacons Robert Mantei; Sean Stack.
Res., 115 N. Cushman St., 99701. Tel: 907-452-3533; Fax: 907-456-3336. [JC]
Catechesis/Religious Programs—Deborah Harris, D.R.E.
Students 164.

3—ST. MARK UNIVERSITY PARISH (1977), Rev. Gerald Ornowski, M.I.C.; Deacon Paul Perreault.
Res., Box 750166, 99775. Tel: 907-474-6776.
Catechesis/Religious Programs—Students 12.

4—ST. RAPHAEL'S (1991), Rev. Patrick D. Bergquist.
Res., P.O. Box 10508, 99710. Tel: 907-457-6603; Fax: 907-457-4461.
Catechesis/Religious Programs—Gloria Slagle, D.R.E., (Grades K-12).
Students 130.

OUTSIDE CITY OF FAIRBANKS

Alakanuk, St. Ignatius (1954) (Yup'ik), Rev. Thomas G. Provinsal, S.J.; Deacons Joseph Phillip, (Retired); Emmanuel Stanislaus; Denis Shelden; Charles Clyde Smith.
Res., P.O. Box 53, 99554. Tel: 907-238-3914. [CEM][JC]
Mission—Sheldon Point, St. Peter's, P.O. Box 45, Sheldon Point, 99666. Tel: 907-498-4246.

Aniak, St. Theresa (1935) (Yup'ik). Unassigned.
Res., P.O. Box 308, 99557. Tel: 907-675-4448. [CEM]
Mission—Kalskag, Box 11, Kalskag, 99607. Tel: 907-471-2298. Sr. Anne Hogan, S.S.J., Pastoral Admin.

Barrow, North Slope Borough, St. Patrick (1954). Unassigned.
Mailing Address: P.O. Box 389, 99723. Tel: 907-852-3515. [JC]

Bethel, Immaculate Conception (1942), Rev. Eugene P. Delmore, S.J.; Deacon Peter Aluska.
Res., 790 River St., P.O. Box 428, 99559. Tel: 907-543-2464.
Catechesis/Religious Programs—Susan Murphy, D.R.E.
Students 120.

Chefornak, St. Catherine (1937) (Yup'ik), Rev. Mark A. Hoelsken, S.J.; Agnes Kairaiuak, Acting Parish Admin.; Deacons David Panruk; Joe Avugiak; Cyril Alexie, (Retired); David Erik, (Retired).
Res., P.O. Box 90, 99561. Tel: 907-867-8702. [CEM]
Catechesis/Religious Programs—Students 134.

Chevak, Sacred Heart (1952) (Cup'ik), Rev. Gregg D. Wood, S.J.; Doris A. Atchak, Acting Parish Admin.; Deacons Frank Smart; David Boyscout.
Res., P.O. Box 249, 99563. Tel: 907-858-7826. [CEM]
Catechesis/Religious Programs—Students 87.

Delta Junction, Our Lady of Sorrows (1959), Rev. William E. Cardy, O.F.M.
Res., 2565 Deborah St., Box 446, 99737. Tel: 907-895-5232.
Catechesis/Religious Programs—Students 39.
Mission—Tok, Holy Rosary, P.O. Box 369, Tok, 99780. Tel: 907-883-4111. Sr. Frances McCarron, I.B.V.M., Pastoral Admin.
Stations—Northway, St. Ann.; Eagle, St. Francis Xavier.

Emmonak, Sacred Heart (1953) (Yup'ik), Rev. Thomas G. Provinsal, S.J.; Deacons Bart Agathluk, Sr.; Raymond Waska.
Res., P.O. Box 190, 99581. Tel: 907-949-1012. [JC]
Catechesis/Religious Programs—Dorothy Kameroff, D.R.E.
Students 175.

Galena, St. John Berchman (1923) (Athabascan), Rev. Andrew Maslanka; Bro. Justin Huber, O.F.M.
Res., P.O. Box 131, 99741. Tel: 907-656-1240; Fax: 907-656-1240.
Catechesis/Religious Programs—Students 36.
Station—Huslia, St. Francis Regis, Tel: 907-829-2234.

Healy, Holy Mary of Guadalupe (1984), Rev. Jack de Verteuil; Barbara Walters, Pastoral Min.
Mailing Address: P.O. Box 32, 99743.
Church—P.O. Box 32, 99743. Tel: 907-683-2535; 683-1018 (Rectory).
Mission—Cantwell. [JC]

Holy Cross, Holy Family (1888). Unassigned.
Res., P.O. Box 101, 99602. Tel: 907-476-7144; Fax: 907-476-7144.

Hooper Bay, Little Flower of Jesus (1928) (Yup'ik), Rev. Gregg D. Wood, S.J.; Deacon James Gump, (Retired).
Res., P.O. Box 9, 99604. Tel: 907-758-4620; Fax: 907-758-4620. [JC]
Catechesis/Religious Programs—Students 25.

Kaltag, St. Teresas (Athabaskan), Rev. Joseph Hemmer, O.F.M.
Res., P.O. Box 69, 99748. Tel: 907-534-2218. [JC]
Catechesis/Religious Programs—Students 39.

Kotlik, St. Joseph (1949) (Yup'ik), Rev. Rene Astruc, S.J.; Deacons Henry Teeluk, (Retired); Raymond Teeluk, (On Leave); Aloysius Wasuli.
Church—P.O. Box 20228, 99620. Tel: 907-899-4715.
Catechesis/Religious Programs—Students 144.

Kotzebue, Northwest Arctic Borough, St. Francis Xavier (1929), Rev. John B. Martinek.
Res., Box 358, 99752. Tel: 907-442-3239; Fax: 907-442-3239. [CEM][JC]

Koyukuk, St. Patrick (Athabascan), Rev. Andrew Maslanka.
Res., P.O. Box 54101, 99754. Tel: 907-927-2240.

Marshall, Immaculate Heart of Mary (1930) (Yup'ik). Unassigned. Deacon Alvin Owletuck, (Retired); Ms. Clara Shorty, Parish Admin.
Mailing Address: P.O. Box 69, 99585. Tel: 907-679-6639; Fax: 907-679-6639.
Catechesis/Religious Programs—Students 47.
Mission—Russian Mission, Wade Hampton Co., Our Lady of Guadalupe Russian Mission, P.O. Box 56, Russian Mission, 99657. Tel: 907-584-5173.

McGrath, St. Michael (1960). Unassigned.
Res., P.O. Box 141, 99627. Tel: 907-524-3928.
Station—Takotna, Tel: 907-298-2328.

Mountain Village, Northwest Arctic Borough, St. Lawrence (1918) (Yup'ik), Rev. Rene Astruc, S.J.; Deacon Elmer Beans; Susie Luke, Parish Admin.
Res. & Mailing Address—P.O. Box 32205, 99632. Tel: 907-591-2348.

Nenana, St. Theresa (1922). Served out of Healy, AK. Sr. Agnes Anne Wilcox, S.M.S.M., Pastoral Admin.; Rev. Jack deVerteuil, Visiting Priest.
P.O. Box 312, 99760. Tel: 907-832-5617. [JC]
Catechesis/Religious Programs—Students 13.

Newtok, Holy Family (1950) (Yup'ik), Rev. Mark A. Hoelsken, S.J.; Deacons Larry Charles; Mark Tom; Ignatius Tommy, Parish Admin.
Res., P.O. Box WWT, 99559. Tel: 907-237-2427. [CEM]
Catechesis/Religious Programs—Sophie John, D.R.E.
Students 70.

Nightmute, Our Lady of Perpetual Help (1950) (Yup'ik), Rev. David Anderson, S.J.; Cecilia Anthony, Acting Parish Admin.; Deacons Thomas Jumbo; Camillus Tulik.
Res., 99690. Tel: 907-647-6428. [CEM]
Catechesis/Religious Programs—Students 70.

Nome, St. Joseph (1901), Rev. John Hinsvark.
Res., P.O. Box 1010, 99762. Tel: 907-443-5527; Fax: 907-443-5757. [CEM]
Catechesis/Religious Programs—Students 21.
Mission—Diomede, St. Jude.

North Pole, North Star Borough, St. Nicholas (1975), Rev. J. Albert Levitre, Jr.; Deacon Walt Gelinas.
Res., 707 St. Nicholas Dr., 99705. Tel: 907-488-2595; Fax: 907-488-9625.
Catechesis/Religious Programs—Susan Hurley, D.R.E.
Students 130.
Station—Manley Hot Springs.

Nulato, Our Lady of the Snows (1877) (Athabascan), Rev. Andrew Maslanka; Bro. Robert Ruzicka, O.F.M.
Res., P.O. Box 89, 99765. Tel: 907-898-2242.
Catechesis/Religious Programs—Students 50.

Pilot Station, St. Charles Spinola (1914) (Yup'ik). Unassigned.
Mailing Address: P.O. Box 5120, 99650. Tel: 907-549-3231; Fax: 907-549-3231. [JC]
Catechesis/Religious Programs—Students 65.

Ruby, St. Peter-in-Chains (1912) (Athabascan), Rev. Joseph Hemmer, O.F.M.
Res., P.O. Box 207, 99768. Tel: 907-468-4482; 468-4413. [JC]

St. Marys, Church of the Nativity, Rev. Theodore E. Kestler, S.J.; Deacon Patrick L. Beans, Sr., (Retired).
Res., P.O. Box 105, 99658. Tel: 907-438-2133; Fax: 907-438-2146. [CEM]
Catechesis/Religious Programs—Students 70.

St. Michael, St. Michael (1895) (Yup'ik), Rev. Ward W. Walker.
Res., P.O. Box 29, 99659. Tel: 907-923-3151. [JC]
Catechesis/Religious Programs—Students 28.

Scammon Bay, Blessed Sacrament (1930) (Yup'ik), Darlene Cholok, Admin.; Rev. Gregg D. Wood, S.J., Itinerant Min.; Deacon Francis Charlie.
Res., P.O. Box 133, 99662. Tel: 907-558-5229. [JC]

Stebbins, St. Bernard (1908) (Yup'ik), Rev. Ward W. Walker; Margaret Marlin, Acting Admin.
Res., 99671. Tel: 907-934-3151. [JC]
Catechesis/Religious Programs—Students 22.

Tanana, St. Aloysius (1887) (Athabascan), Bro. Kirby Boone, C.F.X., Pastoral Min.; Rev. Joseph Laudwein, S.J., Visiting Priest.
Res., P.O. Box 6, 99777. Tel: 907-366-7238. [JC]

Teller, St. Ann (1909), Rev. John Hinsvark.
Res., P.O. Box 529, 99778. Tel: 907-642-3831.

Tok, Holy Rosary (1949), Rev. William E. Cardy, O.F.M.; Sr. Frances McCarron, I.B.V.M., Pastoral Admin.
Res., P.O. Box 369, 99780. Tel: 907-883-4111; Fax: 907-883-4111.

Toksook Bay, St. Peter the Fisherman (1964) (Central Yup'ik), Deacon James Charlie; Rev. David J. Anderson, S.J.; Deacons Joseph Asuluk, Sr.; Nick Therchik, Sr.; Gregory Charlie; Maggie John, Acting Parish Admin.
P.O. Box 37046, 99637. Tel: 907-427-7813. [CEM]
Catechesis/Religious Programs—Tel: 907-427-7826; Fax: 907-427-7820. Maria Abraham, D.R.E.
Students 179.
Station—Umkumute.

Tununak, Northwest Arctic Borough, St. Joseph (Yup'ik), Rev. David J. Anderson, S.J.; Josephine Link, Acting Admin.; Deacons Dick Lincoln, (Retired); Mike Angaiak, (Retired).
Res., P.O. Box 09, 99681. Tel: 907-652-6214; Fax: 907-652-6214. [CEM]
Catechesis/Religious Programs—Tel: 907-652-6237.
Students 108.

Unalakleet, Northwest, Church of the Holy Angels (1952), Rev. Ward W. Walker.
Res., P.O. Box 152, 99684. Tel: 907-624-3711.
Catechesis/Religious Programs—Students 17.

Leave of Absence:
Reverend Fathers—
Wallner, Gerhard

Permanent Deacons:
Agathluk, Bart, Sacred Heart, Emmonak
Alexie, Cyril, St. Catherine's, Chefornak
Aluska, Peter, Sr., Immaculate Conception, Bethel
Angaiak, Michael, St. Joseph Church, Tununak
Asuluk, Joe, St. Peter Fisherman, Toksook Bay
Avugiak, Joe, St. Catherine, Chefornak
Barnard, Robert, Fairbanks - Fort Wainwright
Beans, Elmer, St. Lawrence Church, Mountain Village
Beans, Patrick L., Church of the Nativity, St. Mary
Boyscout, David, Sacred Heart Church, Chevak

Charles, Larry, Holy Family Church, Newtok
Charlie, Francis, Blessed Sacrament, Scammon Bay
Charlie, Gregory, St. Peter the Fisherman, Toksook Bay
Charlie, James, St. Peter the Fisherman, Toksook Bay
Dourte, William, Sacred Heart Cathedral, Fairbanks
Edwards, Patrick, St. Charles Spinola, Pilot Station
Eric, David, St. Catherine's, Chefornak
Gelinas, Walt, St. Nicholas, North Pole
Gump, James, Little Flower Mission, Hooper Bay
Jumbo, Thomas, Our Lady of Perpetual Help, Nightmute
Lincoln, Dick, St. Joseph's, Tununak
Mantei, Robert, Immaculate Conception, Fairbanks
Mazonna, Alvin, Sacred Heart Cathedral, Fairbanks
Panruk, David, St. Catherine, Chefornak
Perreault, Paul, Sacred Heart Cathedral, Fairbanks
Phillip, Joseph, St. Ignatius, Alakanuk
Shelden, Denis, St. Ignatius, Alakanuk
Smart, Frank, Sacred Heart Church, Chevak
Smith, Clyde, St. Ignatius, Alakanuk
Stack, Sean, Immaculate Conception, Fairbanks
Stanislaus, Emmanuel, St. Ignatius, Alakanuk
Steve, Charlie, St. Bernard Church, Stebbins
Teeluk, Henry, St. Joseph Church, Kotlik
Therchik, Nick, St. Peter the Fisherman, Toksook Bay
Tom, Mark, Holy Family, Newtok
Tulik, Camillus, Our Lady of Perpetual Help, Nightmute
Waska, Ray, Sacred Heart, Emmonak
Wasuli, Aloysius, St. Joseph, Kotlik

INSTITUTIONS LOCATED IN THE DIOCESE

[A] HIGH SCHOOLS, DIOCESAN

FAIRBANKS. *Monroe Catholic Junior-Senior High School*, 615 Monroe St., 99701. Tel: 907-452-2044; Fax: 907-456-7481.
E-mail: monroehs@polarnet.com
Web site: www.catholic-schools.org
Mr. John Hoffman, Prin.; Rev. Normand A. Pepin, S.J. Priests 1; Lay Teachers 22; Religious 1; Students 218.

[B] GRADE SCHOOLS, DIOCESAN

FAIRBANKS. *Immaculate Conception Grade School*, 715 Monroe St., 99701. Tel: 907-456-4574; Fax: 907-456-7481.
E-mail: monroehs@polarnet.com
Ms. Nancy Cook, Prin. Sisters 2; Lay Teachers 19; Students 234.

[C] RESIDENCES FOR PRIESTS AND BROTHERS

FAIRBANKS. *Jesuit Residence*, 2890 N. Kobuk Ave., 99709. Tel: 907-474-9320; Fax: 907-479-9073. Revs. Joseph Laudwein, S.J., Supr.; Richard D. Case, S.J.; Normand A. Pepin, S.J.; Louis L. Renner, S.J.; Richard L. McCaffrey, S.J.; Bro. Michael Bennett, S.J. Regional Offices of the Society of Jesus, Alaska.

[D] CONVENTS AND RESIDENCES OF SISTERS

FAIRBANKS. *Diocesan Convent*, 1316 Peger Rd., 99709. Tel: 907-474-9538. Sr. Maria Teresa Boulet, O.P.; Sr. Marita Soucy, O.P.; Sr. Marilyn Marx, S.N.J.M. Sisters 3.

Immaculate Conception Convent, 615 Betty St., 99701. Tel: 907-452-2750. Sr. Felicitas Farrell, O.P.; Sr. Michele Kaelin, C.S.J.; Sr. Patricia Mayer, S.C. Sisters 3.

Xavier Hall, 417 Monroe St., 99701. Tel: 907-452-1322.

NOME. *Little Sisters of Jesus*, Box 845, 99762. Tel: 907-443-2094. Sr. Odette, L.S.J.; Sr. Damiene, L.S.J.; Sr. Yoshie, L.S.J. Sisters 3.

[E] MISCELLANEOUS LISTINGS

FAIRBANKS. *Bishop's Attic, III*, 4523 Old Airport Way, 99709. Tel: 907-474-0209; Fax: 907-474-0204.
E-mail: treasure@cbna.org
Web site: www2.polarnet.com/~cbna/

House of Prayer, 1316 Peger Rd., 99709. Tel: 907-474-9379. Rev. Normand A. Pepin, S.J., Dir.; Sr. Marie Teresa Boulet, O.P.

Monroe Foundation, Inc., P.O. Box 71620, 99707. Tel: 907-456-7970; Fax: 907-456-7481.
E-mail: hipow@ptialaska.net
Nancy Cook, Exec. Dir., 718 Betty St., 99701.

Voice in the Wilderness Prayer Community, 2501 Airport Rd., 99709.

NOME. *Alaska Radio Mission, Station KNOM*, Box 988, 99762. Tel: 907-443-5221; Fax: 907-443-5757.
E-mail: busch@knom.org
Web site: www.knom.org
Thomas Busch, Gen. Mgr. Total Staff 11; Total in Residence 4.

ST. MARYS. *Brother Joe Prince Jesuit Community*, P.O. Box 49, 99658. Tel: 907-438-2536; Fax: 907-438-2146.
E-mail: mhoelsken@juno.com
Revs. Mark A. Hoelsken, S.J., Supr., Pastoral Ministry, Chefornak & Newton, AK; David J. Anderson, S.J., Pastoral Ministry, Toksook Bay, Tununak & Nightmute, AK; Rene Astruc, S.J., Pastoral Ministry, Mountain Village & Kotlik, AK; Eugene P. Delmore, S.J., Pastor, Immaculate Conception, Bethel, AK; Henry G. Hargreaves, S.J., Pastoral Ministry, Bethel, AK; Theodore E. Kestler, S.J., Asst. in Native Ministry Training Program, Pastoral Ministry, St. Mary's, AK; Thomas G. Provinsal, S.J., Pastoral Ministry, Alakunak, Emmonak, & Sheldon Point, AK; Gregg D. Wood, S.J., Pastoral Ministry, Hooper Bay, Scammon Bay, & Chevak, AK.

Native Ministry Training Program, P.O. Box 29, 99658-0029. Tel: 907-438-2832; Fax: 907-438-2832.
E-mail: nmtp@juno.com
Sr. Ellen Callaghan, O.S.F., Dir.; Rev. Theodore E. Kestler, S.J.; L. William Naneng; Pamela A. Tweto. Total Staff 4; Total in Residence 4.

St. Marys Conference Center, P.O. Box 172, 99658. Tel: 907-438-2712; Fax: 907-438-2823.
E-mail: weingarth@juno.com
Erik Weingarth, Admin. Total in Residence 7; Total Staff 12.

RELIGIOUS INSTITUTES OF MEN REPRESENTED IN THE DIOCESE

For further details refer to the corresponding bracketed number in the Religious Institutes of Men or Women section.

[0200]—*Benedictine Monks.*—O.S.B.
[0520]—*Franciscan Friars and Brothers.*—O.F.M.
[0690]—*Jesuit Fathers and Brothers.*—S.J.
[0740]—*Marian Fathers.*—M.I.C.
[1350]—*Xaverian Brothers.*—C.F.X.

RELIGIOUS INSTITUTES OF WOMEN REPRESENTED IN THE DIOCESE

[1070-03]—*Dominican Sisters.*—O.P.
[1070-05]—*Dominican Sisters.*—O.P.
[2370]—*Institute of the Blessed Virgin Mary.*—I.B.V.M.
[2330]—*Little Sisters of Jesus.*—L.S.J.
[2420]—*Missionary Sisters Society of Mary.*—S.M.S.M.
[0590]—*Sisters of Charity of Saint Elizabeth, Convent Station.* (Northern Prov.).—S.C.
[1650]—*The Sisters of St. Francis of Philadelphia.*—O.S.F.
[3830-12]—*Sisters of St. Joseph.* Ogdensburg.—S.S.J.
[3850]—*Sisters of St. Joseph of Carondelet.*—C.S.J.
[1990]—*Sisters of the Holy Names of Jesus and Mary.*—S.N.J.M.

NECROLOGY

(No Deaths)

Diocese of Fall River

(Dioecesis Riverormensis)

Most Reverend

SEAN O'MALLEY, O.F.M.CAP., PH.D.

Bishop of Fall River; ordained August 29, 1970; named Coadjutor May 30, 1984; appointed Bishop of St. Thomas, Virgin Islands; ordained August 2, 1984; installed October 16, 1985; appointed Bishop of Fall River June 16, 1992; installed August 11, 1992.

ESTABLISHED MARCH 12, 1904.

Square Miles 1,194.

Comprises Bristol, Barnstable, Dukes and Nantucket Counties, and the Towns of Marion, Mattapoisett and Wareham in Plymouth County, Massachusetts.

For legal titles of parishes and diocesan institutions, consult the Chancery Office.

Chancery Office: Box 2577, Fall River, MA, 02722. Tel.: *508-675-1311; Fax: 508-679-9220.*

E-mail address: Chancery@dioc-fr.org

STATISTICAL OVERVIEW

Personnel	
Bishop	1
Priests: Diocesan Active in Diocese	134
Priests: Active Outside Diocese	1
Priests: Diocesan in Foreign Missions	2
Priests: Retired, Sick or Absent	30
Number of Diocesan Priests	167
Religious Priests in Diocese	130
Ordinations:	
Diocesan Priests	6
Religious Priests	1
Transitional Deacons	8
Permanent Deacons in Diocese	62
Total Brothers	26
Total Sisters	314
Parishes	
Parishes	106
With Resident Pastor:	
Resident Diocesan Priests	89
Resident Religious Priests	11
Without Resident Pastor:	
Administered by Priests	6
Missions	11
New Parishes Created	1
Closed Parishes	4
Professional Ministry Personnel:	
Brothers	1
Sisters	10
Lay Ministers	54
Welfare	
Catholic Hospitals	1
Total Assisted	85,270
Health Care Centers	1
Total Assisted	102
Homes for the Aged	5
Total Assisted	1,000
Residential Care of Children	1
Total Assisted	160
Day Care and Extended Day Care Centers	2
Total Assisted	105
Specialized Homes	4
Total Assisted	210
Special Centers for Social Services	6
Total Assisted	42,007
Educational	
Diocesan Students in Other Seminaries	16
Students Religious	10
Total Seminarians	26
Colleges and Universities	1
Total Students	2,165
High Schools, Diocesan and Parish	4
Total Students	2,731
Elementary Schools, Diocesan and Parish	24
Total Students	5,987
Catechesis/Religious Education:	
High School Students	5,603
Elementary Students	32,270
Total Students Under Catholic Instruction	48,782
Teachers in the Diocese:	
Priests	22
Brothers	4
Sisters	23
Lay Teachers	676
Vital Statistics	
Receptions into the Church:	
Infant Baptism Totals	4,920
Adult Baptism Totals	121
Received into Full Communion	233
First Communions	4,847
Confirmations	3,737
Marriages:	
Catholic	1,535
Interfaith	373
Total Marriages	1,908
Deaths	6,073
Total Catholic Population	348,549
Total Population	787,876

Former Bishops—Most Rev. WILLIAM STANG, D.D., ord. June 15, 1878; appt. March 12, 1904; cons. May 1, 1904; died Feb. 2, 1907.—Most Rev. DANIEL F. FEEHAN, D.D., ord. Dec. 20, 1879; appt. July 2, 1907; cons. Sept. 19, 1907; died July 19, 1934.—Most Rev. JAMES E. CASSIDY, D.D., ord. Sept. 8, 1898; appt. Titular Bishop of Ibora and Auxiliary, March 21, 1930; cons. May 27, 1930; succeeded to the See, July 28, 1934; died May 17, 1951.—Most Rev. JAMES L. CONNOLLY, D.D., D.Sc.H., ord. Dec. 21, 1923; appt. Titular Bishop of Mylasa and Coadjutor "cum jure successionis," April 18, 1945; cons. May 24, 1945; succeeded to See, May 17, 1951; retired Oct. 30, 1970; died Sept. 12, 1986.—Most Rev. DANIEL A. CRONIN, D.D., S.T.D., ord. Dec. 20, 1952; appt. Titular Bishop of Egnatia and Auxiliary Bishop of Boston, June 10, 1968; cons. Sept. 12, 1968; transferred Fall River, Oct. 30, 1970; installed Dec. 16, 1970; transferred Hartford, Dec. 9, 1991.

Vicar General—Rev. Msgr. GEORGE W. COLEMAN, V.G., *P.O. Box 2577, Fall River, 02722.*

Cabinet Secretaries—

Secretary for Community Service—Rev. EDWARD J. HEALEY, *327 Second St., Fall River, 02721.* Tel: 508-673-2833; Fax: 508-672-0667.

Secretary for Health Care—Rev. Msgr. EDMUND J. FITZGERALD, V.F., *368 N. Main St., Fall River, 02720.* Tel: 508-679-8154; Fax: 508-679-1422.

Secretary for Spiritual Development/Apostolates—Rev. Msgr. THOMAS J. HARRINGTON, J.C.L., *121 Mt. Pleasant St., New Bedford, 02745.* Tel: 508-992-3184.

Secretary for Youth—Rev. GEORGE E. HARRISON, *984 Taunton Ave., Seekonk, 02771.* Tel: 508-336-9022; Fax: 508-336-9010.

Secretary for Temporalities—Rev. MICHAEL K. MCMANUS, *P.O. Box 2577, Fall River, 02722.* Tel: 508-675-1311; Fax: 508-730-2447.

Secretary for Communications—Rev. Msgr. JOHN F. MOORE, *P.O. Box 7, Fall River, 02720.* Tel: 508-675-0211; Fax: 508-675-7048.

Secretary for Education/Evangelization—Rev. Msgr. JOHN J. OLIVEIRA, P.A., *106 Illinois St., New Bedford, 02745.* Tel: 508-995-3593; Fax: 508-995-2453.

Secretary for Ministerial Personnel—Rev. Msgr. JOHN A. PERRY, *P.O. Box 718, E. Freetown, 02717.* Tel: 508-763-2240; Fax: 508-763-3040.

Chancery—450 Highland Ave., Fall River, 02745., Mailing Address: P.O. Box 2577, Fall River, 02722-2577. Tel: 508-675-1311; Fax: 508-730-2447.

Chancellor—Rev. MICHAEL K. MCMANUS.

Secretary to the Bishop—Rev. RICHARD D. WILSON, *394 Highland Ave., Fall River, 02720.*

Diocesan Tribunal—887 Highland Ave., Fall River, 02720. Tel: 508-675-7150; Fax: 508-675-7295.

Judicial Vicar—Rev. JAY T. MADDOCK, J.C.L.

Adjutant Judicial Vicar—Rev. PAUL F. ROBINSON, O.Carm., J.C.D.

Promoter Justitiae—Rev. Msgr. DANIEL F. HOYE, J.C.L.

Judges—Rev. Msgr. HENRY T. MUNROE, P.A.; Revs. RICHARD W. BEAULIEU; THOMAS L. RITA; GERARD A. HEBERT, J.C.L.; MARK R. HESSION, J.C.L.; THOMAS E. MCGLYNN, J.C.L.; Deacon VICTOR HADDAD, J.C.L.

Defenders of the Bond—Rev. ROLAND BOUSQUET, S.T.L.; Rev. Msgr. THOMAS J. HARRINGTON, J.C.L.; Rev. Msgr. DANIEL F. HOYE, J.C.L.

Advocates—Revs. MARC H. BERGERON; BRUCE M. NEYLON; Rev. Msgr. JOHN J. OLIVEIRA, P.A.; Revs. LUCIO B. PHILLIPINO; HORACE J. TRAVASSOS.

Advocate/Auditor—Revs. DAVID M. ANDRADE; JOSE M. SOUSA, J.C.L.

Auditors—Revs. DANIEL W. LACROIX; JOHN J. PERRY; HENRY J. DAHL; Deacons PAUL FOURNIER; ROBERT LEMAY; ROBERT SURPRENANT.

Notaries—DENISE BERUBE; HELENE BEAUDOIN.

Diocesan Consultors—Rev. PAUL E. CANUEL; Rev. Msgr. GEORGE W. COLEMAN, V.G.; Rev. Msgr. EDMUND J. FITZGERALD, V.F.; Revs. EDWARD J. HEALEY; MICHAEL K. MCMANUS; JOHN J. OLIVEIRA; Rev. Msgr. JOHN A. PERRY.

Presbyteral Council—Rev. Msgr. EDMUND J. FITZGERALD, V.F., Chm.; Revs. MAURICE O. GAUVIN, Vice Chm. CRAIG A. PREGANA, Sec., *P.O. Box 2577, Fall River, 02722.* Members: Very Rev. HENRY S. ARRUDA, V.F.; Rev. Msgr. STEPHEN J. AVILA; Revs. GEORGE C. BELLENOIT; JOSEPH BLYSKOSZ; ROMAN CHWALISZEWSKI, O.F.M.Conv.; RICHARD L. CHRETIEN; Rev. Msgr. GEORGE W. COLEMAN, V.G.; Revs. JAMES W. FAHEY; JAMES FERRY; Very Rev. BENTO R.

FRAGA, V.F.; Revs. JOHN A. GOMES; BRIAN J. HARRINGTON; TERENCE F. KEENAN; MICHAEL K. MCMANUS; Very Rev. ROBERT A. OLIVEIRA, V.F.; Rev. Msgr. JOHN A. PERRY, V.F.; Rev. THOMAS L. RITA.

Deans—Fall River Deanery: Rev. Msgr. EDMUND J. FITZGERALD, V.F., *945 Main Rd., P.O. Box 3328, Westport, 02790.* Taunton Deanery: Very Rev. BENTO R. FRAGA, V.F., *261 Tremont St., Taunton, 02780.* Attleboro Deanery: Very Rev. ROBERT A. OLIVEIRA, V.F., *P.O. Box 430, Norton, 02766.* Cape Cod Deanery: Rev. Msgr. JOHN A. PERRY, V.F., *511 Main St., P.O. Box 569, Falmouth, 02541-0569.* New Bedford Deanery: Very Rev. HENRY S. ARRUDA, V.F., *230 Bonney St., New Bedford, 02744.*

Diocesan Offices and Directors

Apostolate for Persons with Disabilities—Vacant, *243 Forest St., Fall River, 02721.* Tel: 508-679-8373; 674-5741, Ext. 2270.

Campus Ministry—

Bristol Community College—Rev. LUCA BRANCOLINI, F.S.C.B.; Sr. ANNETTE BIBEAU, S.S.A., *777 Elsbree St., Fall River, 02720.* Tel: 508-678-2811, Ext. 301.

University of Massachusetts Dartmouth—Rev. CRAIG A. PREGANA; Sr. MADELEINE TACY, O.P. Tel: 508-999-8872.

Wheaton College—Rev. LUCA BRANCOLINI, F.S.C.B.

Massachusetts Maritime Academy—Vacant.

Cape Cod Community College—Vacant.

Catholic Youth Organization—Rev. JAY T. MADDOCK, Dir., *403 Anawan St., Fall River, 02720.*

Catholic Charities Appeal—Rev. Msgr. THOMAS J. HARRINGTON, Dir., Office: *450 Highland Ave., Fall River, 02720.*

Diocesan Apostolate to Hispanics—Rev. RICHARD D. WILSON, Diocesan Dir., *P.O. Box 2577, Fall River, 02722.* Tel: 508-675-1311; Fax: 508-679-9220. Area Offices, Fall River: Revs. EDWARD J. HEALEY, Rector; RAMON DOMINGUEZ, Dir.; Sr. AIDA SANSOR, M.G-.Sp.S., Pastoral Assoc., *327 Second St., Fall River, 02721.* Tel: 508-672-9303. Attleboro: Rev. MICHAEL CARVILL, F.S.C.B., Dir. Tel: 508-222-1730. Sr. ANA GABRIELA CASTRO, M.G.Sp.S., Pastoral Assoc. Tel: 508-997-8729; 222-1730. Taunton: Rev. FRANCIS T. ZLOTKOWSKI, C.S.C., Dir. Tel: 508-822-7116; Fax: 508-822-7117. Sr. SANDRA CAMPOS, M.G.Sp.S. Tel: 508-997-8729; 880-5062., *14 St. Mary's Square, Taunton, 02780.* New Bedford: Rev. KEVIN J. HARRINGTON, Dir.; Sr. CANDELARIA HERNANDEZ, M.G-.Sp.S, Pastoral Assoc. Tel: 508-997-8729; Fax: 508-997-4537., *P.O. Box 40605, New Bedford, 02744.* Tel: 508-996-5862; Fax: 508-992-2208. Cape Cod: Rev. RICHARD WILSON, Dir., *P.O. Box 2577, Fall River, 02722.* Tel: 508-675-1311; Fax: 508-679-9220. Sr. OBDULIA OLIVAR, M.G.Sp.S., Pastoral Assoc., *St. Francis Xavier Church, 347 South St., Hyannis, 02601.* Tel: 508-771-2658; 997-8729.

Director of Ministry to Sick, Retired, and Senior Priests—Rev. JOHN P. CRONIN, *818 Middle St., Fall River, 02721.*

Director of Portuguese Ministry—Rev. JOHN J. OLIVEIRA, *344 Country St., New Bedford, 02740.*

Diocesan Archives—Rev. BARRY W. WALL, *P.O. Box 2577, Fall River, 02722.*

Diocesan Office of Communications—Rev. Msgr. JOHN F. MOORE, Dir. JOHN E. KEARNS, JR., Assoc. Dir. STEPHEN J. MEDEIROS, Asst. Dir., *887 Highland Ave., Fall River, 02720.* Tel: 508-675-7151., *Mailing Address: P.O. Box 7, Fall River, 02722.*

Diocesan Director of Cemeteries—Rev. JOHN P. CRONIN, *818 Middle St., Fall River, 02721.* Tel: 508-673-0377.

Diocesan Education Center—Rev. WILLIAM T. GARLAND, O.S.A., Dir. Schools; JAMES A. MCNAMEE, Supt. Schools; Deacon BRUCE J. BONNEAU, Dir. Rel. Educ. LISA M. GULINO, Dir. Adult Educ., *Office, 423 Highland Ave., Fall River, 02720.* Tel: 508-678-2828; Fax: 508-674-4218.

Diocesan Department of Pastoral Care for the Sick—Rev. EDWARD J. HEALEY, Dir.; Sr. SHIRLEY AGNEW, R.S.M., Asst. Dir., Office: *327 Second St., Fall River, 02721.* Tel: 508-673-2833; Fax: 508-672-0667. Rev. ROBERT A. ROCHON; Sr. CAROLE V.M. MELLO, O.P.; Sr. LORNA RIORDAN, O.P.; Sr. MARY ANN GORELCZENKO, M.S.B.T., *St. Anne's Hospital, 795 Middle St., Fall River, 02721.* Revs. MAREK S. TUPTYNSKI; BRIAN ALBINO; Sr. JACQUELINE DUBOIS, S.S.A.; Sr. LUCILLE SOCCIARELLI, R.S.M., *Charlton Memorial Hospital, Fall River, 02721.* Revs. VINCENT NAGLE; CHRISTOPHER STANIBULA; Sr. ANNETTE LANGLOIS, S.A.S.V., *Sturdy Memorial Hospital, Attleboro, 02703.* Rev. GREGORY MATHIAS; Mrs. KATHERINE SULLIVAN, *Cape Cod Hospital, Hyannis, 02601.* Revs. FRANCIS J. MCMANUS, S.J.; HENRY J. DAHL; Sr. ROBERTA O'CONNELL, F.C.J.; Sr. KATHLEEN SCHMITH, R.S.M.; Sr. M. HOPE HUGHES, R.S.M., *St. Luke's Hospital, New Bedford, 02745.* Revs. PAUL LAMB; JOHN DIAS, C.S.C.; Sr. NOELLA LUSSIER, P.M., *Morton Hospital, Taunton, 02780.* Sr. SHIRLEY AGNEW, R.S.M., *Tobey Hospital, Wareham and Rehabilitation Hospital of Cape & Islands, Sandwich, 02563.* Rev. JOSEPH MAURITZEN, *Falmouth Hospital, Falmouth, 02540.*

Diocesan Department of Catholic Social Services and Special Apostolates—ARLENE A. MCNAMEE, Exec. Dir., Office: *783 Slade St., Box M, S. Station, Fall River, 02724.* Tel: 508-674-4681; Fax: 508-675-2224.

Diocesan Finance Council—Most Rev. SEAN O'MALLEY, O.F.M.Cap., Chm.; Rev. Msgr. HENRY T. MUNROE, P.A.; Rev. Msgr. JOHN J. OLIVEIRA, P.A.; FREDERIC J. TORPHY, Esq.; LAURENCE T. FLYNN, C.P.A., Consultant, *P.O. Box 2577, Fall River, 02722.* Tel: 508-675-1311.

Diocesan Guild for the Blind—Rev. BRUCE M. NEYLON, *385 Central Ave., Seekonk, 02771.* Tel: 508-399-8440.

Diocesan Health Facilities—Rev. Msgr. EDMUND J. FITZGERALD, V.F., Dir., Office: *368 N. Main St., Fall River, 02720.* Tel: 508-679-8154; Fax: 508-679-1422.

Diocesan Insurance Department—JOSEPH A. FIGLOCK, Benefits Mgr. & Insurance Coord., *P.O. Box 2577, Fall River, 02722.* Tel: 508-675-3850; Fax: 508-672-3802.

Diocesan Newspaper, "The Anchor"—Rev. Msgr. JOHN F. MOORE, Editor, Office: *887 Highland Ave., Fall River, 02722.* Tel: 508-675-7151., *Mailing Address: P.O. Box 7, Fall River, 02722.*

Ecumenical Officer—Rev. MARC H. BERGERON, *818 Middle St., Fall River, 02721.* Tel: 508-674-5651.

Episcopal Representative for Religious—Sr. ELAINE HEFFERNAN, R.S.M., *500 Slocum Rd., North Dartmouth, 02747.* Tel: 508-992-9921.

Family Ministry—Rev. THOMAS A. FRECHETTE, Dir., *Family Life Center, 500 Slocum Rd., North Dartmouth, 02747.* Tel: 508-999-6420.

Holy Childhood Association, The—Rev. Msgr. JOHN J. OLIVEIRA, P.A., Dir., *106 Illinois St., New Bedford, 02745.* Tel: 508-995-3593.

In Support of Life Program—Sr. ELAINE HEFFERNAN, R.S.M., Contact Person, *Family Life Center, 500 Slocum Rd., North Dartmouth, 02747.* Tel: 508-999-6420.

Missionary Cooperative Plan—Rev. Msgr. JOHN J. OLIVEIRA, P.A., Dir, *106 Illinois St., New Bedford, 02745.* Tel: 508-995-3593.

Office for Divine Worship—Rev. Msgr. STEPHEN J. AVILA, *157 Middleboro Rd., P.O. Box 718, East Freetown, 02717.* Tel: 508-763-2240; Fax: 508-763-3040.

Office of AIDS Ministry, Inc.—KRYSTEN WINTER-GREEN, Ph.D., Exec. Dir., *243 Forest St., Clemence Hall, Rm. 225, Fall River, 02721.* Tel: 508-674-5600, Ext. 2295.

Office of Pastoral Planning & Urban Ministry—Rev. Msgr. RONALD A. TOSTI, Dir. ROSE SIMPSON, Assoc., *4451 Old Falmouth Rd., Rte.28, Cotuit, 02635., Mailing Address: P.O. Box 1800, Mashpee, 02649.* Tel: 508-428-9557; 428-9157; Fax: 508-428-9526.

Permanent Diaconate Program—Rev. Msgr. JOHN F. MOORE, Dir.; Rev. CRAIG A. PREGANA, Assoc. Dir.; Deacon LAWRENCE A. ST. ONGE, Asst. Dir., *500 Slocum Rd., North Dartmouth, 02747.* Tel: 508-993-9935; 993-9938; Fax: 508-993-9950.

Pro-Life Apostolate—Rev. STEPHEN A. FERNANDES, Dir.; Mrs. MARIAN DESROSIERS, Asst., *500 Slocum Rd., North Dartmouth, 02747.* Tel: 508-997-2290; Fax: 508-997-2923.

Propagation of the Faith—Rev. Msgr. JOHN J. OLIVEIRA, P.A., Dir., Office: *106 Illinois St., New Bedford, 02745.* Tel: 508-995-3593; Fax: 508-995-2453.

St. Vincent De Paul Society—Rev. DAVID A. COSTA, *58 Church St., P.O. Box 470, North Attleboro, 02761-0470.* Tel: 508-699-8383; Fax: 508-699-7016.

Television Apostolate—Rev. Msgr. STEPHEN J. AVILA, Coord., *157 Middleboro Rd., P.O. Box 718, East Freetown, 02717.* Tel: 508-763-2240; Fax: 508-763-3040.

Vocations—Rev. CRAIG A. PREGANA, Dir., *450 Highland Ave., Fall River, 02720.* Tel: 508-675-1311; Fax: 508-730-2887.

Youth-Office of Youth Ministry—LOUIS MILLER, Dir., *P.O. Box 1167, Fall River, 02722.* Tel: 508-675-3847; 675-3867.

Commissions and Councils

Campaign for Human Development—ARLENE A. MCNAMEE, *P.O. Box M, S. Station, Fall River, 02724.* Tel: 508-674-4681; Fax: 508-675-2224.

Catholic Scouting Program—Rev. STEPHEN B. SALVADOR, Dir., *250 Snell St., Fall River, 02721.* Tel: 508-676-8463; Fax: 508-678-8070.

Continuing Education of the Clergy—Rev. MARK R. HESSION, Dir., *230 S. Main St., Centerville, 02632.* Tel: 508-775-5744; Fax: 508-771-0170.

Mentoring Program for Priests—Rev. JOHN J. OLIVEIRA, Dir., *344 County St., New Bedford, 02740.* Tel: 508-992-7727; Fax: 508-997-1462.

Diocesan Council of Catholic Nurses—Rev. MARK R. HESSION, Moderator, *230 S. Main St., Centerville, 02632.* Tel: 508-775-5744; Fax: 508-771-0170.

Diocesan Council of Catholic Women—Rev. THOMAS E. MORRISSEY, Moderator, *249 Whittenton St., Taunton, 02780.* Tel: 508-824-7794.

Diocesan Liaison with Marriage Encounter—Vacant.

Diocesan Liaison with Charismatic Groups—Rev. ROBERT S. KASZYNSKI, Dir., *36 Rockland St., Fall River, 02724.* Tel: 508-672-0423.

Diocesan Liaison with Cursillo—Rev. BRUCE M. NEYLON, *385 Central Ave., Seekonk, 02771.* Tel: 508-399-8440.

Diocesan Pastoral Council—Rev. Msgr. GEORGE W. COLEMAN, V.G., *P.O. Box 2577, Fall River, 02722.*

Legion of Mary—Rev. BARRY W. WALL, *120 Beattie St., Fall River, 02723.* Tel: 508-672-7232.

CLERGY, PARISHES, MISSIONS AND PAROCHIAL SCHOOLS

CITY OF FALL RIVER
(Bristol County)

1—CATHEDRAL OF ST. MARY OF THE ASSUMPTION (1838), Revs. Edward J. Healey, Rector; Ramon Dominguez. In res., Revs. Michael Kuhn; Thomas E. McGlynn.

Res., 327 Second St., 02721. Tel: 508-673-2833; Fax: 508-672-0667.

Catechesis/Religious Programs—467 Spring St., 02721. Tel: 508-672-5531.

Students 125.

2—BLESSED SACRAMENT (1902) (French), Rev. Gerald P. Barnwell.

Res., 2492 S. Main St., 02724. Tel: 508-672-5473.

Catechesis/Religious Programs—Students 90.

3—ESPIRITO SANTO (1904) (Portuguese), Revs. James Ferry; Roger J. Landry, Vicar; Deacon John de Amaral Moniz.

Res., 311 Alden St., 02723. Tel: 508-672-3352; Fax: 508-645-1787.

School—143 Everett St., 02723. Tel: 508-672-3362; Fax: 508-672-7724. Mrs. Patricia Benoit, Prin.

Lay Teachers 14; Students 250.

Catechesis/Religious Programs—Beverly Tavares, D.R.E.

Students 386.

4—HOLY CROSS (1916) (Polish). Merged with SS. Peter & Paul, Fall River.

5—HOLY NAME (1923), Revs. Francis L. Mahoney; Edward A. Murphy.

Res., 709 Hanover St., 02720. Tel: 508-679-6732; Fax: 508-675-4755.

School—850 Pearce St., 02720. Tel: 508-674-9131; Fax: 508-679-0571.

Religious Sisters of Mercy 1; Lay Teachers 14; Students 225.

Catechesis/Religious Programs—Tel: 508-679-3127.

Students 480.

6—HOLY TRINITY (2000), Rev. David M. Andrade.

Res., 951 Stafford Rd., 02721. Tel: 508-672-3200; Fax: 580-673-5518.

School—64 Lamphor St., 02721. Tel: 508-673-6772; Fax: 508-730-1864. Kathleen Barboza, Prin.

Lay Teachers 16; Students 256.

Catechesis/Religious Programs—Tel: 508-672-8340; Fax: 508-673-0512. Patricia Pasternak, D.R.E.

Students 215.

7—NOTRE DAME DE LOURDES (1874) (French), Rev. Richard L. Chretien. In res., Revs. Leonard Hindsley, O.P.; Marek S. Tuptynski.

Res., 529 Eastern Ave., 02723. Tel: 508-679-1991; Fax: 508-676-5276.

School—34 St. Joseph St., 02723. Tel: 508-672-5461; Fax: 508-673-8430.

Lay Teachers 15; Students 198.

Catechesis/Religious Programs—Students 200.

8—OUR LADY OF THE ANGELS (1915) (Portuguese), Rev. Fred Babiczuk, Admin.; Deacon John F. Branco.

Res., 221 Kilburn St., 02724. Tel: 508-676-8883; Fax: 508-673-1280.

Catechesis/Religious Programs—Tel: 508-677-4702. D.R.E.: Marion Carrier, (Gr. 1-6); Deborah Jozak, (Gr. 7-8).

Students 230.

9—OUR LADY OF HEALTH (1924) (Portuguese), Rev. Jose A.F. dos Santos; Deacon Robert A. Faria.

Res., 642 Cambridge St., 02721. Tel: 508-672-2793.

Catechesis/Religious Programs—49 Somerset St., 02721. Tel: 508-673-8987.
Students 230.

10—OUR LADY OF THE HOLY ROSARY (1904) (Italian), Rev. Barry W. Wall.
Res., 120 Beattie St., 02723. Tel: 508-672-7232; Fax: 508-672-1506.
Catechesis/Religious Programs—84 Beattie St., 02723. Tel: 508-672-7262. Robert T. Houghton, D.R.E.
Students 102.

11—OUR LADY OF THE IMMACULATE CONCEPTION (1882), Rev. Kenneth J. Delano.
Res., 15 Thomas St., P.O. Box 4127, 02723. Tel: 508-673-2122; Fax: 508-730-1694.
Catechesis/Religious Programs—Tel: 508-672-3254. Mrs. Colleen Laliberte, D.R.E.
Students 132.

12—SACRED HEART (1872), Rev. Raymond Cambra; Sr. Eugenia Margaret Ready, S.U.S.C., Pastoral Asst. In res., Rev. Craig A. Pregana.
Res., 160 Seabury St., 02720. Tel: 508-673-0852; Fax: 508-678-0873.
Catechesis/Religious Programs—Mrs. Maureen Costa, D.R.E.
Students 142.

13—ST. ANNE'S (1869) (French), Revs. Marc H. Bergeron; Pierre E. Lachance, O.P.; Ramon Dominguez.
Res., 818 Middle St., 02721. Tel: 508-674-5651; 678-5322; Fax: 508-672-0939.
School—Tel: 508-678-2152; Fax: 508-674-5190. Mr. Felipe M. Felipe, Prin.
Sisters 1; Lay Teachers 24; Students 434.
Catechesis/Religious Programs—Tel: 508-678-1510. Susan Chapdelaine, D.R.E.
Students 320.

14—ST. ANTHONY OF PADUA (1911) (Portuguese), Rev. John C. Martins.
Res., 48 Sixteenth St., 02723. Tel: 508-673-2402; Fax: 508-730-2519.
Catechesis/Religious Programs—Tel: 508-764-1986. D.R.E.: Deborah Polselli; John Janeiro.
Students 315.

15—ST. ELIZABETH'S (1915). Merged with St. Jean Baptiste and St. William to form Holy Trinity.

16—ST. JEAN BAPTISTE (1901). Merged with St. Elizabeth and St. William to form Holy Trinity Parish.

17—ST. JOSEPH'S (1873), Rev. John J. Perry. In res., Rev. Msgr. George W. Coleman, V.G.
Res., 1335 N. Main St., 02720. Tel: 508-673-1123; Fax: 508-673-7230.
Catechesis/Religious Programs—Students 265.

18—ST. LOUIS (1885). Closed. Sacramental records can be found at St. Mary's Cathedral.

19—ST. MICHAEL'S (1902) (Portuguese), Revs. Luis A. Cardoso; Dermot Rodgers.
Res., 189 Essex St., 02720. Tel: 508-672-6713; Fax: 508-679-1841. [CEM]
School—Tel: 508-678-0266.
Religious of the Holy Union of the Sacred Hearts 1; Lay Teachers 10; Students 195.
Catechesis/Religious Programs—Tel: 508-678-0266.
Students 385.

20—ST. PATRICK'S (1873), Revs. Freddie Babiczuk; Jose Sousa.
Res., 1598 S. Main St., 02724-2596. Tel: 508-672-2302; Fax: 508-673-1280.
Catechesis/Religious Programs—Tel: 508-677-4702. D.R.E. Marion Carrier, (Gr. 1-6); Deborah Jezak, (Gr. 7-8).
Students 150.

21—SS. PETER AND PAUL (1882), Rev. Stephen B. Salvador.
Res., 250 Snell St., 02721. Tel: 508-676-8463; Fax: 508-678-8070.
Worship Space: Holy Cross Church: 47 Pulaski St., 02721.
School—(Grades (PreK-8)) 240 Dover St., 02721. Tel: 508-672-7258; Fax: 508-674-6042.
Lay Teachers 15; Students 210.
Catechesis/Religious Programs—Tel: 508-672-3720.
Students 156.

22—ST. STANISLAUS (1898) (Polish), Rev. Robert S. Kaszynski; Deacon Franciszek W. Mis.
Res., 36 Rockland St., P.O. Box 111, 02724. Tel: 508-672-0423; Fax: 508-677-1378.
School—37 Rockland St., 02724. Tel: 508-674-6771; Fax: 508-677-1622. Mrs. Denita Tremblay, Prin.
Lay Teachers 11; Students 184.
Catechesis/Religious Programs—Students 75.

23—ST. WILLIAM'S (1905). Merged with St. Elizabeth and St. Jean Baptiste to form Holy Trinity Parish.

24—SANTO CHRISTO (1891) (Portuguese), Revs. Gastao A. Oliveira; Brian Albino.
Res., 185 Canal St., 02721. Tel: 508-676-1184; Fax: 508-676-9701.
Catechesis/Religious Programs—Tel: 508-675-3007. Mr. Osvaldo Pacheco, D.R.E.
Students 616.

OUTSIDE THE CITY OF FALL RIVER

Acushnet, Bristol Co., St. Francis Xavier's (1915), Rev. Richard M. Beaulieu; Deacon Michael P. Guy.
Res., 125 Main St., 02743. Tel: 508-995-7600; Fax: 508-995-1794.
School—223 Main St., 02743. Tel: 508-995-4313; Fax: 508-995-0456. Mrs. Susan Boulay, Prin.
Religious 1; Lay Teachers 18; Students 233.
Catechesis/Religious Programs—Tel: 508-998-7445.
Students 340.

Assonet, Bristol Co., St. Bernard's (1978), Rev. Timothy J. Goldrick; Deacon Lawrence A. St. Onge.
Res., 32 S. Main St., P.O. Box 370, 02702. Tel: 508-644-5585; Fax: 508-644-2136.
Catechesis/Religious Programs—Tel: 508-644-2032. John G. Lanctot, D.R.E.
Students 476.

Attleboro, Bristol Co.,

1—ST. JOHN THE EVANGELIST, (1883), Rev. Msgr. Daniel F. Hoye; Deacon A. Anthony Cipriano.
Res., One St. John Pl., 02703-2251. Tel: 508-222-1206; Fax: 508-226-6461. [CEM]
School—13 Hodges St., 02703. Tel: 508-222-5062; Fax: 508-223-1737. Mrs. Claire Powers, Prin.
Lay Teachers 15; Students 261.
Catechesis/Religious Programs—Tel: 508-222-0707; Fax: 508-222-0701.
Students 870.

2—ST. JOSEPH'S, (1905), Rev. Michael Carvill, F.S.C.B. In res., Revs. Vincent Nagle, F.S.C.B.; Luca Brancolini.
Res., 208 S. Main St., 02703. Tel: 508-226-1115; Fax: 508-226-0234.
Catechesis/Religious Programs—10 Maple St., Tel: 508-222-1730.
Students 199.

3—ST. STEPHEN'S, (1875), Rev. William L. Boffa.
Res., 683 S. Main St., 02703-6397. Tel: 508-222-0641; Fax: 508-222-1815. [CEM]
Catechesis/Religious Programs—Mr. Stephen Wujcik, D.R.E.
Students 286.

4—HOLY GHOST, (1921), Rev. Steven R. Furtado; Deacon Paul M. Fournier.
Res., 71 Linden St., 02703. Tel: 508-222-3266; Fax: 508-222-3292.
Catechesis/Religious Programs—Tel: 508-222-6756. Jacqueline DaSilva, Coord.
Students 136.

5—ST. THERESA OF THE CHILD JESUS, (1925), Rev. James W. Fahey.
Res., 18 Baltic St., S. Attleboro, 02703. Tel: 508-761-8111; Fax: 508-761-5475.
Catechesis/Religious Programs—Tel: 508-761-5367. Mrs. Theresa Paquette, D.R.E.
Students 351.

Attleboro Falls, Bristol Co., St. Mark's (1967), Rev. Peter N. Graziano.
Res., 105 Stanley St., Box 1240, 027630240. Tel: 508-699-7566; Fax: 508-643-0103.
Catechesis/Religious Programs—Tel: 508-695-7773. Mrs. Elaine Corvese, D.R.E.
Students 855.

Brewster, Barnstable Co., Our Lady of the Cape (1961), Revs. Bernard Baris, M.S.; William Kaliyadan, M.S.; Henry Brodeur, M.S.; Deacons R. Donald Biron; James Leavitt; William Ladroga.
Res., Stony Brook Rd., P.O. Box 1799, 02631. Tel: 508-385-3252; Fax: 508-385-6864.
Catechesis/Religious Programs—Tel: 508-385-2115. Elizabeth M. McCullough, D.R.E.
Students 597.
Mission—East Brewster, Barnstable Co., Immaculate Conception, Rte. 6A, 02631.

Buzzards Bay, Barnstable Co., St. Margaret (1915), Rev. James C. Tuxbury, O.F.M.
Res., 141 Main St., 02532. Tel: 508-759-7777; Fax: 508-759-3920. [JC]
School—Tel: 508-759-2213; Fax: 508-759-8776.
Lay Teachers 13; Students 241.
Catechesis/Religious Programs—Tel: 508-759-2065. Constance Carbone, D.R.E.
Students 415.
Mission—Onset, St. Mary Star of the Sea.

Centerville, Barnstable Co., Our Lady of Victory (1957), Revs. Mark R. Hession; James H. Morse; Marek Chmurski; Deacons Joseph P. Stanley; James M. Barrett.
Res., 230 S. Main St., 02632. Tel: 508-775-5744; Fax: 508-771-0170.
Catechesis/Religious Programs—Tel: 508-771-1614. D.R.E.: Jessie duMont; Claudia Anderson.
Students 1,255.
Mission—West Barnstable, Barnstable Co., Our Lady of Hope, Rte. 6A, West Barnstable, 02668. Tel: 508-362-8122.

Chatham, Barnstable Co., Holy Redeemer (1955), Revs. James F. Buckley; George B. Scales; Deacons Joseph F. Mador; Gabriel M. Liegey, Jr.
Res., 57 Highland Ave., Box 687, 02633. Tel: 508-945-0677; Fax: 508-945-3186. [JC]
Catechesis/Religious Programs—Students 102.
Mission—South Chatham, Barnstable Co., Our Lady of Grace, P.O. Box 687, 02633.

Dighton, Bristol Co., St. Peter's (1904), Rev. Thomas A. Frechette, Admin.
Res., 2039 County St., 02715. Tel: 508-669-6463; Fax: 508-669-6463.
Catechesis/Religious Programs—Tel: 508-669-6925; Fax: 508-669-6925.
Students 180.

East Falmouth, Barnstable Co., St. Anthony's (1923), Rev. William M. Costello.
Res., 167 E. Falmouth Hwy., 02536. Tel: 508-548-0108; Fax: 508-457-1723. [CEM]
Catechesis/Religious Programs—Tel: 508-548-3515; Fax: 508-548-3515.
Students 404.

East Freetown, Bristol Co., St. John Neumann (1984), Rev. Msgr. Stephen J. Avila; Deacon Bruce J. Bonneau.
Res., 157 Middleboro Rd., Box 718, 02717. Tel: 508-763-2240; Fax: 508-763-3040.
Catechesis/Religious Programs—Tel: 508-763-8122. D.R.E.: Dr. Doris Thibault; Mrs. Madeleine Oliver.
Students 515.

East Taunton, Bristol Co., Holy Family (1900), Rev. Jay T. Maddock; Deacon John J. Fitzpatrick.
Res., 370 Middleboro, P.O. Box 619, 02718. Tel: 508-824-5707; Fax: 508-824-5665.
Catechesis/Religious Programs—Tel: 508-824-3578; Fax: 508-824-5665. Margaret Ormond, D.R.E.
Students 534.

Edgartown, Dukes Co., St. Elizabeth (1925), Revs. Michael R. Nagle, D.Min.; John C. Ozug.
Res., 86 Main St., P.O. Box 156, 02539. Tel: 508-627-5017; Fax: 508-627-6021.
Catechesis/Religious Programs—School St., Oak Bluffs, 02557. Tel: 508-693-0342; Fax: 508-693-8517.
Students 115.

Fairhaven, Bristol Co., St. Joseph's (1905), Revs. William Heffron, SS.CC.; William Penderghest, SS.CC. In res., Rev. Frederick Meyers, SS.CC.
Res., 41 Walnut St., 02719. Tel: 508-994-9714; Fax: 508-979-4659.
School—Spring St. and Homestead Ave., 02719. Tel: 508-996-1983; Fax: 508-996-1998. Sr. Muriel Ann Lebeau, SS.CC., Prin.
Sisters 1; Lay Teachers 11; Students 208.
Catechesis/Religious Programs—Tel: 508-994-8679.
Students 275.

St. Mary's (1933), Revs. Robert Charlton, SS.CC.; Patrick Killilea, SS.CC., Vicar.
Res., 41 Harding Rd., 02719. Tel: 508-992-7300; Fax: 508-992-0685.
Catechesis/Religious Programs—Tel: 508-992-8721. Sr. Eleanor Cyr, SS.CC., D.R.E.
Students 346.

Falmouth, Barnstable Co., St. Patrick's (1899), Rev. Msgr. John A. Perry; Revs. Tedeusz Pacholczyk; Joseph H. Mauritzen; Deacon Patrick J. Mahoney.
Res., 511 Main St., P.O. Box 569, 02541. Tel: 508-548-1065; Fax: 508-495-0875. [CEM]
Catechesis/Religious Programs—Tel: 508-548-2306. Cynthia O'Connor, D.R.E.
Students 435.
Chapel—Falmouth Heights, St. Thomas, Tel: 508-548-8539.

Hyannis, Barnstable Co., St. Francis Xavier's (1904), Revs. Stephen A. Fernandes; Thomas M. Kocik, Vicar; William M. Rodrigues; Deacon Richard M. Dresser.
Res., 347 South St., 02601. Tel: 508-775-0818; Fax: 508-771-5940. [JC 2]
Catechesis/Religious Programs—Tel: 508-775-6200. Mrs. Mary Offiler, D.R.E.
Students 200.
School—Tel: 508-771-7200; Fax: 508-771-7233. Robert H. Deburro, Headmaster.
Lay Teachers 16; Students 205.
Mission—Yarmouth Port, Barnstable Co., Sacred Heart Chapel, Summer St., Yarmouth Port, 02675.

Mansfield, Bristol Co., St. Mary's (1894), Revs. George C. Bellenoit; Daniel W. Lacroix; Dariusz Kalinowski; Sr. Ann William Publicover, M.S.B.T., Pastoral Min.; Deacons Thomas P. Palanza; Walter D. Thomas.
Res., 330 Pratt St., 02048-1581. Tel: 508-339-2981; Fax: 508-339-0612. [CEM]

Catechesis/Religious Programs—Tel: 508-339-4621. Mrs. Ellen Westlund, D.R.E.
Students 2,056.

Marion, Plymouth Co., St. Rita's (1972), Rev. William G. Campbell.
Res., 113 Front St., Box 902, 02738. Tel: 508-748-1497; Fax: 508-748-0604.
Catechesis/Religious Programs—Tel: 508-748-0576.
Students 246.

Mashpee, Barnstable Co., Christ The King (1984), Rev. Msgr. Ronald A. Tosti; Deacons Robert D. Lemay; Bernard D. Tolassi; Frank D. Fantasia. In res., Rev. Gregory A. Mathias.
Res., The Commons, P.O. Box 1800, 02649. Tel: 508-477-7700; Fax: 508-477-8158.
Catechesis/Religious Programs—Tel: 508-477-6565. D.R.E.: Sr. Annette Roach, O.P.; Sr. Claire Sinotte, O.P.
Students 1,030.

Mattapoisett, Plymouth Co., St. Anthony's (1908), Rev. Leonard M. Mullaney; Deacon Robert L. Surprenant.
Mailing Address: P.O. Box 501, 02739-0501. Fax: 508-758-3019.
Res., 22 Barstow St., 02739. Tel: 508-758-3719. [CEM]
Catechesis/Religious Programs—Tel: 508-758-3735. Mrs. Natalie Taber, D.R.E.
Students 391.

Nantucket, Nantucket Co., St. Mary's, Our Lady of the Isle (1903), Rev. Paul A. Caron; Deacon Donald L. Battiston.
Res., 6 Orange St., P.O. Box 1168, 02554. Tel: 508-228-0100; Fax: 508-325-7991. [CEM]
Catechesis/Religious Programs—Tel: 508-257-9868. Ms. Elaine Boehm, D.R.E.
Students 256.
Station—Siasconset.

New Bedford, Bristol Co.,

1—HOLY NAME. Merged with Sacred Heart, New Bedford to form Holy Name of the Sacred Heart of Jesus, New Bedford.

2—HOLY NAME OF THE SACRED HEART OF JESUS, (1999), Rev. Msgr. Thomas J. Harrington; Deacon Eugene H. Sasseville.
Res., 121 Mt. Pleasant St., 02740. Tel: 508-992-3184; Fax: 508-984-3406.
Catechesis/Religious Programs—Tel: 508-996-8654. D.R.E.: Mrs. Nancy Davis; Mrs. Heidi Kuliga.
Students 275.

3—NUESTRA SENORA DE GUADALUPE, (1993) (Hispanic), Rev. Kevin J. Harrington.
Mailing Address: P.O. Box 40605, 02744-0006.
Res., 110 Summer St., 02740. Tel: 508-996-5862; Fax: 508-992-2208.
Catechesis/Religious Programs—Tel: 508-997-8729. Sr. Candelaria Hernandez, M.G.Sp.S., D.R.E.
Students 87.

4—OUR LADY OF THE ASSUMPTION, (1905) (Cape Verdean), Rev. Richard Lifrak, SS.CC.; Deacons Eduardo M. Pacheco; Antonio M. Da Cruz.
Res., 54 S. 6th St., 02740. Tel: 508-994-0106; Fax: 508-994-9461.
Parish Center—47 S. 6th St., 02740. Tel: 508-994-7602.
Catechesis/Religious Programs—Tel: 508-994-7602.
Students 195.

5—OUR LADY OF FATIMA, (1966), Rev. James F. Greene.
Res., 4256 Acushnet Ave., 02745. Tel: 508-995-7351; Fax: 508-995-4401.
Parish Center—980 Tobey St., New Bedord, 02745.
Catechesis/Religious Programs—Tel: 508-995-6685. Mrs. Pearl Enos, D.R.E.
Students 254.

6—OUR LADY OF THE IMMACULATE CONCEPTION, (1914) (Portuguese), Revs. Daniel O. Reis; Timothy Paul Driscoll.
Res., 136 Earle St., 02746. Tel: 508-992-9892; Fax: 508-992-9907.
Catechesis/Religious Programs—156 Davis St., 02746. Tel: 508-990-0249.
Students 735.

7—OUR LADY OF MT. CARMEL, (1902) (Portuguese), Very Rev. Henry S. Arruda; Revs. Michael Camara, O.F.M.; Scott A. Ciosek; Deacons Paul Macedo; Abilio Pires. In res., Rev. Antonino C. Tavares, (Retired).
Res., 230 Bonney St., 02744. Tel: 508-993-4704; Fax: 508-991-5536.
School—103 Crapo St., 02744. Tel: 508-997-9612; Fax: 508-997-2485. Mrs. Rosemary da Silva, Prin.
Lay Teachers 11; Students 125.
Catechesis/Religious Programs—Tel: 508-984-7097.
Students 900.

8—OUR LADY OF PERPETUAL HELP, (1905) (Polish), Revs. Roman Chwaliszewski, O.F.M.Conv.; Sebastian Slesinski, O.F.M.Conv. In res., Revs. Isidore Kowalski, O.F.M.Conv.; Charles Porada, O.F.M.Conv.
Res., 235 N. Front St., 02746. Tel: 508-992-9378; Fax: 508-993-4881.
Catechesis/Religious Programs—Students 46.

9—SACRED HEART, (1874) (French). Merged With Holy Name, New Bedford to form Holy Name of the Sacred Heart of Jesus, New Bedford.

10—ST. ANNE, (1908) (French), Rev. Martin L. Buote; Deacon Marcel Morency.
Res., 890 Brock Ave., 02744. Tel: 508-997-9271.
Catechesis/Religious Programs—Students 13.

11—ST. ANTHONY OF PADUA'S, (1895) (French), Rev. Msgr. Edmond R. Levesque.
Res., 1359 Acushnet Ave., 02746. Tel: 508-993-1691; Fax: 508-999-4775.
School—109 Ashley Blvd., 02746. Tel: 508-994-5121; Fax: 508-979-5923. Mrs. Elizabeth Lavigne, Prin.
Lay Teachers 20; Students 385.
Catechesis/Religious Programs—Students 84.
Convent—106 Bullard St., 02746. Tel: 508-990-1751. Mother of God
Sisters of Capuchin Recollect 8.

12—ST. CASIMIR, (1927) (Polish), Rev. Henry K. Kropiwnicki.
Res., 2048 Acushnet Ave., 02745-6139. Tel: 508-995-0345; Fax: 508-998-5787.
Catechesis/Religious Programs—Students 10.

13—ST. FRANCIS OF ASSISI, (1928) (Italian), Rev. Albert J. Ryan.
Res., 247 North St., 02740. Tel: 508-997-7732; Fax: 508-991-6630.
Catechesis/Religious Programs—Mrs. Pamela Herbert, D.R.E.
Students 35.

14—ST. HEDWIG, (1908) (Polish), Rev. Kevin J. Harrington.
Mailing Address: P.O. Box 40605, 02744-0006.
Res., 110 Summer St., 02740. Tel: 508-996-8703; Fax: 508-992-2208.

15—ST. JAMES, (1888), Rev. Edward E. Correia; Deacon Lawrence St. Onge. In res., Revs. Herbert T. Nichols; Francis J. McManus, S.J., Chap.
Res., 233 County St., 02740. Tel: 508-992-9408; Fax: 508-990-0575.
School—St. James-St. John, 180 Orchard St., 02740. Tel: 508-996-0534.
Sisters of Mercy 2; Lay Teachers 10; Students 267.
Catechesis/Religious Programs—Tel: 508-992-7122.
Students 200.

16—ST. JOHN THE BAPTIST, (1871) (Portuguese), Rev. John J. Oliveira. In res., Rev. Henry J. Dahl.
Res., 344 County St., 02740. Tel: 508-992-7727; Fax: 508-997-1462. [CEM]
School—See listing for St. James, New Bedford.
Catechesis/Religious Programs—Tel: 508-996-3087. Ms. Marge Ferreira, D.R.E.
Students 213.

17—ST. JOSEPH, (1910). Merged with St. Theresa, New Bedford to form St. Joseph-St. Therese, New Bedford.

18—ST. JOSEPH-ST. THERESE, (1999), Rev. Roger J. Levesque; Deacons Maurice Lavallee; Leo Racine.
Res., 51 Duncan St., 02745-6108. Tel: 508-995-5235; Fax: 508-998-7404.
School—35 Kearsarge St., 02745-6117. Tel: 508-995-2264. Paulette S. Dansereau, Prin.
Lay Teachers 11; Students 225.
Catechesis/Religious Programs—Students 167.

19—ST. KILIAN, (1896), Revs. Jose G. Giunta, I.V.E.; Jose Del Val.
Res., 306 Ashley Blvd., 02746. Tel: 508-992-7587.
Catechesis/Religious Programs—Fax: 508-994-0281.
Students 85.

20—ST. LAWRENCE MARTYR, (1821), Rev. John P. Driscoll. In res., Rev. Kevin J. Harrington.
Res., 110 Summer St., 02740. Tel: 508-992-4251; Fax: 508-993-8277.
School—Holy Family-Holy Name, 91 Summer St., 02740. Tel: 508-993-3547. Ms. Cecilia Felix, Prin. & D.R.E.
Sisters 2; Lay Teachers 12; Students 270.
Catechesis/Religious Programs—Tel: 508-993-3577.
Students 245.

21—ST. MARY'S, (1923), Rev. Msgr. John J. Oliveira, P.A.; Rev. Paul Cark Fedar; Deacon Claude A. Leblanc.
Res., 106 Illinois St., 02745. Tel: 508-995-3593; Fax: 508-995-2453.
School—115 Illinois St., 02745. Tel: 508-995-3696; Fax: 508-995-0840.
Lay Teachers 12; Students 239.
Catechesis/Religious Programs—Students 350.

22—ST. THERESA, (1926) (French). Merged with St. Joseph's, New Bedford to form St. Joseph-St. Therese, New Bedford.

North Attleboro, Bristol Co., St. Mary's (1890), Rev. James M. Fitzpatrick; Deacon James J. Meloni, Jr.
Mailing Address: 14 Park St, 02760. Tel: 508-695-6161; Fax: 508-695-5248.
Res., 14 Park St., 02760. Tel: 508-695-6161. [CEM]
School—See St. Mary-Sacred Heart. Tel: 508-695-3072.
Catechesis/Religious Programs—14 Park St., 02761. Tel: 508-695-3823.
Students 419.
Convent—125 Broad St., 02760. Tel: 508-695-7989. Sisters of the Holy Union 4.

Sacred Heart (1904) (French), Rev. David A. Costa.
Res., 58 Church St., P.O. Box 470, 02761-0470. Tel: 508-699-8383; Fax: 508-699-7016.
School—St. Mary's-Sacred Heart Consolidated School, 57 Richards Ave., 02760. Tel: 508-695-3072; Fax: 508-695-9074. Mrs. Denise M. Peixoto, Prin.
Sisters 1; Lay Teachers 17; Students 233.
Catechesis/Religious Programs—Tel: 508-643-9009.
Students 233.

North Dartmouth, Bristol Co., St. Julie Billiart (1969), Revs. Brian J. Harrington; Robert J. Powell, O.S.B.Cam.
Res., 494 Slocum Rd., 02747. Tel: 508-993-2351; Fax: 508-993-2437.
Catechesis/Religious Programs—Tel: 508-990-0287. Ms. Jane Ayer, D.R.E.
Students 664.

North Dighton, Bristol Co., St. Joseph's (1913), Rev. James McLellan.
Res., 499 Spring St., P.O. Box 564, 02764-0564. Tel: 508-822-1425; Fax: 508-822-3886.
Catechesis/Religious Programs—Tel: 508-824-6581. Sr. Judith Costa, S.S.D., D.R.E.
Students 326.

North Easton, Bristol Co., Immaculate Conception (1871), Rev. Thomas C. Lopes. In res., Rev. Thomas E. Lawton, C.S.C.
Res., 193 Main St., 02356. Tel: 508-238-3232; Fax: 508-238-7849. [CEM]
Catechesis/Religious Programs—Tel: 508-238-3230; Fax: 508-238-7849. Maryann Dziekiewicz, D.R.E.
Students 563 (Gr. 1-9).

North Falmouth, Barnstable Co., St. Elizabeth Seton (1977), Rev. Msgr. John F. Moore; Deacons Paul K. Roma; Willam A. Martin.
Res., 481 Quaker Rd., Box 861, 02556. Tel: 508-563-7770; Fax: 508-563-7794.
Catechesis/Religious Programs—Tel: 508-563-7774.
Students 357.

Norton, Bristol Co., St. Mary's (1925), Very Rev. Robert A. Oliveira; Deacon Michael E. Murray.
Res., 133 S. Worcester St., Box 430, 02766-0430. Tel: 508-285-4462; Fax: 508-285-5589.
Catechesis/Religious Programs—Tel: 508-285-3237. Mrs. Rose E. Collette, D.R.E.
Students 1,295.

Oak Bluffs, Dukes Co., Sacred Heart (1880), Revs. Michael R. Nagle; John C. Ozug.
Res., 156 Circuit Ave., P.O. Box 1565, 02557. Tel: 508-693-0342; Fax: 508-696-8408. [CEM]
Catechesis/Religious Programs—Fax: 508-693-8517.
Students 150.

Orleans, Barnstable Co., St. Joan of Arc (1947), Rev. Richard M. Roy; Deacons Norman McEnaney; John Twerago.
Res., 61 Canal Rd., P.O. Box 336, 02653. Tel: 508-255-0170; Fax: 508-240-6741.
Catechesis/Religious Programs—Tel: 508-255-7442. Judith Burt Walker, D.R.E.
Students 270.

Osterville, Barnstable Co., Our Lady of the Assumption (1906), Rev. Philip A. Davignon.
Res., 76 Wianno Ave., P.O. Box E., 02655. Tel: 508-428-2011; Fax: 508-428-2891.
Catechesis/Religious Programs—Tel: 508-428-1337.
Students 177.

Pocasset, Barnstable Co., St. John the Evangelist (1969), Rev. Robert C. Donovan; Deacon Leonard C. Dexter, Jr.
Res., 15 Virginia Rd., P.O. Box 1558, 02559. Tel: 508-563-3121; 563-5887; Fax: 508-563-3102.
Catechesis/Religious Programs—841 Shore Rd., P.O. Box 1558, 02559. Tel: 508-563-5536; Fax: 508-563-5536. Liz Henry, D.R.E.
Students 311.

Provincetown, Barnstable Co., St. Peter the Apostle (1874), Rev. John A. Raposo; Deacon Chester O. Cook.

Res., 11 Prince St., 02657. Tel: 508-487-0095; Fax: 508-487-2564. [CEM]
Catechesis/Religious Programs—Students 105.
Mission—N. Truro, Our Lady of Perpetual Help.

Raynham, Bristol Co., St. Ann (1961), Revs. Michael K. McManus; David A. Pregana; Deacon John Welch.
Res., 660 N. Main St., P.O. Box 247, 02768. Tel: 508-823-9833; 823-9834; Fax: 508-823-8935.
Catechesis/Religious Programs—725 N. Main St. Box 247, Raynham Center, 02768. Tel: 508-824-9021. Donna Martyniak, D.R.E.
Students 803.

Sandwich, Barnstable Co., Corpus Christi (1830), Revs. Marcel H. Bouchard; John M. Murray; Andrzej Jacek Kozanko; Deacons Richard J. Murphy, Sr.; John J. Emmert; Robert Alence.
Res., 251 Service Rd., P.O. Box 1170, East Sandwich, 02537-2170. Tel: 508-888-0209; Fax: 508-888-8961. [CEM]
Parish Center—324 Quaker Meetinghouse Rd., East Sandwich, 02537.
Catechesis/Religious Programs—Tel: 508-888-8267. Sr. Doreen Donegan, D.R.E.
Students 1,350.
Mission—Sagamore, Barnstable Co., St. Theresa.

Seekonk, Bristol Co., Our Lady of Mt. Carmel (1922), Revs. George E. Harrison; David Sharland; Hernando Herrera.
Res., 984 Taunton Ave., 02771. Tel: 508-336-9022; Fax: 508-336-9010.
Catechesis/Religious Programs—1040 Taunton Ave., 02771. Tel: 508-336-8608. D.R.E.: Mr. Stephen Byers; Sr. Irene Rivard, F.C.S.C.J.
Students 700.

St. Mary's (1906), Revs. Bruce M. Neylon; Christopher Stanibula.
Res., 385 Central Ave., 02771. Tel: 508-399-8440; Fax: 508-399-7398.
Catechesis/Religious Programs—Tel: 508-399-7534.
Students 685.

Somerset, Bristol Co., St. John of God (1928) (Portuguese), Rev. Raul M. Lagoa. In res., Rev. Luciano J. de M. Pereira, (Retired).
Res., 996 Brayton Ave., Box 113, 02726. Tel: 508-678-5513; Fax: 508-678-6458.
Catechesis/Religious Programs—1036 Brayton Ave., 02726. Tel: 508-678-5139. D.R.E.: Edward Medeiros; Jason Kenney.
Students 431.

St. Thomas More (1949), Rev. Edward J. Byington; Deacon Victor Haddad.
Res., 386 Luther Ave., 02726. Tel: 508-673-7831; Fax: 508-730-1396.
Catechesis/Religious Programs—Tel: 508-679-1236. Mr. Dennis Eriffin, D.R.E.
Students 346.

St. Patrick's (1883), Rev. Marc P. Tremblay; Deacon Edward Hussey.
Res., 306 South St., 02726-5617. Tel: 508-672-1523; Fax: 508-675-5787. [CEM]
Catechesis/Religious Programs—Tel: 508-675-1073.
Students 285.

South Dartmouth, Bristol Co., St. Mary's (1930), Revs. Terence Keenan; Michael S. Racine; Deacon Jeremiah J. Reardon.
Res., 783 Dartmouth St., 02748. Tel: 508-992-7163; Fax: 508-992-5209.
Catechesis/Religious Programs—Tel: 508-992-7505. Theresa Lewis, D.R.E.
Students 500.

South Easton, Bristol Co., Holy Cross (1967), Revs. Richard C. Hockman, C.S.C.; John M. Santone, C.S.C.
Res., 225 Purchase St., 02375. Tel: 508-238-2235; Fax: 508-238-0500.
Catechesis/Religious Programs—Tel: 508-238-2131. D.R.E.: Deacon George Zarella; Lorraine Gryniuk; Janet Merriam.
Students 1,293.

South Yarmouth, Barnstable Co., St. Pius Tenth (1954), Rev. Msgr. John J. Smith; Rev. Paul Bernier; Deacons David Akin; Richard J. Hasey; Thomas Bailey; Richard Zeich.
Res., 5 Barbara St., 02664. Tel: 508-398-2248; Fax: 508-398-7233.
Catechesis/Religious Programs—Station Ave., 02664. Tel: 508-394-0709; 0708. D.R.E.: Mrs. Joan Robinson; Mrs. Jean Kelly.
Students 598.
Chapel—Bass River, Our Lady of the Highway, Tel: 508-760-3332.

Swansea, Bristol Co.,

1—St. Dominic's, (1911), Rev. Joseph F. Viveiros.
Res., 1277 Grand Army Hwy., P.O. Box 205, 02777. Tel: 508-675-7206; Fax: 508-675-4626.
Catechesis/Religious Programs—Tel: 508-675-7002.
Students 302.

2—St. Louis de France, (1928) (French), Rev. Roger D. LeDuc; Deacon Robert G.L. Normandin.
Res., 56 Buffington St., 02777. Tel: 508-674-1103; Fax: 508-672-8889.
Catechesis/Religious Programs—66 Buffington St., 02777. Tel: 508-672-0615. Mrs. Paulette J. Normandin, D.R.E.
Students 418.

3—St. Michael's, (1922), Revs. Richard R. Gendreau; Philip N. Hamel; Deacon Thomas F. Prevost.
Res., 270 Ocean Grove Ave., 02777. Tel: 508-673-2808; Fax: 508-672-1642.
Catechesis/Religious Programs—Tel: 508-674-0024.
Students 281.

4—Our Lady of Fatima, (1958), Rev. George F. Almeida; Deacon Mark G. Shea.
Res., 530 Gardner Neck Rd., 02777-3109. Tel: 508-676-1541; Fax: 508-676-0289.
Catechesis/Religious Programs—Tel: 508-678-7011. Sr. Mary Denisita Sullivan, R.S.M., D.R.E.
Students 189.

Taunton, Bristol Co.,

1—Our Lady of the Holy Rosary, (1909) (Polish), Rev. David M. Stopyra, O.F.M.Conv.
Res., 80 Bay St., 02780. Tel: 508-823-3046; Fax: 508-823-0585. [JC]
Catechesis/Religious Programs—Tel: 508-824-3910.
Students 91.

2—Our Lady of the Immaculate Conception, (1883), Rev. Richard E. Degagne.
Res., 387 Bay St., 02780-1718. Tel: 508-824-8794; Fax: 508-821-7616.
Catechesis/Religious Programs—Tel: 508-824-4545. Mrs. Kathleen A. Peterson, D.R.E.
Students 222.

3—Our Lady of Lourdes, (1905) (Portuguese), Rev. John A. Gomes; Deacon Joseph Medeiros.
Res., 49 First St., 02780. Tel: 508-822-0357; Fax: 508-823-4999.
School—52 First St., 02780. Tel: 508-822-3746; Fax: 508-822-1450. Mrs. Arleen Booker, Prin.
Sisters 2; Lay Teachers 6; Students 199.
Catechesis/Religious Programs—Students 235.
Convent—55 First St., 02780. Tel: 508-822-9206.

4—Sacred Heart, (1873), Rev. Jon-Paul Gallant.
Res., 311 Somerset Ave., 02780. Tel: 508-823-2521; Fax: 508-823-2522.
Catechesis/Religious Programs—29 First St., 02780. Tel: 508-824-6791.
Students 328.

5—St. Anthony's, (1910) (Portuguese), Revs. Manuel P. Ferreira; Maurice O. Gauvin; Deacon Thomas J. Souza.
Res., 126 School St., 02780. Tel: 508-822-0714; Fax: 508-828-5844.
Catechesis/Religious Programs—Students 375.

6—St. James, (1904) (French), Rev. Thomas E. Morrissey.
Res., 249 Whittenton St., 02780. Tel: 508-824-7794; Fax: 508-822-8014.
Catechesis/Religious Programs—Tel: 508-824-7808.
Students 132.
Convent—279 Whittenton St., 02780. Tel: 508-824-8946.

7—St. Joseph's, (1896), Rev. Timothy P. Reis.
Res., 19 Kilmer Ave., 02780. Tel: 508-824-5435; Fax: 508-880-1903.
Catechesis/Religious Programs—Tel: 508-823-6819.
Students 211.

8—St. Mary's, (1828), Rev. Francis Zlotkowski, C.S.C.
Res., 14 St. Mary's Square, 02780. Tel: 508-822-7116; Fax: 508-822-7117.
School—Tel: 508-822-9480; Fax: 508-822-7164. Mr. Brian Cote, Prin.; Mrs. Sandra Parker, Asst. Prin.
Lay Teachers 21; Students 443.
Catechesis/Religious Programs—Tel: 508-880-5062.
Students 181.
Dolan Parish Center—Tel: 508-880-5062.

9—St. Paul's, (1904), Very Rev. Bento R. Fraga, V.F.; Deacons Robet J. Hill; John H. Schondek.
Res., 261 Tremont St., 02780. Tel: 508-824-7166; Fax: 508-822-9618.
Catechesis/Religious Programs—Tel: 508-822-9672.
Students 381.

Vineyard Haven, Dukes Co., St. Augustine (1962), Revs. Michael R. Nagle, D.Min.; John C. Ozug.
Res., 56 Franklin St., P.O. Box 1058, 02568. Tel: 508-693-0103; Fax: 508-693-8517.
Catechesis/Religious Programs—School St., Oak Bluffs, 02557. Tel: 508-693-0342; Fax: 508-696-8408.
Students 142.

Wareham, Plymouth Co., St. Patrick's (1911), Revs. Arnold R. Medeiros; Hugh J. McCullough.
Res., 82 High St., P.O. Box 271, 02571-0271. Tel: 508-295-2411; Fax: 508-295-2417. [CEM]
Catechesis/Religious Programs—Tel: 508-295-0780; Fax: 508-295-2417. Mrs. Priscilla Silva, D.R.E.
Students 600.
Mission—West Wareham, Plymouth Co., St. Anthony, P.O. Box 271, 02571-0271.

Wellfleet, Barnstable Co., Our Lady of Lourdes (1910), Rev. John F. Andrews.
Res., 335 Main St., P.O. Box 1414, 02667-1414. Tel: 508-349-2222; Fax: 508-349-9612. [CEM 2]
Catechesis/Religious Programs—Students 28.
Mission—North Eastham, Visitation Church, 930 Massasoit Rd., North Eastham, 02651.

Westport, Bristol Co., Our Lady of Grace (1954), Rev. Horace J. Travassos.
Res., 569 Sanford Rd., 02790. Tel: 508-674-6271; Fax: 508-675-4128.
Catechesis/Religious Programs—Tel: 508-675-5857.
Students 464.

St. George's (1914), Rev. Gerard A. Hebert.
Res., 12 Highland Ave., 02790. Tel: 508-636-4965; Fax: 508-636-4188.
Catechesis/Religious Programs—Tel: 508-636-4909.
Students 275.

St. John the Baptist (1930), Rev. Msgr. Edmund J. Fitzgerald.
Res., 945 Main Rd., Box 3328, 02790. Tel: 508-636-2251; Fax: 508-636-8306.
Catechesis/Religious Programs—924 Main Rd., P.O. Box 3328, 02790. Tel: 508-636-5506.
Students 276.

West Harwich, Barnstable Co., Holy Trinity (1918), Revs. Thomas L. Rita; Joseph J. Blyskosz; Michael O'Hearn. In res., Deacons Ralph F. Cox; Dana G. McCarthy; Vincent P. Walsh.
Res., S. Main St., 02671. Tel: 508-432-4000; Fax: 508-432-3494.
School—Tel: 508-432-8216.
Sisters 2; Lay Teachers 8; Students 196.
Catechesis/Religious Programs—Tel: 508-432-2898. Marie Mann, D.R.E.
Students 420.
Mission—Dennis Port, Barnstable Co., Our Lady of the Annunciation, P.O. Box 428, Dennis Port, 02639. [CEM]

Woods Hole, Barnstable Co., St. Joseph's (1882), Rev. Bernard R. Kelly.
Res., 33 Millfield St., P.O. Box 3, 02543. Tel: 508-548-0990.
Catechesis/Religious Programs—Tel: 508-540-3723.
Students 40.

Chaplains of Public Institutions

Barnstable. *Barnstable County House of Correction.* Deacon Richard J. Murphy, Coord., 347 South St., Hyannis, 02601.

New Bedford. *Bristol Co. House of Correction & Eastern Massachusetts Correctional Alcohol Center.* Rev. Matthew Sullivan, SS.CC., 3 Adams St., P.O. Box 111, Fairhaven, 02719. Tel: 508-993-2442.

Special Assignment:
Reverend Fathers—
Bowen, Donald J., St. James Society, Latin America
Canuel, Paul E., St. Rose of Lima & St. Francis of Assisi, Casa Cural, Guaimaca, Honduras

Graduate Studies:
Reverend Fathers—
O'Connor, Gerard, Pontifical North American College, Via Del Gianicolo, 14, Vatican City State, 00120

Absent on Leave:
Reverend Fathers—
Andrade, Richard G.
Baker, William F.
Boulet, Norman J., 2402 Highland Ave., Fall River, MA 02720
Faria, Andre H., Jr.
Robillard, Raymond A., 2402 Highland Ave., Fall River, MA 02720
Sousa, Douglas H.

Absent on Sick Leave:
Reverend Fathers—
de Mello, Arthur T., P.O. Box 40905, New Bedford, MA 02744-0005
Landry, David J.

Retired:
Reverend Monsignors—
Munroe, Henry T., P.A., P.O. Box 1310, Sagamore Beach, MA 02542
Reverend Fathers—
Boivin, Louis R., 375 Elsbree St., Fall River, MA 02720
Boule, Roland B., 375 Elsbree St., Fall River, MA 02720
Bousquet, Roland, 53 California St., Fall River, MA 02723
Burns, Edward J., 375 Elsbree St., Fall River, MA
Chabot, Bertrand R., 57 Wilfin Rd., South Yarmouth, MA 02135
Connors, Francis B., Marian Manor, 33 Summer St., Taunton, MA 02780
Denehy, John F., 460 Grant Ave., Satellite Beach, FL 32937
Dufour, Clement E., 77 Cottonwood St., Fairhaven, MA 02740-5596
Freitas, Daniel L., P.O. Box 411154, Melbourne, FL 32941-1154
Jussaume, Andre P., 32 Churchill Rd., Lakeville, MA 02347
Jussaume, Lucien, 2400 S. Main St., Fall River, MA 02724
Kirby, Robert F., P.O. Box 169, Cotuit, MA 02635
Lyons, James F., 287 Cory St., Fall River, MA 02720
Maguire, Joseph D., P.O. Box 750, North Falmouth, MA 02556-0750
McCarthy, James, P.O. Box 3176, Pocasset, MA 02559
McIsaac, Edward F., 2446 Highland Ave., Fall River, MA 02720
Murphy, Clarence, 375 Elsbree St., Fall River, MA 02720
Murphy, John J., 375 Elsbree St., Fall River, MA 02720
Pereira, Luciano J., 996 Brayton Ave., Somerset, MA 02721
Phillipino, Lucio B., P.O. Box 1884, No. Falmouth, MA 02556
Robida, Raymond A., 375 Elsbree St., Fall River, MA 02720
Shovelton, Gerald T., 34 Frost Ave., P.O. Box 545, West Yarmouth, MA 02673-0545
Shovelton, William J., 34 Frost Ave., P.O. Box 545, West Yarmouth, MA 02673-0545
Tavares, Antonino C., 230 Bonney St., New Bedford, MA 02744
Tetrault, Ralph D., 375 Elsbree St., Fall River, MA 02720
Wallace, Francis X., P.O. Box 3737, Pocasset, MA 02559

Permanent Deacons:
Akin, David P., St. Pius X, South Yarmouth
Alence, Robert Boston, MA, Corpus Christi, East Sandwich
Bailey, Thomas C. Hartford, CT, St. Pius Tenth, South Yarmouth
Barrett, James M., Jr., Our Lady of Victory, Centerville
Battiston, Donald L. Hartford, CT, St. Mary/O.L. of the Isle, Nantucket
Biron, Donald R. Boston, MA, Our Lady of the Cape, Brewster
Bonneau, Bruce J., St. John Neumann, East Freetown
Bousquet, Louis A., St. Anne, Fall River
Branco, John F., Our Lady of the Angels, Fall River
Camacho, Francis, Florida
Cipriano, A. Anthony, St. John the Evangelist, Attleboro
Cook, Chester O., St. Peter the Apostle, Provincetown
Cox, Ralph F. Galveston-Houston, TX, Holy Trinity, West Harwich
Cwiekowski, John W., (Retired)
daCruz, Antonio, Our Lady of the Assumption, New Bedford
Dexter, Leonard C., Jr., St. John the Evangelist, Pocasset
Dresser, Richard M., St. Francis Xavier, Hyannis
Drinkwater, Oscar T., So. Carolina
Emmert, John J., Corpus Christi, East Sandwich
Fantasia, Frank D., Christ the King, Mashpee
Faria, Robert A., Our Lady of Health, Fall River
Fitzpatrick, John J., Holy Family, East Taunton
Fournier, Paul M., Holy Ghost, Attleboro
Guy, Michael P., St. Francis Xavier, Acushnet
Haddad, Victor, St. Thomas More, Somerset
Hassey, Richard J. Boston, MA, St. Pius Tenth, So. Yarmouth
Hill, Robert J., St. Paul, Taunton
Hussey, Edward J., St. Patrick, Somerset
Ladroga, William Worcester, MA, Our Lady of the Cape, Brewster
Lavallee, Maurice, St. Joseph, New Bedford
Leavitt, James P. Boston, MA, Our Lady of the Cape, Brewster
LeBlanc, Claude A., St. Mary, New Bedford
Lemay, Robert D., Christ the King, Mashpee
Liegey, Gabriel J. New York, NY, Holy Redeemer, Chatham
Macedo, Paul J., St. John the Baptist, New Bedford
Mador, Joseph F., Holy Redeemer, Chatham
Mahoney, Patrick J. Hartford, CT, St. Patrick, Falmouth
Martin, William A., St. Elizabeth Seton, North Falmouth
Marzelli, James, Jr., Mission Parish of Guaymaca - Archdiocese of Tegucigalpa, Honduras
McCarthy, Dana G., Holy Trinity, West Harwich
McEnaney, Norman F., St. Joan of Arc, Orleans
Medeiros, Joseph P., Our Lady of Lourdes, Taunton
Meloni, James J., Jr., St. Mary's, North Attleboro
Metilly, Paul, Florida
Mis, Franciszek W., St. Stanislaus Church, Fall River
Moniz, John de A., Espirito Santo, Fall River
Morency, Marcel G., St. Anne, New Bedford
Murphy, Richard J., St. Francis Xavier, Hyannis
Murray, Michael E., St. Mary, Norton
Nogueira, Benjamin, Fitchburg, MA
Normandin, Robert G.L., St. Louis de France, Swansea
Pacheco, Eduardo M., Our Lady of the Assumption, New Bedford
Palanza, Thomas P., St. Mary, Mansfield
Pelland, Robert W., (Unassigned)
Pires, Abilio dos A., Our Lady of Mt. Carmel, New Bedford
Prevost, Thomas F., St. Michael, Swansea
Racine, Leo W., St. Joseph-St. Therese, New Bedford
Raymond, Robert, (Retired), Arizona
Reardon, Jeremiah J., St. Mary, South Dartmouth
Roma, Paul K., St. Elizabeth Seton, North Falmouth
Sasseville, Eugene H., Holy Name of the Sacred Heart of Jesus, New Bedford
Schondek, John H., St. Paul, Taunton
Shea, Mark G., Our Lady of Fatima, Swansea
Souza, Thomas J., St. Anthony, Taunton
St. Onge, Lawrence A., St. James, New Bedford
Stanley, Joseph P., Our Lady of Victory, Centerville
Surprenant, Robert L., St. Anthony, Mattapoisett
Thomas, Walter D., St. Mary, Mansfield
Tolassi, Bernard D. Hartford, CT, Christ the King, Mashpee
Twerago, John P. Hartford, CT, St. Joan of Arc, Orleans
Wallace, Forrest, Cincinnati, Ohio
Walsh, Vincent, Holy Trinity, West Harwich
Welch, John, St. Ann, Raynham
Zarella, George H., Holy Cross, South Easton
Zeich, Richard C. Paterson, NJ, St. Pius X, South Yarmouth

INSTITUTIONS LOCATED IN THE DIOCESE

[A] COLLEGES AND UNIVERSITIES

EASTON. *Villa Nazareth USA, Inc.*, 320 Washington St., 02537. Tel: 508-230-5738; Fax: 508-565-1420.
E-mail: rrossi@stonehill.edu
For a complete listing, refer to the Colleges and Universities section.

NORTH EASTON. *Holy Cross Fathers Religious*, 480 Washington St., 02356. Tel: 508-238-5942; Fax: 508-230-7455.
E-mail: bbeaupre@stonehill.edu
For a complete listing, refer to the Colleges and Universities section.
Stonehill College, 02357. Tel: 508-565-1000; Fax: 508-238-1297.
E-mail: bbeaupre@stonehill.edu
Web site: www.stonehill.edu
For a complete listing, refer to the Colleges and Universities section.

[B] HIGH SCHOOLS, DIOCESAN

FALL RIVER. *Bishop Connolly High School*, 373 Elsbree St., 02720. Tel: 508-676-1071; Fax: 508-676-8594.
E-mail: bchs@bishopconnolly.com
Web site: www.bishopconnolly.com
Mr. Anthony S. Nunes, Prin.; Bro. Richard J. Lunny, C.F.X., Academic Vice Prin.; Rev. Roger J. Landry, Chap. Brothers 3; Lay Teachers 37; Students 400.

ATTLEBORO. *Bishop Feehan High School*, 70 Holcott Dr., 02703. Tel: 508-226-6223; Fax: 508-226-7696.
E-mail: webmaster@bishopfeehan.com
Web site: www.bishopfeehan.com
Mr. George Milot, Prin.; Rev. Michael F. Kuhn, Chap. Priests 1; Sisters 4; Lay Teachers 69; Students 930.
Our Lady of Mercy Convent, 70 Holcott Dr., 02703. Tel: 508-226-4608; Fax: 508-226-7696. Sr. Rose Angela McLellan, R.S.M., Supr. Sisters 15.

NORTH DARTMOUTH. *Bishop Stang High School*, 500 Slocum Rd., 02747-2999. Tel: 508-996-5602; Fax: 508-994-6756.
E-mail: office@bishopstang.com
Web site: http://www.bishopstang.com
Theresa E. Dougall, Pres.; Mary Ann Miskel, Academic Prin.; Michael P. O'Brien, Prin. of Students; Rev. Paul C. Fedak, Chap. Priests 1; Lay Teachers 56; Support Staff 17; Students 675.

TAUNTON. *Coyle and Cassidy High School*, 2 Hamilton St., 02780. Tel: 508-823-6164; Fax: 508-823-2530.
E-mail: coyle@aol.com
Web site: http://www.coylecassidy.com
Mr. Dennis R. Poyant, Headmaster; Rev. Hernando Herrera. Priests 1; Sisters 2; Lay Teachers 66; Students 726.

[C] ELEMENTARY SCHOOLS, DIOCESAN

TAUNTON. *Taunton Catholic Middle School*, 61 Summer St., 02780. Tel: 508-822-0491; Fax: 508-824-0469.
Web: catholicmiddle.com
Kathleen A. Simpson, Prin.; Rev. Maurice Gauvin, Chap. Sisters 1; Lay Teachers 12; Students 310.

[D] RESIDENTIAL CHILD CARE FACILITIES

FALL RIVER. *St. Vincent's Home Corp.*, Main Campus: 2425 Highland Ave., 02720. Tel: 508-679-8511; Fax: 508-672-2558.
Web site: www.stvincentshome.org
Mr. John T. Weldon, Exec. Dir. Sisters 10; Total Staff 483; Children Residents 160.

[E] NURSERIES

NEW BEDFORD. *St. Saviour's Day Nursery*, 405 County St., 02740-4935. Tel: 508-997-0233. Sr. Marcella Rostkowski, C.R., Supr. Sisters of the Resurrection 6; Students 30.

[F] GENERAL HOSPITALS

FALL RIVER. *Saint Anne's Health Care Management Services, Inc.*, 795 Middle St., 02721-1798. Tel: 508-674-5741; Fax: 508-675-5647
For a complete listing, refer to the Hospitals section.
Saint Anne's Health Care System, Inc., 795 Middle St., 02721-1798. Tel: 508-674-5741; Fax: 508-675-5647
For a complete listing, refer to the Hospitals section.
Saint Anne's Hospital, 795 Middle St., 02721-1798. Tel: 508-674-5741; Fax: 508-675-5647
For a complete listing, refer to the Hospitals section.

[G] SPECIAL HOSPITALS AND SANATORIA FOR INVALIDS

FALL RIVER. *Rose Hawthorne Lathrop Home*, 1600 Bay St., 02724. Tel: 508-673-2322; Fax: 508-679-5830
For a complete listing, refer to the Special Care Facilities section.

[H] HOMES FOR AGED

FALL RIVER. *Catholic Memorial Home Inc.*, 2446 Highland Ave., 02720-4599. Tel: 508-679-0011; Fax: 508-672-5858
For a complete listing, refer to the Special Care Facilities section.

FAIRHAVEN. *Our Lady's Haven of Fairhaven Inc.*, 71 Center St., 02719. Tel: 508-999-4561; Fax: 508-997-0254.
Web site: www.dhfo.org
For a complete listing, refer to the Special Care Facilities section.

NEW BEDFORD. *Sacred Heart Home*, 359 Summer St., 02740. Tel: 508-996-6751; Fax: 508-992-3145.
Web site: www.dhfo.org
For a complete listing, refer to the Special Care Facilities section.

NORTH ATTLEBORO. *Madonna Manor Inc.*, 85 N. Washington St., 02760. Tel: 508-699-2794; Fax: 508-699-0481.
E-mail: ekanuse@dhfo.org
Web site: www.dhfo.org
For a complete listing, refer to the Special Care Facilities section.

TAUNTON. *Bethany House Adult Day Care*, 72 Church Green, 02780. Tel: 508-822-9200
For a complete listing, refer to the Special Care Facilities section.
Marian Manor Inc., 33 Summer St., 02780. Tel: 508-822-4885; Fax: 508-677-4361
For a complete listing, refer to the Special Care Facilities section.

[I] MONASTERIES AND RESIDENCES OF PRIESTS AND BROTHERS

FALL RIVER. *Brothers of Christian Instruction*, 555 Eastern Ave., 02723. Tel: 508-672-5763. Bros. Daniel Caron, Prov.; Walter Zwierchowski, Supr.; Roger Millette; Norman Simoneau. Brothers 4; Faculty of Bishop Connolly High 3.

Cardinal Medeiros Residence-Retirement Facility for Priests, 375 Elsbree St., 02720-7211. Tel: 508-675-1050; Fax: 508-675-2181.

Dominican House, 818 Middle St., 02721. Tel: 508-678-5322. Rev. Pierre E. Lachance, O.P., Supr.

Priests' Hostel, 2402 Highland Ave., 02720. Tel: 508-672-1632; Fax: 508-679-1422. In res. Revs. Raymond A. Robillard; Norman J. Boulet; William Norton; Bernard Vanasse.

St. John Vianney House, 818 Middle St., 02721-1734. Tel: 508-673-0377; Fax: 508-672-0939. Revs. John P. Cronin, Dir.; Pierre E. Lachance, O.P.; Marc H. Berger; Melchor M. Ferrer, S.D.B.; Ramon Dominguez. Priests 5; Total Staff 2.

ATTLEBORO. *La Salette Missionary Association*, 947 Park St., 02703. Tel: 508-222-0027. Very Rev. Dennis J. Loomis, M.S., Dir.

La Salette Provincial House, 947 Park St., P.O. Box 2965, 02703-0965. Tel: 508-222-6682; Fax: 508-222-6178.
Web site: www.lasalette.org
Immaculate Heart of Mary Province. Very Rev. Dennis J. Loomis, M.S., Prov. Supr.
Priests of the Province serving outside the U.S.: Rev. Gerard Comeau, M.S., Sanctuario de Nuestra Senora de LaSalette Siador-Silleda, Ponte Vedra, Espana. Rev. Camille Doucet, M.S., 3535 Park Ave., Montreal, Canada, PQ H2X 2H8. Tel: 514-499-9312; Fax: 514-288-7681. Rev. George Dube, M.S., Our Lady of LaSalette, 3535 Park Ave., Quebec H2Z-2H8, Canada. Tel: 514-499-9312; Fax: 514-288-7681. Rev. Andre Lussier, M.S., La Salette Fathers, P.O. Box AC 59, Quezon City 1100, Philippines. Rev. Joseph Gosselin, M.S., 229 Cadillac St., Ontario N8Y-2S8, Canada. Tel: 519-253-4784; Fax: 519-252-5640. Rev. Fernand Langevin, M.S., 270 Deragon St., Granby, Canada, PQ J2G 5J5. Tel: 450-776-7839; Fax: 450-372-1982. Rev. Paul M. Roy, M.S., Missionari di N.S. de La Salette, Piazza Madonna della Salette, 3, Roma, Italy, 00152. Rev. Robert Vachon, M.S., 4917 St. Urbain, Montreal, PQ H2T-2W1, Canada. Tel: 514-288-7229; Fax: 514-844-6800. Rev. Theodule Richard, M.S., 200 Roberts Boul., Granby, Canada, PQ J2G 9I6. Tel: 450-372-5125. Rev. Roland Vandal, M.S., 3535 Park Ave., Montreal, Quebec H2X-2H8, Canada. Tel: 514-499-9139; Fax: 514-288-7681.

La Salette Shrine, 947 Park St., 02703. Tel: 508-222-5410; Fax: 508-222-6770. Revs. Raymond Vaillancaurt, M.S., Supr.; Andre A. Pateraude, M.S., Dir.; Dennis J. Loomis, M.S., Prov. Sup. In res. Revs. George Brennan, M.S.; Paul Dalbec, M.S.; Fernand Cassista, M.S.; Gerald Forest, M.S.; Ernest J. Carriveau, M.S.; Joseph Fredette, M.S.; Richard Lavaie, M.S.; Richard Landry, M.S.; Raymond Moquin, M.S.; Thomas Paris, M.S.; Manuel Pereira, M.S.; Roger Leraux, M.S.; Donald Paradis, M.S.; Normand Theraux, M.S.; Bros. Lucien Brodeur, M.S.; Charles Caillouette, M.S.; Roger Moreau, M.S.; Leonard Melanson, M.S.; Robert Nichols, M.S.; Ronald Taylor, M.S.; Raymond Tetreault, M.S.; Paul Boucher, M.S.; Jean-Paul Champagne, M.S.; Roger St. Germain, M.S. Priests 17; Brothers 10.

FAIRHAVEN. *National Center of the Enthronement*, P.O. Box 111, 02719-01111. Tel: 508-999-2680; Fax: 508-993-8233.
E-mail: necenter@juno.com
Web site: http://www.sscc.org
Rev. Columban Crotty, SS.CC., Natl. Dir. Total Staff 2.

Sacred Hearts Provincial House, 77 Adams St., P.O. Box 111, 02719-0111. Tel: 508-993-2442; Fax: 508-996-5499.
Web site: www.sscc.org
Congregation of the Sacred Hearts of Jesus and Mary. Very Rev. David P. Reid, SS.CC., Prov.; Bro. Paul R. Alves, SS.CC., Treas.; Revs. Gabriel Healy, SS.CC., Mission Procurator & Dir. Devel.; David Lupo, SS.CC., Vocation Dir.; Matthew Sullivan, SS.CC.; Columban Crotty, SS.CC.; Albert Dagnoli, SS.CC.; Richard McNally, SS.CC. Fathers 5. Damien Residence, 73 Adams St., P.O. Box 111, 02719-0111. Tel: 508-999-0500; Fax: 508-990-7173. Congregation of the Sacred Hearts of Jesus and Mary. Revs. Benedict Folgeri, SS.CC., Dir.; William Davis, SS.CC.; Albert Evans, SS.CC.; William Mitchell, SS.CC.; Roy Yurco, SS.CC.; Rene Gaudin, SS.CC.; Owen Goodwin, SS.CC.; Henry Creighton, SS.CC.; Brian Marggraf, SS.CC.; Daniel J. McCarthy, SS.CC.; Leo King, SS.CC.; Jude Morgan, SS.CC.; Bro. Damien O'Hare, SS.CC. Fathers 12; Brothers 1.
Priests of the Province Serving Abroad - In Japanese Missions: Very Rev. John Yamada, SS.CC., Vice Prov.; Revs. Michael Coleman, SS.CC.; Cornelius Biffar, SS.CC.; Michael Narita, SS.CC.; Lawrence Craig, SS.CC.; William Ducey, SS.CC.; Louis Kawamata, SS.CC.; Edward Keeney, SS.CC.; Augustine Kobayashi, SS.CC.; Peter Kusunoki, SS.CC.; James E. McDonough, SS.CC.; Philip Murphy, SS.CC.; Kenji Honma, SS.CC.; Michiaki Chihara, SS.CC.; Bro. Francis Nakazawa, SS.CC.
In the Philippines: Rev. Andrew Healey, SS.CC.
In Nassau, Bahamas: Revs. Martin Gomes, SS.CC.; Michael Kelly, SS.CC.; Patrick F. Fanning, SS.CC.; Christopher Santangelo, SS.CC.
In Abaco, Bahamas: Rev. Stanley Kolasa, SS.CC.
In India: Revs. William Petrie, SS.CC.; Michael Shanahan, SS.CC.; Subal Nayak, SS.CC.; Bro. James Rukavina, SS.CC.
In Rome, Italy: Rev. William Donegan, SS.CC., General Councillor.
Chaplains in Military Facilities: Rev. James Keefe, SS.CC., William Beaumont Army Medical Center, Chaplains Office, P.O. Box 70005, El Paso, TX, 79920-0005. Tel: 915-569-2978; Fax: 915-569-2376. Rev. Austin Nagel, SS.CC., V.A. Hospital, Belmont St., Brockton, 02401-5599. Tel: 508-587-6737.

NEW BEDFORD. *Franciscans of Primitive Observance*, Immaculate Conception Friary, 107 Rivet St., 02744. Revs. David M. Engo, F.P.O.; Peter Giroux, F.P.O.; Francis Joseph Kelly, F.P.O.; Joseph Paul Medio, F.P.O.; John M. Sweeney, F.P.O.

Marian Friary of Our Lady, Queen of the Seraphic Order, 600 Pleasant St., 02740-6299. Tel: 508-996-8274; Fax: 508-996-8296.
E-mail: ffi@marymediatrix.com
Web site: www.marymediatrix.com
Mailing Address: P.O. Box 3003, 02741-3003. Revs. George M. Roth, F.F.I., Guardian; Martin M. Fonte, F.F.I., Vicar; Alphonsus M. Sutton, F.F.I.; Maximilian M. Warnisher, F.F.I.; Angelo Michael M. Guarin, F.F.I. Priests 5; Brothers 16.

NORTH DARTMOUTH. *Holy Cross Mission House*, 824 Tucker Rd., 02747. Tel: 508-993-2238. Residence for Religious Priests and Brothers. Revs. Charles L. Wallen, C.S.C.; Thomas L. Campbell, C.S.C.; J. Marc Herbert, C.S.C.; Thomas J. Tobin, C.S.C.; John F. Dias, C.S.C.; Francis E. Grogan, C.S.C., Dir.; Bro. Joseph L. Morris, C.S.C.

St. Joseph's Hall, 800 Tucker Rd., 02747-3599. Tel: 508-996-2413.
E-mail: cscda@aol.com
Revs. J. Robert Rioux, C.S.C., Dir.; William Condon, C.S.C. Tel: 508-993-1302; Albert A. Croce, C.S.C.; John F. Dias, C.S.C.; Bro. Joseph Morris, C.S.C. Priests 4; Brothers 1.

ONSET. *St. Joseph Friary-Franciscan Friars*, 46 Robinwood Rd., P.O. Box 63, 02558. Tel: 508-759-7280; Fax: 508-743-9551. Revs. Richard Passeri, O.F.M., Guardian; Frank Genevive, O.F.M., Parochial Asst., St. Margaret Church, Buzzard Bay, MA. In res. Rev. Berard Tufo, O.F.M. Total Staff 2; Total in Residence 3.

[J] CONVENTS AND RESIDENCES FOR SISTERS

FALL RIVER. *Bishop's Residence Convent*, 394 Highland Ave., 02720. Tel: 508-675-1311. Sisters of St. Jeanne d'Arc. Sisters 3.

Convent of Dominican Sisters of Hope, 37 Park St., 02721. Tel: 508-676-3096. Sr. Philomena Marie McCartney, O.P.H., Prioress Gen.

St. Patrick's Convent, 55 Tuttle St., 02724. Tel: 508-673-0796. Sr. M. Romana Murphy, R.S.M., Coord. Sisters 6.

ATTLEBORO. *Our Lady of Mercy Convent*, 70 Holcott Dr., 02703. Tel: 508-226-4608; Fax: 508-222-2713. Sr. Rose Angela McLellan, R.S.M., Local Coord. Sisters 17.

DIGHTON. *Dominican Sisters of Charity of the Presentation of the Blessed Virgin*, 3012 Elm St., 02715. Tel: 508-669-5425; 669-5023 (Novitiate); Fax: 508-669-6521.
E-mail: domsis@webcombo.net
Sr. Joanna Fernandes, O.P., Prov. Supr. Provincial House-Residence, Residence for Aged Sisters, Novitiate. Sisters 23.

FAIRHAVEN. *Franciscan Sisters of the Immaculate*, 382 Main St., 02719. Tel: 508-992-0482.
E-mail: fsi@ici.net
Web site: http://www.connix.com/'/.FIsisters/

Sisters of the Sacred Hearts. Regional Headquarters, 35 Huttleston Ave., 02719-3154. Tel: 508-994-9341; Fax: 508-990-1967.
E-mail: srdolorespavao@cs.com
Legal Title: *Sisters of the Sacred Hearts of Jesus and Mary and of Perpetual Adoration, SS.CC.* Sr. Dolores Pavao, SS.CC., Regional Supr., 44 Adams St., 02719. Tel: 508-994-5917. Sr. Lillian Cookson, SS.CC., Local Supr., 491 Hood St., Fall River, 02720. Tel: 508-675-7716. Sr. Eleanor Cyr, SS.CC., Local Supr. Sisters in Region 10.

HARWICHPORT. *Contemplative Sisters of the Good Shepherd*, 88 Bank St., 02646. Tel: 508-432-5582; Fax: 508-432-6293.
E-mail: abehrend@capecod.net

NEW BEDFORD. *Misioneras Guadalupanas del Espiritu Santo*, 2 Acushnet Ave., 02744. Tel: 508-997-8729; Fax: 508-997-4537.
E-mail: guadalupananb@jaol.com
Sr. Aida Sansor A., M.G.Sp.S.; Sr. M. Candelaria Hernandez; Sr. Sandra Luz Campos, Supr.; Sr. Ana Gabiela Castro; Sr. Obdulia Olivar. Sisters 5.

Our Lady of Mercy Convent, 14 Summer St., 02740. Tel: 508-992-3694. Sr. Jeannette Thomas, R.S.M., Coord. Sisters 4.

Sisters of Mercy, 15 Lemos St., 02740. Tel: 508-992-4947. Sr. M. Nathan Doherty, R.S.M., Contact Person. Sisters 3.

NORTH DARTMOUTH. *Diocesan Family Life Center*, 500 Slocum Rd., 02747. Tel: 508-993-4930; Fax: 508-999-6430. Total Staff 3.

Dominican Sisters of Hope, 856 Tucker Rd., 02747. Tel: 508-996-1305. Sisters 6.

TAUNTON. *Our Lady of Lourdes Convent*, 55 First St., 02780. Tel: 508-822-9206. Sr. M. Margretta Sol, Contact Person. Sisters of Mercy of the Union 3.

Villa Fatima, 90 County St., 02780. Tel: 508-822-6282; Fax: 508-823-0825. Sisters of St. Dorothy. Sr. Rosalie Patrello, S.S.D., Local Coord. Professed Sisters 8.

WAREHAM. *St. Patrick's Missionary Cenacle*, 86 High St., 02571. Tel: 508-295-0780. Outreach to the homebound handicapped.

[K] RETREAT HOUSES

ATTLEBORO. *La Salette Center for Christian Living*, 947 Park St., 02703-0965. Tel: 508-222-8530; Fax: 508-222-8558.
E-mail: lasalett@ma.ultranet.com
Web site: http://www.ultranet.com/~lasalett
Revs. Richard Landry, M.S., Dir.; Fernand Cassista, M.S.; Sr. Mary Hammill, R.S.M.; Bro. Roger A. Moreau, M.S.; Mrs. Karen Laroche. In res. Rev. Normand Theroux, M.S. Priests 2; Total Staff 12; Total Assisted 4,200.

EAST FREETOWN. *Cathedral Camp and Retreat Center*, 167 Middleboro Rd., P.O. Box 428, 02717-0428. Tel: 508-763-3394; Fax: 508-763-3768.
E-mail: joseph_marie2@juno.com
Sr. Joseph Marie Levesque, O.P., Dir. Total Staff 7; Total in Residence 2.

Cathedral Camp Retreat Center, 167 Middleboro Rd., P.O. Box 428, 02717-0428. Tel: 508-763-3994; Fax: 508-763-3768.
E-mail: joseph_marie2@juno.com
Sr. Joseph Marie Levesque, O.P., Dir. Total Staff 7; Total in Residence 2.

NORTH EASTON. *Holy Cross Fathers Retreat House*, 490 Washington St., 02356-1294. Tel: 508-238-2051; Fax: 508-238-0164.
E-mail: jfcal@hotmail.com
Rev. Joseph F. Callahan, C.S.C., Spiritual Dir. In res. Rev. Richard H. Sullivan, C.S.C. Priests 2.

WAREHAM. *Sacred Hearts Retreat Center*, 226 Great Neck Rd., 02571. Tel: 508-295-0100; 295-1450.
E-mail: retreats@sscc.org
Web site: http://www.sscc.org/wareham
Congregation of the Sacred Hearts of Jesus and Mary and of the Perpetual Adoration of the Most Blessed Sacrament. Revs. Thomas McElroy, SS.CC., Dir.; Gabriel Healy, SS.CC.; David Lupo, SS.CC.; Bro. Joseph Fandel, SS.CC. Priests 3; Brothers 1; Sisters 1.

[L] DEPARTMENT OF CATHOLIC SOCIAL SERVICES AND SPECIAL APOSTOLATES

FALL RIVER. *Catholic Social Services of Fall River*, 783 Slade St., P.O. Box M-S, Station, 02724. Tel: 508-674-4681; Fax: 508-675-2224.
E-mail: arlmac@aol.com
Arlene A. McNamee, Exec. Dir. Program Directors: Mary Lou Mancini, M.Ed., L.C.S.W., Pregnancy & Adoption Services; Maria C. Pereira, M.S.W., L.I.C.S.W., Counseling Services; Susan E. Desrosiers, M.S.W., L.I.S.W., Sexual Abuse Prevention; Lydia Brekon, Ph.D, Immigration Services; Eileen White, M.Div, Women's Residency.

Catholic Social Services of Attleboro, 10 Maple St., Attleboro, 02703. Tel: 508-226-4780; Fax: 508-226-5813.

Catholic Social Services of New Bedford, 230 Bonney St., New Bedford, 02744. Tel: 508-997-7337; Fax: 508-984-1667.

Catholic Social Services of Cape Cod, 261 South St., Hyannis, 02601. Tel: 508-771-6771; Fax: 508-771-4711.

Catholic Social Services of Taunton, 78 Broadway, Taunton, 02780. Tel: 508-824-3264; Fax: 508-880-1903.

Reaching Out, 311 Hooper St., Tiverton, RI, 02878. Tel: 401-624-9270; Fax: 508-675-2224.

Special Apostolates, 783 Slade St., P.O. Box M-S, Station, 02724. Tel: 508-674-4681; Fax: 508-675-2224.
E-mail: aam@CSSDIOC.ORG
Arlene A. McNamee, Executive Dir.

Campaign For Human Development Apostolate. Tel: 508-674-4681; Fax: 508-675-2224.

Office for Persons with Disabilities, 783 Slade St., 02724. Tel: 508-679-8373 (Voice); 679-4277 (TTY). Denise Porche, Coord.; Dennis Canuela, Coord.

Spanish Apostolate, 2 Acushnet Ave., New Bedford, 02744. Tel: 508-997-8729; Fax: 508-992-2208. Gloria Rodriquez; Rev. Paul E. Canuel, Dir., P.O. Box 40605, New Bedford, 02744-0006. Tel: 508-997-8729; Fax: 508-992-2208.

Sr Clare Chabot, 189 Wellington St., 02720. Tel: 508-675-1868.
E-mail: clarechabo@aol.com

HYANNIS. *St. Clare's Residence for Women,* 949 Pitcher's Way, 02601. Tel: 508-775-5096.

[M] CAMPS AND COMMUNITY CENTERS

EAST TAUNTON. *Diocesean Catholic Youth Organization,* P.O. Box 619, 02718. Tel: 508-824-5707; Fax: 508-824-5665. Rev. Jay T. Maddock, Diocesan & Area Dir.

Fall River Area Catholic Youth Organization, Sullivan-McCarrick CYO Center, 403 Anawan St., Fall River, 02720. Tel: 508-672-9644; Fax: 508-824-5665.

New Bedford Area Catholic Youth Organization, Kennedy Youth Center, 377 County St., New Bedford, 02740. Tel: 508-996-0536; Fax: 508-824-5665. Mr. George Viveiros, Acting Area Dir.

Taunton Area Catholic Youth Organization, 61 Summer St., Taunton, 02780. Tel: 508-822-5218; Fax: 508-824-5665. Mr. Donald Morrison, Acting Area Dir.

[N] NEWMAN CENTERS AND CAMPUS MINISTRY

FALL RIVER. *Bristol Community College Newman Center,* 777 Elsbree St., 02720-7395. Tel: 508-678-2811, Ext. 2247; Fax: 508-673-4289.
E-mail: abibeau@bristol.mass.edu
Web site: www.bristol.mass.edu/campusministry/index.htm
Sr. Annette Bibeau, S.S.A., (Full Time); Rev. Luca Brancolini. Total Staff 1.

Diocesan Education Center, 423 Highland Ave., 02720. Tel: 508-678-2828; Fax: 508-674-4218.
E-mail: director@dfrcec.com
Web site: www.dfrcec.com
Rev. William T. Garland, O.S.A., Dir. of Education; Mr. James A. McNamee, Supt. of Schools; Rev. Henry J. Dahl, Dir. of R.C.I.A.; Deacon Bruce Bonneau, Dir. Religious Education; Lisa M. Gulino, Dir. of Adult Education & Evangelization; Bud Miller, Dir. Youth & Young Adult Ministry. Tel: 508-675-3847; Fax: 508-675-3864.

BUZZARDS BAY. *Massachusetts Maritime Academy Newman Center,* 141 Main St., 02532.

NORTH DARTMOUTH. *Catholic Campus Ministry University of Massachusetts Dartmouth,* 285 Old Westport Rd., 02747-2300. Tel: 508-999-8872.
E-mail: cpregana@umassd.edu
Web site: www.ccm.mcc.umass.edu
Campus Ministers: Rev. Craig Pregana; Sr. Madeleine Tacy, O.P. Total Staff 2.

NORTON. *Wheaton College Newman Center.* Tel: 508-725-2668; Fax: 508-226-1115.
E-mail: lbrancolini@non-nobis.org
Web site: www.non-nobis.org/wc
Rev. Luca Brancolini, F.S.C.B., St. Joseph Rectory, 208 S. Main St., Attleboro, 02703. Tel: 508-725-2668; Fax: 508-226-1115.

TAUNTON. *Paul A. Dever State School (For Retarded) Newman Center,* Box 631, 02780. Tel: 508-824-5881.

WEST BARNSTABLE. *Cape Cod Community College Newman Center.*

[O] MISCELLANEOUS LISTINGS

FALL RIVER. *Carmelite Convent of Dartmouth, Inc.,* c/o P.O. Box 2577, 02722.

Community Action for Better Housing, Inc., 783 Slade St., P.O. Box M, S. Station, 02724. Tel: 508-674-4681; Fax: 508-675-2224.
E-mail: AAM@cssdioc.org

Diocesan Facilities Self-Insurance Group, Inc., P.O. Box 1110, 02722.

Saint Mary's Education Fund, Inc., P.O. Box 2577, 02722. Tel: 508-675-1311.

Youth Apostles, c/o Rev. Michael F. Kuhn, 327 2nd St., 02721-2007. Tel: 508-672-2755; Fax: 508-672-2755.
E-mail: yas-fr@excite.com
Web site: www.youthapostles.org
Rev. Michael F. Kuhn, Dir. Total in Residence 4.

ATTLEBORO. *Priestly Fraternity of the Missionaries of St. Charles Borromeo, Inc.,* 208 S. Main St., 02703. Tel: 508-226-1115; Fax: 917-464-9065.
E-mail: mcarvill@sancarlo.org
Web site: www.cancarlo.org
Revs. Michael Carvill; Vincent Nagle; Luca Brancolini.

NEW BEDFORD. *The Institute of the Incarnate Word, Inc.,* 306 Ashley Blvd, 02746. Tel: 508-672-9303; Fax: 508-994-0281.
E-mail: jggiunta@aol.com
Web site: http://www.ive.org
Revs. Jose Giunta, I.V.E.; Jose Del Val, I.V.E.; Gustavo Dominguez, I.V.E.

Missionaries of Charity, 556 County St., 02740. Shelter for homeless women. Total in Residence 4; Total Assisted 54.

St. Mary's Home of New Bedford, Inc. c/o P.O. Box 2577, Fall River, 02722. Tel: 508-675-1311.

RELIGIOUS INSTITUTES OF MEN REPRESENTED IN THE DIOCESE

For further details refer to the corresponding bracketed number in the Religious Institutes of Men or Women section.

[0320]—*Brothers of Christian Instruction.*—F.I.C.
[0330]—*Brothers of the Christian Schools.*
[0600]—*Brothers of the Congregation of Holy Cross.*
[]—*Capuchin Recollects Friars.*
[1330]—*Congregation of the Mission.*—C.M.
[1140]—*Congregation of the Sacred Hearts of Jesus and Mary.*—SS.CC.
[0480]—*Conventual Franciscans.* (Buffalo, NY).—O.F.M.Conv.
[0470]—*Franciscan* (Order of Friars Minor Capuchin). (St. Augustine Prov.).—O.F.M.Cap.
[0520]—*Franciscan Friars.* (Immaculate Conception Prov.).—O.F.M.
[0533]—*Franciscan Friars of the Immaculate.*—F.F.I.
[]—*The Institute of the Incarnate Word.*—I.V.E.
[0690]—*Jesuit Fathers and Brothers.*—S.J.
[0720]—*The Missionaries of Our Lady of La Salette.*—M.S.
[0870]—*Montfort Missionaries.*—S.M.M.
[0430]—*Order of Preachers (Dominicans).*—O.P.
[]—*Priestly Fraternity of the Missionaries of St. Charles Borromeo Order.*—F.S.C.B.
[0610]—*Priests of the Congregation of the Holy Cross.* (Eastern Prov.).—C.S.C.

RELIGIOUS INSTITUTES OF WOMEN REPRESENTED IN THE DIOCESE

[]—*Capuchin Recollects Sisters.*
[0330]—*Carmelite Sisters of the Aged and Infirm.*—O.Carm.
[3815]—*Congregation of the Sisters of St. Joan of Arc.*—S.J.A.
[1830]—*Contemplative Sisters of the Good Shepherd.*—C.G.S.
[0750]—*Daughters of the Charity of the Sacred Heart of Jesus.* (Sacred Heart Prov.).—F.C.S.C.J.
[1070-23]—*Dominican Sisters.*—O.P.
[1100]—*Dominican Sisters of Charity of the Presentation of the Blessed Virgin.*—O.P.
[]—*Dominican Sisters of Hope.*—O.P.
[2580]—*Institute of the Sisters of Mercy of the Americas.* (Hartford, CT; Manchester, NH).—R.S.M.
[3790]—*Institute of the Sisters of St. Dorothy.*—S.S.D.
[2790]—*Missionary Servants of the Most Blessed Trinity.*—M.S.B.T.
[]—*Missioneras Guadalupanas del Espirito Santo.*
[3240]—*Poor Sisters of Jesus Crucified and the Sorrowful Mother.*
[3410]—*Religious of Christian Education.*—R.C.E.
[3450]—*Religious of Jesus and Mary.*—R.J.M.
[2070]—*Religious of the Holy Union of the Sacred Hearts.* (Immaculate Heart and Sacred Heart Provs.).—S.U.S.C.
[3650]—*Servants of Our Lady, Queen of the Clergy.*—S.R.C.
[0560]—*Sisters of Charity of Quebec (Grey Nuns).*—S.C.Q.
[0590]—*Sisters of Charity of Saint Elizabeth (Convent Station).*—S.C.
[0640]—*Sisters of Charity of St. Vincent de Paul (Halifax).*—S.C.
[3000]—*Sisters of Notre Dame De Namur.*—S.N.D.deN.
[3720]—*Sisters of Saint Anne.*—S.S.A.
[1705]—*The Sisters of St. Francis of Assisi.*—O.S.F.
[3830-16]—*Sisters of St. Joseph.*—S.S.J.
[3860]—*Sisters of St. Joseph of Cluny.*—S.J.C.
[2980]—*Sisters of the Congregation of Notre Dame.*—C.N.D.
[3180]—*Sisters of the Cross and Passion.*—C.P.
[1830]—*Sisters of the Good Shepherd.*—R.G.S.
[]—*Sisters of the Holy Cross.*
[]—*Sisters of the Holy Cross and of the Seven Dolors.*—C.S.C.
[3480]—*Sisters of the Resurrection.*—C.R.
[3690]—*Sisters of the Sacred Hearts of Perpetual Adoration.*—SS.CC.
[4048]—*Society of the Sisters, Faithful Companions of Jesus.*—F.C.J.

DIOCESAN CEMETERIES

FALL RIVER. *Notre Dame.*
St. John.
St. Mary.
St. Patrick.
ATTLEBORO. *St. John.*
St. Stephen.
EAST FALMOUTH. *St. Anthony.*
HYANNIS. *St. Francis.*
MANSFIELD. *St. Mary.*
MATTAPOISETT. *St. Anthony.*
NANTUCKET. *St. Mary.*
NEW BEDFORD. *St. John Sacred Heart.*
St. Mary.
NORTH ATTLEBORO. *St. Mary.*
NORTH EASTON. *Immaculate Conception.*
OAK BLUFFS. *Sacred Heart.*
PROVINCETOWN. *St. Peter.*
SANDWICH. *St. Peter.*
SOMERSET. *St. Patrick.*
TAUNTON. *St. Francis.*
St. James.
St. Joseph.
St. Mary.
TRURO. *Sacred Heart.*
WAREHAM. *St. Patrick.*
WELLFLEET. *Our Lady of Lourdes.*
WEST HARWICH. *Holy Trinity.*

NECROLOGY

† Clark, James W., (Retired). —Died Dec. 7, 2000.
† Joseph, Louis John, (Retired). —Died Jan. 8, 2000.
† Tavares, Evaristo, Fall River, MA Our Lady of the Angels Church. —Died Jan. 8, 2000.

Diocese of Fargo

(Dioecesis Fargensis)

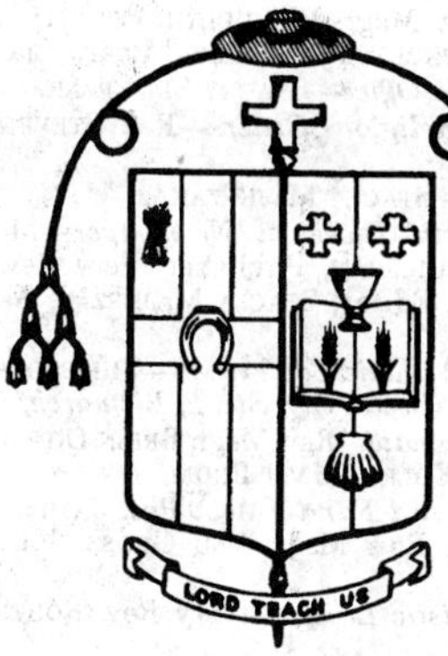

Most Reverend

JAMES S. SULLIVAN, D.D.

Bishop of Fargo; ordained June 4, 1955; consecrated Auxiliary Bishop of Lansing September 21, 1972; appointed Bishop of Fargo April 2, 1985; installed May 30, 1985. *Res., Bishop's House, 608 Broadway, P.O. Box 1750, Fargo, ND, 58107.*

Chancery Office: 1310 Broadway, Box 1750, Fargo, ND, 58107. Tel.: 701-235-6429; Fax: 701-235-0296.

Web site address: www.fargodiocese.org

E-mail address: web@fargodiocese.org

Corporate Title: *The Diocese of Fargo.*

FORMERLY DIOCESE OF JAMESTOWN.

ESTABLISHED NOVEMBER 12, 1889; TRANSFERRED TO FARGO, APRIL 6, 1897.

Square Miles 35,786.

Comprises the Counties of Barnes, Benson, Bottineau, Cass, Cavalier, Dickey, Eddy, Foster, Grand Forks, Griggs, Kidder, LaMoure, Logan, McHenry, McIntosh, Nelson, Pembina, Pierce, Ramsey, Ransom, Richland, Rolette, Sargent, Sheridan, Steele, Stutsman, Towner, Traill, Walsh and Wells in the State of North Dakota.

For legal titles of parishes and diocesan institutions, consult the Chancery Office.

STATISTICAL OVERVIEW

Personnel	
Bishop	1
Priests: Diocesan Active in Diocese	105
Priests: Active Outside Diocese	10
Priests: Diocesan in Foreign Missions	1
Priests: Retired, Sick or Absent	31
Number of Diocesan Priests	147
Religious Priests in Diocese	9
Ordinations:	
Diocesan Priests	5
Permanent Deacons in Diocese	24
Total Brothers	8
Total Sisters	143
Parishes	
Parishes	160
With Resident Pastor:	
Resident Diocesan Priests	83
Resident Religious Priests	9
Without Resident Pastor:	
Administered by Priests	68
New Parishes Created	1
Professional Ministry Personnel:	
Brothers	1
Sisters	7
Lay Ministers	535
Welfare	
Catholic Hospitals	8
Total Assisted	60,798
Health Care Centers	6
Total Assisted	757
Homes for the Aged	5
Total Assisted	485
Day Care and Extended Day Care Centers	35
Total Assisted	280
Residential Care of Disabled	1
Total Assisted	200
Educational	
Seminaries, Diocesan	1
Students from This Diocese	8
Students from Other Diocese	8
Diocesan Students in Other Seminaries	34
Total Seminarians	42
High Schools, Diocesan and Parish	1
Total Students	286
Elementary Schools, Diocesan and Parish	12
Total Students	2,129
Catechesis/Religious Education:	
High School Students	3,856
Elementary Students	7,010
Total Students Under Catholic Instruction	13,323
Teachers in the Diocese:	
Priests	1
Brothers	6
Sisters	4
Lay Teachers	159
Vital Statistics	
Receptions into the Church:	
Infant Baptism Totals	1,231
Adult Baptism Totals	43
Received into Full Communion	172
First Communions	1,314
Confirmations	1,303
Marriages:	
Catholic	320
Interfaith	220
Total Marriages	540
Deaths	809
Total Catholic Population	98,960
Total Population	391,000

Former Bishops—Rt. Rev. JOHN SHANLEY, D.D., ord. 1874; cons. Dec. 27, 1889; died July 16, 1909.—Most Rev. JAMES O'REILLY, D.D., ord. June 24, 1880; cons. May 19, 1910; installed June 1, 1910; died Dec. 19, 1934.—His Eminence ALOISIUS CARDINAL MUENCH, ord. June 8, 1913; appt. Bishop of Fargo, Aug. 10, 1935; cons. Oct. 15, 1935; installed Nov. 6, 1935; appt. Apostolic Visitator for Germany, July 8, 1946; granted personal title of Archbishop, Nov. 1, 1950; appt. Papal Nuncio to Germany, March 10, 1951; created Cardinal Priest and elevated to the Roman Curia, Dec. 14, 1959; died Feb. 15, 1962.—Most Rev. LEO F. DWORSCHAK, ord. May 29, 1926; appt. Coadjutor Bishop of Rapid City, June 23, 1946; cons. August 22, 1946; appt. Auxiliary Bishop of Fargo, April 10, 1947; succeeded to See, May 10, 1960; resigned and retired Sept. 8, 1970; died Nov. 5, 1976.—Most Rev. JUSTIN A. DRISCOLL, ord. July 28, 1945; appt. Bishop of Fargo, Sept. 8, 1970; ord. Bishop of Fargo and installed Oct. 28, 1970; died Nov. 19, 1984.

Chancery Office—1310 Broadway, Box 1750, Fargo, 58107. Tel: 701-235-6429; Fax: 701-235-0296.

Vicar General and Moderator of the Curia—Rev. Msgr. WENDELYN VETTER, V.G.

Vicar for Development—Rev. Msgr. VAL GROSS, V.D.

Vicar for Administration—Very Rev. ROBERT IRWIN, V.A.

Chancellor—Very Rev. ROBERT IRWIN, V.A.

Vice-Chancellor—Rev. DANIEL PILON, J.C.L.

Vice-Chancellor/Priest Secretary to the Bishop—Rev. STEVEN REISKE.

Vice-Chancellor for Supra Diocesan Affairs—J. RITTER HARSY.

Archivist—Very Rev. ROBERT IRWIN, V.A.

Fiscal Officer—SCOTT HOSELTON, C.P.A.

Diocesan Tribunal—2537 S. University Dr., Fargo, 58103. Tel: 701-235-7279.

Officialis—Rev. Msgr. WENDELYN VETTER, V.G.

Vice-Officialis and Tribunal Director—Rev. DANIEL PILON, J.C.L., Adjutant Judicial Vicar.

Promoter Justitiae—Very Rev. VALERIAN PACZEK, J.C.D.

Defensor Vinculi—Very Rev. VALERIAN PACZEK, J.C.D.

Judges—Rev. DANIEL PILON, J.C.L., Presiding Judge; Rev. Msgr. WENDELYN VETTER, V.G.; Rev. Msgr. ALLAN F. NILLES; Very Rev. ROBERT IRWIN, V.A.; Very Rev. CHAD WILHELM; Revs. THOMAS GRANER; JARED KADLEC; AL BITZ.

Advocates—Deacon DONALD TINGUELY; Sr. CELINE FOY; ELLEN O'CONNOR.

Defenders of the Bond—Revs. ANTHONY ODOZI, J.C.D.; EMMANUEL M. OKONMAH, J.C.D., M.C.L.; JAMES MCKINNEY; Sr. PAULA MARIE BLAKE.

Auditor—MARILYN BITTNER.

Notaries—Very Rev. ROBERT IRWIN, V.A.; SCOTT HOSELTON, C.P.A.

Diocesan College of Consultors—Rev. Msgr. WENDELYN VETTER, V.G.; Rev. Msgr. VAL GROSS, V.D.; Very Rev. ROBERT IRWIN, V.A.; Rev. Msgr. JOSEPH SENGER; Rev. Msgr. BRIAN DONAHUE; Revs. DUAINE COTE; STEVE MEYER; FRANKLIN MILLER.

Deans—Southeast: Very Rev. CHAD WILHELM, Lisbon; East Central South: Very Rev. PAUL DUCHSCHERE, Fargo; East Central North: Rev. Msgr. WENDELYN VETTER, Hillsboro; North East: Very Rev. BRIAN BACHMEIER, Walhalla; North Central: Very Rev. MICHAEL SCHOMMER, Langdon; North West: Very Rev. MATT LANZ, Leeds; West Central:; Vacant; South Central: Very Rev. BERNARD PFAU, Jamestown; South West: Very Rev. GARY LUITEN, Ellendale.

Diocesan Pastoral Council—Most Rev. JAMES S. SULLIVAN, Pres.

Priest Representatives—Rev. DONALD A. LEIPHON, Area 1; Rev. RAYMOND COURTRIGHT, Area 2; Rev. LEO KINNEY, Area 3; Very Rev. CHAD WILHELM, Area 4.

Deacon Representatives—Deacon GEORGE ETHIER.

Sister Representatives—Sr. PAULA RINGUETTE, P.B.V.M.; Sr. MARLYSS DIONNE, S.M.P.

Lay Representatives—KATHLEEN SKROCH, Deanery 1; STUART LONGTIN, Deanery 2; SUSAN SPICER, Deanery 3; LAWRENCE J. LATTAISE, Deanery 4; LINDA CULMER, Deanery 5; GAIL TROTTIER, Deanery 6; BETTY REGSTAD, Deanery 7; DARLENE WESHNEVSKI, Deanery 8; GARY HORSAGER, Deanery 9; ALICE POWER, Lay Member at Large; Deacon DAVID EBLEN, Chm. Ex Officio Members: Rev. Msgr. WENDELYN VETTER, V.G.; Very Rev. ROBERT IRWIN, V.A., Chancellor; JO RITTER HARSY, Vice Chancellor & DPC Sec. SCOTT HOSELTON, Fiscal Officer; Rev. GREGORY SCHLESSELMANN, S.T.D.; TERRY KNOEPFLE, Esq. Emeritus Members: ROBERT ARTZ; Revs. PETER HUGHES, C.S.Sp.; JAMES MEYER; BERNIE WAGNER; RALPH ERICKSON.

Diocesan Offices and Directors

Corporate Board—Most Rev. JAMES S. SULLIVAN; Rev. Msgr. WENDELYN VETTER, V.G.; Very Rev. ROBERT IRWIN, V.A.; Very Rev. CHAD WILHELM; SCOTT HOSELTON, C.P.A.; TERRY W. KNOEPFLE, Esq.

Administration Board of Minor Seminary—Rev. Msgr. WENDELYN VETTER, V.G.; Rev. Msgr. VAL GROSS, V.D., Oeconomus; Very Rev. ROBERT IRWIN, V.A., Consilium pro Re Temporali.

Apostleship of Prayer—Rev. ROMAN LUDWIG, Dir.

Diocesan Finance Council—Most Rev. JAMES S. SULLIVAN, Pres.; Rev. Msgr. WENDELYN VETTER, V.G.; Rev. Msgr. VAL GROSS, V.D.; Very Rev. ROBERT IRWIN, V.A.; GERALD F. HAMERLIK; GARY DIETZ; RAY SIMON; SCOTT A. HOSELTON, C.P.A.; TERRY W. KNOEPFLE, Esq.

The Catholic Church Expansion Fund of the Diocese of Fargo—Most Rev. JAMES S. SULLIVAN; Rev. Msgr. WENDELYN VETTER, V.G.; Very Rev. ROBERT IRWIN, V.A.; Very Rev. CHAD WILHELM; SCOTT A. HOSELTON, C.P.A.; TERRY W. KNOEPFLE, Esq.

Censor Librorum—Rev. ROBERT LALIBERTE, Ph.D.

Catholic Family Service—PAUL GRIFFIN, Dir., *2537 S. University Dr., Fargo, 58103.* Tel: 701-235-4457; Fax: 701-239-8266., Grand Forks Office: *505 University Ave., Ste. 1, Grand Forks, 58203.* Tel: 701-775-4196; Fax: 701-775-0129.

Office of Worship and Sacraments—Bro. VINCENT LOMONACO, O.S.F., Dir. Tel: 701-235-6429.

Continuing Education of Priests—Very Rev. PAUL DUCHSCHERE, Chm.

Due Process Board Members (Conciliators)—Rev. Msgr. BRIAN DONAHUE, Chm.

Disaster Response Coordinator—Very Rev. ROBERT IRWIN, V.A.

Ecumenical Commission—Rev. PAUL SCHUSTER.

Vicar for Diocesan Development—Rev. Msgr. VAL GROSS, V.D.

Director of Development—DAVID ZANITSCH. Tel: 701-235-6429.

Director of God's Gift Appeal—DAVID ZANITSCH.

Catholic School Network Office—JERRY BARTHOLOMAY, Supt., *2720 32nd Ave., S.W., Fargo, 58104.* Tel: 701-280-0550.

Diocesan Health Care Director—Very Rev. ROBERT IRWIN, V.A.

Holy Childhood Association—Very Rev. ROBERT IRWIN, V.A., Dir.

Migrant Workers Apostolate—Rev. C. JAMES JEFFREY, Dir., All mail to go to: *P.O. Box 1750, Fargo, 58107.*

Commission for Holy Orders and Ministry—Rev. PHIL ACKERMAN, Chm.; Rev. Msgr. WENDELYN VETTER, V.G.; Very Rev. ROBERT IRWIN, V.A.; Rev. Msgr. BRIAN DONAHUE; Revs. ROBERT SMITH; DENNIS SKONSENG; ROBERT LALIBERTE.

Subcommittee for Holy Orders (Seminarians)—Rev. ROBERT SMITH, Chm.; Rev. Msgr. BRIAN DONAHUE; Revs. DENNIS SKONSENG; ROBERT LALIBERTE.

Subcommittee for Priests (Priests applying to the Fargo Diocese)—Very Rev. ROBERT IRWIN, V.A., Chm.; Rev. Msgr. WENDELYN VETTER, V.G.; Rev. PHILLIP ACKERMAN, Personnel Board Liaison.

Communications Office—STACEY MAJKRZAK.

Committee for Religious Orders—Rev. STEVEN REISKE, Chm.

Media Liaison—STACEY MAJKRZAK.

The "New Earth"-Diocesan Newspaper—Most. Rev. JAMES S. SULLIVAN, Publisher; Very Rev. ROBERT IRWIN, V.A., Editor; STACEY MAJKRZAK, Assoc. Editor.

North Dakota Catholic Conference—CHRISTOPHER DODSON, *227 W. Broadway, Ste. 2, Bismarck, 58501.*

Permanent Diaconate—Rev. Msgr. BRIAN DONAHUE; Deacons DAVE EBLEN; MATT PROM.

Priests Mutual Aid Fund—Most Rev. JAMES S. SULLIVAN, Chm.; Rev. Msgr. VAL GROSS, V.D., Sec. & Treas.

Priests Eucharistic League—Very Rev. ROBERT IRWIN, V.A., Dir.

Priests Personnel Board—Rev. Msgr. VAL GROSS, V.D., Chm.; Revs. PHILLIP ACKERMAN, Sec. ROBERT SMITH; JAMES CHENEY; RAY COURTRIGHT.

Presbyteral Council—Rev. JAMES MEYER, Chm., All mail to go to: *Church of St. John the Baptist, 630 6th St., Wyndmere, 58081.*

Propagation of the Faith—Very Rev. ROBERT IRWIN, V.A., Dir.

Retreats—GEORGE LACHER, Bldg. Dir., *Queen of Peace Retreat Center, 1310 Broadway, Fargo, 58102.* Tel: 701-293-9286.

Rural Life—Rev. THOMAS GRANER, Coord., *P.O. Box 127, Rolette, 58366.* Tel: 701-246-3486. Rev. Msgr. WENDELYN VETTER, V.G., *503 3rd St., S.E., Box 459, Hillsboro, 58045.* Rev. BERNIE SCHNEIDER, *435 E. Main St., Mayville, 58257-1442.*

St. Vincent de Paul Society—Deacon MATT PROM, *316 44th Ave., S., Moorhead, MN, 56560.* ORVILLE KELLY, Pres., *1425 First Ave. S., Fargo, 58102.* Tel: 701-235-5944. DELORES HACKENBERG, *3627 9th Ave. N., Grand Forks, 58203.* Tel: 701-775-9911.

Technology/Computer Office—DAVID WEILER.

Department for Catholic Education and Formation—Rev. GREGORY SCHLESSELMANN, S.T.L.

Evangelization/Catechesis—STELLA JEFFREY.

Youth/Young Adults—JENNIE KORSMO, Dir. KURT GUNWALL, Asst.

Education in Parish Service (EPS)—Deacon DAVID EBLEN.

Department Admin. Asst.-Resource Center—SHARON GUNWALL.

Office for Catholic Schools—THOMAS FREI, Dir.

Vocation Director—Rev. ROBERT SMITH, *Cardinal Muench Seminary, 100-35th Ave., N.E., Fargo, 58102.*

Office of Clerical Formation—Rev. Msgr. BRIAN DONAHUE.

Office of Permanent Deacon Formation—Rev. Msgr. BRIAN DONAHUE.

Diocesan Pension Plan for Lay Employees—SCOTT A. HOSELTON, C.P.A.

Pro-Life—RACHELLE SAUVAGEAU, Coord. Tel: 701-235-6429.

Natural Family Planning (NFP)—PAULINE ECONOMON, Coord. Tel: 701-237-9851.

Catholic Cemeteries—Very Rev. ROBERT IRWIN, V.A.

Diocesan Planning and Survey Board—Very Rev. ROBERT IRWIN, V.A., Coord.; Very Rev. GARY LUITEN; Very Rev. BERNARD PFAU; Very Rev. MICHAEL SCHOMMER; Very Rev. PAUL DUCHSCHERE; Very Rev. CHAD WILHELM; Very Rev. MATT LANZ; Very Rev. BRIAN BACHMEIER; Rev. Msgr. WENDELYN VETTER, V.G.

Diocesan Choir—Bro. VINCENT LOMONACO, O.S.F.

Diocesan Building Committee—Rev. LEONARD LOEGERING, Chm.; Mr. GEORGE LACHER, Sec.

World Apostolate of Fatima (Blue Army)—Rev. STEVEN REISKE.

Cursillo Movement—Very Rev. MATT LANZ.

Engaged Encounter—Rev. GERALD A. MCCARTHY, *304 3rd Ave. W., Box 155, Bisbee, 58317.*

Marriage Encounter—Rev. DALE KINZLER.

Alcohol and Chemical Abuse—Rev. JOHN CAVANAUGH. Tel: 701-282-3321.

Catholic Scouting—KURT GUNWALL.

Apostolate for Spanish Speaking—Rev. C. JAMES JEFFREY, All mail to go to: *P.O. Box 1750, Fargo, 58107.*

Apostolate for Native Americans—Rev. GERALD A. MCCARTHY, *304 3rd Ave. W., Box 155, Bisbee, 58317.*

Beginning Experience Apostolate—Rev. Msgr. WENDELYN VETTER, V.G.

Clergy Credit Union—Rev. KEVIN BOUCHER.

Prison Apostolate—Rev. PAUL SCHUSTER.

Liaison with Charismatic Movement—Revs. ROBERT LALIBERTE, Ph.D.; DONALD LEIPHON.

CLERGY, PARISHES, MISSIONS AND PAROCHIAL SCHOOLS

CITY OF FARGO
(Cass County)

1—ST. MARY'S CATHEDRAL (1880). Also serving Argusville and Merit Care Hospital. Revs. Peter Hughes, C.S.Sp.; Andrew M. Jasinski; Deacon George Loegering.
Office: 619 7th St. N., 58102. Tel: 701-235-4289; 235-4280; Fax: 701-235-2986.
Res., 679 6th Ave. N., 58102. Tel: 701-235-4280. [JC]
Catechesis/Religious Programs—Students 320.
Mission—Argusville, Cass Co., St. William, 105 Drake, Argusville, 58005. Tel: 701-484-5211; Fax: 701-484-5211.

2—HOLY SPIRIT (1951). Also serving Vets' Hospital. Revs. Phillip Ackerman; Joseph Goering; Deacon James Perius.
Res., 1420 N. 7th St., 58102. Tel: 701-232-5900; Fax: 701-232-5902. [JC]
School—1441 8th St. N., 58102. Tel: 701-232-4087; Fax: 701-232-8240. Mrs. Winnie Pratt, Prin.
Lay Teachers 12; Students 150.
Catechesis/Religious Programs—Students 414.

3—NATIVITY (1960). Also serving Manor Care & Villa Maria Nursing Homes, Dakota Heartland Hospital. Revs. Dale Kinzler; Timothy C. Schroeder; Tim Mathern, Parish Admin.
Res., 1825 11th St. S., 58103. Tel: 701-232-2414; Fax: 701-232-4491. [JC]
School—Tel: 701-232-7461; Fax: 701-298-8981. Cindy Hutchins, Prin.
Lay Teachers 20; Students 325.
Catechesis/Religious Programs—Tel: 701-232-2422.
Students 412.

4—SS. ANNE & JOACHIM (1995), Rev. Msgr. Val Gross, V.D.; Rev. David B. Syverson.
3329 S. University Dr., 58104. Tel: 701-235-5757; Fax: 701-235-0651.
Res., 2501 58th Ave. S.W., 58104. Tel: 701-235-1514; Fax: 701-235-0764. [JC]
School—Sullivan Middle School, 2720 32nd Ave., S.W., 58103. Tel: 701-280-0550; Fax: 701-280-0564. Mrs. Winnie Pratt, Prin.
Lay Teachers 14; Students 219.
Catechesis/Religious Programs—Students 280.

5—ST. ANTHONY OF PADUA (1917). Serving Cass County Jail. Revs. James R. Ermer; Quintin Heck; Deacon Math Prom.
Res., 710 S. 10th St., 58103. Tel: 701-237-6063; Fax: 701-237-6064. [JC]
Catechesis/Religious Programs—Tel: 701-232-3995.
Students 350.

6—ST. PAUL NEWMAN CENTER, N.D.S.U. (1928), Rev. Paul Duchschere.
Res., 1141 N. University Dr., 58102. Tel: 701-298-9775.
Church—Tel: 701-235-0142. [JC]
Catechesis/Religious Programs—Students 31.

OUTSIDE THE CITY OF FARGO

Alice, Cass Co., St. Henry (of Alice) (1902) (German). Served from Enderlin. Rev. James F. McKinney.
Mailing Address: 302 Bluff St., Enderlin, 58027.
Church—58003. [CEM]
Catechesis/Religious Programs—Students 20.

Anamoose, McHenry Co., St. Francis Xavier (1899). Also serving Drake. Rev. Leo Kinney.
Res., 605 1st St., W., P.O. Box 49, 58710-0049. Tel: 701-465-3780; Fax: 701-465-0217. [CEM]
Mission—Drake, McHenry Co., St. Margaret Mary, 105 Main St. N., Drake, 58736-0049. Tel: 701-465-3284. [CEM]

Aneta, Nelson Co., Sacred Heart (1908). Served from Cooperstown. Rev. James Cheney.
c/o P.O. Box 217, Cooperstown, 58425. Tel: 701-797-2624. [CEM]
Catechesis/Religious Programs—Students 15.

Ardoch, Walsh Co., St. John the Baptist (1883). Served from Minto.
c/o 629 3rd St., Box 316, Minto, 58261. Tel: 701-248-3589. [CEM]
Catechesis/Religious Programs—Students 18.

Argusville, Cass Co., St. William (1942). Served from St. Mary's Cathedral, Fargo. Revs. Peter Hughes; Andrew M. Jasinski.
Mailing Address: P.O. Box 1, Harwood, 58042.
c/o 619 7th St. N., Fargo, 58102. Tel: 701-235-4289.
Church—107 Drake Ave., 58005. Tel: 701-484-5211. [JC]
Catechesis/Religious Programs—Tel: 701-484-5211.
Students 61.

Ashley, McIntosh Co., St. David (1960) (German-Russian). Served from Zeeland.
c/o P.O. Box 1, Zeeland, 58581. Tel: 701-423-5494.
Catechesis/Religious Programs—Students 21.

Balfour, McHenry Co., St. Joseph's (1906). Closed. For inquiries for parish records please contact the Chancellor.

Balta, Pierce Co., Our Lady of Mount Carmel (1902) (German). Also serving Fulda and Orrin. Rev. Jose Shaji, S.D.B.
Res., Box 428, 58313. Tel: 701-542-3326. [CEM]
Catechesis/Religious Programs—Students 45.
Missions—Fulda, McHenry Co., St. Anselm, Tel: 701-776-5629. [CEM]
Orrin, Pierce Co., Sacred Heart. [CEM]

Bathgate, Pembina Co., St. Anthony (1883). Served from Cavalier.
c/o 201 1st St. S., Box 280, Cavalier, 58220. Tel: 701-265-8877. [CEM]

Bechyne, SS. Peter & Paul (1886) (Czech). Served from Michigan. Rev. Samuel O. Ezeibeke.
c/o P.O. Box 332, Michigan, 58259. Tel: 701-259-2248. [CEM]
Catechesis/Religious Programs—Students 29.

Belcourt, Rolette Co., St. Ann (1885) (Native American), Revs. Dale Craig, S.O.L.T.; Robert J. Cronin, S.O.L.T.; Mark Byrne, S.O.L.T.; Dan Estes, S.O.L.T.; Deacon John Kightlinger.
Res., Box 2000, 58316. Tel: 701-477-5601; Fax: 701-477-0602. [CEM]
Catechesis/Religious Programs—Students 43.
Mission—Belcourt, Rolette Co., St. Anthony Indian Mission, Tel: 701-244-2438. [CEM]

St. Anthony (1895). Attended by St. Ann, Belcourt. Rev. Robert Cronin.
c/o P.O. Box 2000, 58316. Tel: 701-477-5601. [CEM]

Bisbee, Towner Co., Holy Rosary (1889). Served from Rolette. Rev. Thomas M. Graner. In res., Rev. Gerald A. McCarthy, (Retired).
c/o Box 127, Rolette, 58366. Tel: 701-246-3449. [CEM]
Church—P.O. Box 155, 58317. Tel: 701-656-3307; Fax: 701-246-3449.
Catechesis/Religious Programs—Students 32.

Bottineau, Bottineau Co., St. Mark's (1905). Also serving Westhope. Rev. Kevin J. Boucher.
Res., 322 Sinclair St., 58318. Tel: 701-228-3164. [CEM]
Catechesis/Religious Programs—Students 131.
Mission—Westhope, Bottineau Co., St. Andrew, P.O. Box 365, Westhope, 58793. Tel: 701-245-6171.

Bremen, Wells Co., St. Joseph (1896) (German). Served from Fessenden. Rev. Eugene J. Fish.
c/o P.O. Box 325, Fessenden, 58438. Tel: 701-547-3430. [CEM]

Brocket, Ramsey Co., St. Joseph's (1910). Served from Lakota.
c/o 109 East Ave. E., P.O. Box 509, Lakota, 58344. Tel: 701-247-2594. [CEM]

Buchanan, Stutsman Co., St. Margaret (1924). Served from Jamestown.
c/o 622 1st Ave. S., Box 347, Jamestown, 58402. Tel: 701-252-0119; Fax: 701-252-6992. [CEM]
Catechesis/Religious Programs—Tel: 701-252-0478; Fax: 701-252-4453.
Students 31.

Buffalo, Cass Co., St. Thomas (1900) (Norwegian-German). Served from Casselton. Rev. Al Bitz.
Mailing Address: Box 340, Casselton, 58012.
712 2nd St. N., Casselton, 58012. Tel: 701-633-5150. [JC]
Catechesis/Religious Programs—Students 22.

Burnstad, Logan Co., St. Clara (1915). Served from Napoleon.
c/o 401 Broadway, Napoleon, 58561-7013. Tel: 701-754-2860.
Catechesis/Religious Programs—Students 5.

Cando, Towner Co., Sacred Heart (1893), Rev. Edmund Ogbonna.
Res., 310 3rd Ave., P.O. Box 399, 58324. Tel: 701-968-3462. [CEM]
Catechesis/Religious Programs—Tel: 701-968-3830.
Students 99.

Carrington, Foster Co., Sacred Heart (1887), Rev. Lawrence Haas.
Res., 663 1st St. S., P.O. Box 420, 58421. Tel: 701-652-2519. [CEM]
Catechesis/Religious Programs—Tel: 701-652-2072.
Students 184.

Casselton, Cass Co., St. Leo (1880) (German-Norwegian). Also serving Buffalo. Rev. Al Bitz.
Mailing Address: 211 Langer Ave., P.O. Box 340, 58012.
Res., 712 2nd St. N., 58012. Tel: 701-347-4609; Fax: 701-347-5898. [CEM]
St. Leo's Religious Education Center: 211 Langer Ave. N., 58012.
Catechesis/Religious Programs—Students 235.
Mission—Buffalo, Cass Co., St. Thomas, Box 22, Buffalo, 58011. Tel: 701-633-5150.

Cavalier, Pembina Co., St. Bridget's (1881). Also serving Neche. Rev. Anthony Odozi.
Res., 201 First St. S., P.O. Box 280, 58220. Tel: 701-265-8877; Fax: 701-265-8877. [CEM]
Catechesis/Religious Programs—Students 113.
Mission—Neche, Pembina Co., SS. Nereus and Achilleus. [CEM]

Cayuga, Sargent Co., SS. Peter and Paul (1916). Served from Forman. Rev. Francis Quintin Arthur.
c/o Box 175, Forman, 58032-0175. Tel: 701-724-3319; Fax: 701-724-3310.
Catechesis/Religious Programs—Students 9.

Cogswell, Sargent Co., Our Lady of Mercy (1903). Served from Forman. Rev. Francis Quintin Arthur.
c/o Box 175, Forman, 58032-0175. Tel: 701-724-3319; Fax: 701-724-3310. [CEM]
Catechesis/Religious Programs—Students 7.

Conway, Walsh Co., St. Mark (1884) (Czech). Served from Pisek.
c/o Box 27, Pisek, 58273. Tel: 701-284-6060; Fax: 701-284-6331. [CEM]
Catechesis/Religious Programs—Students 16.

Cooperstown, Griggs Co., St. George's (1939). Also serving Aneta, Jessie. Rev. James Cheney.
Res., P.O. Box 217, 58425. Tel: 701-797-2624. [CEM]
Catechesis/Religious Programs—Students 42.
Missions—Jessie, Griggs Co., St. Lawrence. [CEM]
Aneta, Nelson Co., Sacred Heart. [CEM]

Courtenay, Stutsman Co., St. Mary's. Served from Wimbledon.
c/o P.O. Box 9, Wimbledon, 58492. Tel: 701-435-2310. [CEM]
Catechesis/Religious Programs—Students 7.

Crow Hill, St. Jerome. Served from Fort Totten.

Crystal, Pembina Co., St. Patrick (1892). Served from Park River.
505 Park St., E., P.O. Box 110, Park River, 58270. Tel: 701-284-6165; Fax: 701-284-6165. [CEM]
Catechesis/Religious Programs—Students 22.

Dazey, Barnes Co., St. Mary's (1899). Served from Sanborn. Rev. Matthew Attansey (Nigeria).
Church—c/o P.O. Box 35, Sanborn, 58480. Tel: 701-646-6306. [CEM]

Devils Lake, Ramsey Co., St. Joseph's (1884). Also serving Rutten (sometimes called Crary). Revs. Jeffrey Wald; James Gross; Deacon Lawrence Lange.
Res., 515 Fourth St., Box 898, 58301. Tel: 701-662-7558; Fax: 701-662-7559.
School—Tel: 701-662-5016; Fax: 701-662-5017. Tom Burckhard, Prin.
Lay Teachers 11; Students 176.
Catechesis/Religious Programs—8th St. and 10th Ave., Devil's Lake, Tel: 701-662-5071; Fax: 701-662-5017.
Students 348.
Mission—Rutten, Ramsey Co., St. Benedict. [CEM]

Dickey, LaMoure Co., Assumption (1909) (German). Served from LaMoure.
c/o 209 First St., S.E., Box 217, La Moure, 58458. Tel: 701-883-5987; Fax: 701-883-5987. [CEM]
Catechesis/Religious Programs—Students 73.

Drake, McHenry Co., St. Margaret Mary's (1910). Attended by St. Francis Xavier, Anamoose.
Res., 605 Main St., P.O. Box 197, 58736. Tel: 701-465-3281. [CEM]
Catechesis/Religious Programs—Students 66.

Drayton, Pembina Co., St. Edward's (1889). Also serving St. Thomas, St. Thomas and Pembina, Assumption. Rev. William T. Ovsak.
Res., 211 N. Main St., P.O. Box 215, 58225. Tel: 701-454-6171; Fax: 701-454-6171. [CEM]
Catechesis/Religious Programs—Students 62.
Missions—Pembina, Pembina Co., Assumption, 143 Hayden St., Pembina, 58271. Tel: 701-825-6266; Fax: 701-825-6266. [CEM][JC]
St. Thomas, Pembina Co., St. Thomas, P.O. Box 117, St. Thomas, 58276. [CEM]

Dunseith, Rolette Co., St. Louis (1882) (Native American). Also serving Immaculate Heart of Mary (Rolette Co.). Rev. Dale Craig, S.O.L.T.
Res., 112 First St., N.W., Box 160, 58329. Tel: 701-244-5738. [CEM]
Catechesis/Religious Programs—Students 50.
St. Mary's Mission Center—P.O. Box 130, 58329. Tel: 701-244-5784.

Edgeley, LaMoure Co., Transfiguration (1915) (German-Russian). Also serving Nortonville, Manor St. Joseph. Rev. Duaine M. Cote; Deacon Thurston Ham.
Res., 205 Second St., P.O. Box 347, 58433. Tel: 701-493-2387; Fax: 701-493-2387. [CEM]
Catechesis/Religious Programs—Students 94.
Mission—Nortonville, LaMoure Co., Holy Spirit, 705 1st St., 58473.

Ellendale, Dickey Co., St. Helena's (1888). Also serving Fullerton. Very Rev. Gary Luiten.
Res., 421 Second St. N., P.O. Box 796, 58436. Tel: 701-349-3297; Fax: 701-349-3297. [CEM]
Catechesis/Religious Programs—Tel: 701-349-4128.
Students 53.
Mission—Fullerton, Dickey Co., St. Patrick, 421 N. 2nd St., Ellendale, 58436. [CEM]

Enderlin, Ransom Co., St. Patrick's (1901). Also serving Alice, Sheldon. Rev. James F. McKinney.
Res., 302 Bluff St., 58027. Tel: 701-437-2791; Fax: 701-437-2791. [CEM]
Catechesis/Religious Programs—Students 39.
Missions—Alice, Cass Co., St. Henry. [CEM]
Sheldon, Ransom, St. Mary, Our Lady of the Scapular, 118 Cogswell St., Sheldon, 58068. [CEM]

Esmond, Benson Co., St. Boniface (1909), Rev. Daniel J. Hoedl, Admin.
P.O. Box 37, 58332-0033. Tel: 701-249-8360. [CEM]
Catechesis/Religious Programs—Students 61.
Mission—Maddock, Benson Co., St. William.

Fairmount, Richland Co., St. Anthony's (1909). Also serving Carmel Convent. Rev. Donald A. Leiphon.
Res., 204 Second St. N., Box 292, 58030. Tel: 701-474-5518. [CEM]
Catechesis/Religious Programs—Students 60.

Fessenden, Wells Co., St. Augustine's (1896). Also serving Bremen. Rev. Eugene J. Fish.
Res., P.O. Box 325, 58438. Tel: 701-547-3430.
Mission—Bremen, Wells Co., St. Joseph.

Fingal, Barnes Co., Holy Trinity (1889). Attended by St. Bernard, Oriska. Rev. K. S. Kopacz.
c/o 606 Fifth St., Oriska, 58063. Tel: 701-845-3713. [CEM]
Catechesis/Religious Programs—Students 33.

Finley, Steele Co., St. Olaf (1949). Unassigned. Served from Hope.
c/o P.O. Box 99, Hope, 58046. Tel: 701-945-2652. [JC]

Forman, Sargent Co., St. Mary's (1913). Also serving Cayuga, Cogswell, and Milnor. Rev. Francis Quintin Arthur; Deacons Richard Biss; David Gates.
Res., Box 175, 58032-0175. Tel: 701-724-3319; Fax: 701-724-3310. [CEM]
Catechesis/Religious Programs—Students 44.
Missions—Cayuga, Sargent Co., Sts. Peter & Paul, P.O. Box 513, Cayuga, 58013. [JC]
Cogswell, Sargent Co., Our Lady of Mercy, P.O. Box 10, Cogswell, 58017. Tel: 701-724-3943. [CEM]
Milnor, Sargent Co., St. Arnold, P.O. Box 295, Milnor, 58060. Tel: 701-427-9288. [CEM]

Fort Totten, Benson Co., Seven Dolors (1875) (Spirit Lake Dakota). Also serving Crow Hill, Tokio. Rev. Charles J. Leute, O.P.; Deacon Anthony McDonald.
Res., P.O. Box 299, 58335. Tel: 701-766-4314. [CEM]
Catechesis/Religious Programs—Students 5.
Mission—Tokio, Benson Co., Christ the King, c/o Box 299, Fort Totten, 58335-0299.
Memorial Station, Crow Hill, St. Jerome—.

Fried, Stutsman Co., Sacred Heart (1888). Served from Jamestown.
c/o 622 First Ave. S., Box 347, Jamestown, 58402. Tel: 701-252-0119; Fax: 701-252-6992. [CEM]
Catechesis/Religious Programs—Twinned with The Basilica of St. James.

Fulda, McHenry Co., St. Anselm (1901) (German). Served from Balta.
c/o Box 428, Balta, 58313. Tel: 701-542-3326. [CEM]

Fullerton, Dickey Co., St. Patrick (1921) (Irish). Served from Ellendale.
c/o 421 Second St. N., P.O. Box 796, Ellendale, 58436. Tel: 701-349-3297; Fax: 701-349-3297. [CEM]
Catechesis/Religious Programs—Students 24.

Gackle, Logan Co., St. Anne (German). Served from Windsor.
Mailing Address: c/o 207 Washington Ave., Cleveland, 58424. Tel: 701-763-6192; 320-6192 (Cellular).

Geneseo, Sargent Co., St. Martin's (1907) (Polish). Served from Lidgerwood.
c/o 118 Second Ave. N.W., Box 449, Lidgerwood, 58053. Tel: 701-538-4608.
Church—58037. [CEM]
Catechesis/Religious Programs—St. Boniface, Lidgerwood.
Students 148.

Grafton, Walsh Co., St. John the Evangelist's (1881). Also serving State School. Rev. Bert Miller; Deacon Leonard Buresh; Margaret Bruce, Pastoral Assoc.
Res., 344 15th St. W., P.O. Box 636, 58237. Tel: 701-352-1648; Fax: 701-352-1608. [CEM]
St. John's Catechetical Center—58237. D.R.E.: Cindy Jononsek; Rose Marie Kerner.
Students 378.

Grand Forks, Grand Forks Co.,

1—HOLY FAMILY, (1960), Revs. Leonard Loegering; Paul Schuster; Deacon Robert Diebold.
Res., 1018 18th Ave. S., 58201. Tel: 701-746-1454; Fax: 701-746-1456. [JC]
School—Tel: 701-775-9886; Fax: 701-775-0221. Mr. Charles Scherr, Prin.
Lay Teachers 10; Students 125.
Catechesis/Religious Programs—Tel: 701-746-9386; Fax: 701-746-1456.
Students 595.

2—ST. MARY'S, (1915), Rev. Jerald L.C. Finnestad; Deacon Don Litzinger.
216 Belmont Rd., 58201. Tel: 701-775-9318; Fax: 701-775-7568. [JC]
School—Tel: 701-775-4818.
Lay Teachers 8; Students 102.
Catechesis/Religious Programs—Tel: 701-775-2842.
Students 220.

3—ST. MICHAEL'S, (1872), Revs. William C. Sherman; William F. McDermott; Joseph D'Aco.
Res., 520 N. Sixth St., 58203. Tel: 701-772-2624. [JC]

School—Tel: 701-772-1822; Fax: 701-772-0211. Sharon Litchy, Prin.
Lay Teachers 14; Students 128.
St. James Religious Center—410 Cambridge, 58203. Tel: 701-775-4261. Lois Stoltman, Dir.
Catechesis/Religious Programs—Tel: 701-772-2282.
Students 570.

4—St. Thomas Aquinas Parish, UND, (1951), Revs. Raymond P. Courtright; Jason V. Lefor; Deacon Samuel Pupino.
Res., 410 Cambridge St., 58203. Tel: 701-777-6850; Fax: 701-777-8905. [JC]
Catechesis/Religious Programs—Students 56.

Granville, McHenry Co., Our Lady of Perpetual Help (1933) (German-Norwegian). Served from Towner.
c/o 503 First St. S.W., Box 267, Towner, 58788. Tel: 701-537-5133.

Gwinner, Sargent Co., St. Vincent (1908) (German-Scandanavian). Served from Lisbon. Very Rev. Chad F. Wilhelm.
Mailing Address: 701 Oak St., P.O. Box 226, Lisbon, 58054-0226.
707 Oak St., Lisbon, 58054-0226. Tel: 701-683-4620. [CEM]

Hankinson, Richland Co., St. Philip's (1889) (German), Rev. James S. Goodwin.
Res., 612 S. Main, P.O. Box 419, 58041. Tel: 701-242-7327. [CEM]
St. Philip's Religious Education Center—(Grades K-12) St. Francis Convent, Hankison, 58041. Tel: 701-242-7800. Mr. William Hrdlicka, Prin.; Sr. Edwardine O.S.F., D.R.E.
Sisters 4; Lay Teachers 26; Students 131.

Hansboro, Towner Co., Sacred Heart. Closed. For inquiries for parish records please contact the Chancellor.

Harvey, Wells Co., St. Cecilia's (1895) (German-Norwegian). Also serving St. Aloisius Hospital and Selz, St. Anthony's. Rev. Vernon Smith; Deacon Jeffrey M. Faul.
Res., 413 E. Brewster St., 58341. Tel: 701-324-2144; Fax: 701-324-4640. [CEM]
St. Cecilia Religious Education Center—413 E. Brewster St., 58341. Tel: 701-324-2637.
Teachers 16; Students (Grades 1-8) 140; Students (Grades 9-12) 21.
Catechesis/Religious Programs—Students 167.
Mission—Selz, Pierce Co., 29 Girard St., 58341. Tel: 701-324-4059.

Hillsboro, Traill Co., St. Rose of Lima (1892), Rev. Msgr. Wendelyn Vetter, V.G.; Deacon David Eblen.
Res., 503 Third St. S.E., Box 459, 58045. Tel: 701-436-4541; Fax: 701-436-4452. [CEM]
Catechesis/Religious Programs—Students 114.

Hope, Steele Co., St. Agatha's (1907). Also serving Finley and Page. Rev. Cletus Madu.
Res., P.O. Box 99, 58046. Tel: 701-945-2652.
Catechesis/Religious Programs—Students 59.
Missions—Finley, Steele Co., St. Olaf; Page, Cass Co., St. James, 300 Main Ave., 58064.

Hunter, Cass Co., St. Agnes (1898). Attended by Our Lady of Peace, Mayville.
c/o 435 E. Main St., Mayville, 58257. Tel: 701-786-3234.
Catechesis/Religious Programs—Students 52.

Hurdsfield, Wells Co., St. Patrick (1969) (German). Served from Sykeston.
c/o P.O. Box 397, Sykeston, 58486. Tel: 701-984-2266.
Catechesis/Religious Programs—Students 16.

Jamestown, Stutsman Co., The Basilica of St. James (1881). Also serving Buchanan, Fried, and Pingree. Very Rev. Bernard A. Pfau; Revs. Scott Saunter; Jimmy Lim Tiu; Sr. Michaeleen Jantzer, O.S.B., Pastoral Min.; Deacon Timothy Marcy.
Res., 622 First Ave. S., Box 347, 58402. Tel: 701-252-0119; Fax: 701-252-6992. [CEM]
School—St. John's Grade School, Tel: 701-252-3397; Fax: 701-252-4453. Beverly Jacobson, Prin.
Lay Teachers 17; Students (Grades PreK-6) 183.
St. James Religious Education—622 1st Ave. S., P.O. Box 347, 58402-0347. Tel: 701-252-0478; Fax: 701-252-4453. Rita Kenna, D.R.E.
Lay Teachers 40.
Catechesis/Religious Programs—215 5th St., S.E., P.O. Box 347, 58402-0347.
Students 340.
Missions—Fried, Stutsman Co., Sacred Heart, Jamestown,; Buchanan, Stutsman Co., St. Margaret, Jamestown,; Pingree, Stutsman Co., St. Michael, Jamestown. [CEM] Deacon Timothy Marcy.

Jessie, Griggs Co., St. Lawrence (1888). Served from Cooperstown. Rev. James Cheney.
c/o P.O. Box 217, Cooperstown, 58425. Tel: 701-797-2624. [CEM]

Karlsruhe, McHenry Co., SS. Peter and Paul's (1903). Served from Velva.
c/o 201 Second Ave. W., Box K, Velva, 58790-0496. Tel: 701-338-2663. [CEM]

Kensal, Stutsman Co., St. John's (1917). Served by St. Boniface's, Wimbledon.
Mailing Address: c/o P.O. Box 9, Wimbledon, 58492. Tel: 701-435-2310.
Church—58455. Tel: 701-435-2876. [CEM]
Catechesis/Religious Programs—Students 9.

Kindred, Cass Co., St. Maurice (1965). Served from St. John the Baptist, Wyndmere. Rev. James Meyer.
630 6th St. S., Wyndmere, 58081. Tel: 701-439-2200.
Catechesis/Religious Programs—Students 66.

Kintyre, Logan Co., St. Boniface's (1906). Unassigned.
Res., 7013 26th Ave., S.E., 58549. Tel: 701-332-6636. [CEM]
Catechesis/Religious Programs—Students 12.

Knox, Benson Co., St. Mary's (1936). Served from Leeds.
Mailing Address: Box 97, 58343. Tel: 701-583-2808. [CEM]

Lake Williams, Kidder Co., Our Lady of the Lake (1946). Served from Tappen.
c/o 216 1st St. N.E., Tappen, 58487. Tel: 701-327-8344.
Catechesis/Religious Programs—Students 13.

Lakota, Nelson Co., St. Mary's (1902). Also serving Brocket and Tolna. Rev. J. Vincent Fitzpatrick.
Res., 109 East Ave. E., P.O. Box 509, 58344. Tel: 701-247-2594.
Catechesis/Religious Programs—Students 63.
Missions—Brocket, Ramsey Co., St. Joseph. [CEM]
Tolna, Nelson Co., St. Joseph.

La Moure, La Moure Co., Holy Rosary (1890) (German). Also serving Dickey and Marion. Rev. Julian Kupisz.
c/o Assumption: 209 First St. S.E., Box 217, 58458.
Res., 209 First St., S.E., Box 217, 58458. Tel: 701-883-5987; Fax: 701-883-5987. [CEM]
Catechesis/Religious Programs—Students 5.
Missions—Marion, LaMoure Co., St. Francis, (1910) Box 217, 58458.; Dickey, LaMoure Co., Assumption, 58458. [CEM]

Langdon, Cavalier Co., St. Alphonsus (1888). Also serving Nekoma. Very Rev. Michael Schommer.
Res., 1010 Third St., Box 640, 58249. Tel: 701-256-5966; Fax: 701-256-2358. [CEM]
School—Tel: 701-256-2354. Sr. Anne Frawley, P.B.V.M., Prin.
Sisters 3; Lay Teachers 9; Students 74.
Catechesis/Religious Programs—Students 233.
Mission—Nekoma, Cavalier Co., St. Edwards, (1907).

Lankin, Walsh Co., St. Joseph's (1906). Attended by St. John Nepomucene, Pisek.
Church—P.O. Box 27, Pisek, 58273. Tel: 701-284-6060. [CEM]
Catechesis/Religious Programs—Students 12.

Larimore, Grand Forks Co., St. Stephen's (1885), Rev. Thaines Arulandu.
Res., 311 W. Front St., P.O. Box 778, 58251. Tel: 701-343-2377; Fax: 701-343-2316.
Catechesis/Religious Programs—Tel: 701-343-2747.
Students 126.

Leeds, Benson Co., St. Vincent de Paul (1897). Also serving Knox and Minnewaukan. Rev. Mathias F. Lanz.
Res., 315 Central Ave., P.O. Box 307, 58346. Tel: 701-466-2777. [CEM]
Missions—Minnewauken, Benson Co., St. James. [CEM]
Knox, Benson Co., St. Mary, Box 97, Knox, 58351. [CEM]

Leroy, Pembina Co., St. Joseph's (1848) (French-Native American). Served from Walhalla.
Mailing Address: c/o 801 Central Ave., P.O. Box 228, Walhalla, 58282. Tel: 701-549-3750.
Church—58252. [CEM]

Lidgerwood, Richland Co., St. Boniface's (1887). Also serving Geneseo. Rev. Eugene Gilles, S.A.C.
Res., 220 1st St. N.W., P.O. Box 449, 58053. Tel: 701-538-4604;4608 (Rectory). [CEM]
Catechesis/Religious Programs—Tel: 701-538-4604.
Students 189.
Mission—Geneseo, Sargent Co., St. Martin. [CEM]

Lisbon, Ransom Co., St. Aloysius (1884) (German-Irish). Also serving Gwinner. Very Rev. Chad F. Wilhelm.
Mailing Address: 701 Oak St., P.O. Box 226, 58054-0226.
Res., 709 Oak St., 58054-0226. Tel: 701-683-4620; Fax: 701-683-5703. [CEM]
Catechesis/Religious Programs—Tel: 701-683-5703.
Students 165.
Mission—Gwinner, Sargent Co., St. Vincent De Paul, 302 Hwy. 13E, 58040. Tel: 701-678-2239. [CEM]

Lomice, Walsh Co., St. Catherine (1936) (Czech). Served from Michigan, ND. Rev. Samuel Ezeibeke.
c/o P.O. Box 332, Michigan, 58259. Tel: 701-259-2248. [CEM]

Maddock, Benson Co., St. William (1954). Served from Esmond. Rev. Daniel J. Hoedl.
c/o P.O. Box 37, Esmond, 58332. Tel: 701-249-8360.
Catechesis/Religious Programs—Students 26.

Mantador, Richland Co., SS. Peter and Paul's (1881). Served from Mooreton. Rev. Jan Klimek.
Mailing Address: c/o 204 Mooreton Ave. N., Mooreton, 58061. Tel: 701-274-8259.
Church—58058. Tel: 701-242-0001. [CEM]
Catechesis/Religious Programs—Students 36.

Manvel, Grand Forks Co., St. Timothy's (1882). Served from St. Timothy's. Rev. Paul Schuster.
Church—511 Eighth St. W., P.O. Box 28, 58256. Tel: 701-696-2219. [CEM]
Catechesis/Religious Programs—Students 90.

Marion, La Moure Co., St. Francis (1910) (German). Served from LaMoure.
c/o 209 First St., S.E., Box 217, LaMoure, 58458. Tel: 701-883-5987.
Church—58466. [CEM]

Mayville, Traill Co., Our Lady of Peace (1945). Also serving Hunter. Rev. Bernard R. Schneider.
Res., 435 E. Main St., 58257. Tel: 701-786-3234.
Catechesis/Religious Programs—Students 116.
Missions—Hunter, Cass Co., St. Agnes, Box 134, 58048. [CEM]
Mayville, Traill Co., State University Newman Club.

McClusky, Sheridan Co., Holy Family (1932) (German). Served from Sykeston.
c/o P.O. Box 397, Sykeston, 58486. Tel: 701-984-2266.
Catechesis/Religious Programs—Students 9.

McHenry, Foster Co., SS. Peter & Paul (1912). Served from New Rockford. Rev. Jerome Hunkler.
c/o 116 First Ave. N., P.O. Box 389, New Rockford, 58356. Tel: 701-947-5325. [CEM]
Catechesis/Religious Programs—Students 22.

Medina, Stutsman Co., St. Mary (1904). Served from Windsor.
c/o 207 Washington Ave., Cleveland, 58424. Tel: 701-763-6192. [CEM]
Catechesis/Religious Programs—4142 57th Ave. S.E., 58467. Tel: 701-486-3414. Ellen Rau, D.R.E.
Students 16.

Michigan, Nelson Co., St. Lawrence O'Toole (1883) (Irish-Czech). Also serving Bechyne and Lomice. Rev. Samuel Ezeibeke.
Res., P.O. Box 332, 58259. Tel: 701-259-2248.
Catechesis/Religious Programs—Students 49.
Missions—Bechyne, Walsh Co., SS. Peter & Paul. [CEM]
Lomice, Walsh Co., St. Catherine. [CEM]

Milnor, Sargent Co., St. Arnold's (of Milnor) (1905) (German-Bohemian). Attended by St. Mary's, Forman.
c/o Box 175, Forman, 58032-0175. Tel: 701-724-3319; Fax: 701-724-3310.
Church—Box 295, 58060. Tel: 701-427-9288. [CEM]
Catechesis/Religious Programs—Students 68.

Milton, Cavalier Co., St. Clotilde (1893). Served from Wales.
Mailing Address: c/o P.O. Box 127, Wales, 58281. Tel: 701-283-5352; Fax: 701-283-5133. [CEM]

Minnewaukan, Benson Co., St. James (1899). Served from Leeds.
c/o 315 Central Ave., P.O. Box 307, Leeds, 58346. Tel: 701-466-2777. [CEM]

Minto, Walsh Co., Sacred Heart (1905) (Polish-Irish). Also serving Ardoch. Rev. Feliks F. Lubas (Poland).
Res., 629 Third St., P.O. Box 316, 58261. Tel: 701-248-3589. [CEM]
Catechesis/Religious Programs—Students 100.
Mission—Ardoch, Walsh Co., St. John the Baptist, 204 Main St., 58213. Tel: 701-248-3444. [CEM]

Mooreton, Richland Co., St. Anthony's (1885). Also serving Mantador. Rev. Jan Klimek.
Res., 204 Mooreton Ave. N., 58061. Tel: 701-274-8259. [CEM]
Catechesis/Religious Programs—Students 110.
Mission—Mantador, Richland Co., Sts. Peter & Paul, Box 2618, 58058. Tel: 701-242-0001. [CEM]

Mount Carmel, Cavalier Co., Our Lady of Mount Carmel (1888) (German). Served from Wales.
c/o P.O. Box 127, Wales, 58281. Tel: 701-283-5352. [CEM]
Catechesis/Religious Programs—Students 11.

Munich, Cavalier Co., St. Mary's (1916) (German), Rev. Anthony Hession.
Res., P.O. Box 159, 58352. Tel: 701-682-5178; Fax: 701-682-5124. [CEM 3]
Catechesis/Religious Programs—Tel: 701-682-5124.
Students 27.
Mission—Starkweather, Ramsey Co., Assumption of the Blessed Virgin Mary, 502 Main St., P.O. Box 85, Starkweather, 58377. Tel: 701-292-4301.

Napoleon, Logan Co., St. Philip Neri (1906), Rev. James P. Lauerman.
Res., 401 Broadway, 58561-7013. Tel: 701-754-2860. [CEM]
Catechesis/Religious Programs—Students 139.
Mission—Burnstad, Logan Co., St. Clara. [CEM]

Neche, Pembina Co., SS. Nereus and Achilleus (1884). Attended by St. Bridget, Cavalier. Rev. Anthony Odozi.
c/o 201 First St. S., Box 280, Cavalier, 58220. Tel: 701-886-7471; Fax: 701-265-8877. [CEM]

Nekoma, Cavalier Co., St. Edward (1907). Served from Langdon. Very Rev. Michael Schommer.
c/o 1010 Third St., Langdon, 58249. Tel: 701-256-5966; Fax: 701-256-2358. [CEM]
Catechesis/Religious Programs—Students 11.

New Rockford, Eddy Co., St. John's (1896). Also serving McHenry. Rev. Jerome Hunkler.
Res., 116 First Ave. N., P.O. Box 389, 58356. Tel: 701-947-5325. [CEM]
Catechesis/Religious Programs—Students 127.
Mission—McHenry, Foster Co., SS. Peter & Paul, P.O. Box 389, New Rockford, 58356. [CEM]

Nortonville, LaMoure Co., Holy Ghost (Spirit) (1912). Served from Edgeley. Rev. Duaine M. Cote.
c/o 205 Second St., P.O. Box 347, Edgeley, 58433. Tel: 701-493-2387; Fax: 701-493-2387. [JC]
Catechesis/Religious Programs—Students 28.

Oakes, Dickey Co., St. Charles Borromeo (1905). Also serving Oakes Community Hospital, Oakes. Rev. Kevin L. Willis.
Res., 410 N. Seventh St., 58474. Tel: 701-742-2418. [CEM]
Catechesis/Religious Programs—Students 179.
Mission—Verona, LaMoure Co., St. Raphael, Oakes. [CEM]

Oakwood, Walsh Co., Sacred Heart (1881) (French), Rev. David Venganinna.
Res., 7010 County Rd. 4, Grafton, 58237-8860. Tel: 701-352-1392. [CEM]

Olga, Cavalier Co., Our Lady of the Sacred Heart (1882) (French). Served from Walhalla.
Res., H.C. 2, Box 102, Langdon, 58249. Tel: 701-549-2729. [CEM]

Oriska, Barnes Co., St. Bernard's (1908). Also serving Fingal. Rev. K. S. Kopacz.
Res., 606 Fifth St., 58063. Tel: 701-845-3713. [CEM]
Catechesis/Religious Programs—Students 17.
Mission—Fingal, Barnes Co., Holy Trinity.

Orrin, Pierce Co., Sacred Heart (1903). Served from Balta. Rev. Jose Shaji.
Mailing Address: P.O. Box 428, Balta, 58313. Tel: 701-542-3326.
Church—58368. [CEM]

Osnabrock, Cavalier Co., St. Joseph (1909). Served from Wales.
c/o P.O. Box 127, Wales, 58281. Tel: 701-282-5352. [CEM]

Page, Cass Co., St. James (1909). Served from Hope.
c/o Box 99, Hope, 58046. Tel: 701-945-2652.
Church—58064. [CEM]

Park River, Walsh Co., St. Mary's (1888). Also serving St. Ansgar Hospital, Crystal. Rev. Robert P. Unger; Deacon Gerald F. Sobolik.
Res., 505 Park St., E., P.O. Box 110, 58270-0110. Tel: 701-284-6165; Fax: 701-284-6165. [CEM]
Catechesis/Religious Programs—Tel: 701-284-7789.
Students 131.
Mission—Crystal, Pembina Co., St. Patrick, P.O. Box 110, Park River, 58270-0110. [CEM]

Pembina, Pembina Co., Assumption of the Blessed Virgin Mary (1818). Served from Drayton.
Church—143 Hayden St., Box 151, 58271. Tel: 701-825-6266. [JC]
Catechesis/Religious Programs—Students 40.

Penn, Ramsey Co., Immaculate Conception. Closed. For inquiries for parish records contact St. Vincent de Paul, Leeds.

Pingree, Stutsman Co., St. Michael's (1905). Served from Jamestown.
c/o 622 First Ave. S., Box 347, Jamestown, 58402. Tel: 701-252-0119.
Church—58476. [CEM]
Catechesis/Religious Programs—Twinned with St. Margaret's, Buchanan.

Pisek, Walsh Co., St. John Nepomucene (1886) (Czech). Also serving Conway and Lankin. Rev. John Fallon.
Res., Box 27, 58273. Tel: 701-284-6060; Fax: 701-284-6060. [CEM]
Catechesis/Religious Programs—Students 18.
Missions—Conway, Walsh Co., St. Marks, Pisek, 58273. [CEM]
Lankin, Walsh Co., St. Joseph, Pisek, 58273. [CEM]

Reynolds, Grand Forks Co., Our Lady of Perpetual Help (1895). Also serving Thompson. Rev. Kenneth F. Knoke.
Res., 424 Fifth St., Box 96, 58275. Tel: 701-847-2371. [CEM]
Catechesis/Religious Programs—Students 102.
Mission—Thompson, Grand Forks Co., St. Jude. [CEM]

Rock Lake, Towner Co., Immaculate Heart of Mary (1950) (Irish-German). Served from Rolla.
c/o P.O. Box 788, Rolla, 58367. Tel: 701-477-5277.
Catechesis/Religious Programs—Students 23.

Rolette, Rolette Co., Sacred Heart (1918). Also serving Willow City and Bisbee. Rev. Thomas M. Graner; Deacon Conrad A. Schuster.
Res., P.O. Box 127, 58366. Tel: 701-246-3449; Fax: 701-246-3449. [CEM 3]
Catechesis/Religious Programs—Students 43.
Missions—Willow City, Bottineau Co., Notre Dame, 225 1st St. N., Willow City, 58384. Tel: 701-366-4771; Fax: 701-246-3449. [CEM 2]
Bisbee, Towner Co., 304 3rd. Ave., W., P.O. Box 155, Bisbee, 58317. Tel: 701-656-3307; Fax: 701-246-3449. [CEM]

Immaculate Heart of Mary (1948) (Native American). Attended by St. Louis, Dunseith.
c/o 112 First St., N.W., Box 160, Dunseith, 58329. Tel: 701-244-5738. [CEM]
Catechesis/Religious Programs—Twinned with St. Louis, Dunseith.

Rolla, Rolette Co., St. Joachim's (1894). Also serving Rock Lake and Rolla Community Hospital. Rev. Jared C. Kadlec.
Res., 207 Second Ave. N.E., P.O. Box 788, 58367. Tel: 701-477-5277. [CEM]
St. Joachim Religious Education Center—P.O. Box 788, 58367. Tel: 701-477-3568.
Catechesis/Religious Programs—Tel: 701-477-3568.
Students 105.
Mission—Rock Lake, Towner Co., Immaculate Heart of Mary, 3 Eller Ave., Rock Lake, 58365. Tel: 701-266-5615.

Rugby, Pierce Co., St. Therese, Little Flower (1910) (German-Norwegian), Revs. Andrew J. Dudzinski; Augustine Alilonu.
Res., 218 Third St., S.E., 58368. Tel: 701-776-5327. [CEM]
School—306 Third Ave., S.E., 58368. Tel: 701-776-6740; Fax: 701-776-6740. Mr. Dennis DeCoteau, Prin.
Sisters of St. Francis of the Immaculate Heart of Mary (Hankinson, ND) 2; Lay Teachers 9; Students 103.
Little Flower Parish School of Religious Education—306 Third Ave., S.E., 58368. Tel: 701-776-6258.
Lay Teachers 16.
Catechesis/Religious Programs—Tel: 701-776-7640.
Students 250.

Rutten, Ramsey Co., St. Benedict (1910). Served from Devils Lake. Rev. Jeffrey Wald.
c/o 515 Fourth St., Box 898, Devils Lake, 58301. Tel: 701-662-7558. [CEM]
Catechesis/Religious Programs—Students 25.

St. John, Rolette Co., St. John the Baptist (1882). Also serving St. Benedict Indian Mission (Rolette Co.). Rev. Armand L. (Bud) Brooks.
Church—Box 170, 58369. Tel: 701-477-3081. [CEM]
Catechesis/Religious Programs—Students 46.
Mission—Belcourt, Rolette Co., St. Benedict, Box 388, 58316. Tel: 701-244-5026. [CEM]

St. Michael, Benson Co., St. Michael's (1874), Rev. Edward Sherman.
Res., P.O. Box 84, 58370. Tel: 701-766-4151. [CEM]

St. Thomas, Pembina Co., St. Thomas (1886). Served from Drayton.
Mailing Address: c/o 211 N. Main St., P.O. Box 215, Drayton, 58225. Tel: 701-454-6171.
Church—58276. Tel: 701-257-6492. [CEM]
Catechesis/Religious Programs—Students 34.

Sanborn, Barnes Co., Sacred Heart (1904) (German). Also serves Dazey. Rev. Matthew Attansey; Deacon Harry Didier.
Res., P.O. Box 35, 58480. Tel: 701-646-6306. [CEM]
Catechesis/Religious Programs—Students 49.
Mission—Dazey, Barnes Co., St. Mary, 58429. [CEM]

Selz, Pierce Co., St. Anthony's (1917) (German-Russian). Served from Harvey.
c/o 29 Girard St., Harvey, 58341-7316. Tel: 701-324-4059. [CEM]
Catechesis/Religious Programs—Tel: 701-324-2637.
Twinned with St. Cecilia's, Harvey.

Sheldon, Ransom Co., St. Mary, Our Lady of the Scapular (1884). Served from Enderlin.
Mailing Address: c/o Rev. James McKinney, 302 Bluff St., Enderlin, 58027. Tel: 701-437-2791.
Church—58068. [CEM]
Catechesis/Religious Programs—Students 45.

Starkweather, Ramsey Co., Assumption of the Blessed Virgin Mary (1905). Served from Munich. Rev. Anthony Hession.
Mailing Address: 502 Main St., P.O. Box 85, 58377.
c/o Box 159, Munich, 58352. Tel: 701-682-5178; Fax: 701-682-5124.
Church—58377. Tel: 701-292-4301. [CEM]
Catechesis/Religious Programs—Students 25.

Steele, Kidder Co., St. Francis de Sales (1958). Served from Tappen.
216 1st St. N.E., Tappen, 58487. Tel: 701-327-8344. [CEM]
Catechesis/Religious Programs—Students 84.

Stirum, Sargent Co., St. Vincent. Closed. 1986. For inquiries for parish records contact St. Aloysius, Lisbon.

Sykeston, Wells Co., St. Elizabeth's (1905) (German). Also serving Hurdsfield and McCluskey. Rev. Matthew Pamplaniyil.
Res., P.O. Box 397, 58486. Tel: 701-984-2266. [CEM]
Catechesis/Religious Programs—Students 52.
Missions—Hurdsfield, Wells Co., St. Patrick, Sykeston, 58486.; McClusky, Sheridan Co., Holy Family, Sykeston, 58486.

Tappen, Kidder Co., St. Paul's (1908). Also serving Lake Williams and Steele. Rev. Thomas J. Krupich.
Res., 216 1st St. N.E., 58487. Tel: 701-327-8344.
Catechesis/Religious Programs—Students 16.
Missions—Lake Williams, Kidder Co., Our Lady of the Lake. [CEM]
Steele, Kidder Co., St. Francis de Sales. [CEM]

Thompson, Grand Forks Co., St. Jude's (1895). Served from Reynolds.
c/o 424 Fifth St., Box 96, Reynolds, 58275. Tel: 701-847-2371.
Church—58278. Tel: 701-599-2574. [CEM]
Catechesis/Religious Programs—Students 151.

Tokio, Benson Co., Christ the King (1938) (Indian Mission). Served from Fort Totten. Rev. Charles J. Leute, O.P.
c/o P.O. Box 299, Fort Totten, 58335. Tel: 701-766-4314.
Catechesis/Religious Programs—Students 9.

Tolna, Nelson Co., St. Joseph's (1911). Served from Lakota.
c/o 109 E. E Ave., Box 509, Lakota, 58344.
Church—58380. [CEM]

Towner, McHenry Co., St. Cecilia's (1906). Also serving Granville. Rev. Ronald Yee Mon.
Res., 503 First St., S.W., Box 267, 58788. Tel: 701-537-5133. [CEM]
Catechesis/Religious Programs—Students 96.
Mission—Granville, McHenry Co., Our Lady of Perpetual Help, Tel: 701-728-6507.

Valley City, Barnes Co., St. Catherine's (1882) (German). Also serving Newman Center. Rev. H. Gerard Braun; Deacons Arlie Braunberger; Raphael Grim; Eugene Klein.
524 Third Ave., N.E., 58072. Tel: 701-845-0354; Fax: 701-845-3761. [CEM]
School—(Grades K-6). Tel: 701-845-1453; Fax: 701-845-0556. Mr. Ralph Dyrness, Prin.
Lay Teachers 6; Students 58.
St. Catherine's Parish Education Center—540 Third Ave., N.E., 58072. Ralph Dyrness, Parish Education Dir.
Lay Teachers 18.
Catechesis/Religious Programs—Kelley Utt, D.R.E. Students 204.

Velva, McHenry Co., St. Cecilia's (1906). Also serving Karlsruhe. Rev. Daniel Miho Minarevic.
Res., 201 Second Ave. W., P.O. Box K, 58790-0496. Tel: 701-338-2663. [CEM]
Catechesis/Religious Programs—Students 105.
Mission—Karlsruhe, McHenry Co., Sts. Peter & Paul, 501 Main, Karlsruhe, 58744. [CEM]

Verona, LaMoure Co., St. Raphael (1898). Served from Oakes. Rev. Kevin L. Willis.
c/o 410 N. Seventh St., Oakes, 58474. Tel: 701-742-2418. [CEM]
Catechesis/Religious Programs—Students 14.

Veseleyville, Walsh Co., St. Luke (1880) (Czech). Served from Warsaw. Rev. Damian J. Hils. In res., Rev. Joseph Allen.

Mailing Address: 14207 63rd St., N.E., Grafton, 58237. Tel: 701-248-3981; Fax: 701-248-3961. [CEM]
Catechesis/Religious Programs—Tel: 701-352-0026.
Students 37.

Wahpeton, Richland Co., St. John's (1876), Revs. Dale Lagodinski; Roman G. Neva, (Retired); Deacons George Ethier, (Retired); Ignatz Zach.
Mailing Address: Office, 115 Second St. N., 58075. Tel: 701-642-6982; Fax: 701-642-2601. [CEM]
Res., 222 Dakota Ave., 58075. Tel: 701-642-4985.
School—122 Second St. N., 58075. Tel: 701-642-6116; Fax: 701-642-9134. Wilfred Sauer, Prin.
Lay Teachers 11; Students 141.
St. John Day Care Center—Tel: 701-642-4922. Christi Pelvit, Dir.
Staff 29; Students 120.
Catechesis/Religious Programs—Students 288.

Wales, Cavalier Co., St. Michael's (1905). Also serving Mount Carmel, Milton, and Osnabrock. Rev. Emmanuel Okonmah.
Res., P.O. Box 127, 58281. Tel: 701-283-5352. [CEM]
Missions—Mount Carmel, Cavalier Co., Our Lady of Mount Carmel. [CEM]
Milton, Cavalier Co., St. Clothilde. [CEM]
Osnabrock, Cavalier Co., St. Joseph. [CEM]

Walhalla, Pembina Co., St. Boniface's (1850), Rev. Brian Bachmeier; Deacon Alan Storey.
Res., 801 Central Ave., Box 228, 58282. Tel: 701-549-2729. [CEM]
Missions—Leroy, Pembina Co., St. Joseph, c/o St. Boniface, 58282. [CEM]
Olga, Cavalier Co., Our Lady of the Sacred Heart, R.R. 2, Box 102, Langdon, 58249. Tel: 701-549-3465. [CEM]

Warsaw, Walsh Co., St. Stanislaus (1882) (Polish). Also serves Veselyville. Rev. Damian J. Hils.
6098 County Rd. 4, 58261. Tel: 701-248-3981; Fax: 701-248-3961. [CEM]
Catechesis/Religious Programs—Students 23.

West Fargo, Cass Co., Blessed Sacrament (1945), Rev. John Cavanaugh.
Res., 210 Fifth Ave. W., 58078-1799. Tel: 701-282-3321; Fax: 701-282-6503. [CEM]
Catechesis/Religious Programs—Tel: 701-282-4554; Fax: 701-282-6503.
Students 251.

Holy Cross (1981), Rev. James A. Leith, J.C.D.; Ruth Wirtzfield, Pastoral Assoc.; Deacon James Uline.
Res., 1420 Cross Way, 58078-3445. Tel: 701-282-7217; Fax: 701-282-2753. [CEM]
Catechesis/Religious Programs—Students 516.

Westhope, Bottineau Co., St. Andrew's (1904). Served from Bottineau.
Mailing Address: Box 365, 58793. Tel: 701-245-6171. [CEM]
Catechesis/Religious Programs—Students 51.

Wild Rice, Cass Co., St. Benedict's (1870) (French Canadian), Rev. Daniel J. Pilon; Sr. Ann O'Brien, Pastoral Assoc.
Res., 11705 38th St. S., Horace, 58047. Tel: 701-588-4288; Fax: 701-588-4154. [CEM]
Catechesis/Religious Programs—Tel: 701-588-9290.
Students 151.

Willow City, Bottineau Co., Notre Dame des Victoires (1895). Attended by Sacred Heart, Rolette. Rev. Thomas M. Graner.
c/o Box 127, Rolette, 58366. Tel: 701-246-3449; Fax: 701-246-3449.
Church—P.O. Box 115, 58384. Tel: 701-366-4601. [CEM 2]
Catechesis/Religious Programs—Students 13.

Wimbledon, Barnes Co., St. Boniface's (1886). Also serving Courtenay. Rev. Steven J. Meyer.
P.O. Box 9, 58492. Tel: 701-435-2310. [CEM]
Catechesis/Religious Programs—Students 53.

Windsor, Stutsman Co., St. Mathias (1910) (Polish). Also serving Gackle and Medina. Rev. Joseph Okogba.
Res., 207 Washington Ave., Cleveland, 58424. Tel: 701-763-6192; 320-6192 (Cellular). [CEM]
Missions—Medina, Stutsman Co., St. Mary, Medina, 58467. [CEM]
Gackle, Logan Co., St. Anne, Gackle, 58442.

Wishek, McIntosh Co., St. Patrick (1952), Rev. Kevin L. Willis.
Mailing Address: P.O. Box 293, 58495.
314 6th St., 58495. Tel: 701-452-2970. [CEM]
Catechesis/Religious Programs—Students 67.
Mission—Kintyre, Emmons Co., St. Boniface.

Wyndmere, Richland Co., St. John the Baptist (1912) (German). Also serving St. Maurice, Kindred. Rev. James A. Meyer.
Res., 630 Sixth St., 58081. Tel: 701-439-2200. [CEM]
Catechesis/Religious Programs—Students 175.
Mission—Kindred, Cass Co., St. Maurice, Box 272, Kindred, 58051.

Zeeland, McIntosh Co., St. Andrew's (1906) (German-Russian). Also serving Ashley. Rev. John Lewandowski.
Res., P.O. Box 1, 58581. Tel: 701-423-5494. [CEM 2]
Catechesis/Religious Programs—Students 45.
Mission—Ashley, McIntosh Co., St. David, P.O. Box 330, Ashley, 58413.

INDIAN MISSIONS

Turtle Mountain Reservation, (Chippewa Indians), *Missions*—Belcourt, St. Ann. Revs. Dale Craig, S.O.L.T.; Robert J. Cronin, S.O.L.T.; Mark Byrne, S.O.L.T.; Bro. John DeMay, S.O.L.T.; St. Anthony, Rolette Co., St. Anthony. Served from Belcourt.

Fort Totten Reservation, (Sioux Indians) (1875), *Missions*—Tokio, Benson Co., Christ the King, (1938) Fort Totten, 58335. Tel: 701-766-4314. Rev. Charles J. Leute, O.P.; Fort Totten, Benson Co., St. Jerome's, (1892). (Crow Hill District) c/o Box 299, 58334-0299. Tel: 701-766-4314; Fort Totten Reservation, Benson Co., Seven Dolors Indian Mission. Also serving Crow Hill, Tokio. Seven Sorrows Dr., Box 299, 58335-0299. Tel: 701-766-4314. [CEM]
Rev. Charles J. Leute, O.P.

St. Michael, St. Michael's Indian Mission, Rev. Edward Sherman; Bro. Roman Sleger, O.S.B.

Chaplains of Public Institutions

FARGO. *Meritcare Hospital in Fargo*. Served from St. Mary Cathedral, Fargo. 619 N. Seventh St., 58102.
Prairie Psychiatric Center 501 4th St., S., 58102. Rev. John Evans, II.
Veterans Administration Facility. Rev. Phillip Ackerman, Res., Holy Spirit Church, 1420 N. Seventh St., 58102.

DEVILS LAKE. *School for the Deaf*. Rev. Jeffrey Wald, Res., St. Joseph's Rectory, 515 Fourth St., Box 898, 58301.

GRAFTON. *Grafton State School*. Rev. Bert Miller, Res., St. John the Evangelist Church, 344 15th St. W., P.O. Box 636, 58237.

GRAND FORKS. *Grand Forks Air Force Base*. Rev. Gary R. Breig, Res., 1699 J. St., GFAFB, 58205.
School for the Blind. Rev. William C. Sherman, Res., St. Michael Church, 520 N. 6th St., 58203.

JAMESTOWN. *State Hospital*. Rev. Jimmy Tiu.

LISBON. *Soldier's Home*. Very Rev. Chad F. Wilhelm, Res., St. Aloysius Church, 707 Oak St., Box 226, 58054.

Special Assignment:
Reverend Fathers—
Donahue, Brian G., Cardinal Muench Seminary, 100 35th Ave. N.E., Fargo, ND 58102
Evans, John, II, Dir. Pastoral Care, Praire Psychiatric Center, 501 4th St., S., Fargo, ND 58102
Fischer, Charles M., Jr., Cardinal Muench Seminary, 100 35th Ave, N.E., Fargo, ND 58102
Gross, Richard J., Chap., Altro Hospital, 1220 S. Columbia Rd., Grand Forks, ND 58201
Irwin, Robert P., Chancellor, 608 Broadway, P.O. Box 1750, Fargo, ND 58102
Laliberte, Robert L., Cardinal Muench Seminary, 100 35th Ave. N.E., Fargo, ND 58102
Miller, Franklin, (Sabbatical), P.O. Box 1750, Fargo, ND 58107
Reiske, Steven, Vice-Chancellor, 1129 N. University Dr., Fargo, ND 58102
Schlesselmann, Gregory, Dir. Catholic Education & Formation, 1129 N. University Dr., Fargo, ND 58102
Skonseng, Dennis A., Cardinal Muench Seminary, 100 35th Ave. NE, Fargo, ND 58102
Vos, Jude, P.O. Box 1750, Fargo, ND 58107

On Duty Outside the Diocese:
Reverend Fathers—
Bachmeier, Bernard A., Mercy Hospital & Medical Center, 4077 Fifth Ave., San Diego, CA 92103
Cosentino, Jack A., St. Ambrose, P.O. Box 999, Deerfield Beach, FL 33441
Davis, John E., Apartado 134, Chimbote, Peru
Goellen, Richard, 260 Hidden Meadow Ln., Trinidad, CO 81082
Graven, John P., St. Polycarp Church, 8100 Chapman Ave., Stanton, CA 90680
LaCorte, Richard P., St. John the Cross Rectory, 950 82nd Ave., Vero Beach, FL 32966
McCauley, David, 475 University Ave., St. Paul, MN 55103
Mikes, Pavel, Church of Tesetice, 783 46 Tesetice 6, Czech Republic

---

Military Chaplains:
Reverend Fathers—
Herron, Jack B. (CPT), Chap., USACHCS, CHOAC, 95-001, Fort Monmouth, NJ 07703-5612
Kawczynski, Ronald (LT), Chap., Asst. Regt Chaplains, 3942 Roebling Ln., Virginia Beach, VA 23452

Absent on Leave:
Reverend Fathers—
Feltis, Jerome
Haenke, Roger, 5501 Queens Ave. S., Minneapolis, MN 55410
Pietrus, Henryk

Retired:
Reverend Monsignors—
Nilles, Allan F., 200 8th St. S., #402, Fargo, ND 58103. Tel: 701-239-5939
Reverend Fathers—
Aleksonis, Vladas, Riverview Pl., 5300 12th St. S., # 303A, Fargo, ND 58104
Allmaras, Alfred, P.O. Box 1750, Fargo, ND 58107
Anderson, John D., 12th St. S., #217, Fargo, ND 58104
Campbell, Joseph, 4 Lakeview Ave., Bella Vista, AR 72714
Conway, John, 3500 Dupont Ave. S., #203, Minneapolis, MN 55408
Cullen, Martin T., 779 37th Ave. N., Fargo, ND 58102-1093
Dickinson, Stephen, P.O. Box 667, Valley City, ND 58072-0667
Grady, Peter W., Riverview Pl., 5220-12th St. S, #206C, Fargo, ND 58104
Huebsch, Joseph R., 514 First Ave., S.W., P.O. Box 98, Hankinson, ND 58041
Jeffrey, James C., P.O. Box 1117, Boqueron, PR 00622
Koehler, Paul L., St. Gerard Nursing Home, P.O. Box 448, Hankinson, ND 58041
Krile, George F., Brentwood West, 3104 E. Broadway, #211, Mesa, AZ 85204
Lang, Julius, P.O. Box 126, Naples, FL 34106
Lommel, George D., 509 Almeron Ave., Drayton, ND 58225
McCarthy, Gerald A., 304 3rd Ave. W., P.O. Box 155, Bisbee, ND 58317
Mehok, William J., S.J., Riverview Place, 5320 12th St. S., #218, Fargo, ND 58104
Mentel, Joseph C., 404 2nd St., W. #4, Napoleon, ND 58561
Moore, John E., Riverview Pl., 5320 12th St. S., #322, Fargo, ND 58104
Mullins, Robert J., 1451 Third St., S.E., Apt. 306B, St. Cloud, MN 56301
Neva, Roman G., 7975 County Rd. #7, Wahpeton, ND 58075
Paczek, Valerian, 24 Third Ave. S.W., Lidgerwood, ND 58053
Potter, Gerald, 615 39th St. N., #204C, Grandforks, ND 58203
Richard, Antonio J., 5532 E. Aspen Ave., Meza, AZ 85206-1436
Sandell, John, 2115 32nd Ave. S., Fargo, ND 58103
Schill, Victor J., P.O. Box 12, Walhalla, ND 58282
Schneider, George D., 1020 Devine Ave. #5, Harvey, ND 58341
Schue, Dennis L., Mercy Hospital, 1031 Seventh St., Devils Lake, ND 58301
Sinner, Richard W., 5210 S. 12th St., #202B, Fargo, ND 58104
Snell, Roger K., P.O. Box 305, Edgeley, ND 58433
Stelten, Leo F., Rte. 3, Box 651, Frazee, MN 56544
Studzinski, Lambert V., St. Gerard's Nursng Home, Box 448, Hankinson, ND 58041
Walz, Julius J., 2959 Elias Ct., Chicago, IL 60608
Wild, David D., 321 Prairiewood Cir., #202, Fargo, ND 58103

Permanent Deacons:
Biss, Richard, St. Arnold, Milnor
Braumberger, Arlie, St. Catherine, Valley City
Buresh, Leonard, St. John the Evangelist, Grafton
Carpenter, Stanley, St. Boniface, Walhalla
Davis, Francis R., St. Ann, Belcourt
Didier, Harry, Jr., Sacred Heart, Sanborn
Eberle, Edward, St. Therese Little Flower, Rugby
Eblen, David, St. Rose of Lima, Hillsboro
Faul, Jeffrey, St. Cecilia, Harvey
Gates, David, St. Arnold, Milnor
Grim, Raphael, St. Catherine, Valley City
Ham, Thurston, Transfiguration, Edgeley
Hoefs, Gene, St. John, Wahpeton
Hunkler, Howard, St. Philip Neri, Napolean
Klein, Eugene, St. Catherine, Valley City
La Rocque, Dorian, St. Boniface, Walhalla
Lange, Lawrence, St. Joseph's, Devils Lake
Litzinger, Donald, St. Mary, Grand Forks
Loegering, George, St. Mary Cathederal, Fargo
Marcy, Timothy, Sacred Heart, Fried
McDonald, Anthony, Seven Dolors, Fort Totten
Perius, James, Holy Spirit, Fargo
Prom, Mathias, St. Anthony, Fargo

Pupino, Samuel, St. Thomas Aquinas Newman Center, Grand Forks
Schuster, Conrad, Notre Dame, Willow City
Sobolick, Gerald, St. Mary, Park River
Storey, Alan, St. Boniface, Walhalla
Tinguely, Donald, St. Leo, Casselton
Uline, James, Holy Cross, West Fargo
West, James, St. Jude, Thompson
Zach, Ignatz, St. John, Wahpeton

INSTITUTIONS LOCATED IN THE DIOCESE

[A] SEMINARIES, DIOCESAN

FARGO. *Cardinal Muench Seminary*, 100 35th Ave., N.E., 58102. Tel: 701-232-8969; Fax: 701-271-1250.
E-mail: cms@cardinalmuench.org
Web site: www.cardinalmuench.org
Corporate Title: The Cardinal Muench Seminary. Rev. Msgr. Brian G. Donahue, Rector & Pres.; Revs. Dennis A. Skonseng; Robert L. Laliberte; Charles M. Fischer. Sisters 1; Priests 4; Lay Teachers 4; 4-year College Students 15; High School 1.

[B] HIGH SCHOOLS, DIOCESAN

FARGO. *Fargo Catholic Schools Network*, 2710 - 32nd Ave., S.W., 58103. Tel: 701-293-7910; Fax: 701-293-0729. Most Rev. James S. Sullivan, Pres.; Rev. James R. Ermer, Chair; Elaine Borud, Bus. Mgr.; Don Fischer, Transportation Supr.; John Wharthaby, Athletic Dir. Total Enrollment 974.

Shanley High School, 705 13th Ave. N., 58102. Tel: 701-235-5581; Fax: 701-293-3613.
E-mail: rgendrea@sendit.nodak.edu
Web site: www.fcsp.k12.nd.us
Rev. Dale Kinzler, Pres.; Mr. Roger Gendreau, Prin.; Rev. James A. Meyer, Chap. Priests 1; Brothers 1; Lay Teachers 20; Students 288.

[C] PROTECTIVE INSTITUTIONS

FARGO. *Villa Nazareth dba Friendship, Inc.*, 3004 S. 11th St., 58103. Tel: 701-235-8217; Fax: 701-235-7538
For a complete listing, refer to the Special Care Facilities section.

[D] GENERAL HOSPITALS

FARGO. *Prairie Psychiatric Center*, 501 4th St. S., 58102. Tel: 701-476-7200
For a complete listing, refer to the Hospitals section.

BOTTINEAU. *St. Andrew's Health Center*, 316 Ohmer St., 58318. Tel: 701-228-2255; Fax: 701-228-2255.
E-mail: sahc@ndak.net
Web site: bottineau.com/health.htm
For a complete listing, refer to the Hospitals section.

CARRINGTON. *Carrington Health Center*, 800 N. Fourth St., 58421. Tel: 701-652-3141
For a complete listing, refer to the Hospitals section.

DEVILS LAKE. *Mercy Hospital*, 1031 Seventh St., 58301-2798. Tel: 701-662-2131; Fax: 701-662-9651.
E-mail: marlenekrein@chi-midwest.org
For a complete listing, refer to the Hospitals section.

HARVEY. *St. Aloisius Medical Center*, 325 E. Brewster St., 58341. Tel: 701-324-4651; Fax: 701-324-4651.
E-mail: ruolk@stacoisius.com
Web site: www.stacoisius.com
For a complete listing, refer to the Hospitals section.

OAKES. *Oakes Community Hospital*, 314 S. Eighth St., 58474. Tel: 701-742-3291.
E-mail: bradburris@chi-midwest.org
For a complete listing, refer to the Hospitals section.

ROLLA. *Presentation Medical Center*, 213 Second Ave., N.E., P.O. Box 759, 58367. Tel: 701-477-5564.
E-mail: pmc@utma.com
For a complete listing, refer to the Hospitals section.

VALLEY CITY. *Mercy Hospital*, 570 Chautauqua Blvd., 58072. Tel: 701-845-6400; Fax: 701-845-6413.
E-mail: janeabissel@chi-midwest.org
For a complete listing, refer to the Hospitals section.

[E] HOMES FOR AGED

FARGO. *Riverview Place*, 5300 12th St. S., 58103. Tel: 701-237-4700; Fax: 701-235-5738.
E-mail: riverjerry@juno.com
For a complete listing, refer to the Special Care Facilities section.

EDGELEY. *Manor St. Joseph*, 404 Fourth Ave., 58433. Tel: 701-493-2477; Fax: 701-493-2477
For a complete listing, refer to the Special Care Facilities section.

ELLENDALE. *Prince of Peace Care Center*, 201 8th St. N., 58436. Tel: 701-349-3312; Fax: 701-349-3944
For a complete listing, refer to the Special Care Facilities section.

GRAND FORKS. *St. Anne's Guest Home*, 524 N. 17th St., 58203. Tel: 701-746-9401; Fax: 701-795-7825.
E-mail: stannes@corpcomm.net
For a complete listing, refer to the Special Care Facilities section.

HANKINSON. *St. Gerard Community Nursing Home*, 613 First Ave. S.W., 58041. Tel: 701-242-7891; Fax: 701-242-7896
For a complete listing, refer to the Special Care Facilities section.

LA MOURE. *St. Rose Care Center*, Hwy. 13, P.O. Box 627, 58458. Tel: 701-883-5363; Fax: 701-883-5711.
E-mail: tchanson@bhshealth
For a complete listing, refer to the Special Care Facilities section.

ROLETTE. *Presentation Care Center*, 304 John St., 58366. Tel: 701-246-3786
For a complete listing, refer to the Special Care Facilities section.

WAHPETON. *St. Catherine's Living Center*, 1307 N. Seventh St., 58075. Tel: 701-642-6667; Fax: 701-642-2485
For a complete listing, refer to the Special Care Facilities section.

[F] MONASTERIES AND RESIDENCES FOR PRIESTS AND BROTHERS

FARGO. *St. Francis Friary*. Franciscan Brothers of the Sacred Heart, 705 13th Ave. N., P.O. Box 5072, 58105-5072. Tel: 701-298-3009; Fax: 701-298-3010.
E-mail: brothers@fargocity.com
Web site: http://www.fargodiocese.org/brothers.html
Bros. Vincent Lomonaco, O.S.F., Supr.; Timothy Nelson, O.S.F.; Anthony Keidl, O.S.F. Brothers 3.

PISEK. *Franciscan Friars of Mary Immaculate*, St. Francis Friary, 119 Clement Avenue, 58273-7301. Tel: 701-284-6880; Fax: 701-284-6882.
E-mail: ofmi@polarcomm.com
Web site: www.ofmi-ofmi.org
Rev. Steven Reiske, Official Representative with the Bishop, P.O. Box 1750, Fargo, 58107. Revs. Joachim Mudd, O.F.M.I.; David Ladislaus Przedwiecki, O.F.M., In Res., (Pulaski Province); Paul Ruge, O.F.M.I.; Joseph Christensen, O.F.M.I., Vicar General. Novices: Bros. Pio Dull, O.F.M.I.; Pius Maria Harrington, O.F.M.I.; Anthony Valerian Biegler, O.F.M.I.

[G] CONVENTS AND RESIDENCES FOR SISTERS

FARGO. *Prairieland Home Health Agency, Inc.*, 1102 Page Dr., S.W., P.O. Box 10007, 58106-0006. Tel: 701-235-5750; Fax: 701-235-0906.
E-mail: cptbruced@aol.com
Bruce L. Davidson, Pres.

Presentation Center-Sacred Heart Convent, 1101 32nd Ave. S., 58103. Tel: 701-237-4857; Fax: 701-237-9822.
E-mail: psister@rrnet.com
Web site: rrnet.com/~psisters/pbvm.htm
Sr. Paula Ringuette, Pres. Sisters 62.

BELCOURT. *Queen of Peace Monastery*. Sisters of St. Benedict, P.O. Box 370, 58316. Tel: 701-477-6167; Fax: 701-477-5575.
E-mail: qop@utma.com
Sr. Judith Emge, O.S.B., Prioress. Sisters 7.

HANKINSON. *Sisters of St. Francis of the Immaculate Heart of Mary*, P.O. Box 447, 58041-0447. Tel: 701-242-7195; Fax: 701-242-7198.
E-mail: isfhank@means.net
Web site: www.massintransit.com/nd/francnvnt-nd-hnk/index.html
Sr. Donna Welder, O.S.F., Prov. Sisters 62; Novices 2.

VALLEY CITY. *Sisters of Mary of the Presentation*, 11550 River R. Rd., 58072. Tel: 701-845-2864; Fax: 701-845-0805.
E-mail: srmarlyss@fargodiocese.org
Sr. Marlyss Dionne, S.M.P., Prov. Supr.; Rev. John Odermann, O.S.B., Chap. Sisters 56.

WAHPETON. *Carmel of Mary*, 17765 78th St. S.E., 58075. Tel: 701-642-2360. Carmelite Nuns of the Ancient Observance. Mother Margaret Mary of the Sacred Heart, O.Carm., Prioress; Rev. Donald A. Leiphon, Chap. Solemn Professed Nuns 9; Junior Professed Nuns 2; Novices 1.

[H] RETREAT HOUSES

FARGO. *Presentation Prayer Center*, 1101 32nd Ave. S., 58103. Tel: 701-237-4857; Fax: 701-237-9822.
E-mail: saarendt@Juno.com
Web site: rrnet.com/~psisters/pbvm.htm
Sr. Andrea Arendt, P.B.V.M., Dir. Sisters 2.

Queen of Peace Retreat Center, 1310 Broadway, 58102. Tel: 701-293-9286; Fax: 701-235-0296.
E-mail: george@fargodiocese
Web site: www.fargodiocese.org
Diocesan sponsored retreat house operated by the Diocese of Fargo. George Lacher, Bldg. Dir.

[I] NEWMAN FOUNDATIONS

FARGO. *St. Paul's Catholic Chapel*, 1141 N. University Dr., 58102. Tel: 701-235-0142.
E-mail: ndsu-newman-center@ndsu.nodak.edu
Web site: www.acm.ndsu.nodak.edu/ndsu-newman/
Very Rev. Paul Duchschere, Dir. Campus Ministry. Staff 3.

GRAND FORKS. *Univ. of North Dakota Newman Center*, St. Thomas Aquinas Parish, UND. Tel: 701-777-6850; Fax: 701-775-0911.
E-mail: rcourtri@sage.und.nodak.edu
Web site: www.und.nodak.edu/dept.newman
St. Thomas Aquinas Newman Center, UND, 410 Cambridge St., 58203. Tel: 701-777-6850; Fax: 701-775- 0911. Revs. Raymond P. Courtright; Jason Lefor. Staff 4; Catholic Students 2,500.

WAHPETON. *State College of Science Newman Student Parish*, 701 N. Seventh St., 58075. Tel: 701-642-3415; Fax: 701-642-2601. Rev. Dale Lagodinski.

[J] MISCELLANEOUS LISTINGS

FARGO. *Catholic Chaplains Association*, c/o Chancery, 1310 Broadway, Box 1750, 58107. Tel: 701-235-6429; Fax: 701-235-0296.
E-mail: frirwin@fargodiocese.org

Catholic Development Foundation. c/o Chancery 1310 Broadway, Box 1750, 58107. Tel: 701-235-6429; Fax: 701-235-0296.
E-mail: dzanitsch@fargodiocese.org
Web site: www.fargodiocese.org
A non-profit foundation for religious charitable and educational purposes.

Catholic Family Service, 2537 S. University Dr., 58103. Tel: 701-235-4457; Fax: 701-239-8266.
E-mail: fargo@cfsnd.org
Web site: www.cfsnd.org
Statewide social service agency, providing Adoption Services, Child Welfare, Family Life Programs, Guardianship Services, Pregnancy Services and Rural Support. Staff 32.

Catholic School Network Foundation, Office, 705-13th Ave. N., P.O. Box 2085, 58107-2085. Tel: 701-293-7605; Fax: 701-293-7402. A nonprofit foundation for religious charitable and educational purposes. The Foundation is organized to financially support, assist, promote, expand and strengthen religious educational institutions affiliated with and under the governance of the Fargo Catholic Schools Network.

The Presentation Foundation, Sacred Heart Convent, 1101 32nd Ave. S., 58103. Tel: 701-237-4857; Fax: 701-237-9822.
E-mail: psisters@rrnet.com
Web site: rrnet.com/~psisters/pbvm.htm
Sr. Paula Ringuette, Supr. & Pres.

BATHGATE. *Bethlehem Community*, 10194 Garfield St., S., 58216. Tel: 701-265-3717; Fax: 701-265-3716.
E-mail: joe@bethlehembooks.com
Lydia Reynolds, Contact Person.

BOTTINEAU. *Minot State University-Bottineau*, c/o St. Mark, 322 Sinclair St., 58318. Rev. Kevin J. Boucher. Catholic Students 70.

DEVILS LAKE. *UND-Lake Region*, c/o St. Joseph's, 515 Fourth St., P.O. Box 898, 58301. Tel: 701-662-7558; Fax: 701-662-7559.
E-mail: stjosephchurch@stellarnet.com
Rev. Jeffrey Wald. Catholic Students 90.

DRAYTON. *Friends of the International Seminary John Paul II*, 211 W. Main St., P.O. Box 215, 58225. Tel: 701-454-3860. A non-profit foundation for the sole purpose of raising funds in order to financially support, assist, promote, expand and strengthen the International Seminary John Paul II whose primary purpose is to prepare young men from the third world and eastern Europe for the priesthood. The seminary is located in Rome, Italy. Rev. William Ovsak.

GRAND FORKS. *Air Force Base, Our Lady of the Snows Catholic Community*, 319 ARW/HC, 345 6th Ave. (Prairie Rose Chapel), 58205-6335. Tel: 701-747-3147; Fax: 701-747-4102.
E-mail: breigg@thequest.net
Web site: www.grandforks.af.mil
Rev. Gary R. Breig, Catholic Chap.

Grand Forks Catholic Schools Association, 216 Belmont Rd., 58201. Tel: 701-775-4818; Fax: 701-775-7568. Pamela Neppel, Sec. A non-profit organization developing, curriculum study, scholarship, transportation, personnel and fund raising.

JAMESTOWN. *Jamestown College*, 6052 College Ln., 58405. Rev. Bernard A. Pfau; Sr. Michaeleen Jantzer, O.S.B., Pastoral Min. & Campus Min. Catholic Students 247.

PARK RIVER. *Presentation Sisters Rural Outreach Ministry (Center)*, 115 Vivian St., 58270. Sr. Paula Ringuette, P.B.V.M., Pres.

VALLEY CITY. *Valley City State University*, St. Catherine's, 58072. Tel: 701-845-0354; Fax: 701-845-0556.
E-mail: gbraun@rrnet.com
Kelley Utt, Dir. Catholic Students 220.

RELIGIOUS INSTITUTES OF MEN REPRESENTED IN THE DIOCESE

For further details refer to the corresponding bracketed number in the Religious Institutes of Men or Women section.

[0200]—*Benedictine Monks.* (St. Meinrad, Meinrad, IN).—O.S.B.

[0512]—*Franciscan Brothers of the Sacred Heart.*—O.S.F.

[0534]—*Franciscan Friars of Mary Immaculate.*—O.F.M.I.

[0650]—*Holy Ghost Fathers.*—C.S.Sp.

[0430]—*Order of Preachers-Dominicans.*—O.P.

[1190]—*Salesians of Don Bosco.*—S.D.B.

[0975]—*Society of Our Lady of the Holy Trinity.*—S.O.L.T.

[0990]—*Society of the Catholic Apostolate.* (Mater Dei Prov.).—S.A.C.

RELIGIOUS INSTITUTES OF WOMEN REPRESENTED IN THE DIOCESE

[0230]—*Benedictine Sisters of the Pontifical Jurisdiction.* (Belcourt, ND).—O.S.B.

[0300]—*Calced Carmelites.*—O.Carm.

[1310]—*Franciscan Sisters of Little Falls, MN.*

[2575]—*Institute of the Sisters of Mercy of the Americas.* (Omaha, NE).—R.S.M.

[3510]—*Sister Servants of Christ the King.*

[2450]—*Sisters of Mary of the Presentation.* (Maryvale, R.F.D. 1).—S.M.P.

[1590]—*Sisters of St. Francis of the Immaculate Heart of Mary.* (Hankinson, ND).—O.S.F.

[3320]—*Sisters of the Presentation of the B.V.M.* (Fargo, ND).—P.B.V.M.

[]—*Sisters of the Presentation of the Blessed Virgin Mary.* (Aberdeen, South Dakota).

NECROLOGY

† Axtmann, Joseph S, Munich, ND St. Mary. —Died July 4, 2000.

† Bacevicius, John A, Kintyre, ND St. Boniface. —Died March 15, 2000.

† Binder, Albert H., (Retired). —Died Feb. 27, 2000.

† Duffy, Patrick, (Retired). —Died Dec. 30, 1999.

† Filteau, Jerome E., (Retired). —Died March 19, 2000.

† Proeller, Ulric J., (Retired). —Died April 15, 2000.

† Scheller, Raymund, (Retired). —Died July 30, 2000.

† Skarohild, Robert F, Lakota, ND St. Mary. —Died Feb. 20, 2000.

Diocese of Fort Wayne - South Bend

(Dioecesis Wayne Castrensis-South Bendensis)

Most Reverend

JOHN M. D'ARCY, D.D., M.A., S.T.D.

Bishop of Fort Wayne-South Bend; ordained February 2, 1957; appointed Auxiliary Bishop of Boston and Titular Bishop of Mediana December 31, 1974; consecrated February 11, 1975; appointed Bishop of Fort Wayne-South Bend February 26, 1985; installed May 1, 1985. *Mailing Address: P.O. Box 390, Fort Wayne, IN, 46801.*

Chancery Office: 1103 S. Calhoun St., P.O. Box 390, Fort Wayne, IN, 46801. Tel.: 219-422-4611; Fax: 219-423-3382.

Web site address: www.diocesefwsb.org

E-mail address: jkoch@fw.diocesefwsb.org

Most Reverend

DANIEL R. JENKY, C.S.C.

Auxiliary Bishop of Fort Wayne-South Bend; ordained April 6, 1974; appointed Auxiliary Bishop of Fort Wayne-South Bend and Titutar Bishop of Amantia October 21, 1997; consecrated December 16, 1997. *Res., St. Matthew's Cathedral, 1701 Miami St., South Bend, IN, 46613.*

Most Reverend

JOSEPH R. CROWLEY, D.D.

Retired Auxiliary Bishop of Fort Wayne-South Bend; ordained May 1, 1953; appointed Titular Bishop of Maraguia June 16, 1971; consecrated August 24, 1971; retired July 15, 1990. *Mailing Address: 1240 Honan Dr., South Bend, IN, 46614.* Tel.: 219-299-9155.

Most Reverend

JOHN R. SHEETS, S.J.

Retired Auxiliary Bishop of Fort Wayne-South Bend; completed theological studies at St. Mary Jesuit School in Kansas and was ordained in 1953; received his Doctorate in Theology in 1957 in Innsbruck, Austria; ordained to the Episcopacy for the Diocese of Fort Wayne-South Bend on June 25, 1991; and Titular Bishop of Murkona, Province of Maurtitania Cesariense; retired September 21, 1997. *Res., St. Matthew Cathedral, 1701 Miami St., South Bend, IN, 46613.* Tel.: 219-289-5539.

ESTABLISHED SEPT. 22, 1857.

Square Miles 5,792.

REDESIGNATED DIOCESE OF FORT WAYNE-SOUTH BEND ON JULY 22, 1960.

Comprises the Counties of Adams, Allen, Dekalb, Elkhart, Huntington, Kosciusko, La Grange, Marshall, Noble, St. Joseph, Steuben, Wabash, Wells, Whitley in the State of Indiana.

For legal titles of parishes and diocesan institutions, consult the Chancery Office.

STATISTICAL OVERVIEW

Personnel	
Bishop	1
Auxiliary Bishops	1
Retired Bishops	2
Priests: Diocesan Active in Diocese	70
Priests: Active Outside Diocese	1
Priests: Retired, Sick or Absent	24
Number of Diocesan Priests	95
Religious Priests in Diocese	170
Extern Priests in Diocese	22
Ordinations:	
Diocesan Priests	2
Religious Priests	2
Permanent Deacons in Diocese	22
Total Brothers	100
Total Sisters	656
Parishes	
Parishes	87
With Resident Pastor:	
Resident Diocesan Priests	55
Resident Religious Priests	19
Without Resident Pastor:	
Administered by Priests	13
Pastoral Centers	2
Professional Ministry Personnel:	
Brothers	2
Sisters	21
Lay Ministers	94
Welfare	
Catholic Hospitals	5
Total Assisted	375,430
Health Care Centers	1
Total Assisted	20,000
Homes for the Aged	4
Total Assisted	28
Day Care and Extended Day Care Centers	2
Total Assisted	648
Specialized Homes	1
Total Assisted	43
Special Centers for Social Services	4
Total Assisted	18,836
Educational	
Diocesan Students in Other Seminaries	11
Seminaries, Religious	1
Students Religious	37
Total Seminarians	48
Colleges and Universities	5
Total Students	14,811
High Schools, Diocesan and Parish	4
Total Students	3,020
Elementary Schools, Diocesan and Parish	41
Total Students	11,164
Catechesis/Religious Education:	
High School Students	1,860
Elementary Students	10,319
Total Students Under Catholic Instruction	41,222
Teachers in the Diocese:	
Priests	2
Brothers	1
Sisters	21
Lay Teachers	761
Vital Statistics	
Receptions into the Church:	
Infant Baptism Totals	2,799
Adult Baptism Totals	458
Received into Full Communion	480
First Communions	3,132
Confirmations	3,069
Marriages:	
Catholic	558
Interfaith	426
Total Marriages	984
Deaths	1,466
Total Catholic Population	166,108
Total Population	1,170,337

Former Bishops—Rt. Rev. JOHN HENRY LUERS, D.D., cons. Jan. 10, 1858; died June 29, 1871.—Rt. Rev. JOSEPH DWENGER, C.PP.S., D.D., cons. April 14, 1872; died Jan. 27, 1893.—Rt. Rev. JOSEPH RADEMACHER, D.D., cons. Bishop of Nashville, June 24, 1883; transferred to Fort Wayne, July 14, 1893; died Jan. 12, 1900.—Rt. Rev. HERMAN JOSEPH ALERDING, D.D., cons. Nov. 30, 1900; died Dec. 6, 1924.—Most Rev. JOHN FRANCIS NOLL, D.D., cons. June 30, 1925; promoted to rank of Archbishop "ad personam," Sept. 2, 1953; died July 31, 1956.—Most Rev. LEO A. PURSLEY, D.D., cons. Sept. 19, 1950; retired Oct. 19, 1976; died Nov. 15, 1998.—Most Rev. WILLIAM E. MCMANUS, D.D., ord. April 15, 1939; appt. Auxiliary Bishop of Chicago, June 21, 1967; appt. Bishop of Fort Wayne, Aug. 31, 1976; installed as 7th Bishop of Fort Wayne, Oct. 19, 1976; retired Feb. 25, 1985; died March 3, 1997.

Diocese of Fort Wayne-South Bend, Inc.—(Incorporated Aug. 29, 1955). *Board of Directors:* Most Rev. JOHN M. D'ARCY, D.D., M.A., S.T.D., Pres.; Rev. ROBERT C. SCHULTE, Vice Pres. JOSEPH RYAN, Sec. & Treas. *Finance Council:* Most Rev. JOSEPH CROWLEY; Rev. ROBERT C. SCHULTE; Mr. JOSEPH RYAN; ARTHUR DECIO; Sr. JANE MARIE KLEIN, O.S.F.; Mr. JERRY HAMMES; JOSEPH DAHM; MICHAEL HAMMES; THOMAS BLEE; RICHARD DOERMER; VINCENT TIPPMANN; Mr. JERRY KEARNS; ALICE KOPFE; SCOTT MALPAS; RONALD KAUFMAN.

Chancery Office—1103 S. Calhoun St., P.O. Box 390, Fort Wayne, 46801. Tel: 219-422-4611; Fax: 219-423-3382. Office Hours: Mon.-Fri. 8:30-4:30. Other times by appointment.

Vicar General-Chancellor—Rev. ROBERT C. SCHULTE.

Vicar for Retired Clergy—Rev. Msgr. J. WILLIAM LESTER, P.A.

Episcopal Vicar for Education—1103 S. Clinton St., Box 390, Fort Wayne, 46801. Tel: 219-422-4611; Fax: 219-423-3382.

South Bend Chancery—114 W. Wayne St., South Bend, 46624. Tel: 219-234-0687; Fax: 219-232-8483.

Diocesan Tribunal—1103 S. Calhoun St., P.O. Box 390, Fort Wayne, 46801. Tel: 219-422-4611., South Bend Office: *114 W. Wayne St, P.O. Box 1432, South Bend, 46624.* Tel: 219-287-6531; Fax: 219-423-3382.

Judicial Vicar—Rev. BRUCE PIECHOCKI.

Defenders of the Bond—SANDRA LA VIOLETTE; Rev. VIGNY J. BELLERIVE.

Pro-Synodal Judges—Revs. PHILIP DEVOLDER; JAMES G. KARAFFA, C.S.C.; LAWRENCE KRAMER; GARY SIGLER; ELDEN MILLER; BRUCE PIECHOCKI.

Court Consultants—PHIL SUTTON, Ph.D.

Fort Wayne Office Secretary—JANICE BRELL. Office Auditors: VICKI FERRIER; MONICA KLUESNER; BONDA TUTWILER.

Canonist—Rev. VIGNY J. BELLERIVE.

Notary—JANICE BRELL.

South Bend Office Secretary—DIANA HEIDT. Office Auditors: ELIZABETH LIES; ANGELA SARELL; PATRICIA BORS.

Consultors—Rev. Msgr. J. WILLIAM LESTER, P.A.; Rev. Msgr. JAMES J. WOLF; Rev. Msgr. JOHN N. SUELZER; Revs. BRUCE PIECHOCKI; WILLIAM HODDE; RAYMOND BALZER; BERNARD GALIC.

Diocesan Offices and Directors

Business Administration Office—JOSEPH RYAN, Chief Fin. Officer, *P.O. Box 390, Fort Wayne, 46801.* Tel: 219-422-4611.

Buildings and Improvements—Advisory Board: Rev. ROBERT SCHULTE; Rev. Msgr. JAMES WOLF; Revs. DOMINIQUE CARBONEAU; DERRICK SNEYD; WILLIAM SULLIVAN; ANTHONY SZAKALY, C.S.C.; JOHN OVERMYER; DALE BAUMAN; LAURENCE TIPPMANN; DAVID CARKENORD; ELDEN J. MILLER; Mr. JOSEPH RYAN; JAMES SCHENKEL.

Budget Committee—Revs. ROBERT C. SCHULTE; JOHN PFISTER; Rev. Msgr. JOHN SUELZER; Rev. BERNARD GALIC; Mr. JOSEPH RYAN.

Diocesan Services Agency—JOHN KLEIN; MARY LOU O'KEEFFE, Purchasing, *P.O. Box 390, Fort Wayne, 46801.* Tel: 219-422-4611; 800-856-4611.

Diocesan Office of Development—HARRY W. VERHILEY, Dir., *1328 W. Dragoon Trail, Mishawaka, 46544.* Tel: 219-258-6571; Fax: 219-256-2709.

Campus Ministry—LINDA FURGE, Dir., *1330 E. Washington Center Rd., Fort Wayne, 46825.* Tel: 219-483-3661; Fax: 219-483-1881.

Campaign for Human Development—Rev. THOMAS O'CONNOR, *P.O. Box 11383, 1101 S. Lafayette St., Fort Wayne, 46857-1383.* Tel: 219-424-8231; Fax: 219-426-2406.

Catholic Charities—KATHLEEN DONNELLAN, Dir., *315 E. Washington, Fort Wayne, 46802.* Tel: 219-439-0242; 800-686-7459; Fax: 219-439-0250.

Censor Librorum—Rev. MICHAEL HEINTZ, *1701 Miami St., South Bend, 46613.* Tel: 219-289-5539; Fax: 219-289-0227.

Cemeteries—Rev. DAVID CARKENORD, Dir., *1098 County Rd. 39, Waterloo, 46793.* Tel: 219-837-7115; 800-570-8080; Fax: 219-837-7727.

Catholic Cemetery Association of Fort Wayne, Inc.—*3500 Lake Ave., Fort Wayne, 46805.* Tel: 219-426-2044.

Charismatic Movement—Deacon KEVIN RANAGHAN, *1003 St. Vincent, South Bend, 46617.* Tel: 219-234-2465.

Clergy Relief Association—Revs. PHILLIP WIDMANN, Pres. JOHN PFISTER, Vice Pres. DANIEL LEEUW, Sec. THOMAS SHOEMAKER, Treas. Directors: Revs. JACOB GALL; JAMES SECULOFF. Nominating Committee: Revs. ELDEN MILLER. Audit Committee: Revs. BERNARD GALIC; CAMILLO TIRABASSI.

Communications—CHRISTINE BONAHOOM-NIX, Dir., *150 Doan Dr., Fort Wayne, 46816.* Tel: 219-744-0012; Fax: 219-744-1473.

Continuing Education of the Clergy—Rev. ROBERT C. SCHULTE, *P.O. Box 390, Fort Wayne, 46801.* Tel: 219-422-4611; Fax: 219-423-3382.

Council of Priests—Most Rev. DANIEL JENKY, C.S.C.; Rev. ROBERT C. SCHULTE; Rev. Msgr. JAMES J. WOLF; Revs. STEPHEN COLCHIN; JAMES SHAFER; MICHAEL HEINTZ; EDWARD ERPELDING; WILLIAM SCHOOLER; THOMAS LEMOS, C.S.C.; THOMAS SHOEMAKER; TIMOTHY WROZEK; LAWRENCE KRAMER; ROBERT DOMBROWSKI; TERRY FISHER; MARK GURTNER.

Cursillo—Rev. PAUL BUETER. Tel: 219-267-5842 (Spanish); 219-268-1030. Rev. JAMES STOYLE. Tel: 219-291-0570 (English).

Hispanic Ministry Services—Rev. PAUL R. BUETER, Diocesan Coord., *125 N. Harrison, Warsaw, 46580.* Tel: 219-267-5842; Fax: 219-268-1030.

Bremen—Deacon VICTOR CARRILLO, *St. Dominic, 803 W. Bike St., Bremen, 46506.* Tel: 219-546-3601.

Elkhart—Deacon RICARDO MEDINA, III, *St. Vincent de Paul, 1108 S. Main St., Elkhart, 46516.* Tel: 219-293-8231.

Fort Wayne—Rev. GLENN KOHRMAN; Deacon JUSTO DONIAS, *St. Paul, 416 W. Washington Blvd., Fort Wayne, 46802.* Tel: 219-422-0118.

Goshen—Deacon RAMIRO REYES, *St. John the Evangelist, 114 W. Monroe St., Goshen, 46526-3957.* Tel: 219-533-3385.

LaGrange—Vacant, *St. Joseph, 0050N - 100E, P.O. Box 69, LaGrange, 46761.* Tel: 219-463-3472.

Ligonier—Deacon RAMIRO REYES, *St. Patrick, 300 Ravine Park Dr., Ligonier, 46767-1301.* Tel: 219-894-4946.

Milford—Rev. PAUL R. BUETER, *Our Lady of Guadalupe, 4th & Main St., P.O. Box 605, Milford, 46542.* Tel: 219-658-9384; 293-5056.

Plymouth—Deacon VICTOR CARRILLO, *St. Michael, 612 N. Walnut St., Plymouth, 46563.* Tel: 219-936-4935.

South Bend—Rev. THOMAS LEMOS, C.S.C., *St. Stephen, 1102 W. Thomas St., South Bend, 46601.* Tel: 219-287-7681.

Religious Education—LOURDES SILVA.

Youth Minister—NIKI GONZALEZ.

La Casa de Amistad, Inc.—LILIANA SILVESTRY, Dir., *746 S. Mead St., South Bend, 46619.* Tel: 219-233-2120.

Diocesan Council of Catholic Women—Rev. EDWARD NARCOWICH, *5790 E. 1100 S., Geneva, 46740.* Tel: 219-997-6558. GEORGETTA GUNTHORP, Interim Pres., *0240 N. 850 E., LaGrange, 46761.* Tel: 219-367-2359.

Diocesan Family Life—FRED EVERETT; LISA EVERETT, *114 W. Wayne St., South Bend, 46601.* Tel: 219-234-0687; Fax: 219-232-8483.

Ecumenical Affairs—Rev. ROBERT C. SCHULTE, Dir., East, *P.O. Box 390, Fort Wayne, 46801.* Tel: 219-422-4611; Fax: 219-423-3382. DEIRDRE MCQUADE, Dir., West. Tel: 219-234-0687; Fax: 219-232-8483.

Human Development Commission—Rev. THOMAS O'CONNOR, *P.O. Box 11383, Fort Wayne, 46857-1383.* Tel: 219-424-8231; Fax: 219-426-2406.

Liturgical Commission—Revs. WILLIAM KUMMER; PETER ROCCA, C.S.C.; JAMES SHAFER; WILLIAM SCHOOLER, Chm.; Deacon ART BLEAU; JAMES FITZPATRICK; Rev. MICHAEL DRISCOLL; GERVAISE BASTIAN; JUDY MOCKENHAUPT; BEVERLY RIEGER; JUDITH THROM; Mr. STEVE WARNER.

Environment and Art—Revs. CHRISTOPHER SCHENKEL; JAMES FLANIGAN, C.S.C., Chm. RICHARD BULLENE, C.S.C.; DAVID CARKENORD; Sr. AGNES MARIE REGAN, O.S.F.; SAM JONES, A.I.A.; BEVERLY RIEGER.

Diocesan Music Committee—Sr. PHYLLIS GRZECZKA, S.S.N.D.; TOM FARWELL; KEVIN DEMETROFF; RICHARD CLAWSON; TIM ROBISON; JUDY THROM, Chm. RENEE PARSON.

Diocesan Initiation Committee—Ms. GERVAISE BASTIAN, Chm. MARY BARNES; CAROL CONE; Sr. EILEEN DAUDLIN, S.S.N.D.; DONNA MACINO; CHRIS MILLER; JUDY MOCKENHAUPT; Rev. JOHN OVERMYER; GUS ZUEHLKE; REGINA WILSON.

Office of Worship—BEVERLY RIEGER, Dir., *1103 S. Calhoun St., Box 390, Fort Wayne, 46801.* Tel: 219-422-4611.

Official Publication "Today's Catholic"—WILLIAM CONE, Editor; TIMOTHY JOHNSON, Asst. Editor, *150 Doan Dr., Fort Wayne, 46816., Mailing Address: P.O. Box 11169, Fort Wayne, 46856.* Tel: 219-456-2824; Fax: 219-744-1473.

Permanent Diaconate—Rev. WILLIAM KUMMER, *St. John Church, 4525 Arlington Ave., Fort Wayne, 46807.* Tel: 219-744-4393.

Priests' Eucharistic League—Vacant, *P.O. Box 390, Fort Wayne, 46801.* Tel: 219-422-4611.

Pro-Life—FRED EVERETT; LISA EVERETT, *114 W. Wayne St., South Bend, 46601.* Tel: 219-234-0687., Birthline phones: Tel: 219-422-1818 (Fort Wayne); 356-3322 (Huntington); 289-1034 (South Bend).

Propagation of the Faith and Holy Childhood Association—Rev. PHILLIP WIDMANN, *St. Peter Catholic Church, 518 E. DeWald St., Fort Wayne, 46803.* Tel: 219-744-2765; Fax: 219-744-1972.

Office of Catechesis—Sr. M. JANE CAREW, O.V., Diocesan Dir., Religious Education Fort Wayne: DONNA MACINO, Assoc. Dir., *P.O. Box 390, Fort Wayne, 46801.* Tel: 219-422-4611.

South Bend-Mishawaka Area Office of Religious Education—KIM CUNNINGHAM, Assoc. Dir. Religious Education, *1328 W. Dragoon Trail, Mishawaka, 46554.* Tel: 219-259-9994; Fax: 219-256-2709.

Refugee Resettlement Program—KATHLEEN DONNELLAN, Dir., *315 E. Washington, Fort Wayne, 46802.* Tel: 219-422-7511; 800-686-7459; Fax: 219-439-0250.

Retired Clergy Committee—Rev. Msgr. J. WILLIAM LESTER, P.A.; Revs. RAYMOND BALZER; WILLIAM HODDE; ROBERT HOEVEL; JOHN SUELZER; RICHARD URBINE; JAMES WOLF.

Retired Senior Volunteer Program (RSVP)—Auburn: PATTI SHEPPARD, Coord., *500 E. 7th St., Auburn, 46706.* Tel: 219-925-0917.

Serra International—Rev. JOHN SKEVINGTON, Pres., *3221 Rockwood Dr., Fort Wayne, 46815.* Tel: 219-483-2748. Rev. GLENN KOHRMAN, Chap., *St. Patrick Catholic Church, 2120 Harrison St., Fort Wayne, 46802.* Tel: 219-744-1450; Fax: 219-744-6231. Rev. ROBERT YAST, Chap., *225 S. Mill St., Mishawaka, 46544.* Tel: 219-255-6134. South Bend Office; Dr. JOHN B. TOEPP, Pres. Tel: 219-291-3181.

Single Catholic Adult Club—Vacant, *1103 S. Calhoun St., P.O. Box 390, Fort Wayne, 46801.* Tel: 219-422-4611.

Schools—Dr. JEANETTE KAM, Supt. JOSEPH DANO, Area Supt. JOHN GAUGHAN, Asst. Dir. High Schools, *1102 S. Clinton St., Box 390, Fort Wayne, 46801.* Tel: 219-422-4611; Fax: 219-420-6306. South Bend Office: BARBARA JEMIELITY, Area Supt., *1328 W. Dragoon Trail, Mishawaka, 46544.* Tel: 219-255-1387; Fax: 219-256-2709.

School Board, Diocesan—Most Rev. JOHN M. D'ARCY; Rev. TERRY FISHER; Sr. ELAINE BROTHERS, O.S.F.; Dr. JEANETTE KAM; BARBARA JEMIELITY; JOHN GAUGHAN; ELIZABETH BROWN; WILLIAM EHINGER; MARIJO KELLY; JOHN ROSENTHAL; JANE BAKER.

Catholic Schools Office—Dr. JEANETTE KAM; JOSEPH DANO; JOHN GAUGHAN.

Ex Officio Member—Most Rev. JOHN M. D'ARCY, D.D., M.A., S.T.D.

Scouting—Fort Wayne: Rev. CHRISTOPHER YOUNG, Chap., *St. Charles Borromeo Church, 4916 Trier Rd., Fort Wayne, 46815.* Tel: 219-482-2186. South Bend: Rev. ELDEN J. MILLER, Chap., *Queen of Peace, 4508 Vistula Rd., Mishawaka, 46555.* Tel: 219-255-9674; Fax: 219-255-1029.

St. Vincent de Paul Society—Rev. THOMAS O'CONNOR, *1101 S. Lafayette St., Fort Wayne, 46802-3202.* Tel: 219-424-8231; Fax: 219-426-2406., *Mailing Address: P.O. Box 11383, Fort Wayne, 46857-1383.*

Spiritual Development—Fort Wayne: Sr. ANN KIHSLINGER S.S.N.D., Co-Dir.; Sr. JOLENE HEIDEN, S.S.N.D., South Bend: Sr. MARY BROOKS, Co-Dir., *114 W. Wayne St., South Bend, 46601.* Tel: 219-234-0687.

Office of Youth Ministry and Spiritual Development—STEVEN J. WEIGAND, Assoc., *P.O. Box 390, Fort Wayne, 46801.* Tel: 219-422-4611; Fax: 219-420-6306.

Vocations—Rev. BERNARD GALIC, Dir., *114 W. Wayne St., South Bend, 46601.* Tel: 219-234-0687; Fax: 219-232-8483.

Youth Organizations—Vacant, Moderator.

CYO Office—AVA MEYER, Business Mgr., *P.O. Box 445, Monroeville, 46773.* Tel: 219-623-6007; Fax: 219-623-6007. BOB TOMLINSON, Pres., *1124 Ludwig Park Dr., Fort Wayne, 46825.* Tel: 219-489-9672.

Inter City Catholic League—Rev. PETER A. JARRET, C.S.C., Moderator, *St. Pius X Parish, 52553 Fir Rd., Granger, 46530.* Tel: 219-272-8462. TONY VIOLI, Pres., *225 Omer Ave., Mishawaka, 46545.* Tel: 219-259-1638; 255-9776; Fax: 219-259-0995.

CLERGY, PARISHES, MISSIONS AND PAROCHIAL SCHOOLS

CITY OF FORT WAYNE

(Allen County)

1—CATHEDRAL OF THE IMMACULATE CONCEPTION (1836). (Calhoun, between Lewis and Jefferson Sts.). Revs. Robert C. Schulte, Rector; John Bosco Perera (Sri Lanka); Paul Coutinita; Sr. Sally Soules, S.F.C.C., Pastoral Min.; Deacon Joseph R. Zickgraf. In res., Rev. Msgr. J. William Lester.

Res., 1122 Clinton St., P.O. Box 10898, 46854. Tel: 219-424-1485; Fax: 219-423-3382.

Catechesis/Religious Programs—Students 150.

Chapel—MacDougall Memorial Chapel.

2—ST. ANDREW (1910), Rev. Phillip A. Widmann; Sr. Patricia Ann Murray, O.S.F., Pastoral Assoc.
518 E. DeWald, 46803. Tel: 219-422-0380.
Res., 2610 New Haven Ave., 46803. Tel: 219-422-0380.

3—ST. CHARLES BORROMEO (1957), Rev. Msgr. John N. Suelzer; Revs. Christopher Joseph Young; John Klimczyk; Rev. Msgr. Edward I. Hession, Pastor Emeritus, (Retired); Sr. Kathleen Morrissey, O.P., Pastoral Assoc.; Doris Schultz, Business Admin.
Res., 4916 Trier Rd., 46815. Tel: 219-482-2186; Fax: 219-471-2144.
School—4910 Trier Rd., 46815. Tel: 219-484-3392; Fax: 219-482-2006. Mrs. Michelle Hittie, Prin. Franciscan Sisters of the Sacred Heart 3; Lay Teachers 41; Students 804.
Catechesis/Religious Programs—Tel: 219-484-7322. Kathy Monagle, D.R.E. Students 300.

4—ST. ELIZABETH ANN SETON (1988), Revs. James A. Shafer; Dominique Andrew Carboneau; Eugene Eburuche, S.M.M.M. (Nigeria).
Office: 10700 Aboite Center Rd., 46804. Tel: 219-432-0268; Fax: 219-436-5851.
Res., 10517 Unita Dr., 46804. Tel: 219-436-9819.
Catechesis/Religious Programs—Tel: 219-432-0268; Fax: 219-436-5851. Michelle Kriss, D.R.E. Students 860.

5—St. Henry (1956), Rev. Thomas Shoemaker.
Res., 2929 E. Paulding Rd., 46816. Tel: 219-447-4100; Fax: 219-447-4100.
Catechesis/Religious Programs—4643 Gaywood Dr., Ft. Wayne, 46806.
Students 85.

6—St. Hyacinth (1910). Closed. For inquiries for parish records contact the Chancery.

7—St. John Baptist (1929), Rev. William Kummer; Mary L. Glowaski, Pastoral Assoc.
Res., 4525 Arlington Ave., 46807. Tel: 219-744-4393; Fax: 219-456-3072.
School—4500 Fairfield Ave., 46807. Tel: 219-456-3321. Mr. John E. Grote, Prin.
Sisters 1; Lay Teachers 22; Students 375.
Catechesis/Religious Programs—4501 Arlington Ave., 46807. Tel: 219-744-3578. Elizabeth Balbo-Ryan, D.R.E.
Students 84.

8—St. Joseph (1914) (Italian), Rev. Laurence Tippmann. In res., Rev. Adam Schmitt, (Retired).
Res., 1910 Hale Ave., 46802. Tel: 219-432-5113; Fax: 219-432-4711.
School—2213 Brooklyn Ave., 46802. Tel: 219-432-4000; Fax: 219-432-8642. Ms. Mary Schreiber, Prin.
Sisters of St. Agnes 2; Lay Teachers 16; Students 435.

9—St. Joseph (1851) (German), Rev. Robert A. Van Kempen.
Res., 11337 Old U.S. 27 S., 46816. Tel: 219-639-3748; Fax: 219-639-3675. [CEM]
School—11521 Old U.S. 27 S., 46816. Tel: 219-639-3580. Miss Lois Widner, Prin.
Lay Teachers 12; Students 210.
Catechesis/Religious Programs—Students 49.

10—St. Jude (1929), Revs. William C. Schooler; Robert D'Souza (India); Mary Pohlman, Pastoral Assoc.; Deacon Fred J. Larson.
Res., 2130 Pemberton Dr., 46805. Tel: 219-484-6609; Fax: 219-969-1607.
School—2110 Pemberton Dr., 46805. Tel: 219-484-4611. Sr. Kathleen Marie Knueven, Prin.
Sisters of Notre Dame 3; Lay Teachers 38; Students 657.
Catechesis/Religious Programs—Tel: 219-484-6609. Mary Barnes, D.R.E.
Students 270.

11—St. Mary (1848), Rev. Thomas P. O'Connor.
Mailing Address: P.O. Box 11383, 46857-1383. Tel: 219-424-8231; Fax: 219-426-2604.
Res., 1101 S. Lafayette St., 46802.

12—Most Precious Blood (1897), Rev. John C. Mencsik, C.PP.S.; Deacon Peter Loving.
Res., 1515 Barthold St., 46808. Tel: 219-424-5535.
School—1529 Barthold St., 46808. Tel: 219-424-4832. Corinne Tessman, Prin.
Lay Teachers 12; Students 230.
Catechesis/Religious Programs—Students 60.

13—Our Lady of Good Hope (1969), Rev. David Voors.
Res., 7215 St. Joe Rd., 46835. Tel: 219-485-9615; Fax: 219-485-4463.
Catechesis/Religious Programs—Tel: 219-485-3732. Mary Kay Matasky, D.R.E.
Students 317.

14—St. Patrick (1889) (Vietnamese), Rev. Glenn Kohrman. In res., Revs. Daniel Chukwuleta (Nigeria); Angel Lopez, O.F.M. (Mexico).
Res., 2120 S. Harrison St., 46802. Tel: 219-744-1450; Fax: 219-744-6231.
Catechesis/Religious Programs—Students 60.

15—St. Paul (1865) (Hispanic), Revs. Glenn Kohrman; Angel L. Valdez (Mexico); Deacon Justo Donias.
Mailing Address: Office, 416 W. Washington Blvd., 46802. Tel: 219-422-0118; Fax: 219-422-0118.
Res., 2120 S. Harrison Ave., 46802. Tel: 219-744-1450; Fax: 219-744-6231.
Catechesis/Religious Programs—Tel: 219-422-0118; Fax: 219-422-0118.
Students 174.

16—St. Peter (1872), Rev. Phillip A. Widmann.
Res., 518 E. De Wald St., 46803. Tel: 219-744-2765; Fax: 219-744-1972.

17—Queen of Angels (1947), Rev. John F. Pfister. In res., Rev. Bruce Piechocki.
Res., 1500 W. State St., 46808. Tel: 219-482-9411; Fax: 219-471-0005.
School—1600 W. State Blvd., 46808. Tel: 219-483-8214. Mrs. Marsha Jordan, Prin.
Lay Teachers 19; Students 400.
Catechesis/Religious Programs—Students 85.

18—Sacred Heart (1947), Rev. Thomas Shoemaker.
Res., 4643 Gaywood Dr., 46806. Tel: 219-744-2519; Fax: 219-744-2519.
School—Julian Benoit Academy, 3029 E. Paulding Rd., 46816. Tel: 219-447-5121; Fax: 219-447-4606.
Catechesis/Religious Programs—Tel: 219-447-4100; Fax: 219-447-4100.
Students 50.

19—St. Therese (1947), Rev. Joseph A. Rulli.
Res., 2304 Lower Huntington Rd., 46819. Tel: 219-747-9139; Fax: 219-747-1494.
School—2222 Lower Huntington Rd., 46819. Tel: 219-747-2343; Fax: 219-747-4767. Charles A. Grimm, Prin.
Lay Teachers 13; Students 212.
Catechesis/Religious Programs—Tel: 219-747-9139.
Students 80.

20—St. Vincent de Paul (1846), Rev. John M. Kuzmich; Rev. Joseph Gaughan; Rev. Mark Allen Gurtner. Pastoral Assocs.: Sr. Mary Catherine Jarema, S.S.N.D.; Paul O. Schirmeyer, Admin.; Mrs. Judy Mockenhaupt.
Res., 8669 Auburn Rd., 46825. Tel: 219-489-3537; Fax: 219-497-9405. [CEM]
School—8753 Auburn Rd., 46825. Tel: 219-489-4591; Fax: 219-489-5318. Mrs. Sandra Guffey, Prin.
Lay Teachers 32; Students 697.
Catechesis/Religious Programs—Tel: 219-489-1684. Vicky Luetzelschwab, D.R.E.
Students 525.

CITY OF SOUTH BEND
(St. Joseph County)

1—St. Matthew Cathedral (1921), Most Rev. Daniel R. Jenky, D.D., Rector; Rev. Michael Heintz; Deacon Emilio Gizzi; David Laux, Business Mgr.
Res., 1701 Miami St., 46613. Tel: 219-289-5539; Fax: 219-289-0227.
School—1015 E. Dayton, 46613. Tel: 219-289-4535. Ms. Mary Ann Retseck, Prin.
Lay Teachers 23; Students 428.
Catechesis/Religious Programs—1721 Miami St., 46613. Tel: 219-289-0940.
Students 105.

2—St. Adalbert (1910) (Polish), Rev. Daryl Rybicki; Sr. M. Anthony Kubat, C.S.S.F., Pastoral Min.; Rev. Paulinus Ozodor, C.S.Sp (Nigeria). In res., Rev. James Fahey, C.S.C.
Res., 2420 W. Huron St., 46619. Tel: 219-288-5708; Fax: 219-251-2786.
School—519 S. Olive St., 46619. Tel: 219-288-6645; Fax: 219-251-2788. Sr. Dian Majsterek, S.S.J.-T.O.S.F., Prin.
Felician Sisters 1; Sisters of St. Joseph 1; Lay Teachers 8; Students 125.
Catechesis/Religious Programs—Students 25.

3—St. Anthony de Padua (1949), Rev. Terry Fisher; Deacon Brian Miller.
Res., 2120 E. Jefferson Blvd., 46617. Tel: 219-282-2308; Fax: 219-288-8877.
School—2310 E. Jefferson Blvd., 46615. Tel: 219-233-7169; Fax: 219-288-8877. Ms. Martha Lewallen, Prin.
Lay Teachers 22; Students 446.
Catechesis/Religious Programs—Tel: 219-282-2308.
Students 55.

4—St. Augustine (1928) (African American), Rev. Daryl Rybicki; Deacon Paul Baumgartner; Rev. Paulinus Odozor, C.S.Sp (Nigeria).
Mailing Address: P.O. Box 3198, 46619-0198. Tel: 219-234-6334; Fax: 219-251-2786.
Res., 1130 W. Thomas St., 46601. Tel: 219-234-0295.
Catechesis/Religious Programs—Students 20.

5—St. Casimir (1899) (Polish), Rev. Thomas F. Lemos, C.S.C. In res., Rev. Robert C. Steigmeyer, C.S.C.
Res., 1308 W. Dunham St., 46619. Tel: 219-287-9551; Fax: 219-287-9551.
Catechesis/Religious Programs—Students 17.

6—Christ the King (1933), Revs. Thomas J. Jones, C.S.C.; Terrence P. Ehrman, C.S.C.; Deacon Steve Kempinger, C.S.C.
Res., 52473 Indiana State Rte. 933, 46637. Tel: 219-272-3113; Fax: 219-273-6702.
School—Tel: 219-272-3922. Laura Hager, Assoc. Prin.
Lay Teachers 25; Students 500.
Catechesis/Religious Programs—Students 125.

7—Corpus Christi (1961), Rev. Camillo Tirabassi. In res., Rev. Walter J. Bly.
Res., 2822 Corpus Christi Dr., 46628. Tel: 219-272-9982; Fax: 219-272-2545.
School—2817 Corpus Christi Dr., 46628. Tel: 219-272-9868; Fax: 219-272-9894. Mrs. Marilyn Gibbs, Prin.
Daughters of Divine Charity 1; Lay Teachers 26; Students 561.
Catechesis/Religious Programs—Students 25.

8—St. Hedwig (1877) (Polish), Rev. Leonard F. Chrobot.
Res., 331 S. Scott St., 46601. Tel: 219-287-8932; Fax: 219-232-9787.

9—Holy Cross (1929), Revs. Michael Belinski, C.S.C.; Stephen J. Sedlock, C.S.C.; Jacob Freel Landry, Pastoral Assoc. In res., Rev. James G. Karaffa, C.S.C.
Res., 1520 Vassar Ave., 46628. Tel: 219-233-2179; Fax: 219-237-6736.
School—(Grades PreK-8) 1020 Wilber St., 46628. Tel: 219-234-3422; Fax: 219-237-6725. Mrs. Angela Budzinski, Prin.
Lay Teachers 26; Students 387.
Catechesis/Religious Programs—920 Wilber St., 46628. Tel: 219-233-2954. Gloria Kucela, D.R.E.
Students 58.

10—Holy Family (1945), Revs. Bernard J. Galic; Robert McGuire (Ireland); Deacon Eugene Szynski, Pastoral Assoc.
Res., 56405 Mayflower Rd., 46619. Tel: 219-282-2317; Fax: 219-282-2318. [JC]
School—Tel: 219-289-7375; Fax: 219-289-7386. Sr. Joan Marie Shillinger, C.S.S.F., Prin.
Felician Sisters of Livonia, MI 2; Lay Teachers 18; Students 437.
Catechesis/Religious Programs—Tel: 219-289-7375. Ann Schramm, D.R.E.
Students 183.

11—St. John the Baptist (1956), Rev. Terry E. Place.
Res., 3526 St. John Way, 46628. Tel: 219-233-5414.
School—3616 St. John Way, 46628. Tel: 219-232-9849. Sr. Connie Bach, Prin.
Lay Teachers 10; Students 204.
Catechesis/Religious Programs—Students 60.

12—St. Joseph (1853), Revs. Anthony V. Szakaly, C.S.C.; Michael C. Mathews, C.S.C.; Regina Wilson, M.Div., Pastoral Assoc. In res., Bro. Steve Nani, C.S.C.
Res., 226 N. Hill St., 46617. Tel: 219-234-3135.
Parish Office: 211 N. St. Louis Blvd., 46617. Tel: 219-234-3134; Fax: 219-234-2822.
School—216 N. Hill St., 46617. Tel: 219-234-0451; Fax: 219-234-0524. Mrs. Suzanne Wiwi, Prin.
Lay Teachers 25; Students 405.
Catechesis/Religious Programs—Students 55.

13—St. Jude (1948), Rev. James F. Stoyle.
Res., 19704 Johnson Rd., 46614. Tel: 219-291-0570; Fax: 219-299-3051.
School—19657 Hildebrand St., 46614. Tel: 219-291-3820. Ms. Judi Cole, Prin.
Lay Teachers 10; Students 256.
Catechesis/Religious Programs—Tel: 219-291-2797; Fax: 219-299-3051.
Students 106.

14—St. Mary of the Assumption (1882) (German), Rev. Paul McCarthy.
Res., 3501 S. Locust Rd., 46614. Tel: 219-287-0225; Fax: 219-287-8781.
School—3402 S. Locust Rd., 46614. Tel: 219-287-1472; Fax: 219-287-9883.
Lay Teachers 10; Students 150.
Catechesis/Religious Programs—Students 10.

15—Our Lady of Hungary (1921), Revs. Thaddeus Kwak; Peter Kaija (Uganda); Deacon Ervin Kuspa.
Res., 829 W. Calvert St., 46613. Tel: 219-287-1700; Fax: 219-289-6704. [CEM]
School—735 W. Calvert St., 46613. Tel: 219-289-3272; Fax: 219-289-3272. Mr. Clem Wroblewski, Prin.
Lay Teachers 9; Students 165.
Catechesis/Religious Programs—Students 10.

16—St. Patrick (1858), Rev. Charles J. Lavely, C.S.C. In res., Revs. Richard A. Laurick, C.S.C.; Donald J. Bielby, C.S.C. (Canada).
Res., 309 S. Taylor St., 46625. Tel: 219-232-5839; Fax: 219-232-5830. [JC]
Catechesis/Religious Programs—Tel: 219-289-3700.
Students 85.

17—Faith & Hope & Charity Chapel (1975), Revs. James F. Blaes, C.S.C.; Raymond F. Cour, C.S.C.; William A. Botzum, C.S.C.
Res., 114 W. Wayne St., P.O. Box 143, 46624. Tel: 219-289-4263.

18—St. Stanislaus (1899) (Polish), Revs. David J. Porterfield, C.S.C.; Ronald R. Tripi, C.S.C.; Daniel C. Coughlin, C.S.C.; Sr. Linda Bellemore, C.S.C., Pastoral Assoc.
Res., 415 N. Brookfield St., 46628. Tel: 219-233-1217; Fax: 219-233-1940.

19—St. Stephen (1909) (Hispanic-Hungarian), Rev. Thomas F. Lemos, C.S.C. In res., Rev. Robert C. Steigmeyer, C.S.C.
Res., 1102 W. Thomas St., 46601. Tel: 219-287-7681; Fax: 219-287-7695.
Catechesis/Religious Programs—Tel: 219-287-7681. Lourdes Silva, D.R.E., Pastoral Min.
Students 330.

20—St. Therese, Little Flower (1937), Revs. Donald F. Guertin, C.S.C.; James A. Bracke, C.S.C.
54191 N. Ironwood Dr., 46637. Tel: 219-272-7070; Fax: 219-243-3434.
Res., 18160 Bailey, 46637. Tel: 219-243-5421.
Catechesis/Religious Programs—Tel: 219-272-7070.
Students 270.

OUTSIDE THE CITIES OF FORT WAYNE AND SOUTH BEND

Albion, Noble Co., Blessed Sacrament (1875), Rev. Dale Bauman; Deacon Ramiro Reyes.
Res., 300 Ravine Park Dr., Ligonier, 46767-1301. Tel: 219-894-4946. [JC]
Church—State Rd. 9 S., Box 102, 46701-0102. Tel: 219-636-2072.
Catechesis/Religious Programs—Students 91.

Angola, Steuben Co., St. Anthony (1926), Rev. Fred Pasche, O.F.M.Conv. In res., Revs. Conrad L. Schweibold, O.F.M.Conv.; Philip Schneider, O.F.M.Conv.
Res., 700 W. Maumee St., 46703. Tel: 219-665-2259; Fax: 219-665-2268.
Catechesis/Religious Programs—Cathy Bryan, D.R.E.
Students 314.
Mission—Clear Lake, Steuben Co., St. Paul Chapel, 46703.

Arcola, Allen Co., St. Patrick (1846), Rev. Matthew Kafka.
Res., 12305 Arcola Rd., Fort Wayne, 46818. Tel: 219-625-4151. [CEM]
Catechesis/Religious Programs—Students 92.

Auburn, De Kalb Co., Immaculate Conception (1872), Rev. Charles A. Herman.
Res., 500 E. 7th St., 46706. Tel: 219-925-3930; Fax: 219-925-3186. [CEM]
Catechesis/Religious Programs—Tel: 219-925-1621. D.R.E.: Phyllis Gurtner; Karen Wrona.
Students 242.

Avilla, Noble Co., St. Mary of the Assumption (1853), Rev. Daniel Durkin.
Res., 228 N. Main St., Box 700, 46710-0700. Tel: 219-897-3261; Fax: 219-897-3261. [CEM]
School—232 N. Main St., 46710. Tel: 219-897-3481; Fax: 219-897-3706. Mrs. Kathy Garlitz, Prin.
Franciscan Sisters of the Sacred Heart 2; Lay Teachers 6; Students 180.
Catechesis/Religious Programs—Students 109.

Besancon, Allen Co., St. Louis (1846) (French), Rev. Stephen E. Colchin.
Res., 15535 Lincoln Hwy. E., New Haven, 46774. Tel: 219-749-4525. [CEM 2]
School—(Grades PreK-7) 15529 Lincoln Hwy. E., New Haven, 46774. Tel: 219-749-5815. Ms. Agnes Hart, Prin.
Lay Teachers 6; Students 80.
Catechesis/Religious Programs—15412 Dawkins Rd., New Haven, 46774. Tel: 219-749-9396. Mrs. Elizabeth A. Lomont, D.R.E.
Students 168.

Big Long Lake, LaGrange Co., St. Mary of the Angels (1937), Rev. Conrad L. Schweibold, O.F.M.Conv.
Res., St. Anthony Rectory, 700 W. Maumee, Angola, 46703. Tel: 219-665-2259. [JC]
Church—Hudson, 46747. Tel: 219-351-2404.
Catechesis/Religious Programs—Tel: 219-351-2964.
Students 39.

Bluffton, Wells Co., St. Joseph (1875), Rev. Lawrence A. Kramer.
Res., 1700 N. Main St., 46714. Tel: 219-824-1380; Fax: 219-824-2792. [JC]
Catechesis/Religious Programs—Students 160.

Bremen, Marshall Co., St. Dominic (1947), Rev. Robert J. Dombrowski.
Church—212 N. Maryland St., 46506. Tel: 219-546-3601; Fax: 219-546-3659.
Catechesis/Religious Programs—803 W. Bike St., 46506.
Students 275.

Bristol, Elkhart Co., St. Mary of the Annunciation (1942), Rev. James F. Seculoff.
Res., 411 W. Vistula St., Box 245, 46507. Tel: 219-848-4305; Fax: 219-848-4305.
Catechesis/Religious Programs—Students 401.

Churubusco, Whitley Co., St. John Bosco (1971), Rev. Danny Pinto (Sri Lanka) Admin.
Res., 216 N. Main St., 46723. Tel: 219-693-9578; Fax: 219-693-1608.
Catechesis/Religious Programs—Tel: 219-693-3332.
Students 176.

Clear Lake, Steuben Co., St. Paul Chapel (1941), Rev. Philip Schneider, O.F.M.Conv., Admin.
Res., St. Anthony Rectory, 700 W. Maumee, Angola, 46703. Tel: 219-665-2259; Fax: 219-665-2268.
Church—8780 E. 700 N., 46703. Tel: 219-495-9913.
Catechesis/Religious Programs—Tel: 517-238-2047.
Students 33.

Columbia City, Whitley Co., St. Paul of the Cross (1860), Rev. Sextus Don (Sri Lanka) Admin.
Res., 307 S. Line St., 46725. Tel: 219-244-5723; Fax: 219-244-3797. [CEM][JC]
Catechesis/Religious Programs—Fax: 219-244-2833.
Students 164.

Culver, Marshall Co., St. Mary of the Lake, Rev. Jeffery Largent.
Res., 124 College Ave., 46511. Tel: 219-842-2522.
Catechesis/Religious Programs—Tel: 219-842-3667; Fax: 219-842-2549.
Students 110.

Decatur, Adams Co., St. Mary (1840) (German), Rev. Philip DeVolder; Sr. Margaret Rose Donnelly, S.S.N.D., Pastoral Assoc.
Res., 414 W. Madison St., P.O. Box 207, 46733. Tel: 219-724-9159; Fax: 219-724-8948. [CEM]
School—St. Joseph, 127 N. Fourth St., 46733. Tel: 219-724-2765; Fax: 219-724-4953. Mr. Mark Mugg, Prin.
Lay Teachers 20; Students 377.
Catechesis/Religious Programs—Tel: 219-724-9159; Fax: 219-724-9380. Teresa Schurger, D.R.E.
Students 220.

Ege, Noble Co., Immaculate Conception (1876). Attended by St. John Bosco, Churubusco. Rev. Danny Pinto (Sri Lanka) Admin.
216 N. Main St., Churubusco, 46723. Tel: 219-693-9578; Fax: 219-693-1608. [CEM]
Catechesis/Religious Programs—Students 82.

Elkhart, Elkhart Co., St. Thomas the Apostle (1949), Revs. William Sullivan; Thomas Ryan (Ireland). Pastoral Assocs.: Sr. Marcianne Targonski, C.S.S.F.; Sr. Lorenzo Wolak, C.S.S.F.
Res., 1405 N. Main St., 46514. Tel: 219-262-1505; Fax: 219-264-4186. [JC]
School—1331 N. Main St., 46514. Tel: 219-264-4855; Fax: 219-262-8477.
Felician Sisters 2; Lay Teachers 25; Students 400.
Catechesis/Religious Programs—Tel: 219-264-0491.
Students 200.

St. Vincent de Paul (1868), Rev. John Overmyer.
Res., 1108 S. Main St., 46516. Tel: 219-293-8231; Fax: 219-293-1105. [CEM]
School—(Grades PreK-6) 1114 S. Main St., 46516. Tel: 219-293-8451; Fax: 219-293-1105. Mrs. Donna Quinn, Prin.
Lay Teachers 8; Students 176.
Catechesis/Religious Programs—Tel: 219-293-8071. D.R.E.: Miss Lisa Kloska; Mrs. Nancy DeMarco.
Students 450.

Garrett, De Kalb Co., St. Joseph (1876), Rev. Thomas Lombardi; Deacon Harris Hoeffel.
Office: 300 W. Houston, 46738-1424. Tel: 219-357-3122.
Res., 307 S. Ijams St., 46738. Tel: 219-357-3122. [CEM]
School—(Grades K-6) 301 W. Houston, 46738. Tel: 219-357-5137; Fax: 219-357-5138. Ms. Linda Speer, Prin.
Lay Teachers 7; Students 140.

Geneva, Adams Co., St. Mary of the Presentation (1883), Rev. Edward Narcowich.
Res., 5790 E. 1100 S., 46740-9132. Tel: 219-997-6558; Fax: 219-997-6558. [CEM]
Catechesis/Religious Programs—Students 33.

Goshen, Elkhart Co., St. John the Evangelist (1840), Rev. John H. Delaney; Deacons N. Arthur Bleau; Ricardo Medina, III.
Res., 109 W. Monroe St., 46526. Tel: 219-533-3385; Fax: 219-533-1814. [CEM]
School—117 W. Monroe, 46526. Tel: 219-533-9480. Michael A. Ronzone, Prin.
Sisters 1; Lay Teachers 5; Students 120.
Catechesis/Religious Programs—Marsha Myer, D.R.E.
Students 90.

Granger, St. Joseph Co., St. Pius X (1955), Revs. Peter A. Jarret, C.S.C.; William J. Neidhart, C.S.C.; Deacon William G. Gray.
Res., 52553 Fir Rd., 46530. Tel: 219-272-8462; Fax: 219-272-8493.
Catechesis/Religious Programs—Tel: 219-277-5760; Fax: 219-272-8493.
Students 1,041.

Huntington, Huntington Co., St. Mary (1896), Rev. Gary L. Sigler.
Office: 903 N. Jefferson St., 46750. Tel: 219-356-4398; Fax: 219-356-3529.
Res., 939 N. Jefferson St., 46750. Tel: 219-356-7497. [JC]
School—Huntington Catholic School. (Consolidated with SS. Peter and Paul) Primary Building, 820 Cherry St., 46750. Tel: 219-356-2320.
Lay Teachers 10; Students 220.
Middle Building: 960 Warren St., 46750. Tel: 219-356-1926; Fax: 219-356-8419. Mr. Jason Schiffli, Prin.
Catechesis/Religious Programs—Students 147.

SS. Peter and Paul (1843), Rev. Ronald Rieder, O.F.M.Cap.
Res., 860 Cherry St., 46750. Tel: 219-356-4798; Fax: 219-356-7154. [JC]
School—Huntington Catholic School. (See St. Mary for details). Tel: 219-356-2320; Fax: 219-359-8419.
Catechesis/Religious Programs—Sr. Miriam Gill, S.S.N.D., D.R.E.
Students 222.

Kendallville, Noble Co., Immaculate Conception (1867), Rev. Jacob M. Gall.
Res., 319 E. Diamond St., 46755. Tel: 219-347-2522; Fax: 219-347-9829.
Catechesis/Religious Programs—Tel: 219-347-2635.
Students 87.

LaGrange, LaGrange Co., St. Joseph (1930), Rev. Paul Faroh, O.F.M.Conv.
Res., 050 N. 100 E., 46761. Tel: 219-463-3472. [JC]
Catechesis/Religious Programs—Students 98.

Lagro, Wabash Co., St. Patrick (1838). Closed. For inquiries for parish records contact the Chancery.

Lakeville, St. Joseph Co., Sacred Heart (1932), Rev. Thomas King, C.S.C.
Res., 63568 U.S. 31 S., South Bend, 46614-9409. Tel: 219-291-2826; Fax: 219-291-3775. [JC]
Catechesis/Religious Programs—Tel: 219-784-2579.
Students 73.

Ligonier, Noble Co., St. Patrick (1860), Rev. Dale Bauman; Deacon Ramiro Reyes.
Res., 300 Ravine Park Dr., 46767-1301. Tel: 219-894-4946. [JC]
Catechesis/Religious Programs—Students 280.

Milford, Kosciusko Co., Our Lady of Guadalupe (1972) (Hispanic), Rev. Paul Bueter.
Res. & Church: P.O. Box 605, 46542. Tel: 219-658-9384.
Catechesis/Religious Programs—Students 45.

Mishawaka, St. Joseph Co.,

1—St. Bavo, (1903), Rev. Barry C. England; Gus Zuehlke, Pastoral Assoc.; Deacon Kevin M. Ranaghan.
Res., 511 W. 7th St., 46544. Tel: 219-255-1437; Fax: 219-255-0404.
School—513 W. 7th St., 46544. Tel: 219-259-4214. Mr. Jerry Kleinert, Prin.
Lay Teachers 13; Students 270.
Catechesis/Religious Programs—Students 115.

2—St. Joseph, (1848), Rev. Robert A. Yast; Deacon Ronald Moser.
Res., 225 S. Mill St., 46544. Tel: 219-255-6134; Fax: 219-255-6387. [CEM]
School—220 W. 4th St., 46544. Tel: 219-255-5554; Fax: 219-255-6381. Mrs. Mary Geist, Prin.
Lay Teachers 13; Students 227.
Catechesis/Religious Programs—Students 85.

3—St. Monica, (1915), Rev. Derrick Sneyd.
Res., 222 W. Mishawaka Ave., 46545. Tel: 219-255-2247; Fax: 219-255-8375.
Ministries Bldg.: 214 W. Mishawaka Ave., 46545. Tel: 219-255-1957.
School—223 W. Grove St., 46545. Tel: 219-255-0709; Fax: 219-258-5969. Sr. Pat Gavin, S.S.N.D., Prin.
Sisters 1; Lay Teachers 16; Students 233.
Catechesis/Religious Programs—Jane Cors Smith, D.R.E.
Students 110.

4—Queen of Peace, (1957), Revs. Elden J. Miller; Michael Okoye (Nigeria); Carol Cone, Pastoral Assoc.
Res., 4508 Vistula Rd., 46544. Tel: 219-255-9674; Fax: 219-255-9675.
Catechesis/Religious Programs—Tel: 219-255-0392.
Students 32.

5—St. Michael Ukrainian Catholic Church, (1916) (Ukrainian), Rev. Thomas R. Dobrowolski.
Res., 712 E. Lawrence St., 46545-6835. Tel: 219-259-7173. [JC]

Monroeville, Allen Co., St. Rose of Lima (1888), Rev. Babasino Fernandes (India) Admin.
Res., P.O. Box 406, 46773. Tel: 219-623-6437; Fax: 219-623-2370. [CEM]
School—St. Joseph, 209 Mulberry St., 46773. Tel: 219-623-3447; Fax: 219-623-3447. Ms. Carolyn Kirkendall, Prin.
Lay Teachers 5; Students 92.
Catechesis/Religious Programs—Tel: 219-749-2841.
Students 30.

Napanee, Elkhart Co., St. Isidore. Closed. For inquiries for parish records contact the Chancery.

New Carlisle, St. Joseph Co., St. Stanislaus Kostka (1884) (Polish), Rev. Lourdino Fernandes (India) Admin.

Res., 55756 Tulip Rd., 46552. Tel: 219-654-3781; Fax: 219-654-3781.
Catechesis/Religious Programs—Tel: 219-654-8738. Lorrie Applegate, D.R.E.
Students 102.

New Haven, Allen Co., St. John the Baptist (1859), Revs. Richard Hire; Damien Anuka (Nigeria).
Res., 943 Powers St., 46774. Tel: 219-493-4553; Fax: 219-749-6164. [CEM]
School—206 Rufus St., 46774. Tel: 219-749-9903; Fax: 219-749-6047. Robert Sordelet, Prin.
Lay Teachers 15; Students 397.
Catechesis/Religious Programs—Tel: 219-493-3044.
Students 250.

Nix Settlement, Whitley Co., St. Catharine (1850), Rev. Kenneth J. Sarrazine.
Res., St. Joseph Rectory, 641 N. Main St., P.O. Box 250, Roanoke, 46783-0250. Tel: 219-672-2838; Fax: 219-672-3069.
Church—Ind. Hwy. 9 & Whitley Co. Rd., 1,000 S., 46783. Tel: 219-672-2838. [CEM]
Catechesis/Religious Programs—Dr. Kathleen Schneider, D.R.E.
Students 35.

North Manchester, Wabash Co., St. Robert Bellarmine (1963), Rev. Ronald Ramenaden.
Res., 1203 State Rd., 114 E., 46962. Tel: 219-982-4404. [JC]
Catechesis/Religious Programs—Students 56.

Notre Dame, St. Joseph Co., Sacred Heart (1842), Rev. John Patrick Riley, C.S.C. In res., Rev. James B. Gillis, C.S.C.
Res., 104 The Presbytery, 46556-5658. Tel: 219-631-7511; 7512; Fax: 219-631-9687. [CEM][JC]
Catechesis/Religious Programs—Tel: 219-631-9436; Fax: 219-631-8080.
Students 30.

Pierceton, Kosciusko Co., St. Francis Xavier (1841), Rev. Bruce Piechocki.
Mailing Address: P.O. Box 376, 46562. Tel: 219-594-5750; Fax: 219-594-2347.
Church—408 W. Catholic St., 46562. [CEM]
Catechesis/Religious Programs—Students 73.

Plymouth, Marshall Co., St. Michael (1862), Revs. Anthony Gillespie (Ireland) Admin.; Expedito Muwonge (Uganda); Deacon Victor Carrillo.
Res., 612 N. Walnut St., 46563. Tel: 219-936-4935; Fax: 219-936-9293. [CEM]
School—(PreK-6) 612 N. Center St., 46563. Tel: 219-936-4329; Fax: 219-936-1151. Miss Gertrude Nawara, Prin.
Lay Teachers 12; Students 194.
Catechesis/Religious Programs—Sr. Rose Andre Miller, D.R.E.
Students 177.

Roanoke, Huntington Co., St. Joseph (1867), Rev. Kenneth J. Sarrazine.
Res., 641 N. Main St., P.O. Box 250, 46783-0250. Tel: 219-672-2838; Fax: 219-672-3069. [CEM]
Catechesis/Religious Programs—Dr. Kathleen Schneider, D.R.E.
Students 55.

Rome City, Noble Co., St. Gaspar del Bufalo (1957), Rev. Charles F. Mullen, C.PP.S.
Res., 10871 N. State Rd. 9, 46784. Tel: 219-854-3100. [CEM]
Catechesis/Religious Programs—Tel: 219-854-2106.
Students 80.

Syracuse, Kosciusko Co., St. Martin de Porres (1966), Rev. Edward Erpelding.
Res., 6941 E. Waco Dr., 46567-9496. Tel: 219-457-3528; Fax: 219-457-3542.
Catechesis/Religious Programs—Tel: 219-457-8176.
Students 140.

Wabash, Wabash Co., St. Bernard (1864), Rev. Timothy A. Wrozek; Deacon Ted Krizman.
Res., 207 N. Cass St., 46992. Tel: 219-563-4750; Fax: 219-563-0313.
School—(PreK-6) 191 N. Cass St., 46992. Tel: 219-563-5746; Fax: 219-563-4898. Mr. Richard A. Musi, Prin.
Lay Teachers 8; Students 91.
Catechesis/Religious Programs—Tel: 219-563-4495.
Students 156.

Walkerton, St. Joseph Co., St. Patrick (1856), Rev. Michael J. Winkowski, C.PP.S.
Res., 801 Tyler St., 46574. Tel: 219-586-7404.
School—811 Tyler St., 46574. Tel: 219-586-7405. Mrs. Judith Miller, Prin.
Sisters of St. Joseph of the Third Order of St. Francis 1; Lay Teachers 4; Students 59.
Catechesis/Religious Programs—Tel: 219-586-3590.
Students 63.

Warsaw, Kosciusko Co., Sacred Heart (1852), Rev. Msgr. James J. Wolf; Mary Jo Gremling, Pastoral Min.
Res., 125 N. Harrison St., 46580. Tel: 219-267-5842; Fax: 219-268-1030. [JC]
School—135 N. Harrison, 46590. Tel: 219-267-5874; Fax: 219-267-5136. Miss Judy Mugg, Prin.
Lay Teachers 13; Students 210.
Catechesis/Religious Programs—Fax: 219-268-1030.
Students 326.

Waterloo, DeKalb Co., St. Michael the Archangel (1880), Rev. David Carkenord.
Res., 1098 County Road 39, 46793-9779. Tel: 219-837-7115; Fax: 219-837-7727. [CEM]
Catechesis/Religious Programs—Students 182.

Yoder, Allen Co., St. Aloysius (1859), Rev. William G. Hodde.
Res., 14623 Bluffton Rd., 46798-9741. Tel: 219-622-4491. [CEM]
School—14607 Bluffton Rd., 46798-9741. Tel: 219-622-7151. Mary Czech, Prin.
Lay Teachers 7; Students 123.
Catechesis/Religious Programs—Students 78.

Chaplains of Public Institutions

FORT WAYNE. *Lutheran Hospital*. Rev. Eugene Eburuche (Nigeria); Roseann Bloomfield Tel: 219-435-7001.
Parkview Memorial Hospital Tel: 219-484-6636, Ext. 26311. Rev. Robert D'Souza (India) Chap.
St. Joseph Medical Center 700 Broadway, 46802-1402. Tel: 219-425-3000. Rev. Daniel Chukwuleta, Chap.
Veterans Administration Hospital. Rev. Daniel Leeuw, Chap.

On Duty Outside the Diocese:
Reverend Fathers—
Kruger, Brent Allan, C.S.C., Andre House, Phoeniz, AZ
Martelli, Jose M., C.S.C., California
Wilbright, Stephen Sullivan, C.S.C., St. John Vianney, Goodyear, AZ

On Special Assignment:
Reverend Fathers—
McNulty, Patrick J., Madonna House, Combermere, Ontario K0J 1L0
Piechocki, Bruce, Officialis of Diocese, Chancery

Retired:
Reverend Monsignors—
Contant, Robert, St. Charles Seminary, Carthagena, OH 45822. Tel: 419-925-4516, Ext. 304
Faber, William, (Summer) 728 S. Main, Kendallville, IN 46755. Tel: 219-347-5041(summer); 813-791-0856 (winter)
Hession, Edward I., 4827 Woodmark Ct., Fort Wayne, IN 46815. Tel: 219-483-2567
Lester, J. William, P.A., Cathedral of the Immaculate Conception, 1122 S. Clinton St., P.O. Box 10898, Fort Wayne, ID 46854-0898. Tel: 219-424-1485
Reverend Fathers—
Bell, Milford C., Vindobona Nursing Home, P.O. Box 318, Braddock Heights, MD 21714-0318. Tel: 301-371-7160
Cardinali, Fred, 4520 S. Hanna St., Fort Wayne, IN 46806. Tel: 219-456-6889
Cis, James, Albertine Home, 1501 Hoffman St., Hammond, IN 46327. Tel: 219-933-4378
Doriot, Thomas E., 2637 Fulton Ave., #232, Sacramento, CA 95821. Tel: 916-484-6145
Gillig, John, 612 N. Second St., Decatur, IN 46733. Tel: 219-724-3545
Hammond, Robert, St. Anne Home, 1900 Randallia Dr., Fort Wayne, IN 46805. Tel: 219-482-7954
Hoevel, Robert J., 1104 New England Dr., Fort Wayne, IN 46815. Tel: 219-749-8245
Jacobs, Joseph A., 2722 Rock Maple Ct., South Bend, IN 46628. Tel: 219-271-1288
Kazmekcziak, Eugene, 1407 Vans Rd., Fulton, IL 61252. Tel: 309-887-9506
Krason, Edward J., 3602 S. Ironwood Dr. Apt. 314-W, South Bend, ID 46614. Tel: 219-231-1292
Miller, Paul D., 1023 Daly Dr., New Haven, IN 46774
Molnar, Anthony, Healthwin, 20531 Darden Rd., South Bend, IN 46637
O'Connor, James J., 6006 Chapel Pines Run, Fort Wayne, IN 46804. Tel: 219-436-1703
Peil, William, 1841 N. Anthony, Fort Wayne, IN 46805. Tel: 219-422-1950
Rose, James, 2781 Huycks, Coldwater, MI 49036
Ruetz, Edward J., 621 Portage, South Bend, IN 46616. Tel: 219-234-5652
Schmitt, Adam, St. Joseph Church, 190 Hale Ave., Fort Wayne, IN 46802. Tel: 219-432-5113
Sienkiewicz, Matthew, 1080 Three Oaks Rd., Three Oaks, MI 49128. Tel: 616-756-6316
Traub, Robert, Saint Anne Home, 1900 Randallia Dr., Fort Wayne, IN 46805
Urbine, Richard, 533 S. Main St., Bourbon, IN 46504. Tel: 219-342-8012

Permanent Deacons:
Baumgartner, Paul E., 417 Howard St., South Bend, IN 46617
Bleau, N. Arthur, 64429 Pleasant Pl., Goshen, IN 46526
Carrillo, Victor, 803 W. Bike St., Bremen, IN 46506
Dits, Paul, 17433 Battles Rd., Mishawaka, IN 46544
Donias, Justo, Jr., 1829 Third St., Fort Wayne, IN 46808
Egendoerfer, Eugene, 1302 Cantondale Ln., Mishawaka, IN 46544
Folds, Milton, 3286 West, #50, Columbia City, IN 46725
Gizzi, Emilio, 238 Eckman, South Bend, IN 46614
Gray, William G., 905 Handlebar, Mishawaka, IN 46544
Hilger, Edward, 30865 Hunters Dr., Apt. 2, Farmington Hills, MI 48334
Hoeffel, Harris H., 401 S. Harrison, Garrett, IN 46738
Krizman, Ted, Box 134 W. Sinclair, Wabash, IN 46992
Kuspa, Ervin, 434 S. Liberty, South Bend, IN 46619
Larson, Fred J., 1001 Bell, New Haven, IN 46774
Lenzo, Carl, 15632 Windingbrook Dr., Mishawaka, IN 46545
Loving, Peter, 3730 Stillwater Pl., Fort Wayne, IN 46808
Lyczak, Edward, 4645 Mariner Blvd., Spring Hill, FL 34609-1944
McDougall, Louis, 3419 Sanibel Dr., Fort Wayne, IN 46815
Moser, Ronald J., 51812 Whitestable, South Bend, IN 46637
Ranaghan, Kevin, 1003 St. Vincent, South Bend, IN 46617
Reyes, Ramiro, 300 Ravine Park Dr., Ligonier, IN 46767-1301
Salinas, Rogelio, 30492 Co. Rd. 38, Wakarusa, IN 46573
Sanborn, Phillip J., R.R. 2, 814 Apple Hill, Angola, IN 46703
Walsh, Francis, 814 Apple Hill, P.O. Box 283, Angola, IN 46703
Walsh, James M., 2212 Broadmoor Dr., Elkhart, IN 46514
Zickgraf, Joseph R., 289 N. Columbia Pkwy, Columbus City, IN 46725

INSTITUTIONS LOCATED IN THE DIOCESE

[A] SEMINARIES, RELIGIOUS, OR SCHOLASTICATES

NOTRE DAME. *Moreau Seminary*, P.O. Box 668, 46556. Tel: 219-631-7735; Fax: 219-631-9233. This is a college level and Theological Seminary run by the Indiana Province of the Congregation of Holy Cross for Religious Priesthood and Brotherhood candidates.
Formation Staff: Revs. Wilson D. Miscamble, C.S.C., Supr. & Rector; Patrick M. Neary, C.S.C., Asst. Supr.; Charles B. Gordon, C.S.C.; Peter D. Rocca, C.S.C.; James Flanigan, C.S.C.; James K. Foster, C.S.C.; Bro. Edward C. Luther, C.S.C; Sr. Jean Lenz, O.S.F.; Sr. Susan Bruno, O.S.F.; Mrs. Nancy Cavadini. In res. Bros. James E. Gormley, C.S.C.; James Lakofka, C.S.C.; John Platte, C.S.C.; Chester Ziemba, C.S.C.; Robert Ewald, C.S.C.; Richard Kyle, C.S.C.; Thomas Dziekan, C.S.C.; Revs. James R. Trepanier, C.S.C.; James T. Rahilly, C.S.C.; Charles B. Gordon, C.S.C.; Mark B. Thesing, C.S.C.; Paul V. Kollman, C.S.C.; David B. Burrell, C.S.C.; James T. Rahilly, C.S.C.; Charles W. Kohlerman, C.S.C.; Alfred F. D'Alonzo, C.S.C.; Wilson D. Miscamble, C.S.C.; Patrick Neary, C.S.C.; Martin Lan Nguyen, C.S.C.; Peter D. Rocca, C.S.C.
Vocations Office: Revs. James B. King, C.S.C., Dir.; William A. Wack, C.S.C., Asst. Dir., Mailing Address: Moreau Seminary, Box 541, 46556. Priests 13; Seminarians 29; Total Staff 10.

Old College.
E-mail: Charles.B.Gordon.20@nd.edu
Web site: www.nd.edu/
7Evocation/OldCollege.html
Mailing Address: Box 638, 46556-0638. Tel: 219-631-7881; Fax: 219-631-1011. College candidates study here for up to three years before entering Moreau Seminary. Rev. Charles B. Gordon, C.S.C., Dir. & Contact Person. Priests 1; Brothers 1; Lay Teachers 2; Candidates for the Priesthood in the First Three Years of Undergraduate Formation 19.

[B] COLLEGES AND UNIVERSITIES

FORT WAYNE. *University of Saint Francis*, 2701 Spring St., 46808-3994. Tel: 219-434-3100; Fax: 219-434-3183.
E-mail: ekriss@sf.edu
Web site: www.sf.edu
For a complete listing, refer to the Colleges and Universities section.

DONALDSON. *Ancilla Domini College*. Tel: 219-936-8898; Fax: 219-935-1773.
Web site: www.ancilla.edu
Mailing Address: P.O. Box 1, 46513.
For a complete listing, refer to the Colleges and Universities section.

NOTRE DAME. *Holy Cross College, Holy Cross College, Inc.*, 54515 State Rd., 933 N., 46556-0308. Tel: 219-239-8400; Fax: 219-233-7427.
E-mail: rgilman@hcc-nd.edu
Web site: www.hcc-nd.edu
For a complete listing, refer to the Colleges and Universities section.

Saint Mary's College, 46556. Tel: 219-284-4556; Fax: 219-284-4707.
E-mail: 1hitch@saintmarys.edu
Web site: www.saintmarys.edu
For a complete listing, refer to the Colleges and Universities section.

University of Notre Dame Du Lac, (1842) Provost Office, 300 Main Bldg., 46556. Tel: 219-631-5000; 631-5090 (Provost); Fax: 219-631-6897.
E-mail: hubbard.4@nd.edu
Web site: www.nd.edu
For a complete listing, refer to the Colleges and Universities section.

[C] HIGH SCHOOLS, DIOCESAN

FORT WAYNE. *Bishop Dwenger High School*, 1300 E. Washington Center Rd., 46825. Tel: 219-496-4700; Fax: 219-496-4702.
E-mail: bdhs@bishopdwenger.com
Web site: www.bishopdwenger.com
Mr. J. Fred Tone, Prin.; Mr. Dan Swygart, Asst. Prin. Priests 1; Lay Teachers 57; Students 954; Total Staff 91.

Bishop Luers High School, 333 E. Paulding Rd., 46816. Tel: 219-456-1261; Fax: 219-456-1262. Mary Keefer, Prin.; Jo Ann Roscoe, Asst. Prin. Chaplains: Revs. Lawrence A. Kramer; Dominique Carboneau; Thomas Shoemaker. Priests 1; Lay Teachers 40; Students 582.

SOUTH BEND. *Saint Joseph's High School*, 1441 N. Michigan St., 46617. Tel: 219-233-6137; Fax: 219-232-3482.
E-mail: sbdstjoehs@impresso.com
Mr. Michael F. Cassidy, Prin.; Mrs. Kathleen Ratliff, Vice Prin. Academics; Mr. Jim Fitzpatrick, Vice Prin. Operations; Revs. Walter J. Bly; Michael Heintz. Priests 2; Brothers of Holy Cross 2; Sisters of the Holy Cross 2; Lay Teachers 58; Students 746.

MISHAWAKA. *Marian High School*, 1311 S. Logan St., 46544. Tel: 219-259-5257.
E-mail: cmoretti@marianhs.org
Mr. Joseph Brettnacher, Prin.; Carol Miller, Pastoral Min. Priests 1; Sisters 3; Lay Teachers 50; Students 727.

[D] DIOCESAN ELEMENTARY SCHOOLS

FORT WAYNE. *Monsignor Julian Benoit Academy*, 3029 E. Paulding Rd., 46816. Tel: 219-447-5121; Fax: 219-447-4606.
E-mail: benoit@fwi.com
Ms. Jeanette Donovan, Prin. (Consolidation of Sacred Heart, St. Patrick's & St. Henry's Schools.). Sisters 1; Lay Teachers 11; Students 230.

[E] CONSOLIDATED SCHOOL DAY CARE CENTER RESIDENTIAL TREATMENT CENTER

FORT WAYNE. *Catholic Charities Children's Services*, 2820 Reed St., 46806. Tel: 219-745-4929; Fax: 219-456-6100. Theresa Harvey, Dir. Lay Teachers 13; Aides 7; Enrollment 120.

The Children's Cottage, 2820 Reed St., 46806. Tel: 219-745-4929; Fax: 219-456-6100. Licensed day care facility with a capacity for 82 children, ages 2 to 12. Serves families of all faiths. Lay Teachers 13; Aides 7.

[F] GENERAL HOSPITALS

SOUTH BEND. *Our Lady of Peace Hospital, Inc.*, 801 E. LaSalle Ave., 46617. Tel: 219-237-7457.
E-mail: voordec@sjrmc.com
For a complete listing, refer to the Hospitals section.

Saint Joseph's Regional Medical Center, 801 E. LaSalle St., 46617. Tel: 219-237-7111; Fax: 219-271-7077.
E-mail: breedenm@sjrmc.com
Web site: www.sjmed.com
For a complete listing, refer to the Hospitals section.

St. Mary's Medical Plaza, 2515 E. Jefferson Blvd., 46615. Tel: 219-288-8311; Fax: 219-257-2831.
E-mail: khobgood@skynet.net
Web site: http://www.ancillahealthcare.org
For a complete listing, refer to the Hospitals section.

MISHAWAKA. *St. Joseph Community Hospital*, 215 W. 4th St., 46544. Tel: 219-259-2431; Fax: 219-257-2831.
E-mail: khabgood@skynet.net
Web site: http://www.ancillahealthcare.org
For a complete listing, refer to the Hospitals section.

PLYMOUTH. *Saint Joseph's Regional Medical Center - Plymouth Campus*, 1915 Lake Ave., P.O. Box 670, 46563. Tel: 219-936-3181; Fax: 219-935-2235
For a complete listing, refer to the Hospitals section.

[G] SPECIAL HOSPITALS

NOTRE DAME. *University Health Services*, 46556. Tel: 219-239-8013; Fax: 219-631-6047.
E-mail: Ann.E.Thompson.49@nd.edu
For a complete listing, refer to the Special Care Facilities section.

[H] HOMES FOR THE AGED

FORT WAYNE. *Saint Anne Home & Retirement Community*, 1900 Randallia Dr., 46805. Tel: 219-484-5555; Fax: 219-482-8929.
E-mail: sah1900@aol.com
Web site: www.saintannehome.com
For a complete listing, refer to the Special Care Facilities section.

St. Anne Home of the Diocese of Fort Wayne - South Bend, Inc., 1900 Randalia Dr., 46805. Tel: 219-484-5555; Fax: 219-482-8929.
E-mail: sah1900@aol.com
Web site: www.stannehome.com
For a complete listing, refer to the Special Care Facilities section.

AVILLA. *Provena LaVerna Terrace*, 517 N. Main St., 46710. Tel: 219-897-2093; Fax: 219-897-2086
For a complete listing, refer to the Special Care Facilities section.

Provena Sacred Heart Home, 515 N. Main St., 46710-9602. Tel: 219-897-2841; Fax: 219-897-3724
For a complete listing, refer to the Special Care Facilities section.

[I] PERSONAL PRELATURES

SOUTH BEND. *Prelature of the Holy Cross and Opus Dei*, Windmoor Center, 1121 N. Notre Dame Ave., 46617. Tel: 219-232-0550; Fax: 219-287-4798.
Web site: www.opusdei.org
Rev. David Cavanagh. Staff 4; Total in Residence 11.

[J] MONASTERIES AND RESIDENCES OF PRIESTS AND BROTHERS

SOUTH BEND. *Congregation of Holy Cross, Indiana Province, Provincial House*, 1304 E. Jefferson Blvd., 46617. Tel: 219-289-6850; Fax: 219-287-7307.
Web site: www.nd.edu/~vocation
Legal Title: *Priests of Holy Cross, Indiana Province, Inc.* Revs. William D. Dorwart, C.S.C., Prov.; Robert L. Epping, C.S.C., First Asst. Prov.; Kenneth M. Molinaro, C.S.C., Second Asst. Prov. Councilors: Revs. E. William Beauchamp, C.S.C.; David L. Guffey, C.S.C.; John A. Herman, C.S.C.; Peter A. Jarret, C.S.C.; Wilson D. Miscamble, C.S.C.; Robert S. Pelton, C.S.C.; David T. Tyson, C.S.C.; Bro. Edward C. Luther, C.S.C.
Holy Cross Priests Serving in Foreign Countries:
Chile:

Congregacion de Santa Cruz, Casilla 1271, Santiago 1, Chile. Tel: 56-2-672-1402; Fax: 56-2-672-1402. Revs. Jorge A. Canepa, C.S.C., District Supr.; Jose E. Ahumanda, C.S.C.; Sergio E. Concha, C.S.C.; Charles A. Delaney, C.S.C.; Fermin J. Donoso, C.S.C.; Joseph A. Dorsey, C.S.C.; Donald G. Fetters, C.S.C.; Erwin A. Fonseca, C.S.C.; Roberto M. Gilbo, C.S.C.; Malcolm D. Johnson, C.S.C.; Gerald T. Papen, C.S.C.; Pedro Parra, C.S.C.; Moises Perez, C.S.C.; Bro. Joaquin R. Parada, C.S.C.; Revs. Jorge Urtubia, C.S.C.; Robert L. Plasker, C.S.C.; Romulo E. Vera, C.S.C.; Gerald J. Whelan, C.S.C.
Peru: Rev. Diego J. Yrrarrazaval, C.S.C.

Instituto de Estudios Aymaras, Apartado 295, Puno, Peru; Fax: 011-51-54-351574. Rev. Philip T. Devlin, C.S.C., Apartado 3872, Lima 100, Peru. Rev. Gerald R. Barmasse, C.S.C., Apartado 317, Chimbote, Peru. Tel: 011-51-44-329509; Fax: 011-51-44-329509.
District of East Africa (Uganada): Holy Cross Bugembe, P.O. Box 1037, Jinja, Uganda. Tel: 011-256-43-120013; Fax: 011-256-43-121322. Revs. George J. Lucas, C.S.C., District Supr.; William G. Blum, C.S.C.; Robert T. Hesse, C.S.C.; James E. Kelly, C.S.C.; H. Thomas McDermott; Russell K. McDougall, C.S.C.; Francis J. Murphy, C.S.C.; Richard L. Potthast, C.S.C.; Richard J. Wunsch, C.S.C.
District of East Africa (Kenya): P.O. Box 50813, Nairobi, Kenya. Tel: 011-254-2-601014; Fax: 011-254-2-601014. Revs. James J. Ferguson, C.S.C.; Stephen P. Newton, C.S.C.; Cornelius J. Ryan, C.S.C.; Richard E. Stout, C.S.C.
Tanzania: St. Brendan, P.O. Box 39, Karatu, Arusha, Tanzania. Rev. Thomas W. Smith, C.S.C.
On Leave for Higher Studies: Rev. James Burasa, C.S.C., Congregazione di Santa Croce, 85 Via Framura, Rome, Italy, 00168. Tel: 011-39-06-627-6920. Rev. Robert A. Dowd, C.S.C.

St. Monica's Parish, 725 California Ave., Santa Monica, CA, 90403. Tel: 310-393-9287. Rev. Mark R. Ghyselinck, C.S.C., St. Augustine Cathedral, 542 W. Michigan Ave., Kalamazoo, MI, 49007. Tel: 616-345-5147; Fax: 616-349-0166. Rev. Paul V. Kollman, C.S.C, Moreau Seminary, Notre Dame, 46556. Tel: 219-631-4146. Rev. James M. Lies, C.S.C., 2115 Summit Ave., Apt. 4151, St. Paul, MN, 55105. Tel: 651-962-8716; Fax: 612-624-8277. Rev. William M. Lies, C.S.C., The Christian Brothers, 4720 Fifth Ave., Pittsburgh, PA, 15213. Tel: 412-208-3538; Fax: 412-208-1915. Rev. Felipe Morel, C.S.C., Corby Hall, P.O. Box 514, Notre Dame, 46556. Tel: 219-631-7870. Rev. Randall C. Renter, C.S.C., Corpus Christi, 529 W. 121st St., New York, NY, 10027. Tel: 212-666-9350. Rev. Mark B. Thesing, C.S.C., Corby Hall, P.O. Box 514, Notre Dame, 46556. Tel: 219-631-7559.
Military Chaplains: Rev. S. Douglas Smith, C.S.C., CHC, USNR Commander, Amphibious Squadron Eleven (N01C), Unit 25507, FPO, AP, 66001-7002. Tel: 011-956-24-1111, Ext. 3577. Rev. Robert E. Roetzel, C.S.C., 711 N. Broadway St., Apt. 512, Leavenwoth, KS, 66040. Tel: 913-651-2447.
Priests of the Province in Residences Not Listed Elsewhere: Rev. Maurice E. Amen, C.S.C., Columba Hall, P.O. Box 47, Notre Dame, 46556. Tel: 219-631-8440. Rev. James T. Burtchaell, C.S.C., Holy Cross Center, 2597 Virginia St., Berkeley, CA, 94709. Tel: 510-548-8515. Rev. Lawrence E. Calhoun, C.S.C., 13645 Riverside Dr., Sherman Oaks, CA, 91423. Tel: 818-386-1931. Rev. LeRoy E. Clementich, C.S.C., Archdiocese of Anchorage, 225 Cordova St., Anchorage, AK, 99501. Tel: 907-297-7734. Rev. Charles W. Corso, C.S.C., Box 3908, Fremont, CA, 94539. Tel: 510-659-9717. Rev. Harry C. Cronin, C.S.C., Holy Cross Center, 2597 Virginia St., Berkeley, CA, 94709. Tel: 510-548-8515; Fax: 510-548-7903. Rev. James J. Denn, C.S.C., Oratoire Saint-Joseph, 3800 chemin Queen Mary, Montreal, OC, H3V 1H6. Tel: 514-733-8211; Fax: 514-733-1461. Rev. Ralph F. Dunn, C.S.C., 655 W. Irving Park Rd., Apt. 3916, Chicago, IL, 60613. Tel: 773-528-1407; Fax: 773-528-1407. Rev. Thomas F. Elliott, C.S.C., St. Vincent's Medical Center, P.O. Box 6016, Bridgeport, CT, 06606. Tel: 203-576-6922. Rev. Bernard P. Foley, C.S.C., Brothers of the Holy Cross, 426 N. San Felipe St., San Antonio, TX, 78228. Tel: 210-434-9100; Fax: 210-433-1666. Rev. John T. Ford, C.S.C., Mailing Address: Catholic University, Cardinal Station, Box 236, Washington, DC, 20064. Rev. William W. Faiella, C.S.C., Emmanuel House, 73-441 Fred Waring Dr., Palm Desert, CA, 92260. Tel: 760-772-1243; Fax: 760-772-1543. Rev. Lawrence J. Henry, C.S.C., Le Mans Academy, P.O. Box 7, Rolling Prarie, 46371. Tel: 219-778-2521; Fax: 219-778-4801. Rev. James W. Irwin, C.S.C., c/o Calle Puebla 844 Norte, Ciudad Obregon, Mexico. Tel: 011-91-641-77721. Rev. Michael W. Glockner, C.S.C., St. Paul's Retirement Community, 3602 S. Ironwood Dr., 46614. Tel: 219-291-8205; Fax: 219-291-0858. Rev. John P. Keefe, C.S.C., Hispanic Ministry, 384 S. Reese St., P.O. Box 428, Battle Mountain, NV, 89820-0428. Tel: 775-635-2576; Fax: 775-635-5729. Rev. Edward C. Krause, C.S.C., Gannon University, Erie, PA, 16541. Tel: 814-871-7702. Rev. Robert J. Lochner, C.S.C., 325 Arthur Ave., Cocoa Beach, FL, 32931. Tel: 407-799-8383; Fax: 407-783-6312. Rev. John W. Lubbers, C.S.C., Brothers of Holy Cross, 426 N. San Felipe St., San Antoinio, TX, 78228. Tel: 210-434-9100. Rev. Jose M. Martelli, C.S.C., Valley Missionary Program, 52-565 Oasis Palms St., Coachella, CA, 92236. Tel: 760-398-9277. Rev. Walter L. McInerney, C.S.C., 51 Joan Rd., Centerville, MA, 02632. Tel: 508-771-1928. Rev. John M. Mulcahy, C.S.C., Morris Camp, Box 550, Ontario, Canada. Tel: 807-929-2341; Fax: 807-929-7181.

Most Rev. Charles A. Schleck, C.S.C., Piazza di Spagna 48, 00187, Rome, Italy. Tel: 011-39-6-679-6941. Rev. Norbert J. Sinski, C.S.C., 319 Ave. C, Apt. 2B, New York, NY, 10009. Tel: 212-673-1101. Rev. John A. Struzzo, C.S.C., Mission Hospital Regional Medical Center, 27700 Medical Center Rd., Mission Viejo, CA, 92691. Tel: 949-364-1400; Fax: 949-388-6069. Rev. John V. VandenBossche, C.S.C., St. Francis High School, 1885 Miramonte Ave., Mountain View, CA, 94040. Tel: 650-967-2530. Rev. David H. Verhalen, C.S.C., The Hermitage, Rte. 3, Box 3575, Palestine, TX, 75801. Tel: 903-549-2467. Rev. James N. Watzke, C.S.C., 400 E. Randolph St., Apt. 3230, Chicago, IL, 60601. Tel: 312-861-0651. Rev. Herbert C. Yost, C.S.C., Solitude of the Savior, 9033 N. County Rd., 600E, Rolling Prairie, 46371. Tel: 219-778-2345. Rev. Francis D. Zagorc, C.S.C., St. Edward High School, 13500 Detroit Ave., Lakewood, OH, 44107-4697. Tel: 216-221-2096. Rev. Richard P. Zang, C.S.C., All Saints Parish, Huttenweg 46, 14195 Berlin, Germany. Tel: 011-49-30-813-2026; Fax: 011-49-30-813-2047.

Holy Cross House, P.O. Box 1048, Notre Dame, 46556. Tel: 219-631-6337; Fax: 219-631-5172. Revs. Andre E. Leveille, C.S.C., Supr.; William P. Melody, C.S.C., Asst. Supr.; Lawrence T. Bauer, C.S.C.; William J. Beston, C.S.C.; Paul E. Beichner, C.S.C.; James F. Blaes, C.S.C.; Leon J. Boarman, C.S.C.; Claude L. Boehm, C.S.C.; William A. Botzum, C.S.C.; Edward A. Buenger, C.S.C.; Jeremiah R. Buttomer, C.S.C.; Joseph H. Fey, C.S.C.; Casimir F. Grabarz, C.S.C.; G. Carl Hager, C.S.C.; Arthur S. Harvey, C.S.C.; Norbert F. Hess, C.S.C.; William F. Hickens, C.S.C.; George G. Kahle, C.S.C.; William F. Keegan, C.S.C.; Anthony J. Lauck, C.S.C.; Jerome R. Lawyer, C.S.C.; Gregory J. Lombardo, C.S.C.; Michael G. O'Brien, C.S.C.; Augustine J. Peverada, C.S.C.; Paul B. Rankin, C.S.C.; Bernard E. Ransing, C.S.C.; Joseph W. Rehage, C.S.C.; Joseph A. Rogusz, C.S.C.; George E. Schidel, C.S.C.; William M. Schreiner, C.S.C.; G. Michael Scully, C.S.C.; Chester A. Soleta, C.S.C.; John H. Wilson, C.S.C.; Bros. Remy Aydt, C.S.C.; Clarence J. Breitenbach, C.S.C.; Thomas J. Combs, C.S.C.; Andrew Corsini Fowler, C.S.C.; Orlando Gozdowski, C.S.C.; Paul H. Loos, C.S.C.; Thomas Mahon, C.S.C.; Beatus Schlenker, C.S.C.

NOTRE DAME. *Congregation of Holy Cross, Midwest Province*, Provincial Admin., 54515 State Rd. 933 North, P.O. Box 460, 46556-0460. Tel: 219-251-2222; Fax: 219-289-0487.
E-mail: dgibbs@hcc-nd.edu
Legal Title: *Brothers of Holy Cross, Inc.* Bros. Donald Gibbs, C.S.C., Prov.; Robert Fillmore, C.S.C., Asst. Prov. & Vicar; William Dygert, C.S.C., Prov. Steward; Jerome Meyer, C.S.C., Prov. Sec. Provincial Councilors: Bros. Kenneth Haders, C.S.C.; Donald Stabrowski, C.S.C.; Chester Freel.

Holy Cross Brothers Center, P.O. Box 716, 46556. Bros. Joseph Fox, C.S.C., Supr.; Rex Hennel, C.S.C., Asst. Supr.; Rev. Kenneth Grabner, C.S.C., Chap. Total in Residence 25.

Dujarie House, Infirmary, P.O. Box 706, 46556. Tel: 219-287-1838; Fax: 219-289-7277. Stephen Kastner, Admin. Total in Residence 20.

Helen D. Schubert Villa, Assisted Living, P.O. Box 1020, 46556-1020. Tel: 219-287-1986; Fax: 219-289-7277. Stephen Kastner, Admin. Total in Residence 16.

Columba Hall, P.O. Box N, 46556. Tel: 219-631-6284; Fax: 219-631-9882. Bros. Thomas Shaughnessy, C.S.C., Supr.; James Linscott, C.S.C., Asst. Supr.; Rev. Maurice Amen, C.S.C., Chap. Total in Residence 35.

Holy Cross Community, Corby Hall, University of Notre Dame, 46556. Tel: 219-631-7325; Fax: 219-631-6715. Revs. Robert J. Austgen, C.S.C.; Nicholas Ayo, C.S.C.; Leonard N. Banas, C.S.C.; Ernest J. Bartell, C.S.C.; Michael J. Baxter, C.S.C.; E. William Beauchamp, C.S.C.; Thomas E. Blantz, C.S.C.; Richard S. Bullene, C.S.C.; Gary Chamberland, C.S.C.; Austin I. Collins, C.S.C.; John E. Conley, C.S.C.; Michael E. Connors, C.S.C.; Raymond F. Cour, C.S.C.; Paul F. Doyle, C.S.C.; Thomas P. Doyle, C.S.C.; John S. Dunne, C.S.C.; Clarence R. Durbin, C.S.C.; Carl F. Ebey, C.S.C.; Mark J. Fitzgerald, C.S.C.; James K. Foster, C.S.C.; Patrick Gaffney, C.S.C.; Thomas E. Gaughan, C.S.C.; James B. Gillis, C.S.C.; Charles B. Gordon, C.S.C.; Eugene F. Gorski, C.S.C.; Bro. Francis J. Gorch, C.S.C.; Revs. Gregory A. Green, C.S.C.; Daniel Groody, C.S.C.; Bro. Edward Hagus, C.S.C.; Revs. John A. Herman, C.S.C.; Theodore M. Hesburgh, C.S.C.; Bro. Louis F. Hurcik, C.S.C.; Revs. John I. Jenkins, C.S.C., Religious Supr.; Edmund P. Joyce, C.S.C.; Thomas P. King, C.S.C.; Jim B. King, C.S.C.; Jerome E. Knoll, C.S.C.; John Lahey, C.S.C.; Bro. Edward C. Luther, C.S.C.; Revs. James E. McDonald, C.S.C., Steward; James J. McGrath, C.S.C.; Most Rev. Mark G. McGrath, C.S.C., Panama; Revs. Donald P. McNeill, C.S.C.; Edward A. Malloy, C.S.C.; Patrick H. Maloney, C.S.C.; Leon J. Mertensotto, C.S.C.; Bros. Dennis Meyers, C.S.C.; Jerome Meyer, C.S.C.; Revs. Matthew M. Miceli, C.S.C.; Felipe Morel, C.S.C.; Robert H. Moss, C.S.C.; Michael J. Murphy, C.S.C.; Edward D. O'Connor, C.S.C.; John H. Pearson, C.S.C.; Robert S. Pelton, C.S.C.; Mark L. Poorman, C.S.C.; Herman R. Reith, C.S.C.; James L. Riehle, C.S.C.; James A. Rigert, C.S.C.; John P. Riley, C.S.C.; George A. Rozum, C.S.C.; David J. Scheidler, C.S.C.; Timothy R. Scully, C.S.C.; William D. Seetch, C.S.C., Rel. Supr. Corby Hall; William Simmons, C.S.C.; Thomas G. Streit, C.S.C.; Michael Bruce Sullivan, C.S.C.; Thomas Tallarida, C.S.C.; Mark Thesing, C.S.C.; Merwyn J. Thomas, C.S.C.; Bro. Thomas P. Tucker, C.S.C.; Revs. William A. Wack, C.S.C.; Joseph L. Walter, C.S.C.; Richard V. Warner, C.S.C.; Charles Weiher, C.S.C.; Oliver F. Williams, C.S.C.; George C. Wiskirchen, C.S.C.

[K] CONVENTS AND RESIDENCES OF SISTERS

FORT WAYNE. *Marian Convent.* (St. Joseph Hospital), 4138 S. Harrison, 46807. Tel: 219-745-4041.
E-mail: MarianConvent@juno.com
Sr. Loretta Schleper; Sr. Mary Conrad Kirchhoff, S.J.H.; Sr. Julienne Smith, S.J.H.; Sr. Laura Banet; Sr. Helen Watkins. Poor Handmaids of Jesus Christ 5.

Sisters of Providence Residences, 813 1-2 Kinnaird Ave., 46807-1829. Tel: 219-744-0780. Other Location: 2440 Fairfield Ave., Apt. 212, 46807-1250. Tel: 219-744-5586.

Sisters of St. Benedict. Mailing Address: 802 E. Tenth St., Ferdinand, 47532-9239. Tel: 812-367-1411; Fax: 812-367-2313.
E-mail: sisters@thedome.org
Web site: www.thedome.org

Sisters of St. Joseph of the Third Order of St. Francis Residences S.S.J.-T.O.S.F., 2425 Chestnut St., 46803. Tel: 219-422-6675. Sisters 3. Other Location: 2419 Chestnut St., 46803. Tel: 219-424-5084. Sisters 2.

SOUTH BEND. *Handmaids of the Most Holy Trinity Monastery-Hermitage*, 23089 Adams Rd., 46628-9674. Tel: 219-272-9425. Sr. Mary Emmanuel Baggoo, H.T., Rep. Contemplative Community; Prayer Ministry; Prayer Witness which includes Retreats and Spiritual Direction.

St. Joseph High School Convent. The Upper Room Ministry, 1445 N. Michigan, 46617. Tel: 219-234-0149. Legal Title: *Sisters of the Holy Cross, Inc.* Sisters of the Holy Cross Convents, 1104 N. Notre Dame Ave., 46617. Tel: 219-288-2665. Sisters 3. Legal Title: *Sisters of the Holy Cross, Inc.* 919 St. Vincent St., 46617. Tel: 219-232-6084. Sisters 2. 52700 Shellbark Ave., 46628. Tel: 219-277-1877; 277-1646. Sisters 4. 831 W. Colfax St., 46601. Tel: 219-246-0673. Sisters 4. 303 Waterfall Dr., Box 50, Ekhart, 46516. 190 Village Dr., Mishawa, 46545. Tel: 219-258-5974. St. Joseph's Towers, 316 S. St. Joseph's St., #116, 46601-2342. Tel: 219-232-8170. Sisters 4.

The Sisters of St. Joseph of the Third Order of St. Francis Central Offices, S.S.J.-T.O.S.F., 1208 Thomas St., 46601. Sr. Rose Margaret Firkus, Novice Min.

AVILLA. *St. Mary Convent*, 226 N. Main St., P.O. Box 109, 46710. Tel: 219-897-3484; Fax: 219-897-3706.
E-mail: stmarynun@F.W.I.com
Franciscan Sisters of the Sacred Heart. Sr. M. Debrah, Funfsinn, O.S.F.; Sr. Theresa Renninger, O.S.F., Supr. Sisters 2.

DONALDSON. *Convent Ancilla Domini*, 46513. Tel: 219-936-9936; Fax: 219-935-1785.
E-mail: sjolisem@poorhandmaids.org
Web site: www.poorhandmaids.org
Provincialate, Poor Handmaids of Jesus Christ (The Ancilla Domini Sisters). Sr. Jolise May, P.H.J.C., Prov. Professed Sisters 43.

Catherine Kasper Home. Tel: 219-935-1742; Fax: 219-935-1755. Retired Sisters 55.

Ancilla Domini Hospitals Insurance Trust. Tel: 219-947-8544; Fax: 219-947-5274.

Maria Center. Senior Apartments (Efficiency and Singles), 46513. Tel: 219-936-9936; Fax: 219-935-1790. Apartments 15.

Poor Handmaids of Jesus Christ Community Support Trust. Tel: 219-936-9936; Fax: 219-935-1785.

Ancilla College. Tel: 219-936-8898; Fax: 219-935-1773.

Lindenwood, Retreat & Conference Center. Tel: 219-935-1780; Fax: 219-935-1728.

St. Joseph Community Foundation, Ft. Wayne. Tel: 219-969-2001; Fax: 219-969-2004.

HUNTINGTON. *Victory Noll—Motherhouse of Our Lady of Victory Missionary Sisters*, 1900 W. Park Dr., Box 109, 46750. Tel: 219-356-0628; Fax: 219-358-1504, Ext. 157.
E-mail: victorynoll@olvm.org
Web site: www.olvm.org
Rev. Thomas C. Fahey, Chap.; Sr. Jeanette Halbach, O.L.V.M.
Legal Holding: Victory Noll Sisters Community Support Trust. Sr. Mary Elise Allmaras, O.L.V.M.; Sr. Margarita Aragon, O.L.V.M.; Sr. Helen Marie Beall, O.L.V.M.; Sr. Louise Marie Berand, O.L.V.M.; Sr. Jean Brosnan, O.L.V.M.; Sr. Marie Jane Chettle, O.L.V.M.; Sr. Helen Collis, O.L.V.M.; Sr. Camilla Cray, O.L.V.M.; Sr. Kathleen Cummings, O.L.V.M.; Sr. Marjorie Curran, O.L.V.M.; Sr. Adriana Daskoski, O.L.V.M.; Sr. Evelyn Marie Davis, O.L.V.M.; Sr. Denise Dean, O.L.V.M.; Sr. Madeline DeGroot, O.L.V.M.; Sr. Mary Barbara Desch, O.L.V.M.; Sr. Theresa Egidy, O.L.V.M.; Sr. Marie Celine Ernst, O.L.V.M.; Sr. Sharon Rose Eshleman, O.L.V.M.; Sr. Carmela Farley; Sr. Celestine Feik, O.L.V.M.; Sr. Folty, O.L.M.V.; Sr. Mary Paula Fortier, O.L.V.M.; Sr. Agnes Ganse; Sr. Mary Joan Ginsterblum, O.L.V.M.; Sr. Rose Francis Gilmore, O.L.M.V.; Sr. Antoinette Golabowski, O.L.V.M.; Sr. Victoria Grabler, O.L.V.M.; Sr. Margaret Gutierrez; Sr. Jeanette Holbach, O.L.V.M.; Sr. Elizabeth Hann, O.L.V.M.; Sr. Mary Magdelan Heim, O.L.V.M.; Sr. Veronica Hirjak, O.L.V.M.; Sr. Rose Elizabeth Hohner, O.L.V.M.; Sr. Carolyn Issenmann, O.L.V.M.; Sr. Mary Karl, O.L.V.M.; Sr. Isabelle Kestler, O.L.V.M.; Sr. Justine Kiefer, O.L.V.M.; Sr. Josephine Konrad, O.L.V.M.; Sr. Mary Dolores Kotas, O.L.V.M.; Sr. Marian Kozlowski; Sr. Martin Ksycki; Sr. Vivian Lembeck, O.L.V.M.; Sr. Dorothy Anne Lengerich, O.L.V.M.; Sr. Mary Rosella Lengerich, O.L.V.M.; Sr. Callista Ley, O.L.V.M.; Sr. Florentine Lohr, O.L.V.M.; Sr. Florence Luechtefeld, O.L.V.M.; Sr. Trinidad Luna, O.L.V.M.; Sr. William Ann Maloney, O.L.V.M.; Sr. Mary Bernardo Marquez, O.L.V.M.; Sr. Barbara McCord, O.L.V.M.; Sr. Lurlien McCoy, O.L.V.M.; Sr. Delores McGinley, O.L.V.M.; Sr. Otilia Mendoza, O.L.M.V.; Sr. Mary Rafael Mendoza, O.L.V.M.; Sr. Frances Meyer, O.L.V.M.; Sr. Anna Rita Montoya, O.L.V.M.; Sr. Carmen Montoya, O.L.V.M.; Sr. Evelyn Mourey, O.L.V.M.; Sr. Carolyn Louise Neff, O.L.V.M.; Sr. Mary Cecelia Niehaus, O.L.V.M.; Sr. Melanie Perscke, O.L.V.M.; Sr. Marcella Poydock, O.L.V.M.; Sr. John Francis Radler, O.L.V.M.; Sr. Lucy Regaldo, O.L.V.M.; Sr. Anna Marie Richter, O.L.V.M.; Sr. Mary Lawrence Rochel, O.L.V.M.; Sr. Fidelis Roels, O.L.V.M.; Sr. Mary Helen Rogers, O.L.V.M.; Sr. Mary Esther Rosenbeck, O.L.V.M.; Sr. Rose Zita Rosonke; Sr. Florence Russell; Sr. Gertrude Salitrik, O.L.V.M.; Sr. Grace Marie Samblanet, O.L.V.M.; Sr. Marilyn Sckatz, O.L.V.M.; Sr. Marie Schene, O.L.V.M.; Sr. Clare Marie Schnedecker, O.L.V.M.; Sr. Martha Sijota, O.L.V.M.; Sr. Helena Smith; Sr. Rita Snyder, O.L.M.V.; Sr. Gertrude Spetter, O.L.V.M.; Sr. Mary Matilda Spetter, O.L.V.M.; Sr. Germaine Stadler, O.L.V.M.; Sr. Joachim Stetar, O.L.V.M.; Sr. Elaine Sullivan; Sr. Gertrude Sullivan; Sr. Mary John Sullivan, O.L.V.M.; Sr. Regina Torzewski, O.L.V.M.; Sr. Rose Ann Trudell, O.L.V.M.; Sr. Monica Ulibarri, O.L.V.M.; Sr. Margaret Urhausen, O.L.V.M.; Sr. Lucy Marie Vega, O.L.V.M.; Sr. Amelia Villanueva, O.L.V.M.; Sr. Mildred Weber, O.L.V.M.; Sr. Marie Welter, O.L.V.M.; Sr. Henrietta Wilke, O.L.V.M.; Sr. Barbara Marie Witt, O.L.V.M.; Sr. Marlene Wolf, O.L.V.M.; Sr. Dorothy Louise Wortmann, O.L.V.M.
FORT WAYNE: Sr. Karen Kneckt, O.L.M.V.; Sr. Rita Musante, O.L.V.M.; Sr. Judith Ann Turnock, O.L.V.M.; Sr. Martha Wordeman, O.L.V.M.
SYRACUSE: Sr. Dolores Carlos, O.L.V.M. Professed Sisters 99.

MISHAWAKA. *Our Lady of the Angels Convent*, 1515 Dragoon Tr., P.O. Box 766, 46546-0766. Tel: 219-259-5427. Convent for retired and infirm sisters. Sr. M. Elizabeth Ann, O.S.F., Supr.; Rev. Dacian Bluma, O.F.M., Chap. Sisters 48.

St. Francis Provincialate, 1515 Dragoon Tr., Box 766, 46546-0766. Tel: 219-259-5427; Fax: 219-256-0822.
Web site: www.ssfpa.org
Sisters of St. Francis of Perpetual Adoration, Inc. St. Francis Convent and Novitiate of Immaculate Heart of Mary Province. Sr. M. Blanche Rausch, O.S.F., Prov.; Rev. Francis Affelt, O.F.M., Chap. Sisters 40; Novices 1; Postulants 3.

NOTRE DAME. *Saint Mary's of the Immaculate Conception*, Bertrand Hall, 46556. Tel: 219-284-5550; Fax: 219-284-5779. Sr. Aline Marie, C.S.C., Pres.; Sr. Joan Marie Steadman, C.S.C., Vice Pres.; Sr. Mary Eliza, C.S.C., Leadership Team, Finance; Sr. Marilyn Zugish, C.S.C., Leadership Team, Ministry; Sr. Veronique, C.S.C., Leadership Team, Holistic Living; Sr. Anna Mae Golden, C.S.C., Leadership Team, Holistic Living. Professed Sisters in Congregation 585; Temporarily Incorporated 26; Novices 23. Generalate, Candidate Program, Associate Program. Legal Title: *Sisters of the Holy Cross, Inc.; Sisters of the Holy Cross, Inc. dba CSC Consultation Services; Holy Cross Health System Corporation; The Corporation of Saint Mary's College, Notre Dame; Holy Cross Services Corporation.*

Sisters of the Holy Cross Other Residences and Programs:
Andre House-East. Tel: 219-284-5644. Sisters 3.
Andre House-West. Tel: 219-284-5645. Sisters 3.
Immaculata Convent. Tel: 219-284-5818. Sisters 3.
Lourdes Convent. Tel: 219-284-5589. Sisters 22.
Marian Convent. Tel: 219-284-5710. Sisters 7.
Mary's Solitude. Tel: 219-284-5599.
Moreau Convent. Tel: 219-284-5663. Sisters 4.
Queen of Peace Convent. Tel: 219-284-5579. Sisters 11.
Rosary Convent. Tel: 219-284-5845. Sr. John Margaret, Supr. Sisters 34.
Shalem House. Tel: 219-284-5358. Sisters 3.
St. Bridget's Convent. Tel: 219-232-2683. Sisters 2.
St. John's Convent. Tel: 219-284-5695. Sisters 4.
St. Joseph's Convent. Tel: 219-284-5719. Sisters 2.
Bethany House. Tel: 219-284-5674. Sisters 4.
Saint Mary's Convent. Tel: 219-284-5688; 5689; 284-5736. Sr. Mary Brassil, C.S.C., Supr.; Sr. Marian Daniel, C.S.C., Asst. Supr. Sisters 85.
Loretto Convent. Tel: 219-284-5667. Sisters 6.
Holy Spirit Convent, Saint Mary's. Tel: 219-284-5715. Sisters 3.
Kateri Convent, Saint Mary's, 46556. Tel: 219-284-5993. Sisters 4.
Madonna Convent, St. Mary's, 46556. Tel: 219-284-5890. Sisters 3.
Nazareth Convent, Saint Mary's, 46556. Tel: 219-284-5822. Sisters 2.
Saint Ann's Convent, Saint Mary's, 46556. Tel: 219-284-5713. Sisters 3.
Saint Ann's West, Saint Mary's. Tel: 219-284-5717. Sisters 3.
Saint Claire Convent, Saint Mary's, 46556. Tel: 219-284-5892. Sisters 2.
Saint Theresa's Convent, Saint Mary's, 46556. Tel: 219-284-5892. Sisters 2.
Visitation Convent, Saint Mary's, 46556. Tel: 219-284-5820. Sisters 4.
Sisters of the Holy Cross, P.O. Box 327, University of Notre Dame, 46556. Tel: 219-631-7072.

[L] MISSION HOUSES

NOTRE DAME. *Holy Cross Mission House,* 46556. Tel: 219-232-6005. Revs. William B. Simmons, C.S.C., Supr.; Stephen C. Gibson, C.S.C.; Andrew Guljas, C.S.C.; Robert Hoffman, C.S.C.; Roman Ladewski, C.S.C.; Walter Michulik, C.S.C.; Paul G. Wendel, C.S.C., Asst. Supr.

[M] RETREAT HOUSES & EDUCATIONAL CENTERS

DONALDSON. *Lindenwood Retreat,* PHJC Ministry Center. Tel: 219-935-1780; Fax: 219-935-1728.
E-mail: lw@lindenwood.org
Web site: www.lindenwood.org
Mailing Address: P.O. Box 1, 46513. Tel: 219-935-1780; Fax: 219-935-1728. Carole Wielosinski, Dir. Overnight facilities for 100, Conference rooms for 250, Handicapped accessibility. Total Staff 10; Total in Residence 1.

NOTRE DAME. *Mary's Solitude,* St. Mary's, 100 Lourdes Hall, 46556-5014. Tel: 219-284-5599; Fax: 219-284-5701.
E-mail: msolitude@cscsisters.org
Sr. Virginia M. Stasim, S.S.N.D., Dir.; Mary Frances Duffy, Asst. Dir. A retreat and conference center offering: Spiritual direction, days and evenings of reflection, week-end retreats, individually directed retreats, private and group retreats, Scripture, and special interest programs, 30-day directed retreats and the Nineteenth Annotation. Sixteen rooms are available; 14 single and 2 double. Total Staff 7.
Our Lady of Fatima Retreat Center, P.O. Box 929, 46556-0929. Tel: 219-631-8288; Fax: 219-631-5239.
E-mail: nd.fatima.1@nd.edu
Web site: www.nd.edu/~Fatima
Directors: Revs. Ronald Patrick Raab, C.S.C., Dir.; Stephen C. Gibson, C.S.C.; Paul G. Wendel, C.S.C., Spiritual Dir. in Res.; Sr. Rose Edward Goodrow, C.S.C. Retreats for men, women, husbands and wives, special interest groups, professional groups, youth groups and religious. Total Staff 4; Total in Residence 10.

[N] MISCELLANEOUS

FORT WAYNE. *Cathedral Museum,* McDougal Chapel, lower level, Catherdral Square, 46854. Tel: 219-744-2765; Fax: 219-744-1972. Mailing Address: P.O. Box 10898, Fort Waye, 46854. Rev. Phillip A. Widmann, Dir.
Catholic Charities. Tel: 219-439-0242; Fax: 219-439-0250.
E-mail: fwoffice@fw.diocesefwsb.org
Fort Wayne Community Service Center, 315 E. Washington Blvd., 46802. Tel: 219-439-0242; Fax: 219-439-0250. Kathleen Donnellan, M.S.W., Exec. Dir. Total Staff 85; Total Assisted 15,280.
South Bend Community Service Center, 425 N. Michigan, Ste. 222, South Bend, 46601. Tel: 219-234-3111; Fax: 219-289-1034. Total Staff 25; Total Assisted 3,556.
Elkhart Community Service Center, 201 S. Second St., Elkhart, 46516. Tel: 219-295-5284; Fax: 219-294-1428.
Villa of the Woods-Catholic Charities Residential Living, 5610 Noll Ave., 48606. Tel: 219-745-7039; Fax: 219-744-4887. Cheryl Smith, Admin. Total Staff 10; Residents 27. Residential facilities for the elderly including housing, meals, laundry services and planned activities.
Crosier Fathers of Fort Wayne, 1721 Magnavox Way, 46802. Tel: 320-532-5225.
E-mail: ABecker@Crosiers.org
William G. Niezer, Registered Agent. Total Staff 1.
The Diocese of Fort Wayne-South Bend, Endowment Trust, Inc., 1103 S. Calhoun Street, P.O. Box 390, 46801. Tel: 219-422-4611; Fax: 219-423-3382.
E-mail: jkoch@fw.diocesefwsb.org
Most Rev. John M. D'Arcy, Contact Person.
Foundation For Catholic Secondary Schools of Fort Wayne, Inc., P.O. Box 11632, 46859-1632. Tel: 219-424-8112; Fax: 219-424-7630. Donald J. Mauch, Pres.; Michael E. Millikan, Dir. & Contact Person.
The St. Joseph Community Health Foundation, Inc., 500 W. Main St., 46802. Tel: 219-969-2001; Fax: 219-969-2004.
E-mail: mdistler@fwi.com
Meg Distler, Exec. Dir. Total Staff 2.
St. Vincent de Paul Society Store, 1600 S. Calhoun St., 46802. Tel: 219-456-3561. Steve R. App, Mgr. Total Staff 10; Total Assisted 1000.
The Christ Child Society of Fort Wayne, Inc., 1103 S. Calhoun St., 46802. Tel: 219-422-4611; Fax: 219-423-3382.
E-mail: jeannemirro@hotmail.com
Shirley Vorndran, Contact Person.

SOUTH BEND. *Chiara Home, Inc.,* 1105 W. Jefferson Blvd., 46601-2618. Tel: 219-287-5435; Fax: 219-287-3184. Sr. Gretchen Clark, S.S.J.-T.O.S.F., Contact Person. Respite Care for people with special needs. Total Staff 4; Total Families Assisted 174.
Christ Child Society of South Bend. Tel: 219-288-6028. Mailing Address: P.O. Box 1286, 46624. Total Assisted 3,401.
Holy Cross Care Services, Inc., 105 Jefferson Ctr., Ste. 700, 46601-1916. Tel: 219-232-3512; Fax: 219-239-4908.
Web site: www.hccsiweb.org
Edward B. Newman, Pres. & CEO. Total Staff 1,000; Total in Residence 1,200.
Holy Cross Community Services, Inc., 610 N. Michigan, Ste. 310, 46601. Tel: 219-232-9534; Fax: 219-232-8968. Sr. Jeannine Curtis, L.C.S.W., Exec. Dir.; Bro. Donald Gibbs, C.S.C., Pres. Board of Dir. Total Staff 21; Total Assisted 750.
Holy Cross Resources, Inc., 3575 Moreau Ct., 46628-4320. Tel: 219-283-4701; Fax: 219-283-4709.
E-mail: jlong@hcri.org
Web site: www.hcri.org
Mr. David L. Burk, Pres. & CEO.
Saint Joseph's Care Foundation, Inc., 919 E. Jefferson, Ste. 408, 46617. Tel: 219-239-6140; Fax: 219-288-4735.
E-mail: sextont@sjrmc.com
Web site: www.sjmed.com
Saint Joseph's Regional Medical Center, Inc., 801 E. LaSalle, 46617. Tel: 219-237-7989; Fax: 219-237-7077.
E-mail: breedenm@sjrmc.com
Web site: www.sjmed.com
Robert L. Beyer, Pres. & CEO. Total Staff 196.
St. Vincent de Paul Referral Services, 3408 Ardmore Tr., 46628. Tel: 219-234-6211; Fax: 219-234-6248.
Web site: www.stvinnie.org
Mrs. Joan M. Eash, Exec. Dir. Total Staff 7; Volunteers 200; Total Assisted 19,000.
St. Vincent de Paul Society of St. Joseph County, Inc., 3408 Ardmore Tr., 46628. Tel: 219-234-6211; Fax: 219-234-6248.
Web site: www.stvinnie.org
Total Staff 7; Volunteers 200; Total Assisted 19,000.
St. Vincent de Paul Thrift Shop, 3408 Ardmore Tr., 46628-1302. Tel: 219-234-6009; Fax: 219-234-6248.
Web site: www.stvinnie.org
Alicia McMurtrie, Mgr.

GRANGER. *Jesuit Community,* 16203 Candlewycke Ct., 46530. Tel: 219-243-0601; Fax: 219-631-8092.
E-mail: neyrey.1@nd.edu
Web site: www.nd.edu/~jneyrey11
Rev. Jerome H. Neyrey, S.J., Contact Person.
St. Joseph's Farm, 52682 Current Rd., 46530. Tel: 219-272-0962. Brothers of the Congregation of Holy Cross, South-West Province. Bro. Donald Dunleavy, C.S.C., Dir. This farm is operated in the interests of the Congregation of Holy Cross, South-West Province. Brothers 1; Total Staff 2.

HUNTINGTON. *Our Sunday Visitor, Inc.,* 200 Noll Plaza, 46750. Tel: 219-356-8400; Fax: 219-359-9117.
E-mail: osvinc@osv.com
Web site: www.osv.com
Publishers of Catholic Periodicals, Books, Religious Education Materials and Offering Envelopes. Most Rev. John M. D'Arcy, Chm. Bd.

MISHAWAKA. *Ancilla Health Care, Inc.* Tel: 219-259-2431; Fax: 219-257-2831.
E-mail: khabgood@skynet.net
Web site: www.ancillahealthcare.org
dba St. Joseph Community Hospital of Mishawaka. Tel: 219-259-2431; Fax: 219-257-2831.
dba St. Mary Community Hospital, South Bend. Tel: 219-288-8311; Fax: 219-257-2831. 215 W. Fourth St., 46544. Tel: 219-259-2431; Fax: 219-257-2831. Mary Roos, Pres. & CEO; Sr. Pauline Bridegroom, P.H.J.C., Vice Pres. Mission Effectiveness.
Catholic Health Midwest Inc., 1515 Dragoon Tr., P.O. Box 1290, 46546-1290. Tel: 219-256-3935. Sr. M. Angela Mellady, O.S.F., Admin.
Alverno Health Corporation, 1515 Dragoon Tr., P.O. Box 1290, 46546-1290.
Alverno Memphis Corporation, 1515 Dragoon Tr., P.O. Box 1290, 46546-1290.
Sisters of St. Francis Health Services, Inc. Mailing Address: P.O. Box 1290, 46546-1290.
St. Anthony Medical Center Foundation, 1515 Dragoon Tr., P.O. Box 1290, 46546-1290. Tel: 219-256-3935.
The Foundation of Ancilla Health Care, Inc., 215 W. Fourth St., 46544. Tel: 219-257-2897; Fax: 219-258-1506.
E-mail: BKillilea@ancilla.org
Mr. William B. Killilea, Vice Pres.
Saint Joseph's Visiting Nurse Association, Inc., 810 E. Park Pl., P.O. Box 5006, 46546-5006. Tel: 219-271-2125; Fax: 219-271-2100.
E-mail: guzickim@sjrmc.com
Web site: www.sjuna.org
Mr. Mark Guzicki, Exec. Dir. Total Staff 184; Total Assisted 2,267.
Sisters of St. Francis of Perpetual Adoration, Inc., Mailing Address: P.O. Box 766, 46546-0766. Tel: 219-259-5427; Fax: 219-256-0822.
Web site: www.ssfpa,org
Sisters of St. Francis of Perpetual Adoration, Inc., Medical Benefits Trust.
Sisters of St. Francis of Perpetual Adoration, Inc. Capital Improvements Trust, 1515 Dragoon Tr., Box 766, 46546-0766. Tel: 219-259-5427.
Web site: www.ssfpa.org
Sisters of St. Francis Charitable Mission Trust.
Sisters of St. Francis Retirement Fund.
SSFPA Ministry Corporation, 1515 Dragoon Trail, P.O. Box 766, 46546. Tel: 219-258-5048; 258-5427. Sr. M. Blanche Rausch, O.S.F., Prov. Supr.
St. Margaret Mercy Health Care Center, Inc., 1515 Dragoon Tr., 46546. Tel: 219-256-3935.
Yves R. Simon Institute, 508 Travers Cir., 46545. Tel: 219-259-1864.
E-mail: aosimon@michiana.org
Mr. Anthony O. Simon, Dir. & Contact Person. Catholic academic institute. Total Staff 2.

NOTRE DAME. *Andre Residential Services, Inc.,* Dujarie House-200 W. River Ridge Rd., P.O. Box 706, 46556-0706. Tel: 219-287-1838; Fax: 219-289-7277. Stephen Kastner, Admin.; Bro. Donald Gibbs, C.S.C., Pres. of Board. Sponsored by Brothers of the Holy Cross, Inc. Purpose: to establish and maintain a health facility for members and persons associated with the Congregation.
Association of St. Joseph, Mailing Address: P.O. Box 985, 46556-0985. Tel: 219-631-7830. Bro. Flavius Ellison, C.S.C., Contact Person.
Ave Maria Press, Inc., P.O. Box 428, 46556. Tel: 219-287-2831; Fax: 219-239-2904.
E-mail: avemariapress.1@nd.edu
Frank J. Cunningham, Pres. & Publisher. Owned and operated by the Congregation of Holy Cross, Indiana Province, Inc.
Brothers of Holy Cross Life Development Trust, Mailing Address: P.O. Box 460, 46556. Tel: 219-251-2222; Fax: 219-289-0487. Trustees: Bros. Donald Bailer; William Dygert; Paul Kelly; Stanley Olszowka; Lawrence Skitzki.
Holy Cross Associates, Mailing Address: Moreau Seminary, P.O. Box 668, 46556. Tel: 219-631-5521; Fax: 219-631-3444.
E-mail: nd.hcassoc.1.@nd.edu
Web site: www.nd.edu/~hcassoc/
John Pinter, Contact Person-Dir. Total Staff 3; Total in Residence 55.
Holy Cross Ministry Net-Work, Inc., Bertrand Hall - St. Mary's, 46556-5000. Tel: 219-284-5551; Fax: 219-284-5779. Sr. Mary Eliza Martin, C.S.C., Admin.
Holy Cross Services Corp., Bertrand Hall, St. Mary's, 46556. Tel: 219-284-5551; Fax: 219-284-5779.
E-mail: maryeliza@cscsisters.org
Sisters of the Holy Cross.
Holy Cross Village at Notre Dame, Inc., 54515 State Rd. 933 N., P.O. Box 460, 46556-0460. Tel: 219-251-3250; Fax: 219-287-0487. Bro. Donald Gibbs, C.S.C., Prov.

PLYMOUTH. *Catherine Kasper Life Center, Inc.*, 9601 Union Rd., 46563. Tel: 219-936-9936.
E-mail: sjolisem@poorhandmaids.org
Sponsored by the Poor Handmaids of Jesus Christ. Sr. Jolise May, P.H.J.C., Pres. & Prov.; Linda Burt, Vice Pres.; Patricia DeMunck, Sec.
Purpose: To provide quality care and address the spiritual, emotional, and physical needs of the aged, sick and disabled.

Earthworks, Inc., 9815 Union Rd., 46563. Tel: 219-935-4164.
E-mail: earthworks@skyenet.net
Web site: www.earthwrks.org
H. L. Potts, Dir. An environmental education center; a sponsored entity of the Poor Handmaids of Jesus Christ (P.H.J.C.) affiliated with Convent Ancilla Domini, Donaldson, IN.

RELIGIOUS INSTITUTES OF MEN REPRESENTED IN THE DIOCESE

For further details refer to the corresponding bracketed number in the Religious Institutes of Men or Women section.

[0600]—*Brothers of the Congregation of Holy Cross.* (Midwest Province).—C.S.C.
[0470]—*The Capuchin Friars.* (Prov. of St. Joseph).—O.F.M.Cap.
[0480]—*Conventual Franciscans.* (Prov. of Our Lady of Consolation).—O.F.M.Conv.
[0520]—*Franciscan Friars.* (Prov. of St. John the Baptist).—O.F.M.
[0690]—*Jesuit Fathers and Brothers.*—S.J.
[0610]—*Priests of the Congregation of Holy Cross.* (Indiana Province).—C.S.C.
[1060]—*Society of the Precious Blood.* (Cincinnati Province).—C.PP.S.

RELIGIOUS INSTITUTES OF WOMEN REPRESENTED IN THE DIOCESE

[0230]—*Benedictine Sisters of Pontifical Jurisdiction.* (Ferdinand, IN).—O.S.B.
[3710]—*Congregation of the Sisters of Saint Agnes.*—C.S.A.
[1920]—*Congregation of the Sisters of the Holy Cross.*—C.S.C.
[1710]—*Congregation of the Third Order of St. Francis of Mary Immaculate.* (Joliet, IL).—O.S.F.
[0760]—*Daughters of Charity of St. Vincent de Paul.* (East Central Province).—D.C.
[0790]—*Daughters of Divine Charity.* (Holy Trinity Province).—F.D.C.
[1070-03]—*Dominican Sisters.*—O.P.
[1070-13]—*Dominican Sisters.*—O.P.
[1170]—*Felician Sisters.* (Presentation of the B.V.M. Province).—C.S.S.F.
[1450]—*Franciscan Sisters of the Sacred Heart.*—O.S.F.
[]—*Handmaids of the Most Holy Trinity.*—H.T.
[3130]—*Our Lady of Victory Missionary Sisters.*—O.L.V.M.
[3230]—*Poor Handmaids of Jesus Christ.*—P.H.J.C.
[2970]—*School Sisters of Notre Dame.*—S.S.N.D.
[2990]—*Sisters of Notre Dame.* (Province of Toledo).—S.N.D.
[3000]—*Sisters of Notre Dame de Namur.* (Chesapeake Province).—S.N.D.deN.
[3360]—*Sisters of Providence of Saint Mary-of-the-Woods, Indiana.*—S.P.
[1640]—*Sisters of St. Francis of Perpetual Adoration.* (Province of the Immaculate Heart of Mary).—O.S.F.
[3830]—*Sisters of St. Joseph.*—C.S.J.
[3880]—*Sisters of St. Joseph of Medaille.* (New Orleans).—C.S.J.
[3930]—*Sisters of St. Joseph of the Third Order of St. Francis.*—S.S.J.-T.O.S.F.
[2110]—*Sisters of the Humility of Mary.*—H.M.
[3260]—*Sisters of the Precious Blood.* (Dayton, OH).—C.PP.S.

DIOCESAN CEMETERY

FORT WAYNE. *Catholic*, 3500 Lake Ave., 46805. Tel: 219-426-2044.

NECROLOGY

† Gieranowski, William, (Retired). —Died April 24, 2000.
† Hinckley, Christopher J., (Retired). —Died May 9, 2000.
† Horvath, Martin A., (Retired). —Died Sept. 20, 2000.
† Lange, Matthew J., (Retired). —Died Dec. 31, 1999.
† Urbine, Richard, (Retired). —Died Oct. 31, 2000.
† Voors, Rev. Msgr. William J., (Retired). —Died March 9, 2000.

Diocese of Fort Worth

(Dioecesis Arcis-Vorthensis)

Most Reverend

JOSEPH P. DELANEY, D.D.

Bishop of Fort Worth; ordained December 18, 1960; appointed Bishop of Fort Worth July 10, 1981; ordained Bishop September 13, 1981. *Mailing Address: 800 West Loop 820 S., Fort Worth, TX, 76108.* Tel.: 817-560-3300.

ESTABLISHED AUGUST 22, 1969.

Square Miles 23,950.

Comprises the following twenty-eight Counties in the State of Texas: Archer, Baylor, Bosque, Clay, Comanche, Cooke, Denton, Eastland, Erath, Foard, Hardeman, Hill, Hood, Jack, Johnson, Knox, Montague, Palo Pinto, Parker, Shackleford, Stephens, Somervell, Tarrant, Throckmorton, Wichita, Wilbarger, Wise and Young.

For legal titles of parishes and diocesan institutions, consult the Chancery Office.

The Catholic Center: 800 West Loop 820 S., Fort Worth, TX, 76108. Tel.: 817-560-3300; Fax: 817-244-8839.

Web site address: www.fwdioc.org

E-mail address: rwilson@fwdioc.org

STATISTICAL OVERVIEW

Personnel	
Bishop	1
Priests: Diocesan Active in Diocese	46
Priests: Active Outside Diocese	4
Priests: Diocesan in Foreign Missions	1
Priests: Retired, Sick or Absent	9
Number of Diocesan Priests	60
Religious Priests in Diocese	55
Extern Priests in Diocese	9
Ordinations:	
Diocesan Priests	2
Transitional Deacons	2
Permanent Deacons in Diocese	63
Total Brothers	13
Total Sisters	100
Parishes	
Parishes	86
With Resident Pastor:	
Resident Diocesan Priests	33
Resident Religious Priests	23
Without Resident Pastor:	
Administered by Priests	22
Administered by Deacons	3
Administered by Professed Men Religious	1
Administered by Women Religious	1
Missions	3
Professional Ministry Personnel:	
Brothers	4
Sisters	50
Lay Ministers	160
Welfare	
Catholic Hospitals	1
Total Assisted	160,000
Health Care Centers	1
Total Assisted	2,394
Homes for the Aged	5
Total Assisted	754
Day Care and Extended Day Care Centers	1
Total Assisted	80
Special Centers for Social Services	16
Total Assisted	35,000
Educational	
Diocesan Students in Other Seminaries	12
Total Seminarians	12
High Schools, Diocesan and Parish	4
Total Students	1,560
Elementary Schools, Diocesan and Parish	14
Total Students	4,887
Elementary Schools, Private	1
Total Students	260
Catechesis/Religious Education:	
High School Students	8,273
Elementary Students	19,333
Total Students Under Catholic Instruction	34,325
Teachers in the Diocese:	
Priests	1
Scholastics	4
Brothers	11
Lay Teachers	484
Vital Statistics	
Receptions into the Church:	
Infant Baptism Totals	6,015
Adult Baptism Totals	470
Received into Full Communion	793
First Communions	4,974
Confirmations	2,798
Marriages:	
Catholic	797
Interfaith	451
Total Marriages	1,248
Deaths	1,109
Total Catholic Population	228,649
Total Population	2,490,147

Former Bishops—Most Rev. JOHN J. CASSATA, D.D., ord. Dec. 8, 1932; Titular Bishop of Bida and Auxiliary of Dallas-Fort Worth; appt. March 20, 1968; cons. June 5, 1968; first Bishop, Fort Worth; appt. Aug. 22, 1969; retired Sept. 16, 1980; died Sept. 8, 1989.

Vicar General—Rev. Msgr. JOSEPH A. SCHUMACHER.

Chancellor and Moderator of the Curia—Rev. ROBERT WILSON.

Deans—Rev. Msgr. CHARLES KING, North; Rev. LIAM SWEENEY, S.A.C., Southwest; Rev. IVOR KOCH, Northwest; Rev. KEN ROBINSON, East; Rev. Msgr. HUBERT NEU, Central.

Diocesan Pastoral Advisory Council—(Includes Presbyteral Council listed below). Lay Persons: Ms. MARY ALVAREZ; Mr. JAMES GAGLIARDO; Mr. ROBERT GARRISON; Mr. PETE GUERRERO; Ms. JO ANN HARRIS; Ms. JOSIE HERNANDEZ; Ms. JENNIFER JONES; Ms. KAY KEGLOVITS; Mr. RUSSELL OVERBY. Career Ministers: Ms. SHARON CASTLEBERRY; Mr. PAUL COMBEST; Ms. MARY HELEN FRANKO; Ms. KAY FUHRMAN; Sr. BERNICE KNAPEK, S.S.M.N.; Mr. RALPH MCCLOUD; Bro. PAUL MCMULLEN, T.O.R.; Deacon JAMES POOLE; Ms. CHARMAINE WILLIAMS, Facilitator.

Presbyteral Council and Consultors—Revs. STEPHEN JASSO, T.O.R.; RAYMUND MULLAN; WARREN MURPHY, T.O.R.; KEN ROBINSON; JOSEPH SCANTLIN; KARL SCHILKEN; JOSEPH A. SCHUMACHER; ROBERT WILSON.

Diocesan Finance Council—Mr. CHUCK BARTUSH, JR.; Mr. JOHN HERNANDEZ; Rev. PHILIP L. JOHNSON; Ms. BARBARA MAY; Mr. DAVID MORITZ; Ms. ELAINE PETRUS; Mr. ROBERT SCHUMACHER; Mr. EARLE SHIELDS, JR.; Mr. PETER FLYNN, Staff; Rev. ROBERT WILSON, Ex Officio; Rev. Msgr. JOSEPH A. SCHUMACHER, Chm. Ex Officio.

Catholic Foundation of North Texas—Mr. PETER FLYNN, Exec. Dir.; Mr. CHUCK BARTUSH, JR.; Mr. JOHN HERNANDEZ; Rev. PHILIP L. JOHNSON; Ms. BARBARA MAY; Mr. DAVID MORITZ; Ms. ELAINE PETRUS; Mr. ROBERT SCHUMACHER; Mr. EARLE SHIELDS, JR.; Rev. ROBERT WILSON; Rev. Msgr. JOSEPH A. SCHUMACHER.

Catholic Schools' Trust—Mr. EARLE SHIELDS, JR., Chm.; Mr. KEVIN SHORT; Mr. HOWARD RATTLIFF; Mrs. ELAINE EVANS; Mr. TIM CONNOLLY; Mr. GLENN POLK; Mrs. JANELLE KAVANAUGH, Sec.; Sr. MARGUERITE CONNORS, S.H.Sp., Supt. of Schools; Mr. PETER FLYNN, Exec. Officer; Ms. JANELLE KAVANAUGH, Sec.

Catholic Cemeteries Trust—Mr. HENRY PENNARTZ; Mr. BILL METZLER; Mr. DAN SHINE; Mr. PAUL HOLUB; Mr. JOHN ECKELKAMP; Ms. JOLEEN RAMPY; Mr. RAY LINDEMANN; Mr. MALCOLM GORRIE, Staff.

St. Joseph's Health Care Trust—Rev. ROBERT W. WILSON.

North Texas San Benito, Inc.—Mr. PETER FLYNN.

Division Directors, Diocesan Offices

Christian Formation—Dr. DAN LUBY.

Clergy and Religious Personnel Services—Rev. Msgr. JOSEPH A. SCHUMACHER.

Executive Services—Rev. ROBERT WILSON.

Financial Services—Mr. PETER FLYNN.

Pastoral and Community Services—Mr. RALPH MCCLOUD.

Pastoral Planning and Human Resources—Mrs. CHARMAINE WILLIAMS.

Schools—Sr. MARGUERITE CONNORS, S.H.Sp.

The Catholic Center—800 West Loop 820 S., Fort Worth, 76108. Tel: 817-560-3300; Fax: 817-244-8839. Departments and programs below, which are part of one of the divisions above, are listed alphabetically. Unless specifically noted the address and phone numbers are as above.

Boards and Associations

Board of Arbitration and Conciliation—Mr. PHIL RECORD, Chm.; Ms. SANDRA LEIGHTON; Mr. STEVE WILCOX; Mr. CLE ROYAL; Ms. THERESA TAYLOR.

Building Commission—Rev. Msgr. HUBERT NEU, Chm. Emeritus; Rev. Msgr. JOSEPH A. SCHUMACHER, Chm.; Mr. JACK DREWETT; Ms. DEBORAH GAGLIARDI; Mr. CREIGHTON PICKETT; Mr. BRAD RUPAY; Mr. DAVID FLEMING; Mr. GARY FRAGOSSO, Staff.

Diocesan Pastoral Finance Council (Budgets)—Rev. ROBERT WILSON, Chm.

Diocesan School Advisory Council—Mr. MICHAEL CASEY.

Mission Council—Sr. MARGUERITE CONNORS, S.H.Sp.; Mr. PETER FLYNN; Mr. GARY GARZA; Rev. PHILIP JOHNSON; Dr. DAN LUBY; Mr. RALPH MCCLOUD; Mr. JOHN MCKONE; Sr. DOROTHY POWERS; Revs. JOSEPH SCANTLIN; ROBERT W. WILSON.

Priests' Personnel Board—Rev. JOSEPH SCANTLIN, Chm., *2100 N. Davis Dr., Arlington, 76012-1803.* Tel: 817-460-2751.

Priests' Retirement Board—Rev. Msgr. JOSEPH A. SCHUMACHER, Chm.; Ms. BARBARA MAY; Mr. FRANKLIN MOORE; Rev. Msgr. HUBERT NEU; Mr. JAMES O'TOOLE; Mr. EARLE SHIELDS; Mr. MARK SIMEROTH.

Diocesan Programs

Christian Formation—Dr. DAN LUBY, Div. Dir.
Adult Formation—Dr. DAN LUBY, Dir.
Campus Ministry—Mr. PAUL COMBEST, Contact Person.
Children's Catechesis—Sr. DOROTHY POWERS, S.S.M.N., Dir.; Ms. TERRI CASEY, Dir.
Cursillo—Rev. FRANCIS X. FERNANDEZ, O.F.M.Cap., *Cursillo Center, 2221 N.W. 26th St., Fort Worth, 76106.* Tel: 817-624-9411.
Hispanic Pastoral Services—Mr. ANDRES ARANDA, Dir.
Synod and Permanent Diaconate Formation—Ms. CHELA GONZALEZ, Hispanic Specialist.
Rural Hispanic Ministry—Vacant, Dir.
Light of Christ Institute for Lay Ministry Development—Mr. PEDRO MORENO, Dir.
Media Library—Ms. RITA PHELPS; Ms. STEPHANI ALLEN.
Permanent Diaconate Formation Program—Dr. ANN HEALEY, Dir.
Scouting—Rev. JOHN GREMMELS, *2016 Willis Ln., Keller, 76248.* Tel: 817-431-3857.
Diocesan Synod—Ms. SHARON PERKINS, Coord.
Worship—Ms. MARY MCLARRY, Dir.
Young Adult Ministry—Mr. PAUL COMBEST, Dir.
Youth Ministry and Adolescent Catechesis—Mr. KEVIN PREVOU, Dir.

Clergy and Religious Personnel Services—Rev. Msgr. JOSEPH A. SCHUMACHER, Div. Dir.
Clergy Relief Association—Rev. Msgr. JOSEPH A. SCHUMACHER.
Continuing Pastoral Formation—Rev. JOSEPH PEMBERTON.
Permanent Deacon Formation—Ms. ANN HEALEY, Dir.
Permanent Diaconate, Office of—Deacon JOSEPH MILLIGAN, Dir.
Seminarians—Sr. DONNA FERGUSON, S.S.M.N., Dir.
Vicar for Religious—Sr. THERESA KHIRALLAH, S.S.N.D.
Vocations—Rev. ANH TRAN, Dir.

Executive Services—Rev. ROBERT WILSON, Div. Dir.
Development Office—Vacant.
Foundation Relations—Vacant.
Annual Appeal—Ms. MARY MILLS, Dir.; Ms. MARY PESQUEDA, Coord. Stewardship & Planning for Spanish Speaking.
Newspaper "North Texas Catholic"—Mr. JEFF HENSLEY, Editor; Ms. MARY MARTIN, Assoc. Editor.
Propagation of the Faith—Rev. ROBERT WILSON, Dir.
Tribunal—Rev. TIMOTHY THOMPSON, Judicial Vicar; Mrs. SANDRA LEIGHTON, Dir.

Financial Services—Mr. PETER FLYNN, Div. Dir.; Mr. MALCOLM GORRIE, Assoc. Dir.
Accounting/Budgeting—Ms. CAROLYN JONES.
Construction and Property Management—Mr. GARY FRAGOSSO, Dir.
Cemeteries—Mr. MALCOLM GORRIE, Dir.

Planning and Human Resources—Ms. CHARMAINE WILLIAMS, Div. Dir.
Pastoral Planning Office—Ms. CHARMAINE WILLIAMS, Dir.
Benefits Coordinator—Ms. SHARON FIELDER.
Parish Pastoral Planning—Mr. JOE RODRIGUEZ.
Personnel Officer—Mr. STEVE LANDON.

Pastoral and Community Services—Mr. RALPH MCCLOUD, Div. Dir.
African American Ministries—Mr. RALPH MCCLOUD, Dir.
Catholic Women, Council of—Rev. IVOR KOCH, *Sacred Heart Parish, 1504 10th St., Wichita Falls, 76301.* Tel: 817-723-5288.
Campaign for Human Development—Mr. RALPH MCCLOUD.
Ecumenism, Office of—Rev. Msgr. CHARLES KING, *St. John the Apostle, 7341 Glenview Dr., Fort Worth, 76180.* Tel: 817-284-4811.
Family Life and Pre-Cana—Deacon RICHARD STOJAK.
Hospital Chaplaincy—Rev. VINCENT ELSEN, O.F.M., *St. Mary of the Assumption, 509 W. Magnolia Ave., Fort Worth, 76104.* Tel: 817-923-1911. Sr. TERESA NASCHE, S.H.Sp., *3416 Brady, Fort Worth, 76109.* Tel: 817-926-7180.
Jail Ministry—Mr. RALPH MCCLOUD, Dir.
Laotian Pastoral Center—3508 Maurice Ave., Fort Worth, 76111. Tel: 817-831-4404.
Peace and Justice Office—Mr. RALPH MCCLOUD, Coord.
Prolife—Deacon RICHARD STOJAK.
Rural Life—Mr. RALPH MCCLOUD, Contact Person.
St. Vincent de Paul—Deacon JOE RAETZ, *5013 Emerald Dr., Fort Worth, 76103.* Tel: 817-457-6948.
Wichita Falls-United Regional Health Care System-Chaplain—Rev. AIDAN DONLON, S.A.C., *1600 11th St., Wichita Falls, 76301.* Tel: 817-723-4111.

Schools—Sr. MARGUERITE CONNORS, S.H.Sp., Div. Dir. & Supt. of Catholic Schools.
Associate Superintendent—Sr. BERNICE KNAPEK, S.S.M.N.
Holy Childhood Association—Sr. MARGUERITE CONNORS, S.H.Sp., Dir.

CLERGY, PARISHES, MISSIONS AND PAROCHIAL SCHOOLS

CITY OF FORT WORTH
(Tarrant County)

1—ST. PATRICK CATHEDRAL (1870), Rev. Msgr. Hubert Neu; Revs. Albert Tyl; Robert Strittmatter.
Res., 1206 Throckmorton St., 76102. Tel: 817-332-4915; Fax: 817-338-1988.
Catechesis/Religious Programs—Tel: 817-338-4441.
Students 411.

2—ALL SAINTS (1902) (Hispanic), Revs. Stephen Jasso, T.O.R.; Bernardo Nicolau, T.O.R. (Spain); Sr. Maxine Torres, M.C.D.P.
Res., 214 N.W. 20th St., 76106. Tel: 817-626-3055; Fax: 817-626-3050.
School—2006 N. Houston St., 76106-8195. Tel: 817-624-2670; 624-3471; Fax: 817-624-1221.
Sisters 1; Lay Teachers 11; Students 113.
Catechesis/Religious Programs—2022 Houston St., 76106. Tel: 817-626-1711.
Students 880.

3—HOLY FAMILY (1942), Rev. Joseph Pemberton; Deacon Joseph L. Milligan, Jr.
Res., 6150 Pershing Ave., 76107. Tel: 817-737-6768; Fax: 817-737-6876.
School—Tel: 817-737-4201.
Lay Teachers 14; Students 211.
Catechesis/Religious Programs—Students 245.

4—HOLY NAME OF JESUS (1952), Rev. Lawrence Breedlove.
Res., 2637 Avenue L., 76105. Tel: 817-536-9604.
Catechesis/Religious Programs—Tel: 817-535-8495.
Students 547.

5—IMMACULATE HEART OF MARY (1961), Revs. Domingo Romero, O.F.M.Cap.; Greg Goicoechea, O.F.M.; Antonio Bandres, O.F.M.
Res., 100 E. Pafford St., 76110. Tel: 817-923-6323; Fax: 817-923-6523.
Catechesis/Religious Programs—Tel: 817-923-8582.
Students 1,747.

6—OUR LADY OF GUADALUPE (1977) (Hispanic), Revs. Claudio Zudaire, O.F.M.Cap.; Francis Garces, O.F.M.Cap.; Roberto Garcia, O.F.M.Cap. In res., Revs. Eric Azcona, O.F.M.Cap.; Francis Fernandez, O.F.M.Cap.
Res., 4100 Blue Mound Rd., 76106. Tel: 817-626-7421; Fax: 817-626-4461.
Catechesis/Religious Programs—Tel: 817-624-3240.
Students 862.

7—OUR MOTHER OF MERCY (1929) (African American), Rev. Michael J. Farrell, S.S.J.
Res., 1007 E. Terrell Ave., 76104-3788. Tel: 817-335-1695.
School—1003 E. Terrell Ave., 76104-3799. Tel: 817-336-2880; Fax: 817-338-4227.
Sisters of the Holy Spirit 2; Sisters of St. Mary of Namur 1; Lay Teachers 8; Students 212.

8—ST. ANDREW (1953), Revs. Warren Murphy, T.O.R.; Carl Szura. In res., Revs. Benjamin Medeiros, T.O.R.; Theodore J. Bradower, T.O.R.; Luke Robertson, T.O.R.
Res., 46 Chelsea Dr., 76134. Tel: 817-927-5383; Fax: 817-927-8507.
School—St. Andrew Catholic School, 3304 Dryden Rd., 76109. Tel: 817-924-8917; Fax: 817-927-8507.
Lay Teachers 38; Students 683.
Catechesis/Religious Programs—Students 684.

9—ST. BARTHOLOMEW (1969), Revs. Richard Beaumont; Gary Geurtz; Deacon Gerald M. Barry.
Res., 3601 Altamesa Blvd., 76133. Tel: 817-292-7703; Fax: 817-292-2568.
Catechesis/Religious Programs—Students 341.

10—ST. GEORGE (1941), Bro. Paul McMullen, T.O.R., Pastoral Admin.; Deacon Ruben Curiel. In res., Rev. Raphael Eagle, T.O.R.
Res., 825 Karnes, 76111. Tel: 817-831-4404; Fax: 817-834-0121.
School—824 Hudgins St., 76111. Tel: 817-222-1221; Fax: 817-838-0424.
Lay Teachers 10; Students 147.
Catechesis/Religious Programs—Tel: 817-831-4404.
Students 394.

11—ST. JOHN THE APOSTLE (North Richland Hills) (1964), Revs. D. Timothy Thompson; John Swistovich; Gilbert Pansza.
Res., 7341 Glenview Dr., 76180. Tel: 817-284-4811; Fax: 817-284-1729.
School—7421 Glenview Dr., 76180. Tel: 817-284-2228; Fax: 807-284-1800.
Lay Teachers 41; Students 570.
Catechesis/Religious Programs—Tel: 817-590-0915.
Students 1,200.

12—ST. MARY OF THE ASSUMPTION (1909), Rev. Gerald Haby, S.M. In res., Rev. Vincent Elsen, O.F.M.
Res., 509 W. Magnolia Ave., 76104. Tel: 817-923-1911; Fax: 817-923-0769.
Catechesis/Religious Programs—Students 491.

13—ST. PAUL (1952), Rev. Ellsworth T. Wigginton; Deacon Ron Aziere.
Res., 925 Yale St., 76114. Tel: 817-738-9925; Fax: 817-735-8579.
Church—5508 Black Oak Ln., 76114.
Catechesis/Religious Programs—Students 102.

14—ST. PETER THE APOSTLE (1952), Rev. James Hart; Mrs. Fran Bresler, Pastoral Assoc.; Deacons Louis Poth; Pat Bresler.
Office: 1201 S. Cherry Ln., 76108. Tel: 817-246-3622; Fax: 817-246-4900.
Res., 7828 Abbott, 76108. Tel: 817-246-3442.
School—Tel: 817-246-2032; Fax: 817-246-3686. Mrs. Deborah Herrera, Prin.
Lay Teachers 18; Students 215.
Catechesis/Religious Programs—Students 238.

15—ST. RITA (1910), Revs. Richard Flores; Ignatius Duong.
Res., 5550 E. Lancaster, 76112. Tel: 817-451-9395; Fax: 817-451-9421.
School—712 Weiler Blvd., 76112. Tel: 817-451-9383.
Lay Teachers 18; Students 194.
Catechesis/Religious Programs—Students 194.

16—ST. THOMAS (1937), Rev. Salvator Stefula, T.O.R.
Res., 2920 Azle Ave., 76106. Tel: 817-624-2184; Fax: 817-624-9688.
Catechesis/Religious Programs—Students 452.
Mission—Azle, Tarrant Co., Holy Trinity, 800 Highcrest, Azle, 76020. Tel: 817-444-3063; Fax: 817-444-2217.
Mailing Address: P.O. Box 136038, Forth Worth, 76136.

17—ST. THOMAS MORE, Rev. Edward James Hart.
Res., 2901 Merida Ave., 76109. Tel: 817-927-2414.

18—SAN MATEO (1939) (Hispanic), Sr. Lucia Soledad Flores, M.C.
Rectory—2909 Photo Ave., 76107. Tel: 817-737-5470.
Res., 2640 Avenue L., 76105. Tel: 817-535-8495.
Catechesis/Religious Programs—Students 138.

19—CHRIST THE KING. (Quasi-Parish). Rev. Hilary Khanh, C.M.C. In res., Rev. Anthony Pham.
Res., 1112 Eagle Dr., 76111. Tel: 817-831-7200; Fax: 817-222-3410.

OUTSIDE THE CITY OF FORT WORTH

Abbott, Hill Co., Immaculate Heart of Mary (1946), Rev. Ronald Scheible, O.S.A. In res., Rev. James G. Ryan, O.S.A.
Res., 601 W. Houston St., 76621. Tel: 254-582-3092; Fax: 254-582-7222. [CEM]
Catechesis/Religious Programs—Students 70.

Albany, Shackelford Co., Jesus of Nazareth (1970), Deacon Ruben L. Castaneda.
Res., P.O. Box 1584, 76430. Tel: 915-762-2632. [JC]
Catechesis/Religious Programs—Students 63.

Arlington, Tarrant Co.,

1—CHURCH OF ST. MARY THE VIRGIN, (1994), Rev. Allan R.G. Hawkins.
Res., 1408 N. Davis Dr., 76012. Tel: 817-460-2278; Fax: 817-277-9927.

2—CHURCH OF THE VIETNAMESE MARTYRS, (2000), Revs. Hilary Tran Cong Ly, C.M.C.; Louis Minh Nhien, C.M.C.
801 E. Mayfield Rd., 76014. Tel: 817-557-6885.

3—Most Blessed Sacrament, (1978), Rev. Joseph S. Scantlin.
Res., 2100 N. Davis Dr., 76012. Tel: 817-460-2751; Fax: 817-460-2761.
Catechesis/Religious Programs—Students 690.

4—St. Joseph's, (1988), Rev. James Miller; Deacon G. Timothy Dorsey, Pastoral Assoc.
Office: 1927 S.W. Green Oaks Blvd., 76017-2734. Tel: 817-472-5181; Fax: 817-467-9319.
Res., 5108 Winterberry, 76018. Tel: 817-468-7521.

5—St. Maria Goretti, (1941), Revs. James Gigliotti, T.O.R.; Raymond Nedimyer, T.O.R.
Res., 1200 S. Davis Dr., 76013. Tel: 817-274-0643; Fax: 817-277-4193.
School—Tel: 817-275-5081.
Lay Teachers 24; Students 464.
Catechesis/Religious Programs—Tel: 817-460-0048.
Students 375.

6—St. Matthew, (1964), Rev. Msgr. Joseph A. Schumacher; Revs. Hilary M. Tran-cong-Ly, C.M.C.; John Robert Skeldon; Deacons Eduardo Garcia; Benito Serenil.
Res., 2021 New York Ave., 76010-6097. Tel: 817-860-0130; Fax: 817-277-7159.
Catechesis/Religious Programs—Students 1,298.

7—St. Vincent de Paul, (1976), Rev. Philip L. Johnson; Deacons George R. Nicklas, Jr.; Charles Castleberry.
Res., 5819 W. Pleasant Ridge Rd., 76016. Tel: 817-478-8206; Fax: 817-478-8513.
Catechesis/Religious Programs—Tel: 817-478-8208.
Students 1,601.

Bedford, Tarrant Co., St. Michael (1977), Revs. James O'Toole; Steven Berg; David Bristow; Deacons Harry Heinz; Lonnie Weaver.
Res., 3713 Harwood, 76021-4097. Tel: 817-283-8746; Fax: 817-283-9306.
Catechesis/Religious Programs—Students 1,349.

Bowie, Montague Co., St. Jerome (1986). Attended by St. Mary, Henrietta. Rev. John S. Stasiowski.
Mailing Address: 105 S. Barrett, Henrietta, 76365. Tel: 940-538-4214.
Catechesis/Religious Programs—Students 30.

Breckenridge, Stephens Co., Sacred Heart (1920), Rev. George Foley.
Res., 208 S. Miller St., 76424. Tel: 254-559-2860; Fax: 254-559-5289.
Catechesis/Religious Programs—Students 128.

Bridgeport, Wise Co., St. John the Baptizer (1889), Rev. Gonzalo Morales.
Res., 1801 Irvin, 76426. Tel: 940-683-2743; Fax: 940-683-2743.
Catechesis/Religious Programs—Students 95.

Burkburnett, Wichita Co., St. Jude Thaddeus (1965), Rev. Severius Blank.
Res., 600 Davey Dr., 76354. Tel: 817-569-1222.
Catechesis/Religious Programs—Students 58.

Burleson, Tarrant Co., St. Ann (1971), Rev. John Hennessy.
Res., 100 S.W. Alsbury Blvd., 76028. Tel: 817-295-5621; Fax: 817-295-5482.
Catechesis/Religious Programs—Tel: 817-295-5482; Fax: 807-295-3521.
Students 364.

Carrollton, Denton Co., St. Catherine of Siena (1981), Revs. George Thennattil, T.O.R.; Thomas Panickaruparampil, T.O.R.; Deacons Philip Webb; Robert Stuart.
Mailing Address: 1705 Peters Colony, 75007-3704. Tel: 972-492-3237; Fax: 972-394-0676.
Catechesis/Religious Programs—Students 847.

Cisco, Eastland Co., Holy Rosary (1920). Attended by St. Rita, Ranger. Rev. Leo Bonsall, O.S.B.
1109 Blackwell St., Ranger, 76470. Tel: 254-647-3167.

Cleburne, Johnson Co., St. Joseph (1888), Rev. Sergio Rizo.
Mailing Address: 807 N. Anglin St., 76031. Tel: 817-645-4478.
Catechesis/Religious Programs—Tel: 817-558-9938.
Students 275.

Clifton, Bosque Co., Holy Angels (1954), Rev. Danny Kelley.
Church—1915 W. Fifth St., 76634. Tel: 254-675-8877; Fax: 254-675-2298.
Catechesis/Religious Programs—Tel: 254-675-3165.
Students 40.

Colleyville, Tarrant Co., Good Shepherd (1992), Rev. Vincent Elsen, O.F.M. Administrators: Sr. Dorothy Eggering, S.S.N.D.; Sr. Theresa Khirallah, S.S.N.D. 1000 Tinker Rd., 76034. Tel: 817-421-1387; Fax: 817-421-4709.
Catechesis/Religious Programs—Students 905.

The Colony, Denton Co., Holy Cross (1981), Rev. Publius Xuereb.
Church—7000 Morning Star, P.O. Box 560156, 75056. Tel: 972-625-5252; Fax: 972-370-5524.
Catechesis/Religious Programs—Students 420.

Comanche, Comanche Co., Sacred Heart (1964). Attended by St. Brendan, Stephenville.
Church—1444 W. Washington Ave., Stephenville, 76401. Tel: 254-965-5693.
Catechesis/Religious Programs—Students 75.

Crowell, Foard Co., St. Joseph (1910). Attended by Holy Family, Vernon. Rev. Oren W. Key, S.J.
Church—2200 Roberts, P.O. Box 1377, Vernon, 76384. Tel: 940-552-2895; 940-552-9870 (Rel. Ed.); Fax: 940-552-6084.

Decatur, Wise Co., Assumption of the Blessed Virgin Mary (1938), Rev. Gonzalo Morales.
Res., 1305 Deer Park Rd., 76234-9701. Tel: 940-627-3307; Fax: 940-683-2743.
Church Rectory: 1801 Irvin, Bridgeport, 76426. Tel: 817-627-2561.
Catechesis/Religious Programs—Tel: 940-683-2743.
Students 185.

De Leon, Comanche Co., Our Lady of Guadalupe (1975). Attended by St. Brendan, Stephenville.
Mailing Address: c/o St. Brendan, 1444 W. Washington, Stephenville, 76401. Tel: 254-965-5693.
Church—Hwy. 16, 2 miles S. of Hwy. 6, 76444. Tel: 817-893-5511.
Catechesis/Religious Programs—Students 46.

Denton, Denton Co., Immaculate Conception (1894), Rev. Msgr. Charles King; Deacon Popo Gonzalez; Rev. Mel Bessellieu.
Res., 1215 N. Elm St., 76201. Tel: 940-565-1770; Fax: 940-382-7939.
Catechesis/Religious Programs—Sr. Helen Stejskal, S.S.N.D., D.R.E.
Students 1,020.

St. Mark (1995), Rev. Eugene Sweeney, S.M. In res., Rev. Robert M. Lewandowski, S.M.
2800 Pennsylvania, 76205. Tel: 940-387-6223; Fax: 940-382-1641.
Catechesis/Religious Programs—Students 201.

Dodson Prairie, Palo Pinto Co., St. Boniface (1913). Closed. For inquiries for parish records contact the Chancery.

Dublin, Erath Co., St. Mary (1916). Attended by St. Brendan, Stephenville.
1444 W. Washington Ave., Stephenville, 76401. Tel: 254-965-5693.
Catechesis/Religious Programs—Students 150.

Eastland, Eastland Co., St. Francis Xavier (1920). Attended by St. Rita, Ranger. Rev. Leo Bonsall, O.S.B.
1109 Blackwell St., Ranger, 76470. Tel: 254-647-3167; Fax: 254-647-3167.

Electra, Wichita Co., St. Paul (1966), Deacon Patrick Burke, Admin.
Mailing Address: P.O. Box 991, 76360.
Office: 1008 First St., Iowa Park, 76367. Tel: 940-592-2802; Fax: 940-592-2802.
Res., 709 W. Rebecca St., Iowa Park, 76367. Tel: 940-592-2930. [JC]
Church—500 N. Bailey, 76360. Tel: 940-495-3464; 592-2802.

Gainesville, Cooke Co., St. Mary (1879), Rev. Reinhard Sternemann, O.S.A. In res., Rev. Edward Andrews, O.S.A.
Res., 805 N. Weaver St., 76240. Tel: 940-665-5395, Ext. 2; Fax: 940-665-0957.
School—931 N. Weaver St., 76240. Fax: 940-668-1881.
Lay Teachers 17; Students 193.
Catechesis/Religious Programs—Tel: 817-665-5395.
Students 295.
Convent—825 N. Weaver St., 76240.

Glen Rose, Somervell Co., St. Rose of Lima (1969). Attended by St. Frances Cabrini. Rev. Juan Rivero. P.O. Box 757, Granbury, 76048. Tel: 254-326-2131; Fax: 817-326-3211. [JC]
2301 Acton Hwy., Granbury, 76049.

Graford, Palo Pinto Co., St. Francis of Assisi (1949). Attended by Sacred Heart, Breckenridge. Rev. William J. Hopkins.
Res., P.O. Box 404, 76449. Tel: 254-779-2023.

Graham, Young Co., St. Mary (1922), Rev. Raymund A. Mullan.
Res., 1218 S. Rodgers Dr., Box 547, 76450. Tel: 940-549-4314. [JC]
Catechesis/Religious Programs—Students 175.

Granbury, Hood Co., St. Frances Cabrini (1976), Rev. Juan Rivero; Deacon Ed Bevers.
Res., 812 Shadygrove Dr., 76049. Tel: 817-326-2131; Fax: 817-326-3211. [JC]
Catechesis/Religious Programs—76048. Tel: 817-326-2131.
Students 249.

Grapevine, Tarrant Co., St. Francis of Assisi (1949), Revs. Ken Robinson; Hoa Nguyen.
Res., 861 Wildwood, 76051-3361. Tel: 817-481-2685; Fax: 817-488-3169.
Catechesis/Religious Programs—Students 1,303.

Henrietta, Clay Co., St. Mary (1879), Rev. John S. Stasiowski.
Res., 105 S. Barrett St., 76365. Tel: 940-538-4214. [CEM]

Hillsboro, Hill Co., Our Lady of Mercy (1887), Rev. Alfred LaFleur, O.S.A.
Res., Interstate 35, P.O. Box 567, 76645. Tel: 254-582-5640; Fax: 254-582-0347.
Catechesis/Religious Programs—Students 132.

Iowa Park, Wichita Co., Christ the King (1980), Deacon Patrick Burke, Admin.
Mailing Address: P.O. Box 239, 76367.
Office: 1008 First St., 76367. Tel: 940-592-2802.
Res., 709 W. Rebecca St., 76367. Tel: 940-592-2930; Fax: 940-592-2802.
Catechesis/Religious Programs—Students 44.

Jacksboro, Jack Co., St. Mary (1911), Rev. Gonzalo Morales.
Mailing Address: c/o St. John the Baptizer, 1801 Irvin St., Bridgeport, 76426. Tel: 940-683-2743; 683-2743 (Rel. Ed.); Fax: 940-683-2743; 683-2743 (Rel. Ed.).
Church—Hwy. 148 N., 76458.

Keller, Tarrant Co., St. Elizabeth Ann Seton (1985), Revs. John Gremmels; Dennis Smith; Deacons Klaus Gutbier; Donald E. Werner.
Office: 2016 Willis Ln., 76248. Tel: 817-431-3857; Fax: 817-431-9568.
School—(Grades PreK-4). Tel: 817-431-4845. Kay Burrell, Prin.
Catechesis/Religious Programs—Tel: 817-431-6023; Fax: 817-431-3871.
Students 1,515.

Knox City, Knox Co., Santa Rosa (1948). Attended by St. Joseph, Rhineland. Rev. Leo Schloemer, Glmy.; Deacon Julian Estrada.
Mailing Address: P.O. Box 428, 79529. Tel: 940-658-5062.
Church—N. 3rd and Ave. G, 79521. Tel: 940-658-5062. [JC]
Catechesis/Religious Programs—Students 53.

Lewisville, Denton Co., St. Philip the Apostle (1976), Rev. Jonathan Scalone; Deacon Raymond G. Lamarre.
Office: 1897 W. Main St., 75067. Tel: 972-436-9581; Fax: 972-436-5302.
Catechesis/Religious Programs—Students 1,386.

Lindsay, Cooke Co., St. Peter (1902), Rev. Sebastian Beshoner, O.S.B.
Res., 424 Main St., P.O. Box 148, 76250. Tel: 940-668-7609; Fax: 940-668-7723. [CEM]
Catechesis/Religious Programs—P.O. Box 95, 76250. Tel: 940-665-6763.
Students 300.

Mansfield, Tarrant Co., St. Jude (1898), Rev. Karl Schilken.
Res., 500 E. Dallas St., 76063. Tel: 817-473-6709; Fax: 817-477-2088. [CEM]
Parish Hall: Tel: 817-473-9463.
Catechesis/Religious Programs—Tel: 817-473-0768.
Students 559.

Megargel, Archer Co., St. Mary (1909). Attended by Sacred Heart, Seymour. Rev. Richard Eldredge, T.O.R.
207 W. Pecan, Seymour, 76380. Tel: 940-889-5252; Fax: 940-889-2136. [CEM]

Mineral Wells, Palo Pinto Co., Our Lady of Lourdes (1960), Rev. William J. Hopkins.
Res., 108 N.W. 4th Ave., P.O. Box 1327, 76068. Tel: 940-325-4789; Fax: 940-327-8170.
Catechesis/Religious Programs—Students 275.

Montague, Montague Co., St. William (1899). Attended by St. Mary, Henrietta. Rev. John S. Stasiowski.
Mailing Address: 105 S. Barrett, Henrietta, 76365. Tel: 940-538-4214. [CEM]
Catechesis/Religious Programs—Students 57.

Morgan, Bosque Co., Our Lady of Guadalupe (1987), Rev. Danny Kelley.
Mailing Address: 304 Charles St., P.O. Box 441, 76661. Tel: 254-635-0145; Fax: 254-675-2298.

Muenster, Cooke Co., Sacred Heart (1889), Rev. John Ohner, O.S.A.
Res., 714 N. Main St., 76252. Tel: 940-759-2511; Fax: 940-759-4422. [CEM]
Preschool—.
Lay Teachers 2; Students 25.
School—Tel: 940-759-4121.
Benedictine Sisters 2; Lay Teachers 13; Students 172.

High School—Benedictine Sisters 2; Lay Teachers 12; Students 226.
Catechesis/Religious Programs—Tel: 940-759-2511, Ext. 37.
Students 231.

Nocona, Montague Co., St. Joseph (1948). Attended by St. Mary, Henrietta. Rev. John S. Stasiowski.
105 S. Barrett, Henrietta, 76365. Tel: 940-538-4214.

Olney, Young Co., St. Theresa of the Infant Jesus (1935). Attended by St. Mary, Graham. Rev. Raymund A. Mullan.
Mailing Address: P.O. Box 547, Graham, 76450. Tel: 940-549-4314. [JC]
Church—Oak & Ave. E, 76374. Tel: 940-564-5426.

Penelope, Hill Co., Nativity of the Blessed Virgin Mary (1909), Rev. Ronald Scheible, O.S.A.
Mailing Address: P.O. Box 98, 76676. Tel: 254-533-2325. [CEM 2]
Catechesis/Religious Programs—Tel: 254-533-2486.
Students 57.

Pilot Point, Denton Co., St. Thomas Aquinas (1891), Rev. Donald Brennan, O.S.A.
Res., 925 N. Charcut, 76258. Tel: 940-686-2088; Fax: 940-686-3044. [CEM]
Catechesis/Religious Programs—400 E. Gibbons, 76258. Tel: 940-686-2360.
Students 260.

Quanah, Hardeman Co., St. Mary (1914). Attended by Holy Family, Vernon. Rev. Oren W. Key, S.J.
2200 Roberts, P.O. Box 1377, Vernon, 76384. Tel: 940-552-2895; Fax: 940-552-6084. [JC]

Ranger, Eastland Co., St. Rita (1919), Rev. Leo Bonsall, O.S.B.
Res., 1109 Blackwell St., 76470. Tel: 254-647-3167; Fax: 254-647-3167.

Rhineland, Knox Co., St. Joseph (1895), Rev. Leo Schloemer, Glmy.; Deacon Julian Estrada.
Res., Rte. 2, P.O. Box 15, Rhineland, Munday, 76371. Tel: 940-422-4994; Fax: 940-422-4994. [CEM]
Catechesis/Religious Programs—Students 113.

Scotland, Archer Co., St. Boniface (1911). Attended by St. Mary, Windthorst. Rev. David Kraeger, T.O.R.
Church—76379. Tel: 940-423-6687; Fax: 940-423-6657. [CEM]

Seymour, Baylor Co., Sacred Heart (1910), Rev. Richard Eldredge.
Res., 207 W. Pecan St., 76380. Tel: 940-889-5252. [CEM]
Sacred Heart Pastoral Center—207 W. Pecan, 76380. Fax: 940-889-2136.
Catechesis/Religious Programs—Students 129.

Stephenville, Erath Co., St. Brendan (1958), Rev. Philip McNamara, S.A.C.; Deacon William Bolf.
Res., 1444 W. Washington Ave., 76401. Tel: 254-965-5693.
Catechesis/Religious Programs—Students 283.

Strawn, Palo Pinto Co., St. John (1912). Attended by St. Rita. Rev. Leo Bonsall, O.S.B.
Res., 1109 Blackwell Rd., Ranger, 76470. Tel: 254-647-3167.

Throckmorton, Throckmorton Co., San Patricio (1964). Attended by Sacred Heart, Breckenridge. Rev. George Foley.
Mailing Address: 208 S. Miller, Breckenridge, 76024. Tel: 254-559-2860; Fax: 254-559-5289.

Valley View, Cooke Co., St. John (1946), Rev. Bart Landwermeyer.
Res., 709 Lee St., 76272. Tel: 940-726-3524. [JC]

Vernon, Wilbarger Co., Holy Family (1891), Rev. Oren W. Key, S.J.
Res., 2200 Roberts, P.O. Box 1377, 76384. Tel: 940-552-2895; Fax: 940-552-6084.
Catechesis/Religious Programs—Students 180.

Weatherford, Parker Co., St. Stephen (1882), Rev. Liam Sweeney, S.A.C.
Mailing Address: P.O. Box 1743, 76086.
Office: 1802 Bethel Rd., 76086. Tel: 817-596-9585.
Res., 105 E. Columbia St., 76086. Tel: 817-596-9586.
Catechesis/Religious Programs—Students 655.

Wichita Falls, Wichita Co., Our Lady of Guadalupe (1927) (Hispanic), Rev. Hector Medina; Deacon Anastasio Perez.
Res., 421 Marconi, 76301. Tel: 940-766-2735; Fax: 940-766-4052. [JC]
Parish Hall: Tel: 817-322-0143.
Catechesis/Religious Programs—Students 327.
Our Lady Queen of Peace (1956), Rev. Chris Davis; Deacons Richard A. Arndt; Larry W. Bills.
Res., 4040 York Ave., 76309. Tel: 940-696-1253; Fax: 940-696-1216. [JC]
Catechesis/Religious Programs—Students 250.
Sacred Heart (1891), Revs. Ivor Koch; Atanasio M. Linh Uy, C.M.C.; Deacon Russell W. Detwiler.
Mailing Address: 1504 Tenth St., 76301. Tel: 940-723-5288; Fax: 940-767-0160.
Res., 1505 Ninth St., 76301. Tel: 940-723-5288; Fax: 940-767-0160.
Catechesis/Religious Programs—Students 350.
Mission—Wichita Falls, Wichita Co., The Assumption of Mary, 909 Lincoln St., 76304. Tel: 940-322-2500. [CEM][JC]

Windthorst, Archer Co., St. Mary (1892), Rev. David Kraeger, T.O.R.; Deacon Andres Lunca.
Res., P.O. Drawer 230, 76389. Tel: 940-423-6687; Fax: 940-423-6657. [CEM]
Catechesis/Religious Programs—Students 320.

Chaplains of Public Institutions

DENTON. *State School* 1215 E. Elm St., 76201. Tel: 817-387-1755. Rev. Juan Rivero.

GAINESVILLE. *Texas Youth Council Youth Facility*. Vacant. 805 N. Weaver, 76240. Tel: 817-665-2413.

WICHITA FALLS. *State Hospital* Tel: 817-723-4111. Rev. Aidan Donlon, S.A.C.

On Duty Outside the Diocese:
Reverend Fathers—
Olson, Michael
Renteria, Rudy, 4050 Glenridge Rd., Dallas, TX 75220
Spong, William, Ogdensburg, NY
Thames, Robert, Residencia de Arzobispado, Casilla 25, Santa Cruz, Bolivia, Bolivia

---

Retired:
Reverend Fathers—
Boyle, James A., Wildwood Springs, 305 Springdale Village, Bradenton, FL 34207
Cooney, Gerald, c/o 1824 Clark Rd., Crowley, TX 76036-9714
Curtsinger, George, 3015 Lubbock #5, Fort Worth, TX 76109
Edwards, Dale
Landwermeyer, Bart, St. Francis Village, 148 St. Anthony St., Crowley, TX 76036
Magaldi, Philip, c/o The Catholic Center, 800 W. Loop 820 S., Fort Worth, TX 76108
Miranda, Luke, 3240 Daniels, Apt. 101, Dallas, TX 75205
Perez, Salvador, Calle 22 #678, N. con Avenida Guerrero, Torreon, Coah 27000 Mexico
Stephens, Gerald, 208 Martin St., Wylie, TX 75098

Permanent Deacons:
Amos, Clarence
Armknecht, William
Arndt, Richard
Aziere, Ronald
Barry, Gerald
Bell, James
Benoit, Roland
Bevers, Eddy
Bills, Larry
Bolf, William
Bowden, Edgar
Bressler, Patrick
Burke, Patrick
Casias, Arturo
Castaneda, Ruben
Castellon, Damaso
Castleberry, Charles
Crowley, Norman
Curiel, Ruben
Detwiler, Russell
Dorsey, Tim
Eschbach, Franklin
Estrada, Julian
Falbo, Tony
Firth, John
Friedman, William
Garcia, Eduardo
Garcia, Raul
Giovannitti, Thomas
Gonzalez, Emilio
Greene, Clifford
Griego, Richard
Gutbier, Klaus
Guzman, John
Hatch, Larry
Heinz, Harry
Junginger, George
Kunath, Wolfgang
Lamarre, Raymond
Laremore, Robert
Luna, Andres
Marquez, Mario
McDermott, John
Milligan, Joseph
Nelson, Bob
Nicklas, George
Novak, Jim
Perez, Anastasio
Poole, James
Poth, Louis J.
Raetz, Joseph
Ruiz, Jesus
Salva, Hector
Serenil, Benito
Stojak, Richard
Stuart, Robert
Tassin, Terry
Torrez, Simon
Warner, Don
Weaver, Lonnie, Jr.
Webb, Philip
Wolf, George
Wuenschel, Douglas F.

INSTITUTIONS LOCATED IN THE DIOCESE

[A] COLLEGES & UNIVERSITIES

FORT WORTH. *The College of St. Thomas More*, 3013 Lubbock St., 76109.

[B] HIGH SCHOOLS, DIOCESAN

FORT WORTH. *Cassata Learning Center*. (Coed Secondary). 1400 Hemphill St., 76104-4796. Tel: 817-926-1745; Fax: 817-926-3132.
E-mail: cassata@hotmail.com
Web site: www.expage.com/page/cassata
Ms. Cynthia Morton, Exec. Dir. Teachers 12; Students 390.
Nolan Catholic High School. (Grades 7-12). (Coed), 4501 Bridge St., 76103. Tel: 817-457-2920; Fax: 817-496-9775.
E-mail: meyerpet@lenet.edu
Web site: www.nolancatholics.org
Society of Mary. Bros. Eugene Meyerpeter, S.M., Pres.; Oscar Vasquez, S.M., Prin.; Rev. James Mueller, S.M. Priests 1; Brothers 8; Sisters 4; Lay Teachers 84; Students 1,097.
Nolan School Trust.

WICHITA FALLS. *Notre Dame Middle-High School*, 2821 Lansing Blvd., 76309. Tel: 940-692-6041; Fax: 940-692-2811. Mr. James M. Anderson, Prin. Lay Teachers 24; Students 217.

[C] HIGH SCHOOLS, PAROCHIAL

MUENSTER. *Sacred Heart School*. (Grades Prek-12), 141 E. Sixth, Box 588. Mr. Jack Murdock, Prin. Priests 1; Olivetan Benedictine Sisters 3; Lay Teachers 20; Students 297.
Sacred Heart Teachers Trust Fund.

[D] ELEMENTARY AND SECONDARY SCHOOLS, PAROCHIAL

ARLINGTON. *Holy Rosary Catholic School*, 2015 S.W. Green Oaks Blvd., 76017. Tel: 817-419-6800; Fax: 817-459-7080. Mr. Lowell L. Day, Prin. Total Staff 25; Students 313.

DENTON. *Immaculate Conception Catholic School*, 1212 Bolivar, 76201. Tel: 940-381-1155; Fax: 940-381-1837.
E-mail: eschad@escll.net
Web site: www.catholicschooldenton.org
Ms. Elaine Schad, Prin. Lay Teachers 13; Students 207.

GRAPEVINE. *Holy Trinity Catholic School*,. Mailing Address: 3750 William D. Tate Ave., 76051. Tel: 817-421-8000; Fax: 817-421-4468.
E-mail: htcs2@airmail.net
Web site: azone.net/users/holytrinity
Mr. Ed Doherty, Prin. Lay Teachers 35; Students 500.

WICHITA FALLS. *Notre Dame Elementary School*, 4060 York Ave., 76309. Mr. Joseph Cluley, Prin. Sisters 1; Lay Teachers 13; Students 260.

[E] ELEMENTARY SCHOOLS, PRIVATE

FORT WORTH. *Our Lady of Victory Elementary*, 3320 S. Hemphill St., 76110. Tel: 817-924-5123; Fax: 817-922-6598. Sisters 2; Lay Teachers 11; Students 260.

[F] CHILDREN'S GROUP CARE

FORT WORTH. *Catholic Charities, Inc.* An Independent Corporation Founded by the Diocese of Fort Worth. 2701 Burchill Rd. N., 76105-3012. Tel: 817-534-0814; Fax: 817-535-8779.
E-mail: webmaster@ccdofw.org
Web site: www.ccdofw.org
Karen Spicer, LMSW-ACP, Exec. Dir.
Emergency Financial Assistance, 1404 Hemphill,

76104. Tel: 817-921-5381; Fax: 817-923-6818. Carolyn Henry, Div. Dir. Provides direct financial and material assistance to families in financial crisis. Office Sites: 401 W. Sanford, Arlington, 76011. Tel: 817-274-2560; Fax: 817-274-1797. Harvest House. 349 N.W. Renfro, Burleson, 76028. Tel: 817-295-6252. Westaid. 4701 Bryant Irwin Rd. N., Ste. 100, 76107. Tel: 817-737-9338; Fax: 817-732-6936. 3540 E. Rosedale, 76105. Tel: 817-531-2873; Fax: 817-534-6423.

Special Services Department. 2701 Burchill Rd. N., 76105-3012. Tel: 817-534-0814; Fax: 817-535-8779. Administers residential programs for the elderly, disabled, and additional programs for special populations.

Program Sites: Nuestro Hogar, Inc., 709 Magnolia St., Arlington, 76012. Tel: 817-216-0608; Fax: 817-861-6178. CASA, Inc., 3201 Sondra Dr., 76107. Tel: 817-332-7276; Fax: 817-877-0487. CASA Brendan & CASA II, Inc., 1300 Hyman St., Stephenville, 76401. Tel: 817-965-6964; Fax: 817-968-3072.

Department of Health & Family Services, 2701 Burchill Rd. N., 76105. Tel: 817-534-0814; Fax: 817-535-8779. Mary Smith, LMSW-ACP, Div. Dir. Provides a wide range of clinical and supportive services.

Program Sites: St. Teresa's Group Home, 2701 Burchill Rd. N., 76105-3012. Tel: 817-534-0814; Fax: 817-535-8779. Assessment Center of Tarrant County. (Children's Shelter), 2000 McKenzie, 76105. Tel: 871-534-0814. Extended Day Treatment & Family Support Services, 2701 Burchhill Rd., 76105. Tel: 817-534-0814. Therapeutic Foster and Respite Care, 2701 Burchill Rd. N., 76105. Tel: 817-534-0814. Family Preservation Unit, 1208 W. Magnolia, 76104. Anne Simon Reeves Children's Center, 2641 Ave. L, 76105. Tel: 817-534-0814.

Clinical Counseling Department, 1216 W. Magnolia, 76104. Tel: 817-536-6857; Fax: 817-923-8211.

Immigration and Refugee Services Department, 1216 W. Magnolia, 76104. Tel: 817-338-0774; Fax: 817-335-9749. Katy Burns, LMSW-ACP, Dept. Dir. Immigration Counseling, Refugee Resource Center and Refugee Resettlement. Assistance in migration matters: family reunification, adjustment of status, naturalization, ESL, and employment services.

Community Support Services Department, 1404 Hemphill, 76104. Tel: 807-921-5381; Fax: 817-923-6818. Carolyn Henry, LMSW-AP, Dept. Dir. Coordinates the Emergency Assistance Association of Tarrant County, Social Concerns, Holiday Network, Disaster Relief, Public Relations.

[G] GENERAL HOSPITALS

WICHITA FALLS. *United Regional Health Care System,* Eleventh Street Campus, 1600 Eleventh St., 76301. Tel: 940-723-4111.
E-mail: dwitcker@urhcs.org
Web site: www.urhcs.org
For a complete listing, refer to the Hospitals section.

[H] RETIREMENT & DISABILITY HOUSING

FORT WORTH. *Casa del Cor, Inc.,* 2701 Burchill Rd. N., 76105. Tel: 817-534-0814; Fax: 817-535-8779.
E-mail: webmaster@ccdofw.org
Web site: www.ccdofw.org
For a complete listing, refer to the Special Care Facilities section.

Casa, Inc. Housing for the Elderly and Handicapped, 3201 Sondra Dr., 76107. Tel: 817-332-7276.
E-mail: casal@flash.nt
Web site: www.ccdofw.org
For a complete listing, refer to the Special Care Facilities section.

ARLINGTON. *Nuestro Hogar, Inc. Catholic Charities,* 709 Magnolia St., 76012. Tel: 817-261-0608.
E-mail: nuestrol@flash.net
Web site: www.ccdofw.org
For a complete listing, refer to the Special Care Facilities section.

CROWLEY. *St. Francis Village, Inc.,* 1 Chapel Plaza, 76036. Tel: 817-292-5786; Fax: 817-294-2989.
Web site: www.saintfrancisvillage.com
For a complete listing, refer to the Special Care Facilities section.

STEPHENVILLE. *CASA Brendan & CASA II, Inc. Catholic Charities,* 1300 Hyman, 76401. Tel: 254-965-6964.
E-mail: casab@our-town.net
Web site: www.ccdofw.org
For a complete listing, refer to the Special Care Facilities section.

[I] MONASTERIES AND RESIDENCES OF PRIESTS AND BROTHERS

CROWLEY. *St. Maximilian Kolbe Friary* (Fort Worth), One Marquard Cir. & Two Marquard Cir., St. Francis Village, 76036. Tel: 817-370-9747; Fax: 817-361-9522.
E-mail: maxkolby@aol.com
Revs. Peter Fritz, O.F.M.; Raymar Bobber, O.F.M.; Vincent Elsen, O.F.M; Jovian Lang, O.F.M; Michael Ewert, O.F.M; Donald Werr, O.F.M.; Augustine Healey, O.C.D.; Bros. Camillas Smith, O.F.M., Guardian; Allan Haiar, O.F.M.

[J] CONVENTS AND RESIDENCES FOR SISTERS

FORT WORTH. *Hermanas Catequistas Guadalupanas,* 1001 Altamont Dr., 76106. Tel: 817-740-0038. Sisters 3.

Missionary Catechists of the Sacred Hearts of Jesus and Mary, 2640 Avenue L., 76105. Tel: 817-535-8495. Sr. Lucia Flores, Supr. Sisters 4.

Provincialate, Our Lady of Victory Center, 909 W. Shaw St., 76110. Tel: 817-923-8393; Fax: 817-921-5064.
E-mail: smargm@airmail.net
Web site: web2.airmail.net/ssmn
Provincial House of the Western Province, Sisters of St. Mary of Namur. Sr. Joan Markey, S.S.M.N., Prov. Supr.

Sisters of St. Mary Namur, 909 W. Shaw, 76110. Tel: 817-921-0305; 923-8393; Fax: 817-921-5064.
E-mail: smargm@airmail.net
Web site: web2.airmail.net/ssmn
Sisters of St. Mary of Namur.

ARLINGTON. *Monastery of the Most Holy Trinity, Discalced Carmelites,* 5801 Mt. Carmel Dr., 76017. Tel: 817-468-1781; Fax: 817-468-1782.
E-mail: arcarmel@ix.netcom.com
Web site: www.carmelnuns.com
Mother Anne Teresa Kulinski, O.C.D., Prioress. Solemn Professed Nuns 9; Novices 2.

WICHITA FALLS. *Mercy Convent,* 3000 Lansing Blvd., 76309. Tel: 940-692-9770; Fax: 940-696-1216.
E-mail: mercycom@aol.com
Web site: web2.airmail.net/ssmn
Sisters 2; Associates 1.

Notre Dame House of Prayer and Hospitality, 2820 Lansing Blvd., 76309. Tel: 940-692-2043; Fax: 940-696-3924. Sisters 2.

[K] RETREAT HOUSES

LAKE DALLAS. *Montserrat Jesuit Retreat House,* 600 N. Shady Shores Rd., P.O. Box 398, 75065. Tel: 940-321-6020; 321-6030; Fax: 940-321-6040.
E-mail: retreat1@airmail.net
Web site: web2.airmail.net/retreat1
Revs. George Wiltz, S.J.; Walter C. McCauley, S.J., Assoc. Dir.

Montserrat Foundation, Inc. Tel: 940-321-6020; Fax: 940-321-6040.
Board Members: Rev. George Wiltz, S.J.; Mr. Vic Muse; Mr. Michael Grimshaw; Mr. Bill Brookman.

[L] RENEWAL CENTERS

FORT WORTH. *The Catholic Renewal Center of North Texas, Inc.,* 4503 Bridge St., 76103. Tel: 817-429-2920 (Metro); Fax: 817-492-8668.
E-mail: crcstaff@juno.com
Ms. Gail Schatzman, Dir.

Beginning Experience. Tel: 817-429-2920; Fax: 817-492-8668.

Retorno. Tel: 817-485-9764.

Special Days for Special People. Tel: 807-429-2920; Fax: 817-492-8668.

National Marriage Encounter of North Texas. Tel: 817-451-6005.

Engaged Encounter of North Texas. Tel: 817-429-2920; Fax: 817-492-8668.

CRC Ministries Outreach. Sr. Pat Miller, S.S.N.D.; Sr. Kay Kolb, S.S.N.D.

[M] SOCIETY OF ST. VINCENT DE PAUL

FORT WORTH. *St. Vincent de Paul Diocesan Council of Fort Worth,* 3005 Phoenix Dr., 76116. Tel: 817-244-4624; Fax: 817-244-4626.
E-mail: rehassel@aol.com
Mr. Ralph E. Hassel, Pres.

WICHITA FALLS. *Particular Council of Wichita Falls, St. Vincent de Paul Society,* 4516 Lake Park Dr., 76302. Tel: 817-322-2920. Mr. Walter Brady.

[N] NEWMAN CENTERS

FORT WORTH. *Texas Christian University Catholic Community,* TCU Station, P.O. Box 297310, 76129-0001. Tel: 817-257-7830; Fax: 817-257-7333.
E-mail: c.calabrese@tcu.edu
Web site: www.catholic.tcu.edu/catholic
Rev. Charles L. Calabrese (STU).

ARLINGTON. *University of Texas at Arlington,* 303 Lampe, 76010. Tel: 817-460-1155; Fax: 817-244-8839.
E-mail: egray@fwdioc.org
Legal Title: *University of Texas at Arlington University Catholic Community.*

DENTON. *University of North Texas and Texas Woman's University,* 1303 Eagle Dr., 76201. Tel: 940-566-0004; Fax: 817-244-8839.
E-mail: egray@fwdioc.org
Web site: orgs.unt.edu/unt_ccm
Rev. Robert M. Lewandowski, S.M., Chap.; Mr. Eric Gray, Campus Min. Legal Title: *University of North Texas and Texas Woman's University.*

HILLSBORO. *Hill College Newman Center.* Attended from Our Lady of Mercy as United Christian Fellowship. P.O. Box 567, 76645. Tel: 817-582-5640. Deacon Jim Poole, Campus Min.

WICHITA FALLS. *Catholic Campus Ministry,* Midwestern State University, 3410 W. Louis Rodriguez Dr., 76308. Tel: 817-692-9778.
E-mail: msucatholiccampuscenter@hotmail.com
Web site: www.mwsu.edu/htmldocs/departments/organizations/catholic/framehomepage.htm
Ms. Debbie Neely.

[O] MISCELLANEOUS

FORT WORTH. *Community Hospice of Texas,* 6100 Western Place, Ste. 500, 76107. Tel: 817-870-2795; Fax: 817-878-3713.
E-mail: agreen@chot.org
Ms. Andrea Green.

Ministry to Gay & Lesbians, 3312 Dryden Rd., 76109. Tel: 817-927-5383; Fax: 817-927-8507.
Web site: www.webvalldy.com/standrew
Rev. Warren L. Murphy, T.O.R.

North Texas San Benito, Inc., The Catholic Center, 800 W. Loop, 820 S., 76108. Tel: 817-560-3300; Fax: 817-244-8839.
E-mail: pflynn@fwdioc.org
Web site: www.fwdioc.org

Sister of St. Mary of Namur Marian House, 3353 College Ave., 76110. Tel: 817-927-2240.

GRAPEVINE. *Magnificat, Grapevine Chapter,* 2112 Winding Creek S., 76051. Tel: 817-481-6815. Ms. Charmain Singleton, Sec.

RELIGIOUS INSTITUTES OF MEN REPRESENTED IN THE DIOCESE

For further details refer to the corresponding bracketed number in the Religious Institutes of Men or Women section.

[0140]—*The Augustinians.*—O.S.A.
[0200]—*Benedictine Monks.*—O.S.B.
[0470]—*The Capuchin Friars.*—O.F.M.Cap.
[0520]—*Franciscan Friars.*—O.F.M.
[0690]—*Jesuit Fathers and Brothers.*—S.J.
[]—*Priests and Brothers of the Mother Coredemptrix.*—C.M.C.
[0760]—*Society of Mary (Marianists).*—S.M.
[0990]—*Society of the Catholic Apostolate.*—S.A.C.
[0560]—*Third Order Regular of Saint Francis.*—T.O.R.

RELIGIOUS INSTITUTES OF WOMEN REPRESENTED IN THE DIOCESE

[0100]—*Adorers of the Blood of Christ.*—A.S.C.
[0230]—*Benedictine Sisters of Pontifical Jurisdiction.*—O.S.B.
[]—*Congregation of Missionary Catechists of the Sacred Heart of Jesus and Mary.*—M.C.
[0420]—*Discalced Carmelite Nuns.*—O.C.D.
[1170]—*Felician Sisters.*—C.S.S.F.
[1900]—*Hermanas Catequistas Guadalupanas.*—H.C.G.
[2970]—*School Sisters of Notre Dame.*—S.S.N.D.
[3950]—*Sisters of Saint Mary of Namur.*—S.S.M.N.
[1970]—*Sisters of the Holy Family of Nazareth.*—C.S.F.N.
[2050]—*Sisters of the Holy Spirit and Mary Immaculate.*—S.H.Sp.
[1110]—*Cabra Dominican Sisters.*—O.P.
[0460]—*Congregation of Sisters of Charity of the Incarnate Word.*—C.C.V.I.

NECROLOGY

† Boyle, James A., (Retired). —Died Dec. 26, 2000.

Diocese of Fresno

(Dioecesis Fresnensis)

Most Reverend

JOHN T. STEINBOCK, D.D.

Bishop of Fresno; ordained May 1, 1963; appointed Titular Bishop of Midila and Auxiliary Bishop of Orange May 29, 1984; consecrated July 14, 1984; installed as Bishop of Santa Rosa March 31, 1987; installed as Bishop of Fresno November 24, 1991. *Office: 1550 N. Fresno St., Fresno, CA, 93703-3788.* Tel.: 559-488-7400; Fax: 559-488-7464.

ESTABLISHED DECEMBER 15, 1967.

FORMERLY DIOCESE OF MONTEREY-FRESNO.

Square Miles 35,239.

Comprises the Counties of Fresno, Inyo, Kern, Kings, Madera, Mariposa, Merced and Tulare in the State of California.

Diocesan Patroness: St. Therese of the Child Jesus.

Legal titles of parishes and institutions, the Roman Catholic Bishop of Fresno, a Corporation Sole, Diocese of Fresno Education Corporation (for schools).

Chancery Office: 1550 N. Fresno St., Fresno, CA, 93703-3788. Tel.: 559-488-7400; Fax: 559-488-7464.

STATISTICAL OVERVIEW

Personnel	
Bishop	1
Priests: Diocesan Active in Diocese	86
Priests: Active Outside Diocese	1
Priests: Retired, Sick or Absent	27
Number of Diocesan Priests	114
Religious Priests in Diocese	37
Extern Priests in Diocese	23
Ordinations:	
Diocesan Priests	1
Transitional Deacons	4
Permanent Deacons	1
Permanent Deacons in Diocese	9
Total Brothers	4
Total Sisters	121
Parishes	
Parishes	85
With Resident Pastor:	
Resident Diocesan Priests	71
Resident Religious Priests	9
Without Resident Pastor:	
Administered by Priests	5
Missions	40
Professional Ministry Personnel:	
Brothers	4
Sisters	121
Lay Ministers	175
Welfare	
Catholic Hospitals	3
Total Assisted	743,635
Homes for the Aged	2
Total Assisted	215
Specialized Homes	1
Total Assisted	120
Special Centers for Social Services	14
Total Assisted	382,431
Educational	
Diocesan Students in Other Seminaries	26
Seminaries, Religious	1
Total Seminarians	26
High Schools, Diocesan and Parish	2
Total Students	1,423
Elementary Schools, Diocesan and Parish	23
Total Students	5,423
Catechesis/Religious Education:	
High School Students	7,343
Elementary Students	26,067
Total Students Under Catholic Instruction	40,282
Teachers in the Diocese:	
Priests	2
Sisters	29
Lay Teachers	326
Vital Statistics	
Receptions into the Church:	
Infant Baptism Totals	15,789
Adult Baptism Totals	581
Received into Full Communion	458
First Communions	9,730
Confirmations	3,847
Marriages:	
Catholic	1,975
Interfaith	385
Total Marriages	2,360
Deaths	3,264
Total Catholic Population	360,574
Total Population	2,324,650

Former Prelates of Diocese of Monterey-Fresno—Most Rev. JOHN B. MACGINLEY, ord. June 8, 1895; cons. May 10, 1910; First Bishop of Monterey-Fresno, July 31, 1924; resigned Sept. 30, 1932; died Oct. 19, 1969.—Most Rev. PHILIP G. SCHER, ord. June 6, 1903; appt. April 28, 1933; cons. June 29, 1933; died Jan. 3, 1953.—Most Rev. ALOYSIUS J. WILLINGER, C.Ss.R., ord. July 2, 1911; cons. Bishop of Ponce, Puerto Rico, Oct. 28, 1929; Coadjutor Bishop of Monterey/Fresno *"cum jure successionis,"* Dec. 17, 1946; succeeded to the See, Jan. 3, 1953; resigned Oct. 25, 1967; died July 25, 1973.—Most Rev. HARRY ANSELM CLINCH, D.D., ord. June 6, 1936; appt. Auxiliary to the Bishop of Monterey-Fresno, Dec. 5, 1956; transferred to the See of Monterey, Dec. 14, 1967.

Former Bishops of Fresno—His Eminence TIMOTHY CARDINAL MANNING, D.D., appt. Titular Bishop of Lesvi and Auxiliary of Los Angeles, Aug. 3, 1946; cons. Oct. 15, 1946; installed as First Bishop of Fresno, Dec. 15, 1967; elevated to Coadjutor Archbishop of Los Angeles *"cum jure successionis,"* June 11, 1969; succeeded to the See, Jan. 21, 1970; created Cardinal, March 5, 1973; died June 23, 1989.—Most Rev. HUGH A. DONOHOE, D.D., ord. June 14, 1930; appt. Auxiliary in San Francisco, Aug. 2, 1947; cons. Oct. 7, 1947; appt. Bishop of Stockton, Feb. 21, 1962; appt. Second Bishop of Fresno, Aug. 28, 1969; resigned July 1, 1980; died Oct. 26, 1987.—His Eminence ROGER CARDINAL MAHONY, D.D., ord. May 1, 1962; appt. Auxiliary, Jan. 7, 1975; ord. Bishop, March 19, 1975; transferred to Diocese of Stockton, April 17, 1980; appt. Archbishop of Los Angeles, July 16, 1985; created Cardinal, June 28, 1991.—Most Rev. JOSEPH J. MADERA, D.D., cons. March 4, 1980; succeeded to the See on July 1, 1980; transferred to Archdiocese for the Military Services, Washington, DC May 28, 1991.

Vicar General and Moderator of the Curia—Rev. MYRON COTTA, V.G.

Chancellor—Sr. SANDRA ANN SILVA, S.H.F.

Chancery Office—1550 N. Fresno St., Fresno, 93703-3788. Tel: 559-488-7400; Fax: 559-488-7464.

Diocesan Tribunal—NANCY STEVENS, J.C.L., Dir. Tribunal; Rev. MICHAEL BURCHFIELD, J.C.L., Asst. Dir., *1550 N. Fresno St., Fresno, 93703-3788.* Tel: 559-488-7490; Fax: 559-488-7498.

Judicial Vicar—Rev. Msgr. STEPHEN A. FROST, J.C.L., Office of the Tribunal, *Christ the King Center - Bakersfield.* Tel: 661-391-4640; Fax: 661-391-4649.

Adjutant Judicial Vicar—Rev. Msgr. HERBERT ELMLINGER; Rev. MICHAEL BURCHFIELD, J.C.L., Fresno.

Promoter of Justice—NANCY STEVENS, J.C.L.

Defensores Vinculi—Rev. Msgr. MICHAEL R. BRAUN; Rev. Msgr. THOMAS G. KLEINHANS; Rev. PATRICK MCCORMICK.

Judges—Most Rev. GABINO ZAVALA, D.D.; Rev. Msgr. RICHARD RYAN, J.C.D.; Rev. Msgr. HERBERT ELMLINGER; Revs. STEPHEN A. FROST, J.C.L.; THOMAS FRANSISCUS, J.C.L.; MICHAEL BURCHFIELD, J.C.L.

Notaries—Revs. PERRY KAVOOKJIAN; THOMAS M. TIMMINGS; Mrs. NANCY CLEMONS; Mrs. GLORIA MARY MARSCHALL.

Approved Advocates—Rev. Msgr. JOHN ESQUIVEL; Rev. Msgr. WALTER MINHOTO; Revs. JOHN GRIESBACH; CHARLES F. SMITH; RICHARD URIZALQUI.

Diocesan Consultors—Rev. Msgr. PATRICK FLOOD; Rev. Msgr. JOHN MORETON, V.U.; Revs. STEPHEN BULFER, V.F.; MYRON COTTA, V.G.; ROBERT WENZINGER, V.F.; JOHN GRIESBACH, V.F.; RICHARD URIZALQUI, V.F.

Vicars Forane—Rev. Msgr. JOHN MORETON, V.U.; Revs. JOHN GRIESBACH, V.F.; RICHARD URIZALQUI, V.F.; ROBERT WENZINGER, V.F.; STEPHEN BULFER, V.F.

Diocesan Offices and Directors

Catholic Charities—ERNIE VELASQUEZ, *149 N. Fulton, Fresno, 93701.* Tel: 559-237-0851; Fax: 559-237-7144.

Channel 49 (KNXT)—MARV HARRISON, Gen. Mgr., *1550 N. Fresno St., Fresno, 93703-3788.* Tel: 559-488-7440; Fax: 559-488-7444.

Continuing Formation of Priests—Rev. MYRON COTTA, V.G., *1550 N. Fresno St., Fresno, 93703.* Tel: 559-488-7400. Rev. JEAN-MICHAEL LASTIRI, *P.O. Box 2087, Merced, 95344.* Tel: 209-383-3924.

Cursillo Movement—Rev. RONALD ALVES, C.M.F., *2494 S. Chestnut Ave., Fresno, 93725.* Tel: 559-255-4260.

Department of Education—RICHARD SEXTON, Supt.; Miss PATRICIA BAILEY, Asst. Supt.

Diocesan Advisory Board of Education—Mr. MICHAEL O'DELL, Pres., *1510 N. Fresno St., Fresno, 93703-3711.* Tel: 559-488-7429; Fax: 559-488-7422.

Diocese of Fresno Education Corporation—1550 N. Fresno St., Fresno, 93703-3788.

Diocesan Newspaper—BILL LUCIDO, Editor, *"Central California Catholic Life", 1550 N. Fresno St., Fresno, 93703-3788.*

Ecumenical Affairs—Rev. DAVID J. NORRIS, *4875 N. Belmont, Fresno, 93727.* Tel: 559-255-3871.

Finance Committee—Rev. MYRON COTTA, V.G.; Rev. Msgr. J. WAYNE HAYES, P.A.; Rev. Msgr. MICHAEL BRAUN; LEROY GILSDORF; GARY BETHKE; LARRY STEFANI; GARY RENNER; PAUL R. WORSLEY, JR., *1550 N. Fresno St., Fresno, 93703-3788.* Tel: 559-488-7400.

Deposit and Loan Fund—Rev. MYRON COTTA, V.G.; Rev. Msgr. MICHAEL BRAUN; Rev. Msgr. J. WAYNE HAYES, P.A.; Mr. JAMES F. SWEENEY; Mrs. ROSEMARY MCCAVE; Mr. GARY BETHKE.

Detention Ministry—Sr. JOAN ALLEM, C.S.C., *1550 N. Fresno St., Fresno, 93703-3788.* Tel: 559-493-2851.

Hispanic Apostolate—Mr. ZEFERINO GONZALES, Coord. Migrant Prog., *1530 N. Fresno St., Fresno, 93703-3788.* Tel: 559-488-7455.

Holy Childhood, Pontifical Association—Rev. MYRON COTTA, V.G., Dir., *1550 N. Fresno St., Fresno, 93703-3788.* Tel: 559-488-7400; Fax: 559-488-7464.

Italian Catholic Federation—Rev. Msgr. J. WAYNE HAYES, P.A., Diocesan Chap.

Legion of Mary—Rev. Msgr. LASERIAN BYRNE, Diocesan Dir., *5770 N. Maroa, Fresno, 93704.* Tel: 559-439-0124.

Marian Federation of Guadalupe—Rev. Msgr. DANIEL LOPEZ, Diocesan Chap., *2441 Dockery Ave., Selma, 93662.*

Ministry to Priests—Rev. MYRON COTTA, V.G.

Newman Apostolate—Rev. PERRY KAVOOKJIAN, *1572 E. Barstow Ave., Fresno, 93710.* Tel: 559-436-3434.

Office of Development—BILL LUCIDO, *1550 N. Fresno St., Fresno, 93703-3788.* Tel: 559-488-7414.

Office of Diocesan Properties—TIM TILLMAN, *1550 N. Fresno St., Fresno, 93703-3788.* Tel: 559-488-7470.

Office of Finances—GARY BETHKE, Fiscal Mgr., *1550 N. Fresno St., Fresno, 93703-3788.* Tel: 559-488-7426; Fax: 559-488-7461.

Office of Insurance and Human Resources—PAT GORDON, S.P.H.R., Dir., *1550 N. Fresno St., Fresno, 93703-3788.* Tel: 559-488-7488.

Office of Ministries—Sr. CLARA ANN BUDENZ, O.P.; PAUL MENTLEWSKI, Admin. Asst. Tel: 559-488-7474. JAMES GRANT, Coord. Catechetical Ministries. Tel: 559-488-7476.

Campesino Ministry (Spanish)—Mr. ZEFERINO GONZALEZ. Tel: 559-488-7455.

Youth Ministry and Family Life (English)—Vacant. Tel: 559-488-7463.

Youth Ministry and Family Life (Spanish)—PATRICIA RODRIGUEZ, Dir. Tel: 559-488-7424.

Lay Ministry Formation Coord.—Sr. CLARA ANN BUDENZ, O.P. Tel: 559-488-7496.

Office of Liturgy—Rev. PATRICK MCCORMICK, Dir., *4636 W. Dakota, Fresno, 93722.* Tel: 559-275-2022.

Pastoral Center—TIM TILLMAN, *1530 N. Fresno St., Fresno, 93703.* Tel: 559-488-7470.

Permanent Diaconate Office—Deacon EDWARD HARMON, Dir., *1550 N. Fresno St., Fresno, 93703-3788.* Tel: 559-493-2840.

Personnel Committee—Rev. Msgr. JOHN MORETON, V.U.; Rev. Msgr. JAMES LOGAN; Revs. JOSEPH HEFFERNAN; JOHN GRIESBACH; MYRON COTTA, V.G.; PATRICK MCCORMICK; ROBERT WENZINGER; RICHARD URIZALQUI; PERRY KAVOOKJIAN; STEPHEN BULFER.

Priests' Council—Rev. Msgr. JOHN MORETON, V.U.; Revs. JOHN GRIESBACH, V.F.; ROBERT WENZINGER, V.F.; RICHARD URIZALQUI, V.F.; STEPHEN BULFER, V.F.; Rev. Msgr. RAYMOND C. DREILING; Rev. Msgr. JOHN ESQUIVEL, Chm.; Rev. Msgr. RONALD SWETT; Rev. Msgr. PATRICK FLOOD; Revs. MYRON COTTA, V.G.; WARREN HENGEL; VITO DI MARZIO, R.S.J.

Propagation of the Faith and St. Peter Society—Rev. MYRON COTTA, V.G., *1550 N. Fresno St., Fresno, 93703-3788.*

Retreats—Retreat Masters: Revs. LARRY DUNPHY, O.F.M., Dir. PEDRO UMANA, O.F.M.; RICHARD JUZIX, O.F.M.; Bros. MARION ALFONSO, O.F.M.; VICTOR HUNTER, O.F.M.; GERALD CHUMIK, O.F.M., *P.O. Box 249, Three Rivers, 93271.* Tel: 559-561-4595.

Scouting—Rev. ROD CRAIG, *1550 N. Fresno St., Fresno, 93703-3788.*

Vicar for Insurance and Retirement Affairs—Rev. Msgr. J. WAYNE HAYES, P.A., *1621 Center Ave., Los Banos, 93635.* Tel: 209-826-4246; Fax: 209-826-5335.

Vicar for Religious—Sr. SANDRA SILVA, S.H.F., *1550 N. Fresno St., Fresno, 93703.* Tel: 559-488-7400; Fax: 559-488-7464.

Vocations—Rev. ROD CRAIG, Dir., *1550 N. Fresno St., Fresno, 93703-3788.* Tel: 559-488-7400; Fax: 559-488-7475.

CLERGY, PARISHES, MISSIONS AND PAROCHIAL SCHOOLS

CITY OF FRESNO
(Fresno County)

1—ST. JOHN CATHEDRAL (1882), Rev. Msgr. John Esquivel, Rector; Revs. Gaspar Bautista; Jorge Gomez. In res., Rev. Msgr. Walter F. Minhoto, (Retired).
Res., 2814 Mariposa St., 93721. Tel: 559-485-6210; Fax: 559-485-8409.
Catechesis/Religious Programs—Students 1,283.
Mission—Fresno, St. Francis, Ninth & Lowe, 93702. Tel: 559-485-9467. Rev. Joseph Nguyen, (Vietnamese Ministry).

2—HOLY SPIRIT (1981), Rev. Msgr. James T. Logan; Esther Aquino, Business Mgr.
Mailing Address: 355 E. Champlain Dr., 93720-1273. Tel: 559-434-7701; Fax: 559-434-7734.
Res., 8781 N. Millbrook, 93720-1718. Tel: 559-435-2278 (Rectory).
Catechesis/Religious Programs—Tel: 559-434-3522. Judy Bedrosian, D.R.E.
Students 335.
Missions—Pinedale, Fresno Co., St. Agnes, 111 W. Birch St., Pinedale, 93650. Tel: 559-439-2100; Fax: 559-439-0248; Auberry, Infant Jesus of Prague, Tollhouse, Auberry, 93602. Tel: 559-855-5011.
Station—Tollhouse, Shaver Lake, Tel: 559-841-3524.

3—OUR LADY OF MT. CARMEL, Rev. Warren Hengel, Jr.
Office: 816 Pottle Ave., 93706. Tel: 559-264-2587; Fax: 559-264-2539.
Catechesis/Religious Programs—1207 E. Trinity, 93706. Tel: 559-233-1010.
Students 145.

4—OUR LADY OF VICTORY (1950), Rev. Msgr. John Moreton.
Res., 1215 W. Michigan Ave., 93705. Tel: 559-226-1163.
Parish Center—2850 N. Crystal, 93705. Fax: 559-226-2093.
School—1626 W. Princeton Ave., 93705. Tel: 559-229-0205; Fax: 559-229-3230. Mr. Terry Lane, Prin.
Lay Teachers 11; Students 228.
Catechesis/Religious Programs—Tel: 559-229-0024.
Students 420.

5—SACRED HEART (1947), Revs. Charles F. Smith; Miguel Flores.
Res., 2240 N. Cedar Ave., 93703-2668. Tel: 559-237-4121; Fax: 559-237-0122.
School—4460 E. Yale, 93703. Tel: 559-251-3171; Fax: 559-251-7778. Victor M. Suarez, Prin.
Sisters of the Love of God 3; Lay Teachers 6; Students 177.
Catechesis/Religious Programs—Tel: 559-237-4365.
Students 452.
Convent—4305 E. Union, 93703. Tel: 559-454-1864.

6—ST. ALPHONSUS, Rev. Raul Sanchez.
351 E. Kearney Blvd., 93706.

7—ST. ANTHONY OF PADUA (1953), Rev. Msgr. John Harguindeguy; Rev. Loren Blessing, O.F.M.
Office: 5770 N. Maroa St., 93704. Tel: 559-439-0124; Fax: 559-439-3050.
School—Tel: 559-435-0700; Fax: 559-435-6749. Mr. Shawn Carey, Prin.
Lay Teachers 24; Students 620.
Catechesis/Religious Programs—5770 N. Maroa St., 93704. Tel: 559-439-0124.
Students 875.

8—ST. ANTHONY MARY CLARET (Calwa Area) (1952), Revs. Ronald Alves, C.M.F.; Robert Billett, C.M.F. In res., Revs. Fernando Vega, C.M.F.; Cecil Barron, C.M.F.
Res., 2494 S. Chestnut Ave., 93725. Tel: 559-255-4260; Fax: 559-255-4264.
Catechesis/Religious Programs—Students 2,000.
Mission—Malaga, Fresno Co., Christ the King, 3565 Calvin St., 93725.

9—ST. GENEVIEVE (1938), Rev. Vincent Lau (Hong Kong).
Res., 1127 Tulare St., 93706. Tel: 559-486-2988; Fax: 559-486-2988. [CEM]

10—ST. HELEN (1955), Revs. David J. Norris, D.Min.; Miguel Flores. In res., Revs. Joseph Nguyen Hoan (Vietnam); Gerald Amerando.
Office: 4875 E. Grant Ave., 93727.
Res., 4870 E. Belmont, 93727. Tel: 559-255-3871; Fax: 559-255-7625.
School—4888 E. Belmont, 93727. Tel: 559-251-5855; Fax: 559-251-5948. Dr. Toni Amodio, Prin.
Lay Teachers 13; Students 310.
Junior Kindergarten:—Tel: 209-251-2422. Mrs. Linda Stuart, Dir.
Catechesis/Religious Programs—Students 210.

11—ST. MARY (1967), Rev. Patrick Joseph McCormick.
Res., 4636 W. Dakota, 93722. Tel: 559-275-2022; Fax: 559-275-2040. [CEM]
Catechesis/Religious Programs—Tel: 559-271-1459.
Students 363.

12—ST. PAUL (1964), Rev. Perry Kavookjian.
Church—California State University, St. Paul Newman Center, 1572 E. Barstow St., 93710. Tel: 559-436-3434; Fax: 559-436-3430.
Catechesis/Religious Programs—Students 339.

13—ST. THERESE (1927), Rev. Msgr. E. James Petersen; Rev. John Congdon.
Mailing Address: 1444 N. Wishon, 93728. Tel: 559-268-6388; Fax: 559-268-0852.
Res., 855 E. Floradora Ave., 93728. Tel: 559-485-2199.
Catechesis/Religious Programs—Students 125.

OUTSIDE THE CITY OF FRESNO

Arvin, Kern Co., St. Thomas (1939), Rev. Lucas Azpericueta.
Res., 350 E. Bear Mountain Blvd., 93203. Tel: 661-854-6150; Fax: 661-854-2564.
Catechesis/Religious Programs—Students 145.

Atwater, Merced Co., St. Anthony (1909), Rev. Thomas Timmings.
Office: 1799 Winton Way, 95301. Tel: 209-358-5743; Fax: 209-358-2423.
Res., 1999 Juniper Ave., 95301.
School—Tel: 209-358-3341. Miss Dianne Silva, Prin.
Lay Teachers 7; Students 135.
Preschool:—Tel: 209-358-3341. Mrs. Debbie Flores, Dir.
Catechesis/Religious Programs—Tel: 209-358-3382.
Students 825.
Mission—Buhach, Merced Co., Immaculate Conception, 1799 Winton Way, 95301.

Avenal, Kings Co., St. Joseph (1941), Rev. Gregory Kareta, O.F.M. Con.
Res., P.O. Box 219, 93204. Tel: 559-386-9523; Fax: 559-386-1068.
Catechesis/Religious Programs—Students 70.
Mission—Kettleman City, St. Cecilia, Milham & 8th St., Kettleman City 93239.

Bakersfield, Kern Co.,

1—OUR LADY OF GUADALUPE, (1925), Revs. James Catalano, O.S.J.; Chummar Chirayath, O.S.J. (India); Victor Mendoza, O.S.J. (Mexico).
Res., 601 E. California Ave., 93307. Tel: 661-323-3148; Fax: 661-323-6016.
School—609 E. California Ave., 93307. Tel: 661-323-6059. Sr. Teresa Juarez, S.J.S., Prin.
Sisters 3; Lay Teachers 6; Students 230.
Catechesis/Religious Programs—Tel: 661-323-7642. Luis Maldonado, D.R.E.
Students 560.
Missions—Bakersfield, Kern Co., Holy Spirit, 720 E. Belle Terrace, 93307. Tel: 661-834-7095; Bakersfield, Kern Co., St. Jude, 825 Chapman, 93307. Tel: 661-323-2347.

2—OUR LADY OF PERPETUAL HELP, (1948), Rev. Msgr. Michael R. Braun.
Res., 124 Columbus St., 93305. Tel: 661-323-3108; Fax: 661-325-7067.
School—Tel: 805-327-7741. Mrs. Eleanor Etcheverry, Prin.
Lay Teachers 13; Students 273.
Catechesis/Religious Programs—Tel: 661-327-0712.
Students 358.
Mission—Bakersfield, Kern Co., San Clemente, 1305 Water St., 93305. Tel: 661-871-9190. Rev. Jim Kudilil.

3—SACRED HEART, (1952), Rev. Dan Coyle.
Res., 9915 Ramos St., 93307. Tel: 661-831-8905; Fax: 661-837-8075.
Catechesis/Religious Programs—Tel: 661-831-6223.
Students 309.

4—ST. FRANCIS, (1881), Revs. Craig F. Harrison; Titus Rodrigo, O.S.B.; Deacon Peter Gutierrez.
Res., 900 H St., 93304. Tel: 661-327-4734; Fax: 661-327-4930.
School—2516 Palm St., 93304. Tel: 661-326-7955; Fax: 661-327-0395. Mrs. Cynthia Meek, Prin.
Lay Teachers 21; Students 480.
Daycare/Preschool—Tel: 661-326-7958. Mrs. Mary Johnson, Dir.
Students 55.
Catechesis/Religious Programs—2424 Palm St., 93304. Tel: 661-323-8800. Mrs. Alice Fry, D.R.E.
Students 480.

5—ST. JOSEPH, (1907), Revs. Robert D. Wenzinger; Hilary Silva, O.M.I.
Res., 1515 Baker St., 93305. Tel: 661-327-2744; Fax: 661-327-0133.
Catechesis/Religious Programs—Tel: 661-325-2581.
Students 1,704.

6—ST. PHILIP THE APOSTLE, (1968), Rev. Msgr. Ronald J. Swett; Rev. Michael Moore.
Mailing Address: 7100 Stockdale Hwy., 93309-1399. Tel: 661-834-7483; Fax: 661-834-2214.
Preschool:—Mrs. Debi Anderson, Dir.

Catechesis/Religious Programs—Leila Hinzman, D.R.E.
Students 1,220.

Bass Lake, Madera Co., Our Lady of the Sierra, Rev. Herman O. Bezunartea.
Res. & Mailing Address: P.O. Box 410, 93604. Tel: 559-642-3452; Fax: 559-642-3452.; 40180 Indian Springs Rd., Oakhurst, 93644.
Missions—North Fork, Madera Co., St. Joseph the Worker, 56522 Rd. 200, North Fork, 93643.; Bass Lake, Madera Co., St. Dominic Savio, (1961) 40077 Rd. 222, 93604.

Bishop, Inyo Co., Our Lady of Perpetual Help (1947), Rev. Charles Casale.
Res., 849 N. Home St., 93514. Tel: 760-872-7231; Fax: 760-872-9222.
Catechesis/Religious Programs—Tel: 760-873-8862; Fax: 760-873-8862.
Students 294.
Mission—Big Pine, Inyo Co., St. Stephen, 461 S. Main St., Bishop 93513. Tel: 760-938-2724.

Boron, Kern Co., St. Joseph (1969), Rev. John Gracey.
Mailing Address: Drawer 1080, 93596. Tel: 760-762-5453; Fax: 760-373-2206.
Catechesis/Religious Programs—Karen Thomas, D.R.E. (California City).
Students 12.
Mission—California City, Kern Co., Our Lady of Lourdes, 93505. Tel: 760-373-2256.
Station—California City, Our Lady of Lourdes, Tel: 760-373-2256.

Buttonwillow, Kern Co., St. Mary (1941), Rev. Msgr. Loydell J. Marth, Admin.
Res., 420 N. Main St., Box 875, 93206. Tel: 661-764-5486.
Catechesis/Religious Programs—Students 45.

Chowchilla, Madera Co., St. Columba (1921), Rev. Kenneth J. Bozzo.
Res., 213 Orange Ave., 93610. Tel: 559-665-3376. [JC]
Catechesis/Religious Programs—Tel: 559-665-5104.
Students 200.

Clovis, Fresno Co., Our Lady of Perpetual Help (1929), Rev. Msgr. Raymond C. Dreiling; Rev. Jose Sierra.
Res., 929 Harvard, 93612. Tel: 559-299-4270; Fax: 559-299-7126.
Church—Ninth & DeWitt.
School—836 DeWitt, 93612. Tel: 559-299-7504; Fax: 559-299-4627.
Immaculate Conception Sisters 5; Lay Teachers 7; Students 270.
Catechesis/Religious Programs—Tel: 559-297-8506.
Students 805.

Coalinga, Fresno Co., St. Paul The Apostle (1907), Rev. Nobert Rackensperger, O.F.M.Conv.
Res., 637 Sunset St., P.O. Box 812, 93210. Tel: 559-935-1872; Fax: 559-935-3763. [JC]
Catechesis/Religious Programs—Students 210.

Corcoran, Kings Co., Our Lady of Lourdes (1939), Rev. Gerald F. Chavez.
Res., 1404 Hanna, 93212. Tel: 559-992-4414; Fax: 559-992-2512.
Catechesis/Religious Programs—Tel: 559-992-4698.
Students 620.

Cutler, Tulare Co., St. Mary (1953), Rev. Jose Luis Vega.
Res., 12588 Avenue 407, P.O. Box 6, 93615. Tel: 559-528-3566.
Catechesis/Religious Programs—Tel: 559-528-3077.
Students 330.

Delano, Kern Co., St. Mary's of the Miraculous Medal (1920), Revs. Rick Fierros, M.Div.; James Kyrie, O.F.M.
Res., 916 Lexington St., 93215. Tel: 661-725-8456; Fax: 661-725-8485.
School—Tel: 661-725-9055; Fax: 661-725-3224. Mrs. Ruth Meadows, Prin.
Sisters 1; Lay Teachers 9; Students 132.
Catechesis/Religious Programs—Tel: 805-725-9041.
Students 515.
Mission—Richgrove, Tulare Co., St. Vincent, 1716 11th Ave., 93215.

Our Lady of Guadalupe (1954), Revs. Emerito Gomez, O.F.M.; Ervan Beers, O.F.M.
Res., 1015 Clinton St., 93215. Tel: 661-725-9087; 725-9115; Fax: 661-725-5128.
Catechesis/Religious Programs—Tel: 661-725-2777; Fax: 661-725-7129.
Students 520.

Del Rey, Fresno Co., St. Katherine. (Quasi-parish included with St. Mary, Sanger). Rev. Vito DiMarzio, R.C.J.
Res., 828 "O" St., P.O. Box 335, Sanger, 93657. Tel: 559-888-2889; 875-2025.
Catechesis/Religious Programs—Students 75.

Dinuba, Tulare Co., St. Catherine (1948), Rev. Msgr. Anthony Janelli; Rev. Abel Quispe.
Res., 356 N. Villa Ave., 93618. Tel: 559-591-0931; Fax: 559-591-2965.
Catechesis/Religious Programs—Tel: 559-591-2988. D.R.E.: Tomi Castilleja; Laura Rico; Maria Medina; Victoria Contreras; Ray Montanez; Rigoberto Medina.
Students 507.

Dos Palos, Merced Co., Sacred Heart (1924), Rev. Robert R. Vanoncini.
Res., 1655 Lucerne, 93620-2623. Tel: 209-392-2724; Fax: 209-392-1037.
Catechesis/Religious Programs—Students 400.

Earlimart, Tulare Co., St. Jude Thaddeus (1968), Revs. Antero Sachez, M.S.C. (Mexico); Jorge Luis de la Torre, M.S.C. (Mexico).
Mailing Address: P.O. Box 12187, 93219. Tel: 661-849-3170; Fax: 661-849-0704.
Res., 964 Dove St., 93219. Tel: 661-849-2858.
Catechesis/Religious Programs—Students 144.

Easton, Fresno Co., St. Jude Mission, Rev. Roderick L. Craig.
208 W. Jefferson, 93706. Tel: 559-485-3870; Fax: 559-485-3880.
Catechesis/Religious Programs—Students 137.

Exeter, Tulare Co., Sacred Heart (1950), Rev. Msgr. Nicolas Herrero.
Res., 417 North E St., 93221. Tel: 559-592-2465; Fax: 559-592-6075.
Catechesis/Religious Programs—Tel: 559-592-1020.
Students 579.
Mission—Farmersville, Tulare Co., St. Anthony of Egypt, 821 W. Visalia Rd., Farmersville, 93223. Tel: 559-747-0234.

Firebaugh, Fresno Co., St. Joseph (1950), Rev. Patrick Joel Davadilla, Jr.
Res., 1558 12th St., 93622. Tel: 559-659-2225; Fax: 559-659-0408.
School—1900 Saipan, 93622. Tel: 559-659-2841.
Lay Teachers 9; Students 100.
Catechesis/Religious Programs—Students 190.

Fowler, Fresno Co., St. Lucy (1965), Rev. Joaquin S. Arriaga; Deacon Ed Harmon, III.
Res., 512 S. 5th, 93625. Tel: 559-834-2624; Fax: 559-834-6814.
Catechesis/Religious Programs—Tel: 559-834-9124.
Students 197.

Frazier Park, Kern Co., Our Lady of the Snows. (Quasi-parish). Rev. Angel Sotelo.
7115 Lakewood Dr. Lake of the Woods, P.O. Box 995, 93225. Tel: 661-245-3741; Fax: 661-245-6404.
Catechesis/Religious Programs—Students 90.

Goshen, Tulare Co., St. Thomas the Apostle (1963), Revs. Raphael G. Farrow; Ramon Orozco; Deacon Julian Ponce.
Res., 1908 N. Court, Visalia, 93291. Tel: 559-732-8089; Fax: 559-732-0969. [CEM]

Gustine, Merced Co., Our Lady of Miracles (1919), Rev. Leonard J. Trindade; Mary Aguirre, Parish Admin.
Res., 370 Linden Ave., 95322. Tel: 209-854-6692; Fax: 209-854-1344.
School—Tel: 209-854-3180. Mr. Michael Gillitzer, Prin.
Lay Teachers 10; Students 198.
Preschool:—Tel: 209-854-3180. Mrs. Connie Rayan, Dir.
Catechesis/Religious Programs—Tel: 209-854-2834. Mrs. Val Knittle, D.R.E.
Students 240.

Hanford, Kings Co., St. Brigid (1886), Revs. Daniel C. Avila; Xavier Pappalliyil, O.C.D. (India).
Office & Mailing Address: 200 E. Florinda, 93230. Tel: 559-582-2533; Fax: 559-582-9193.
Res., 1005 N. Douty St., 93230. Tel: 559-582-2533. [CEM]
School—St. Rose-McCarthy Catholic School, 1000 N. Harris St., 93230. Tel: 559-584-5218; Fax: 559-584-5273. Ms. Debra Cabral, Prin.
Sisters of Our Lady of Nazareth 1; Lay Teachers 9; Students 215.
Catechesis/Religious Programs—Tel: 559-582-6563; Fax: 559-582-9193.
Students 425.

Immaculate Heart (1948), Revs. Victor V. Piansay; Jose Luis Varo.
Res., 10355 Hanford Armona Rd., 93230. Tel: 559-584-8576; Fax: 559-584-0436.
Catechesis/Religious Programs—Tel: 559-582-5688.
Students 345.

Hilmar, Merced Co., Holy Rosary (1948), Rev. A. Joseph Heffernan.
Res., P.O. Box 429, 95324. Tel: 209-667-8961; Fax: 209-667-5239.
Catechesis/Religious Programs—Tel: 209-632-7163.
Students 311.
Mission—Stevinson, Merced Co., St. Mary, 95374.

Huron, Fresno Co., St. Frances Cabrini (1961), Rev. Stephen M. Devine.
Res., 36986 Los Angeles St., P.O. Box 939, 93234. Tel: 559-945-2507.
Catechesis/Religious Programs—Students 162.

Kerman, Fresno Co., St. Patrick (1943), Rev. John Griesbach.
Mailing Address: P.O. Box 375, 93630. Tel: 559-846-8190; Fax: 559-846-7705.
Res., 567 S. Sixth St., 93630.
Catechesis/Religious Programs—Tel: 559-846-9106.
Students 350.

Kingsburg, Fresno Co., Holy Family (1950), Rev. Ricardo Magdaleno.
Res., 1301 Smith St., P.O. Box 798, 93631-0798. Tel: 559-897-5953; Fax: 559-897-8599. [JC]
Catechesis/Religious Programs—Tel: 559-897-7620.
Students 292.
Missions—London, Tulare Co., Santa Cruz, 5625 Ave. 378, 93631.; Traver, Tulare Co., St. John the Baptist Educational Center, 4204 Merritt Dr., Traver, 93673.

Lamont, Kern Co., St. Augustine (1962), Rev. John Schmoll.
Res., 10601 Myrtle Ave., 93241-2198. Tel: 661-845-0003; Fax: 661-845-0259.
Catechesis/Religious Programs—Tel: 805-845-3622.
Students 1,356.

Laton, Fresno Co., Shrine of Our Lady of Fatima (1953), Rev. Timothy A. Gallemore.
Res., P.O. Box 119, 93242. Tel: 559-923-4935; Fax: 559-923-2284.
Catechesis/Religious Programs—Tel: 559-923-3715.
Students 360.

Lemoore, Kings Co., St. Peter (1912), Rev. Eric Swearingen.
Res., 19 Follett St., 93245. Tel: 559-924-2562; Fax: 559-924-5727.
School—884 N. Lemoore Ave., 93245. Tel: 559-924-3424; Fax: 559-924-7848. Sr. Marion Abraham, C.S.S.T., Prin.
Carmelite Sisters of St. Teresa 4; Lay Teachers 6; Students 243.
Catechesis/Religious Programs—Tel: 559-924-2826. Edna Rowell, D.R.E.
Students 345.
Missions—Stratford, Kings Co., St. Joseph, 19359 Empire St., Stratford, 93266.; Tache Indian Reservation, Kings Co., St. Rosa, 16111 Alkaki, 93245. [CEM]
Chapel—St. Rose of Lima.

Lindsay, Tulare Co., Sacred Heart (1925), Rev. Alex C. Ignacio.
Res., 217 Lindero Ave., 93247-2623. Tel: 559-562-4008; Fax: 559-562-5511.
Catechesis/Religious Programs—Tel: 559-562-2082.
Students 355.
Missions—Tonyville, St. Anthony Church, 21631 Brooks Ave., 93247.; Strathmore, Tulare Co., St. James Catholic Church, 19752 Guthrie Rd., Strathmore, 93267. Tel: 559-568-0435.
Station—Plainview.

Livingston, Merced Co., St. Jude Thaddeus (1937), Rev. Harvey Fonseca.
Res., 330 Franci St., 95334. Tel: 209-394-7512; Fax: 209-394-3089.
Catechesis/Religious Programs—Tel: 209-394-7516. Rosa Maria Mercado, D.R.E.
Students 1,074.
Mission—Delhi, Merced Co., Teresa of Calcutta, P.O. Box 68, Delhi, 95315. Tel: (209) 667-7742.

Lone Pine, Inyo Co., Santa Rosa (1919), Rev. Francis P. Simeone, Admin.
Res., P.O. Box 246, 93545. Tel: 760-876-4350; Fax: 760-876-4350.
Catechesis/Religious Programs—Students 30.
Missions—Shoshone-Tecopa, Inyo Co., St. John the Baptist, P.O. Box 246, 93545.; Independence, Inyo Co., St. Vivian.
Station—Lone Pine, Death Valley.

Los Banos, Merced Co., St. Joseph (1905), Rev. Msgr. J. Wayne Hayes, P.A.; Rev. John Rodriguez.
Res., 1545 Center Ave., 93635. Tel: 209-826-4246; Fax: 209-827-3457.
School—Tel: 209-826-2709; Fax: 209-826-7320. Ms. Connie McGhee, Prin.
Franciscan Sisters 1; Lay Teachers 9; Students 249.
Catechesis/Religious Programs—1625 Center Ave., 93635. Tel: 209-826-1512.
Students 472.

Madera, Madera Co., St. Joachim (1881), Revs. Larry Toschi, O.S.J.; Guadalupe Sanchez, O.S.J.; Carlos Esquivel, O.S.J.
Res., 401 W. Fifth St., 93637. Tel: 559-673-3290; Fax: 559-673-6471.
School—Tel: 559-674-7628; Fax: 559-674-8770. Sr. Carmen Santuiste, R.C.M., Prin.
Immaculate Conception Sisters 2; Lay Teachers 7; Students 276.
Catechesis/Religious Programs—Tel: 559-674-5871.
Students 1,790.
Missions—Madera, Madera Co., St. Agnes, 7308 Hwy. 145, 93637.; Raymond, Madera Co., St. Anne, Raymond-Knowles, Raymond, 93653.

Mariposa, Mariposa Co., St. Joseph (1857), Rev. Stephen C. Bulfer.
Mailing Address: P.O. Box 215, 95338-0215. Tel: 209-966-2522; Fax: 209-966-2522.
Res., 4985 Bullion St. [CEM 3]
Catechesis/Religious Programs—Students 125.
Mission—Hornitos, Mariposa Co., St. Catherine of Sienna.

McFarland, Kern Co., St. Elizabeth (1966), Revs. Antero Sanchez, M.S.C., Admin.; Jorge Luis de la Torre, M.S.C.
Res., 835 E. Perkins, 93250. Tel: 661-792-3225; Fax: 661-792-5645.
Catechesis/Religious Programs—Tel: 661-792-3429. Socorro Munoz, D.R.E.
Students 353.

Mendota, Fresno Co., Our Lady of Guadalupe (1953), Rev. Msgr. Ricardo Barajas.
Res., P.O. Box 248, 93640. Tel: 559-655-3631; 4237 (Rectory).
Catechesis/Religious Programs—Students 107.
Mission—Three Rocks, Fresno Co., Our Lady of Lourdes, 161015 S. Derrick, Three Rocks, 93608. Tel: 559-829-3358.

Merced, Merced Co., Our Lady of Mercy/St. Patrick's, Revs. Jean-Michael Lastiri; Onyema Okorie.
Mailing Address: P.O. Box 2087, 95344.
Churches—Our Lady of Mercy, (1867), 435 W. 21st St., 95340. Tel: 209-383-3924; 383-3930 (Mass Recording); Fax: 209-723-6510. [JC]
St. Patrick, (1968), 671 E. Yosemite, 95340. Tel: 209-726-3216.
Res., 334 & 338 Snowhaven Ct., 95348. Tel: 209-383-3924; Fax: 209-723-6510.
School—Our Lady of Mercy Elementary, 1400 E. 27th St., 95340. Tel: 209-722-7496; Fax: 209-722-7532. Mrs. Brenda Feehan, Prin.
Lay Teachers 22; Students 489.
Preschool:—Tel: 209-722-6657. Mrs. Jill Serpa, Dir.
Catechesis/Religious Programs—Tel: 209-723-8888. Sr. Mary Kinsinger, D.R.E.
Students 695.
Mission—Hopeton, St. John the Baptist.

Sacred Heart (1945), Rev. Jose M. Montiel.
Res., 1220 M St., 95340. Tel: 209-383-6604; Fax: 209-383-6147.
Catechesis/Religious Programs—Tel: 209-383-1528. Sr. Gabriel Ann Tamayo, D.R.E.
Students 535.
Missions—Merced, Merced Co., El Nido, 95340.; Merced, Merced Co., St. George.

Oildale, Kern Co., Christ the King (1952), Rev. Msgr. Stephen A. Frost, J.C.L.
Res., 1800 Bedford Way, 93308. Tel: 661-391-4640; Fax: 661-391-4649.
Catechesis/Religious Programs—Tel: 661-399-1956.
Students 176.

Orange Cove, Fresno Co., St. Isidore the Farmer (1978), Rev. Robert Davis.
Mailing Address: P.O. Box 309, 93646. Tel: 559-626-4943; Fax: 559-626-4648.
Res., 480 Adams Ave., 93646.
Catechesis/Religious Programs—Students 335.
Mission—Squaw Valley, Fresno Co., St. Rita, 30673 George Smith Rd., Squaw Valley, 93675.

Parlier, Fresno Co., Our Lady of Sorrows (1963), Rev. Raul Diaz.
Res., 830 Tulare St., 93648. Tel: 559-646-2161; Fax: 559-646-9511.
Catechesis/Religious Programs—Students 280.

Planada, Merced Co., Sacred Heart (1939), Rev. Edgar A. Jimenez (Mexico).
Res., 9317 Amistad, P.O. Box 278, 95365. Tel: 209-382-0459; 382-0814. [JC]
Catechesis/Religious Programs—Students 130.
Mission—Le Grand, Merced Co., Our Lady of Lourdes.

Porterville, Tulare Co., St. Anne (1896), Revs. Scott Daugherty; Martin A. McGagh; Ignacio Villafan; Deacon Guilliermo Preciado.
Res., 378 North F St., 93257. Tel: 559-784-2800; Fax: 559-784-4338.
School—369 North F St., 93257. Tel: 559-784-4096. Sr. Rosario Mediavilla, R.A.D., Prin.
Sisters of the Love of God 4; Lay Teachers 8; Students 198.
Preschool:—Tel: 559-781-8614. Mrs. Rhonda Dotters, Dir.
Catechesis/Religious Programs—Students 650.
Missions—Porterville, Our Lady of Guadalupe, 217 S. Wallace, 93257.; Tule Indian Reservation, Tulare Co., Mater Dolorosa, Tel: 559-784-2800; Terra Bella, Tulare Co., Blessed Miguel Agustin Pro, 9120 Rd. 236, Terra Bella, 93270.
Station—At Methodist Church, 35725 Hwy. 190, Springville, 93265.

Reedley, Fresno Co., St. Anthony (1906), Rev. Msgr. Francis G. Tasy, V.S.; Rev. Angel Gonzalez, S.P.
Res., P.O. Box 188, 93654. Tel: 559-638-2012; Fax: 559-638-8211.
Schools—LaSalle Preschool / Child Care Center, Tel: 559-638-2621; Fax: 559-638-5542. Sr. Lucy Cassarino, Dir.; St. La Salle Grammar School, 404 E. Manning Ave., 93654. Tel: 559-638-2621; Fax: 559-638-5542.
Sisters 3; Lay Teachers 12; Students 249.
Catechesis/Religious Programs—Tel: 559-638-5608. Sr. Kathleen Garcia, S.H.F., D.R.E.
Students 574.

Ridgecrest, Kern Co., St. Ann (1946), Rev. Robert E. Gamel.
Res., 446 W. Church St., P.O. Box 127, 93556. Tel: 760-375-2110; Fax: 760-375-6345. [JC]
School—(Grades K-8). Tel: 760-375-4713.
Lay Teachers 9; Students 177.
Catechesis/Religious Programs—Students 263.
Mission—Randsburg, Kern Co., Santa Barbara, 72 Lexington Ave., Randsburg, 93554.

Riverdale, Fresno Co., St. Ann (1928), Revs. Raymond J. Duffy; Pedro M. Mancilla.
Res., P.O. Box 335, 93656. Tel: 559-867-3035; Fax: 559-867-7205. [JC]
Catechesis/Religious Programs—Tel: 559-867-4996.
Students 380.
Missions—Diener Ranch At Five Points, Fresno Co., Holy Family Chapel; Riverdale, Fresno Co., Our Lady of the Assumption, West & Herndon, P.O. Box 335, 93656-0335.

Rosamond, Kern Co., St. Mary, Rev. Leslie F. Shenoy.
Mailing Address:—3100 Fifteenth St., 93501. Fax: 661-256-7127.
Catechesis/Religious Programs—Students 120.
Mission—Mojave, Kern Co., St. Francis of Assisi Church, 15382 Myer Rd., Mojave, 93501. Tel: 805-256-4505.

Sanger, Fresno Co., St. Mary (1922), Revs. Vito Di Marzio, R.C.J.; Fillippo Puntrello, R.C.J. In res., Rev. Rodolfo D'Agostino, R.C.J.
Res., 828 O St., P.O. Box 335, 93657. Tel: 559-875-2025; Fax: 559-875-1281. [JC]
Catechesis/Religious Programs—2590 North Ave., 93657. Tel: 559-875-6340.
Students 1,019.
Mission—Del Rey, Fresno Co., St. Katherine's, 5375 Carmel, Del Rey, 93616. Tel: 559-888-2889; Fax: 559-888-2889.

Selma, Fresno Co., St. Joseph (1913), Rev. Msgr. Daniel Lopez; Deacon Ed Harmon, III.
Res., 2441 Dockery Ave., 93662. Tel: 209-896-1052; Fax: 209-896-3975.
Catechesis/Religious Programs—Tel: 559-896-2620.
Students 500.

Shafter, Kern Co., St. Therese (1952), Rev. Thomas O'Neill.
Res., 300 W. Lerdo, P.O. Box 1448, 93263. Tel: 661-746-4471; Fax: 661-746-0945.
Catechesis/Religious Programs—Tel: 661-746-9937.
Students 423.

Taft, Kern Co., St. Mary (1918), Rev. Msgr. Loydell J. Marth.
Res., 110 E. Woodrow St., 93268. Tel: 661-765-4292.
Catechesis/Religious Programs—Students 35.

Tehachapi, Kern Co., St. Malachy (1887), Rev. Msgr. Joseph C. Barnes.
Res., 407 W. "E" St., 93561-1642. Tel: 661-822-3060; Fax: 661-822-3159.
Catechesis/Religious Programs—Tel: 661-822-6327.
Students 265.

Tipton, Tulare Co., St. John The Evangelist (1945), Rev. Gregory Beaumont.
Res., 232 S. Adams Rd., Box 159, 93272. Tel: 559-752-4544; Fax: 559-752-1409.
Catechesis/Religious Programs—Students 437.
Mission—Woodville, Tulare Co., St. Francis of Assisi, 16410 Ave. 168, Woodville, 93258.
Station—Tipton, Pixley.

Tranquillity, Fresno Co., St. Paul (1924), Rev. Arturo Gomez.
Res., P.O. Box 575, 93668. Tel: 559-698-7429; Fax: 559-698-1059.
Catechesis/Religious Programs—Students 150.
Mission—San Joaquin, Fresno Co., St. Vincent de Paul.

Tulare, Tulare Co., St. Aloysius (1905), Revs. Richard Urizalqui; Raul Marta; Deacon Robert Smith.
Res., 125 E. Pleasant Ave., 93274. Tel: 559-688-1796; 1797; Fax: 559-688-0948.
School—Tel: 559-686-6250; Fax: 559-686-0479. Sr. Kay O'Brien, O.P., Prin.
Dominican Sisters of Tacoma, WA 1; Lay Teachers 9; Students 214.
Catechesis/Religious Programs—Tel: 559-688-8644.
Students 550.

St. Rita (1967), Rev. Timothy N. Cardoza.
Res., 954 S. O St., 93274. Tel: 559-686-3847; Fax: 559-686-9672.
Catechesis/Religious Programs—Students 613.

Visalia, Tulare Co., Holy Family (1950), Revs. Raphael G. Farrow; Ramon Orozco; Deacon Julian Ponce.
Res., 1908 N. Court St., 93291. Tel: 559-732-8089; Fax: 559-732-0969. [JC]
Catechesis/Religious Programs—Tel: 559-732-9651. James Rooney, D.R.E.
Students 993.
Mission—Ivanhoe, Tulare Co., San Felipe de Jesus, 32809 Rd. 159, Ivanhoe, 93235. Tel: 559-798-1359.

St. Mary (1861), Rev. Msgr. Thomas G. Kleinhans; Rev. Douglas Walker.
Res., 608 N. Church St., P.O. Box 287, 93279. Tel: 559-734-9522; Fax: 559-734-3435.
School—George McCann Memorial School, 200 E. Race St., 93291. Tel: 559-732-5831; Fax: 559-741-1562. Mrs. Lorraine Brown, Prin.
Lay Teachers 9; Students 202.
Catechesis/Religious Programs—Tel: 559-733-3929; Fax: 559-733-1255. Mrs. Joan Bell, D.R.E.
Students 900.

Wasco, Kern Co., St. John the Evangelist (1919), Rev. John P. Fluetsch.
Res., 1300 Ninth Pl., 93280. Tel: 661-758-6688; Fax: 661-758-7751.
School—Tel: 661-758-6467. Mrs. Joanne Todd, Prin.
Lay Teachers 5; Students 69.
Preschool:—Tel: 661-758-6829. Mrs. Donna Ward, Dir.
Catechesis/Religious Programs—Students 283.
Mission—Blackwell's Corner, Kern Co., Nuestra Senora de la Paz, 14846 Hwy. 33, Lost Hills, 93249.

Wofford Heights, Kern Co., St. Jude (1969), Rev. Patrick Persinger.
Res., 86 Nellie Dent Dr., 93285. Tel: 760-376-2416; Fax: 760-376-2416.
Catechesis/Religious Programs—Students 35.

Woodlake, Tulare Co., St. Frances Cabrini (1963), Rev. Jesse C. Venzor.
Res., 599 N. Valencia Blvd., P.O. Box 459, 93286. Tel: 559-564-2647.
Catechesis/Religious Programs—Students 321.
Mission—Three Rivers, Tulare Co., St. Clair, Alta Acres Dr., Three Rivers, 93271.

Yosemite National Park, Mariposa Co., Our Lady of the Snows (1963), Rev. Dennis M. Alvernaz.
Res., P.O. Box 457, 95389. Tel: 209-372-4729; Fax: 209-372-4767.
Station—Yosemite National Park, Wawona.

Chaplains of Public Institutions

FRESNO. *Community Hospital, Veterans' Hospital & University Medical Center.* Attended by Capuchin Fathers. Revs. David LaPierre, O.F.M.Cap., Supr.; Alejandro Magallanes, O.F.M.Cap.; Donal Burke, O.F.M.Cap.; Alan Wilson, O.F.M.Cap.
Valley Children's Hospital. Rev. James Cairns, C.M.

AVENAL. *California State Prison, Kings Co.* Deacon Ned Quigley.

BAKERSFIELD. *Kern Medical Center, Bakersfield Memorial Hospital & San Joaquin Community Hospital.* Rev. David Johnson, O.F.M.

BORON. *Federal Prison Camp.* Vacant. P.O. Box 500, 93561.

CALIFORNIA CITY. *California City Correctional Center* P.O. Box 2590, 93550. Deacon Gerald Fitzgerald.

CHOWCHILLA. *Department of Corrections, Central California Women's Facility.* Vacant.
Valley State Prison for Women P.O. Box 99, 93610-9361. Sr. Mary Adele Appleby, B.V.M.

COALINGA. *Pleasant Valley State Prison* 601 C Washington, 93210. Rev. James R. Cadera.

CORCORAN. *Calif. State Prison* Tel: 559-992-8800. Rev. John J. Moore.
California Substance Abuse Treatment Facility & State Prison - Corcoran 900 Quebec Ave., P.O. Box 7100, 93212. Sr. Carolyn Whited, S.H.F.; Sr. Christine McNamara, S.S.L.

DELANO. *North Kern State Prison.* Vacant Tel: 661-721-2345, Ext. 6862.

MARIPOSA. *Mt. Bullion Conservation Camp* P.O. Box 5006, 95338. Rev. Jose Montiel.

PORTERVILLE. *Developmental Center* P.O. Box 2000, 93258. Sr. Patrick Malani, S.O.L.M.

TAFT. *Correctional Institution* P.O. Box 7000, 93268. Tel: 661-763-2510. Rev. Francisco Diaz.

TEHACHAPI. *California Correctional Institution* P.O. Box 426, 93581. Tel: 661-822-4402, Ext. 4387. Rev. Hermengildo Adolfo, Chap.

WASCO. *Prison Facility* P.O. Box 8800, 93280-8800. Tel: 661-758-8400. Rev. Daniel Bringas.

On Special Assignment:
Reverend Fathers—
Amerando, Jerry, Chap., San Joaquin Memorial H.S.
Burchfield, Michael, J.C.L., Asst. Tribunal Dir. & Adjutant Vicar, Canada
Congdon, John, Chap., Hinds Hospice, Fresno, CA
Cotta, Myron, V.G., 1550 N. Fresno St., Fresno, CA 93703-3788

Faculties Only:
Reverend Fathers—
Drieci, Pat, C.SS.R.
Vogt, William

On Duty Outside the Diocese:
Reverend Fathers—
Flickinger, Don D., 15333 Woodard Rd., San Jose, CA 95124

Absent on Sick Leave:
Reverend Fathers—
Bray, Kevin

On Leave:
Reverend Monsignors—
Belluomini, Ralph
Reverend Fathers—
Smith, Richard

Retired:
Reverend Monsignors—
Balker, Joseph W., 2401 N. Kaweah, Exeter, CA 93221
Byrne, Laserian, 5770 N. Marda, Fresno, CA 93704
Cleary, Kevin, P.O. Box 1407, Ridgecrest, CA 93556
Doherty, Patrick G., 2121 N. 1st. St., Fresno, CA 93703
Elmlinger, Herbert, 188A W. Barstow, Fresno, CA 93704
Flood, Patrick, 2121 N. 1st. St., Fresno, CA 93703
Herdegen, Anthony, 5660 N. River Forrest Dr., Milwaukee, WI 53209
Lahey, Maurice, 2121 N. 1st St., Fresno, CA 93703
Lee, Howard T.
Meyer, Gilbert, P.O. Box 117, Olancha, CA 93548
Minhoto, Walter F., 2814 Mariposa, Fresno, CA 93721
O'Connor, Michael
O'Friel, John, 181 W. Bush St., Lemoore, CA 93245
Pointek, Francis J., P.O. Box 1240, Tehachapi, CA 93581
Poschen, Ed, 390 N. Winchester Blvd., 5-4A, Santa Clara, CA 95050
Riccomini, Dino, 440 Kerwin, Cambria, CA 93428
Reverend Fathers—
Alabart, Francis X., 722 Dover Pl., Delano, CA 93215
Barron, Cecil, C.M.F., 2494 S. Chestnut, Fresno, 93725
Cummins, Timothy, 2121 N. First St., Fresno, CA 93703
Dreici, Patrick, C.SS.R., 3456 140 Marks, Apt. 103, Fresno, 93722
Gonzalez, Antonio, 715 E. Elm St., Tulare, CA 93274
Leitheiser, Douglas, P.O. Box 639, Lindsay, CA 93247
McGagh, Martin A., P.O. Box 52, Porterville, CA 93258
McKee, John, c/o Hugent Summerhill, Athlone, Ireland
Orozco, Rodolfo, c/o M.A. Vallejo, 1970 Bergen Ct., Kingsburg, CA 93631
Pascual, Manuel, 4701 S. Mooney Blvd., Sp.R7, Visalia, CA 93277
Raffel, Godfrey, P.O. Box 387, Tehachapi, CA 93581

INSTITUTIONS LOCATED IN THE DIOCESE

[A] HIGH SCHOOLS, DIOCESAN

FRESNO. *San Joaquin Memorial High School*, 1406 N. Fresno St., 93703. Tel: 559-268-9251; Fax: 559-268-1351.
E-mail: DOFSJM@impresso.com
John Eckman, Prin. Lay Teachers 44; Students 705.

BAKERSFIELD. *Garces Memorial High School*, 2800 Loma Linda Dr., 93305. Tel: 661-327-2578; Fax: 661-327-5427.
E-mail: jkvasnicka@onemain.com
Web site: www.garces.org
John Kvasnicka, Prin.; David West, Dir. Campus Ministry. Lay Teachers 40; Students 725.

[B] GENERAL HOSPITALS

FRESNO. *Saint Agnes' Medical Center*, 1303 E. Herndon, 93720. Tel: 559-449-3000; Fax: 559-449-5699
For a complete listing, refer to the Hospitals section.

BAKERSFIELD. *Catholic Healthcare West Central California*, 2215 Truxtun Ave., 93301. Tel: 661-632-5000; Fax: 661-327-2592.
Web site: www.chw.edu
For a complete listing, refer to the Hospitals section.

MERCED. *Mercy Hospital & Health Services*, 2740 M St., 95340. Tel: 209-384-6444; Fax: 209-722-2902
For a complete listing, refer to the Hospitals section.

[C] HOMES FOR INVALID AND AGED

FRESNO. *Nazareth House*, 2121 N. First St., 93703. Tel: 559-237-2257; Fax: 559-237-1958.
E-mail: PSNRose@earthlink.net
For a complete listing, refer to the Special Care Facilities section.

LOS BANOS. *New Bethany*, 93635 1441 Berkeley Dr. Tel: 209-827-8933.
E-mail: JDF2003@grid.com
For a complete listing, refer to the Special Care Facilities section.

[D] CATHOLIC CHARITIES

FRESNO. *Catholic Charities of the Diocese of Fresno*, 149 N. Fulton St., 93701. Tel: 559-264-6434; Fax: 559-237-7144.
E-mail: velas@ccdof.org
Mr. Ernest Velasquez, Diocesan Dir.

Catholic Charities Thrift Store, 149 N. Fulton St., 93701-1607. Tel: 559-237-0851; Fax: 559-264-0655. Sandi Fournet, Prog. Mgr. Total Staff 2.

Catholic Social Services, 149 N. Fulton St., 93701. Tel: 559-237-0851; Fax: 559-264-0655.
E-mail: socialservices@ccdof.org
Web site: www.ccdof.org
Sandra Fournet, Prog. Mgr. Total Staff 1; Total Assisted 5,584.

Francis X. Singleton Emergency Food Assistance Program, 149 N. Fulton St., 93701. Tel: 559-237-0851; Fax: 559-264-0655. Peter P. Hagel, Prog. Mgr. Total Staff 2; Total Assisted 96,500.

Immigration & Refugee Services, 149 N. Fulton St., 93701. Tel: 559-264-6400.
E-mail: FRESM@lightspeed.net
Total Staff 3; Total Assisted 102,500.

Senior Companion Program. Tel: 559-498-6377.
E-mail: ecaples@ccdof.org
Catherine Caples, Prog. Mgr. Total Staff 6; Total Assisted 324.

BAKERSFIELD. *Bakersfield Big Brothers*, 525 18th St., 93301. Tel: 661-281-2130; Fax: 661-281-2139.
E-mail: drodri@ccdof.org
David Rodriguez, Prog. Mgr. Staff 1; Total Assisted 75.

Catholic Social Services, 525 18th St., 93301. Tel: 661-281-2130; Fax: 661-281-2139.
E-mail: vcabaz@ccdof.org
Virginia Cavazos, Prog. Mgr. Total Staff 2; Total Assisted 78,000.

Homemaker Program, Cabrini League, 631 E. Calif, 93307. Tel: 661-325-2995; Fax: 661-325-4382. Dan Miller, Coord. Staff 6; Total Assisted 250.

Immigration & Refugee Services, 525 18th St., 93301. Tel: 661-281-2130; Fax: 661-281-2139. Delfina Granados, Immigration Counselor. Total Staff 1; Total Assisted 1,200.

Junipero Serra Inn-Half Way House, 700 19th St., 93301. Tel: 661-324-6125; 323-4646; Fax: 661-324-5723. Hassan Kowwasar, Prog. Mgr. Halfway/Work Furlough Community Correctional Re-entry Center (CCRC). Total Staff 17; Total Assisted 120.

FARMERSVILLE. *St. Vincent de Paul Center*, 468 E. Visalia Rd., P.O. Box 106, 93223. Tel: 559-594-4932; Fax: 559-594-5632. Mary G. Flores, Prog. Mgr. Total Staff 3; Total Assisted 2,100.

MERCED. *Catholic Charities*, 366 W. Main #1, 95340. Tel: 209-383-2494; 383-5220; Fax: 209-383-3975. Ramiro Coronado, Deputy Dir. Total Staff 5; Total Assisted 21,898.

Direct Services, 366 W. Main, #1, 95340. Tel: 209-383-2494; Fax: 209-383-3975. Ramiro Coronado, Deputy Dir.

Migrant and Refugee Services, 336 W. Main St., Ste. 1, 95340. Tel: 209-383-0283; Fax: 209-383-3975. Ramiro Coronado, Deputy Dir. Tel: 209-383-5220.

PORTERVILLE. *Catholic Social Services*, 1309 W. Main, Bldg. B, 93257. Tel: 559-781-5778; Fax: 559-781-3415. Mary Meisel, Prog. Mgr. Total Staff 3; Total assisted annually 42,650.

VISALIA. *Catholic Social Services*, 1638 N. Dinuba Blvd., 93294. Tel: 559-734-1572; Fax: 559-734-4921. Sr. Kenneth Quinn, D.C., M.S.W., Dir. Total Staff 13; Total Assisted 94,000.

Good News Medical Clinic, 1638 N. Dinuba Blvd., 93291. Tel: 559-734-0483; Fax: 559-738-8922. Total Assisted Annually 32,500.

Good News Center (Sr. Ursula's Kitchen & Thrift Store), 1638 N. Dinuba Blvd., 93291. Tel: 559-738-8922.

Good News Inn (Shelter), 1718 & 1722 N. Dinuba Blvd., 93291. Tel: 559-734-6470; Fax: 559-734-4921. Total Assisted Annually 150.

[E] CONVENTS AND RESIDENCES FOR SISTERS

FRESNO. *Franciscan Hospitallers of the Immaculate Conception (FHIC)*, 6020 N. Flora Ave., 93722. Tel: 559-261-1782.

Poor Sisters of Nazareth, 2121 N. First St., 93703. Tel: 559-237-2257. Sr. Antionette Farrell, P.S.N., Supr. Sisters 6.

St. Agnes Hospital Convent, 1261 E. Los Altos Ave., 93710. Tel: 559-431-3376. Sisters of the Holy Cross, Inc. 8.

Sister Disciples of the Divine Master, 3700 N. Cornelia Ave., 93722. Tel: 559-275-1656; Fax: 559-275-2725. Sr. M. Lucille VanHoogmoed, P.D.D.M., Supr. Sisters 13.

Sisters of the Love of God (RAD), 4305 E. Union Ave., 93703. Tel: 559-454-1864. Sisters 5.

ATWATER. *Our Lady of the Atonement Convent*, 1694 Grove Ave., 95301. Tel: 209-358-2109. Sr. Louise Silva, S.A.; Sr. Mary Kinsinger, S.A.; Sr. Maureen Murphy, S.A. Franciscan Sisters of the Atonement 3.

BAKERSFIELD. *Sister Servants of the Blessed Sacrament (SJS)*, 1100 S. Kern St., 93307. Tel: 661-631-1061 (Convent); 323-6059; 323-6050 (School); Fax: 661-323-6050. Sisters 5.

CLOVIS. *Sisters of the Immaculate Conception (RCM)*, 859 Harvard Ave., 93612. Tel: 559-299-8407.
Web site: www.rg.net/conception
Sisters 5.

LEMOORE. *Carmelite Sisters of St. Teresa (CSST)*, 884 N. Lemoore Ave., 93245. Tel: 559-924-2347. Sisters 5.

LOS BANOS. *Franciscan Hospitallers of the Immaculate Conception (FHIC)*, 1441 Berkeley Dr., 93635. Tel: 209-826-0770.
E-mail: jdf2003@yahoo.com
Sisters 13.

MADERA. *Sisters of the Immaculate Conception (RCM)*, 224 N. J St., 93637. Tel: 559-674-4085; Fax: 559-674-4085. Sisters 3.

MERCED. *Daughters of the Holy Spirit (DHS)*, 2987 Tahoe Dr., 95340. Tel: 209-384-2705. Sisters 3.

Dominican Sisters, 2635 Piedmont Dr., 95340-9679. Tel: 209-723-6564; Fax: 209-388-9423. Sisters 2.

Dominican Sisters (OP), 2635 Piedmont Dr., 95340-9679. Sisters 3.

PORTERVILLE. *Sisters of the Love of God (RAD)*, 385 N. F St., 93257. Tel: 559-784-6889; Fax: 559-784-4338.
E-mail: Mediavilla@triax.com
Sisters 5.

REEDLEY. *Daughters of Divine Zeal (FDZ)*, 379 E. Manning Ave., 93654. Tel: 559-638-1916; Fax: 559-638-5542.
E-mail: dofstlasalle@impresso.com

THREE RIVERS. *Daughters of Charity of St. Vincent de Paul (DC)*, 40534 Cherokee Oaks Dr., 93271-9743. Tel: 559-561-1204.
E-mail: doc3riv@thegrid.net
Sisters 3.

[F] RETREAT HOUSES

THREE RIVERS. *St. Anthony's Retreat House*, P.O. Box 249, 93271. Tel: 559-561-4595; Fax: 559-561-4493. Revs. Larry Dunphy, O.F.M., Dir.; Pedro Umana, O.F.M., Retreat Master; Richard Juzix; Bros. Gerald Chumik, O.F.M.; Victor Hunter, O.F.M.; Marion Alfonso, O.F.M. Priests 2; Brothers 3.

[G] NEWMAN CENTERS

FRESNO. *St. Paul Newman Center*, 1572 E. Barstow Ave., 93710. Tel: 559-436-3434; Fax: 559-436-3430.
E-mail: pkavookjian@hotmail.com

Web site: http://www.csufnewman.com
Rev. Perry Kavookjian; Sr. Joanne Bauer, C.S.C., Campus Min.
California State University at Fresno.
Fresno City College.

BAKERSFIELD. *Bakersfield College Newman Center,* 710 Stockdale Hwy., 93309-1399. Tel: 661-834-7483. Rev. Michael Moore, Chap.

[H] SOCIETY OF ST. VINCENT DE PAUL

FRESNO. *Fresno District Council,* 149 N. Fulton St., 93701. Alice M. Thoms, Trustee.
Kern District Council, 1515 Baker St., Bakersfield, 93305. Rev. Robert Wenzinger, Mod.
Merced-Mariposa District Council, 131 W. Main St., Merced, 95340. Tel: 209-723-6077. Dolores Schwerdferger, Pres.

[I] MISCELLANEOUS & AGENCIES

MERCED. *Catholic Professional & Business Breakfast Club of the Fresno Diocese.* Mailing Address: P.O. Box 775, Atwater, 95301. Tel: 209-394-7984; Fax: 209-394-4988. 1550 N. Fresno St., Fresno, 93703-3788. Jeff Winder, Pres.; Rev. Msgr. Laserian Byrne, Chap.

SANGER. *Fr. Hannibal House Social Service Center,* 1501 14th St., P.O. Box 37, 93657. Tel: 559-875-0564; Fax: 559-875-1281.
E-mail: rogusa@aol.com
Total Assisted: Food Distribution 11,853.

RELIGIOUS INSTITUTES OF MEN REPRESENTED IN THE DIOCESE

For further details refer to the corresponding bracketed number in the Religious Institutes of Men or Women section.

[0200]—*Benedictine Monks.*—O.S.B.
[0470]—*The Capuchin Friars.*—O.F.M.Cap.
[]—*Carmelite.*—O.C.D.
[0360]—*Claretian Missionaries.* (Western Prov.).—C.M.F.
[0480]—*Conventual Franciscans.* (St. Joseph Cupertino Prov.).—O.F.M.Conv.
[0260]—*Discalced Carmelite Friars.*—O.C.D.
[0520]—*Franciscan Friars.* (St. Barbara Prov.).—O.F.M.
[0650]—*Holy Ghost Fathers.* (Western Prov.).—C.S.Sp.
[0690]—*Jesuit Fathers and Brothers.*—S.J.
[]—*Missioneros del Sagrado Corazon y Santa Maria de Guadalupe.*—M.S.C.
[0910]—*Oblates of Mary Immaculate.*—O.M.I.
[0930]—*Oblates of St. Joseph.* (Asti, Italy).—O.S.J.
[0430]—*Order of Preachers.*—O.P.
[1050]—*Pontifical Institute for Foreign Missions.*—P.I.M.E.
[1070]—*Redemptorists.*—C.SS.R.
[1090]—*Rogationist Fathers.*—R.C.J.
[1200]—*Society of the Divine Savior.*—S.D.S.
[1330]—*Vincentians (Congregation of the Mission).*—C.M.

RELIGIOUS INSTITUTES OF WOMEN REPRESENTED IN THE DIOCESE

[0230]—*Benedictine Sisters of Pontifical Jurisdiction.* (Mt Angel, OR).—O.S.B.
[]—*Carmelite Sisters of St. Teresa.* (Gidellahalli, Bangalore-India).—C.S.S.T.
[1010]—*Congregation of Divine Providence of San Antonio, Texas.* (Helotes, TX).—C.D.P.
[3935]—*Congregation of the Sisters of St. Louis.* (Juilly, Monaghan).—S.S.L.
[1920]—*Congregation of the Sisters of the Holy Cross.* (Notre Dame, IN).—C.S.C.
[0760]—*Daughters of Charity of St. Vincent de Paul.* (Los Altos Hills, CA) (Western Prov.).—D.C.
[0795]—*Daughters of Divine Zeal.* (Rome, Italy).—F.D.Z.
[0820]—*Daughters of the Holy Spirit.* (France) (Putnam, CT Prov. House).—D.H.S.
[1070-20]—*Dominican Sisters.* (Congregation of St. Thomas Aquinas, Marymount, Tacoma, WA).—O.P.
[1070-25]—*Dominican Sisters.* (Congregation of the Dominican Sisters of St. Catherine of Siena of Kenosha).—O.P.
[1270]—*Franciscan Hospitaller Sisters of the Immaculate Conception.* (San Jose, CA).—F.H.I.C.
[1190]—*Franciscan Sisters of the Atonement.* Garrison, NY).—S.A.
[2180]—*Immaculate Heart Community.* (Los Angeles, CA).—I.H.M.
[2570]—*Institute of the Sisters of Mercy of the Americas.* (Burlingame, CA).—R.S.M.
[2690]—*Missionary Catechists of Divine Providence.* (San Antonio, TX).—M.C.D.P.
[0980]—*Pious Disciples of the Divine Master.* (Staten Island, NY).—P.D.D.M.
[3242]—*Poor Sisters of Nazareth.* (Los Angeles, CA).—P.S.N.
[2970]—*School Sisters of Notre Dame.* (St. Louis, MO).—S.S.N.D.
[3499]—*Servants of the Blessed Sacrament.* (El Segundo, CA).—S.J.S.
[0430]—*Sisters of Charity of Blessed Virgin Mary.* (Dubuque, IA).—B.V.M.
[]—*Sisters of Our Lady of Nazareth.* (Fiji, South Pacific).—S.O.L.N.
[3840]—*Sisters of St. Joseph of Carondelet.* (Los Angeles, CA).—C.S.J.
[1960]—*Sisters of the Holy Family.* (Mission San Jose, CA).—S.H.F.
[2130]—*Sisters of the Immaculate Conception.* (San Francisco, CA).—R.C.M.
[]—*Sisters of the Love of God.* (La Puente, CA).—R.A.D.
[4120-06]
[]—*Ursuline Nuns of the Congregation of Paris.* (Toledo, OH).—O.S.U.

DIOCESAN CEMETERIES

FRESNO. *Fresno Catholic Cemeteries,* 264 N. Blythe, 93706. Tel: 559-488-7449; Fax: 559-488-7466. Michael Orlando, Dir.

NECROLOGY

(No Deaths)

Diocese of Gallup

(Diocesis Gallupiensis)

Most Reverend

DONALD E. PELOTTE, S.S.S., D.D., PH.D.

Bishop of Gallup; ordained September 2, 1972; appointed Coadjutor Bishop of Gallup February 24, 1986; consecrated May 6, 1986; succeeded to See, March 20, 1990. *Office: P.O. Box 1338, Gallup, NM, 87305. Res., 433 Camino Del Sol, P.O. Box 1317, Gallup, NM, 87305.* Tel.: 505-722-3047.

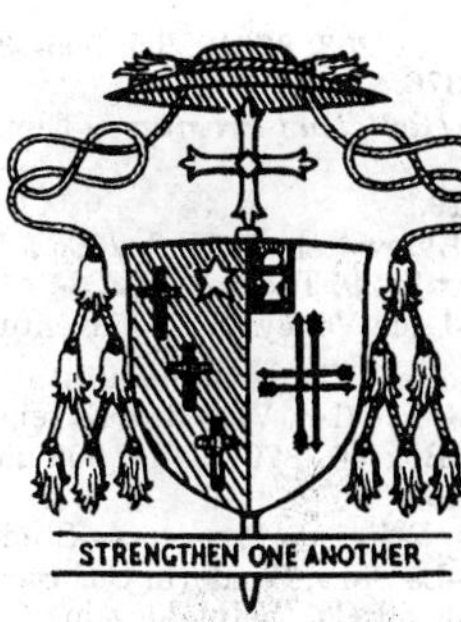

Chancery: 711 S. Puerco Dr., P.O. Box 1338, Gallup, NM, 87305. Tel.: 505-863-4406; Fax: 505-722-9131.

ESTABLISHED DECEMBER 16, 1939.

Square Miles 55,468.

Comprises Apache, Navajo and those parts of the Navajo and Hopi Reservations in Coconino Counties in the State of Arizona; San Juan, McKinley, Catron, Cibola and those parts of Rio Arriba, Sandoval, Bernalillo and Valencia Counties lying west of 106, 52', 41" meridian in the State of New Mexico.

Legal Title: New Mexico: Roman Catholic Church of the Diocese of Gallup. Arizona: Bishop of the Roman Catholic Church of the Diocese of Gallup.

For legal titles of parishes and diocesan institutions, consult the Chancery Office.

STATISTICAL OVERVIEW

Personnel	
Bishop	1
Priests: Diocesan Active in Diocese	32
Priests: Active Outside Diocese	10
Priests: Retired, Sick or Absent	21
Number of Diocesan Priests	63
Religious Priests in Diocese	28
Extern Priests in Diocese	3
Ordinations:	
Diocesan Priests	2
Permanent Deacons	2
Permanent Deacons in Diocese	26
Total Brothers	13
Total Sisters	139
Parishes	
Parishes	56
With Resident Pastor:	
Resident Diocesan Priests	23
Resident Religious Priests	19
Without Resident Pastor:	
Administered by Priests	10
Administered by Deacons	1
Administered by Women Religious	1
Completely Vacant	2
Missions	35
Professional Ministry Personnel:	
Brothers	3
Sisters	35
Lay Ministers	11
Welfare	
Homes for the Aged	1
Total Assisted	60
Day Care and Extended Day Care Centers	3
Total Assisted	66
Specialized Homes	2
Total Assisted	78
Special Centers for Social Services	24
Total Assisted	30,861
Other Institutions	1
Total Assisted	40,314
Educational	
Diocesan Students in Other Seminaries	4
Total Seminarians	4
High Schools, Private	3
Total Students	357
Elementary Schools, Private	10
Total Students	1,540
Catechesis/Religious Education:	
High School Students	1,345
Elementary Students	3,771
Total Students Under Catholic Instruction	7,017
Teachers in the Diocese:	
Priests	2
Sisters	31
Lay Teachers	135
Vital Statistics	
Receptions into the Church:	
Infant Baptism Totals	962
Adult Baptism Totals	267
Received into Full Communion	119
First Communions	974
Confirmations	647
Marriages:	
Catholic	166
Interfaith	71
Total Marriages	237
Deaths	639
Total Catholic Population	54,306
Total Population	379,555

Former Bishop—Most Rev. BERNARD T. ESPELAGE, O.F.M., D.D., ord. May 16, 1918; appt. Bishop of Gallup, July 20, 1940; cons. Oct. 9, 1940; resigned Sept. 3, 1969; died Feb. 19, 1971.—Most Rev. JEROME J. HASTRICH, D.D., ord. Feb. 9, 1941; cons. Auxiliary Bishop of Madison and Titular Bishop of Gurza, July 31, 1963; transferred to the See of Gallup, Sept. 3, 1969; installed Dec. 3, 1969; retired March 20, 1990; died May 12, 1995.

Vicar General—Rev. Msgr. LEO GOMEZ, V.G.

Vicar for Indian Affairs—Rev. CARON VOLLMER, O.F.M.

Office of the Bishop—711 S. Puerco Dr., P.O. Box 1338, Gallup, 87305. Tel: 505-863-4406.

Chancery—711 S. Puerco Dr., P.O. Box 1338, Gallup, 87305. Tel: 505-863-4406; Fax: 505-722-9131. Office Hours: Mon.-Thurs. 8:30-12 & 1-4:30; Fri. 8:30-12.

Chancellor—Sr. CONSOLTA BEECHER, S.B.S.

Financial Secretary—Mrs. ANNA J. DIGREGORIO.

Diocesan Tribunal (First Instance)—711 S. Puerco Dr., P.O. Box 1338, Gallup, 87305. Tel: 505-863-4406; Fax: 505-722-9324.

Judicial Vicar—Rev. LAWRENCE J. O'KEEFE, J.C.D.

Adjutant Judicial Vicar—Rev. ALFRED A. TACHIAS, J.C.L.

Judges—Rev. ALFRED A. TACHIAS, J.C.L.; Deacon JIM HOY.

Defenders of the Bond—Revs. THOMAS MAIKOWSKI, Ph.D.; EMERIC NORDMEYER, O.F.M.

Notary—MARY ALICE SALAZ.

Episcopal Vicars—Very Rev. WALTER OPALEWSKI, V.F., McKinley Vicariate; Very Rev. MARTAN RADEMAKER, O.F.M., V.F., Apache Vicariate; Rev. DANIEL HUSSEY, V.F., Navajo Vicariate; Very Rev. ALBERTO AVELLA, V.F., Lower Arizona Vicariate; Very Rev. GENEBOWSKI, San Juan Vicariate; Very Rev. EMERIC NORDMEYER, O.F.M., Cibola Vicariate.

Vicaress for Religious—Sr. MARGUERITE MCGRANAHAN, R.S.M.

Presbyteral Council—Most Rev. DONALD E. PELOTTE, S.S.S., D.D., Ph.D.; Rev. Msgr. LEO GOMEZ, V.G.; Very Rev. LAWRENCE O'KEEFE, Moderator; Revs. DIEGO MAZON, O.F.M.; EMERIC NORDMEYER, O.F.M.; Very Revs. ALBERTO AVELLA; DANIEL HUSSEY; LOUIS FRANZ, C.M.; WALTER OPULEWSKI; Revs. TIMOTHY FARRELL; THOMAS MAIKOWSKI; PATRICK UNIVERSAL; GENE BOWSKI; MELDON HICKEY, O.F.M.; Sr. CONSOLATA BEECHER, S.B.S., Sec., *P.O. Box 1338, Gallup, 87305.*

Diocesan Consultors—Rev. Msgr. LEO GOMEZ, V.G.; Revs. LAWRENCE O'KEEFE; DANIEL HUSSEY; EDWARD FRONSKE, O.F.M.; THOMAS MAIKOWSKI; Very Rev. DIEGO MAZON, O.F.M.; Rev. LOUIS FRANZ, C.M.

Diocesan Navajo Mission Board—Most Rev. DONALD E. PELOTTE, S.S.S.; Very Rev. MARTAN RADEMAKER, O.F.M.; Revs. CARON VOLLMER, O.F.M.; DAVIN VON HAGEL, O.F.M.

Diocesan Offices and Directors

Archivist—Sr. CONSOLATA BEECHER, S.B.S.

Boy Scouts—Rev. THOMAS MAIKOWSKI, Ph.D., Dir. & Chap., *P.O. Box 1028, Gallup, 87305.* Tel: 505-863-3563.

Budget and Finance—Deacon JAMES P. HOY, Dir.

Cemeteries—Vacant, *Box 2840, Farmington, 87401.*

Catholic Charities—Sr. BETTY MARIE DUNKEL, D.C., Dir., *Main Office, Gallup, P.O. Box 1589, Gallup, 87305.* Tel: 505-722-5272. Chinle: *P.O. Box 417, Chinle, AZ, 86053.* Tel: 520-674-3238. Grants-Milan: *2595 W. Hwy. 66, P.O. Box 124, Grants, 87020.* Tel: 505-285-5451. Farmington: *119 W. Broadway, Farmington, 87401.* Tel: 505-325-3724. Holbrook: *P.O. Box 41, Holbrook, AZ, 86025.* Tel: 520-524-9720. White Mountain: *P.O. Box 600, McNary, AZ, 85930.* Tel: 520-334-2219.

Cursillos—Rev. MELDON HICKEY, O.F.M., *P.O. Box 680, St. Michael's, AZ, 86511.* Tel: 520-871-4171.

Diocesan Pastoral Council—Most Rev. DONALD E. PELOTTE, S.S.S., D.D., Ph.D.; VALDO LAWRENCE, Chm. MARY ANN MONTOYA, Vice Chm. ANDRE BORG, Sec.; Revs. THOMAS MAIKOWSKI; PATRICK UNIVERSAL; Deacon ROY STRINGFELLOW; Sr. CONSOLATA BEECHER, S.B.S.; MARILYN BECENTI; MARIA CLASSAY; Sr. BETTY DUNKEL, D.C.; Sr. MARY FRATE, D.C., Alternate; Sr. ADELAIDE LINK, O.S.F.; BETTY PEDERLICK; ROMY RODRIGUEZ; ERNST D. TSOSIE, JR.

Native American Lay Ministry and Diaconate Program—Rev. BLANE GREIN, O.F.M., Dir.

Director of Education, (Catholic Schools and Religious Education)—Rev. THOMAS MAIKOWSKI, Ph.D., Dir. Educ., *P.O. Box 1028, Gallup, 87305.* Tel: 505-863-3563.

Ecumenical Affairs in Arizona, Arizona Ecumenical Council—Rev. ALBERTO AVELLA, *P.O. Box 1449, Showlow, 85901.* Tel: 520-537-2543.

Ecumenical Affairs in New Mexico, New Mexico Council of Churches—Rev. DANIEL DALEY, *307 N. Church St., Bloomfield, 87413.* Tel: 505-632-2014.

Newspaper—"Voice of the Southwest"; Rev. TIMOTHY FARRELL, *P.O. Box 1338, Gallup, 87305.* Tel: 505-863-4406.

Permanent Deacon Program—Most Rev. DONALD E. PELOTTE, S.S.S., D.D., Ph.D.; Deacons TIMOTED P.

LUJAN, Deacon Dir. JIM HOY, Asst. Dir.; Mrs. LINDA HOY, Asst. Dir.

Priests' Retirement Fund—WILLIAM DAY, Chm.; Revs. ROBERT MATHIEU; WILLIAM SAUTER; OLIVER CURRAN; ALBERTO AVELLA.

Propagation of the Faith—Deacon JOSEPH F. KRIKAWA, Dir., *P.O. Box 1338, Gallup, 87305.*

Radio and Television—Rev. CORMAC ANTRAM, O.F.M., *P.O. Box 517, Kayenta, AZ, 86033.*

Search—TED GOMEZ, Dir., *2103 Lynwood Dr., Farmington, 87401.*

Serra Club—Vacant.

Social Justice and Outreach—Sr. BETTY MARIE DUNKEL, D.C., *P.O. Box 1589, Gallup, 87305.*

Vocations—For Priesthood: Rev. JOACHIM BLONSKI, *414 N. Allen Ave., Farmington, 87401.* Deacon Vocations: Deacon TIMOTED LUJAN, *P.O. Box 2612, Milan, 87021-2612.* Vicaress of Religious: Sr. MARGUERITE MCGRANAHAN, R.S.M.

Youth Ministry—DOUGLAS CLAPPER; LENA CLAPPER, *P.O. Box 1615, Aztec, 87410.*

CLERGY, PARISHES, MISSIONS AND PAROCHIAL SCHOOLS

CITY OF GALLUP
(McKinley County)

1—CATHEDRAL OF THE SACRED HEART (1939). (Dedicated June 19, 1955). Revs. Patrick J. Universal, Rector; James E. Walker.
Res. & Mailing Address: 415 E. Green Ave., 87301. Tel: 505-722-6644; Fax: 505-722-6645.
Catechesis/Religious Programs—Tel: 505-722-5485. Barbara Kozeliski, D.R.E.
Students 350.

2—ST. FRANCIS OF ASSISI (1943) (Hispanic), Revs. Diego Mazon, O.F.M.; Ulric Pax, O.F.M.; Bro. Maynard Shurley, O.F.M.
Res., 411 N. Second, 87301. Tel: 505-863-3033; Fax: 505-863-6887.
Catechesis/Religious Programs—Tel: 505-863-5291. Sr. Ana Lilie Zuniga, H.N.S.G., D.R.E.
Students 350.
Mission—Gamerco, St. Joseph the Worker.

3—ST. JEROME. Closed. For inquiries for parish records contact the Chancery.

4—ST. JOHN VIANNEY (1973), Rev. Walter Opalewski; Deacon Timothy Kelley.
Res., 3408 Zia Dr., 87301. Tel: 505-722-3361.
Catechesis/Religious Programs—Tel: 505-722-5085.
Students 142.

OUTSIDE THE CITY OF GALLUP, NEW MEXICO

Acoma, Cibola Co., San Esteban, Acoma Catholic Indian Mission (1629) (Native American), Revs. Berard Doerger, O.F.M.; Lawrence C. Smith, S.J. Pastoral Team: Ernest Vallo; Miriam Pritchard; Romalda Allen.
Res., P.O. Box 448, Pueblo of Acoma, 87034-0448. Tel: 505-552-6403. [CEM]
Catechesis/Religious Programs—Students 46.
Missions—Acomita, Cibola Co., St. Anne, P.O. Box 448, 87034.; McCartys, Cibola Co., Santa Maria de Acoma, 87034.

Aragon, Catron Co., Santo Nino (1910) (Hispanic), Rev. Thomas Coleman; Deacon Juan Aragon.
Res., P.O. Box 489, Reserve, 87830-0489. Tel: 505-533-6240.
Missions—Lower San Francisco, Catron Co., San Isidro; Reserve, Catron Co., St. Francis; Horse Springs, Catron Co., St. Anne.
Station—Apache Creek.

Aztec, San Juan Co., St. Joseph (1946) (Hispanic), Revs. Joachim Blonski; Michael Kugler; Deacon Charles Peterson.
Res., 500 N. Mesa Verde St., 87410. Tel: 505-334-6535.
Catechesis/Religious Programs—Tel: 505-334-3542. Sr. Sara Marie Gomez, O.S.U., D.R.E.
Students 250.

Blanco, San Juan Co., St. Rose of Lima, Rev. Daniel P. Daley.
Res., 307 N. Church St., Bloomfield, 87413. Tel: 505-632-2014.
Catechesis/Religious Programs—Students 102.; *Catechesis/Religious Programs*—D.R.E.: Joann Valdez; Monique Bryant.
Students 75.
Mission—Los Martinez, Our Lady of Guadalupe.

Bloomfield, San Juan Co., St. Mary, Rev. Daniel P. Daley.
Res., 307 N. Church St., 87413. Tel: 505-632-2014.
Catechesis/Religious Programs—Roselie Valdez, D.R.E.
Students 200.

Chichiltah, McKinley Co., St. Patrick (1965) (Navajo), Rev. Jeffrey King.
Res., P.O. Box 267, Vanderwagon, 87326. Tel: 505-778-5410.
Catechesis/Religious Programs—Students 6.
Mission—Good Shepherd Catholic Mission.

Church Rock, McKinley Co., St. Philip Benizi. Unassigned.
Res., P.O. Box 310, 87311. Tel: 505-488-5515.
Station—Pinedale.

Crownpoint, McKinley Co., St. Paul (1961) (Navajo), Revs. Patrick J. Universal; John Boland. Pastoral Administrators: Sr. Barbara Smith, A.S.C.; Sr. Maureen Farrar, A.S.C.
Res., P.O. Box 268, 87313. Tel: 505-786-5376; Fax: 505-786-5376. [JC]
Catechesis/Religious Programs—Christine Smith, D.R.E.
Students 19.
Mission—Bluewater, McKinley Co., Risen Savior, HC 62, Box 7129, Thoreau, 87323-9410.
Stations—Lake Valley.; St. Bonaventure, Thoreau.

Cuba, Sandoval Co., Immaculate Conception (Nacimiento) (1914), Very Rev. Eugene Bowski.
Res., P.O. Box 40, 87013. Tel: 505-289-3803; Fax: 505-289-3236.
Catechesis/Religious Programs—Students 65.
Missions—La Jara, Sandoval Co., Santo Nino; San Luis, Sandoval Co., Saint Aloysius Gonzaga; Cabezon, Sandoval Co., San Jose.

Farmington, San Juan Co., Sacred Heart (1929), Rev. Timothy Farrell. In res., Rev. Raymond Mahlmann.
Res., 414 N. Allen Ave., 87401. Tel: 505-325-9743; Fax: 505-325-8860.
Catechesis/Religious Programs—Tel: 505-564-8164. Cindy Blanco, D.R.E.
Students 405.

St. Mary's (1976) (Hispanic), Rev. Msgr. Leo Gomez; Rev. Timothy Cervantes; Deacon Frank Chavez.
Res., P.O. Box 2840, 87499-2840. Tel: 505-325-0287; Fax: 505-564-8515.
Catechesis/Religious Programs—Tel: 505-325-0287, Ext. 147. Sr. Ruth Battagila, D.R.E.
Students 428.

Flora Vista, San Juan Co., Holy Trinity (1986) (Hispanic), Revs. Joachim Blonski; Michael Kugler; Deacon Charles Peterson.
Res., 500 N. Mesa Verde Ave., Aztec, 87410. Tel: 505-334-6535.

Fort Wingate, McKinley Co., St. Eleanor. Closed. For inquiries for parish records contact the Chancery.
Station—Iyanbito.

Grants, Cibola Co., St. Teresa (1942), Rev. Emeric Nordmeyer, O.F.M. In res., Revs. Maurus Pax, O.F.M.; Godfrey Blank, O.F.M.; Deacons Larry Chavez; Paul Sanchez.
Res., 213 Smith St., P.O. Box 668, 87020. Tel: 505-285-6645; Fax: 505-285-6646.
Catechesis/Religious Programs—Tel: 505-287-3549. Socorro Jackson, D.R.E.
Students 445.

Laguna, Cibola Co., St. Joseph (Laguna Indian Pueblo) (1699), Rev. Berard Doerger, O.F.M. In res., Rev. Gilbert Schneider, O.F.M.
Res., P.O. Box 1000, 87026. Tel: 505-552-9330.
Catechesis/Religious Programs—Tel: 505-552-7464; Fax: 505-552-9429. D.R.E.: Sr. Marcia Huber, S.M.I.C., (Youth); Sr. Virginia Adler, C.S.A, (Adult).
Students 72.
Missions—Encinal, Nativity of the Blessed Virgin Mary; Mesita, Sacred Heart; Paguate, St. Elizabeth; Paraje, St. Mary Margaret; Seama, St. Anne.

Lumberton, Rio Arriba Co., St. Francis of Assisi (1910) (Hispanic-Native America), Rev. Donald J. Richardson.
Res., H.C. 71, P.O. Box 68, 87528. Tel: 505-759-1307; Fax: 505-759-1392. [CEM]
Catechesis/Religious Programs—Tel: 505-759-3002. Sr. Kim Kasakaitas, M.S.B.T, D.R.E.
Students 85.
Mission—Dulce, Rio Arriba Co., St. Anthony. 3760 Sandhill.

Milan, Cibola Co., St. Vivian (1969), Rev. Gil Mangampo, Admin.
Res., P.O. Box 145, San Rafael, 87051. Tel: 505-287-8164.

Navajo, McKinley Co., St. Berard (1963) (Navajo), Rev. Niles E. Kraft, O.F.M.; Deacon Wilson Gorman. In res., Rev. Davin W. Von Hagel, O.F.M.
Res., P.O. Box 1284, 87328. Tel: 505-777-2251.
Catechesis/Religious Programs—Tel: 505-777-2490. D.R.E.: Sr. Marquerite Bartz; Rita Bia; Julia Gorman.
Students 55.
Mission—Sawmill, Apache Co., St. Francis Mission, P.O. Box 41, Sawmill, AZ 86549. Tel: 602-729-5224.
Station—Crystal.

Pinehaven, McKinley Co., Good Shepherd Catholic Mission (1972) (Navajo), Rev. Jeffrey King.
Res., P.O. Box 2170, Gallup, 87305. Tel: 505-778-5658.
Catechesis/Religious Programs—Students 5.
Convent—Box 267, Vanderwagen, 87326. Tel: 505-778-5740. Missionaries of Charity
Sisters 4.

Quemado, Catron Co., Sacred Heart (1951) (Hispanic), Rev. Robert E. Mathieu.
Res., P.O. Box 339, 87829. Tel: 505-773-4631.

San Fidel, Cibola Co., St. Joseph Mission (1920) (Hispanic). Attended by Acoma, NM.
Res., P.O. Box 448, Acoma, 87034. Tel: 505-552-6403. [CEM]

San Mateo, Cibola and McKinley Cos., San Mateo, Rev. Gil Mangampo, Admin.
Mailing Address: P.O. Box 2938, Milan, 87021. Tel: 505-287-9327.
Res., P.O. Box 2938, Milan, 87021.

San Rafael, Cibola Co., San Rafael, Rev. Gil Mangampo, Admin.
Res., P.O. Box 145, 87051. Tel: 505-287-8164.

Seboyeta, Cibola Co., Our Lady of Sorrows (1974) (Hispanic), Deacon William P. Beaton, Admin.
Res., H.C. 77, P.O. Box 13, 87014. Tel: 505-552-6301.
Missions—Bibo, Our Lady of Loretto; Moquino, Santa Rosalia.
Station—Marquez.

Shiprock, San Juan Co., Christ the King (1924) (Native American), Rev. John Sauter.
Res., P.O. Box 610, 87420. Tel: 505-368-4532.
Catechesis/Religious Programs—Tel: 505-368-5845.
Students 58.

Thoreau, McKinley Co., St. Bonaventure, Rev. John Boland.
Res., P.O. Box 1389, 87323. Tel: 505-862-7449.
Station—Smith Lake, Holy Spirit.

Tinaja, Cibola Co., San Lorenzo (1935) (Hispanic-Navajo). Attended by Chichiltah, NM. Rev. Jeffrey King.
Res., State Rte. 2, Box 47, Ramah, 87321. Tel: 505-783-4301.
Catechesis/Religious Programs—Students 5.
Mission—Fence Lake, El Morro.

Tohatchi, McKinley Co., St. Mary Church (1920) (Navajo), Rev. John Mittelstadt, O.F.M.; Bro. Michael Haag, O.F.M.; Deacon Sherman Manuelito.
Res., Box 39, 87325. Tel: 505-733-2243; Fax: 505-733-2243. [CEM]
Catechesis/Religious Programs—Tel: 505-733-2468. Sr. Marlene Kochert, O.S.F., D.R.E.
Students 105.
Mission—Naschitti, St. Anthony, Tel: 505-732-4344.
Stations—Coyote Canyon.; Mexican Springs.; Twin Lakes.; Sheep Springs.; Chuska.

Waterflow, San Juan Co., Sacred Heart (1917), Rev. Patrick Wedeking, Admin.
Res., 9 Rd. 6820, 87421. Tel: 505-598-5454.
Catechesis/Religious Programs—Sr. Ann Reges Barrett, M.S.B.T.
Students 70.
Missions—Kirtland, San Juan Catholic Center, P.O. Box 857, 87417. Tel: 505-598-6799; Ojo Amarillo, Sacred Heart Missionary Cenacle, P.O. Box 1037, Fruitland, 87416. Tel: 505-598-9856. Sr. Ann Regis Barrett, M.S.B.T., Dir.

Zuni, McKinley Co., St. Anthony, Our Lady of Guadalupe (Zuni Indian Pueblo) (1923), Rev. Sean Murnan, O.F.M.; Sr. Clara Scherr, S.C.L., Pastoral Min. In res., Rev. Terance Rhoades, O.F.M.
Res., P.O. Box 486, 87327. Tel: 505-782-2888; Fax: 505-782-2888.
Catechesis/Religious Programs—Students 15.

ARIZONA

Alpine, Apache Co., St. Helena (1971), Rev. Msgr. Arthur F. MacDonald.
Res., P.O. Box 229, 85920. Tel: 520-339-4363.
Catechesis/Religious Programs—Students 6.
Mission—Glenwood, Catron Co., Santo Nino, P.O. Box 284, Glenwood, NM 88039.

Chinle, Apache Co., Our Lady of Fatima (1905) (Navajo), Rev. Blane Grein, O.F.M.

Res., P.O. Box 2119, 86503. Tel: 520-674-5413; Fax: 520-674-5813.
Missions—Many Farms, Apache Co., St. Anthony, P.O. Box 578, Many Farms, 86538. Tel: 520-781-6350; Pinon, Navajo Co., St. Mary of the Rosary, P.O. Box 432, Pinon, AZ 86510. Tel: 520-725-3365.
Catechesis/Religious Programs—Tel: 520-674-5029.
Students 25.

Cibecue, Navajo Co., St. Catherine (1929) (Apache), Rev. Bernard Green, S.D.S., Admin.
Res., P.O. Box 80156, 85911. Tel: 520-332-2311; Fax: 520-332-2528.
Mission—Cedar Creek, St. Anthony. (TUC).

Concho, Apache Co., San Rafael (1977), Rev. Frank Chacon.
Church—P.O. Drawer C, 85924. Tel: 520-337-2515.

Fort Defiance, Apache Co., Our Lady of Blessed Sacrament (1915) (Navajo), Revs. Martan Rademaker, O.F.M.; Meldon Hickey, O.F.M., Assoc.; Deacon Dan Martin.
Res., P.O. Box 70, 86504-0070. Tel: 520-729-5068.
Catechesis/Religious Programs—Sr. Mary Hotten Roth, S.B.S., D.R.E.
Students 74.

Ganado, Apache Co., All Saints (1968) (Navajo), Rev. Flann O'Neil, O.F.M.
Res., P.O. Box 119, 86505. Tel: 520-755-3401.
Catechesis/Religious Programs—Tel: 520-652-3236; Fax: 520-652-3236. Sr. Monica Dubois, O.P., D.R.E.
Students 68.
Mission—Klagetoh, Apache Co., St. Anne, Tel: 520-652-3264. Bro. John Hotstream, S.C. Tel: 520-654-3236. In res., Bros. Dwight Kenney, S.C.; David Landry, S.C.
Mission—Greasewood, Our Lady of the Rosary, #50, HC 58, Box 70, 86505. Bro. Paul O'Brien, O.F.M.
Stations—Cornfields.; Wide Ruins.

Holbrook, Navajo Co., Our Lady of Guadalupe (1923), Rev. Lawrence O'Keefe; Deacons Robert Dedecker; Robert Racicot.
Res., 212 E. Arizona St., P.O. Box 849, 86025. Tel: 520-524-3261; Fax: 520-524-1507.
Catechesis/Religious Programs—Students 242.

Houck, Apache Co., St. John the Evangelist (Tekakwitha Mission) (1927) (Navajo), Rev. Cormac Antram, O.F.M.
Res., P.O. Box 48, 86506. Tel: 520-688-2921.
Catechesis/Religious Programs—Students 29.
Mission—Pine Springs, St. Rose.

Kayenta, Navajo Co., Our Lady of Guadalupe (1967), Rev. Jerome Herff, C.M.
Res., P.O. Box 517, 86033. Tel: 520-697-3429.
Catechesis/Religious Programs—Students 20.

Keams Canyon, Navajo Co., St. Joseph's Indian Mission (1920) (Hopi-Navajo), Rev. Clayton F. Kilburn, C.M.
Res., P.O. Box 128, 86034. Tel: 520-738-2325; Fax: 520-738-2325.
Station—Toyei.

Lukachukai, Apache Co., St. Isabel (1910) (Navajo), Rev. Caron Vollmer, O.F.M.
Res., P.O. Box 128, 86507. Tel: 520-787-2322.
Catechesis/Religious Programs—Students 8.
Missions—Round Rock, Our Lady of Guadalupe; Tsaile, St. Ann; Wheatfields, Our Lady of the Lake.

McNary, Apache Co., St. Anthony (1922), Rev. Cyril Levy.
Res., P.O. Box 628, 85930. Tel: 520-334-2394.
Catechesis/Religious Programs—Students 3.
Stations—Hawley Lake.; Vernon. (Summer).; Sunrise Ski Lodge. (Winter).

Overgaard, Navajo Co., Our Lady of Assumption (1982), Rev. William F. Day.
Res., P.O. Box 628, 85933. Tel: 520-535-5329.
Catechesis/Religious Programs—Students 18.

Page, Coconino Co., Immaculate Heart of Mary (1958), Rev. Mark Ford, C.M.; Deacon Roy Stringfellow.
Res., P.O. Box 1387, 86040. Tel: 520-645-2301; Fax: 520-645-1261.
Catechesis/Religious Programs—Students 110.

Pinetop, Navajo Co., St. Mary of the Angels (1974), Rev. Oliver Curran; Deacons Russell Majesky; Richard Conn.
Res., Box 819, 85935. Tel: 520-367-2080; Fax: 520-367-2085.
Catechesis/Religious Programs—Mindy Savoia, D.R.E.
Students 240.

Pinon, Navajo Co., St. Mary of the Rosary (1937) (Navajo). Attended by Chinle, AZ.
Res., P.O. Box 432, 86510. Tel: 520-725-3365.
Catechesis/Religious Programs—Students 12.
Stations—Tachee.; Blue Gap.; Forest Lake.; Whippoorwill Spring.; Hardrock.; Kits'iiLi.

Show Low, Navajo Co., St. Rita (1962), Rev. Alberto Avella; Deacon John Heal.
Res., P.O. Box 1449, 85901. Tel: 520-537-2543; Fax: 520-537-2543.
Catechesis/Religious Programs—Susan Olsen, D.R.E.
Students 70.

Snowflake, Navajo Co., Our Lady of the Snows (1963), Rev. William J. Welch; Deacon William J. Rogers.
Res., 1654 S. Main St., 85937. Tel: 520-536-4559; Fax: 520-536-5852.
Catechesis/Religious Programs—Mrs. John M. Heal, D.R.E.
Students 63.

Springerville, Apache Co., St. Peter (1880) (Hispanic), Rev. Robert E. Mathieu; Deacon George Campos.
Res., P.O. Box 1566, 85938. Tel: 520-333-4423; Fax: 520-333-4423.
Catechesis/Religious Programs—; Students 100.

St. Johns, Apache Co., St. John the Baptist (1890), Rev. Frank Chacon; Deacon Filomeno Ulibarri.
Res., P.O. Box 309, 85936. Tel: 520-337-4390.
Catechesis/Religious Programs—Tel: 520-337-4461.
Students 230.

St. Michaels, Apache Co., St. Michael (1898) (Navajo), Revs. Martan Rademaker, O.F.M.; Meldon Hickey, O.M.F. In res., Bros. John Friebel, O.F.M.; Francis Evans, O.F.M.
Res., P.O. Box 680, 86511-0680. Tel: 520-871-4171; Fax: 520-871-4172.
Catechesis/Religious Programs—Tel: 520-871-4173. D.R.E.: Sr. Josephine Goebel, C.S.A.; Sr. Frances Rose Dinkel, C.S.A.
Students 96.
Mission—St. Michaels, St. Michael's Mission for Navajo Indians.

Tuba City, Coconino Co., St. Jude (1956), Rev. J. Godden Menard, C.M.
Res., P.O. Box 248, 86045. Tel: 520-283-5391.
Catechesis/Religious Programs—Students 54.

Whiteriver, Navajo Co., St. Francis (1921) (Apache), Rev. Edward Fronske, O.F.M.
Res., P.O. Box 679, 85941. Tel: 520-338-4432; Fax: 520-338-1568.
Catechesis/Religious Programs—Mary Christen, D.R.E.
Students 80.

Winslow, Navajo Co., St. Joseph's (1896), Revs. Daniel C. Hussey; Jakov Juric.
Res., 300 W. Hillview St., 86047. Tel: 520-289-2350; Fax: 520-289-9226.
Catechesis/Religious Programs—Students 168.
Madre de Dios (1950) (Hispanic), Rev. Daniel C. Hussey.
Res., 300 W. Hillview St., 86047. Tel: 520-289-2350; Fax: 520-289-9226.
Catechesis/Religious Programs—Carol Gilliam, D.R.E.
Students 72.

Chaplains of Public Institutions

GALLUP. *Gallup Area Hospitals & Nursing Homes* 506 W. 66 Ave., 87301. Tel: 505-722-0999. Rev. Hugh O'Neill.

FARMINGTON. *Farmington Area Hospitals* 414 N. Allen Ave., 87401. Tel: 505-325-9743. Rev. Raymond Mahlmann.

Special Assignment:
Reverend Fathers—
Maikowski, Thomas R., Dir. of Education

On Duty Outside of Diocese:
Reverend Fathers—
Bezzina, Benjamin, St. Mary's Catholic Church, 56 Burton St., Concord, New South Wales 2137 Australia
Casimano, Santino, Chap., Navsubase Nlon, Groton, CT 06349-5013
Coutu, Joseph, Most Holy Trinity Monastery, Dugway Rd., Petersham, MA 01366
DeGante, Adalberto, 917 W. 7th Ave., Fort Morgan, CO 80701. Tel: 970-867-2885
Llano, Isidoro
Morello, Peter, VA Medical, 650 E. Indian School Rd., Phoenix, AZ 85012
Sanchez, Raul, Ch. Capt., USAF, 6933 Borderbrook Dr., Apt. 1313, San Antonio, TX. Tel: 210-670-7373
Turner, Robert, Blessed Sacrament Parish, 3100 S. 41st St., Milwaukee, WI 53215
Vigil, Michael A., Catholic University of America, Washington, DC

Absent on Leave:
Reverend Fathers—
Buckley, James, P.O. Box 71037, Sanger, TX 76266
Finnegan, Kevin
Kassis, Daniel, P.O. Box 4742, Laguna Beach, CA 92652-4742
Lopez, Adolfo
McConvey, Michael, 3 Argyll Ave., Bustin Brae Larne, Co. Antrim, Ireland
McNeill, Douglas, 488 7th Ave., Brooklyn, NY 11215
Mesley, Jerry
Obersteiner, Ernest, 67-918 Arden Dr., Cathedral City, CA 92234
Wollersheim, David, 1222 A Washington St., Apt. 1, Manitowoc, WI 54220

Retired:
Reverend Fathers—
Budai, Frank A., 149530 Seneca Tr., P.O. Box 2709, Big River, CA 92242
Burns, James, P.O. Box 2155, Wickenburg, AZ 85378
Downie, Arley T., #15 Rd. 6015, Farmington, NM 87401
Doyle, Gerald, P.O. Box 2131, Swansboro, NC 28584
Hart, William, P.O. Box 413, Castine, ME 04421
Konechne, Louis, Villa Guadalupe, 1900 Mark Ave., Gallup, NM 87301
Lindenmeyer, James, 4600 San Medina, Farmington, NM 87401
Manero, Ismael, Eladio Perlado 26-8C, Burgos, 09007
Pispeky, Steve
Rodriguez, Jose H.
Smith, Norman, Mullen Home, 3629 W. 29th Ave., Denver, CO 80211
Stanfield, Francis E., 309 E. Logan Ave., Gallup, NM 87301

Permanent Deacons:
Aragon, Juan, Gen. Del., Aragon, NM
Aragon, Vidal, 324 Jane N.E., Albuquerque, NM 87123
Beaton, William P., P.O. Box 425, San Fidel, NM 87049
Berhost, Paul, 2104 E. 17th St., Farmington, NM 87020
Bloomfield, John, P.O. Box 5024, Gallup, NM 87305
Campos, George, P.O. Box 1254, Eagar, AZ 85925
Chavez, Frank, 341 Arnold Dr., Aztec, NM 87410
Chavez, Larry, P.O. Box 1883, Grants, NM 87020
Dedecker, Robert
Dooley, Paul
Gorman, Wilson C., P.O. Box 218, Fort Defiance, AZ 86504-0218
Guoladdle, Bobby
Heal, John, P.O. Box 1429, Snowflake, AZ 85937
Hernandez, Arnold, St. Edwards Church, 610 W. Stevens, Carlsbad, NM 88220
Hoy, James, P.O Box 1084, Gallup, NM 87305
Kelley, Timothy, 416 Valentina Dr., Gallup, NM 87301
Krikawa, Joseph, P.O. Box 651, Gallup, NM 87305
Lane, John F.
Lucero, Levy, 414 San Andreas, Alamogordo, NM 88310
Lujan, Timoteo, P.O. Box 2612, Milan, NM 87021-2612
Majesky, Russel, P.O. Box 139, Greer, AZ 85927
Manuelito, Sherman, P.O. Box 296, Tohatchi, NM 87325-0296
Martin, Daniel Nez, P.O. Box 724, Window Rock, AZ 86515
Moffett, Stephen, P.O. Box 4383, North Las Vegas, NV 89036
Peterson, Charles, 28 Rd. 3009, Aztec, NM 87410
Racicot, Robert, P.O. 892, Holbrook, AZ 86025-0892
Resendes, Daniel, 4514 N. Carlin Springs Rd., Arlington, VA 22203
Rogers, Earl, P.O. Box 283, La Plata, NM 87418
Rogers, William, P.O. Box 217, Taylor, AZ 85939-0217
Sanchez, Paul, 203 N. Nimitz, Grants, NM 89020
Scarabino, Anthony
Stando, Matthew, 2446 Harlem Rd., Cheektowaga, NY 14225
Starrs, William, 4580 N. Aqua Fria Dr., #A, Prescott Valley, AZ 86314
Stringfellow, Roy, P.O. Box 2559, Page, AZ 86040
Tafoya, Samuel, P.O. Box 38, San Rafael, NM 87051-0038
Ulibarri, Fiomeno, P.O. Box 453, Concho, AZ 85924
Valencia, Ernest, P.O. Box 461, Blanco, NM 87412

INSTITUTIONS LOCATED IN THE DIOCESE

[A] SEMINARIES, DIOCESAN

GALLUP. *Diocesan Diaconate and Lay Ecclesial Ministry Formation Program*, P.O. Box 1338, 87305. Tel: 505-863-4406.
E-mail: dcntimo@cia-g.com
Most Rev. Donald E. Pelotte; Deacon Timoteo Lujan, Dir. Assoc. Directors: Deacon James P. Hoy; Linda Hoy. Faculty: Revs. Alfred A. Tachias; Lawrence O'Keefe; Berard Doerger, O.F.M.; Meldon Hickey, O.F.M.; Jerome Herff, C.M.; James E. Walker; Sr. Rene Bache, C.S.A.; Sr. Sarah Page, O.S.F., Ed.D; Sr. Michael Claire Wilson, O.P.; Sr. Annette O'Donnell, S.B.S., Ed.D.; Sr. Mary Frate, D.C.; Sr. Ruth Battaglia, O.S.A.; Deacon James P. Hoy; Dr. Emerine Glowienka, Ph.D. Diaconate Students 9; Lay Eccelesial Ministry Students 8; Other Students 7.

CHINLE, AZ. *Native American Lay Ministry and Diaconate Program*, P.O. Box 2119, 86503. Tel: 520-674-5413; Fax: 520-674-5813. Rev. Blane Grein, O.F.M., Dir. Faculty: Rev. John Sauter; Bro. John Hotstream, S.C.; Sr. Maureen Farrar, A.S.C.; Sr. Barbara Smith, A.S.C.; Sr. Gloria Davis, S.B.S.; Sr. Marcia Huber, S.M.I.C.; Sr. Mildred Speed, O.S.F.; Sr. Annette O'Donnell, S.B.S.; Shirley Britt; Chris Rayner. Students 65.

[B] HIGH SCHOOLS, PRIVATE

GALLUP. *Gallup Catholic High School*, 515 Park Ave., 87301. Tel: 505-863-6652; Fax: 505-726-8147.
E-mail: gcschool@cnetco.com
Donald Sparks, Prin. Lay Teachers 6; Students 76.

ST. MICHAELS, AZ. *St. Michael High School*, P.O. Box 650, 86511. Tel: 520-871-4443; Fax: 520-871-3191. John K. Reilly, Prin. Sisters 3; Lay Teachers 11; Students 190.

THOREAU. *St. Bonaventure High School*, 25 Navarre Blvd., Box 909, 87323. Tel: 505-862-7466; Fax: 505-862-7798.
E-mail: tpepe@cnctco.com
Web site: www.sbms.kiz.nm.us
Roy Heusel, Prin. Sisters 1; Lay Teachers 8; Students 91.

[C] ELEMENTARY SCHOOLS, PRIVATE

GALLUP. *Gallup Catholic School*. (Grades PreK-8), 515 Park Ave., 87301. Tel: 505-863-6652; Fax: 505-726-8142. Donald Sparks, Prin. Lay Teachers 11; Students 211.

St. Francis of Assisi School, 215 W. Wilson, 87305. Tel: 505-863-3145; Fax: 505-863-8150. Rev. Thomas R. Maikowski, Ph.D., Prin. Sisters 10; Lay Teachers 1; Students 140.

CUBA. *Immaculate Conception School*. (Grades K-3), P.O. Box 218, 87013. Tel: 505-289-3749. Sheryl A. Crawford, Prin. Lay Teachers 2; Students 12.

FARMINGTON. *Sacred Heart School*. (Grades K-6), 404 N. Allen Ave., 87401. Tel: 505-325-7152. Bill Francis, Prin. Sisters 1; Lay Teachers 9; Students 160.

GRANTS. *St. Teresa of Avila School*. (Grades K-8), P.O. Box 729, 87020. Tel: 505-287-2261; Fax: 505-285-4350. Jerry Garcia, Prin. Lay Teachers 10; Students 166.

LUMBERTON. *St. Francis School*. (Grades K-8), HC 71, Box 26, 87528. Tel: 505-759-3252; Fax: 505-759-3844.
E-mail: lumbertonschool@yahoo.com
Teresita R. Mangampo-Yu, Prin. Lay Teachers 7; Students 93.

ST. MICHAELS, AZ. *St. Michael Elementary School*, P.O. Box 650, 86511. Tel: 520-871-4636; Fax: 520-871-3027.
Web site: www.rc.net/gallup/stmichael
Sr. Kathleen Kajer, Prin. Sisters 7; Lay Teachers 7; Students 260.

SAN FIDEL. *St. Joseph School*. (Grades K-8), P.O. Box 370, 87049. Tel: 505-552-6362; Fax: 505-552-6362.
E-mail: stjosephmissionschool@hotmail.com
Sr. Michelle Geerken, Prin. Sisters 1; Lay Teachers 7; Students 104.

THOREAU. *St. Bonaventure School*. (Grades PreK-12), 25 Navarre Blvd., W., P.O. Box 909, 87323. Tel: 505-862-7847; Fax: 505-862-7029.
Web site: sbms.kk12.nm.us
Sr. Natalie Bussiere, S.N.D.deN., Prin. Sisters 2; Faculty 17; Students 189.

ZUNI. *St. Anthony Indian School*, P.O. Box 486, 87327. Tel: 505-782-4596; Fax: 505-782-2013. Charles R. Glover, Prin. Lay Teachers 10; Students 205.

[D] CONVENTS AND RESIDENCES FOR SISTERS

GALLUP. *Carmelite Monastery*, P.O. Box 690, 191 Twin Buttes Rd., 87305-0690. Tel: 505-722-4516; Fax: 505-863-2186. Discalced Carmelite Nuns. Mother Mary of the Angels, O.C.D., Prioress. Sisters 6; Novices 1.

Casa Reina, 217 E. Wilson, 87301. Tel: 505-722-5511; Fax: 505-863-0075. Sisters of Guadalupe and St. Joseph. Mother Magda, H.N.S.G., Supr.
Perpetual Adoration Chapel. Immigration and Naturalization Services, Hispanic Ministry. Sisters 16.

Catholic Indian Center, 506 W. 66th Ave., 87301. Tel: 505-722-0999; Fax: 505-722-7512.
E-mail: bdunkeldc@usa.net
Web site: cnetco.com/~catholiccharities
Sr. Betty Marie Dunkel, D.C., Exec. Dir.

Our Lady of Mt. Carmel, 208 Cedar Ave., 87301. Tel: 505-722-9411; Fax: 505-863-5017. Sr. Rose Marie Holden, O.S.F., Dir. Residence for Indian girls. Total Assisted 50; Staff 12.

[E] HOMES FOR THE AGED

GALLUP. *Villa Guadalupe Home for the Aged*, 1900 Mark Ave., 87301. Tel: 505-863-6894; Fax: 505-722-4121. Sr. Celine Therese, L.S.P.; Rev. Alfred A. Tachias, Chap. Little Sisters of the Poor 8. Total Assisted 60; Total Staff 50.

[F] MISCELLANEOUS LISTINGS

GALLUP. *Blue Army*. (Fatima Apostolate), 217 E. Wilson Ave., 87301. Tel: 505-722-5511. Mrs. Lillie Yepez, Pres.; Sr. Magda Leticia Garcia, Spiritual Dir. Contact Persons: Sr. M. Magda Garcia, H.N.S.G.; Sr. Lorena Osuna, H.N.S.G.

Casa San Martin, 411 W. Wilson St., 87301. Tel: 505-722-5156. Soup Kitchen & Shelter for Native American Clients. Missionaries of Charity. Sr. Annie Teresa, M.C., Supr. Convent, 207 E. Wilson Ave., 87301. Tel: 505-722-5261. Total Assisted 40,341.

Catholic Peoples' Initiatives, Inc., P.O. Box 369, 87305. Tel: 505-726-8295; Fax: 505-726-8295.
E-mail: cpi@cia-g.com
Rev. Mike Mack, Exec. Dir.

Gallup Catholic School Foundation, Inc., 515 Park Ave., 87301. Tel: 505-722-6966; Fax: 505-726-8142.
E-mail: gcshoolfdn@cnetco.com
Elizabeth Sparks, Dir.

Sacred Heart Retreat, Zuni Hwy. S., P.O. Box 1989, 87305. Tel: 505-722-6755. Sr. Sarah Page, O.S.F.

Southwest Indian Foundation, 100 W. Coal Ave., P.O. Box 307, 87305. Tel: 505-863-9568.
E-mail: swif@cia-g.com
Mr. William McCarthy, Exec. Dir. Board of Directors: Most Rev. Donald E. Pelotte, S.S.S., Ex Officio; Mr. James Mason, Pres.; Mr. John Dowling, Vice Pres.; Mrs. Mary Constant, Sec.; Revs. Conall P. Lynch, O.F.M.; Caron Vollmer, O.F.M.; Joe Blonski; Sr. Angela Aldi, O.S.F.; Hon. Judge Marie Nezwood; Mr. Martin Neal; Mr. Leonard Shirley; Mrs. Fred Melton.

CHINLE, AZ. *Talbot House-Catholic Charities*, P.O. Box 417, 86503. Tel: 520-674-3238; Fax: 520-674-5813.
E-mail: ThCC@cybertrails.com
Web site: www.cnetco.com/catholiccharities
Sr. Adelaide Link, S.F.P., C.I.S.W., Dir. (Affiliated with Catholic Charities). Total Assisted 1585; Staff 4.

GRANTS-MILAN. *Casa San Jose*, 2595 W. Hwy. 66, 87020-9626. Tel: 505-285-5451; Fax: 505-285-6436.
E-mail: casa@7cities.com
Sr. Francine Schuster, A.S.C., Admin. Residence of Pregnant teenagers. Operated by Catholic Charities. Sisters Adorers of the Blood of Christ 2; Sinsinawa Dominican of the Most Holy Rosary 1; Total Staff 6; Total Assisted 28.

PINETOP, AZ. *St. Vincent DePaul Society*. Thrift Shop & Emergency Aid Office. St. Mary of the Angels, P.O. Box 819, 85935. Tel: 520-367-2029; 3057. Ann C. Schultz, Pres.; Bill Schultz, Shop Mgr.; Barbara Parris, Emergency Aid Contact Person. Total Assisted 1048; Total Staff 2.

THOREAU. *St. Bonaventure Indian Mission & School*, 25 Navarre Blvd. W., P.O. Box 610, 87323. Tel: 505-862-7847; Fax: 505-862-7029.
E-mail: boconnell@sbms.kiz.nm.us
Web site: www.sbms.kiz.nm.us
Paul Leche, Chm.; Barbara Morales, Sec.; Suzanne Slankard, Vice Chm.; Frank Thompson, Treas.

WINSLOW, AZ. *La Casa de Nuestra Senora*. Mission of Madonna House Apostolate Combermere, Ontario, Canada. 213 Jefferson St., 86047. Tel: 520-289-9284. Janet Bourdet, Dir.
Prayer and Community Service Center. Total Residents 6.

RELIGIOUS INSTITUTES OF MEN REPRESENTED IN THE DIOCESE

For further details refer to the corresponding bracketed number in the Religious Institutes of Men or Women section.

[1100]—*Brothers of the Sacred Heart.*—S.C.
[1330]—*Congregation of the Mission.*—C.M.
[0520]—*Franciscan Friars.* (Provs. of Our Lady of Guadalupe & St. Barbara).—O.F.M.
[0590]—*Missionaries of the Holy Apostles.*—M.Ss.A.
[1200]—*Society of the Divine Savior.*—S.D.S.

RELIGIOUS INSTITUTES OF WOMEN REPRESENTED IN THE DIOCESE

[0100]—*Adorers of the Blood of Christ.*—A.S.C.
[3710]—*Congregation of the Sisters of Saint Agnes.*—C.S.A.
[0760]—*Daughters of Charity of St. Vincent de Paul.*—D.C.
[0420]—*Discalced Carmelite Nuns.*—O.C.D.
[1070-13]—*Dominican Sisters (Adrian, MI).*—O.P.
[1070-14]—*Dominican Sisters (Grand Rapids, MI).*—O.P.
[1070-06]—*Dominican Sisters (Newburgh, NY).*—O.P.
[1070-09]—*Dominican Sisters (Racine, WI).*—O.P.
[1070-12]—*Dominican Sisters (San Jose, CA).*—O.P.
[1070-03]—*Dominican Sisters (Sinsinawa, WI).*—O.P.
[1120]—*Dominican Sisters of the Roman Congregation.*—O.P.
[1390]—*Franciscan Missionary Sisters of Our Lady of Sorrow.*—O.S.F.
[1350]—*Franciscan Missionary Sisters of the Immaculate Conception.*—O.S.F.
[1425]—*Franciscan Sisters of Peace.*—F.S.P.
[2340]—*Little Sisters of the Poor.*—L.S.P.
[2470]—*Maryknoll Sisters of St. Dominic.*—M.M.
[2710]—*Missionaries of Charity.*—M.C.
[2790]—*Missionary Servants of the Most Blessed Trinity.*—M.S.B.T.
[2760]—*Missionary Sisters of the Immaculate Conception of the Mother of God.*—S.M.I.C.
[2850]—*Missionary Sisters of the Precious Blood.*—C.P.S.
[1640]—*Poor Sisters of St. Francis Seraph of the Perpetual Adoration.*—O.S.F.
[2970]—*School Sisters of Notre Dame.*—S.S.N.D.
[]—*Sisters for Christian Community.*—S.F.C.C.
[0480]—*Sisters of Charity of Leavenworth, KS.*—S.C.L.
[2570]—*Sisters of Mercy.* (Erie, PA).—R.S.M.
[3000]—*Sisters of Notre Dame de Namur.*—S.N.D.deN.
[]—*Sisters of Our Lady of Guadalupe and St. Joseph, Inc.*
[1510]—*Sisters of St. Francis.*—O.S.F.
[1730]—*Sisters of St. Francis of Oldenburg.*—O.S.F.
[1650]—*The Sisters of St. Francis of Philadelphia.*—O.S.F.
[0260]—*Sisters of the Blessed Sacrament for Indians and Colored People.*—S.B.S.
[1030]—*Sisters of the Divine Savior.*—S.D.S.
[1830]—*The Sisters of the Good Shepherd.*—R.G.S.
[2940]—*Sisters of the Most Holy Sacrament.*—M.H.S.
[1440]—*Sisters of the Poor of St. Francis.*—S.F.P.
[3260]—*Sisters of the Precious Blood.* (Dayton, OH).—C.PP.S.
[1800]—*Sisters of the Third Order Regular.*—O.S.F.
[4120-05]—*Ursuline Nuns of the Congregation of Paris.*—O.S.U.

NECROLOGY

(No Deaths)

Diocese of Galveston—Houston

(Dioecesis Galvestoniensis Houstoniensis)

Most Reverend

JOSEPH A. FIORENZA, D.D.

Bishop of Galveston-Houston; ordained May 29, 1954; appointed Bishop of San Angelo September 4, 1979; consecrated and installed October 25, 1979; appointed Bishop of Galveston-Houston December 18, 1984; installed February 18, 1985. *Office: 1700 San Jacinto, Houston, TX, 77002-8291. Mailing Address: P.O. Box 907, Houston, TX, 77001-0907.* Tel.: 713-659-5461.

Most Reverend

JAMES A. TAMAYO, D.D.

Auxiliary Bishop of Galveston-Houston; ordained June 11, 1976; appointed Titular Bishop of Ita and Auxiliary Bishop of Galveston-Houston January 26, 1993; consecrated March 10, 1993. *Mailing Address: P.O. Box 907, Houston, TX, 77001-0907. Office: 1700 San Jacinto, Houston, TX, 77002-8291.* Tel.: 713-659-5461.

ESTABLISHED IN 1847.

Square Miles 8,880.

REDESIGNATED DIOCESE OF GALVESTON-HOUSTON ON JULY 25, 1959.

Comprises the Counties of Walker, San Jacinto, Galveston, Grimes, Montgomery, Waller, Harris, Fort Bend, Brazoria and Austin in the State of Texas.

For legal titles of parishes and diocesan institutions, consult the Chancery Office.

Chancery Office: P.O. Box 907, Houston, TX, 77001-0907. Tel.: 713-659-5461; Fax: 713-759-9151.

STATISTICAL OVERVIEW

Personnel	
Bishop	1
Auxiliary Bishops	1
Priests: Diocesan Active in Diocese	143
Priests: Active Outside Diocese	6
Priests: Diocesan in Foreign Missions	1
Priests: Retired, Sick or Absent	48
Number of Diocesan Priests	198
Religious Priests in Diocese	212
Extern Priests in Diocese	40
Ordinations:	
Diocesan Priests	2
Religious Priests	2
Transitional Deacons	3
Permanent Deacons in Diocese	296
Total Brothers	11
Total Sisters	498
Parishes	
Parishes	151
With Resident Pastor:	
Resident Diocesan Priests	98
Resident Religious Priests	51
Without Resident Pastor:	
Administered by Priests	2
Missions	8
Pastoral Centers	17
Welfare	
Catholic Hospitals	3
Total Assisted	455,315
Health Care Centers	5
Total Assisted	75,879
Homes for the Aged	3
Total Assisted	395
Residential Care of Children	3
Total Assisted	2,508
Day Care and Extended Day Care Centers	38
Total Assisted	4,025
Specialized Homes	4
Total Assisted	3,283
Special Centers for Social Services	10
Total Assisted	811,278
Educational	
Seminaries, Diocesan	1
Students from This Diocese	11
Students from Other Diocese	35
Diocesan Students in Other Seminaries	20
Seminaries, Religious	3
Students Religious	35
Total Seminarians	66
Colleges and Universities	1
Total Students	2,897
High Schools, Diocesan and Parish	2
Total Students	328
High Schools, Private	6
Total Students	3,216
Elementary Schools, Diocesan and Parish	44
Total Students	14,051
Elementary Schools, Private	6
Total Students	11,946
Catechesis/Religious Education:	
High School Students	14,803
Elementary Students	66,255
Total Students Under Catholic Instruction	113,562
Teachers in the Diocese:	
Priests	35
Sisters	29
Lay Teachers	1,493
Vital Statistics	
Receptions into the Church:	
Infant Baptism Totals	19,630
Adult Baptism Totals	1,374
Received into Full Communion	1,078
First Communions	16,392
Confirmations	8,062
Marriages:	
Catholic	2,957
Interfaith	1,020
Total Marriages	3,977
Deaths	3,631
Total Catholic Population	951,360
Total Population	4,528,005

Former Bishops—Rt. Rev. J. M. ODIN, C.M., D.D., cons. Bishop of Claudiopolis and Vicar-Apostolic of Texas, March 6, 1842; transferred to Galveston 1847; promoted to New Orleans in 1861; died in Ambierle, France, May 25, 1870; Rt. Rev. C. M. DUBUIS, D.D., cons. Nov. 23, 1862; resigned 1881 remained Titular Bishop of Galveston till 1892, when he was promoted to an Archbishopric *i.p.i.; died May 21, 1895* at Vernaison, France; Rt. Rev. P. DUFAL, C.S.C., D.D., cons. Nov. 25, 1860; Bishop of Delcon, and Vicar-Apostolic of Eastern Bengal; transferred to Galveston as Coadjutor of Rt. Rev. C. M. DUBUIS, *cum jure successionis,* May 14, 1878; resigned 1880; died in Paris 1898; Rt. Rev. NICHOLAS A. GALLAGHER, D.D., cons. Titular Bishop of Canopus, April 30, 1882; succeeded to Galveston, Dec. 16, 1892; died Jan. 21, 1918; Most Rev. CHRISTOPHER E. BYRNE, D.D., appt. July 18, 1918; cons. Nov. 10, 1918; made Assistant at the Pontifical Throne, May 8, 1941; died April 1, 1950.—Most Rev. WENDELIN J. NOLD, S.T.D., appt. Nov. 29, 1947; cons. Feb. 25, 1948; died Oct. 1, 1981; Most Rev. JOHN L. MORKOVSKY, S.T.D., ord. Dec. 5, 1933; Titular Bishop of Hieron and Auxiliary Bishop of Amarillo; appt. Dec. 22, 1955; cons. Feb. 22, 1956; succeeded to See Aug. 18, 1958; transferred to Galveston-Houston as Titular Bishop of Tigava and Coadjutor and Apostolic Administrator *"cum jure successionis"*April 1963; installed June 11, 1963; succeeded to the See of Galveston-Houston, April 22, 1975; retired Aug. 16, 1984; died March 24, 1990.

Chancery Office—1700 San Jacinto St., Houston, 77002-8291., P.O. Box 907, Houston, 77001-0907. Office Hours: Mon.-Fri. 8:30-4:30. Tel: 713-659-5461; Fax: 713-759-9151.

Chancellor and Moderator of the Curia—Rev. FRANK H. ROSSI, S.T.L., *1700 San Jacinto St., Houston, 77002-8291., P.O. Box 907, Houston, 77001-0907.* Tel: 713-659-5461.

Vice Chancellor—Rev. R. TROY GATELY, *1700 San Jacinto St., Houston, 77002-8291., P.O. Box 907, Houston, 77001-0907.* Tel: 713-659-5461.

Vicar General—Rev. Msgr. VINCENT M. RIZZOTTO, P.A., *11720 Joan of Arc, Houston, 77024-2602.* Tel: 713-465-3414.

Ethnic Vicars—Vacant, Vicar of African American Catholics; Vacant, Vicar of Hispanic Catholics; Rev. ANTHONY CHINH QUANG DAO, O.P., Vicar of Vietnamese Catholics; Rev. Msgr. SETH HERMOSO, Vicar of Filipino Catholics.

Vicar for Religious—Sr. M. ADELINE O'DONOGHUE, C.C.V.I., *6510 Lawndale, Houston, 77023.* Tel: 713-928-6053.

Director of Ministry to Priests—Rev. PHIL NEGLEY, M.S., *5918 Wigton Dr., Houston, 77096.* Tel: 713-729-3906.

Finance Officer and Business Manager—Mr. THOMAS B. O'TOOLE, *1700 San Jacinto St., Houston, 77002-8291., P.O. Box 907, Houston, 77001-0907.* Tel: 713-659-5461.

Diocesan Tribunal—

Judicial Vicar—Rev. LAWRENCE JOZWIAK, J.C.L., *Chancery Bldg., P.O. Box 907, Houston, 77001-0907.* Tel: 713-659-5461.

Adjutant Judicial Vicar—Rev. FRED CHALUPA, J.C.L., *P.O. Box 907, Houston, 77001-0907.* Tel: 713-659-5461.

Diocesan Judges—Rev. Msgr. T. JOSEPH CULVER; Rev. Msgr. PHILIPPE LE-XUAN THUONG, J.C.D.; Revs. TRUNG V. NGUYEN, J.C.L.; ERIC PITRE; ROBERT RAMON, M.Div.; ANTON SHELTZ; STEPHEN P. ZIGRANG, J.C.L.; Sr. ROSEMARY SMITH, S.C., J.C.D.; Ms. MEG ROMANO-HOGAN, J.C.L.

Promoter of Justice—Rev. Msgr. VINCENT M. RIZZOTTO, J.C.L.

Defender of the Bond—Rev. Msgr. DAVID KENNEDY, J.C.L.; Rev. Msgr. WILLIAM PICKARD, J.C.D.; Rev. JOHN E. CAHOON, J.C.L.

Censor Librorum—Rev. TERENCE BRINKMAN, S.T.D., *2302 Oak Shores Dr., Kingwood, 77339-1801.* Tel: 281-358-6637.

Deans and Vicariates—

Central Vicariate—Rev. Msgr. PATRICK WELLS, Episcopal Vicar Pro-Tem. Tel: 713-659-5461. Rev. ISIDORE GARCIA, O.M.I., V.F., Central Dean. Tel: 713-224-5291. Rev. ITALO DELL'ORO, V.F., Northeast Dean. Tel: 713-672-6141. Rev. PAUL CHOVANEC, V.F., Southeast Dean. Tel: 713-645-6614.

Northern Vicariate—Rev. Msgr. GEORGE A. SHELTZ, Episcopal Vicar. Tel: 409-273-6979. Rev. Msgr. DAVID W. KENNEDY, V.F., Northern Dean. Tel: 409-756-8186. Rev. JOHN A. ZABELSKAS, V.F., Eastern Dean. Tel: 281-843-2422. Rev. PAUL PROCELLA, V.F., San Jacinto Dean. Tel: 281-446-8211.

Southern Vicariate—Rev. Msgr. T. JOSEPH CULVER, E.V., Episcopal Vicar. Tel: 409-938-7000. Rev. Msgr. MILAM E. KLEAS, V.F., Galveston-Mainland Dean. Tel: 281-337-4112. Rev. Msgr. REGINALD R. NESVADBA, V.F., Bay Area Dean. Tel: 281-471-2000. Rev. Msgr. LEO WLECZYK, V.F., Southern Dean. Tel: 409-297-3041.

Western Vicariate—Rev. Msgr. ED RANDALL, E.V., Episcopal Vicar. Tel: 713-774-7475. Rev. DANIEL WARDEN, V.F., Western Dean. Tel: 281-342-3089. Rev. Msgr. BILL YOUNG, V.F., Southwest Dean. Tel: 713-789-1250. Rev. Msgr. DANIEL SCHEEL, V.F., Northwest Dean. Tel: 281-955-7324. Rev. ROBERT BARRAS, V.F., Bluebonnet Dean. Tel: 409-826-2275.

Secretariat Directors—

Secretariat For Pastoral and Educational Ministries—Bro. JIM BARRETTE, S.M., Dir., *2403 Holcombe, Houston, 77021-2099.* Tel: 713-741-8786.

Secretariat for Social Concerns—Mrs. SUSAN STROMATT, Dir., *2403 Holcombe, Houston, 77021-2099.* Tel: 713-741-8769.

Secretariat For Administration—Mr. THOMAS B. O'TOOLE, Dir., *1700 San Jacinto St., Houston, 77002-8291., P.O. Box 907, Houston, 77001-0907.* Tel: 713-659-5461.

Secretariat For Communication—Mrs. ANNETTE GONZALES-TAYLOR, *1700 San Jacinto St., Houston, 77002-8291., P.O. Box 907, Houston, 77001-0907.* Tel: 713-659-5461.

Secretariat For Clergy Formation and Chaplaincy Services—Rev. Msgr. FRANK H. ROSSI, Dir., *1700 San Jacinto St., Houston, 77002-8291., P.O. Box 907, Houston, 77001-0907.* Tel: 713-659-5461.

Diocesan Councils, Commissions and Committees—

Diocesan Presbyteral Council—1700 San Jacinto St., Houston, 77002-8291., P.O. Box 907, Houston, 77001-0907. Tel: 281-498-4653.

Presbyteral Council—Revs. DON NESTI, C.S.Sp.; MARIO ARROYO; DOUGLAS J. HYPOLITE, S.J.; Rev. Msgr. GEORGE A. SHELTZ; Rev. Msgr. ED RANDALL; Revs. ANTHONY DAO, O.P.; TOM RAFFERTY; Rev. Msgr. T. JOSEPH CULVER; Revs. DAVID CARDENAS; DON KUDER, C.S.B.; JOHN T. WEYER; STEVE ZIGRANG; WILLIAM BARTNISKI; Rev. Msgr. VINCENT M. RIZZOTTO; Rev. Msgr. FRANK H. ROSSI; Rev. DAN WARDEN; Rev. Msgr. CHESTER L. BORSKI; Rev. Msgr. PATRICK R. WELLS.

College of Consultors—Rev. Msgr. T. JOSEPH CULVER; Rev. Msgr. WILLIAM M. PICKARD, J.C.D.; Rev. Msgr. VINCENT M. RIZZOTTO, J.C.L.; Rev. Msgr. DANIEL SCHEEL; Rev. Msgr. FRANK H. ROSSI, S.T.L.; Rev. Msgr. GEORGE A. SHELTZ; Rev. JOHN WEYER; Rev. Msgr. ED RANDALL.

Priests Personnel Committee—Rev. Msgr. VINCENT M. RIZZOTTO, J.C.L., Chm., *11720 Joan of Arc, Houston, 77024-2602.* Tel: 713-465-3414. Rev. Msgr. REGINALD R. NESVADBA; Rev. ERIC PITRE; Rev. Msgr. FRANK H. ROSSI; Revs. DOMINIC PISTONE; STEVE TIEMANN; PHIL M. NEGLEY, M.S.

Building Commission—Rev. Msgr. CHARLES C. DOMEC, Chm., *26777 Glen Loch Rd., The Woodlands, 77381-2921.* Tel: 281-367-9885. Rev. Msgr. T. JOSEPH CULVER; Rev. Msgr. EDWARD RANDALL; Rev. ANTON SHELTZ; Mr. JAMES GRIBBLE; Mr. TONY ROURKE; Mr. STANLEY SARMAN.

Board of Education—Mrs. ANA CUMMINGS, Pres., *Chancery Bldg., at St. Dominic Center.* Tel: 713-741-8786.

Ecumenism and Interreligious Affairs Commission—Mrs. GARLAND POHL, Chm., *8003 Mobud, Houston, 77036-6403.* Tel: 713-774-0097.

Liturgical Commission—Rev. DON NEUMANN, Chm.

Diocesan Departments and Offices

Archives—Ms. LISA MAY, Dir., *1700 San Jacinto St., Houston, 77002-8291., P.O. Box 907, Houston, 77001-0907.* Tel: 713-659-5461.

Accounting Department—Mrs. LIZ TORRES, Dir., *1700 San Jacinto St., Houston, 77002-8291., P.O. Box 907, Houston, 77001-0907.* Tel: 713-659-5461.

African American Ministry—Ms. CHAROLETTE DAVIS, Dir., *2403 Holcombe, Houston, 77021-2098.* Tel: 713-741-8733.

Aging Ministry—Sr. DOROTHY SACHNIK, C.V.I., Dir., *2403 Holcombe, Houston, 77021-2098.* Tel: 713-741-8712.

Apostleship of Prayer—Vacant.

Apostleship of the Sea (Port Ministry)—Rev. RIVERS PATOUT, Houston Dir., *9217 E. Ave. L., Houston, 77012-2727.* Tel: 713-923-5843; 926-7669 (Rectory)., *Houston International Seaman's Center, P.O. Box 9506, Houston, 77261.* Tel: 713-672-0511. Galveston: Mrs. KAREN LAI, *2002 Mechanic, Galveston, 77550.* Tel: 409-762-0021.

Boy and Girl Scouts—Rev. Msgr. WILLIAM L. YOUNG, Dir., *3600 Brinkman Rd., Houston, 77018-6329.* Tel: 713-692-9123.

Campaign for Human Development—Mrs. STEPHANIE WEBER, Dir., *2403 Holcombe, Houston, 77021-2098.* Tel: 713-741-8731.

Young Adult and Campus Ministry— Mr. WILLIAM CORK, Dir., *2403 Holcombe, Houston, 77021-2098.* Tel: 713-741-8786.

Catholic Cemeteries—Mr. TERRANCE D. MULCARE, Dir., *P.O. Box 965 (Gulf Fwy. at Hughes Rd.), Dickinson, 77539.* Tel: 281-337-1641; 409-948-1455.

Catholic Chaplain Corps (Hospital Chaplains)—Vacant, *4206 MacGregor Way S., Houston, 77021-1598.* Tel: 713-526-6438.

Associated Catholic Charities—ANNA M. BABIN, C.P.A., Pres. & CEO, *2900 Louisiana St., P.O. Box 66508, Houston, 77266.* Tel: 713-526-4611; Fax: 713-526-1546.

Program Services—BOB FLEMING. Tel: 713-874-6739.

Finance and Support Services—MICHAEL J. PIERI, C.P.A., Vice Pres.

Fund Development/Marketing—RIC ARMSTRONG, Dir.

Children Services—VALERIE PERALES, L.M.S.W.-A.C.P., Admin.

Children Placement Services Adoption and Foster Care—SHARON JORGESON, L.M.S.W., Supvr.

Services to Pregnant Adolescents and Their Families—MICHELLE MITCHELL, L.M.S.W.-A.C.P., A.C.S.W., C.C.A. Supvr.

Post Adoption Services—LILLIAN SALINAS, L.M.S.W. Tel: 800-BABY-DUE.

Community Outreach Services—GREG PATIN, Admin.

Diocesan AIDS Ministry—Sr. MARY BRENDA, O.P., Supvr., *2900 Louisiana St., Houston, 77266.* Tel: 713-526-4611.

Guadalupe Area Social Services—YOLANDA GUTIERREZ, L.M.S.W., Site Coord., *326 S. Jensen, Houston, 77003-1599.* Family Assistance Program, La Casita, Villa Guadalupe-Transitional Housing for Women.

Parish Social Ministry—ESMERALDA CERVANTES, Coord. Tel: 713-526-4611.

Services to the Alone and Frail Elderly—NYDIA CORTEZ, Supvr. Tel: 713-520-7835.

Family Counseling—VALERIE PERALES, L.M.S.W., A.C.P., Admin. ENCARNITA GOMEZ, M.S., L.M.F.T., L.C.D.C., Lead Clinician. Tel: 713-668-5763; 526-4611, Ext. 3500 (Appointments); Fax: 713-527-9198 (Family Counseling).

Immigration and Refugee Services—JANET WAITES, Admin.

Texas Center for Immigrant Legal Assistance—MAGALI CANDLER, Supvr. Tel: 713-526-4611, Ext. 3406.

Refugee Resettlement Services—NHO NGUYEN, Supvr. Tel: 713-526-4611.

Undocumented and Unaccompanied Juvenile Foster Care—CONNIE HIDALGO, Supvr. Tel: 713-526-4611.

Serenity House—NYDIA CORTEZ. Tel: 713-526-4611, Ext. 3268.

Catholic Charities Galveston—ELIZABETH KINARD, Case Mgr., *4418 Ave. M, Galveston, 77550-3726.* Tel: 409-762-2143; Fax: 409-762-2088.

Catholic Relief Services—Mrs. HILDA HERNANDEZ, Dir., *Chancery Bldg., 1700 San Jacinto St., Houston, 77002-8921., P.O. Box 907, Houston, 77001-0907.* Tel: 713-659-5461.

Computer Network Manager—Mr. ED HERRERA, *Chancery Bldg., 1700 San Jacinto St., Houston, 77002-8921., P.O. Box 907, Houston, 77001-0907.* Tel: 713-659-5461.

Community Relations—Mrs. SUSAN STROMATT, *2403 Holcombe, Houston, 77021-2099.* Tel: 713-741-8731.

Continuing Christian Education—Mrs. ANNE COMEAUX, Dir., *2403 Holcombe, Houston, 77021-2099.* Tel: 713-741-8730.

Construction/Preventative Maintenance—Mr. TONY ROURKE, Dir., *Chancery Bldg., 1700 San Jacinto St., Houston, 77002-8291., P.O. Box 907, Houston, 77001-0907.* Tel: 713-659-5461. Mr. MICHAEL ZIKOGIANNIS, Preventive Maintenance.

Correctional Ministries (Jail Chaplains)—Rev. RONALD F. CLOUTIER, Dir. (Chaplain Office at Harris County Jail), Office and Mailing Address: *2403 E. Holcombe, Houston, 77021-2098.* Tel: 713-869-1449., *215 E. 10th St., Houston, 77008-7025.* Tel: 713-864-2653.

Council of Catholic Women—Rev. Msgr. DANIEL SCHEEL, Dir., *3600 Brinkman Rd., Houston, 77018-6329.* Tel: 713-692-9123.

Cursillos in Christianity—Rev. JOSE MARIA FERNANDEZ, Dir., *4419 N. Main, Houston, 77009-5199.* Tel: 713-869-1449., *St. Paul Cursillo Center, 4000 Belk St., Houston, 77087.* Tel: 713-643-7682.

Deaf Apostolate—Ms. CARLA HOLMES, Dir., *St. Dominic Center, 2401 Holcombe Blvd., Houston, 77021-2099.* Tel: 713-741-8721.

Development Office—Rev. CARL PIEBER, C.M., Dir., *1700 San Jacinto St., Houston, 77002-8291., P.O. Box 907, Houston, 77001-0907.* Tel: 713-659-5461.

Diaconal Formation/Diaconal Ministry—Rev. Msgr. JACK M. DINKINS, Dir., *1530 Norwalk Dr., Katy, 77450-4999.* Tel: 281-578-0707.

Permanent Deacons—Mr. FRED SHETZ, Dir., *1700 San Jacinto St., Houston, 77002-8291., P.O. Box 907, Houston, 77001-0907.* Tel: 713-659-5461.

Diocesan Services Fund—Southwest Bank of Texas, Diocese of Galveston-Houston, Lock Box 4681, Houston, 77210-4681. 1700 San Jacinto St., Houston, 77002-8291. Tel: 713-659-5461.

Disaster Relief—Rev. Msgr. FRANK H. ROSSI, S.T.L., Dir., *St. Mary, Star of the Sea Church, 1019 W. 6th St., Freeport, 77541-5423.* Tel: 409-233-5271.

Family Life Ministry—Mrs. WINIFRED HONEYWELL, Dir., *St. Dominic Center, 2403 Holcombe, Houston, 77021-2099.* Tel: 713-741-8710.

Hispanic Ministry—Mr. JORGE DELGADO, Dir., *2403 E. Holcombe, Houston, 77021-2099.* Tel: 713-741-8727.

Insurance & Risk Manager—MEREDITH B. SMITH, CPCU, ARM Dir., *1700 San Jacinto St., Houston, 77002-8291., P.O. Box 907, Houston, 77001-0907.* Tel: 713-659-5461.

Legal Services—Mr. ROBERT SCAMARDO, Dir. Gen. Council, *Chancery Bldg., 1700 San Jacinto St., Houston, 77002-8291., P.O. Box 907, Houston, 77001-0907.* Tel: 713-659-5461.

Internal Auditor—WILLIAM PRIME, *1700 San Jacinto St., Houston, 77002-8291., P.O. Box 907, Houston, 77001-0907.* Tel: 713-659-5461.

Real Estate—Mr. KEN SYKES, *1700 San Jacinto St., Houston, 77002-8291., P.O. Box 907, Houston, 77001-0907.* Tel: 713-659-5461.

Marian Activities—Vacant, *St. Dominic Center, 2403 Holcombe, Houston, 77021-2099.* Tel: 281-741-8721.

Media Center—Mrs. DIANE O'CONNOR, Sec., *2403 E. Holcombe, Houston, 77021-2099.* Tel: 713-741-8781.

Mission Office—Mrs. HILDA HERNANDEZ, Dir., *Chancery Bldg., 1700 San Jacinto St., Houston, 77002-8291., P.O. Box 907, Houston, 77001-0907.* Tel: 713-659-5461. Holy Childhood, Propagation of the Faith.

Oremus Pro Invicem—Rev. Msgr. FRANCIS G. WEARDEN, Dir., *1100 Parthenon Pl., New Caney, 77357-3039.* Tel: 281-399-0270.

Parish Accounting Services (PAS)—Mrs. JANIE MORALES, Dir., *1700 San Jacinto St., Houston, 77002-8291., P.O. Box 907, Houston, 77001-0907.* Tel: 713-659-5461.

Catholic Campaign for Human Development—Ms. STEPHANIE WEBER, *Chancery at St. Dominic's Diocesan Center, 2403 E. Holcombe, Houston, 77021-2099.* Tel: 713-741-8730.

Personnel—Mr. FRED SHETZ, Dir., *1700 San Jacinto St., Houston, 77002.* Tel: 713-659-5461.

Benefits—Mrs. DAWN GIBLIN, Dir., *1700 San Jacinto St., Houston, 77002.* Tel: 713-659-5461.

Radio—Mrs. MADELINE JOHNSON, Dir., *1700 San Jacinto St., Houston, 77002-8291., P.O. Box 907, Houston, 77001-0907.* Tel: 713-659-5461.

Records—Miss MARY ANN ACOSTA, Dir., *1700 San Jacinto St., Houston, 77002-8291., P.O. Box 907, Houston, 77001-0907.* Tel: 713-659-5461.

Respect Life Office—Mrs. MARCELLA COLBERT, Dir., *2403 Holcombe, Houston, 77021-2098.* Tel: 713-225-5826; 741-8730 (Main Tel.).

Claims Risk Manager—LEIZA LONG, Dir., *2403 Holcombe, Houston, 77021-2099.* Tel: 713-741-8758; 800-856-4040; Fax: 713-748-3205.

Rural Life Bureau—Rev. Msgr. FRANK H. ROSSI, S.T.L., *1700 San Jacinto St., Houston, 77002-8291., P.O. Box 907, Houston, 77001-0907.* Tel: 713-659-5461.

Seminarian Support—Rev. CLINT RESSLER, Dir., *1700 San Jacinto St., Houston, 77002-8291., P.O. Box 907, Houston, 77001-0907.* Tel: 713-659-5461.

Catholic School Office—Mr. NORMAN GLISSMAN, Supt., *2403 Holcombe, Houston, 77021-2099.* Tel: 713-741-8704.

School of Environmental Education - Camp Kappe—Sr. THOMAS ANN LACOUR, O.P., Dir., *Rte. 2, Box 3197, Navasota, 77868.* Tel: 409-894-2141.

St. Dominic Diocesan Center—Mr. WAYNE KNIGHT, Mgr., *2401 E. Holcombe, Houston, 77021-2024.* Tel: 713-741-8741.

St. Vincent de Paul Society—Mrs. DIERDRE WORKMAN, Dir., *2403 Holcombe, Houston, 77021-2099.* Tel: 713-741-8783.

Stewardship—Mr. TONY OLTREMARI, Dir., *1700 San Jacinto St., Houston, 77002-8291.* Tel: 713-659-5461., *P.O. Box 907, Houston, 77001-0907.*

Texas Catholic Herald—Mr. ERIC NORIEGA, Editor, *1700 San Jacinto St., Houston, 77002-8291., P.O. Box 907, Houston, 77001-0907.* Tel: 713-659-5461. Saturdays & Holidays. Tel: 713-659-3702; Fax: 713-659-3444.

Vocations Office—Rev. CLINT RESSLER, Dir., *1700 San Jacinto St., Houston, 77002-8291., P.O. Box 907, Houston, 77001-0907.* Tel: 713-659-5461.

Worship—*2403 Holcombe, Houston, 77021-2099.* Tel: 713-741-8760.

Youth Ministry—Mr. BRIAN JOHNSON, *2403 Holcombe, Houston, 77021-2099.* Tel: 713-741-8723.

Special Youth Services (Juvenile Detention Ministry)—MARILU BALLOW, Dir., *2403 Holcombe, Houston, 77021-2099.* Tel: 713-527-1894; 762-7192 (Pager).

CLERGY, PARISHES, MISSIONS AND PAROCHIAL SCHOOLS

CITY OF GALVESTON
(Galveston County)

1—ST. MARY'S CATHEDRAL BASILICA (1847), Rev. John N. LaBauve, S.V.D. In res., Revs. Raymond James Guidry, S.V.D.; Gerald Lewis, S.V.D.; Deacon John S. Pistone.
Res., 2011 Church St., 77550-2091. Tel: 409-762-9611; Fax: 409-765-8585.

2—HOLY ROSARY (1888), Rev. Paul H. Banet, S.S.J. In res., Revs. Charles H. Banet, C.PP.S.; Aloysius Udo.
Res., 1420 31st St., 77550-4399. Tel: 409-762-2478; Fax: 409-762-8383.
Catechesis/Religious Programs—Tel: 409-935-4372. Thomasine Allen, D.R.E.
Students 55.

3—OUR LADY OF GUADALUPE. Closed. August 1992. Contact St Patrick, Galveston for further information.

4—ST. PATRICK (1870), Revs. John Bok, O.F.M.; Joseph Rigali, O.F.M.; Deacon Tom Hunter.
Mailing Address: 1010 35th St., 77550-4058. Tel: 409-762-9646; Fax: 409-765-7636.
Res., 3420 Avenue K, 77550.
Church—34th and Avenue K, 77550.
Catechesis/Religious Programs—Jo Anita Jefferies, D.R.E.
Students 256.
Mission—Galveston, Galveston Co., Queen of Peace Mission, 706 51st St., 77551-4106. Tel: 409-762-2833; Fax: 409-765-7747. Rev. Serafin Cejudo.

5—ST. PETER THE APOSTLE (1965), Rev. William D. Bartniski; Deacons William J. Bobb; Henry Becker, Jr.; Louis Sam Dell'Olio.
1804 69th St., 77551-1326.
Res., 1805 Driftwood Ln., 77551-1326. Tel: 409-744-3561; Fax: 409-744-4286.
Catechesis/Religious Programs—Tel: 409-744-7250. Randy Adams, D.R.E.
Students 155.
Mission—Jamaica Beach, Galveston Co., Mary, Star of the Sea.

6—SACRED HEART (1884), Rev. Frank T. Fabj.
Res., 1302 Broadway, 77550-6198. Tel: 409-762-6374; Fax: 409-762-0919.
Catechesis/Religious Programs—Tel: 409-765-9531. Michelle Gonzalez, D.R.E.
Students 158.

CITY OF HOUSTON
(Harris County)

1—SACRED HEART CO-CATHEDRAL (1896), Revs. R. Troy Gately; Trung Nguyen; Edmund Eduarte; Deacon Marvin R. Fikac.
Res., 1111 Pierce St., 77002-8195. Tel: 713-659-1561; Fax: 713-739-1185.
Catechesis/Religious Programs—Tel: 281-447-4848. Jim Hodge, D.R.E.
Students 90.

2—ALL SAINTS (1908), Rev. Msgr. Adam S. McClosky; Deacon Frank Matula. In res., Rev. Ronald F. Cloutier.
Res., 215 E. 10th St., 77008-7025. Tel: 713-864-2653; Fax: 713-864-0761.
Catechesis/Religious Programs—Natalia Pena, D.R.E.
Students 270.

3—ST. ALBERT OF TRAPANI (1970), Rev. Philip A. Wilhite, S.T.L.; Deacons Carlito Buhay; Alvaro Casas. In res., Rev. Joseph Manapuram.
Res., 11027 S. Gessner Dr., 77071-3599. Tel: 713-771-3596; Fax: 713-270-0441.
Catechesis/Religious Programs—Peggy Popkey, D.R.E.
Students 377.

4—ST. ALPHONSUS (1966), Rev. Rivers A. Patout, Coord. Port Min.; Sr. Lucinda Gonzalez, Admin. & Pastoral Assoc.
Res., 9217 E. Ave. L, 77012-2727. Tel: 713-923-5843; Fax: 713-923-5866.
Catechesis/Religious Programs—Tel: 713-644-7008. D.R.E.: Ophelia Martinez; V. Gutierrez.
Students 316.

5—ST. AMBROSE (1958), Revs. Benjamin Smaistrla; Juan Pablo Pena. In res., Rev. Franklin Simmons.
Res., 4213 Mangum Rd., 77092-5599. Tel: 713-686-3497; Fax: 713-686-6604.
School—Tel: 713-686-6990; Fax: 713-686-6902. Mrs. Mary Kay Volker, Prin.
Sisters 1; Lay Teachers 27; Students 498.
Catechesis/Religious Programs—Tel: 713-686-3857. Alicia I. Perez, D.R.E.
Students 438.

6—ST. ANDREW KIM (1977) (Korean), Rev. Augustine Hyeok-Ku Yeo.
Res., 1706 Bingle Rd., 77055-2336. Tel: 713-465-2682; Fax: 713-465-5974.
Catechesis/Religious Programs—Students 137.

7—ST. ANNE (1925), Revs. John F. Robbins, C.S.B.; Thomas J. McReavy, C.S.B.; Thomas B. Mailloux, C.S.B.; Charles E. Lynch, C.S.B.; Deacons Jean-Paul Budinger; William Garrett.
Res., 2140 Westheimer, 77098-1496. Tel: 713-526-3276; Fax: 713-526-3079.
School—Tel: 713-526-3279. Kathy Burns, Prin.
Sisters 1; Lay Teachers 29; Students 348.
Catechesis/Religious Programs—Tel: 713-526-2936. D.R.E.: Arlene Holm; Maria Gongora.
Students 592.

8—ST. ANNE DE BEAUPRE (1948), Rev. Eliseus Ibeh, M.S.P.
Res., 2810 Link Rd., 77009-1196. Tel: 713-869-1319; Fax: 713-869-2569.
Catechesis/Religious Programs—Tel: 713-682-6787. Sara Kirby, D.R.E.
Students 50.

9—ANNUNCIATION (1869), Rev. Msgr. James L. Golasinski; Deacons Joseph Jachimcyk; Robert Alexander. In res., Rev. Patrick Cummings.
Mailing Address: P.O. Box 214, 77001-0214. Tel: 713-222-2289; Fax: 713-222-2280.
Res., 1618 Texas Ave., 77003.
Catechesis/Religious Programs—Students 64.

10—ASCENSION CHINESE MISSION (1988) (Chinese), Rev. Louis C. Zee.
Res., 4605 Jetty Ln., 77072-1222. Tel: 713-575-8855; Fax: 713-575-8866.
Catechesis/Religious Programs—Carol Chang, D.R.E.
Students 62.

11—ASSUMPTION (1948), Revs. Italo Dell'Oro, C.R.S. (Italy); Narciso Bordignon, C.R.S.; John Peter Borsari, C.R.S.; Deacon Albert Bottjer.
Res., 901 Rose Ln., 77037-4699. Tel: 281-447-6381; Fax: 281-447-6382.
Catechesis/Religious Programs—Rachael Gil, D.R.E.
Students 688.

12—ST. AUGUSTINE (1955), Rev. Msgr. Seth Hermoso, (Vicar for Filipinos); Rev. Francisco Ordonez.
Res., 5560 Laurel Creek Way, 77017-6729. Tel: 713-946-8968; Fax: 713-946-0080.
School—5500 Laurel Creek Way, 77017. Tel: 713-946-9050; Fax: 713-943-3444. Patricia Mulvey, Prin.
Lay Teachers 22; Students 282.
Catechesis/Religious Programs—Tel: 713-946-7636. Karen Jones, D.R.E.
Students 436.

13—ST. BENEDICT THE ABBOT (1963), Revs. Gabriel Kitira, C.S.Sp.; Benoit Mukamba, C.S.Sp.; Deacon Frank Laugermann.
Office: 4025 Grapevine, 77045-6320. Tel: 713-433-9836; Fax: 713-433-3949.; Rectory: 3931 Grapevine, 77045.
Catechesis/Religious Programs—Tel: 713-433-2436.
Students 295.

14—ST. BERNADETTE SOUBIROUS (1977), Revs. Joseph J. McCarthy, O.Carm.; Adrian Wilde, O.Carm.; Deacon Bob Rumford.
Mailing Address: 15500 El Camino Real, 77062. Tel: 281-486-0337; Fax: 281-486-7664.
Catechesis/Religious Programs—Tel: 281-486-0337. D.R.E.: Sheryl Dalpe; Barbara Aubushon.
Students 1,389.

15—CHRIST, THE INCARNATE WORD (1997) (Vietnamese), Rev. Msgr. Philippe Le-Xuan Thuong, J.C.D.; Rev. Joseph Bui-Tien; Deacon Joseph Bach Si Nguyen.
Res., c/o 7720 Boone Rd., 77072-3595. Tel: 281-495-2510; Fax: 281-879-1527.
Catechesis/Religious Programs—Tel: 281-444-2181.
Students 407.

16—BLESSED SACRAMENT (1910), Revs. Jose Isidore Garcia, O.M.I., V.F.; Roberto Pena, O.M.I. In res., Rev. Cornelius Scanlan, O.M.I.
Res., 4015 Sherman Ave., 77003-2695. Tel: 713-224-5291; Fax: 713-224-5292.
Catechesis/Religious Programs—Tel: 713-947-2515. Mary T. Martinez, D.R.E.
Students 215.

17—ST. CATHERINE OF SIENA (1975), Rev. Michael J. Carmody; Deacons John Coussirat; F. J. Vocelka. In res., Rev. Pierre Nguyen Van Thong.
Mailing Address: 10688 Shadow Wood Dr., 77043-2826. Tel: 713-467-8170; Fax: 713-467-7149.
Catechesis/Religious Programs—Christine Twardowski, D.R.E.
Students 136.

18—ST. CECILIA (1956), Rev. Msgr. Vincent M. Rizzotto, J.C.L., Vicar Gen.; Rev. Octavio A. Muguerza; Deacons Don Bradley; Cade Nelms. In res., Rev. Jacques Weber, S.J., S.T.L., M.S.
Res., 11720 Joan of Arc, 77024-2602. Tel: 713-465-3414; Fax: 713-465-1305.
School—Tel: 713-468-9515; Fax: 713-468-4698. Ms. Bridget Collins, Prin.
Lay Teachers 37; Students 490.
Catechesis/Religious Programs—Lettie Gillespie, D.R.E.
Students 996.

19—ST. CHARLES BORROMEO (1962), Revs. John E. Cahoon; Nicholas J. Harding; Deacon Rodrigo Lozano.
Res., 501 Tidwell, 77022-2121. Tel: 713-692-6303; Fax: 713-692-6314.
School—Tel: 713-692-4898; Fax: 713-692-1376. Mrs. Shelly McKinley, Prin.
Sisters 2; Lay Teachers 14; Students 270.
Catechesis/Religious Programs—Tel: 281-442-1334. Linda Schulle, D.R.E.
Students 560.

20—CHRIST THE KING (1928), Rev. Stephen B. Reynolds; Deacons Gerardo Garcia; Rasco Watkins. In res., Rev. Jose Maria Fernandez.
Res., 4419 N. Main St., 77009-5199. Tel: 713-869-1449; Fax: 713-869-1491.
School—Dr. Maritza Cano Roman, Prin. Lay Teachers 3; Students 30.
Catechesis/Religious Programs—Tel: 713-869-3140. Daniel Schwieterman, D.R.E.
Students 1,120.

21—CHRIST THE REDEEMER (1980), Revs. Dominic A. Peluse, S.C.J.; Leonard F. Elder, S.C.J.; Deacons Jim Osterhaus; Thomas Reich.
Church and Mailing Address: 11507 Huffmeister Rd., 77065-1051. Tel: 281-469-5533; Fax: 281-469-8441.
Res., 12402 Bexhill, 77065.
Catechesis/Religious Programs—Tel: 281-469-5533. Fredna Kilcomming, D.R.E.
Students 1,177.

22—ST. CHRISTOPHER (1924), Revs. Paul R. Chovanec, B.A., M.Th.; Eugene Doboz. In res., Rev. Raul A. Marterior, O.P.; Deacon Merce C. Leal, Jr.
Res., 8150 Park Place Blvd., 77017-3033. Tel: 713-645-6614; Fax: 713-640-1640.
School—8134 Park Place Blvd., 77017. Tel: 713-649-0009; Fax: 713-649-1104. Jo Ann Prater, Prin.
Sisters 3; Lay Teachers 19; Students 283.
Catechesis/Religious Programs—Gloria Leal, D.R.E.
Students 748.

23—ST. CLARE OF ASSISI (1990), Rev. John H. Kappe; Deacons Don Durden; Daniel Q. Guerra.
Res., 15922 Hillside Falls Tr., 77062.
Mailing Address: 3131 El Dorado Blvd., 77059-5100. Tel: 281-286-7729; Fax: 281-286-1256.
School—Tel: 281-286-3395. Brenda Fricks, Prin.
Lay Teachers 7; Students 91.

Catechesis/Religious Programs—Tel: 281-486-0874. Celia Guadiano, D.R.E.
Students 652.

24—ST. CYRIL OF ALEXANDRIA (1963), Revs. Mario J. Arroyo; Isaac O. Francis; Christopher Shackelford; Deacon Edward Thompson.
Res., 10503 Westheimer Rd., 77042-3502. Tel: 713-789-1250; Fax: 713-780-0967.
Catechesis/Religious Programs—Tel: 713-789-1250. Margaret McDermott, D.R.E.
Students 689.

25—CORPUS CHRISTI (1956), Revs. Dominic Phuc Nguyen Thuan, S.S.S.; John Thomas Lane, S.S.S.; Frederico-Joseph G. Ablog, S.S.S.; Thomas A. Weisse, S.S.S.; Deacon Joseph Bourgeois.
Res., 9900 Stella Link Rd., 77025-4798. Tel: 713-667-0497; Fax: 713-668-4742.
School—4005 Cheena St., 77025. Tel: 713-664-3351; Fax: 713-664-6095. Theresa Rourke, Prin.
Lay Teachers 20; Students 240.
Catechesis/Religious Programs—Peggy Marroquin, D.R.E.
Students 495.

26—ST. DOMINIC (1965), Rev. Anton R. Sheltz, M.Th.; Deacon Philip Arlen Wiles.
Res., 8215 Reservoir St., 77049-1728. Tel: 281-458-2910; Fax: 281-458-7114.
Catechesis/Religious Programs—Tel: 713-564-6719; 713-453-6719. George T. McDonald, D.R.E.
Students 186.

27—ST. ELIZABETH ANN SETON (1977), Rev. Frank Wittouck, S.C.J.; Deacons Francis Adams; Charles G. Pennell; Brian Lambert; Ed Tripp; Joe Zamora. In res., Rev. Ralph J. Intranuovo.
Res., 6646 Addicks-Satsuma Rd., 77084-1599. Tel: 281-463-7878; Fax: 281-463-4822.
School—Tel: 281-463-1444. Jan Krametbauer, Prin.
Lay Teachers 9; Students 131.
Catechesis/Religious Programs—Tel: 281-463-7356. Carm Cline, D.R.E.
Students 1,966.

28—ST. FRANCES CABRINI (1962), Revs. Norbert J. Maduzia, Jr.; Vincent-Vuong Nguyen; Deacons Frank Moreno; Robert Gregory Stevens; Fernando Ramirez; Charles Roessler.
Mailing Address: 10727 Hartsook St., 77034-3523. Tel: 713-946-5768; Fax: 713-946-3282.
Res., 10726 Bessemer St., 77034.
8105 Avenelle St., 77034.
Catechesis/Religious Programs—D.R.E.: Patricia Weimer; Joan Whorton.
Students 976.

29—ST. FRANCIS DE SALES (1962), Revs. Joseph A. Limanni; Ralph O. Roberts; Joseph Phiet The Nguyen; Deacons Albert G. Bothe; Hugo Klein.
Res., 8018 Roos Rd., 77036. Tel: 713-774-7475; Fax: 713-774-6591.
School—8100 Roos Rd., 77036. Tel: 713-774-4447; Fax: 713-271-6744. Sandra Mendez, Prin.
Lay Teachers 31; Students 538.
Catechesis/Religious Programs—Tel: 713-774-9631. Diane Wooten, D.R.E.
Students 1,269.

30—ST. FRANCIS OF ASSISI (1950), Rev. Msgr. Patrick R. Wells; Deacons Ignatius Joseph; Michael St. Julian.
Res., 5102 Dabney St., 77026-3015. Tel: 713-672-7773; Fax: 713-673-1913.
School—5100 Dabney St., 77026. Tel: 713-674-1966; Fax: 713-674-9901. Stephanie C.M. Murphy, Prin.
Sisters 1; Lay Teachers 15; Students 185.
Catechesis/Religious Programs—Tel: 713-674-5314. Shirley M. Rene, D.R.E.
Students 129.

31—ST. FRANCIS XAVIER (1952), Rev. Kenneth Howard, S.S.J.; Deacons Daniel W. Gilbert; Albert Henry; Michael V. Jenkins.
Res., 4600 Reed Rd., 77051-2857. Tel: 713-738-2311; Fax: 713-738-3337.
Catechesis/Religious Programs—Tel: 713-731-2775 (Office). Grenda Williams, D.R.E.
Students 192.

32—ST. GREGORY THE GREAT (1962), Rev. Francis Huan Ngo; Deacons Julio Ramirez; Abner Brown.
Res., 10500 Nold Dr., 77016-2921. Tel: 713-631-3681; Fax: 713-631-6114.
Catechesis/Religious Programs—Tel: 713-631-0058. D.R.E.: Sr. Ann Theresa; Mary Rocha; Al Landry.
Students 360.

33—HOLY CROSS CHAPEL (Downtown) (1981), Rev. Michael Barrett.
Chapel—905 Main St., 77002-6408. Tel: 713-650-1323; Fax: 713-650-8836.

34—HOLY GHOST (1946), Revs. Leonard Broniak, C.Ss.R.; Gan Minh Peter Nguyen, C.Ss.R.; Peter H. Voelker, C.Ss.R.; Scott R. Katzenberger, C.Ss.R. In res., Revs. Edward Glebe, C.Ss.R.; A. J. Chandonnet, C.Ss.R.; Bro. Michael Rhodes, C.Ss.R.; Deacons Robert Brueggerhoff; James Meshell.
Res., 6921 Chetwood Dr., 77081-5697. Tel: 713-668-0463; Fax: 713-661-4645.
School—6920 Chimney Rock, 77081. Tel: 713-668-5327. Susan Sanchez, Prin.
Lay Teachers 16; Students 244.
Catechesis/Religious Programs—Tel: 713-668-8001. Anne W. Brown, D.R.E.
Students 894.

35—HOLY NAME (1920), Rev. Charles Kelly, S.C.J.
Res., 1917 Cochran St., 77009-8497. Tel: 713-222-1255; Fax: 713-222-1260.
School—1912 Marion St., 77009-8649. Tel: 713-227-9529; Fax: 713-227-0224. Sr. Angelica Garza, S.S.C.J., Prin.
Sisters 3; Lay Teachers 12; Students 178.
Catechesis/Religious Programs—Tel: 713-223-4059. Mrs. Alicia Bernal, D.R.E.
Students 525.

36—HOLY ROSARY (1913), Revs. Joseph D. Konkel, O.P.; William H. Brenda, O.P.; Joseph Nguyen Ngoc Tu, O.P. In res., Rev. Albert Moraczewski, O.P.
Res., 3600 Travis St., 77002-9591. Tel: 713-529-4854; Fax: 713-522-3967.

37—IMMACULATE CONCEPTION (1911), Revs. Charles J Borski, O.M.I.; James Miller, O.M.I.; Deacons Joseph G. Morin; Leslie Bart Hock; Luis A. Rodriguez.
Res., 7250 Harrisburg Blvd., 77011-4791. Tel: 713-921-1261; Fax: 713-921-2304.
Catechesis/Religious Programs—Tel: 713-645-5932. Ms. Nora Ponce, D.R.E.
Students 744.

38—IMMACULATE HEART OF MARY (1926), Revs. William Davis, O.M.I.; John Lasseigne, O.M.I.
Res., 7539 Ave. K, 77012-1033. Tel: 713-923-2394; Fax: 713-923-2395.
School—7535 Ave. L, 77012-1098. Tel: 713-921-5431; Fax: 713-923-2395. Dora Tillman, Prin.
Sisters 1; Lay Teachers 6; Students 65.
Catechesis/Religious Programs—Tel: 713-928-5238. Rosalinda Carbajal, D.R.E.
Students 572.

39—ST. JEROME (1960), Rev. Msgr. Daniel Scheel, S.T.L., M.Ch.A.; Revs. Douglas Smith; Edwin Coreas; Deacons Alden Knobloch; Jim Rutledge.
Res., 8825 Kempwood, 77080-4199. Tel: 713-468-9555; Fax: 713-464-0325.
School—Tel: 713-468-7946. Sharon Makulski, Prin.
Sisters 3; Lay Teachers 19; Students 349.
Catechesis/Religious Programs—Tel: 713-464-5029. Sr. Imelda Alcober, D.R.E.
Students 887.

40—ST. JOHN NEUMANN (1977), Rev. Msgr. Eugene G. Francis, M.R.E.; Rev. Charles J. Samperi; Deacons Klaus W. Petereit; Richard L. Leach.
2730 Nelwood Dr., 77038-1025. Tel: 281-931-0684 (Res); Fax: 281-931-5363 (Res).
Catechesis/Religious Programs—Tel: 281-931-0684. Mrs. Kathy Kimich, D.R.E.
Students 380.

41—ST. JOHN VIANNEY (1966), Revs. John N. Morfin; Niall Nolan; Mercurio Montenegro, M.S.C.; Deacons Dale Steffes; Albert Vacek, Jr.; Fred Kosegi.
Res., 625 Nottingham Oaks Tr., 77079-6299. Tel: 281-497-1500; Fax: 281-584-2024.
Catechesis/Religious Programs—Tel: 281-497-6665. Frances Contello, D.R.E.
Students 1,387.

42—ST. JOSEPH (1880), Revs. A. Ferdinand Derrera, S.J.; Edgar J. Tiblier, S.J.; Bro. Walter A. Eckler, S.J.; Deacons Geronimo Flores; Martin Sanchez.
Res., 1505 Kane St., 77007-7711. Tel: 713-222-6193; Fax: 713-222-1729.
Catechesis/Religious Programs—Marina Ramirez, D.R.E.
Students 280.

43—ST. JUSTIN MARTYR (1982), Revs. Thomas F. Rafferty; Dominic Chinh Van Pham, C.Ss.R.; Deacons Robert C. Keller; Gene Festa; Cornelius C. Llorens; J. M. Baker, C.S.
Res., 13350 Ashford Point Dr., 77082-5100. Tel: 281-556-5116; Fax: 281-556-6932.
Rectory: 12809 Sunset Dunes, 77082.
Catechesis/Religious Programs—Carole Polzer, D.R.E.
Students 935.

44—ST. LEO THE GREAT (1973), Revs. Louis Piran, C.S.; Carlo Titotto, C.S.
Res., 2131 Lauder Rd., 77039-3199. Tel: 281-449-2344; Fax: 281-449-3664.
Catechesis/Religious Programs—Alicia Perez, D.R.E.
Students 520.

45—ST. LUKE THE EVANGELIST (1975), Revs. Stephen R. Horn, M.Div.; Doa Kim Nguyen; Deacons John E. Devine, Jr.; James Sharpless; Paul J. Robison, Jr.; Jerry Coenen; Jesse Tollett.
11011 Hall Rd., 77089-2999. Fax: 281-481-8780.
Res., 10914 Sagemeadow, 77089. Tel: 281-481-6816; Fax: 281-481-8969.
Catechesis/Religious Programs—Tel: 281-481-4735.
Students 910.

46—ST. MARK THE EVANGELIST (1974), Rev. Roosevelt Martin; Deacons John Benoit; Marcelino Villarreal.
Church and Mailing Address: 5430 W. Ridgecreek Dr., Houston, 77053-3211.
Res., 5302 Castlecreek Ln., Houston, 77053. Tel: 281-437-9114; 437-4828; Fax: 281-835-6303.
Catechesis/Religious Programs—Tel: 281-438-0350. Zulema Perez, D.R.E.
Students 318.

47—ST. MARY OF THE PURIFICATION (1929), Revs. Alvin Dixon, S.V.D.; Paul Kahan, S.V.D. In res., Rev. Stanley J. Gootee, S.V.D.
Res., 3006 Rosedale Ave., 77004-6199. Tel: 713-528-0571; Fax: 713-528-0572.
School—3002 Rosedale, 77004. Tel: 713-522-9276; Fax: 713-522-1879. Mae Smith, Ed.D., Prin.
Lay Teachers 18; Students 232.
Catechesis/Religious Programs—Tel: 281-437-4110. Mrs. Evelyn Hunter, D.R.E.
Students 150.

48—ST. MATTHEW THE EVANGELIST (1974), Revs. Robert Tucker, S.C.J.; Jack Cavanaugh, S.C.J.; Deacon John Adams.
Res., 9915 Hollister Dr., 77040-1702. Tel: 713-466-4030; Fax: 713-896-7235.
Catechesis/Religious Programs—Tel: 713-466-4030. Virginia Diehl, D.R.E.
Students 730.

49—ST. MAXIMILIAN KOLBE (1983), Rev. John Ulm; Deacons Ronald J. Frazier; Auburn Higgins.
Church and Mailing Address: 10135 West Rd., 77064-5361. Tel: 281-955-7324; Fax: 281-955-7328.
Res., 10218 Great Plains, 77064.
Catechesis/Religious Programs—Ginger Tamborello, D.R.E.
Students 932.

50—ST. MICHAEL (1925), Rev. Msgr. Edward Randall, V.F.; Revs. Sean P. Horrigan; Stephen V. Cooley, O.Carm.; Deacons Woods Martin; Thomas C. Newhouse.
Res., 1801 Sage Rd., 77056-3598. Tel: 713-621-4370; Fax: 713-850-8341.
School—1833 Sage Rd., 77056-3599. Tel: 713-621-6847; Fax: 713-877-8812. Stephen P. Parson, Prin.
Lay Teachers 39; Students 604.
Catechesis/Religious Programs—Tel: 713-840-8213. Gabrielle Baginskie, D.R.E.
Students 604.

51—ST. RAPHAEL THE ARCHANGEL (1961), Rev. James C. Arrambide, C.Ss.R.; Deacon Antonio Marquez.
Mailing Address: P.O. Box 630787, 77263-0787. Tel: 713-781-9511; Fax: 713-278-9705.
Res., 3915 Ocee, 77063-5417.
Catechesis/Religious Programs—Ana Oliva, D.R.E.
Students 384.

52—ST. MONICA (1960), Rev. Alphonsus Bakyil, S.O.L.T.
Res., 8421 W. Montgomery Rd., 77088-7116. Tel: 281-447-5837; Fax: 281-447-8410.
Catechesis/Religious Programs—Jennifer Sims, D.R.E.
Students 170.

53—ST. NICHOLAS (1887), Rev. Donatus U. Anosike, M.S.P.
Res., 2508 Clay Ave., 77003-4498. Tel: 713-223-5210; Fax: 713-222-0424.
Catechesis/Religious Programs—Synthia Martell, D.R.E.
Students 22.

54—NOTRE DAME (1969), Revs. Nicholas Pasadilla; Antonio Castro; Deacons Francis Ostrowski; Ernest Abadejos. In res., Rev. Mark Horacek.
Res., 11226 Pompano Ln., 77072-3595.
Church—7720 Boone Rd., 77072-3595. Tel: 281-498-4653; Fax: 281-879-1527.
Catechesis/Religious Programs—D.R.E.: Cynthia O'Connor; Josephine Lowell.
Students 436.

55—OUR LADY OF CZESTOCHOWA (1982) (Polish), Rev. Jerzy Frydrych, S.Ch.
Res., 1712 Oak Tree, 77080-7240. Tel: 713-973-1081; Fax: 713-984-9501.
Church—1731 Blalock Rd., 77080.
Catechesis/Religious Programs—Students 10.

56—OUR LADY OF GUADALUPE (1912), Revs. James D. Steffes, S.C.J.; Peter Mastrobuono, S.C.J.; Francis Strafalace, S.C.J.; Deacon Guadalupe Gonzalez.
Res., 2405 Navigation Blvd., 77003-1510. Tel: 713-222-0203; Fax: 713-225-2235. [JC]
School—Tel: 713-224-6904; Fax: 713-225-2122. Chris Skowronek, Prin.
Brothers 1; Sisters 6; Lay Teachers 12; Students 283.

Catechesis/Religious Programs—Sr. Lelia Martinez, M.C.D.P., D.R.E.
Students 994.

57—OUR LADY OF LAVANG CHURCH (1985) (Vietnamese), Revs. Anthony Chinh Quang Dao, O.P., Vicar for Vietnamese; Joseph Luc Do, O.P.; Bro. Peter Mai Van To, O.P.; Deacon Michael Nguyen K. Khanh.
Res., 12320 Old Foltin Rd., 77086-3513. Tel: 281-999-1672; Fax: 281-820-7095.
Catechesis/Religious Programs—Nam Hoang Luong, D.R.E.
Students 441.

58—OUR LADY OF LOURDES (1994), Revs. Dominic Huy The Trinh, O.P.; Peter Van Hoang Thien, O.P.; Deacon Joseph Chuong Nguyen Do.
Mailing Address: 6550 Fairbanks N. Houston, 77040-4307. Tel: 713-939-1906; Fax: 713-939-0771.
Catechesis/Religious Programs—Students 428.

59—OUR LADY OF MT. CARMEL (1953), Rev. Ronald Oakham, O.Carm.; Deacons Fred Guajardo; John Motley; Terrance Mulcare. In res., Rev. Mark Schaffner, O.Carm.
Res., 6723 Whitefriars Dr., 77087-6598. Tel: 713-645-6673; Fax: 713-645-6674.
Church—6725 Reed Rd., 77087.
School—6703 Whitefriars Dr., 77087. Tel: 713-643-0676; Fax: 713-645-6674. Jeanette Bradley, Prin.
Lay Teachers 15; Students 225.
Catechesis/Religious Programs—Tel: 713-645-6010. Esperanza Moterrubio, D.R.E.
Students 310.

60—OUR LADY OF ST. JOHN (1947), Rev. Armando J. Rodriguez; Deacon Julio Suriano.
Res., 7500 Hirsch Rd., 77016-6215. Tel: 713-631-0810; Fax: 713-631-0781.
Catechesis/Religious Programs—Students 192.

61—OUR LADY OF SORROWS (1936), Rev. Norberto Conde.
Res., 3006 Kashmere St., 77026-5999. Tel: 713-673-5622; Fax: 713-673-5667.
Catechesis/Religious Programs—Diana Ruiz, D.R.E.
Students 201.

62—OUR LADY OF WALSINGHAM (1984), Rev. James T. Moore; Deacon James Barnett.
Mailing Address: 7809 Shady Villa Ln., 77055-5011. Tel: 281-821-0423; Fax: 713-683-1518.
Res., 21806 Galewood Lane, 77073.
Catechesis/Religious Programs—Students 40.

63—OUR MOTHER OF MERCY (1930), Revs. Roger Caesar, S.S.J.; Walter Cerbin, S.S.J. In res., Deacons Charles Allen, Sr.; Irvin Johnson, Jr.
Res., 4000 Sumpter St., 77020-2497. Tel: 713-672-0026; Fax: 713-672-2031.
School—Tel: 713-673-1862; Fax: 713-674-8575. Linda Mabrie, Prin.
Sisters 5; Lay Teachers 10; Students 187.
Catechesis/Religious Programs—Tel: 713-672-2037. Sr. Theresa Healy, S.H.Sp., D.R.E.
Students 328.

64—OUR LADY STAR OF THE SEA (1950), Rev. John O'Rourke, S.S.J. In res., Rev. Eugene R. Moynihan, S.S.J.
Res., 1401 Fidelity St., 77029-4624. Tel: 713-674-9206; Fax: 713-675-7842.
Catechesis/Religious Programs—Daisy Fields, D.R.E.
Students 62.

65—ST. PATRICK (1880), Rev. Henry B. Walker, O.M.I.
Res., 4918 Cochran St., 77009-2117. Tel: 713-695-0631; Fax: 713-695-6255.
Catechesis/Religious Programs—Beatrice Perez, D.R.E.
Students 740.

66—ST. PAUL (1964), Rev. Dominic J. Pistone, Jr. In res., Revs. Walter N. Sheffield; Edward DeRussy, S.J.; Deacons Richard Labrecque; Robert G. Alexander.
Church—18223 Point Lookout Dr., 77058-3594. Tel: 281-333-3891; Fax: 281-333-3815.
Rectory: 18326 Point Lookout Dr., 77058.
Catechesis/Religious Programs—Tel: 281-335-5701. Sara Fontana, D.R.E.
Students 682.

67—ST. PETER THE APOSTLE (1941), Revs. Paul N. Ofoha, M.S.P.; Frederick Isek, M.S.P.; Deacon Clarence Johnson.
Res., 6220 La Salette Dr., 77021-1323. Tel: 713-747-7800; Fax: 713-747-9671.
School—Tel: 713-747-9484; Fax: 713-747-2621. Mr. Lucius M. Guillory, Prin.
Lay Teachers 10; Students 125.
Catechesis/Religious Programs—Tel: 713-747-4535. D.R.E.: Helen Kinard; Virgie Ricardo.
Students 81.

68—ST. PETER CLAVER (1964), Rev. Rawlin B. Enette, S.S.J.; Deacon Raymond Despania.
Mailing Address: 6005 N. Wayside Dr., 77028-4494. Tel: 713-674-3338; Fax: 713-674-6524.
Catechesis/Religious Programs—Helen Wilson, D.R.E.
Students 165.

69—ST. PHILIP NERI (1961), Rev. Tom Byrne, C.S.Sp., D.Min.; Deacon Ronald Simon. In res., Rev. Elvio Nery Alves, C.S.Sp.
Res., 10960 Martin Luther King Jr. Blvd., 77048-1815.
Mailing Address: P.O. Box 330190, 77233-0190. Tel: 713-734-0320; Fax: 713-734-0331.
School—Tel: 713-733-2343. Melina G. Harris, Prin.
Sisters 1; Lay Teachers 7; Students 101.
Catechesis/Religious Programs—Tel: 713-734-0320. Mrs. Mary Freeman, D.R.E.
Students 125.

70—ST. PHILIP OF JESUS (1958), Rev. Miguel A. Soloranzo; Deacon Roy Breaux.
Mailing Address: P.O. Box 9818, 77213-9818.
Res., 3526 La Retama Dr., 77013-3818. Tel: 713-672-6141; Fax: 713-672-8675.
Church—9700 Villita St., 77013-3851.
Catechesis/Religious Programs—Tel: 713-674-1664. Alberto Patetta, D.R.E.
Students 499.

71—PRINCE OF PEACE (1971), Revs. John Keller; Thomas V. Ponzini; Deacons George Trosclair; Bob Dalecki; Charles Duck; Chuck Butler; Jeronimo Bazan.
Res., 8300 Dorrcrest Ln., 77070-3510.
Church—19222 Tomball Pkwy., 77070-3510. Tel: 281-469-2686; Fax: 281-469-8418.
Catechesis/Religious Programs—Dominica Weir, D.R.E.
Students 1,650.

72—QUEEN OF PEACE (1942), Revs. Christian H.F. Riesbeck; Daren Bryk; Deacon Jose Liendo. In res., Revs. Francis A. Frankovich; Ed Wade; Sean A. Wenger.
Res., 3011 Telephone Rd., 77023-5395. Tel: 713-921-6127; Fax: 713-921-6128.
School—Tel: 713-921-1558. Theresa Cutrer, Prin.
Sisters 2; Lay Teachers 8; Students 94.
Catechesis/Religious Programs—Tel: 713-921-1917. Sr. Gisela Rivera, C.M.S.T., D.R.E.
Students 901.

73—RESURRECTION (1920), Revs. David J. Cardenas; Blas P. Herrador; Deacons Gregory Garcia; Jose J. Ramirez.
Res., 915 Zoe St., 77020-6898. Tel: 713-675-5333; Fax: 713-673-3605.
School—916 Majestic St., 77019. Tel: 713-674-5545. Dora Tillman, Prin.
Sisters 1; Lay Teachers 12; Students 168.
Catechesis/Religious Programs—Tel: 713-674-2151. Gloria Hewitt, D.R.E.
Students 293.
Station—Port Houston, La Divina Providencia.

74—ST. ROSE OF LIMA (1947), Rev. Msgr. James Anderson; Rev. Thuy Quang Nguyen.
Res., 3600 Brinkman St., 77018-6329. Tel: 713-692-9123; Fax: 713-692-5638.
School—Mr. Paul Boer, Prin. Lay Teachers 21; Students 385.
Catechesis/Religious Programs—Students 216.

75—ST. STEPHEN (1941), Revs. Ignacio Garzon, M.J.; Jesus E. Flores, M.J.
Mailing Address: 2019 Center St., 77007-6106.
Res., 1910 Center St., 77007. Tel: 713-864-4075; Fax: 713-880-8611.
Catechesis/Religious Programs—Tel: 281-445-8830. Sr. Esperanza Mendoza, C.M.S.T., D.R.E.
Students 312.

76—ST. THERESA (1946), Revs. Benjamin Smaistrla; Francis M. Macatangay; Deacons Larry A. Vaclavik; John M. Baker. In res., Rev. Dennis L. Peterson.
Res., 6622 Haskell St., 77007-2097. Tel: 713-869-3783; Fax: 713-869-3784.
School—Tel: 713-864-4536. Mrs. Judy Fritsch, Prin.
Lay Teachers 18; Students 228.
Catechesis/Religious Programs—Tel: 713-869-9725. Betty Blazek, D.R.E.
Students 293.

77—ST. THOMAS MORE (1963), Rev. Msgr. William L. Young, III; Revs. Albert Walsh; Alberto Rodriguez. In res., Rev. Thomas Joseph Medayil; Deacons Anthony Alessi; Edwin Gosline; Edward Stoessel; John Pelletier.
Res., 10330 Hillcroft, 77096-4795. Tel: 713-729-0221; Fax: 713-729-3294.
School—5927 Wigton, 77096. Tel: 713-729-3434. Mrs. Nadine Mouser, Prin.
Lay Teachers 32; Students 638.
Catechesis/Religious Programs—Tel: 713-729-3435. Barbara Mackie, D.R.E.
Students 750.

78—ST. VINCENT DE PAUL (1939), Rev. Msgr. James A. Jamail; Revs. Phi Thanh Nguyen; Romanus O. Muoneke. In res., Deacons Dr. Joseph Lorino; George Sheltz.
Res., 6800 Buffalo Speedway, 77025-1499. Tel: 713-667-9111; Fax: 713-667-3453.
School—6802 Buffalo Speedway, 77025. Tel: 713-666-2345; Fax: 713-663-3562. Mary Getschow, Prin.
Sisters 3; Lay Teachers 32; Students 527.
Catechesis/Religious Programs—Tel: 713-667-3524. Sr. Jean Marie Goukas, C.V.I., D.R.E.
Students 650.

79—VIETNAMESE MARTYRS (1986) (Vietnamese), Rev. John Hoang Minh Toan; Deacon Joseph Nguyen Pham.
10612 Kingspoint Rd., 77075-4114.
Res., 10614 Kingspoint Rd., 77075-4114. Tel: 713-941-0521; Fax: 713-941-0521.
Church—10610 Kingspoint Rd., 77075-4114.

OUTSIDE THE CITIES OF GALVESTON AND HOUSTON

Alvin, Brazoria Co., St. John the Baptist (1952), Revs. Daniel McKenna, O.M.I.; Adolph Kaler, O.M.I.; Deacons Robert Kacz; David Bowman.
Res., 110 E. South St., 77511-3500. Tel: 281-331-3751; Fax: 281-331-5430.
Catechesis/Religious Programs—Sr. Charles Marie Flores, S.S.C.J., D.R.E.
Students 794.

Anderson, Grimes Co., St. Stanislaus (1866), Rev. Louis S. Sikorski; Deacons Anton Sicinski; Peter Sechelski.
Res., P.O. Box 210, 77830-0210. Tel: 936-873-2291; Fax: 936-873-3304. [CEM]
Church—1511 Hwy. 90 S., 77830.
Catechesis/Religious Programs—Students 118.

Angleton, Brazoria Co., Most Holy Trinity (1960), Revs. Vincent Dulock, C.S.B.; Enrique Bravo, C.S.B.; Deacon Andrew J. Shefts.
Res., 1713 N. Tinsley, 77515-3598. Tel: 979-849-2421; Fax: 979-849-2425.
Catechesis/Religious Programs—Tel: 979-849-1764. Lina Ramirez, D.R.E.
Students 522.

Barrett Station, Harris Co., St. Martin de Porres (1944), Rev. Anthony Ekanem, M.S.P.; Deacon Steve Arceneaux, Jr.
Mailing Address: P.O. Box 3459, 77532-2459. Tel: 281-328-4451; Fax: 281-328-7306. [JC]
Res., 12606 Crosby-Lynchburg Rd., 77532-2459.
Catechesis/Religious Programs—Tel: 281-328-1972. Mrs. Louis Salandy, D.R.E.
Students 232.

Beasley, Ft. Bend Co., St. Wenceslaus Mission (1923). (Independent Mission). Rev. Henry C. Rachunek.
Res., P.O. Box 121, Hungerford, 77448-0121. Tel: 979-532-4747; Fax: 979-532-8713. [CEM]
Catechesis/Religious Programs—Students 132.

Baytown, Harris Co., St. John the Evangelist (1974), Rev. William A. Oliver; Deacons Justin Wewer; John William Singer, Jr.; Bob Hennessy.
Res., 800 W. Baker Rd., 77521-2311. Tel: 281-837-8180; Fax: 281-837-8181.
Catechesis/Religious Programs—Tel: 281-837-0532. Jan Allison, D.R.E.
Students 320.

St. Joseph (1924), Rev. Stephen A. Mandry, S.T.D.; Deacon John William Singer, Jr.
Res., 1907 Carolina St., 77520-6098. Tel: 281-420-3588; Fax: 281-422-3044.
School—1811 Carolina St., 77520-6099. Tel: 281-422-3044. Robert Schieffer, Prin.
Sisters 1; Lay Teachers 8; Students 112.
Catechesis/Religious Programs—Tel: 281-427-5720. Jude Arceneaux, D.R.E.
Students 235.

Our Lady of Guadalupe (1958), Revs. Luis E. Hernandez, O.S.A.; Miguel Angel Ruiz, O.S.A.; Deacons Fernando Gonzalez; Rudy Venegas; George Rincon.
Res., 1124 Beech St., 77520-4198. Tel: 281-428-1507; Fax: 281-422-4554.
Catechesis/Religious Programs—Tel: 281-427-5836. Dahlia & Hector Meza, D.R.E.
Students 510.

Bellville, Austin Co., SS. Peter & Paul (1860), Rev. Timothy P. Bucek, M.Th.
Res., P.O. Box 176, 77418-0176. Tel: 979-865-2368; Fax: 979-865-9929.
Catechesis/Religious Programs—Tel: 979-865-8601. Cristina Pier, D.R.E.
Students 230.
Mission—Industry, Austin Co., Immaculate Conception, (1875).

Brazoria, Brazoria Co., St. Joseph on the Brazos (1840), Rev. Tin Cosmas Kim Pham; Deacons Raul A. Castillo; Jimmy Smith.
Res., 219 Country Rd. 762, 77422-8699. Tel: 409-798-2288; Fax: 409-798-2271.

Mailing Address: Rte. 4, Box 4100, 77422-8699.
Catechesis/Religious Programs—Jimmy Smith, D.R.E.
Students 157.

Channelview, Harris Co., St. Andrew (1970), Rev. Stephen P. Zigrang, J.C.L.; Deacons Jack Rook; John Santos; Steve Miller; Javier Gomez; Nick Thompson.
Res., 827 Sheldon Rd., 77530-3511. Tel: 281-452-9865; Fax: 281-452-2157.
Catechesis/Religious Programs—Tel: 281-452-0618. Sr. Helen Spanos, D.R.E.
Students 1,014.

Clute, Brazoria Co., St. Jerome (1969), Rev. James F. Lynes; Deacon Julio Garcia.
Mailing Address: 201 N. Lazy Ln., 77531-4001. Tel: 979-265-5179; Fax: 979-265-4601.
Catechesis/Religious Programs—Tel: 979-266-8634. Dina Tonche, D.R.E.
Students 323.

Conroe, Montgomery Co., Sacred Heart (1916), Rev. Msgr. David W. Kennedy, V.F.; Rev. Manuel La Rosa-Lopez; Deacons Leo St. Aubin; John Ehrman.
Res., 109 N. Frazier St., 77301-2889. Tel: 936-756-8186; Fax: 936-756-8105.
School—615 McDade, 77301-2890. Tel: 936-756-3848. Gerard Kubelka, Prin.
Sisters 2; Lay Teachers 12; Students 311.
Spanish Ministry—Tel: 936-756-8288.
Catechesis/Religious Programs—Students 676.

Crosby, Harris Co., Sacred Heart (1935), Rev. Msgr. Fred P. O'Connor.
Res., 915 Runnenburg Rd., 77532-5826. Tel: 281-328-4871; Fax: 281-328-1075.
School—907 Runneberg Rd., 77532. Tel: 281-328-6561; Fax: 281-462-0072. Deborah Francis, Prin.
Sisters 3; Lay Teachers 12; Students 155.
Catechesis/Religious Programs—Margaret Benham, D.R.E.
Students 245.

Damon, Brazoria Co., Sts. Cyril and Methodius (1925), Rev. James Ramsey.
Res. & Mailing Address: P.O. Box 309, 77430-0309. Tel: 979-742-3383; Fax: 979-742-3383. [CEM]
Church—603 Parrott Ave., 77430-0309.
Catechesis/Religious Programs—Tel: 979-345-3976. Tricia Wleczyk, D.R.E.
Students 54.

Danbury, Brazoria Co., St. Anthony de Padua (1911), Rev. Msgr. Boleslaus Zientek; Deacon Gerald Peltier.
Res., P.O. Box 299, 77534-0299. Tel: 979-922-1240; Fax: 979-922-8643. [CEM]
Catechesis/Religious Programs—Tel: 979-922-1241. Mary LeCompte, D.R.E.
Students 128.

Deer Park, Harris Co., St. Hyacinth (1965), Revs. Richard Baker; Kenneth Heberlein, Admin.; Deacons Dennis M. Hickey; Richard F. Camunez.
Res., 2921 Center St., 77536-4997. Tel: 281-479-4298; Fax: 281-479-4132.
Catechesis/Religious Programs—Tel: 281-479-8832. Mary Wilson, D.R.E.
Students 998.

Dickinson, Galveston Co., Shrine of the True Cross (1909), Rev. Msgr. Milam E. Kleas; Rev. Robert C. Ramon; Deacon Sam Ausmus, III. In res., Rev. Kenneth E. Mikulik.
Mailing Address: P.O. Box 687, 77539-0687.
Res., 3720 Spruce, 77539. Tel: 281-337-4112; Fax: 281-337-5779.
Church—300 Pine Dr., 77539.
School—400 Pine Dr., 77539. Tel: 281-337-5212. Susan Callaway, Prin.
Lay Teachers 13; Students 302.
Catechesis/Religious Programs—Tel: 281-337-3130. Jane Hebert, D.R.E.
Students 553.

Freeport, Brazoria Co., St. Mary: Star of the Sea (1925), Rev. William Sommerville; Deacon Wallace Shaw.
Mailing Address: 1019 West 6th St., 77541-5423.
Res., 914 W. 7th St., 77541. Tel: 979-233-5271; Fax: 979-233-5272.
Catechesis/Religious Programs—Tel: 979-233-1726. Marilyn Saccomanno, D.R.E.
Students 268.

St. Henry (1932), Rev. Jose M. Sanchez.
Mailing Address: P.O. Box 857, 77542-0857.
Res., 318 E. 5th St., 77541-5913. Tel: 979-233-2887; Fax: 979-233-0293.
Catechesis/Religious Programs—Tel: 979-233-4374. Margaret Garcia, D.R.E.
Students 111.

Friendswood, Galveston Co., Mary, Queen (1964), Revs. Paul Mandziuk, M.S.; Ronald Beauchemin, M.S.; Deacon Darrell Moulton. In res., Rev. Ronald Groschen, M.S.
Res., P.O. Box 207, 77549-0207. Tel: 281-482-1391; Fax: 281-482-4886.
Catechesis/Religious Programs—Donna Patlach, D.R.E.
Students 901.

Frydek, Austin Co., St. Mary's (1908), Rev. Bernard C. Snock.
Res., 124 Zaruba Rd., Sealy, 77474-9801. Tel: 979-885-3131; Fax: 979-885-4555. [CEM]
Catechesis/Religious Programs—Tel: 979-885-3178. Leona Buchala, D.R.E.
Students 122.

Galena Park, Harris Co., Our Lady of Fatima (1946), Revs. Robert D. Carlson; Agerico L. Galang; Deacons Jerry Kulhanek, Sr.; Hector Morales. In res., Rev. Rivers A. Patout.
Res., 1705 Eighth St., P.O. Box 644, 77547-0644. Tel: 713-675-0981; Fax: 713-675-0982.
School—1702 Ninth St., 77547. Tel: 713-674-5832; Fax: 713-674-3877. Sr. Martini Hoare, S.H.Sp., Prin.
Sisters 1; Lay Teachers 11; Students 185.
Catechesis/Religious Programs—Rachel Gonzalez, D.R.E.
Students 432.

Hempstead, Waller Co., Mary, Mother of God (1879), Rev. James M. Burkart.
Mailing Address: P.O. Box 576, 77445-0576. Tel: 979-826-2275; Fax: 979-826-8057. [CEM]
Res., 604 14th St., 77445.
Catechesis/Religious Programs—D.R.E.: Carmen Karisch; Rosemary Thompson; Lucille Pavlock.
Students 330.

Highlands, Harris Co., St. Jude Thaddeus (1946), Rev. John A. Zabelskas.
Res., 800 S. Main St., 77562-4236. Tel: 281-843-2422; Fax: 281-426-3671.
Catechesis/Religious Programs—Tel: 281-426-6800. Reecie Plocheck, D.R.E.
Students 196.

Hitchcock, Galveston Co., Our Lady of Lourdes (1954), Rev. Peter A. Ferguson.
Res., 10114 Hwy. 6, 77563-4515. Tel: 409-925-3579; Fax: 409-925-5094.
School—Tel: 409-925-3224. Teresa "Terry" Bogar, Prin.
Sisters 2; Lay Teachers 6; Students 152.
Catechesis/Religious Programs—Sr. Mary Anne Hollmann, C.V.I., D.R.E.
Students 252.

Huffman, Harris Co., St. Philip the Apostle (1977), Rev. George J. Olsovsky, M.Th.
Mailing Address: P.O. Box 292, 77336-0292. Tel: 281-324-1478; Fax: 281-324-2775.
Res., 2308 Third St., 77336.
Catechesis/Religious Programs—Tel: 281-334-4401. Maureen Schuster, D.R.E.
Students 203.

Humble, Harris Co., St. Mary Magdalene (1911), Rev. Msgr. Paul Procella; Rev. Hernan J. Sanchez; Deacons James N. Caruso; Tom McKinney; Robert A. MacFarlane.
Mailing Address: 527 S. Houston Ave., 77338-4763.
Res., 525 S. Houston Ave., 77338-4763. Tel: 281-446-8211; Fax: 281-446-8213.
Catechesis/Religious Programs—Tel: 281-446-2933. Deborah Jones, D.R.E.
Students 985.

Huntsville, Walker Co., St. Thomas the Apostle (1963), Rev. Stephen J. Payne; Deacons Frank Ortego; Ivy Floyd; Ricard Lopez.
Res., 1323 16th St., 77340-4431. Tel: 936-295-8159; Fax: 936-295-3543.
Catechesis/Religious Programs—Tel: 936-295-2298. Sharyn Pezan, D.R.E.
Students 255.

Katy, Harris Co., St. Bartholomew the Apostle (1965), Rev. Alberto A. Maullon, Jr.; Deacons William C. Wagner; L. William Hamilton; Arthur Chin-Fatt.
Res., 5356 11th St., 77493-1748. Tel: 281-391-4758; Fax: 281-391-3978.
Catechesis/Religious Programs—Tel: 281-391-0839. Bill Wagner, D.R.E.
Students 998.

St. Edith Stein (1999), Rev. Robert Barras; Deacons John Rooney; Leonard Broussard.
Res., 3311 N. Fry Rd., 77449. Tel: 281-492-7500; Fax: 281-492-0266.
Catechesis/Religious Programs—Students 350.

Epiphany of the Lord (1981), Rev. Msgr. Jack M. Dinkins; Deacon Don Kish.
Res., 1530 Norwalk Dr., 77450-4999. Tel: 281-578-0707; Fax: 281-578-9161.
Catechesis/Religious Programs—Tel: 281-578-8271.
Students 2,216.

Kingwood, Harris Co., St. Martha (1979), Revs. Terence Brinkman, S.T.D.; Dwight M. Canizares; Frank V. Du Preez.
Res., 2302 Oak Shores Dr., 77339-1801. Tel: 281-358-6637; Fax: 281-358-7973.
School—P.O. Box 6354, 77325-6354. Tel: 281-358-5523.
Sisters 1; Lay Teachers 19; Students 197.
Catechesis/Religious Programs—Tel: 713-358-1959. Carla Lewton, D.R.E.
Students 1,770.

Lake Jackson, Brazoria Co., St. Michael (1966), Rev. Msgr. Leo Wleczyk, V.F.
Res., 100 Oak Dr. S., 77566-5630. Tel: 979-297-3041; Fax: 979-297-7895.
Catechesis/Religious Programs—Tel: 979-297-3043. Marsha Jacklitsch, D.R.E.
Students 847.

La Marque, Galveston Co., Our Lady Queen of Peace (1951), Rev. Msgr. T. Joseph Culver, E.V.; Deacon James Bonura. In res., Rev. A. Peter Whitney.
Mailing Address: 1224 Cedar Dr., 77568.
Res., 626 Laurel, 77568. Tel: 409-938-7000; Fax: 409-935-9791.
Church—1200 Cedar Dr., 77568.
Catechesis/Religious Programs—Tel: 409-935-3535. Armando Tapia, D.R.E.
Students 268.

La Porte, Harris Co., St. Mary of the Immaculate Conception (1954), Rev. Eric Pitre; Deacons Hector Cantu; Thomas Lewis.
Res., 816 Park Dr., 77571-5811. Tel: 281-471-2000; Fax: 281-471-9365.
Catechesis/Religious Programs—Tel: 281-471-2316. Diane Koonce, D.R.E.
Students 390.

League City, Galveston Co., St. Mary (1910), Rev. Msgr. Eugene Cargill; Deacons Robert Garza; Jerome McAllister; George Blanford.
Res., 1612 E. Walker St., 77573-4137. Tel: 281-332-3031; Fax: 281-332-8328.
School—Tel: 281-332-4014.
Lay Teachers 20; Students 208.
Catechesis/Religious Programs—Tel: 281-332-7459. Theresa Thomas, D.R.E.
Students 721.

Magnolia, Montgomery Co., St. Matthias the Apostle (1978), Rev. Frank W. Jones; Deacon George Trosclair.
Res., 302 S. Magnolia Blvd., 77355-8535. Tel: 281-356-2000; Fax: 281-356-7818.
Catechesis/Religious Programs—Barbara Bezub, D.R.E.
Students 374.

Manvel, Brazoria Co., Sacred Heart of Jesus (1945), Revs. James J. Gaunt, C.S.B.; John S. Broussard, C.S.B.; Deacon Robert Leicht, Jr.
Res., 6502 Co. Rd. 48, 77578-2908. Tel: 281-489-8720; Fax: 281-489-8727.
Catechesis/Religious Programs—Tel: 281-489-7603. Theresa Garza, D.R.E.
Students 553.

McNair, Harris Co., Holy Family (1945), Rev. Rodrick J.D. Coates, S.S.J.
Res. and Mailing Address: 7122 Whiting Rock Dr., Baytown, 77521-1124. Tel: 281-426-8448; Fax: 281-426-8449. [JC]
Catechesis/Religious Programs—Tel: 281-383-2324. Mary Norman, D.R.E.
Students 79.

Missouri City, Ft. Bend Co., Holy Family (1915), Revs. Thaddeus T. Valencia, C.S.B.; David Zapalac, C.S.B.; Hugh J. Curran, C.S.B.; Deacon William Seifert. In res., Rev. Anthony Nirappel.
Res., 1510 Fifth St., 77489-1298. Tel: 281-499-9688; Fax: 281-499-9680.
Catechesis/Religious Programs—Tel: 281-499-4612. Yolanda Pena, D.R.E.
Students 472.

Navasota, Grimes Co., Christ Our Light (1869), Rev. Paul G. Felix; Deacons Grant E. Holt; Gregory N. Jelinek, M.D.
Mailing Address: 510 Manley St., 77868-3926.
Res., 615 Church St., 77868-3905. Tel: 936-825-3920; Fax: 936-825-7612.
Church—9677 Hwy. 6, 77868.
Catechesis/Religious Programs—Margie Terrell, D.R.E.
Students 220.

Needville, Fort Bend Co., St. Michael (1926), Rev. James Ramsey.
Res., P.O. Box 95, 77461-0095. Tel: 979-793-4477; Fax: 979-793-7456. [CEM]
Church—9202 Main St., 77461.
Catechesis/Religious Programs—Lynn Sury, D.R.E., Tel: 281-232-4006 (Res.).
Students 538.

New Caney, Montgomery Co., St. John of the Cross (1989), Rev. Gary A. Rickles.
Mailing Address: 20000 Loop 494, 77357-9804. Tel: 281-399-9008; Fax: 281-399-9008.
Catechesis/Religious Programs—Tel: 281-399-9127. Debbie Davis, D.R.E.
Students 291.

New Waverly, Walker Co., St. Joseph (1869), Rev. Joseph K. Kalladan; Deacons Jose Trujillo; Klaus Petereit.
Church and Res.: 101 Elmore, 77358-4105. Tel: 936-344-6104 (Res); Fax: 936-344-2818 (Res). [CEM 2]
Catechesis/Religious Programs—Tel: 936-856-3713.
Students 135.
Mission—Point Blank, St. Stephen the Martyr.

Pasadena, Harris Co., St. Pius the Fifth (1941), Revs. Hubert J. Kealy; Stanislaus Bieniek; Deacons Leon Arceneaux; Arturo Gomez.
Res., 824 Main St., 77506-3532. Tel: 713-473-9484; Fax: 713-473-2731.
School—812 S. Main St., Pasaena, 77506. Tel: 713-472-5172.
Lay Teachers 25; Students 182.
Catechesis/Religious Programs—D.R.E.: Sr. Felice Mojica, M.C.D.P.; Sr. Frances Jean Terrazas, M.C.D.P.
Students 1,250.

Blessed Juan Diego (1954) (Hispanic). (Formerly Guardian Angel). Revs. J. Francisco Leon, O.S.A.; Leonel Martinez, O.S.A. (Mexico); Deacon Valeriano Leija.
Res., 3301 Pasadena Blvd., 77503-3201. Tel: 713-477-6693; Fax: 713-477-0523.
Catechesis/Religious Programs—Tel: 713-472-0356. Beatrice Canas, D.R.E.
Students 412.

Pattison/Brookshire, Waller Co., Sacred Heart (1914), Rev. David DuBois.
Mailing Address: P.O. Box 300, Pattison, 77466-0300.
Res., 4445 F.M. 359 N., Pattison, 77466. Tel: 281-375-6799; Fax: 281-375-5799.
Catechesis/Religious Programs—Tel: 281-375-6638. Mrs. Marie Pattison, D.R.E.
Students 189.

Pearland, Brazoria Co., St. Helen (1966), Rev. Msgr. Reginald Nesvadba; Revs. Wayne Wilkerson; Thomas Ponmelil; Deacon Darvin Bordelon.
Res., 2209 Old Alvin Rd., 77581. Tel: 281-485-2421; Fax: 281-485-6789.
School—2213 Old Alvin Rd., 77581. Tel: 281-485-2845; Fax: 281-485-7607. Mary Margaret Hitt, Prin.
Lay Teachers 4; Students 60.
Catechesis/Religious Programs—Patsy Morales, D.R.E.
Students 1,534.

Plantersville, Grimes Co., St. Mary (1894), Rev. Edward C Kucera, Jr.
P.O. Box 388, 77363-0388. [CEM]
Res., 8227 County Rd. 205, 77363. Tel: 936-894-2223; Fax: 936-894-2223.
Catechesis/Religious Programs—Students 156.
Mission—Stonehan, Grimes Co., St. Joseph.

Port Bolivar, Galveston Co., Our Mother of Mercy (1968), Rev. John J. Connolly.
Mailing Address: P.O. Drawer C, 77650-0703.
Church—18th St. at Madison, Port Boliver, 77650.
Res., 1313 18th St., 77650-0703. Tel: 409-684-8962; Fax: 409-684-8962.
Catechesis/Religious Programs—Students 23.
Mission—Crystal Beach, Galveston Co., St. Therese of Lisieux, (1994) 2400 Hwy. 87, Crystal Beach, 77650. Tel: 409-684-6824.

Prairie View, Waller Co., St. Martin de Porres (1962), Rev. James M. Burkart.
Res., F.M. 1098, P.O. Box 3027, 77446-3027. Tel: 936-857-3351; Fax: 936-857-8057.
Church—708 Thompson Dr., 77446. [CEM]
Catechesis/Religious Programs—Tel: 936-857-3538. Mary Hawkins, D.R.E.
Students 20.

Richmond, Fort Bend Co., Sacred Heart (1935), Rev. Howard E. Drabek; Deacons Don Ries; Joe Kelly; Emiliano Gonzales; Brick Hodge.
Res., 507 S. Fourth St., 77469-3599. Tel: 281-342-3609; Fax: 281-342-9833.
Catechesis/Religious Programs—Tel: 281-342-8371. Virginia Ewald, D.R.E.
Students 1,125.

St. John Fisher (1952), Rev. Wencil C. Pavlovsky, C.S.B.; Deacon Ben Munguia.
Mailing Address: 410 Clay St., 77469-1708.
Res., 610 North Fourth St., 77469. Tel: 281-342-5092; Fax: 281-232-2607.
Catechesis/Religious Programs—Tel: 281-342-8371. Virginia Ewald, D.R.E.
Students 276.

Rosenberg, Fort Bend Co., Holy Rosary (1911), Rev. Daniel L. Warden, V.F.
Res., 1416 George St., 77471-3198. Tel: 281-342-3089; Fax: 281-342-7688.
School—1408 James St., 77471. Tel: 281-342-5813; Fax: 281-762-3013. Mrs. Elizabeth Anthony, Prin.
Lay Teachers 13; Students 241.
Catechesis/Religious Programs—Barbara Respondek, D.R.E., Tel: 281-342-3089 Ext. 106.
Students 296.

Our Lady of Guadalupe (1936), Revs. James Blocker, C.S.B.; Francis Launtrie, C.S.B.; William L. May, C.S.B.
Mailing Address: 514 Carlisle St., 77471-1822. Tel: 281-342-4008; Fax: 281-342-4008. [CEM]
Catechesis/Religious Programs—Tel: 281-232-4322. Dolores Yanz, D.R.E.
Students 776.

Sealy, Austin Co., Immaculate Conception (1889), Rev. Octavio A. Muguerza; Deacons Frank Laredo; Jerome Losack.
Mailing Address: P.O. Box 337, 77474-0337.
Res., 517 Fifth St., 77474-0337. Tel: 979-885-3868; Fax: 979-885-2246.
Church—525 5th St., 77474. [CEM]
Catechesis/Religious Programs—Tel: 979-885-6902. Donna Brown, D.R.E.
Students 346.

South Houston, Harris Co., Our Lady of Grace (1971), Rev. Jose Maria Asenjo.
Mailing Address: P.O. Box 164, 77587-0164.
Church—1211 Michigan Ave., 77587.
Res., 1204 Michigan St., 77587. Tel: 979-946-6461; Fax: 979-946-0647.
Catechesis/Religious Programs—Tel: 281-461-9417. Amalia D. Parra, D.R.E.
Students 249.

Spring, Harris Co.,

1—CHRIST THE GOOD SHEPHERD, (1978), Rev. Msgr. William P. Robertson; Rev. John C. Upton; Deacons Steve La Bonte; Pat Camerino.
Res., 18511 Klein Church Rd., 77379-4998. Tel: 281-376-6831; Fax: 281-376-8945.
Catechesis/Religious Programs—K. Kelley, D.R.E.
Students 1,012.

2—ST. EDWARD, (1969), Rev. Joseph A. Gietl; Deacon Kenneth Martin.
Res., 2601 Spring Stuebner Rd., 77389-4824. Tel: 281-353-9774; Fax: 281-353-9786.
School—Tel: 281-353-4570; Fax: 281-353-8255. Ann Henthorn, Prin.
Lay Teachers 22; Students 385.
Catechesis/Religious Programs—Tel: 281-353-4930. Joe Wappelhorst, D.R.E.
Students 554.

3—ST. IGNATIUS OF LOYOLA, (1985), Revs. Francis X. Pistorius, S.J.; Daniel Creagan, S.J.; Joseph M. Nasser, S.J.; Deacons Glen Cupier; Jim Hite.
Church—7810 Cypresswood Dr., 77379-7101. Tel: 281-370-3401 (Office); Fax: 281-370-9306.
Catechesis/Religious Programs—Joe Wappelhorst, D.R.E.
Students 1,894.

4—ST. JAMES THE APOSTLE, (1976), Revs. Francisco X. Quezada; Marcial Gadingan.
Res., 22800 Aldine Westfield Rd., 77373-6500. Tel: 281-353-5053; Fax: 281-355-8847.
Catechesis/Religious Programs—Tel: 281-353-3497. Jan Skrehot, D.R.E.
Students 773.

Sugar Land, Fort Bend Co., St. Laurence (1985), Revs. John T. Weyer, B.A., M.Th.; William Andrew Wood; Chacko Puthumayil; Deacons Lee Tollett; Bob Dunham.
Res., 3100 Sweetwater Blvd., 77479-2630. Tel: 281-980-9812; Fax: 281-980-0686.
School—2630 Austin Pkwy., 77479. Tel: 281-980-0550; Fax: 281-980-0026. Nancy Taylor, Prin.
Lay Teachers 28; Students 537.
Catechesis/Religious Programs—Tel: 281-265-5774. Eleanor Notz, D.R.E.
Students 1,815.

St. Theresa (1924), Revs. Robert J. Matzinger, C.S.B.; Robert G. Ritz, C.S.B.; George E. Silvester, C.S.B.; Deacons Don Burns; Frank Cromer.
Res., 115 Seventh St., P.O. Box 968, 77487-0968. Tel: 281-494-1156; Fax: 281-242-1393.
Catechesis/Religious Programs—Tel: 281-494-2717. Christy Wright, D.R.E.
Students 1,799.

St. Thomas Aquinas (1978), Rev. Kevin C. Thissen, O.P.; Deacons Sam Dunning; Bob Kirkpatrick.
Church & Mailing Address:—12627 W. Bellfort, 77478-1844. Tel: 281-240-6721; Fax: 281-240-6733.
Catechesis/Religious Programs—Students 584.

Sweeny, Brazoria Co., Our Lady of Perpetual Help (1954), Rev. Lee Flores.
Res., N. McKinney St., 77480-2899. Tel: 979-548-2020; Fax: 979-548-2020.
Catechesis/Religious Programs—Tel: 979-548-4470. Marcia Smith, D.R.E.
Students 207.
Mission—West Columbia, Brazoria Co., St. John the Apostle, 807 Loggins, West Columbia, 77486-3843. Tel: 979-345-3600.

Texas City, Galveston Co., St. Mary (1911), Rev. Ralph G. Schmidt, Jr. In res., Rev. Msgr. Thomas J. Cullen (MOB); Deacon Michael Satterwhite.
Mailing Address: 1604 Ninth Ave. N., 77590-5468.
Res., 722 Third Ave. N., 77590. Tel: 409-948-8448; Fax: 409-945-8662.
School—Our Lady of Fatima, 1600 Ninth Ave. N., 77590. Tel: 409-945-3326. Mary Ann Cullen, Prin.
Lay Teachers 20; Students 163.
Catechesis/Religious Programs—Joe Hensley, D.R.E.
Students 491.

The Woodlands, Montgomery Co., Sts. Simon and Jude (1979), Rev. Msgr. Charles C. Domec; Rev. Hai Duc Dang; Deacons Ken Carlson; Robert Flynn; Fred Shetz; Sid Sandiford.
Res., 26777 Glen Loch Dr., 77381-2921. Tel: 281-367-9885; Fax: 281-367-9888.
Catechesis/Religious Programs—Tel: 281-292-9801. D.R.E.: Robin Walker; Bill Wilson.
Students 1,512.

St. Anthony of Padua (1997), Rev. Msgr. George Sheltz; Deacons Joe Mignogna; Tom Reich; Michael Schmidt.
7801 Bay Branch Dr., 77382-5312.
Res., 75 W. Sandalbranch Cir., 77382. Tel: 281-296-2800; Fax: 281-296-7238.
Catechesis/Religious Programs—Laurie Thompson, D.R.E.
Students 1,302.

Tomball, Harris Co., St. Anne (1964), Rev. Fred Valone.
Res., 1111 S. Cherry St., 77375-6675. Tel: 281-351-8106; Fax: 281-351-8142.
School—Tel: 281-351-0093. Theresa Rourke, Prin.
Lay Teachers 23; Students 274.
Catechesis/Religious Programs—Katherine Raniowski, D.R.E.
Students 387.

Wallis, Austin Co., Guardian Angel (1892), Rev. Richard A. Johnston, S.C.J.
Mailing Address: P.O. Box 487, 77485-0487. Tel: 979-478-6532; Fax: 979-478-7275. [CEM]
Church and Res.: 5610 Demel St., 77485.
Catechesis/Religious Programs—Tel: 979-478-6717. Steve Williams, D.R.E.
Students 193.

Chaplains of Public Institutions

Prison Chaplains

GALVESTON. *Galveston County Jail*. Vacant. 715 19th St., 77550. Tel: 409-766-2315.
John Sealy Hospital, Prison Unit Tel: 409-772-6108. Deacon Earl Llewellyn.

HOUSTON. *Federal Correctional Center* 1200 Texas Ave., 77002. Tel: 713-755-5326. Rev. Ronald G. Cloutier.

ANGLETON. *Brazoria County Jail* Tel: 409-849-2441. Evelyn Nachtegaele.
Pam Lychner State Jail. Deacon Javier Gomez, 2350 Atoscocita Rd., Humble, 77396. Tel: 281-454-5036, Ext. 358.
Retrieve Unit. Vacant. Rte. 4, Box 1500, 77515. Tel: 409-849-9306.

BRAZORIA. *Clemens Unit*. Vacant. Rte. 1, Box 1077, 77422. Tel: 409-798-2188.

HUNTSVILLE. *Diagnostic Unit*. Anthony Velasquez, P.O. Box 100, 77340. Tel: 409-295-8459.
Eastham Unit. Rev. Virginio C. Vazquez, P.O. Box 1974, 77342. Tel: 409-636-7321.
Ellis I Unit. Vacant. Rt. 6, 77343. Tel: 409-295-5756, Ext. 217.
Estelle Unit. Vacant. 77343. Tel: 409-291-4200, Ext. 2274.
Goree Unit. Mr. Anthony Velasquez, Box 38, 77340. Tel: 409-295-8159.
Huntsville Walls Unit. Vacant. P.O. Box 32, 77340. Tel: 409-295-8159; 291-4200, Ext. 149.
Texas Department of Criminal Justice 2503 Lake Rd., Ste. #19, 77340. Tel: 409-294-6548 (Regl. Program Admin.). Deacon Richard Lopez.
Walls Unit. Vacant. Box 32, 77340. Tel: 409-295-8159.
Wynne Unit. Deacon Jose Trujillo, Rte. 1, Box 1, 77340. Tel: 409-295-8159.

MIDWAY. *Ferguson Unit*. Vacant. Rte. 2, Box 20, Huntsville, 75852. Tel: 409-348-3751, Ext. 333.

NAVASOTA. *Pack I Unit*. Deacon Peter Sechelski, Rte. 3, Box 300, 77686. Tel: 409-825-3728.
Pack II Unit. Deacon Peter L. Sechelski, Rte. 1, Box 1000, 77686. Tel: 409-825-7548.

RICHMOND. *Jester I, II, III, IV Unit*. Rev. Donald McNally, O.M.I., Rte. 2, 77469. Tel: 281-277-3700.

ROSHARON. *Darrington Unit*. Deacon Darrell Moulton, Rte. 3, Box 59, 77583. Tel: 281-595-2465, Ext. 275.
Ramsey I Unit. Deacon Gerry Garcia, Rte. 4, Box 1100, 77583. Tel: 281-595-3491.
Ramsey II Unit. Deacon Gerry Garcia, Rte. 4, Box 1200, 77583. Tel: 281-595-3413.
Ramsey III Unit. Deacon Bob Leicht, Rte. 4, Box 1300, 77583. Tel: 281-595-3481.

SUGAR LAND. *Central Unit.* Deacon Tom McKinney, Vacant. One Circle Dr., Richmond, 77478. Tel: 281-491-2146.

Jail Chaplains

HOUSTON. *Harris County Jail.* Rev. Ronald F. Cloutier Tel: 713-755-5326, Res., 215 E. 10th St., 77008. Tel: 713-755-5326. 701 Bldg. Tel: 713-755-8562.
Juvenile Detention Center. Special Youth Svcs. Ms. Marilu Ballow Tel: 713-741-8779.

CONROE. *Montgomery County Jail.* Deacon Leo St. Alban Tel: 409-756-8186.

On Special or Other Diocesan Assignment:
Reverend Fathers—
Gately, R. Troy, Vice Chancellor
Jozwiak, Lawrence, Tribunal
Nguyen, Trung, Tribunal
Rossi, Frank H., Chancellor
Russler, Clint, Vocation Dir.

On Duty Outside the Diocese:
Reverend Monsignors—
Broussard, William L., Texas Catholic Conference
Fruge, Donald J., P.O. Box 13327, Capitol Station, Austin, TX 78711
Reverend Fathers—
Cantu, Oscar, Casa Santa Maria, Via dell'Umilta, 30 00187, Rome, Italy. Tel: (06) 68-69-441
Corrigan, Michael T., St. Anne, 300 Ashton Ave., Kingstree, SC 29556. Tel: 803-354-7798
McGinnis, Jack P., Chap., P.O. Box 2456, Idyllwild, CA 92549-2456
Nguyen, Trung, Divine Word College, Catholic University of America, Washington, D.C.
Perez, Joseph, The Chancery, P.O. Box 907, Houston, TX 77001

Retired:
Reverend Monsignors—
Alleman, C. J., 501 13th St., Galveston, TX 77550-5034. Tel: 409-763-2588
Barzyk, Robert R., 212 Oakdale, Shoreacres, TX 77571-7347
Beck, Albert, Holy Cross Chapel, Houston, TX
Beck, George A., 8045 Holiday, Houston, TX 77075
Braden, Leroy H., Pope John XXIII Residence, 2407 Holcombe Blvd., Houston, TX 77021-2023. Tel: 713-440-7540
Crosthwait, Joseph H., P.O. Box 1302, New Ulm, TX 78950. Tel: 409-992-3821
Donovan, Thomas A., Pope John XXIII Residence, 2407 Holcombe Blvd., Houston, TX 77021-2023. Tel: 713-741-9471
Fuchs, Sylvester, Lost Prairie Villa, 9901 FM 2086, Temple, TX 76501-3528. Tel: 817-984-2312
Jones, John B., Pope John XXIII Residence, 2407 E. Holcombe Blvd., Houston, TX 77021-2023. Tel: 713-747-1746
Lagana, Frank A., Pope John XXIII Residence, 2407 E. Holcombe Blvd., Houston, TX 77021-2023. Tel: 713-748-7022
Madden, James J., Pope John XXIII Residence, 2407 E. Holcombe Blvd., Houston, TX 77021-2023. Tel: 713-748-1761
Peguero, Lawrence, Pope John XXIII Residence, 2407 E. Holcombe Blvd., Houston, TX 77021-2023. Tel: 713-741-8326
Rhein, George V., 2407 Holcombe Blvd., Houston, TX 77021-2023. Tel: 713-747-7308
Schoppe, Charles K. Tel: 713-748-4596
Wearden, Francis G., 1100 Parthenen Pl., New Caney, TX 77357-3039. Tel: 713-399-0270
Reverend Fathers—
Antle, Nicholas C., Pope John XXIII Residence, 2407 Holcombe Blvd., Houston, TX 77021-2023. Tel: 713-748-1553
Burns, Charles E., 343 Bobolink, New Braunfels, TX 78130-3868
Burns, David E.
Carreon, Albert S., P.O. Box 15836, Santa Ana, CA 92705
Chu, Peter Ngoc Thanh, Pope John XXIII Residence, 2407 Holcombe Blvd., Houston, TX 77021-2023. Tel: 713-747-8774
Connelly, Laurence D., 7 Tourney Cove, Austin, TX 78738-1119
Daigle, Robert E., 6505 O'Bannon Dr., Las Vegas, NV 89102-0854
del Val, Feliciano, St. Dominic Village, Maloney Hall, 2409 Holcombe Blvd., Houston, TX 77021-2023. Tel: 713-741-8701
Dougherty, George Patrick, 7228 Comanche Trail, Austin, TX 78732-1011. Tel: 512-266-2186
Ferguson, Carlos, c/o Chancery. Tel: 713-748-4608
Freret, Warren Joseph, P.O. Box 8691, Gulfport, MS 39506. Tel: 228-868-1687
Gillece, Eugene J., Pope John XXIII, 2407 Holcombe Blvd., Houston, TX 77021-2023. Tel: 713-748-7201
Greenwald, Alfred E., 630 N. Via Lucia, Tucson, AZ 85745. Tel: 602-792-0122
Guillermo, Rodrigo J., M.S.Ch.E., M.B.A., c/o Chancery
Hebert, Marvin A., c/o Mr. Jude C. Hebert, 415 Jeannette Dr., Bridge City, TX 77611-3742
Hughes, Royce, 745 E. U.S. Hwy. 90, Schulenberg, TX 78956-5233. Tel: 409-743-3722
Kellick, John W., 6517 Burdock Dr., Santa Fe, TX 77510-9340. Tel: 409-925-6817
Lee, Lawrence, Pope John XXIII Residence, 2407 Holcombe Blvd., Houston, TX 77021-2023. Tel: 713-741-7267
Linan, Jesse S., P.O. Box 250, Anderson, TX 77830-0250. Tel: 409-873-2945
Lynch, Denis
Natho, Clifton J., 8326 Autumn Wind Dr., Houston, TX 77040-1474. Tel: 713-856-8469
O'Malley, Joseph T., St. Thomas More, 10330 Hillcroft Ave., Houston, TX 77096-4795. Tel: 713-729-0021
Schwarting, Donald J., 3972 Jackdaw #115, San Diego, CA 92103. Tel: 619-298-5464
Stredny, Anthony G., B.A.
Tran, John Chinh Chan, 8138 Lynn St., Houston, TX 77017-3050. Tel: 713-645-2834
Walker, Anselm, 1815 Parker, Houston, TX 77093. Tel: 713-697-7109

Permanent Deacons:
Abadejos, Ernesto, Notre Dame, Houston
Abram, Alfred, Sr., Unassigned
Acosta, Angel R., St. Mary, Texas City
Adame, David, Annunciation/St. Joseph Hospital, Houston
Adams, Francis E., St. Elizabeth Anne Seton, Houston
Adams, John W., St. Matthew the Evangelist, Houston
Aiuvalasit, Anthony George, St. John Vianney, Houston
Alessi, Anthony V., St. Thomas More, Houston
Alexander, Robert George, Annunciation and St. Paul, Houston
Allen, Charles J., Sr., Our Mother of Mercy, Houston
Aranda, Jose Francisco, St. Christopher, Houston
Arceneaux, Leon M., Jr., St. Pius V, Pasadena
Arceneaux, Steve, Jr., St. Martin de Porres, Barrett Station
Arellano, Jose, Immaculate Heart of Mary, Houston
Ausmus, Sam, III, Shrine of the True Cross, Dickinson
Baker, J. M., St. Theresa and St. Justin Martyr, Houston
Baker, Theodore Otis, St. Matthias the Apostle, Magnolia
Barnett, James, Our Lady of Walsingham, Houston
Bart, James, St. Augustine, Houston
Bazan, Jeronimo, Prince of Peace, Houston
Becker, Henry, St. Peter the Apostle, Galveston
Betancourt, Manuel, Unassigned
Birsinger, Alvin, St. Luke the Evangelist, Houston
Blanford, George, St.Mary, League City
Bobb, William J., St. Peter the Apostle, Galveston
Bonura, James L., Sr., TDC/Queen of Peace, La Marque
Bordelon, Darvin A., St. Helen, Pearland
Bothe, Albert G., St. Francis de Sales, Houston
Bottjer, Albert, Assumption, Houston; Ben Taub Hospital; Jail Chap.
Bowman, David, St. John the Baptist, Alvin
Bradley, Donald E., St. Cecilia, Houston
Breaux, Roy, St. Phillip of Jesus, Houston
Brinkman, Fred H., TDC-Ramsey Units I, II, III/Drug Trustee Camp
Broussard, Leonard J., Epiphany of the Lord, Katy; Holy Name Retreat Center, Houston
Brown, Albert, Sr., St. Gregory
Brueggerhoff, Robert T., Holy Ghost, Houston
Budinger, Jean-Paul, St. Anne, Houston
Buhay, Carlito, St. Albert, Houston
Burns, Don, St. Theresa, Sugar Land
Butler, Charles, Prince of Peace, Houston
Cabler, Paul Stephen, Unassigned
Calonge, Elie, Texas Dept. of Corrections, Palestine, TX
Calvo, Clement S., Hispanic Ministry Office, Houston
Camerino, Pat W., Christ the Good Shepherd, Spring
Camunez, Richard F., St. Hyacinth, Deer Park
Cantu, Hector, St. Mary, La Porte
Carlson, Kenneth D., Sts. Simon & Jude, The Woodlands
Caruso, James, St. Mary, Humble
Casas, Alvaro, Jr., St. Albert, Houston
Castaneda, Guillermo F., Jr., Diocese of Brownsville
Castillo, Raul A., St. Joseph, Brazoria
Charnisky, John E., Jr., Diocese of Beaumont
Chin-Fatt, Arthur, St. Bartholomew
Coehen, Jerry, St. Luke the Evangelist, Houston
Cooper, Leslie F., Unassigned
Coussirat, John F., St. Catherine, Houston
Crawford, J. R., St. Anne, Tomball
Cromer, Frank P., St. Theresa, Sugarland
Cuiper, Glen H., St. Ignatius of Loyola, Spring
Dalecki, Robert, Prince of Peace, Houston
Davis, Roger, St. Luke the Evangelist, Houston
Dell-Olio, L. S., St. Peter, Galveston
Despania, Raymond L., Sr., St. Peter Claver, Houston
Devine, John E., Jr., St. Luke the Evangelist, Houston
Do, Joseph Chuong Nguyen, Our Lady of Lourdes, Houston
Duck, Charles, Prince of Peace, Houston
Dunham, Robert K., St. Laurence, Sugarland
Dunning, Sam, St. Thomas
Duplan, Jose, Jr., St. Mary's, Texas City
Dupont, Gerald W., St. Theresa, Sugar Land
Durden, Jonathon, St. Clare
Ehrman, John W., Jr., Sacred Heart, Conroe
Evon, William J., Sr., St. Ignatius of Loyola, Spring
Festa, Gene, St. Justin Martyr, Houston
Fikac, Marvin R., Sacred Heart Co-Cathedral, Houston
Flores, Geronimo, St. Joseph, Houston
Floyd, Ivy C., St. Thomas the Apostle, Huntsville
Flynn, Robert E., Sr., Sts. Simon & Jude, The Woodlands
Fraser, Ronald J., St. Maximilian Kolbe, Houston
Garcia, Gerardo J., Christ the King, Houston
Garcia, Gregory C., Resurrection, Houston
Garcia, Julio, St. Jerome, Clute
Garrett, William, St. Anne, Houston
Garza, Robert, St. Mary, League City
Gilbert, Daniel W., St. Francis Xavier, Houston
Glor, Richard J.L., Unassigned
Gomez, Arturo M., Notre Dame, Houston
Gomez, Javier, St. Andrew, Channelview
Gonzales, Emiliano, TDC Prison Chaplain, Houston
Gonzalez, Enrique, St. Charles Borromeo, Houston
Gonzalez, Guadalupe, Our Lady of Guadalupe, Houston
Gonzalez Bangs, Fernando, Our Lady of Guadalupe, Baytown
Gosline, Edwin F., St. Thomas More, Houston
Graham, Michael G., Unassigned
Gramann, Henry T., St. Christopher, Houston
Granado, Alfred E., Jr., Leave of Absence
Griesmyer, Steven, Sr., St. James the Apostle, Spring
Guajardo, Fredrico, Our Lady of Mt. Carmel, Houston
Guerra, Daniel, Sr., St. Clare of Assisi, Houston
Gutierrez, Diego, Sr., St. John the Baptist, Alvin
Hall, Raymond J., Unassigned
Hamilton, L. William, St. Bartholomew, Katy
Hargraves, Wilfred J., Jr., Transfer to Austin, TX
Harper, Stephen Edwin, St. Laurence, Sugarland
Hennessy, Robert, St. John the Evangelist, Baytown
Henry, Albert, St. Francis Xavier, Houston
Herrera, Rolando, Archdiocese of San Antonio
Hickey, Dennis, St. Hyacinth, Deer Park
Higgins, Auburn, St. Maximilian Kolbe, Houston
Hite, James, St. Ignatius Loyola, Spring
Hock, Leslie Bart, Immaculate Conception, Houston
Hodapp, Cyril J., St. Bernadette, Houston
Hodge, Brick, Sacred Heart, Richmond
Holt, Grant E., Christ Our Light, Navasota
Horbowy, Thaddeus J., Chap. Fed. Bureau of Prisons and Medical Center, Lexington, KY
Horr, Louis Eugene, St. Jerome, Houston
Housholder, John, St. Helen, Pearland
Hubisz, John, St. Laurence
Hunter, Thomas Alexander, Hospital Port St. Patrick, Galveston
Husch, John M., Unassigned
Jachimczyk, Joseph A., Annunciation, Houston
Jackson, Clifford X., Our Lady of Sorrows, Houston
Jelinek, Gregory N., M.D., Christ Our Light-Navasota; O.C. Luther TDC
Jenkins, Michael V., St. Francis Xavier, Houston
Johnson, Clarence B., St. Peter the Apostle, Houston
Johnson, Irvin, Jr., Our Mother of Mercy, Houston
Joseph, Ignatius, St. Francis of Assisi, Houston
Kacz, Robert, St. John the Baptist, Alvin
Kelleher, Peter J., St. Christopher, Houston
Keller, Robert C., St. Justin Martyr, Houston
Kelly, Joseph R., Sr., Sacred Heart, Richmond
Kish, Don, Epiphany of the Lord, Katy
Klein, Hugo L., St. Francis de Sales, Houston
Knobloch, Alden J., St. Jerome, Houston
Koch, William E., Sr., Unassigned
Kulhanek, Jerry Peter, Sr., Our Lady of Fatima, Galena Park
Kutach, Emil W., Leave of Absence

LaBonte, Stephen L., Christ the Good Shepherd, Spring
Labrecque, Richard, St. Paul, Houston
Landry, Burke J., St. Elizabeth Ann Seton, Madisonville
Lansch, John, St. Justin Martyr, Houston
Laredo, Frank, Immaculate Conception, Sealy
Laugermann, Frank J., Jr., St. Benedict the Abbot, Houston
Leach, Richard L., Christ the Redeemer; St. John Neumann, Houston
Leal, Merce C., Jr., St. Christopher, Houston
Leblanc, Irvin, Unassigned
Leicht, Robert, Sacred Heart, Manvel
Leija, Valeriano, Blessed Juan Diego, Pasadena
Lerma, Pedro, Sr., Blessed Sacrament, Houston
Lewis, Edward Thomas, St. Mary, La Porte
Liendo, Jose L., Queen of Peace, Houston
Llewellyn, Earl, Jr., TDCJ Hospital Chaplain, Galveston; Queen of Peace, LaMarque
Llorens, Cornelius C., St. Justin Martyr, Houston
Lopez, Richard, St. Thomas the Apostle, Huntsville
Lorino, Joseph E., St. Vincent de Paul, Houston
Losack, Jerome, Immaculate Conception, Sealy
Lozano, Rodrigo, St. Charles Borromeo, Houston
Lugo, Loni G., Unassigned
Lynch, Philip F., Unassigned
MacFarlane, Robert, St. Mary, Humble
Marquez, Antonio, St. Raphael, Houston
Martin, Henry Woods, St. Michael, Houston
Martin, Kenneth, St. Edward, Spring
Matula, Francis L., All Saints, Houston
McAllister, Jerome, St. Mary, League City
McKinney, Thomas K., Ellis Unit TDC; St. Mary Magdalene, Humble
Meshell, James, Holy Ghost, Houston
Mignogna, Joe, St. Anthony of Padua, The Woodlands
Miller, Arthur, Unassigned
Miller, Stephen, St. Andrew, Channelview
Mitchell, David D., Holy Rosary, Rosenberg
Morales, Hector Hernando, Our Lady of Fatima, Galena Park
Moreno, Aurelio Frank, Jr., St. Frances Cabrini, Houston
Moreno, Leopold R., Catholic Charismatic Center, Houston
Morin, Joseph G., Immaculate Conception, Houston
Motley, John M., Unassigned
Moulton, Darrell, Mary Queen, Friendswood; Covenant House, Houston
Mulcare, Terrance D., St. Christopher, Houston
Munguia, Ben, St. John, Fischer
Navarro, Raul G., Immaculate Heart of Mary, Houston
Nelms, D. Cade, St. Cecilia, Houston
Newhouse, Thomas C., St. Michael, Houston
Nguyen Kim Khanh, Michael, Our Lady of Lavang, Houston
Nguyen Pham, Joseph, Vietnamese Martyrs, Houston
Nguyen Si Bach, Joseph, Christ the Incarnate Word, Houston
O'Brien, Alfred J., Prison Chaplain Stiles Unit-Beaumont
Ortego, Frank P., St. Thomas the Apostle, Huntsville
Osterhaus, James H., Christ the Redeemer, Houston
Ostrand, Gerard, St. Martha, Kingwood
Ostrowski, F. L., Notre Dame, Houston
Pareja, Juan Francisco, St. Jerome, Houston
Parr, Kenneth, Catholic Charismatic Center, Houston
Payne, George, Leave of Absence
Pelletier, John, St. Thomas More, Houston
Peltier, Gerald, St. Anthony, Danbury
Pennell, Charles G., St. Elizabeth Ann Seton, Houston
Petereit, Klaus, St. John Newmann, Houston
Pistone, John Salvadore, St. Mary's Cathedral Basilica, Galveston
Provenzano, Luis, St. Justin Martyr, Houston
Ramirez, Fernando, St. Frances Cabrini, Houston
Ramirez, Jose J., Resurrection, Houston
Ramirez, Julio M., St. Gregory the Great, Houston
Ramirez, Leonard, Holy Family, Missouri City
Rapp, Donald, St. Thomas More, Houston
Reish, Thomas, Christ the Redeemer, Houston
Ries, Donald G., Sacred Heart, Richmond
Rincon, George, Our Lady of Guadalupe, Baytown
Robison, Paul L., Jr., St. Luke the Evangelist, Houston
Rodriguez, Luis, Immaculate Conception, Houston
Roessler, Charles F., Jr., St. Frances Cabrini, Houston
Romeu, Hector J., St. John Vianney, Houston
Rook, R. Jack, St. Andrew, Channelview
Rooney, John, St. Frances Cabrini, Houston
Rowan, Vincent A., St. Michael, Lake Jackson
Rumford, Robert, St. Bernadette
Rutledge, James E., St. Jerome, Houston
Salazar, Mariano, St. Joseph, Houston
Saltzmann, Peter, Catholic Charismatic Center, Houston
Sanchez, Martin G., St. Joseph, Houston
Sanders, Raymond L., Jr., Diocese of Austin
Sandiford, Sid, Sts. Simon & Jude, The Woodlands
Santos, John, St. Andrew, Channelview
Satterwhite, Michael, St. Mary, Texas City
Schmidt, Glendon Michael, St. James, Spring
Sechelski, Peter, TDC/St. Stanislaus, Anderson
Seifert, William E., Jr., Holy Family, Missouri City
Sharpless, James, St. Luke the Evangelist, Houston
Shaw, Wallace, St. Mary Star of the Sea, Freeport
Sheffield, William Leonard, Christ Our Light, Navasota; St. Matthias, Magnolia
Shefts, Andrew, St. Basil, Angleton
Sheltz, George A., Sr., St. Joseph Hospital/St. Vincent de Paul, Houston
Shetz, Fred T., Dir. Perm. Deacons, Sts. Simon & Jude, The Woodlands
Sicinski, Anton, St. Stanislaus, Anderson
Simon, Ronald, St. Philip Neri, Houston
Singer, John William, Jr., St. Joseph, Baytown
Smaistrla, Denis J., St. Mary's Seminary, Houston
Smith, Jimmy, St. Joseph, Brazoria
St. Aubin, Leo F., Sacred Heart, Conroe
St. Julian, Michael, St. Francis of Assisi
Steffes, Dale W., St. John Vianney, Houston
Stevens, Robert Gregory, St. Francis Cabrini, Houston
Stoessel, Edward T., St. Thomas More, Houston
Sullivan, John, Queen of Peace, Houston
Suriano, Julio S., Our Lady of St. John, Houston
Thompson, Edward, St. Cyril
Thomson, Nicholas, St. Andrew, Channelview
Tollett, Jesse, St. Luke, Houston
Tollett, Lee Joseph, St. Laurence, Sugar Land
Tripp, Edwin, St. Elizabeth, Houston
Trosclair, George, Prince of Peace, Houston; St. Mary, Plantersville
Vacek, Albert E., Jr., St. John Vianney, Houston
Vaclavik, Larry A., St. Theresa, Houston
Vanderslice, Ron, Diocese of Tulsa
Venegas, Rudy, Our Lady of Guadalupe
Vicknair, Tom Jude, Catholic Charismatic Center, Houston
Villarreal, Gilbert R., St. Helen, Pearland
Villarreal, Marcelino, St. Benedict the Abbot, Houston
Vocelka, Frank Jay, Jr., St. Theresa, Houston
Wagner, William C., St. Bartholomew, Katy
Waterman, John H., St. Anthony of Padua, The Woodlands
Watkins, Rollo J., Christ the King, Houston
Weaver, William A., St. Elizabeth Ann Seton, Houston
Wewer, Justin J., St. John the Evangelist, Baytown
Wiles, Philip Arlen, St. Dominic, Houston
Wright, Jim, Unassigned
Zamora, Joe, St. Augustine, Houston
Zuk, Adolph J., St. Matthew the Evangelist, Houston

INSTITUTIONS LOCATED IN THE DIOCESE

[A] SEMINARIES, DIOCESAN

HOUSTON. *St. Mary's Seminary*, 9845 Memorial Dr., 77024-3498. Tel: 713-686-4345; Fax: 713-681-7550. Rev. Msgr. Chester L. Borski, Rector; Revs. Leon Streider (AUS), Vice Rector; Luis Narro, S.J.; Brendan Cahill; Raphael Davila, M.M.; Edward Abell; John Kha Tran; Ivan C. Marsh, O.Carm; Sr. Barbara Tovar, M.C.D.P., Dir. Cultural Formation; Deacon Denis J. Smaistrla, Treas. & Plant Mgr.; Rev. Louis T. Brusatti, C.M., Dean School of Theology. Priests 12; Sisters 2; Lay Teachers 8; Diocesan Seminarians 46; Religious Seminarians 9; Total Enrollment 55.

[B] SEMINARIES, RELIGIOUS OR SCHOLASTICATES

HOUSTON. *Casa San Basilio*, 1910 W. Alabama, 77098. Tel: 713-522-1736; Fax: 713-522-1917.
E-mail: sinasac@earthlink-net
Rev. Alvin A. Sinasac, C.S.B., Dir.
Purpose: House of formation for Hispanic men in Religious life discernment. Apostolate of the Basilian Fathers. Total Enrollment 2.

Holy Ghost Fathers and Brothers, Holy Spirit Seminary, 4410 Yoakum Blvd., 77006-5820. Tel: 713-529-0405; Fax: 713-529-4236.
Web site: www.spiritans.org
Revs. John J. Walsh, C.S.Sp.; Philip D. Evanstock, C.S.Sp., Dir.; Bro. Robert W. Hassel, C.S.Sp. Priests 2; Consecrated Religious 6.

SUGAR LAND. *Basilian Fathers House of Prayer*, 106 Fifth St., 77478. Tel: 281-491-8700; Fax: 281-491-8700. Priests 1.

[C] COLLEGES AND UNIVERSITIES

HOUSTON. *University of St. Thomas*, 3800 Montrose Blvd., 77006-4696. Tel: 713-522-7911; Fax: 713-525-2125.
E-mail: president@stthom.edu
Web site: www.stthom.edu
For a complete listing, refer to the Colleges and Universities section.

[D] HIGH SCHOOLS, DIOCESAN

GALVESTON. *O'Connell Catholic High School*, 1320 Tremont St., 77550-4513. Tel: 409-765-5534; Fax: 409-765-5536. Rev. Frank T. Fabj; Mr. Patrick Danesi, Prin. Priests 1; Lay Teachers 15; Total Staff 23; Students 135.

HOUSTON. *Mt. Carmel High School*, 6700 Mt. Carmel Dr., 77087-6699. Tel: 713-649-2745; Fax: 713-649-6851. Mr. William Knapick, Prin. Priests 1; Sisters 1; Lay Teachers 18; Total Staff 28; Students 192.

[E] JUNIOR HIGH SCHOOLS, DIOCESAN

HOUSTON. *Seton Catholic Jr. High School*, 801 Rose Ln., 77037-4696. Tel: 281-447-2132; Fax: 281-447-1825. Mr. Patrick W. Clark, Prin. Sisters 2; Principals 1; Assistant Principals; 1; Counselors 1; Development Directors 1; Lay Teachers 13; Total Staff 16; Students 264.

[F] HIGH SCHOOLS, PRIVATE

HOUSTON. *Duchesne Academy of the Sacred Heart*, 10202 Memorial Dr., 77024-3299. Tel: 713-468-8211; Fax: 713-465-9809.
E-mail: Jan_Dunn@duchesne.org
Web site: www.duchesne.org
Religious of the Sacred Heart. Sr. Jan Dunn, R.S.C.J., Headmistress. Sisters 2; Lay Teachers 81; Girls (Grades 9-12) 228; Total Enrollment (Grades PK-12) 648.

Incarnate Word Academy, 609 Crawford St., 77002-3668. Tel: 713-227-3637; Fax: 713-227-1014.
E-mail: rpurcell@incarnateword.org
Web site: www.incarnateword.org
Sisters of the Incarnate Word and Blessed Sacrament. Principals: Sr. M. Rosalia Purcell, C.V.I.; Mrs. Susan Sanchez. Sisters 7; Lay Teachers 15; Girls 233.

St. Agnes Academy, 9000 Bellaire Blvd., 77036-4683. Tel: 713-219-5400; Fax: 713-219-5499.
E-mail: sjmeyer@st-agnes.org
Web site: www.st-agnes.org
Sr. Jane Meyer, O.P., Prin. Tel: 713-219-5400; Fax: 713-219-5499. Dominican Sisters 1; Lay Teachers 48; Girls 745.

St. Pius X High School, Inc., 811 W. Donovan, 77091-5699. Tel: 713-692-3581; Fax: 713-692-5725.
E-mail: pollardd@stpiusx.org
Web site: www.stpiusx.org
Sr. Donna M. Pollard, O.P., Prin. Priests 1; Dominican Sisters 2; Lay Teachers 50; Total Staff 53; Students 670.

St. Thomas High School, 4500 Memorial Dr., 77007-7332. Tel: 713-864-6348 (School); 868-9209 (Residence); Fax: 713-864-5750.
Web site: www.sths.org
Basilian Residence, Basilian Fathers. Revs. Jack H. Hanna, C.S.B., Supr.; Carl L. Belisch, C.S.B.; Edward A. Doser, C.S.B.; William Vela, C.S.B.; Ronald G. Schwenzer, C.S.B.; Albert R. Gaelens, C.S.B.; Richard A. Wahl, C.S.B.; Priests 5; Lay Teachers 54; Total Staff 60; Total Enrollment 585.

Strake, Jesuit College Preparatory Inc., 8900 Bellaire Blvd., 77036-4699. Tel: 713-774-7651; Fax: 713-774-6427.
E-mail: strakejesuit.org
Web site: www.strakejesuit.org
Mr. Richard Nevle, Prin. & Pres.; Revs. Christopher A. Billac, S.J.; John N. Folzenlogen, S.J.; Douglas J. Hypolite, S.J., Rector; Joseph B. Leininger, S.J.; D. Richard Toye, S.J. Scholastics: Rafael V. D. Baylon; Flavio I. Bravo; Bro. Castenzio A. Ferlita, S.J.
Teachers: Priests 5; Brothers 1; Scholastics 2; Lay Teachers 54; Boys 765.

[G] ELEMENTARY SCHOOLS, PRIVATE

HOUSTON. *Duchesne Academy of the Sacred Heart*, 10202 Memorial Dr., 77024-3299. Tel: 713-468-8211; Fax: 713-465-9809.
E-mail: Jan_Dunn@duchesne.org
Web site: www.duchesne.org
Sr. Jan Dunn, R.S.C.J., Headmistress. Sisters 2; Lay Teachers 81; Total Staff 120; Girls 648.

John Paul II Catholic School, 1400 Parkway Plaza Dr., 77077-1503. Tel: 281-496-1500; Fax: 281-496-2943.
E-mail: principal@jp2.org
Web site: jp2.org
Debra Haney, Prin.; Nancy Moore, Asst. Prin. Lay Teachers 39; Students 639.

The Regis School, 7330 Westview Dr., 77055-5122. Tel: 713-682-8383; Fax: 713-682-8388.
E-mail: regis@theregisschool.org
Web site: www.theregisschool.org
Catholic School for Boys. Anne Storey Carty, Headmistress. Lay Teachers 25; Students 173.

St. Catherine's Montessori, 2510 Westridge, 77054-1508. Tel: 713-665-2195; Fax: 713-665-1478.
E-mail: scms@io.com
Judy McCullough, Prin. Lay Teachers 11; Students 198.

[H] ELEMENTARY SCHOOLS, CONSOLIDATED

GALVESTON. *Galveston Catholic School*, 2601 Ursuline Ave., 77550-4398. Tel: 409-765-6607; Fax: 409-765-5154. Mrs. Mary Frances Bernardoni, Prin. Sisters 1; Lay Teachers 28; Students 324.

NAVASOTA. *School of Environmental Education - Camp Kappe*. (Grades 5), Rte. 2, Box 3197, 77868-9604. Tel: 936-894-2141; Fax: 936-894-2198.
E-mail: STALSEE@aol.com
Sr. Thomas Ann LaCour, O.P., Prin. Sisters 1; Lay Teachers 3; Total Enrollment 1,400.

RICHWOOD. *Our Lady Queen of Peace*, 1600 Hwy. 2004, 77531. Tel: 979-265-3909; Fax: 979-265-9780.
E-mail: olqp@tgn.net
Web site: www.olqpschool.org
Mr. Jack Hawthorne, Prin. Lay Teachers 29; Students 368.
Serving the parishes of St. Basil; St. Jerome, Clute; St. Anthony, Danbury; St. Henry; St. Mary, Star of the Sea, Freeport; St. Michael, Lake Jackson; Our Lady of Perpetual Help, Sweeney; St. John the Apostle Mission, West Columbia; St. Joseph's, Brazoria, TX.

[I] SOCIAL AGENCIES CATHOLIC CHARITIES

HOUSTON. *Associated Catholic Charities of the Diocese of Galveston-Houston*, 2900 Louisiana St., P.O. Box 66508, 77266. Tel: 713-526-4611; Fax: 713-526-1546.
Web site: www.catholiccharities.org
Anna M. Babin, Pres. Total Assisted 72,339.

Diocesan AIDS Ministry. Tel: 713-526-4611; Fax: 713-526-1546.

Catholic Charities, Galveston. Tel: 409-762-2143; Fax: 409-762-2064.

Guadalupe Area Social Services. (Family Assistance). Tel: 713-227-9981; Fax: 713-225-1242.

Children's Placement Services. (Adoption and Foster Care). Tel: 713-526-4611; Fax: 713-526-1546.

Services to Pregnant and Parenting Adolescents. Tel: 713-526-4611; Fax: 713-526-1546.

Post Adoption Services. Tel: 713-526-4611; Fax: 713-526-1546.

Family Counseling. Tel: 713-526-4611; Fax: 713-526-1546.

Texas Center for Immigrant Legal Assistance. Tel: 713-526-4611; Fax: 713-526-1546.

Refugee Resettlement Program. Tel: 713-526-4611; Fax: 713-526-1546.

Unaccompanied Juvenile Foster Care Program. Tel: 713-526-4611; Fax: 713-526-1546.

Services to the Alone and Frail Elderly. Tel: 713-526-4611; Fax: 713-526-1546.

Serenity House. Tel: 713-526-4611; Fax: 713-526-1546.

Parish Social Ministry/Family Pathfinders. Tel: 713-526-4611; Fax: 713-526-1546.

Villa Guadalupe. (Transitional Housing). Tel: 713-227-4971; Fax: 713-225-1242.

[J] HEALTH AND HOSPITALS

HOUSTON. *CHRISTUS Health*, 2600 N. Loop W., 77092. Tel: 713-680-4835; Fax: 713-812-6867.
Web site: www.christushealth.org
For a complete listing, refer to the Hospitals section.

CHRISTUS Health Gulf Coast, 1919 LaBranch, 77002. Tel: 713-756-5008; Fax: 713-657-7123.
Web site: CHRISTUShealth.org
For a complete listing, refer to the Hospitals section.

Sisters of Charity of the Incarnate Word, Houston, Texas, 6510 Lawndale Ave., 77223-0969. Tel: 713-928-6053; Fax: 713-928-8148.
E-mail: obordelon@ccvi-vdm.org
For a complete listing, refer to the Hospitals section.

[K] CATHOLIC CHAPLAIN CORPS

HOUSTON. *The Catholic Chaplain Corps*, 4206 S. MacGregor Way, 77021-1598. Tel: 713-526-6438; Fax: 713-747-3642.
Houston Hospitals: St. Luke's Episcopal, Texas Heart Institute, Texas Children's Hospital, Methodist, M. D. Anderson Cancer Center - Hospital of University of Texas, Diagnostic, Shriners Hospital for Crippled Children, The Institute of Rehabilitation and Research, Ben Taub Hospital, Hermann Memorial Hospital, Diagnostic Center Hospital, Vencor Hospital.

Catholic Chaplain Corps, Texas Medical Center. Tel: 713-526-6438; Fax: 713-747-3642. Revs. Alcuin E. Greenburg; Joseph Doan; Elias E. Doroin; Bruce H. Noble; David H. Noble; Don A. Neumann; Donald E. Kuder, C.S.B.; Teodoro Tim Y. Prado; Sr. Beatrice Cruz, I.W.B.S.; Revs. Patrick Cummings; Hung Tran, O.P.; Sr. Josephine Nolan, C.V.I.; Page Polk.

Chaplain Corps, Memorial Southwest Center Complex, 10330 Hillcroft, 77096-4795. Tel: 713-776-5000; Fax: 713-776-5369. Rev. Joseph Medayil, C.M.I.

Chaplain Corps, Lyndon B. Johnson Hospital. Tel: 713-636-5000 (24-hour paging); Fax: 713-747-3642. Rev. A. Ed Doser, C.S.B.; Sr. Martha Christina Mejia, C.V.I.

Chaplain Corps. Tel: 713-526-6438 (24 hour paging); Fax: 713-747-3642. Rev. Franklin Simmons.
Memorial City/Spring Branch Medical Complexes: Memorial City Medical Center Hospital.

Chaplain Corps: John Sealy Medical Center, U.T.M.B. Hospital, 2011 Ave. F (Church St.), Galveston, 77550-2091. Tel: 409-762-9612; Fax: 409-762-9612. Revs. Gerald Lewis, S.V.D.; Raymond J. Giudry, S.V.D.

[L] CLINICS

HOUSTON. *San Jose Clinic*, 301 Hamilton St., 77002. Tel: 713-228-9411; Fax: 713-228-6371. Nona Fain, Exec. Dir. Patients assisted annually 25,032; Lay Staff 35.

[M] PROTECTIVE INSTITUTIONS

HOUSTON. *Casa de Esperanza, De Los Ninos, Inc.*, Mailing Address: P.O. Box 66581, 77266-6581. Tel: 713-529-0639; Fax: 713-529-9179.
E-mail: casa@casahope.org
For a complete listing, refer to the Special Care Facilities section.

Casa Juan Diego, 4818 Rose, 77007. Tel: 713-869-7376; Fax: 713-864-4994.
E-mail: info@cjd.org
Web site: www.cjd.org
For a complete listing, refer to the Special Care Facilities section.

Casa Maria de Guadalupe Medical Clinic and Social Service Center, 6101 Edgemoor, 77081. Tel: 713-995-9414; Fax: 713-864-4994.
E-mail: info@cjd.org
Web site: www.cjd.org
For a complete listing, refer to the Special Care Facilities section.

Covenant House Texas, 1111 Lovett Blvd., 77006. Tel: 713-523-2231; Fax: 713-523-6904.
E-mail: RRobinson@ghg.net
Web site: covenanthousetx.org
For a complete listing, refer to the Special Care Facilities section.

Santa Maria Hostel, 807 Paschall St., 77009. Tel: 713-228-0125; Fax: 713-222-0595.
E-mail: cempey@hotmail.com
For a complete listing, refer to the Special Care Facilities section.

[N] HOMES FOR THE AGED

HOUSTON. *St. Dominic Village*, 2401 Holcombe Blvd., 77021-2099. Tel: 713-741-8701; Fax: 713-741-9811
For a complete listing, refer to the Special Care Facilities section.

[O] RESIDENTIAL TREATMENT AND RENEWAL CENTERS

SPLENDORA. *Shalom Center, Inc.*, 13516 Morgan Dr., 77372-3121. Tel: 281-399-0520; Fax: 281-399-3366. A residential treatment center for clergy and men and women religious. Sr. Gina Marie Iadanza, M.S.C., Exec. Dir.

[P] PERSONAL PRELATURES

HOUSTON. *Opus Dei*. Prelature of the Holy Cross and Opus Dei, 5505 Chaucer Dr., 77005-2631. Tel: 713-528-4081; Fax: 713-523-6829.
Web site: www.opusdei.org
Very Rev. Jose Gomez, Vicar of the delegation of Texas; Revs. Gerald Kolf; Michael Manz; Michael Barrett.

[Q] MONASTERIES AND RESIDENCES OF PRIESTS AND BROTHERS

HOUSTON. *Carmelite Priory*, Casa Santa Teresita, 6725 Reed Rd., 77087-6830. Tel: 713-644-8400; Fax: 713-649-6955.
E-mail: casa@carmelnet.org
Revs. Gregory Houck, O.Carm., Dir. & Prior; John Long, O.Carm. Pre-novitiate house for students in the Most Pure Heart Province of the Carmelite Order (O.Carm.). Students 5; Total in Residence 7; Total Staff 1.

Companions of the Cross (Texas), 1949 Cullen Blvd., P.O. Box 230287, 77023-5395. Tel: 713-236-9977; Fax: 713-236-0073.
E-mail: fafrankovich@yahoo.com
Web site: www.companionscross.ca
Rev. Francis A. Frankovich, Dir.

Congregation of the Passion, Holy Name Retreat Center, 430 Bunker Hill Rd., 77024-6399. Tel: 713-464-4932; Fax: 713-932-7303. Very Rev. Alexander Steinmiller, C.P., Local Supr.; Revs. Simon Herbers, C.P.; Christopher Gibson, C.P.; John P. Conley, C.P.; John Schork, C.P., Retreat Dir.; Bernard Weber, C.P.; Robert Bovenzi, C.P.; E. John Hilgert, C.P.; Deacon James Griffith.

Dillon House, 1302 Kipling, 77006-4297. Tel: 713-529-3994; Fax: 713-942-7623. Basilian Fathers. Revs. Paul F. O'Connor, C.S.B., Supr.; Norbert H. Clemens, C.S.B., (Retired); Wilfred S. Canning, C.S.B., (Retired); William E. Coughlin; Joseph B. Courtney, C.S.B., (Retired); Gerald F. Dillon, C.S.B.; William L. Morin; William L. Moran, C.S.B.

Dominican Fathers and Brothers, St. Mark Priory, Inc., 1702 Bolsover Rd., 77005-1726. Tel: 713-526-6411; Fax: 713-528-6795.
E-mail: isid@juno.com
Revs. Isidore V. Vicente, O.P., Subprior; Robert A. Bordenkircher, O.P.; Thomas A. Clifford, O.P.; Brian G. Donovan, O.P.; Richard Martin Patrick, O.P.; Joseph Ngoc Tu Nguyen, O.P.; John J. Boll, O.P.; Anthony Hung Ngoc Tran, O.P.
Assigned to St. Mark Priory, Residing Elsewhere: Revs. Joseph D. Konkel, O.P., Prior; William H. Brenda, O.P.; Albert S. Moraczewski, O.P.; John D. Logan, O.P.

Franciscan Friars, Kolbe Friary, 4643 Wild Indigo, #409, 77027-7058. Tel: 713-355-1319. Mailing Address: P.O. Box 27530, 77227. Bro. Robert Hozie, O.F.M., Supr.

Marianist Community, 6409 Brookside Dr., 77023-3323. Tel: 713-926-5925.
E-mail: WNVW88B@worldnet.att.net
Web site: marianist.udayton.edu
Society of Mary. Rev. Robert E. Hackel, S.M.; Bro. James E. Barrette, S.M.

Maryknoll Fathers and Brothers, 2360 Rice Blvd., 77005-2652. Tel: 713-529-1912; Fax: 713-529-0372.
E-mail: mklhouston@aol.com
Web site: www.maryknoll.org
Rev. Joseph Kowalczyk, M.M.; Bros. Mark Gruenke, M.M., Dir.; Leo Shedy, M.M.
Priests Residing Elsewhere: Rev. Rafael R. Davila, M.M., St. Mary Seminary, 9845 Memorial Dr., 77024-3498. Tel: 713-686-6844. Rev. Richard E. Paulissen, M.M., P.O. Box 9592, 77261. Tel: 713-921-2736.

Residence of the Basilian Fathers of the University of St. Thomas, 4019 Yoakum Blvd., 77006-4833. Tel: 713-525-3515; Fax: 713-529-0844. Revs. Dennis M. Andrews, C.S.B., Supr.; Edward A. Bader, C.S.B.; Edward J. Baenziger, C.S.B.; Patrick O. Braden, C.S.B.; Victor B. Brezik, C.S.B.; Daniel D. Callam, C.S.B.; Robert W. Crooker, C.S.B.; George H. Hosko, C.S.B.; James J. Keon, C.S.B.; Joseph L. Meyers, C.S.B.; J. Michael Miller, C.S.B.; Harold V. O'Leary, C.S.B.; Richard J. Schiefen, C.S.B.; Jefferson M. Thompson, C.S.B.; T. Patrick Warden, C.S.B.; Walter M. Werbylo, C.S.B.; William J. Young, C.S.B.; Janusz Ihnatowicz (Poland).

Western Province of the Congregation of the Holy Ghost, 1700 West Alabama St., 77098-2808. Tel: 713-522-2882; Fax: 713-522-8063.
E-mail: spiritans@aol.com
Web site: www.spiritans.org
Very Rev. Donald S. Nesti, C.S.Sp., Supr. Total in Residence 2.

BARRETT STATION. *Missionary Society of St. Paul, Inc. - U.S. Region*. Rev. Paul N. Ofoha, M.S.P., Local Supr.

MANVEL. *The Basilian Fathers' Monastery of Citeaux*, Mailing Address: 6502 County Rd. 48, 77578-2908. Tel: 281-489-0852; Fax: 281-489-8727.
E-mail: Gauntjim@yahoo.com
Rev. James J. Gaunt, C.S.B., Dir.

NEW CANEY. *Congregation of the Mother Coredemptrix*, 23404 Oak Shadows Pl., 77357-8516. Tel: 281-354-4764. Rev. Joseph Doan Huy Chuong. Total in Residence 1.

SUGAR LAND. *Basilian Mission Center*, 414 Main St., P.O. Box 708, 77487-0708. Tel: 218-242-3148; Fax: 281-242-3149.
E-mail: basmissions@earthlink.net
Revs. John R. Whitley, C.S.B., Mission Procurator, Treas.; Robert J. Klem, C.S.B.; Joseph P. Shannon, C.S.B.; Roy J. Oggero, C.S.B., Supr.
Priests Serving in Foreign Missions: Revs. Francis A. Amico, C.S.B.; Ernesto Arriaga, C.S.B.; Robert J.

Barringer, C.S.B.; John L. Boscoe, C.S.B.; M. Marciano Dominguez, C.S.B.; Thomas P. Dugan, C.S.B.; Rene J. Espejel, C.S.B.; Alberto A. Ferrara, C.S.B.; William J. Frankenberger, C.S.B.; Marco A. Hernandez, C.S.B.; Francis J. Launtrie, C.S.B.; Rafael I. Lopera, C.S.B.; Francisco S. Mauricio, C.S.B.; W. Lawrence Moran, C.S.B.; Francois J. Morfin, C.S.B.; Bernard C. Owens, C.S.B.; Roberto P. Rojas, C.S.B.; Alejandro Romero, C.S.B.; Robert J. Seguin, C.S.B.; Thomas W. Sepulveda, C.S.B.; J. Vincent Thompson, C.S.B.; Clarence E. Watrin, C.S.B. Associates 16; Scholastics 8; Novices 4.

[R] CONVENTS AND RESIDENCES FOR SISTERS

HOUSTON. *Carmelite Sisters of the Sacred Heart (C.S.H.)*, 22 Farrell, 77022. Tel: 713-697-6020. Sr. Antonia Albarran, Supr. Total Staff 6.

Casa de Esperanza, P.O. Box 66581, 77266. Tel: 713-529-0639; Fax: 713-529-9179.
E-mail: casa@casahope.org
Web site: www.casahope.org

Casa Providencia, 3907 Rotman, 77003. Tel: 713-227-2555; Fax: 713-923-5866.

Congregation of Divine Providence (C.D.P.), 2008 Southgate, 77030-2126. Tel: 713-659-5461; Fax: 713-759-9151.
E-mail: Karstedt@diocese-gal-hou.org
Web site: www.diocese-gal-hou.org
Other Addresses: 2800 West T.C. Jester, No. 15, 77018. Tel: 713-683-9762. 1111 Blalock #61, 77055. Tel: 713-621-4370.

Congregation of the Incarnate Word & Blessed Sacrament (C.V.I.) (Houston), Incarnate Word Convent, 3400 Bradford Pl., 77025-1398. Tel: 713-668-0423; Fax: 713-668-1857. Casa Pacis Convent, 3428 Bradford Pl., 77025. Tel: 713-661-3785. Sisters 2. Incarnate Word Academy, 609 Crawford St., 77002. Tel: 713-223-4143. Sisters 8. St. Christopher Convent, 8711 Glen Loch, 77061. Tel: 713-649-4700. Sisters 2. Visitation Convent, 3418A Bradford Pl., 77025-1398. Tel: 713-664-8370. Sisters 4. Our Lady of Lourdes Convent, 10114 Hwy 6, Hitchcock, 77563. Tel: 409-925-7237. Sisters 3. Sacred Heart Convent, 615 McDade, Conroe, 77301. Tel: 936-756-3051. Sisters 2. St. Joseph Convent, 1811 Carolina, Baytown, 77520. Tel: 281-422-7700. St. Michael Convent, 5515 W. 43rd, 77092. Tel: 713-682-2242. Sisters 35.

Congregation of the Lovers of the Cross of Thaibinh Diocese, N. Vietnam, 8138 Lynn St., 77017. Tel: 713-643-3694. Sisters 2.

Congregation of the Sisters of Charity of the Incarnate Word (C.C.V.I.), 6510 Lawndale, P.O. Box 230969, 77223-0969. Tel: 713-928-6053; Fax: 713-928-8148.
E-mail: MGTA@CCVI-VDM.org
Web site: sistersofcharity.org
Total Sisters in Congregation (professed sisters) 226. St. Jeanne Convent. Tel: 713-928-6053; Fax: 713-928-8148. Sisters 2. Marian Convent. Tel: 713-928-8148; Fax: 713-928-8148. Sisters 18. St. Anne Convent. Tel: 713-928-6053; Fax: 713-921-1070. Sisters 14. Ruah Community. Tel: 713-928-6053; Fax: 713-928-9962. Sisters 5. Villa de Matel. Tel: 713-928-6053; Fax: 713-928-8148. Sisters 12. St. Placidus Convent, 1500 S. Wayside Dr., P.O. Box 230969, 77223-0969. Tel: 713-928-6053; Fax: 713-928-8148. Sisters 28. Edith Stein Convent, 6405 Pinehurst, 77023. Tel: 713-926-6024. Sisters 3. Dubuis Convent, 6510 Lawndale Ave., P.O. Box 230696, 77223-0969. Tel: 713-748-8814; Fax: 713-928-8148. Sisters 4. St. Joseph Convent, 1919 La Branch St., 77002. Tel: 713-757-7485; Fax: 713-756-5232. Sisters 15. St. John Convent, 1623 Antigua Ln., 77058. Tel: 713-333-9363; Fax: 281-333-2489. Sisters 3. St. Mary's Convent, 4400 Ave. N., Galveston, 77550. Tel: 409-763-1971; Fax: 409-762-0599. Sisters 2.

Incarnate Word Charitable Trust, 6510 Lawndale, P.O. Box 230969, 77223-0969. Tel: 713-928-6053; Fax: 713-926-3085. Sr. Ann Margaret Savant, C.C.V.I., Chairperson.

Congregation of the Sisters of Charity of the Incarnate Word (C.C.V.I.), Mailing Address: P.O. Box 230969, 77223-0969. Tel: 713-928-6053; Fax: 713-928-8148.
E-mail: OBordelon@ccvi-vdm.org
Villa de Matel, 6510 Lawndale Ave., 77023. Tel: 713-928-6053; Fax: 713-928-8148.

Incarnate Word Charitable Trust. Tel: 713-928-6053; Fax: 713-928-8148.

Dominican Sisters of Houston, Motherhouse Complex & Administrative Offices: 6501 Almeda Rd., 77021-2095. Tel: 713-747-3310; Fax: 713-747-4707.
E-mail: houstonop@domhou.org
Web site: www.op.org/houstonop
Legal Title: *Dominican Sisters of Houston, Texas Inc. (O.P.)*. The Sacred Heart Convent Retirement Trust. Sr. Heloise Cruzat, O.P., Prioress.
St. Agnes Academy, Inc.; St. Agnes Academy Foundation, Inc.; St. Pius X High School, Inc.; St. Pius X High School Foundation, Inc.; The Sacred Heart Convent Retirement Trust.

Dominican Sisters-Vietnamese (O.P.), Inc., Provincial House, 5250 Gasmer Dr., 77035. Tel: 713-723-8250; Fax: 713-723-0924. Sisters 57. Vietnamese Dominican Sisters House of Study, 5250 Gasmer Dr., 77035. Tel: 713-723-8250; 723-8208; Fax: 713-723-8229. Mary Immaculate Convent, 5900 Chippewa Blvd., 77086. Tel: 281-445-9574; Fax: 281-445-6716. Sisters 10. Our Lady of the Rosary Convent (Novititate), 1602 Adams St., Missouri City, 77489. Tel: 281-403-9300; Fax: 281-403-9300. Sisters 15.

Eucharistic Missionaries of St. Theresa-Mexico (M.E.S.T.), St. John of the Cross Convent, 430 Bunker Hill, 77024-6399. Tel: 713-461-8337. Sr. Evangelina Ceja, M.E.S.T., Supr. Sisters 4.

Handmaids of the Sacred Heart of Jesus (H.S.H.), St. Andrew Kim Convent, 1706 Bingle Rd., 77055. Tel: 713-465-1196.
Web site: www.stakim.org
Rev. Augustine H.K. Yeo. Sisters 2.

Incarnate Word Convent, 3400 Bradford Pl., 77025-1398. Tel: 713-668-0423; Fax: 713-668-1857.
E-mail: mbcummins@incarnateword.org

Maryknoll Sisters of St. Dominic (M.M.), 7490 Brompton, No. 265, 77025. Tel: 713-793-2480 (Office); 666-5245 (Home); Fax: 713-666-5245.

Missionary Carmelites of St. Teresa (C.M.S.T.), Holy Family Provincial House, 9548 Deer Trail Dr., 77038. Tel: 281-445-5520; Fax: 281-445-5748. Sisters 5. Divine Providence Convent, 9600 Deer Trail Dr., 77038. Tel: 281-847-3328. Sisters 7. Mt. Carmel House of Prayer, 9600 Deer Trail Dr., 77038. Tel: 281-445-8830. Sisters 7. St. Therese Novitiate, 9608 Deer Trail Dr., 77038. Tel: 281-820-3732. Sisters 6.

Missionary Catechists of the Sacred Hearts of Jesus and Mary (M.C.S.H.S.M.). Our Lady of Guadalupe Convent, 502 Carlisle St., Rosenberg, 77471. Tel: 281-232-5500; Fax: 281-342-4008. Sisters 3.

Missionary Sisters of the Immaculate Conception (S.M.I.C.), 6414 Ludington Dr., 77035-3919. Tel: 713-729-6971.
E-mail: angmenta@hal-pc.org

Our Lady of the Cenacle (R.C.), Cenacle Retreat House, 420 N. Kirkwood, 77079. Tel: 281-497-3131; Fax: 281-497-7632.
E-mail: cenacle.retreat@pdg.net
Web site: www.cenacleretreathouse.org
Sr. Lois Dideon; Sr. Mary Dennison; Sr. Thressa Heard; Sr. Elizabeth Mozina; Sr. Dorothy Briscoe; Sr. Fran Tan. Sisters 6.

Religious of the Sacred Heart (R.S.C.J.), Duchesne Community, 10204 Memorial Dr., 77024. Tel: 713-467-5312; Fax: 713-465-9809.
Web site: rscj.org
Sisters 5. 2020 Harvard, 77008. Tel: 713-868-9607. Sisters 3.

School Sisters of Notre Dame (S.S.N.D.) Community, 4010 Linkwood Dr., #902, 77025-3405. Tel: 713-660-9317.
E-mail: schirish@yahoo.com
Sisters 2.

Sisters for Christian Community (S.F.C.C.). SFCC Community, 109 N. Frazier, Conroe, 77301. Tel: 409-756-3051; Fax: 409-756-8105. Sacred Heart Convent, 105 N. Frazier St., 77301. Tel: 936-756-3051; Fax: 936-756-8105. St. Gregory the Great Convent, 5123 Calgary, 77016. Sr. Natalia Adame, S.F.C.C., 2200 Fountainview, #60, 77057. Sr. Ginny Braniff, S.F.C.C., Sacred Heart Convent, 105 N. Frazier, Conroe, 77301. Tel: 936-756-8288; Fax: 936-756-8105. Sr. Isidra Hernandez, S.F.C.C., 3709 Lila, 77026. Sr. Juanita Martinez, S.F.C.C., 502 29th Ave. N., Texas City, 77590. Sr. Laurine Murragh, S.F.C.C.

Sisters of Providence of St. Mary of the Woods (Indiana) (S.P.), 4727 Oakshire, No. 2, 77027. Tel: 713-850-1687; Fax: 713-745-0349.

Sisters of the Holy Family (S.S.F.), Our Mother of Mercy Convent, 2000 Benson St., 77020. Tel: 713-674-6560. Sisters 4.

Sisters of the Holy Spirit and Mary Immaculate (S.H.Sp.), St. Charles Borromeo Convent, 9601 McGallon, 77076. Tel: 713-694-4264; Fax: 713-692-6314.
E-mail: ceciel@juno.com
Sr. Veronica Cahill, S.H.Sp., Gen. Supr. Tel: 210-533-5149; 533-5522; Fax 210-533-3434; Sr. Muriel Clarke, Our Lady of Fatima Convent, 1701 Ninth St., 77547. Tel: 713-674-1811.

Sisters of the Sacred Heart (S.S.C.J.), Holy Name Convent, 1217 Hogan, 77009. Tel: 713-228-4500; Fax: 713-227-0224.

MISSOURI CITY. *Schoenstatt Sisters of Mary (I.S.S.M.)*, Holy Family Church, 1510 Fifth St., 77489. Tel: 281-499-6246, Ext. 339; Fax: 281-499-9680. Sr. M. Carmen Rodriguez, Coord., Social Min.

NEW CANEY. *Discalced Carmelite Nuns (O.C.D.) Carmel of the Holy Trinity*, 1100 Parthenon Pl., 77357-3039. Tel: 281-399-0270; Fax: 281-689-3615. Sisters 10.

[S] RETREAT HOUSES

HOUSTON. *Cenacle Retreat House*, 420 N. Kirkwood, 77079. Tel: 281-497-3131; Fax: 281-497-7632.
E-mail: cenacle.retreat@pdq.net
Web site: cenacleretreathouse.org
Congregation of Our Lady of the Retreat in the Cenacle. Sr. Dorothy Briscoe; Sr. Lois Dideon; Sr. Mary Dennison; Sr. Thressa Heard, Ministry Co-ord.; Sr. Elizabeth Mozina. Sisters 6.

Holy Name Retreat Center, 430 Bunker Hill Rd., 77024-6399. Tel: 713-464-0211; Fax: 713-464-0671.
E-mail: holyname@pdq.met
Revs. John Schork, C.P., Retreat Dir.; Robert Bovenzi, C.P., Assoc. Dir.; Christopher Gibson, C.P., Retreat Staff. Total in Residence 1; Total Staff 3.

Shalom House of Prayer, 6510 Lawndale Ave., P.O. Box 230969, 77223. Tel: 921-5305. Sr. Genevieve Marheineke, Hermit. Total in Residence 2.

DICKINSON. *Christian Renewal Center*, 1515 Hughes Rd., P.O. Box 699, 77539-0635. Tel: 281-337-1312 (Center); Fax: 281-337-2615.
E-mail: crc1515@wt.net
Revs. Eugene Canas, O.M.I., Dir.; William Clark, O.M.I., Assoc. Dir. In res. Revs. Richard Beck, O.M.I.; Manuel Villarreal, O.M.I.; John Ward, O.M.I. Total in Residence 5; Total Staff 17.

[T] NEWMAN CENTERS

GALVESTON. *Galveston Newman Center*, 1402 Broadway, 77550-4938. Tel: 409-762-4202; Fax: 409-762-4233.
Texas A & M University at Galveston; University of Texas Medical Branch; Galveston College; College of the Mainland.

HOUSTON. *Catholic Newman Association at the University of Houston Central Campus*, Catholic Center, 4805 Calhoun Rd., 77004. Tel: 713-748-2529; Fax: 713-748-8412.
E-mail: catholic@uh.edu
Web site: www.uh.edu/catholic

Satellite Office, 203 AD Bruce Religion Center, 77204. Tel: 713-748-2529; 748-2342; Fax: 713-748-8412. Revs. John J. Boll, O.P., Campus Min. & Dir.; Paul Gallagher, O.F.M., Campus Min.; Eileen Halm, Sec.

Rice University / Texas Medical Center Schools; Catholic Student Center, 1703 Bolsover Rd., 77005. Tel: 713-526-3809; Fax: 713-526-6010.
E-mail: cathcen@rice.edu
Web site: www.rice.edu/catholic
Sr. Antoinette "Kitty" Carter, O.P., Dir. Total Staff 3.

Texas Southern University Catholic Newman Hall, 3535 Wheeler, 77004. Tel: 713-747-9595; Fax: 713-747-3193.
E-mail: newmantsu@aol.com
Rev. Donatus U. Anosike, M.S.P. Total in Residence 1; Total Staff 4.

University of St. Thomas Campus Ministry, 3800 Montrose Blvd., 77006. Tel: 713-525-3589; Fax: 713-525-3524.
E-mail: thompson@stthom.edu
Web site: www.stthom.edu
Rev. Jefferson M. Thompson, C.S.B., Dir., Campus Ministry.

HUNTSVILLE. *Catholic Student Center, S.H.S.U.*, 1310 17th St., 77340-4415. Tel: 409-291-2620; Fax: 409-291-2620.
E-mail: donna_rowe@hotmail.com
Web site: www.shsu.edu/~org.cath/
Donna Rowe, Dir. Total Assisted 275; Total Staff 3.

PRAIRIE VIEW. *Prairie View A & M University Catholic Center*, P.O. Box 3027, 77446-3027. Tel: 936-857-3351; Fax: 979-826-8057. Rev. James M. Burkart. Total Staff 1.

[U] MISCELLANEOUS

GALVESTON. *The Bishop's Palace*, 1402 Broadway, 77550. Tel: 409-762-2475. Rev. William D. Bartniski, Exec. Dir.

HOUSTON. *Asociacion Nacional de Sacerdotes Hispanos*, 5505 Chaucer Dr., 77005. Tel: 713-528-6517; Fax: 713-528-6379.
E-mail: info@ansh.org
Web site: www.ansh.org
Rev. Jose H. Gomez, Exec. Dir.

Catholic Charismatic Center, 1949 Cullen P.O. Box 230287, 77223-0287. Tel: 713-236-9977; Fax: 713-236-0073.
E-mail: fafrankovich@yahoo.com
Web site: catholiccharismatic.com
Revs. Francis A. Frankovich, Dir.; Ed Wade, Assoc. Dir.; Sean A. Wenger, Assoc. Dir.

Catholic Clerical Student Fund, 9845 Memorial, 77024. Tel: 713-686-4345, Ext. 273; Fax: 713-681-7550.
E-mail: caroleupdyke@att.net
Most Rev. Joseph A. Fiorenza, Chm.; Carole Updyke, Pres. Higher learning for the priesthood.

The Catholic Endowment Foundation of Galveston-Houston, P.O. Box 907, 77001-0907. Tel: 713-963-8008. Mr. Harold Hidalgo, Pres.
Charity Guild of Catholic Women, 1203 Lovett Blvd., 77006. Tel: 713-529-0995; Fax: 713-529-9263.
Charity Guild of St. Joseph, P.O. Box 570728-319, 77257-0728. Tel: 713-965-0965. Alice Marie Geaccone, Pres.
Equestrian Order of the Holy Sepulchre of Jerusalem, 309 Knipp Rd., 77024. Tel: 713-468-5602; Fax: 713-468-1218.
E-mail: AnneKendall@compuserve.com
Mr. F. Russell Kendall, Knight of the Collar, Vice Gov. Gen. of Honor; Mr. Michael Earthman, Lt.
Southwestern Lieutenancy, Equestrian Order of the Holy Sepulchre of Jerusalem, 2240 Chilton Rd., 77019-1402. Tel: 713-523-5442; Fax: 713-523-5442.
Jesuit Volunteer Corps: South, P.O. Box 3126, 77253-3126. Tel: 713-756-5095; Fax: 713-756-8928.
E-mail: jvcsouth@jesuitvolunteers.org
Web site: jesuitvolunteers.org
Ms. Pam Krinock, Dir. Volunteer service organizations.
Kolbe Project, Inc., 1030 Heights Blvd., 77008-6914. Tel: 713-861-1800; Fax: 713-861-7212.
E-mail: info@kolbeproject.org
Web site: www.kolbeproject.com
P.O. Box 7765, 77270-7765. Tel: 713-861-1800; Fax: 713-861-7212.
Martha's Kitchen Food Services, 322 S. Jensen Dr., 77003. Tel: 713-224-2522; Fax: 713-224-7814. Rev. Terence P. Brinkman, S.T.D. Sisters 2.
Sacred Military Constantinian Order of Saint George, American Delegation, 302 Gessner Rd., 77024. Tel: 713-888-0242; Fax: 713-888-0345.
E-mail: usa@twosicilies.org
Web site: www.twosicilies.org
Mr. L. Charles Scholz, Chancellor.
St. Dominic Center, Inc., 2401 E. Holcombe, 77021. Tel: 713-741-8743; Fax: 713-741-8705. Wayne Knight, Facility Admin.
St. Francis de Sales School Foundation, 8100 Roos, 77036. Tel: 713-774-4447; Fax: 713-271-6744.
E-mail: webmaster@st-francis-de-sales.org
Web site: www.st-francis-de-sales.org
St. Mary's Children's Relief Fund, Chancery Bldg., 1700 San Jacinto, P.O. Box 907, 77001-0907. Tel: 713-659-5461; Fax: 713-759-9151. Most Rev. Joseph A. Fiorenza, Pres.; Rev. Msgr. Frank A. Lagana, Vice Pres.
St. Pius X High School Foundation, Inc., 811 W. Donovan, 77091-5699. Tel: 713-692-3581; Fax: 713-692-5725.
E-mail: pollardd@stpiusx.org
Web site: www.stpiusx.org
Harold Hidalgo, Pres.
Sociedad San Martin de Porres, P.O. Box 7788, 77270-7788. Tel: 713-869-0999; Fax: 713-880-0091.
Southern Dominican Volunteer Program.
Corporate Office: 6501 Almeda Rd., 77021-2095. Tel: 713-747-3310; Fax: 713-747-4707.

CONROE. *Dogwood Foundation, Inc.*, P.O. Box 2774, 77305-2774. Tel: 936-588-2078. Ben J. Petru, Pres.

RELIGIOUS INSTITUTES OF MEN REPRESENTED IN THE DIOCESE

For further details refer to the corresponding bracketed number in the religious Institutes of Men or Women section.

[0140]—*The Augustinians*.—O.S.A.
[0170]—*Basilian Fathers*. (Toronto, Canada).—C.S.B.
[0470]—*The Capuchin Friars*.—O.F.M.Cap.
[0270]—*Carmelite Fathers & Brothers*. (Prov. of Most Pure Heart of Mary).—O.Carm.
[0275]—*Carmelites of Mary Immaculate*.—C.M.I.
[0360]—*Claretian Missionaries*.—C.M.F.
[0220]—*Congregation of the Blessed Sacrament*.—S.S.S.
[1330]—*Congregation of the Mission*. (Southern Prov.).—C.M.
[]—*Congregation of the Mother Coredemptrix*.—C.M.C.
[1000]—*Congregation of the Passion*. (Chicago).—C.P.
[1130]—*Congregation of the Priests of the Sacred Heart*.—S.C.J.
[0520]—*Franciscan Friars*.—O.F.M.
[0650]—*Holy Ghost Fathers*. (Western Prov.).—C.S.Sp.
[0690]—*Jesuit Fathers and Brothers*. (New Orleans Prov.).—S.J.
[0800]—*Maryknoll*.—M.M.
[0720]—*The Missionaries of Our Lady of La Salette*. (Prov. of Mary Queen).—M.S.
[]—*Missionaries of St. Joseph*. (Mexico).—M.J.
[]—*Missionaries of St. Paul*.—M.S.P.
[1110]—*Missionaries of the Sacred Heart*.—M.S.C.
[0910]—*Oblates of Mary Immaculate*.—O.M.I.
[0920]—*Oblates of St. Francis de Sales*.—O.S.F.S.
[0430]—*Order of Preachers-Dominicans*. (Prov. of St. Albert the Great).—O.P.
[1070]—*Redemptorist Fathers*. (New Orleans Vice Prov.).—C.SS.R.
[0700]—*St. Joseph's Society of the Sacred Heart*. (Baltimore, MD).—S.S.J.
[]—*Scalabrinians*.—C.S.
[1260]—*Society of Christ*.—S.Ch.
[0975]—*Society of Our Lady of the Most Holy Trinity*.—S.O.L.T.
[0420]—*Society of the Divine Word*.—S.V.D.
[]—*Society of the Precious Blood Sanguinist Fathers*.—C.P.P.S.
[1250]—*Somascan Fathers*.—C.R.S.

RELIGIOUS INSTITUTES OF WOMEN REPRESENTED IN THE DIOCESE

[0230]—*Benedictine Sisters of the Sacred Heart*.—O.S.B.
[0390]—*Carmelite Missionaries of St. Teresa*.—C.M.S.T.
[]—*Carmelite Sisters of the Sacred Heart*.—C.S.C.
[]—*Communidad Apostolica de Maria Siempre Virgen*.—C.A.M.S.V.I.
[1010]—*Congregation of Divine Providence*.—C.D.P.
[3110]—*Congregation of Our Lady of the Retreat in the Cenacle*.—R.C.
[3830-08]—*Congregation of St. Joseph*. (Cleveland, OH).—C.S.J.
[3830-01]—*Congregation of St. Joseph*. (Boston, MA).—C.S.J.
[]—*Congregation of the Lovers of the Cross*. (N. Vietnam).—H.C.L.
[]—*Daughters of Divine Love*. (Nigeria).—D.D.L.
[0420]—*Discalced Carmelite Nuns*.—O.C.D.
[1070-13]—*Dominican Sisters*. (Adrian, MI).—O.P.
[1070-21]—*Dominican Sisters*. (Edmonds, WA).—O.P.
[1070-19]—*Dominican Sisters, Congregation of the Sacred Heart*. (Houston).—O.P.
[]—*Eucharistic Missionaries of St. Theresa*. (Mexico).—M.E.S.T.
[]—*Handmaids of the Holy Child Jesus*. (Nigeria).—H.H.C.J.
[]—*Handmaids of the Sacred Heart*. (N. Korea).—H.S.H.
[2410]—*Marianites of the Holy Cross*.—M.S.C.
[2470]—*Maryknoll Sisters of St. Dominic*.—M.M.
[2690]—*Missionary Catechists of Divine Providence*.—M.C.D.P.
[2700]—*Missionary Catechists of the Sacred Hearts of Jesus and Mary*.—M.C.SS.CC.J.M.
[2760]—*Missionary Sisters of the Immaculate Conception*.—S.M.I.C.
[2860]—*Missionary Sisters of the Sacred Heart*.—M.S.C.
[1145]—*The Religious Missionaries of St. Dominic, Inc.*—O.P.
[4070]—*Religious of the Sacred Heart*.—R.S.C.J.
[4110]—*Roman Union of the Order of St. Ursula*.—O.S.U.
[]—*Schoenstatt Sisters of Mary*.—I.S.S.M.
[2970]—*School Sisters of Notre Dame*.—S.S.N.D.
[]—*Sisters for Christian Community*.—S.F.C.C.
[0440]—*Sisters of Charity*. (Cincinnati, OH).—S.C.
[0590]—*Sisters of Charity of St. Elizabeth*. (Northern Prov.).—S.C.
[0470]—*Sisters of Charity of the Incarnate Word*. (Houston).—C.C.V.I.
[0460]—*Sisters of Charity of the Incarnate Word*. (San Antonio).—C.C.V.I.
[3360]—*Sisters of Providence*. (St. Mary of the Woods, IN).—S.P.
[]—*Sisters of St. Francis of the Providence of God*. (Whitehall, PA).—O.S.F.
[]—*Sisters of St. Joseph*. (Boston).—C.S.J.
[3830-08]—*Sisters of St. Joseph*. (Cleveland, OH).—C.S.J.
[3950]—*Sisters of St. Mary of Namur*.—S.S.M.N.
[1950]—*Sisters of the Holy Family*.—S.S.F.
[2050]—*Sisters of the Holy Spirit and Mary Immaculate*.—S.H.Sp.
[2150]—*Sisters of the Immaculate Heart of Mary*.—I.H.M.
[2190]—*Sisters of the Incarnate Word and Blessed Sacrament*. (Houston).—C.V.I.
[2200]—*Sisters of the Incarnate Word and Blessed Sacrament*. (Corpus Christi).—I.W.B.S.
[2205]—*Sisters of the Incarnate Word and Blessed Sacrament*. (Victoria).—I.W.B.S.
[3310]—*Sisters of the Presentation of Mary*.—P.M.
[3670]—*Sisters of the Sacred Heart of Jesus*.—S.S.C.J.
[]—*Vietnamese Dominican Sisters*.—O.P.

DIOCESAN CEMETERIES

GALVESTON. *Old Catholic, Calvary.*
HOUSTON. *Holy Cross.*
St. Vincent.
DICKINSON. *Mount Olivet.*

NECROLOGY

† DeForke, John C., (Retired). —Died Sept. 15, 2000.
† Doga, Rev. Msgr. Allen R., Spring, TX St. Edward. —Died Dec. 15, 1999.

Diocese of Gary

(Dioecesis Gariensis)

Most Reverend

DALE J. MELCZEK, D.D.

Bishop of Gary; ordained June 6, 1964; appointed Auxiliary Bishop of Detroit and Titular Bishop of Trau December 3, 1982; consecrated January 27, 1983; appointed Apostolic Administrator of Gary August 19, 1992; appointed Coadjutor Bishop of Gary October 20, 1995; succeeded to the See of Gary June 1, 1996. *Office: 9292 Broadway, Merrillville, IN, 46410.* Tel.: 219-769-9292; Fax: 219-769-2066.

ESTABLISHED DECEMBER 17, 1956.

Square Miles 1,807.

Comprises the Counties of Lake, LaPorte, Porter and Starke in the State of Indiana.

For legal titles of parishes and diocesan institutions, consult the Chancery.

Chancery: 9292 Broadway, Merrillville, IN, 46410. Tel.: 219-769-9292; Fax: 219-738-9034.

Web site address: www.chancery@dcgary.org

STATISTICAL OVERVIEW

Personnel	
Bishop	1
Priests: Diocesan Active in Diocese	84
Priests: Active Outside Diocese	5
Priests: Diocesan in Foreign Missions	1
Priests: Retired, Sick or Absent	33
Number of Diocesan Priests	123
Religious Priests in Diocese	47
Extern Priests in Diocese	8
Ordinations:	
Diocesan Priests	1
Transitional Deacons	1
Permanent Deacons	11
Permanent Deacons in Diocese	39
Total Brothers	15
Total Sisters	117
Parishes	
Parishes	75
With Resident Pastor:	
Resident Diocesan Priests	67
Resident Religious Priests	4
Without Resident Pastor:	
Administered by Priests	4
Missions	4
Pastoral Centers	6
Professional Ministry Personnel:	
Brothers	2
Sisters	12
Lay Ministers	58
Welfare	
Catholic Hospitals	6
Total Assisted	830,567
Homes for the Aged	3
Total Assisted	449
Residential Care of Children	3
Total Assisted	93
Day Care and Extended Day Care Centers	2
Total Assisted	500
Specialized Homes	1
Total Assisted	700
Special Centers for Social Services	7
Total Assisted	10,000
Educational	
Diocesan Students in Other Seminaries	9
Seminaries, Religious	1
Students Religious	4
Total Seminarians	13
Colleges and Universities	1
Total Students	978
High Schools, Diocesan and Parish	3
Total Students	1,705
Elementary Schools, Diocesan and Parish	27
Total Students	7,350
Elementary Schools, Private	1
Total Students	112
Catechesis/Religious Education:	
High School Students	705
Elementary Students	11,950
Total Students Under Catholic Instruction	22,813
Teachers in the Diocese:	
Priests	3
Brothers	4
Sisters	19
Lay Teachers	489
Vital Statistics	
Receptions into the Church:	
Infant Baptism Totals	2,473
Adult Baptism Totals	200
Received into Full Communion	285
First Communions	2,504
Confirmations	2,082
Marriages:	
Catholic	499
Interfaith	315
Total Marriages	814
Deaths	1,985
Total Catholic Population	186,800
Total Population	761,912

Former Bishops—Most Rev. ANDREW GREGORY GRUTKA, D.D., ord. Dec. 5, 1933; appt. Bishop of Gary Dec. 29, 1956; cons. February 25, 1957; retired July 9, 1984; died Nov. 11, 1993.—Most Rev. NORBERT F. GAUGHAN, D.D., Ph.D., ord. Nov. 4, 1945; appt. Auxiliary Bishop of Greensburg April 2, 1975; cons. June 26, 1975; appt. Bishop of Gary July 9, 1984; retired June 1, 1996; died Oct. 1, 1999.

Vicar General—Rev. STANLEY J. DOMINIK.

Deans—Rev. DOMINIC V. BERTINO, Gary-Hobart Deanery; Rev. STANLEY J. DOMINIK, North Lake County Deanery; Rev. DENNIS J. TELES, South Lake County Deanery; Rev. GERALD H. SCHWEITZER, Porter-Starke County Deanery; Rev. RICHARD H. AMELING, LaPorte County Deanery.

Chancery—9292 Broadway, Merrillville, 46410. Tel: 219-769-9292; Fax: 219-738-9034.

Administrative Assistant to the Bishop—Rev. JON J. PLAVCAN.

Bishop's Delegate for Sexual Abuse Matters—Rev. Msgr. JOHN J. SIEKIERSKI, J.C.L.

Director of Finance and Administration—KARL P. DYTRYCH.

Secretary to the Bishop—VALERIE D. MCMANUS. Tel: 219-769-9181; Fax: 219-769-2066.

Diocesan Tribunal—9292 Broadway, Merrillville, 46410. Tel: 219-769-9292.

Judicial Vicar—Very Rev. JAMES W. MEADE, J.D., S.T.L., J.C.L.

Judges—Rev. MATTHEW C. IWUJI, J.U.D.; Sr. THERESE GUERIN SULLIVAN, S.P., D.Min., J.C.L.

Second Instance—Rev. Msgr. RALPH G. HOFFMANN; Rev. Msgr. EDWARD F. LITOT; Rev. Msgr. VINCENT L. LENGERICH; Rev. RONALD WALTERS, O.F.M., J.C.L.

Defenders of the Bond—Rev. Msgr. JOHN J. SIEKIERSKI, J.C.L.; Rev. SAMMIE L. MALETTA, J.D., J.C.L.

Auditors—Rev. MICHAEL L. MAGINOT, S.T.L., J.C.L.; Sr. EVELYN OVALLES, S.P., B.A., LL.B.; Deacons nameSherman Brown ROBERT BONTA; DONNA V. CALLAWAY; LINDA PLANER.

Notaries—VALERIE MCMANUS; MARY ANN O'CONNELL; JEAN DAVID.

Bishop's Council of Priests—Revs. RICHARD H. AMELING; DOMINIC V. BERTINO; DERRICK F. DUDASH; PATRICK J. KALICH; JOHN E. KALICKY, C.PP.S.; STANLEY J. DOMINIK; EDWARD J. KENNEDY; STEPHEN D. KOSINSKI; JAMES P. MCGROGAN; JAMES W. MEADE; PETER J. MUHA; WILLIAM F. O'TOOLE; JON J. PLAVCAN; GERALD H. SCHWEITZER; DENNIS J. TELES; STEPHEN J. TITKO; JOHN J. STREBIG; JOSEPH E. VAMOS; JOHN R. WINTERLIN.

Consultors—Revs. GERALD H. SCHWEITZER; DOMINIC V. BERTINO; STANLEY J. DOMINIK; DENNIS J. TELES; RICHARD H. AMELING; JON J. PLAVCAN.

Priests' Personnel Board—Rev. Msgr. JOSEPH F. SEMANCIK, M.S.W., Ph.D.; Rev. GERALD H. SCHWEITZER; Rev. Msgr. DON C. GRASS; Revs. DENNIS J. TELES; RICHARD H. AMELING; STANLEY J. DOMINIK; DOMINIC V. BERTINO; JON J. PLAVCAN; DOUGLAS J. MAYER; PATRICK J. CONNOLLY; TERRENCE R. CHASE.

Diocesan Offices and Directors

African American Catholic Ministry—PEARLETTE SPRINGER, Coord., *9292 Broadway, Merrillville, 46410.* Tel: 219-769-9292; Fax: 219-738-9034.

Blue Army—Rev. MARK G. MAZZA, Chap., *303 Keller Ave., North Judson, 46366.* Tel: 219-896-2195.

Boy Scouts Liaison—Rev. RONALD WALTERS, O.F.M., Chap. SUSAN BARRIBALL, Chm., *919 Foxpoint Dr., Chesterton, 46304.* Tel: 219-926-3028.

Campaign for Human Development—Rev. THOMAS M. GANNON, S.J., *7128 Arizona Ave., Hammond, 46323.* Tel: 219-844-7515; Fax: 219-844-7566.

Campus Ministry—St. Teresa of Avila Catholic Student Center (Valparaiso University); Rev. KEVIN P. MCCARTHY, Chap., *1511 LaPorte St., Valparaiso, 46383.* Tel: 219-464-4042. Indiana University Northwest; Rev. JOHN T. AMBRE, Chap., *501 W. Ridge Rd., Gary, 46408.* Tel: 219-887-0514.

Catholic Services Appeal/Development Office—JOYCE ILLYES; URIEL MARTINEZ, *9292 Broadway, Merrillville, 46410.* Tel: 219-769-9292; Fax: 219-738-9034.

Catholic Youth Organization (CYO) Office—CHUCK CONNORS, Dir., *7725 Broadway, Ste. G, Merrillville, 46410.* Tel: 219-736-8931; Fax: 219-736-9457.

Cemeteries—Rev. STANLEY J. DOMINIK, Dir., *1731 LaPorte Ave., Whiting, 46394.* Tel: 219-659-0733.

Charismatic Apostolate—Rev. JOHN V. SCOTT, Dir., *406 E. Washington St., Knox, 46534.* Tel: 219-772-4134.

Charities—KENNETH M. FLANAGAN, M.S.W., Ph.D., Dir., *973 W. Sixth Ave., Gary, 46402.* Tel: 219-882-2720.

Communications Office—BRIAN T. OLSZEWSKI, Dir., *9292 Broadway, Merrillville, 46410.* Tel: 219-769-9292; Fax: 219-738-9034.

Council of Catholic Women—Rev. ROY T. BEECHING, Diocesan Moderator, *5304 Hohman Ave., Hammond, 46320.* Tel: 219-932-0702.

Cursillos in Christianity—Revs. JUAN GONZALEZ, C.PP.S., Chap. (Spanish); EDWARD J. KENNEDY, (English), *11000 W. 133rd Ave., Cedar Lake, 46303.* Tel: 219-374-7160.

Diaconate—Rev. MICHAEL J. YADRON, Deacon Formation Dir., *526 S. Woodland Ave., Michigan City, 46360.* Tel: 219-872-9196. Deacon JOHN D. ROSCOE, SR., Diaconate Dir. - Post Ordination, *2402 Willowwood Ave., Valparaiso, 46383.* Tel: 219-477-3616.

Ecumenical Officer—Mr. MARK PLAISS, *4137 W. Andrea Dr., LaPorte, 46350.* Tel: 219-324-6026.

Employee Benefits—KAREN WALSH, Coord., *9292 Broadway, Merrillville, 46410.* Tel: 219-769-9292; Fax: 219-738-9034.

Engaged Encounter—GREG CASIMER; LISA CASIMER, *6365 Venus Ave., Portage, 46368.* Tel: 219-762-2039.

Family Life Ministry—RITA MAYER, Coord., *973 W. Sixth Ave., Gary, 46402.* Tel: 219-882-2720.

Finance Council—DENNIS BIELFELDT; CALVIN E. BELLAMY; T. CLIFFORD FLEMING; JOSEPH F. GLOTZBACH, C.P.A.; KARL DYTRYCH; FELICIA FLOWERS SMITH; Rev. JOSEPH M. PAWLOWSKI; DENISE CARRASQUILLO.

Girl Scout Liaison—Rev. THEODORE A. NORDQUIST, *109 C St., LaPorte, 46350.* Tel: 219-362-9595.

Heartland Center—Revs. THOMAS M. GANNON, S.J.; JAMES W. SCHULZ, S.J., *7128 Arizona Ave., Hammond, 46323.* Tel: 219-844-7515; Fax: 219-844-7566.

Holy Childhood Association—cf. Mission Office.

Hispanic Diocesan Ministries—Coordinators: ANGEL TORRES; ADELINE TORRES, *P.O. Box 3027, East Chicago, 46312.* Tel: 219-397-2125; Fax: 219-397-2168.

Indiana Catholic Conference—Rev. JAMES W. SCHULZ, S.J., Diocesan Coord., *7128 Arizona Ave., Hammond, 46323.* Tel: 219-844-7515; Fax: 219-844-7566.

Lay Ministry Formation Office—ANNE VERBEKE, Coord., *9292 Broadway, Merrillville, 46410.* Tel: 219-769-9292; Fax: 219-738-9034.

Legal Counsel—ROBERT M. SCHWERD, *2637 45th St., Highland, 46322.* Tel: 219-924-2427.

Marriage Dispensations—Rev. GERALD H. SCHWEITZER, *P.O. Box 386, Wanatah, 46390.* Tel: 219-733-2955.

Marriage Encounter—BRIAN OTTO; DEBBIE OTTO, *0674 E. 600 N., LaPorte, 46350.* Tel: 219-778-4712.

Ministry with the Physically and Mentally Challenged—Rev. JOHN J. ZEMELKO, Coord., Ministry to Hearing Impaired, *1340 121st St., Whiting, 46394.* Tel: 219-659-3848.

Mission Office—Rev. JOSEPH E. VAMOS, Dir., *9292 Broadway, Merrillville, 46410.* Tel: 219-769-9292.

Newspaper—"Northwest Indiana Catholic", BRIAN T. OLSZEWSKI, Editor; CAROL MACINGA, Circulation Mgr., *9292 Broadway, Merrillville, 46410.* Tel: 219-769-9292; Fax: 219-738-9034.

Parish Pastoral Councils—ANNE VERBEKE, Coord., *9292 Broadway, Merrillville, 46410.* Tel: 219-769-9292; Fax: 219-738-9034.

Peace and Social Justice, Office of—Rev. THOMAS M. GANNON, S.J., Coord., *7128 Arizona Ave., Hammond, 46323.* Tel: 219-844-7515; Fax: 219-844-7566.

Priestly Life—Rev. EDWARD J. KENNEDY, Coord., *11000 W. 133rd Ave., Cedar Lake, 46303.* Tel: 219-374-7160.

Pro-Life Activities—Rev. THEODORE J. MENS, Diocesan Coord., *525 N. Broad St., Griffith, 46319.* Tel: 219-924-4163.

Propagation of the Faith and Holy Childhood Association—cf. Mission Office.

Religious Education Office—FRANK J. ZOLVINSKI, Coord., *9292 Broadway, Merrillville, 46410.* Tel: 219-769-9292; Fax: 219-738-9034.

Religious, Liaison for Women and Men—Sr. JACINTA KRECEK, O.S.F., *5454 Hohman Ave., Hammond, 46320.* Tel: 219-933-2059.

Retirement Plan of the Diocese of Gary, Indiana—JOSEPH F. GLOTZBACH, C.P.A., *9292 Broadway, Merrillville, 46410.* Tel: 219-769-9292.

Rural Life Conference—Rev. ANTHONY L. SPANLEY, Coord., *P.O. Box 230, Hamlet, 46532.* Tel: 219-867-2461.

St. Vincent de Paul Society—DIANE MCKERN, Pres., *7132 Arizona Ave., Hammond, 46324.* Tel: 219-845-7531.

Schools Office—KIM PRYZBYLSKI, Supt. Schools, *9292 Broadway, Merrillville, 46410.* Tel: 219-769-9292.

Spiritual Life / Seimetz Center—*1441 Hoffman St., Hammond, 46327.* Tel: 219-932-8321.

Stewardship—ANNE VERBEKE, Coord., *9292 Broadway, Merrillville, 46410.* Tel: 219-769-9292; Fax: 219-738-9034.

Vocations—Rev. IAN J. WILLIAMS, Dir., *1247 171st Pl., Hammond, 46324.* Tel: 219-989-7948; Fax: 219-391-8999.

Worship and Spirituality, Office of—Rev. MARTIN J. DOBRZYNSKI, Coord. JULIE VOLKMANN, Assoc., *9292 Broadway, Merrillville, 46410.* Tel: 219-769-9292; Fax: 219-738-9034.

Youth Ministry—COLLEEN CLARK, Coord., *9292 Broadway, Merrillville, 46410.* Tel: 219-769-9292; Fax: 219-738-9034.

CLERGY, PARISHES, MISSIONS AND PAROCHIAL SCHOOLS

CITY OF GARY
(Lake County)

1—CATHEDRAL OF HOLY ANGELS (1907), Rev. Robert P. Gehring.
Res., 640 Tyler St., 46402-2299. Tel: 219-882-6079; Fax: 219-882-0133.
Catechesis / Religious Programs—Students 27.

2—BLESSED SACRAMENT (1947), Rev. Krzysztof S. Bugno, S.D.S (Poland); Deacon Joseph Kwitko.
Res., 1775 W. 41st Ave., 46408. Tel: 219-980-3081; Fax: 219-980-5646.
School—Tel: 219-980-5635.
Poor Handmaids of Jesus Christ 2; Lay Teachers 12; Students 222.
Catechesis / Religious Programs—Mrs. Lucille Highsmith, D.R.E.
Students 20.

3—HOLY FAMILY (1926) (Polish), Rev. Stanley J. Milewski.
Res., 416 E. Ridge Rd., 46409. Tel: 219-884-1733.

4—HOLY ROSARY (1931), Rev. Frank D. Torres; Deacons Martin Gomez; Frederick Romanski, (On leave).
Res., 719 Clark Rd., 46406. Tel: 219-944-1084; Fax: 219-949-7465.
Catechesis / Religious Programs—Mary Ellen Sendejas, D.R.E.
Students 61.

5—HOLY TRINITY (1911) (African American). Closed. For inquiries for parish records contact Cathedral of Holy Angels, Gary.

6—SACRED HEART (1918) (Polish). Closed. For inquiries for parish records contact Cathedral of Holy Angels, Gary.

7—ST. ANN (1942), Rev. Stephen D. Kosinski.
Res., 6025 W. 25th Ave., 46406. Tel: 219-844-2448; Fax: 219-844-2897.

8—ST. ANTHONY (1918). Closed. For inquiries for parish records contact Cathedral of Holy Angels, Gary.

9—ST. CASIMIR (1916) (Lithuanian). Closed. For inquries for parish records contact Holy Angels Cathedral.

10—ST. EMERIC (1911). Closed. For inquiries for parish records contact Holy Trinity (Hungarian), East Chicago.

11—ST. HEDWIG (1908) (Polish),
Serviced by Salvatorian Fathers. 1746 Pennsylvania St., 46407. Tel: 219-882-2584.; 5755 Pennsylvania St., Merrillville, 46410. Tel: 219-884-0714; Fax: 219-981-9224. [JC]

12—ST. JOSEPH THE WORKER (1912) (Croatian), Revs. Stephen Loncar, O.F.M.Conv.; Benedict Benakovic, O.F.M.Conv.
Res., 330 E. 45th Ave., 46409. Tel: 219-980-1846.

13—ST. LUKE (1917). See St. Monica, Gary.

14—ST. MARK (1921), Rev. John T. Ambre.
Res., 501 W. Ridge Rd., 46408. Tel: 219-887-0514; Fax: 219-887-0515.
Catechesis / Religious Programs—Students 20.
Convent—509 W. Ridge Rd., 46408. Tel: 219-886-0266.
Missionaries of Charity 4.

15—ST. MARY OF THE LAKE (1929), Rev. Thomas E. Mischler.
Res., 6060 Miller Ave., 46403. Tel: 219-938-1373; Fax: 219-938-1316.
Catechesis / Religious Programs—Tel: 219-938-9115. Mary K. Mauer, D.R.E.
Students 50.

16—SS. MONICA-ST. LUKE (1927; 1917), Rev. J. Patrick Gaza; Deacons Melvin Clark; Michael Richardson.
Res., 645 Rhode Island, 46402. Tel: 219-883-1861.
Catechesis / Religious Programs—Students 42.

OUTSIDE THE CITY OF GARY

Beverly Shores, Porter Co., St. Ann (1956) (Lithuanian), Rev. John B. Barasinski.
Res., P.O. Box 727, 46301. Tel: 219-879-7565; Fax: 219-879-8893.

Cedar Lake, Lake Co., Holy Name (1859), Rev. Edward J. Kennedy.
Res., 11000 W. 133rd Ave., 46303. Tel: 219-374-7160; Fax: 219-374-7165. [CEM]
Parish Center—13209 Schneider St., 46303. Tel: 219-374-8798.
Catechesis / Religious Programs—Tel: 219-374-8798.
Students 260.

Chesterton, Porter Co., St. Patrick (1858), Revs. Lawrence S. Heeg; Eduardo Malagon; Deacons Nicholas Juracevich; William Jones.
Res., 638 N. Calumet Rd., 46304. Tel: 219-926-1282; Fax: 219-395-1560. [CEM]
School—640 N. Calumet Rd., 46304. Tel: 219-926-1707; Fax: 219-921-1922. Ruth McCullough, Prin.
Lay Teachers 11; Students 235.
Catechesis / Religious Programs—Tel: 219-926-1265. Norma Dvorscak, D.R.E.
Students 615.

Crown Point, Lake Co., St. Mary (1865) (German), Rev. Msgr. Don C. Grass; Rev. Patrick J. Kalich.
Res., 321 E. Joliet St., 46307. Tel: 219-663-0044; Fax: 219-663-0676. [CEM]
School—405 E. Joliet St., 46307. Tel: 219-663-0676. Suzan LaPeer, Prin.
Lay Teachers 22; Students 575.
Catechesis / Religious Programs—Mrs. Jan Mucha, D.R.E.
Students 263.

St. Matthias (1967), Rev. Terrence J. Steffens; Deacon Gregory Fabian.
Mailing Address: 101 W. Burrell Dr., 46307. Tel: 219-663-2201; Fax: 219-663-2567.
Res., 12505 Marshall St., 46307.
Catechesis / Religious Programs—Tel: 219-663-4281. Christine Nienhaus, D.R.E.
Students 246.

Dyer, Lake Co., St. Joseph (1867), Rev. Mark S. Pavlina.
Res., 440 Joliet St., 46311. Tel: 219-865-2271; Fax: 219-865-2350. [CEM]
School—Tel: 219-865-2750; Fax: 219-865-2750. Mr. Bill Davis, Prin.
Lay Teachers 14; Students 188.
Catechesis / Religious Programs—430 Joliet St., 46311. Tel: 219-865-2355.
Students 315.

St. Maria Goretti (1977), Rev. Alfred J. Dettmer.
Res., 500 Northgate Dr., 46311. Tel: 219-865-8956; Fax: 219-322-1670.
Catechesis / Religious Programs—Tel: 219-322-6124. Joyce Peterson, D.R.E.
Students 275.

East Chicago, Lake Co.,

1—ASSUMPTION, (1915) (Slovak). Closed. For inquiries for parish records contact St. Patrick, East Chicago.

2—HOLY TRINITY, (1916) (Croatian), Rev. Msgr. Paul P. Bogovich.
Res., 4754 Carey St., 46312. Tel: 219-398-3061.

3—HOLY TRINITY, (1906) (Hungarian), Rev. Alphonse Skerl.
Res., 4759 McCook Ave., 46312. Tel: 219-397-1907.

4—IMMACULATE CONCEPTION, (1933) (Italian). Closed. For inquiries for parish records contact St. Stanislaus, East Chicago.

5—OUR LADY OF GUADALUPE, (1927) (Hispanic), Revs. Juan Gonzalez, C.PP.S.; Diego J. Gettig, C.PP.S.; Bro. Jerry Schwieterman, C.PP.S., Pastoral Assoc.
Res., 3510 Deodar St., P.O. Box 3400, 46312. Tel: 219-398-0253; Fax: 219-398-0266.
School—Interparochial Consolidated, Tel: 219-397-1122; Fax: 219-397-1972.
Catechesis / Religious Programs—3916 Pulaski St., IL 46312. Tel: 219-397-3293. D.R.E.: Monica Vitela; Guadalupe Figueroa; Edith A. Downes.
Students 75.

6—SACRED HEART, (1926) (Slovak), Rev. Msgr. Joseph F. Semancik.
Res., 4423 Olcott Ave., 46312. Tel: 219-397-5857.
Catechesis / Religious Programs—Students 16.

7—ST. FRANCIS, (1913) (Lithuanian). Closed. For inquiries for parish records contact St. John Cantius, East Chicago.

8—ST. JOHN CANTIUS, (1906) (Polish), Rev. Joseph R. Niezgoda.
Res., 3903 Main St., 46312. Tel: 219-398-1370.
School—Indiana Harbor Catholic Elementary School, Tel: 219-397-1122; Fax: 219-397-1972.

9—ST. JOSEPH, (1916) (Polish). Closed. For inquiries for parish records contact St. John Cantius, East Chicago.

10—ST. JUDE, (1933). Closed. For inquiries for parish records contact Our Lady of Guadalupe, East Chicago.

11—St. Mary, (1890), Rev. Stephen G. Gibson.
822 W. 144th St., 46312. Tel: 219-398-2409; Fax: 219-391-8999.
School—Tel: 219-397-4404; Fax: 219-397-0924. Mr. Michael Ritchie, Prin.
Lay Teachers 3; Students 45.
Catechesis/Religious Programs—Students 250.

12—St. Patrick, (1902) (Hispanic), Rev. Fernando de Cristobal; Sr. Irene DeMeulenaere, Pastoral Assoc.
Res., 3810 Grand Blvd., 46312. Tel: 219-398-1036; Fax: 219-398-1036.
School—Interparochial, Tel: 219-397-1122.
Catechesis/Religious Programs—3916 Pulaski St., 46312. Tel: 219-397-3293.
Students 81.

13—St. Stanislaus, (1900) (Polish), Rev. Msgr. John J. Siekierski.
Res., 808 W. 150th St., 46312. Tel: 219-398-2341; Fax: 219-398-2388.
School—4930 Indianapolis Blvd., 46312. Tel: 219-398-1316; Fax: 219-398-9080. Michael Ritchie, Prin.
Lay Teachers 15; Students 240.
Catechesis/Religious Programs—Students 14.
Convent—4940 Indianapolis Blvd., 46312. Tel: 219-397-7059.

East Gary, Lake Co., . (Name change - refer to Lake Station, Lake Co., IN, for all information.).

Fish Lake, La Porte Co., St. Anthony (1948), Rev. Michael G. Heimer.
Res., (Fish Lake) 7732 E. State Rd. 4, Walkerton, 46574. Tel: 219-369-1210.
Catechesis/Religious Programs—Students 12.

Griffith, Lake Co., St. Mary (1928), Rev. Theodore J. Mens. In res., Rev. Charles A. Mosley.
Res., 525 N. Broad St., 46319. Tel: 219-924-4163; Fax: 219-922-2291.
School—Tel: 219-924-8633. Sr. Anita Holzmer, Prin.
Sisters of St. Francis of Perpetual Adoration 4; Lay Teachers 16; Students 324.
Catechesis/Religious Programs—Tel: 219-922-2277.
Students 335.
Convent—508 N. Lafayette St., 46319. Tel: 219-922-2278.

Hamlet, Starke Co., Holy Cross (1888), Rev. Anthony L. Spanley.
Res., P.O. Box 230, 46532. Tel: 219-867-2461. [CEM]
Catechesis/Religious Programs—Students 15.
Mission—Koontz Lake, Starke Co., St. Dominic, (1981) P.O. Box 230, 46532.

Hammond, Lake Co.,

1—All Saints, (1896), Rev. J. Antonio Valtierra.
Res., 570 Sibley St., P.O. Box 836, 46325-0836. Tel: 219-932-0204; Fax: 219-932-4507.
Catechesis/Religious Programs—Josephine Perez, D.R.E.
Students 160.

2—Our Lady of Perpetual Help, (1937), Rev. John R. Winterlin; Deacon Thomas Kreidler.
Res., 7132 Arizona St., 46323. Tel: 219-844-3438; Fax: 219-844-3580.
Catechesis/Religious Programs—7128 Arizona St., 46323. Ruth Rossi, D.R.E.
Students 241.

3—St. Casimir, (1890) (Polish), Revs. Vladimir Janeczek; Andrew Malarz.
Res., 4340 Johnson St., 46327. Tel: 219-931-2589.
School—4329 Cameron St., 46327. Tel: 219-932-2686. Mrs. Stasia Krempa, Prin.
Lay Teachers 12; Students 271.
Catechesis/Religious Programs—Tel: 219-931-8466.
Students 50.

4—St. Catherine of Siena, (1956), Rev. Larry J. Kew; Sr. Margaret Urban, P.H.J.C., Pastoral Assoc.
Res., 6605 Kentucky Ave., 46323. Tel: 219-845-1939; Fax: 219-845-4772.
School—6525 Kentucky Ave., 46323. Tel: 219-845-1217; Fax: 219-845-1591. Christine Nielsen, Prin.
Poor Handmaids of Jesus Christ 1; Lay Teachers 9; Students 185.
Catechesis/Religious Programs—Tel: 219-845-2207. Mrs. Shirley Brown, D.R.E.
Students 70.
Convent—Tel: 219-845-5341.

5—St. John Bosco, (1934), Revs. Richard Orlinski; Ian J. Williams; Deacon Robert DeVore.
Res., 7113 Columbia Ave., 46324. Tel: 219-844-9027; Fax: 219-844-6986.
Pastoral Center: 1247-171st Pl., 46324. Fax: 219-989-7947.
School—(Grades K-8) 1231-171st Pl., 46324. Tel: 219-845-6226; Fax: 219-989-7946. James O'Donnell, Prin.
Lay Teachers 12; Students 225.
Catechesis/Religious Programs—Tel: 219-844-9027, Ext. 305. Mrs. Vickie Blackwood, D.R.E.
Students 68.

6—St. Joseph, (1879), Rev. Roy T. Beeching.
Res., 5304 Hohman Ave., 46320. Tel: 219-932-0702; Fax: 219-932-0059.
Catechesis/Religious Programs—Tel: 219-932-7294. Joan Crist, D.R.E.
Students 89.

7—St. Margaret Mary, (1947), Rev. Matthew C. Iwuji.
Res., 1445 Hoffman St., 46327. Tel: 219-931-5229; Fax: 219-937-4357.

8—St. Mary, (1912) (Polish). Unassigned.
Res., 931 Merrill St., 46320. Tel: 219-838-3680.
Church—Morris & Tapper Aves., 46320. Tel: 219-933-9772.
Catechesis/Religious Programs—Tel: 219-844-9027; Fax: 219-989-7947.
Students 3.

Hebron, Porter Co., St. Helen (1946), Rev. Derrick F. Dudash.
Res., 302 N. Madison St., 46341. Tel: 219-996-4611.
Catechesis/Religious Programs—Tel: 219-996-4612. D.R.E.: Susan Witt; Karen Yankauskas.
Students 109.

Highland, Lake Co., Our Lady of Grace (1949), Revs. Edward J. Moszur; Kevin R. Huber. In res., Rev. Jon J. Plavcan.
Office: 3005 Condit St., 46322. Tel: 219-838-0395; Fax: 219-972-6372.
School—3025 Highway Ave., 46322. Tel: 219-838-2901; Fax: 219-972-6389. Marilyn Tomko, Prin.
Lay Teachers 14; Students 243.
Catechesis/Religious Programs—Tel: 219-838-6790. Alice Lewinski, D.R.E.
Students 203.

St. James the Less (1967), Revs. Francis M. Lazar; Lys Florival, C.S.Sp.; Deacons Martin Denkhoff; Raymond Dec.
Mailing Address: 9640 Kennedy Ave., 46322.
Res., 2703 45th St., 46322. Tel: 219-924-4220; Fax: 219-924-4295.
Catechesis/Religious Programs—Tel: 219-924-4222. Barbara Letts, D.R.E.
Students 427.

Hobart, Lake Co., St. Bridget (1873), Revs. Dominic V. Bertino; Dave W. Kime; Deacon Richard W. Huber.
Res., 568 E. Second St., 46342. Tel: 219-942-6441; Fax: 219-942-4573.
School—(Grades PreK-8) 107 Main St., 46342. Tel: 219-942-1894. Sr. Rita Marie Malachinski, S.S.J., Prin.
Lay Teachers 13; Students 285.
Catechesis/Religious Programs—219-945-0186
Students 199.

Kingsford Heights, La Porte Co., Immaculate Heart of Mary (1953). Closed. For inquiries for parish records contact St. Anthony, Fish Lake.

Knox, Starke Co., St. Thomas Aquinas (1923), Rev. John V. Scott.
Res., 406 E. Washington St., 46534. Tel: 219-772-4134.
Catechesis/Religious Programs—Students 76.

Kouts, Porter Co., St. Mary (1884), Rev. Thomas T. Tibbs.
Res., P.O. Box 663, 46347. Tel: 219-766-3680. [CEM]
Catechesis/Religious Programs—Susan Keller, D.R.E.
Students 110.

Lake Station, Lake Co., St. Francis Xavier (1930), Rev. Robert B. Evers; Deacon Leonard Holland.
Res., 2447 Putnam St., 46405. Tel: 219-962-8626; Fax: 219-962-8627. [CEM]
School—2453 Putnam St., 46405. Tel: 219-962-4507. Carol Brendza, Prin.
Lay Teachers 5; Students 115.
Catechesis/Religious Programs—Laverne Papich, D.R.E.
Students 155.

La Porte, La Porte Co., St. Joseph (1858), Rev. Theodore A. Nordquist; Deacon Robert Bucheit.
Res., 109 C St., 46350. Tel: 219-362-9595. [CEM]
School—101 C St., 46350. Tel: 219-362-6472; Fax: 219-362-2707. Sr. M. James Kuzell, Prin.
Sisters of St. Francis of Perpetual Adoration 3; Lay Teachers 10; Students 218.
Catechesis/Religious Programs—Students 156.
Convent—102 B St., 46350. Tel: 219-362-2587.

St. Peter (1853), Rev. George M. Vrabely.
Res., 1104 Monroe St., 46350. Tel: 219-362-6186.
Catechesis/Religious Programs—1110 Monroe St., 46350. Tel: 219-362-2509; Fax: 219-362-2748. Patricia Poleski, D.R.E.
Students 357.

Sacred Heart (1912) (Polish), Rev. Gerald A. Sroka.
Res., 130 Bach St., 46350. Tel: 219-362-2815; Fax: 219-362-4822. [JC]
Catechesis/Religious Programs—Joan Kowalczyk, D.R.E.
Students 123.

Lowell, Lake Co., St. Edward (1870), Rev. Peter J. Muha.
Res., 216 S. Nichols St., 46356. Tel: 219-696-7307; Fax: 219-696-3525. [CEM]
School—210 S. Nichols St., 46356. Tel: 219-696-9876; Fax: 219-696-2524.
Lay Teachers 11; Students 135.
Catechesis/Religious Programs—Tel: 219-696-4282; Fax: 219-696-3525. Maureen Margis, D.R.E.
Students 250.
Mission—Shelby, Lake Co., St. Theresa, 23315 Shelby Rd., Shelby, 46377.

Merrillville, Lake Co.,

1—Our Lady of Consolation, (1947), Rev. Joseph E. Vamos; Deacon Robert E. Gill.
Res., 8303 Taft St., 46410. Tel: 219-769-2785; Fax: 219-769-2177.
Catechesis/Religious Programs—Tel: 219-769-1755. Bernadette Burosh, D.R.E.
Students 347.

2—St. Andrew, (1965), Rev. Terrence R. Chase; Deacon George V. Modrak.
Res., 801 W. 73rd Ave., 46410. Tel: 219-769-8534; Fax: 219-769-8543.
School—Tel: 219-769-2049. June Kachur, Prin.
Lay Teachers 10; Students 180.
Catechesis/Religious Programs—Tel: 219-769-2049.
Students 225.
Mission—Gary, St. Hedwig, 1746 Pennsylvania St., 46407.

3—St. Joan of Arc, (1968), Rev. Sammie L. Maletta.
Res., 200 E. 78th Ave., 46410. Tel: 219-769-1973; Fax: 219-769-9056.
Catechesis/Religious Programs—Tel: 219-769-2037. Bunny Callahan, D.R.E.
Students 88.
St. Joan of Arc Center—.

4—Ss. Peter and Paul, (1841), Rev. Dennis J. Teles.
Res., 5885 Harrison St., 46410. Tel: 219-980-2693; Fax: 219-980-2851. [CEM]
Catechesis/Religious Programs—Tel: 219-887-2940. Paula Burrell, D.R.E.
Students 103.

5—St. Stephen, Martyr, (1968), Rev. Michael L. Maginot.
Res., 5920 Waite St., 46410. Tel: 219-980-9348; Fax: 219-980-9354.
Catechesis/Religious Programs—5885 Harrison, 46410. Tel: 219-887-2940.
Students 25.

Michigan City, La Porte Co.,

1—St. Mary of the Immaculate Conception, (1849), Rev. James P. McGrogan. In res., Rev. James Meade.
Res., 411 W. 11th St., 46360. Tel: 219-874-7231.
School—(Grades PreK-8) 321 W. 11th St., 46360. Tel: 219-873-1321; Fax: 219-873-1329. Dorothy Murphy, Prin.
Lay Teachers 11; Students 222.
Mission—Michigan City, Sacred Heart, 1001 W. Eighth St., 46360.
Catechesis/Religious Programs—Students 22.

2—Notre Dame, (1953), Rev. Richard H. Ameling.
Res., 1010 Moore Rd., 46360. Tel: 219-872-4844; Fax: 219-872-2510.
School—(Grades PreK-8). Tel: 219-872-6216; Fax: 219-872-6216. Mrs. Karen Breen, Prin.
Lay Teachers 18; Students 252.
Catechesis/Religious Programs—Students 23.

3—Queen of All Saints, (1950), Revs. Michael J. Yadron; Andrew J. Corona.
Res., 606 S. Woodland Ave., 46360. Tel: 219-872-9196; Fax: 219-872-9176.
School—1715 E. Barker Ave., 46360. Tel: 219-872-4420; Fax: 219-872-1943. Chet A. Nordyke, Prin.
Sisters of Holy Cross 1; Lay Teachers 20; Students 390.
Catechesis/Religious Programs—Tel: 219-878-9348. Kathy Schroeder, D.R.E.
Students 260.
Convent—Tel: 219-872-5401.

4—St. Stanislaus Kostka, (1891) (Polish), Rev. Walter M. Ciesla; Deacon Daniel Bowmar.
Res., 109 Ann St., 46360. Tel: 219-879-9281; Fax: 219-879-6501.
School—1506 Washington St., 46360. Tel: 219-872-2258; Fax: 219-872-2295.
Lay Teachers 9; Students 162.
Catechesis/Religious Programs—203 Benton St., 46360. Tel: 219-872-1257. Antoinette Sajewski, D.R.E.
Students 76.

5—Sacred Heart Mission, (1915) (Lebanese), Rev. James P. McGrogan, Admin.
Res., 1001 W. Eighth St., 46360. Tel: 219-874-7231; Fax: 219-873-1329.
Catechesis/Religious Programs—Students 50.

Munster, Lake Co., St. Thomas More (1945), Revs. Richard A. Emerson; William F. O'Toole; Lee R. Purcell; Deacon Joseph Sobek.
Res., 8501 Calumet Ave., 46321. Tel: 219-836-8610; Fax: 219-836-9185.
School—Tel: 219-836-9151; Fax: 219-836-0982. Kevin T. Zajdel, Ed.D., Prin.
Lay Teachers 30; Students 565.
Catechesis/Religious Programs—Tel: 219-836-9152. Sr. Marilyn Hettinger, D.R.E.
Students 669.

New Chicago, Lake Co., Assumption of the Blessed Virgin Mary (P.O. Hobart) (1917) (Polish), Rev. Martin J. Dobrzynski.
Res., 3530 Illinois St., Hobart, 46342. Tel: 219-962-1073.
Catechesis/Religious Programs—Tel: 219-962-6678.
Students 50.

North Judson, Starke Co., Ss. Cyril and Methodius (1881), Rev. Mark G. Mazza.
Res., 303 Keller Ave., 46366. Tel: 219-896-2195. [CEM]
Catechesis/Religious Programs—Students 60.

Otis, La Porte Co., St. Mary (1873) (Polish), Rev. Joseph E. Pusateri.
Res., 101 N. Church St., 46391. Tel: 219-785-2212; Fax: 219-785-4743. [CEM]
Catechesis/Religious Programs—Tel: 219-785-2160; Fax: 219-785-4743.
Students 52.

Portage, Porter Co., Nativity of Our Savior (1964), Revs. Walter J. Rakoczy; Robert T. Naglich, S.C.J.; Deacons Robert J. Bonta; Alexander A. Saims; Sr. Kay Kelly, S.P., Pastoral Assoc.
Res., 2949 Willowcreek Rd., 46368. Tel: 219-762-4858; Fax: 219-762-3094.
School—2929 Willowcreek Rd., 46368. Tel: 219-763-2400. Jo Ann Abbott, Prin.
Lay Teachers 10; Students 232.
Catechesis/Religious Programs—Marian Weeks, D.R.E.
Students 623.

Rolling Prairie, Laporte Co., St. John Kanty (1888) (Polish), Rev. Michael G. Heimer, Admin.
Res., 7732 E. State Rd. 4, Walkerton, 46574. Tel: 219-369-1210. [CEM]
Catechesis/Religious Programs—Students 48.

Saint John, Lake Co., St. John Evangelist (1839), Revs. Stephen J. Titko; James E. Wozniak.
Mailing Address: P.O. Box 360, 46373.
Res., 11211 W. 93rd St., 46373. Tel: 219-365-5678; Fax: 219-365-2703. [CEM]
Parish Office: 11301 W. 93rd Ave., P.O. Box 360, St. John, 46373.
School—9400 Wicker Ave., St. John, 46373. Tel: 219-365-5451; Fax: 219-365-6173. Patricia Panozzo, Prin.
Lay Teachers 22; Students 380.
Catechesis/Religious Programs—Tel: 219-365-3709. Colleen Anderson, D.R.E.
Students 275.
Convent—11340 School St., 46373. Tel: 219-365-3882.

San Pierre, Starke Co., All Saints (1858), Rev. William J. Spranger.
Res., P.O. Box 56, 46374. Tel: 219-828-4281. [CEM]
Catechesis/Religious Programs—Students 7.

Schererville, Lake Co., St. Michael (1874), Revs. Patrick J. Connolly; Keith M. Virus.
Res., One Wilhelm St., 46375. Tel: 219-322-4505; Fax: 219-322-4508. [CEM]
Preschool—(Good Shepherd Program). Tel: 219-322-3077.
Students 13.
School—16 W. Wilhelm St., 46375. Tel: 219-322-4531; Fax: 219-322-1710.
Franciscan Sisters of the Sacred Heart 1; Lay Teachers 14; Students 319.
Catechesis/Religious Programs—Tel: 219-322-3077.
Students 665.

Shelby, Lake Co., St. Theresa (1939), Revs. Peter J. Muha; Bede Hepnar, O.F.M.
Res., 216 S. Nichols St., Lowell, 46356. Tel: 219-696-7307; Fax: 219-696-3525.

Valparaiso, Porter Co., Our Lady of Sorrows (South Haven) (1967), Rev. Douglas J. Mayer; Deacon Sherman Brown.
Res., 356 W. Seven Mile Rd., 46385. Tel: 219-759-2400.
Catechesis/Religious Programs—Tel: 219-759-2286.
Students 133.

St. Paul (1858), Rev. Joseph M. Pawlowski; Deacons John McGuckin; John Roscoe; Michael Foster.
Mailing Address: P.O. Box 1475, 46384-1475. Tel: 219-464-4831; Fax: 219-464-4833.
Res., 452 W. Chicago St., 46383. Tel: 219-465-3723. [CEM]
Church—P.O. Box 1475, 46384-1475. Tel: 219-464-4831; Fax: 219-464-4833.
School—352 W. Chicago St., 46383. Tel: 219-462-3374; Fax: 219-477-1763. Mary Knarr, Prin.
Lay Teachers 13; Students 184.
Catechesis/Religious Programs—Tel: 219-464-8502.
Students 715.
Child Development Center—Tel: 219-465-0882; Fax: 219-531-2047. Janet McCorkle, Dir.
St. Agnes Day Service Center—1859 Harrison Blvd., 46383. Tel: 219-477-5433. Barbara Kubiszak, Dir.

St. Elizabeth Seton (1978), Rev. David H. Gosnell; Deacons James J. Keough; Michael Prendergast.
Res., 509 W. Division Rd., 46385. Tel: 219-464-1624; Fax: 219-465-7673.
Catechesis/Religious Programs—Tel: 219-462-2202.
Students 449.

Wanatah, La Porte Co., Sacred Heart (1887), Rev. Gerald H. Schweitzer; Deacon Dale Walsh.
Res., 202 N. Ohio St, P.O. Box 386, 46390. Tel: 219-733-2955; Fax: 219-733-0001. [CEM]
Catechesis/Religious Programs—Tel: 219-733-2315.
Students 150.
Mission—LaCrosse, LaPorte Co., St. Martin, (1860) Lowell & Dominic Sts., LaCrosse, 46348.

Whiting, Lake Co.,

1—Immaculate Conception, (1922) (Slovak), Rev. Stanley J. Dominik, Admin.
Res., 2006 Schrage Ave., 46394. Tel: 219-659-0724.

2—Sacred Heart, (1889), Rev. Stanley Dominik.
Res., 1731 Laporte Ave., 46394. Tel: 219-659-0733; Fax: 219-659-0195.

3—St. Adalbert, (1902) (Polish), Rev. John J. Zemelko.
Res., 1340 121st St., 46394. Tel: 219-659-3848; Fax: 219-473-0133.

4—St. John the Baptist, (1897) (Slovak), Revs. John E. Kalicky, C.PP.S.; Edward C. Homco, C.PP.S.; Gary Scherer, C.PP.S.; Deacons David Hajduch; Joseph Manchak. In res., Rev. Leon Flaherty, C.PP.S.
Res., 1849 Lincoln Ave., P.O. Box 711, 46394. Tel: 219-659-0023; Fax: 219-473-7551.
School—1844 Lincoln Ave., 46394. Tel: 219-659-3042; Fax: 219-473-7553. Thomas J. Puplava, Prin.
Lay Teachers 22; Students 521.
Catechesis/Religious Programs—Tel: 219-659-1889; Fax: 219-473-7553. Miss Lenore R. Lazur, D.R.E.
Students 134.

5—Sts. Peter and Paul, (1910), Rev. Charles W. Niblick.
Res., 1709 Center St., 46394. Tel: 219-659-1291.

Winfield Township, Lake Co., Holy Spirit (1998), Rev. Joseph V. Murphy.
Res., 7667 E. 109th Ave., Crown Point, 46307. Tel: 219-661-0644; Fax: 219-661-0645.
Catechesis/Religious Programs—Students 180.

Chaplains of Public Institutions

Michigan City. *Indiana State Prison*. Rev. Paul LeBrun, C.S.C., P.O. Box 929, Notre Dame, 46556.

Rolling Prairie. *Sharing Meadows*. Dennis J. Blaney, P.O. Box 400, 46371. Tel: 219-778-9130.

Westville. *Westville Correctional Center*. Rev. Walter M. Ciesla, Coord., 109 Ann St., Michigan City, 46360. Tel: 219-879-9281.

On Duty Outside the Diocese:
Reverend Monsignors—
Charlebois, Robert L., 161 E. Chicago Ave., Chicago, IL 60611
Reverend Fathers—
Angotti, Joseph A., 975 Lincoln St., Fort Benning, GA 31995
Coriden, James A., 6896 Laurel St., N.W., Washington, DC 20012
Hand, Dennis M., Parroquia de los Santos Inocentes, Apartado Postal #102, La Libertad, El Salvador Central America
Hendricks, Clare, 1428 Lyon St., Columbia, TN 38401

Military Chaplains:
Reverend Fathers—
Nondorf, Aloysius J., 1962 Bay City Pl., El Paso, TX 79936

Absent on Sick Leave:
Reverend Fathers—
Murzyn, John A., P.O. Box 6189, Hilo, HI 96720

Retired:
Reverend Monsignors—
Charlebois, John J., P.O. Box 2342, Chesterton, IN 46304
Doody, Timothy F., 1501 Hoffman St., Hammond, IN 46327
Fowerbaugh, F. Raymond, 1501 Hoffman St., Hammond, IN 46327
Hoffmann, Ralph, 2103 Hawthorne Ln., Chesterton, IN 46304
Lengerich, Vincent L., 7329 E. Edgewood Ave., Indianapolis, IN 46239
Litot, Edward F., 317 Waverly Rd., La Porte, IN 46350
Martin, William F., 419 Autumn Tr., Michigan City, IN 46360
Melevage, F. J., 3214 Milestone Creek Ct., Valparaiso, IN 46383
Morales, John F., 333 N. Palm Dr., #305, Beverly Hills, CA 90210
Tomaszewski, Michael J., 2605 Hermoine Dr., Michigan City, IN 46360
Urbonas, Ignatius L., 14911-127th St., Lemont, IL 60439
Van Nevel, Albert H., 11652 Patterson St., Cedar Lake, IN 46303
Witte, John C., 3713 S. State Rd. 104, La Porte, IN 46350
Zollinger, Richard, 301 South Main St., Knox, IN 46534
Reverend Fathers—
Bargielski, John C., Albertine Home, 1501 Hoffman St., Hammond, IN 46327
Danforth, Clarence E., 1501 Hoffman St., Hammond, IN 46327
Daniels, John W., 425 Birch St., N.W., DeMotte, IN 46310
Doyle, Charles E., 105 Autumn Tr., Michigan City, IN 46360
Hogan, John A., 11620 N. Quicksilver, Tucson, AZ 46534
Kashmer, George B., 2501 Chelwood, N.E., Albuquerque, NM 87112
Kish, Matthew J., 1501 Hoffman St., Hammond, IN 46327
Kronkowski, Leonard J., 1 Cambridge Ct., Apt. 8, Michigan City, IN 46360
Lukaszewski, Leonard, 1877 W. 84th Dr., Apt. G163, Merrillville, IN 46410
Meneghello, Serafino, Via Oliosi, 13 San Massimo, Verona, Italy
Minnich, John F., P.O. Box 537, Georgetown, IN 47122
Peil, William L., 1841 N. Anthony Blvd., Fort Wayne, IN 46805
Pogorzelski, Eugeniusz, 1501 Hoffman St., Hammond, IN 46327
Strebig, John J., 135 Kingsbury Ave., LaPorte, IN 46350
Till, Joseph E., 417 Autumn Trail S., Michigan City, IN 46360
Vogt, William E., 2121 North First St., Fresno, Ca 93703
Zimmerman, Albert J., Albertine Home, 1501 Hoffman St., Hammond, IN 46327

Permanent Deacons:
Bacon, John
Bonta, Robert J.
Bowmar, Daniel L.
Brown, Sherman W.
Bucheit, Robert J.
Cichoracki, Eugene
Clark, Melvin
Codespoti, Joseph
Dec, Raymond
Delgado, Victor
Denkhoff, Martin J.
DeVore, Robert S.
Etter, James, On Leave
Fabian, Gregory G.
Foster, Michael
Gill, Robert E.
Gomez, Martin
Hajduch, David A.
Haugh, James
Hawkins, Dennis
Holland, Leonard D.
Huber, Richard
Janowski, Victor
Jefferson, Melvin
Jones, William E., Jr.
Jurasevich, Nicholas J.
Keough, James J.
Kozub, Edward
Kreidler, Thomas
Kwitko, Joseph
Lunsford, Malcolm
Maldonado, Felipe
Manchak, Joseph C.
McGuckin, John D.
Modrak, George V.

Patrick, Charles
Perez, Gilberto, On Duty Outside the Diocese
Prendergast, Michael
Richardson, Michael E.
Romanski, Frederick, On Leave
Roscoe, John
Saims, Alexander
Sobek, Joseph J., Sr.
Walsh, Dale

INSTITUTIONS LOCATED IN THE DIOCESE

[A] COLLEGES AND UNIVERSITIES

WHITING. *Calumet College of St. Joseph*, 2400 New York Ave., 46394. Tel: 219-473-7770; Fax: 219-473-4259.
Web site: www.ccsj.edu
For a complete listing, refer to the Colleges and Universities section.

[B] HIGH SCHOOLS, DIOCESAN

HAMMOND. *Bishop Noll Institute*, 1519 Hoffman St., 46327. Tel: 219-932-9058; Fax: 219-853-1736.
E-mail: sowen.bni@ash.palni.edu
Web site: www.bishopnoll.com
Diane Marie Collins, O.S.F. Priests 2; Lay Teachers 45; Students 692.

MERRILLVILLE. *Andrean High School*, 5959 Broadway, 46410. Tel: 219-887-5281; Fax: 219-981-5072. Rev. Paul E. Quanz, C.S.B., Prin.; Sr. Fabian Philothea, S.S.C.M., Asst. Prin.; Rev. John J. Fiore, C.S.B. Basilian Fathers 2; Sisters of Sts. Cyril and Methodius 4; Lay Teachers 48; Students 783.

MICHIGAN CITY. *Marquette Catholic High School*, 306 W. Tenth St., 46360. Tel: 219-873-1325; Fax: 219-873-1327.
E-mail: mhsoff@adsnet.com
Web site: www.marquette-hs.org
Patrick Cannon, Prin. Priests 1; Lay Teachers 23; Students 245.

[C] ELEMENTARY SCHOOLS, DIOCESAN

GARY. *Sr. Thea Bowman Elementary School*, 975 W. Sixth Ave., 46402-1799. Tel: 219-883-1331; Fax: 219-883-1350.
E-mail: Thea@connectinc.com
Sr. Lucy Williams, O.S.F. Sisters 1; Lay Teachers 8; Total Staff 16; Students 134.

[D] ELEMENTARY SCHOOLS, PRIVATE

ROLLING PRAIRIE. *Le Mans Academy.* (Grades 5-9), 46371. Tel: 219-778-2521; Fax: 219-778-4801.
E-mail: LMASpartan@aol.com
Web site: www.lemansacademy.org
Private boarding school for boys. Bro. William Dygent, C.S.C., Pres.; Mr. Steve Cash, Headmaster. Priests 1; Brothers 7; Lay Teachers 9; Total Staff 50; Enrollment 112.

[E] ELEMENTARY SCHOOLS, INTERPAROCHIAL

EAST CHICAGO. *Indiana Harbor Catholic Elementary School*, 3916 Pulaski St., 46312. Tel: 219-397-1122; Fax: 219-397-1972.
E-mail: FPIHCES3916@aol.com
Mrs. Francisca C. Phelps, Prin. Lay Teachers 5; Students 132. Serving the parishes of Our Lady of Guadalupe, St John Cantius, and St. Patrick in East Chicago.

[F] GENERAL HOSPITALS

CROWN POINT. *St. Anthony Medical Center of Crown Point*, 1201 S. Main St., 46307-8483. Tel: 219-738-2100; Fax: 219-757-6242
For a complete listing, refer to the Hospitals section.

DYER. *St. Margaret Mercy Healthcare Centers, South Campus*, 24 Joliet, 46311. Tel: 219-865-2141
For a complete listing, refer to the Hospitals section.

EAST CHICAGO. *St. Catherine Hospital*, 4321 Fir St., 46312. Tel: 219-392-1700; Fax: 219-392-7002.
Web site: www.StCatherineHospital.org
For a complete listing, refer to the Hospitals section.

HAMMOND. *St. Margaret Mercy Healthcare Centers - North Campus*, 5454 Hohman Ave., 46320. Tel: 219-932-2300
For a complete listing, refer to the Hospitals section.

HOBART. *St. Mary Medical Center*, 1500 S. Lake Park Ave., 46342. Tel: 219-942-0551; Fax: 219-947-6037.
Web site: www.stmary-hobart.com
For a complete listing, refer to the Hospitals section.

MICHIGAN CITY. *St. Anthony Memorial Health Centers*, 301 W. Homer St., 46360. Tel: 219-879-8511; Fax: 219-877-1409.
E-mail: SAMHC.ORG
Web site: www.SAMHC.ORG
For a complete listing, refer to the Hospitals section.

[G] PROTECTIVE INSTITUTIONS

EAST CHICAGO. *Carmelite Home for Girls*, 4840 Grasselli Ave., 46312. Tel: 219-397-1085; Fax: 219-392-3574
For a complete listing, refer to the Special Care Facilities section.

HAMMOND. *St. Joseph's Home for Boys, Inc.*, 4007 Sheffield Ave., 46327. Tel: 219-931-6451; Fax: 219-931-2241.
E-mail: stjoseph@netnitco.net
For a complete listing, refer to the Special Care Facilities section.

[H] HOMES FOR THE AGED

CROWN POINT. *Franciscan Home Care Services, Inc.*, 203 Franciscan Dr., 219-757-6423
For a complete listing, refer to the Special Care Facilities section.

Franciscan Homes & Community Services, Inc., 203 Franciscan Dr., 46307-4824. Tel: 219-757-6281; Fax: 219-757-6236.
Web site: www.franciscancommunities.com
For a complete listing, refer to the Special Care Facilities section.

HAMMOND. *Albertine Home*, 1501 Hoffman St., 46327. Tel: 219-937-0575.
E-mail: albertineusa@aol.com
For a complete listing, refer to the Special Care Facilities section.

SAN PIERRE. *Holy Cross Care Services dba Little Company of Mary Health Facility, Inc.*, 7520 S. U.S. Hwy. 421, 46374-4275. Tel: 219-828-4111; Fax: 219-828-4275
For a complete listing, refer to the Special Care Facilities section.

[I] PERSONAL PRELATURES

VALPARAISO. *Opus Dei*, 359 West 200 North, 46383. Tel: 219-462-6594; 462-0931; Fax: 219-465-6241.
E-mail: shellbourne@juno.com
Prelature of the Holy Cross and Opus Dei, Shellbourne Conference Center.

[J] MONASTERIES AND RESIDENCES OF PRIESTS AND BROTHERS

CEDAR LAKE. *Our Lady of Lourdes Friary*, 12915 Parrish St., P.O. Box 156, 46303. Tel: 219-374-5931. Franciscan Friars of the Assumption of the B.V.M. Province (Order of Friars Minor). Revs. Anthony F. Janik, O.F.M.; Francis Appelt; Bede Hepnar, O.F.M.; Bronislaus Jaskulski, O.F.M.; Myron Lowisz, O.F.M., Guardian; Clarence Mazur, O.F.M.; Andrew Meronek; Bert Pepowski; Dacian Bluma. Priests 9; Brothers 2.

San Damiano Friary, 12921 Parrish St., P.O. Box 500, 46303. Tel: 219-374-5741; Fax: 219-374-9650. Cedar Lake Franciscan Friars (Order of Friars Minor). Interprovinicial Novitiate. Revs. James G. Gannon, O.F.M., Guardian; Edward G. Tlucek, O.F.M., Dir. Novices; Ronald F. Walters, O.F.M., J.C.L., Treas. & Vicar; Theophane Ballman, O.F.M. Priests 4; Novices 4.

EAST CHICAGO. *Roque Gonzalez Residence-Jesuit Fathers*, 3905 Fir St., 46312. Tel: 219-397-1885; 397-3906; Fax: 219-932-8321.
E-mail: xctb29c@prodigy.com
Revs. Thomas M. Gannon, S.J.; James W. Schulz, S.J.

MERRILLVILLE. *Basilian Fathers Residence*, 5959 Broadway, 46410. Tel: 219-887-5284; Fax: 219-981-5072. Revs. John J. Fiore, C.S.B., Rector; Paul E. Quanz, C.S.B., Treas. Priests 2.

Salvatorian Fathers (Society of the Divine Savior), 5755 Pennsylvania St., 46410. Tel: 219-884-0714; Fax: 219-981-9224.
E-mail: zenekb@iname.com
Web site: www.sds.org
Mission House for Polish Priests and Brothers. Revs. Krzysztof Bugno; Joseph R. Zuziak, S.D.S., Vice Supr.; Edward Kawa, S.D.S.; Zenon Boczek, S.D.S.; Walter M. Pawlik, S.D.S.; Andrzej Muchla, S.D.S.; Bro. Marek Miazga, S.D.S. Priests 6; Brothers 1.

MUNSTER. *Discalced Carmelite Fathers Monastery*, 1628 Ridge Rd., 46321. Tel: 219-838-7111; Fax: 219-838-7214.
E-mail: carmel@netnitco.net
Revs. Sylwan Zielinski, O.C.D., Prior; Bronislaw F. Socha, O.C.D., Subprior; Jacek Palica, O.C.D., Second Consultor; Waclaw L. Lech, O.C.D., Sec. & Treas.; John Baptista Kolaczek, O.C.D.; Casimir Adalbert Borcz, O.C.D.; Joseph Ivans, O.C.D.; Edward C. Spyrka, O.C.D.; Thomas I. Balys, O.C.D.; Richard C. Nitschke, O.C.D.; Michael G. Veneklase, O.C.D.; John Benedict M. Merren, O.C.D.; Bro. Tomasz S. Paczek, O.C.D. Priests 12; Brothers 1.

[K] CONVENTS AND RESIDENCES OF SISTERS

GARY. *Missionaries of Charity, St. Mark Convent*, 501 W. Ridge Rd., 46408. Tel: 219-884-2140. Sr. M. Davis, M.C., Supr. Sisters 4.

EAST CHICAGO. *St. Catherine Convent*, 4325 Elm St., 46312. Tel: 219-398-0403; Fax: 219-398-9232.
E-mail: STCATHEC@aol.com
Web site: poorhandmaids.org
Poor Handmaids of Jesus Christ 5; Dominican Sister 1.

Saint Patrick Convent, 3814 Grand Blvd., 46312. Tel: 219-398-1983. Teaching and Parish Ministry, Our Lady of Victory Missionary Sisters.

HAMMOND. *Albertine Sisters (Prov. of Krakow, Poland)*, 1501 Hoffman St., 46327. Tel: 219-937-0575.
E-mail: ALBERTINEUSA@AOL.COM
Sr. Sigmunda Wojtusiak, Supr. Sisters 12.

MERRILLVILLE. *Andrean H.S. Sisters' Residence*. Sisters of SS. Cyril and Methodius, 5959 Broadway, 46410. Tel: 219-887-5287. Teaching at Andrean High School. Sisters 4.

[L] RETREAT HOUSES

EAST CHICAGO. *Bethany Retreat House*, 2202 Lituanica Ave., 46312. Tel: 219-398-5047; Fax: 219-398-9329.
E-mail: bethanyrh@sprynet.com
Web site: bethanyretreathouse.org
Sr. Joyce Diltz, P.H.J.C. Total Staff 2; Guests 269.

MICHIGAN CITY. *Angela House*, 412 W. 10th St., 46360. Tel: 219-873-1324.
E-mail: angela@ads.com
Sr. Anna Clare O'Connor, C.S.C., Dir.; Sr. Cyril Dubala, C.S.C. Total Staff 2; Total in Residence 2.

[M] DIOCESAN CHARITIES

GARY. *Catholic Charities*, 973 W. Sixth Ave., 46402. Tel: 219-882-2720; Fax: 219-886-2428.
Web site: www.catholic-charities.org/
Kenneth M. Flanagan, M.S.W., Ph.D., Diocesan Dir.

Catholic Family Service, 973 W. Sixth Ave., 46402. Tel: 219-882-2723; Fax: 219-886-2428. Marcella Walters, M.S.W., Dir., 1128 Broadway, 46402. Tel: 219-880-0280; Fax: 219-880-0281. 3901 Fir St., East Chicago, 46312. Tel: 219-397-5803; Fax: 219-397-5804. 6919 Indianapolis Blvd., Hammond, 46324. Tel: 219-844-4883; Fax: 219-844-4885. 2967 Willowcreek Rd., Portage, 46368. Tel: 219-762-1177; Fax: 219-762-1827. 1501 Franklin St., Michigan City, 46360. Tel: 219-879-9312; Fax: 219-879-9073. 166 S. West St., Crown Point, 46307. Tel: 219-662-7677; Fax: 219-662-7678.

Family Life Ministry. Tel: 219-882-2759; Fax: 219-886-2428. Legal Title: *Family Life Ministry, Refugee Assistance Program, Marriage Preparation, Rainbows, Pastor's Emergency Fund, Elizabeth Ministry and Project Respect.* 973 W. Sixth Ave., 46402. Tel: 219-882-2720; Fax: 219-886-2428.

Services to the Aging, Retired & Senior Volunteer Program. Tel: 219-882-2737; Fax: 219-886-2428. LaPorte & Starke Co., 1501 Franklin St., Michigan City, 46360. Tel: 219-874-8195; Fax: 219-879-9073. Lake Co., 973 W. Sixth Ave., 46402. Tel: 219-882-2737; Fax: 219-886-2428.

Senior Companion Program. Tel: 219-882-7331; Fax: 219-886-2428. Lake Co., 973 W. Sixth Ave., 46402. Tel: 219-882-7331; Fax: 219-886-2428.

Foster Grandparent Program, 973 W. 6th Ave., 46402. Tel: 219-882-2720; Fax: 219-886-2428.

[N] NEWMAN APOSTOLATES

GARY. *Indiana University Northwest*, 501 W. Ridge Rd., 46408. Tel: 219-887-0514.
E-mail: nsuman@juno.com
Rev. John T. Ambre. For Catholic students attending Indiana University, Northwest. Students 5,000.

VALPARAISO. *Newman Apostolate-Valparaiso University*, 1511 La Porte Ave., 46383-5818. Tel: 219-464-4042; Fax: 219-462-2711.
E-mail: KMccarth@valpo.edu
Web site: www.balpo.edu/student/stt/
St. Teresa, Catholic Student Center of Avila. Chapel and Center for Students attending Valparaiso University. Rev. Kevin P. McCarthy, Chap. Students 836.

[O] MISCELLANEOUS

GARY. *Sojourner Truth House*, 410 W. 13th Ave., 46407. Tel: 219-885-2282; Fax: 219-885-1984.
E-mail: STHphic@aol.com
Web site: STHjopeg@aol.com
A ministry for women and children (Professional Clothes Closet, Computer, Parenting, Lifeskill

Classes, Transitional Housing, Hospitality Center, Laundry Facilities, connection to agencies.).

DYER. *Amicare Home Health Services, Inc.*, 24 Joliet St., 46311. Tel: 219-322-1323. Mr. Gary Baum, Pres.

EAST CHICAGO, IL. *Health Visions Midwest*, 4522 Indianapolis Blvd., 46312. Tel: 219-397-4335; Fax: 219-397-4651.
E-mail: akampwerth@hvwsa.org
Mr. Donald G. Barnes, Pres. & CEO.

Office of Hispanic Ministry, 1709 E. 138th St., P.O. Box 3027, 46312. Tel: 219-397-2125; Fax: 219-397-2168.
E-mail: atorresedcgary.org
Web site: www.dcgary.org
Angel Torres, Dir.; Adeline Torres, Asst.

St. Catherine Hospital of East Chicago, 4321 Fir St., 46312. Tel: 219-392-7009; Fax: 219-392-7037.
E-mail: tshropshire@ancilla.org
Affiliate of Ancilla Systems, Inc. Sponsored by the Poor Handmaids of Jesus Christ.

HAMMOND. *Alverno Clinical Laboratories, Inc. (ACL)*, 2434 Interstate Plaza, 46324-3361. Tel: 219-989-3800.

Alverno-Hammond Corporation. 1515 Dragoon Tr., P.O. Box 1290, Mishawaka, 46546-1290.

The Beginning Experience, St. John Bosco Parish Center, 1247 171st Pl., 46324. Tel: 219-989-8915; Fax: 219-989-8916.
E-mail: imc@beimc.attmail.com
Web site: www.beinfo.com

Heartland Center, 7128 Arizona Ave., 46323. Tel: 219-844-7515; Fax: 219-844-7566.
E-mail: heartlandc@aol.com
Web site: www.thetimesonline.com/org/Heartland
Office of Peace and Social Justice of the Diocese of Gary. Revs. Thomas M. Gannon, S.J.; James W. Schulz, S.J. Total Staff 4.

Spiritual Life/Seimetz Center, 1441 Hoffman St., 46327. Tel: 219-932-8321; Fax: 219-932-8321.
E-mail: xctb29c@prodigy.com
Total Staff 6.

HOBART. *Ancilla Systems Incorporated*, 1000 S. Lake Park Ave., 46342. Tel: 219-947-8500; Fax: 219-947-4037.
E-mail: KQuinn@ancilla.org
Web site: www.ancilla.org

Ancilla Systems Foundation, Inc., 46342. Tel: 219-947-8516; Fax: 219-947-4037.

MICHIGAN CITY. *Alverno-Michigan City Corp.* 1515 Dragoon Tr., P.O. Box 1290, Mishawaka, 46546-1290.

VALPARAISO. *Camp Lawrence.* Diocesan Spiritual Center and Youth Camp. 68 E. 700 N., 46383. Tel: 219-462-8243; 462-5261; Fax: 219-477-4452.
E-mail: thorstand@gte/net
Catholic Youth Organization, 5284 Broadway, Merrillville, 46410. Tel: 219-887-9581.

RELIGIOUS INSTITUTES OF MEN REPRESENTED IN THE DIOCESE

For further details refer to the corresponding bracketed number in the Religious Institutes of Men or Women section.

[0170]—*Basilian Fathers.* (Toronto).—C.S.B.

[0200]—*Benedictine Monks.*—O.S.B.

[0600]—*Brothers of the Congregation of Holy Cross.*—C.S.C.

[1130]—*Congregation of the Priests of the Sacred Heart.*—S.C.J.

[0480]—*Conventual Franciscans.* (Croatia).—O.F.M.Conv.

[0260]—*Discalced Carmelite Friars.* (Holy Ghost Prov., Poland).—O.C.D.

[0520]—*Franciscan Friars.* (Prov. of Assumption of B.V.M.; Prov. of St. John the Baptist; Prov. of the Sacred Heart).—O.F.M.

[0690]—*Jesuit Fathers .*—S.J.

[0610]—*Priests of the Congregation of Holy Cross.*—C.S.C.

[1200]—*Society of the Divine Savior.*—S.D.S.

[1060]—*Society of the Precious Blood.*—C.PP.S.

RELIGIOUS INSTITUTES OF WOMEN REPRESENTED IN THE DIOCESE

[]—*Albertine Sisters.* (Prov. of Krakow, Poland).—C.S.A.

[0230]—*Benedictine Sisters of the Pontifical Jurisdiction.*—O.S.B.

[0360]—*Carmelite Sisters of the Divine Heart of Jesus.*—Carmel D.C.J.

[3710]—*Congregation of the Sisters of Saint Agnes.*—C.S.A.

[1920]—*Congregation of the Sisters of the Holy Cross.*—C.S.C.

[1070-03]—*Dominican Sisters.*—O.P.

[1070-13]—*Dominican Sisters.*—O.P.

[1210]—*Franciscan Sisters of Chicago.*—O.S.F.

[1450]—*Franciscan Sisters of the Sacred Heart.*—O.S.F.

[2710]—*Missionaries of Charity.*—M.C.

[3130]—*Our Lady of Victory Missionary Sisters.*—O.L.V.M.

[3230]—*Poor Handmaids of Jesus Christ.*—P.H.J.C.

[2970]—*School Sisters of Notre Dame.*—S.S.N.D.

[3340]—*Sisters of Providence.*—S.P.

[3780]—*Sisters of Saints Cyril and Methodius.*—SS.C.M.

[]—*Sisters of St. Anne of Bangalore.*—S.A.B.

[1640]—*Sisters of St. Francis of Perpetual Adoration.*—O.S.F.

[3930]—*Sisters of St. Joseph of the Third Order of St. Francis.* (Immaculate Conception Prov.).—S.S.J.-T.O.S.F.

DIOCESAN CEMETERIES

HAMMOND. *Saint John-Saint Joseph*, 1547 167th St., 46324. Tel: 219-844-9475.

MICHIGAN CITY. *Saint Stanislaus*, 1015 Greenwood, 46360. Tel: 219-874-4310.

NECROLOGY

† Ficko, Anthony D, Whiting, IN Immaculate Conception. —Died Aug. 23, 2000.

† McGinnity, Ambrose T., (Retired). —Died Feb. 27, 2000.

Diocese of Gaylord

(Dioecesis Gaylordensis)

Most Reverend

PATRICK R. COONEY, S.T.D., S.T.L.

Bishop of Gaylord; ordained December 20, 1959; appointed Titular Bishop of Hodelm and Auxiliary Bishop of Detroit December 3, 1982; consecrated January 27, 1983; appointed Bishop of Gaylord November 21, 1989; installed January 28, 1990. *Res., 1665 W. M-32, Seton Building, Gaylord, MI, 49735.*

ESTABLISHED JULY 20, 1971.

Square Miles 11,171.

Comprises the following 21 Counties in the State of Michigan: Alcona, Alpena, Antrim, Benzie, Charlevoix, Cheboygan, Crawford, Emmet, Grand Traverse, Iosco, Kalkaska, Leelanau, Manistee, Missaukee, Montmorency, Ogemaw, Oscoda, Otsego, Presque Isle, Roscommon and Wexford.

For legal titles of parishes and diocesan institutions, consult the Chancery Office.

Diocesan Pastoral Center: 1665 W. M-32, Gaylord, MI, 49735. Tel.: 517-732-5147; Fax: 517-732-1706.

Web site address: www.dioceseofgaylord.org

E-mail address: msteffel@dioceseofgaylord.org

STATISTICAL OVERVIEW

Personnel	
Bishop	1
Priests: Diocesan Active in Diocese	46
Priests: Active Outside Diocese	2
Priests: Retired, Sick or Absent	25
Number of Diocesan Priests	73
Religious Priests in Diocese	16
Extern Priests in Diocese	6
Ordinations:	
Diocesan Priests	1
Transitional Deacons	2
Permanent Deacons in Diocese	12
Total Brothers	1
Total Sisters	49
Parishes	
Parishes	81
With Resident Pastor:	
Resident Diocesan Priests	44
Resident Religious Priests	11
Without Resident Pastor:	
Administered by Priests	16
Administered by Deacons	5
Administered by Women Religious	3
Administered by Lay People	2
Professional Ministry Personnel:	
Brothers	1
Sisters	12
Lay Ministers	53
Welfare	
Catholic Hospitals	3
Total Assisted	369,365
Residential Care of Children	2
Total Assisted	29
Specialized Homes	1
Total Assisted	633
Special Centers for Social Services	19
Total Assisted	4,433
Educational	
Diocesan Students in Other Seminaries	9
Total Seminarians	9
High Schools, Diocesan and Parish	4
Total Students	596
Elementary Schools, Diocesan and Parish	17
Total Students	2,686
Catechesis/Religious Education:	
High School Students	1,888
Elementary Students	5,423
Total Students Under Catholic Instruction	10,602
Teachers in the Diocese:	
Sisters	6
Lay Teachers	210
Vital Statistics	
Receptions into the Church:	
Infant Baptism Totals	1,078
Adult Baptism Totals	177
Received into Full Communion	155
First Communions	1,134
Confirmations	1,539
Marriages:	
Catholic	319
Interfaith	212
Total Marriages	531
Deaths	944
Total Catholic Population	82,835
Total Population	458,130

Former Bishops—Most Rev. EDMUND C. SZOKA, J.C.L., D.D., First Bishop of Gaylord; ord. June 5, 1954; cons. July 20, 1971; installed July 20, 1971; appt. Archbishop of Detroit March 28, 1981; installed May 17, 1981; named Cardinal Priest May 29, 1988; elevated June 28, 1988 Assigned to the Vatican, 1990—Most Rev. ROBERT J. ROSE, S.T.L., D.D., ord. Dec. 21, 1955; appt. Bishop of Gaylord Oct. 13, 1981; installed Dec. 6, 1981; transferred to Diocese of Grand Rapids July 11, 1989; installed Aug. 30, 1989.

Vicar General—Rev. EDWIN A. THOME.

Diocesan Offices and Departments

Diocesan Pastoral Center—611 W. North St., Gaylord, 49735-8349. Tel: 989-732-5147; Fax: 989-705-3589. Office Hours: Mon.-Fri. 8-4:30 All business should be directed to this office.

Consultors, Diocesan Board of—Revs. JAMES L. BRUCKSCH; ANDREW G. BUVALA, O.F.M.; FRANCIS J. MURPHY; THOMAS A. NEIS; DENNIS R. STILWELL; EDWIN A. THOME.

Members of the Presbyteral Council—

Elected Members—Revs. ALEXANDER BORUTA, O.F.M.; ANDREW G. BUVALA, O.F.M.; CHARLES DONAJKOWSKI; GERALD F. MICKETTI; ISADORE J. MIKULSKI; FRANCIS J. MURPHY; THOMAS A. NEIS; FRANCIS C. PARTRIDGE; DENNIS R. STILWELL.

Appointed Members—Revs. JAMES L. BRUCKSCH; JAMES A. HOLTZ; EDWIN A. THOME; JOHN E. MCCRACKEN.

Vicars (by region)—Rev. DONALD R. GEYMAN, Alpena; Rev. ANTHONY M. CITRO, Gaylord; Rev. MICHAEL P. CONNER, Manistee; Rev. JAMES A. SUCHOCKI, Petoskey; Rev. JAMES K. GARDINER, Traverse City; Rev. J. AUGUST FRANCZEK, West Branch.

Administrative Services, Secretariat for—MICHAEL E. STEFFEL, Dir., *611 W. North St., Gaylord, 49735.* Tel: 989-732-5147.

Audio-Visual Resource Center—Ms. TERI HALL, *611 W. North St., Gaylord, 49735.* Tel: 989-732-5147.

Archivist—Rev. GERALD F. MICKETTI, *611 W. North St., Gaylord, 49735.* Tel: 989-732-5147.

Catechesis—(See Faith Formation of Children and Youth.).

Communications, Secretariat for—CANDACE NEFF, Dir., *611 W. North St., Gaylord, 49735.* Tel: 989-732-5147.

Council of Catholic Women, Diocesan—BETTY PRESEAU, Pres., *2894 Levering Rd., Cheboygan, 49721.* Tel: 231-627-4885.

Cursillo—Rev. ANTHONY CITRO, *P.O. Box 248, Roscommon, 48653.* Tel: 989-275-5212.

Ecumenical and Interreligious Affairs, Delegate for—Rev. JOSEPH P. GRAFF, *St. Anne Parish, 817 Sable, Alpena, 49707.* Tel: 989-356-0622.

Faith Formation of Adults, Secretariat for—Miss MARLENE PEPLINSKI, Dir., *611 W. North St., Gaylord, 49735.* Tel: 989-732-5147.

Faith Formation of Children and Youth, Secretariat for—Revs. JOHN E. MCCRACKEN, Dir. DANIEL B. GALLAGHER, Staff, *611 W. North St., Gaylord, 49735-8349.* Tel: 989-732-5147.

Finance Council, Diocesan—Most Rev. PATRICK R. COONEY; Rev. EDWIN A. THOME; BARBARA BENSON; HOWARD MCCOLLEY; EDWARD CARLSON; WILLIAM CORBETT; DACIA DENTON; ROSEMARY BURMEISTER; KIM SMITH.

Holy Childhood Pontifical Association—Rev. Msgr. GERARD F. GUZIKOWSKI, *371 Fifth St., Manistee, 49660.* Tel: 231-723-2165.

Native American Apostolate—Rev. ANDREW G. BUVALA, O.F.M., Coord., *Blessed Kateri Tekakwitha Parish, P.O. Box 369, Suttons Bay, 49682.* Tel: 231-271-6651.

Knights of Columbus—MICHAEL J. STANCHINA, Eastern Diocesan Prog. Dir., *937 Joyce Court, Mio, 48647.* Tel: 989-848-5322. ROGER HANSEN, Western Diocesan Prog. Dir., *2853 Victoria Dr., Traverse City, 49684.* Tel: 231-947-6884.

Worship and Liturgical Formation, Secretariat for—Sr. ARLENE BENNETT R.S.M., Dir.; Rev. DUANE A. WACHOWIAK, Staff, *611 W. North St., Gaylord, 49735.* Tel: 989-732-5147.

Marriage Enrichment, Secretariat for—Sr. ARLENE BENNETT, R.S.M., Dir., *611 W. North St., Gaylord, 49735.* Tel: 517-732-5147.

Migrant Apostolate—Rev. CHAD W. ZIELINSKI, Pastor, Admin. of Diocese Mission for Hispanics, *P.O. Box 257, Empire, 49630.* Tel: 231-326-5255. Rev. REYNALDO GARCIA, S.J., Pastor, Pastoral Matters of Diocesan Mission for Hispanics, *St. Wenceslaus Church, 8500 E. Kolarik, Suttons Bay, 49682.* Tel: 231-271-3574.

Parish Social Ministries—Vacant, Dir., *611 W. North St., Gaylord, 49735.* Tel: 989-732-5147.

Pastoral Care of Priests, Pastoral Administrators and Permanent Deacons—Rev. JOHN E. MCCRACKEN, Delegate, *611 W. North St., Gaylord, 49735.* Tel: 989-732-5147.

Priests' Retirement Fund—Most Rev. PATRICK R. COONEY, Chm. Board of Directors. Elected Members: Revs. THOMAS M. DOMINIAK; ROBERT W. NALLEY; EDWIN A. THOME; JAMES P. HAYDEN. Appointed Members: MARGE WAGNER; Rev. JOHN E. MCCRACKEN.

Vocations and Pastoral Care of Seminarians, Delegate for—Rev. JAMES P. HAYDEN, *Diocese of Gaylord, 611 W. North St., Gaylord, 49735.* Tel: 989-732-5147.

Propagation of the Faith—Rev. Msgr. GERARD F. GUZIKOWSKI, Dir., *Guardian Angels Parish, 317 Fifth St., Manistee, 49660.* Tel: 231-723-2165.

St. Vincent De Paul, Society of—Particular Council of Tawas, *115 First St., Tawas City, 49763.* Roscommon County, *Box 644, Prudenville, 48651.* Tel: 989-366-7613. *1028 Hannah, Traverse City, 49684.* Frederic Ozanam Council of St. Vincent de Paul, *821 Lake St., P.O. Box 37, Roscommon, 48653.* Tel: 989-275-3036. JAMES C. HODGES, Dir. BERNARD S. SCHWARTZ, Volunteer Also particular councils in Cheboygan, Hillman, Hale, Prescott, Mikado and Alpena.

Spiritual Formation—MICHAEL FONSECA, Dir., *611 W. North St., Gaylord, 49735.* Tel: 989-732-5147.

Tribunal Diocesan—Rev. ROBERT W. NALLEY, Judicial Vicar. Judges: Revs. DENNIS R. STILWELL; R. DALE MAGOON; WILLIAM L. ZWIEFKA; Revs. JAMES A. HOLTZ, Defender of the Bond. Procurators-Advocates: JAMES P. HAYDEN; CHARLES G. DONAJKOWSKI; PATRICIA WARD, Auditor; MARY DICKERSON, Notary Inquiries may be made through the local pastors or directed to this office: *611 W. North St., Gaylord, 49735.* Tel: 989-732-5147.

CLERGY, PARISHES, MISSIONS AND PAROCHIAL SCHOOLS

CITY OF GAYLORD
(Otsego County)

1—ST. MARY CATHEDRAL, Revs. John E. McCracken, Rector; Garth L. Hilmer; Sr. Cecilia Faber, O.P., Pastoral Min.
Res., 606 N. Ohio Ave., 49735. Tel: 989-732-5448; Fax: 989-705-3585. [CEM]
Catechesis/Religious Programs—Students 486.

OUTSIDE THE CITY OF GAYLORD

Acme, Grand Traverse Co., Christ the King, Rev. Duane A. Wachowiak, Admin.
Res., P.O. Box 95, 49610. Tel: 231-938-9214; Fax: 231-938-3266.
Church—3801 Shore Rd., 49610.
School—Grand Traverse Area Schools. See separate listing under Institutions Located in the Diocese.
Catechesis/Religious Programs—Patricia Cesere, D.R.E.
Students 394.

Afton, Cheboygan Co., St. Monica, Rev. Thomas M. Dominiak.
Res., P.O. Box 130, Onaway, 49765. Tel: 989-733-4043; Fax: 989-733-6053. [CEM]
Church—M-68, 49705.

Alpena, Alpena Co.,

1—ST. ANNE, Revs. Joseph P. Graff; Wladyslaw Marczynski.
Res., 817 Sable, 49707. Tel: 989-356-0622; Fax: 989-354-3918. [JC]
Church—201 S. Ninth Ave., 49707.
Catechesis/Religious Programs—Sylvia Owens, D.R.E.
Students 218.

2—ST. BERNARD, Rev. David E. Greka.
Res., 322 Chisholm St., 49707. Tel: 989-354-2676; Fax: 989-354-5142. [JC]
Catechesis/Religious Programs—Tel: 989-354-8018. Geraldine LaCross, D.R.E.
Students 27.

3—ST. JOHN THE BAPTIST, Rev. Kenneth R. Stachnik.
Res., 2550 S. First Ave., 49707. Tel: 989-354-3019; Fax: 989-358-9079.

4—ST. MARY, Rev. Donald R. Geyman.
Res., 516 N. Second Ave., 49707. Tel: 989-354-2322; Fax: 989-356-9637. [JC]
Catechesis/Religious Programs—Tel: 989-354-8655. Mrs. Cherie Smigelski, D.R.E.
Students 145.
Convent—120 E. Miller St., 49707. Tel: 989-354-2505.

Alverno, Cheboygan Co., St. Francis of Assisi. Closed. For sacramental records contact St. Mary-St. Charles Parish, Cheboygan.

Atlanta, Montmorency Co., Jesus the Good Shepherd, Rev. Vianney C. Sipulski, O.F.M.
Res., P.O. Box 216, Hillman, 49746. Tel: 989-742-4542; Fax: 989-742-8090.
Church—4521 County Rd. 491, 49746.

Bay Shore, Emmet Co., St. Francis Solanus, Rev. James A. Suchocki.
Res., 513 State St., Petoskey, 49770. Tel: 231-347-4133; Fax: 231-347-4134.
Church—Townline Rd., 49770.

Beaver Island, Charlevoix Co., Holy Cross. Unassigned.
Res., P.O. Box 145, St. James, 49782. [CEM]
Church—St. James, Kings Hwy., 49782. Tel: 231-448-2230; Fax: 231-448-2230.

Bellaire, Antrim Co., St. Luke, Sr. Celine Goessl, S.C.S.C., Admin.; Sr. Kathy Lange, S.C.S.C., Pastoral Assoc.
Res., 3078 M-88, P.O. Box 799, 49615-0799. Tel: 231-533-8121; Fax: 231-533-8759.

Black River, Alcona Co., St. Gabriel, Rev. Lawrence A. Kelleher.
Res., 2188 W. Nicholson Hill Rd., Ossineke, 49766-9736. Tel: 989-471-2555; Fax: 989-471-3221. [CEM]
Church—5570 N. Lake Shore Dr., 48721.

Boyne City, Charlevoix Co., St. Matthew, Rev. Francis C. Partridge.
Res., 1303 Boyne Ave., 49712. Tel: 231-582-7718; Fax: 231-582-7490. [JC]
Catechesis/Religious Programs—Tel: 231-582-6589. Suzanne Dzwik, D.R.E.
Students 125.

Boyne Falls, Charlevoix Co., St. Augustine, Rev. Francis C. Partridge.
Res., 1303 Boyne Ave., Boyne City, 49712. Tel: 231-582-7718; Fax: 231-582-7490. [CEM]
Church—Grove St., 49713. Tel: 231-549-2350.
Catechesis/Religious Programs—Frank Wasylewski, D.R.E.
Students 52.

Burt Lake, Cheboygan Co., Assumption of St. Mary, Rev. Sylvester Micek, O.F.M.
Res., P.O. Box 122, Pellston, 49769. Tel: 231-539-8805.

Cadillac, Wexford Co., St. Ann, Revs. Francis J. Murphy; Daniel B. Gallagher; Sr. Hilda Sucher, R.S.M., Pastoral Min.
Res., 800 W. 13th St., 49601-9281. Tel: 231-775-2471; Fax: 231-775-0161. [CEM]

Cedar, Leelanau Co., Holy Rosary, Deacon John Moeggenberg, Admin.
Res., 3919 E. Gatzke Rd., 49621. Tel: 231-228-5429; Fax: 231-228-5529. [CEM]

Charlevoix, Charlevoix Co., St. Mary, Rev. Thomas A. Neis.
Res., 102 W. Garfield, 49720. Tel: 231-547-6652.
Catechesis/Religious Programs—Students 116.

Cheboygan, Cheboygan Co., St. Mary-St. Charles, Rev. Dennis R. Stilwell. Pastoral Assocs.: Deacon Stan Szczepanski; Mrs. Patricia Watson.
Mailing Address: P.O. Box 40, 49721. Tel: 231-627-2105; Fax: 231-627-5362. [JC]
Catechesis/Religious Programs—Students 261.

Copemish, Manistee Co., St. Raphael, Rev. Richard A. Kosterman.
Res., P.O. Box 204, 49625. Tel: 231-378-2984; Fax: 231-378-4953. [CEM]
Church—M-115, 49765.

Cross Village, Emmet Co., Holy Cross, Deacon Joseph Nelson, Pastoral Admin.
Res., 6624 N. Lake Shore, 49740-9745. Tel: 231-526-2030. [CEM]

East Jordan, Charlevoix Co., St. Joseph, Rev. Herbert J. William, Admin.
Res., P.O. Box 379, 49727. Tel: 231-536-2934; Fax: 231-536-2988. [CEM]

East Tawas, Iosco Co., St. Joseph. Merged with Immaculate Heart of Mary, Tawas City to form Holy Family, East Tawas.

Elk Rapids, Antrim Co., Sacred Heart, Rev. Robert J. Zuchowski.
Res., 143 Charles St., 49629. Tel: 231-264-8087; Fax: 231-264-6350. [CEM]
Catechesis/Religious Programs—Sandra S. Boals, D.R.E.
Students 176.

Elmira, Antrim Co., St. Thomas Aquinas, Rev. Richard T. Hannon.
Res., P.O. Box 128, 49730. Tel: 231-546-3326. [CEM]
Church—M-32, 49730.

Empire, Leelanau Co., St. Philip Neri, Rev. Chad W. Zielinski.
Res., P.O. Box 257, 49630. Tel: 231-326-5255; Fax: 231-326-5839. [CEM]
Church—11411 La Core Ave., 49630.

Fife Lake, Grand Traverse Co., St. Aloysius, Rev. James A. Holtz.
Res., 0438 County Rd. 612, Kalkaska, 49646. Tel: 231-258-5021; Fax: 231-258-2842. [CEM]
Church—Merritt St., 49633. Tel: 231-258-2752.

Frankfort, Benzie Co., St. Ann, Rev. James M. Bearss.
Res., P.O. Box 1168, 508 Crystal Ave., 49635. Tel: 231-352-4421; Fax: 231-352-9940.
Catechesis/Religious Programs—Tel: 231-352-4541.
Students 42.

Gills Pier, Leelanau Co., St. Wenceslaus, Rev. Reynaldo Garcia, S.J.
Res., 8500 E. Kolarik Rd., Suttons Bay, 49682. Tel: 231-271-3574. [CEM]
Church—County Rds. 637 & 626, 49682.

Glennie, Alcona Co., St. Francis of Assisi. Closed. For inquiries for parish records contact the Chancery.

Good Hart, Emmet Co., St. Ignatius, Deacon Joseph Nelson, Pastoral Admin.
Res., 6624 N. Lake Shore Dr., Cross Village, 49740. Tel: 231-526-2030. [CEM]

Grayling, Crawford Co., St. Mary, Rev. Robert W. Nalley.
Res., 708 Peninsular St., 49738. Tel: 989-348-7291; 348-7657 (Office); Fax: 989-348-7658.
Catechesis/Religious Programs—Students 55.

Hale, Iosco Co., St. Pius X, Rev. J. August Franczek.
Res., P.O. Box 428, 48739. Tel: 989-728-2278; Fax: 989-728-7487.
Church—3900 M-65, 48739.
Catechesis/Religious Programs—Tel: 989-728-2278; Fax: 989-728-7487. Karol Shellenbarger, D.R.E.
Students 25.

Hannah, Grand Traverse Co., St. Mary, Rev. Albin J. Gietzen.
Res., 2962 M-113 West Rd., Kingsley, 49649. Tel: 231-263-5640. [CEM]
Catechesis/Religious Programs—Sr. Geneva Marie Schaub, O.P., D.R.E.
Students 47.
Convent—2912 M-113 West Rd., Kingsley, 49649. Tel: 616-263-5287.

Harbor Springs, Emmet Co., Holy Childhood of Jesus, Rev. Frank Kordek, O.F.M.; Bro. Patrick Kendrick, O.F.M. In res., Rev. Albert Langheim, O.F.M.
Res., 150 W. Main St., 49740. Tel: 231-526-2017; Fax: 231-526-9299. [CEM]
Catechesis/Religious Programs—Tel: 616-526-7181. Ginny Day, D.R.E.
Students 110.

Harrietta, Wexford Co., St. Edward, Rev. Francis J. Murphy.
Res., 800 W. 13th St., Cadillac, 49601-9281. Tel: 231-775-2471; Fax: 231-775-2452.
Church—207 W. Gaston, 49638.

Harrisville, Alcona Co., St. Anne, Rev. Lawrence E. Boks.
Res., P.O. Box 345, 48740. Tel: 989-724-6713. [CEM]
Church—110 State St., 48740.

Herron, Alpena Co., St. Rose of Lima, Deacon Robert Goetz, Admin.
Church—3439 Herron Rd., 49744. Tel: 989-379-4316.

Higgins Lake, Roscommon Co., St. Hubert, Rev. Gregory P. McCallum.
Res., P.O. Box 75, 48627. Tel: 989-821-5591; Fax: 989-821-5895.
Church—7612 W. Higgins Lake Dr., 48627.

Hillman, Montmorency Co., St. Augustine, Rev. Vianney C. Sipulski, O.F.M.
Res., P.O. Box 216, 49746. Tel: 989-742-4542; Fax: 989-742-8090. [CEM]
Church—24140 Veterans Memorial Hwy., 49746.
Catechesis/Religious Programs—Patty Gressick, D.R.E.
Students 69.

Houghton Lake, Roscommon Co., St. James, Rev. Gregory P. McCallum.
Res., P.O. Box 75, Higgins Lake, 48627. Tel: 989-821-5591; Fax: 989-821-5895.
Church—7878 E. Houghton Lake Dr., 48629. Tel: 989-422-3925.

Indian River, Cheboygan Co., Cross in the Woods Catholic Shrine, Revs. Donard Paulus, O.F.M.; Flavius Czuba, O.F.M.; Elstan Coghill, O.F.M.; Harry Speckman, O.F.M.; Deacon John B. Wallace.
Res., 7078 M-68, 49749. Tel: 231-238-8973; Fax: 231-238-7012. [CEM]
Catechesis/Religious Programs—49749. Tel: 231-238-8542. Mrs. Kenya Swiss, D.R.E.
Students 135.

Kalkaska, Kalkaska Co., St. Mary of the Woods, Rev. James A. Holtz.
Res., 0438 County Rd. 612, 49646. Tel: 231-258-5021; Fax: 231-258-2842. [CEM]
Catechesis/Religious Programs—Robert Bowersox. Students 60.

Klacking Creek, Ogemaw Co., Holy Family, Rev. Miro Wiese, O.F.M.
Res., 402 W. Peters Rd., West Branch, 48661. Tel: 989-345-3422. [CEM]
Catechesis/Religious Programs—Glen Painter, D.R.E.
Students 47.

Lake City, Missaukee Co., St. Stephen, Rev. Roy Zebrowski, O.F.M.
Res., P.O. Box 379, 49651. Tel: 231-839-2121; Fax: 231-839-3755.
Church—506 Union St., 49651.
Catechesis/Religious Programs—Students 31.

Lake Leelanau, Leelanau Co., St. Mary, Rev. Gerard A. Hunko.
Mailing Address: P.O. Box 340, 49653. Tel: 231-256-9676; Fax: 231-256-7812.
Res., 307 S. St. Mary St., 49653. [CEM]
Church—403 S. St. Mary St., 49653.

Larks Lake, Emmet Co., St. Nicholas, Deacon Joseph Nelson, Pastoral Admin.
Res., 6624 N. Lake Shore Dr., Cross Village, 49740. Tel: 231-526-2030. [CEM]

Lewiston, Montmorency Co., St. Francis of Assisi, Rev. Gregory Kurutz, O.F.M.
Res., P.O. Box 182, 49756. Tel: 989-786-2235; Fax: 989-786-7685. [CEM]
Church—4086 Salling Ave., 49756. Tel: 989-786-3081.
Catechesis/Religious Programs—Eva Claeys, D.R.E. Students 35.

Mackinaw City, Emmet Co., St. Anthony of Padua, Sr. Chris Herald, O.P., Pastoral Admin.
Res., P.O. Box 460, 49701. Tel: 231-436-5561; 436-5601; Fax: 231-436-5699. [CEM]
Church—600 W. Central Ave., 49701.

Mancelona, Antrim Co., St. Anthony, Rev. R. Dale Magoon.
Mailing Address: P.O. Box 677, 49659-0677.
Church—209 Jefferson St., 49659. Tel: 231-587-8401. [CEM]

Manistee, Manistee Co., Guardian Angels, Rev. Msgr. Gerard Guzikowski.
Res., 371 Fifth St., 49660. Tel: 231-723-2165. [JC]
Convent—501 Michael St., 49660. Tel: 231-723-6332.

St. Joseph, Revs. William L. Zwiefka; Alex Mugonya.
Res., 254 Sixth St., 49660. Tel: 231-723-2619; Fax: 231-723-6827. [JC]
Catechesis/Religious Programs—Tel: 231-723-3732. Shirley Skiera, D.R.E.
Students 140.

St. Mary of Mt. Carmel Shrine, Rev. Gabriel Fox.
Res., 260 St. Mary Pkwy., 49660. Tel: 231-723-3345; Fax: 231-723-2157. [JC]
Catechesis/Religious Programs—Sr. Ann Porter, O.P., D.R.E.
Students 113.

Manton, Wexford Co., St. Theresa, Rev. Roy Zebrowski, O.F.M.
Res., P.O. Box 379, Lake City, 49651. Tel: 231-839-2121.
Church—9475 14th & 1/4 Rd., 49663.

Maple City, Leelanau Co., St. Rita-St. Joseph, Rev. Chad W. Zielinski.
Mailing Address: P.O. Box 75, 49664-0075. Tel: 231-228-5823; Fax: 231-228-5823.
Church—8707 Hill St., 49664. Tel: 231-228-5823.

Mapleton, Grand Traverse Co., St. Joseph, Rev. Patrick J. Barrett.
Mailing Address: 13400 Center Rd., Traverse City, 49686. Tel: 231-223-4303. [CEM]
Catechesis/Religious Programs—Peggy Stinnet, D.R.E.
Students 125.

McBain, Missaukee Co., St. Rita. Closed. For inquiries for parish records contact the Chancery.

Metz, Presque Isle Co., St. Dominic, Sr. Rita Epple, R.S.M., Pastoral Admin.
Res., 9269 County Rd. 441, Posen, 49776. Tel: 989-766-2694; Fax: 989-766-2694. [CEM]
Catechesis/Religious Programs—Carolyn Haske, D.R.E.
Students 36.

Mikado, Alocona Co., St. Raphael, Rev. Lawrence E. Boks.
Res., P.O. Box 345, Harrisville, 48740. Tel: 989-724-6713. [CEM]
Church—2531 E. Mikado Rd., 48745. Tel: 989-736-6071.

Mio, Oscoda Co., St. Mary, Rev. Mark Szych, O.F.M.
Res., P.O. Box 189, 48647. Tel: 989-826-5509; Fax: 989-826-1333.
Ministry Office—Tel: 989-826-6057.

Northport, Leelanau Co., St. Gertrude, Rev. Wayne H. Dziekan.
Res., P.O. Box 9, Suttons Bay, 49682. Tel: 231-271-3744.
Church—701 Warren, 49670.

Onaway, Presque Isle Co., St. Paul, Rev. Thomas M. Dominiak.
Res., 3856 Oak St., P.O. Box 130, 49765. Tel: 989-733-4043; Fax: 989-733-6053. [CEM]

Onekama, Manistee Co., St. Joseph, Rev. Michael P. Conner.
Res., P.O. Box 150, 49675. Tel: 231-889-4254; Fax: 231-889-3706. [CEM]
Church—8380 Fifth St., 49675.

Oscoda, Iosco Co., Sacred Heart, Rev. James L. Bruck-sch.
Res., 5300 N. U.S.-23, 48750. Tel: 989-739-9511; Fax: 989-739-3010. [CEM]
Catechesis/Religious Programs—Tel: 989-739-5523. Mrs. Jackie Welles, D.R.E.
Students 109.

Ossineke, Alpena Co., St. Catherine, Rev. Lawrence A. Kelleher.
Res., 2188 W. Nicholson Hill Rd., 49766-9736. Tel: 989-471-2556; Fax: 989-471-3221. [CEM]
Catechesis/Religious Programs—Tel: 989-471-5121. D.R.E.: Ann Skuse; Valerie LaBell.
Students 147.

Pellston, Emmet Co., St. Clement, Rev. Sylvester Micek, O.F.M.
Res., P.O. Box 122, 49769. Tel: 231-539-8805; Fax: 231-539-8572. [CEM]
Church—202 Maple, 49769.

Peshabestown, Leelanau Co., Blessed Kateri Tekak-witha, Rev. Andrew Buvala, O.F.M.
Res., P.O. Box 369, Suttons Bay, 49682. Tel: 231-271-6651; Fax: 231-271-4954.

Petoskey, Emmet Co., St. Francis Xavier, Revs. James A. Suchocki; Joseph A. Blasko.
Res., 513 Howard St., 49770. Tel: 231-347-4133; Fax: 231-347-4134. [CEM]
School—414 Michigan St., 49770. Tel: 231-347-3651. Pamela Dickerson, Prin.
Students 207.
Catechesis/Religious Programs—Tel: 231-347-2681.
Students 170.

Posen, Presque Isle Co., St. Casimir, Rev. Stanislaw J. Bereda.
Res., P.O. Box 217, 49776. Tel: 989-766-2660. [CEM]
Church—10075 M-65 North, 49776-0217.
Catechesis/Religious Programs—Joan Chappa, D.R.E.
Students 123.

Praga, Antrim Co., St. John Nepomucene, Rev. Herbert J. Willman, Admin.
Res., P.O. Box 379, East Jordan, 49727. Tel: 231-536-2934; Fax: 231-536-2988. [CEM]

Prudenville, Roscommon Co., Our Lady of the Lake, Rev. John O. Ladd.
Res., 1037 W. Houghton Lake Dr., P.O. Box 800, 48651. Tel: 989-366-5533; Fax: 989-366-5988.
Catechesis/Religious Programs—Lea Ann Ander-son, D.R.E.
Students 100.
Convent—1039 W. Houghton Lake Dr., 48651. Tel: 989-366-5592.

Riggsville, Cheboygan Co., Sacred Heart, Rev. Leonard Jocys.
Mailing Address: P.O. Box 490, Cheboygan, 49721. Tel: 231-627-9663 (Parish); Fax: 231-627-7836.
Church—4989 Polish Line Rd., Cheboygan, 49721.

Rogers City, Presque Isle Co., St. Ignatius, Rev. Charles G. Donajkowski.
Mailing Address: 585 S. Third St., 49779. Tel: 989-734-3388; Fax: 989-734-7671. [CEM]
Business Office: 585 S. Third St., 49779. Tel: 989-734-3605.
Catechesis/Religious Programs—Tel: 989-734-7768. Robert Chapdelaine, D.R.E.
Students 158.
Convent—585 S. Third St., 49779. Tel: 989-734-3605.

Roscommon, Roscommon Co., St. Michael, Rev. Anthony M. Citro.
Res., 104 N. 6th St., P.O. Box 248, 48653. Tel: 989-275-5212; Fax: 989-275-9020.
Catechesis/Religious Programs—Tel: 989-275-5212. Kathleen Butler, D.R.E.
Students 217.

St. Helen, Roscommon Co., St. Helen, Rev. Albert Couturier.
Res., 737 N. M-76, 48646. Tel: 989-389-3495; 389-4959 (Office); 389-3441 (Church); Fax: 989-389-3495.

Skidway Lake, Ogemaw Co., St. Stephen of Hungary, Rev. Alexander Boruta, O.F.M.
Res., 2811 E. Greenwood Rd., Prescott, 48756. Tel: 989-873-3340; Fax: 989-873-5209.

Suttons Bay, Leelanau Co., St. Michael the Archangel, Rev. Wayne H. Dziekan.
Res., P.O. Box 9, 49682. Tel: 231-271-3744. [CEM]
Church—315 Broadway, 49682.

Tawas City, Iosco Co., Holy Family. Consolidation of St. Joseph, East Tawas and Immaculate Heart of Mary, East Tawas. Rev. Ronald V. Gronowski.
Mailing Address: P.O. Box 472, East Tawas, 48730.
Church—516 W. Lincoln, East Tawas, 48730. Tel: 989-362-3162; Fax: 989-362-9077.

Immaculate Heart of Mary. Merged with St. Joseph, East Tawas to form Holy Family, East Tawas.

Traverse City, Grand Traverse Co., Immaculate Conception, Revs. James P. Hayden; Paul Megge.
Res., 720 W. Second, 49684. Tel: 231-946-4211; Fax: 231-946-0567.
Catechesis/Religious Programs—Tel: 231-946-2782. Dannie Brzezinski, D.R.E.
Students 350.

St. Francis of Assisi, Rev. James K. Gardiner; Sr. Katherine Murphy, R.S.M., Pastoral Assoc. In res., Rev. William W. Lipscomb.
Res., 1025 S. Union St., 49684. Tel: 231-947-4620; Fax: 231-947-4693.

St. Patrick, Rev. Gerald F. Micketti.
Res., 630 W. Silver Lake Rd. S., 49684-8526. Tel: 231-943-4633; Fax: 231-943-8886.
Catechesis/Religious Programs—Students 204.

Vanderbilt, Otsego Co., Holy Redeemer, Rev. John E. McCracken.
Res., 606 N. Ohio St., Gaylord, 49735. Tel: 989-732-5448.

West Branch, Ogemaw Co., St. Joseph, Rev. Robert H. Bissot.
Res., 907 Houghton Ave., 48661. [CEM]
Business Office: 961 W. Houghton, 48661. Tel: 989-345-0064; Fax: 989-345-8757.
School—Tel: 989-345-0220; Fax: 989-345-3030.
Catechesis/Religious Programs—Tel: 989-345-0670.
Students 90.

Whittemore, Iosco Co., St. James, Rev. James Kras-man, O.F.M.
Res., P.O. Box 206, 48770. Tel: 989-756-2591; Fax: 989-756-3255. [CEM]
Church—202 E. Sherman, 48770.

Special Assignment:
Reverend Fathers—
Cotter, Raymond C., On Duty in the Diocese of Marquette
Derylo, Walter W., Ministry with Food for the Poor; Res in Diocese of Grand Rapids

Absent on Leave:
Reverend Monsignors—
Gemuend, David W.
Reverend Fathers—
Greene, John C.

Retired:
Reverend Fathers—
Gaj, Zygmut, 2733 Bullock Rd., Bay City, MI 48708
Harnish, Lionel, 4039 26th St., Dorr, MI 49323
Jocys, Leonard, 71 Chelsea Ln., Cheboygan, MI 49721
Kluonius, Joseph V., 2013 Hess, Holiday, FL 34691
Machcinski, Anthony J., 7826 Homer Ave., Hudson, FL 34667
Marek, Walter, P.O. Box 203, Whitehall, MI 49461
Mausolf, James H., 1421 Veterans Dr., Traverse City, MI 49684
Mikulski, Isadore J., 7718 Westwood Dr., Oscoda, MI 48750
Mulka, Arthur C., 2388 Emmett, Alpena, MI 49707
Mulka, Raymond C., 300 Washington, Alpena, MI 49707
Pilarski, Raymond J., P.O. Box 26, Alpena, MI 49707
Reitz, Joseph A., 52 Marble Rd., Lowell, MI 49331
Rushman, John, P.O. Box 646, East Tawas, MI 48730
Sarosiek, John H., 4468 Lincoln, Dearborn Heights, MI 48125
Seifferly, Richard R., P.O. Box 422, West Branch, MI 48661-0422
Sitar, Richard T., 12039 Leer Rd., Posen, MI 49776

Smolinski, Clarence D., 14692 Lakeside Dr., Presque Isle, MI 49777
Tamulis, John J., 1189 S. 35 Mile Rd., Cadillac, MI 49601
Thome, Edwin A., P.O. Box 412, Acme, MI 49610
Tupper, John B., P.O. Box 262, Conway, MI 49722
Wiekierak, Joseph F., 1470 West Norton, Apt. H-5, Muskegon, MI 49441-4362
Zawacki, Casimir J., 305 Fifth Ave., #4, Manistee, MI 49660

Permanent Deacons:
Bousmara, Thomas, Immaculate Conception, Traverse City
Friend, Harry, St. Philip, Empire
Goetz, Robert, St. Rose of Lima, Herron
LePain, Andrew, Unassigned
LoVetere, Arthur, Jesus the Good Shepherd, Atlanta
Moeggenberg, John, Holy Rosary, Cedar
Nelson, Joseph B., Holy Cross, Cross Village
Szczepanski, Stanley T., St. Mary-St. Charles, Cheboygan
Trapp, Richard, Unassigned
Vondra, Edward, Unassigned
Wallace, John, Catholic Shrine, Indian River
Wendell, Max, Unassigned

INSTITUTIONS LOCATED IN THE DIOCESE

[A] INTERPAROCHIAL SCHOOLS

CHEBOYGAN. *Bishop Baraga Elementary.* (Grades PreK-6), 421 State St., 49721.
E-mail: principal@nmo.net
James Leinbach, Prin. Lay Teachers 15; Preschool 60; Students 196. Preschool, 120 C St., 49721.

MANISTEE. *Manistee Catholic Central Schools.* (Grades PreK-12), 1200 U.S. 31 South (at 12th St.), 49660. Tel: 231-723-2529. Gina Hagen, Prin. Sisters 1; Lay Teachers 20; Students 289; Preschool 49.

TRAVERSE CITY. *Elizabeth Ann Seton Middle School.* (Grades 6-8), 1601 Three Mile Rd. N., 49686. Tel: 231-932-4810. Kenneth Knudsen, Prin.; Deborah Haase, Sec. Lay Teachers 14; Students 275.
Grand Traverse Area Catholic Schools, 123 E. 11th St., 49684. Tel: 231-946-8100. Michael R. Buell, Supt. Sisters 2; Lay Teachers 57; Students 1,131.
Holy Angels Elementary. (Grades K-2), 130 E. 10th, 49684. Tel: 231-946-5961. Maureen DeYoung, Prin. Lay Teachers 11; Students 245.
Immaculate Conception Elementary School. (Grades 3-5), 218 Vine, 49684. Tel: 231-947-1252.
E-mail: icebridges@aol.com
Rob Bridges, Prin. Sisters 1; Lay Teachers 14; Students 301.
St. Francis High School, 123 E. 11th St., 49684. Tel: 231-946-8038; Fax: 231-946-1878.
E-mail: mesper@gtacs.org
Web site: www.gtacs.org
Mark Esper, Prin. Sisters 1; Lay Teachers 18; Students 310.

[B] PAROCHIAL SCHOOLS

GAYLORD. *St. Mary Cathedral Elementary School.* (Grades K-6), 321 N. Otsego Ave., 49735. Deanna Couture, Prin. Lay Teachers 17; Students 267.
St. Mary Cathedral High School. (Grades 7-12), 310 W. Mitchell, 49735.
E-mail: stmarys@northland.lib.mi.us
Mr. James Kerfoot, Prin. Lay Teachers 9; Students 219.

ALPENA. *St. Anne Elementary.* (Grades K-5), 205 S. 9th, 49707. Tel: 989-354-4911; Fax: 989-354-3918.
E-mail: stanne2@alpena.cc.mi.us
Mr. William Morford, Jr., Prin. Lay Teachers 7; Students 153.
St. Mary Elementary. (Grades K-6), 500 N. Second, 49707. Sr. Mary Edwardine Stoppa, C.S.S.F., Prin. Lay Teachers 6; Students 59.

CADILLAC. *St. Ann Elementary.* (Grades K-5), 800 W. 13th, 49601. Tel: 231-775-1301; Fax: 231-775-0161. Mary Ann Palacios, Prin. Lay Teachers 7; Students 145.

CHARLEVOIX. *St. Mary Elementary.* (Grades K-6), 1005 Bridge St., 49720. Tel: 231-547-9441; Fax: 231-547-0141.
E-mail: stmary@freeway.net
Janet M. Troppman, Prin. Sisters 2; Lay Teachers 5; Students 77.

EAST TAWAS. *Holy Family Elementary School.* (Grades K-6), 411 N. Wilkinson, 48730. Edward Eppert, O.P., Prin. Sisters 1; Lay Teachers 8; Students 103.

HANNAH. *St. Mary's Hannah School.* (Grades K-8), 2912 M-113, 49649. Mary Beecy, Prin. Sisters 1; Lay Teachers 8; Students 88.

LAKE LEELANAU. *St. Mary's Schools.* (Grades K-12), 303 S. St. Mary St., 49653. Tel: 231-256-9636; Fax: 231-256-7239.
E-mail: stmarys@microageetc.com
Mailing Address: P.O. Box 340, 49653. Patrick Gaudard, Prin. Lay Teachers 13; Students 217.

PETOSKEY. *St. Francis Xavier Elementary.* (Grades K-8), 414 Michigan, 49770. Pamela Dickerson, Prin. Lay Teachers 14; Students 186.

PRUDENVILLE. *Our Lady of the Lake Elementary.* (Grades K-8), 1039 W. Houghton Lake, 48651. Tel: 989-366-5592; Fax: 989-366-1348.
E-mail: olls@freeway.net
Elizabeth Kindermann, Prin. Lay Teachers 6; Students 83.

ROGERS CITY. *St. Ignatius Elementary.* (Grades 1-8), 545 S. Third, 49779. Tel: 989-734-3443; Fax: 989-734-7768. Charles Taylor, Prin. Lay Teachers 9; Students 111.

WEST BRANCH. *St. Joseph Elementary.* (Grades K-8), 935 W. Houghton Ave., 48661. Tel: 989-345-0220; Fax: 989-345-3030. Lorrene Spaulding, Prin. Lay Teachers 9; Students 192.

[C] GENERAL HOSPITALS

CADILLAC. *Mercy Hospital*, 400 Hobart St., 49601. Tel: 231-779-7200
For a complete listing, refer to the Hospitals section.

GRAYLING. *Mercy Hospital*, 1100 E. Michigan Ave., 49738. Tel: 989-348-5461; Fax: 989-348-0479
For a complete listing, refer to the Hospitals section.

TAWAS CITY. *St. Joseph Health System*, 200 Hemlock, M-55, 48764-0659. Tel: 989-362-3411; 362-4611; Fax: 989-362-7277
For a complete listing, refer to the Hospitals section.

[D] CONVENTS AND RESIDENCES FOR SISTERS

CONWAY. *Sacramentine Monastery of Perpetual Adoration*, 49722. Tel: 231-347-0447. Sr. Mary Rosalie, O.S.S., Prioress. Sacamentine Sisters 4.

TRAVERSE CITY. *Infant Jesus of Prague Monastery*, 3501 Silver Lake Rd., 49684-8949. Tel: 231-946-4960; Fax: 231-947-7729. Rev. George B. Billman, Chap. Tel: 231-947-6935. Carmelite Nuns 9; Solemn Vows 5.

[E] CHILD CARE FACILITIES

ALPENA. *Huron House / Boysville of Michigan, Inc.*, 4761 U.S. 23 N., 49707. Tel: 989-356-3573; Fax: 989-356-4910. Mailing Address: Boysville of Michigan, 8759 Clinton-Macon Rd., Clinton, 49236. Residential and community-based treatment programs for troubled youth and families, with facilities located throughout the state of Michigan and three in the state of Ohio under the auspices of the Brothers of the Holy Cross at Notre Dame. Parent company, Boysville of Michigan, Inc. Bro. Francis Boylan, C.S.C., Exec. Dir.; Joseph Martinus, Pastoral Min.; Rick Boone, Regional Dir. Boys 14; Staff 17.

ONAWAY. *Russell House*, P.O. Box 599, 49765. Tel: 989-733-5201; Fax: 989-733-8678. Boys 15; Staff 17.

TRAVERSE CITY. *Non-Secure Detention / Boysville of Michigan, Inc.*, 207 W. Grandview Pkwy., Ste. 200, 49684. Tel: 231-922-9664; 800-235-9664; Fax: 231-922-9675.
Web site: www.boysville.org
Bro. Francis Boylan, C.S.C., Exec. Dir.; Rick Boone, Regional Dir. Youth 633.

[F] RETREAT CENTERS AND CAMPS

GAYLORD. *Camp Sancta Maria*, P.O. Bo 338, 49734. Tel: 231-546-3878; Fax: 231-546-3171.
E-mail: office@campsanctamaria.org
Web site: www.campsanctamaria.org
Michael Hickey, Exec. Dir.; James Berigan, Contact Person. Staff 45; Campers 470.

CONWAY. *Augustine Center*, P.O. Box 84, 49722-0084. Tel: 231-347-3657; Fax: 231-347-9502.
E-mail: hubenyop@freeway.net
Sr. Barbara Hubeny, O.P., Dir.

ST. JAMES. *Brother Damian Lodge* (Beaver Island), 49782. Tel: 231-448-2204. Open June, July and August. Bro. Paul Ackerman, F.S.C., Dir.

[G] CATHOLIC SOCIAL SERVICE AGENCIES

GAYLORD. *Catholic Human Services*, 611 W. North St., 49735. Tel: 989-732-5147; Fax: 989-705-3589.
E-mail: chshast@freeway.net
Mr. David Martin, Pres. & CEO.
Area Offices: 154 S. Ripley Blvd., Alpena, 49707. Tel: 989-356-6385; Fax: 989-356-4909. Julie Deno, Administrative Coord., 421 S. Mitchell, Cadillac, 49601. Tel: 231-775-6581; Fax: 231-775-5421. Mr. David Martin, Admin., 1169 Elkview #3, 49735. Tel: 989-732-6761; Fax: 989-732-6763. Kathy Arndt, Admin., 1000 Hastings St., Traverse City, 49686. Tel: 231-947-8110; Fax: 231-947-3522. Mr. David Martin, Admin.

[H] MISCELLANEOUS

GAYLORD. *Northern Michigan Catholic Foundation, Inc.*, 611 W. North St., 49735. Tel: 989-732-5147; Fax: 989-705-3589.
E-mail: msteffel@dioceseofgaylord.org
H. Charles Nelson, Pres.; Ken Kleinrichert, Vice Pres.; Joel Myler, Sec.; James Kelly, Treas. Members: Most Rev. Patrick R. Cooney; Ann Mawby; David M. Penrod.

ALPENA. *Madonna House Apostolate*, 309 Lockwood, 49707. Tel: 989-354-4073. Rosemary Horan, Dir.

HARBOR SPRINGS. *Christ Child Society of Northern Michigan, Inc.*, P.O. Box 132, 49740-0132. Tel: 231-526-7271. Patti Forman, Pres.

JOHANNESBURG. *Stella Maris Hermitage*, 19920 Black River Rd., 49751-9645. Tel: 989-732-9580.
E-mail: rwkropf@freeway.net
Web site: stelamar.cjb.net
Rev. Richard Kropf.

PRESCOTT. *House of the Holy Shroud*, 1629 Beach Rd., 48756. Tel: 989-873-4000. Bro. Michael W. Whitman, Dir.

RELIGIOUS INSTITUTES OF MEN REPRESENTED IN THE DIOCESE

For further details refer to the corresponding bracketed number in the Religious Institutes of Men or Women section.

[0520]—*Franciscan Friars.* (Assumption, Sacred Heart Provs.).—O.F.M.
[0690]—*Jesuit Fathers and Brothers.*—S.J.

RELIGIOUS INSTITUTES OF WOMEN REPRESENTED IN THE DIOCESE

[0420]—*Discalced Carmelite Nuns.*—O.C.D.
[1070]—*Dominican Sisters.*—O.P.
[1170]—*Felician Sisters.*—C.S.S.F.
[2580]—*Institute of the Sisters of Mercy of the Americas.*—R.S.M.
[3490]—*Sacramentine Nuns.*—O.S.S.
[3560]—*Servants of Jesus.*—S.J.
[2630]—*Sisters of Mercy of the Holy Cross.* (Merill, WI).—S.C.S.C.
[3830]—*Sisters of St. Joseph.*—S.S.J.

NECROLOGY

† Adomaitis, John J, Mackinaw City, MI St. Anthony of Padua. —Died Nov. 10, 1999.
† Frederick, Edwin J., (Retired). —Died Jan. 4, 2000.
† Marciulionis, Benedict J., (Retired). —Died May 5, 2000.

Diocese of Grand Island

(Dioecesis Insulae Grandis)

Most Reverend

LAWRENCE J. McNAMARA, D.D., S.T.L.

Bishop of Grand Island; ordained May 30, 1953; appointed January 10, 1978; consecrated and installed March 28, 1978. *Mailing Address: Box 1531, Grand Island, NE, 68802.*

Most Reverend

JOHN L. PASCHANG, D.D., PH.D., J.C.D.

Retired Bishop of Grand Island; ordained June 12, 1921; appointed July 28, 1951; consecrated October 9, 1951. *Res., 320 E. Decatur St., West Point, NE, 68788.*

ERECTED AT KEARNEY, MARCH 8, 1912; SEE TRANSFERRED TO GRAND ISLAND, APRIL 11, 1917.

Square Miles 40,000.

Comprises the Counties of Arthur, Banner, Blaine, Box Butte, Brown, Buffalo, Cherry, Cheyenne, Custer, Dawes, Deuel, Garden, Garfield, Grant, Greeley, Hooker, Howard Keyapaha, Kimball, Logan, Loup, McPherson, Morrill, Rock, Scotts Bluff, Sheridan, Sherman, Wheeler, Sioux, Thomas, Valley, and those portions of Dawson, Hall, Lincoln and Keith lying north of the South Platte River in the State of Nebraska.

For legal titles of parishes and diocesan institutions, consult the Chancery Office.

Chancery Office: 311 W. 17th St., P.O. Box 996, Grand Island, NE, 68802. Tel.: 308-382-6565; Fax: 308-382-6569.

STATISTICAL OVERVIEW

Personnel	
Bishop	1
Retired Bishops	2
Priests: Diocesan Active in Diocese	47
Priests: Active Outside Diocese	2
Priests: Retired, Sick or Absent	27
Number of Diocesan Priests	76
Total Sisters	91
Parishes	
Parishes	43
With Resident Pastor:	
Resident Diocesan Priests	43
Missions	40
Welfare	
Health Care Centers	2
Total Assisted	164,473
Homes for the Aged	1
Total Assisted	75
Educational	
Diocesan Students in Other Seminaries	6
Total Seminarians	6
High Schools, Diocesan and Parish	4
Total Students	808
Elementary Schools, Diocesan and Parish	7
Total Students	871
Catechesis/Religious Education:	
High School Students	3,263
Elementary Students	5,361
Total Students Under Catholic Instruction	10,309
Teachers in the Diocese:	
Priests	1
Sisters	4
Lay Teachers	129
Vital Statistics	
Receptions into the Church:	
Infant Baptism Totals	1,063
Adult Baptism Totals	123
Received into Full Communion	175
First Communions	1,179
Confirmations	773
Marriages:	
Catholic	195
Interfaith	213
Total Marriages	408
Deaths	608
Total Catholic Population	56,879
Total Population	295,176

Former Bishops—Most Rev. JAMES ALBERT DUFFY, D.D., cons. April 16, 1913; resigned See, May 7, 1931; appt. Titular Bishop of Silando; died Feb. 12, 1968.—Most Rev. STANISLAUS V. BONA, D.D., appt. Bishop of Grand Island, Dec. 18, 1931; cons. Feb. 25, 1932; appt. Coadjutor Bishop of Green Bay and Titular Bishop of Mela, Dec. 2, 1944; succeeded to See, March 3, 1945; died Dec. 1, 1967.—Most Rev. EDWARD J. HUNKELER, D.D., ord. June 14, 1919; appt. March 10, 1945; cons. May 1, 1945; transferred to Kansas City in Kansas, March 31, 1951; died Oct. 1, 1970.—Most Rev. JOHN L. PASCHANG, D.D., Ph.D., J.C.D., ord. June 12, 1921; appt. July 28, 1951; cons. October 9, 1951; resigned July 25, 1972; died March 21, 1999.—Most Rev. JOHN J. SULLIVAN, D.D., ord. Sept. 23, 1944; appt. July 25, 1972; cons. Sept. 19, 1972; transferred to Kansas City-St. Joseph in Missouri, Aug. 17, 1977.

Vicar General—Rev. JAMES D. O'KANE, *St. Agnes, Scottsbluff, 69363.* Tel: 308-632-3541.

Chancery Office—311 W. 17th St., P.O. Box 996, Grand Island, 68802. Tel: 308-382-6565; Fax: 308-382-6569. Office Hours: 9-5.

Chancellor—Rev. MICHAEL F. MCDERMOTT.

Vice Chancellor—LINDA L. WEMHOFF.

Moderator of the Curia—Rev. RICHARD L. PIONTKOWSKI, JR., S.T.L., J.C.L.

Diocesan Tribunal—P.O. Box 5405, Grand Island, 68802. Tel: 308-382-6364.

Vicar-Judicial—Rev. MICHAEL F. MCDERMOTT, J.C.L.

Adjutant Vicars-Judicial—Revs. RICHARD L. PIONTKOWSKI, JR., S.T.L., J.C.L.; CHARLES L. TORPEY, S.T.L., J.C.L.

Defenders of the Bond—Revs. THOMAS RYAN; DONALD E. LARMORE, J.C.D.

Promoter Justitiae—Rev. DONALD E. LARMORE, J.C.D.

Judges—Revs. CHARLES L. TORPEY, S.T.L., J.C.L.; RICHARD PIONTKOWSKI, JR., S.T.L., J.C.L.; MICHAEL F. MCDERMOTT, J.C.L.

Procurator—Rev. JAMES M. HUNT.

Advocates—Rev. JAMES M. HUNT; CONNIE RUHLMAN; KATHLEEN HAHN.

Associate Director-Notary—RUTH NOZISKA.

Diocesan Consultors—Revs. JOHN E. SCHLAF; DON BUHRMAN; CHARLES L. TORPEY, S.T.L., J.C.L.; JOSEPH HANNAPPEL; MICHAEL F. MCDERMOTT, S.T.L., J.C.L.; JAMES D. O'KANE.

Vicar for Religious Communities of Women—Rev. FRANK L. HOELCK.

Diocesan Offices and Directors

Building Committee—Revs. ANDREW GONDA; STANLEY GORAK; JOHN SCHLAF; JAMES D. O'KANE.

Charismatic Renewal—Rev. HAROLD KURTENBACH, Dir., *2136 W. 11th St., Grand Island, 68802.*

Charities—Rev. JOSEPH M. WALSH, Dir., Catholic Soc. Svc. Bureau; JAMES R. BLUE, Asst. Dir., Catholic Soc. Svcs., *301 S. 70th St., Ste. 300, Lincoln, 68510.* Tel: 402-489-1834.

Communications—Rev. DONALD E. LARMORE, Dir., *Grand Island, 68801.* Tel: 308-384-0532.

Continuing Education for the Clergy—Revs. ARTHUR FAESSER, *P.O. Box 427, North Platte, 69103.* ROBERT ROONEY, *P.O. Box 123, Ord, 68862.*

Council of Catholic Women, Diocesan—Rev. STEPHEN F. DEAVER, Diocesan Moderator.

Hispanic Ministry—

Justice and Peace Office—Mr. MARIO DELGADO, Dir., *P.O. Box 651, North Platte, 69103.* Tel: 308-532-2707. Rev. PAUL J. COLLING, Asst. Dir., *1103 12th Ave., Scottsbluff, 69361.* Tel: 308-632-2845.

Liturgical Commission—Revs. CHARLES L. TORPEY, S.T.L., J.C.L., Chm. JAMES D. O'KANE, Vice Chm.

Newspaper—"The West Nebraska Register", MARY PARLIN, Editor. Address all correspondence to: *P.O. Box 608, Grand Island, 68802.* Tel: 308-382-4660; Fax: 308-382-4746.

Personnel Board—Revs. BRYAN D. ERNEST; JOHN R. RADEMACHER; CHARLES L. TORPEY; JOHN E. SCHLAF; JAMES H. HEITHOFF; JAMES R. GOLKA.

Priests' Advisory Board (Presbyteral Council)—Revs. MICHAEL F. MCDERMOTT; RAYMOND M. KOSMICKI; PAUL J. COLLING; JOHN E. SCHLAF; CHARLES L. TORPEY; LOUIS NOLLETTE; NEAL NOLLETTE; EDWARD CORTNEY; JAMES O'KANE; JAMES P. WARNER; REGINALD A. URBAN; MARTIN L. EGGING; JAMES E. NOVAKOWSKI.

Catholic Relief Services—Most Rev. LAWRENCE J. MCNAMARA, Dir.

Priests' Pension and Welfare Board—Address all mail to: Rev. JAN SMUTNY, *P.O. Box 194, Pleasanton, 68866.*

Propagation of the Faith—Rev. MICHAEL D. MCDONALD, Dir., *1210 E. 11th, Kearney, 68847.* Tel: 308-236-9171.

Remex-Media Center—CYNTHIA MUENCHRATH, Dir., *214 W. 5th St., P.O. Box 1617, North Platte, 69103.* Tel: 308-532-2707.

Religious Education—DONALD KURRE, Dir. CYNTHIA MUENCHRATH, Assoc. Dir., *214 W. 5th St., P.O. Box 1617, North Platte, 69103.* Tel: 308-532-2707.

Rural Life Conference—Rev. NEAL P. NOLLETTE, Dir., *P.O. Box 530, Elm Creek, 68836.*

Schools—Rev. THOMAS A. RYAN, Diocesan Supt. of Schools, *311 W. 17th, P.O. Box 996, Grand Island, 68802.* Tel: 308-682-6565; Fax: 308-382-6569.

Vocations—Rev. BRYAN D. ERNEST, Dir., *1104 Cheyenne Ave., Alliance, 69301.* Tel: 308-762-1418.

Youth & Young Adult—JENNIFER HOSTLER, Dir. JAMES RYAN, Assoc. Dir., *P.O. Box 1721, Grand Island, 68802.* Tel: 308-382-4660; Fax: 308-382-4746.

CLERGY, PARISHES, MISSIONS AND PAROCHIAL SCHOOLS

CITY OF GRAND ISLAND (Hall County)

1—CATHEDRAL OF THE NATIVITY OF THE BLESSED VIRGIN MARY (1864), Revs. Thomas A. Ryan; Jose M. Chavez.
Res., 207 S. Elm St., 68801. Tel: 308-384-2523; Fax: 308-384-2527.
Catechesis/Religious Programs—502 West Division, 68801. Tel: 308-382-1198. Sr. Barbara Bader, C.S.J., D.R.E.
Students 570.

2—BLESSED SACRAMENT (1949), Revs. Donald E. Larmore; Frank L. Hoelck.
Res., 1724 N. Walnut, 68801. Tel: 308-384-0568.
Church—518 W. State St., 68801. Tel: 308-384-0532; Fax: 308-384-0424.
Catechesis/Religious Programs—518 W. State St., 68801. Tel: 308-395-8521. Ms. Debra Wetzel, D.R.E.
Students 420.
Chapel—Geer-Sterne, 801 Stoeger Dr., 68803.

3—RESURRECTION (1973), Rev. James C. Schmitt.
Res., 4110 Cannon Rd., 68803. Tel: 308-382-8644.
Catechesis/Religious Programs—Tel: 308-382-0976. Therese Stump, D.R.E.
Students 297.

4—ST. LEO (1972), Rev. John R. Rademacher; Sr. Leona Augustyn, Pastoral Min.
Res., 2410 S. Blaine, 68801. Tel: 308-382-4753.
Catechesis/Religious Programs—Lisa Bianco, D.R.E.
Students 501.

OUTSIDE THE CITY OF GRAND ISLAND

Ainsworth, Brown Co., St. Pius X, Rev. James M. Hunt.
Res., P.O. Box 7, 69210. Tel: 402-387-1275.
Catechesis/Religious Programs—Tel: 402-387-2260. D.R.E.: Linda Schumacher, (St. Pius X); Sue Jilg, (Holy Cross).
Students 133.
Mission—Bassett, Rock Co., Holy Cross, P.O. Box 7, Bassett 69210. Tel: 402-684-3640.

Alliance, Box Butte Co., Holy Rosary (1894), Revs. Bryan D. Ernest; James R. Golka.
Parish Offices: 1104 Cheyenne Ave., 69301. Tel: 308-762-2009; Fax: 308-762-7474.
Res., 916 Cheyenne Ave., 69301. Tel: 308-762-1418. [CEM]
School—St. Agnes Academy, Tel: 308-762-2315.
Sisters 3; Lay Teachers 14; Students 160.
Catechesis/Religious Programs—Tel: 308-762-2830. Noreen Placek, D.R.E. (Grades K-5).
Students 375.

Anselmo, Custer Co., St. Anselm's (1905), Rev. Mark A. Maresh.
Res., P.O. Box 157, 68813. Tel: 308-749-2254. [CEM]
Catechesis/Religious Programs—D.R.E.: Brenda Stupka, (High School); Peggy Anderson, (High School); Cindy Hempstead, (Elementary).
Students 104.
Mission—Merna, Custer Co., St. Paul, P.O. Box 157, 68813. [CEM]

Bridgeport, Morrill Co., All Souls (1919), Rev. Christopher R. Keith.
Res., P.O. Box 250, 69336-0250. Tel: 308-262-0709. [CEM]
Catechesis/Religious Programs—D.R.E.: Sheri Hopkins; April Pohl; Janet Dailey; Dot Hall.
Students 180.
Missions—Dalton, Cheyenne Co., St. Mary, P.O. Box 346, 69131-0346. Tel: 308-377-2440; Bayard, Morrill Co., Sacred Heart, P.O. Box 190, 69334-0190. Tel: 308-586-1160.

Broadwater, Cheyenne Co., St. Dominic. Closed. For inquiries for parish records contact the Chancery.

Broken Bow, Custer Co., St. Joseph's (1888), Rev. Todd K. Philipsen.
Mailing Address: P.O. Box 405, 68822. Tel: 308-872-5809 (Office); Fax: 308-872-5809.
Res., 1407 S. E St., 68822. Tel: 308-872-5716; Fax: 308-872-5809. [CEM]
Catechesis/Religious Programs—Frances Peterson, D.R.E.
Students 144.
Missions—Ansley, Custer Co., Sacred Heart, 68822.; Mason City, Custer Co., St. Thomas, 68822.

Burwell, Garfield Co., Sacred Heart (1910), Rev. Bernard M. Berger.
Res., 747 I St., P.O. Box 667, 68823. Tel: 308-346-4190; Fax: 308-346-5480.
Catechesis/Religious Programs—Tel: 308-346-4366. Betty Kovarik, D.R.E.
Students 94.
Mission—Ericson, Wheeler Co., St. Theresa of the Child Jesus, 68823.
Catechesis/Religious Programs—Students 52.
Mission—Sargent, Custer Co., Assumption of the Blessed Virgin Mary, P.O. Box 397, Sargent, 68874. [CEM]
Catechesis/Religious Programs—Students 55.

Chadron, Dawes Co., St. Patrick's (1886), Rev. Edward P. Cortney.
Office: 340 Cedar St., P.O. Box 231, 69337. Tel: 308-432-2626; Fax: 308-432-4969. [CEM]
Catechesis/Religious Programs—Tel: 308-432-2161. Linda Yeradi, D.R.E.
Students 166.

Chappell, Deuel Co., St. Joseph's (1909), Rev. Martin L. Egging.
Office: Tel: 308-874-3407.
Res., 1049 2nd St., P.O. Box 586, 69129. Tel: 308-874-3221. [CEM]
Catechesis/Religious Programs—Students 36.
Mission—Oshkosh, Garden Co., St. Elizabeth, 300 W. 4th, P.O. Box 17, 69154. Tel: 308-772-3221.
Catechesis/Religious Programs—Tel: 308-722-3445.
Students 50.
Mission—Lisco, Garden Co., St. Gall, 307 1st St., 69148.

Cozad, Dawson Co., Christ the King (1951), Rev. Donald J. O'Brien; Sr. Juana O'Brien, O.P., Pastoral Assoc., Tel: 308-537-3364.
Res., 1220 Ave. M, 69130. Tel: 308-784-3959.
Catechesis/Religious Programs—512 E. 19th, Tel: 308-784-2696. Donna Kolbo, D.R.E.
Students 206.
Mission—Gothenburg, Dawson Co., Our Lady of Good Counsel, Gothenburg, 69138.

Crawford, Dawes Co., St. John the Baptist (1896) (German-Irish), Rev. Loren Pohlmeier.
Res., 808 4th St., 69339. Tel: 308-665-1584. [CEM]
Catechesis/Religious Programs—Tel: 308-665-2240. Linda Moloney, D.R.E.
Students 69.
Mission—Harrison, Sioux Co., Church of the Nativity of the Blessed Virgin Mary, 426 Kate St., Harrison 69339. Tel: 308-668-2181.

Elm Creek, Buffalo Co., Immaculate Conception (1879), Rev. Neal P. Nollette.
Res., P.O. Box 530, 68836. Tel: 308-856-4375; Fax: 308-856-4375. [CEM]
Catechesis/Religious Programs—Students 135.
Missions—Overton, Dawson Co., Holy Rosary, 6th and D, Overton, 68863. Tel: 308-987-2379; Amherst, Buffalo Co., St. John Capistran, Jefferson & Ash, Amherst, 68812.; Eddyville, Custer Co., St. Patrick, 2nd St. and Hwy. 40, 68834. [CEM]

Elyria, Valley Co., St. Mary's. Closed. For inquiries for parish records contact the Chancery.

Farwell, Howard Co., St. Anthony of Padua (1877), Rev. Lawrence W. Coulter.
Res., 103 Kearns Ave., Box 156, 68838. Tel: 308-336-3323. [CEM 3]
Catechesis/Religious Programs—D.R.E.: Kathy Gorecki Tel: 308-336-3351; Victor Dush Tel: 308-968-3421; Sharon Krzycki Tel: 308-738-2167.
Students 204.
Missions—Elba, Howard Co., St. Joseph, 68838. Tel: 308-336-3323; Ashton, Sherman Co., St. Francis, Ashton, 68817. [CEM]
Catechesis/Religious Programs—Mrs. Eddy Krzycki, D.R.E.
Students 56.
Mission—Paplin, Howard Co., Our Lady of Mount Carmel, 68838.

Gering, Scotts Bluff Co., Christ the King (1958), Rev. Gerald J. Harr.
Res., 1730 N St., P.O. Box 33, 69341. Tel: 308-436-4000; Fax: 308-436-2923.
Catechesis/Religious Programs—18th & N St., P.O. Box 33, 69341. Tel: 308-436-2290. Micki Walker, D.R.E. & Dir. Youth Ministry.
Students 300.

Gordon, Sheridan Co., St. Leo's (1887), Rev. Robert A. Karnish.
Res., 228 N. Maverick, 69343. Tel: 308-282-0427. [JC]
Catechesis/Religious Programs—Students 102.
Missions—Rushville, Sheridan Co., Immaculate Conception, 606 Church St., 69360. Tel: 308-327-2430; Hay Springs, Sheridan Co., St. Columbkille, 545 N. Main, 69347.

Greeley, Greeley Co., Sacred Heart (1893) (Irish), Rev. Gerald J. Carlson.
Res., 302 W. Wicklow, P.O. Box 99, 68842. Tel: 308-428-2855. [JC]
School—Students 33.
Catechesis/Religious Programs—Tel: 308-428-3015.
Students 98.
Missions—Scotia, Greeley Co., St. Patrick, 68842.; O'Connor, Greeley Co., Our Lady of the Visitation, 68842.

Hemingford, Box Butte Co., St. Bridget (1888), Rev. Hubert J. Spanel.
Res., 801 Niobrara Ave., P.O. Box 67, 69348. Tel: 308-487-3617. [CEM]
Catechesis/Religious Programs—Kathie Gettert, D.R.E.
Students 114.
Mission—Hay Springs, Sheridan Co., Sacred Heart, 69347.

Kearney, Buffalo Co., St. James (1881), Revs. Charles L. Torpey; Tim Stoner; Sr. Jackie Thorn, O.S.M., Assoc. Admin.
3801 Ave. A, P.O. Box 128, 68847. Tel: 308-234-5536.
Res., 7 Sioux Ln., 68847. Tel: 308-233-5051. [JC]
High School—Kearney Catholic, (Grades 6-12). Tel: 308-234-2610; Fax: 308-234-4986. Mr. Terrence Torson, Admin.
Sisters 1; Lay Teachers 24; Students 306.
Catechesis/Religious Programs—Tel: 308-234-9695. Deb Kratochvil, D.R.E.
Students 845.
Prince of Peace (1986), Rev. Michael D. McDonald; Sr. Mary Chamberlain, O.S.M., Pastoral Min.
Res., 1210 E. 11th St., 68847. Tel: 308-236-9171.
Catechesis/Religious Programs—Ms. Carolynn Smallcomb, D.R.E.
Students 169.

Kimball, Kimball Co., St. Joseph's (1921), Rev. Francis T. Curran.
Res., 507 S. Howard, 69145. Tel: 308-235-2162.
Catechesis/Religious Programs—Students 93.

Lexington, Dawson Co., St. Ann's (1883), Rev. Donald A. Buhrman; Sr. Dottie Moss, C.S.J., Pastoral Min., Tel: 308-324-2450.
Res., 303 E. 6th St., P.O. Box 578, 68850. Tel: 308-324-4648. [CEM]
Catechesis/Religious Programs—St. Ann's Parish Center, 10th & Taft St., 68850. Tel: 308-324-2616; Fax: 308-324-5320. Joan Karre, D.R.E. (Grades K-5).
Students 565.

Loup City, Sherman Co., St. Josaphat's (1882) (Polish), Rev. Reginald A. Urban.
Res., P.O. Box 626, 68853. Tel: 308-745-0315.
Catechesis/Religious Programs—Tel: 308-745-1235.
Students 174.

Merriman, Cherry Co., St. Elizabeth. Closed. For inquiries for parish records contact the Chancery.

Minatare, Scotts Bluff Co., St. Mary. Closed. For inquiries for parish records contact the Chancery.

Mitchell, Scotts Bluff Co., St. Theresa's (1930), Rev. Stephen F. Deaver.
Res., 1715 17th St., 69357. Tel: 308-623-1745.
Catechesis/Religious Programs—Tel: 308-623-2245.
Students 50.
Missions—Morrill, Scotts Bluff Co., St. Ann, Hwy. 26 & Walsh, Morrill, 69358. Tel: 308-247-3238; Lyman, Scotts Bluff Co., Sacred Heart, 69352.

Mullen, Hooker Co., St. Mary's, Rev. James L. Warner.
Res., 302 S. Blaine, P.O. Box 191, 69152. Tel: 308-546-2250; Fax: 308-546-2250.
Catechesis/Religious Programs—Students 94.
Missions—Brownlee, Cherry Co., St. Joan of Arc, 69152.; Hyannis, Grant Co., All Saint's, 69152.; Thedford, Thomas Co., St. Thomas of Canterbury, 69152.

North Platte, Lincoln Co., Holy Spirit (1973), Rev. Arthur A. Faesser.
Res., P.O. Box 427, 69103. Tel: 308-534-4334; 534-7906; Fax: 308-534-6525.

Catechesis/Religious Programs—Tel: 308-534-6623. Traci McKeon, D.R.E.
Students 157.

St. Patrick (1875), Rev. Richard L. Piontkowski, Jr.
Res., 415 N. Chestnut, P.O. Box 399, 69103. Tel: 308-532-0942; Fax: 308-532-0944. [CEM]
School—(Grades K-6). Tel: 308-532-0622; Fax: 308-532-8015. Mr. Rick Carpenter, Prin.
Lay Teachers 17; Students 244.
High School—(Grades 7-12). Tel: 308-532-1874; Fax: 308-532-1875. Mr. William McGahan, Jr., Supt.
Lay Teachers 17; Students 209.
Catechesis/Religious Programs—Tel: 308-532-6388. Teresa Titchen, D.R.E.
Students 97.

Ogallala, Keith Co., St. Luke's (1887), Rev. John E. Schlaf.
Res., 417 E. Third, 69153. Tel: 308-284-3196. [JC]
School—Tel: 308-284-4841.
Lay Teachers 4; Students 67.
Catechesis/Religious Programs—Lay Teachers 22; Students 165.

Ord, Valley Co., Our Lady of Perpetual Help (1908), Rev. Rob Rooney.
Res., P.O. Box 123, 68862. Tel: 308-728-3351. [CEM]
School—Tel: 308-728-5389.
Sisters 1; Lay Teachers 5; Students 76.
Catechesis/Religious Programs—Students 152.

Pleasanton, Buffalo Co., St. Mary's (1909) (German), Rev. Louis A. Nollette.
Res., 504 N. Sycamore St., Box 134, 68866. Tel: 308-388-2181. [CEM][JC]
Catechesis/Religious Programs—Tel: 308-388-3062. D.R.E.: Sue Riessland; Claudette Sekutera; Janet Schmitz; Lisa Kennedy.
Students 114.
Missions—Hazard, Sherman Co., St. Gabriel, Market St. & DeWitt St., 68844.; Prairie Center, Buffalo Co., St. Mary, 31325 190 Rd., Kearney 68847. Tel: 308-237-0857. [CEM]

Ravenna, Buffalo Co., Our Lady of Lourdes (1887) (German), Rev. Rodney Lee A. Pruss.
Res., 515 Sicily Ave., Box 90, 68869. Tel: 308-452-3314.
Catechesis/Religious Programs—Tel: 308-452-3109; Fax: 308-452-9102.
Students 148.
Mission—Rockville, Sherman Co., St. Mary's, 406 Fair St., Rockville, 68871. [CEM]

St. Libory, Howard Co., St. Libory's (1884), Rev. David L. Rykwalder.
Res., P.O. Box 7, 68872. Tel: 308-687-6276; Fax: 308-687-6093. [CEM]
Catechesis/Religious Programs—Students 130.
Mission—Wolbach, Greeley Co., St. Joseph's, 713 Elm St., Wolbach, 68882.

St. Paul, Howard Co., SS. Peter and Paul (1878), Rev. Michael F. McDermott.
Res., 405 7th St., 68873. Tel: 308-754-4649; Fax: 308-754-4002. [JC]
Catechesis/Religious Programs—713 Elm St., 68873. Tel: 308-754-4002. Sr. Maria del Rey Mangan, O.P., D.R.E.
Students 118.

Scottsbluff, Scotts Bluff Co., St. Agnes (1912), Rev. James D. O'Kane.
Res., 2314 3rd Ave., P.O. Box 349, 69363. Tel: 308-632-2541; Fax: 308-632-2146.
School—Tel: 308-632-6918; Fax: 308-632-6918.
Lay Teachers 9; Students 107.
Catechesis/Religious Programs—Kathleen Roehl, D.R.E.
Students 146.

Our Lady of Guadalupe (1955) (Hispanic), Rev. Paul J. Colling.
Res., 1103 12th Ave., 69361. Tel: 308-632-2845; Fax: 308-632-7356. [CEM]
Catechesis/Religious Programs—Elizabeth Salazar, D.R.E.
Students 207.

Sidney, Cheyenne Co., St. Patrick's (1878), Rev. Ted A. Nekoliczak; Sr. Marietta Spenner, O.S.F., Pastoral Assoc.
Res., 1039 14th Ave., P.O. Box 99, 69162. Tel: 308-254-2828; Fax: 308-254-2830. [JC]
Catechesis/Religious Programs—D.R.E.: Sr. Marietta Spenner, O.S.F.; Pat Mertz.
Students 305.

Spalding, Greeley Co., St. Michael's (1887), Rev. Joseph A. Hannappel.
Res., 68665. Tel: 308-497-2662. [CEM 2]
Schools—Spalding Academy, Tel: 308-497-2103; Fax: 308-497-2105.
Sisters of St. Dominic 2; Lay Teachers 13; Students 84; (Grades K-6).
Lay Teachers 5; Students 44.
High School—Lay Teachers 9; Students 38.
Catechesis/Religious Programs—Students 110.

Stapleton, Logan Co., St. John the Evangelist (1913) (German), Rev. James E. Novakowski.
Res., P.O. Box 309, 69163. Tel: 308-636-2421. [CEM]
Catechesis/Religious Programs—Marie Chapman, D.R.E.
Students 75.
Mission—Arnold, Custer Co., St. Agnes, Box 309, Arnold 69163. Tel: 308-848-2442.
Catechesis/Religious Programs—Mary Becker Harvey, D.R.E.
Students 50.
Mission—Stapleton, St. Boniface.
Catechesis/Religious Programs—D.R.E.: Gerry Dodge; Joyce Brestel.
Students 62.
Mission—Oconto, St. Mary, 69163.

Sutherland, Lincoln Co., Sacred Heart, Rev. James J. Janovec.
Res., 69165. Tel: 308-386-4300.
Catechesis/Religious Programs—Tel: 308-386-2401.
Students 252.
Missions—Paxton, Keith Co., St. Patrick, P.O. Box 398, 69165.; Hershey, Lincoln Co., Our Lady of Guadalupe, 69165. [JC]

Valentine, Cherry Co., St. Nicholas (1893), Rev. James H. Heithoff.
Res., 69201. Tel: 402-376-1672; Fax: 402-376-1673. [JC]
Catechesis/Religious Programs—Tel: 402-376-1938. Mary Lou Stauffer, D.R.E.
Students 160.
Mission—Nenzel, Cherry Co., St. Mary, P.O. Box 510, 69201. [CEM]

Wood River, Hall Co., St. Mary's (1884), Rev. Raymond M. Kosmicki.
Res., P.O. Box 37, 68883. Tel: 308-583-2464. [CEM]
Catechesis/Religious Programs—Students 120.
Mission—Shelton, Buffalo Co., Sacred Heart, P.O. Box 190, 68876.
Catechesis/Religious Programs—Students 100.

Chaplains of Public Institutions

GRAND ISLAND. *Nebraska Veterans Home*. Rev. James C. Schmitt.
U.S. Veterans' Hospital. Rev. Walter M. Phelan.
KEARNEY. *Youth Development Center* W. Hwy. 30, 68847. Tel: 308-237-3181. Rev. Michael D. McDonald, Chap.

On Duty Outside the Diocese:
Reverend Fathers—
Whalen, Joseph E., 512 Gibson Ave., Lexington, KY 40517

Military Chaplains:
Reverend Fathers—
Borzych, Alexander J.

Retired:
Reverend Monsignors—
Hayden, Carl T., 111 Emerson #1225, Denver, CO 80218
Portrey, Lawrence A., Linden Manor, 420 W. 4th St., North Platte, NE 69101
Reverend Fathers—
Abele, Joseph P., Box 168, Oshkosh, NE 69154
Augustyn, Andrew M., 2517 W. Phoenix, Grand Island, NE 68803
Bauer, Jacob F., 2106 W. Cottage, Grand Island, NE 68803
Chamberlain, Robert F., Box 803, Sutherland, NE 69165
Cook, John N., Box 242, Greeley, NE 68842
Dennett, John A., Box 1323, Lusk, WY 82225
Dillon, Thomas J., 1200 S. Oak, Apt. 2C, North Platte, NE 69101
Dowd, Thomas M., 2516 Commerce Ave., Grand Island, NE 68801
Ferris, Carl A., Valentine, NE 69201
Gonda, Andrew, 1111 E. Nebraska Ave., Grand Island, NE 68801
Gorak, Stanley C., 318 E. 22nd St., Kearney, NE 68847
Guevara, Miguel H., Box 399, North Platte, NE 69103
Koprowski, Mitchell J., Mullen, NE 69152
Kremeier, James, 200 Swink Ave., Rocky Ford, CO 81067
Krystosek, Robert H., Box 425, Clara City, MN 56222
Kurtenbach, Harold R., 2136 W. 11th St., Grand Island, NE 68803
Mullowney, Thomas E., 2801 Grand Ave. #170, Kearney, NE 68847
Murphy, James E., Rte. 1, Box 131, Spalding, NE 68665
Phelan, Walter M., 515 N. Cluster, Grand Island, NE 68803
Phillips, Walter W., 701 Student Dr., Ogallala, NE 69153
Smutny, Jan, Box 194, Pleasanton, NE 68866
Snyder, Frederick, St. Mary's Convent, 2649-US20, Swanton, OH 43558
Szczesny, Michael S., 205 Franciscan Dr., Apt. 326, Crown Point, IN 46307
Whalen, James R., 314 East E, Ogallala, NE 69153

INSTITUTIONS LOCATED IN THE DIOCESE

[A] HIGH SCHOOLS, DIOCESAN

GRAND ISLAND. *Central Catholic Schools*. (Grades 6-12), 1200 Ruby Ave., 68803. Tel: 308-384-2440; Fax: 308-389-3274.
E-mail: rripp@genie.esu10.k12.ne.us
Dr. R. L. Ripp, Supt.; John Golka, Prin.; Howard Schumann, Asst. Prin.; Rev. Frank L. Hoelck..Sisters 1; Lay Teachers 35; Students 413.

[B] GENERAL HOSPITALS

GRAND ISLAND. *Saint Francis Medical Center*, 2620 W. Faidley Ave., P.O. Box 9804, 68802. Tel: 308-384-4600; Fax: 308-389-5589.
E-mail: dsanders@sfmc-gi.org
Web site: www.sfmc-gi.org
For a complete listing, refer to the Hospitals section.

KEARNEY. *Good Samaritan Health Systems dba Good Samaritan Hospital*, 10 E. 31st St., P.O. Box 1990, 68848-1990. Tel: 308-865-7100
For a complete listing, refer to the Hospitals section.

[C] HOMES FOR THE AGED

KEARNEY. *Mount Carmel Home-Keens' Memorial*, 412 W. 18th St., 68847. Tel: 308-237-2287; Fax: 308-236-9380.
E-mail: marycarmelite@hotmail.com
Web site: www.carmelites.org/corpuschristi.htm
For a complete listing, refer to the Special Care Facilities section.

[D] NEWMAN CENTERS

CHADRON. *Chadron State College-Newman Club*, 907 Main St., 69337. Tel: 308-432-4286; 432-3846.
E-mail: newmancsc@bbc.net
Mr. J. Colby Thomazin. Total in Residence 1; Total Staff 1.

KEARNEY. *University of Nebraska at Kearney Newman Apostolate*, 821 W. 27th St., 68845. Tel: 308-234-1539; Fax: 308-233-5718.
E-mail: cathnewman@nebi.com
Web site: www.unk.edu/related/newman
Shirley Wallace, Dir.; Rev. Michael McDonald. Total in Residence 6; Total Staff 4.

RELIGIOUS INSTITUTES OF WOMEN REPRESENTED IN THE DIOCESE

For further details refer to the corresponding bracketed number in the Religious Institutes of Men or Women section.

[0350]—*Carmelite Sisters (Corpus Christi)*.—O.Carm.
[1070-01]—*Dominican Sisters*.—O.P.
[1070-13]—*Dominican Sisters*.—O.P.
[3580]—*Servants of Mary*. (Omaha, NE).—O.S.M.
[3710]—*Sisters of St. Agnes*.—C.S.A.
[0230]—*Sisters of St. Benedict*. (Colorado Springs, CO).
[1630]—*Sisters of St. Francis of Penance and Christian Charity*.—O.S.F.
[1640]—*Sisters of St. Francis of Perpetual Adoration*.—O.S.F.
[3830]—*Sisters of St. Joseph*.—C.S.J.
[3930]—*Sisters of St. Joseph of the Third Order of St. Francis P*.—S.S.J.-T.O.S.F.
[2110]—*Sisters of the Humility of Mary*.—H.M.
[4120-03]—*Ursuline Nuns of the Congregation of Paris*. (Louisville, KY).—O.S.U.

NECROLOGY

† Foster, Robert L., (Retired). —Died Dec. 27, 2000.
† Hargarten, Joseph F., (Retired). —Died Jan. 29, 2000.
† McSweeny, James, (Retired). —Died Jan. 22, 2000.

Diocese of Grand Rapids

(Dioecesis Grandormensis)

Most Reverend

ROBERT J. ROSE, S.T.L., D.D.

Bishop of Grand Rapids; ordained December 21, 1955; appointed Bishop of Gaylord October 13, 1981; consecrated December 6, 1981; appointed Bishop of Grand Rapids July 11, 1989; installed August 30, 1989. *Office: 660 Burton St., S.E., Grand Rapids, MI, 49507.* Tel.: 616-243-0491.

Most Reverend

JOSEPH M. BREITENBECK, D.D.

Retired Bishop of Grand Rapids; ordained May 30, 1942; appointed Titular Bishop of Tepelta and Auxiliary of Detroit October 18, 1965; consecrated December 20, 1965; appointed Bishop of Grand Rapids October 15, 1969; installed December 2, 1969; retired August 3, 1989. *Mailing Address: 660 Burton St., S.E., Grand Rapids, MI, 49507.*

Most Reverend

JOSEPH C. McKINNEY, D.D.

Titular Bishop of Lentini and Auxiliary of Grand Rapids; ordained December 20, 1953; appointed Auxiliary July 24, 1968; consecrated September 26, 1968. *Res., Villa Maria #5110, 1315 Walker, N.W., Grand Rapids, MI, 49504.* Tel.: 616-776-8506; Fax: 616-776-8413.

ESTABLISHED MAY 19, 1882.

Square Miles 6,795.

Comprises the following Counties of the Lower Peninsula of the State of Michigan: Ionia, Kent, Lake, Mason, Mecosta, Montcalm, Muskegon, Newaygo, Oceana, Osceola, Ottawa.

For legal titles of parishes and diocesan institutions, consult the Chancery Office.

Administrative Office of Diocese of Grand Rapids: 660 Burton St., S.E., Grand Rapids, MI, 49507. Tel.: 616-243-0491; Fax: 616-243-4910.

Web site address: www.dioceseofgrandrapids.org

STATISTICAL OVERVIEW

Personnel	
Bishop	1
Auxiliary Bishops	1
Retired Bishops	1
Priests: Diocesan Active in Diocese	86
Priests: Active Outside Diocese	4
Priests: Retired, Sick or Absent	31
Number of Diocesan Priests	121
Religious Priests in Diocese	20
Extern Priests in Diocese	14
Ordinations:	
Diocesan Priests	1
Religious Priests	1
Permanent Deacons in Diocese	18
Total Brothers	2
Total Sisters	294
Parishes	
Parishes	91
With Resident Pastor:	
Resident Diocesan Priests	88
Resident Religious Priests	3
Missions	12
Pastoral Centers	2
Professional Ministry Personnel:	
Brothers	2
Sisters	29
Lay Ministers	61
Welfare	
Catholic Hospitals	2
Total Assisted	397,374
Homes for the Aged	1
Total Assisted	140
Specialized Homes	1
Total Assisted	529
Special Centers for Social Services	15
Total Assisted	222,840
Other Institutions	6
Total Assisted	30,055
Educational	
Seminaries, Diocesan	1
Students from This Diocese	5
Diocesan Students in Other Seminaries	13
Total Seminarians	18
Colleges and Universities	1
Total Students	2,605
High Schools, Diocesan and Parish	4
Total Students	1,916
Elementary Schools, Diocesan and Parish	41
Total Students	8,133
Catechesis/Religious Education:	
High School Students	2,120
Elementary Students	14,863
Total Students Under Catholic Instruction	29,655
Teachers in the Diocese:	
Brothers	1
Sisters	11
Lay Teachers	509
Vital Statistics	
Receptions into the Church:	
Infant Baptism Totals	3,137
Adult Baptism Totals	298
First Communions	2,928
Confirmations	2,352
Marriages:	
Catholic	533
Interfaith	449
Total Marriages	982
Deaths	1,410
Total Catholic Population	158,050
Total Population	1,167,900

Former Bishops—Most Rev. HENRY JOSEPH RICHTER, D.D., cons. April 22, 1883; died Dec. 26, 1916.—Most Rev. MICHAEL JAMES GALLAGHER, D.D., ord. March 19, 1893; appt. titular Bishop of Tipasa and Coadjutor Bishop of Grand Rapids July 5, 1915; cons. Sept. 8, 1915; succeeded to the Diocese of Grand Rapids, Dec. 26, 1916; transferred to the See of Detroit, July 18, 1918; died Jan. 20, 1937.—Most Rev. EDWARD D. KELLY, ord. June 16, 1886; cons. auxiliary Bishop of Detroit, Jan. 26, 1911; transferred to the See of Grand Rapids, Jan. 16, 1919; died March 26, 1926.—Most Rev. JOSEPH G. PINTEN, D.D., ord. Nov. 1, 1890; cons. Bishop of Superior May 3, 1922; transferred to See of Grand Rapids June 25, 1926; resigned and appt. Titular Bishop of Sela Nov. 1, 1940; died Nov. 6, 1945.—Most Rev. JOSEPH CASIMIR PLAGENS, ord. July 5, 1903; cons. Sept. 30, 1924, Auxiliary Bishop of Detroit and Titular Bishop of Rhodiopolis; transferred to See of Marquette Nov. 16, 1935; transferred to See of Grand Rapids Dec. 16, 1940; installed as Bishop of Grand Rapids Feb. 18, 1941; died March 31, 1943.—Most Rev. FRANCIS J. HAAS, D.D., ord. June 11, 1913; appt. Sept. 26, 1943; cons. and installed as Bishop of Grand Rapids, Nov. 18, 1943; died Aug. 29, 1953.—Most Rev. ALLEN J. BABCOCK, D.D., ord. March 7, 1925; appt. Titular Bishop of Irenopolis and Auxiliary of Detroit Feb. 15, 1947; cons. March 25, 1947; appt. to Grand Rapids March 23, 1954; died June 27, 1969.

Administrative Office of Diocese of Grand Rapids—660 Burton St., S.E., Grand Rapids, 49507. Tel: 616-243-0491; Fax: 616-243-4910. Office Hours: Mon.-Fri. 8-4:30 All official communications to be directed to this office.

Moderator of the Curia—Rev. Msgr. TERRENCE L. STEWART.

Chancellor—SR. PATRICE KONWINSKI, O.P.

Vice Chancellor—Rev. WILLIAM H. DUNCAN.

Director of Finance—JOHN S. CZACHORSKI.

Vicars General—Most Rev. JOSEPH C. MCKINNEY, *1315 Walker Rd., N.W., #5110, Grand Rapids, 49504.* Tel: 616-776-8506; Fax: 616-776-8413. Rev. Msgr. TERRENCE L. STEWART, *660 Burton St., S.E., Grand Rapids, 49507.* Tel: 616-243-0491.

Clergy Fund—Rev. R. LOUIS STASKER. Tel: 616-949-4170.

Deans—Rev. DANIEL C. AERTS, Big Rapids, *831 S. Chestnut, Reed City, 49677.* Tel: 231-832-5544. Rev. JOSEPH W. KENSHOL, Grand Rapids North, *1 Maple St., P.O. Box 140, Sand Lake, 49343.* Tel: 616-636-5671. Rev. THEODORE KOZLOWSKI, Grand Rapids South, *101 Hall, S.E., Grand Rapids, 49507.* Tel: 616-243-0222. Rev. JAMES KOWALSKI, Grand Rapids East, *6477 Ada Dr., P.O. Box 369, Ada, 49301.* Tel: 616-676-9111. Rev. STEVEN D. CRON, Grand Rapids West, *733 Bridge, N.W., Grand Rapids, 49504.* Tel: 616-458-3213. Rev. THOMAS F. BOUFFORD, Ionia, *531 Jordan Lake St., Lake Odessa, 48849.* Tel: 616-374-7253. Rev. THOMAS C. NIEDZWIECKI, Ludington, *1 Oak St., P.O. Box 155, Irons, 49644.* Tel:

231-266-5155. Rev. RICHARD J. VAN LENTE, Montague, *510 Iroquois, Fremont, 49412.* Tel: 231-924-0160. Rev. JAMES WYSE, Muskegon, *1292 Jefferson St., Muskegon, 49441-2027.* Tel: 231-722-2793.

Presbyteral Council—Rev. RICHARD J. VAN LENTE, *P.O. Box 248, Fremont, 49412.* Tel: 231-924-0160.

Finance Council—Most Rev. ROBERT J. ROSE, *660 Burton St., S.E., Grand Rapids, 49507.* Tel: 616-243-0491.

Vicar For Religious—Vacant.

Catholic Services Appeal—660 Burton St., S.E., Grand Rapids, 49507. Tel: 616-243-0491.

Tribunal Office—Rev. DENNIS A. WAGNER, Officialis, *265 Sheldon Ave., S.E., Grand Rapids, 49503.* Tel: 616-459-4509.

Vicar For Priests—Rev. DONALD E. WEBER, *1630 Godfrey, S.W., Wyoming, 49509.* Tel: 616-241-6489.

Moderator of the Curia—Rev. Msgr. TERRENCE L. STEWART, *660 Burton St., S.E., Grand Rapids, 49507.* Tel: 616-243-0491.

Secretariat for Christian Life and Ministry Formation

Secretary—Vacant.

Bishop Baraga Bookstore and Religious Education Resource Center—MARGARET A. DEVITO, Coord. Tel: 616-245-2251.

Youth, Young Adult and Family—Mr. MARK MANN. Tel: 616-243-0491, Ext. 539.

Worship and Spirituality—Vacant.

Permanent Diaconate—Rev. DONALD HEYDENS. Tel: 616-243-0491, Ext. 551.

Director of Spiritual Formation—Rev. PHILLIP SHANGRAN.

Christopher House—Rev. MICHAEL DANNER, *723 Rosewood Ave., S.E., East Grand Rapids, 49506.* Tel: 616-243-6538.

Leadership and Professional Formation—Dr. WILLIAM JOHNSTON, Coord. Tel: 616-243-0491, Ext. 540.

Volunteer Formation—Vacant.

Continuing Formation of Priests—Rev. MARK C. PRZYBYSZ, *760 Gladston, S.E., Grand Rapids, 49506.* Tel: 616-243-8998.

Vocation Director—Rev. PAUL MILANOWSKI, *600 Burton, S.E., Grand Rapids, 49507.* Tel: 616-243-0491, Ext. 530.

Pastoral Council Formation—Rev. DENNIS A. WAGNER, Dir.

Secretariat for Diocesan Schools

Secretary—JAMES O'DONNELL.

Supt. of Schools—JAMES O'DONNELL, *600 Burton St., S.E., Grand Rapids, 49507.* Tel: 616-243-0491.

Associate Supt.—Vacant.

Secretariat for Social Justice

Secretary—JAMES RADEMAKER, Dir., *650 Burton St., S.E., Grand Rapids, 49507.* Tel: 616-243-0491.

Catholic Social Services, Grand Rapids—RICHARD V. LIBERATORE, Exec. Dir., *1152 Scribner, N.W., Grand Rapids, 49504.* Tel: 616-456-1443.

Catholic Social Services, Muskegon—ROBERT H. MILLS, Exec. Dir., *1095 Third St., Ste. 125, Muskegon, 49441.* Tel: 616-726-4735.

Catholic Human Development Outreach—SUSAN COOK, Exec. Dir., *650 Burton St., S.E., Grand Rapids, 49507.* Tel: 616-248-3030.

Christian Community Center—540 E. Hackley, Muskegon, 49444. Tel: 231-725-7579.

Rose Haven Ministry—245 Griggs, S.E., Grand Rapids, 49507. Tel: 616-246-6445; Fax: 616-246-8020.

Office of Social Justice—650 Burton St., S.E., Grand Rapids, 49507. Tel: 616-243-0491.

Bishops Overseas Appeal—

Catholic Relief Services—

Project Rachel—PATRICIA RYAN, *650 Burton St., S.E., Grand Rapids, 49507.* Tel: 616-243-0491, Ext. 520.

Office of Black Catholic Ministry—650 Burton St., S.E., Grand Rapids, 49507. Tel: 616-243-0491.

Native American Ministry—SHARRON DETZ, Staff Coord., *650 Burton St., S.E., Grand Rapids, 49507.* Tel: 616-243-0491, Ext. 517.

Hispanic Ministry—LUIS BETETA, *650 Burton S.W., Grand Rapids, 49507.* Tel: 616-243-0491, Ext. 557.

Vietnamese Ministry—Rev. PETER NGHIEM, *Our Lady of Lavang, 2420 Avon, S.W., Wyoming, 49509.* Tel: 616-531-5213.

Prison/Jail Ministry—JUDITH GRANSTROM, Dir., *650 Burton St., S.E., Grand Rapids, 49507.* Tel: 616-243-0491.

Secretariat for Administration

Secretary—Sr. PATRICE KONWINSKI, O.P., *660 Burton St., S.E., Grand Rapids, 49507.* Tel: 616-243-0491.

Archivist—Rev. DENNIS W. MORROW, *660 Burton St., S.E., Grand Rapids, 49507.* Tel: 616-243-0491.

Building and Planning Committee—Sr. PATRICE KONWINSKI, O.P., *660 Burton St., S.E., Grand Rapids, 49507.* Tel: 616-243-0491.

Cemeteries—ROBERT MENZEL, *4100 Clyde Park, S.W., Wyoming, 49509-0063.* Tel: 616-531-9320. Resurrection Cemetery; Mt. Calvary Cemetery; St. Andrew Cemetery; Holy Cross Cemetery: ROBERT R. MENZEL, Mgr., *Res., 4100 Clyde Park, S.W., Grand Rapids, 49509.* Tel: 616-531-9320.

Director of Finance—JOHN S. CZACHORSKI, *660 Burton St., S.E., Grand Rapids, 49507.* Tel: 616-243-0491.

Self-Insurance Program—Sr. PATRICE KONWINSKI, O.P., *660 Burton St., S.E., Grand Rapids, 49507.* Tel: 616-243-0491.

Tribunal—Rev. DENNIS A. WAGNER, Officialis, *265 Sheldon, S.E., Grand Rapids, 49503.* Tel: 616-459-4509.

Council of Catholic Women—HELEN WEISNECK, *650 Burton St., S.E., Grand Rapids, 49507.* Tel: 616-243-0491.

Ecumenical Commission—Rev. CHARLES R. DAUTREMONT, *50 Bellevue St., S.W., Wyoming, 49548-3144.*

Hospital Apostolate—Rev. MARK E. MITCHELL, Chap., *Res., 628 Diamond N.E., Grand Rapids, 49503.* Tel: 616-242-4832.

Director of Communications—MARY HAARMAN.

Director of Stewardship/Development—SHARRON REYNOLDS.

Director of Research & Planning—KEVIN WOODS.

CLERGY, PARISHES, MISSIONS AND PAROCHIAL SCHOOLS

CITY OF GRAND RAPIDS
(Kent County)

1—CATHEDRAL OF ST. ANDREW, Rev. M. Thomas Bolster.
Res., 267 Sheldon Ave., S.E., 49503. Tel: 616-456-1454. [CEM]
School—305 Sheldon Ave., S.E., 49503.
Sisters 4; Lay Teachers 14; Students 188.
Catechesis/Religious Programs—Students 140.

2—BASILICA OF ST. ADALBERT (Polish), Rev. Thomas J. De Young.
Parish Office: Box 1, Basilica Center, 671 Davis, N.W., 49504-5137. Tel: 616-458-3065; Fax: 616-458-0563. [JC]

3—ST. ALPHONSUS, Revs. Thomas Donaldson, C.SS.R.; Bernard Rooney, C.SS.R.; Rudy Papes, C.SS.R.; Thomas O'Connor, C.SS.R.; Robert Balser, C.SS.R.; Durkin Fitzgerald.
Res., 224 Carrier St., N.E., 49505. Tel: 616-451-3043. [JC]
School—228 Carrier St., N.E., 49505. Tel: 616-454-4904.
Brothers 1; Sisters 1; Lay Teachers 20; Students 375.
Catechesis/Religious Programs—Lucio Caruso, D.R.E.
Students 215.

4—ST. ANTHONY OF PADUA, Revs. Edmund Goldbach, O.F.M.Conv.; Peter Nickels, O.F.M. Conv. In res., Rev. Raymond Oosdyke, O.F.M.Conv.
Res., 2510 Richmond St., N.W., 49504. Tel: 616-453-8229; Fax: 616-453-8053.
School—Tel: 616-453-4062. Paul R. Guild, Prin.
Lay Teachers 19; Students 371.
Catechesis/Religious Programs—Tel: 616-453-6647. Sandra Ten Hagen, D.R.E.
Students 362.

5—BLESSED SACRAMENT, Rev. John J. Wisneski; Deacon George LeMire.
Res., 2275 Diamond Ave., N.E., 49505-4313. Tel: 616-361-7339; Fax: 616-361-1327. [JC]
School—2233 Diamond, N.E., 49505-4313. Tel: 616-364-9453; Fax: 616-361-6991.
Lay Teachers 17; Students 307.
Catechesis/Religious Programs—Tel: 616-361-7738. Jody DeGraw, D.R.E.
Students 96.

6—ST. FRANCIS XAVIER, Rev. Jose Quintana.
Res., 250 Brown St., S.E., 49507. Tel: 616-241-2485; Fax: 616-241-2079. [JC]
School—240 Brown St., S.E., 49507. Tel: 616-241-5474; Fax: 616-241-5493. Mr. Tom Priest, Prin.
Lay Teachers 11; Students 180.
Catechesis/Religious Programs—Angie Ciccone, D.R.E.
Students 60.

7—HOLY NAME OF JESUS, Rev. Donald E. Weber.
Res., 1630 Godfrey Ave., S.W., 49509. Tel: 616-241-6489; Fax: 616-241-6480. [JC]
School—1650 Godfrey Ave., S.W., 49509. Tel: 616-243-1126; Fax: 616-243-0862. Sr. Adele Labiotka, Prin.
Sisters 1; Lay Teachers 12; Students 162.
Catechesis/Religious Programs—Tel: 616-245-3359.
Students 157.

8—HOLY SPIRIT, Rev. Leonard Sudlik; Daryl E. Nowicki, Business Mgr.
Res., 2230 Lake Michigan Dr., N.W., 49504. Tel: 616-453-6369; Fax: 616-453-0244.
School—Tel: 616-453-2772; Fax: 616-453-0018.
Lay Teachers 27; Students 517.
Catechesis/Religious Programs—Tel: 616-453-1591.
Students 195.

9—IMMACULATE HEART OF MARY, Rev. Julian Reginato; Deacon Virgil Glocheski.
Res., 1935 Plymouth Rd., S.E., 49506. Tel: 616-241-4477; Fax: 616-241-2832.
School—Tel: 616-241-4633; Fax: 616-241-4418.
Lay Teachers 20; Students 424.
Catechesis/Religious Programs—Tel: 616-241-0863. Teri D'Orazio, D.R.E.
Students 133.

10—ST. ISIDORE'S (Polish), Rev. Donald E. Lomasiewicz.
Res., 628 Diamond Ave., N.E., 49503. Tel: 616-459-4731; Fax: 616-454-5832. [JC]
School—625 Spring Ave., N.E., 49503. Tel: 616-454-1236.
Lay Teachers 12; Students 142.
Catechesis/Religious Programs—Students 56.

11—ST. JAMES, Rev. Steven D. Cron; Norm Szubinski, Pastoral Assoc.
Res., 733 Bridge St., N.W., 49504. Tel: 616-458-3213; Fax: 616-458-9002.
School—751 First St., N.W., 49504. Tel: 616-454-2567.
Lay Teachers 13; Students 121.
Catechesis/Religious Programs—671 Davis N.W., 49504. Tel: 616-451-4215; Fax: 616-451-4215.
Students 90.

12—ST. JOHN VIANNEY, Rev. Larry King.
Res., 4135 Clyde Park, S.W., 49509. Tel: 616-534-5449; Fax: 616-530-8224. [JC]
School—Tel: 616-532-7001; Fax: 616-532-1884. Catherine Prietz, Prin.
Lay Teachers 23; Students 434.
Catechesis/Religious Programs—Tel: 616-532-2397.
Students 289.

13—ST. JOSEPH THE WORKER, Rev. Pedro V. Garcia.
Res., 333 Rumsey St., S.W., 49503-4935. Tel: 616-456-7982; Fax: 616-456-1445.

14—ST. DOMINIC, Rev. Charles R. Dautremont.
Office: 50 Bellevue, S.W., 49548-3144. Tel: 616-531-1480; Fax: 616-531-0759.
Catechesis/Religious Programs—Students 43.

15—ST. JUDE, Rev. Thomas S. Vesbit.
Office: 1120 Four Mile, N.E., 49505. Tel: 616-363-6885; Fax: 616-363-1470.
School—Tel: 616-363-7725; Fax: 616-363-3086.
Lay Teachers 16; Students 226.
Catechesis/Religious Programs—1110 Four Mile, N.E., 49505. Tel: 616-363-6897; Fax: 616-363-1470. Patricia Cebelak, D.R.E.
Students 294.

16—ST. MARY'S, Rev. Dick Host.
Res., 423 First St., N.W., 49504. Tel: 616-459-7390; Fax: 616-459-9630.
Catechesis/Religious Programs—Tel: 616-451-4215. Dick Bulkowski, D.R.E.
Students 48.

17—ST. MARY MAGDALEN, Rev. Louis L. Anderson; Sr. Beverly Pety, O.P., Pastoral Assoc.; Deacon Michael L. Wood.
Res., 1213 52nd St., S.E., 49508. Tel: 616-455-9310; Fax: 616-455-4139.
Catechesis/Religious Programs—Tel: 616-455-1110.
Students 555.

18—OUR LADY OF SORROWS (Italian), Rev. Theodore Kozlowski.
Res., 101 Hall St., S.E., 49507. Tel: 616-243-0222.
Catechesis/Religious Programs—Tony Bulgarella, D.R.E.
Students 104.

19—ST. PAUL THE APOSTLE, Rev. Msgr. Ernest Schneider; Deacon Richard Radecki; Daniel J. Donnelly, Pastoral Assoc.
Res., 2750 Burton St., S.E., 49546. Tel: 616-949-4170; Fax: 616-949-5295.
School—Tel: 616-949-1690; Fax: 616-949-0836.
Lay Teachers 16; Students 259.
Catechesis/Religious Programs—Beth Kolenda, D.R.E.
Students 20.

20—SS. PETER AND PAUL (Lithuanian), Rev. Dennis Morrow; Deacon Manuel E. Herrera.
Res., 520 Myrtle St., N.W., 49504. Tel: 616-454-6000; Fax: 616-454-4532. [CEM]
School—1433 Hamilton Ave., N.W., 49504. Lori Salva, Prin.
Lay Teachers 8; Students 95.
Catechesis/Religious Programs—Students 26.

21—SACRED HEART, Rev. Edward A. Hankiewicz; Sr. Marie Bernarde Salazar, O.P., Pastoral Assoc. In res., Rev. Msgr. James P. Moran, P.A.
Res., 156 Valley Ave., S.W., 49504. Tel: 616-459-8362. [JC]
School—Tel: 616-459-0948; Fax: 616-459-0899. Richard E. Kosla, Prin.
Lay Teachers 9; Students 170.
Catechesis/Religious Programs—Barbara Velte, D.R.E.
Students 57.

22—ST. STEPHEN'S, Rev. Mark C. Przybysz.
Res., 750 Gladstone Ave., S.E., 49506. Tel: 616-243-8998; Fax: 616-245-7360. [JC]
School—740 Rosewood Ave., S.E., 49506. Fax: 616-243-0451. Nannette Swanson, Prin.
Lay Teachers 12; Students 290.
Catechesis/Religious Programs—Mrs. Rhonda Lomonaco, D.R.E.
Students 400.

23—ST. THOMAS THE APOSTLE, Rev. James A. Chelick.
Res., 1449 Wilcox Park Dr., S.E., 49506. Tel: 616-459-4662; Fax: 616-458-4047. [JC]
School—Tel: 616-458-4228; Fax: 616-458-4583. David A. Faber, Prin.
Lay Teachers 14; Students 292.

OUTSIDE THE CITY OF GRAND RAPIDS

Ada, Kent Co., St. Robert, Revs. R. Louis Stasker; James C. Kowalski. Pastoral Assocs.: Sr. Joan Brown, O.P.; Sr. Ann Michael Farnsworth, O.P.
Res., P.O. Box 369, 49301. Tel: 616-676-9111; Fax: 616-676-0950.
Catechesis/Religious Programs—Tel: 616-676-1488. Mary Ann Snyder, D.R.E.
Students 1,148.

Alpine, Kent Co., Holy Trinity, Rev. Daniel R. DePew.
Res., 1200 Alpine Church Rd., N.W., 49321. Tel: 616-784-0677; Fax: 616-784-0678.
School—Comstock Park, 49321. Tel: 616-784-0696. Nancy Kryger, Prin.
Lay Teachers 9; Students 220.
Catechesis/Religious Programs—Tel: 616-784-3242. Jackie Lyals, D.R.E.
Students 235.

Baldwin, Lake Co., St. Ann's, Rev. Joseph J. Fix.
Res., 740 E. Ninth St., 49304. Tel: 231-745-7997; Fax: 231-745-9844.
Mission—Luther, St. Ignatius.

Belding, Ionia Co., St. Joseph's, Rev. Troy Nevins.
Office: 409 S. Bridge St., 48809. Tel: 616-794-2145; Fax: 616-794-2145. [CEM]
School—St. Joseph-St. Mary, Tel: 616-794-1910. Kathy Rand, Prin.
Lay Teachers 4; Students 62.

Belmont, Kent Co., Assumption of the Blessed Virgin Mary, Rev. James M. Bozung, Admin.
Res., 6369 Belmont Ave., 49306. Tel: 616-361-5126; Fax: 616-361-5503. [CEM]
School—6393 Belmont Ave., 49306. Tel: 616-361-5483; Fax: 616-361-2553. Sr. Rosemary Smith, R.S.M., Prin.
Lay Teachers 9; Students 217.

Big Rapids, Mecosta Co., St. Mary's, Rev. Michael G. McKenna; Beth Dake, Pastoral Assoc.
1009 Marion Ave., 49307. Tel: 231-796-5202; Fax: 231-796-9231. [CEM]
School—Tel: 231-796-6731; Fax: 231-976-9293. Patricia A. Knapp, Prin.
Lay Teachers 9; Students 129.
Catechesis/Religious Programs—Fax: 231-796-9123.
Students 11.

St. Paul's Campus Parish, Rev. Wayne B. Wheeler, Jr.
Res., One Damascus Rd., 49307. Tel: 231-796-7393; Fax: 231-796-3990.
Catechesis/Religious Programs—Students 171.

Brunswick, Newaygo Co., St. Michael's, Rev. Donn P. Tufts.
Res., 10224 Maple Island Rd., R.R. #5, Fremont, 49412. Tel: 231-924-3389; 924-9803; Fax: 231-924-0402. [CEM]
School—Tel: 231-924-0268; Fax: 231-924-0268. Sr. M. Theresa Pelky, R.S.M.
Sisters 3; Lay Teachers 4; Students 77.
Catechesis/Religious Programs—Students 102.
Mission—Hesperia, Christ the King.

Byron Center, Kent Co., St. Sebastian's, Rev. Msgr. Gaspar F. Ancona.
Res., 9408 Wilson, 49315. Tel: 616-878-1893; Fax: 616-878-4019. [CEM]
Catechesis/Religious Programs—Tel: 616-878-1619; Fax: 616-878-0715. Theresa Dekker, D.R.E.
Students 204.

Caledonia, Kent Co., Holy Family, Rev. David E. LeBlanc.
Res., 9669 Kraft Ave., S.E., 49316. Tel: 616-891-1160; 891-9259 (Office); Fax: 616-891-1346. [CEM 3]
Catechesis/Religious Programs—Tel: 616-891-8867. Judy France, D.R.E.
Students 617.

Carson City, Montcalm Co., St. Mary's, Rev. William J. Reitz.
Res., 404 N. Division St., 48811. Tel: 517-584-3553. [CEM]
Catechesis/Religious Programs—Tel: 517-981-6668. Kathleen Copp, D.R.E.
Students 70.

Conklin, Ottawa Co., St. Francis Xavier, Rev. John F. Porter.
Res., 2044 Gooding Rd., 49403. Tel: 616-899-2471; Fax: 231-853-2191.
Catechesis/Religious Programs—Students 85.

Coopersville, Ottawa Co., St. Michael's, Rev. John Vallier.
Res., 17151 88th Ave., 49404. Tel: 616-837-8792; 837-8158 (Parish Office); Fax: 616-837-7893.
School—Tel: 616-837-6346. Kevin Varner, Prin.
Lay Teachers 5; Students 90.
Catechesis/Religious Programs—Tel: 616-837-8580.
Students 90.

Custer, Mason Co., St. Mary's, Rev. Isidro Gargatiel (Philippines).
Res., 85 S. Madison, P.O. Box 68, 49405. Tel: 231-757-4709. [CEM]
Catechesis/Religious Programs—Tel: 231-757-3078. Roberta Edel, D.R.E.
Students 53.

Edmore, Montcalm Co., St. Margaret Mary, Rev. Vincent Bryce, O.P.
Res., 1051 E. Howard City Rd., 48829. Tel: 517-427-5645; Fax: 517-427-3268.
Catechesis/Religious Programs—Students 50.

Evart, Osceola Co., Sacred Heart, Rev. Joseph J. Fix.
Res., 9878 E. US 10, P.O. Box 778, 49631. Tel: 231-734-3171; Fax: 231-734-6880.
Catechesis/Religious Programs—Students 30.

Free Soil, Mason Co., St. John Cantius, Rev. Thomas C. Niedzwiecki.
Res., 2845 E. Michigan, 49411-9602. Tel: 231-464-5672. [CEM]
Catechesis/Religious Programs—Tel: 231-464-5567. Mary Kovalcik, D.R.E.
Students 38.

Fremont, Newaygo Co., All Saints, Rev. Richard J. Van Lente.
Res., 510 Iroquois Dr., P.O. Box 248, 49412. Tel: 231-924-0160; Fax: 231-924-0996.
Catechesis/Religious Programs—Tel: 231-924-5520.
Students 125.

Grand Haven, Ottawa Co., St. Patrick's, Rev. William A. Langlois; Deacon Dale Hollern.
Res., 920 Fulton St., 49417. Tel: 616-842-0001.
Catechesis/Religious Programs—Tel: 616-842-8230. Jeff Andrini, D.R.E.
Students 303.
Mission—Robinson Township, St. Anthony, 13421 Green St., 49417.

Grandville, Kent Co., St. Pius X, Rev. George E. Darling; Deacon Norman Riksen, Pastoral Assoc.
Res., 3937 Wilson Ave., S.W., 49418. Tel: 616-532-9344; Fax: 616-538-6340.
Catechesis/Religious Programs—Tel: 616-538-2600. Linda Vanden Berg, D.R.E.
Students 573.

Greenville, Montcalm Co., St. Charles, Rev. G. Fredrick Brucker.
Res., 505 S. Lafayette, 48838. Tel: 616-754-4194; Fax: 616-754-2357. [CEM]
School—502 S. Franklin St., 48838. Tel: 616-754-3416; Fax: 616-754-9262. Sr. David Therese Korson, O.P., Prin.
Sisters of St. Dominic, Grand Rapids, MI 1; Lay Teachers 8; Students 137.
Catechesis/Religious Programs—Tel: 616-754-3196. Joseph Velie, D.R.E.
Students 125.
Mission—Harvard, Kent Co., St. Margaret, 10195 16 Mile Rd., Cedar Springs, 49319. Tel: 616-696-3904. [CEM]

Hart, Oceana Co., St. Gregory's, Rev. Ronald F. Schneider.
Res., 316 Peach St., 49420. Tel: 231-873-2660; Fax: 231-873-7601.
Catechesis/Religious Programs—Andrea Bosse, D.R.E.
Students 110.
Mission—Elbridge, St. Joseph Church.

Holland, Ottawa Co., St. Francis de Sales, Rev. Stephen S. Dudek; Sr. M. Therese Harum, I.H.M., Pastoral Assoc.; Deacon Juan Garcia.
Office: 195 W. 13th St., 49423. Tel: 616-396-7641; Fax: 616-392-2474.
Res., 454 Melrose Dr. E., 49423. Tel: 616-392-3985.
School—Holland Area Catholic Schools 12100 Quincy St., 49424. Tel: 616-994-9864; Fax: 616-994-9870. Mitri Zainea, Prin.
Lay Teachers 13; Students 286.
Catechesis/Religious Programs—195 W. 13th St., 49423. Tel: 616-392-6700. Marilyn Torborg, D.R.E.
Students 370.

Our Lady of the Lake, Rev. William H. Duncan.
Res., 480 152nd Ave., 49424. Tel: 616-399-1062; Fax: 616-399-5766.
Catechesis/Religious Programs—Mark E. Peacock, D.R.E.
Students 406.

Howard City, Montcalm Co., Christ the King, Rev. Phillip A. Sliwinski.
Res., 9596 Reed Rd., 49329. Tel: 231-937-5757; Fax: 231-937-9268.
Catechesis/Religious Programs—Katherine P. Miller, D.R.E.
Students 70.

Hubbardston, Ionia Co., St. John the Baptist, Rev. William J. Reitz.
Res., 404 N. Division, Carson City, 48811. Tel: 517-584-3553. [CEM]
Catechesis/Religious Programs—Tel: 517-981-6668. Kathleen Copp, D.R.E.
Students 68.

Ionia, Ionia Co., SS. Peter and Paul, Rev. Melvin E. Fox; Deacon Zenon Cardenas, Sr.
Parish Office: 434 High St., 48846. Tel: 616-527-3610; Fax: 616-527-3697. [CEM]
School—317 Baldie, 48846. Tel: 616-527-3561; Fax: 616-527-3562.
Lay Teachers 12; Students 189.
Catechesis/Religious Programs—Students 135.

Irons, Lake Co., St. Bernard's, Rev. Thomas C. Niedzwicki.
Res., One Oak St., P.O. Box 155, 49644. Tel: 231-266-5155; Fax: 231-266-8948.
Catechesis/Religious Programs—Students 13.

Jenison, Ottawa Co., Holy Redeemer, Rev. Richard J. Lawie.
Res., 2700 Baldwin Dr., 49428. Tel: 616-669-9220; Fax: 616-669-9360.
Catechesis/Religious Programs—Tel: 616-669-0820. Therese Carroll-Caruso, D.R.E.
Students 719.

Lake Odessa, Ionia Co., St. Edward's, Rev. Thomas F. Boufford.
Res., 531 Jordan Lake St., 48849-6200. Tel: 616-374-7253; Fax: 616-374-1559.
Catechesis/Religious Programs—Dee Manshum, D.R.E.
Students 110.

Lakeview, Montcalm Co., St. Francis de Sales, Rev. Phillip A. Sliwinski.
Res., 9596 N. Reed Rd., Howard City, 49329. Tel: 231-937-5757; Fax: 231-937-9268.
Church—829 E. Richardson, 48850. Tel: 517-352-7293.
Catechesis/Religious Programs—Tel: 517-352-6716.
Students 35.

Lakewood Club, Muskegon Co., St. Mary of the Woods, Rev. Paul T. Johnson.
Res., 150 Church St., Twin Lake, 49457. Tel: 231-894-5887.

Lowell, Kent Co., St. Mary's, Rev. George J. Fekete.
Res., 402 Amity St., 49331-1308. Tel: 616-897-9820; Fax: 616-897-9683. [CEM]
Catechesis/Religious Programs—Maggie Walsh, D.R.E.
Students 160.

Ludington, Mason Co., St. Simon's, Rev. Kenneth H. Schichtel.
Res., 702 E. Bryant Rd., 49431. Tel: 231-843-8606; Fax: 231-843-2052. [CEM]
School—Tel: 231-843-3188. Collin Thompson, Prin.
Lay Teachers 10; Students 194.
Catechesis/Religious Programs—Tel: 231-843-3497; Fax: 231-843-3497.
Students 350.

St. Stanislaus, Rev. Dennis O'Donnell.
Res., 503 Third St., 49431. Tel: 231-845-7666. [JC]

Marion, Osceola Co., St. Agnes, Rev. Joseph J. Fix.
Res., P.O. Box 778, Evart, 49631. Tel: 231-734-3171.
Church—Tel: 231-743-6401; Fax: 231-734-6880.

Marne, Ottawa Co., St. Mary's, Rev. Msgr. Terrence L. Stewart; Sr. Bernadine Gazda, S.S.J., Pastoral Assoc.
Res., 15164 Juniper Dr., 49435. Tel: 616-677-3934;

Fax: 616-677-5866. [CEM]
Catechesis/Religious Programs—Tel: 616-677-3753.
Students 166.

Miriam, Ionia Co., St. Mary's, Rev. Troy Nevins.
Office: 409 S. Bridge St., Belding, 48809. Tel: 616-794-2145; Fax: 616-794-2145. [CEM]
School—St. Joseph-St. Mary. See St. Joseph, Belding. 616-794-1910.

Montague, Muskegon Co., St. James, Rev. Chris Rouech.
Res., 5179 Dowling St., 49437. Tel: 231-893-3085; Fax: 231-894-9929. [CEM]
School—Tel: 231-893-2972. Mitzi Luttrull, Prin.
Lay Teachers 7; Students 78.
Catechesis/Religious Programs—Tel: 616-894-8771. Brenda Runyan, D.R.E.
Students 130.
Mission—Claybanks, St. John. 5179 Dowling St.

Muskegon, Muskegon Co.,

1—Our Lady of Grace, Rev. Michael P. Olson; Michael A. Pekar, Jr., Pastoral Assoc.
Res., 451 S. Getty St., 49442. Tel: 231-722-2803; Fax: 231-722-3622. [JC]
Catechesis/Religious Programs—Students 85.

2—St. Francis de Sales, Revs. Thomas G. Simons; Thomas J. Brown; Deacon William McCabe.
Res., 2929 McCracken St., 49441. Tel: 231-755-1953; Fax: 231-759-7074.
Catechesis/Religious Programs—Tel: 231-755-1307. Terry Klages, D.R.E.
Students 170.

3—St. Jean Baptiste, Rev. James B. Wyse; T. J. Achatz, Pastoral Assoc.
Res., 1292 Jefferson St., 49441. Tel: 231-722-2793; Fax: 231-726-5976. [JC]
Catechesis/Religious Programs—Barbara Miles, D.R.E.
Students 130.

4—St. Joseph's, Rev. David Harpe.
Res., 1224 Fifth St., 49441. Tel: 231-722-2556. [CEM]

5—St. Mary's, Rev. Ernest J. Bernott, Admin.
Res., 239 W. Clay Ave., 49440-1213. Tel: 231-722-2844; Fax: 231-722-0733. [JC]

6—St. Michael's, Rev. Thomas J. Hack.
Res., 1716 Sixth St., 49441. Tel: 231-722-3071; Fax: 231-722-3243. [JC]
Catechesis/Religious Programs—Sr. Agnes Mary Wojtkowiak, O.P., D.R.E.
Students 627.

7—St. Thomas the Apostle, Rev. Phillip J. Witkowski; Deacon David Kasprzyk.
Office: 3252 Apple Ave., 49442. Tel: 231-773-3160; Fax: 231-777-7866.
Catechesis/Religious Programs—Students 175.

Muskegon Heights, Muskegon Co., Sacred Heart, Rev. Norman P. Droski.
Res., 150 E. Summit Ave., 49444. Tel: 231-733-2440; Fax: 231-733-5128.
Catechesis/Religious Programs—Tel: 231-733-2455.
Students 35.
Convent—2900 Leahy St., 49444.

Newaygo, Newaygo Co., St. Bartholomew's, Rev. Loc Trinh.
Res., 599 Brooks St., 49337. Tel: 231-652-1286; Fax: 231-652-6669. [CEM]
Catechesis/Religious Programs—Jearise Havenga, D.R.E.
Students 261.
Mission—Grant, Our Lady of Guadalupe Church.

North Muskegon, Muskegon Co., Prince of Peace, Rev. Robert A. Hart; Deacon Wesley Hewitt, Pastoral Assoc.
Res., 1110 Dykstra, 49445. Tel: 231-744-3321; Fax: 231-744-4859.
Catechesis/Religious Programs—Tel: 231-744-5445. John Graveline, D.R.E.
Students 60.

Parnell, Kent Co., St. Patrick's, Rev. Ronald D. Hutchinson.
Res., 4351 Parnell Ada, 49301. Tel: 616-691-8541; Fax: 616-691-6309. [CEM]
School—Tel: 616-691-8833. Suzanne Dengaw, Prin.
Students 184.

Pewamo, Ionia Co., St. Joseph's, Rev. Charlon O. Mason, Admin.
Res., 106 East St., 48873. Tel: 517-593-3440. [CEM]
School—Tel: 517-593-3400. Lorie Salisbury, Prin.
Lay Teachers 5; Students 105.
Catechesis/Religious Programs—840 N. Norway Dr., P.O. Box 372, Fowler, 48835. Tel: 517-593-3488. Aaron Epkey.
Students 99.

Portland, Ionia Co., St. Patrick's, Revs. Charles D. Hall; Peter Vu.
Res., 140 Church St., 48875. Tel: 517-647-6505; Fax: 517-647-7807.
School—122 West St., 48875. Tel: 517-647-7551; Fax: 517-647-4545.
Lay Teachers 15; Students 352.
High School—Lay Teachers 16; Students 120.
Catechesis/Religious Programs—Tel: 517-647-0040. Thomas Jandernoa, D.R.E.
Students 280.

Ravenna, Muskegon Co., St. Catherine, Rev. John F. Porter.
Res., 49451. Tel: 231-853-6222; Fax: 231-853-2191. [CEM]
School—Tel: 231-853-6743. Sr. Peter Mary Korson, O.P., Prin.
Lay Teachers 4; Students 43.
Catechesis/Religious Programs—Tel: 231-853-6222.
Students 53.

Reed City, Osceola Co., St. Philip Neri, Rev. Daniel C. Aerts.
Res., 831 S. Chestnut, 49677. Tel: 231-832-5544; Fax: 231-832-5545. [CEM]
Catechesis/Religious Programs—Elizabeth Marek, D.R.E.
Students 118.
Mission—Paris, Mecosta Co., St. Anne, 49338.

Remus, Mecosta Co., St. Michael's, Rev. William F. Zink.
Res., 5045 Nine Mile Rd., 49340. Tel: 517-967-3520; Fax: 517-967-8246. [CEM]
School—(Grades PreK-6). Mr. Deborah Tyson, Prin.
Sisters 2; Lay Teachers 9; Students 160.
Catechesis/Religious Programs—Robert Cathcart, D.R.E.
Students 134.

Rockford, Kent Co., Our Lady of Consolation, Revs. Thomas P. Page; Anthony S. Russo; Mary Ellen Koziol, Pastoral Assoc.
Office: 5001 Eleven Mile Rd., 49341. Tel: 616-866-0931; Fax: 616-866-3668.
School—(Grades PreK-6). Tel: 616-866-2427; Fax: 616-866-5475. Carolyn Hardy, Prin.
Lay Teachers 10; Students 235.
Catechesis/Religious Programs—Tel: 616-866-2577. Amy Sue Paquin, D.R.E.
Students 950.

Rothbury, Oceana Co., Our Lady of the Assumption, Rev. Mark F. Bauer.
Res., 1372 S. Oceana Dr., Shelby, 49455. Tel: 231-861-2620.
Church—3000 Winston Rd., P.O. Box 8, 49452. Tel: 231-893-0905.

Sand Lake, Kent Co., Mary Queen of Apostles, Rev. Joseph W. Kenshol.
Res., P.O. Box 140, 49343. Tel: 616-636-5671; Fax: 616-636-4570. [CEM 2]
Catechesis/Religious Programs—Tel: 616-636-5923. Pat Patin, D.R.E.
Students 204.
Mission—Coral, St. Clara, 4584 N. Bailey Rd., 49322.

Saranac, Ionia Co., St. Anthony, Rev. Norbert L. Leyrita (Phillipines).
Res., 3927 Jackson Rd., 48881. Tel: 616-642-6119.
Catechesis/Religious Programs—Tel: 616-642-6402. D.R.E.: Janice Diaz; Sharon Bassett.
Students 73.

Scottville, Mason Co., St. Jerome, Rev. Isidro T. Gargantiel.
Res., 203 W. State St., 49454. Tel: 231-757-2855.
Catechesis/Religious Programs—Kathy Papes, D.R.E.
Students 62.

Shelby, Oceana Co., Our Lady of Fatima, Rev. Mark F. Bauer.
Res., 1372 S. Oceana Dr., 49455. Tel: 231-861-2620.
Catechesis/Religious Programs—Paula Michalko, D.R.E.
Students 70.

Sparta, Kent Co., Holy Family, Rev. Philip A. Shangraw.
Res., 425 S. State St., 49345. Tel: 616-887-8222; Fax: 616-887-0681.
Catechesis/Religious Programs—Tel: 616-887-8857.
Students 255.

Spring Lake, Ottawa Co., St. Mary's, Rev. Anthony C. Vainavicz.
Res., 406 E. Savidge, 49456. Tel: 616-842-1702; Fax: 616-842-3392.
School—Tel: 616-842-1282. Wendy Sipka, Prin.
Dominican Sisters 3; Lay Teachers 11; Students 219.
Catechesis/Religious Programs—Tel: 616-842-2840. Peggy Secory, D.R.E.
Students 285.
Convent—421 E. Exchange St., 49456. Tel: 616-842-1615.

Stanton, Montcalm Co., St. Bernadette of Lourdes, Rev. Vincent Bryce, O.P.
Res., 1051 E. Howard City, Edmore, 48829. Tel: 517-427-5645; Fax: 517-427-3268.
Catechesis/Religious Programs—Students 75.

Weare Twp., Oceana Co., St. Joseph's, Rev. Charles D. Brown.
Res., 2380 W. Jackson Rd., Hart, 49420. Tel: 231-873-2683; Fax: 231-873-5327. [CEM]
Catechesis/Religious Programs—Tel: 231-869-5231. Clara Jean Monton, D.R.E.
Students 110.
Mission—Pentwater, St. Vincent, 637 E. Sixth, 49449. Tel: 231-869-2601.

White Cloud, Newaygo Co., St. Joseph's, Rev. Richard J. VanLente, Admin.
965 Newell St., 49349. Tel: 231-689-6061; Fax: 231-689-6225. [CEM]

Wright Township, Ottawa Co., St. Joseph's, Rev. Leo S. Rosloniec.
Res., 18876 Eighth Ave., Conklin, 49403. Tel: 616-899-2286; Fax: 616-899-2212.
School—Tel: 616-899-5300; Fax: 616-899-5491. Mrs. Ann Rutowski, Prin.
Dominican Sisters 1; Lay Teachers 5; Students 75.
Catechesis/Religious Programs—Students 132.

Wyoming, Our Lady of LaVang (1999), Rev. Peter Nghiem.
2420 Avon S.W., 49509. Tel: 616-531-5213; Fax: 616-261-9906.

CHAPELS

Grand Rapids. *Chapel of Our Lady of Aglona, Latvian Apostolate* 507 Broadway Ave., N.W., 49504. Tel: 616-363-2337.

Chapel of St. Paul-Catholic Information Center 246 Ionia, N.W., 49503. Tel: 616-459-7267. Revs. Robert Cary, C.S.P.; Joseph W. Gallagher, C.S.P.; Charles Cunniff, C.S.P.; John Kenny, C.S.P.; Deacon Michael Mauer.

Michigan Veterans' Facility Catholic Chapel 3000 Monroe Ave., N.E., 49505. Tel: 616-364-5323.

On Special Assignment:

Reverend Monsignors—

Stewart, Terrence L., Moderator of the Curia & Vicar Gen., 660 Burton, S.E., Grand Rapids, MI 49507. Tel: 616-243-0491

Reverend Fathers—

Bolster, M. Thomas, In charge of Hispanic Community, Our Lady of Guadalupe, 267 Sheldon, S.E., Grand Rapids, MI 49503. Tel: 616-456-1454

Brucker, G. Fredrick, Tribunal Office. Tel: 616-459-4509

Danner, Michael A., Dir. Christopher House, Christopher House, 723 Rosewood, S.E., Grand Rapids, MI 45906. Tel: 616-243-6538

Darling, George E., Rural Life Dir., 409 S. Bridge St., Belding, MI 48809. Tel: 616-794-2145

Dudek, Stephen S., Assoc. Dir. Hispanic Apostolate, Res., 3252 Apple Ave., Muskegon, MI 49442. Tel: 616-777-1621

Duncan, William H., Vice Chancellor, 660 Burton, S.E., Grand Rapids, MI 49507. Tel: 616-243-0491

Fekete, George J., Dir. Missions, 402 Amity, Lowell, MI 49331. Tel: 616-897-9820

Hankiewicz, Edward, Tribunal Office. Tel: 616-459-4509

Heydens, Donald J., Dir. of Permanent Diaconate, Tribunal Office. Tel: 616-459-4509; 243-0491

Milanowski, Paul A., Dir. of Priestly Vocations. Tel: 616-243-0491

Mitchell, Mark E., Chap., Blodgett & Butterworth Hospitals, 628 Diamond, N.E., Grand Rapids, MI 49503. Tel: 616-242-4832

Morrow, Dennis, Adjutant Judicial Vicar for the Tribunal; Diocesan Archivist; Chap. Grand Rapids Fire Dept. & Grand Rapids Police Dept.

Najdowski, John A., Vicar for Priests Emeritus

Nghiem, Peter Hoan-Xuan, Dir. Vietnamese Apostolate, National service to community of Vietnamese Clergy and Religious; Serving Vietnamese Catholic Federation of USA., 2420 Avon S.W., Grand Rapids, MI 49509. Tel: 616-531-5213

Nguyen, Phillip D., Chap. U.S. Air Force

Page, Thomas P., Diocesan Coord. Campus Ministry, Assoc. Vicar for Priests. Tel: 616-866-0931

Porter, John, Officialis Diocesan Tribunal. Tel: 616-459-4509

Przybysz, Mark C., Dir. of Continuing Formation of Priests. Tel: 616-243-8998, Ext. 201

Shangraw, Philip A., Coord. Planning & Direction Diocesan Third Millenium Prog. Tel: 616-887-8222

Wagner, Dennis A., Officialis, Diocesan Tribunal Office, 265 Sheldon, S.E., Grand Rapids, MI 49503. Tel: 616-459-4509

Weber, Donald E., Vicar Priests. Tel: 616-241-6489

On Duty Outside the Diocese:
Reverend Fathers—
Cook, Daniel
Kurylowicz, Martin
Nguyen, Phillip D.
Pham, Phong Q.
Turner, Robert

Retired:
Reverend Monsignors—
Brophy, Charles D., 1247 Rennslaer, N.W., Grand Rapids, MI 49504
Giammona, John J., 3803 Old Elm Dr. SE, Kentwood, MI 49512
Jude, Walter F., 105 W.11 Mile Rd., Irons, MI 49644
Moran, James P., 156 Valley, S.W., Grand Rapids, MI 49504
Powers, William E., 7015 Carnation St., #108, Richmond, VA 23235
Zerfas, Herman H., 3888 44th St., S.W., Grandville, MI 49418
Reverend Fathers—
Allen, Joseph A., 1631 Ferdinand, Detroit, MI 48209
Antekeier, Charles R.
Baudone, Louis
Bernott, Albert R., 1409 Quarry, N.W., Grand Rapids, MI 49504
Bielskas, Edward J., 4101 Clyde Park, S.W., Wyoming, MI 49509
Bruck, Raymond E., 876 17 Mile Rd., Bitley, MI 49309
Cawley, Patrick, c/o General Delivery, Vanderbilt, MI 49795
Cusack, James C., 2168 Wildfield Dr. NE, Grand Rapids, MI 49505
Dondzila, Henry J., 6369 Belmont Ave. N.E., Belmont, MI 49306
Farrell, Edmund J., 307 57th St. Ct., West Bradenton, FL 34209
Feltman, Harold R., 504 S.E. 14 Ter., Cape Coral, FL 33990
Gillespie, Robert B., 2110 Leonard N.E., Apt. 214, Grand Rapids, MI 49505
Golas, Eugene S., 2110 Leonard N.E., Apt. #416, Grand Rapids, MI 49505
Hall, Bernard, St. Ann's Home, 2161 Leonard NW, Grand Rapids, MI 49504
Kubiak, Edward J., 437 First St., N.W., Grand Rapids, MI 49504
La Goe, John P., 3119 Scenic Dr., N. Muskegon, MI 49445
McKinney, Thomas A., St. Ann's Home, 2161 Leonard NW, Rm. 109, Grand Rapids, MI 49504
McKnight, William, 425 Sanborn, Big Rapids, MI 49307
Nash, Denis P., 4487 Glenhollow, Hudsonville, MI 49426
Pettit, Joseph J.
Schiller, Thomas A., 3816 Fountain R., Ludington, MI 49431
Tolis, Martin, 3028 Piney Ridge Rd., Ludington, MI 49431
Wing, Kenneth A., 2093 Barclay, #209, Muskegon, MI 49441
Yager, James P., 3062 W. Leonard St., Grand Rapids, MI 49504

Permanent Deacons:
Cardenas, Zenon, SS. Peter and Paul, Ionia
Fett, Richard, Jail Ministry, Ottawa Co.
Garcia, Juan, St. Francis de Sales, Holland
Glocheski, Virgil, Immaculate Heart of Mary, Grand Rapids
Herrera, Manuel E., SS. Peter and Paul, Grand Rapids
Hewitt, Wesley, Prince of Peace, North Muskegon
Hollern, Dale, St. Patrick, Grand Haven
Jankowski, Leon, (Retired)
Jurek, Thomas, Holy Name of Jesus, Wyoming, MI
Kasprzyk, David, St. Thomas the Apostle, Muskegon
LeMire, George, Blessed Sacrament, Grand Rapids
Mauer, Michael J., Catholic Information Center, Grand Rapids
McCabe, William, St. Francis de Sales, Muskegon
McGinnity, Michael, All Saints, Fremont
Radecki, Richard, St. Paul the Apostle, Grand Rapids
Riksen, Norman, St. Pius X, Grandville
Scheid, Howard, St. Joseph, Belding
Wood, Michael, St. Mary Magdalen, Grand Rapids

INSTITUTIONS LOCATED IN THE DIOCESE

[A] SEMINARY, DIOCESAN

GRAND RAPIDS. *Christopher House-College Department of St. Joseph's Seminary*, 723 Rosewood Ave., S.E., 49506. Tel: 616-243-6538; Fax: 616-243-3041.
E-mail: dannermike@aol.com
Rev. Michael A. Danner, Dir. Students 6.
Students attend area colleges.

[B] COLLEGES AND UNIVERSITIES

GRAND RAPIDS. *Aquinas College*, 1607 Robinson Rd., S.E., 49506. Tel: 616-459-8281, Ext. 4417; Fax: 616-732-4589
For a complete listing, refer to the Colleges and Universities section.

[C] HIGH SCHOOLS, DIOCESAN

GRAND RAPIDS. *Catholic Central High School*, 319 Sheldon Ave., S.E., 49503. Tel: 616-459-4559; Fax: 616-459-0257.
Web site: www.remc8.k12.mi.us/cathsec/cchome
Mr. Steve Passinault, Prin.; Tom Maj, Asst. Prin. Sisters of St. Dominic 3; Lay Teachers 49; Students 975.

West Catholic High School, 1801 Bristol, N.W., 49504. Tel: 616-453-4467. Mr. Bernard T. Stanko, Prin. Lay Teachers 32; Students 580.

MUSKEGON. *Muskegon Catholic Middle and High School*. Greater Muskegon Catholic Schools. 1145 W. Laketon, 49441. Tel: 231-755-2201; Fax: 231-755-2415. Thomas Powers, Chief School Officer & Exec. Dir.; Patricia O'Toole, Prin., High School; Julie Whelan, Prin., Middle School. Brothers 1; Lay Teachers 45; High School Students 270; Middle School Students 220.

[D] GRADE SCHOOL INTERPAROCHIAL

MUSKEGON. *St. Francis de Sales Elementary School*. (Grades PreK-5). Greater Muskegon Consolidated Catholic School. 2947 McCracken Ave., 49441. Tel: 231-755-1045; Fax: 231-759-7009. Mrs. Marcy Henehan, Prin. Lay Teachers 10; Students 227.

St. Michael Elementary School. (Grades PreK-5). Greater Muskegon Consolidated School. 215 W. Dale Ave., 49441. Tel: 231-722-4666; Fax: 231-725-7282. Cindy Thomas, Prin. Lay Teachers 7; Students 180.

[E] GENERAL HOSPITALS

GRAND RAPIDS. *St. Mary's Health Services*, 200 Jefferson, S.E., 49503. Tel: 616-752-6090
For a complete listing, refer to the Hospitals section.

MUSKEGON. *Mercy Hospital*, 1500 E. Sherman Blvd., P.O. Box 358, 49443. Tel: 231-739-9341; Fax: 231-733-0957
For a complete listing, refer to the Hospitals section.

[F] HOMES FOR THE AGED

GRAND RAPIDS. *St. Ann's Home*, 2161 Leonard St., N.W., 49504. Tel: 616-453-7715; Fax: 616-453-7359
For a complete listing, refer to the Special Care Facilities section.

[G] MONASTERIES AND RESIDENCES OF PRIESTS AND BROTHERS

MUSKEGAN. *Dominican Friars*, 1145 West Laketon, 49441. Tel: 231-755-5238.
E-mail: brobenop@aol.com
Dominicans Province of St. Albert the Great, U.S.A. Bro. Benedict Baer, O.P.

[H] CONVENTS AND RESIDENCES FOR SISTERS

GRAND RAPIDS. *Aquinata Hall*, 2025 E. Fulton, 49503-3894. Tel: 616-456-5038; Fax: 616-454-6105. Sisters 42; Beds 54.

Dominican Center, 2025 E. Fulton St., 49503-3895. Tel: 616-454-1241; Fax: 616-454-2861. Mark Clarke, Dir.

Motherhouse of the Dominican Sisters, Marywood, 2025 E. Fulton St., 49503-3895. Tel: 616-459-2910. Motherhouse and Novitiate for the Sisters of the Order of St. Dominic of the Congregation of Our Lady of the Sacred Heart. Legal Titles: *Sisters of St. Dominic of the Congregation of Our Lady of the Sacred Heart (The Religious Institute).*; *Sisters of the Order of St. Dominic of Grand Rapids, Michigan (The Corporation).* Sr. Maribeth Holst, O.P., Prioress; Rev. Paul Colloton, O.P., Coord. Pastoral Life; Sr. Carmelita Switzer, O.P., Coord. Pastoral Life; Sr. Darlene Sikorski, O.P., Treas. Sisters 334.

ADA. *Discalced Carmelite Nuns, Monastery of Our Lady of Guadalupe* Parnell, 4300 Mount Carmel Dr., N.E., 49301-9784. Tel: 616-691-7625. Mother Agnes Therese, O.C.D., Prioress. Professed Carmelite Nuns 17; Extern Sisters 2; Novices 1.

BELMONT. *Motherhouse of the Consolata Missionary Sisters*, 6801 Belmont Rd., P.O. Box 371, 49306. Tel: 616-361-2072; Fax: 616-361-2049.
E-mail: REUSA.mc@pcn.net
Web site: www.consolatasisters.org
Sr. Cecilia Clara Zamboni, M.C., Supr. Consolata Sisters 14.

[I] RETREAT HOUSES

SPRING LAKE. *St. Lazare Retreat House*, 18600 W. Spring Lake Rd., 49456-0462. Tel: 616-842-3370; Fax: 616-842-6815.
E-mail: mjsstlazare@triton.net
Revs. Michael J. Shea, C.M.; Richard J. Kehoe, C.M.

[J] NEWMAN CENTERS

COOPERSVILLE. *Grand Valley State University Catholic Campus Ministry*, Allendale Campus, 17150-88th Ave., 49404-9413. Tel: 616-837-8158; Fax: 616-837-7893. Rev. John F. Vallier, Campus Priest.

EDMORE. *Montcalm Community College Newman Center*, 1051 E. Howard City Rd., 48829. Rev. Vincent Bryce, O.P.

[K] MISCELLANEOUS LISTINGS

GRAND RAPIDS. *Basilica of St. Adalbert Education Foundation*, 671 Davis Ave., N.W., Box 1 - Basilica Center, 49504. Tel: 616-458-3065; Fax: 616-458-3065.
E-mail: basilica@iserv.net

Bishops' Housing Corporation, 660 Burton St., S.E., 49507. Tel: 616-243-0491; Fax: 616-243-4910.

The Catholic Foundation of West Michigan, 660 Burton, S.E., 49507. Tel: 616-243-0491; Fax: 616-243-4910. Sr. Patrice Konwinski, O.P.

Educational Foundation of St. Francis Xavier School, Inc., 240 Brown St., S.E., 49507. Tel: 616-241-5474; Fax: 616-241-5493.
Web site: saintfrancisxavier.org

The Foundation for Catholic Education of Greater Grand Rapids, Inc., 410 Bridge St., N.W., 49504. Tel: 616-454-2682.

Fund for Faith, 660 Burton St., S.E., 49507. Tel: 616-243-0491; Fax: 616-243-4910. Foundation established in 1976 for various apostolic works.

Marywood Academy, 2025 E. Fulton St., 49503-3895. Tel: 616-454-2910; Fax: 616-454-6105.

Ministry Ventures, 2025 E. Fulton St., 49503-3895. Tel: 616-454-4548.
E-mail: dsikorski@grdominicans.org
Sr. Darlene Sikorski, Treas.; Carole Nugent, Opers. Admin.

SS. Peter and Paul Parish Education Endowment Fund, 520 Myrtle St., N.W., 49504. Tel: 616-454-6000.

Sisters of St. Dominic Charitable Trust, 2025 E. Fulton Rd., 49503-3895. Tel: 616-459-2910; Fax: 616-454-6105. Sr. Maribeth Holst, O.P. Legal Title: *Sisters of St. Dominic of the Congregation of Our Lady of the Sacred Heart Charitable Trust (The Trust).*

Steepletown Neighborhood Services, Inc., 671 Davis, N.W., Basilica Center Box #2, 49504. Tel: 616-451-4215; Fax: 616-451-4215. Special Center for Social Service and Assistance.

LOWELL. *Franciscan Life Process Center*, 11650 Downes St., 49331-9489. Tel: 616-897-7842; Fax: 616-897-7054. Sr. Colleen Ann Nagle, F.S.E., Dir.

MUSKEGON HEIGHTS. *Christian Community Center*, 540 E. Hackley, 49444. Tel: 231-725-7579.

Madonna House Apostolate, 3201 Peck St., 49444. Tel: 231-733-1129. Prayer-Listening House. Total in residence 2.

PORTLAND. *The Father Flohe Foundation*, 140 Church St., 48875. Tel: 517-647-6505; Fax: 517-647-7807.

VESTABURG. *Emmaus Monastery*, 7001 Tamarack, 48891. Tel: 517-268-5494; Fax: 517-268-5373.
E-mail: emmaus@sensible-net.com
Web site: www.nethawk.com/emmaus
Sr. Linda-Susan Beard, Contact Person.

RELIGIOUS INSTITUTES OF MEN REPRESENTED IN THE DIOCESE

For further details refer to the corresponding bracketed number in the Religious Institutes of Men or Women section.

[1330]—*Congregation of the Mission.* (Eastern Prov.).—C.M.

[0480]—*Conventual Franciscans.* (Louisville).—O.F.M.Conv.

[0430]—*Order of Preachers-Dominicans.* (Central Prov.).—O.P.

[1030]—*Paulist Fathers.*—C.S.P.

[]—*Priests of the Holy Cross.* (Indiana Prov.).—C.S.C.

[1070]—*Redemptorist Fathers.* (Prov. of St. Louis).—C.SS.R.

RELIGIOUS INSTITUTES OF WOMEN REPRESENTED IN THE DIOCESE

[0360]—*Carmelite Sisters of the Divine Heart of Jesus.*—Carmel.D.C.J.

[0720]—*Consolata Missionary Sisters.*—M.C.

[0420]—*Discalced Carmelite Nuns.*—O.C.D.

[1070-14]—*Dominican Sisters.*—O.P.

[1250]—*Institute of the Franciscan Sisters of the Eucharist.*—F.S.E.

[2575]—*Institute of the Sisters of Mercy of the Americas.*—R.S.M.

[2970]—*School Sisters of Notre Dame.*—S.S.N.D.

[3560]—*Servants of Jesus.*—S.J.

[1530]—*Sisters of St. Francis.*—O.S.F.

[]—*Sisters for Christian Community*S.F.C.C.

[0460]—*Sisters of Charity of the Incarnate Ward*—C.C.V.I.

[2990]—*Sisters of Notre Dame*—S.N.D.

[3830-11]—*Sisters of St. Joseph of Nazareth.*—S.S.J.

[1830]—*Sisters of the Good Shepherd*—R.G.S.-C.G.S.

[2150]—*Sisters of the Immaculate Heart of Mary.*—I.H.M.

[3260]—*Sisters of the Precious Blood.*—C.PP.S.

NECROLOGY

† Najdowski, Rev. Msgr. John A., (Retired). —Died Oct. 26, 2000.

† Statkus, Edward, (Retired). —Died Dec. 26, 1999.

Diocese of Great Falls—Billings

(Dioecesis Magnocataractensis-Billingensis)

Most Reverend

ANTHONY M. MILONE, D.D.

Bishop of Great Falls-Billings; ordained December 15, 1957; appointed Titular Bishop Plestia and Auxiliary of Omaha November 10, 1981; Episcopal ordination January 6, 1982; appointed Bishop of Great Falls-Billings December 14, 1987; installed February 23, 1988. *Office: 121-23rd St. S., Great Falls, MT, 59401.* Tel.: 406-727-6683.; (Corporation title: "Roman Catholic Bishop of Great Falls, Montana, a corporation sole.").

Pastoral Office: 121 23rd St. S., Great Falls, MT, 59401-3997. Mailing Address: P.O. Box 1399, Great Falls, MT, 59403-1399. Tel.: 406-727-6683; 800-332-9998 (Toll Free Montana Only); Fax: 406-454-3480.

Web site address: www.mcn.net/~dioceseofgfb

E-mail address: dioceseofgfb@mcn.net

ERECTED MAY 18, 1904.

Square Miles 94,158.

Comprises the eastern part of the State of Montana and is made up of the following Counties: Big Horn, Blaine, Carbon, Carter, Cascade, Chouteau, Custer, Daniels, Dawson, Fallon, Fergus, Garfield, Golden Valley, Hill, Judith Basin, Liberty, McCone, Musselshell, Park, Petroleum, Phillips, Powder River, Prairie, Richland, Roosevelt, Rosebud, Sheridan, Stillwater, Sweet Grass, Treasure, Valley, Wibaux, Yellowstone and parts of Toole.

For legal titles of parishes and diocesan institutions, consult the Pastoral Office .

STATISTICAL OVERVIEW

Personnel	
Bishop	1
Priests: Diocesan Active in Diocese	31
Priests: Active Outside Diocese	7
Priests: Retired, Sick or Absent	31
Number of Diocesan Priests	69
Religious Priests in Diocese	14
Extern Priests in Diocese	7
Permanent Deacons in Diocese	3
Total Brothers	1
Total Sisters	77
Parishes	
Parishes	66
With Resident Pastor:	
Resident Diocesan Priests	33
Resident Religious Priests	10
Without Resident Pastor:	
Administered by Priests	18
Administered by Women Religious	3
Administered by Lay People	2
Missions	47
Closed Parishes	2
Professional Ministry Personnel:	
Brothers	1
Sisters	16
Lay Ministers	44
Welfare	
Catholic Hospitals	2
Total Assisted	153,629
Health Care Centers	1
Total Assisted	18,507
Day Care and Extended Day Care Centers	7
Total Assisted	609
Special Centers for Social Services	3
Total Assisted	22,745
Educational	
Diocesan Students in Other Seminaries	6
Total Seminarians	6
Colleges and Universities	1
Total Students	1,054
High Schools, Diocesan and Parish	2
Total Students	375
High Schools, Private	1
Total Students	166
Elementary Schools, Diocesan and Parish	8
Total Students	1,430
Elementary Schools, Private	4
Total Students	1,204
Catechesis/Religious Education:	
High School Students	2,085
Elementary Students	4,518
Total Students Under Catholic Instruction	10,838
Teachers in the Diocese:	
Priests	2
Sisters	7
Lay Teachers	215
Vital Statistics	
Receptions into the Church:	
Infant Baptism Totals	945
Adult Baptism Totals	164
Received into Full Communion	176
First Communions	1,044
Confirmations	2,396
Marriages:	
Catholic	173
Interfaith	140
Total Marriages	313
Deaths	776
Total Catholic Population	57,429
Total Population	391,360

Former Bishops—Most Rev. MATHIAS C. LENIHAN, D.D., ord. Dec. 20, 1879; cons. First Bishop of Great Falls, Sept. 21, 1904; resigned Jan. 18, 1930; created Titular Archbishop of Preslavo, Feb. 14, 1930; died Aug. 19, 1943.—Most Rev. EDWIN V. O'HARA, D.D., ord. June 10, 1905; appt. Aug. 1, 1930; cons. Oct. 28, 1930; appt. Bishop of Kansas City April 15, 1939 made asst. at the Pontifical Throne Jan. 5, 1949; appt. Archbishop "Ad Personam" June 29, 1954; died Sept. 11, 1956, Milan, Italy.—Most Rev. WILLIAM J. CONDON, D.D., ord. Oct. 14, 1917; appt. Aug. 5, 1939; cons. Oct. 18, 1939 asst. at the Pontifical Throne Dec. 9, 1964; died Aug. 17, 1967.—Most Rev. ELDON BERNARD SCHUSTER, D.D., ord. May 27, 1937; appt. Titular Bishop of Amblada; cons. Dec. 21, 1961; appt. Bishop of Great Falls Dec. 2, 1967; resigned Dec. 27, 1977; died Sept. 4, 1998.—Most Rev. THOMAS JOSEPH MURPHY, S.T.D., D.D., appt. Bishop of Great Falls July 5, 1978 Episcopal ordination and installation Aug. 21, 1978; appt. coadjutor Archbishop of Seattle May 26, 1987; died June 26, 1997.

Vicar General—Rev. JAY PETERSON, V.G.

Pastoral Office—121 23rd St. S., P.O. Box 1399, Great Falls, 59403. Tel: 406-727-6683; 800-332-9998 (Montana Toll Free Number Only); Fax: 406-454-3480. All applications for dispensations and official communications should be addressed to this office.

Chancellor—Sr. MARY MURRAY, O.P.,Direct all Matrimonial Correspondence to the Tribunal.

Moderator of the Curia—Rev. JAY PETERSON, V.G.

Business Manager/Fiscal Officer—JOSEPH LONCKI.

Diocesan Tribunal—121 23rd St. S., P.O. Box 1399, Great Falls, 59403. Tel: 406-727-6683; 800-332-9998 (Montana Toll Free Number Only).

Judicial Vicar—Rev. ROBERT D. GROSCH, J.C.L.

Promoter of Justice—Rev. JOHN W. ROBERTSON, J.C.L.

Defenders of the Bond—Rev. ROBERT FOX; MARGARET ROMANO-HOGAN.

Director of the Tribunal—TERRYAL ANN REAVLEY.

Notary—TERRYAL ANN REAVLEY.

Diocesan Consultors—Revs. ANTHONY GREGORI; GILBERT HEMAUER, O.F.M.Cap.; JAMES O'NEIL; JOSEPH JERUZAL, O.F.M.Cap.; LEO McDOWELL; RICHARD OSTERMAN; RICHARD SCHLOSSER; MICHAEL SCHNEIDER; ANTHONY SCHUSTER.

Personnel Board—Most Rev. ANTHONY M. MILONE; Revs. JERRY CONNOLLY; DAN O'ROURKE; JAMES O'NEIL; THOMAS HARNEY; THAD KOZIKOWSKI; ROGER VEIK, O.F.M.Cap., Vicar of Clergy Personnel (Ex Officio); JAY PETERSON.

Vicars Forane—Rev. ROGER VEIK, O.F.M.Cap., Billings; Rev. RICHARD SCHLOSSER, Great Falls; Rev. MARCEL VOGEL, Havre; Rev. GILBERT HEMAUER, O.F.M.Cap., Miles City; Rev. STEPHEN ZABROCKI, Wolf Point.

Cemetery Board—Rev. JAY PETERSON, V.G., Great Falls; JOSEPH LONCKI.

Vicar of Clergy Personnel—Rev. ROGER VEIK, O.F.M.Cap., *1122 N. 30th St., Billings, 59101.* Tel: 406-259-9902.

Cum Christo/Cursillo—Rev. FRANCIS McINNIS, Spiritual Dir., *P.O. Box 1248, Great Falls, 59403.* Tel: 406-453-0258.

Vicar for Ministry to Native Americans—Rev. PETER E. GUTHNECK, *Rocky Boy CPU-Box 3009, Box Elder, 59521-3009.* Tel: 406-395-4380.

Diocesan Offices and Directors

Boy Scouts—Rev. LEO McDOWELL, Chap., *P.O. Box 160, Circle, 59215-0160.* Tel: 406-485-3520.

Catholic Campaign for Human Development—BRUCE DAY, Diocesan Dir., *121 23rd St. S., Great Falls, 59401., P.O. Box 1399, Great Falls, 59403.* Tel: 406-727-6683; Fax: 406-454-3480.

Stewardship Committee—STELLA ZIEGLER, Chm.

Catechesis—PAUL F. KAISER, Dir., *Pastoral Center, P.O. Box 1399, Great Falls, 59403.* Tel: 406-727-3386. Sr. BARBARA BROWN, O.P., Assoc. Dir., *1109 Orr St., Miles City, 59301.* Tel: 406-232-2116.

Catholic Relief Services—BRUCE DAY, Dir.

Catholic University, Friends of—Rev. ROBERT J. FOX, S.T.L., Ph.D., *P.O. Box 53, Poplar, 59255.*

Clerical Benefit Association—Most Rev. ANTHONY M. MILONE, Ex Officio; Revs. JAMES BIRKMAIER; PATRICK ZABROCKI; THOMAS HARNEY, Sec. JAMES SIKORA, Pres. LOTHAR KRAUTH, Sec. TERRANCE REGAN, Vice

Pres. JOSEPH LONCKI, Consultant; Rev. MICHAEL GUINAN, Retired Priests' Rep.

Continuing Education for Clergy—Rev. JOHN J. HOULIHAN, *St. Patrick's Co-Cathedral, 215 N. 31st St., Billings, 59101-9920.*

Diocesan Pastoral Council—Sr. MARY MURRAY, O.P., Exec. Coord. LUKE LARSON, Chm., *121 23rd St. S., P.O. Box 1399, Great Falls, 59403-1399.* Tel: 406-727-6683; Fax: 406-454-3480.

Diocesan School Board—Sr. JEAN M. DAWSON, S.C.L., Supt. BARBARA DERWINSKI-ROBINSON, Chm., *P.O. Box 31158, Billings, 59107-1158.* Tel: 406-252-9595; Fax: 406-252-9875.

D.C.C.W.—KATHLEEN O'NEAL, Pres.; Most Rev. ANTHONY M. MILONE, Episcopal Moderator.

Ecumenical Officer—PAUL F. KAISER.

Education—Sr. JEAN DAWSON, S.C.L., Diocesan School Supt., *P.O. Box 31158, Billings, 59107.* Tel: 406-252-9595; 800-682-2218 (Montana Toll Free Number Only); Fax: 406-252-9875.

Finance Council—Most Rev. ANTHONY M. MILONE; JOSEPH LONCKI, Consultant; Rev. JAY PETERSON, V.G.; MARILYN HARMON; THOMAS LANE; JOHN NELSON; ALBERT MARTENS; THOMAS PELATT; MARILYN ROSE; ELLEN SOLEM; Rev. LEO MCDOWELL.

Holy Childhood Association—Rev. JAY H. PETERSON, V.G.

Lay Ministry Programs—Sr. EILEEN HURLEY, S.C.L.

Liturgical Commission—CAROL FALBO; CARRIE GRACE; Sr. LEANDRA KOSMOSKI, S.S.J.; Revs. THEODORE SZUDERA; STEPHEN ZABROCKI; Mr. JOE SULLIVAN; JAN WOOD, Vice Chm.; ANN O'BRIEN; Most Rev. ANTHONY MILONE.

Office of Worship—Vacant.

Newspaper—"Harvest"; Rev. JAY PETERSON, V.G.

Social Justice and Peace Office—BRUCE DAY, Dir., *P.O. Box 1399, Great Falls, 59403-1399.* Tel: 406-727-6683; Fax: 406-454-3480.

RCIA—Vacant.

Pastoral Outreach—Rev. JAY PETERSON, V.G., Coord. PAUL F. KAISER; Sr. BARBARA BROWN, O.P.; Sr. MARY MURRAY, O.P.; BRUCE DAY; SUZANNE JOHNSON.

Priests' Council—Most Rev. ANTHONY M. MILONE; Revs. RICHARD SCHLOSSER; JAY PETERSON, V.G.; JOSEPH JERUZAL, O.F.M.Cap.; ANTHONY GREGORI; PASCHAL SILER, O.F.M.Cap.; LEO MCDOWELL; RICHARD OSTERMAN; ANTHONY SCHUSTER; JAMES O'NEIL, Chm. GILBERT HEMAUER, O.F.M.Cap.; MICHAEL SCHNEIDER.

Sister's Council—Vacant.

Director of Vocations—Rev. DALE E. YURKOVIC, *St. Mary's Church, P.O. Box 646, Livingston, 59047.* Tel: 406-222-1393; Fax: 406-222-1405.

Inter-Diocesan Organizations

Montana Catholic Conference—SHARON HOFF-BRODOWY, Dir., *P.O. Box 1708, Helena, 59624.* Tel: 406-442-5761; Fax: 406-442-9047.

Catholic Social Services of Montana—ROSEMARY MILLER, Dir., *P.O. Box 907, Helena, 59624.* Tel: 406-442-4130. Provides adoption and counseling services for families, children and infants.

Billings Office—BECKY HUBBERT, *2703 11th Ave. N., Ste. 2, Billings, 59101.* Tel: 406-252-3399.

Great Falls Office—KYLA KALANICK, *P.O. Box 7410, Great Falls, 59403.* Tel: 406-771-7805.

Helena Office—Sr. NOEL BRUCH; SHIRLEY COLE, *P.O. Box 907, Helena, 59601.* Tel: 406-442-4130.

Missoula Office—BETSY ROBEL-GOMEZ, *St. Patrick's Hospital, 554 W. Broadway, Missoula, 59802.* Tel: 406-329-5629.

Montana Association of Churches—Rev. JESSICA CRIST, Pres. MARGARET E. MACDONALD, Exec. Dir., *180-24th St. W., Ste. G, Billings, 59102.* Tel: 406-656-9779.

CLERGY, PARISHES, MISSIONS AND PAROCHIAL SCHOOLS

CITY OF GREAT FALLS
(Cascade County)

1—ST. ANN'S CATHEDRAL, Most Rev. Anthony M. Milone, D.D.; Rev. Oliver Doyle, Admin.; Domenico Pizzonia, Pastoral Assoc.
Res., 715 Third Ave. N., P.O. Box 1708, 59403. Tel: 406-761-5456; Fax: 406-761-5457.

2—HOLY SPIRIT, Rev. Richard Schlosser; Rev. Msgr. Joseph Gluszek, (Retired); Sr. Catherine Kinsella, O.P., Pastoral Assoc.
Parish Office: 2816 Central Ave., 59401-3498. Tel: 406-452-6491(Office); 761-4805 (Worship Center); Fax: 406-452-6495 (Office).
School—(Grades PreK-8) 2820 Central Ave., 59401. Tel: 406-761-5775; Fax: 406-761-5887. Linda Traxinger, Prin.
Lay Teachers 20; Students 252.
Catechesis/Religious Programs—Chris Hueth, D.R.E.
Students 177.
Chapels—St. Gerard's, 2211-5th Ave. N., 59401.; Holy Family, 2800 Central Ave., 59401.
Sts. Peter & Paul Worship Center: 200-44th St. S., 59405.

3—ST. GERARD MAJELLA. Closed. See Holy Spirit.

4—HOLY FAMILY. Closed. See Holy Spirit.

5—STS. PETER & PAUL. Closed. See Holy Spirit.

6—ST. JOSEPH'S, Rev. Patrick R. Zabrocki; Jean Sobolik, Pastoral Assoc.
Church and Res.: 500-2nd. Ave., S.W., 59404. Tel: 406-453-5558 (Church); 453-9331 (Res.).
Catechesis/Religious Programs—Tel: 406-453-9331. Carmen Thorsen, D.R.E.
Students 142.

7—OUR LADY OF LOURDES, Rev. Lothar Krauth; Sr. Marian Lorang, O.S.U., Pastoral Assoc.
Res., 409 13th St. S., 59405. Tel: 406-452-6464; Fax: 406-761-7180.
School—(Grades PreK-8) 1305 Fifth Ave. S., 59405. Tel: 406-452-0551. Mrs. Sherri Schmitz, Prin.
Ursuline Nuns1; Lay Teachers 18; Students 225.
Catechesis/Religious Programs—Sena Bozlee, D.R.E.
Students 106.

8—ST. LUKE THE EVANGELIST, Rev. Patrick R. Zabrocki. Pastoral Assocs.: Donna Wilson; Mary Lynn Wojtowick.
Res., 420 22nd Ave. N.E., 59404. Tel: 406-453-6546; Fax: 406-453-0323.
Catechesis/Religious Programs—Jeanne Tonkovich, D.R.E.
Students 289.

CITY OF BILLINGS
(Yellowstone County)

1—ST. PATRICK'S CO-CATHEDRAL, Revs. John J. Houlihan; Richard J. Hopkins; Robert Sewvello.
Res., 215 N. 31st St., 59101. Tel: 406-259-3389; Fax: 406-248-1185.
Catechesis/Religious Programs—Tel: 406-259-7611. Jean Ott, D.R.E.
Students 57.

2—HOLY ROSARY, Sr. Leandra Kosmoski, S.S.J., Pastoral Admin.; Virginia Jeanotte, Pastoral Assoc.; Deacon Melvin A. Melius.
Office: 521 Custer Ave., 59101. Tel: 406-259-7611; Fax: 406-248-8921.
Catechesis/Religious Programs—Jean Ott, D.R.E.
Students 55.

3—LITTLE FLOWER, Rev. Paul Reichling, O.F.M.Cap.
Res., 209 S. 35th St., 59101. Tel: 406-245-4717.
Catechesis/Religious Programs—Tel: 406-259-7611. Jean Ott, D.R.E.
Students 55.

4—ST. BERNARD'S, Rev. David Reichling, O.F.M.Cap.
Office: 226 Wicks Ln., 59105. Tel: 406-259-4350; Fax: 406-259-0443.
Catechesis/Religious Programs—D.R.E.: Sandra Stokoe; Stacy Brensdal.
Students 530.
Mission—Ballantine, Sts. Cyril & Methodius.

5—OUR LADY OF GUADALUPE, Rev. Paul Reichling, O.F.M.Cap.
Res., 209 S. 35th St., 59101. Tel: 406-245-4717.
Catechesis/Religious Programs—Tel: 406-259-7611.
Students 50.

6—ST. PIUS X, Rev. Stephen L. Tokarski; Deacon Robert W. Daem; Bob Bender, Pastoral Assoc.
Parish Center: 717 18th St. W., 59102. Tel: 406-656-2522; Fax: 406-656-2584.
Catechesis/Religious Programs—Cheryl Daem, D.R.E.
Students 380.

7—ST. THOMAS THE APOSTLE, Rev. William A. Hogan. Pastoral Assocs.: Jim Downs; Sr. Genevieve Garvin, R.S.M.
Res., 2101-24th St. W., 59102. Tel: 406-656-5578.
Church—2055 Woody Dr., 59102. Tel: 406-656-5800; Fax: 406-656-8260.
Catechesis/Religious Programs—Joyce Hollowell, D.R.E.
Students 318.

OUTSIDE THE CITIES OF GREAT FALLS AND BILLINGS

Ashland, Rosebud Co., St. Labre's, Rev. Paschal Siler, O.F.M.Cap.
Res., Tongue River Rd., P.O. Box 228, 59003. Tel: 406-784-4536.
Station—Ashland, Birney Post.

Baker, Fallon Co., St. John the Evangelist, Rev. Thomas Tobin.
Res., P.O. Box 1519, 59313. Tel: 406-778-2297.
Catechesis/Religious Programs—Norma Losing, D.R.E.
Students 136.
Missions—Ekalaka, St. Joan of Arc; Plevna, St. Anthony. [CEM]

Belt, Cascade Co., St. Mark the Evangelist, Rev. Ted F. Szudera.
Res., P.O. Box 213, 59412. Tel: 406-277-3537.
Catechesis/Religious Programs—Tel: 406-277-3366. Brenda Danks, D.R.E.
Students 60.
Missions—Monarch, St. Clement; Raynesford, St. Mary.
Chapel—St. Jane Frances, Highwood, 59450.

Big Sandy, Chouteau Co., St. Margaret Mary, Rev. Peter E. Guthneck; Sr. Margaret Mary O'Doherty, O.P., Pastoral Assoc. & D.R.E.; Sr. Kathleen Kane, O.P., Pastoral Assoc.
Res., St. Mary's Rocky Boy Indian Reservation, Rocky Boy CPU-Box 3009, Box Elder, 59521. Tel: 406-395-4380.
Catechesis/Religious Programs—Students 46.
Missions—Box Elder, St. Anthony; Rocky Boy Indian Reservation, St. Mary.

Big Timber, Sweet Grass Co., St. Joseph, Tom Schleder, Pastoral Admin.
Res., P.O. Box 871, 59011. Tel: 406-932-4728.

Black Eagle, Cascade Co., Most Blessed Sacrament, Rev. Raymond J. Nyquist.
Res., 1325 Smelter Ave., 59414. Tel: 406-453-8425; Fax: 406-453-8425.
Catechesis/Religious Programs—Students 12.

Bridger, Carbon Co., Sacred Heart, Sr. Mary Lou Mendel, S.C.L., Pastoral Admin.
Res., P.O. Box 309, 59014-0309. Tel: 406-662-3550.
Catechesis/Religious Programs—Students 112.
Missions—Fromberg, St. Joseph; Joliet, St. John.

Broadus, Powder River Co., St. David's, Rev. Chester Poppa, O.F.M.Cap.
Mailing Address: P.O. Box 52, 59317. Tel: 406-436-2348. [CEM]

Centerville, Cascade Co., Holy Trinity, Rev. Ted Szudera.
Mailing Address: P.O. Box 125, Stockett, 59480-0125. Tel: 406-736-5491.
Res., P.O. Box 213, Belt, 59412.
Catechesis/Religious Programs—Tel: 406-736-5114. Margie Prill, D.R.E.
Students 56.

Chester, Liberty Co., St. Mary's, Rev. Joseph Diekhans; Natalie Ghekiere, Parish Coord.
Res., P.O. Box 647, 504 Main, 59522. Tel: 406-759-5377; Fax: 406-759-5568.
Catechesis/Religious Programs—Tel: 406-759-5389. D.R.E.: Natalie Ghekiere; Dianne Folk.
Students 135.
Missions—Hingham, Our Lady of Ransom; Inverness, Sacred Heart; Rudyard, Holy Family Center.

Chinook, Blaine Co., St. Gabriel's, Rev. Marcel J. Vogel.
Res., 152 Eighth St., P.O. Box 1089, 59523. Tel: 406-357-2073; Fax: 406-357-2173.
Catechesis/Religious Programs—D.R.E.: Mrs. Ellen Pyette, (Elementary); Mrs. Norma Fritz, (High School).
Students 77.
Missions—Harlem, Blaine Co., St. Thomas the Apostle, P.O. Box 819, Harlem, 59526. Tel: 406-353-4643; Hogeland, Blaine Co., St. Thomas Aquinas, c/o Mary Ann Olszewski, HC 80-Box 1, Hogeland, 59529. Tel: 406-379-2582.

Circle, McCone Co., St. Francis Xavier, Rev. Leo McDowell.
Res., 1102 C Ave., P.O. Box 160, 59215-0160. Tel: 406-485-3520; Fax: 406-485-3519.
Catechesis/Religious Programs—Students 88.
Missions—Jordan, St. John the Baptist, Tel: 406-557-6135; Richey, St. Francis de Sales.

Colstrip, Rosebud Co., St. Margaret Mary, William Medved, Pastoral Admin.; Jeanette Bartel, Pastoral Assoc.
Res., P.O. Box 305, 59323. Tel: 406-748-2234; Fax: 406-748-2234.
Catechesis/Religious Programs—Sue McKamey, D.R.E.
Students 95.

Columbus, Stillwater Co., St. Mary's, Rev. Charles Gorman, Admin.
Mailing Address: P.O. Box 956, 59019. Tel: 406-322-5541.
Catechesis/Religious Programs—D.R.E.: Jeanne Harsha; Peggy Joki; Laura Kane.
Students 96.
Mission—Absarokee, St. Michael.

Crow Agency, Big Horn Co., St. Dennis, Rev. Charles Robinson, O.F.M.Cap.; Sr. Loretta Sedlmayer, R.S.M., Pastoral Assoc.
Res., P.O. Box 57, 59022. Tel: 406-638-2641.
Catechesis/Religious Programs—Students 85.
Mission—St. Xavier, St. Francis Xavier, P.O. Box 138, St. Xavier, 59075. Tel: 406-666-2380. Coleen Couture, Pastoral Assoc.

Culbertson, Roosevelt Co., St. Anthony's, Rev. Thomas Pittappilly.
Res., P.O. Box 30, 59218. Tel: 406-787-6666.
Catechesis/Religious Programs—Students 39.
Missions—Bainville, Sacred Heart; Froid, Immaculate Conception.

Forsyth, Rosebud Co., Immaculate Conception, Rev. Jerry Connolly.
Res., 591 N. 12th Ave. N., P.O. Box 166, 59327. Tel: 406-356-2101 (Church); 356-9239 (Parish Center).
Catechesis/Religious Programs—Renee Steinberger, D.R.E.
Students 70.
Mission—Hysham, St. Joseph.

Fort Benton, Chouteau Co., Immaculate Conception, Rev. Denis J. Keane; Trish Eklund, Pastoral Assoc.
Res., P.O. Box 868, 59442. Tel: 406-622-3726.
Catechesis/Religious Programs—Tel: 406-622-5288. Vicky O'Hara, D.R.E.
Students 45.
Mission—Geraldine, St. Margaret.

Fort Shaw, Cascade Co., St. Ann, Rev. Eugene P. Hruska.
Res., 13327 MT. Hwy 200, 59443. Tel: 406-264-5554.
Catechesis/Religious Programs—D.R.E.: JoAnn Holmes, (St. Ann), Tel: 406-264-5495; David Konecny, (Sacred Heart), Tel: 406-468-2368.
Students 107.
Mission—Cascade, Sacred Heart.

Glasgow, Valley Co., St. Raphael's, Rev. Thad Kozikowski.
Office: 412 Third Ave. N., P.O. Box 1047, 59230. Tel: 406-228-4651.
Catechesis/Religious Programs—Tel: 406-228-4651. Margaret Chambers, D.R.E.
Students 129.
Missions—Fort Peck, Our Lady of the Lake; Hinsdale, St. Albert; Nashua, Queen of the Angels.

Glendive, Dawson Co., Sacred Heart, Rev. Joseph Ponessa.
Res., 316 W. Benham St., P.O. Box 36, 59330. Tel: 406-365-2585; Fax: 406-365-4033.
Catechesis/Religious Programs—Tel: 406-365-4569. D.R.E.: Monica Christianson, (Sacred Heart); Glen Fitzpatrick, (St. Peter).
Students 240.
Missions—Wibaux, St. Peter, P.O. Box 217, Wibaux, 59353. Tel: 406-795-2215; Wibaux, St. Philip, P.O. Box 217, Wibaux, 59353. Tel: 406-795-8188.

Hardin, Big Horn Co., St. Joseph's, Rev. Fabian Fehring, O.F.M.Cap.
Res., 710 N. Custer, P.O. Box 510, 59034. Tel: 406-665-1432.
Catechesis/Religious Programs—Students 95.
Mission—Custer, St. Mary.

Havre, Hill Co., St. Jude Thaddeus, Rev. Robert D. Grosch; Timothy Maroney, Pastoral Assoc.
Res., 624 Fourth St., P.O. Box 407, 59501. Tel: 406-265-4261; Fax: 406-265-4408.
School—(Grades PreK-8). Tel: 406-265-4613. Mrs. Therese Cowdery, Prin.
Lay Teachers 12; Students 221.
Catechesis/Religious Programs—Mary Pat Bebee, D.R.E.
Students 139.
Mission—Cottonwood, St. John the Baptist.

Hays, Blaine Co., St. Paul's Indian Mission, Rev. Joseph R. Retzel, S.J.; Sr. Barbara Bogenschutz, O.P., Pastoral Assoc.
Res., P.O. Box 40, 59527. Tel: 406-673-3300.
School—Tel: 406-673-3123. Sr. Helen Durso, O.P., Prin.
Sisters 3; Lay Teachers 5; Students 100.
Catechesis/Religious Programs—Students 162.
Missions—Zortman, St. Joseph; Dodson, St. Thomas, Lodgepole Rte., Dodson, 59524. Tel: 406-673-3454; Fax: 406-673-3454. Sr. Laura Fucito, O.P., Pastoral Assoc.; Fort Belknap Agency, Sacred Heart, P.O. Box 429, Harlem, 59526. Tel: 406-353-2927; Fax: 406-353-2927. Sr. Nancy Maclean, S.P., Pastoral Assoc.

Lame Deer, Rosebud Co., Blessed Sacrament, Rev. Joseph Jeruzal, O.F.M.Cap.
Res., P.O. Box 100, 59043. Tel: 406-477-6384; Fax: 406-477-6224.
Catechesis/Religious Programs—Students 14.
Mission—Busby, Christ the King.

Laurel, Yellowstone Co., St. Anthony's, Rev. Thomas C. Harney.
Res., P.O. Box 955, 59044. Tel: 406-628-7182. [CEM]
Catechesis/Religious Programs—Tel: 406-628-7484. Barb Hoppel, D.R.E.
Students 230.

Lewistown, Fergus Co., St. Leo's, Rev. Daniel O'Rourke; Sr. Anne Walch, O.S.F.
Res., P.O. Box 421, 59457. Tel: 406-538-9306; Fax: 406-538-7624. [CEM]
Catechesis/Religious Programs—D.R.E.: Judy Marxer, (Grades K-6); Denise Goodwyn, (Grades 7-12).
Students 390.
Mission—Winifred, Holy Family.
Chapels—Danvers, St. Wenceslaus.; Hilger, St. Victor.; Roy, Sacred Heart.

Livingston, Park Co., St. Mary's, Rev. Dale E. Yurkovic; Joannie Lee, Pastoral Assoc.
Res., S. F St., P.O. Box 646, 59047-0646. Tel: 406-222-1393; Fax: 406-222-1405. [CEM]
School—(Grades PreK-8). Tel: 406-222-3303. Michelle Moore, Prin.
Lay Teachers 13; Students 139.
Catechesis/Religious Programs—Students 57.
Missions—Clyde Park, St. Margaret; Gardiner, St. William.

Lodge Grass, Big Horn Co., Our Lady of Loretto, Rev. James Antoine, O.F.M.Cap.
Res., P.O. Box N, 59050. Tel: 406-639-2254; Fax: 406-639-2254.
Catechesis/Religious Programs—Rosaline Old Bear, D.R.E.
Students 40.
Mission—Wyola, Blessed Kateri Tekakwitha.

Malta, Phillips Co., St. Mary's, Rev. James O'Neil.
Res., 27 S. Seventh St. W., P.O. Box 70, 59538. Tel: 406-654-1446; Fax: 406-654-1467.
Catechesis/Religious Programs—Tel: 406-654-1311. Dianne Salsbery, D.R.E.
Students 125.
Missions—Dodson, Sacred Heart; Saco, St. Francis of Assisi; Whitewater, St. John.

Miles City, Custer Co., Sacred Heart, Revs. Gil Hemauer, O.F.M.Cap.; Wilfred Splonskowski; Mrs. Carol Green, Pastoral Assoc.
Mailing Address: P.O. Box 1016, 59301. Tel: 406-232-1691; Fax: 406-232-5687.
Church—110 N. Montana, Tel: 406-232-7585.
School—(Grades K-8). Tel: 406-232-3850. Bart Freese, Prin.
Lay Teachers 7; Students 71.
Catechesis/Religious Programs—Mrs. Janice Wood, D.R.E.
Students 175.
Mission—Terry, Sacred Heart, P.O. Box 526, Terry, 59349. Tel: 406-637-5569.
Stations—Pine Hills School, Tel: 406-232-1377; Fax: 406-232-7432; Holy Rosary Extended Care, Tel: 406-233-2600; Fax: 406-233-2621; Holy Rosary Hospital.; Veterans' Administration Hospital, Tel: 406-232-3060; Miles City, Friendship Villa Rest Home, Tel: 406-232-2687.

Plentywood, Sheridan Co., St. Joseph's, Rev. Benjamin R. Lobo; Kordelia French, Admin. Asst.
Res., P.O. Box 6, 59254. Tel: 406-765-2250; Fax: 406-765-2345.
Catechesis/Religious Programs—Tel: 406-765-2251. Barb Golterman, D.R.E.
Students 154.
Mission—Medicine Lane, St. Patrick.
Chapel—Outlook, St. Boniface.

Poplar, Roosevelt Co., Our Lady of Lourdes, Rev. Michael Schneider; Sr. Mary Hourigan, O.P., Pastoral Assoc.
Res., P.O. Box 187, 59255. Tel: 406-768-3244 (Rectory); 768-3305 (Office); Fax: 406-768-5703.
Catechesis/Religious Programs—Val Gorder, D.R.E.
Students 85.
Mission—Brockton, St. Thomas.
Chapel—Fort Kipp, St. Anthony.

Pryor, Big Horn Co., St. Charles Borromeo Mission, Rev. Randolph Graczyk, O.F.M.Cap.
Res., P.O. Box 29, 59066. Tel: 406-259-9747; Fax: 406-259-7092.
School—(Grades K-8). Tel: 406-259-9976; Fax: 406-259-7092. Pat Townsend, Prin.
Sisters 1; Lay Teachers 16; Students 110.

Red Lodge, Carbon Co., St. Agnes, Rev. Richard D. Osterman.
Res., P.O. Box 1067, 59068. Tel: 406-446-1237; Fax: 406-446-1237.
Catechesis/Religious Programs—Students 60.

Roundup, Musselshell Co., St. Benedict's, Rev. Anthony Schuster.
Res., 503 Main St., 59072. Tel: 406-323-1019.
Catechesis/Religious Programs—Ann Newell, D.R.E.
Students 65.
Missions—Melstone, Our Lady of Mercy; Winnett, St. Aloysius; Broadview, Little Flower; Ryegate, St Mathias.
Chapel—St. Honorata, Musselshell, 59059.

Scobey, Daniels Co., St. Philip Bonitus, Rev. Gary R. Norman.
Res., P.O. Box 827, 59263. Tel: 406-487-5525.
Catechesis/Religious Programs—D.R.E.: Carol Fauhy; Del Henderson; Terry Risa.
Students 64.
Missions—Flaxville, St. Louis; Glentana, Holy Family; Peerless, St. Ann. [CEM]

Sidney, Richland Co., St. Matthew, Rev. Greg Staudinger; Linda Latka, Parish Admin.
Res., 219 Seventh St. S.E., 59270. Tel: 406-482-1068; Fax: 406-482-4373. [CEM]
Catechesis/Religious Programs—Tel: 406-482-2510. D.R.E.: Barbara Olson; Gary Rauchendorfer; Yvonne Volkman.
Students 540.
Missions—Fairview, Richland Co., St. Catherine, P.O. Box 494, Fairview, 59221. Tel: 406-747-5293; Lambert, Richland Co., St. Theresa, P.O. Box 153, Lambert, 59243. Tel: 406-774-3360; Charley Creek, St. Bernard's; Savage, Richland Co., St. Michael, P.O. Box 95, Savage, 59262.

Stanford, Judith Basin Co., St. Rose of Lima, Rev. Terrence P. Regan.
P.O. Box 250, 59479. Tel: 406-566-2531.
Catechesis/Religious Programs—Students 100.
Missions—Denton, St. Anthony, P.O. Box 384, Denton, 59430. Tel: 406-567-2438; Geyser, St. Cyril, P.O. Box 35, Geyser, 59447. Tel: 406-735-4388; Moore, St. Mathias, P.O. Box 104, Moore, 59464. Tel: 406-374-2477; Hobson, Sacred Heart, P.O. Box 286, Hobson, 59452. Tel: 406-423-5613.

Wolf Point, Roosevelt Co., Immaculate Conception, Rev. Stephen J. Zabrocki.
Res., 500 Fifth Ave. S., P.O. Box 789, 59201. Tel: 406-653-2610. [CEM]
Catechesis/Religious Programs—Linda Johnson, D.R.E.
Students 150.
Missions—Frazer, St. Joseph; Vida, St. Ann; Riverside, Sacred Heart.

Special Assignment:
Reverend Fathers—
Cote, David P., 315 72nd St. N., Malmstrom AFB, MT 59402-7514
Doyle, Oliver, St. Ann's Cathedral, P.O. Box 1708, Great Falls, MT 59403
Norman, Gary, St. Philip Bonitus, P.O. Box 827, Scobey, MT 59263-0827
Pittapilly, Thomas, St. Anthony's, P.O. Box 30, Culbertson, MT 59218-0030
Sewvello, Robert, P.O. Box 21271, Billings, MT 59104-1271
Taylor, Jon, University of Great Falls, 1302 20th St. S., Great Falls, MT 59405
Vogel, Marcel J., St. Gabriel's Church, P.O. Box 1089, Chinook, MT 59523-1089

On Duty Outside of the Diocese:
Reverend Fathers—
Cawley, William M., St. Patrick Rectory, 231 S. Beaver St., York, PA 17403-5499
Christofferson, Kevin, 102 S. Washington St., Butte, MT 59701-1638
Dobbin, Jay D., St. Ignatius House of Studies, P.O. Box 20516 GMF, Barrigada, Guam 96921-0516
Kirkness, Michael D., 104 Palm Court Dr., Santa Maria, CA 93454-6644
Krier, John P., Immaculate Conception Church, P.O. Box 910, Davenport, WA 99122-0910

Military Chaplains:
Reverend Fathers—
Munsell, Richard F., 8FW/HC, PSC 2 Box 923, APO, AP 96264-0010

Sabbatical:
Reverend Fathers—
Pittard, Wayne M., c/o Diocese of Great Falls-Billings, P.O. Box 1399, Great Falls, MT 59403-1399

Retired:
Reverend Monsignors—
Gluszek, Joseph, 2810 Central Ave., Great Falls, MT 59401-3412
Reverend Fathers—
Arbanas, Harold P., 3475 16th St., #6, San Francisco, CA 94114-1751
Beggin, Thomas M., 1242 Custer Ave., Billings, MT 59102-5218
Bofto, Robert C., 3001 S. 288th St., #230, Federal Way, WA 98003-8017
Bourke, Nathaniel J., 2101-24th St., W., Billings, MT 59201-2246

Clausen, Kenneth J., 3729 Second Ave. S., Billings, MT 59101-3603
Coady, John, 5734 E.19th St., Tucson, AZ 85711-5163
Dimke, John, P.O. Box 42, Neihart, MT 59465-0042
Fisher, Martin, 507 Parkhill Dr., Billings, MT 59102-3619
Fox, Robert J., P.O. Box 53, Poplar, MT 59255-0053
Gedvila, Izidorius, 1718 Haverhill Cir., Chipley, FL 32428-3179
Gorman, Charles L., P.O. Box 956, Columbus, MT 59019-0956
Gregori, Anthony F., 1711 Smelter Ave., Great Falls, MT 59414-1222
Guinan, Michael, 1701 26th St. S., #4, Great Falls, MT 59405-5173
Hoffman, Emmett G., P.O. Box 687, Ashland, MT 59003-0687
Hopkins, Richard J., St. Patrick's Co-Cathedral, 215 N. 31st St., Billings, MT 59101-1908
Hruska, Eugene P., 13327 MT Hwy. 200, Fort Shaw, MT 59443-9409
Janson, Leo F., Regina Cleri, 2003 Woody Dr., No. 1, Billings, MT 59102-2891
Kaminski, Joseph M., 649 21st St., Black Eagle, MT 59414-1119
Kelly, Frank F., 1701 26th St. S., #1, Great Falls, MT 59405-5173
McInnis, Francis L., 1701-26th St. S. #3, Great Falls, MT 59404-5173
McTague, Thomas, P.O. Box 225, Hysham, MT 59038-0225
Moore, John J., 18140 Medford Ave., Stratford, CA 93266-9748
Moran, Patrick A., 1464 Green Trails Dr., No. 1, Naperville, IL 60540-8380
O'Hanlon, Michael A., Danesfort, Dromahane Mallow, County Cork, Ireland
O'Reilly, Patrick J., 823 Leisure World, Mesa, AZ 85206-2406
Papes, Joseph T., 5201 Raubinger Rd., Swartz Creek, MI 48473
Rutan, Albert E., P.O. Box 50, Liberty Center, IA 50145-0050
Sampson, Patrick, 2003 Woody Dr., #4, Billings, MT 59102-2891
Shinnick, Edward P., RR 2 - Box 156A, Savage, MT 59262-9706
Tarrant, Patrick J., P.O. Box 275, Yarmouth Port, MA 02675-0275

Permanent Deacons:
Birkle, Timothy J., 1216 Claim Jumper, Billings, MT 59101-614
Daem, Robert W., 220 34th St. W., Billings, MT 59102-4473
Melius, Melvin A., 1437 Avenue D, Billings, MT 59102-3124

INSTITUTIONS LOCATED IN THE DIOCESE

[A] COLLEGES AND UNIVERSITIES

GREAT FALLS. *University of Great Falls,* (1932) 1301 20th St. S., 59405. Tel: 406-761-8210; Fax: 406-791-5393.
E-mail: adminrec@ugf.edu
Web site: www.ugf.edu
For a complete listing, refer to the Colleges and Universities section.

[B] HIGH SCHOOLS, DIOCESAN

BILLINGS. *Central Catholic High School,* 3 Broadwater Ave., 59101. Tel: 406-245-6651; Fax: 406-259-3124.
E-mail: sprigler@myvista.com
Tom Sprigler, Prin.; Mr. Donald Dundas, Assoc. Prin. Sisters 1; Lay Teachers 26; Students 349.

[C] HIGH SCHOOLS, PRIVATE

ASHLAND. *St. Labre Indian Catholic High School,* Mission Rd., 59003. Tel: 406-784-4500; Fax: 406-784-4565. Dr. Russell Alexander, Dir. of Schools & Prin. Lay Teachers 18; Students 165.

[D] ELEMENTARY SCHOOLS, DIOCESAN

BILLINGS. *St. Francis Intermediate School.* (Grades 3-5), 1734 Yellowstone Ave., 59102. Tel: 406-656-2300; Fax: 406-656-2301. Chris Read, Prin. Lay Teachers 13; Students 196.
St. Francis Primary School. (Grades PreK-2), 511 Custer Ave., 59101. Tel: 406-259-6421; Fax: 406-245-0176.
E-mail: kpetermann@metnet.mt.gov
Web site: www.bcs.pvt.k12.mt.us
Sr. Elizabeth Young, S.C.L., Head Prin.; Karen Petermann, Assoc. Prin. Lay Teachers 11; Students 280.
St. Francis Upper School. (Grades 6-8), 205 N. 32nd St., 59101. Tel: 406-259-5037; Fax: 406-259-7981.
E-mail: mzauher@metnet.mt.gov
Martha Zauher, Prin. Lay Teachers 13; Students 210.

[E] ELEMENTARY SCHOOLS, PRIVATE

ASHLAND. *St. Labre Indian Catholic Elementary School,* Mission Rd., 59003. Tel: 406-784-4500; Fax: 406-784-4565. Dr. Russell Alexander, Dir. of Schools; Scott Gion, Prin., Middle School; Nocole Trahan, Prin., K-3. Lay Teachers 20; Students 275.
PRYOR. *St. Charles Mission School,* P.O. Box 29, 59066. Tel: 406-259-9976; Fax: 406-259-7092.
E-mail: ptownsend@stlabre.org
Patricia Townsend, Prin. Priests 1; Sisters 1; Lay Teachers 15; Students 107.
ST. XAVIER. *Pretty Eagle Catholic School,* P.O. Box 257, 59075. Tel: 406-666-2215; Fax: 406-666-2245.
E-mail: jhardy@stlabre.org
Joel Hardy, Prin. Sisters 1; Lay Teachers 16; Students 143.

[F] CHILD CARE & YOUTH SERVICES

GREAT FALLS. *St. Thomas Child and Family Center,* 416 23rd St. N., 59401. Tel: 406-761-6538; Fax: 406-727-0670.
E-mail: stthomaskids@mcn.net
Web site: stthomaskids.org
Sisters of Providence. Calvin Moore, Exec. Dir. Child Care Center; Family Life Education; Prevention and Treatment of Child Abuse; Education, Information, and Referral Service; Summer Food Program for Low-Income Children; Before- and After-School Care Programs. Lay Staff 61; Child Care & Nursery Children 360.
BILLINGS. *Little Flower Day Care,* 120 S. 34th St., P.O. Box 31158, 59107. Tel: 406-252-5697; Fax: 406-252-5697. Gail Weber, Dir.
St. Francis Day Care, 511 Custer Ave., 59101. Tel: 406-259-6421; Fax: 406-252-5697. Gail Weber, Dir.
Saint Francis Day Care West, 2821 Augusta Ln., 59102. Tel: 406-256-3562; Fax: 406-252-5697. Gail Weber, Dir.

[G] GENERAL HOSPITALS

GREAT FALLS. *Benefis Health Care,* 500-15th Ave. S., P.O. Box 5013, 59403. Tel: 406-455-5000; Fax: 406-455-4587.
E-mail: benefis@benefis.org
Web site: www.benefis.org
For a complete listing, refer to the Hospitals section.
BILLINGS. *St. Vincent Healthcare,* 1233 N. 30th St., P.O. Box 35200, 59107-5200. Tel: 406-657-7000; Fax: 406-237-3078.
E-mail: 1larson@svhhc.org
Web site: www.svhhc.org
For a complete listing, refer to the Hospitals section.
MILES CITY. *Holy Rosary Healthcare,* 2600 Wilson St., 59301. Tel: 406-233-2600; Fax: 406-233-2611
For a complete listing, refer to the Hospitals section.

[H] CONVENTS AND RESIDENCES FOR SISTERS

GREAT FALLS. *Our Lady of Lourdes Convent,* 319 14th St. S., 59405. Tel: 406-761-6443. Ursuline Nuns 2.
Poor Clares of Montana, Inc., 416-2nd Ave., S.W., 59404-2904. Tel: 406-453-7891; Fax: 406-453-8689.
E-mail: PoorClaresMT@worldnet.att.net
Web site: www.poorclare.org/montana
Sisters 4.
Ursuline Convent, 2300 Central Ave., 59401. Tel: 406-452-8585; Fax: 406-452-8586.
E-mail: ursuline@in-tch.com
Sr. Daniel Ryan, O.S.U., Supr. Ursuline Sisters 7.
BILLINGS. *Mercy Convent,* 2420 Elm St., 59101. Tel: 406-259-2550; Fax: 406-259-2550. Sisters of Mercy 2.
Sisters of Charity of Leavenworth, 1134 N. 31st St., 59101. Tel: 406-252-0395. Sisters 3.

[I] RENEWAL CENTERS

BILLINGS. *Sacred Heart Renewal Center,* 26 Wyoming Ave., P.O. Box 153, 59103-0153. Tel: 406-252-0322.
E-mail: shrc@mcn.net
Kathleen O'Neal, Admin. Dir.; Polly Eaton, Spiritual Dir.

[J] RETREAT HOUSES

GREAT FALLS. *Ursuline Retreat Centre,* 2300 Central Ave., 59401. Tel: 406-452-8585; Fax: 406-452-8586.
E-mail: ursuline@in-tch.com
Harry J. Tholen, Dir.

[K] MISCELLANEOUS LISTINGS

GREAT FALLS. *Cascade County Council of the St. Vincent de Paul Society,* P.O. Box 1562, 500 Central Ave. W., 59403. Tel: 406-761-0870. Dione Leidholt, Opers. Dir.
Catholic Foundation of Eastern Montana, Inc., P.O. Box 1399, 59403-1399. Tel: 406-727-6683; Fax: 406-454-3480.
E-mail: dioceseofgfb@mcn.net
Web site: www.mcn.net/~dioceseofgfb
Joseph Pipinich, Contact Person.
Committee for a Great Falls Catholic High School, P.O. Box 1399, 59403-1399. Tel: 406-727-6683; Fax: 406-454-3480.
E-mail: dioceseofgfb@mcn.net
Web site: www.mcn.net/~dioceseofgfb
Joseph Loncki, Diocesan Finance Officer.
Frank & Isabell Stites Memorial Center. (Retired Priests & Lay People Living). Mailing Address: Pastoral Center, P.O. Box 1399, 59403. Tel: 406-727-6683.
E-mail: dicoeseofgfb@mcn.net
Web site: www.mcn.net/~dioceseofgfb
1701 26th St. S., 59403. Joseph Loncki, Contact Person.
Great Falls City-Wide Ministry to Native Americans, 121 23rd St. S., P.O. Box 1399, 59403. Tel: 406-727-6683; Fax: 406-454-3480.
E-mail: dioceseofgfb@mcn.net
Linda Kovar, Dir.
Heisey Memorial Trust Fund, 313 Seventh St. N., 59401. Tel: 406-453-1211. Mr. Kirby Crosley, Dir.
Heisey Memorial Youth Center, 313 Seventh St. N., 59401. Tel: 406-453-1211. Mr. Kirby Crosley, Dir. Recreation center serving the adults and youth of the community.
Holy Spirit Catholic School Endowment Trust, 2816 Central Ave., 59401-3412. Tel: 406-761-5775; Fax: 406-761-5887.
E-mail: parshscs@hotmail.com
Joseph Sullivan, Pres.
St. Joseph's Education Trust, 500 2nd Ave. S.W., 59404. Tel: 406-453-5558. Rev. Patrick R. Zabrocki, Chm.
Tekakwitha Conference, P.O. Box 6768, 59406. Tel: 406-727-0147; Fax: 406-452-9845.
E-mail: TEKAKWITHA.CONFERENCE@worldnet.att.net
Sr. Kateri Mitchell, S.S.A., Exec. Dir.
BILLINGS. *Billings Area Catholic Education Trust.* (BACET), P.O. Box 31158, 59107-1158. Tel: 406-252-0252; Fax: 406-252-5731.
E-mail: klucas@bcs.pvt.k12.mt.us
Web site: www.bcs.pvt.k12.mt.us
Ms. Karin E. Lucas, Exec. Dir.; Mr. Clay Skurdal, Chair; Ms. Elizabeth Wilmouth, Vice Chair; Mr. Jim Winchell, Treas.
Billings Catholic Engaged Encounter, 2221 - 6th St. W., 59102. Tel: 406-651-9132.
Kateri Indian Ministry, 1015 Broadwater, 59102-5440. Tel: 406-256-5142; Fax: 406-256-5678.
E-mail: kateri2000@juno.com
Bro. Bede Baldry, F.S.C., Dir.
Mayfair Auction, Billings Catholic Schools. Mailing Address: P.O. Box 31158, 59107. Tel: 406-252-5968; Fax: 406-252-9875. Vicki Davison, Exec. Dir.
Newman Center, 1500 N. 30th St., Box 55 MSU-Billings, 59101. Tel: 406-657-2276.
E-mail: blgsnewmancntr@hotmail.com
Regina Cleri. Pastoral Center, P.O. Box 1399, Great Falls, 59403. Tel: 406-727-6683; Fax: 406-454-3480.
E-mail: dioceseofgfb@mcn.net
Web site: www.mcn.net/~dioceseofgfb
2003 Woody Dr., 59102. (Retired Priests Living). Joseph Loncki, Contact Person.
St. Vincent de Paul Society of Yellowstone County, 2610 Montana Ave., 59101-2340. Tel: 406-252-1855.
E-mail: stvincentdpmt@aol.com
Harold W. Merchant, Exec. Dir.; Bro. Bede Baldry, Spiritual Advisor.
Saint Vincent Foundation, P. O. Box 35200, 59107-5200. Tel: 406-237-3600, Ext. 600; Fax: 406-237-3619.
E-mail: cennis@svhhc.org
Carolyn K. Ennis, Exec. Dir.; Paul R. Crellin, M.D., Chm., Bd. of Trustees.
ASHLAND. *St. Labre Indian School Educational Association,* P.O. Box 216, 59003. Tel: 406-784-4500; Fax: 406-784-6161.
Web site: www.stlabre.org
A nonprofit Corporation. Mr. Curtis Yarlott, Pres & Exec. Dir.; Rev. Emmett G. Hoffmann. Four Catholic schools for Native Americans: St. Labre Indian School at Ashland (Grade School Students 275); (High School Students 165); Pretty Eagle Catholic School, St. Xavier (Students 136); St. Charles Mission School, Pryor (Students 107).
St. Labre Youth & Family Services/Youth Group Home, P.O. Box 458, 59003. Tel: 406-784-4521; Fax: 406-784-4527. Clay A. Ramey, Dir. Licensed for 8 children.
HAVRE. *St. Jude's Education Trust,* 1110-7th St., 59501. Tel: 406-265-7174. M. F. Clancey, Chm.

LEWISTOWN. *Big Sky Cum Christo/Cursillo*, P.O. Box 638, 59407-0638. Contact Persons: Bob Meyers. Tel: 406-453-5304; Vern Boyer. Tel: 406-628-4753.

St. Leo's Catholic Education Trust, P.O. Box 421, 59457. Tel: 406-538-9306; Fax: 406-538-7624. E-mail: stleos@tein.net
Rev. Daniel O'Rourke, Chm.

MALTA. *St. Mary's Catholic Education Trust*, P.O. Box 70, 59538. Rev. James O'Neil.

MILES CITY. *Custer County Conference of the Society of Saint Vincent de Paul and Thrift Store*, 407 Main St., 59301. Tel: 406-232-3011. Dorothy Buck, Pres. Store Managers: Jane O'Donnell; Phebe Beeler; Marcia Rudolph; Mrs. Marjorie Shipp.

MONARCH. *Thieltges-St. Thomas Camp*, P.O. Box 46, 59463. Tel: 406-236-5385.

RELIGIOUS INSTITUTES OF MEN REPRESENTED IN THE DIOCESE

For further details refer to the corresponding bracketed number in the Religious Institutes of Men or Women section.

[0200]—*Benedictine Monks.* (Assumption Abbey, Richardton, ND; Cleveland, OH).—O.S.B.

[0330]—*Brothers of the Christian Schools.* (Midwest Province).—F.S.C.

[0470]—*The Capuchin Friars.* (Prov. of St. Joseph, Detroit).—O.F.M.Cap.

[0690]—*Jesuit Fathers and Brothers.* (Oregon Prov.).—S.J.

RELIGIOUS INSTITUTES OF WOMEN REPRESENTED IN THE DIOCESE

[0230]—*Benedictine Sisters of Pontifical Jurisdiction.* (Rapid City, SD and St. Paul, MN).—O.S.B.

[2100]—*Congregation of the Humility of Mary.* (Davenport, IA).—C.H.M.

[3830-06]—*Congregation of the Sisters of St. Joseph.* (Buffalo, NY).—S.S.J.

[1730]—*Congregation of the Sisters of the Third Order of St. Francis.* (Oldenburg, IN).—O.S.F.

[1070-10]—*Dominican Sisters of Springfield in Illinois.*—O.P.

[1070-11]—*Dominican Sisters, Congregation of Our Lady of the Rosary.* (Sparkill, NY).—O.P.

[1070-03]—*Dominican Sisters, Sinsinawa Dominican Congregation of the Most Holy Rosary.* (Sinsinawa, WI).—O.P.

[3760]—*Poor Clares of Montana, Inc.* (Great Falls, MT).—O.S.C.

[0480]—*Sisters of Charity of Leavenworth, Kansas.*—S.C.L.

[2560]—*Sisters of Mercy - US Prov.* (Redlands, CA).—R.S.M.

[2575]—*Sisters of Mercy of the Americas.* (Omaha, NE).—R.S.M.

[3350]—*Sisters of Providence.* (Spokane, WA).—S.P.

[]—*Sisters of Sainte Anne.* (Victoria, BC, Canada).—S.S.A.

[3320]—*Sisters of the Presentation of the B.V.M.* (Aberdeen, SD).—P.B.V.M.

[1720]—*Sisters of the Third Order Regular of St. Francis of the Congregation of Our Lady of Lourdes.* (Rochester, MN).—O.S.F.

[4110]—*Ursuline Nuns.* (Santa Rosa, CA).—O.S.U.

DIOCESAN CEMETERIES

GREAT FALLS. *Calvary.*
Mount Olivet.

BILLINGS. *Calvary.*
Holy Cross.

NECROLOGY

† Bedicek, Valerian Vincent, (Retired). —Died April 4, 2000.

† Hanrahan, John Alphonsus, (Retired). —Died Sept. 12, 2000.

Diocese of Green Bay

(Dioecesis Sinus Viridis)

Most Reverend

ROBERT J. BANKS, D.D.

Bishop of Green Bay; ordained December 20, 1952; consecrated September 19, 1985; appointed Auxiliary Bishop to the Archbishop of Boston and Titular Bishop of Taraqua on June 26, 1985; appointed to Green Bay October 16, 1990. *Office: 1910 S. Webster Ave., P.O. Box 23825, Green Bay, WI, 54305-3825.* Tel.: 920-437-7531.

Most Reverend

ALOYSIUS J. WYCISLO, D.D.

Retired Bishop of Green Bay; ordained April 7, 1934; appointed Titular Bishop of Stadia and Auxiliary of Chicago October 17, 1960; consecrated December 21, 1960; appointed to Green Bay March 8, 1968; retired May 10, 1983; appointed Apostolic Administrator of Green Bay Diocese June 16, 1983. *Res., 1825 Riverside Dr., Green Bay, WI, 54301.* Tel.: 920-435-3685.

Most Reverend

ROBERT F. MORNEAU, D.D.

Auxiliary Bishop of Green Bay and Titular Bishop of Massa Lubrense; ordained May 28, 1966; appointed December 19, 1978; consecrated February 22, 1979. *Res., 1825 Riverside Dr., P.O. Box 23825, Green Bay, WI, 54305-3825. Office: 1910 S. Webster, P.O. Box 23825, Green Bay, WI, 54305-3825.* Tel.: 920-437-7531.

Chancery: 1910 S. Webster Ave., P.O. Box 23825, Green Bay, WI, 54305-3825. Tel.: 920-437-7531; Fax: 920-435-1330.

Web site address: www.gbdioc.org

E-mail address: jdewane@gbdioc.org

ESTABLISHED MARCH 3, 1868.

Square Miles 10,728.

Incorporated January 16, 1907.

Legal Title: Catholic Diocese of Green Bay.

Comprises these 16 Counties: Brown, Calumet, Door, Florence, Forest, Kewaunee, Langlade, Manitowoc, Marinette, Menominee, Oconto, Outagamie, Shawano, Waupaca, Waushara and Winnebago in the State of Wisconsin.

For legal titles of parishes and diocesan institutions, consult the Chancery Office.

STATISTICAL OVERVIEW

Personnel	
Bishop	1
Auxiliary Bishops	1
Retired Bishops	1
Abbots	1
Retired Abbots	2
Priests: Diocesan Active in Diocese	139
Priests: Active Outside Diocese	8
Priests: Diocesan in Foreign Missions	4
Priests: Retired, Sick or Absent	69
Number of Diocesan Priests	220
Religious Priests in Diocese	136
Extern Priests in Diocese	5
Ordinations:	
Diocesan Priests	1
Permanent Deacons	5
Permanent Deacons in Diocese	87
Total Brothers	38
Total Sisters	622
Parishes	
Parishes	191
With Resident Pastor:	
Resident Diocesan Priests	109
Resident Religious Priests	23
Without Resident Pastor:	
Administered by Priests	48
Administered by Deacons	1
Administered by Women Religious	6
Administered by Lay People	4
Missions	4
Pastoral Centers	13
Closed Parishes	7
Professional Ministry Personnel:	
Brothers	1
Sisters	73
Lay Ministers	169
Welfare	
Catholic Hospitals	8
Total Assisted	1,074,636
Homes for the Aged	10
Total Assisted	1,132
Day Care and Extended Day Care Centers	1
Total Assisted	60
Specialized Homes	4
Total Assisted	6,965
Special Centers for Social Services	8
Total Assisted	188,437
Residential Care of Disabled	1
Total Assisted	9
Educational	
Diocesan Students in Other Seminaries	11
Seminaries, Religious	1
Students Religious	5
Total Seminarians	16
Colleges and Universities	2
Total Students	6,455
High Schools, Diocesan and Parish	5
Total Students	1,521
High Schools, Private	1
Total Students	757
Elementary Schools, Diocesan and Parish	78
Total Students	12,379
Catechesis/Religious Education:	
High School Students	8,739
Elementary Students	24,325
Total Students Under Catholic Instruction	54,192
Teachers in the Diocese:	
Sisters	42
Lay Teachers	812
Vital Statistics	
Receptions into the Church:	
Infant Baptism Totals	4,844
Adult Baptism Totals	206
Received into Full Communion	298
First Communions	4,900
Confirmations	3,535
Marriages:	
Catholic	1,315
Interfaith	494
Total Marriages	1,809
Deaths	3,247
Total Catholic Population	388,093
Total Population	924,032

Former Bishops—Rt. Rev. JOSEPH MELCHER, D.D., cons. July 12, 1868; died Dec. 20, 1873.—Rt. Rev. FRANCIS XAVIER KRAUTBAUER, D.D., cons. June 29, 1875; died Dec. 17, 1885.—Rt. Rev. FREDERICK XAVIER KATZER, D.D., appt. July 13, 1886; cons. Sept. 21, 1886; appt. Archbishop of Milwaukee, Jan. 30, 1891; died July 20, 1903.—Rt. Rev. SEBASTIAN GEBHARD MESSMER, D.D., cons. Bishop of Green Bay, March 27, 1892; appt. Archbishop of Milwaukee, Nov. 28, 1903; died Aug. 4, 1930.—Rt. Rev. JOSEPH J. FOX, D.D., cons. Bishop of Green Bay, July 25, 1904; resigned Dec. 4, 1914; appt. Titular Bishop of Ionopolis; died March 14, 1915.—Most Rev. PAUL P. RHODE, D.D., ord. June 17, 1894; cons. Titular Bishop of Barca and Auxiliary to the Archbishop of Chicago, July 29, 1908; transferred to the See of Green Bay, July 5, 1915; died March 3, 1945.—Most Rev. STANISLAUS V. BONA, D.D., ord. Nov. 1, 1912; appt. Bishop of Grand Island, NE Dec. 18, 1931; cons. Feb. 25, 1932; appt. Coadjutor Bishop of Green Bay, Dec. 2, 1944; succeeded to See, March 3, 1945; died Dec. 1, 1967.—Most Rev. ALOYSIUS J. WYCISLO, D.D., ord. April 7, 1934; appt. Titular Bishop of Stadia and Auxiliary Bishop of Chicago Oct. 17, 1960; cons. Dec. 21, 1960; appt. to Green Bay, March 8, 1968; retired May 10, 1983.—Most Rev. ADAM J. MAIDA, J.C.L., J.D., S.T.L., ord. May 26, 1956; appt. to Green Bay, Nov. 8, 1983; cons. Jan. 25, 1984; installed as Archbishop of Detroit, June 12, 1990; created Cardinal on Nov. 26, 1994.

Vicars General—Most Rev. ROBERT F. MORNEAU, D.D.; Rev. Msgr. JOHN B. DEWANE, M.A., S.T.L., D.Min.

Chancery—1910 S. Webster Ave., P.O. Box 23825, Green Bay, 54305-3825. Tel: 920-437-7531; Fax: 920-435-1330. Office Hours: Mon.-Fri. 9-5; other times by appointment only.

Vicar for Administration—Rev. Msgr. JOHN B. DEWANE, M.A., S.T.L., D.Min.

Chancellor—Sr. MARY BRIDE GRUBBS, A.N.G., M.P.S.

Vice-Chancellor—Rev. Msgr. JOHN H. SCHUH.

Assistant Chancellor—Rev. JOHN DOERFLER, J.C.L., S.T.L.

Archivist—Vacant.

Secretary to Bishop—TERRI WICKMAN, , Ext. 8194.

Chancery Secretary—MARY JO KRUEGER, , Ext. 8188.

Diocesan Tribunal—Mailing Address: *1910 S. Webster Ave., P.O. Box 23825, Green Bay, 54305-3825.* Tel: 920-437-7531.

Presiding Judge and Officialis—Rev. ROBERT J. KABAT, J.C.L.

Vice-Officialis and Assoc. Presiding Judge—Rev. RICHARD GETCHEL, J.C.L.

Defenders of the Bond—Revs. LEE J. KAHRS; PHILIP HOFFMANN.

Prosynodal Judges—Rev. Msgr. DENNIS M. LALLY; Rev. Msgr. ROY M. KLISTER, J.C.L.; Revs. ARTHUR J. DANKS; JOHN DOERFLER, J.C.L., S.T.L.; JAMES B. HERRING, O.Praem.; GARY NEVILLE, O.Praem., J.C.D.; RICHARD C. SHAFER, M.A.; WILLIAM L. VAN DE KREEKE, J.C.L.

Notaries—BARBARA BOWER; MARGIE GANTZ; KATHLEEN SCHUMACHER.

Diocesan Consultors—Most Rev. ROBERT F. MORNEAU; Rev. Msgr. JOHN B. DEWANE; Rev. Msgr. JAMES DILLENBURG; Rev. Msgr. JAMES FEELY; Rev. Msgr. PETER KLAUCK; Rev. Msgr. PAUL KOSZAREK; Rev. Msgr. ROY KLISTER; Revs. JOHN BERGSTADT; MICHAEL O'ROURKE.

Secretary to Consultors—Sr. MARY BRIDE GRUBBS, A.N.G.

Pastor Consultors—Rev. Msgr. PETER N. KLAUCK; Rev. Msgr. CARL E. STEINER; Revs. JOHN P. BERGSTADT; JAMES A. HABLEWITZ; JOSEPH A. MATTERN; PAUL A. SCHUMACHER; WILLARD J. VAN DE LOO.

Regional Vicars—Revs. RALPH J. GILLIS, Vicariate I; LEONARD M. EVERS, Vicariate II; JOHN M. GALLAGHER, Vicariate III; PHILIP DINH-VAN-THIEP, Vicariate IV; DENNIS M. RYAN, Vicariate V; DAVID J. PLIER, Vicariate VI; ANTHONY J. BIRDSALL, Vicariate VII; DAVID J. KOCH, Vicariate VIII; DENNIS L. BERGSBAKEN, Vicariate IX; MICHAEL R. KOCH, Vicariate X; RALLEN H. STENCIL, Vicariate XI; RONALD A. COLOMBO, Vicariate XII.

Diocesan Pastoral Council—Rev. Msgr. JOHN B. DEWANE, Contact Person.

Presbyteral Council—Rev. Msgr. JAMES DILLENBURG, Chm.

Appointed Representatives—Rev. Msgr. PETER KLAUCK; Rev. Msgr. PAUL KOSZARCK; Revs. JOHN DOERFLER; PATRICK GAWRYLEWSKI, O.F.M.; ROBERT KOLLATH; GERY MEEHAN, O.Praem.; JEROME PASTORS; MICHAEL O'ROURKE.

Elected Representatives—Rev. JOSEPH DORNER, Vicariate I; Rev. MICHAEL CARROLL, Vicariate II; Rev. JOHN GALLAGHER, Vicariate III; Rev. Msgr. MARK SCHOMMER, Vicariate IV; Rev. GERALD PRUSAKOWSKI, O.F.M., Vicariate V; Rev. Msgr. JAMES DILLENBURG, Vicariate VI; Rev. WILLIAM KUHR, Vicariate VII; Rev. JOHN BERGSTADT, Vicariate VIII; Rev. DAVID SCHMIDT, Vicariate IX; Rev. Msgr. JAMES FEELY, Vicariate X; Rev. GARY NEW, S.D.S., Vicariate XI; Rev. MATTHEW SIMONAR, Vicariate XII. Ex Officios: Most Rev. ROBERT F. MORNEAU; Rev. Msgr. JOHN B. DEWANE.

Bishop's Finance Council—Rev. ROBERT K. FINNEGAN, O.Praem.; MARY STAUDENMAIER; MICHAEL ARIENS; JAMES LIETHEN; JOHN F. BERGSTROM; ROBERT C. GALLAGHER; WILLIAM FRIEDER.

Resource—Most Rev. ROBERT F. MORNEAU; THOMAS KURKOWSKI.

Ministry Personnel

Vicar for Religious—Rev. Msgr. JOHN H. SCHUH, *P.O. Box 23825, Green Bay, 54305-3825.* Tel: 920-437-7531, Ext. 8179.

Representative for Religious—Sr. MARY JO KIRT, *P.O. Box 23825, Green Bay, 54305-3825.* Tel: 920-437-7531, Ext. 8292.

Vicar for Priests—Rev. WILLARD J. VAN DE LOO, *P.O. Box 23825, Green Bay, 54305-3825.* Tel: 920-437-7531, Ext. 8322.

Vicar for Senior Priests—Rev. PHILIP HOFFMANN, *P.O. Box 23825, Green Bay, 54305-3825.* Tel: 920-437-7531, Ext. 8183.

Ministry to Priests Program—Rev. WILLARD J. VAN DE LOO, Dir., *P.O. Box 23825, Green Bay, 54305-3825.* Tel: 920-437-7531, Ext. 8322.

Department of the Permanent Diaconate—Deacon MAURICE REED, Dir., Prog. Coord. & Vicar for Deacons, *P.O. Box 23825, Green Bay, 54305-3825.* Tel: 920-437-7531, Ext. 8290.

Vocations—Rev. DOUGLAS LECAPTAIN, Dir., *P.O. Box 23825, Green Bay, 54305-3825.* Tel: 920-437-7531, Ext. 8293.

Department for Parish Ministers—Sr. FLORENCE YOUNGWIRTH, A.N.G., Dir., *P.O. Box 23825, Green Bay, 54305-3825.* Tel: 920-437-7531, Ext. 8268.

Education

Total Catholic Education Department—Mr. LELAND NAGEL, Dir., *1825 Riverside Dr., P.O. Box 23825, Green Bay, 54305-3825.* Tel: 920-437-7531, Ext. 8309; Fax: 920-437-0694.

Consultants—

Youth Ministry—TONY PICHLER, Ext. 8281.

Scouts—Rev. ROGER STREBEL, *P.O. Box 10, Townsend, 54175-0010.*

Administrative Development—Sr. PAT MCCORMICK, Ext. 8271.

Administrative Services—ANN FOX, Ext. 8273.

Educational Leadership/School Program Development—Sr. PATRICIA BECKMAN, Ext. 8284.

Staff Development/Educational Programs—CHRIS BROSLAVICK, Ext. 8283.

Young Adult/Adult Catechesis—Sr. PEG GABIK, Ext. 8274.

Religious Education (K-6)—ANDREA SABOR, Ext. 8270.

Liaisons-Office of Education—

Priests Eucharistic League—Rev. DONALD FELLER, *2496 Mary Jo Dr., Green Bay, 54311-5208.* Tel: 920-465-3460.

The Diocesan Charismatic Renewal Center—Rev. Msgr. JAMES VANDEN HOGEN, *St. John Nepomucene Parish, 323 S. Pine St., Little Chute, 54140-1854.* Tel: 920-788-9061.

Serra Clubs—Rev. DOUGLAS LECAPTAIN, *P.O. Box 23825, Green Bay, 54305-3825.* Tel: 920-437-7531.

Blue Army - World Apostolate of Fatima—Rev. ARTHUR DANKS, *2616 He-Nis-Ra Ln., Green Bay, 54304-1308.* Tel: 920-499-9309.

Cursillo—Rev. DAVID PLEIER, *2040 Hillside Ln., Green Bay, 54302-4098.* Tel: 920-468-4811.

Xavier Guild—Rev. DENNIS M. RYAN, Chap., *St. Nicholas Parish, N4088 Cty. Rd. E., Kaukauna, 54130-7592.* Tel: 920-788-1492.

Diocesan Council of Catholic Women—DELLA GORDON, Pres., *1756 River St., Niagara, 54151.* Tel: 715-251-4148.

Pastoral Services

Pastoral Services—*1825 Riverside Dr., P.O. Box 23825, Green Bay, 54305-3825.* Tel: 920-437-7531; Fax: 920-437-0694. MARK MOGILKA, Dir., Ext. 8297.

Family Life Department (Voice & TDD)—TOM RINKOSKI, Dir., Ext. 8304.

Marriage Preparation, Parenting—MARY STUBLER, Ext. 8315.

Consultants—

Ecumenism—Rev. PHILIP HOFFMANN, Ecumenical Officer, Ext. 8183.

Evangelization/Renew 2000—JACKIE STALEY, Ext. 8316.

Ministry with Persons with Disabilities—SUE PERRAULT, Ext. 8306.

Parish Planning & Collaboration—DIANE VANDER HEIDEN, Consultant, Ext. 8286.

Pastoral Care—MARY SHERMAN, Ext. 8300.

Respect Life—MARY SHERMAN, Ext. 8300.

Rural Life—Vacant.

Social Concerns—PAUL GRIMM, Consultant, Ext. 8299.

Worship Department—DIANN WIMMER, Dir., Ext. 8311.

RCIA—ANISSA WILLKOM, Consultant, Ext. 8301.

Sacred Music—PAUL GRIMM, Consultant, Ext. 8299.

Campus Ministry—Rev. ROBERT KOLLATH, Dir., *717 W. Irving, Oshkosh, 54901.* Tel: 920-233-5555.

Holy Name Retreat House—Tel: 920-437-7531, Ext. 8296.

Evangelization Commission—JACKIE STALEY.

Liturgical Commission—DIANN WIMMER.

Ecumenical Commission—Rev. PHILIP HOFFMAN.

Justice & Peace Commission—Deacon PAUL GRIMM.

Community Services

Catholic Charities, Diocese of Green Bay, Inc.—KAREN JOHNSTON, Dir., *1825 Riverside Dr., P.O. Box 23825, Green Bay, 54305-3825.* Tel: 920-437-7531, Ext. 8234; Fax: 920-437-0694.

Department of Catholic Social Services—KAREN JOHNSTON, Dir. JANE KOEFERL, Clinical Svcs. Coord., Ext. 8234.

Department of Refugee, Migration and Hispanic Services—BARBARA B. BIEBEL, Dir., Ext. 8252.

Apostleship of the Sea—Deacon GLENN TESKE, Port Chap., *2839 S. Broadway, Green Bay, 54304-5309.* Tel: 920-499-0035.

Diocesan Health Services—Rev. RICHARD KLINGEISEN, Coord., *1110 S. 10th St., Manitowoc, 54220-5288.* Tel: 920-684-3718.

McCormick Memorial Home for the Aged—*212 Iroquois St., Green Bay, 54301-1995.* Tel: 920-437-0883. JAMES GENRICH, Admin.; Rev. THADDEUS J. KOSZAREK, Chap.

Liaisons - Community Services—

Sign of God Deaf Ministry—MARY E. ZUPANSIC, Pastoral Assoc., *1016 N. Broadway, De Pere, 54115-2697.* Tel: 920-337-9454 (V/TDD).

Society of St. Vincent de Paul—JAMES MATOUSEK, Pres. & Trustee; Rev. Msgr. ROY M. KLISTER, Chap. (Council of the Green Bay Diocesan, Society of St. Vincent de Paul, Inc.); EVERETT JOHNSON, Exec. Sec., *834 Gross Ave., Green Bay, 54304.*

Knights of Columbus—MEL STEINER, *830 B Blackstone Rd., Kiel, 53042.* Tel: 920-894-4530. Rev. STANLEY BROWNE, Chap.

Our Lady of Charity Center, Inc.—Sr. DEANA KOHLMAN, O.L.C., Dir., *2560 Shawano Ave., P.O. Box 10357, Green Bay, 54307-0357.* Tel: 920-434-8208.

Catholic Veterans of War—RAYMOND WOZNICK, Commander, *418 Forrest Ave., Fond du Lac, 54935.* JOSEPH RICKERT, District 3 Commander, *936 W. Marquette St., Appleton, 54911.* Tel: 920-734-9684.

Menominee Pastoral Program—Rev. DAVID S. BARRETT, *St. Michael Church, P.O. Box 610, Keshena, 54135-0160.* Tel: 715-799-3811.

Support Services

Support Services—*P.O. Box 23825, Green Bay, 54305-3825.* Tel: 920-437-7531; Fax: 920-435-1330. Rev. Msgr. JOHN B. DEWANE, M.A., S.T.L., D.Min., Vicar for Admin., Ext. 8171.

Department of World Mission Services—CLAIRE THOMAS, Dir., *P.O. Box 23825, Green Bay, 54305-3825.* Tel: 920-437-7531, Ext. 8192; Fax: 920-435-1330.

Agencies—Propagation of the Faith, St. Peter the Apostle, Holy Childhood Association, Catholic Relief Services.

Annual Bishop's Appeal—RON SHAHA, Ext. 8196.

Medical Insurance and Benefits—MARY VANKAUWENBERG, *Box 23825, Green Bay, 54305-3825.* Tel: 920-437-7531, Ext. 8260.

Bishop's Charities Game—JAMES HOGAN, *P.O. Box 23825, Green Bay, 54305-3825.* Tel: 920-437-7531, Ext. 8219.

Camp Tekawitha—ROBERTA LARSON, *P.O. Box 23825, Green Bay, 54305-3825.* Tel: 920-437-7531, Ext. 8511.

Cemeteries—JON RUATTI, *1825 Riverside Dr., P.O. Box 23825, Green Bay, 54305-3825.* Tel: 920-437-7531, Ext. 8229.

Communications—*P.O. Box 23825, Green Bay, 54305-3825.* Tel: 920-437-7531. TONY KUICK, Dir., Ext. 8214. SARA ELIASON, Pub. Rels. Coord., Ext. 8213.

Diocesan Newspaper—*"The Compass", P.O. Box 23825, Green Bay, 54305-3825.* Tel: 920-437-7531. Appleton Area: Tel: 920-233-5555. TONY KUICK, Gen. Mgr., Ext. 8214. ANTON STALEY, Editor, Ext. 8210.

Computer Services—TONY KUICK, Dir. BEA SEIDL, Database Admin., Ext. 8255. DAN LEE, P.C. Specialist, , Ext. 8253., *Box 23825, Green Bay, 54305-3825.* Tel: 920-437-7531.

Financial Services—THOMAS KURKOWSKI, Dir., Ext. 8267. MIKE SPEEL, Sr. Acct., Ext. 8259., *P.O. Box 23825, Green Bay, 54305-3825.* Tel: 920-437-7531.

Personnel—JAMES HOGAN, Dir., *P.O. Box 23825, Green Bay, 54305-3825.* Tel: 920-437-7531, Ext. 8219.

Property Management and Real Estate—KEVIN M. BRUNNER, Dir. Diocesan Properties, *P.O. Box 23825, Green Bay, 54305-3825.* Tel: 920-437-7531, Ext. 8277.

Sacred Heart Seminary, Inc.—*P.O. Box 23825, Green Bay, 54305-3825.* Tel: 920-437-7531.

Sacrificial Giving Program—CINDI BRAWNER, Dir., *P.O. Box 23825, Green Bay, 54305-3825.* Tel: 920-437-7531, Ext. 8173.

St. Joseph Corporation and Central Services—VINCE PELLETIER, *P.O. Box 23825, Green Bay, 54305-3825.* Tel: 920-437-7531, Ext. 8246.

Stewardship and Development—CINDI BRAWNER, *P.O. Box 23825, Green Bay, 54305-3825.* Tel: 920-437-7531, Ext. 8173.

Priests' Personnel Board—Revs. JOHN H. VAN DEUREN, Chm. RONALD BELITZ; RALPH MERKATORIS; MICHAEL INGOLD; WILLIAM RICKERT; JOHN MULLARKEY; Rev. Msgr. JOHN H. SCHUH; Rev. WILLARD J. VAN DE LOO, Resource Person.

Conciliation and Arbitration Board—Rev. JOHN T. MULLARKEY, Pres. ROBERT J. KABAT, Clerk, *P.O. Box 23825, Green Bay, 54305-3825.* Tel: 920-437-7531.

Liaisons—Personnel—

Association of Pastoral Associates—Sr. FLORENCE YOUNGWIRTH, *P.O. Box 23825, Green Bay, 54305-3825.* Tel: 920-437-7531, Ext. 8268.

Leo Benevolent Association—Rev. WILLIAM J. SPALDING, Chm., *228 S. Sawyer St., #4, Shawano, 54166-2469.* Tel: 715-524-5904.

Clergy Credit Union—Rev. CHARLES W. MOCCO, Treas., *St. Joseph Church, 526 Louisiana St., Sturgeon Bay, 54235-1738.* Tel: 920-743-2062.

Community of Our Lady—Rev. REGIS N. BARWIG, Prior, *2804 Oakwood Ln., Oshkosh, 54904-8406.* Tel: 920-233-5633.

A New Genesis—Sr. DIANE BAUMANN, Moderator, *1324 N. Perkins St., #9, Appleton, 54914.* Tel: 920-993-1963. Most Rev. ALOYSIUS J. WYCISLO, Chap.

CLERGY, PARISHES, MISSIONS AND PAROCHIAL SCHOOLS

CITY OF GREEN BAY
(Brown County)

1—ST. FRANCIS XAVIER CATHEDRAL. Also serves St. John, Green Bay. Rev. Msgr. Roy Klister; Deacon Paul Plantico.
Res., 139 S. Madison St., 54301-4501. Tel: 920-432-4348; Fax: 920-435-5068.
School—St. Thomas More, 650 S. Irwin Ave., 54301. Tel: 920-432-8242. Barbara Schneider, Prin.
Catechesis/Religious Programs—Associated with St. John, Green Bay. 413 St. John St., 54301. Tel: 920-436-6380. Patricia Detaege, D.R.E.
Students 77.

2—NATIVITY OF OUR LORD, Revs. James A. Hablewitz; Donald Everts; Deacon Michael Schmidt.
Res., 2270 S. Oneida St., 54304-4712. Tel: 920-499-5156; Fax: 920-490-9285.
Catechesis/Religious Programs—Tel: 920-499-6012. D.R.E.: L. Cann; M. Loberger; T. Herbert; M. Schlender.
Students 1,433.

3—ST. AGNES, Rev. Richard Getchel; Deacon Robert Nooker.
Res., 1484 9th St., 54304-3061. Tel: 920-494-2534.
School—Holy Family, 1204 S. Fisk St., 54304. Tel: 920-494-1931. Sr. Kathryn Klackner, O.S.F., Prin.
Franciscan Sisters of Christian Charity 4; Lay Teachers 26; Students 477.
Catechesis/Religious Programs—Tel: 920-494-6450. D.R.E.: R. Nooker; E. Mommaerts; M. Neckuty.
Students 377.
Convent—1208 S. Fisk St., 54304.

4—ANNUNCIATION OF THE BLESSED VIRGIN MARY. Served from St. Jude, Green Bay. Revs. Ronald C. Belitz; Thomas Hagendorf, O.Praem.
Mailing Address: 1423 Kellogg St., 54303-3113. Tel: 920-496-2160; Fax: 920-496-2167.
Res., 401 Gray St., 54303-3013. Tel: 920-499-2333.
School—Trinity Catholic Schools, (Grades 5-8) 1087 Kellogg St., 54303. Tel: 920-499-1919. Dan O'Rourke, Prin.
Lay Teachers 12; Students 221.
Catechesis/Religious Programs—Tel: 920-496-2164. Carolyn Whitcomb, D.R.E.
Students 111.

5—ST. BERNARD, Revs. David Pleier; Jerome Pastors; Deacons John Laurant; Larry Mastalish.
Res., 2040 Hillside Ln., 54302-4055. Tel: 920-468-4811; Fax: 920-468-1396.
School—2020 Hillside Ln., 54302. Tel: 920-468-5026. Sr. Patricia Clement, Prin.
Sisters 1; Lay Teachers 20; Students 488.
Catechesis/Religious Programs—Tel: 920-468-4390. Sr. Mary Ramone Blahnik, D.R.E.
Students 752.

6—ST. JOHN. Served from St. Francis Xavier Cathedral, Green Bay. Rev. Msgr. Roy M. Klister.
Res., 413 St. John St., 54301-4116. Tel: 920-436-6380.
Catechesis/Religious Programs—Associated with St. Francis Xavier Cathedral, Green Bay.

7—ST. JOSEPH, Rev. Michael Ingold.
Res., 936 9th St., 54304-3439. Tel: 920-497-7042; Fax: 920-497-7240.
School—1224 12th Ave., 54304. Tel: 920-497-7085. Jeanne Pischke, Prin.
Lay Teachers 13; Students 174.
Catechesis/Religious Programs—1434 12th Ave., 54304. Eugene Mailhiot, D.R.E.
Students 128.

8—ST. JUDE, Revs. Ronald C. Belitz; Thomas Hagendorf, O.Praem.
Res., 1423 Kellogg St., 54303-3113. Tel: 920-496-2160; Fax: 920-496-2167.
School—Trinity Catholic Schools, (Grades PreK-4) 1420 Division St., 54303-3113. Tel: 920-296-2162. Jane Schueller, Prin.
Religious 1; Lay Teachers 14; Students 259.
Catechesis/Religious Programs—Tel: 920-496-2164. Carolyn Whitcomb, D.R.E.
Students 246.

9—HOLY MARTYRS OF GORCUM, Rev. Robert E. Rhyner; Deacon William Burkel.
Res., 3562 Finger Rd., 54311-7733. Tel: 920-468-5718; Fax: 920-468-5713. [CEM]
School—3542 Finger Rd., 54311-7733. Tel: 920-468-7262. Sr. Therese Kulas, Prin.
Lay Teachers 9; Students 141.
Catechesis/Religious Programs—Mary Holzberger, D.R.E.
Students 138.

10—ST. MARY OF THE ANGELS, Revs. Albert Lis, O.F.M.; Nathan Jaskulski, O.F.M.; Deacon Paul Umentum. In res., Rev. Maynard Kolodziej, O.F.M.
Res., 645 S. Irwin Ave., 54301-3397. Tel: 920-437-1979; Fax: 920-437-8990.
School—St. Thomas More, (Grades PreK-8). Consolidated with Cathedral and Ss. Peter & Paul. 650 S. Irwin, 54301. Tel: 920-432-8242. Barbara Schneider, Prin.
Religious 1; Lay Teachers 22; Students 255.
Catechesis/Religious Programs—High school associated with St. John. Tel: 920-432-2747. Mary (Nelson) Sedlacek, D.R.E.
Students 105.

11—ST. MATTHEW, Rev. David R. Baeten.
Res., 130 Saint Matthews St., 54301-2910. Tel: 920-435-6811; Fax: 920-435-0065.
School—2575 S. Webster Ave., 54301. Tel: 920-432-5223. Elizabeth Berg, Prin.
Religious 1; Lay Teachers 15; Students 198.
Catechesis/Religious Programs—D.R.E.: T. Cibula; A. Westenberg; P. Hein; J. Wichlacz.
Students 275.

12—ST. PATRICK, Rev. Msgr. Brian P. Coleman, Admin.
Res., 211 N. Maple Ave., 54303-2749. Tel: 920-437-3911; Fax: 920-437-3274.
Catechesis/Religious Programs—D.R.E.: M. Vander Steeg; P. Vander Steeg; S. Appleby; D. Leisgang; V. Hill.
Students 165.

13—SS. PETER AND PAUL, Revs. Thomas Farrell; John G. VanDerHorst; Deacon Kenneth Kopydlowski.
Res., 710 N. Baird St., 54302-1902. Tel: 920-435-7548; Fax: 920-432-1321.
Schools—St. Thomas More Elementary. Consolidation of SS. Peter & Paul, St. Mary & Cathedral. Tel: 920-432-0621. Mrs. Barbara Schneider, Prin.
Sisters 1; Lay Teachers 24; SSPP Students 81; St. Thomas More School System, (Grades PreK-8) 650 S. Irwin Ave., 54301.
Lay Teachers 7; SSPP Students 42.
Catechesis/Religious Programs—Associated with Holy Martyrs (for Confirmation). 1420 Harvey St., 54302. Tel: 920-437-0651. Mike Vincent, D.R.E.
Students 234.

14—ST. PHILIP THE APOSTLE, Rev. Lawrence J. Canavera; Deacon Terry Dineen.
Res., 312 Victoria St., 54302-2818. Tel: 920-468-7848; Fax: 920-468-1025.
School—Tel: 920-468-7755. Sr. Carol Seidl, O.S.F., Prin.
Sisters 2; Lay Teachers 14; Students 279.
Catechesis/Religious Programs—Tel: 920-468-4368.
Students 354.
Convent—312 Victoria St., 54302. Franciscan Sisters of Christian Charity

15—RESURRECTION, Rev. Paul E. Demuth; Deacon Timothy Reilly.
Res., 333 Hilltop Dr., 54301-2799. Tel: 920-336-7768; Fax: 920-336-1949.
School—Tel: 920-336-3230. Brian Jones, Prin.
Lay Teachers 18; Students 229.
Catechesis/Religious Programs—D.R.E.: Jane Lyon; Barb Mogilka; Mary Vanden Busch.
Students 374.

16—ST. ELIZABETH ANN SETON, Rev. Msgr. James E. Dillenburg; Rev. John H. VanDeuren; Deacon James Gauthier.
Res., 2771 Oakwood Dr., 54304-1618. Tel: 920-499-1546; Fax: 920-499-2207.
School—Holy Family. Consolidated with St. Agnes. 1204 Fisk St., 54304. Tel: 920-494-1931. Sr. Kathryn Klackner, Prin.
Religious 5; Lay Teachers 26; Students 259.
Catechesis/Religious Programs—Carol Vanden Bush, D.R.E.
Students 675.

17—ST. WILLEBRORD, Rev. Kenneth J. DeGroot, O.Praem.; Deacon Luis Sanchez.
Res., 209 S. Adams St., 54301-4513. Tel: 920-435-2016; Fax: 920-435-2039.

OUTSIDE THE CITY OF GREEN BAY

Abrams, Oconto Co., St. Louis. Served from St. John Cantius, Sobieski. Rev. Gerald Prusakowski, O.F.M.
Mailing Address: 6051 Noble St., Sobieski, 54171-9724. Tel: 920-826-7425; Fax: 920-822-1859. [JC]
Catechesis/Religious Programs—Associated with St. John Cantius, Sobieski. Tel: 920-822-8795. Donna Rae VanKauwenbergh.
Students 65.

Algoma, Kewaunee Co., St. Mary, Rev. William M. Kuhr, Admin.
Res., 118 Church St., 54201-1033. Tel: 920-487-5005; Fax: 920-487-5002. [CEM]
School—214 Church St., 54201-1035. Tel: 920-487-5004. Mrs. Mary Mayheu, Prin.
Lay Teachers 9; Students 115.
Catechesis/Religious Programs—Roseann Kubicek, D.R.E.
Students 130.

Alverno, Manitowoc Co., St. Joseph. Merged with St. Casimir, Northeim; St. Isidore, Osman and St. Wendel, Cleveland to form St. Thomas the Apostle, Northeim.

Amberg, Marinette Co., St. Agnes. Served from St. Augustine, Wausaukee. Rev. Joseph E. Dorner, Admin.
Mailing Address: 507 Church St., P.O. Box 375, Wausaukee, 54177-9749. Tel: 715-856-5276.

Aniwa, Shawano Co., St. Boniface. Served from St. Philomena, Birnamwood. Rev. Everard S. Scesney, O.F.M.
Res., P.O. Box K, Birnamwood, 54414-0911. Tel: 715-449-2104. [CEM]
Catechesis/Religious Programs—Kataie Waldrogel, D.R.E.
Students 84.

Antigo, Langlade Co., St. Hyacinth, Rev. Msgr. Paul P. Koszarek.
Res., 819 3rd Ave., 54409-1930. Tel: 715-623-5255. [JC]
School—All Saints, 419 Fulton St. & 723 Deleglise St., 54409. Tel: 715-623-4835. Sr. Carol Jean Zais, Prin.
Catechesis/Religious Programs—D.R.E.: S. Brettingen; L. Ourada; L. Arrowood.
Students 74.

St. John, Rev. Charles G. Hoffmann.
Res., 426 Hudson St., 54409-2197. Tel: 715-623-2024; Fax: 715-627-0234. [JC]
School—All Saints, 420 Fulton St., 54409. Tel: 715-623-4835; Fax: 715-627-2969. Sr. Carol Jean Zais, Prin.
Lay Teachers 12; Students 261.
Catechesis/Religious Programs—Joyce Wagner, D.R.E.
Students 249.

St. Mary. (Also serves St. Wencaslaus, Neva). Rev. Jeremiah F. Worman; Deacon Thomas J. Hanley.
Res., 735 Deleglise St., 54409-1497. Tel: 715-623-2522.
School—All Saints. (St. Mary site) 723 Deleglise St., 54409. Tel: 715-623-5629. Sr. Carol Jean Zais, Prin.
Sisters of Mercy of the Holy Cross 1; Lay Teachers 5; Students 71.
Catechesis/Religious Programs—734 Deleglise St., 54409. Tel: 715-623-4938. Thomas J. Hanley, D.R.E.
Students 94.

Appleton, Outagamie Co.,

1—ST. BERNADETTE, Rev. Harold Berryman.
Church—2331 E. Lourdes Dr., 54915-3698. Tel: 920-739-4157; Fax: 920-739-2795.
School—Tel: 920-739-5391. Jennifer Rohlf, Prin.
Lay Teachers 26; Students 218.
Catechesis/Religious Programs—Tel: 920-734-7502. D.R.E.: Shirley Riley; Peter Gagnon.
Students 510.

2—ST. BERNARD, Rev. John Bergstadt; Deacons Maurice Reed; Robert Vincent. In res., Rev. Michael F. Simonini.
Parish Center: 1617 W. Pine St., 54914-5118. Tel: 920-739-0331; Fax: 920-749-9771.
Catechesis/Religious Programs—Barbara Conder, D.R.E.
Students 697.

3—ST. JOSEPH, Rev. John Holly, O.F.M.Cap.; Deacons Peter Reinl; Roy Baumruk. In res., Rev. Kenneth Reinhart, O.F.M.Cap.
Res., 404 W. Lawrence St., 54911-5855. Tel: 920-734-7195; Fax: 920-734-0227.
School—Appleton Catholic Education System, 300 N. Woods Edge Dr., 54914. Tel: 920-735-9380. William O'Brien, Exec. Dir.
Catechesis/Religious Programs—Associated with St. Mary's, Appleton. Tel: 920-738-7413. M. A. Bayer, D.R.E.
Students 167.

4—ST. MARY, Rev. Michael K. O'Rourke; Deacon William Burke.
Church—312 S. State St., 54911-5926. Tel: 920-739-5119; Fax: 920-739-5111. [CEM]
School—Catholic Central. Member of Appleton Catholic Education System. 313 S. State St., 54911. Tel: 920-733-3709; Fax: 920-733-8142. Rosemary Perrino, Prin.
Religious 1; Lay Teachers 23; Students 226.
Catechesis/Religious Programs—Associated with St. Joseph-St. Mary Interparish. 404 W. Lawrence St., 54911. Tel: 920-738-7413. Mary Ann Bayer, D.R.E.
Students 307.

5—ST. PIUS X, Revs. Donald M. Zuleger; Mark Vander Steeg.
Office: 500 W. Marquette St., 54911-1997. Tel: 920-733-0575.
School—Tel: 920-733-4918. Sr. Carol Jean Peterson, C.S.J., Prin.
Lay Teachers 16; Students 332.

Catechesis/Religious Programs—Tel: 920-733-4919. Laura Fiorello, D.R.E.
Students 726.

6—Sacred Heart, Rev. Robert J. Karuhn, Admin.; Deacons Gilbert Schmidt; Donald Gigure.
Res., 222 E. Fremont St., 54915-1827. Tel: 920-739-3196; Fax: 920-739-4062.
Preschool—1810 W. Prospect Ave., 54914. Tel: 920-735-9380.
Catechesis/Religious Programs—Debbie Peters, D.R.E.
Students 304.

7—St. Theresa, Rev. Daniel C. Gilsdorf; Deacon Patrick Whitcomb.
Office: 213 E. Wisconsin Ave., 54911-4875. Tel: 920-733-8568; Fax: 920-954-5727.
School—Member of Appleton Catholic Education System. 1810 W. Prospect Ave., 54914. Tel: 920-735-9380.
Catechesis/Religious Programs—Tel: 920-739-0794. Bro. Allen Broeckman, S.S.S., D.R.E.
Students 133.

8—St. Thomas More, Rev. Gerald R. Falk; Deacons Craig Merrick; Donald Wetzel; Reinhart Wessing; Paul Klein.
Res., 1810B N. McDonald St., 54911-3450. Tel: 920-739-7758; Fax: 920-739-2376.
School—1810 N. McDonald St., 54911. Tel: 920-739-7826; Fax: 920-739-2376. Mr. David Callan, Prin.
Sisters 2; Lay Teachers 19; Students 229.
Catechesis/Religious Programs—Tel: 920-739-8172. D.R.E.: I. Skarban; P. VandeHey; A. Vosters.
Students 415.
Convent—1226 E. Pauline St., 54911.

Argonne, Forest Co., St. Mary. Served from St. Joseph, Crandon, St. Michael Station, Hiles and St. Ambrose, Wabeno. Rev. Ralph J. Gillis.
Res., 208 N. Park Ave., Crandon, 54520-1351. Tel: 715-478-3396. [CEM]
Catechesis/Religious Programs—Associated with St. Joseph, Crandon. Lynn Edwards-Barker, D.R.E.

Armstrong Creek, Forest Co., St. Stanislaus Kostka. (Also serves St. Joan of Arc, Goodman). Rev. Edward S. Nowakowski.
Mailing Address: P.O. Box 39, 54103-0039. Tel: 715-336-2334.
Catechesis/Religious Programs—Associated with St. Joan of Arc, Goodman. Deborah Thompson, D.R.E.
Students 67.

Askeaton, Brown Co., St. Patrick, Rev. Allen Geiser.
Res., 7815 Saint Patrick Church Rd., Greenleaf, 54126-9611. Tel: 920-532-6665. [CEM]

Aurora, Florence Co., Sacred Heart. Served from St. Anthony, Niagara. Rev. Michael E. Betley (Niagara).
Mailing Address: P.O. Box 85, Florence, 54121-0085.
Res., 308 Florence Ave., Florence, 54121-0085. Tel: 715-528-3310; Fax: 715-528-3052.
Catechesis/Religious Programs—Tel: 715-528-4992.
Students 63.

Baileys Harbor, Door Co., St. Mary of the Lake. Served from St. John the Baptist, Egg Harbor. Rev. Mathew Simonar.
Mailing Address: P.O. Box 49, Egg Harbor, 54209-0049. Tel: 920-839-2041. [CEM]
Station—Washington Island, Door Co., St. Michael. (Also serves St. Rosalia, Sister Bay).

Bay Settlement, Brown Co., Holy Cross, Rev. Timothy D. Shillcox, O.Praem.
Res., 3009 Bay Settlement Rd., Green Bay, 54311-7301. Tel: 920-468-0595; Fax: 920-468-4764. [CEM]
School—3002 Bay Settlement Rd., Green Bay, 54311. Tel: 920-468-0625; Fax: 920-468-0625. Mrs. Jane Wicker, Prin.
Lay Teachers 10; Students 193.
Catechesis/Religious Programs—Tel: 920-468-6554. D.R.E.: Christopher Merle; Patricia Davister.
Students 195.

Bear Creek, Outagamie Co., St. Mary. Attended by St. Rose, Clintonville. Rev. Msgr. Mark J. Schommer.
Mailing Address: P.O. Box 27, 54922-0027. Tel: 715-752-4177; Fax: 715-752-3249. [CEM]
School—P.O. Box 216, 54922-0027. Tel: 715-752-4168. Sr. Jane Resop, Prin.
Sisters 1; Lay Teachers 2; Students 35.
Catechesis/Religious Programs—Associated with St. Rose, Clintonville. Joe Lehman, D.R.E.
Students 68.
Convent—Tel: 715-752-3585.

Birnamwood, Shawano Co., St. Philomena. (Also serves St. Boniface, Aniwa). Rev. Everard S. Scesney, O.F.M.
Res., P.O. Box K, 54414-0911. Tel: 715-449-2104. [CEM]
Catechesis/Religious Programs—Mary Resch, D.R.E.
Students 170.

Black Creek, Outagamie Co., St. Mary, Rev. Paul Paider.
Res., P.O. Box 217, 54106-0217. Tel: 920-984-3319. [CEM]

Brillion, Calumet Co., St. Mary. (Also serves St. Mary-St. Patrick, Reedsville/Maple Grove). Rev. W. Thomas Long.
Res., 215 Center St., 54110-1222. Tel: 920-756-2535; Fax: 920-756-3695. [CEM 2]
School—209 N. Custer St., 54110. Tel: 920-756-2502. Judy Phillip, Prin.
Lay Teachers 11; Students 115.
Catechesis/Religious Programs—Tel: 920-756-9015. D.R.E.: Bobbie Whittaker; Theresa Lambrecht.
Students 228.

Brussels, Door Co., St. Francis-St. Mary Parish. (St. Francis Xavier, Brussels and St. Mary, Namur merged.) Rev. Pius Cotter, O.F.M.Cap., Admin.
Res., 9716 Cemetery Rd., 54204-9749. Tel: 920-825-7555; Fax: 920-825-1492. [CEM 3]
Catechesis/Religious Programs—Sue Johnson, D.R.E.
Students 247.

Casco, Kewaunee Co., Holy Trinity. Merged with Mission of St. Adalbert, Slovan. Rev. John F. Doerfler.
Res., 506 Church Ave., 54205-9712. Tel: 920-837-7234; Fax: 920-837-2361. [CEM]
School—510 Church Ave., 54205-9700. Tel: 920-837-7531. Mrs. Kaye Jacobs, Prin.
Lay Teachers 7; Students 111.
Catechesis/Religious Programs—Students 152.

Cecil, Shawano Co., St. Martin. Attended by Sacred Heart, Shawano. Rev. Leonard M. Evers, Mod.; Deacon Thomas Craig, Parish Dir.
P.O. Box 144, 54111-0144. Tel: 715-745-6681.
Mailing Address: 321 S. Sawyer St., Shawano, 54111. Tel: 715-526-2023.
Church—107 S. Warrington, P.O. Box 157, 54111. [CEM]
Catechesis/Religious Programs—Associated with Sacred Heart, Shawano.

Champion, Brown Co., St. Joseph. Served from Immaculate Conception, Luxemburg. (Has records from St. Amand, Walhain, St. Martin, Tonet and St. Odile, Thiry Daems.) Rev. Milton M. Suess, Admin.
Mailing Address: 5996 County Rd. K, New Franken, 54229-9456. Tel: 920-866-9961. [CEM]
Catechesis/Religious Programs—Roxanne Zellner, D.R.E.
Students 125.

Charlesburg, Calumet Co., St. Charles Borromeo. (Linked with St. Mary, Chilton; St Augustine, Chilton; St. Elizabeth, Kloten; St, Martin, Chatlstown; Holy Trinity, Jericho). Revs. Gary New, S.D.S.; Glen Sayers, S.D.S.
Mailing Address: 62 E. Main St., Chilton, 53014-1499. Tel: 920-849-9363; Fax: 920-849-7270. [CEM]
School—Chilton Catholic. (Consolidated). Tel: 920-849-4141. Patricia Leuknecht, Prin.
Catechesis/Religious Programs—Associated with Chilton area parishes. See St. Mary, Chilton. Tel: 920-849-4613. Clairemary McDermott, D.R.E.

Charlestown, Calumet Co., St. Martin. Served from St. Mary, Chilton. Revs. Gary New, S.D.S.; Glen Sayers, S.D.S.
Mailing Address: 62 E. Main St., Chilton, 53014-1499. Tel: 920-849-9363; Fax: 920-849-7270. [CEM]
School—Chilton Catholic. (Consolidated). Tel: 920-849-4141. Patricia Leuknecht, Prin.
Catechesis/Religious Programs—Associated with Chilton area parishes. See St. Mary, Chilton. Tel: 920-849-4613. Clairemary McDermott, D.R.E.

Chase, Oconto Co., St. Joseph. Attended by St. John Cantius, Sobieski. Rev. Gerald Prusakowski, O.F.M.
Res., 6051 Noble St., Sobieski, 54171-9724. Tel: 920-822-5255. [CEM]
Catechesis/Religious Programs—Associated with St. John Cantius, Sobieski. Tel: 920-822-8795. Donna Rae VanKauwenbergh, D.R.E.

Chilton, Calumet Co., St. Augustine. Served from St. Mary, Chilton. Revs. Gary New, S.D.S.; Glen Sayers, S.D.S.
Mailing Address: 62 E. Main St., 53014-1499. Tel: 920-849-9363; Fax: 920-849-7270. [CEM]
School—Chilton Catholic, 60 E. Washington St., 53014. Tel: 920-849-4141. Patricia Leuknecht, Prin.
Catechesis/Religious Programs—Associated with Chilton area parishes. See St. Mary, Chilton. 920-849-4613. Clairemary McDermott, D.R.E.

St. Mary. Also serves St. Augustine, Chilton; St. Charles Borromeo, Charlesburg; St. Elizabeth, Kloten; St. Martin, Charlstown; Holy Trinity, Jericho). Revs. Gary New, S.D.S.; Glen Sayers, S.D.S.
Res., 62 E. Main St., 53014-1499. Tel: 920-849-9363; Fax: 920-849-7270. [CEM]
School—Chilton Catholic School. (Consolidated) 60 E. Washington St., 53014. Tel: 920-849-4141. Patricia McDermott, Prin.
Sisters 1; Lay Teachers 10; Students 155.
Catechesis/Religious Programs—Consolidated with all area parishes. Tel: 920-849-4613. Clairemary McDermott, D.R.E.
Students 574.
Convent—(Catholic Inter-Parish Ministry of Chilton includes the following parishes: St. Charles, Charlesburg; St. Martin, Charlestown; St. Elizabeth, Kloten; Holy Trinity, Jericho; St. Augustine and St. Mary, Chilton.) 38 E. Washington St., 53014. School Sisters of St. Francis

Clarks Mills, Manitowoc Co., Immaculate Conception, Rev. John F. Conrad.
Res., 15 S. County Rd. J, Cato, 54230-8329. Tel: 920-775-4365; Fax: 920-775-4365. [CEM]
School—St. Mary, 19 S. County Rd. J, Cato, 54230. Tel: 920-775-4366. Sr. Marie Bernadette Dorn, Prin.
Franciscan Sisters of Christian Charity 4; Lay Teachers 5; Students 88.
Catechesis/Religious Programs—Teresa Pederson (Valders).
Students 116.

Cleveland, Manitowoc Co., St. Wendel. Merged with St. Isidore, Osman; St. Joseph, Alverno and St. Casimir, Northeim to form St. Thomas the Apostle, Northeim.

Clintonville, Waupaca Co., St. Rose. Also serves St. Mary, Bear Creek. Rev. Msgr. Mark J. Schommer; Deacon Thomas Jozwiak.
Res., 24 7th St., 54929-1733. Tel: 715-823-3416; Fax: 715-823-3402. [CEM]
School—140 Auto St., 54929. Tel: 715-823-4360; Fax: 715-823-7160. Dennis Bessette, Prin.
Lay Teachers 9; Students 77.
Catechesis/Religious Programs—Tel: 715-823-5266. Dawn Kratzke, D.R.E.
Students 149.

Coleman/Klondike, Marinette Co., Ss. Francis/Wenceslaus. (Has records for St. Leo, Pound and St. John, Coleman.) Rev. John Hephner.
Res., 228 E. Main St., Coleman, 54112-9407. Tel: 920-897-3226; Fax: 920-897-4677. [CEM 2]
Catechesis/Religious Programs—Joyce Woulf, D.R.E.
Students 221.

Combined Locks, Outagamie Co., St. Paul, Rev. Robert H. Vandenberg; Deacon George Schraufnagel.
Res., 410 Wallace St., 54113-1128. Tel: 920-788-4553; Fax: 920-788-6822. [CEM]
Catechesis/Religious Programs—Tel: 920-788-5711. J. Angha, D.R.E.
Students 254.

Cooperstown, Manitowoc Co., St. James. Served from All Saints, Denmark. Rev. Ronald A. Colombo, Admin.; Deacon Clarence Naidl.
Res., 18228 County Rd. R, Denmark, 54208-9554. Tel: 920-863-2585; Fax: 920-863-5445. [CEM]
Catechesis/Religious Programs—D.R.E.: Joan Lindahl; Nancy Van Elzen.
Students 224.

Crandon, Forest Co., St. Joseph. Also serves St. Mary, Argonne, St. Ambrose, Wabeno and St. Michael at Hiles. Rev. Ralph J. Gillis.
Res., 208 N. Park Ave., 54520-1351. Tel: 715-478-3396.
Catechesis/Religious Programs—Associated with St. Mary, Argonne. Lynn Edwards-Barker, D.R.E.
Students 155.

Crivitz, Marinette Co., St. Mary, Rev. Donald R. Burkart.
Mailing Address: P.O. Box 159, 54114-0159. Tel: 715-854-2501. [CEM]
Catechesis/Religious Programs—Students 265.
Station—Caldron Falls.

Darboy, Outagamie Co. (Appleton P.O.), Holy Angels, Rev. Thomas Pomeroy.
Res., W5831 County Road KK, Appleton, 54915-9345. Tel: 920-733-6214; Fax: 920-733-5440. [CEM]
School—W2796 KK, Appleton, 54915-9407. Tel: 920-733-2651. Mary Vanden Busch, Prin.
Religious 1; Lay Teachers 16; Students 280.
Catechesis/Religious Programs—Tel: 920-734-6470. Sr. Elise Cholewinski, D.R.E.
Students 311.

Denmark, Brown Co., All Saints, Rev. Ronald A. Colombo.
Res., P.O. Box 787, 54208-0787. Tel: 920-863-2357; Fax: 920-863-5425. [CEM]
Office: Tel: 414-863-5256.
School—Tel: 920-863-2449. Lynn Moreau, Prin.
Lay Teachers 8; Students 112.

Catechesis/Religious Programs—Associated with Holy Trinity, New Denmark. Mary Burns, D.R.E. Students 191.
Mission—New Denmark, Holy Trinity.

De Pere, Brown Co.,

1—St. Francis Xavier, Rev. V. Anthony Dolski.
Res., 220 S. Michigan St., 54115-2730. Tel: 920-336-1813. [JC]
School—Notre Dame of De Pere Middle School. Consolidated with St. Mary, De Pere. 221 S. Wisconsin St., 54115. Tel: 920-337-1100. William Matchefts, Prin.
Religious 1; Lay Teachers 26; Students 243.
Catechesis/Religious Programs—Students 274.

2—St. Mary, Rev. John H. Harper; Deacons Earl Charlier; Frank W. Kremer, Sr.
Mailing Address: P.O. Box 70, 54115-0070. Tel: 920-337-2330; Fax: 920-337-2332. [JC]
School—Notre Dame. Consolidated with St. Francis Xavier, De Pere. 100 S. Huron St., 54115. Tel: 920-337-1100. William Matchefts, Prin.
Sisters of St. Francis of the Holy Cross 1; Lay Teachers 26; Students 484.
Catechesis/Religious Programs—Tel: 920-337-2334. Marge Frase, D.R.E.
Students 266.

3—St. Joseph. Merged with St. Boniface, De Pere to form Our Lady of Lourdes, De Pere.

4—St. Boniface. Merged with St. Joseph, De Pere to form Our Lady of Lourdes, De Pere.

5—Our Lady of Lourdes, (1996), Revs. Conrad J. Kratz, O. Praem.; James T. Baraniak, O. Praem.; Deacon Harvey Quinette.
Res., 1307 Lourdes Ave., 54115-1018. Tel: 920-336-4033; Fax: 920-336-3910.
School—1305 Lourdes Ave., 54115-1099. Tel: 920-336-3091. Mrs. Susan Sands, Prin.
Lay Teachers 25; Students 311.
Catechesis/Religious Programs—Tel: 920-337-0443. Mrs. Karen Nienhaus, D.R.E.
Students 407.

6—St. Norbert Campus Ministry, Revs. Gery G. Meehan, O.Praem.; Sal Cuccia, O.Praem.
Mailing Address: Campus Ministry, St. Norbert College, 100 Grant St., 54115-2099.
Res., 402 3rd St., 54115-2142. Tel: 920-403-3010; Fax: 920-403-4432.
Catechesis/Religious Programs—Tel: 920-403-3559. Judy Van Caster, D.R.E.
Students 78.

Dyckesville, Kewaunee Co., St. Louis, Revs. Timothy D. Shillcox, O.Praem., Mod.; Joseph L. Bestler; Sr. Marlene M. Dimmerling, O.P., Dir.
Res., N8726 County Line Rd., Luxemburg, 54217-8629. Tel: 920-866-2410. [CEM 2]
School—N8710 Cty. Line Rd., Luxemburg, 54217. Tel: 920-866-2611. Mrs. Mary Rechek, Prin.
Lay Teachers 6; Students 60.
Catechesis/Religious Programs—Tel: 920-866-2842. Mrs. Kathy Cornette, D.R.E.
Students 125.

Eaton, Brown Co., SS. Cyril and Methodius. Merged with Our Lady Queen of Peace, Humboldt to form St. Thomas the Apostle, Humboldt.

Egg Harbor, Door Co., St. John the Baptist. Also serves St. Mary of the Lake, Baileys Harbor, St. Paul, Fish Creek, St. Michael, Jacksonport, St. Rose, Sister Bay and the Station Bay and the Station at Washington Island. Rev. Mathew Simonar.
Mailing Address: P.O. Box 49, 54209-0049. Tel: 920-868-3241. [CEM]
Catechesis/Religious Programs—Tel: 920-743-4274. D.R.E.: Nancy Stubenvoll; Pat Gureski.
Students 60.

Eland, Shawano Co., St. William. Merged Holy Family, Wittenberg. Rev. Michael Carroll, Admin.
Res., 106 N. Ellms St., Wittenberg, 54499-9099. Tel: 715-253-2050.

Elcho, Langlade Co., Holy Family. (also serves St. Mary Mission, Pickerel). Rev. Jerome J. Taddy, Admin.
Mailing Address: P.O. Box 128, 54428-0128. Tel: 715-275-3750. [CEM]
Mission—Pickerel, St. Mary.

Fish Creek, Door Co., St. Paul. Served from St. John the Baptist, Egg Harbor. Rev. Mathew Simonar.
Mailing Address: P.O. Box 49, Egg Harbor, 54209-0049. Tel: 920-868-3241.
Catechesis/Religious Programs—Associated with St. John the Baptist, Egg Harbor.

Flintville, Brown Co., SS. Edward and Isidore, Rev. David D. Kasperek; Deacon Earl Kunzer.
Res., 3667 Flintville Rd., Green Bay, 54313-8330. Tel: 920-865-7844; Fax: 920-865-4375. [CEM]
Rectory: 3752 Elm Tree Rd., Green Bay, 54313. Tel: 920-865-7019.
Catechesis/Religious Programs—Tel: 920-865-7677. D.R.E.: Nancy Nelson; Dianne Jaworski.
Students 656.

Florence, Florence Co., Immaculate Conception. Served from St. Anthony, Niagara. Rev. Michael E. Bentley.
Res., P.O. Box 166, 54121-0166. Tel: 715-528-3310; Fax: 715-528-3310. [CEM]
Catechesis/Religious Programs—Tel: 715-582-4992. D.R.E.: M. Schalow; D. Schuch.
Students 139.

Francis Creek, Manitowoc Co., St. Anne. (Also serves St. Augustine, Kossuth.) Rev. Theodore J. Hendricks.
Res., P.O. Box 217, 54214-0217. Tel: 920-682-6640. [CEM]
School—202 Packer Dr., 54214. Tel: 920-682-1454. Mr. Charles Vaughan, Prin.
Franciscan Sisters of Christian Charity 4; Lay Teachers 4; Students 95.
Catechesis/Religious Programs—803 Forest Home Dr., 54214. Tel: 920-682-4393. Linda Klessig, D.R.E.
Students 109.

Freedom, Outagamie Co., St. Nicholas, Rev. Dennis M. Ryan; Deacon Donald Newhouse.
Res., N4088 County Rd. E., Kaukauna, 54130-7592. Tel: 920-788-1492. [CEM]
School—W2035 County Rd. S., Kaukauna, 54130. Tel: 920-788-9371. Phyllis Techlin, Prin.
Lay Teachers 12; Students 189.
Catechesis/Religious Programs—Tel: 920-788-1451. Sr. Charlene Hockers, D.R.E.
Students 355.

Gillett, Oconto Co., St. John, Rev. John M. Gallagher.
Res., P.O. Box 377, 54124-0377. Tel: 920-855-2542. [CEM]
Catechesis/Religious Programs—Wendy Wozniak, D.R.E.
Students 122.

Glenmore, Brown Co., Immaculate Conception. Merged with St. Mary, Stark.

Goodman, Marinette Co., St. Joan of Arc. Served from St. Stanislaus Kostka, Armstrong Creek. Rev. Edward S. Nowakowski.
Mailing Address: P.O. Box 39, Armstrong Creek, 54103-0039. Tel: 715-336-2334.
Catechesis/Religious Programs—Associated with St. Stanislaus Kosta, Armstrong Creek. Deborah Thompson, D.R.E.
Students 50.

Greenleaf, Brown Co., St. Mary, Rev. Robert J. Kabat.
Res., 2212 Day St., 54126-9200. Tel: 920-864-2550; Fax: 920-864-2979. [CEM 2]
School—2218 Day St., 54126-9200. Tel: 920-864-2586. Gloria Kennedy, Prin.
Religious 1; Lay Teachers 6; Students 64.
Catechesis/Religious Programs—Tel: 920-864-2585. Mike Lotto, D.R.E.
Students 159.

Greenville, Outagamie Co., St. Mary, Rev. John Zickert, O.F.M.Cap.; Deacon Richard Miech.
Mailing Address: N2385 Municipal Dr., 54942. Tel: 920-757-6555; Fax: 920-757-6560. [CEM]
Res., N2343 Municipal Dr., 54942. Tel: 920-757-6333; Fax: 920-757-6560.
School—(Grades PreK-8) N2387 Municipal Dr., 54942. Tel: 920-757-5516. Steve Langl, Prin.
Lay Teachers 10; Students 158.
Catechesis/Religious Programs—Tel: 920-757-6519. Jamie Whalen, D.R.E.
Students 305.

Gresham, Shawano Co., St. Francis Solanus. Served from St. Mary, Keshena. Rev. David S. Barrett, Admin.
Mailing Address: P.O. Box 177, 54128-0177. Tel: 715-787-3250. [CEM]
Catechesis/Religious Programs—Tel: 715-787-3377. Sr. Mary S. Brunner, D.R.E.
Students 63.

Hilbert, Calumet Co., St. Mary, Rev. Rallen H. Stencil.
Res., P.O. Box 386, 54129-0386. Tel: 920-853-3252. [CEM]
School—154 S. 6th St., P.O. Box 249, 54129-0249. Tel: 920-853-3216. Sr. Jodene Wydeven, Prin.
Religious 1; Lay Teachers 4; Students 51.
Catechesis/Religious Programs—Students 155.

Hofa Park, Shawano Co., St. Stanislaus. Served from Assumption BVM, Pulaski. Rev. Patrick Gawrylewski, O.F.M., Admin.
Res., N1302 Maple Rd., Seymour, 54165-9506. Tel: 920-822-5512; Fax: 920-822-8030. [CEM]
Catechesis/Religious Programs—Tel: 920-822-5203. Linda Rosek, D.R.E.
Students 69.

Hollandtown, Brown Co., St. Francis, Rev. John T. Mullarkey.
Res., 433 County Rd. CE, Kaukauna, 54130-8964. Tel: 920-766-1222. [CEM]
School—431City Rd. CE, Kaukauna, 54130. Tel: 920-766-3469. Mrs. Jennie Eggleston, Prin.
Franciscan Sisters of Christian Charity 2; Lay Teachers 5; Students 54.

Catechesis/Religious Programs—Associated with St. Aloysius, Kaukauna.
Students 58.

Hortonville, Outagamie Co., SS. Peter and Paul, Rev. David J. Funk, O.F.M.Cap.; Deacon Kenneth D. Bilgrien.
Res., P.O. Box 238, 54944-0238. Tel: 920-779-6133; Fax: 920-779-6133. [CEM]
School—107 N. Olk St., 54944. Tel: 920-779-4425; Fax: 920-799-4425. Robert Bootz, Prin.
Sisters of St. Agnes 1; Lay Teachers 8; Students 110.
Catechesis/Religious Programs—Tel: 920-779-0551. Sr. Clarice Sevegney, D.R.E.
Students 214.

Howard, Brown Co., St. John the Baptist, Revs. William Swichtenberg, Co-Pastor; Gregory J. Smith, Co-Pastor; Deacon Nicholas Williams.
Res., 2597 Glendale Ave., Green Bay, 54313-6899. Tel: 920-434-2145; Fax: 920-434-5015. [CEM]
School—2561 Glendale Ave., Green Bay, 54313. Tel: 920-434-3822; Fax: 920-434-5016. Kay L. Franz, Prin.
Lay Teachers 21; Students 342.
Catechesis/Religious Programs—880 Cardinal Lane, Green Bay, 54313. Tel: 920-434-2417. D.R.E.: P. Vanden Boogaard; M. Schiffer.
Students 652.

Humboldt, Brown Co., Our Lady Queen of Peace. Merged with SS. Cyril & Methodius, Eaton to form St. Thomas the Apostle, Humbolt.

Humbolt, Brown Co., St. Thomas the Apostle. Also serves St. Kilian, New Franken. (Has records for SS. Cyril & Methodius, Eaton and Our Lady Queen of Peace, Humboldt.). Rev. Dean H. Dombroski.
Res., 5930 Humboldt Rd., Luxemburg, 54217-9325. Tel: 920-863-6113; Fax: 920-845-5180. [JC 4]
Catechesis/Religious Programs—3041 S. Co. Rd. T, Green Bay, 54311. Tel: 920-863-5297. D.R.E.: Anne Charneski; Laurie Davister.
Students 229.

Institute, Door Co., SS. Peter and Paul. Served from St. Joseph, Sturgeon Bay. Rev. Charles W. Mocco, Admin.; Deacon Roger Madsen.
Res., 4767 Dunn Rd., Sturgeon Bay, 54235-8822. Tel: 920-743-4842; Fax: 920-743-3885. [CEM]
School—4761 Dunn Rd., Sturgeon Bay, 54235. Tel: 920-743-6335; Fax: 920-743-3885. Gina Morgan-Sauve, Prin.
Sisters of St. Francis of the Holy Cross 1; Lay Teachers 6; Students 119.

Isaar, Outagamie Co., St. Sebastian, Rev. David K. Ashbeck, Admin.
Res., N9269 Isaar Rd., Seymour, 54165-9428. Tel: 920-833-2558. [CEM]
Catechesis/Religious Programs—D.R.E.: Mary Wilinski; Linda Haase.
Students 161.

Jacksonport, Door Co., St. Michael. Served from St. John the Baptist, Egg Harbor. Rev. Mathew Simonar.
Mailing Address: P.O. Box 49, Egg Harbor, 54209-0049. Tel: 920-868-3241. [JC]

Jericho, Calumet Co., Holy Trinity. Served from St. Mary, Chilton. Revs. Gary New, S.D.S.; Glen Sayers, S.D.S.
Mailing Address: 62 E. Main St., Chilton, 53014-1428. Tel: 920-849-9363; Fax: 920-849-7270. [CEM]
School—Chilton Catholic. Consolidated with all 6 Chilton area parishes. See St. Mary, Chilton. Tel: 920-849-4141. Patricia Leuknecht, Prin.
Catechesis/Religious Programs—Associated with Chilton area parishes. See St. Mary, Chilton. Tel: 920-849-4613. Clairemary McDermott, D.R.E.

Kaukauna, Outagamie Co., Holy Cross. Also serves St. Francis, Hollandtown. Revs. John T. Mullarkey; James Lucas.
Res., 309 Desnoyer St., 54130-2103. Tel: 920-766-3773; Fax: 920-766-3774. [CEM]
School—Kaukauna Catholic Schools System, Tel: 920-766-0186. Sr. Camilla Wolfgram, Prin.
Sisters 5; Lay Teachers 14; Students 237.
Catechesis/Religious Programs—Tel: 920-766-3510. Elaine Huss, D.R.E.
Students 502.

St. Aloysius, Rev. David Schmidt, Admin.
Res., 2401 Main Ave., 54130-3518. Tel: 920-766-5111; Fax: 920-766-5229.
School—Kaukauna Catholic Schools System, Tel: 920-766-5199. Gayle Reider, Prin.
Franciscan Sisters of Christian Charity 3; Lay Teachers 12; Students 125.
Catechesis/Religious Programs—Tel: 920-766-5379. D.R.E.: Maxine Geiger; Jane Schaefer.
Students 309.

St. Mary of the Annunciation, Rev. Robert Udulutsch, O.F.M.Cap.; Deacon Steven VandeHey. In res., Revs. Leopold Gleissner, O.F.M.Cap.; Kieran Hickey, O.F.M.Cap.; Irvin Udulutsch, O.F.M.Cap.

Res., 119 W. 7th St., 54130-2356. Tel: 920-766-1445; Fax: 920-766-1476. [JC]
School—Kaukauna Catholic Schools System, 112 W. 8th St., 54130. Tel: 920-766-1545; Fax: 920-766-1476. Mrs. Rita Schmidt, Prin.
Sisters 1; Lay Teachers 13; Students 153.
Catechesis/Religious Programs—Tel: 920-766-5997. D.R.E.: Jean Olsen; Jane Schaefer.
Students 369.
Convent—Tel: 414-766-2952. Franciscan Sisters of Christian Charity

Kellnersville, Manitowoc Co., St. Joseph, Rev. Ronald A. Colombo, Mod.; Rev. Msgr. Robert F. Gulig; Sr. Marlene Greatens, A.N.G., Parish Dir.
Res., P.O. Box 27, 54215-0027. Tel: 920-732-3770. [CEM 2]
Catechesis/Religious Programs—Tel: 920-732-3462. Jane Kalies, D.R.E.
Students 68.

Keshena, Menominee Co., St. Michael (Indian). Also serves St. Francis Solanus, Gresham and St. Joseph of the Lake Mission, South Branch. Rev. David S. Barrett.
Mailing Address: P.O. Box 610, 54135-0610. Tel: 715-799-3811. [CEM]
Catechesis/Religious Programs—Tel: 715-799-3234. Sr. Kathleen Walli, O.P.
Students 113.
Mission—St. Joseph of the Lake, South Branch.

Kewaunee, Kewaunee Co., Holy Rosary, Rev. Daniel Dewane.
Res., 521 Juneau St., 54216-1336. Tel: 920-388-2285; Fax: 920-388-3822. [CEM]
School—519 Kilbourn St., 54216. Tel: 920-388-2431. Caniel Malmberg, Prin.
Lay Teachers 11; Students 175.
Catechesis/Religious Programs—D.R.E.: Terri Vandervest; Patty Walecka.
Students 178.

Kiel, Manitowoc Co., SS. Peter and Paul, Rev. Loren G. Nys, S.D.S. In res., Rev. Cletus LeMere, S.D.S.
Res., 413 Fremont St., 53042-1316. Tel: 920-894-3553; Fax: 920-894-4462. [CEM]
School—423 Fremont St., 53042. Tel: 920-894-3533; Fax: 920-894-4462. Dr. Carl Bronowski, Prin.
Sisters 2; Lay Teachers 9; Students 135.
Catechesis/Religious Programs—Tel: 920-894-2280. D.R.E.: Mary Jo Meyer; Karen Miller.
Students 254.

Kimberly, Outagamie Co., Holy Name of Jesus, Rev. Dennis L. Bergsbaken.
Res., 602 E. Kimberly Ave., 54136-1599. Tel: 920-788-7640; Fax: 920-788-7658. [CEM]
School—614 E. Kimberly Ave., 54136. Tel: 920-788-7650. Jeanine Leege-Jankowski, Prin.
Lay Teachers 24; Students 276.
Catechesis/Religious Programs—Tel: 920-788-7655. D.R.E.: M. A. Jasaik; A. Lemmers.
Students 436.

King, Waupaca Co., St. George. Closed. For inquiries for parish records contact the Chancery.

Klondike, Oconto Co., St. Wenceslaus. Merged with St. Francis of Assisi, Coleman, to form Ss. Francis of Assisi and Wenceslaus.

Kloten, Calumet Co., St. Elizabeth. Served from St. Mary, Chilton. Revs. Gary New, S.D.S.; Glen Sayers, S.D.S.
Mailing Address: 62 E. Main St., Chilton, 53014-1499. Tel: 920-849-9363; Fax: 920-849-7270. [CEM]
School—Chilton Catholic. Consolidated with all 6 Chilton area parishes. See St. Mary, Chilton. Tel: 920-849-4141. Patricia Leuknecht, Prin.
Catechesis/Religious Programs—Associated with Chilton area parishes. See St. Mary, Chilton. Clairemary McDermott, D.R.E.

Kossuth, Manitowoc Co., St. Augustine. Attended by St. Anne, Francis Creek. Rev. Theodore J. Hendricks.
Mailing Address: P.O. Box 217, Francis Creek, 54214-0217. Tel: 920-682-6640. [CEM]
Catechesis/Religious Programs—Associated with St. Anne, Francis Creek.

Krakow, Shawano Co., St. Casimir, Rev. James J. Esser, O.F.M.
Mailing Address: P.O. Box 66, 54137-0066. Tel: 920-899-3621. [CEM]
Catechesis/Religious Programs—Cathy Sikorski, D.R.E.
Students 106.

Krok, St. John. Merged with St. Joseph, Montpelier to form St. Joseph-St. John, Montpelier.

Lakewood, Oconto Co., St. Mary of the Lake. (Stations at Crooked Lake and Silver Cliff.) Rev. Stanley T. Browne; Deacon Harold Orlowski.
Res., P.O. Box 219, 54138-0219. Tel: 715-276-7364. [CEM]
Stations—Crooked Lake.; Silver Cliff.

Catechesis/Religious Programs—D.R.E.: M. Anderle; N. Gardebrecht.
Students 75.

Langlade, Langlade Co., St. Stanislaus Kostka. Merged with St. James, White Lake to form SS. James and Stanislaus, White Lake.

Laona, Forest Co., St. Leonard. (Also serves St. Norbert, Long Lake and St. Hubert Mission, Newald). Rev. John W. Cerkas.
Res., Rte. 1, Box 344, 54541-9641. Tel: 715-674-3241; Fax: 715-674-3401. [JC]
Catechesis/Religious Programs—Patrice Hawks, D.R.E.
Students 137.
Mission—Newald, Argonne Co., St. Hubert. (Also serves St. Norbert, Long Lake).

Lebanon Township, Waupaca Co., St. Patrick, Rev. Msgr. Dennis Lally, Admin.
Res., N5705 County Rd. T, New London, 54961-8464. Tel: 920-982-5475. [CEM]
Catechesis/Religious Programs—Students 99.

Lena, Oconto Co., Holy Cross. (Has records for St. Charles Borromeo, Lena and Sacred Heart, Spruce.). Rev. Frank Schrage, Admin.
Res., P.O. Box 30, 54139-0030. Tel: 920-829-5222; Fax: 920-829-5222. [JC 2]
School—221 E. Main St., 54139. Tel: 920-829-6027. Barbara Brodahl, Prin.
Lay Teachers 4; Students 68.
Catechesis/Religious Programs—Jim Brill, D.R.E.
Students 211.

Leopolis, Shawano Co., St. Mary, Rev. Harry G. Hafeman.
Res., P.O. Box 39, 54948-0039. Tel: 715-787-3377. [CEM]
Catechesis/Religious Programs—Students 64.

Lincoln, Kewaunee Co., St. Peter. Merged with St. Hubert, Rosiere.

Little Chute, Outagamie Co., St. John, Rev. Msgr. James VandenHogen; Rev. John Schuetze; Deacon Vincent M. DeGroot.
Res., 323 Pine St., 54140-1854. Tel: 920-788-9061; Fax: 920-687-0851. [CEM]
School—328 Grand Ave., 54140. Tel: 920-788-9082. Sisters 4; Lay Teachers 25; Students 584. Prins.: Holly Rottier; Mary Terrien.
Catechesis/Religious Programs—Tel: 920-788-9033. D.R.E.: Nancy Schmoll; Melissa Breault; Vicki Van Vreede.
Students 533.

Little Suamico, Oconto Co., St. Pius. Served from St. Benedict, Suamico. Rev. Gary J. Dantinne.
Mailing Address: P.O. Box 66, Suamico, 54173-0066. Tel: 920-434-2024; Fax: 920-622-2301.
Catechesis/Religious Programs—Joan Koehne, D.R.E.
Students 80.

Long Lake, Florence Co., St. Norbert. Served from St. Leonard, Laona and St. Hubert Mission, Newald. Rev. John W. Cerkas.
Res., R.R.1, Box 344, Laona, 54541-9641. Tel: 715-674-3241.
Catechesis/Religious Programs—Associated with St. Leonard, Laona. (Lanoa also serves St. Hubert Mission, Newald).

Montpelier, Kewaunee Co., St. Joseph-St. John. Merged with St. Lawrence, Stangelville to form St. Therese de Lisieux, Stangelville.

Luxemburg, Kewaunee Co., Immaculate Conception. (also serves St. Joseph, Champion). Rev. Milton M. Suess.
Res., 1412 Main St., 54217-1308. Tel: 920-845-2056. [CEM]
School—St. Mary, 1406 Main St., 54217-1308. Tel: 920-845-2224. Lyn Gaus, Prin.
Lay Teachers 8; Students 161.
Catechesis/Religious Programs—Mary Jacques, D.R.E.
Students 232.

Mackville, Outagamie Co., St. Edward, Rev. Charles R. Brooks.
Res., N2926 State Rd. 47, Appleton, 54915-9564. Tel: 920-733-9266; Fax: 920-733-7964. [CEM]
School—N2944 State Rd. 47, Appleton, 54915. Tel: 920-733-6276. Candee Schmalzer, Prin.
Lay Teachers 6; Students 45.
Catechesis/Religious Programs—Mary Lee Lehr, D.R.E.
Students 232.

Manawa, Waupaca Co., Sacred Heart. Attended by SS. Peter and Paul, Weyauwega. Rev. Bertin L. Samsa, O.F.M.Cap., Admin.
Res., P.O. Box 10, 54949-0010. Tel: 920-596-3323; Fax: 920-596-3323. [JC]
Catechesis/Religious Programs—Sr. Toni Jendrasiak, D.R.E.
Students 118.

Manitowoc, Manitowoc Co.,

1—St. Boniface. Served from St. Andrew, Manitowoc. Rev. Camillus W. Janas, O.F.M.
Res., 1110 S. 10th St., 54220-5212. Tel: 920-684-3718; Fax: 920-652-0659.
School—Member of MACS. See Consolidated Schools under Institutions Located in the Diocese. 1418 Grand Ave., 54220. Tel: 920-683-6888. Linda Bender (Xavier), Prin.
Religious 2; Lay Teachers 9; Students 40.
Catechesis/Religious Programs—Associated with St. Paul, St. Mary & St. Andrew. 1001 Marshall St., 54220. Tel: 920-683-3897. D.R.E.: Chris Kouba; Jim Modl.
Students 60.
Convent— Franciscan Sisters of Christian Charity
Holy Family Conservatory—1015 S. 11th St., 54220.

2—Holy Innocents, Rev. Gerald J. Foley; Deacons Richard Bahnaman; Paul Kieffer; Ken Nelesen.
Res., 1121 N. 14th St., 54220-3236. Tel: 920-682-0031; Fax: 920-682-1096.
School—St. Francis de Sales. See Consolidated Schools under Institutions Located in the Diocese. 1408 Waldo Blvd., 54220. Tel: 920-683-6892. Sr. Paulyn Vanden Hogen, Prin.
Religious 1; Lay Teachers 22; Students 381.
Catechesis/Religious Programs—1122 N. 14th St., 54220. Tel: 920-684-4313. Claudia Malley, D.R.E.
Students 354.

3—St. Mary, Rev. Roman Zbieranski, O.F.M.; Deacon Robert Drobka.
Res., 1114 S. 21st St., 54220-4917. Tel: 920-684-3558; Fax: 920-684-3255.
School—St. Frances Cabrini (MACS). See Consolidated Schools under Institutions Located in the Diocese. 2109 Marshall St., 54220. Tel: 920-683-6884. James Clark, Prin.
Lay Teachers 20; Students 229.
Catechesis/Religious Programs—Associated with St. Boniface, Manitowoc. 1110 S. 10th St., 54220. Tel: 920-683-3867. D.R.E.: Chris Kouba; James Modl.
Students 210.

4—Sacred Heart, Rev. David Hoffman.
Res., 520 N. 7th St., 54220-4043. Tel: 920-684-8692. [JC]
School—member of MACS.
Catechesis/Religious Programs—702 State St., 54220. Tel: 920-683-2165. Sr. Rose Marie Buscemi, D.R.E.
Students 220.

5—St. Andrew. (also serves St. Boniface, Manitowoc). Rev. Camillus W. Janas, O.F.M., Admin.
Res., 1416 Grand Ave., 54220-6199. Tel: 920-682-0023; Fax: 920-682-1452.
School—St. Francis Xavier. See Consolidated Schools under Institutions Located in the Diocese. 1418 Grand Ave., 54220. Tel: 920-683-6888. Mrs. Linda Bender, Prin.
Religious 2; Lay Teachers 11; Students 216.
Catechesis/Religious Programs—Associated with St. Boniface, St. Paul, St. Mary, and St. Andrew. 1001 Marshall St., 54220. Tel: 920-683-3897. Chris Kouba, D.R.E.
Students 60.

6—St. Paul, Rev. Ronald P. Reimer; Deacons Alan Boeldt; William D. Klein.
Res., 712 S. 24th St., 54220-4498. Tel: 920-684-6714.
School—Member of MACS, 1418 Grand Ave., 54220-6130. Tel: 920-683-6880.
Catechesis/Religious Programs—Associated with St. Boniface, St. Mary, St. Andrew. 1110 S. 10th St., 54220. Tel: 920-684-3718. D.R.E.: Chris Kouba; Jim Modl.
Students 72.

Maple Grove, Manitowoc Co., St. Patrick. Merged with St. Mary, Reedsville. Rev. Nicholas A. Johannes; Deacon Donald Schneider.
Mailing Address: P.O. Box 248, Reedsville, 54230-0248. Tel: 414-754-4665. [CEM]

Maplewood, Door Co., St. Mary, Rev. Wilbert L. Buhl.
Mailing Address: P.O. Box 308, 54226-0308. Tel: 920-856-6440. [CEM 2]
Catechesis/Religious Programs—Laurie Duquaine, D.R.E.
Students 209.

Marchand, Door Co., St. Francis de Paul (Duvall). Closed. For inquiries for parish records contact St. Louis, Dyckesville.

Marinette, Marinette Co.,

1—Holy Family. (Has records for St. Anthony, St. Joseph, Our Lady of Lourdes and Sacred Heart-,Marinette.) Rev. Lawrence T. Marto; Deacons Mark Gribowski; Jerry Thetreau; Byron Otradovec.
Office: 1223 Carney Blvd., 54143-2512. Tel: 715-735-9100; Fax: 715-735-9650. [CEM 2]
School—1232 Garfield Ave., 54143. Tel: 715-735-7174. Mrs. Judith Urbanski, Prin.
Students 210.

Catechesis/Religious Programs—Kathryn Lieburn, D.R.E.
Students 470.

2—OUR LADY OF LOURDES. Merged with Holy Family Parish.

3—ST. JOSEPH. Merged with Holy Family Parish.

4—SACRED HEART CONGREGATION. Merged with Holy Family Parish.

5—ST. ANTHONY. Merged with Holy Family Parish.

Marion, Waupaca Co., St. Mary. Served from St. Anthony, Tigerton. Rev. Michael R. Carroll, Admin.
Mailing Address: P.O. Box 206, 54950. Tel: 715-754-2116; Fax: 715-754-2116. [CEM]
Catechesis/Religious Programs—Associated with St. Anthony, Tigerton. Jon Ann Kasson, D.R.E.
Students 87.

Mattoon, Shawano Co., Holy Family. Served from St. Anthony, Neopit and St. Joseph, Phlox. Rev. R. David Kiefer; Deacon Thomas Hartman.
Mailing Address: P.O. Box 21, 54450-0021. Tel: 715-756-2361. [CEM]

Menasha, Winnebago Co., St. John, Rev. Paul J. Radetski, Admin.
Res., 516 Depere St., 54952-2899. Tel: 920-722-8922; Fax: 920-729-9248. [CEM]
School—628 Fifth St., 54952. Tel: 920-722-9370. Mr. Lawrence Konetzke, Prin.
Lay Teachers 15; Students 168.
Catechesis/Religious Programs—Tel: 920-722-4830. Debra Spielbauer, D.R.E.
Students 163.

St. Mary, Revs. Robert Lussier, S.S.S.; Dana G. Pelotte, S.S.S.; Deacon Gerald Cross. In res., Bros. Allen Broeckman, S.S.S.; Michael Galligan, S.S.S.
Res., 212 Appleton St., 54952-3120. Tel: 920-725-7714; Fax: 920-725-7612. [CEM]
School—(Grades PreK-5) 540 Second St., 54952. Tel: 920-725-5351; Fax: 920-722-5940. Michael Buss, Prin.
Lay Teachers 17; Students 187.
Catechesis/Religious Programs—Tel: 920-722-6491. Cathy Hein, D.R.E.
Students 175.

St. Patrick, Rev. Roy J. Geenen; Deacon Howard Bricco.
Res., 324 Nicolet Blvd., 54952-3334. Tel: 920-725-8381; Fax: 920-725-5544. [JC]
School—Seton Catholic Middle School, 312 Nicolet Blvd., 54952. Tel: 920-727-0279; Fax: 920-727-1215. Ms. Monica Bausom, Prin.
Lay Teachers 16; Students 160.
Catechesis/Religious Programs—Barb Mauthe, D.R.E.
Students 205.

Mishicot, Manitowoc Co., Holy Cross, Rev. John C. Neuser.
Res., 423 S. Main St., 54228-9777. Tel: 920-755-2550. [CEM]
School—423 Church St., 54228. Tel: 920-755-2487. Joseph Linsmeier, Prin.
Lay Teachers 6; Students 102.
Catechesis/Religious Programs—3210 Tannery Rd., Two Rivers, 54241. Tel: 920-793-1755.
Students 180.

Montpelier, Kewaunee Co., St. Joseph/St. John. Merged with St. Lawrence, Stangelville and St. Hedwig, West Kewaunee to form St. Therese de Lisieux, Stangelville.

Namur, Door Co., St. Mary. Closed. See St. Frances and St. Mary, Brussels, for details.

Navarino, Shawano Co., St. Lawrence, Rev. Paul Paider, Mod.; Sr. Charlotte Rebbe, O.P., Parish Dir.
Res., W5125 State Hwy. 156, Bonduel, 54107-8614. Tel: 715-758-8161; Fax: 715-758-7562. [CEM]
Catechesis/Religious Programs—Sr. Charlotte Rebbe, D.R.E.
Students 90.

Neenah, Winnebago Co., St. Gabriel, Rev. Richard L. Allen.
Res., 900 Geiger St., 54956-2302. Tel: 920-722-4914; Fax: 920-722-2566. [JC]
School—Tel: 920-725-4161. Selene Finch, Prin.
Lay Teachers 18; Students 224.
Catechesis/Religious Programs—Tel: 920-725-0660. D.R.E.: K. Grube; J. Schneider; D. Koeller.
Students 688.

St. Margaret Mary, Rev. David J. Koch; Deacon Norman Spielbauer.
Res., 439 Washington Ave., 54956-3340. Tel: 920-729-4560; Fax: 920-729-4572. [JC]
Church—666 Division St., 54956-3398.
School—610 Division St., 54956. Tel: 920-729-4565. Kathy Burke, Prin.
Lay Teachers 18; Students 169.
Catechesis/Religious Programs—Tel: 920-729-4562. D.R.E.: Sr. Diane Baumann; Cindy Kylers.
Students 230.

Neopit, Menominee Co., St. Anthony. (Also serves St. Joseph, Phlox, and Holy Family, Mattoon). Rev. R. David Kiefer; Deacon Thomas Hartman.
Mailing Address: P.O. Box 241, 54150-0241. Tel: 715-756-2361. [CEM]
Catechesis/Religious Programs—Tel: 715-756-2321. Sr. Charlotte Ann Wagner, D.R.E.
Students 104.

Neva, Langlade Co., St. Wenceslaus. Served from St. Mary, Antigo. Rev. Jeremiah F. Worman; Deacon Thomas Hanley.
Mailing Address: P.O. Box 50, Deerbrook, 54424-0050. Tel: 715-627-2126.
735 Deleglise St., Antigo, 54409-1425. Tel: 715-623-2522.
Res., N5340 Church Rd., Deerbrook, 54424-9413. Tel: 715-623-7019. [CEM]
School—All Saints Catholic School, Tel: 715-623-4835. Sr. Carol Jean Zais, S.D.S., Prin.
Catechesis/Religious Programs—Students 160.

Newald, Argonne Co., St. Hubert. Served from St. Leonard, Laona. Rev. John W. Cerkas.
Res., R.R. 1, Box 344, Laona, 54541-9641. Tel: 715-674-3241; Fax: 715-674-3401.
Mission—Laona, St. Leonard.

New Denmark, Brown Co., Holy Trinity. Served from All Saints, Denmark. Rev. Ronald A. Colombo.
Res., P.O. Box 787, Denmark, 54208-0787. Tel: 920-863-2357; Fax: 920-863-5425. [CEM]
Mission—Denmark, All Saints.

New Franken, Brown Co., St. Kilian. Served from St. Thomas the Apostle, Humboldt. Rev. Dean H. Dombroski.
Res., P.O. Box 83, 54229-0083. Tel: 920-866-2285. [CEM]
Catechesis/Religious Programs—Tel: 920-866-3541. Mrs. Nancy Meltzer, D.R.E.
Students 122.

New Holstein, Calumet Co., Holy Rosary. (Also serves St. Ann, St. Anna). Rev. Frank Weber.
Res., 1724 Madison St., 53061-1326. Tel: 920-898-4884; Fax: 920-898-4884. [CEM]
School—1814 Madison St., 53061-1347. Tel: 920-898-4210. Sr. Valerie Lemansky, Prin.
Sisters 4; Lay Teachers 10; Students 150.
Catechesis/Religious Programs—Tel: 920-898-9248. Andrew Glaza, D.R.E.
Students 158.

New London, Waupaca Co., Most Precious Blood, Rev. David J. Lewis, Admin.
Res., 808 S. Pearl St., 54961-1863. Tel: 920-982-2346. [CEM]
School—102 E. Washington St., 54961. Tel: 414-982-2134.
Lay Teachers 12; Students 156.
Catechesis/Religious Programs—Ellen Clarke, D.R.E.
Students 332.

Niagara, Marinette Co., St. Anthony. Also serves St. Margaret, Pembine, Immaculate Conception, Florence and Sacred Heart, Aurora. Rev. Michael E. Betley, Admin.
Res., 1432 River St., 54151-1544. Tel: 715-251-3879; Fax: 715-251-3875.
Catechesis/Religious Programs—D.R.E.: D. Johnson; D. Sonnenberg; P. Kinsella.
Students 251.

Norman, Kewaunee Co., St. Joseph. Served from Nativity BVM, Tisch Mills. Rev. Joseph R. Coopmans, O.Praem., Admin.
Res., E3295 County Rd. G, Kewaunee, 54216-9538. Tel: 920-776-1555. [CEM]
Catechesis/Religious Programs—D.R.E.: (Grades 9-12 associated with Nativity, Tisch Mills.) Gloria Urban; Crystal Wavrunek.

Northeim, Manitowoc Co., St. Casimir. Merged with St. Joseph, Alverno; St. Wendel, Cleveland and St. Isidore, Osman to form St. Thomas the Apostle, Northeim.

St. Thomas the Apostle, Manitowo Co., (2000). (Has records for St. Joseph, Alverno, St. Wendel, Cleveland, and St. Isidore, Osman.) Rev. David B. Beaudry.
Res., 8109 Northeim Rd., Newton, 53063-9630. Tel: 920-726-4228; Fax: 920-726-4229. [CEM]
School—St. Joseph School, 2143 S. Alverno Rd., Manitowoc, 54220. Tel: 920-682-4217. Pam Fischer, Prin.

Oconto, Oconto Co., Holy Trinity (1996). (Has records for St. Joseph and St. Peter, Oconto.) Rev. David Ruby; Deacon Walter Kaszynski.
Res., 716 Madison St., 54153-1668. Tel: 920-834-5900; Fax: 920-834-5907.
School—310 Arbutus Ave., 54153. Tel: 920-834-5910.

St. Joseph. Merged with St. Peter, Oconto to form Holy Trinity Parish, Oconto.

St. Peter. Merged with St. Joseph, Oconto to form Holy Trinity Parish, Oconto.

Oconto Falls, Oconto Co., St. Anthony. Served from St. Patrick, Stiles. Revs. John J. Hephner, Priest Moderator; Harold Beerntsen; Mrs. Patricia DeGroot, Parish Dir.
Church—239 N. Franklin St., 54154-1042. Tel: 920-846-2152; Fax: 920-846-8254. [CEM]
School—253 N. Franklin St., 54154. Tel: 414-846-2276. Ms. Rosemary Marifke, Prin.
Lay Teachers 5; Students 48.
Catechesis/Religious Programs—Associated with St. Patrick, Stiles. Mary Holzberger, D.R.E.
Students 191.

Omro, Winnebago Co., St. Mary, Rev. Joseph A. Mattern.
Res., 233 E. Scott, 54963-1705. Tel: 920-685-2258; Fax: 920-685-7343.
Catechesis/Religious Programs—Janet Abalan, D.R.E.
Students 218.

Oneida, Brown Co., St. Joseph, Rev. George G. Lenzner.
Res., 145 St. Joseph Dr., 54155-8914. Tel: 920-869-2244. [CEM]
Catechesis/Religious Programs—Tel: 920-862-2219. D.R.E.: Mary Van Schyndel; Darlene Wertel.
Students 258.

Oneida Township, Outagamie Co., Immaculate Conception, Rev. Richard L. Thomas, Admin.
Res., N5589 County Rd. E., De Pere, 54115-8529. Tel: 920-869-2626. [CEM]
Catechesis/Religious Programs—Tel: 920-788-6569. Shelley Bastien, D.R.E.
Students 83.

Oshkosh, Winnebago Co.,

1—ST. PETER, Rev. John J. Becker; Deacon Gerald Kuborn.
Res., 449 High Ave., 54901-4790. Tel: 920-231-9782; Fax: 920-231-9808. [JC]
School—Please see Unified Catholic Schools of Oshkosh under section [E] Consolidated Schools in the Institution section.
Catechesis/Religious Programs—Tel: 920-235-6156. D.R.E.: Kevin Feyen; Patricia Birling.
Students 274.

2—ST. MARY, Sr. Judith Miller, Parish Dir.; Revs. John J. Becker, Priest Moderator; Robert Stegmann; Deacon Robert Penzenstadler.
Res., 442 Monroe St., 54901-5146. Tel: 920-231-5317; Fax: 920-231-1344.
School—St. Francis Cabrini Elementary. Part of the Unified Catholic Schools of Oshkosh. Includes St. Vincent, St. Peter & St. Raphael. 619 Merritt Ave., 54901-5100. Tel: 920-235-0637. Sr. Michelle Wronkowski, S.S.J., Prin.
Lay Teachers 12; Students 227.
Catechesis/Religious Programs—Tel: 920-235-4266. Karen Pettibone, D.R.E.
Students 150.
Convent—441 Boyd St., 54901-5135. Tel: 414-231-3388.

3—ST. JOSAPHAT, Rev. Robert Stegmann.
Res., 1333 Walnut St., 54901-3699. Tel: 920-235-3363; Fax: 920-235-3863.
Catechesis/Religious Programs—M. Wichmann, D.R.E.
Students 173.

4—ST. VINCENT DE PAUL. Served from St. John, Oshkosh. Rev. William L. Van De Kreeke; Deacon Raymond Brandenstein.
Res., 216 W. South Park Ave., 54902-6598. Tel: 920-231-8855. [JC]
School—St. Elizabeth Seton Elementary. (Part of the Unified Catholic Schools of Oshkosh. Includes St. Vincent, St. Peter, St. Raphael, and St. Mary.) 1207 Oregon St., 54901. Tel: 920-235-4060. Mrs. Pamela Beach, Prin.
Religious 1; Lay Teachers 10; Students 233.
Catechesis/Religious Programs—James Rasmussen, D.R.E.
Students 109.

5—ST. JOHN. (Also serves St. Vincent de Paul, Oshkosh). Rev. William L. Van De Kreeke.
Res., 434 W. South Park Ave., 54902-6597. Tel: 920-231-8596; Fax: 920-235-3863. [JC]
Catechesis/Religious Programs—450 W. 12th Ave., 54902. Tel: 920-231-7526. Robin Flanigan, D.R.E.
Students 232.

6—SACRED HEART, Rev. Msgr. James B. Feely.
Res., 1020 W. 6th Ave., 54902-5794. Tel: 920-235-2073; Fax: 920-235-7412. [CEM]
School—Please see Unified Catholic Schools of Oshkosh under section [E] Consolidated Schools in the Institution section.
Catechesis/Religious Programs—Tel: 920-235-5236. Cindy Hable, D.R.E.
Students 112.

7—ST. RAPHAEL, Rev. Daniel J. Felton.
Church & Mailing Address: 830 S. Westhaven Dr., 54904-7977. Tel: 920-233-8044; Fax: 920-233-2360.; 2355 W. Ninth Ave., 54904. Tel: 920-235-7158. [JC]
School—Please see Unified Catholic Schools of Oshkosh under [E] Consolidated Schools in the Institution section. Steven Roy, Pres.
Catechesis/Religious Programs—D.R.E.: Amy Matz; Brian Mitchell.
Students 785.

Osman, Manitowoc Co., St. Isidore. Merged with St. Wendel, Cleveland; St. Joseph, Alverno and St. Casimir, Northeim to form St. Thomas the Apostle, Northeim.

Pembine, Marinette Co., St. Margaret. Served from St. Anthony, Niagara. Rev. Michael E. Betley.
Mailing Address: P.O. Box 235, 54156-0235.
Res., 1432 River St., Niagara, 54151-1544. Tel: 715-324-5849; Fax: 715-324-6571.

Peshtigo, Marinette Co., St. Mary, In res., Rev. David Zimmerman, Admin.
Res., 600 Thompson St., 54157-1430. Tel: 715-582-3876; Fax: 715-582-1165.
School—141 S. Wood, 54157. Tel: 715-582-4041. Linda Wilke, Prin.
Sisters 1; Lay Teachers 7; Students 89.
Catechesis/Religious Programs—Tel: 715-582-4897. Alice Boyce, D.R.E.
Students 251.

Phlox, Langlade Co., St. Joseph. Served from St. Anthony, Neopit and Holy Family, Mattoon. Rev. R. David Kiefer; Deacon Tom Hartman.
Mailing Address: P.O. Box 73, 54464-0073. Tel: 715-489-3330. [CEM]
Catechesis/Religious Programs—Eileen Hartl, D.R.E.
Students 83.

Pine Grove, Brown Co., Holy Trinity, Rev. Ralph C. Merkatoris.
Res., 4767 Stagecoach Rd., Denmark, 54208-9181. Tel: 920-863-2545. [CEM]
Catechesis/Religious Programs—D.R.E.: K. Lemmens; J. Melotte; J. Adrians; K. Naidl.
Students 340.

Plainfield, Waushara Co., St. Paul, Rev. Faustin Misakabo, O.Praem., Admin.
Res., 622 S. Beach St., 54966-9637. Tel: 715-335-4314. [CEM]
Catechesis/Religious Programs—Tel: 715-335-4144. Marge Feyrer, D.R.E.
Students 200.

Poy Sippi, Waushara Co., Sacred Heart of Jesus. Served from St. Mark, Redgranite. Rev. Raymond J. Conard, Admin.
Mailing Address: P.O. Box 273, Redgranite, 54970-0273. Tel: 920-566-4442.

Pulaski, Brown Co., Assumption of the Blessed Virgin Mary. (Also serves St. Stanislaus, Hofa Park). Revs. Patrick Gawrylewski, O.F.M., Admin.; Brendan Wroblewski, O.F.M.; Deacon William Doran.
Res., P.O. Box 379, 54162-0379. Tel: 920-822-3279; Fax: 920-822-8030. [CEM]
School—109 E. Pulaski St., 54162. Tel: 920-822-5650. Mrs. Deanne Wilinski, Prin. & D.R.E.
Sisters 2; Lay Teachers 10; Students 125.
Catechesis/Religious Programs—Staci Karcz, D.R.E.
Students 290.

Redgranite, Waushara Co., St. Mark. (Also serves Sacred Heart of Jesus, Poy Sippi). Rev. Raymond J. Conrad, Admin.
Mailing Address: P.O. Box 273, 54970-0273. Tel: 920-566-4442; Fax: 920-566-4559.
Catechesis/Religious Programs—Sr. Virginia Pfaller, D.R.E.
Students 72.

Reedsville/Maple Grove, Manitowoc Co., St. Mary-St. Patrick. Served from St Mary, Brillion. Rev. W. Thomas Long.
Res., P.O. Box 248, Reedsville, 54230-0248. Tel: 920-754-4665. [CEM 3]
School—628 Menasha St., Reedville, 54230. Tel: 920-754-4124. Debra Nate, Prin.
Lay Teachers 8; Students 118.
Catechesis/Religious Programs—Tel: 920-756-9015. Bobbi Whittaker, D.R.E.
Students 152.

Rosiere, Kewaunee Co., St. Peter and St. Hubert. Merged with St. Peter, Lincoln. Rev. Dennis G. Drury.
Res., E3085 County Rd. X, Casco, 54205-9787. Tel: 920-837-2852. [CEM 4]
Catechesis/Religious Programs—D.R.E.: D. Bredael; L. Yunk; L. Veeser.
Students 279.

St. Anna, Calumet Co., St. Ann. Served from Holy Rosary, New Holstein. Rev. Frank Weber.
Res., N188 School St., New Holstein, 53061-9776. Tel: 920-894-3147; Fax: 920-894-3147. [CEM]
Catechesis/Religious Programs—Tel: 920-894-3166. June Winkel, D.R.E.
Students 54.

St. John, Calumet Co., St. John the Baptist. Merged with Sacred Heart, Sherwood, to form St. John-Sacred Heart, Sherwood/St. John.

St. Nazianz, Manitowoc Co., St. Gregory. (Also serves Holy Trinity, School Hill). Rev. Gerald Sirois, S.D.S.; Deacon James Steffen.
Mailing Address: P.O. Box 199, 54232-0199. Tel: 920-773-2511. [CEM]
School—212 School St., 54232. Tel: 920-773-2530. Jane Graves, Prin.
Lay Teachers 10; Students 90.
Catechesis/Religious Programs—Tel: 920-849-9045. Rosie Bartel, D.R.E.
Students 154.

School Hill, Manitowoc Co., Holy Trinity. Served from St. Gregory, St. Nazianz. Rev. Gerald Sirois, S.D.S.; Deacon James Steffen.
Res., 11928 Marken Rd., Kiel, 53042-9731. Tel: 920-773-2380. [CEM]
Catechesis/Religious Programs—N4061 Riverview Hts. Ct., Chilton, 53014. Tel: 920-849-9045. Rosie Bartel, D.R.E.
Students 168.

Seymour, Outagamie Co., St. John, Rev. Martin F. Fox, Admin.; Deacons Paul Grimm; Orvell DeBruin.
Mailing Address: 915 Ivory St., 54165-1629.
Res., 904 S. Main St., 54165. Tel: 920-833-6140; Fax: 920-833-7098. [CEM]
School—928 S. Main St., 54165. Tel: 920-833-2122. Jaclyn Behnke, Prin.
Lay Teachers 8; Students 109.
Catechesis/Religious Programs—1002 S. Main St., 54165. Tel: 920-833-2504. Mary Carter, D.R.E.
Students 222.

Shawano, Shawano Co., Sacred Heart. (Also serves St. Martin, Cecil). Rev. Leonard M. Evers.
Office & Mailing: 321 S. Sawyer St., 54166-2437. Tel: 715-526-2023.
Res., 325 S. Main St., 54166. Tel: 715-526-4106. [CEM 2]
School—324 E. Center St., 54166. Tel: 715-526-5328. Peter Young, Prin.
Lay Teachers 13; Students 220.
Catechesis/Religious Programs—Mary Ellen Waldvogel, D.R.E.
Students 350.

Sherwood/St. John, Calumet Co., St. John-Sacred Heart. (St. John the Baptist, St. John, and Sacred Heart, Sherwood merged.) Rev. Kenneth R. Frozena.
Res., N369 Military Rd., P.O. Box 58, Sherwood, 54169. Tel: 920-989-1515. [CEM]
School—N361 Military Rd., P.O. Box 78, Sherwood, 54169. Tel: 920-989-1373. Kerry Sievert, Prin.
Lay Teachers 9; Students 125.
Catechesis/Religious Programs—Patti Sevela, D.R.E.
Students 113.

Shiocton, Outagamie Co., St. Denis. Served from St. Patrick, Stephensville. Rev. David J. Funk, O.F.M.Cap., Priest Moderator; Mrs. Karin Posdal, Parish Dir.
Mailing Address: N5591 2nd St., 54170-8652. Tel: 920-986-3369; Fax: 920-986-3634. [JC]
Catechesis/Religious Programs—Tel: 920-757-5090. Mrs. Donna Cherry, D.R.E.
Students 166.

Sister Bay, Door Co., St. Rosalia. Served from St. John the Baptist, Egg Harbor. Rev. Mathew Simonar.
Mailing Address: P.O. Box 49, Egg Harbor, 54209. Tel: 920-854-5264. [CEM]
Catechesis/Religious Programs—Sandy Sohns, D.R.E.
Students 95.

Slovan, Kewaunee Co., St. Adalbert. Merged with Holy Trinity, Casco.

Sobieski, Oconto Co., St. John Cantius. (Also serves St. Joseph, Chase, and St. Louis, Abrams). Rev. Gerald Prusakowski, O.F.M.
Res., 6051 Noble St., 54171-9724. Tel: 920-822-5255; Fax: 920-822-1859. [CEM]
Catechesis/Religious Programs—Tel: 920-822-8795. Donna Rae VanKauwenbergh, D.R.E.
Students 101.

South Branch, Menominee Reservation, St. Joseph of the Lake. Served from St. Michael, Keshena. Rev. David S. Barrett.
Mailing Address: P.O. Box 610, Keshena, 54135-0610. Tel: 715-799-3811. [CEM]
Catechesis/Religious Programs—Associated with St. Michael, Keshena. Tel: 715-799-3234. Sr. Kathleen Walli, O.P., D.R.E.

Spruce, Oconto Co., Sacred Heart of Jesus. Merged with St. Charles Borromeo, Lena.

Stangelville, Kewaunee Co., St. Lawrence. Merged with St. Joseph-St. John, Montpelier and St. Hedwig, West Kewaunee to form St. Therese de Lisieux, Stangelville.
St. Therese de Lisieux (2000). (Holding records for St. Joseph-St. John, Montpelier/Krok and St. Hedwig, West Kewaunee.). Rev. Terrence LaCombe, Admin.
Mailing Address: N2085 County Rd. AB, Denmark, 54208-7705. Tel: 920-863-8747. [JC]

Stark, Brown Co., St. Mary, Rev. Lee J. Kahrs.
Mailing Address: 5840 Big Apple Rd., De Pere, 54115-9746. Tel: 920-864-7641. [CEM 2]

Stephensville, Outagamie Co., St. Patrick. (Also serves St. Denis, Shiocton). Revs. David J. Funk, O.F.M.Cap., Priest Moderator; John Kastenholz, O.Praem.; Karin Posdal, Parish Dir.
Res., N3686 State Rd. 76, Hortonville, 54944-8320. Tel: 920-757-5090; Fax: 920-986-3634. [CEM]
Catechesis/Religious Programs—Donna Cherry, D.R.E.
Students 120.

Stiles, Oconto Co., St. Patrick. Served from St. Anthony, Oconto Falls. Revs. John J. Hephner, Priest Moderator; Harold Beerntsen; Patricia DeGroot, Parish Dir.
Res., 5246 St. Patrick Rd., Lena, 54139-9105. Tel: 920-834-2575. [JC]
Catechesis/Religious Programs—Associated with St. Anthony, Oconto Falls. 253 N. Franklin, Oconto Falls, 54154. Tel: 920-846-2276. Linda Patzke, D.R.E.
Students 51.

Stockbridge, Calumet Co., St. Mary, Rev. Leander F. Nickel.
Res., P.O. Box 8, 53088-0008. Tel: 920-439-1515. [CEM]
Catechesis/Religious Programs—D.R.E.: J. Propson; N. Wilson.
Students 125.

Sturgeon Bay, Door Co., St. Joseph, Rev. Charles W. Mocco, Admin.; Deacon Kenneth Hunsader.
Res., 526 Louisiana St., 54235-1738. Tel: 920-743-2062; Fax: 920-743-6786.
School—130 N. 5th Ave., 54235. Tel: 920-743-9219; Fax: 920-743-9297. Sr. Janette Wicker, O.P., Prin.
Lay Teachers 11; Students 112.
Catechesis/Religious Programs—D.R.E.: Sr. Sandra Peterson; Pam Marsh.
Students 263.
Corpus Christi, Rev. Anthony J. Birdsall; Deacons Richard Nowak; Paul Zenefski.
Mailing Address: & Oratory: 25 N. Elgin Ave., 54235-2963. Tel: 920-743-4716; Fax: 920-743-3711. [JC]
Res., 722 W. Maple St., 54235. [JC]
School—15 N. Elgin Ave., 54235. Tel: 920-743-4144. Mr. Hugh LeVoy, Prin.
Lay Teachers 9; Students 171.
Catechesis/Religious Programs—Amy Alberts, D.R.E.
Students 169.

Suamico, Brown Co., St. Benedict. (Also serves St. Pius, Little Suamico). Rev. Gary J. Dantinne; Deacon John Maloney.
Mailing Address: P.O. Box 66, 54173-0066. Tel: 920-434-2024. [CEM]
Catechesis/Religious Programs—Tel: 920-434-1219. D.R.E.: L. Hollister; P. Hendricks; E. Nier.
Students 143.

Suring, Oconto Co., St. Michael. (also serves Chute Lake Station, Chute Lake). Revs. John Gallagher, Priest Moderator; Michael J. Clifford; Sr. Karen Vollmer, O.P., Parish Dir.
Mailing Address: P.O. Box 248, 54174-0248. Tel: 920-842-2580. [CEM]
Catechesis/Religious Programs—Tel: 920-842-9825.
Students 128.
Station—Chute Lake.

Thiry Daems, Kewaunee Co., St. Odile. Closed. For inquiries for parish records contact the Chancery.

Tigerton, Shawano Co., St. Anthony. (Also serves St. Mary, Marion and Holy Family-St. William, Wittenberg-Eland.) Rev. Michael R. Carroll, Admin.; Deacons Ken Sambs; Hilary Hayek.
Mailing Address: P.O. Box 106, 54486-0106. Tel: 715-535-2571; Fax: 715-535-2953.
Catechesis/Religious Programs—Rosalie Dudzik, D.R.E.
Students 70.

Tisch Mills, Manitowoc Co., Nativity of the Blessed Virgin Mary. (Also serves St. Joseph, Norman). Rev. Joseph R. Coopmans, O.Praem.
Mailing Address: 18424 Tisch Mills Rd., Denmark, 54208-9508. Tel: 920-776-1555. [CEM]
Catechesis/Religious Programs—D.R.E.: Robert Wavrunek; Linda French.
Students 145.

Tonet, Kewaunee Co., St. Martin. Closed. For inquiries for parish records contact the Chancery.

Two Rivers, Manitowoc Co.,

1—St. Luke. (Also serves St. Mark, Two Rivers). Rev. Larry J. Seidl; Deacons Jim Sustman; Kenneth Coenen.
Res., 1814 Jefferson St., 54241-2699. Tel: 920-793-2236; Fax: 920-793-2236.
School—Two Rivers Catholic Central. Consolidated with St. Mark, Two Rivers. 2203 12th St., 54241. Tel: 920-794-7266.
Lay Teachers 16; Students 255. Principals: Kay Franz; Josephine Vermillion.
Catechesis/Religious Programs—Associated with Holy Redeemer, Two Rivers. 3218 Tannery Rd., 54241. Tel: 920-793-4531. D.R.E.: Sr. Maria; Dorothy Boutin.
Students 93.

2—Sacred Heart. Merged with Most Holy Redeemer, Two Rivers to form Sacred Heart-Most Holy Redeemer, Two Rivers.

3—Holy Redeemer - Sacred Heart, (2000), Rev. William O'Brien.
Church—3218 Tannery Rd., 54241-1648. Tel: 920-793-1755; Fax: 920-793-8067. [CEM]

4—St. Mark. Served from St. Luke, Two Rivers. Rev. Larry J. Seidl; Deacons James Sustman; Kenneth Coenen.
Mailing Address: 2214 11th St., 54241-3718. Tel: 920-794-1717.
School—Two Rivers Catholic Central. Consolidated with St. Luke, Two Rivers. 2203 12th St., 54241. Tel: 920-794-7622. Josephine Vermillion, Prin.
Students 95.
Catechesis/Religious Programs—Associated with Most Holy Redeemer, Two Rivers. Tel: 920-793-4531. D.R.E.: Sr. Judanne Stratman; Sr. Andrene Flasch.
Students 128.

5—Most Holy Redeemer. Merged with Sacred Heart, Two Rivers to form Sacred Heart-Most Holy Redeemer, Two Rivers.

Wabeno, Forest Co., St. Ambrose. (Served from St. Joseph, Crandon). Rev. Ralph J. Gillis.
Mailing Address: P.O. Box 280, Lakewood, 54566-0280. Tel: 715-473-2511; Fax: 715-473-2131. [CEM]
Catechesis/Religious Programs—Linda McEwen, D.R.E.
Students 67.

Wagner, Marinette Co., St. Edward. Attended by St. Joseph, Walsh. Rev. Roger Strebel, Admin.
Res., W3308 County Rd. G, Porterfield, 54159-9736. Tel: 715-789-2254. [CEM]
Catechesis/Religious Programs—Students 37.

Walhain, Kewaunee Co., St. Amand. Closed. For inquiries for parish records contact the Chancery.

Walsh, Marinette Co., St. Joseph. (Also serves St. Edward, Wagner). Rev. Roger Strebel, Admin.
Res., W3308 County Rd. G, Porterfield, 54159-9736. Tel: 715-789-2254; Fax: 715-789-2293. [CEM]
Catechesis/Religious Programs—W5303 Cty. Rd. G, Porterfield, 54159. Tel: 715-854-7216. D.R.E.: Kathy Gajewski; Donna McVane.
Students 106.

Waupaca, Waupaca Co., St. Mary Magdalene. (Has records for St. George, King.). Rev. James F. Vennix.
Office and Mailing Address: 223 S. Division St., 54981-1594. Tel: 715-258-3000; Fax: 715-258-5708. [CEM]
Res., E. 1277 Cleghorn Rd., 54981. Tel: 715-258-4928.
Catechesis/Religious Programs—Tel: 715-258-8752. D.R.E.: Betty Manion; Cathy Miller.
Students 440.

Wausaukee, Marinette Co., St. Augustine. (Also serves St. Agnes, Amberg). Rev. Joseph E. Dorner, Admin.
Mailing Address: 507 Church St., 54177-9749. Tel: 715-856-5276.
Catechesis/Religious Programs—Tel: 715-856-5066. Mrs. Sherry Ledvina, D.R.E.
Students 170.

Wautoma, Waushara Co., St. Joseph, Rev. Philip Dinh-Van-Thiep.
Res., 364 S. Cambridge St., 54982-8101. Tel: 920-787-3848; Fax: 920-787-4781. [CEM]
Catechesis/Religious Programs—Ellen Scheibe, D.R.E.
Students 236.

West Kewaunee, Kewaunee Co., St. Hedwig. Merged with St. Joseph-St.John, Montpelier and St. Lawrence, Stangelville to form St. Therese de Lisieux, Stangelville.

Weyauwega, Waupaca Co., SS. Peter and Paul. (Also serves Sacred Heart, Manawa). Rev. Bertin L. Samsa, O.F.M.Cap.
Res., P.O. Box 548, 54983-0548. Tel: 920-867-2179; Fax: 920-867-2179. [CEM]
Catechesis/Religious Programs—Tel: 920-867-2170. Sr. Marie Rose Van Deurzen, S.S.N.D., D.R.E.
Students 175.

White Lake, Langlade Co., Ss. James & Stanislaus. (St. James, Whitelake and St. Stanislaus, Langlade merged.). Rev. Omer C. Kelley, Priest Moderator.
Mailing Address: P.O. Box 36, 54491-0036. Tel: 715-822-2551. [CEM 2]
Res., 252 Bissell St., 54491.

Whitelaw, Manitowoc Co., St. Michael, Rev. Richard H. Heymen.
Mailing Address: P.O. Box 206, 54247-0206. Tel: 920-732-3901. [CEM]
School—132 W. Menasha Ave., 54247. Tel: 920-732-4442. Mrs. Arlene Rhein, Prin.
Lay Teachers 5; Students 53.
Catechesis/Religious Programs—110 W. Menasha Ave., 54247.
Students 124.

Winneconne, Winnebago Co., St. Mary, Rev. Leroy R. Smet.
Res., 205 Pleasant Dr., 54986-0640. Tel: 920-582-4246; Fax: 920-582-0181.
Church—P.O. Box 640, 54986-0640. [JC]
Catechesis/Religious Programs—Tel: 920-582-4601. Jenny Thorn, D.R.E.
Students 291.

Wittenberg, Shawano Co., Holy Family. Merged with St. William, Eland to form Holy Family-St. William, Wittenberg.

Holy Family-St. William (2000). Served from St. Anthony, Tigerton. Rev. Michael R. Carroll, Admin.
Res., 106 N. Ellms St., 54499-9099. Tel: 715-253-2050. [CEM]

Wrightstown, Brown Co., St. Paul, Revs. Dennis L. Bergsbaken, Mod.; Robert J. Kabat; Sr. Lisa Lucht, O.P., Parish Dir.
Res., 437 Main St., P.O. Box 187, 54180-0187. Tel: 920-532-4374. [JC]
School—425 Main St., 54180. Tel: 920-532-4833. Mrs. Carol Hoard, Prin.
Lay Teachers 8; Students 105.
Catechesis/Religious Programs—Tel: 920-532-0319. Rosemary Reedy, D.R.E.
Students 131.

Special Assignment:
Reverend Monsignors—
Dewane, John B., P.O. Box 23825, Green Bay, WI 54305-3825
Gulig, Robert, 224 Iroquois Ave., #7, Green Bay, WI 54301-1998
Maufort, Richard A., Charlestown Pointe I, 1975 Ridgeway Dr., Apt. 30, De Pere, WI 54115-4109
Schuh, John H., P.O. Box 23825, Green Bay, WI 54305-3825
Reverend Fathers—
Carr, Martin P., 1965 Oshkosh Ave., Oshkosh, WI 54901-2659
Clifford, Michael J., 4775 Pine Ridge Tr., Abrams, WI 54101
Gilsdorf, Gordon J., Notre Dame de la Baie Academy, 610 Maryhill Dr., Green Bay, WI 54303-2092
Gilsdorf, Richard W., N9599 Bay Shore Ln., Luxemburg, WI 54217-9630
Golden, Thomas, 1162 McCormick St., Green Bay, WI 54301
Groher, Robert C., 6202 Dogwood Ln., Oconto, WI 54153-9590
Hoffmann, Philip A., P.O. Box 23825, Green Bay, WI 54305-3825
Koch, Michael R., Chap. for Sisters of the Sorrowful Mother, Oshkosh, 890 Graceland Dr., Apt. 8, Oshkosh, WI 54904
Kollath, Robert, Newman Center, 717 W. Irving, Oshkosh, IN 54901-4319
Krutzik, Norman, 622 E. Pershing St., Appleton, WI 54911-8270
Reinke, Frank, 1820 Ridgeway Dr., Apt. 12B, DePere, WI 54115
Samter, James, P.O. Box 23825, Green Bay, WI 54305-3825
Smith, Ivan E., 3416 County Rd. V, Sturgeon Bay, WI 54235-8832
Van De Loo, Willard, P.O. Box 23825, Green Bay, WI 54305-3825
Van Deuren, John H., 1490 Capitol Dr., Green Bay, WI 54303-2250
Ver Bust, Richard M., 824 Voelker St., De Pere, WI 54115-3618

On Duty Outside the Diocese:
Reverend Monsignors—
Dewane, Frank J., Pontificio Consiglio Cor Unum, 00120 Vatican City, Rome, Italy. Tel: 011-396-6988-7331
Polc, Jaroslav, Tha Kurova 3, 16000 Prague 6, Czech Republic
Reverend Fathers—
Hoffmann, William A., Parroquia Cathedral, San Juan Bautista, c/o Duarte No. 42, San Juan de la Maguana, Dominican Republic
Mayefske, Thomas J., 833 Arizona, S.E., Albuquerqe, NM 87108
Rank, Robert F., 203 Dunne Ave., Robstown, TX 78380-3501
Reuter, John F., Apartado 46, Tlaxiaco, Oaxaca Mexico
Schiavone, Robert W., 8537 W. Forest Hill Ave., Franklin, WI 53132-9705
Seis, Michael, Casa Curiel, Pannoquia Santa Teresa, Elias Pina, Dominican Republic
Taylor, Peter, 3520 N. Grovers Ave., Glendale, AZ 85308
Vander Heyden, William F., Chap., V.A. Medical Center, 3001 Green Bay Rd., North Chicago, IL 60064-3049

Graduate Studies:
Reverend Fathers—
Barta, William, 1025 Michigan Ave., N.E., Washington, DC 20017-1895

Military Chaplains:
Reverend Fathers—
Dory, Michael, Lt. Cmdr., 303 Market St., Apt. 527, San Diego, CA 92101-6861

Absent on Leave:
Reverend Fathers—
Bauschka, Joseph
Blaha, John
Eberhardy, William
Massart, James
Mastalir, Peter
Pawelski, John
Schneider, Ronald
Shebuski, Charles
Somers, Michael

Retired:
Most Rev.—
Wycislo, Aloysius, P.O. Box 23825, Green Bay, WI 54305-3825
Reverend Monsignors—
Hotchkiss, Eugene, 1400 S. Park Ave., Neenah, WI 54956-4651
Klauck, Peter, 825 East River Dr., Apt. 1, De Pere, WI 54115
Rose, Donald, 865 Mill Rd., Sturgeon Bay, WI 54235-9267
Schneider, Alfred, 224 Iroquois Ave., #11, Green Bay, WI 54301-1999
Steiner, Carl, 1053 Main St., Wrightstown, WI 54180
Reverend Fathers—
Barcome, Earl, 1326 S. Fisk St., Green Bay, WI 54304-3055
Bedessem, Henry W., 1851 Eldorado Dr., Apt. 6, Green Bay, WI 54302-5554
Beerntsen, Harold, 10544 W. Rost Lake Rd., Coleman, WI 54112
Bernardy, Patrick, P.O. Box 86, Crandon, WI 54520
Bestler, Joseph, 224 Iroquois Ave., #14, Green Bay, WI 54301-1969
Danks, Arthur J., 2616 He Nis Ra Ln., Green Bay, WI 54304-1308
Dawling, Raymond, 3404 American Dr., #3201, Lago Vista, TX 78645
DuCharme, Paul, 224 Iroquois Ave., #8, Green Bay, WI 54301-1998
Feeney, John P., 3333 W. 2nd St., 56/123, Los Angeles, CA 90004-6149
Feller, Donald J., 2496 Mary Jo Dr., Green Bay, WI 54311-5208
Flatley, Eugene T., 2153 Calle Buena Ventura, Oceanside, CA 92056-3216
Fuller, Donald, 500 W. Marquette St., Appleton, WI 54911-1917
Geigel, Francis, Rte. 1, Box 396, Wabeno, WI 54566-9742
Gerend, Lawrence, 216 Catherine St., Kaukauna, WI 54130-3126
Gomulka, Henry J., Mother Theresa Home, 1270 Franciscan Dr., Rm. 231, Lemont, IL 60439
Hogan, LeRoy, 220 W. 4th St., Kaukauna, WI 54130
Jacobs, James T., P.O. Box 86, Crandon, WI 54520-0086
Johanek, John, 224 Iroquois Ave., #9, Green Bay, WI 54301
Kelley, Omer C., P.O. Box 33, White Lake, WI 54491-0033
Kerscher, Francis, 2408 W. River St., Two Rivers, WI 54241-1943
Kilsdonk, Edward, 2249 W. Cortland Dr., Appleton, WI 54914-1932

Knier, Aloysius M., 1910 W. Ohio Ave., Room 251, Milwaukee, WI 53215-4933
Koehne, David, 224 Iroquois Ave., #12, Green Bay, WI 54301-1970
Kolbasz, Stanley, 3031 Fond du Lac Rd., Oshkosh, WI 54902
Koszarek, Thaddeus J., 224 Iroquois Ave., #1, Green Bay, WI 54301-1994
Kutiuk, Casimir, 1246 W. 20th Ave., Oshkosh, WI 54901-6620
Laux, Donald, P.O. Box 219, Birnamwood, WI 54414-0219
Lessard, Leo, 17725 Munger Lake Lane, P.O. Box 24, Lakewood, WI 54138
Lexa, Robert, 2320 Woodrow Ct., #7, Appleton, WI 54915
Marquardt, Donald, 224 Iroquois Ave., #3, Green Bay, WI 54301-1994
Mauthe, Richard, 315 Breezy Acres, Luxemburg, WI 54127
McLaughlin, John, 427 Fairview Ct., Green Bay, WI 54303
Melchior, Frank, E2783 Rockledge Rd., Casco, WI 54205
O'Brien, John, 502 N. Front St., Apt. 4, De Pere, WI 54115
Peeters, R. Thomas, 224 Iroquois Ave., #6, Green Bay, WI 54301-1998
Resheske, Florian, 224 Iroquois Ave., #15, Green Bay, WI 54301-1969
Rickert, William, 224 Iroquois Ave., #5, Green Bay, WI 54301-1998
Rodgers, Kenneth, 441 St. Mary Blvd., Green Bay, WI 54301-2607
Sammut, Tito, 985 N. Broadway, #64, De Pere, WI 54115
Schmidt, Eugene, 2650 Vinland Rd., Oshkosh, WI 54901-1524
Schmitt, John P., 2819 35th St., Two Rivers, WI 54241-1521
Schreiter, Daniel A., 4616 Basswood St., Land O'Lakes, FL 34639-5603
Schuh, Earl, 2470 Mary Jo Dr., Green Bay, WI 54311-5208
Schumacher, Paul, 2427 County Rd. J, Abrams, WI 54101
Shafer, Richard, 1515 Capitol Dr., #105, Green Bay, WI 54303-2246
Sladek, Robert, 1025 Pine Beach Rd., #205, Marinette, WI 54143-4248
Spalding, William, 228 S. Sawyer St., #4, Shawano, WI 54166-2469
Staudenmaier, Wilbert, 214 E. Summer St., Appleton, WI 54911-4863
Stengel, William, W8445 Germantown Rd., Crivitz, WI 54114
Stingle, Lawrence A., 2777 He Nis Ra Ln., Green Bay, WI 54304-1357
Vanden Hogen, Paul, 689 Evans St., Apt. 8, Waupaca, WI 54981
Werner, Justin, N1682 Ridgeway Dr., Greenville, WI 54942
Worzalla, Dennis A., St. Peter Parish, 800 4th Ave., Stevens Point, WI 54481-1627

Permanent Deacons:
Andrastek, Phil, 1607 Hamilton St., Manitowoc, WI 54220-5029
Asmuth, James, (Retired), 1615 Nicolet Blvd., Neenah, WI 54956-2984
Bahnaman, Richard, Holy Innocents Church, Manitowoc
Baumruk, Roy, St. Joseph Church, Appleton
Bilgrien, Kenneth, Ss. Peter & Paul Church, Hortonville
Boeldt, Alan, St. Paul Church, Manitowoc
Boucher, Paul, (Retired), N 7323 County Rd., G, Gresham, WI 54128-8998
Brandenstein, Raymond, St. Vincent de Paul Church, Oshkosh
Bricco, Howard, St. Patrick Church, Menasha
Burke, William, St. Mary Church, Appleton
Burkel, William, Holy Martyrs of Gorcum Church, Green Bay
Charlier, Earl, St. Mary, De Pere
Coenen, Kenneth, St. Luke and St. Mark Churches, Two Rivers
Craig, Thomas, Parish Dir., St. Martin, Cecil
Cross, Gerald, St. Mary Church, Menasha
De Bruin, Orvell, St. John Church, Seymour
De Groot, Vincent M., St. John Church, Little Chute
DeYoung, David
Dineen, Terry, St. Philip the Apostle Church, Green Bay
Doran, William, Assumption BVM Church, Pulaski
Drobka, Robert, St. Mary Church, Manitowoc
Ellis, Robert, 1372 Nienhaus Dr., DePere, WI 54115-8600
Garcia, Benjamin, (Retired)
Gauthier, James, St. Elizabeth Ann Seton Church, Green Bay
Gigure, Donald, Sacred Heart Church, Appleton
Gribowski, Mark, Holy Family Church, Marinette
Grimm, Paul, St. John Church, Seymour
Hanley, Thomas, St. Mary Church, Antigo and St. Wenceslaus Church, Neva
Hartman, Thomas, St. Joseph Church, Phlox; Holy Family Church, Mattoon; St. Anthony Church, Neopit
Hayek, Hilary, St. Anthony Church, Tigerton
Hunsader, Kenneth, St. Joseph Church, Sturgeon Bay
Jacqmin, Robert, (Retired)
Jozwiak, Thomas, St. Rose Church, Clintonville
Kaszynski, Walter, Holy Trinity Church, Oconto
Kieffer, Paul, Holy Innocents Church, Manitowoc
Klein, Paul, St. Thomas More Church, Appleton
Klein, William, St. Paul Church, Manitowoc
Kopydlowski, Kenneth, SS. Peter & Paul Church, Green Bay
Kremer, Frank, Jr., (Retired), 309 S. Webster Ave., De Pere, WI 54115-3421
Kuborn, Gerald, St. Peter Church, Oshkosh
Kunzer, Earl, Ss. Edward/Isidore Church, Flintville
Laurant, John, St. Bernard Church, Green Bay
Le Mere, David, W10742 Upper Lake Rd., Cresham, WI 54128-4126
Lobdell, Donald, N1796 Dawn Dr., Waupaca, WI 54981-9767
Lowe, Russ, (Retired), N2280 Country Ln., Waupaca, WI 54981-9526
Madsen, Roger, Ss. Peter/Paul Church, Institute
Maloney, John, St. Benedict Church, Suamico
Mastalish, Larry, St. Bernard Church, Green Bay
Meich, Richard, St. Mary, Greenville
Meidl, Richard, 8117 W. Pamela Ln., Peoria, AZ 85345
Merrick, Craig, St. Thomas More Church, Appleton
Naidl, Clarence, St. James, Cooperstown
Nass, Donald, (Retired), 946 Debbie Ln., Redgranite, WI 54970-9521
Nelesen, Ken, Holy Innocents Church, Manitowoc
Newhouse, Don, St. Nicholas Church, Freedom
Nooker, Robert, St. Agnes Church, Green Bay
Nowak, Richard, Corpus Christi, Sturgeon Bay
Orlowski, Harold, St. Mary/Lake Church, Lakewood
Otradovec, Byron, 8147 Belgian Rd., Lena, WI 54139
Penzenstadler, Robert, St. Mary Church, Oshkosh; Holy Name Retreat House, Chambers Island
Plantico, Paul, St. Francis Xavier Cathedral, Green Bay
Proulx, Rahlf, 1240 N. 10th St., Manitowoc, WI 54220-1906
Quinette, Harvey, Our Lady of Lourdes Church, De Pere
Reed, Maurice, Dir. Office of Permanent Diaconate, St. Bernard Church, Appleton
Reilly, Timothy, Ressurection Church, Green Bay
Reinl, Peter, St. Joseph Church, Appleton
Rocchi, Steven, (Retired), N4297 Cty. WW, Wild Rose, WI 54984-9418
Sambs, Kenneth, St. Anthony Church, Tigerton
Sanchez, Luis, St. Willebrord, Green Bay
Schmidt, Gilbert, Sacred Heart Church, Appleton
Schmidt, Michael, Nativity of Our Lord, Green Bay
Schraufnagel, George, St. Paul Church, Combined Locks
Spielbauer, Norman, St. Margaret Mary Church, Neenah
Steffen, James, Holy Trinity Church, School Hill and St. Gregory Church, St. Nazianz
Sustman, James, St. Luke and St. Mark Churches, Two Rivers
Swinford, Norval, (Retired), N1764 County Rd. D, Hortonville, WI 54944-9802
Teske, Glenn, Port Chap., Apostleship of the Sea
Thetreau, Jerome, Holy Family Church, Marinette
Umentum, Paul, St. Mary of the Angels, Green Bay
Vande Hey, Steven, St. Mary Church, Kaukauna
Vanden Heuvel, Lee P., St. Raphael the Archangel Church, Oshkosh
Vincent, Robert, St. Bernard Church, Appleton
Wessing, Reinhart, St. Thomas More Church, Appleton
Wetzel, Donald, St. Thomas More Church, Appleton
Whitcomb, Patrick, St. Theresa Church, Appleton
Wildenberg, Clay, 115 Professional Plaza, Apt. 138, Neenah, WI 54956-4064
Williams, Nicholas, St. John the Baptist Church, Howard
Zenefski, Paul, Corpus Christi Church, Sturgeon Bay

INSTITUTIONS LOCATED IN THE DIOCESE

[A] SEMINARIES, RELIGIOUS OR SCHOLASTICATES

GREEN BAY. *St. Mary of the Angels Friary*, 645 S. Irwin Ave., 54301-3397. Tel: 920-437-7411; Fax: 920-437-7411. Bro. James Buda, O.F.M., Guardian. Priests 4; Brothers 2.

DE PERE. *St. Norbert Abbey*, 1016 N. Broadway, 54115-2697. Tel: 920-337-4300; Fax: 920-337-4328.
E-mail: gjn@netnet.net
Web site: www.norbertines.org
Rt. Revs. E. Thomas De Wane, O.Praem., Abbot; Benjamin T. Mackin, O.Praem., Abbot Emeritus; Jerome G. Tremel, O.Praem., Abbot Emeritus; Very Rev. David M. Komatz, Prior; Revs. Gary J. Neville, O.Praem., Provisor, Sec. & Treas.; James T. Baraniak, O.Praem., Vocation Coord.; Ambrose J. Peters, O.Praem., Subprior & House Supr.; Andrew G. Cribben, O.Praem., Dir. Formation & Novice Master; Thomas O. Muelemans, O.Praem., Mission Procurator; John L. Bostwick, O.Praem., Dir. Norbertine Center for Spirituality. Priests 75; Brothers 6; Seminarians 5; Total Staff 86.

[B] COLLEGES AND UNIVERSITIES

DE PERE. *St. Norbert College*, 54115-2099. Tel: 920-337-3181; Fax: 920-403-4096.
E-mail: kinnae@mail.snc.edu
Web site: www.snc.edu
For a complete listing, refer to the Colleges and Universities section.

MANITOWOC. *Silver Lake College of the Holy Family*, 2406 S. Alverno Rd., 54220-9319. Tel: 920-684-6691; Fax: 920-684-7082.
E-mail: silver.sl.edu
Web site: www.sl.edu
For a complete listing, refer to the Colleges and Universities section.

[C] HIGH SCHOOLS, DIOCESAN

APPLETON. *Xavier High School*. Coed, 1600 W. Prospect Ave., 54914. Tel: 920-733-6632; Fax: 920-733-5513.
E-mail: mreynebeau@xavier.k12.wi.us
Web site: www.xavier.k12.wi.us
Mr. Matt Reynebeau, Prin.; Mrs. Donna Fahrenkrug, Assoc. Prin.; Andrew Mahoney, Dir. Guidance Dept.; Ms. Sarah Simon, Campus Min. Lay Teachers 42; Students 551.

MANITOWOC. *Roncalli High School*, 2000 Mirro Dr., 54220-6799. Tel: 920-682-8801; Fax: 920-686-8110. Christian Brothers and Franciscan Sisters of Christian Charity. Co-Principals: Mr. Tim Olson; Mr. Mark Schmitt; Mrs. Jennifer Nooker, Campus Min. Brothers 3; Sisters 2; Lay Teachers 25; Students 383.

MARINETTE. *Marinette Catholic Central High School*, 1200 Main St., 54143-2594. Tel: 715-735-7481; Fax: 715-735-3375. Rose Adler, Prin. Lay Teachers 14; Students 103.

NEENAH/MENASHA. *St. Mary Central High School*. 1050 Zephyr Dr., Neenah, 54956-1389. Tel: 920-722-7796; Fax: 920-722-5940. Mrs. Sue Simonsen, Prin. Lay Teachers 24; Students 278.

OSHKOSH. *Lourdes High School*. (Coed.), 110 N. Sawyer St., 54901-5696. Tel: 920-235-5670; Fax: 920-235-7453.
E-mail: Lourdes@vbe.com
Web site: www.vbe.com/~Lourdes
(Part of Unified Catholic Schools of Oshkosh). Bro. Roger Betzold, F.S.C., Prin.; Mr. Tom Baum, Vice Prin. Lay Teachers 21; Students 206.

[D] HIGH SCHOOLS, PRIVATE

GREEN BAY. *Notre Dame de la Baie Academy*, 610 Maryhill Dr., 54303-2092. Tel: 920-498-6464; Fax: 920-498-6456.
E-mail: mschmidt@mail.wiscnet.net
Web site: www.geocities.com/athens/6330/
Timothy M. Schumacher, Prin. Priests 2; Lay Teachers 48; Students 793.

[E] CONSOLIDATED SCHOOLS

APPLETON. *Appleton Catholic Educational System (ACES)*, 300 N. Woods Edge Dr., #3, 54914. Tel: 920-735-9380; Fax: 920-735-1787.
E-mail: aces@athenet.net
Web site: acesys.org
William O'Brien, Exec. Dir. Lay Teachers 85; Total Enrollmen 1,705.

MANITOWOC. *Manitowoc Area Catholic System (MACS)*, 1418 Grand Ave., 54220-6130. Tel: 920-683-6880; Fax: 920-683-6881.
E-mail: jjohnson9@mps.k12.wi.us
Jeffrey Johnson, MACS System Admin.
St. Francis de Sales School. (Grades K-5), 1408 Waldo Blvd., 54220-2610. Tel: 920-683-6892; Fax: 920-683-6889. Sr. Paulyn Vanden Hogen, Prin.

St. Francis Xavier School. (Grades PreK-5), 1418 Grand Ave., 54220-6197. Tel: 920-683-6888; Fax: 920-683-6881. Mrs. Linda Bender, Prin.

St. Frances Cabrini Middle School. (Grades 6-8), 2109 Marshall St., 54220-4959. Tel: 920-683-6884; Fax: 920-683-6882. Mr. James Clark, Prin. Consolidation of Holy Innocents, Sacred Heart, St. Andrew, St. Paul, St. Mary and St. Boniface grade schools in Manitowoc. Sisters 5; Lay Teachers 48; Total Enrollment 690.

NEENAH/MENASHA. *Twin Cities Catholic Educational System (TCCES).* Tel: 920-722-7922; Fax: 920-722-1838. 312 Nicolet Blvd., Menasha, 54952-3334. Tel: 920-722-7922; Fax: 920-722-1838. Julie Klein, Contact Person. Consolidation of St. Gabriel, St. Margaret Mary, St. Mary Elementary, Seton Catholic Middle School and St. Mary Central High School. Lay Teachers 100; Total Enrollment 1058.

OSHKOSH. *Unified Catholic Schools of Oshkosh,* 110 N. Sawyer St., 54901. Tel: 920-426-3626. Brothers 1; Sisters 4; Lay Teachers 145; Total Enrollment 767.

TWO RIVERS. *Two Rivers Catholic Schools (TRCCS),* 2203 12th St., 54241. Tel: 920-794-7266; Fax: 920-794-7622. Consolidation of St. Luke and St. Mark Schools. Josephine Vermillion, Prin. Lay Teachers 17; Students 211.

[F] GENERAL HOSPITALS

GREEN BAY. *Libertas Treatment Center for Chemically Dependent,* 1701 Dousman St., 54303-3282. Tel: 920-498-8600; Fax: 920-496-2027
For a complete listing, refer to the Hospitals section.

St. Mary's Hospital-Medical Center, 1726 Shawano Ave., 54303-3282. Tel: 920-498-4200; Fax: 920-498-1861.
Web site: www.stmgb.org
For a complete listing, refer to the Hospitals section.

St. Vincent Hospital, P.O. Box 13508, 54307-3508. Tel: 920-433-0111; 433-8162; Fax: 920-431-3275.
E-mail: mbush@stvgb.org
For a complete listing, refer to the Hospitals section.

ANTIGO. *Langlade Memorial Hospital,* 112 E. 5th Ave., 55409. Tel: 715-623-2331; Fax: 715-623-9359
For a complete listing, refer to the Hospitals section.

APPLETON. *St. Elizabeth Hospital,* 1506 S. Oneida St., 54915-1305. Tel: 920-738-2000; Fax: 920-738-8913.
E-mail: Bturner@affinityhealth.org
For a complete listing, refer to the Hospitals section.

KEWAUNEE. *St. Mary Kewaunee Area Memorial Hospital,* 810 Lincoln St., 54216. Tel: 920-388-2210; Fax: 920-388-1166
For a complete listing, refer to the Hospitals section.

MANITOWOC. *Holy Family Memorial, Inc.,* 2300 Western Ave., P.O. Box 1450, 54221-1450. Tel: 920-684-2011; Fax: 920-684-2522.
E-mail: services@hfmhealth.org
Web site: www.hfmhealth.org
For a complete listing, refer to the Hospitals section.

OSHKOSH. *Mercy Medical Center,* 500 S. Oakwood Rd., P.O. Box 3370, 54902-3370. Tel: 920-236-2000; Fax: 920-223-0508.
E-mail: kphillip@affinityhealth.org
For a complete listing, refer to the Hospitals section.

STURGEON BAY. *Door County Memorial Hospital,* 323 S. 18th Ave., 54235. Tel: 920-743-5566; Fax: 920-743-8165.
E-mail: gworrick@dcmh.org
Web site: www.ministryhealth.org
For a complete listing, refer to the Hospitals section.

[G] PROTECTIVE INSTITUTIONS

GREEN BAY. *McClosky Program, Inc.,* 2560 Shawano Ave., P.O. Box 10357, 54313. Tel: 920-434-8208; Fax: 920-662-0047
For a complete listing, refer to the Special Care Facilities section.

Our Lady of Charity Center, Inc., 2560 Shawano Ave., P.O. Box 10357, 54313. Tel: 920-434-8208; Fax: 920-662-0047
For a complete listing, refer to the Special Care Facilities section.

OSHKOSH. *The Convent Project, Inc.,* 471 High Ave., 54901. Tel: 920-233-1894
For a complete listing, refer to the Special Care Facilities section.

TWO RIVERS. *Sisters Treatment Group Home,* 3904 Martin Ln., 54241. Tel: 920-794-1524; Fax: 920-794-1524
For a complete listing, refer to the Special Care Facilities section.

[H] HOMES FOR AGED

GREEN BAY. *The McCormick Memorial Home for the Aged,* 212 Iroquois Ave., 54301-1918. Tel: 920-437-0883; Fax: 920-437-2696
For a complete listing, refer to the Special Care Facilities section.

APPLETON. *Franciscan Care and Rehabilitation Center, Inc.,* 2915 N. Meade St., 54911-1598. Tel: 920-831-8700; Fax: 920-731-3206.
E-mail: nbassett@affinityhealth.org
For a complete listing, refer to the Special Care Facilities section.

KAUKAUNA. *St. Paul Elder Services, Inc.,* 316 E. Fourteenth St., 54130. Tel: 920-766-6020; Fax: 920-766-7945.
Web site: stpaulelders.org
For a complete listing, refer to the Special Care Facilities section.

MANITOWOC. *Felician Village Inc.,* 1700 S. 18th St., 54220. Tel: 920-683-8811; Fax: 920-683-9292
For a complete listing, refer to the Special Care Facilities section.

St. Mary's Home for the Aged, 2005 Division St., 54220-5699. Tel: 920-684-7171; Fax: 920-684-0240.
E-mail: stmarys@lakefield.net
For a complete listing, refer to the Special Care Facilities section.

NEENAH. *Assisi Homes of Neenah, Inc.,* 210 Byrd Ave., 54956. Tel: 920-722-5100; Fax: 920-722-5171
For a complete listing, refer to the Special Care Facilities section.

Villa Saint Clare, Inc., 130 Byrd Ave., 54946. Tel: 920-722-5100; Fax: 920-722-5171
For a complete listing, refer to the Special Care Facilities section.

NEW LONDON. *St. Joseph Residence, Inc., New London,* 107 E. Beckert Rd., 54961. Tel: 920-982-5354; Fax: 920-982-5420.
E-mail: sjradm@athenet.net
For a complete listing, refer to the Special Care Facilities section.

NIAGARA. *Maryhill Manor (SNF),* 501 Madison Ave., 54151. Tel: 715-251-3178; Fax: 715-251-1200
For a complete listing, refer to the Special Care Facilities section.

[I] MONASTERIES AND RESIDENCES OF PRIESTS AND BROTHERS

GREEN BAY. *St. Mary of the Angels Friary,* 645 S. Irwin Ave., 54301-3303. Tel: 920-437-7411; 437-1979 (Res.); Fax: 920-437-7411. Franciscan Friars, Assumption of the Blessed Virgin Mary Province (Order of Friars Minor). Revs. Albert Lis, O.F.M.; Nathan Jaskulski, O.F.M., In Res. Revs. Campion Kluczynski; Maynard Kolodziej, O.F.M.; Bros. James Buda, O.F.M., Guardian; Stephen Dupuis, O.F.M., Vicar. Priests 4; Brothers 2.

APPLETON. *St. Fidelis Friary,* 1100 N. Ballard Rd., 54911-5100. Tel: 920-954-8954; Fax: 920-954-1095. Order of Friars Minor Capachin. Revs. Loran Miller, O.F.M.Cap., Guardian; David Belongea, O.F.M.Cap.; Benjamin Adams, O.F.M.Cap.; William Alcuin, O.F.M.Cap.; Claude Pulvermacher, O.F.M.Cap.; Bruce Riski, O.F.M.Cap.; Patrick Berther, O.F.M.Cap.; Camilus Doerfler, O.F.M.Cap.; Joseph Doefler, O.F.M.Cap.; Donald Brody, O.F.M.Cap.; Ambrose De Groot, O.F.M.Cap.; Silas Baumann, O.F.M.Cap.; Pius Pulvermacher, O.F.M.Cap.; Reynold Rynda, O.F.M.Cap.; Ambrose Simon, O.F.M.Cap.; Giles Soyka, O.F.M.Cap.; Vianney Thibedeau, O.F.M.Cap.; Grigion Wenning, O.F.M.Cap.; Bros. Carmel Labadie, O.F.M.Cap.; Cyrus Toschik, O.F.M.Cap.; John Gau, O.F.M.Cap.; Conrad Heinen, O.F.M.Cap. Priests 18; Brothers 4; Staff 3.

St. Joseph Friary, 404 W. Lawrence St., 54911-5855. Tel: 920-734-7195; Fax: 920-734-0227.
Web site: www.stjosephparish.org
Order of Friars Minor Capuchin. Revs. John Holly, O.F.M.Cap.; Kenneth Reinhart, O.F.M.Cap.

DE PERE. *St. Joseph Priory,* 103 Grant St., 54115-2001. Tel: 920-403-3572 (Office). Residence for Norbertine Community. Revs. James T. Baraniak, O.Praem.; John Bostwick, O.Praem.; Robert J. Cornell, O.Praem.; Rowland C. De Peaux, O.Praem.; Jay M. Fostner, O.Praem.; Conrad J. Kratz, O.Praem., House Supr.; Brendan J. McKeough, O.Praem.; Gery G. Meehan, O.Praem.; Thomas O. Meulemans, O.Praem.; Gilbert Mihayli, O.Praem.; Dane Radecki, O.Praem.; Joseph S. Rekasi, O.Praem.; Timothy D. Shillcox, O.Praem.; Harvey H. Toonen, O.Praem.; Robert Vande Hey, O.Praem. Priests 15.

St. Norbert Abbey, 1016 N. Broadway, 54115-2697. Tel: 920-337-4300; Fax: 920-337-4328.
E-mail: gjn@netnet.net
Web site: www.norbertines.org
Canons Regular of Premontre. Legal Titles: *The Premonstratensian Fathers.*; *NORBERT & CO., a nominee of The Premonstratensian Fathers, Norbertine Fathers.*; *St. Norbert Abbey, Inc.*; *Augustine Stewardship Fund Trust.*; *Norbertine Retirement Fund Trust.*; *St. Norbert Abbey Seminary and Education Fund Trust.*; *The Walnut Markets, Inc.*; *Los Amigos del Peru, Inc.* Rt. Revs. E. Thomas De Wane, O.Praem., Abbot; Benjamin T. Mackin, O.Praem., Abbot Emeritus; Sylvester M. Killeen, O.Praem., Abbot Emeritus; Jerome G. Tremel, O.Praem., Abbot Emeritus; Very Rev. David M. Komatz, O.Praem., Prior; Revs. Gary J. Neville, O.Praem., Provisor & Sec.-Treas.; Ambrose J. Peeters, O.Praem., Subprior & House Supr.; Thomas O. Meulemans, O.Praem., Mission Procurator; Bartholomew A. Agar, O.Praem.; Jordan R. Blecha, O.Praem.; Bernard M. Brunette, O.Praem.; Robert E. Carson, O.Praem.; Angelo J. Feldkamp, O.Praem.; Roderick R. Fenzl, O.Praem.; Robert K. Finnegan, O.Praem.; Michael F. Frisch, O.Praem., Graduate Studies, Univ. of MI, Ann Arbor, MI; Guy E. Guyon, O.Praem; Robert L. Hyde, O.Praem.; Gilbert H. Jacobs, O.Praem.; John P. Kastenholz, O.Praem.; Gerald B. Kemper, O.Praem.; Laurence A. Mayer, O.Praem.; Alfred A. McBride, Weston, MA; Faustin Misakabo Mulenga, O.Praem. (Kinshasa, Congo); Conan P. Mulrooney, O.Praem.; Richard D. Mulroy, O.Praem.; James P. Nielson, O.Praem.; Donald C. Noel, O.Praem.; Peter J. Renard, O.Praem.; Robert B. Reppen, O.Praem.; Julian C. Resch, O.Praem.; William H. Ribbens, O.Praem.; Joseph A. Rohlinger, O.Praem; Stephen J. Rossey, O.Praem.; Glen F. Siebers, O.Praem; Roman R. Vanasse, O.Praem.; Steven J. Vanden Boogard, O.Praem, (Chap. United States Navy, Monterey, CA); Achilles E. Van Hoof, O.Praem., (Tongerlo, Belgium); Albin V. Veszelovszky, O.Praem., (Godollo, Hungary); Michael J. Weber, O.Praem., (Chap., United States Air Force, Travis AFB, CA); Bros. Robert J. Craanen, O.Praem.; Steven J. Herro, O.Praem.; Gerlac J. Riess, O.Praem.; Clement G. Tourangeau, O.Praem. Brothers 6; Priests 75; Priests at St. Norbert Abbey 37; Seminarians 5.
Retreats, Missions and Renewals: Rev. Robert E. Carson, O.Praem.; Rt. Rev. Jerome G. Tremel, O.Praem.
Priests serving in foreign countries: Archdiocese of Lima, Peru, Padres Norbertinos, Correo Las Flores, Lima 36, Lima, Peru, South America. Tel: 011-511-992-4323 (Cellular); 011-511-458-0715 (Regular); Fax: 011-511-459-5905. Archdiocese of Iquitos, Peru, Santa Clotilde, Rio Napo, Apartado 216, Iquitos, Peru, South America. Tel: 011-51-94-25-1932; Fax: 011-51-94-25-1932. Revs. Lambert C. Baeten, O.Praem.; John P. MacCarthy, O.Praem.

NEW HOLSTEIN. *Salvatorian Center Residence,* 53061-0001. Tel: 920-898-5635. Brothers 4.

Salvatorian Public Relations, Salvatorian Center, 53062. Tel: 920-898-4201; Fax: 920-898-4736. Rev. Gregory Coulthardt, S.D.S.

Salvatorian Mission Warehouse, 53061. Tel: 920-898-5898; Fax: 920-898-4736. Bro. Regis Fust, S.D.S., Dir. Mission Supply Prog.

OSHKOSH. *Community of Our Lady.* (Diocesan Pious Union), 2804 Oakwood Ln., 54904-8406. Tel: 920-233-5633; Fax: 920-233-5604. Very Rev. Regis N. Barwig, Prior; Revs. Eugene E. Kalinski; Augustine Serafini.

PULASKI. *Assumption of B.V.M. Friary,* 143 E. Pulaski St., P.O. Box 100, 54162-0100. Tel: 920-822-5422; Fax: 920-822-5423.
E-mail: abvm@execpc.com
Web site: www.ofm.abvm.org
Headquarters of Franciscan Friars Assumption BVM Province, Inc. (Order of Franciscan Fathers, Order of Friars Minor). Revs. Thomas Luczak, O.F.M., Prov. Min.; Thomas Wojciechowski, O.F.M., Prov. Vicar; John Cella, O.F.M., Treas.; Eliot Bacia, O.F.M., Prov. Sec.; Gregory Plata, O.F.M., Voc. Dir.

Friary, 54162. Tel: 414-822-8125. Revs. Melvin Wierzbicki, O.F.M.; Finian Zaucha, O.F.M.; Bros. Herman-Joseph Peplinski, O.F.M.; Anthony Gancarz, O.F.M.; Peter Rydza, O.F.M.; Gregory Stasinski, O.F.M.; David Typek, O.F.M.; Henry Kolbok, O.F.M.; Austin Mysliwiec, O.F.M.; Andrew Brophy, O.F.M., Guardian; Michael Janiak, O.F.M.; Andrew Giba, O.F.M.
Retired-Infirm - Elsewhere: St. Mary's Home, Manitowoc: Revs. Thomas Wojciechowski, O.F.M., Chap.; Herman J. Ziemba, O.F.M.; Josaphat Ledwon, O.F.M.; Sylvester E. Makarewicz, O.F.M.; Arent Julian, O.F.M.; Patrick Szemla, O.F.M.; Humphrey Tobias, O.F.M.; Bros. Louis Modiszewski, O.F.M.; Otto Janowiak, O.F.M.; Eugene Lacny, O.F.M.; Miles Brainer, O.F.M., Villa Alverna, N. 11450 Rademaker Rd., Wausaukee, 54177. Tel: 715-732-6612. Franciscan Friars, Assumption Prov. Bro. David Typek, O.F.M., Dir.
Outside of Diocese: Revs. Ladislaus Szepe, S.F.O., Sarasota, FL; Lazarus Macior, O.F.M., Univ. of Akron, Biology Dept., Akron, OH, 44325-3908. Rev. Adam Szufel, O.F.M., Warner Robins, GA, 31088. Rev. Robert Kroll, McAllen, TX 78501-4304; Bros. John Brice, O.F.M., South Africa; Mario Nagy, O.F.M., Novo Sibirsk, Russia; Andre Lemay, O.F.M., Las Vegas, NV; Augustine Fraszczak, O.F.M., Philippines.
Priests of the Province Serving Abroad: Revs. Sergius Wroblewski, O.F.M., South Africa; Lyle Chrobak, O.F.M., Guaymas, Mexico; Arcadius Smolinski, O.F.M., Europe; Henry Howaniec, O.F.M.,

Kazakstan; James Heinsch, O.F.M., Holy Land; Barnabas Gorski, O.F.M., Morocco.
Military Chaplains: Revs. Conrad Targonski, O.F.M.; Randall Roberts, O.F.M.
Franciscan Publishers and Printers, Inc. Tel: 920-822-5833.

ST. NAZIANZ. *Religious House of the Society of the Divine Savior S.D.S.* Salvatorian Community. 206 Church, 54232. Tel: 920-773-2794. Bros. Thaddeus Huebner, S.D.S.; Florian Schueth, S.D.S. Brothers 2.

[J] CONVENTS AND RESIDENCES FOR SISTERS

GREEN BAY. *Hospital Sisters of the Third Order of St. Francis.* Sr. Maureen O'Connor, O.S.F., Prov. Sec. & Treas., 304 David Dr., 54303. Tel: 920-497-1882. Sisters 2. 1015 S. Webster St., 54305. Tel: 920-432-1337. Sisters 3.
St. Francis Convent of Sisters of St. Francis of the Holy Cross, 3025 Bay Settlement Rd., 54311-7301. Tel: 920-468-1828; Fax: 920-468-1207.
E-mail: sistersosf@gbonline.com
Sr. Sally Ann Brickner, Pres. Sisters 86; In Diocese 83.
Sisters of Our Lady of Charity of the North American Union, Inc., 2560 Shawano Ave., P.O. Box 10357, 54313. Tel: 920-434-8208; Fax: 920-662-0047. Sr. Patrick Dolan, Supr. Sisters 19.

MANITOWOC. *Holy Family Convent of Franciscan Sisters of Christian Charity.* Motherhouse and Novitiate dedicated to the Holy Family, 2409 S. Alverno Rd., 54220-9320. Tel: 920-682-7728; Fax: 920-682-4195. Revs. DePaul Sobotka, O.F.M., Chap.; Samuel D. Jadin, O.Praem.; Sr. Paula Vanden Hogen, Community Dir. Sisters 471; In Diocese 344; Novices 1; Total in Residence 180.
St. Clare Convent, 3 Riverview Dr., 54220. Tel: 920-682-5145.
E-mail: smnbrown@juno.com
Sr. Michael Majeskie, Dir. Franciscan Sisters of Christian Charity. Sisters 8.
St. Francis Convent, 6835 Hwy. 151, 54220. Tel: 920-684-7884; Fax: 920-682-4195. Sr. Debra Shepeck, Sec. Franciscan Sisters of Christian Charity. Sisters 45.

NEW FRANKEN. *Monastery of the Holy Name of Jesus, Ltd.* Discalced Carmelite Nuns, 4047 Chapel Dr., 54229-9768. Tel: 920-866-1815.
E-mail: holynamecarmel@juno.com
Mother Mary Elizabeth, Prioress. Total 10.

OSHKOSH. *SSM Franciscan Courts,* 815 S. Westhaven Dr., 54904-7978. Tel: 920-426-2440; Fax: 920-426-3196.
E-mail: franct@athenet.net
Sisters of the Sorrowful Mother. Steve Komp, Admin.; Brenda Retzlaff, Human Resources Mgr.; Tammi Reiner, Administrative Coord.; Rev. Michael R. Koch, Chap. Sisters 43.

ST. NAZIANZ. *St. Mary's Convent-Sisters of the Divine Savior.* (Home for retired sisters), 300 S. 2nd Ave., 54232. Tel: 920-773-2515. Sr. Jane Barman, S.D.S., Coord. Sisters 5.

[K] CAMPS AND COMMUNITY CENTERS

SHAWANO. *Camp Tekawitha.* (Located on Loon Lake, Shawano). Mailing Address: P.O. Box 23825, Green Bay, 54305-3825. Tel: 715-526-2316, Ext. 8511. Mrs. Roberta Larson, Dir. Capacity 160. (Boys & Girls ages 7 to 14).

[L] SHRINES

ROBINSONVILLE. *The Chapel of Our Lady of Good Help (Diocesan Shrine)-Robinsonville,* 4047 Chapel Dr., 54229-9768. Tel: 920-866-2571.

[M] RETREAT HOUSES

APPLETON. *Monte Alverno Retreat Center,* 1000 N. Ballard Rd., 54911-5148. Tel: 920-733-8526; Fax: 920-733-7562.
E-mail: montealverno@juno.com
The Province of St. Joseph of the Capuchin Order, Inc. Revs. Werner Wolf, O.F.M.Cap., Dir.; Lester Bach, O.F.M.Cap.; Timon Costello, O.F.M.Cap.; Ellis Zimmer, O.F.M.Cap.; Bro. John Kocian, O.F.M.Cap. Priests 4; Brothers 1; Retreatants Annually 2,700; Total in residence 5; Total Staff 16.

BAILEYS HARBOR. *St. Joseph Retreat Center,* 3035 O'Brien Rd., 54202-9132. Tel: 920-839-2391; Fax: 920-839-2391.
E-mail: malbert.mail@rtol.com
Sr. Mary Anne Albert, S.S.S.F., Dir.; Rev. Byron Haaland, S.C.J., Admin. Retreat & Coord. Community; Sr. Lorraine Aspenleiter, S.S.S.F.; Bros. John Monek, S.C.J.; Andrew Lewandowski, S.C.J. In res. Rev. Joseph Dean, S.C.J. Priests 2; Brothers 2; Sisters 2; Total in residence 6; Total Staff 12.

CHAMBERS ISLAND. *Holy Name Retreat House.* Mailing Address: 1825 Riverside Dr., P.O. Box 23825, Green Bay, 54305-3825. Tel: 920-437-7531; Fax: 920-437-0694. Conducted by Diocese of Green Bay.

DE PERE. *Norbertine Center for Spirituality.* (An Apostolate of the Norbertine Fathers), St. Norbert Abbey, 1016 N. Broadway, 54115-2697. Tel: 920-337-4315; Fax: 920-337-4328.
E-mail: norbertinecenter@yahoo.com
Web site: www.norbertines.org
Rev. John L. Bostwick, O.Praem., Dir. Total in residence 2; Total Staff 6.

MENASHA. *Mount Tabor Center,* 522 2nd St., 54952-3112. Tel: 920-722-8918; Fax: 920-722-8918. Theresa Collier, Administrative Asst.; Sr. Mary Jo Kirt, Admin. Youth Ministers: Lisa Ann Krutzik; Dick Lauer. Total Staff 4.

OSHKOSH. *Jesuit Retreat House,* 4800 Fahrnwald Rd., Hwy. 45, 54902-7598. Tel: 920-231-9060. Society of Jesus. Revs. Richard F. McCaslin, S.J., Dir.; Robert Dufford, S.J.; Orville J. Catuso, S.J.; Sr. Marie Schwan, C.S.J.; Revs. Eugene F. Zimmerman, S.J.; Eugene C. Kollasch, S.J.

[N] NEWMAN CENTERS

GREEN BAY. *Ecumenical Center-UWGB,* 2420 Nicolet Dr., 54311-7001. Tel: 920-465-5133; Fax: 920-465-0128.
E-mail: ecumenical2@itol.com
Web site: ecumenical-center.org
Lawrence University Newman Center. (Appleton).
University of Wisconsin Manitowoc Campus Newman Center. (Manitowoc). Tel: 920-684-6691.
University of Wisconsin Marinette Campus Newman Center. (Marinette).
University of Wisconsin Fox Valley Campus Newman Center. (Menasha).
University of Wisconsin Newman Center, 717 W. Irving Ave., Oshkosh, WI, 54901-4319. Tel: 920-233-5555. Rev. Robert Kollath, Dir. & Chap.

[O] MISCELLANEOUS LISTINGS

GREEN BAY. *The Catholic Foundation of the Diocese of Green Bay, Inc.,* 1910 S. Webster Ave., P.O. Box 23825, 54305-3825. Tel: 920-437-7531, Ext. 8173; Fax: 920-435-1330.
E-mail: cbrawner@gbdioc.org
Web site: www.gbdioc.org
Cindi Brawner, Exec. Dir.
The Diocesan Charismatic Renewal Center, 1227 13th Ave., 54304. Tel: 920-405-1960. Rev. Msgr. James Vanden Hogen, Liaison; Mrs. Karen Wautlet, Asst. Liaison; Judy Goolsbey, Office Mgr.
Green Bay Area Catholic High School Foundation, L.T.D., P.O. Box 23825, 54305-3825. Tel: 920-437-7531. Mr. Dick White, Pres.; Rev. Edward J. Smith, O.Praem., Exec. Dir.
A New Genesis (ANG). An Association of the Faithful, 1825 S. Riverside Dr., P.O. Box 23825, 54305-3825. Tel: 920-437-7531; Fax: 920-437-0694.
E-mail: dbaumann@athenet.net
Sr. Diane Baumann, Mod., St. Joseph Chapel; Most Rev. Aloysius J. Wycislo. Total Members 29.
Notre Dame de la Baie Foundation, Inc., 610 Maryhill Dr., 54303. Tel: 920-429-6100.
E-mail: grossm@notredameacademy.com
Web site: www.NDAFdn.org
Dr. Michael Gross, Pres.
Sacred Heart Seminary, Inc., P.O. Box 23825, 54305-3825. Tel: 920-437-7531; Fax: 920-435-1330. Rev. Msgr. John B. Dewane, Admin.; Sr. Mary Bride Crubbs, Chancellor.
St. Joseph Corporation, Diocesan Central Offices, P.O. Box 23825, 54305-3825. Tel: 920-437-7531; Fax: 920-437-0694.
E-mail: vpelle@gbdioc.orgtier
Web site: www.gbdioc.org
Mr. Vincent Pelletier, Admin.
Teens Encounter Christ (TEC), Green Bay Chapter, P.O. Box 23825, 54305-3825. Tel: 920-437-7531; Fax: 920-437-0694.
E-mail: tpichler@gbdioc.org
Mr. Tony Pichler, Diocesan Liaison.

APPLETON.
Christ Child Society of Appleton Wisconsin, Inc., 522 N. Union St., 54911. Tel: 920-733-1275. Co-Presidents: Midge Schweitzer; Betty Milhaupt; Tottie Oudenhoven, Sec.; Germaine Goudemans, Treas.
St. Elizabeth Hospital Community Foundation, Inc., 1506 S. Oneida St., 54915-1397. Tel: 920-738-2859; Fax: 920-738-0949.
E-mail: Lweiner@affinityhealth.org
Franciscan Sisters, Daughters of the Sacred Heart of Jesus and Mary (Wheaton, IL). Mr. Kevin Nolan, CEO Affinity Health System; Lisa Weiner, Exec. Dir. & Pres.

DE PERE. *Augustine Stewardship Fund Trust,* 1016 N. Broadway, 54115-2697. Tel: 920-337-4300; Fax: 920-337-4328.
E-mail: gjn@netnet.net
Web site: www.norbertines.org
Canons Regular of Magnovarad, Ltd., 1016 N. Broadway, 54115-2697. Tel: 920-337-4300; Fax: 920-337-4328. Rev. Albin V. Veszelovszky, O.Praem., Pres.; Rt. Rev. Jerome G. Tremel, O.Praem., Vice Pres.; Revs. Joseph S. Rekasi, O.Praem.; Robert K. Finnegan, O.Praem., Sec. & Treas.
Los Amigos del Peru, Inc., 1016 N. Broadway St., 54115-2697. Tel: 920-337-4300; Fax: 920-337-4328.
NORBERT & CO. A nominee of The Premonstratensian Fathers, 1016 N. Broadway, 54115-2697. Tel: 920-337-4300; Fax: 920-337-4328.
E-mail: gjn@netnet.net
Web site: www.norbertines.org
Rt. Rev. E. Thomas DeWane, O.Praem.; Very Rev. David M. Komatz, O.Praem.; Rev. Gary J. Neville, O.Praem.
Norbertine Generalate, Inc., 1016 N. Broadway, 54115-2697. Tel: 920-337-4300; Fax: 920-337-4328.
E-mail: rkfinn@netnet.net
Web site: www.premontre.org
Most Rev. Hermenegild J. Noyens, O.Praem., Pres., Rome, Italy; Rt. Rev. Benjamin T. Mackin, O.Praem., Vice Pres.; Rev. Robert K. Finnegan, O.Praem., Sec. & Treas.
Norbertine Retirement Fund Trust, 1016 N. Broadway, 54115-2697. Tel: 920-337-4300; Fax: 920-337-4328.
E-mail: gjn@netnet.net
Web site: www.norbertines.org
St. Norbert Abbey Seminary and Education Fund Trust, 1016 N. Broadway, 54115-2697. Tel: 920-337-4300; Fax: 920-337-4328.
E-mail: gjn@netnet.net
Web site: www.norbertines.org

DEERBROOK.
Living Waters International, Inc., N7544 County Rd. S., 54424. Tel: 715-627-4782; Fax: 715-627-4782.
E-mail: livinh20@antigopro.net
Dr. Stephen L. Zimmerman, Ph.D., Pres. Total in residence 4; Staff 4.

MANITOWOC. *Franciscan Sisters of Christian Charity HealthCare Ministry, Inc.,* 1415 S. Rapids Rd., 54220-9302. Tel: 920-684-7071; Fax: 920-684-6417.
E-mail: lwolf@fhcm.org
Web site: www.fhcm.org
Sr. Laura J. Wolf, O.S.F., Pres.

MENASHA. *Affinity Health System,* 1570 Midway Place, 54952. Tel: 920-720-1713; Fax: 920-720-1907.
E-mail: Knolan@affinityhealth.org
Web site: www.affinity.org
Kevin Nolan, Pres. & CEO. Sponsored by Wheaton Franciscan Services, Inc. (Wheaton, IL) and Ministry Health Care, Inc. (Milwaukee, WI).

NEENAH. *Global Outreach, Inc.,* 433 Hawthorne St., 54956. Tel: 920-727-1207.
E-mail: globalmom@aol.com
Gary Elmer, Pres.; Joseph Jankowski, Vice Pres. & Treas.; Jeanine Jankowski, Sec.; Mary Piette, Dir.
St. Mary High School Foundation, Inc., 1050 Zephyr Dr., 54956-1389.

OSHKOSH. *Villa St. Theresa, Inc.,* 1255 W. 18th Ave., 54901. Tel: 920-231-7701. Total Assisted Annually 70.

[P] CLOSED PARISHES

GREEN BAY. *Green Bay Diocesan Archives,* 1910 S. Webster Ave., P.O. Box 23825, 54305-3825. Tel: 920-437-7531, Ext. 8186. Parish sacramental records for parishes that have closed or merged can be found at the locations listed below. As the location of sacramental records can change periodically, inquiries for records of parishes on this list should be directed to the above address.
St. Joseph, Alverno. Please see St. Thomas the Apostle, Northeim.
St Wendel, Cleveland. Please see St. Thomas the Apostle, Northeim.
St. John the Baptist, Coleman. Please see Ss. Francis and Wenceslaus, Coleman/Klondike.
St. Francis of Assisi, Coleman/Pound. Please see Ss. Francis and Wenceslaus, Coleman/Klondike.
St. Boniface, De Pere. Please see Our Lady of Lourdes, De Pere.
St. Joseph, De Pere. Please see Our Lady of Lourdes, De Pere.
SS. Cyril and Methodius, Eaton. Please see St. Thomas the Apostle, Humboldt.
St. William, Eland. Please see Holy Family-St. William, Wittenberg.
Our Lady Queen of Peace, Humboldt. Please see St. Thomas the Apostle, Humboldt.
St. George, King. Please see St. Mary Magdalene, Waupaca.
St. Wenceslaus, Klondike. Please see Ss. Francis and Wenceslaus, Coleman/Klondike.
St. John, Krok. Please see St. Therese de Lisieux, Stangelville.

St. Stanislaus Kostka, Langlade. Please see Ss. James and Stanislaus, White Lake/Langlade.
St. Charles Borromeo, Lena. Please see Holy Cross, Lena/Spruce.
St. Peter, Lincoln. Please see St. Peter and St. Hubert, Rosiere/Lincoln.
St. Patrick, Maple Grove. Please see St. Patrick, Reedsville/Maple Grove.
St. Francis De Paul, Marchand/Duvall. Please see St. Louis, Dyckesville.
Our Lady of Lourdes, Marinette. Please see Holy Family, Marinette.
Sacred Heart of Jesus, Marinette. Please see Holy Family, Marinette.
St. Anthony, Marinette. Please see Holy Family, Marinette.
St. Joseph, Marinette. Please see Holy Family, Marinette.
St. Joseph, Montpelier. Please see St. Therese de Lisieux, Stangelville.
St. Joseph-St. John, Montpelier/Krok. Please see St. Therese de Lisieux Stangelville.
St. Mary, Namur. Please see St. Francis and St. Mary, Brussels/Namur.
St. Casimir, Northeim. Please see St. Thomas the Apostle, Northeim.
St. Joseph, Oconto. Please see Holy Trinity, Oconto.
St. Peter, Oconto. Please see Holy Trinity, Oconto.
St. Isidore, Osman. Please see St. Thomas the Apostle, Northeim.
St. Leo, Pound. Please see Ss. Francis and Wenceslaus, Coleman/Klondike.
St. Adalbert, Slovan. Please see Holy Trinity, Casco/Slovan.
Sacred Heart, Spruce. Please see Holy Cross, Lena/Spruce.
St. John the Baptist, St. John. Please see St. John-Sacred Heart, Sherwood/St. John.
St. Lawrence, Stangelville. Please see St. Therese de Lisieux, Stangelville.
St. Mary, Stark. Please see St. Mary, Glenmore/Stark.
St. Odile, Thiry Daems. Please see St. Joseph, Champion.
St. Martin, Tonet. Please see St. Joseph, Champion.
Sacred Heart, Two Rivers. Please see Holy Redeemer-Sacred Heart, Two Rivers.
St. Amand, Walhain. Please see St. Joseph, Champion.
St. Hedwig, West Kewaunee. Please see St. Therese de Lisieux, Stangelville.

RELIGIOUS INSTITUTES OF MEN REPRESENTED IN THE DIOCESE

For further details refer to the corresponding bracketed number in the Religious Institutes of Men or Women section.

[0330]—*Brothers of the Christian Schools*.—F.S.C.
[0900]—*Canons Regular of Premontre*.—O.Praem.
[0470]—*The Capuchin Friars*. (Province of St. Joseph).—O.F.M.Cap.
[0220]—*Congregation of the Blessed Sacrament*.—S.S.S.
[1130]—*Congregation of the Priests of the Sacred Heart*.—S.C.J.
[0690]—*Franciscan Friars*.—O.F.M.
[0305]—*Institute of Christ the King*.
[0690]—*Jesuit Fathers and Brothers*. (Wisconsin Province).—S.J.
[0910]—*Oblates of Mary Immaculate*.—O.M.I.
[1200]—*Society of the Divine Savior*.—S.D.S.

RELIGIOUS INSTITUTES OF WOMEN REPRESENTED IN THE DIOCESE

[3710]—*Congregation of the Sisters of St. Agnes*.—C.S.A.
[0420]—*Discalced Carmelite Nuns*.—O.C.D.
[1070-03]—*Dominican Sisters*.—O.P.
[1070-09]—*Dominican Sisters*.—O.P.
[1070-13]—*Dominican Sisters*.—O.P.
[1070-14]—*Dominican Sisters*.—O.P.
[1170]—*Felician Sisters*.—C.S.S.F.
[1230]—*Franciscan Sisters of Christian Charity*.—O.S.F.
[1240]—*Franciscan Sisters, Daughters of the Sacred Hearts of Jesus and Mary*.—O.S.F.
[1820]—*Hospital Sisters of the Third Order of St. Francis*.—O.S.F.
[3070]—*North American Union Sisters of Our Lady of Charity*.—N.A.U.-O.L.C.
[3440]—*Religious Hospitallers of Saint Joseph*.—R.H.S.J.
[2970]—*School Sisters of Notre Dame*.—S.S.N.D.
[1680]—*School Sisters of St. Francis*.—O.S.F.
[0500]—*Sisters of Charity of Nazareth*.—S.C.N.
[0430]—*Sisters of Charity of the Blessed Virgin Mary*.—B.V.M.
[2630]—*Sisters of Mercy of the Holy Cross*.—S.C.S.C.
[3800]—*Sisters of St. Elizabeth*.—S.S.E.
[1705]—*The Sisters of St. Francis of Assisi*.—O.S.F. - S.S.S.F.
[1550]—*Sisters of St. Francis of the Holy Cross*.—O.S.F.
[3840]—*Sisters of St. Joseph of Carondelet*. (Prov. of St. Louis).—C.S.J.
[3880]—*Sisters of St. Joseph of Medaille*.—C.S.J.
[3930]—*Sisters of St. Joseph of the Third Order of St. Francis*.—S.S.J.-T.O.S.F.
[1030]—*Sisters of the Divine Savior*.—S.D.S.
[4100]—*Sisters of the Sorrowful Mother (Third Order of St. Francis)*.—S.S.M.

DIOCESAN CEMETERIES

GREEN BAY. *Diocesan Cemeteries*, P.O. Box 23825, 54305-3825. Tel: 920-437-7531, Ext. 8229. Mr. John C. Nelson, Diocesan Dir.
Allouez Catholic Cemetery, 2121 Riverside Dr., 54301.
Allouez Chapel Mausoleum, 2121 Riverside Dr., 54301.
Queen of Peace Cemetery & Mausoleum, Box 535, Antigo, 54409.
St. Joseph Cemetery, P.O. Box 2676, Appleton, 54913-2676.
Mount Calvary Cemetery, 1307 Lourdes Ave., De Pere, 54115.
Mount Olivet Cemetery, S. Erie St., De Pere, 54115.
Calvary Cemetery & Calvary Chapel Mausoleum, 2601 S. 14th St., Manitowoc, 54220-6467.
Oconto Catholic Cemetery, c/o 716 Madison St., Oconto, 54153. Tel: 414-834-5750.
Oshkosh Catholic Cemetery, 1905 Roosevelt Ave., Oshkosh, 54901.
St. Joseph Cemetery & Mausoleum, 25 N. Elgin, Sturgeon Bay, 54235.

NECROLOGY

† Bablitch, Michael, (Retired). —Died Jan. 29, 2000.
† Hietpas, Raymond W., (Retired). —Died April 20, 2000.
† Reimer, Elroy, Wrightstown, WI St. Paul. —Died July 19, 2000.
† Scanlan, Lambert D., (Retired). —Died July 9, 2000.
† Steckbauer, Linus, (Retired). —Died April 21, 2000.
† Thompson, Robert B., (On Duty Outside Diocese). —Died Nov. 26, 1999.
† Zimmer, William H., Manitowoc, WI Sacred Heart. —Died Nov. 25, 1999.

Diocese of Greensburg

(Dioecesis Greensburgensis)

Most Reverend

ANTHONY G. BOSCO, D.D., J.C.L.

Bishop of Greensburg; ordained June 7, 1952; appointed Auxiliary Bishop of Pittsburgh and Titular Bishop of Labico May 14, 1970; consecrated June 30, 1970; appointed Bishop of Greensburg April 14, 1987; installed June 30, 1987. *Office: 723 E. Pittsburgh St., Greensburg, PA, 15601.*

Pastoral Center: 723 E. Pittsburgh St., Greensburg, PA, 15601. Tel.: 724-837-0901; Fax: 724-837-0857.

Web site address: www.catholicgbg.org

ESTABLISHED MARCH 10, 1951.

Square Miles 3,334.

Comprises the Counties of Armstrong, Fayette, Indiana and Westmoreland in the State of Pennsylvania.

For legal titles of parishes and diocesan institutions, consult the Chancery Office.

STATISTICAL OVERVIEW

Personnel	
Bishop	1
Abbots	1
Priests: Diocesan Active in Diocese	101
Priests: Active Outside Diocese	12
Priests: Retired, Sick or Absent	38
Number of Diocesan Priests	151
Religious Priests in Diocese	77
Ordinations:	
Diocesan Priests	1
Religious Priests	2
Total Brothers	27
Total Sisters	409
Parishes	
Parishes	105
With Resident Pastor:	
Resident Diocesan Priests	81
Resident Religious Priests	9
Without Resident Pastor:	
Administered by Priests	15
Professional Ministry Personnel:	
Brothers	1
Sisters	15
Lay Ministers	78
Welfare	
Catholic Hospitals	1
Total Assisted	110,488
Homes for the Aged	2
Total Assisted	132
Special Centers for Social Services	7
Total Assisted	3,982
Residential Care of Disabled	1
Total Assisted	40
Other Institutions	2
Total Assisted	5
Educational	
Diocesan Students in Other Seminaries	5
Seminaries, Religious	1
Students Religious	20
Total Seminarians	25
Colleges and Universities	2
Total Students	2,559
High Schools, Diocesan and Parish	2
Total Students	771
Elementary Schools, Diocesan and Parish	24
Total Students	5,543
Elementary Schools, Private	3
Total Students	220
Catechesis/Religious Education:	
High School Students	3,787
Elementary Students	10,476
Total Students Under Catholic Instruction	23,381
Teachers in the Diocese:	
Priests	23
Brothers	6
Sisters	34
Lay Teachers	562
Vital Statistics	
Receptions into the Church:	
Infant Baptism Totals	1,993
Adult Baptism Totals	134
Received into Full Communion	373
First Communions	2,375
Confirmations	2,503
Marriages:	
Catholic	579
Interfaith	426
Total Marriages	1,005
Deaths	2,699
Total Catholic Population	188,710
Total Population	680,152

Former Bishops—Most Rev. HUGH L. LAMB, S.T.D., First Bishop of Greensburg; ord. May 29, 1915; appt. Titular Bishop of Helos and Auxiliary of Philadelphia Dec. 19, 1935; cons. March 19, 1936; promoted to Greensburg May 28, 1951; installed Jan. 16, 1952; died Dec. 8, 1959.—Most Rev. WILLIAM G. CONNARE, D.D., ord. June 14, 1936; appt. Feb. 23, 1960; cons. May 4, 1960; retired Jan. 20, 1987; died June 12, 1995.

Pastoral Center—723 E. Pittsburgh St., Greensburg, 15601-2697. Tel: 724-837-0901; Fax: 724-837-0857. Office Hours: Mon.-Fri. 8:45-5.

Vicar General / General Executive Director, Moderator of the Curia—Rev. ROGER A. STATNICK, V.G., S.T.L., Ph.D. Tel: 724-837-9521.

Chancellor / Associate General Executive Director—Rev. LAWRENCE T. PERSICO, J.C.L. Tel: 724-837-9522.

Executive Director of Finance—Mr. MICHAEL J. MCGEE.

Deaneries—Rev. JAMES T. GASTON, V.F., Deanery 1; Rev. Msgr. WILLIAM G. CHARNOKI, V.F., Deanery 2; Rev. Msgr. JOHN L. CONWAY, V.F., Deanery 3; Rev. JOSEPH P. MADDALENA, V.F., Deanery 4; Rev. JOHN R. CINDRIC, V.F., Deanery 5; Rev. KENNETH G. ZACCAGNINI, V.F., Deanery 6.

Director for Religious—Vacant, Office: *723 E. Pittsburgh St., Greensburg, 15601-2697.*

Tribunal—Address all correspondence to, *723 E. Pittsburgh St., Greensburg, 15601-2697.* Tel: 724-837-9523.

Judicial Vicar—Rev. WILLIAM R. RATHGEB, J.C.L.

Defender of Bond—Rev. LAWRENCE T. PERSICO, J.C.L.

Judges—Revs. LAWRENCE T. PERSICO, J.C.L.; WILLIAM R. RATHGEB, J.C.L.; RICHARD J. KOSISKO, J.C.L.; Rev. Msgr. WILLIAM G. CHARNOKI, J.C.L., V.F.; Bro. DAVID KELLY, O.S.B., J.C.L.

Advocates—Rev. DANIEL C. MAHONEY; Sr. MARY HALLORAN, S.C.

Notaries—Mrs. CINDY J. OZZELLO; Ms. KATHLEEN POLOSKY.

Assesor—Vacant.

Advisory Bodies

Board of Consultors—Most Rev. ANTHONY G. BOSCO, Presider; Revs. ROGER A. STATNICK, V.G.; THADDEUS J. KACZMAREK; Rev. Msgr. JOHN L. CONWAY, V.F.; Revs. LAWRENCE R. KINIRY; RICHARD G. CURCI; MICHAEL J. BEGOLLY; JAMES D. TRINGHESE; GEORGE W. SWAST.

Diocesan Pastoral Council—In process of restructuring.

Bishop's Priests Council—Rev. ROGER A. STATNICK, V.G.; Rev. Msgr. JOHN L. CONWAY, V.F.; Revs. JOSEPH P. MADDALENA, V.F.; JAMES T. GASTON, V.F.; Rev. Msgr. WILLIAM G. CHARNOKI, V.F.; Rev. KENNETH G. ZACCAGNINI, V.F.; Rev. Msgr. ROBERT J. SHUDA; Revs. J. EDWARD MCCULLOUGH; GEORGE K. ALDERSON; JOHN A. MOINEAU; JOHN R. CINDRIC, V.F.; ALEXANDER L. PLEBAN; RICHARD E. MACKIEWICZ; RONALD L. SIMBOLI; LARRY J. KULICK.

Finance Council—Most Rev. ANTHONY G. BOSCO; Rev. ROGER A. STATNICK, V.G.; Mr. JOSEPH G. KLOCEK; Mr. JOHN A. ROBERTSHAW, JR.; Mrs. NORMA F. SCHERER; Rev. THADDEUS J. KACZMAREK; Mr. CHARLES A. FAGAN, III; Sr. GERTRUDE FOLEY, S.C.; Mr. B. PATRICK COSTELLO.

Diocesan Offices, Commissions and Special Programs

The Catholic Foundation Trust for the Diocese of Greensburg—Under Declaration of Trust dated 1st day of November, 1988, as amended 2nd day of November 1992 having as its purpose the support of any Roman Catholic benevolent, charitable, educational or missionary undertaking. Most Rev. ANTHONY G. BOSCO, D.D., J.C.L., Chm. Board of Trustees; Revs. ROGER A. STATNICK, V.G., S.T.L., Ph.D., Vice Chm. LAWRENCE T. PERSICO, J.C.L., Assoc. Vice Chm.; Mr. JOHN A. ROBERTSHAW, JR., Pres.; Mr. CHARLES A. FAGAN, III, Sec.; Mr. MICHAEL J. MCGEE, Treas.; Mrs. HELEN D. FRENDE, *723 E. Pittsburgh St., Greensburg, 15601-2697.*

The Catholic Institute of Greensburg—A Corporation, not-for-profit, incorporated under the law of the Commonwealth of Pennsylvania on the 4th day of June, 1954 having as its purpose the support of any Roman Catholic benevolent, charitable, educational or missionary undertaking.

Board Members of the Corporation—Most Rev. ANTHONY G. BOSCO, D.D., J.C.L., Pres.; Revs. ROGER A. STATNICK, V.G., Vice Pres. LAWRENCE T. PERSICO, Sec.

Board of Trustees—Mr. J. PATRICK HALL, Pres.; Mr. MICHAEL J. MCGEE, Sec. Trustees: Rev. RICHARD G. CURCI; Mr. MARK E. LOPUSHANSKY; Mr. LAWRENCE S. BUSCH; Mrs. SHEILA R. MURRAY, Financial Officer, *723 E. Pittsburgh St., Greensburg, 15601-2697.*

Greensburg Catholic Accent and Communications, Inc.—A corporation, not-for-profit, under the laws of the Commonwealth of Pennsylvania having as its purpose the support of any Roman Catholic benevolent, charitable, educational or missionary undertaking. Most Rev. ANTHONY G. BOSCO, D.C., J.C.L., CEO; Rev. ROGER A. STATNICK, V.G., Vice Pres.; Mr. MICHAEL J. MCGEE, Treas., *723 E. Pittsburgh St., Greensburg, 15601-2697.* Tel: 724-837-0901.

Catholic Charities of the Diocese of Greensburg, PA, Inc.—A corporation not-for-profit incorporated under the law of the Commonwealth of Pennsylvania on the 27th day of August, 1954, having as its purpose, the support of any Roman Catholic benevolent, charitable, educational or missionary undertaking. Most Rev. ANTHONY G. BOSCO, D.D., J.C.L., Chm. Bd. Members of the Corp.; Rev. JOSEPH P. TRAYNOR, Pres. Bd. of Trustees; Rev. RAYMOND E. RIFFLE, Exec. Dir., *711 E. Pittsburgh St., Greensburg, 15601-2697.* Tel: 724-837-1840; Fax: 724-837-4077.

Archives—Ms. ALBINA GUERRIERI, Sec.

Catholic Charities—Rev. RAYMOND E. RIFFLE, M.S.W., M.P.A., Exec. Dir.; Mr. ROBERT MCHENRY, Dir. Oper. & Finance; Mrs. JUDY MODECKI, Dir. Devel., *711 E. Pittsburgh St., Greensburg, 15601-2636.* Tel: 724-837-1840; Fax: 724-837-4077.

Catholic Relief Services Representative—Rev. Msgr. DAVID L. FISHER, *723 E. Pittsburgh St., Greensburg, 15601-2697.* Tel: 724-837-0901.

Communications—Ms. ANGELA J. BURROWS, Exec. Dir., *723 E. Pittsburgh St., P.O. Box 850, Greensburg, 15601-2697.* Tel: 724-834-4010; Fax: 724-836-5650.

Office of Information Technology—Ms. KAREN CORNELL, Dir.; Mr. STEVE PATTEN, Sr. Systems Analyst; Mr. BRIAN LOOSZ, Network Analyst; Mr. TONY KRANCE, Lotus Notes Admin.; Mrs. NINA MANNO, Instructional Technology Analyst.

Purchasing and Services Office—Mr. RICHARD LITTLE, Coord., *723 E. Pittsburgh St., Greensburg, 15601-2697.* Tel: 724-837-0901; Fax: 724-837-0857.

Office of Pastoral Life—Ms. MARY ANN GUBISH, Dir.; Sr. SUSAN JENNY, S.C., Assoc. Dir., *723 E. Pittsburgh St., Greensburg, 15601-2697.* Tel: 724-837-0901; Fax: 724-837-0857.

Department of Education and Spiritual Formation—Sr. MARGARET HILLARY, O.P., Exec. Dir., *723 E. Pittsburgh St., Greensburg, 15601-2697.* Tel: 724-837-0901; Fax: 724-837-0857.

Office of Catholic Schools—Sr. MARGUERITE COYNE, C.S.J., Supt.; Mr. JOHN BECK, Assoc. Supt.; Ms. DEBORAH WOJCIECHOWSKI, Coord. Govt. Programs & Technology; Miss THERESE TELEPAK, Coord. Drug & Alcohol Prevention, *723 E. Pittsburgh St., Greensburg, 15601-2697.* Tel: 724-836-1281; Fax: 724-837-0857.

Office of Worship and Word—Mr. MICHAEL J. GRAMMER, Dir.; Sr. JOAN SUPEL, O.P., Assoc. Dir. Catechesis; Miss THERESE TELEPAK, Assoc. Dir. for Youth Formation; Mrs. SALLY LOUGHRAN, Coord. Marriage Formation; Mr. ANGELO DIPPOLITO, Coord. Athletics; Rev. LAWRENCE L. MANCHAS, Coord. Scouts; Mrs. MARIE KONOPKA, Diocesan Liturgy Coord., *723 E. Pittsburgh St., Greensburg, 15601-2697.* Tel: 724-837-0901; Fax: 724-837-0857.

Office Ministry Formation—Ms. MARSHA KABLE, Dir.; Rev. LARRY J. KULICK, Consultant Priestly Vocations; Rev. JOSEPH P. MADDALENA, V.F., Consultant Continuing Clergy Formation, *723 E. Pittsburgh St., Greensburg, 15601-2697.* Tel: 724-837-0901; Fax: 724-837-0857.

Missions—Society for the Propagation of the Faith and Holy Childhood, Rev. Msgr. DAVID L. FISHER, *723 E. Pittsburgh St., Greensburg, 15601-2697.* Tel: 724-837-0901; Fax: 724-837-0857.

Newspaper—*"The Catholic Accent", 723 E. Pittsburgh St., P.O. Box 850, Greensburg, 15601-2697.* Tel: 724-834-4010; Fax: 724-836-5650. Mr. VINCENT A. CAPOZZI, Editor; Mr. JEROME ZUFELT, Mng. Editor.

Engineering and Facility Management Office—Mr. EDGAR R. TURNER, Dir.; Mr. RUSSELL FORAN, Assoc. Dir., *723 E. Pittsburgh St., Greensburg, 15601-2697.* Tel: 724-837-0901; Fax: 724-836-5592.

Stewardship—Mr. JAMES A. SCHUCOLSKY, Assoc. Dir. Stewardship & Devel.; Mrs. JUDY MODECKI, Dir. Devel. for Catholic Charities, *723 E. Pittsburgh St., Greensburg, 15601-2697.* Tel: 724-837-0901; Fax: 724-837-0857.

SPECIAL PROGRAMS

Apostleship of Prayer—Rev. J. EDWARD MCCULLOUGH, Dir., *459 Ranch Rd., Dunbar, 15431.* Tel: 724-277-4236; Fax: 724-277-0192.

Apostolate for the Deaf—Rev. JOSEPH P. TRAYNOR, Dir., *349 Morris St., Clymer, 15728.* Tel: 724-254-3041.

Catholic Business and Professional Women's Association—Vacant, *723 E. Pittsburgh St., Greensburg, 15601-2697.* Tel: 724-837-0901; Fax: 724-837-0857.

Catholic Daughters of America—Rev. Msgr. DAVID L. FISHER, Dir., *201 Church St., P.O. Box 398, Penn, 15675.* Tel: 724-523-3450.

Cemeteries—*723 E. Pittsburgh St., Greensburg, 15601-2697.* Tel: 724-837-0901.

Charismatic—Sr. ANN INFANGER, S.C., Moderator, *Seton Hill College, Greensburg, 15601.* Tel: 724-834-2200, Ext. 374.

Cursillo—Vacant.

Diocesan Council of Catholic Women—Rev. DONALD J. MONDELLO, Dir., *1204 Ligonier St., Latrobe, 15650.* Tel: 724-539-9751.

Holy Childhood Association—Rev. Msgr. DAVID L. FISHER, Dir., *723 E. Pittsburgh St., Greensburg, 15601-2697.* Tel: 724-837-0901; Fax: 724-837-0857.

Holy Name Society—Rev. PATRICK J. O'CONNOR, Dir., *61 Mill St., Uniontown, 15401.* Tel: 724-438-2341.

Legion of Mary—Rev. HENRY P. DINICCO, Dir., *135 Carriage Dr., North Huntington, 15642.* Tel: 724-861-5424.

Pilgrimages—Rev. J. EDWARD MCCULLOUGH, Dir., *459 Ranch Rd., Dunbar, 15431.* Tel: 724-277-4236.

Priests' Eucharistic League—Rev. J. EDWARD MCCULLOUGH, *459 Ranch Rd., Dunbar, 15431.* Tel: 724-277-4236.

St. Thomas More Guild for Lawyers—*723 E. Pittsburgh St., Greensburg, 15601-2697.* Tel: 724-837-0901.

St. Vincent de Paul Society—Rev. JOHN A. SEDLAK, Spiritual Dir., *St. Hedwig Church, Church St., Box 251, Smock, 15480.* Tel: 724-677-2110.

CLERGY, PARISHES, MISSIONS AND PAROCHIAL SCHOOLS

CITY OF GREENSBURG
(Westmoreland County)

1—BLESSED SACRAMENT CATHEDRAL, Revs. Michael J. Begolly, D.Min.,M.A.; William J. Lechnar, M.Div.; Jonathan J. Wisneski, M.Div., M.A.; Helene Paharik, Pastoral Assoc.; Jack W. Simon, Bus. Mgr.
Res., 300 N. Main St., 15601. Tel: 724-834-3710; Fax: 724-834-1518. [CEM]
Convent—350 N. Main St., 15601. Tel: 724-834-0894. Sisters of Charity
School—Aquinas Academy. See separate listing under Elementary Schools in the Institution section.

2—ST. BRUNO, Rev. Blane L. Resko, O.S.B.
Res., 1707 Poplar St., 15601. Tel: 724-836-0690.
School—Aquinas Academy. See separate listing under Elementary Schools in the Institution section.

3—OUR LADY OF GRACE, Revs. Lawrence R. Kiniry; Daniel L. Blout; Joseph V. Trupkovich.
Res., 1001 Mount Pleasant Rd., 15601. Tel: 724-838-9480; Fax: 724-838-1842.
School—Aquinas Academy. See separate listing under Elementary Schools in the Institution section.

4—ST. PAUL, Rev. Daniel C. Mahoney.
Res., 820 Carbon Rd., 15601. Tel: 724-834-6880; Fax: 724-834-1492.
School—Aquinas Academy. See separate listing under Elementary Schools in the Institution section.

OUTSIDE THE CITY OF GREENSBURG

Apollo, Armstrong Co., St. James the Greater, Rev. John T. Sweeney.
Res., 109 Owens View, 15613. Tel: 724-478-4958; Fax: 724-478-3551.

Arnold, Westmoreland Co., All Saints (Slovak), Rev. Richard G. Curci, Admin.
Res., 1700 Leishman Ave., 15068. Tel: 724-335-8232.

Avonmore, Westmoreland Co., St. Ambrose, Rev. William J. Homolak.
Res., P.O. Box 617, 505 Cambria Ave., 15618. Tel: 724-697-4129; Fax: 724-697-5116.

Belle Vernon, Westmoreland Co., St. Sebastian, Revs. John R. Cindric, V.F.; Donald P. Trexler.
Res., 801 Broad Ave., 15012. Tel: 724-929-9300; Fax: 724-930-7611.
School—815 Broad Ave., 15012. Tel: 724-929-5143; Fax: 724-929-3038. Dr. Mathew F. Harris, Prin. Sisters of St. Francis Millvale 1; Lay Teachers 9; Students 242.
Chapel—Newell, Our Lady of Perpetual Help.

Blairsville, Indiana Co., SS. Simon and Jude, Rev. Chester J. Raimer.
Res., 155 N. Brady St., 15717. Tel: 724-459-7103; Fax: 724-459-5314.

Bovard, Westmoreland Co., St. Bede, Rev. Brinstan G. Takach, O.S.B.
Res., c/o St. Vincent Archabbey, 300 Fraser Purchase Rd., Latrobe, 15650. Tel: 724-532-6629; 837-3690.

Brady's Bend, Armstrong Co., St. Patrick, Rev. Thomas A. Federline.
Res., R.D. 1, Box 78, 16028. Tel: 724-526-5079; Fax: 724-526-3028. [CEM 2]
Chapel—Sugar Creek, Chapel of St. Patrick, Brady's Bend, Tel: 724-445-2459. [CEM]

Brownsville, Fayette Co., St. Peter, Rev. Vincent J. Gigliotti.
Res., 304 Shaffner Ave., 15417. Tel: 724-785-7781; Fax: 724-785-0844. [CEM 2]
Convent—302 Shaffner Ave., 15417. Tel: 724-785-7172.
St. Mary (Slovak), Rev. Vincent J. Gigliotti.
Res., 118 Church St., 15417. Tel: 724-785-7781; Fax: 724-785-0844. [CEM]

Cadogan, Armstrong Co., St. Lawrence, Rev. Edward Volz, O.S.P.P.E.
Res., Box 114, 16212. Tel: 724-763-1089. [CEM]
Chapel—Nicholson Run, Guardian Angel Cemetery and Chapel.

Calumet, Westmoreland Co., St. Stanislaus (Polish), Rev. John M. Foriska, Admin.
Res., P.O. Box 56, 15621. Tel: 724-423-4052; Fax: 724-423-4438. [CEM]

Cardale, Fayette Co., Madonna of Czestochowa (Polish), Rev. Ronald J. Rutkowski.
Res., 212 Filbert-Orient Rd., New Salem, 15468. Tel: 724-246-9657. [CEM]

Clymer, Indiana Co., Church of the Resurrection, Revs. Micah E. Kozoil; Joseph P. Traynor; Dennis E. Sheehy.
Administration Center: 349 Morris St., 15728-1266. Tel: 724-254-3041; Fax: 724-254-3045. [CEM]
Chapel—Camerons Bottom, Chapel of Church of the Resurrection, Clymer.

Connellsville, Fayette Co.,

1—IMMACULATE CONCEPTION, Rev. Michael J. Sciberras.
Res., 148 E. Crawford Ave., 15425. Tel: 724-628-8550; Fax: 724-628-3410. [CEM 5]
School—Conn-Area Catholic School. See separate listing under Elementary Schools in the Institution section.
Chapel—Dawson, Sacred Heart Chapel.

2—HOLY TRINITY, (Polish), Rev. John M. Butler, Admin.
Res., 109 N. Seventh St., 15425. Tel: 724-628-7061. [CEM]
School—Conn-Area Catholic School. See seperate listing under Elementary Schools in the Institution section.

3—ST. JOHN THE EVANGELIST, (Slovak), Rev. John M. Butler.
Res., 908 W. Crawford Ave., 15425. Tel: 724-628-2112. [CEM]
School—Conn-Area Catholic School. See separate listing under Elementary Schools in the Institution section.

4—ST. RITA, (Italian), Rev. Francis A. Lesniowski.
Res., 116 S. Second St., 15425. Tel: 724-628-4015. [CEM]
School—Conn-Area Catholic School. See separate listing under Elementary Schools in the Institution section.

Coral, Indiana Co., St. Francis, Rev. Lawrence L. Happe, Ph.D.
Res., Box G, 15731. Tel: 724-479-9161; Fax: 724-479-0449. [CEM]
Chapel—Blacklick, Chapel of St. Francis, Coral.

Crabtree, Westmoreland Co., St. Bartholomew, Rev. Luke Policicchio, O.S.B.
Res., P.O. Box A, 15624. Tel: 724-834-0709; Fax: 724-832-3768. [CEM]

Delmont, Westmoreland Co., St. John Baptist de La Salle, Rev. William C. McGuirk.
Res., 497 Athena Dr., 15626. Tel: 724-468-4221; Fax: 724-468-6206.

Derry, Westmoreland Co., St. Joseph, Rev. Stephen C. West.
Rectory: 117 S. Ligonier St., 15627. Tel: 724-694-5359; Fax: 724-694-2024. [CEM]
St. Joseph Residence: 209 Broad St., 15627. Tel: 724-694-0320; Fax: 724-694-0320. Rev. Roger A. Statnick, V.G., S.T.L., Ph.D.

Donegal, Westmoreland Co., St. Raymond of the Mountains, Rev. John J. Harrold.
Res., P.O. Box 330, 15628. Tel: 724-593-7479; Fax: 724-593-5934. [CEM]

Dunbar, Fayette Co., St. Aloysius, Rev. J. Edward McCullough.
Res., 459 Ranch Rd., 15431. Tel: 724-277-4236; Fax: 724-277-0192. [CEM]

East Vandergrift, Westmoreland Co., Our Lady, Queen of Peace, Rev. Joseph Minsterman.
Res., 400 Kennedy Ave., 15629. Tel: 724-567-7603.

Ernest, Indiana Co., Church of the Assumption. Closed. For inquiries for parish records contact Church of the Resurrection, Clymer.

Everson, Fayette Co., St. Joseph (Polish), Rev. Robert M. Washko.
Res., 201 Painter St., 15631. Tel: 724-887-6714. [CEM]

Export, Westmoreland Co., St. Mary, Rev. Dismas Young, O.F.M.Cap. In res., Revs. John Carey, O.F.M.Cap.; Charles Knoll, O.F.M.Cap.; Bro. John Donatelli, O.F.M.Cap.
Res., 5900 Kennedy Ave., 15632. Tel: 724-327-0647; Fax: 724-325-3784.

Fairchance, Fayette Co., SS. Cyril and Methodius, Rev. David Nazimek.
Res., 50 Morgantown St., 15436. Tel: 724-564-7436; Fax: 724-564-7435. [CEM]
Chapel—Shoaf, Chapel of SS. Cyril & Methodius, Fairchance.

Farmington, Fayette Co., St. Joan of Arc, Rev. Paul A. Whalen.
Res., P.O. Box 92, 15437. Tel: 724-329-4522; Fax: 724-329-4955. [CEM]

Fayette City, Fayette Co., Holy Spirit, Rev. Leonard McAlpin.
Res., P.O. Box 639, 139 S. High St., 15438. Tel: 724-326-4352; Fax: 724-326-4221.

Footedale, Fayette Co., St. Thomas (Polish), Rev. James L. Popochock, Admin.
Res., P.O. Box 547, New Salem, 15468. Tel: 724-245-9244; Fax: 724-245-9289. [CEM]

Forbes Road, Westmoreland Co., St. Mary, Rev. Anthony J. Burlas, O.S.B.
Res., c/o St. Vincent Archabbey, 300 Fraser Purchase Rd., Latrobe, 15650. Tel: 724-539-9761; 532-6648.

Ford City, Armstrong Co., St. Mary, Revs. Terry A. Hercik, Co-Pastor; Edward J. Lewis, Co-Pastor.
Res., 718 Fourth Ave., 16226. Tel: 724-763-1631. [CEM]
School—Divine Redeemer School. See separate listing under Elementary Schools in the Institution section.

St. Francis of Paola (Polish), Revs. Terry A. Hercik, (Co-Pastor); Edward J. Lewis, (Co-Pastor).
Res., P.O. Box 327, 736 Fifth Ave., 16226. Tel: 724-763-1196. [CEM]
School—Divine Redeemer School. See separate listing under Elementary Schools in the Institution section.

Holy Trinity (Slovak), Revs. Terry A. Hercik, (Co-Pastor); Edward J. Lewis, (Co-Pastor).
Res., 1008 Sixth Ave., 16226. Tel: 724-763-9141. [CEM]
School—Divine Redeemer School. See separate listing under Elementary Schools in the Institution section.
Convent— Vincentian Sisters of Charity

Freeport, Armstrong Co., St. Mary, Rev. George K. Alderson.
Res., 608 High St., 16229. Tel: 724-295-2281; Fax: 724-295-3090. [CEM]
School—610 High St., 16229. Tel: 724-295-3003; Fax: 724-295-2790. Mrs. Adrienne Ofcharsky, Prin.
Lay Teachers 6; Students 98.

Glen Campbell, Indiana Co., St. Michael. Closed. For inquiries for parish records contact Church of the Resurrection, Clymer.

Grindstone, Fayette Co., St. Cecilia (Slovak), Rev. John A. Sedlak, Admin.
c/o P.O. Box 251, Smock, 15480. Tel: 724-677-2110; Fax: 724-677-0146.

Harrison City, Westmoreland Co., St. Barbara, Revs. V. Paul Fitzmaurice; Robert T. Lubic.
Res., 34 Raymaley Rd., 15636. Tel: 724-744-7474; Fax: 724-744-3056. [CEM]

Heilwood, Indiana Co., St. John the Baptist. Closed. For inquiries for parish records contact Church of the Resurrection, Clymer.

Herminie, Westmoreland Co., St. Edward, Rev. Lawrence L. Manchas.
Res., 87 Sixth St. Ext., 15637. Tel: 724-446-5197; Fax: 724-446-1433.
School—89 Sixth St. Ext., 15637. Tel: 724-446-5381. Sr. MaryLou Witkowski, S.H.S., Prin.
Sisters of the Holy Spirit 2; Lay Teachers 9; Students 170.
Convent—89 Sixth St. Ext., 15637. Tel: 724-446-5359. Sisters of the Holy Spirit

Indiana, Indiana Co., St. Bernard, Rev. Msgr. William G. Charnoki, J.C.L., V.F.; Rev. Michael Sikon.
Res., 200 Clairvaux Dr., 15701. Tel: 724-465-2210; Fax: 724-465-0422. [CEM]
School—300 Clairvaux Dr., 15701. Tel: 724-465-7139; Fax: 724-465-0803. Mrs. Maria Hastings, Prin.
Lay Teachers 14; Students 177.

St. Thomas More University Parish. (Newman Center). Rev. Michael J. Crookston.
Res., Indiana University of PA, 1200 Oakland Ave., 15701. Tel: 724-463-2277; Fax: 724-463-7116.

Irwin, Westmoreland Co., Immaculate Conception, Rev. Msgr. John L. Conway, V.F.; Rev. Thomas Trupkovich, Regional Curate, Tel: 724-863-2626.
Res., 305 Second St., 15642. Tel: 724-863-9550; Fax: 724-863-9552. [CEM]
School—Queen of Angels Regional Catholic School. See separate listing under Elementary Schools in the Institution section.

Iselin, Indiana Co., Holy Cross. Closed. For inquiries for parish records contact Church of the Good Shepherd, Kent.

Jeannette, Westmoreland Co., Sacred Heart, Revs. William A. Beaver, O.S.B.; James H. Loew, O.S.B.; Bro. James Cartwright, O.S.B., Parish Min. In res., Rev. Dominic J. Petroy, O.S.B.
Res., 504 Cowan Ave., 15644. Tel: 724-523-2560; Fax: 724-523-9400. [CEM]

Ascension (Italian), Rev. Msgr. Nicholas A. Mitolo.
Res., 615 Division Ave., 15644. Tel: 724-523-6567; 6568.

Kent, Indiana Co., Church of the Good Shepherd, Rev. Larry J. Kulick.
Res., P.O. Box 99, 15752. Tel: 724-479-3881; Fax: 724-479-3882.

Kittanning, Armstrong Co., St. Mary, Our Lady of Guadalupe, Rev. Emil S. Payer.
Res., 101 W. High St., 16201. Tel: 724-548-7640; 548-7649; Fax: 724-543-2938. [CEM]
Convent—348 N. Water St., 16201. Tel: 724-543-4518. Sisters of St. Joseph

Maxwell, Fayette Co., St. James, Rev. James F. Petrovsky.
Res., Box 247, LaBelle, 15450. Tel: 724-785-3617.
Chapel—Isabella, Chapel of St. James, Maxwell.

Latrobe, Westmoreland Co.,

1—Holy Family, Revs. Donald J. Mondello; Alan W. Grote.
Res., 1204 Ligonier St., 15650. Tel: 724-539-9751; Fax: 724-539-8044. [CEM]
School—Christ the Divine Teacher School. See separate listing under Elementary Schools in the Institution section.

2—St. Vincent Basilica, Revs. Athanasius C. Cherry, O.S.B.; Philip M. Kanfush, O.S.B.; Stanley T. Markiewicz, O.S.B.
Res., 300 Fraser Purchase Rd., 15650. Tel: 724-539-8629; Fax: 724-539-3810. [CEM]
School—Christ the Divine Teacher School. See separate listing under Elementary Schools in the Institution section.

3—St. John the Evangelist, Rev. Thomas M. Lukac.
Res., 306 St. John Dr., 15650. Tel: 724-537-8909; Fax: 724-537-2788.
School—Christ the Divine Teacher School. See separate listing under Elementary Schools in the Institution section.

4—St. Rose, Rev. William P. Donahue.
Res., 1112 Hillview Ave., 15650. Tel: 724-537-3709. [CEM]
School—Christ the Divine Teacher School. See separate listing under Elementary Schools in the Institution section.

5—St. Boniface. (Chestnut Ridge). Rev. Simon J. Toth, O.S.B. Tel: 724-532-6735.
Res., c/o St. Vincent Archabbey, 300 Fraser Purchase Rd., 15650. Tel: 724-532-6600.
School—Christ the Divine Teacher School. See separate listing under Elementary Schools in the Institution section.

Leckrone, Fayette Co., Our Lady of Perpetual Help (St. Mary), Rev. Andrew M. Kawecki.
Res., P.O. Box 248, 15454. Tel: 724-737-5736; Fax: 724-737-1042. [CEM]

Leechburg, Armstrong Co.,

1—St. Catherine of Alexandria. Closed. For inquiries for parish records contact the Chancery.

2—Christ The King, Rev. Joseph E. Bonafed.
Administrative Center: 630 Second St., 15656. Tel: 724-845-8191; 842-1791; Fax: 724-845-5480. [CEM]

3—Church of the Assumption. Closed. For inquiries for parish records contact the Chancery.

4—St. Martha, (Slovak). Closed. For inquiries for parish records contact the Chancery.

Leisenring, Fayette Co., St. Vincent de Paul, Rev. Peter L. Peretti.
Res., Box 24, 15455. Tel: 724-628-7361. [CEM]

Ligonier, Westmoreland Co., Holy Trinity, Rev. Joseph P. Maddalena, S.T.L., V.F.
Res., 342 W. Main St., 15658. Tel: 724-238-6434; Fax: 724-238-6688. [CEM]
School—327 W. Vincent St., 15658. Tel: 724-238-6430; Fax: 724-238-6341. Mrs. Barbara Sabo, Prin.
Lay Teachers 8; Students 117.
Chapel—Wilpen, Chapel of Holy Trinity, Ligonier.

Lower Burrell, Westmoreland Co., St. Margaret Mary, Revs. James T. Gaston; Richard E. Mackiewicz, Regional Curate, Tel: 724-335-7433.
Res., 201 Park Dr., 15068. Tel: 724-335-2336; Fax: 724-337-6676.
School—3055 Leechburg Rd., 15068. Tel: 724-335-6700; Fax: 724-335-8982. Mrs. Darlene Scopel, Prin.
Lay Teachers 9; Students 143.

Lucernemines, Indiana Co., St. Louis, Rev. James M. Goldberg.
Res., P.O. Box 197, 15754. Tel: 724-479-9542; Fax: 724-479-0983. [CEM]

Marguerite, Westmoreland Co., St. Benedict, Rev. Stephen R. Honeygosky, O.S.B.
Res., R.D. 8, Box 560, Greensburg, 15601. Tel: 724-834-9045; Fax: 724-834-1880.

Masontown, Fayette Co., All Saints, Rev. James F. Bump.
Res., 101 W. Church Ave., 15461. Tel: 724-583-7866; Fax: 724-583-0373. [CEM]
School—100 S. Washington St., 15461. Tel: 724-583-2141; Fax: 724-583-2141. Paul E. Polink, Prin.
Lay Teachers 10; Students 140.
Chapel—McClellandtown, Chapel of All Saints, Masontown.

Monessen, Westmoreland Co., The Epiphany of Our Lord, Revs. Paul A. Lisik; E. George Saletrik.
Res., 618 Knox Ave., 15062. Tel: 724-684-7661; Fax: 724-684-8981. [CEM 2]
School—701 Schoonmaker Ave., 15062. Tel: 724-684-5610; Fax: 724-684-5464. Mrs. Tamara Bojsen, Prin.
Lay Teachers 7; Students 88.

Mount Pleasant, Westmoreland Co., St. Pius X, Rev. Michael W. Matusak.
Res., 216 Spruce St., 15666. Tel: 724-547-1911; Fax: 724-542-7147. [CEM]

Transfiguration (Polish), Rev. Michael W. Matusak, Admin. In res., Rev. James W. Clark.
Res., 35 N. Hitchman St., 15666. Tel: 724-547-2556. [CEM]

Visitation of the Blessed Virgin Mary (Slovak), Rev. Anthony W. Ditto.
Res., 740 Walnut St., 15666. Tel: 724-547-5735; Fax: 724-547-2630. [CEM]

Murrysville, Westmoreland Co., Mother of Sorrows, Revs. John A. Moineau; Ronald L. Cyktor, Jr.
Res., 4200 Old William Penn Hwy., 15668. Tel: 724-733-8870; Fax: 724-733-8108.
School—3264 Evergreen Dr., 15668. Tel: 724-733-8840; Fax: 724-733-8807. Patricia A. Sheahan, Ed.D., Prin.
Lay Teachers 23; Students 350.

New Alexandria, Westmoreland Co., St. James, Rev. Lawrence T. Persico, J.C.L.
Res., R.D. 3, Box 400, 15670. Tel: 724-668-2829; Fax: 724-668-7327.

New Derry, Westmoreland Co., St. Martin, Rev. Arthur Holtz, O.S.B.
Res., R.D. 1, Box 100, 15671. Tel: 724-694-5716. [CEM]

New Kensington, Westmoreland Co., St. Mary of Czestochowa (Polish), Revs. Richard P. Karenbauer; Richard E. Mackiewicz, Regional Curate, Tel: 724-335-7433; Sr. Mary Roberta Debski, C.S.S.F., Pastoral Min.
Res., 857 Kenneth Ave., 15068. Tel: 724-335-8212; Fax: 724-335-1314. [CEM]
Convent—837 Kenneth Ave., 15068. Tel: 724-339-9868. Felician Sisters Sr. Mary Roberta Debski, C.S.S.F., Pastoral Min.

St. Joseph, Revs. George W. Swast; Richard E. Mackiewicz, Regional Curate, Tel: 724-335-7433.
Res., 1125 Leishman Ave., 15068. Tel: 724-337-6412; Fax: 724-337-4022.
School—1129 Leishman Ave., 15068. Tel: 724-339-4411; Fax: 724-337-6457. Sr. Marie Corde Denny, C.S.J., Prin.
Sisters 4; Lay Teachers 11; Students 170.

Mt. St. Peter (Italian), Revs. Richard G. Curci; Charles P. Esposito.
Res., 100 Freeport Rd., 15068. Tel: 724-335-9877; Fax: 724-335-9138.
School—Tel: 724-335-5911. Sr. Mariella Bradley, R.S.M., Prin.
Sisters of Mercy 2; Lay Teachers 16; Students 306.

New Salem, Fayette Co., St. Procopius, Rev. James L. Popochock.
Res., 20 Church St., P.O. Box 547, 15468. Tel: 724-245-9244; Fax: 724-245-9289. [CEM]

North Huntingdon, Westmoreland Co., St. Agnes, Rev. Thaddeus J. Kaczmarek. In res., Rev. Thomas S. Trupkovich, Regional Curate.
Res., 11400 St. Agnes Ln., 15642. Tel: 724-863-2626; 863-2630; Fax: 724-863-1057.

School—Queen of Angels Catholic School. See separate listing under Elementary Schools in the Institution section.
Convent—12240 Rte. 30, Apt. F, 15642. Tel: 724-863-1670. Sisters of St. Joseph

St. Elizabeth Ann Seton, Revs. Richard J. Kosisko; Thomas S. Trupkovich, Regional Curate, Tel: 724-863-2626.
Res., 200 Leger Rd., 15642. Tel: 724-864-6364; Fax: 724-864-4580.

Palmer, Fayette Co., St. Albert, Rev. Ronald J. Rutkowski.
Res., Box 295, Adah, 15410. Tel: 724-737-6720.

Parker, Armstrong Co., St. Mary, Our Lady of the Snows, Rev. Thomas A. Federline, Admin.
Res., c/o R.D. 1, Box 78, Brady's Bend, 16028. Tel: 724-526-5079; Fax: 724-526-3028.

Penn, Westmoreland Co., St. Boniface, Rev. Msgr. David L. Fisher.
Res., 201 Church St., Box 398, 15675. Tel: 724-523-3450; Fax: 724-523-6468. [CEM]

Perryopolis, Fayette Co., St. John the Baptist, Rev. John T. Euker.
Res., P.O. Box 606, 15473. Tel: 724-736-4442; Fax: 724-736-8403. [CEM]

Point Marion, Fayette Co., St. Hubert, Rev. Joseph L. Sredzinski, M.Div.
Res., 9 Sadler St., 15474. Tel: 724-725-3655.

Republic, Fayette Co., Holy Rosary, Rev. Stephen R. Bugay.
Res., Main St., P.O. Box 400, 15475. Tel: 724-246-9639; Fax: 724-246-8081. [CEM]
School—Abigail St., P.O. Box 797, 15475. Tel: 724-246-9083; Fax: 724-246-2500. Sr. Corrine Giel, V.S.C., Prin.
Sisters 2; Lay Teachers 9; Students 173.
Convent—P.O. Box 797, 15475. Vincentian Sisters of Charity

Rossiter, Indiana Co., St. Francis of Assisi. Closed. For inquiries for parish records contact the Church of the Resurrection, Clymer.

Rostraver, Westmoreland Co., St. Anne, Rev. Ronald L. Simboli.
Res., 1870 Rostraver Rd., Belle Vernon, 15012. Tel: 724-872-3555; Fax: 724-872-3373.

Sagamore, Armstrong Co., Sacred Heart, Rev. Robert E. Moslener, Admin.
Res., c/o Box 327, Yatesboro, 16263. Tel: 724-783-7191; Fax: 724-783-7783. [CEM]

Saltsburg, Indiana Co., St. Matthew (Italian), Rev. Gregory J. Flohr.
Res., 703 Indiana Ave., 15681. Tel: 724-639-3690. [CEM]

Scottdale, Westmoreland Co., St. John the Baptist, Rev. Leonard W. Stoviak.
Res., 416 S. Broadway, 15683. Tel: 724-887-6321; Fax: 724-887-6324. [CEM]
School—504 S. Broadway, 15683. Tel: 724-887-9550; Fax: 724-887-9553. Joseph Dreliszak, Prin.
Benedictine Sisters 3; Lay Teachers 16; Students 203.
Convent—408 S. Broadway, 15683. Tel: 724-887-6612. Benedictine Sisters

Seward, Westmoreland Co., Holy Family, Rev. John E. Wilt.
Res., Box 481, 15954. Tel: 814-446-5759; Fax: 814-446-4481. [CEM 3]
Chapels—New Florence, Chapel of Holy Family, Seward, Tel: 724-235-2290; Bolivar, Chapel of Holy Family, Seward, Tel: 724-676-4781.

Slickville, Westmoreland Co., St. Sylvester, Rev. Raymond E. Riffle, M.S.W., M.P.A.
Res., Box 307, 15684. Tel: 724-468-5794; Fax: 724-468-5765.

Smithton, Westmoreland Co., St. Timothy, Rev. Paul R. Stivason, Admin.
Res., Center & Hill Streets, Box 308, Yukon, 15698. Tel: 724-722-3141; Fax: 724-722-3140. [CEM]
Parish Administration Center: Tel: 724-722-3141; Fax: 724-722-3140.

Smock, Fayette Co., St. Hedwig (Slovak), Rev. John A. Sedlak.
Res., Box 251, 15480. Tel: 724-677-2110; Fax: 724-677-0146. [CEM 2]
Chapel—Keisterville, Chapel of St. Hedwig, Smock, Tel: 724-437-6667; Fax: 724-677-0146.

Starford, Indiana Co., St. Elizabeth. Closed. For inquiries for parish records contact Church of the Resurrection, Clymer.

Sutersville, Westmoreland Co., St. Charles Borromeo, Rev. James Vasil.
Res., Fifth Ave., P.O. Box 413, 15083. Tel: 724-872-5286; Fax: 724-872-3650.

Trafford, Westmoreland Co., St. Regis, Rev. James D. Tringhese.
Res., 517 Homewood Ave., 15085. Tel: 412-372-4577; Fax: 412-373-5979.
Convent—424 Edgewood Ave., 15085. Tel: 412-372-3198. Sisters of Charity

Trauger, Westmoreland Co., Forty Martyrs (Hungarian), Rev. Aaron N. Buzzelli, O.S.B.
Res., c/o St. Vincent Archabbey, 300 Fraser Purchase Rd., Latrobe, 15650. Tel: 724-423-3282; 532-6767; Fax: 724-537-4554. [CEM]

Uniontown, Fayette Co.,

1—St. John The Evangelist, Rev. William J. Kiel.
Res., 50 Jefferson St., 15401. Tel: 724-437-7569; Fax: 724-437-6277.
School—84 Pennsylvania Ave., 15401. Tel: 724-438-8598; Fax: 724-438-8585. Christine Roskovensky, Prin.
Sisters 2; Lay Teachers 14; Students 281.
Convent—88 Pennsylvania Ave., 15401. Tel: 724-438-5271. School Sisters of St. Francis

2—St. Joseph, (Polish), Rev. Alexander L. Pleban, S.T.L.
Res., 180 Old Walnut Hill Rd., 15401. Tel: 724-437-3927; Fax: 724-437-5354. [CEM]

3—Nativity of the Blessed Virgin Mary, (Slovak), Rev. Msgr. Andrew A. Chupela.
Res., 61 N. Mount Vernon Ave., 15401. Tel: 724-437-1512; Fax: 724-437-7482. [CEM]
School—17 Gilmore St., 15401. Tel: 724-438-8471; Fax: 724-438-8338. Melvyn Sepic, Prin.
Sisters 1; Lay Teachers 11; Students 230.
Convent—7 Gilmore St., 15401. Tel: 724-437-5478; Fax: 724-439-9328. Vincentian Sisters of Charity
Chapel—Lemont Furnace, Chapel of St. Mary, Uniontown.

4—St. Therese, the Little Flower of Jesus, (Italian), Rev. Kenneth G. Zaccagnini. In res., Rev. Patrick J. O'Connor.
Res., 61 Mill St., 15401. Tel: 724-438-2341; Fax: 724-438-2361.

United, Westmoreland Co., St. Florian, Rev. John M. Foriska.
Res., P.O. Box 187, 15689. Tel: 724-423-4431; Fax: 724-423-4438. [CEM]
School—P.O. Box 188, 15689. Tel: 724-423-4437; Fax: 724-423-2207. Mrs. Lucy Hastings, Prin.
Lay Teachers 8; Students 135.

Vandergrift, Westmoreland Co., St. Gertrude, Revs. Thaddeus E. Rettger, O.S.B.; Leo Rothrauff O.S.B.
Res., 303 Franklin Ave., 15690. Tel: 724-568-2331. [CEM]
School—315 Franklin Ave., 15690. Tel: 724-568-3304; Fax: 724-567-1900. Mr. Robert Fornatley, Prin.
Lay Teachers 10; Students 98.

West Newton, Westmoreland Co., Holy Family, Rev. John A. Regoli.
Res., 225 N. Second St., 15089. Tel: 724-872-6123; Fax: 724-872-6133.

Whitney, Westmoreland Co., St. Cecilia, Rev. Chad R. Ficorilli, O.S.B.
Res., P.O. Box 80, 15693. Tel: 724-423-3777; 423-2289; Fax: 724-423-3778.

Yatesboro, Armstrong Co., St. Mary, Rev. Robert E. Moslener.
Res., P.O. Box 327, 16263. Tel: 724-783-7191; Fax: 724-783-7783. [CEM]

Youngstown, Westmoreland Co., Sacred Heart, Revs. Chad R. Ficorilli, O.S.B.; Ralph Tajak, O.S.B.
Res., P.O. Box 328, 15696. Tel: 724-537-7358; Fax: 724-537-6988.
School—P.O. Box 328, 15696. Tel: 724-539-5561; Fax: 724-539-6338. Sr. Grace Marie Spera, C.S.S.F., Prin.
Felician Sisters 2; Lay Teachers 5; Students 129.
Convent—Main St., P.O. Box 328, 15696. Tel: 724-537-8958. Felician Sisters

Youngwood, Westmoreland Co., Holy Cross, Rev. John S. Szczesny.
Res., 701 Depot St., 15697. Tel: 724-925-7811; Fax: 724-925-6170.
School—S. Eighth St., 15697. Tel: 724-925-7253; Fax: 724-925-7707.
Lay Teachers 6; Students 131.
Chapel—Hunker, Chapel of Holy Cross, Youngwood.

Yukon, Westmoreland Co., Seven Dolors, Rev. Paul R. Stivason.
Res., Center St. & Hill St., P.O. Box 308, 15698. Tel: 724-722-3141; 722-3140 (Hall); Fax: 724-722-3140. [CEM]

Chaplains of Public Institutions

Greensburg. *Westmoreland Hospital* Tel: 724-832-4000. Rev. Jacques de Paul Daley, O.S.B., Chap., Assoc. Chaplains: Rev. Msgr. Robert J. Shuda; Revs. Robert R. Byrnes; Justin Withrow, O.S.B.

Brownsville. *Brownsville General Hospital*. Attended by St. Peter, Brownsville, Tel: 724-785-7200; 785-7781 (Res.).

Connellsville. *Highlands Hospital & Health Center* Tel: 724-628-1500. Rev. James W. Clark, Chap., Tel: 724-547-2556 (Res.).

Indiana. *Indiana Hospital*. Attended by St. Bernard, Indiana, Tel: 724-357-7000; 724-465-2210 (Res.). Tel: 724-357-7000.

Jeannette. *Jeannette District Memorial Hospital* Tel: 724-527-3551. Revs. Dominic J. Petroy, O.S.B., Chap., Tel: 724-523-2560 (Res.); Justin Withrow, O.S.B., Assoc. Chap., Tel: 724-539-9761 (Res.).
Monsour Medical Center Tel: 724-527-1511. Revs. Dominic J. Petroy, O.S.B., Chap., Tel: 724-523-2560 (Res.); Justin Withrow, O.S.B., Assoc. Chap., Tel: 724-539-9761 (Res.).

Kittanning. *Armstrong County Hospital* Tel: 724-543-8500. Rev. Raphael K. Glinkowski, O.S.P.P.E., Chap., Tel: 724-763-1375 (Res.).

Latrobe. *Latrobe Area Hospital* Tel: 724-537-1000. Rev. Ermin R. Smith, O.S.B., Chap., Assoc. Chaplains: Revs. Justin Withrow, O.S.B.; Michael A. McIlwain, O.S.B. Tel: 724-539-9761 (Res.).

Mount Pleasant. *Frick Community Health Center* Tel: 724-547-1500. Rev. James W. Clark, Chap., Tel: 724-547-2556 (Res.).

New Kensington. *Citizens General Hospital*. Attended by St. Mary, New Kensington, Tel: 724-335-8212 (Res.); St. Joseph, New Kensington, Tel: 724-337-6412 (Res.); Mount St. Peter, New Kensington, Tel: 724-335-9877 (Res.). Tel: 724-337-3541.

Torrance. *Torrance State Hospital* Tel: 724-459-8000. Rev. Chester J. Raimer, Chap., Tel: 724-459-7103 (Res.).

Uniontown. *Uniontown Hospital* Tel: 724-430-5000. Rev. Marion L. Herrick, O.F.M., Chap., Tel: 724-438-0500 (Res.).

On Duty Outside the Diocese:
Reverend Monsignors—
DeAndrea, Joseph A., Via Del Mascherino 72, 00193 Rome, Italy. Tel: 011-39-6-66162662
Dylag, Michael R., One Kenberton Dr., Pleasant Ridge, MI 48069. Tel: 248-547-2006
Reverend Fathers—
Conroy, Donald B., Dir., Nat'l. Institute for Family, 3019 4th St., N.E., Washington, DC 20017. Tel: 202-462-2591
Preneta, Henry S., St. Paul Church, 128 N. McKean St., Butler, PA 16001
Survil, Bernard, Convento Santo Domingo, Primer Ave. 1-31, Zona 3, 16001 Coban Ave., Guatemala C.A.
Waczula, Michael F., 1415 Main St. #252, Dunedin, FL 34698

Military Chaplains:
Reverend Fathers—
Koser, Rudolph J., Jr., Maj. CH., 71 FTW/HC, 195 Fields St., Vance, AFB, OK 73705-5025. Tel: 580-213-7211
Mandock, Patrick H., CH. (LTC), 1271 E. Buckhorn Dr., Sierra Vista, AZ 85631-1357
Sinclair, Roger A., 428 Hyde Park Ave., Apt 3, Roslindale, MA 02131

Retired:
Reverend Monsignors—
Garred, John L., Neumann House, 2900 Seminary Dr., Greensburg, PA 15601
Hanicak, Robert A., Neumann House, 2900 Seminary Dr., Greensburg, PA 15601
McCarren, Stephen A., 247 Avenue of Barons, Nokomis, FL 34275
Ramellini, P. Lino, 19 Rex Blvd., Monessen, PA 15062
Reverend Fathers—
Bahleda, Aloysius J., Neumann House, 2900 Seminary Dr., Greensburg, PA 15601
Bienia, Michael A., Neumann House, 2900 Seminary Dr., Greensburg, PA 15601
Borkowski, Aloysius J., R.D. 3, Box 138D, Derry, PA 15627
Bratus, Walter N., 723 East Pittsburgh St., Greensburg, PA 15601
Bucci, Michael J., 1319 Walnut St., South Connellsville, PA 15425
Casaliggi, John R., Casa Del Clero Cerati, Via Torta 28, 29100 Piacenza, Italy
Charnoki, Andrew J., St. Anne Home, 685 Angela Dr., Greensburg, PA 15601
Cheatham, Louis W., Neumann House, 2900 Seminary Dr., Greensburg, PA 15601
Curry, Edward V., P.O. Box 14697, Jacksonville, FL 32238-4097
Dinnico, Henry P., 135 Carriage Dr., North Huntington, PA 15642
Drab, Stephen J., 232 W. Pennsville St., Connellsville, PA 15425
Gearing, Edward P., 37 Pocono Dr., Pittsburgh, PA 15220

Higgins, Edward F., 230 Countryview Dr., Lower Burrell, PA 15068
Hirt, Edwin H., St. Anne Home, 685 Angela Dr., Greensburg, PA 15601
Horvath, Andrew B., St. Anne Home, 685 Angela Dr., Greensburg, PA 15601
Marzilli, Raphael, Chap. to the Franciscan Missionaries of Mary, 399 Fruit Hill Ave., North Providence, RI 02911-2842. Tel: 401-354-4254
Murphy, Harry J., Nazareth House-St. Michael's, 6333 Rancho Mission Rd., San Diego, CA 92108-2099
Oris, Fabian G., RD 2, Box 476E, Uniontown, PA 15401
Rivi, Geno G., Sailwind Condo #416, 1200 Shoreline Dr., Gulf Breeze, FL 32561
Stofcik, John A., 304 Stacey Dr., Mount Pleasant, PA 15666
Weiksner, Jerome M., P.O. Box 875, Greensburg, PA 15601

INSTITUTIONS LOCATED IN THE DIOCESE

[A] SEMINARIES, RELIGIOUS OR SCHOLASTICATES

LATROBE. *St. Vincent Seminary*, 300 Fraser Purchase Rd., 15650. Tel: 724-537-4592; Fax: 724-532-5052.
E-mail: acklin@stvincent.edu
Web site: www.benedictine.stvincent.edu/seminary
Very Rev. Thomas Acklin, O.S.B., Rector; Revs. Kurt Belsole, O.S.B., Interim Rector; Justin M. Matro, O.S.B., Dir. Spiritual Life; William J. Fay, Vice Rector; Alan E. Thomas, Dean of Students; Sr. Cecilia Murphy, R.S.M., Academic Dean; Rev. Richard B. Michel, O.S.B., Dir. of Field Education. Professors 30; Theology Students 15; Seminarians 78; Benedictines 18.

[B] COLLEGES AND UNIVERSITIES

GREENSBURG. *Seton Hill College*, 15601. Tel: 724-834-2200; Fax: 724-830-4611.
E-mail: admit@setonhill.edu
Web site: www.setonhill.edu
For a complete listing, refer to the Colleges and Universities section.

LATROBE. *Saint Vincent College*, 300 Fraser Purchase Rd., 15650-2690. Tel: 724-539-9761; Fax: 724-537-4587
For a complete listing, refer to the Colleges and Universities section.

[C] HIGH SCHOOLS, DIOCESAN

GREENSBURG. *Greensburg Central Catholic High School*, 901 Armory Dr., 15601. Tel: 724-834-0310; Fax: 724-834-2472. Sr. Brigid Marie Grandey, S.C., Prin.; Rev. Daniel L. Blout, Pres. Priests 1; Sisters 2; Lay Teachers 33; Students 448.

CONNELLSVILLE. *Geibel Catholic High School*, 611 E. Crawford Ave., 15425. Tel: 724-628-5600; Fax: 724-626-5700.
E-mail: geibelhs@telerama.com
John Beck, Acting Prin.; Mr. Vincent Mascia, Vice Prin.; Rev. Gregory F. Premoshis, Pres. Priests 1; Sisters 1; Lay Teachers 27; Students 299.

[D] ELEMENTARY SCHOOLS, INTER-PAROCHIAL

GREENSBURG. *Aquinas Academy*, 330 N. Main St., 15601. Tel: 724-834-7940; Fax: 724-836-0497.
E-mail: sbeolaag@all-lines-tech.com
Sr. Brycelyn Eyler, S.C., Prin.; Mr. Daniel Mahoney, Vice-Prin. Sisters 1; Lay Teachers 43; Students 672.

CONNELLSVILLE. *Conn-Area Catholic School*, 110 N. Prospect St., 15425. Tel: 724-628-5090; Fax: 724-628-5023.
E-mail: connarea@cvzoom.net
Sr. Catherine Meinert, S.C., Prin. Lay Teachers 11; Students 204.

FORD CITY. *Divine Redeemer School*, 726 Fourth Ave., 16226. Tel: 724-763-3761; Fax: 724-763-4112. Joseph A. Mauro, Prin. Lay Teachers 9; Students 234.

JEANNETTE. *Queen of Angels Regional Catholic School*, 320 N. 7th St., 15644. Tel: 724-523-3780; 863-9581; Fax: 724-523-3783.
E-mail: qofaschool@aol.com
Web site: www.queenofangelssch.org
Sr. Grace Hartzog, S.C., Prin. Sisters 1; Lay Teachers 23; Students 510.

LATROBE. *Christ the Divine Teacher School*. (Grades PreK-8), 323 Chestnut St., 15650. Tel: 724-539-1561; Fax: 724-532-3873.
E-mail: cdt@cdtschool.org
Sr. Donna Marie Palya, V.S.C., Prin. Sisters 1; Lay Teachers 23; Students 405.

[E] SPECIAL EDUCATION

GREENSBURG. *Clelian Heights School for Exceptional Children*, R.D. 9, Box 607, 15601. Tel: 724-837-8120; Fax: 724-837-6480.
E-mail: clelian@aol.com
Web site: www.clelianheights.org
Apostles of the Sacred Heart of Jesus. Sr. M. Adrianne DiLonardo, A.S.C.J., Dir.; Sr. Linda Pettinella, A.S.C.J., Prin.; Rev. William R. Rathgeb, J.C.L., Chap. Sisters 10; Lay Teachers 6; Students 45.
Elizabeth Seton Montessori School of Westmoreland County, Inc., R.D. 7, P.O. Box 268, 15601. Tel: 724-837-8500; Fax: 724-836-0772. Sisters of Charity. Sr. Anita Schulte, S.C., Dir. Sisters 1; Lay Teachers 3; Students 50.

MOUNT PLEASANT. *Verna Montessori School*, 268 Prittstown Rd., 15666. Tel: 724-887-8810; Fax: 724-887-2977.
E-mail: vmsami@a1usa.net
Ivrea Sisters of Charity of the Immaculate Conception. Sr. M. Letizia Tribuzio, S.C.I.C., Prin.; Sr. Maria Letizia Garruba, Admin. Sisters 5; Lay Teachers 3; Students 132.

[F] GENERAL HOSPITALS

JEANNETTE. *Jeannette District Memorial Hospital*, Jefferson Ave., 15644. Tel: 724-527-3551; Fax: 724-527-9430.
E-mail: ram1@jdmh.org
Web site: jdmh.org
For a complete listing, refer to the Hospitals section.

[G] HOMES FOR AGED

GREENSBURG. *Neumann House*, 2900 Seminary Dr., 15601. Tel: 724-834-7350; Fax: 724-834-7351.
E-mail: jbertig@dioceseofgreensburg.org
For a complete listing, refer to the Special Care Facilities section.
St. Anne Home, 685 Angela Dr., 15601. Tel: 724-837-6070; Fax: 724-837-6099
For a complete listing, refer to the Special Care Facilities section.

[H] MONASTERIES AND RESIDENCES OF PRIESTS AND BROTHERS

BOLIVER. *Mount Carmel Hermitage*, RR #1 Box 3300, 15923. Tel: 724-238-0423. Revs. Bede J.K. Mulligan, O.Carm.; Simeon D. Marro, O.Carm. Priests 2.

KITTANNING. *Pauline Fathers Monastery*, Bunker Hill Rd., P.O. Box 66, 16201. Tel: 724-763-1375; Fax: 724-763-8100. Revs. Edward Volz, O.S.P.P.E., Prior; Raphael K. Glinkowski, O.S.P.P.E., Admin. Priests 2.

LATROBE. *Saint Vincent Archabbey*, 300 Fraser Purchase Rd., 15650-2686. Tel: 724-532-6600; Fax: 724-539-2110.
E-mail: nowicki@acadl.stvincent.edu
Web site: benedict.stvincent.edu/archabbey
Legal Titles: *The Benedictine Society of Westmoreland County.*; *Saint Vincent College Corporation.*; *The Wimmer Corporation.*; *The Saint Vincent Cemetery Corporation.* Rt. Revs. Douglas R. Nowicki, O.S.B., Archabbot; Paul R. Maher, O.S.B., Archabbot (Retired); Very Rev. Earl J. Henry, O.S.B., Prior; Bro. Anthony Kirsch, O.S.B., Subprior; Revs. Sebastian A. Samay, Master of Novices; Reginald G. Bender, O.S.B., Procurator; Thomas Acklin, O.S.B., Rector of the Seminary; Martin R. Bartel, O.S.B.; Aelred J. Beck, O.S.B.; Kurt J. Belsole, O.S.B.; Joseph P. Bronder, O.S.B.; Gilbert J. Burke, O.S.B.; Godfrey F. Burkhardt, O.S.B.; Anthony J. Burlas, O.S.B.; Aaron N. Buzzelli, O.S.B.; Andrew S. Campbell, O.S.B.; Athanasius C. Cherry, O.S.B.; Wulfstan F. Clough, O.S.B.; Cyprian G. Constantine, O.S.B.; Patrick T. Cronauer, O.S.B.; Vincent de Paul Crosby, O.S.B.; Jacques de Paul Daley, O.S.B.; Thomas W. Devereux, O.S.B.; Alvin T. Downey, O.S.B.; Demetrius R. Dumm, O.S.B.; Marion J. Emling, O.S.B.; John R. Erickson, O.S.B.; Augustine A. Flood; Clair F. Gannon, O.S.B.; Campion P. Gavaler, O.S.B.; David R. Griffin, O.S.B., Dir. of College Campus Ministry; Anthony J. Grossi, O.S.B.; Mark F.X. Gruber, O.S.B.; Thomas M. Hart, O.S.B.; Bede J. Hasso, O.S.B.; Clement J. Heid, O.S.B.; Roland L. Heid, O.S.B.; Lawrence H. Hill, O.S.B.; Vernon A. Holtz, O.S.B.; Cuthbert A. Jack, O.S.B.; Philip Michael Kanfush, O.S.B.; Myron M. Kirsch, O.S.B.; Omer U. Kline, O.S.B., Admin. Asst. to the Archabbot; Rene M. Kollar, O.S.B.; Germain L. Lieb, O.S.B.; Joel R. Lieb, O.S.B.; Stanley T. Markiewicz, O.S.B.; Justin M. Matro, O.S.B., Spiritual Dir. (Seminary); Michael A. McIlwain, O.S.B.; Michael McKay, O.S.B.; Alphonse H. Meier, O.S.B.; Richard B. Michel, O.S.B.; Nathan J. Munsch, O.S.B.; Jonathan J. Murrman, O.S.B.; Warren D. Murrman, O.S.B.; John F. Murtha, O.S.B.; Justin Nolan, O.S.B.; Daniel Paul O'Keefe, O.S.B.; Emeric J. Pfiester, O.S.B.; Jerome J. Purta, O.S.B.; Donald Raila, O.S.B.; Roland R. Ripoli, O.S.B.; Kieran J. Rodgers, O.S.B.; Noel H. Rothrauff, O.S.B., Dir. of Foreign Missions; Paul E. Rubadue, O.S.B.; Chrysostom V. Schlimm, O.S.B.; Louis S. Sedlacko, O.S.B.; Paulinus J. Selle, O.S.B.; Thomas More Sikora, O.S.B.; Paul-Alexander Shutt, O.S.B.; Brendan L. Smetana, O.S.B.; Ermin R. Smith, O.S.B.; Brinstan G. Takach, O.S.B.; Paul R. Taylor, O.S.B.; Simon J. Toth, O.S.B.; Damian J. Warnock, O.S.B.; Mark Edward Wenzinger, O.S.B.; Justin Withrow, O.S.B.; Flavian G. Yelinko, O.S.B.
Priests of the Archabbey Serving Abroad: Very Rev. Lucas Torrell deAlmeida Costa, O.S.B., Prior; Revs. Mauro de Souza Fernandes, O.S.B.; Claudio Moraes, O.S.B.
Priests on Leave: Revs. Cristiano Aparecido Brito, O.S.B.; Becket G. Senchur, O.S.B.; William Wurm, O.S.B.; Millard Cook, O.S.B.; Mark Peters, O.S.B.; Daniel-Zachary Waldspurger, O.S.B.
Priests on Loan: Revs. Cornelius P. Chang, O.S.B., Archdiocese of New York; Christian G. Le Frois, O.S.B., Diocese of Savannah. Priests in Archabbey 78; Community: Priests 136; Deacons 4; Solemn Professed Choir-Monks 24; Junior Professed Monks 11; Choir Novices 3; Brothers 6.

UNIONTOWN. *St. Anthony Friary*, 115 Oakland Ave., 15401-2818. Tel: 724-438-0500; Fax: 724-438-4251. Friars Richard A. Portasik, O.F.M., Local Min.; Joseph L. Portasik, O.F.M.; Bros. Damien Murkley, O.F.M., Vicar; Joseph Haley, Assistance.

[I] CONVENTS AND RESIDENCES FOR SISTERS

GREENSBURG. *Apostles of the Sacred Heart of Jesus*, Clelian Heights Convent, R.D. 9, Box 607, 15601. Tel: 724-837-8120; Fax: 724-837-6480.
E-mail: clelian@aol.com
Web site: www.clelianheights.org
Sr. M. Adrianne DiLonardo, A.S.C.J., Local Supr.; Rev. William R. Rathgeb, J.C.L., Chap. Sisters 11.
Benedictine Sisters (Eichstatt, Bavaria), St. Emma Monastery, 1001 Harvey Ave., 15601-1494. Tel: 724-834-3060; Fax: 724-834-5772.
E-mail: benedictinenuns@stemma.org
Web site: www.stemma.org
Mother Mary Anne Noll, O.S.B., Prioress; Rev. Msgr. Robert J. Shuda, Chap. Sisters 19; Postulants 2.
Doran Hall, 443 Mount Thor Rd., 15601. Tel: 724-837-8645; Fax: 724-836-0766. Sisters of Charity 26.
Ennis Hall, 447 Mount Thor Rd., 15601. Tel: 724-836-7940. Sisters of Charity 11.
Regina House. (Sisters of Charity Generalate), 465 Mt. Thor Rd., 15601. Tel: 724-836-0406; Fax: 724-836-8280. Sr. Gertrude Foley, S.C., Pres. Sisters 486; Postulants 11.
Sisters of Charity, Caritas Christi, Motherhouse, 465 Mount Thor Rd., 15601. Tel: 724-853-7948; Fax: 724-838-1512. Sr. Mary Janice Grindle, Dir. Community Life. Sisters 94.
Sisters of Charity, Marian Hall, 451 Mount Thor Rd., 15601. Tel: 724-837-5863. Sisters of Charity 3.
Sisters of Charity of Seton Hill, Greensburg, Pennsylvania, 463 Mount Thor Rd., 15601. Tel: 724-836-0406; Fax: 724-836-8280. Res. Regina House, 465 Mt. Thor Rd. DePaul Center. Administrative offices.463 Mt. Thor Rd. Tel: 724-836-0406; Fax: 724-836-8280.
Caritias Christi. Tel: 724-853-7948.
Doran Hall. Tel: 724-837-8645.
Ennis Hall. Tel: 724-836-7940.
Marian Hall. Tel: 724-837-5863.
Bayley House. Tel: 724-836-6398. Sisters 486; Novices 22; Postulants 11. A Pennsylvania non-profit corporation.
Sisters of Mary Immaculate (Krishnagar, India), St. Joseph Center Convent, 2900 Seminary Dr., 15601. Tel: 724-836-0449. Sr. Tracy Vattakuzhiyil, S.M.I., Local Supr. Sisters 2.

LATROBE. *Discalced Carmelite Nuns*, Carmel of the Assumption, R.D. 6, Box 28, Center Dr., 15650. Tel: 724-539-1056. Sr. Barbara Sitter, O.C.D., Prioress; Rev. Michael A. McIlwain, O.S.B., Chap. Professed Nuns of Solemn Vows 13; Extern 1.

LEECHBURG. *Sisters of Mary Immaculate (West Bengal, India)*, R.D. 5, Box 1231, 15656. Tel: 724-845-2828; Fax: 724-845-1658.
E-mail: smi@kiski.net
Sr. Tracy Vattakuzhiyil, S.M.I., Local Supr. Sisters 4.

MOUNT PLEASANT. *Ivrea Sisters of Charity of the Immaculate Conception*, Immaculate Virgin of Miracles Convent, R.D. 2, Box 348, 15666. Tel: 724-887-6753; Fax: 724-887-0220.
E-mail: scicusapa@worldnet.att.net
Sr. Letizia Garruba, S.C.I.C., Local Supr. Sisters 10.

[J] RETREAT HOUSES

GREENSBURG. *St. Emma Retreat House*, 1001 Harvey Ave., 15601. Tel: 724-834-3060; Fax: 724-834-5772.
E-mail: benedictinenuns@stemma.org
Web site: www.stemma.org
Benedictine Sisters (Eichstatt, Bavaria). Mother Mary Anne Noll, O.S.B., Prioress.

[K] MISCELLANEOUS LISTINGS

GREENSBURG. *Gilbert Straub Plaza*, 620 Reamer Ave., 15601. Tel: 724-832-2280; Fax: 724-832-9511. Sisters of Charity. Sr. Andrew Mary, S.C., Mgr. Sisters 1.

St. Joseph Center, 2900 Seminary Dr., 15601. Tel: 724-834-7350; Fax: 724-834-7351.
E-mail: jbertig@dioceseofgreensburg.org
Mr. Gerald R. Bertig, Dir. Facilities Mgmt.

INDIANA. *Clairvaux Commons*, 100 Clairvaux Dr., 15701. Tel: 724-349-2920; Fax: 724-349-2921. Sisters of St. Joseph 2.

LEECHBURG. *Bishop Morrow Personal Care Home*, R.D. #5, Box 1231, 15656. Tel: 724-845-2828; Fax: 724-845-1658.
E-mail: smi@kiski.net
Sisters of Mary Immaculate. Sr. Tracy Vattakuzhiyil, S.M.I., Dir.

SMOCK. *Ladies of Charity*, Box 251, 15480. Tel: 724-677-2110; Fax: 724-677-0146. Rev. John A. Sedlak, Spiritual Dir.

RELIGIOUS INSTITUTES OF MEN REPRESENTED IN THE DIOCESE

For further details refer to the corresponding bracketed number in the Religious Institutes of Men or Women section.

[0200]—*Benedictine Monks.* (St. Vincent Archabbey).—O.S.B.
[0270]—*Carmelite Fathers and Brothers.*—O.Carm.
[0520]—*Franciscan Friars.*—O.F.M.
[1010]—*Pauline Fathers.*—O.S.P.P.E.

RELIGIOUS INSTITUTES OF WOMEN REPRESENTED IN THE DIOCESE

[0130]—*Apostles of the Sacred Heart of Jesus.*—A.S.C.J.
[0190]—*Benedictine Sisters.*—O.S.B.
[0230]—*Benedictine Sisters of Pontifical Jurisdiction.*—O.S.B.
[0420]—*Discalced Carmelite Nuns.*—O.C.D.
[1070]—*Dominican Sisters, St. Mary of the Springs.* (Columbus, OH).—O.P.
[1170]—*Felician Sisters.*—C.S.S.F.
[2575]—*Institute of the Sisters of Mercy of the Americas.* (Pittsburgh, PA).—R.S.M.
[1690]—*School Sisters of the Third Order of St. Francis.*—O.S.F.
[0570]—*Sisters of Charity of Seton Hill, Greensburg, Pennsylvania.*—S.C.
[0450]—*Sisters of Charity of the Immaculate Conception of Ivrea.*—S.C.I.C.
[0990]—*Sisters of Divine Providence.* (St. Peter Prov.).—C.D.P.
[2440]—*Sisters of Mary Immaculate.*—S.M.I.
[1660]—*Sisters of Saint Francis of the Providence of God.*—O.S.F.
[1620]—*Sisters of Saint Francis, Millvale, Pennsylvania.*—O.S.F.
[3830-13]—*Sisters of St. Joseph.*—C.S.J.
[2040]—*Sisters of the Holy Spirit.*—S.H.S.
[3730]—*Sisters of the Order of St. Basil the Great.*—O.S.B.M.
[4160]—*Vincentian Sisters of Charity.*—V.S.C.

NECROLOGY

† Babula, Benjamin S., Connellsville, PA Holy Trinity. —Died July 6, 2000.

Diocese of Harrisburg

(Dioecesis Harrisburgensis)

Most Reverend

NICHOLAS C. DATTILO, D.D.

Bishop of Harrisburg; ordained May 31, 1958; appointed Eighth Bishop of Harrisburg November 21, 1989; consecrated January 26, 1990. *Res., 4800 Union Deposit Rd., P.O. Box 2153, Harrisburg, PA, 17105.* Tel.: 717-657-4804.

LOVE LIFE AND DO GOOD

ESTABLISHED MARCH 3, 1868.

Square Miles 7,660.

Comprises the Counties of Dauphin, Lebanon, Lancaster, York, Adams, Franklin, Cumberland, Perry, Juniata, Mifflin, Snyder, Northumberland, Union, Montour and Columbia in the State of Pennsylvania.

PATRON OF DIOCESE: St. Patrick, Bishop and Confessor.

For legal titles of parishes and diocesan institutions, consult the General Secretariat.

Diocesan Center: P.O. Box 2153, Harrisburg, PA, 17105-2153. Tel.: 717-657-4804; Fax: 717-657-2453.

Web site address: www.hbgdiocese.org

E-mail address: general@hbgdiocese.org

STATISTICAL OVERVIEW

Personnel	
Bishop	1
Priests: Diocesan Active in Diocese	116
Priests: Active Outside Diocese	10
Priests: Retired, Sick or Absent	34
Number of Diocesan Priests	160
Religious Priests in Diocese	36
Extern Priests in Diocese	13
Ordinations:	
Diocesan Priests	4
Transitional Deacons	3
Permanent Deacons in Diocese	61
Total Sisters	491
Parishes	
Parishes	89
With Resident Pastor:	
Resident Diocesan Priests	77
Resident Religious Priests	12
Without Resident Pastor:	
Administered by Priests	3
Missions	8
Welfare	
Catholic Hospitals	1
Total Assisted	168,827
Homes for the Aged	4
Total Assisted	828
Residential Care of Children	1
Total Assisted	123
Specialized Homes	5
Total Assisted	270
Special Centers for Social Services	11
Total Assisted	1,674
Educational	
Diocesan Students in Other Seminaries	19
Total Seminarians	19
High Schools, Diocesan and Parish	7
Total Students	3,784
Elementary Schools, Diocesan and Parish	39
Total Students	11,162
Elementary Schools, Private	1
Total Students	114
Catechesis/Religious Education:	
High School Students	2,164
Elementary Students	21,218
Total Students Under Catholic Instruction	38,461
Teachers in the Diocese:	
Priests	1
Sisters	72
Lay Teachers	808
Vital Statistics	
Receptions into the Church:	
Infant Baptism Totals	3,272
Adult Baptism Totals	337
Received into Full Communion	534
First Communions	3,564
Confirmations	3,226
Marriages:	
Catholic	512
Interfaith	611
Total Marriages	1,123
Deaths	2,238
Total Catholic Population	240,495
Total Population	1,940,954

Former Bishops—Rt. Rev. JEREMIAH F. SHANAHAN, D.D., cons. July 12, 1868; died Sept. 24, 1886.—Rt. Rev. THOMAS MCGOVERN, D.D., cons. March 11, 1888; died July 25, 1898.—Rt. Rev. JOHN W. SHANAHAN, D.D., cons. May 1, 1899; died Feb. 19, 1916.—Most Rev. PHILIP R. MCDEVITT, D.D., cons. Sept. 21, 1916; died Nov. 11, 1935.—Most Rev. GEORGE L. LEECH, D.D., J.C.D., appt. Auxiliary of Harrisburg July 6, 1935; cons. Oct. 17, 1935; succeeded to See Dec. 19, 1935; retired Oct. 19, 1971; died March 12, 1985.—Most Rev. JOSEPH T. DALEY, D.D., cons. Jan. 7, 1964; appt. Coadjutor Bishop July 31, 1967; succeeded to See Oct. 19, 1971; died Sept. 2, 1983.—Most Rev. WILLIAM H. KEELER, ord. July 17, 1955; cons. Sept. 21, 1979; appt. Bishop of Harrisburg, Nov. 10, 1983; succeeded to See Jan. 4, 1984; transferred Baltimore May 23, 1989.

Diocese of Harrisburg Officials

Bishop—Most Rev. NICHOLAS C. DATTILO, D.D., *P.O. Box 2153, Harrisburg, 17105-2153.* Tel: 717-657-4804.

Vicar General—Very Rev. JAMES M. LYONS, M.Div., M.Ed., *4800 Union Deposit Rd., Box 2153, Harrisburg, 17105-2153.* Tel: 717-657-4804.

General Secretary—Very Rev. JAMES M. LYONS, M.Div., M.Ed., *P.O. Box 2153, Harrisburg, 17105-2153.*

Secretary for Canonical Services—Very Rev. WILLIAM J. KING, J.C.L., M.Div., M.A., *P.O. Box 2557, Harrisburg, 17105-2557.* Tel: 717-657-4804.

Secretary for Catholic Charities—Rev. Msgr. FRANCIS M. KUMONTIS, M.S.W., M.B.A., Ph.D., *P.O. Box 3551, Harrisburg, 17105-3551.* Tel: 717-657-4804.

Secretary for Clergy and Religious Life—Very Rev. J. MICHAEL MCFADDEN, *P.O. Box 2161, Harrisburg, 17105-2161.*

Secretary for Communications—Very Rev. T. RONALD HANEY, M.A., *4800 Union Deposit Rd., P.O. Box 2555, Harrisburg, 17105-2555.* Tel: 717-657-4804.

Secretary for Education—Very Rev. EDWARD J. QUINLAN, III, M.Div., M.A., M.S., *P.O. Box 3553, Harrisburg, 17105-3553.* Tel: 717-657-4804; 921-2363 (Res.).

Secretary for Parish and Special Ministries—Very Rev. WILLIAM C. FORREY, M.A., M.Div., *P.O. Box 3557, Harrisburg, 17105-3557.* Tel: 717-657-4804.

Judicial Vicar—Very Rev. WILLIAM J. KING, J.C.L., M.A., M.Div., *P.O. Box 2557, Harrisburg, 17105-2557.* Tel: 717-657-4804.

Chancellor—CAROL HOUGHTON, S.T.D., J.C.D., *P.O. Box 2557, Harrisburg, 17105-2557.* Tel: 717-657-4804.

Diocesan Offices, Commissions, Boards and Programs

Adult Religious Formation, Department for—Dr. MARY ANN BOYARSKI, Dir., *P.O. Box 2161, Harrisburg, 17105-2161.*

Archives—KATHLEEN SIGNOR, Archivist, *4800 Union Deposit Rd., P.O. Box 2153, Harrisburg, 17105-2153.* Tel: 717-657-4804.

Black Catholic Ministry—GWEN SUMMERS, Coord., *4800 Union Deposit Rd., P.O. Box 3557, Harrisburg, 17105.* Tel: 717-657-4804.

Buildings and Properties—LES ZIMMERMAN, Dir., *4800 Union Deposit Rd., P.O. Box 3651, Harrisburg, 17105.* Tel: 717-657-4804.

Campus Ministry—Very Rev. WILLIAM C. FORREY, M.A., M.Div., Coord., *P.O. Box 3557, Harrisburg, 17105.* Tel: 717-657-4804.

Catholic Charities Administration, Department for—MATTHEW ZABOLOTNY, Dir., *P.O. Box 3551, Harrisburg, 17105.*

Catholic Charities Counseling/Field Services, Department for—Reg. Directors: PETER BIASUCCI, L.S.W.; FRANK KOEBER, M.S., M.F.; THOMAS THORPE, *P.O. Box 3551, Harrisburg, 17105.*

Catholic Schools, Department for—Sr. SUE ANN STEVES, I.H.M., Supt., *P.O. Box 3553, Harrisburg, 17105.*

The "Catholic Witness"—Very Rev. T. RONALD HANEY, Exec. Editor, *4800 Union Deposit Rd., Box 2555, Harrisburg, 17105.* Tel: 717-657-4804.

Catholic Women, Diocesan Council of—PATRICIA LEONE, *17 Clover Lane, Mechanicsburg, 17055.* Tel: 717-766-2599.

Cemeteries—EDWARD G. FARADAY, Dir., *4800 Union Deposit Rd., Box 3651, Harrisburg, 17105.* Tel: 717-652-0539.

Charismatic Movement—Rev. FRANCIS KARWACKI, Liaison, *732 E. Main St., Lykens, 17048.*

Consultors, College—Revs. JOHN BATEMAN; ROBERT GILLELAN; Rev. Msgr. LAWRENCE OVERBAUGH; Very Rev. PATRICK A. DEVINE, V.F.; Very Rev. PAUL C. HELWIG; Very Rev. KENNETH F. LAWRENCE, V.F.; Very Rev. JAMES M. LYONS, V.G.; Revs. J. MICHAEL MCFADDEN; SAMUEL HOUSER; THOMAS LANGAN; ROBERT YOHE; CHESTER A. SNYDER.

Cursillo Movement—Rev. Msgr. THOMAS H. SMITH, Moderator.

Deans—Very Rev. JOSEPH C. HILBERT, V.F., Adams Deanery; Very Rev. RICHARD P. WALDRON, V.F., Cumberland/Perry Deanery; Rev. Msgr. WILLIAM M. RICHARDSON, V.F., Dauphin Deanery; Rev. Msgr. THOMAS R. BRENNER, V.F., Franklin Deanery; Very Rev. KENNETH F. LAWRENCE, V.F., North Lancaster Deanery; Rev. Msgr. THOMAS H. SMITH, V.F., South Lancaster Deanery; Very Rev. DAVID T. MCANDREW, V.F., Lebanon Deanery; Very Rev. PATRICK A. DEVINE, V.F., Northern Deanery; Very Rev. THOMAS R. HOKE, V.F., York Deanery.

Diocesan Center—LES ZIMMERMAN, Coord., *4800 Union Deposit Rd., P.O. Box 3651, Harrisburg, 17105.* Tel: 717-657-4804.

Ecumenical and Interreligious Affairs—Deacon CHARLES CLARK, Dir., *P.O. Box 3557, Harrisburg, 17105.*

Family Ministries, Department for—VICTORIA LASKOWSKI, J.D., Dir., *P.O. Box 3557, Harrisburg, 17105.* Tel: 717-657-4804.

Finance Council—

Financial Administration, Department for—EDWARD G. FARADAY, Dir., *4800 Union Deposit Rd., P.O. Box 3651, Harrisburg, 17105.* Tel: 717-657-4804.

Health Care Ministry—*P.O. Box 3557, Harrisburg, 17105.*

Holy Name Societies—NORMAND RABOIN, Liaison, *334 Frederick St., Hanover, 17331.* Tel: 717-637-6491.

Knights of Columbus—PATRICK MONAGHAN, Pres., *1304 Foerster Dr., New Cumberland, 17070.* Tel: 717-774-3489.

Ministry Development, Department for—MARY ANN O'DONNELL, Dir., *4800 Union Deposit Rd., P.O. Box 3557, Harrisburg, 17105.* Tel: 717-657-4804.

Lay Personnel, Department for—Very Rev. JAMES M. LYONS, M.Div., M.Ed., *Box 2153, Harrisburg, 17105.* Tel: 717-657-4804.

Legion of Mary—Rev. WALTER SEMPKO, Moderator, *1051 Avila Rd., Harrisburg, 17109.* Tel: 717-652-5900.

Missions, Office of (Home and Foreign)—Rev. ROBERT F. SHARMAN, S.T.L., Dir., *P.O. Box 3657, Harrisburg, 17105.* Tel: 717-657-4804.

Pastoral Council, Diocesan—ANNA BIANCO; DANIEL P. ERNST; VERONICA FABIAN; LAWRENCE P. GEMMELL; Very Rev. WILLIAM C. FORREY; Deacon MICHAEL A. GRELLA; Dr. CAROL L. HOUGHTON; SARAH C. KANASKIE; ERNEST P. KLINE; JOSEPH C. LAMONT; NINH V. LE; BLANDINA LECCE; Very Rev. JAMES M. LYONS; Dr. HUGH F. MCKEEGAN; LORRAINE MITRICK; ALBERTA COSTA NORTON; MARY ANN O'DONNELL; Rev. EDWARD J. QUINLAN, III; THOMAS ROBEL; Dr. WALTER SEVERS; Rev. ROBERT F. SHARMAN; Sr. MARY AGNES SHURER, S.C.C.

Permanent Diaconate, Office for—Very Rev. J. MICHAEL MCFADDEN, Dir., *P.O. Box 2161, Harrisburg, 17105.* Tel: 717-657-4804.

Deanery Primary—Rev. THOMAS F. LANGAN, Adams; Rev. CHESTER P. SNYDER, Cumberland/Perry; Rev. DANIEL C. MITZEL, Dauphin; Rev. ROBERT A. YOHE, JR., Franklin; Rev. ANDREW P. MARINAK, Lebanon; Rev. RAYMOND COLLINS, C.SS.R., North Lancaster; Very Rev. BERNARDO PISTONE, South Lancaster; Rev. THOMAS A. SCALA, Northern; Rev. Msgr. LAWRENCE R. OVERBAUGH, Northumberland; Rev. ROBERT M. GILLELAN, York.

Appointed—Revs. JOHN B. BATEMAN; SYLVAN P. CAPITANI, D.Min.; Very Rev. PATRICK A. DEVINE, V.F.; Revs. PAUL C. HELWIG; MICHAEL E. HOMOLA; SAMUEL E. HOUSER; Very Rev. KENNETH F. LAWRENCE, V.F.; Revs. DANIEL F.X. POWELL; JOHN D. SCHMALHOFER.

Prison Ministry—*P.O. Box 3557, Harrisburg, 17105.*

Project: Head, Elder Council—VICTORIA LASKOWSKI, Coord., *P.O. Box 3557, Harrisburg, 17105.*

Respect Life/Human Growth and Development, Office for—MARY SHRIVER, M.A., Dir., *P.O. Box 3553, Harrisburg, 17105.*

Public Relations, Department for—Very Rev. T. RONALD HANEY, M.A., Dir., *P.O. Box 2555, Harrisburg, 17105.*

Religious Education (CCD), Department for—Vacant, *P.O. Box 3553, Harrisburg, 17105.*

Religious Life, Department for—*P.O. Box 2161, Harrisburg, 17105.*

Saint Thomas More Society—GINA M. D'ALFONSO, Esq., *P.O. Box 8212, Harrisburg, 17105.* Tel: 717-787-7213.

Saint Vincent de Paul Society—JOSEPH MERLINA, Pres., *40 Hickorytown Rd., Carlisle, 17013.* Tel: 717-243-1090.

Spanish Speaking Ministry—Very Rev. BERNARDO PISTONE, Vicar, *Assumption B.V.M., 119 S. Prince St., Lancaster, 17603.* Tel: 717-392-2578.

Special Ministries, Department for—Very Rev. WILLIAM C. FORREY, Dir., *P.O. Box 3557, Harrisburg, 17105.*

Telecommunications—JOSEPH APONICK, Dir., *4800 Union Deposit Rd., Box 2555, Harrisburg, 17105.* Tel: 717-657-4804.

Tribunal—*4800 Union Deposit Rd., P.O. Box 2557, Harrisburg, 17105.* Tel: 717-657-4804; Fax: 717-657-1573.

Judicial Vicar—Very Rev. WILLIAM J. KING, J.C.L.

Adjutant Judicial Vicar—Rev. EDWARD C. MALESIC, J.C.L.

Case Services Administrator—Mrs. BARBARA A. ROTH.

Diocesan Judges—Rev. Msgr. MERCURIO A. FREGAPANE; Rev. Msgr. RICHARD A. YOUTZ, J.C.L.; CAROL L. HOUGHTON, S.T.D., J.C.D.

Defender of the Bond—Rev. EDWARD R. LAVELLE, S.T.L.

Promoter of Justice—CAROL L. HOUGHTON, S.T.D., J.C.D.

Advocates—Rev. Msgr. THOMAS J. KUJOVSKY; Rev. MICHAEL A. MESSARO, M.SS.CC.; Mr. ROBERT F. O'DONNELL; BARBARA A. ROTH.

Notaries—CAROL WILK; KATHRYN GOULDY; RITA PATACKIS.

Vietnamese Ministry—Rev. JOSEPH HOA VAN NGUYEN, Coord., *Our Lady of the Blessed Sacrament, 2121 N. Third St., Harrisburg, 17110.* Tel: 717-233-1014.

Vocations, Office for—Rev. THOMAS J. ROZMAN, S.T.B., Dir., *P.O. Box 2161, Harrisburg, 17105.* Tel: 717-657-4804.

World Apostolate of Fatima—Rev. JOHN A. SZADA, JR., Spiritual Moderator, *St. Francis of Assisi, 1439 Market St., Harrisburg, 17103.* Tel: 717-232-1003.

Worship, Office of—Mrs. PATRICIA BOGDAN, Dir., *P.O. Box 2161, Harrisburg, 17105.* Tel: 717-657-4804.

Youth and Young Adult Ministry, Department for—ROBERT WILLIAMS, Dir., *4800 Union Deposit Rd., Box 3551, Harrisburg, 17105.* Tel: 717-657-4804.

CLERGY, PARISHES, MISSIONS AND PAROCHIAL SCHOOLS

CITY OF HARRISBURG
(Dauphin County)

1—CATHEDRAL PARISH OF ST. PATRICK (1995), Rev. Msgr. William M. Richardson, V.F.; Deacons J. Leo Dunn; Charles W. Clark. In res., Very Rev. J. Michael McFadden.
Res., 212 State St., 17101. Tel: 717-232-2169; Fax: 717-232-2799.
Catechesis/Religious Programs—Students 105.

2—ST. CATHERINE LABOURE (1948). (Shrine of the Miraculous Medal). Rev. Msgr. Hugh A. Overbaugh; Rev. Leo M. Goodman, III; Deacons Thomas H. Flannery; William E. Whale; Thomas A. Fedor. In res., Rev. Curtis R. Delarm; Very Rev. James M. Lyons, V.G.; Rev. Msgr. Vincent J. Topper.
Res., 4000 Derry St., 17111. Tel: 717-564-1321; Fax: 717-564-8822.
School—4020 Derry St., 17111. Tel: 717-564-1760; Fax: 717-564-3010. Sr. Suzanne Duzen, SS.C.M., Prin.
Sisters of SS. Cyril and Methodius 5; Lay Teachers 32; Students 593.
Catechesis/Religious Programs—Sr. Carol Marie, SS.C.M., D.R.E.
Students 391.
Convent—4010 Derry St., 17111. Tel: 717-564-0721.

3—ST. FRANCIS OF ASSISI (1901), Rev. Daniel C. Mitzel; Hilda Gomez, Pastoral Assoc.; Deacons Miguel Marroquin; Francis Enderle. In res., Rev. John Szada.
Res., 1439 Market St., 17103. Tel: 717-232-1003; Fax: 717-232-4536.
Catechesis/Religious Programs—Tel: 717-233-7912.
Students 53.

4—HOLY FAMILY (1958), Rev. Bernard P. McGinley, M.A.
Church—555 S. 25th St., 17104. Tel: 717-232-4237; Fax: 717-232-9661.
Rectory: 2501 Barkley Ln., 17104. Tel: 717-561-8250.
School—Tel: 717-232-2551. Sr. Joseph Marie Carter, I.H.M., Prin.
Sisters Servants of the Immaculate Heart of Mary 2; Lay Teachers 9; Students 213.
Catechesis/Religious Programs—Students 282.
Convent—2473 Adrian St., 17104. Tel: 717-564-7236.

5—HOLY NAME OF JESUS (Lower Paxton Twp.) (1960), Revs. Daniel J. Mahoney; David S. Keller; Francis M. Lahout, (Retired); Deacons Jerome Foerster; Joseph J. Wrabel.
Res., 6150 Allentown Blvd., 17112. Tel: 717-652-4211; Fax: 717-652-2033.
School—(Grades K-8). (Lower Paxton Twp.) 6190 Allentown Blvd., 17112. Tel: 717-657-1704; Fax: 717-697-8834. Tom Nissley, Prin.
Sisters of St. Joseph 1; Lay Teachers 53; Students 856.
Catechesis/Religious Programs—Tel: 717-545-1154; Fax: 717-545-1154. Evelyn Alviani, D.R.E.
Students 1,543.
Convent—Tel: 717-545-4357.
Pastoral Associates 2; Teachers 1; Diocesan Administrators 2.

6—ST. LAWRENCE (1859) (German). Closed. See St. Patrick Cathedral, Harrisburg.

7—ST. MARGARET MARY ALACOQUE (Penbrook) (1948), Revs. John G. Allen; Wesley M. Mash; Mrs. Karen Hurley, Pastoral Assoc.
Res., 2848 Herr St., 17103-1817. Tel: 717-233-3062; Fax: 717-238-5633.
School—Tel: 717-232-3771; Fax: 717-232-0776. Mrs. Joyce Haug, Prin.
Sisters of Mercy 2; Lay Teachers 19; Students 365.
Catechesis/Religious Programs—Tel: 717-232-3800. Mrs. Suzanne Fonner, D.R.E.
Students 163.

8—OUR LADY OF THE BLESSED SACRAMENT (1906), Revs. Paul R. Shuda; Michael Laicha; Deacon John Mowery, (Retired); Cecelia Jackson, Pastoral Assoc. In res., Rev. Joseph Hoa Nguyen.
Res., 2121 N. Third St., 17110-1812. Tel: 717-233-1014; Fax: 717-234-5652.
Catechesis/Religious Programs—Tel: 717-234-8656.
Students 41.

9—SACRED HEART OF JESUS (1901). Closed. See St. Patrick Cathedral, Harrisburg.

OUTSIDE THE CITY OF HARRISBURG

Abbottstown, York Co., Immaculate Heart of Mary (1809), Rev. Thomas F. Langan; Deacon Raymond J. Smith. In res., Rev. Msgr. Robert C. Gribbin.
Res., R.D. 1, Box 343, Canal Rd., 17301-9051. Tel: 717-259-0611; Fax: 717-259-6371. [CEM]
Catechesis/Religious Programs—Tel: 717-259-9426.
Students 249.

Annville, Lebanon Co., St. Paul the Apostle (1928), Rev. John D. Peck, O.S.B.
Res., 125 S. Spruce St., 17003. Tel: 717-867-1525; Fax: 717-867-5318.
Catechesis/Religious Programs—Tel: 717-867-7471.
Students 256.
Stations—Fort Indiantown Gap, Our Lady of Victory, Tel: 717-861-2241; Lebanon Valley College, Miller Chapel, Tel: 717-867-6135.

Berwick, Columbia Co., Immaculate Conception of the Blessed Virgin Mary (1906), Rev. Francis J. Tamburro.
Res., 1730 Fowler Ave., 18603-1462. Tel: 717-759-8113; Fax: 717-759-6637. [CEM]
School—Holy Family Consolidated School, Tel: 717-752-2021; Fax: 717-752-2914.
Catechesis/Religious Programs—Tel: 717-759-9225.
Students 217.

St. Joseph's (1928), Rev. Dennis G. Dalessandro; Sr. M. Carmelina, D.M., Pastoral Assoc.
Res., 721 Monroe St., 18603. Tel: 570-752-5684.
School—Holy Family Consolidated School, Tel: 570-752-2021; Fax: 570-752-5623. Sr. M. Judith Tarozzi, D.M., Prin.
Catechesis/Religious Programs—Students 130.
Convent—728 Washington St., 18603. Tel: 570-752-2112. Daughters of Mercy
Sisters 4.

Bloomsburg, Columbia Co., St. Columba (1882) (Irish), Rev. Patrick A. Devine.
Mailing Address: P.O. Box 829, 17815. Tel: 570-784-0801; Fax: 570-387-2604. [CEM]
Res., 42 E. Third St., 17815. [CEM]
School—(Grades PreK-6) 40 E. Third St., 17815. Tel: 570-784-5932. Mrs. Margaret Jessick, Prin.
Sisters 1; Lay Teachers 6; Students 163.
Catechesis/Religious Programs—Tel: 570-387-4068.
Students 350.
Convent—342 Iron St., 17815. Tel: 570-784-1385.
Mission—Benton, Columbia Co., Christ the King, Mendenhall Ln., Benton, 17814. Tel: 570-925-6969.

Blue Ridge Summit, Franklin Co., St. Rita (1919), Revs. Michael A. Messaro, M.SS.CC.; John J. Cavanaugh, M.SS.CC.
Mailing Address: Immaculate Conception, P.O. Box 704, Fairfield, 17320. Tel: 717-642-8815; Fax: 717-642-9616. [JC]
Catechesis/Religious Programs—Students 48.

Bonneauville, Adam Co., St. Joseph (1859), Rev. Philip DeChico; Deacon Richard J. Weaver.
Res., 12 E. Hanover St., Gettysburg, 17325-7750. Tel: 717-334-2510; Fax: 717-337-1968. [CEM]
Catechesis/Religious Programs—Students 50.

Buchanan Valley, Adams Co., St. Ignatius Loyola (Orrtanna) (1817), Rev. Carl J. Steffen.
Res., 1095 Church Rd., Orrtanna, 17353. Tel: 717-677-8012. [CEM]
Catechesis/Religious Programs—Tel: 717-677-8012.
Students 80.

Camp Hill, Cumberland Co., Good Shepherd (1951), Revs. Paul C. Helwig; Neil S. Sullivan; Deacon Francis Gorman. In res., Very Rev. William J. King.
Res., 3435 Trindle Rd., 17011. Tel: 717-761-1167; Fax: 717-761-5313.
School—Tel: 717-737-7261; Fax: 717-761-4673. Mrs. Maretta K. Schmidt, Prin.
Lay Teachers 16; Students 248.
Catechesis/Religious Programs—3400 Market St., 17011. Tel: 717-737-8216. Mrs. Lucille Smith, D.R.E.
Students 286.

Carlisle, Cumberland Co., St. Patrick (1779), Revs. Andrew J. Fontanella; Edward J. Keating; Andre J. Meluskey; Deacon Gerard J. Kole. In res., Rev. Daniel J. Menniti.
Res., 140 E. Pomfret St., 17013. Tel: 717-243-4411; Fax: 717-258-9281. [CEM 2]
School—87 Marsh Dr., 17013. Tel: 717-249-4826; Fax: 717-245-0522. Sr. Karen Washabaugh, S.S.J., Prin.; Marilynn Noel, Asst. Prin.
Lay Teachers 27; Students 475.
Catechesis/Religious Programs—Tel: 717-243-4891. Mrs. Helen Richards, D.R.E.
Students 351.
Chapel—Pine Grove Furnace, St. Eleanor Regina.

Centralia, Columbia Co., St. Ignatius (1869). Closed. See Our Lady of Mount Carmel, Mount Carmel.

Chambersburg, Franklin Co., Corpus Christi (1792), Rev. Msgr. Thomas R. Brenner, V.F.; Revs. Daniel F. Lawler, S.J.; Luis R. Rodriguez.
Res., 320 Philadelphia Ave., 17201. Tel: 717-264-6317; Fax: 717-264-1787. [CEM]
School—305 N. Second St., 17201. Tel: 717-263-5036; Fax: 717-263-6079. Mr. Robert G. Dortenzo, Prin.
Lay Teachers 21; Students 331.
Catechesis/Religious Programs—Tel: 717-263-9541. Mr. David C. Cheslock, D.R.E.
Students 234.
Mission—Doylesburg, Franklin Co., Our Lady of Refuge, 21169 Cross Rd., Doylesburg, 17219. Tel: 717-349-7953. Rev. John R. Campion, Admin.
Station—Scotland School for Veterans' Children, Tel: 717-264-7187; Fax: 717-264-0322.

Coal Township, North Thumberland Co., Our Lady of Hope, Very Rev. Philip G. Burger, V.F.; Rev. Charles L. Persing.
Res., 863 W. Chestnut St., 17866-1995. Tel: 570-648-4432; Fax: 570-648-8944.
Catechesis/Religious Programs—Students 138.

St. Stephen Protomartyr, Northumberland Co., (1898) (Polish). Closed. See Our Lady of Hope, Coal Township.

Columbia, Lancaster Co., St. Peter (1828), Rev. Kenneth G. Smith; Sr. George Ann Biscan, A.S.C., Pastoral Assoc.
Res., 121 S. Second St., 17512. Tel: 717-684-7070. [CEM 2]
School—Our Lady of the Angels, 215 Union St., 17512-1725. Tel: 717-684-2433; Fax: 717-684-2664. Mrs. Theresa M. Burg, Prin.
Lay Teachers 21; Students 343.
Catechesis/Religious Programs—Tel: 717-684-7070. Richard Groff, D.R.E.
Students 70.
Convent—Tel: 717-684-2707.
Mission—Wrightsville, York Co., Mother of Holy Purity, 217 Maple St., 17368. Tel: 717-252-3806.

Holy Trinity (1860), Very Rev. Kenneth F. Lawrence; Sr. Anna Cosgrave, O.S.F., Pastoral Assoc.
Res., 409 Cherry St., 17512. Tel: 717-684-2711; Fax: 717-684-9612. [CEM]
School—(Consolidated) 404 Cherry St., 17512. Tel: 717-684-2664; Fax: 717-684-5039. Theresa Burg, Prin.
Lay Teachers 21; Students 317.
Catechesis/Religious Programs—Tel: 717-684-2232.
Students 149.
Convent—548 Cherry St., 17512. Tel: 717-684-2232. Sisters of St. Francis of Philadelphia

Conewago Township, Adams Co., Basilica of the Sacred Heart of Jesus (1730), Rev. Lawrence J. McNeil, D.Min.
Res., 30 Basilica Dr., Hanover, 17331-8924. Tel: 717-637-2721. [CEM]
School—Tel: 717-632-8715. Sr. Eileen Kean, Prin.
Sisters of St. Joseph 4; Lay Teachers 8; Students 265.
Convent—55 Basilica Dr., Hanover, 17331. Tel: 717-637-3370. Sisters of St. Joseph
Sisters 6.

Cornwall, Lebanon Co., Sacred Heart of Jesus (1886), Rev. Andrew P. Marinak.
Res., 2596 Cornwall Rd., P.O. Box 136, 17016-0136. Tel: 717-273-1574. [CEM]
Parish Center—Tel: 717-274-3239.
Catechesis/Religious Programs—Tel: 717-273-2160. Sr. Helen Ann Gaidos, D.R.E.
Students 106.

Dallastown, York Co., St. Joseph (1850), Rev. Robert S. Panza; Deacon John Weaver.
Res., 251 E. Main St., 17313. Tel: 717-246-3007; Fax: 717-244-5278. [CEM][JC]
School—271 E. Main St., 17313. Tel: 717-244-9386; Fax: 717-244-9478. Donna Phillips, Prin.
Lay Teachers 10; Students 230.
Catechesis/Religious Programs—Tel: 717-244-6279.
Students 1,267.

Danville, Montour Co., St. Joseph (1848), Revs. William M. Weary; Lawrence C. Gross.
Res., 18 E. Center St., 17821. Tel: 570-275-2512; Fax: 570-275-6840. [CEM 3]
School—511 Ferry St., 17821. Tel: 717-275-2435.
Sisters 1; Lay Teachers 8; Students 170.
Catechesis/Religious Programs—Students 404.
Convent—9 Bloom St., 17821. Tel: 570-275-5933.

Dauphin, Dauphin Co., St. Matthew, Apostle and Evangelist (1976), Very Rev. Edward J. Quinlan; Deacon Richard Aull.
Res., 420 Stony Creek Rd., P.O. Box 459, 17018. Tel: 717-921-2363; Fax: 717-921-2364.
Catechesis/Religious Programs—Students 74.

Doylesburg, Franklin Co., Our Lady of Refuge Mission (1802), Rev. John R. Campion, Admin. (Retired).
Res., 21169 Cross Rd., 17219. Tel: 717-349-7953; Fax: 717-349-7255. [CEM]
Catechesis/Religious Programs—Students 12.

Elizabethtown, Lancaster Co., St. Peter (1752), Rev. David L. Danneker, Ph.D. In res., Rev. Msgr. Thomas J. Kujovsky; Deacon Richard A. Ryan.
Parish Office: 1840 Marshall Dr., 17022. Tel: 717-367-1255; Fax: 717-367-1270.
Res., 1 Saint Peter's Pl., 17022-1956. [CEM]
School—61 E. Washington St., 17022. Tel: 717-367-1678. Mrs. Paula Fish, Prin.
Lay Teachers 6; Students 107.
Catechesis/Religious Programs—Students 212.

Elysburg, Northumberland Co., Queen of the Most Holy Rosary (1950), Rev. Charles R. Slough.
Res., 103 W. Center St., 17824. Tel: 750-672-2302; Fax: 570-672-3310. [JC]
Catechesis/Religious Programs—Tel: 570-672-9930.
Students 215.

Enhaut, Dauphin Co., St. John the Evangelist (1902). Closed. See Prince of Peace, Steelton.

Enola, Cumberland Co., Our Lady of Lourdes (1926), Rev. John A. Acri; Ms. Celeste Hamilton, Pastoral Assoc.; Deacon Edwin L. Fitzpatrick.
Res., 225 Salt Rd., 17025. Tel: 717-732-9642; Fax: 717-732-8184.
Catechesis/Religious Programs—Students 433.

Ephrata, Lancaster Co., Mother of Perpetual Help (1914), Very Rev. Raymond F. Collins, C.SS.R.; Revs. Brendan P. Greany, C.SS.R.; William G. Geiger, C.SS.R.; John J. Dorff, C.SS.R.; Deacon Robert Robertson.
Church Office: 320 Church Ave., 17522. Tel: 717-733-9641; Fax: 717-733-2119.
Res., 300 W. Pine St., P.O. Box 209, 17522. Tel: 717-733-6596; Fax: 717-733-0502. [JC]
School—330 Church Ave., 17522. Tel: 717-738-2414; Fax: 717-738-3280. Sr. Marie Gayda, O.S.F., Prin.
Bernardine Sisters of the Third Order of St. Francis 4; Lay Teachers 10; Students 328.
Catechesis/Religious Programs—Tel: 717-738-4517; Fax: 717-733-2119.
Students 427.
Convent—310 Church Ave., 17522. Tel: 717-733-1291.

Fairfield, Adams Co., Immaculate Conception of the Blessed Virgin Mary (1823), Revs. Michael A. Messaro, M.SS.CC.; John J. Cavanaugh, M.SS.CC. 256 Tract Rd., P.O. Box 704, 17320.
Res., 17320. Tel: 717-642-8815; Fax: 717-642-9616. [CEM][JC]
Catechesis/Religious Programs—Students 120.

Gettysburg, Adams Co., St. Francis Xavier's (1831), Very Rev. Joseph C. Hilbert, V.F.; Revs. Michael E. Messner; Jeffrey F. Thomas; Deacons James Sneeringer; Leonard Cain.
Res., 22 W. High St., 17325. Tel: 717-334-3919; 334-7711; Fax: 717-338-0831. [CEM]
School—45 W. High St., 17325. Tel: 717-334-4221; Fax: 717-334-8883. Sr. Phyllis R.S.M., Prin.
Sisters of Mercy 2; Sisters of St. Joseph; l; Lay Teachers 15; Students 261.
Catechesis/Religious Programs—Tel: 717-334-1221.
Students 522.
Convents—Tel: 717-334-4310. Sisters of Mercy Convent
Sisters 4; Tel: 717-338-0844. Sisters of St. Joseph Convent
Sisters 2.

Greencastle, Franklin Co., St. Mark the Evangelist (1965), Rev. Joseph L. Stahura.
Res., 395 S. Ridge Ave., P.O. Box 218, 17225. Tel: 717-597-2705. [JC]
Catechesis/Religious Programs—Tel: 717-597-2705.
Students 209.
Mission—Mercersburg, Franklin Co., St. Luke the Evangelist, Overhill Dr. & Black Rd., 17236.

Hanover, York Co., St. Joseph (1864), Revs. Joseph F. Gotwalt; John R. Bateman.
Res., 244 Baltimore St., 17331. Tel: 717-637-5236; Fax: 717-637-6615. [CEM]
School—236 Baltimore St., 17331. Tel: 717-632-1335; Fax: 717-632-5147. Mrs. Susan M. Mummert, Prin.
Lay Teachers 16; Students 254.
Catechesis/Religious Programs—Tel: 717-637-7028.
Students 653.
Convent—252 Baltimore St., 17331. Tel: 717-637-4233.

St. Vincent (1904), Rev. Bernard Quinn.
Res., 220 Third St., 17331. Tel: 717-637-4625; Fax: 717-637-6650. [CEM]
School—224 Third St., 17331. Tel: 717-637-5190.
Lay Teachers 8; Students 201.
Catechesis/Religious Programs—Students 60.

Hershey, Dauphin Co., St. Joan of Arc (1920), Rev. Msgr. Leo N. Bierster; Revs. Caesar A. Belchez; Martin Aitsebaomo, O.P.; Deacon Thomas S. Oliver. In res., Rev. Msgr. Francis M. Kumontis.
Res., 359 W. Areba Ave., 17033. Tel: 717-533-7168; Fax: 717-520-0526.
School—329 W. Areba Ave., 17033. Tel: 717-533-2854; Fax: 717-534-0755. Sr. Eileen M. McGowan, Prin.
Daughters of Our Lady of Mercy 2; Lay Teachers 21; Students 333.
Catechesis/Religious Programs—Tel: 717-533-8578.
Students 688.
Convent—Tel: 717-533-2864.
Sisters 3.

Kulpmont, Northumberland Co., Assumption of the Blessed Virgin Mary (1909). Closed. See Holy Angels, Kulpmont.

St. Casimir (1915). Closed. See Holy Angels, Kulpmont.

Holy Angels (1995), Rev. Raymond J. Orloski.
Res., 855 Scott St., 17834. Tel: 570-373-1221; Fax: 570-373-1226. [CEM 3]
Catechesis/Religious Programs—863 Scott St., 17834. Tel: 570-373-1512.
Students 220.

Lancaster, Lancaster Co.,

1—St. Anne, (1923), Rev. Gerald A. Lytle; Rev. Msgr. Leo A. Beierschmitt; Deacons Frank Eckman; Joseph L. Anders.
Res., 929 N. Duke St., 17602. Tel: 717-392-2225.
School—Cherry & Liberty St., 17602. Tel: 717-394-6711; Fax: 717-394-8628.
Lay Teachers 11; Students 263. Principals: Donna Power, (Elementary); Dermot Garrett, (High School).
Catechesis/Religious Programs—Tel: 717-397-8755. Mrs. Suzanne Ganse, D.R.E.
Students 110.

2—St. Anthony of Padua, (1870), Revs. Patrick. McGarrity, C.SS.R.; James Small, C.SS.R.; Patrick Flynn, C.SS.R.
Res., 501 E. Orange St., 17602. Tel: 717-394-0669; Fax: 717-394-4507. [CEM]
School—Resurrection. See Assumption of the Blessed Virgin Mary, Lancaster, and report of Resurrection School for details. Tel: 717-397-3136; Fax: 717-295-8475.
Catechesis/Religious Programs—Tel: 717-392-2930. Patricia Meyer, D.R.E.
Students 129.
Convent—533 E. Orange St., 17602. Tel: 717-397-1043. Sisters of the Holy Cross
Stations—Lancaster, Lancaster County Prison, Tel: 717-299-7800; Conestoga View Nursing Home, Tel: 717-299-7850.

3—Assumption of the Blessed Virgin Mary, (1741), Very Rev. Bernardo Pistone; Revs. Thomas J. Gralinski; Allan F. Wolfe; Ignacio Palomino (Peru); Mrs. Frances Sescilla, Pastoral Assoc.; Deacon Manuel Velazquez.
Res., 119 S. Prince St., 17603. Tel: 717-392-2578; Fax: 717-394-6549.

School—Resurrection. Consolidation of St. Anthony, St. Joseph and St. Mary. 32 W. Vine St., 17603. Tel: 717-397-3136. Mary Jo Moczulski, Prin. Religious 2; Lay Teachers 20; Students 450.
Catechesis/Religious Programs—Ann Bleistine, D.R.E.
Students 250.

4—ST. JOHN NEUMANN, (1978), Rev. Msgr. Richard A. Youtz, J.C.L.; Rev. David M. Hereshko; Sr. Helen E. McCormac, Pastoral Assoc.; Deacon William J. Jordan.
Res., 601 E. Delp Rd., 17601. Tel: 717-569-8531; Fax: 717-569-2135.
Catechesis/Religious Programs—Tel: 717-569-8533. Mrs. Patty Zanghi, D.R.E.
Students 1,173.

5—ST. JOSEPH, (1849), Rev. Msgr. Thomas H. Smith; Rev. Msgr. Cletus H. Wagman, Senior Priest; Mrs. Patricia Weaver, Pastoral Assoc.
Res., 440 St. Joseph St., 17603-5298. Tel: 717-397-6921. [CEM]
School—Resurrection. See Assumption of the Blessed Virgin Mary, Lancaster, for details.
Catechesis/Religious Programs—Students 118.

6—SACRED HEART OF JESUS, (1900), Rev. Michael J. Grab.
Res., 558 W. Walnut St., 17603. Tel: 717-394-0757; Fax: 717-394-3589.
School—235 Nevin St., 17603. Tel: 717-393-8433. Sr. Patricia McKee, I.H.M., Prin.
Servants of the Immaculate Heart of Mary 4; Lay Teachers 13; Students 239.
Catechesis/Religious Programs—Sr. Mary Elizabeth Schmidt, I.H.M., D.R.E.
Students 85.
Convent—565 W. Walnut St., 17603. Tel: 717-392-4522.

Lebanon, Lebanon Co.,

1—ASSUMPTION OF THE BLESSED VIRGIN MARY, (1810), Very Rev. David T. McAndrew, V.F.; Rev. Stan U. Ukwe, O.P.; Deacon Richard Wentzel. In res., Rev. Walter A. Halaburda.
Office & Res.: 2 N. Eighth St., 17046. Tel: 717-272-5674; Fax: 717-270-2734. [CEM][JC]
Catechesis/Religious Programs—Debra Herr, D.R.E.
Students 335.
Mission—Lebanon, Lebanon Co., Our Lady of Fatima, 2 N. 8th St., 17046.

2—ST. BENEDICT THE ABBOT, (1995), Rev. Msgr. Mercurio A. Fregapane.
Res., 1300 Lehman St., 17046-3331. Tel: 717-272-0623; Fax: 717-270-6926.
Catechesis/Religious Programs—Tel: 717-272-1242.
Students 168.

3—ST. CECILIA, (1995), Revs. Joseph T. Scanlin; Walter A. Sempko, (Retired).
Res., 202 E. Lehman St., 17046. Tel: 717-272-4412; Fax: 717-272-3966. [CEM]
Catechesis/Religious Programs—Tel: 717-272-4352.
Students 170.

4—ST. GERTRUDE, (1906). Closed. See St. Cecilia, Lebanon.

5—ST. GREGORY THE GREAT, (1965). Closed. See St. Cecilia, Lebanon.

6—SS. CYRIL AND METHODIUS, (1905) (Slavonic). Closed. See St. Benedict the Abbot, Lebanon.

Lewisburg, Union Co., Sacred Heart of Jesus (1935), Revs. William J. Nessel, O.S.F.S.; Patrick J. Shannon.
Res., 814 St. Louis St., 17837. Tel: 570-523-3104; Fax: 570-524-5156.
Catechesis/Religious Programs—D.R.E.: Sr. Karen Wilson, SS.C.M.; Sr. Thomas More Dzurnak, SS.C.M., Pastoral Sister.
Students 380.
Mission—Mifflinburg, Union Co., Saint George Church, 999 Buffalo Rd., Mifflinburg, 17844.

Lewistown, Mifflin Co., Sacred Heart of Jesus (1830), Revs. Thomas C. Marickovic; Lawrence Coakley.
Res., 106 N. Dorcas St., 17044. Tel: 717-242-2781; Fax: 717-248-0260. [CEM]
School—110 N. Dorcas St., 17044. Tel: 717-248-5351; 248-0260; Fax: 717-248-5351.
Lay Teachers 12; Students 119.

Lititz, Lancaster Co., St. James (1977), Rev. Gerard J. Szymkowiak, C.SS.R.
Res., 505 Woodcrest Ave., 17543. Tel: 717-626-5580; Fax: 717-626-2146.
Catechesis/Religious Programs—Tel: 717-626-0244. Joseph Trainor, D.R.E.
Students 480.

Littlestown, Adams Co., St. Aloysius (1884), Rev. James M. Sterner.
Res., 29 S. Queen St., 17340. Tel: 717-359-4513; Fax: 717-359-0683. [CEM]

Catechesis/Religious Programs—Faith Redding, D.R.E.
Students 164.

Locustdale, Columbia Co., St. Joseph (1913). Closed. See Our Lady of Mount Carmel, Mount Carmel.

Locust Gap, Northumberland Co., St. Joseph (1870). Closed. See Our Lady of Mount Carmel, Mount Carmel.

Lykens, Dauphin Co., Our Lady Help of Christians (1853), Rev. Francis J. Karwacki, M.Ed., M.Div.
Res., 732 E. Main St., 17048. Tel: 717-453-7895. [CEM 2][JC 3]
Catechesis/Religious Programs—Tel: 717-453-9931.
Students 229.
Mission—Williamstown, Dauphin Co., Sacred Heart of Jesus, 140 E. Market St., Williamstown, 17098. Tel: 717-647-2645; 647-2447.

McSherrystown, Adams Co., Annunciation of the Blessed Virgin Mary (1899), Rev. Lawrence W. Sherdel; Deacon Joseph F. Lawrence. In res., Rev. George J. Koychick.
Res., 26 N. Third St., 17344. Tel: 717-637-1191; Fax: 717-637-1715. [CEM]
School—316 North St., 17344. Tel: 717-637-3135. Sr. Ann Marie Wierman, S.S.J., Prin.
Lay Teachers 18; Students 386.
Catechesis/Religious Programs—Students 110.

Manheim, Lancaster Co., St. Richard (1978), Rev. Robert Plociennik, O.F.M.Conv.
Res., 201 Adele Ave., 17545. Tel: 717-665-2465; Fax: 717-665-7119. [JC]
Catechesis/Religious Programs—Jeannette Mastromatteo, D.R.E.
Students 72.

Marietta, Lancaster Co., Presentation of the Blessed Virgin Mary (1869). Closed. See Mary, Mother of the Church, Mount Joy.

Marion Heights, Northumberland Co., Our Lady of Perpetual Help (1905). Closed. See Holy Angels, Kulpmont.

Marysville, Perry Co., Our Lady of Good Counsel (1956), Rev. Thomas J. Rozman. In res., Very Rev. William C. Forrey, Jr.
Res., 121 William St., 17053. Tel: 717-957-2662; Fax: 717-957-4247.
Catechesis/Religious Programs—D.R.E.:, Tel: 717-957-9218. Sally Rebert; Shirley Moore.
Students 160.
Mission—Duncannon, Perry Co., St. Bernadette, (1954) 901 High St., Duncannon, 17020.

Mechanicsburg, Cumberland Co., Saint Katharine Drexel (1988), Rev. James R. O'Brien; Deacons Melvin Dowdy; Joseph Gorini. In res., Rev. Msgr. Vincent J. Smith.
Res., One Peter Drive, 17050. Tel: 717-697-8716; Fax: 717-697-3702.
Mailing Address: One Peter Dr., 17055.
Catechesis/Religious Programs—Tel: 717-795-8572. Christopher Adams, D.R.E.
Students 431.

St. Elizabeth Ann Seton (1977), Very Rev. Richard P. Waldron, V.F. In res., Rev. Edward C. Malesic.
Res., 310 Hertzler Rd., 17055. Tel: 717-697-2614; Fax: 717-795-0800.
Catechesis/Religious Programs—Tel: 717-697-3545. D.R.E.: Carol Holder; Judy Olinger.
Students 591.

St. Joseph (1950), Revs. Chester P. Snyder; Stephen D. Weitzel; Rose Baker, Pastoral Assoc.; Deacon Jack Paruso; William Reilly, Parish Mgr.
Res., 200 S. Filbert St., P.O. Box 2012, 17055. Tel: 717-766-9433; Fax: 717-795-9123.
Church—400 E. Simpson St., 17055.
School—410 E. Simpson St., 17055. Tel: 717-766-2564; Fax: 717-766-1226.
Sisters of SS. Cyril and Methodius 2; Lay Teachers 19; Students 490.
Catechesis/Religious Programs—Tel: 717-766-2472; Fax: 717-766-2856. Sr. Joseph Therese, D.R.E.
Students 521.
Convent—302 S. Chestnut St., 17055.

Middletown, Dauphin Co., Seven Sorrows of the Blessed Virgin Mary (1855), Revs. Louis P. Ogden; John Trigilio, Jr., Ph.D.
Res., 280 N. Race St., 17057. Tel: 717-944-3133; Fax: 717-944-1170. [CEM]
School—(Grades PreK-8) Race & Conewago St., 17057. Tel: 717-944-5371; Fax: 717-944-5419. Mr. Thomas Yurkovic, Prin.
Lay Teachers 14; Students 203.
Catechesis/Religious Programs—Students 300.

Mifflintown, Juniata Co., St. Jude (1959), Rev. Thomas C. Marickovic; Deacon John A. Rocco.
Res., Box 187, 17059. Tel: 717-436-6722.

Millersburg, Dauphin Co., Queen of Peace (1952), Rev. Paul R. Fisher, O.Praem.
Res., 202 Zimmerman, 17061. Tel: 717-692-3504.
Catechesis/Religious Programs—Tel: 717-692-3504. Mrs. Cynthia Miskinis, D.R.E.
Students 115.

Millersville, Lancaster Co., St. Philip the Apostle (1965), Rev. Brian P. Conrad; Deacons Martin C. Light, Sr.; Ross Beighley.
Res., 2111 Millersville Pike, Lancaster, 17603. Tel: 717-872-2166; Fax: 717-872-2587.
Catechesis/Religious Programs—Tel: 717-872-5653. Miss Christine M. Miller, D.R.E.
Students 385.

Milton, Northumberland Co., St. Joseph (1805), Rev. Thomas A. Scala.
Res., 109 Broadway, 17847. Tel: 717-742-4356; Fax: 717-742-9171. [CEM]
Catechesis/Religious Programs—Tel: 717-742-4481. Belinda Stefl, D.R.E.
Students 182.

Mount Carmel, Northumberland Co.,

1—DIVINE REDEEMER, (1995), Revs. Joseph M. Pease; Darius G.C. Moss.
Res., 438 West Ave., 17851. Tel: 570-339-3450; Fax: 570-339-5759. [CEM 4]
Catechesis/Religious Programs—250 West Ave., 17851. Tel: 570-339-4420.
Students 79.

2—HOLY CROSS, (1892) (Lithuanian). Closed. See Divine Redeemer, Mount Carmel.

3—ST. JOHN THE BAPTIST, (1892) (Slovak). Closed. See Divine Redeemer, Mount Carmel.

4—ST. JOSEPH, (1875) (Polish). Closed. See Our Lady of Mount Carmel, Mount Carmel.

5—OUR LADY OF MOUNT CARMEL, (1886), Rev. Msgr. Lawrence R. Overbaugh; Rev. Ronald J. Moratelli.
Res., 47 S. Market St., 17851. Tel: 717-339-1031; Fax: 717-339-4814. [JC 4]
Catechesis/Religious Programs—Tel: 717-339-4420. Ms. Victoria Calabretta, D.R.E.
Students 159.

6—OUR MOTHER OF CONSOLATION, (1895) (Polish). Closed. See Divine Redeemer, Mount Carmel.

7—ST. PETER, (1905) (Italian). Closed. See Divine Redeemer, Mount Carmel.

Mount Joy, Lancaster Co., Assumption of B.V.M. (1979). Closed. See Mary, Mother of the Church, Mount Joy.

Mary, Mother of the Church (1995), Rev. Paul T. Rindos.
Res., 625 Union School Rd., 17552-9712. Tel: 717-653-4903; Fax: 717-653-4058.
Catechesis/Religious Programs—Students 180.

Myerstown, Lebanon County, Mary, Gate of Heaven (1926), Rev. Robert F. Berger.
Res., 188 W. McKinley Ave., P.O. Box 227, 17067. Tel: 717-866-5640.
Catechesis/Religious Programs—Students 153.

New Bloomfield, Perry Co., St. Bernard (1942), Rev. Robert F. Sharman.
Res., 120 W. McClure St., P.O. Box 25, 17068. Tel: 717-582-4113; Fax: 717-582-3797.
Catechesis/Religious Programs—Alice Vilk, D.R.E.
Students 250.

New Cumberland, Cumberland Co., St. Theresa of the Infant Jesus (1928), Rev. Msgr. Robert E. Lawrence; Rev. Michael C. Letteer; Deacon Joseph J. Kramer. In res., Very Rev. Thomas R. Haney.
Res., 1300 Bridge St., 17070. Tel: 717-774-5918; Fax: 717-774-5915.
School—1210 Bridge St., 17070. Tel: 717-774-7464; Fax: 717-774-3154.
Lay Teachers 30; Students 488. Principals: Sr. Bernadette Bergen, R.S.M., (Elementary); Sr. Francine Gagne, I.H.M., (High School).
Catechesis/Religious Programs—Tel: 717-774-7296.
Students 487.

New Freedom, York Co., St. John the Baptist (1841), Revs. Sylvan P. Capitani; Michael P. Reid, II; Deacon Michael Bahn.
Res., 315 N. Constitution Ave., 17349. Tel: 717-235-2156; Fax: 717-235-2223. [CEM]
Catechesis/Religious Programs—Tel: 717-235-2439.
Students 615.

New Holland, Lancaster Co., Our Lady of Lourdes (1972), Rev. John D. Schmalhofer.
Res., 737 Walnut St., 17557. Tel: 717-354-2540; Fax: 717-354-4170.
Catechesis/Religious Programs—Tel: 717-354-3338.
Students 350.

New Oxford, Adams Co., Immaculate Conception of the Blessed Virgin Mary (1852), Rev. Msgr. Francis J. Hudak.
Res., 106 Carlisle St., 17350. Tel: 717-624-4121; Fax: 717-624-4221. [CEM]
School—101 N. Peter St., 17350. Tel: 717-624-2061;

Fax: 717-624-9711. Dianne Giampietro, Prin.
Lay Teachers 13; Students 207.
Catechesis/Religious Programs—Tel: 717-624-7531. Sr. Paula Mary Aumen, D.R.E.
Students 111.
Convent—5 Carlisle St., 17350. Tel: 717-624-7531.

Northumberland, Northumberland Co., St. Thomas More (1955). Closed. See St. Monica, Sunbury.

Palmyra, Lebanon Co., Holy Spirit (1955), Rev. James F. Podlesny, O.S.B.
Res., 245 W. Pine St., 17078. Tel: 717-838-3369; Fax: 717-838-3065.
Catechesis/Religious Programs—Mrs. Helen Remington, D.R.E.
Students 219.

Quarryville, Lancaster Co., St. Catherine of Siena (1843), Rev. Joseph C. Coyne.
Res., 955 Robert Fulton Hwy., 17566-9543. Tel: 717-786-2695; Fax: 717-786-0374. [CEM]
Catechesis/Religious Programs—Mrs. Diane Dalgaard, D.R.E.
Students 248.

Ranshaw, Northumberland Co., St. Anthony of Padua (1919). Closed. See Mother Cabrini, Shamokin.

Roaring Creek, Columbia Co., Our Lady of Mercy (1923), Rev. Thomas Ignatius Mannion.
Res., 304 Slabtown Rd., Catawissa, 17820. Tel: 570-799-5642. [CEM]
Catechesis/Religious Programs—Mrs. Margaret Jessick, D.R.E.
Students 81.

Rohrerstown, Lancaster Co., St. Leo the Great (1964), Very Rev. William J. Sullivan, V.F.; Rev. Charles E. Ukwe, O.P. (Nigeria); Deacon Eugene Vannucci.
Res., 2427 Marietta Ave., Lancaster, 17601. Tel: 717-394-1742; Fax: 717-394-1779.
School—Tel: 717-392-2441; Fax: 717-392-4080. Mrs. Joyce Redington, Prin.
Lay Teachers 17; Students 268.
Catechesis/Religious Programs—Tel: 717-394-7354.
Students 559.

Selinsgrove, Snyder Co., St. Pius X (1964), Rev. Joseph A. Celia.
Res., 610 University Ave., 17870. Tel: 570-374-4113; Fax: 570-374-4113.
Catechesis/Religious Programs—Students 212.
Missions—Selinsgrove, Snyder Co., Susquehanna University, 610 University Ave., 17870. Tel: 570-372-4113; Selinsgrove, Snyder Co., Selinsgrove Center, 17870.; Selinsgrove, Snyder Co., Snyder County Prison.

Shamokin, Northumberland Co.,

1—Assumption of the Blessed Virgin Mary, (1892) (Slovak). Closed. See Mother Cabrini, Shamokin.

2—St. Edward, (1866). Closed. See Mother Cabrini, Shamokin.

3—St. Joseph, (1913). Closed. See Our Lady of Hope, Coal Township.

4—St. Michael Archangel, (1894) (Lithuanian). Closed. See Mother Cabrini, Shamokin.

5—Mother Cabrini, (1995), Revs. Dennis Grumsey, O.F.M.Conv.; Gerald Kedziora, O.F.M.Conv.; Robert Grybowski, O.F.M.Conv.; John Voytek, O.F.M.Conv.
Res., 214 N. Shamokin St., 17872. Tel: 717-648-4512; Fax: 717-648-1209. [JC 4]

6—St. Stanislaus Kostka, (1874) (Polish). Closed. See Mother Cabrini, Shamokin.

Shippensburg, Cumberland Co., Our Lady of the Visitation (1950), Rev. Robert A. Yohe, Jr.
Res., 305 N. Prince St., 17257. Tel: 717-532-2912; Fax: 717-532-3905.
Catechesis/Religious Programs—Students 133.

South Mountain, Franklin Co., Most Holy Rosary. Closed. See St. Ignatius, Buchannon Valley.

Spring Grove, York Co., Sacred Heart (1976), Rev. Hugh J. McLaughlin.
Res., 152 N. Main St., Box 42, 17362. Tel: 717-225-1704; Fax: 717-225-9570.
Catechesis/Religious Programs—Tel: 717-225-1997. Peggy Rizzuto, D.R.E.
Students 122.

Steelton, Dauphin Co.,

1—St. Ann, (1901) (Italian). Closed. See Prince of Peace, Steelton.

2—Assumption of the Blessed Virgin Mary, (1898) (Croatian). Closed. See Prince of Peace, Steelton.

3—St. James, (1878). Closed. See Prince of Peace, Steelton.

4—St. Peter, (1909) (Slovenian). Closed. See Prince of Peace, Steelton.

5—Prince of Peace, (1995), Revs. Samuel E. Houser; Daniel P. O'Brien; Deacons Michael Grella; Frank Kenski.
Res., 815 S. Second St., 17113. Tel: 717-985-1330; Fax: 717-985-1333.
School—245 Reynders St., 17113. Tel: 717-939-6357; Fax: 717-939-3660. Mr. James Collins, Prin.
Catechesis/Religious Programs—Students 100.

Sunbury, Northumberland Co., St. Michael Archangel (1863). Closed. See St. Monica, Sunbury.
St. Monica (1995), Rev. William T. Haviland.
Res., 20 N. Front St., 17801. Tel: 570-286-0761; Fax: 570-286-8588.
School—109 Market St., 17801. Tel: 570-286-5983; Fax: 570-286-7351. Theodore J Andrewlevich, Prin.
Lay Teachers 13; Students 225.
Catechesis/Religious Programs—Mrs. Peggy Walker, D.R.E.
Students 163.

Trevorton, Northumberland Co., St. Patrick (1850), Revs. Philip G. Burger; Charles L. Persing.
Res., 331 W. Shamokin St., 17881-1523. Tel: 570-797-8251; Fax: 570-797-3990. [CEM]
Catechesis/Religious Programs—Tel: 570-648-8437. Mrs. Margaret Conrad, D.R.E.
Students 84.

Waynesboro, Franklin Co., St. Andrew (1893), Rev. Thomas J. Hemler.
Res., 12 N. Broad St., P.O. Box 167, 17268. Tel: 717-762-1914; Fax: 717-762-3319. [CEM]
School—213 E. Main St., 17268. Tel: 717-762-3221. Mrs. Eileen M. Sullivan, Prin.
Lay Teachers 12; Students 151.
Catechesis/Religious Programs—Tel: 717-762-5958; Fax: 717-762-3319. Margaret E. Wagaman, D.R.E.
Students 185.

Williamstown, Dauphin Co., Sacred Heart of Jesus (1875), Rev. Francis J. Karwacki.
Res., 140 E. Market St., 17098. Tel: 717-647-2645. [CEM][JC]
Catechesis/Religious Programs—Tel: 717-647-2447. Sr. Carlotta R.S.M., D.R.E.
Students 90.

York, York Co.,

1—Immaculate Conception of the Blessed Virgin Mary, (1852), Rev. Robert M. Gillelan, Jr. Pastoral Assocs.: Deacon Catalino Gonzalez; Mrs. Marilynn Trauger.
Res., 309 S. George St., 17403. Tel: 717-845-7629; Fax: 717-845-2433. [CEM][JC]
Catechesis/Religious Programs—Tel: 717-846-6001. Mrs. Jane Kerchner, D.R.E.
Students 108.
Convent—26 E. College Ave., 17403. Tel: 717-848-1232.

2—St. Joseph, (1913), Revs. John Daya, O.F.M.Cap.; Robert E. McCreary, O.F.M.Cap.; John McCloskey, O.F.M.Cap. In res., Revs. Victor Kriley, O.F.M.Cap.; James Froehlich, O.F.M.Cap.
Res., 2935 Kingston Rd., 17402-4003. Tel: 717-755-7503; Fax: 717-757-1900.
School—2945 Kingston Rd., 17402. Tel: 717-755-1797; Fax: 717-751-0136. Sr. Dorita Slaughter, O.S.F., Prin.; Mrs. Patricia A. Byrnes, Asst. Prin.
Sisters 3; Lay Teachers 21; Students 380.
Catechesis/Religious Programs—Tel: 717-757-1707. D.R.E.: Sr. Jean Holtz, S.S.J.; Mrs. Jeanne Strittmatter.
Students 808.
Convent—405 Quaker Dr., 17402. Tel: 717-757-3667. Sisters of St. Francis
Sisters 3.

3—St. Patrick, (1776), Rev. C. Anthony Miller; Deacon Sam Moschella; Sr. Monica Imgrund, R.S.M., Pastoral Assoc. In res., Rev. William M. Cawley (GF).
Res., 231 S. Beaver St., 17403. Tel: 717-848-2007; Fax: 717-843-4533. [CEM]
School—235 S. Beaver St., 17403. Tel: 717-854-8263; Fax: 717-846-6049. Sr. Noreen Joseph, I.H.M., Prin.
Sisters, Servants of the Immaculate Heart of Mary 2; Lay Teachers 12; Students 187.
Catechesis/Religious Programs—Tel: 717-854-6653. Mrs. Connie Egan, D.R.E.
Students 183.
Convent—Tel: 717-848-1911. Sisters, Servants of the Immaculate Heart of Mary
Sisters 7.

4—St. Rose of Lima, (1907), Very Rev. Thomas R. Hoke, V.F.; Rev. Norman C. Hohenwarter, Jr.; Deacon Joseph Sferrella. In res., Rev. Carl T. Tancredi.
Res., 950 W. Market St., 17404. Tel: 717-846-4935; Fax: 717-699-0715. [JC]
School—459 W. King St., 17404. Tel: 717-854-7979; Fax: 717-843-4391. Robert L. Savidge, Prin.
Sisters of St. Joseph 2; Lay Teachers 12; Students 220.
Catechesis/Religious Programs—Tel: 717-843-3043. Sr. Jane Keller, S.S.J., D.R.E.
Students 430.
Convent—944 W. Market St., 17404. Tel: 717-854-0378. Sisters of St. Joseph
Sisters 7.

York Haven, York Co., Holy Infant (1972), Rev. Clarence A. Olszewski; Rebecca Papa, Pastoral Asst.
Res., 34 Third St., 17370. Tel: 717-266-5286; Fax: 717-266-2177.
Catechesis/Religious Programs—Students 176.

Chaplains of Public Institutions

Harrisburg. *Community General Osteopathic Hospital*. Vacant.
Harrisburg Hospital Tel: 717-782-3333. Rev. John A. Szada, Jr. Tel: 717-233-1014.
Polyclinic Medical Clinic Tel: 717-782-4141. Rev. John A. Szada, Jr. Tel: 717-233-1014.
State Hospital Pouch A, 17105. Tel: 717-787-9232. Deacon Frank Parr.

Camp Hill. *State Correctional Institution* P.O. Box 200, 17011. Tel: 717-737-4531, Ext. 307. Deacon Manuel Velazquez.

Danville. *Geisinger Medical Center* Tel: 717-275-2512. Rev. Lawrence C. Gross.
State Hospital P.O. Box 219, 17821. Tel: 717-275-7011. Rev. Thomas Ignatius Mannion Tel: 717-799-5642.

Hershey. *Milton J. Hershey Medical Center* 500 University Blvd., 17033. Tel: 717-534-8177.

Lancaster. *Lancaster County Prison* 625 E. King St., 17602. Tel: 717-534-8177. Deacon William J. Jordan.
Lancaster General Hospital and Lancaster Community Hospital. Rev. James Muthuplakel.

Lebanon. *Veterans Administration Hospital* R.D. No. 1, 17042. Tel: 717-272-6621. Rev. Dennis M. Young.

Lewisburg. *U.S. Penitentiary* Tel: 717-523-1251. Sr. Patricia Weidman, Chap.

Selinsgrove. *Selinsgrove Center* Box 500, 17870. Tel: 717-374-2911, Ext. 425. Rev. Joseph A. Celia; Deacon Samuel Sica.

South Mountain. *Restoration Center* Tel: 717-749-5773. Rev. Joeseph C. Carolin.

York. *York Hospital* 1001 S. George St., 17405. Tel: 717-771-2345. Rev. Carl T. Tancredi.

On Duty Outside the Diocese:
Reverend Fathers—
Barrett, Edward J., Wadsworth VA Hospital, Los Angeles, CA 90073
Blackwell, Edward A., 520 N.E. 20th St., #408, Fort Lauderdale, FL 33305-2195
Kemper, John C., S.S., Sts. Cyril & Methodius Seminary, 3535 Indian Tr., Orchard Lake, MI 48324
McLernon, Thomas M., Sacred Heart University, 5151 Park Ave., Fairfield, CT 06432-1000
Sperber, Timothy (MIA), St. Gregory Church, 200 N. University Dr., Plantation, FL 33324-2085
Topper, Charles J., 467 Bloomfield Ave., Bloomfield, CT 06002

Graduate Studies:
Rev.—
LaVoie, Raymond J., Pontificial North American College, 00120 Vatican City State, Europe

---

Absent on Leave:
Reverend Fathers—
Bennett, Michael X.

Retired:
Reverend Monsignors—
Kujovsky, Thomas J.
McGovern, Damian E.
Smith, Vincent J.
Topper, Vincent J.
Reverend Fathers—
Beeman, James W.
Burakowski, Anthony E., 13 Pratt St., Fairfield, CT 06430
Farace, Frederick A., P.O. Box 276, Mount Carmel, PA 17851
Fennessy, Joseph H.
Greaney, John
McGinley, Anthony J.
Miller, Paul
Sawdy, Wallace E., 115 North St., Harrisburg, PA 17101
Zangari, Salvatore V.

Permanent Deacons:
Anders, Joseph L., St. Anne, Lancaster
Aull, Richard H., St. Matthew's, Dauphin
Bahn, Michael P., St. Joseph, York
Bankos, Stephen, St. Mary, York
Beighley, Ross W., St. Catherine of Siena, Quarryville
Bertollo, Edward L., Jr., Immaculate Conception BVM, Berwick
Clark, Charles W., St. Patrick, Harrisburg
Colonell, Arthur W., Our Mother of Perpetual Help, Ephrata

Culley, Matthew P., St. John Neumann, Lancaster
Dunn, J. Leo, St. Patrick, Harrisburg
Eckman, Frank M., St. Anne, Lancaster
Fedor, Thomas A., Holy Family, Harrisburg
Fine, Andrew V., St. Joseph, Mechanicsburg
Fitzpatrick, Edwin L., Our Lady of Lourdes, Enola
Flannery, Thomas H., St. Catherine, Harrisburg
Foerster, Jerome T., Holy Name of Jesus, Harrisburg
Gonzales, Catalino, Spanish-Speaking Apostolate, Harrisburg; Cristo Salvador, York
Gorman, Francis, Good Shepherd, Camp Hill
Grella, Michael A., St. Peter, Steelton
Hackman, Donald D., St. James, Lititz
Hayes, Arthur Hull, Jr.
Jordan, William J., Lancaster County Prison & St. Anthony of Padua, Lancaster
Kenski, Francis G., Holy Spirit Hospital, Camp Hill; Our Lady of Good Counsel, Marysville
Kole, Gerard J., Chap., County Nursing Home, Cumberford; County Prison, Carlisle
Kramer, Joseph J., St. Theresa, New Cumberland
Lawrence, Joseph F., Annunciation BVM, McSherrystown
Leszczynski, Edward A., St. Catherine of Siena, Quarryville
Light, Martin C., St. Philip, Millersville
Lydon, Michael, St. Peter, Columbia
MacAdam, Morris D., Sacred Heart of Jesus, Harrisburg
Mack, Robert P., St. Edward, Shamokin
Marroquin, Miguel, Spanish-Speaking Apostolate, Harrisburg
Miller, Gene R., Immaculate Conception BVM, New Oxford
Mordecai, Philip B.
Moschella, Sabino E., St. Patrick, York
Mowery, John, Our Lady of the Blessed Sacrament, Harrisburg
Oliver, Thomas S., St. Joan of Arc, Hershey
Parr, Frank J., Harrisburg State Hospital, Harrisburg
Paruso, John L., St. Joseph, Mechanicsburg
Ramos, Felix, San Juan Bautista, Lancaster
Rocco, John, St. Jude Thaddeus, Mifflintown; Sacred Heart, Lewistown
Runkle, Ralph H., St. Patrick, York
Ryan, Richard A., St. Paul the Apostle, Annville
Sahd, Joseph A., St. Joseph Hospital, Lancaster
Santiago, Expidito, San Juan Bautista, Lancaster
Sferrella, Joseph, St. Rose of Lima, York
Sica, Samuel A., St. Pius X & Selinsgrove Center, Selinsgrove
Smith, Raymond, Immaculate Heart, Abbottstown
Sneeringer, James, St. Francis Xavier, Gettysburg
Vannucci, Eugene D., St. Leo the Great, Rohrerstown
Velazquez, Manuel, Camp Hill State Correctional Institution, Camp Hill
Weaver, John A., St. Joseph, Dallastown
Weaver, Richard J., St. Joseph, Bonneauville
Weaver, Robert E., St. Joseph Hospital, Lancaster
Wentzel, Richard W., Assumption BVM & Lebanon Catholic High School, Lebanon
Whale, William E., St. Catherine Laboure, Harrisburg
Wrabel, Joseph J., Holy Name, Harrisburg

INSTITUTIONS LOCATED IN THE DIOCESE

[A] HIGH SCHOOLS

HARRISBURG. *Bishop McDevitt High School*, 2200 Market St., 17103-2499. Tel: 717-236-7973; Fax: 717-234-1270.
E-mail: mcdevitthbg@juno.com
Web site: www.bishopmcdevitt.org
Mr. John D. Brixius, Prin. Sisters 7; Lay Teachers 48; Students 738.

CAMP HILL. *Trinity High School*, 3601 Simpson Ferry Rd., 17011. Tel: 717-761-1116; Fax: 717-761-7309.
E-mail: fgagne@trinityhs.k12.pa.us
Web site: www.trinityhs.k12.pa.us
Sr. Francine Gagne, I.H.M., Prin. Sisters 5; Lay Teachers 43; Students 614.

COAL TOWNSHIP. *Our Lady of Lourdes Regional High School*, 2001 Clinton Ave., 17866-1699. Tel: 570-644-0375; Fax: 570-644-7655.
E-mail: lourdes@postoffice.ptd.net
Web site: http://home.ptd.net/ lourdes/
Sr. Rita O'Leary, I.H.M., Prin. Sisters 4; Lay Teachers 24; Students 231.

LANCASTER. *Lancaster Catholic High School*, 650 Juliette Ave., 17601. Tel: 717-509-0315; Fax: 717-509-0312.
E-mail: dgarrett@lancatholichs.pvt.k12.pa.us
Mr. Dermot Garrett, Prin. Sisters 3; Lay Teachers 43; Students 733.

LEBANON. *Catholic Junior-Senior High School*, 1400 Chestnut St., 17042. Tel: 717-273-3731; Fax: 717-274-5167. Thomas Beazley, Prin. Sisters of St. Joseph 2; Lay Teachers 25; Students 270; Total Staff 6.

YORK. *York Catholic High School*, 601 E. Springettsbury Ave., 17403. Tel: 717-846-8871; Fax: 717-843-4588.
E-mail: yorkcatholic@blazenet.net
Web site: www.yorkcatholic.org
Rev. William M. Cawley (GF), Teacher. Priests 1; Sisters 3; Lay Teachers 42; Total Staff 75; Students 636.

[B] CONSOLIDATED ELEMENTARY SCHOOLS

HARRISBURG. *Cathedral School*, 212 State St., 17101. Tel: 717-234-3797; Fax: 717-213-2000.
E-mail: cathedralcs@paonline.com
Web site: www.paonline.com/cathedrl
Sr. Mary Agnes Shurer, S.C.C., Prin.
Upper School. (Includes Kindergarten). Sisters 1; Lay Teachers 6.
Lower School. Total Students 185. Sisters 1; Lay Teachers 3.

LEBANON. *Our Lady of the Valley School*, 740 Willow St., 17042. Tel: 717-272-8961; Fax: 717-274-8466. Mrs. Karen Smoker, Prin. Lay Teachers 19; Total Staff 28; Students 306.

MOUNT CARMEL. *Holy Spirit Consolidated School*, 250 West Ave., 17851. Tel: 570-339-3823; Fax: 570-339-0606.
E-mail: dove@sunlink.net also hss@sunlink.net
Web site: www.sunlink.net/~dove
Sr. Mary Rene Procopio, Prin. Sisters 2; Lay Teachers 11; Students 177.

SHAMOKIN. *Queen of Peace Consolidated School*. (Grades K-8), 201 N. Shamokin St., 17872. Tel: 570-648-6672; 648-0182 (Convent); Fax: 570-644-0502.
E-mail: squeenofpeace@hbgdiocese.org
Sr. Jeanne Patrick, I.H.M., Prin. Serves the parishes of Our Lady of Hope, Coal Township; Queen of the Most Holy Rosary, Elysburg; Mother Cabrini, Shamokin; and St. Patrick, Treverton. Sisters 4; Lay Teachers 12; Students 220.

[C] PRESCHOOLS AND DAY NURSERIES

MCSHERRYSTOWN. *St. Joseph Academy Preschool*, 90 Main St., 17344. Tel: 717-630-9990.
E-mail: stjoes@mail.cvn.net
Sisters of St. Joseph. Sr. Anne Leonard Freed, S.S.J., Dir. Sisters 1; Students 36.

YORK. *Holy Child Nursery*, 1141 E. Market St., 17403. Tel: 717-848-1691; Fax: 717-848-5181.
E-mail: hcn1141@juno.com
Daughters of Our Lady of Mercy. Sr. M. Ambrogina, D.M., Admin. Sisters 5; Lay Aides 4; Students 48.

[D] RELIGIOUS RESOURCE CENTERS

CAMP HILL. *Trinity High School*, 17011. Tel: 717-761-1116; Fax: 717-761-7309.
E-mail: fgagne@trinityhs.k12.pa.us
Web site: www.trinityhs.k12.pa.us

DANVILLE. *Villa Sacred Heart*, 17821-1698. Tel: 570-275-3581; Fax: 570-275-5997.
Web site: www.sscm.org

[E] CATHOLIC CHARITIES COUNSELING & FIELD SERVICES

HARRISBURG. *Department for Catholic Charities Administrative Office*, P.O. Box 3551, 17105. Tel: 717-657-4804; Fax: 717-657-8683.
E-mail: msgrkumontis@hbgdiocese.org
Web site: www.hbgdiocese.org
Adoption Services, 214 State St., 17101. Tel: 717-238-5944; Fax: 717-238-6050. Kay Eisenhour, M.S.W., L.S.W., Prog. Dir.
Capital Region Office, 223 North St., 17101. Tel: 717-233-7978; Fax: 717-233-4194. Larry Belmont, L.S.W., Dir.
Cenacle Youth Shelter, 1611 Boas St., 17103. Tel: 717-236-8211; Fax: 717-236-8140. Jocelyn Valentin, Prog. Dir.
Evergreen House Program, 100 Evergreen St., 17104. Tel: 717-238-6343; Fax: 717-238-4161. Sue Rogers, Program Dir.
Specialized Foster Care, 806-C South 29th St., 17111. Tel: 717-654-7115; Fax: 717-564-7180. Nancy Jamison, M.S.W., Prog. Dir.
Immigration and Refugee Services, 900 N. 17th St., 17103. Tel: 717-232-0568; Fax: 717-234-1742. Norman Lederer, M.A., Prog. Dir.
Interfaith Shelter for Homeless Families, Harrisburg St. Hospital, Hemlock Bldg. #26, 17105. Tel: 717-236-6783; Fax: 717-236-3271. Michele O'Neill, Prog. Dir.
Lourdeshouse Maternity Services, 100 B. Livingston St., Enhaut, 17113. Tel: 717-986-9510; Fax: 717-986-1030. Annette Perry, Prog. Dir.
Paradise School, 6156 West Canal Rd., Abbottstown, 17301. Tel: 717-259-9537; Fax: 717-259-9262. Michael Langley, M.S., Prog. Dir.
Chambersburg Office, 336 Philadelphia Ave., Chambersburg, 17201. Tel: 717-263-3765; Fax: 717-263-3226. Carolyn George, M.Div., Dir.
Chambersburg Family Outreach, 336 Philadelphia Ave., Chambersburg, 17201. Tel: 717-264-2332; Fax: 717-264-0654. Craig Cordell, M.S., Prog. Dir.
Lancaster Office, 925 N. Duke St., Lancaster, 17602. Tel: 717-299-3659; Fax: 717-299-1328. Kirk Reider, A.C.S.W., L.S.W., Dir.
Intensive Day Treatment, 47 S. Mulberry St., Lancaster, 17603. Tel: 717-295-9630; Fax: 717-295-9525. Claire E. Spalla, M.S.W., L.S.W., Prog. Dir.
Lancaster In-Home Intensive Services, 417 Poplar St., Lancaster, 17603. Tel: 717-392-3619; Fax: 717-392-4198. Chris Vandenberg, M.H.S., Prog. Dir.
Lebanon Office, 1431 Walnut St., Lebanon, 17042. Tel: 717-273-8514; Fax: 717-273-7518. Heather Teter, M.S.W., L.S.W., Prog. Dir.
Lebanon Family FOCUS, 1431 Walnut St., Lebanon, 17042. Tel: 717-273-3011; Fax: 717-273-8518. D.J. Dunlap, L.S.W., Prog. Dir.
Northern Office, 815 W. Chestnut St., Coal Township, 17872. Tel: 570-648-6431; Fax: 570-648-9610. Loretta Stefanovage, M.S.W., L.S.W., Dir.
York Office, 253 E. Market St., York, 17403. Tel: 717-845-2696; Fax: 717-843-3941. Donna Dillon, M.S., Dir.
York Intensive Family Services, 253 E. Market St., York, 17403. Tel: 717-843-7986; Fax: 717-699-0020. Connie Krout, M.H.S., Prog. Dir.
HOPE House, 1509 Cresent Ave., Lancaster, 17601. Tel: 717-293-9089; Fax: 717-293-1425. Sr. Marie Aimee Finnegan, R.S.M., Program Dir. Total Staff 300; Total Assisted 9,700.

[F] GENERAL HOSPITALS

CAMP HILL. *Holy Spirit Hospital and Community Mental Health Center*, 503 N. 21st St., 17011-2288. Tel: 717-763-2100; Fax: 717-763-2183.
E-mail: jfegan@hsh.org
Web site: www.hsh.org
For a complete listing, refer to the Hospitals section.

[G] CONVALESCENT & RETIREMENT HOMES

HARRISBURG. *Villa Teresa Nursing Home*, 1051 Avila Rd., 17109. Tel: 717-652-5900; Fax: 717-652-5941.
E-mail: villateresa@panetwork.com
For a complete listing, refer to the Special Care Facilities section.

COLUMBIA. *St. Anne's Home*, 3952 Columbia Ave., 17512-9715. Tel: 717-285-5443; Fax: 717-285-5950.
E-mail: stannadm@supernet.com
For a complete listing, refer to the Special Care Facilities section.

DANVILLE. *Holy Family Convent and Infirmary*, One Montour St., 17821. Tel: 717-275-3141
For a complete listing, refer to the Special Care Facilities section.
Maria Hall, Maria Hall Dr., 17821. Tel: 570-275-1120; Fax: 570-275-1134.
E-mail: sscmarhl@aol.com
For a complete listing, refer to the Special Care Facilities section.
Maria Joseph Manor, 875 Montour Blvd., 17821. Tel: 570-275-4221; Fax: 570-275-4711.
E-mail: meadows@mail.ptdprolog.net
For a complete listing, refer to the Special Care Facilities section.

YORK. *Misericordia Convalescent Home*, 998 S. Russell St., 17402. Tel: 717-755-1964; Fax: 717-840-0010.
E-mail: misericordia@computerlynx.net
For a complete listing, refer to the Special Care Facilities section.

[H] MONASTERIES AND RESIDENCES OF PRIESTS AND BROTHERS

EPHRATA. *St. Clement's Mission House*, P.O. Box 209, 17522-0209. Tel: 717-733-6596; Fax: 717-733-0502.
E-mail: omph@ptd.net
Redemptorist Fathers and Brothers. Very Rev. Raymond Collins, C.SS.R.; Revs. John J. Creaven, C.SS.R.; Gerard J. Szymkowiak, C.SS.R.; John J. Dorff, C.SS.R.; John H. Wright; William Geiger, C.SS.R.; Brendan Greany, C.SS.R.
Mission Preaching Band: Revs. Arthur J. Mahoney, C.SS.R.; John W. Kelly, C.SS.R.; Paul Bryan, C.SS.R. Total in Residence 10.

[I] CONVENTS AND RESIDENCES FOR SISTERS

HARRISBURG. *Bishops' Residence*, 4800-A Union Deposit Rd., 17105. Tel: 717-671-9323. Sr. Elsa Moore, S.C.C., Supr. Sisters of Christian Charity 2.

Immaculate Heart of Mary Convent, 603 N. Second St., 17101. Tel: 717-236-4821. Sr. Edward Marie Dougherty, I.H.M., Supr. Sisters, Servants of the Immaculate Heart of Mary 11.

St. Joseph Convent, 605 N. Second St., 17101. Tel: 717-232-0204.
E-mail: mashurer@paonline.com
Sisters of Christian Charity. Sr. Mary Agnes Shurer, S.C.C., Supr. Sisters of St. Francis (Aston, PA) 1; Total in Residence 8; Total Staff 8.

Saint Margaret Mary Convent, 2836 Herr St., 17103. Tel: 717-232-0204; 717-230-9411.
E-mail: pmarian@desupernet.net
Adorers of the Blood of Christ. Total in Residence 5; Total Staff 5.

COLUMBIA. *Adorers of the Blood of Christ*, 3950 Columbia Ave., 17512-9714. Tel: 717-285-4536; Fax: 717-285-9789.
E-mail: agathagrft@redrose.net
Web site: www.adorers.org
Province Center of the Adorers of the Blood of Christ. Sr. Agatha Marie Groft, A.S.C., Prov. Supr.

The Precious Blood Spiritual Center, 3950 Columbia Ave., 17512-9714. Tel: 717-285-2215; Fax: 717-285-4415.
E-mail: pbsc@redrose.net
S. Constance Sophy, R.S.M., Dir. Columbia Province 75.

DANVILLE. *Villa Sacred Heart*, 17821-1698. Tel: 570-275-3581; 275-4929; Fax: 570-275-5997.
Web site: www.sscm.org
Motherhouse of the Sisters of SS. Cyril and Methodius. Sr. Pamela Smith, SS.C.M., Gen. Supr.; Rev. Francis Malinowski, C.S.Sp., Chap. Sisters 36.

Villa Sacred Heart Formation Center. Tel: 570-275-3702; Fax: 570-275-5997. Vocation Office/SCA Spiritual Center. Tel: 570-275-1093; Fax: 570-275-5997. Sr. Virginia DeWan, SS.C.M., Vocation Dir.

Villa Sacred Heart Music Conservatory, 17821-1698. Tel: 570-275-5185; Fax: 570-275-5997. Sr. M. Michaelette, SS.C.M., Dir.

St. Cyril Academy Preschool and Kindergarten, 17821-1698. Tel: 570-275-1667; Fax: 570-275-8303. Sr. Judy Therese, SS.C.M., Prin.

ELYSBURG. *Carmelite Monastery*, 70 Monastery Rd., 17824-9697. Tel: 570-672-2935; Fax: 570-672-0278. Discalced Carmelite Nuns. Sr. Christine O'Brien, O.C.D., Prioress. Nuns in Solemn Vows 16.

LANCASTER. *Monastery of the Dominican Nuns of the Perpetual Rosary*, 1834 Lititz Pike, 17601-6585. Tel: 717-569-2104; Fax: 717-569-1598.
E-mail: monihm@juno.com
Mother Mary Veronica, O.P., Prioress; Rev. Francis R. Mullin, O.P., Chap. Solemnly Professed Nuns 12; Novices 1.

St. Francis Convent, 903 W. Walnut St., 17603. Tel: 717-392-1740; Fax: 717-392-0010.
E-mail: srssfran@lancnews.inf.net
Sisters of St. Francis of Philadelphia 6.

[J] QUASI-PARISHES

LANCASTER. *Iglesia de San Juan Bautista*, 425 S. Duke St., 17602. Tel: 717-392-4118.
E-mail: p127sanjuan@hbgdocese.org
Very Rev. Bernardo Pistone, Diocesan Vicar for the Hispanics; Revs. Ignacio Palomino; Allan F. Wolfe; Sr. Therese Marie Smith, A.S.C., Pastoral Asst.; Deacons Expedito Santos; Manuel Velazquez; Felix Ramos.

[K] NEWMAN CENTERS

HARRISBURG. *Catholic Campus Ministry*, P.O. Box 3557, 17105-3557. Tel: 717-657-4804; Fax: 717-657-4041.
E-mail: frforrey@hbgdiocese.org
Web site: www.hbgdiocese.org
Very Rev. William C. Forrey, Jr.

Lebanon Valley College, 125 S. Spruce St., Annville, 17003. Tel: 717-867-1525. Rev. John D. Peck, O.S.B.

Bloomsburg University of Pennsylvania, 353 College Hill, Bloomsburg, 17815. Tel: 570-784-3123; Fax: 570-784-3123. Rev. Alfred P. Sceski; Anita McGowan.

Dickinson School of Law, 140 E. Pomfret St., Carlisle, 17013. Tel: 717-243-4411. Rev. Edward J. Keating, Jr.

Wilson College Chambersburg, Corpus Christi, 320 Philadelphia Ave., Chambersburg, 17201. Tel: 717-264-6317. Rev. Msgr. Thomas R. Brenner.

Elizabethtown College, 1840 Marshall Dr., Elizabethtown, 17022. Tel: 717-367-1255. Rev. David L. Danneker; Judith McAllister.

Gettysburg College, 12 E. Hanover St., Gettysburg, 17325-0136. Tel: 717-334-2510. Rev. Philip DeChico; Susan Collinge.

Hershey Medical Center, St. Joan of Arc, 359 W. Areba Ave., 17033. Tel: 717-533-7168.

Messiah College, One College Ave., Grantham, 17027. Tel: 717-766-2511.

Franklin and Marshall College, Lancaster, 227 N. George St., Millersville, 17551. Tel: 717-872-3350. Rev. Daniel F.X. Powell.

Bucknell University, Newman Center, 610 St. George St., Lewisburg, 17837. Tel: 570-524-7951. Rev. Martin O. Moran, III.

Penn State University, Harrisburg Campus, Seven Sorrows BVM, 401 Conewago St., Middletown, 17057. Tel: 717-944-3133. Rev. Louis P. Ogden.

Millersville University, Newman Center, 227 N. George St., Millersville, 17551. Tel: 717-872-3350. Rev. Daniel F.X. Powell.

Susquehanna University Catholic Campus Ministry, 610 University Ave., Selinsgrove, 17870. Tel: 570-374-4113. Rev. Joseph A. Celia.

Shippensburg University, 305 N. Prince St., Shippensburg, 17257. Tel: 717-477-1244. Rev. Robert A. Yohe; Roxanne Dennis.

Penn State University, Mont Alto Campus, South Mountain, 1 Campus Dr., Mont Alto, 17237. Tel: 717-749-6135. Roxanne Dennis.

Penn State University, York Campus, 931 S. Pershing Ave., York, 17403. Tel: 717-873-5163. Rev. Carl T. Tancredi, D.Min.

York College, 931 S. Pershing Ave., York, 17403. Tel: 717-846-7591. Rev. Carl T. Tancredi, D.Min.

[L] MISCELLANEOUS LISTINGS

HARRISBURG. *Pennsylvania Catholic Conference*, 223 North St., P.O. Box 2835, 17105. Tel: 717-238-9613; Fax: 717-238-1473.
E-mail: staff@pacatholic.org
Web site: www.pacatholic.org

Pennsylvania Catholic Health Association, 223 North St., P.O. Box 2835, 17105. Tel: 717-238-9613; Fax: 717-238-1473.
E-mail: PCHA@pacatholic.org
Web site: www.pacatholic.org
Sr. Clare Christi Schiefer, O.S.F., Pres.

ELYSBURG. *Carmelite Monastery Foundation of Wheeling*, c/o Carmelite Monastery, 70 Monastery Rd., 17824-9697. Sr. Christine O'Brien, Pres.

LANCASTER. *Bachmann Realty Corporation*, 830 Marietta Ave., 17603. Tel: 610-358-4548.

Saint Joseph Health Ministries & Saint Joseph Hospital Foundation, 832 Marietta Ave., 17603. Tel: 717-291-8551; Fax: 717-291-1963. John K. Tolmie, Pres.

PHILADELPHIA. *St. Joseph Village Corporation*, Mount Saint Joseph Convent, 9701 Germantown Ave., 19118-2694. Tel: 215-248-7200; Fax: 215-248-7277.
E-mail: msvc19118@aol.com
Sisters of St. Joseph. Village location, 90 Main St., McSherrystown, 17344. Tel: 717-637-2227. Sr. Eugenie Madeleine Gaddi, Gen. Sec. Residence for Senior Citizens. Total Staff 3; Total in Residence 40.

RELIGIOUS INSTITUTES OF MEN REPRESENTED IN THE DIOCESE

For further details refer to the corresponding bracketed number in the Religious Institutes of Men or Women section.

[0200]—*Benedictine Monks*.—O.S.B.
[0470]—*The Capuchin Friars*.—O.F.M.Cap.
[0480]—*Conventual Franciscans*. (Buffalo, NY).—O.F.M.Conv.
[0650]—*Holy Ghost Fathers*. (Eastern Prov.).—C.S.Sp.
[0690]—*Jesuit Fathers and Brothers*.—S.J.
[1120]—*Missionaries of the Sacred Hearts of Jesus and Mary*.—M.SS.CC.
[0920]—*Oblates of St. Francis De Sales*. (American Prov.).—O.S.F.S.
[0430]—*Order of Preachers (Dominicans)*.—O.P.
[1070]—*Redemptorist Fathers*. (Baltimore Prov.).—C.SS.R.
[0700]—*St. Joseph's Society of the Sacred Heart*.—S.S.J.
[1060]—*Society of the Precious Blood*. (Cincinnati Prov.).—C.PP.S.
[0560]—*Third Order Regular of Saint Francis*. (Prov. of the Most Sacred Heart).—T.O.R.

RELIGIOUS INSTITUTES OF WOMEN REPRESENTED IN THE DIOCESE

[0100]—*Adorers of the Blood of Christ*.—A.S.C.
[1810]—*Bernardine Sisters of the Third Order of St. Francis*.—O.S.F.
[1920]—*Congregation of the Sisters of Holy Cross*.—C.S.C.
[0890]—*Daughters of Our Lady of Mercy*.—D.M.
[0420]—*Discalced Carmelite Nuns*.—O.C.D.
[1050]—*Dominican Contemplative Nuns*.—O.P.
[1170]—*Felician Sisters*.—C.S.S.F.
[1470]—*Franciscan Sisters of St. Joseph*.—F.S.S.J.
[2575]—*Institute of the Sisters of Mercy of the Americas*.—R.S.M.
[2970]—*School Sisters of Notre Dame*.—S.S.N.D.
[0660]—*Sisters of Christian Charity*.—S.C.C.
[3780]—*Sisters of Saints Cyril and Methodius*.—SS.C.M.
[1650]—*The Sisters of St. Francis of Philadelphia*.—O.S.F.
[3830-13]—*Sisters of St. Joseph*.—C.S.J.
[2110]—*Sisters of the Humility of Mary*.—H.M.
[2170]—*Sisters, Servants of the Immaculate Heart of Mary*.—I.H.M.

NECROLOGY

† Blasovich, Joseph D, Elizabethtown, PA St. Peter. —Died Dec. 12, 1999.
† Halaburda, Walter A, Lebanon, PA Assumption of the B.V.M. —Died Oct. 22, 2000.
† Kobularik, Robert J, New Freedom, PA St. John the Baptist. —Died Dec. 30, 1999.

Archdiocese of Hartford

(Archidioecesis Hartfortiensis)

Most Reverend

DANIEL A. CRONIN, S.T.D.

Archbishop of Hartford; ordained December 20, 1952; appointed Titular Bishop of Egnatia and Auxiliary Bishop of Boston June 10, 1968; ordained Bishop September 12, 1968; transferred to Fall River October 30, 1970; installed December 16, 1970; transferred to Hartford December 10, 1991; installed January 28, 1992. *Office: 134 Farmington Ave., Hartford, CT, 06105-3784.* Tel.: 860-541-6491; Fax: 860-541-6293.

Most Reverend

PETER A. ROSAZZA, D.D., V.G.

Auxiliary Bishop of Hartford and Titular Bishop of Oppido Nuovo; ordained June 29, 1961; appointed February 28, 1978; ordained Bishop June 24, 1978. *Office & Res.: 1450 Chapel St., New Haven, CT, 06511.* Tel.: 203-789-5970.

Most Reverend

CHRISTIE A. MACALUSO, D.D., V.G.

Auxiliary Bishop of Hartford and Titular Bishop of Grassy Valley; ordained May 22, 1971; appointed March 18, 1997; ordained Bishop June 10, 1997. *Office: 134 Farmington Ave., Hartford, CT, 06105-3784.* Tel.: 860-541-6491; Fax: 860-541-6293.

ESTABLISHED NOVEMBER 28, 1843; CREATED ARCHDIOCESE AUGUST 6, 1953.

Square Miles 2,288.

Corporate Title: *"The Hartford Roman Catholic Diocesan Corporation."*

Comprises the Counties of Hartford, Litchfield and New Haven in the State of Connecticut.

For legal titles of parishes and archdiocesan institutions, consult the Chancery Office.

Chancery Office: 134 Farmington Ave., Hartford, CT, 06105-3784. Tel.: 860-541-6491; Fax: 860-541-6309.

Web site address: www.archdiocese-hartford.org

E-mail address: chancllr@connix.com

STATISTICAL OVERVIEW

Personnel	
Archbishop	1
Auxiliary Bishops	2
Priests: Diocesan Active in Diocese	281
Priests: Active Outside Diocese	12
Priests: Diocesan in Foreign Missions	1
Priests: Retired, Sick or Absent	86
Number of Diocesan Priests	380
Religious Priests in Diocese	138
Extern Priests in Diocese	19
Ordinations:	
Diocesan Priests	2
Permanent Deacons in Diocese	308
Total Brothers	48
Total Sisters	941
Parishes	
Parishes	218
With Resident Pastor:	
Resident Diocesan Priests	186
Resident Religious Priests	22
Without Resident Pastor:	
Administered by Priests	10
Missions	3
New Parishes Created	1
Closed Parishes	2
Professional Ministry Personnel:	
Brothers	43
Sisters	45
Lay Ministers	105
Welfare	
Catholic Hospitals	3
Total Assisted	777,990
Health Care Centers	1
Total Assisted	60
Homes for the Aged	2
Total Assisted	328
Residential Care of Children	1
Total Assisted	69
Day Care and Extended Day Care Centers	3
Total Assisted	170
Specialized Homes	1
Total Assisted	58
Educational	
Seminaries, Diocesan	1
Students from This Diocese	6
Seminaries, Religious	1
Students Religious	114
Total Seminarians	120
Colleges and Universities	2
Total Students	5,706
High Schools, Diocesan and Parish	4
Total Students	1,947
High Schools, Private	6
Total Students	3,106
Elementary Schools, Diocesan and Parish	67
Total Students	17,882
Elementary Schools, Private	3
Total Students	380
Catechesis/Religious Education:	
High School Students	12,422
Elementary Students	59,416
Total Students Under Catholic Instruction	100,979
Teachers in the Diocese:	
Priests	18
Brothers	43
Sisters	45
Lay Teachers	105
Vital Statistics	
Receptions into the Church:	
Infant Baptism Totals	10,194
Adult Baptism Totals	330
Received into Full Communion	363
First Communions	10,421
Confirmations	7,830
Marriages:	
Catholic	2,321
Interfaith	535
Total Marriages	2,856
Deaths	8,841
Total Catholic Population	745,069
Total Population	1,805,278

Former Bishops—Rt. Rev. WILLIAM TYLER, D.D., first Bishop; cons. March 17, 1844; died June 18, 1849.—Rt. Rev. BERNARD O'REILLY, D.D., second Bishop; cons. Nov. 10, 1850; perished at sea, Jan., 1856.—Rt. Rev. FRANCIS P. MCFARLAND, D.D., third Bishop; cons. March 14, 1858; died Oct. 12, 1874.—Rt. Rev. THOMAS GALBERRY, D.D., fourth Bishop; cons. March 19, 1876; died Oct. 10, 1878.—Rt. Rev. LAWRENCE S. MCMAHON, D.D., fifth Bishop; cons. Aug. 10, 1879; died Aug. 21, 1893.—Rt. Rev. MICHAEL TIERNEY, D.D., sixth Bishop; cons. Feb. 22, 1894; died Oct. 5, 1908.—Most Rev. JOHN J. NILAN, D.D., seventh Bishop; cons. April 28, 1910; died April 13, 1934.—Most Rev. MAURICE F. MCAULIFFE, D.D., eighth Bishop; ord. July 29, 1900; appt. Auxiliary to the Bishop of Hartford, Dec. 17, 1925; cons. April 28, 1926; appt. Bishop of Hartford, April 25, 1934; installed May 29, 1934; died Dec. 15, 1944.—Most Rev. HENRY J. O'BRIEN, D.D., ninth Bishop, first Archbishop; ord. July 8, 1923; appt. Titular Bishop of Sita and Auxiliary to Bishop of Hartford, March 19, 1940; cons. May 14, 1940; appt. Bishop of Hartford, April 7, 1945; appt. Archbishop of Hartford, Aug. 6, 1953; appt. at Pontifical Throne, April 29, 1955; resigned and appt. Titular Archbishop of Utina, Nov. 20, 1968; Given title "Former Archbishop of Hartford", Nov. 14, 1970; died July 23, 1976.—Most Rev. JOHN F. WHEALON, D.D., S.T.L., S.S.L., tenth Bishop, second Archbishop; ord. May 26, 1945; appt. Titular Bishop of Andrapa and Auxiliary of Cleveland, June 2, 1961; cons. July 6, 1961; appt. Bishop of Erie, Nov. 30, 1966; installed March 7, 1967; appt. Archbishop of Hartford, Dec. 28, 1968; installed March 19, 1969; died Aug. 2, 1991.

Vicars General—Most Rev. PETER A. ROSAZZA, D.D.; Most Rev. CHRISTIE A. MACALUSO, D.D.

Episcopal Vicars—Rev. Msgr. DANIEL J. PLOCHARCZYK, Hartford Vicariate; Rev. Msgr. JAMES G. COLEMAN, New Haven Vicariate; Rev. Msgr. JOHN D. REGAN, Waterbury Vicariate.

Chancery Office—134 Farmington Ave., Hartford, 06105-3784. Tel: 860-541-6491; Fax: 860-541-6293 (Bishop's Office); Fax: 860-541-6309 (Chancery). All applications for dispensations and correspondence on diocesan business should be sent to this address. Office Hours: Mon.-Fri. 8:30-4:30.

Moderator of the Curia—Most Rev. CHRISTIE A. MACALUSO.

Chancellor—Rev. Msgr. THOMAS M. GINTY.

Vice-Chancellor—Rev. ROBERT B. VARGO, J.C.L.

Archbishop's Delegate for Special Needs—Sr. HELEN MARGARET FEENEY, C.S.J.

Archdiocesan Liturgical Consultant—Sr. MARY KATHLEEN RONAN, R.S.M., . Fax: 860-541-6521.

Archivist—Sr. MARJORIE FALLON, R.S.M.

Fiscal Officer—Most Rev. CHRISTIE A. MACALUSO, D.D., Finance Officer; MICHAEL R. ST. DENIS, C.P.A., Fiscal Coord., Internal Affairs; THERESA MROCZKOWSKI, Accounts Mgr. PATRICIA TORMAY, Accounts Payable; LESLI-ANN ANDERSON, Group Benefits; MATTHEW A. BYRNE, C.P.A., Fiscal Coord., External Affairs; BRENDA ROCK, Asst. to Fiscal Coord., External Affairs; DOROTHY ARDEN, Fiscal Office Sec.

Secretary to the Archbishop—Rev. Msgr. THOMAS M. GINTY.

Metropolitan Tribunal—134 Farmington Ave., Hartford, 06105-3784. Tel: 860-541-6491.

Judicial Vicar (Officialis)—Rev. ALVIN J. LEBLANC, J.C.L.

Defenders of the Bond—Revs. CHRISTOPHER M. FORD, J.C.L.; MICHAEL H. GOSSELIN, S.T.M., J.C.L.

Promoter of Justice—Rev. ROBERT B. VARGO, J.C.L.

Judges—Rev. Msgr. JOHN J. MCCARTHY, J.C.D., J.D.; Rev. Msgr. WILLIAM J. MULLEN, J.C.D.; Revs. LAWRENCE G. WRENN, J.C.D.; JAMES F. KINNANE, J.C.L.; THOMAS J. BARRY, J.C.L.

Accessor—Sr. MARY NIKA SCHAUMBER, R.S.M., J.C.L.

Auditors (Part-time Case Instructors)—Revs. LAWRENCE R. BOCK; HENRY P. CODY; MICHAEL J. DOLAN; JOHN F. EDWARDS; RONALD A. FERRARO; GENE E. GIANELLI; VITTORIO GUERRERA; BERNARD KILLEEN; LEONARD KVEDAS; DANIEL J. MCLEAREN; TIMOTHY A. O'BRIEN; THOMAS E. PTASZYNSKI; THOMAS J. SAS; BRIAN A. SHAW; RONALD T. SMITH; ADAM C. SUBOCZ; ROBERT F. TUCKER; Deacons PAUL B. LAUER; MARTIN O'CONNOR; Sr. EILEEN FUCITO, C.P.; Mr. HENRY FORGIONE; Mr. ANTHONY SYLVESTER; Ms. DIAN GRANT.

Secretary—CAROL M. HATTEN.

College of Consultors—Most Rev. PETER A. ROSAZZA, D.D., V.G.; Most Rev. CHRISTIE A. MACALUSO, D.D., V.G.; Rev. Msgr. JOHN D. REGAN; Rev. Msgr. THOMAS M. GINTY; Rev. Msgr. JAMES G. COLEMAN; Revs. JAMES B. GUNNOUD; JAMES H. SMITH.

Deans—Hartford Vicariate: Rev. RICHARD R. RUSSELL, Farmington Valley; Rev. JOSEPH V. NAPOLITANO, New Britain; Rev. WILLIAM P. PRZYBYLO, Hartford; Rev. JOHN F. EDWARDS, Suburban Hartford; Rev. JEFFREY T. WALSH, Manchester; Rev. ROBERT T. O'GRADY, Enfield New Haven Vicariate: Rev. ROBERT G. HEFFERNAN, Hamden-North Haven; Rev. VINCENT A. BROWN, East Shore Line; Rev. GEORGE F. LAURETTI, Meriden; Rev. LAWRENCE S. SYMOLON, West Shore Line; Rev. WILLIAM M. BURBANK, New Haven Waterbury Vicariate: Rev. JOHN M. COONEY, Suburban Waterbury; Rev. LEONARD J. KVEDAS, Ansonia-Derby; Rev. EDWARD F. HYLAND, Waterbury; Rev. ROBERT F. TUCKER, Litchfield; Rev. ROBERT J. ROUSSEAU, Bristol; Rev. JAMES B. GUNNOUD, Naugatuck-Cheshire.

Ecumenical Affairs, Commission for—Rev. KENNETH H. SHINER, Ecumenical Officer, *St. Mary Star of the Sea Rectory, 16 Bidwell Square, Unionville, 06085-1116.* Tel: 860-673-2422.

Evangelization Office—Rev. Msgr. MICHAEL J. MOTTA, Dir., *650 Willard Ave., Newington, 06111-2614.* Tel: 860-667-0891; Fax: 860-667-2595.

Holy Childhood Association—Rev. BRIAN W. MONNERAT, Dir., *467 Bloomfield Ave., Bloomfield, 06002-2999.* Tel: 860-243-9184; Fax: 860-243-9460.

Office for Divine Worship—Rev. Msgr. THOMAS M. GINTY, Dir. LUCY ZOCCO, Asst. to the Dir., *467 Bloomfield Ave., Bloomfield, 06002-2999.* Tel: 860-242-4020; Fax: 860-286-0513.

Newspaper—"The Catholic Transcript"; Rev. CHRISTOPHER M. TIANO, Exec. Editor, *467 Bloomfield Ave., Bloomfield, 06002-2999.* Tel: 860-286-2828; 800-726-2391; Fax: 860-726-0000. Most Rev. DANIEL A. CRONIN, D.D., Pres. & Publisher; CAROLE CRONSELL, Business Mgr. ELISA KROCHMALNYCKYI, Assoc. Editor; Rev. Msgr. DAVID Q. LIPTAK, Consulting Editor; SUSAN MELLOON, Graphic Design & Layout Mgr. JOYCE H. BOUDREAU, Circulation Supvr. ROY J. ROWLAND, Advertising Mgr.

Office for AIDS Ministries—Sr. DOROTHY STRELCHUN, S.N.D.deN., *Catholic Charities, 467 Bloomfield Ave., Bloomfield, 06002-2999.* Tel: 860-242-9577.

Office for Black Catholics—Mr. MYLES N. HUBBARD, Dir. St. Thomas Seminary, *467 Bloomfield Ave., Bloomfield, 06002-2999.* Tel: 860-243-0648; Fax: 860-243-0648.

Office of Continuing Formation of Priests—Rev. GERARD G. SCHMITZ, Dir., *134 Farmington Ave., Hartford, 06105-3784.* Tel: 860-541-6491.

Office of Radio and Television—Rev. JOHN P. GATZAK, Exec. Dir., *15 Peach Orchard Rd., Prospect, 06712-1052.* Tel: 203-758-7367; Fax: 203-758-7371.

Office of Family Life, Marriage and Family Apostolate—Co-Directors: DONALD PAGLIA; CHRISTINE PAGLIA, *412 Ridge Rd., Hamden, 06517-2941.* Tel: 203-230-2460; Fax: 203-230-2472.

Archbishop's Annual Appeal—Rev. DOUGLAS P. CLANCY, Exec. Dir. BERNADETTE FOLEY, Sec., *134 Farmington Ave., Hartford, 06105-3784.* Tel: 860-541-6268; Fax: 860-541-6289.

Office of Religious Education (CCD)—Rev. Msgr. MICHAEL J. MOTTA, Dir., *650 Willard Ave., Newington, 06111-2614.* Tel: 860-667-0891; Fax: 860-667-2595.

Priests Eucharistic League—Rev. THOMAS E. MCCARTHY, Dir., *St. Ann, 289 Arch Rd., Avon, 06001-4209.* Tel: 860-673-9858; Fax: 860-675-4350.

Commission for Priests' Retreats—Revs. FREDERICK M. ANIELLO, Chm. EARL KEATING, C.P.; GERARD G. SCHMITZ; DANIEL JEREMIAH SULLIVAN.

Office of Ministry for Priests—Rev. Msgr. JOHN P. CONTE, Min. for Priests, *St. Thomas Seminary, 467 Bloomfield Ave., Bloomfield, 06002-2999.* Tel: 860-286-8644; Fax: 860-286-7651.

Mission Cooperative Planning Office—Sr. HELEN MARGARET FEENEY, C.S.J., *Chancery, 134 Farmington Ave., Hartford, 06105-3784.* Tel: 860-541-6491.

Pro-Life Activities—Rev. JAMES J. CRONIN, Dir., *70 Gulf St., P.O. Box 230, Milford, 06460-0230.* Tel: 203-878-3571.

Propagation of the Faith, Society for—(The Catholic Mission Aid Society of Hartford)—Rev. BRIAN W. MONNERAT, Dir., *467 Bloomfield Ave., Bloomfield, 06002-2999.* Tel: 860-243-9184; Fax: 860-243-9460.

Radio Apostolate—Radio Station WJMJ—JOHN L. ELLINGER, Station Mgr., *467 Bloomfield Ave., Bloomfield, 06002-2999.* Tel: 860-242-8800. Licensed by St. Thomas Seminary, Bloomfield. (Hartford).

Office of Catholic Schools—Rev. ZIGFORD J. KRISS, Supt.; Dr. JOSEPH A. BOUND, Asst. Supt. Spec. Svcs. & Secondary Schools; Sr. LORETTA FRANCIS MANN, O.S.F., Asst. Supt. Elementary Educ. JEANNINE V. DASH, Dir. Devel., *467 Bloomfield Ave., Bloomfield, 06002-2999.* Tel: 860-242-4362; Fax: 860-242-8683.

Diocesan Labor Institute—Rev. DANIEL E. JOHNSON, Dir., *115 Pond Hill Rd., Wallingford, 06492-4836.* Tel: 203-265-1694.

Social Service—PATRICK J. JOHNSON, Dir., *467 Bloomfield Ave., Bloomfield, 06002-2999.* Tel: 860-242-9577; Fax: 860-286-2800.

Office for Catholic Relief Services—PATRICK J. JOHNSON, Coord., *467 Bloomfield Ave., Bloomfield, 06002-2999.* Tel: 860-242-9577; Fax: 860-286-2800.

Vocations—Rev. JOHN J. DIETRICH, Dir., *Pope Paul VI House of Formation, 469 Bloomfield Ave., Bloomfield, 06002-2903.* Tel: 860-286-7670; Fax: 860-242-9701.

Office of the Permanent Diaconate—Deacon RICHARD L. SANTELLO, Dir., *467 Bloomfield Ave., Bloomfield, 06002-2999.* Tel: 860-243-8005; Fax: 860-243-5287.

Office for Religious—Rev. JAMES F. KINNANE, Vicar; Sr. HELEN MARGARET FEENEY, C.S.J., Dir., *134 Farmington Ave., Hartford, 06105-3784.* Tel: 860-541-6491; Fax: 860-541-6309.

Office of Vicar For Priests—Rev. Msgr. CHARLES B. JOHNSON, *467 Bloomfield Ave., Bloomfield, 06002-2999.* Tel: 860-242-2510; Fax: 860-242-3785.

Censor Librorum—Rev. Msgr. DAVID Q. LIPTAK.

Archdiocesan Offices and Directors

Archdiocesan Dispute Resolution Office—Most Rev. CHRISTIE A. MACALUSO, D.D., Moderator of the Curia, *134 Farmington Ave., Hartford, 06105-3784.* Tel: 860-541-6491.

Archdiocesan Office of Urban Affairs—P. JOSEPH SMYTH, Exec. Dir., *81 Saltonstall Ave., New Haven, 06513-4356.* Tel: 203-777-7279; Fax: 203-776-3233.

Office for Hispanic Evangelization—Most Rev. PETER A. ROSAZZA, D.D., Vicar; Deacon RAFAEL LOPEZ, Dir. LYNNETTE COLON, Office Mgr., *467 Bloomfield Ave., Bloomfield, 06002-2999.* Tel: 860-243-0940; Fax: 860-286-2797.

Cana Conferences—DONALD PAGLIA; CHRISTINE PAGLIA, *412 Ridge Rd., Hamden, 06517-2941.* Tel: 203-230-2460; Fax: 203-230-2472.

Catholic Cemeteries Association—Rev. Msgr. DAVID M. WALKER, Dir. ROBERT S. MAREK, Exec. Dir., *700 Middletown Ave., P.O. Box 517, North Haven, 06473-0517.* Tel: 203-239-2557; Fax: 203-239-5035.

Catholic Deaf Apostolate—Rev. Msgr. ROBERT D. BERGIN, Dir.; Sr. MAURA JOSEPH, R.S.M., Coord., *243 Steele Rd., W. Hartford, 06117-2797.* Tel: 860-523-7530 (TDD or Voice); 236-3503.

Catholic Library and Information Center—Rev. EDWARD J. MCLEAN, Dir., *125 Market St., Hartford, 06103-1397.* Tel: 860-522-0602; 246-5628; 800-308-3300; Fax: 860-247-3490.

Connecticut Catholic Conference—Dr. MARIE HILLIARD, Exec. Dir., *134 Farmington Ave., Hartford, 06105-3784.* Tel: 860-524-7882; Fax: 860-525-0750.

Office for People with Disabilities—GEORGE DUCHARME, Ph.D., Co-Dir. MARY N. MCGRATH, Co-Dir., *467 Bloomfield Ave., Bloomfield, 06002-2999.* Tel: 860-242-3304.

Small Christian Communities—Bro. ROBERT K. MORIARTY, S.M., Coord., *467 Bloomfield Ave., Bloomfield, 06002-2999.* Tel: 860-243-9642; Fax: 860-286-0289.

Cursillo Movement, Archdiocesan Director of—Rev. JOHN M. COONEY, Dir., *St. John the Evangelist, 21 Academy Hill, Watertown, 06795-2101.* Tel: 860-274-8836.

Computer Services, Ministry of—Rev. EUGENE J. CHARMAN, Archdiocesan Consultant, *Computer Learning Center, P.O. Box 455, Plantsville, 06479-1111.* Tel: 203-272-0897; Fax: 203-439-7014.

CLERGY, PARISHES, MISSIONS AND PAROCHIAL SCHOOLS

CITY OF HARTFORD
(Hartford County)

1—CATHEDRAL OF ST. JOSEPH (1872), Rev. Msgr. Daniel J. Plocharczyk. In res., Revs. John P. Gatzak; Michael H. Gosselin, (Retired); George J. Ziezulewicz, (Retired).
Res., 140 Farmington Ave., 06105-3708. Tel: 860-249-8431; Fax: 860-249-5910.

2—HOLY TRINITY (1900) (Lithuanian), Rev. Msgr. John P. Conte, Admin.
Res., 53 Capitol Ave., 06106-1798. Tel: 860-246-4162.

3—IMMACULATE CONCEPTION (1899). Closed. For inquiries for parish records contact the Chancery. For inquiries for sacramental records contact St. Anne-Immaculate Conception, Hartford.

4—OUR LADY OF FATIMA (1957) (Portuguese), Rev. Jose D. Silva.
Res., Fatima Sq., 06106-2042. Tel: 860-236-1443; Fax: 860-236-1443.

5—OUR LADY OF SORROWS (1895), Revs. Joseph M. O'Neil, M.S., Co-Pastor & Admin.; Francis C. Cooney, M.S., Co-Pastor; Deacons Peter J. Klimanowski; Carmelo Hernandez.
Res., 16 Greenwood St., 06106-2109. Tel: 860-233-4424; Fax: 860-236-0149.
Church—79 New Park Ave., 06106-2109.
Catechesis/Religious Programs—Students 85.

6—SACRED HEART (1872) (Spanish), Revs. Albert Zanatta, C.R.S.; Giulio Veronesi, C.R.S.; Deacons Isidro DeJesus; Edwin Ortiz.
Res., 49 Winthrop St., 06103-1030. Tel: 860-527-6459; Fax: 860-527-6450.
Catechesis/Religious Programs—Students 125.

7—ST. ANNE (1889) (French). Closed. For inquiries for sacramental records contact St. Anne-Immaculate Conception, Hartford.

8—ST. ANNE-IMMACULATE CONCEPTION (French-Spanish), Rev. James J. Aherne, M.S., Admin. In res., Rev. Louis S. Paturzo.
Res., 820 Park St., 06106-2388. Tel: 860-728-7445; Fax: 860-727-8748.
Catechesis/Religious Programs—Students 525.

9—ST. AUGUSTINE (1902), Revs. Nicholas J. Cesaro; Charles E. Jacobs; Deacons Valentin Perez; John F. Dempsey.
Res., 10 Campfield Ave., 06114-1832. Tel: 860-522-7128; Fax: 860-246-1753.
School—20 Clifford St., 06114-1798. Tel: 860-249-5661; Fax: 860-293-2981. Sr. Patricia Dora, C.S.J., Prin.
Priests 1; Brothers 1; Sisters 2; Lay Teachers 15; Students 340.
Catechesis/Religious Programs—Tel: 860-249-3430; Fax: 860-246-1753.
Students 80.

10—SS. CYRIL AND METHODIUS (1902) (Polish), Revs. William P. Przybylo; Kazimierz Heisig (Poland).
Res., 55 Charter Oak Ave., 06106-1902. Tel: 860-522-9157; Fax: 860-524-9433.
School—35 Groton St., 06106. Tel: 860-522-8490; Fax: 860-493-7409.
Sisters 5; Lay Teachers 8; Students 230.
Catechesis/Religious Programs—Tel: 860-527-3775.
Students 259.
Convent—45 Groton St., 06106. Tel: 860-527-3775. Felician Sisters

11—ST. JUSTIN (1924) (African American/West Indian), Rev. Christopher M. Ford.
Res., 230 Blue Hills Ave., 06112-1836. Tel: 860-246-6897; Fax: 860-246-6898.

Catechesis/Religious Programs—Students 90.

12—ST. LAWRENCE O'TOOLE (1885), Revs. Joseph T. Devine; Paul F. Kenefick; Deacon Dominic Delgado. Res., 494 New Britain Ave., 06106-3797. Tel: 860-522-1129; Fax: 860-549-4261.
Catechesis/Religious Programs—Students 100.

13—ST. LUKE (1930), Rev. Frederick M. Aniello; Deacon James E. Hickey, Jr. In res., Rev. Msgr. Charles W. Daly.
Res., 66 Bolton St., 06114. Tel: 860-296-8681.
Catechesis/Religious Programs—Students 115.

14—ST. MICHAEL (1900) (African American-Hispanic), Rev. Stuart H. Pinette, Temporary Admin.; Deacon Thomas F. Breen, III.
Res., 98 Capen St., 06120-2075. Tel: 860-522-6184; Fax: 860-278-8410.
Catechesis/Religious Programs—Tel: 860-522-6184; Fax: 860-278-8410.
Students 51.

15—ST. PATRICK-ST. ANTHONY (1829), Revs. James F. Hynes, O.F.M.; John Murphy, O.F.M.; Andrew Giardino, O.F.M.; Frank Sevola, O.F.M.; Bro. Kevin McGoff, O.F.M. Pastoral Assocs.: Sr. Regina Whalen, S.N.D.; Sr. Elaine Bane, O.S.F.
Franciscan Center for Urban Ministry: 285 Church St., 06103. Tel: 860-756-4034; Fax: 860-249-6487.
Catechesis/Religious Programs—Students 232.

16—ST. PETER (1859) (Irish), Rev. Michael S. Galasso.
Res., 160 Main St., 06106-1894. Tel: 860-525-2683.
Catechesis/Religious Programs—Tel: 860-525-2684.
Students 350.
Convent—11 Charter Oak Pl., 06106. Tel: 860-522-8428. Sisters of Mercy Mercedarian Missionary Sisters (Spanish).

OUTSIDE THE CITY OF HARTFORD

Ansonia, New Haven Co.,

1—ASSUMPTION, (1870), Team Ministry: Revs. George P. Burnett; Robert F. Condron; Deacons John F. Brady, Jr.; Robert C. Johnson. In res., Rev. Albert J. Zanavich.
Res., 61 N. Cliff St., 06401-1698. Tel: 203-735-7857; Fax: 203-734-5521.
School—Tel: 203-734-0855; Fax: 203-734-5521. Mrs. Kathleen Molner, Prin.
Lay Teachers 11; Students 272.
Catechesis/Religious Programs—51 N. Cliff St., 06401. Tel: 203-735-2701; Fax: 203-734-5521.
Students 279.

2—HOLY ROSARY, (1908) (Italian), Revs. Ronald L. Genua; Carlos Garces-Henao; Deacon Mario DiRienzo. In res., Rev. Raymond F. Paul.
Res., Fr. Salemi Dr., 06401-2396. Tel: 203-735-7875; Fax: 203-732-2212.
Catechesis/Religious Programs—Tel: 203-736-0242; Fax: 203-732-2212. Verna Ingrassia, D.R.E.
Students 226.

3—ST. ANTHONY'S, (1915) (Lithuanian), Rev. Patrick J. Berkery.
Res., 199 N. Main St., 06401-1696. Tel: 203-734-4759; Fax: 203-734-2259.
Catechesis/Religious Programs—Students 30.

4—ST. JOSEPH'S, (1925) (Polish), Revs. Marek W. Sobczak; Joseph Szpilski, C.M. In res., Rev. Henry Czekala, C.M.
Res., 32 Jewett St., 06401-2499. Tel: 203-734-0402.
School—36 Jewett St., 06401. Tel: 203-734-3821; Fax: 203-734-4884. Mrs. Carmel Brown, Prin.
Lay Teachers 10; Students 130.
Catechesis/Religious Programs—Students 107.

Avon, Hartford Co., St. Ann's (1917), Revs. Thomas E. McCarthy; Vittorio Guerrera; Deacons Alan D. Campbell; John J. Mylott.
Res., 289 Arch Rd., 06001-4209. Tel: 860-673-9858; Fax: 860-675-4350. [CEM]
Catechesis/Religious Programs—Tel: 860-673-2137; Fax: 860-675-4350. Patricia Piano, D.R.E.
Students 745.

Bantam, Litchfield Co., Our Lady of Grace (1970), Rev. John H. McCann, S.M.M., Admin.
Res., P.O. Box 427, Rte. 202, 06750. Tel: 860-567-9522; Fax: 860-567-9522. [CEM]
Catechesis/Religious Programs—Students 51.
Mission—Morris, Litchfield Co., Our Lady of Hope, Rte. 109, 06763. Tel: 860-567-5717.

Beacon Falls, New Haven Co., St. Michael's (1899), Rev. Leonard J. Kvedas; Deacon Victor M. Lembo.
Res., 25 Maple Ave., 06403-1145. Tel: 203-729-2504.
Catechesis/Religious Programs—Tel: 203-729-2504.
Students 354.

Bethlehem, Litchfield Co., Church of the Nativity (1921), Rev. Richard L. Shellman; Deacon Daniel A. Camerota.
Res., 48 East St., Box 192, 06751-0192. Tel: 203-266-5211.
Catechesis/Religious Programs—Tel: 203-266-5212.
Students 244.

Bloomfield, Hartford Co., Christ the King (1936). Closed. For inquiries for sacramental records contact Sacred Heart, Bloomfield.

Sacred Heart (1878), Rev. Aidan N. Donahue; Deacon Barrry T. Skipp.
Rectory—25 Foothills Way, 06002-2488. Tel: 860-242-1942; Fax: 860-286-0044.
Church—26 Wintonbury Ave., 06002. Tel: 860-242-4142; Fax: 860-286-0044.
Catechesis/Religious Programs—Students 125.

Branford, New Haven Co., St. Elizabeth (1966), Rev. Ralph M. Colicchio; Deacon Joseph F. Coyne.
Res., 65 Burban Dr., 06405. Tel: 203-488-1661; Fax: 203-483-9248.
Catechesis/Religious Programs—Tel: 203-483-1997; Fax: 203-483-9248.
Students 254.

St. Mary (1868), Revs. Vincent A. Brown; Robert F. Birmingham; Deacons Paul V. Prete; Robert P. Tartaris.
Res., 731 Main St., 06405-3693. Tel: 203-488-1607; Fax: 203-483-9208. [CEM 2]
School—(Grades PreK-8). Tel: 203-488-8386; Fax: 203-488-2347.
Lay Teachers 16; Students 235.
Catechesis/Religious Programs—Tel: 203-488-7412.
Students 701.

St. Therese (1947), Rev. Raymond J. Barry; Deacons Paul C. Eschrich, (Retired); Gerald S. Walton.
Office: 105 Leetes Island Rd., 06405. Tel: 203-488-2998; Fax: 203-488-8542.
Res., 39 Acorn Rd., 06405. Tel: 203-483-9304.
Catechesis/Religious Programs—Students 305.

Bristol, Hartford Co.,

1—ST. ANN, (1908) (French), Revs. Robert J. Rousseau; Dennis C. Nicholas-Gingras; Deacons Joseph E. Levesque; Albert Lozier.
Res., 215 West St., 06010-5754. Tel: 860-582-8169; Fax: 860-585-7139.
Catechesis/Religious Programs—Tel: 860-582-3524. Carol Gignac, D.R.E.
Students 198.

2—ST. ANTHONY'S, (1920) (Italian), Revs. Nicholas P. Melo; Joseph G.M. Kurnath; Deacon Laurent J. Cote.
Res., 111 School St., 06010-6078. Tel: 860-583-1349; Fax: 860-582-3861.
School—30 Pleasant St., 06010. Tel: 860-582-7874; Fax: 860-582-3861.
Lay Teachers 16; Students 317.
Catechesis/Religious Programs—20 Pleasant St., 06010. Tel: 860-583-4495; Fax: 860-582-3861.
Students 215.

3—ST. GREGORY'S, (1957), Revs. John J. Georgia; Joseph H. Keating; Christopher Meade; Deacon Roger Albert.
Res. & Mailing Address: St. Gregory Rectory, Maltby St., 06010-3892. Tel: 860-589-2295; Fax: 860-589-6692.
Catechesis/Religious Programs—1043 Stafford Ave., 06010. Tel: 860-589-4232; Fax: 860-584-4786. Barbara Sergio, D.R.E.
Students 1,125.

4—ST. JOSEPH, (1864), Revs. James F. Leary; James C. Manship; Deacon Robert M. Pallotti.
Res., 149 Goodwin St., 06010-5115. Tel: 860-583-1369; Fax: 860-589-5374. [CEM]
School—335 Center St., 06010. Tel: 860-582-8696; Fax: 860-584-9907. Mark J. Monnerat, Prin.
Lay Teachers 19; Students 383.
Catechesis/Religious Programs—Tel: 860-582-2888.
Students 332.

5—ST. STANISLAUS, (1919) (Polish), Rev. Brian A. Shaw, D.Min.; Rev. Msgr. John P. Wodarski, S.T.D., (Retired); Rev. Lech Kuna (Poland); Deacons Roy C. Dungan; Leonard R. Lewandoski.
Res., 510 West St., P.O. Box 1860, 06011-1860. Tel: 860-583-4242; Fax: 860-583-9464.
Catechesis/Religious Programs—Tel: 860-584-5378.
Students 250.

Broad Brook, Hartford Co., St. Catherine's (1886), Rev. Msgr. David Q. Liptak; Deacon Vincent Motto.
Res., 6 Windsorville Rd., P.O. Box 359, 06016-0359. Tel: 860-623-4636; Fax: 860-623-4636. [CEM]
Catechesis/Religious Programs—7 Rye St., 06016. Tel: 860-623-1974.
Students 281.

Canaan, Litchfield Co., St. Joseph's (1920), Rev. James Merlino, O.F.M.; Deacon John A. Catsoris.
Res., 4 Main St., P.O. Box 845, 06018-2459. Tel: 860-824-7078; Fax: 860-824-7078. [CEM][JC]
Mission—Falls Village, Litchfield Co., St. Patrick, (1851) Beebe Hill Rd. [CEM][JC]
Catechesis/Religious Programs—Students 140.

Cheshire, New Haven Co., Church of the Epiphany (1967), Rev. Norman L. Brockett; Deacons Edward J. Pantalena; Thomas Giaimo.
Res., 1777 Old Waterbury Rd., 06410-1399. Tel: 203-272-5211.
Church & Parish Center—1750 Huckins Rd., 06410. Tel: 203-272-4355; Fax: 203-272-4878.
Catechesis/Religious Programs—Tel: 203-272-4355, Ext. 2.
Students 250.

St. Bridget's (1871), Revs. James B. Gunnoud; John K. Lynch; Robert P. Ricciardi; Deacon Richard Wilber.
Res., 175 Main St., 06410-2446. Tel: 203-272-3531; Fax: 203-271-3356. [CEM]
Parish Center—Tel: 203-271-9994.
Catechesis/Religious Programs—Tel: 203-272-6504.
Students 1,058.

St. Thomas Becket (1971), Rev. Eugene J. Charman; Deacon Francis J. Casey.
Res., 511 Sharon Dr., 06410-4244. Tel: 203-272-3324; Fax: 203-271-9210.
Catechesis/Religious Programs—Tel: 203-272-5777.
Students 445.

Collinsville, Hartford Co., St. Patrick's (1856), Rev. Ronald P. May; Deacon Robert N. Blair.
Res., 7 Burlington Ave., P.O. Box 287, 06022-0287. Tel: 860-693-8727; Fax: 860-693-4538. [CEM][JC 2]
Catechesis/Religious Programs—Tel: 860-693-1068; Fax: 860-693-4538.
Students 528.

Cornwall Bridge, Litchfield Co., St. Bridget (1883), Rev. John P. Gwozdz, Admin.
Res., 7 River Rd., P.O. Box 52, 06754-1903. Tel: 860-672-6515; Fax: 860-364-9893. [CEM]
Catechesis/Religious Programs—Students 52.

Derby, New Haven Co., St. Jude (1961), Rev. William J. Killeen; Deacon Michael J. Impellitteri.
Res., 71 Pleasant View Rd., 06418-2455. Tel: 203-735-8725; Fax: 203-735-4402.
Catechesis/Religious Programs—Tel: 203-735-8725; Fax: 203-735-4402.
Students 103.

St. Mary's (1851), Revs. James H. Smith; Peter G. Mitchell, Pastor Emeritus; Deacon Frederick M. Grant.
Res., 212 Elizabeth St., 06418-1834. Tel: 203-735-3341; Fax: 203-736-6492.
School—St. Mary-St. Michael, (Grades K-8) St. Mary Campus, 14 Seymour Ave., P.O. Box 397, 06418. Tel: 203-735-6471; Fax: 203-732-9009.
Lay Teachers 14; Students 236.
Catechesis/Religious Programs—Students 300.

St. Michael (1905) (Polish), Revs. Ronald A. Wiktor, C.M.; Walenty Pieczka, C.M.; John Kuczynski, C.M.
Res., 75 Derby Ave., 06418-2098. Tel: 203-734-0005. [CEM]
School—St. Mary-St. Michael, (Grades 4-8) St. Michael Campus, 73 Derby Ave., P.O. Box 397, 06418. Tel: 203-734-2017.
Lay Teachers 6; Students 172.
Catechesis/Religious Programs—Fax: 203-736-2044.
Students 172.

East Berlin, Hartford Co., Sacred Heart (1896), Rev. Thomas C. Culotta.
Res., 48 Cottage St., 06023. Tel: 860-828-0159; Fax: 860-828-5305.
Church—66 Cottage St., 06023. Tel: 860-828-0154; Fax: 860-828-5305.
Catechesis/Religious Programs—Students 220.

East Hartford, Hartford Co.,

1—BLESSED SACRAMENT, (1948), Rev. Jeffrey T. Walsh.
Res., 36 Cambridge Dr., P.O. Box 380057, 06138-0057. Tel: 860-568-2747; Fax: 860-568-4133.
Catechesis/Religious Programs—Tel: 860-568-7997.
Students 139.

2—OUR LADY OF PEACE, (1971), Rev. James J. Nock; Deacon Raymond A. Parenteau.
Res., 370 May Rd., 06118-3496. Tel: 860-568-4414.
Catechesis/Religious Programs—Students 205.

3—ST. CHRISTOPHER, (1965), Revs. James G. Fanelli; William E. McGrath, Pastor Emeritus; Sr. Joan Bernier, S.N.D., Pastoral Assoc.; Deacon William J. Gilles.
Res., 538 Brewer St., 06118-2399. Tel: 860-568-5240; Fax: 860-568-0673.
School—570 Brewer St., 06118. Tel: 860-568-4100; Fax: 860-568-1070. Sr. Valerie Noone, O.P., Prin.
Lay Teachers 19; Students 296.
Catechesis/Religious Programs—Tel: 860-568-0546 (Rel. Educ.); 895-8692 (Youth Min.); Fax: 860-568-0242.
Students 350.

4—ST. ISAAC JOGUES, (1964), Rev. Emilio P. Padelli.
Res., 1 Community St., 06108-2808. Tel: 860-528-6749; Fax: 860-282-2730.
Catechesis/Religious Programs—Tel: 860-528-7976.
Students 163.

5—ST. MARY'S, (1873), Revs. Martin J. Scholsky; Frank E. Papa, S.O.L.T.; Deacon Ronald R. Daigle.
Res., 15 Maplewood Ave., 06108-4021. Tel: 860-289-7916.
Parish Center—30 Maplewood Ave., 06108. Tel: 860-289-7510.
Catechesis/Religious Programs—Students 137.

6—ST. ROSE'S, (1920), Rev. Thomas R. Mitchell; Deacon Rafael Lopez.
Res., 33 Church St., 06108-3794. Tel: 860-289-8616; Fax: 860-289-3966.
School—Tel: 860-528-4169; Fax: 860-528-4160.
Lay Teachers 9; Students 193.
Catechesis/Religious Programs—Students 207.

East Haven, New Haven Co., Our Lady of Pompeii (1947), Revs. Dennis R. Hussey; Matthew R. Shanley; Deacon Joseph W. LaPierre.
Res., Foxon Rd., 06513. Tel: 203-469-0764; Fax: 203-469-3645.
Catechesis/Religious Programs—Tel: 203-469-9350.
Students 738.

St. Clare (1947), Rev. Ralph M. Colicchio; Deacon Wayne E. Sandford.
Res., 234 Coe Ave., 06512-4112. Tel: 203-467-5136; Fax: 203-469-0241.
Catechesis/Religious Programs—Fax: 203-469-0552.
Students 335.

St. Vincent de Paul's (1915), Revs. Gary F. Simeone; Robert J. Burbank, Pastor Emeritus; Alphonso R. Fontana; Deacons Norman H. Singer; William Eyles.
Res., 80 Taylor Ave., 06512. Tel: 203-467-6394; Fax: 203-467-6716.
School—35 Bishop St., 06512. Tel: 203-467-1606; 467-1607; Fax: 203-467-8851.
Lay Teachers 10; Students 254.
Catechesis/Religious Programs—Students 552.

East Windsor, Hartford Co., St. Philip's (1959), Rev. Adam C. Subocz.
Res., 150 S. Main St., 06088-9760. Tel: 860-623-0408; Fax: 860-623-8937.
Catechesis/Religious Programs—Students 98.

Enfield, Hartford Co.,

1—HOLY FAMILY, (1965), Rev. Francis T. Kerwan; Deacon Arthur J. Dickman. In res., Rev. William J. Hilliard.
Res., 23 Simon Rd., 06082-5903. Tel: 860-741-2101; Fax: 860-741-7411.
Catechesis/Religious Programs—Tel: 860-745-1018. D.R.E.: Elizabeth McGivney; Carole Frappier.
Students 1,152.

2—ST. ADALBERT'S, (1915) (Polish), Rev. Edmund M. O'Brien; Deacon Robert E. Lambert. In res., Rev. Anthony J. Bruno Tel: 860-745-9966.
Res., 90 Alden Ave., 06082-2865. Tel: 860-745-4837; Fax: 860-745-1787. [CEM]
School—Tel: 860-745-6135.
Sisters 3; Lay Teachers 7; Students 163.
Catechesis/Religious Programs—Students 70.
Convent—82 Alden Ave., 06082. Tel: 860-745-4169. Felician Sisters

3—ST. BERNARD'S, (1870), Revs. Joseph E. Vujs; William F. O'Keefe; Deacons J. Gerard Mon; Donald H. Pond.
Res., 426 Hazard Ave., 06082-4719. Tel: 860-749-8353; Fax: 860-749-6456. [CEM]
School—Tel: 860-749-8182 (East Campus); 745-5275 (West Campus); Fax: 860-749-8182.
Sisters 2; Lay Teachers 23; Students 431.
Catechesis/Religious Programs—Tel: 860-749-2993.
Students 239.
Convent—376 Hazard Ave., 06082. Tel: 860-749-4214. Felician Sisters

4—ST. MARTHA'S, (1961), Revs. John B. O'Connell; Stanley Smolenski; Deacon Robert Bernd.
Res., 214 Brainard Rd., 06082-2609. Tel: 860-745-5616.
School—Tel: 860-745-3833.
Felician Sisters 1; Lay Teachers 11; Students 260.
Catechesis/Religious Programs—Tel: 860-745-5616.
Students 350.

5—ST. PATRICK'S, (1866), Revs. Francis J. Browne, C.Ss.R.; Thomas G. Sullivan, C.Ss.R.
Res., 64 Pearl St., 06082-3594. Tel: 860-745-2411; Fax: 860-253-9483. [CEM]
Catechesis/Religious Programs—Tel: 860-741-0572.
Students 330.

Farmington, Hartford Co., St. Patrick's (1871), Rev. James F. Pilon; Deacon William A. Farrell.
Res., 110 Main St., P.O. Box 523, 06034-0523. Tel: 860-677-2639; Fax: 860-677-2672.
Catechesis/Religious Programs—Fax: 860-677-2672.
Students 644.

Forestville, Hartford Co., St. Matthew (1891), Revs. Brian W. Monnerat; Arthur J. Audet; Sr. Judith Mulhall, C.S.J., Pastoral Assoc.; Deacons John E. Pahl; Michael P. Szumigala.
Res., 120 Church Ave., Box 9216, 06011-9216. Tel: 860-583-1833; Fax: 860-582-6152.
School—Welch Dr., 06010. Tel: 860-583-5214; Fax: 860-314-1541.
Sisters 4; Lay Teachers 9; Students 314.
Parish Resource Center—101 Church Ave., 06010. Tel: 860-583-1241.
Catechesis/Religious Programs—Tel: 860-583-7806.
Students 655.
Convent—119 Church Ave., 06010. Tel: 860-583-2004. Sisters, Servants of the Immaculate Heart of Mary

Glastonbury, Hartford Co., St. Dunstan (1971), Rev. William L. Traxl.
Res., 1345 Manchester Rd., 06033-2604. Tel: 860-633-3317; Fax: 860-659-8611.
Catechesis/Religious Programs—Tel: 860-633-6876.
Students 715.

St. Paul's (1954), Revs. L. Randall Blackall; Michael F. X. Hinkley; Deacon Peter J. Klein.
Res., 2577 Main St., 06033-2023. Tel: 860-633-9419; Fax: 860-633-0040.
Catechesis/Religious Programs—Tel: 860-659-3029. Joan Flannery, D.R.E.
Students 668.

Goshen, Litchfield Co., St. Thomas of Villanova (1880), Rev. Raymond G. Proulx; Deacons Nick Diorio; Kenneth Dos Santos.
Res., 71 North St., P.O. Box 177, 06756-0177. Tel: 860-491-2756. [CEM]
Catechesis/Religious Programs—Tel: 860-491-9276.
Students 203.

Granby, Hartford Co., St. Therese's (1958), Rev. Ronald R. Yelle; Deacon Robert D. Newbery.
Res., 120 W. Granby Rd., 06035-2907. Tel: 860-653-3371.
Catechesis/Religious Programs—Tel: 860-653-5780.
Students 450.

Guilford, New Haven Co., St. George (1870), Rev. Msgr. James G. Coleman; Revs. Dominic Thomas, M.C.B.S.; John P. Melnick; Deacons Adam J. Michaele; James F. O'Neill.
Res., 33 Whitfield St., 06437-2698. Tel: 203-453-2788; Fax: 203-458-1937. [CEM]
Catechesis/Religious Programs—Tel: 203-453-3496.
Students 1,201.

Hamden, New Haven Co.,

1—ASCENSION, (1964), Rev. Thomas J. O'Rourke; Deacon Kenneth McCusker.
Res., 1040 Dunbar Hill Rd., 06514-1410. Tel: 203-288-7516.
Catechesis/Religious Programs—Tel: 203-288-5761.
Students 126.

2—BLESSED SACRAMENT, (1939), Rev. David M. McDonald; Deacons James A. Tripp, Sr.; Joseph R. Ryzewski.
Res., 321 Circular Ave., 06514-3428. Tel: 203-288-1652; Fax: 203-248-0873.
Catechesis/Religious Programs—306 Circular Ave., 06514. Tel: 203-288-5228.
Students 317.

3—OUR LADY OF MT. CARMEL, (1869), Revs. Daniel G. Keefe; Daniel James Sullivan; Deacons John O'Donovan; James H. Stanley.
Res., 2819 Whitney Ave., 06518-2598. Tel: 203-248-0141; Fax: 203-248-8658. [CEM]
Parish Center—2809 Whitney Ave., 06518. Tel: 203-287-9017.
Catechesis/Religious Programs—Tel: 203-287-9017. Sr. Ann O'Neill, R.S.M., D.R.E.
Students 928.

4—ST. ANN'S, (1919) (Italian), Rev. Kenneth P. Bonadies.
Res., 930 Dixwell Ave., 06514-4990. Tel: 203-865-0886.
Catechesis/Religious Programs—Students 50.

5—ST. JOAN OF ARC, (1971), Rev. Robert G. Heffernan; Deacon Paul T. Koch.
Res., 450 W. Todd St., 06518. Tel: 203-288-4543; Fax: 203-288-1130.
Catechesis/Religious Programs—Tel: 203-230-1926.
Students 251.

6—ST. RITA'S, (1928), Rev. Msgr. David M. Walker; Rev. Philip J. Sharkey. In res., Rev. Geoffrey C. Smith.
Res., 1620 Whitney Ave., 06517. Tel: 203-248-5513; Fax: 203-248-2684.
School—1601 Whitney Ave., 06517. Tel: 203-248-3114; Fax: 203-248-1016.
Priests 1; Dominican Sisters of St. Mary of the Springs 2; Apostles of the Sacred Heart 4; Lay Teachers 23; Students 491.
Catechesis/Religious Programs—Tel: 203-281-7522; Fax: 203-248-2684. Dianne Breen, D.R.E.
Students 464.

7—ST. STEPHEN'S, (1953), Rev. David J. Baranowski; Deacon Richard Santello.
Res., 400 Ridge Rd., 06517-2941. Tel: 203-288-6439; Fax: 203-288-4152.
School—Tel: 203-288-6792.
Sisters of Mercy 2; Lay Teachers 10; Students 243.
Catechesis/Religious Programs—Students 95.

Harwinton, Litchfield Co., Immaculate Heart of Mary (1956), Rev. Allan J. Hill; Deacon Gerald Wootton.
Res., 78 Litchfield Rd., 06791-2230. Tel: 860-485-1588; Fax: 860-485-1004.
Catechesis/Religious Programs—Tel: 860-485-9264. Christine Rousseau, D.R.E.
Students 393.

Kensington, Hartford Co., St. Paul's (1878), Team Ministry: Revs. Herman Czaster, O.F.M.Conv.; Herbert Obijiski, O.F.M.Conv.; Thomas Lavin, O.F.M.Conv.; Deacon Carmen Guzzardi.
Res., 479 Alling St., 06037-2170. Tel: 860-828-0331; Fax: 860-828-7620.
Parish Center—467 Alling St., Kesington, 06037-2170.
School—(Grades PreK-8). Tel: 860-828-4343; Fax: 860-828-1226. Mrs. Patricia O'Neil Tiezzi, Prin.
Lay Teachers 19; Students 278.
Catechesis/Religious Programs—Tel: 860-828-1934. Louann Warren, D.R.E.
Students 1,190.

Kent, Litchfield Co., Sacred Heart (1970), Rev. Thomas E. Berberich; Deacon Roland Miller.
Res., 90 Cobble Rd., P.O. Box 186, 06757-0186. Tel: 860-927-3003; Fax: 860-927-3985. [CEM]
Church—17 Bridge St., 06757.
Catechesis/Religious Programs—Students 84.

Lakeville, Litchfield Co., St. Mary's (1874), Rev. Thomas Kelly.
Res., 76 Sharon Rd., 06039-0466. Tel: 860-435-2659; Fax: 860-435-1042. [CEM]
Catechesis/Religious Programs—Students 127.

Litchfield, Litchfield Co., St. Anthony's (1882), Rev. Robert F. Tucker; Deacon John R. Maffeo.
Res., 49 South St., P.O. Box 97, 06759-0097. Tel: 860-567-5209; Fax: 860-567-2052. [CEM]
Catechesis/Religious Programs—Tel: 860-567-4188.
Students 435.

Madison, New Haven Co., St. Margaret (1937), Revs. Gerard G. Schmitz; Francis R. Fador; Deacons Joseph M. Regan; William A. Elder.
Res., 24 Academy St., P.O. Box 814, 06443-2647. Tel: 203-245-7301; Fax: 203-245-8568.
Catechesis/Religious Programs—Tel: 203-245-7971.
Students 1,149.

Manchester, Hartford Co.,

1—ASSUMPTION, (1955), Rev. John F. Brinsmade; Deacon J. Fernand Chamberland.
Res., 285 W. Center St., 06040-4898. Tel: 860-643-2195; Fax: 860-646-4360.
School—Tel: 860-649-0889. Sr. Mary Mark Prin.
Sisters 3; Lay Teachers 8; Students 202.
Catechesis/Religious Programs—Tel: 860-643-7596.
Students 202.
Convent—21 S. Adams St., 06040. Tel: 860-643-0452. Sisters of Charity of Our Lady, Mother of the Church

2—ST. BARTHOLOMEW'S, (1958), Rev. Thomas A. Sievel; Deacon Edward J. Giard.
Res., 45 Ludlow Rd., 06040-4542. Tel: 860-646-1613; Fax: 860-646-7121.
Catechesis/Religious Programs—Tel: 860-643-9178.
Students 380.

3—ST. BRIDGET'S, (1870), Revs. Joseph T. Donnelly; Dennis J. Vincenzo.
Res., 80 Main St., 06040-3180. Tel: 860-643-2403; Fax: 860-646-6936.
School—74 Main St., 06040. Tel: 860-649-7731.
Lay Teachers 16; Students 265.
Catechesis/Religious Programs—Tel: 860-643-5454.
Students 440.

4—ST. JAMES, (1874), Rev. Msgr. Douglas P. Clancy; Revs. William F. Lynch; Louis D. Cremonie; Deacon William J. Brown.
Res., 896 Main St., 06040-6079. Tel: 860-643-4129; Fax: 860-643-4130.
School—Tel: 860-643-5088; Fax: 860-649-6462. Mrs. Patricia Kanute, Prin.
Sisters 2; Lay Teachers 23; Students 457.
Catechesis/Religious Programs—73 Park St., 06040. Tel: 860-643-9605.
Students 341.

Marlborough, Hartford Co., St. John Fisher (1972), Rev. Mario P. Pepe; Deacon John W. McKaig.
Res., 24 Cheney Rd., 06447-1327. Tel: 860-295-0067; 295-0001(Office).
Catechesis/Religious Programs—Tel: 860-295-0067.
Students 319.

Meriden, New Haven Co.,

1—OUR LADY OF MOUNT CARMEL, (1894) (Italian), Rev. David J. Borino; Deacon Robert Gale.
Res., 109 Goodwill Ave., 06451-3000. Tel: 203-235-6381; Fax: 203-238-3629.
School—Tel: 203-235-2959.
Sisters 2; Lay Teachers 9; Students 220.
Catechesis/Religious Programs—Students 218.
Convents—109 Goodwill Ave., 06451-3000. Tel: 203-235-3622. Apostles of the Sacred Heart of Jesus
Sisters 3; 17 North St., Tel: 203-686-0916. The Dominicans

2—ST. JOSEPH, (1900), Revs. Mark R. Jette; Robert P. Roy.
Res., 22 Goodwill Ave., 06451. Tel: 203-237-5593.
School—Tel: 203-237-6800; Fax: 203-238-2963. Sr. Georgeann Vumbaco, Prin.
Sisters of Mercy 5; Lay Teachers 8; Students 240.
Catechesis/Religious Programs—Tel: 203-237-5593.
Students 390.

3—ST. LAURENT, (1880) (French), Rev. Joseph V. DiSciacca.
Res., 121 Camp St., 06450-3279. Tel: 203-634-1583; Fax: 203-630-4403.
Catechesis/Religious Programs—Students 65.

4—ST. MARY, (1890) (German), Revs. Mark R. Jette; Robert P. Roy.
Res., 5 Sherman Pl., 06451. Tel: 203-235-0519. [CEM]
School—Tel: 203-237-2931; Fax: 203-237-9013.
Lay Teachers 9; Students 112.
Catechesis/Religious Programs—Students 6.

5—ST. ROSE OF LIMA, (1848), Revs. Paul Rotondi, O.F.M.; Isaac J. Calicchio, O.F.M.; Deacons Charles E. Cunniff, Jr.; Jacinto Ortiz.
Res., 35 Center St., 06450-5685. Tel: 203-235-1644; Fax: 203-235-1360.
Catechesis/Religious Programs—Tel: 203-235-6887.
Students 375.

6—ST. STANISLAUS, (1891) (Polish), Revs. Edmund S. Nadolny; Joseph K. Parzymies.
Res., 82 Akron St., 06450-5796. Tel: 203-235-6341; Fax: 203-235-6342. [CEM]
School—Tel: 203-235-1005.
Sisters of St. Joseph of the Third of St. Francis (Garfield Heights, OH) 3; Lay Teachers 25; Students 430.
Catechesis/Religious Programs—Tel: 203-235-6341.
Students 200.

Middlebury, New Haven Co., St. John of the Cross (1904), Rev. Msgr. John D. Regan; Rev. Joseph F. Keough.
Res., 1089 Whittemore Rd., P.O. Box 361, 06762-0361. Tel: 203-758-2659; Fax: 203-758-1121.
Catechesis/Religious Programs—Tel: 203-758-1326.
Students 476.

Milford, New Haven Co.,

1—CHRIST THE REDEEMER, (1966), Rev. John T. Moskus. In res., Rev. Stephen A. Krugel; Deacon George A. Puskas.
Res., 325 Oronoque Rd., 06460-1798. Tel: 203-878-7431; Fax: 203-878-0677.
Catechesis/Religious Programs—Students 160.

2—ST. ANN'S, (1924), Rev. Thomas J. Baylis.
Res., 501 Naugatuck Ave., 06460-5095. Tel: 203-874-0634.
School—Tel: 203-878-2738.
Lay Teachers 10; Students 170.
Catechesis/Religious Programs—Tel: 203-878-8130.
Students 280.

3—ST. GABRIEL, (Wildemere Beach) (1946), Rev. Maurice J. Maroney; Deacons Calvin Croll; Henry Doyle.
Res., 26 Shorefront, 06460-5968. Tel: 203-877-6096; Fax: 203-878-9700.
School—(Grades PreK-8) 1 Tudor Rd., 06460. Tel: 203-874-3811; Fax: 203-874-0416.
Religious 1; Lay Teachers 16; Students 230.
Catechesis/Religious Programs—Tel: 203-876-9355; Fax: 203-876-9355.
Students 80.

4—ST. MARY'S, (Wildemere Beach) (1874), Revs. James J. Cronin; Frederick M. Langlois; Deacons Paul E. Sabo; Richard M. Sennett; Paul Lauer.
Res., 70 Gulf St., Box 230, 06460-0230. Tel: 203-878-3571; Fax: 203-877-8741. [CEM]
School—Tel: 203-878-6539; Fax: 203-878-1866.
Sisters of Mercy 2; Lay Teachers 30; Students 480.
Catechesis/Religious Programs—Tel: 203-877-5874. Sue Marra, D.R.E.
Students 900.

Naugatuck, New Haven Co., St. Francis of Assisi (1866), Revs. William J. Brenza; Faron Calumba (Philippines).
Res., 318 Church St., 06770. Tel: 203-729-4543; Fax: 203-729-6216.
School—Tel: 203-729-2247; Fax: 203-729-0512. Mrs. Margaret Carabelli, Prin.
Lay Teachers 11; Students 234.
Catechesis/Religious Programs—D.R.E.: Mr. Joseph Guarino; Mr. John Paret.
Students 614.

St. Vincent Ferrer (1975), Rev. Jeremiah N. Murasso; Deacon Nicholas J. Iassogna, Jr.; Sr. Susan Carlin, R.S.M., Pastoral Min.
Res., 1006 New Haven Rd., 06770-4731. Tel: 203-723-7497; Fax: 203-729-2978.
Catechesis/Religious Programs—Agnes Dann, D.R.E.
Students 450.

New Britain, Hartford Co.,

1—ALL SAINTS, (1918) (Slovak), Rev. Christopher M. Tiano.
Res., 15 Wilcox St., 06051. Tel: 860-229-0135; Fax: 860-224-4283.

2—HOLY CROSS, (1927) (Polish), Revs. Peter S. Sobiecki; Darius Gosciniak; Edward Ziemnicki. In res., Revs. Henry P. Fiedorczyk; Edward M. LaRose.
Res., 31 Biruta St., 06053-2899. Tel: 860-229-2011; Fax: 860-826-5887.
School—221 Farmington Ave., 06053. Tel: 860-225-4275; Fax: 860-225-5073.
Sisters of St. Joseph of the Third Order of St. Francis 4; Lay Teachers 25; Students 350.
Catechesis/Religious Programs—Students 178.

3—SACRED HEART OF JESUS, (1894) (Polish), Rev. Paul P. Wysocki.
Res., 158 Broad St., 06053-4195. Tel: 860-229-0081; Fax: 860-826-4721. [CEM]
School—Tel: 860-229-7663. Sr. M. Alma Sakowicz, Prin.
Daughters of Mary of the Immaculate Conception 2; Lay Teachers 20; Students 435.
Catechesis/Religious Programs—.
Students 318.

4—ST. ANDREW'S, (1895) (Lithuanian), Rev. Ronald T. Smith.
Res., 396 Church St., Box 515, 06050-0515. Tel: 860-224-0341; Fax: 860-826-6201.

5—ST. ANN, (1938) (Italian), Rev. Christopher M. Tiano; Deacon Carl Lickwar. In res., Rev. Augustine H. Giusani.
Res., 47 Clark St., 06051-1903. Tel: 860-225-7625; Fax: 860-224-4283.
Catechesis/Religious Programs—Tel: 860-229-1929.
Students 138.

6—ST. FRANCIS OF ASSISI, (1941), Rev. Paul R. Guido, O.F.M. In res., Rev. Richard J. Donovan, O.F.M.
Res., 1755 Stanley St., 06053-2099. Tel: 860-225-6449; Fax: 860-225-2315.
Middle School—Tel: 860-225-8729.
School Sisters of Notre Dame 3; Lay Teachers 10; Students 155.
Catechesis/Religious Programs—Students 110.

7—ST. JEROME'S, (1958), Rev. Thomas J. Cieslikowski; Deacon Reginald Roy.
Res., 1010 Slater Rd., 06053-1698. Tel: 860-224-2411; Fax: 860-224-6838.
Catechesis/Religious Programs—Students 176.

8—ST. JOHN THE EVANGELIST, (1916), Rev. Harold D. Heinrich.
Res., 655 East St., 06051-2108. Tel: 860-223-3667; 3668; Fax: 860-348-1488.
Catechesis/Religious Programs—Students 102.

9—ST. JOSEPH'S, (1896), Rev. Thomas F. Gaffney.
Res., 195 S. Main St., 06051-3199. Tel: 860-229-4851; Fax: 860-225-1403.
School—Tel: 860-223-5959.
Lay Teachers 10; Students 231.
Catechesis/Religious Programs—Students 154.

10—ST. MARY'S, (1848), Rev. Salvatore J. Rosa; Deacons Ronald Camden; John E. Thayer.
Res., 544 Main St., 06051-1814. Tel: 860-229-4894; Fax: 860-223-2756.
Catechesis/Religious Programs—Students 180.

11—ST. MAURICE, (1946), Rev. Joseph V. Napolitano.
Res., 100 Wightman Rd., 06052-1597. Tel: 860-225-8419; Fax: 860-224-1947.
Catechesis/Religious Programs—Tel: 860-225-4477. Linda E. Tower, D.R.E.
Students 245.

12—ST. PETER'S, (1873) (German-French), Rev. Daniel H. Connaghan.
Catechesis/Religious Programs—Students 28.
Res., 98 Franklin Sq., 06051-2607. Tel: 860-224-1446; Fax: 860-223-8717.

New Hartford, Litchfield Co., Immaculate Conception (1869), Rev. Kevin J. Gray.
Res., 60 Town Hill Rd., 06057. Tel: 860-379-5215. [CEM]
Catechesis/Religious Programs—Tel: 860-379-0144; Fax: 860-738-4836.
Students 359.

New Haven, New Haven Co.,

1—SACRED HEART, (1876), Revs. Robert V. Newman, S.C.; James Richardson, S.C. In res., Rev. Paul Shamsher; Deacon Jose Rivera.
Res., 74 Liberty St., 06519-2299. Tel: 203-562-7592; Fax: 203-562-1737.
School—208 Columbus Ave., 06519. Tel: 203-777-8137; Fax: 203-776-5018.
Lay Teachers 13; Students 220.
Catechesis/Religious Programs—Students 175.

2—ST. AEDAN'S, (1900), Revs. Joseph H. McCann; Cyriac Maliekal; Deacon Edward Taddei.
Res., 112 Fountain St., 06515-0156. Tel: 203-389-2619; Fax: 203-389-1235.
School—Tel: 203-387-5693; Fax: 203-387-1609. Miss Nancy Bourgoin, Prin.
Lay Teachers 17; Students 247.
Catechesis/Religious Programs—Students 120.

3—ST. ANTHONY'S, (1904) (Italian), Revs. Joseph G. Moffo, C.S.; Antonio Licastro.
Res., 25 Gold St., 06519. Tel: 203-624-1418; Fax: 203-624-3420.

4—ST. BERNADETTE'S, (1938), Rev. Howard J. Nash; Deacon Martin J. O'Connor.
Res., 385 Townsend Ave., 06512-3998. Tel: 203-467-1007; Fax: 203-467-3719.
School—Tel: 203-469-2271.
Lay Teachers 9; Students 196.
Catechesis/Religious Programs—Tel: 203-467-8763.
Students 177.

5—ST. BONIFACE'S, (1868) (German), Rev. John D. Casey. In res., Rev. Johannes B. Hari Kustanto, S.J. (Indonesia).
Res., 630 State St., 06511-6599. Tel: 203-865-3365.
Catechesis/Religious Programs—Students 6.

6—ST. BRENDAN'S, (1913), Rev. Donald J. French; Deacon Robert Brunell.
Res., 455 Whalley Ave., 06511-3080. Tel: 203-865-0561; Fax: 203-865-0562.
School—342 Ellsworth Ave., 06511. Tel: 203-562-6128; Fax: 203-562-6129.
Sisters 6; Lay Teachers 5; Students 225.
Convent—455 1/2 Whalley Ave., 06511. Tel: 203-787-4631. Sisters of Our Lady of the Garden

7—ST. CASIMIR'S, (1912) (Lithuanian), Rev. John D. Casey.
Res., 339 Greene St., 06511-6599. Tel: 203-624-8085.

8—ST. DONATO'S, (1915) (Italian), Rev. Louis Anthony Evangelisto.
Res., 505 Lombard St., 06513-2910. Tel: 203-789-1576.

9—ST. FRANCIS, (1868), Rev. Daniel J. McLearen. In res., Rev. William M. Burbank; Deacon Henry Lotto.
Res., 397 Ferry St., 06513-3698. Tel: 203-777-5356; Fax: 203-777-0874.
School—Tel: 203-777-5352; Fax: 203-865-1271. Mr. Frank P. Smith, Prin.
Religious 2; Lay Teachers 10; Students 255.
Catechesis/Religious Programs—Tel: 203-865-5179.
Students 58.

10—ST. JOHN THE BAPTIST, (1893), Rev. John J. Keane; Deacons Ronald Gurr; Jose A. Rivera. In res., Rev. Daniel J. Scott, M.S.
Res., 782 Dixwell Ave., 06511-1098. Tel: 203-624-3097; Fax: 203-562-0433.
Parish Center—20 Elizabeth St., 06511. Tel: 203-562-3908. Sr. Rosalie Shields, O.P., Pastoral Min.
Catechesis/Religious Programs—Tel: 203-562-5587.
Students 41.

11—ST. JOHN THE EVANGELIST. Closed. For inquiries for sacramental records contact Sacred Heart, New Haven.

12—ST. JOSEPH'S, (1900), Rev. John P. Sullivan, Temp. Admin.
Res., 129 Edwards St., 06511-2299. Tel: 203-777-2548.
Catechesis/Religious Programs—Students 30.

13—SAINT MARTIN DE PORRES, (1942) (African American), Rev. Joseph M. Elko.
Res., 136 Dixwell Ave., 06511-3400. Tel: 203-624-9944.

14—ST. MARY'S PRIORY, (1832), Very Rev. Carleton Parker Jones, O.P., Prior; Rev. Paul A. Bernardin, O.P. In res., Revs. John Farren, O.P.; William Holt, O.P.; Bernard T. Confer, O.P.; William B. Ryan, O.P.; John A. Gregory Maturi, O.P.; Bro. Gerard Thayer, O.P.
Mailing Address: P.O. Box 1202, 06505-1202.
Res., 5 Hillhouse Ave., 06511. Tel: 203-562-6193; Fax: 203-562-1273.
Shrine—The Shrine of the Infant Prague (Inc.), Tel: 203-562-9326; Fax: 203-562-1273.

15—ST. MICHAEL'S, (1889) (Italian), Rev. Andrew Brizzolara, C.S.
Res., 29 Wooster Pl., 06511-6998. Tel: 203-562-7178; Fax: 203-752-0157.
Parish Center—Tel: 203-789-9453.

16—ST. PETER, (1902). Closed. For inquiries for sacramental records contact Sacred Heart, New Haven.

17—ST. ROSE OF LIMA, (1907), Rev. William Burbank; Deacon Julius Marcarelli.
Res., 115 Blatchley Ave., 06513-4298. Tel: 203-865-6149; Fax: 203-865-6140.
School—12 Richard St., 06513. Tel: 203-624-5075; Fax: 203-624-1586. Mary Joy Walsh, Prin.
Lay Teachers 10; Students 192.
Catechesis/Religious Programs—Students 120.

18—ST. STANISLAUS, (1901) (Polish), Revs. Waclaw Hlond, C.M.; Boleskew Potemski, C.M.; Roman Kmiec, C.M.
Res., 9 Eld St., 06511-3815. Tel: 203-562-2828; Fax: 203-752-0217.
Catechesis/Religious Programs—Students 73.
Convent—15 Eld St., 06511. Tel: 203-562-2751. Sisters Minor of Mary Immaculate

Newington, Hartford Co., Holy Spirit (1964), Revs. James F. Kinnane; Lawrence R. Bock; Piotr J. Dwornik; Deacons James H. Shiels; James Fortier. In res., Rev. Raymond S. Smialowski.
Res., 183 Church St., 06111-4898. Tel: 860-666-5671; Fax: 860-666-9784.
Catechesis/Religious Programs—Tel: 860-666-3562. D.R.E.: Virginia Marchese; Mary Grace Messana.
Students 722.

St. Mary (1924), Revs. Thomas J. Barry; Michael J. Dolan; Deacon Bruce R. Thompson.
Res., 626 Willard Ave., 06111. Tel: 860-666-1591; Fax: 860-666-5720.
School—Tel: 860-666-3844; Fax: 860-666-5570. Religious 1; Lay Teachers 14; Students 267.
Maryhouse—(Sisters of Mercy) 21 Hartford Ave., #9, 06111. Tel: 860-666-1085.
Catechesis/Religious Programs—Tel: 860-666-6347.
Students 763.
Convent—168 Cedar St., 06111. Tel: 860-667-1790; Fax: 860-667-9881. Sisters of Charity

New Milford, Litchfield Co., St. Francis Xavier's (1871), Revs. Mario F. Julian, O.F.M.; Jack W. Hoak, O.F.M.; Deacon George H. Streib.
Mailing Address: 1 Elm St., 06776-4009.
Res., 48 Old Park Ln., 06776-2508. Tel: 860-354-2202; 350-1611; Fax: 860-355-9485.
Catechesis/Religious Programs—Tel: 860-354-5372.
Students 784.

Our Lady of the Lakes (1990), Rev. Thomas E. Ptaszynski; Deacon Robert E. Muro Tel: 860-350-6002.
Res., 3 Old Town Park Rd., 06776-4212. Tel: 860-354-5239; Fax: 860-354-2968.
Catechesis/Religious Programs—Tel: 860-355-5365.
Students 492.

Norfolk, Litchfield Co., Immaculate Conception (1889), Rev. John S. Ahern.
Res., 4 North St., P.O. Box 583, 06058-0583. Tel: 860-542-5442. [CEM]
Catechesis/Religious Programs—Students 103.

North Branford, New Haven Co., St. Augustine (1941), Rev. Daniel F. McSheffery.
Res., 30 Caputo Rd., 06471-1027. Tel: 203-484-0403; Fax: 203-484-0132.
Catechesis/Religious Programs—Students 724.

Northford, New Haven Co., St. Monica's (1964), Rev. Joseph Parel; Mrs. Judith Derbacher, Pastoral Assoc.; Deacons Louis P. Fusco; William B. Bergers.
Res., 1331 Middletown Ave., Box 160, 06472-0160. Tel: 203-484-9226; Fax: 203-484-1189.
Catechesis/Religious Programs—Tel: 203-484-2434.
Students 418.

North Haven, New Haven Co., St. Barnabas (1922), Revs. Hugh J. MacDonald; John J. Daly, Pastor Emeritus; Deacon Joseph Cretella.
Res., 44 Washington Ave., 06473-1799. Tel: 203-239-5378; Fax: 203-239-3510.
Catechesis/Religious Programs—Tel: 203-239-3804. Karin Tierney, D.R.E.
Students 367.

St. Frances Cabrini (1967), Rev. Robert J. St. Martin; Deacons George R. Stephens; James P. Taylor.
Res., 6 Welch Rd., 06473-2896. Tel: 203-239-5700; Fax: 203-239-6463.
Church & Parish Center—Pond Hill Rd., 06473. Tel: 203-239-5644.
Catechesis/Religious Programs—94 Chapel Hill Rd., 06473. Tel: 203-239-8012.
Students 394.
Nursery School—90 Chapel Hill Rd., 06473. Tel: 203-239-8012.
Convent— Sisters of the Sacred Heart of Jesus

St. Therese (1925), Revs. Timothy A. Meehan; Alexander J. Cherukarakunnel (India); Deacons Louis J. Florio; Carmine Angeloni.
Res., 555 Middletown Ave., 06473-4000. Tel: 203-239-1671; Fax: 203-234-2220.
Catechesis/Religious Programs—Tel: 203-234-9287.
Students 578.

Oakville, Litchfield Co., St. Mary Magdalen (1900), Revs. Joseph T. Kaminsky; William O. Seery; Deacon Neil Culhane.
Res., 145 Buckingham St., 06779-1797. Tel: 860-274-9273; Fax: 860-274-2013.
School—Tel: 860-945-0621; Fax: 860-945-6162.
Lay Teachers 12; Students 294.
Catechesis/Religious Programs—Students 447.

Orange, New Haven Co., Holy Infant (1952), Revs. Peter S. Dargan; Mathew Kappalumakkel; Bernard D. Killeen, (Retired); Deacons Americo Bichi; Bernard J. Hayden; Harold J. Hoffman; Joseph D. Sullivan.
Res., 450 Race Brook Rd., 06477. Tel: 203-799-2379; Fax: 203-799-9720.
Catechesis/Religious Programs—Tel: 203-777-2417.
Students 883.

Oxford, New Haven Co., St. Thomas the Apostle (1966), Rev. Dominic J. Valla.
Res., 733 Oxford Rd., 06478. Tel: 203-888-2382; Fax: 203-881-5518.
Catechesis/Religious Programs—Tel: 203-888-4951.
Students 704.

Plainville, Hartford Co., Our Lady of Mercy (1881), Revs. Richard P. McGann; Edmund K Karwowski; Deacon Gerald Geraci. In res., Rev. Sebastian Kochupurkal.
Res., 15 S. Canal St., 06062-2799. Tel: 860-793-1399; Fax: 860-747-5407. [CEM]
Parish Center: 19 S. Canal St., 06062. Tel: 860-747-6825.
Catechesis/Religious Programs—Tel: 860-747-6010. Jeanne Gionfriddo, D.R.E.
Students 230.

Plantsville, Hartford Co., Mary Our Queen (1961), Rev. Arthur J. DuPont; Deacons James P. Quinn; Paul J. Kulas.
Res., 248 Savage St., P.O. Box 46, 06479-0046. Tel: 860-628-4901; Fax: 860-621-0610.
Catechesis/Religious Programs—Tel: 860-628-0437.
Students 509.

St. Aloysius (1961), Rev. John P. Blanchfield. In res., Rev. Donald J. O'Leary; Deacon Angelo J. Coppola.
Res., 254 Burritt St., 06479-1426. Tel: 860-276-9208; Fax: 860-628-7650. [JC]
Catechesis/Religious Programs—Tel: 860-621-2454.
Students 560.

Poquonock, Hartford Co., St. Joseph's (1874), Rev. Robert B. Vargo, Admin.; Deacon Leo R. LaRocque.
Res., 1747 Poquonock Ave., P.O. Box 253, 06064-0253. Tel: 860-688-9566; Fax: 860-683-2225. [CEM]
Catechesis/Religious Programs—Tel: 860-683-0366. Sr. Elizabeth Ann Seton, S.F.C.C., D.R.E.
Students 439.

Prospect, New Haven Co., St. Anthony's (1939), Revs. Philip J. Cascia; Joseph R. DeCarolis; Deacons Domenic Stolfi; George Dinkle.
Res., 4 Union City Rd., P.O. Box 7117, 06712-0117. Tel: 203-758-4056; Fax: 203-758-4594.
Catechesis/Religious Programs—Tel: 203-758-4848.
Students 895.

Rocky Hill, Hartford Co., St. James (1880), Rev. Thomas B. Shepard; Deacon Michael Shelto.
Res., 767 Elm St., 06067-1902. Tel: 860-529-8655; Fax: 860-257-1754.
Catechesis/Religious Programs—(Grades K-10). Tel: 860-529-1274. Thomas Sacerdote, D.R.E.
Students 680.

St. Elizabeth Seton (1985), Rev. James A. Shanley.
Res., 280 Brook St., 06067-0485. Tel: 860-529-3222; Fax: 860-529-6421.
Catechesis/Religious Programs—Students 443.

Seymour, New Haven Co., Good Shepherd (1967), Revs. Edward S. Jaksina; Robert P. Ricciardi; Deacons Frank J. Krasnicki; Alan C. Baldwin.
Res., 135 Mountain Rd., 06483-2038. Tel: 203-888-9243.
Catechesis/Religious Programs—D.R.E.:, Tel: 203-735-3190. Glenn Durette; Debra Durette.
Students 447.

St. Augustine's (1866), Rev. Brian E. Jeffries; Deacons John R. Saffo, Sr.; Richard Renker.
Res., 35 Washington Ave., 06483-3198. Tel: 203-888-2081; Fax: 203-888-9681. [CEM]
Catechesis/Religious Programs—Tel: 203-888-7003.
Students 232.

Sharon, Litchfield Co., St. Bernard's (1885), Rev. John P. Gwozdz, Admin.
Res., 52 New St., Box 218, 06069-0218. Tel: 860-364-5244; Fax: 860-364-9893. [CEM]
Catechesis/Religious Programs—Students 38.

Simsbury, Hartford Co., St. Mary's (1921), Revs. William R. Metzler; John W. McHugh; Deacons John Sweeney; Joseph Gabriele.
Res., 940 Hopmeadow St., P.O. Box 575, 06070-0575. Tel: 860-658-7627; Fax: 860-658-7626.
Parish Offices—3 Massaco St., P.O. Box 575, 06070.
School—St. Mary School, 946 Hopmeadow St., 06070. Tel: 860-658-9412; Fax: 860-658-1737. Mrs. Maria Maynard, Prin.
Lay Teachers 14; Students 295.
Catechesis/Religious Programs—Tel: 860-658-5919.
Students 1,001.

Southbury, New Haven Co., Sacred Heart (1884), Rev. Mark F. Flynn; Deacons Joseph Lavoie, (Retired); Vincent Cassidy; Charles Dietsch; Michael Kulas.
Res., 68 Georges Hill Rd., 06488-0686. Tel: 203-264-5071; Fax: 203-264-9562. [CEM]
Catechesis/Religious Programs—Tel: 203-264-5065. Eileen Dignazio, D.R.E.
Students 962.
Station—Southbury, Southbury Training School, Tel: 203-264-8231.

South Glastonbury, Hartford Co., St. Augustine (1877), Rev. Kevin P. Cavanaugh; Deacon Stephen L. Weaver.
Res., 55 Hopewell Rd., P.O. Box 175, 06073-0175. Tel: 860-633-9505; Fax: 860-633-1341. [CEM]
Catechesis/Religious Programs—Hopewell School, (Grades K-8). Tel: 860-633-9505.
Students 275.

Southington, Hartford Co., Immaculate Conception (1915) (Polish), Rev. David J. Lewandowski.
Res., 130 Summer St., 06489. Tel: 203-628-2181. [CEM]
Catechesis/Religious Programs—Judy Telesmanic, D.R.E.
Students 211.
Father Kolbe Catechetical Center—152 Summer St., Plantsville, 06479. Tel: 860-628-6973.

St. Dominic (1971), Rev. Henry C. Frascadore; Deacons John L. Crowley; Eugene P. Nebiolo. In res., Rev. John T. O'Connor, (Retired); Sr. Ann Kane, C.S.J., D.Min., Pastoral Assoc.
Res., 1050 Flanders Rd., 06489-1344. Tel: 860-628-0349; Fax: 860-276-8390.
Catechesis/Religious Programs—Tel: 860-628-5159. Jacqueline Marenholz, D.R.E.
Students 750.

St. Thomas (1860), Revs. George F. Lauretti; James T. Gregory; Deacon Wesley F. Baxter.
Res., 99 Bristol St., 06489-4599. Tel: 860-628-4713; Fax: 860-628-7341. [CEM]
School—Tel: 860-628-2485. Mrs. Joan Murphy, Prin.
Lay Teachers 8; Students 159.
Catechesis/Religious Programs—Tel: 860-628-9679.
Students 435.

South Meriden, New Haven Co., Holy Angels (1887), Rev. Roland M. LaPlante; Deacon Donald H. Smith.
Res., 915 Main St., 06451-4999. Tel: 203-235-5311 (Rectory); 235-3822 (Office); Fax: 203-630-3041.
Catechesis/Religious Programs—585 Main St., 06451. Tel: 203-237-8697. Stephen N. Filippo, D.R.E.
Students 178.

South Windsor, Hartford Co., St. Francis of Assisi (1941), Rev. John P. Rohan.
Res., 673 Ellington Rd., 06074-4166. Tel: 860-528-8288; Fax: 860-528-1685.
Catechesis/Religious Programs—Tel: 860-289-3671. Mark F. Cerrato, D.R.E.
Students 570.

St. Margaret Mary (1961), Revs. Daniel Jeremiah Sullivan; Francis V. Krukowski; Deacons Thomas J. Conklin; David Dwyer.
Res., 80 Hayes Rd., 06074-1499. Tel: 860-644-2411; Fax: 860-644-5765.
Catechesis/Religious Programs—Tel: 860-644-2549.
Students 1,150.

Suffield, Hartford Co., Sacred Heart (1884), Rev. Theodore T. Raczynski.
Res., 446 Mountain Rd., P.O. Box 626, 06078-0626. Tel: 860-668-4246; Fax: 860-668-1337. [JC]
Catechesis/Religious Programs—Tel: 860-668-7766.
Students 805.

St. Joseph's (1916) (Polish), Rev. William L. Baldyga; Deacon Edward Szewczyk.
Res., 140 S. Main St., 06078-2218. Tel: 860-668-2880. [CEM]
Catechesis/Religious Programs—Students 40.
Convent—156 S. Main St., 06078. Tel: 860-668-2503. Felician Sisters

Tariffville, Hartford Co., St. Bernard's (1878), Rev. Thomas A. Flower; Deacons Andrew J. Anthony; Thomas P. Scanlon.
Res., 7 Maple St., P.O. Box 85, 06081-0085. Tel: 860-658-5142; Fax: 860-658-2804. [CEM]
Catechesis/Religious Programs—Students 158.

Terryville, Litchfield Co., Immaculate Conception (1882), Rev. Gerald H. Dziedzic; Deacon John W. Makara.
Res., 21 Maple St., 06786-1197. Tel: 860-583-4697. [CEM 2]
Catechesis/Religious Programs—Students 154.

St. Casimir (1906), Rev. Gerald H. Dziedzic.
Mailing Address: 21 Maple St.
Res., 19 Allen St., 06786-1503. Tel: 860-583-4697.
Catechesis/Religious Programs—Students 101.

Thomaston, Litchfield Co., St. Thomas (1869), Revs. Harold M. Kearns; John E. Cockayne; Deacons Jose L. Dlugokinski; Robert Gordon.
Parish Center—(CEM) 19 Electric Ave., 06787-1651. Tel: 860-283-5817; Fax: 860-283-1009.
School—30 N. Main St., 06787. Tel: 860-283-5955; Fax: 860-283-4326.
Lay Teachers 11; Students 155.
Catechesis/Religious Programs—Tel: 860-283-4296.
Students 443.

Torrington, Litchfield Co.,

1—St. Francis of Assisi, (1877), Revs. Robert W. Ladish; John G. Weaver; Deacon Edward Dickson; Sr. Helen Marie Clark, R.S.M., Pastoral Assoc.
Res., 160 Main St., 06790-5299. Tel: 860-482-5571; Fax: 860-489-1590.
School—Tel: 860-489-4177. Mr. Joseph Meaney, Prin.
Lay Teachers 9; Students 205.
Catechesis/Religious Programs—360 Prospect St., 06790. Tel: 203-482-3121.
Students 473.

2—Sacred Heart, (1910) (Slovak), Revs. Gerard G. Masters; Stephen M. Sledesky; Deacon John L. Dembishack.
Res., 116 Grove St., 06790-5047. Tel: 860-482-8246; Fax: 860-482-1863.
Parish Center—119 Grove St., 06790. Tel: 860-489-4070.
Catechesis/Religious Programs—Students 77.

3—St. Mary's, (1919) (Polish), Revs. Robert W. Ladish; John G. Weaver.
Res., 61 Forest Ct., 06790-4698. Tel: 860-482-3583.
Catechesis/Religious Programs—Students 112.

4—St. Peter's, (1910) (Italian), Revs. Gerard G. Masters; Stephen M. Sledesky.
Res., 107 E. Main St., 06790-5493. Tel: 860-482-4433; Fax: 860-482-1891.
School—Tel: 860-489-8735; Fax: 860-482-9406.
Maestre Pie Filippini 2; Lay Teachers 12; Students 160.
Catechesis/Religious Programs—Students 155.

Union City, New Haven Co., St. Hedwig (Naugatuck) (1906) (Polish), Revs. Stephen H. Bzdyra; Ronald P. Zepecki; Deacon Thomas J. Clifford.
Res., 32 Golden Hill St., 06770-3099. Tel: 203-729-2490; Fax: 203-720-2161.
School—Tel: 203-729-2403. Ms. Patricia Dayner, Prin.
Lay Teachers 9; Students 140.
Catechesis/Religious Programs—Students 100.

St. Mary's (Naugatuck) (1907), Rev. Richard M. Taberski, Admin.; Deacon Earle A. Kimball.
Res., 338 N. Main St., 06770-3235. Tel: 203-729-2279; Fax: 203-729-2270.
Catechesis/Religious Programs—Students 173.

Unionville, Hartford Co., St. Mary's (1874), Rev. John S. Golas.
Res., 16 Bidwell Sq., 06085-1116. Tel: 860-673-2422; Fax: 860-673-2001. [CEM]
Catechesis/Religious Programs—Tel: 860-675-8522.
Students 800.

Wallingford, New Haven Co., Holy Trinity (1869), Revs. Charles J. MacDonald; Luis M. Jaramillo; Edward G. Pfnausch; Deacons Raul Cardona; Eugene Riotte.
Res., 68 N. Colony St., 06492-3696. Tel: 203-269-8791; Fax: 203-269-0880.
School—11 N. Whittlesey Ave., 06492. Tel: 203-269-4476; Fax: 203-294-4983. Sr. Kathleen Kelly, R.S.M., Prin.
Sisters of Mercy 1; Lay Teachers 9; Students 271.
Catechesis/Religious Programs—Tel: 203-265-6300. Frances Selmecki, D.R.E.
Students 901.

Resurrection (1963), Rev. Msgr. John J. McCarthy; Rev. Daniel E. Johnson, Pastor Emeritus. In res., Rev. Mark J. Bonsignore (Peru); Deacon Wayne F. Griffin.
Res., 115 Pond Hill Rd., 06492-4836. Tel: 203-265-1694; Fax: 203-284-9766.
Catechesis/Religious Programs—Tel: 203-269-4683. Mary Ann Marchitto, D.R.E.
Students 610.

SS. Peter and Paul (1924), Rev. Daniel J. Karpiey; Deacon Louis P. Sill, Jr.
Res., 139 N. Orchard St., 06492-3617. Tel: 203-269-4617; Fax: 203-265-6751. [CEM]
Catechesis/Religious Programs—Tel: 203-269-0271.
Students 102.

Washington Depot, Litchfield Co., Our Lady of Perpetual Help (1893), Rev. Thomas F. Bennett.
Res., 34 Green Hill Rd., P.O. Box 303, 06794. Tel: 860-868-2600. [CEM]
Catechesis/Religious Programs—Students 163.
Mission—Roxbury, Litchfield Co., St. Patrick's, Church St., Roxbury 06783.

Waterbury, New Haven Co.,

1—Blessed Sacrament, (1911), Revs. Walter A. Vichas; Nathaniel C. Labarda; Deacon William M. McGrath.
Res., 182 Robbins St., 06708. Tel: 203-753-3149; Fax: 203-596-0740.
School—Tel: 203-756-5313; Fax: 203-756-5313.
Sisters 3; Lay Teachers 9; Students 266.
Catechesis/Religious Programs—Tel: 203-757-1656.
Students 78.
Convent—407 Robinwood Rd., 06708. Tel: 203-753-1472. Sisters of the Third Order Regular of St. Francis

2—Immaculate Conception, (1848), Revs. John J. Bevins; George M. White, O.M.I.; John Curry Gay; Maximo Asencios-Pablo, M.Ss.A.; Thomas Simon, M.Ss.A; Saysiri Leonard (Sri Lanka); Deacon Carl Vecca. In res., Rev. Michael Burke.
Res., 74 W. Main St., 06721-1670. Tel: 203-574-0017; Fax: 203-756-8748.
School—St. Mary's, Tel: 203-753-2574; Fax: 203-596-2498.
Lay Teachers 18; Students 500.
Catechesis/Religious Programs—Students 500.
Convent—55 Cole St., 06702. Tel: 203-754-2913. Maryknoll Sisters

3—Our Lady of Fatima, (1971) (Portuguese), Rev. Nelson Ribeiro, C.M.
Res., 2071 Baldwin St., 06706. Tel: 203-753-1424; Fax: 203-753-1424.
Catechesis/Religious Programs—Students 411.

4—Our Lady of Loreto, (1971), Rev. Msgr. Joseph A. Devine.
Res., 12 Ardsley Rd., 06708-1825. Tel: 203-757-6112; Fax: 203-756-9656.
Catechesis/Religious Programs—Students 278.

5—Our Lady of Lourdes, (1899) (Italian), Rev. Ronald A. Ferraro; Deacon George M. Pettinico.
Res., 309 S. Main St., 06706-1090. Tel: 203-754-4134; Fax: 203-755-0456.
Catechesis/Religious Programs—Students 55.

6—Our Lady of Mt. Carmel, (1923) (Italian), Revs. Carmine B. Raneri; Ronald Mikasauskas, M.Ss.A.
Res., 785 Highland Ave., 06708-4199. Tel: 203-756-8981; Fax: 203-756-2074.
School—645 Congress Ave., 06708. Tel: 203-755-6809. Mrs. Robin A. Booth, Prin.
Lay Teachers 10; Students 256.
Catechesis/Religious Programs—Tel: 203-753-1713.
Students 310.
Convent—656 Congress Ave., 06708.

7—Sacred Heart, (1855), Rev. Kevin G. Donovan, Admin. In res., Rev. Richard C. Bollea.
Res., 13 Wolcott St., 06702-1790. Tel: 203-757-8737; Fax: 203-754-5862.

8—St. Anne, (1886) (French), Rev. Alvin J. LeBlanc, Admin.; Deacons Francis X. Bandeira; Gaspard D. LeBlanc.
Res., 515 S. Main St., 06706-1089. Tel: 203-756-4439; Fax: 203-754-3244.
Catechesis/Religious Programs—Students 29.

9—St. Cecilia's, (1893) (German), Rev. John C. Blackall, (Spanish Apostolate); Deacon Alejandro Lopez.
Res., 83 Cherry St., 06702-1699. Tel: 203-574-5156.
Catechesis/Religious Programs—Tel: 203-754-1124.
Students 367.

10—St. Francis Xavier's, (1896), Rev. Paul J. Pace; Deacon Donald E. Cruess.
Res., 625 Baldwin St., 06706-1597. Tel: 203-756-7804.
School—605 Baldwin St., 06706. Tel: 203-753-3197; Fax: 203-574-0128. Mr. J. Brian Lally, Prin.
Lay Teachers 10; Students 248.
Catechesis/Religious Programs—Tel: 203-754-6996.
Students 170.

11—St. Joseph, (1894) (Lithuanian), Rev. Kevin J. Forsyth.
Res., 46 Congress Ave., 06708. Tel: 203-754-1557; Fax: 203-754-6337.
School—Tel: 203-755-1985; Fax: 203-756-0179.
Lay Teachers 10; Students 200.
Catechesis/Religious Programs—Students 220.

12—St. Leo the Great, (1974), Rev. Joseph F. Gorman; Deacons Modesto Rosello; Charles Colella.
Res., 14 Bentwood Dr., 06705-3612. Tel: 203-573-0511.
Catechesis/Religious Programs—Students 223.

13—St. Lucy's, (1926) (Italian), Rev. Paul Mangiafico.
Res., 24 Branch St., 06704-3626. Tel: 203-574-5903; Fax: 203-574-2906.
School—58 Griggs St., 06704. Tel: 203-756-3831; Fax: 203-759-0438. Mr. John J. Petto, Prin.
Lay Teachers 10; Students 218.
Parish Center: 64 Division St., 06704. Tel: 203-755-8420.
Catechesis/Religious Programs—Students 60.

14—St. Margaret's, (1910) (Hispanic), Rev. Joseph E. Looney; Deacon Paul P. Iadarola.
Res., 289 Willow St., 06710. Tel: 203-754-6101; Fax: 203-754-2006.
School—Tel: 203-753-3708; Fax: 203-753-1360. Donna Binkoski, Prin.
Lay Teachers 11; Students 249.
Catechesis/Religious Programs—Students 133.

15—St. Michael, (1897), Rev. Ronald Gliatta, O.F.M.; Deacon George D. Hajjar.
Res., 62 St. Michael Dr., 06704-1295. Tel: 203-753-0689; Fax: 203-573-9101.
Catechesis/Religious Programs—Students 184.

16—St. Patrick, (1880) (Irish), Rev. John L. Williams; Deacon Thomas F. Johnson.
Mailing Address: P.O. Box 271, 06720-0271. Tel: 203-756-8837; Fax: 203-756-4690.
Res., 50 Charles St., 06708. Tel: 203-756-8837.
Catechesis/Religious Programs—645 Highland Ave., 06708. Tel: 203-753-1713.
Students 26.

17—SS. Peter and Paul, (1920), Revs. Edward F. Hyland; Shawn T. Daly; Joseph R. Cronin.
Res., 67 Southmayd Rd., 06705. Tel: 203-756-7919; Fax: 203-755-3535.
School—Tel: 203-755-0881. Janet Curry, Prin.
Lay Teachers 12; Students 283.
Catechesis/Religious Programs—114 Beecher Ave., 06705. Tel: 203-753-4242.
Students 218.

18—St. Stanislaus Kostka, (1913) (Polish), Revs. Stephen H. Bzdyra, Admin.; Ronald P. Zepecki.
Res., 86 East Farm St., 06704. Tel: 203-574-0871; Fax: 203-575-0107.

19—St. Thomas, (1898). Closed. For inquiries for sacramental records contact St. Michael, Waterbury.

Watertown, Litchfield Co., St. John the Evangelist (1878), Rev. John M. Cooney; Deacons George Simonin; John Chartes.
Res., 21 Academy Hill, 06795-2101. Tel: 860-274-8836; Fax: 860-274-8837. [CEM]
School—Tel: 860-274-9208; Fax: 860-945-1082. Margaret Whalen, Prin.
School Sisters of Notre Dame 3; Lay Teachers 8; Students 223.

Catechesis/Religious Programs—Tel: 860-274-4123. Theresa N. Morgado, D.R.E.
Students 636.

West Hartford, Hartford Co.,

1—ST. BRIGID'S, (1919), Revs. Edward J. McLean; Francis T. Carter. In res., Rev. Msgr. Charles B. Johnson.
Res., 1088 New Britain Ave., 06110-2489. Tel: 860-236-5965; Fax: 860-233-8016.
School—100 Mayflower St., 06110. Tel: 860-561-2130; Fax: 860-561-0011.
Sisters 1; Lay Teachers 18; Students 246.
Catechesis/Religious Programs—Tel: 860-521-8523.
Students 296.

2—ST. HELENA, (1966), Revs. Francis P. Johnson; Eugene M. Kilbride; Deacon Robert J. Hilliard. In res., Rev. Zigford J. Kriss.
Res., 30 Echo Ln., 06107-3698. Tel: 860-521-1921.
Catechesis/Religious Programs—Tel: 860-521-3661.
Students 285.

3—ST. JOHN THE EVANGELIST, (1942) (Spanish). Closed. For inquiries for sacramental records contact St. Lawrence O'Toole, Hartford.

4—ST. MARK THE EVANGELIST, (1942), Team Ministry: Rev. Thomas J. Sas; Rev. Msgr. William J. Mullen; Deacon Raymond J. Fugere.
Res., 467 S. Quaker Ln., 06110-1042. Tel: 860-233-1269.
Catechesis/Religious Programs—491 Quaker Ln., 06110. Tel: 860-236-3545. Catherine Umanetz, D.R.E.
Students 270.

5—ST. PETER CLAVER, (1966), Rev. Joseph P. McGarry.
Res., 47 Pleasant St., 06107-1600. Tel: 860-561-4235; Fax: 860-561-4235(4).
Catechesis/Religious Programs—Tel: 860-521-2904.
Students 657.

6—ST. THOMAS THE APOSTLE CHURCH, (1921), Revs. Arthur J. Murphy; Patrick J. Curran (SLC); Edward M. Moran. In res., Rev. John J. Stack.
Res., 872 Farmington Ave., 06119-1499. Tel: 860-233-8269; Fax: 860-523-8794.
School—25 Dover Rd., 06119. Tel: 860-236-6257; Fax: 860-236-8865.
Lay Teachers 29; Students 310.
Catechesis/Religious Programs—Tel: 860-523-4209; Fax: 860-570-0273.
Students 240.

7—ST. TIMOTHY'S, (1958), Rev. Henry P. Cody.
Res., 1116 N. Main St., 06117-1209. Tel: 860-233-5131; Fax: 860-232-2189.
School—St. Timothy Middle School, 225 King Philip Dr., 06117. Tel: 860-236-0614; Fax: 860-920-0293.
Lay Teachers 15; Students 141.
Catechesis/Religious Programs—Tel: 860-232-3952.
Students 254.

West Haven, New Haven Co.,

1—OUR LADY OF VICTORY, (1935), Revs. Mark S. Suslenko; Ronald J. Osborne. In res., Rev. Gregory M. Altermatt.
Res., 600 Jones Hill Rd., 06516-6399. Tel: 203-934-6357; Fax: 203-932-3315.
School—Tel: 203-932-6457; Fax: 203-932-6456.
Lay Teachers 16; Students 390.
Catechesis/Religious Programs—Tel: 203-933-0044.
Students 692.

2—ST. JOHN VIANNEY, (1965), Rev. Timothy A. O'Brien; Deacons Frank J. Bevvino, Jr.; Charles W. Parlee, Jr.
Res., 300 Capt. Thomas Blvd., 06516-5974. Tel: 203-934-6000; Fax: 203-934-5677.
Catechesis/Religious Programs—Tel: 203-933-8471.
Students 211.

3—ST. LAWRENCE'S, (1886), Team Ministry: Revs. James V. Hickey; Simon Lee, S.J.; Deacons Anthony P. Solli; John E. Wheeler. In res., Rev. Chacko K. Kumplam (India).
Res., 207 Main St., 06516-4599. Tel: 203-934-8351; Fax: 203-937-7858.
School—233 Main St., 06516. Tel: 203-933-2518; Fax: 203-932-2058. Mrs. Paul Wirkus, Dir.
Lay Teachers 11; Students 249.
Catechesis/Religious Programs—231 Main St., 06516. Tel: 203-933-2519.
Students 175.

4—ST. LOUIS, (1886) (French Territorial), Rev. Peter J. Pinto; Deacons Salvatore DeFilippo; Edward J. Mancini.
Res., 89 Bull Hill Ln., 06516-3998. Tel: 203-934-5249; Fax: 203-934-5240.
Catechesis/Religious Programs—Students 114.

5—ST. PAUL'S, (1916), Revs. Lawrence Symolon; Augustine Mangalath (India); Deacons George Schiro; Richard Fournier.
Res., 41 Alling St., 06516-2799. Tel: 203-933-1024; Fax: 203-931-9416.
Catechesis/Religious Programs—Tel: 203-934-1357. Patricia Sastor, D.R.E.
Students 330.
Parish Center: 45 Alling St., 06516. Tel: 203-934-1357.
Mission—West Haven, Our Lady of Mt. Carmel Chapel, Fenwick St., 06516. Tel: 203-389-6384.

West Simsbury, Hartford Co., St. Catherine of Siena (1971), Rev. Richard R. Russell; Deacon Thomas F. Delehanty.
Res., Box 184, 06092. Tel: 860-658-1642.
Catechesis/Religious Programs—Students 400.

Wethersfield, Hartford Co., Corpus Christi (1941), Team Ministry: Revs. Thomas B. Campion, Co-Pastor; David W. Lonergan, Co-Pastor; Deacon Seth M. English. In res., Rev. Bradford Colton, Pastor Emeritus.
Res., 84 Somerset St., 06109-3031. Tel: 860-529-2545; Fax: 860-529-5861.
School—Tel: 860-529-5487; Fax: 860-257-9106. Mrs. Eileen Sampiere, Prin.
Religious 1; Lay Teachers 29; Students 541.
Catechesis/Religious Programs—581 Silas Deane Hwy., 06109. Tel: 860-721-9419.
Students 605.

Incarnation (1963), Revs. John F. Edwards; James M. Moran; Deacon Robert J. D'Efemia. In res., Rev. Msgr. Michael J. Motta.
Res., 544 Prospect St., 06109-3696. Tel: 860-529-2533; Fax: 860-721-6595.
Catechesis/Religious Programs—Tel: 860-529-6765. Noranne Wamester, D.R.E.
Students 549.

Sacred Heart (1876), Team Ministry: Revs. Thomas B. Campion, Co-Pastor; David W. Lonergan, Co-Pastor; Deacon Cornelius D. O'Connell.
Res., 56 Hartford Ave., 06109-1800. Tel: 860-529-1991.
Catechesis/Religious Programs—Tel: 860-529-0815.
Students 159.

Windsor, Hartford Co., St. Gabriel's (1894), Revs. Richard J. Neumann; Robert J. Grant; Deacons Joseph J. Cooke; Ronald M. Biamomte.
Res., 379 Broad St., 06095-3004. Tel: 860-688-4905; Fax: 860-688-2638.
School—77 Bloomfield Ave., 06095. Tel: 860-688-6401; Fax: 860-298-8668.
Lay Teachers 12; Students 255.
Catechesis/Religious Programs—Students 286.

St. Gertrude's (1947), Rev. Maurice J. Barry; Deacon Vincent Thorney.
Res., 550 Matianuck Ave., 06095-3599. Tel: 860-522-6163; Fax: 860-525-2320.
Catechesis/Religious Programs—Students 159.

Windsor Locks, Hartford Co., St. Mary (1852), Revs. Robert A. O'Grady; Francis P. McDonnell; Deacons Donald Norton; Benedict L. Winiarski.
Res., 42 Spring St., 06096-2311. Tel: 860-623-2524; Fax: 860-623-5684. [CEM]
Parish Center—45 Church St., 06096. Tel: 860-627-9469.
Catechesis/Religious Programs—Students 600.

St. Robert Bellarmine (1962), Rev. Thomas F. Farrell.
Res., 52 S. Elm St., P.O. Box 315, 06096-0315. Tel: 860-623-0240; Fax: 860-623-0240.
Catechesis/Religious Programs—Students 76.

Winsted, Litchfield Co., St. Joseph's (1853), Revs. Anthony F. Moore, O.F.M.; Leon Ristuccia, O.F.M.; Deacon William H. Wilcox.
Res., 31 Oak St., P.O. Box 808, 06098-0808. Tel: 860-379-3369; Fax: 860-379-4194. [CEM]
School—St. Anthony's, 55 Oak St., 06098. Tel: 860-379-7521; Fax: 860-379-7522. Sr. Fidelis Shepherd, F.M.D.M., Prin.
Lay Teachers 10; Students 250.
Catechesis/Religious Programs—Tel: 860-379-5968.
Students 333.

Wolcott, New Haven Co., St. Pius X (1955), Rev. Henry A. Balchunas; Deacon Stephen J. Kelly.
Res., 525 Woodtick Rd., 06716-2898. Tel: 203-879-2544; Fax: 203-879-2545.
Catechesis/Religious Programs—Tel: 203-879-9030.
Students 711.

St. Maria Goretti (1973), Rev. William R. Sokolowski.
Res., 1300 Woodtick Rd., P.O. Box 6291, 06716-0291. Tel: 203-879-4608; Fax: 203-879-4609.
Catechesis/Religious Programs—Tel: 203-879-5242.
Students 416.

Woodbridge, New Haven Co., Church of the Assumption (1924), Revs. Gene E. Gianelli; Vincent J. Curran; Deacon Joseph P. Borland.
Res., 81 Center Rd., 06525-1699. Tel: 203-387-7119; Fax: 203-387-4281.
Catechesis/Religious Programs—Tel: 203-389-9863. D.R.E.: Sr. Dorellen Sullivan, R.S.M.; Deacon John J. Conte, Jr.
Students 685.

Woodbury, Litchfield Co., St. Teresa's (1902), Rev. Robert M. Kwiatkowski.
Res., P.O. Box A, 11 Washington Ave., 06798-0417. Tel: 203-263-2008.
Catechesis/Religious Programs—Students 420.

Woodmont, New Haven Co., St. Agnes (1906), Rev. Francis X. Callahan. In res., Rev. George J. Raffaeta, (Retired).
Res., 400 Merwin Ave., 06460-7198. Tel: 203-878-1617; Fax: 203-878-5545.
Catechesis/Religious Programs—Students 513.

Yalesville, New Haven Co., Our Lady of Fatima (1960), Revs. Salvatore F. Cavagnuolo; Kevin M. Dillon. In res., Revs. Leo J. Daily, (Retired); Dawson D. Trenchard, (Retired).
Res., 382 Hope Hill Rd., 06492-2270. Tel: 203-265-0961; Fax: 203-269-9386.
Catechesis/Religious Programs—Tel: 203-265-6426; 265-6818 (Youth Minister). Tracy Blum, D.R.E.
Students 772.

Chaplains of Public Institutions

HARTFORD. *Hartford Hospital* 80 Seymour St., 06102-5037. Tel: 860-545-2251; Fax: 860-545-3594. Chaplains: Rev. Gerard Pelletier, S.M.; Deacon Paul Koch.

BRISTOL. *Bristol Hospital* Brewster Rd., 06011-0977. Tel: 860-585-3431. Rev. J. Richard Fowler, Interfaith Chap.

CHESHIRE. *Connecticut Correctional Institution* 900 Highland Ave., 06410-1698. Tel: 203-250-2787. Chaplains: Rev. Stephen A. Krugel; Deacon Robert P. Gale.

Manson Youth Institution 42 Jarvis St., 06510. Tel: 203-272-5391. Deacon Robert Blair.

ENFIELD. *Carl Robinson Correctional Institution* P.O. Box 1400, 06083-1400. Tel: 860-763-6200. Chaplains: Rev. William H. Hilliard; Deacon Robert P. Gale.

Community Correctional Institution 426 Hazard Ave., 06082-4719. Tel: 203-789-7111. Rev. Stephen A. Krugel, Chap., 426 Hazard Ave., 06082-4719. Tel: 203-789-7111.

NEW BRITAIN. *New Britain General Hospital* 100 Grand St., 06050. Tel: 860-224-5011. Rev. Ronald T. Smith, Chap., Res., 396 Church St., 06051.

NEW HAVEN. *Yale-New Haven Hospital* 20 York St., 06504-1001. Tel: 203-688-2152. Rev. Geoffrey C. Smith, Chap.

NEWINGTON. *Department of Veteran Affairs Medical Center* 555 Willard Ave., 06111. Tel: 860-666-6951. Rev. Francis M. Vella, Chap.

ROCKY HILL. *Veterans' Home and Hospital* West St., 06067. Tel: 860-529-2571. Rev. Joseph F. Whalen, M.S.

SUFFIELD. *Macdougall Correctional Institute* 1153 E. St. S., 06080-0002. Tel: 860-627-2148; Fax: 860-627-2152. Rev. Louis S. Paturzo, Chap., Res., 90 Alden Ave., Enfield, 06082-2865. Tel: 860-745-9966.

WATERBURY. *Waterbury Hospital* 64 Robbins St., 06708. Tel: 203-573-7213; Fax: 203-573-7326. Rev. Richard C. Bollea, Chap.

WEST HAVEN. *V.A. CT Health Care System* 950 Campbell Ave., 06516. Tel: 203-932-5711. Rev. Daniel V. Scott, M.S.

Special and other Archdiocesan Assignment:
Reverend Monsignors—
Bergin, Robert D., Dir., Deaf Apostolate, Mercyknoll, 243 Steele Rd., West Hartford, CT 06117
Conte, John P., Min., Office of Ministry for Priests, 467 Bloomfield Ave., Bloomfield, CT 06002
Ginty, Thomas M., Sec. to the Archbishop, Chancellor, Dir. Office for Divine Worship, 467 Bloomfield Ave., Bloomfield, CT 06002
Johnson, Charles B., Vicar for Priests, St. Thomas Seminary, 467 Bloomfield Ave., Bloomfield, CT 06002
Liptak, David Q., Consulting Editor, "The Catholic Transcript", 785 Asylum Ave., Hartford, CT 06105
Motta, Michael J., Dir., Office of Religious Education, Newington, CT 06111
Reverend Fathers—
Charman, Eugene J., Archdiocesan Computer Consultant, Plantsville, CT 06479
Couturier, George M., Coord., Office to Study Restructuring Parishes and Asst. to Vicar for Priests, St. Thomas Seminary, 467 Bloomfield Ave., Bloomfield, CT 06002
Dietrich, John J., Vocations Dir., St. Thomas Seminary, 469 Bloomfield Ave., Bloomfield, CT 06002

Donohue, Aidan N., Rector & Pres., St. Thomas Seminary, 467 Bloomfield Ave., Bloomfield, CT 06002
Gatzak, John P., Dir., Office of Communications (Radio/Television), 785 Asylum Ave., Hartford, CT 06105
Kinnane, James F., J.C.L., Vicar for Religious, 134 Farmington Ave., Hartford, CT 06105-3784
Kriss, Zigford J., Supt. of Schools, 467 Bloomfield Ave., Bloomfield, CT 06002
LeBlanc, Alvin J., Judicial Vicar (Officialis), Chancery Tribunal, 134 Farmington Ave., Hartford, CT 06105
McLean, Edward J., Dir., Catholic Library and Information Center, 125 Market St., Hartford, CT 06103
Tiano, Christopher M., Exec. Editor, "The Catholic Transcript", 785 Asylum Ave., Hartford, CT 06105
Vargo, Robert B., Vice Chancellor, 134 Farmington Ave., Hartford, CT 06105-3784
Wrenn, Lawrence G., Judicial Vicar for the Court of Appeals, Tribunal Office, 134 Farmington Ave., Hartford, CT 06105

On Duty Outside the Archdiocese:
Reverend Monsignors—
Sokolowski, Robert S., Catholic University of America, 401 Michigan Ave., N.E., Washington, DC 20064
Reverend Fathers—
Charbonneau, William R., HGB/HC, 1411 Jefferson Davis Hwy., Ste. 9502, Arlington, VA 22202-3231
Cwiekowski, Frederick J., S.S., St. Patrick Seminary, 320 Middlefield Rd., Menlo Park, CA 94025
Goekler, Thomas F., Apartado Postal 2127, San Pedro Sula, Honduras
Leavitt, Robert F., S.S., St. Mary Seminary, 5400 Roland Ave., Baltimore, MD 21210
Matera, Frank J., Catholic University of America, 401 Michigan Ave., N.E., Washington, DC 20017
McBrien, Richard P., University of Notre Dame, Notre Dame, IN 46556
Morrison, Douglas A., 24 Courthouse Sq., Apt. 805, Rockville, MD 20850-2340
Thayer, David D., S.S., Theological College of Catholic University of America, 401 Michigan Ave., N.E., Washington, DC 20064

Military Chaplains:
Reverend Fathers—
Hanley, Dennis P., U.S. Air Force, 10427 Kuter Ave., 3WG/HC, Elmendorf AFB, AK 99506
Hellwig, Lee W., U.S. Navy, 2199 John C. Stennis (CVN 74), Box 8 Crmd., FPO AP, 96615-2894

Retired:
Reverend Monsignors—
Daly, Charles W., St. Luke Rectory, 66 Bolton St., Hartford, CT 06114-2698
Fries, Francis A., 42 Blakeslee St., Bristol, CT 06010
Wodarski, John P., St. Stanislaus Rectory, 510 West St., Bristol, CT 06010
Reverend Fathers—
Archambault, James H., 2003 49th St. W., Bradenton, FL 34209
Bieluch, Chester A., St. Mary Home, 2021 Albany Ave., West Hartford, CT 06117-2701
Boyle, James M., 2021 Albany Ave., West Hartford, CT 06117-2701
Castellani, John J., 81 Reservoir Ridge Dr., Southington, CT 06489-1356
Colton, Bradford, Corpus Christi Rectory, 84 Somerset St., Wethersfield, CT 06109
Cook, John P., 45 Jefferson Rd., Bldg. 3, Apt. 15, Branford, CT 06082
Cronin, W. Vincent, St. Mary Home, 2021 Albany Ave., West Hartford, CT 06117
Croteau, Francois A., St. Mary Home, 2021 Albany Ave., West Hartford, CT 06117
Crowley, Stephen L., 156 Circular Ave., Hamden, CT 06514
Curran, John F., 355 Captain Thomas Blvd., Apt. 51, West Haven, CT 06516
Daily, Leo J., Our Lady of Fatima Rectory, 382 Hope Hill Rd., Yalesville, CT 06492
DeMuro, S. Patrick, 1229 Winsted Rd., #91, Torrington, CT 06790
Dery, Henry R., St. Thomas Seminary, 467 Bloomfield Ave., Bloomfield, CT 06002
Dilion, Joseph A., 13 Leeway Dr., Westbrook, CT 06498
Donahue, Joseph P., St. Francis Manor, 6448 Main St., Trumbull, CT 06611-2078
Emerling, James R., P.O. Box 243, East Otis, MA 01029-0243
Ferrigno, Denis P., Our Lady of Good Counsel Rectory, 56 Center St., Folly Beach, SC 29439
Fiedorczyk, Henry P., Holy Cross Rectory, 31 Biruta St., New Britain, CT 06053
Fitzgerald, Neil F., 41 Concord St., Hamden, CT 06514
Flynn, Joseph A., Harborside Healthcare Madison House, 34 Wildwood Ave., Madison, CT 06443
Frisbie, Kenneth J., St. Thomas Seminary, 467 Bloomfield Ave., Bloomfield, CT 06002
Gengras, Joseph C., St. Thomas Seminary, 467 Bloomfield Ave., Bloomfield, CT 06002
Giusani, Augustine H., St. Ann, 47 Clark St., New Britain, CT 06051
Gosselin, Michael H., Cathedral of St. Joseph Rectory, 140 Farmington Ave., Hartford, CT 06105
Graziani, Joseph A., 380 Lake Plymouth Blvd., Plymouth, CT 06728
Hannon, John P., 21 Pleasant Rd., Enfield, CT 06082
Hayes, William J., St. Ann, 47 Clark St., New Britain, CT 06051
Hewitt, Charles L., St. Joseph Manor, 6448 Main St., Trumbull, CT 06611
Horgan, John A., P.O. Box 5021, New Haven, CT 06525
Jaenicke, Alfred J., Caixa Postal 162, 56300-000, Petrolina, PE Brazil
Kaminski, Ladislaus J., St. Lucian's Residence, 532 Burritt St., New Britain, CT 06503
Karvelis, Francis V., 14 Deepwood Dr., Southington, CT 06489-3442
Keane, Martin T., St. Mary Home, 2021 Albany Ave., West Hartford, CT 06117
Keating, Joseph H., 574 Easton St., New Haven, CT 06513
Ladamus, Robert G., P.O. Box 90, Milford, CT 06460
Laliberte, George G., 948 Villeroy Greens Dr., Sun City Center, FL 33573
LaRose, Edward M., Holy Cross Rectory, 31 Biruta St., New Britain, CT 06053
LeClair, Lawrence J., Spring Lake Village, 661 Ledgeview Ct., Southington, CT 06489
Maguire, Felix H., 95 Harbour Close, New Haven, CT 06519
Malley, Michael A., 9 Sunset Ave., Terryville, CT 06786
Maynard, Leo E., 123 Maple St., Somers, CT 06071
McDonald, John F., St. Thomas Seminary, 467 Bloomfield Ave., Bloomfield, CT 06002
McGrath, Robert D., 873 Durham Rd., Madison, CT 06443
McGrath, William E., St. Christopher Rectory, 538 Brewer St., East Hartford, CT 06118-2399
Muha, Edward J., 236 Fairlawn Dr., Torrington, CT 06790
Mullins, Charles R., 2 Willowbrook Rd., West Hartford, CT 06107-1638
Murphy, Joseph G., Heritage Cove Condo, 85 River Rd., N1, Essex, CT 06426
Nazzaro, Stanley J., 135 West Ave., Great Barrington, MA 01230
O'Connor, John T., St. Dominic Rectory, 1050 Flanders Rd., Southington, CT 06489
O'Leary, Donald J., St. Aloysius Rectory, 254 Burritt St., Plantsville, CT 06479
Paul, Raymond F., Holy Rosary Rectory, Fr. Salemi Dr., Ansonia, CT 06401
Pettit, Joseph H., 433 Lakeview Dr., Southington, CT 06489
Ptaszynski, Stephen F., 90 Wolcott St., Box 1271, Bristol, CT 06011-1271
Quinn, John J., 150 Pheasant Ln., Branford, CT 06405
Quinn, Thomas P., 218 Mountain Rd., Windsor, CT 06095
Raffaeta, George J., St. Agnes Rectory, 400 Merwin Ave., Woodmont, Ct 06460
Rikteraitis, John E., 1039 Maple Ave, P.O. Box 341361, Hartford, CT 06134-1361
Rush, James C., 161 Brunswick Ave., West Hartford, CT 06107-1715
Russo, Robert T., P.O. Box 567, Broad Brook, CT 06016-0567
Sabulis, Paul P., St. Mary Home, 2021 Albany Ave., West Hartford, CT 06117-2701
Shamsher, Paul, Sacred Heart Rectory, 74 Liberty St., New Haven, CT 06519-2299
Shaw, Charles E., P.O. Box 10158, Phoenix, AZ 85064
Sherer, Richard B.
Sheridan, Philip A., St. Joseph Manor, 20 Carmel Ridge Estates, Trumbull, CT 06611-2072
Smith, William C., 82 W. Rocks Rd., Norwalk, CT 06851
Speer, Patrick J., St. Joseph Manor, 6448 Main St., Trumbull, CT 06611
Spodnik, A. Leo, P.O. Box 456, Higganum, CT 06441
Testa, Genaro J., 5233 S.W. 11th Ct., Cape Coral, FL 33914
Thuer, William J., (Mailing Address: P.O. Box 1027, Woodbury, CT 06798), Visitation Plaza, 100 Jefferson Sq., Apt. 6-A, Waterbury, CT 06706
Toscano, Pasquale A., St. Joseph Residence, 1365 Enfield St., Enfield, CT 06082-4900
Tracy, John P., St. Thomas Seminary, 467 Bloomfield Ave., Bloomfield, CT 06002
Trenchard, Dawson D.
Ventura, Anthony C., St. Thomas Seminary, 467 Bloomfield Ave., Bloomfield, CT 06002
Vitka, Stephen G., 2448 Columbia Dr., Apt. 66, Clearwater, FL 33763
Zanavich, Albert J., Assumption Rectory, 61 N. Cliff St., Ansonia, CT 06401
Ziezulewicz, George F., Cathedral of St. Joseph Rectory, 140 Farmington Ave., Hartford, CT 06105

Permanent Deacons:
Abdalla, John, (Retired)
Aconfora, Ralph A., (Retired)
Albert, Roger R., St. Gregory the Great, Bristol
Angeloni, Carmine, (Retired)
Anthony, Andrew, Leave of Absence
Arena, Paul, Leave of Absence
Azzaro, Gabriel S., (Retired)
Baldwin, Alan C., Good Shepherd, Seymour
Bandeira, Francis, St. Anne, Waterbury
Bartlett, William, Jr., (Retired)
Battiston, Donald, (Retired)
Baxter, Wesley F., St. Thomas, Southington
Bergers, William, St. Monica, Northford
Bernd, Robert E., St. Martha, Enfield
Bevvino, Frank J., Jr., St. John Vianney, West Haven
Biamonte, Ronald, St. Gabriel, Windsor
Bichi, Americo, Holy Infant, Orange
Blair, Robert N., St. Patrick, Collinsville
Borland, Joseph P., Assumption, Woodbridge
Brady, John F., Assumption, Ansonia
Breen, Thomas F., III, St. Michael, Hartford
Brown, George S., (Retired)
Brown, William J., St. James, Manchester
Brunell, Robert J., St. Brendan, New Haven
Camerota, Daniel A., Nativity, Bethlehem
Campbell, Alan D., St. Ann, Avon
Cardona, Raul, Holy Trinity, Wallingford
Carey, Edward J., (Retired)
Carrero, Adolfo G., St. Anne-Immaculate Conception, Hartford
Carroll, Michael E., SS. Peter & Paul, Waterbury
Casey, Francis J., St. Thomas Becket, Cheshire
Cassidy, Vincent, Sacred Heart, Southbury
Catsoris, John A., St. Joseph, Canaan
Chamberland, J. Fernand, Assumption, Manchester
Charles, John H., St. John the Evangelist, Watertown
Clifford, Thomas J., St. Hedwig, Union City
Colella, Charles, St. Leo the Great, Waterbury
Colella, Guy A., (Retired)
Conklin, Thomas J., St. Margaret Mary, South Windsor
Conte, John J.M., Jr., Assumption, Woodbridge
Cooke, Joseph J., St. Gabriel, Windsor
Coppola, Angelo J., St. Aloysius, Plantsville
Cote, Laurent L., St. Anthony, Bristol
Coyne, Joseph F., St. Elizabeth, Branford
Cretella, Joseph J., Jr., St. Barnabas, North Haven
Croll, Calvin S., St. Gabriel, Milford
Crowley, John, St. Dominic, Southington
Cruess, Donald E., (Retired)
Culhane, Neil, St. Mary Magdalen, Oakville
Cunniff, Charles E., Jr., St. Rose, Meriden
D'Efemia, Robert J., Incarnation, Wethersfield
Daigle, Ronald R., St. Mary, East Hartford
DeFilippo, Salvatore A., St. Louis, West Haven
DeHippolytis, Albert J., Unassigned
DeJesus, Efrain, (Retired)
DeJesus, Isidiro, Sacred Heart, Hartford
DelCorte, Nicholas, (Retired)
Delehanty, Thomas F., St. Catherine of Siena, West Simsbury
Delgado, Domingo, St. Lawrence O'Toole, Hartford
Dembishack, John L., Sacred Heart and St. Peter, Torrington
Dempsey, John F., St. Augustine, Hartford
Dickman, Arthur J., Holy Family, Enfield
Dickson, Edward, St. Francis of Assisi, Torrington
Dietsch, Charles C., Sacred Heart, Southbury
DiMauro, Joseph, (Retired)
Dinkle, George J., St. Anthony, Prospect
Diorio, Nicholas J., St. Thomas, Goshen
DiPiro, Joseph L., (Retired)
DiRienzo, Mario, Holy Rosary, Ansonia
Dlugokinski, Jose L., St. Thomas, Thomaston
DosSantos, Kenneth, St. Thomas Villanova, Goshen
Doyle, Henry, St. Gabriel, Milford
Driscoll, Frank M., Unassigned
Dungan, Roy C., St. Stanislaus, Bristol

Dwyer, David F., St. Margaret Mary, South Windsor
Elder, William A., St. Margaret, Madison
English, Seth M., Corpus Christi, Wethersfield
Eschrich, Paul C., (Retired)
Eyles, William H., St. Vincent de Paul, East Haven
Farrell, William A., St. Patrick, Farmington
Fiederlein, Frank H., (Retired)
Fitzgerald, Robert W., (Retired)
Florio, Louis J., St. Therese, North Haven
Fortier, James A., Holy Spirit, Newington
Fournier, Richard G., St. Paul, West Haven
Fracasso, Robert G., (Retired)
Fugere, Raymond J., St. Mark the Evangelist, West Hartford
Fusco, Louis P., St. Monica, Northford
Gabriele, Joseph G., St. Mary, Simsbury
Gale, Robert P., Our Lady of Mt. Carmel, Meriden
Geraci, Gerald S., Our Lady of Mercy, Plainville
Giaimo, Thomas, Epiphany, Cheshire
Giard, Edward J., St. Bartholomew, Manchester
Gilles, William J., St. Christopher, East Hartford
Giordano, William D., (Retired)
Giusto, Oreste M., (Retired)
Gordon, Robert D., Unassigned
Grant, Frederick M., St. Mary, Derby
Griffin, Wayne F., Resurrection, Wallingford
Gurr, Ronald, St. John the Baptist, New Haven
Guzzardi, Carmelo A., St. Paul, Kensington
Hajjar, George D., St. Michael, Waterbury
Hart, John L., St. Augustine, North Branford
Hayden, Bernard J., Holy Infant, Orange
Hernandez, Carmelo, Our Lady of Sorrows, Hartford
Hickey, James E., Jr., St. Luke, Hartford
Hilliard, Robert J., St. Helena, West Hartford
Hoffman, Harold, Holy Infant, Orange
Iadarola, Paul P., St. Margaret, Waterbury
Iassogna, Nicholas J., Jr., St. Vincent Ferrer, Naugatuck
Impellitteri, Michael, Sr., (Retired)
Jacques, J. Martin, (Retired)
Johnson, Robert C., Assumption, Ansonia
Johnson, Thomas F., St. Patrick, Waterbury
Kane, Joseph E., (Retired)
Kelly, Stephen J., St. Pius X, Wolcott
Kieda, Rene J., Leave of Absence
Kimball, Earle A., St. Mary, Union City
Klein, Peter J., Jr., St. Paul, Glastonbury
Klimanowski, Peter J., Our Lady of Sorrows, Hartford
Klimas, Vincent A., (Retired)
Koch, Paul T., St. Joan of Arc, Hamden
Krasnicki, Frank J., Good Shepherd, Seymour
Kraussman, George A., (Retired)
Kulas, Michael J., Sacred Heart, Southbury
Kulas, Paul J., Mary Our Queen, Plantsville
Lambert, Robert E., St. Adalbert, Enfield
LaPierre, Joseph W., Our Lady of Pompeii, East Haven
LaRocque, Leo R., St. Joseph, Poquonock
Lauer, Paul B., St. Mary, Milford
Lavoie, Joseph V., (Retired)
LeBlanc, Gaspard D., St. Anne, Waterbury
Lembo, Victor M., St. Michael, Beacon Falls
Lepkowski, Henry M., (Retired)
Levesque, Joseph J., St. Ann, Bristol
Lewandoski, Leonard R., St. Stanislaus, Bristol
Lickwar, R. Carl, St. Ann, New Britain
Linehan, F. Robert, (Retired)
Locorotondo, Frank S., (Retired)
Lopatosky, Thomas J., (Retired)
Lopez, Alejandro, St. Cecilia, Waterbury
Lopez, Rafael, St. Rose, East Hartford
Lotto, Henry, St. Francis, New Haven
Lovelace, William, St. Augustine, North Branford
Lowe, Burdon G., (Retired)
Lozier, Albert J., St. Ann, Bristol
Maffeo, John R., St. Anthony of Padua, Litchfield
Makara, John W., Immaculate Conception, Terryville
Mancini, Edward J., St. Louis, West Haven
Marcarelli, Julius R., St. Rose of Lima, New Haven
Masucci, Ernest J., (Retired)
McCusker, Kenneth F., Ascension, Hamden
McGivney, Raymond J., Jr., Unassigned
McGrath, William M., Blessed Sacrament, Waterbury
McInnis, John P., (Retired)
McKaig, John W., St. John Fisher, Marlborough
Michaele, Adam J., St. George, Guilford
Miller, Roland G., Sacred Heart, Kent
Mingrone, William F., (Retired)
Mon, Joseph J.G., St. Bernard, Enfield
Motto, Vincent J., St. Catherine, Broad Brook
Muro, Robert E., Sr., Our Lady of the Lakes, New Milford
Murphy, James R., (Retired)
Mylott, John J., St. Ann, Avon
Navickas, Robert D., St. Therese, Granby
Nebiolo, Eugene, (Retired)
Newbery, Robert D., St. Therese, Granby
Norton, Donald E., St. Mary, Windsor Locks
O'Connell, Cornelius D., Sacred Heart, Wethersfield
O'Connor, Martin J., St. Bernadette, New Haven
O'Donovan, John, Our Lady of Mt. Carmel, Hamden
O'Neill, James F., St. George, Guilford
O'Toole, Michael J., (Retired)
Ortiz, Edwin, Sacred Heart, Hartford
Ortiz, Jacinto, St. Rose of Lima, Meriden
Pahl, John E., St. Matthew, Forestville
Pallotti, Robert M., St. Joseph, Bristol
Pantalena, Edward J., Epiphany, Cheshire
Parenteau, Raymond A., Our Lady of Peace, East Hartford
Parlee, Charles, St. John Vianney, West Haven
Perez, Valentin, St. Augustine, Hartford
Pettinico, George, Our Lady of Lourdes, Waterbury
Phaneuf, Eugene E., (Retired)
Poland, James K., (Retired)
Pond, Donald H., Jr., St. Bernard, Enfield
Prete, Paul V., St. Mary, Branford
Puskas, George A., Christ the Redeemer, Milford
Quinn, James P., Mary Our Queen, Plantville
Ramos, Edmund J., St. Ann, Milford
Regan, Joseph M., Jr., St. Margaret, Madison
Renker, Richard E., St. Augustine, Seymour
Rescildo, Ralph, St. Teresa, Woodbury
Riotte, Eugene C., St. Augustine, Seymour
Rivera, Jose A., St. John the Baptist, New Haven
Rivera, Pedro L., St. Anne-Immaculate Conception, Hartford
Rogers, Joseph K., (Retired)
Rogers, Thomas D., (Retired)
Rolando, Joseph E., (Retired)
Rosello, Modesto A., St. Leo the Great, Waterbury
Roy, Reginald, St. Jerome, New Britain
Ruiz, Candelario, (Retired)
Ryzewski, Joseph R., Blessed Sacrament, Hamden
Sabo, Paul E., Our Lady of Victory, West Haven
Saffo, John R., Sr., St. Augustine, Seymour
Sandford, Wayne E., St. Clare, East Haven
Santello, Richard L., Dir. Office Permanent Diaconate, St. Stephen, Hamden
Scanlon, Thomas P., St. Bernard, Tariffville
Schiro, George J., St. Paul, West Haven
Sennett, Richard M., St. Mary, Milford
Serafini, Ferdinand T., (Retired)
Shelto, Michael A., St. James, Rocky Hill
Shiels, James H., Holy Spirit, Newington
Sill, Louis P., Jr., SS. Peter and Paul, Wallingford
Simonin, George A., St. John the Evangelist, Watertown
Singer, Norman H., St. Vincent de Paul, East Haven
Skipp, Barry T., St. Mary, Newington
Sloan, Daniel A., (Retired)
Sloan, Joseph S., Unassigned
Smith, Donald H., Jr., Holy Angels, South Meridan
Solli, Anthony P., St. Lawrence, West Haven
Sponzo, Michael T., (Retired)
Stadtlander, Hobart, (Retired)
Stanley, James H., Our Lady of Mt. Carmel, Hamden
Stephens, George R., St. Francis Cabrini, North Haven
Stolfi, Domenic N., St. Anthony, Prospect
Streib, George H., St. Francis Xavier, New Milford
Sullivan, Joseph, Holy Infant, Orange
Suzio, John J., (Retired)
Sweeney, John M., St. Mary, Simsbury
Szewczyk, Edward J., St. Joseph, Suffield
Szumigala, Michael P., St. Matthew, Forestville
Taddei, Edward D., (Retired)
Talbot, Oral A., (Retired)
Tartaris, Robert P., St. Mary, Branford
Taylor, James P., St. Francis Cabrini, North Haven
Thayer, John E., St. Mary, New Britain
Thompson, Bruce R., St. Mary, Newington
Thorney, Vincent M., St. Gertrude, Windsor
Tomasiello, Frank R., (Retired)
Tripp, James A., Sr., Blessed Sacrament, Hamden
Vecca, Carl M., Immaculate Conception, Waterbury
Violette, Carroll, Unassigned
Wallin, Robert F., SS. Peter & Paul, Waterbury
Walton, Gilbert E., Jr., St. Therese, Branford
Weaver, Stephen L., St. Augustine, South Glastonbury
Weir, John, (Retired)
Wheeler, John E., St. Lawrence, West Haven
Wilber, Richard, St. Bridget, Cheshire
Wilcox, William H., St. Joseph, Winsted
Winiarski, Benedict L., St. Mary, Windsor Locks
Wootton, Gerald R., Immaculate Heart of Mary, Harwinton

INSTITUTIONS LOCATED IN THE ARCHDIOCESE

[A] SEMINARIES, ARCHDIOCESAN

BLOOMFIELD. *St. Thomas Seminary*, 467 Bloomfield Ave., 06002-2999. Tel: 860-242-5573; Fax: 860-242-4886. Rev. Aidan N. Donahue, Rector & Contact. In res. Most Rev. Christie A. Macaluso, D.D.; Revs. George M. Couturier; John F. McDonald; Henry R. Dery; Ivan Ferguson; Stephen C. Foley; Kenneth J. Frisbie; Joseph C. Gengras; Alvin J. LeBlanc; Stanley J. Sikora; John P. Tracy; Anthony Ventura. Fathers 13.

Pope Paul VI House of Formation, 469 Bloomfield Ave., 06002. Tel: 860-286-7670. Rev. John J. Dietrich, Dir. Students 7; Candidates for Diaconate Studies 36.

[B] SEMINARIES, RELIGIOUS OR SCHOLASTICATES

CHESHIRE. *Novitiate of the Legion of Christ*, 475 Oak Ave., 06410. Tel: 203-271-0805; Fax: 203-271-3845.
E-mail: chehire@legionaries.org
Rev. Julio Marti, L.C., Rector. Vice Rectors: Bro. Paul Moreau, L.C.; Revs. Jose Felix Medina, L.C.; Anthony Bailleres, L.C., Asst. to the Natl. Dir. Instructors of Novices: Rev. Christopher Brackett, L.C. Studies: Revs. Owen Kearns, L.C.; Anthony Rodriguez, L.C.; Tarciscio Samaniego, L.C.; Jeffrey Bowker, L.C.; Walter Schu, L.C. Priests 9; Religious 11; Juniors 54; Novices 60. (Center Harbor, N.H.).

[C] COLLEGES AND UNIVERSITIES

HAMDEN. *Mt. Sacred Heart College*, 265 Benham St., 06514-2801. Tel: 203-248-4225; Fax: 203-230-8341.
E-mail: srpasej@aol.com
For a complete listing, refer to the Colleges and Universities section.

NEW HAVEN. *Albertus Magnus College*, 700 Prospect St., 06511-1189. Tel: 203-773-8550; Fax: 203-785-8652.
E-mail: admissions@albertus.edu
Web site: www.albertus.edu
For a complete listing, refer to the Colleges and Universities section.

WEST HARTFORD. *Saint Joseph College*, 1678 Asylum Ave., 06117. Tel: 860-232-4571; Fax: 860-233-5695.
E-mail: info@mercy.sjc.edu
Web site: www.sjc.edu
For a complete listing, refer to the Colleges and Universities section.

[D] HIGH SCHOOLS, ARCHDIOCESAN

BRISTOL. *St. Paul Catholic High School*, 1001 Stafford Ave., 06010-3894. Tel: 860-584-0911; Fax: 860-585-8815.
E-mail: stpaulchs@erols.com
Web site: www.stpaulchs.com
Joseph A. Bischof, Prin.; Jo-Ann Thomas, Asst. Prin. Faculty: Sisters 1; Lay Teachers 38; Students 389.

MANCHESTER. *East Catholic High School*, 115 New State Rd., 06040. Tel: 860-649-5336; Fax: 860-649-7191.
E-mail: pegsieg@aol.com
Web site: ECHS.com
Peggy Siegmund, Prin. Sisters of Notre Dame de Namur 5; Lay Teachers 48; Priests 1; Students 577.

WATERBURY. *Sacred Heart High School*, 142 S. Elm St., 06722. Tel: 203-753-1605; Fax: 203-597-1686.
E-mail: heart2@weconn.net
Rev. Craig Drezek, Prin.; Mrs. Eileen Regan, Dir. Devel.; Mrs. Jacqueline Jennings, Vice Prin. Priests 1; Lay Teachers 36; Students 489.

WEST HARTFORD. *Northwest Catholic High School*, 29 Wampanoag Dr., 06117. Tel: 860-236-4221; Fax: 860-586-0911.
Web site: www.nwcath.org
Dr. Michael S. Griffin, Pres.; Mrs. Margaret R. Williamson, Prin.; Mr. Richard Callahan, Vice Prin. Priests 1; Lay Teachers 55; Students 570.

[E] HIGH SCHOOLS, PRIVATE

HAMDEN. *Sacred Heart Academy*, 265 Benham St., 06514-2833. Tel: 203-288-2309; Fax: 203-230-9680.
E-mail: Principal@SHA-Excelsior.org
Apostles of the Sacred Heart of Jesus. Sr. Ritamary Schultz, A.S.C.J., Prin. & Contact. Sisters 8; Lay Teachers 38; Students 480.

MILFORD. *Academy of Our Lady of Mercy*, Lauralton Hall, 200 High St., 06460. Tel: 203-877-2786; Fax: 203-876-9760.
E-mail: dkosiewicz@lauraltonhall.org
Web site: www.lauraltonhall.org
Sisters of Mercy. Mrs. Karen Yardley, Pres. & Contact. Sisters 3; Lay Teachers 47; Students 454.

NEW BRITAIN. *Mary Immaculate Academy*, Osgood Ave. and Corbin Ave., 06053. Tel: 860-229-1747; Fax: 860-229-9185. Daughters of Mary of the Immaculate Conception. Sr. Mary Jennifer Carroll, Prin. &

Contact. Sisters 5; Lay Teachers 18; Students 150.

NEW MILFORD. *Canterbury School*, Aspetuck Ave., 06776-1739. Tel: 860-210-3800; Fax: 860-350-4425. Coed. Boarding and day students. Thomas J. Sheehy, III, HeadMaster; Patricia L. Hiro, Headmaster's Asst. & Contact; Rev. Sebastian Leonard, O.S.B., Chap. Priests 1; Lay Teachers 65; Students 330.

WATERBURY. *Holy Cross High School*, 587 Oronoke Rd., 06708. Tel: 203-757-9248; Fax: 203-757-3423.
Web site: HolyCrosshs-ct.com
Brothers of the Congregation of Holy Cross. Bro. Jerome Donnelly, C.S.C., Chief Admin. & Head of School & Contact; Mr. Timothy McDonald, Prin. Brothers 1; Sisters 4; Lay Teachers 71; Students 1,000.

WEST HAVEN. *Notre Dame High School*, 24 Ricardo St., 06516. Tel: 203-933-1673; Fax: 203-933-2474.
E-mail: ralph@notredamehs.com
Web site: www.notredamehs.com
Holy Cross Brothers. Bro. James Branigan, C.S.C., Headmaster; Mr. Ralph Proto, Prin.; Mr. Patrick Clifford, Asst. Prin. for Academics; Mr. Thomas Marcucci, Asst. Prin. for Student Life; Mr. Joseph Ramirez, Dir. of Guidance; Mrs. Gail Bellucci, Campus Min. Brothers 5; Sisters 1; Lay Teachers 51; Students 680.
Notre Dame Loyalty & Endowment Fund, Inc., 24 Ricardo St., 06516.

[F] ELEMENTARY SCHOOLS, PRIVATE

MADISON. *Our Lady of Mercy School, Incorporated*, 149 Neck Rd., 06443-2728. Tel: 203-245-4393; Fax: 203-245-3498.
E-mail: olmschool.homestead.com
Dr. Joan E. Venditto, Prin. & Contact. Sisters of Mercy 2; Lay Teachers 17; Students 172.

WEST HARTFORD. *Cedar Court School, Inc.*, 27 Park Rd., 06119. Tel: 860-523-0060; Fax: 860-523-1310.
E-mail: cedarcourt@juno.com
Sr. Phyllis Campoli, Prin. Sisters of St. Joseph of Chambery 3; Lay Teachers 9; Children 102.

[G] SPECIALIZED CHILD CARING HOME

NEW BRITAIN. *Marian Educational Clinic*, 314 Osgood Ave., 06053. Tel: 860-223-0501
For a complete listing, refer to the Special Care Facilities section.

NEW HAVEN. *St. Francis Home for Children, Inc.*, 651 Prospect St., 06511. Tel: 203-777-5513; Fax: 203-777-0644
For a complete listing, refer to the Special Care Facilities section.

[H] DAY CARE CENTER

HAMDEN. *Clelian Adult Day Center*, 261 Benham St., 06514. Tel: 203-288-4151; Fax: 203-288-0551. Sr. Shawn Lyons, A.S.C.J., Dir. & Contact. Apostles of the Sacred Heart of Jesus. A day health care facility for elderly and disabled adults. Total Assisted 86 per week; Total Staff 20.
Sacred Heart Manor Nursery and Kindergarten, 261 Benham St., 06514. Tel: 203-230-4889.
E-mail: sealat@yahoo.com
Sr. Elaine Ann Lattanzi, Contact. Apostles of the Sacred Heart of Jesus 1; Lay Teachers 4; Students 105; Total Assisted 98.

WEST HARTFORD. *Park Village Child Development Center*, 27 Park Rd., 06119. Tel: 203-523-1482. Sisters of St. Joseph of Chambery 1; Children 30.

[I] GENERAL HOSPITALS

HARTFORD. *Saint Francis Hospital and Medical Center*, 114 Woodland St., 06105-1299. Tel: 860-714-4000; Fax: 860-714-7809.
E-mail: pastoralcare@stfranciscare.org
Web site: www.stfranciscare.org
For a complete listing, refer to the Hospitals section.

NEW HAVEN. *Hospital of St. Raphael*, 1450 Chapel St., 06511. Tel: 203-789-3000; Fax: 203-789-3107.
E-mail: mcanavan@srhs.org
Web site: www.srhs.org
For a complete listing, refer to the Hospitals section.
Saint Regis Health Center, Inc., 1354 Chapel St., 06511. Tel: 203-867-8300; Fax: 203-867-8370.
E-mail: rhellrige@grhs.org
For a complete listing, refer to the Hospitals section.

WATERBURY. *St. Mary Hospital*, 56 Franklin St., 06706. Tel: 203-574-6000; Fax: 203-597-3238.
Web site: stmh.org
For a complete listing, refer to the Hospitals section.

[J] SPECIAL HOSPITALS

WEST HARTFORD. *Saint Agnes Home, Inc.*, 104 Mayflower St., 06110. Tel: 860-521-7516; Fax: 860-521-6160.
E-mail: safc@aol.com
For a complete listing, refer to the Special Care Facilities section.

[K] HOMES FOR AGED

ENFIELD. *The Home for the Aged of the Little Sisters of the Poor*, 1365 Enfield St., 06082-4900. Tel: 860-741-0791; Fax: 860-741-3982
For a complete listing, refer to the Special Care Facilities section.

NEW BRITAIN. *Monsignor Bojnowski Manor, Inc.*, 50 Pulaski St., 06053. Tel: 860-229-0336; Fax: 860-229-3252.
E-mail: dblados@snet.net
Web site: mbmanor.org
For a complete listing, refer to the Special Care Facilities section.
St. Lucian's Residence, Inc., 532 Burritt St., 06053-3699. Tel: 860-223-2123; Fax: 860-612-0321
For a complete listing, refer to the Special Care Facilities section.

WEST HARTFORD. *Saint Mary Home*, 2021 Albany Ave., 06117. Tel: 860-570-8200; Fax: 860-570-8205
For a complete listing, refer to the Special Care Facilities section.

[L] HEALTH CARE CENTERS FOR AGED

WEST HARTFORD. *McAuley Center, Inc.*, 275 Steele Rd., 06117. Tel: 860-920-6300; Fax: 860-232-4077
For a complete listing, refer to the Hospitals section.

[M] MONASTERIES AND RESIDENCES OF PRIESTS AND BROTHERS

HARTFORD. *Missionaries of LaSalette, Provincial Secretary*, 915 Maple Ave., 06114-2330. Tel: 860-956-8870; Fax: 860-956-8849.
E-mail: mlsadmin@aol.com
Province of Our Lady of Seven Dolors. Legal Title: *Missionaries of La Salette Corp.* Revs. James H. Kuczynski, M.S., Prov. Supr.; James A. Henault, M.S., Vicar & Prov. Sec. & Vocation Dir.; John J. O'Neill, M.S., Asst.; Bro. G. Peter Collins, M.S., Treas. Priests 3.
Religious Trust of the Missionaries of Our Lady of LaSalette. Legal Title: *Religious Trust of the Missionaries of Our Lady of LaSalette Province of Our Lady of Seven Dolors (MLS Trust).*
Missionaries of LaSalette, 85 New Park Ave., 06106-2184. Tel: 860-523-8275; Fax: 860-586-0754. Revs. Richard R. Boucher, M.S., Supr. & Treas.; Salvatore D. Altavista, M.S.; Michael J. Cox, M.S.; William H. Crane, M.S.; Stephen G. Dressell, M.S.; Frederick R. Flaherty, M.S.; Joseph J. Horgan, M.S.; Stanley T. Kennedy, M.S.; William J. Kinney, M.S.; William W. Mulcair, M.S.; John R. Nuelle, M.S.; James P. O'Reilly, M.S.; Daniel J. Scott, M.S.; John G. Toner, M.S.; Gerald R. Biron, M.S.; Joseph F. Kettner, M.S.; Joseph F. Whalen, M.S.; Bros. Ronald R. Beaudoin, M.S.; G. Peter Collins, M.S.; David J. Cook, M.S.; Alexander J. Delaney, M.S.; Mark L. Gallant, M.S.; Andre J. Hamel, M.S.; Paul Maceyka; Bonaventure Russell, M.S.; Francis X. Smith, M.S.; Peter Staskiewicz, M.S.; Alfred D. Tetrault, M.S.; Donald J. Wininski, M.S. Priests 18; Brothers 11; Oblates 1.
Military Chaplains: Rev. Robert F. Ippolito, M.S., P.O. Box 65987, Langley AFB, VA, 23665-5987. Tel: 757-764-7801.
Priests-Brothers of Province Serving Abroad:
Missionaries in Argentina: Revs. Robert R. Butler, M.S.; Eugene P. Brennan, M.S.; John M. Garvey, M.S.; James T. Lowery, M.S.; John J. McCarthy, M.S.; John P. Sullivan, M.S.
Bolivia: Revs. Norman H. Butler, M.S.; John F. Higgins, M.S.
St. Anne-Immaculate Conception, 820 Park St., 06106-2388. Tel: 860-728-7445; Fax: 860-728-1973. Rev. James J. Aherne, M.S.
Our Lady of Sorrows Rectory, 16 Greenwood St., 06106-2109. Tel: 860-233-4424; Fax: 860-236-0149. Co-Pastors: Revs. Joseph M. O'Neil, M.S.; Francis C. Cooney, M.S.
North American La Salette Mission Center, 85 New Park Ave., 06106-2184. Tel: 860-523-4017; Fax: 860-523-4074. Rev. John R. Nuelle, M.S., Dir.; Bro. Mark L. Gallant, M.S., Asst.
Sacred Heart Rectory, 49 Winthrop St., 06103-1030. Tel: 860-527-6459; Fax: 860-527-6450.
E-mail: sheart@snet.net
Somascan Fathers. Total in Residence 2; Total Staff 2.
St. Patrick-St. Anthony Friary (Holy Name Prov.), 285 Church St., 06103-1105. Tel: 860-246-6874; Fax: 860-249-6487.
Web site: stpatrick-stanthony.org
Franciscan Friars.
St. Joseph Rectory, 31 Oak St., P.O. Box 808, Winsted, 06098-1715. Tel: 860-379-3369; Fax: 860-379-4194.

BLOOMFIELD. *Brothers of the Sacred Heart*, 1153 Blue Hills Ave., 06002-1971. Tel: 860-242-3342. Total in Residence 3.

CHESHIRE. *Legionaries of Christ*, 475 Oak Ave., 06410. Tel: 203-271-0805; Fax: 203-271-3845.
E-mail: cheshire@legionaries.org
393 Derby Ave., Orange, 06477. Tel: 203-795-2800; Fax: 203-795-2808.

EAST HARTFORD. *Society of Our Lady of the Most Holy Trinity*, 15 Maplewood Ave., 06108. Tel: 860-289-7916.

ENFIELD. *St. Patrick Rectory*, 64 Pearl St., 06082. Tel: 860-745-2411; Fax: 860-253-9483.
E-mail: fjbrowne@aol.com
Redemptorist Fathers and Brothers. Priests 2; Brothers 1.

LITCHFIELD. *Montfort Missionaries*, 83 Montfort Rd., P.O. Box 667, 06759. Tel: 860-567-8434; Fax: 860-567-9670. Revs. Thomas Poth, S.M.M., Supr. & Novice Dir.; Eugene Lynch, S.M.M., Contact; Donald Lasalle, S.M.M. Priests 3.
Lourdes in Litchfield. Tel: 860-567-1041. Legal Title: *Lourdes Shrine Guild, Inc.*
Montfort House (Center for Spiritual Renewal). Tel: 860-567-8434; Fax: 860-567-9670.
Monfort Novitiate. Revs. Thomas Poth, S.M.M., Supr. & Novice Dir.; Eugene Lynch, S.M.M., Contact Person; Donald Lasalle, S.M.M. Priests 3.

MANCHESTER. *DePaul Provincial Residence*. (Vincentian Fathers and Brothers), 234 Keeney St., 06040-7048. Tel: 860-643-2828; Fax: 860-533-9462.
E-mail: nepcm@snet.net
Congregation of the Mission, New England Province. Very Rev. John S. Sledziona, C.M., Prov. & Contact; Revs. George J. Dabrowski, C.M., Supr.; Anthony F Kuzia, C.M., Asst. Prov.; Chester R. Mrowka, C.M., Procurator; Julian Szumilo, C.M.; Bros. Richard Glinski, C.M.; Henry Wojtkiewicz, C.M. Legal Title: *The New England Province of the Congregation of the Mission Incorporated.*
Charitable Trust of the New England Province of the Congregation of the Mission.
Special Assignments: Revs. Martin Cymbrowski, C.M.; Henry Czekala, C.M.; Edward Gicewicz, C.M.; Casimir Kiczuk, C.M.; Joseph C. Paciorek, C.M.; Stanley Staniszewski, C.M.; Bro. Joseph S. Zurowski, C.M.
St. Joseph Rectory, 32 Jewett St., Ansonia, 06401-2499. Tel: 203-734-0402.
St. Michael the Archangel Rectory, 75 Derby Ave., Derby, 06418-2098. Tel: 203-734-0005.
St. Stanislaus Rectory, 9 Eld St., New Haven, 06511-3899. Tel: 203-562-2828; Fax: 203-752-0217.

MILFORD. *The Augustinians*, 26 Shorefront, 06460. Tel: 203-877-6096; Fax: 203-878-9700. Bro. John N. Konwerski, O.S.A. Total in Residence 1.
Brothers of the Congregation of Holy Cross.
E-mail: lar587@aol.com
Brothers of Holy Cross. Bro. Lawrence Lussier, C.S.C., Contact, 400 Merwin Ave., 06460. Tel: 203-876-9355; Fax: 203-876-9355.
E-mail: lar587@aol.com
Bro. Thomas Gorman, C.S.C., Contact.
24 Ricardo St., West Haven, 06516-2499. Tel: 203-932-2101. Bro. Jerome Donnelly, C.S.C., Contact.
236A Cherry St., Naugatuck, 06770. Tel: 203-723-5137.

NEW BRITAIN. *Conventual Franciscans*, 548 Burritt St., 06053-2869. Tel: 860-225-5786. Rev. Augustine Pilatowski, O.F.M.Conv., Supr.-Delegate & Contact. Chaplains: Revs. Walter Leon Mruk, O.F.M.Conv.; Gilbert Wdzieczyny, O.F.M.Conv. Daughters of Mary Motherhouse.
St. Paul Friary, 479 Alling St., Kensington, 06037-2100. Tel: 860-828-0331; Fax: 860-828-7620.

NEW HAVEN. *Priests of the Congregation of Holy Cross*, 203 Maple St., 06511. Tel: 203-776-2405.
E-mail: JLMYoung@poe.net
Rev. Wilfred J. Raymond, C.S.C., Prov.
Sacred Heart Rectory, 74 Liberty St., 06519-2299. Tel: 203-562-7592; Fax: 203-562-1737.
E-mail: rnewman@snet.net
Sons of Charity.
St. Anthony Rectory, 25 Gold St., 06519. Tel: 203-624-1418; Fax: 203-624-3420.
E-mail: revmoffosaol.com
Missionaries of St. Charles-Scalabrinians.
St. Michael Rectory, 29 Wooster Pl., 06511. Tel: 203-562-7178; Fax: 203-752-0157.
St. Mary Priory, 5 Hillhouse Ave., 06505-1202. Tel: 203-562-6193; Fax: 203-562-1273.
Web site: http://www.connix/~mcs/stjos/stjoes.htm
Rev. Carleton Parker Jones, O.P., Contact. Order of Preachers (Dominicans). Total in Residence 10.

NEW MILFORD. *Canterbury School*, Aspetuck Ave., 06776. Tel: 860-355-4891.
E-mail: admissions@canterbury.pvt.k12.ct.us
Web site: www.canterbury.pvt.k12.ct.us
Benedictine Monks.

NORTH GUILFORD. *Our Lady of Grace Monastery*, 11 Race Hill Rd., 06437. Tel: 203-457-0599. Sr. Lee, O.P., Contact. Order of Preachers (Dominicans). Total in Residence 44.

WATERBURY. *Immaculate Conception Rectory*, 74 W. Main St., 06702. Tel: 203-574-0017; Fax: 203-756-8748. Missionaries of the Holy Apostles; Oblates of Mary Immaculate;.

St. Michael Rectory (Immaculate Conception Prov.), 62 St. Michael Dr., 06704-1295. Tel: 203-753-0689; Fax: 203-573-9101.

WEST HARTFORD. *Holy Family Monastery/Retreat*, 303 Tunxis Rd., 06107. Tel: 860-521-0440; Fax: 860-521-0883 (Community); 521-1929. Congregation of the Passion of Jesus Christ. Bro. Edward Hall, C.P., Provincial Vicar; Rev. Ronan Callahan, C.P., Asst. Supr.
Monastery Staff: Revs. Quentin Amrhein, C.P.; Cajetan Bendernagel, C.P.; Louis Bouchard, C.P.; Victor Donovan, C.P.; Jude Dowling; Kiernan Earley, C.P.; Conrad Federspiel, C.P.; Daniel Free, C.P.; Nicholas Gill, C.P.; Peter Hallisy, C.P.; Cormac Kinkead, C.P.; John Francis McLoughlin, C.P.; Julian Morgan, C.P.; Columkille O'Grady, C.P.; Florian Pekar, C.P.; John Baptist Pesce, C.P.; Owen Sharkey, C.P.; Basil Trahon, C.P.; Simon Paul Wood, C.P.; Bros. Frederick Barton, C.P.; Gabriel Chilbert, C.P.; Charles Dell; William Drotar, C.P.; Edward Hall; Joseph Rogers, C.P.
Retreat House. Revs. David Cinquegrani, C.P.; Earl Keating, C.P.; Alexis Paul, C.P.

WOLCOTT. *Maryknoll*, 8 S. View St., 06716. Tel: 203-879-3936.

[N] CONVENTS AND RESIDENCES FOR SISTERS

HARTFORD. *Dominican Oblates of Jesus*, 510 New Britain Ave., 06106. Tel: 860-249-2912; 249-3735. Sisters 4.
Medical Mission Sisters, 92 Sherman St., 06105. Tel: 860-233-0875; Fax: 860-509-9509.
E-mail: mms@hartsem.edu
Web site: www.medicalmissionsisters.org
St. Peter Convent, 11 Charter Oak Pl., 06106. Tel: 860-522-8428. Franciscans Sisters of Allegany, Sisters of Mercy of the Americas of Connecticut, Sisters of Notre Dame de Namur.
SS. Cyril & Methodius Convent, 45 Groton St., 06106. Tel: 860-527-3775. Felician Sisters of the Order of St. Francis of Connecticut. Rev. William P. Przybylo.
Sisters of Notre Dame de Namur, 18 Dover St., 06114. Tel: 860-296-5498. 217 Laurel St., 06105. Tel: 860-246-0678.
Sisters of St. Joseph of Chambery. 27 Park Rd., West Hartford, 06119. Tel: 860-233-5126; Fax: 860-232-4649. 145 Elizabeth St., 06105. Tel: 860-523-5704. 40 Clifford St., 06114. Tel: 860-246-4086; Fax: 860-722-6817.
Shalom Community, 33 Freeman St., 06114. Tel: 860-956-9247. 35B Freeman St., 06114. Tel: 860-956-9248. 35A Freeman St., 06114. Tel: 860-956-8157; Fax: 860-525-2439.
Spirit of Mercy Community, 410 Campfield Ave., 06114-2807. Tel: 860-956-3030.
Bethany Community/Formation Center, 7 Charter Oak Pl., 06106-1915. Tel: 860-728-0851.

BEACON FALLS. *Sisters of St. Joseph of the Third Order of St. Francis*, 68 Cambridge Ct., 06403. Tel: 203-729-9415.

BETHLEHEM. *Abbey of Regina Laudis*, 237 Flanders Rd., 06751. Tel: 203-266-7727. Benedictine Nuns of the Primitive Observance. Benedictine Nuns (Cloistered). Mothers Benedict Duss, O.S.B., Abbess Emerita; David Serna, O.S.B., Abbess & Mailing Contact. In res. Rev. Basil Rettenburg, O.S.B. Professed Nuns 28; In First Vows 5; Novices 3; Postulants 3.
St. Catherine's Convent of Mercy, 63 Crane Hollow Rd., 06751. Tel: 203-266-5411; Fax: 203-266-5421.
E-mail: rsmbeth@wtco.net
Religious Sisters of Mercy (Alma, MI). Sisters 4.

BLOOMFIELD. *Sisters of Mercy of the Americas of Connecticut*, 5 Garrison Ter., 06002. Tel: 860-243-8524.
Sisters of Notre Dame de Namur. (Connecticut Province), 5 Garrison Ter., 06002. Tel: 860-243-8524.
E-mail: sndbloom@aol.com
Holy Innocents House, 546 Bloomfield Ave., 06002. Tel: 860-243-2542. Total in Residence 3.

BRISTOL. *Queen of Apostles Provincial House*, 474 East Rd., 06010. Tel: 860-584-2138; Fax: 860-582-1119.
E-mail: Ltflower@Erols.com
Web site: queenofapostles.com
Religious Teachers Filippini. Sr. Christine Spirito, M.P.F., Prov. Supr.; Sr. Josephine Riccio, M.P.F., Community Archivist & Contact. Sisters in Diocese 19.
Sisters of Mercy of the Americas of Connecticut, 50 South St. Ext., 06010. Tel: 860-584-2418.

CHESHIRE. *Sisters of St. Joseph of Chambery*, 441 E. Mitchell Ave., 06410. Tel: 203-699-9421.

EAST HARTFORD. *Sisters of Notre Dame de Namur*, 21 Highview St., 06108. Tel: 860-289-5295.
E-mail: smrsnd@aol.com
50 Larrabee St. #F, 06108. Tel: 860-528-1024. 50 Larrabee St. #G, 06108. Tel: 860-289-2421. 52 Elms Village Rd., 06118. Tel: 860-569-0022. 908 Forbes St., 06118. Tel: 860-568-6958.

EAST HAVEN. *Provincial House*, 520 Thompson Ave., 06512. Tel: 203-469-7872; Fax: 203-469-8819.
E-mail: scmm_eh@snet.net
87 Gerrish Ave., 06512. Tel: 203-469-5584; Fax: 203-468-9112.

ENFIELD. *Felician Sisters - Our Lady of the Angels*, Provincial House, 1315 Enfield St., 06082-4929. Tel: 860-745-7791; 745-4946; Fax: 860-741-0819.
E-mail: cssfct@aol.com
Felician Sisters of the Order of St. Francis of Connecticut. Sr. Mary Laureann Alexandrowicz, C.S.S.F., Contact.
Provincial House and Novitiate. Tel: 860-745-7791; Fax: 860-741-0819. Sr. Mary Laureann Alexandrowicz, C.S.S.F., Prov. Min. Felician Sisters. Rev. Adolphe T. Renkiewicz, Chap.
In Province: Professed Sisters 126.
Felician Adult Day Care, 1333A Enfield St., 06082-4929. Tel: 860-745-2542; Fax: 860-745-2542.
E-mail: fadcmail@juno.com
Total Assisted 25; Total Staff 13. Felician Sisters. Sr. Patricia Marie Iagrosso, C.S.S.F., Dir. A day respite health care facility for Caregivers of the Frail, elderly and Alzheimer Clients.
Felician Sisters Infirmary, 1315 Enfield St., 06082-4929. Tel: 860-745-0217; Fax: 860-741-6474.
E-mail: snmfs@netzero.net
Mother Angela Residence, 1333-B Enfield St., 06082-4929. Tel: 860-745-5705.
E-mail: angela.res@snet.net
Child Jesus Convent, 1370 Enfield St., 06082-5526. Tel: 860-745-5847; Fax: 860-745-2010.
Enfield Montessori School, 1370 Enfield St., 06082-5526. Tel: 860-745-5847; Fax: 860-745-2010.
E-mail: Montessori@SNET.net
Sr. Mary Anastasia, C.S.S.F., Contact. Students 113.
St. Bernard Convent, 376 Hazard Ave., 06082-4709. Tel: 860-749-4214; Fax: 860-745-0167 (at school).
E-mail: st.bernards.west@snet.net
St. Adalbert Convent, 1315 Enfield St., 06082-4929. Tel: 860-745-4169; Fax: 860-745-6135.
Little Sisters of the Poor, 1365 Enfield St., 06082-4900. Tel: 860-741-0791; Fax: 860-741-3982.
St. Patrick Convent, 33 Spring St., 06082. Tel: 860-745-5174.
E-mail: maryoneillrsm@juno.com
Sisters of Mercy of the Americas of Connecticut. Total in Residence 2.

FARMINGTON. *St. Gabriel House*, 31 Colton St., 06032. Tel: 860-678-7274.
Sisters of the Cross and Passion, St. Gabriel's House, 31 Colton St., 06032. Tel: 860-678-7274; Fax: 860-677-2873.
Web site: www.cptryon.org/scp
Sisters 3.

FORESTVILLE. *Daughters of Wisdom*, 45 Hawthorne St. D-2, 06010.
St. Matthew Convent, 119 Church Ave., 06010. Tel: 860-583-2004; Fax: 860-314-1541.
E-mail: stmatt@ct2.nai
Sisters, Servants of the Immaculate Heart of Mary.
Sisters of St. Joseph of the Third Order of St. Francis, 105 Kenney St., 06010. Tel: 860-582-1635.
E-mail: ctmlw@aol.com
Web site: ssj-tosf.org
82 Kenney St., 06010. Tel: 860-584-2985. Total in Residence 7; Total Staff 14.

HAMDEN. *Daughters of Wisdom*, 95 Kaye Vue Dr., Apt. 2E, 06514. Tel: 203-281-7800.
E-mail: dwhamden@aol.com
Total in Residence 2.
Dominican Sisters of Hope, 1204 Whitney Ave., #217, 06517. Tel: 203-248-2601.
Mary, Mother of the Church Convent, 115 Denslow Hill Rd., 06514. Tel: 203-407-1042. Sisters 6.
Mount Sacred Heart Provincial House and Novitiate, 265 Benham St., 06514. Tel: 203-248-4225; Fax: 203-230-8341.
E-mail: srpascj@aol.com
Web site: http://www.ascj.org
Sister: Sr. Deborah Lopez, Prov. Supr.; Sr. Rosemary Zaffuto, Vicaress. Sisters in Province 175. Residents in Convent: Sisters 17.
St. Rita Convent, 30 Gillies Rd., 06517. Tel: 203-288-4707.
E-mail: melboyle32@hotmail.com
Dominican Sisters (Columbus, OH).
Sisters of Mercy of the Americas of Connecticut, 2809 Whitney Ave., 06518-2544. Tel: 203-287-9017.
St. Stephen Convent, 412 Ridge Rd., 06517. Tel: 203-288-7270.

LITCHFIELD. *Daughters of Wisdom*, 229 E. Litchfield Rd., 06759. Tel: 860-567-3163; Fax: 860-567-3166.
E-mail: info@wisdomhouse.org
Web site: www.wisdomhouse.org

MADISON. *Sisters of Mercy of the Americas of Connecticut*, 149 Neck Rd., 06443. Tel: 203-245-4261.
Sisters of St. Joseph of Brentwood, 62 Kelsey Pl., 06443. Tel: 203-245-1329.

MANCHESTER. *Assumption Convent*, 21 S. Adams St., 06040. Tel: 860-643-0452; Fax: 860-643-0559. Sisters of Charity of Our Lady, Mother of the Church.
Sisters of Notre Dame de Namur, 9 Plano Pl., 06040-4907. Tel: 860-647-8544.
Web site: www.snadden.org
1218B2 Middle Tpke. W., 06040-7920. Tel: 860-528-5091. 117 Prospect St., 06040. Tel: 860-649-6891. 1 Main St., Apt. B-6, 06040-3154. Tel: 860-432-2423. Total in Residence 4.
Sisters of St. Joseph of Chambery, 241E New State Rd., 06040. Tel: 860-645-9750.

MERIDEN. *Generalate and Motherhouse of the Franciscan Sisters of the Eucharist*, 405 Allen Ave., 06451. Tel: 203-238-2243; Fax: 203-237-3734.
E-mail: fsecommunity.org
The Institute of the Franciscan Sisters of the Eucharist. Sr. Suzanne Gross, F.S.E., Contact. Legal Title: *Franciscan Sisters of the Eucharist, Inc.* Mother Rosemae Pender, F.S.E., Mother General. Professed 20 (in CT), 78 (in Community); Novices 4. 275 Finch Ave., 06451. Tel: 203-238-2400; Fax: 203-237-3739. 269 Finch Ave., 06451. Tel: 203-630-1771; Fax: 203-630-1776.
Mt. Carmel Convent, 109 Goodwill Ave., 06451. Tel: 203-235-3622. Apostles of the Sacred Heart of Jesus.
St. Joseph Convent, 19 Goodwill Ave., 06451. Tel: 203-235-8551.
St. Stanislaus Convent, 70 Akron St., 06450. Tel: 203-237-1559. Sisters of St. Joseph of the Third Order of St. Francis, Sisters of Mercy.
Ursuline Sisters of the Congregation of Tildonk, Belgium, 64 Springdale Ave., 06451. Tel: 203-686-1702.

MILFORD. *Franciscan Sisters of the Atonement*, 245 Orange Ave., 06460. Tel: 203-876-2902.
Sisters of Mercy of the Americas of Connecticut, 23 Jones Ct., 06460. Tel: 203-877-1170.
E-mail: Patsio@aol.com
St. Mary Convent, 74 Gulf St., 06460. Tel: 203-874-8427.

NAUGATUCK. *Sisters of Mercy of the Americas of Connecticut*, 1006 New Haven Rd., 06770. Tel: 203-723-8735; Fax: 203-729-2978.
E-mail: stvinferr@aol.com

NEW BRITAIN. *Cana*, 1190 Slater Rd., 06053. Tel: 860-826-1655. Total in Residence 2. Sisters of St. Joseph of Chambery.
Holy Cross Convent, 225 Farmington Ave., 06053-2929. Tel: 860-229-0677. Sisters of St. Joseph of the Third Order of St. Francis.
Miriam House of Formation, 643 Burritt St., 06053. Tel: 860-826-6112.
E-mail: dmvocdir@snet.net
Web site: www.crossfire.org/daughtersofmary
Sr. Mary Christine, Sec.
Motherhouse of Daughters of Mary of the Immaculate Conception, 314 Osgood Ave., 06053. Tel: 860-225-9406; Fax: 860-225-4321.
Web site: www.crossfire.org/daughtersofmary
Daughters of Mary of the Immaculate Conception. Mother Mary Mark Pizzotti, D.M., Supr. Gen.; Sr. Mary Christine, D.M., Sec. & Contact; Rev. Walter Leon Mruk, O.F.M.Conv., Chap. Tel: 860-225-5786. Sisters in Community 62; Residence at the Motherhouse 24.
Sacred Heart Convent, 23 Orange St., 06053. Tel: 860-225-3989.
Msgr. Bojnowski Manor, 50 Pulaski St., 06053. Tel: 860-229-0336; Fax: 860-229-3252.
St. Lucian Home, 532 Burritt St., 06053. Tel: 860-223-2123; Fax: 860-612-0321.
Marian Educational Clinic, 314 Osgood Ave., 06053. Tel: 860-223-0501.
St. Francis of Assisi Convent, School Sisters of Notre Dame, 1757 Stanley St., 06053. Tel: 860-225-7143.
E-mail: stfrancis@snet.net
Sisters 3.
Sisters of Mercy of the Americas, 37 Carlton St., 06053. Tel: 860-229-7575.
The Sisters of St. Francis of Philadelphia, 15 Wilcox St., 06051. Tel: 860-229-0463; Fax: 860-242-8683.
E-mail: lmann@adh-ocs.org
Sisters of the Cross and Passion, 25 Streamside Ln., 06052. Tel: 860-224-1193.

NEW HARTFORD. *Missionary Servants of the Most Blessed Trinity*, 595 Town Hill Rd., 06057. Tel: 860-379-4329; Fax: 860-379-4329.
E-mail: msbtphl@aol.com
Total in Residence 3.

NEW HAVEN. *St. Brendan Convent*, 455 1/2 Whalley Ave., 06511. Tel: 203-787-4631; Fax: 203-785-1781.
E-mail: marineap@hotmail.com
Sisters of Our Lady of the Garden.
St. Joseph Convent, 135 Edwards St., 06511. Tel: 203-562-9202.
E-mail: peggy.sause@juno.com
Web site: www.odc.edu/sisters
15 Lincoln St., 06511. Tel: 203-865-7305.
E-mail: dom.allen@juno.com
1914 Chapel St., 06515. Tel: 203-389-9428.

Albertus Magnus College, 790 Prospect St., 06511. Tel: 203-777-7484; Fax: 203-773-3117.
Sisters of Charity of St. Elizabeth, Convent Station, 1450 Chapel St., 06511. Tel: 203-789-3377. 450 Central Ave., 06515. Tel: 203-397-5243. 80 Whittier Ave., 06515. Tel: 203-389-4400.
Sisters of Charity of St. Elizabeth, Convent Station, 1450 Chapel St., 06511. Tel: 203-789-5116.
Sisters of Notre Dame de Namur. 311 Eastern St. #901E, 06513. Tel: 203-469-5093. 311 Eastern St. #917E, 06513. Tel: 203-469-8385. 311 Eastern St. #1704, 06513. Tel: 203-469-9934. 83 Porter St., 06519. Tel: 203-498-7011.
Sisters of St. Joseph of Chambery, 83 Porter St., 06519. Tel: 203-498-9569.

NEWINGTON. *Maryhouse*, 21 Hartford Ave. #9, 06111. Tel: 860-666-1085; Fax: 860-666-5720. Sisters of Mercy of the Americas.
St. Mary Convent, 168 Cedar St., 06111. Tel: 860-667-1790. Sisters of Charity of St. Elizabeth, Convent Station. Total in Residence 3.
Sisters of Notre Dame de Namur, 42 E. Robbins Ave., 06111.

NORTH BRANFORD. *Sisters of Mercy of the Americas of Detroit*, 1739 Foxon Rd., #G-7, 06471-1566. Tel: 203-488-0692; Fax: 203-488-0692.
E-mail: margaret.farley@yale.edu

NORTH GUILFORD. *Monastery of Our Lady of Grace*, 11 Race Hill Rd., 06437-1099. Tel: 203-457-0599; Fax: 203-457-1248. Dominican Nuns. A contemplative community with solemn vows and papal enclosure. Perpetual Adoration. Sr. Lee, O.P., Prioress & Contact; Rev. Thomas B. Confer, O.P., Chap. Tel: 203-457-0595. Professed Sisters 41. Dominican Contemplative Nuns (Cloistered). Sr. Lee, O.P., Prioress; Rev. Thomas B. Confer, O.P., Chap. Professed Sisters 41.

NORTH HAVEN. *St. Francis Cabrini Convent*, 94 Chapel Hill Rd., 06473. Tel: 203-239-8012. Sisters of the Sacred Heart of Jesus of Ragura. Total in Residence 3.

NORTHFORD. *Sisters of St. Joseph of Chambery*, 30 Mansfield Dr. #1603, 06472. Tel: 203-484-7018.

SOUTHINGTON. *Congregation of Notre Dame*, 96 Summer St., 06489. Tel: 860-628-4506.
E-mail: cndsouthington@juno.com
Total in Residence 3.

SUFFIELD. *St. Joseph Convent*, 156 S. Main St., 06078. Tel: 860-668-2503.

TERRYVILLE. *Daughters of Wisdom*, Marie Louise Convent, 25 Allen St., 06786-6301. Tel: 860-583-8786. Our Lady of Providence Convent, 41 Allen St., 06786-6301. Tel: 860-582-7676.

TORRINGTON. *St. Francis of Assisi Convent*, 93 Marcia Dr., 06790. Tel: 860-489-7405. Sisters of Mercy of the Americas of Connecticut.
St. Peter Convent, 25 St. John Pl., 06790. Tel: 860-489-4035. Religious Teachers Filippini.
School Sisters of Notre Dame, 106 Mill Ln., 06790. Tel: 860-489-1741.

WALLINGFORD. *Holy Trinity Convent*, 247 S. Main St., 06492. Tel: 203-265-6999; Fax: 203-294-4983. Sisters of Mercy of the Americas of Connecticut, Sisters of Notre Dame de Namur.
Sisters of Mercy of the Americas of Connecticut, 1043 North Farms Rd., 06492. Tel: 203-265-6624.

WATERBURY. *Anawim Community*, 129 Grandview Ave., 06708. Tel: 203-753-0867.
E-mail: chuot2@juno.com
Daughters of the Holy Spirit. 27 State St., 06702. Tel: 203-754-0844. 44 Kramer, Ave., 06705. Tel: 203-754-4825.
E-mail: rachelledhs@juno.com
Franciscan Sisters of Allegany, NY, 407 Robinwood Rd., 06708. Tel: 203-753-1472.
Holy Land Convent, 60 Slocum St., 06706. Tel: 203-755-2456. Religious Teachers Filippini.
Maryknoll Sisters of St. Dominic, 55 Cole St., 06706. Tel: 203-754-2913. Total in Residence 8.
Notre Dame Convent, 119 Southmayd Rd., 06705. Tel: 203-753-1095; Fax: 203-753-4431. Sisters of the Congregation of Notre Dame. Sr. Rita Corley, C.N.D., Contact; Sr. Lena Mastroianni, C.N.D.; Sr. Edith Laflamme, C.N.D.; Sr. Pauline Dufresne, C.N.D.; Sr. Jewel Renna, C.N.D. Sisters 8. 587 Oronoke Rd., 06708. Tel: 203-755-8828. Sisters 2. 109 Highland Ave., 06708. Tel: 203-753-3073. Sisters 2.
St. Mary Hospital, 56 Franklin St., 06706. Tel: 203-574-6455. Sisters of St. Joseph of Chambery. 284 Windy Dr., 06705. Tel: 203-574-6374. 31 Marita Dr., 06705. Tel: 203-753-4503.
Sisters of Charity of St. Elizabeth, Convent Station. 100 Jefferson Sq. #6H, 06706. Tel: 203-596-1331.
Sisters of Mercy of the Americas, 1054 Meriden Rd., 06705-3137. Tel: 203-753-3507.
Visitation Plaza, 100 Jefferson Sq. #7J, 06706. Tel: 203-755-7236. 36 Irving St. #2, 06710. Tel: 203-753-4503.
Sisters of Notre Dame de Namur, 131 Herschel Ave., 06708. Tel: 203-757-1444. 38 Summer St., 06704. Tel: 203-755-0012.

WATERTOWN. *St. John the Evangelist Convent*, 9 Academy Hill, 06795. Tel: 860-274-1820. School Sisters of Notre Dame. Sisters 3.

WEST HARTFORD. *Convent of Mary Immaculate, Provincial House of the Sisters of St. Joseph of Chambery*. (North American Province), 27 Park Rd., 06119. Tel: 860-233-5126; 232-8252; Fax: 860-232-4649.
E-mail: csjusa@juno.com
Sisters of St. Joseph of Chambery. Legal Title: *The Sisters of St. Joseph Corporation*. Sr. Mary Kelly, C.S.J., Prov. Supr.; Sr. Presentation Hoye, C.S.J., Contact. In Community: Professed Sisters 176.
Religious Trust of the Sisters of St. Joseph of Chambery (the "Trust").
Canticle Hall, 27 Park Rd., 06119. Tel: 860-232-2797.
Caritas, 27 Park Rd., 06119. Tel: 860-233-5126, Ext. 249.
Euphrasia Hall, 27 Park Rd., 06119. Tel: 860-233-1697.
Mercyknoll, Incorporated, 243 Steele Rd., 06117. Tel: 860-236-3503; Fax: 860-233-1737.
E-mail: amanning-mk@mchct.org
Sisters of Mercy of the Americas, Connecticut Regional Community. A retirement and health care facility of the Sisters of Mercy; skilled nursing open to all. Anne Manning, Admin. & Contact; Rev. Msgr. Robert D. Bergin, Chap. Bed Capacity 88; Skilled Nursing 58; RHNS 1; HFA 29.
St. Mary Home, 2021 Albany Ave., 06117. Tel: 860-236-1924; Fax: 860-570-8293.
Sisters of Mercy of the Americas. Connecticut Regional Community.
Mercy Administrative Office, 249 Steele Rd., 06117-2796. Tel: 860-232-8602; Fax: 860-233-0065.
E-mail: rsmct.mercy@snet.net
Sr. Judith A. Carey, R.S.M., Regl. Pres. Sisters in Community 241.
Sisters of Mercy of the Americas of Connecticut, 132 Milton St., 06119. Tel: 860-523-0707.
St. Joseph College, Lourdes Hall, 1678 Asylum Ave., 06117. Tel: 860-232-6730.
Convent of the Holy Spirit, 243 Steele Rd., 06117. Tel: 860-236-7805.
Catherine McAuley Unit, 243 Steele Rd., 06117. Tel: 860-236-3503.
St. Paul Convent, 243 Steele Rd., 06117. Tel: 860-232-7745.
Trocaire, 243 Steele Rd., 06117. Tel: 860-233-2195.
Sacred Heart Convent, 243 Steele Rd., 06117. Tel: 860-236-3503.
Maranatha, 243 Steele Rd., 06117. Tel: 860-236-9448. 25 Beechwood Rd., 06107. Tel: 860-561-5997. 27 Park Rd., 06119. Tel: 860-236-5626. 54 Boulanger Ave. #1, 06110. Tel: 860-231-8472. 54 Boulanger Ave. #2, 06110. Tel: 860-233-6679. 98 Caya Ave., 06110. Tel: 860-236-2051.
Sisters of Mercy of the Americas of Vermont, 54 Clifford Dr., 06107. Tel: 860-561-5997.
Sisters of Notre Dame de Namur, 21 Prescott St., 06110. Tel: 860-231-7979.
Sisters of St. Joseph. (Springfield, MA), 50 Crescent St., 06119. Tel: 860-233-8708.
Vietnamese Dominican Sisters, 78 Westpoint Ter., 06107. Tel: 860-521-8296; Fax: 860-521-8296. Sr. Magdalene Nguyen, O.P., Supr. & Contact. Total in Residence 3.

WEST HAVEN. *Our Lady of Victory Convent*, 634 Jones Hill Rd., 06516. Tel: 203-934-8601. Ursuline Sisters of the Congregation of Tildonk, Belgium.
St. Paul Parish Center, 45 Alling St., 06516. Tel: 203-934-1357; Fax: 203-931-9416.
Sisters of the Assumption, 491 Washington Ave. #3W, 06516. Tel: 203-932-6449; Fax: 203-777-0144.
E-mail: jo-ann.veillette@yale.edu
Web site: www.sasv.org

WETHERSFIELD. *Daughters of Wisdom*, 78 Fairlane Dr., 06109. Tel: 860-529-8419.
Maryknoll Sisters of St. Dominic, 547 Goff Rd., 06109. Tel: 860-529-1483. 96 Victoria Rd., Hartford, 06114. Tel: 860-296-1826.
Sisters of Notre Dame de Namur, 98-1 Folly Brook Blvd., 06109. Tel: 860-529-3525.
E-mail: tkreibick@aol.com

WINCHESTER CENTER. *Villa Ferretti, Religious Teachers Filippini*, 438 Winchester Rd., Box 55, 06094. Tel: 860-379-3279.

WINDSOR. *Sisters of Notre Dame de Namur*, Province Center, 468 Poquonock Ave., 06095-2473. Tel: 860-688-1832; Fax: 860-683-1741.
E-mail: sndct@aol.com
Web site: www.sndden.org
Administrative Team: Sr. Joan Farley, S.N.D. Tel: 860-285-0554; Sr. Elizabeth McLaughlin, S.N.D., Contact. Tel: 860-285-8901; Sr. Marilyn Pechillo, S.N.D. Tel: 860-285-8441.
Community, 468 Poquonock Ave., 06095-2473. Tel: 860-285-0038; Fax: 860-683-1741.
Julie House, 425 Poquonock Ave., 06095-2465. Tel: 860-298-8320; Fax: 860-683-1351. Assisted living home for S.N.D.'s only. Residents 17; Staff 4.
Sisters of St. Joseph of Chambery, 67 Bloomfield Ave., 06095. Tel: 860-285-0890; Fax: 860-285-0883.
E-mail: windwomen@aol.com

WINDSOR LOCKS. *Sisters of Notre Dame de Namur*, 34 Ellis St., 06096-1704. Tel: 860-627-8002.
E-mail: ellisnd@aol.com
Total in Residence 4.

WINSTED. *St. Anthony Convent*, 66 Oak St., 06098. Tel: 860-379-8375; Fax: 860-379-7522.
E-mail: sas-principal@snet.net
Franciscan Missionaries of the Divine Motherhood. Sisters 3.

WOLCOTT. *Daughters of Wisdom*, 18 Munson Rd. #2, 06716. Tel: 203-879-3432.
E-mail: dm.guekette@gateway.net

[O] COUNSELING CENTERS

MERIDEN. *Franciscan Life Center*, 271 Finch Ave., 06451. Tel: 203-237-8084; Fax: 203-639-1333. Legal Title: *Franciscan Life Center Network, Inc.* Sr. Shaun Vergauwen, F.S.E., Dir. & Contact. Franciscan Sisters of the Eucharist 7; Total Assisted 1,200; Total Staff 3.

[P] ADOPTION SERVICES-HOME CARE

MERIDEN. *Franciscan Family Care Center*, 267 Finch Ave., 06451. Tel: 203-237-8084; Fax: 203-639-1333
For a complete listing, refer to the Special Care Facilities section.

[Q] RETREAT HOUSES-RENEWAL CENTERS

FARMINGTON. *Our Lady of Calvary Retreat House*. Conducted by the Sisters of the Cross and Passion for Religious and Lay Persons, 31 Colton St., 06032. Tel: 860-677-8519; Fax: 860-677-2873.
E-mail: olcret@juno.com
Retreat Team: Sr. Joanne Fahey, C.P., Admin. & Contact; Sr. Ann Rodgers, C.P., Prog. Dir.; Sr. Jeanne Snyder, C.P., Asst. Admin.; Joanne Ceccarelli-Egan; Marie DiBenedetto; Hanna Grymek; Beverly Montana; Sr. Mary O'Brien, C.P.; Sr. Pauline Semkow, R.S.M.

LITCHFIELD. *Wisdom House Retreat Center*, 229 E. Litchfield Rd., 06759-3002. Tel: 860-567-3163; Fax: 860-567-3166.
E-mail: info@wisdomhouse.com
Web site: www.wisdomhouse.org
A retreat center for spiritual and human development programs. Use of space is available for programs in education, spirituality and the arts, and for non-profit organizations when their purpose corresponds to the Mission of Wisdom House. The Center is a ministry of the Daughters of Wisdom. Sr. Rosemarie Greco, D.W., Admin.

MADISON. *Mercy Center, Incorporated*, 167 Neck Rd., P.O. Box 191, 06443. Tel: 203-245-0401; Fax: 203-245-8718.
E-mail: mercymad@aol.com
Web site: www.mercyctrmadison.com
Sisters of Mercy. Sr. Eugenie Guterch, R.S.M., Exec. Dir. & Contact. Sisters 10; Total in Residence 7; Total Staff 25.

NEW HARTFORD. *Trinita*, 595 Town Hill Rd., Rte. 219, 06057. Tel: 860-379-4329. Total in Residence 3; Total Staff 5. Mailing Address: 3501 Solly Ave., Philadelphia, PA, 19136. Missionary Servants of the Most Blessed Trinity.

WEST HARTFORD. *Holy Family Retreat Center*, 303 Tunxis Rd., 06107. Tel: 860-521-0440; Fax: 860-521-1929.
E-mail: holyfamret@aol.com
Web site: cptryon.org/holyfamily
For laymen and laywomen. Conducted by the Passionist Community. Rev. David Cinguegrani, C.P., Retreat Dir. Assoc. Directors: Revs. Earl Keating, C.P.; Alexis Paul, C.P.; Sr. Mary Ann Strain, C.P.; Mr. Darrell Paulsen. Priests 3; Sisters 1; Lay Staff 1.

[R] NEWMAN CENTERS

HARTFORD. *University of Hartford Newman Center*, 200 Bloomfield Ave., 06117. Tel: 860-768-4899. Rev. Raymond S. Smialowski, Chap., Holy Spirit Rectory, 183 Church St., 06111. Trinity College Chapel, 300 Summit St., 06106. Tel: 860-297-2015.

HAMDEN. *Catholic Community at Quinnipac College*, P.O. Box 340, 06518-1908. Tel: 203-582-8257. Rev. Louis Anthony Evangelisto, Chap. & Contact.

NEW BRITAIN. *Central Connecticut State University Newman House*, 145 Paul J. Manafort Dr., 06053-2552. Tel: 860-832-3795; Fax: 860-225-2315.
E-mail: donovanr@ccsu.edu
Rev. Richard J. Donovan, O.F.M. Total Staff 1.
St. Francis of Assisi Friary, 1755 Stanley St., 06053. Tel: 860-225-6449; Fax: 860-225-2315.

NEW HAVEN. *Southern Connecticut State University Catholic Center*, 129 Edwards St., 06511. Tel: 203-392-5331; 624-5297.
E-mail: sullivan_j@scsudctstateu.edu
Rev. John P. Sullivan.

Yale University-St. Thomas More Catholic Center and Chapel, 268 Park St., 06511. Tel: 203-777-5537; Fax: 203-777-0144. Rev. Robert L. Beloin, Ph.D., Chap. & Contact; Sr. Jo-Ann Veillette, S.A.S.V., Assoc. Chap.

[S] ORGANIZED CHARITIES

HARTFORD. *Catholic Charities-Catholic Family Services (Archdiocese of Hartford)*. Central Office. Archdiocesan Center, 467 Bloomfield Ave., Bloomfield, 06002-2999. Tel: 860-242-9577. Patrick J. Johnson, Jr., A.C.S.W., Dir. Charities & Exec. Dir.; Sr. Dorothy Strelchum, Assoc. Dir.; Linda S. Smith, C.I.S.W., Asst. Exec. Dir. Programs; Edgar Bernier, C.P.A., Controller; Francis Laffin, Dir. Group Home Svcs.

Network Connecticut, Inc., c/o Catholic Charities, 467 Bloomfield Ave., Bloomfield, 06002-2999. Tel: 860-242-9577. Patrick J. Johnson, Jr., Dir. Charities.

Capitol Region:

Hartford, 896 Asylum Ave., 06105. Tel: 860-522-8241. John R. Morrison, Regl. Dir.

Corpus Christi Child Development Center, 449 Silas Deane Hwy., 06109. Tel: 203-563-3747. Elizabeth Went, Contact Person.

Family Counseling Service, St. Bernard Church, 426 Hazard Ave., Enfield, 06082. Tel: 860-745-1727.

Institute for the Hispanic Family, 80 Jefferson St., 06105. Tel: 860-527-1124. Galo Rodriguez, Dir.

The Hispanic Child Guidance Clinic, 80 Jefferson St., 06105. Tel: 860-524-8974.

South Region:

New Haven, 478 Orange St., New Haven, 06502. Tel: 203-787-2207. Patricia Nere, A.C.S.W., Regl. Dir.

Project Apoyo, 790 Grand Ave., New Haven, 06511. Tel: 203-772-1131.

Centro San Jose, Inc., 290 Grand Ave., New Haven, 06513. Tel: 203-562-3135.

Ansonia, 205 Wakelee Ave., P.O. Box 364, Ansonia, 06401. Tel: 203-735-7483.

Meriden, 220 Colony St., Meriden, 06450. Tel: 203-235-2707.

Milford, 203 High St., P.O. Box 147, Milford, 06460. Tel: 203-874-6270.

Guilford Office, 57 Whitfield St., Guilford, 06437.

West Region: New Britain, 90 Franklin Sq., New Britain, 06051. Tel: 860-225-3561. Gregory Paleologos, A.C.S.W., Regl. Dir.

Torrington, 132 Grove St., Torrington, 06790. Tel: 860-482-5558.

Waterbury, 56 Church St., Waterbury, 06702. Tel: 203-755-1196.

Bristol Office, 300 Main St., Bristol, 06010. Tel: 860-589-8662.

Southbury Office, 88 Main St., Southbury, 06488.

Migration and Refugee Service, 125 Market St., 06103. Tel: 860-548-0059. Robert Snyder, Dir.

[T] SOCIAL SERVICE CENTERS FOR SPANISH-SPEAKING AND BLACK PEOPLE

BLOOMFIELD. *Office for Hispanic Evangelization*, 467 Bloomfield Ave., 06002-2999. Tel: 860-243-0940; Fax: 860-286-2797.
E-mail: hispanic.evnglztn@snet.net
Most Rev. Peter A. Rosazza, Vicar Hispanics; Deacon Rafael Lopez, Dir.

WATERBURY. *Spanish-Speaking Center*, 83 Cherry St., 06702. Tel: 203-574-5156. Rev. John C. Blackall, Contact. Total Assisted 350; Total Staff 1.

[U] SOCIETY OF ST. VINCENT DE PAUL

HARTFORD. *Particular Council of the St. Vincent de Paul Society*. Greater Hartford, 134 Farmington Ave., 06105-3784. Tel: 860-541-6491. Legal Title: *Particular Council of the St. Vincent de Paul Society of the Archdiocese of Hartford.*

[V] MISCELLANEOUS

HARTFORD. *Mercy Housing & Shelter Corporation*, 211 Wethersfield Ave., 06114. Tel: 860-724-7988; Fax: 860-548-0692. Patricia McKeon, R.S.M., Pres. & Exec. Dir.; Amy Lynn Silverman, Contact. Special Centers for Social Service and Assistance. Total Assisted 10,000; Total Staff 65.

North American La Salette Mission Center, Inc., 85 New Park Ave., 06106-2184. Tel: 860-523-4017; Fax: 860-523-4074.
E-mail: lasalettemission@aol.com
Rev. John R. Nuelle, M.S., Pres. & Exec. Dir.; Bro. Mark L. Gallant, M.S., Asst. Dir.

Religious Trust of the Missionaries of Our Lady of LaSalette. Province of Our Lady of Seven Dolors, (MLS Trust), 915 Maple Ave., 06114-2330. Tel: 860-956-8870; Fax: 860-956-8849.
E-mail: mlsadmin@aol.com
Bro. G. Peter Collins, M.S., Contact.

BLOOMFIELD. *Archdiocesan Spiritual Life Center*, 467 Bloomfield Ave., 06002-2903. Tel: 860-243-2374; Fax: 860-242-7914.
E-mail: spiritlifectr@juno.com
Sr. Mary Costello, R.S.M., Assoc. Dir.; Cathleen Murtha, D.W., Contact.

Foundation for the Advancement of Catholic Schools, 467 Bloomfield Ave., 06002-2999. Tel: 860-242-4362; Fax: 860-242-8683.
E-mail: jdash@adh-ocs.org
Peter G. Carey, Pres.; Jeannine V. Dash, Exec. Dir. & Contact.

CHESHIRE. *Logos, Inc.*, 475 Oak Ave., 06410. Tel: 203-271-0805; Fax: 203-271-3845.
E-mail: cheshire@legionaries.org
Bro. Juan Sabadell, L.C., Contact.

LITCHFIELD. *Lourdes Shrine Guild, Inc.*, 83 Montfort Rd., 06759. Tel: 860-567-1041; Fax: 860-567-9670. Rev. Gerald Fitzsimmons, S.S.M., Prov. & Contact Person.

MERIDEN. *Franciscan Life Center Network, Incorporated*, 405 Allen Ave., 06451. Tel: 203-237-8084; Fax: 203-639-1333.

Franciscan Life Center, 271 Finch Ave., 06451. Tel: 203-237-8084; Fax: 203-639-1333.

Franciscan Life Process Center, 11650 Downes St., Lowell, MI, 49331. Tel: 616-897-7842; Fax: 616-897-7054.

Franciscan Montessori Earth School, 14750 S.E. Clinton St., Portland, OR, 97236. Tel: 503-760-8220; Fax: 503-760-8333.

Franciscan Northwoods Computer Center, 5601 Lilac Hill Rd., Duluth, MN, 55810. Tel: 218-624-5478; Fax: 218-624-4649.

John S. Duss Memorial Music Center, 2211 Greysolon Rd., Duluth, MN, 55812. Tel: 2218-724-6912; Fax: 218-724-3318.

Franciscan Cre-Act School, 526 Grant St., P.O. Box 723, Pocatello, ID, 83204. Tel: 208-233-4747.

Franciscan Family Life Center, 1745 Pocatello Creek Rd., Pocatello, ID, 83201. Tel: 208-233-9383.

Creative Acting, 526 S. Grant St., Pocatello, ID, 83204. Tel: 208-233-4747.

NEW HAVEN. *The Children's Foundation at St. Francis Home, Inc.*, 651 Prospect St., 06505. Tel: 203-777-5513; Fax: 203-777-0644.
E-mail: psalerno1@aol.com
Mr. Peter T. Salerno, Exec. Dir.

NEW MILFORD. *Our Lady of the Lakes Corporation*, 3 Old Town Park Rd., 06776-4212. Tel: 860-354-5239; Fax: 860-354-2968.
E-mail: byrdolol@aol.com

ORANGE. *Helping Hand Investments, Inc*, 393 Derby Ave., 06477. Tel: 203-795-2800. Rev. Juan Sabadell, L.C., Contact.

Horizons Institute, Inc., 393 Derby Ave., 06477. Tel: 203-795-2800; Fax: 203-795-2808. Rev. Juan Sabadell, L.C., Contact.

Legion of Christ, Inc., 393 Derby Ave., 06477. Tel: 203-795-2800; Fax: 203-795-2808.
E-mail: vhiggins@legionaries.org
Rev. Anthony Bannon, L.C., Territorial Dir.; Bro. Vincent Higgins, L.C., Sec. Assistants: Revs. Emilio Diaz Torre, L.C.; Anthony Bailleres, L.C. Priests 4; Religious 3.

LUX ET VITA, INC., 393 Derby Ave., 06477. Tel: 203-795-2800. Rev. Juan Sabadell, L.C., Contact.

Racebrook, Inc., 393 Derby Ave., 06477. Tel: 203-795-2800; Fax: 203-795-2808. Rev. Emilio Diaz-Toree, L.C., Contact.

Rossotto, Inc., 393 Derby Ave., 06477. Tel: 203-795-2800. Rev. Juan Sabadell, L.C., Sec. & Contact.

WEST HARTFORD. *Mercy Community Health, Inc.*, 2021 Albany Ave., 06117-2796. Tel: 860-570-8300; Fax: 860-233-8849.
E-mail: rkisner@mchct.org
Sr. Maureen Reardon, R.S.M., Bd. Chm.

Mercy Community Home Care Services, Inc., 275 Steele Rd., 06117. Tel: 860-586-8418; 586-8318.
E-mail: nancytracy@snet.net
Nancy Tracy, R.N., M.S.N., Admin. & COO.

Mercy Services, Inc., 2021 Albany Ave., 06117-2796. Tel: 860-570-8300; Fax: 860-233-8849.
E-mail: rkisner@mchct.org
Mr. Richard J. Kisner, Pres.

Project Hope, Inc. Business Office & Mailing Address, 27 Park Rd., 06119. Tel: 860-233-5126; 953-2443; Fax: 860-953-2443. Center Location, 873 New Britain Ave., Hartford, 06106. Tel: 860-953-2443; Fax: 860-953-2443. Sr. Helen Hart, C.S.J. Total Enrollment 72; Total Staff 4. Sisters of St. Joseph of Chambery.

WINDSOR. *The Connecticut Province of the Sisters of Notre Dame de Namur, Inc.*, 468 Poquonock Ave., 06095-2473. Tel: 860-688-1832; Fax: 860-683-1741.
E-mail: sndct@aol.com
Web site: www.sndden.org
Sr. Elizabeth McLaughlin, S.N.D.deN., Contact.

RELIGIOUS INSTITUTES OF MEN REPRESENTED IN THE ARCHDIOCESE

For further details refer to the corresponding bracketed number in the Religious Institutes of Men or Women section.

[0140]—*The Augustinians.*—O.S.A.
[0200]—*Benedictine Monks.*—O.S.B.
[0600]—*Brothers of the Congregation of Holy Cross.* (Notre Dame, IN).—C.S.C.
[1100]—*Brothers of the Sacred Heart.*—S.C.
[1330]—*Congregation of the Mission (Vincentian Fathers).*—C.M.
[1000]—*Congregation of the Passion.* (Prov. of St. Paul of the Cross).—C.P.
[0480]—*Conventual Franciscans.* (St. Anthony of Padua Prov.).—O.F.M.Conv.
[0520]—*Franciscan Friars.* (Immaculate Conception, Holy Name Provs.).—O.F.M.
[0690]—*Jesuit Fathers and Brothers.*—S.J.
[0730]—*Legionaries of Christ.*—L.C.
[0780]—*Marist Fathers.*—S.M.
[0800]—*Maryknoll.*—M.M.
[0720]—*The Missionaries of Our Lady of La Salette.* (Prov. O.L. of Seven Dolors).—M.S.
[1210]—*Missionaries of St. Charles-Scalabrinians.*—C.S.
[0590]—*Missionaries of the Holy Apostles.*—M.S.A.
[0860]—*Missionhurst Congregation of the Immaculate Heart of Mary.*—C.I.C.M.
[0870]—*Montfort Missionaries.*—S.M.M.
[0910]—*Oblates of Mary Immaculate.*—O.M.I.
[0430]—*Order of Preachers-Dominicans.* (Eastern Prov.).—O.P.
[0610]—*Priests of the Congregation of Holy Cross.*—C.S.C.
[1070]—*Redemptorist Fathers.* (Baltimore Prov.).—C.SS.R.
[0760]—*Society of Mary (Marianists).*—S.M.
[0975]—*Society of Our Lady of the Most Holy Trinity.*—S.O.L.T.
[1250]—*Somascan Fathers.*—C.R.S.
[]—*Sons of Charity.*—S.C.

RELIGIOUS INSTITUTES OF WOMEN REPRESENTED IN THE ARCHDIOCESE

[0130]—*Apostles of the Sacred Heart of Jesus.*—A.S.C.J.
[0180]—*Benedictine Nuns of the Primitive Observance.*—O.S.B.
[0860]—*Daughters of Mary of the Immaculate Conception.*—D.M.
[0820]—*Daughters of the Holy Spirit.*—D.H.S.
[0960]—*Daughters of Wisdom.*—D.W.
[1050]—*Dominican Contemplative Nuns.*—O.P.
[]—*Dominican Oblates of Jesus.* (Madrid, Spain).—D.O.O.P.
[1070-02]—*Dominican Sisters (Congregation of St. Mary of the Springs).*—O.P.
[]—*Dominican Sisters (Vietnamese Congregation of St. Catherine of Siena).*—O.P.
[]—*Dominican Sisters of Fatima.*—O.P.
[1070-15]—*Dominican Sisters of Hope.*—O.P.
[1170]—*Felician Sisters.* (Our Lady of the Angels Province).—C.S.S.F.
[]—*Franciscan Missionaries of the Divine Motherhood.*—F.M.D.M.
[1180]—*Franciscan Sisters of Alleghany, New York.*—O.S.F.
[1250]—*Institutes of the Franciscan Sisters of the Eucharist.*—F.S.E.
[2340]—*Little Sisters of the Poor.*—L.S.P.
[2470]—*Maryknoll Sisters of St. Dominic.*—M.M.
[2490]—*Medical Mission Sisters.*—M.M.S.
[2790]—*Missionary Servants of the Most Blessed Trinity.*—M.S.B.T.
[2519]—*Religious Sisters of Mercy of Alma.* (MI).—R.S.M.
[3430]—*Religious Teachers Filippini.*—M.P.F.
[2970]—*School Sisters of Notre Dame.*—S.S.N.D.
[]—*Sisters Minor of Mary Immaculate.*—S.M.M.I.
[0520]—*Sisters of Charity of Our Lady, Mother of Mercy.*—S.C.M.M.
[0530]—*Sisters of Charity of Our Lady, Mother of the Church.*—S.C.M.C.
[0590]—*Sisters of Charity of Saint Elizabeth, Convent Station.*—S.C.
[2575]—*Sisters of Mercy of the Americas.* (Albany, Vermont, Detroit & Connecticut).—R.S.M.
[3000]—*Sisters of Notre Dame de Namur.* (Connecticut, Boston, California & Base Community).—S.N.D.deN.
[]—*Sisters of Our Lady of the Garden.*—O.L.G. [3720]—Sisters of Saint Anne.—S.S.A.
[1650]—*Sisters of St. Francis of Philadelphia.*—O.S.F.

[3830-16]—*Sisters of St. Joseph.* (Springfield).—S.S.J.
[3830-05]—*Sisters of St. Joseph of Brentwood.*—C.S.J.
[3850]—*Sisters of St. Joseph of Chambery.*—C.S.J.
[3930]—*Sisters of St. Joseph of the Third Order of St. Francis.*—S.S.J.-T.O.S.F.
[0150]—*Sisters of the Assumption B.V.*—S.A.S.V.
[2980]—*Sisters of the Congregation de Notre Dame.*—C.N.D.
[3180]—*Sisters of the Cross and Passion.*—C.P.
[]—*Sisters of the Sacred Heart of Jesus of Ragura.*—S.S.H.J.
[2170]—*Sisters, Servants of the Immaculate Heart of Mary.*—I.H.M.
[4060]—*Society of the Holy Child Jesus.*—S.H.C.J.
[4130]—*Ursuline Sisters of The Congregation of Tildonk, Belgium.*—O.S.U.

ARCHDIOCESAN CEMETERIES

HARTFORD. *Catholic Cemeteries Association of the Archdiocese of Hartford, Inc.* 700 Middletown Ave., P.O. Box 517, North Haven, 06473-0517. Tel: 203-239-2557. Rev. Arthur J. DuPont, Dir.; Robert Marek, Exec. Dir.
Holy Trinity.
St. Patrick.

ANSONIA. *Old St. Mary.*
St. Mary.
BLOOMFIELD. *Mount Saint Benedict.*
DERBY. *Mount St. Peter.*
Old St. Mary.
EAST HARTFORD. *St. Mary.*
MANCHESTER. *St. Bridget.*
St. James.
MERIDEN. *Sacred Heart.*
St. Patrick.
NAUGATUCK. *St. Francis.* (New Haven Region).
St. James.
NEW BRITAIN. *Old St. Mary.*
St. Mary.
NEW HAVEN. *St. Bernard.*
St. Lawrence.
NORTH HAVEN. *All Saints.*
TORRINGTON. *Old St. Francis.*
St. Francis.
St. Peter.
WALLINGFORD. *Holy Trinity.*
St. John.
WATERBURY. *Calvary.*
Old St. Joseph.
St. Joseph.
WATERTOWN. *Mount Olivet.*

NECROLOGY

† Bray, William A., (Retired). —Died Nov. 15, 2000.
† Flynn, Vincent J., (Retired). —Died Nov. 8, 2000.
† Foran, Edward R., (Retired). —Died May 23, 2000.
† Guandalini, Julius S., (Retired). —Died Jan. 19, 2000.
† Kennedy, Rev. Msgr. John S., (Retired). —Died Oct. 3, 2000.
† Lesco, Francis J., (Retired). —Died July 6, 2000.
† O'Dea, James J., Beacon Falls, CT St. Michael. —Died Oct. 4, 2000.
† Peruti, John J., Hartford, CT St. Luke. —Died Sept. 28, 2000.
† Pitruzzello, Raymond S., Waterbury, CT Immaculate Conception. —Died Jan. 7, 2000.
† Sullivan, James J., (Retired). —Died Aug. 13, 2000.
† Ventresca, A. Andrew, (Retired). —Died Sept. 14, 2000.
† Yuskauskas, Raymond B., (Retired). —Died Feb. 12, 2000.

Diocese of Helena

(Dioecesis Helenensis)

Most Reverend

ROBERT C. MORLINO, S.T.D.

Bishop of Helena; ordained June 1, 1974; appointed July 6, 1999; consecrated and installed September 21, 1999. *Office: P.O. Box 1729, Helena, MT, 59624-1729.* Tel.: 406-442-5820; Fax: 406-442-1085. *E-mail address: bishop@diocesehelen.org. Res., 710 Linden St., Helena, MT, 59601.* Tel.: 406-442-7212; Fax: 406-442-4035.

ERECTED MARCH 7, 1884.

Square Miles 51,922.

Comprises the western part of the State of Montana, and is made up of the following Counties: Lewis and Clark, Glacier, Pondera, Flathead, Lake, Lincoln, Missoula, Mineral, Sanders, Powell, Granite, Ravalli, Deer Lodge, Silver Bow, Jefferson, Broadwater, Gallatin, Madison, Beaverhead, Meagher, Wheatland and parts of Teton and Toole.

Diocesan Legal Title—*Roman Catholic Bishop of Helena, Montana, a Corporation Sole.*

For legal titles of parishes and diocesan institutions, consult the Chancery Office.

Chancery and Diocesan Pastoral Office: 515 North Ewing, P.O. Box 1729, Helena, MT, 59624. Tel.: 406-442-5820; Fax: 406-442-5191.

E-mail address: chancery@diocesehelena.org

STATISTICAL OVERVIEW

Personnel	
Bishop	1
Priests: Diocesan Active in Diocese	48
Priests: Active Outside Diocese	8
Priests: Diocesan in Foreign Missions	1
Priests: Retired, Sick or Absent	25
Number of Diocesan Priests	82
Religious Priests in Diocese	10
Extern Priests in Diocese	5
Ordinations:	
Diocesan Priests	1
Religious Priests	1
Transitional Deacons	1
Permanent Deacons	7
Permanent Deacons in Diocese	34
Total Brothers	1
Total Sisters	48
Parishes	
Parishes	58
With Resident Pastor:	
Resident Diocesan Priests	40
Resident Religious Priests	4
Without Resident Pastor:	
Administered by Priests	9
Administered by Deacons	1
Administered by Women Religious	4
Missions	39
Pastoral Centers	14
Professional Ministry Personnel:	
Brothers	1
Sisters	26
Lay Ministers	28
Welfare	
Catholic Hospitals	3
Total Assisted	180,996
Day Care and Extended Day Care Centers	3
Total Assisted	130
Educational	
Seminaries, Diocesan	1
Students from This Diocese	3
Diocesan Students in Other Seminaries	4
Total Seminarians	7
Colleges and Universities	1
Total Students	1,292
High Schools, Diocesan and Parish	2
Total Students	418
Elementary Schools, Diocesan and Parish	4
Total Students	889
Catechesis/Religious Education:	
High School Students	1,692
Elementary Students	5,669
Total Students Under Catholic Instruction	9,967
Teachers in the Diocese:	
Priests	10
Sisters	10
Lay Teachers	200
Vital Statistics	
Receptions into the Church:	
Infant Baptism Totals	1,060
Adult Baptism Totals	185
Received into Full Communion	125
First Communions	1,078
Confirmations	763
Marriages:	
Catholic	140
Interfaith	136
Total Marriages	276
Deaths	871
Total Catholic Population	67,500
Total Population	424,372

Former Bishops—Rt. Rev. JOHN B. BRONDEL, cons. Bishop of Victoria, V.I., Dec. 14, 1879; appt. Vicar Apostolic of Montana, April 17, 1883; Bishop of Helena, March 7, 1884; died Nov. 3, 1903.—Rt. Rev. JOHN P. CARROLL, D.D., cons. Bishop of Helena, Dec. 21, 1904; died Nov. 4, 1925.—Most Rev. GEORGE J. FINNIGAN, C.S.C., D.D., cons. Bishop of Helena, Aug. 1, 1927; died Aug. 14, 1932.—Most Rev. RALPH L. HAYES, D.D., cons. Bishop of Helena, Sept. 21, 1933; transferred to Rectorship North American College, Rome, Italy, September 11, 1935; transferred to Titular See of Hierapolis, Oct. 26, 1935; transferred to Davenport, Nov. 16, 1944; appt. Assistant at the Pontifical Throne, April 30, 1958; transferred to Titular See of Naraggara and retired, Oct. 20, 1966; died July 4, 1970.—Most Rev. JOSEPH M. GILMORE, S.T.D., cons. Bishop of Helena, Feb. 19, 1936; died April 2, 1962.—Most Rev. RAYMOND G. HUNTHAUSEN, ord. June 1, 1946; appt. July 8, 1962; cons. Bishop of Helena, Aug. 30, 1962; transferred to Archdiocese of Seattle, Feb. 25, 1975; installed Archbishop of Seattle, May 22, 1975; retired Aug. 21, 1991.—Most Rev. ELDEN F. CURTISS, D.D., ord. May 24, 1958; appt. March 4, 1976; cons. Bishop of Helena, April 28, 1976; transferred to Archdiocese of Omaha, May 4, 1993; installed Archbishop of Omaha, June 25, 1993.—Most Rev. ALEXANDER J. BRUNETT, Ph.D., ord. July 13, 1958; appt. April 19, 1994; cons. Bishop of Helena, July 6, 1994; transferred to Archdiocese of Seattle Oct. 28, 1997; installed Archbishop of Seattle Dec. 18, 1997.

Vicar General—Very Rev. KEVIN S. O'NEILL, V.G.

Liaison to Senior Status Priests—Rev. Msgr. JOSEPH D. HARRINGTON, *Carroll College, Helena, 59625.* Tel: 406-447-4459.

Episcopal Vicar for Canonical Services—P.O. Box 1729, Helena, 59624. Tel: 406-442-5820; Fax: 406-442-5191.

Chancery and Diocesan Pastoral Office—515 N. Ewing St., P.O. Box 1729, Helena, 59624. Tel: 406-442-5820; Fax: 406-442-5191.

Moderator of the Curia—Very Rev. KEVIN S. O'NEILL, V.G.

Chancellor—Mr. MYLES GROTBO.

Director of Pastoral Office—Deacon J. ANTHONY DUVERNAY.

Archivist—Sr. DOLORES BRINKEL, S.C.L.

Business Administration Office—PETER MCNAMEE, Diocesan Finance Officer, *515 N. Ewing St., P.O. Box 1729, Helena, 59624.* Tel: 406-442-5820.

Development Office—Deacon GERALD KUHL, Dir., *P.O. Box 1729, Helena, 59624.* Tel: 406-442-5820.

Western Montana Catholic Foundation—PHILIP GREANY, Pres.; Deacon GERALD KUHL, Contact Person, *P.O. Box 1729, Helena, 59624.* Tel: 406-442-5820.

Diocesan Tribunal—515 N. Ewing St., P.O. Box 1729, Helena, 59624. Tel: 406-442-5820; Fax: 406-442-5191.

Judicial Vicar—Rev. JOHN W. ROBERTSON.

Associate Judges—Revs. JEFFREY FLEMING; RAYMOND V. GILMORE; THOMAS HAFFEY; MATTHEW HUBER; PATRICK MCGURK.

Promoter of Justice—Rev. ROBERT GROSCH, J.C.L.

Defenders of the Bond—Revs. ROBERT BEAULIEU; EMMETT KELLY; ROBERT NOONAN; KEVIN O'NEILL; GARY RELLER.

Notaries—PAULA HOUSE; GERALDINE ROBINSON.

Diocesan Consultors—Very Rev. KEVIN S. O'NEILL, V.G.; Revs. THOMAS F. HEALY, S.J.; THOMAS HAFFEY; MATTHEW HUBER; CHARLES ROMAN; Rev. Msgr. DONALD SHEA; Rev. JEREMIAH SULLIVAN.

Presbyteral Council—Very Rev. KEVIN S. O'NEILL, V.G.; Revs. THOMAS F. HEALY, S.J.; JOHN J. DARRAGH; THOMAS HAFFEY; EDWARD HISLOP; MATTHEW HUBER; ROBERT NOONAN; JOHN ROBERTSON; CHARLES ROMAN; Rev. Msgr. DONALD SHEA; Rev. JEREMIAH SULLIVAN; Mr. MYLES GROTBO, Chancellor, Sec.

Diocesan Finance Council—JEANNE AHMANN; TONI BROADBENT; ROBERT BUGNI; EDWARD CASNE; THOMAS DOWNEY; MYLES GROTBO; PETER JOHNSON; Very Rev. KEVIN S. O'NEILL, V.G.; MICHAEL RIELEY; HUGH MCWHORTER; Rev. DANIEL SHEA.

Vicariates—Rev. ROBERT NOONAN, Conrad; Rev. WILLIAM J. GREYTAK, Helena; Rev. MATTHEW HUBER, Missoula; Rev. GARY W. RELLER, Kalispell; Rev. THOMAS HAFFEY, Butte.

Personnel Board—Very Rev. KEVIN S. O'NEILL, V.G.; Revs. THOMAS P. HAFFEY; EDWARD G. KOHLER; JOHN MURRAY; THOMAS M. O'DONNELL; DANIEL SHEA.

Diocesan Pastoral Council—ERIN BUTTS; MICHAEL BUTTS; MARTIN CHABOT; DANIEL DOYLE; Rev. WILLIAM GREYTAK; MYLES GROTBO; Rev. THOMAS HAFFEY; PATRICK HAGGARTY; Revs. EDWARD HISLOP; MATTHEW HUBER; Deacon ROBERT LANE; FRANK LOCH; MARIE LOCH; JAMES MCNEELY; Deacon DONALD

MARKS; JAMES MCDEVITT; ROSE NISTLER; Sr. ELIZABETH OLSEN, B.V.M.; Very Rev. KEVIN S. O'NEILL, V.G.; Revs. LEO PROXELL; GARY RELLER; STEPHEN ROWAN; JOHN RUSSELL; ERIC SCHIEDERMEYER; MARY SECCOMBE; DON SHAUGHNESSY; Sr. SHARON SMITH, S.C.L.; DEANNA SULLIVAN-ZANGENBERG; DENICE VOLESKY; SANDI WAVEREK.

Inter-Diocesan Organizations

Montana Catholic Conference—SHARON HOFF-BRODOWY, *P.O. Box 1708, Helena, 59624.* Tel: 406-442-5761; Fax: 406-442-9047.

Board of Directors—Most Rev. ROBERT C. MORLINO, (Helena); Most Rev. ANTHONY MILONE, (Great Falls); KIM LARSEN, (Great Falls); Rev. JAY PETERSON, (Great Falls); Sr. MARY JOE MCDONALD, S.C.L., (Butte).

Catholic Social Services for Montana, Inc.—ROSEMARY MILLER, Dir., *22 S. Ewing St., P.O. Box 907, Helena, 59601.* Tel: 406-442-4130; Fax: 406-442-4192. Coordinates and supervises all Catholic Social welfare in the State of Montana.

Board of Directors—Most Rev. ROBERT C. MORLINO, (Helena); Most Rev. ANTHONY MILONE, (Great Falls); JULIE FRENCH, (Great Falls); MYLES GROTBO, (Helena); LINDA MCCAULEY, (Helena).

Helena Office—ROSEMARY MILLER, Dir., Adoptions; Sr. MARY NOEL BRUCH, S.C.L., Social Worker, *22 S. Ewing, P.O. Box 907, Helena, 59624.* Tel: 406-442-4130.

Billings Office—Social Workers: BECKY HUBBERT, (Billings); SUSAN BARTON, (Billings); SAM HUBBERT, (Columbus), *St. Vincent's Hospital, 2703 11th Ave. N., Billings, 59101.* Tel: 406-252-3399.

Great Falls Office—KYLA KALANICK, Social Worker, *1601 Second Ave. N., Ste. 640, Great Falls, 59401.* Tel: 406-771-7805.

Missoula Office—BETSY ROBEL-GOMEZ, Social Worker, *420 W. Pine St., Missoula, 59802.* Tel: 406-728-5429.

Montana Association of Churches—MARGARET MACDONALD, Exec. Dir., *180 24th St. W., Ste. G, Billings, 59102.* Tel: 406-656-9779. Rev. GARY W. RELLER, Diocesan Ecumenical Officer, *P.O. Box 1477, Polson, 59860.* Tel: 406-883-4607.

Diocesan Offices and Organizations

Borromeo Pre-Seminary Program—Rev. WILLIAM GREYTAK, *Carroll College, Helena, 59625.* Tel: 406-447-4350.

Catholic Campaign for Human Development—Deacon J. ANTHONY DUVERNAY, *P.O. Box 1729, Helena, 59624.* Tel: 406-442-5820.

Catholic Committee on Scouting—JAMES TUCKER, Contact, *P.O. Box 1729, Helena, 59624.* Tel: 406-442-5820.

Catholic Youth Coalition—Deacon DAN MCGRATH, *P.O. Box 1729, Helena, 59624.* Tel: 406-442-5820.

Charismatic Renewal—Diocesan Pastoral Office, P.O. Box 1729, Helena, 59624.

Christian Family Movement—Diocesan Pastoral Office, P.O. Box 1729, Helena, 59624.

Clergy Senior Status and Security Trust Board—Rev. ROBERT J. BEAULIEU; Rev. Msgr. JOSEPH HARRINGTON; Revs. PATRICK MCGURK; JOSEPH OBLINGER; KEVIN O'NEILL; DANIEL SHEA.

Continuing Formation of the Clergy—Rev. THOMAS P. HAFFEY, Dir., *2100 Farragut, Butte, 59701.* Tel: 406-723-4303.

Assembly of Women Religious—Sr. JOAN MARGRET SCHWAGER, R.S.M., Pres., *835 2nd Ave. E., Kalispell, 59901.* Tel: 406-752-6303.

Cursillo Movement, Journey and Search—Deacon J. ANTHONY DUVERNAY, Diocesan Dir., *Diocesan Pastoral Office, P.O. Box 1729, Helena, 59624.* Tel: 406-442-5820.

Daughters of Isabella—SUSAN COSTLE, State Regent, *1019 E. 5th St., Anaconda, 59711.*

Diocesan Attorney—WARD SHANAHAN, *Gough, Shanahan, Johnson & Waterman, P.O. Box 1715, Helena, 59624.* Tel: 406-442-8560.

Diocesan Buildings—SCOTT FITZPATRICK, Mgr., *P.O. Box 1729, Helena, 59624.*

Diocesan Council of Catholic Women—SUSAN PORROVECCHIO, Pres., *3155 Swan Hwy., Bigfork, 59911.*

Diocesan Ecumenical Officer—Rev. GARY W. RELLER, *P.O. Box 1477, Polson, 59860.* Tel: 406-883-4607.

Friends of The Catholic University—Rev. Msgr. JOSEPH HARRINGTON, Chm., *Carroll College, Helena, 59625.* Tel: 406-447-4459.

Guatemala Missions—Deacon J. ANTHONY DUVERNAY, Dir., *P.O. Box 1729, Helena, 59624.* Tel: 406-442-5820.

Holy Childhood Association—Rev. JOSEPH L. BYRNE, Dir., *P.O. Box 610, Townsend, 59644.* Tel: 406-266-3973.

Legendary Lodge (Diocesan Summer Camp)—JAMES TUCKER, *P.O. Box 1729, Helena, 59624.* Tel: 406-442-5820.

Marriage Encounter—DAN PHILLIPS; MARY BETH PHILLIPS, *4614 A Ironwood, Great Falls, 59405.*

Office of Due Process—Contact Judicial Vicar, *P.O. Box 1729, Helena, 59624.* Tel: 406-442-5820.

Permanent Deacons—Deacon J. ANTHONY DUVERNAY, Dir., *P.O. Box 1729, Helena, 59624.* Tel: 406-442-5820.

Program of Formation for Lay Ministry—JAMES TUCKER, *P.O. Box 1729, Helena, 59624.* Tel: 406-442-5820.

Program of Formation for the Permanent Diaconate—Deacon J. ANTHONY DUVERNAY, Coord., *P.O. Box 1729, Helena, 59624.* Tel: 406-442-5820.

Office of Worship—Rev. EDWARD HISLOP, Liturgy Consultant; Sr. MARY JO QUINN, Liturgical Music Consultant, *1700 Missoula Ave., Helena, 59601.* Tel: 406-442-5268.

Propagation of the Faith—Rev. JOSEPH L. BYRNE, Diocesan Dir., *P.O. Box 610, Townsend, 59644.* Tel: 406-266-3973.

Religious Education—JAMES TUCKER, Dir., *515 N. Ewing St., P.O. Box 1729, Helena, 59624.* Tel: 406-442-5820.

Resource Center—KATHY WARD, Mgr., *515 N. Ewing St., P.O. Box 1729, Helena, 59624.* Tel: 406-442-5820.

Vicar for Catholic Schools—Rev. JOHN W. ROBERTSON, *515 N. Ewing St., P.O. Box 1729, Helena, 59624.* Tel: 406-442-5820; Fax: 406-442-5191.

Third Order of St. Francis—KATHY POELMAN, S.F.O., *1702 Peosta, Helena, 59601.*

Vocations Office—*P.O. Box 1729, Helena, 59624.* Tel: 406-442-5820. Rev. THOMAS O'DONNELL, Dir., *P.O. Box 1110, East Helena, 59635.* Tel: 406-227-5334.

"Montana Catholic" (Diocesan Newspaper)—ALEX LOBDELL, Editor; M. CATHERINE TILZEY, Asst. Editor, *515 N. Ewing St., P.O. Box 1729, Helena, 59624.* Tel: 406-442-5820; Fax: 406-442-5191.

CLERGY, PARISHES, MISSIONS AND PAROCHIAL SCHOOLS

CITY OF HELENA
(Lewis and Clark County)

1—CATHEDRAL OF ST. HELENA (1866), Very Rev. Kevin S. O'Neill, V.G., Rector; Rev. Rudolph C. Bullman; Deacons Fritz Roos; J. Anthony Duvernay. Pastoral Assocs.: Bro. Stephen Hale, C.F.C.; Tracey Johnson; Lorraine Tucker.
Office: 530 N. Ewing St., 59601. Tel: 406-442-5825; 442-7094 (after hours); Fax: 406-449-5113.
Good Samaritan Thrift Store—(Assistance to those in need.) 1388 N. Hannaford, 59601. Tel: 406-442-0780.

2—ST. MARY (1910), Rev. Edward J. Hislop. Pastoral Assocs.: Sr. Mary Jo Quinn, S.C.L.; Sr. Patricia Sullivan, S.C.L.; Joanie Volesky; Janice Nankivel.
Office: 1700 Missoula Ave., 59601. Tel: 406-442-5268; Fax: 406-449-0860.

3—OUR LADY OF THE VALLEY, Rev. Daniel B. Shea; Deacons Richard Miller; Randy Fraser.
Office: 1502 Shirley Rd., 59601. Tel: 406-458-6114; Fax: 406-458-8179.
Missions—Wolf Creek, Lewis and Clark Co., Sacred Heart; Marysville, Lewis and Clark Co., Our Lady of Lourdes.

OUTSIDE THE CITY OF HELENA

Anaconda, Deer Lodge Co.,

1—ANACONDA CATHOLIC COMMUNITY, (1980). Serves the entire community of Anaconda. Revs. John E. Murray; Daniel Driscoll. Pastoral Assocs.: Sr. Eileen Johnson, S.C.L.; Sr. Constance Howe, R.S.M.; Mr. John McKenna, Admin.
Office: 217 W. Pennsylvania, 59711. Tel: 406-563-8406; Fax: 406-563-5912.
Res., 405 Alder St., 59711. Tel: 406-563-6633.
Churches—Holy Family, 217 W. Pennsylvania, 58711.; St. Peter, 401 Alder St., 59711.
Station—Anaconda, Georgetown Lake.

2—ST. JOSEPH'S, (1957). Closed 1977. For inquiries for parish records contact Anaconda Catholic Community, Anaconda.

3—ST. PAUL'S, (1888). Closed 1980. For inquiries for parish records contact Anaconda Catholic Community, Anaconda.

4—ST. PETER'S, (1898). Closed 1980. For inquiries for parish records contact Anaconda Catholic Community, Anaconda.

Bigfork, Flathead Co., St. Catherine (1958), Rev. Richard H. Sodja; Deacons James Butts, Pastoral Assoc.; Anthony Martin.
Res., P.O. Box 277, 59911. Tel: 406-837-4846; Fax: 406-837-4909.
Church—105 Oliver Ln., 59911.
Mission—Somers, St. Ann.

Bonner, Missoula Co., St. Ann (1940), Rev. Raymond V. Gilmore.
Res., P.O. Box 1008, 59823. Tel: 406-258-6815; Fax: 406-258-2943.
Mission—Seeley Lake, Missoula Co., Living Water Mission, 465 Highland Dr., P.O. Box 995, Seeley Lake, 59868.

Boulder, Jefferson Co., St. Catherine (1894), Rev. William Greytak.
Res., 214 S. Elder St., P.O. Box 205, 59632. Tel: 406-225-3222; Fax: 406-225-9152.
Mission—Boulder Valley, Jefferson Co., St. John the Evangelist.

Bozeman, Gallatin Co., Holy Rosary (1885), Rev. Robert J. Beaulieu. Pastoral Assocs.: Sr. Patricia Toeckes, S.C.L.; Laurie Croghan; Timothy Bell.
Office: 220 W. Main St., P.O. Box 96, 59771-0096. Tel: 406-587-4581; Fax: 406-582-0248.
Resurrection (1965). (Newman Parish). Rev. Robert Hall; Deacon Michael Certalic. Pastoral Assocs.: Marge O'Leary; Diane Dwyer.
Office: 1725 S. 11th, 59715. Tel: 406-586-9243; 406-587-8667 (Res.); Fax: 406-586-2886.

Browning, Glacier Co., Church of the Little Flower (1904), Revs. Edward Kohler; Michael McHugh, S.J.; Sr. Edna Hunthausen, S.C.L., Pastoral Assoc.; Deacons Robert Bremner; John Gobert.
Office: P.O. Box 519, 59417. Tel: 406-338-5775; Fax: 406-338-5506.
Church—204 First St. N.W., 59417.
Missions—Babb, St. Mary, Queen of the World; Starr School, Sacred Heart; East Glacier, Church of the Ascension.

Butte, Silver Bow Co.,

1—BUTTE CATHOLIC COMMUNITY NORTH. Includes Immaculate Conception, St. Joseph, and St. Patrick Parishes. See individual listings. Rev. Msgr. Donald W. Shea; Rev. Kevin Christofferson (GF); Sr. Patricia Field, S.C.L., Pastoral Assoc. In res., Rev. Harry Butori; Deacons Ronald Fournier; Stan Gould.
Office and Res.: 102 S. Washington St., 59701. Tel: 406-723-5407; Fax: 406-782-8082.

2—HOLY SAVIOR, (1904). Closed 1974. For inquiries for parish records contact Butte Catholic Community North, Butte.

3—HOLY SPIRIT, (1978), Sr. Sharon Smith, S.C.L., Pastoral Admin.; Deacon Dan McGrath.
Office: 3930 East Lake, 59701. Tel: 406-494-5078; Fax: 406-494-5726.

4—IMMACULATE CONCEPTION, (1907). (Butte Catholic Community North). Rev. Msgr. Donald W. Shea; Rev. Kevin Christofferson (GF).
Office and Res.: 102 S. Washington, 59701. Tel: 406-723-5407; Fax: 406-782-8082.
Church—Western & Caledonia St., 59701.

5—SACRED HEART PARISH, (1903). Closed 1970. For inquiries for parish records contact Butte Catholic Community North, Butte.

6—ST. ANN, (1917), Rev. Thomas P. Haffey; Sr. Mary Jo McDonald, S.C.L., Pastoral Assoc.; Deacon H. J. Johnson.
Res., 2100 Farragut, 59701. Tel: 406-723-4303; Fax: 406-723-5172.

7—ST. HELENA, (1921). Closed 1966. For inquiries for parish records contact Butte Catholic Community North, Butte.

8—ST. JOHN THE EVANGELIST, (1917), Rev. Edward Courtney. Pastoral Assocs.: John McPherson; Kathy Walter.
Office: 1500 Cobban Ave., 59701.
Res., 2040 Whitman, 59701. Tel: 406-782-8349; Fax: 406-782-1660.
Church—1500 Majors Ave., 59701.

9—ST. JOSEPH, (1905). (Butte Catholic Community North). Rev. Msgr. Donald W. Shea; Rev. Kevin Christofferson (GF).
Office and Res.: 102 S. Washington, 59701. Tel: 406-723-5407 (Office); Fax: 406-782-8082.
Church—Utah & Second St., 59701.

10—ST. MARY, (1903). Closed 1986. For inquiries for parish records contact Butte Catholic Community North, Butte.

11—ST. PATRICK, (1881). (Butte Catholic Community North). Rev. Msgr. Donald W. Shea; Rev. Kevin Christofferson (GF).
Office and Res.: 102 S. Washington St., 59701. Tel: 406-723-5407; Fax: 406-782-8082.
Church—Mercury & Washington St., 59701.

Choteau, Teton Co., St. Joseph (1898), Rev. Robert C. Noonan, Pastor.
Res., P.O. Box 640, 59422. Tel: 406-466-2961; Fax: 406-466-5157.
Church—320 Main St., 59422.

Columbia Falls, Flathead Co., St. Richard (1941), Rev. Joseph P. Moran; Deacon Robert Pearce.
Res., P.O. Box 2073, 59912. Tel: 406-892-5142; Fax: 406-892-2147.
Church—1210 Ninth St. W., 59912.
Mission—West Glacier, Flathead Co.
Station—Columbia Falls, Apgar.

Conrad, Pondera Co., St. Michael (1909), Rev. Leo Proxell.
Res., 106 S. Maryland St., 59425. Tel: 406-278-7517; Fax: 406-278-9106.
Station—Conrad, Stations Brady Ledger.

Cut Bank, Glacier Co., St. Margaret (1914), Rev. Stanley Popowski; Kathy Campbell, Pastoral Assoc.; Deacon James E. Hayes.
Res., 207 Second St., S.E., 59427. Tel: 406-873-4413; Fax: 406-873-9256.

Deer Lodge, Powell Co., Immaculate Conception (1911), Rev. Patrick McGurk.
Res., 605 Clark St., P.O. Box 786, 59722. Tel: 406-846-1444; Fax: 406-846-1444.
Mission—Avon, Powell Co., St. Theodore.

Dillon, Beaverhead Co., St. Rose of Lima (1901), Rev. Robert G. Porter (SFD); Cecilia Tarleton, Pastoral Assoc.
Office: 226 S. Atlantic St., 59725. Tel: 406-683-4391; 683-6753 (Rectory); Fax: 406-683-4391.
Missions—Melrose, Silver Bow Co., St. John The Apostle; Wisdom, Beaverhead Co., Our Lady of Wisdom.

Drummond, Granite Co., St. Michael (1919), Rev. Herbert J. Pins (Seattle).
Res., P.O. Box 329, 59832. Tel: 406-288-3847; Fax: 406-288-3847.
Mission—Goldcreek, Powell Co., St. Mary.

Dutton, Teton Co., St. William (1962), Rev. Leo Proxell, Sacramental Min.; Sr. Johanna Rickl, C.H.M., Pastoral Admin.
Res., 107-1st Ave. N.E., 59433. Tel: 406-476-3429; Fax: 406-476-3392.
Mission—Power, Guardian Angel.

East Helena, Lewis and Clark Co., SS. Cyril and Methodius (1907), Rev. Thomas M. O'Donnell; Deacon Gerald Kuhl.
Res., 214 W. Riggs St., P.O. Box 1110, 59635. Tel: 406-227-5334; Fax: 406-227-5891.
Missions—Canyon Ferry, Our Lady of the Lake; Clancy, St. John's.
Station—East Helena, Alhambra.

Eureka, Lincoln Co., Our Lady of Mercy (1916), Rev. Henry Steinhoff (B); Deacon Dan Casazza, Pastoral Admin.
Res., 500 Dewey Ave., P.O. Box 626, 59917. Tel: 406-296-2118; Fax: 406-296-5247.

Fairfield, Teton Co., St. John (1941), Rev. Robert C. Noonan.
Res., 514 First Ave. S., P.O. Box 397, 59436. Tel: 406-467-2481.
Mission—Augusta, Lewis and Clark Co., St. Matthias.

Frenchtown, Missoula Co., St. John the Baptist (1884), Rev. Dougald J. McCallum; Deacon Van Wolverton.
Res., P.O. Box 329, 59834. Tel: 406-626-4492; Fax: 406-626-1970. [CEM]
Missions—Superior, St. Mary Queen of Heaven; Alberton, Mineral Co., St. Albert the Great.

Hamilton, Ravalli Co., St. Francis (1896), Rev. John J. Darragh; Sr. Margaret Hogan, S.C.L., Pastoral Assoc.; Deacon Roland Peterson.
Res., 411 S. Fifth St., 59840. Tel: 406-363-1385; Fax: 406-375-0967.
Mission—Darby, Ravalli Co., St. Philip Benizi.

Harlowton, Wheatland Co., St. Joseph (1909), Rev. Michael P. Poole, Admin.
Res., 26 Third St., N.W., Box 286, 59036. Tel: 406-632-5538; Fax: 406-632-4897.
Missions—Judith Gap, Wheatland Co., Immaculate Conception; Shawmut, Wheatland Co., Blessed Sacrament.

Heart Butte, Glacier Co., St. Anne (1911), Rev. Daniel Powers, S.J. Pastoral Assocs.: Bev Bullshoe; Deacon Melvin Rutherford.
Res., Blackfeet Reservation, P.O. Box 160, 59448. Tel: 406-338-2312; Fax: 406-338-2362.
Mission—Heart Butte, Glacier Co., Holy Family Mission. [CEM]

Helmville, Powell Co., St. Thomas (1889), Rev. Kevin Ryan, O.S.B.; Kathy Daniels, Pastoral Assoc.
Res., P.O. Box 90, 59843. Tel: 406-793-5697; Fax: 406-793-5697. [CEM]
Mission—Lincoln, Lewis and Clark Co., St. Jude's.

Kalispell, Flathead Co., St. Matthew (1895), Rev. Victor E. Langhans; Deacon Fred Topp, Pastoral Assoc.
Office: 602 S. Main St., 59901. Tel: 406-752-6788; Fax: 406-756-8248.
Res., 644 First Ave. W., 59901. Tel: 406-755-1357.
Risen Christ (1978), Rev. James Connor.
Res., 65 W. Evergreen Dr., 59901. Tel: 406-752-4219; Fax: 406-752-4226.

Libby, Lincoln Co., St. Joseph (1911), Rev. Raymond J. Hannigan; Deacons Andy Dorrington; David Weisbeck.
Res., 719 Utah Ave., P.O. Box 1467, 59923. Tel: 406-293-4322; Fax: 406-293-7231.
Mission—Troy, Immaculate Conception.

Madison, Madison Co., Madison County Catholic Community. Comprised of St. Mary of the Assumption, Laurin; St. Joseph, Sheridan; and St. Patrick, Ennis. Rev. Edward L. Stupca. Pastoral Assocs.: Laurie Bartoletti; Kathy Miller; Roberta McKay.
Res., 105 Poppleton, P.O. Box 17, Sheridan, 59749. Tel: 406-842-5588; Fax: 406-842-7433.

Missoula, Missoula Co.,

1—Christ the King, (1966). (Newman Parish). Rev. James J. Hogan; Dianne Peterson, Campus Min.; Sue Monroe, Parish Admin.
Office: 1400 Gerald Ave., 59801. Tel: 406-728-3845; Fax: 406-829-8797.

2—Holy Family, (1972), Rev. Matthew Huber; Deacon Thomas McCarthy. Pastoral Assocs.: Sr. Ursula Keough, C.H.M; Sr. Kathleen O'Sullivan, B.V.M.
Res., 4616 Gharrett St., 59803. Tel: 406-251-2692; Fax: 406-251-0324.
Mission—Lolo, Missoula Co., Spirit of Christ, 4200 Farm Ln., P.O. Box 743, Lolo, 59847. Tel: 406-273-2748.

3—Pope John XXIII, (1971), Rev. Frank McCormick. Pastoral Assocs.: Beckie Hasse; Chris Kappes.
Office: 1475 Eaton St., 59801. Tel: 406-721-2405; Fax: 406-721-0025.

4—St. Anthony, (1921), Rev. John P. Miller. Pastoral Assocs.: Terry Jimmerson; Linda McKnight; Maggie Hammond.
Office: 217 Tremont St., 59801. Tel: 406-543-3129; Fax: 406-549-6009.

5—St. Francis Xavier, (1881), Revs. Kevin T. Clarke, S.J.; James Meehan, S.J.; Deacons Michael Bloomdahl; Carlton Quamme. In res., Revs. Roger E. Blanchette, S.J.; John S. Harrington, S.J.; Thomas F. Healy, S.J.
Office: 420 W. Pine St., 59802. Tel: 406-542-0321; Fax: 406-327-8537.

Philipsburg, Granite Co., St. Philip (1892), Rev. Herbert J. Pins (Seattle).
Res., 307 W. Kearney, P.O. Box 397, 59858. Tel: 406-859-3908; Fax: 406-859-3960.

Plains, Sanders Co., St. James (1889), Rev. Kenneth E. Fortney; Deacon Lynn F. McAtee.
Res., 107 Meany St., P.O. Box 745, 59859. Tel: 406-826-3668; Fax: 406-826-0029.
Mission—Hot Springs, Sacred Heart.

Polson, Lake Co., Immaculate Conception (1909), Rev. Gary W. Reller; Deacons Wesley Vert; Daniel Gullotta.
Res., 908 Fifth Ave. E., P.O. Box 1477, 59860. Tel: 406-883-4607; 883-2506 (Office); Fax: 406-883-4607. [CEM 3]
Church—1002 Fourth Ave. E., 59860.

Ronan, Lake Co., Sacred Heart (1911), Rev. Gary W. Keller; Sr. Barbara Bell, O.P., Pastoral Admin.
Res., 325 Round Butte W., 59864. Tel: 406-676-4511; Fax: 406-676-4515.
Mission—Charlo, Mount Lake Co., St. Joseph's.

St. Ignatius, Lake Co., St. Ignatius Mission (1854), Rev. Gustav H. Schmidt, S.J. Pastoral Assocs.: Sr. Dolores Shortal, O.P.; Sr. Joan Bartin, O.P.
Res., #1 Church St., P.O. Box 667, 59865. Tel: 406-745-2768; Fax: 406-745-0010.
Missions—Arlee, Lake Co., Sacred Heart, 434 HI Francis, Arlee, 59821. Tel: 406-726-3450; Fax: 406-726-0012; Jocko, Lake Co., St. John Berchman's.

Shelby, Toole Co., St. William (1924), Rev. William F. Vernon.
Res., 531 Main St., 59474. Tel: 406-434-2988; Fax: 406-434-9133.
Mission—Sunburst, St. Thomas Aquinas, (1917).

Stevensville, Ravalli Co., St. Mary (1842), Rev. Michael M. Smith.
Res., 333 Charlos St., 59870. Tel: 406-777-5574; Fax: 406-777-1032. [CEM]
Mission—Florence, Ravalli Co., St. Joseph.

Swan Valley, Lake Co., Swan Valley Catholic Community, Rev. Dusan A. Okorn, Admin.; Michelle Jenkins, Pastoral Assoc.
Res., The Sycamore Tree, Swan Lake, 59911. Tel: 406-754-2429; Fax: 406-754-2429.

Thompson Falls, Sanders Co., St. William (1955), Rev. Kenneth E. Fortney; Deacon Ronald Kazmierezak.
Res., 416 Preston Ave., P.O. Box 186, 59873. Tel: 406-827-4433; Fax: 406-827-4422.
Mission—Noxon.

Three Forks, Gallatin Co., Holy Family (1886), Rev. John F. Ward; Deacon Robert Lane.
Res., 104 Birch St., P.O. Box 99, 59752. Tel: 406-285-3592; Fax: 406-285-0838.
Mission—Belgrade, Valley of Flowers, 609 Quaw Blvd., Belgrade, 59714.

Townsend, Broadwater Co., Holy Cross (1903), Rev. Joseph L. Byrne; Deacon Donald Marks.
Res., 101 S. Walnut, P.O. Box 610, 59644. Tel: 406-266-4811; Fax: 406-266-4811.
Mission—Toston, Broadwater Co., Immaculate Conception.
St. Joseph's Historical Church—Canton.

Valier, Pondera Co., St. Francis (1909), Rev. Stanley Popowski; Mary Jean Brophy, Pastoral Assoc.
Res., 701-4th St., P.O. Box 338, 59486. Tel: 406-279-3327.
Mission—Dupuyer, Pondera Co., Holy Cross.

Walkerville, Silver Bow Co., St. Lawrence O'Toole (1896). Closed 1986. For inquiries for parish records contact Butte Catholic Community North, Butte.

West Yellowstone, Gallatin Co., Our Lady of the Pines, Rev. Joseph B. Oblinger, (Retired); Sr. Anne Marie Burke, S.C.L., Pastoral Admin.
Res., Madison Ave. & Geyser St., P.O. Box 577, 59758. Tel: 406-646-7755; Fax: 406-646-4590.
Mission—Big Sky.

Whitefish, Flathead Co., St. Charles (1890), Rev. Charles Roman.
Res., 230 Baker, P.O. Box 128, 59937. Tel: 406-862-2051; Fax: 406-862-9897.

Whitehall, Jefferson Co., St. Teresa (1911), Revs. Francis J. Wiegenstein; Joseph Finnegan; Charlene Dillon, Parish Coord.
Res., 109 Second Ave. E., P.O. Box 430, 59759. Tel: 406-287-3893; Fax: 406-287-9213.
Mission—Twin Bridges, Jefferson Co., Notre Dame.

White Sulphur Springs, Meagher Co., St. Bartholomew (1916), Rev. Michael P. Poole, Admin.
Res., 407 Second Ave. S.E., P.O. Box 422, 59645. Tel: 406-547-3737; Fax: 406-547-2581.

DIOCESAN MISSIONS

Guatemala, Santo Tomas La Union,
10017 Departmento Suchitepequez. Rev. James Hazelton; Sr. Mary Waddell, B.V.M., Clinic Dir.; Sr. Anna Priester, B.V.M., D.R.E.

Helena, Guatemala Mission Medical Fund,
Supplies for needs of mission personnel, medicines, medical supplies, and health care needs to people in the mission area in Guatemala. Donations may be forwarded to the Fund at P.O. Box 1729, Helena, MT 59624.

Chaplains of Public Institutions

Helena. *U.S. Veteran's Hospital.* Served by Helena Area Parishes. Fort Harrison.

Boulder. *Boulder River School and Hospital.* Attended from St. Catherine, Boulder. Rev. William Greytak.

Deer Lodge. *Montana State Prison.* Rev. Herbert J. Pins (SEA).

Warm Springs. *Warm Springs State Hospital.* Rev. Herbert J. Pins (SEA).

Special Assignments:
Reverend Fathers—
Dornbos, William, Diocesan Chancery, Mailing Address: P.O. Box 1729, Helena, MT 59624
Dumais, George J., S.J., Dir., Rochmont, Inc., 1700 Madeline, Missoula, MT 59801
Finnegan, Joseph, Mailing Address: P.O. Box 503, Whitehall, MT 59759
Malnar, Stan, 4220 W. Fremont Rd., Spokane, WA 99204
Robertson, John W., Judicial Vicar, Vicar for Canonical Concerns & Vicar for Catholic Schools, Mailing Address: P.O. Box 1729, Helena, MT 59624

On Duty Outside the Diocese:
Reverend Monsignors—
McCarthy, John F., P.A., Oblates of Wisdom, P.O. Box 8027, Ponce, Puerto Rico 00732
Reverend Fathers—
Driscoll, Michael, Notre Dame University, Department of Theology, Notre Dame, IN 46556
Flynn, Thomas, Emory University, 1278 Oakdale Rd., N.E., Atlanta, GA 30307
Hazelton, James, Santo Tomas La Union, Departmento Suchitepequez, Guatemala 10017
Sullivan, James M., Creighton University, 2500 California St., Omaha, NE 68178

On Leave of Absence:
Reverend Fathers—
McCarthy, James C.

Military Chaplains:
Reverend Fathers—
Diphe, Juan, U.S. Air Force
Hightower, O. Lee., U.S. Army
Patton, Patrick G., U.S. Army

Retired:
Reverend Monsignors—
Brown, Anthony M., 30 Penny Ln., Butte, MT 59701
Harrington, Joseph D., Carroll College, Helena, MT 59625
Mavsar, Joseph, P.A., P.O. Box 1167, East Helena, MT 59635
Reverend Fathers—
Burke, Gregory, 105 Rampart Dr., #215, Butte, MT 59701
Burns, Ernest, 100 E. Broadway #601, Butte, MT 59701
Butori, Harry, 102 S. Washington St., Butte, MT 59701
Fenlon, Thomas J., 100 E. Broadway, Butte, MT 59701
Hunthausen, John F., Carroll College, Helena, MT 59625
Kelly, Emmett, 4309 Gharrett, Missoula, MT 59803
Kirsch, John B., P.O. Box 893, Sheridon, MT 59749
Koenig, Bernard, P.O. Box 765, Ronan, MT 59864
Lynam, Gerald J., 915 Saddle Dr., #115, Helena, MT 59625
McCarthy, Bernard, 202 Waterford Way, Butte, MT 59701
O'Sullivan, Sarsfield, 410 N. Western Ave., Butte, MT 59701
Oblinger, Joseph B., 2400 Durston Rd., #37, Bozeman, MT 59715
Okorn, Dusan A., Sycamore Tree, Swan Lake, MT 59701
Plummer, J. Bruce, 261 Half Circle Way, Polson, MT 59860
Simons, Lawrence D., P.O. Box 696, Honaunau, HI 96726
Strom, Charles W., 341 Lupfer Ave., Whitefish, MT 59937
Sullivan, J. Bernard, 915 Saddle Dr., #309, Helena, MT 59601
Tallman, Stephen, 5630 Lower Woodchuck Rd., Florence, MT 59833
Vadakkekudy, Jacob (India), P.O. Box 1181, La Junta, CO 81050
Waggenor, William L., 2828 Saratoga Tr., Billings, MT 59105
Wang, John, 425 Ford St., Missoula, MT 59801

Permanent Deacons:
Bloomdahl, Michael, St. Francis Xavier, Missoula
Bremner, Robert, Sr., Little Flower, Browning
Britton, Michael, (Retired)
Butts, James, St. Catherine, Bigfork
Certalic, Michael, Resurrection, Bozeman
Cline, Donald, St. Anthony, Missoula
Curry, James, (Retired)
Dorrington, Andy, St. Joseph, Libby
Duvernay, J. Anthony, Dir. Diocesan Pastoral Office, St. Helena Cathedral
Fournier, Ronald, Catholic Community North, Butte
Fraser, Randall, Our Lady of the Valley, Helena
Gobert, John, Little Flower, Browning
Gould, Stanley F., St. Patrick, Butte
Gullotto, Daniel, Immaculate Conception, Polson
Hayes, James E., St. Margaret, Cut Bank
Johnson, H. J., St. Ann's, Butte
Kazmierczak, Ronald, St. William, Thompson Falls
Kelley, Robert, (Leave Of Absence)
Kuhl, Gerald, Sts. Cyril and Methodius, East Helena
Lane, Robert, Holy Family, Three Forks
Marks, Donald, Holy Cross, Townsend
Martin, Anthony, St. Catherine, Bigfork
McAtee, Lynn F., St. James, Plains
McCarthy, Thomas, Holy Family, Missoula
McGrath, Daniel, Holy Spirit, Butte; Diocesan Youth Minister
Miller, Richard, Our Lady of the Valley, Helena
Pearce, Robert, St. Richard, Columbia Falls
Peterson, Roland, St. Francis Parish, Hamilton
Quamme, Carlton, St. Francis, Missoula
Roos, Fritz, Cathedral of St. Helena, Helena
Rutherford, Melvin, (On Duty Outside the Diocese)
Topp, Frederick, St. Matthew, Kalispell
Vert, Wesley, Immaculate Conception, Polson
Weisbeck, David, St. Joseph, Libby
Wolverton, Van, St. John the Baptist, Frenchtown

INSTITUTIONS LOCATED IN THE DIOCESE

[A] SEMINARIES, DIOCESAN

HELENA. *Carroll College*, 1601 N. Benton Ave., 59625. Rev. William Greytak, Dir. Diocesan Pre-Seminary Program. Students 3.

[B] COLLEGES AND UNIVERSITIES

HELENA. *Carroll College*, (1909) 1601 N. Benton Ave., 59625. Tel: 406-447-4300; Fax: 406-447-4533
For a complete listing, refer to the Colleges and Universities section.

[C] HIGH SCHOOLS, DIOCESAN

BUTTE. *Central High School*, 9 S. Idaho St., 59701. Tel: 406-782-6761; Fax: 406-723-3873.
E-mail: joellen39@yahoo.com
JoEllen Estenson, Prin. Priests 1; Lay Teachers 18; Students 187.

MISSOULA. *Loyola Sacred Heart High School*. (Missoula Catholic Schools), 320 Edith St., 59801. Tel: 406-549-6101; Fax: 406-542-1432.
E-mail: lsh@montana.com
Web site: www.montana.com/loyola/index,html/loyola.htm
Patrick Haggarty, Prin. & Pres. of the Missoula Catholic Schools; Sheldon Hanser, Dean. Priests 1; Lay Teachers 26; Students 231.

[D] SCHOOLS, ELEMENTARY

BUTTE. *Central Elementary School*. (Grades PreK-5), 1100 Delaware, 59701. Tel: 406-782-4500; Fax: 406-723-4845.
E-mail: bcelem@in-tch.com
Sr. Mary Jane Schmitz, S.C.L., Prin. Sisters 3; Lay Teachers 15; Students 265.
After School Care. Tel: 406-782-4500; Fax: 406-723-4845. Mary Carol Hagart, Dir. Students (Ages 5-12) 25.

Central Junior High School. (Grades 6-8), 400 W. Park, 59701. Tel: 406-782-1233; Fax: 406-723-4645.
E-mail: bcjhs@in-tch.com
JoEllen Estenson, Prin.; Rene Knapp, Building Supvr. Lay Teachers 10; Students 98.

KALISPELL. *St. Matthew School*, 602 S. Main St., 59901. Tel: 406-752-6303; Fax: 406-756-8248. Eugene Boyle, Prin. Sisters 2; Lay Teachers 16; Students 223.
Day Care Center. (Ages 2-6). Tel: 406-752-6303; Fax: 406-756-8248. Ginger Jay, Dir. Students 60.

MISSOULA. *St. Joseph Elementary School*. (Missoula Catholic Schools), 503 Edith St., 59801. Tel: 406-549-1290; Fax: 406-543-4034.
Web site: www.montana.com/stjoe
Scott Anderson, Prin. Lay Teachers 15; Students 303.
Child Care Center. (Ages 2-12). Tel: 406-549-1290; Fax: 406-543-4034. Evalie Hankinson, Dir.

[E] GENERAL HOSPITALS

BUTTE. *St. James Healthcare, Sisters of Charity of Leavenworth Healthcare Corporation*, 400 S. Clark St., 59701. Tel: 406-723-2500; Fax: 406-723-2443.
Web site: www.sj-mt.org
For a complete listing, refer to the Hospitals section.

MISSOULA. *St. Patrick Hospital and Health Sciences Center, Sisters of Providence of Montana Corporation*, 500 W. Broadway, 59802. Tel: 406-543-7271; Fax: 406-329-5693.
E-mail: white@saintpatrick.org
Web site: www.saintpatrick.org
For a complete listing, refer to the Hospitals section.

POLSON. *St. Joseph Hospital Corporation*, #6 Thirteenth Ave. E., P.O. Box 1010, 59860. Tel: 406-883-5377; Fax: 406-883-8488.
Web site: saintjoes.org
For a complete listing, refer to the Hospitals section.

[F] CONVENTS AND RESIDENCES OF SISTERS

COLUMBIA FALLS. *Epiphany Monastery*, P.O. Box 8177, 59912. Tel: 406-892-4670. Monastery dependent upon St. Martin Monastery, Rapid City, SD. Sisters 2.

[G] HOUSES OF PRAYER

SWAN LAKE. *The Sycamore Tree Contemplative Prayer Center*, 59911. Tel: 406-754-2429. Rev. Dusan A. Okorn, Dir.; Michelle Jenkins, Asst.

[H] NEWMAN CHAPLAINS

BOZEMAN. *Montana State University*. (Resurrection Parish), Office: 1725 S. Eleventh, 59715-4218. Tel: 406-586-9243; Fax: 406-586-2886. Rev. Robert Hall; Deacon Michael Certalic, Campus Min.

BUTTE. *Montana College of Mineral Science and Technology*, Office: 102 S. Washington St., 59701. Tel: 406-723-5407; Fax: 406-723-8082. Rev. Msgr. Donald Shea; Deacon Ronald Fournier, Campus Min.

DILLON. *Western Montana College*, 226 S. Atlantic St., 59725. Tel: 406-683-4391. Rev. Robert G. Porter.

MISSOULA. *University of Montana*. (Christ the King Parish), 1400 Gerald Ave., 59801-4230. Tel: 406-728-3845; Fax: 406-829-8797. Rev. James J. Hogan; Diane Peterson, Campus Min.

[I] MISCELLANEOUS

HELENA. *The St. Helena Cathedral Foundation, Inc.*, 530 N. Ewing St., 59601-4001. Tel: 406-442-5825; Fax: 406-449-5113. Marty Heller, Pres.

BUTTE. *Central Education Foundation*, P.O. Box 634, 59703-0634. Tel: 406-723-6706; Fax: 406-723-3873. Don Peoples, Jr., Exec. Dir.

Maternal Life International, 434 N. Main St, 59701-8804. Tel: 406-782-1719.
E-mail: usacares@in-tch.com
Web site: Maternallifeintl.com
Dr. George Mulcaire-Jones, Medical Dir. & Board Pres.

St. Vincent de Paul Thrift Store, 123 E. Park St., 59701. Tel: 406-782-0233. Wayne Thomas, Mgr.

MISSOULA. *Loyola-Sacred Heart High School Foundation*, 300 Edith St., 59801-3916. Tel: 406-728-2367; 728-2353; Fax: 406-542-9900.
E-mail: lshftjf@montana.com
Julia Jones, Pres.; Tim Furey, Exec. Dir.

STEVENSVILLE. *Historic St. Mary's Mission*, P.O. Box 211, 59870-0211. Tel: 406-777-5734.

RELIGIOUS INSTITUTES OF MEN REPRESENTED IN THE DIOCESE

For further details refer to the corresponding bracketed number in the Religious Institutes of Men or Women sections.

[0200]—*Benedictine Monks (Swiss-American Congregation, St. Meinrad Archabbey)*.—O.S.B.

[0330]—*Brothers of the Christian Schools*. (Midwest Prov.).—F.S.C.

[0690]—*Jesuit Fathers and Brothers*. (Oregon Prov.).—S.J.

RELIGIOUS INSTITUTES OF WOMEN REPRESENTED IN THE DIOCESE

[0230]—*Benedictine Sisters of Pontifical Jurisdiction*. (Rapid City).—O.S.B.

[2100]—*Congregation of the Humility of Mary*.—C.H.M.

[1070-03]—*Dominican Sisters*.—O.P.

[1070-11]—*Dominican Sisters*.—O.P.

[1070-13]—*Dominican Sisters*.—O.P.

[2575]—*Institute of the Sisters of Mercy of the Americas*. (Cedar Rapids, IA).—R.S.M.

[0440]—*Sisters of Charity of Cincinnati, Ohio*.—S.C.

[0480]—*Sisters of Charity of Leavenworth, Kansas*.—S.C.L.

[0430]—*Sisters of Charity of the Blessed Virgin Mary*.—B.V.M.

[3350]—*Sisters of Providence*. (Mother Joseph Prov.).—S.P.

[3840]—*Sisters of St. Joseph of Carondelet*.—C.S.J.

[3960]—*Sisters of St. Mary of Oregon*.—S.S.M.O.

[1720]—*Sisters of the Third Order Regular of St. Francis of the Congregation of Our Lady of Lourdes*.—O.S.F.

DIOCESAN CEMETERIES

HELENA. *Resurrection*, 3700 N. Montana Ave., P.O. Box 5029, 59604. Tel: 406-442-1782; Fax: 406-443-7036. Scott Fitzpatrick, Dir. Cemeteries; Laura Disney, Office Mgr.

Resurrection Cemetery Association. (Corporate Name for Diocesan Cemeteries), 3700 N. Montana Ave., P.O. Box 5029, 59604. Tel: 406-442-1782; Fax: 406-443-7036. Mr. Scott Fitzpatrick, Exec. Dir.; Laura Disney, Office Mgr.

BUTTE. *Holy Cross*, Office: 4700 Harrison Ave., 59701. Tel: 406-494-3812.

St. Patrick, Office: 4700 Harrison Ave., 59701. Tel: 406-494-3812.

MISSOULA. *St. Mary*, Office: 641 Turner St., 59802. Tel: 406-543-7951.

NECROLOGY

† Courtney, Humphrey, (Retired). —Died Nov. 22, 1999.

† Provost, James H., Washington, D.C. The Catholic University of America. —Died Aug. 26, 2000.

Diocese of Honolulu

(Dioecesis Honoluluensis)

Most Reverend

FRANCIS X. DILORENZO, D.D., S.T.D.

Bishop of Honolulu; ordained May 18, 1968; appointed Titular Bishop of Tigia and Auxiliary Bishop of Scranton January 26, 1988; consecrated March 8, 1988; appointed Apostolic Administrator October 12, 1993; succeeded to See November 29, 1994. *Mailing Address: Chancery Office, 1184 Bishop St., Honolulu, HI, 96813; Fax: 808-537-1860.*

Chancery Office: 1184 Bishop St., Honolulu, HI, 96813. Tel.: 808-533-1791; Fax: 808-521-8428.

Web site address: www.pono.net

E-mail address: bishop@pono.net

Most Reverend

JOSEPH A. FERRARIO, D.D.

Retired Bishop of Honolulu; ordained May 19, 1951; appointed Titular Bishop of Cuse and Auxiliary November 8, 1977; ordained Bishop January 13, 1978; succeeded to See June 25, 1982; retired October 12, 1993. *Mailing Address: Catholic Chancery Office, 1184 Bishop St., Honolulu, HI, 96813-2858.*

Corporate Title: *The Roman Catholic Church In The State Of Hawaii.*

Comprises all of the Hawaiian Islands.

The Hawaiian Islands were annexed as a Territory of the United States in 1898. Hawaii became the 50th State of the Union on August 21, 1959.

Square Miles 6,435.

In 1826, a Prefecture-Apostolic was erected for the Hawaiian Islands, then called Sandwich Islands, and entrusted to the Fathers of the Sacred Hearts of Jesus and Mary (Picpus). The Very Rev. Alexis Bachelot, SS.CC., was the first Prefect-Apostolic. He arrived with his companions at Honolulu on the 7th of July, 1827. In 1844, the Islands were erected a Vicariate. Diocese erected Sept. 10, 1941.

For legal titles of parishes and diocesan institutions, consult the Chancery Office.

STATISTICAL OVERVIEW

Personnel	
Bishop	1
Retired Bishops	1
Priests: Diocesan Active in Diocese	36
Priests: Active Outside Diocese	15
Priests: Retired, Sick or Absent	19
Number of Diocesan Priests	70
Religious Priests in Diocese	72
Permanent Deacons in Diocese	32
Total Brothers	54
Total Sisters	155
Parishes	
Parishes	66
With Resident Pastor:	
Resident Diocesan Priests	34
Resident Religious Priests	28
Without Resident Pastor:	
Administered by Priests	3
Administered by Deacons	1
Missions	24
Professional Ministry Personnel:	
Brothers	2
Sisters	22
Lay Ministers	37
Welfare	
Catholic Hospitals	2
Total Assisted	365,373
Health Care Centers	15
Total Assisted	35,136
Homes for the Aged	1
Total Assisted	49
Day Care and Extended Day Care Centers	1
Total Assisted	105
Specialized Homes	1
Total Assisted	71
Special Centers for Social Services	13
Total Assisted	12,016
Other Institutions	30
Total Assisted	16,046
Educational	
Seminaries, Religious	1
Students Religious	1
Total Seminarians	1
Colleges and Universities	1
Total Students	2,812
High Schools, Diocesan and Parish	3
Total Students	1,173
High Schools, Private	5
Total Students	2,406
Elementary Schools, Diocesan and Parish	32
Total Students	7,386
Elementary Schools, Private	3
Total Students	406
Catechesis/Religious Education:	
High School Students	2,223
Elementary Students	8,034
Total Students Under Catholic Instruction	24,441
Teachers in the Diocese:	
Priests	59
Brothers	8
Sisters	83
Lay Teachers	817
Vital Statistics	
Receptions into the Church:	
Infant Baptism Totals	2,502
Adult Baptism Totals	302
Received into Full Communion	226
First Communions	1,970
Confirmations	1,052
Marriages:	
Catholic	263
Interfaith	491
Total Marriages	754
Deaths	1,447
Total Catholic Population	124,987
Total Population	1,185,497

Former Prelates—Very Rev. Alexis Bachelot, SS.CC., Pref. Apost. died Dec. 5, 1837.—Very Rev. Louis Maigret, SS.CC., Pref. Apost. till 1844.—Rt. Rev. Vincent Ferrier Duboize, SS.CC., resigned before he was consecrated.—Rt. Rev. Louis Maigret, SS.CC., Titular Bishop of Arathia; cons. at Santiago, Oct. 31, 1847; died June 11, 1882.—Rt. Rev. Herman Koeckemann, SS.CC., Titular Bishop of Olba; cons. at San Francisco Aug. 21, 1881; died Feb. 18, 1892.—Rt. Rev. Gulstan Ropert, SS.CC., Titular Bishop of Panopolis; cons. at San Francisco, Sept. 25, 1892; died Jan. 3, 1903.—Rt. Rev. Libert H. Boeynaems, SS.CC., Titular Bishop of Zeugma; cons. at San Francisco, July 25, 1903; died May 13, 1926.—Most Rev. Stephen P. Alencastre, SS.CC., Titular Bishop of Arabissus; cons. at Los Angeles, Aug. 24, 1924; died Nov. 9, 1940.—Most Rev. James J. Sweeney, D.D., ord. June 20, 1925; appt. May 20, 1941; cons. at San Francisco, July 25, 1941; died June 19, 1968.—Most Rev. John J. Scanlan, D.D., Retired Bishop of Honolulu; ord. June 22, 1930; succeeded to see March 6, 1968; retired June 30, 1981; died Jan. 31, 1997.—Most Rev. Joseph A. Ferrario, D.D., Retired Bishop of Honolulu; ord. May 19, 1951; succeeded to see June 25, 1982; retired Oct. 12, 1993.

Vicar General—Very Revs. Joseph A. Grimaldi, J.C.L.; Thomas L. Gross.

Moderator of the Curia—Vacant.

Chancery Office—1184 Bishop St., Honolulu, 96813-2858. Tel: 808-533-1791; Fax: 808-521-8428; 585-3382 (Chancellor's Office). Office Hours: Mon.-Fri. 8-4.

Chancellor—John N. Ringrose, J.C.L.

Vice-Chancellor—Very Rev. Joseph A. Grimaldi, J.C.L.

Tribunal—1184 Bishop St., Honolulu, 96813-2858. Tel: 808-533-1791; Fax: 808-585-3382. Office Hours: Mon.-Fri 8-4.

Judicial Vicar—Very Rev. Joseph A. Grimaldi, J.C.L.

Promoter of Justice—Rev. Robert Maher, O.F.M.Cap.

Defender of the Bond—Revs. Arnold L. Dagcuta, J.C.L.; William O'Connell, S.M.

Defender of the Bond Ad Hoc—Sr. Grace Dorothy Lim, M.M., J.C.L.

Judges—Very Rev. Joseph A. Grimaldi, J.C.L.; Revs. Matthew Lochs, SS.CC., S.T.L.; Robert Maher, O.F.M.Cap.; John N. Ringrose, J.C.L.

Notaries and Secretaries—Nettie Lou Peiler; Kathy Sniffen.

Diocesan Theologian—Rev. Marc Alexander, S.T.D.

Diocesan Theological Commission—Rev. Marc R. Alexander, S.T.D. Commission Members: David Coleman, M.A.; Revs. Joseph Grimaldi, M.A.,

J.C.L.; HALBERT WEIDNER, C.O., M.A., D.Phil.; Sr. GRETCHEN GILROY, O.S.F., School Admin. CELESTE O'BRIEN, M.A. Rel. Ed., M.A. Ed. Admin.; Bro. JAMES CHRISTIANA, S.M., M.A., Ph.D.

Master of Ceremonies for Episcopal Functions—Rev. Msgr. TERRENCE WATANABE.

Coordinator of Diocesan Major Events—Rev. Msgr. TERRENCE WATANABE.

Administrative Council—Most Rev. FRANCIS X. DILORENZO, D.D., S.T.D.; Very Revs. JOSEPH A. GRIMALDI, J.C.L.; THOMAS L. GROSS.

Bishop's Administrative Advisory Council—Very Revs. JOSEPH A. GRIMALDI, J.C.L.; THOMAS L. GROSS; Rev. Msgr. TERRENCE WATANABE; Rev. MICHEL DALTON, O.F.M.Cap.; Deacon WALTER YOSHIMITSU; WILLIAM BURTON; PATRICIA S. TOSSEY.

Vicar for Clergy—Rev. GARY SECOR.

Associate Vicar for Clergy—Vacant.

Vocations Director—Rev. GARY SECOR.

Clergy Personnel Board—Rev. GARY SECOR, Chm. Members: Very Revs. JOSEPH A. GRIMALDI, J.C.L.; THOMAS L. GROSS; Revs. CLARENCE L. FISHER; KONELIO FALETOI; ROLAND PACUDAN; Deacon LAUREN WONG.

Permanent Deacon Council—Deacon LAUREN WONG, Chm.

Permanent Deacon Formation—Coordinators: Deacon WILLIAM MCPEEK; FLORENCE MCPEEK.

Priestly Life and Ministry Committee—Revs. GARY SECOR, Chm. MICHAEL CROSBY, O.F.M.

Consulting Pastors—Revs. MICHEL DALTON, O.F.M.Cap.; ETUALE ETUALE.

College of Consultors—Very Revs. JOSEPH A. GRIMALDI, J.C.L.; THOMAS L. GROSS; Revs. JAMES BERRY; MICHAEL DALTON, O.F.M.Cap.; WILLIAM F. MATTIMORE; RAYMOND MALLEY, S.M.; PAUL MCLEOD, SS.CC.; ROBERT SCHWARZHAUPT; HALBERT WEIDNER, C.O.; Rev. Msgr. TERRENCE WATANABE.

Finance Committee—Most Rev. FRANCIS X. DILORENZO, D.D.; Very Rev. JOSEPH A. GRIMALDI, J.C.L.; ALFRED FERNANDES; REGINALD MALDONADO; ROBERT BRUCE GRAHAM, JR.; ROBERT HASTINGS; DAVID HOULE; LETIA QUERY; JAMES SEVERSON; PHYLLIS SHEA; EUGENE TIWANAK; JOHN TOLMIE, SR.; MELVIN VENTURA; LENORA NOBRIGA WEE.

Diocesan Planning and Building Commission—Deacon WALTER YOSHIMITSU, Chm.; Rev. Msgr. TERRENCE WATANABE; Sr. HELENE WOOD, SS.CC.; GARY BATCHELLER; WILLIAM BURTON; Rev. GARY COLTON; MICHAEL DARCY; Rev. SCOTT BUSH; LUKE YASAKA; MARK LIVELY; DANIEL PARKER; ANNE KUSAO; FRANK FELIX, JR.

Vicar for Ethnic Ministries—Sr. GRACE DOROTHY LIM, M.M., J.C.L., Dir.

Chinese Ministry—Rev. ANDREW NG, S.D.B., Coord.

Japanese Ministry—Rev. FRANCIS NAKAGAWA, S.M., Coord.

Filipino Ministry—Sr. GRACE DOROTHY LIM, M.M., Dir.; Rev. Msgr. EDGAR BRILLANTES; Revs. REAN ENRIQUEZ; GAUDELIO DONATO; CALIXTO PABLO; EDGAR SERRANO.

Hispanic Ministry-Oahu—Rev. JAMES MCFADDEN, M.M., Coord.

Hispanic Ministry-Kailua Kona—Rev. JACK RYAN.

Hispanic Ministry-Maui—Rev. BERNARD GATLIN.

Korean Ministry—Rev. JOHN KANG, Coord.

Samoan Ministry—Rev. SEBASTIAN CHACKO, Coord.

Tongan Ministry—Rev. LANE AKIONA, SS.CC., Coord.

Vietnamese Ministry—Rev. VINCENT KIEN NGUYEN, Coord. (Hsin-Chu).

Business Office—1184 Bishop St., Honolulu, 96813-2858. Tel: 808-533-1791; Fax: 808-521-8428. Office Hours: Mon.-Fri. 8-4.

Business Manager—WILLIAM L. BURTON, JR.

Diocesan Offices and Directors

Archivist—JOHN N. RINGROSE, J.C.L.

Censor Liborum—Rev. MARC R. ALEXANDER, S.T.D.

Vicars Forane—Rev. HALBERT WEIDNER, C.O., East Honolulu; Rev. Msgr. TERRENCE WATANABE, West Honolulu; Rev. MICHEL DALTON, O.F.M.Cap., Leeward; Rev. WILLIAM MATTIMORE, Windward; Rev. JAMES BERRY, West Hawaii Island; Rev. ROBERT SCHWARZHAUPT, East Hawaii Island; Rev. PAUL MCLEOD, SS.CC., Kauai; Rev. RAYMOND MALLEY, S.M., Maui, Molokai, Lanai.

Presbyteral Council—Very Revs. JOSEPH A. GRIMALDI, J.C.L.; THOMAS GROSS; Revs. MARC ALEXANDER, S.T.D.; LANE AKIONA, SS.CC.; JAMES BERRY; KONELIO FALETOI; PAUL MCLEOD, SS.CC.; ALAPAKI KIM, C.S.P.; MICHAEL HILL, O.F.M.; DENNIS KOSHKO; RAYMOND MALLEY S.M.; MICHEL DALTON, O.F.M.Cap.; GARY COLTON; GARY SECOR; HALBERT WEIDNER, C.O.; ROBERT SCHWARZHAUPT; WILLIAM F. MATTIMORE; Rev. Msgr. TERRENCE WATANABE.

Diocesan Pastoral Council—CATHERINE WONG, Contact, *78 Kaikaina St., Kailua, 96734.* Tel: 808-381-2057.

Delegate of the Bishop for Religious—Sr. BEATRICE TOM, O.S.F.

Associate Delegate of the Bishop for Religious—Bro. THOMAS SPRING, S.M.

Senior Priests' Committee—Revs. GARY SECOR, Chm. ANTHONY BOLGER; JOSEPH CARROLL; Rev. Msgr. DANIEL DEVER; Revs. CLARENCE L. FISHER; DENNIS KOSHKO; MARVIN SAMIANO; Rev. Msgr. TERRENCE WATANABE; Very Rev. JOSEPH GRIMALDI, J.C.L.; Revs. JAMES BERRY; LOUIS H. YIM; WILLIAM BURTON.

Hawaii Catholic Herald—1184 Bishop St., Honolulu, 96813-2858. Tel: 808-533-1791; Fax: 808-521-8428. Most Rev. FRANCIS X. DILORENZO, Publisher; PATRICK DOWNES, Editor.

Saint Stephen Diocesan Center—6301 Pali Hwy., Kaneohe, 96744-5298. Tel: 808-263-8844; Fax: 808-261-7022. Office Hours: Mon.-Fri, 8-4; Deacon WALTER YOSHIMITSU, Admin.

Religious Education—Ext. 341. Sr. KATHLEEN MARIE SHIELDS, C.S.J., Dir.

Servant Leadership Education Program—Sr. KATHLEEN MARIE SHIELDS, C.S.J., Dir.

Hawaii Catholic Conference—Most Rev. FRANCIS X. DILORENZO; ERROL J. CHRISTIAN, Program Dir. PATRICK DOWNES; JEROME E. RAUCKHORST; ANA ROSAL; Sr. BEATRICE TOM, O.S.F.; Dr. SUE WESSELKAMPER; CARMEN HIMENES.

Hawaii Catholic Schools—Ext. 364. CARMEN HIMENES, Supt. LOUISE WONG, Assoc. Supt.

Office of Development—ROBERT J. STILLWELL, Ed.D., Ext. 323.

Diocesan Development Committee—JOAN BICKSON; R. CHARLES BOCKEN; JOHN BROGAN, Chm.; ROBERT BRUCE GRAHAM, JR.; STANLEY HONG; JON THOMAS HUNTER; WILLIAM BURTON; ROBERT STILLWELL.

Office for the Welcoming Parish—, Ext. 333. SHARON CHIARUCCI, Coord.

Office of Worship—Ext. 328. Sr. HELENE WOOD, SS.CC., Dir.

Diocesan Liturgical Commission—Rev. JOHN BERGER; ROSE BRITO; BARBARA ISODA; ROBERT MONDOY; CORA ROLLINS; LINDA MAGNO; WENDELL APOSTOL; CECIL FARIN; JONILA KIM.

Respect Life Office—Ext. 322. Deacon GEORGE THORP, Dir.

Natural Family Planning—TED BORN; HOLLY BORN; ED CODA; BETTY CODA; WALTER YOSHIMITSU; FRANCES YOSHIMITSU.

Other Diocesan Offices—

Apostleship of the Sea—579-D Keolu Dr., Kailua, 96734. Tel: 808-262-5422. Rev. JOHN G. NEWTON, Chap.

Campaign for Human Development—3300 Ala Laulani St., Honolulu, 96818. Tel: 808-839-1876. Rev. Msgr. TERRENCE WATANABE, Dir.

[*]Catholic Charities—250 S. Vineyard St., Honolulu, 96813-2495. Tel: 808-537-6321; Fax: 808-523-8773. JEROME E. RAUCKHORST, Dir., Ext. 301.

Board of Trustees—Most Rev. FRANCIS X. DILORENZO, D.D., Pres.; Very Rev. JOSEPH A. GRIMALDI, J.C.L.; JEROME RAUCKHORST, Dir. WILLIAM BURTON; WILLIAM POWELL; CLIFF K. CISCO; JAMES WALSH, Chm.

Board of Directors—Most Rev. FRANCIS X. DILORENZO, D.D., Pres. JAMES WALSH, Bd. Chm. DOUGLAS SMITH, Vice Chm. ROBERT TONG, Treas.; Very Rev. JOSEPH A. GRIMALDI, J.C.L.; Revs. JOSEPH BUKOSKI, III, SS.CC.; GARY SECOR; Mr. DAVID BELLO; MARY LOU BROGAN; JEFFREY CASE; CLIFF K. CISCO; Dr. LESLIE CORREA; LISA DOHRN; ROSE DOMONDON; BRANDT FARIAS; WILLIAM BURTON; WILLIAM GILARDY; PATRICK GRIGGS; PAULA HARRIS; ALAN ITO; LYNNE KANESHIRO; Dr. KENT KEITH; Sr. ALICIA DAMEN LAU, O.S.F.; MICHAEL MAGAOAY; LINDA MCKENZIE; SANDRA OHARA; WILLIAM POWELL; CATHY SEKIGUCHI; ROGER WALL; SHARON WEINER.

Catholic Charities Community Services—MORRIS MASUDA, Exec. Dir. Tel: 808-536-5774, Ext. 13.

Catholic Charities Elderly Services—2745 Pali Hwy., Honolulu, 96817. Tel: 808-595-0077; Fax: 808-595-0811. STELLA WONG, Exec. Dir.

Catholic Charities Housing Development Corporation—250 Vineyard St., Honolulu, 96813-2495. Tel: 808-537-6321. JEROME RAUCKHORST, Dir.

Catholic Charities Immigrant Services—Sr. ERNEST CHUNG, M.M., Social Policy Dir., *250 Vineyard St., Honolulu, 96813-2495.* Tel: 808-537-6321, Ext. 326; Fax: 808-523-8773.

Catholic Charities Family Services—200 N. Vineyard Blvd., Ste. 200, Honolulu, 96817. Tel: 808-536-1794; Fax: 808-599-8761. ANA ROSAL, Exec. Dir.

Hospital Ministry—1717 Ala Wai Blvd. #1806, Honolulu, 96815. Tel: 808-941-4979. Revs. PAUL SMITH, Dir. TEODULO GAQUIT.

Prison Ministry—1184 Bishop St., Honolulu, 96813. Tel: 808-533-1791, Ext. 341. Deacon WALTER YOSHIMITSU, Diocesan Representative.

Leadership Association of Religious Congregations—125 Ainoni St., Kailua, 96734. Sr. DOLORES ROSSO, M.M., Coord.

Office for Social Ministry—140 B Holomua St., Hilo, 96720. Tel: 808-935-3050; Fax: 808-935-3794. Toll Free: 1-877-935-3050; CAROL IGNACIO, Diocesan Dir.

Oahu Branch—6301 Pali Hwy., Kaneohe, 96744-5298. Tel: 808-263-8844, Ext. 334. Vacant, Program Dir.

Maui County Branch—95 Mahalani St., Wailuku, 96793. Tel: 808-244-8106; Fax: 808-244-8106. Sr. ROSELANI ENOMOTO, C.S.J., Program Dir.

Hawaii Island Branch—CAROL IGNACIO, Program Dir.

Care-a-Van—MIA FERREIRA, Program Dir.

Catholic Relief Services—CAROL IGNACIO, Diocesan Dir.

Hawaii Island Food Bank—MATTHEW J. PIPPIN, Admin.

Mobile Health Care Van—KAYE LUNDBURG, Coord.

Ministry to Persons with Disabilities—IWIE TAMASHIRO, Program Dir.

Development Director and Grants Manager—HEATHER BRIEN.

Boards and Commissions—

Bishop's Advisory Board for Persons with Disabilities—Members: MAGGIE BAXTER; SHARON CHIARUCCI; Sr. ROSELANI ENOMOTO, C.S.J.; JUDY CABANTING; JIM STEIBER; CAROLE SUAPAIA; TRACEY HEMASA; JOHN MAHER; LINDA DEVERA; CAROL IGNACIO, Staff Representative; PATRICIA TOSSEY, Bishop's Representative.

Diocesan Board of Education—Most Rev. FRANCIS X. DILORENZO, D.D., Pres. Members: Sr. JOHN JOSEPH GILLIGAN, C.S.J., Chm. ROEANA ALEXANDER; Dr. MARIANNE AU; ANTHONY BOQUER; Very Rev. THOMAS L. GROSS; Dr. MARY SHERIDAN, Ex Officio; Dr. HAROLD KOZUMA; Revs. CLARENCE GUERREIRO, SS.CC.; KONELIO FALETOI; Sr. JOAN OF ARC SOUZA, O.S.F.; Deacon JOSEPH BORGES; Dr. EDWARD KLEIN; CAROLA SOUZA; MICHAEL WEAVER; CAROL WEST.

Ecumenical Commission—Rev. Msgr. DANIEL DEVER; Revs. CLARENCE L. FISHER; HAL WEIDNER, C.O., Chm.; Sr. CLAUDIA WONG, C.S.J.; GAIL LEONG; REGINA PFEIFFER.

Diocesan Synod Implementation Committee—Deacon WALTER YOSHIMITSU, Coord.

Women's Concerns Committee—Co-Coordinators: JUDI BRAMLETT; Sr. CHRISTINE HILLIARD, C.S.J.

Lay Associations—

Apostleship of Prayer—Vacant.

Basic Christian Community of Hawaii—Spiritual Directors: Rev. MICHAEL SAWYER, O.S.B.; Sr. MARY JO MCENANY, O.S.B.

Beginning Experience-Hawaii—Rev. BERNARD CASSIDY, S.J., Spiritual Dir.

Catholic Committee on Scouting—712 N. School St., Honolulu, 96817. Tel: 808-521-1700; Fax: 808-599-3629. Rev. DANIEL SENGER, O.F.M., Chap.

Catholic Daughters of America—2124 Pauoa Rd., Honolulu, 96813. Tel: 808-531-6980. Rev. MARK A. CONSALVI, SS.CC., Chap.

Catholic Women's Guild—1511 Nuuanu Ave, Prince Tower 30, Honolulu, 96817-3758. Tel: 808-524-4385. Rev. FRANCIS PETERSON, Chap.

Chinese Catholic Club—4470 Aliiikoa St., Honolulu, 96821. Tel: 808-734-0396. Rev. Msgr. ROY PETERS, Spiritual Dir.

Confraternity of Our Lady of Mt. Carmel—P.O. Box 219, Hana, 96713. Tel: 808-248-8030. Rev. PAUL ZEGERS, SS.CC.

Confraternity of the Most Holy Rosary—4524 Waikui St., Honolulu, 96821. Tel: 808-548-4613. Deacon ANDREW GERAKAS, Pres.

Cursillos of Hawaii—1525 Waimano Home Rd., Pearl City, 96782. Tel: 808-455-9039. Rev. ANDREW MANETTA, O.F.M.Cap., Spiritual Dir.

Engaged Encounter—130 Ohua Ave., Honolulu, 96815. Tel: 808-923-7024. Rev. LANE AKIONA, SS.CC, Spiritual Dir.

Filipino Catholic Clubs, Diocesan Congress of—94-675 Farrington Hwy., Waipahu, 96797. Tel: 808-677-4276. Rev. JOVEN JUNIO, M.S., Diocesan Dir.

Oahu—1403 A California Ave., Wahiawa, 96786. Tel: 808-621-5109. Rev. CLARENCE L. FISHER, Spiritual Dir.

Kauai—P.O. Box 487, Kalaheo, 96741. Tel: 808-332-8011. Rev. CALIXTO PABLO, Spiritual Dir.

Maui—40 Kuhinia St., Wailuku, 96793. Tel: 808-244-3284. Deacon JAMES R. GONSALES, Spiritual Dir.

Hawaii Catholic Charismatic Renewal—6301 Pali Hwy., Kaneohe, 96744. Tel: 808-263-8844, Ext. 342. Rev. ANDREW MANETTA, O.F.M.Cap., Diocesan Liaison.

Holy Childhood Association—Vacant.

Holy Name Society, Diocesan Union of the—1124 7th Ave., Honolulu, 96816. Tel: 808-732-0281. Rev. GERARD LEICHT, SS.CC., Spiritual Dir.

Knights of Columbus—Most Rev. FRANCIS X. DILORENZO, D.D., State Chap.; Most Rev. JOSEPH FERRARIO, State Chap. Emeritus; WILLIAM JOHNSON, JR., State Deputy.

Legion of Mary—

Oahu—1124 7th Ave., Honolulu, 96816. Tel: 808-732-0281. Rev. GERARD LEICHT, SS.CC., Spiritual Dir.

Missionary Basic Christian Community of Hawaii—1184 Bishop St., Honolulu, 96813. Tel: 808-533-1791. Sr. GRACE DOROTHY LIM, M.M., Spiritual Dir.

Nocturnal Adoration Society—800 Kaheka St., Honolulu, 96814. Tel: 808-941-0675; Fax: 808-945-0689. Rev. Msgr. ROY PETERS, Spiritual Dir.

Reparation of the Immaculate Heart of Mary Association—1124 7th Ave., Honolulu, 96816. Tel: 808-732-0281. Rev. EDWIN DUFFY, Spiritual Dir.

St. Francis Xavier Clubs—

Oahu—1184 Bishop St., Honolulu, 96813. Tel: 808-536-7036. Rev. FRANCIS NAKAGAWA, S.M.

Maui—1627-A Mill St., Wailuku, 96793-1999. Tel: 808-244-4148. Rev. CHARLES OYABU, S.M.

St. Vincent de Paul Society—Honolulu District Council, 1708 Hoohulu St., Pearl City, 96782. Tel: 808-456-1029. HENRY SUMIDA, Dir.

Secular Franciscan Order—99-312 Moanalua Rd., Honolulu, 96701. Tel: 808-487-2414. Rev. ANDREW MANETTA, O.F.M.Cap., Reg. Spiritual Asst.

Secular Order of Discalced Carmelites—1514 Keolu Dr., Kailua, 96734. Tel: 808-262-0362. GWENDOLYN B. LAW, O.C.D.S., Group Leader.

Serra Club of Honolulu—1184 Bishop St., Honolulu, 96813. Tel: 808-623-3332. Rev. GARY L. SECOR, Chap.

Society for the Propagation of the Faith—Vacant.

Third Order of Mary/Companions of Mary—4470 Aliikoa St., Honolulu, 96821. Tel: 808-732-3481. Rev. JOHN SULLIVAN, S.M.

Worldwide Marriage Encounter—1511 Nuuanu Ave., Prince Tower 30, Honolulu, 96817-3758. Tel: 808-524-4385. Rev. FRANCIS PETERSON, Spiritual Dir.

Young Ladies' Institute—

Honolulu Institute No. 84—Rev. Msgr. RAYMOND NISHIGAYA, J.C.L., Spiritual Dir.

Ana Malia Institute No. 208—Rev. PATRICK FREITAS, Spiritual Dir.

Kailua Institute No. 213—Rev. GARY SECOR, Spiritual Dir.

Young Men's Institute—Rev. GARY SECOR, Chap.

CLERGY, PARISHES, MISSIONS AND PAROCHIAL SCHOOLS

ISLAND OF OAHU
CITY OF HONOLULU

1—CATHEDRAL OF OUR LADY OF PEACE (1843) (Portuguese-Filipino), Most Rev. Francis DiLorenzo, D.D.; Revs. Gary Secor, Rector; Arnold Dagcuta, J.C.L.; John Berger; Mrs. Ann Hannan, M.R.E., Pastoral Assoc. & D.R.E. In res., Rev. Robert Hannan.
Res., 1184 Bishop St., 96813-2838. Tel: 808-536-7036; Fax: 808-536-7039.
School—Cathedral School, 1728 Nuuanu Ave., 96817. Tel: 808-533-2069; Fax: 808-533-2069. Mrs. Mary Ann Lopes, Prin.
Lay Teachers 13; Students 147.
Catechesis/Religious Programs—Students 22.

2—CO-CATHEDRAL OF ST. THERESA OF THE CHILD JESUS (1931) (Filipino), Revs. Michael W. Hill, O.F.M.; Daniel W. Senger, O.F.M. In res., Rev. Michael Crosby, O.F.M.
Res., 712 N. School St., 96817. Tel: 808-521-1700; Fax: 808-599-3629.
School—Tel: 808-536-4703; Fax: 808-524-6861. Sr. John Joseph Gilligan, C.S.J., Prin.
Sisters 13; Lay Teachers 15; Students 517.
Catechesis/Religious Programs—Students 105.
Convent—Tel: 808-533-3101. Sisters of St. Joseph of Carondelet

3—ST. ANTHONY (1916) (Filipino), Rev. Napoleon Andres, M.S. In res., Rev. Teodulo Gaquit.
Res., 640 Puuhale Rd., 96819. Tel: 808-845-3255; Fax: 808-845-3664.
School—Tel: 808-845-2769; Fax: 808-853-2234. Sr. Ruth Linaac, R.V.M., Prin.
Sisters 5; Lay Teachers 6; Students 142.
Catechesis/Religious Programs—Students 150.
Convent—702 Puuhale Rd., 96819. Tel: 808-845-4888.
Religious of the Blessed Virgin Mary (R.V.M.) Sisters 5.

4—ST. AUGUSTINE (1854), Rev. Thomas Choo, SS.CC., Admin.
Res., 130 Ohua Ave., 96815. Tel: 808-923-7024; Fax: 808-922-4086.
Catechesis/Religious Programs—Students 33.

5—BLESSED SACRAMENT (1938), Rev. Mark Consalvi, SS.CC.; Deacons Ronald Choo; Roy Matsuo.
Res., 2124 Pauoa Rd., 96813. Tel: 808-531-6980.
Catechesis/Religious Programs—Tel: 808-538-7461. Mr. Francis Aiu, D.R.E.
Students 29.

6—HOLY FAMILY (1950), Rev. Maurice McNeely.
Res., 830 Main St., 96818. Tel: 808-422-1135; Fax: 808-421-1702.
School—Tel: 808-422-9612; Fax: 808-422-5030. Antonio J. Boquer, Prin.
Lay Teachers 51; Students 575.
Catechesis/Religious Programs—D.R.E.: Ann Amrich; Deborah Naone.
Students 162.

7—NEWMAN CENTER-HOLY SPIRIT PARISH (1981), Rev. Randall H. Roche, S.J., Dir.
Mailing Address: 1941 East West Road, 96822-2321. Tel: 808-988-6222; Fax: 808-988-7627.
Res., Jesuit House, 2727 Pamoa Rd., 96822-1838. Tel: 808-988-3464; Fax: 808-988-3464.
Catechesis/Religious Programs—Students 16.

8—HOLY TRINITY (1939), Rev. Halbert Weidner, C.O.; Deacons Paul Lee; Samuel Taylor.
Res., 5919 Kalanianaole Hwy., 96821. Tel: 808-396-0551; Fax: 808-396-1380.
School—Tel: 808-396-8466; Fax: 808-396-3310. Monica Des Jarlais, Prin.
Sisters 2; Lay Teachers 13; Students 160.
Catechesis/Religious Programs—Elizabeth Kekoa, D.R.E.
Students 140.

9—ST. JOHN THE BAPTIST (1844) (Filipino-Samoan), Rev. Msgr. Edgar B. Brillantes, Admin.; Rev. Jim McFadden, M.M., Hispanic Min.
Res., 2324 Omilo Ln., 96819. Tel: 808-845-0984; Fax: 808-841-6643. [CEM]
School—Tel: 808-841-5551; Fax: 808-842-6104. Mary Lou Superio, Prin.
Dominican Sisters 6; Lay Teachers 7; Students 178.
Catechesis/Religious Programs—Tel: 808-845-3304.
Students 125.
Convent—2330 Omilo Ln., 96819. Tel: 808-845-2622.
Dominican Sisters of the Most Holy Rosary 6; Sisters of the Holy Family 1.

10—OUR LADY OF THE MOUNT (1870), Rev. Jose R. Nacu, M.S. In res., Rev. Mario Raquepo.
Res., 1614 Monte St., 96819. Tel: 808-845-0828; Fax: 808-845-0828. [CEM]
Catechesis/Religious Programs—Tel: 808-845-0223.
Students 126.

11—ST. PATRICK (1929), Rev. Lane K. Akiona, SS.CC. In res., Rev. Paul Zaccone, O.M.
Res., 1124 Seventh Ave., 96816. Tel: 808-732-5565; Fax: 808-737-2477. Please refer to the listing for St. Patrick Monastery under Monasteries and Residences for Priests and Brothers for additional residents.
School—Tel: 808-734-8979; Fax: 808-732-2851. Sr. Rose Miriam Schillinger, C.S.J., Prin.
Sisters 5; Lay Teachers 30; Students 536.
Catechesis/Religious Programs—Tel: 808-735-0252.
Students 138.

12—ST. PHILOMENA (1942), Rev. Msgr. Terrence A.M. Watanabe. In res., Rev. Patrick Freitas.
Res., 3300 Ala Laulani St., 96818-2837. Tel: 808-839-1876; Fax: 808-834-6888.
School—Tel: 808-833-8080; Fax: 808-834-3438. Angeline A.V. Thomas, Prin.
Lay Teachers 11; Teacher Aids 17; Students 180.
Catechesis/Religious Programs—Students 130.

13—SACRED HEART (1914), Revs. Marc R. Alexander, S.T.D.; Steve Nguyen; Deacon Sidney Townsley, Ph.D.
Res., 1701 Wilder Ave., 96822. Tel: 808-973-2211; Fax: 808-973-2209.
School—Maryknoll Grade School, 1526 Alexander St., 96822. Tel: 808-952-8400; 952-7100; Fax: 808-972-7101. Paul O'Brien, Prin.
Teacher Aides 5; Lay Teachers 42; Students 826.
High School—1402 Punahou St., 96822. Tel: 808-952-7200; Fax: 808-952-7201. Mr. Andrew Corcoran, Prin.
Sisters 2; Lay Teachers 56; Students 564.
Catechesis/Religious Programs—Tel: 808-952-7120; Fax: 808-952-7121. Rose Anne Petro, D.R.E.
Students 115.

14—ST. STEPHEN (1932), Rev. Alan Nagai.
Res., 2747 Pali Hwy., 96817. Tel: 808-595-3105; Fax: 808-590-2719.
Catechesis/Religious Programs—Students 32.

15—STAR OF THE SEA (1946), Revs. John Sullivan, S.M.; John F. McGregor, S.M.; Andrew Ng, S.D.B.; Bro. Roy Madigan, S.M.; Deacons Thomas Rienzi; Andrew Gerakas. In res., Rev. Vincent Nguyen.
Res., 4470 Aliikoa St., 96821. Tel: 808-734-0396; Fax: 808-735-6017.
School—Tel: 808-734-0208; Fax: 808-735-9790. Carola Souza, Prin.
Lay Teachers 23; Students 268.
Early Learning Center—Tel: 808-734-3840; Fax: 808-732-1738. Lisa Foster, Prin.
Lay Teachers 10; Assistants 11; Students 147.
Catechesis/Religious Programs—Tel: 808-735-0259. Darlene Ah Yo, D.R.E.
Students 200.

16—ST. PIUS X (1958), Revs. Marc R. Alexander, S.T.D.; Steve Nguyen; Sandy Campus, Pastoral Assoc. In res., Rev. John Kang, Korean Ministry; Deacon Dominic Kang.
Mailing Address: 2821 Lowrey Ave., 96822-1644. Tel: 808-988-3308; 988-3321; Fax: 808-988-9313.
Res., 1701 Wilder Ave., 96822-4999. Tel: 808-973-2211; Fax: 808-972-2209.
Catechesis/Religious Programs—Maria Minkel, D.R.E.
Students 15.

17—SAINTS PETER AND PAUL (1969), Rev. David O. Travers, S.J., Admin.; Rev. Msgr. Roy V. Peters; Deacon Richard Port.
Mailing Address: 800 Kaheka St., 96814. Tel: 808-941-0675; Fax: 808-945-0689.
Res., 1561 Kanunu St., #1006, 96814. Tel: 808-955-8830.
Catechesis/Religious Programs—Students 60.

OUTSIDE THE CITY OF HONOLULU
County of Honolulu

Aiea, St. Elizabeth (1926), Revs. Michel Dalton, O.F.M.Cap.; Robert Maher, O.F.M.Cap. In res., Rev. Gordon Combs, O.F.M.Cap.
Res., 99-312 Moanalua Rd., 96701. Tel: 808-487-2414; Fax: 808-487-2168.
School—Tel: 808-488-5322; Fax: 808-486-0856. Sr. Mark Berdin, O.P., Prin.
Sisters 4; Lay Teachers 8; Students 256.
Catechesis/Religious Programs—Tel: 808-487-7994. D.R.E.: Will Layden; Missy Layden.
Students 236.
Convent—99-310 Moanalua Rd., 96701. Tel: 808-487-3131.
Dominican Sisters of the Most Holy Rosary 4.

Ewa, Immaculate Conception (1929) (Filipino), Rev. Frank Bourgeois, M.S. In res., Rev. Rean Frederick Enriquez, M.S.
Res., 91-1298 Renton Rd., 96706. Tel: 808-681-3701; Fax: 808-681-3117.
Catechesis/Religious Programs—Students 117.

Ewa Beach, Our Lady of Perpetual Help (1969), Revs. Konelio Faletoi; Robert Batoon.
Res., 91-1004 North Rd., 96706-2796. Tel: 808-689-8681; Fax: 808-689-8681.
School—91-1010 North Rd., 96706. Tel: 808-689-0474; Fax: 808-689-4847. Mr. Dennis Sasaki, Prin.
Lay Teachers 9; Students 193.
Catechesis/Religious Programs—Tel: 808-689-8563. Janese Akins, D.R.E.
Students 295.

Kahuku, St. Roch (1928) (Filipino-Hawaiian), Rev. Sydney Fernandes, Admin.
Res., P.O. Box 295, 96731. Tel: 808-293-5026; Fax: 808-293-1737. [CEM]
Catechesis/Religious Programs—Students 86.
Mission—Punaluu, Honolulu Co., St. Joachim, (1917) P.O. Box 295, 96731. Tel: 808-293-8590.

Kailua, St. Anthony (1933), Revs. Dennis Koshko; Marvin Samiano; Deacon Clarence DeCaires.
Res., 114 Makawao St., 96734. Tel: 808-266-2222; Fax: 808-266-2229.
School—148 Makawao St., 96734. Tel: 808-261-3331; Fax: 808-263-3518. Mrs. Lovey DeRego, Prin.
Sisters 1; Lay Teachers 25; Students 323.
Catechesis/Religious Programs—Tel: 808-266-2231. D.R.E.: Sr. Ruth Faisca, S.H.F.; Mrs. Kanani Asing.
Students 205.

St. John Vianney (1962), Rev. Thomas L. Gross; Deacons Lauren S.F. Wong; Walter H. Yoshimitsu.
Res., 920 Keolu Dr., 96734. Tel: 808-262-8317; Fax: 808-261-4039.
School—940 Keolu Dr., 96734. Tel: 808-261-4651; Fax: 808-263-0505. Mr. Michael Chu, Prin.
Lay Teachers 22; Staff 11; Students 290.
Catechesis/Religious Programs—Maria Brasher, D.R.E.
Students 157.

Kaneohe, St. Ann (1841), Revs. Clarence L. Guerreiro, SS.CC.; Bertram Lock, SS.CC. In res., Rev. Herman Gomes, SS.CC.

Res., 46-129 Haiku Rd., 96744. Tel: 808-247-3092; Fax: 808-235-0717. [CEM]
School and Early Learning Center—46-125 Haiku Rd., 96744. Tel: 808-247-3492 (School); 247-3324 (Early Learning Center). Sr. Anne Clare DeCosta, SS.CC., Dir., Tel: 808-235-5682; Mrs. Daphne Kauhane, Prin. (School); Mrs. Frances Vasquez, Prin. (Early Learning Center); Mr. Michael Pa'ekukui, Prin. (Religious Ed.).
Sisters 1; Lay Teachers 37; Students 462.
Catechesis/Religious Programs—Tel: 808-235-5682.
Students 265.

Makakilo, St. Jude (1988), Rev. Roland Pacudan.
Res., 92-455 Makakilo Dr., Kapolei, 96707. Tel: 808-672-8669; Fax: 808-672-3779.
Church—92-455 Makakilo Dr., Kapolei, 96707.
Catechesis/Religious Programs—Tel: 808-672-8669, Ext. 2. Caren Argenzia, D.R.E.
Students 212.

Mililani Town, St. John Apostle and Evangelist (1969), Rev. Gordian J. Carvalho, Jr.; Deacon Wally Mitsui. In res., Rev. Thomas B. Killackey, M.M.
Res., 95-370 Kuahelani Ave., 96789. Tel: 808-623-3332, Ext. 100; Fax: 808-623-3286.
St. John Catholic Preschool—Tel: 808-623-3332, Ext. 200; Fax: 808-623-6496. Monica Caldeira, Prin.
Catechesis/Religious Programs—Tel: 808-623-3332, Ext. 204, 205. Sandra Beltran, D.R.E.
Students 417.

Nanakuli, St. Rita (1963) (Hawaiian), Rev. Alapaki Kim, C.S.P.
Res., 89-318 Farrington Hwy., 96792. Tel: 808-668-7833; Fax: 808-668-7716.
Catechesis/Religious Programs—Tel: 808-682-5359. Cathy Agor, D.R.E.
Students 130.

Pearl City, Our Lady of Good Counsel (1958), Revs. John Niland, O.F.M.Cap; Paul Minchak, O.F.M.Cap. In res., Revs. Andrew Mannetta, O.F.M.Cap.; Eymard McKinnon, O.F.M.Cap.
Office: 1525 Waimano Home Rd., 96782. Tel: 808-455-3012; Fax: 808-456-9443. [CEM]
School—1530 Hoolana St., 96782. Tel: 808-455-4533; Fax: 808-455-5587. Mrs. Cindy Olaso, Prin.
Lay Teachers 16; Students 264.
Catechesis/Religious Programs—Ms. Leilani Asuncion, D.R.E.
Students 356.
Friary: 1530 #2 Hoolana St., 96782.

Wahiawa, Our Lady of Sorrows (1939), Rev. Clarence L. Fisher; Deacons Benjamin A. Awana; George Kagehiro.
Res., 1403-A California Ave., 96786-2595. Tel: 808-621-5109; Fax: 808-622-5073.
School—Tel: 808-621-8951; Fax: 808-621-8951. Mrs. Deborah Bee, Prin.
Lay Teachers 11; Students 149.
Catechesis/Religious Programs—Mrs. Janice Vannatta, D.R.E.
Students 241.

Waialua, St. Michael (1853), Rev. Albert Garcia, SS.CC.
Res., 67-390 Goodale Ave., 96791. Tel: 808-637-4040; Fax: 808-637-4287.
School—67-340 Haona St., 96791. Tel: 808-637-7772; Fax: 808-637-7722. Sr. William Marie Eleniki, O.S.F., Prin.
Sisters 2; Lay Teachers 11; Students 192.
Catechesis/Religious Programs—Tel: 808-637-4040, Ext. 5. Priscilla Tampon, D.R.E.
Students 146.
Convent—Tel: 808-637-7772; Fax: 808-637-7722.
Sisters 2.
Mission—Waimea Bay, Honolulu Co., SS. Peter and Paul, 67-390 Goodale, 96791.

Waianae, Sacred Heart (1838), Rev. Sebastian Chacko, Admin.
Res., 85-786 Old Government Rd., 96792. Tel: 808-696-3773; Fax: 808-696-2242. [CEM]
Parish Outreach—Tel: 808-696-3746.
Catechesis/Religious Programs—Tel: 808-696-2242.
Students 156.

Waikane, Our Lady of Mt. Carmel (1850), Rev. Eugene L. Keusal, Admin.
Res., 48-422 Kamehaineha Hwy., Kaneohe, 96744. Tel: 808-239-9269; Fax: 808-239-8561. [CEM]
Catechesis/Religious Programs—Students 60.

Waimanalo, St. George (1960), Rev. William F. Mattimore, Admin.; Deacon Ernest Carlbom.
Res., 41-1323 Kalanianaole Hwy., 96795. Tel: 808-259-7188; Fax: 808-259-0169.
Catechesis/Religious Programs—Students 95.

Waipahu, St. Joseph (1940) (Filipino), Revs. Joven Junio, M.S.; Rene Bisaillon; Augustine Cheerakathil, M.S.
Res., 94-675 Farrington Hwy., 96797. Tel: 808-677-4276; Fax: 808-671-3215. [CEM]
School—Tel: 808-677-4475; Fax: 808-677-8937. Miss Beverly Sandobal, Prin.
Sisters 1; Lay Teachers 23; Students 342.
Catechesis/Religious Programs—Tel: 808-676-3493; Fax: 808-676-3493. Geraldine Simbahon, D.R.E.
Students 664.
Convent—91-807 Poowai Pl., Ewa Beach, 96706. Tel: 808-681-4610. Sisters of St. Joseph of Carondelet

Waipio, Resurrection of the Lord (1986), Rev. Ronald J. Burke.
Mailing Address: 94-1260 Lumikula St., Waipahu, 96797. Tel: 808-676-4700; Fax: 808-676-4534.
Catechesis/Religious Programs—Yuko D. Ornellas, D.R.E.
Students 179.

ISLAND OF HAWAII
County of Hawaii

Hilo, St. Joseph (1860), Revs. Scott Bush; Enrique Cabante; Deacons LeRoy Andrews; Harvey Kawaihae; Don Aanavi.
Res., 43 Kapiolani St., 96720. Tel: 808-935-1465; Fax: 808-969-1665. [CEM]
School—1000 Ululani St., 96720. Tel: 808-935-4935; Fax: 808-969-9019. Ms. Barbara Austen, Prin. (Elementary); Deacon Leroy Andrews, Prin. (Junior-Senior High School).
Franciscan Sisters of Third Order 4; Lay Teachers 44; Students 385.
Catechesis/Religious Programs—Tel: 808-935-1202. Patrick Hurney, D.R.E.
Students 190.
Convent—49 Iiwipolena Rd., 96720. Tel: 808-935-1388.

Hawi, Sacred Heart (1926), Rev. Maurice Cardinal, M.S., Admin.
Res., P.O. Box 220, 96719. Tel: 808-889-6436; Fax: 808-889-5698. [CEM 2]
Catechesis/Religious Programs—Tel: 808-889-5353. Sr. Yolanda Francisco, S.H.F.
Students 140.
Mission—Halaula, Hawaii Co., Our Lady of Grace.

Honaunau, St. Benedict (1899), Rev. Ronald E. Clubb.
Res., Box 209, 96726. Tel: 808-328-2227; Fax: 808-328-8482. [CEM 5][JC 5]
Catechesis/Religious Programs—Marjorie Fujimoto, D.R.E.
Students 72.
Missions—Kealakekua, Honaunau Co., P.O. Box 209, 96726. Tel: 808-323-3711; Milolii, Honaunau Co., P.O. Box 209, 96726.

Honokaa, Our Lady of Lourdes (1870), Rev. Anastacio Postrano.
Mailing Address: P.O. Box 129, 96727. Tel: 808-775-9591; Fax: 808-775-0591.
Res., 45-5028 Plumeria St., 96727. [CEM 6]
Catechesis/Religious Programs—Students 143.
Mission—Paauilo, Hawaii Co., St. Joseph.

Kailua-Kona, St. Michael The Archangel (1840), Revs. James A. Berry; Jack Ryan; Deacon John K. Shuster. In res., Rev. John B. Stawasz.
Res.: 75-5769 Alii Dr., 96740. Tel: 808-326-7771; Fax: 808-326-7096. [CEM 4]
Catechesis/Religious Programs—Rev. Jack Ryan, D.R.E.
Students 109.
Missions—Kalaoa, Holy Rosary; Holualoa, Immaculate Conception; Honalo, St. Paul; Kahaluu, St. Peter.

Kamuela, Church of the Annunciation (1965), Rev. Robert F. Wynne, M.M.; Deacon William McPeek.
Res., P.O. Box 301, 96743. Tel: 808-885-4196; Fax: 808-885-4196. [CEM]
Catechesis/Religious Programs—Tel: 808-887-1203.
Students 170.
Mission—Puako, Church of the Ascension, Puako, 96743.

Keaukaha, Hilo, Malia Puka'O Kalani (Mary Gate of Heaven) (1929) (Hawaiian), Rev. George De Costa.
Res., 326 Desha Ave., 96720. Tel: 808-935-9338; Fax: 808-935-3865.
Montessori Preschool—Coordinators: Marie Roberts, Prin. & D.R.E.; Joseph Camacho.
Catechesis/Religious Programs—Students 120.

Mountain View, St. Theresa (1930) (Portuguese-Filipino), Rev. Edgardo C. Bonghanoy, Admin.
Res., P.O. Box 37, 96771. Tel: 808-968-6233; Fax: 808-968-6233.
Catechesis/Religious Programs—Students 105.
Mission—Keaau, Holy Rosary.

Naalehu, Sacred Heart (1846), Rev. Stephen A. Macedo.
Office: P.O. Box 150, 96772. Tel: 808-929-7474; Fax: 808-929-7474. [CEM]
Catechesis/Religious Programs—Tel: 808-929-7686. Margorie Pedra, D.R.E.
Students 44.

Pahala, Holy Rosary (1885), Rev. Stephen A. Macedo.
Res., P.O. Box 760, 96777. Tel: 808-929-8208; Fax: 808-929-8208. [CEM]
Catechesis/Religious Programs—Tel: 808-928-9054. Jovena Moses, D.R.E.
Students 78.

Pahoa, Sacred Heart (1882), Rev. Etuale Etuale; Sr. Eva Joseph Mesina, C.S.J.
Res., P.O. Box 17, 96778. Tel: 808-965-8202; Fax: 808-965-8202. [CEM 2]
Catechesis/Religious Programs—Tel: 808-965-8202. Sr. Eva Joseph Mesina, D.R.E.
Students 144.

Papaaloa, St. Anthony (1926), Rev. Edgar Serrano, Admin.
Oratory—Laupahoehoe, P.O. Box 339, 96813. Tel: 808-962-6538; Fax: 808-962-6538. [CEM 2]
Catechesis/Religious Programs—Fax: 808-962-6538. D.R.E.: Kay Lundberg; Carol Mendes.
Students 28.

Papaikou, Immaculate Heart of Mary (1950), Rev. Robert Schwarzhaupt.
Church—P.O. Box 79, 96781. Tel: 808-964-1240; 963-5434; Fax: 808-964-1240.
Catechesis/Religious Programs—Laura Kanoa, D.R.E.
Students 110.
Mission—Honomu, Hawaii Co., Good Shepherd, 96728.

ISLAND OF KAUAI
County of Kauai

Kalaheo, Holy Cross (1909) (Portuguese-Filipino), Rev. Christopher Keahi, SS.CC., Admin. In res., Rev. Calixto Pablo.
Res., 2-2370 Kaumualii Hwy., 96741. Tel: 808-332-8011; Fax: 808-332-7749. [CEM]
Catechesis/Religious Programs—Students 203.
Mission—Eleele, Kauai Co., Sacred Heart, P.O. Box 487, 96741.

Kapaa, St. Catherine (1887), Revs. Bruce Lery, S.M.; Daniel Seccomb, S.M.
Res., 5021-A Kawaihau Rd., 96746. Tel: 808-822-4804; 882-7900 (Office); Fax: 808-822-3014. [CEM 2]
School—Tel: 808-822-4212; Fax: 808-822-0991. Carol West, Prin.
Lay Teachers 12; Students 120.
Catechesis/Religious Programs—Tel: 808-822-0665. Mrs. Donna Charron, D.R.E.
Students 143.
Missions—Kilauea, Kauai Co., St. Sylvester, Kolo Rd., Kilauea, 96754. Tel: 808-828-2818; Hanalei, Kauai Co., St. William, 5292 Kuhio Hwy., Hanalei, 96714. Tel: 808-826-4163.

Kekaha, St. Theresa (1944), Rev. Alphonse Larochelle, M.S.
Res., P.O. Box 159, 96752. Tel: 808-337-1784 (Rectory); 337-1548 (Office); Fax: 808-337-1548. [JC]
School—8311 Kaumualii Hwy, 96752. Tel: 808-337-1351.
Sisters 5; Lay Teachers 5; Students 124.
Catechesis/Religious Programs—Tel: 808-338-1725. Beverly Johnston, D.R.E.
Students 89.
Convent—P.O. Box 277, 96752. Tel: 808-337-9661. Sr. Kathleen Murphy, Supr.
Franciscan Sisters of Christian Charity 5.
Missions—Waimea, Kauai Co., Sacred Hearts of Jesus & Mary, 9500 Kaumualii Hwy., Waimea, 96796.; Kaumakani, Kauai Co., St. Joseph, Village Main St., Kaumakani, 96747.

Koloa, St. Raphael (1841), Rev. Felix J. Vandebroek, SS.CC.
Res., 3011 Hapa Rd., 96756. Tel: 808-742-1955; Fax: 808-742-1845. [CEM 2]
Catechesis/Religious Programs—Students 85.

Lihue, Immaculate Conception (1884) (Filipino-Portuguese), Rev. Paul McLeod, SS.CC.
Res., 4453 Kapaia Rd., 96766. Tel: 808-245-2432; Fax: 808-246-2571. [CEM 2]
Catechesis/Religious Programs—Fax: 808-245-5628. Sr. Florence Remata, O.S.F., D.R.E.
Students 185.

ISLAND OF LANAI

Lanai City, Sacred Hearts (1930), Rev. Michael Owens, Admin.
Res., P.O. Box 784, 96763. Tel: 808-565-6837; Fax: 808-565-6897.
Catechesis/Religious Programs—D.R.E.: Priscilla Felipe; Rosita Camero.
Students 65.

ISLAND OF MAUI
County of Maui

Haiku, St. Rita (1950), Rev. Gary Colton; Deacon Patrick Constantino.

Res., 655 Haiku Rd., 96708. Tel: 808-575-2601; Fax: 808-575-2063. [CEM]
Catechesis/Religious Programs—Sandra Silva, D.R.E.
Students 77.
Mission—Keanae, Maui Co., St. Gabriel, 655 Haiku Rd., 96708. Tel: 808-248-8658; Fax: 808-248-7097.

Hana, St. Mary (1859), Rev. Paul A. Zegers, SS.CC.
Res., P.O. Box 219, 96713. Tel: 808-248-8030; Fax: 808-248-7654. [CEM][JC 2]
Catechesis/Religious Programs—Esse Sinenci, D.R.E.
Students 58.
Missions—Puuiki, Maui Co., St. Peter; Kipahulu, Maui Co., St. Paul; Kaupo, Maui Co., St. Joseph.

Kahului, Christ the King (1932), Rev. William Shannon; Deacon Frank R. Singson, Sr., Pastoral Assoc. In res., Rev. Gaudelio Donato, (Filipino Min.).
Res., 20 W. Wakea Ave., 96732. Tel: 808-877-6098; Fax: 808-871-6296.
School—(Grades PreK-6). Tel: 808-877-6618; Fax: 808-871-8101. Mr. Isacc Balicanta, Prin.
Sisters 5; Lay Teachers 10; Students 164.
Catechesis/Religious Programs—Tel: 808-877-7783. Sr. Angela Laurenzo, C.S.J, D.R.E.
Students 210.
Convent—211 S. Kaulawahine St., 96732. Tel: 808-877-0790. Sisters of St. Joseph of Carondelet

Kihei, St. Theresa (1908), Revs. Anthony Bolger; Teodoro Magpayo.
Res., 25 W. Lipoa St., 96753. Tel: 808-879-2649; Fax: 808-879-0045. [CEM]
Catechesis/Religious Programs—Students 297.

Kula, Our Lady Queen of the Angels (1944) (Portuguese), Rev. Thomas R. Heinzel.
Res., R.R. 2, Box 211, 96790. Tel: 808-878-1261; Fax: 808-878-3105. [CEM 2]
Catechesis/Religious Programs—Tel: 808-878-6924. Mrs. Maureen Rompasky, D.R.E.
Students 80.
Missions—Waiakoa, Maui Co., Holy Ghost, 9 Lower Kula Rd., Waiakoa, 96790. Tel: 808-878-1091; Ulupalakua, Maui Co., St. James the Less.

Lahaina, Maria Lanakila (1846), Revs. Joseph Bukoski, III, SS.CC., J.C.L.; Francis Schellemans, SS.CC., Pastoral Assoc.
Res., 712 Wainee St., 96761-1511. Tel: 808-661-0552; Fax: 808-661-1670. [CEM]
School—Tel: 808-661-4720; Fax: 808-661-1670. Paul Lohmann, Prin.
Lay Teachers 12; Students 260.
Catechesis/Religious Programs—Tel: 808-661-6607.
Students 127.
Mission—Honokahua (Kapalua), Maui Co., Sacred Hearts of Jesus and Mary, Office Rd., Honokahua, 96761. Tel: 808-669-7022.

Makawao, St. Joseph (1851), Revs. Donald Macgregor, Admin.; Alfred Rebuldelha; Deacon Albert Phillips, Jr.
Res., 1294 Makawao Ave., 96768. Tel: 808-572-7652; Fax: 808-573-2278. [CEM]
School—(Grades PreK-6). Tel: 808-572-8675; Fax: 808-572-0748. Tamara Johnson, Prin.
Sisters 4; Lay Teachers 7; Students 112.
Catechesis/Religious Programs—Sr. Rosario Tuvida, O.P., D.R.E.
Students 151.
Convent—57 Dominican Ln., 96768. Tel: 808-572-8454.
Dominican Sisters of the Most Holy Rosary 4.

Paia, Holy Rosary (1915) (Portuguese-Filipino), Rev. Gary Colton; Deacon Patrick Constantino.
Church—954 Baldwin Ave., 96779-9605. Tel: 808-579-9551; Fax: 808-579-8714. [CEM]
Catechesis/Religious Programs—Tel: 808-579-9551; Fax: 808-575-2063.
Students 40.

Waihee, St. Ann (1935), Deacon James R. Gonsalves, Admin. In res., Rev. Bernard Gatlin (LA).
Res., 40 Kuhinia St., 96793-9216. Tel: 808-244-3284; Fax: 808-244-3284, Ext. 51. [CEM][JC]
Catechesis/Religious Programs—Students 21.
Missions—Waikapu, St. Joseph, 96793. [CEM][JC] Kahakuloa, St. Francis Xavier, 96793. [CEM][JC]

Wailuku, St. Anthony (1846), Revs. Raymond E. Malley, S.M.; Charles Oyabu; Deacon Joseph Borges.
Res., 1627 B Mill St., 96793-1999. Tel: 808-244-4148; Fax: 808-242-9375. [CEM]
School—(Grades PreK-6). Tel: 808-244-4976; 242-9024 (PreK); Fax: 808-244-7950. Mrs. Winona Martinez, Prin.; Mrs. Carlene Santos, Dir. (PreK).
Lay Teachers 18; Students 244.
Catechesis/Religious Programs—Tel: 808-242-6040. Kay Stone, D.R.E.
Students 337.

ISLAND OF MOLOKAI

Kalaupapa, St. Francis (1873) (Hawaiian), Rev. Joseph Hendriks, SS.CC.
Res., 96742. Tel: 808-567-6238.
Mission—Kalawao, Molokai Co., St. Philomena, P.O. Box 9, 96742.

Kaunakakai, Molokai Catholic Community (1874). Attended by Our Lady of Sorrows, Kalua'aha; St. Joseph, Kamalo; St. Sophia, Kaunakakai; and St. Vincent, Maunaloa. Rev. James Orsini.
Mailing Address: P.O. Box 1948, 96748-1948. Tel: 808-553-5220; Fax: 808-553-5556. [CEM 2]
Office: 115 Ala Malama St., 96748.
Catechesis/Religious Programs—Students 163.

Chaplains of Public Institutions

HONOLULU. *Prison Ministry* 1184 Bishop St., 96813. Tel: 808-533-1791, Ext. 341. Deacon Walter Yoshimitsu, Diocesan Rep.

On Duty Outside the Diocese:
Reverend Fathers—
Butler, John
Coughlin, Thomas
Drew, James F.
Farrell, Jeremiah
Guerrero, Robert
Lee, William, Chicago, IL

Military Chaplains:
Reverend Fathers—
Blazek, Eugene E., U.S. Air Force
Evers, Paul, U.S. Navy
Gervacio, Adrian R., U.S. Navy
Lanuevo, Victor, U.S. Navy
Santry, Robert, U.S. Army

On Sabbatical:
Reverend Fathers—
Carter, Eli
McNichol, Daniel

Leave of Absence:
Reverend Fathers—
DeOtero, Roberto
DeRego, Frank
Kaleikoa, Charles
O'Mahony, James

Retired:
Reverend Monsignors—
Dever, Daniel J., 6301 Pali Hwy., Kaneohe, HI 96744
Eikmeier, Bernard J., 801 S. King St. # 1006, Honolulu, HI 96813
Marzen, Francis A., P.O. Box 4935, Kaneohe, HI 96744
Reverend Fathers—
Carroll, Joseph, 801 S. King St. # 1007, Honolulu, HI 96813
Ching, Herbert, 86-660 Lualualei Homestead, Maili, HI 96792
daPonte, Robert, 4730 N. Mesa St. #59, El Paso, TX 79912
Duffy, Edwin J., Alexander Towers, 1226 Alexander St., Apt. 601, Honolulu, HI 96826
Halloran, John, Our Lady of Peace, 2800 Mission College Blvd., Santa Clara, CA 95054
Hannon, Robert E., 1184 Bishop St., Honolulu, HI 96813
Nishigaya, Raymond J., 801 S. King St. # 1011, Honolulu, HI 96813
O'Brien, Arthur, 94-1390 Kulewa Lp #D, Waipahu, HI 96797
O'Leary, Bartholomew J., Nazareth House, Dromahane, Mallow, County Cook Ireland
Pascale, Anthony, 801 S. King St. # 1009, Honolulu, HI 96813
Peterson, Francis, 1511 Nuuanu Ave., PT 122, Honolulu, HI 96817
Sabog, Henry, 2909 Kalihi St., Honolulu, HI 96819
Siu, Robert K.C., P.O. Box 1047, Lander, WY 82520
Stawasz, James, 75-5769 Alii Dr., Kailua-Kona, HI 96740
Thomas, Donald, P.O. Box 0358, Haleiwa, HI 96812
Turner, Edward, 2723 Avenida De Anita, #102, Carlsbad, CA 92008
Yim, Louis H., 801 S. King St. #1002, Honolulu, HI 96813

Permanent Deacons:
Aanavi, Don, St. Joseph Church, P.O. Box 165, Ninole, HI 96773
Andrews, LeRoy, St. Joseph, 136 Ululani St., Hilo, HI 96720
Awana, Benjamin A., Our Lady of Sorrows, Wahiawa, 89-104 A Haleakala Ave., Nannakuli, HI 96792
Borges, Joseph W., St. Anthony, 299 Lilolilo St., Wailuku, HI 96793
Carlbom, Ernest F., St. George, 41-865 Mahailua St., Waimanalo, HI 96795
Choo, Ronald T.Y., Blessed Sacrament, 46-144 Hilinama St., Kaneoha, HI 96744
Constantino, Patrick R., Holy Rosary, Paia; St. Rita, Haiku, 3188 Kilani Pl., Pukalani, HI 96734
DeCaires, Clarence, Jr., St. Anthony, 1131 Kupau St., Kailua, HI 96734
Gerakas, Andrew J., Star of the Sea, 4524 Waikui St., Honolulu, HI 96821
Gonsalves, James R., St. Ann, Waihee, Maui, 2534 Main St., Wailuku, HI 96793
Hart, Christopher L., On Leave
Ignacio, Lawrence, St. Anthony, Papaaloa, P.O. Box 317, Paauilo, HI 96776
Kagehiro, George K., Our Lady of Sorrows, 916 Lemi St., Wahiawa, HI 96786
Kang, Dominic, St. Pius X, 2750 Kalawao St., Honolulu, HI 96822
Kawaihae, Harvey, St. Joseph, 24 Poni Mai Pl., Hilo, HI 96720
Lee, Paul, Holy Trinity, Honolulu, 360 Opihikao Pl., Mahani
Matsuo, Roy T., Blessed Sacreament, 1755 Mahani, LP, Honolulu, HI 96819
McPeek, William, Anunciation Parish, Kamuela, P.O. Box 278, Kapaau, HI 96755
Mitsui, Wallace M., St. John Apostle & Evangelist, 95-690 Lewanuu St., Mililani, HI 97689
Miyashiro, Thomas H., Our Lady of Good Counsel, 2054 Hoohai St, Pearl City, HI 96782
Phillips, Albert C., St. Joseph, Makaweo, Maui, 3297 Haleakala Hwy., Pukalani, HI 96788
Port, Richard J., Sts. Peter and Paul, 1600 Ala Moana Blvd., #3100, Honolulu, HI 96815
Rienzi, Thomas M., Star of the Sea, 676 Elepaio St., Honolulu, HI 96819
Seagraves, On duty outside the Diocese
Shuster, John K., St. Michael, P.O. Box 2495, Kealakekua, HI 96759
Singson, Frank, Christ the King, 468 Kipuka Pl., Kahului, Maui 96732
Taylor, Samuel, Holy Trinity, 7218 Pikoni Pl., Honolulu, HI 96825
Thorp, George, 1459 Akamai St., Kailua, HI 96734
Townsley, Sidney J., Sacred Heart/St Pius X, 1717 Mott-Smith Dr., Honolulu, HI 96822
Waldemar, Donald, On duty outside the Diocese, St. Catherine, P.O. Box 401, Kilauea, HI 96754
Wong, Lauren H., St. John Vianney, 1309 Kupau St., Kailua, HI 96734
Yoshimitsu, Walter H., St. John Vianney, 681 Akoakoa St., Kailua, HI 96734

INSTITUTIONS LOCATED IN THE DIOCESE

[A] COLLEGES AND UNIVERSITIES

HONOLULU. *Chaminade University of Honolulu*, 3140 Waialae Ave., 96816. Tel: 808-735-4711; Fax: 808-735-7748.
E-mail: cuhadm@lava.net
Web site: www.chaminade.edu
For a complete listing, refer to the Colleges and Universities section.

[B] HIGH SCHOOLS, DIOCESAN AND PAROCHIAL

HONOLULU. *Maryknoll School*, 1526 Alexander St., 96822. Tel: 808-952-7330; Fax: 808-952-7331.
E-mail: admissions@maryknollschool.org
Web site: www.maryknollschool.org
Michael E. Baker, Pres.; Paul O'Brien, Prin.; Kathleen W. Shimabukuro, Contact Person. Sisters 2; Lay Teachers 103; Students 1,393.

HILO. *St. Joseph Junior-Senior High School*, 1000 Ululani St., 96720. Tel: 808-935-4936; Fax: 808-969-9019.
E-mail: sjadmin@interpac.net
Web site: www.sjhshilo.org
Deacon LeRoy M. Andrews, Prin. Sisters 2; Deacons 1; Lay Teachers 25; Students 228; Total Staff 27.

WAILUKU. *St. Anthony Junior-Senior High School*, 1618

Lower Main St., 96793. Tel: 808-244-4190; Fax: 808-242-8081.
E-mail: sas@ccmaui.com
Web site: www.sasmaui.org/
Daina Collins, Prin. Sisters 2; Lay Teachers 29; Students 380.

[C] HIGH SCHOOLS, PRIVATE

HONOLULU. *Damien Memorial High School*, 1401 Houghtailing St., 96817. Tel: 808-841-0195; Fax: 808-847-1401.
E-mail: odonnell@damien.edu
Web site: www.damien.edu
Congregation of Christian Brothers. Legal Title: *Congregation of Christian Brothers of Hawaii, Inc.* Bro. Gregory O'Donnell, C.F.C., Pres.; Michael Weaver, Prin.; Bro. F. Louis Frick, Community Leader. Brothers 6; Sisters 1; Lay Teachers 23; Boys 412.

Sacred Hearts Academy. (Grades JK-12), 3253 Waialae Ave., 96816. Tel: 808-734-5058; Fax: 808-737-7067.
E-mail: bwhite@sacredhearts.org
Web site: www.sacred.pvt.k12.hi.us
Mrs. Betty White, Prin. Sisters 6; Lay Teachers 67; Girls 1,046; Support Staff, Counselors, Administrators 26.

St. Francis School. (Grades 6-12), 2707 Pamoa Rd., 96822. Tel: 808-988-4111; Fax: 808-988-5497.
E-mail: admin@stfrancis-oahu.org
Web site: www.stfrancis@stfrancis-oahu.org
Sr. Joan of Arc Souza, O.S.F., Prin.; Louise Gerboc, Contact Person. Sisters 13; Lay Teachers 31; Girls 426.

St. Francis School. (Grades 7-12). (Kaua'i Campus). 3343 Kanakolu St., Lihue, 96766. Tel: 808-246-3802; Fax: 808-245-3680.
E-mail: saintfr@aloha.net
Robert Bodnar, Prin. Lay Teachers 8; Students 94.

Saint Louis School, 3142 Waialae Ave., 96816-1578. Tel: 808-739-7777; Fax: 808-739-4853.
E-mail: jdelong123@aol.com
Web site: www.stlouishon.org
Chaplains: Revs. James Allen DeLong, S.M., Pres.; William O'Connell, S.M. Priests 2; Brothers 2; Lay Teachers 59; Boys 897.

[D] PRESCHOOL CENTERS

HONOLULU. *St. Philomena Early Learning Center*, 3300 Ala Laulani St., 96818. Tel: 808-833-8080; Fax: 808-834-6888; 808-834-3438.
E-mail: stphilomenaelc@aol.com
Angie A. Thomas, Prin. Lay Teachers 20; Students 180; Total Staff 26.

HILO. *Hale O Kamalii Montessori Preschool*, 326 Desha Ave., 96720. Tel: 808-935-9338. Co-Directors: Marie Roberts; Joe Camacho. Students 10; Total Staff 4.

MILILANI TOWN. *St. John Catholic Preschool*, 95-370 Kuahelani Ave., 96789. Tel: 808-623-3332, Ext. 200; Fax: 808-623-6496. Monica Caldeira, Dir. Total Staff 12; Lay Teachers 4; Students 72.

[E] GENERAL HOSPITALS

HONOLULU. *St. Francis Healthcare System of Hawaii*, P.O. Box 29380, 96820. Tel: 808-547-6883; Fax: 808-547-6616.
Web site: www.sfhs.hi.org
For a complete listing, refer to the Hospitals section.

[F] SPECIAL HOSPITALS AND SANATORIA FOR INVALIDS

KALAUPAPA. *Kalaupapa Settlement*, Molokai, 96742. Tel: 808-567-6911; Fax: 808-567-6916
For a complete listing, refer to the Special Care Facilities section.

[G] MONASTERIES AND RESIDENCES OF PRIESTS AND BROTHERS

HONOLULU. *Congregation of Christian Brothers*, 1401 Houghtailing St., 96817. Tel: 808-845-2330; Fax: 808-847-1401.
E-mail: frick@damien.edu
Bro. F. Louis Frick, C.F.C., Supr. Brothers 12.

Jesuit Fathers House, 2727 Pamoa Rd., 96822-1838. Tel: 808-988-3464; Fax: 808-988-7627.
E-mail: bcassidy@calprov.org
Revs. Randall H. Roche, S.J., Reg. Supr.; Bernard F. Cassidy, S.J.; Thomas J. Griffen-Smolenski, S.J.; Joseph E. Specht, S.J.

Marianist Communities, 1184 Bishop St., 96813-2857. Tel: 808-536-7036. Rev. Francis Nakagawa, S.M.

Center Marianist Community, 3140 Waialae Ave., 96816. Tel: 808-735-2711; Fax: 808-734-3117. Revs. Allen DeLong, S.M.; Timothy Eden, S.M. Priests 2; Brothers 12; Total in Residence 14.

Marianist Hall Community, 3140 Waialae Ave., 96816. Tel: 808-739-8300; Fax: 808-739-8320. Revs. William O'Conell, S.M., Dir.; Joseph Priestly, S.M. Priests 2; Brothers 10.

Chaminade Pohaku Marianist Community, 3140 Waialae Ave., 96816. Tel: 808-735-4857; Fax: 808-739-8333. Bro. Thomas Spring, S.M., Dir. Priests 1; Brothers 1.

Wailuku Marianist Community, 1627 B Mill St., Wailuku, 96793. Tel: 808-244-4148; Fax: 808-242-9375. Revs. Raymond E. Malley, S.M.; Charles Oyabu, S.M. Priests 2.

Maryknoll Fathers House (M.M.), Honolulu Society House, 1721 Dole St, 96822. Tel: 808-949-7737. Revs. Charles W. Schmidt, M.M.; Elias Tederous, M.M.; Bro. Venard F. Ruane, M.M., Dir., Annunciation Church, P.O. Box 301, Kamuela, 96743. Rev. Robert F. Wynne, M.M., Holy Trinity Church, 5919 Kalanianaole Hwy., 96821. Revs. Robert W. Donnelly, M.M.; James J. McFadden, M.M., 1721 Dole St., 96822-4906. Rev. Thomas B. Killackey, M.M., St. John Apostle and Evangelist, 95-370 Kuahelani Ave., Mililani, 96789. Priests 4; Brothers 1; Total in Residence 5; Total Staff 1.

KANEOHE. *Congregation of the Sacred Hearts of Jesus and Mary (Hawaii Province SS.CC.)*, P.O. Box 797, 96744. Tel: 808-247-5035; Fax: 808-235-8849.
E-mail: fatherclyde@aol.com
Very Rev. Clyde Guerreiro, SS.CC., Prov. Priests 35; Brothers 8.

Sacred Hearts Center, P.O. Box 787, 96744. Tel: 808-247-3647; Fax: 808-235-8849. Revs. Clyde Guerreiro, SS.CC., Prov.; Mark Consalvi, SS.CC.; Nobincio Fernandez, SS.CC.; Bros. Charles Kaahanui, SS.CC.; Richard Kupo, SS.CC., Supr.

St. Patrick's Monastery, 1124-A Seventh Ave., Honolulu, 96816. Tel: 808-732-0281. Revs. Gaston Diels, SS.CC.; Gerard Leicht, SS.CC.; Clement Geysen, SS.CC.; Timothy Jacobs, SS.CC.; Matthew Lochs, SS.CC.; Albert Miechielsen, SS.CC.; Anthony O'Brien, SS.CC.; Raphael Smulders, SS.CC.; Gabriel Vanden Brouke, SS.CC.; Alfred Vann, SS.CC.; Stephen Van den Eynde, SS.CC., Supr.; Ildephonse Kuntz, SS.CC.; Bros. James Dunn, SS.CC.; Leo Vendiola, SS.CC.; Patrick Hughes, SS.CC; Dominic Stone, SS.CC.; George Apo, SS.CC. Total in Residence 18; Total Staff 6.

WAIALUA, OAHU. *Benedictine Monastery of Hawaii/ Retreat Center*, 67-290 Farrington Hwy., P.O. Box 490, 96791. Tel: 808-637-7887; Fax: 808-637-8601.
E-mail: benedicthi@aol.com
Benedictine Congregation of Our Lady of Mounte Oliveto, O.S.B. Revs. Michael Sawyer, O.S.B.; Timothy Ottman, O.S.B.; David Barfknecht, O.S.B., Supr.; Sr. Mary Jo McEnany, O.S.B.; Bros. Gregory Foret, O.S.B.; Richard Morgado, O.S.B.

[H] CONVENTS AND RESIDENCES FOR SISTERS

HONOLULU. *Congregation of the Sacred Hearts and of Perpetual Adoration*, 1120 Fifth Ave., 96816. Tel: 808-737-5822; Fax: 808-735-0878.
E-mail: regina-jenkins@worldnet.att.net
Web site: www.glauco.it/sscc
Sisters of the Congregation of the Sacred Hearts of Jesus and Mary of Perpetual Adoration SS.CC. Sr. Regina Mary Jenkins, Pres. & Prov. Supr.; Sr. Katherine Francis Miller, SS.CC., Auditor; Sr. Rose Kathleen Lenchanko, Sec.; Sr. Anne Clare DeCosta, Vice Pres.; Sr. Mary Josephine Araki, Treas.; Sr. Regina M. Jenkins, Contact Person. Sisters 8.
The following are listings of residences and the number of sisters residing at each:

Paewalani Community, 45-901 Wailele Rd., 96744. Tel: 808-247-3688; Fax: 808-235-0717. Sr. Anne Clare DeCosta, SS.CC., Contact Person. Sisters 4.

Malia o ka Malu Community, 1117 Fourth Ave., 96816. Tel: 808-734-2048. Sr. Helene Wood, SS.CC., Contact Person. Sisters 11.

Na Leo Ho'onani Community, 2151 Kauhana St., 96816. Tel: 808-739-5566. Sr. Irene Barboza, SS.CC., Contact Person. Sisters 4.

Maryknoll Sisters of St. Dominic M.M.
E-mail: mksrscpr@lava.net
125 Ainoni St., Kailua, 96734-2138. Tel: 808-261-0267; Fax: 808-261-1283. Sr. Dolores Rosso, M.M., Contact Person.
The following are listings of residences and the number of sisters residing at each:

Maryknoll Sisters, 2880 Oahu Ave., 96822-1726. Tel: 808-988-6540; Fax: 808-988-7938.
E-mail: mkmanoa@lava.net
Sisters 4.

Maryknoll Sisters, 125 Ainoni St., Kailua, 96734-2138. Tel: 808-261-6356.

Maryknoll Sisters, 1570 Mokulua Dr., Kailua, 96734-3254. Tel: 808-261-1674. Sisters 3.

Maryknoll Sisters, 87-204 Holomalia Pl., Nanakuli, 96792-3706. Tel: 808-668-1603. Sisters 3.

Maryknoll Sisters, St. Anthony Convent, 702 Puuhale Rd., 96819. Tel: 808-841-5652.

Maryknoll Sisters, P.O. Box 996, Pepeekeo, 96783. Tel: 808-964-3032. Sisters 2.

St. Anthony Retreat Center, 3351 Kalihi St, 96819. Tel: 808-845-4353; Fax: 808-848-2696. Sr. Rose Kathleen Lenchanko, SS.CC., Contact. Sisters 6.

Sisters of St. Joseph of Carondelet CSJ, Hawaii Vice-Province. Administration Center, 5311 Apo Dr., 96821-1829. Tel: 808-373-2096; 808-841-4519 (Res.); 808-852-4379 (Pager); Fax: 808-373-5341.
E-mail: palencsj@aol.com
Sr. Brenda Lau, C.S.J., Dir.
The following are listings of residences and the number of sisters residing at each:

Carondelet Community, 5311 Apo Dr., 96821-1829. Tel: 808-373-3850; Fax: 808-373-5341.
E-mail: csjh@hgea.org
Sisters 2.

Hale Medaille Community, 2220 E. Kalaiwa Way #19, 96819-2711. Tel: 808-847-7807.
E-mail: srrose@aol.com
Sisters 3.

Ho'omaluhia Community, 1735 Ala Aolani St., 96819-1413. Tel: 808-836-8575.
E-mail: maluhiaa@lava.net
Sisters 2.

Mana'Olana Community, 1046 6th Ave., 96816-1644. Tel: 808-737-2130; Fax: 808-732-2851.
E-mail: srm@kahala.net
Sisters 3.

St. Theresa Community, 712 N. School St., 96817-3098. Tel: 808-533-3101.
E-mail: stcesj@pixi.com
Sisters 9.

Christ the King Community, 211 A. South Kaulawahine St., Kahului, 96732-2200. Tel: 808-877-0790.
E-mail: ctkcsj@ccmaui.com
Sisters 6.

Hale Iokepa Community, 828 Analioa St., Waiehu, 96793-9610. Tel: 808-244-8123; Fax: 808-244-5474.
E-mail: haleiokepa@hotmail.com
Sisters 2.

La'ialoha Community, P.O. Box 23858, 96823-3514. Tel: 808-833-5264; Fax: 808-833-5264.
E-mail: compassionatecounseling@iName.com

Sisters of the Third Franciscan Order; Hawaii Region, St. Francis Convent, 2715 Pamoa Rd., 96822-1885. Tel: 808-988-4432; Fax: 808-988-1486. Franciscan Sisters of Syracuse (O.S.F.). Sisters 21.
The following are listings of residences and the number of sisters residing at each:

Marianne Cope Convent, 2102 Liliha St., 96817-1642. Tel: 808-538-1526. Sisters 7.

St. Elizabeth Convent, Bishop Home and Hospital, Kalaupapa, 96742-0129. Tel: 808-567-6079. Sisters 3.

St. Joseph Convent, 49 Iwipolina Rd., Hilo, 96720-1777. Tel: 808-935-1388. Sisters 4.

St. Francis Medical Center - West, St. Clare Convent, 91-1048 A'awa Dr., Ewa Beach, 96706-3900. Tel: 808-687-3420. Sisters 5.

St. Michael Convent, 67-340 Haona St., Waialua, 96791-9689. Tel: 808-637-5606; 637-7772. Sisters 2.

KANEOHE. *Carmel of the Holy Trinity (Carmelite Monastery)*, 6301 Pali Hwy., 96744-5224. Tel: 808-261-6542. Order of Discalced Carmelite Nuns of Our Lady of Mount Carmel (O.C.D.). Sr. Agnes Marie Wong, Prioress. Sisters 6.

WAIPAHU. *Dominican Center Hawaii*, 94-1249 Lumikula St., 96797. Tel: 808-676-1452; 677-1202; Fax: 808-676-1452.
E-mail: srmauraliaop@juno.com
Web site: www.ophawiiregion.com
Sr. M. Aurelia Sanchez, O.P., Reg. Supr.
Please refer to the following parish convents for additional residences: St. Elizabeth, Aiea; St. John, Honolulu; St. Catherine, Kapaa; St. Joseph, Makawao. Sisters 8.

Sisters of Charity of the Blessed Virgin Mary, 94-1031 Kaukahi Pl., Apt. G7, 96797. Tel: 808-676-4433. Sr. Joan Madden, Contact Person.

[I] MISCELLANEOUS

HONOLULU. *Catholic Charities Housing Development Corporation*, 250 S. Vineyard St., 96813. Tel: 808-537-6321; Fax: 808-523-8773. Jerome E. Rauckhorst, Diocesan Dir.

Marianist Center of Hawaii, 3140 Waialae Ave., 96816. Tel: 808-739-4738; Fax: 808-732-3374. Total Staff 3.

Our Lady the Mystical Rose Chapel. (Oratory). Rev. William O'Connell, S.M., Pastor, Marianist Center of Hawaii, 3140 Waialae Ave., 96816. Tel: 808-739-4738; Fax: 808-732-3374.

KANEOHE. *Augustine Educational Foundation*, St. Stephen Diocesan Center, 6301 Pali Hwy., 96744. Tel: 808-230-2440, Ext. 336; Fax: 808-230-2441.
E-mail: aef@aloha.net
Web site: www.planet-hawaii.com/~aef/
Most Revs. Francis X. DiLorenzo, Pres.; Joseph A. Ferrario, D.D., Chm.; Rev. Msgr. Daniel J. Dever, Sec.; Anna Ordenstein, Second Vice Pres.; Lawrence S.L. Ching, Treas.; Wendall K. Pang, Asst. Treas.; Susan Ferandin, Assoc. Dir.

PEARL CITY. *St. Vincent de Paul Society Honolulu District Council*, 1708 Hoohulu St., 96782. Tel: 808-456-1029; Fax: 808-455-4225.
E-mail: Hwestp9845@aol.com
Henry Sumida, Lay Dir.

WAILUKU. *Maui Helio Endowment Fund*, c/o St. Anthony Church, 1627-B Mill St., 96793. Tel: 808-572-4593. Kurt Wright, Pres.

RELIGIOUS INSTITUTES OF MEN REPRESENTED IN THE DIOCESE

For further details refer to the corresponding bracketed number in the Religious Institutes of Men or Women section.

[0200]—*Benedictine Monks.* (Olivetan).—O.S.B.
[0470]—*The Capuchin Friars.*—O.F.M.Cap.
[0310]—*Congregation of Christian Brothers.*—C.F.C.
[1140]—*Fathers of the Sacred Hearts.* (Hawaii Prov.).—SS.CC.
[0520]—*Franciscan Friars.*—O.F.M.
[0690]—*Jesuit Fathers and Brothers.*—S.J.
[0780]—*Marist Fathers.*—S.M.
[0800]—*Maryknoll.*—M.M.
[0720]—*The Missionaries of Our Lady of La Salette.* (Pacific Region).—M.S.
[0950]—*Oratorians.*—C.O.
[1030]—*Paulist Fathers.*—C.S.P.
[0760]—*Society of Mary.* (Prov. of the Pacific).—S.M.

RELIGIOUS INSTITUTES OF WOMEN REPRESENTED IN THE DIOCESE

[]—*Benedictine Congregation of Our Lady of Mounte Oliveto.*—O.S.B.
[0870]—*Congregation of the Daughters of Mary Immaculate (Marianist Sisters).*—F.M.I.
[0950]—*Daughters of Saint Paul.*—F.S.P.
[0420]—*Discalced Carmelite Nuns.*—O.C.D.
[1070-03]—*Dominican Sisters of the Most Holy Rosary.*—O.P.
[1230]—*Franciscan Sisters of Christian Charity.*—O.S.F.
[1780]—*Franciscan Sisters of Perpetual Adoration.*—F.S.P.A.
[2420]—*Marist Missionary Sisters.*—S.M.S.M.
[2470]—*Maryknoll Sisters of St. Dominic.*—M.M.
[]—*Religious of the Blessed Virgin Mary.*—R.V.M.
[0430]—*Sisters of Charity of the Blessed Virgin Mary.*—B.V.M.
[3000]—*Sisters of Notre Dame de Namur.*—S.N.D.deN.
[3840]—*Sisters of St. Joseph of Carondelet.*—C.S.J.
[1960]—*Sisters of the Holy Family.*—S.H.F.
[3690]—*Sisters of the Sacred Hearts and of Perpetual Adoration.*—SS.CC.
[1490]—*Sisters of the Third Franciscan Order.* (Syracuse, NY).—O.S.F.

NECROLOGY

(No Deaths)

Diocese of Houma-Thibodaux

(Dioecesis Humensis-Thibodensis)

Most Reverend

MICHAEL JARRELL, D.D.

Bishop of Houma-Thibodaux; ordained June 3, 1967; appointed December 29, 1992; consecrated and installed March 4, 1993. *Address: Chancery Office, 2779 Hwy. 311, Schriever, LA, 70395. Mailing Address: P.O. Box 505, Schriever, LA, 70395.* Tel.: 504-868-7720.

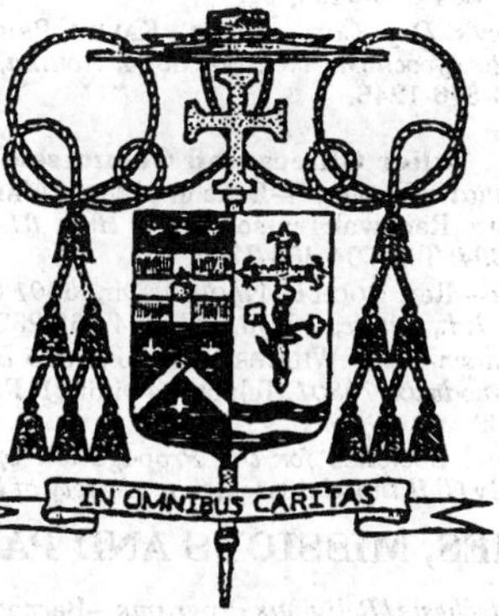

ERECTED JUNE 5, 1977.

Square Miles 3,440.

Comprises the parishes of Lafourche, Terrebonne, parts of St. Mary and Jefferson.

For legal titles of parishes and diocesan institutions, consult the Chancery Office.

Address all Chancery correspondence to: P.O. Box 505, Schriever, LA, 70395. Tel.: 504-868-7720; Fax: 504-868-7727.

E-mail address: htchancellor@archdiocese-no.org

STATISTICAL OVERVIEW

Personnel	
Bishop	1
Priests: Diocesan Active in Diocese	43
Priests: Active Outside Diocese	1
Priests: Retired, Sick or Absent	34
Number of Diocesan Priests	78
Religious Priests in Diocese	5
Ordinations:	
Diocesan Priests	1
Permanent Deacons in Diocese	29
Total Brothers	7
Total Sisters	32
Parishes	
Parishes	39
With Resident Pastor:	
Resident Diocesan Priests	31
Resident Religious Priests	8
Without Resident Pastor:	
Administered by Women Religious	1
Missions	5
Welfare	
Day Care and Extended Day Care Centers	1
Total Assisted	96
Specialized Homes	3
Total Assisted	65
Special Centers for Social Services	4
Total Assisted	22,000
Educational	
High Schools, Diocesan and Parish	3
Total Students	1,937
Elementary Schools, Diocesan and Parish	10
Total Students	4,233
Catechesis/Religious Education:	
High School Students	2,910
Elementary Students	6,545
Total Students Under Catholic Instruction	15,625
Vital Statistics	
Receptions into the Church:	
Infant Baptism Totals	1,759
Adult Baptism Totals	48
Received into Full Communion	147
First Communions	1,573
Confirmations	1,304
Marriages:	
Catholic	399
Interfaith	75
Total Marriages	474
Deaths	1,013
Total Catholic Population	126,000
Total Population	202,000

Former Bishops—Most Rev. WARREN L. BOUDREAUX, J.C.D., D.D., Retired Bishop of Houma-Thibodaux; ord. May 30, 1942; retired Dec. 29, 1992; died Oct. 6, 1997.

Chancery

Address all correspondence to: P.O. Box 505, Schriever, 70395. Office: *2779 Hwy. 311, Schriever, 70395.* Tel: 504-868-7720; Fax: 504-868-7727. Office Hours: Mon.-Fri. 8-5

Vicar General—Rev. Msgr. JOSEPH N. LATINO.

Chancellor—Sr. MIRIAM MITCHELL, S.H.Sp.

Diocesan Tribunal

Address all correspondence to: P.O. Box 505, Schriever, 70395. Office: *2779 Hwy. 311, Schriever, 70395.* Tel: 504-850-3126

Departments of the Diocesan Curia

Department of Administration Ministries

Judicial Vicar—Rev. VICENTE DELA CRUZ.

Judges—Rev. Msgr. WILLIAM KONINKX; Revs. BRENDAN FOLEY; JOHN A. GALLEN.

Defenders of the Bond—Rev. Msgr. JOSEPH N. LATINO; Revs. DANIEL M. POCHE; ROLAND TIMBRE; Deacon CHARLES GIROIR.

Counselor—Sr. KATERI BATTAGLIA, M.S.C.

Priests Council and College of Consultors—Rev. Msgr. JOSEPH N. LATINO; Revs. WILMER TODD; CHARLES PERKINS; JAMES MORRISON; DANIEL POCHE; DEAN DANOS; JEROME WEBER; PATRICK O'BRIEN; CLYDE MAHLER; ROBERT CRUZ, *Mailing Address: P.O. Box 505, Schriever, 70395. 2779 Hwy. 311, Schriever, 70395.*

Deans—Upper Lafourche Deanery: Very Rev. WILMER TODD, *815 Barbier Ave., Thibodaux, 70301.* South Lafourche Deanery: Rev. DEAN DANOS, *P.O. Box 10, Larose, 70373.* Terrebonne Deanery: Very Rev. PATRICK O'BRIEN, *409 Funderburk Ave., Houma, 70364-1895.*

Diocesan Finance Council—DOUGLAS P. TOUPS; Rev. Msgr. FREDERIC J. BRUNET; Rev. Msgr. JOSEPH N. LATINO; Rev. PATRICK O'BRIEN; A. J. CHAMPAGNE, JR.; ROBERT NAQUIN; Mr. LEE RINGEMAN; ANN BARKER.

Coordinator—DOUGLAS P. TOUPS, *2779 Hwy. 311, Schriever, 70395, Mailing Address: P.O. Box 505, Schriever, 70395.* Tel: 504-868-7720.

Accounting, Business Office, Finance, Insurance—DOUGLAS P. TOUPS, Business Mgr., *2779 Hwy. 311, Schriever, 70395, Mailing Address: P.O. Box 505, Schriever, 70395.* Tel: 504-868-7720.

Archives and Historical Research Center—Sr. MIRIAM MITCHELL, S.H.Sp., *205 Audubon St., Thibodaux, 70301.* Tel: 504-446-2383.

Building Commission—JAMES J. DANOS, Dir., *2779 Hwy. 311, Schriever, 70395, Mailing Address: P.O. Box 505, Schriever, 70395.* Tel: 504-868-7720.

Cemeteries—GEORGE COOKE, Dir., *949 Menard St., Thibodaux, 70301.* Tel: 504-446-0280.

Legal Services—Rev. Msgr. JOSEPH N. LATINO, Dir., *2779 Hwy. 311, Schriever, 70395, Mailing Address: P.O. Box 505, Schriever, 70395.* Tel: 504-868-7720. Attorneys: KENNETH WATKINS; DANIEL WALKER, *501 Roussell St., P.O. Box 5095, Houma, 70361.* Tel: 504-868-2333.

Stewardship and Development—JEREMY BECKER, Dir., *2779 Hwy. 311, Schriever, 70395, Mailing Address: P.O. Box 505, Schriever, 70395.* Tel: 504-868-7720.

Department for Clergy and Religious

Coordinator—Rev. Msgr. JOSEPH N. LATINO, *2779 Hwy. 311, Schriever, 70395, Mailing Address: P.O. Box 505, Schriever, 70395.* Tel: 504-868-7720.

Clergy Personnel—Rev. Msgr. JOSEPH N. LATINO, *Mailing Address: P.O. Box 505, Schriever, 70395.* Tel: 504-868-7720.

Continuing Education of the Clergy-Ministry to Priests Program—Rev. WILMER TODD, *815 Barbier Ave., Thibodaux, 70301.*

Vicar for Priests—Rev. Msgr. FRANCIS LEGENDRE, *15300 W. Main St., Cutoff, 70345.* Tel: 504-632-3858.

Permanent Diaconate—Deacon ROBERT DUSSE, *514 Gaynell Dr., Houma, 70364.* Tel: 504-876-5122., *2779 Hwy. 311, Schriever, 70395, Mailing Address: P.O. Box 505, Schriever, 70395.* Tel: 504-868-7720.

Vocations—Rev. JAMES MORRISON, Dir. Seminarians; Bro. STEPHEN SYNAN, F.M.S., Ph.D., *2779 Hwy. 311, Schriever, 70395, Mailing Address: P.O. Box 505, Schriever, 70395.* Tel: 504-868-7720.

Women Religious—Sr. MIRIAM MITCHELL, S.H.Sp., *P.O. Box 505, Schriever, 70395.* Tel: 504-850-3121.

Department of Formation Ministries

Coordinator—LOUIS G. AGUIRRE, *2779 Hwy. 311, Schriever, 70395, Mailing Address: P.O. Box 505, Schriever, 70395.* Tel: 504-868-7720.

Campus Ministry—Rev. VICENTE DE LA CRUZ, Dir., N.S.U., *Box 2051, Thibodaux, 70310.* Tel: 504-446-6201.

Catholic Schools—Sr. IMMACULATA PAISANT, M.S.C., Supt., *2779 Hwy. 311, Schriever, 70395, Mailing Address: P.O. Box 505, Schriever, 70395.* Tel: 504-868-7720.

Communications, Public Relations, Publications, Radio & Television—LOUIS G. AGUIRRE, Dir., *2779 Hwy. 311, Schriever, 70395, Mailing Address: P.O. Box 505, Schriever, 70395.* Tel: 504-868-7720.

Religious Education—Sr. FIONNUALA QUINN, O.P., Dir., *2779 Hwy. 311, Schriever, 70395, Mailing Address: P.O. Box 505, Schriever, 70395.* Tel: 504-868-7720.

Pastoral Staffing—Dr. MARIAN SCHWAB, Dir., *2779 Hwy. 311, Schriever, 70395., Mailing Address: P.O. Box 505, Schriever, 70395.* Tel: 504-868-7720.

"The Bayou Catholic"—(Diocesan Newspaper)—LOUIS G. AGUIRRE, Editor, *2779 Hwy. 311, Schriever, 70395, Mailing Address: P.O. Box 505, Schriever, 70395.* Tel: 504-868-7720.

Family Ministries/Respect Life—Sr. MARY KATERI BATTAGLIA, M.S.C., *2779 Hwy. 311, Schriever, 70395, Mailing Address: P.O. Box 505, Schriever, 70395.* Tel: 504-868-7720.

Worship—Sr. MARLENE BERTHELOT, O.P., Dir., *2779 Hwy. 311, Schriever, 70395, Mailing Address: P.O. Box 505, Schriever, 70395.* Tel: 504-868-7720.

Youth Ministry—Bro. DOMINICK PUJIA, F.M.S., Dir., *2779 Hwy. 311, Schriever, 70395, Mailing Address: P.O. Box 505, Schriever, 70395.* Tel: 504-868-7720.

Department of Social Ministries

Coordinator—Sr. MIRIAM MITCHELL, S.H.Sp., *2779 Hwy. 311, P.O. Box 505, Schriever, 70395.* Tel: 504-850-3121.

Assisi Bridge House—ROBERT D. GORMAN, A.C.S.W., B.C.S.W., Exec. Dir., *Bull Run Rd., Schriever, 70395.* Tel: 504-872-5529. GERMAINE JACKSON, Assoc. Dir., *1220 Aycock St., P.O. Box 883, Houma, 70361.* Tel: 504-876-0490.

Campaign for Human Development—ROBERT GORMAN, Diocesan Dir., *1220 Aycock St., P.O. Box 3894, Houma, 70361.* Tel: 505-876-0490. Liaison for Catholic Relief Service. Sr. MIRIAM MITCHELL, S.H.Sp.

Catholic Social Services; Justice & Peace—ROBERT D. GORMAN, A.C.S.W., B.C.S.W., Dir. GERMAINE JACKSON, Assoc. Dir., *1220 Aycock St., P.O. Box 3894, Houma, 70361.* Tel: 504-876-0490.

Disaster Relief—ROBERT D. GORMAN, A.C.S.W., B.C.S.W., Dir., *1220 Aycock St., P.O. Box 3894, Houma, 70361.* Tel: 504-876-0490.

St. Lucy's Day Care Center—KAREN PRICE, Admin., *1220 Aycock St., P.O. Box 3894, Houma, 70361.* Tel: 504-876-1246.

Other Offices and Commissions

Charismatic Renewal—Deacon MELVIN MARTS, Charismatic Renewal Liaison, *2779 Hwy. 311, Schriever, 70394.* Tel: 504-868-7720.

Cursillo—Rev. ROCH R. NAQUIN, Dir., *5101 Grand Caillou Rd., Dulac, 70353.* Tel: 504-563-2325.

Ecumenism—Rev. WILMER TODD, Dir., *815 Barbier Ave., Thibodaux, 70301.* Tel: 504-446-5571; Fax: 504-449-1939.

Pontifical Societies for the Propagation of the Faith; Holy Childhood Association; Society of St. Peter the Apostle—Rev. NGUYEN VAN TY, Dir., *1027 Hwy. 308, Thibodaux, 70301.* Tel: 504-446-6663.

Scouting—Bro. DOMINIC PUJIA, F.M.S., Dir., *2779 Hwy. 311, Schriever, 70395, Mailing Address: P.O. Box 505, Schriever, 70395.* Tel: 504-868-7720.

Organizations

Catholic Daughters of the Americas—Rev. GREGORY FRATT, Diocesan Advisor to State Court Officers, *15300 W. Main, Cut Off, 70345.* Tel: 504-632-3858.

Diocesan Council of St. Vincent de Paul Societies—AL JACKSON, Pres., *107 Point St., Houma, 70360.* Tel: 504-872-9373.

Knights of Columbus—Rev. Msgr. JOSEPH N. LATINO, Diocesan Chap., *P.O. Box 4014, Houma, 70361.* Tel: 504-876-6904.

Legion of Mary—ROSE M. MARCEAUX, Pres.; Rev. Msgr. JOSEPH N. LATINO, Spiritual Dir.

St. Vincent de Paul Store—Mrs. CORRINE CLARK, Pres.; Mr. FRANCIS FREDRICK, Vice Pres.; Mr. DRUREY BOUDREAUX, *107 Point St., Houma, 70360.* Tel: 504-872-9373.

Serra Club of South Lafourche—Mr. BOBBY CHERAMIE, Pres.

Anawim—EVELYN RUCKSTUHL, Pres., *501 Grinage St., Houma, 70360.* Tel: 504-872-4761.

CLERGY, PARISHES, MISSIONS AND PAROCHIAL SCHOOLS

CITY OF HOUMA
(Parish Terrebonne)

1—CATHEDRAL OF ST. FRANCIS DE SALES (1847), Rev. Msgr. Joseph N. Latino; Rev. Roger Villarubia.
Res., P.O. Box 4014, 70361. Tel: 504-876-6904; Fax: 504-851-4204. [CEM 2]
School—300 Verret St., 70361. Tel: 504-868-6646; Fax: 504-851-5896.
Lay Teachers 31; Students 782.
Catechesis/Religious Programs—Students 165.
Convent—501 Grinage St., 70361. Tel: 504-876-7260.

2—ANNUNZIATA (1963), Rev. James R. Morrison. In res., Rev. Lonnie Cheramie.
Res., 2011 Acadian Dr., 70363. Tel: 504-876-2971; Fax: 504-868-6414.
Catechesis/Religious Programs—Tel: 504-876-2865.
Students 360.

3—MARIA IMMACOLATA (1963), Rev. Caesar Silva; Deacon Douglas Authement.
Administration Office: 246 Corporate Dr., 70360. Tel: 504-876-3313; Fax: 504-879-2137.
Res., 326 Estate Dr., 70360. Tel: 504-868-4915.
School—324 Estate Dr., 70360. Tel: 504-876-1631; Fax: 504-876-1608.
Lay Teachers 19; Students 228.
Catechesis/Religious Programs—Students 317.

4—OUR LADY OF THE MOST HOLY ROSARY (1948). (Holy Rosary Church). Revs. Bert Heise, O.F.M.; Paul Desch, O.F.M. In res., Revs. Edwin Deane, O.F.M (CIN); Duane Stenzel, (Retired); Deacons Raymond LeBouef; Harold Kurtz.
Res., 8594 Main St., 70363. Tel: 504-876-7652; Fax: 504-876-7647. [CEM]
Catechesis/Religious Programs—Tel: 504-876-7647. D.R.E.: Kathy Lirette; Debbie Hotard.
Students 549.

5—ST. BERNADETTE (1958), Very Rev. Patrick O'Brien; Rev. Alexander Francisco.
Res., 409 Funderburk Ave., 70364. Tel: 504-879-1506; Fax: 504-876-9654.
School—309 Funderburk Ave., 70364. Tel: 504-872-3854.
Lay Teachers 28; Students 493.
Catechesis/Religious Programs—Mrs. April Crochet, D.R.E.
Students 570.

6—ST. GREGORY BARBARIGO (1963), Rev. Wilfredo G. Decal.
Mailing Address: P.O. Box 1066, 70361.
Res., 439 Sixth St., 70364. Tel: 504-876-2003.
Administration Bldg.: 1005 Williams Ave., 70364. Tel: 504-876-2047; Fax: 504-876-0628.
School—441 Sixth St., 70364. Tel: 504-876-2038; Fax: 504-879-2789.
Lay Teachers 11; Students 286.
Catechesis/Religious Programs—Students 321.

7—ST. LOUIS (1965), Rev. Thomas R. Bouterie.
Res., 2226 Bayou Blue Rd., 70364. Tel: 504-876-3449; Fax: 504-876-6810. [CEM]
Catechesis/Religious Programs—Tel: 504-876-6686. Nancy P. Champton, D.R.E.
Students 321.

8—ST. LUCY, Rev. Bert Heise, O.F.M (CIN).
Mailing Address: P.O. Box 3508, 70361. Tel: 504-879-2632; Fax: 504-876-4054.
Res., 8594 Main Street, 70360. Tel: 504-879-2623.
Church—1222 Aycock St., 70360.
Catechesis/Religious Programs—Bernadette Travis, D.R.E.
Students 69.

CITY OF THIBODAUX
(Lafourche Parish)

1—ST. JOSEPH CO-CATHEDRAL (1817), Revs. Oscar Solis; John Ruiz; Robert-Joel T. Cruz; Deacon Willie R. Orgeron.
Res., 721 Canal Blvd., P.O. Box 966, 70302. Tel: 504-446-1387; Fax: 504-446-6571.
School—501 Cardinal Dr., 70301. Tel: 504-446-1346; Fax: 504-449-0760.
Lay Teachers 35; Students 696.
Catechesis/Religious Programs—Students 213.

2—ST. CHARLES BORROMEO (1912), Rev. Nguyen Van Ty.
Res., 1027 Hwy. 308, 70301. Tel: 504-446-6663; Fax: 504-447-3348. [CEM]
Catechesis/Religious Programs—Students 175.

3—CHRIST THE REDEEMER (1983), Revs. John Gallen; Scott Dugas.
Res., 720 Talbot Ave., 70301. Tel: 504-447-2013; Fax: 504-447-4422. [CEM]
Catechesis/Religious Programs—Students 344.

4—ST. GENEVIEVE (1959), Very Rev. Wilmer L. Todd; Rev. Clyde Mahler.
Res., 815 Barbier Ave., 70301. Tel: 504-446-5571; Fax: 504-449-1939.
School—807 Barbier Ave., 70301. Tel: 504-447-9291; Fax: 504-447-9883.
Lay Teachers 26; Students 448.
Catechesis/Religious Programs—Tel: 504-446-5127.
Students 209.

5—ST. JOHN THE EVANGELIST (1919), Revs. John Gallen; Scott Dugas; Deacon Charles Giroir.
Res., 2085 St. Mary St., 70301. Tel: 504-447-3995; Fax: 504-447-2092. [CEM]
Catechesis/Religious Programs—Linda Traigle, D.R.E.
Students 320.

6—ST. LUKE, Rev. Oscar Solis; Sr. Nancy McNemar, S.S.N.D., Pastoral Assoc.
Office: P.O. Box 1819, 70302. Tel: 504-446-0487; Fax: 504-446-4080.
Catechesis/Religious Programs—Students 65.

7—ST. THOMAS AQUINAS (1970), Very Rev. Vicente de La Cruz.
Res., Nicholls Sta., NSU Box 2051, 70310. Tel: 504-446-6201; Fax: 504-449-0710.

OUTSIDE THE CITIES OF HOUMA AND THIBODAUX

Amelia, St. Mary Parish, St. Andrew (1965), Rev. Charles J. Perkins.
Res., P.O. Box 310, 70340. Tel: 504-631-2333; Fax: 504-631-2334. [CEM]
Catechesis/Religious Programs—Students 132.
Thanh Gia (1981). Personal Parish for Vietnamese Community. Rev. Francis Bui.
Res., 711 Magnolia St., Morgan City, 70380. Tel: 504-631-3194; Fax: 504-631-2634.
Catechesis/Religious Programs—Students 109.
Domus Dei Institute, Inc.—1002 Aycock St., Houma, 70360. Tel: 504-851-1351.

Bayou Black, Terrebonne Parish, St. Anthony (1876), Rev. Gerard C. Hayes.
Res., 3897 Bayou Black Dr., Houma, 70360. Tel: 504-872-0922; Fax: 504-872-2001.
Catechesis/Religious Programs—Students 265.

Bourg, Terrebonne Parish, St. Ann (1908), Rev. Guy P. Zeringue; Deacon Gerald Belanger.
Res., 4355 Hwy. 24, P.O. Box 700, 70343. Tel: 504-594-3548; Fax: 504-594-3570. [CEM]
Catechesis/Religious Programs—Tel: 504-594-5088.
Students 475.

Chacahoula, Terrebonne Parish, St. Lawrence (1848), Rev. Michael Bergeron.
Res., P.O. Box 259, Gibson, 70356. Tel: 504-575-3087; Fax: 504-575-8243. [CEM]

Chackbay, Lafourche Parish, Our Lady of Prompt Succor (1892), Rev. Roland Timbre.
Res., 529 Hwy. 20, Thibodaux, 70301. Tel: 504-633-2903; Fax: 504-633-9225. [CEM 2]
Catechesis/Religious Programs—Students 385.

Chauvin, Terrebonne Parish, St. Joseph (1948), Rev. Msgr. Frederic J. Brunet; Rev. Joseph Tu Tran.
Res., 5232 Hwy. 56, 70344. Tel: 504-594-5859; Fax: 504-594-2116. [CEM]
Catechesis/Religious Programs—Sharon Picou, D.R.E.
Students 550.
Missions—Cocodrie, Our Lady of the Gulf; Upper Little Caillou, Our Lady of Prompt Succor.

Cut-Off, Lafourche Parish, Sacred Heart (1923), Rev. Msgr. Francis J. Legendre; Rev. Gregory Perkins Fratt.
Res., 15300 W. Main, 70345. Tel: 504-632-3858; Fax: 504-632-4452. [CEM]
Catechesis/Religious Programs—Tel: 504-632-6322.
Students 497.

Galliano, LaFourche Parish, St. Joseph (1958), Rev. Shenan J. Boquet.
Res., P.O. Box 519, 70354. Tel: 504-632-7321; Fax: 504-632-7345. [CEM]
Catechesis/Religious Programs—Students 283.

Gheens, LaFourche Parish, Community of St. Anthony. (Quasi Parish). Rev. Daniel M. Poche, Admin.
Res., P.O. Box 12, Mathews, 70375. Tel: 504-532-6497.
Catechesis/Religious Programs—Tel: 504-537-6002; Fax: 504-337-4408.
Students 145.

Gibson, Terrebonne Parish, St. Patrick (1920). Merged with St. Lawrence, Chacahoula.

Golden Meadow, LaFourche Parish, Our Lady of Prompt Succor (1916), Rev. Carl Collins.
Res., 723 N. Bayou Dr., 70357. Tel: 504-475-5428; Fax: 504-475-7699. [CEM]
Catechesis/Religious Programs—Students 351.

Grand Caillou, Terrebonne Parish, Holy Family (1952), Revs. Jerome Weber; Joseph Pilola.
Res., 6641 Grand Caillou Rd., Dulac, 70353. Tel: 504-563-2325; Fax: 504-563-4980. [CEM 2]
Catechesis/Religious Programs—Students 226.

Grand Isle, West Jefferson Parish, Our Lady of the Isle (1933), Rev. Warren F. Chassaniol.
Res., P.O. Box 885, 70358. Tel: 504-787-2385; Fax: 504-787-4530. [CEM]
Catechesis/Religious Programs—Students 99.

Kraemer, Lafourche Parish, St. Lawrence the Martyr (1962), Rev. Domingo Cruz.
Res., 3723 Hwy. 307, Thibodaux, 70301. Tel: 504-633-9431; Fax: 504-633-5706. [JC 2]
Mission—Choctaw, St. James, 1278 Choctaw Rd., Thibodaux, 70301. Tel: 504-633-9855. [CEM]

Catechesis/Religious Programs—Tel: 504-633-5714.
Students 170.

Larose, Lafourche Parish, Our Lady of the Rosary (1873), Revs. Dean F. Danos; Nghia Dink; Sr. Claire M. Rodrigue, C.I.C., Pastoral Assoc.
Res., Box 10, 70373. Tel: 504-693-3433; Fax: 504-693-7551. [CEM]
School—P.O. Box 40, 70373. Tel: 504-693-3342; Fax: 504-693-3348.
Sisters 1; Lay Teachers 15; Students 359.
Catechesis/Religious Programs—Tel: 504-693-3125. Camile Gautreaux, D.R.E.
Students 520.

Lockport, Lafourche Parish, Holy Savior (1850), Rev. Florentino Santiago.
Res., 612 Main St., 70374. Tel: 504-532-3533; Fax: 504-532-2010. [CEM]
School—201 Church St., 70374. Tel: 504-532-2536; Fax: 504-532-2269.
Lay Teachers 29; Students 353.
Catechesis/Religious Programs—Students 373.

Montegut, Terrebonne Parish, Sacred Heart (1864), Rev. Robert C. Rogers.
Res., P.O. Box 2, 70377. Tel: 504-594-5856; Fax: 504-594-8087. [CEM 2]
Catechesis/Religious Programs—Students 100.

Morgan City, St. Mary Parish, Sacred Heart of Jesus (1859), Rev. Sabino B. Rebosura, II.
Res., 415 Union St., P.O. Box 632, 70381. Tel: 504-385-0770; Fax: 504-384-7176.
Catechesis/Religious Programs—Tel: 504-384-8108.
Students 315.

Holy Cross (1964), Rev. Jay Baker; Deacon Andrew Dragna.
Res., 2100 Cedar St., Unit 3, 70380. Tel: 504-384-3551; Fax: 504-384-5790.
School—2100 Cedar St., Unit 2, 70381. Tel: 504-384-1933.
Lay Teachers 18; Students 384.
Catechesis/Religious Programs—Students 259.
Mission—Morgan City, St. Martin Parish, St. Rosalie, 1315 Stephensville Rd., 70380. Tel: 504-385-5713.

Pointe-Aux-Chenes, LaFourche Parish, St. Charles Borromeo (1971), Rev. Robert C. Rogers.
Mailing Address: P.O. Box 54, Montegut, 70377.
Res., 531 Hwy. 665, Montegut, 70377. Tel: 504-594-6801; Fax: 504-594-6802. [CEM]
Catechesis/Religious Programs—Students 147.

Raceland, LaFourche Parish, St. Hilary of Poitiers (1965), Rev. Daniel M. Poche.
Res., 333 Twin Oaks, 70394. Tel: 504-537-6002; Fax: 504-537-4408.
Catechesis/Religious Programs—Students 361.

St. Mary's Nativity (1850), Rev. Msgr. Donald L. Ledet; Rev. Lawrence Cavell. In res., Rev. Msgr. Stanislaus J. Manikowski.
Res., 3500 Hwy. 1, 70394. Tel: 504-537-3204; Fax: 504-537-3235. [CEM]
School—(Grades PreK-6) P.O. Box K, 70394. Tel: 504-537-7544; Fax: 504-537-4020.
Lay Teachers 9; Students 278.
Catechesis/Religious Programs—Students 154.

Schriever, Terrebonne Parish, St. Bridget (1912), Rev. Michael Bergeron; Sr. Mary Teresa O'Donnell, R.S.M.; Deacon James V. Didier.
Res., 100 Hwy. 311, 70395. Tel: 504-446-6801; Fax: 504-448-2764. [CEM]
Catechesis/Religious Programs—Students 302.

Theriot, Terrebonne Parish, St. Eloi (1875), Revs. Jerome Weber; Joseph Pilola; Deacons Glenn Porche; Daniel Bascle.
Res., 1335 Bayou Dularge Rd., 70397. Tel: 504-872-2946; Fax: 504-872-9961.
Catechesis/Religious Programs—Tel: 504-851-6893.
Students 213.

Chaplains of Public Institutions

HOUMA. *Terrebonne Parish General Hospital*. Rev. Van Constant.

THIBODAUX. *Nicholls State University*. Rev. Vicente de La Cruz.
Thibodaux General Hospital. Rev. Carlos S. Talavera.

On Duty Outside the Diocese:
Reverend Fathers—
Cao, John

On Leave:
Reverend Fathers—
Chaisson, Louis
Charpentier, Dale
Coyne, Joseph
Decell, Stephen
McCool, Malachy
Melancon, Robert
Violette, Tex

Retired:
Reverend Monsignors—
Bergeron, Albert G., Hollywood Park Apartments, 4000 West Bank Expwy., Apt. 65, Marrero, LA 70072
Koninkx, William, P.O. Box 1066, Houma, LA 70361
Landry, George A., 1016 France St., New Orleans, LA 70117
Manikowski, Stanislaus J., P.O. Box 527, Raceland, LA 70394
Newfield, John L., 2832 Burdette St., Apt. 428, New Orleans, LA 70125-2514
Songy, James B., 410 Ninth St., Lockport, LA 70374
Whitney, Philip, 1201 Cardinal Dr., Thibodaux, LA 70302
Reverend Fathers—
Amedee, Francis, 725 St. Phillips St., Thibodaux, LA 70301
Brewerton, Peter H., P.O. Box 1404, Thibodaux, LA 70302
Broussard, Hubert C., Chateau Creole, 220 Monarch Dr., Apt. J13, Houma, LA 70360
Daigle, H.C. Paul, 1915 Branard St., Apt. 16, Houston, TX 77098
Foley, Brendan P., 182 E. 110th St., Galliano, LA 70354
Fossier, Emile, P.O. Box 4014, Houma, LA 70361
Loresco, Alfredo, 155 Church St., Lockport, LA 70374
Luu, Joseph
Naquin, Roch, 539 Island Rd., Montegut, LA 70377
Pol, Dom Te, 3596 Friendswood, Apt. #6, Houma, LA 70363
Prince, Gerald
Toth, Victor, 57 Marcus Mitchell Rd., Picayune, MS 39466

Permanent Deacons:
Authement, Douglas, Maria Immacolata, Houma
Bascle, Daniel, St. Eloi, Theriot
Blanchard, Edward, St. Mary's Nativity, Raceland
Blanchard, Gerald, St. Ann, Bourg
Burregi, Sammy, Sacred Heart, Cut Off
Cantrelle, Michael, Holy Rosary, Larose
Didier, James V., St. Bridget, Schriever
Domangue, Kurt J., Holy Family, Grand Caillou
Dragna, Andrew J., Holy Cross, Morgan City
Dufrene, Roland, St. Hilary of Poitiers, Raceland
Dusse, Robert, St. Bernadette, Houma
Duthu, James, Annunziata, Houma
Fanguy, Bernard A. Harold, Holy Family, Grand Caillou
Frazier, Eldon, Cut-Off
Giroir, Charles, Christ the Redeemer, Thibodaux
Kurtz, Harold, Our Lady of the Most Holy Rosary, Houma
Landry, Alduce, St. Charles, Thibodaux
LeBouef, Raymond, Holy Rosary, Houma
Legendre, Paul Joseph, Jr., St. Genevieve, Thibodaux
Marts, Melvin, St. Joseph, Galliano
Messina, Nick, St. Anthony, Bayou Black
Orgeron, Willie R., St. Joseph Co-Cathedral, Thibodaux
Porche, Glenn, St. Eloi, Theriot
Pujals, Pedro P., St. Thomas Aquinas, Thibodaux
Rabalais, Bertrand A., Annunziata, Houma
Uzee, Dickey, St. Mary's Nativity, Raceland

INSTITUTIONS LOCATED IN THE DIOCESE

[A] HIGH SCHOOLS, DIOCESAN

HOUMA. *Vandebilt Catholic High*, 209 S. Hollywood Rd., 70360. Tel: 504-876-2551; Fax: 504-868-9774.
E-mail: vchs@archdiocese-no.org
Web site: www2.cajun.net/~vchs
Brothers of the Sacred Heart. Mr. David Keife, Prin.; Bro. Carl Evans, S.C., Chap. Brothers 3; Lay Teachers 75; Junior High Students 449; Senior High Students 510.

THIBODAUX. *Edward Douglas White Catholic High*. (Coed), 555 Cardinal Dr., 70301. Tel: 504-446-8486; Fax: 504-448-1275.
E-mail: edwhitehi@archdiocese-no.org
Brothers of the Sacred Heart. Mr. David Boudreaux, Prin. Brothers 2; Lay Teachers 52; Students 779.
E.D. White Catholic High School Foundation, Inc. Tel: 504-449-1859; Fax: 504-448-1275.
E.D. White Catholic High School Alumni Association. Tel: 504-446-8486; Fax: 504-448-1275.

MORGAN CITY. *Central Catholic High*, 2100 Cedar St., 70380. Tel: 504-385-5372; Fax: 504-385-3444.
E-mail: centcathi@archdiocese-no.org
Web site: www.cchseagles.com
Mr. Rory Rafferty, Prin.; Patricia Roland, Guidance Counselor. Lay Teachers 21; Students 209.

[B] DAY CARE CENTERS

HOUMA. *St. Lucy Day Care and Child Development Center*, P.O. Box 3894, 70361. Tel: 504-876-1246.
E-mail: enfants@mobiltel.com
Staff 11; Children 65.

[C] RETREAT CENTERS

SCHRIEVER. *Lumen Christi Retreat Center*, 100 Lumen Christi Ln., Hwy. 311, 70395. Tel: 504-868-1523; Fax: 504-868-1525. Rev. Rock Travnikar, O.F.M., Dir.

[D] CONVENTS

LOCKPORT. *Monastery of the Heart of Jesus*, 155 Church St., 70374. Tel: 504-532-2411. Dominican Contemplative Sisters of the Heart of Jesus of the Diocese of Houma-Thibodaux. Sr. Mary Henry McKanna, O.P., Prioress.

[E] MISCELLANEOUS

THIBODAUX. *The Diocese of Houma-Thibodaux Historical Research Center*, 205 Audubon Ave., 70301. Tel: 504-446-2383; Fax: 504-449-0574.
E-mail: htchancllor@htdiocese.org
Sr. Miriam Mitchell, S.H.Sp., Chancellor & Archivist.
Magnificat of the Houma-Thibodaux Diocese, 830 Laurel Jalley Rd., P.O. Box 1422, 70301. Tel: 504-446-5001; Fax: 504-447-4261. Mrs. Mina McKee, Coord., Bayou River Chapter.
St. Joseph Manor. (Retirement Community), 1201 Cardinal Dr., 70301. Tel: 504-446-9050; Fax: 504-449-0047.
E-mail: annt@stjosephmanor.com
Web site: www.stjosephmanor.com
Ann Thibodaux, Admin.

SCHRIEVER. *Cemeteries Trust*, P.O. Box 505, 70395. Tel: 504-850-3149; Fax: 504-850-3164.
E-mail: pbreaux@htdiocese.org

RELIGIOUS INSTITUTES OF MEN REPRESENTED IN THE DIOCESE

For further details refer to the corresponding bracketed number in the Religious Institutes of Men or Women section.

[1100]—*Brothers of the Sacred Heart*.—S.C.
[0520]—*Franciscan Friars*.—O.F.M.
[0770]—*Marist Brothers*.—F.M.S.

RELIGIOUS INSTITUTES OF WOMEN REPRESENTED IN THE DIOCESE

[0400]—*Congregation of Our Lady of Mount Carmel*.—O.Carm.
[2550]—*Sisters of Mercy*.—R.S.M.
[2410]—*Congregation of the Marianites of Holy Cross*.—M.S.C.
[]—*Dominican Contemplative Sisters*.—O.P.
[]—*Dominican Sisters*. (Cabra, Ireland).—O.P.
[1140]—*Eucharistic Missionaries of St. Dominic*.—O.P.
[2970]—*School Sisters of Notre Dame*.—S.S.N.D.
[3830]—*Sisters of St. Joseph*.—C.S.J.
[2050]—*Sisters of the Holy Spirit and Mary Immaculate*.—S.H.Sp.
[2120]—*Sisters of the Immaculate Conception*.—C.I.C.

NECROLOGY

(No Deaths)

Archdiocese of Indianapolis

(Archidioecesis Indianapolitana)

Most Reverend

DANIEL MARK BUECHLEIN, O.S.B., D.D.

Archbishop of Indianapolis; ordained May 3, 1964; appointed to Memphis January 20, 1987; consecrated Bishop March 2, 1987; installed March 2, 1987; appointed Archbishop of Indianapolis July 13, 1992; installed September 9, 1992.

The Archbishop Edward T. O'Meara Catholic Center: 1400 N. Meridian St., P.O. Box 1410, Indianapolis, IN, 46206. Tel.: 317-236-1400; Fax: 317-236-1401.

Web site address: www.archindy.org

E-mail address: chancery@archindy.org

ESTABLISHED A DIOCESE IN 1834; ESTABLISHED AN ARCHDIOCESE DECEMBER 19, 1944. BY DECREE OF POPE PIUS XII

Square Miles 13,757.7

Comprises the Counties of Bartholomew, Brown, Clark, Clay, Crawford, Dearborn, Decatur, Fayette, Floyd, Franklin, Hancock, Harrison, Hendricks, Henry, Jackson, Jefferson, Jennings, Johnson, Lawrence, Marion, Monroe, Morgan, Ohio, Orange, Owen, Parke, Perry, Putnam, Ripley, Rush, Scott, Shelby, Switzerland, Union, Vermillion, Vigo, Washington and Wayne, and the township of Harrison in Spencer County, in the southern part of Indiana.

For legal titles of parishes and archdiocesan institutions, consult the Chancery Office.

STATISTICAL OVERVIEW

Personnel	
Archbishop	1
Abbots	1
Retired Abbots	2
Priests: Diocesan Active in Diocese	123
Priests: Active Outside Diocese	2
Priests: Diocesan in Foreign Missions	1
Priests: Retired, Sick or Absent	35
Number of Diocesan Priests	161
Religious Priests in Diocese	115
Extern Priests in Diocese	11
Ordinations:	
Diocesan Priests	2
Total Brothers	48
Total Sisters	758
Parishes	
Parishes	139
With Resident Pastor:	
Resident Diocesan Priests	91
Resident Religious Priests	13
Without Resident Pastor:	
Administered by Priests	24
Administered by Women Religious	10
Administered by Lay People	1
Missions	13
New Parishes Created	1
Professional Ministry Personnel:	
Brothers	3
Sisters	25
Lay Ministers	146
Welfare	
Catholic Hospitals	2
Total Assisted	1,259,463
Homes for the Aged	5
Total Assisted	887
Day Care and Extended Day Care Centers	3
Total Assisted	110
Specialized Homes	3
Total Assisted	734
Special Centers for Social Services	7
Total Assisted	125,311
Educational	
Diocesan Students in Other Seminaries	24
Seminaries, Religious	1
Students Religious	6
Total Seminarians	30
Colleges and Universities	2
Total Students	3,226
High Schools, Diocesan and Parish	6
Total Students	3,236
High Schools, Private	3
Total Students	2,025
Elementary Schools, Diocesan and Parish	62
Total Students	18,125
Catechesis/Religious Education:	
High School Students	2,994
Elementary Students	13,197
Total Students Under Catholic Instruction	42,833
Teachers in the Diocese:	
Priests	4
Brothers	7
Sisters	42
Lay Teachers	1,345
Vital Statistics	
Receptions into the Church:	
Infant Baptism Totals	4,196
Adult Baptism Totals	844
Received into Full Communion	920
First Communions	3,967
Confirmations	3,093
Marriages:	
Catholic	700
Interfaith	678
Total Marriages	1,378
Deaths	2,148
Total Catholic Population	227,501
Total Population	2,359,104

The Diocese of Vincennes (now Indianapolis) was established by decree of Pope Gregory XVI, May 6, 1834, and the See was fixed at Vincennes. The territory then comprised the entire State of Indiana and the eastern third of Illinois. By decree of Pius IX, January 8, 1857, the northern half of the State became the Diocese of Fort Wayne. The southern half of the State remained the Diocese of Vincennes.

The second Bishop of Vincennes, by Apostolic Brief, was permitted to establish his residence either at Vincennes, Madison, Lafayette or Indianapolis; the See city, however, was to remain at Vincennes. This permission was renewed to the fourth Bishop, with the exception of Lafayette. On the appointment of the fifth Bishop, he was directed to fix his residence at Indianapolis, but the Cathedral and title of the See were continued at Vincennes. By an Apostolic Brief dated March 28, 1898, the title of the Diocese was changed to that of "Diocese of Indianapolis" with the city of Indianapolis as the Episcopal See. By the same Brief the Patron Saint of the Diocese was to remain St. Francis Xavier, the title of the old Cathedral in Vincennes.

On December 19, 1944, Most Reverend Amleto Giovanni Cicognani, Apostolic Delegate to the United States, solemnly proclaimed the Papal Decree of Pope Pius XII in SS. Peter and Paul Cathedral, Indianapolis, elevating Indianapolis to the status of an Archdiocese, the State of Indiana being the Metropolitan Area. The Dioceses of Evansville and Lafayette-in-Indiana were created by the same decree and were made Suffragan Sees of Indianapolis. Upon the establishment of the Diocese of Gary on December 17, 1956, it too became a Suffragan See.

Former Bishops—Rt. Rev. SIMON GABRIEL BRUTE, S.S., D.D., cons. 1834; died 1839.—Rt. Rev. CELESTINE DE LA HAILANDIERE, D.D., cons. 1839; resigned 1847; died in France, 1882.—Rt. Rev. JOHN S. BAZIN, D.D., cons. 1847; died 1848.—Rt. Rev. MAURICE DE ST. PALAIS, D.D., cons. Jan. 14, 1849; died June 28, 1877.—Rt. Rev. FRANCIS SILAS CHATARD, D.D., cons. May 12, 1878; died Sept. 7, 1918.—Most Rev. JOSEPH CHARTRAND, D.D., cons. Titular Bishop of Flavias and Coadjutor Bishop, Sept. 15, 1910; succeeded to the See of Indianapolis, Sept. 7, 1918; died Dec. 8, 1933.—Most Rev. JOSEPH ELMER RITTER, S.T.D., cons. Titular Bishop of Hippo and Auxiliary Bishop, March 28, 1933; succeeded to the See March 24, 1934; installed as Archbishop Dec. 19, 1944; transferred to Metropolitan See of St. Louis, July 20, 1946; named Cardinal, Jan. 16, 1961; died June 10, 1967.—Most Rev. PAUL C. SCHULTE, D.D., cons. Bishop of Leavenworth, Sept. 21, 1937; appt. Archbishop of Indianapolis, July 20, 1946; installed Oct. 10, 1946; resigned Jan. 14, 1970; died Feb. 17, 1984.—Most Rev. GEORGE J. BISKUP, cons. Titular Bishop of Hermeria and Auxiliary of Dubuque, April 24, 1957; transferred to Des Moines Feb. 3, 1965 transferred to Indianapolis "cum jure successionis," July 26, 1967; succeeded to See Jan. 14, 1970; resigned March 26, 1979; died Oct. 17, 1979.—Most Rev. EDWARD T. O'MEARA, S.T.D., appt. Titular Bishop of Thisiduo and Auxiliary of St. Louis Jan. 28, 1972; cons. in the Basilica of St. Peter, Rome, Feb. 13, 1972; appt. Archbishop of Indianapolis Nov. 27, 1979; installed Jan. 10, 1980; died Jan. 10, 1992.

Archdiocesan Administration—Secretariats/Vicariates/ Agencies and Offices can be contacted through The Archbishop Edward T. O'Meara Catholic Center. *1400 N. Meridian St., Indianapolis, 46202., Address all mail unless otherwise indicated to: P.O. Box 1410, Indianapolis, 46206-1410.* Tel: 317-236-1400; Fax: 317-236-1401.

Vicar General and Moderator of the Curia—Rev. Msgr. JOSEPH F. SCHAEDEL, M.S., M.Div.

Chancellor—SUZANNE L. MAGNANT.

Assistant Chancellor—Rev. WILLIAM STUMPF.

Chief Financial Officer—JEFFREY D. STUMPF.

Board of Consultors—Most Rev. DANIEL M. BUECHLEIN, O.S.B., D.D., Chm.; Rev. Msgr. JOSEPH F. SCHAEDEL, M.S., M.Div.; Rev. Msgr. FRANCIS R. TUOHY; Rev. Msgr. RICHARD LAWLAR; Revs. WILLIAM STUMPF; CLIFFORD VOGELSANG; PAUL ETIENNE; PAUL KOETTER; DANIEL MAHAN; DANIEL STAUBLIN.

Deaneries and Deans—Rev. PATRICK DOYLE, Indianapolis North; Rev. JOSEPH RIEDMAN, Indianapolis East; Rev. Msgr. RICHARD LAWLER, V.F., Indianapolis South; Rev. Msgr. JOHN RYAN, V.F., Indianapolis West; Rev. WILLIAM FARRIS, O.F.M., V.F., Batesville; Rev. CHARLES S. CHESEBROUGH, V.F., Bloomington; Rev. STANLEY J. HERBER, V.F., Connersville; Rev. CLIFFORD VOGELSANG, New Albany; Rev. JOHN MEYER, Seymour; Rev. JEREMY KING, O.S.B., Tell City; Rev. JOSEPH KERN, Terre Haute.

Council of Priests—Most Rev. DANIEL M. BUECHLEIN, O.S.B., D.D., Pres. SUZANNE MAGNANT; Rev. Msgr. JOSEPH F. SCHAEDEL, M.S., M.Div., V.G.; Revs. AL AJAMIE; DANIEL ATKINS; NOAH CASEY, O.S.B.; CLEM DAVIS; STEPHEN GIANNINI; PAUL ETIENNE; ROBERT GILDAY; JEREMY KING, O.S.B.; GERALD KIRKHOFF; RICHARD LAWLER; MICHAEL O'MARA; DANIEL STAUBLIN; ROGER RUDOLF; DANIEL MAHAN; MARTIN PETER; STEVEN SCHAFTLEIN; WILLIAM STUMPF; Rev. Msgr. FRANCIS R. TUOHY; Rev. MICHAEL WELCH, Chm.

Finance Council—Most Rev. DANIEL M. BUECHLEIN, O.S.B., D.D., Chm.; Rev. Msgr. JOSEPH F. SCHAEDEL, M.S., M.Div.; JEFFREY D. STUMPF, C.F.O. L. H. BAYLEY; MICHAEL BINDNER; JAY BREHM; JACKIE BYERS; PATRICK CARR; MICHAEL DILTS; JOSEPH NAUGHTON; DENNIS SCHLICHTE; JAMES SHANAHAN. Tel: 317-236-7325.

Priests' Personnel Board—Most Rev. DANIEL M. BUECHLEIN, O.S.B., D.D.; Revs. THOMAS CLEGG; PATRICK DOYLE; JAMES FARRELL; JOHN GEIS; STAN HERBER; GERALD KIRKHOFF; DANIEL STAUBLIN; WILLIAM STUMPF.

Archdiocesan Pastoral Council—Most Rev. DANIEL M. BUECHLEIN, O.S.B., D.D.; Rev. Msgr. JOSEPH SCHAEDEL, Vicar Gen. SUZANNE MAGNANT, Chancellor; CELINA ACOSTA-TAYLOR; L. H. BAYLEY; MARIA BLAKE; MILLY BREHOB; WILLIAM R. BRUNS; RON DOXSEE; Rev. Msgr. FREDERICK EASTON, J.C.L.; Revs. JAMES FARRELL; JOSEPH FOLZENLOGEN; CHARLES GARDNER; THOMAS GAYBRICK; ROBERT W. GOLOBISH; ANNETTE "MICKEY" LENTZ; Rev. STEVEN SCHAFTLEIN; AMANDA STRONG; JEFFREY STUMPF; Rev. WILLIAM STUMPF. Tel: 317-236-7325.

Secretariat for Catholic Charities and Family Ministries—THOMAS GAYBRICK, M.S.W., Sec. Tel: 317-236-1560.

Family Ministries—DAVID BETHURAM, Assoc. Sec. Tel: 317-236-1596.

Bloomington Catholic Social Services—KAREN BROSIUS, M.S.W., Dir., *635 N. College Ave., Bloomington, 47404.* Tel: 812-332-1262.

Catholic Campaign for Human Development—THOMAS GAYBRICK, Dir. Tel: 317-236-1560.

Catholic Social Services of Central Indiana—DAVID BETHURAM, Exec. Dir. Tel: 317-236-1500.

Multicultural Ministry—Rev. KENNETH TAYLOR, Dir. Tel: 317-236-1596.

New Albany Deanery Catholic Charities—BARBARA WILLIAMS, M.S., Dir., *702 E. Market St., New Albany, 47150.* Tel: 812-948-0438.

Pro-Life Activities—Sr. DIANE CAROLLO, S.G.L., Dir. Tel: 317-236-1569.

St. Elizabeth's—(Pregnancy Services); DAVID J. SILER, M.S.W., Exec. Dir., *2500 Churchman Ave., Indianapolis, 46203.* Tel: 317-787-3412.

St. Elizabeth's Southern Indiana (Regional Maternity Center)—(Pregnancy Services); KEITH E. STORMES, Exec. Dir., *601 E. Market St., New Albany, 47150.* Tel: 812-949-7305.

St. Mary's Child Center—Dr. PATRICIA WELCH, Exec. Dir., *901 Dr. Martin Luther King, Jr. St., Indianapolis, 46202.* Tel: 317-635-1491.

Tell City Catholic Charities—SUSAN HUGHES, Program Supvr., *802 Ninth St., Tell City, 47586.* Tel: 812-547-6414.

Terre Haute Catholic Charities—JOHN ETLING, M.S., Dir., *Corporate Square Annex, 2931 Ohio Blvd., Terre Haute, 47803.* Tel: 812-232-1447.

Youth and Family Ministries—DAVID BETHURAM, Exec. Dir. Tel: 317-236-1439.

Secretariat for Catholic Education and Faith Formation—ANNETTE "MICKEY" LENTZ, Sec./Exec. Dir. Tel: 317-236-1438.

Administration—G. JOSEPH PETERS, Assoc. Exec. Dir. Tel: 317-236-1437.

Faith Formation—Dr. HARRY DUDLEY, Assoc. Exec. Dir. Tel: 317-236-1446.

Catholic Youth Organization—EDWARD TINDER, Exec. Dir., *580 Stevens St., Indianapolis, 46203.* Tel: 317-632-9311.

Secretariat for Communications—WILLIAM R. BRUNS, Sec. Tel: 317-236-1585.

Archdiocesan Newspaper, "The Criterion"—Most Rev. DANIEL M. BUECHLEIN, O.S.B., D.D., Publisher; WILLIAM R. BRUNS, Exec. Editor; GREG A. OTOLSKI, Mng. Editor. Tel: 317-236-1570.

Catholic Communications Center—SUSAN SCHRAMM, Dir. Tel: 317-236-1585.

Secretariat for Finance and Administrative Services—JEFFREY D. STUMPF, Sec. Tel: 317-236-1421.

Accounting Services—Vacant, Controller. Tel: 317-236-1410.

Information Services—TOM O'DROBINAK, Dir. Tel: 317-236-1420.

Management Services—DAVID L. HODDE, Dir. Tel: 317-236-1452.

Catholic Cemeteries—TONY LLOYD, Buchanan Group, *9001 N. Haverstick Rd., Indianapolis, 46240.* Tel: 317-574-8898.

Chief Financial Officer—JEFF STUMPF. Tel: 317-236-7325.

Roman Catholic Archdiocese of Indianapolis Properties—Most Rev. DANIEL M. BUECHLEIN, O.S.B., Pres.; Rev. Msgr. JOSEPH F. SCHAEDEL, Vice Pres. Secretaries: SUZANNE L. MAGNANT; JEFFREY D. STUMPF. Tel: 317-236-1421.

Secretariat for Lay Ministry and Pastoral Services—SUZANNE L. MAGNANT, Sec. Tel: 317-236-7325.

Archives—JANET NEWLAND, Assoc. Archivist. Tel: 317-236-1429.

Archdiocesan Historian—Rev. JACK W. PORTER, Ph.D.

Human Resources—ED ISAKSON, Dir. Tel: 317-236-1594.

Lay Ministry—SUZANNE MAGNANT, Dir. Tel: 317-236-7325.

Parish Planning and Organizational Development—SUZANNE MAGNANT, Dir. Tel: 317-236-7325.

Secretariat for Spiritual Life and Worship—CHARLES GARDNER, Sec. Tel: 317-236-1483.

Archdiocesan Cathedral—Rev. RICHARD GINTHER, Pastor & Rector, *1347 N. Meridian St., Indianapolis, 46202-2396.* Tel: 317-634-4519.

Evangelization Commission—Rev. JOSEPH FOLZENLOGEN, S.J., Coord. Tel: 317-236-1489.

Office of Worship—CHARLES GARDNER, Dir. Tel: 317-236-1483.

Retreat & Renewal Ministries and Fatima Retreat House—KEVIN DEPREY, Dir., *5353 E. 56th St., Indianapolis, 46226.* Tel: 317-545-7681; Fax: 317-545-0095.

Secretariat for Stewardship and Development—JOSEPH THERBER, Sec./Exec. Dir. Tel: 317-236-1415.

Office of Stewardship and Development—REX CAMP, Dir., School & Agency Svcs. Tel: 317-236-1447. Vacant, Dir., Donor & Parish Svcs. Tel: 317-236-1426.

Catholic Community Foundation, Inc.—Most Rev. DANIEL M. BUECHLEIN, O.S.B., D.D., Chm. SANDRA BEHRINGER, Dir. Gift Planning. Tel: 317-236-1427.

Mission Office—Sr. MARIAN T. KINNEY, S.P., Dir. Tel: 317-236-1485.

Vicariate of Clergy and Parish Life Coordinators: Formation and Personnel—Rev. WILLIAM STUMPF, Vicar. Tel: 317-236-1495.

Ministry to Priests—Rev. NOAH CASEY, O.S.B., Dir. Tel: 317-236-1491.

Personnel: Priests and Parish life Coordinators—Rev. WILLIAM STUMPF, Dir. Tel: 317-236-1449.

Priestly and Religious Vocations—Rev. JOSEPH B. MORIARTY, Dir. Tel: 317-236-1490.

Vicariate Judicial Metropolitan Tribunal—Rev. Msgr. FREDERICK EASTON, J.C.L., Judicial Vicar. Tel: 317-236-1460.

Vice Vicars Judicial—Revs. ROBERT J. GILDAY, S.T.B.; PAUL M. SHIKANY, J.C.L.

Judge Instructor—KATHARINE LOZANO, B.A., J.D.

Advocates—SHERIE BERG, B.A., M.T.S.; ANN TULLY, B.S.

Defenders of the Bond—Revs. JAMES R. BONKE, J.C.L.; NATHANIAL REEVES, O.S.B., J.C.L.; JOSEPH W. DOOLEY, S.T.D., Ph.D.

Deputy Defenders of the Bond—Rev. MYLES H. SMITH, J.C.L.; PATRICIA JEFFERS.

Archdiocesan Judges—Revs. CLEMENT DAVIS, M.Div.; JOHN DEDE, J.C.D., Emeritus; HERMAN LUTZ, S.T.L., J.C.L.; RICHARD MUELLER, S.T.L.; Rev. Msgr. FRANCIS TUOHY, J.C.L., P.A.

Auditor—Rev. ROBERT MAZZOLA.

Notaries—KAREN CLEMENT; PEGGY FLECKER; MELODY PEAY.

CLERGY, PARISHES, MISSIONS AND PAROCHIAL SCHOOLS

CITY OF INDIANAPOLIS
(Marion County)

1—SS. PETER AND PAUL CATHEDRAL (1892), Rev. Richard M. Ginther. In res., Revs. James R. Bonke; William F. Stumpf; Joseph F. Schaedel; Dennis M. Duvelius, F.S.S.P.
Res., 1347 N. Meridian St., 46202. Tel: 317-634-4519; Fax: 317-634-0151. [JC]
Catechesis/Religious Programs—Students 50.

2—CHRIST THE KING (1939), Rev. Msgr. Francis R. Tuohy.
Parish Office: 5884 Crittenden Ave., 46220. Tel: 317-255-3666; Fax: 317-475-6579.
Res., 1827 E. Kessler Blvd., 46220. Tel: 317-475-6582.
School—5858 Crittenden Ave., 46220. Tel: 317-257-9366.
Lay Teachers 24; Students 357.
Catechesis/Religious Programs—Tel: 317-255-3666; Fax: 317-475-6579.
Students 117.

3—GOOD SHEPHERD (1993). (St. Catherine, 1909, and St. James the Greater, 1951, were closed, merged, and renamed in 1993). Rev. Thomas Clegg; Thomas Meier, Parish Life Coord.
Church & Parish Office: 1109 E. Cameron St., 46203. Tel: 317-783-3158; Fax: 317-781-5961. [JC]
School—Central Catholic School, 1155 E. Cameron St., 46203. Tel: 317-783-7759; Fax: 317-781-5964.
Students 220.
Catechesis/Religious Programs—Students 21.

4—HOLY ANGELS (1903) (African American), Rev. Clarence R. Waldon.
Res., 740 W. 28th St., 46208-5099. Tel: 317-926-3324; Fax: 317-926-3325. [JC]
School—2822 Dr. Martin Luther King, Jr. St., 46208. Tel: 317-926-5211; Fax: 317-926-5219. Sr. Gerry O'Laughlin, Prin.
Sisters of St. Joseph 2; Sisters of I.H.M. Reparatrix 1; Lay Teachers 11; Students 250.
Catechesis/Religious Programs—Students 30.

5—HOLY CROSS (1895), Rev. Lawrence Voelker.
Church—125 N. Oriental St., 46202. Tel: 317-637-2620; Fax: 317-637-0112.
School—Tel: 317-638-9068; Fax: 317-638-0116.
Lay Teachers 15; Students 221.

6—HOLY ROSARY (1909) (Italian), Rev. Msgr. Joseph Schaedel; Rev. Dennis Duvelius, F.S.S.P.
Office: 520 Stevens St., 46203. Tel: 317-636-4478; Fax: 317-636-2522. [JC]

7—HOLY SPIRIT (1946), Revs. Joseph G. Riedman; Henry F. Tully; J. Nicholas Dant.
Res., 7243 E. 10th St., 46219. Tel: 317-353-9404; Fax: 317-351-1707.
School—7241 E. 10th St., 46219. Tel: 317-352-1243.
Lay Teachers 23; Students 411.
Catechesis/Religious Programs—Tel: 317-357-6915.
Students 588.

8—HOLY TRINITY (1906), Rev. Kenneth E. Taylor.
Res., 2618 W. St. Clair St., 46222. Tel: 317-631-2939; Fax: 317-631-2921. [JC]
School—All Saints. Consolidated. See St. Anthony listing. Tel: 317-636-3739; Fax: 317-636-1928.
Catechesis/Religious Programs—Students 29.

9—IMMACULATE HEART OF MARY (1946), Rev. Jeffery H. Godecker.
Parish Center: 5692 N. Central Ave., 46220. Tel: 317-257-2266; Fax: 317-475-7380. [JC]
Res., 5683 Washington Blvd., 46220. Tel: 317-252-5737.
School—317 E. 57th St., 46220. Tel: 317-255-5468; Fax: 317-475-7379.
Lay Teachers 30; Students 412.

10—NATIVITY OF OUR LORD JESUS CHRIST (1947), Rev. Steven Schwab.
7225 Southeastern Ave., 46239. Tel: 317-357-1200. [JC]
School—3310 S. Meadow Dr., 46239. Tel: 317-357-1459; Fax: 317-357-9175.
Sisters of Providence 2; Lay Teachers 11; Students 267.
Catechesis/Religious Programs—Tel: 317-359-6075.
Students 189.

11—OUR LADY OF LOURDES (1909), Rev. James Farrell; Mr. Charles Eble, Pastoral Assoc. In res., Rev. Joseph Moriarty.
Res., 5333 E. Washington St., 46219. Tel: 317-356-7291; Fax: 317-356-2358.
School—30 S. Downey St., 46219. Tel: 317-357-3316; Fax: 317-357-0980.
Lay Teachers 19; Students 375.
Catechesis/Religious Programs—Students 25.

12—SACRED HEART OF JESUS (1875) (German), Revs. Michael G. Barrett, O.F.M.; Elias Koppert, O.F.M.; Justin Belitz, O.F.M.; Frank Jasper, O.F.M.; Al Jost, O.F.M; Tom Fox, O.F.M.
Res., 1530 S. Union St., 46225. Tel: 317-638-5551, 803-3751 (TTY); Fax: 317-637-9741. [JC]
School—Central Catholic Consolidated. See Good Shepherd Listing. Tel: 317-783-7759.

Catechesis/Religious Programs—Students 24.

13—ST. ANDREW THE APOSTLE (1946), Sr. Marilyn Herber, S.P., Parish Life Coord.; Revs. Pat Kelly; Patrick Doyle, Priest Moderator.
Parish Office: 4052 E. 38th St., 46218-1444. Tel: 317-546-1571; Fax: 317-549-6311.
School—School & Daycare, Tel: 317-546-1571; Fax: 317-549-6306.
Lay Teachers 16; Students 233.
Catechesis/Religious Programs—Students 43.

14—ST. ANN (1917), Rev. Glenn L. O'Connor.
Office & Mailing Address: 2862 S. Holt Rd., 46241. Tel: 317-244-3750; Fax: 317-244-9841.
Res., 2850 S. Holt Rd., 46241. [JC]
Catechesis/Religious Programs—Laura Williams, D.R.E.
Students 71.

15—ST. ANTHONY (1891) (Irish-German), Rev. Msgr. John T. Ryan, V.F.
379 N. Warman Ave., 46222. Tel: 317-636-4828; Fax: 317-636-3140. [JC]
School—All Saints Consolidated, 75 N. Belleview Pl., 46222-4145. Tel: 317-636-3739; Fax: 317-636-1928.
Lay Teachers 14; Students 240.
Catechesis/Religious Programs—Students 60.

16—ST. BARNABAS (1965), Revs. Joseph McNally; Joseph Pesola.
Res., 8300 Rahke Rd., 46217. Tel: 317-882-0724; Fax: 317-887-8932.
School—Tel: 317-881-7422; Fax: 317-887-8933. Paulette Conner, Prin.
Lay Teachers 31; Students 608.
Catechesis/Religious Programs—Students 320.

17—ST. BERNADETTE (1952), Rev. James Farrell. In res., Rev. Noah Casey, O.S.B.
Church & Parish Office: 4838 Fletcher Ave., 46203. Tel: 317-356-5867; Fax: 317-356-2460.
Res., 4826 Fletcher Ave., 46203. Tel: 317-356-5867. [CEM]

18—ST. CHRISTOPHER (Speedway City) (1937), Rev. D. Michael Welch. Pastoral Assocs.: Sr. Sue Bradshaw, O.S.F.; Mr. Bill Szolek Van Valkenburgh; Nancy L. Meyer. In res., Rev. Robert J. Gilday.
Res., 5301 W. 16th St., 46224. Tel: 317-241-6314; Fax: 317-241-6587.
School—5335 W. 16th St., 46224. Fax: 317-244-6678. Mrs. Barbara Leek, Prin.
Lay Teachers 11; Students 272.
Catechesis/Religious Programs—Ms. Therese Brennan, D.R.E.
Students 295.

19—ST. GABRIEL THE ARCHANGEL (1963), Rev. Larry P. Crawford; Sr. Mary Timothy Kavanaugh, O.S.F., Pastoral Assoc. In res., Rev. Msgr. Frederick C. Easton.
Res., 6000 W. 34th St., 46224. Tel: 317-291-7014; Fax: 317-297-6455.
School—(Grades PreK-8). Tel: 317-297-1414; Fax: 317-297-6453.
Teachers 20; Students 246.
Catechesis/Religious Programs—Tel: 317-299-9924.
Students 80.

20—ST. JOAN OF ARC (1921), Rev. Patrick A. Doyle; Mary Breckenridge, Pastoral Assoc.
Res., 4217 Central Ave., 46205. Tel: 317-283-5508; Fax: 317-283-5511. [JC]
School—500 E. 42nd St., 46205. Tel: 317-283-1518; Fax: 317-931-3380.
Lay Teachers 15; Students 220.
Catechesis/Religious Programs—Tel: 317-283-5508; Fax: 317-283-5511.
Students 81.

21—ST. JOHN THE EVANGELIST (1837) (Irish), Rev. Thomas Murphy.
Res., 126 W. Georgia St., 46225. Tel: 317-635-2021; Fax: 317-635-2014. [JC]

22—ST. JOSEPH (1949), Rev. Glenn L. O'Connor. In res., Rev. Mark Tran-Xuan Thanh (Vietnam).
Res., 1375 S. Mickley Ave., 46241. Tel: 317-244-9002; Fax: 317-244-0278. [JC]
School—All Saints Consolidated. See St. Anthony Listing.
Catechesis/Religious Programs—Students 83.

23—ST. JUDE (1959), Rev. Gerald J. Kirkhoff.
Res., 5353 McFarland Rd., 46227. Tel: 317-786-4371; 780-7588; Fax: 317-780-7592.
School—5375 McFarland Rd, 46227. Tel: 317-784-6828.
Sisters of Providence 2; Lay Teachers 20; Students 513.
Catechesis/Religious Programs—Tel: 317-780-7591.
Students 220.

24—ST. LAWRENCE (1949), Revs. John Beitansopf; Augustine Doo Wan Kim, (Korean Community). In res., Revs. Myles H. Smith; William Joseph Brown.
Office: 6944 E. 46th St., 46226. Tel: 317-546-4065; Fax: 317-543-4926.
Res., 4650 N. Shadeland Ave., 46226. Tel: 317-543-4921.
School—6950 E. 46th St., 46226. Tel: 317-543-4923; Fax: 317-543-4924.
Lay Teachers 23; Students 434.
Catechesis/Religious Programs—Tel: 317-543-2935.
Students 350.

25—ST. LUKE (1961), Rev. Daniel J. Mahan.
Res., 7575 Holliday Dr. E., 46260. Tel: 317-259-4373; Fax: 317-254-3210. [JC]
School—7650 N. Illinois St., 46260. Tel: 317-255-3912; Fax: 317254-3210.
Lay Teachers 32; Students 506.
Catechesis/Religious Programs—Tel: 317-479-7373.
Students 315.

26—ST. MARK THE EVANGELIST (1946), Rev. Msgr. Richard C. Lawler.
Res., 535 E. Edgewood, 46227. Tel: 317-787-8246; Fax: 317-781-6466.
School—541 E. Edgewood Ave., 46227. Tel: 317-786-4013.
Lay Teachers 24; Students 342.
Catechesis/Religious Programs—Tel: 317-784-7155.
Students 161.

27—ST. MARY/IMMACULATE CONCEPTION (1858), Rev. Michael E. O'Mara; Sr. Therese Wente, O.S.F., Pastoral Assoc.
Res., 317 N. New Jersey St., 46204. Tel: 317-637-3983; Fax: 317-637-0111. [JC]
Catechesis/Religious Programs—The Marian Center, 311 N. New Jersey St., 46204. Bro. Ricardo Iman Trevino, D.R.E.
Students 105.

28—ST. MATTHEW (1958), Rev. Donald L. Schmidlin. In res., Revs. Richard Hindel, O.S.B.; Robert E. Mazzola.
Res., 4100 E. 56th St., 46220. Tel: 317-257-4297; 479-2382 (Rectory); Fax: 317-479-2381.
School—(Grades PreK-8). Tel: 317-251-3997; Fax: 317-479-2381.
Lay Teachers 29; Students 540.
Catechesis/Religious Programs—Tel: 317-257-9733.
Students 80.

29—ST. MICHAEL THE ARCHANGEL (1948), Rev. Anthony Volz.
Res., 3354 W. 30th St., 46222. Tel: 317-926-7359; Fax: 317-921-3282.
School—3352 W. 30th St., 46222. Tel: 317-926-0516; Fax: 317-921-3280.
Lay Teachers 20; Students 362.
Catechesis/Religious Programs—Tel: 317-925-7597.
Students 126.

30—ST. MONICA (1956), Revs. Paul D. Koetter; Patrick J. Beidelman.
Res., 6131 N. Michigan Rd., 46228. Tel: 317-253-2193; Fax: 317-253-3342.
School—Tel: 317-255-7153; Fax: 317-259-5570.
Lay Teachers 30; Students 458.
Catechesis/Religious Programs—Tel: 317-253-2193.
Students 408.

31—ST. PATRICK (1865) (Irish-Hispanic), Revs. Lawrence Voelker; Al Jost, O.F.M.; Thomas Fox, O.F.M., (Hispanic Ministry).
Church—950 Prospect St., 46203. Tel: 317-631-5824; Fax: 317-631-5828.
School—Consolidated. See Central Catholic Good Shepherd Parish.
Catechesis/Religious Programs—Students 120.

32—ST. PHILIP NERI (1909), Rev. Carlton J. Beever.
Res., 550 N. Rural St., 46201. Tel: 317-631-8746; Fax: 317-632-8161. [JC]
School—545 Eastern Ave., 46201. Tel: 317-636-0134; Fax: 317-636-3231.
Lay Teachers 14; Students 191.
Catechesis/Religious Programs—Students 191.

33—ST. PIUS X (1955), Revs. Martin A. Peter; J. Nicholas Dant.
Res., 7200 Sarto Dr., 46240. Tel: 317-255-4534; Fax: 317-466-3354.
School—Tel: 317-466-3361.
Lay Teachers 28; Students 505.
Catechesis/Religious Programs—Tel: 317-257-1085.
Students 550.

34—ST. RITA (1919), Revs. Anthony Clark, S.V.D.; Alfred Ayem, S.V.D.; Joseph Dao Vu, S.V.D., Dir. Vietnamese Apostolate; Cathy McCrary, Business Mgr. In res., Revs. Charles Smith, S.V.D.; Kenneth Hamilton, S.V.D.; Chester Smith, S.V.D.
Res., 1733 Dr. Andrew J. Brown Ave., 46202. Tel: 317-632-9349; Fax: 317-687-0973. [JC]
School—1816 N. Arsenal Ave., 46218. Tel: 317-636-8580; Fax: 317-636-6041. Bernadette Paradise, Prin.
Lay Teachers 13; Students 141.
Catechesis/Religious Programs—Students 44.

35—ST. ROCH (1922), Rev. James R. Wilmoth.
Res., 3600 S. Pennsylvania St., 46227. Tel: 317-784-1763; Fax: 317-783-9617. [JC]
School—3603 S. Meridian St., 46217. Tel: 317-784-9144.
Lay Teachers 20; Students 306.
Catechesis/Religious Programs—Students 34.

36—ST. SIMON (1961), Rev. Robert W. Sims. In res., Rev. Peter Gallagher.
Res., 8155 Oaklandon Rd., 46236. Tel: 317-826-6000; Fax: 317-826-6010.
School—Tel: 317-826-6000, Ext. 107; Fax: 317-826-6020.
Lay Teachers 33; Students 639.
Catechesis/Religious Programs—Beverly Hansberry, D.R.E.
Students 155.

37—ST. THERESE OF THE INFANT JESUS (LITTLE FLOWER) (1925), Revs. Vincent Lampert; Jonathan Stewart.
Res., 4720 E. 13th St., 46201. Tel: 317-357-8352; Fax: 317-357-5316. [JC]
School—1401 N. Bosart Ave, 46202. Tel: 317-353-2282.
Lay Teachers 22; Students 492.
Catechesis/Religious Programs—Students 640.

38—ST. THOMAS AQUINAS (1939), Rev. William G. Munshower.
Office: 4625 N. Kenwood Ave., 46208. Tel: 317-253-1461; Fax: 317-253-1410.
Res., 4650 N. Illinois St., 46208.
School—4600 N. Illinois St., 46208. Tel: 317-255-6244; Fax: 317-255-6106.
Lay Teachers 14; Students 212.
Catechesis/Religious Programs—Students 32.

OUTSIDE THE CITY OF INDIANAPOLIS

Aurora, Dearborn Co., St. Mary of the Immaculate Conception (1857), Rev. Christopher A. Craig.
Parish Office: 203 Fourth St., 47001. Tel: 812-926-0644; 926-0060; Fax: 812-926-4439.
School—211 Fourth St., 47001. Tel: 812-926-1558; Fax: 812-926-2590.
Lay Teachers 10; Students 169.
Catechesis/Religious Programs—Students 71.

Batesville, Ripley Co., St. Louis (1868) (German), Revs. William J. Farris, O.F.M.; Damian Cesanek, O.F.M.; Alphonse Hoff, O.F.M., (Retired); Benno Heidlage, O.F.M., (Retired).
Res., 13 St. Louis Pl., 47006. Tel: 812-934-3204; Fax: 812-933-0667. [CEM]
School—17 St. Louis Pl., 47006. Tel: 812-934-3310; Fax: 812-934-6202.
Lay Teachers 26; Students 472.
Catechesis/Religious Programs—Prudence McFarland, D.R.E.
Students 360.

Bedford, Lawrence Co., St. Vincent de Paul (1864), Rev. Bernard Cox.
Parish Office: 1723 I St., 47421.
Res., 1711 I St., 47421. Tel: 812-275-6539; Fax: 812-275-3493.
School—923 18th St., 47421. Tel: 812-279-2540.
Lay Teachers 10; Students 230.
Catechesis/Religious Programs—Students 75.

Beech Grove, Marion Co., Holy Name (1908), Rev. Gerald F. Burkert. In res., Rev. Joseph F. Rautenberg.
Res., 89 N. 17th Ave., 46107. Tel: 317-784-5454; Fax: 317-784-1834. [JC]
School—21 N. 17th Ave., 46107. Tel: 317-784-9078; Fax: 317-784-9103. Michael Cleary, Prin.
Lay Teachers 20; Students 263.
Catechesis/Religious Programs—Students 105.

Bloomington, Monroe Co., St. Charles Borromeo (1864), Revs. Charles S. Chesebrough, V.F.; Don Davison, C.P.P.S.
Res., 2222 E. Third St., 47401. Tel: 812-336-6846; Fax: 812-331-6732. [JC]
School—(Grades PreK-8) 2224 E. Third St., 47401. Tel: 812-336-5853; Fax: 812-349-0300.
Lay Teachers 30; Students 507.
Catechesis/Religious Programs—Tel: 812-334-1664.
Students 175.

St. John the Apostle (1970), Rev. Daniel B. Donohoo.
Res., 4607 W. State Rd. 46, 47404-9255. Tel: 812-876-1974; Fax: 812-876-9494.
Catechesis/Religious Programs—Tel: 812-876-0718, Ext. 203. Patricia A. Witt, D.R.E.
Students 205.

St. Paul Catholic Center (1969), Rev. Daniel Atkins.
Res., 1413 E. 17th St., 47408. Tel: 812-339-5561; Fax: 812-333-4846.
Catechesis/Religious Programs—Students 132.

Bradford, Harrison Co., St. Michael (1835), Rt. Rev. Bonaventure Knaebel, O.S.B.
Mailing Address: P.O. Box 22, 47107. Tel: 812-364-6646; Fax: 812-364-6614. [CEM]
Catechesis/Religious Programs—Tel: 812-364-6173.
Students 234.

Brazil, Clay Co., Annunciation of the Blessed Virgin Mary (1865), Rev. Anthony P. Spicuzza.
Res., 19 N. Alabama St., 47834. Tel: 812-448-1901. [CEM]
School—(Grades PreK-5) 415 E. Church St., 47834. Tel: 812-448-1394; Fax: 812-443-3089.
Lay Teachers 6; Students 100.

Bright, Dearborn Co., St. Teresa Benedicta of the Cross (2000), Rev. William Marks.
24486 State Line Rd., Ste. 102, Lawrenceburg, 47025-8372. Tel: 812-656-8700; Fax: 812-656-8777.

Brookville, Franklin Co., St. Michael (1845), Rev. Msgr. Louis E. Schumacher.
Res., 354 High St., P.O. Box J, 47012. Tel: 765-647-5462; Fax: 765-647-5462. [CEM]
School—145 Wallace St., P.O. Box J, 47012. Tel: 765-647-4961; Fax: 317-647-4961.
Sisters of the Third Order Regular of St. Francis 2; Lay Teachers 12; Students 249.
Catechesis/Religious Programs—Tel: 765-647-4353; Fax: 765-647-4353.
Students 78.

Brownsburg, Hendricks Co., St. Malachy (1869), Revs. Daniel J. Staublin; Russell R. Zint.
Parish Center: 326 N. Green St., 46112. Tel: 317-852-3195; Fax: 317-852-8939. [CEM 2]
School—330 N. Green St., 46112. Tel: 317-852-2242; Fax: 317-852-3604.
Lay Teachers 22; Students 407.
Catechesis/Religious Programs—Tel: 317-852-8476.
Students 649.

Brownstown, Jackson Co., Our Lady of Providence (1934). Attended by St. Ambrose, Seymour. Rev. Joseph B. Sheets, Admin.
Mailing Address: c/o St. Ambrose Church, 325 S. Chestnut St., Seymour, 47274.
Res., Hwy. 50, 47220.
Catechesis/Religious Programs—Students 6.

Cambridge City, Wayne Co., St. Elizabeth of Hungary (1852), Rev. John H. Luerman.
Res., 333 W. Maple St., 47327. Tel: 317-478-3242.
Catechesis/Religious Programs—Students 119.

Cannelton, Perry Co., St. Michael (1859), Revs. Benet Amato, O.S.B.; Barnabas Gillespie, O.S.B.
Parish Office: c/o Catholic Ministry Center, 802 Ninth St., Tell City, 47586-2114. Tel: 812-547-7994; Fax: 812-547-6985.
Res., 814 Jefferson St., Tell City, 47586. Tel: 812-547-9901.
Church—Eighth St., 47520. [CEM]

Cedar Grove, Franklin Co., Holy Guardian Angels (1874) (German), Rev. Msgr. Louis E. Schumacher, Admin.
Res., 405 U.S. Hwy. 52, 47016. Tel: 765-647-6981; Fax: 765-647-5462. [CEM]
Res., 354 High St., Brookville, 47012. Tel: 765-647-5462; Fax: 765-647-5462.
Catechesis/Religious Programs—Tel: 765-647-5382.
Students 47.

Charlestown, Clark Co., St. Michael (1860), Rev. Stephen Donahue.
Res., 101 St. Michael Dr., 47111. Tel: 812-256-3200; Fax: 317-256-9066. [CEM]
Child Care Center—(Grades PreK-K) 102 St. Michael Dr., 47111. Tel: 812-256-3503.
Students 80.
Catechesis/Religious Programs—Students 52.
Mission—Henryville, Clark Co., St. Francis Xavier, (1869) Hwy. 31 & 160, P.O. Box 368, Henryville, 47126.

Clarksville, Clark Co., St. Anthony of Padua (1851), Rev. Dismas J. Veeneman, O.F.M.Conv. In res., Revs. Arnold Dearing, O.F.M.Conv.; David Lenz, O.F.M. Conv.; Bro. Ray Ramos, O.F.M.Conv.
Res., 310 N. Sherwood Ave., 47129. Tel: 812-282-2290; Fax: 812-283-3924. [CEM]
School—320 N. Sherwood Ave., 47129. Tel: 812-282-2144.
Sisters of St. Benedict 1; Lay Teachers 22; Students 379.
Catechesis/Religious Programs—Students 38.

Clinton, Vermillion Co., Sacred Heart (1891), Rev. Joseph Villa.
Office: 619 S. Fifth St., 47842-2016. Tel: 765-832-8468; Fax: 765-832-5092.; Rectory: 558 Nebeker St., 47842.
School—(Grades PreK-5) 610 S. Sixth St., 47842. Tel: 317-832-3228.
Lay Teachers 6; Students 73.
Mission—Universal, Vermillion Co., St. Joseph, (1920) Universal, 47884.
Catechesis/Religious Programs—Paulette Davis, D.R.E.
Students 85.

Columbus, Bartholomew Co., St. Bartholomew (1994). St. Bartholomew (1841) and St. Columba (1963) were closed, merged, and renamed St. Bartholomew. Revs. Clement T. Davis; Larry Borders.
St. Bartholomew's Catholic Parish: 845 8th St., 47201. Tel: 812-379-9353; Fax: 812-375-0720.
Res., 1302 27th St., 47201. Tel: 812-372-6453.
Pre-School Center—845 8th St., 47201. Tel: 812-376-0468.
School—(Grades K-8) 1302 27th St., 47201. Tel: 812-372-6830; Fax: 812-376-0377.
Lay Teachers 23; Students 425.
Catechesis/Religious Programs—Tel: 812-372-2207.
Students 402.

Connersville, Fayette Co., St. Gabriel (1851), Rev. Stanley J. Herber, M.A.; Pamela S. Rader, Bus. Mgr.
Res., 232 W. Ninth St., 47331-2099. Tel: 765-825-8578; Fax: 765-825-7060. [JC]
School—(Grades PreK-6) 224 W. Ninth St., 47331. Tel: 765-825-7951; Fax: 765-827-4347. Patricia Whitaker, Prin.
Lay Teachers 7; Students 150.
Catechesis/Religious Programs—220 W. Ninth St., 47331. Tel: 765-825-2944. Beth Luking, D.R.E.
Students 137.

Corydon, Harrison Co., St. Joseph (1896), Rev. Louis Manna.
Res., 312 E. High St., 47112. Tel: 812-738-2742; Fax: 812-738-2718. [CEM]
School—512 N. Mulberry St., 47112. Tel: 812-738-4549; Fax: 812-738-2722.
Lay Teachers 10; Students 155.
Catechesis/Religious Programs—Tel: 812-738-2759.
Students 110.
Missions—New Middletown, Harrison Co., Most Precious Blood, (1880) Corydon-New Middletown Rd., New Middletown, 47160. [CEM]
Elizabeth, Harrison Co., St. Peter, (1849) Buena Vista Rd., Elizabeth, 47117. [CEM]

Danville, Hendricks Co., Mary Queen of Peace (1939), Rev. Thomas K. Stepanski.
Res., 1005 W. Main St., 46122. Tel: 317-745-4284; Fax: 317-745-7090.
Catechesis/Religious Programs—Peg Klein, D.R.E.
Students 231.

Dover, Dearborn Co., St. John the Baptist (1824). Unassigned.
Church & Mailing Address: 25743 State Rte.1, Guilford, 47022. Tel: 812-576-4302; Fax: 812-576-2324. [CEM]
Catechesis/Religious Programs—Students 172.

Edinburgh, Johnson Co., Holy Trinity (1851), Rev. Paul M. Shikany.
Res., Keely Dr. & Main Cross, P.O. Box 216, 46124. Tel: 812-526-9460; Fax: 812-526-2477.

Enochsburg, Decatur Co., St. John the Evangelist (1844) (German), Rev. Gregory Bramlage, Admin.
Mailing Address: 5267 N. Hamburg Rd., Oldenburg, 47036. Tel: 812-934-5854; Fax: 812-934-5854.
Church—9995 E. Base Rd., Greensburg, 47240. [CEM]
Catechesis/Religious Programs—Tel: 812-934-2880; Fax: 812-934-2880.
Students 98.

Fortville, Hancock Co., St. Thomas (1869), Rev. Roger B. Gaudet.
Res., 523 S. Merrill St., 46040. Tel: 317-485-5101; Fax: 317-485-4373.
Catechesis/Religious Programs—Tel: 317-485-5103; Fax: 317-485-0022.
Students 191.

Franklin, Johnson Co., St. Rose of Lima (1868), Rev. Paul M. Shikany; Jean Martin, Pastoral Assoc., Tel: 317-738-2965.
Res., 114 Lancelot Dr., 46131. Tel: 317-738-3929; Fax: 317-738-3583.
School—(Grades PreK-6). Tel: 317-738-3451. Laura Riley, Prin.
Catechesis/Religious Programs—Tel: 317-736-6754.
Students 239.

French Lick, Orange Co., Our Lady of the Springs (1887), Rev. John M. Hall.
Res., 8796 W. State Rd. 56, 47432. Tel: 812-936-4568; Fax: 812-936-4568.
Catechesis/Religious Programs—Students 22.
Mission—Paoli, Orange Co., Our Lord Jesus Christ the King, (1948) East Highway 150, Paoli, 47454. Tel: 812-723-3900.
Catechesis/Religious Programs—Students 22.

Frenchtown, Harrison Co., St. Bernard (1849), Rev. Frederick J. Denison.
Res., 7600 Hwy. 337 N.W., Depauw, 47115. Tel: 812-347-2326. [CEM]
Catechesis/Religious Programs—Students 123.
Mission—Frenchtown, Crawford Co., St. Joseph, (1855) 47115.

Fulda, Spencer Co., St. Boniface (1847), Rev. Jeremy King, O.S.B.; Steve Shockley, O.S.B., Pastoral Assoc.
Mailing Address: P.O. Box 1, 47536. Tel: 812-357-5533; Fax: 812-357-2862. [CEM]
Catechesis/Religious Programs—Students 108.

Greencastle, Putnam Co., St. Paul the Apostle (1853), Rev. Michael C. Fritsch.
Res., 202 E. Washington St., 46135. Tel: 765-653-5678; Fax: 765-653-4377.
Catechesis/Religious Programs—Students 135.

Greenfield, Hancock Co., St. Michael (1860), Rev. Severin Messick, O.S.B.
Res., 519 Jefferson Blvd., 46140. Tel: 317-462-4240; Fax: 317-462-2571.
School—515 Jefferson Blvd., 46140. Tel: 317-462-6380.
Lay Teachers 14; Students 258.
Catechesis/Religious Programs—Students 335.

Greensburg, Decatur Co., St. Mary (1858), Rev. Stephen Schaftlein.
Res., 302 E. McKee St., 47240. Tel: 812-663-8427; Fax: 812-663-6088. [CEM]
School—(Grades PreK-6) 210 S. East St., 47240. Tel: 812-663-2804.
Lay Teachers 16; Students 288.
Catechesis/Religious Programs—Students 255.

Greenwood, Johnson Co., Our Lady of the Greenwood (1948), Revs. Harold L. Knueven; Darvin Edwin Winters, Jr.
Res., 335 S. Meridian St., 46143. Tel: 317-888-2861; Fax: 317-885-5006. [JC]
School—399 S. Meridian St., 46143. Tel: 317-881-1300.
Lay Teachers 23; Students 509.
Catechesis/Religious Programs—Tel: 317-885-5007.
Students 358.

SS. Francis and Clare of Assisi (1993), Rev. Stephen Jarrell.
Church & Parish Office: 5901 Olive Branch Rd., 46143. Tel: 317-859-4673; Fax: 317-859-4678.
Catechesis/Religious Programs—Students 264.

Hamburg, Franklin Co., St. Anne (1869), Rev. Gregory Bramlage.
Res., 5267 N. Hamburg Rd., Oldenburg, 47036. Tel: 812-934-5854; Fax: 812-934-5854. [CEM]
Catechesis/Religious Programs—Students 53.

Henryville, Clark Co., St. Francis Xavier (1869). Attended from St. Michael's, 101 St. Michael Dr., Charlestown, IN 47111. Tel: 812-256-3200. Rev. Stephen Donahue, Admin.
Church—Hwy 31 & Hwy 160, P.O. Box 368, 47126.

Jeffersonville, Clark Co., Sacred Heart (1953), Rev. Raymond E. Schafer. In res., Rev. H. Michael Hilderbrand.
Church & Parish Office: 1840 E. 8th St., 47103. Tel: 812-282-0423; Fax: 812-284-6673.
School—1842 E. 8th St., 47130. Tel: 812-283-3123.
Lay Teachers 20; Students 321.
Catechesis/Religious Programs—Tel: 812-283-6914.
Students 46.

St. Augustine (1851), Rev. Clifford R. Vogelsang.
Res., 315 E. Chestnut St., P.O. Box 447, 47130. Tel: 812-282-2677; Fax: 812-282-8821. [CEM]
Catechesis/Religious Programs—316 E. Maple St., Tel: 812-282-1231; Fax: 812-282-1605.
Students 116.

Knightstown, Henry Co., St. Rose (1872), Sr. Shirley Gerth, Parish Life Coord.; Revs. Joseph F. Rautenberg; Stanley J. Herber.
Mailing Address: P.O. Box 209, 46148. Tel: 765-345-5595.
Church—8144 W. U.S. Hwy. 40, 46148.
Catechesis/Religious Programs—Students 38.

Lanesville, Harrison Co., St. Mary (1843) (German), Rev. Harold A. Ripperger.
Res., 2500 St. Mary's Dr., 47136. Tel: 812-952-2853; Fax: 812-952-2852. [CEM]
Catechesis/Religious Programs—Tel: 812-952-2854.
Students 150.

Lawrenceburg, Dearborn Co., St. Lawrence (1842) (German), Rev. John Hartzer.
Rectory: 526 Walnut St., 47025. Tel: 812-537-1297; Fax: 812-537-3992 (Call first).
School—524 Walnut St., 47025. Tel: 812-537-3690.
Lay Teachers 16; Students 223.
Catechesis/Religious Programs—Tel: 812-537-1112.
Students 163.

Leopold, Perry Co., St. Augustine (1837), Rev. Sean Hoppe, O.S.B.
Res., 18020 Lafayette St., 47551. Tel: 812-843-5143; Fax: 812-843-5143. [CEM]
Catechesis/Religious Programs—Students 180.

Liberty, Union Co., St. Bridget (1854), Rev. John O'Brien, O.S.B.
Res., 404 E. Vine St., 47353. Tel: 765-458-5412. [CEM]
Catechesis/Religious Programs—Students 47.

Madison, Jefferson Co., Prince of Peace (1993). St. Michael (1837), St. Mary (1851), St. Patrick (1853), Madison, and St. Anthony, China (1861) were closed; merged and renamed Prince of Peace. Revs. John A. Meyer; William L. Ehalt.
Mailing Address: Catholic Community Center, 305 W. State St., 47250. Tel: 812-265-4166; Fax: 812-273-3427.
Res., 415 E. Second St., 47250. Tel: 812-265-4166. [CEM 2]
School—Pope John XXIII, (Grades K-6) 221 State St., 47250. Tel: 812-273-3957; Fax: 812-265-4566.
High School—Shawe Memorial Junior-Senior High School. See High Schools, Inter-Parochial, under Institutions Located in the Archdiocese. Tel: 812-273-2150; Fax: 812-273-6694.
Catechesis/Religious Programs—Students 98.

Martinsville, Morgan Co., St. Martin of Tours (1848), Rev. Mark Gottemoeller.
Res., 1709 E. Harrison St., 46151. Tel: 765-342-6379. [CEM]
Catechesis/Religious Programs—Tel: 765-352-0602; Fax: 765-342-1263.
Students 189.

Milan, Ripley Co., St. Charles Borromeo (1908), Rev. Msgr. Bernard R. Schmitz. In res., Rev. John J. Minta, (Retired).
Mailing Address: c/o St. Anthony, P.O. Box 3, Morris, 47033. Tel: 812-654-2009; Fax: 812-934-5936.
Church—213 Ripley St., 47031.
Catechesis/Religious Programs—Students 99.
Mission—St. Pius, Ripley Co., St. Pius, (1859). [CEM]

Millhousen, Decatur Co., Immaculate Conception (1834), Sr. Christine Ernstes, O.S.F., Parish Life Coord.; Revs. William G. Ripperger; Frank Eckstein.
Mailing Address: 2081 E. County Rd., 820 S., Greensburg, 47240-9636. Tel: 812-591-2362.
Mission—St. Denis, Jennings Co., St. Denis, (1894) 12155 N. County Rd., 600 E., Westport, 47283. [CEM]
Catechesis/Religious Programs—Students 129.

Mitchell, Lawrence Co., St. Mary/Assumption (1869), Rev. Bernard Cox.
Res., 777 S. 11th St., 47446. Tel: 812-849-3570; Fax: 812-275-3493.
Catechesis/Religious Programs—Fax: 812-849-6024.
Students 65.

Montezuma, Parke Co., Immaculate Conception (1867). Attended by St. Joseph's, 217 E. Ohio St., Rockville, IN. Tel: 765-569-5406. Rev. Joseph R. Kern, Admin.
Church—Madison & Sycamore St.

Mooresville, Morgan Co., St. Thomas More (1967), Rev. Richard Eldred, Admin.
Res., 1200 N. Indiana St., 46158. Tel: 317-831-4142; Fax: 317-834-2947.
Catechesis/Religious Programs—Tel: 317-831-1431.
Students 315.

Morris, Ripley Co., St. Anthony of Padua (1856), Rev. Msgr. Bernard R. Schmitz.
Mailing Address: P.O. Box 3, 47033. Tel: 812-934-6218; Fax: 812-934-5936. [CEM]
Parish Office: 4781 E. Morris Church St., 47033.
Church—4773 E. Morris Church St., 47033.
Catechesis/Religious Programs—Students 113.

Napoleon, Ripley Co., St. Maurice (1848), Rev. William G. Ripperger.
Mailing Address: 8874 Harrison St., P.O. Box 17, 47034. Tel: 812-852-4237. [CEM]
Catechesis/Religious Programs—Students 138.

Nashville, Brown Co., St. Agnes (1940), Sr. Mildred Wannemuehler, O.S.B., Parish Life Coord.; Rev. William F. Stumpf.
Mailing Address: 602 N. State Rd. 135, P.O. Box 577, 47448. Tel: 812-988-2778; Fax: 812-988-2778. [JC]
Catechesis/Religious Programs—Students 103.

Navilleton, Floyd Co., St. Mary (German) (1845), Rev. Tony Hubler.
Res., 7500 Navilleton Rd., Floyds Knobs, 47119. Tel: 812-923-5419; Fax: 812-923-3430. [CEM]
Catechesis/Religious Programs—Students 250.

New Albany, Floyd Co., Holy Family (1954), Rev. Wilfred E. Day.
Res., 129 W. Daisy Ln., 47150. Tel: 812-944-8283; Fax: 812-945-0180. [JC]
School—217 W. Daisy Ln., 47150. Tel: 812-944-6090; Fax: 812-944-7299.
Lay Teachers 23; Students 425.
Catechesis/Religious Programs—Students 98.

Our Lady of Perpetual Help (1950), Rev. Paul D. Etienne; Tom Yost, Pastoral Assoc.
Res., 1752 Scheller Ln., 47150. Tel: 812-944-1184; Fax: 812-944-1184.
School—Tel: 812-944-7676; Fax: 812-948-2944.
Lay Teachers 23; Students 445.
Catechesis/Religious Programs—Tel: 812-948-0185.
Students 70.

St. Mary (1858) (German), Rev. William W. Ernst, V.F.
Res., 415 E. Eighth St., 47150. Tel: 812-944-0417; Fax: 812-944-9557. [JC]
School—420 E. 8th St., 47150. Tel: 812-944-0888; Fax: 812-945-4770.
Lay Teachers 13; Students 176.
Catechesis/Religious Programs—Carole Strohbeck, D.R.E.
Students 60.

New Alsace, Dearborn Co., St. Paul (1833), Rev. William J. Turner.
Mailing Address: 8044 Yorkridge Rd., Guilford, 47022. Tel: 812-623-3408; Fax: 812-623-4879.
Res., 8044 Yorkridge Rd., Guilford, 47022. Tel: 812-623-3408; 487-2096. [CEM]
School—(Grades K-6) 9775 N. Dearborn Rd., Guilford, 47022. Tel: 812-623-2631; Fax: 812-623-4758.
Lay Teachers 7; Students 80.
Catechesis/Religious Programs—Tel: 812-623-2662.
Students 110.

New Castle, Henry Co., St. Anne (1873), Sr. Shirley Gerth, O.S.F., Parish Life Coord.; Revs. Joseph F. Rautenberg; Stanley J. Herber.
Parish Office: 102 N. 19th St., 47362. Tel: 765-529-0933; Fax: 765-529-8976. [CEM]
Church—1904 Broad St., 47362. Tel: 765-529-7413.
Catechesis/Religious Programs—Students 102.

New Marion, Ripley Co., St. Magdalen (1847). Attended from St. John, Osgood. Rev. Francis Eckstein.
Res., Tel: 812-689-4244.

New Middletown, Harrison Co., Most Precious Blood (1880). Attended from St. Joseph, 312 E. High St., Corydon, IN 47112. Tel: 812-738-2742. Rev. Louis Manna.
Mailing Address: 312 E. High St., Corydan, 47112.
Church—Corydan-New Middletown Rd., 47160. Fax: 812-738-2718. [CEM]
Catechesis/Religious Programs—Tel: 812-738-2759.
Students 7.

North Vernon, Jennings Co., St. Mary/Nativity of the Blessed Virgin Mary (1861), Rev. Herman Lutz.
212 Washington St., 47265. Tel: 812-346-3604; Fax: 812-346-3506. [CEM]
School—209 Washington St., 47265. Tel: 812-346-3445; Fax: 812-346-5930.
Lay Teachers 8; Students 208.
Catechesis/Religious Programs—Students 105.

Oak Forest, Franklin Co., St. Cecilia of Rome/Formerly St. Philomena (1844) (German). Closed. Parish is now an oratory of St. Mary-of-the-Rock Church, St. Mary-of-the-Rock.

Oldenburg, Franklin Co., Holy Family (1837), Rev. Sylvester Heppner, O.F.M. In res., Rev. Raymar Middendorf, O.F.M.
Res., 3027 Pearl St., P.O. Box 98, 47036. Tel: 812-934-3013; Fax: 812-933-0728. [CEM]
Catechesis/Religious Programs—Students 195.

Osgood, Ripley Co., St. John (1867), Rev. Francis Eckstein.
Res., 331 S. Buckeye St., 47037. Tel: 812-689-4244; Fax: 812-689-4244. [CEM]
Mission—New Marion, Ripley Co., St. Mary Magdalen, (1847) 47037. [CEM]
Catechesis/Religious Programs—349 S. Buckeye St., 47037. Tel: 812-689-6670.
Students 153.

Paoli, Orange Co., Our Lord Jesus Christ the King (1948). Attended from Our Lady of the Springs, French Lick. Rev. John M. Hall.
Church—Hwy. 150 E., 47454. Tel: 812-936-4568.

Plainfield, Hendricks Co., St. Susanna (1953), Rev. Kevin Morris.
Res., 1210 E. Main St., 46168. Tel: 317-839-3333; Fax: 317-839-0732.
School—(Grades PreK-6) 1212 E. Main St., 46168. Tel: 317-839-3713; Fax: 317-838-7718.
Lay Teachers 15; Students 259.
Catechesis/Religious Programs—Tel: 317-838-7722.
Students 283.

Richmond, Wayne Co., Holy Family (1953), Revs. Todd M. Riebe; Stanley Pondo.
Mailing Address: 240 S. 6th St., 47374. Tel: 765-962-3902; Fax: 765-966-0820.
Res., 720 N. A St., 47374. Tel: 765-962-3569.
Church—815 W. Main St., 47374.
School—St. Elizabeth Ann Seton, (Grades 4-8) 801 W. Main St., 47374. Tel: 765-962-4877.
Lay Teachers 11; Students 167.
Catechesis/Religious Programs—233 S. 5th St., 47374. Tel: 765-966-0916. Marcy Valentini, D.R.E.
Students 155.

St. Andrew (1846), Revs. Todd M. Riebe; Stanley Pondo.
Mailing Address: 240 S. 6th St., 47374. Tel: 765-962-3902; Fax: 765-966-0820.
Res., 720 A North St., 47374. Tel: 765-962-3569. [JC]
Church—235 S. 5th St., 47374.
Parish Center—233 S. Fifth St., 47374. Tel: 765-966-0916.
Catechesis/Religious Programs—Tel: 765-966-0916. Marcy Valentini, D.R.E.
Students 155.

St. Mary (1859), Revs. Todd M. Riebe; Stanley Pondo.
Mailing Address: 240 S. 6th St., 47374. Tel: 765-962-3902; Fax: 765-966-0820.
Church & Res.: 720 N. A St., 47374. Tel: 765-962-3569. [JC]
School—St. Elizabeth Ann Seton, (Grades K-3) 700 N. A St., 47374. Tel: 317-962-5010.
Lay Teachers 7; Students 208.
Catechesis/Religious Programs—233 S. 5th St., 47374. Tel: 765-966-0916. Marcy Valentini, D.R.E.
Students 155.

Rockville, Parke Co., St. Joseph (1867), Rev. Joseph R. Kern.
Res., 217 E. Ohio St., 47872. Tel: 765-569-5406.
Catechesis/Religious Programs—Tel: 765-597-2474.
Students 60.
Mission—Montezuma, Parke Co., Immaculate Conception, (1867) Madison & Sycamore St., Montezuma, 47872. Tel: 765-245-0232. [CEM]

Rushville, Rush Co., Immaculate Conception/St. Mary (1857), Rev. Roger G. Rudolf.
Res., 512 N. Perkins St., 46173. Tel: 765-932-2588; Fax: 765-932-3639. [CEM]
School—(Grades PreK-6) 226 E. 5th St., 46173. Tel: 765-932-3639; Fax: 765-988-1322.
Lay Teachers 11; Students 243.
Catechesis/Religious Programs—Fax: 765-932-2458.
Students 163.

St. Anne, Jennings Co., St. Anne (1841). Attended from St. Joseph, Jennings Co., 1875 S. County Rd. 700 W., North Vernon, IN 47265. Tel: 812-346-4783. Rev. Joseph L. Brown, C.PP.S., Admin.

St. Croix, Perry Co., Holy Cross (1860), Rev. John B. Schoettelkotte.
Res., State Rd. 62, Gen. Delivery, 47576. Tel: 812-843-5701. [CEM]
Catechesis/Religious Programs—Students 22.

St. Isidore the Farmer (1968). St. John, (1875), and St. Joseph, (1891), Perry Co., were closed; merged and renamed St. Isidore in 1968. Rev. John B. Schoettelkotte.
Res., 6501 St. Isidore Rd., Bristow, 47515. Tel: 812-843-5713. [CEM]
Catechesis/Religious Programs—Students 78.

St. Denis, Jennings Co., St. Denis (1894). Attended by Immaculate Conception, Millhousen. Revs. William Ripperger; Francis Eckstein; Sr. Christine Ernstes, O.S.F., Parish Life Coord.
Church—12155 N. County Rd. 600E, Westport, 47283.
Mailing Address: 2081 E. County Rd. 820S, Greensburg, 47240. Tel: 812-591-2362. [CEM]
Catechesis/Religious Programs—Clustered with Immaculate Conception, Milhousen.

St. Joseph, Crawford Co., St. Joseph (1855). Attended by St. Bernard, Frenchtown. Rev. Frederick J. Denison, Admin.
Mailing Address: 7600 Hwy. 337 N.W., Depauw, 47115. Tel: 812-347-2326.
Church—State Rd. 66, Marengo, 47140. [CEM]
Catechesis/Religious Programs—Students 47.

St. Joseph, Jennings Co., (1850), Rev. Joseph L. Brown, C.PP.S., Admin.
Res., 1875 S. County Rd. 700 W., North Vernon, 47265. Tel: 812-346-4783; Fax: 812-352-9033. [CEM]
Mission—St. Anne, Jennings Co., St. Anne, (1841).
Catechesis/Religious Programs—Students 53.

St. Joseph Hill, Clark Co., St. Joseph (1853), Rev. John Raphael Hadnagy, O.F.M.Conv. In res., Revs. Kent

Biergans, O.F.M.Conv.; Kenneth Gering, O.F.M.Conv.
Res., 2605 St. Joe Rd. W., Sellersburg, 47172. Tel: 812-246-2512; Fax: 812-246-2671. [CEM]
Catechesis/Religious Programs—Tel: 812-246-3969.
Students 143.

St. Leon, Dearborn Co., St. Joseph (1841). Unassigned.
Res., 7536 Church Ln., West Harrison, 47060. Tel: 812-576-3593; Fax: 812-576-2304. [CEM]
Catechesis/Religious Programs—29060 State Rte. 1, West Harrison, 47060. Tel: 812-576-3234. Jesse Garza, D.R.E.
Students 160.

St. Mark, Perry Co., St. Mark (1863) (German), Rev. Sean Hoppe, O.S.B.
Res., Hwy. 145, R.R. 1, Box 324, Tell City, 47586. Tel: 812-836-2481. [CEM][JC]
Catechesis/Religious Programs—Students 104.

St. Mary-of-the-Knobs, Floyd Co., St. Mary-of-the-Knobs (1823), Rev. John F. Geis.
Res., 3033 Martin Rd., Floyds Knobs, 47119. Tel: 812-923-3011; Fax: 812-923-1431. [CEM]
Catechesis/Religious Programs—Tel: 812-932-7258.
Students 528.

St. Mary-of-the-Rock, Franklin Co., St. Mary-of-the-Rock (1844) (German). Unassigned. Sr. Patricia Campbell, Parish Life Coord.
Office: 17440 St. Mary's Rd., Batesville, 47006. Tel: 812-934-4165. [CEM]
Catechesis/Religious Programs—Tel: 812-934-3219.
Students 39.
Oratory—Oak Forest, Franklin Co., St. Cecilia of Rome, (1844) 47006.

St. Mary-of-the-Woods, Vigo Co., St. Mary (1837), Sr. Peggy Lynch, S.P., Parish Life Coord.; Rev. J. Lawrence Richardt.
Mailing Address: P.O. Box 155, 47876. Tel: 812-535-1240; Fax: 812-535-1261. [CEM]
Catechesis/Religious Programs—Tel: 765-828-9213. Elizabeth Davis, D.R.E.
Students 77.

St. Maurice, Decatur Co., St. Maurice (1859), Rev. Gregory Bramlage, Admin.
Mailing Address: 5267 N. Hamburg Rd., Oldenburg, 47036. Tel: 812-934-5854.
Church—1963 N. St. John St., Greensburg, 47240. [CEM]
Catechesis/Religious Programs—Students 141.

St. Meinrad, Spencer Co., St. Meinrad (1854), Rev. Jeremy King, O.S.B.; Steve Shockley, Pastoral Assoc.
Mailing Address: P.O. Box 8, 47577. Tel: 812-357-5533; Fax: 812-357-2862. [CEM]
Catechesis/Religious Programs—Students 162.

St. Nicholas, Ripley Co., St. Nicholas (1836), Rev. Msgr. Bernard R. Schmitz; Rev. William J. Engbers, (Retired).
Res., 6461 E. St. Nicholas Dr., Sunman, 47041. Tel: 812-623-2964; 934-6218; Fax: 812-623-2964. [CEM]
School—(Grades PreK-8) 6459 E. St. Nicholas Dr., Sunman, 47041. Tel: 812-623-2348.
Lay Teachers 11; Students 256.
Catechesis/Religious Programs—Students 83.

St. Peter, Franklin Co., St. Peter (1838), Sr. Margie Niemer, O.S.F., Parish Life Coord.; Revs. Al Hudelpohl, O.F.M.; William J. Farris, O.F.M., Mod.
Res., 1207 East Rd., Brookville, 47012. Tel: 812-623-3670; Fax: 812-623-5261. [CEM]
Catechesis/Religious Programs—Students 82.

St. Peter, Harrison Co., (1849). Attended from St. Joseph, Corydon, St. Peter, 312 E. High St., Corydon, Harrison Co., IN 47112. Rev. Louis Manna.
Mailing Address: 312 E. High St., Corydon, 47112. Tel: 812-738-2742; Fax: 812-738-2718.
Church—Buena Vista Rd., Elizabeth, 47117. [CEM]
Catechesis/Religious Programs—Students 5.

St. Pius, Ripley Co., St. Pius (1859). Attended from St. Charles Borromeo, Milan. Rev. Msgr. Bernard R. Schmitz, Admin.
Mailing Address: P.O. Box 3, Morris, 47033. Tel: 812-934-6218; Fax: 812-934-5936. [CEM]

St. Vincent de Paul, Shelby Co., St. Vincent de Paul (1837), Rev. Paul Landwerlen.
Res., 4218 E. Michigan Rd., Shelbyville, 46176. Tel: 317-398-4028. [CEM]
Catechesis/Religious Programs—Tel: 317-392-3879; Fax: 317-392-3879.
Students 88.
Mission—. [CEM]

Salem, Washington Co., St. Patrick (1942), Rev. Thomas L. Schliessmann.
208 S. Shelby St., P.O. Box 273, 47167. Tel: 812-752-3693. [CEM]
Catechesis/Religious Programs—Tel: 812-883-3589.
Students 75.

Scottsburg, Scott Co., American Martyrs (1938), Rev. Thomas L. Schliessmann.
270 S. Bond St., 47170-2009. Tel: 812-752-3693; Fax: 812-752-3693.
Catechesis/Religious Programs—Students 65.
Mission—Salem, Washington Co., St. Patrick, (1942) 208 S. Shelly St., Salem, 47167.

Seelyville, Vigo Co., Holy Rosary (1908), Rev. Ken Ciano.
Church & Mailing Address: 2585 N. Main, P.O. Box 151, 47878. Tel: 812-877-1279.
Catechesis/Religious Programs—Students 35.

Sellersburg, Clark Co., St. Paul (1948), Rev. Paul F. Richart.
Res., 218 Scheller Ave., 47172. Tel: 812-246-3522; Fax: 812-246-7635.
School—(Grades K-6) 105 St. Paul St., 47172. Tel: 812-246-3266; Fax: 812-246-7632.
Lay Teachers 15; Students 294.
Catechesis/Religious Programs—216 Scheller Ave., 47172. Tel: 812-246-5088.
Students 91.

Seymour, Jackson Co., St. Ambrose (1860), Rev. Joseph B. Sheets.
Res., 325 S. Chestnut St., 47274. Tel: 812-522-5304; Fax: 812-522-8959. [CEM]
School—(Grades K-6) 301 S. Chestnut St., 47274. Tel: 812-522-3522.
Lay Teachers 12; Students 102.
Catechesis/Religious Programs—Tel: 812-522-2686.
Students 130.
Mission—Brownstown, Jackson Co., Our Lady of Providence, (1934) 47274.

Shelbyville, Shelby Co., St. Joseph (1868), Rev. John F. Fink.
Res., 125 E. Broadway, 46176. Tel: 317-398-8227; Fax: 317-392-7820. [CEM][JC]
School—(Grades PreK-5) 127 E. Broadway, 46176. Tel: 317-398-4202; Fax: 317-398-0270.
Lay Teachers 17; Students 210.
Catechesis/Religious Programs—Tel: 317-398-0530.
Students 205.

Siberia, Perry Co., St. Martin of Tours (1869), Rev. Jeremy King, O.S.B.; Steve Shockley, Pastoral Assoc.
Mailing Address: St. Meinrad, P.O. Box 8, St. Meinrad, 47536. Tel: 812-357-5533; Fax: 812-357-2862. [CEM]
Church—HC70, Box 65, 47515.
Catechesis/Religious Programs—Students 44.

Spencer, Owen Co., St. Jude the Apostle (1951), Rev. Paul M. Dede.
300 W. Hillside Ave., P.O. Box 317, 47460. Tel: 812-829-3082; Fax: 812-829-0888.
Catechesis/Religious Programs—Students 50.

Starlight, Clark Co., St. John the Baptist (1861) (German), Rev. Michael H. Kelley.
Res., 8310 St. John's Rd., Floyds Knobs, 47119. Tel: 812-923-5785; Fax: 812-923-2015. [CEM][JC]
Catechesis/Religious Programs—Tel: 812-923-0445; Fax: 812-923-2065.
Students 96.

Tell City, Perry Co., St. Paul (1859), Co-Pastors: Revs. Benet Amato, O.S.B.; Barnabas Gillispie, O.S.B.
Parish Office: Catholic Ministry Center, 802 9th St., 47586. Tel: 812-547-7994; Fax: 812-547-6985.
Church—814 Jefferson St., 47586. Tel: 812-547-9901. [CEM]
Catechesis/Religious Programs—Tel: 812-547-7102.
Students 381.

Terre Haute, Vigo Co.,

1—SACRED HEART OF JESUS, (1924), Rev. Stephen W. Giannini.
Res., 2322 N. 13 1/2 St., 47804. Tel: 812-466-1231; Fax: 812-466-9683.
School—1330 Lafayette Ave., 47804. Tel: 812-232-8901.
Sisters 1; Lay Teachers 9; Students 168.
Catechesis/Religious Programs—Students 111.

2—ST. ANN, (1876), Sr. Constance Kramer, S.P., Parish Life Coord.; Rev. Stephen W. Giannini.
Res., 1440 Locust St., 47807. Tel: 812-232-6832; Fax: 812-232-2444. [JC]
Catechesis/Religious Programs—Students 30.

3—ST. BENEDICT, (1865) (German), Rev. Joel Burget, O.F.M.Conv.
Parish Office: 111 S. Ninth St., 47807. Tel: 812-235-3041; Fax: 812-238-9203. [JC]
Church—118 S. Ninth St., 47807.
Catechesis/Religious Programs—Tel: 812-232-8421.
Students 167.

4—ST. JOSEPH, (1838), Revs. Martin Day, O.F.M.Conv.; Joseph West, O.F.M.Conv.
Res., 113 S. Fifth St., 47807. Tel: 812-232-7011; Fax: 812-232-7012. [JC]
Catechesis/Religious Programs—Students 168.

5—ST. MARGARET MARY, (1920), Rev. Ron Ashmore.
Res., 2405 S. Seventh St., 47802. Tel: 812-232-3512; Fax: 812-232-6921. [JC]
Catechesis/Religious Programs—Students 135.

6—ST. PATRICK, (1881), Rev. Lawrence J. Moran; John Fuller, Pastoral Assoc.
Church—1807 Poplar St., 47803. Tel: 812-232-8518; Fax: 812-234-3312.
School—(Grades PreK-8) 449 S. 19th St., 47803. Tel: 812-232-2157; Fax: 812-478-9384. Sr. Theresa Boland, S.P., Prin.
Lay Teachers 16; Students 305.
Catechesis/Religious Programs—Tel: 812-232-2827.
Students 196.

Troy, Perry Co., St. Pius (1849), Co-Pastors: Revs. Barnabas Gillespie, O.S.B.; Benet Amato, O.S.B.
Parish Office & Mailing Address: Catholic Ministry Center, 802 9th St., Tell City, 47586. Tel: 812-547-7994; Fax: 812-547-6985. [CEM]
Church—State Rd. 66, 47588.

Universal, Vermillion Co., St. Joseph (1920). Attended from Sacred Heart, 619 S. Fifth St., Clinton, IN 47842-2016. Tel: 765-832-8468. Rev. Joseph Villa, Admin.
Church—270 E. Wood Ave., 47884.

Vevay, Switzerland Co., Most Sorrowful Mother of God (1876), Revs. John A. Meyer; William L. Ehalt.
Mailing Address: Catholic Community Center, 305 W. State St., Madison, 47250. Tel: 812-265-4166; Fax: 812-273-3427.
Church—Ferry St., 47043.
Catechesis/Religious Programs—Students 10.

West Terre Haute, Vigo Co., St. Leonard of Port Maurice (1912), Sr. Margaret M. Lynch, S.P., Parish Life Coord.
126 N. Eighth St., 47885. Tel: 812-533-1240.

Yorkville, Dearborn Co., St. Martin (1852), Rev. William J. Turner.
Res., 8044 Yorkridge Rd., Guilford, 47022. Tel: 812-487-2096; 623-3408; Fax: 812-623-4879. [CEM]
Catechesis/Religious Programs—Tel: 812-623-2662.
Students 110.

Chaplains of Public Institutions

INDIANAPOLIS. *Community Hospital North.* Vacant.
Indiana University Hospital/Riley Hospital for Children. Rev. George Henninger.
Indiana Women's Prison. Rev. Lawrence Voelker.
Indianapolis Fire Department. Rev. Thomas Clegg.
Indianapolis International Airport. Rev. Glenn L. O'Connor.
Larue D. Carter Hospital. Vacant.
Marion County Sheriff Department. Rev. James R. Wilmoth.
Methodist Hospital. Rev. David Lawler.
Veterans' Administration Hospital. Revs. Joachim Keine, O.F.M.Conv.; Gordon P. Wagoner.
Winona Medical Center. Vacant.
Wishard Memorial Hospital. Vacant.

PUTNAMVILLE. *Indiana State Farm.* Rev. Michael C. Fritsch.

RICHMOND. *Richmond State Hospital.* Rev. Todd M. Riebe.

TERRE HAUTE. *Regional Hospital/Union Hospital.* Rev. Joel Burget, O.F.M.Conv.
U.S. Penitentiary. Rev. Francis Roof.

On Duty Outside the Archdiocese:
Reverend Monsignors—
Svarczkopf, Mark, Dir. of Institute for Theologian Education, North American College, Rome, Italy
Reverend Fathers—
Banet, Stephen J., Archdiocese of Mechelen-Brussels, Our Lady of Mercy Parish, Brussels, Belgium
Evard, Paul A., Ecuador, South America
Evrard, Donald J., Stuebenville, OH
Happel, Stephen P., The School of Religious Studies, The Catholic University of America., Washington, DC 20064

On Special or Other Archdiocesan Assignment:
Reverend Fathers—
Mazzola, Robert E., Auditor., Metropolitan Tribunal
Porter, Jack W., Archdiocesan Historian
Smith, Myles H., Deputy Defender of the Bond, Metropolitan Tribunal

---

On Disability Leave:
Reverend Fathers—
Mader, Joseph

Retired:
Reverend Monsignors—
Kavanagh, Richard T., St. Paul Hermitage, 501 N. 17th Ave., Beech Grove, IN 46107-1196
Marchino, Louis H., 127 Rossmore Dr., New Albany, IN 47150
Minta, John J., 213 Ripley, P.O. Box 336, Milan, IN 47031
Sweeney, Kenny C., 8431 E. Fairmont Ave., Scottsdale, AZ 85251
Wright, John M., CHC,USN, 7972 Avenida Navidad, #86, San Diego, CA 92112
Reverend Fathers—
Ajamie, Albert, Fatima Retreat House, 5353 E. 56th St., Indianapolis, IN 46226
Armstrong, Daniel F., Christian Brothers University, 650 E. Pkwy. S., Memphis, TN 38104
Arneson, James E., 1868 Shore Dr. S., #114, South Pasadena, FL 33707
Brown, Henry P., St. Paul Hermitage, 501 N. 17th Ave., Beech Grove, IN 46107
Buchanan, LCDR Donald E., CHC, USN, 13575 Sandy Key Dr., Unit 412, Pensacola, FL 32507-9641
Burwinkel, Elmer J., M.Ed., M.Div., 3991 W.C.R. 925 S., Madison, IN 47250
Cleary, William D., 874 W. Bauer Dr., Ninevah, IN 46164
Commons, Patrick M., 2046 S. Country Rd., 675 E., Dillsboro, IN 47018
Dede, James R., 8499 W. U.S. Hwy. 150, Hardensburg, IN 47125
Dede, John F., 2421 S. Seventh St., Terre Haute, IN 47802
Dooley, Joseph W., 8021 Guion Rd., Indianapolis, IN 46268
Engbers, William J., 6457 St. Nicholas Dr., Sunman, IN 47041
Gayso, Edward V., 5235 E. Greenbriar Dr., Apt. 5A, Terre Haute, IN 47802
Head, Bernard, 3461 St. Mary's Rd., #331, West Terre Haute, IN 47885
Kraeszig, Charles J., 7901 Castle Dr., Lakewood Estates, New Port Richey, FL 34653
Meny, Hilary G., P.O. Box 245, Haubstadt, IN 47639
Mueller, Richard J., 2722 B Marquette Manor W. Dr., Indianapolis, IN 46268
O'Riley, James K., 3388 Rothshire Cir., North Vernon, IN 47265
Porter, Jack W., 7432-D Lions Head Dr., Indianapolis, IN 46260-34459
Ripperger, Edward J., 7268 E. State Rd., 144, Mooresville, IN 46158
Rodas, Mauro, 736 Royal St. George Dr., Greenwood, IN 46143
Sciarra, John N., 8300 Rahke Rd., Indianapolis, IN 46217
Sexton, Charles E., St. Paul Hermitage, 501 N. 17th St., Beach Grove, IN 46107
Stineman, William F., 7432-D Lions Head Dr., Indianapolis, IN 46260
Terrill, Richard F., 1391 Gardner Ave., Newago, MI 49337
Zore, Richard I, 5254 McFarland Rd., Indianapolis, IN 46227

INSTITUTIONS LOCATED IN THE ARCHDIOCESE

[A] SEMINARIES, RELIGIOUS OR SCHOLASTICATES

ST. MEINRAD. *St. Meinrad Seminary*, 47577. Tel: 812-357-6611; Fax: 812-357-6964.
E-mail: rector@saintmeinrad.edu
Web site: www.saintmeinrad.edu
School of Theology. Revs. Mark O'Keefe, O.S.B., Pres. & Rector; Justin Duvall, O.S.B., Vice Rector & Provost; John J. Buckel; Bede Cisco, O.S.B.; Patrick Cooney, O.S.B.; Cyprian Davis, O.S.B.; Kenneth Davis, O.F.M.Cap.; Guerric DeBona, O.S.B.; Carl Deitchman, O.S.B.; Damian Dietlein, O.S.B.; Jonathan Fassero, O.S.B.; Harry Hagan, O.S.B.; Eugene Hensell, O.S.B.; Columba Kelly, O.S.B.; Guy Mansini, O.S.B.; Noel Mueller, O.S.B.; Jerome Neufelder (EVN); Matthias Neuman, O.S.B.; Julian Peters, O.S.B.; Nathaniel Reeves, O.S.B.; Thomas Richstatter, O.F.M.; Denis Robinson, O.S.B. (MEM); Damian Schmelz, O.S.B.; Kurt Stasiak, O.S.B.; John Thomas (OWN); Joseph A. Weigman (TOL); Peter Yock, O.S.B. Other Faculty and Staff 26; Students 86.

[B] COLLEGES AND UNIVERSITIES

INDIANAPOLIS. *Marian College*, 3200 Cold Spring Rd., 46222. Tel: 317-955-6000; Fax: 317-955-6048.
Web site: www.marian.edu
For a complete listing, refer to the Colleges and Universities section.

SAINT MARY-OF-THE-WOODS. *Saint Mary-of-the-Woods College*, 47876. Tel: 812-535-5151; Fax: 812-535-4613.
E-mail: smeier@woods.smwc.edu
Web site: www.smwc.edu
For a complete listing, refer to the Colleges and Universities section.

[C] HIGH SCHOOLS, INTER-PAROCHIAL

INDIANAPOLIS. *Bishop Chatard High School*, 5885 N. Crittenden Ave., 46220. Tel: 317-251-1451; Fax: 317-254-5427.
E-mail: umile@aol.com
Web site: www.chatard.org
Bro. Joseph Umile, C.S.C., Pres.; Paul Lockard, Prin.; Rev. William Joseph Brown, Chap. Priests 1; Sisters of St. Benedict 2; Brothers of Holy Cross 1; Lay Teachers 52; Students 750.

Cardinal Ritter High School, 3360 W. 30th St., 46222. Tel: 317-924-4333; Fax: 317-927-7822. Barbara Shuey, Pres.; Jo Hoy, Prin. Priests 2; Sisters 5; Brothers 1; Lay Teachers 25; Students 386.

Father Thomas Scecina Memorial High School, 5000 Nowland Ave., 46201-1836. Tel: 317-356-6377; Fax: 317-322-4289.
E-mail: kmarsg@scecina.org
Web site: www.scecina.org
Mr. Keith A. Marsh, Pres.; Mr. Rich J. Ruhl, Prin.; Rev. J. Peter Gallagher. Priests 1; Lay Teachers 44; Students 441.

Roncalli High School, 3300 Prague Rd., 46227. Tel: 317-787-8277; Fax: 317-788-4095.
E-mail: cweisenbach@yahoo.com
Web site: www.roncalli.org
Mr. Joseph D. Hollowell, Pres.; Charles Weisenbach Prin. Priests 1; Sisters 3; Lay Teachers 65; Students 965.

CLARKSVILLE. *Our Lady of Providence Junior & Senior High School*, 707 W. Hwy. 131, 47129. Tel: 812-945-2538.
Web site: www.providencehigh.com
Dr. Cecil Mattingly, Prin.; Mr. Gerald Wilkinson, Pres.; Mr. Robert Casey, Asst. Prin.; Rev. H. Michael Hilderbrand, Chap. Priests 1; Sisters 1; Lay Teachers 46; Students (Grades 9-12) 595; Students (Grades 7-12) 40.

MADISON. *Shawe Memorial Junior-Senior High School*, 201 W. State St., 47250. Tel: 812-273-2150; Fax: 812-273-6694.
E-mail: shaweprincipal@popeace.org
Larry Truax, Pres.; Sr. Jane Ann Breen, O.S.B., Prin.; Rev. William L. Ehalt, Chap. Lay Teachers 14; Priests 1; Sisters 1; Students 159.

[D] HIGH SCHOOLS, PRIVATE

INDIANAPOLIS. *Brebeuf Jesuit Preparatory School, Inc.*, 2801 W. 86th St., 46268-1925. Tel: 317-872-7050; Fax: 317-876-4732.
E-mail: brebeuf1@iquest.net
Web site: www.brebeuf.indianapolis.in.us
Rev. Benjamin Hawley, S.J., Pres.; Mrs. Linda Skafish, Interim Prin. Society of Jesus Community. 2823 W. 86 St., 46268-1926. Tel: 317-876-4700. Revs. J. Peter Carey, S.J., Rector; J. Paul O'Brien, S.J.; Frederick J. Deters, S.J.; Joseph D. Folzenlogen, S.J.; G. Paul Peterson, S.J.; George R. Menke, S.J.; Benjamin Hawley, S.J.; Bro. John F. Buchman, S.J. Priests 7; Sisters 1; Brothers 1; Lay Teachers 82; Students 765.

Cathedral High School (Cathedral Trustees, Inc.), 5225 E. 56th St., 46226. Tel: 317-542-1418; Fax: 317-543-5050.
E-mail: chsjtp@indy.net
Web site: www.cathedralirish.org
Stephen J. Helmich, M.S., Pres.; Rev. Patrick J. Kelly, M.S., Prin. Sisters 4; Priests 3; Lay Teachers 91; Students 1,075.

OLDENBURG. *Oldenburg Academy of the Immaculate Conception*, One Twister Cir., P.O. Box 200, 47036-0200. Tel: 812-934-4440; Fax: 812-934-4838. Martha J. Kollstedt, Prin. Sisters 4; Lay Teachers 18; Students 182.

[E] RELIGIOUS EDUCATION CENTERS

CLARKSVILLE. *Aquinas Center for Continuing Religious Education*, 707 W. Hwy. 131, 47129. Tel: 812-945-0354; Fax: 812-945-2995.
E-mail: bobnadac@aol.com
Mr. Robert K. Leonard, Dir. Catechetical Ministry & Religious Education; Mr. D. Ray Lucas, Dir. Youth Ministries.

New Albany Deanery / Catholic Youth Ministries. Tel: 812-945-0354; Fax: 812-945-2995.

TERRE HAUTE. *Terre Haute Deanery Pastoral Center*, 2931 Ohio Blvd., 47803. Tel: 812-232-8400; Fax: 812-234-2665.
E-mail: thdeanery@aol.com
Sue Butwin, Dir.; Lois Massinon, Admin. Asst. Total Staff 2.

[F] GENERAL HOSPITALS

INDIANAPOLIS. *St. Vincent Hospital and Health Care Center, Inc.*, 2001 W. 86th St., 46260. Tel: 317-338-7000; Fax: 317-338-7005.
E-mail: jbford@stvincent.org
Web site: www.stvincent.org
For a complete listing, refer to the Hospitals section.

Seton Health Corporation of Central Indiana, 2001 W. 86th St., 46260. Tel: 317-338-7000; Fax: 317-338-7005.
E-mail: jbford@stvincent.org
Web site: www.stvincent.org
For a complete listing, refer to the Hospitals section.

BEECH GROVE. *St. Francis Hospital and Health Centers*, 1600 Albany St., 46107. Tel: 317-787-3311; Fax: 317-782-6731.
Web site: www.stfrancishospitals.org
For a complete listing, refer to the Hospitals section.

[G] PROTECTIVE INSTITUTIONS

TERRE HAUTE. *Gibault School for Boys*, 6301 S. U.S. Hwy. 41, P.O. Box 2316, 47802-0316. Tel: 812-299-1156; Fax: 812-299-0019.
E-mail: gibault@gibault.org
Web site: www.gibault.org
For a complete listing, refer to the Special Care Facilities section.

[H] HOMES FOR AGED

INDIANAPOLIS. *St. Augustine Home, Little Sisters of the Poor*, 2345 W. 86th St., 46260. Tel: 317-872-6420; Fax: 317-875-9883
For a complete listing, refer to the Special Care Facilities section.

BEECH GROVE. *St. Paul Hermitage*, 501 N. 17th Ave., 46107. Tel: 317-786-2261; Fax: 317-782-1411.
E-mail: sphherm@indyweb.net
For a complete listing, refer to the Special Care Facilities section.

NEW ALBANY. *Mercy Long Term Care Initiatives dba Mercy Providence Village*, 4915 Charlestown Rd., 47150. Tel: 812-945-5221; Fax: 812-945-2614
For a complete listing, refer to the Special Care Facilities section.

[I] RETREAT HOUSES

INDIANAPOLIS. *Our Lady of Fatima Retreat House, Inc.*, 5353 E. 56th St., 46226. Tel: 317-545-7681; Fax: 317-545-0095.
E-mail: fatima@archindy.org
Web site: www.archindy.org/fatima
Mr. Kevin V. DePrey, Dir. Priests 1; Total in Residence 1; Total Staff 9.
Used by both clergy and laity.

BEECH GROVE. *Benedict Inn Retreat & Conference Center*, 1402 Southern Ave., 46107-1197. Tel: 317-788-7581; Fax: 317-782-3142.
E-mail: benedict@indy.net
Web site: www.benedictinn.org
Sr. Carol Falkner, O.S.B., Admin. Sisters 4. Retreats and workshops for clergy, religious, and laity.

MOUNT SAINT FRANCIS. *Mount Saint Francis Friary and Retreat Center*, 101 St. Anthony Dr., 47146-9999. Tel: 812-923-8817; Fax: 812-923-0177. Revs. Cyprian Uline, O.F.M.Conv., Retreat Staff; Jim Van Dorn, O.F.M.Conv., Parish Missions; Eliot Comstock, O.F.M.Conv., Treasurer's Office; Simeon Yates, O.F.M.Conv., Retreat Staff; Florian, O.F.M. Conv., Nursing Home Chap.; Kenneth Davis, O.F.M. Conv., Prof., St. Meinrad's. In res. Rev. Maximilian Korecki, O.F.M. Conv., Chap., Little Sisters; Bros. Ambrose Eischens, O.F.M.Conv., Guardian & Retreat Dir.; Angelo Catania, O.F.M.Conv., Retreat Staff; Lawrence Eberhardt, O.F.M.Conv., Archivist; Jeffry Hines, O.F.M.Conv., Sec. of the Province; Michael Austin, O.F.M.Conv., Vocation Promotion & Youth Min.; James Worchuck, O.F.M.Conv., Devel. Office Staff; Aloysius Wagener, O.F.M.Conv., (Retired).

Province of Our Lady of Consolation, Inc. (Provincial Office). Tel: 812-923-8444; Fax: 812-923-8145. Revs. Kent Biergans, O.F.M.Conv., Min. Prov.; Richard Kaley, O.F.M.Conv., Vicar; Bro. Jeffrey Hines, O.F.M.Conv., Sec. of Province. Total Staff 5; Total in Residence 14.

ST. MEINRAD. *Archabbey Guest House*, 47577. Tel: 812-357-6585; 800-581-6905; Fax: 812-357-6325.
E-mail: mzoeller@stmeinrad.edu
Web site: www.saintmeinrad.edu/abbey/ghouse.htm
Retreat House for Men, Women, Couples. Double Rooms 25.

[J] MONASTERIES AND RESIDENCES OF PRIESTS AND BROTHERS

INDIANAPOLIS. *St. Maur Priory*, 4615 N. Michigan Rd., 46228. Tel: 317-925-9095. Very Rev. Charles W. Henry, O.S.B., Prior; Rev. Bernardin Patterson, O.S.B. Priests 2; Brothers 4.

MOUNT SAINT FRANCIS. *Provincial Headquarters for the Conventual Franciscan Province*, 101 Anthony Dr., 47146. Tel: 812-923-8444; Fax: 812-923-8145. Very Rev. Kent Biergans, O.F.M.Conv., Minister Prov.; Rev. Richard Kaley, O.F.M.Conv., Vicar Prov.; Bro. Jeffrey Hines, O.F.M.Conv., Sec. of Province. Priests 2. Legal Title: *Province of Our Lady of Consolation. Vocation Office of the Province*. Tel: 502-933-4439; Fax: 502-933-7747. St. Paul Friary, 6901 Dixie Hwy., Pleasure Ridge Park, KY, 40258. Tel: 502-933-4439; Fax: 502-933-7747. Rev. James Kent, O.F.M.Conv., Vocation Dir.
Priests of the Conventual Franciscan Province of Our Lady of Consolation Teaching or Studying at Universities: Rev. Duane Doherty, O.F.M.Conv., 3695 Lincoln Dr., Bloomfield Hills, MI, 48301. Tel: 248-350-1330. Rev. Basil Heiser, O.F.M.Conv., Curia Generalizia, Piazza Ss. Apostoli, 51, Rome, Italy, 00187. Tel: 0113906699571; Fax: 011390669957321. Rev. Leopold Keffler, O.F.M.Conv., Marian College, 3200 Cold Spring Rd., Indianapolis, 46222. Tel: 317-923-9387. Rev. Wayne Hellmann, O.F.M.Conv., 4030 Flad Ave., St. Louis, MO, 63110. Tel: 314-772-5804.

ST. MEINRAD. *St. Meinrad Archabbey*, 47577-1010. Tel: 812-357-6611; Fax: 812-357-6551.
E-mail: abbot@saintmeinrad.edu
Web site: www.saintmeinrad.edu
Archabbey of the Order of St. Benedict, including School of Theology (St. Meinrad Seminary). Rt. Rev. Lambert Reilly, O.S.B., Archabbot; Revs. Tobias Colgan, O.S.B., Prior; Harry Hagan, O.S.B., Master of Novices & Junior Master; Gavin Barnes, O.S.B.; Alban Berling, O.S.B.; Meinrad Brune, O.S.B.; Adelbert Buscher, O.S.B.; Aelred Cody, O.S.B.; Patrick Cooney, O.S.B.; Joseph Cox, O.S.B. (PEO); Simeon Daly, O.S.B.; Augustine Davis, O.S.B.; Cyprian Davis, O.S.B.; Carl Deitchman, O.S.B.; Justin DuVall, O.S.B.; Jonathan Fassero, O.S.B.; Malachy Fulton, O.S.B.; Rembert Gehant, O.S.B.; Colman Grabert, O.S.B.; Theodore Heck, O.S.B.; Warren Heitz, O.S.B.; Eugene Hensell, O.S.B.; Michael Keene, O.S.B.; Columba Kelly, O.S.B.; Alcuin Leibold, O.S.B.; Alaric Lewis, O.S.B. (SFD); Eric Lies, O.S.B.; Prosper Lindauer, O.S.B.; Conrad Louis, O.S.B.; Simon McTighe, O.S.B.; Guy Mansini, O.S.B.; Noel Mueller, O.S.B.; Louis Mulcahy, O.S.B.; Mark O'Keefe, O.S.B., Pres. & Rector, School of Theology; Rupert Ostdick, O.S.B.; Julian Peters, O.S.B.; Nathaniel Reeves, O.S.B.; Denis Robinson, O.S.B.; Anselm Russell, O.S.B.; Damian Schmelz, O.S.B.; Christopher Shappard, O.S.B.; Stephen Snoich, O.S.B.; Kurt Stasiak, O.S.B.; Germain Swisshelm, O.S.B.; Cyril Vrablic, O.S.B.; Donald Walpole, O.S.B.; Joachim Walsh, O.S.B.; Peter Yock, OS.B. Priests 96; Brothers 38.
Priests of the Archabbey Teaching, Studying at Universities, or on Special Assignment: Rt. Rev. Bonaventure Knaebel, O.S.B., Resigned Archabbot, St. Michael Church, P.O. Box 22, Bradford, 47107. Rev. Benet Amato, O.S.B., St. Paul Parish, 814 Jefferson St., Tell City, 47586. Rev. Aurelius Boberek, O.S.B., The American College, Katholieke Universiteit Leuven, Naamsestraat 100, Leuven B-3000, Belgium. Rev. Adrian Burke, O.S.B., Collegio Sant' Anselmo, Piazza Cavalieri di Malta, 5, Roma, Italy, 1-00153. Rev. Ephrem Carr, O.S.B., Collegio Sant' Anselmo, Piazza Cavalieri di Malta 5, Rome, Italy, I-00153. Rev. Noah Casey, O.S.B., 4826 Fletcher Ave., Indianapolis, 46203. Rev. Gregory D. Chamberlin, O.S.B., St. Benedict Church, 1328 Lincoln Ave., Evansville, 47714-1598. Rev. Bede Cisco, O.S.B., St. Michael Parish, 3354 W. 30th St., Indianapolis, 46222. Rev. Guerric DeBona, O.S.B., Saint Meinrad Archabbey, St Meinrad, 47577. Rev. Camillus Ellspermann, O.S.B., St. Henry Rectory, 1311 W. 1100 S., Ferdinand, 47532. Rev. Cassian Folsom, O.S.B., Il Priorato Maria Sedes Sapientiae, via B. Peruzzi, 19, Rome, Italy, 00153. Rev. Barnabas Gillespie, O.S.B., St. Paul Church, 802 Ninth St., Tell City, 47586. Rev. Harold Hammerstein, O.S.B., 701 S. Boeke, Evansville, 47714. Rev. Boniface Hardin, O.S.B., 2171 Avondale Pl., P.O. Box 18567, Indianapolis, 46218. Rev. Richard Hindel, O.S.B., St. Bartholomew, 845 Eighth St., Columbus, 47201. Rev. Sean Hoppe, O.S.B., St. Augustine Church, General Delivery, Leopold, 47551. Rev. Aidan Kavanagh, O.S.B., 409 Prospect St., Hamden, CT, 06157. Rev. Jeremy King, O.S.B., V.F., St. Meinrad Parish, 47577. Rev. Pius Klein, O.S.B., St. Mary Rectory, 313 Washington St., Huntingburg, 47532. Rev. Micheas Langston, O.S.B., The Hollows, 1300 Longcreek Dr., Apt. 713, Columbia, SC, 29210. Rev. Sebastian Leonard, O.S.B., Canterbury School, Aspetuck Ave., New Milford, CT, 06776. Rev. Edward Linton, O.S.B., 2106 Woodriver Dr., #8, Carbondale, IL, 62901. Rev. Ralph Lynch, O.S.B., St. Paul's Hermitage, 501 N. 17th Ave., Beech Grove, 46107. Rev. Keith J. McClellan, O.S.B., St. Michael Catholic Community, 1 Wilhelm St., Schererville, 46375. Rev. Isaac McDaniel, O.S.B., St. Jerome Parish, 903 Fairdale Rd., Fairdale, KY, 40118. Rev. Alan R. McIntosh, O.S.B., St. Mary of the Assumption, P.O. Box 68, Sainte Marie, IL, 62459. Rev. Severin Messick, O.S.B., St. Michael Church, 519 Jefferson Blvd., Greenfield, 46140. Rev. Benedict Meyer, O.S.B., St. John the Baptist Parish, 203 W. Ash, Brinkley, AR, 72021. Rev. Godfrey Mullen, O.S.B., Saint Benedict Monastery, 9535 Linton Hall Rd., Bristow, VA, 20136. Rev. Matthias Neuman, O.S.B., 1414 Southern Ave., Beech Grove, 46107. Rev. Mel Patton, O.S.B., Sacred Heart Monastery, 1005 W. Eighth St., Yankton, SD, 57078. Rev. David Rabenecker, O.S.B., Holy Trinity Parish, 2818 E. Bennett, Springfield, MO, 65804. Rev. Kevin Ryan, O.S.B., St. Thomas Church, P.O. Box 90, Helmville, MT, 59843. Rev. Raymond Studzinski, O.S.B., Curley Hall, Catholic University of America, Washington, DC, 20064. Rev. Timothy Sweeney, O.S.B., Parish of the Immaculate, 2516 Christie Place, Owensboro, KY, 42301. Rev. Vincent Tobin, O.S.B., Collegio di Sant'Anselmo, Piazza Cavalieri di Malta 5, Rome, Italy, I-00153. Rev. Frederick P. Walsh, O.S.B., Our Lady Queen Monastery, 50352 Antioch Rd., Tickfaw, LA, 70466. Rev. Marion C. Walsh, O.S.B., Our Lady Queen Monastery, 50352 Antioch Rd., Tickfaw, LA, 70466. Rev. Samuel Weber, O.S.B., Wake Forest Divinity School, P.O. Box 7719, Winston-Salem, NC, 27109-7719.

[K] CONVENTS AND RESIDENCES FOR SISTERS

INDIANAPOLIS. *F.I.H. Convent*, 3356 W. 30th St., 46222. Tel: 317-920-1289; Fax: 317-920-1289.
E-mail: franciscansisters@yahoo.com
Sr. Ushatta Mary, F.I.H., Supr. Sisters 7.
Hispanic Education Center, Inc., 580 E. Stevens St., 46203-1740. Tel: 317-634-5022; Fax: 317-634-0442. Total Staff 6; Total Assisted 3,000.
Servants of the Gospel of Life, Inc, 1400 N. Meridian St., 46202. Tel: 317-236-1512.
E-mail: dcarollo@archindy.org
Sr. Diane Carollo, Sr. Servant.
Sisters of Our Lady of Mount Carmel Carmelite Monastery, 2500 Cold Spring Rd., 46222-2323. Tel: 317-926-5654; Fax: 317-926-1492.
E-mail: indycarm@iquest.net
Web site: http//members.iquest.net/~indycarm
Sr. Joanne Dewald, O.C.D., Prioress. Professed Religious 15.

BEECH GROVE. *Charitable Trust of the Monastery of Our Lady of Grace*, 1402 Southern Ave., 46107-1197. Tel: 317-787-3287; Fax: 317-780-2368.
E-mail: srbolg@aol.com
Web site: www.benedictine.com
Legal Title: *Charitable Trust of the Monastery of Our Lady of Grace, Sisters of the Order of St. Benedict.*
Our Lady of Grace Monastery, 1402 Southern Ave., 46107-1197. Tel: 317-787-3287; Fax: 317-780-2368.
E-mail: srbolg@aol.com
Web site: www.benedictine.com
Legal Title: *Sisters of St. Benedict of Beech Grove, IN, Inc.* Rev. Matthias Newman, O.S.B., Chap., 1414 Southern Ave., 46107-1197. Tel: 317-786-0338.
E-mail: mnewman@dellnet.com
Sisters 82.

OLDENBURG. *Motherhouse of the Congregation of the Sisters of the Third Order of St. Francis*, 47036. Tel: 812-934-2475; Fax: 812-933-6403.
E-mail: osf@seidata.com
Sr. Jean Marie Cleveland, O.S.F., Congregational Minister; Revs. Raymar Middendorf, O.F.M.; Sylvester Heppner, O.F.M., Assoc. Chap., Holy Family Friary. Professed Sisters in Congregation 340; Professed Sisters in Archdiocese 229; Total in Residence 136.
Sisters of St. Francis Community Support Trust. Tel: 812-934-2475.
E-mail: osf@seidata.com

SAINT MARY-OF-THE-WOODS. *Sisters of Providence General Administration*, 47876-1089. Tel: 812-535-4193; Fax: 812-535-4727.
Web site: www.sistersof providence.org
Sr. Diane Ris, S.P., Gen. Supr.; Rev. J. Lawrence Richardt, Chap. Professed in Congregation 581; Professed Residing in Archdiocese 352; Novices 3; Postulants 2.
Sisters of Providence Community Support Trust.
Woods Day Care/Preschool, Inc. Tel: 812-535-4610. Total Staff 21; Children 48.
Providence Self-Sufficiency Ministries, Inc., 225 W. Daisy Ln., New Albany, 47150-4538. Tel: 812-948-2053; Fax: 812-948-2053. Sr. Barbara Ann Zeller, Pres. Total Staff 194; Total Assisted 2,968.
St. Mary-of-the-Woods College. Tel: 812-535-5151. Total Staff 221; Total Assisted 1,439.

TERRE HAUTE. *Monastery of St. Joseph, Discalced Carmelites*, 59 Allendale, 47802-4751. Tel: 812-299-1410; Fax: 812-299-5820.
E-mail: carmelth@iquest.net
Mother Mary Clare, O.C.D., Prioress. Solemnly Professed 11; Novices 2; Postulants 1.

[L] ARCHDIOCESAN CHARITIES

INDIANAPOLIS. *Adult Day Services*, 1400 N. Meridian, P.O. Box 1410, 46202-2367. Tel: 317-236-1527; Fax: 317-261-3375.
E-mail: lbaxter@archindy.org
Lula E. Baxter, Prog. Dir.
A Caring Place - Adult Day Care Center, c/o Fairview Presbyterian Church, 4609 N. Capitol Ave., 46208. Tel: 317-466-0015; Fax: 317-251-2246. Sr. Susan Dinnin, Site Mgr.
Holy Trinity Place - Adult Day Care Center, 907 Holmes Ave., 46222. Tel: 317-638-8322; Fax: 317-638-9215. Joan Goore, Site Mgr.
St. Ann's Place. Part-time Respite Center, c/o Gethsemane Lutheran Church, 6810 E. 10th St., 46219. Tel: 317-261-3378; Fax: 317-638-9215. Susan Koehler, Program Coord. Total Assisted 110; Total Staff 12.
Catholic Social Services of Central Indiana, The Catholic Center, 1400 N. Meridian St., P.O. Box 1410, 46206. Tel: 317-236-1500; Fax: 317-261-3375.
E-mail: css@archindy.org
Web site: www.archindy.org
David Bethuram, Dir. Total Staff 55; Total Assisted 13,927.
Holy Family Emergency Shelter, 30 E. Palmer St., 46225. Tel: 317-635-7830; Fax: 317-684-9702.
E-mail: hf-shelter@iquest.net
Amy Moelhman, A.C.S.W., L.C.S.W., Dir. Total Staff 15; Total Assisted 1,206.

NEW ALBANY. *Catholic Charities*, 702 E. Market St., 47150. Tel: 812-948-0438; Fax: 812-948-0400. Barbara K. Williams, M.S., L.S.W., Dir. Total Staff 3; Total Assisted 660.
St. Elizabeth's Regional Maternity Center, 601 E. Market St., 47150. Tel: 812-949-7305; Fax: 812-941-7008.
E-mail: stelizabeths@juno.com
Web site: www.stelizabeths1.org
Full-range maternity home and adoption agency offering residential and outreach services. Keith E. Stormes, Dir. Total Staff 15; Total in Residence 36.

TELL CITY. *Catholic Charities*, 802 Ninth St., 47586. Tel: 812-547-6414.
Rainbow Cottage Latch Key Program. Total Staff 4; Total Assisted 44.

TERRE HAUTE. *Catholic Charities of Terre Haute*, Corporate Square Annex, 2931 Ohio Blvd., 47803. Tel: 812-232-1447; Fax: 812-232-1447.
E-mail: cathchar@1quest.net
Web site: www.abcs.com/ryveshall/thcc.html
John Etling, M.A., Dir. Total Staff 3.
Bethany House, 1402 Locust Ave., 47807. Tel: 812-232-4978. Marty Green, Mgr. Total Staff 3; Total Assisted 10,000.
Christmas House, 829 N. 14th St., 47808. Tel: 812-234-7242. Pat Armstrong, Dir. Total Staff 1; Total Assisted 3,600.
Household Exchange, 829 N. 14th St., 47807. Tel: 812-234-7242. John Etling, M.A., Dir. Total Staff 1; Total Assisted 960.
Ryves Hall Youth Center, 1356 Locust St., 47807. Tel: 812-235-1261. Jim Edwards, Youth Center Dir. Total Staff 6; Total Assisted 1,600.
Simeon House I (St. Patrick Parish), 1801 Poplar St., 47803. Tel: 812-232-6144. Delores Carbon, Dir. Total Staff 4; Total Assisted 175.
Anthony Square - Assisted Living, 400 College Ave., 47802. Tel: 812-232-6533. Harriett Johnson, Dir. Total Staff 4; Total Assisted 300.
Terre Haute Catholic Charities Foodbank, 1356 Locust St., 47807. Tel: 812-232-1447. Pat Etling, Dir. Total Staff 4; Total Assisted 80,000.

[M] CATHOLIC YOUTH ORGANIZATIONS

INDIANAPOLIS. *Catholic Youth Organization*, Related Ministries, 580 E. Stevens St., 46203. Tel: 317-632-9311. Mr. Edward J. Tinder, Exec. Dir.; Mr. Gerald R. Ross, Asst. Exec. Dir. Monsignor Downey Athletic Field. Perkins & Raymond St., 46203.

NASHVILLE. *C.Y.O. Camp Rancho Framasa*, 2230 N. Clay Lick Rd., 47448. Tel: 888-998-2839; Fax: 812-988-4842.
E-mail: cyocamp@aol.com
Web site: www.members.aol.com/cyocamp
Mr. Kevin Sullivan, Camp Dir.

[N] NEWMAN CENTERS

INDIANAPOLIS. *Butler University Newman Center*, 4615 Sunset Ave., 46208. Tel: 317-283-7651. Rev. Don Quinn, Dir. Total Staff 2; Total in Residence 1.

Indiana University-Purdue University, Indianapolis Newman Center, Catholic Student Center, 4615 Sunset Ave., 46208. Tel: 317-283-7651. Rev. Don Quinn, Dir. Total Staff 2; Total in Residence 1.
University of Indianapolis Newman Center, 4615 Sunset Ave., 46208. Tel: 317-283-7651. Rev. Don Quinn, Dir. Total Staff 2; Total in Residence 1.
BLOOMINGTON. *Indiana University, Bloomington Newman Center*, St. Paul's Catholic Center, 1413 E. 17th St., 47408. Tel: 812-339-5561; Fax: 812-333-4846.
Web site: www.st-pauls.org
Rev. Daniel Atkins. Total Staff 9; Total in Residence 5.
FRANKLIN. *Franklin College Newman Center*, 114 Lancelot Dr., 46131. Tel: 317-738-3929. Rev. Paul M. Shikany.
GREENCASTLE. *DePauw Catholic Campus Ministry*, c/o St. Paul Church, 202 E. Washington St., 46135. Tel: 765-653-5678; Fax: 765-653-4377.
E-mail: stpaul@ccrtc
Rev. Michael C. Fritsch.
MADISON. *Hanover College Newman Center*, 305 W. State St., 47250. Tel: 812-265-4166; Fax: 812-273-3427. Revs. John A. Meyer; William L. Ehalt.
RICHMOND. *Earlham College Newman Center*, 240 S. Sixth St., 47374. Tel: 765-962-3902. Rev. Todd M. Riebe. Total in Residence 9; Total Staff 1.
TERRE HAUTE. *Indiana State University, Rose Hulman Institute Newman Center*, St. Joseph University Parish, 113 S. Fifth St., 47807-3577. Tel: 812-232-8088. Sr. Carmen Gillick, S.F.C.C., Pastoral Assoc. for Students.

[O] MISCELLANEOUS

INDIANAPOLIS. *Archdiocesan Black Catholics Concerned*, The Archbishop O'Meara Catholic Center, P.O. Box 1410, 46206-1410. Tel: 317-236-1562. Rev. Kenneth E. Taylor.
Association of Contemplative Sisters, c/o Carmelite Monastery, 2500 Cold Spring Rd., 46222. Tel: 317-926-5654; Fax: 317-926-1492.
E-mail: indycarm@iquest.net
Ms. Rosalie Bertell, Pres. Membership 350.
International Catholic Deaf Association (Chapter No. 38), P.O. Box 1410, 46206. Tel: 317-236-1439. Revs. Joseph W. Dooley, Chap. Tel: 317-872-5485; 800-855-2880(TDD); Joseph G. Pesola; Bernard Cox; David Bethuram, Contact Person, Office Youth & Family Ministries.
Society of St. Vincent de Paul, Archdiocesan Council of Indianapolis, Inc., P.O. Box 19133, 46219. Tel: 317-805-4766; Fax: 317-805-4723.
Web site: www.web.net/stvdepaul/index.html
Mr. Don Striegel, Pres. Total Assisted 35,000.
Vietnamese Catholic Association of Indianapolis & Vicinity, 3746 Paddington Ln., N., 46268. Tel: 317-872-5320. Mr. Nhan Nguyen, Pres.; Trung Q. Ngo, Vice Pres.; Dzuy Nguyen, Treas.
BEECH GROVE. *Alverno-Beech Grove Corp.*, 1600 Albany St., 46107. Tel: 317-783-8133; Fax: 317-782-6731. Mr. Robert J. Brody, Pres. & CEO.
Catholic Health Midwest, Inc. dba Alverno Information Services, 1300 Albany St., 46107. Tel: 317-532-7800; Fax: 317-532-7801.
Web site: www.alverno.org
Mr. William G. Laker, Vice Pres. & CIO. Sponsored by Sisters of St. Francis Health Services, Inc.
MOUNT SAINT FRANCIS. *Mount Saint Francis Sanctuary, Inc.*, 101 St. Anthony Dr., 47146-9999. Tel: 812-923-8817; Fax: 812-923-0177. Mailing Address: Marian College, 3200 Cold Spring Rd., Indianapolis, 46222. Tel: 317-822-6810. Samuel L. Smith, Pres.; David Benedict, Vice Pres.; Thomas A. Smith, O.F.M.Conv., Treas.; Leopold Keffler, Sec.
NEW ALBANY. *New Albany Deanery-Catholic Youth Ministries*, 707 W. Hwy. 131, 47129. Tel: 812-945-0354; Fax: 812-945-2995.
E-mail: nadcym@aye.net

[P] CLOSED PARISHES, SCHOOLS AND OTHER INSTITUTIONS

INDIANAPOLIS. *Archives of the Archdiocese of Indianapolis*, 1400 N. Meridian St., 46202. Tel: 317-236-1429; Fax: 317-236-1406.
E-mail: archives@archindy.org
Sacramental and other records may be found where indicated.
Closed Parishes and Missions:
Indianapolis:
Assumption (1894-1994). Merged with St. Anthony, where sacramental records are kept.
St. Bridget (1880-1994). Merged with SS. Peter & Paul, where sacramental records are kept.
St. Catherine of Siena (1909-1993). Merged with St. James and renamed Good Shepherd, where sacramental records are kept.
St. Francis de Sales (1881-1983). Merged with four neighboring parishes. Sacramental records are located in the archives.
St. James the Greater (1951-1993). Merged with St. Catherine and renamed Good Shepherd, where sacramental records are kept.
St. Joseph (1873-1949). Sacramental records kept at the new St. Joseph parish.
Acton:
St. John the Evangelist (1855-1936).
Adyeville:
St. Jude Thaddeus (1889-1898).
Bainbridge:
St. Patrick (1865-1973).
Blanford:
Queen of the Most Holy Rosary (1917-1942).
Cannelton:
St. Patrick (1847-1902). Merged with St. Michael, Cannelton, where sacramental records are kept.
Carbon:
St. Joseph (1870-1970). Sacramental records are located in the archives.
Centenary:
St. Anthony (1917-1942).
China:
St. Anthony (1861-1993). Merged with Prince of Peace, Madison, where sacramental records are kept.
Columbus:
St. Columba (1963-1994). Merged with St. Bartholomew, Columbus, where sacramental records are kept.
Cypress Dale:
Sacred Heart (1868-1918).
Derby:
St. Mary (1824-1973). Sacramental records kept at St. Augustine, Leopold.
Diamond:
St. John Baptist (Greek Uniate Catholic) (1897-1926). Sacramental records are located in the archives.
St. Mary (1897-1991). Sacramental records are located in the archives.
Dogwood:
St. Michael (1820-1928).
Dugger:
Our Lady of Perpetual Help (1911-1982). Sacramental records kept at St. Mary, Sullivan Co., Diocese of Evansville.
Ellsworth:
St. John (1910-1912).
Eureka:
Mattingly Chapel (1874-1886).
Fontanet:
St. Augustine (1891-1980). Sacramental records are located in the archives.
Hovey:
All Souls Chapel (1900-1915).
Indian Creek:
St. Columban (1848-1868).
Knightsville:
St. Patrick (1868-1890).
Laconia:
Sacred Heart of Mary (1854-1922).
Laurel:
St. Raphael (1869-1958). Sacramental records kept at St. Gabriel, Connersville.
Lexington:
Mother of God (1854-1941).
Locust Point:
St. Joachim (1888-1930).
Madison:
St. Mary (1851-1993). Merged with St. Patrick (1853-1993) and St. Michael (1837-1993) and renamed Prince of Peace, where sacramental records are kept.
McCutcheonville:
St. Patrick (1842-1881).
Mecca:
St. Mary (1905-1936).
Milltown:
St. Joseph (1855-1974). Sacramental records kept at St. Joseph, Crawford Co.
Mount Erin:
St. John Baptist (1852-1885).
Mount Pleasant:
St. Rose (1821-1883).
Nebraska:
St. Bridget (1845-1936).
New Albany:
Holy Trinity (1836-1975). Merged with St. Mary, New Albany, where sacramental records are kept.
Rome:
St. Peter (1868-1885). Sacramental records are located in the archives.
St. Catherine:
St. Catherine (1841-1871). Sacramental records are located in the archives.
St. James:
St. James (1844-1850). Merged with St. Joseph, Perry Co. (1891-1968) and renamed St. Isidore, Perry Co., where sacramental records are kept.
St. Magdalen:
St. Magdalen (1847-1941). Sacramental records kept at St. John, Osgood.
St. Paul:
St. Paul (1859-1996). Sacramental records kept at St. Vincent, Shelby Co.
Perry Co.:
St. Peter.
St. Rose:
St. Rose (1840-1903). Merged with St. Thomas, Knox Co., Diocese of Evansville, where sacramental records are kept.
Salem:
St. Mary (1871-1902).
Scipio:
St. Patrick (1841-1958). Sacramental records are located in the archives.
Shelburn:
St. Ann (1909-1978). Sacramental records kept at St. Mary, Sullivan, Diocese of Evansville.
Shirley:
Mother of God (1900-1920). Sacramental records are located in the archives.
Taylorsville (Selvin):
St. Thomas (1845-1875).
Valley Mills:
St. John the Baptist (1855-1903). Sacramental records are located in the archives.
West Baden Springs:
Our Lady of Lourdes (1900-1929).
Willow Valley:
St. Stephen (1906-1944).
Closed Parish Grade Schools.
Indianapolis:
Assumption, All Saints Catholic School, 337 N. Warman Ave., 46222. Tel: 317-636-3739.
Cathedral, Holy Cross Central School, 125 N. Oriental St., 46201. Tel: 317-638-9068.
Holy Rosary, Holy Rosary Rectory, 520 Stevens St., 46203. Tel: 317-636-4478.
Holy Trinity, All Saints Catholic School, 337 N. Warman Ave., 46222. Tel: 317-636-3739.
Sacred Heart, Sacred Heart Rectory, 1530 Union St., 46225. Tel: 317-638-5551.
St. Ann, St. Ann Rectory, 2862 S. Holt Rd., 46241. Tel: 317-244-3750.
St. Anthony, All Saints Catholic School, 337 N. Warman Ave., 46222. Tel: 317-636-3739.
St. Bernadette.
St. Bridget. Sacramental records are located in the archives.
St. Catherine, Central Catholic School, 1155 Cameron St., 46203. Tel: 317-783-7759.
St. Francis de Sales. Sacramental records are located in the archives.
St. James the Greater, Central Catholic School, 1155 Cameron St., 46203. Tel: 317-783-7759.
St. Joseph, All Saints Catholic School, 337 N. Warman Ave., 46222. Tel: 317-636-3739.
St. Mary, Holy Cross Central School, 125 N. Oriental St., 46201. Tel: 317-638-9068.
St. Patrick, Central Catholic School, 1155 Cameron St., 46203. Tel: 317-783-7759.
Madison:
St. Mary; St. Michael, Pope John XXIII Grade School, 221 State St., Madison, 47250. Tel: 812-273-3957.
Morris:
St. Anthony, St. Anthony Rectory, P.O. Box 3, Morris, 47033. Tel: 812-934-6218.
New Castle:
St. Anne, St. Anne Rectory, 102 N. 19th St., New Castle, 47362. Tel: 765-529-0933.
Richmond:
Holy Family; St. Andrew; St. Mary, Elizabeth Ann Seton School, 801 W. Main St., Richmond, 47374. Tel: 765-962-4877.
Terre Haute:
St. Ann; St. Joseph, Student Services, Vigo County School Corp., P.O. Box 3703, Terre Haute, 47803. Tel: 812-462-4224.
St. Benedict. Sacramental records are located in the archives., Terre Haute.
St. Margaret Mary, St. Margaret Mary Rectory, 2405 S. Seventh St., Terre Haute, 47802. Tel: 812-232-3512.
Closed High Schools and Academies.
Brute Latin School. School records are located in the archives.
Chartrand; Kennedy; Sacred Heart, Roncalli High School, 3300 Prague Rd., 46227. Tel: 317-787-8277.
St. John; St. Agnes; Ladywood; Ladywood/St. Agnes Academies, Sisters of Providence, Records Office - Owens Hall, St. Mary-of-the-Woods, 47876. Tel: 812-535-3131.
St. Mary Academy, Registrar, Franciscan Motherhouse, Oldenburg, 47036. Tel: 812-934-2475.
Our Lady of Grace Academy, Our Lady of Grace Monastery, 1402 Southern Ave., Beech Grove, 46107. Tel: 317-787-3287.

Terre Haute:
Central Catholic High School for Girls.
St. Patrick High School for Girls.
St. Vincent Academy. Renamed St. Joseph Academy.
Schulte High School, Student Services, Vigo County School Corp., P.O. Box 3703, Terre Haute, 47803. Tel: 812-462-4224.
Other Closed Institutions.
Indianapolis:
Sisters of the Good Shepherd Convent. Sacramental records are located in the archives.
Angel Guardian School for Orphans. Entrance records, 1924-1937, are located in the archives.
Marydale School For Girls. Sacramental records, 1875-1953, are located in the archives. For other records contact Sisters of the Good Shepherd, 811 Highland Ave., Ft. Thomas, KY 41075. Tel: 606-572-0713.
New Albany:
St. Edward Hospital, New Albany, Sisters of St. Francis of Perpetual Adoration (O.S.F.), Box 766, Mishawaka, 46546. Tel: 219-259-5427.
Terre Haute:
St. Ann Orphanage For Girls.
St. Anthony Hospital. Baptismal records are located in the archives.

RELIGIOUS INSTITUTES OF MEN REPRESENTED IN THE ARCHDIOCESE

For further details refer to the corresponding bracketed number in the Religious Institutes of Men or Women section.

[0200]—*Benedictine Monks of St. Maur & St. Meinrad.*—O.S.B.
[0600]—*Brothers of the Congregation of Holy Cross (Midwest & Eastern Provinces).*—C.S.C.
[1140]—*Congregation of the Sacred Heart of Jesus & Mary.*—SS.CC.
[0480]—*Conventual Franciscans.* (Our Lady of Consolation Prov.).—O.F.M.Conv.
[0500]—*Franciscan Brothers of Christ the King.*—O.S.F.
[0520]—*Franciscan Friars (St. John the Baptist & Sacred Heart Province).*—O.F.M.
[0690]—*Jesuit Fathers and Brothers.* (Chicago Prov.).—S.J.
[]—*Priestly Fraternity of Saint Peter.*—F.S.S.P.
[0420]—*Society of the Divine Word.* (Chicago Province).—S.V.D.

RELIGIOUS INSTITUTES OF WOMEN REPRESENTED IN THE ARCHDIOCESE

[0230]—*Benedictine Sisters of Pontifical Jurisdiction.* (Ferdinand, IN).—O.S.B.
[1920]—*Congregation of the Sisters of the Holy Cross.*—C.S.C.
[1730]—*Congregation of the Sisters of the Third Order of St. Francis, Oldenburg, IN.*—O.S.F.
[0760]—*Daughters of Charity of St. Vincent De Paul.* (Evansville, IN).—D.C.
[0420]—*Discalced Carmelite Nuns.*—O.C.D.
[1070-03]—*Dominican Sisters.*—O.P.
[]—*Franciscan Sisters of the Immaculate Heart of Mary.* (Quilon, Kerala, India).—F.I.H.
[2340]—*Little Sisters of the Poor.* (Baltimore, MD).—L.S.P.
[2710]—*Missionaries of Charity.*—M.C.
[2820]—*Missionary Sisters of Our Lady of Africa.* (American Headquarters, Winooski, VT).—M.S.O.L.A.
[0440]—*Sisters of Charity of Cincinnati, Ohio.* (Central Region).—S.C.
[0500]—*Sisters of Charity of Nazareth.* (Nazareth, KY).—S.C.N.
[0430]—*Sisters of Charity of the Blessed Virgin Mary.* Dubuque, IA.—B.V.M.
[]—*Sisters of Loretto at the Foot of the Cross.* Nerinx, KY.—S.L.
[3360]—*Sisters of Providence of Saint Mary-of-the-Woods, IN.*—S.P.
[]—*Sisters of St. Benedict of Our Lady of Grace Monastery.* (Beech Grove, IN).—O.S.B.
[1640]—*Sisters of St. Francis of Perpetual Adoration.*—O.S.F.
[3840]—*Sisters of St. Joseph Carondelet.* (St. Louis, MO).—C.S.J.
[]—*Sisters of St. Joseph of Tipton.* (Tipton, IN).—C.S.J.
[1720]—*Sisters of the Third Order Regular of St. Francis of the Congregation of Our Lady of Lourdes.*—O.S.F.
[2150]—*Sisters, Servants of the Immaculate Heart of Mary.* (Monroe, MI).—I.H.M.
[4120-03]—*Ursuline Nuns of the Congregation of Paris.*—O.S.U.

ARCHDIOCESAN CEMETERIES

INDIANAPOLIS. *Catholic Cemeteries*, 9001 Haverstick Rd., 46240.
Indianapolis Deanery.
Holy Cross.
St. Joseph.
Calvary.
Our Lady of Peace.
St. Malachy, Brownsburg.
St. Malachy, Pittsboro.
BATESVILLE. *Batesville Deanery.*
St. Mary, Greensburg.
St. John, Osgood.
St. Charles, Milan.
St. Maurice, Napoleon.
BLOOMINGTON. *Bloomington Deanery.*
Catholic, Martinsville.
CONNERSVILLE. *Connersville Deanery.*
St. Raphael, Laurel.
St. Michael, Brookville.
Holy Family, Oldenburg.
Holy Family Shrine, Oldenburg.
Cemetery North, Brookville.
Calvary, Rushville.
St. Bridget, Liberty.
St. Mary, Richmond.
NEW ALBANY. *New Albany Deanery.*
St. Joseph, Corydon.
St. Michael, Dogwood.
St. Peter, Taylor Twp.
Cemetery South West, Bradford.
St. Bernard, Frenchtown.
St. Joachim, Locust Point.
St. Anthony, Jeffersonville.
Queen of Heaven.
St. Michael.
SEYMOUR. *Seymour Deanery.*
St. Ambrose.
St. Mary, North Vernon.
St. Catherine.
Old St. James.
St. Joseph.
St. Patrick.
St. Magdalen.
TELL CITY. *Tell City Deanery.*
St. Joseph, St. Croix.
St. Croix. (Cemetery on original parish site.), St. Croix.
St. Meinrad, St. Meinrad.
St. Paul.
St. Peter, Cannelton.
TERRE HAUTE. *Terre Haute Deanery.*
Catholic, Brazil.
Calvary.
St. Joseph.
St. Mary of the Woods.

NECROLOGY

† Byrne, James F., (Retired). —Died Jan. 23, 2000.
† Herold, Carl A., (Retired). —Died Nov. 26, 1999.
† Kos, Joseph S., Chap, Indianapolis, IN Wishard Memorial Hospital. —Died Aug. 9, 2000.
† Murphy, Kenneth J., (Retired). —Died Nov. 24, 1999.
† Ross, Rev. Msgr. Charles R., (Retired). —Died Aug. 25, 2000.
† Sexton, Charles E., (Retired). —Died Oct. 18, 2000.
† Strahl, Ernest, (Retired). —Died Jan. 3, 2000.

Diocese of Jackson

(Dioecesis Jacksoniensis)

Most Reverend

WILLIAM R. HOUCK, D.D.

Bishop of Jackson; ordained May 19, 1951; appointed Auxiliary Bishop of Jackson and Titular Bishop of Allessano on March 28, 1979; consecrated May 27, 1979; appointed Bishop of Jackson April 24, 1984; installed June 5, 1984. *Mailing Address: P.O. Box 2248, Jackson, MS, 39225-2248.*

Chancery Office: 237 E. Amite St., P.O. Box 2248, Jackson, MS, 39225-2248. Tel.: 601-969-1880; Fax: 601-960-8455.

Web site address: www.jacksondiocese.org

E-mail address: chancery@jacksondiocese.org

Legal Title: "Catholic Diocese of Jackson".

ESTABLISHED JULY 28, 1837 AS DIOCESE OF NATCHEZ. NAME CHANGED TO DIOCESE.OF NATCHEZ-JACKSON, MARCH 7, 1957. NAME CHANGED TO DIOCESE OF JACKSON, JUNE 6, 1977

Square Miles 37,643.

Comprises 65 Counties in the State of Mississippi, namely: Adams, Alcorn, Amite, Attala, Benton, Bolivar, Calhoun, Carroll, Chickasaw, Choctaw, Claiborne, Clarke, Clay, Coahoma, Copiah, De Soto, Franklin, Grenada, Hinds, Holmes, Humphreys, Issaquena, Itawamba, Jasper, Jefferson, Kemper, Lafayette, Lauderdale, Leake, Lee, Leflore, Lincoln, Lowndes, Madison, Marshall, Monroe, Montgomery, Neshoba, Newton, Noxubee, Oktibbeha, Panola, Pike, Pontotoc, Prentiss, Quitman, Rankin, Scott, Sharkey, Simpson, Smith, Su.nflower, Tallahatchie, Tate, Tippah, Tishomingo, Tunica, Union, Warren, Washington, Webster, Wilkinson, Winston, Yalobusha and Yazoo.

STATISTICAL OVERVIEW

Personnel	
Bishop	1
Priests: Diocesan Active in Diocese	49
Priests: Active Outside Diocese	6
Priests: Diocesan in Foreign Missions	1
Priests: Retired, Sick or Absent	9
Number of Diocesan Priests	65
Religious Priests in Diocese	30
Extern Priests in Diocese	2
Permanent Deacons in Diocese	7
Total Brothers	12
Total Sisters	240
Parishes	
Parishes	74
With Resident Pastor:	
Resident Diocesan Priests	37
Resident Religious Priests	17
Without Resident Pastor:	
Administered by Priests	11
Administered by Deacons	1
Administered by Professed Men Religious	1
Administered by Women Religious	4
Administered by Lay People	3
Missions	29
Professional Ministry Personnel:	
Brothers	3
Sisters	22
Lay Ministers	13
Welfare	
Catholic Hospitals	1
Total Assisted	85,799
Health Care Centers	2
Total Assisted	9,271
Homes for the Aged	1
Total Assisted	225
Residential Care of Children	3
Total Assisted	350
Day Care and Extended Day Care Centers	2
Total Assisted	550
Specialized Homes	7
Total Assisted	2,000
Special Centers for Social Services	5
Total Assisted	12,500
Residential Care of Disabled	3
Total Assisted	60
Other Institutions	3
Total Assisted	60
Educational	
Diocesan Students in Other Seminaries	9
Total Seminarians	9
Colleges and Universities	1
Total Students	24
High Schools, Diocesan and Parish	4
Total Students	1,224
Elementary Schools, Diocesan and Parish	16
Total Students	3,779
Catechesis/Religious Education:	
High School Students	870
Elementary Students	3,980
Total Students Under Catholic Instruction	9,886
Teachers in the Diocese:	
Priests	2
Brothers	2
Sisters	17
Lay Teachers	349
Vital Statistics	
Receptions into the Church:	
Infant Baptism Totals	798
Adult Baptism Totals	161
Received into Full Communion	312
First Communions	667
Confirmations	488
Marriages:	
Catholic	89
Interfaith	201
Total Marriages	290
Deaths	411
Total Catholic Population	47,873
Total Population	1,980,025

Former Bishops—Rt. Rev. JOHN J. CHANCHE, S.S., D.D., cons. March 14, 1841; died July 22, 1852.—Rt. Rev. J. O. VAN DE VELDE, S.J., D.D., transferred from Chicago, July 29, 1853; died Nov. 13, 1855.—Most Rev. WILLIAM HENRY ELDER, D.D., cons. May 3, 1857; transferred to Cincinnati, 1880; died Oct. 31, 1904.—Most Rev. FRANCIS JANSSENS, D.D., cons. May 1, 1881; transferred to New Orleans, Aug. 7, 1888; died June 9, 1897.—Rt. Rev. THOMAS HESLIN, D.D., cons. June 18, 1889; died Feb. 22, 1911.—Rt. Rev. JOHN EDWARD GUNN, S.M., D.D., cons. Aug. 29, 1911; died Feb. 19, 1924.—Most Rev. RICHARD OLIVER GEROW, LL.D., S.T.D., ord. June 5, 1909; appt. June 25, 1924; cons. Oct. 15, 1924; retired Dec. 2, 1967; died Dec. 20, 1976.—Most Rev. JOSEPH B. BRUNINI, D.D., LL.D., J.C.D., ord. Dec. 5, 1933; cons. Jan. 29, 1957; appt. Bishop, Dec. 2, 1967; installed Jan. 29, 1968; retired Jan. 24, 1984; died Jan. 7, 1996.

Chancery Office—237 E. Amite St., P.O. Box 2248, Jackson, 39225-2248. Tel: 601-969-1880; Fax: 601-960-8455. The telephone number for all Diocesan Offices is 601-969-1880, unless otherwise listed. Office Hours: 8:30-4:30.

Office of the Bishop—Most Rev. WILLIAM R. HOUCK, D.D., *237 E. Amite St., P.O. Box 2248, Jackson, 39225-2248.*

Office of Vicar General—Revs. MICHAEL FLANNERY, J.C.L.; FRANCIS J. COSGROVE.

Department of Ecclesiastical Affairs—

Chancellor—Rev. MICHAEL FLANNERY, J.C.L., *237 E. Amite St., P.O. Box 2248, Jackson, 39225-2248.*

Vice Chancellor—Rev. KEVIN SLATTERY, J.C.L.

Director of Vocations—Rev. JOSEPH TONOS.

Director of Permanent Diaconate—Deacon KEVIN J. MCCARTHY.

Propagation of the Faith—Rev. PATRICK FARRELL, Dir., *P.O. Box 57, Jackson, 39205.* Tel: 601-969-3125.

Archivist—JO ANN HAIEN.

Judicial Vicar—Rev. KEVIN SLATTERY, J.C.L.

Engaged Encounter—Rev. KEVIN SLATTERY, J.C.L., Dir.

Ecumenism—Rev. RICHARD SMITH, *St. Michael, P.O. Box 388, Forest, 39074-0388.* Tel: 601-469-1916.

Promoters of Justice—Revs. MICHAEL FLANNERY, J.C.L.; FRANCIS COSGROVE; THOMAS NIEMIRA.

Defenders of the Bond—Revs. MICHAEL FLANNERY, J.C.L.; FRANCIS COSGROVE; THOMAS NIEMIRA; JOHN BOHN; JEFFREY WALDREP; WILLIAM CULLEN; DANIEL GALLAGHER; AEDAN MANNING, S.T., J.C.L.

Notaries—Rev. ROBERT OLIVIER; MARYBETH RABERT.

Diocesan Judges—Rev. Msgr. NOEL G. FOLEY, J.C.L.; Revs. PATRICK FARRELL; KEVIN SLATTERY, J.C.L.

Approved Advocate and Auditors—Revs. THOMAS DELANEY; CHARLES BUCCIANTINI; MEYRL SCHMIT; DON DERIVAUX, S.T.L.

Priests' Council—Most Rev. WILLIAM R. HOUCK, Pres.; Revs. JOSEPH DYER, Chm. MARTIN RUANE, Vice Chm. JEFFREY WALDREP, Sec. KEVIN SLATTERY, Treas. BRIAN CARROLL; DONALD DERIVAUX; PATRICK FARRELL; ROBERT DORE; MICHAEL FLANNERY, J.C.L.; ROBERT OLIVIER; RICHARD SMITH; SAMUEL MESSINA.

Diocesan Consultors—Revs. MICHAEL FLANNERY, J.C.L.; FRANCIS COSGROVE; Rev. Msgr. NOEL FOLEY; Revs. ROBERT OLIVIER; SAM MESSINA; PATRICK FARRELL.

Association of Priests—Most Rev. WILLIAM R. HOUCK, Co-Chm.; Most Rev. JOSEPH L. HOWZE, Co-Chm.; Rev. PATRICK FARRELL, Pres.; Rev. THOMAS CONWAY, Sec. & Treas.; Trustees; Revs. KEN RAMON-LANDRY; ELVIN SUNDS; JEFFREY WALDREP; Rev. Msgr. ANDREW MURRAY.

Diocesan Pastoral Council—Most Rev. WILLIAM R. HOUCK, Pres.

Personnel Board—Revs. MICHAEL FLANNERY, Personnel Dir. THOMAS MCGING; PATRICK FARRELL; Rev. Msgr. NOEL FOLEY; Revs. PATRICK NOONAN; JEFFREY WALDREP.

Department of Administration & Finance—WILLIAM P. DUNNING, Dir., Admin. Affairs, *237 E. Amite St., P.O. Box 2248, Jackson, 39225-2248.*

Income Development—GEORGE ROMAN, Dir.

Department of Catholic Charities and Community Services—

Catholic Charities, Inc.—LINDA RAFF, Dir., *748 N. President St., P.O. Box 2248, Jackson, 39225-2248*. Tel: 601-355-8634; Fax: 601-960-8493.

Parish-Based Ministries—Sr. DONNA GUNN, C.S.J., Dir. Parish Social Ministry. Tel: 601-355-8634. Mrs. LOUISE DILLON, Dir. Family Ministry.

Peace and Justice—LINDA RAFF, Dir., *P.O. Box 2248, Jackson, 39225-2248*.

Department of Educational Services—Rev. WILLIAM CULLEN, Dir., *237 E. Amite St., P.O. Box 2248, Jackson, 39225-2248*.

Holy Childhood Pontifical Association—Sr. KAREN O'KELLY, O.P., Dir.

Superintendent of Schools—Sr. DEBORAH HUGHES, S.S.J.

Assistant Superintendent—Sr. MARY KAREN O'KELLY, O.P.

Early Child Development, Health and Education Projects—Sr. CYRENA HARKINS, R.S.M.

Director of Religious Education—Mr. JOHN VALENTI.

Director of Spring Hill Theology Program—Mr. JOHN VALENTI.

Campus Ministry—Rev. WILLIAM CULLEN, Dir.

Department of Evangelization—Miss MARY WOODWARD, Dir.

Charismatic Renewal—Rev. WILLIAM HENRY.

Cursillo Movement—Rev. ANTHONY QUYET, Spiritual Dir.

Youth Ministry—Rev. JOSEPH TONOS, Diocesan Dir.

Parish Pastoral Councils—Miss MARY WOODWARD, Dir.

"Mississippi Catholic"—JANNA AVALON, Editor.

Black Catholic Ministry—JOYCE HART, Dir.

Hispanic Ministry—Bro. TED DAUSCH, C.F.C., Dir.

Catholic Foundation-Diocese of Jackson—GEORGE ROMAN, Dir., *P.O. Box 2248, Jackson, 39225-2248*.

CLERGY, PARISHES, MISSIONS AND PAROCHIAL SCHOOLS

CITY OF JACKSON
(Hinds County)

1—ST. PETER CATHEDRAL, Rev. Patrick Farrell, Rector. In res., Revs. Michael Flannery; Daniel Gallagher.
Res., 123 N. West St., P.O. Box 57, 39205-0057. Tel: 601-969-3125; Fax: 601-969-3130.

2—ST. MARY, Rev. Richard P. Chiles, O.Praem.
Res., 653 Claiborne Ave., 39209. Tel: 601-353-2292; Fax: 601-944-1606.
School—Tel: 601-353-7357; Fax: 601-352-5164. Ms. Wanda Gosa, Prin.
Lay Teachers 7; Students 152.

3—ST. RICHARD, Rev. Msgr. Noel Foley; Rev. John Joseph Bohn. In res., Rev. Msgr. Michael Glynn.
Res., 1242 Lynnwood Dr., P.O. Box 16547, 39236. Tel: 601-366-2335; Fax: 601-366-0438.
School—Tel: 601-366-1157; Fax: 601-366-4344.
Lay Teachers 33; Students 480.

4—ST. THERESE, Rev. Thomas Lalor. Pastoral Assocs.: Mr. Nick L. Scheller; Evelyn Thibeaux, Ph.D.
Res., 304 Fairhill Dr., 39204. Tel: 601-372-3441.
Church—309 McDowell Rd., P.O. Box 8642, 39284-8642. Tel: 601-372-4481; Fax: 601-376-0094.
School—Tel: 601-372-3323; Fax: 601-372-3365.
Lay Teachers 8; Students 180.

5—HOLY FAMILY, Rev. Edward Balser. In res., Rev. Brian Kaskie.
Res., 381 St. Augustine Dr., Madison, 39110. Tel: 601-853-0441.
Church—820 Forest Ave., 39206-3299. Tel: 601-362-1888.

6—HOLY GHOST, Rev. Ryszard Kalinowski; Deacon Sam Baker.
Res., 1151 Cloister St., 39202. Tel: 601-353-1339.

7—CHRIST THE KING, Rev. Richard P. Chiles, O.Praem.
Res., 2303 J.R. Lynch St., 39209. Tel: 601-948-8867.
School—Preschool and Montessori, Tel: 601-352-5441; Fax: 601-352-5441. Ms. Janie Paige, Asst. Dir.
Students 132.

OUTSIDE THE CITY OF JACKSON

Aberdeen, Monroe Co., St. Francis of Assisi, Rev. Timothy Murphy, Glmy.; Bro. Terry O'Rourke, Glmy., Outreach Worker.
Res., 104 S. James St., P.O. Box 134, 39730-0134. Tel: 662-369-2897; Fax: 662-369-2897.
Mission—Houston, Chickasaw Co., Immaculate Heart of Mary, P.O. Box 309, Houston, 38851. Tel: 662-456-5450. Mission Coordinators: Sr. Rosemary Empen, O.P.; Sr. Pat Sullivan, O.P.
Mission—Okolona, Chickasaw Co., St. Theresa, 116 N. Fleming St., Okolona, 38860. Tel: 662-447-3008. Sr. Elizabeth Brown, C.S.J., Mission Coord.

Amory, Monroe Co., St. Helen, Sr. Florita Rodman, C.D.P., Res. Pastoral Min.; Sr. Mary Agatha Ruhe, C.D.P., Pastoral Assoc.
Res., 401 Eighth Ave. S., P.O. Box 97, 38821-0097. Tel: 662-256-8392; Fax: 662-256-8392.
Mission—Fulton, Itawamba Co., Christ the King, 100 E. Main St., Fulton, 38843-1207. Tel: 662-862-2239; Fax: 662-862-2239. Mr. Jerry Woods, Mission Coord.

Batesville, Panola Co., St. Mary, Rev. Thomas Boyce.
Res., P.O. Box 569, 38606-0569. Tel: 662-563-2273.
Mission—Sardis, St. John the Baptist.

Belzoni, Humphreys Co., All Saints, Rev. Samuel Messina.
Res., 200 Bowles St., 39038-3602. Tel: 662-247-1408; Fax: 662-247-1504.
Mission—Anguilla, Our Mother of Mercy.

Booneville, Prentiss Co., St. Francis of Assisi, Rev. Thomas L. Burns, S.C.J., Admin.; Sr. Dorothy Pashuta, C.S.J., Pastoral Min.
Res., P.O. Box 654, 38829. Tel: 662-728-7509; Fax: 662-728-7509.
Mission—Iuka, Tishomingo Co., St. Mary, P.O. Box 651, Iuka, 38852. Tel: 662-423-9358; Fax: 662-423-9358. Sr. Dolores Partsch, C.S.J., Pastoral Min.

Brandon, Rankin Co., St. Paul, Rev. Brian Carroll; Deacon Frank Agosta.
Res., 108 Twin Oaks Dr., 39047. Tel: 601-992-3222; Fax: 601-992-9972.
Church—5971 Hwy. 25, 39047. Tel: 601-992-9547; Fax: 601-992-9972.
School—Learning Center, Tel: 601-992-2876; Fax: 601-992-8741. Ellen Treadaway, Dir.
Students 102.

Brookhaven, Lincoln Co., St. Francis, Rev. Patrick Noonan.
Res., 227 E. Cherokee St., P.O. Box 196, 39601. Tel: 601-833-1799.
Mission—Meadville, Franklin Co., St. Ann.

Bruce, Calhoun Co., St. Luke The Evangelist. Unassigned.
Res., 204 E. Clay, P.O. Box 230, 38915. Tel: 662-983-2790.

Camden, Madison Co., Immaculate Conception, Rev. John P. McSpiritt, S.T. In res., Bro. Finbarr Ray, S.T.
Res., 1363 Hwy. 17, 39045. Tel: 662-468-2354; Fax: 662-468-2488.
School—Tel: 662-468-2324; Fax: 662-468-2721.
Sisters 2; Lay Teachers 8.

Canton, Madison Co., Sacred Heart, Rev. William Cullen; Sr. Mary Ann Grausam, S.L.W., Pastoral Assoc. In res., Rev. Kevin Slattery.
Res., 238 E. Center St., P.O. Box 361, 39046. Tel: 601-859-3749; Fax: 601-859-8011.

Holy Child Jesus, Rev. William Cullen; Sr. Mary Ann Grausam, S.L.W., Pastoral Assoc.
Res., 315 Garrett St., P.O. Box 366, 39046. Tel: 601-859-2957.
School—Tel: 601-859-4168; Fax: 601-859-4140. Mr. Michael Owen, Prin.
Brothers 1; Lay Teachers 6; Students 102.

Carthage, Leake Co., St. Anne, Revs. William Cullen; Kevin Slattery, S.T.; Sr. Patricia Godri, S.C., Res. Pastoral Min.
Res., 207 Red Dog Rd., 39051. Tel: 601-267-7190; Fax: 601-267-8972.

Charleston, Tallahatchie Co., St. John, Bro. Senan Gallagher, S.T.
Church—304 W. Cypress St., P.O. Box 30, 38921-0030. Tel: 662-647-3170.

Chatawa, Pike Co., St. Teresa, Rev. Robert Dore.
Res., P.O. Box 11, 39632-0011. Tel: 601-783-5931; Fax: 601-783-3984.
Mission—Magnolia, Pike Co., St. James, Bay St., 39652.

Clarksdale, Coahoma Co., St. Elizabeth, Rev. Kent Bowlds.
Res., 130 Florence Ave., 38614-2720. Tel: 662-624-4301; Fax: 662-627-7856.
School—107 Clark St., 38614-2720. Tel: 662-624-4239; Fax: 662-624-2072. Sr. Carolyn Zionce, R.S.M., Prin.
Lay Teachers 9; Students 134.

Immaculate Conception, Rev. Kent Bowlds; Mr. Richard Edelen, Pastoral Assoc.
Res., 510 Ritchie Ave., 38614. Tel: 662-624-4029; Fax: 662-627-4867.
Early Childhood Center—520 Ritchie Ave., 38614. Tel: 662-627-4823; Fax: 662-627-4867. Mrs. Josephine Burk, Dir.
Lay Teachers 5; Students 65.

Cleveland, Bolivar Co., Our Lady of Victories, Rev. Charles Bucciantini.
Res., 215 Bishop Rd., P.O. Box 1450, 38732-1450. Tel: 662-846-6273.
Station—Cleveland, Delta State University.

Clinton, Hinds Co., Holy Savior, Rev. Noel Prendergast.
Res., 714 Lyndale St., P.O. Box 85, 39060-0085. Tel: 601-924-6344.
Mission—Raymond, Immaculate Conception.

Columbus, Lowndes Co., Annunciation, Rev. Gerard Hurley; Sr. Josephine Fogarty, R.S.M., Pastoral Assoc.
Res., 808 College St., 39701. Tel: 662-328-2927; Fax: 662-329-8270.
School—223 N. Browder St., 39701. Tel: 662-328-4479; Fax: 662-328-0430.
Lay Teachers 14; Students 167.

Corinth, Alcorn Co., St. James, Rev. Thomas L. Burns, S.C.J.
Res., 3187 Harper Rd., P.O. Box 660, 38835-0660. Tel: 662-287-1385.
Church—3189 Harper Rd., 38835. Tel: 662-287-1051.

Crystal Springs, Copiah Co., St. John, Rev. Aedan Manning, S.T.
Res., 217 E. Georgetown St., P.O. Box 167, 39059-0167. Tel: 601-892-1717.
Mission—Hazlehurst, St. Martin.

Fayette, Jefferson Co., St. Anne, Rev. Robert Zawacki.
Res., 195 New Harriston Rd., P.O. Box 159, 39069. Tel: 601-445-5700; Fax: 601-442-6030.

Forest, Scott Co., St. Michael, Rev. Richard Smith.
Res., P.O. Box 388, 39074. Tel: 601-469-1916.
Mission—Newton, St. Anne, 608 Decatur St., Newton, 39045.

Greenville, Washington Co., St. Joseph, Revs. Richard Somers; Jerry Alan Mattingly.
Res., 410 Main St., P.O. Box 1220, 38702-1220. Tel: 662-335-5251; Fax: 662-332-1178.
School—Our Lady of Lourdes, (Grades PreK-6). Tel: 662-334-3287; Fax: 662-332-9877. Sr. Marie Elizabeth Alspaugh, S.S.J., Prin.
Sisters 2; Lay Teachers 25; Students 296.
Junior & Senior High School—(Grades 7-12). Tel: 662-378-9711; Fax: 662-378-3496. Mr. Anthony Durso, Prin.
Students 290.

Sacred Heart, Rev. Eric Groner, S.V.D.
Res., 560 E. Gloster St., 38701-3836. Tel: 662-332-0891; Fax: 662-332-0891.

Greenwood, LeFlore Co., Immaculate Heart of Mary, Rev. Thomas Delaney; Sr. Christiana Hofmann, S.C.N., Pastoral Min.
Res., 511 W. Washington St., P.O. Box 313, 38935-0313. Tel: 662-453-3980.
Parish Center—310 Henderson St., 38935-0313. Tel: 662-453-9535.

St. Francis of Assisi, Rev. Hilary Brzezinski, O.F.M.; Bro. Mario Nagy, O.F.M.
Res., 2613 Hwy. 82 E., 38930-5966. Tel: 662-453-0623; Fax: 662-453-9060.
School—2607 Hwy. 82 E., 38930-5966. Tel: 662-453-9511; Fax: 662-453-9060.
Sisters 4; Lay Teachers 9; Students 194.
Convent—2603 Hwy 82 E., 38930-5966. Tel: 662-453-1221. Franciscan Sisters of Christian Charity

Grenada, Grenada Co., St. Peter, Rev. John Brock.
Res., 320 College Blvd., 38901-3808. Tel: 662-226-2490.

Hernando, DeSoto Co., Holy Spirit, Rev. James A. Cunniffe, S.C.J.; Deacon Everell Van Tassel.
Res., P.O. Box 424, 38632-0424. Tel: 662-429-7851; Fax: 662-429-7882.

Holly Springs, Marshall Co., St. Joseph, Revs. Paul M. Casper, S.C.J.; James R. Schifano, S.C.J., Assoc. Pastor.
Church—305 Van Dorn Ave., P.O. Box 430, 38635-0430. Tel: 662-252-3138; Fax: 662-252-1522.
School—Holy Family School, (Grades K-8). Tel: 662-252-1612; Fax: 662-252-3694. Dr. Helen Olivier, Prin.
Students 234.
Holy Family Childcare—Tel: 662-252-1366; Fax: 662-252-1576. Sr. Diane Bauknecht, C.S.A., Dir.
Students 57.

Indianola, Sunflower Co., Immaculate Conception, Rev. Anthony Quyet.
Res., Hwy. 448, P.O. Box 944, 38751-9665. Tel: 662-887-4659.

St. Benedict the Moor, Rev. Anthony Quyet.
Res., 403 Church Ave., P.O. Box 407, 38751. Tel: 662-887-4608; 887-4659.

Kosciusko, Attala Co., St. Therese, Barbara A. Sturbaum, Ph.D., Res. Pastoral Min.
Res., 108 Bell St., P.O. Box 628, 39090. Tel: 662-289-1193.

Leland, Washington Co., St. James, Rev. Sean Atkinson.
Res., 312 E. Third St., P.O. Box 352, 38756-0352. Tel: 662-686-7352; Fax: 662-686-7352.
Mission—Hollandale, Immaculate Conception.

Lexington, Holmes Co., St. Thomas, Rev. Hilary Brzezinski, O.F.M., Admin.
Res., 200 Boulevard St., 39095. Tel: 662-834-4443.
Mission—Winona, Sacred Heart, 304 Jones St., Winona, 38967. Tel: 662-283-1422. Rev. Hilary Brzezinski, O.F.M.

Louisville, Winston Co., Sacred Heart, Barbara A. Sturbaum, Ph.D., Res. Pastoral Min.
Res., 410 Spring Ave., 39339. Tel: 662-773-6062.

McComb, Pike Co., St. Alphonsus, Rev. William Henry.
Church—507 Delaware Ave., P.O. Box 1105, 39648-1105. Tel: 601-684-5648; Fax: 601-684-1924.
School—Elementary and Preschool, Tel: 601-684-1843. Mrs. Kathy Gifford, Prin.
Students 192.

Madison, Madison Co., St. Francis of Assisi, Revs. Francis J. Cosgrove; Brian Kaskie.
Office: 4000 W. Tidewater Ln., 39110-8942. Tel: 601-856-5556; Fax: 601-856-2849.
Learning Center—Tel: 601-856-9494. Sr. Paula Blouin, S.S.N.D., Dir.
Students 155.
Mission—Gluckstadt, St. Joseph, 127 Church Rd., 39110. Tel: 601-856-2054. Sr. Jane Desaulniers, S.S.N.D., Pastoral Assoc.; Deacon Kevin J. McCarthy.

Magee, Simpson Co., St. Stephen, Rev. Robert Goodyear, S.T.
Res., 594 Simpson Hwy. 149, P.O. Box 427, 39111-0427. Tel: 601-849-3237; Fax: 601-849-3398.
Mission—Raleigh, St. Paul, Hwy. 35 S., Raleigh, 39153.

Meridian, Lauderdale Co., St. Patrick, Rev. Elvin Sunds.
Church & Mailing Address: 2601 Davis St., P.O. Box 529, 39302. Tel: 601-693-1321; Fax: 601-484-8953.
Res., 204-39th Ct., 39301. Tel: 601-693-2574.
School—Tel: 601-482-6044; Fax: 601-485-2762.
Lay Teachers 11; Students 196.
Mission—Quitman, Good Shepherd, Hwy. North, 39355.

St. Joseph, Rev. Elvin Sunds; Sr. Andre Burkhart, O.S.F., Pastoral Assoc.
Res., 1914 18th Ave., P.O. Box 532, 39302-0532. Tel: 601-485-5349; Fax: 601-484-8953.

Mound Bayou, Bolivar Co., St. Gabriel, Rev. Don Derivaux; Bro. Pius Kamphefner, F.S.C., Res. Pastoral Min.
Res., P.O. Box 53, 38762-0053. Tel: 662-741-2439.
Pre-School—Tel: 662-741-2395.
Sisters 5; Lay Teachers 5; Students 70.

Natchez, Adams Co., Assumption of the B.V.M., Rev. Michael O'Brien.
Res., 10 Morgantown Rd., 39120-2788. Tel: 601-442-7250.

Holy Family, Rev. Robert Zawacki, S.S.J.
Res., 16 Orange Ave., 39120. Tel: 601-445-5700; Fax: 601-442-6030.
School—Tel: 601-442-3947; Fax: 601-442-6030.
Sisters 2; Lay Teachers 9; Students 126.
Convent—8 Orange Ave., 39120. Tel: 601-445-4257; Fax: 601-442-6030. Sisters of the Holy Spirit
Mission—Cranfield, St. John the Baptist.

St. Mary Basilica, Revs. Alfred L. Camp; Michael O'Brien.
Res., 107 S. Union St., P.O. Box 1044, 39121-1044. Tel: 601-445-5616; Fax: 601-445-5616.
School—Cathedral Unit School. See High Schools, Inter-Parochial under Institutions Located in the Diocese. Tel: 601-442-2531; Fax: 601-442-0960.

New Albany, Union Co., St. Francis of Assisi, Rev. Steven P. Pawelk, Glmy.
Res., 1507 S. Central Ave., P.O. Box 887, 38652-0887. Tel: 662-534-9205; Fax: 662-538-0406.
Church—650 Hwy. 15 S., P.O. Box 887, 38652-0887. Tel: 662-534-4654.
Mission—Pontotoc, Pontotoc Co., St. Christopher, S. Main St., P.O. Box 67, Pontotoc, 38863-0067. Tel: 662-489-7749.

Olive Branch, DeSoto Co., Queen of Peace, Rev. John Young, S.C.J.; Deacon Henry Babin.
Res., 8455 Germantown Rd., P.O. Box 65, 38654-0065. Tel: 662-895-5007; Fax: 662-895-5036.

Oxford, Lafayette Co., St. John, Rev. Joseph Dyer; Deacon Theodore Klingen.
Church: 403 University Ave., 38655-4329. Tel: 662-234-6073; 234-1940 (Res.); Fax: 662-234-6079.

Paulding, Jasper Co., St. Michael, Rev. Richard Smith.
Mailing Address: P.O. Box 388, Forest, 39074-0388. Tel: 601-469-1916.
Church—Star Rte., P.O. Box 15, 39348. Fax: 601-469-1916.

Pearl, Rankin Co., St. Jude, Rev. Martin Ruane.
Res., 399 Barrow St., P.O. Box 5526, 39288-5526. Tel: 601-939-1863; 939-3181 (Office).
Station—Whitfield, Mississippi State Mental Hospital.

Philadelphia, Neshoba Co., Holy Cross, Rev. Kenan Ryan, S.T.
Res., 406 Wilson St., 39350-2906. Tel: 601-656-1841.

Holy Rosary (Tucker Community), Revs. David A. Hamm, S.T.; Raphael F. Toner, S.T.
Res., Hwy. 19, P.O. Box 37, 39350. Tel: 601-656-2880; Fax: 601-656-2829.
Missions—Conehatta, St. Catherine, Tel: 601-775-3900; Philadelphia, St. Theresa, Tel: 601-656-6411.

Port Gibson, Claiborne Co., St. Joseph, Rev. Msgr. Thaddeus Harkins.
Res., 411 Coffee St., P.O. Box 1012, 39150. Tel: 601-437-5790.

Ripley, Tippah Co., Tippah County Catholic Community, Sr. Kate Regan, C.S.J., Mission Coord.
Res., P.O. Box 452, 38663. Tel: 601-837-3529.

Rosedale, Bolivar Co., Sacred Heart, Pastoral Ministry Team: Sr. Celia Evers, O.P.; Sr. Catherine Leamy, S.N.J.M.; Rev. Charles Bucciantini.
Res., P.O. Box 307, 38769. Tel: 662-759-6341.

Senatobia, Tate Co., St. Gregory the Great, Rev. Dermot Twomey, S.C.J., Admin.
Church—P.O. Box 129, 707 Strayhorn St., 38668-0129. Tel: 662-562-5318; Fax: 662-562-6649.

Shaw, Bolivar Co., St. Francis of Assisi, Rev. Donald F. Derivaux.
Res., 303 Dean Blvd., P.O. Box 239, 38773. Tel: 662-754-5561; Fax: 662-754-2362.

Shelby, Bolivar Co., St. Mary, Mrs. Bernadette Johnson, Pastoral Min.; Rev. Paul Wangaih.
Res., 700 Second St., P.O. Box 208, 38774-0208. Tel: 662-398-7964.
Station—Shelby, Parchman State Penitentiary, Tel: 662-745-6611.

Southhaven, DeSoto Co., Christ the King, Revs. Patrick J. Lloyd, S.C.J.; Francis J. Burshnick, S.C.J.; Deacon Lawrence M. Campbell.
Office: 1090 Stateline Rd., W. Southhaven, 38671. Tel: 662-342-1073; Fax: 662-342-7733.
School—Sacred Heart Elementary School, 5150 Tchulahoma Rd., Southaven, 38671. Tel: 662-349-0900; Fax: 662-349-0690.

Starkville, Oktibbeha Co., St. Joseph, Rev. Jeffrey Waldrep.
Res., 607 University Dr., 39759. Tel: 662-323-2257; Fax: 662-323-2258.
Mission—Macon, Corpus Christi.
Chaplaincy—Mississippi State University.

Tupelo, Lee Co., St. James, Rev. Henry Shelton.
Res., 820 Lakeshire Dr., P.O. Box 734, 38802-0734. Tel: 662-842-4881; Fax: 662-844-0327.
Mission—Saltillo, St. Thomas Aquinas.

Vicksburg, Warren Co., St. Paul, Rev. Thomas McGing.
Res., 713 Crawford St., P.O. Box 646, 39180-0646. Tel: 601-636-0140; Fax: 601-638-5021.
High School—Vicksburg Catholic School, (Grades PreK-12). See High Schools, Inter-Parochial under Institutions Located in the Diocese. Tel: 601-636-2256; Fax: 601-631-0430.

St. Mary, Rev. Charles Boykins, S.V.D.
Res., 1512 Main St., 39183. Tel: 601-636-0115; Fax: 601-661-0677.

St. Michael, Rev. James O'Riordan.
Res., 100 St. Michael Pl., 39180. Tel: 601-636-3445; Fax: 601-636-3534.

Walls, DeSoto Co., Sacred Heart, Revs. Dermot J. Twomey, S.C.J., Admin. Pro Tem; Francis J. Burshnick, S.C.J.
Res., 6473 Hwy. 161 N., P.O. Box 60, 38680-0060. Tel: 662-781-0450; Fax: 662-781-7766.
School—Moved to Southhaven, DeSoto Co.
Convent—P.O. Box 237, 38680. Tel: 662-781-9233. School Sisters of St. Francis
Mission—Tunica, Tunica Co., St. Anthony of Padua, P.O. Box 2026, Tunica, 38676. Tel: 662-363-0140; Fax: 662-363-3596.

West Point, Clay Co., Immaculate Conception, Rev. John Vollor.
Res., 617 E. Main, 39773-3007. Tel: 662-494-3486.
Mission—Europa, Webster Co., St. John, 201 W. Roane St., Europa, 39744. Tel: 662-258-7539. Pastoral Coordinators: Gene Grabbe; Mary Helen Grabbe.

Woodville, Wilkinson Co., St. Joseph, Rev. Walter W. Brown, Admin.
Res., 338 Church St., P.O. Box 668, 39669. Tel: 601-888-3261.
Missions—Fort Adams, St. Patrick; Gloster, Amite Co., Holy Family, P.O. Box 548, Gloster, 39638. Tel: 601-225-4171.

Yazoo City, Yazoo Co., St. Mary, Rev. Patrick J. Curley.
Res., 129 N. Washington St., P.O. Box 27, 39194-0027. Tel: 662-746-1680; Fax: 662-746-8407.

St. Francis, Rev. Patrick J. Curley.
Res., 735 E. Powell St., 39194-4398. Tel: 662-746-1680.

Chaplains of Public Institutions

JACKSON. *Institute for the Blind, Institute for the Deaf and Speech Impaired*. Rev. Msgr. Noel Foley.
University of Mississippi Medical Center. Rev. Daniel Gallagher; Sr. Sharon Glumb, S.L.W., Campus Min.
Veterans Administration Hospital. Rev. Daniel Gallagher.

MERIDIAN. *East Mississippi State Hospital*. Rev. Elvin Sunds.

PARCHMAN. *Mississippi State Penitentiary*. Rev. Paul Wangaih.

PEARL. *Rankin County Prison*. Rev. Martin Ruane.

SANATORIUM. *Boswell Retardation Center*. Rev. Robert Goodyear, S.T.

WHITFIELD. *Mississippi State Hospital*. Rev. Martin Ruane.

On Duty Outside the Diocese:
Reverend Fathers—
Johnson, Howard
Lopez, Jose
Madden, Paul
Niemira, Thomas
Quinn, Peter
Rietti, John
Schmit, Meyrl
Spadini, Marian

Retired:
Reverend Monsignors—
Canonici, Paul, P.O. Box 2207, Madison, MS 39130-2207
Glynn, Michael, St. Richard Church, P.O. Box 16547, Jackson, MS 39236-6547
Koury, Joseph A., 105 Abby Oak Dr., Clinton, MS 39056
Reverend Fathers—
Brett, James G., King's Daughters & Sons Rest Home, 6615 Poplar Spring Dr., Apt. #8, Meridian, MS 39305
Carroll, James, Parkview, Oldcastle, Co. Meath, Ireland
Corcoran, Frank
Engelhart, William, 515 Laurel St., McComb, MS 39648
Leonard, John, Vicksburg Apartments, 801 Clay St., Apt. #10-A, Vicksburg, MS 39180
Loyacono, Charles, Williamsburg Retirement Community, Baton Rouge, LA
Maloney, Walter, 200 Dominican Dr. #5108, Madison, MS 39110-8612
Pentony, Liam

Permanent Deacons:
Agosta, Frank, St. Paul, Brandon
Babin, Henry, Queen of Peace, Olive Branch
Baker, Sam, Holy Ghost, Jackson
Campbell, Lawrence M., Christ the King, Southhaven
Klingen, Dr. Theodore, St. John, Oxford
McCarthy, Kevin J., St. Joseph Mission, Gluckstadt
Van Tassel, Everell, Holy Spirit, Hernando

INSTITUTIONS LOCATED IN THE DIOCESE

[A] HIGH SCHOOLS, INTER-PAROCHIAL

GREENVILLE. *St. Joseph Junior-Senior High School*. (Grades 7-12). (Coed), 700 Golf St., 38701. Tel: 601-378-9711; Fax: 601-378-3496.
E-mail: jaxsjg@impresso.com
Mr. Anthony Durso, Prin. Lay Teachers 25; Students 286.

MADISON. *St. Joseph Catholic School*. (Grades 7-12). (Coed), 308 New Mannsdale Rd., P.O. Box 2027, 39130-2027. Tel: 601-898-4800; Fax: 601-898-4689.
E-mail: stjoe@netdoor.com
Web site: www.stjoeonline.com
Mr. William M. Heller, Prin.; Rev. David O'Connor, Dir. Devel. & Business Mgr. Priests 1; Brothers 1; Sisters 1; Lay Teachers 29; Students 353.

NATCHEZ. *Cathedral School*. (Grades PreK-12). (Coed), 701 Martin Luther King, Jr. St., 39120. Tel: 601-442-2531; Fax: 601-442-0960.
E-mail: sfleming@bkbank.com
Dr. Scott Fleming, Prin. Sisters 2; Lay Teachers 60; Students 668.

VICKSBURG. *Vicksburg Catholic School.* (Grades PreK-12). (Coed), 1900 Grove St., 39180. Tel: 601-636-2256; Fax: 601-631-0430.
E-mail: jaxvcs@impresso.com
Mr. Alan Powers, Prin. Sisters 1; Lay Teachers 50; Students 717.

[B] ELEMENTARY SCHOOLS INTER-PAROCHIAL

SOUTHHAVEN. *Southhaven Catholic School.* (Grades PreK-8), 5150 Tchulahoma Rd., 38671. Tel: 662-349-0900; Fax: 662-349-0690.
E-mail: jaxshw@impresso.com
Ms. Kathleen Fuccaro, Prin.

[C] SPECIAL SCHOOLS

JACKSON. *St. Richard's Special Kids Program,* P.O. Box 16172, 39236. Tel: 601-981-4869. John Tracy, Co-ord. Lay Teachers 2; Aides 2; Students 18.

[D] GENERAL HOSPITALS

JACKSON. *St. Dominic-Jackson Memorial Hospital,* 969 Lakeland Dr., 39216. Tel: 601-982-0121; Fax: 601-364-6800.
E-mail: charbarger@stdom.com
Web site: www.stdom.com
For a complete listing, refer to the Hospitals section.

GLENDORA. *Glendora Clinic (Satellite of Tutwiler Clinic),* Gipson & Westbrook Sts., 38928. Tel: 662-375-8878
For a complete listing, refer to the Hospitals section.

TUTWILER. *Tutwiler Clinic, Inc.,* 205 Alma St., P.O. Box 462, 38963-0462. Tel: 662-345-8334; Fax: 662-345-8336
For a complete listing, refer to the Hospitals section.

[E] ORPHANAGES AND INFANT HOMES

JACKSON. *D'Evereaux Hall Home, Inc.,* P.O. Box 2248, 39225. Tel: 601-355-8634
For a complete listing, refer to the Special Care Facilities section.

St. Mary Orphan Home, Inc., P.O. Box 2248, 39225. Tel: 601-355-8634
For a complete listing, refer to the Special Care Facilities section.

[F] MONASTERIES AND RESIDENCES OF PRIESTS AND BROTHERS

JACKSON. *Christian Brothers Residence,* 820 Forest Ave., 39206-3299. Tel: 601-362-3861; Fax: 601-362-1382. Bros. John Brennan, C.F.C.; Theodore Dausch, C.F.C.; Daniel Lauber, C.F.C.; Robert McGovern, C.F.C.
Congregation of Christian Brothers. Tel: 914-636-6194; Fax: 914-636-0021.

Priory of St. Moses the Black, 653 Claiborne Ave., 39209. Tel: 601-354-3287. Canons Regular of Premontre (The Premonstratensian Fathers). Revs. Richard P. Chiles, O.Praem., Prior; Xavier G. Colavechio, O.Praem.; Norbert N'Zilamba, O.Praem.; Jeremy Tobin, O.Praem.; Joseph Tonos; Bros. Chris Akpa; James Herring; Chibuzor Igboanusi; Ugo Nwabueze. Priests 5; Brothers 4.

NESBIT. *St. Michael Community House,* 1360 Nesbit Rd., P.O. Box 38, 38651. Tel: 662-429-8424; Fax: 662-429-8369.
E-mail: jcunniffe@shsm.org
Revs. Francis J. Burshnick, S.C.J.; James A. Cunniffe, S.C.J., Coord.; Thomas Lind, S.C.J.; Patrick J. Lloyd, S.C.J.; Lawrence Rucker, S.C.J.; Kenneth Stoll, S.C.J.; Dermot J. Twomey, S.C.J.; Charles Yost, S.C.J.

[G] CONVENTS AND RESIDENCES FOR SISTERS

JACKSON. *Our Lady of Mount Carmel and Little Flower Monastery,* 2155 Terry Rd., 39204. Tel: 601-373-1460; Fax: 601-372-1369.
E-mail: jm2155jt@aol.com
Sr. Dona Marie Degnan, O.C.D., Prioress. Discalced Carmelites. Nuns with Solemn Vows 4.

BROOKSVILLE. *The Dwelling Place,* 2824 Dwelling Place Rd., 39739-9537. Tel: 662-738-5348; Fax: 662-738-5345.
E-mail: dwellpl@crawdat.com
Web site: dwellingplace.com
Clare Van Lent, Dir.

CHATAWA. *St. Mary of the Pines,* 3129 Old Hwy. 51 S., P.O. Box 38, 39632. Tel: 601-783-3494; Fax: 601-783-3984.
E-mail: smpines@telapex.com
Sr. Suzanne Pescay, S.S.N.D., Admin. Home for the Retired Sisters of the Dallas Province of the School Sisters of Notre Dame. Retreat Center for Lay and Religious Groups. Sisters in Residence 62.

PHILADELPHIA. *Holy Rosary Convent,* P.O. Box 496, 39350. Tel: 601-656-2949.

VICKSBURG. *Sisters of Mercy,* 1625 East Ave., 39180. Tel: 601-638-8636; Fax: 601-638-8636.
E-mail: srfatima@hotmail.com
Sisters of Mercy 2.

[H] NEWMAN CENTERS

JACKSON. *Belhaven College Newman Center,* P.O. Box 57, 39205-0057. Tel: 601-974-1239; Fax: 601-974-1229.
E-mail: glumbs@millsaps.edu
Rev. Patrick Farrell; Sr. Sharon Glumb, S.L.W.

Jackson State University Newman Center, 2303 Lynch St., 32909. Rev. Richard P. Chiles, O.Praem.

Millsaps College Newman Center, P.O. Box 57, 39205-0057. Tel: 601-974-1239; Fax: 601-974-1229.
E-mail: glumbs@millsaps.edu
Rev. Patrick Farrell; Sr. Sharon Glumb, S.L.W.

Tougaloo College Newman Center, Holy Ghost Church, 1151 Cloister St., 39202. Tel: 601-353-1339. Rev. Ryszard Kalinowski, S.V.D.

University of Mississippi Medical Center - Newman Center, P.O. Box 57, 39205-0057. Tel: 601-974-1239; Fax: 601-974-1229.
E-mail: glumbs@millsaps.edu
Rev. Patrick Farrell; Sr. Sharon Glumb, S.L.W.

BOONEVILLE. *Northeast Mississippi Community College Catholic Student Center,* St. Francis of Assisi, P.O. Box 654, 38829. Tel: 662-728-7509; Fax: 662-728-7509. Sr. Dorothy Pashuta, C.S.J.

BROOKHAVEN. *Lincoln Junior College Newman Center,* P.O. Box 196, 39602. Tel: 601-833-1799. Rev. Patrick Noonan.

CLEVELAND. *Delta State University Newman Center,* Our Lady of Victories, 215 Bishop Rd., P.O. Box 1450, 38732-1450. Tel: 662-846-6273. Rev. Charles Bucciantini.

CLINTON. *Mississippi College Newman Center,* Holy Savior Church, P.O. Box 85, 39060. Tel: 601-924-6344. Rev. Noel Prendergast.

COLUMBUS. *Mississippi University for Women Student Center,* Annunciation Church, 808 College St., 39701. Tel: 662-328-2927; Fax: 662-329-8270. Rev. Gerard Hurley.

FOREST. *East Central Community College Newman Center,* St. Michael's Church, P.O. Box 388, 39074. Tel: 601-469-1916; Fax: 601-469-1916.
E-mail: res@localink4.com
Rev. Richard Smith.

GOODMAN. *Holmes Community College Newman Center.* St. Thomas, 200 Boulevard St., Lexington, 39095. Tel: 662-453-0623; Fax: 662-453-9060. Rev. Hilary Brzezinski, O.F.M.

HOLLY SPRINGS. *Rust College Newman Center,* St. Joseph's, P.O. Box 430, 38635. Tel: 662-252-3138. Rev. Ron Trojcak, Chap.

OXFORD. *University of Mississippi Newman Center,* St. John Church, 403 University Ave., 38655. Tel: 662-915-3169; Fax: 662-234-6079.
E-mail: stjohns@watervalley.net
Rev. Joseph Dyer; Deacon Dr. Theodore Klingen.

RAYMOND. *Hinds Community College Catholic Student Organization,* Denise Scifres, P.O. Box 11269 - Hinds Community College, 39154. Tel: 601-857-3302; Fax: 601-857-3406.
E-mail: dlscifres@hinds.cc.ms.us

SENATOBIA. *Northwest Mississippi Community College Newman Center,* St. Gregory Church, P.O. Box 129, 38668-0129. Tel: 662-562-5318. Rev. Dermot Twomey, S.C.J.

STARKVILLE. *Mississippi State University Catholic Student Association,* St. Joseph Church, 607 University Dr., 39759. Tel: 662-323-2257; Fax: 662-323-2258.
E-mail: falavelle@hotmail.com
Web site: www.msstate.edu/org/csa
Rev. Jeffrey Waldrep; Fran Lavelle, Campus Min.

[I] MISCELLANEOUS

JACKSON. *Jackson Diocese Educational Services, Inc.,* P.O. Box 2248, 39225-2248. Tel: 601-969-1880; Fax: 601-960-8469.
E-mail: williamcullen@jacksondiocese.org
Rev. William Cullen, Dir. & Contact Person.

Parroquia De San Miguel Del Arcangel, P.O. Box 2248, 39225-2248. Rev. Msgr. Michael Thornton. Saltillo Mission Sponsored by Dioceses of Jackson and Biloxi. Suc. "A" Apdo. 52, Saltillo, Coahuilla, Mexico, C.P. 25000.

Pax Christi Franciscans, LaVerna House, 2108 Alta Woods Blvd., 39204. Tel: 601-373-4463. Genevieve Feyen, Pres.; Rhoda Kalscheur, House Dir. A Private Association of the Christian faithful, living a consecrated life, engaged in social and educational works. Consecrated Members 7.

ABERDEEN. *Catholic Committee of the South, Inc.,* St. Francis of Assisi, Box 134, 39730. Tel: 662-369-2897; Fax: 662-369-2897.
E-mail: stfa@juno.com
Sr. Mary Priniski, O.P., Coord.

CANTON. *Notre Dame Education Center, Inc.* Mailing Address: P.O. Box 505, 39046. 153 E. Center St., 39046. Tel: 601-859-6826; Fax: 601-859-6898. Res., 519 E. Peace St., 39046. Tel: 601-859-7654.

GREENWOOD. *Pax Christi Franciscans,* St. Francis Information Center, 709 Ave. I, 38930. Tel: 662-453-1465. Genevieve Feyen, Pres.; Bessie Willburn, Center Dir. A Private Association of the Christian faithful, living a consecrated life, engaged in social and educational works. Consecrated Members 8.

MARKS. *DePorres Delta Ministries, Inc.,* 217 Locust St., P.O. Box 207, 38646. Tel: 662-326-2323. George Scheiderman, Exec. Dir.

DePorres Health Center, 411 Poplar St., P.O. Box 376, 38646. Tel: 662-326-9232. Sr. Andrea Balconis, O.P., M.D., Medical Dir.

MOUND BAYOU. *St. Gabriel Center,* P.O. Box 0824, 38762-0824. Tel: 662-741-3255; Fax: 662-741-3494.
E-mail: btom@saintgabriel.org
Bro. Thomas Geraghty, F.S.C., Dir.; Sr. Cyrena Harkins, R.S.M., Coord.
Outreach Program of the Sisters of Mercy Health System (Mercycare) and Educational Services, Inc. Tel: 601-969-2742; Fax: 601-960-8469.

ROSEDALE. *Delta Catholic Ministries,* 113 Railroad St., P.O. Box 307, 38769-0307. Tel: 662-756-6341.
E-mail: dcmsh@juno.com
Directors: Sr. Catherine Leamy, S.N.J.M., Pres.; Sr. Kay Burton, S.N.J.M., Vice Pres.; Sr. Celia Evers, O.P., Sec. & Treas.

WALLS. *Sacred Heart League,* 6050 Hwy. 161 N., P.O. Box 300, 38680-0300. Tel: 662-781-1360; Fax: 662-781-3340.
Web site: www.sacredheartleague.org
Rev. Charles Yost, S.C.J., Spiritual Dir.; Mr. Roger Courts, Dir. & CEO.

Sacred Heart Southern Missions Housing Corporation, P.O. Box 365, 38680-0365. Tel: 662-781-3298; Fax: 662-781-3534.
E-mail: badams@shsm.org
Sr. Elizabeth A. Adams, C.S.J., Dir. of Housing; Mr. Bob Barber, Vice Pres. & Treas.; Mr. Morgan Billingsley, Pres.; Mr. J. Martin Regan, Jr., Sec.

Sacred Heart Southern Missions, Inc., 6473 Hwy. 161 N., P.O. Box 190, 38680-0190. Tel: 662-781-1472; Fax: 662-781-0842.
E-mail: cyost@shl.org

RELIGIOUS INSTITUTES OF MEN REPRESENTED IN THE DIOCESE

For further details refer to the corresponding bracketed number in the Religious Institutes of Men or Women section.

[1350]—*Brothers of St. Francis Xavier.*—C.F.X.
[0330]—*Brothers of the Christian Schools.* (Prov. of St. Louis, MO).—F.S.C.
[0900]—*Canons Regular of Premontre.*—O.Praem.
[0310]—*Congregation of Christian Brothers.*—C.F.C.
[1130]—*Congregation of the Priests of the Sacred Heart.*—S.C.J.
[0520]—*Franciscan Friars.* (Pulaski, WI).—O.F.M.
[0570]—*Glenmary Home Missioners.*—Glmy.
[0840]—*Missionary Servants of the Most Holy Trinity.*—S.T.
[0700]—*St. Joseph's Society of the Sacred Heart.*—S.S.J.
[0420]—*Society of the Divine Word.*—S.V.D.

RELIGIOUS INSTITUTES OF WOMEN REPRESENTED IN THE DIOCESE

[]—*Congregation of Sisters of Charity of St. Charles Borromeo.*—C.B.
[2410]—*Congregation of the Marianites of the Holy Cross.*—M.S.C.
[3710]—*Congregation of the Sisters of Saint Agnes.*—C.S.A.
[1780]—*Congregation of the Sisters of the Third Order of St. Francis of Perpetual Adoration.*—F.S.P.A.
[0760]—*Daughters of Charity of St. Vincent de Paul.*—D.C.
[0420]—*Discalced Carmelite Nuns.*—O.C.D.
[1070-03]—*Dominican Sisters.* (Sinsinawa, WI).—O.P.
[1070-06]—*Dominican Sisters.* (Newburgh, NY).—O.P.
[1070-09]—*Dominican Sisters.* (Racine, WI).—O.P.
[1070-10]—*Dominican Sisters.* (Springfield, IL).—O.P.
[1070-13]—*Dominican Sisters.* (Adrian, MI).—O.P.
[1310]—*Franciscan Sisters of Little Falls, Minnesota.*—O.S.F.
[2575]—*Institute of the Sisters of Mercy of the Americas.* (Rochester, NY; St. Louis, MO).—R.S.M.
[]—*Literary Society of St. Catherine of Sienna Kentucky Dominican.*—O.P.
[2800]—*Missionary Sisters of the Most Sacred Heart of Jesus.*—M.S.C.
[2970]—*School Sisters of Notre Dame.* (Baltimore & Dallas Provs., Mankato).—S.S.N.D.
[1680]—*School Sisters of St. Francis.*—O.S.F.
[0500]—*Sisters of Charity of Nazareth.* (Kentucky).—S.C.N.
[0590]—*Sisters of Charity of Saint Elizabeth, Convent Station.*—S.C.

[0430]—*Sisters of Charity of the Blessed Virgin Mary.* (Dubuque, IA).—B.V.M.

[]—*Sisters of Christian Community.*—S.F.C.C.

[]—*Sisters of Humility of Mary.*—C.H.M.

[]—*Sisters of Mercy of Mississippi, Inc.*—R.S.M.

[3360]—*Sisters of Providence of Saint Mary-of-the-Woods, Indiana.*—S.P.

[1540]—*Sisters of Saint Francis, Clinton, Iowa.*—O.S.F.

[3893]—*Sisters of Saint Joseph of Chestnut Hill, Philadelphia.*—S.S.J.

[]—*Sisters of St. Francis of Sylvania, Ohio.*—O.S.F.

[1550]—*Sisters of St. Francis of the Holy Cross.* (Green Bay).—O.S.F.

[1570]—*Sisters of St. Francis of the Holy Family.* (Dubuque).—O.S.F.

[3830-02]—*Sisters of St. Joseph.* (La Grange Park, IL).—C.S.J.

[3830-15]—*Sisters of St. Joseph.* (Concordia, KS).—C.S.J.

[3840]—*Sisters of St. Joseph of Carondelet.* (St. Louis & St. Paul Provs.).—C.S.J.

[3930]—*Sisters of St. Joseph of the Third Order of St. Francis.* (Marymount Prov.).—S.S.J.-T.O.S.F.

[3950]—*Sisters of St. Mary of Namur.* (Belgium).—S.S.M.N.

[2980]—*Sisters of the Congregation de Notre Dame.* (Ridgefield, CT).—C.N.D.

[1030]—*Sisters of the Divine Savior.*—S.D.S.

[1990]—*Sisters of the Holy Names of Jesus and Mary.* (Albany, NY; Spokane, WA; Los Gatos, CA; Marylhurst, OR; Winnipeg, Canada).—S.N.J.M.

[2050]—*Sisters of the Holy Spirit and Mary Immaculate.*—S.H.Sp.

[2350]—*Sisters of the Living Word.*—S.L.W.

[1760]—*Sisters of the Third Order of St. Francis of Penance and Charity.*—O.S.F.

[2160]—*Sisters, Servants of the Immaculate Heart of Mary.*—I.H.M.

[4120-03]—*Ursuline Nuns, of the Congregation of Paris.*—O.S.U.

NECROLOGY

† Curley, Patrick J., (Retired). —Died May 15, 2000.

Diocese of Jefferson City

(Dioecesis Civitatis Jeffersoniensis)

Most Reverend

JOHN RAYMOND GAYDOS, D.D.

Bishop of Jefferson City; ordained December 20, 1968; appointed June 25, 1997; consecrated August 27, 1997. *Res., Bishop's House, P.O. Box 417, Jefferson City, MO, 65102.*

Chancery: 605 Clark Ave., P.O. Box 417, Jefferson City, MO, 65102. Tel.: 573-635-9127; Fax: 573-635-0386.

Web site address: www.diojeffcity.org

E-mail address: diojeffcity@primelink.com

ESTABLISHED JULY 2, 1956.

Square Miles 22,127.

Comprises the Counties of Adair, Audrain, Benton, Boone, Callaway, Camden, Chariton, Clark, Cole, Cooper, Crawford, Gasconade, Hickory, Howard, Knox, Lewis, Linn, Macon, Maries, Marion, Miller, Moniteau, Monroe, Montgomery, Morgan, Osage, Pettis, Phelps, Pike, Pulaski, Putnam, Ralls, Randolph, Saline, Schuyler, Scotland, Shelby and Sullivan in the State of Missouri.

For legal titles of parishes and diocesan institutions, consult the Chancery Office.

STATISTICAL OVERVIEW

Personnel	
Bishop	1
Retired Bishops	1
Priests: Diocesan Active in Diocese	79
Priests: Active Outside Diocese	3
Priests: Diocesan in Foreign Missions	4
Priests: Retired, Sick or Absent	24
Number of Diocesan Priests	110
Religious Priests in Diocese	9
Extern Priests in Diocese	14
Ordinations:	
Diocesan Priests	1
Permanent Deacons	7
Permanent Deacons in Diocese	63
Total Brothers	5
Total Sisters	89
Parishes	
Parishes	95
With Resident Pastor:	
Resident Diocesan Priests	61
Resident Religious Priests	6
Without Resident Pastor:	
Administered by Priests	21
Administered by Deacons	3
Administered by Women Religious	1
Administered by Lay People	3
Missions	15
Professional Ministry Personnel:	
Sisters	24
Lay Ministers	21
Welfare	
Catholic Hospitals	1
Total Assisted	281,999
Health Care Centers	14
Total Assisted	149,012
Homes for the Aged	2
Total Assisted	210
Special Centers for Social Services	1
Total Assisted	15,573
Educational	
Seminaries, Diocesan	1
Students from This Diocese	19
Students from Other Diocese	7
Diocesan Students in Other Seminaries	13
Total Seminarians	32
High Schools, Diocesan and Parish	2
Total Students	976
Elementary Schools, Diocesan and Parish	37
Total Students	6,536
Non-residential Schools for the Disabled	1
Total Students	37
Catechesis/Religious Education:	
High School Students	2,607
Elementary Students	4,993
Total Students Under Catholic Instruction	15,181
Teachers in the Diocese:	
Priests	5
Brothers	5
Sisters	20
Lay Teachers	454
Vital Statistics	
Receptions into the Church:	
Infant Baptism Totals	1,415
Adult Baptism Totals	245
Received into Full Communion	355
First Communions	1,586
Confirmations	1,603
Marriages:	
Catholic	338
Interfaith	281
Total Marriages	619
Deaths	895
Total Catholic Population	86,826
Total Population	807,921

Former Bishops—Most Rev. JOSEPH M. MARLING, C.PP.S., D.D., ord. Feb. 21, 1929; appt. Auxiliary of Kansas City, June 9, 1947; cons. Aug. 6, 1947; appt. Bishop of Jefferson City, Aug. 24, 1956; retired July 2, 1969; died Oct. 2, 1979.—Most Rev. MICHAEL F. MCAULIFFE, S.T.D., ord. May 31, 1945; appt. July 2, 1969; cons. Aug. 18, 1969; retired August 27, 1997.

Vicar General—Rev. Msgr. MICHAEL J. WILBERS, *P.O. Box 417, Jefferson City, 65102-0417.*

Chancery Office—605 Clark Ave., P.O. Box 417, Jefferson City, 65102-0417. Tel: 573-635-9127; Fax: 573-635-0386. All offices are at this address unless noted otherwise.

Chancellor—Sr. ETHEL-MARIE BIRI, S.S.N.D., M.R.Ed., M.A.

Secretary to the Bishop—Rev. ROBERT A. KURWICKI.

Vice-Chancellors—Revs. BRENDAN DOYLE; GREGORY L. HIGLEY; ROBERT A. KURWICKI.

Moderator of the Curia—Rev. Msgr. MICHAEL J. WILBERS, V.G.

Diocesan Tribunal—

Judicial Vicar—Rev. BRENDAN DOYLE.

Adjutant Judicial Vicar—Rev. GREGORY L. HIGLEY.

Defenders of the Bond—Rev. ROBERT W. DUESDIEKER; Deacon JAMES R. BUTLER; Mrs. CONSTANCE SCHEPERS.

Promoter of Justice—Vacant.

Judges—Rev. Msgr. FRANCIS G. GILLGANNON; Revs. J. JAMES OFFUTT; MARK A. PORTERFIELD, J.C.L.; MICHAEL F. QUINN.

Notaries—Mrs. JULIE LAUNE; Miss LORETTA NEUNER.

Diocesan Consultors—Rev. Msgr. MICHAEL T. FLANAGAN; Revs. PHILIP M. KANE; DANIEL I.J. LUECKENOTTE; THOMAS E. MCGRATH; GREGORY C. MEYSTRIK; Rev. Msgr. MICHAEL J. WILBERS, V.G.

Deans—I. Brookfield: Rev. LEONARD S. MISEY, Dean: Brookfield, Brunswick, Clarence, Indian Grove, Macon (Bevier), Marceline (Hurricane Branch/ Mendon), Salisbury, Shelbina, Wien; II. Columbia: Rev. PATRICK DOLAN, Dean: Boonville, Columbia, Fayette, Moberly, Pilot Grove; III. Hannibal: Rev. WILLIAM F. FLANAGAN, Dean: Canton (La Grange), Ewing, Hannibal, Indian Creek, Kahoka (Wayland), Louisiana (Clarksville), Monroe City, Palmyra, Perry (Paris), St. Clement, St. Patrick; IV. Jefferson City: Rev. DONALD J. ANTWEILER, Dean: California, Holts Summit, Jefferson City, Osage Bend, Russelville, St. Martins, St. Thomas, Taos, Wardsville; V. Kirksville: Rev. JOSEPH HOI, Dean: Baring, Edina, Kirksville (Novinger), Memphis, Milan (Unionville); VI. Lake Ozark: Rev. CLARENCE E. WIEDERHOLT, Dean: Camdenton, Eldon, Laurie (Versailles), Hermitage (Climax Springs), Lake Ozark, Mary's Home, St. Anthony, St. Elizabeth; VII. Marshall: Rev. HENRY J. REICHERT, Dean: Glasgow, Marshall (Sweet Springs), Sedalia, Slater, Tipton, Warsaw (Cole Camp); VIII. Mexico: Rev. THOMAS J. SEIFNER, Dean: Centralia, Fulton, Hermann, Jonesburg, Martinsburg, Mexico, Mokane, Montgomery City, Morrison, Rhineland, Vandalia (Laddonia), Wellsville; IX. Osage: Rev. MICHAEL P. MURPHY, Dean: Argyle (Koeltztown), Bonnots Mill, Chamois, Folk, Frankenstein, Freeburg, Linn, Loose Creek, Meta, Rich Fountain, Westphalia; X. Rolla: Rev. IGNAZIO C. MEDINA, Dean: Belle, Bourbon, Brinktown, Crocker, Cuba, Dixon, Owensville, Richland, Rolla, Rosati, St. James, Steelville, Vienna, Waynesville.

Masters of Ceremonies—

To The Bishop—Revs. ROBERT A. KURWICKI; DAVID J. VEIT.

To The Cathedral—Rev. DANIEL J. MERZ.

Assistant—Rev. JOSEPH HOI.

Personnel Board—Most Rev. JOHN RAYMOND GAYDOS; Revs. FRED J. ELSKAMP; L. JAMES FINDER; Rev. Msgr. MICHAEL T. FLANAGAN; Revs. ROBERT A. KURWICKI; DONALD W. LAMMERS; Rev. Msgr. MICHAEL J. WILBERS, V.G.

Presbyteral Council—Most Rev. JOHN RAYMOND GAYDOS, Pres. Senators: Revs. PHILIP M. MORIARTY; MARK S. SMITH, Sec. DANIEL I.J. LUECKENOTTE, Treas. J. DAVID MAHER; PATRICK J. SHORTT; JAMES R. FUEMMELER; PHILLIP M. KANE; THOMAS J. SEIFNER, V.F.; PAUL M. HARTLEY; JOHN W. GRONER; Revs. THOMAS L. ALBERS, C.PP.S., Rel. Representative; WILLIAM L. FORST, Retired Representative. Appointed Members: Revs. EDWIN J. COLE; MANUS P. DALY; CHRISTOPHER L. CORDES, Vice Chm. JOHN F. DEGNAN; Rev. Msgr. FRANCIS G. GILLGANNON; Rev. MARION J. MAKAREWICZ, Chm. Ex Officio Members: Rev. Msgr. MICHAEL J. WILBERS, V.G.; Rev.

Msgr. MICHAEL T. FLANAGAN, Episcopal Vicar.

Diocesan Offices and Directors

Buildings and Properties—Mr. BARRY VOLLMER.

Campus Ministry—Rev. CHARLES D. PARDEE.

Catholic Relief Overseas Fund—Mrs. ALICE J. WOLTERS, Dir.

Cemeteries—Rev. ROBERT A. KURWICKI, Dir.

Charismatic Renewal Program—Deacon KENNETH BERRY, Diocesan Representative, *201 N. Cottey, Edina, 63537.* Tel: 660-397-2636.

Communication—Mr. MARK D. SAUCIER, Dir.

Cursillo Movement—Mr. JIM SOWASH, Lay Dir.; Rev. PATRICK J. SHORTT, Spiritual Dir., *1211 Torrey Pines, Columbia, 65203.* Tel: 573-442-9084.

Diocesan Excellence in Education Fund, Inc.—Most Rev. JOHN RAYMOND GAYDOS, Chm.; Most Rev. MICHAEL F. MCAULIFFE, S.T.D.; Mr. LOUIS J. LEONATTI, Pres.; Sr. ETHEL-MARIE BIRI, S.S.N.D.; Sr. CORNELIA M. KNEZEK, S.S.C.J.; Mr. JOHN KOLB; Mrs. MILLIE SCHELL; Deacon DONALD W. ORSCHELN, Vice Pres.; Mr. GARY SCHELL; Mr. NORMAN P. STUCKENSCHNEIDER; Rev. Msgr. MICHAEL J. WILBERS, V.G.

Diaconate Office—Rev. FRED J. ELSKAMP, Vicar; Deacon ROBERT RACKERS.

Ecumenical Commission—Rev. Msgr. FRANCIS G. GILLGANNON, Dir.

Engaged Encounter—Coords.: RICHARD SPORLEDER; BERNICE SPORLEDER, *Rte. 3, Box 22, Marshall, 65340.* Rev. MICHAEL F. QUINN, Spiritual Dir.

Evangelization Office—Vacant.

Family Life—Mr. MICHAEL A. VAN GUNDY; Dr. STEPHANA LANDWHER, Pro-Life.

Finance—Mr. STEPHEN J. KOMAROMI, Dir.

Finance Committee—Most Rev. JOHN RAYMOND GAYDOS; Most Rev. MICHAEL F. MCAULIFFE, S.T.D.; Sr. ETHEL-MARIE BIRI, S.S.N.D.; Miss OLIVIA BUERSMEYER; Mr. CHARLES CASSMEYER; Rev. Msgr. MICHAEL T. FLANAGAN; Mr. CHRIS HERMANN; RICHARD KAMPETER; Mr. PAUL KANAGO; Deacon DONALD ORSCHELN; Mrs. HELEN VOSSEN; Rev. Msgr. MICHAEL J. WILBERS, V.G.

Hispanic Ministry—Sr. ELLEN ORF, C.PP.S., Coord., *373 W. Jackson, Marshall, 65340.* Tel: 660-886-3112.

Historical Archivist—Rev. ROBERT A. KURWICKI.

Holy Childhood—(See Mission Office).

Human Development Campaign—Ms. BARBARA ROSS.

Leadership Services—Sr. ETHEL-MARIE BIRI, S.S.N.D.

Legion of Mary—Rev. WILLIAM L. KORTE, *700 Hwy. Z, Fulton, 65251.* Tel: 573-642-5562.

Liturgical Commission—Rev. LOUIS E. DORN, Chm., *6410 Rt. W, Jefferson City, 65101.* Tel: 573-636-4925.

Mediation and Arbitration Board—Rev. LOUIS E. DORN, Vicar, *6410 Rt. W, Jefferson City, 65101.* Tel: 573-636-4925.

Marriage Encounter—Chair Couple: BRITT SMITH; CANDY SMITH; Rev. GREGORY C. MEYSTRIK, Spiritual Dir., *215 Boonville Rd., Jefferson City, 65109.* Tel: 573-636-3712.

Ministry Formation—Rev. GEORGE KRAMER, Dir., *P.O. Box 68, Bonnots Mill, 65016.* Tel: 573-897-2061.

Ministry to Priests—Rev. WILLIAM L. KORTE, Dir.; Most Rev. JOHN RAYMOND GAYDOS; Revs. MANUS P. DALY; JOHN F. DEGNAN; JAMES L. FINDER; Rev. Msgr. FRANCIS G. GILLGANNON; Revs. ROBERT A. KURWICKI; IGNAZIO C. MEDINA; HENRY J. REICHERT.

Mission Office (Peru Missions, Propagation of the Faith, Holy Childhood)—Mrs. ALICE J. WOLTERS, Dir.; Mr. MARK D. SAUCIER, *P.O. Box 551, Jefferson City, 65102.*

Newspaper—"Catholic Missourian"—Mr. JAY NIES, Editor, *P.O. Box 1107, Jefferson City, 65102.*

Planning Commission—Sr. ETHEL-MARIE BIRI, S.S.N.D., Chm.

Priestly and Religious Vocations—Rev. BRIAN DRISCOLL, Dir.

Priests' Eucharistic League—Rev. FRED J. ELSKAMP, Dir.

Priests' Mutual Benefit Society—Board of Trustees: Most Rev. JOHN R. GAYDOS; Most Rev. MICHAEL F. MCAULIFFE, S.T.D., Advisor; Revs. WAYNE M. BOYER; EDWIN J. COLE; Rev. Msgr. MICHAEL T. FLANAGAN; Revs. KEVIN GORMLEY; GREGORY L. HIGLEY, Sec. & Treas.; Rev. Msgr. GERARD L. POELKER, Chm.; Rev. Msgr. MICHAEL J. WILBERS, V.G., Ex Officio.

Priests' Purgatorial Society—Vacant.

Propagation of Faith & Holy Childhood—Mrs. ALICE J. WOLTERS, Dir., *P.O. Box 551, Jefferson City, 65102.*

Religious Education Office—Mr. JAMES M. KEMNA, Dir.; Mr. RANDY H. KOLLARS; Mrs. CAROLYN A. SAUCIER; Mr. MICHAEL A. VAN GUNDY.

Refugee and Immigration Services—Mrs. ALICE J. WOLTERS, Dir.

Residents Encounter Christ—Ms. BARBARA ROSS, Diocesan Liaison; Rev. LOUIS E. DORN, Spiritual Dir.

School Office—Sr. CORNELIA M. KNEZEK, S.S.C.J., Supt. BARBARA SWANSON, Assoc. Supt.

Diocesan Schools Technology Foundation—Sr. CORNELIA M. KNEZEK, S.S.C.J., Supt., *605 Clark Ave., P.O. Box 417, Jefferson City, 65102.* Tel: 573-635-9127; Fax: 573-635-0153.

Scouting—Rev. GREGORY C. MEYSTRIK, Chap., *P.O. Box 8, Loose Creek, 65054.* Tel: 573-897-2922.

Diocesan Sisters' Organization—Sr. VIRGINIA GRUMICH, S.S.N.D., *120 Hayden, Hannibal, 63401.* Tel: 573-221-3241.

Social Concerns Office—Ms. BARBARA ROSS, Dir.; Sr. FRAN BUSCHELL, S.S.N.D., Prison Ministry; Sr. FRAN BUSCHELL, S.S.N.D.

Spiritual Renewal for the Laity—Rev. DAVID G. BUESCHER, Dir.

Stewardship—Ms. JANE RUTTER, Dir.

Teens Encounter Christ (TEC)—Ms. LEE MENZ, Lay Dir.; Rev. MICHAEL A. COLEMAN, Spiritual Dir., *3713 Hwy. 19, Owensville, 65066.* Tel: 573-437-2719.

Youth Ministry—Mr. RANDY H. KOLLARS.

CLERGY, PARISHES, MISSIONS AND PAROCHIAL SCHOOLS

JEFFERSON CITY
(Cole County)

1—ST. JOSEPH CATHEDRAL (1959), Revs. Frederick J. Elskamp, Rector; Daniel Merz; Deacons Robert J. Rackers; Joseph Braddock; Dana K. Joyce.
Office: Tel: 573-635-7991; Fax: 573-635-0842. [JC]
School—2305 W. Main St., 65109. Tel: 573-635-5024; Fax: 573-635-5238.
Lay Teachers 25; Students 429.
Catechesis/Religious Programs—Students 81.

2—ST. PETER (1946), Revs. Donald W. Lammers; Joseph S. Corel; Deacons Robert L. Dulle; Thomas M. Whalen. In res., Rev. Robert H. Fields.
Res., 216 Broadway, 65101. Tel: 573-636-8159; Fax: 573-634-6079. [JC]
School—Tel: 573-636-8922; Fax: 573-636-8410.
Sisters 2; School Sisters of Notre Dame 1; Sisters of Charity of the Incarnate Word 1; Lay Teachers 30; Students 530.
Catechesis/Religious Programs—Students 235.

3—IMMACULATE CONCEPTION (1913), Revs. Gregory L. Higley; Timothy M. Tatro. In res., Rev. Brendan Doyle.
Res., 1206 E. McCarty St., 65101. Tel: 573-635-6143; 6144; Fax: 573-635-6036. [JC]
School—Tel: 573-636-7680; Fax: 573-635-6036.
Sisters 1; Lay Teachers 32; Students 549.
Catechesis/Religious Programs—Students 116.

OUTSIDE JEFFERSON CITY

Argyle, Osage Co., St. Aloysius (1910), Rev. Michael P. Murphy.
Mailing Address: P.O. Box 6, 65001. Tel: 573-728-6212. [CEM 2]
Catechesis/Religious Programs—Students 95.
Mission—Koeltztown, St. Boniface, (1866) P.O. Box 53, 65001. Tel: 314-728-6919. Rev. Msgr. Bernard H. Boessen.

Baring, Knox Co., St. Aloysius (1894). Attended by Edina. Rev. R. William Peckman.
Res., 509 N. Main St., Edina, 63537-1239. Tel: 660-397-2183; Fax: 660-397-3680. [CEM]

Belle, Maries Co., St. Alexander (1908). Attended by Sacred Heart, Rich Fountain. Rev. Mark A. Porterfield.
Mailing Address: 400 W. Third St., P.O. Box 606, 65013. Tel: 573-859-6231.
Church—Tel: 573-859-6427; Fax: 573-859-6231. [CEM]
Catechesis/Religious Programs—Students 25.

Bonnots Mill, Osage Co., St. Louis (1905), Rev. George J. Kramer.
Mailing Address: P.O. Box 68, 65016. Tel: 573-897-2061. [CEM]
Res., 65016. Tel: 573-897-2061.
Catechesis/Religious Programs—Students 14.

Boonville, Cooper Co., SS. Peter and Paul (1856), Rev. Patrick G. Dolan; Deacon David Miller.
Res., 322 7th St., 65233. Tel: 660-882-6468; Fax: 660-882-6757. [CEM]
School—Tel: 660-882-2589; Fax: 660-882-3020.
Sisters 1; Lay Teachers 10; Students 200.
Catechesis/Religious Programs—Tel: 660-882-7920.
Students 200.

Bourbon, Crawford Co., St. Francis (1915), Rev. Robert W. Duesdieker; Mr. Bradley J. Harmon, Pastoral Admin.
Res., 1098 Old Hwy. 66 W., Box 419, 65441. Tel: 573-732-4494; Fax: 573-732-4494. [CEM 2]
Catechesis/Religious Programs—Students 20.

Brinktown, Maries Co., Guardian Angels (1891). Attended by Visitation, Vienna. Rev. John J. Schmitz.
Res. & Mailing Address: P.O. Box 226, Vienna, 65582. Tel: 573-422-3950; Fax: 573-422-3950. [CEM]
Church—37515 Hwy., Tel: 573-422-3105.
Catechesis/Religious Programs—Students 17.

Brookfield, Linn Co., Immaculate Conception (1859), Rev. Thomas Duggan.
Res., 313 N. Livingston St., 64628. Tel: 660-258-2507. [CEM]
Catechesis/Religious Programs—Students 98.

Brunswick, Chariton Co., St. Boniface (1860), Rev. Leonard S. Misey.
Res., 203 E. Vine St., P.O. Box 5, 65236. Tel: 660-548-3267. [CEM]
Catechesis/Religious Programs—Students 42.

California, Moniteau Co., Annunciation (1872), Rev. Francis G. Gillgannon.
Res., 414 W. Patrick St., 65018. Tel: 573-796-4872. [CEM]
Catechesis/Religious Programs—Students 175.

Camdenton, Camden Co., St. Anthony (1946), Rev. James R. Fuemmeler; Deacons Martin J. Towey; Richard A. Von Gunten.
Church—Rt. 2, Box 344-E, 65020. Tel: 573-346-2716; Fax: 573-346-0625.
Catechesis/Religious Programs—Tel: 573-317-1835.
Students 210.

Canton, Lewis Co., St. Joseph (1865), Rev. Thomas L. Alber; Deacon Robert DePyper, Pastoral Admin.
Res., 812 Lewis St., 63435. Tel: 573-288-3198; Fax: 573-288-3198.
Catechesis/Religious Programs—Students 82.
Mission—La Grange, Lewis Co., Notre Dame, (1868) Rte. C, La Grange, 63448. Tel: 573-655-4296.

Centralia, Boone Co., Holy Spirit (1897), Rev. J. James Offutt.
Res., 404 S. Rollins St., 65240. Tel: 573-682-2815.
Catechesis/Religious Programs—Students 78.

Chamois, Osage Co., Most Pure Heart of Mary (1865), Rev. Patrick Dowling.
Res., P.O. Box 156, 65024. Tel: 573-763-5345. [CEM 2]
Catechesis/Religious Programs—Students 57.

Clarence, Shelby Co., St. Patrick (1884), Rev. Christopher L. Cordes.
Mailing address and Res.: 307 E. Chestnut, Shelbina, 63468. Tel: 573-588-4458. [CEM]
Church—32 Grand St., 63437.
Catechesis/Religious Programs—Students 13.

Columbia, Boone Co., Our Lady of Lourdes (1958), Revs. Michael T. Flanagan; David John Veit; Deacon Fred Fritsch.
Res., 903 Bernadette Dr., 65203. Tel: 573-445-7915; Fax: 573-446-7402.
School—817 Bernadette Dr., 65203. Tel: 573-445-6516; Fax: 573-446-7402.
Sisters 1; Lay Teachers 30; Students 505.
Catechesis/Religious Programs—Tel: 573-445-9602.
Students 484.

Sacred Heart (1876), Rev. Edwin J. Cole; Deacon Michael Daly.
Res., 1115 Locust St., 65201. Tel: 573-443-3470; Fax: 573-875-3947.
Catechesis/Religious Programs—Students 112.

St. Thomas More Newman Center, University of Missouri (1963), Revs. Charles D. Pardee, Dir.; Mark S. Smith.
Res., 701 Maryland, 65201. Tel: 573-445-8068.
Church—Tel: 573-449-5514; 449-5424; Fax: 573-874-2777.
Catechesis/Religious Programs—Students 380.

Crocker, Pulaski Co., St. Cornelius (1966). Attended by Dixon. Rev. Walter J. Reisinger, C.M.
Res., P.O. Box 310, Dixon, 65459. Tel: 573-759-7521. [CEM]
Catechesis/Religious Programs—Students 15.

Cuba, Crawford Co., Holy Cross (1880), Rev. Robert W. Duesdieker; Deacon Earl Horsefield.
Res., 415 W. School Ave., 65453. Tel: 573-885-3520; 885-3291 (Rectory). [CEM]
School—407 W. School Ave., 65453. Tel: 573-885-4727; Fax: 573-885-3501.
Lay Teachers 7; Students 52.
Catechesis/Religious Programs—Teresa Leicht, D.R.E.
Students 69.

Dixon, Pulaski Co., St. Theresa (1928), Rev. Walter J. Reisinger, C.M.
Res., P.O. Box 310, 65459. Tel: 573-759-7521. [CEM]
Catechesis/Religious Programs—Students 18.

Edina, Knox Co., St. Joseph (1844), Rev. R. William Peckman; Deacon Kenneth Berry.
Res., 509 N. Main St., 63537-1239. Tel: 660-397-2183. [CEM 2]
Catechesis/Religious Programs—Tel: 660-397-3128; Fax: 660-397-3680.
Students 94.

Eldon, Miller Co., Sacred Heart (1910), Rev. James J. O'Sullivan.
Res., 540 N. Mill St., 65026. Tel: 573-392-5334; Fax: 573-392-3493.
Catechesis/Religious Programs—Students 110.

Ewing, Lewis Co., Queen of Peace (1887), Rev. David D. Cox.
Res., 307 N. Main, P.O. Box 347, 63440. Tel: 573-209-3343. [CEM 2]
Catechesis/Religious Programs—Students 53.

Fayette, Howard Co., St. Joseph (1956), Rev. Donald L. Wallace.
Res., 300 S. Cleveland, 65248. Tel: 660-248-2439; Fax: 660-248-2439.
Catechesis/Religious Programs—Students 40.

Folk, Osage Co., St. Anthony of Padua (1905), Rev. John H. Henderson.
Mailing Address: HCR 65, Box 91, Westphalia, 65085. Tel: 573-455-2888. [CEM]
Catechesis/Religious Programs—Tel: 573-455-2482.
Students 54.

Frankenstein, Osage Co., Our Lady of Help (1863), Rev. George J. Kramer.
Res., P.O. Box 68, Bonnots Mill, 65016. Tel: 573-897-2061. [CEM 2]
School—Tel: 573-897-2567.
Lay Teachers 4; Students 48.
Catechesis/Religious Programs—Students 29.

Freeburg, Osage Co., Holy Family (1904), Rev. Michael P. Murphy.
Res., P.O. Box 97, 65035. Tel: 573-744-5254; Fax: 573-744-5254. [CEM]
School—Tel: 573-744-5200.
Sisters 1; Lay Teachers 3; Students 54.

Fulton, Callaway Co., St. Peter (1875), Rev. William L. Korte.
Parish Center: 700 Hwy. Z, 65251. Tel: 573-642-5562; Fax: 573-642-2861.
School—Tel: 573-642-2839; Fax: 573-642-2839.
Sisters 2; Lay Teachers 8; Students 155.
Catechesis/Religious Programs—Sisters of Christian Charity 3; Students 50.

Glasgow, Howard Co., St. Mary (1866), Rev. Philip M. Kane; Deacon Jerome C. Brucks.
Res., 421 Third St., 65254. Tel: 660-338-2053; Fax: 660-338-2589. [CEM]
School—Tel: 660-338-2258.
Lay Teachers 11; Students 129.
Catechesis/Religious Programs—Students 6.

Hannibal, Marion Co., Holy Family (1845), Rev. Michael F. Quinn; Deacon Emmett E. Pierceall.
Office: 2103 Broadway, 63401. Tel: 573-221-1078; Fax: 573-248-1662. [JC]
School—Tel: 573-221-0456; Fax: 573-221-6357.
Brothers 1; Lay Teachers 13; Students 219.
Catechesis/Religious Programs—1113 Broadway, 63401.
Students 74.

Hermann, Gasconade Co., St. George (1845), Rev. Ambrose German, O.F.M.
Res., 128 W. 4th St., 65041-1099. Tel: 573-486-2723. [CEM]
School—Tel: 573-486-5914; Fax: 573-486-2434.
Lay Teachers 14; Students 196.
Catechesis/Religious Programs—Tel: 573-486-2157.
Students 115.

Hermitage, Hickory Co., St. Bernadette (1973), Rev. Clarence Wiederholt, Admin.
Church—Hwy. 254, P.O. Box 167, 65668. Tel: 417-745-6361.
Res., HCR 67 Box 777, Roach, 65787. Tel: 573-346-2688.
Catechesis/Religious Programs—Students 31.
Mission—Climax Springs, Camden Co., Our Lady of the Snows, P.O. Box 21, Climax Springs, 65324. Tel: 573-345-4223.

Holts Summit, Callaway Co., St. Andrew (1975), Rev. Patrick L. Pierceall; Deacon Lawrence A. Weber.
Res., 400 St. Andrew Dr., 65043. Tel: 573-896-4309. [CEM]
Catechesis/Religious Programs—Students 88.

Ilasco, Ralls Co., Holy Cross. Closed. For inquires for parish records please see Holy Family, Hannibal.

Indian Creek, Monroe Co., St. Stephen (1833), Rev. William Flanagan.
Res., P.O. Box 251, Monroe City, 63456. Tel: 573-735-4033. [CEM]

Indian Grove, Chariton Co., St. Raphael (1886). Attended by Brunswick. Rev. Leonard S. Misey.
Mailing Address: 203 E. Vine St., P.O. Box 5, Brunswick, 65236-0005. Tel: 660-548-3267. [CEM]

Jonesburg, Montgomery Co., St. Patrick (1862), Rev. Gerald J. Kaimann; Ms. Kristin Roth, Pastoral Admin.
Res., 505 First St., 63351. Tel: 636-488-5623; Fax: 636-488-5623. [CEM]
Catechesis/Religious Programs—Students 57.

Kahoka, Clark Co., St. Michael the Archangel (1891), Rev. Brendan Lawless.
Church—622 W. Exchange St., P.O. Box 216, 63445. Tel: 660-727-3472.
Catechesis/Religious Programs—Students 64.
Mission—Wayland, Clark Co., St. Martha, (1887) 202 S. Main St., Wayland, 63472. Tel: 660-754-6011.

Kirksville, Adair Co., Mary Immaculate (1888), Revs. Patrick J. Shortt; William P. Kottenstette; Deacons Thomas Capuano; David D. Ream.
716 E. Washington St., 63501. Tel: 660-665-2466; Fax: 660-665-8955. [CEM]
School—Tel: 660-665-1006; Fax: 660-665-1006.
Lay Teachers 8; Students 134.
Catechesis/Religious Programs—Tel: 660-665-2466.
Students 195.
Mission—Novinger, Adair Co., St. Rose of Lima, (1903) Hwy. 149, Novinger, 63559. Tel: 660-488-6680.

Lake Ozark, Miller Co., Our Lady of the Lake (1940), Rev. Msgr. Michael J. Wilbers, V.G.; Deacon Francis P. Zimmerman.
Church—2411 Bagnell Dam Blvd., P.O. Box 2390, 65049. Tel: 573-365-2241; Fax: 573-365-4458.
Catechesis/Religious Programs—Students 104.

Laurie, Morgan Co., Shrine of St. Patrick (1870), Rev. Fred J. Barnett.
Office: P.O. Box 1098, 65038-1098. Tel: 573-374-7855 (Office); Fax: 573-374-0627. [CEM]
Catechesis/Religious Programs—Students 44.
Mission—Versailles, Morgan Co., St. Philip Benizi, (1963) 17034 Hwy. D, Versailles, 65084. Tel: 573-378-5958; Fax: 573-374-4825. Rev. C. Duane Ryan.
Catechesis/Religious Programs—Students 45.
Shrine—Mary Mother of the Church, P.O. Box 1250, 65038.

Linn, Osage Co., St. George (1866), Rev. Paul M. Hartley.
Res., P.O. Box 49, 65051. Tel: 573-897-2293. [CEM]
School—Tel: 573-897-3645; Fax: 573-897-2148.
Lay Teachers 12; Students 176.
Catechesis/Religious Programs—Students 88.

Loose Creek, Osage Co., Immaculate Conception (1845), Rev. Gregory C. Meystrik.
Res., P.O. Box 8, 65054. Tel: 573-897-2922; Fax: 573-897-4528. [CEM 2]
School—Tel: 573-897-3516; Fax: 573-897-4271.
School Sisters of Notre Dame 2; Lay Teachers 7; Students 96.
Catechesis/Religious Programs—Students 47.

Louisiana, Pike Co., St. Joseph (1865), Rev. Thomas L. Waickman.
Res., 508 N. 3rd St., 63353. Tel: 573-754-4757. [CEM]
Catechesis/Religious Programs—Students 25.
Mission—Clarksville, Pike Co., Mary Queen of Peace, (1951) South Second St., Clarksville, 63336. Tel: 573-242-3730.

Macon, Macon Co., Immaculate Conception (1857), Rev. Russell R. Judge; Deacons Leo Prenger; Bernhard Toll.
Res., 402 N. Rollins St., 63552. Tel: 660-385-3792. [CEM]
School—Tel: 660-385-2711.
Sisters 2; Lay Teachers 3; Students 58.
Catechesis/Religious Programs—Students 58.
Mission—Bevier, Macon Co., Sacred Heart, (1880) Bevier, 63532. Tel: 660-385-3792.

Marceline, Linn Co., St. Bonaventure (1888), Rev. Manus P. Daly.
Res., 409 S. Kansas Ave., 64658-1301. Tel: 660-376-3239. [CEM 2]
School—Tel: 660-376-3580.
Lay Teachers 7; Students 70.
Catechesis/Religious Programs—Students 104.
Mission—Hurricane Branch, Chariton Co., St. Joseph, (1870).

Marshall, Saline Co., St. Peter (1870), Rev. Kevin Gormley.
Res., 1801 S. Miami Ave., P.O. Box 220, 65340. Tel: 660-886-7960; Fax: 660-831-1723. [CEM]
School—Tel: 660-886-6390; Fax: 660-866-6606.
Lay Teachers 10; Students 97.
Catechesis/Religious Programs—Tel: 660-886-3112; Fax: 660-886-6606.
Students 177.
Mission—Sweet Springs, Saline Co., Holy Family, (1945) 200 Ruby St., Sweet Springs, 65351.

Martinsburg, Audrain Co., St. Joseph (1876), Rev. Wayne M. Boyer.
Res., 408 E. Kellett, 65264. Tel: 573-492-6595; Fax: 573-492-6105. [CEM]
School—Tel: 573-492-6283.
Lay Teachers 6; Students 63.
Catechesis/Religious Programs—Students 46.

Mary's Home, Miller Co., Our Lady of the Snows (1883), Rev. Clarence E. Wiederholt.
Res., 274 Hwy. H, Eugene, 65032. Tel: 573-498-3820; Fax: 573-498-3779. [CEM]
School—Tel: 573-498-3574; Fax: 573-498-3776.
Lay Teachers 5; Students 59.
Catechesis/Religious Programs—Students 129.

Memphis, Scotland Co., St. John (1952), Rev. William P. Kottenstette.
Rectory: Rte. 1, Box 34 H, 63555. Tel: 660-465-7130. [CEM]
Res., c/o Mary Immaculate Parish Newman Center, 716 E. Washington, Kirksville, 63501. Tel: 660-665-5269; 665-2466. [CEM]

Meta, Osage Co., St. Cecilia (1904), Rev. John J. Schutty.
Res., P.O. Box 96, 65058-0096. Tel: 573-229-4811; Fax: 573-229-4699. [CEM]
Catechesis/Religious Programs—Students 80.

Mexico, Audrain Co., St. Brendan (1857), Rev. Allan Stetz, O.S.B.
Res., 615 S. Washington St., 65265. Tel: 573-581-4720; Fax: 573-581-4720. [CEM]
School—Tel: 573-581-2443.
Lay Teachers 10; Students 158.
Catechesis/Religious Programs—Mary Beardslee, D.R.E.
Students 90.

Milan, Sullivan Co., St. Mary (1868), Rev. Joseph Hoi; Deacon Terence L. Reibenspies.
Res., 101 W. Baker St., P.O. Box 147, 63556. Tel: 660-265-4110; Fax: 660-265-4110. [CEM 2]
Catechesis/Religious Programs—Tel: 660-265-4110.
Students 50.
Mission—Unionville, Putnam Co., St. Mary, (1868). Tel: 660-947-2599.

Moberly, Randolph Co., St. Pius X (1888), Rev. Michael A. Coleman.
Res., 217 S. Williams St., P.O. Box 310, 65270. Tel: 660-263-5243; Fax: 660-263-0101. [CEM]
School—Tel: 660-263-5500; Fax: 660-263-5744.
Lay Teachers 17; Students 232.
Catechesis/Religious Programs—Tel: 660-263-0427.
Students 126.

Mokane, Callaway Co., St. Jude Thaddeus (1900), Rev. Thomas J. Seifner; Deacon Lawrence A. Weber.
Church—P.O. Box 128, 65059. Tel: 573-676-3238.
Mailing Address: 605 Bluff St., Rhineland, 65069. Tel: 573-236-4390; Fax: 573-236-4747.
Catechesis/Religious Programs—401 Adams, 65059.
Students 30.

Monroe City, Monroe Co., Holy Rosary (1884), Rev. William Flanagan; Deacon Harold L. Parn.
Res., 405 S. Main St., 63456. Tel: 573-735-4718. [CEM]
School—Tel: 573-735-2422.
Sisters of St. Dominic 1; Lay Teachers 10; Students 170.
Catechesis/Religious Programs—Students 115.

Montgomery City, Montgomery Co., Immaculate Conception (1861), Rev. Gerald J. Kaimann.
Res., 307 N. Walker, 63361. Tel: 573-564-2375; Fax: 573-564-2375. [CEM 2]
School—407 W. Third St., 63361. Tel: 573-564-2679.
Lay Teachers 5; Students 42.
Catechesis/Religious Programs—Students 74.

Morrison, Gasconade Co., Assumption (1875). Attended by Chamois. Rev. Patrick Dowling.
Mailing Address: P.O. Box 156, Chamois, 65024. Tel: 573-763-5345. [CEM 2]
Catechesis/Religious Programs—Students 18.

Osage Bend, Cole Co., St. Margaret of Antioch (1907), Rev. Louis E. Dorn; Deacons Larry G. Hildebrand; Robert Smerek, Pastoral Admin.
Mailing Address: 12025 Rte. W., Jefferson City, 65101. Tel: 573-496-3404. [CEM]
Catechesis/Religious Programs—Students 50.

Owensville, Gasconade Co., Immaculate Conception (1893), Rev. L. James Finder.
Res., 404 S. First St., 65066. Tel: 573-437-2494; Fax: 573-437-7494. [CEM 2]
Catechesis/Religious Programs—Tel: 573-437-3086.
Students 201.

Palmyra, Marion Co., St. Joseph (1866), Rev. Daniel I. J. Lueckenotte; Sr. Marlene Buese, S.S.N.D., Pastoral Min.
Res., 411 S. Lane St., P.O. Box 606, 63461. Tel: 573-769-3270; Fax: 573-769-3176.

Catechesis/Religious Programs—Tel: 573-769-2837.
Students 180.

Perry, Ralls Co., St. William (1901), Rev. Kenneth E. Brockel.
Res., P.O. Box 339, 63462. Tel: 573-565-2852; Fax: 573-565-8012. [CEM]
Catechesis/Religious Programs—Students 69.
Missions—Paris, Monroe Co., St. Frances Cabrini, (1953) Hwy. 24, Paris, 65275. Tel: 660-327-4448; Center, Ralls Co., St. Paul (Historic Church), Hwy. EE, Center, 63436.

Pilot Grove, Cooper Co., St. Joseph (1894), Rev. Eric A. Schlachter.
Res., 407 Harris St., 65276. Tel: 660-834-4251. [CEM 3]
School—Tel: 660-834-5600.
Lay Teachers 5; Students 51.
Catechesis/Religious Programs—Students 123.
Station—Clear Creek, St. John the Baptist, (1840). (Mass).

Rhineland, Montgomery Co., Church of the Risen Savior (1979), Rev. Thomas J. Seifner; Deacons Joseph E. Horton; Gerald W. Korman.
Res., 605 Bluff St., 65069. Tel: 573-236-4390; Fax: 573-236-4747. [CEM 2]
Catechesis/Religious Programs—Students 79.
Pilgrimage Site—(1888), Shrine of Our Lady of Sorrows, Starkenburg, Montgomery Co., Tel: 573-236-4390.

Rich Fountain, Osage Co., Sacred Heart (1838), Rev. Mark A. Porterfield.
Res., Rte. 1, Box 118, 65035. Tel: 573-744-5987. [CEM]
School—Tel: 573-744-5898; Fax: 573-744-5761.
Sisters of Notre Dame 1; Lay Teachers 6; Students 106.
Catechesis/Religious Programs—Students 73.

Richland, Pulaski Co., St. Jude (1972), Rev. John W. Groner.
Res. & Mailing Address: 367 Old Hwy. 66, St. Robert, 65584. Tel: 573-336-3662.
Church—P.O. Box 8, 65556.

Rolla, Phelps Co., St. Patrick (1862), Rev. Ignazio C. Medina; Deacons Michael S. Brooks; Thomas C. Manion.
Res., 17 St. Patrick Ln., 65401. Tel: 573-364-1435; 341-9004; Fax: 573-364-2073. [CEM]
School—Tel: 573-364-1162; Fax: 573-364-2073.
Sisters of St. Francis of Our Lady of Perpetual Help 1; Lay Teachers 11; Students 175.
Catechesis/Religious Programs—Students 160.

Rosati, Phelps Co., St. Anthony (1908), Rev. Ignazio Medina, Admin.
Res., 21670 County Rd. 3640, St. James, 65559. Tel: 573-265-7247; Fax: 573-265-1191. [CEM]

Russellville, Cole Co., St. Michael (1906), Rev. Brendan Doyle; Sr. Donna Eggering, O.S.F., Pastoral Admin.; Deacon Gary Christhoff.
Res., 13321 Railroad Ave., 65074-9447. Tel: 573-782-4503; Fax: 573-782-8280. [CEM]
Catechesis/Religious Programs—Tel: 573-782-3171.
Students 58.

St. Anthony, Miller Co., St. Anthony (1906), Rev. John J. Schutty.
Church—132 Main St., Iberia, 65486. Tel: 573-793-6550; Fax: 573-793-6550. [CEM]
Catechesis/Religious Programs—Students 60.

St. Clement, Pike Co., St. Clement (1871), Rev. Richard W. Frank.
Res., 21509 Hwy. J, Bowling Green, 63334. Tel: 573-324-5545; Fax: 573-324-5155. [CEM]
School—Tel: 573-324-2166; Fax: 573-324-6159.
Lay Teachers 7; Students 106.
Catechesis/Religious Programs—Students 100.

St. Elizabeth, Miller Co., St. Lawrence (1871), Rev. John F. Degnan.
Res., P.O. Box 128, 65075. Tel: 573-493-2301. [CEM]
Catechesis/Religious Programs—Tel: 573-493-2301.
Students 144.

St. James, Phelps Co., Immaculate Conception (1870), Rev. Ignazio Medina, Admin.
Oratory—St. James, 316 E. Scioto, 65559. Tel: 573-265-7250; Fax: 573-265-1191. [CEM]
Catechesis/Religious Programs—Tel: 573-265-7247.
Students 77.

St. Martins, Cole Co., St. Martin (1885), Rev. Edwin A. Schmidt; Deacon Francis Butel.
Res., 7148 St. Martins Ave., Jefferson City, 65109. Tel: 573-893-2923; Fax: 573-893-3865. [CEM]
School—Tel: 573-893-3519; Fax: 573-893-7404.
Lay Teachers 12; Students 199.
Catechesis/Religious Programs—Tel: 573-893-2352.
Students 58.

St. Patrick, Clark Co., The Shrine of St. Patrick (1839). Attended by Canton. Rev. Thomas L. Alber; Deacon Robert DePyper, Pastoral Admin.
Parish Office: 812 Lewis St., Canton, 63435. Tel: 573-288-3198; Fax: 573-228-3198. [CEM]
Catechesis/Religious Programs—Students 12.

St. Thomas, Cole Co., St. Thomas the Apostle Church (1869), Rev. Donald J. Antweiler.
Res., 14814 Rt. B, P.O. Box 146, 65076. Tel: 573-477-3315. [CEM]
School—P.O. Box 211, 65076. Tel: 573-477-3322.
Lay Teachers 6; Students 60.
Catechesis/Religious Programs—Tel: 573-477-3398.
Students 47.

Salisbury, Chariton Co., St. Joseph (1870), Rev. William D. Debo.
Res., 301 W. Williams, 65281. Tel: 660-388-5590; Fax: 660-388-6088. [CEM]
School—Tel: 660-388-5518; Fax: 660-388-5518.
Sisters of Charity of Leavenworth 2; Lay Teachers 9; Students 113.
Catechesis/Religious Programs—Tel: 660-388-6180.
Students 81.

Sedalia, Pettis Co., St. Patrick (1866), Revs. Thomas Albers, C.PP.S.; Timothy J. Guthridge, C.PP.S.; Paul L. Becquet, C.PP.S.; David Matz, C.PP.S.; Deacons Jerome Connery; G. Robert Watson.
Res., 415 E. Fourth St., 65301. Tel: 660-826-2062; Fax: 660-829-1085.
Catechesis/Religious Programs—Students 89.
Station—Clifton City, St. Joseph. (Mass).

Sacred Heart (1882), Revs. Thomas L. Albers, C.PP.S.; John M. Behen, C.PP.S.; David Matz, C.PP.S.; Timothy J. Guthridge, C.PP.S.; Paul L. Becquet, C.PP.S.; Deacons G. Robert Watson; Jerome Connery.
Res., 421 W. Third St., 65301. Tel: 660-827-2311; Fax: 660-827-3941. [CEM]
School—Tel: 660-827-3800; Fax: 660-827-3806.
Sisters of Divine Providence 1; Congregation of Sisters of the Sacred Heart of Jesus of Saint-Jacut 1; Lay Teachers 11; Students 305.
High School—Lay Teachers 20; Students 125.
Catechesis/Religious Programs—Students 63.
Mission—Bahner, Pettis Co., St. John, (1845).
Station—Spring Fork, St. Patrick, (1876). (Mass).

Shelbina, Shelby Co., St. Mary (1879), Rev. Christopher L. Cordes.
Res., 307 E. Chestnut St., 63468. Tel: 573-588-4498; Fax: 573-588-4728. [CEM]
Catechesis/Religious Programs—Students 75.

Slater, Saline Co., St. Joseph (1882). Attended by Glasgow. Rev. Philip M. Kane.
Res., 325 W. Emma St., 65349. Tel: 660-529-2588.
Catechesis/Religious Programs—Students 17.

Steelville, Crawford Co., St. Michael (1949), Rev. Robert W. Duesdieker; Mr. Bradley Harmon, Pastoral Admin.
Mailing Address: 1098 Old Hwy. 66 W., Box 419, Bourbon, 65441. Tel: 573-732-4494; Fax: 573-732-4494.
Church—Hwy. 8 E., 65565.
Catechesis/Religious Programs—Students 24.

Taos, Cole Co., St. Francis Xavier (1838), Rev. J. David Maher; Deacon James E. Skahan.
Res., 7319 Rte. M, Jefferson City, 65101. Tel: 573-395-4401; Fax: 573-395-4302. [CEM]
School—Tel: 573-395-4612; Fax: 573-395-4612.
Lay Teachers 14; Students 225.
Catechesis/Religious Programs—Students 50.

Tipton, Moniteau Co., St. Andrew (1857), Rev. Henry J. Reichert.
Res., 106 W. Cooper St., P.O. Box 598, 65081. Tel: 660-433-2162. [CEM]
School—Tel: 660-433-2232; Fax: 660-433-5432.
Lay Teachers 10; Students 118.
Catechesis/Religious Programs—Students 87.

Vandalia, Audrain Co., Sacred Heart (1891), Rev. Thomas J. Seifner, Admin.
Res., 203 W. Home, 63382. Tel: 573-594-2717; Fax: 573-594-2556.
Catechesis/Religious Programs—Students 71.
Mission—Laddonia, Audrain Co., St. John, (1889) 7th and Elm, Laddonia, 63352. Tel: 573-373-5351; Fax: 573-373-2221.

Vienna, Maries Co., Visitation (1867), Rev. John J. Schmitz.
Res., 105 N. Main St., P.O. Box 171, 65582. Tel: 573-422-3950; Fax: 573-422-3950. [CEM]
School—105 N. Coffey St., P.O. Box 269, 65582. Tel: 573-422-3375; Fax: 573-422-3950.
Sisters of Sacred Heart of Jesus 1; Lay Teachers 5; Students 76.

Wardsville, Cole Co., St. Stanislaus (1880), Rev. Louis E. Dorn. In res., Rev. Brian J. Driscoll.
Res., 6410 Rte. W., Jefferson City, 65101. Tel: 573-636-4925; Fax: 573-636-2534. [CEM]
School—Tel: 573-636-7802; Fax: 573-635-4782.
Lay Teachers 18; Students 314.
Catechesis/Religious Programs—Tel: 573-496-3404.
Students 14.

Warsaw, Benton Co., St. Ann (1945), Rev. Richard Colbert, C.PP.S.
Res., Rte. 2, Box 29-20, 65355. Tel: 660-438-3844 (Church); 438-5870 (Rectory). [CEM]
Catechesis/Religious Programs—Students 50.
Mission—Cole Camp, Benton Co., SS. Peter & Paul, (1878) Rte. 2, P.O. Box 248, Cole Camp, 65325. Tel: 660-668-3952.

Waynesville, Pulaski Co., St. Robert Bellarmine (1941), Rev. John W. Groner.
Res., 367 Old Hwy. 66, St. Robert, 65584. Tel: 573-336-3662. [CEM]
Catechesis/Religious Programs—Students 124.

Wellsville, Montgomery Co., Resurrection (1873), Rev. Wayne M. Boyer; Deacon Vincent Garufi.
Church—409 E. Bates, 63384.
Res., 408 E. Kellett, Martinsburg, 65264. Tel: 573-492-6595; Fax: 573-492-6105. [CEM]
Catechesis/Religious Programs—Students 55.

Westphalia, Osage Co., St. Joseph (1835), Rev. Robert A. Kurwicki.
Res., P.O. Box 116, 65085-0116. Tel: 573-455-2320; Fax: 573-455-2984. [CEM]
School—Tel: 573-455-2339; Fax: 573-455-2287.
Lay Teachers 9; Students 116.
Catechesis/Religious Programs—Students 70.

Wien, Chariton Co., St. Mary of the Angels (1876), Rev. Philip M. Moriarty.
Res., Rte. 1, Box 65, New Cambria, 63558. Tel: 660-226-5243. [CEM 2]
Catechesis/Religious Programs—Students 75.
Station—Hamden, Immaculate Conception. (Mass).

Chaplains of Public Institutions

Prisons

JEFFERSON CITY. *Central Missouri Correctional Center.* Vacant. Hwy. 179, 65109. Tel: 573-751-2053.
Jefferson City Correctional Center P.O. Box 900, 65102. Tel: 573-751-3224. Rev. John A. Henderson, Chap., Tel: 573-455-2888; Sr. Ruth Heaney, O.S.B., Chap., Tel: 573-635-8123.
Missouri Intermediate Reformatory. (Algoa) Algoa Rd., 65101. Tel: 573-751-3911. Chaplains: Rev. Sylvester W. Bauer Tel: 573-744-5913; Sr. Fran Buschell, S.S.N.D. Tel: 573-635-9127.

BOONVILLE. *Boonville Correctional Center.* E. Morgan St., 65233. Tel: 660-882-6521. Rev. John A. Henderson, Chap., Tel: 573-455-2888.

BOWLING GREEN. *Northeast Correctional Center* 13698 Pike 46, Airport Rd., 63334. Tel: 573-324-9975. Rev. Richard W. Frank, Chap.

FULTON. *Diagnostic and Reception Center* P.O. Box 581, 65251. Tel: 573-592-4040. Deacon Robert L. Dulle, Chap.

MOBERLY. *Missouri Training Center For Men* P.O. Box 7, 65270. Tel: 660-263-3778. Rev. Michael A. Coleman, Chap., Tel: 660-263-5243.

TIPTON. *State Correctional Pre-Release Center* 65081. Tel: 660-433-2031. Rev. Henry J. Reichert, Chap., Tel: 660-433-2162.

VANDALIA. *Women's Eastern Missouri Reception, Diagnostic and Correctional Center* P.O. Box 300, 63382. Tel: 573-594-6686. Chaplains: Sr. Fran Buschell, S.S.N.D. Tel: 573-635-9127; Sr. Cathryn Kever, S.S.S.F. Tel: 573-594-6686 Ext. 2752.

Hospitals and Schools

JEFFERSON CITY. *Capital Region Medical Center* 1125 Madison St., 65101. Tel: 573-635-7100. Rev. David G. Buescher.

COLUMBIA. *Boone Hospital Center* 1600 E. Broadway, 65201. Tel: 573-875-4545.
Columbia Regional Hospital 404 Keene St., 65201. Tel: 573-875-9000.
Ellis Fischel State Cancer Hospital 115 Business Loop 70 W., 65201. Tel: 573-882-2100.
Mid-Missouri Mental Health Center 3 Hospital Dr., 65201. Tel: 573-449-2511.
Rusk Rehabilitation Center 315 Business Loop 70 W., 65203. Tel: 573-817-2703.
University Hospital & Clinics One Hospital Dr., 65201. Tel: 573-882-4141.
Chaplains for the Columbia Hospitals listed above: Revs. Edwin J. Cole, Dir., Tel: 578-443-2892; Donald L. Wallace Tel: 660-248-2439; Eleanor Braddock, M.D. Tel: 573-445-6701; Sr. Florence Seib, A.S.C. Tel: 573-499-3810.
Veterans' Administration Medical Center. (Harry S. Truman Memorial) 800 Stadium Rd., 65201. Tel: 573-443-2511. Rev. Edwin J. Cole, Chap., Tel: 573-443-2892.

FULTON. *Fulton State Hospital* Fifth St., 65251. Tel: 573-642-3311. Deacon Robert L. Dulle, Chap.

Missouri School for the Deaf E. Fifth St., 65251. Tel: 573-642-3301. Rev. William L. Korte, Chap., Tel: 573-642-5562.

MARCELINE. *Pershing Regional Health Care Center.* Attended by St. Boniventure Rectory, 409 S. Kansas, Marceline, 64658. Tel.:660-376-3239. 225 W. Hayden, 64658. Tel: 660-376-3521.

MARSHALL. *Marshall State School-Hospital* E. Slater St., 65340. Tel: 660-886-2202. Rev. Kevin Gormley, Chap., Tel: 660-886-7960.

ST. JAMES. *Missouri Veterans' Home.* Vacant. 620 N. Jefferson St., 65559. Tel: 573-265-3271.

On Duty Outside the Diocese:
Reverend Fathers—
Hereford, Thomas D.
Palmieri, Luigi
Porterfield, Mark A.
Stockman, Gerald

Missionary Assignment in Peru:
Reverend Fathers—
Dlabal, Norbert
Griffey, Brendan M.
Keyes, Raphael
Lawlor, Joseph
Niemeyer, James J.

Absent on Leave:
Reverend Fathers—
Behan, Hugh F.
Clohessy, Kevin P.
Crosby, Donald W.
Doyle, Edward A.
Faletti, Stephen L.
Keogh, William
Linnebur, Vincent
McGrath, Thomas E.
Siciliano, Donald E.
Smith, Mark C.

Retired:
Reverend Monsignors—
Poelker, Gerard L., P.O. Box 39, Holts Summit, MO 65043. Tel: 573-896-4748
Sommer, Jerome, Regina Cleri, 7850 Kenrick Rd., St. Louis, MO 63119. Tel: 314-961-0271

Reverend Fathers—
Bonn, Ferdinand C., Wyandott Apartments, 2717 Wyandotte A5, Las Vegas, NV 89102
Buhman, Leo T., 1513 43rd St., St. Joseph, MO 64506. Tel: 816-233-7775
Chenoweth, Robert, 917 Country Club Dr., St. Louis, MO 63121
Cronin, Richard, c/o Mr. & Mrs. Tim O'Leary, 8 Ashleigh Dr., Skehard Rd., Cork City, Ireland. Tel: 011-353-21-292006
Forst, William, 965 Dietrick Rd., P.O. Box 5, Foristell, MO 63348-0005. Tel: 636-673-1052
Konrad, Erwin, 901 Missouri Blvd., PMB 107, Jefferson City, MO 65109-1759
Long, John, Tara, Curragheen Rd., Bishopstown, Cork Ireland. Tel: 011-353-21-870373
Mersinger, Arthur, 7913 Colleen, St. Louis, MO 63123
Robl, Eugene J., 907 Clayton, Columbia, MO 65203. Tel: 573-443-0423
Stangl, Frank J., 4229 Shelly Dr., Rocky Mount, NC 27804
Starmann, Joseph W., 25 Ackermann Rd., Winfield, MO 63389-3106. Tel: 636-566-8420
Walsh, Peter, 97 New St., Ballinrobe, Co. Mayo Ireland. Tel: 011-353-92-42371
Wheeler, Clarence, M.S., 612 Norris Dr., Jefferson City, MO 65109. Tel: 573-635-0648

Permanent Deacons:
Agniel, Harry M., (Retired)
Anderberg, Peter K., (Retired)
Berry, Kenneth
Bilgrien, Kenneth D., On Duty Outside Diocese
Braddock, Joseph
Breazile, James E., On Duty Outside Diocese
Brooks, Michael
Brown, William J., (Retired)
Brucks, Jerome C.
Butel, Francis J.
Butler, James R., On Duty Outside Diocese
Capuano, Tom
Chaplin, Mark, On Duty Outside Diocese
Christoff, Gary
Connery, Jerome
Daly, Michael M.
Davis, Howard E., On Duty Outside Diocese
Dodds, Michael, On Duty Outside Diocese
Dulle, Robert L.
Fritsch, Frederick
Garufi, Vincent E.
Gerling, Thomas J., On Duty Outside Diocese
Heidlage, Walter F., (Retired)
Hildebrand, Larry
Himmelberg, Robert L., (Retired)
Horsefield, Earl R.
Horton, Joseph E.
Houston, John D., On Duty Outside Diocese
Joyce, Dana K.
Kazmierczak, Eugene S.
Kinney, William J., (Retired)
Korman, Gerald W.
Luebbering, Richard H.
Manion, Thomas C.
McEvoy, Tim, On Duty Outside Diocese
Miller, David
Nordmeyer, Charles, (Retired)
Orscheln, Donald W., (Retired)
Osman, Robert C., (Retired)
Parn, Harold L.
Pierceall, Eugene E.
Prenger, Leo F.
Rackers, Robert J.
Ream, David D.
Reibenspies, Terence L.
Reuter, Ralph V., (Retired)
Rockhold, Jess L., (Retired)
Shumake, Lindell P., (Retired)
Skahan, James E.
Snooks, Richard W., On Duty Outside Diocese
Spalding, George T., (Retired)
Tebbe, John J., (Retired)
Toll, Bernhard F.
Towey, Martin G.
Visot, Luis R., On Duty Outside Diocese
Von Gunten, Richard A.
Warden, Donald E.
Watson, G. Robert
Weber, Lawrence A.
Weisel, Fred M., Leave of Absence
Whalen, Tom
Wilmarth, Albert W., Leave of Absence
Zimmerman, Francis P.

INSTITUTIONS LOCATED IN THE DIOCESE

[A] SEMINARIES, DIOCESAN

HANNIBAL. *St. Thomas Aquinas Seminary,* P.O. Box 858, 245 N. Levering Ave., 63401. Tel: 573-221-4330; Fax: 573-221-5401.
E-mail: stasem@socket.net
Web site: members.sockets.net/~stasem/
Very Rev. Marion J. Makerewicz, Rector; Rev. Thomas L. Alber; Rev. Msgr. James J. Wenting; Rev. Msgr. Louis W. McCorkle; Revs. David D. Cox; P. Gregory Oligschlaeger; Bro. Christian J. Guertin, F.F.S.C.; Mr. Robert Catalpa; Mr. Dominic Geinosky. Students 26.

[B] HIGH SCHOOLS, DIOCESAN

JEFFERSON CITY. *Helias High School,* 1305 Swift's Hwy., 65109. Tel: 573-635-6139; Fax: 573-635-5615. Mr. Stan Ochsner, Dean of Students; Sr. Jean Dietrich, Prin.; Mr. Dennis Hughes, Admin.; Mr. Ron Vossen, Campus Ministry; Rev. Brendan Doyle. Brothers of the Christian Schools 3; School Sisters of Notre Dame 1; Lay Teachers 47; Students 872.

[C] GENERAL HOSPITALS

JEFFERSON CITY. *St. Marys Health Center,* 100 St. Marys Medical Plaza, 65101. Tel: 573-761-7000
For a complete listing, refer to the Hospitals section.

[D] NURSING HOMES

JEFFERSON CITY. *St. Joseph's Home,* 1306 W. Main St., 65109. Tel: 573-635-0166; Fax: 573-635-1405
For a complete listing, refer to the Special Care Facilities section.

Villa Marie Skilled Nursing Facility, 1030 Edmonds St., 65109. Tel: 573-761-6700
For a complete listing, refer to the Special Care Facilities section.

[E] CONVENTS AND RESIDENCES FOR SISTERS

JEFFERSON CITY. *Discalced Carmelite Monastery,* 2201 W. Main St., 65109. Tel: 573-636-3364. Mother Therese Dubois, O.C.D., Prioress. Professed of Solemn Vows 8.

Franciscan Sisters of Mary, Jericho Community, 202 Binder Dr., 65109-0815. Tel: 573-635-8123. Franciscan Sisters of Mary 3.

BRINKTOWN. *Guardian Angel Convent,* 65443. Tel: 573-422-3921. Franciscan Sisters of Mary.

COLUMBIA. *Our Lady of Peace Monastery,* 3710 W. Broadway Blvd., 65203-0116. Tel: 573-446-2300; Fax: 573-446-2312.
E-mail: administration@benedictinesister.org
Web site: www.benedictinesister.org
Sr. Rose Maria Birkenfeld, O.S.B., Prioress. Benedictine Sisters of Pontifical Jurisdiction 11.

MARCELINE. *Our Lady of the Rosary Community,* 200 W. Bigger St., 64658-1070. Tel: 660-376-3969. Franciscan Sisters of Mary. Sisters 2.

[F] NEWMAN CENTERS

JEFFERSON CITY. *Lincoln University-Newman Center,* 708 Marshall St., 65101. Tel: 573-635-9356.
E-mail: newmanctr@mail.ultraweb.net
Darryl Cook, Dir.

COLUMBIA. *University of Missouri-Columbia, Campus Ministry,* 701 Maryland, 65201. Tel: 573-449-5424; Fax: 573-874-2777.
E-mail: pardeech@tranquility.net
Web site: www.students.missouri.edu~newman
Revs. Charles D. Pardee, Dir. & Pastor; Mark S. Smith.

FAYETTE. *Central Methodist College,* c/o St. Joseph Church, 300 S. Cleveland, 65248. Tel: 660-248-2439; Fax: 660-248-2439.
E-mail: don1835@hotmail.com
Rev. Donald Wallace, Dir.

KIRKSVILLE. *Catholic Newman Center, Truman State University,* 709 S. Davis, 63501. Tel: 660-665-4357.
E-mail: tsnewman@kvmo.net
Web site: www.kvmo.net/~newman/
Mrs. Bettie Lesczynski, Dir.; Rev. William P. Kottenstette, Chap.

ROLLA. *University of Missouri-Rolla,* 2 Vichy Rd., 65401. Tel: 573-364-2133; Fax: 573-364-2073.
E-mail: newman@umr.edu
Web site: www.umr.edu/~newman
Sr. Renita Brummer, O.S.F., Dir.

[G] SOCIAL SERVICES

JEFFERSON CITY. *Samaritan Center,* 1310 E. McCarty St., P.O. Box 1687, 65102. Tel: 573-634-7776; Fax: 573-761-5948.
E-mail: samlady@socket.net
Marylyn DeFeo, Exec. Dir.

[H] MISCELLANEOUS

JEFFERSON CITY. *Diocesan Excellence in Education Fund, Inc.,* P.O. Box 417, 65102. Tel: 573-635-9127.

Missouri Catholic Conference, 600 Clark Ave., P.O. Box 1022, 65102. Tel: 573-635-7239; Fax: 573-635-7431.
E-mail: MoCatholic@aol.com
Web site: www.members.aol.com/MoCatholic
Lawrence A. Weber, Exec. Dir.

St. Marys Health Center, Jefferson City, Missouri, Foundation, 100 St. Marys Medical Plaza, 65101. Tel: 573-761-7198. Member of the SSM Health Care. Ms. Beverly Stafford, Dir.

ST. LOUIS. *Residents Encounter Christ,* Missouri State Board, 7522 Big Bend Blvd., 63119. Tel: 314-647-7060; Fax: 314-647-8380. Mr. Joseph Hedley, Exec. Dir.

RELIGIOUS INSTITUTES OF MEN REPRESENTED IN THE DIOCESE

For further details refer to the corresponding bracketed number in the Religious Institutes of Men or Women section.

[0330]—*Brothers of the Christian Schools.* (Midwest Prov.).—F.S.C.

[1330]—*Congregation of the Mission.* (Midwest Prov.).—C.M. [0510]—Franciscan Brothers of the Holy Cross.—F.F.S.C.

[0520]—*Franciscan Friars.* (Sacred Heart Prov.).—O.F.M.

[0720]—*The Missionaries of Our Lady of La Salette.* (Prov. of Mary Queen).—M.S.

[]—*Order of St. Benedict.* (Conception Abbey).

[1060]—*Society of the Precious Blood.* (Kansas City Prov.).—C.PP.S.

RELIGIOUS INSTITUTES OF WOMEN REPRESENTED IN THE DIOCESE

[0100]—*Adorers of the Blood of Christ.* (Wichita).—A.S.C.

[0230]—*Benedictine Sisters of Pontifical Jurisdiction.* (Columbia, MO).—O.S.B.

[0360]—*Carmelite Sisters of the Divine Heart of Jesus.*—Carmel.D.C.J.

[3670]—*Congregation of the Sacred Heart of Jesus of Saint Jacut.* (San Antonio, TX).—S.S.C.J.

[0460]—*Congregation of the Sisters of Charity of the Incarnate Word.*—C.C.V.I.

[1730]—*Congregation of the Sisters of the Third Order of St. Francis.* (Oldenburg, IN).—O.S.F.

[0420]—*Discalced Carmelite Nuns.*—O.C.D.

[1070-11]—*Dominican Sisters.* (Sparkill, NY).—O.P.

[1415]—*Franciscan Sisters of Mary.* (St. Louis Prov.).—F.S.M.

[1430]—*Franciscan Sisters of Our Lady of Perpetual Help.*—O.S.F.

[2970]—*School Sisters of Notre Dame.* (Milwaukee Prov.).—S.S.N.D.

[2970]—*School Sisters of Notre Dame.* (St. Louis Prov.).—S.S.N.D.

[2970]—*School Sisters of Notre Dame.* (Dallas, TX Prov.).—S.S.N.D.

[1680]—*School Sisters of St. Francis.* (Milwaukee, WI).—O.S.F.

[0480]—*Sisters of Charity of Leavenworth, Kansas.* (Leavenworth, KS).—S.C.L.

[0660]—*Sisters of Christian Charity.* (Wilmette, IL).—S.C.C.

[0990]—*Sisters of Divine Providence.* (St. Louis Prov.).—C.D.P.

[2549]—*Sisters of Mercy.* (Co. Sligo, Ireland).—R.S.M.

[3840]—*Sisters of St. Joseph of Carondelet.* (St. Paul, MN).—C.S.J.

[3270]—*Sisters of the Most Precious Blood.* (O'Fallon, MO).—C.PP.S.

DIOCESAN CEMETERIES

JEFFERSON CITY. *St. Peter's Catholic Cemetery Association,* c/o Resurrection Cemetery, 3015 W. Truman Blvd., 65109. Tel: 573-893-2751. Mr. James Cox, Pres.

NECROLOGY

† Hunkins, Richard C., Stoutsville, MO Special Ministry. —Died April 27, 2000.

† Kutz, Rev. Msgr. Ralph G., Argyle, MO St. Aloysius. —Died July 5, 2000.

† Quinn, J. Patrick, Rich Fountain, MO Sacred Heart; Belle, MO St. Alexander. —Died Nov. 17, 1999.

Diocese of Joliet in Illinois

(Dioecesis Joliettensis in Illinois)

Most Reverend

JOSEPH L. IMESCH, D.D.

Bishop of Joliet; ordained December 16, 1956; ordained Auxiliary Bishop of Detroit April 3, 1973; appointed Bishop of Joliet June 30, 1979; installed August 28, 1979. *Res., 425 Summit St., Joliet, IL, 60435.*

Most Reverend

ROGER L. KAFFER, D.D.

Auxiliary Bishop of Joliet; Titular Bishop of Dusa; ordained May 1, 1954; appointed April 25, 1985; consecrated June 26, 1985. *Res., 425 Summit St., Joliet, IL, 60435.*

ESTABLISHED BY BULL DATED DECEMBER 11, 1948.

CANONICALLY ERECTED MARCH 24, 1949.

Square Miles 4,218.

Comprises the Counties of Du Page, Kankakee, Will, Grundy, Ford, Iroquois and Kendall in the State of Illinois.

PATRON OF DIOCESE: St. Francis Xavier.

For legal titles of parishes and diocesan institutions, consult the Chancery.

Chancery: 425 Summit St., Joliet, IL, 60435. Tel.: 815-722-6606; Fax: 815-722-6602.

E-mail address: dojchan@aol.com

STATISTICAL OVERVIEW

Personnel	
Bishop	1
Auxiliary Bishops	1
Abbots	1
Retired Abbots	1
Priests: Diocesan Active in Diocese	148
Priests: Active Outside Diocese	11
Priests: Diocesan in Foreign Missions	1
Priests: Retired, Sick or Absent	34
Number of Diocesan Priests	194
Religious Priests in Diocese	101
Extern Priests in Diocese	10
Ordinations:	
Diocesan Priests	4
Religious Priests	1
Transitional Deacons	3
Permanent Deacons in Diocese	152
Total Brothers	92
Total Sisters	669
Parishes	
Parishes	120
With Resident Pastor:	
Resident Diocesan Priests	101
Resident Religious Priests	14
Without Resident Pastor:	
Administered by Priests	7
Missions	12
Professional Ministry Personnel:	
Brothers	3
Sisters	66
Lay Ministers	191
Welfare	
Catholic Hospitals	3
Total Assisted	669,656
Homes for the Aged	12
Total Assisted	7,359
Day Care and Extended Day Care Centers	4
Total Assisted	991
Specialized Homes	1
Total Assisted	1,300
Special Centers for Social Services	5
Total Assisted	25,011
Residential Care of Disabled	1
Total Assisted	120
Educational	
Diocesan Students in Other Seminaries	28
Total Seminarians	28
Colleges and Universities	3
Total Students	11,375
High Schools, Diocesan and Parish	4
Total Students	2,556
High Schools, Private	4
Total Students	3,279
Elementary Schools, Diocesan and Parish	56
Total Students	19,549
Catechesis/Religious Education:	
High School Students	4,723
Elementary Students	54,338
Total Students Under Catholic Instruction	95,848
Teachers in the Diocese:	
Priests	20
Brothers	24
Sisters	43
Lay Teachers	1,659
Vital Statistics	
Receptions into the Church:	
Infant Baptism Totals	10,284
Adult Baptism Totals	370
Received into Full Communion	999
First Communions	10,218
Confirmations	7,571
Marriages:	
Catholic	1,582
Interfaith	679
Total Marriages	2,261
Deaths	3,627
Total Catholic Population	591,706
Total Population	1,609,740

Former Bishops—Most Rev. MARTIN D. MCNAMARA, D.D., appt. first Bishop of Joliet; ord. Dec. 3, 1922; appt. Dec. 17, 1948; cons. March 7, 1949; died May 23, 1966.—Most Rev. ROMEO BLANCHETTE, D.D., appt. Auxiliary Bishop of Joliet and Titular Bishop of Maxita Feb. 8, 1965; cons. April 3, 1965; appt. Bishop of Joliet July 19, 1966; installed Aug. 31, 1966; resigned Jan. 30, 1979; died Jan. 10, 1982.

Chancery—*425 Summit St., Joliet, 60435.* Tel: 815-722-6606; Fax: 815-722-6602. Office Hours: Mon.-Fri. 8:30-4:30.

Vicar General—Most Rev. ROGER L. KAFFER, D.D., J.C.L.

Chancellor—Sr. JUDITH A. DAVIES, O.S.F.

Moderator of the Curia—Rev. JOSEPH TAPELLA.

Director of Administration—JAMES P. LYNCH.

Director of Finance—GUY A. SELL.

Matrimonial Tribunal—*310 Bridge St., Joliet, 60435.* Tel: 815-722-2256.

Judicial Vicar—Rev. JOSEPH TAPELLA, J.C.L.

Adjutant Judicial Vicar—Rev. MICHAEL GINTER, J.C.L.

Notaries—LORRAINE A'HEARN; SYLVIA CARBONI; MARIE SMEETS; BETTY JOUTRAS; HELEN MILCHERSKA.

Defender of the Bond—Sr. MARILYN PHILLIPS, O.S.F., Ph.D., J.C.D.

Judges—Revs. JOSEPH TAPELLA, J.C.L.; MICHAEL W. GINTER, J.C.L.; Mr. THOMAS E. KERBER, J.C.L.

Advocates—Mrs. VIRGINIA L. LAUTZ; Sr. CLARE VAN VOOREN, O.S.F.

Diocesan Offices and Directors

Board of Conciliation and Arbitration—*425 Summit St., Joliet, 60435.*

Campaign for Human Development—ELIZABETH FRANKLIN, *St. Charles Borromeo Pastoral Center, 402 S. Independence Blvd., Romeoville, 60441.* Tel: 815-834-4027.

Catholic Cemeteries—KEVIN DELABRE, Dir., *St. Charles Borromeo Pastoral Center, 402 S. Independence Blvd., Romeoville, 60441.* Tel: 815-838-0395.

Catholic Charities—Legal Title: *Catholic Charities of the Diocese of Joliet.* KATHLEEN MCGOWAN, Exec. Dir., *203 N. Ottawa St., Joliet, 60432.* Tel: 815-723-3405.

The Catholic Education Foundation of the Diocese of Joliet—MAME BYRNE, Foundation Dir., *St. Charles Borromeo Pastoral Center, 402 S. Independence Blvd., Romeoville, 60441.* Tel: 815-834-4033.

Catholic Relief Services—THOMAS GARLITZ, Dir., *St. Charles Center, 402 S. Independence Blvd., Romeoville, 60441.* Tel: 815-834-4026.

Council of Catholic Women—Mrs. JOAN DILLON, Dir., Office: *St. Charles Borromeo Pastoral Center, 402 S. Independence Blvd., Romeoville, 60441.* Tel: 815-834-4070.

Communications Office—*Chancery, 425 Summit St., Joliet, 60435.* Tel: 815-722-6606.

Cursillo Movement—Rev. JOSEPH SHIMANEK, Moderator, *St. Charles Borromeo Pastoral Center, 405 S. Independence Blvd., Romeoville, 60441.* Tel: 815-838-8100.

Deans—Rev. WILLIAM CONWAY, East Dupage; Rev. JOEL FORTIER, West Dupage Kendall; Rev. JAMES FITZGERALD, East Will; Rev. JAMES DOUGHERTY, West Will; Rev. CHARLES WHEELER, Kankakee-Grundy; Rev. F. LEE RYAN, Ford-Iroquois.

Development—KEVIN DELABRE, Dir., *St. Charles Borromeo Pastoral Center, 402 S. Independence Blvd., Romeoville, 60441.* Tel: 815-838-8515.

Coordinator for Health Affairs—Sr. JUDITH A. DAVIES, O.S.F., *Chancery, 425 Summit St., Joliet, 60435.* Tel: 815-722-6606.

Vicar for Religious—Sr. JEAN OKROI, I.B.V.M., *St. Charles Borromeo Pastoral Center, 402 S. Independence Blvd., Romeoville, 60441.* Tel: 815-834-4009.

Diaconate—Deacon WILL WORDEN, Dir., *St. Charles Borromeo Pastoral Center, 402 S. Independence Blvd., Romeoville, 60441.* Tel: 815-834-4091.

Divine Worship—Sr. SHARON MARIE STOLA, O.S.B., Dir., *St. Charles Borromeo Pastoral Center, 402 S. Independence Blvd., Romeoville, 60441.* Tel: 815-834-4010.

Ecumenism—Rev. STANLEY ORLIKIEWICZ, Dir., *St. Raymond Cathedral, 604 N. Raynor Ave., Joliet, 60435.* Tel: 815-722-6653.

Family Ministry—Dr. JAMES HEALY, Dir., *St. Charles Borromeo Pastoral Center, 402 S. Independence Blvd., Romeoville, 60441.* Tel: 815-838-5334.

Hispanic Ministry—Sr. JUDY CALLAHAN, B.V.M., Dir., *St. Charles Borromeo Center, 402 S. Independence Blvd., Romeoville, 60441.* Tel: 815-834-4037.

Catholic Explorer—MARY BRESLIN, Editor, Office: *St. Charles Borromeo Pastoral Center, 402 S. Independence Blvd., Romeoville, 60441.* Tel: 815-838-6475; Fax: 815-834-4068.

Diocesan Life Office—FRAN FORTIER, Dir., *St. Charles Borromeo Pastoral Center, 402 S. Independence Blvd., Romeoville, 60441.* Tel: 815-838-1002.

Marriage Encounter—Leadership Couple: LUIS TAMEZ; LISA TAMEZ, *1006 Windemere, Naperville, 60565.* Tel: 630-236-7438.

Marriage Preparation—Dr. JAMES HEALY, Dir., *St. Charles Borromeo Pastoral Center, 402 S. Independence Blvd., Romeoville, 60441.* Tel: 815-838-5334.

Ministry Formation—Dr. JEAN BOHR, Dir., *St. Charles Borromeo Pastoral Center, 402 S. Independence Blvd., Romeoville, 60441.* Tel: 815-834-4001.

College Campus Ministry—Bro. JOHN DORNBOS, C.F.C., Dir., *402 S. Independence Blvd., Romeoville, 60446-2264.* Tel: 815-834-4022.

Peace and Social Justice Ministry—THOMAS GARLITZ, Dir. Tel: 815-834-4026., *St. Charles Borromeo Pastoral Center, 402 S. Independence Blvd., Romeoville, 60441.*

Personnel—Mr. MICHAEL SVACH, Dir. Tel: 815-834-4077.

Presbyteral Council—Rev. ERNEST NORBECK, Pres., *425 Summit, Joliet, 60435.* Tel: 815-722-6606.

Propagation of the Faith—Rev. DAMIEN GRAZIANO, Dir., *15314 Summit St., Oakbrook Terrace, 60181.* Tel: 708-629-5810.

Religious Education—Sr. MARILYN ELLERT, O.S.F., Dir., *430 N. Center St., Joliet, 60435.* Tel: 815-727-6411.

Rural Life—Rev. LEE BACCHI, *St. Peter, 450 E. 3rd, P.O. Box 25, Clifton, 60927.* Tel: 815-694-2027.

St. Vincent de Paul Society—*213 Main St., West Chicago, 60185.* Tel: 630-293-9420.

Catholic Schools—Sr. HELEN JEAN KORMELINK, O.S.B., Supt., *425 Summit St., Joliet, 60435.* Tel: 815-727-4674.

Scouts—Rev. JOHN DOYLE, Office: *St. Anne Parish, 1702 N. Dearborn, Joilet, 60435.* Tel: 815-722-3222.

Stewardship—MARIANNE MURPHY, Dir., *St. Charles Borromeo Pastoral Center, 402 S. Independence Blvd., Romeoville, 60441.* Tel: 815-834-4030.

Vocations—Rev. JOHN REGAN, Dir., *St. Charles Borromeo, 402 S. Independence Blvd., Romeoville, 60441.* Tel: 815-834-4002.

CLERGY, PARISHES, MISSIONS AND PAROCHIAL SCHOOLS

CITY OF JOLIET
(Will County)

1—THE CATHEDRAL OF ST. RAYMOND (1917), Revs. Stanley Orlikiewicz; Joseph Siegel. In res., Rev. Joseph J. Tapella.
Res., 604 N. Raynor Ave., 60435. Tel: 815-722-6653; Fax: 815-722-6175.
School—713 Douglas St., 60435. Tel: 815-722-6626; Fax: 815-727-4668.
Sisters 1; Lay Teachers 27; Students 507.
Catechesis/Religious Programs—Students 260.

2—HOLY CROSS, Rev. Chris Groh.
Res., 901 Elizabeth St., 60435. Tel: 815-722-0785; Fax: 815-723-0679. [CEM]

3—HOLY FAMILY (1959), Rev. John L. Dennerlein.
Church—600 N. Brookforest Ave., Shorewood, 60431. Tel: 815-725-6880; Fax: 815-725-8649.
Res., 604 Edgebrook Dr., Shorewood, 60431. Tel: 815-725-6880.
School—Tel: 815-725-8149.
Lay Teachers 12; Students 290.
Catechesis/Religious Programs—Tel: 815-729-2243.
Students 515.

4—MOUNT CARMEL (1939) (Mexican American), Revs. Raymond Corkery, O.Carm.; Felix Rivera, O.Carm.
Res., 409 Irving St., 60432. Tel: 815-726-5208; Fax: 815-727-7225.
Catechesis/Religious Programs—Tel: 815-727-7187.
Students 330.

5—SACRED HEART (1886) (African American), Rev. Raymond C. Lescher; Deacon Ralph Bias.
Res., 337 S. Ottawa St., 60436. Tel: 815-722-0295; Fax: 815-722-6088.
Catechesis/Religious Programs—Students 45.

6—ST. AMBROSE (1965), Rev. John J. Doyle.
Res., 1711 Burry Cir., Crest Hill, 60435. Tel: 815-722-3748; Fax: 815-722-4950.
Catechesis/Religious Programs—Tel: 815-722-9193.
Students 230.

7—ST. ANNE (1953), Rev. John J. Doyle.
Res., 1702 N. Dearborn St., Crest Hill, 60435. Tel: 815-722-3222; Fax: 815-722-1955.
Catechesis/Religious Programs—Students 125.

8—ST. ANTHONY (1902) (Italian), Rev. Arthur LaPore.
Res., 100 N. Scott St., 60431-1210. Tel: 815-722-1057; Fax: 815-722-9805.

9—ST. BERNARD (1921), Rev. Richard Ross.
Res., 1313 Ridgewood Ave., 60432. Tel: 815-726-4474.
Catechesis/Religious Programs—Clustered with St. Mary Magdalene, Joliet. Tel: 815-722-7653.

10—SS. CYRIL AND METHODIUS (1900) (Slovak), Rev. Branislav Caniga, Admin.
Res., 704 Landau Ave., 60432. Tel: 815-722-3586; Fax: 815-722-7276.
Catechesis/Religious Programs—Tel: 815-723-0061.
Students 62.

11—ST. JOHN THE BAPTIST (1852) (Hispanic), Revs. Edward Shea, O.F.M.; Medard Buvala, O.F.M.; Deacon Jose Lopez. In res., Revs. Lawrence Jagelfeld, O.F.M.; Louis B. Antl, O.F.M.; Bros. John Sweeney, O.F.M.; Terence Santiapillai, O.F.M.
Res., 404 N. Hickory St., 60435. Tel: 815-727-4788; Fax: 815-740-1521. [CEM]
Catechesis/Religious Programs—403 N. Hickory St., 60435. Fax: 815-727-1729.
Students 265.

12—ST. JOSEPH (1891) (Slovenian), Rev. George F. Klepec.
Res., 416 N. Chicago St., 60432. Tel: 815-727-9378; Fax: 815-722-1213.
School—409 N. Scott St., 60432. Tel: 815-722-1005.
Sisters 2; Lay Teachers 12; Students 230.
Catechesis/Religious Programs—Students 60.

13—ST. JUDE (1954), Rev. James A. Schwab; Deacons Raymond Clark; William Hetzel.
Res., 2212 McDonough St., 60436. Tel: 815-725-2209; Fax: 815-741-8844.
School—2204 McDonough St., 60436. Tel: 815-729-0288; Fax: 815-729-0344.
Sisters of St. Francis of Mary Immaculate 1; Lay Teachers 15; Students 288.
Catechesis/Religious Programs—Tel: 815-729-0288; Fax: 815-729-0344.
Students 285.

14—ST. MARY. Closed. For inquiries for parish records contact the Chancery.

15—ST. MARY MAGDALENE (1953), Rev. Ron P. Neitzke.
Res., 127 S. Briggs St., 60433. Tel: 815-722-7653; Fax: 815-724-1720.
School—Tel: 815-727-9079; Fax: 815-727-2059.
Lay Teachers 8; Students 150.
Catechesis/Religious Programs—Students 125.

16—ST. MARY NATIVITY (1906) (Croatian), Revs. Christopher Groh; Dennis Paul; John T. McGeean.
Res., 706 N. Broadway, 60435. Tel: 815-726-4031; Fax: 815-727-4393.
School—702 N. Broadway, 60435. Tel: 815-722-8518.
Sisters of St. Francis of Christ the King 3; Lay Teachers 15; Students 311.
Catechesis/Religious Programs—Tel: 815-726-4073.
Students 130.

17—ST. PATRICK (1838), Rev. James M. Lennon; Deacons Paul Kolodziej; Charles Peterson. In res., Rev. Eugene Bucciferro.
Res., 710 W. Marion St., 60436. Tel: 815-727-4746; Fax: 815-727-4798.
School—110 Willow Ave., 60436. Tel: 815-726-2924; Fax: 815-726-9289.
Lay Teachers 15; Students 312.
Catechesis/Religious Programs—Tel: 815-727-4746.
Students 120.

18—ST. PAUL THE APOSTLE (1950), Revs. James Dougherty; Peter Jankowski; Deacons James Bouldin; William Bevan; Alex Krostenko.
Res., 18 Woodlawn Ave., 60435. Tel: 815-725-1527; Fax: 815-730-9907.
School—130 N. Woodlawn Ave., 60435. Tel: 815-725-3390; Fax: 815-725-3180.
Lay Teachers 15; Students 403.
Catechesis/Religious Programs—120 Woodlawn Ave., 60435. Tel: 815-725-6927.
Students 225.

19—ST. THADDEUS (1927) (Polish), Rev. Edward P. Rowland.
Res., 501 Liberty St., 60432. Tel: 815-727-7212.
Hall—510 Columbia St., 60432. Tel: 815-727-7806.

OUTSIDE THE CITY OF JOLIET

Addison, Du Page Co., St. Joseph (1956), Revs. James T. Kempfer; Michael Pennock; Deacons Dino J. Franch; Gabriel Gamboa.
Res., 330 E. Fullerton, 60101. Tel: 630-279-6553; Fax: 630-279-4925.
School—Tel: 630-279-4211; Fax: 630-279-4032. Mrs. Mary Rehfield, Prin.
Lay Teachers 14; Students 214.
Catechesis/Religious Programs—Tel: 630-832-5514. Mrs. Joni Giammarino, D.R.E.
Students 675.

St. Philip The Apostle (1963), Revs. Tom Sularz; Robert H. Noesen; Deacons Philip Hertz; James Dixon.
Res., 1223 W. Holtz Ave., 60101. Tel: 630-628-0900; Fax: 630-543-9858.
School—Tel: 630-543-4130; Fax: 630-458-8750.
Lay Teachers 16; Students 349.
Catechesis/Religious Programs—Tel: 630-543-1754.
Students 491.

Ashkum, Iroquois Co., Assumption of the Blessed Virgin Mary (1903), Rev. James Holup.
Res., N. Second St., Box 218, 60911. Tel: 815-698-2262; Fax: 815-698-2262. [CEM][JC 2]
Mission—L'Erable, Iroquois Co., St. John the Baptist, (1856) Box 218, 60911. Tel: 815-698-2262.
Catechesis/Religious Programs—Tel: 815-698-2224.
Students 130.

Aurora, Du Page Co., Our Lady of Mercy (1988), Revs. Hugh Fullmer; Albert Heidecke, Vicar. Pastoral Assocs.: Sr. Louise Staszewski, O.S.M.; Sr. Marianne Talian, O.S.M.
Res., 801 S. Eola Rd., 60504. Tel: 630-851-3444; Fax: 630-851-3468.
Catechesis/Religious Programs—Students 1,500.

Beaverville, Iroquois Co., St. Mary (1857) (French), Rev. Robert J. Coleman.
Res., 308 St. Charles St., P.O. Box 152, 60912. Tel: 815-435-2432. [CEM]
Catechesis/Religious Programs—Students 36.

Bensenville, Du Page Co., St. Alexis (1926), Revs. William Conway; Agustin Ortega; Sr. Laurina Kahne, C.S.J., Pastoral Assoc. In res., Rev. Raymond Davis.
Res., 400 W. Wood St., 60106. Tel: 708-766-3530; Fax: 708-766-3536.
Catechesis/Religious Programs—410 W. Wood St., 60106. Tel: 708-766-4417. Mrs. Trudy Anderson, D.R.E.
Students 411.

St. Charles Borromeo (1959), Rev. Don E. McLaughlin; Sr. Margaret Barrett, R.S.M., Pastoral Assoc.; Deacon Michael Principe.
Res., 1135 Daniel, 60106. Tel: 630-860-1120; Fax: 630-860-5029.
School—Tel: 630-766-0116; Fax: 630-766-0181.
Lay Teachers 9; Students 273.
Catechesis/Religious Programs—Tel: 630-766-8822; Fax: 630-766-0181.
Students 320.
Mission—Bensenville, Polish Catholic Pastoral Mission, 1135 Daniel Dr., 60106-3484. Tel: 630-860-7724. Rev. Janusz Zych, S.Ch., Dir.

Bloomingdale, DuPage Co., St. Isidore (1920), Revs. Joel F. Fortier; Peter Jarosz; Luis Gutierrez; Sr. Helen Mantovani, O.P., Pastoral Assoc.; Deacons Ken Jackson; John Freund; Terry Cummiskey; Dan Randolph.

Res., 427 W. Army Trail Rd., 60108. Tel: 630-529-3045; Fax: 630-529-2940. [CEM]
School—Tel: 630-529-9323; Fax: 630-529-2940.
Religious 1; Lay Teachers 17; Students 347.
Catechesis/Religious Programs—Tel: 630-529-9191.
Students 1,550.

Bolingbrook, Will Co., St. Dominic (1964), Revs. Mark Jendrysik; Thomas Cargo; Deacons Thomas Ross; John Knapstein; Robert Wallace; Paul Walen; James Kelly.
Res., 440 E. Briarcliff Rd., 60440. Tel: 630-739-5703; Fax: 630-739-2036.
School—420 E. Briarcliff Rd., 60440. Tel: 630-739-1633; Fax: 630-739-5989.
Sisters of St. Francis of Christ the King 1; Lay Teachers 16; Students 354.
Catechesis/Religious Programs—Tel: 630-739-2102.
Students 670.

St. Francis of Assisi (1980), Revs. David Hankus; Michael Pennock; Mario Quejadas; Deacons Raymond Hamilton; Terrance Hanley, Sr.; Rudulfo Molano; Thomas Fricke; Marco Lorero.
Res., 325 Whitewater Dr., 60440. Tel: 630-759-7588; Fax: 630-759-5257.
Catechesis/Religious Programs—Tel: 630-759-7611. D.R.E.: Sr. Mary Jane Petzel, O.S.F.; Sr. Jeanette Pitts, O.S.F.
Students 605.

Bourbonnais, Kankakee Co., Maternity of the Blessed Virgin Mary (1847), Revs. Charles Bolser, C.S.V.; John N. Peeters, C.S.V.; Donald F. Lund, C.S.V.; Deacons Euchrist J. Marcotte; Francis Chamness.
Res., 308 E. Marsile St., 60914. Tel: 815-933-8285; Fax: 815-933-8289. [CEM]
School—Tel: 815-933-7758; Fax: 815-933-1884.
Sisters of the Congregation of Notre Dame 1; Lay Teachers 15; Students 244.
Catechesis/Religious Programs—Tel: 815-933-8226; Fax: 815-933-1884.
Students 420.

Bradley, Kankakee Co., St. Joseph (1904), Rev. William G. Dewan; Deacons Bob LaMotte; Leon Fritz. In res., Rev. John Antczak.
Res., 211 N. Center Ave., 60915. Tel: 815-939-3573; Fax: 815-939-3138.
School—Tel: 815-933-8013; Fax: 815-933-2775.
Sisters 3; Lay Teachers 15; Students 309.
Catechesis/Religious Programs—247 N. Center Ave., 60915. Tel: 815-937-9340.
Students 265.
Convent—247 N. Center Ave., 60915. Tel: 815-932-0112.

Braidwood, Will Co., Immaculate Conception (1869) (Irish-Italian), Rev. Steven Bondi.
Res., 110 S. School St., 60408. Tel: 815-458-2125; Fax: 815-458-2836. [CEM]
Catechesis/Religious Programs—Students 300.

Cabery, Ford Co., St. Joseph (1867) (German), Rev. Richard F. Kostelz.
Res., 112 W. Main St., P.O. Box 77, 60919. Tel: 815-949-1568. [CEM]
Mission—Reddick, Kankakee Co., St. Mary, (1899) 216 E. Lincoln, Reddick, 60961.

Carol Stream, Du Page Co., Corpus Christi (1989), Rev. Charles A. Gemskie; Sr. M. Laurentia Fenlon, O.P., Pastoral Assoc. In res., Rev. Henry Wilkening, (Retired).
Res., 1415 Lies St., 60188-0453. Tel: 630-483-4673; Fax: 630-483-4679.
Catechesis/Religious Programs—Tel: 630-483-4222.
Students 986.

St. Luke (1963), Rev. Thomas Schutter; Sr. Barbara Rowan, S.S.S.F., Pastoral Assoc.
Res., 421 Cochise Ct., 60188. Tel: 630-668-1325; Fax: 630-668-1356.
Catechesis/Religious Programs—Tel: 630-665-2322.
Students 675.

Channahon, Will Co., St. Ann Parish (1990), Rev. Richard Smith.
Res., 25050 W. Eames St., 60410. Tel: 815-467-6962; Fax: 815-467-2320.
Catechesis/Religious Programs—Tel: 815-467-6992.
Students 350.

Chebanse, Iroquois Co., SS. Mary and Joseph's (1869), Rev. Lee F. Bacchi.
Res., 525 S. Chestnut, P.O. Box 5, 60922. Tel: 815-697-2654. [CEM]
Catechesis/Religious Programs—Students 85.

Clarendon Hills, Du Page Co., Notre Dame (1954), Revs. Robert J. Schuler; Venard Kommer, O.F.M.; Deacons Neill Carson; Frank Foys; David Lifka; Alan Symonanis.
Res., 64 Norfolk Ave., 60514. Tel: 630-654-3365; Fax: 630-654-8701.
School—Tel: 630-323-1642; Fax: 630-654-3255.
Lay Teachers 17; Students 285.
Catechesis/Religious Programs—Tel: 630-654-8701; Fax: 630-654-3365, Ext. 233.
Students 465.

Clifton, Iroquois Co., St. Peter's (1869), Rev. Lee F. Bacchi.
Res., 450 E. Third Ave., Box 25, 60927. Tel: 815-694-2027. [CEM][JC]
Catechesis/Religious Programs—Students 110.

Coal City, Grundy Co., Assumption (1889), Rev. Donald O'Connor, S.V.D.; Sr. Dorothy Wolsiffer, S.P., Pastoral Assoc.
Res., 245 S. Kankakee St., 60416. Tel: 815-634-4171; Fax: 815-634-4186.
Catechesis/Religious Programs—Tel: 815-634-8020. Patricia Keefer, D.R.E.
Students 400.

Darian, Du Page Co., Our Lady of Korean Martyrs Mission, Rev. Suk-Mo Hwang.
7121 Clarendon Hills Rd., Darien, 60561. Tel: 630-794-0203.

Darien, Du Page Co., Our Lady of Peace (1970), Revs. Alphonse Micka, M.I.C.; Anthony Kelpsas, M.I.C.; William Hayward, M.I.C.; Deacons Frank Bina; Paul Brachle; Walter Schmidt; Dennis Stolarz.
Res., 701 Plainfield Rd., 60561. Tel: 630-323-4333; Fax: 630-323-4354.
School—709 Plainfield Rd., 60561. Tel: 630-325-9220; Fax: 630-325-1995.
Sisters of St. Casimir 1; Lay Teachers 27; Students 560.
Catechesis/Religious Programs—Tel: 630-986-8430; 986-8446; Fax: 630-986-1214.
Students 708.

Our Lady of Mount Carmel (1970), Revs. Gavin Quinn, O.Carm.; Russell Gavin, O.Carm.; Kevin Shanley, O.Carm.; Lambert Zulkie, O.Carm.; Deacon John Farrell.
Res., 8404 Cass Ave., 60561. Tel: 630-852-3303; Fax: 630-852-5227.
Catechesis/Religious Programs—Tel: 630-963-3053.
Students 1,523.

Downers Grove, Du Page Co., Divine Savior (1968), Rev. Robert E. Pietras. In res., Rev. Leonard J. Guz.
Res., 6700 Main St., 60516. Tel: 630-969-1532; Fax: 630-969-1724.
Catechesis/Religious Programs—Tel: 630-969-1673.
Students 710.

St. Joseph (1907), Revs. Paul Hottinger; Jerome Kish.
Res., 4824 Highland, 60515. Tel: 630-964-0216; Fax: 630-964-0867.
School—Franklin & Highland, 60515. Tel: 630-969-4306; Fax: 630-969-3946.
Lay Teachers 22; Students 520.
Catechesis/Religious Programs—Tel: 630-971-1740; Fax: 630-964-0867.
Students 625.

St. Mary of Gostyn (1891), Revs. Thomas Paul; Keith V. Werling.
Res., 444 Wilson St., 60515. Tel: 630-969-1063; Fax: 630-969-1259.
School—444 Prairie Ave., 60515. Tel: 630-968-6155; Fax: 630-968-6208.
Felician Sisters 2; Lay Teachers 25; Students 587.
Catechesis/Religious Programs—Tel: 630-960-3565; Fax: 630-969-1289.
Students 842.

Elmhurst, Du Page Co., Immaculate Conception (1876), Revs. James Murphy; Raymond Garbin; Brad Baker; Deacons John S. Cole; Thomas Goebel.
Res., 134 Arthur St., 60126. Tel: 630-530-8515; Fax: 630-530-9346.
School—Tel: 630-530-3490; Fax: 630-530-9787. Helen Kwasmiewski, Prin.
Sisters 1; Lay Teachers 24; Students 635.
High School—217 Cottage Hill Ave., 60126. Tel: 630-530-3460; Fax: 630-530-2290. Sr. Maureen Field, I.H.M.
Lay Teachers 21; Students 291.
Catechesis/Religious Programs—Tel: 630-530-3480.
Students 625.

Mary, Queen of Heaven (1957), Rev. John Barrett. In res., Rev. Thomas Wolter; Deacons John Maloney; Thomas Nolan.
Res., 426 N. West Ave., 60126. Tel: 630-279-5700; Fax: 630-279-4667.
Catechesis/Religious Programs—442 N. West Ave., 60126. Tel: 630-832-8962.
Students 450.

Visitation (1953), Revs. Michael Lane; William DeSalvo; Deacons Dominic Cuzzone; Jay Janousek; Anthony Spatafore.
Res., 779 S. York St., 60126. Tel: 630-834-6700; Fax: 630-834-6711.
School—Tel: 630-834-4931; Fax: 630-834-4936.
Sisters of St. Adrian Dominican 4; Lay Teachers 23; Students 540.
Catechesis/Religious Programs—851 S. York, 60126. Tel: 630-279-7058.
Students 690.

Frankfort, Will Co., St. Anthony (1929), Revs. Thomas A. Corbino; John Ouper; Katie Augustynowicz, Pastoral Assoc.; Deacons Donald Berkey; Daniel Danahey; Richard Rosko.
Res., 7659 W. Sauk Trail, 60423. Tel: 815-469-3750; Fax: 815-469-6514.
Catechesis/Religious Programs—Tel: 815-469-6072; Fax: 815-469-6514.
Students 1,608.

Gibson City, Ford Co., Our Lady of Lourdes (1875), Rev. William F. Smith.
Res., 534 N. Wood St., 60936. Tel: 217-784-4671.
Catechesis/Religious Programs—Students 74.
Mission—Melvin, Ford Co., St. George.

Gilman, Iroquois Co., Immaculate Conception, Rev. John Balluff.
Res., 224 N. Secor St., 60938. Tel: 815-265-7236. [CEM]
Catechesis/Religious Programs—Tel: 815-265-7315.
Students 98.
Mission—Onarga, Iroquois Co., Our Lady of Guadalupe, 504 W. Seminary Ave., Onarga, 60955.

Glendale Heights, Du Page Co., St. Matthew (1960), Revs. David Dillon, O.Carm.; Felix Prior, O.Carm.; Deacon Ronald Darschewski.
Res., 1555 Glen Ellyn Rd., 60139. Tel: 630-469-6300; Fax: 630-469-6302.
School—Tel: 630-858-3112; Fax: 630-858-0623.
Lay Teachers 22; Students 402.
Catechesis/Religious Programs—Tel: 630-469-5178; Fax: 630-469-6302.
Students 715.

Glen Ellyn, Du Page Co., Queenship of Mary (1993) (Vietnamese), Rev. Nguyen Huy Quyen.
Res., 23W371 Armitage, 60137. Tel: 630-469-7494; Fax: 630-752-0332.
Catechesis/Religious Programs—Tel: 630-752-0332.
Students 123.

St. Petronille (1925), Revs. Michael A. O'Keefe; John Sullivan; Gerald Simonelli; Deacons Ronald Yurcus; John Spiezio. In res., Rev. Nguyen Huy Quyen.
Res., 425 Prospect Ave., 60137. Tel: 630-469-0404; Fax: 630-469-0412.
School—Tel: 630-469-5041; Fax: 630-469-5071.
Lay Teachers 33; Students 528.
Catechesis/Religious Programs—Tel: 630-858-3796; Fax: 630-858-6232.
Students 1,140.

St. James the Apostle (1965), Revs. John M. Sebahar; Jeff Stoneberg.
Res., 480 S. Park Blvd., 60137. Tel: 630-469-7540; Fax: 630-469-7590.
School—Tel: 630-469-8060; Fax: 630-469-1107.
Lay Teachers 25; Students 301.
Catechesis/Religious Programs—490 S. Park Blvd., 60137. Tel: 630-858-5646; Fax: 630-858-5687.
Students 900.

Goodrich, Kankakee Co., Sacred Heart (1895), Rev. Paul F. Jasinski, C.S.V.; Deacon John R. Reville.
Res., 588 S. 10000 W. Road, Bonfield, 60913-7019. Tel: 815-426-2221. [CEM]
Catechesis/Religious Programs—Tel: 815-426-2770.
Students 41.

Herscher, Kankakee Co., St. Margaret Mary, Rev. Ronald Hart.
Res., 207 E. Fifth St., 60941. Tel: 815-426-2153; Fax: 815-426-2136. [CEM]
Catechesis/Religious Programs—Tel: 815-426-2720.
Students 124.

Hinsdale, Du Page Co., St. Isaac Jogues (1930) (Irish-Italian), Revs. Theodore Weitzel; Matthew Hughes.
Res., 306 W. Fourth St., 60521. Tel: 630-323-1248; Fax: 630-323-6373.
School—Tel: 630-323-3244; Fax: 630-655-6676.
Religious 1; Lay Teachers 42; Students 686.
Catechesis/Religious Programs—421 S. Clay St., 60521. Tel: 630-323-0265.
Students 1,030.

Hopkins Park, Kankakee Co., Sacred Heart (1939) (African American), Rev. Denis E. White.
Res. & Mailing Address: 119 Market St., Momence, 60954. Tel: 815-944-5562; Fax: 815-472-3043.
Catechesis/Religious Programs—16485 E. Birch, P.O. Box 557, 60944.
Students 7.

Irwin, Kankakee Co., St. James The Apostle, Rev. Ronald Hart.
Res., 4372 Main St., Kankakee, 60901. Tel: 815-933-8807; Fax: 815-426-2136. [CEM]

Catechesis/Religious Programs—Tel: 815-933-5443.
Students 74.

Itasca, Du Page Co., St. Andrew Kim (1981) (Korean), Rev. Mathias Lee.
Res., 1275 Arlington Hts. Rd., 60143. Tel: 630-250-0576; Fax: 630-250-2502.

St. Peter the Apostle (1956), Revs. Donald P. Pock; Joseph Stalzer.
Res., 524 N. Rush St., 60143-1698. Tel: 630-773-1272; Fax: 630-773-1720.
School—500 N. Cherry St., 60143-1699. Tel: 630-773-1979; Fax: 630-773-2826.
Lay Teachers 12; Students 226.
Catechesis/Religious Programs—Tel: 630-773-1959; Fax: 630-773-2624.
Students 307.

Kankakee, Kankakee Co.,

1—St. Martin of Tours, (1950), Rev. Dennis F. Settles.
Res., 953 S. Ninth Ave., 60901. Tel: 815-933-7177; Fax: 815-933-2171. [JC]
School—907 S. Ninth Ave., 60901. Tel: 815-932-7911; Fax: 815-932-7296.
Lay Teachers 11; Students 161.
Catechesis/Religious Programs—Students 225.

2—St. Patrick, (1893) (Irish), Revs. Richard Pighini, C.S.V.; Donald R. Wehnert. Pastoral Assocs.: Marilyn Mulcahy; Deacon Joseph Cotugno; Sr. Theresa Galvan, C.N.D., Pastoral Min. In res., Revs. Joseph Tremonti, C.S.V.; Francis Cerwronka, C.S.V.; Bro. Daniel Belanger, C.S.V.
Res., 428 S. Indiana Ave., 60901. Tel: 815-932-6716; Fax: 815-932-2585.
School—Tel: 815-932-8124; Fax: 815-932-0485.
Lay Teachers 14; Students 235.
Catechesis/Religious Programs—Students 206.

3—St. Rose of Lima, (1855), Rev. Charles Wheeler.
Res., 486 W. Merchant St., 60901. Tel: 815-933-9391; Fax: 815-933-9393.
Catechesis/Religious Programs—Students 77.

4—St. Stanislaus, (Polish). Closed. For inquiries for parish records contact the Chancery.

5—St. Teresa, (1949), Rev. Anthony Taschetta. Pastoral Assocs.: Barbara Staniszeski; Sr. Mary McElmeel, B.V.M.
Res., 361 N. St. Joseph Ave., 60901. Tel: 815-933-7683; Fax: 815-933-7692.
Lisieux Pastoral Center—371 St. Joseph Ave., 60901. Tel: 815-939-2913.
School—School and Religious Program combined with St. Patrick, Kankakee. Tel: 815-932-8124.

Kinsman, Grundy Co., Sacred Heart (1880), Rev. Robert Maternoski, Admin.
Res., 219 Emmett St., P.O. Box 824, 60437. Tel: 815-392-4245; Fax: 815-392-4307. [JC]
Catechesis/Religious Programs—Students 54.

Lisle, Du Page Co., St. Joan of Arc (1924), Revs. Gerald Tivy; Kenneth Zigmond, O.S.B.; Thomas Bothroyd; Deacons Denis Stucko; Joseph Dalpiaz.
Office: 820 Division St., 60532. Tel: 630-963-4500; Fax: 630-963-4568.
School—Tel: 630-969-1732; Fax: 630-963-9070.
Lay Teachers 24; Students 692.
Catechesis/Religious Programs—Students 450.

Lockport, Will Co.,

1—St. Bernard, (1978), Rev. Richard B. Prodehl; Sr. Mary Carr, O.P., Pastoral Assoc.
Res., 14135 Parker Rd., 60441. Tel: 708-301-3020; Fax: 708-301-0738.
Catechesis/Religious Programs—14724 S. Arboretum Dr., 60441. Tel: 708-301-6952; Fax: 708-301-8870.
Students 882.

2—St. Dennis, (1846), Revs. Jim Curtin; Thomson Panakal; Sr. Joanne Vallaro, C.S.J., Pastoral Assoc.; Deacons Rob Weierman; William Uffman.
Res., 1214 Hamilton St., 60441. Tel: 815-838-0704; Fax: 815-838-2401.
School—1201 S. Washington St., 60441. Tel: 815-838-4494; Fax: 815-838-5435.
Lay Teachers 11; Students 260.
Catechesis/Religious Programs—Students 852.

3—St. John Vianney, (1958), Rev. Andrew L. Buczyna.
Res., 401 Brassel, 60441. Tel: 815-723-3291.
Catechesis/Religious Programs—Students 15.

4—St. Joseph, (1868), Rev. Thomas McGivney, Jr.; Dr. Jeanne M. Cosgrove, Pastoral Assoc. In res., Rev. Don Harkabus.
Res., 410 S. Jefferson St., 60441. Tel: 815-838-0187; Fax: 815-838-5379.
School—529 Madison, 60441. Tel: 815-838-8173; Fax: 815-838-0504.
Franciscan Sisters of the Sacred Heart 2; Lay Teachers 11; Students 265.
Catechesis/Religious Programs—529 Madison St., 60441. Tel: 815-838-2112.
Students 322.
Convent—531 E. Fourth St., 60441. Tel: 815-838-0186.

5—Our Mother of Good Counsel, (1996), Revs. Thomas Osborne, O.S.A.; Donald Lewandowski, O.S.A.
Church—16043 S. Bell Rd., 60441. Tel: 708-301-6246; Fax: 708-301-6356.
Catechesis/Religious Programs—Students 460.

Lombard, Du Page Co., Christ the King (1960), Rev. James Dvorscak; Deacon Wayne Storrs.
Res., 1501 S. Main St., 60148. Tel: 630-629-1717; Fax: 630-629-1717.
School—Tel: 630-627-0640; Fax: 630-627-0640.
Lay Teachers 16; Students 183.
Catechesis/Religious Programs—Tel: 630-629-1717, Ext. 16; Fax: 630-629-1717, Ext. 6.
Students 340.

Sacred Heart (1912), Revs. Arno A. Dennerlein; Jess Testa; Deacon Thomas Bailey.
Res., 114 S. Elizabeth St., 60148. Tel: 630-627-0687; Fax: 630-627-0688.
School—Tel: 630-629-0536; Fax: 630-629-4752.
Lay Teachers 11; Students 300.
Catechesis/Religious Programs—328 W. Maple St., 60148. Tel: 630-495-0843.
Students 489.

St. Pius X (1954), Revs. Herbert Essig; Gregory Rothfuchs; Sr. Pauline Schutz, O.S.F., Pastoral Assoc.; Deacons Thomas Rachubinski; Ron Knecht; William Crane; Larry Lissak.
Res., 1025 E. Madison, 60148. Tel: 630-627-4526; Fax: 630-495-5926.
School—Tel: 630-627-2353; Fax: 630-627-1810. Patricia Walther, Prin.
Lay Teachers 29; Students 464.
Catechesis/Religious Programs—Tel: 630-627-1551. Sr. Helen Susan, D.R.E.
Students 520.

Manhattan, Will Co., St. Joseph (1891), Rev. Edward J. O'Malley.
Res., 235 W. North, P.O. Box 25, 60442. Tel: 815-478-3341; Fax: 815-478-5258. [CEM 2]
School—Tel: 815-478-3951; Fax: 815-478-7412.
Lay Teachers 11; Students 133.
Catechesis/Religious Programs—Tel: 815-478-4419.
Students 395.

Manteno, Kankakee Co., St. Joseph (1855), Rev. Ed Grotovsky; Deacons Francis Henrisey; John Hindes; Richard Balgeman.
Res., 207 S. Main St., 60950. Tel: 815-468-3403; Fax: 815-468-7089. [CEM][JC]
Catechesis/Religious Programs—Tel: 815-468-8116.
Students 384.

Martinton, Iroquois Co., St. Martin (1899), Rev. Robert J. Coleman.
Res., P.O. Box 152, Beaverville, 60912. Tel: 815-435-2432. [CEM]
Catechesis/Religious Programs—Students 28.

Minooka, Grundy Co., St. Mary (1862) (Irish), Rev. Mark Fracaro.
Res., 303 St. Mary St., P.O. Box 456, 60447. Tel: 815-467-2233; Fax: 815-467-1760. [CEM]
Catechesis/Religious Programs—Tel: 815-467-2769.
Students 529.

Mokena, Will Co., St. Mary Church (1864), Revs. James Fitzgerald; Scott McCawley; Sr. Dolores Zemont, O.S.F., Pastoral Assoc.; Deacons Jim Fitzgerald; Donald Bernardin.
Res., 19517 S. 115th Ave., P.O. Box 2, 60448. Tel: 708-479-3380; Fax: 708-479-8403.
School—Tel: 708-479-3383; Fax: 708-479-4985.
Franciscan Sisters of the Sacred Heart 1; Lay Teachers 10; Students 309.
Catechesis/Religious Programs—11409 W. 195th St., 60448. Tel: 708-479-3385.
Students 1,650.

Momence, Kankakee Co., St. Patrick (1859), Revs. Denis E. White; Michael Powell, Temporary Admin.; Deacon Dan Hessling.
Res., 119 Market St., 60954. Tel: 815-472-2864; Fax: 815-472-3043. [CEM]
School—404 W. Second St., 60954. Tel: 815-472-2469.
Lay Teachers 5; Students 120.
Catechesis/Religious Programs—Students 170.

Monee, Will Co., St. Boniface (1868) (Irish-Polish), Rev. Mark Menezes; Deacon Robert Jossey.
Res., 5301 W. Main St., P.O. Box 217, 60449. Tel: 708-534-9682; Fax: 708-534-9683.
Catechesis/Religious Programs—Students 140.

Morris, Grundy Co., Immaculate Conception of the Blessed Virgin Mary (1852), Rev. Robert A. Hoffenkamp; Deacon Robert Stansberry, Jr.
Res., 516 E. Jackson St., 60450. Tel: 815-942-0620; Fax: 815-942-3171. [CEM]
School—Tel: 815-942-4111; Fax: 815-942-5094.
Lay Teachers 15; Students 254.
Catechesis/Religious Programs—505 E. North St., 60450. Tel: 815-942-4177.
Students 369.

Naperville, DuPage Co.,

1—Holy Spirit Catholic Community, (1998), Rev. Richard Bennett.
Res., 2228 Snow Creek Rd., 60564. Tel: 630-922-0081; Fax: 630-922-0085.
Catechesis/Religious Programs—Students 1,141.

2—St. Elizabeth Seton, Du Page Co., (1986), Revs. Ernest Norbeck; James Radek; Deacons Thomas Sheridan; Bart Federici.
Res., 2220 Lisson Rd., 60565. Tel: 630-416-3325; Fax: 630-416-3642.
Catechesis/Religious Programs—Tel: 630-416-1992; Fax: 630-416-4086.
Students 1,833.

3—Sts. Peter and Paul, (1856), Revs. James Burnett; Gregor Gorsic; Gordon Mahoney; Slawomir Ignasik. Pastoral Assocs.: Sr. Aniceta Skube, O.P.; Sr. Kathleen Hook, O.S.F.; Deacons William Girard; Manuel J. Solis.
Res., 36 N. Ellsworth St., 60540. Tel: 630-355-1081; Fax: 630-355-1179. [CEM]
School—201 E. Franklin, 60540. Tel: 630-355-0113; Fax: 630-355-9803. Mr. Frank Glowaty, Prin.
Sisters 2; Lay Teachers 25; Students 622.
Catechesis/Religious Programs—36 N. Ellsworth St., Ste. 104, 60540. Tel: 630-357-2436; Fax: 630-357-2458.
Students 1,250.

4—St. Raphael, (1963), Revs. William E. Donnelly; Philip Danaher; Deacons William Blessing; John McHugh; Andrew Repak; Charles Woods.
Mailing Address: 1215 Modaff Rd., 60540-7818. Tel: 630-355-4545; Fax: 630-355-7470.
Res., 416 Gartner, 60540. Tel: 630-355-4545; Fax: 630-355-7470.
School—Tel: 630-355-4545, Ext. 135; Fax: 630-428-4974.
Lay Teachers 22; Students 314.
Catechesis/Religious Programs—Tel: 630-355-4545, Ext. 121.
Students 2,516.

5—St. Margaret Mary, (1980), Revs. William J. O'Shea; Danilo Soriano, C.P.; Sr. Madelyn Gould, S.S.S.F., Pastoral Assoc.; Deacons Kenneth J. Miles; Frederick E. Straub.
1450 Green Trails Dr., 60540. Tel: 630-369-0777; Fax: 630-369-1493.
Catechesis/Religious Programs—Tel: 630-369-0833.
Students 1,743.

6—St. Thomas the Apostle, (1984), Revs. Donald Kenny; Richard Lundgren; Sr. Ann James Murray, O.S.F., Pastoral Assoc.; Deacons William Worden; Charles Lane.
Res., 1500 Brookdale Rd., 60563. Tel: 630-355-8980; Fax: 630-355-0521.
Catechesis/Religious Programs—Tel: 630-305-6318.
Students 1,753.

New Lenox, Will Co., St. Jude (1934), Revs. Michael Slattery, O.S.A.; David Brecht, O.S.A.; R. William Sullivan, O.S.A.; John P. Murphy, O.S.A. In res., Rev. John Merkelis, O.S.A.; Bro. Robert Fisher, O.S.A.; Deacons Robert Fitt; William Ciston.
Res., 241 W. Second Ave., 60451. Tel: 815-485-8049; Fax: 815-485-7754.
School—Tel: 815-485-2549; Fax: 815-485-7754.
Lay Teachers 12; Students 274.
Catechesis/Religious Programs—Tel: 815-485-4852.
Students 1,574.

Oakbrook Terrace, DuPage Co., Ascension of Our Lord (1967), Rev. J. Damien Graziano; Roger Grant, Pastoral Assoc.; Deacon William J. Tansey, M.D.
Res., 1 S 314 Summit Ave., 60181. Tel: 630-629-5810; Fax: 630-953-8251.
Catechesis/Religious Programs—Tel: 630-629-5810, Ext. 215; 216.
Students 225.

Oswego, Kendall Co., St. Anne (1963), Revs. Daniel F. Stempora; Robert Collogan; Deacons David Brockman; William Dunn.
Res., 551 Boulder Hill Pass, P.O. Box 670, 60543. Tel: 630-554-3331; Fax: 630-554-0530.
Catechesis/Religious Programs—(Grades K-8). Tel: 630-554-1425.
Students 1,137.

Park Forest, Will Co., St. Mary (1953), Rev. John Ryan.
Res., 212 Monee Rd., 60466. Tel: 708-747-1600; Fax: 708-748-6907.
School—227 Monee Rd., 60466-2403. Tel: 708-748-6686.
Franciscan Sisters of the Sacred Heart 1; Lay Teachers 10; Students 197.

Paxton, Ford Co., St. Mary, Rev. James Heramb.
Res., 407 W. Pells, 60957. Tel: 217-379-4033.
Mission—Loda, Iroquois Co., St. Joseph, c/o St. Mary, 407 W. Pells, 60957.
Catechesis/Religious Programs—Students 153.

Peotone, Will Co., St. Paul the Apostle (1961), Rev. Michael Ginter.
Res., 501 N. Conrad St., P.O. Box 700, 60468-0700. Tel: 708-258-6917; Fax: 708-258-3031.
Catechesis/Religious Programs—Tel: 708-258-9580.
Students 260.

Piper City, Ford Co., St. Peter (1887), Rev. John Balluff.
Res. & Mailing Address: 212 Pine St., 60959. Tel: 815-686-2595.
Mission—Roberts, Immaculate Conception. [CEM 2]

Plainfield, Will Co., St. Mary Immaculate (1909), Revs. Anthony A. Nugent; Richard Dochstader. Pastoral Assocs.: Sr. Margaret Ann Spagnola, O.S.M.; David Medow; Deacons James Sossong; Terry Sakfo; James Walters; Jerry Krupowicz.
Mailing Address: 129 S. Division St. (Rte. 59), 60544.
Res., 116 Frederick, 60544. Tel: 815-436-2651; Fax: 815-436-5017. [CEM]
School—129 S. Division St., 60544-8806. Tel: 815-436-3953.
Lay Teachers 21; Students 500.
Catechesis/Religious Programs—Tel: 815-436-4501.
Students 1,641.

Plano, Kendall Co., St. Mary (1885), Revs. Jerome A. Zalonis, M.I.C.; Boniface Vaisnoras, M.I.C.; Deacons Dale Metcalf; Santos Martinez.
Res., 901 N. Center St., 60545. Tel: 630-552-3448; Fax: 630-552-3450. [CEM]
School—817 N. Center Ave., 60545. Tel: 630-552-3345; Fax: 630-552-4385.
Lay Teachers 9; Students 258.
Catechesis/Religious Programs—810 N. Center Ave., 60545. Tel: 630-552-1505. Sr. Kathryn Frankovich, O.S.F., D.R.E.
Students 550.
Mission—Bristol, Kendall Co., St. Patrick, 406 Walnut St., Yorkville, 60560. Tel: 708-553-6671; Fax: 708-553-2695. [CEM]

Rockdale, Will Co., St. Joseph (1914), Rev. John J. Zanoni.
Res., 1329 Belleview Ave., 60436. Tel: 815-725-4469.
Catechesis/Religious Programs—Tel: 815-729-9149.
Students 70.

Romeoville, Will Co., St. Andrew the Apostle (1959), Revs. Richard Walsh; Millard O'Keefe; Deacons David Raskowski; Stephen Clancy. In res., Rev. John Driscoll; Deacon Leo Borkowicz.
Res., 219 Arlington Dr., 60446. Tel: 815-886-4165; Fax: 815-886-6119.
School—Tel: 815-293-2016.
Sisters 2; Lay Teachers 13; Students 305.
Catechesis/Religious Programs—505 Kingston Dr., 60446. Tel: 815-886-5962.
Students 701.

Roselle, Du Page Co., St. Walter (1946), Revs. Francis B. McDonald; John Guiney, S.M.A.; Doug Hauber; Deacons Ron Searls; Evan Lysaght.
Res., 130 W. Pine Ave., 60172. Tel: 630-894-2461; Fax: 630-582-4206.
School—201 W. Maple Ave., 60172. Tel: 630-529-1721; Fax: 630-529-9290.
Lay Teachers 28; Students 758.
Catechesis/Religious Programs—140 W. Pine, 60172. Tel: 630-894-5880; Fax: 630-582-4206. Sr. Jane Haslwanter, B.V.M., D.R.E.
Students 1,003.

St. Anne, Kankakee Co., St. Anne (1872), Rev. James Fanale, C.S.V.
Res., 230 N. Sixth Ave., 60964. Tel: 815-427-8265.
Catechesis/Religious Programs—Students 55.

St. George, Kankakee Co., St. George (1853) (French Canadian), Rev. Kenneth Yarno, C.S.V.
Res., 5272 E. 5000 North Rd., Bourbonnais, 60914-9725. Tel: 815-939-1851; Fax: 815-939-2777. [CEM]
Catechesis/Religious Programs—Students 56.

South Wilmington, Grundy Co., St. Lawrence (1904), Rev. Robert Maternoski; Deacon Joseph Riggi.
Res., 165 Rice St., Box 190, 60474. Tel: 815-237-2230; Fax: 815-237-2201.
Catechesis/Religious Programs—Students 100.

Steger, Will Co., St. Liborius (1902), Revs. Joseph Burns; Roger Kutzner; Deacon Len Olszak.
Res., 71 W. 35th St., 60475. Tel: 708-754-1363; Fax: 708-754-7577.
School—(Steger Campus) 3436 Halsted Blvd., 60475. Tel: 708-754-0192.
Lay Teachers 15; Students 246.
Catechesis/Religious Programs—Tel: 708-754-3460.
Students 440.

Villa Park, Du Page Co., St. Alexander (1924), Rev. Tuan Van Nguyen; Deacons John Boyle; Christopher Cochran; James Krueger; John Gibbons.
Res., 300 S. Cornell Ave., 60181. Tel: 630-833-7730; Fax: 630-833-3127.
School—136 S. Cornell Ave., 60181. Tel: 630-834-3787; Fax: 630-834-1961.
Lay Teachers 19; Students 300.
Catechesis/Religious Programs—130 S. Cornell Ave., 60181. Tel: 630-832-0506.
Students 410.

St. John the Apostle (1959), Rev. Robert Duda.
Res., 330 N. Westmore, 60181. Tel: 630-279-7404; Fax: 630-530-9910.
Catechesis/Religious Programs—Tel: 630-832-7588; Fax: 630-832-7588.
Students 125.

Warrenville, Du Page Co., St. Irene (1927), Rev. James Antiporek. Pastoral Assocs.: Sr. Roseann Eck, C.S.J.; Annette Kubalanza; Deacons William Murphy; Robert True; Joseph Urso.
Res., 28 W. 441 Warrenville Rd., 60555. Tel: 630-393-2400; Fax: 630-393-9680.
School—3S601 Warren Ave., 60555. Tel: 630-393-9303. Beverly Murphy, Prin.
Lay Teachers 13; Students 238.
Catechesis/Religious Programs—Tel: 630-393-2400, Ext. 22.
Students 353.

Watseka, Iroquois Co., St. Edmund (1872), Rev. F. Lee Ryan.
Res., 219 E. Locust St., 60970. Tel: 815-432-3274.
Catechesis/Religious Programs—Tel: 815-432-5569.
Students 193.
Mission—Crescent City, Iroquois Co., St. Joseph, P.O. Box 173, 60928.

Wayne, Du Page Co., Resurrection, Rev. Laurian Janicki, O.F.M.
Res., 30 W. 350 Army Tr., 60184. Tel: 630-289-5400; Fax: 630-289-5407.
Catechesis/Religious Programs—Tel: 630-289-5400, Ext. 215; 216.
Students 724.

West Chicago, Du Page Co., St. Mary (1894), Revs. Vernon Arseneau; Reynaldo Treyes.
Res., 140 N. Oakwood Ave., 60185. Tel: 630-231-0013; Fax: 630-293-2671. [CEM]
School—147 Garden St., 60185. Tel: 630-231-1776.
Lay Teachers 12; Students 221.
Catechesis/Religious Programs—Tel: 630-231-5704.
Students 410.

Westmont, Du Page Co., Holy Trinity (1938), Revs. James A. Nowak; John Sponder.
Res., 111 S. Cass Ave., 60559. Tel: 630-968-1366; Fax: 630-968-7846.
School—108 S. Linden, 60559. Tel: 630-971-0184; Fax: 630-971-1175.
Lay Teachers 18; Students 405.
Catechesis/Religious Programs—Tel: 630-968-5978.
Students 380.

Wheaton, Du Page Co., St. Daniel the Prophet Church (1989), Rev. Thomas J. White. Pastoral Assocs.: Sr. Josephine Sincak; Sr. Mary Potthast; Sr. Margaret M. Ivers, I.B.V.M.
Res., 231 Danada Dr., 60187. Tel: 630-682-5003; Fax: 630-682-5004.
Catechesis/Religious Programs—Tel: 630-682-5002.
Students 724.

St. Mark (1962), Rev. John Ducaji.
Res., 303 E. Parkway Dr., 60187. Tel: 630-665-0030; Fax: 630-665-0303.
Catechesis/Religious Programs—300 E. Cole St., 60187. Tel: 630-668-4614.
Students 145.

St. Michael (1882), Revs. Martin Gabel; Raymond Stonich; M. Selvan Augustine, S.J.; Deacons John Cozzens; William Stroner; David Meador.
Res., 315 W. Illinois St., 60187. Tel: 630-665-2250; Fax: 630-665-6820. [CEM]
School—314 W. Willow Ave., 60187. Tel: 630-653-1454; Fax: 630-665-1491.
Notre Dame Sisters of Toledo 2; Lay Teachers 27; Students 620.
Catechesis/Religious Programs—Tel: 630-682-3650; Fax: 630-690-3324.
Students 979.

Wilmington, Will Co., St. Rose (1844), Rev. Frank Vitus; Sr. Ann Ellen Quirk, B.V.M., Pastoral Assoc.; Deacon Don Dyer.
Res., 603 S. Main St., 60481. Tel: 815-476-7491; Fax: 815-476-1085. [CEM]
School—Tel: 815-476-6220; Fax: 815-476-2154.
Lay Teachers 11; Students 190.
Catechesis/Religious Programs—Students 181.

Wilton Center, Will Co., St. Patrick (1905) (Irish), Rev. S. C. Giunta.
Res., 14936 Wilmington Peotone Rd., Manhattan, 60442. Tel: 815-478-3440. [CEM]
Catechesis/Religious Programs—Students 33.

Winfield, Du Page Co., St. John the Baptist (1867), Revs. Guy Vaccaro; Michael Valente; John Bosco Panakal; Deacon Andrew Nielo.
Res., O.S. 233 Church St., 60190. Tel: 630-668-0918; Fax: 630-668-1074. [CEM]
School—O.S. 259 Church St., 60190. Tel: 630-668-2625; Fax: 630-668-7176. Carl Macaione, Prin.
Lay Teachers 20; Students 333.
Catechesis/Religious Programs—Tel: 630-682-4400; Fax: 630-668-1074. Maureen Brennan, D.R.E.
Students 950.

Wood Dale, Du Page Co., Holy Ghost (1946), Rev. Kevin R. Farrell.
Res., 254 N. Wood Dale Rd., 60191. Tel: 630-860-2975; Fax: 630-860-9482.
School—Tel: 630-766-4508; Fax: 630-860-7697.
Lay Teachers 19; Students 233.
Catechesis/Religious Programs—Tel: 630-766-1045.
Students 525.

Woodridge, Du Page Co., Christ The Servant Parish (1990), Rev. Dennis Lewandowski.
Mailing Address: 8700 Havens Dr., 60517. Tel: 630-910-0770; Fax: 630-910-6060.
Catechesis/Religious Programs—Students 88.

St. Scholastica (1962), Revs. Gerald Riva; David Lawrence; Sr. Regina Ann Weissmann, O.S.B., Pastoral Assoc.; Deacons Roger Schmith; Robert Varra.
Res., 7800 S. Janes Ave., 60517. Tel: 630-985-2351; Fax: 630-985-8770.
School—Tel: 630-985-2515; Fax: 630-985-2395. Gail Kueper, Prin.
Lay Teachers 12; Students 293.
Catechesis/Religious Programs—7720 Janes Ave., 60517. Tel: 630-985-9255. Sr. Suzanne Lesniewski, O.S.F., D.R.E.
Students 888.

Chaplains of Public Institutions

JOLIET. *Dept. of Corrections* McDonough St., 60436. Rev. Richard Ross.
Illinois State Penitentiary 404 N. Hickory St., P.O. Box 112, 60435. Jerry Bowman.
Illinois Youth Commission, Reception and Diagnostic Center McDonough St., 60436. Deacon Joseph O'Connor.
Joliet Correctional Depot Collins St. Revs. John J. Doyle; Joseph F. Kilas.
Silver Cross Hospital 1200 Maple Rd., 60432. Rev. Andrew L. Buczyna.

ELMHURST. *Elmhurst Memorial Hospital* 200 Berteau Ave., 60126. Rev. Thomas Wolter.

HINSDALE. *Hinsdale Hospital* 120 N. Oak, 60521. Rev. James Walton, O.F.M.

KANKAKEE. *Riverside Medical Center* 350 N. Wells, 60901. Rev. John Antczak.
Shapiro Development Center 100 E. Jeffrey, 60901. Rev. Richard Jacklin.

NAPERVILLE. *Edward Hospital* S. Washington St., 60540. Rev. Philip Dedera.

WINFIELD. *Central DuPage Hospital* 0N025 Winfield, 60190. Rev. Michael Valente.

On Duty Outside the Diocese:
Reverend Fathers—
Butters, Joseph, St. Patrick, 501 Fair Oaks Ave., Box 860, Arroyo Grande, CA 93421
Caruso, Carmen A., St. Isabel, 3559 Sanibel-Captiva Rd., Sanibel, FL 33957
Dieter, Thomas, St. Catherine of Siena, 1955 S. Belcher Rd., Clearwater, FL 34624
Hemrick, Eugene F., U.S.C.C., Department of Education, 1312 Massachusetts, N.W., Washington, DC 20005
Howlin, Carroll, Good Shepherd Catholic Services, P.O. Box 550, Whitley City, KS 42653
Meis, J. Anthony, St. Louis, MO
Moriarty, John, Society of St. James the Apostle, 24 Clark St., Boston, MA 02109
Schoenstene, Robert L., St. Mary of the Lake Seminary, Mundelein, IL 60060

Graduate Studies:
Reverend Fathers—
Martis, Douglas, L'Institut Catholique, Rome
Milota, Thomas, North American College, Rome

Absent on Sick Leave:
Reverend Fathers—
Best, Richard
Joyce, Edwin
Massacavalo, Bruno

Absent on Leave:
Reverend Fathers—
Blanchette, Michael
Collins, Michael J.

Retired:
Reverend Monsignors—
Podesta, John F., 5555 N. Sheridan Rd., Apt. 1412, Chicago, IL 60640
Reverend Fathers—
Bowden, Lloyd, 115 N. May St., Joliet, IL 60540
Corley, Thomas, St. John Vianney Villa, 1464 Green Trails Dr., Naperville, IL 60450
Cullen, William, 6267 Trinity Dr., #2D, Lisle, IL 60532
Davis, Raymond, St. Alexis, 400 W. Wood St., Bensenville, IL 60106-2496
Driscoll, John, St. Andrew the Apostle, 219 Arlington Dr., Romeoville, IL 60446
Duffy, James
Fischer, Lowell, Motherhouse, 9201 W. St. Francis Rd., Frankfort, IL 60423
Fleming, Thomas, St. John Vianney Villa, 1464 Green Trails Dr., Naperville, IL 60540
Flynn, George, 2012E Lincoln, Apt. 210, Bloomington, IL 61701
Formusa, Salvatore, P.O. Box 46010, Chicago, IL 60046
Hurley, George, 5 Oak Brook Dr., Oakbrook, IL 60521-1314
Kloepfer, John S., Box 1742, Clarksville, VA 23927
Maher, Arthur, 1115 Lorraine Rd., #326, Wheaton, IL 60187
Memenas, Vytas, 29 S. Delaplaine Rd., Riverside, IL 60546
Morrissette, Dominic, P.O. Box 851, Indian Springs, NV 89018
Mulloy, Sylvester, St. Patrick Residence, 1400 Brookdale, Naperville, IL 60563-2126
Novak, John, Countryside Villas, Rte. 1, Box 7-1A, Clifton, IL 60927
Ryan, William, St. John Vianney Villa, 1464 Green Trails Dr., Naperville, IL 60540
Shimanek, Joseph, 438 N. LaGrange Rd., LaGrange Park, IL 60525
Stockinger, Tony, St. John the Baptist, 05233 Church St., Winfield, IL 60190
Valentino, Dominic, 1230 E. East St., St. John Rd., Phoenix, AZ 85022
Wilkening, Henry, Corpus Christi, 1415 Lies Rd., Carol Stream, IL 60188-4841

Permanent Deacons:
Accardi, Rodger F., Central DuPage Hospital, Winfield
Agurkis, Albert, St. Mary of Gostyn, Downers Grove
Anchor, Robert, On Duty Outside Diocese
Anderson, Roy D., Residing Outside Diocese
Bailey, Thomas, Sacred Heart, Lombard
Balgeman, Richard, St. Joseph, Manteno
Beabout, Norman, On Duty Outside Diocese
Berkey, Donald, St. Anthony, Frankfort
Bernardin, Donald, St. Mary, Mokena
Bevan, William F., III, St. Paul the Apostle, Joliet
Bias, Ralph, Sacred Heart, Joliet
Bina, Frank, Our Lady of Peace, Darien
Blessing, William, St. Raphael, Naperville
Borkowicz, Leo M., St. Andrew the Apostle, Romeoville
Bouldin, James, St. Paul the Apostle, Joliet
Boyle, John R., St. Alexander, Villa Park
Brachle, Paul L., Jr., Our Lady of Peace, Darien
Brockman, David, St. Anne, Oswego
Carlson, Bruce, St. Mary, West Chicago
Carson, Neill, Notre Dame, Claredon Hills
Casey, William, Holy Trinity, Westmont
Chambers, Frank A., On Duty Outside Diocese
Chamness, Francis J., Maternity BVM, Bourbonnais
Christensen, Gerald G., Leave of Absence
Ciston, William, St. Jude, New Lenox
Clancy, Steven, St. Andrew, Romeoville
Clark, Raymond, St. Jude, Joliet
Clodi, Gregory, St. Martin of Tours, Kankakee
Cochran, Christopher, St. Alexander, Villa Park
Cole, John, Immaculate Conception, Elmhurst
Cook, Michael, Cathedral of St. Raymond, Joliet
Cooley, Stephen, On Duty Outside Diocese
Cotugno, Joseph, St. Patrick, Kankakee
Cozzens, John, St. Michael, Wheaton
Crane, William H., St. Pius X, Lombard
Cummiskey, Terry, St. Isidore, Bloomingdale
Cuzzone, Dominic, Visitation, Elmhurst
Dalpiaz, Joseph C., St. Joan of Arc, Lisle
Danahey, Daniel, St. Anthony, Frankfort
Darschewski, Ronald, St. Matthew, Glendale Heights
Dixon, James A., St. Philip, Addison
Donahue, James, St. Mary, Downers Grove
Dougherty, Michael, On Duty Outside Diocese
Drinan, Russell, St. Isaac Jogues, Hinsdale
Dunn, William, St. Anne, Oswego
Dyer, Donald L., St. Rose, Wilmington
Eastburn, Lloyd D., On Duty Outside Diocese
Ellman, Edward, On Duty Outside Diocese
Farrell, John, Our Lady of Mt. Carmel, Darien
Federici, Bart, St. Elizabeth Seton, Naperville
Fitt, Robert, St. Jude, New Lenox
Fitzgerald, James P., Jr., St. Mary, Mokena
Foys, Frank F., Notre Dame, Clarendon Hills
Franch, Dino J., St. Joseph, Addison
Freund, John, St. Isidore, Bloomington
Fricke, Thomas E., St. Francis of Assisi, Bolingbrook
Fritz, Leon P., St. Joseph, Bradley
Gamboa, Gabriel, St. Joseph, Addison
Gavin, Philip, (Retired)
Gibbons, John, St. Alexander, Villa Park
Girard, William, Sts. Peter and Paul, Naperville
Goebel, Thomas, St. Pius X, Lombard
Hamilton, Raymond, St. Francis of Assisi, Bolingbrook
Hamrlick, James, On Duty Outside Diocese
Hanley, Terrance R., St. Francis of Assisi, Bolingbrook
Heitz, Philip, St. Philip, Addison
Henrissey, Francis R., St. Joseph, Manteno
Hessling, Danny E., Sacred Heart Seminary, Hales Corner, WI
Hetzel, William, St. Jude, Joliet
Hindes, John T., St. Joseph, Manteno
Jackson, Kenneth, St. Isidore, Bloomingdale
Jacob, Jeffrey, St. Patrick, Momence
Jagielo, Thomas, Holy Trinity, Westmont
Janousek, Jay, Visitation, Elmhurst
Jazdzewski, Melvin J., Unassigned
Jossey, Robert, St. Boniface, Monee
Kelly, James, St. Dominic, Bolingbrook
Kenes, Michael, Annunciation Byzantine Catholic, Lockport
Knapstein, John W., St. Dominic, Bolingbrook
Knecht, Ronald, St. Pius X, Lombard
Kolodziej, Paul, St. Patrick, Joliet
Kowalski, Henry, St. Joseph, Downers Grove
Krostenko, Alexander, St. Paul the Apostle, Joliet
Krueger, James, St. Alexander, Villa Park
Krupowicz, Jerome, St. Mary Immaculate, Plainfield
LaLonde, James A., St. Joseph, Downers Grove
Lamon, John D., On Duty Outside Diocese
LaMotte, Robert, St. Joseph, Bradley
Lane, Charles, St. Thomas, Naperville
Lifka, David, Notre Dame, Clarendon Hills
Lissak, Lawrence, St. Pius X, Lombard
Lopez, Jose L., St. John the Baptist, Joliet
Lovero, Marco, St. Francis of Assisi, Bolingbrook
Lysaght, Evan, St. Walter, Roselle
Maloney, John, Mary Queen of Heaven, Elmhurst
Mangen, Richard
Marcotte, Euchrist, Maternity B.V.M., Bourbonnais
Marrow, Philip J., St. John the Apostle, Villa Park
Martinez, Santos H., St. Mary, Plano
Mathieu, Donulus, Sr., (Retired)
McHugh, John, St. Raphael, Naperville
Meador, David, St. Michael, Wheaton
Metcalfe, Dale R., St. Patrick, Plano
Miles, Kenneth J., Jr., St. Margaret Mary, Naperville
Molano, Rodulfo N., St. Francis of Assisi, Bolingbrook
Molinaro, Serafin, Resurrection, Wayne
Murphy, William E., St. Irene, Warrenville
Murray, John, St. Mary Magdalene, Joliet
Naso, James, Christ the Servant, Woodridge
Neher, Norman, Sacred Heart, Hopkins Park
Nielo, Andrew, St. John the Baptist, Winfield
Nolan, Thomas J., Mary, Queen of Heaven, Elmhurst
Nowak, Richard, On Duty Outside Diocese
Nunez, Charles, Mary Queen of Heaven, Elmhurst
O'Connor, Joseph, St. Joseph, Downers Grove
Olszak, Leonard, St. Liborius, Steger
Ouska, Gregory, St. Joseph Downers Grove
Pecka, Lawrence, St. Mary, Downers Grove
Pellack, Robert J., On Duty Outside Diocese
Petak, Edwin, Cathedral of St. Raymond, Joliet
Peterson, Charles M., St. Patrick, Joliet
Principe, Michael, St. Charles Borromeo, Bensenville
Rachubinski, Thomas, St. Pius X, Lombard
Randolph, Donald, St. Isidore, Bloomingdale
Raskowski, David, St. Andrew, Romeoville
Renville, John, Sacred Heart, Goodrich
Riggi, Joseph, St. Lawrence, South Wilimington
Rosko, Richard, St. Anthony, Frankfort
Ross, Thomas, St. Dominic, Bolingbrook
Ruiz, Victor
Safko, Terry L., St. Mary, Plainfield
Scavone, Emmanuel J., (Retired)
Schimandle, John, Assumption, Coal City
Schlund, James, On Duty Outside Diocese
Schmidt, Walter F., On Leave
Schmith, Roger, St. Scholastica, Woodridge
Schneider, Paul A., On Duty Outside Diocese
Schubert, Anthony, On Duty Outside Diocese
Schumacher, Carl N.J., St. Joseph, Downers Grove
Searls, Ronald, St. Walter, Roselle
Sheaffer, Harry, St. Mary, West Chicago
Sheridan, Thomas, St. Elizabeth Seton, Naperville
Sipek, Sr., Robert, Holy Trinity, Westmont
Siwek, Raymond, (Retired)
Solis, Joseph, Sts. Peter and Paul, Naperville
Sossong, James R., St. Mary Immaculate, Plainfield
Spatafore, Anthony, Visitation, Elmhurst
Spiezio, John, St. Petronille, Glen Ellyn
Stansberry, Robert T., Jr., Immaculate Conception, Morris
Stevens, Richard R., On Duty Outside Diocese
Stolarz, Dennis, Our Lady of Peace, Darien
Storrs, Wayne, Christ the King, Lombard
Straub, Fred, St. Margaret Mary, Naperville
Stroner, William, St. Michael, Wheaton
Stucko, Denis, St. Joan of Arc, Lisle
Sullivan, Robert, St. Joseph, Downers Grove
Symonanis, Alan, Notre Dame, Clarendon Hills
Tansey, William, Ascension, Oakbrook Terrace
Tetrault, Robert L., On Duty Outside Diocese
True, Robert, St. Irene, Warrenville
Uffmann, William, St. Dennis, Lockport
Urso, Joseph, St. Irene, Warrenville
Valdez, George, St. Mary, West Chicago
Van Dril, William, On Duty Outside Diocese
Vavra, Robert, St. Scholastica, Woodridge
Walen, Paul J., Sr., St. Dominic, Bolingbrook
Wallace, Robert, St. Dominic, Bolingbrook
Walsh, Thomas, On Duty Outside Diocese
Walters, James C., St. Mary, Plainfield
Weierman, Robert, St. Dennis, Lockport
Wood, Charles, St. Raphael, Naperville
Worden, William, St. Thomas the Apostle, Naperville
Yarshen, Richard, Holy Family, Joliet
Yurcus, Ronald J., St. Petronille, Glen Ellyn

INSTITUTIONS LOCATED IN THE DIOCESE

[A] COLLEGES AND UNIVERSITIES

JOLIET. *University of St. Francis*, 500 N. Wilcox, 60435. Tel: 815-740-3360; Fax: 815-740-4285.
Web site: www.stfrancis.edu
For a complete listing, refer to the Colleges and Universities section.

LISLE. *Benedictine University*, 5700 College Rd., 60532-0900. Tel: 630-829-6000; Fax: 630-960-1126.
Web site: www.ben.edu
For a complete listing, refer to the Colleges and Universities section.

ROMEOVILLE. *Lewis University*, One University Pkwy., 60446. Tel: 815-838-0500; Fax: 815-838-1267.
E-mail: wassbeca@lewis.edu
Web site: www.lewisu.edu/
For a complete listing, refer to the Colleges and Universities section.

[B] HIGH SCHOOLS, DIOCESAN

KANKAKEE. *Bishop McNamara High School*, 550 W. Brookmont, 60901. Tel: 815-932-7413; Fax: 815-932-0926.
E-mail: McNamarasmj@hotmail.com
Web site: www.McNamara.org
Sr. Madeleine LaMarre, C.N.D. Sisters 1; Lay Teachers 33; Students 448; Total Staff 59.

[C] HIGH SCHOOLS, PRIVATE

JOLIET. *Joliet Catholic Academy*. (Coed), 1200 N. Larkin Ave., 60435. Tel: 815-741-0500; Fax: 815-741-8825.
E-mail: Tim@JCA-online.org
Web site: www.JCA-online.org
Carmelites & Joliet Franciscans. Sr. Faith Szambelanczyk, O.S.F., Pres. & CEO; Rev. Timothy P. Andres, O.Carm., Prin. & COO; Dr. Robert Jenkins, Asst. Prin. Priests 2; Sisters 4; Brothers 1; Lay Teachers 56; Students 865.

ADDISON. *Driscoll Catholic High School*, 555 N. Lombard Rd., 60101. Tel: 630-543-6310; Fax: 630-543-2913.
E-mail: smarth@driscollcatholic.com
Web site: www.driscollcatholic.com
Mr. Stephen A. Marth, Prin. & Acting. Pres.; Mr. Michael Neis, Asst. Prin.; Mr. Peter Lewek, Admin. Asst.; Mr. Tim Racki, Dean; Mrs. Laraine Parker, Campus Minister. Brothers of Christian Schools 2; Lay Teachers 34; Students 480.

LISLE. *Benet Academy*, 2200 Maple Ave., 60532. Tel: 630-969-6550; Fax: 630-719-0929.
E-mail: webmaster@benet.org
Web site: www.benet.org
Rt. Rev. Hugh R. Anderson, O.S.B., Chancellor; Rev. Jude D. Randall, O.S.B., Pres.; Mr. Ernest Stark, Prin.; Mr. James Brown, Asst. Prin.; Mr. Tim Turner, Dir. Devel.; Rev. Anthony J. Jacob, O.S.B., Business Mgr. Priests 6; Sisters 2; Brothers 4; Lay Teachers 64; Students 1,285.

LOMBARD. *Montini Catholic High School*, 19 W. 070 16th St., 60148-4797. Tel: 630-627-6930; Fax: 630-627-0537.
Web site: www.montini.org
Bro. Thomas A. Harding, F.S.C., Pres. Brothers of the Christian Schools 3; Lay Teachers 50; Students 655.

NEW LENOX. *Providence Catholic High School*. (Coed), 1800 W. Lincoln Hwy., 60451. Tel: 815-485-2136; Fax: 815-485-2709.
E-mail: fmcg123@aol.com
Web site: www.providencecatholic.org
Rev. Richard J. McGrath, O.S.A., Pres.; Ms. Judith Legan, Asst. Prin.; Revs. Roland F. Follmann, O.S.A.; Donald Lewandowski, O.S.A.; Gerald A. Nicholas, O.S.A. Priests 4; Brothers 2; Lay Teachers 68; Students 1,162.

WHEATON. *St. Francis High School*, 2130 W. Roosevelt Rd., 60187. Tel: 630-668-5800; Fax: 630-668-5893.
Web site: www.stfrancishighschool.org
Mrs. Beth Sullivan, Prin. Lay Teachers 49; Students 657.

[D] AGENCIES AND INSTITUTIONS OF THE CHARITIES OF THE DIOCESE

JOLIET. *Catholic Charities*, 203 N. Ottawa St., 60432. Tel: 815-723-3405; Fax: 815-723-3452.
E-mail: kmcgowan@cc-doj.org
Kathleen McGowan, Exec. Dir. Diocesan Administrative Office and Regional Office for Will and Grundy Counties.

KANKAKEE. *Catholic Charities*, 270 N. Schuyler Ave., 60901. Tel: 815-933-7791; Fax: 815-932-3030. Regional Office for Kankakee, Ford, and Iroquois Counties.

LOMBARD. *Catholic Charities*, 26 W. St. Charles Rd., 60148. Tel: 708-495-9850; Fax: 708-495-9854. Regional Office for DuPage and Kendall Counties.

[E] PROTECTIVE INSTITUTIONS

JOLIET. *Guardian Angel Home*, 1550 Plainfield Ave., 60435. Tel: 815-729-0930; Fax: 815-744-6087.
E-mail: sas726@aol.com
Web site: www.guardianangelhome.org
For a complete listing, refer to the Special Care Facilities section.

MOMENCE. *Good Shepherd Manor*, P.O. Box 260, 60954. Tel: 815-472-6492; Fax: 815-472-2160.
E-mail: gsm@keynet.net
Web site: www.GoodShepherdManor.Org.
For a complete listing, refer to the Special Care Facilities section.

[F] DAY CARE LEARNING CENTERS

JOLIET. *Franciscan Learning Center*, 1734 Theodore St., 60435. Tel: 815-744-7634; Fax: 815-744-2152.
E-mail: lillppl@megsinet.net
Sr. Margaret McGuckin, Dir. Students 88.

Vilaseca Josephine Center, 351 N. Chicago St., 60432. Tel: 815-727-1467; Fax: 815-727-1480. Students 88. Josephine Sisters.

BOURBONNAIS. *Provena Fortin Villa Learning Center*, 615 S. Main St., 60914. Tel: 815-932-8411; Fax: 815-932-9002. Rhonda K. Greene, Dir. Childcare with Preschool for children 15 months to 12 years. Staff 20; Students 100.

[G] GENERAL HOSPITALS

JOLIET. *Provena Saint Joseph Medical Center*, 333 N. Madison St., 60435-6595. Tel: 815-741-7236; Fax: 815-741-7579.
E-mail: name@provena.org
Web site: www.provenasaintjoe.org
For a complete listing, refer to the Hospitals section.

FRANKFORT. *Provena Health (Jol)*, 9223 West St. Francis Rd., 60423. Tel: 815-469-4888; Fax: 815-469-4864.
Web site: www.Provena.Org
For a complete listing, refer to the Hospitals section.

Provena Hospitals (Jol), 9223 West Saint Francis Rd., 60423. Tel: 815-469-4888.
Web site: www.Provena.Org
For a complete listing, refer to the Hospitals section.

KANKAKEE. *Provena St. Mary's Hospital*, 500 West Court St., 60901. Tel: 815-937-2490; Fax: 815-937-8772
For a complete listing, refer to the Hospitals section.

[H] REHABILITATION CENTERS

WHEATON. *Marianjoy Rehabilitation Hospital & Clinics*, 26 W. 171 Roosevelt Rd., P.O. Box 795, 60189. Tel: 630-462-4000; Fax: 630-462-0112.
Web site: www.marianjoy.org
Franciscan Sisters, Daughters of the Sacred Hearts of Jesus and Mary (Wheaton, IL). Sr. Mariette Kalbac, Chap. Bed Capacity 120; Patients assisted annually 3,500. Legal Title: *Marianjoy, Inc.*

[I] HOMES FOR AGED

JOLIET. *Our Lady of Angels Retirement Home*, 1201 Wyoming, 60435. Tel: 815-725-6631; Fax: 815-725-1451
For a complete listing, refer to the Special Care Facilities section.

Provena Villa Franciscan, 210 N. Springfield, 60435. Tel: 815-725-3400; Fax: 815-725-2160
For a complete listing, refer to the Special Care Facilities section.

St. Elizabeth Home, 704 W. Marion St., 60436. Tel: 815-727-0125; Fax: 815-723-3452
For a complete listing, refer to the Special Care Facilities section.

BOURBONNAIS. *Provena Our Lady of Victory*, 20 Briarcliff Ln., 60914. Tel: 815-937-2022; Fax: 815-936-3231
For a complete listing, refer to the Special Care Facilities section.

CLIFTON. *Merkle-Knipprath Countryside Home*, 1190 E. 2900 N Rd., 60927-7103. Tel: 815-694-2306
For a complete listing, refer to the Special Care Facilities section.

CRETE. *St. James Manor & Villas*, 1251 Richton Rd., 60417. Tel: 708-672-6700; Fax: 708-672-4939.
E-mail: dstrutynski@franciscancommunities.com
For a complete listing, refer to the Special Care Facilities section.

DARIEN. *Carmelite Carefree Retirement Village*, 8419 Bailey Rd., 60561-5361. Tel: 630-960-4060; Fax: 630-960-4071
For a complete listing, refer to the Special Care Facilities section.

KANKAKEE. *Provena Heritage Village*, 901 North Entrance Ave., 60901. Tel: 815-939-4506; Fax: 815-939-4761
For a complete listing, refer to the Special Care Facilities section.

Provena Meadowview Lodge, 995 North Entrance Ave., 60901. Tel: 815-939-4506; Fax: 815-939-4761
For a complete listing, refer to the Special Care Facilities section.

LISLE. *Villa St. Benedict*, 1920 Maple Ave., 60532. Tel: 630-852-5360; Fax: 630-852-3196.
E-mail: glenntrem@aol.com
Web site: www.Qopc.net
For a complete listing, refer to the Special Care Facilities section.

NAPERVILLE. *St. John Vianney Villa*, 1464 Green Trails Dr., 60540-8372. Tel: 630-983-0533; Fax: 630-983-6375
For a complete listing, refer to the Special Care Facilities section.

St. Patrick's Residence, 1400 Brookdale Rd., 60563-2125. Tel: 630-416-6565; Fax: 630-416-8755.
E-mail: stpatres@earthlink.net
Web site: Stpatricksresidence.org
For a complete listing, refer to the Special Care Facilities section.

OAK BROOK. *Mayslake Village*, 1801 35th St., 60521. Tel: 630-850-8232; Fax: 630-850-8233.
E-mail: mayslakvlg@aol.com
Web site: www.mayslake.com
For a complete listing, refer to the Special Care Facilities section.

WHEATON. *Marian Park, Inc.*, 2126 W. Roosevelt Rd., 60187. Tel: 630-665-9100; Fax: 630-665-9357
For a complete listing, refer to the Special Care Facilities section.

[J] MONASTERIES AND RESIDENCES OF PRIESTS AND BROTHERS

JOLIET. *Congregation of Christian Brothers, Brother Rice Province Center*, 958 Western Ave., 60435-6954. Tel: 815-723-5464; Fax: 815-723-5278.
E-mail: gattone@brrice.chi.il.us
Web site: www.brprovince.org
Legal Title: *The Christian Brothers of Ireland, Inc.* Bros. Charles J. Gattone, C.F.C., Prov. Leader; James Keane, C.F.C. Councillors: Bros. Charles D. McKenna, C.F.C.; Donald D. Murray, C.F.C.; Michael S. Segvich, C.F.C. In res. Bros. John Dornbos, C.F.C.; Daniel Casey, C.F.C.

St. Elias Carmelites, 3504 Lake Shore Dr., 60431-8819. Tel: 815-439-8246; Fax: 815-439-8633. Revs. Joseph Maisonneuve, O.Carm., Prior; Raymond Foster, O.Carm.; Rocco DiLeonardi, O.Carm., (Retired); Louis Rogge, O.Carm.; Leopold Glueckert, O.Carm.; Timothy P. Andres, O.Carm. Priests 6.

St. John the Baptist Friary, 404 N. Hickory St., 60435. Tel: 815-727-9783; Fax: 815-740-1521. Revs. Edward Shea, O.F.M.; Lawrence Jagdfeld, O.F.M.; Louis B. Antl, O.F.M.; Medard Buvala, O.F.M.; Jason Kommer, O.F.M.; Gerold Schubert, O.F.M.; Venard Kommer, O.F.M.; Bros. John Sweeney, O.F.M.; Terence Santiapillai, O.F.M. Priests 7; Brothers 2.

BURR RIDGE. *Christian Brothers Provincial Office (Midwest Province)*, 7650 County Line Rd., 60521-6950. Tel: 630-323-3725; Fax: 630-323-3779.
E-mail: info@cbmidwest.org
Web site: www.cbmidwest.org
Bros. Thomas Johnson, F.S.C., Prov.; Francis Carr, F.S.C., Auxiliary Prov.; Michael Fehrenbach, F.S.C., Auxiliary Prov.; Ms. Marge Beauvais, Dir. Lasallian Family; Mr. Leo Hirsch, Dir. Devel.; Bros. Joseph Saurbier, F.S.C., Dir. Finance; Thomas Sullivan, F.S.C., Dir. Vocations & Formation; Nicholas Schumer, F.S.C., Dir. St. La Salle Auxiliary.

DARIEN. *Carmelite Community*, St. Simon Stock Priory, 8501 Bailey Rd., 60561. Tel: 630-241-1802. Rev. Kevin Shanley, O.Carm., Prior; Bros. Robert Murphy, O.Carm.; Charles Kwiatkowski, O.Carm.; Revs. Robert E. Lee, O.Carm.; Roy Ontiveros, O.Carm.; Leo McCarthy, O.Carm.; Robert E. Colaresi, O.Carm.; Roger Bonneau, O.Carm. Priests 6; Brothers 2.

Carmelite Provincial Office, 1317 Frontage Rd., 60561. Tel: 630-971-0050; Fax: 630-971-0195.
E-mail: provincial@carmelnet.org
Web site: www.carmelnet.org
Legal Title: *Society of Mt. Carmel of Illinois.* Very Rev. Leo McCarthy, O.Carm., Prior Prov.; Revs. Daniel O'Neill, O.Carm., Prov. Procurator; Joseph Wallroth, O.Carm., Military Chap. Carmelites Serving In Italy: Revs. Raul Maravi, O.Carm.; Craig Morrison, O.Carm.; Joachim Smet, O.Carm. Carmelites serving in Canada: Revs. Bruce Baker, O.Carm.; Terrence Cyr, O.Carm.; Leonard Gilman, O.Carm.; Thomas Hakala, O.Carm.; Leo Huard, O.Carm.; Anthony McNamara, O.Carm.; Joseph O'Brien, O.Carm.; Jordon Rooney, O.Carm.; Ferdinand Schaefer, O.Carm.; Malachy Smith, O.Carm.; Bros. Robert Holt, O.Carm.; Lawrence Fidelus, O.Carm.; Gabriel Murray, O.Carm. Carmelites serving in Peru: Prelate Nullius, Sicuani, Peru. Tel: 011-51-8-435-11611; Fax: 011-51-8-435-1089. Most Rev. Michael LaFay, O.Carm.; Revs. Salvador Bartolo, O.Carm.; Michael Brown, O.Carm.; Michael Sgarioto, O.Carm.; Kevin Lafey, O.Carm.; Gerald Payea, O.Carm.; Alban Quinn, O.Carm.; Joseph Lucchesi, O.Carm.; Enrique Laguna-Vargas, O.Carm.; James Geaney, O.Carm.; Edward Adelmann, O.Carm.; Bros. Miguel Angel Bonfilla, O.Carm.; Miguel Bacigalupo-Del Corrall, O.Carm.; Jorge Villegas, O.Carm.; Juan Carlos Llerena, O.Carm.; Carlos Valdez, O.Carm.; Eduardo Rivero, O.Carm. Carmelites serving elsewhere: Revs. Noel Ahrens, O.Carm.; Jeffry Fairfield, O.Carm.; Gregory Klein, O.Carm.; Patrick Gleeson, O.Carm.; Michael Greenwell, O.Carm.; Devin Griffin, O.Carm.; Henry Ormond, O.Carm.; John F. Donohue, O.Carm.; Blaise McInerney, O.Carm.; Venard Poslusney, O.Carm.; Warren Carlin, O.Carm.; Barry Kremer, O.Carm.; Frank Weil, O.Carm.; Myron Judy, O.Carm.; Albert P. Koppes, O.Carm.; Matthew Sprouffske, O.Carm.; Andrew Skotnicki, O.Carm.; Charles Kurgan, O.Carm.; Anton Kollar, O.Carm.; Robert Primozic, O.Carm.; Timothy Moore, O.Carm.; James Lewis, O.Carm. Carmelites serving in Mexico: Revs. Peter Hinde, O.Carm.; Joel Moelter, O.Carm.; John Hertel, O.Carm.; Thomas Jordan, O.Carm.; Thomas Alkire, O.Carm.; Charles Countie, O.Carm.; William Smith, O.Carm.; Bros. Jose Luis Torres P., O.Carm.; Rodolfo Aznaran, O.Carm.; Emilio Rodriguez, O.Carm.

LISLE. *St. Procopius Abbey*, 5601 College Rd., 60532. Tel: 630-969-6410; Fax: 630-969-6426.
Web site: http://www.procopius.org
Benedictine Monks. Rt. Rev. Hugh R. Anderson, O.S.B., Abbot; Very Rev. Columban Trojan, O.S.B., Prior; Revs. Thomas Chisholm, O.S.B., Subprior; James Flint, O.S.B., Master of Novices & Juniors; Kevin J. Sheeran, O.S.B., Procurator & Business Mgr.; Gabriel Baltes, O.S.B.; Frederic J. Beller, O.S.B.; Christian W. Ceplecha, O.S.B.; Joseph Chang, O.S.B.; Odilo Crkva, O.S.B.; Ivan Dobnikar, O.S.B.; Jerome Dobry, O.S.B.; Julian von Duerbeck, O.S.B.; Terence Fitzmaurice, O.S.B.; T. Becket Franks, O.S.B.; Roman Galiardi, O.S.B.; Rt. Rev. Thomas J. Havlik, O.S.B., Abbot, (Retired); Revs. Paschal D. Honner, O.S.B.; Alban Hrebic, O.S.B.; Zachary Hrisko, O.S.B.; Anthony J. Jacob, O.S.B.; Dismas B. Kalcic, O.S.B.; Michael E. Komechak, O.S.B.; Edward Kucera, O.S.B.; Timothy R. Marceau, O.S.B.; Jude D. Randall, O.S.B., Pres., Benet Academy; Rt. Rev. Valentine Skluzacek, O.S.B., Abbot, (Retired); Revs. James Saul, O.S.B.; Clement Sobr, O.S.B.; Theodore D. Suchy, O.S.B.;

Philip S. Timko, O.S.B.; David Turner, O.S.B.; Mel R. Uzdrowski, O.S.B.; Stanley G. Vesely, O.S.B.; Kenneth Zigmond, O.S.B.; Francis Lawrence; Most Rev. Daniel W. Kucera, O.S.B., (Retired) Archbishop of Dubuque, IA. Monks 55; Priests 35; Brothers 16; Bishops 1; Oblates 3.

Benedictine Chinese Mission, 24 W. 350 Maple Ave., Naperville, 60540. Tel: 630-968-4264. Rev. James Saul, O.S.B., Dir.

Slav Missions, 5601 College Dr., 60532. Tel: 630-969-6410; Fax: 630-969-6426.

Benedictine University, 5700 College Rd., 60532. Tel: 630-829-6000; Fax: 630-829-6242.

Benet Academy, 2200 Maple Ave., 60532. Tel: 630-969-6550; Fax: 630-719-0929.

St. Scholastica Mission House. Missionary Oblates of St. Benedict, 24 W. 350 Maple Ave., Naperville, 60540. Tel: 630-968-4264.

St. Procopius Abbey Endowment, 5601 College Rd., 60532. Tel: 630-969-6410; Fax: 630-969-6426.

MOMENCE. *Brother Mathias Barrett Inc. of Illinois*, P.O. Box 260, 60954. Tel: 815-472-3700; Fax: 815-472-2160. Bro. Alphonsus Brown, Pres. Brothers 3.

NEW LENOX. *Augustinian Friary*, 1800 W. Lincoln Hwy., 60451. Tel: 815-485-6880; Fax: 815-485-2709.
(See separate listing for Providence High School).
In res. Revs. Richard J. McGrath, O.S.A., Pres.; Roland F. Follmann, O.S.A.; Gerald A. Nicholas, O.S.A., Prior; Bros. John E. Newton, O.S.A.; John Patrick Currier, O.S.A.

ROMEOVILLE. *Christian Brothers Center*, 200 De La-Salle Dr., 60446-1899. Tel: 815-838-8903; Fax: 815-838-7089. Bro. Nick Schumer, F.S.C., Dir. Brothers 14.

De La Salle Hall, Lewis University Student Res., 200 De LaSalle Dr., 60441. Tel: 815-838-8902; Fax: 815-838-7089.
E-mail: VESELSRO@ Lewisu.Edu
Bro. Robert Veselsky, Dir. Student Residents 59; Brothers 1.

La Salle House Community, 100 Faculty Lane, 60446. Tel: 815-836-5463; Fax: 815-836-5858.
E-mail: dupreth@lewisu.edu
Bro. Thomas Dupre, F.S.C., Dir. Brothers 17.

[K] CONVENTS AND RESIDENCES FOR SISTERS

JOLIET. *Josephine Sisters*, 351 N. Chicago St., 60432. Tel: 815-727-1467; Fax: 815-727-1480. Josephine Sisters of Mexico (Hermanas Josefinas). Sisters 7.

St. Francis Convent (Motherhouse), 520 Plainfield Ave., 60435. Tel: 815-727-3686; Fax: 815-727-9435. Congregation of the Third Order of St. Francis of Mary Immaculate, Joliet, IL. Sr. Maria Pesavento, O.S.F., Pres.; Sr. Joan Clare Wisner, Building Admin. Sisters 46. Legal Title: *Retirement Plan Trust of the Congregation of the Third Order of St. Francis of Mary Immaculate*.

FRANKFORT. *Franciscan Sisters of the Sacred Heart*, St. Francis Woods, 9201 W. St. Francis Rd., 60423-8335. Tel: 815-469-4895; Fax: 815-464-3809.
E-mail: smeimler@aol.com
Web site: http://www.fssh.com
Legal Title: *An Association of Franciscan Sisters of the Sacred Heart and the Franciscan Sisters of the Sacred Heart in California*. Co-sponsors with Servants of the Holy Heart of Mary, Holy Family Prov., U.S.A. Sr. Mary Elizabeth Imler, Gen. Supr.; Rev. Lowell Fischer, Chap. Sisters 139.

KANKAKEE. *St. Clare House of Prayer*, 2041 W. Rte. 113, 60901-7411. Tel: 815-933-3945. Sisters of St. Francis of Mary Immaculate 5.

Servants of the Holy Heart of Mary, Holy Family Prov., U.S.A., Provincial Administration, 485 W. Merchant St., 60901. Tel: 815-937-2380; Fax: 815-937-5520.
E-mail: KathleenMMulchay@ProvenaHealth.com
Web site: inil.com/users/hatton
Legal Title: *Servants of the Holy Heart of Mary Charitable Trust*. Co-Sponsors: Provena Health with Franciscan Sisters of the Sacred Heart and Sisters of Mercy of the Americas Regional Community of Chicago. Sr. Kathleen Mulchay, Prov. Supr. Professed Sisters 56. Provena Health including 7 hospitals and 13 long term care institutions.

LISLE. *Benedictine Sisters of the Sacred Heart, Sacred Heart Monastery*, 1910 Maple Ave., 60532-2164. Tel: 630-969-7040; Fax: 630-969-5814.
E-mail: jheble@aol.com
Web site: www.shmlisle.org
Sr. Judith Ann Heble, O.S.B., Prioress; Rev. Becket Franks, Chap. Professed Sisters 50. Legal Title: *Benedictine Sisters of the Sacred Heart Charitable Trust*.

MINOOKA. *The Poor Clares of Joliet, Annunciation Monastery*, 6200 E. Minooka Rd., 60447. Tel: 815-467-0032; Fax: 815-467-0032. Sr. M. Dorothy Urschalitz, P.C., Contact Person. Cloistered Sisters 8; Extern Sisters 1; Novices 2.

NEW LENOX. *Mother of Good Counsel Monastery*. Augustinian Sisters from St. Louis. 440 Marley Rd., 60451. Tel: 815-463-9662; Fax: 815-463-9662. Sr. Mary Grace Kuppe, O.S.A., Prioress.

PLAINFIELD. *Mantellate Sisters Servants of Mary of Plainfield*, 16949 S. Drauden Rd., 60544-9219. Tel: 815-436-5796; Fax: 815-436-7486. Sr. Francis Gresser, O.S.M., Regional Supr. Sisters 9.
Ministry in the field of Academic Education, Parish Ministry, Social Work, Nursing, Homes for the Aged, and Foreign Missions. Homes for the Aged and Foreign Missions.

WHEATON. *Convent of Our Lady of the Angels Motherhouse and Novitiate*. Franciscan Sisters, Daughters of the Sacred Hearts of Jesus and Mary (Wheaton, IL), P.O. Box 667, 60189-0667. Tel: 630-462-7422; Fax: 630-462-7148.
E-mail: leadership@franciscanswheaton.org
Sr. Margaret Grempka, O.S.F., Prov. Dir. Sisters 118. Legal Title: *Wheaton Franciscan Sisters Corp.*

Loretto Convent, Religious of the Institute of the Blessed Virgin Mary, P.O. Box 508, 60189. Tel: 630-653-4740; Fax: 630-653-4886. Sr. Mary Catherine Spatz. Sisters 27.

Loretto Conference Center. Tel: 630-653-7918; Fax: 630-653-4886.

Wheaton Franciscan Sisters Religious Charitable Trust, 26 W. 171 Roosevelt Rd., P.O. Box 667, 60189-0667. Tel: 630-462-7422; Fax: 630-462-7148.

[L] HOUSES OF RETREAT/PRAYER

DARIEN. *Carmelite Spiritual Center*, 8433 Bailey Rd., 60561. Tel: 630-969-4141; Fax: 630-969-3376.
E-mail: CSCRETREAT@aol.com
Revs. Kevin Shanley, O.Carm.; Robert E. Colaresi, O.Carm., Dir. Total Staff 16.

DOWNERS GROVE. *Mayslake Marmion Ministries, Inc.*, 4832 Main St., 60515. Tel: 630-719-1620; Fax: 630-719-1621.
E-mail: Mayslake-Ministries@Juno.com
Rev. Jonathan D. Foster, O.F.M. Priests 1; Lay Staff 3.

FRANKFORT. *Portiuncula Center for Prayer*, 9263 W. St. Francis Rd., 60423-8330. Tel: 815-464-3880; Fax: 815-469-4880.
E-mail: PORTC4P@aol.com
Web site: www.PORTC4P.com

PLANO. *La Salle Manor Christian Brothers Retreat House*, 12480 Galena Rd., 60545. Tel: 630-552-3224; Fax: 630-552-9160.
E-mail: LSManor@aol.com
Robert Dressel, Pres.

WARRENVILLE. *Congregation of Our Lady of the Retreat in the Cenacle*, 29W012 Batavia Rd., P.O. Box 797, 60555-0797. Tel: 630-393-1231; Fax: 630-393-2646.
E-mail: cenaclemin@aol.com
Web site: www.cenacle.org
Sr. Mary Sharon Riley, R.C., Supr. Sisters 12.

[M] MISCELLANEOUS

JOLIET. *St. Vincent Thrift Shop*, 307 N. Chicago St., 60432. Tel: 815-722-1140. 211 Main St., West Chicago, 60185. Tel: 630-293-9755; Fax: 630-293-9881.

AURORA. *Assisi Homes - Constitution House, Inc.*, 401 Constitution Dr., 60506. Tel: 630-396-2100; Fax: 630-896-0313. Mailing Address: Franciscan Ministries, Inc., 26 W. 171 Roosevelt Rd., P.O. Box 667, Wheaton, 60189-0667.

BURR RIDGE. *Christian Brothers Fund, Inc.*, 7650 S. County Line Rd., 60521-6950. Tel: 630-323-3725; Fax: 630-323-3779.
E-mail: info@cbmidwest.org
Web site: cbmidwest.org
Bro. Thomas Hetland, Pres.

CAROL STREAM. *Assisi Homes - Colony Park, Inc.*, 550 E. Thornhill Dr., 60188. Tel: 630-682-9000; Fax: 630-682-9008. Mailing Address: Franciscan Ministries, Inc., 26 W. 171 Roosevelt Rd., P.O. Box 667, Wheaton, 60189-0667.

DARIEN. *Carmelite Mission Office*, 1317 Frontage Rd., 60561. Tel: 630-969-5220; Fax: 630-971-0195.
E-mail: JEMMALLEY@Juno.com
Web site: www.carmelnet.org/missions/missions/HTM
Rev. John Malley, O.Carm., Dir.

National Shrine of St. Therese, 8501 Bailey Rd., 60561. Tel: 630-969-3311; Fax: 630-969-5536.
E-mail: webmaster@littleflower.org
Web site: www.Saint-Therese.org
Rev. Roger Bonneau, O.Carm., Dir.

Provincial Office of Lay Carmelites and Scapular Confraternity, 8501 Bailey Rd., 60561. Tel: 630-969-5050; Fax: 630-969-7519.
E-mail: laycarmelites@carmelnet.org
Web site: carmelnet.org
Sr. Libby Dahlstrom, O.Carm., Assoc. Dir.; Rev. Robert E. Lee, O.Carm., Assoc. Dir.

Society of the Little Flower, 1313 Frontage Rd., 60561-5341. Tel: 630-968-9400; Fax: 630-968-9542.
E-mail: webmaster@littleflower.org
Web site: http://www.littleflower.org
Rev. Robert E. Colaresi, O.Carm., Dir.

GURNEE. *Assisi Homes of Gurnee, Inc.*, 3495 W. Grand Ave., 60031. Tel: 847-336-4428; Fax: 847-336-3778. Mailing Address: Franciscan Ministries, Inc., 26 W. 171 Roosevelt Rd., P.O. Box 667, Wheaton, 60189-0667.

KANKAKEE. *Lisieux Pastoral Outreach Center*, 371 N. St. Joseph Ave., 60901-2741. Tel: 815-939-2913; Fax: 815-933-7692.
E-mail: lisieuxpc@aol.com

Provena Senior Services, 200 E. Court St., Suite 200, 60901. Tel: 815-937-2034; Fax: 815-928-6150.
Web site: www.Provena.org
Ms. Connie March, Pres.

LISLE. *Catholic CEO Health Care Connection (CCHC)*, 3333 Warrenville Rd, Ste. 200, 60532. Tel: 630-799-8315; Fax: 630-799-8316.
E-mail: rnbutler@compuserve.com
Roger N. Butler, Exec. Dir.

National Association of Catholic Nurses-U.S.A., P.O. Box 3016, 60532-3016. Tel: 610-558-1192.
E-mail: dianaml@bellatlantic.net
Web site: www.nacn-usa.org
Mailing Address: P.O. Box 3016, 60532. Diane M.L. Newman, R.N., Ed.D., Pres.

MOMENCE. *B.G.S. Charitable Trust*, P.O. Box 736, 60954-0736. Tel: 815-472-3131; Fax: 815-472-6914. Michael Brown, Contact Person.

Little Brothers of the Good Shepherd, Inc. of Illinois, 4129 N. Dixie Hwy., P.O. Box 736, 60954. Tel: 815-472-3131; Fax: 815-472-6914.
E-mail: jabrinkman@aol.com
Web site: www.LBGS.org
Bro. Richard MacPhee, Treas. Gen.; Judy Brinkmann, Dir. of Finance.

OAK BROOK. *Catholic Community Investment Retirement Trust*. Christian Brothers of the Midwest, Inc. 915 Harger Rd., Ste. 250, 60523. Tel: 630-571-2182. Bro. Joseph Saurbier, F.S.C.

ROMEOVILLE. *Charitable Trust of the Brothers of the Christian Schools*, 1205 Windham Pkwy., 60446-1679. Tel: 630-378-2900; Fax: 630-378-2501.
E-mail: info@cbservices.org
Web site: www.cbservices.org

Christian Brothers Employee Benefit Trust, 1205 Windham Pkwy., 60446-1679. Tel: 630-378-2900; Fax: 630-378-2501.
E-mail: info@cbservices.org
Web site: www.cbservices.org

Christian Brothers Employee Retirement Plan Trust, 1205 Windham Pkwy., 60446-1679. Tel: 630-378-2900; Fax: 630-378-2501.
E-mail: info@cbservices.org
Web site: www.cbservices.org

Christian Brothers Religious Community Deductible Trust, 1205 Windham Pkwy., 60446-1679. Tel: 630-378-2900; Fax: 630-378-2501.
E-mail: info@cbservices.org
Web site: www.cbservices.org

Christian Brothers Religious Comprehensive Trust, 1205 Windham Pkwy., 60446-1679. Tel: 630-378-2900; Fax: 630-378-2501.
E-mail: info@cbservices.org
Web site: www.cbservices.org

Christian Brothers Retirement Savings Plan Trust, 1205 Windham Parkway, 60446-1679. Tel: 630-378-2900. Bro. William Walz, F.S.C., Contact Person.

Christian Brothers Services, 1205 Windham Pkwy., 60446-1679. Tel: 630-378-2900; Fax: 630-378-2501.
E-mail: info@cbservices.org
Web site: www.cbservices.org
Bro. William Walz, F.S.C.

Religious & Charitable Risk Pooling Trust of the Brothers of the Christian Schools, 1205 Windham Pkwy., 60446-1679. Tel: 630-378-2900; Fax: 630-378-2501.
E-mail: info@cbservices.org
Web site: www.cbservices.org

WEST CHICAGO. *Society of St. Vincent de Paul*, Diocesan Council of Joliet, 211 Main St., 60185. Tel: 630-293-9755; Fax: 630-293-9881.
E-mail: thomassvdp@yahoo.com

WHEATON. *Assisi Homes of Illinois, Inc.* Mailing Address: Franciscan Ministries, Inc., 26 W. 171 Roosevelt Rd., P.O. Box 667, 60189-0667.

Canticle Place Ministries, Inc., 26 W. 171 Roosevelt Rd., 60189. Tel: 630-588-9165; Fax: 630-588-9167.
E-mail: brad@canticleplace.org
Web site: www.canticleplace.org
Brad Ogilvie, Contact Person. Tel: 630-784-2722.

Canticle Place, Inc., 26 W. 105 Roosevelt Rd., #13, 60187. Tel: 630-588-9165; Fax: 630-588-9167.
E-mail: brad@canticleplace.org
Web site: www.canticleplace.org
Mailing Address: Franciscan Ministries, Inc., 26 W. Roosevelt Rd., P.O. Box 667, 60189-0667.

Clara Pfaender Fund, Inc., 26 W. 171 Roosevelt Rd., P.O. Box 667, 60189. Tel: 630-462-9271; Fax: 630-462-4977. Sr. Patricia Norton, Chairperson/Pres. Franciscan Sisters, Daughters of the Sacred Hearts of Jesus and Mary (Wheaton, IL).

Franciscan Health & Education Corp., Inc., 26 W. 171 Roosevelt Rd., P.O. Box 667, 60189. Tel: 630-462-9065; Fax: 630-462-7422.

Franciscan Ministries, Inc. Property & Mailing Address: P.O. Box 667, 26 W. 171 Roosevelt Rd., 60189-0667. Tel: 630-462-9271; Fax: 630-462-4977.

Institute of the Blessed Virgin Mary Charitable Trust, P.O. Box 508, 60189. Tel: 630-653-6113; Fax: 630-653-4886.
E-mail: ibvmjfryel@aol.com
Web site: ibvm.org

Marionjoy Rehablink Corporation, 26 W. 171 Roosevelt Rd., P.O. Box 667, 60189. Tel: 630-462-9271; Fax: 630-462-0112. Kathleen Yosko, Pres. & CEO.

Wheaton Franciscan Services, Inc., 26 W. 171 Roosevelt Rd., P.O. Box 667, 60189. Tel: 630-462-9271; Fax: 630-462-4977. Sr. Patricia Norton, Chm.; John D. Oliverio, Pres. & CEO.

RELIGIOUS INSTITUTES OF MEN REPRESENTED IN THE DIOCESE

For further details refer to the corresponding bracketed number in the Religious Institutes of Men or Women section.

[0140]—*The Augustinians.* (Mother of Good Counsel Prov.).—O.S.A.
[0200]—*Benedictine Monks.*—O.S.B.
[0330]—*Brothers of the Christian Schools.* (Midwest Prov.).—F.S.C.
[0580]—*Brothers of the Good Shepherd.*—B.G.S.
[0270]—*Carmelite Fathers & Brothers.* (Prov. of Pure Heart of Mary).—O.Carm.
[1320]—*Clerics of St. Viator.*—C.S.V.
[0310]—*Congregation of Christian Brothers.*—C.F.C.
[0430]—*Dominicans.* (Prov. of Albert the Great).—O.P.
[0520]—*Franciscan Friars.* (Sacred Heart, Assumption Provs.).—O.F.M.
[0540]—*Franciscan Missionary Brothers of the Sacred Heart of Jesus.*—O.S.F.
[0520]—*Franciscans.* (Order of Friars Minor, Sacred Heart Prov.).—O.F.M.
[0740]—*Marian Fathers.* (Prov. of St. Casimer).—M.I.C.
[0610]—*Priests of the Congregation of Holy Cross.*—C.S.C.
[0110]—*Society of African Missions.*—S.M.A.
[0690]—*Society of Jesus.* (Chicago and St. Louis Prov.).—S.J.

RELIGIOUS INSTITUTES OF WOMEN REPRESENTED IN THE DIOCESE

[0230]—*Benedictine Sisters of Pontifical Jurisdiction.* (Lisle, IL; Ferdinand, IN).—O.S.B.
[0330]—*Carmelite Sisters for the Aged and Infirm.* (Germantown, NY).—O.Carm.
[0400]—*Congregation of Our Lady of Mount Carmel.* (Lacombe, LA).—O.Carm.
[3110]—*Congregation of Our Lady of the Retreat in the Cenacle.*—R.C.
[3710]—*Congregation of the Sisters of Saint Agnes.*—C.S.A.
[1920]—*Congregation of the Sisters of the Holy Cross.*—C.S.C.
[1710]—*Congregation of the Third Order of St. Francis of Mary Immaculate, Joliet, IL.*—O.S.F.
[1070-01]—*Dominican Sisters.* (St. Catharine, KY).—O.P.
[1070-03]—*Dominican Sisters.* (Sinsinawa).—O.P.
[1070-10]—*Dominican Sisters.* (Springfield).—O.P.
[1070-13]—*Dominican Sisters.* (Adrian).—O.P.
[1170]—*Felician Sisters.*—C.S.S.F.
[1780]—*Franciscan Sisters of Perpetual Adoration.* (Woodruff, WI).—F.S.P.A.
[1450]—*Franciscan Sisters of the Sacred Heart.*—O.S.F.
[1240]—*Franciscan Sisters, Daughters of the Sacred Hearts of Jesus and Mary.*—O.S.F.
[1910]—*Hermanas Josefinas.*—H.J.
[2370]—*Institute of the Blessed Virgin Mary (Loretto Sisters).*—I.B.V.M.
[2575]—*Institute of the Sisters of Mercy of the Americas.* (Chicago, IL).—R.S.M.
[3570]—*Mantellate Sisters, Servants of Mary.* (Plainfield, IL).—O.S.M.
[]—*Missionary Sisters of the Holy Family.* (Komorrow-Warsaw, Poland).—M.S.H.F.
[3760]—*Order of St. Clare.*—P.C.C.
[2970]—*School Sisters of Notre Dame.* (Chicago Prov.).—S.S.N.D.
[1680]—*School Sisters of St. Francis.* (U.S. Prov.).—O.S.F.
[3590]—*Servants of Mary.* (Ladysmith, WI).—O.S.M.
[3520]—*Servants of the Holy Heart of Mary.*—S.S.C.M.
[0430]—*Sisters of Charity of the Blessed Virgin Mary.*—B.V.M.
[1010]—*Sisters of Divine Providence of San Antonio.* Texas.—C.D.P.
[2990]—*Sisters of Notre Dame.* (Toledo, OH).—S.N.D.
[3000]—*Sisters of Notre Dame de Namur.* (Cincinnati Prov.).—S.N.D.deN.
[3360]—*Sisters of Providence of Saint Mary-of-the-Woods, IN.*—S.P.
[3740]—*Sisters of St. Casimir.*—S.S.C.
[1540]—*Sisters of St. Francis.* (Clinton, IA).—O.S.F.
[1705]—*The Sisters of St. Francis of Assisi.* (St. Francis).—O.S.F.
[1520]—*Sisters of St. Francis of Christ the King.*—O.S.F.
[1570]—*Sisters of St. Francis of Dubuque.* (Iowa).—O.S.F.
[3830-02]—*Sisters of St. Joseph.*—C.S.J.
[3930]—*Sisters of St. Joseph of the Third Order of St. Francis.* (Prov. of Immaculate Conception).—S.S.J.-T.O.S.F.
[2980]—*Sisters of the Congregation de Notre Dame.*—C.N.D.
[1720]—*Sisters of the Third Order Regular of St. Francis of the Congregation of Our Lady of Lourdes.* (Rochester, MN).—O.S.F.
[2150]—*Sisters Servants of the Immaculate Heart of Mary.*—I.H.M.

DIOCESAN CEMETERIES

JOLIET. *Holy Cross*, Theodore St. Tel: 815-838-0395.
Mount Olivet, 1320 E. Cass St. Tel: 815-838-0395.
St. John the Baptist, Ruby St. & Clemet St. Tel: 815-838-0395.
St. Mary Nativity, Caton Farm Rd. & Oakland Ave. Tel: 815-838-0395.
St. Patrick, Hunter St. & Jefferson St. Tel: 815-838-0395.
SS. Cyril and Methodius, Rte. 6 & Maple Rd. Tel: 815-838-0395.

BOURBONNAIS. *All Saints*, 1839 W. Rte. 102. Tel: 815-936-9378.
Maternity/BVM, Canberry Ln. Tel: 815-933-2342.

CAROL STREAM. *St. Stephen*, St. Charles Rd. Tel: 630-668-3313.

DOWNERS GROVE. *St. Bernard*, Hobson & Belmont Roads. Tel: 630-668-3313.

ELMHURST. *St. Mary*, Alexander Blvd. Tel: 630-668-3313.

KANKAKEE. *Mt. Calvary*, 2000 E. Court St. Tel: 815-933-2342.
St. Rose, Rte. 50. Tel: 815-933-2342.

LOCKPORT. *Calvary*, Rte. 171 & High Rd. Tel: 815-838-0395.

LOCKPORT SOUTH. *St. Dennis*, 16th St. & Washington St. Tel: 815-838-0395.

LOMBARD. *St. Mary*, Finley Rd. Tel: 630-668-3313.

NAPERVILLE. *SS. Peter & Paul*, Columbia St. & North Ave. Tel: 630-668-3313.

ROMEOVILLE. *Resurrection*, 135th St. & Rte. 53. Tel: 815-838-0395.
St. Charles Borromeo, 402 S. Independence Blvd., 60446-2264. Tel: 815-838-0395.

WHEATON. *Assumption*, One S. 510 Winfield Rd. Tel: 630-668-3313.

WINFIELD. *St. John the Baptist*, Summit Rd. & Gary Mill Rd. Tel: 630-668-3313.

NECROLOGY

† Kinzig, James J., (Retired). —Died May 2, 2000.
† Richter, Raynor, (Retired). —Died Feb. 8, 2000.
† Slikas, William, Joliet, IL Holy Cross. —Died Oct. 22, 2000.
† Stalzer, David, Joliet, IL St. Mary Magdalene. —Died June 18, 2000.

Diocese of Juneau

(Dioecesis Junellensis)

Most Reverend

MICHAEL W. WARFEL

Bishop of Juneau; ordained April 26, 1980; appointed November 19, 1996; installed December 17, 1996.

ESTABLISHED JUNE 23, 1951.

Square Miles 37,566.

Corporate Title: "Corporation of the Catholic Bishop of Juneau."

Comprises the entire southeastern part of the State of Alaska known legally as The First Judicial District.

For legal titles of parishes and diocesan institutions, consult the Chancery Office.

Chancery: 419 Sixth St., #200, Juneau, AK, 99801. Tel.: 907-586-2227; Fax: 907-463-3237.

Web site address: www.juneau-diocese.addr.com

E-mail address: junodio@gci.net

STATISTICAL OVERVIEW

Personnel	
Bishop	1
Priests: Diocesan Active in Diocese	5
Priests: Active Outside Diocese	2
Number of Diocesan Priests	7
Religious Priests in Diocese	2
Extern Priests in Diocese	1
Permanent Deacons in Diocese	5
Total Sisters	7
Parishes	
Parishes	10
With Resident Pastor:	
Resident Diocesan Priests	5
Resident Religious Priests	4
Without Resident Pastor:	
Administered by Priests	1
Missions	14
Professional Ministry Personnel:	
Sisters	3
Lay Ministers	10
Welfare	
Catholic Hospitals	1
Total Assisted	50,105
Homes for the Aged	1
Total Assisted	128
Day Care and Extended Day Care Centers	1
Total Assisted	100
Special Centers for Social Services	1
Total Assisted	7,829
Other Institutions	1
Total Assisted	10,688
Educational	
Seminaries, Religious	2
Total Seminarians	2
Elementary Schools, Diocesan and Parish	1
Total Students	100
Catechesis/Religious Education:	
High School Students	237
Elementary Students	599
Total Students Under Catholic Instruction	938
Teachers in the Diocese:	
Lay Teachers	9
Vital Statistics	
Receptions into the Church:	
Infant Baptism Totals	107
Adult Baptism Totals	20
Received into Full Communion	12
First Communions	116
Confirmations	216
Marriages:	
Catholic	13
Interfaith	11
Total Marriages	24
Deaths	24
Total Catholic Population	5,453
Total Population	73,302

Former Bishops—Most Rev. DERMOT O'FLANAGAN, D.D., ord. Aug. 27, 1929; appt. Bishop July 9, 1951; cons. Oct. 3, 1951; resigned June 19, 1968; appt. Titular Bishop of Trecalae; died Dec. 31, 1972.—Most Rev. FRANCIS T. HURLEY, D.D., ord. June 16, 1951; appt. Titular Bishop of Daimlaig and Auxiliary of Juneau, Feb. 4, 1970; cons. March 19, 1970; Ordinary of See, July 20, 1971; appt. Archbishop of Anchorage, May 4, 1976.—Most Rev. MICHAEL H. KENNY, D.D., ord. March 30, 1963; appt. March 20, 1979; cons. May 27, 1979; installed June 15, 1979; died Feb. 19, 1995.

Diocesan Pastoral Center

Chancery—419 Sixth St., #200, Juneau, 99801. Tel: 907-586-2227; Fax: 907-463-3237.

Chancellor—Rev. PATRICK J. TRAVERS, J.C.L., J.D.

Diocesan Consultors—Rev. PETER GORGES; MICHAEL NASH; PERRY KENASTON; PATRICK J. TRAVERS, J.C.L., J.D.; MICHAEL SCHWARTE; ANTHONY B. DUMMER, O.M.I.

Tribunal—433 Jackson St., Ketchikan, 99901. Tel: 907-247-2755; Fax: 907-225-2571.

Judicial Vicar—Rev. PATRICK J. TRAVERS, J.C.L., J.D.

Defender of the Bond—Sr. CAROLYN ROEBER, O.P., J.C.L., J.D.

Auditor—Ms. DONNA M. STEINFORT.

Notaries—Ms. ROBERTA IZZARD; Ms. DONNA M. STEINFORT; Mr. JAMES M. WINGREN, SR.

Administration—419 Sixth St., #200, Juneau, 99801. Tel: 907-586-2227; Fax: 907-463-3237.

Business Manager and Finance Officer—SKIP ELLIOTT.

Director of Administrative Services—ROBERTA IZZARD.

Assistant to the Finance Officer—DENISE GRANT.

Finance Council—Rev. PETER GORGES; SKIP ELLIOTT; HUGH GRANT; WIN GERMAIN; CATHY BARRETT; CHRIS MILLER; DENISE LICCIOLI.

Diocesan Offices and Directors

Apostleship of the Sea—Port Chaplains: Revs. MICHAEL NASH, *416 Fifth St., Juneau, 99801.* PATRICK TRAVERS, *433 Jackson St., Ketchikan, 99801.* PETER GORGES, *P.O. Box 495, Sitka, 99835.* MICHAEL SCHWARTE, *Box 469, Wrangell, 99929.* MICHAEL SCHWARTE, *P.O. Box 47, Petersburg, 99833.*

Catholic Community Service, Inc.—ROSEMARY HAGEVIG, Exec. Dir., *419 Sixth St., CCS Wing, Juneau, 99801.* Tel: 907-463-6151.

Board of Directors—Most Rev. MICHAEL W. WARFEL, Pres.; DAN AUSTIN; Mr. LOREN GERHARD; MARY GORE; JOHN GREELEY; SHARON KELLY; MARJORIE MENZI; THOMAS SLAGLE; KEVIN SULLIVAN; BEVERLY WARD; JOHN WILLIAMS.

Southeast Senior Services—Vacant, Prog. Dir., *419 Sixth St., CCS Wing, Juneau, 99801.* Tel: 907-463-6153.

Child Care & Family Resources—Vacant, Prog. Dir., *520 Harris St., Juneau, 99801.* Tel: 907-463-6153.

Diocesan Publication "Inside Passage"—LOUISE MILLER, Editor, *419 Sixth St., #200, Juneau, 99801.* Tel: 907-586-2237, Ext. 32.

Ministry Support Center—Directors: Sr. JILL JAEB, O.S.U.; Sr. JOSEPHINE ALORALREA, O.S.U.; MICHAEL PRICE, *419 Sixth St., #200, Juneau, 99801.* Tel: 907-586-2227.

Commission on Liturgy & Spiritual Life—Sr. JILL JAEB, O.S.U., *419 6th St., #200, Juneau, 99801.* Tel: 907-586-1513.

Commission on Charity, Justice and Peace—PETE HOKKY, *419 Sixth St., Juneau, 99801.* Tel: 907-586-2227, Ext. 29.

Commission on Christian Formation—CHARLES ROHRBACHER, *416 Fifth St., Juneau, 99801.* Tel: 907-586-8046.

Permanent Deacon Program—Deacon CHARLES SESLAR, *4133 Columbia Blvd., Juneau, 99801.* Tel: 907-789-2262.

School—TOM SHIVELY, Prin., *Holy Name School, 433 Jackson St., Ketchikan, 99901.* Tel: 907-225-2400.

Shrine of St. Therese—THOMAS FITTERER, *5933 Lund St., Juneau, 99801.* Tel: 907-780-6112. Caretakers: JODIE LILIEDAHL; MARCIA LILIEDAHL, *8695 Short Ct., Juneau, 99801.* Tel: 907-789-9815.

St. Vincent de Paul Society—DAN AUSTIN, *8617 Teal St., Juneau, 99801.* Tel: 907-789-5535.

Special Collections and Archivist—Deacon GARY HORTON, *419 6th St., #200, Juneau, 99801.* Tel: 907-586-2227, Ext. 36.

Vocations—Sr. ZITA SIMON, Dir., *P.O. Box 170, Craig, 99921.* Tel: 907-755-2345.

CLERGY, PARISHES, MISSIONS AND PAROCHIAL SCHOOLS

CITY AND BOROUGH OF JUNEAU

1—CATHEDRAL OF THE NATIVITY OF THE BLESSED VIRGIN MARY, Rev. Michael Nash, Rector.
Res., 416 Fifth St., 99801. Tel: 907-586-1513; Fax: 907-586-8091.

2—ST. PAUL THE APOSTLE, Revs. Anthony B. Dummer, O.M.I.; Juan Gomez.
Res., 9055 Atlin Ave., 99801. Tel: 907-789-2648 (Rectory); 789-7307 (Office); Fax: 907-790-3430.

OUTSIDE THE CITY AND BOROUGH OF JUNEAU

Craig, St. John by the Sea, Rev. Jean-Paulin Lockulu; Sr. Zita Simon, O.P., Pastoral Assoc.
Res., P.O. Box 170, 99921. Tel: 907-755-2345; Fax: 907-755-2350.
Missions—Thorne Bay, P.O. Box 19150, Thorne Bay, 99919. Tel: 907-828-3324; Coffman Cove; Hydaburg; Klawock; Throne Bay; Kasaan; Whale Pass; Naukati; Hollis.

Haines, Sacred Heart, Rev. Jim Blaney, O.M.I.
Res., Box 326, 99827. Tel: 907-766-2241.

Hoonah, Sacred Heart, In res., Deacon Francis Mackin.
Res., P.O. Box 368, 99829. Tel: 907-945-3323.

Ketchikan, Holy Name, Rev. Patrick J. Travers, J.C.L., J.D.
Res., 433 Jackson St., 99901. Tel: 907-225-2570; 225-5352 (Rectory); Fax: 907-247-0041.
School—Tel: 907-225-2400.
Lay Teachers 7; Students 100.
Mission—Metlakatla, Holy Family, P.O. Box 228, Metlakatla, 99926. Fax: 907-247-0041.

Petersburg, St. Catherine of Siena, Rev. Michael Schwarte.
Res., P.O. Box 508, 99833. Tel: 907-772-3257; Fax: 907-772-3020.
Mission—Kake.

Sitka, St. Gregory of Nazianzen, Rev. Peter Gorges; Sr. Maggie Butler, S.S.J., Pastoral Assoc.
Res., P.O. Box 495, 99835. Tel: 907-747-8371; 747-6997; Fax: 907-747-8051.
Mission—Angoon.

Skagway, St. Therese of the Child Jesus, Rev. Jim Blaney, O.M.I.
Res., Box 496, 99840. Tel: 907-983-2271.

Wrangell, St. Rose of Lima, Rev. Michael Schwarte.
Res., Box 469, 99929. Tel: 907-874-3771; Fax: 907-874-3744.

Yakutat, St. Ann, Rev. Perry Kenaston; Sr. Josephine Abralrea, O.S.U., Parish Admin.
Res., P.O. Box 323, 99689. Tel: 907-784-3406.
Missions—Hobart Bay; Cube Cove; Elfin Cove; Gustavus; Pelican; Tenakee Springs.

On Duty Outside the Diocese:
Reverend Fathers—
Finn, William, 11056 N.E. 33rd Pl., #C-2, Bellevue, WA 98005
Gutierrez, Javier, P.O. Box 6315, Chula Vista, CA 92011
Saba, Joseph, 5660 W. Placita Del Risco, Tuscon, AZ 85745

Retired:
Reverend Fathers—
Cronin, James D., 1870-A Vista del Sur, Sante Fe, NM 87505
Frister, Jerome, 3621 Vista Campana S. #70, Oceanside, CA 92057
Ryan, James, 2828 Sloat Rd., Pebble Beach, CA 93953

Permanent Deacons:
Horton, Gary, Cathedral of the Nativity of the Blessed Virgin Mary, Juneau
Johnson, Charles, St. Gregory's, Sitka
Mackin, Francis, St. Gregory's, Sitka
Paradis, Paul, (Retired)
Seslar, Charles, Cathedral of the Nativity of the Blessed Virgin Mary, Juneau

INSTITUTIONS LOCATED IN THE DIOCESE

[A] NURSING HOMES

JUNEAU. *St. Ann's Care Center, Inc.*, 415 Sixth St., 99801. Tel: 907-586-3883
For a complete listing, refer to the Special Care Facilities section.

[B] HOSPITALS

KETCHIKAN. *Ketchikan General Hospital*, 3100 Tongass, 99901. Tel: 907-225-5171; Fax: 907-228-8334
For a complete listing, refer to the Hospitals section.

[C] CONVENTS AND RESIDENCES FOR SISTERS

JUNEAU. *St. Joseph Convent*, 2971 Douglas Hwy., 99801. Tel: 907-586-2085. Intercommunity residence of various religious orders of women. Sisters 2.

KETCHIKAN. *Sisters of St. Joseph of Peace*, 130 Bryant St., #108, 99901. Tel: 907-225-9357.

RELIGIOUS INSTITUTES OF WOMEN REPRESENTED IN THE DIOCESE

For further details refer to the corresponding bracketed number in the Religious Institutes of Women section.

[1070]—*Dominican Sisters.*—O.P.
[3893]—*Sisters of St. Joseph.*—S.S.J.
[3890]—*Sisters of St. Joseph of Peace.*—C.S.J.P.
[]—*Sisters of the Holy Names.*—S.N.J.M.
[]—*Ursuline Sisters of the Roman Union.*—O.S.U.

NECROLOGY

(No Deaths)

Diocese of Kalamazoo

(Dioecesis Kalamazuensis)

Most Reverend

JAMES A. MURRAY

Bishop of Kalamazoo; ordained June 7, 1958; appointed Bishop of Kalamazoo November 18, 1997; ordained and installed January 27, 1998.

Most Reverend

PAUL V. DONOVAN, D.D.

Former Bishop of Kalamazoo; ordained May 20, 1950; appointed Bishop of Kalamazoo June 15, 1971; ordained and installed July 21, 1971; resigned November 22, 1994. *Mailing Address: 238 Falkirk Ct., Kalamazoo, MI, 49006.*

ESTABLISHED JULY 21, 1971.

Square Miles 5,337.

Comprises the following nine Counties in the State of Michigan: Allegan, Barry, Berrien, Branch, Calhoun, Cass, Kalamazoo, St. Joseph and Van Buren.

For legal titles of parishes and diocesan institutions, consult the Chancery.

Chancery: 215 N. Westnedge Ave., Kalamazoo, MI, 49007-3760. Tel.: 616-349-8714; Fax: 616-349-6440.

STATISTICAL OVERVIEW

Personnel	
Bishop	1
Retired Bishops	1
Priests: Diocesan Active in Diocese	39
Priests: Retired, Sick or Absent	17
Number of Diocesan Priests	56
Religious Priests in Diocese	13
Extern Priests in Diocese	12
Ordinations:	
Transitional Deacons	1
Permanent Deacons in Diocese	23
Total Brothers	3
Total Sisters	155
Parishes	
Parishes	46
With Resident Pastor:	
Resident Diocesan Priests	37
Resident Religious Priests	5
Without Resident Pastor:	
Administered by Deacons	2
Administered by Women Religious	2
Missions	13
Pastoral Centers	1
Professional Ministry Personnel:	
Brothers	3
Sisters	12
Lay Ministers	38
Welfare	
Catholic Hospitals	3
Total Assisted	628,992
Day Care and Extended Day Care Centers	8
Total Assisted	293
Specialized Homes	2
Total Assisted	246
Special Centers for Social Services	5
Total Assisted	30,825
Educational	
Diocesan Students in Other Seminaries	12
Total Seminarians	12
High Schools, Diocesan and Parish	3
Total Students	827
Elementary Schools, Diocesan and Parish	22
Total Students	3,672
Catechesis/Religious Education:	
High School Students	767
Elementary Students	5,461
Total Students Under Catholic Instruction	10,739
Teachers in the Diocese:	
Sisters	5
Lay Teachers	286
Vital Statistics	
Receptions into the Church:	
Infant Baptism Totals	1,644
Adult Baptism Totals	295
First Communions	1,586
Confirmations	1,522
Marriages:	
Catholic	304
Interfaith	254
Total Marriages	558
Deaths	922
Total Catholic Population	117,523
Total Population	917,327

Former Bishops—Most Rev. PAUL V. DONOVAN, D.D., ord. May 20, 1950; appt. Bishop of Kalamazoo June 15, 1971; installed July 21, 1971; resigned Nov. 22, 1994.—Most Rev. ALFRED J. MARKIEWICZ, D.D., ord. June 6, 1953; appt. Titular Bishop of Afufenia and Auxiliary to the Bishop of Rockville Centre, July 7, 1986; ord. Bishop, Sept. 17, 1986; appt. Bishop of Kalamazoo, Nov. 22, 1994; installed Jan. 31, 1995; died Jan. 9, 1997.

Vicar General—Rev. EUGENE A. SEARS, *211 Church St., St. Joseph, 49085.* Tel: 616-983-1575; Fax: 616-983-1576.

Chancery—215 N. Westnedge Ave., Kalamazoo, 49007-3760. Tel: 616-349-8714; Fax: 616-349-6440. Office Hours: 8:30-4; Address all communications to this office.

Chancellor—Mr. T. EDWARD CAREY, JR., *215 N. Westnedge Ave., Kalamazoo, 49007.* Tel: 616-349-8714, Ext. 116; Fax: 616-349-6440.

Diocesan Tribunal—215 N. Westnedge Ave., Kalamazoo, 49007-3760. Tel: 616-349-8714, Ext. 115; Fax: 616-349-6440.

Judicial Vicar—MICHAEL A. OSBORN, J.C.L.

Adjutant Judicial Vicar—LEONARD A. BOGDAN, J.C.D.

Defenders of the Bond—Revs. MICHAEL A. HACK, J.C.D.; JEFFREY A. KASSIAN, J.C.O.L.

Promoter of Justice—Rev. MICHAEL A. HACK, J.C.D.

Judges—Revs. KENNETH W. SCHMIDT, J.C.D.; EDWARD A. HANKIEWICZ, J.C.L.; THOMAS A. MARTIN, J.C.D.; Sr. JOYCE HOBEN, S.N.D., J.C.L.

Advocate—Mr. MARK MILLER, J.D.

Chief Notary and Administrative Assistant—Mrs. MARLENE J. PRANSKATIS.

Notaries—Mrs. NANCY L. BOOTHBY; Mrs. AUDREY J. ARENDARSKI.

Archivist—Rev. ROBERT F. CREAGAN, *209 S. Brown St., Paw Paw, 49079.* Tel: 616-657-4459; Fax: 616-657-4260.

Diocesan Consultors—Revs. DAVID C. ADAMS; WILLIAM J. FITZGERALD; MICHAEL D. HAZARD; JAMES A. MORRIS; JAMES S. O'LEARY; EUGENE A. SEARS; MARK J. VYVERMAN.

Vicar for Religious—Sr. MARY JOAN WALSH, S.S.J., *4111 Nazareth Rd., Kalamazoo, 49004.* Tel: 616-226-4839.

Diocesan Offices and Directors

Campaign for Human Development—Sr. SUSAN RIDLEY, O.P., Dir., *215 N. Westnedge Ave., Kalamazoo, 49007-3760.* Tel: 616-349-8714, Ext. 238; Fax: 616-349-6440.

Catholic Family Services—Mrs. FRANCES H. DENNY, Exec. Dir., *1819 Gull Rd., Kalamazoo, 49001.* Tel: 616-381-9800; Fax: 616-381-2932.

Catholic Relief Services—Sr. SUSAN RIDLEY, O.P., Dir., *215 N. Westnedge Ave., Kalamazoo, 49007-3760.* Tel: 616-349-8714, Ext. 238; Fax: 616-349-6440.

Cemeteries—Mr. T. EDWARD CAREY, JR., *215 N. Westnedge Ave., Kalamazoo, 49007.* Tel: 616-349-8714, Ext. 116; Fax: 616-349-6440.

Diocesan Cemetery - Kalamazoo—Mt. Olivet.

Children & Adult Catechesis—Mr. D. J. FLORIAN, Dir., *215 N. Westnedge Ave., Kalamazoo, 49007-3760.* Tel: 616-349-8714, Ext. 227; Fax: 616-349-6440.

Christian Service—Sr. SUSAN RIDLEY, O.P., Dir., *215 N. Westnedge Ave., Kalamazoo, 49007-3760.* Tel: 616-349-8714, Ext. 238; Fax: 616-349-6440.

Common Ministry—Mrs. MARY JANE DOERR, Dir., *215 N. Westnedge Ave., Kalamazoo, 49007-3760.* Tel: 616-349-8714, Ext. 246; Fax: 616-349-6440.

Communications—Mrs. SUSAN H. HAJEC, *215 N. Westnedge Ave., Kalamazoo, 49007-3760.* Tel: 616-349-8714, Ext. 230.

Audio-Visual Resources—Mr. D. J. FLORIAN, Coord., *215 N. Westnedge Ave., Kalamazoo, 49007-3760.* Tel: 616-349-8714, Ext. 227.

Diocesan Council of Catholic Women (D.C.C.W.)—Rev. DONALD P. KLINGER, Spiritual Dir. ROSETTA "KITTY" CHASE, Pres., *Sacred Heart Parish, Bangor, 11131 CR 215, Grand Junction, 49056.* Tel: 616-434-6856.

Diocesan Development Office—Mr. DAVID BAERWALDE, Dir., *215 N. Westnedge Ave., Kalamazoo, 49007-3760.* Tel: 616-349-8714, Ext. 349.

Diocesan Pastoral Council—Vacant, *215 N. Westnedge Ave., Kalamazoo, 49007-3760.* Tel: 616-349-8714.

Diocesan-Parish Council Ministry—Vacant, *215 N. Westnedge Ave., Kalamazoo, 49007-3760.* Tel: 616-349-8714.

Diocesan Pilgrimages—Rev. ROBERT F. CREAGAN, Diocesan Coord., *209 S. Brown St., Paw Paw, 49079.* Tel: 616-657-4459; Fax: 616-657-4260.

Education—FRANK C. WIPPEL, Ed.D., Supt. of Schools. Associate Superintendents: Mrs. MARGARET ERICH, Ext. 239. Sr. MARY ANN DALTON, S.S.J., Ext. 248., *215 N. Westnedge Ave., Kalamazoo, 49007-3760.* Tel: 616-349-8714, Ext. 235; Fax: 616-349-6440. Rev. WILLIAM J. FITZGERALD, Consultant-Resource Person on Educational Matters, *92 Capital Ave., N.E., Battle Creek, 49017.* Tel: 616-968-6645.

Finance Council—Rev. DAVID C. ADAMS; Mr. T. EDWARD CAREY, JR.; Mr. ED EDWARDS; Mr. ED KOWIESKI; Mr. DANIEL KUNITZER; Mr. JERRY B. LOVE; Mr. JOHN A. PANFIL; Mr. BRUCE RAGAN; Mr. LEO A. SWIAT.

Holy Childhood Association—Rev. ROBERT F. CREAGAN, Dir., *215 N. Westnedge Ave., Kalamazoo, 49007-3760.* Tel: 616-349-8714, Ext. 119.

Inner City Ministry—Sr. RITA SCHAFER, S.S.J.; Sr. MARY PUNG, S.S.J., *Catholic Community Center, 589 Pearl St., Benton Harbor, 49022.* Tel: 616-926-6424; Fax: 616-926-2870.

Jail Ministry—Sr. MARILYN SULLIVAN, S.S.J., Coord., *215 N. Westnedge Ave., Kalamazoo, 49007-3760.* Tel: 616-349-8714.

Knights of Columbus—Rev. ROBERT F. CREAGAN, Diocesan Chap., *209 S. Brown St., Paw Paw, 49079.* Tel: 616-657-4459; Fax: 616-657-4260.

Marriage and Family Ministry, Office of—Mr. JOE SCHMITT, Dir. Tel: 616-349-8714, Ext. 112. Mrs. MARCELLA V. KELEMEN, Admin. Dir. Tel: 616-349-8714, Ext. 113., *215 N. Westnedge Ave., Kalamazoo, 49007-3760;* Fax: 616-349-6440.

Ministry Formation—Sr. MARLENE HALPIN, O.P., Dir., *215 N. Westnedge Ave., Kalamazoo, 49007-3760.* Tel: 616-349-8714, Ext. 233.

Ministry with Persons with Disabilities—Miss ANN SHERZER, Dir., *215 N. Westnedge Ave., Kalamazoo, 49007-3760.* Tel: 616-349-7276, Ext. 229.

Missions—Rev. ROBERT F. CREAGAN, Dir., *215 N. Westnedge Ave., Kalamazoo, 49007-3760.* Tel: 616-349-8714, Ext. 119; Fax: 616-349-6440.

Natural Family Planning Center of Southwestern Michigan—Mrs. MARY CULP, Exec. Dir., *165 N. Washington St., Battle Creek, 49017.* Tel: 616-964-9474; Fax: 616-964-0431.

Permanent Diaconate—Mr. D. J. FLORIAN, Chm., *215 N. Westnedge Ave., Kalamazoo, 49007-3760.* Tel: 616-349-8714, Ext. 227; Fax: 616-349-6440.

Presbyteral Council—Revs. DAVID C. ADAMS; WILLIAM J. FITZGERALD; MICHAEL D. HAZARD; JAMES A. MORRIS; JAMES S. O'LEARY; EUGENE A. SEARS; MARK J. VYVERMAN.

Priestly Life and Ministry Office—Rev. MICHAEL D. HAZARD, Dir., *936 Lake St., Kalamazoo, 49001.* Tel: 616-343-6256; Fax: 616-343-1214.

Respect Life—Sr. SUSAN RIDLEY, O.P., Dir., *215 N. Westnedge Ave., Kalamazoo, 49007-3760.* Tel: 616-349-8714, Ext. 238; Fax: 616-349-6440.

St. Vincent DePaul Society—Rev. LAWRENCE W. KROLL, Spiritual Advisor, *534 W. Kilgore Rd., Kalamazoo, 49008.* Tel: 616-345-4389; Fax: 616-345-5211.

Scouting Apostolate—Deacon JERRY MIX, Chap., *62012 Bayshore Dr., Sturgis, 49091.* Tel: 616-467-8100.

Spanish-Speaking Apostolate—Ms. FANNY TABARES, Dir., *215 N. Westnedge Ave., Kalamazoo, 49007-3760.* Tel: 616-349-8714, Ext. 236; Fax: 616-349-6440.

Vocations—Rev. ROBERT F. CREAGAN, Dir., *215 N. Westnedge Ave., Kalamazoo, 49007-3760.* Tel: 616-349-8714, Ext. 242; Fax: 616-349-6440.

Worship and Initiation, Office of—Mr. DAVID J. REILLY, Dir., *215 N. Westnedge Ave., Kalamazoo, 49007-3760.* Tel: 616-349-8714, Ext. 245; Fax: 616-349-6440.

Youth and Young Adult Ministry—Miss LISA IRWIN, Dir., *215 N. Westnedge Ave., Kalamazoo, 49007-3760.* Tel: 616-349-8714, Ext. 228; Fax: 616-349-6440.

Address communications for all other offices to Chancery, Diocese of Kalamazoo. *215 N. Westnedge Ave., Kalamazoo, 49007-3760;* Fax: 616-349-6440.

CLERGY, PARISHES, MISSIONS AND PAROCHIAL SCHOOLS

CITY OF KALAMAZOO
(Kalamazoo County)

1—ST. AUGUSTINE CATHEDRAL (1856), Revs. Mark J. Vyverman; Mark Ghyselinck, C.S.C.; A. Thomas Fernando (India).
Res., 542 W. Michigan Ave., 49007. Tel: 616-345-5147; Fax: 616-349-0166.
School—600 W. Michigan Ave., 49007. Tel: 616-349-1945; Fax: 616-349-1085.
Lay Teachers 23; Students 301.
Catechesis/Religious Programs—Tel: 616-345-6055.
Students 90.

2—ST. JOSEPH (1904), Revs. Michael D. Hazard; Robert F. Dentzman, O.F.M.; Deacon John Bodway.
Res., 936 Lake St., 49001. Tel: 616-343-6256; Fax: 616-343-1214.
School—930 Lake St., 49001. Tel: 616-342-9441; Fax: 616-343-1214.
Lay Teachers 13; Students 138.
Catechesis/Religious Programs—Tel: 616-343-6258.
Students 181.

3—ST. MARY (1935), Rev. Stephen E. Naas.
Res., 939 Charlotte Ave., 49048. Tel: 616-342-0621.
School—929 Charlotte Ave., 49048. Tel: 616-342-2884.
Lay Teachers 11; Students 116.
Catechesis/Religious Programs—Students 89.

4—ST. MONICA (1935), Revs. Lawrence W. Kroll; Michael Rejent, O.S.F.S. In res., Rev. Gaylord Shimnowski.
Res., 534 W. Kilgore Rd., 49008. Tel: 616-345-4389; Fax: 616-345-5211.
School—530 W. Kilgore Rd., 49008. Tel: 616-345-2444; Fax: 616-345-8534.
Sisters of St. Joseph 1; Lay Teachers 22; Students 475.

5—ST. THOMAS MORE STUDENT PARISH (1956), Rev. Kenneth W. Schmidt.
Office: 421 Monroe St., 49006. Tel: 616-381-8917; Fax: 616-381-0195.
Catechesis/Religious Programs—936 Lake St., 49001. Tel: 616-343-6256; Fax: 616-343-1214.
Students 61.

OUTSIDE THE CITY OF KALAMAZOO

Albion, Calhoun Co., St. John the Evangelist (1873), Rev. Gordon L. Greene.
Office: 879 Finley Dr., 49224-9712. Tel: 517-629-4532; Fax: 517-629-5462. [CEM]
School—1020 Irwin Ave., 49224-1507. Tel: 517-629-6132; Fax: 517-629-8806.
Lay Teachers 5; Students 83.
Catechesis/Religious Programs—Students 57.

Allegan, Allegan Co., Blessed Sacrament (1934), Rev. Jerome M. Heyman, O.S.A.
Res., 422 Hubbard St., 49010-1246. Tel: 616-673-4455; Fax: 616-673-5869. [CEM]
Church—110 Cedar St., 49010-1244.
Catechesis/Religious Programs—Students 155.

Bangor, Van Buren Co., Sacred Heart of Jesus (1932), Rev. Thomas Seidel, C.S.C., Admin.
Res., 201 S. Walnut St., 49013. Tel: 616-427-7514; Fax: 616-427-5558. [CEM]
Catechesis/Religious Programs—Tel: 616-427-8202.
Students 68.
Chapel—Grand Junction, St. Cyril. (summer).

Battle Creek, Calhoun Co., St. Jerome (1955), Deacon Albert W. Patrick.
Res., 229 Collier Ave., 49017. Tel: 616-968-2218; Fax: 616-968-2233. [JC]

St. Joseph (1942), Revs. James S. O'Leary; Zdzislaw Gnat (Poland); Stephen Rodrigo (India). In res., Rev. Donn J. Taylor.
Res., 61 N. 23rd St., 49015. Tel: 616-962-0165; Fax: 616-962-5937. [JC]
School—63 N. 24th St., 49015. Tel: 616-965-7749; Fax: 616-965-0790.
Lay Teachers 17; Students 313.
Catechesis/Religious Programs—Tel: 616-465-4079.
Students 295.

St. Philip (1869), Revs. William J. Fitzgerald; Jaya Rao Polimera (India); Anthaiah Bitchapogu (India).
Office: 126 Capital Ave., N.E., 49017. Tel: 616-968-6645; Fax: 616-968-0632.
Res., 92 Capital Ave., N.E., 49017. [CEM]
School—(Grades 6-12) 20 Cherry St., 49017. Tel: 616-963-4935; Fax: 616-963-5590.
Lay Teachers 24; Students 186.
Catechesis/Religious Programs—Tel: 616-962-9506.
Students 129.

Benton Harbor, Berrien Co., Ss. John & Bernard (1996), Rev. David C. Adams.
Res., 600 Columbus Ave., 49022. Tel: 616-925-2425; Fax: 616-925-4678. [CEM]
Catechesis/Religious Programs—220 Church St., St. Joseph, 49085. Tel: 616-983-7797.
Students 34.

St. Bernard. Merged with St. John, Benton Harbor.

St. John the Evangelist. Merged with St. Bernard, Benton Harbor.

Bridgman, Berrien Co., Our Lady Queen of Peace (1939), Rev. Raymond J. Barth.
Res., 3903 Lake St., P.O. Box 747, 49106-0747. Tel: 616-465-6252; Fax: 616-465-4930.
Catechesis/Religious Programs—Students 99.

Bronson, Branch Co., St. Mary's (1867) (Polish), Rev. Richard A. Fritz.
Res., 602 W. Chicago, 49028. Tel: 517-369-2120; Fax: 517-369-5101. [CEM]
School—204 Albers Rd., 49028. Tel: 517-369-4625; Fax: 517-369-1652.
Lay Teachers 8; Students 89.
Mission—Colon, St. Joseph Co., St. Barbara.
Catechesis/Religious Programs—Students 39.

Buchanan, Berrien Co., St. Anthony (1963), Rev. Charles T. Page.
Res., 509 W. 4th St., 49107. Tel: 616-695-3863; Fax: 616-695-3864.
Catechesis/Religious Programs—Students 72.

Byron Center, Kent Co., St. Mary's Visitation (1866), Rev. Richard L. Altine.
Res., 2459 146th Ave., 49315. Tel: 616-681-9701; Fax: 616-681-9919. [JC 2]
School—2455 146th Ave., 49315.
Lay Teachers 6; Students 120.
Catechesis/Religious Programs—Students 171.

Cassopolis, Cass Co., St. Ann (1915), Rev. Donald G. Potts.
Res., 313 N. Broadway, P.O. Box 247, 49031. Tel: 616-445-3000; Fax: 616-445-5787.
Church—421 N. Broadway, P.O. Box 247, 49031. Tel: 616-445-3000; Fax: 616-445-5787.
Catechesis/Religious Programs—Students 52.

Coldwater, Branch Co., St. Charles Borromeo (1849), Rev. Brian L. Stanley.
Res., 150 Taylor St., 49036. Tel: 517-278-2650; Fax: 517-278-5800.
School—79 Harrison St., 49036. Tel: 517-279-0404; Fax: 517-278-0505.
Lay Teachers 8; Students 118.
Catechesis/Religious Programs—Students 104.
Mission—Union City, Branch Co., Our Lady of Fatima, Tel: 517-741-7275.

Decatur, Van Buren Co., Holy Family (1938), Deacon Bartholomew E. Connolly.
Res., 500 W. St. Mary Blvd., 49045. Tel: 616-423-3151; Fax: 616-423-7755.
Catechesis/Religious Programs—Students 41.

Delton, Barry Co., St. Ambrose (1950), Rev. Richard G. Valls.
Res., 11252 Floria Rd., 49046. Tel: 616-623-2490; Fax: 616-623-2498.
Catechesis/Religious Programs—Students 74.
Mission—Lacey, Barry Co., Our Lady of Great Oak, 6547 Lacey Rd., Lacey, 49021. Tel: 616-758-3636.

Dorr, Allegan Co., St. Stanislaus (1892) (Polish), Rev. James Vinh Le.
Res., 1871 136th Ave., 49323. Tel: 616-793-7268; Fax: 616-793-7268. [CEM]
School—1861 136th Ave., 49323. Tel: 616-793-7204; Fax: 616-793-3264.
Lay Teachers 6; Students 135.
Catechesis/Religious Programs—Students 98.
Mission—Watson, Allegan Co., Sacred Heart. [CEM]

Douglas, Allegan Co., St. Peter (1894), Rev. Ronald R. Turchich, O.S.A.
Res., St. Peter's Dr., 49406. Tel: 616-857-7951; 857-8175; Fax: 616-857-8164.

Dowagiac, Cass Co., Holy Maternity of Mary (1892), Rev. Leo A. Taubitz.
Res., 210 N. Front St., 49047. Tel: 616-782-2808; Fax: 616-782-3558. [CEM]
Catechesis/Religious Programs—Students 109.

Edwardsburg, Cass Co., Our Lady of the Lake (1923), Rev. David C. Otto.
Res., 24832 U.S. 12 E., 49112. Tel: 616-699-5870; Fax: 616-699-5474.
Catechesis/Religious Programs—Students 167.

Gobles, Van Buren Co., St. Jude (1985), Sr. Theresa V. MacIntyre, S.S.J., Pastoral Min.
Church and Mailing Address: 13809 M-40 N., P.O. Box 102, 49055. Tel: 616-628-2219; Fax: 616-628-2219.
Res., 405 S. Slate St., Apt. 2, 49055. Tel: 616-628-4424.
Catechesis/Religious Programs—Students 38.

Gull Lake, Kalamazoo Co., St. Ann (1958), Rev. Michael A. Osborn.
Res., 12648 E. D Ave., Augusta, 49012. Tel: 616-731-4721; Fax: 616-731-4147.
Catechesis/Religious Programs—Tel: 616-731-0295; Fax: 616-731-4147.
Students 315.

Hartford, Van Buren Co., Immaculate Conception (1946) (Hispanic), Rev. German Perez Diaz.
Res., 63559 60th Ave., P.O. Box 185, 49057. Tel: 616-621-4106; Fax: 616-621-2138.
Catechesis/Religious Programs—Students 156.

Hastings, Barry Co., St. Rose of Lima (1873), Rev. Charles H. Fischer.
Res., 805 S. Jefferson Ave., 49058. Tel: 616-945-4246; Fax: 616-945-0005. [CEM]
School—707 S. Jefferson St., 49058. Tel: 616-945-3164.
Sisters of St. Joseph 1; Lay Teachers 6; Students 144.
Catechesis/Religious Programs—Students 113.
Mission—Nashville, Barry Co., St. Cyril, 203 N. State St., Nashville, 49073.

Marshall, Calhoun Co., St. Mary (1852), Rev. James L. Barrett.
Res., 212 Hanover St., 49068. Tel: 616-781-3949; 781-7341; Fax: 616-781-3632. [CEM]

Mattawan, Van Buren Co., St. John Bosco (1952), Rev. Bogdan Werra (Poland).
Res., 23830 Front Ave., 49071. Tel: 616-668-3312; Fax: 616-668-3313.
Catechesis/Religious Programs—Students 270.
Mission—Marcellus, Cass Co., St. Margaret Mary, 296 E. Dibble St., Marcellus, 49067.

Mendon, St. Joseph Co., St. Edward (1872), Rev. Thomas A. Martin.
Res., 332 W. State, P.O. Box 368, 49072. Tel: 616-496-3525; Fax: 616-496-8640. [CEM]
Catechesis/Religious Programs—Students 79.

New Buffalo, Berrien Co., St. Mary of the Lake (1857), Rev. Thomas F. DeVita.
Res., 718 W. Buffalo St., 49117. Tel: 616-469-2637; Fax: 616-469-7393.
School—704 W. Merchant St., 49117. Tel: 616-469-1515; Fax: 616-469-3772.
Lay Teachers 10; Students 217.
Catechesis/Religious Programs—Students 27.

Niles, Berrien Co., St. Mark (1955), Rev. Joseph W. Koma, C.S.C.
Res., 3 N. 19th St., 49120. Tel: 616-683-8650; Fax: 616-683-9314.
Catechesis/Religious Programs—Tel: 616-684-4855.
Students 64.

St. Mary (1870), Rev. Canon Marian M. Kencik (Poland); Rev. Stanley Witek (Poland).
Res., 211 S. Lincoln Ave., 49120. Tel: 616-683-5087; Fax: 616-683-5089. [CEM 2]
School—217 S. Lincoln Ave., 49120. Tel: 616-683-9191.
Sisters 1; Lay Teachers 7; Students 143.
Catechesis/Religious Programs—Students 158.
Convent—219 S. State St., 49120. Tel: 616-683-8630.
Mission—Berrien Springs, Berrien Co., St. Gabriel Mission Church, 429 Rose Hill, Berrien Springs, 49103. Tel: 616-471-2424.

Otsego, Allegan Co., St. Margaret (1887), Rev. Donald P. Klingler.
Res., 245 Court St., 49078. Tel: 616-694-6311; Fax: 616-694-5415. [CEM]
School—736 S. Farmer, 49078. Tel: 616-694-2951; Fax: 616-694-4520.
Lay Teachers 10; Students 147.
Catechesis/Religious Programs—Tel: 616-694-9708.
Students 205.

Parchment, Kalamazoo Co., St. Ambrose (1955), Rev. Carl F. Peltz (STU).
Res., 1628 E. G Ave., 49004. Tel: 616-385-4152; Fax: 616-385-2527.
Catechesis/Religious Programs—Students 133.

Paw Paw, Van Buren Co., St. Mary (1887), Revs. Robert F. Creagan; Jeffrey A. Kassian (STN).
Res., 500 Paw Paw St., 49079. Tel: 616-657-4459; Fax: 616-657-4260. [CEM]
School—508 Paw Paw St., 49079. Tel: 616-657-3750; Fax: 616-657-4260.
Lay Teachers 8; Students 141.
Catechesis/Religious Programs—Tel: 616-657-3497.
Students 238.
Mission—Gobles, Van Buren Co., St. Jude's Church.

Pearl, Allegan Co., San Felipe de Jesus (1986) (Hispanic), Mr. Ricardo Martinez, Pastoral Coord.
Mailing Address: P.O. Box 588, Fennville, 49408. Tel: 616-561-5029.
Catechesis/Religious Programs—Students 28.

Portage, Kalamazoo Co., St. Catherine of Siena (1966), Revs. Robert E. Flickinger; Kevin A. Covert, O.F.M.Cap. In res., Revs. John M. Grathwohl; Alfred Russell, O.S.F.S.
Res., 1150 W. Centre St., 49024-5385. Tel: 616-327-5962; Fax: 616-327-7266.
Catechesis/Religious Programs—Tel: 616-327-0861.
Students 1,197.

St. Joseph, Berrien Co., St. Joseph (1720), Revs. Eugene A. Sears; James A. Morris; Mark J. Nojek (Poland); Deacons John F. DeStazio; Alfred Lazaga; Michael Gallagher.
Res., 211 Church St., 49085. Tel: 616-983-1575; Fax: 616-983-6305. [CEM]
Annex: Stevensville, 5353 S. Roosevelt Rd., 49085. Tel: 616-489-1074.

Silver Creek, Cass Co., Sacred Heart of Mary (1838) (Native American), Sr. Monica Marie Ruoff, S.S.J., Pastoral Coord.
Res., 51841 Leach Rd., Dowagiac, 49047. Tel: 616-782-5740; Fax: 616-782-5692. [CEM]
Catechesis/Religious Programs—Students 66.

South Haven, Van Buren Co., St. Basil (1900), Rev. John E. Young.
Res., 513 Monroe Blvd., 49090. Tel: 616-637-2404; Fax: 616-637-8374.
School—94 Superior St., 49090. Tel: 616-637-3529; Fax: 616-639-1242.
Lay Teachers 9; Students 155.
Catechesis/Religious Programs—Students 65.

Sturgis, St. Joseph Co., Holy Angels (1921), Rev. Leon H. Pohl.
Res., 402 S. Nottawa St., 49091. Tel: 616-651-5200; Fax: 616-659-8366.
School—Tel: 616-651-2088.
Lay Teachers 9; Students 163.

Three Oaks, Berrien Co., St. Mary of the Assumption (1880), Rev. Donald Suberlak, C.R.
Res., 28 W. Ash St., 49128. Tel: 616-756-2041; Fax: 616-756-2212.
Catechesis/Religious Programs—Students 60.
Mission—Sawyer, Berrien Co., St. Agnes.

Three Rivers, St. Joseph Co., Immaculate Conception (1885), Rev. Mathew K. Illikattil; Deacon Robert Pellack.
Res., 645 S. Douglas Ave., 49093. Tel: 616-273-8953; Fax: 616-273-2114.
School—601 S. Douglas Ave., 49093-2044. Tel: 616-273-2085; Fax: 616-273-2114.
Lay Teachers 8; Students 95.
Catechesis/Religious Programs—Tel: 616-273-8953. Diann Robinson, D.R.E.
Students 50.
Mission—Centreville, St. Clare.

Vicksburg, Kalamazoo Co., St. Martin (1951), Sr. Marjorie Manning, C.S.C., Pastoral Coord.
Res., 5855 E. W Ave., 49097. Tel: 616-649-1629; Fax: 616-649-2877.
Catechesis/Religious Programs—5835 East W. Ave., 49097. Tel: 616-649-3626.
Students 229.

Watervliet, Berrien Co., St. Joseph (1896), Rev. Donald A. Wieber.
Res., 179 Lucinda Ln., Box 157, 49098. Tel: 616-463-5470; Fax: 616-463-4642. [CEM]
School—Tel: 616-463-3941; Fax: 616-463-4525.
Lay Teachers 8; Students 190.
Catechesis/Religious Programs—Tel: 616-463-5540.
Students 95.

Wayland, Allegan Co., St. Therese (1942), Rev. Gary W. Pamment.
Res., 128 Cedar St., 49348. Tel: 616-792-2138; 792-9315; Fax: 616-792-2908.
School—Tel: 616-792-2016.
Lay Teachers 5; Students 85.
Catechesis/Religious Programs—Tel: 616-792-9138.
Students 179.

SS. Cyril and Methodius (1917), Sr. Marie Beaulac, S.S.J., Pastoral Coord.
Church—150-131st Ave., 49348. Tel: 616-792-2889; Fax: 616-792-6244. [CEM]
Catechesis/Religious Programs—Students 56.

White Pigeon, St. Joseph Co., St. Joseph (1832), Sr. Maxine McGee, S.S.J., Pastoral Coord.
Res., 16603 E. U.S. 12, P.O. Box 344, 49099-0344. Tel: 616-483-7621; Fax: 616-483-7891. [CEM]
Catechesis/Religious Programs—Students 46.

Chaplains of Public Institutions

COLDWATER. *Camp Branch*. Rev. Brian L. Stanley, Volunteer Chap., St. Charles Church, 150 Taylor St., 49036. Tel: 517-278-2650; Fax: 517-278-5800.
Florence Crane Correctional Facility for Women. Rev. Brian L. Stanley, Volunteer Chap.
Lakeland Correctional Facility for Men. Rev. Brian L. Stanley, Volunteer Chap.

Retired:
Reverend Fathers—
Atchison, Donald W., 5021 Gilead Shores, Bronson, MI 49028
Bogdan, Leonard A., P.O. Box 5753, Sun City Center, AZ 85376-5753
Burger, Frank J., P.O. Box 143, Grand Junction, MI 49506
Consani, Robert E., 1604 Laughton Pl., Sun City Center, FL 33573
Crenner, William A., 465 Gladys, Apt. J, Kalamazoo, MI 49002
Crowley, Charles J., 1516 Vassar Dr., Kalamazoo, MI 49001
Ginther, Benjamin H., 1328 E. V.W. Ave., Box 10, Vicksburg, MI 49097
Grathwohl, John M., St. Catherine Church, 1150 W. Centre St., Portage, MI 49024
Hengesbach, Julius L., 13599 Jason Rd., Portland, MI 48875
Limbert, William G., 11859 Marquette Dr., New Buffalo, MI 49117
Sonefeld, Raymond G., 814 Engleman St., Manistee, MI 49660
Spillane, Walter J., 63 Centennial Dr., #17, Norwood, MA 02062
Steffey, John M., 9160 E. D Ave., Apt. 502, Richland, MI 49083
Taylor, Donn J., 61 N. 23rd St., Battle Creek, MI 49015
Thachet, Joseph, House 21, Skyline Park Villas, Cherukode, TVM, Peyad 695-573 Kerala, India
Weller, Joseph W., P.O. Box 231, New Buffalo, MI 49117
White, Leroy E., 317 N. Dayton St., Davison, MI 48423
Wieber, Elmer F., 3317 N. Stewart, Tucson, AZ 85716

Permanent Deacons:
Barbosa, Juan, San Felipe de Jesus, Pearl
Bartholomew, David, St. Monica, Kalamazoo
Bodway, John, St. Joseph, Kalamazoo
Carroll, Edward, St. Mary of the Lake, New Buffalo
Connolly, Bart, Holy Family, Decatur
DeStazio, John F. (TOL), St. Joseph, St. Joseph
Gallagher, Michael, St. Joseph, St. Joseph
Lazaga, Alfred C. (MI), St. Joseph, St. Joseph
Mathias, James, St. Philip, Battle Creek
Mix, Jerome (CHI), Holy Angels, Sturgis
Moreno, Michael, St. Joseph, Battle Creek
Morsaw, Art, Immaculate Conception, Hartford
Patrick, Albert W., St. Jerome, Battle Creek
Pellack, Robert, Immaculate Conception, Three Rivers
Prendergast, John (RCK), St. Catherine of Siena, Portage
Provot, Alvin (DET), St. Charles, Coldwater
Rauner, James D. (FTW), St. Joseph, Watervliet
Rodriguez, Maximino, San Felipe de Jesus, Pearl
Smoker, Gerald J., St. Mary, Bronson
Stevens, Robert, St. Monica, Kalamazoo
Van Dril, William, Blessed Sacrament, Allegan
Whitehouse, Howard (DET), St. Mary, Niles
Wright, Gary, St. Jerome, Battle Creek

INSTITUTIONS LOCATED IN THE DIOCESE

[A] HIGH SCHOOLS, DIOCESAN

KALAMAZOO. *Msgr. Hackett Catholic Central High School*, 1000 W. Kilgore Rd., 49008. Tel: 616-381-2646; Fax: 616-381-3919.
E-mail: Hackett@KRESANET.ORG
Mr. James Miner, Prin. Lay Teachers 25; Students 477.

BATTLE CREEK. *St. Philip Catholic Central High School*, 20 Cherry St., 49017. Tel: 616-963-4503; Fax: 616-963-5590. Mr. Mike Low, Prin. Sisters 1; Lay Teachers 11; Students 161.

ST. JOSEPH. *Lake Michigan Catholic Junior High and High School*. (Grades 7-12), 915 Pleasant St., 49085. Tel: 616-983-2511; Fax: 616-983-0883.
E-mail: dbooth@remcII.k12.MI.US
Mr. Philip Brooks, Prin. Adrian Dominican Sisters of Immaculate Conception Province 1; Lay Teachers 17; Students 293.

[B] GRADE SCHOOLS, INTERPAROCHIAL

ST. JOSEPH. *Lake Michighan Catholic Schools*. (Grades PreK-6), 3165 Washington Ave., 49085. Tel: 616-429-0227; Fax: 616-429-1461.
E-mail: diokazoolme@Impresso.com
Mrs. Karla J. Cook, Prin. Lay Teachers 21; Students 390.

[C] CATHOLIC SOCIAL AGENCIES

KALAMAZOO. *Catholic Family Services*, 1819 Gull Rd., 49048. Tel: 616-381-9800; Fax: 616-381-2932.
E-mail: fdennyacsw@aol.com
Web site: www.telecity.org/cfs
Mrs. Frances H. Denny, A.C.S.W., Exec. Dir.

[D] GENERAL HOSPITALS

KALAMAZOO. *Borgess Medical Center*, 1521 Gull Rd., 49048-1640. Tel: 616-226-7000; Fax: 616-226-7396.
E-mail: rstasik@borgess.com
For a complete listing, refer to the Hospitals section.

BATTLE CREEK. *Battle Creek Health System*, 300 North Ave., 49016. Tel: 616-966-8000; Fax: 616-966-8010
For a complete listing, refer to the Hospitals section.

DOWAGIAC. *Lee Memorial Hospital*, 420 W. High St., 49047. Tel: 616-782-8681; Fax: 616-782-7611
For a complete listing, refer to the Hospitals section.

[E] RESIDENCES OF PRIESTS AND BROTHERS

KALAMAZOO. *St. Philip Neri House*, 219 Woodward Ave., 49007. Tel: 616-385-9933; Fax: 616-553-9497.
E-mail: rsirico@acton.org
Rev. Robert Sirico; Bros. David Grondz; Joseph Pawlanta; Jordan Chua.

DOUGLAS. *Order of St. Augustine*. (Chicago Prov.), St. Peter Dr., 49406. Tel: 616-857-8175; 857-7951 (Parish); Fax: 616-857-8164. Rev. Ronald R. Turcich, O.S.A.; Bro. Lawrence Sparacino, O.S.A., Parish Sec. Brothers 2.

[F] HOMES FOR SENIOR CITIZENS

KALAMAZOO. *Borgess Nursing Home*, 537 Chicago Ave., 49048. Tel: 616-382-2392; Fax: 616-382-0843
For a complete listing, refer to the Special Care Facilities section.

BATTLE CREEK. *Mercy Pavilion Skilled Nursing Home and Senior Care Residence*, 80 N. 20 St., 49015. Tel: 616-964-5400; Fax: 616-964-5559
For a complete listing, refer to the Special Care Facilities section.

DOWAGIAC. *Dowagiac Nursing Home*, 610 Uneta St., 49047. Tel: 616-782-3471; Fax: 616-782-1681
For a complete listing, refer to the Special Care Facilities section.

NAZARETH. *Dillon Complex for Independent Living, Inc.*, 49074. Tel: 616-342-0263; Fax: 616-342-1814.
E-mail: rheynssj@complink.net
For a complete listing, refer to the Special Care Facilities section.

OTSEGO. *Otsego Senior Apts., Inc.*, Baraga Manor, 301 Washington St., 49078. Tel: 616-694-9711; Fax: 616-694-5857
For a complete listing, refer to the Special Care Facilities section.

[G] CONVENTS AND RESIDENCES FOR SISTERS

NAZARETH. *Motherhouse and Novitiate of the Sisters of St. Joseph*, 49074. Tel: 616-381-6290; Fax: 616-381-4909.
E-mail: ssjnaz@aol.com
Sr. Janet Fleischhacker, S.S.J., Pres. Congregation; Rev. Michael J. Howell, Chap. Sisters in the Community 309.

[H] NEWMAN CENTERS

KALAMAZOO. *Western Michigan University, Kalamazoo College-Kalamazoo Valley Community College*, St. Thomas More Student Parish, 421 Monroe St., 49006. Tel: 616-381-8917; Fax: 616-381-0195.
E-mail: st_toms@wmich.edu
Web site: www.sttomskazoo.oerg
Rev. Kenneth W. Schmidt. Pastoral Assocs.: Sr. Sue McCrery, S.S.J.; Marion Nelson.

[I] MISCELLANEOUS LISTINGS

KALAMAZOO. *Borgess Health Alliance, Inc.*, 1521 Gull Rd., 49048. Tel: 616-226-7000; Fax: 616-226-7396.
Web site: www.borgess.com
Integrated Health Care System sponsored by the Sisters of St. Joseph which operates Borgess Ambulatory Care, Inc., Borgess Foundation, Borgess Medical Center, Borgess Nursing Home, Inc., Borgess-Pipp Health Center, Doctor's Hospital, Dowagiac Nursing Home, Lee Memorial Hospital Corp., ProMed Healthcare, Inc., Preferred Partners, Visiting Nurse & Hospice Services; VNA Home Care, Borgess Health Partners, LLC., Preferred Network, Preferred Access Ins. Co., Textile Systems, Inc., Lee Memorial Jackson Foundation and Jackson Medical Services. Incorporated in the State of Michigan. R. Timothy Stack, Pres. & CEO; Mr. Michael Alfred, Exec. Dir., Business Dev. & Public Rels.; James Devlin, Chair; Bryan Dunlop, M.D., Vice Chair; Sidney B. Williams, Jr., Sec. & Treas.

Kalamazoo Regional Catholic Schools Foundation, 1000 W. Kilgore Rd., 49008. Tel: 616-381-2646; Fax: 616-381-3919.
Web site: hackettcc.org

Secular Franciscan Order, 2903 E. Main St., 49001. Tel: 616-342-0989. Mr. Lawrence Verdon, Spiritual Asst.

BATTLE CREEK. *BCACS Foundation, Inc.* (Battle Creek Area Catholic Schools Foundation, Inc.), 63 N. 24th St., 49015. Tel: 616-963-4771; Fax: 616-963-3917.
E-mail: BCHCS@voyager.net

Diocesan Council of St. Vincent dePaul, 136 E. Hill, 49017. Tel: 616-660-9579; Fax: 616-372-0908.
E-mail: MFC7@home.com
Mr. Fred Clark, Pres.

HASTINGS. *St. Rose Lima Trust Fund*, 805 S. Jefferson St., 49058. Tel: 616-945-4246.

ST. JOSEPH. *Twin-City Area Catholic School Fund, Inc.*, 220 Church St., 49085. Tel: 616-983-5529; Fax: 616-983-5520.

SOUTH HAVEN. *St. Basil Educational Endowment Fund*, 94 Superior St., 49090. Tel: 616-637-3529.

STURGIS.

Holy Angels School Foundation, Inc., P.O. Box 24, 49091-0024. Tel: 616-467-8114.

RELIGIOUS INSTITUTES OF MEN REPRESENTED IN THE DIOCESE

For further details refer to the corresponding bracketed number in the Religious Institutes of Men or Women section.

[0140]—*The Augustinians.*—O.S.A.

[0200]—*Benedictine Monks.*—O.S.B.

[0470]—*The Capuchin Friars.* (Province of St. Joseph, Det.).—O.F.M.Cap.

[1080]—*Congregation of the Resurrection.*—C.R.

[0520]—*Franciscan Friars.* (Prov. of the Sacred Heart).—O.F.M.

[0920]—*Oblates of St. Francis deSales.* (Toledo-Detroit Prov.).—O.S.F.S.

[0610]—*Priests of the Congregation of the Holy Cross.* (Indiana Prov.).—C.S.C.

RELIGIOUS INSTITUTES OF WOMEN REPRESENTED IN THE DIOCESE

[1920]—*Congregation of the Sisters of the Holy Cross.*—C.S.C.

[1070-05]—*Dominican Sisters.*—O.P.

[1070-13]—*Dominican Sisters.*—O.P.

[1070-14]—*Dominican Sisters.*—O.P.

[2575]—*Sisters of Mercy of the Americas.*—R.S.M.

[3830-11]—*Sisters of St. Joseph.* (Nazareth, MI).—S.S.J.

[3840]—*Sisters of St. Joseph of Carondelet.* (St. Paul, MN).—C.S.J.

[3930]—*Sisters of St. Joseph of the Third Order of St. Francis.*—S.S.J.-T.O.S.F.

[3260]—*Sisters of the Precious Blood.* (Dayton, OH).—C.PP.S.

[2150]—*Sisters, Servants of the Immaculate Heart of Mary.* (Monroe, MI).—I.H.M.

NECROLOGY

† O'Meara, James, (Retired). —Died Aug. 18, 2000.

Archdiocese of Kansas City in Kansas

(Archidioecesis Kansanopolitana in Kansas)

Most Reverend

JAMES P. KELEHER, S.T.D.

Archbishop of Kansas City in Kansas; ordained April 12, 1958; appointed Bishop of Belleville October 23, 1984; consecrated December 11, 1984; transferred to Kansas City in Kansas September 8, 1993. *Office: 12615 Parallel Pkwy., Kansas City, KS, 66109.* Tel.: 913-721-1570.

Catholic Chancery Offices: 12615 Parallel Pkwy., Kansas City, KS, 66109. Tel.: 913-721-1570; Fax: 913-721-1577.

Web site address: www.archkck.org

E-mail address: archkck@archkck.org

Most Reverend

IGNATIUS J. STRECKER, D.D., S.T.D.

Former Archbishop of Kansas City in Kansas; ordained December 19, 1942; appointed Bishop of Springfield-Cape Girardeau April 7, 1962; consecrated June 20, 1962; transferred to Kansas City September 10, 1969; retired September 8, 1993. *Res., 3408 Minnesota Ave., Kansas City, KS, 66101.*

Most Reverend

MARION F. FORST, D.D.

Former Auxiliary Bishop of Kansas City in Kansas; ordained June 10, 1934; consecrated Bishop of Dodge City, March 24, 1960; installed April 5, 1960; resigned from Dodge City; appointed Auxiliary October 16, 1976; retired December 23, 1986. *Res., 16600 W. 126th, Olathe, KS, 66062.*

ESTABLISHED VICARIATE APOSTOLIC JULY 19, 1850. DIOCESE OF LEAVENWORTH ESTABLISHED MAY 22, 1877. SEE CHANGED TO KANSAS CITY IN KANSAS MAY 10, 1947; CREATED ARCHDIOCESE AUGUST 9, 1952.

Square Miles 12,524.

Comprises the following 21 Counties of Kansas: Anderson, Atchison, Brown, Coffey, Doniphan, Douglas, Franklin, Jackson, Jefferson, Johnson, Leavenworth, Linn, Lyon, Marshall, Miami, Nemaha, Osage, Pottawatomie, Shawnee, Wabaunsee and Wyandotte.

PATRONS OF THE DIOCESE: I. Blessed Virgin Mary (Immaculate Conception); II. St. John Baptist Vianney.

STATISTICAL OVERVIEW

Personnel	
Archbishop	1
Retired Archbishops	1
Retired Bishops	1
Abbots	1
Retired Abbots	2
Priests: Diocesan Active in Diocese	78
Priests: Active Outside Diocese	1
Priests: Diocesan in Foreign Missions	1
Priests: Retired, Sick or Absent	20
Number of Diocesan Priests	100
Religious Priests in Diocese	66
Ordinations:	
Religious Priests	2
Transitional Deacons	3
Total Brothers	16
Total Sisters	712
Parishes	
Parishes	119
With Resident Pastor:	
Resident Diocesan Priests	61
Resident Religious Priests	15
Without Resident Pastor:	
Administered by Priests	43
Professional Ministry Personnel:	
Sisters	21
Lay Ministers	71
Welfare	
Catholic Hospitals	4
Total Assisted	491,040
Health Care Centers	4
Total Assisted	21,168
Homes for the Aged	4
Total Assisted	440
Special Centers for Social Services	10
Total Assisted	15,500
Residential Care of Disabled	1
Total Assisted	229
Educational	
Diocesan Students in Other Seminaries	22
Students Religious	2
Total Seminarians	24
Colleges and Universities	3
Total Students	3,489
High Schools, Diocesan and Parish	5
Total Students	3,320
High Schools, Private	2
Total Students	277
Elementary Schools, Diocesan and Parish	43
Total Students	11,684
Elementary Schools, Private	1
Total Students	30
Catechesis/Religious Education:	
High School Students	3,844
Elementary Students	14,772
Total Students Under Catholic Instruction	37,440
Teachers in the Diocese:	
Sisters	23
Lay Teachers	990
Vital Statistics	
Receptions into the Church:	
Infant Baptism Totals	4,256
Adult Baptism Totals	457
Received into Full Communion	805
First Communions	4,051
Confirmations	3,353
Marriages:	
Catholic	669
Interfaith	528
Total Marriages	1,197
Deaths	1,362
Total Catholic Population	197,190
Total Population	1,174,500

Predecessors—Rt. Rev. J. B. MIEGE, S.J., cons. Bishop of Messenia, Vicar-Apostolic, March 25, 1851 resignation accepted by Pope Pius IX Nov. 8, 1874; died July 21, 1884.—Rt. Rev. LOUIS M. FINK, O.S.B., D.D., cons. Bishop of Eucarpia June 11, 1871; appt. first Bishop of Leavenworth May 22, 1877; died March 17, 1904.—Rt. Rev. THOMAS F. LILLIS, O.D., cons. Bishop of Leavenworth, Dec. 27, 1904; appt. Coadjutor Bishop of Kansas City, with right of succession March 14, 1910; succeeded to the See of Kansas City, Feb. 21, 1913.—Rt. Rev. JOHN WARD, D.D., ord. July 17, 1884; appt. Bishop of Leavenworth Nov. 25, 1910; cons. Feb. 22, 1911; died April 20, 1929.—Most Rev. FRANCIS JOHANNES, D.D., LL.D., cons. May 1, 1928; succeeded to the See, April 20, 1929; died March 13, 1937.—Most Rev. PAUL C. SCHULTE, D.D., ord. June 11, 1915; appt. Bishop of Leavenworth May 29, 1937; cons. Sept. 21, 1937; appt. Archbishop of Indianapolis July 20, 1946; installed Oct. 10, 1946.—Most Rev. GEORGE J. DONNELLY, S.T.D., ord. June 12, 1921; appt. Titular Bishop of Coela and Auxiliary of St. Louis March 19, 1940; cons. April 23, 1940; appt. Bishop of Leavenworth Nov. 9, 1946; died Dec. 13, 1950.—Most Rev. EDWARD J. HUNKELER, D.D., ord. June 14, 1919; appt. Bishop of Grand Island March 10, 1945; cons. May 1, 1945; transferred to Kansas City March 28, 1951; elevated to Archiepiscopal dignity Aug. 9, 1952; retired Sept. 10, 1969; died Oct. 1, 1970.—Most Rev. IGNATIUS J. STRECKER, D.D., S.T.D., ord. Dec. 19, 1942; appt. Bishop of Springfield-Cape Girardeau April 7, 1962; cons. June 20, 1962; transferred to Kansas City Sept. 10, 1969; retired Sept. 8, 1993.

Catholic Chancery Offices—12615 Parallel Pkwy., Kansas City, 66109. Tel: 913-721-1570; Fax: 913-721-1577. Office Hours: 8:30-5.

Vicars General—Revs. CHARLES MCGLINN; THOMAS TANK.

Chancellor—Rev. THOMAS TANK.

Vice-Chancellor—Rev. RAYMOND BURGER.

Metropolitan Tribunal—12615 Parallel Pkwy., Kansas City, 66109. Tel: 913-721-1570; Fax: 913-721-1577.

Judicial Vicar—Rev. PHILIP KENDALL, C.S.V., J.C.D.

Pro-Synodal Judges—Revs. PHILIP E. KENDALL, C.S.V., J.C.D.; GEORGE BERTELS, J.C.L.

Defenders of the Bond—Rev. GARY APPLEGATE, J.C.L.; Sr. VIRGINIA BARTOLAC, S.C.L., J.C.D.

Advocates—Selected priests, Sr. MARY ANN BARTOLAC, S.C.L.,selected Lay Advocates.

Director Notary—JOAN DEBAUGE.

Archdiocesan Consultors—Revs. RAYMOND DAVERN; THOMAS TANK; Rt. Rev. BARNABAS SENECAL, O.S.B.; Revs. FRANCIS KRISCHE; CHARLES MCGLINN; NORBERT LICKTEIG.

Archdiocesan Council on Finances—Rev. THOMAS TANK, Chancellor; Mr. RICHARD ANDERSON; Mr. JERRY

MAYNE; Mr. FRANK SABATINI; Mr. JOHN MEGHINI.

Archdiocesan Finance Officer—JERRY MAYNE.

Regional Pastoral Leaders—Rev. GERARD SENECAL, O.S.B., Atchison; Rev. GERALD VOLZ, Emporia; Rev. FRANK BURGER, Johnson Co.; Rev. DENNIS SCHMITZ, Lawrence; Rev. GARY APPLEGATE, Leavenworth; Rev. RONALD CORNISH, Nortonville; Rev. HARRY SCHNEIDER, Topeka; Rev. THOMAS KEARNS, Garnett; Rev. RODERIC GILLER, O.S.B., Nemah-Marshall; Rev. EARL DEKAT, St. Mary's; Rev. CHARLES ANDALIKIEWICZ, Wyandotte Co.

Archdiocesan Administrative Team—Mr. MIKE ALEX; Rev. CHARLES MCGLINN; Mr. BLAKE MULVANY; Mr. JERRY MAYNE; Rev. THOMAS TANK; Mr. MARK HENKE.

Catholic Foundation of Northeast Kansas—12615 Parallel Pkwy., Kansas City, 66109.

Catholic Education Foundation—12615 Parallel Pkwy., Kansas City, 66109.

Minister to Priests—Rev. JAMES WHITE, S.J., *12600 Hollingsworth Rd., Kansas City, 66109.* Tel: 913-721-3966.

Archdiocesan Archivist—Rev. LEO COOPER.

Archdiocesan Offices and Directors

Savior Pastoral Center—12601 Parallel, Kansas City, 66109. Tel; 913-721-1097.

Black Catholics—REGINA BARGER, Dir., *2203 Parallel, Kansas City, 66104.* Tel: 913-321-1958.

Department of Parish Ministries—Rev. THOMAS TANK, Dir., *12615 Parallel Pkwy., Kansas City, 66109.* Tel: 913-721-1570.

Adult Faith Formation—Mr. LAWRENCE LIVINGSTON.

Deaf—Sr. ANN ALBRECHT, C.S.J.

Family Life—Mrs. JACKI CORRIGAN.

Liturgy—Rev. FRANCIS HUND.

Peace and Justice—Sr. BARBARA MCCRACKEN, O.S.B.

Religious Education—Mrs. JEANNE BRADY.

Youth—Mr. DANA NEARMYER.

Hispanic Ministry—Rev. PETER JARAMILLO.

Administrative Services/Human Resources—Mrs. SUSAN CARROLL.

Stewardship and Development Office—Mr. MIKE ALEX, Dir., *12615 Parallel Pkwy., Kansas City, 66109.* Tel: 913-721-1570.

Apostleship of Prayer—Vacant.

Catholic Youth Organization—DAVE NICK, Athletic Dir., *5041 Reinhardt Dr., P.O. Box 721, Shawnee Mission, 66201.* Tel: 913-384-7377.

Catholic Charities—Mr. MARK HENKE, Dir., *2220 Central Ave., Kansas City, 66102.* Tel: 913-621-1504.

Council for Catholic Charismatic Renewal—Rev. MARK MERTES.

Catholic Community Service—2220 Central Ave., Kansas City, 66102. Tel: 913-621-1504.

Communications—12615 Parallel Pkwy., Kansas City, 66109. Tel: 913-721-1570.

Catholic Scouts—Rev. MARK BROSKI, O.S.B., Chap.

Holy Childhood Association—Rev. NORBERT LICKTEIG, *12615 Parallel Pkwy., Kansas City, 66109.* Tel: 913-721-1570.

Hospitals—Rev. JEREMIAH L. SPENCER, Dir., *16 S. Iowa, Kansas City, 66101.*

Kansas Catholic Conference—Mr. MIKE FARMER; Exec. Dir., *6301 Antioch, Shawnee Mission, 66202.* Tel: 913-722-6633.

Legion of Mary—Rev. ROBERT BURGER, Dir., *13520 W. 92nd, Lenexa, 66215.*

Missions—Rev. NORBERT LICKTEIG, *12615 Parallel Pkwy., Kansas City, 66109.*

Newspaper "The Leaven"—Rev. MARK GOLDASICH, Editor, *12615 Parallel Pkwy., Kansas City, 66109.* Tel: 913-721-1570; Fax: 913-721-5276.

Nurses Association—Rev. JEREMIAH L. SPENCER, Dir., *16 S. Iowa, Kansas City, 66103.*

Priests' Council—Rev. NORBERT LICKTEIG, Chm.

Propagation of the Faith—Rev. NORBERT LICKTEIG, *12615 Parallel Pkwy., Kansas City, 66109.*

Respect Life—Mr. MARK HENKE, Coord.

Schools—BLAKE MULVANY, Supt. KATHY O'HARA, Assoc. Supt.; Sr. KATHLEEN CONDRY, O.S.U., Asst. Supt., *12615 Parallel Pkwy., Kansas City, 66109.* Tel: 913-721-1570.

Vocations Office—Directors: Revs. DENNIS SCHMITZ; MICHAEL MULLEN, *12615 Parallel Pkwy., Kansas City, 66109.* Tel: 913-721-1570.

CLERGY, PARISHES, MISSIONS AND PAROCHIAL SCHOOLS

CITY OF KANSAS CITY
(Wyandotte County)

1—CATHEDRAL OF ST. PETER THE APOSTLE, Revs. Thomas Tank; Philip Kendall, C.S.V.; John Torrez.
Res., 409 N. 15th St., 66102. Tel: 913-371-2345; Fax: 913-371-2151.
Business Office: 431 N. 15th St., 66102. Tel: 913-371-0840; Fax: 913-371-2151.
School—422 N. 14th, 66102. Tel: 913-371-8101.
Lay Teachers 20; Students 237.

2—BLESSED SACRAMENT, Rev. William McEvoy.
Res., 2203 Parallel Ave., 66104. Tel: 913-321-1958; Fax: 913-321-1997.

3—CHRIST THE KING, Rev. Raymond J. Davern.
Res., 3024 N. 53rd St., 66104. Tel: 913-287-8823; Fax: 913-287-8711.
School—3027 N. 54th St., 66104. Tel: 913-287-8883; Fax: 913-287-7409.
Lay Teachers 15; Students 242.

4—HOLY FAMILY (Slovene), Rev. Msgr. Heliodore Mejak.
Res., 274 Orchard Ave., 66101. Tel: 913-371-1561.
School—St. John and Holy Family. (Consolidated). See separate listing under St. John the Baptist. Tel: 913-371-3923.

5—HOLY NAME, Rev. Jeremiah L. Spencer.
Res., 16 S. Iowa St., 66103. Tel: 913-236-9219; Fax: 913-236-4559.
School—1007 S.W. Blvd., 66103. Tel: 913-722-1032; Fax: 913-722-4175.
Lay Teachers 8; Students 145.

6—SACRED HEART. Attended by St. John the Evangelist, Kansas City. Rev. Charles Andalikiewicz.
Res., 2910 Strong Ave., 66106. Tel: 913-677-4621.
Church—2646 S. 34th, 66106. Tel: 913-677-1277.
School—Our Lady of Unity. See separate listing. Tel: 913-262-7022; Fax: 913-262-7836.

7—OUR LADY AND ST. ROSE. Attended by Blessed Sacrament, Kansas City.
Mailing Address: 2203 Parallel, 66104.
Church—2300 N. Eighth St., 66101. Tel: 913-321-1958; Fax: 913-321-1997.

8—ST. MARY-ST. ANTHONY, Rev. Matt J. Horvat.
Res., 615 N. Seventh St., 66101. Tel: 913-371-1408.

9—SS. CYRIL AND METHODIUS (Slovak). Attended by St. Joseph-St. Benedict, Kansas City. Rev. Michael Hermes.
Res., 801 Vermont, 66101. Tel: 913-371-3549; Fax: 913-621-2709.

10—ST. JOHN THE BAPTIST (Croatian), Rev. Francis Horvat.
Res., 708 N. Fourth St., 66101. Tel: 913-371-0627; Fax: 913-342-3324.
School—St. John the Baptist and Holy Family. (Consolidated) 515 Ohio, 66101. Tel: 913-371-3923; Fax: 913-321-0649.
Lay Teachers 12; Students 145.

11—ST. JOHN THE DIVINE (Mexican). (Stational Church).

12—ST. JOHN THE EVANGELIST, Rev. Charles Andalikiewicz.
Res., 2910 Strong Ave., 66106. Tel: 913-677-4621.
School—Our Lady of Unity. Consolidated with Sacred Heart. See separate listing for further details.

13—ST. JOSEPH AND ST. BENEDICT, Rev. Michael Hermes.
Res., 801 Vermont Ave., 66101. Tel: 913-371-1837; Fax: 913-621-2709.
School—All Saints. (Consolidated). See separate listing.

14—ST. PATRICK'S, Revs. Michael Mullen; Samuel Opoku-Sarkodie (Ghana) Associate.
Res., 1086 N. 94th St., 66112. Tel: 913-299-3370; Fax: 913-299-3422.
School—1066 N. 94th, 66112. Tel: 913-299-8131; Fax: 913-299-2845.
Sisters 1; Lay Teachers 23; Students 367.

15—ST. THOMAS THE APOSTLE. Closed. For inquiries for parish records contact the Chancery.

OUTSIDE THE CITY OF KANSAS CITY

Alma, Wabaunsee Co., Holy Family. Attended by Paxico. Rev. John C. Reynolds.
Church—66401. Tel: 785-636-5547; Fax: 785-636-5538.

Atchison, Atchison Co., St. Benedict's, Rev. Gerard Senecal, O.S.B.
Res., 1001 N. Second St., 66002. Tel: 913-367-0671; Fax: 913-367-0797. [JC]
School—Atchison Catholic Elementary. (Consolidated). See separate listing.
Sacred Heart, Rev. Gerard Senecal, O.S.B.
Res., 1001 N. Second St., 66002. Tel: 913-367-0387; Fax: 913-367-0797. [JC]
School—Atchison Catholic Elementary. (Consolidated). See separate listing.
St. Joseph's, Rev. Bertrand LaNoue, O.S.B.
Res., 705 Spring Garden St., 66002. Tel: 913-367-4271. [JC]
School—Atchison Catholic Elementary. (Consolidated). See separate listing.

Axtell, Marshall Co., St. Michael's, Rev. Thomas H. Dolezal.
Mailing Address: P.O. Box K, 66403. Tel: 785-736-2220; Fax: 785-736-2230.
School—605 Elm St., 66403. Tel: 785-736-2257.
Lay Teachers 4; Students 36.

Baileyville, Nemaha Co., Sacred Heart, Rev. Albert J. Fey, C.PP.S.
Church—Box 36, 66404. Tel: 785-336-6464. [CEM]

Baldwin, Douglas Co., Annunciation. Attended by Assumption, Edgerton. Rev. William Fisher.
Church—P.O. Box 293, 66006. Tel: 785-594-3700. [CEM]

Basehor, Leavenworth Co., Holy Angels, Rev. Linus J. Evers, C.PP.S.
Res., 15440 Leavenworth Rd., Box 295, 66007. Tel: 913-724-3122; 724-1665 (Offices); Fax: 913-724-3114. [CEM]

Beattie, Marshall Co., St. Malachy's. Attended by St. Gregory, Marysville. Rev. George Bertels.
Church—1012 Main St., 66406. Tel: 785-353-2280.

Bendena, Doniphan Co., St. Benedict's. Attended by St. Joseph, Wathena. Rev. Phillip J. Winkelbauer.
Church—P.O. Box 128, 66008. Tel: 785-359-6725; Fax: 785-989-2313. [CEM]

Blaine, Pottawatomie Co., St. Columbkille. Attended by St. Vincent de Paul, Onaga. Rev. Jude Burbach, O.S.B.
Church—66480.

Blue Rapids, Marshall Co., St. Elizabeth. Attended by Annunciation, Frankfort. Rev. William Bruning.

Burlington, Coffey Co., St. Francis Xavier's, Rev. Michael Hawken.
Res., 214 Juniatta, 66839. Tel: 316-364-2416; Fax: 316-364-2416. [CEM]

Corning, Nemaha Co., St. Patrick's. Attended by St. Mary's, St. Benedict. Rt. Rev. Ralph Koehler, O.S.B. Tel: 785-336-3174.
Res., St. Mary, R.R. 1, Box 59, Seneca, 66538. Tel: 785-868-2790. [CEM]

Delia, Jackson Co., Sacred Heart of Jesus. (Stational Church).

Doniphan, Doniphan Co., St. John's. (Stational Church).

Easton, Leavenworth Co., St. Lawrence, Rev. Kyle Haden.
Res., P.O. Box 129, 66020. Tel: 913-773-5712. [CEM]

Edgerton, Johnson Co., Assumption of the Blessed Virgin Mary, Rev. William Fisher.
Church—P.O. Box 74, 66021. Tel: 913-893-6272; Fax: 785-594-3700. [CEM]

Effingham, Atchison Co., St. Ann's, Rt. Rev. Owen Purcell, O.S.B.
Res., 301 William, Box 54, 66023. Tel: 913-833-5660. [CEM]

Emerald, Anderson Co., St. Patrick's. Served by St. Francis Xavier, Burlington. Rev. Michael Hawken.
Church—Williamsburg P.O., 66095. Tel: 316-364-2416; Fax: 316-364-2416.

Emmett, Pottawatomie Co., Holy Cross. Attended by Immaculate Conception, St. Marys. Rev. Earl M. Dekat.

Emporia, Lyon Co., Sacred Heart, Rev. Daniel L. Gardener.
Office: 101 Cottonwood St., 66801. Tel: 316-342-1061; Fax: 316-342-0450. [CEM]
School—102 Cottonwood St., 66801. Tel: 316-343-7394; Fax: 316-343-7395.
Lay Teachers 11; Students 171.
Rectory—123 Cottonwood St., 66801. Tel: 316-342-3328; Fax: 316-342-3328.
St. Catherine. Attended by Sacred Heart, Emporia. Rev. Daniel L. Gardener.
Church—205 S. Lawrence St., 66801. Tel: 316-342-1061. [CEM]

Eskridge, Wabaunsee Co., St. John Vianney. Attended by Sacred Heart, Paxico. Rev. John C. Reynolds.

Eudora, Douglas Co., Holy Family, Rev. Paul W. Miller.
Res., P.O. Box H, 66025-0808. Tel: 785-542-2788. [CEM]

Fidelity, Brown Co., St. Augustine's. Attended by Sacred Heart, Sabetha. Rev. Donald Redmond, O.S.B.

Flush, Pottawatomie Co., St. Joseph's. Attended by St. Bernard, Wamego. Rev. Thomas N. Hesse Tel: 785-494-8234.

Fort Leavenworth, Leavenworth Co., St. Ignatius Chapel, Rev. William F. Carey, Military Services Army Chap. [Natl. CEM].
Church—66027. Tel: 913-684-3000.

Frankfort, Marshall Co., Annunciation, Rev. William Bruning.
Res., 213 E. Fifth St., 66427. Tel: 785-292-4462; Fax: 785-292-5095. [CEM]

Gardner, Johnson Co., Sacred Heart, Rev. Gerald E. Sheeds.
Res., 122 E. Warren, 66030. Tel: 913-856-7781; Fax: 913-856-7781. [CEM]

Garnett, Anderson Co., Holy Angels, Rev. George A. Matz.
Res., 514 E. Fourth, 66032. Tel: 785-448-3846. [CEM]
School—530 E. Fourth, 66032. Tel: 785-448-3423; Fax: 785-448-3423.
Sisters 1; Lay Teachers 4; Students 59.

Greeley, Anderson Co., St. John the Baptist's. Attended by Holy Angels, Garnett. Rev. George A. Matz.
Res., 66033. Tel: 785-867-3120. [CEM]
School—Tel: 785-867-2680; Fax: 785-867-3160.
Sisters 1; Lay Teachers 3; Students 47.

Hartford, Lyon Co., St. Mary's. Attended by St. Joseph's, Olpe. Rev. Timothy A. Haberkorn.

Hiawatha, Brown Co., St. Ann's, Rev. Terence Sullivan, O.S.B.
Res., 800 Hiawatha Ave., 66434. Tel: 785-742-3010.

Holton, Jackson Co., St. Dominic's, Rev. Ronald Cornish.
Res., 416 Ohio Ave., 66436. Tel: 785-364-3262. [CEM]
Mission—Potawatomi Reservation, Our Lady of Snows.

Horton, Brown Co., St. Leo's, Rev. Keith Lunsford.
Res., 1340 First Ave. E., 66439. Tel: 785-486-3971; Fax: 785-486-2402. [CEM 3]

Kelly, Nemaha Co., St. Bede's (1901). Attended by St. Mary, St. Benedict. Rt. Rev. Ralph Koehler, O.S.B. Tel: 785-336-3174. [CEM]
Catechesis/Religious Programs—Students 100.

LaCygne, Linn Co., Our Lady of Lourdes. Attended by St. Philip Neri, Osawatomie. Rev. Joseph Cramer.
Church—66040.

Lansing, Leavenworth Co., St. Francis de Sales, Rev. Michael C. Stubbs.
Res., 119 Woodland Rd., 66043. Tel: 913-727-3768.
Church—900 Ida St., 66043. Tel: 913-727-3742; Fax: 913-727-3742. [JC]

Lapeer, Douglas Co., St. Francis. Attended by St. Patrick, Osage City. Rev. Michael Mulvany. [CEM]

Lawrence, Douglas Co., Corpus Christi, Rev. James E. Shaughnessy.
Church & Office: 6001 W. 15th, 66049-5200. Tel: 785-843-6286; Fax: 785-865-3933.
Res., 3209 Harvard Rd., 66049. Tel: 785-749-4724. [JC]
School—The Lawrence Catholic School. (Consolidated). See separate listing.

St. John the Evangelist, Rev. Charles Polifka, O.F.M.Cap.
Office: 1229 Vermont St., 66044. Tel: 785-843-0109; Fax: 785-749-5064. [CEM]
School—The Lawrence Catholic School. (Consolidated). See separate listing.

Leavenworth, Leavenworth Co.,

1—IMMACULATE CONCEPTION. (Old Cathedral). Revs. David McEvoy, O.Carm.; Fergus Lickteig, O.Carm.
Office: 747 Osage, 66048. Tel: 913-682-3953; Fax: 913-682-5599.
Church—711 N. 5th St., 66048.
School—Xavier Elementary. (Consolidated). See separate listing.
Rectory, 300 N. Broadway, 66048. Tel: 913-682-0809.

2—SACRED HEART OF JESUS, Rev. Gary Applegate.
Res., 1401 Second Ave., 66048. Tel: 913-772-1787.
School—Xavier Elementary. (Consolidated). See separate listing. Tel: 913-682-3135.

3—ST. CASIMIR'S, (Polish), Rev. Gary Applegate.
Res., 1401 Second Ave., 66048. Tel: 913-772-1787.
School—Xavier Elementary. (Consolidated). See separate listing. Tel: 913-682-3135.

4—ST. JOSEPH'S, Revs. David McEvoy, O.Carm; Fergus Lickteig, O.Carm.
Office: 747 Osage, 66048. Tel: 913-682-3953; 682-0809 (Res.); Fax: 913-682-5599.
School—Xavier Elementary. (Consolidated). See separate listing.

5—ST. JOSEPH OF THE VALLEY. Attended by St. Lawrence, Easton. Rev. Kyle Haden.
Mailing Address: P.O. Box 129, Easton, 66020. Tel: 913-773-5712.
Church—31151 207th St., 66048.

Leawood, Johnson Co., Church of the Nativity, Revs. Alfred Rockers; Craig Maxim.
Church—3800 W. 119th St., 66209. Tel: 913-491-5017; Fax: 913-491-5065.
School—3700 W. 119th St., 66209. Tel: 913-338-4330; Fax: 913-338-2050.
Lay Teachers 36; Students 704.
Christian Formation Office: Tel: 913-338-4367; Fax: 913-338-0285.

Cure of Ars, Revs. Charles McGlinn; Brian Schieber.
Res., 9401 Mission Rd., 66206. Tel: 913-649-1337; Fax: 913-649-1339.
School—9403 Mission Rd., 66206. Tel: 913-648-2620; Fax: 913-648-3810.
Lay Teachers 40; Students 667.
Vianney Center for Ministries—Tel: 913-649-8625; Fax: 913-649-1339.

St. Michael the Archangel,
Church—14200 Mission Rd., 66224. Tel: 913-402-8101; Fax: 913-681-8566. Rev. William Porter.

Lenexa, Johnson Co., Holy Trinity, Rev. Raymond Burger. In res., Revs. Robert Burger, (Retired); Robert Pflumm, (Retired).
Office: 9150 Pflumm Rd., 66215. Tel: 913-888-2770; Fax: 913-888-4403.
School—13600 W. 92nd St., 66215. Tel: 913-888-3250; Fax: 913-438-2572.
Lay Teachers 37; Students 724.

Lillis, Marshall Co., St. Joseph's. Attended by St. Vincent de Paul, Onaga. Rev. Jude Burbach, O.S.B. Tel: 785-889-4896. [CEM]

Louisburg, Miami Co., Immaculate Conception, Rev. Anthony Lickteig.
Res., Box 118, 66053. Tel: 913-837-2295; Fax: 913-837-3309. [CEM]

Marysville, Marshall Co., St. Gregory's, Rev. George Bertels.
Res., 204 N. 13th, 66508. Tel: 785-562-3302; Fax: 785-562-4039. [CEM]
School—207 N. 14th, 66508. Tel: 785-562-2831; Fax: 785-562-4039.
Lay Teachers 8; Students 130.

Mayetta, Jackson Co., St. Francis Xavier. Attended by St. Dominic, Holton. Rev. Ronald Cornish.
Tel: 785-364-3262.

Meriden, Jefferson Co., St. Aloysius. Attended by St. Theresa, Perry. Rev. Francis Hund.
Res., P.O. Box 364, 66512. Tel: 785-484-3312. [CEM]

Mission, Johnson Co., St. Pius X, Rev. Robert Hasenkamp.
Res., 5601 Woodson Ave., 66202. Tel: 913-432-4808; Fax: 913-432-4855.
School—5500 Woodson, 66202. Tel: 913-432-9355; Fax: 913-432-2086.
Lay Teachers 15; Students 200.

Mooney Creek, Jefferson Co., Corpus Christi. Attended by St. Lawrence, Easton. Rev. Kyle Haden.
Mailing Address: P.O. Box 129, Easton, 66020. Tel: 913-773-5712. [CEM]

Mound City, Linn Co., Sacred Heart Shrine to St. Philippine Duchesne. Attended by St. Philip Neri, Osawatomie. Rev. Joseph Cramer.
Res., 66056. Tel: 913-795-2724.

Nortonville, Jefferson Co., St. Joseph's, Rev. Thomas Cawley, C.M.
Res., 221 N. Sycamore St., 66060. Tel: 913-886-2030. [CEM]
School—222 N. Sycamore St., 66060-4014. Tel: 913-886-3510.
Lay Teachers 2; Students 20.

Olathe, Johnson Co., St. Paul's, Rev. Anthony C. Williams.
Office: 900 S. Honeysuckle, 66061. Tel: 913-764-0323; Fax: 913-782-2998.
Res., 840 Larkspur, 66061. Tel: 913-782-6062.
School—920 W. Honeysuckle, 66061. Tel: 913-764-0619; Fax: 913-768-6040.
Lay Teachers 10; Students 206.

Prince of Peace, Revs. Frank Burger; Jon Hullinger.
Res., Tel: 913-782-8864; Fax: 913-780-9658.
School—16000 W. 143rd St., 66062. Tel: 913-764-0650.
Sisters 3; Lay Teachers 24; Students 540.

Olpe, Lyon Co., St. Joseph's, Rev. Timothy A. Haberkorn.
Res., P.O. Box 165, 66865. Tel: 316-475-3326; Fax: 316-475-3711. [CEM]
School—Tel: 316-475-3416.
Lay Teachers 5; Students 65.

Onaga, Pottawatomie Co., St. Vincent de Paul, Rev. Jude Burbach, O.S.B.
Res., Box 396, 66521. Tel: 785-889-4896.

Osage City, Osage Co., St. Patrick's, Rev. Michael Mulvany.
Res., 309 S. Sixth St., 66523. Tel: 785-528-3424; Fax: 785-528-3381. [CEM]

Osawatomie, Miami Co., St. Philip Neri, Rev. Joseph Cramer.
Church—500 Parker Ave., 66064. Tel: 913-755-2652.
Chaplaincy—State Hospital for Mentally Ill, 66064.

Ottawa, Franklin Co., Sacred Heart, Rev. Steven Beseau, S.T.L.
Res., 408 S. Cedar St., 66067. Tel: 785-242-2174. [CEM]
School—426 S. Cedar, 66067. Tel: 785-242-4297; Fax: 785-242-4297.
Lay Teachers 6; Students 91.

Overland Park, Johnson Co.,

1—CHURCH OF THE ASCENSION, Revs. Lawrence Albertson; Joseph Lopez.
Res., 9510 W. 127th St., 66213. Tel: 913-681-3348; Fax: 913-681-3517.
School—Tel: 913-851-2531; Fax: 913-851-2518.
Lay Teachers 30; Students 516.

2—HOLY CROSS, Rev. Mark Mertes. In res., Rev. Msgr. Thomas Culhane.
Office: 8311 W. 93rd St., 66212. Tel: 913-381-2755; Fax: 913-381-2766.
Res., 8315 W. 93rd St., 66212. Tel: 913-341-5618; Fax: 913-381-2766.
School—8101 W. 95th, 66212. Tel: 913-381-7408; Fax: 913-381-1312.
Lay Teachers 29; Students 419.

3—HOLY SPIRIT, Revs. Albert Hauser, O.S.B.; William A. Finnerty.
Res., 11300 W. 103rd St., 66214. Tel: 913-492-7318; Fax: 913-492-7370.
School—Tel: 913-492-2582; Fax: 913-492-9613.
Lay Teachers 24; Students 463.

4—QUEEN OF THE HOLY ROSARY, Rev. Ronald Livojevich.
Res., 7023 W. 71st St., 66204. Tel: 913-432-4616; Fax: 913-432-0620.
School—6915 W. 71st, 66204. Tel: 913-432-6350; Fax: 913-432-5081.
Lay Teachers 15; Students 201.

Paola, Miami Co., Holy Trinity, Rev. Thomas Kearns.
Res., 505 E. Chippewa, 66071. Tel: 913-557-2067; Fax: 913-294-9607. [CEM]
School—Tel: 913-294-3286; Fax: 913-294-9286.
Lay Teachers 10; Students 137.

Paxico, Wabaunsee Co., Sacred Heart, Rev. John C. Reynolds.
Res., 66526. Tel: 785-636-5547; Fax: 785-636-5538. [CEM]

Perry, Jefferson Co., St. Theresa's, Rev. Francis Hund.
Res., 66073. Tel: 785-597-5656. [CEM]

Prairie Village, Johnson Co., St. Ann's, Rev. William M. Haegelin.
Res., 7231 Mission Rd., 66208. Tel: 913-362-2817; Fax: 913-362-2678.
School—7241 Mission Rd., 66208. Tel: 913-362-7008; Fax: 913-362-7059.
Lay Teachers 33; Students 529.

Purcell, Doniphan Co., St. Mary's. Attended by St. Leo's, Horton. Rev. Keith Lunsford.
446 Hwy 137, 66041. Tel: 785-486-3971; Fax: 785-486-2402. [CEM]

Reading, Lyon Co., Assumption. Closed. For inquiries for parish records contact the Chancery.

Richmond, Franklin Co., St. Therese. Attended by St. Boniface, Scipio. Rev. Emil Agostino, O.Carm.
Res., 32320 N.E. Nevada Rd., Garnett, 66032. Tel: 785-835-6273; Fax: 785-835-6112.

Roeland Park, Johnson Co., St. Agnes, Revs. Donald Cullen; John H. Wisner.
Res., 5250 Mission Rd., 66205. Tel: 913-262-2400; Fax: 913-262-1050.
School—5130 Mission Rd., 66205. Tel: 913-262-1686; Fax: 913-384-1567.
Lay Teachers 31; Students 473.

Rossville, Shawnee Co., St. Stanislaus. Attended by Immaculate Conception, St. Marys. Rev. Earl M. Dekat.

Sabetha, Nemaha Co., Sacred Heart, Rev. Donald Redmond, O.S.B.
Res., 1042 S. 14th, 66534. Tel: 785-284-3068.

St. Benedict, Nemaha Co., St. Mary's, Rt. Rev. Ralph Koehler, O.S.B.
Res., R.R. 1, Box 59, Seneca, 66538. Tel: 785-336-3174. [CEM]

St. Louis, Atchison Co., St. Louis. Attended by St. Ann's, Effingham. Rt. Rev. Owen Purcell, O.S.B.
Mailing Address: c/o St. Ann's, 301 William, Box 54, Effingham, 66023. Tel: 913-833-5660.
Church—11321 Morton Rd., Atchison, 66002. Tel: 913-847-6849. [CEM]

St. Marys, Pottawatomie Co., Immaculate Conception, Rev. Earl M. Dekat.
Res., 208 W. Bertrand, 66536. Tel: 785-437-2408; Fax: 785-437-2938. [CEM]

St. Patrick, Atchison Co., St. Patrick's. Attended by St. Joseph. Rev. Bertrand LaNoue, O.S.B. [CEM]

Scipio, Anderson Co., St. Boniface, Rev. Emil Agostino, O.Carm. In res., Rev. Bernard Lickteig, O.Carm.
Res., 32320 N.E. Nevada Rd., Garnett, 66032. Tel:

785-835-6273; Fax: 785-835-6112. [CEM]

Scranton, Osage Co., St. Patrick's. Attended by St. Patrick's, Osage City. Rev. Michael Mulvany. Tel: 785-528-3424. [CEM]

Seneca, Nemaha Co., SS. Peter and Paul's, Rev. Roderic Giller, O.S.B.
Res., 66538. Tel: 785-336-2208; Fax: 785-336-3666. [CEM]
School—401 Pioneer, 66538. Tel: 785-336-2727. Benedictine Sisters 1; Lay Teachers 13; Students 182.

Shawnee, Johnson Co., Good Shepherd, Rev. George Seuferling.
Office: 12800 W. 75th St., 66216. Tel: 913-631-7116; Fax: 913-631-3539.
Res., 7124 Bond, 66203. Tel: 913-631-5661.
School—12800 W. 75th St., 66216. Tel: 913-631-0400.
Lay Teachers 17; Students 219.
Parish Center: 12800 W. 75th St., 66216.
Sacred Heart, Rev. Patrick Jerome.
Office: 21801 Johnson Dr., 66226. Tel: 913-422-5520; Fax: 913-422-5723.
School—Tel: 913-422-5520; Fax: 913-422-5723.
Lay Teachers 12; Students 243.
St. Joseph's, Rev. Msgr. Robert Bergman; Rev. Richard McDonald.
Res., 5832 King St., 66203. Tel: 913-631-5983; Fax: 913-631-5973.
School—(Grades 1-8) 5901 Flint St., 66203. Tel: 913-631-7730; Fax: 913-631-3608.
Lay Teachers 43; Students 643.
Early Education Center—(Day Care, Preschool & Kindergarten) 5900 Bond St., 66203. Tel: 913-631-0004; Fax: 913-631-4364.
Auxiliary Teachers 41; Students 329.

Summerfield, Marshall Co., Holy Family. Attended by St. Michael's, Axtell. Rev. Thomas H. Dolezal.
Church—P.O. Box 136, 66541. Tel: 785-736-2220.

Tonganoxie, Leavenworth Co., Sacred Heart, Rev. Mark Goldasich.
Res., 703 E. River, P.O. Box 539, 66086-0539. Tel: 913-369-2851.

Topeka, Shawnee Co.,

1—ASSUMPTION, Rev. John F. Rossiter.
Res., 204 S.W. Eighth Ave., 66603. Tel: 785-232-2907; Fax: 785-232-8147. [JC]
School—735 S.W. Jackson, 66603. Tel: 785-235-0953; Fax: 785-235-5809.
Sisters 3; Lay Teachers 10; Students 193.

2—CHRIST THE KING, Rev. Norbert Lickteig.
Res., 5972 W. 25th St., 66614. Tel: 785-273-0710; 273-0715; Fax: 785-273-4766.
School—5973 S.W. 25th St., 66614. Tel: 785-272-2220; Fax: 785-273-4766.
Lay Teachers 29; Students 345.

3—HOLY NAME, Rev. Harold Schneider.
Res., 1114 W. 10th Ave., 66604. Tel: 785-232-7744; Fax: 785-232-2341.
School—934 Clay St., 66606. Tel: 785-233-1727; Fax: 785-232-2341.
Sisters of Charity of Leavenworth 1; Lay Teachers 14; Students 222.

4—MOST PURE HEART OF MARY, Revs. Francis Krische; Michael Kantanka (Ghana); Prasad Rao Maddela (India).
Church Office: 1800 S.W. Stone, 66604. Tel: 785-272-5590; Fax: 785-272-2801.
School—1750 S.W. Stone, 66604. Tel: 785-272-4313; Fax: 785-272-1138.
Lay Teachers 31; Students 490.

5—OUR LADY OF GUADALUPE, (Mexican), Rev. Raymond May.
Res., 1008 N.E. Atchison Ave., 66616. Tel: 785-232-5088; Fax: 785-232-5166.
School—210 N.E. Branner St., 66616. Tel: 785-233-9171; Fax: 785-232-8683.
Sisters of Charity of Leavenworth 1; Lay Teachers 11; Students 139.

6—SACRED HEART, Rev. John Erickson.
Res., 333 N.E. Freeman Ave., 66616. Tel: 785-234-3338.
School—1733 Seward Ave., 66616. Tel: 785-234-8980; Fax: 785-234-8980.
Lay Teachers 10; Students 142.

7—ST. JOSEPH'S, Rev. Carl Dekat.
Res., 227 S.W. Van Buren St., 66603. Tel: 785-232-2863; Fax: 785-357-7844.

8—ST. MATTHEW, Rev. Patric Riley.
Res., 2700 S.E. Virginia Ave., 66605. Tel: 785-232-5012; Fax: 785-232-0028.
School—Tel: 785-235-2188.
Lay Teachers 14; Students 225.

Troy, Doniphan Co., St. Charles. Attended by St. Joseph's, Wathena. Rev. Phillip J. Winkelbauer.
Church—133 S. Park, 66087. Tel: 785-985-2271. [CEM]

Valley Falls, Jefferson Co., St. Mary's Immaculate Conception. Attended by St. Joseph's, Nortonville.
Church—Broadway at Linn, 66088. Tel: 913-945-3544. [CEM]

Wamego, Pottawatomie Co., St. Bernard's, Rev. Thomas N. Hesse.
Res., 1006 8th St., 66547. Tel: 785-456-7869; Fax: 785-456-7862. [CEM]

Waterville, Marshall Co., St. Monica's. Attended by Annunciation, Frankfort. Rev. William Bruning.

Wathena, Doniphan Co., St. Joseph's, Rev. Phillip J. Winkelbauer.
Res., P.O. Box 159, 66090. Tel: 785-989-4818; Fax: 785-989-2313. [CEM]

Waverly, Coffey Co., St. Joseph's. Attended by St. Francis Xavier, Burlington. Rev. Michael Hawken. Tel: 316-364-2416; Fax: 316-364-2416.

Wea, Miami Co., Queen of the Holy Rosary (Bucyrus P.O.), Rev. Kenneth W. Kelly.
Res., 22779 Metcalf Rd., Bucyrus, 66013. Tel: 913-533-2285; Fax: 913-533-2200. [CEM]
School—22705 Metcalf Rd., Bucyrus, 66013. Tel: 913-533-2462.
Lay Teachers 11; Students 93.

Westphalia, Anderson Co., St. Teresa's. Attended by St. Francis Xavier, Burlington. Rev. Michael Hawken. Tel: 316-364-2416; Fax: 316-364-2416.

Wetmore, Nemaha Co., St. James. Attended by Sacred Heart, Sabetha. Tel.: 785-284-3068. Rev. Donald Redmond, O.S.B.

Wheaton, Pottawatomie Co., St. Michael's. Closed. For inquiries for parish records contact the Chancery.

Chaplains of Public Institutions

KANSAS CITY. *K.U. Medical Center and Chapel* Holy Name Church. Rev. Jeremiah L. Spencer, Chap.

LAWRENCE. *Haskell Institute.* (Government Indian School). Rev. Duane F. Reinert, O.F.M.Cap.

TOPEKA. *Kansas Neurological Institute and Kansas Reception and Diagnostic Center.* Rev. William Guthman (OM) Chap.
Topeka State Hospital. State Reform School attended from Holy Name Church. Menninger Clinic attended from Holy Name Church. Veterans Administration Hospital.

Special Assignment:
Reverend Fathers—
Chontos, Joseph, 901 N. 52nd St., Kansas City, KS 66102
Cooper, Leo, Archdiocesan Archivist, 12615 Parallel, Kansas City, KS 66109
Hays, Edward, Prison Ministry, 251 Muncie Rd., Leavenworth, KS 66048
Park, Benedict, Korean Ministry, 10418 Pflumm Rd., Apt. 717, Lenexa, KS 66215
Wait, Dennis, Sanctuary of Hope, 2601 Ridge Ave., Kansas City, KS 66102-4617

On Duty Outside the Archdiocese:
Reverend Fathers—
Tillia, Marc, Bahia, Brazil

Military Chaplains:
Reverend Fathers—
Ludwikoski, James E., U.S.A.F.

On Leave of Absence:
Reverend Fathers—
McGinn, Charles
Richardson, Barry

Absent on Sick Leave:
Reverend Fathers—
Melchior, Thomas
Pecinovsky, Albert

On Sabbatical:
Reverend Fathers—
O'Sullivan, Peter

Retired:
Reverend Monsignors—
Culhane, Thomas, Overland Park, KS
Loncaric, Stanley, Olathe, KS
Trompeter, Arthur J., Topeka, KS
Reverend Fathers—
Blaufuss, Tony, Garnett, KS
Burger, Robert, Lenexa, KS
Dunnivan, John, Overland Park, KS
Gardner, Maurice, Kansas City, KS
Klasinski, George, Topeka, KS
O'Grady, James, Lawrence, KS
Pflumm, Robert, Overland Park, KS
Pool, Robert, Mound City, KS
Schepers, Frank, Olathe, KS
Schwalm, Donald, Minnesota
Stitz, John, Leavenworth, KS
Wempe, Richard C., Seneca, KS
Wickey, Harold, Bonner Springs, KS

INSTITUTIONS LOCATED IN THE ARCHDIOCESE

[A] COLLEGES AND UNIVERSITIES

KANSAS CITY. *Donnelly College*, 608 N. 18th St., 66102. Tel: 913-621-6070; Fax: 913-621-0354.
E-mail: kgibson@donnelly.cc.ks.us
Web site: www.Donnelly.cc.ks.us
For a complete listing, refer to the Colleges and Universities section.

ATCHISON. *Benedictine College*, 66002. Tel: 913-367-5340; Fax: 913-367-3673.
E-mail: peylar@raven.benedictine.edu
Web site: www.benedictine.edu
For a complete listing, refer to the Colleges and Universities section.

LEAVENWORTH. *Saint Mary College*, 66048. Tel: 913-682-5151; Fax: 913-758-6140.
E-mail: admis@hub.smcks.edu
Web site: www.smcks.edu
For a complete listing, refer to the Colleges and Universities section.

[B] HIGH SCHOOLS, INTERPAROCHIAL

KANSAS CITY. *Bishop Miege High School*. 5041 Reinhardt Dr., Shawnee-Mission, 66205. Tel: 913-262-2700; Fax: 913-262-3754.
E-mail: bmiege3@idir.net
Web site: www.bishopmiege.com
Joseph Passantino, Ed.D., Pres.; Stanley Herbic, Prin. Sisters 2; Lay Teachers 57; Students 860.
Bishop Miege High School Foundation. Tel: 913-262-2700; Fax: 913-262-3754.
Bishop Ward High School, 708 N. 18th St., 66102. Tel: 913-371-1201; Fax: 913-371-2145.
E-mail: wardhigh@wardhigh.org
Web site: www.wardhigh.org
Mr. Timothy Mulvany, Pres.; Dr. Robert Runnebaum, Prin.; Rev. John Torrez, Chap. Sisters of Charity of Leavenworth 5; Lay Teachers 35; Students 479.
Bishop Ward High School Foundation. Tel: 913-371-1201; Fax: 913-371-2145.

LEAVENWORTH. *Immaculata High School*, 66048. Tel: 913-682-3900; Fax: 913-682-9036.
E-mail: dessert@archkckcs.org
Rolland Dessert, C.E.A.; Michael Connelly, Prin. Lay Teachers 22; Students 199.

OVERLAND PARK. *Saint Thomas Aquinas High School, Inc.*, 11411 Pflumm Rd., 66215. Tel: 913-345-1411; Fax: 913-345-2319.
E-mail: wpford@stasaints.net
Web site: www.stasaints.net
Adam Holden, Prin.; Dr. William P. Ford, Pres.; Rev. Jon Hullinger, Chap. Sisters 2; Lay Teachers 77; Students 1,212.
St. Thomas Aquinas High School Foundation. Tel: 913-345-1411; Fax: 913-345-2319.

TOPEKA. *Hayden High School*, 401 Gage Blvd., 66606. Tel: 785-272-5210; Fax: 785-272-2975.
E-mail: streckerr@haydenhigh.org
Web site: www.haydenhigh.org
Mr. Rick Strecker, Pres.; Mr. Mark Madsen, Prin. Religious 1; Lay Teachers 39; Students 570.
Hayden High School Foundation. Tel: 785-272-5210; Fax: 785-272-2975.

[C] HIGH SCHOOLS, PRIVATE

ATCHISON. *Maur Hill Prep School*, 66002. Tel: 913-367-5482; Fax: 913-367-5096.
E-mail: head@maurhill.com
Web site: www.maurhill.com
Mr. Patrick Cairney, Pres.; Mr. Richard Hunninghake, Headmaster; Mr. Rob Stevens, Res. Dir.; Rev. Camillus Wurtz, O.S.B.; Bro. Marjon Charboneau, O.S.B. Religious 2; Lay Teachers 24; Students 160.
Domestic Department. Misioneras Guadalupanas de Cristo Rey, O.S.B. Sisters 12.
Mount St. Scholastica Academy, 810 R St., 66002. Tel: 913-367-1334; Fax: 913-367-5108.
E-mail: mssa@best.com
Web site: www.mountstscholastica.com
Sisters of St. Benedict. Girls boarding and day high school. Sr. Dorothy Wolters, O.S.B., Pres. Sisters 2; Lay Teachers 14; Students 117.

[D] ELEMENTARY SCHOOLS, INTERPAROCHIAL

KANSAS CITY. *All Saints School*. Consolidated, 809 Vermont, 66101. Tel: 913-342-3669; Fax: 913-342-3705.
E-mail: mdelac@archkckcswy.org
Mary Delac, Prin. Lay Teachers 15; Students 341.

Our Lady of Unity School, 2646 S. 34th, 66106. Tel: 913-262-7022; Fax: 913-262-7836.
E-mail: sdrlong@hotmail.com
Sr. Delores Long, Prin. Sisters 2; Lay Teachers 9; Students 138.

St. John/Holy Family School. (Consolidated), 515 Ohio & 420 Barnett, 66101. Tel: 913-321-0649; Fax: 913-321-5001.
E-mail: sthohn_holyfamily@yahoo.com
Mary Staley, Prin. Lay Teachers 13; Students 155.

ATCHISON. *Atchison Catholic Elementary*, 201 Division, 66002. Tel: 913-367-3503; Fax: 913-367-0797. Mr. Keith Mispagel, Prin. Lay Teachers 21; Students 315.

LAWRENCE. *The Lawrence Catholic School.*

Corpus Christi Campus, 6001 W. 15th St., 66049. Tel: 785-331-3374; Fax: 785-331-3904. Lay Teachers 2; Students 23.

St. John Campus, 1208 Kentucky St., 66044. Tel: 785-843-9511; Fax: 785-843-7143. Pat Newton, Prin. Lay Teachers 18; Students 320.

LEAVENWORTH. *Xavier Elementary School*, Admin. Office, 320 N. Broadway, 66048. Tel: 913-682-3135; Fax: 913-682-5262.
E-mail: teachxvr@idir.net
Consolidation of the following parishes: St. Casimir (Grades PreK-K); Sacred Heart (Grades 1-3); St. Joseph (Grades 7-8); and Immaculate Conception (Grades 4-6), St. Ignatius, St. Francis de Sales, St. Lawrence, and St. Joseph of the Valley. Mr. Rolly Dessert, Chief Exec. Admin.; Margaret O'Sullivan, Admin. Sisters 1; Lay Teachers 24; Students 477.

[E] ELEMENTARY AND SECONDARY SCHOOLS, PRIVATE

MAPLE HILL, KS. *Our Lady of Compassion*, P.O. Box 236, 66507. Tel: 785-256-4500. Rev. Michael Irwin, F.S.S.P. Priests 1; Lay Teachers 3; Students 30.

[F] GENERAL HOSPITALS

KANSAS CITY. *Bethany Medical Center, Inc.*, 51 N. 12th St., 66102. Tel: 913-281-8400; Fax: 913-281-8494.
E-mail: scbones@pmc-sjh.org
Web site: www.pmc-sjh.org
For a complete listing, refer to the Hospitals section.

Providence Medical Center, 8929 Parallel Pkwy., 66112. Tel: 913-596-4000; Fax: 913-596-4098
For a complete listing, refer to the Hospitals section.

LEAVENWORTH. *Saint John Hospital*, 3500 S. 4th St., 66048. Tel: 913-680-6000; Fax: 913-680-6013
For a complete listing, refer to the Hospitals section.

TOPEKA. *St. Francis Hospital and Medical Center*, 1700 W. 7th St., 66606. Tel: 785-295-8000
For a complete listing, refer to the Hospitals section.

[G] NURSING AND REST HOMES

KANSAS CITY. *Marian Hall*, 1920 Tauromee, 66102. Tel: 913-621-4302; Fax: 913-621-1824
For a complete listing, refer to the Special Care Facilities section.

Providence Place, 8909 Parallel, 66112. Tel: 913-596-4200; Fax: 913-596-4901.
E-mail: tallin@medmgmt.com
For a complete listing, refer to the Special Care Facilities section.

OLATHE. *Villa St. Francis, Inc.*, 16600 W. 126th St., 66062. Tel: 913-829-5201; Fax: 913-829-5390
For a complete listing, refer to the Special Care Facilities section.

OVERLAND PARK. *Villa St. Joseph Nursing Home*, 11901 Rosewood, 66209. Tel: 913-345-1745; Fax: 913-345-1346
For a complete listing, refer to the Special Care Facilities section.

[H] MONASTERIES AND RESIDENCES FOR PRIESTS AND BROTHERS

ATCHISON. *St. Benedict's Abbey*, 1020 N. 2nd St., 66002. Tel: 913-367-7853; Fax: 913-367-6230.
E-mail: barnabas@benedictine.edu
Web site: www.benedictine.edu/abbey/index.html
Rt. Revs. Barnabas Senecal, O.S.B., Abbot; Owen Purcell, O.S.B., (Retired Abbot); Ralph Koehler, O.S.B., (Retired Abbot); Very Rev. Michael Santa, O.S.B., Prior; Revs. Meinrad Miller, O.S.B., Subprior; Maurice Haefling, O.S.B., Business Mgr.; James Albers, O.S.B.; Mark Broski, O.S.B.; Eugene Dehner, O.S.B.; James Downey, O.S.B.; Basil Finken, O.S.B.; Thomas Flaherty, O.S.B.; Timothy Fry, O.S.B.; Matthew Habiger, O.S.B.; Regis Hickey, O.S.B.; Hugh Keefer, O.S.B.; Benedict J. LaRocque, O.S.B.; Anselm Llewellyn, O.S.B.; Stephen McCann, O.S.B.; Denis Meade, O.S.B.; Conrad Pillar, O.S.B.; Brendan Rolling, O.S.B.; Augustine Rottering, O.S.B.; Blaine Schultz, O.S.B.; Paul Steingreaber, O.S.B.; Benjamin Tremmel, O.S.B.; Gilbert Wolters, O.S.B.; Michael Zoellner, O.S.B.; Bros. Lawrence Bradford, O.S.B.; Martin Burkhard, O.S.B.; Dominic Cason, O.S.B.; Marion Charboneau, O.S.B.; Robert Heiman, O.S.B.; John Kaighin, O.S.B.; Gabriel Landis, O.S.B.; Columba McNeill, O.S.B.; Francis Mutter, O.S.B.; John Peto, O.S.B.; Joseph Ryan, O.S.B.; Gregory Viscek, O.S.B.; Anthony Vorwerk, O.S.B. Bishops 1; Priests 44; Brothers 15.

LAWRENCE. *St. Conrad's Friary.* (Capuchins), 745 Tennessee, 66044. Tel: 785-843-0188.
Web site: www.capuchins.org
In res. Revs. James Moster, O.F.M.Cap.; Duane F. Reinert, O.F.M.Cap.; Charles Polifka, O.F.M.Cap.; Bro. Joseph McGlynn, O.F.M.Cap. Total in Residence 4.

[I] CONVENTS AND RESIDENCES FOR SISTERS

KANSAS CITY. *Convent of the Sisters, Servants of Mary*, 800 N. 18th St., 66102. Tel: 913-371-3423; Fax: 913-621-4962. Ministers to the Sick, Motherhouse of the Congregation for the United States. Nurses, private duty, and visiting nursing in the homes. Mother Alfonsa Bellido, S.M., Prov. Supr.; Sr. Carmela Sanz, S.M., Local Supr.; Rev. Philip Kendall, C.S.V., Chap., St. Peters Cathedral. Professed 47.

ATCHISON. *Dooley Center, Inc.*, 801 S. Eighth St., 66002. Tel: 913-360-6200; Fax: 913-360-6275. Benedictine Sisters of Mount St. Scholastica, Inc., Atchison, KS. Nursing care facility for the aged/infirm members of this religious community.

Mount St. Scholastica, 801 S. 8th St., 66002. Tel: 913-360-6200; Fax: 913-360-6190.
E-mail: collinsm@benedictine.edu
Web site: www.benedictine.edu/mount.html
Motherhouse of the Sisters of St. Benedict. Sr. Mary Collins, O.S.B., Prioress.
In community: Professed Sisters 209; Novices 5; Postulants 1. Attended from St. Benedict's Abbey.

LEAVENWORTH. *Motherhouse of the Sisters of Charity of Leavenworth*, 66048-5054. Tel: 913-758-6501; Fax: 913-682-2128.
E-mail: smiller@scls.org
Web site: www.scls.org
Sr. Joan Sue Miller, S.C.L., Community Dir.; Sr. Lucy Walter, S.C.L., Local Coord.; Sr. Rita Smith, S.C.L., Local Admin.; Rev. Michael Zoellner, O.S.B., Chap. Sisters 414; Total in Residence 134.

PAOLA. *Our Lady of Lourdes Convent*, 901 E. Miami St., 66071. Tel: 913-557-2349; Fax: 913-557-2340.
E-mail: ursuline@paolaursuline.org
Web site: www.paolaursuline.org
Motherhouse of the Ursuline Sisters. Sr. Patricia Lynch, O.S.U., Supr.; Rev. Aaron Peters, O.S.B., Chap. Sisters 36.

[J] CAMPUS MINISTRY

EMPORIA. *Didde Catholic Campus Center, Emporia State University*, Office: 1415 Merchant, 66801. Tel: 316-343-6765; Fax: 316-343-6792.
E-mail: dccc@osprey.net
Web site: www.emporia.edu/dccc
Rev. Jerry Volz, Chap., 1102 Neosho St., 66801. Tel: 316-342-8727. Total Staff 9.

LAWRENCE. *Haskell Catholic Campus Center*, 2301 Barker Ave., 66046-4813. Tel: 785-842-2401.
E-mail: DEN1588@aol.com
Bro. Joseph McGlynn, O.F.M.Cap., Dir.; Rev. Duane F. Reinert, O.F.M.Cap., Chap. Total Staff 2.

St. Lawrence Center Foundation.

St. Lawrence Catholic Campus Center at the University of Kansas and Residence, 1631 Crescent Rd., 66044. Tel: 785-843-0357.
Web site: www.st-lawrence.org
Revs. Vincent E. Krische; John Pilcher. Total Staff 20.

TOPEKA. *Catholic Campus Center of Washburn University*, 1633 Jewell, 66604. Tel: 785-233-2204.

[K] MISCELLANEOUS LISTINGS

KANSAS CITY. *Casa Juan Diego Centro de Evangelization*, 229 S. 8th, 66101.

The Catholic Foundation of Northeast Kansas. (Formerly known as Archdiocesan Foundation), 12615 Parallel, 66109. Tel: 913-721-1570; Fax: 913-721-1577.
E-mail: stewdev@archkck.org

Catholic Housing of Wyandotte County, Security Bank Bldg., Ste. M4, 707 Minnesota Ave., 66101. Tel: 913-342-7580; Fax: 913-342-7581.
E-mail: chwc@primary.net

Duchesne Clinic, 636 Tauromee, 66101. Tel: 913-321-2626; Fax: 913-321-2651.
E-mail: caritas@birch.net
Sr. Ann McGuire, Exec. Dir.; Sr. Janet Cashman, Mgr. A division of Caritas Clinics, Inc., Leavenworth, KS. Total Staff 7; Total Patients 7,255.

El Centro, Inc., 1333 S. 27th, 66106. Tel: 913-677-0100; Fax: 913-362-8250; 362-8513. Mr. Richard Ruiz, Dir. Sisters 5. 1330 S. 30th St., 66106. Tel: 913-677-1115.

The Gardner Institute, 2215 Parallel Ave., 66104. Tel: 913-371-8254; Fax: 913-371-8510.
E-mail: srickie@gardnerkcks.org

Lay Employee's Retirement Plan of the Archdiocese of Kansas City in Kansas, 12615 Parallel Pkwy., 66109. Tel: 913-721-1570; Fax: 913-721-1577.
E-mail: insure@archkck.org
Web site: www.archkck.org

Priest's Retirement Plan of the Archdiocese of Kansas City in Kansas, 12615 Parallel Pkwy., 66109. Tel: 912-721-1570; Fax: 912-721-1577.
E-mail: insure@archkck.org
Web site: www.archkck.org

Providence Medical Center Foundation, 8929 Parallel Pkwy., 66112. Tel: 913-596-4151; Fax: 913-596-4098.
E-mail: kcuda@pmc-sjh.org
Web site: www.pmc-sjh.org

Shalom Catholic Worker House, 2100 N. 13th, 66104. Tel: 913-321-2206. Total Staff 4; Total Assisted 2,000.

ATCHISON. *The Maur Hill Prep School Endowment Association, Inc.*, 1000 Green St., 66002. Tel: 913-367-5482.

The Mount Community Center, Inc., 751 S. 8th St., 66002. Tel: 913-360-6200; Fax: 913-360-6152. Sr. Laura Hang, O.S.B., Program Dir.

EASTON. *Shantivanam Archdiocesan House of Prayer*, 22019 Meagher Rd., 66020. Tel: 913-773-8255.
E-mail: wnepps@lvnworth.com
Jennifer Sullivan, Dir. Total in Residence 5; Total Staff 9.

EMPORIA. *Community Service Center*, 116 W. 12th, 66801. Tel: 316-343-2296; Fax: 316-342-9517. Total Assisted 578; Staff 18.

LAWRENCE. *Catholic Community Services*, 320 Main St., P.O. Box 342, 66044. Tel: 785-841-0307; Fax: 785-832-1710.

LEAVENWORTH. *Caritas Clinics, Inc.*, 511 S. Fifth St., 66048. Tel: 913-651-8860; Fax: 913-682-4409.
E-mail: caritas@birch.net
Sisters of Charity of Leavenworth. Ann Zimmerman, Pres.; Sr. Ann McGuire, Exec. Dir. Administrative structure for St. Vincent Clinic, Leavenworth, Duchesne Clinic, Kansas City, Mobile Clinic "Care a Van", Wyandotte and Leavenworth Co. Total Staff 5; Total Patients 813.

Catholic Community Services, 716 N. 5th St., 66048. Tel: 913-651-8060; Fax: 913-651-9350.
E-mail: leavenworthccs@juno.com
Staff 7; Patients assisted annually 4,001.

Catholic School Foundation of the Leavenworth Region, Inc., 320 N. Broadway, 66048. Tel: 913-682-7801; Fax: 913-682-6019.
E-mail: lcsdev@archkckcs.org
Rolly Dessert, Chief Exec. Admin.

Saint Vincent Clinic. (A division of Caritas Clinics, Inc., Leavenworth, KS.), 422 Walnut, 66048. Tel: 913-651-8860; Fax: 913-682-4409.
E-mail: caritas@birch.net
Sr. Ann McGuire, Exec. Dir.; Mary Sullivan, Mgr. Total Staff 4; Total Patients 3,100.

Sisters of Charity of Leavenworth Health System, Inc., 4200 S. 4th St., 66048. Tel: 913-682-1338; Fax: 913-682-1052.
E-mail: sclhsc@sclhsc.org
Web site: www.sclhsc.org
Mr. William M. Murray, Pres. & CEO.

MAYETTA. *Our Lady of the Snows Catholic Shrine*, Potawatomi Reservation, 66509.

OLATHE. *Catholic Community Services*, 333 E. Poplar, 66061. Tel: 913-782-4077; Fax: 913-782-0983.

PAOLA. *Lakemary Center, Inc.*, 100 Lakemary Dr., 66071-0449. Tel: 913-557-4000; Fax: 913-557-4910.
E-mail: bcraig@lakemaryctr.org
Web site: www.lakemaryctr.org
Ursuline Sisters. Dr. William R. Craig, Pres. Serves children and adults with mental retardation. Total Staff 235; Total Assisted 229.

Ursuline Sisters Charitable Trust, 901 E. Miami, 66071. Tel: 913-557-2349; Fax: 913-557-2340.
E-mail: ursuline@paolaursuline.org
Web site: www.paolaursuline.org

TOPEKA. *Catholic Community Services Inc.*, 306 SW VanBuren, 66603. Tel: 785-233-6300.

Catholic Health Association of Kansas, P.O. Box 2308, 66601. Tel: 785-233-7436.

El Centro de Servicios Para Hispanos, 216 N.E. Branner, 66616. Tel: 785-232-8207; Fax: 785-232-8834.

Marian Clinic, Inc., Medical Plaza Bldg., 1001 S.W. Garfield, 66604. Tel: 785-233-8081; Fax: 785-233-8952.
E-mail: mpage@cynetworks.com
Affiliate of Sisters of Charity of Leavenworth Health Services Corp. Mr. William M. Murray, Pres.; Marilyn Page, Exec. Dir. Total Patients 10,000.

St. Francis Hospital Foundation, 1700 W. 7th St., 66606. Tel: 785-295-5356; Fax: 785-295-5479.
E-mail: bjuozitis@stfrancistopeka.org

RELIGIOUS INSTITUTES OF MEN REPRESENTED IN THE ARCHDIOCESE

For further details refer to the corresponding bracketed number in the Religious Institutes of Men or Women section.

[0200]—*Benedictine Monks.*—O.S.B.

[0470]—*The Capuchin Friars.* (Holy Family).—O.F.M.Cap.

[0270]—*Carmelite Fathers & Brothers.* (American Prov.).—O.Carm.

[1320]—*Clerics of St. Viator.*—C.S.V.

[0520]—*Franciscan Friars.* (Cincinnati, OH.).—O.F.M.

[]—*Priestly Fraternity of St. Peter.*—F.S.S.P.

[]—*Society of Jesus.*—S.J.

[1060]—*Society of the Precious Blood.*—C.PP.S.

[]—*Vincentian Fathers.*—C.M.

RELIGIOUS INSTITUTES OF WOMEN REPRESENTED IN THE ARCHDIOCESE

[0100]—*Adorers of the Blood of Christ.*—A.S.C.

[0230]—*Benedictine Sisters of Pontifical Jurisdiction.*—O.S.B.

[1170]—*Felician Sisters.*—C.S.S.F.

[1430]—*Franciscan Sisters of Our Lady of Perpetual Help.*—O.S.F.

[3130]—*Our Lady of Victory Missionary Sisters.*—O.L.V.M.

[0480]—*Sisters of Charity of Leavenworth, Kansas.*—S.C.L.

[1520]—*Sisters of St. Francis of Christ the King.*—O.S.F.

[1570]—*Sisters of St. Francis of the Holy Family.*—O.S.F.

[3840]—*Sisters of St. Joseph of Carondelet.* (St. Louis, MO).—C.S.J.

[3830-18]—*Sisters of St. Joseph of Wichita.*—C.S.J.

[3600]—*Sisters, Servants of Mary.*—S.M.

[4120]—*Ursuline Nuns, of the Congregation of Paris.*—O.S.U.

ARCHDIOCESAN CEMETERIES

KANSAS CITY. *Gate of Heaven.*

St. John's, Mount Calvary, Resurrection, St. Joseph's, Shawnee, and St. John, Lenexa.

ATCHISON. *Mount Calvary.*

LEAVENWORTH. *Mount Calvary.*

LENEXA. *Holy Trinity.*

TOPEKA. *Mount Calvary.*

NECROLOGY

(No Deaths)

Diocese of Kansas City-St. Joseph

(Dioecesis Kansanopolitanae Sancti Josephi)

Most Reverend

RAYMOND J. BOLAND, D.D.

Bishop of Kansas City-St. Joseph; born February 8, 1932; ordained June 16, 1957; appointed Bishop of Birmingham February 2, 1988; consecrated March 25, 1988; appointed Bishop of Kansas City-St. Joseph June 22, 1993; installed September 9, 1993. *Mailing Address: P.O. Box 419037, Kansas City, MO, 64141-6037.*

Most Reverend

JOHN J. SULLIVAN, D.D.

Former Bishop of Kansas City-St. Joseph; born July 5, 1920; ordained September 23, 1944; appointed Bishop of Grand Island July 25, 1972; consecrated September 19, 1972; installed Grand Island September 21, 1972; appointed Bishop of Kansas City-St. Joseph June 27, 1977; installed August 17, 1977; retired September 9, 1993. *Res., 8745 James A. Reed Rd., Kansas City, MO, 64138.*

Diocese of Kansas City Established September 10, 1880; Diocese of St. Joseph Established March 3, 1868.

Redesignated Diocese of Kansas City-St. Joseph August 29, 1956.

Square Miles 15,429.

Comprises the Counties of Andrew, Atchison, Bates, Buchanan, Caldwell, Carroll, Cass, Clay, Clinton, Daviess, DeKalb, Gentry, Grundy, Harrison, Henry, Holt, Jackson, Johnson, Lafayette, Livingston, Mercer, Nodaway, Platte, Ray, Saint Clair, Vernon and Worth in the State of Missouri.

For legal titles of parishes and diocesan institutions, consult the Chancery Office.

Chancery: P.O. Box 419037, Kansas City, MO, 64141-6037. Tel.: 816-756-1850; Fax: 816-756-0878.

Web site address: www.diocese-kcsj.org

STATISTICAL OVERVIEW

Personnel	
Bishop	1
Retired Bishops	1
Abbots	1
Retired Abbots	1
Priests: Diocesan Active in Diocese	74
Priests: Active Outside Diocese	3
Priests: Diocesan in Foreign Missions	2
Priests: Retired, Sick or Absent	43
Number of Diocesan Priests	122
Religious Priests in Diocese	94
Extern Priests in Diocese	3
Ordinations:	
Religious Priests	1
Permanent Deacons in Diocese	57
Total Brothers	32
Total Sisters	279
Parishes	
Parishes	85
With Resident Pastor:	
Resident Diocesan Priests	61
Resident Religious Priests	18
Without Resident Pastor:	
Administered by Deacons	1
Administered by Women Religious	3
Administered by Lay People	1
Missions	14
Welfare	
Catholic Hospitals	3
Total Assisted	263,364
Homes for the Aged	16
Total Assisted	1,134
Day Care and Extended Day Care Centers	13
Total Assisted	346
Special Centers for Social Services	2
Total Assisted	24,000
Residential Care of Disabled	1
Total Assisted	25
Educational	
Diocesan Students in Other Seminaries	14
Seminaries, Religious	1
Students Religious	3
Total Seminarians	17
Colleges and Universities	2
Total Students	5,163
High Schools, Diocesan and Parish	4
Total Students	1,515
High Schools, Private	3
Total Students	1,941
Elementary Schools, Diocesan and Parish	34
Total Students	10,364
Elementary Schools, Private	1
Total Students	338
Catechesis/Religious Education:	
High School Students	998
Elementary Students	8,992
Total Students Under Catholic Instruction	29,328
Teachers in the Diocese:	
Priests	3
Brothers	2
Sisters	17
Lay Teachers	861
Vital Statistics	
Receptions into the Church:	
Infant Baptism Totals	2,572
Adult Baptism Totals	328
Received into Full Communion	480
First Communions	2,746
Confirmations	1,958
Marriages:	
Catholic	507
Interfaith	473
Total Marriages	980
Deaths	1,259
Total Catholic Population	158,089
Total Population	1,394,040

Former Bishops—Rt. Rev. John Joseph Hogan, D.D., ord. April 10, 1852; cons. Bishop of St. Joseph, MO, Sept. 13, 1868; transferred to Kansas City, Sept. 10, 1880; died Feb. 21, 1913.—Most Rev. Thomas F. Lillis, D.D., ord. Aug. 15, 1885; cons. Bishop of Leavenworth, Dec. 27, 1904; appt. Coadjutor to the Bishop of Kansas City, *"cum jure successionis,"* March 14, 1910 Bishop of Kansas City, Feb. 21, 1913; appt. assistant at the Pontifical Throne, Aug. 19, 1935; died Dec. 29, 1938.—Most Rev. Edwin V. O'Hara, D.D., ord. June 10, 1905; appt. Bishop of Great Falls, MT, August 1, 1930; cons. Oct. 28, 1930; transferred to the See of Kansas City, April 15, 1939 made assistant at the Pontifical Throne, Jan. 5, 1949; appt. Archbishop "ad personam," June 29, 1954; died Sept. 11, 1956.—His Eminence John Cardinal Cody, S.T.D., ord. Dec. 8, 1931; appt. Titular Bishop of Appollonia and Auxiliary Bishop of St. Louis, May 14, 1947; cons. July 2, 1947; promoted to coadjutor of St. Joseph *"cum jure successionis,"* Jan. 27, 1954; appt. to Diocese of Kansas City-St. Joseph, Aug. 24, 1956; succeeded to Sept. 11, 1956; transferred to Archdiocese of New Orleans as Coadjutor Archbishop *"cum jure successionis,"* Aug. 10, 1961; acceded the See of New Orleans, Nov. 8, 1964; transferred to the Archdiocese of Chicago, June 16, 1965; created Cardinal Priest, June 26, 1967; died April 25, 1982.—Most Rev. Charles H. Helmsing, D.D., ord. June 10, 1933; appt. Titular Bishop of Axomis and Auxiliary Bishop of St. Louis, March 17, 1949; cons. April 19, 1949; appt. Bishop of Springfield-Cape Girardeau, Aug. 24, 1956; transferred to Diocese of Kansas City-St. Joseph, Jan. 27, 1962; retired Aug. 17, 1977; died Dec. 20, 1993.—Most Rev. John J. Sullivan, D.D., ord. Sept. 23, 1944; appt. Bishop of Grand Island, July 25, 1972; cons. Sept. 19, 1972; installed Grand Island, Sept. 21, 1972; appt. Bishop of Kansas City-St. Joseph, June 27, 1977; installed Aug. 17, 1977; retired Sept. 9, 1993.

Former Bishops of Diocese of St. Joseph, MO—Rt. Rev. John J. Hogan, D.D., ord. April 10, 1852; appt. first Bishop of St. Joseph, March 3, 1868; cons. Sept. 13, 1868; transferred to See of Kansas City, Sept. 10, 1880; administrator of St. Joseph until 1893; died Feb. 21, 1913.—Rt. Rev. Maurice F. Burke, D.D.,born May 5, 1844; ord. May 22, 1875; appt. first Bishop of Cheyenne, WY, Aug. 9, 1887; cons. Oct. 28, 1887; transferred to St. Joseph, June 19, 1893; died March 17, 1923.—Most Rev. Francis Gilfillan, D.D.,born Feb. 16, 1872; ord. June 24, 1895; appt. titular Bishop of Spigas and Coadjutor with the right of succession to the See of St. Joseph, July 8, 1922; cons. Nov. 8, 1922; succeeded to the See of St. Joseph, March 17, 1923; died Jan. 13, 1933.—Most Rev. Charles H. LeBlond, D.D., ord. Oct. 27, 1909; appt. Bishop of St. Joseph, July 21, 1933; cons. Sept. 21, 1933; resigned as Bishop of St. Joseph and appointed Titular Bishop of Orcistus, Aug. 24, 1956; died Dec. 30, 1958.

Vicar General—Rev. Patrick R. Rush.

Chancery—*P.O. Box 419037, Kansas City, 64141-6037.* Tel: 816-756-1850; Fax: 816-756-0878. All official

matters should be sent to this address.
Chancellor—GEORGE M. NOONAN.
Vice Chancellor—Sr. JEAN BESTE, B.V.M.
Diocesan Finance Officer—DAVID A. MALANOWSKI.
Diocesan Tribunal—*P.O. Box 419037, Kansas City, 64141-6037*. Tel: 816-756-1850.
Tribunal Director—Sr. VIRGINIA BARTOLAC, S.C.L., J.C.D.
Judicial Vicar—Rev. C. MICHAEL COLEMAN, J.C.L.
Adjutant Judicial Vicar—Rev. JOSEPH H. MATT, J.C.L.
Defender of the Bond—Sr. RITA KILLACKEY, O.S.B.
Procurators—DONNA EISENBARTH; JANET DIXON.
Secretary of the Tribunal—CAROLYN RAMM.
Diocesan Consultors—Revs. J. KENNETH CRIQUI; JAMES HART; JOSEPH B. POWERS; ROBERT A. ROST; PATRICK J. RUSH; MICHAEL E. TIERNEY; JOHN WEISS; DONALD HELFREY; MICHAEL ROACH; JAMES E. SHEA, C.SS.R.
Presbyteral Council—Revs. KEN RILEY, Chm. ANTHONY PILEGGI, Sec. & Treas.
Deans—Rev. DONALD P. FARNAN, Deanery I; Rev. JAMES E. SHEA, C.SS.R., Deanery II; Rev. DONALD HELFREY, Deanery III; Rev. JOHN WEISS, Deanery IV; Rev. KENNETH RILEY, Deanery V; Rev. MICHAEL CLARY, Deanery VI; Rev. ANTHONY PILEGGI, Deanery VII; Rev. KENNETH CRIQUI, Deanery VIII; Rev. ROBERT KERR, Deanery IX; Rev. DANIEL PETSCHE, O.S.B., Deanery X; Rev. ROBERT ROST, Deanery XI; Rev. THOMAS LUDWIG, Deanery XII; Rev. MICHAEL ROACH, Deanery XIII; Rev. JOSEPH MANCUSO, Deanery XIV.

Diocesan Offices and Directors

Archivist—Rev. C. MICHAEL COLEMAN, J.C.L.
Building Commission—Revs. MICHAEL RICE; PATRICK J. RUSH, V.G.; DANIEL KENNALEY; Mr. BERNARD J. GRAM, Chm. WILLIAM TURNER; BERNARD JACQUINOT; STEPHEN F. OBARSKI; DAVID A. MALANOWSKI; Sr. JEAN BESTE, B.V.M.; THOMAS REDMOND; WILLIAM FAGAN; WAYNE ROY; ALLEN MILLER; HERMAN JOHANNESMEYER, (See Property Mgmt. Office).
The "Catholic Key" Diocesan Newspaper—ALBERT DE ZUTTER, Editor.
Cemetery (Catholic Cemeteries Associated, Diocese of Kansas City-St. Joseph, Inc.)—Rev. ROBERT M. CAMERON, Diocesan Dir., *7601 Blue Ridge, Kansas City, 64138*. Diocesan Cemeteries: Kansas City, Mt. Olivet; Mt. St. Mary; Resurrection; St. Joseph, Mt. Olivet.
Censor Librorum—Rev. Msgr. WILLIAM J. BLACET, J.C.L.
Catholic Charities Foundation—Vacant, Exec. Dir, *301 E. Armour Blvd., Ste. 620, Kansas City, 64111*. Tel: 816-756-1850, Ext. 563; Fax: 816-756-5022.
Catholic Charities of Kansas City-St. Joseph, Inc.—*1112 Broadway, Kansas City, 64105-1574*. Tel: 816-221-4377; Fax: 816-221-9116. MICHAEL W. HALTERMAN, CEO; GEORGE HANS, Chief Financial Officer; SUSAN COOK, Children and Family Services, Dir. LAURA WHITE, Executive Assistant to the Chief Executive Officer; ANN PAVLICH, Human Resources/CQI Manager; ROB SNEAD, Customer Services/MIS Manager; LYNN FLAHERTY, Director of Community Relations, *301 E. Armour Blvd., Ste. 620, Kansas City, 64111*. Tel: 816-756-1850, Ext. 560. Northern Diocesan Branch Office: MARTIN J. GOEDKEN, Dir., *1302 Faraon, St. Joseph, 64501*. Tel: 816-232-2885. Southern Diocesan Branch Office: SUSAN LOYD, A.C.S.W., L.I.C.S.W., Dir., *123 E. Gay St., Ste. A1-A, Warrensburg, 64093*. Tel: 660-747-2241.
Center for Pastoral Life and Ministry—DENISE SIMEONE, Dir.
Ministry Formation—Catechist Formation: TONY BUTEL. Continuing Education: CLARA DINA HINOJOSA. Loyola: CELE BREEN. New Wine: DENISE SIMEONE. Parish Life Summer Institute: TONY BUTEL. Ministry Formation Classes: TONY BUTEL.
Parish Life Development—Christian Initiation: CELE BREEN. Evangelization: DALE MOONEY. Hispanic Ministry: DALE MOONEY. Pastoral Leadership Councils: ROSE THERESE HUELSMAN. Pastoral Leadership Staff: CELE BREEN. Religious Education: BIAGIO MAZZA. Small Christian Communities: ROSE THERESE HUELSMAN.
Central City School Fund Office—Vacant, Dir. MELANIE MARTIN, Assoc. Dir.
Diocesan Annual Appeal—THOMAS MINGES, Dir.
Diocesan Development—THOMAS MINGES, Dir.
Diocesan Ecumenical Officer—GEORGE M. NOONAN.
Diocesan Finance Council—Revs. ROBERT STEWART; JOHN WANDLESS; Sr. HELEN FLEMINGTON; MICHAEL BROSNAHAN; JAMES STACY; MARGO SHEPARD; MARYELLEN CONNOR; DAVID A. MALANOWSKI, Staff Representative; JOHN DESTEFANO; JOHN HOULEHAN; THOMAS MCCULLOUGH; ED MCSHANE; THOMAS MINGES; THERESA HUPP; MONICA ADAMS, Staff Representative.
Diocesan Finance Office—DAVID A. MALANOWSKI, Finance Officer; MONICA ADAMS, Internal Auditor; BARBARA VOLZ, Accounting Mgr.
Diocesan Insurance Office—MONICA ADAMS, Risk Mgr. ROSALEE WIETHARN, Benefits Coord.
Diocesan Ministry for Persons With Disabilities—JUDY SHUTE, Exec. Sec., *4101 E. 105th Ter., Kansas City, 64137*. Tel: 816-767-0058.
Education Office—JUDY WARREN, Supt., Schools; Sr. CAROL ANN PETERSON, O.S.B., Assoc. Supt. THOMAS BLAKE, Assoc. Supt. Tel: 816-756-1850.
Family Life Office—KENNETH GREENE, Dir.
Holy Childhood Association—Rev. ROBERT M. CAMERON, Dir.; Deacon ROSS BEAUDOIN, Coord.
Legion of Mary—Rev. DONALD STURM, Dir.
Office of the Diaconate—Deacon ROSS BEAUDOIN, Dir.
Office of Social Concerns—NEAL COLBY, JR., Dir.
Office of Personnel and Planning—Sr. JEAN BESTE, B.V.M., Dir.
Peace and Justice Office—JOCELE MCENANY, Dir. JEAN CHRISTENSEN, R.S.M., Assoc. Dir.; Rev. FRANCIS SCHUELE, Assoc. Dir. Tel: 816-756-1850; Fax: 816-756-5221.
Priests' Purgatorial Society—Rev. ROBERT M. CAMERON, Sec.
Priests' Pension Plan—Administrative Committee: Rev. Msgr. HENRY G. BAUER; Revs. ROBERT M. CAMERON; C. MICHAEL COLEMAN; DAVID A. MALANOWSKI.
Propagation of the Faith—(Pontifical Society for the Propagation of the Faith, Missionary Union of the Clergy and Religious, The Pontifical Society of St. Peter the Apostle for Native Clergy, and Daily World missionaries); Rev. ROBERT M. CAMERON, Dir.
Property Management—WAYNE ROY, Diocesan Property Mgr. CINDY FOERSCHLER, Coord. AL MILLER, Construction Mgr., . Fax: 816-756-5572.
Respect Life Activities—KENNETH GREENE, Coord.
St. Vincent De Paul Particular Council—Sr. PATRICIA BACHMAN, D.C., Moderator.
Vocations—Revs. ROBERT STEWART, Dir. JOSEPH CISETTI, Assoc. Dir.
Office of Worship—STEPHEN F. OBARSKI, Dir. MARIE RUBIS BAUER, Assoc. Dir.
Youth Office—MARY KELLY MUELLER, Dir.

CLERGY, PARISHES, MISSIONS AND PAROCHIAL SCHOOLS

KANSAS CITY
(Jackson County)

1—CATHEDRAL OF IMMACULATE CONCEPTION (1882). See listing for Old St. Patrick's. Rev. Msgr. Ernest J. Fiedler; Rev. Martin DeMeulenaere, O.S.B.
Res., 416 W. 12th St., 64105. Tel: 816-842-0416; Fax: 816-842-3849.

2—ST. ALOYSIUS (1886) (Hispanic), Rev. John L. Hix.
Res., 2611 E. 11th St., 64127. Tel: 816-231-1886; Fax: 816-241-7010.
Catechesis/Religious Programs—Students 55.

3—ST. ANTHONY (1991), Rev. John Schuele.
Res., 318 Benton Blvd., 64124. Tel: 816-231-5445; Fax: 816-231-5446.

4—ST. BERNADETTE'S (1958), Rev. Kenneth A. Riley; Deacon Emory Corrigan.
Res., 9020 E. 51st Ter., 64133. Tel: 816-356-3700.
School—Tel: 816-356-3702; Fax: 816-737-3447.
Lay Teachers 16; Students 170.
Catechesis/Religious Programs—Students 76.

5—BLESSED SACRAMENT. Closed. For inquiries for parish records contact St. Monica, Kansas City.

6—ST. CATHERINE OF SIENA (1926), Rev. Robert Stone; Deacon William Markey. Pastoral Assocs.: Veronica Ward; Diana Rose. In res., Rev. John P. Coleman.
Res., 4101 E. 105th Ter., 64137-1649. Tel: 816-761-5483; Fax: 816-761-8795.
School—Our Lady of Peace Consolidated School, 10526 Grandview Rd., 64137-1699. Tel: 816-761-5605; Fax: 816-761-2797.
Catechesis/Religious Programs—Students 94.

7—ST. CHARLES BORROMEO (1947), Revs. John Wolf, C.PP.S.; Keith Branson, C.PP.S.; Garry Richmeier, C.PP.S.; Bro. Robert Herman, C.PP.S.; Deacons Jerry Williams; Frank Peak; John Koch.
Res., 900 N.E. Shady Lane Dr., Oakview, 64118-4742. Tel: 816-436-0880; Fax: 816-436-0103.
School—804 N.E. Shady Lane Dr., Oakview, 64118. Tel: 816-436-1009; Fax: 816-436-6293.
Lay Teachers 31; Students 450.
Catechesis/Religious Programs—Students 528.

8—CHRIST THE KING (1938), Revs. John C. Weiss; John Wandless; Jose G. Herrera (STV).
Res., 8510 Wornall Rd., 64114. Tel: 816-363-4888; Fax: 816-363-2315.
School—(Grades K-8) 425 W. 85th St., 64114. Tel: 816-363-1113; Fax: 816-363-2889.
Lay Teachers 21; Students 245.
Preschool:—(Infant/Toddler & Preschool). Tel: 816-363-5313.
Lay Teachers 21; Students 62.
Catechesis/Religious Programs—Students 45.

9—ST. ELIZABETH'S (1917), Revs. Robert S. Gregory; James Schrader, C.PP.S.; Deacon Donald Schmit. In res., Rev. Martin DeMeulenaere, O.S.B.
Res., 7444 Main St., 64114. Tel: 816-523-2405; Fax: 816-444-9858.
School—Tel: 816-523-7100; Fax: 816-523-2566.
Lay Teachers 31; Students 483.
Catechesis/Religious Programs—Students 20.

10—ST. FRANCIS SERAPH. Closed. For inquiries for parish records contact St. Anthony, Kansas City.

11—ST. FRANCIS XAVIER (1910), Rev. Timothy M. McMahon, S.J.
Res., 1001 E. 52nd St., 64110. Tel: 816-523-5115; Fax: 816-333-0082.
School—5220 Troost Ave., 64110. Tel: 816-523-2258; Fax: 816-523-2272.
Lay Teachers 17; Students 185.
Catechesis/Religious Programs—Students 60.

12—ST. GABRIEL ARCHANGEL (1956), Rev. Karl Barmann, O.S.B.
Res., 4737 N. Cleveland Ave., 64117. Tel: 816-453-1183; Fax: 816-453-6254.
School—Tel: 816-453-4443.
Lay Teachers 16; Students 222.
Early Childhood Learning Center—Tel: 816-453-4555.
Lay Teachers 23; Students 120.
Catechesis/Religious Programs—Students 531.

13—GUARDIAN ANGELS (1909), Margaret Lima, Pastoral Admin.; Rev. Glenn R. Mueller, S.J.
Parish Office: 1310 Westport Rd., 64111. Tel: 816-931-4351; Fax: 816-531-6396.
Schools—Our Lady of the Angels School, 211 W. Linwood, 64111. Tel: 816-931-1693; Fax: 816-753-3606.; Our Lady of Guadalupe School, 2310 Madison, 64111. Tel: 816-221-2539; Fax: 816-283-3315.
Catechesis/Religious Programs—Students 36.

14—HOLY CROSS (1902), Revs. Thomas Holder; Raymond Tu; Deacon Charles DiMartino.
Res., 5106 St. John Ave., 64123. Tel: 816-231-4845; Fax: 816-483-0900.

15—HOLY FAMILY (1981), Rev. Robert H. Stewart.
Res., 919 N.E. 96th St., 64155. Tel: 816-436-9200; Fax: 816-436-8049.
Catechesis/Religious Programs—Students 337.

16—CHURCH OF THE HOLY MARTYRS (1991) (Vietnamese), Revs. Joseph Phan Trong Hanh; Raymond Tu.
Res., 7801 Paseo, 64131. Tel: 816-333-3214; Fax: 816-523-8168.
Catechesis/Religious Programs—Tel: 816-333-5349.
Students 320.

17—HOLY ROSARY (1891) (Italian), Rev. Joseph Vicentini, C.S. In res., Rev. Firmo Mantoovrni, C.S., Northeast Hispanic Ministry.
Res., 911 Missouri Ave., 64106. Tel: 816-842-5440; Fax: 816-221-3806.
Catechesis/Religious Programs—913 Pacific Ave., 64106. Tel: 816-421-5537.
Students 16.

18—HOLY TRINITY. Closed. For inquiries for parish records contact Our Lady of Peace, Kansas City.

19—ST. JAMES (1906), Rev. Al Ebach, C.PP.S.
Res., 3909 Harrison St., 64110. Tel: 816-561-8512; Fax: 816-561-1452.
Catechesis/Religious Programs—Students 47.

20—ST. JOHN THE BAPTIST. Closed. For inquiries for parish records contact St. Anthony, Kansas City, Tel: 816-231-5445.

21—ST. JOHN FRANCIS REGIS (1964), Rev. Paul Turner; Deacons Edwin Bonnarens; Marvin Mason.
Res., 8941 James A. Reed Rd., 64138. Tel: 816-761-1608; Fax: 816-966-1350.
School—Tel: 816-763-5837.
Lay Teachers 21; Students 297.
Catechesis/Religious Programs—Tel: 816-763-1366.
Students 121.

22—ST. MONICA (1995) (African American), Rev. Philip Egan.
Res., 1616 The Paseo, 64108. Tel: 816-471-3696; Fax: 816-471-1111.

23—St. Louis (1919) (African American), Rev. Donald Farnan.
Res., 5930 Swope Pkwy., 64130. Tel: 816-444-6535.
Catechesis/Religious Programs—Tel: 816-333-1204; Fax: 816-444-6027.
Students 220.

24—St. Matthew The Apostle (1964), Rev. James Taranto; Deacon Joseph Ofenloch.
Res., 8001 Longview Rd., 64134. Tel: 816-763-0208; Fax: 816-765-2617.
School—Our Lady of Peace Consolidated School, 10526 Grandview Rd., 64134. Tel: 816-761-5605; Fax: 816-761-2797.
Catechesis/Religious Programs—Tel: 816-765-7381.
Students 80.

25—St. Michael Archangel. Closed. For inquiries for parish records contact Our Lady of Peace, Kansas City, Tel: 816-231-1653.

26—Old St. Patrick's (1869). Public Oratory associated with Cathedral of the Immaculate Conception. Rev. Msgr. Ernest J. Fiedler.
Res., The Cathedral House, 416 W. 12th St., 64105. Tel: 816-842-0416; Fax: 816-842-3849.

27—Our Lady of Good Counsel (1866), Rev. Msgr. William J. Blacet. In res.,
Res., 3934 Washington, 64111-2904. Tel: 816-561-0400; Fax: 816-561-1551.

28—Our Lady of Guadalupe. Closed. For inquiries for parish records contact Sacred Heart - Guadalupe, Kansas City, Tel: 816-842-6146.

29—Sacred Heart-Guadalupe (1887) (Hispanic), Rev. James G. Betzen, C.PP.S.
Res., 907 Cesar Chavez Ave., 64108. Tel: 816-842-6146; Fax: 816-471-7540.
Catechesis/Religious Programs—Students 86.

30—Our Lady of Peace (1991) (Hispanic), Rev. Donald Helfrey; Deacon Al Ohmes.
Res., 1029 Bennington Ave., 64126-2299. Tel: 816-231-0953; Fax: 816-231-8911.
School—Consolidated School St. Stephen's Academy. See separate listing. Tel: 816-231-5227; Fax: 816-231-2824.
Catechesis/Religious Programs—Students 47.

31—Our Lady of Perpetual Help (1878), Revs. James Shea, C.Ss.R.; Frank Kriski, C.Ss.R.; Ivan Dawson, C.Ss.R.; Bros. James Burke, C.Ss.R.; Charles Long, C.Ss.R.; Michael Schnittker. In res., Revs. Joseph Curalli, C.Ss.R.; Edward Kane, C.Ss.R.; Eugene Oates, C.Ss.R.; Patrick Power, C.Ss.R.
Res., 3333 Broadway, 64111. Tel: 816-561-3771; Fax: 816-561-3704.
School—Our Lady of the Angels, 211 W. Linwood Blvd., 64111. Tel: 816-931-1693; Fax: 816-753-3606. Mary Kallman, Prin.
Sisters 2; Lay Teachers 22; Students 251.

32—Our Lady of Sorrows (1891), Revs. Thomas W. Wiederholt; Ambrose G. Karels, Chap. of Latin Mass Community, Tel: 816-931-1030.
Res., 2552 Gillham Rd., 64108. Tel: 816-421-2112; Fax: 816-421-6037.

33—St. Patrick (1924), Rev. Gerald Waris; Deacon Michael Lewis, Pastoral Assoc.
Res., 1357 N.E. 42nd Ter., 64116. Tel: 816-453-5510; Fax: 816-453-4458.
School—1401 N.E. 42nd Ter., 64116. Tel: 816-453-0971; Fax: 816-453-5451.
Lay Teachers 18; Students 273.
Catechesis/Religious Programs—Students 182.

34—St. Peter's (1927), Rev. Joseph M. Sharbel. In res., Rev. Patrick J. Rush, V.G.
Res., 6415 Holmes St., 64131. Tel: 816-363-2320; Fax: 816-363-2492; 363-8157.
School—6400 Charlotte St., 64131. Tel: 816-523-4899; Fax: 816-523-1248.
Sisters 2; Lay Teachers 35; Students 602.
Catechesis/Religious Programs—Students 54.

35—St. Raphael the Archangel (1963), Rev. Alexander B. Sinclair.
Res., 7952 N.E. 54th St., 64119. Tel: 816-454-2338.
Catechesis/Religious Programs—Students 47.

36—St. Stanislaus. Closed. For inquiries for parish records contact Our Lady of Peace, Kansas City, Tel: 816-231-0953.

37—St. Therese Little Flower (1925) (African American), Rev. Donald Farnan, Sac. Min.; Sr. Helen Flemington, C.S.J., Pastoral Admin.
Res., 5814 Euclid Ave., 64130. Tel: 816-444-5406; Fax: 816-444-9345.
Catechesis/Religious Programs—Students 40.

38—St. Therese Parish (Kansas City North) (1949), Revs. Michael Roach; Patrick Tobin.
Res., 7207 Hwy. 9, N.W., 64152. Tel: 816-741-2800; Fax: 816-741-4959.
School—7277 Hwy. 9 N.W., 64152. Tel: 816-741-5400.
Lay Teachers 31; Students 658.
Catechesis/Religious Programs—Tel: 816-741-3957.
Students 634.

39—St. Thomas More (1964), Revs. William A. Bauman; Thomas Borkowski; Henry Piacitelli.
Res., 11822 Holmes St., 64131. Tel: 816-942-2492; Fax: 816-942-8803.
School—Tel: 816-942-5581; Fax: 816-941-2450.
Lay Teachers 40; Students 680.
Catechesis/Religious Programs—Students 30.

40—Visitation of the Blessed Virgin Mary (1915), Revs. Norman Rotert; Steven Cook.
Mailing Address: 5141 Main St., 64112. Tel: 816-753-7422; Fax: 816-753-5505.
Res., 2 E. 51st, 64112. Tel: 816-753-6968.
School—Tel: 816-531-6220; Fax: 816-531-8045.
Lay Teachers 29; Students 475.
Catechesis/Religious Programs—Preschool 50; Students 58.

CITY OF ST. JOSEPH
(Buchanan County)

1—St. Joseph's Co-Cathedral (1845), Rev. Richard Dierkes; Deacons William Dattilo; Richard W. Snooks.
Res., 519 N. 10th St., 64501. Tel: 816-232-7763; Fax: 816-232-2460.
School—518 N. 11th St., 65401. Tel: 816-232-8486; Fax: 816-232-8793.
Lay Teachers 18; Students 268.
Catechesis/Religious Programs—Students 30.

2—Our Lady of Guadalupe (1981), Rev. Gregory Haskamp; Jeanne Sample, Bus. Mgr.; Kathryn Powers, Pastoral Assoc.
Church—4503 Frederick, 64506. Tel: 816-232-2847; Fax: 816-232-0269.
Catechesis/Religious Programs—Tel: 816-232-0112. Toni Hamera, D.R.E.
Students 250.

3—St. Francis Xavier (1890), Revs. Michael Volkmer, C.PP.S.; Thomas Ozanne, C.PP.S. In res., Rev. Bernard Diekhoff, C.PP.S.
Res., 2618 Seneca St., 64507. Tel: 816-232-8449; Fax: 816-232-8440.
School—2614 Seneca St., 64507. Tel: 816-232-9411.
Lay Teachers 23; Students 427.
Catechesis/Religious Programs—Students 97.

4—St. James (1900), Rev. Vincent Rogers; Deacon Robert Farris.
Res., 5814 King Hill Ave., 64504. Tel: 816-238-0853; Fax: 816-238-1758.
School—120 Michigan Ave., 64504. Tel: 816-238-0281.
Lay Teachers 9; Students 210.
Catechesis/Religious Programs—Students 86.

5—St. Mary's (1891), Rev. Thomas K. Ludwig.
Res., 1606 N. 2nd St., 64505. Tel: 816-279-1154; Fax: 816-279-4078.
Catechesis/Religious Programs—Students 65.

6—St. Patrick's (1869), Rev. Matthew Brumleve; Deacon Elmer Hoppins.
Office: 1723 S. 12th St., 64503. Tel: 816-279-2594; Fax: 816-232-0744.
School—1813 S. 12th St., 64503. Tel: 816-232-9001; Fax: 816-232-7904.
Lay Teachers 11; Students 150.
Catechesis/Religious Programs—Students 53.

7—Queen of the Apostles. Closed. For inquiries for parish records contact the Co-Cathedral of St. Joseph, Kansas City, Tel: 816-232-7763.

OUTSIDE THE CITIES OF KANSAS CITY AND ST. JOSEPH

Belton, Cass Co., St. Sabina's (1944), Rev. Joseph H. Matt.
Res., 700 Trevis Ave., 64012. Tel: 816-331-4713; Fax: 816-322-6196.
Catechesis/Religious Programs—Students 358.

Bethany, Harrison Co., Blessed Sacrament (1945), Sr. Mary Ann T. Schmieding, O.S.F., Pastoral Admin.
Res., 1208 S. 25th St., 64424. Tel: 660-425-8160; Fax: 660-425-0114.
Catechesis/Religious Programs—Students 20.
Mission—Cainsville, Harrison Co., St. Mary's, 1208 S. Hwy. 69, 64424.

Blue Springs, Jackson Co., St. John La Lande (1938), Rev. Michael O. Clary.
Res., 805 NW R.D. Mize Rd., 64015. Tel: 816-229-3378; Fax: 816-229-1362.
School—801 NW R.D. Mize Rd., 64015. Tel: 816-228-5895.
Lay Teachers 23; Students 383.
Catechesis/Religious Programs—Tel: 816-228-4511.
Students 311.

St. Robert Bellarmine (1983), Rev. Lloyd E. Opoka.
Res., 4313 S.W. State Rte. 7, 64014-5701. Tel: 816-229-5168; Fax: 816-229-3981.
Catechesis/Religious Programs—Students 465.

Buckner, Jackson Co., Church of the Santa Fe (1965), Rev. Ralph L. Kaiser.
Res., P.O. Box 317, 64016. Tel: 816-650-9341.

Butler, Bates Co., St. Patrick's, Rev. Richard Ducate.
Res., 400 W. Nursery St., 64730. Tel: 660-679-4482.
Catechesis/Religious Programs—Tel: 660-679-5476.
Students 70.

Cameron, Clinton Co., St. Munchin (1867) (German-Irish), Rev. Alvin L. Herber, C.PP.S.
Res., 316 W. Third St., 64429. Tel: 816-632-2768. [CEM 2]
Catechesis/Religious Programs—Tel: 816-632-6276.
Students 145.
Mission—Maysville, DeKalb Co., St. Aloysius, 301 S. Water, Maysville, 64469.

Carrollton, Carroll Co., St. Mary's (1867), Rev. Kenneth Criqui.
Res., 211 E. Shanklin St., 64633. Tel: 660-542-1259; Fax: 660-542-1259. [CEM]
Catechesis/Religious Programs—Students 124.
Mission—Norborne, Carrollton Co., Sacred Heart.

Chillicothe, Livingston Co., St. Columban (1857), Rev. J. Matthew Rotert; Deacons Lawrence Schneider, (Retired); Joseph Crookshanks; Jerry Davis.
Res., 1111 Trenton St., 64601. Tel: 660-646-0190. [CEM 2]
School—Bishop Hogan Memorial School, 1112 Trenton St., 64601. Tel: 660-646-0705.
Lay Teachers 10; Students 103.
Catechesis/Religious Programs—Students 99.

Clinton, Henry Co., Holy Rosary (1875), Rev. Thomas W. Hermes.
Res., 610 S. 4th St., 64735. Tel: 660-885-4523.
School—400 E. Wilson, 64735. Tel: 660-885-4412.
Lay Teachers 6; Students 79.
Catechesis/Religious Programs—Students 65.
Missions—Osceola, St. Clair Co., St. Catherine's, Hwy. WW, Osceola, 64776. Tel: 417-646-2217; Windsor, Henry Co., St. Bartholomew, 504 E. Benton, Windsor, 65360. Tel: 660-647-2613.

Conception Junction, Nodaway Co., St. Columba (1860), Rev. Augustine Dreiling, O.S.B.; Deacon Martin Goedken.
Res., 311 Roosevelt, P.O. Box 27, 64434. Tel: 660-944-2301. [CEM]
Catechesis/Religious Programs—Students 160.

Easton, Buchanan Co., St. Joseph's (1830), Rev. Matthew Brumleve; Sr. Barbara Jennings, C.S.J., Pastoral Admin.
Res., P.O. Box 197, 64443. Tel: 816-473-2011. [CEM]
Catechesis/Religious Programs—Students 54.

Excelsior Springs, Clay Co., St. Ann (1889), Rev. William Caldwell, S.T.B., Admin.; Deacon John Lauhoff.
Res., 1503 Tracy, 64024. Tel: 816-630-6659.
Catechesis/Religious Programs—Tel: 816-630-5874. Connie Davis, D.R.E.
Students 197.

Gladstone, St. Andrew the Apostle (1964), Rev. Joseph A. Mancuso.
Res., 6415 N.E. Antioch Rd., 64119. Tel: 816-453-2089; Fax: 816-453-2442.
School—(Grades PreK-1).
Students 95.
Catechesis/Religious Programs—Tel: 816-453-5179.
Students 115.

Grandview, Jackson Co., Coronation of Our Lady (1958), Rev. Robert Murphy.
Res., 13000 Bennington, 64030. Tel: 816-761-8811; Fax: 816-761-8812. [CEM]
Catechesis/Religious Programs—Students 254.

Hamilton, Caldwell Co., Sacred Heart (1921), Rev. Robert Kerr.
Res., 205 E. Middle St., 64644. Tel: 816-583-4413.
Catechesis/Religious Programs—Students 51.
Mission—Gallatin, Daviess Co., Mary Immaculate, 409 S. Main, Gallatin, 64640. Rev. Robert Kerr.

Harrisonville, Cass Co., Our Lady of Lourdes (1941), Rev. Bradley S. Offutt.
Res., 2700 N. Hwy. 7, 64701. Tel: 816-380-5744; Fax: 816-380-5132.
Catechesis/Religious Programs—Students 214.
Mission—Pleasant Hill, Cass Co., St. Bridget, (1884) P.O. Box 247, 64701.

Higginsville, Lafayette Co., St. Mary's (1879) (German-Irish), Deacon Ron Elliott, Pastoral Admin.
Res., 400 W. 29th, 64037. Tel: 660-584-3038; Fax: 660-584-5081. [CEM]
Catechesis/Religious Programs—Students 89.

Hirlingen, Buchanan Co., Seven Dolors (1872), Rev. Donald E. Sturm.
Res., 2830 Angelique, St. Joseph, 64501. Tel: 816-671-1510. [CEM]
Catechesis/Religious Programs—Students 20.

Holden, Johnson Co., St. Patrick's (1896), Rev. Ernest L. Gauthier.
Res., 703 S. Olive St., 64040. Tel: 816-732-4516; Fax: 816-732-5595. [CEM]
Catechesis/Religious Programs—Tel: 816-850-4510. Jo Engert, D.R.E.
Students 70.

Independence, Jackson Co.,

1—St. Ann's, (1917), Rev. Terry Bruce.
Res., 10113 Lexington Ave., 64053. Tel: 816-252-1160; Fax: 816-252-1161.
School—Tel: 816-252-1024; Fax: 816-504-6234.
Sisters of St. Francis of the Holy Eucharist 1; Sisters of Charity 1; Benedictine Sisters; 1; Lay Teachers 14; Students 175.

2—St. Joseph the Worker, (1976), Rev. John E. Leitner.
Res., 2200 N. Blue Mills Rd., 64058. Tel: 816-796-6877; Fax: 816-796-6876.
Catechesis/Religious Programs—Barbara Ganz, D.R.E.
Students 73.

3—St. Mark, (1965), Rev. James E. Healy; Deacon Gary Walczak.
Res., 3736 Lee's Summit Rd., 64055. Tel: 816-373-2600; Fax: 816-373-3816.
Catechesis/Religious Programs—Joyce Arthur, D.R.E.
Students 450.

4—St. Mary's, (1845), Rev. Charles F. Jones; Deacon Thomas D. Powell.
Res., 611 N. Liberty St., 64050. Tel: 816-252-0121; Fax: 816-461-8153. [CEM]
Catechesis/Religious Programs—Students 66.

5—Nativity of the Blessed Virgin Mary, (1938), Rev. Robert A. Rost, D.Min.; Deacons Donald L. McCandless; Justin M. McMenamy.
Res., 10017 E. 36th Ter., 64052. Tel: 816-353-2184; Fax: 816-358-4155.
School—10021 E. 36th Ter., 64052. Tel: 816-353-0284; Fax: 816-969-5251.
Lay Teachers 14; Students 237.
Catechesis/Religious Programs—Tel: 816-353-1638.
Students 70.

Kearney, Clay Co., Church of the Annunciation (1980), Rev. Thomas A. Conway, C.PP.S.
Mailing Address: P.O. Box 599, 64060-0599. Tel: 816-628-5030; Fax: 816-628-4279.
Catechesis/Religious Programs—Students 162.

Lee's Summit, Jackson Co., St. Margaret's Catholic Community, Rev. Michael D. Rice; Sue Nichols, Bus. Mgr.
Res., 1134 N.E. Birchwood Pl., 64086. Tel: 816-246-6800; Fax: 816-246-9858.
Catechesis/Religious Programs—Cathie Liccar, D.R.E.
Students 215.

Our Lady of the Presentation (1896), Revs. James Hart; Charles N. Rowe; Deacons Joseph Stueve; Del Wilkinson; Mark Fountain.
Parish Office: 130 N.W. Murray Rd., 64081. Tel: 816-251-1100; Fax: 816-251-1199.
School—150 N.W. Murray Rd., 64081. Tel: 816-251-1150; Fax: 816-251-1155.
Lay Teachers 25; Students 416.
Catechesis/Religious Programs—Tel: 816-251-1135.
Students 505.

Holy Spirit (1979), Rev. Michael E. Tierney; Ann Hayles, Pastoral Assoc.
Res., 800 S.W. Hwy. 150, 64082. Tel: 816-537-6990; Fax: 816-537-8104.
Catechesis/Religious Programs—Tel: 816-537-6990.
Students 264.

Lexington, Lafayette Co., Immaculate Conception (1842), Rev. Terrell M. Finnell.
Res., 107 N. 18th St., 64067. Tel: 660-259-3043; Fax: 660-259-3043. [CEM]
Catechesis/Religious Programs—MaryJo Wynne, D.R.E.
Students 79.
Chapel—Chapel of Ease, Lexington.

Liberty, Clay Co., St. James (1840), Revs. Ronald Will, C.PP.S.; Dien Troung, C.PP.S.
Res., 309 S. Stewart Rd., 64068. Tel: 816-781-4343; Fax: 816-792-8691.
School—Tel: 816-781-4428; Fax: 816-781-0747.
Lay Teachers 19; Students 301.
Catechesis/Religious Programs—Tel: 816-781-4343, Ext. 205.
Students 477.

Maryville, Nodaway Co., St. Gregory Barbarigo (1860), Revs. Chuck Tobin; Donald S. Miller; Deacons Roy Seipel; Martin Schieber.
Res., 333 S. Davis St., 64468. Tel: 660-582-3833. [CEM 2][JC]
School—315 S. Davis St., 64468. Tel: 660-582-2462; Fax: 660-582-2496.
Lay Teachers 13; Students 212.
Newman Center—606 College Ave., 64468. Tel: 660-582-7373; Fax: 660-582-7373.
Catechesis/Religious Programs—Tel: 660-582-5914.
Students 194.

Montrose, Henry Co., Immaculate Conception (1876) (German), Rev. Philip Watanabe (Japan).
Res., 606 Kansas Ave., 64770-9601. Tel: 660-693-4651; Fax: 660-693-4713. [CEM][JC 2]
School—St. Mary School, Tel: 660-693-4502.
Lay Teachers 4; Students 35.
Mission—Urich, Henry Co., Holy Trinity, 1372 N.W. Grahm Rd., Urich, 64788. Tel: 660-638-4715.
Catechesis/Religious Programs—Students 45.

Nevada, Vernon Co., St. Mary's (1887), Rev. Anthony J. Pileggi.
Res., 330 N. Main St., 64772. Tel: 417-667-5604. [CEM]
School—Tel: 417-667-7517.
Lay Teachers 3; Students 35.
Catechesis/Religious Programs—Students 80.
Mission—Rich Hill, Bates Co., St. Bridget's.

Odessa, Lafayette Co., St. George (1882), Rev. Peter M. Savidge; Deacon Harry Rodman.
Res., 716 S. Third, 64076. Tel: 816-230-4127.
Mission—Oak Grove, Jackson Co., St. Jude the Apostle, 2001 S. Broadway, P.O. Box 590, Oak Grove, 64075. Tel: 816-690-3165.
Catechesis/Religious Programs—Students 38.

Parnell, Nodaway Co., St. Joseph's (1891), Rev. Roland Carbone, O.S.B.
Res., P.O. Box 78, 64475. Tel: 660-986-3305. [CEM][JC]
Catechesis/Religious Programs—Students 96.

Plattsburg, Clinton Co., St. Ann's (1866) (Irish), Rev. Robert E. Crider.
Res., 700 Maple St., 64477. Tel: 816-539-2634; Fax: 816-539-2964. [CEM]
Catechesis/Religious Programs—Students 83.

Raytown, Jackson Co., Our Lady of Lourdes (1948), Rev. Joseph Powers; Deacon Jerry Williams.
Res., 7009 Blue Ridge Blvd., 64133. Tel: 816-353-2380; Fax: 816-353-5737.
School—8812 E. Gregory Blvd., 64133. Tel: 816-353-7062; Fax: 816-353-7650.
Sisters of St. Joseph 1; Lay Teachers 15; Students 200.
Catechesis/Religious Programs—Students 65.

Richmond, Ray Co., Immaculate Conception (1869), Rev. Joseph I. Cisetti.
Res., 602 S. Camden, 64085. Tel: 660-470-2268; Fax: 816-470-9967. [CEM]
Catechesis/Religious Programs—Students 70.

Savannah, Andrew Co., St. Rose of Lima (1898), Rev. Mark A. Honhart.
Mailing Address: 707 Hall Ave., 64485. Tel: 816-324-5700.
Res., 705 S. Hall Ave., 64485. Tel: 816-324-3231.
Catechesis/Religious Programs—Students 112.
Mission—Forest City, Holt Co., St. Patrick, 303 Grand Ave., Forest City, 64451. Tel: 660-446-2045.

Smithville, Clay Co., Church of the Good Shepherd (1974), Rev. Bernard E. Branson.
Res., 1103 S. Commercial, P.O. Box 653, 64089. Tel: 816-532-4344 (Church); 532-0522 (Res.); Fax: 816-532-0019.
Catechesis/Religious Programs—Tel: 816-734-8925.
Students 225.

Stanberry, Gentry Co., St. Peter's (1880), Rev. Daniel Petsche, O.S.B.
Res., 614 N. Alanthus Ave., 64489. Tel: 660-783-2159. [CEM]
Catechesis/Religious Programs—Students 125.
Mission—Ford City, Gentry Co., St. Patrick's, King City, 64463.

Sugar Creek, Jackson Co., St. Cyril (1912) (Croatian-Slovak), Rev. Walter J. Pilecki.
Res., 11231 Chicago Ave., 64054. Tel: 816-252-9564.
Catechesis/Religious Programs—Students 12.

Tarkio, Atchison Co., St. Paul the Apostle (1890), Rev. Reginald Sander, O.S.B.
Res., 908 Elm St., 64491. Tel: 660-736-4342. [JC]
Catechesis/Religious Programs—Students 6.
Mission—Burlington Junction, Nodaway Co., St. Benedict Catholic Church, Burlington Junction, 64428. Tel: 660-725-4407.

Trenton, Grundy Co., St. Joseph's (1872), Rev. Edgar Probstfield, O.S.B.
Res., 1728 St. Joseph Ave., 64683. Tel: 660-359-2841. [CEM]
Mission—Princeton, Mercer Co., Immaculate Heart of Mary Church, 1728 St. Joseph Ave., 64683. [JC]
Catechesis/Religious Programs—Students 46.

Warrensburg, Johnson Co., Sacred Heart (1865), Rev. Dennis Schaab, C.PP.S.
Res., 300 S. Ridgeview Dr., P.O. Box 926, 64093. Tel: 660-747-6154; Fax: 660-747-5965.
Catechesis/Religious Programs—Tel: 660-747-5965; Fax: 660-747-7623.
Students 225.

Weston, Platte Co., Holy Trinity (1842), Rev. Thomas Hawkins.
Res., 407 Cherry St., 64098. Tel: 816-640-2206. [JC]
Catechesis/Religious Programs—Students 119.

Special Assignment:
Reverend Fathers—
Cameron, Robert, Cememteris & Mission Office Dir., 7601 Blue Ridge, Kansas City, MO 64138
Coleman, C. Michael, J.C.L., Judicial Vicar & Diocesan Archivist, P.O. Box 419037, Kansas City, MO 64141-6037
Deming, Robert N., P.O. Box 32227, Kansas City, MO 64111
Herrera, Jose G. (STV), Dir. Young Adult & Campus Ministry, Christ the King, 8510 Wornall Rd., Kansas City, MO 64114
Jankowski, Marcellus A., Hospital Chap., 2909 Vista Court, Independence, MO 64057
Mahoney, Robert J., 4550 Warwick, Kansas City, MO 64111
Moscaritolo, Mario, 4019 Warwick, Kansas City, MO 64111
Rush, Patrick J., V.G., P.O. Box 419037, Kansas City, MO 64141-6037
Schuele, Francis J., Assoc. Dir. Peace & Justice Office, 8300 E. 88th Ter., #3002, Kansas City, MO 64138
Verhaeghe, Ronald, Hospital Chap., 2800 Independence Ave., Apt. 3W, Kansas City, MO 64124

On Duty Outside the Diocese:
Reverend Fathers—
Cronin, Thomas
Holloway, David L.
Reardon, Daniel, Military Chap.

Mission Duty:
Reverend Fathers—
Gillgannon, Michael, Casilla 12162, La Paz, Bolivia, S.A.
Walker, Michael, Parroquia San Pedro, Yepocapa Chimaltenango, Guatemala, C.A. Guatemala, C.A.

Leave of Absence:
Reverend Fathers—
Arciga, Michael
Evers, Paul K.
Monahan, Hugh F.
Townsend, C. Frederick
Turner, Thomas W.

Retired:
Reverend Monsignors—
Bauer, Henry, 6425 Woodson, Kansas City, MO 64133
Froeschl, Martin H., P.O. Box 201, Oregon, MO 64473
Huhmann, John F., 10515 Bridlespur Dr., Kansas City, MO 64114-4712
Kearney, Vincent L., 12655 State Line, Kansas City, MO 64145
O'Brien, Thomas J., 615 E. 117th St., Kansas City, MO 64131-3807
Summers, R. Emmett, Jeanne Jugan Center, 8300 E.88th Terr., Apt. 2008, Kansas City, MO 64138
Reverend Fathers—
Blaes, Paul, M.A., Ph.D., 1589 Carrollwood Dr., Sarasota, FL 34232-3309
Boyle, Leo A., 4291 Richmond Rd., Cleveland, OH 44122
Carney, Richard F., 1100 W. 101st Terr.# B, Kansas City, MO 64114
Cleary, Donald R., 411 E. 79th St., Kansas City, MO 64131
Coleman, John P., 4101 E. 105th Ter., Kansas City, MO 64137
Eldringhoff, John P., 2607 Quail Creek Dr., Independence, MO 64055
Faller, Henry E., Jeanne Jugan Center, 8745 James A. Reed Rd., Kansas City, MO 64138
Giacopelli, John A., # 5B Birchwood Ct., Whiting, NJ 08759
Hoppe, Sylvester J., 918 S. Noyes Blvd., St. Joseph, MO 64507
Jakubowski, Joseph J., 8745 James A. Reed Rd., Kansas City, MO 64138
Karels, Ambrose G., P.O. Box 410834, Kansas City, MO 64141

Lyons, James P., 9001 James A. Reed Rd., Kansas City, MO 64138
McCarthy, Thomas H., USAA Parklane West Rm. 324A, San Antonio, TX 78209
McCormack, John, 8300 E. 88th Ter., #2010, Kansas City, MO 64138-4490
McGlynn, Francis, 700 E. Eigth St., #910, Kansas City, MO 64106
McQuinn, Maurice, 115 W. 99th Terrace, No 102, Kansas City, MO 64114
Meisburger, Joseph C., 611 N. Liberty, Independence, MO 64050
Miller, Donald S., 333 S. Davis, Maryville, MO 64468
Miller, Roger F., 2440 N.W. Shady Bend, Lee's Summit, MO 64081
Moser, Victor G., 2102 Blue Mills Rd., Independence, MO 64058
Mullin, Hugh J., 10901 Johnson Blvd. J 712, Seminole, FL 33772
O'Connor, Patrick, Rte. 3, Box 32, Butler, MO 64730
Paa, Donald R., 1500 W. 23rd Ter., Apt. 3, Independence, MO 64050
Pecoraro, James A., 410 W. 104th St., Apt. A., Kansas City, MO 64114
Powell, Harold W., 720 E. 17th St. Apt D., Cheyenne, WY 82001
Russ, Francis J., 12900 E. 62nd, Kansas City, MO 64133
Ryan, C. Duane, Rte. 2, Box 335, Sunrise Beach, MO 65079
Saale, Richard T., 8800 Buckingham Ln., Apt. 14, Kansas City, MO 64138
Speichinger, Lawrence, 10914 Old Hwy. 190, Chillicothe, MO 64601
Ward, Thomas, 3600 Poplar, Independence, MO 64052

Permanent Deacons:
Barry, James Timothy
Beaudoin, Philip Ross
Bode, William
Bonnarens, Edwin
Browning, Melvin, (Retired)
Cathers, Calvin
Clark, Joseph P.
Corrigan, Emory S.
Crookshanks, Joseph V.
Dattilo, William
Davis, F. Jerry
DiMartino, Charles, (Retired)
Elliot, Ronald
Ernst, John H.
Falcon, Francis L., (Retired)
Falcon, Louie P., (Retired)
Farris, Robert E.
Fountain, Mark J.
Goedken, Martin J.
Guerra, Manuel P.
Henggeler, Francis J., (Retired)
Hoppins, Elmer E.
Koch, John J.
Kopp, George C., (Retired)
Kopp, Harold G., Sr., (Retired)
Kratofil, Lawrence
Langdon, Harry
Lauhoff, John D., (Retired)
Lewis, Michael
Lickteig, Wayne A.
Madden, Donald
Maloney, John J., (Retired)
Markey, William R., (Retired)
Mason, Marvin M.
McArdle, Paul
McCandless, Donald L.
McCoy, Warren W.
McKay, Clarence W.
McMenamy, Justin M.
Muraski, Richard J.
Ofenloch, Joseph C., (Retired)
Ohmes, Albert J.
Peak, Francis L.
Powell, D. Thomas
Riead, John
Rodman, Harold M.
Sandoval, Antonio J.
Santellan, Alfred M.
Schieber, Martin L., (Retired)
Schmit, Donald A., (Retired)
Schneider, Lawrence, (Retired)
Seipel, Leroy
Snooks, Richard W., (Retired)
Stoetzer, Jerome P., (On Leave of Absence)
Stueve, Joseph E.
Thompson, John R., (Retired)
Williams, Jerry

INSTITUTIONS LOCATED IN THE DIOCESE

[A] SEMINARIES, RELIGIOUS OR SCHOLASTICATES

KANSAS CITY. *Gaspar Mission House*, 5221 Rockhill Rd., 64110. Tel: 816-333-7980. Revs. Lac Pham, C.PP.S.; Al Ebach, C.PP.S.; David Matz, C.PP.S.; Bro. Daryl Charron, C.PP.S. Priests 3; Brothers 1; Students 2.

CONCEPTION. *Conception Seminary College*, 37174 State Hwy., P.Ol. Box 502, 64433. Tel: 660-944-2218; Fax: 660-944-2829.
E-mail: seminary@conception.edu
Web site: conceptionabbey.org
Rt. Rev. Gregory Polan, O.S.B., Chancellor; Revs. Benedict Neenan, O.S.B., Pres. & Rector; Sebastian Allgaier, O.S.B.; Albert Bruecken, O.S.B.; Roland Carbone, O.S.B.; Patrick Caveglia, O.S.B.; Donald Grabner, O.S.B.; James Jones, O.S.B.; Quentin Kathol, O.S.B.; Aidan McSorley, O.S.B.; Xavier Nacke, O.S.B.; Daniel Petsche, O.S.B.; James Polich (Des Moines); Kenneth Reichert, O.S.B.; Duane F. Reinert, O.F.M.Cap.; Samuel Russell, O.S.B.; Timothy Schoen, O.S.B.; Isaac True, O.S.B.; Peter Ullrich, O.S.B.; Jerome Werth, O.S.B. Priests 19; Brothers 8; Sisters 1; Lay Professors 6; Students 97.

LIBERTY. *Precious Blood Center*. (Kansas City Province), 2110-2140 Hughes Rd., 64068. Tel: 816-781-4344; Fax: 816-781-3639.
E-mail: KCPROV@aol.com
Bro. Stephen Ohnmacht, C.PP.S., Local Dir. Priests 9; Brothers 2.

Society of the Precious Blood Provincial Offices, P.O. Box 339, 64069-0339. Tel: 816-781-4344; Fax: 816-781-3639.
E-mail: KCProv@aol.com
Revs. William P. Walter, C.PP.S., Prov. Vice; Mark Miller, C.PP.S., Prov. Dir.; Garry Richmeier, C.PP.S., Prov. Sec.; William Dineen, C.PP.S., Prov. Treas. Students 2.

[B] COLLEGES AND UNIVERSITIES

KANSAS CITY. *Avila College*, 11901 Wornall Rd., 64145-1698. Tel: 816-942-8400; Fax: 816-942-3362.
Web site: www.avila.edu
For a complete listing, refer to the Colleges and Universities section.

Rockhurst University, 1100 Rockhurst Rd., 64110-2561. Tel: 816-501-4000; Fax: 816-501-4293.
E-mail: cathy.dubois@rockhurst.edu
Web site: www.rockhurst.edu
For a complete listing, refer to the Colleges and Universities section.

[C] HIGH SCHOOLS, DIOCESAN

KANSAS CITY. *Archbishop O'Hara High School*. (Coed), 9001 James A. Reed Rd., 64138. Tel: 816-763-4800; Fax: 816-763-0156.
E-mail: postmaster@oharahs.org
Mr. Walter Bowman, Prin. Christian Brothers 2; Lay Teachers 47; Students 605.

St. Pius X High School, 1500 N.E. 42nd Ter., 64116. Tel: 816-453-3450; Fax: 816-452-7099.
E-mail: NCARLIN@stpiusedu.com
Edward P. Carlin, Ph.D., Prin. Sisters 2; Lay Teachers 31; Students 413.

ST. JOSEPH. *Bishop LeBlond High School*, 3529 Frederick Ave., 64506. Tel: 816-279-1629; Fax: 816-279-5488.
E-mail: leblond@ccp.com
Web site: leblond.saint-joseph.mo.us
Sr. Corrine Connelly, R.S.M., Prin.; Rev. Thomas K. Ludwig, Chap. Priests 1; Sisters 1; Lay Teachers 25; Students 255.

INDEPENDENCE. *St. Mary's Diocesan High School-Bundschu Memorial*, 622 N. Main St., 64050. Tel: 816-252-8733; Fax: 816-252-2780.
E-mail: gjonas@stmhs.org
Web site: stmhs.org
Trudy Jonas, Prin. Sisters 1; Lay Teachers 16; Students 241.

[D] HIGH SCHOOLS, PRIVATE

KANSAS CITY. *De La Salle Academy*, 3732 Paseo, 64109. Tel: 816-531-6561; Fax: 816-756-3916.
E-mail: dalejuan@juno.com
Special Educational Programs & LaSallian Tutorial Programs. Christian Brothers, F.S.C. and LaSallian Volunteers. Christian Brothers 4; LaSallian Volunteers 2; Students 60.

Notre Dame de Sion High School, 10631 Wornall Rd., 64114. Tel: 816-942-3282; Fax: 816-942-4052.
E-mail: amunninghoff@ndsion.com
Web site: www.sion-kc.edu
Affiliated with Sisters of Notre Dame de Sion. Alice Munninghoff, Head of School; Michelle Olson, Prin. Lay Teachers 40; Students 435.

Rockhurst High School, 9301 State Line Rd., 64114-3229. Tel: 816-363-2036; Fax: 816-363-3764.
E-mail: tpesci@rockhursths.edu
Web site: www.rockhursths.edu
Revs. Thomas A. Pesci, S.J., Pres.; Mark J. Daves, S.J.; Gerard E. Menard, S.J.; Mark A. Kramer, Scholastic. Jesuit Priests 3; Lay Teachers 70; Students 1,000.

St. Teresa's Academy, 5600 Main St., 64113. Tel: 816-501-0011; Fax: 816-523-0232.
E-mail: nnhand@n2education.com
Web site: st-teresas-academy.pvt.k12.mo.us
Affiliated with Sisters of St. Joseph of Carondelet. Dr. Faith Wilson, Ph.D., Pres.; Mary Anne Hoecker, M.A., Assoc. Prin.; Nancy Hand, M.A., Assoc. Prin. Sisters 2; Lay Teachers 42; Students 505.

[E] CONSOLIDATED SCHOOLS

KANSAS CITY. *Bishop John J. Sullivan Preschool*, 3208 Lexington, 64124. Tel: 816-231-6769. Leslie Bales, Dir. Lay Teachers 8; Students 61.

Holy Cross School, 121 N. Quincy, 64123-1399. Tel: 816-231-8874; Fax: 816-231-7258. Christine Higgins, Prin. Sisters 1; Lay Teachers 14; Students 222.

Our Lady of Guadalupe School, 2310 Madison, 64108. Tel: 816-221-2539; Fax: 816-283-3315. Connie Bowman, Prin. Lay Teachers 5; Students 100.

Our Lady of Peace School. (Grades PreK-8), 10526 Grandview Rd., 64137. Tel: 816-761-5605; Fax: 816-761-2797.
Web site: http://www.kansascity.com/.schools
Ms. Barbara J. Becker, Prin. Consolidated with Coronation, St. Catherine's, St. Matthew's, and St. Sabina's to form Our Lady of Peace School. Lay Teachers 22; Students 396; Preschool Students 43.

Our Lady of the Angels School. (Grades PreK-8), 211 W. Linwood Blvd., 64111. Tel: 816-931-1693; Fax: 816-753-3606. Mary Kallman, Prin. Sisters 2; Lay Teachers 16; Students 223.

St. Monica School. (Grades PreK-8), Elementary: 5809 Michigan, 64130. Tel: 816-444-6736.
E-mail: stmonica@earthlink.net
Charles E. Monckton, Prin. Consolidated with St. Monica of Africa, St Therese Little Flower, St. Louis, and St. James to form St. Monica's School. Sisters 1; Lay Teachers 18; Students 220.

St. Stephen's Academy, 1001 Bennington Ave., 64126. Tel: 816-231-5227; Fax: 816-231-2824.
E-mail: maripatkc@aol.com
Mari Pat Brooks, Prin. Consolidation of Our Lady of Peace, St. Anthony's, Holy Cross, Holy Rosary & St. Aloysius. Sisters 2; Brothers 1; Lay Teachers 14; Students 179.

[F] ELEMENTARY SCHOOLS, PRIVATE

KANSAS CITY. *Notre Dame de Sion Elementary School*, 3823 Locust St., 64109. Tel: 816-753-3810; Fax: 816-753-0806.
E-mail: loc@nds.net
Web site: www.sion-kc.edu
Affiliated with Sisters of Notre Dame de Sion. Alice Munninghoff, Head of School; Catherine Butel, Prin.; Barbara Altergott, Asst. Prin. & Admissions Dir. Lay Teachers 32; Students 338.

[G] GENERAL HOSPITALS

KANSAS CITY. *Saint Joseph Health Center*, 1000 Carondelet Dr., 64114. Tel: 816-942-4400; Fax: 816-943-2840.
Web site: www.carondelethealth.org
For a complete listing, refer to the Hospitals section.

BLUE SPRINGS. *St. Mary's Hospital of Blue Springs*, 201 W. R.D. Mize Rd., 64014. Tel: 816-228-5900; Fax: 816-655-5408
For a complete listing, refer to the Hospitals section.

MARYVILLE. *St. Francis Hospital & Health Services*, 2016 S. Main, 64468. Tel: 660-562-2600; Fax: 660-562-7911
For a complete listing, refer to the Hospitals section.

[H] SPECIAL CARE UNITS

KANSAS CITY. *Carondelet Manor*, 621 Carondelet Dr., 64114. Tel: 816-943-4777
For a complete listing, refer to the Special Care Facilities section.

BLUE SPRINGS. *St. Mary's Manor*, 111 Mock Ave., 64014. Tel: 816-228-5655; Fax: 816-228-8480.
E-mail: pkelley@carondelet.com
For a complete listing, refer to the Special Care Facilities section.

LIBERTY. *Immacolata Manor*, 2101 Hughes Rd., 64068-9397. Tel: 816-781-4332; Fax: 816-781-8820.
E-mail: immanor@crn.org
For a complete listing, refer to the Special Care Facilities section.

[I] HOMES FOR THE ELDERLY

KANSAS CITY. *Brighton Place*, 2429 Brighton, 64127. Tel: 816-483-8299
For a complete listing, refer to the Special Care Facilities section.

Cathedral Square Towers, 444 W. 12th St., 64105. Tel: 816-471-6555; Fax: 816-421-1279
For a complete listing, refer to the Special Care Facilities section.

Columbus Park Plaza, 801 Pacific, 64106. Tel: 816-472-0887; Fax: 816-472-6105.
E-mail: columbus@planetkc.com
For a complete listing, refer to the Special Care Facilities section.

Jeanne Jugan Center, 8745 James A. Reed Rd., 64138. Tel: 816-761-4744; Fax: 816-761-4724
For a complete listing, refer to the Special Care Facilities section.

Marlborough Manor, 1818 E. 79th St., 64132. Tel: 816-333-7761; Fax: 816-523-2388.
E-mail: marlborough@planetKC.com
For a complete listing, refer to the Special Care Facilities section.

Red Bridge Place, 11300 Colorado, 64137. Tel: 816-761-4667; Fax: 816-761-4769
For a complete listing, refer to the Special Care Facilities section.

Tremont Place, 6161 N. Chatham, 64151. Tel: 816-587-7707; Fax: 816-587-7637.
E-mail: tremont@crn.org
For a complete listing, refer to the Special Care Facilities section.

CAMERON. *St. Patrick's Manor*, 514 Northland Dr., 64429. Tel: 816-632-1684; Fax: 816-632-7624
For a complete listing, refer to the Special Care Facilities section.

LIBERTY. *Our Lady of Mercy Country Home*, 2205 Hughes Rd., 64068. Tel: 816-781-5711; Fax: 816-781-7276.
Web site: ourladyofmercy.net
For a complete listing, refer to the Special Care Facilities section.

SAVANNAH. *La Verna Heights Retirement Center, Inc.*, 104 E. Park Ave., P.O. Box 488, 64485-0488. Tel: 816-324-3179; Fax: 816-324-6512.
E-mail: osf@ccp.com
For a complete listing, refer to the Special Care Facilities section.

La Verna Village Apartments, 1000-1005 Hall Ave., 64485. Tel: 816-324-3179; Fax: 816-324-7264
For a complete listing, refer to the Special Care Facilities section.

La Verna Village Nursing Home, 904 Hall Ave., P.O. Box 279, 64485. Tel: 816-324-3185; Fax: 816-324-4097
For a complete listing, refer to the Special Care Facilities section.

[J] MONASTERIES AND RESIDENCES OF PRIESTS

KANSAS CITY. *Redemptorists of Kansas City*, 3333 Broadway Blvd., 64111. Tel: 816-561-3771; Fax: 816-561-3704.
E-mail: jshea@olph-kc.org
Very Rev. James Shea, C.SS.R., Rector; Revs. Frank Kriski, C.SS.R.; Joseph Curalli, C.SS.R.; Edward Kane, C.SS.R.; Eugene Oates, C.SS.R.; Patrick Power, C.SS.R.; Ivan Dawson, C.SS.R.; Bros. James Burke, C.SS.R.; Charles Long, C.SS.R.; Michael Schnittker, C.SS.R. Priests 7; Brothers 3.

Rockhurst Jesuit Community, 5133 Forest Ave., 64110-2513. Tel: 816-501-3300; Fax: 816-501-3250. Revs. John J. Callahan, S.J., Rector; Dirk J. Dunfee, S.J., Minister; Martin J. Bredeck, S.J.; Edward K. Burger, S.J.; Robert R. Burke, S.J.; Luke J. Byrne, S.J.; Thomas J. Casey, S.J.; Mark J. Daues, S.J.; Thomas F. Denzer, S.J.; Edward Kinerk, S.J.; Mark A. Kramer, Scholastic; Revs. Wilfred L. LaCroix, S.J.; Timothy M. McMahon, S.J.; Gerard E. Menard, S.J.; Glenn R. Mueller, S.J.; Francis J. Murphy, S.J.; Louis J. Oldani, S.J.; Thomas A. Pesci, S.J.; Christopher P. Pinne, S.J.; James D. Wheeler, S.J.; Bros. E. Glenn Kerfoot, S.J.; John R. Olson, S.J.; Gerard A. Schroeder, S.J. Total in Residence 22.

St. Francis Xavier - Jesuit Community, 1001 E. 52nd St., 64110. Tel: 816-523-5142. Total in Residence 1.

Vincentian Parish Mission Center, 2100 N. Noland Rd., 64050. Tel: 816-254-3000; Fax: 816-836-9922.
E-mail: mm@therapist.net
Web site: www.thevincentians.org
Revs. Richard Gielow, C.M.; Ronald J. Hoye, C.M.; Francis Crowley, C.M.; Richard O'Brien, C.M.; Charles Prost, C.M.; Michael Mulhearn, C.M.; Carl G. Schulte, C.M., Supr. Total in Residence 7.

CONCEPTION. *Conception Abbey*, 64433. Tel: 660-944-2211; Fax: 660-944-2800.
E-mail: communications@conception.edu
Web site: www.ConceptionAbbey.org
Rt. Rev. Gregory Polan, O.S.B., Abbot; Very Rev. Kenneth Reichert, O.S.B., Prior; Bro. Bernard Montgomery, O.S.B., Subprior; Rt. Rev. James Jones, O.S.B., Retired Abbot; Revs. Sebastian Allgaier, O.S.B.; Jerome Werth, O.S.B.; Walter Heeney, O.S.B.; Albert Bruecken, O.S.B.; Patrick Caveglia, O.S.B.; Malachy Riley, O.S.B.; Karl Barmann, O.S.B., St. Gabriel Parish, 4737 N. Cleveland Ave., Kansas City, 64117. Tel: 816-453-1183. Rev. Martin DeMeulenaere, O.S.B., Pastoral Care, St. Joseph Hospital, St. Elizabeth Parish, 7444 Main St., Kansas City, 64114. Revs. Lawrence Gidley, O.S.B.; Donald Grabner, O.S.B.; Quentin Kathol, O.S.B.; Aidan McSorley, O.S.B.; Xavier Nacke, O.S.B.; Alexander Luetkemeyer, O.S.B.; Benedict Neenan, O.S.B., Seminary Pres., Rector; Daniel Petsche, O.S.B., St. Peter Parish, 614 N. Alanthus Ave., Stanberry, 64489. Tel: 660-783-2159. Revs. Regis Probstfield, O.S.B.; Aelred Rosser, O.S.B.; Samuel Russell, O.S.B.; Adam Ryan, O.S.B.; Norbert Schappler, O.S.B.; Joachim Schieber, O.S.B.; Timothy Schoen, O.S.B.; Philip Schuster, O.S.B.; Gilbert Stack, O.S.B., Dir. Pilgrimages, 8332 Belleview, Kansas City, 64114. Tel: 816-444-9031. Revs. Augustine Stock, O.S.B.; Hugh Tasch, O.S.B.; Paschal Thomas, O.S.B.; Isaac True, O.S.B.; Peter Ullrich, O.S.B. Benedictine Monks. Priests 52; Brothers 21.

LIBERTY. *Precious Blood Center*, 2130 Hughes Rd., 64068. Tel: 816-781-4344; Fax: 816-781-3639.
E-mail: kcprov@aol.com
Bro. Stephen Ohnmacht, C.PP.S., Supr.; Revs. Bernard Mullen, C.PP.S.; Ralph Bushell, C.PP.S.; Thomas A. Conway, C.PP.S.; David Dougherty, C.PP.S.; Edmund Weigel, C.PP.S.; Ronald Will, C.PP.S.; William Dineen, C.PP.S.; Dien Truong, C.PP.S.; Leonard Goettemoeller, C.PP.S.; Bro. Joseph Mary Hrezo.

Precious Blood Society Provincial Office, P.O. Box 339, 64069-0339. Tel: 816-781-4344; Fax: 816-781-3639.
E-mail: KCProv@aol.com
Very Rev. Mark Miller, C.PP.S., Prov. Dir.; Revs. Garry Richmeier, C.PP.S., Prov. Sec.; William Dineen, C.PP.S., Prov. Treas. Priests 9; Brothers 1.

[K] CONVENTS AND RESIDENCES FOR SISTERS

KANSAS CITY. *Sisters of Notre Dame de Sion*, 3629 Gillham Rd., #57, 64111. Tel: 816-531-1374.

Sisters of the Society of Our Lady of the Most Holy Trinity, 3738 Tracy, 64109. Tel: 816-561-8849. Society of Apostolic Life. Sisters 4.

BLUE SPRINGS. *Franciscan Sisters of Mary*, Our Lady of the Springs Community, 731 N. Sixth St., 64014-2404. Tel: 816-228-3739. Sisters 3.

CLYDE. *Benedictine Convent of Perpetual Adoration*, 64432. Tel: 660-944-2221; Fax: 660-944-2133.
E-mail: srsean@grm.net
Web site: www.benedictinesisters.org
Sisters 45. Attended by Conception Abbey.

INDEPENDENCE. *St. Francis Convent Novitiate and Prayer Center*, 2100 N. Noland Rd., 64050. Tel: 816-252-1673; Fax: 816-252-5574. Motherhouse of the Sisters of St. Francis of the Holy Eucharist. Sr. M. Connie Boulch, O.S.F., Supr. Sisters 19.

LIBERTY. *Mercedarian Missionaries of Berriz (M.M.B.)*, 2209 Hughes Rd., 64068. Tel: 816-415-3024. Sr. Jacinta Fernandez, M.M.B., Local Coord. Sisters 4.

Mercedarian Missionaries of Berriz (M.M.B.), 2213 Hughes Rd., 64068. Tel: 816-415-3133. Sr. Sandra Thibeau, M.M.B., Local Coord. Sisters 3.

Mercederian Missionaries of Berriz, U.S. Regional Headquarters, 2205 Hughes Rd., #101B, 64068-7985. Tel: 816-781-8202; Fax: 816-781-8205.
E-mail: mmbzonekc@microlink.net
Sr. Betty Preston, M.M.B., Reg. Coord. Mercedarian Missionaries of Berriz 10.

Queen of Angels Monastery - Benedictine Sisters, 23615 N.E.100th St., 64068. Tel: 816-750-4618; Fax: 816-750-4641.
E-mail: qofamonlib@aol.com
Sr. Mary Imelda Koch, O.S.B., Prioress. Sisters 9; Total in Residence 12.

SAVANNAH. *Congregation of the Sisters of St. Anne*, 104 E. Park Ave., P.O. Box 488, 816-324-3179. Tel: 816-324-3179; Fax: 816-324-7294. Sisters 2.

La Verna Heights Provincial House, 104 E. Park, Box 488, 64485-0488. Tel: 816-324-3179; Fax: 816-324-7264.
E-mail: osf@ccp.com
Web site: sistersofstfrancis.org
Sisters of St. Francis of Savannah, MO. Motherhouse and Novitiate. Rev. Alexander Luetkemeyer, O.S.B., Chap. Sisters 22.

Maintenance and Custodial Care Trust of the Franciscan Sisters of Savannah, MO. Tel: 816-324-3179; Fax: 816-324-7264.

[L] SERVICES

KANSAS CITY.
Seton Center Family & Health Services, 2816 E. 23 St., 64127. Tel: 816-231-3955.
E-mail: rasaro@pei.edu
Rachel A. Asaro, Dir. Total Assisted 14,000; Total Staff 24.

[M] NEWMAN CENTERS

KANSAS CITY. *Avila College Campus Ministry*, 11901 Wornall Rd., 64145. Tel: 816-501-2423, Ext. 2423; Fax: 816-501-2454.
E-mail: hubersj@mail.avila.edu
Web site: www.avila.edu
Stephen Huber, Dir. Campus Ministry.

Bishop Sullivan Center, 6435 Truman Rd., 64126. Tel: 816-231-0984; Fax: 816-231-3096.
E-mail: tturner@crn.org
Rev. Thomas W. Turner, Dir. Total Assisted 10,000; Total Staff 10.

MARYVILLE. *Newman Catholic Center, Northwest Missouri State University*, 606 College Ave., 64468. Tel: 660-582-7373. Marie de Young, Dir.

WARRENSBURG. *Central Missouri State University Newman Center*, 106 Broad St., 64093. Tel: 660-747-6997; Fax: 305-489-8102.
E-mail: newman@iland.net
Web site: www.begemot.net/newman
William Kriege, Dir.

[N] MISCELLANEOUS

KANSAS CITY. *Camp Little Flower*, 300 E. 36th St., P.O. Box 419037, 64141. Tel: 816-756-1850. Rose-Mary Montemore, Pres.

Catholic Charities Foundation, 301 E. Armour Blvd.-Suite 620, 64111. Tel: 816-756-1850; 756-1858, Ext. 562; Fax: 816-756-5022. Bob Frazier, Exec. Dir.

Diocesan Council of Catholic Women, 300 E. 36th St., P.O. Box 419037, 64141. Tel: 816-756-1850.
E-mail: kcdietch@aol.com
Rev. Joseph A. Mancuso, Diocesan Moderator; Elizabeth Dietrich, 1st Vice Pres.

Diocesan Education Endowment Trust Fund, 300 E. 36th St., P.O. Box 419037, 64111. Tel: 816-756-1850. Mr. Thomas Minges, Contact Person.

Friends, Inc., 300 E. 36th St., P.O. Box 419037, 64141-6037. Tel: 816-756-1850.

Immacolata Retreat Center, 300 E. 36th St., P.O. Box 419037, 64141-6037. Tel: 816-756-1850.

Knights of St. Peter Claver (K.P.C.). Ladies Auxiliary of St. Peter Claver. 1616 Paseo, St. Monica Parish, 64108. Tel: 816-471-3696.

Ladies of Charity of Metropolitan Kansas City, P.O. Box 480753, 64148-0753. Tel: 816-968-9046. Mrs. Mary Fern, Pres. A group of volunteers who work and raise money to help the poor and those in need through Seton Center and other agencies.

Marillac Home for Children, P.O. Box 419037, 64141-6037.

Our Lady of Perpetual Help Charitable Trust, 3333 Broadway, 64111. Tel: 816-561-3771; Fax: 816-561-3704.
E-mail: jshea@olph-kc.org
Rev. James Shea, C.SS.R., Contact Person.

St. Anthony's Home, 300 E. 36th St., P.O. Box 419037, 64141-6037. Tel: 816-756-1850.

St. John's Seminary, Inc., P.O. Box 419037, 64141-6037.

Siena Club, 300 E. 36th St., P.O. Box 419037, 64141. Tel: 816-756-1850.

Society of Our Lady of the Most Holy Trinity, 3704 Tracy, 64109. Tel: 816-931-9131. Rev. John M. Fiala, S.O.L.T.

CONCEPTION. *Conception Benedictine Trust*, 64433. Tel: 660-944-2857; Fax: 660-944-2800.
E-mail: albert@conception.edu
Web site: www.conceptionabbey.org
Rt. Rev. Gregory J. Polan, O.S.B., Pres.; Bro. Mark Kosiba, O.S.B., Vice Pres.; Rev. Albert Bruecken, O.S.B., Sec. & Treas.

LEE'S SUMMIT. *Mercy Midwest Properties.* Mailing Address: Mercy Housing Midwest, 7262 Mercy Rd., Ste. 102, Omaha, NE, 68124-2348. Tel: 402-398-6614; Fax: 402-398-6370.
E-mail: ccoffey@mercyhousing.org
Mercy Midwest Properties, 920 Northeast Ridgeview Dr., #A, 64086. Tel: 816-525-0990; Fax: 816-525-0078. Sr. Carolyn Coffey, R.S.M., Regl. Pres. Affordable service enriched housing for individuals and families who are economically poor. Total Assisted 141; Total Staff 3.

LIBERTY. *Our Lady of Mercy Home*, 2205 Hughes Rd., 64068-9469. Tel: 816-781-5711; Fax: 816-781-7276.

St. Gaspar Society, P.O. Box 339, 64069. Tel: 816-781-4344; Fax: 816-781-3639.
E-mail: kcprov@aol.com
Revs. Ralph Bushell, C.PP.S., Sec.; William Dineen, Treas.

MARYVILLE. *St. Francis Hospital Foundation*, 2016 S. Main, 64468. Tel: 660-562-2600. Member of SSM Health Care.

RELIGIOUS INSTITUTES OF MEN REPRESENTED IN THE DIOCESE

For further details refer to the corresponding bracketed number in the Religious Institutes of Men or Women section.

[0200]—*Benedictine Monks.* (Conception Abbey).—O.S.B.

[0330]—*Brothers of the Christian Schools.* (St. Louis, MO).—F.S.C.

[]—*Christian Brothers of the Midwest, Burr Ridge, FSC.*

[1330]—*Congregation of the Mission.* (Western Prov.).—C.M.

[1210]—*Congregation of the Missionaries of St. Charles.*—C.S.

[0690]—*Jesuit Fathers and Brothers.* (Missouri Prov.).—S.J.

[0800]—*Maryknoll.*—M.M.

[1070]—*Redemptorist Fathers.* (St. Louis Prov.).—C.SS.R.

[]—*Society of Our Lady of Most Holy Trinity.*—S.O.L.T.

[1060]—*Society of the Precious Blood.* (Kansas City Prov.).—C.PP.S.

RELIGIOUS INSTITUTES OF WOMEN REPRESENTED IN THE DIOCESE

[3320]—*Sisters of the Presentation*—(Dubuque, IA).—P.B.V.M.

[0100]—*Adorers of the Blood of Christ.*—A.S.C.

[0230]—*Benedictine Sisters of Pontifical Jurisdiction.* (Atchinson, KS; Columbia, MO; Liberty, MO).—O.S.B.

[]—*Congregation of Mary Queen.* (Springfield, MO).—C.M.R.

[2950]—*Congregation of Notre Dame de Sion.*—N.D.S.

[0220]—*Congregation of the Benedictine Sisters of Perpetual Adoration of Pontifical Jurisdiction.*—O.S.B.

[0760]—*Daughters of Charity of St. Vincent de Paul.*—D.C.

[]—*Dominican Sisters.* (Sinsinawa, WI).—O.P.

[1415]—*Franciscan Sisters of Mary.*—F.S.M.

[2575]—*Institute of the Sisters of Mercy of the Americas.* (Omaha, NE).—R.S.M.

[2340]—*Little Sisters of the Poor.*—L.S.P.

[]—*Maryknoll Sisters of St. Dominic.* (Maryknoll, NY).—M.M.

[2510]—*Mercedarian Missionaries of Berriz.*—M.M.B.

[]—*Notre Dame Sisters.* (Omaha, NE).—N.D.

[]—*School Sisters of St. Francis.* (Milwaukee, WI).—O.S.F.

[]—*Sister Servants of Immaculate Heart of Mary.* (Monroe, MI).—I.H.M.

[0480]—*Sisters of Charity of Leavenworth, Kansas.*—S.C.L.

[0430]—*Sisters of Charity of the Blessed Virgin Mary.*—B.V.M.

[2360]—*Sisters of Loretto at the Foot of the Cross.*—S.L.

[]—*Sisters of St. Anne* . (Provincialate - Marlborough, MA).—S.A.T.

[1540]—*Sisters of St. Francis.* (Clinton, IA).—O.S.F.

[1670]—*Sisters of St. Francis of Savannah, MO.*—O.S.F.

[1560]—*Sisters of St. Francis of the Holy Eucharist.* (Independence, MO).—O.S.F.

[]—*Sisters of St. Francis of the Holy Eucharist Foundation.*

[3830-15]—*Sisters of St. Joseph.* (Concordia, KS).—C.S.J.

[3830-18]—*Sisters of St. Joseph.* (Wichita, KS).—C.S.J.

[3840]—*Sisters of St. Joseph of Carondelet.*—C.S.J.

[]—*Society of Our Lady of the Most Holy Trinity.*—S.O.L.T.

[4120-02]—*Ursuline Nuns.* (Paola, KS).—O.S.U.

[4120-04]—*Ursuline Nuns.* (Cleveland, OH).—O.S.U.

[4120-05]—*Ursuline Nuns.* (Maple Mount, KY).—O.S.U.

DIOCESAN CEMETERIES

KANSAS CITY. *Mount Olivet & Mount St. Mary.*

ST. JOSEPH. *Mount Olivet.*

KANSAS CITY NORTH. *Resurrection.*

NECROLOGY

† Bachnak, Francis J., (Retired). —Died April 16, 2000.

† Carson, Paul C., (Retired). —Died Feb. 23, 2000.

† Hughes, Joseph, Savannah, MO St. Rose of Lima. —Died July 13, 2000.

† Lackamp, Franklin J., (Retired). —Died June 26, 2000.

Diocese of Knoxville

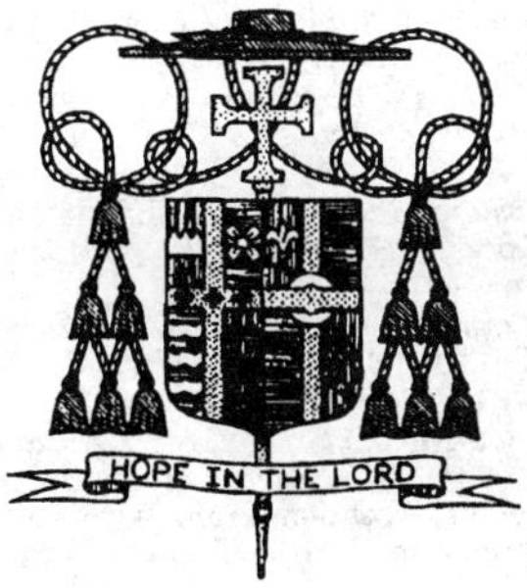

Most Reverend

JOSEPH E. KURTZ, D.D.

Bishop of Knoxville; ordained 1972; appointed October 26, 1999; ordained and installed December 8, 1999. *Office: 805 Northshore Dr.,S.W., P.O. Box 11127, Knoxville, TN, 37939-1127.*

ESTABLISHED SEPTEMBER 8, 1988.

Square Miles 14,242.

Comprises the Counties of Anderson, Bledsoe, Blount, Bradley, Campbell, Carter, Claiborne, Cocke, Cumberland, Fentress, Grainger, Greene, Hamblen, Hamilton, Hancock, Hawkins, Jefferson, Johnson, Knox, Loudon, McMinn, Marion, Meigs, Monroe, Morgan, Pickett, Polk, Rhea, Roane, Scott, Sequatchie, Sevier, Sullivan, Unicoi, Union and Washington in the State of Tennessee.

For legal titles of parishes and diocesan institutions, consult the Chancery Office.

Chancery Office: 805 Northshore Dr., S.W., P.O. Box 11127, Knoxville, TN, 37939-1127. Tel.: 865-584-3307.

STATISTICAL OVERVIEW

Personnel	
Bishop	1
Priests: Diocesan Active in Diocese	40
Priests: Active Outside Diocese	4
Priests: Retired, Sick or Absent	7
Number of Diocesan Priests	51
Religious Priests in Diocese	17
Extern Priests in Diocese	8
Ordinations:	
Diocesan Priests	1
Transitional Deacons	2
Permanent Deacons in Diocese	20
Total Brothers	13
Total Sisters	42
Parishes	
Parishes	44
With Resident Pastor:	
Resident Diocesan Priests	30
Resident Religious Priests	6
Without Resident Pastor:	
Administered by Priests	7
Administered by Lay People	1
Missions	2

Pastoral Centers	2
Professional Ministry Personnel:	
Sisters	3
Lay Ministers	22
Welfare	
Catholic Hospitals	2
Total Assisted	616,932
Health Care Centers	1
Total Assisted	189
Homes for the Aged	1
Total Assisted	513
Specialized Homes	1
Total Assisted	320
Special Centers for Social Services	6
Total Assisted	42,451
Educational	
Diocesan Students in Other Seminaries	10
Total Seminarians	10
High Schools, Diocesan and Parish	2
Total Students	1,041
Elementary Schools, Diocesan and Parish	8
Total Students	2,717
Catechesis/Religious Education:	

High School Students	1,296
Elementary Students	3,575
Total Students Under Catholic Instruction	8,639
Teachers in the Diocese:	
Priests	2
Brothers	1
Sisters	7
Lay Teachers	272
Vital Statistics	
Receptions into the Church:	
Infant Baptism Totals	780
Adult Baptism Totals	162
Received into Full Communion	223
First Communions	1,069
Confirmations	859
Marriages:	
Catholic	115
Interfaith	151
Total Marriages	266
Deaths	350
Total Catholic Population	47,232
Total Population	2,012,885

Former Bishops—Most Rev. ANTHONY J. O'CONNELL, ord. 1963; appt. Bishop of Knoxville May 27, 1988; installed Sept. 8, 1988; appt. Bishop of Palm Beach Nov. 11, 1998.

Vicar General—Rev. FRANCIS XAVIER MANKEL, V.G., S.T.L.

Deans of the Diocese—Revs. WILLIAM H. GAHAGAN, Five Rivers Deanery; MICHAEL CRESON, Chattanooga Deanery; MICHAEL SWEENEY, Cumberland Mtn. Deanery; T. ALLEN HUMBRECHT, Smoky Mtn. Deanery.

Chancery Office—*805 Northshore Dr. S.W., P.O. Box 11127, Knoxville, 37939-1127.* Tel: 865-584-3307; Fax: 865-584-7538. Office Hours: Mon-Fri 9-5. All official business should be directed to this office.

Chancellor—Rev. J. VANN JOHNSTON, JR., J.C.L.

Auditors—All priests on assignment in the diocese.

Presbyteral Council—All priests on assignment in the diocese.

Diocesan Consultors—Revs. DAVID BOETTNER; JOSEPH J. BRANDO; WILLIAM C. CASEY; WILLIAM H. GAHAGAN; ROBERT J. HOFSTETTER; T. ALLEN HUMBRECHT; FRANCIS XAVIER MANKEL, V.G., S.T.L.; CHRIS MICHELSON; TOM VOS, O.F.M.

Diocesan Finance Council—DORMAN BLAINE; J. MICHAEL CONNOR, Chm. LARRY COOL, Ex Officio, Diocesan Finance Officer; SHARON FOLK; SAL GERACI; TERRY TORRICELLI, Ex Officio, Diocesan Dir. Stewardship & Devel.; Rev. FRANCIS XAVIER MANKEL, V.G., S.T.L., Ex Officio; Rev. CHRIS MICHELSON; JOHN T. O'CONNOR, Ex Officio, Diocesan Attorney; PAUL PREMO; SOCRATES SABATER; DAVE SANTI; Rev. GEORGE E. SCHMIDT, JR.; SUZANNE SCHRIVER; WILLIAM SWAIN; FRAN THIE, Vice Chm. FRANK VARALLO; GEORGE WARNE.

Diocesan Offices and Directors

Adult Christian Living—Rev. EVAN ECKHOFF, O.F.M., Dir., *805 Northshore Dr., S.W., Knoxville, 37919.* Tel: 865-584-3307.

Appalachian Community Development—MARIE CIRILLO, Dir., *281 Roses Creek, Clairfield, 37715.* Tel: 423-784-6832. Participants in CORE-Appalachian Ministries, a joint project of Dioceses of Covington, Knoxville, Lexington, Nashville, Richmond and Wheeling-Charleston.

Associated Catholic Charities of East Tennessee, Inc.—Rev. RAGAN SCHRIVER, Exec. Dir., *119 Dameron Ave., Knoxville, 37917.* Tel: 865-524-9896; Fax: 865-971-3575. The umbrella agency for all Catholic charities of the diocese.

Catholic Campaign for Human Development—Rev. RAGAN SCHRIVER, Dir., *119 Dameron Ave., Knoxville, 37917.* Tel: 865-524-9896.

Campus Ministries—

East Tennessee State University—Rev. WILLIAM H. GAHAGAN, Chap., *Catholic Center, 734 W. Locust St., Johnson City, 37604.* Tel: 423-926-7061.

University of Tennessee-Chattanooga—Rev. MICHAEL LINDER, Dir., *514 Palmetto St., Chattanooga, 37403.* Tel: 423-267-3064.

University of Tennessee-Knoxville—Rev. TERRENCE RYAN, C.S.P., Dir., *1710 Melrose Pl., Knoxville, 37916.* Tel: 865-523-7931.

Catholic Schools Office—Dr. AURELIA MONTGOMERY, Supt., *805 Northshore Dr., S.W., Knoxville, 37919.* Tel: 865-584-3307.

Catholic Charities (Chattanooga Area)—LYNDA DIPRIMA, Admin., *859 McCallie Ave., Chattanooga, 37403.* Tel: 423-267-1297.

Catholic Charities (Knoxville Area)—VICKIE STOVALL, Admin., *119 Dameron Ave., Knoxville, 37917.* Tel: 865-524-9896.

Catholic Charities (Upper East Tennessee Area)—DEBBIE WOLLARY, Admin., *703 East Jackson Blvd., P.O. Box 323, Jonesborough, 37659.* Tel: 423-753-3001.

Cemeteries—LARRY COOL, Dir., *805 Northshore Dr., S.W., Knoxville, 37919.* Tel: 865-584-3307. Rev. GEORGE E. SCHMIDT, JR., Contact, Mt. Olivet Cemetery in Chattanooga. Tel: 423-266-1618. Rev. JAMES A. HALEY, C.S.P., Contact, Calvary Cemetery in Knoxville. Tel: 865-522-1508.

Chancellor—Rev. J. VANN JOHNSTON, JR., J.C.L., *805 Northshore Dr., S.W., Knoxville, 37919.* Tel: 865-584-3307.

Censor Librorum—Rev. ROBERT J. HOFSTETTER, *930 Ashland Ter., Chattanooga, 37415.* Tel: 423-870-2386.

Deaf Ministry—Rev. MICHAEL CUMMINS, Dir., *Sacred Heart Cathedral, 711 Northshore Dr., S.W., Knoxville, 37919.* Tel: 865-558-4144.

Diocesan Council of Catholic Women—Rev. FRANCIS XAVIER MANKEL, V.G., S.T.L., Diocesan Spiritual Moderator, *P.O. Box 3936, Knoxville, 37927.* Tel: 865-482-1191.

Ecumenism—Rev. T. ALLEN HUMBRECHT, Dir., *805 Northshore Dr., S.W., Knoxville, 37919.* Tel: 865-584-3307.

Evangelization—Sr. ALBERTINE PAULUS, R.S.M., Dir., *805 Northshore Dr., S.W., Knoxville, 37919.* Tel: 865-584-3307.

Finance Office—LARRY COOL, Diocesan Finance Officer, *805 Northshore Dr., S.W., Knoxville, 37919.* Tel: 865-584-3307.

Hispanic Ministry—JACK KRAMER, Dir., *119 Dameron Ave., Knoxville, 37917.* Tel: 865-637-4769.

Justice - Peace - Integrity of Creation—Co-Directors: MARCUS KEYES; GLENDA STRUSS-KEYES, *119 Dameron Ave., Knoxville, 37917.* Tel: 865-540-8348.

Marriage Tribunal—Rev. DEXTER BREWER, J.C.L. J.V., *2400 21st Ave. S., Nashville, 37212-5387*. Tel: 615-383-6393. Diocesan marriage tribunal is shared with the Diocese of Nashville.

Ministries of the Chattanooga Deanery—Rev. MICHAEL CRESON, Dean; PATRICIA APPLETON, Exec. Dir., *859 McCallie Ave., Ste. 302, Chattanooga, 37403*. Tel: 423-267-9878.

Ministries of the Five Rivers Deanery—Rev. WILLIAM H. GAHAGAN, Dean, *2211 E. Lakeview Dr., Johnson City, 37601*. Tel: 423-282-6367.

Ministries of the Cumberland Mtn. Deanery—Rev. MICHAEL SWEENEY, Dean, *535 Margrave St., Harriman, 37748*. Tel: 865-882-9838.

Ministries of the Smoky Mtn. Deanery—Rev. T. ALLEN HUMBRECHT, Dean, *711 Northshore Dr., S.W., Knoxville, 37919*. Tel: 865-588-0249.

Diaconate—Rev. GREGORY BOISVERT, A.A., Dir., *P.O. Box 1861, Fairfield Glade, 38558*. Tel: 931-484-3628.

Priestly Life and Ministry—Rev. ROBERT J. HOFSTETTER, Dir., *930 Ashland Ter., Chattanooga, 37415*. Tel: 423-870-2386.

Propagation of the Faith—Rev. J. VANN JOHNSTON, JR., J.C.L., Dir., *805 Northshore Dr., S.W., Knoxville, 37919*. Tel: 865-584-3307.

Religious Education—CATHY QUALLS, Dir., *212 Mt. Bethel Rd., Greeneville, 37745*. Tel: 800-553-0284.

Religious Education Resource Center—CATHY QUALLS, Dir., *212 Mt. Bethel Rd., Greeneville, 37745*. Tel: 800-553-0284.

Scouting—Deacon OTTO PRESKE, Scout Chap., *535 Buckhorn Rd., Gatlinburg, 37738*. Tel: 865-436-5339.

Stewardship and Development—TERRY TORRICELLI, Dir., *805 Northshore Dr., S.W., Knoxville, 37919*. Tel: 865-584-3307.

Strategic Pastoral Planning—PAUL TERHAAR, Dir., *805 Northshore Dr., S.W., Knoxville, 37919*. Tel: 865-584-3307.

"The East Tennessee Catholic"—(Diocesan Newspaper). APRIL PARTIN, Editor, *805 Northshore Dr., S.W., Knoxville, 37919*. Tel: 865-584-3307.

Vocations—805 Northshore Dr., S.W., Knoxville, 37919. Tel: 865-584-3307. Revs. MICHAEL CRESON, Dir. Seminarians, Vocation Promotion; MICHAEL CUMMINS, Cumberland Mtn. Deanery Vocation Coord., Vocation Promotion Coord. WILLIAM H. GAHAGAN, Five Rivers Deanery Vocation Coord. T. ALLEN HUMBRECHT, Smoky Mtn. Deanery Vocation Coord. MICHAEL NOLAN, Chattanooga Deanery Vocation Coord. Assoc. Vocation Promoters: Revs. KWAKU JOHN APPIAH; RAGAN SCHRIVER.

Worship and Liturgy—Rev. ALEX WARAKSA, Dir., *805 Northshore Dr., S.W., Knoxville, 37919*. Tel: 865-584-3307.

Youth Ministry—Rev. MICHAEL CUMMINS, Diocesan Coord., *711 Northshore Dr., S.W., Knoxville, 37919*. Tel: 865-558-4144. PAT RIECKE, Coord. Chattanooga Deanery, *859 McCallie Ave., Ste. 302, Chattanooga, 37403*. Tel: 423-267-9878. LINDA D. MURASKI, Coord., Five Rivers Deanery, *159 Carden Dr., Elizabethton, 37643*. Tel: 423-543-7449. ANNE MCGAUGH, Coord., Cumberland Mtn. Deanery, *327 Vermont Ave., Oak Ridge, 37830*. Tel: 865-483-7519. THOMAS MIKLUSICAK, Coord., Smoky Mtn. Deanery, *711 Northshore Dr., S.W., Knoxville, 37919*. Tel: 865-558-8348.

CLERGY, PARISHES, MISSIONS AND PAROCHIAL SCHOOLS

CITY OF KNOXVILLE
(Knox County)

1—CATHEDRAL OF THE SACRED HEART OF JESUS (1956), Revs. T. Allen Humbrecht; Christian Mathis; Deacon James Lawson, Pastoral Assoc. In res., Rev. Michael Cummins.
Res., 711 Northshore Dr., S.W., 37919. Tel: 865-588-5189; Fax: 865-558-9671. [JC]
School—Tel: 865-588-0415; Fax: 865-558-4139. Pamela Bernards, Prin.
Brothers 1; Sisters 1; Lay Teachers 62; Students 689.
Catechesis/Religious Programs—Tel: 865-584-4528. Joanne Romeo, D.R.E.
Students 215.

2—ALL SAINTS CATHOLIC CHURCH (1994), Revs. Chris Michelson; Samuel L. Sturm. In res., Rev. Ragan Schriver.
Mailing Address: 620 N. Cedar Bluff Rd., 37923. Tel: 865-531-0770; Fax: 865-531-1009.
Catechesis/Religious Programs—Students 450.

3—IMMACULATE CONCEPTION (1852) (Irish), Revs. James A. Haley, C.S.P.; Broderick M. Walsh, C.S.P.
Res., 414 W. Vine Ave., 37902. Tel: 865-522-1508; Fax: 865-524-8514. [CEM]
Catechesis/Religious Programs—Betty Krusenklaus, D.R.E.
Students 177.

4—JOHN XXIII UNIVERSITY PARISH/CATHOLIC CENTER (1968). (Non-territorial parish for the University of Tennessee at Knoxville). Revs. Terrence P. Ryan, C.S.P.; Eric P. Andrews, C.S.P.; Ruth Queen Smith, Pastoral Assoc.
Res., 1710 Melrose Pl., 37916. Tel: 865-523-7931; Fax: 865-523-7979.
Catechesis/Religious Programs—Students 55.

5—HOLY GHOST (1908), Revs. F. Xavier Mankel, V.G., S.T.L.; J. Vann Johnston, Jr., J.C.L.
Res., 111 Hinton Ave., 37917. Tel: 865-522-2205; Fax: 865-525-6051. [JC]
School—St. Joseph, 1810 Howard Rd., 37918. Tel: 865-689-3424; Fax: 865-687-7885. Joan Turbyville, Prin.
Sisters 1; Lay Teachers 32; Students 272.
Catechesis/Religious Programs—Betty Krusenklaus, D.R.E.
Students 156.

6—ST. JOHN NEUMANN (1977), Revs. John R. Dowling; John Joseph Campbell; Deacons Donald Amelse; Marquis Syler.
Church—St. John Neumann, 225 Jamestowne Blvd., 37922. Tel: 865-966-4540; Fax: 865-966-4541.
Res., 300 Dominion Cir., 37922. Tel: 865-966-8924.
School—625 St. John Ct., 37922. Tel: 865-777-0077; Fax: 865-777-0087. Sr. Mary Janice Brink, R.S.M., Prin.
Catechesis/Religious Programs—Peggy Phares, D.R.E.
Students 517.

OUTSIDE THE CITY OF KNOXVILLE

Alcoa, Blount Co., Our Lady of Fatima (1950), Rev. Alex J. Waraksa.
Res., 860 Louisville Rd., 37701. Tel: 865-982-3672; Fax: 865-977-4183.
Catechesis/Religious Programs—Tel: 865-981-2676; Fax: 865-983-3563. LuAnne Zelasko, D.R.E.
Students 325.
Mission—Townsend, Blount Co., St. Francis of Assisi, 7717 River Rd., Townsend, 37882. Tel: 865-448-6070. Rev. Joseph W. Julius; Deacon Michael G. Nestor.
Catechesis/Religious Programs—Students 24.

Athens, McMinn Co., St. Mary (1968), Rev. David A. Boettner.
Res., 2007 Congress Pkwy., 37303. Tel: 423-745-4277; Fax: 423-745-4277.
Catechesis/Religious Programs—Tel: 423-476-7869. Joyce Spurlin, D.R.E.
Students 164.

Chattanooga, Hamilton Co.,

1—SS. PETER AND PAUL, (1852), Rev. George E. Schmidt, Jr.; Deacon James Wilson.
Res., 214 E. 8th St., 37402. Tel: 423-266-1618. [JC]
Catechesis/Religious Programs—Students 42.

2—OUR LADY OF PERPETUAL HELP, (1937), Revs. Michael F. Nolan; James L. Vick; Deacons Mark Gang, Jr.; William Oleck.
Res., 501 S. Moore Rd., 37412. Tel: 423-622-7232; Fax: 423-624-2686. [CEM]
School—505 S. Moore Rd., 37412. Tel: 423-622-1418; Fax: 423-622-2016. Mrs. Ray Ann Kurtz, Prin.
Sisters of Charity of the Blessed Virgin Mary 1; Lay Teachers 32; Students 436.
Catechesis/Religious Programs—Tel: 423-622-7232; Fax: 423-624-2686. Lois Colosia, D.R.E.
Students 101.
Convent—511 S. Moore Rd., 37412. Tel: 423-698-3274.

3—ST. JUDE, (1958), Revs. Robert J. Hofstetter; John B. Charles O'Neill. In res., Rev. Pio Palad.
Res., 930 Ashland Ter., 37415. Tel: 423-870-2386; Fax: 423-876-8960. [JC]
School—Tel: 423-877-6022; Fax: 423-875-8920. JoAnne Bollman, Prin.
Lay Teachers 33; Students 444.
Catechesis/Religious Programs—Students 165.

4—ST. STEPHEN, (1961), Rev. P. J. McGinnity. In res., Rev. John Appiah.
Res., 7111 Lee Hwy., 37421. Tel: 423-892-1261; Fax: 423-892-3242. [JC]
Catechesis/Religious Programs—Tel: 423-892-2957.
Students 184.

Cleveland, Bradley Co., St. Therese of Lisieux (1914), Rev. Phillip F. Thoni; Sr. Marian Ruede, Pastoral Assoc.
Res., 900 Clingan Ridge Dr., N.W., 37312. Tel: 423-476-8123; Fax: 423-479-3339.
Catechesis/Religious Programs—David Wilson, D.R.E.
Students 267.

Clinton, Anderson Co., St. Therese (1971), Rev. Dan G. Whitman; Sr. Yvette Gillen, R.S.M., Pastoral Assoc.
Church & Res.—701 S. Charles G. Seivers Blvd., 37716. Tel: 865-457-4073 (Church); 457-1317 (Res.); Fax: 865-463-9734.
Catechesis/Religious Programs—Students 75.

Copperhill, Polk Co., St. Catherine Laboure (1977). Attended by St. Mary, Athens. In res., Rev. Paul A. Hostettler.
Mailing Address: Box 566, 37317. Tel: 423-496-3498.
Catechesis/Religious Programs—Tel: 706-374-6362.
Students 6.

Crossville, Cumberland Co., St. Alphonsus (1948), Rev. Patrick P. Brownell.
Res., 426 Sparta Dr., 38555. Tel: 931-484-2358 (Office); 456-5005 (Res.) ; Fax: 931-484-7407.
Catechesis/Religious Programs—Tel: 931-456-5227. Sara Carey, D.R.E.
Students 106.

Dayton, Rhea Co., St. Bridget (1969), Rev. John Milewski, K.H.S.; Deacon Tom Kiefer.
Res., 320 Walnut Grove Church Rd., 37321. Tel: 423-775-2664 (Church); 775-5542 (Rectory); Fax: 423-775-1545.
Catechesis/Religious Programs—Students 54.

Dunlap, Sequatchie Co., Shepherd of the Valley (1997). (Quasi Parish). Rev. Thomas W. Moser.
Res., 110 Old York Hwy., P.O. Box 1747, 37327. Tel: 423-949-6903; Fax: 423-837-7793.

Elizabethton, Carter Co., St. Elizabeth (1982), Rev. R. R. Archer, O.P.
Res., 510 W. C St., 37643. Tel: 423-543-3412.
Catechesis/Religious Programs—Donna Townsend, D.R.E.
Students 50.

Fairfield Glade, Cumberland Co., St. Francis of Assisi (1983), Rev. Gregory Boisvert, A.A.; Deacons Mark Fredrick; Mark White.
Res., Peavine Rd., P.O. Box 1861, 38558. Tel: 931-484-3628; Fax: 931-707-0186.
Catechesis/Religious Programs—Students 5.

Gatlinburg, Sevier Co., St. Mary (1935), Rev. Herbert W. Prescott, Admin. Pro Tem; Deacon Otto Preske.
Res., 304 Historic Nature Tr., 37738. Tel: 865-436-4907.
Catechesis/Religious Programs—Students 23.
Mission—Pigeon Forge, Sevier Co., Holy Cross, (1992) 144 Wears Valley Rd., Pigeon Forge, 37863. Tel: 865-429-5587; Fax: 865-453-8951. Rev. Jay Flaherty, Admin. pro tem.
Catechesis/Religious Programs—Students 86.

Greeneville, Greene Co., Notre Dame (1955), Rev. James P. Harvey. In res., Rev. Joseph Mary Hammond, C.H.S.
Res., 212 Mt. Bethel Rd., 37745. Tel: 423-639-9381; Fax: 423-638-5219.
Catechesis/Religious Programs—Tel: 423-638-5514. D.R.E.: Diana Thompon, (Elementary); Mary Ann Connell, (Elementary); Margeret Ayers, (High School).
Students 95.

Harriman, Roane Co., Blessed Sacrament (1908), Rev. Michael Sweeney.
Res., 535 Margrave St., 37748. Tel: 865-882-9838; Fax: 865-882-3786.
Catechesis/Religious Programs—Students 77.
Mission—Jamestown, Fentress Co., Mission Catholic Community of Fentress County, c/o Jim Romer, 204 Tinch Ave., Jamestown, 38556-5221. Tel: 931-879-8144; Fax: 931-879-8145.
Catechesis/Religious Programs—Students 12.
Stations—Brushy Mountain Prison, Tel: 865-346-6641; Morgan County Regional Correctional Facility.

Helenwood, Scott Co., St. Jude Parish (1982). Attended by St. Therese, Clinton. Rev. Dan G. Whitman; Sr. Patricia Soete, R.S.M., Pastoral Assoc.
Mailing Address: 13067 Scott Hwy; P.O. Box 555, 37755. Tel: 423-569-3492; 569-9584 (Church).
Catechesis/Religious Programs—Students 6.

Jefferson City, Jefferson Co., Holy Trinity Catholic Church (1997), Rev. G. Patrick Garrity; Deacon Gerald James Fage.
475 N. Hwy. 92, P.O. Box 304, 37760. Tel: 865-471-0347; Fax: 865-471-0349.
Catechesis/Religious Programs—Students 46.

Johnson City, Washington Co., St. Mary (1906), Revs. William H. Gahagan; Gerard Finucane.
Res., 2211 E. Lakeview Dr., 37601. Tel: 423-282-8696; Fax: 423-282-6145.
School—Tel: 423-282-3397; Fax: 423-282-0224. Sr. Mary Jane Jansen, S.S.N.D., Prin.
Sisters 1; Lay Teachers 16; Students 188.

Catechesis/Religious Programs—Tel: 423-282-6367. Sr. Mary Jane Jansen, S.S.N.D., D.R.E. Students 354.

Kingsport, Sullivan Co., St. Dominic (1941), Revs. Charles Burton; Dennis Kress; Deacon Milton Robelot.
Res., 2517 John B. Dennis Hwy., 37660. Tel: 423-288-2773; Fax: 423-288-7183.
School—Tel: 423-245-0362; Fax: 423-245-2907. Debbie DePollo, Prin.
Lay Teachers 11; Students 93.
Catechesis/Religious Programs—Tel: 423-288-8101. Shirley Parsons, D.R.E.
Students 305.

LaFollette, Campbell Co., Our Lady of Perpetual Help (1905), Rev. Greg Neuzil.
Mailing Address: 1142 E. Elm St., P.O. Box 1704, 37766. Tel: 423-562-0312; Fax: 423-562-0312.
Catechesis/Religious Programs—Tel: 423-562-9165.
Students 23.

Lancing, Morgan Co., St. Ann (1982). Attended by Blessed Sacrament, Harriman. Rev. Michael Sweeney.
Mailing Address: P.O. Box 77, 37770-0077. Tel: 865-346-6260; Fax: 865-882-3786.
Catechesis/Religious Programs—Tel: 865-882-3786.
Students 12.

Lenoir City, Loudon Co., St. Thomas the Apostle (1973), Rev. Steve LaPrad; Deacon Jose Rivera.
Res., 2500 Harrison Rd., 37771. Tel: 865-986-9885; Fax: 865-986-1503.
Catechesis/Religious Programs—Students 65.

Madisonville, Monroe Co., Monroe County Catholic Church (1992). (Quasi Parish). Paul Witte, Pastoral Coord., Tel: 423-442-5530.
Mailing Address: 4263 Hwy. 411, 37354. Tel: 423-442-7273; Fax: 423-442-7273.

Morristown, Hamblen Co., St. Patrick (1959), Revs. G. Patrick Garrity; Joseph Hammond; Deacon Gerald James Fage.
Res., 2518 W. Andrew Johnson Hwy., 37814. Tel: 423-586-9174; Fax: 423-318-7044.
Catechesis/Religious Programs—Tel: 423-586-4091. Patricia Holmes, D.R.E.
Students 225.

Mountain City, Johnson Co., St. Anthony of Padua Catholic Church (1995). (Quasi Parish). Rev. Thomas Vos, O.F.M.
Res., 833 W. Main St., 37683. Tel: 423-727-7870; Fax: 423-727-5017.

Newport, Cocke Co., Good Shepherd (1967). Attended by Notre Dame, Greeneville. Rev. James P. Harvey, II; Mr. Dennis H. Bible, Parish Coord.
Mailing Address: 659 E. Broadway, 37821. Tel: 423-623-5051.
School—Students 30.
Catechesis/Religious Programs—Students 33.

Norris, Anderson Co., St. Joseph (1949), Rev. Frank X. Brett.
Res., 3452 Andersonville Hwy. 61, P.O. Box 387, 37828. Tel: 865-494-7746; Fax: 865-426-8759.
Catechesis/Religious Programs—Laura Seymour, D.R.E.
Students 80.

Oak Ridge, Anderson Co., St. Mary (1943), Revs. Michael A. Woods; Gilbert Diaz.
Res., 327 Vermont Ave., 37830. Tel: 865-482-2875; Fax: 865-482-0443.
School—323 Vermont Ave., 37830. Tel: 865-482-9700; Fax: 865-482-8305. Sr. Bernadette Mathieson, O.P., Prin.
Sisters 3; Lay Teachers 19; Students 223.
Catechesis/Religious Programs—Tel: 865-481-8106; Fax: 865-482-0443.
Students 275.

Rogersville, Hawkins Co., St. Henry (1981), Rev. Michael T. Jennings.
Res., 112-114 Hwy. 70 N., 37857. Tel: 423-272-6897.
Catechesis/Religious Programs—Students 21.

Seymour, Sevier Co., Holy Family (1984), Rev. Thomas P. O'Connell.
Mailing Address: 407 Overlook Dr., 37865. Tel: 865-609-1081; Fax: 865-579-3645.
Catechesis/Religious Programs—Tel: 865-577-3881. D.R.E.: Valerie Priddy; Carol Idol.
Students 70.

Signal Mountain, Hamilton Co., St. Augustine (1938), Rev. Paul Valleroy; Deacon Gordon Kilburn.
Res., 1716 Anderson Pike, P.O. Box 10, 37377. Tel: 423-886-3424; Fax: 423-886-3451. [JC]
Catechesis/Religious Programs—Students 170.

Sneedville, Hancock Co., St. James the Apostle (1982). Attended by St. Henry, Rogersville. Rev. Mike Jennings.
Mailing and Res.: P.O. Box 93, 37869. Tel: 423-272-6897.
Catechesis/Religious Programs—Students 1.

Soddy Daisy, Hamilton Co., Holy Spirit Catholic Church (1999). (Quasi-parish). Rev. Michael Creson.
Res. & Mailing Address: 10812 Dayton Pike, P.O. Box 1015, 37384. Tel: 423-332-5300; Fax: 423-332-5391.
Catechesis/Religious Programs—Students 38.

South Pittsburg, Marion Co., Our Lady of Lourdes (1899), Rev. Thomas W. Moser.
Res., 700 Holly Ave., P.O. Box 288, 37380. Tel: 423-837-7068; Fax: 423-837-7793.
Mission—Marian, Marian Co., Virgin of the Poor Shrine.
Catechesis/Religious Programs—Students 38.

Tazewell, Claiborne Co., Christ the King (1990), Rev. Greg Neuzil.
Mailing Address: P.O. Box 404, 37879.
Res., 1142 E. Elm St., LaFollette, 37766. Tel: 423-562-0312.
Catechesis/Religious Programs—Students 25.

Townsend, Blount Co., St. Francis of Assisi (1961). Attended by Our Lady of Fatima, Alcoa. In res., Rev. Joseph W. Julius (NSH).
Mailing Address: 7717 River Rd., 37882. Tel: 423-448-6070.
Catechesis/Religious Programs—Students 321.

Retired:
Reverend Monsignors—
Siener, Leo C., Alexian Village Health Care Center, 100 James Blvd., Rm. 728, Signal Mtn., TN 37377-1816
Reverend Fathers—
Bowes, David, P.O. Box 9325, Pensacola, FL 32513
Casey, William, 670 Shakerag Rd., Greenville, TN 37743
Hostettler, Paul A., P.O. Box 566, Copperhill, TN 37317
Junod, Louis J., 1414 Continental Dr., Apt. 207, Chattanooga, TN 37405
Prescott, Herbert W., P.O. Box 15341, Chattanooga, TN 37415
Thoni, Philip F., (Retired LTC), 900 Clingan Ridge Dr., N.W., Cleveland, TN 37312

Permanent Deacons:
Amelse, Donald, St. John Neumann, Knoxville
Bresler, Thomas, St. Augustine Chapel, Signal Mountain; Alexian Village
Diesing, William
Fage, Gerald J., II, St. Patrick, Morristown
Fischer, Robert W., St. Elizabeth Church, Elizabethton
Fredrick, Mark A., St. Francis of Assisi, Fairfield Glade
Gang, Mark, Jr., Our Lady of Perpetual Help, Chattanooga
Kiefer, Thomas, St. Bridget, Dayton
Kilburn, Gordon, St. Augustine, Signal Mountain
Lawson, James, Sacred Heart Cathedral
Nestor, Michael, St. Francis of Assisi, Townsend
Oleck, William A., Our Lady of Perpetual Help, Chattanooga
Preske, Otto F., St. Mary, Gatlinburg
Rivera, Jose, St. Thomas the Apostle, Lenoir City
Robelot, Milton P., St. Dominic, Kingsport
Syler, Marquis E., St. John Neumann, Knoxville
Torrelli, Ralph, St. Alphonsus, Crossville
White, Mark F., St. Francis of Assisi, Fairfield Glade
Wilson, James E., SS. Peter and Paul, Chattanooga

INSTITUTIONS LOCATED IN THE DIOCESE

[A] HIGH SCHOOLS, DIOCESAN

KNOXVILLE. *Knoxville Catholic High School* (1932), 9245 Fox Lonas Rd., 37923. Tel: 865-560-0313; Fax: 865-560-0314.
E-mail: kchs@esper.com
Web site: members.tripod.com/knoxcatholic/Main.htm
Philip M. Dampf, III, Prin. Priests 2; Lay Teachers 29; Students 468.
Knoxville Catholic High School Development Board of Trust. Tel: 865-560-0509; Fax: 865-560-0314.

CHATTANOOGA. *Notre Dame High School* (1876). (Grades 9-12), 2701 Vermont Ave., 37404. Tel: 423-624-4618; Fax: 423-624-4621.
E-mail: P.StoreyNDHS@juno.com
Web site: www.chattanooga.net/notredame
Mr. Perry Storey, Prin. Priests 2; Lay Teachers 51; Students 575; Staff 19.
Notre Dame High School Financial Board of Trustees.

[B] GENERAL HOSPITALS

KNOXVILLE. *St. Mary's Health System, Inc.*, (1930) 900 E. Oak Hill Ave., 37917. Tel: 865-545-8000; Fax: 865-545-6732.
E-mail: rwilliams@stmaryshealth.com
Web site: www.stmaryshealth.com
For a complete listing, refer to the Hospitals section.

CHATTANOOGA. *Memorial Hospital*, (1952) 2525 DeSales Ave., 37404. Tel: 423-495-2525.
Web site: memorial.org
For a complete listing, refer to the Hospitals section.

[C] SPECIAL HOSPITALS

SIGNAL MOUNTAIN. *Alexian Village Health Care Center*, (1938) 100 James Blvd., 37377. Tel: 423-886-0100; Fax: 423-886-0470.
E-mail: AVTCEO@aol.com
Web site: www.alexianvillage.com
For a complete listing, refer to the Special Care Facilities section.

[D] HOMES FOR THE AGED

SIGNAL MOUNTAIN. *Alexian Village of Tennessee*, 100 James Blvd., 37377. Tel: 423-886-0100; Fax: 423-886-0470.
E-mail: AVTCEO@aol.com
Web site: www.alexianvillage.com
For a complete listing, refer to the Special Care Facilities section.

[E] PROTECTIVE INSTITUTIONS

KNOXVILLE. *Columbus Home, Inc.*, 119 Dameron Ave., 37917. Tel: 865-971-3570; Fax: 865-546-0433.
E-mail: inglecolumbus@aol.com
For a complete listing, refer to the Special Care Facilities section.

[F] MONASTERIES AND RESIDENCES OF PRIESTS AND BROTHERS

KNOXVILLE. *Brothers of Holy Cross*, 816 Creswell Ct., 37919-7444. Tel: 865-588-5566. Bro. Roland Driscoll, C.S.C., (Retired). Total in Residence 1; Total Staff 1.
Presentation Brothers of Mary, 1409 Buxton Dr., 37922. Tel: 865-694-3135; Fax: 865-694-5080.
E-mail: brgerard@usa.net
Web site: www.presentationbrothers.org
Bros. Gerard Despathy, F.P.M.; Pat Stack, F.P.M.; Francis Sebo, F.P.M. Total in Residence 3.

LANCING. *Brothers of Holy Cross*, 297 Davidson Rd., 37770. Tel: 423-965-3392. Bro. Paul Bray, C.S.C., Dir.

MOUNTAIN CITY. *Franciscan Friars*, Alverna Friary, 513 Hickory St., 37683. Tel: 423-727-7870; Fax: 423-727-5017. Revs. Evan Eckhoff, O.F.M.; Thomas Vos, O.F.M.

SIGNAL MOUNTAIN. *Alexian Brothers*, 198 James Blvd., 37377. Tel: 423-886-0380; Fax: 423-886-0381.
E-mail: eyochim@aol.com
Bros. Edward Walsh, C.F.A., Supr. Gen.; Anthony J. Ragucci, C.F.A.; Edward Yochim, C.F.A., Dir. Community; Cajetan Gavranich, C.F.A., Asst. Dir.; Ewald Herb, C.F.A., (Health Center); James Johnston, C.F.A.; Simeon Pytel, C.F.A., Sec. (Generalate); Bernard Riley, C.F.A.; Andrew Thome, C.F.A.; Rev. Maro Cannon, C.F.A. Brothers 9.

[G] CONVENTS AND RESIDENCES FOR SISTERS

KNOXVILLE. *Sisters of Mercy*. (Cincinnati Region).
E-mail: SERiney@notes.mercy.com
St. Mary's Medical Center, 900 E. Oak Hill Ave., 37917. Tel: 865-545-8000; Fax: 865-545-6732. Sisters 9.

APISON. *Sisters of the Presentation of the Blessed Virgin Mary*, 10996 Apison Pike, 37302. Tel: 423-236-5385. Sr. Mary Dennis Lentsch, P.B.V.M.

BUTLER. *Sisters of St. Joseph, Third Order of St. Francis*, 254 Pine Orchard Rd., 37640. Tel: 423-768-2842. Sr. Barbara Hathaway, S.S.J.-T.O.S.F.

CHATTANOOGA. *Missionary Sisters of the Sacred Heart of Jesus "Ad Gentes"*, 430 Glenwood Dr., 37404. Sr. Catalina Delores Garcia Rosas, M.A.G.; Sr. Maria Lina Ramos, M.A.G.; Sr. Celia Sanchez, M.A.G. Sisters 3.
Sisters of Charity of Nazareth, 425 Glenwood Dr., 37404. Tel: 423-624-2293. Sr. Marie Anne Ballard, S.C.N.; Sr. Frances Josephine Smith, S.C.N. Sisters 2.
Sisters of Charity of the Blessed Virgin Mary, 511 S. Moore Rd., 37412-2949. Tel: 423-698-3274.
E-mail: fsch4002@netzero.net
Web site: www.bvmcong.org
Sr. Mary Zita Henkel, S.C.N.; Sr. Frances Schaeffer, B.V.M.; Sr. Helen Sherrard, B.V.M. Sisters 3.

CLEVELAND. *Sisters of Charity of Cincinnati - St. Therese Lisieux Church*, 2701 Hilltop Dr., N.W., 37312. Tel: 423-476-5972; Fax: 423-479-3339.
E-mail: ruede@juno.com

CLINTON. *St. Therese Convent*, 701 S. Charles G. Seivers Blvd., 37716. Tel: 865-463-9734.

COPPERHILL. *Monastery of Our Lady of Little Citeaux*, Box 1799 McGee Rd., 37317. Tel: 423-496-7373. Sr. Veronica Sweeney; Sr. Angela Ferry. Sisters 2.

HELENWOOD. *Sisters of Mercy*, P.O. Box 555, 13071 Scott Hwy., 37755. Tel: 423-569-3492.

LANCING. *Sisters of Holy Cross*, 641 Island Ford Rd., 37770. Tel: 423-965-3923. Sr. Rita Bray, C.S.C.; Sr. Julie Marie Jacomet, C.S.C. Sisters 2.

OAK RIDGE. *Dominican Sisters (St. Cecilia Congregation)*, St. Mary's Convent, 323 Vermont Ave., 37830. Tel: 865-483-9700; Fax: 865-483-8305. Sr. Mary Therese Brooks, O.P.; Sr. Mary Celeste D'Souza, O.P.; Sr. Bernadette Mathieson, O.P. Sisters 3.

[H] RETREAT HOUSES

KNOXVILLE. *The Mountaincrest Spiritual Center*, 1310 Luttrell St., 37917. Tel: 865-524-0068. Dr. Johanna C. Humphrey, Dir.

[I] CAMPS AND COMMUNITY CENTERS

NEWCOMB.
Crazy Quilt Friendship Center, 2967 Hwy. 297, 37819. Tel: 423-784-6022; Fax: 423-784-9732. Community center, crafts co-op and clothing store. Total Assisted 1,450; Total Staff 4.

[J] NEWMAN CENTERS

KNOXVILLE. *UT-Knoxville, Newman Foundation, Inc.*, John XXIII University Parish/Catholic Center, 1710 Melrose Pl., 37916. Tel: 423-523-7931. Revs. Terrence P. Ryan, C.S.P.; Eric P. Andrews, C.S.P.

CHATTANOOGA. *Newman Foundation of Chattanooga, Inc.*, Catholic Student Center, 514 Palmetto St., 37403. Tel: 423-267-3064. Rev. Michael Linder; Becky Lewis, Assoc. Campus Min. Total Staff 2.

GREENEVILLE. *Tusculum College Newman Center.* Attended by Notre Dame Church, Greeneville. c/o Notre Dame Church, 212 Mt. Bethel Rd., 37745.

JOHNSON CITY. *ETSU-Catholic Center*, 734 W. Locust St., 37604. Tel: 423-926-7061.
E-mail: ccenter@planetconnect
Web site: www.etsu.edu/newman
Rev. William H. Gahagan, Chap.; Daniel Reese, Resident Dir. of Campus Ministry. Total Staff 1.

[K] MISCELLANEOUS

KNOXVILLE. *The Catholic Diocese of Knoxville Foundation, Inc.*, 805 Northshore Dr., S.W., 37919. Tel: 865-584-3307; Fax: 865-584-7538.

Catholic Foundation of East Tennessee, 805 Northshore Dr., S.W., 37919. Tel: 865-584-3307; Fax: 865-584-7538.

Diocesan Council of Catholic Women, 805 Northshore Dr., S.W., 37919. Tel: 865-482-1191. Rev. F. Xavier Mankel, V.G., S.T.L., Diocesan Spiritual Moderator. Deanery Spiritual Moderators: Revs. William H. Gahagan, Five Rivers; Robert J. Hofstetter, Chattanooga; F. Xavier Mankel, V.G., S.T.L., Smoky Mountain; Dan G. Whitman, Cumberland Mountain.

Ladies of Charity, 1031 Central Ave., 37917. Tel: 865-522-6341; 524-0538; Fax: 865-546-5863. Rev. F. Xavier Mankel, V.G., S.T.L., Spiritual Moderator. Total Assisted 19,000; Total Staff 4.

CHATTANOOGA. *Ladies of Charity*, 1800 E. Main St., 37404. Tel: 423-624-3222; Fax: 423-698-2606. Gives emergency assistance in the form of food, medicine, clothing, Lifeline, meals on wheels, layettes to newborn, payment on utilities, rent, glasses, dental work, etc. Total Assisted 11,000.

RELIGIOUS INSTITUTES OF MEN REPRESENTED IN THE DIOCESE

For further details refer to the corresponding bracketed number in the Religious Institutes of Men or Women section.

[0120]—*Alexian Brothers.*—C.F.A.
[0130]—*Assumptionists.*—A.A.
[0600]—*Brothers of the Congregation of Holy Cross.*—C.S.C.
[]—*Crusaders of the Holy Spirit.*—C.H.S.
[0520]—*Franciscan Friars.*—O.F.M.
[0570]—*The Glenmary Home Missioners.*—Glmy.
[0840]—*Missionary Servants of the Most Holy Trinity.*—S.T.
[0430]—*Order of Preachers-Dominicans.*—O.P.
[1030]—*Paulist Fathers.*—C.S.P.
[]—*Presentation Brothers of Mary.*—F.P.M.

RELIGIOUS INSTITUTES OF WOMEN REPRESENTED IN THE DIOCESE

[1920]—*Congregation of the Sisters of Holy Cross.*—C.S.C.
[1070-07]—*Dominican Sisters (St. Cecilia Congregation).*—O.P.
[2575]—*Institute of the Sisters of Mercy of the Americas.* (Cincinnati Prov.).—R.S.M.
[]—*Missionary Sisters of the Sacred Heart of Jesus "Ad Gentes".*—M.A.G.
[2970]—*School Sisters of Notre Dame.*—S.S.N.D.
[0440]—*Sisters of Charity of Cincinnati, OH.*—S.C.
[0500]—*Sisters of Charity of Nazareth.*—S.C.N.
[0430]—*Sisters of Charity of the Blessed Virgin Mary.*—B.V.M.
[2360]—*Sisters of Loretto at the Foot of the Cross.*—S.L.
[1510]—*Sisters of St. Francis.*—O.S.F.
[3930]—*Sisters of St. Joseph, Third Order of St. Francis.*—S.S.J.-T.O.S.F.
[0970]—*Sisters of the Divine Compassion.*—R.D.C.
[3320]—*Sisters of the Presentation of the B.V.M.*—P.B.V.M.

INTERPAROCHIAL CEMETERIES

KNOXVILLE. *Calvary*, Martin Luther King Blvd., 37915. Tel: 865-522-1508. Rev. James A. Haley, C.S.P.

CHATTANOOGA. *Mount Olivet*, Ringgold Rd., 37412. Tel: 423-266-1618. Rev. George E. Schmidt, Jr.

NECROLOGY

† Schilling, Francis X., Gatlinburg, TN St. Mary. —Died July 9, 2000.

Diocese of La Crosse

(Dioecesis Crossensis)

Most Reverend

RAYMOND L. BURKE, D.D., J.C.D.

Bishop of La Crosse; ordained June 29, 1975; appointed to the Residential See of La Crosse December 10, 1994; consecrated January 6, 1995; installed as Eighth Bishop of La Crosse February 22, 1995. *Res., 3720 East Ave., S., La Crosse, WI, 54602-4004. Mailing Address: P.O. Box 4004, La Crosse, WI, 54602-4004.* Tel.: 608-788-7700.

Most Reverend

JOHN J. PAUL, D.D.

Retired Bishop of La Crosse; ordained January 24, 1943; appointed Titular Bishop of Lambese and Auxiliary Bishop of La Crosse May 17, 1977; consecrated August 4, 1977; appointed to the Residential See of La Crosse October 18, 1983; installed as Seventh Bishop of La Crosse December 5, 1983; retired December 10, 1994. *Res., Holy Cross Diocesan Center, P.O. Box 4004, La Crosse, WI, 54602-4004.* Tel.: 608-788-8395; 788-7700.

ERECTED MARCH 3, 1868. SUBDIVIDED MAY 3, 1905. SUBDIVIDED JANUARY 15, 1946.

Square Miles 15,078.

Comprises the following 19 Counties in the State of Wisconsin: Adams, Buffalo, Chippewa, Clark, Crawford, Dunn, Eau Claire, Jackson, Juneau, La Crosse, Marathon, Monroe, Pepin, Pierce, Portage, Richland, Trempealeau, Vernon and Wood.

For legal titles of parishes and diocesan institutions, consult the Chancery Office.

Chancery Office: 3710 East Ave. S., P.O. Box 4004, La Crosse, WI, 54602-4004. Tel.: 608-788-7700; Fax: 608-788-8413.

Web site address: www.dioceseoflacrosse.com

E-mail address: mailbox@dioceseoflacrosse.com

STATISTICAL OVERVIEW

Personnel	
Bishop	1
Retired Bishops	1
Retired Abbots	1
Priests: Diocesan Active in Diocese	120
Priests: Active Outside Diocese	8
Priests: Diocesan in Foreign Missions	2
Priests: Retired, Sick or Absent	71
Number of Diocesan Priests	201
Religious Priests in Diocese	27
Extern Priests in Diocese	19
Ordinations:	
Diocesan Priests	2
Permanent Deacons	10
Permanent Deacons in Diocese	35
Total Brothers	6
Total Sisters	494
Parishes	
Parishes	168
With Resident Pastor:	
Resident Diocesan Priests	97
Resident Religious Priests	11
Without Resident Pastor:	
Administered by Priests	48
Administered by Deacons	3
Administered by Women Religious	4
Administered by Lay People	1
Completely Vacant	3
New Parishes Created	2
Closed Parishes	4
Professional Ministry Personnel:	
Sisters	14
Lay Ministers	40
Welfare	
Catholic Hospitals	9
Total Assisted	582,416
Homes for the Aged	12
Total Assisted	1,319
Day Care and Extended Day Care Centers	2
Total Assisted	200
Specialized Homes	6
Total Assisted	12,204
Special Centers for Social Services	2
Total Assisted	3,125
Residential Care of Disabled	2
Total Assisted	175
Educational	
Seminaries, Diocesan	1
Students from This Diocese	3
Students from Other Diocese	5
Diocesan Students in Other Seminaries	39
Total Seminarians	42
Colleges and Universities	1
Total Students	2,106
High Schools, Diocesan and Parish	7
Total Students	1,745
Elementary Schools, Diocesan and Parish	76
Total Students	9,817
Catechesis/Religious Education:	
High School Students	8,448
Elementary Students	15,855
Total Students Under Catholic Instruction	38,013
Teachers in the Diocese:	
Priests	5
Sisters	27
Lay Teachers	752
Vital Statistics	
Receptions into the Church:	
Infant Baptism Totals	2,874
Adult Baptism Totals	122
Received into Full Communion	341
First Communions	3,464
Confirmations	3,328
Marriages:	
Catholic	840
Interfaith	465
Total Marriages	1,305
Deaths	2,063
Total Catholic Population	209,426
Total Population	831,042

Former Bishops—Most Rev. MICHAEL HEISS, D.D., cons. Sept. 6, 1868; appt. Titular Archbishop of Hadrianople, and coadjutor to the Metropolitan of Milwaukee March 14, 1880; promoted to Milwaukee, Sept. 1881; died March 26, 1890.—Rt. Rev. KILIAN CASPAR FLASCH, D.D., cons. Aug. 24, 1881; died Aug. 3, 1891.—Rt. Rev. JAMES SCHWEBACH, D.D., cons. Feb. 25, 1892; died June 6, 1921.—Most Rev. ALEXANDER J. MCGAVICK, D.D., LL.D., cons. Titular Bishop of Marcopolis and Auxiliary Bishop of Chicago, May 1, 1899; transferred to See of La Crosse, Nov. 21, 1921; died Aug. 25, 1948.—Most Rev. JOHN P. TREACY, S.T.D., cons. Titular Bishop of Metelis and Coadjutor of La Crosse "cum jure successionis," Oct. 2, 1945; succeeded to the See, July 23, 1946; died Oct. 11, 1964.—Most Rev. FREDERICK W. FREKING, D.D., J.C.D., cons. Bishop of Salina, KS, November 30, 1957; transferred to the See of La Crosse, Dec. 30, 1964; installed La Crosse, Feb. 24, 1965; retired May 10, 1983; died Nov. 28, 1998.—Most Rev. JOHN J. PAUL, D.D., appt. Titular Bishop of Lambese and Auxiliary Bishop of La Crosse, May 17, 1977; cons. Aug. 4, 1977; appt. to the Residential See of La Crosse, Oct. 18, 1983; installed as Bishop of La Crosse, Dec. 5, 1983; retired Dec. 10, 1994.

Vicar General—Very Rev. JOSEPH J. RAFACZ S.T.L., *Mary Mother of the Church Parish, 2006 Weston St., La Crosse, 54601.*

Chancery Office—3710 East Ave. S., P.O. Box 4004, La Crosse, 54602-4004. Tel: 608-788-7700; Fax: 608-788-8413. Office Hours: Mon.-Fri. 8-4:30.

Chancellor—Sr. MARLENE WEISENBECK, F.S.P.A., J.C.L.

Vice-Chancellor—Rev. LEON A. POWELL.

Moderator of the Curia—Rev. MICHAEL J. GORMAN, J.C.L.

Secretary to the Bishop—Rev. RICHARD W. GILLES, J.C.L.

Archivist—Sr. MARLENE WEISENBECK, F.S.P.A., J.C.L.

Assistant Archivist—Rev. ROBERT T. ALTMANN.

Finance Officer—SONDRA RIEDER.

Ecclesiastical Notaries—Revs. RICHARD W. GILLES; MICHAEL J. GORMAN; LEON A. POWELL; Sr. MARLENE WEISENBECK, F.S.P.A.; KELLY MCCARTHY; SHERYL STAPLETON; SUSAN VLASAK, *P.O. Box 4004, La Crosse, 54602-4004.*

Diocesan Tribunal—3710 East Ave. S., P.O. Box 4004, La Crosse, 54602-4004. Tel: 608-788-7700. (Address all rogatory commissions to the Chancellor).

Judicial Vicar—Very Rev. ROBERT P. HUNDT, J.C.L.

Promoter of Justice—GEORGE E. NIX, J.C.L.

Defensores Vinculi—Sr. MARLENE WEISENBECK, F.S.P.A., J.C.L.; GEORGE E. NIX, J.C.L.
Auditors—GEORGE E. NIX, J.C.L.; SHERYL STAPLETON.
Diocesan Judges—Revs. MICHAEL J. GORMAN, J.C.L.; RICHARD W. GILLES, J.C.L.

College of Consultors—Very Revs. JOSEPH J. RAFACZ, V.G.; ROBERT J. COOK; Revs. WILLIAM N. GREVATCH; EUGENE A. KLINK; JOHN L. PARR; MARK R. PIERCE; ROGER J. SCHECKEL; MICHAEL J. GORMAN, Sec.

Deans—Very Rev. LEONARD G. KAISER, Arcadia; Very Rev. WILLIAM P. FELLIX, Chippewa Falls; Very Rev. THOMAS J. DONALDSON, Durand; Very Rev. PAUL R. GITTER, Eau Claire; Very Rev. ROGER J. SCHECKEL, La Crosse; Very Rev. CHARLES D. STOETZEL, Marshfield; Very Rev. G. RICHARD ROBERTS, Mauston; Very Rev. EUGENE J. WOLF, Prairie du Chien; Very Rev. WAYNE R. KIDD, Richland Center; Very Rev. JAMES P. MCNAMEE, Sparta; Very Rev. DONALD L. PRZYBYLSKI, Stevens Point; Very Rev. ROMAN F. KAISER, Thorp; Very Rev. WILLIAM N. GREVATCH, Wausau; Very Rev. R. JOHN SWING, Wisconsin Rapids.

Diocesan Offices and Directors

Apostolate for the Indians—Vacant.

Boy Scouts—Rev. ANTHONY J. WOLF, *112 E. 11th St., Marshfield, 54449-4216.* Tel: 715-384-3213.

Building Commission—CHRISTOPHER CARSTENS; Very Rev. J. FLOYD DWYER; Revs. ALLAN L. SLOWIAK; MICHAEL J. GORMAN; Sr. MARLENE WEISENBECK, F.S.P.A.; SONDRA RIEDER; DONALD NOVOTNEY.

Catholic Women, Council of—Rev. DONALD M. BERG, Moderator, *207 N. Third Ave., P.O. Box 386, Edgar, 54426-0386.* Tel: 715-352-3444.

Central Wisconsin Hispanic Ministry—P.O. Box 4004, La Crosse, 54602-4004. Tel: 608-788-7700.

Department of Catholic Education—ROBERT J. LECHELER, Dir. Catechesis & Evangelization; VIRGINIA HALBUR, Asst. Dir. Catechesis & Evangelization; DONALD F. NOVOTNEY, Dir. Schools; DIANA ROBERTS, Asst. Dir. Schools; BOUA NENG YANG, LaCrosse Area Hmong Catechist, *3710 East Ave. S., P.O. Box 4004, La Crosse, 54602-4004.* Tel: 608-788-7707.

Office of Family Life—SUE GILBERT, Dir., *P.O. Box 4004, La Crosse, 54602-4004.* Tel: 608-788-7700.
Natural Family Planning—Coordinators: JEFF HEINZEN; ALICE HEINZEN, *711 24th St. N.E., Menomonie, 54751.* Tel: 715-235-6226.

Holy Childhood Association—Very Rev. JOSEPH J. RAFACZ, Dir., *P.O. Box 4004, La Crosse, 54602-4004.* Tel: 608-788-7700.

Hospitals and Health Affairs—Co-Coordinators: Rev. EDMUND J. KLIMEK, *Sacred Heart Hospital, 900 W. Clairemont Ave., Eau Claire, 54701.* Tel: 715-839-4121. Rev. LAWRENCE G. DUNKLEE, *St. Charles Borromeo Parish, P.O. Box 292, Genoa, 54632.* Tel: 608-689-2646.

Newman Campus Ministry—Rev. MARK R. PIERCE, Co-ord., *1732 State St., La Crosse, 54601.* Tel: 608-784-4994.

Office of Communications and Public Relations—ROSE A. HAMMES, Dir., *P.O. Box 4004, La Crosse, 54602-4004.* Tel: 608-788-7700.

Office of the Consecrated Life—Sr. MARLENE WEISENBECK, F.S.P.A., Dir., *P.O. Box 4004, La Crosse, 54602-4004.* Tel: 608-788-7700.

Office of Ecumenism—Rev. STEVEN J. BRICE, Diocesan Officer, Ecumenical Questions, *110 N. 6th St., Wausau, 54401.* Tel: 715-675-9749.

Office of Justice and Peace—Dr. ARTHUR HIPPLER, Dir., *P.O. Box 4004, La Crosse, 54602-4004.* Tel: 608-788-7700. Justice and Peace Commission Office.

Office of Ministries—Rev. ERIC R. BERNS, Dir., *P.O. Box 4004, La Crosse, 54602-4004.* Tel: 608-788-7700. Office of Ministries consists of Vocation Office, Permanent Diaconate, Lay Ministries & Clergy Continuing Education.

Office for Pastoral Planning—Vacant, Dir., *P.O. Box 4004, La Crosse, 54602-4004.* Tel: 608-788-7700.

Office of Sacred Worship—Rev. MICHAEL GORMAN, Acting Dir.; Mr. CHRISTOPHER CARSTENS, Asst. Dir., *P.O. Box 4004, La Crosse, 54602-4004.* Tel: 608-788-7700. Sacred Worship Commission-confer Office.

Office of Youth Ministry—DENNIS KURTZ, Dir., *P.O. Box 1062, Eau Claire, 54702-1062.* Tel: 715-834-7079.

Pastoral Council—Most Rev. RAYMOND L. BURKE, Pres.; Very Rev. JOSEPH J. RAFACZ, V.G., Exec. Sec., *P.O. Box 4004, La Crosse, 54602-4004.* Tel: 608-788-7700.

Personnel Council—Most Rev. RAYMOND L. BURKE, Pres.; Revs. WILLIAM G. MENZEL, Chm.; DAVID C. KUNZ, Sec.; Very Revs. THOMAS J. DONALDSON; JOSEPH J. RAFACZ, V.G.; Revs. ERIC R. BERNS; LAWRENCE G. DUNKLEE; MICHAEL J. GORMAN; T. MICHAEL SCHELBLE; LYLE L. SCHULTE, *P.O. Box 4004, La Crosse, 54602-4004.* Tel: 608-788-7700.

Presbyteral Council—Most Rev. RAYMOND L. BURKE, Pres. Elected Members: Revs. ANDREW K. KAROBLIS; ALBERT W. SONNBERGER; JOHN A. WISNESKI; THOMAS J. RUDOLPH; CHARLES J. HIEBL; THOMAS J. DONALDSON; ALLAN L. SLOWIAK; MARK R. PIERCE; FRANK CORRADI; JOHN T. MCHUGH; ARNOLD F. REUTER; BERNARD MCCOY, O.Cist.
Ex Officio Members—Very Rev. JOSEPH J. RAFACZ, V.G.; Rev. MICHAEL J. GORMAN, Moderator of the Curia. Consultors: Very Revs. ROBERT J. COOK; WILLIAM N. GREVATCH; ROGER J. SCHECKEL; Revs. EUGENE A. KLINK; JOHN L. PARR.

Propagation of the Faith—Very Rev. JOSEPH J. RAFACZ, V.G., Dir., *P.O. Box 4004, La Crosse, 54602-4004.* Tel: 608-788-7700.

Rural Life Conference and Community Development—P.O. Box 4004, La Crosse, 54602-4004. Tel: 608-788-7700.

St. Joseph's Priest Fund, Inc., (Benevolent Society)—Rev. MICHAEL J. GORMAN, Exec. Sec., *P.O. Box 4004, La Crosse, 54602-4004.* Tel: 608-788-7700.

"Times Review": Diocesan Newspaper—THOMAS A. SZYSZKIEWICZ, Editor, *P.O. Box 4004, La Crosse, 54602-4004.* Tel: 608-788-1524.

CLERGY, PARISHES, MISSIONS AND PAROCHIAL SCHOOLS

CITY OF LA CROSSE
(La Crosse County)

1—ST. JOSEPH THE WORKMAN CATHEDRAL, Very Rev. Robert J. Cook, Rector.
Res., 530 Main St., 54601. Tel: 608-782-0322; Fax: 608-782-8228. [CEM 2]
School—Coulee Catholic Schools. See Unified Catholic School Systems under Institutions Located in the Diocese.

2—BLESSED SACRAMENT, Very Rev. Robert P. Hundt; Rev. John A. Potaczek.
Res., 130 Losey Blvd. S., 54601. Tel: 608-782-2953; Fax: 608-785-1064. [CEM 2]
School—Coulee Catholic Schools. See Unified Catholic School Systems under Institutions Located in the Diocese.

3—HOLY CROSS. Closed. For inquiries for parish records contact St. Joseph the Workman Cathedral, La Crosse.

4—HOLY TRINITY, Rev. Lawrence B. Berger.
Res., 1333 S. 13th St., 54601. Tel: 608-782-2028. [CEM 2]
School—Coulee Catholic Schools. See Unified Catholic School Systems under Institutions Located in the Diocese.

5—ST. JAMES THE LESS, Rev. Roger J. Scheckel. In res., Rev. John Kowalski (Poland).
Res., 1032 Caledonia St., 54603. Tel: 608-782-7557; Fax: 608-796-0086. [CEM 2]
School—Coulee Catholic Schools. See Unified Catholic School Systems under Institutions Located in the Diocese.

6—ST. JOHN THE BAPTIST. Closed. For inquiries for parish records contact St. James, La Crosse.

7—ST. MARY. Closed. For inquiries for parish records contact St. Joseph the Workman Cathedral, La Crosse.

8—ST. PIUS X. Closed. For inquiries for parish records contact Mary, Mother of the Church, La Crosse.

9—MARY, MOTHER OF THE CHURCH, Very Rev. Joseph J. Rafacz, V.G.
Res., 2006 Weston St., 54601. Tel: 608-788-5483; Fax: 608-788-4070. [CEM 4]
School—Coulee Catholic Schools. See Unified Catholic School Systems under Institutions Located in the Diocese.

10—RONCALLI NEWMAN PARISH, Rev. Mark R. Pierce.
Res., 1732 State St., 54601. Tel: 608-784-4994; Fax: 608-784-0230.

11—ST. THOMAS MORE. Closed. For inquiries for parish records contact Mary, Mother of the Church, La Crosse.

12—ST. WENCESLAUS. Closed. For inquiries for parish records contact St. Joseph the Workman Cathedral, La Crosse.

OUTSIDE THE CITY OF LA CROSSE

Abbotsford, Clark Co., St. Bernard. Attended by Holy Rosary, Owen. Rev. Allen F. Jakubowski; Sr. Mary Jo Donaldson, O.S.B., Pastoral Assoc.
Res., 101 W. Cedar St., 54405-9558. Tel: 715-223-3331. [JC]

Adams, Adams Co., St. Joseph. Also serves St. Ann, Brooks. Rev. Dennis P. Stanchik; Deacon David Kennedy (MIL).
Res., Box 310, 53910. Tel: 608-339-3485; Fax: 608-339-0225. [CEM]

Alma, Buffalo Co., St. Lawrence. Also serves St. Boniface, Waumandee. Rev. John W. Steiner.
Res., P.O. Box 246, 54610. Tel: 608-685-3253; Fax: 608-685-3253.

Alma Center, Jackson Co., Immaculate Conception. Attended by St. Joseph, Fairview. Rev. David A. Ziegelmaier.
Mailing Address: Box 188, 54611. Tel: 715-964-5201.
Res., N13740 Fairview Rd., Fairchild, 54741-8514. Tel: 715-334-2202. [CEM]

Almond, Portage Co., Holy Guardian Angels. Closed. For inquiries for parish records contact St. Maximilian Maria Kolbe, Southeastern Portage County.

Altdorf, Wood Co., St. Joseph. Closed. For inquiries for parish records contact St. Joachim, Pittsville.

Altoona, Eau Claire Co., St. Mary, Rev. Norbert J. Wilger.
Res., 1827 Lynn Ave., 54720. Tel: 715-835-8813; Fax: 715-855-8664. [JC]
School—Catholic Area Schools of the Eau Claire Deanery. See Unified Catholic School Systems under Institutions Located in the Diocese.

Amherst, Portage Co., St. James. Also serves St. Mary of Mount Carmel, Fancher. Rev. Robert F. Pedretti.
Res., 453 S. Main, Box 280, 54406-0280. Tel: 715-824-3455; Fax: 715-824-3455. [CEM]

Arcadia, Trempealeau Co., Holy Family, Rev. Patrick A. Umberger.
Res., 223 E. Maple St., 54612. Tel: 608-323-7116.
Our Lady of Perpetual Help. Closed. For inquiries for parish records contact Holy Family, Arcadia.
St. Stanislaus. Closed. For inquiries for parish records contact Holy Family, Arcadia.

Arkansaw, Pepin Co., St. Joseph, Rev. Matthew J. Molinaro.
Res., W. 7805 County Rd. Z, 54721. Tel: 715-285-5313. [CEM 2]

Arpin, Wood Co., St. Francis. Closed. For inquiries for parish records contact St. James, Vesper.

Athens, Marathon Co., St. Anthony de Padua. Also serves Holy Family, Poniatowski. Rev. Charles J. Hiebl.
Res., 417 Caroline St., Box 206, 54411-0206. Tel: 715-257-7684. [JC]
School—Tel: 715-257-7541.
Sisters 1; Lay Teachers 5; Students 90.

Auburndale, Wood Co., Nativity of the Blessed Virgin Mary. Also serves St. Michael, Hewitt. Rev. T. Michael Schelble.
Res., 5866 Main St., P.O. Box 177, 54412-0177. Tel: 715-652-2806; Fax: 715-652-8020. [CEM 2]
School—Tel: 715-652-2196; Fax: 715-652-8020.
Franciscan Sisters of Perpetual Adoration, F.S.P.A. 1; Sisters of Notre Dame 1; Lay Teachers 6; Students 70.

Augusta, Eau Claire Co., St. Anthony de Padua. Closed. For inquiries for Parish Records contact St. Raymond of Penafort, Southeastern Eau Claire County.

Babcock, Wood Co., All Saints. Closed. For inquiries for Parish Records contact Sacred Heart of Jesus, Nekoosa.

Bakerville, Wood Co., Corpus Christi. Attended by Sacred Heart, Marshfield. Rev. Anthony J. Wolf. In res., Rev. Charles P. Schumacher Tel: 715-676-2824.
Mailing Address: 10075 Hwy. BB, Marshfield, 54449. Tel: 715-676-3658.
Res., 112 E. 11th St., Marshfield, 54449-4216. Tel: 715-384-3213. [CEM]

Bangor, La Crosse Co., St. Mary. Attended by St. Leo the Great, West Salem. Rev. Robert S. Hegenbarth. In res., Rev. Paul L. Sankoorikal.
Mailing Address: 210 W. Hamlin St., West Salem, 54669. Tel: 608-786-0610. [CEM]
Res., P.O. Box 290, 54614-0290. Tel: 608-486-2033.

Bear Valley, Richland Co., St. Kilian. Closed. For inquiries for parish records contact Nativity, B.V.M., Keyesville.

Bevent, Marathon Co., St. Ladislaus. Attended by St. Joseph, Galloway. Rev. Rex A. Zimmerman; Sr. Mary Ellen Diermeier, S.S.J.-T.O.S.F., Pastoral Assoc.
Mailing Address: 6455 State Hwy. 153, Hatley, 54440. Tel: 715-446-3060; Fax: 715-446-2668. [CEM]

Big River, Pierce Co., Nativity of the Blessed Virgin Mary, Rev. John W. Beckfelt.
Res., W10137 570th Ave., River Falls, 54022. Tel: 715-425-5806. [CEM 2]

Black River Falls, Jackson Co., St. Joseph, Rev. Michael C. Braun.
Res., 507 Main St., 54615-1699. Tel: 715-284-5613. [CEM]

Blair, Trempealeau Co., St. Ansgar. Attended by St. John the Apostle, Whitehall. Rev. James Arthur.
Mailing Address: 35900 Lee St., Whitehall, 54773. Tel: 715-538-4607; Fax: 715-538-2224.

Blenker, Wood Co., St. Kilian. Attended by St. Wenceslaus, Milladore. Rev. John A. Wisneski.
Mailing Address: Box 100, Milladore, 54454. Tel: 715-457-2314. [CEM]

Bloomer, Chippewa Co., St. Paul. Also serves St. Jude, New Auburn. Rev. Norman D. Boneck.
Res., 1222 Main St., 54724. Tel: 715-568-3255. [CEM 3]
School—1210 Main St., 54724. Tel: 715-568-3233; Fax: 715-568-3244.
Sisters 2; Lay Teachers 11; Students 189.
Convent—1205 13th Ave., 54724. Tel: 715-568-3266.

Boyceville, Dunn Co., St. Luke. Attended by St. Joseph, Menomonie. Rev. Lyle L. Schulte; Sr. Judith Kramer, O.S.B., Min.
Mailing Address: 919 Center St., P.O. Box 316, 54725. Tel: 715-232-4922.
Res., St. Bede Monastery, P.O. Box 66, Eau Claire, 54702-0066. Tel: 715-834-3176; Fax: 715-834-4292. [JC]

Boyd, Chippewa Co., Sacred Heart of Jesus-St. Joseph. Attended by Holy Family, Stanley. Rev. Robert W. Nelson. In res., Rev. Eugene P. Smith Tel: 714-667-3038.
Res., 719 Patten St., P.O. Box 10, 54726-0010. Tel: 715-667-3341. [CEM 2]
School—Tel: 715-667-3346.
Lay Teachers 7; Students 75.

Brackett, Eau Claire Co., Holy Guardian Angels. Closed. For inquiries for Parish Records contact St. Raymond of Penafort, Southeastern Eau Claire County.

Brooks, Adams Co., St. Ann. Attended by St. Joseph, Adams. Rev. Dennis P. Stanchik.
Mailing Address: P.O. Box 132, Oxford, 53952. Tel: 608-584-4900. [CEM]

Buena Vista, Portage Co., St. Martin. Closed. For inquiries for parish records contact St. Maximilian Maria Kolbe, Southeastern Portage County.

Cadott, Chippewa Co., St. Rose of Lima. Also serves St. Anthony, Drywood. Rev. Thomas F. Crowley.
Res., Box 160, 54727. Tel: 715-289-4551. [CEM]
School—Tel: 715-289-4985.
Lay Teachers 6; Students 48.

Camp Douglas, Juneau Co., St. James. Also serves St. Michael, Indian Creek. Rev. William J. Blazewicz.
Res., Box 289, 54618. Tel: 608-427-6762. [CEM]

Cashton, Monroe Co., Sacred Heart of Jesus. Attended by Nativity of the Blessed Virgin Mary, St, Mary's Ridge. Revs. Joseph W. Hirsch Tel: 608-654-7619; Scott A. Bauer.
Res., 26400 CTH U, 54619-9757. Tel: 608-823-7906; Fax: 608-823-7272. [CEM 3]
School—Sacred Heart of Jesus School, 1223 Front St., 54619. Tel: 608-654-7733; Fax: 608-654-7733.
Lay Teachers 7; Students 59.

Cassel, Marathon Co., Sacred Heart. Also serves St. Patrick, Halder. Rev. Joseph Batkiewicz.
Res., 3372 County Rd. S., Marathon City, 54448. Tel: 715-443-3675. [CEM]

Cazenovia, Richland Co., St. Anthony de Padua. Also serves Sacred Heart, Lone Rock; and St. Mary, Keyesville. Rev. Daniel J. Kiedinger.
Res., Rte. 2, Box 175, 53924. Tel: 608-983-2367. [CEM]
School—Tel: 608-983-2786.
Lay Teachers 4; Students 34.

Chili, Clark Co., St. Stephen. Closed. For inquiries for Parish Records contact St. Mary's Parish, Neillsville, WI.

Chippewa Falls, Chippewa Co., Holy Ghost. Also serves St. Bridget, Springfield. Revs. Edmund J. Doerre; Charles J. Scherman, S.J.
Res., 412 S. Main St., 54729. Tel: 715-723-4890; Fax: 715-723-7358. [JC]
School—Chippewa Falls Area Catholic Schools. See Unified Catholic School Systems under Institutions Located in the Diocese.

Notre Dame, Rev. Jerome R. Robinson. In res., Rev. Brian J. Jazdzewski.
Res., 117 Allen St., 54729-2899. Tel: 715-723-7108; Fax: 715-723-7523. [JC]
School—Chippewa Falls Area Catholic Schools. See Unified Catholic School Systems under Institutions Located in the Diocese.

St. Charles Borromeo. Also serves St. John the Baptist, Cooks Valley; St. Peter, Tilden. Revs. William P. Felix; Eric G. Linzmaier.
Res., 810 Pearl St., 54729. Tel: 715-723-4088; Fax: 715-723-2195. [JC]
School—Chippewa Falls Area Catholic Schools. See Unified Catholic School Systems under Institutions Located in the Diocese.

Colby, Clark Co., St. Mary Help of Christians, Rev. John E. Malik.
Res., 205 S. 2nd St., P.O. Box 436, 54421. Tel: 715-223-3048; Fax: 715-223-0223. [CEM]
School—Tel: 715-223-3033; Fax: 715-223-0223.
Lay Teachers 12; Students 126.

Cooks Valley, Chippewa Co., St. John the Baptist. Attended by St. Charles Borromeo, Chippewa Falls. Revs. William P. Felix; Eric G. Linzmaier.
Mailing Address: 4540 State Hwy. 40, Bloomer, 54724. Tel: 715-568-3778.
Res., 810 Pearl St., Chippewa Falls, 54729. Tel: 715-723-4088. [CEM]

Coon Valley, Vernon Co., St. Mary, Rev. Zbigniew Kucharski (Poland).
Res., 904 Central Ave., 54623. Tel: 608-452-3841; Fax: 608-452-3841. [CEM]

Cornell, Chippewa Co., Holy Cross. Also serves Sacred Heart, Jim Falls. Rev. Jeremiah Cashman.
Res., 107 S. 8th St., P.O. Box 68, 54732. Tel: 715-239-6826. [CEM 2]

Custer, Portage Co., Immaculate Conception, Rev. Robert A. Schaller.
Res., 800 4th St., Stevens Point, 54481. Tel: 715-544-6115. [CEM]
Parish Address: 7176 Co. Q, 54432. Tel: 715-592-4330.

Czestochowa, Clark Co., St. Mary of Czestochowa. Closed. For inquiries for parish records contact Holy Family, Stanley.

De Soto, Crawford Co., Sacred Heart. Closed. For inquiries for parish records contact St. Charles Borromeo, Genoa.

Dilly, Vernon Co., St. John Nepomucene. Closed. For inquiries for parish records contact St. Aloysius, Hillsboro.

Dorchester, Clark Co., St. Louis, Rev. James F. Schaefer.
Res., 133 N. 3rd St., 54425-9577. Tel: 715-654-5089. [JC]
School—134 N. 4th St., 54425. Tel: 715-654-5467.
Lay Teachers 4; Students 21.

Drywood, Chippewa Co., St. Anthony. Attended by St. Rose of Lima, Cadott. Rev. Thomas F. Crowley; Deacon Bob Anderson.
Res., P.O. Box 68, Jim Falls, 54748. Tel: 715-382-4422. [CEM]

Durand, Pepin Co., St. Mary's Assumption. Served from Holy Rosary, Lima. Deacon James Weingart.
Mailing Address: 911 W. Prospect St., P.O. Box 188, 54736-1049. Tel: 715-672-5640; Fax: 715-672-4193. [CEM]
Res., N6235 CTH V, 54736.
School—901 W. Prospect St., 54736. Tel: 715-672-5617; Fax: 715-672-3931.
Lay Teachers 10; Students 132.

Eastman, Crawford Co., St. Wenceslaus, Rev. John V. Cassidy.
Res., P.O. Box 109, 54626. Tel: 608-874-4151. [CEM]

Eau Claire, Eau Claire Co.,

1—Immaculate Conception, Rev. Eugene A. Klink.
Res., 1712 Highland Ave., 54701. Tel: 715-835-9935; Fax: 715-835-9459.
School—Catholic Area Schools of the Eau Claire Deanery. See Unified Catholic School Systems under Institutions Located in the Diocese.

2—Newman Community, Revs. George R. Szews; Edmund J. Klimek; Thomas J. Krieg.
Res., 110 Garfield Ave., 54701-4042. Tel: 715-834-3399. [JC]

3—Sacred Heart of Jesus. Merged with St. Patrick, Eau Claire to form Sacred Heart of Jesus-St. Patrick, Eau Claire. For inquiries for parish records contact Sacred Heart of Jesus-St. Patrick, Eau Claire.

4—Sacred Heart of Jesus-St. Patrick. Attended by St. Raymond of Penafort, Fall Creek. Very Rev. Paul R. Gitter; Rev. Kurt J. Apfelbeck; Deacon Larry Agema.
318 Fulton St., 54703-5399. Tel: 715-832-0925; Fax: 715-835-4658. [CEM 2]
Res., 510444 Hwy. 53, Fall Creek, 54742.

5—St. James the Greater, Rev. John A. Schultz.
Res., 2502 Eleventh St., 54703-2700. Tel: 715-835-5887; Fax: 715-835-3110. [JC]
School—Catholic Area Schools of the Eau Claire Deanery. See Unified Catholic School Systems under Institutions Located in the Diocese.

6—St. Olaf, Rev. Frank Corradi, S.C.
Res., 2408 North Ln., 54703-0960. Tel: 715-832-2504; Fax: 715-832-0742. [JC]
School—Catholic Area Schools of the Eau Claire Deanery. See Unified Catholic School Systems under Institutions Located in the Diocese.

7—St. Patrick. Merged with Sacred Heart of Jesus, Eau Claire to form Sacred Heart of Jesus-St. Patrick, Eau Claire. For inquiries for parish records contact Sacred Heart of Jesus-St. Patrick, Eau Claire.

Eau Galle, Dunn Co., St. Henry, Rev. Roy L. Mish.
Res., N. 460 CTH D, 54737. Tel: 715-283-4448. [CEM]

Edgar, Marathon Co., St. John the Baptist, Rev. Bernard L. Raschke; Deacon Herman Schulz.
Res., 103 N. Fourth Ave., P.O. Box 35, 54426. Tel: 715-352-3011; Fax: 715-352-3011. [CEM]
School—Tel: 715-352-3000.
Lay Teachers 10; Students 132.

Edson, Chippewa Co., Sacred Heart of Jesus. Merged with St. Joseph, Boyd to form Sacred Heart of Jesus-St. Joseph, Boyd.

Elk Mound, Dunn Co., St. Joseph, Rev. Henry R. Hoerburger.
Res., P.O. Box 275, 54739. Tel: 715-879-5332. [CEM]

Ellsworth, Pierce Co., St. Francis of Assisi, Very Rev. Thomas J. Donaldson.
Res., 264 S. Grant St., P.O. Box 839, 54011. Tel: 715-273-4066; Fax: 715-723-4060. [CEM]
School—Box 250, 54011. Tel: 715-273-4391.
Sisters of St. Benedict 1; Lay Teachers 8; Students 158.

Elmwood, Pierce Co., Sacred Heart. Also serves Sacred Heart of Jesus, Spring Valley. Rev. Varkey V. Joseph, S.A.C. (India).
114 W. Wilson Ave., 54740. Tel: 715-639-2741; Fax: 715-639-6031. [CEM]

Elroy, Juneau Co., St. Patrick. Attended by St. Joseph, Kendall. Very Rev. James P. McNamee.
Res., 307 Spring St., Box 155, Kendall, 54638. Tel: 608-462-5875; Fax: 608-462-5876. [CEM]

Ettrick, Trempealeau Co., St. Bridget. Also serves St. Kevin, Melrose. Rev. Thomas J. McInnis.
Res., 22650 Washington St., 54627. Tel: 608-525-3811. [CEM]

Fairchild, Eau Claire Co., St. John Cantius. Attended by St. Joseph, Fairview. Rev. David A. Ziegelmaier.
Res., N13740 Fairview Rd., 54741-8514. Tel: 715-334-2202.

Fairview, Eau Claire Co., St. Joseph. Also serves Immaculate Conception, Alma Center; and St. John Cantius, Fairchild. Rev. David A. Ziegelmaier.
Res., N13740 Fairview Rd., Fairchild, 54741-8514. Tel: 715-334-2202.

Fall Creek, Eau Claire Co., St. John the Apostle. Closed. For inquiries for Parish Records contact St. Raymond of Penafort, Southeastern Eau Claire Country.

St. Raymond of Penafort. Also serves Sacred Heart-St. Patrick, Eau Claire. Revs. Paul R. Gitter; Kurt J. Apfelbeck.
S10444 Hwy. 53, 54732. Tel: 715-878-4183. [CEM]

Fancher, Portage Co., St. Mary of Mount Carmel. Attended by St. James, Amherst. Rev. Robert F. Pedretti.
Res., P.O. Box 280, 453 S. Main St., Amherst, 54406. Tel: 715-824-3455; Fax: 715-824-3455. [CEM]

Fountain City, Buffalo Co., Immaculate Conception, Rev. Douglas C. Robertson.
Res., One Wall St., P.O. Box 218, 54629-0218. Tel: 608-687-3496. [CEM]

Galesville, Trempealeau Co., St. Mary. Attended by St. Bartholomew, Trempealeau. Rev. Robert J. Wagner.
Mailing Address: 20354 W. Ridge Ave., P.O. Box 68, 54630-0068. Tel: 608-582-2365.
Res., 11646 South St., Trempealeau, 54461-8238. Tel: 608-534-9760.

Galloway, Marathon Co., St. Joseph. Also serves St. Ladislaus, Bevent. Rev. Rex A. Zimmerman; Sr. Mary Ellen Diermeier, S.S.J.-T.O.S.F., Pastoral Assoc.
Res., 8846 CTH C, Wittenberg, 54499-8936. Tel: 715-454-6431. [CEM]

Gays Mills, Crawford Co., St. Mary. Also serves St. Philip, Rolling Ground. Rev. Thomas E. Langer.
Res., 115 E. School St., 54631. Tel: 608-735-4420. [JC]

Genoa, Vernon Co., St. Charles Borromeo, Rev. Lawrence G. Dunklee.
Res., P.O. Box 130, 54632. Tel: 608-689-2646; Fax: 608-689-2811. [CEM]
School—Tel: 608-689-2642.
Lay Teachers 6; Students 61.

Germantown, Juneau Co., Our Lady of the Lake. Attended by St. Paul, New Lisbon. Rev. Steven H. Baures.
Res., 408 W. River St., New Lisbon, 53950. Tel: 608-562-3125. [CEM]

Greenwood, Clark Co., St. Mary Help of Christians. Also serves Holy Family, Willard. Rev. A. Joseph Follmar.
Res., 123 N. Main St., P.O. Box 129, 54437. Tel: 715-267-6282. [CEM]
School—Tel: 715-267-6477.
Lay Teachers 3; Students 52.

Halder, Marathon Co., St. Patrick. Attended by Sacred Heart, Cassel. Rev. Joseph Batkiewicz.
Mailing Address: 3158 Halder Dr., Mosinee, 54455. Tel: 715-693-2765. [CEM]
Res., Sacred Heart Rectory, 3372 County Rd. S., Marathon City, 54448-0068. Tel: 715-443-3675.

Hatley, Marathon Co., St. Florian, Rev. Thomas J. Abraham.
Res., 500 Church Ln., P.O. Box 100, 54440. Tel: 715-446-2252; 446-3085 (Office). [CEM]
School—Tel: 715-446-3950.
Lay Teachers 5; Students 72.

Heffron, Portage Co., St. John the Baptist. Closed. For inquiries for parish records contact St. Maximilian Maria Kolbe, Southeastern Portage County.

Hewitt, Wood Co., St. Michael. Attended by St. Mary, Auburndale. Rev. T. Michael Schelble.
Office: 11086 Main St., 54441. Tel: 715-384-7676; Fax: 715-384-7675.
Res., 5866 Main St., Box 177, Auburndale, 54412. Tel: 715-652-2806; Fax: 715-652-8020. [JC]

Hillsboro, Vernon Co., St. Aloysius, Rev. Wayne R. Kidd.
Res., 545 Prairie Ave., P.O. Box 466, 54634. Tel: 608-489-2580. [JC]

Holmen, La Crosse Co., St. Elizabeth Ann Seton, Rev. Delbert J. Malin; Sr. Bridget Donaldson, O.S.B., Pastoral Assoc.
Office: 515 N. Main St., 54636. Tel: 608-526-4424; Fax: 608-526-3177.
Res., 704 Hillcrest Dr., 54636.

Independence, Trempealeau Co., SS. Peter and Paul. Also serves St. Michael, North Creek. Very Rev. Leonard G. Kaiser.
Res., 36028 Osseo Rd., P.O. Box 428, 54747-0428. Tel: 715-985-2227; Fax: 715-985-5288. [CEM]
School—Tel: 715-985-3719.
Lay Teachers 10; Students 136.

Indian Creek, Monroe Co., St. Michael. Attended by St. James, Camp Douglas. Rev. William J. Blazewicz.
Mailing Address: P.O. Box 289, Camp Douglas, 54618. Tel: 608-427-6762. [CEM]

Jim Falls, Chippewa Co., Sacred Heart. Attended by Holy Cross, Cornell. Rev. Jeremiah Cashman; Deacon Bob Anderson.
Res., Box 68, 54748. Tel: 715-382-4422.

Junction City, Portage Co., St. Michael. Attended by St. Wenceslaus, Milladore. Rev. John A. Wisneski.
Res., P.O. Box 100, Milladore, 54454. Tel: 715-457-2314. [CEM]

Kendall, Monroe Co., St. Joseph. Also serves St. Patrick, Elroy, and St. John the Baptist, Wilton. Very Rev. James P. McNamee.
Res., 307 Spring St., P.O. Box 155, 54638. Tel: 608-463-7120. [CEM]

Keyesville, Richland Co., Nativity of the Blessed Virgin Mary. Attended by St. Anthony, Cazenovia. Rev. Daniel J. Kiedinger.
Mailing Address: 32605 Durst Ln., Richland Center, 53581. Tel: 608-585-4846. [CEM]
Res., 32505 Hwy. V, Cazenovia, 53924. Tel: 608-983-2367.

Knowlton, Marathon Co., St. Francis Xavier. Also serves St. John the Baptist, Peplin. Rev. Joseph A. Grassl.
Res., 651 Mead Ln., Mosinee, 54455. Tel: 715-693-3120. [CEM]

Lanark, Portage Co., St. Patrick. Closed. For inquiries for parish records contact St. Maximilian Maria Kolbe, Southeastern Portage County.

Lima, Pepin Co., Holy Rosary. Also serves St. Mary's Assumption, Durand and Sacred Heart of Jesus, Mondovi. Deacon James Weingart.
Res., N6235 CTH V, Durand, 54736.
Mailing Address: 911 W. Prospect St., Box 188, Durand, 54736-1048. Tel: 715-672-5640. [CEM]
School—Tel: 715-672-4276.
Lay Teachers 5; Students 74.

Lone Rock, Richland Co., Sacred Heart. Attended by St. Anthony, Cazenovia. Rev. Daniel J. Kiedinger.
Mailing Address: Rte. 2, Box 175, Cazenovia, 53924. Tel: 608-983-2367.

Loyal, Clark Co., St. Anthony of Padua, Very Rev. Roman F. Kaiser.
Res., 407 N. Division St., P.O. Box 69, 54446-0069. Tel: 715-255-8017; Fax: 715-255-8017. [CEM]
School—212 W. Spring St., Tel: 715-255-8636.
Lay Teachers 7; Students 57.

Lyndon Station, Juneau Co., St. Mary, Rev. Ronald T. Zinkle, S.J.
Res., 117 Juneau St. N., P.O. Box 303, 53944. Tel: 608-666-2421. [CEM]

Marathon City, Marathon Co., Nativity of the Blessed Virgin Mary, Revs. Joseph Diermeier, O.F.M.Cap.; Robert Thorn, O.F.M. Cap.
Res., 712 Market St., Box 7, 54448-0007. Tel: 715-443-2045; Fax: 715-443-3045. [CEM]
School—Tel: 715-443-3430.
Franciscan Sisters of Perpetual Adoration 1; Lay Teachers 15; Students 241.

Marshfield, Wood Co., Our Lady of Peace, Very Rev. James J. Logan.
Res., 1414 W. 5th St., 54449. Tel: 715-384-9414; Fax: 715-384-6606. [JC]
School—1300 W. 5th St., 54449. Tel: 715-384-5474; Fax: 715-387-8697.
Sisters of Notre Dame 2; Lay Teachers 20; Students 257.

Sacred Heart of Jesus. Also serves Corpus Christi, Bakerville. Rev. Anthony J. Wolf.
Res., 112 E. 11th St., 54449-4216. Tel: 715-384-3213. [JC]
School—1117 S. Central Ave., 54449. Tel: 715-384-3939.
Lay Teachers 4; Students 34.

St. John the Baptist. Also serves Christ the King, Spencer. Revs. Charles D. Stoetzel; Todd A. Misna. In res., Rev. Brian D. Konopa.
Res., 201 W. Blodgett St., P.O. Box 644, 54449-0644. Tel: 715-384-3252; Fax: 715-384-5131. [JC]
School—Tel: 715-384-4989.
Lay Teachers 13; Students 210.

Mauston, Juneau Co., St. Patrick, Very Rev. G. Richard Roberts.
Res., 401 Mansion St., 53948-1393. Tel: 608-847-6054; Fax: 608-847-3288. [CEM 2]
School—325 Mansion St., 53948. Tel: 608-847-5844; Fax: 608-847-4103.
Lay Teachers 11; Students 198.

Melrose, Jackson Co., St. Kevin. Attended by St. Bridget, Ettrick. Rev. Thomas J. McInnis.
Mailing Address: St. Bridget, 22650 Washington, Ettrick, 54627. Tel: 608-525-3811. [JC]

Menomonie, Dunn Co., St. Joseph. Also serves St. Luke, Boyceville. Rev. Lyle L. Schulte.
Res., 910 Wilson Ave., 54751. Tel: 715-232-4922; Fax: 715-232-4923. [CEM]
School—Tel: 715-232-4920; Fax: 715-232-4923.
Lay Teachers 8; Students 141.

Middle Ridge, La Crosse Co., St. Peter. Also serves St. Joseph, St. Joseph Ridge. Rev. Robert T. Altmann.
Res., Box 101, W695 Hwy. 33, Rockland, 54653. Tel: 608-486-2180. [CEM]

Milan, Marathon Co., St. Thomas. Attended by St. John the Baptist, Wuerzburg. Rev. Leonard C. Stashek.
Mailing Address: 1506 Wuerzburg Rd., Athens, 54411. Tel: 715-257-7092. [CEM]

Mill Creek, Portage Co., St. Bartholomew. Attended by St. Stephen, Stevens Point. Rev. Daniel E. Kozlowski.
Res., 1401 Clark, Stevens Point, 54481. Tel: 715-344-3003. [CEM]

Milladore, Wood Co., St. Wenceslaus. Also serves St. Kilian, Blenker & St. Michael, Junction City. Rev. John A. Wisneski.
Res., 146 Main St., Box 100, 54454. Tel: 715-457-2314. [CEM]

Mondovi, Buffalo Co., Sacred Heart of Jesus. Attended by Holy Rosary, Lima. Deacon James Weingart.
Mailing Address: P.O. Box 188, Durand, 54736. Tel: 715-672-5640.
Res., N6235 CTH V, Durand, 54736. [CEM 2]

Mosinee, Marathon Co., St. Paul, Rev. Jerome G. Hoeser.
Res., 603 Fourth St., 54455. Tel: 715-693-2650; Fax: 715-693-1332. [CEM]
School—404 High St., 54455. Tel: 715-693-2675; Fax: 715-693-1332.
Lay Teachers 13; Students 156.

Necedah, Juneau Co., St. Francis of Assisi, Rev. James J. Lesczynski.
Res., 202 W. 5th St., 54646-8142. Tel: 608-565-2488. [CEM]
Church—Main at Sixth, 54646.

Neillsville, Clark Co., St. Mary, Rev. Joseph N. Henseler.
Res., 1813 Black River Rd., 54456. Tel: 715-743-3840; Fax: 715-743-3840. [CEM]

Nekoosa, Wood Co., Sacred Heart of Jesus. Also serves St. Alexander, Port Edwards. Very Rev. R. John Swing.
Res., 711 Prospect Ave., 54457. Tel: 715-886-3422; Fax: 715-886-4722. [JC]
School—Wisconsin Rapids Area Catholic Schools. See Unified Catholic School Systems under Institutions Located in the Diocese.

New Auburn, Chippewa Co., St. Jude. Attended by St. Paul, Bloomer. Rev. Norman D. Boneck.
Mailing Address: 1222 Main St., Bloomer, 54724. Tel: 715-568-3255; Fax: 715-568-3255. [JC]

New Lisbon, Juneau Co., St. Paul. Also serves Our Lady of the Lake, Germantown. Rev. Steven H. Baures.
Res., 408 W. River St., 53950. Tel: 608-562-3125. [CEM]

North Creek, Trempealeau Co., St. Michael. Attended by SS. Peter and Paul, Independence. Very Rev. Leonard G. Kaiser.
Mailing Address: 36028 Osseo Rd., Independence, 54747. Tel: 715-985-2227; Fax: 715-985-5288. [CEM]

Norwalk, Monroe Co., St. Augustine of Hippo. Attended by Nativity of the Blessed Virgin Mary, St. Mary's Ridge. Revs. Joseph W. Hirsch; Scott A. Bauer. In res., Rev. James H. Miller.
Res., 26400 CTH U, Cashton, 54619-9757. Tel: 608-823-7906; Fax: 608-823-7272. [CEM]

Onalaska, La Crosse Co., St. Patrick, Rev. William J. Matzek; Deacon Frank Abnet. In res., Rev. Edwin J. Thome.
Res., 1031 Main St., 54650. Tel: 608-783-5535.
School—Coulee Catholic Schools.
See Unified Catholic School Systems under Institutions Located in the Diocese.

Owen, Clark Co., Holy Rosary. Also serves St. Bernard, Abbotsford. Rev. Allen F. Jakubowski.
Res., 415 W. 3rd St., P.O. Box 309, 54460-0309. Tel: 715-229-2747.
School—Tel: 715-229-2348.
Lay Teachers 5; Students 53.

Peplin, Marathon Co., St. John the Baptist. Attended by St. Francis Xavier, Knowlton. Rev. Joseph A. Grassl. In res., Rev. Wladyslaw J. Kowalski (SUP).
Mailing Address: 651 Mead Ln., Mosinee, 54455. Tel: 715-693-3120. [CEM]

Pine Creek, Trempealeau Co., Most Sacred Heart, Rev. Robert F. Polcyn, O.F.M.Cap., Parochial Admin.
Res., N20555 CTH G, Dodge, 54625-9721. Tel: 608-539-3704. [CEM]

Pittsville, Wood Co., St. Joachim. Also serves St. James, Vesper and Holy Rosary, Sigel. Rev. James T. Benzmiller.
Res., 5312 Third Ave., P.O. Box 69, 54466-0069. Tel: 715-884-6815. [CEM]

Plover, Portage Co., St. Bronislava, Rev. James F. Trempe.
Res., 3200 Plover Rd., P.O. Box 158, 54467-0158. Tel: 715-344-4326; Fax: 715-344-6121. [CEM]
School—3301 Willow Dr., 54467. Tel: 715-342-2015; Fax: 715-342-2016.

Plum City, Pierce Co., St. John the Baptist, Rev. Ambrose J. Blenker.
Res., 212 Church Rd., P.O. Box 206, 54761-0206. Tel: 715-647-2301. [CEM]
School—Tel: 715-647-2901.
Lay Teachers 5; Students 50.

Polonia, Portage Co., Sacred Heart. Attended by St. Adalbert, Rosholt.
Res., 7375 Church St., Custer, 54423. Tel: 715-592-4221; Fax: 715-592-4189. [CEM]
School—7379 Church St., Custer, 54423. Tel: 715-592-4902.
Lay Teachers 4; Students 48.
Convent—7381 Church St., Custer, 54423. Tel: 715-592-4213.

Poniatowski, Marathon Co., Holy Family. Attended by St. Anthony de Padua, Athens. Rev. Charles J. Hiebl; Deacon LeRoy Knauf.
Mailing Address: R444 Hwy. U, Edgar, 54426. Tel: 715-352-3033. [CEM]

Port Edwards, Wood Co., St. Alexander, Very Rev. R. John Swing; Sr. Catherine Kaiser, F.S.P.A., Pastoral Assoc.
Church—880 First St., 54469. Tel: 715-887-3012; Fax: 715-887-3748.

Prairie du Chien, Crawford Co., St. Gabriel, Revs. William F. Gerut, S.J.; James B. Warosh, S.J.; John W. Wambach, S.J.
Office: 506 N. Beaumont Rd., P.O. Box 176, 53821-0176. Tel: 608-326-2404. [CEM 2]
School—Prairie Catholic Schools, 515 N. Beaumont Rd., 53821. Tel: 608-326-8624.
Lay Teachers 22; Students 323.

St. John Nepomucene, Revs. William F. Gerut, S.J.; James B. Warosh, S.J.; John W. Wambach, S.J.
Res., 710 S. Wacouta St., P.O. Box 28, 53821-0028. Tel: 608-326-6511; Fax: 608-326-4876.
School—Prairie Catholic Schools, 720 S. Wacouta St., 53821. Tel: 608-326-4400.

Prescott, Pierce Co., St. Joseph, Rev. Edward J. Shuttleworth.
Res., 269 Dakota St. S., P.O. Box 245, 54021-0245. Tel: 715-262-5310. [CEM]
School—281 Dakota St. S., 54021. Tel: 715-262-5912; Fax: 715-262-5912.
Franciscan Sisters of Perpetual Adoration 2; Lay Teachers 8; Students 189.
Convent—268 Dakota St. S., 54021. Tel: 715-262-5105.

Richland Center, Richland Co., St. Mary (Assumption of B.V.M.). Served from St. Aloysius, Hillsboro. Very Rev. Wayne R. Kidd; Rev. Emmanuel Famiyeh.

160 W. 4th St., P.O. Box 456, 53581. Tel: 608-647-2621; Fax: 608-647-6029. [CEM]
Res., P.O. Box 466, Hillsboro, 54634.
School—155 W. 5th St., 53581. Tel: 608-647-2422. Lay Teachers 12; Students 124.
Convent—789 N. Central Ave., 53581. Tel: 608-647-4933.

Rising Sun, Crawford Co., St. James. Closed. For inquiries for parish records contact St. Mary, Viroqua.

Rock Falls, Dunn Co., St. Joseph, Rev. Anton L. Lecheler.
Res., E. 9265 STH 85, Mondovi, 54755-8857. Tel: 715-875-4539. [CEM]

Rolling Ground, Crawford Co., St. Philip. Attended by St. Mary, Gays Mills. Rev. Thomas E. Langer.
Mailing Address: 115 E. School St., Gays Mills, 54631-0036. Tel: 608-735-4420. [CEM]

Rosholt, Portage Co., St. Adalbert. Also serves Sacred Heart, Polonia. Rev. Marcin Mankowski, O.P.
Res., 3315 St. Adalbert Rd., 54473. Tel: 715-677-4519. [CEM]
School—3314 St. Adalbert Rd., 54473. Tel: 715-677-4517.
Religious 1; Lay Teachers 5; Students 38.

Rothschild, Marathon Co., St. Mark, Rev. Allan L. Slowiak; Deacon Patrick McKeough.
Res., 602 Military Rd., 54474-1523. Tel: 715-359-5206.
School—Wausau Area Catholic Schools. See Unified Catholic School Systems under Institutions Located in the Diocese.

St. Therese of the Child Jesus, Rev. Robert A. Streveler.
Res., 113 W. Kort St., 54474-1094. Tel: 715-359-2421; Fax: 715-355-3088. [CEM]
School—Wausau Area Catholic Schools. See Consolidated Elementary Schools under Institutions Located in the Diocese.

Rozellville, Marathon Co., St. Andrew. Attended by St. Joseph, Stratford. Rev. Thomas J. Rudolph. In res., Rev. Arthur S. Redmond Tel: 715-384-7932.
Res., Box 106, Stratford, 54484. Tel: 715-687-2404. [CEM]

Rudolph, Wood Co., St. Philip. Attended by St. Lawrence, Wisconsin Rapids. Rev. John P. Hogan. In res., Rev. Douglas C. Robertson.
Office: 6957 Grotto Ave., Box 165, 54475. Tel: 715-435-3286. [CEM]
Res., 530 Tenth Ave. N., Wisconsin Rapids, 54495. Tel: 715-421-5777.
School—Wisconsin Rapids Area Catholic Schools. See Unified Catholic School Systems under Institutions Located in the Diocese.

Saint Joseph Ridge, La Crosse Co., St. Joseph. Attended by St. Peter, Middle Ridge. Rev. Robert T. Altmann.
Res., W2601 Hwy. 33, La Crosse, 54601. Tel: 608-788-1646. [CEM]

Saint Mary's Ridge, Monroe Co., Nativity of the Blessed Virgin Mary. Also serves St. Augustine, Norwalk; St. John the Baptist, Summit; Sacred Heart of Jesus, Cashton. Revs. Joseph W. Hirsch; Scott A. Bauer.
Res., 26400 CTH U, Cashton, 54619-9157. Tel: 608-823-7906; Fax: 608-823-7272. [CEM]
School—Tel: 608-823-7577.
Lay Teachers 5; Students 55.

Seneca, Crawford Co., St. Patrick. Also serves Sacred Heart, Wauzeka. Very Rev. Eugene J. Wolf.
Res., Box 18, 54654. Tel: 608-734-3931. [CEM]

Sigel, Wood Co., Holy Rosary. Attended by Joachim, Pittsville. Rev. James T. Benzmiller.
Mailing Address: P.O. Box 69, Pittsville, 54466-0069. [CEM]

Southeastern Portage County, Portage Co., St. Maximilian Maria Kolbe, Rev. Daniel H. Farley.
Mailing Address: P.O. Box 69, Pittsville, 54466-0069. [CEM]
Res., 1632 Oak St., Box 99, Almond, 54909-0099. Tel: 715-366-2811. [CEM 4]

Sparta, Monroe Co., St. Patrick, Rev. James Leary, O.F.M.Cap.
Res., 319 W. Main St., 54656-2143. Tel: 608-269-2655; Fax: 608-269-3084. [CEM]
School—318 W. Oak St., 54654. Tel: 608-269-4748.
Lay Teachers 11; Students 150.

Spaulding-City Point, Jackson Co., North American Martyrs. Closed. For inquiries for parish records contact St. Joachim, Pittsville.

Spencer, Marathon Co., Christ the King. Attended by St. John, Marshfield. Revs. Charles D. Stoetzel; Todd A. Mlsna.
Res., 201 W. Blodgett, Box 644, Marshfield, 54449-0644. Tel: 715-659-4480; Fax: 715-384-5131. [JC]

Spring Valley, Pierce Co., Sacred Heart of Jesus. Attended by Sacred Heart, Elmwood. Brett A. Swearingen, Pastoral Assoc.
Res., S. 105 Sabin Ave., P.O. Box 456, 54767-0456. Tel: 715-778-5519; Fax: 715-778-4591. [CEM 2]

Springfield, Eau Claire Co., St. Bridget. Attended by Holy Ghost, Chippewa Falls. Revs. Edmund J. Doerre; Charles J. Scherman, S.J.
Office: 412 S. Main, Chippewa Falls, 54729. Tel: 715-723-4890. [CEM]

Stanley, Chippewa Co., Holy Family. Also serves Sacred Heart of Jesus-St. Joseph, Boyd. Rev. Robert W. Nelson.
Office: P.O. Box 125, 54768. Tel: 715-644-5435.
Res., 226 E. 3rd Ave., P.O. Box 125, 54768. Tel: 715-644-5435. [CEM]
School—136 3rd Ave., 54768. Tel: 715-644-3602.
Lay Teachers 9; Students 87.

Stevens Point, Portage Co.,

1—Newman University Parish, Rev. Thomas F. Lindner.
Office: 2108 Fourth Ave., 54481. Tel: 715-345-6500.
Res., 1301 6th Ave., #5, 54481. Tel: 715-342-5930. [JC]

2—St. Casimir. Also serves St. Mary, Torun. Rev. Donald J. Walczak.
Res., 203 W. Casimir Rd., 54481. Tel: 715-344-9582. [CEM]

3—St. Joseph, Rev. Alan T. Burkhardt.
Res., 1709 Wyatt Ave., 54481-3699. Tel: 715-341-1617; Fax: 715-341-2623. [JC]
School—Stevens Point Area Catholic Schools. See Unified Catholic School Systems under Institutions Located in the Diocese.

4—St. Peter, Rev. Robert A. Schaller. In res., Revs. Dennis A. Worzalla (GB); Michael E. Klos.
Res., 800 4th Ave., 54481-1627. Tel: 715-344-6115. [JC]
School—Stevens Point Area Catholic Schools. See Unified Catholic School Systems under Institutions Located in Diocese.

5—St. Stanislaus, Very Rev. Donald L. Przybylski; Deacons Hugh Walker; Donald Borski.
Res., 838 N. Fremont St., 54481. Tel: 715-344-9117; Fax: 715-344-1771. [JC]
School—Stevens Point Area Catholic Schools. See Unified Catholic School Systems under Institutions Located in the Diocese.

6—St. Stephen. Also serves St. Bartholomew, Mill Creek. Rev. Daniel E. Kozlowski; Deacon Robert Hensen.
Res., 1401 Clark St., 54481. Tel: 715-344-3319; Fax: 715-344-6101. [CEM]
School—Stevens Point Area Catholic Schools. See Unified Catholic School Systems under Institutions Located in the Diocese.

Stratford, Marathon Co., St. Joseph. Also serves St. Andrew, Rozellville. Rev. Thomas J. Rudolph.
Res., 420 Larch St., Box 6, 54484. Tel: 715-687-2404; Fax: 715-687-2404. [CEM 3]
School—P.O. Box 6, 54484. Tel: 715-687-4145; Fax: 715-687-4343.
Lay Teachers 11; Students 113.

Summit, Monroe Co., St. John the Baptist. Attended by Nativity of the Blessed Virgin Mary, St. Mary's Ridge. Revs. Joseph W. Hirsch; Scott A. Bauer.
Mailing Address: 26400 CTH U, Cashton, 54619-9757. Tel: 608-823-7906; Fax: 608-823-7272. [CEM]

Thorp, Clark Co., St. Bernard-St. Hedwig Parish, Rev. John W. Puerner.
Res., Box 329, 54771. Tel: 715-669-5526; Fax: 715-669-5754. [CEM]
School—Box 369, 54771. Tel: 715-669-5530.
Sisters of St. Joseph 1; Lay Teachers 11; Students 112.

Tilden, Chippewa Co., St. Peter. Attended by St. Charles Borromeo, Chippewa Falls. Revs. William P. Felix; Eric G. Linzmaier.
Mailing Address: 11358 CTH Q, Chippewa Falls, 54729-6115. Tel: 715-288-6484; Fax: 715-723-2195.
Res., 11358 CTU Q, Chippewa Falls, 54729-6115. Tel: 715-723-4088; Fax: 715-723-2195. [CEM]
School—(Grades 1-8) 11370 CTH Q, 54729. Tel: 715-288-6250; Fax: 715-288-6250.
Lay Teachers 5; Students 76.

Tomah, Monroe Co., St. Mary (Immaculate Conception). Also serves St. Andrew, Warrens. Rev. Richard C. Dickman.
Res., 203 W. Monroe St., 54660. Tel: 608-372-4516; Fax: 608-372-4506. [CEM]
School—315 W. Monroe St., 54660. Tel: 608-372-5765.
Lay Teachers 14; Students 190.

Torun, Portage Co., St. Mary. Attended by St. Casimir, Stevens Point. Rev. Donald J. Walczak.
Res., 5589 Dewey Dr., Stevens Point, 54481. Tel: 715-344-2599. [CEM]

Trempealeau, Trempealeau Co., St. Bartholomew. Also serves St. Mary, Galesville. Rev. Robert J. Wagner.
Res., 11646 South St., 54661-8238. Tel: 608-534-6652. [CEM 2]

Union Center, Juneau Co., St. Theresa of Avila. Closed. For inquiries for parish records contact St. Jerome, Wonewoc.

Vesper, Wood Co., St. James. Attended by St. Joachim, Pittsville. Rev. James T. Benzmiller.
Res., P.O. Box 69, Pittsville, 54489.
6623 N. Church St., Box 68, 54489. Tel: 715-569-4412. [CEM]

Viroqua, Vernon Co., Annunciation of the Blessed Virgin Mary, Rev. Steven J. Kachel.
Res., 400 Congress Ave., 54665. Tel: 608-637-7711.

Warrens, Monroe Co., St. Andrew. Attended by St. Mary (Immaculate Conception), Tomah. Rev. Richard C. Dickman.
Mailing Address: 24798 Atlas Ave., 54666. Tel: 608-378-4397.
Res., 203 W. Monroe St., Tomah, 54660. Tel: 608-372-4516.

Waumandee, Buffalo Co., St. Boniface. Also serves St. Lawrence, Alma. Rev. John W. Steiner.
Res., Box 962, 54622-0962. Tel: 608-626-2621; Fax: 608-685-3253. [CEM 2]
School—Tel: 608-626-2611.
Students 43.

Wausau, Marathon Co.,

1—Church of the Resurrection, Rev. Stephen F. Gross.
Mailing Address: 621 2nd St., 54403. Tel: 715-845-6715; 845-5379; Fax: 715-845-4120. [JC]

2—Holy Name of Jesus. Attended by St. Matthew, Wausau. Revs. John L. Parr; Anthony Dichoso; Mrs. Patricia Gaska, Pastoral Assoc.
Res., 2700 Westwood Dr., 54401. Tel: 715-842-4543; Fax: 715-845-5059.
School—Wausau Area Catholic Schools. See Unified Catholic School Systems under Institutions Located in the Diocese.

3—St. Anne, Revs. Steven J. Brice; Keith B. Apfelbeck.
Res., 700 W. Bridge St., 54401. Tel: 715-849-3930; Fax: 715-849-4679. [JC]
School—Wausau Area Catholic Schools. See Unified Catholic School Systems under Institutions Located in the Diocese.

4—St. James the Greater. Closed. For inquiries for Parish Records contact Resurrection of Our Lord Jesus Christ, Wausau.

5—St. Mary (Immaculate Conception). Closed. For inquiries for Parish Records contact Resurrection of Our Lord Jesus Christ, Wausau.

6—St. Matthew. Also serves Holy Name of Jesus, Wausau. Revs. John L. Parr; Anthony Dichoso.
Res., 2700 Westwood Dr., 54401. Tel: 715-842-3148.
School—Wausau Area Catholic Schools. See Consolidated Elementary Schools under Institutions Located in the Diocese.
St. Matthew Parish Education Center—221 S. 28th Ave., 54401. Tel: 715-845-2938.

7—St. Michael, Very Rev. William N. Grevatch.
Res., 1315 6th St., 54403-3599. Tel: 715-842-4283; 842-2344; Fax: 715-849-2509. [CEM]
School—Wausau Area Catholic Schools. See Unified Catholic School Systems under Institutions Located in the Diocese.
Convent—611 Stark, 54403. Tel: 715-845-6885.

Wauzeka, Crawford Co., Sacred Heart. Attended by St. Patrick, Seneca. Very Rev. Eugene J. Wolf; Sr. Donna Weber, F.S.P.A., Pastoral Assoc.
Res., 711 E. Main St., P.O. Box 237, 53826. Tel: 608-875-5401. [CEM]

West Salem, La Crosse Co., St. Leo the Great. Also serves St. Mary, Bangor. Rev. Robert S. Hegenbarth.
Res., 210 W. Hamlin St., 54669. Tel: 608-786-0610.

Weston, Marathon Co., St. Agnes. Served from St. Therese of the Child Jesus, Rothschild. Rev. Robert A. Streveler.
6101 Zinser St., 54476. Tel: 715-359-5675; Fax: 715-359-4392. [CEM]
Res., 113 Kort St., Rothschild, 54474. Tel: 715-359-2421.

Whitehall, Trempealeau Co., St. John the Apostle. Also serves St. Ansgar, Blair. Rev. James Arthur.
Res., 35900 Lee St., P.O. Box 127, 54773-0127. Tel: 715-538-4607; Fax: 715-538-2224.

Willard, Clark Co., Holy Family. Attended by St. Mary Help of Christians, Greenwood. Rev. A. Joseph Follmar.
Res., 123 N. Main St., Greenwood, 54437. Tel: 715-267-6282; 267-6760. [CEM]

Wilson, Eau Claire Co., St. Peter. Closed. For inquiries for parish records contact Sacred Heart-St. Joseph, Boyd.

Wilton, Monroe Co., St. John the Baptist. Attended by St. Joseph, Kendall. Very Rev. James P. McNamee.
Res., Box 155, Kendall, 54638. Tel: 608-463-7120. [CEM]

Wisconsin Rapids, Wood Co.,

1—OUR LADY, QUEEN OF HEAVEN, Rev. Dennis J. Lynch. Res., 750 10th Ave. S., 54494. Tel: 715-423-1251; Fax: 715-423-9407. [JC]
School—Wisconsin Rapids Area Catholic Schools. See Unified Catholic School Systems under Institutions Located in the Diocese.

2—ST. LAWRENCE. Also serves St. Philip, Rudolph. Rev. John P. Hogan; Deacon James L. Landry.
Res., 530 10th Ave. N., 54495. Tel: 715-421-5777; 424-2651. [JC]
School—Wisconsin Rapids Area Catholic Schools. See Unified Catholic School Systems under Institutions Located in the Diocese.

3—ST. VINCENT DE PAUL, Rev. William G. Menzel.
Res., 820 13 St. S., 54494-5336. Tel: 715-423-2111; Fax: 715-423-4227.
School—Wisconsin Rapids Area Catholic Schools. See Unified Catholic School Systems under Institutions Located in the Diocese.

4—SS. PETER AND PAUL, Rev. Andrew K. Karoblis.
Res., 1150 2nd St. N., 54494. Tel: 715-423-1351. [CEM]

Wonewoc, Juneau Co., St. Jerome. Attended by St. Aloysius, Hillsboro. Rev. Wayne R. Kidd.
Office: 528 N. Center St., R.R. 2, Box 87A, 53968. Tel: 608-464-7713; 462-5875. [CEM]

Wuerzburg, Marathon Co., St. John the Baptist. Also serves St. Thomas, Milan. Rev. Leonard C. Stashek.
Res., 1506 Wuerzburg Rd., Athens, 54411. Tel: 715-257-7092. [CEM]

Yuba, Richland Co., St. Wenceslaus. Closed. For inquiries for parish records contact St. Aloysius, Hillsboro.

Chaplains of Public Institutions

OXFORD. *Federal Correctional Institute.* Vacant Tel: 608-584-5511.

TOMAH. *Veterans Administration Medical Center* 54660. Tel: 608-372-3971. Rev. Sebastian A. Ugochukwu.

WAUSAU. *Wausau Hospital Center* 333 Pine Ridge Blvd., 54401. Tel: 715-847-2121; 847-2840. Rev. Michael J. Lynch, Res., 4303 Lake Shore Dr., 54401. Tel: 715-355-4499.

Special Assignment:
Reverend Fathers—
Berns, Eric P., Dir Vocations, P.O. Box 4004, La Crosse, WI 54602-4004. Tel: 608-788-7700; 788-3681
Gilles, Richard W., Secretary to the Diocesan Bishop, P.O. Box 4004, La Crosse, WI 54602-4004. Tel: 608-788-7700;788-6671
Gorman, Michael J., Moderator of the Curia, P.O. Box 4004, La Crosse, WI 54602-4004
McHugh, John T., Dir. of Holy Cross Seminary House of Formation, P.O. Box 4004, La Crosse, WI 54602-4004. Tel: 608-788-9095
Powell, Leon A., Vice Chancellor, P.O. Box 4004, La Crosse, WI 54602-4004. Tel: 608-788-7700; 788-4625
Rafacz, Joseph J., Vicar Gen. & Dir. Diocesan Mission Office, St. Thomas More Parish, 2006 Weston St., La Crosse, WI 54601. Tel: 608-788-5483

On Duty Outside the Diocese:
Reverend Fathers—
Fliss, Richard L., 8531 S.W. 185th Terrace, Miami, FL 33157. Tel: 305-969-9964
Heagle, John L., Tara Center, 1037 S. 102nd St., Seattle, WA 98168. Tel: 206-763-8721
Kunz, David C., Immaculate Heart of Mary Seminary, 700 Terrace Heights #43, Winona, MN 55987-1399. Tel: 507-457-7377
Louis, Kevin C., Pontifical College Josephinum, 7625 N. High St., Columbus, OH 43235-1498. Tel: 614-885-5585
Mason, James E., 233 S. Kane St., Burlington, WI 53105
Monti, Robert M., 3003 Terramar St., Apt. 201, Fort Lauderdale, FL 33304-4037. Tel: 954-561-5908
Neis, William P., C.H.C., U.S.N.R., Greater Antilles Section, U.S.C.G., P.O. Box 9022029, San Juan, PR 00902-2029
O'Lenny, Patrick J., Pastor of Holy Family Chapel, N. Yorkshire, U.K., PSC 45, Box 1503, APO, APE, 09468 U.S.A.

Foreign Missions:
Reverend Fathers—
Flock, Robert H., Parroquia de la Santa Cruz, Casilla 713, Santa Cruz, Bolivia. Tel: 011-591-332-6302
Kolodziejczyk, Sebastian J., Casa Hogar Juan Pablo II, Lurin 16, Peru. Tel: 011-5114-30-5646

On Leave of Absence:
Reverend Fathers—
Konopacky, Joseph R.

Retired:
Reverend Monsignors—
Dall, Norbert P., W5735 Timber Trail, New Lisbon, WI 53950. Tel: 608-565-7714
Finucan, James P., Holy Cross Diocesan Center, 3710 E. Ave. S., P.O. Box 4004, La Crosse, WI 54602-4004. Tel: 608-788-7151
Reverend Fathers—
Abts, Cletus, Box 402, Tomahawk, WI 54487. Tel: 715-453-3079
Berg, Donald M., P.O. Box 386, Edgar, WI 54426. Tel: 715-352-3444
Binkowski, James P., Holy Cross Diocesan Center, 3710 E. Ave. S., P.O. Box 4004, LaCrosse, WI 54602-4004. Tel: 608-788-2904
Blecha, Charles A., 420 Heller Rd., Apt. 322, Menomonie, WI 54751. Tel: 715-235-1860
Bornbach, Raymond H., 215 W. Upham St., Marshfield, WI 54449. Tel: 715-384-7571; 608-643-8361
Connolly, Robert V., Bethany-St. Joseph Care Center, 2501 Shelby Rd., La Crosse, WI 54601. Tel: 608-788-5700
Cosgrove, J. Kelly, 4182 Mt. Vernon Ave., Titusville, FL 32780. Tel: 407-267-8601
Devine, Patrick T., 1020 Balsam St., La Crescent, MN 55947
Dockendorff, Carl J., 1092 Queensway, Nekoosa, WI 54457. Tel: 715-325-6125
Doyle, Mark A., 2230 14th St. S., Wisconsin Rapids, WI 54494. Tel: 715-424-2298
Dwyer, J. Floyd, Holy Cross Diocesan Center, 3710 East Ave. S., P.O. Box 4004, La Crosse, WI 54602-4004. Tel: 608-788-6935
Faber, Emmet N., 77 Cynthia Dr., Bastrop, TX 78602
Ferron, Joseph B., 5 Buenos Aires, Fort Pierce, FL 34951-1252. Tel: 828-682-0822
Finucan, J. Thomas, 315 S. 14th St., LaCrosse, WI 54601. Tel: 608-785-3167
Fisher, Gerald E., Holy Cross Diocesan Center, 3710 Gast Ave. S., P.O. Box 4004, La Crosse, WI 54602-4004. Tel: 608-787-8735
Garthwaite, Thomas F., 28183 Cty. Hwy. 4, Cashton, WI 54619. Tel: 608-758-6946
Geissler, Lloyd F., 309 Hwy. 107 N., Marathon, WI 54448. Tel: 715-443-3287
Geissler, Ralph J., Angelus Retirement Community, 510 W. Wausau St., Apt. 01, Colby, WI 54421
Gerum, Jerome G., 1601 N. Palmetto Ave., P.O. Box 673, Marshfield, WI 54449-0673. Tel: 715-387-4783
Greatorex, Robert W., 1300 Maria Dr., Stevens Point, WI 54481
Hansen, Robert H., St. Joseph Nursing Home, 2902 East Ave. S., La Crosse, WI 54601. Tel: 608-788-3918
Hemmersbach, Alfred F., Holy Cross Diocesan Center, 3710 East Ave. S., P.O. Box 4004, La Crosse, WI 54602-4004. Tel: 608-788-8326
Henseler, Joseph N., 502 W. Second St., Neillsville, WI 54456. Tel: 715-743-7760
Herrmann, Richard J., 309 W. Blodgett St., Marshfield, WI 54449. Tel: 715-384-5039
Kamla, Jerome J., 8316 E. Calypso Ave., Mesa, AZ 85208. Tel: 602-984-2344
Keating, Joseph R., 40 Spring Mount Rd., Schwenksville, PA 19473-1739
Kelly, Bernard T., W. 7407 CTH Z, R.R. 2, Box 284, Onalaska, WI 54650. Tel: 608-781-0281
Kelly, Daniel J., 417 Thomas St., P.O. Box 162, Westfield, WI 53964. Tel: 608-206-3170
King, Norbert E., 135 Charles St., Schofield, WI 54476-1202. Tel: 715-359-7367
Knauf, Edwin L., 836 Leroy Ln., River Falls, WI 54022-1291. Tel: 715-425-9377
Kulovits, Fred A., 221 Scott St., Apt. 412, Wausau, WI 54403. Tel: 715-842-4823
Lee, Henry H., 817 Macomber St., Chippewa Falls, WI 54729. Tel: 715-723-1151
Leisle, Charles E., 3141 Mayer Rd., Eau Claire, WI 54701. Tel: 715-831-0922
Leketas, Peter J., 109 North Oak Ave., Apt. M, Marshfield, WI 54449. Tel: 715-384-8331
Mannion, Thomas J., 10 Ardsallaghmore, Roscomain, Ireland
Mauel, John N., 5533 Woodland St., Stevens Point, WI 54481. Tel: 715-342-0132
McGarty, Bernard O., 109 S. 9th St., La Crosse, WI 54601. Tel: 608-784-4473
Mertens, Michael G., Holy Cross Diocesan Center, 3710 East Ave. S., P.O. Box 4004, La Crosse, WI 54602-4004. Tel: 608-788-0311
Miller, James H., St. Augustine Rectory, W. 109 CTH U, Norwalk, WI 54648. Tel: 608-823-7643
Moczarny, Chester B., Holy Cross Diocesan Center, 3710 East Ave. S., P.O. Box 4004, La Crosse, WI 54602-4004. Tel: 608-787-5834
Nowak, Bernard J., Keeler Park Apartments, 601 Seneca Manor Dr., Apt. 14L, Rochester, NY 14621
Oberwinder, Robert J., Bethany-St. Joseph Care Center, 2501 Shelby Rd., La Crosse, WI 54601. Tel: 608-788-5700
Osowski, Chester J., St. Philip Rectory, 6597 Grotto Ave., P.O. Box 165, Rudolph, WI 54475. Tel: 715-569-4412
Papiernik, Roman J., 3460 Woodbridge Ct., La Crosse, WI 54601. Tel: 608-787-6027
Pedretti, Raymond J., St. Mary of Mt. Carmel Rectory, 3995 Cty. Rd. K, Amherst, WI 54406. Tel: 715-824-3455
Penchi, Edward J., Casilla 713, Santa Cruz, Bolivia. Tel: 011-591-343-0302
Reardon, Thomas J., 405 Grote St., Mauston, WI 53948. Tel: 608-847-2633
Redmond, Arthur S., St. Andrew Rectory, D1876 CTHC, P.O. Box 106, Stratford, WI 54484-0106
Reuter, Arnold F., Holy Cross Diocesan Center, 3710 East Ave. S., P.O. Box 4004, La Crosse, WI 54602-4004. Tel: 608-788-0717
Schreiber, Bernard G., Bethany-St. Joseph Care Center, 2501 Shelby Rd., La Crosse, WI 54601. Tel: 608-788-5399
Schulte, Oswald W., Bethany-St. Joseph Care Center, 2501 Shelby Rd., La Crosse, WI 54601. Tel: 608-788-5700
Schumacher, Charles P., Corpus Christi, 10775 Hwy. BB, Marshfield, WI 54449. Tel: 715-676-2824
Simmons, Hilary F., (Summer) 2972 Wausau Rd., Rhinelander, WI 54501. Tel: 751-282-5751
Simmons, Hilary F., (Winter) 2731 S.W. 11th Ct., Ft. Lauderdale, FL 33312. Tel: 305-583-8725
Smith, Eugene P., St. Joseph Rectory, P.O. Box 10, Boyd, WI 54726-0010. Tel: 715-667-3038
Sonnberger, Albert W., St. John the Baptist Rectory, 4540 5th 40, Bloomer, WI 54724. Tel: 715-568-3778
Szczerbicki, Thaddeus P., 5319 Greenview Ln., Stevens Point, WI 54481. Tel: 715-341-4616
Theisen, Donald J., 1025 Pine Beach Rd., Apt. 207, Marinette, WI 54143. Tel: 715-735-3199
Thome, Edwin J., St. Patrick Rectory, 1031 Main St., Onalaska, WI 54650. Tel: 608-783-5535
Wagner, Raymond J., Holy Cross Diocesan Center, 3710 E. Ave South, P.O. Box 4004, LaCrosse, WI 54602-4004. Tel: 608-788-1172
Walijewski, Joseph A., Casa Hogar Juan Pablo II, Lurin 16, Peru. Tel: 011-5114-30-5646
Walljasper, Mark A., 505 W. Division, Sparta, WI 54656. Tel: 608-269-7801
Wozniak, Aloysius A., Holy Cross Diocesan Center, 3710 East Ave. S., P.O. Box 4004, La Crosse, WI 54602-4004
Zoromski, Herbert P., 8490 Padre Dr., Wittenberg, WI 54499. Tel: 715-454-6994
Zvinklys, Antanas, St. Joseph's Rehabilitation Center, 2902 East Ave. S., La Crosse, WI 54602-4004. Tel: 608-788-2539

Permanent Deacons:
Abnet, Frank, St. Patrick, Onalaska
Agema, Larry, Sacred Heart, Eau Claire
Anderson, Robert, Sacred Heart, Jim Falls
Ashenbrenner, David, St. Joseph, Galloway, St. Ladislaus, Bevent
Barnum, John, Sun City, AZ.
Beck, Guy, Waverly, IA
Borski, Donald, St. Stanislaus, Stevens Point
Brunner, Norbert, St. Vincent de Paul, Wisconsin Rapids
Burek, Peter, Wausau, WI
Chittendon, Robert, St. Olaf, Eau Claire
Delgado, Juan (Gary), Mauston
Ebben, Ronald, (Retired)
Hensen, Robert, St. Stephen, Stevens Point
Hite, James, Houston, TX
Hurrish, Florian, (Retired)
Jirous, Thomas, St. James, Amherst, St. Mary of Mt. Carmel, Fancher
Jolliffe, Garry, Arizona
Kennedy, David (MIL), St. Joseph, Adams
Knauf, LeRoy, Holy Family, Poniatowski
Kostner, Richard, St. Paul, Bloomer, St. Jude, New Auburn
Koza, J. Michael, La Crescent, MN
Landry, James, St. Lawrence, Wisconsin Rapids
McKeough, Patrick, St. Mark, Rothschild

Proulx, Rahlf, Holy Family Medical Center, Manitowoc
Richard, Gordon, Winona, MN
Rivers, Dennis, Holy Cross, Cornell
Sage, Richard, La Crosse
Schaller, Arthur, Immaculate Conception, Custer
Schulz, Herman, St. John the Baptist, Edgar
Skrade, Fredrick, Rockford, IL
Slason, Stillman, St.Patrick, Sparta
Stack, William, Oregon
Walker, Hugh, St. Stanislaus, Stevens Point
Waterman, John (RCK), St. Mary, Torun, St. Casimir, Stevens Point
Weingart, James, St. Mary's Assumption, Durand; Holy Rosary, Lima; Sacred Heart, Mondovi

INSTITUTIONS LOCATED IN THE DIOCESE

[A] SEMINARIES, DIOCESAN

LA CROSSE. *Holy Cross Seminary House of Formation*, 3710 East Ave. S., P.O. Box 4004, 54602-4004. Tel: 608-788-9095; Fax: 608-788-8413. Revs. John T. McHugh, Dir.; Michael J. Gorman, Asst. Dir.; Richard W. Gilles, Spiritual Dir.; Mr. Michael P. Gallagher, Prefect. Tel: 608-788-0238. Students 8.

[B] COLLEGES AND UNIVERSITIES

LA CROSSE. *Viterbo University*, 815 Ninth St. South, 54601-8802. Tel: 608-796-3000; Fax: 608-796-3050.
E-mail: admission@viterbo.edu
Web site: www.viterbo.org
For a complete listing, refer to the Colleges and Universities section.

[C] UNIFIED CATHOLIC SCHOOL SYSTEMS

LA CROSSE. *Coulee Catholic Schools*. Central Office: 521 S. 13th St., 54601. Tel: 608-784-8585; Fax: 608-784-9988. John R. Carlucci, Pres.; Rev. Roger J. Scheckel, Dean CCS.

Aquinas Middle School North, 127 11th North, Onalaska, 54650. Tel: 608-783-5483. Mrs. Patricia A. Gallagher-Kosmatka, Prin. Lay Teachers 7; Students 48.

Aquinas Middle School South, 315 S. 11th St., 54601. Tel: 608-784-0156. Mrs. Patricia A. Gallagher-Kosmatka, Prin.

Aquinas High School, 315 S. 11th St., 54601. Tel: 608-784-0287.
E-mail: jbrengman@aquinas.la-crosse.wi.us
Web site: www.centuryinter.net/aquinas
Jeffrey Brengman, Prin.; Rev. John McHugh, Chap. Priests 1; Lay Teachers 37; Students 509.

Blessed Sacrament School, 2404 King St., 54601. Tel: 608-782-5564. Kay Berra, Prin. Lay Teachers 21; Students 290.

Holy Trinity School, 1417 S. 13th St., 54601. Tel: 608-782-1040. Victor Kapusinski, Prin. Lay Teachers 8; Students 127.

Mary, Mother of the Church School, 3710 East Ave. S., 54601. Tel: 608-788-6919. Charles Burnett, Prin. Lay Teachers 17; Students 200.

Mary, Mother of the Church Early Childhood Center, 2000 Weston St., 54601. Tel: 608-788-5225. Charles Burnett, Prin. Students 75.

St. James School, 716 Windsor St., 54603. Tel: 608-784-6167. Patricia Tschumper, Prin. Lay Teachers 10; Students 129.

St. Joseph Cathedral School, 1319 Ferry St., 54601. Tel: 608-782-5998. John Stellflue, Prin. Lay Teachers 10; Students 175.

St. Patrick School, 127 11th Ave. N., Onalaska, 54650. Tel: 608-783-5483. Sharon Tempke, Prin. Lay Teachers 11; Students 228.

CHIPPEWA FALLS. *Chippewa Falls Area Catholic Schools*. Central Office: 1316 Bel Air Blvd., 54729. Tel: 715-723-0538; Fax: 715-723-1501.
E-mail: msully99@hotmail.com
Michael Sullivan, Pres.

Holy Ghost Elementary School. (Grades 3-5), 436 S. Main St., 54729. Tel: 715-726-8788. Mary T. Selz, Prin. Lay Teachers 12; Students 167.

McDonnell High School, 1316 Bel Air Blvd., 54729. Tel: 715-723-9126; Fax: 715-723-1501. John Flanagan, Prin.; Rev. Brian J. Jazdzewski, Chap. Priests 1; Lay Teachers 22; Students 249.

Notre Dame Middle School. (Grades 6-8), 22 S. Prairie, 54729. Tel: 715-723-4777. Sue Goslyn, Prin.; Rev. Eric G. Linzmaier, Chap. Lay Teachers 13; Students 171.

St. Charles Primary School. (Grades PreK-2), 429 W. Spruce St., 54729. Tel: 715-723-5827. Mary Selz, Prin. Students 207.

EAU CLAIRE. *Catholic Area Schools of the Eau Claire Deanery (C.A.S.E.)*. Central Office: 448 N. Dewey St., 54703. Tel: 715-830-2273; Fax: 715-835-4658. Dr. Terry Sheridan, Pres.

Genesis Child Development Center, 418 N. Dewey St., 54701. Tel: 715-830-2275. Gayle Flaig, Dir.

Immaculate Conception School. (Grades K-6), 1703 Sherwin Ave., 54701. Tel: 715-830-5816. Sr. Dorothy Brenner, F.S.P.A., Prin. Lay Teachers 18; Students 289.

Regis Child Devel. Center, 2100 Fenwick Ave., 54701. Tel: 715-830-2274; Fax: 715-830-2270. Gayle Flaig, Dir.

Regis Middle School. (Grades 7-8), 2100 Fenwick Ave., 54701. Tel: 715-830-1327. Renee Cassidy, Prin.; Rev. Jeffrey D. Burrill, Chap. Lay Teachers 10; Students 122.

Regis High School, 2100 Fenwick Ave., 54701. Tel: 715-830-2271; Fax: 715-830-5461. Earl A. Larson, Prin.; Rev. Jeffrey D. Burrill, Chap. Priests 1; Lay Teachers 15; Students 200.

St. James School. (Grades K-6), 2502 Eleventh St., 54703. Tel: 715-830-2277. Lay Teachers 9; Students 119.

St. Mary School. (Grades K-6), 1828 Lynn Ave., Altoona, 54720. Tel: 715-830-2278; Fax: 715-830-9573.

St. Olaf School. (Grades K-6), 2407 North Ln., 54703. Tel: 715-830-2279. Faculty 11; Students 120.

MARSHFIELD. *Columbus High School*, 710 Columbus Ave., 54449. Tel: 715-387-1177; Fax: 715-384-4535.
E-mail: chs@wctc.net
Web site: www.columbus.marshfield.wi.us
Rev. Paul Lauzon, S.D.S., Prin. Priests 2; Lay Teachers 21; Students 164.

Holy Family Middle School. (Grades 7-8), 710 Columbus Ave., 54449. Tel: 715-384-7184; Fax: 715-384-4535.
E-mail: hfms@wctc.net
Web site: www.columbus.marshfield.wi.us/hfms
Revs. Paul Lauzon, S.D.S., Prin.; Brian D. Konopa, Chap. Priests 2; Lay Teachers 8; Students 81.

STEVENS POINT. *Stevens Point Area Catholic Schools*. Central Office: 1408 Ellis St., 54481. Tel: 715-341-2445; Fax: 715-342-2001.
E-mail: ghansel@spacs.k12.wi.us
Web site: www.spacs.k12.wi.us
Mr. Gregg Hansel, Pres.

St. Bronislava School. (Grades K-5), 3301 Willow Dr., Plover, 54467. Tel: 715-342-2015. Laura Barnett, Prin. Lay Teachers 7; Students 133.

Pacelli High School, 1301 Maria Dr., 54481. Tel: 715-341-2442. Rebecca Lindahl, Prin.; Rev. Michael E. Klos, Chap. Priests 1; Sisters 3; Lay Teachers 30; Students 301.

St. Joseph School Early Childhood Center, 1901 Lincoln Ave., 54481. Tel: 715-341-2878. Laura Barnett, Prin. Lay Teachers 3; Students 95.

St. Peter Middle School. (Grades 6-8), 708 First St., 54481. Tel: 715-344-1890; Fax: 715-342-2005. Anne Rogalski, Prin.; Rev. Michael E. Klos, Chap. Lay Teachers 15; Students 216.

St. Stanislaus School. (Grades K-2), 2150 High St., 54481. Tel: 715-344-3086; Fax: 715-342-2014. Joyce Trebatoski, Prin. Lay Teachers 9; Students 166.

St. Stephen School. (Grades 3-5), 1335 Clark St., 54481. Tel: 715-344-3751; Fax: 715-342-2013. Joyce Trebatoski, Prin. Lay Teachers 13; Students 187.

WAUSAU. *Wausau Area Catholic Schools*. Central Office: 602 N. Second St., 54403. Tel: 715-845-5735; Fax: 715-848-3582. Mark Watson, Pres.

Holy Name School. (Grades PreK-5), 1122 S. 9th Ave., 54401-5910. Tel: 715-848-3281. Jeanne Lang, Prin. Lay Teachers 11; Students 135. Sisters of the Divine Saviour.

Newman High School, 1130 W. Bridge St., 54401. Tel: 715-845-8274; Fax: 715-842-1302. Carolyn Beckman, Prin.; Rev. David Olson, Chap. Priests 1; Lay Teachers 29; Students 247.

St. Anne School. (Grades PreK-5), 604 N. 6th Ave., 54401. Tel: 715-845-5754. Sandra Gilge, Prin. Lay Teachers 16; Students 303.

St. Mark School, 602 Military Rd., Rothschild, 54474. Tel: 715-359-9662. Vicki Koeppel, Prin. Lay Teachers 9; Students 158.

St. Matthew Middle School. (Grades 6-8), 225 S. 28th Ave., 54401. Tel: 715-842-4857. Janet Klosinski, Prin.; Rev. Anthony Dichoso, Chap. Lay Teachers 19; Students 248.

St. Michael School. (Grades PreK-5), 614 Steuben St., 54403. Tel: 715-848-0206. Lucille McCarthy, Prin. Felician Sisters 1; Lay Teachers 11; Students 122.

St. Therese School. (Grades 4-6), 112 W. Kort St., Schofield, 54476. Tel: 715-359-2131. Vicki Koeppel, Prin. Lay Teachers 5; Students 68. Franciscan Sisters of St. Joseph.

WISCONSIN RAPIDS. *Wisconsin Rapids Area Catholic Schools*. Central Office: 711 Hill St., 54494. Tel: 715-422-0900; Fax: 715-422-0903.
E-mail: jsteepleton_WRACS@hotmail.com
Joseph Steepleton, Pres.

Assumption Middle School, 440 Mead, 54494. Tel: 715-422-0950. Thomas Reichenbacher, Prin.; Rev. Samuel Martin, Chap.

Assumption High School, 445 Chesnut St., 54494. Tel: 715-422-0910.
E-mail: cjmahs@wctc.net
Joseph S. Dente, Jr., Prin.; Rev. Samuel Martin, Chap. Priests 1; Lay Teachers 21; Students 173.

Our Lady Queen of Heaven School, 750 Tenth Ave. S., 54495. Tel: 715-422-0980; Fax: 715-424-2972. Brenda Walczak, Prin. Lay Teachers 11; Students 168.

Sacred Heart of School, 710 Vilas Ave., Nekoosa, 54457. Tel: 715-886-3761; Fax: 715-886-3745. Jean Stelzer, Prin. Lay Teachers 7; Students 78.

St. Lawrence Early Childhood Center, 551 Tenth Ave. N., 54495. Tel: 715-422-0990; Fax: 715-424-1124. Carol Olson, Prin. Lay Teachers 6; Students 72.

St. Philip School, 6975 Grotta Ave., Rudolph, 54475. Tel: 715-435-3386. Carol Olson, Prin. Lay Teachers 7; Students 69.

St. Vincent de Paul School, 831 12th St. S., 54494. Tel: 715-422-0960; Fax: 715-422-0963. Lay Teachers 16; Students 154.

[D] GENERAL HOSPITALS

LA CROSSE. *Franciscan Skemp Healthcare, Mayo Health System, La Crosse Campus Medical Center*, 700 West Ave. S., 54601-4796. Tel: 608-785-0940; Fax: 608-791-9429
For a complete listing, refer to the Hospitals section.

ARCADIA. *Franciscan Skemp Healthcare, Mayo Health System, Arcadia Campus Hospital*, 464 S. St. Joseph Ave., 54612. Tel: 608-323-3341; Fax: 608-323-3694
For a complete listing, refer to the Hospitals section.

CHIPPEWA FALLS. *St. Joseph's Hospital*, 2661 County Hwy. I, 54729. Tel: 715-723-1811; Fax: 715-726-3204.
Web site: www.stjoeschipfalls.com
For a complete listing, refer to the Hospitals section.

EAU CLAIRE. *Sacred Heart Hospital*, 900 W. Clairemont Ave., 54701-6122. Tel: 715-839-4121; Fax: 715-839-8417.
E-mail: shec.hshs/org
Web site: www.sacredhearthospital-ec.org
For a complete listing, refer to the Hospitals section.

HILLSBORO. *St. Joseph's Memorial Hospital, Inc.*, 400 Water Ave., P.O. Box 527, 54634. Tel: 608-489-2211
For a complete listing, refer to the Hospitals section.

MARSHFIELD. *Saint Joseph's Hospital of Marshfield, Inc.*, 611 St. Joseph Ave., 54449. Tel: 715-387-1713; Fax: 715-387-8601.
Web site: www.ministryhealth.org
For a complete listing, refer to the Hospitals section.

SPARTA. *Franciscan Skemp Healthcare, Mayo Health System, Sparta Campus Hospital*, 310 W. Main St., 54656-2142. Tel: 608-269-2132
For a complete listing, refer to the Hospitals section.

STANLEY. *Victory Medical Center, Inc.*, 230 E. Fourth Ave., 54768. Tel: 715-644-5571; Fax: 715-644-5665.
Web site: www.ministryhealth.org
For a complete listing, refer to the Hospitals section.

STEVENS POINT. *St. Michael's Hospital of Stevens Point, Inc.*, 900 Illinois Ave., 54481. Tel: 715-346-5000; Fax: 715-346-5077.
E-mail: jm@smhosp.org
Web site: www.ministryhealth.org
For a complete listing, refer to the Hospitals section.

[E] REHABILITATION FACILITIES

LA CROSSE. *St. Francis Community Programs, Inc.*, 700 West Ave. S., 54601-4796. Tel: 608-791-9582; Fax: 608-784-7084. Adult Day Care Center 82; Special Centers for Social Services & Assistance 350; Total Staff 45.

Gerard Hall. 8 bed home for single mothers. Tel: 608-791-3985; Fax: 608-784-7084.

St. Francis Community Housing, Inc. Apartment units for chronically mentally ill; 8 bed apartment unit in Dodgeville, WI; and 12 bed apartment unit in Prairie du Chien, WI. Tel: 608-792-9488; Fax: 608-782-2779.

St. Francis Housing Alternatives, Inc. Apartment units for the chronically mentally ill; 8 bed apartment unit in Arcadia, WI; 8 bed apartment unit in Black River Falls, WI; and 8 bed apartment unit in Mauston, WI. Tel: 608-791-9488; Fax: 608-782-2779.

Siena Hall. 20 bed home for mentally ill adults. Tel: 608-784-6010; Fax: 608-784-7084.

LAAR House. 24 bed home for chemically dependent adults. Tel: 608-782-7700; Fax: 608-784-6010.

Scarseth House. 8 bed home for chemically dependent adolescents. Tel: 608-785-1270; Fax: 608-784-7084.

Pinecrest Center. 32 bed home for chemically dependent adults. Tel: 608-462-8434; Fax: 608-462-8969.

Villa Success, Prairie du Chien, 53821.

CHIPPEWA FALLS. *Libertas-L.E. Phillips Treatment Center for the Chemically Dependent*, 2661 County Hwy. I, 54729. Tel: 715-723-5585; Fax: 715-726-3504.
Web site: www.stjoeschipfalls.com
Hospital Sisters Health System, Hospital Sisters of the Third Order of St. Francis. David B. Fish, Exec. Vice Pres.; Larry W. Monson, Prog. Coord. Bed Capacity 43; Patients assisted annually 12,628.

Transitus House, 1830 Wheaton St., 54729. Tel: 715-723-1155. Hospital Sisters of the Third Order of St. Francis. David B. Fish, Chm.; Susan J. Anderson, Ph.D., Prog. Coord. Transitional living facility for women recovering from chemical dependency. Legal Title: *Hospital Sisters HealthCare-West, Inc.* Beds 20; Assisted annually 67.

[F] HOMES FOR AGED

LA CROSSE. *Bethany-St. Joseph Care Center*, 2501 Shelby Rd., 54601. Tel: 608-788-5700
For a complete listing, refer to the Special Care Facilities section.

Elder Care of North La Crosse, Inc. (Village on St. James), 800 St. James St., 54603. Tel: 608-791-9784
For a complete listing, refer to the Special Care Facilities section.

Franciscan Elder Care, Inc., 800 West Avenue S., 54601-4796. Tel: 608-791-9505; Fax: 608-782-2779
For a complete listing, refer to the Special Care Facilities section.

Franciscan Skemp Healthcare, Mayo Health System, La Crosse Campus Nursing Home, 620 S. 11th St., 54601. Tel: 608-791-9787; Fax: 608-791-9716
For a complete listing, refer to the Special Care Facilities section.

St. Joseph's Nursing Home, 2902 East Ave. S., 54601. Tel: 608-788-9870
For a complete listing, refer to the Special Care Facilities section.

ARCADIA. *Franciscan Skemp Healthcare, Mayo Health System, Arcadia Campus Nursing Home*, 464 S. St. Joseph Ave., 54612. Tel: 608-323-3341; Fax: 608-323-3694
For a complete listing, refer to the Special Care Facilities section.

EAU CLAIRE. *St. Francis Apartment*, 851 University Dr., 54701. Tel: 715-834-1388
For a complete listing, refer to the Special Care Facilities section.

HILLSBORO. *St. Joseph's Nursing Home*, P.O. Box 527, 54634
For a complete listing, refer to the Special Care Facilities section.

ONALASKA. *Franciscan Skemp Healthcare, Mayo Health System, Onalaska Nursing Home*, 1600 Main St., 54650. Tel: 608-783-4681
For a complete listing, refer to the Special Care Facilities section.

SPARTA. *Elder Care of Sparta, Inc.*, 622 S. Court, 54656. Tel: 608-791-9505
For a complete listing, refer to the Special Care Facilities section.

Franciscan Skemp Healthcare, Mayo Health System, Sparta Campus Nursing Home, 310 W. Main St., P.O. Box 529, 54656-2142. Tel: 608-269-2132; Fax: 608-269-1017
For a complete listing, refer to the Special Care Facilities section.

WAUSAU. *Marywood Convalescent Center*, 1821 N. 4th Ave., 54401. Tel: 715-675-9451; Fax: 715-675-9051
For a complete listing, refer to the Special Care Facilities section.

[G] RETREAT HOUSES

LA CROSSE. *Franciscan Spirituality Center*, 920 Market St., 54601-8809. Tel: 608-791-5295; Fax: 608-782-6301.
E-mail: fscenter@fspa.org
Web site: www.fspa.org
Sisters of the Third Order of St. Francis of Perpetual Adoration. Vince Hatt, Dir.

CUSTER. *St. Clare Center for Spirituality*, 7381 Church St., 54423. Tel: 715-592-4099.
E-mail: stclare@coredcs.com
Felician Sisters. Sr. Mary Therese Lukas, C.S.S.F., Dir.

EAU CLAIRE. *Saint Bede Retreat and Conference Center*, 1190 Priory Rd., P.O. Box 66, 54702-0066. Tel: 715-834-8642; Fax: 715-834-4292.
Web site: www.saintbede.org
Benedictine Sisters. Sr. Hildegarde Geraets, O.S.B., Dir.; Mary Traynor, Asst. Dir.

MARATHON CITY. *St. Anthony Retreat Center*, 300 E. 4th St., 54448-9602. Tel: 715-443-2236; Fax: 715-443-2235.
E-mail: info@sarcenter.com
Web site: www.sarcenter.com
The Province of St. Joseph of the Capuchin Order, Inc. Rev. Dan Crosby, O.F.M.Cap., Leadership Team. Priests 3; Brothers 1.

[H] MONASTERIES AND RESIDENCES OF PRIESTS AND BROTHERS

LA CROSSE. *Holy Cross (Seminary) Diocesan Center*, 3710 East Ave. S., P.O. Box 4004, 54602-4004. Tel: 608-788-7700. Mr. John J. Newman, Dir. In res. Most Rev. John J. Paul. Tel: 608-788-8395; Rev. Msgr. James P. Finucan. Tel: 608-788-7151; Very Rev. J. Floyd Dwyer. Tel: 608-788-6935; Revs. Eric R. Berns. Tel: 608-788-3681; James P. Binkowski. Tel: 608-788-2904; Gerald Fisher. Tel: 608-787-8735; Richard W. Gilles. Tel: 608-788-6671; Michael J. Gorman. Tel: 608-788-4578; Alfred F. Hemmersbach. Tel: 608-788-8326; Maryon Jordan, O.S.B. Tel: 608-787-6838; John T. McHugh. Tel: 608-788-9095; Michael G. Mertens. Tel: 608-788-0311; Chester B. Moczarny. Tel: 608-787-5834; Leon A. Powell. Tel: 608-788-4625; Arnold F. Reuter. Tel: 608-788-0717; Thomas J. Smith. Tel: 608-788-4555; Raymond J. Wagner. Tel: 608-788-1172; Aloysius Wozniak.

CASHTON. *Institute of Christ the King - Sovereign Priest*, American Headquarters: Immaculate Conception Priory, 26384 CTHU, 54619-9757. Tel: 608-823-7992; Fax: 608-823-7274.
E-mail: inst.christ.king@centuryinter.net
Web site: www.institute-christ-king.org
Rev. R. Michael Schmitz.

DE SOTO. *Brothers of St. Pius X*, P.O. Box 217, 54624-0217. Tel: 608-648-2087. Bro. Charles Bisenius, Dir.

MARATHON CITY. *St. Anthony Retreat Center*, 300 E. Fourth St., 54448-9602. Tel: 715-443-2236; Fax: 715-443-2235.
E-mail: info@sarcenter.com
Web site: www.sarcenter.com
The Province of St. Joseph of the Capuchin Order, Inc. Revs. Dan Crosby, O.F.M.Cap., Leadership Team; Peter Hesse, O.F.M.Cap.; Marty Pable, O.F.M. Cap.; Florian Ruskamp, O.F.M.Cap. Priests 3; Brothers 1.

ST. MARY'S RIDGE. *Immaculate Conception Priory.* 26384 CTH U, Cashton, 54619-9757. Tel: 608-823-7992; 823-7892; Fax: 608-823-7852. Institute of Christ the King-Sovereign Priest. Rev. R. Michael Schmitz.

SPARTA. *Our Lady of Spring Bank, Cistercian Abbey*, 17304 Havenwood Rd., 54656-9536. Tel: 608-269-8138; Fax: 608-269-2800.
E-mail: Porter@MonksOnline.org
Web site: www.MonksOnline.org
Legal Office for Cistercian Monasteries Auxiliary. Revs. Robert Keffer, O.Cist., Prior Admin.; Bernard McCoy, O.Cist., Subprior & Cellerar; Rt. Rev. Blaise Fuez, O.Cist., Abbott Emeritus; Rev. Gregory Norman, O.Cist. Solemnly Professed 4; Simple Professed 1.

[I] CONVENTS AND RESIDENCES FOR SISTERS

LA CROSSE. *St. Rose Convent*, 912 Market St., 54601. Tel: 608-782-5610; Fax: 608-782-6301.
E-mail: fspa@fspa.org
Web site: www.fspa.org
Motherhouse and Novitiate of the Congregation of the Franciscan Sisters of Perpetual Adoration. Sr. Marla Lang, F.S.P.A., Pres.
In community: Professed 459; Transfers 5.
In Motherhouse: Sisters 99.

Villa St. Joseph, W2658 State Rd. 33, 54601-2625. Tel: 608-788-5100; Fax: 608-788-7360.
E-mail: mkerwin@pressenter.com
A Retirement home for aged and convalescent Sisters. Franciscan Sisters of Perpetual Adoration. Sr. Maris Kerwin, F.S.P.A., Admin. Sisters 10; Lay Staff 100; Under Care 108.

CHIPPEWA FALLS. *St. Francis Convent*, 2509 County Hwy. I, 54729. Tel: 715-723-7476. Hospital Sisters of the Third Order of St. Francis. Sr. Frances E. Schmitz, O.S.F., Coord. Professed Sisters 4.

St. Joseph Convent, 5085 176th St., 54729. Tel: 715-723-7479. Hospital Sisters of the Third Order of St. Francis.

EAU CLAIRE. *Sacred Heart Hospital Franciscan Sisters Convent*, 901 University Ave., 54701. Tel: 715-839-8725; Fax: 715-831-9670.
E-mail: sisteras@juno.com
Hospital Sisters of the Third Order of St. Francis. Sr. Augusta Sperl, O.S.F., Coord. Professed Sisters 5.

St. Bede Monastery, 1190 Priory Rd., P.O. Box 66, 54702-0066. Tel: 715-834-3176; Fax: 715-834-4292.
E-mail: sisters@saintbede.org
Web site: www.saintbede.org
Motherhouse of Sisters of the Order of St. Benedict. Retreat and Conference Center. Sr. Margaret Michaud, O.S.B., Prioress; Rev. Thomas J. Krieg, Chap. Professed 45.

Sisters of St. Benedict, The Clairemont, 2120 Heights Dr., 54701. Residence for Sisters of the Order of St. Benedict. Sr. Michaela Hedican, O.S.B., Health Care & House Coord. Sisters 9.

POLONIA. *St. Clare Convent*, 7381 Church St., 54423. Tel: 715-592-4213. Sr. M. Christella Butrymowicz, Local Min. Felician Sisters 5.

STEVENS POINT. *St. Joseph Congregational Home*, 1300 Maria Dr., 54481. Tel: 715-344-2830; Fax: 715-344-2380.
E-mail: marise@coredcs.com
Residence of the Sisters of St. Joseph of the Third Order of St. Francis. Rev. Robert W. Greatorex, Chap. Tel: 715-344-8346. Coordinators: Sr. Marise Zielinski, S.S.J.-T.O.S.F.; Sr. Janet Smolinski, S.S.J.-T.O.S.F. Sisters 65.

[J] SOCIAL SERVICE AGENCIES

LA CROSSE. *Catholic Charities of the Diocese of La Crosse, Inc.*, 128 S. 6th St., P.O. Box 266, 54601. Tel: 608-782-0710; Fax: 608-782-0702.
E-mail: info@catholiccharitieslax.org
Web site: catholiccharities.org
Counseling and Mental Health Services, Financial Counseling, Pregnancy & Parenting Services, Adoption Placement, Emergency Services, Immigration & Refugee Services. Most Rev. Raymond Burke, J.C.D., Pres.; Rev. Michael J. Gorman, J.C.L., Vice Pres. & Treas.; Sr. Marlene Weisenbeck, F.S.P.A., J.C.L., Sec.; Daniel Idzikowski, Exec. Dir. Total Staff 25.

Catholic Residential Services, Inc., 505 King St., Ste. 010, P.O. Box 2394, 54602-2394. Tel: 608-784-5323; Fax: 608-784-7522. Mr. Robert Laubach, Exec. Dir.; Sr. Joan Moran, Bd. Pres.; Josephine Smieja, Bd. Vice Pres.; John Newman, Bd. Sec. Total Staff 171; Patients assisted annually 420.

WAUSAU. *Northland House*, 102 McClellan St., 54402-0231. Tel: 715-845-4898. Operated by Catholic Residential Services, Inc., Diocese of La Crosse. Residential Care of Children. Janet R. Nissen, Admin.

[K] NEWMAN CAMPUS MINISTRY

LA CROSSE. *Roncalli Newman Parish.* Serving University of Wisconsin-La Crosse and Western Wisconsin Technical College. 1732 State St., 54601. Tel: 608-784-4994; Fax: 608-784-0280.
E-mail: newmanuw-l@juno.com
Web site: perth.uwlax.edu/newman
Rev. Mark R. Pierce, Pastor; Jon Stuttgen, Campus Min.

EAU CLAIRE. *Newman Parish.* Serving University of Wisconsin-Eau Claire and Chippewa Valley Technical College. 110 Garfield Ave., 54701-4042. Tel: 715-834-3399.
E-mail: georges128@aol.com
Web site: www.newmanec.com
Revs. George R. Szews, Pastor; Edmund J. Klimek, Assoc.; Thomas J. Krieg, Assoc.

MENOMONIE. *The Ministry to the University of Wisconsin-Stout*, 108 3rd Ave. W., 54751. Tel: 715-235-4258. Rev. Thomas J. Krieg, Chap.; Dulcie Holtz, Campus Min.

STEVENS POINT. *Newman University Parish.* Serving University of Wisconsin-Stevens Point. 2108 Fourth Ave., 54481. Tel: 715-345-6500.
E-mail: TomLNewman@aol.com
Web site: www.uwsp.edu/stuorg/newman
Rev. Thomas F. Lindner, Pastor.

[L] FOUNDATIONS, FUNDS & TRUSTS

LA CROSSE. *Aquinas High School and Aquinas Schools Foundation*, 315 S. 11th St., 54601. Tel: 608-784-0287; Fax: 608-782-8851.
E-mail: jbrengman@aquinas.la-crosse.wi.us
Web site: www.centuryinter.net/aquinas/

Bishop's Education Endowment Trust, P.O. Box 4004, 54602-4004. Tel: 608-788-7700.

Blessed Sacrament Parish Endowment Trust, 130 S. Losey Blvd., 54601. Tel: 608-782-2953; Fax: 608-785-1064.

Cathedral of St. Joseph the Workman Endowment Trust, 530 Main St., 54601. Tel: 608-782-0322.

Father Joseph Walijewski Orphanage Endowment Trust, 3710 E. Ave S., 54601. Tel: 608-788-7700; Fax: 608-788-8413. Most Rev. Raymond L. Burke, Chm.; Very Rev. Joseph J. Rajacz, V.C., Exec. Sec.

Franciscan Skemp Foundation, Inc., 700 W. Ave. South, 54601-4796. Tel: 608-784-6449; Fax: 608-791-9799. Peter Grabow, Dir.

Holy Cross Seminary Education Fund Endowment Trust, P.O. Box 4004, 54602-4004. Tel: 608-788-7700; Fax: 608-788-8413.

Holy Trinity Catholic Church Endowment Trust, 1333 S. 13th St., 54601. Tel: 608-782-2028.

La Crosse Deanery Catholic Education Endowment Trust, P.O. Box 4004, 54602-4004.

Mary, Mother of the Church Parish Endowment Trust, 2006 Weston St., 54601.

Roncalli Newman Parish Student Endowment Trust, 1732 State St., 54601. Tel: 608-784-4994; Fax: 608-784-0230.
E-mail: newmanuw-l@juno.com
Web site: perth.uwlax.edu/newman

St. James Parish Endowment Trust, 1032 Caledonia St., 54603. Tel: 608-782-7557; Fax: 608-796-0086. E-mail: scheckel@execpc.com

ALTOONA. *St. Mary Parish Endowment Trust*, 1812 Lynn Ave., 54720. Tel: 715-855-1294; Fax: 715-855-8664. E-mail: stmary1827@myexcel.com

ARCADIA. *Arcadia Catholic School Endowment Trust Fund*, 341 S. Washington St., 54612. Tel: 608-323-3676; Fax: 608-323-3780. E-mail: acs@winbright.net Web site: www.holyfam.com

Franciscan Skemp Foundation of Arcadia, Inc., 464 S. St. Joseph Ave., 54612. Tel: 608-323-3341; Fax: 608-323-3694. E-mail: tracey.robert@mayo.edu Robert Tracey, Ex-Officio.

AUBURNDALE. *St. Mary Education Endowment Trust*, Box 177, 54412-0177. Tel: 715-652-2806; Fax: 715-652-8020.

BIG RIVER. *The St. Mary's-Big River Endowment Trust*. W10139 570th Ave., River Falls, 54022. Tel: 715-425-5806.

BLAIR. *The St. Ansgar Catholic Church Endowment Trust*. 35900 Lee St., Whitehall, 54773. Tel: 715-538-4607; Fax: 715-538-2224.

CADOTT. *St. Rose of Lima Catholic Church Endowment Trust*, Box 160, 54727. Tel: 715-289-4551.

CHIPPEWA FALLS. *The Chippewa Area Catholic Schools Endowment Trust*, 1316 Bel Air Blvd., 54729. Tel: 715-723-0538; Fax: 715-723-1501.

The Education/Sustaining Endowment Trust, 412 Main St., 54729. Tel: 715-723-4890; Fax: 715-723-7358.

Friends of St. Joseph's Foundation, St. Joseph's Hospital, 2661 County Hwy. I, 54729. Tel: 715-723-3392; Fax: 715-726-3302. E-mail: bswanson@sjcf.hshs.org Web site: www.stjoeschipfalls.com

Notre Dame Children's Endowment Trust, 117 Allen St., 54729-2899. Tel: 715-723-7108; Fax: 715-723-7523.

Notre Dame Parish Endowment Trust, 117 Allen St., 54729-2899. Tel: 715-723-7108; Fax: 715-723-7523.

St. Charles Future Fund Trust, 810 Pearl St., 54729. Tel: 715-723-4088; Fax: 715-723-2195.

COLBY. *St. Mary's Catholic School, Colby Endowment Trust*, P.O. Box 436, 54421.

DURAND. *St. Mary Catholic School Endowment Trust*, 901 W. Prospect St., 54736-1049. Tel: 715-672-5617.

EAU CLAIRE. *Educational Endowment Trust of Eau Claire Coordinated Catholic Schools*, 448 N. Dewey St., 54703. Tel: 715-830-2273; Fax: 715-835-4658.

Friends of St. James the Greater Catholic School at Eau Claire Tuition Endowment Trust, 2502 11th St., 54703-2700. Tel: 715-835-5887; Fax: 715-835-3110. E-mail: stjameseac@aol.com

The Newman Parish - Eau Claire Endowment Trust, 110 Garfield Ave., 54701-4042. Tel: 715-834-3399. E-mail: pastor@newmanec.com Web site: www.newmanec.com

Regis High School Foundation, 2100 Fenwick Ave., 54701-4498. Tel: 715-830-2271; Fax: 715-830-5461.

The Sacred Heart Parish Endowment Trust, 318 Fulton St., 54703. Tel: 715-832-0925.

The St. James the Greater Catholic Church Endowment Trust, 2502 11th St., 54703-2700. Tel: 715-835-5887; Fax: 715-835-3110. E-mail: stjameseac@aol.com

St. Olaf Parish Endowment Trust, 2408 North Ln., 54703-0960.

St. Patrick Parish of Eau Claire Endowment Trust, 318 Fulton St., 54703-5399. Tel: 715-832-0925.

ELLSWORTH. *The St. Francis Parish Endowment Trust*, 264 S. Grant, Box 839, 54011. Tel: 715-273-4774; Fax: 715-273-4066. E-mail: francis@pressenter.com

HOLMEN. *St. Elizabeth Ann Seton Endowment Trust*, 515 N. Main St., 54636. Tel: 608-526-4424; Fax: 608-526-3177. E-mail: seas@aol.com

INDEPENDENCE. *The SS. Peter & Paul Parish-Independence Education Endowment Trust*, 36028 Osseo Rd., P.O. Box 428, 54747-0428. Tel: 715-985-2227; Fax: 715-985-5288.

LYNDON STATION. *Troy Quasi-Endowment Trust*, P.O. Box 303, 53944. Tel: 60/-666-2421.

MARATHON CITY. *Nativity of the Blessed Virgin Mary, Marathon Endowment Trust*, 712 Market, Box 7, 54448=0007.

MARSHFIELD. *Columbus High School Foundation*, 710 S. Columbus Ave., 54449. Tel: 715-387-2444; Fax: 715-384-4535. E-mail: chs@wctc.net Web site: www.columbus.marshfield.wi.us Michelle Keffer, Dir. Devel.

Foundation of Saint Joseph's Hospital of Marshfield, Inc., 611 St. Joseph Ave., 54729. Tel: 715-389-4072; Fax: 715-389-3993. E-mail: bosona@stjosephs-marshfield.org

The Our Lady of Peace Endowment Trust, 1414 W. 5th St., 54449. Tel: 715-384-9414; Fax: 715-384-6606.

St. John the Baptist Educational Endowment Trust, 201 W. Blodgett, Box 644, 54449-0644. Tel: 715-384-3252; Fax: 715-384-5131. E-mail: fr-stoetzel@tznet.com

St. John the Baptist Maintenance Endowment Trust, 201 W. Blodgett, Box 644, 54449-0644. Tel: 715-384-3252; Fax: 715-384-5131. E-mail: fr-stoetzel@tznet.com

MAUSTON. *St. Patrick's Congregation Trust*, 401 Mansion St., 53948-1393. Tel: 608-847-6054; Fax: 608-847-3288. E-mail: patrick@mwt.net Web site: www.stpatrickmauston.com

MENOMONIE. *The St. Joseph School at Menomonie Endowment Trust*, 910 Wilson Ave., 54747. Tel: 715-232-4922; Fax: 715-232-4923.

MOSINEE. *St. Paul Parish Endowment Trust*, 603 4th St., 54455. Tel: 715-693-2650; Fax: 715-693-1332.

NEILLSVILLE. *The St. Mary's Catholic Church Endowment Trust*, 1813 Black River Rd., 54456. Tel: 715-743-3840. E-mail: stmaryneillsville@tds.net

ONALASKA. *Charles Simpson of St. Patrick Parish, Onalaska Endowment Trust*, 1031 Main St., 54650.

Father John Rossiter and Friends Endowment Trust of St. Patrick Parish, 1031 Main St., 54650. Tel: 608-783-5535.

PITTSVILLE. *St. Joachim's Parish Endowment Trust*, P.O. Box 69, 54466-0069. Tel: 715-884-6815.

PLOVER. *St. Bronislava Parish, Plover Endowment Trust*, 3200 Plover Rd., P.O. Box 158, 54467-0158. Tel: 715-344-4326; Fax: 715-344-6121. E-mail: stbrons@stbrons.com Web site: stbrons.com Most Rev. Raymond L. Burke, Chm.; Rev. James F. Trempe, Exec. Sec.

PRAIRIE DU CHIEN. *The St. Gabriel's Endowment Trust*, 506 N. Beaumont Rd., P.O. Box 176, 53821-0176. Tel: 608-326-2404.

The St. John's Endowment Trust, 710 S. Wacouta St., P.O. Box 28, 53821-0028. Tel: 608-326-6511; Fax: 608-326-4876.

RICHLAND CENTER. *The Assumption of the Blessed Virgin Mary Parish Endowment Trust*, 160 W. 4th St., Box 456, 53581. Tel: 608-647-2621; Fax: 608-647-6029. Web site: www.mwtnet/~st.marys

ROTHSCHILD. *The St. Mark Catholic Parish Endowment Trust*, 602 Military Rd., 54474-1523.

St. Therese Catholic Church Endowment Fund, 113 Kort St., 54474. Tel: 715-359-2421; Fax: 715-355-3088.

ST. JOSEPH RIDGE. *St. Joseph Endowment Trust*. W2602 Hwy. 33, Rte. 1, La Crosse, 54601. Tel: 608-788-1646.

ST. MARY'S RIDGE. *Holy Family Endowment Trust Fund*. Rectory, 26400 CTH U, Cashton, 54619-9757. Tel: 608-823-7906; Fax: 608-823-7272. E-mail: SMR1856@centurytel.com

SPARTA. *Endowment Trust of the Friends and Parishioners of St. Patrick Parish*, 319 W. Main St., 54656-2143. Tel: 608-269-2655.

Franciscan Skemp Foundation of Sparta, Inc., 310 W. Main St., 54656-2142. Tel: 608-269-2132; Fax: 608-269-4562. Robert M. Tracey, Admin.

STEVENS POINT. *Catholic Schools Endowment Trust in Portage County, Wisconsin*, 1408 Ellis St., 54481. Tel: 715-341-2445; Fax: 715-342-2001. E-mail: ghansel@spacs.k12.wi.us Web site: www.spacs.k12.wi.us

Community Foundation of Saint Michael's Hospital, 900 Illinois Ave., 54481. Tel: 715-346-5337; Fax: 715-346-5298. E-mail: devlinp@smhosp.org Phyllis A. Devlin, Dir.

Pacelli High School Foundation, 1301 Maria Dr., 54481. Tel: 715-341-2442.

St. Joseph's Congregation, Stevens Point Endowment Trust, 1709 Wyatt Ave., 54481-3699. Tel: 715-344-3319; Fax: 715-341-2623. Most Rev. Raymond L. Burke, Chm.; Rev. Alan T. Burkhardt, Exec. Sec.

St. Stanislaus Kostka Congregation, Stevens Point Endowment Trust, 838 Fremont St., 54481. Tel: 715-344-9117; Fax: 715-344-1771. E-mail: ststan@coredcs.com Most Rev. Raymond L. Burke, Chm.; Rev. Donald L. Przyblyski, Exec. Sec.

St. Stephen Parish Endowment Trust, 1401 Clark St., 54481. Tel: 715-344-3319; Fax: 715-344-6101. E-mail: ststephen@wctc.net Web site: www.geocities.com/dol_saintstephens

STRATFORD. *St. Joseph Parish Endowment Trust*, Box 6.

TILDEN. *St. Peter Parish Endowment Trust*, 11358 CTH Q. Tel: 715-288-6484; Fax: 715-723-2195. Chippewa Falls, 54729-6115.

TOMAH. *The St. Mary's Catholic Church Educational Endowment Trust*, 203 W. Monroe St., 54660. Tel: 608-372-4516.

WAUMANDEE. *St. Boniface Parish Catholic School Endowment Trust Fund*, Box 962, 54622-0962. Tel: 608-626-2621. E-mail: stbon@mwt.net Web site: www.mwt.net/~stbon

WAUSAU. *St. Michael Parish Endowment Trust*, 1315 6th St., 54403-3599. Tel: 715-842-4283; Fax: 715-849-2509. E-mail: stmichael@dwave.net

Wausau Area Catholic Schools Endowment Trust, 602 Second St., 54403. Tel: 715-845-5735. Marian Wolaver, Admin.

WHITEHALL. *St. John Parish Endowment Trust*, 35900 Lee St., 54773. Tel: 715-538-4607; Fax: 715-538-2224.

WILLARD. *Holy Family Parish, Willard Endowment Trust*, 54493.

WISCONSIN RAPIDS. *St. Lawrence Parish, Wisconsin Rapids Endowment Trust*, 530 10th Ave. N., 54495-2566. Tel: 715-421-5777. Most Rev. Raymond L. Burke, Pres.; Rev. John P. Hogan, Contact Person.

Wisconsin Rapids Area Catholic Schools Endowment Trust, 711 Hill St., 54494. Most Rev. Raymond L. Burke, Pres.; Joseph Steepleton, Contact Person.

[M] ASSOCIATIONS OF THE FAITHFUL

PRESCOTT. *Franciscan Servants of Jesus*, Shekinah House of Prayer, 122 Court St., 54021. Tel: 715-262-3697; Fax: 715-262-4144. E-mail: amberlit@pressenter.com Web site: www.pressenter.com/namberlit Sr. Julie Green, F.S.J., Co-Director; Sr. Anne LeBlanc, F.S.J., Co-Director. In Formation 2.

TILDEN. *Institute of St. Joseph*. 11386 CTH Q, Chippewa Falls, 54729-6115. Tel: 715-288-6272; Fax: 715-288-6008. E-mail: jmj@discover-net.net Rev. William P. Felix, Moderator.

[N] SOCIETY FOR APOSTOLIC LIFE

CASHTON. *Institute of Christ the King-Sovereign Priest*, American Headquarters: Immaculate Conception Priory, 26384 CTHU, 54619-9757. Tel: 608-823-7992; 823-7892; Fax: 608-823-7274. Rev. R. Michael Schmitz, Vicar Gen. & Supr.

[O] MISCELLANEOUS LISTINGS

LA CROSSE. *The Association of Marian Catechists of the Diocese of La Crosse*, P.O. Box 4004, 54602-4004. Tel: 608-788-5752. Mary Kelemen, Acting Dir.

Franciscan Skemp Healthcare, Inc., Mayo Health System, Corporate Office, 700 West Ave. S., 54601-4796. Tel: 608-785-9710; Fax: 608-791-9429. Glenn S. Forbes, M.D., Pres. & CEO, Integrated Healthcare Delivery System. Sponsored by the Congregation of the Sisters of the Third Order of St. Francis of Perpetual Adoration (Franciscan Sisters of Perpetual Adoration) and Mayo Foundation.

Franciscan Skemp Healthcare, Mayo Health System, La Crosse Campus Clinic, 800 West Ave. S., 54601. Tel: 608-782-9760; Fax: 608-791-9429. Glenn S. Forbes, M.D., Pres. & CEO. Total Staff 525; Patient Visits 396,000.

Franciscan Skemp Medical Center, Inc., 700 West Ave. S., 54601-4796. Tel: 608-785-0940; Fax: 608-791-9429. Glenn S. Forbes, M.D., Pres. & CEO.

Mater Redemptoris House of Formation, 3730 East Ave. S., 54602. Tel: 608-788-2128. Sr. M. Stephania Newell, O.S.F., Dir.

Shrine of Our Lady of Guadalupe of the Diocese of La Crosse, Inc., 3710 East Ave. S., 54601. Tel: 608-788-7700. Julie Hogan, Admin.

ARCADIA. *Franciscan Skemp Healthcare, Mayo Health System, Arcadia Campus Clinic*, 464 St. Joseph Ave., 54612. Tel: 608-323-3341; Fax: 608-323-3694. E-mail: tracey.robert@mayo.edu Robert Tracey, Admin.

CHIPPEWA FALLS. *Northern Wisconsin Center for the Developmentally Disabled*. State Institution for the Developmentally Disabled, East Park Ave., 54729. Tel: 715-723-5542.

EAU CLAIRE. *Hospital Sisters Health Care-West, Inc.*, St. Francis Apartments, 851 University Dr., 54701. Tel: 715-834-1338.

GENOA. *The Hermitage of St. Mary, Inc.*, W1498 Spring Coulee Rd., 54632. Tel: 608-689-2753. Sr. Mary Dawiczyk, Pres. & Treas.; Rev. Gregory Norman, O.Cist., Vice Pres. & Sec.

HILLSBORO. *St. Joseph's Community Health Services*, 400 Water Ave., P.O. Box 527, 54634. Tel: 608-489-2211; Fax: 608-489-4249. E-mail: k.beaver.stjoseph@mwt.net

St. Joseph's Clinic. Tel: 608-489-4151; Fax: 608-489-4249.

St. Joseph's Nursing Home. Tel: 608-489-4236; Fax: 608-489-4249.

St. Joseph's Memorial Hospital. Tel: 608-489-2211; Fax: 608-489-2211.

MARSHFIELD.
Ministry Home Care, 611 St. Joseph Ave., 54449.

SPARTA. *Franciscan Skemp Healthcare, Mayo Health System, Sparta Campus Clinic*, 310 W. Main St., 54656-2142. Tel: 608-269-2132; Fax: 608-269-4562.
E-mail: thompson.kaye@mayo.edu
Robert M. Tracey, Admin.

STEVENS POINT. *Ministry Behavioral Health of St. Michael's Hospital, Inc.*, 209 Prentice St. N., 54481. Tel: 715-344-4611; Fax: 715-344-8127.
E-mail: josteven@coredcs.com
JoAnne Stevens, Exec. Dir. Corporate Sponsor: Ministry Healthcare, Inc. (Milwaukee, WI); Sponsored by Sisters of the Sorrowful Mother.

TOMAH. *Assisi Homes - Eldr Manor, Inc.*, 1500 Lincoln Ave., 54660. Tel: 608-372-5890. Franciscan Sisters, Daughters of the Sacred Hearts of Jesus and Mary of Wheaton, IL. Sr. Susan Dillberg, O.S.F., Pres. Purpose: to acquire or develop and operate housing projects for low income families and elderly persons.

WILLARD. *The Christine Center*, W8291 Mann Rd., 54493. Tel: 715-267-7507; Fax: 715-267-7512.
E-mail: christinecenter@hotmail.com
Sr. Johanna Seubert, F.S.P.A., Pres.

RELIGIOUS INSTITUTES OF MEN REPRESENTED IN THE DIOCESE

For further details refer to the corresponding bracketed number in the Religious Institutes of Men or Women section.

[0200]—*Benedictine Monks, Corpus Christi Abbey.* (Sandia, TX).—O.S.B.
[1180]—*Brothers of Saint Pius X.* (La Crosse).—C.S.P.X.
[0470]—*The Capuchin Friars.* (St. Joseph's Prov., Detroit).—O.F.M.Cap.
[0340]—*Cistercian Fathers.* (Sparta, WI).—O.Cist.
[1130]—*Congregation of the Priests of the Sacred Heart.* (U.S. Province).—S.C.J.
[0690]—*Jesuit Fathers and Brothers.* (Missouri Prov. & Wisconsin Prov.).—S.J.
[0430]—*Order of Preachers.* Cracow, Poland Province).—O.P.
[]—*Secular Institute of Schoenstadt of Mary.* (Waukesha, WI).
[0990]—*Society of the Catholic Apostolate.* (India Province).—S.S.C.
[1200]—*Society of the Divine Savior.* (Milwaukee).—S.D.S.

RELIGIOUS INSTITUTES OF WOMEN REPRESENTED IN THE DIOCESE

[0230]—*Benedictine Sisters of Pontifical Jurisdiction.* (Eau Claire, WI).—O.S.B.
[1010]—*Congregation of Divine Providence.* (San Antonio,TX).—C.D.P.
[0470]—*Congregation of Sisters of Charity of the Incarnate Word.* (San Antonio, TX).—C.C.V.I.
[1070-09]—*Congregation of St. Catherine of Siena.* (Racine, WI).—O.P.
[1170]—*Congregation of the Sisters of St. Felix of Cantalice, of the III Order of St. Francis.* (Chicago, IL).—C.S.S.F.
[1780]—*Congregation of the Sisters of the Third Order of St. Francis of Perpetual Adoration.* (La Crosse, WI).—F.S.P.A.
[]—*Daughters of the Redeemer.* (Zambia).
[1310]—*Franciscan Sisters of Little Falls, Minnesota.*—O.S.F.
[1240]—*Franciscan Sisters, Daughters of the Sacred Hearts of Jesus and Mary.* (Wheaton, IL).—O.S.F.
[1820]—*Hospital Sisters of the Third Order of St. Francis.* (Springfield, IL).—O.S.F.
[2970]—*School Sisters of Notre Dame.* (Milwaukee Prov.).—S.S.N.D.
[1680]—*School Sisters of St. Francis.* (Milwaukee, WI).—O.S.F.
[3590]—*Servants of Mary.* (Ladysmith, WI).—O.S.M.
[1070-03]—*Sinsinawa Dominican Congregation of the Most Holy Rosary.*—O.P.
[2630]—*Sisters of Mercy of the Holy Cross.* (Merrill, WI).
[1620]—*Sisters of St. Francis of Millvale.* (Pittsburgh, PA).—O.S.F.
[1570]—*Sisters of St. Francis of the Holy Family.* (Dubuque, IA).—O.S.F.
[1600]—*Sisters of St. Francis of the Martyr St. George.* (Alton, IL, Prov. of St. Elizabeth).—O.S.F.
[1720]—*Sisters of St. Francis of the Third Order Regular of St. Francis of the Congregation of Our Lady of Lourdes.* (Rochester, MN).—O.S.F.
[3930]—*Sisters of St. Joseph - Third Order Regular.* (Stevens Point, WI).—S.S.J.-T.O.S.F.
[1030]—*Sisters of the Divine Savior.*—S.D.S.
[4100]—*Sisters of the Sorrowful Mother.* (U.S./Carribean Prov.).—S.S.M.
[1705]—*Sisters of the Third Order of St. Francis of Assisi of Penance and Charity.* (Milwaukee, WI).—O.S.F.
[]—*Tertiary Sisters of St. Francis.* (Cameroon Province).

DIOCESAN CEMETERIES

LA CROSSE. *Catholic*, 519 Losey Blvd. S., 54601. Tel: 608-782-0238. Jeffrey Reinhart, Supt.
Gate of Heaven Cemetery; French Island Cemetery.
Woodlawn, 3636 Mormon Coulee Rd., 54601. Tel: 608-788-0980. John Reinhart, Supt.

CHIPPEWA FALLS. *Hope Cemetery and Mausoleum*, 418 N. State St., 54729. Tel: 715-723-0792. Walter Hurt, Supt.

EAU CLAIRE. *Calvary Cemetery and Mausoleum*, P.O. Box 755, 54702-0755. Tel: 715-832-1411. Rodney Sorenson, Mgr.

MARSHFIELD. *Gate of Heaven*, 1803 S. Maple Ave., 54449. Tel: 715-384-3869. Marvin Fait, Pres.; Monica Herman, Sec.; Michael Boltus, Maintenance.

STEVENS POINT. *Stevens Point Area Catholic Cemetery Association, Inc.*, P.O. Box 497, 54481. Tel: 715-341-3236. Jack Okonek, Supt.; Shirley Suplicki, Exec. Sec. & Treas.

NECROLOGY

† Curtiss, John B., (Retired). —Died Sept. 8, 2000.
† Ennis, James E., Hillsboro, WI St. Aloysius Parish. —Died Feb. 11, 2000.
† Leinfelder, Philip, (Retired). —Died May 2, 2000.
† Murphy, John T., (Retired). —Died July 23, 2000.
† Nikolai, William V., (Retired). —Died Oct. 19, 2000.
† Peters, Raymond, (Retired). —Died June 27, 2000.

Diocese of Las Cruces

(Dioecesis Las Cruces)

Most Reverend

RICARDO RAMIREZ, C.S.B., D.D.

Bishop of Las Cruces; ordained December 10, 1966; appointed Titular Bishop of Vatarba and Auxiliary of San Antonio October 27, 1981; consecrated December 6, 1981; appointed First Bishop of Las Cruces August 31, 1982; installed October 18, 1982. *Res., 455 W. Palmer Rd., Las Cruces, NM, 88005.*

ESTABLISHED OCTOBER 18, 1982.

Square Miles 44,483.

Comprises the Counties of Dona Ana, Hidalgo, Grant, Luna, Sierra, Otero, Lincoln, Chaves, Eddy and Lea in the State of New Mexico.

For legal titles of parishes and diocesan institutions, consult The Pastoral Center.

The Pastoral Center: 1280 Med Park Dr., Las Cruces, NM, 88005. Tel.: 505-523-7577; Fax: 505-524-3874.

Web site address: www.zianet.com/diocese/

E-mail address: diocese@zianet.com

STATISTICAL OVERVIEW

Personnel	
Bishop	1
Priests: Diocesan Active in Diocese	20
Priests: Retired, Sick or Absent	11
Number of Diocesan Priests	31
Religious Priests in Diocese	51
Extern Priests in Diocese	3
Permanent Deacons in Diocese	25
Total Brothers	2
Total Sisters	45
Parishes	
Parishes	44
With Resident Pastor:	
Resident Diocesan Priests	16
Resident Religious Priests	24
Without Resident Pastor:	
Administered by Priests	1
Administered by Deacons	1
Administered by Women Religious	3
Missions	45
Pastoral Centers	2
Professional Ministry Personnel:	
Brothers	1
Sisters	8
Lay Ministers	27
Welfare	
Health Care Centers	3
Total Assisted	35,000
Day Care and Extended Day Care Centers	3
Total Assisted	226
Special Centers for Social Services	1
Total Assisted	7,600
Educational	
Diocesan Students in Other Seminaries	1
Total Seminarians	1
Elementary Schools, Diocesan and Parish	4
Total Students	624
Catechesis/Religious Education:	
High School Students	2,564
Elementary Students	8,333
Total Students Under Catholic Instruction	11,522
Teachers in the Diocese:	
Sisters	2
Lay Teachers	60
Vital Statistics	
Receptions into the Church:	
Infant Baptism Totals	2,414
Adult Baptism Totals	232
Received into Full Communion	94
First Communions	2,142
Confirmations	1,664
Marriages:	
Catholic	363
Interfaith	80
Total Marriages	443
Deaths	984
Total Catholic Population	132,646
Total Population	484,637

The Pastoral Center—1280 Med Park Dr., Las Cruces, 88005. Tel: 505-523-7577; Fax: 505-524-3874. Office Hours: Mon.-Fri. 8:00-4:30.

Bishops Administrative Council—Most Rev. RICARDO RAMIREZ, C.S.B.; Very Rev. Msgr. JOHN E. ANDERSON; Revs. ROBERT POWER, C.S.B.; DENIS TEJADA; Sr. CATHERINE DARCY, R.S.M.; DAVID MCNAMARA.

Vicar General—Very Rev. Msgr. JOHN E. ANDERSON.

Episcopal Vicar for Clergy and Personnel—Very Rev. Msgr. ROBERT L. GETZ.

Chancellor—Sr. CATHERINE DARCY, R.S.M.

Director of Clergy Personnel—Very Rev. Msgr. JOHN E. ANDERSON.

Diocesan Tribunal—Rev. JOHN S. WEBER, O.F.M.Conv., J.C.L., Judicial Vicar; Sr. CATHERINE C. DARCY, R.S.M., J.C.D., Admin. Dir., *1280 Med Park Dr., Las Cruces, 88005.*

Promoter of Justice—Very Rev. DANIEL R. BARFIELD, S.J.

Judges—Very Revs. GILES CARIE, O.F.M.Conv.; JOHN M. WILSON, C.S.B., J.C.L.; Rev. ENRIQUE LOPEZ-ESCALERA, J.C.L.; Deacon ALPHONSO F. BOWERS; Sr. CATHERINE C. DARCY, R.S.M., J.C.D.

Defenders of the Bond—Very Rev. DANIEL R. BARFIELD, S.J.; Very Rev. Msgr. JOHN E. ANDERSON, V.G.; Revs. DAVID BERGS; RICHARD CATANACH; MICHAEL LINDSAY; NOEL KRAMER, O.F.M.Conv.

Canonical Assistant—IRENE PORTILLO.

Assesors—JUDITH MONTES; DANIEL MONTES; CHARLOTTE KINCH.

Advocates—Sr. JANE KERNS, S.H.C.J.; JUDY MONTES; DAN MONTES.

Notaries—IRENE V. PORTILLO; VELIA SALINAS.

Vicars—Revs. ROBERT POWER, C.S.B.; RICHARD CATANACH; VALENTINE JANKOWSKI, O.F.M.Conv.; DENNIS FOUNTAIN, O.F.M.Conv.; ANDRES ALAVA, O.A.R.; DAVID BERGS.

Diocesan Consultors—Very Rev. Msgr. JOHN E. ANDERSON; Very Rev. Msgr. ROBERT L. GETZ; Revs. ANDRES ALAVA, O.A.R.; RICHARD CATANACH; DENNIS FOUNTAIN, O.F.M.Conv.; VALENTINE JANKOWSKI, O.F.M.Conv.; MICHAEL LINDSAY; CONRADO PYTLIK; ART ROBERTS; DENIS TEJADA.

Presbyteral Council—Revs. RICHARD CATANACH, Pres. WILLIAM MCCANN, Vice Pres. ALFRED GALVAN, Sec.; Very Rev. Msgr. JOHN E. ANDERSON; Very Rev. Msgr. ROBERT L. GETZ; Revs. ANDRES ALAVA, O.A.R.; DAVID BERGS; DENNIS FOUNTAIN, O.F.M.Conv.; VALENTINE JANKOWSKI, O.F.M.Conv.; NOEL KRAMER, O.F.M.Conv.; MICHAEL LINDSAY; ED HERRERA; ANTHONY CLARK; DONALD ADAMSKI, O.F.M.Conv.; ENRIQUEZ LOPEZ; ROBERT POWER, C.S.B.; CONRADO PYTLIK; ART ROBERTS, C.S.B.; DENIS TEJADA; ROBERT YOUNG, O.F.M.; JOHN WEBER, O.F.M.Conv., J.C.L.; THOMAS DEVINE, O.A.R.; MICHAEL CERRETO, C.S.B.; PAUL BOTENHAGEN, O.F.M.

Priests Personnel Board—Most Rev. RICARDO RAMIREZ, C.S.B.; Very Rev. Msgr. JOHN E. ANDERSON; Very Rev. Msgr. ROBERT L. GETZ; Revs. MICHAEL LINDSAY; RODERICK NICHOLS; ENRIQUE LOPEZ; DENIS TEJADA; Deacon DANIEL CHECK; Sr. CATHERINE DARCY, R.S.M.

Priestly Life and Ministry Committee—Most Rev. RICARDO RAMIREZ, C.S.B.; Very Rev. Msgr. ROBERT L. GETZ; Revs. DAVID BERGS; RICHARD CATANACH; FRANKLIN EICHHORST, O.F.M.Cap; RICARDO HINOJAL, O.A.R.; VALENTINE JANKOWSKI, O.F.M.Conv.; MICHAEL LINDSAY; ROBERT POWER, C.S.B.; JOHN TICKLE.

Pastoral Center Personnel Committee—Sr. CATHERINE DARCY, R.S.M.; MAGGIE CANDIA; MARGARET FLORES; ARTHUR E. JIRON; IRENE PORTILLO; DEBBIE ISHAM MOORE; SUSAN ROBERTS; PHILIP ALVAREZ.

Priests Retirement Fund Committee—Very Rev. Msgr. ROBERT L. GETZ; Revs. DAVID BERGS; MICHAEL LINDSAY; WILLIAM MCCANN; Mr. DANIEL DOLAN; FELIPE SALCIDO, JR.

Permanent Deacon Council—Deacons JOHN LUCERO, Chm. WILLIAM HOLGUIN, Sec. DANIEL CHECK; SAM NAVARETTE; PETE VELOTT; BENJAMIN VIGIL.

Deacon Formation—Deacon PETE VELOTT, Dir.

Comptroller—FELIPE SALCIDO, JR.

Finance Council—Most Rev. RICARDO RAMIREZ, C.S.B.; Very Rev. Msgr. JOHN E. ANDERSON; Rev. RICHARD CATANACH; Sr. CATHERINE DARCY, R.S.M.; SAM ACOSTA; DON BEASLEY; DAN DOLAN; RICHARD FORCE; GILBERT GOMEZ; HAROLD GRANDI; DAVID MCNAMARA; EDWARD PILLAR; CHARLENE WARD.

Office of Development and Foundation—SUSAN ROBERTS, Exec. Dir. PATRICIA PADILLA-TORRES, Devel. Assoc.

Office of Insurance—MARTA ROMERO, Insurance Dir.

Office of Buildings and Properties—Rev. DENIS TEJADA, Dir. MANUEL LEYVA, Asst.

Diocesan Ministries Offices and Directors

Office of Director of Ministries—DAVID MCNAMARA.

Office of Adult Catechesis—DAVID MCNAMARA.

Office of Vocations—Rev. Enrique Lopez, Dir.
Art and Environment Committee—Sr. Lucy Meissen, C.PP.S.
Attorney—Daniel Dolan.
Campus Ministry—Revs. Mitchell Dowalgo, C.S.B.; Marcos Reyna, O.F.M.Conv.
Judicial Vicar—Rev. John Weber, O.F.M.Conv., J.C.L.
Office of Catholic Social Ministry—Antonio Lujan, Dir. Carlos Corral, Assoc. Dir.
Colonias Development Council—Diana Bustamante, Dir.
Office of Parish 2000—David McNamara, Dir.
Cursillo Secretariat—Victor Rodriguez, Pres. Blanca Luna, Treas. Vicente Luna, Sec.
Office of Elementary Catechesis—David McNamara, Dir.
Lay Ministry Formation—William Rademacher, Dir.
Ecumenical Liaison—Sr. Jane Kerns, S.H.C.J.
Hispanic Ministry—Rev. Robert Power, C.S.B.
Holy Childhood Association—Very Rev. Msgr. John E. Anderson.
Hospital Ministry—Minerva Romero.
Office of Liturgical Education—Sr. Lucy Meissen, C.PP.S.
Propogation of the Faith—Very Rev. Msgr. John E. Anderson.
Order of Christian Initiation—Sr. Lucy Meissen, C.PP.S., Adult; David McNamara, Children; Sr. Jane Marie Kerns, S.H.C.J.; Romelia Enriquez; Esteban Roal; Sally Harper.
Office of Adolescent Catechesis and Youth Ministry—Kevin Vigil.
Pastoral Councils—David McNamara; Antonio Lujan; Sr. Catherine Darcy, R.S.M.; William Rademacher.
Diocesan Resource Center—David McNamara, Coord. Dolores Diaz, Librarian.
Diocesan Archives—Joanna Harmon, Archivist.
Charismatic Renewal Liaisons—Leo Marrufo, (East); Mr. Sam Tome, (West); Mrs. Enedina Tome, (West).
Agua Viva—Christy Anchondo, Editor; David McNamara, Special Projects.
Agua Viva Editorial Advisory Board—Rev. Robert Power, C.S.B.; Sr. Catherine C. Darcy, R.S.M.; Philip Alvarez; Ruben Abeyta; Christy Anchondo; Lala Gonzalez; Manuel Leyva; Antonio Lujan; David McNamara; Betty Moreno.
Office of Jail and Prison Ministry—Richard Petrillo, Coord. Carmely Hamilton, Dir. Training.
Office of Marriage and Family Life—Richard Petrillo, Coord.
Office of Catholic Schools—Sr. Joan Berninger, M.M., Supt.
Pro-Life Coordinators—Joseph Behnke; Elizabeth Behnke.

CLERGY, PARISHES, MISSIONS AND PAROCHIAL SCHOOLS

CITY OF LAS CRUCES
(Dona Ana County)

1—Cathedral of Immaculate Heart of Mary, Revs. Robert E. Power, C.S.B., Rector; John Tickle; Michael Cerreto, C.S.B.
Office: 1240 S. Espina St., 88001. Tel: 505-524-8563; Fax: 505-523-2252.
Campus—Las Cruces Area Catholic School, 865 E. Idaho, 88001. Tel: 505-524-8563.
Lay Teachers 11; Students 106.

2—Holy Cross (1970), Very Rev. Msgr. John E. Anderson; Rev. Manuel Ibarra.
Office: 1327 N. Miranda St., 88005. Tel: 505-523-0167; Fax: 505-523-8023.
Campus—Las Cruces Area Catholic School, 1331 N. Miranda, 88001. Tel: 505-526-2517; Fax: 505-523-8023.
Sisters 1; Lay Teachers 23; Students 234.

3—Our Lady of Health (1956), Revs. Ricardo Hinojal, O.A.R.; Dionisio Gutierrez, O.A.R.
Res., 1178 N. Mesquite, 88001. Tel: 505-526-9545; Fax: 505-526-9545.

4—St. Albert the Great Newman Parish. Serving New Mexico State University. Revs. Mitchell G. Dowalgo, C.S.B.; Mark Gazin, C.S.B.; Deacon Pete Velott.
Res., 2615 S. Solano, 88001. Tel: 505-522-6202; Fax: 505-521-3453.

5—St. Genevieve (1859), Revs. Denis Tejada; Juan Moreno; Martin Cordero.
Res., 100 S. Espina, 88001. Tel: 505-524-9649. [CEM]

6—Santa Rosa de Lima, Rev. Jesus Espinosa, O.A.R.
Church—5035 Holsome Rd., 88011. Tel: 505-382-8123.

OUTSIDE THE CITY OF LAS CRUCES

Alamogordo, Otero Co., Immaculate Conception, Revs. Bryant Hausfeld, O.F.M.; Gregg D. Petri, O.F.M.; Bruce Hausfeld, O.F.M.; Deacons Levy Lucero; Donald Dichman.
Res., 705 Delaware Ave., 88310. Tel: 505-437-3291; Fax: 505-437-3239. [CEM]
School—Rev. James B. Hay, 1000 E. Eighth St., 88310. Tel: 505-437-7821. Gilbert Candelaria, Prin.
Lay Teachers 6; Students 105.
Missions—Boles Acres, Our Lady of the Desert; La Luz, Our Lady of the Light; Cloudcroft, Sacred Heart.

St. Jude (1965), Very Rev. Daniel R. Barfield, S.J.; Deacon Adam Sanchez.
Office: 1404 College Ave., 88310. Tel: 505-437-0238; Fax: 505-437-0267.

Anthony, Dona Ana Co., St. Anthony's (1899), Revs. Thomas J. Devine, O.A.R.; Juan Almarza, O.A.R.
Res., P.O. Box 2624, 88021. Tel: 505-882-2239; Fax: 505-882-2239. [CEM]
Church—224 Lincoln St., 88021. Tel: 505-882-2239.
Convent—Chaparral, MN 88021. Tel: 505-824-0508. Hermanas Dominicas de la Doctrina Cristiana
Missions—Chaparral, St. Thomas More, 528 E. Paseo, Chaparral, 88021. Tel: 505-824-4433. Rev. Miguel Echeverria, O.A.R.; La Union, Our Lady of Refuge, Rte. 1, Box 484A, La Union, 88021. Tel: 505-589-0542. Sr. Mary Ellen Quinn, R.S.M., Parish Life Coord.; Berino, Immaculate Conception, San Benito Rd., P.O. Box 155, Berino, 88024.

Artesia, Eddy Co., St. Anthony, Rev. Dennis Fountain.
Res., 502 S. Ninth St., 88210. Tel: 505-746-4471.

Our Lady of Grace (1942), Revs. Vincent Petersen, O.F.M.Conv.; Alcuin Hunter, O.F.M. Conv.; Deacon Pablo Metjil.
Res., 1111 N. Roselawn Ave., 88210. Tel: 505-748-1356; Fax: 505-748-1049.
Catechesis/Religious Programs—Martha Shoemaker, D.R.E.
Students 452.

Bayard, Grant Co., Our Lady of Fatima (1950), Revs. Paulus Kao; Virgilio Flores.
Res., P.O. Box 1425, 88023. Tel: 505-537-2421.
Missions—Fierro, Grant Co., St. Anthony; Hanover, Grant Co., Holy Family; San Lorenzo, Grant Co., San Lorenzo. Deacon Alfonso Alvarado, Parish Life Coord.

Carlsbad, Eddy Co., St. Edward (1893), Rev. Noel R. Kramer, O.F.M.Conv. In res., Rev. Maurus Hauer, O.F.M. Conv.
Office: 209 N. Guadalupe St., 88220. Tel: 505-885-6600; Fax: 505-885-9992.
Res., 610 W. Stevens, 88220. Tel: 505-887-6486.
School—(Grades K-5) 805 Walter St., 88220. Tel: 505-885-4620; Fax: 505-885-7706. Bob Porter, Prin.
Lay Teachers 6; Students 82.

San Jose (1902), Rev. Valentine Jankowski, O.F.M. Conv.
Res., 1002 DeBaca, 88220. Tel: 505-885-5792; Fax: 505-887-3553.
Religious Education Center—Tel: 505-887-1346. Patsy Grantner, D.R.E.
Students 241.

Carrizozo, Lincoln Co., St. Rita, Rev. David J. Bergs.
Res., Box 727, 88301. Tel: 505-648-2853; Fax: 505-648-2853.
Missions—Capitan, Sacred Heart; Corona, St. Therese of the Little Flower.

Santa Clara, Grant Co., Santa Clara (1888), Rev. Michael P. Lindsay.
Res., P.O. Box 215, 88026. Tel: 505-537-3713; Fax: 505-537-3472.

Chamberino, Dona Ana Co., San Luis Rey (1959), Rev. Robert Villegas, C.S.C.
Res., P.O. Box 230, 88027. Tel: 505-882-2045.
Convent—920 Convent Rd., P.O. Box 149, 88027. Tel: 505-882-5811. Our Lady of Guadalupe Franciscan Missionaries of Mary 4.

Deming, Luna Co., Holy Family (1905), Rev. David Bentley, Admin.
Res., 612 S. Copper Ave., 88030. Tel: 505-546-3356; Fax: 505-546-0123.

St. Ann's (1918), Rev. Richard Catanach.
Res., 400 S. Ruby St., 88030. Tel: 505-546-3343.
Catechesis/Religious Programs—901 S. Pearl (Fr. Stanley Hall), 88030. Tel: 505-546-3905. Teresita D. Scully, D.R.E.
Students 309.
Mission—Deming, Luna Co., Holy Family, 400 S. Ruby St., 88030. Tel: 505-531-2373.

Dexter, Chavez Co., Immaculate Conception, Deacon Jesus Herrera, Admin.
Res., 400 W. Fifth, P.O. Box 189, 88230. Tel: 505-734-5478.
Missions—Lake Arthur, Our Lady of Guadalupe, 204 Broadway, Lake Arthur, 88253.; Hagerman, St. Catherine, 200 S. Texas, Hagerman, 88232.

Dona Ana, Dona Ana Co., Our Lady of the Purification, Rev. Miguel Macaya; Deacons Daniel Check; Rigoberto Chavez.
Mailing Address: P.O. Box 706, 88032. Tel: 505-526-2114. [JC]
Mission—San Isidro, Dona Ana Co., San Isidro.

Garfield, Dona Ana Co., San Isidro (1945), Sr. Marie Paule Willem, F.M.M., Parish Life Coord.
Res., H.C. 31, Box 43, 87936-9701. Tel: 505-267-5111; Fax: 505-267-1887.
Missions—San Jose, Sierra Co., Arrey; Hillsboro, Sierra Co., Our Lady of Guadalupe.

Hatch, Dona Ana Co., Our Lord of Mercy (1889), Rev. William McCann.
Res., Box 321, 87937. Tel: 505-267-4983; Fax: 505-267-4983.
Mission—Rincon, Dona Ana Co., Our Lady of All Nations.

Hobbs, Lea Co., Our Lady of Guadalupe, Rev. Jose Pedro Valdez; Deacon Samuel Navarrette.
Office: 914 S. Selman, 88240. Tel: 505-393-4991; Fax: 505-397-1480.

St. Helena (1951), Revs. Donald J. Adamski, O.F.M.Conv.; Jose Reyes, O.F.M.Conv. Pastoral Assocs.: Sr. Margaret McTaggert, S.S.C.; Sr. Delphine Grigas, S.S.C.
Res., 100 E. Bender Blvd., 88240. Tel: 505-392-7551; 7552; Fax: 505-392-3333.
School—Tel: 505-392-5405; Fax: 505-392-0128. Mrs. Libby Isselharo, Head Teacher.
Lay Teachers 7; Students 81.
Convent—110 E. Bender, 88240. Tel: 505-392-8115.

Hurley, Grant Co., Infant Jesus (1916), Rev. Daniel Porter.
Res., Box 97, 88043. Tel: 505-537-3691; 536-9405.
Missions—San Juan, Grant Co., San Juan; Faywood, Luna Co., San Jose.

Jal, Lea Co., St. Cecilia (1941), Rev. Dr. Roderick J. Garvey, C.SS.R.
Res., P.O. Box 430, 300 N. Nevada St., 88252. Tel: 505-395-2431; 505-395-2238 (Hall); Fax: 505-395-2431.

La Mesa, Dona Ana Co., San Jose, Revs. Andres Alava, O.A.R.; Jesus Perez-Recio, O.A.R.
Res., P.O. Box 278, 88044. Tel: 505-233-3191.
Mission—Vado, Dona Ana Co., San Pedro Del Cerro, P.O. Box 281, La Mesa, 88048. Tel: 505-233-3977.

Lordsburg, Hidalgo Co., St. Joseph (1900), Rev. Anthony Clark.
Res., 416 E. Second St., 88045. Tel: 505-542-3268.
Missions—Cotton City, St. Jude; Rodeo, San Felipe; Playas, St. Augustine; Hachita, St. Catherine.

Loving, Eddy Co., Our Lady of Grace, Rev. Valentine Jankowski.
Res., 301 4th St., P.O. Box 428, 88256. Tel: 505-745-3341.
Mission—Malaga, Cristo Rey.

Lovington, Lea Co., St. Thomas Aquinas, Rev. Franklin Eichhorst, O.F.M.Cap.
Res., 1301 N. Ninth St., 88260. Tel: 505-396-4206; Fax: 505-396-4206.
Mission—Tatum, Our Lady of the Holy Rosary.

Mescalero, Otero Co., St. Joseph (1895) (Apache Indian Mission), Rev. Paul Botenhagen, O.F.M.; Bro. Peter Boegel, O.F.M.; Sr. Robert Ann Hecker, O.S.F.
Res., Box 187, 88340. Tel: 505-671-4473; Fax: 505-671-1511.
Missions—Bent, Our Lady of Guadalupe, 123 Mission Trail, Bent, 88340.; Three Rivers, Otero Co., St. Patrick. P.O. Box 187.

Mesilla, Dona Ana Co., St. Albino (1852), Rev. Conrad E. Pytlik.
Res., P.O. Box 26, 88046. Tel: 505-526-9349; Fax: 505-647-1619.
Mission—Fairacres, Dona Ana Co., San Jose Mission, P.O. Box 502, Fairacres, 88033. Tel: 505-647-1979. Rev. John Weber.

Mesilla Park, Dona Ana Co., Shrine and Parish of Our Lady of Guadalupe, Rev. Ivan Rohloff, O.F.M.Conv.; Deacon Al Bowers.
Res., Box 298, 88047. Tel: 505-526-8171; Fax: 505-523-1175.

Roswell, Chaves Co., St. Peter (1903), Rev. Dennis Fountain, O.F.M. In res., Revs. Ramon Smith, O.F.M.; John Lanzrath, O.F.M.; Lawrence Schreiber, O.F.M.
Res., 111 E. Derning, 88201. Tel: 505-622-5742; Fax: 505-623-9228.

St. John the Baptist (1903) (Hispanic), Rev. Juan Montoya, O.F.M.; Deacon Jesus Herrera.
Res., 506 S. Lincoln, 88201. Tel: 505-622-3531; Fax: 505-623-8933.

Assumption of the Blessed Virgin Mary (1963), Rev. Msgr. Robert Getz.
Res., 2808 N. Kentucky, 88201. Tel: 505-622-9895; Fax: 505-622-6845.

Ruidoso, Lincoln Co., St. Eleanor (1939), Rev. Alfred Galvan; Deacon Benjamin Vigil.
Res., P.O. Box 8300, 120 Junction Rd., 88355. Tel: 505-257-2330; Fax: 505-257-7062.
Missions—San Patricio, St. Jude Thaddeus; Lincoln, San Juan; Fort Stanton, Sacred Heart; Picacho, St. Joseph; Glenco, San Ysidro.

San Miguel, Dona Ana Co., San Miguel, Rev. Jose Luis Duenas, O.A.R.
Res., Drawer E, 88058. Tel: 505-233-2453; Fax: 505-233-2453.
Augustinian Recollects: P.O. Box 310, Mesilla, 88046. Tel: 505-523-7030; Fax: 505-233-7030.
Mission—Mesquite, Our Lady of Perpetual Help, P.O. Box 48, 88048. Tel: 505-233-4695.

Silver City, Grant Co., St. Vincent de Paul (1874), Rev. Rodrick Nichols; Deacons William Holguin; Johnnie Perez.
Res., 414 Bayard St., P.O. Box 1189, 88061. Tel: 505-538-9373; Fax: 505-388-0870.
Missions—Gila, Grant Co., St. Isidore; Pinos Altos, Grant Co., Holy Cross.
St. Francis Newman Center Parish. Serving Western New Mexico University. Rev. Marcos Reyna, O.F.M.Conv., Admin.
Res., 914 W. 13th St., 88061. Tel: 505-538-3662; Fax: 505-534-1059.

Sunland Park, Dona Ana Co., St. Martin de Porres (1964), Rev. Edward Herrera; Deacons Jesus Favela; Jesus Medina.
Res., P.O. Box 248, 88063. Tel: 505-589-2106.

Tularosa, Otero Co., St. Francis de Paula (1868), Revs. Clifford Herle, O.F.M.; Peter A. Verheggen, O.F.M.
Res., 303 Encino, 88352. Tel: 505-585-2793; Fax: 505-585-3005. [CEM]

Truth or Consequences, Sierra Co., Our Lady of Perpetual Help (1916), Revs. Art Roberts, C.S.B.; Donald Hyatt, C.S.B.; Sean Garrity, C.S.B.
Res., 103 E. Sixth Ave., 87901. Tel: 505-894-7804; Fax: 505-894-0451.
Missions—Cuchillo, Sierra Co., St. Joseph; Las Palomas, Sierra Co., San Ysidro; Montecello, Sierra Co., St. Ignatius; Placitas, Sierra Co., San Lorenzo.
Chapels—St. Gregory, Chapels Chise.; San Miguel, Rancho de San Miguel.; Winston, St. Jude.

Special Assignment:
Reverend Fathers—
Anderson, Joe, O.S.B.
Morgan, Arthur

Absent On Leave:
Reverend Fathers—
Amezaga, Louis

Absent On Sick Leave:
Reverend Fathers—
Beggane, Thomas

Retired:
Reverend Monsignors—
Lynch, Richard
Milano, James
VonderHaar, Roland
Reverend Fathers—
Griffith, Edwin
Lafrenz, James

Permanent Deacons:
Alvarado, Alfonso, Blackrange Stations, San Lorenzo
Bowers, Al, Our Lady of Guadalupe, Mesilla Park
Chavez, Rigoberto, Our Lady of Purification, Dona Ana
Check, Daniel
Crowder, Richard, (Retired)
Daniel, Gregory T., St. Helena, Hobbs
Dickman, Donald, Our Lady of the Light, La Luz
Dougil, Edward, (Retired)
Favela, Jesus, San Martin de Porres, Sunland Park
Gale, Howard, (Retired)
Herrera, Jesus, Immaculate Conception, Dexter
Holguin, William, St. Vincent de Paul, Silver City
Lucero, John S., Holy Cross, Las Cruces
Lucero, Levy, Immaculate Conception, Alamogordo
Luevano, Manuel, Outside Diocese
Medina, Jesus, San Martin de Porres, Sunland Park
Merjil, Pablo, Our Lady of Grace, Artesia
Narvaez, Arthur, (Retired)
Navarrette, Sam, Our Lady of Guadalupe, Hobbs
Perez, Johnnie, St. Vincent de Paul, Silver City
Polson, Charles, On Sabbatical
Roane, Tom, St. Helena, Hobbs
Sanchez, Adam L., St. Jude, Alamogordo
Schretlen, Frank, (Retired)
Velott, Pete, St. Albert Newman Center, Las Cruces
Vigil, Benjamin, St. Eleanors, Ruidoso

INSTITUTIONS LOCATED IN THE DIOCESE

[A] CLINICS

CARLSBAD. *St. Mary's Health Care Center*, 2330 West Pierce, 88220. Tel: 505-887-0516; Fax: 505-885-8239
For a complete listing, refer to the Special Care Facilities section.

HOBBS. *St. Mary Medical Center*, 2410 North Fowler, 88240. Tel: 505-392-5572; Fax: 505-392-4848
For a complete listing, refer to the Special Care Facilities section.
St. Mary's Family Health Care Center, 515 East Main, 88240. Tel: 505-393-1096; Fax: 505-393-3758
For a complete listing, refer to the Special Care Facilities section.

[B] MONASTERIES & RESIDENCES OF PRIESTS AND BROTHERS

LAS CRUCES. *Basilian Fathers*, 1682 Alta Vista Pl., 88011. Tel: 505-522-1263; Fax: 505-505-2042.
Web site: www.basilian.org
Revs. Mitchell G. Dowalgo, C.S.B., Rector; Robert E. Power, C.S.B.; Michael Cerretto, C.S.B.; Mark R. Gazin, C.S.B.

MESILLA. *Augustinian Recollect Fathers*. Province of St. Nicholas of Tolentine, Provincial Delegation in the South of U.S.A. San Alypius House, P.O. Box 310, 88046. Tel: 505-523-7030. Revs. Andres Alava, O.A.R.; Antonio Martinez, O.A.R; Jose Luis Duenas, O.A.R.; Jose Luis Garayoa, O.A.R.

[C] CONVENTS AND RESIDENCES FOR SISTERS

ANTHONY. *Sisters of Mercy of the Americas (Omaha Region)*, 301 Lincoln St., P.O. Box 2411, 88021. Tel: 505-882-5553; Fax: 505-882-7312. Sisters 3.

CHAMBERINO. *Franciscan Missionaries of Mary*, P.O. Box 149, 88027. Tel: 505-882-5811; Fax: 505-882-5374.
E-mail: FMMLupe@aol.com

CHAPPARAL. *Dominicas De La Doctrina Cristiana*, 124 Tornillo, 88021. Tel: 505-824-0508. Professed 5; Novices 6.

DEMING. *Daughters of the Heart of Mary*, P.O. Box 1531, 88030. Tel: 505-546-7599.
E-mail: nazhouse@swnm.com

GARFIELD. *Franciscan Missionaries of Mary*, Loma Parade St., 2003, 87936-9701. Tel: 505-267-5111; Fax: 505-267-1887.

LAUNION. *Sisters of Mercy - Omaha Region*, 1320 Mercantile Ave., 88021. Tel: 505-874-2967; Fax: 505-589-0542.
E-mail: MEQ@Flash.net
Sisters of Mercy - New Jersey/Vermont, 2675 Salome Hernandez St., La Union, 88021. Tel: 505-589-0852.
E-mail: darcyrsm@flash.net

ROSWELL. *Poor Clare Monastery of Our Lady of Guadalupe*, 809 E. 19th St., 88201. Tel: 505-622-0868. Mothers M. Francis, P.C.C., Abbess; Mary Jeannine, P.C.C., Vicaress. Professed Nuns 26; Novices 2; Postulants 1.

SILVER CITY. *Sisters of St. Joseph*, St. Mary's Center, 1801 N. Alabama, 88061. Tel: 505-538-3350; Fax: 505-538-0495. 1803 N. Alabama, 88061. Tel: 505-388-3684; Fax: 505-538-0495.
E-mail: rkfarrell@juno.com

[D] RETREAT CENTERS

MESILLA PARK. *Holy Cross Retreat and Friary*, P.O. Box 158, 88047. Tel: 505-524-3688; Fax: 505-524-3811.
E-mail: Franciscan@zianet.com
Web site: www.zianet.com/franciscan
Rev. Sebastian Cunningham, O.F.M.Conv.

[E] MISCELLANEOUS

LAS CRUCES. *Catholic Diocese of Las Cruces Foundation, Inc.*, 1280 Med Park Dr., 80005. Tel: 505-523-7577; Fax: 505-524-3874. Susan Roberts, Exec. Dir.
Family Unity and Citizenship Program, 1485 N. Main, Ste. 11, 88001. Tel: 505-525-6779. Veronica Campos, Dir.
Our Lady of Guadalupe Prayer Center, Inc., P.O. Box 6772, 88006. Tel: 505-522-5250.
E-mail: OLOGPC@Catholic.org
The Priests' Retirement Plan of the Catholic Diocese of Las Cruces, Inc., 1280 Med Park Dr., 88005. Tel: 505-523-7577; Fax: 505-524-3874.

SAN PATRICIO. *Benedictine Center*, P.O. Box 158, 88348. Tel: 505-653-4709; 653-4215. Rev. Colman Heffern, O.S.B.

RELIGIOUS INSTITUTES OF MEN REPRESENTED IN THE DIOCESE

For further details refer to the corresponding bracketed numbers in the Religious Institutes of Men or Women section.

[0170]—*Basilian Fathers*.—C.S.B.
[0200]—*Benedictine Monks*.—O.S.B.
[0470]—*Capuchin Friars*. (St. Bonaventure).—O.F.M.Cap.
[0480]—*Conventual Franciscans*. (Our Lady of Guadalupe Custody).—O.F.M.Conv.
[0520]—*Franciscan Friars*. (St. John the Baptist, Our Lady of Guadalupe, St. Barbara Provs.).—O.F.M.
[0690]—*Jesuit Fathers and Brothers*. (New Orleans, Wisconsin Provs.).—S.J.
[0150]—*Order of the Augustinian Recollects*.—O.A.R.
[0610]—*Priests of the Congregation of Holy Cross*. (Southwest Prov.).—C.S.C.

RELIGIOUS INSTITUTES OF WOMEN REPRESENTED IN THE DIOCESE

[0460]—*Congregation of the Sisters of Charity of the Incarnate Word*.—C.C.V.I.
[0810]—*Daughters of the Heart of Mary*.—D.H.M.
[1110]—*Dominican Sisters of Our Lady of the Rosary and of Saint Catherine of Siena, Cabra*.—O.P.
[1070]—*Dominicas de la Doctrina Cristiana*.—O.P.
[1370]—*The Franciscan Missionaries of Mary*.—F.M.M.
[1430]—*Franciscan Sisters of Our Lady of Perpetual Help*.—O.S.F.
[2470]—*Maryknoll Sisters of St. Dominic*.—M.M.
[2490]—*Medical Mission Sisters*.—M.M.S.
[2710]—*Missionaries of Charity*.—M.C.
[3130]—*Our Lady of Victory Missionary Sisters*.—O.L.V.M.
[3760]—*Poor Clares Monastery of Our Lady of Guadalupe*.—P.C.C.
[]—*Sisters for Christian Community*.
[0440]—*Sisters of Charity of Cincinnati, Ohio*.—S.C.
[2575]—*Sisters of Mercy of the Americas*. (Omaha, Vermont, Cincinnati, New Jersey).—R.S.M.
[3740]—*Sisters of St. Casimir*.—S.S.C.
[1570]—*Sisters of St. Francis of the Holy Family*.—O.S.F.
[3830-15]—*Sisters of St. Joseph*.—C.S.J.
[3830-03]—*Sisters of St. Joseph of Orange*.—C.S.J.
[3270]—*Sisters of the Most Precious Blood (O'Fallon, MO)*.—C.PP.S.
[4060]—*Society of the Holy Child Jesus*.—S.H.C.J.

NECROLOGY

(No Deaths)

Diocese of Las Vegas

(Dioecesis Campensis)

ERECTED BY HIS HOLINESS POPE PIUS XI MARCH 27, 1931.

REDESIGNATED DIOCESE OF RENO-LAS VEGAS BY POPE PAUL VI, OCTOBER 13, 1976.

REDESIGNATED DIOCESE OF LAS VEGAS BY HIS HOLINESS POPE JOHN PAUL II MARCH 21, 1995.

Square Miles 39,688.

For legal titles of parishes and diocesan institutions, consult the Chancery Office.

(Vacant See)

Chancery Office: 336 Cathedral Way, Las Vegas, NV, 89109. Mailing Address: P.O. Box 18316, Las Vegas, NV, 89114-8316. Tel.: 702-735-3500; Fax: 702-735-8941.

STATISTICAL OVERVIEW

Personnel	
Priests: Diocesan Active in Diocese	24
Priests: Active Outside Diocese	1
Priests: Retired, Sick or Absent	6
Number of Diocesan Priests	31
Religious Priests in Diocese	21
Extern Priests in Diocese	25
Permanent Deacons in Diocese	7
Total Brothers	3
Total Sisters	26
Parishes	
Parishes	24
With Resident Pastor:	
Resident Diocesan Priests	14
Resident Religious Priests	4
Without Resident Pastor:	
Administered by Priests	6
Administered by Women Religious	1
Missions	7
Professional Ministry Personnel:	
Brothers	1
Sisters	2
Lay Ministers	53
Welfare	
Catholic Hospitals	1
Total Assisted	101,528
Day Care and Extended Day Care Centers	1
Total Assisted	8,400
Special Centers for Social Services	19
Total Assisted	1,000,000
Other Institutions	1
Total Assisted	101
Educational	
Diocesan Students in Other Seminaries	7
Total Seminarians	7
High Schools, Diocesan and Parish	1
Total Students	996
Elementary Schools, Diocesan and Parish	7
Total Students	2,531
Catechesis/Religious Education:	
High School Students	2,433
Elementary Students	10,124
Total Students Under Catholic Instruction	16,091
Teachers in the Diocese:	
Priests	1
Lay Teachers	177
Vital Statistics	
Receptions into the Church:	
Infant Baptism Totals	4,997
Adult Baptism Totals	296
Received into Full Communion	221
First Communions	3,233
Confirmations	1,044
Marriages:	
Catholic	574
Interfaith	165
Total Marriages	739
Deaths	780
Total Catholic Population	406,000
Total Population	1,400,000

Chancery Office—336 Cathedral Way, Las Vegas, 89109. Tel: 702-735-3500; Fax: 702-735-8941. Office Hours: Mon.-Fri. 8:30-12 & 1-4:30, *Mailing Address: P.O. Box 18316, Las Vegas, 89114-8316.*

Diocesan Administrator—Rev. Msgr. PATRICK LEARY.

Chancellor—Rev. ROBERT E. STOECKIG. Tel: 702-735-9605.

Diocesan Tribunal Office-Judicial Vicar—Rev. PETER ROMEO, J.C.L. Tel: 702-735-1210; Fax: 702-735-5146.

Notary-Secretary—Mrs. SIDNEY MARSH; Mrs. CECELIA CAMMARANO.

Promoter of Justice—Rev. Msgr. MICHAEL MORAN, J.C.D.

Defender of the Bond—Rev. Msgr. ADRIAN DWYER, J.C.D.; ROBERT J. FLUMMERFELT, J.C.L.

Diocesan Judges—Revs. MARK ROBERTS, M.A., J.C.L.; KEVIN MCAULIFFE, M.A., J.C.L.; JOHN SULLIVAN, M.A., J.C.L.; DAVID I. FULTON, S.T.D., J.C.L.

Diocesan Advocates—Revs. TOM FRANSISCUS, J.C.L.; PHILIP ACQUARO, J.C.L.; MARY JO GRETZINGER, J.C.D.

Presbyteral Council for the Diocese of Las Vegas—Vacant.

Diocesan Offices and Directors

Building Committee—Bro. JOHN DODD, C.S.V.; Revs. KEVIN MCAULIFFE, J.C.L.; ROBERT STOECKIG; TOM MCCORMICK.

Catholic Charities of Southern Nevada—ED SKONICKI, Exec. Dir., *808 S. Main St., Box 1926, Las Vegas, 89125.* Tel: 702-385-2662.

Chief Financial Officer—Bro. JOHN DODD, C.S.V. Tel: 702-735-7865.

Development Office—Ms. PATSY VINCENT. Tel: 702-735-1109.

Education Department—

Director of Clergy Education—Rev. ROBERT STOECKIG.

Schools Superintendent—RICHARD FACCIOLO. Tel: 702-697-5918.

Newman Center Apostolate—Rev. FRED LUCCI, O.P. Tel: 702-736-0887.

Office of Catechetical Ministries—Sr. PAT MCGINLEY, S.S.J., Dir. Tel: 702-735-6044. ANDREA OWEN, Assoc. Dir. Tel: 702-735-6044.

Office of Youth Ministries—GRACE CASSETTA, Dir. Tel: 702-735-3500.

Office of Peace and Social Justice—Rev. CAESAR J. CAVIGLIA.

Home and Foreign Missions—Rev. Msgr. PATRICK LEARY. Tel: 702-735-9605.

Hospital Apostolate—Rev. JESSE CORTEZ, West Side. Tel: 702-870-2767.

Information, Communications and Media—Rev. BEDE WEVITA. Tel: 702-657-0200; Fax: 702-648-2327.

Italian Catholic Federation—Rev. Msgr. ELWOOD LAVOY.

Native American and Colored People Commission—Rev. Msgr. PATRICK LEARY.

Newsletter—DESERT CLARION.

Pontifical Association of the Holy Childhood—Rev. ROBERT STOECKIG.

Priests' Pension Board—Rev. JAMES BEVAN, JR.; Rev. Msgr. PATRICK LEARY; Revs. PHILIP O'DONNELL; ROBERT STOECKIG; FRANCIS VIVONA; Bro. JOHN DODD, C.S.V.

Priests' Personnel Board—Rev. Msgr. PATRICK LEARY; Revs. PHILIP O'DONNELL; WILLIAM KENNY; JOSEPH ANTHONY; ROBERT STOECKIG.

Property Management—Bro. JOHN DODD, C.S.V.

Vocations—Rev. ANTHONY VERCELLONE.

Respect Life Liaison—KATHLEEN MILLER, *P.O. Box 18316, Las Vegas, 89114.*

Fertility Care—MICKEY BACHMAN, R.N., C.N.F.P.P. Tel: 702-566-7550.

CLERGY, PARISHES, MISSIONS AND PAROCHIAL SCHOOLS

CITY OF LAS VEGAS
(Clark County)

1—GUARDIAN ANGEL CATHEDRAL (1963), Revs. James Crilly, C.S.V., Rector; Francis P. White, C.S.V.; Stewart R. Schramko, C.S.V.; Thomas G. Langenfeld, C.S.V.; Sr. Timothy Malone, C.H.S., Pastoral Assoc.

302 Cathedral Way, 89109. Tel: 702-735-5241; Fax: 702-734-7086.

2—CHRIST THE KING (1978), Revs. William J.M. Kenny; Leo Coughlin.

Mailing Address: 4925 S. Torrey Pines, 89118. Tel:

702-871-1904; Fax: 702-251-4935.
Res., 5122 S. Torrey Pines, 89118.
Catechesis/Religious Programs—Tel: 702-871-1904, Ext. 230. Beth Summers, D.R.E.
Students 640.
Mission—Sandy Valley, Clark Co., St. Catherine of Siena, P.O. Box 19789, Jean, 89019.

3—HOLY FAMILY (1975), Revs. Clarence J.D. Savial; Gary L. Vollmer.
Mailing Address: 4490 Mountain Vista, 89121.
Office & Res.: 4528 E. Harmon Ave., 89121-6548. Tel: 702-458-2211 (Office); 458-5997 (Res.); Fax: 702-458-0966 (Office).
Catechesis/Religious Programs—Tel: 702-458-3575.
Students 428.

4—OUR LADY OF LAS VEGAS (1957), Revs. Robert P. Petekiewicz, Admin.; Brian Highfill; Joseph Trong; Jesse Cortes; Deacon Louis Guastella. In res., Rev. Bill Duff.
Office: 3050 Alta Dr., 89107. Tel: 702-870-2767; Fax: 702-870-1267.
Res., 3104 Alta Dr., 89107.
School—3046 Alta Dr., 89107. Tel: 702-878-6841; Fax: 702-880-5758. Karen Murphy, Prin.
Lay Teachers 20; Students 530.
Catechesis/Religious Programs—Tel: 702-870-1882.
Students 644.

5—PRINCE OF PEACE (1981), Revs. Francis Timoney (Scotland); Mario Garcia (Mexico); Deacon James Whittle.
Office: 5485 E. Charleston Blvd., 89142. Tel: 702-431-2233; Fax: 702-431-2234.
Res., 653 Los Feliz, 89110. Tel: 702-452-5524; Fax: 702-459-2702.
Catechesis/Religious Programs—Students 1,131.

6—ST. ANNE (1948), Revs. John Andrew Sullivan, J.C.L.; Alberto Alzate (Colombia).
Office & Res.: 1901 S. Maryland Pkwy., 89104. Tel: 702-735-0510; Fax: 702-735-5582.
School—1813 S. Maryland Pkwy., 89104. Tel: 702-735-2586; Fax: 702-735-8357. Phyllis Joyce, Prin.
Lay Teachers 14; Students 340.
Catechesis/Religious Programs—Tel: 702-735-2985; Fax: 702-735-9237.
Students 690.

7—ST. BRIDGET (1945), Rev. James L. Swenson.
Office: 220 N. 14th St., 89101-4312. Tel: 702-384-3382; Fax: 702-382-9467.
Res., 215 N. 14th St., 89101. Tel: 702-384-7201.
Catechesis/Religious Programs—Tel: 702-384-4264.
Students 62.

8—ST. ELIZABETH ANN SETON (1992), Revs. Kevin W. McAuliffe, J.C.L.; Jon D. Besinga; Jerome E. Nadine (BRK); Deacons Joe Deegan; Frank Pemper; Howard Tirgrath. In res., Rev. Francis M. Vivona.
Office: 1811 Pueblo Vista Dr., 89128. Tel: 702-228-8311; Fax: 702-228-8310.
Res., 2109 Golden Lotus Dr., 89134.
School—1807 Pueblo Vista Dr., 89128. Tel: 702-804-8328; Fax: 702-228-8906. Tim Curtin, Prin.
Lay Teachers 11; Students 177.
Catechesis/Religious Programs—Tel: 702-228-8311; Fax: 702-228-2154.
Students 1,172.

9—ST. FRANCIS DE SALES (1964) (Hispanic), Revs. James J. Bevan, Jr.; Frank S. Yncierto; Manuel Quintero.
Office: 1111 Michael Way, 89108. Tel: 702-647-3440; Fax: 702-646-3587.
Res., 1628 Desert Fort, 89128. Tel: 702-233-1010.
School—Tel: 702-647-2828; Fax: 702-647-0284. Mrs. Catherine Thompson, Prin.
Lay Teachers 14; Students 307.
Catechesis/Religious Programs—Tel: 702-646-2266; Fax: 702-647-6701.
Students 668.

10—ST. JAMES THE APOSTLE (1942) (African American), Rev. Michael Blackburn, O.F.M.; Sr. Deborah Lockwood, O.S.F., Pastoral Assoc. & D.R.E.
Office: 820 N. H St., 89106. Tel: 702-648-6606; Fax: 702-648-0352.
Res., 1420 W. Bartlett, 89106. Tel: 702-648-2798; Fax: 702-648-2798.
Catechesis/Religious Programs—Tel: 702-648-6606; Fax: 702-648-0352.
Students 85.

11—ST. JOAN OF ARC (1908), Rev. Philip O'Donnell.
Office & Res.: 315 S. Casino Center Blvd., 89101. Tel: 702-382-9909; Fax: 702-382-6655.
School—1300 Bridger Ave., 89101. Tel: 702-384-6909; Fax: 702-386-0249. Mrs. Lynda Ballard, Prin.
Lay Teachers 10; Students 233.
Catechesis/Religious Programs—Clustered with St. Bridget's, Las Vegas.

12—ST. JOSEPH, HUSBAND OF MARY (1989), Revs. Joseph L. Anthony; Patrick Rudolph; Thomas E. Gallenbach; Oneil A. Monzillo; Deacon Michael J. Heidenreich. In res., Rev. Frank Tinajero, S.V.D.
Mailing Address: Office, 7260 W. Sahara Ave., 89117. Tel: 702-363-1902; Fax: 702-363-7976.
Res., 10261 Rarity Ave., 89135.
Catechesis/Religious Programs—Tel: 702-363-3658; Fax: 702-363-0142. Cynthia O'Connell, D.R.E.
Students 913.

13—ST. MARY THE VIRGIN (1983). Closed. For inquiries for parish records contact the Chancery.

14—ST. PAUL JUNG-HA-SANG (1987) (Korean), Rev. Msgr. Patrick R. Leary, Admin., Tel: 702-735-3500. 5225 Meikle Ln., 89115. Tel: 702-453-0033; Fax: 702-876-2989.

15—ST. VIATOR (1954), Revs. Richard A. Rinn, C.S.V.; Wayne G. Dupuis, C.S.V.; William F. Haesaert, C.S.V.; Bro. Michael Rice, C.S.V.
Office: 2461 E. Flamingo Rd., 89121. Tel: 702-733-8323; Fax: 702-733-8154.
School—Tel: 702-732-4477; Fax: 702-732-4418. Mrs. Kathleen Daulton, Prin.
Lay Teachers 25; Students 662.
Catechesis/Religious Programs—Tel: 702-732-0459. Carol Russell, D.R.E.
Students 325.

16—SHRINE OF THE MOST HOLY REDEEMER (1991), Rev. Msgr. Patrick R. Leary, Admin., Tel: 702-735-3500. Office: 55 E. Reno Ave., 89119. Tel: 702-891-8600; Fax: 702-891-0339.

OUTSIDE THE CITY OF LAS VEGAS

Amargosa Valley, Nye Co., Christ of the Desert Catholic Church (1987) (Hispanic), Sr. Jacinta Kaiser, Admin.
Office & Res.: P.O. Box 218, Amargosa, 89020. Tel: 775-372-5337. [JC]
Catechesis/Religious Programs—Students 13.

Boulder City, Clark Co., St. Andrew's (1931), Rev. Joseph P. Annese.
1399 San Felipe Dr., 89005. Tel: 702-293-7500; Fax: 702-293-4419.
Catechesis/Religious Programs—Sondra Hoffman, D.R.E.
Students 184.

Bunkerville, Clark Co., La Virgen de Guadalupe (1992), Rev. Gustavo Cruz.
Mailing Address: P.O. Box 7309, 89007. Tel: 702-346-7065; Fax: 702-346-0648.
Res., 121 Falcon St., Mesquite, 89027.
Corner of 1st W. and 1st S., 89007.
Catechesis/Religious Programs—Students 282.

Caliente, Lincoln Co., Holy Child (1870), Rev. Leo Slatterie.
P.O. Box 708, 89008-0708. Tel: 775-726-3669; Fax: 775-726-3669.
Res., 90 Culverwell St., 89008-0708. [CEM]
Catechesis/Religious Programs—Students 20.

Ely, White Pine Co., Sacred Heart (1869), Very Rev. Timothy Clark Wehn, V.F.
Mailing Address & Office: P.O. Box 26, 89301. Tel: 775-289-8111; Fax: 775-289-2207.
Res., 515 Murry St., 89301.
Catechetical Ministry Center—1100 Park Ave., P.O. Box 26, 89301.
Catechesis/Religious Programs—Students 180.
Mission—McGill, White Pine Co., St. Michael's, P.O. Box 26, Ely, 89301.

Henderson, Clark Co., St. Peter the Apostle (1943), Revs. Mark Roberts; Peter Romeo.
Office & Res.: 204 S. Boulder Hwy., 89015. Tel: 702-565-8406; Fax: 702-565-8731.
Catechesis/Religious Programs—Tel: 702-565-0284.
Students 903.
St. Thomas More (1986), Revs. Dan Nolan, C.S.V.; Michael Keliher, C.S.V.; Ken Morris, C.S.V.; Robert Bolser, C.S.V.; Deacon George Flaherty.
130 N. Pecos Rd., 89014. Tel: 702-361-3022; Fax: 702-361-7784.
Catechesis/Religious Programs—Tel: 702-361-8840; Fax: 702-361-5992. Juliann Dwyer, D.R.E.
Students 1,480.

Laughlin, Clark Co., St. John the Baptist Catholic Mission (1992), Rev. Ray Schultz.
P.O. Box 31230, 89028. Tel: 702-298-0440; Fax: 702-298-0279.
Res., 3115 Terrace View, 89029.
Catechesis/Religious Programs—Students 22.

North Las Vegas, Clark Co., St. Christopher (1953), Revs. Gregory W. Gordon; Bruno R. Mauricci.
Mailing Address: 1840 N. Bruce St., 89030. Tel: 702-642-1154; Fax: 702-642-0719.
Res., 1401 Flower Ave., 89030.
School—Tel: 702-657-8008; Fax: 702-642-2461. Mrs. Carol Haeberlin, Prin.
Lay Teachers 11; Students 284.
Catechesis/Religious Programs—Tel: 702-657-6779; Fax: 702-657-8406. Mrs. Sharon Pauli, D.R.E.
Students 2,215.
St. John Neumann (1999),
Mailing Address: 4519 Simmons St., 89031. Tel: 702-657-0200; Fax: 702-648-2327.
Res., 912 Whitehollow Ave., 89031. Tel: 702-642-6750. Rev. Bede Wevita, Admin.
Catechesis/Religious Programs—Students 303.

Overton, Clark Co., St. John the Evangelist (1959), Rev. Brian Stenson.
Mailing Address: P.O. Box 457, 89040.
Office: 150 N. Moapa Valley Blvd., 89040. Tel: 702-397-8096; Fax: 702-397-8264.
Res., 425 W. Joan St., 89040.
Catechesis/Religious Programs—Tel: 702-397-2009.
Students 144.

Pahrump, Nye Co., Our Lady of the Valley (1985), Rev. John H. Lima.
Res., 781 E. Gamebird, 89048. Tel: 775-727-4044; Fax: 775-727-4044.
Mailing Address: 781 E. Gamebird, 89048.
Catechesis/Religious Programs—Students 38.
Mission—Pahrump.

Tonopah, Nye Co., St. Patrick (1902) (Native American), Rev. James P. McCauley, S.J.
Mailing Address: P.O. Box 468, 89049. Tel: 775-482-6746; Fax: 775-482-6746.
Res., 144 South St., 89049. Tel: 775-775-6716. [JC]
Catechesis/Religious Programs—Students 35.
Missions—Round Mountain, Nye Co., St. Barbara, P.O. Box 1710, Hadley, 89045.; Fish Lake, Esmeralda Co., Our Lady of Guadalupe.

Military Chaplains:
Reverend Fathers—
Diphe, Juan, Chap., Our Lady of the Skies, 4302 N. Washington Blvd., Nellis AFB, NV 89191
McNulty, Jerry, Wing Chap., Dept. of Veterans Affairs, VAMC - 125, 1700 Vegas Dr., Las Vegas, NV 89107. Tel: 702-385-3700
ReVello, James P., Wing Chap., Our Lady of the Skies, 4302 N. Washington Blvd., Nellis AFB, NV 89191

Retired:
Reverend Fathers—
Caviglia, Caesar
Duff, William
Franzinell, Benjamin
Lavoy, Elwood
McVeigh, John J.
Slatterie, Leo

Permanent Deacons:
Deegan, Joseph
Flaherty, George
Guastella, Louis
Heidenreich, Mike
Pemper, Frank
Tirgrath, Howard
Whittle, James

INSTITUTIONS LOCATED IN THE DIOCESE

[A] HIGH SCHOOLS, DIOCESAN

LAS VEGAS. *Bishop Gorman High School*, 1801 Maryland Pkwy., 89104. Tel: 702-732-1945; Fax: 702-732-2856.
E-mail: bghs@wizard.com
Web site: http://members.aol.com/bghslv/
Connie Gerber, Prin.; Rev. Norbert P. Bibeault, C.S.V..Priests 1; Lay Teachers 69; Students 996.

[B] GENERAL HOSPITALS

HENDERSON. *St. Rose Dominican Hospital*, 102 Lake Mead Dr., 89015. Tel: 702-564-2622; Fax: 702-564-4699.
E-mail: vdalesan@chw.edu
For a complete listing, refer to the Hospitals section.

[C] DAY NURSERIES

LAS VEGAS. *Catholic Charities Child Care Center*, 451 E. Twain, 89109. Tel: 702-735-4358; Fax: 702-735-6659.
E-mail: childcare@catholiccharities.com
Connie Johnson, Dir.; Barbara Gray, Admin.

Sponsor: Catholic Charities. Enrollment Capacity 163.

[D] MONASTERIES AND RESIDENCES OF PRIESTS AND BROTHERS

LAS VEGAS. *Clerics of St. Viator Retirement Home,* 4219 Pinecrest Cir. E., 89121. Tel: 702-456-8512. Revs. Robert F. Cooney, C.S.V., Dir.; Norbert P. Bibeault, C.S.V. Priests 2.

Dominican Rectory, Fra Angelico House. (Western Dominican Province), 1701 Chapman Dr., 89104. Tel: 702-369-1215; Fax: 702-369-3742.

[E] CONVENTS AND RESIDENCES FOR SISTERS

LAS VEGAS. *The Franciscan Sisters of Perpetual Adoration.* Tel: 702-735-0640.
E-mail: lorforster@aol.com
Mailing Address: 1304 E. St. Louis Ave., 89104-3466. Tel: 702-735-0640. Sisters 2.

Holy Family Convent, 5276 S. Lookout St., 89120. Tel: 702-435-1526; Fax: 702-647-4703.
E-mail: srmjulie@333aol.com
Sisters of the Holy Family 2.

HENDERSON. *Convent of the Sisters of St. Joseph Chestnut Hill, Philadelphia,* 507 Chestnut View Pl., 89052-2821. Tel: 702-260-4928; Fax: 702-697-5917.
E-mail: mcginley@dioceseoflasvegas.org
Sr. Patricia McGinley, S.S.J., Dir., Catechetical Min.

[F] RETREAT HOUSES

CALIENTE. *Monastery of Christ in the Mountains,* P.O. Box 708, 89008. Tel: 775-726-3669; Fax: 775-726-3669.

[G] MISCELLANEOUS

LAS VEGAS. *Catholic Charities of Southern Nevada,* 808 S. Main St., P.O. Box 1926, 89125. Tel: 702-385-2662; Fax: 702-384-0677.
E-mail: community@catholiccharities.com
Web site: www.catholiccharities.com

Adoption Services. Tel: 702-385-3351; Fax: 702-388-8723.

Crossroads Transitional Housing for Senior Men. Tel: 702-385-2777; Fax: 702-383-8243.

Deferred Giving Program. Tel: 702-385-2662; Fax: 702-384-0677.

Department of Pastoral Ministry, 1501 Las Vegas Blvd., N., 89101. Tel: 702-383-0700; Fax: 702-383-8243. Rev. John McShane, Chap.

Catholic Charities Child Care Center. Tel: 702-735-4358; Fax: 702-735-6659.

Immigration Services. Tel: 702-383-8387; Fax: 702-385-7748.

Marian Transitional Housing for Senior Women. Tel: 702-565-5388; Fax: 702-565-7711.

Migration and Refugee Services. Tel: 702-383-8387; Fax: 702-385-7748.

Regina Hall. Tel: 702-565-0688; Fax: 702-564-4823.

Respite Care Referral Service. Tel: 702-385-5284; Fax: 702-385-3206.

RSVP (Retired & Senior Volunteer Program). Tel: 702-385-5284; Fax: 702-385-3206.

Senior Community Employment Service. Tel: 702-385-5284; Fax: 702-385-3206.

Senior Companion. Tel: 702-385-5284; Fax: 702-385-3206.

Senior Nutrition & Meals-on-Wheels. Tel: 702-385-5284; Fax: 702-385-3206.

Social Ministry. Tel: 702-383-0766; Fax: 702-383-9031.

Social Services. Tel: 702-383-0766; Fax: 702-383-9031.

Lied Dining Facility. Tel: 702-385-7801; Fax: 702-383-8243.

St. Vincent Shelter and Employment Services Center. Tel: 702-383-0700; Fax: 702-383-8243.

Catholic Charities Thrift Stores. Tel: 702-385-2662; Fax: 702-384-0677.

NCWB Housing, Inc. Tel: 702-873-3071; Fax: 702-873-0629.

CCSN Mojave Project, Inc. Tel: 702-873-3071; Fax: 702-873-0629.

CCSN-CTS Annex, Inc. Tel: 702-873-3071; Fax: 702-873-0629.

CCSN McFarland Housing Development Corporation, Inc. Tel: 702-255-0282; Fax: 702-255-0283.

CCSN McFarland Housing, Inc., 2021 Loro Ct., 89117. Tel: 702-255-0282; Fax: 702-255-0283. David Elnes, Project Coord.

Diocesan Residence, 5155 W. Tropicana, Unit 2186, 89103. Tel: 702-735-3500; Fax: 702-735-8941.
E-mail: lvpriest@aol.com

Serra House (Formation Residence), 1212 E. Oakey Blvd., 89104. Rev. Anthony Vercellone, Vocations Dir.

HENDERSON. *Saint Therese Center,* 67 E. Lake Mead Blvd., 89009. Tel: 702-564-4224; Fax: 702-564-0604.
E-mail: aidsproject@dioceseoflasvegas.org
Rev. Joseph O'Brien, O.P., Exec. Dir. HIV/AIDS Outreach Program.

RELIGIOUS INSTITUTES OF MEN REPRESENTED IN THE DIOCESE

For further details refer to the corresponding bracketed number in the Religious Institutes of Men or Women section.

[1320]—*Clerics of St. Viator.*—C.S.V.
[0520]—*Franciscan Friars.*—O.F.M.
[0690]—*Jesuit Fathers & Brothers.*—S.J.
[]—*Western Dominican Province.*—O.P.

RELIGIOUS INSTITUTES OF WOMEN REPRESENTED IN THE DIOCESE

[1780]—*Congregation of the Sisters of the Third Order of St. Francis of Perpetual Adoration.*—F.S.P.A.
[1070-04]—*Dominican Sisters.*—O.P.
[1190]—*Franciscan Sisters of the Atonement.*—S.A.
[1630]—*Sisters of St. Francis of the Penance and Christian Charity.* (St. Francis Prov.).—O.S.F.
[3893]—*Sisters of St. Joseph of Chestnut Hill.*—S.S.J.
[1960]—*Sisters of the Holy Family.*—S.H.F.

NECROLOGY

(No Deaths)

Diocese of Lafayette in Indiana

(Diocesis Lafayettenis in Indiana)

Most Reverend

WILLIAM L. HIGI, D.D.

Bishop of Lafayette in Indiana; ordained May 30, 1959; appointed Bishop of Lafayette in Indiana April 7, 1984; consecrated and installed June 6, 1984. *Res., 610 Lingle Ave., P.O. Box 260, Lafayette, IN, 47902-0260.*

Office of Bishop and Chancery: P.O. Box 260, Lafayette, IN, 47902-0260. Tel.: 765-742-0275; Fax: 765-742-7513.

Web site address: www.dioceseoflafayette.org

CANONICALLY ERECTED OCTOBER 21, 1944.

Square Miles 9,832.

Comprises the Counties of Benton, Blackford, Boone, Carroll, Cass, Clinton, Delaware, Fountain, Fulton, Grant, Hamilton, Howard, Jasper, Jay, Madison, Miami, Montgomery, Newton, Pulaski, Randolph, Tippecanoe, Tipton, Warren and White in the State of Indiana.

For legal titles of parishes and diocesan institutions, consult the Bishop's Office (Chancery).

STATISTICAL OVERVIEW

Personnel	
Bishop	1
Priests: Diocesan Active in Diocese	82
Priests: Active Outside Diocese	21
Priests: Retired, Sick or Absent	19
Number of Diocesan Priests	122
Religious Priests in Diocese	19
Extern Priests in Diocese	1
Permanent Deacons in Diocese	5
Total Brothers	2
Total Sisters	88
Parishes	
Parishes	63
With Resident Pastor:	
Resident Diocesan Priests	52
Resident Religious Priests	4
Without Resident Pastor:	
Administered by Priests	7
Professional Ministry Personnel:	
Sisters	13
Lay Ministers	91
Welfare	
Catholic Hospitals	7
Total Assisted	698,740
Homes for the Aged	3
Total Assisted	334
Educational	
Diocesan Students in Other Seminaries	6
Total Seminarians	6
Colleges and Universities	3
Total Students	9,338
High Schools, Diocesan and Parish	1
Total Students	339
Elementary Schools, Diocesan and Parish	24
Total Students	4,760
Catechesis/Religious Education:	
High School Students	3,505
Elementary Students	10,321
Total Students Under Catholic Instruction	28,269
Teachers in the Diocese:	
Lay Teachers	266
Vital Statistics	
Receptions into the Church:	
Infant Baptism Totals	1,887
Adult Baptism Totals	361
Received into Full Communion	381
First Communions	2,198
Confirmations	1,967
Marriages:	
Catholic	290
Interfaith	298
Total Marriages	588
Deaths	845
Total Catholic Population	96,791
Total Population	1,144,222

Former Bishops—Most Rev. JOHN GEORGE BENNETT, D.D., LL.D., ord. June 27, 1914; appt. First Bishop of Lafayette Nov. 11, 1944; cons. Jan. 10, 1945; died Nov. 20, 1957.—His Eminence JOHN CARDINAL CARBERRY, D.D., ord. July 28, 1929; appt. Coadjutor with Right of Succession Aug. 22, 1956; appt. Bishop of Lafayette in Indiana Nov. 20, 1957; transferred to Diocese of Columbus, Jan. 20, 1965; transferred to the Archdiocese of St. Louis March 24, 1968; created Cardinal April 28, 1969; retired July 31, 1979; died June 17, 1998.—Most Rev. RAYMOND J. GALLAGHER, D.D., ord. March 25, 1939; appt. Bishop of Lafayette in Indiana June 23, 1965; cons. Aug. 11, 1965; installed Aug. 23, 1965; resigned Oct. 26, 1982; retired April 13, 1983; died March 7, 1991.—Most Rev. GEORGE A. FULCHER, S.T.D., D.D., ord. Feb. 28, 1948; appt. Auxiliary Bishop of Columbus, OH and Titular Bishop of Morosbido May 24, 1976; cons. July 18, 1976; appt. Bishop of Lafayette in Indiana Feb. 8, 1983; installed April 14, 1983; died Jan. 25, 1984.

Vicar General—Rev. Msgr. ROBERT L. SELL, III, J.C.L.

Chancellor and Moderator of the Curia—Rev. Msgr. ROBERT L. SELL, III, J.C.L.

Office of Bishop and Chancery—P.O. Box 260, Lafayette, 47902-0260. Tel: 765-742-0275; Fax: 765-742-7513.

Deans—Rev. DANIEL B. GARTLAND, Lafayette Deanery; Rev. ROBERT L. WILLIAMS, Anderson Deanery; Rev. THOMAS E. FOX, Fowler Deanery; Rev. THOMAS H. METZGER, Carmel Deanery; Rev. PHILIP S. HASLINGER, Logansport Deanery; Rev. WILLIAM R. GRADY, Muncie Deanery.

Diocesan Consultors—Rev. Msgr. ROBERT L. SELL, III, J.C.L., V.G.; Revs. WILLIAM R. GRADY, V.F.; DONALD L. GROSS, V.F.; THEODORE D. ROTHROCK; MICHAEL J. MCKINNEY; DOMINIC G. YOUNG.

Diocesan Pastoral Office for Administration—ROBERT H. QUINN, Finance Officer, *P.O. Box 260, Lafayette, 47902-0260.* Tel: 765-742-4852.

Diocesan Pastoral Office for Planning and Communication—THOMAS A. RUSSELL, Dir., *610 Lingle Ave., P.O. Box 1603, Lafayette, 47902-1603.* Tel: 765-742-2050.

Publisher- "The Catholic Moment"—LAURIE CULLEN, Asst. Editor; AMY SCHNEIDAU, Contributing Editor; MARY MANCHA, Reporter; CAROLYN MCKINNEY, Administrative Asst. Advertising.

Diocesan Pastoral Office for Social Ministry—DAVID R. WILSON, Dir., *836 S. Purdum, Kokomo, 46901-5533.* Tel: 765-457-1172. Assists parishes in developing parish social ministry; co-ordinates the work of the Campaign for Human Development and the Indiana Catholic Conference; liaison with St. Elizabeth Home (Indianapolis) relative to adoption services, Pro-Life Service Centers, St. Vincent dePaul and Ladies of Charity, and coordinates the Premarital Evaluation program.

Diocesan Pastoral Office for Formation—Rev. Msgr. ROBERT L. SELL, III, V.G., *Catholic Pastoral Center, 2300 S. Ninth St., Lafayette, 47909-2400.* Tel: 765-474-6644; Fax: 765-474-3403. Coordinates marriage preparation conferences and programs, Natural Family Planning, Separated-Divorced Catholic programs, Sacramental preparation with families, implementation of Family Perspective and Family Catechesis. Additional responsibilities include all programs (Catholic Schools, Religious Education, Youth Ministry, Pre-schools, Sacramental Preparation, Scouts, Athletics, etc.) for young people in the local church. That responsibility extends to the formation of those who minister to young people as catechists, teachers, coaches, youth leaders and administrators.

Diocesan Tribunal—Catholic Pastoral Center, 2300 S. Ninth St., Lafayette, 47909-2400. Tel: 765-474-0506.

Judicial Vicar—Rev. DAVID L. RASNER, J.C.L.

Adjutant Judicial Vicar—Rev. RICHARD E. MILLER, J.C.L.

—First Instance:

Presiding Judge—Rev. DAVID L. RASNER, J.C.L.

Associate Judge—Rev. PETER VANDERKOLK.

Defenders of the Bond—Revs. DAVID J. BUCKLES, J.C.L.; DONALD L. GROSS; WILLIAM R. VATH.

Deputy Defender—Sr. KATHRYN KIRK.

Ecclesiastical Notary—VERNA S. MEEK.

Full-Time Advocates—BRIDGET O'BRIEN; LOU CUFFING.

Periti—PHILLIP M. SUTTON, Ph.D.; MICHAEL MILLARD, Ph.D.

—Second Instance:

Presiding Judge—Rev. RICHARD E. MILLER, J.C.L.

Associate Judges—Rev. Msgr. JOHN C. DUNCAN; Rev. Msgr. FRED E. POTTHOFF; Revs. MELVIN BENNETT; GERALD J. BORAWSKI; JAMES R. GOODRUM; FRED H. GSCHWIND; DONALD B. VERNON; EDWARD F. DHONDT; THOMAS J. ZIMMER.

Defender of the Bond—Rev. JOSEPH W. DOOLEY.

Ecclesiastical Notary—PEGGY FLETCHER.

Advocates—Refer to Court of First Instance.

Lay Advocates—Refer to Court of First Instance.

Periti—Refer to Court of First Instance.

Administrative Causes—Rev. Msgr. ROBERT L. SELL, III, J.C.L.

Diocesan Offices and Directors

Archivist—Vacant.

Building Commission—KEN MCGINITY, Chm.; Rev. THEODORE ROTHROCK; Rev. Msgr. ROBERT SELL; ROBERT

GLOYESKE; Dr. DOUGLAS SUTTON; WILL WRIGHT; NORBERT STRANSKY; DANIEL MADER; EUGENE HATKE; DENNIS G. PAGE.

Finance Officer—ROBERT H. QUINN, *P.O. Box 260, Lafayette, 47902-0260.* Tel: 765-742-4852.

Administration—Refer to Diocesan Pastoral Office.

Corporation—Roman Catholic Diocese of Lafayette in Indiana, Inc.(Incorporated, March 21, 1958.); Most Rev. WILLIAM L. HIGI, Pres. & Treas.; Rev. Msgr. ROBERT L. SELL, III, J.C.L., Vice Pres. & Sec.; Mr. ROBERT H. QUINN, Asst. Sec. & Treas.

Director of Development—PAMELIA STORMS-BARRETT, *Bishop's Office, P.O. Box 1687, Lafayette, 47902-1687.* Tel: 765-742-7000; Fax: 765-742-7513.

Director of Planned Giving—JOSEPH A. BONNER, *Bishop's Office, P.O. Box 1687, Lafayette, 47902-1687.* Tel: 765-742-7000; Fax: 765-742-7513.

Fruitful Harvest Office—P.O. Box 1687, Lafayette, 47902. Tel: 765-742-4852.

Finance Council—Most Rev. WILLIAM L. HIGI; Rev. Msgr. ROBERT L. SELL, III, J.C.L., V.G.; ROBERT H. QUINN, Dir. Pastoral Office for Admin. LEON CYR; BEVERLY SOKOLEK; LEE SNIDER; DON GOETZ; EDWARD LOPKE; JOHN F. BODLE, Legal Counsel.

Human Resources Department—HELEN BENDER, *P.O. Box 260, Lafayette, 47902-0260.* Tel: 765-742-4852.

Legal Council—JOHN C. DUFFEY, *Life Building, P.O. Box 1010, Lafayette, 47902.* Tel: 765-423-1561; Fax: 765-742-8175.

Presbyteral Council—Revs. T. EDWARD KACENA, Chm. DANIEL B. GARTLAND, V.F., Vice Chm.

Members—Rev. Msgr. ROBERT L. SELL, III, J.C.L., V.G.; Revs. BRIAN A. DUDZINSKI; WILLIAM R. GRADY, V.F.; PHILIP S. HASLINGER, V.F.; DANIEL B. GARTLAND, V.F.; JOSEPH E. JACOB; THOMAS H. METZGER, V.F.; ROBERT L. WILLIAMS, V.F.; THOMAS E. FOX, V.F.; MELVIN J. BENNETT; PAUL WICKLUM; PAUL W. COCHRAN; THEODORE ROTHROCK.

Catholic Relief Services—Vacant.

Censor Librorum—Rev. DAVID L. RASNER, J.C.L., *Catholic Pastoral Center, 2300 S. Ninth St., Lafayette, 47909-2400.* Tel: 765-474-0506.

Aquinas Educational Foundation, Inc.—Rev. DANIEL C. DAVIS, O.P., Res. Agent, *535 State St., West Lafayette, 47906.* Tel: 765-743-4653.

Clergy Relief Association—Board of Directors: Revs. RICHARD J. WEISENBERGER, Pres.; THEODORE ROTHROCK, Vice Pres.; PHILIP BOWERS, Sec.; THOMAS FOX, Treas.

Members—Revs. DENNIS GOTH; CHARLES KLINE; PAUL R. WICKLUM.

Catholic Charities Central Office—Refer to Diocesan Pastoral Office.

Social Ministry—DAVID R. WILSON, Diocesan Dir., *Diocesan Catholic Offices, 836 S. Purdum, Kokomo, 46901.* Tel: 765-457-1172.

Superintendent for Catholic Schools—Sr. LOIS ANN MEYER, S.N.D.deN., *The Catholic Pastoral Center, 2300 S. Ninth St., Lafayette, 47909-2400.* Tel: 765-474-6644.

Society of St. Vincent de Paul—DAVID R. WILSON, Diocesan Dir., *Diocesan Catholic Offices, 836 S. Purdum St., Kokomo, 46901.* Tel: 765-457-1172.

Association of Ladies of Charity—DAVID R. WILSON, Dir., *Diocesan Catholic Offices, 836 Purdum St., Kokomo, 46901.* Tel: 765-457-1172.

Liturgical Commission—Refer to Diocesan Pastoral Office.

Eucharistic League—The Chancery, *P.O. Box 260, Lafayette, 47902.*

Greater Lafayette Catholic School Board—DAVID WORLAND. Tel: 765-474-2496.

Greater Lafayette Catholic School Foundation, Inc.—JOSEPH BONNER, *2410 S. Ninth St., Lafayette, 47905.*

Holy Childhood Association—Vacant.

Diocesan Board of Education—In process of reorganization & formation.

D.C.C.W.—Vacant.

Ministry to Priests' Program—Rev. DONALD L. GROSS, Dir., *Sacred Heart Church, 107 E. Main St., Fowler, 47944-1148.* Tel: 765-884-1818.

Newman Apostolate, Purdue University—Rev. DANIEL C. DAVIS, O.P., Dir., *535 State St., West Lafayette, 47906.* Tel: 765-743-4652.

Newman Foundation, Ball State, Inc.—Rev. JOHN J. KEIFER, Dir., *800 Riverside Ave., Muncie, 47303.* Tel: 765-288-6180.

Newman Apostolate, Wabash College—Rev. MELVIN BENNETT, Dir., *310 S. Grant Ave., Crawfordsville, 47933.* Tel: 765-362-6121.

Newspaper "The Catholic Moment"—LAURIE CULLEN, Acting Editor; AMY SCHNEIDAU, Contributing Editor; MARY MANCHA, Reporter; CAROLYN CASE, Advertising, Editorial Office, *P.O. Box 1603, Lafayette, 47902.* Tel: 765-742-2050.

Office of the Apostolate to the Spanish Speaking—Deacon DOMINGO CASTILLO, Assoc. Dir., *917 Branson St., Marion, 46952.* Tel: 317-662-3288., *Guadalupe Center.* Tel: 765-664-3710.

Propagation of the Faith—DAVID WILSON, Refer to Pastoral Office for Social Ministry.

Religious Education Dept.—Refer to Pastoral Office for Formation.

Rural Life Program—Rev. FRED H. GSCHWIND, Dir., *340 N. Mill St., Tipton, 46072.* Tel: 765-675-2422.

Schools—See Superintendent listing.

St. Joseph Memorial Hospital Foundation, Inc.—PEGGY CALDWELL, Exec. Dir., *1907 W. Sycamore St., Kokomo, 46901.* Tel: 765-456-5425.

Vicar for Clergy—Vacant.

Vicar for Religious—Vacant.

Vocation Director—Rev. BRIAN DOERR, Dir., *St. Mary Cathedral, 1212 South St., Lafayette, 47901-1576.* Tel: 765-742-4440.

CLERGY, PARISHES, MISSIONS AND PAROCHIAL SCHOOLS

CITY OF LAFAYETTE
(Tippecanoe County)

1—ST. MARY CATHEDRAL (1843), Revs. Robert Klemme; Brian M. Doerr. In res., Rev. Joseph J. Bruetsch.
Res., 1207 Columbia St., 47901-1522. Tel: 765-742-4440; Fax: 765-742-8933. [JC]
School—(Grades PreK-3). Tel: 765-742-6302.
Lay Teachers 11; Students 205.
Catechesis/Religious Programs—Tel: 765-742-8336.
Students 110.

2—ST. ANN (1884), Revs. Michael J. McKinley; Maurice R. Miller.
Res., 612 Wabash Ave., 47905-1096. Tel: 765-742-7031; Fax: 765-429-5690. [JC]
Catechesis/Religious Programs—Tel: 765-423-4635.
Students 167.

3—ST. BONIFACE (1853) (German), Rev. Timothy M. Alkire; Deacon Ron Nevinger. In res., Rev. William R. Vath.
Res., 318 N. Ninth St., 47904-2597. Tel: 765-742-5063; Fax: 765-742-5018. [CEM]
School—Lafayette Catholic Middle School, (Grades 4-6). Tel: 765-742-7913; Fax: 765-423-4988.
Sisters 3; Lay Teachers 4; Students 148. Principals: Sr. M. Lois DeLee, O.S.F.; Sr. M. Lenore Schwartz, O.S.F.
Catechesis/Religious Programs—Tel: 765-742-1351.
Students 411.

4—ST. LAWRENCE (1895), Revs. Daniel B. Gartland; Jack Trippel. In res., Rev. Anthony Pogorelc, S.M (STL).
Res., 1916 Meharry St., 47904-1442. Tel: 765-742-2107; Fax: 765-742-1347.
School—1902 Meharry St., 47904-1497. Tel: 765-742-4450. Mrs. Pam Peroutky, Prin.
Lay Teachers 14; Students 271.
Catechesis/Religious Programs—Tel: 765-423-2396. Susan Schmitz, D.R.E.
Students 275.

OUTSIDE THE CITY OF LAFAYETTE

Alexandria, Madison Co., St. Mary (1896), Rev. Paul W. Cochran.
Res., 820 W. Madison St., 46001-1520. Tel: 765-724-2483; 724-4459; Fax: 765-724-9711.
School—Tel: 765-724-4459.
Sisters 2; Lay Teachers 5; Students 82.
Catechesis/Religious Programs—Students 80.

Anderson, Madison Co., St. Ambrose (1947), Rev. Edward F. Dhondt.
Res., 2801 Lincoln St., 46016-5067. Tel: 765-644-5956; 642-9439.
School—Tel: 765-642-8428; Fax: 765-642-7348.
Lay Teachers 14; Students 163.
Catechesis/Religious Programs—Students 216.

St. Mary (1858), Rev. Robert L. Williams; Mrs. Mary Pat Marstall, Pastoral Assoc.
Res., 1115 Pearl St., 46016-1789. Tel: 765-644-8467. [CEM]
School—Tel: 765-642-1848; Fax: 765-642-1828. Mr. Richard D. Mathena, Prin.
Lay Teachers 15; Students 176.
Station—Anderson, St. John Medical Center Chapel, Tel: 765-649-2511.
Catechesis/Religious Programs—Tel: 765-642-5339.
Students 148.

Attica, Fountain Co., St. Francis Xavier (1890), Rev. Charles Kline.
Res., 407 S. Perry St., P.O. Box 55, 47918-0001. Tel: 765-762-3330; Fax: 765-762-1810. [CEM]
Catechesis/Religious Programs—Students 92.

Bryant, Jay Co., Holy Trinity (1860) (German), Rev. Robert C. Reinhart, C.PP.S.
Res., 7321 E. SR 67, 47326-9637. Tel: 219-997-6450. [CEM]
Catechesis/Religious Programs—Tel: 219-997-6450.
Students 166.

Carmel, Hamilton Co., Our Lady of Mount Carmel (1955), Rev. Msgr. John C. Duncan; Revs. Michael A. Ondo; Richard J. Doerr; Deacon William Rahill.
Office: 1045 W. 146th St., 46032-1198. Tel: 317-846-3475; Fax: 317-846-3477. [JC]
School—Tel: 317-846-1118; Fax: 317-582-2375.
Sisters of Notre Dame 4; Lay Teachers 40; Students 683.
Catechesis/Religious Programs—Tel: 317-846-3878; Fax: 317-582-2375.
Students 1,300.

St. Elizabeth Ann Seton (1981), Revs. Theodore D. Rothrock; Fred A. Schroeder; Anthony W. Levi.
Res., 10655 Haverstick Rd., 46033-3800. Tel: 317-846-3850; 846-6073; Fax: 317-846-3710.
Catechesis/Religious Programs—Fax: 317-846-3850.
Students 1,199.

Cicero, Hamilton Co., Sacred Heart (1898) (German-Irish), Rev. W. Michael Kettron.
Res., 429 S. Main St., 46034-9680. Tel: 317-984-5117; Fax: 317-984-5117.
Catechesis/Religious Programs—Tel: 317-984-2115.
Students 101.

Covington, Fountain Co., St. Joseph (1861), Rev. Charles Kline.
Res., 308 Pearl St., 47932-1062. Tel: 765-793-3289. [CEM]
Catechesis/Religious Programs—Tel: 765-793-8923.
Students 62.

Crawfordsville, Montgomery Co., St. Bernard (1859), Rev. Melvin J. Bennett; Sr. Nora Klewicki, Pastoral Assoc.
Res., 1306 E. Main St., P.O. Box 719, 47933-0719. Tel: 765-362-6121; Fax: 765-361-0796. [CEM]
Catechesis/Religious Programs—Tel: 765-362-5472.
Students 261.

Delphi, Carroll Co., St. Joseph (1859), Rev. Peter J. Vanderkolk.
Res., 207 N. Washington St., 46923-1297. Tel: 765-564-2407. [CEM]
Catechesis/Religious Programs—Tel: 765-564-3439.
Students 160.

De Motte, Jasper Co., St. Cecilia (1952), Rev. Paul R. Wicklum.
Res., 334 Fifteenth St., S.W., 46310-9269. Tel: 219-987-3511; Fax: 219-987-7755. [CEM]
Catechesis/Religious Programs—Tel: 219-987-3514.
Students 171.

Dunkirk, Jay Co., St. Mary (1896), Rev. Rick Tucker.
Res., 346 S. Broad St., 47336-1310. Tel: 765-768-6157.
Catechesis/Religious Programs—Students 43.

Dunnington, Benton Co., St. Mary (1876), Rev. Donald Gross.
Mailing Address: 2961 South SR71, Ambia, 47917. Tel: 765-884-1818. [CEM]
Catechesis/Religious Programs—Students 40.

Earl Park, Benton Co., St. John the Baptist (1888). Merged with St. Joseph, Kentland.

Elwood, Madison Co., St. Joseph (1889) (Irish-German), Rev. Kenneth T. Raczek.
Res., 1306 S. A St., 46036-1941. Tel: 765-552-6753. [CEM][JC]
Catechesis/Religious Programs—Tel: 765-552-6753. Mary Pat Miller, D.R.E.
Students 179.

Fishers, Hamilton Co., Holy Spirit Church (1991), Revs. Phillip T. Bowers; T. Edward Kacena.
Mailing Address: 10350 Glaser Way, 46038. Tel: 317-849-9245; Fax: 317-849-9388.
Res., 10868 Geist Woods Ln., Indianapolis, 46256. Tel: 317-845-0992.
Catechesis/Religious Programs—Tel: 317-849-8016.
Students 1,550.

St. Louis de Montfort (1978), Revs. Herbert Woolson; Timothy D. Kroeger.
Res., 11441 Hague Rd., 46038-1876. Tel: 317-842-6778; 842-6358; Fax: 317-576-1932.
Catechesis/Religious Programs—Students 843.

Fowler, Benton Co., Sacred Heart of Jesus (1872), Rev. Donald L. Gross.
Res., 107 E. Main St., 47944-1148. Tel: 765-884-1818; Fax: 765-884-1583. [CEM]

School—Tel: 765-884-0710; Fax: 765-884-0710. Mrs. Terri Goodman, Prin.
Lay Teachers 8; Students 138.
Catechesis/Religious Programs—Students 102.

Francesville, Pulaski Co., St. Francis Solano (1867), Rev. Paul R. White, C.PP.S., Admin.
Res., St. Joseph's College, P.O. Box 852, Rensselaer, 47978. Tel: 219-866-6271.
Catechesis/Religious Programs—Students 24.

Frankfort, Clinton Co., St. Mary (1875), Rev. Gerald J. Borawski.
Res., 600 St. Mary's Ave., 46041-0181. Tel: 765-654-5796; Fax: 765-654-6589. [CEM]
Preschool—Tel: 765-659-3914.
Catechesis/Religious Programs—Students 292.

Gas City, Grant Co., Holy Family (1908), Rev. David J. Newton.
Res., 325 E. North A St., 46933-1431. Tel: 765-674-2605; Fax: 765-674-2605.
Catechesis/Religious Programs—Students 130.

Goodland, Newton, SS. Peter and Paul (1880). Merged with St. Joseph, Kentland.

Hartford City, Blackford Co., St. John the Evangelist (1865), Rev. Robert E. Moran.
Res., 209 S. Spring St., 47348-2551. Tel: 765-348-3123.
School—Tel: 765-348-3889; Fax: 765-348-4399.
Lay Teachers 5; Students 70.
Catechesis/Religious Programs—Students 61.

Kentland, Newton, St. Joseph (1864), Rev. Robert J. Bernotas.
Res., 409 E. Allen St., P.O. Box 131, 47951-1322. Tel: 219-474-5514. [CEM]
School—Tel: 219-474-5614.
Lay Teachers 6; Students 45.
St. Joseph School Foundation, Inc.—Tel: 219-474-5514.
Catechesis/Religious Programs—Tel: 219-474-5614.
Students 129.

Kewanna, Fulton Co., St. Ann (1857), Rev. Joseph E. Jacob, Admin.
Res., P.O. Box 235, 46939-0181. Tel: 219-653-2520. [CEM]
Catechesis/Religious Programs—Students 7.

Kokomo, Howard Co., St. Joan of Arc (1927), Revs. Dennis J. O'Keeffe; Alejandro M. Paternoster.
Res., 900 S. Purdum, 46901-5598. Tel: 765-457-9371; Fax: 765-454-7241.
School—Sts. Joan of Arc & Patrick. (Consolidated School) 824 S. Purdum St., 46901-5500. Tel: 765-452-1610 (St. Joan); 459-4769 (St. Patrick); Fax: 765-454-7245.
Lay Teachers 22; Students 343.
Catechesis/Religious Programs—923 S. Jay St., 46901. Tel: 765-457-1375; Fax: 765-454-7241.
Students 385.

St. Patrick (1859), Rev. Francis I. Kilcline; Tom Shook, Business Mgr.
Office and Mailing Address—320 W. Broadway, 46901-2898. Tel: 765-452-6021; Fax: 765-868-8384.
Res., 1229 N. Washington, 46901-2898. [JC]
Schools—(Grades K-8). Tel: 765-459-4769; Fax: 765-457-3096.
Lay Teachers 23; Students 355; SS. Joan of Arc & Patrick. (South Campus) 824 S. Purdum St., 46901-5500. Tel: 765-452-1610; Fax: 765-454-7245. (North Campus) 1230 N. Armstrong St., 46901.
Catechesis/Religious Programs—Pete Wiggins, D.R.E.
Students 181.

Lake Village, Newton, St. Augusta (1947), Rev. John J. Cummings.
Res., 3228 W. St. Rd. 10, 46349-9706. Tel: 219-992-3220; Fax: 219-992-9332. [JC]
Catechesis/Religious Programs—Students 78.

Lebanon, Boone Co., St. Joseph (1862), Rev. Thomas H. Metzger.
Mailing Address: P.O. Box 309, 46052-0309. Tel: 765-482-5558; Fax: 765-482-1436.
Res., 319 E. South St., 46052-2684. Tel: 765-482-5558. [CEM]
Catechesis/Religious Programs—Sr. Barbara James, D.R.E.
Students 180.

Logansport, Cass Co., All Saints (1985). Consolidation of the following three parishes (Legal Titles): St. Bridget (1875); St. Joseph (1868); and St. Vincent de Paul (1838). Revs. John Zahn; Leo J. Haigerty; Kay White, Pastoral Assoc.
Parish Office: 112 E. Market St., 46947-2922. Tel: 219-722-4080; Fax: 219-722-5426.
Res., 114 E. Market St., 46947. Tel: 219-753-3020. [JC]
School—All Saints Elementary, 107 Eel River Ave., 46947-3188. Tel: 219-753-3410.
All Saints Middle School—620 Wilkinson St., 46947. Tel: 219-722-5622; Fax: 219-722-5519.
Lay Teachers 16; Students 281.
Catechesis/Religious Programs—Tel: 219-722-4080; Fax: 219-722-5426. Lori Eubank, D.R.E.
Students 162.
Convent—700 Wheatland Ave., 46947. Tel: 219-753-3684.
Mission—Lucerne, Cass Co., St. Elizabeth of Hungary, P.O. Box 86, 46950.

Lucerne, Cass Co., St. Elizabeth (1953), Rev. John H. Zahn, Admin.
Mailing Address: 112 East Market, Logansport, 46947. Tel: 219-753-3020.
Office: P.O. Box 86, 46950. [CEM]

Marion, Grant Co., St. Paul (1868), Rev. Richard J. Weisenberger.
Res., 46952-2098. Tel: 765-664-6345; Fax: 765-664-5953.
School—1009 Kem Rd., 46952. Tel: 765-662-2883. Mrs. Jackie Certain, Prin.
Lay Teachers 15; Students 179.
Catechesis/Religious Programs—Tel: 765-664-6345.
Students 156.

Our Lady of Guadalupe (Hispanic). Closed. For inquiries for parish records contact St. Paul, Marion.

Medaryville, Pulaski Co., St. Henry (1868), Rev. Paul R. White, C.PP.S., Admin.
Res., St. Joseph's College, P.O. Box 852, Rensselaer, 47978. Tel: 219-866-6271. [CEM]
Catechesis/Religious Programs—Students 10.

Monterey, Pulaski Co., St. Anne (1851) (German), Rev. Dominic Young.
Res., Church St., P.O. Box 96, 46960-0096. Tel: 219-542-2061. [CEM]
School—Tel: 219-542-4711; Fax: 219-542-4711.
Lay Teachers 4; Students 50.
Catechesis/Religious Programs—Tel: 219-542-4711.
Students 24.

Monticello, White Co., Our Lady of the Lakes (1948), Rev. James R. Goodrum.
Res., 543 S. Main St., 47960-2948. Tel: 219-583-5724; Fax: 219-583-4112.
Catechesis/Religious Programs—Tel: 219-583-6790.
Students 208.

Montpelier, Blackford Co., St. Margaret of Scotland (1864), Rev. Robert E. Moran, Admin.
Res., 207 W. Huntington St., P.O. Box 247, 47359. Tel: 765-728-5757. [CEM]

Muncie, Delaware Co., St. Francis of Assisi (1972). (Ball State University Parish). Revs. John D. Kiefer; Michael A. McKinney.
Res., 1200 W. Riverside Ave., 47303-3650. Tel: 765-288-6180; Fax: 765-288-7777.
Catechesis/Religious Programs—Students 185.

St. Lawrence (1869), Rev. Dennis J. Goth.
Res., 820 E. Charles St., 47305-2699. Tel: 765-288-9223; Fax: 765-289-9262.
School—2801 E. 16th St., 47302. Tel: 765-282-9353; Fax: 765-282-0457.
Lay Teachers 12; Students 152.
Catechesis/Religious Programs—Students 79.

St. Mary (1930), Revs. William R. Grady; Brian A. Dudzinski. In res., Revs. James T. Keane; Anthony J. Prosen.
Res., 2300 W. Jackson St., 47303-4797. Tel: 765-288-5308.
School—2301 W. Gilbert St., 47303-4797. Tel: 765-288-5878; Fax: 765-284-3685.
Lay Teachers 21; Students 270.
Catechesis/Religious Programs—Students 148.

Noblesville, Hamilton Co., Our Lady of Grace (1944), Revs. James R. Bates; Patrick R. Click; Gordon P. Wagoner, M.A., S.T.L.
Res., 9900 E. 191st St., 46060-1998. Tel: 317-773-4275; Fax: 317-773-9344.
School—Tel: 317-770-5660; Fax: 317-770-5663. Margaret Bailey, Prin.
Lay Teachers 10; Students 88.
Catechesis/Religious Programs—Tel: 317-773-0297.
Students 910.

Otterbein, Benton Co., St. Charles (1902), Rev. David L. Rasner.
Res., 108 N. Meadow St., Box 661, 47970-0661. Tel: 765-583-4641. [JC]
Catechesis/Religious Programs—Students 125.

Oxford, Benton Co., St. Patrick (1867) (Irish), Rev. Donald Eder.
Res., 502 S. Michigan St., 47971-8562. Tel: 765-385-2587; Fax: 765-385-0225. [CEM][JC]
Catechesis/Religious Programs—Students 84.

Peru, Miami Co., St. Charles Borromeo (1860), Rev. Philip S. Haslinger.
Res., 58 W. Fifth St., 46970-2100. Tel: 765-473-5543; Fax: 765-472-2632. [CEM]
School—(Grades PreK-6). Tel: 765-473-5669.
Lay Teachers 8; Students 148.
Catechesis/Religious Programs—80 W. Fifth St., 46970. Tel: 765-473-5544; Fax: 765-472-2692.
Students 126.

Portland, Jay Co., Immaculate Conception (1876) (German), Rev. Martin J. Sandhage.
Res., 506 E. Walnut St., 47371-1599. Tel: 219-726-7341. [JC]
Catechesis/Religious Programs—Tel: 219-726-7055.
Students 236.

Remington, Jasper Co., Sacred Heart (1875), Rev. Thomas E. Fox.
Res., 124 New York St., P.O. Box 159, 47977-0159. Tel: 219-261-2302. [CEM]
Catechesis/Religious Programs—Tel: 317-279-2656.
Students 79.

Rensselaer, Jasper Co., St. Augustine (1883), Revs. Mark R. Peres, C.PP.S.; Leonard J. Kostka, C.PP.S., Pastoral Assoc.
Res., 318 N. McKinley St., 47978-2599. Tel: 219-866-5351. [CEM]
School—Tel: 219-866-5480; Fax: 219-866-5663.
Religious 1; Lay Teachers 6; Students 125.
Catechesis/Religious Programs—Tel: 219-866-5351.
Students 145.

Reynolds, White Co., St. Joseph (1866), Rev. Richard E. Miller.
Res., 601 South Kenton St., 47980-8098. Tel: 219-984-5401. [CEM]
Catechesis/Religious Programs—Students 88.

Rochester, Fulton Co., St. Joseph (1900), Rev. Joseph E. Jacob, Admin.
Res., 1310 Main St., 46975-2108. Tel: 219-223-2808; Fax: 219-224-2808. [JC]
Catechesis/Religious Programs—Tel: 219-223-3246.
Students 108.
Mission—Kewanna, Fulton Co., St. Ann, P.O. Box 235, Kewanna, 46939. Tel: 219-653-2520.

Star City, Pulaski Co., St. Joseph (1851), Rev. Ronald J. Schiml, C.PP.S.
Res., 5895 S. SR 119, 46985-8826. Tel: 219-595-7198. [CEM 2][JC]
Catechesis/Religious Programs—Students 87.

Tipton, Tipton Co., St. John the Baptist (1866), Rev. Leroy G. Kinnaman.
Res., 340 N. Mill St., 46072-1403. Tel: 765-675-2422. [CEM]
School—(Grades PreK-5). Tel: 765-675-4741; Fax: 765-675-2163.
Lay Teachers 10; Students 128.
Catechesis/Religious Programs—Students 110.

Union City, Randolph Co., St. Mary (1865) (Irish-German), Rev. C. Alan Funk.
Res., 425 W. Hickory St., 47390-1301. Tel: 765-964-4202. [CEM]
Catechesis/Religious Programs—Tel: 765-964-4767.
Students 75.

Westfield, Hamilton Co., St. Maria Goretti (1995), Rev. Kevin J. Haines; Stephen Miller, Business Mgr.
Res., 17102 Springmill Rd., 46074. Tel: 317-867-3213; Fax: 317-867-3263.
School—Tel: 317-896-5582; Fax: 317-867-0783.
Lay Teachers 20; Students 395.
Catechesis/Religious Programs—Connie Anderson, D.R.E.
Students 81.

West Lafayette, Tippecanoe Co., Blessed Sacrament (1957), Rev. David M. Douglas.
Res., 2224 Sacramento Ave., 47906-1998. Tel: 765-463-5733; Fax: 765-497-7866.
Catechesis/Religious Programs—Students 381.
Stations—Indiana Veterans' Home, Tel: 765-463-1502; Mary Queen of the Universe Chapel.

St. Thomas Aquinas (1951). (Purdue University Parish). Revs. Dan Davis, O.P.; Steve Kuhlman, O.P.; Andrew Pavlak, O.P.
Office: 535 State St., 47906-3592. Tel: 765-743-4652; Fax: 765-743-0426.
Catechesis/Religious Programs—Eileen Strater, D.R.E.
Students 363.

Wheatfield, Jasper Co., Sorrowful Mother (1887), Rev. Philip A. Mahalic.
Res., P.O. Box 248, 46392-0248. Tel: 219-956-3343; Fax: 219-956-3343. [CEM]
Church Hall: Tel: 219-956-4648.
Catechesis/Religious Programs—Students 137.

Winamac, Pulaski Co., St. Peter (1859), Rev. John J. Hoying, C.PP.S.
Res., 401 N. Monticello St., 46996-1327. Tel: 219-946-4906; Fax: 219-946-4962. [CEM]
Catechesis/Religious Programs—424 N. Market St., 46996. Tel: 219-946-6804.
Students 178.

Winchester, Randolph Co., St. Joseph (1952), Rev. Louis S. Heitz.
Res., 425 W. North St., 47394-1502. Tel: 765-584-2861.
Catechesis/Religious Programs—Tel: 765-584-1084.
Students 60.

Zionsville, Boone Co., St. Alphonsus (1945), Rev. Douglas McCormack.
Res., 1870 W. Oak, 46077-1894. Tel: 317-873-2885; 873-2700; Fax: 317-873-8746. [JC]
Catechesis/Religious Programs—Tel: 317-873-9418.
Students 418.

Chaplains of Public Institutions

LAFAYETTE. *Indiana Veterans' Home, Queen of the Universe Chapel*. Attended from Blessed Sacrament Church, West Lafayette.

GRISSOM. *Grissom Air Force Base, St. Michael's Chapel* 46971. Tel: 765-688-2191. Rev. Philip S. Hascinger, Auxiliary Civilian Chap.

LOGANSPORT. *Logansport State Hospital*. Vacant.

MARION. *U.S. Veteran's Hospital*. Revs. James Rose (FTW) Chap.; Joseph W. Grace, Auxiliary Chap.

PENDLETON. *Correctional Industrial Complex Ecumenical Chapel* P.O. Box 601, 46064. Tel: 765-778-8011. Rev. Anthony J. Prosen.
Indiana State Reformatory, St. Christopher Chapel P.O. Box 28, 46064. Tel: 765-778-2107. Rev. Anthony J. Prosen.

Special Assignment:
Reverend Monsignors—
Sell, Robert L., III, J.C.L., Vicar Gen., Chancellor & Moderator of the Curia, 1128 E. State St., Lafayette, IN 47905. Tel: 765-742-1665
Reverend Fathers—
Buckles, David, J.C.L., Diocesan Tribunal, 2300 S. 9th St., Lafayette, IN 47905. Tel: 765-474-0506
Doerr, Brian, Vocation Dir., 1212 South St., Lafayette, IN 47901-1576. Tel: 765-742-4440
Miller, Richard E., J.C.L., Diocesan Tribunal, 2300 S. 9th St., Lafayette, IN 47905. Tel: 765-474-0506
Prosen, Anthony J., 1315 W. University St., Muncie, IN 47303. Tel: 765-288-6180
Rasner, David L., J.C.L., Treas., Clergy Relief Association
Vath, William R., Diocesan Tribunal, 2300 S. 9th St., Lafayette, IN 47905. Tel: 765-474-0506

On Duty Outside the Diocese:
Reverend Fathers—
Clegg, Timothy, 3635 Westchester Dr., Holiday, FL 34691
Comeau, Ronald R., 6 Johnson Rd., Aurora, Ontario L4C 2A2. Tel: 416-772-1965
Cover, Phillip B., 1600 S. Eads St., #923-S, Arlington, VA 22202
Cox, Alan B., P.O. Box 10, Post Falls, ID 83877-0010. Tel: 208-773-4715
Gross, Barry, 1601 Georgia Ave., Wheaton, MD 20902
Holbrook, William M., 6210 W. Bell Plaine, Chicago, IL 60634
Mannion, John H., St. Francis Hospital, Pastoral Care Department, 1600 Albany St., Beechgrove, IN 46107. Tel: 317-787-3311
Plaster, George F., 1751 - 8436 Viburnum Ct., Indianapolis, IN 46260. Tel: 317-251-9249
Schultz, John C., P.O. Box 415, Danville, IL 61834. Tel: 217-443-3936
Westfall, Joseph B., P.O. Box 45715, Kansas City, MO 64171

Military Chaplains:
Reverend Fathers—
Kinney, John M., 2520 Crested Hills, Schertz, TX 78154. Tel: 210-658-6825

Leave of Absence:
Reverend Fathers—
Bohlinger, Kenneth

Unassigned:
Reverend Fathers—
Colletti, Joseph A.
Courtney, Patrick E.
DiGeronimo, Richard
Hagan, Paul
Lutkenhoff, Bernard

Retired:
Reverend Monsignors—
Foley, Maurice D., Albertine Home, 1501 Hoffman St., Hammond, IN 46327-1764. Tel: 219-937-9211
Potthoff, Fred E., 37 Wea Oaks St., Lafayette, IN 47905-3406. Tel: 765-474-7152
Reverend Fathers—
Bruetsch, Joseph J., St. Mary Cathedral, 1212 South St., Lafayette, IN 47901-1576. Tel: 765-742-4440
Eckert, Carl E., Century Village Healthcare, 705 N. Meridan St., Rm. 501, Greentown, IN 46936-1246. Tel: 765-628-3377
Fosselman, Robert J., 3554 E. Bailey Rd., Monticello, IN 47960-7040. Tel: 219-253-7406
Funcheon, Gerald A., 6106 Desoto Ave., New Port Richey, FL 34653
Hardebeck, Donald E., 5243 N. Crab Apple Loop, Monticello, IN 47960-7056. Tel: 219-583-6417
Matuszak, Edward S., 619 1/2 E. 10th St., Erie, PA 16503-1315. Tel: 814-455-1166
Puetz, Richard W., St. Elizabeth Healthcare Center, 701 Armory Rd., Rm. 409, Delphi, IN 46923-1915. Tel: 765-564-2182
Remaklus, Charles W., 708 N. Mohee Dr., Hartford City, IN 47348-8603. Tel: 765-348-1998
Ruffing, Joseph R., 204 Cedar Creek Rd., Princeton, KY 42445-2341. Tel: 502-365-2932
Schiavone, Jeldo J., P.O. Box 13484, Tampa, FL 33681-3484. Tel: 813-835-0377
Schott, Victor P., 3706 E. Wilson Rd., Muncie, IN 47303-6203. Tel: 765-284-7355
Weller, Harold E., P.O. Box 235, Kewanna, IN 46939. Tel: 219-223-2305
Zimmer, Thomas J., 3814 Sunray Dr., Holiday, FL 34691-3239. Tel: 813-943-5112

Permanent Deacons:
Castillo, Domingo, St. Paul, Marion
Cloud, H. William, St. Alphonsus, Zionsville
Miller, Mark, Our Lady of Grace, Noblesville
Nevinger, Ronald, St. Boniface, Lafayette
Rahill, William, Our Lady of Mount Carmel, Carmel

INSTITUTIONS LOCATED IN THE DIOCESE

[A] COLLEGES AND UNIVERSITIES

RENSSELAER. *Saint Joseph's College*, P.O. Box 909, 47978. Tel: 219-866-6000; Fax: 219-866-6100.
Web site: www.saintjoe.edu
For a complete listing, refer to the Colleges and Universities section.

[B] HIGH SCHOOLS, INTER-PAROCHIAL

LAFAYETTE. *Central Catholic Junior-Senior High School*, 2410 S. Ninth St., 47909-2499. Tel: 765-474-2496; Fax: 765-474-8752.
E-mail: worland@lcss.org
Web site: www.lcss.org/cc/cc_centralcatholic/html
David L. Worland, Prin.; Mrs. Susan Hoefer, Campus Min. Lay Teachers 27; Students 339.

[C] GENERAL HOSPITALS

LAFAYETTE. *St. Elizabeth Medical Center*, 1501 Hartford St., P.O. Box 7501, 47903. Tel: 765-423-6011; Fax: 765-423-6040.
E-mail: pr@glhsi.org
Web site: www.ste.org
For a complete listing, refer to the Hospitals section.

ANDERSON. *Saint John's Health System*, 2015 Jackson St., 46016. Tel: 765-646-8745; Fax: 765-646-8373
For a complete listing, refer to the Hospitals section.

CARMEL. *St. Elizabeth Ann Seton Hospital of Central Indiana, Inc.*, 13500 N. Meridian St., 46032. Tel: 317-582-8560; Fax: 317-582-8565.
E-mail: phalexan@stvincent.org
For a complete listing, refer to the Hospitals section.

ELWOOD. *St. Vincent Mercy Hospital, Inc.*, 1331 South A St., 46036-1942. Tel: 765-552-4600; Fax: 765-552-4700.
E-mail: rjcoughl@stvincent.org
For a complete listing, refer to the Hospitals section.

KOKOMO. *St. Joseph Hospital & Health Center of Kokomo, Indiana, Inc.*, 1907 W. Sycamore St., 46901. Tel: 765-452-5611.
Web site: www.stjhhc.org
For a complete listing, refer to the Hospitals section.

[D] NURSING HOMES

LAFAYETTE. *St. Anthony Health Care*, 1205 N. 14th St., 47904. Tel: 765-423-4861; Fax: 765-742-8790
For a complete listing, refer to the Special Care Facilities section.

DELPHI. *St. Elizabeth Healthcare Center*, 701 Armory Rd., 46923. Tel: 765-564-6380; Fax: 765-564-6384.
E-mail: SEHC@gte.net
Web site: www.franciscanservices.com
For a complete listing, refer to the Special Care Facilities section.

[E] MONASTERIES AND RESIDENCES OF PRIESTS AND BROTHERS

LAFAYETTE. *Emmaus House*, 2500 S. Ninth St., 47905. Tel: 317-477-6441.

[F] CONVENTS AND RESIDENCES FOR SISTERS

LAFAYETTE. *Monastery of the Precious Blood*, 1106 State St., E., 47905-1219. Tel: 765-742-8227; Fax: 765-420-7361.
E-mail: saotproc@aol.com
Web site: members.aol.com/saotproc/index.htm
Sr. Jacqueline Hayden, A.P.B., Supr.; Rev. John A. Bach, Chap., Res., 155 Durkee's Run Dr., 47905. Sisters Adorers of the Precious Blood. Professed 7; Novice 1.

ANDERSON. *Sisters of the Holy Cross*, 1007 Raible Ave., 46011. Tel: 765-642-6117. Sisters 2.
Additional addresses for Sisters of the Holy Cross: 2115 Meridian St., 46016. Tel: 765-642-2427. Sisters 2.
Sisters of the Holy Cross, Inc.

KOKOMO. *Maria Regina Mater Monastery*, 1175 N. 300 W., 46901-1799. Tel: 765-457-5743. Monastery of Poor Clares of the Reform of St. Colette. Mother Miriam, Abbess; Rev. Method Wilson, O.F.M., Chap. Solemnly Professed Nuns in Cloister 8; Perpetually Professed Extern Sister 1; Postulants 1; Novice 1 ; Temporarily Professed 1.

TIPTON. *St. Joseph Center: Sisters of St. Joseph*, 1440 W. Division Rd., 46072-8584. Tel: 765-675-4146; Fax: 765-675-7471.
E-mail: csjtip@tiptontel.com
Web site: www.sistersstjo-tipton.org
Sr. Martin McEntee, C.S.J., Pres. Sisters Resident at Motherhouse 20; Total in Residence 22; Total Staff 3. Tel: 765-675-6203; Fax: 765-675-7471. Rev. Fred H. Gschwind, Chap.

[G] RETREAT HOUSES

HARTFORD CITY. *John XXIII Center*, 407 W. McDonald St., 47348. Tel: 765-348-4008; Fax: 765-348-5819.
E-mail: john23rd@netusa1.net
Web site: www.netusa1.net/~john23rd
Rev. Keith P. Hosey, Dir.; Sr. Maureen Mangen, C.PP.S., Asst. Dir.

[H] NEWMAN CENTERS

CRAWFORDSVILLE. *Newman Center at Wabash College*, 310 S. Grant Ave., P.O. Box 601, 47933-0601. Tel: 765-362-8105. Rev. Melvin J. Bennett.

MUNCIE. *St. Francis of Assisi University Church*, Newman Center, 1200 W. Riverside Ave., 47303. Tel: 765-288-6180; Fax: 765-288-7777.
E-mail: frjohnkiefer@Juno.com
Rev. Michael A. McKinney. Total in Residence 8; Total Staff 8.

WEST LAFAYETTE. *St. Thomas Aquinas Parish and Foundation for Catholic Students Attending Purdue University*, 535 State St., 47906. Tel: 765-743-4652; Fax: 765-743-0426.
E-mail: sttomaq@sttoms-purdue.org
Web site: www.sttoms-purdue.org
Revs. Daniel C. Davis, O.P., Pastor & Dir., Newman Apostolate; Steven Kuhlmann, O.P., Assoc. Pastor; Andrew Pavlac, O.P.

[I] MISCELLANEOUS

LAFAYETTE. *Catholic Foundation of Northcentral Indiana, Inc.*, P.O. Box 1687, 47902-1687. Tel: 765-742-7000; Fax: 765-742-7513.
E-mail: pbarrett@dioceseoflafayette.org
Web site: www.dioceseoflafayette.org/staff-deveolopent.html

ANDERSON. *Saint John's Foundation, Inc.*, 2015 Jackson St., 46016. Tel: 765-646-8373; Fax: 765-646-8504.
E-mail: dlapple@sjhsnet.org
Mr. Jerry D. Brumitt, Pres. & CEO.

CARMEL. *Our Lady of Mount Carmel Parochial School*, 1047 W. 146 St., 46032. Tel: 317-846-3475; Fax: 317-846-3477.
E-mail: DuncanJ@olmc1.org
Web site: olmc1.org
Rev. Msgr. John C. Duncan, Contact Person.

CRAWFORDSVILLE,. *St. Clare Medical Center*, 1710 Lafayette Rd., 46933-1099. Tel: 765-362-2800; Fax: 765-364-3189.
Web site: www.stclaremedical.org

RELIGIOUS INSTITUTES OF MEN REPRESENTED IN THE DIOCESE

For further details refer to the corresponding bracketed number in the Religious Institutes of Men or Women section.

[0520]—*Order of St. Francis Minors.*—O.F.M.
[1060]—*Society of the Precious Blood.*—C.PP.S.

RELIGIOUS INSTITUTES OF WOMEN REPRESENTED IN THE DIOCESE

[1920]—*Congregation of the Sisters of the Holy Cross.*—C.S.C.

[1070-09]—*Dominican Sisters.*—O.P.

[1780]—*Franciscan Sisters of Peace.*—F.S.P.A.

[4150]—*Irish Ursuline Union.*—O.S.U.

[0240]—*Olivetan Benedictine Sisters.*—O.S.B.

[3230]—*Poor Handmaids of Jesus Christ.*—P.H.J.C.

[2970]—*School Sisters of Notre Dame.*—S.S.N.D.

[0110]—*Sisters Adorers of the Precious Blood.*—A.P.B.

[0430]—*Sisters of Charity of the Blessed Virgin Mary.*—B.V.M.

[2990]—*Sisters of Notre Dame.* (Toledo Prov.).—S.N.D.

[3000]—*Sisters of Notre Dame de Namur.*—S.N.D.deN.

[3360]—*Sisters of Providence of Saint Mary-of-the-Woods, IN.*—S.P.

[]—*Sisters of St. Francis.* (Sylvania, OH).—O.S.F.

[1640]—*Sisters of St. Francis of Perpetual Adoration.*—O.S.F.

[3830-10]—*Sisters of St. Joseph.*—C.S.J.

[3260]—*Sisters of the Precious Blood.* (Dayton, Ohio).—C.PP.S.

NECROLOGY

† Carr, Bernard J., Anza, CA Sacred Heart. —Died Dec. 1, 2000.

† Klein, Rev. Msgr. Sylvester P., Tipton, IN St. Joseph Center. —Died Sept. 6, 2000.

Diocese of Lafayette

(Dioecesis Lafayettensis)

Most Reverend

EDWARD JOSEPH O'DONNELL, D.D.

Bishop of Lafayette; ordained April 6, 1957; appointed Titular Bishop of Britonia and Auxiliary Bishop of St. Louis December 6, 1983; consecrated February 10, 1984; appointed fifth Bishop of Lafayette November 8, 1994; installed December 16, 1994. *Mailing Address: P.O. Box 3387, Lafayette, LA, 70502.*

Most Reverend

GERARD LOUIS FREY, D.D.

Retired Bishop of Lafayette; ordained April 2, 1938; appointed Bishop of Savannah May 31, 1967; consecrated August 8, 1967; transferred to Lafayette November 7, 1972; installed January 7, 1973; retired May 13, 1989. *Office: 1408 Carmel Ave., Lafayette, LA, 70501.* Tel.: 337-261-5613.

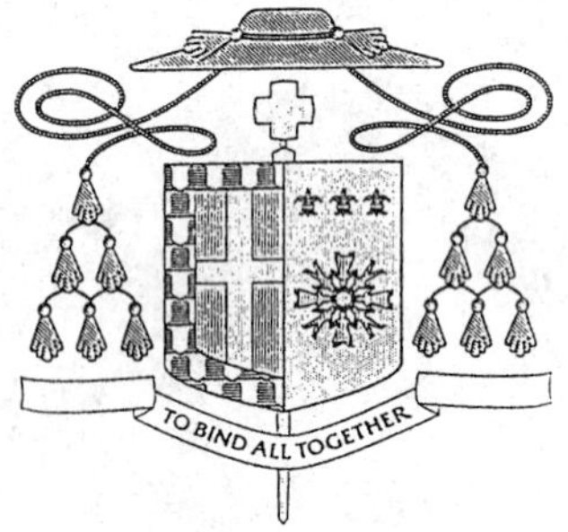

ESTABLISHED JANUARY 11, 1918.

Square Miles 5,777.

Comprises the civil parishes (Counties) of Acadia, Evangeline, Iberia, Lafayette, St. Landry, St. Martin and St. Mary (west of Atchafalaya River) and Vermilion in the south central part of the State of Louisiana.

For legal titles of Diocese, parishes and diocesan institutions, consult the Chancery Office.

Administrative Offices: Diocesan Office Building, 1408 Carmel Ave., Lafayette, LA, 70501. Tel.: 337-261-5500; Fax: 337-261-5635.

Web site address: www.dol-louisiana.org

E-mail address: robins@dol-louisiana.org

STATISTICAL OVERVIEW

Personnel	
Bishop	1
Retired Bishops	1
Priests: Diocesan Active in Diocese	98
Priests: Active Outside Diocese	3
Priests: Diocesan in Foreign Missions	1
Priests: Retired, Sick or Absent	39
Number of Diocesan Priests	141
Religious Priests in Diocese	57
Extern Priests in Diocese	8
Ordinations:	
Diocesan Priests	2
Transitional Deacons	4
Permanent Deacons	23
Permanent Deacons in Diocese	76
Total Brothers	27
Total Sisters	148
Parishes	
Parishes	121
With Resident Pastor:	
Resident Diocesan Priests	88
Resident Religious Priests	23
Without Resident Pastor:	
Administered by Priests	7
Administered by Deacons	5
Missions	32
Professional Ministry Personnel:	
Brothers	4
Sisters	19
Lay Ministers	70
Welfare	
Catholic Hospitals	1
Total Assisted	81,000
Health Care Centers	1
Total Assisted	16,000
Homes for the Aged	5
Total Assisted	1,200
Specialized Homes	7
Total Assisted	2,300
Special Centers for Social Services	6
Total Assisted	188,000
Educational	
Diocesan Students in Other Seminaries	36
Seminaries, Religious	1
Students Religious	7
Total Seminarians	43
High Schools, Diocesan and Parish	9
Total Students	3,775
High Schools, Private	1
Total Students	133
Elementary Schools, Diocesan and Parish	29
Total Students	10,485
Elementary Schools, Private	2
Total Students	664
Catechesis/Religious Education:	
High School Students	10,771
Elementary Students	21,468
Total Students Under Catholic Instruction	43,564
Teachers in the Diocese:	
Brothers	2
Sisters	21
Lay Teachers	926
Vital Statistics	
Receptions into the Church:	
Infant Baptism Totals	5,578
Adult Baptism Totals	204
Received into Full Communion	305
First Communions	4,954
Confirmations	4,143
Marriages:	
Catholic	1,618
Interfaith	282
Total Marriages	1,900
Deaths	3,480
Total Catholic Population	335,700
Total Population	546,000

Former Bishops—Most Rev. JULES B. JEANMARD D.D., LL.D., ord. June 11, 1903; appt. first Bishop of Lafayette, July 18, 1918; cons. Dec. 8, 1918; installed as first Bishop of Lafayette, Dec. 12, 1918; appt. Assistant at the Pontifical Throne, Dec. 8, 1943; resigned and named Titular Bishop of Bareta, March 13, 1956; died Feb. 23, 1957.—Most Rev. ROBERT E. TRACY, D.D., Auxiliary Bishop of Lafayette, March 18, 1959; appt. first Bishop of Baton Rouge, Aug. 10, 1961.—Most Rev. WARREN L. BOUDREAUX, D.D., J.C.D., Auxiliary Bishop of Lafayette, May 19, 1962; appt. second Bishop of Beaumont, Texas, June 4, 1971.—Most Rev. MAURICE SCHEXNAYDER, D.D., ord. April 11, 1925; appt. Titular Bishop of Tuscamia and Auxiliary of Lafayette, Dec. 11, 1950; cons. Feb. 22, 1951; appt. second Bishop of Lafayette, March 13, 1956; installed May 24, 1956; resigned Nov. 7, 1972; died Jan. 23, 1981.—Most Rev. GERARD L. FREY, D.D., appt. third Bishop of Lafayette, Nov. 7, 1972; installed Jan. 7, 1973; resigned May 13, 1989.—Most Rev. HARRY J. FLYNN, D.D., ord. May 28, 1960; appt. Coadjutor Bishop of Lafayette, April 19, 1986, fourth Bishop of Lafayette, May 13, 1989; appt. Coadjutor Archbishop of St. Paul, Minneapolis, Feb. 22, 1994.

Bishop's Office—Diocesan Office Building, P.O. Box 3387, Lafayette, 70502. Tel: 337-261-5614; Fax: 337-261-5603.

Administrative Offices—Diocesan Office Building, 1408 Carmel Ave., Lafayette, 70501. Tel: 337-261-5500; Fax: 337-261-5635.

Vicars General—Rev. Msgr. H. ALEXANDRE LARROQUE, J.C.D., *P.O. Box 3387, Lafayette, 70502.* Tel: 337-261-5613. Rev. Msgr. RONALD BROUSSARD, *P.O. Box 3387, Lafayette, 70502.* Tel: 337-261-5536.

Chancellor and Director of Administration—Sr. JOANNA VALONI, S.S.N.D., *P.O. Box 3387, Lafayette, 70502.* Tel: 337-261-5611.

Episcopal Vicars—Very Rev. Msgr. L. MICHAEL HERPIN, Lafayette Region; Very Rev. THOMAS JAMES, S.V.D., South Region; Very Rev. Msgr. J. ROBERT ROMERO, North Region; Very Rev. Msgr. FREDERICK O. SWENSON, West Region.

Vicar for Religious—Sr. MILDRED LEONARDS, C.D.P., *1408 Carmel Ave., Lafayette, 70501.* Tel: 337-261-5634.

Vicar for Priests—Rev. RUSSELL HARRINGTON, *P.O. Drawer V, Lafayette, 70501.* Tel: 337-268-9677; Fax: 337-261-5545.

Tribunal—P.O. Box 3387, Lafayette, 70502. Tel: 337-261-5623; Fax: 337-261-5646.

Judicial Vicar—Very Rev. Msgr. J. DOUGLAS COURVILLE, J.C.L.
Adjutant Judicial Vicars—Revs. ROBIE ROBICHAUX, J.C.L.; ARTHUR M. WARREN.
Advocates—Revs. A. REX BROUSSARD; BILL JOHN MELANCON; ROBERT COURVILLE; JULES ARCENEAUX; PAUL BROUSSARD; JEFFERSON DEBLANC; MITCHELL GUIDRY; KEITH LABOVE; MARK LEDOUX; W. CURTIS MALLET; MALCOLM O'LEARY, S.V.D.; JOSEPH SIMON, S.V.D.
Promoter of Justice—Vacant.
Assessor—Mrs. KAROL MEYNARD.
Judges—Rev. Msgr. GLEN JOHN PROVOST; Rev. Msgr. H. ALEXANDRE LARROQUE, J.C.D.; Revs. GRADY ESTILETTE; HERBERT MAY.
Defenders of the Bond—Revs. OVERTON JOSEPH BREAUX; KENNETH R. MORVANT, J.C.L.
Notaries—Mrs. EULA B. LANDRY; Rev. AUSTIN LEGER.

Diocesan Offices and Directors

Adult Catechesis—GLORIA CLARK, *1408 Carmel Ave., Lafayette, 70501.* Tel: 337-261-5550.
Alcohol & Drug Abuse—BEVERLY MIRE, *1408 Carmel Ave., Lafayette, 70501.* Tel: 337-261-5674.
Archives—BARBARA C. DEJEAN, *1408 Carmel Ave., Lafayette, 70501.* Tel: 337-261-5639; 261-5667.
Auxiliary Services—PATSY ARWOOD, *1408 Carmel Ave., Lafayette, 70501.* Tel: 337-261-5600.
Bishop's Services Appeal—CONNIE KLEINPETER, *1408 Carmel Ave., Lafayette, 70501.* Tel: 337-261-5641.
Black Catholics—Revs. CHESTER ARCENEAUX; RONALD BROUSSARD, V.G., *1408 Carmel Ave., Lafayette, 70501.* Tel: 337-261-5536.
Catholic Social Services—PAULA MILNER, *1408 Carmel Ave., Lafayette, 70501.* Tel: 337-261-5654.
Catholic Foundation of the Diocese of Lafayette—CONNIE KLEINPETER, *1408 Carmel Ave., Lafayette, 70501.* Tel: 337-261-5641.
Catholic Charismatic—Rev. ALBERT G. NUNEZ, *P.O. Box 40, Carencro, 70520.* Tel: 337-896-7732.
Christian Formation—Sr. LORRAINE LANDRY, S.S.N.D., *1408 Carmel Ave., Lafayette, 70501.* Tel: 337-261-5565.
Clergy Health Care & Retirement—BEVERLY BROUSSARD, *1408 Carmel Ave., Lafayette, 70501.* Tel: 337-261-5629.
Communications—Newspaper—*"Acadiana Catholic"*, THOMAS SUMMERS, Editor, *1408 Carmel Ave., Lafayette, 70501.* Tel: 337-261-5513; 261-5511; 261-5518. *Radio-TV*—DAVID MERGIST, Producer & Dir., *1408 Carmel Ave., Lafayette, 70501.* Tel: 337-261-5626.
Community Services—J. BERNEL FONTENOT, *1408 Carmel Ave., Lafayette, 70501.* Tel: 337-261-5650.
Data Processing—ROBIN STEVENSON, *1408 Carmel Ave., Lafayette, 70501.* Tel: 337-261-5516.
Deaf Apostolate—MYRA MOUTON, *1408 Carmel Ave., Lafayette, 70501.* Tel: 337-261-5548.
Development—CONNIE KLEINPETER, *1408 Carmel Ave., Lafayette, 70501.* Tel: 337-261-5641.
Education / Communication—GERALD DILL, *1408 Carmel Ave., Lafayette, 70501.* Tel: 337-261-5526.
Family Life—BARBARA WALLEY, M.S.W., Mailing Address: *1408 Carmel Ave., Lafayette, 70501.* Tel: 337-261-5653.
Fiscal Administration—MARY PARKER, *P.O. Box 3387, Lafayette, 70502.* Tel: 337-261-5629.
Hispanic Ministry—Rev. ARTURO LOZANO, S.J., *1408 Carmel Ave., Lafayette, 70501.* Tel: 337-261-5535; 261-5542.
Institutions—J. BERNEL FONTENOT, *1408 Carmel Ave., Lafayette, 70501.* Tel: 337-261-5650.
Justice and Peace—UNA HARGRAVE, *1408 Carmel Ave., Lafayette, 70501.* Tel: 337-261-5545.
Migration Refugee Services—TINA QUESADA, *1408 Carmel Ave., Lafayette, 70501.* Tel: 337-261-5535.
Office for Persons with Disabilities—MYRA MOUTON, *1404 Carmel Ave., Lafayette, 70501.* Tel: 337-261-5548.
Parish Services—Sr. LORRAINE LANDRY, S.S.N.D., *1408 Carmel Ave., Lafayette, 70501.* Tel: 337-261-5565.
Parish Finances—JEANNINE REYNOLDS, Mgr., *P.O. Box 3387, Lafayette, 70502.* Tel: 337-261-5632.
Permanent Diaconate—Deacon RONALD A. BOREL, *1408 Carmel Ave., Lafayette, 70501.* Tel: 337-261-5609.
Pro-Life Issues—BRENDA DESORMEAUX, *1408 Carmel Ave., Lafayette, 70501.* Tel: 337-261-5607.
Prison Ministry—*1408 Carmel Ave., Lafayette, 70501.* Tel: 337-261-5545.
Religious Education and Pastoral Ministry—Sr. CARMELITA LATIOLAIS, *1408 Carmel Ave., Lafayette, 70501.* Tel: 337-261-5674.
Religious Personnel—Sr. MILDRED LEONARDS, C.D.P., Vicar, *1408 Carmel Ave., Lafayette, 70501.* Tel: 337-261-5634.
Schools—ANNA LARRIVIERE, Supt., *1408 Carmel Ave., Lafayette, 70501.* Tel: 337-261-5529.
Seminarians—Rev. RUSSELL HARRINGTON, *1408 Carmel Ave., Lafayette, 70501.* Tel: 337-261-5690.
Vocations—Rev. THOMAS VOORHIES, *206 W. Church St., Delcambre, 70528.* Tel: 337-685-4426.
Youth Ministry—KATHY STELLY, *1408 Carmel Ave., Lafayette, 70501.* Tel: 337-261-5551.
Worship—Rev. JASON MOUTON, *1408 Carmel Ave., Lafayette, 70501.* Tel: 337-261-5536.

Diocesan Commissions and Boards

Building Review Board—Sr. JOANNA VALONI, S.S.N.D., *1408 Carmel Ave., Lafayette, 70501.* Tel: 337-261-5611.
Campus Ministry—Rev. W. CURTIS MALLET, Dir., *Our Lady of Wisdom Catholic Student Center, P.O. Box 43271, Lafayette, 70504.* Tel: 337-232-8742.
Catholic Daughters of America—Rev. CEDRIC SONNIER, *St. John Cathedral, P.O. Drawer V, Lafayette, 70502.* Tel: 337-232-1322.
Catholic Relief Services—UNA HARGRAVE, *1408 Carmel Ave., Lafayette, 70501.* Tel: 337-261-5545.
Clergy Personnel Advisory Board—Rev. LOUIS RICHARD, *St. Michael Church, P.O. Box 406, Crowley, 70527.* Tel: 337-783-7394.
Clergy Welfare Commission—Rev. Msgr. PAUL METREJEAN, Chm., *P.O. Box 176, Mermentau, 70556.* Tel: 337-824-2278.
Continuing Formation of the Clergy—Rev. RUSSELL HARRINGTON, *1408 Carmel Dr., Lafayette, 70501.* Tel: 337-261-5690.
Credit Union—*116 St. Jules St., Lafayette, 70506.* Tel: 337-261-1151.
Cursillo—Rev. Msgr. LOUIS J. MELANCON, *P.O. Box 8, Duson, 70529-0008.* Tel: 337-873-4962.
Diocesan Council of Catholic Women—Rev. Msgr. J. GUY LEMOINE, Diocesan Moderator, *St. Peter Church, P.O. Box 12507, New Iberia, 70562.* Tel: 337-369-3816.
Diocesan Pastoral Council—Sr. LORRAINE LANDRY, S.S.N.D., Coord., *1408 Carmel Ave., Lafayette, 70501.* Tel: 337-261-5565.
Ecumenism—Rev. HERBERT DELAUNAY, *1112 Saturn Rd., Morgan City, 70380.* Tel: 504-395-2470.
Finance Advisory Board—LEON K. POCHE, K.S.G., *633 W. 17th St., Crowley, 70526.* Tel: 337-783-0650.
Holy Childhood—ANNA LARIVIERRE, *1408 Carmel Ave., Lafayette, 70501.* Tel: 337-261-5534.
Holy Name Society—Vacant.
Hospitals—Vacant, Coord. Health Affairs, *P.O. Box 3387, Lafayette, 70502.* Tel: 337-261-5613.
Knights of Columbus—Rev. MICHAEL GUIDRY, Diocesan Chap., *Our Lady of Perpetual Help, P.O. Box 10110, New Iberia, 70562.* Tel: 337-365-5481.
Legion of Mary—Vacant.
Parish Boundaries and Future Parish Development Board—Sr. JOANNA VALONI, S.S.N.D., *1408 Carmel Ave., Lafayette, 70501.* Tel: 337-261-5611.
Retreats—Rev. KENNETH BUDDENDORFF, S.J., *Our Lady of the Oaks Retreat House, P.O. Box D, Grand Coteau, 70541.* Tel: 337-662-5410. Rev. ALBERT LOUAPRE, S.J., Dir., *Jesuit Spirituality Center, P.O. Box C, Grand Coteau, 70541.* Tel: 337-662-5251.
Scouting—Rev. MITCHELL GUIDRY, Chap., *St. Anthony, P.O. Box 31, Eunice, 70535.* Tel: 337-457-5285. ROBERT MARCEAUX, Lay Chm., *101 Bellridge Dr., Lafayette, 70506.* Tel: 337-984-1767.
Society for the Propagation of the Faith—Sr. MILDRED LEONARDS, C.D.P., *P.O. Box 3387, Lafayette, 70502.* Tel: 337-261-5634.

CLERGY, PARISHES, MISSIONS AND PAROCHIAL SCHOOLS

CITY OF LAFAYETTE
(Lafayette Parish)

1—CATHEDRAL OF ST. JOHN THE EVANGELIST (1821), Revs. Keith J. DeRouen; C. Nicholas Trahan; Deacon James Guilbeau. In res., Rev. Joseph Kurian Kanat (India).
Res., 515 Cathedral St., P.O. Drawer V, 70502. Tel: 337-232-1322; Fax: 337-232-1379. [CEM]
Church—914 St. John St., 70501.
School—Cathedral-Carmel Elementary, 848 St. John St., 70502. Tel: 337-235-5577; Fax: 337-261-9493. Mrs. Adele H. Nunez, Prin.
Sisters of Mt. Carmel 4; Brothers of the Christian Schools 3; Lay Teachers 50; Students 828.
Catechesis / Religious Programs—Tel: 337-232-1325; Fax: 337-232-1379.
Students 113.

2—ST. PAUL THE APOSTLE (1911), Rev. Robert Seay.
Res., 326 S. Washington St., 70501. Tel: 337-235-0272; Fax: 337-235-3100.
Catechesis / Religious Programs—Students 150.
Mission—Lafayette, Lafayette Parish, Our Lady of Good Hope, E. Convent, 70501.

3—HOLY CROSS (1965), Rev. Martin Borcherding; Deacons Michael Clark; Norbert Luke.
Res., 505 Broadmoor Blvd., 70503. Tel: 337-984-9636; Fax: 337-988-3790.
Catechesis / Religious Programs—Tel: 337-984-9643.
Students 924.

4—IMMACULATE HEART OF MARY (1934) (African American), Revs. Francis Borgia Aubespin, S.V.D.; Vincentius Alexius, S.V.D.; Jaison G. Mangalath, S.V.D.; Deacon Anthony Ozene. In res., Rev. Charles Heskamp, S.V.D.
Res., 818-12th St., P.O. Box 2398, 70502. Tel: 337-235-4618; Fax: 337-235-4775. [CEM]
School—800-12th St., 70502. Tel: 337-235-7843; Fax: 337-233-0070. Germaine Ozene, Prin.
Sisters of Holy Family 2; Lay Teachers 10; Students 225.
Catechesis / Religious Programs—Tel: 337-235-6323.
Students 460.

5—OUR LADY OF FATIMA (1949), Rev. Msgr. Glen John Provost; Rev. Paul Broussard.
Res., 2319 Johnston St., 70503. Tel: 337-232-8945; Fax: 337-232-0323.
School—2315 Johnston St., 70503. Tel: 337-235-2464; Fax: 337-235-1320. Mr. Lloyd Guiberteau, Prin.
Lay Teachers 60; Students 932.
Catechesis / Religious Programs—Students 1,067.

6—OUR LADY OF WISDOM, UNIVERSITY OF LOUISIANA (1942), Revs. W. Curtis Mallet; Isaac Opara; Deacon Samuel Theriot. In res., Rev. Thomas Finley.
Mailing Address: P.O. Box 42371, 70504. Tel: 337-232-8741; Fax: 337-236-6737.

7—OUR LADY QUEEN OF PEACE (1969) (African American), Rev. Thomas Jason Mouton; Deacon Louis J. Lloyd.
Res., 145 Martin Luther King Jr. Dr., 70501. Tel: 337-233-1591; Fax: 337-232-5961. [CEM]
Catechesis / Religious Programs—Tel: 337-237-6225.
Students 350.

8—ST. ANTHONY (1955) (African American), Rev. Robert B. Fisher, S.V.D.; Deacon Albert Marcel.
Res., 615 Edison St., 70501. Tel: 337-234-5855; Fax: 337-264-1507.
Catechesis / Religious Programs—Students 285.

9—ST. EDMOND (1974), Rev. Gary Schexnayder; Deacons Paul D. Matte; Timothy Borbas.
Res., 4131 W. Congress St., 70506. Tel: 337-981-0874; Fax: 337-989-1417.
Catechesis / Religious Programs—Brenda Labbe, D.R.E.
Students 661.

10—ST. ELIZABETH SETON (1975), Rev. Harold Trahan.
Office: 610 Raintree Tr., 70507. Tel: 337-235-1483; Fax: 337-235-9645.
Res., 603 Raintree Tr., 70507. Tel: 337-232-7365.
Catechesis / Religious Programs—Students 247.

11—ST. GENEVIEVE (1929), Revs. Jody Simoneaux; Richard Dale Broussard.
Res., 417 E. Simcoe St., P.O. Box 90307, 70509. Tel: 337-234-5147; Fax: 337-234-8654. [CEM]
School—201 Elizabeth St., 70501. Tel: 337-234-5257; Fax: 337-237-6065. Mrs. Susan Stephen, Prin.
Lay Teachers 25; Students 400.
Catechesis / Religious Programs—Students 241.
Mission—Lafayette, Lafayette Parish, Gift of Mary Chapel, Raine St., 70501.

12—ST. JULES (1962), Rev. Msgr. J. Douglas Courville.
Res., 116 St. Jules St., 70506. Tel: 337-234-2727; Fax: 337-232-1544.
Catechesis / Religious Programs—Students 116.

13—ST. LEO THE GREAT (1960), Rev. Paul G. Bienvenu. In res., Rev. John Vianney Choorackunnel.
Res., 300 W. Alexander St., 70501. Tel: 337-232-2404; Fax: 337-261-0801.
School—Sts. Leo-Seton, 502 St. Leo St., 70501. Tel: 337-234-5510; Fax: 337-234-3676. William Butcher, Prin.
Sisters 1; Lay Teachers 25; Students 546.
Catechesis / Religious Programs—Tel: 337-667-7050; Fax: 337-667-6434.
Students 168.

14—ST. MARY, MOTHER OF THE CHURCH (1976), Rev. Robie Robichaux, J.C.L.; Deacon Julian Judice.
Res., 419 Doucet Rd., 70503. Tel: 337-981-3379; Fax: 337-981-5445.
School—St. Mary Early Learning Center, (Grades Pre-K). Tel: 337-984-3750. Amy Robideaux, Prin.
Students 140.
Catechesis / Religious Programs—Tel: 337-984-5396.
Students 337.

15—ST. PATRICK (1952), Rev. Howard Blessing.
Res., 406 E. Pinhook Rd., 70501. Tel: 337-237-0988; Fax: 337-233-8868.
Catechesis / Religious Programs—Students 20.

16—St. Pius X (1968), Rev. Msgr. Richard von Phul Mouton.
Res., 200 E. Bayou Pkwy., P.O. Box 80489, 70598. Tel: 337-232-4656; Fax: 337-233-9468. [JC]
School—201 E. Bayou Pkwy., 70508. Tel: 337-237-3139; Fax: 337-232-3455. Dr. Catherine James, Prin.
Lay Teachers 25; Students 365.
Catechesis/Religious Programs—Tel: 337-237-5059.
Students 515.

OUTSIDE THE CITY OF LAFAYETTE

Abbeville, Vermilion Parish, St. Mary Magdalen (1844), Revs. Donald C. Theriot; Cedric Sonnier.
Mailing Address: P.O. Box 1507, 70511. Tel: 337-893-0244; 0245; Fax: 337-893-0427. [CEM]
High School—Vermilion Catholic, 425 Park Ave., 70511. Tel: 337-893-6636; Fax: 337-893-8718. Mr. Alvin Lasseigne, Prin.
Lay Teachers 18; Students 250.
Catechesis/Religious Programs—Students 427.

St. Therese of the Child Jesus (1959), Revs. Chester Arceneaux; Herbert Bennerfield, III; Deacon Benny Morello.
Mailing Address: P.O. Box 609, 70511. Tel: 337-893-5631; Fax: 337-893-9168.
Catechesis/Religious Programs—Students 321.

Arnaudville, St. Landry Parish, St. Francis Regis (1853), Rev. William Ruskoski.
Mailing Address: 212 Main St., P.O. Box 649, 70512. Tel: 337-754-5912; Fax: 337-754-7203. [CEM]
Catechesis/Religious Programs—Students 750.

St. Catherine (1949) (African American), Rev. William Ruskoski; Deacon R. M. Balderas, Pastoral Assoc.
Mailing Address: P.O. Box 53, 70512. Tel: 337-754-7754.
Catechesis/Religious Programs—Tel: 337-754-5912.
Students 605.

Baldwin, St. Mary Parish, Sacred Heart (1906), Rev. Mitchell G. Guidry; Deacons Harold Achee; Harry Darce.
Mailing Address: P.O. Box 308, 70514. Tel: 337-923-7781; Fax: 337-923-4966. [CEM]
Catechesis/Religious Programs—Tel: 337-923-4966.
Students 161.

Basile, Evangeline Parish, St. Augustine (1921) (Acadian-African American), Rev. Kenneth Domingue.
Res., 2717 Third St., 70515. Tel: 337-432-6817; Fax: 337-432-5203. [CEM]
Catechesis/Religious Programs—Tel: 337-432-5608.
Students 380.
Mission—Basile, Evangeline Parish, Assumption, Glasper St., Basile 70515.

Bayou Vista, St. Mary Parish, St. Bernadette (1963), Rev. Barry F. Crochet.
Res., 1112 Saturn Rd., Morgan City, 70380. Tel: 504-395-2470; Fax: 504-395-6514.
Catechesis/Religious Programs—Students 200.

Berwick, St. Mary Parish, St. Stephen (1950), Rev. Emmanuel Fernandez.
Res., 3217 Second St., 70342. Tel: 504-385-1280; Fax: 504-385-1279.
Catechesis/Religious Programs—Tel: 504-385-1283.
Students 187.

Breaux Bridge, St. Martin Parish, St. Bernard (1848), Revs. Donald Leger; Allen Breaux; Deacons Harold Richard; Marcel P. Hebert, Jr.; Bob McDonner; Jim Davis.
Res., 204 N. Main St., 70517. Tel: 337-332-2159; Fax: 337-332-2276. [CEM 2][JC 2]
School—251 E. Bridge St., 70517. Tel: 337-332-5350; Fax: 337-332-5894. Jeannine Menard, Prin.
Sisters 1; Lay Teachers 24; Students 507.
Catechesis/Religious Programs—219 E. Bridge St., 70517. Tel: 337-332-4488; Fax: 337-332-4488.
Students 350.

St. Francis of Assisi (1923) (African American), Rev. Richard F. Wagner, S.S.J.
Res., 610 N. Main St., 70517. Tel: 337-332-2250; Fax: 337-332-2052. [CEM]
Catechesis/Religious Programs—Students 370.

Broussard, Lafayette Parish, Sacred Heart of Jesus (1883), Rev. Msgr. L. Michael Herpin.
Mailing Address: P.O. Box 737, 70518. Tel: 337-837-1864; Fax: 337-837-1703. [CEM]
School—St. Cecilia, P.O. Box 309, 70518. Tel: 337-837-6363; Fax: 337-837-3688. Mr. George Fontenot, Prin.
Lay Teachers 31; Students 460.
Catechesis/Religious Programs—Students 440.

St. Joseph (1952) (African American), Rev. Michael M. Sucharski, S.V.D. In res., Rev. Philipus Pito Karnogora, S.V.D.
Mailing Address: P.O. Box 278, 70518. Tel: 337-837-6218; Fax: 337-837-2072. [CEM 2]
Res., 232 St. DePorres St., 70518.
Catechesis/Religious Programs—Students 110.
Mission—Cade, St. Anthony.

Cankton, St. Landry Parish, St. John Berchmans (1925), Rev. Mario Romero.
Res., 552 Main St., 70584-9722. Tel: 337-668-4413; Fax: 337-668-4505. [CEM]
Catechesis/Religious Programs—Students 159.

Carencro, Lafayette Parish, St. Peter (1874), Rev. Bill Melancon; Deacon Eugene Maguespack.
Mailing Address: P.O. Box 40, 70520. Tel: 337-896-9408; Fax: 337-896-9414. [CEM]
School—Carencro Catholic, 200 W. St. Peter St., 70520. Tel: 337-896-8973. Mrs. Julie Breaux, Prin.
Lay Teachers 28; Students 529.
Catechesis/Religious Programs—Tel: 337-896-8488.
Students 600.

Our Lady of the Assumption (1925) (African American), Rev. Paul J. LaFleur; Deacon John Thibodeaux.
Res., 410 N. Michaud St., P.O. Box 130, 70520-0130. Tel: 337-896-8304. [CEM]
Catechesis/Religious Programs—Tel: 337-896-5874.
Students 75.

Catahoula, St. Martin Parish, St. Rita (1952), Rev. Donald Pelous.
Res., 1006 St. Rita Hwy., St. Martinville, 70582. Tel: 337-394-4679; Fax: 337-394-7020. [CEM]
Catechesis/Religious Programs—Students 235.

Cecilia, St. Martin Parish, St. Joseph (1893), Rev. Lloyd F. Benoit.
Mailing Address: P.O. Box 279, 70521. Tel: 337-667-6344; Fax: 337-667-7073. [CEM][JC]
Catechesis/Religious Programs—Tel: 337-667-7073.
Students 377.

St. Rose of Lima (1944) (African American), Rev. Norbert W. Stein, S.S.J.
Mailing Address: P.O. Box 126, 70521. Tel: 337-667-6555; Fax: 337-667-6686. [CEM]
Catechesis/Religious Programs—Students 232.

Centerville, St. Mary Parish, St. Joseph (1953), Rev. Oneil Anthony Landry, (Retired).
Res., 70522. Tel: 337-836-5659; Fax: 337-836-4600. [CEM]
Catechesis/Religious Programs—P.O. Box 280, 70522.
Students 150.

Charenton, St. Mary Parish, Immaculate Conception (1844), Rev. William Crumley, C.S.C.
Mailing Address: P.O. Box 278, 70523. Tel: 337-923-4281. [CEM]
Catechesis/Religious Programs—Students 58.

Chataignier, Evangeline Parish, Our Lady of Mount Carmel (1869), Rev. Thomas Montelaro; Deacon Thomas J. Richard. In res., Rev. T. Alcide Sonnier, (Retired).
Mailing Address: P.O. Box 100, 70524. Tel: 337-885-3223; Fax: 337-885-3223. [CEM]
Catechesis/Religious Programs—Students 124.

Church Point, Acadia Parish, Our Lady of the Sacred Heart (1873), Rev. Frederick O. Swenson; Deacon James G. Cormier.
Res., 118 N. Rogers St., P.O. Box 403, 70525. Tel: 337-684-5494; Fax: 337-684-2133. [CEM 3][JC]
School—Our Mother of Peace, 218 N. Rogers St., 70525. Tel: 337-684-5780; Fax: 337-684-5780. Mrs. Joni Duos, Prin.
Lay Teachers 15; Students 258.
Catechesis/Religious Programs—Students 423.
Chapel—Lewisburg, St. John.

Our Mother of Mercy (1941) (African American), Rev. Francis Butler, S.S.J.
Res., 693 N. Main St., P.O. Box 237, 70525. Tel: 337-684-2319; Fax: 337-684-3086. [JC]
Catechesis/Religious Programs—Students 168.

Coteau, Iberia Parish, Our Lady of Prompt Succor (1934), Rev. Matthew P. Higginbotham.
Res., 2409 Coteau Rd., New Iberia, 70560. Tel: 337-369-6993; Fax: 337-560-4475. [CEM]
Catechesis/Religious Programs—Students 450.

Coteau Holmes, St. Martin Parish, St. Elizabeth (1956), Rev. Thomas Edapaddy, C.M.I. (India).
Office: 1006 St. Elizabeth St., St. Martinville, 70582. Tel: 337-394-6684; 394-7530; Fax: 337-394-6684. [CEM]
Catechesis/Religious Programs—Students 80.

Cow Island, Vermilion Parish, St. Anne (1933), Rev. William G. Rogalla; Deacon Chris Mouton.
Res., 17315 Lionel Rd., Abbeville, 70510. Tel: 337-643-7714; Fax: 337-643-1021. [CEM][JC 3]
Catechesis/Religious Programs—Students 217.
Missions—Forked Island, Vermilon Parish, Immaculate Conception, 22102 Church Rd., Abbeville, 70510.; Pecan Island, Vermilion Parish, Sacred Heart, 28220 W. Hwy. 82, Kaplan, 70548.

Crowley, Acadia Parish, St. Michael Archangel (1895), Rev. Louis J. Richard.
Mailing Address: P.O. Box 406, 70527. Tel: 337-783-7394; Fax: 337-788-0237.
School—805 E. Northern Ave., 70527. Tel: 337-783-1410; Fax: 337-783-8547. Mrs. Myra Broussard, Prin.
Lay Teachers 28; Students 448.
Catechesis/Religious Programs—Tel: 337-783-7393.
Students 225.

Immaculate Heart of Mary (1959), Revs. Gerry Siebold, C.S.S.R.; Joseph Greenwell, C.SS.R.
Res., 901 E. Elm St., 70526. Tel: 337-783-3498; Fax: 337-783-7444.
School—Redemptorist Grade School, 606 South Ave. N., 70526. Tel: 337-783-4466; Fax: 337-788-0961. Brenda Savoy, Prin.
Lay Teachers 18; Students 293.
Catechesis/Religious Programs—Tel: 337-783-5759.
Students 150.

St. Theresa (1920) (African American), Rev. Richard Sadlier, S.S.J.
Res., 417 W. 3rd St., 70526. Tel: 337-783-1880; Fax: 337-783-1880.
Catechesis/Religious Programs—Tel: 337-783-1311.
Students 267.

Delcambre, Vermilion Parish, Our Lady of the Lake (1897), Rev. Thomas P. Voorhies.
Res., 206 W. Church St., 70528. Tel: 337-685-4426; Fax: 337-685-4426. [CEM]
Catechesis/Religious Programs—Castel School of Religion, 208 South St. Peter St., 70528. Tel: 337-685-2549.
Students 378.

Saint Martin de Porres (1948) (African American), Rev. Thomas P. Voorhies.
Res., 206 W. Church St., 70528. Tel: 337-685-4426; Fax: 337-685-4426. [JC]
Catechesis/Religious Programs—Castel School of Religion, 208 S. Peter St., 70528. Tel: 337-685-2549.
Students 30.

Duralde, Evangeline Parish, Annunciation of the B.V.M. (1964) (Acadian), Deacon Theo Landry, Admin.
Res., 4476 Duralde Hwy., Eunice, 70535. Tel: 337-457-4849; Fax: 337-457-4502.
Catechesis/Religious Programs—Students 105.

Duson, Lafayette Parish, St. Theresa of the Child Jesus (1928), Rev. O. Joseph Breaux.
Mailing Address: P.O. Box 8, 70529. Tel: 337-873-4962; Fax: 337-873-3023. [CEM]
Catechesis/Religious Programs—Tel: 337-873-4488.
Students 192.

St. Benedict the Moor (African American), Very Rev. Ronald Broussard, V.G.
Mailing Address: 9135 Cameron St., P.O. Box 127, 70529. Tel: 337-873-6772. [CEM]
Catechesis/Religious Programs—Students 140.

Erath, Vermilion Parish, Our Lady of Lourdes (1928), Rev. Wayne J. Duet; Deacon Ron J. Bodin, Pastoral Assoc.
Res., 700 S. Broadway, 70533. Tel: 337-937-6888; Fax: 337-937-8650. [CEM 2]
Catechesis/Religious Programs—Students 513.

Eunice, St. Landry Parish, St. Anthony of Padua (1902), Revs. Joseph J. Alexander; Gregory Semien; Deacon Chuck Ortego.
Mailing Address: P.O. Box 31, 70535. Tel: 337-457-5285; Fax: 337-457-7904. [CEM]
School—St. Edmund Elementary, 331 N. 3rd St., 70535. Tel: 337-457-5988; Fax: 337-457-5989. Sr. Stephanie Brignac, M.S.C., Prin.
High School—St. Edmund High, 351 W. Magnolia St., 70535. Tel: 337-457-2592; Fax: 337-457-2648. Mr. Harry Summerlin, Prin.
Lay Teachers 40; Students: Elementary 367; High School 249.
Catechesis/Religious Programs—Tel: 337-457-7505.
Students 266.

St. Mathilda (1939) (African American), Rev. Joseph V. Tyson, S.S.J.
Mailing Address: P.O. Box 346, 70535. Tel: 337-457-3286. [CEM]
Res., 800 E. Laurel Ave., 70535.
Catechesis/Religious Programs—Tel: 337-457-0108.
Students 182.

St. Thomas More (1967), Rev. Matthew G. Roussel; Deacon David Guillory.
Mailing Address: P.O. Box 1022, 70535. Tel: 337-457-8107; Fax: 337-457-1735.

Catechesis/Religious Programs—337-457-8101. Tel: 337-457-8224.
Students 363.

Evangeline, Acadia Parish, St. Joseph (1938), Rev. Kenneth M. Mayne.
Mailing Address: P.O. Box 183, 70537. Tel: 337-824-4995; Fax: 337-824-4995. [CEM]
Catechesis/Religious Programs—Students 289.
Mission—Petit Mamou, Acadia Parish, St. Jules, Tel: 337-824-7088.

Four Corners, St. Mary Parish, St. Peter the Apostle (1960), Rev. Mitchell Guidry, Admin. In res., Rev. Abraham Kunnakkattu.
Res., 1325 Big Four Corners Rd., Franklin, 70538. Tel: 337-276-5256; Fax: 337-276-5256.
Catechesis/Religious Programs—Tel: 337-276-2348.
Students 54.
Mission—Glencoe, St. Joan of Arc.

Franklin, St. Mary Parish, Assumption B.V.M. (1852), Rev. Michael Russo; Deacon Douglas Hebert.
Mailing Address: 211 Iberia St., 70538. Tel: 337-828-3869; Fax: 337-828-3872.
School—St. John Elementary, 924 Main St., 70538. Tel: 337-828-2648; Fax: 337-828-2112. Mrs. Gayle Clements, Prin.
Lay Teachers 18; Students 298.
High School—Hanson High School, 903 Anderson St., 70538. Tel: 337-828-3487; Fax: 337-828-7431. Ms. Lynn Gordey, Prin.
Lay Teachers 30; Students 360.
Catechesis/Religious Programs—Tel: 337-828-9499.
Students 102.

St. Jules (1950), Rev. John Kanjiramkuzhy; Deacons Edward Bodin; Joseph Thomas.
Res., 601 Magnolia St., 70538. Tel: 337-828-1714; Fax: 337-828-1734. [CEM]
Catechesis/Religious Programs—Students 180.
Mission—Verdunville, St. Mary Parish, Immaculate Conception, 601 Magnolia, 70538.

Grand Coteau, St. Landry Parish, St. Charles Borromeo (1819), Revs. David L. Andrus, S.J.; John Welsh, S.J.; Norman J. Rogge, S.J.; Bro. John Puza, S.J.; Deacon Samuel Henry.
Mailing Address: P.O. Drawer A, 70541. Tel: 337-662-5279; Fax: 337-662-5270.
Res., 174 Church St., 70541. [CEM][JC]
School—St. Ignatius, P.O. Drawer J, 70541. Tel: 337-662-3325; Fax: 337-662-3349. Mr. Russell Erickson, Prin.
Brothers 1; Lay Teachers 22; Students 339.
Catechesis/Religious Programs—Tel: 337-662-5271.
Students 379.
Mission—Bellevue, St. Landry Parish, Christ the King, 369 Christ the King Rd., Opelousas 70570. Tel: 337-942-6888.

Grand Prairie, St. Landry Parish, St. Peter (1951), Rev. Msgr. Louis J. Melancon.
Res., 1074 Hwy. 748, Washington, 70589. Tel: 337-826-3870; Fax: 337-826-5635. [CEM]
Catechesis/Religious Programs—Students 155.
Mission—Plaisance, St. Landry Parish, St. Andrew.

Gueydan, Vermilion Parish, St. Peter (1907), Rev. Grady J. Estilette.
Res., 603 Main St., P.O. Box 28, 70542. Tel: 337-536-9258. [JC]
School—513 6th St., 70542. Tel: 337-536-9460. Sr. Ann Louise Arno, M.S.C., Prin.
Sisters 2; Lay Teachers 9; Students 147.
Catechesis/Religious Programs—Students 200.
Mission—Mulvey, Vermilion Parish, St. David, P.O.Box 28, Gueydan, 70542.

Henderson, St. Martin Parish, Our Lady of Mercy (1962), In res., Rev. Joseph Stemman.
Res., Henderson Sta., P.O. Box 587, Breaux Bridge, 70517. Tel: 337-228-2352; Fax: 337-228-2372. [CEM][JC]
Catechesis/Religious Programs—Students 261.
Mission—Butte La Rose, St. Martin Parish, Sacred Heart.

Henry, Vermilion Parish, St. John (1939) (French-Acadian), Rev. Cedric Sonnier.
Res., 18534 La. Hwy. 689, Erath, 70533. Tel: 337-937-5108; Fax: 337-937-0002. [CEM]
Catechesis/Religious Programs—Students 245.
Mission—Esther, Vermilion Parish, St. James.

Iota, Acadia Parish, St. Joseph (1892), Rev. F. David Broussard.
Mailing Address: P.O. Box 710, 70543. Tel: 337-779-2627; Fax: 337-779-2627.
School—St. Francis, P.O. Box 870, 70543. Tel: 337-779-2527. Mark Shamburger, Prin.
Lay Teachers 13; Students 189.
Catechesis/Religious Programs—Students 350.
Mission—Egan, Acadia Parish, St. Michael, P.O. Box 298, Egan, 70531. Tel: 337-788-0529.

Jeanerette, Iberia Parish, St. John the Evangelist (1879), Rev. Edward Degeyter; Deacon Gerald Bourg.
Res., 1510 Church St., 70544. Tel: 337-276-4576; Fax: 337-276-5804. [CEM]
School—St. Joseph, 10917 Old Jeanerette Rd., 70544. Tel: 337-276-3615; Fax: 337-276-3616. Dr. Corinne Hebert, Prin.
Lay Teachers 15; Students 125.
Catechesis/Religious Programs—Tel: 337-276-6944.
Students 189.

Our Lady of the Rosary (1945), Rev. Joseph E. Detig, S.V.D.
Res., 11200 Old Jeanerette Rd., 70544. Tel: 337-276-6900; Fax: 337-276-6900. [CEM][JC]
Catechesis/Religious Programs—Students 120.

Judice, Lafayette Parish, St. Basil (1970), Rev. Henry J. Broussard.
Res., 1803 Duhon Rd. (Judice), Duson, 70529. Tel: 337-984-2179; Fax: 337-988-3793. [CEM 2]
Catechesis/Religious Programs—Tel: 337-988-2655.
Students 296.

Kaplan, Vermilion Parish, Our Lady of the Holy Rosary (1896), Revs. William C. Blanda; Mark Patrick Ledoux; Deacons Paul R. Eleazar; Kendal James Faulk. In res., Rev. John D.S. Nwagbaraicga.
Mailing Address: P.O. Box 429, 70548. Tel: 337-643-6472; Fax: 337-643-2516. [JC]
School—Maltrait Memorial, One Crusader Square, 70548. Tel: 337-643-7765; Fax: 337-643-2516. Mrs. Renee C. Meaux, Prin.
Lay Teachers 10; Students 111.
Catechesis/Religious Programs—701 N. Boudreaux Ave., P.O. Box 429, 70548. Tel: 337-643-2309.
Students 683.
Mission—Kaplan, Vermilion Parish, St. Frances Xavier Cabrini, 705 N. Frederick, P.O. Box 429, 70548.

Krotz Springs, St. Landry Parish, St. Anthony (1958), Rev. Robert W. Courville.
Mailing Address: P.O. Box 425, 70750. Tel: 337-566-3527; Fax: 337-566-2803. [CEM]
Catechesis/Religious Programs—Students 124.

Lawtell, St. Landry Parish, St. Bridget (1920), Rev. Daniel Picard.
Mailing Address: P.O. Box 156, 70550. Tel: 337-543-7591; Fax: 337-543-7593. [CEM]
Catechesis/Religious Programs—Students 206.
Mission—Prairie Ronde, St. Landry Parish, Sacred Heart.

Holy Family (1953) (African American), Revs. Denis A. Osuagwn (Nigeria); Jude M. Obiechina (Nigeria).
Mailing Address: P.O. Box 310, 70550. Tel: 337-543-2366; Fax: 337-543-8281. [CEM]
Catechesis/Religious Programs—Students 220.

Lebeau, St. Landry Parish, Immaculate Conception (1897) (African American), Rev. Alfred Umaga, M.S.P.
Mailing Address: P.O. Box 6, 71345. Tel: 337-623-4783; Fax: 337-623-4783. [CEM]
Catechesis/Religious Programs—Students 106.
Mission—Rideau Settlement, St. Landry Parish, Sacred Heart.

Leonville, St. Landry Parish, St. Leo the Great, Rev. Msgr. Paul Metrejean.
Mailing Address: P.O. Box 8, 70551. Tel: 337-879-2365; Fax: 337-879-3050. [CEM][JC]
Catechesis/Religious Programs—Students 258.

St. Catherine (1952), Rev. Raymond Hannah, S.V.D.
Mailing Address: P.O. Box 547, 70551. Tel: 337-879-2940; Fax: 337-879-2940.
Catechesis/Religious Programs—Students 107.
Mission—Prairie Laurent, St. Landry Parish, St. Jules.

Leroy, Vermilion Parish, Our Lady of Perpetual Help (1922), Rev. A. Rex Broussard.
Res., 12995 Louisiana Hwy. 699, Maurice, 70555. Tel: 337-893-0610; Fax: 337-893-0694. [CEM]
Catechesis/Religious Programs—Tel: 337-893-5306.
Students 116.

Loreauville, Iberia Parish, St. Joseph (1873), Rev. Aaron Melancon.
Mailing Address: P.O. Box 365, 70552. Tel: 337-229-4254; Fax: 337-229-4255. [CEM][JC 2]
Catechesis/Religious Programs—Tel: 337-229-6728.
Students 388.

Our Lady of Victory (1953) (African American), Rev. Aaron Melancon.
Mailing Address: P.O. Box 387, 70552. Tel: 337-229-8284; Fax: 337-229-4255. [JC]
Catechesis/Religious Programs—Tel: 337-229-6329.
Students 125.

Louisa, St. Mary Parish, St. Helena, Rev. Thomas Thanh Nguyen; Deacon Tam Minh Trah.
Res., 108 St. Helen's Church Ln., Franklin, 70538. Tel: 337-867-4378.

Lydia, Iberia Parish, St. Nicholas (1867), Rev. Richard Fabre; Deacon L. J. Freyou.
Mailing Address: P.O. Box 369, 70569. Tel: 337-364-5228; Fax: 337-364-5251. [CEM]
Catechesis/Religious Programs—Tel: 337-367-0562.
Students 548.

Lyons Point, Acadia Parish, St. John the Baptist (1952), Rev. Albert G. Nunez; Deacon Rodless Leleux.
Res., 8021 Lyons Point Highway, Crowley, 70526. Tel: 337-783-2457; Fax: 337-783-9015. [CEM]
Catechesis/Religious Programs—Tel: 337-783-9875.
Students 105.

Mallet, St. Landry Parish, St. Ann (1856) (African American), Revs. Denis A. Osuagwn (Nigeria); Jude M. Obiechina (Nigeria).
Mailing Address: P.O. Box 310, Lawtell, 70550. Tel: 337-543-2385; Fax: 337-543-8281. [CEM]
Catechesis/Religious Programs—Tel: 337-543-2366.
Students 256.

Mamou, Evangeline Parish, St. Ann (1914), Revs. Timothy Richard; Pius Vallooran, C.M.I.
Parish Center: 716 Sixth St., 70554. Tel: 337-468-3159; Fax: 337-468-3427. [CEM]
Catechesis/Religious Programs—Students 252.
Mission—Vidrine, Evangeline Parish, Holy Spirit.

Maurice, Vermilion Parish, St. Alphonsus (1893), Rev. Martin C. Leonards.
Res., 8700 Maurice Ave., P.O. Box 190, 70555. Tel: 337-893-4099; Fax: 337-893-2474. [CEM]
Catechesis/Religious Programs—Tel: 337-893-2474.
Students 323.

St. Joseph (1946) (African American), Rev. Joseph D. Simon, S.V.D.
Mailing Address: P.O. Box 250, 70555. Tel: 337-893-5428; Fax: 337-893-5428. [JC]

Melville, St. Landry Parish, St. John the Evangelist (1931), Rev. Jose L.F. Padinjarepeedika, C.M.I. (India).
Mailing Address: 318 First St., P.O. Box 256, 71353-0256. Tel: 337-623-4957; Fax: 337-623-4970. [CEM]
Catechesis/Religious Programs—Students 20.
Mission—Palmetto, St. Landry Parish, St. Thomas, the Apostle, 340 E. Railroad Ave., Palmetto 71358.

Mermentau, Acadia Parish, St. John the Evangelist (1882), Rev. Msgr. Paul Metrejean.
Mailing Address: P.O. Box 176, 70556. Tel: 337-824-2278; Fax: 337-824-9624. [CEM]
Catechesis/Religious Programs—Students 220.
Mission—Estherwood, Acadia Parish, St. Margaret.

Milton, Lafayette Parish, St. Joseph (1977), Rev. M. Keith LaBove; Deacon Cody Miller.
Mailing Address: P.O. Box 299, 70558. Tel: 337-856-5997; Fax: 337-856-5955. [CEM]
Catechesis/Religious Programs—Students 542.

Mire, Acadia Parish, Assumption of the Blessed Virgin Mary (1954), Rev. Msgr. Russell J. Harrington, V.E.; Deacon J. Douglas Melancon.
Res., 6080 Mire Hwy., Church Point, 70525. Tel: 337-873-6574; Fax: 337-873-3777. [CEM]
Catechesis/Religious Programs—Tel: 337-873-3777.
Students 248.

Morrow, St. Landry Parish, St. Peter (French), Rev. George Thychary.
Mailing Address: P.O. Box 319, 71356. Tel: 318-346-7010. [CEM]
Mission—Whiteville, Resurrection.

Morse, Acadia Parish, Immaculate Conception (1956), Rev. Donald Pousson.
Mailing Address: P.O. Box 297, 70559. Tel: 337-783-2968.
Catechesis/Religious Programs—Students 111.
Mission—Midland, St. Aloysius.

Mowata, Acadia Parish, St. Lawrence (1905), Rev. George Heffner, S.V.D.
Res., 29031 Crowley-Eunice Hwy., Eunice, 70535. Tel: 337-457-2739; Fax: 337-457-2739. [CEM 2]
Catechesis/Religious Programs—Students 87.

New Iberia, Iberia Parish,

1—St. Peter, (1838) (Hispanic-Acadian), Revs. Charles Langlois; Jude Halphen; Deacons Ronald H. Broussard; James Wilson; Wade Joseph Broussard; Kenneth Waguespack, Pastoral Assoc. In res., Rev. Msgr. John H. Disch; Rev. Msgr. J. Guy Lemoine.
Mailing Address: P.O. Box 12507, 70562. Tel: 337-369-3816; Fax: 337-369-3192. [CEM][JC]
Catechesis/Religious Programs—Students 450.

2—NATIVITY OF OUR LADY, (1964), Rev. Michael Arnaud; Deacon John George Sarkies. In res., Rev. Albert J. Boumans, (Retired).
Res., Richelieu Circle, 70560. Tel: 337-364-8360; Fax: 337-364-1509. [CEM]
Catechesis/Religious Programs—Tel: 337-365-3759.
Students 507.

3—OUR LADY OF PERPETUAL HELP, (1949), Revs. Michael Guidry; Mark Derise; Deacons Ulysse J. Boudreaux; Ronald Borel; George Sikes.
Res., 1303 St. Jude Ave., 70560. Tel: 337-365-5481; Fax: 337-365-5483. [JC]
Catechesis/Religious Programs—St. Ann, Tel: 337-365-3783.
Students 369.

4—ST. EDWARD, (1917), Revs. Thomas James, S.V.D.; Sebastian Myladiyil, S.V.D. In res., Bro. Dismas Mauk, S.V.D.
Res., 175 Ambassador W. Lemelle Dr., 70560. Tel: 337-369-3101; Fax: 337-369-3118. [CEM][JC]
School—175 Porter St., 70560. Tel: 337-369-6764; Fax: 337-369-9534. Sr. Michelle Callanan, S.B.S., Prin.
Sisters of the Blessed Sacrament 3; Lay Teachers 16; Students 375.
Catechesis/Religious Programs—Tel: 337-365-3762.
Students 325.
Mission—New Iberia, Iberia Parish, St. Jude, 4408 Old Jeanerette Rd., 70560. Tel: 337-364-2907.

5—SACRED HEART OF JESUS, (1960), Rev. Steven C. LeBlanc.
Res., 2514 Old Jeanerette Rd., 70560. Tel: 337-364-4439; Fax: 337-364-4474.
Catechesis/Religious Programs—Students 459.

Opelousas, St. Landry Parish,

1—ST. LANDRY, (1776), Rev. Eugene R. Tremie; Deacons Carlo Cannatella; John W. Miller.
Res., 1020 N. Main St., 70570. Tel: 337-942-6552; Fax: 337-948-1295. [CEM][JC]
Catechesis/Religious Programs—Students 79.

2—OUR LADY OF MERCY, (1942), Rev. Jefferson J. DeBlanc, Jr. In res., Rev. James Vellankal.
Res., 124 N. Camille St., 70570. Tel: 337-942-4174; Fax: 337-942-1476.
Catechesis/Religious Programs—Tel: 337-942-9404.
Students 253.

3—OUR LADY QUEEN OF ANGELS, (1967), Rev. Angelo Cremaldi.
Res., 2136 S. Union St., P.O. Box 508, 70570. Tel: 337-942-5628; Fax: 337-942-9708. [JC]
Catechesis/Religious Programs—Tel: 337-942-7831.
Students 498.

4—HOLY GHOST, (1920) (African American), Rev. Malcolm O'Leary, S.V.D. In res., Rev. Raymond Jones, S.V.D.
Res., 788 N. Union St., 70570. Tel: 337-942-2732; Fax: 337-948-4108. [JC]
Catechesis/Religious Programs—Students 618.

Parks, St. Martin Parish, St. Joseph (1938), Rev. Gregory P. Cormier.
Mailing Address: P.O. Box 2810, 70582. Tel: 337-845-4168; Fax: 337-845-5079.
Mission—Parks, St. Louis, Tel: 337-845-4681.

Patterson, St. Mary Parish, St. Joseph, Rev. Richard Greene.
Res., 1011-1st St., P.O. Box 219, 70392. Tel: 504-395-3616; Fax: 504-395-3616. [CEM]

Pine Prairie, Evangeline Parish, St. Peter (1924), Rev. Brendan Murphy, S.V.D.
Mailing Address: P.O. Box 230, 70576. Tel: 337-599-2224. [CEM]
Mission—St. Landry, St. Theresa.
Catechesis/Religious Programs—Students 210.

Plaisance, St. Landry Parish, St. Joseph (1949) (African American), Revs. Thomas Montelaro; Michael Moody, S.V.D.; Deacon Thomas J. Richard.
Res., 3283 Hwy. 167, Opelousas, 70570. Tel: 337-826-3395. [CEM]
Catechesis/Religious Programs—Students 60.
Mission—Frilot Cove, St. Ann, Tel: 337-826-3394.

Port Barre, St. Landry Parish, Sacred Heart of Jesus (1871), Rev. Michael Hebert.
Mailing Address: P.O. Box 129, 70577. Tel: 337-585-2279; Fax: 337-585-2276. [CEM][JC]
Catechesis/Religious Programs—Students 430.

St. Mary (1952) (African American), Rev. Raymond Jones, S.V.D.; Deacon Alvin DeJean, Parish Life Coord.
Mailing Address: P.O. Box 338, 70577. Tel: 337-585-2315; Fax: 337-585-2315. [CEM][JC]
Catechesis/Religious Programs—Tel: 337-585-2863.
Students 100.

Rayne, Acadia Parish, St. Joseph (1872), Rev. Jules M. Arceneaux, II, (Retired); Deacons Mike Clark, Pastoral Assoc.; Adam Sonnier.
Mailing Address: P.O. Box 199, 70578. Tel: 337-334-2193; Fax: 337-334-2199. [CEM 2][JC 2]
School—Rayne Catholic Elementary, 407 S. Polk St., 70578. Tel: 337-334-5657; 5658; Fax: 337-334-3301. Dr. Sherry Cormier, Prin.
Lay Teachers 18; Students 384.
Catechesis/Religious Programs—Tel: 337-334-9849.
Students 553.

Shrine of Our Mother of Mercy (1924) (African American), Rev. Joseph McKinley, S.S.J., Admin.; Deacons Coley Bellamy; Nolton Senegal, Sr.
Mailing Address: P.O. Box 468, 70578. Tel: 337-334-3516; Fax: 337-334-4416. [CEM]
Res., 707 Lyman Ave., 70578.
Catechesis/Religious Programs—Tel: 337-334-4909.
Students 281.

Richard, Acadia Parish, St. Edward, Rev. J. Daniel Edwards.
Res., 1463 Charlene Hwy., Church Point, 70525. Tel: 337-684-2870; Fax: 337-684-0189. [CEM][JC]
Catechesis/Religious Programs—Students 200.
Mission—Savoy, St. Landry Parish, St. Thomas. Tasso Loop.

Robert's Cove, Acadia Parish, St. Leo IV (1883) (German), Rev. Francis L. Bourgeois.
Res., 7166 Roberts Cove Rd., Rayne, 70578-8912. Tel: 337-334-5056; Fax: 337-334-0832. [CEM]
Catechesis/Religious Programs—Tel: 337-334-7458.
Students 105.
Mission—Branch, French Parish, St. Edmund.

Rynella, Iberia Parish, St. Marcellus (1960), Rev. C. Conley Bertrand.
Res., 6100 Avery Island Rd., New Iberia, 70560. Tel: 337-364-0818; Fax: 337-364-0824. [CEM]
Catechesis/Religious Programs—Tel: 337-364-9419.
Students 239.

St. Martinville, St. Martin Parish, St. Martin of Tours (1765) (Acadian), Revs. P. Austin Leger; Kenneth A. Bienvenu, (Retired). In res., Rev. Jean Marie Jammes.
Res., 133 S. Main St., P.O. Drawer 10, 70582. Tel: 337-394-6021; Fax: 337-394-6020. [CEM]
Catechesis/Religious Programs—Students 262.

Notre Dame de Perpetuel Secours (1938) (African American), Rev. Thomas A. Mullally, S.V.D.; Deacon Carlton Lee.
Res., 240 Gary St., 70582. Tel: 337-394-3084; Fax: 337-394-5380. [CEM][JC]
Catechesis/Religious Programs—Tel: 337-394-4749.
Students 600.

Scott, Lafayette Parish, SS. Peter and Paul (1904), Rev. Gilbert J. Dutel.
Mailing Address: P.O. Box 610, 70583. Tel: 337-235-2433; Fax: 337-233-4868. [CEM]
Catechesis/Religious Programs—Tel: 337-232-6167.
Students 785.

Saint Martin de Porres (1961) (African American), Rev. George H. Simon.
Mailing Address: P.O. Box 1347, 70583-1347. Tel: 337-232-1968; Fax: 337-232-1968. [CEM]
Catechesis/Religious Programs—Students 104.

Ville Platte, Evangeline Parish, Sacred Heart of Jesus (1854), Very Rev. Msgr. J. Robert Romero, V.E.; Rev. Donavan Labbe; Deacon Harris Soileau.
Res., 708 E. Main St., 70586. Tel: 337-363-2989; Fax: 337-363-3500. [CEM]
School—Sacred Heart Elementary, 532 E. Main St., 70586. Tel: 337-363-3322; Fax: 337-363-2318. Paula Landreneau, Prin.
High School—Sacred Heart High, 114 S. Trojan Ln., 70586. Tel: 337-363-1475; Fax: 337-363-0348. Paula Landreneau, Prin.
Lay Teachers 48; Students: Elementary 573; High School 298.
Catechesis/Religious Programs—Tel: 337-363-7788; Fax: 337-363-3500.
Students 168.
Mission—Belaire Cove, Sacred Heart, 70586.

Our Lady Queen of All Saints (1969), Rev. Randall Moreau; Deacon Eugene Le Boeuf.
Res., 211 Parkview St., P.O. Drawer E, 70586. Tel: 337-363-5167; Fax: 337-363-5179.
Catechesis/Religious Programs—Students 144.

St. Joseph (1947) (African American), Very Rev. Msgr. J. Robert Romero, V.E.
Res., 1107 Martin L. King Dr., 70586. Tel: 337-363-1051. [CEM]

Washington, St. Landry Parish, Immaculate Conception (1756) (French-German), Rev. William J. Gearheard, Jr.
Mailing Address: P.O. Box 116, 70589. Tel: 337-826-7396; Fax: 337-826-0099.
Catechesis/Religious Programs—Students 117.

Holy Trinity (1950) (African American), Rev. William Gearheard; Deacon Alvin R. DeJean, Parish Life Coord.
Mailing Address: P.O. Box 186, 70589. Tel: 337-826-3376; Fax: 337-826-3376.

Youngsville, Lafayette Parish, St. Anne (1859), Rev. Louis Lam Vu.
Mailing Address: P.O. Box 410, 70592. Tel: 337-856-8212; Fax: 337-856-8277. [CEM]
Catechesis/Religious Programs—Tel: 337-856-8242.
Students 578.

On Special Assignment:
Reverend Fathers—
Abara, Lawrence N., Chap. (extern-diocesan), Our Lady of Lourdes Regional Med. Ctr., 611 St. Landry St., Lafayette, LA 70506
Boyer, Millard G., Chap., Lafayette General Medical Center, 210 Long Plantation Blvd., Lafayette, LA 70508. Tel: 337-289-7483
Champagne, Michael, Chap., Hospitals/Health Care Facilities, Community of Jesus Crucified, 421 1/2 Carmen Ave., Lafayette, LA 70501
Choorackunnel, John Vianney, C.M.I., Chap., Medical Center, S.W., St. Leo, 300 W. Alexander St., Lafayette, LA 70501
Finley, John Thomas, Chap., Bethany Health Care, 231 General Gardiner Ave., Lafayette, LA 70501
Frey, Jerome V., Community of Jesus Crucified, 421 1/2 Carmel Ave., Lafayette, LA 70501
Hemphil, Anthony, S.V.D., Chap., University Med. Center, Mailing Address: St. Anthony Church, 615 Edison St., Lavayette, LA 70501
Heskamp, Charles, S.V.D., Immaculate Heart of Mary, P.O. Box 2398, Lafayette, LA 70502-2398
Jones, Raymond, S.V.D., Holy Ghost, 732 N. Main St., Opelousas, LA 70570
Kamenski, Thomas, O.F.M., Chap., Our Lady of Lourdes Hospital, P.O. Box 4027-C, Lafayette, LA 70506
Kanat, Joseph Kurian (India), Chap. (extern-diocesan), Diocesan Prison Ministry, Res., Cathedral of St. John the Evangelist, P.O. Drawer V, Lafayette, LA 70502
Lozano, Arturo, S.J., Dir. Hispanic Ministry, 1408 Carmel Ave., Lafayette, LA
Luberti, Richard A., C.SS.R., Disabilities Office, 1408 Carmel Ave., Lafayette, WI 70501
Morvant, Kenneth R., Office of the Tribunal, P.O. Box 3387, Lafayette, LA 70502-3387
O'Rourke, John J., S.S.J., Swing Man, St. Rose of Lima, P.O. Box 126, Cecilia, LA 70521
Sibley, Bryce Andrew, Pontificial North American College, 00120 Vatican City State
Vellankal, James, Chap. (extern-diocesan), Opelousas General Hospital and Doctors Hospital, Our Lady of Mercy, 150 Camille St., Opelousas, LA 70570

On Duty Outside the Diocese:
Reverend Fathers—
Boudreaux, John S., Corpus Christi Church, 6300 McKenna Dr., Mobile, AL 36608
Hampton, Davis, Notre Dame Seminary, 2901 S. Carrolton Ave., New Orleans, LA 70118-4391
Meaux, Glenn, Haiti Mission, P.O. Box 46802, Gladstone, MO 64118
Voorhies, Bennett J., St. Anthony, HC70 Box 23, Pecos, NM 87552. Tel: 505-757-6345

Military Chaplains:
Reverend Fathers—
Vidrine, Richard, Chapel of Hope, 1172 Vaughan St., New Port, RI 02841

On Sabbatical:
Reverend Fathers—
Downs, Gregory T., P.O. Box 641634, Kenner, LA 70064

Absent on Sick Leave:
Reverend Fathers—
Delauney, Herbert C.
Montelaro, Thomas, Sacramental Min., Our Lady of Mount Carmel, P.O. Box 471, Eunice, LA 70535

Absent on Leave:
Reverend Fathers—
Broussard, Kenneth M.
Coupar, David A.

Retired:
Reverend Monsignors—
Angelle, Robert G., 205 N. Anita St., Lafayette, LA 70501

Barsen, Herman J., 130 N. Richelieu Circle, New Iberia, LA 70560. Tel: 337-365-0616
Benefiel, Harry E., 301 Eraste Landry Rd., Lafayette, LA 70506. Tel: 337-235-4373
Disch, John H., P.O. Box 12507, New Iberia, LA 70562
Mallet, Charles J., 40 Audobon Oaks Blvd., Lafayette, LA 70506
Martin, Ignatius, Rte. 2, Box 785, Maurice, LA 70555. Tel: 337-893-8931
Mouton, Charles Burton, Basilica St. Mary Major, Vatican City State, 00120 Europe
Richard, Wayne R., 317 Guilbeau Rd., Apt. 202-B, Lafayette, LA 70506
Van Boxel, W. H., Apollolaan 454, NL-2324 CG Leiden, The Netherlands

Reverend Fathers—
Bergeron, C. Paul, 402 Wayside Dr., Houma, LA 70360
Bienvenu, Kenneth A., 1017 Alan Dr., St. Martinville, LA 70582
Boumans, Albert, Nativity of Our Lady, 130 B. Richelieu, New Iberia, LA 70560
Bourg, Edwin, 108B Margaret St., Lafayette, LA 70501
Brennan, Joseph F., 203 Bocage Circle, Lafayette, LA 70503
Calais, Floyd J., 313 Rue Louis XIV, Apt. H, Lafayette, LA 70508. Tel: 337-988-6278
DeLeeuw, John, 526 Raintree Tr., Lafayette, LA 70507. Tel: 337-235-5706
Desilets, Viateur, 2319 E. Main St., New Iberia, LA 70560
Dugas, Willard, 520 Dugas Rd., Lafayette, LA 70507
Dutra, Luis C., (Extern-diocesan), 522 Carmel Ave., Lafayette, LA 70501
Edwards, Roy D., P.O. Box 280, Carencro, LA 70520
Fontaine, Edouard, (Extern), 784 Soileau Rd., Eunice, LA 70535
Hebert, T. J., 202 Stanford St., Apt. B, Lafayette, LA 70503. Tel: 337-981-8113
Herbert, Lloyd P., 39100 Orchard Ave., Cherry Valley, CA 92223
Jammes, Jean Marie, P.O. Drawer 10, St. Martinville, LA 70582. Tel: 337-394-6021
Landry, Oneil Anthony, 198 Elm St., Centerville, LA 70522
Landry, Ralph James, 2603 Bodin Rd., New Iberia, LA 70562
Ledoux, Louis Vernon, (Retired Armed Forces), P.O. Box 4026, McChord AFB, WA 98438-4026
Maraist, Martin, 5690 Resweber Hwy., St. Martinsville, LA 70582
Matt, J. Wilson, Res., St. Landry Church, 1020 N. Main St., Opelousas, LA 70570
Mau, Joseph, 3142 Lambert Dr., Baton Rouge, LA 70805
Robitaille, Raymond, 2319 Main St., New Iberia, LA 70560
Senneville, Eugene Joseph, P.O. Box 9, Port Barre, LA 70577
Sonnier, T. Alcide, P.O. Box 100, Chataignier, LA 70524
Spekschate, John, Kapelaanspad, 24, NL-5801 BN Venray, B.N. 5801 The Netherlands
Speyrer, Jules, 105 White St., Basile, LA 70515-0212. Tel: 337-432-5054
Stemmann, Joseph, Our Lady of Mercy, P.O. Box 587, Breaux Bridge, LA 70517
Thibodeaux, Paul, Res., St. Jules Church, 116 St. Jules St., Lafayette, LA 70506
Warren, Arthur, Tribunal Office, 1408 Carmel Ave., Lafayette, LA 70501

Permanent Deacons:
Achee, Harold L., Sr., (Retired)
Bellamy, Coley M., Mother of Mercy, Rayne
Benedetto, Joseph, (Retired)
Bergeron, Harris, Our Lady of Mercy, Henderson
Bodin, Edward J., St. Jules Church, Franklin
Bodin, Ronnie J., Our Lady of Lourdes, Erath
Borbas, Timothy, St. Edmond, Lafayette
Borel, Ronald, Our Lady of Perpetual Help, New Iberia; Chancery, Lafayette
Boudreaux, Ulysse, Our Lady of Perpetual Help, New Iberia
Bourg, Gerald J., Sacred Heart, Baldwin; St. John, Jeanerette
Broussard, Ronald H., St. Peter, New Iberia
Broussard, Wade, St. Peter, New Iberia
Cannatella, Carlo, St. Landry, Opelousas
Clark, Michael, Holy Cross, Lafayette; St. Joseph, Rayne
Collins, Jerome, Our Lady Queen of Angels, Opelousas
Comeaux, Joseph, St. Stephen, Berwick
Cormier, James, Our Lady of the Sacred Heart, Church Point
Davis, James, St. Bernard, Breaux Bridge
Dejean, Alvin Ray, St. Mary, Port Barre; Holy Trinity, Washington
Doumit, Christopher, St. Joseph, Loreauville
Eleazar, Paul R., Holy Rosary, Kaplan
Faulk, Kendal, Our Lady of the Holy Rosary, Kaplan
Freyou, Leonard J., St. Nicholas Church, Lydia
Green, Justin, St. Genevieve, Lafayette
Guilbeau, James, (Retired)
Guillory, David, St. Thomas More, Eunice
Hanemann, Louis, Fayetteville
Hebert, Douglas J., Assumption, Franklin
Hebert, Marcel, St. Bernard, Breaux Bridge
Henry, Samuel, St. Charles, Grand Coteau
Jacobs, Lawrence, St. Francis of Assisi, Breaux Bridge
Joubert, Ulysse, Our Lady of Mercy, Opelousas
Judice, Julian, St. Mary, Lafayette
Kincel, James, Sts. Peter and Paul, Scott
Landry, Theodule, Annunciation of the BVM, Duralde
Lebouef, Eugene J., Queen of All Saints, Ville Platte
Lee, Carlton J., Sr., Notre Dame, St. Martinville
Lejeune, Joseph L., St. John the Evangelist, Mermentau
Leleux, Rodless, St. John the Baptist, Lyons Point; St. Michael, Crowley
Lindsey, Thomas, Our Lady of Mercy, Opelousas
Lloyd, Louis, Our Lady Queen of Peace, Lafayette
Luke, Norbert, Holy Cross, Lafayette
Marcel, Albert, St. Anthony, Lafayette
Mason, Jonas E., (Retired)
Matte, Paul, St. Edmond, Lafayette
McDonner, Robert, Unassigned
Melancon, J. Douglas, Assumption, Mire
Melancon, Roy, Our Lady of Mercy, Henderson
Miller, Cody, St. Joseph, Milton
Miller, John W., St. Landry, Opelousas
Morello, Benedict, St. Theresa, Abbeville
Moulton, Chris, St. Mary Magdalen, Abbeville
Mouton, Melvin, Pasadena, TX
Ortego, Charles, St. Anthony of Padua, Eunice
Ozene, Anthony Leroy, Immaculate Heart of Mary, Lafayette
Perron, Roderick P., (Retired)
Picard, Richard, Holy Cross, Lafayette
Richard, Harold, St. Bernard, Breaux Bridge
Richard, Thomas, Our Lady of Mount Carmel, Chataignier; St. Joseph, Plaisance
Royston, John, Unassigned
Sarkies, John, Nativity of Our Lady, New Iberia
Senegal, Nolton, Our Mother of Mercy, Rayne
Sikes, George, Our Lady of Perpetual Help, New Iberia
Simon, Steve, St. Theresa, Duson
Soileau, Harris, Sacred Heart of Jesus, Ville Platte
Sonnier, Adam, (Retired)
Theriot, Samuel, Our Lady of Wisdom, Lafayette
Thibodeaux, John, Assumption, Carencro
Thomas, Joseph, St. Jules, Franklin
Trahan, Joseph, Sacred Heart, Broussard
Tran, Tam, St. Helena, Louisa
Waguespack, Eugene, St. Peter, Carencro
Waguespack, Kenneth, St. Peter, New Iberia
Wilson, James, St. Peter, New Iberia

INSTITUTIONS LOCATED IN THE DIOCESE

[A] SEMINARIES, RELIGIOUS OR SCHOLASTICATES

GRAND COTEAU. *St. Charles College*, P.O. Box C, 70541-1003. Tel: 337-662-5251; Fax: 337-662-3187. Novitiate of New Orleans Province of the Society of Jesus. Revs. Francis W. Huete, S.J., Novice Dir. & Supr. of Community; Warren J. Broussard, S.J., Asst. Novice Dir. Priests 2; Novices 8.

[B] HIGH SCHOOLS, INTERPAROCHIAL

LAFAYETTE. *St. Thomas More*, 450 E. Farrel Rd., 70508. Tel: 337-988-3700; Fax: 337-988-2911.
Web site: www.stm.k12.la.us/index.html
Mr. Ray Simon, Prin. Brothers 1; Lay Teachers 67; Students 980.

Teurlings Catholic High, 139 Teurlings Dr., 70501. Tel: 337-235-5711; Fax: 337-234-8057.
E-mail: mboyer@tcac.net
Web site: www.tchs.net
Mr. Michael H. Boyer, Prin. Lay Teachers 41; Students 697.

CROWLEY. *Notre Dame High School of Acadia Parish*, 910 N. Eastern Ave., 70526. Tel: 337-783-3519; Fax: 337-788-2115.
E-mail: Pios5224@aol.com
Mr. John E. Dailey, Prin. Lay Teachers 38; Students 543.

NEW IBERIA. *Catholic High School*. (Grades 4-12), 1301 DeLaSalle Dr., 70560. Tel: 337-364-5116; Fax: 337-364-5041.
E-mail: chspanthers.com
Dave J. Cavalier, Jr., Prin. Lay Teachers 60; Total Staff 77; Students 922.

OPELOUSAS. *Opelousas Catholic School*. (Grades PreK-12), 428 E. Prudhomme Ln., 70570. Tel: 337-942-5404; Fax: 337-942-5922.
E-mail: ocsvikings@yahoo.com
Web site: www.asd.com(#8706)
Mrs. Karen Domengeaux, Prin. Elementary: (PreK-5). Lay Teachers 14; Students 247. High School: (6-12). Lay Teachers 30; Students 432.

[C] ELEMENTARY SCHOOLS, INTERPAROCHIAL

LAFAYETTE. *Holy Family School*, 200 St. John St., 70501. Tel: 337-235-0267. Sisters of the Holy Family. Sisters 3; Lay Teachers 12; Students 126.

ST. MARTINVILLE. *Trinity Catholic School*. (Grades PreK-8), 242 Gary St., 70582. Tel: 337-394-6693; Fax: 337-394-3394.
E-mail: trinity_catholic@stmartin.k12.la.us
Miss Rosemary Pierre, Prin. Priests 2; Sisters 2; Lay Teachers 20; Total Staff 38; Students 445.

[D] ELEMENTARY SCHOOLS, PRIVATE

ABBEVILLE. *Mt. Carmel Elementary School*, 405 Park, 70510. Tel: 337-898-0859; Fax: 337-893-5968.
E-mail: carmel@acadian.net
Web site: www.acadian.net/~carmel
Sr. Janet LeBlanc, O.Carm., Prin. Sisters of Mt. Carmel 3; Lay Teachers 24; Students 513.

[E] HIGH AND ELEMENTARY SCHOOLS, PRIVATE

GRAND COTEAU. *Academy of the Sacred Heart*. (Grades PreK-12), P.O. Box 310, 70541. Tel: 337-662-5275; Fax: 337-662-3011.
E-mail: chaggarty@ashcoteau.org
Web site: www.ashcoteau.org
Day School for girls. Boarding facilities for girls 8th-12th grade. Sr. Carol Haggarty, R.S.C.J., Prin. Religious of the Sacred Heart 3; Lay Teachers 39; Students 349.

[F] GENERAL HOSPITALS

LAFAYETTE. *Our Lady of Lourdes Regional Medical Center, Inc.*, 611 St. Landry St., P.O. Box 4027, 70502. Tel: 337-289-2100; Fax: 337-289-2574.
Web site: www.lourdes.net
For a complete listing, refer to the Hospitals section.

[G] HOMES FOR THE AGED INFIRM

LAFAYETTE. *Bethany M.H.S. Health Care Center*, P.O. Box 2308, 70502. Tel: 337-234-2459; Fax: 337-234-9483
For a complete listing, refer to the Special Care Facilities section.

Village du Lac, Inc., 1404 Carmel Ave., 70501. Tel: 337-234-5106
For a complete listing, refer to the Special Care Facilities section.

NEW IBERIA. *Consolata Home*, 2319 E. Main St., 70560. Tel: 337-365-8226; Fax: 337-365-8626.
E-mail: HDLANDRY@aisp.Net
For a complete listing, refer to the Special Care Facilities section.

OPELOUSAS. *C'est La Vie Center of the Sisters Marianites of Holy Cross*, 960 E. Prudhomme St., 70570. Tel: 337-942-8154; Fax: 337-942-8279.
E-mail: olpsnh@eatel.net
For a complete listing, refer to the Special Care Facilities section.

Our Lady of Prompt Succor Home, 954 E. Prudhomme St., 70570. Tel: 337-948-3634; Fax: 337-942-8279.
E-mail: olpsnh@eatel.net
For a complete listing, refer to the Special Care Facilities section.

[H] MONASTERIES AND RESIDENCES PRIESTS AND BROTHERS

LAFAYETTE. *De La Salle Christian Brothers*, 1522 Carmel Dr., 70501. Tel: 337-235-3576; Fax: 337-261-0765. Retired Brothers Home. Bros. Louis Welker, F.S.C., Dir.; Jerry Vincent, F.S.C., Sub-Dir.; C. Daniel Duplantis, F.S.C., Coord.; Rev. Luiz C. Dutra, Chap. Brothers 16.

De La Salle Christian Brothers Provincialate, 1522 Carmel Dr., 70501. Tel: 337-234-1973; Fax: 337-261-1014.
E-mail: nosf@BellSouth.net
Headquarters for the New Orleans-Santa Fe District. Legal Title: *Brothers of the Christian Schools of Lafayette LA, Inc.* Bros. Clarence Fioke, F.S.C.,

Prov.; James Brown, F.S.C., Auxiliary Prov. and Finance Dir.; Brendan Hayden, F.S.C., Prov. Bookkeeper.

OPELOUSAS. *Mother of the Redeemer Monastery*, 168 Monastery Ln., 70570. Tel: 337-543-2237; Fax: 337-543-7752. Priests 1; Brothers 2; Candidates 1.

[I] CONVENTS AND RESIDENCES FOR SISTERS

LAFAYETTE. *Discalced Carmelites*. Monastery of Mary, Mother of Grace. 1250 Carmel Ave., 70501. Tel: 337-232-4651; Fax: 337-232-3540. Mother Regina Mullins, O.C.D., Prioress; Rev. Msgr. H. Alexandre Larroque, Chap. Cloistered Nuns 17; Extern Sisters 4.

Franciscan Missionaries of Our Lady.
E-mail: l
Our Lady of Lourdes Hospital, P.O. Box 4027, 70502. Tel: 337-289-2100 (Convent); 289-2100 (Hospital); Fax: 337-289-2574.
E-mail: lyonsb@lourdesrmc.com
Web site: www.lourdes.net
611 St. Landry St., 70506. Students 2.

Marianites of Holy Cross, 1417 St. John St., 70506. Tel: 337-234-5454.
E-mail: SrRaymsc@aol.com
Sisters 2.

Missionaries of Charity, 911 St. John St., 70501. Tel: 337-233-3929. Sisters 4.

School Sisters of Notre Dame, 105 Dogwood, 70501. Tel: 337-232-6975; Fax: 337-261-5556. Sisters 2.

Sisters of Divine Providence, 317 Guilbeau Rd., Apt. 101-E, 70506. Tel: 337-984-8520; Fax: 337-261-5635.
Other Addresses: P.O. Box 298, Egan, 70531-0298. Tel: 337-788-0529. 220 Wilkle St., Apt. 863, 70506. Tel: 337-234-4546.

Sisters of Mt. Carmel, 309 Evangeline Dr., 70501. Tel: 337-235-8687. Sisters 3.
Other Addresses: 506 Surrey St., 70501. Tel: 337-235-1837. Sisters 2. 415 N. Domingue Ave., Apt. 42, 70506. Tel: 337-988-5456. 317 Guilbeau Rd., Apt. 206A, 70506. Tel: 337-981-4378.

Sisters of the Most Holy Sacrament, Convent Generalate, 313 Corona Dr., 70503-4757. Tel: 337-981-8475; Fax: 337-981-9128. Sr. Judine Theriot, M.H.S., Major Supr. Sisters 2. Administrative Offices, P.O. Box 90037, 70509-0037.
Other Addresses: 317 St. Patrick St., No. 1, 70506-4565. Tel: 337-234-6724. 317 St. Patrick St., No. 3, 70506-4565. Tel: 337-264-1948. Sisters 2. 317 St. Patrick St., No. 4, 70506-4565. Tel: 337-232-3443. 317 St. Patrick St., No. 5, 70506-4565. Tel: 337-264-1921. 317 St. Patrick St., No. 6, 70506-4565. Tel: 337-235-1755. 107 Wisteria Dr., 70506-6858. Tel: 337-989-9817. Sisters 2. Maison Faller Residence, 406 St. Julien St., 70506-4622. Tel: 337-235-4711. Sisters 4. St. Anne's Annex, P.O. Box 2308, 70502-2308. Tel: 337-233-8901. Sisters 2. Bethany MHS Health Care Center, P.O. Box 2308, 70502-2308. Sisters 8.

ABBEVILLE. *Sisters of Mt. Carmel*, 108 Petain St., 70510. Tel: 337-898-0140.
Other Addresses: 2326 Camella, 70510. Tel: 337-898-1807. Sisters 2. 108 W. St. Victor St., 70510. Tel: 337-893-0138.

ARNAUDVILLE. *Sisters of Mt. Carmel*, P.O. Box 53, 70512. Tel: 337-754-7754; Fax: 337-754-7754.
E-mail: Sr.Paula@Juno.com

BREAUX BRIDGE. *Sisters of the Most Holy Sacrament*, 221 Berard St., 70517. Tel: 337-332-1951.

CHURCH POINT. *Sisters of the Blessed Sacrament*, 695 N. Main St., 70525. Tel: 337-684-2120. Sisters 3.

CROWLEY. *Marianites of the Holy Cross*, 516 N. Ave. E, 70526. Tel: 337-783-1550.

Sisters of Divine Providence, 516 N. Ave. E, 70526. Tel: 337-783-1550.

Sisters of the Most Holy Sacrament, P.O. Box 695, 70527. Tel: 337-783-3675. Mailing Address: P.O. Box 90037, Lafayette, 70509-0037.

DUSON. *Eucharistic Missionaries of St. Dominic*, P.O. Box 725, 70529. Tel: 318-873-4159.

GRAND COTEAU. *Religious of the Sacred Heart*, P.O. Box 292, 70541. Tel: 337-942-1551. Sisters 3.
Other Addresses: P.O. Box 446, 70541. Tel: 337-662-5526. Sisters 4. P.O. Box 308, 70541. Tel: 337-662-5453. Sisters 4.

LEBEAU. *Sisters of the Holy Spirit*, P.O. Box 115, 71345. Tel: 337-623-5540.

NEW IBERIA. *Sisters of Providence*, 213 Oak Hill Rd., 70563. Tel: 337-364-3142.

OPELOUSAS. *Sisters of the Holy Family*, 317 Congress, 70570. Tel: 337-942-2052. Sisters 4.

RAYNE. *Sisters of Mt. Carmel*, 411 S. Polk St., 70578. Tel: 337-334-3403. Sisters 5.

Sisters of the Blessed Sacrament, 710 Malvern Ave., 70578-4632. Tel: 337-334-3606.
E-mail: Roselle6@Juno.com
Web site: Slavin2@Juno.com
Sisters 2.

ST. MARTINVILLE. *Sisters of Mercy of the Americas*, P.O. Box 674, 70582. Tel: 337-394-14486.

Sisters of the Blessed Sacrament, 201 Gary St., 70582. Tel: 3378-394-3036. Sisters 3.

SUNSET. *Sisters of Mt. Carmel*, P.O. Box 1734, 70584-1734. Tel: 337-662-7178.

[J] RETREAT HOUSES

GRAND COTEAU. *Jesuit Spirituality Center (St. Charles College)*, P.O. Box C, 70541-1003. Tel: 337-662-5251; Fax: 337-662-3187.
E-mail: jespirtcen@aol.com
Web site: members.aol.com/jespitcen/
Year-round directed retreats of 3, 5, 8, or 30 days plus a variety of weekend retreats and/or programs open to men and women. Revs. Albert C. Louapre, S.J., Dir.; Louis A. Arceneaux, C.M.; Peter Bayhi, S.J.; John J. Cazenavette, S.J.; Thomas J. Jenniskens, S.J.; Arturo Lozano, S.J.; Henry R. Montecino, S.J.; Fred G. Reynolds, S.J.; Norman J. Rogge, S.J.; Bro. George A. Murphy, S.J.; Sr. Consuelo Champagne, M.S.C. Priests 9; Brothers 1; Sisters 2.

Our Lady of the Oaks Retreat House, P.O. Box D, 70541. Tel: 337-662-5410; Fax: 337-662-5331.
E-mail: olorhgc@BellSouth.net
Preached retreats for men, women and married couples. Jesuit Fathers. Rev. Kenneth Buddendorff, S.J., Dir. Assoc. Directors: Revs. Francis J. Coco, S.J.; John T. Condry, S.J.; Joseph P. McGill, S.J.

[K] CURSILLO CENTERS

OPELOUSAS. *Cursillo Center*, 3651 Hwy. 104, 70570. Tel: 337-543-2100. Rev. Msgr. Louis J. Melancon, Spiritual Dir.

[L] NEWMAN CENTERS

LAFAYETTE. *Our Lady of Wisdom Catholic Student Center*, University of Southwestern Louisiana, P.O. Box 43271, 70505. Tel: 337-232-8741; 232-8742. Rev. W. Curtis Mallet.

EUNICE. *Catholic Student Center-Louisiana State Univ.*, P.O. Box 1129, 70535. Tel: 337-457-8668. Total Staff 2; Total in Residence 1.

[M] MISCELLANEOUS

LAFAYETTE. *Brothers of the Christian Schools of Lafayette - Retirement Trust*, 1522 Carmel Ave., 70501. Tel: 337-234-1973; Fax: 337-261-1014.
E-mail: nosf@BellSouth.net
Total Staff 9; Total in Residence 22.

Come Lord Jesus, 1804 W. University Ave., 70506. Tel: 337-233-6277; Fax: 337-233-6144.
E-mail: comelord@BellSouth.net
Rev. Conley Bertand, Dir.; Ms. Victoria Bordelon, Admin. Asst.

Community of Jesus Crucified, 421 1/2 Carmel Dr., 70501. Tel: 337-232-7491; Fax: 337-261-5294. Revs. Jerome V. Frey, Spiritual Dir.; Michael Champagne.

St. Augustine Trust Fund, P.O. Box 90037, 70509-0037. Tel: 337-981-8475; Fax: 337-981-9128. Sisters of the Most Holy Sacrament.

St. La Salle Auxiliary, 1522 Carmel Dr., 70501. Tel: 337-234-1973; Fax: 337-261-1014.
E-mail: nosf@bellsouth.net
The St. LaSalle Auxiliary is a development project of "Brothers of the Christian Schools of Lafayette, LA, Inc.," a non-profit organization. Brothers of the Christian Schools.

Sisters of the Eucharistic Covenant, 105 Upperline Ave., 70501. Tel: 337-233-2226; Fax: 337-233-2308.
E-mail: clarroqu@bellsouth.net
Sr. Celeste D. Larroque, S.E.C., Pres.

NEW IBERIA. *Progressive Education Program, Inc.*, P.O. Box 10237, 70562-0237. Tel: 337-365-0933; Fax: 337-364-2555.
E-mail: pepi@aisp.net
Sr. Rosarine Gonzales, S.S.N.D., Dir.

[N] SOCIAL SERVICE CENTERS

LAFAYETTE. *Lafayette Catholic Service Centers, Inc.*, 409 St. John St., P.O. Box 3177, 70501. Tel: 337-235-4972; Fax: 337-234-0953.
Service Centers: Albert J. Glaude, Exec. Dir.
Boustany Square Apartments.
Msgr. A. O. Sigur Service Center. Tel: 337-233-7788.
St. Joseph Shelter for Men. Tel: 337-237-1866.
St. Joseph Diner. Tel: 337-232-8434.
Shalom House Family Shelter. Tel: 337-261-1320.
Emmanuel House Family Apts.
St. Joseph Distribution Center. Tel: 337-232-1166.
The Bishop Harry J. Flynn Hospitality Center. Tel: 337-235-6971. Total Assisted Annually 245,450.

ABBEVILLE. *Christian Service Center*, 701 Chevis St., 70510. Tel: 337-893-9756; 893-3114.

CROWLEY. *Crowley Christian Care Center*, 825 N. Ave. F, P.O. Box 686, 70527-0686. Tel: 337-783-5811. Total Staff 50; Total Assisted 4,800.

NEW IBERIA. *Social Service Center*, 432 Bank Ave., 70560. Tel: 337-369-6384. Paul H. DeClouet, Dir. Total Staff 30; Total Families Assisted 7,179.

OPELOUSAS. *Opelousas Housing Corporation*, 411 E. Landry St., P.O. Box 7045, 70571. Tel: 337-948-3161; Fax: 337-948-0011.

New Life Center, 411 E. Landry St., 70570. Shelter for women & children operated under the direction of the Lafayette Catholic Services Center, Inc.

Even Start Program. (Childcare/Preschool Birth-5yrs), 110 S. Walnut, 70570.

VILLE PLATTE. *Christian Care and Share Center*, 129 W. Main St., P.O. Box 901, 70586. Tel: 337-363-8041. Mr. Eugene S. Fontenot, Chm. Total Staff 12.

RELIGIOUS INSTITUTES OF MEN REPRESENTED IN THE DIOCESE

For further details refer to the corresponding bracketed number in the Religious Institutes of Men or Women section.

[0200]—*Benedictines (Olivetan, Subiaco Congregation)*.—O.S.B.

[0330]—*Brothers of the Christian Schools*. (New Orleans Prov.).—F.S.C.

[]—*Carmelites of Mary Immaculate*.—C.M.I.

[]—*Congregation of St. Theresa of the Child Jesus*.—C.S.T.

[0520]—*Franciscan Friars*.—O.F.M.

[0690]—*Jesuit Fathers and Brothers*. (New Orleans Prov.).—S.J.

[]—*Missionaries of St. Paul*. (Nigeria).—M.S.P.

[0610]—*Priests of the Congregation of Holy Cross*.—C.S.C.

[1070]—*Redemptorist Fathers*.—C.SS.R.

[0700]—*St. Joseph's Society of the Sacred Heart*. (Baltimore Prov.).—S.S.J.

[0420]—*Society of the Divine Word*.—S.V.D.

RELIGIOUS INSTITUTES OF WOMEN REPRESENTED IN THE DIOCESE

[0400]—*Congregation of Our Lady of Mount Carmel*.—O.Carm.

[2410]—*Congregation of the Marianites of Holy Cross*.—M.S.C.

[1950]—*Congregation of the Sisters of the Holy Family*.—S.S.F.

[0750]—*Daughters of Charity of the Sacred Heart of Jesus*.—F.C.S.C.J.

[0420]—*Discalced Carmelite Nuns*.—O.C.D.

[1140]—*Eucharistic Missionaries of St. Dominic*.—O.P.

[1380]—*Franciscan Missionaries of Our Lady*.—O.S.F.

[2575]—*Institute of the Sisters of Mercy of the Americas*.—R.S.M.

[2710]—*Missionaries of Charity*. (Bronx, NY).—M.C.

[4070]—*Religious of the Sacred Heart*.—R.S.C.J.

[2970]—*School Sisters of Notre Dame*. (South Central).—S.S.N.D.

[0990]—*Sisters of Divine Providence*. (San Antonio, TX).—C.D.P.

[3360]—*Sisters of Providence of Saint Mary-of-the-Woods, Indiana*. (Prov. of St. Joseph).—S.P.

[3880]—*Sisters of St. Joseph of Medaille*.—C.S.J.

[0260]—*Sisters of the Blessed Sacrament for Indians and Colored People*.—S.B.S.

[2050]—*Sisters of the Holy Spirit and Mary Immaculate*.—S.H.Sp.

[2120]—*Sisters of the Immaculate Conception*.—C.R.

[2940]—*Sisters of the Most Holy Sacrament*.—M.H.S.

NECROLOGY

† Schexnayder, Daniel, Leonville, LA St. Leo the Great. —Died June 19, 2000.

Diocese of Lake Charles

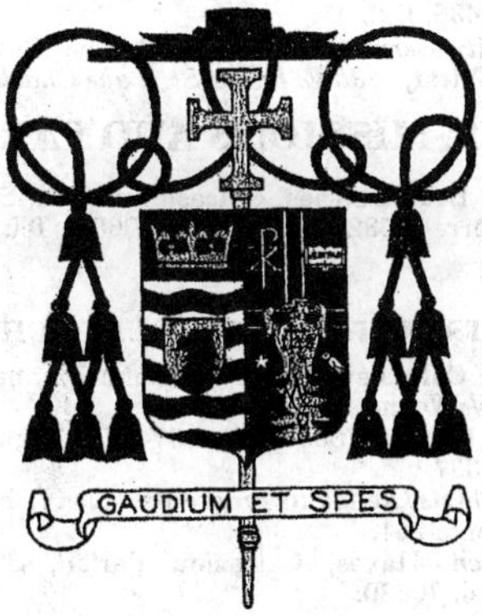

Most Reverend

EDWARD K. BRAXTON

Bishop of Lake Charles; ordained May 13, 1970; appointed Auxiliary Bishop of St. Louis March 28, 1995; ordained Auxiliary Bishop of St. Louis May 17, 1995; appointed Bishop of Lake Charles December 12, 2000; installed Bishop of Lake Charles February 22, 2001.

Chancery Office: 414 Iris St., P.O. Box 3223, Lake Charles, LA, 70602. Tel.: 337-439-7400; Fax: 337-439-7413.

Web site address: lcdiocese.laol.net

E-mail address: lcdiocese@laol.net

ESTABLISHED APRIL 25, 1980.

Square Miles 5,313.

Comprises the civil parishes (or counties) of Allen, Beauregard, Calcasieu, Cameron and Jefferson Davis in the State of Louisiana.

For legal titles of parishes and diocesan institutions, consult the Chancery Office.

STATISTICAL OVERVIEW

Personnel	
Bishop	1
Priests: Diocesan Active in Diocese	37
Priests: Active Outside Diocese	3
Priests: Retired, Sick or Absent	6
Number of Diocesan Priests	46
Religious Priests in Diocese	12
Extern Priests in Diocese	12
Ordinations:	
Permanent Deacons	3
Permanent Deacons in Diocese	24
Total Brothers	1
Total Sisters	25
Parishes	
Parishes	36
With Resident Pastor:	
Resident Diocesan Priests	28
Resident Religious Priests	8
Missions	25
Professional Ministry Personnel:	
Brothers	1
Sisters	4
Lay Ministers	28
Welfare	
Catholic Hospitals	1
Total Assisted	117,653
Homes for the Aged	1
Total Assisted	62
Day Care and Extended Day Care Centers	1
Total Assisted	65
Special Centers for Social Services	1
Total Assisted	11,781
Educational	
Total Seminarians	10
High Schools, Diocesan and Parish	1
Total Students	574
Elementary Schools, Diocesan and Parish	7
Total Students	2,594
Catechesis/Religious Education:	
High School Students	2,656
Elementary Students	6,492
Total Students Under Catholic Instruction	12,316
Teachers in the Diocese:	
Lay Teachers	221
Vital Statistics	
Receptions into the Church:	
Infant Baptism Totals	1,479
Adult Baptism Totals	103
Received into Full Communion	223
First Communions	1,367
Confirmations	1,271
Marriages:	
Catholic	305
Interfaith	160
Total Marriages	465
Deaths	936
Total Catholic Population	80,199
Total Population	259,425

Diocesan Board of Administration (Legal Title - *Society of the Roman Catholic Church of the Diocese of Lake Charles, LA*)—Most Rev. JUDE SPEYRER; Rev. HENRY MANCUSO; Rev. Msgr. VINCENT A. SEDITA; Rev. Msgr. JAMES GADDY; Deacon GEORGE A. STEARNS.

Bishop's Office—414 Iris St., P.O. Box 3223, Lake Charles, 70602. Tel: 337-439-7400, Ext. 14.

Chancery Office—414 Iris St., P.O. Box 3223, Lake Charles, 70602. Tel: 337-439-7400; Fax: 337-439-7413. Office Hours: Mon.-Fri. 8:30-4:30.

Perry Building—411 Iris St., Lake Charles, 70601. Tel: 337-439-7426; Fax: 337-439-7428. Office Hours: Mon.-Fri. 8:30-4:30.

Vicar General—Rev. Msgr. VINCENT SEDITA, V.G., *P.O. Box 3223, Lake Charles, 70602.* Tel: 337-439-7400, Ext. 14.

Chancellor—Deacon GEORGE STEARNS, *P.O. Box 3223, Lake Charles, 70602.* Tel: 337-439-7400, Ext. 14.

Assistant Chancellor—Rev. Msgr. HARRY GREIG, *P.O. Box 3223, Lake Charles, 70602.* Tel: 337-439-7400, Ext. 14.

Vicar Judicial—Rev. JACE ESKIND, J.C.L., *P.O Box 3223, Lake Charles, 70607.* Tel: 337-439-7400, Ext. 20.

Tribunal—414 Iris St., P.O. Box 3223, Lake Charles, 70602. Tel: 337-439-7400, Ext. 20.

Judges—Rev. JACE ESKIND, J.C.L.; Rev. Msgr. VINCENT SEDITA; Revs. JOHN A. POERIO; ALBERT BOREL, J.C.L.; Sr. BONNIE KOEHNE, S.E., J.C.L.

Advocates—Rev. Msgr. VINCENT SEDITA; Revs. JOHN POERIO; JOSEPH MCGRATH; T. L. HERLONG.

Defenders of the Bond—Rev. Msgr. HARRY GREIG; Rev. JAMES DOYLE.

Notary—PATRICIA SIGUR.

Episcopal Vicars—Rev. HENRY MANCUSO, West Deanery; Rev. Msgr. JAMES GADDY, East Deanery; Rev. JACE ESKIND, Tribunal; Rev. Msgr. IRVING DEBLANC, Spec. Svcs.; Rev. Msgr. VINCENT SEDITA, Vicar Gen.

Vicars—Deacon EDWARD LAVINE, Black Catholics; Sr. ROSE ANN BLAIR, C.D.P., Religious; Mrs. SANDRA GAY, Christian Formation.

Priest's Senate—Revs. HERBERT MAY, Chm. KARL FUSELIER; WAYNE LEBLEU; JOSEPH MCGRATH; DANIEL TORRES.

Diocesan Consultors—Rev. Msgr. LOUIS MELANCON; Rev. Msgr. CHARLES J. DUBOIS; Rev. Msgr. IRVING DEBLANC, Spec. Svcs.; Rev. Msgr. VINCENT SEDITA, Vicar Gen.; Rev. Msgr. HARRY GREIG; Rev. HENRY MANCUSO; Rt. Rev. HERBERT J. MAY, JR., J.C.L.; Revs. JOHN GILES; KARL FUSELIER; JACE ESKIND, J.C.L.; AUBREY GUILBEAU; AUGUSTINE MULANJANANY; Rev. Msgr. JAMES GADDY.

Offices, Boards, Commissions, Committees

Black Catholics—Deacon EDWARD LAVINE, *P.O. Box 3223, Lake Charles, 70601.* Tel: 337-439-7436, Ext. 11.

Charismatic Renewal—Rev. ORIS BROUSSARD, *2409 2nd St., Lake Charles, 70601.* Tel: 337-439-1898.

Christian Formation—Mrs. SANDRA GAY, *411 Iris St., Lake Charles, 70601.* Tel: 337-439-7426, Ext. 19.

Clergy Formation—Rev. DON PIRARO, *5121 Sam Houston Jones Pkwy., Lake Charles, 70611.* Tel: 337-855-1232.

Communications—MORRIS LEBLEU, *P.O. Box 3223, Lake Charles, 70601.* Tel: 337-439-7400, Ext. 24.

Counseling—Rev. WHITNEY MILLER, *P.O. Box 3223, Lake Charles, 70601.* Tel: 337-439-7400.

Deaf Apostolate—Rev. AUBREY GUILBEAU, *418 Iris St., Lake Charles, 70601.* Tel: 337-439-4373.

Development Office—MORRIS LEBLEU, *P.O. Box 3223, Lake Charles, 70602.* Tel: 337-439-7400, Ext. 24.

Diocesan Building Commission—Deacon GEORGE STEARNS, Chm., *P.O. Box 3223, Lake Charles, 70602.* Tel: 337-439-7400, Ext. 14.

Diocesan Pastoral Council—Most Rev. JUDE SPEYRER, Chm., *P.O. Box 3223, Lake Charles, 70602.* Tel: 337-439-7400, Ext. 14.

Diocesan Religious Council—Sr. ROSE ANN BLAIR, C.D.P., *1806 Westwood St., Lake Charles, 70601.* Tel: 337-491-7739.

Director of Seminarians—Rev. AUBREY GUILBEAU, *P.O. Box 3223, Lake Charles, 70601.* Tel: 337-439-7426, Ext. 17.

Education—Deacon MICHAEL MATHEWS, Supt., *P.O. Box 3223, Lake Charles, 70601.* Tel: 337-439-7426, Ext. 18.

Evangelization—GLENN HARMON, *411 Iris St., Lake Charles, 70601.* Tel: 337-439-7426, Ext. 10.

Fiscal Administration—Ms. PATRICIA MYERS, *P.O. Box 3223, Lake Charles, 70602.* Tel: 337-439-7400, Ext. 15.

Hispanic Ministry—Rev. CARLOS GARCIA-CARDOVA, *St. Philip Neri Church, P.O. Box 146, Kinder, 70648.* Tel: 337-738-5612.

Office For Worship—Rev. JACE ESKIND, *221 Aqua Dr., Lake Charles, 70605.* Tel: 337-477-1434.

Parish Boundaries Commission—Deacon GEORGE STEARNS, Chm., *P.O. Box 3223, Lake Charles, 70602.* Tel: 337-439-7400, Ext. 14.

Permanent Diaconate—Deacon EDWARD LAVINE, *2333 E. Broad St., Lake Charles, 70601.* Tel: 337-439-7436, Ext. 11.

Personnel Board—Rev. WILLIAM MILLER, Chm., *P.O. Box 849, Iowa, 70647.* Tel: 337-582-3503.

Propagation of the Faith & Holy Childhood Association—Rev. V. WAYNE LEBLEU, Dir., *P.O. Box 3223, Lake Charles, 70602.* Tel: 337-439-7400.

Religious Education—Mrs. SANDY GAY, *411 Iris St., Lake Charles, 70601.* Tel: 337-439-7426, Ext. 19.

Relief Services Catholic—Rev. V. WAYNE LEBLEU, Dir., *P.O. Box 3223, Lake Charles, 70602.* Tel: 337-439-7400.

St. Charles Retreat Center—Rev. DON PIRARO, Dir., *2151 Sam Houston Jones Pkwy., Lake Charles, 70611.* Tel: 337-855-1232.

Sea, Apostleship of the—ARCHIE THOMAS, *160 Marine St., Lake Charles, 70601.* Tel: 337-436-1315.

Social Services, Catholic—Deacon EDWARD LAVINE, Dir., *2333 E. Broad St., Lake Charles, 70601.* Tel: 337-439-7436, Ext. 11.

Community Services, Catholic—Deacon EDWARD LAVINE, Vicar, *2333 E. Broad St., Lake Charles, 70601.* Tel: 337-439-7436, Ext. 11.

Scouting—Rev. MAURICE J. MARTINEAU, *P.O. Drawer P, Lake Arthur, 70591.* Tel: 337-774-2614.

Seminary Advisory Board—Rev. AUBREY GUILBEAU, *411 Iris St., Lake Charles, 70601.* Tel: 337-439-7426, Ext. 17.

Vocation Director—Rev. TIMOTHY GOODLY, *411 Iris St., Lake Charles, 70601.* Tel: 337-439-7426, Ext. 17.

CLERGY, PARISHES, MISSIONS AND PAROCHIAL SCHOOLS

LAKE CHARLES
(Calcasieu Parish)

1—IMMACULATE CONCEPTION CATHEDRAL (1869), Rev. Msgr. Harry D. Greig, II; Deacons H. E. Wagner; Milton P. White; Michael Mathews. In res., Rev. Whitney Miller.
Mailing Address: P.O. Box 1029, 70602. Tel: 337-436-7251; Fax: 337-436-7240.
Church—935 Bilbo, 70601. [CEM]
School—Tel: 337-433-3497; Fax: 337-436-8294. Mr. John Augustine, Prin.
Lay Teachers 27; Students 340.

2—IMMACULATE HEART OF MARY (1953) (African American), Revs. Michael J. Barras; Karl Fuselier.
Res., 2031 Opelousas St., 70601. Tel: 337-436-8093; Fax: 337-436-8033.
Catechesis/Religious Programs—Tel: 337-436-8513.
Students 381.
Mission—Lake Charles, Calcasieu Parish, Our Lady of Fatima Chapel, 1700 Graham St., 70601.

3—SACRED HEART OF JESUS (1919) (African American), Revs. Henry Mancuso; Whitney G. Harris; Deacon Ed Lavine. In res., Rev. Alfredo Marco.
Res., 612 Louisiana Ave., 70601. Tel: 337-439-2646; Fax: 337-439-2650. [CEM]
School—Tel: 337-436-3588; Fax: 337-433-1761. Mr. Herman Metoyer, Prin.
Lay Teachers 12; Students 139.
Catechesis/Religious Programs—Tel: 318-439-9923. Willa Golden, D.R.E.
Students 175.

4—ST. HENRY (1942), Revs. Joseph Angadiath, C.M.I.; Timothy Goodly; Deacon Ray Granger.
Res., 1021 Eighth Ave., 70601. Tel: 337-436-7223; Fax: 337-436-4614. [JC]
Catechesis/Religious Programs—Tel: 337-433-6119. Mrs. Anne R. Jacobs, D.R.E.
Students 350.

5—ST. MARGARET (1940), Revs. Aubrey Guilbeau; Alan P. Trouille; Deacons Dan Landry; Vic Bonnaffee. In res., Rev. Scott DesOrmeaux.
Res., 2500 Enterprise Blvd., 70601. Tel: 337-439-4585; Fax: 337-433-3186.
School—Tel: 337-436-7959; Fax: 337-436-9932. Mrs. Priscilla Courville, Prin.
Sisters 1; Lay Teachers 40; Students 406.
Catechesis/Religious Programs—Tel: 337-436-6358. D.R.E.: Betty Timpa; Joanne Schwem.
Students 310.

6—ST. THEODORE'S (1974), Rev. Msgr. Charles J. Dubois; Deacon Jack Reynolds. In res., Revs. James Doyle; T.L. Herlong.
Res., 786 Sam Houston Jones Pkwy., 70611. Tel: 337-855-6662; Fax: 337-855-6663.
School—(Grades PreK-6). Tel: 337-855-9465. Mrs. Connie Dronette, Prin.
Lay Teachers 18; Students 215.
Catechesis/Religious Programs—Tel: 337-855-6664. Victoria Hogan, D.R.E.
Students 582.

7—OUR LADY OF GOOD COUNSEL (1957), Rev. Jace Eskind.
Res., 221 Aqua Dr., 70605. Tel: 337-477-1434; Fax: 337-479-2129.
Catechesis/Religious Programs—Gloria Taylor, D.R.E.
Students 135.

8—OUR LADY QUEEN OF HEAVEN (1957), Rev. Msgr. Ronald Groth; Rev. Msgr. Irving A. DeBlanc; Revs. John H. Giles, Jr.; Simon Palathingal.
Mailing Address: P.O. Box 5940, 70606.
Res., 617 W. Claude St., 70605. Tel: 337-477-1236; Fax: 337-478-3451. [CEM]
School—(Grades K-8). Tel: 337-477-7349; Fax: 337-477-7384. Mrs. Mary Ann Hipp, Prin.
Lay Teachers 41; Students 768.
Preschool and Day Care—Tel: 337-477-8438.
Students 65.
Catechesis/Religious Programs—3909 Creole St., 70605. Tel: 337-477-3937. D.R.E.: Mrs. Nancy Chehotsky, (Grades 7-12); Mrs. Robin Suire, (Grades 1-6).
Students 1,318.
Missions—Lake Charles, Calcasieu Parish, Christ the King, 7680 Gulf Hwy., 70605. Tel: 337-478-0213; Lake Charles, Calcasieu Parish, St. Martin de Porres, 5326 Elliot Rd., 70605. Tel: 337-478-3845.

OUTSIDE THE CITY OF LAKE CHARLES

Bell City, Calcasieu Parish, St. John Vianney (1939), Rev. V. Wayne LeBleu.
Res., Box 10, 70630. Tel: 337-622-3255; Fax: 337-622-3337. [CEM]
Catechesis/Religious Programs—Lisa Reber, D.R.E.
Students 261.
Mission—Hayes, Calcasieu Parish, St. Daniel Chapel, 70630.

Big Lake, Cameron Parish, St. Mary of the Lake (1938), Rev. John A. Poerio.
Res., 11054 Hwy. 384, 70607. Tel: 337-598-3101; Fax: 337-598-4298.
Catechesis/Religious Programs—Students 200.
Mission—Sweet Lake, St. Patrick's.

Cameron, Cameron Parish, Our Lady Star of the Sea (1961), Rev. Alphonse M. Volpe.
Res., 135 Our Lady's Road, 70631. Tel: 337-775-5342; Fax: 337-775-7042.
Catechesis/Religious Programs—Students 114.

Creole, Cameron Parish, Sacred Heart of Jesus (1890), Rev. E. Joseph McGrath.
Res., P.O. Drawer 9, 70632. Tel: 337-542-4795; Fax: 337-542-4641. [CEM 3]
Catechesis/Religious Programs—Tel: 337-542-4871. Stephanie Rodrigue, D.R.E.
Students 280.
Mission—Cameron, Cameron Parish, St. Rose of Lima, 2267 Trosclair Rd., Cameron, 70631. Tel: 337-542-4795.

De Quincy, Calcasieu Parish, Our Lady of La Salette (1922) (African American), Rev. John L. Blumm, M.S.
Res., 203 S. Grand, P.O. Box 236, 70633. Tel: 337-786-3500; Fax: 337-786-3500.
Catechesis/Religious Programs—Tel: 337-786-3205.
Students 366.
Mission—Ragley, Beauregard Parish, St. Pius X, 16816 Hwy. 171, Ragley, 70657. Tel: 337-725-3719.

De Ridder, Beauregard Parish, St. Joseph's (1938), Revs. Daniel Torres; Thomas Panthalani; Deacon Sumner Kohlhund.
Res., 1125 Blankenship Dr., 70634. Tel: 337-463-6878; Fax: 337-463-6875.
Catechesis/Religious Programs—Sr. Rita Deschenes, S.S.J., D.R.E.
Students 288.
Missions—Merryville, Beauregard Parish, St. Bridget; De Ridder, Beauregard Parish, St. Jude, 5072 Hwy. 113, Tel: 337-328-8476. Rev. Susil Fernando.

Elton, Jefferson Davis Parish, St. Paul (1913), Rev. Marshall Boulet; Deacon John Eaves.
Res., P.O. Box 129, 70532. Tel: 337-584-2818; Fax: 337-584-2818. [CEM]
Catechesis/Religious Programs—Cathy Hollingsworth, D.R.E.
Students 199.

St. Joseph's (1950) (African American), Rev. Jose Vattakunnel; Deacon John Eaves.
Res., P.O. Box 789, 70532. Tel: 337-584-2038; Fax: 337-584-2038. [CEM]
Catechesis/Religious Programs—Tel: 337-584-2642. D.R.E.: Mary Jane Thomas; Carroll Sue Gobert.
Students 55.

Fenton, Jefferson Davis Parish, St. Charles Borromeo (1980), Rev. Augustine Mulanjanany.
Res., P.O. Box 309, 70640. Tel: 337-756-2529.
Catechesis/Religious Programs—Beverly Cornier, D.R.E.
Students 80.

Grand Chenier, Cameron Parish, St. Eugene (1962), Rev. Vincent Vadakkedath.
Res., 5035 Grand Chenier Hwy., 70643. Tel: 337-538-2245; Fax: 337-538-2438. [CEM]
Catechesis/Religious Programs—Students 78.
Mission—Grand Chenier, Cameron Parish, Immaculate Conception, 70643.

Hackberry, Cameron Parish, St. Peter Apostle (1955), Rev. Eugene F. McKenna, M.S.
Res., 1210 Main St., P.O. Box 236, 70645. Tel: 337-762-3365.
Catechesis/Religious Programs—Tel: 337-762-4255. Tamra Welch, D.R.E.
Students 221.
Mission—Holly Beach, Holy Trinity. Rev. Roland Vaughn.
Res., 6470 Gulf Beach Hwy., Holly Beach, 70631-9607. Tel: 337-569-2132.
Mission—Johnson Bayou, Our Lady of the Assumption.

Iowa, Calcasieu Parish, St. Raphael (1931), Rev. William Miller.
Res., P.O. Drawer 849, 70647. Tel: 337-582-3503; Fax: 337-582-6326. [CEM]
Catechesis/Religious Programs—Students 547.
Missions—Lacassine, Jefferson Davis Parish, St. John the Evangelist, 70647-0849. Tel: 337-588-4606; Le Bleu Settlement, Calcasieu Parish, St. Joseph, 70647-0849. Tel: 337-582-3483.

Jennings, Jefferson Davis Parish, Our Lady Help of Christians (1891), Rev. Msgr. James Gaddy; Deacon Ed McNally.
Res., 710 State St., P.O. Drawer 1170, 70546. Tel: 337-824-0168; Fax: 337-824-7597. [CEM]
School—600 Roberts Ave., 70546. Tel: 337-824-1743; Fax: 337-824-1743. Mrs. Susan Daigle, Prin.
Lay Teachers 25; Students 433.
Catechesis/Religious Programs—Tel: 337-824-0168. Janet Guidry, D.R.E.
Students 252.

Immaculate Conception (1956), Rev. Oris Broussard.
Res., 515 Bryan St., P.O. Box 358, 70546. Tel: 337-824-1164; Fax: 337-824-1717.
Catechesis/Religious Programs—Bennett McNeal, D.R.E.
Students 187.

Our Lady of Perpetual Help (1941), Rev. Peter Nkedife.
Res., 920 S. Broadway, P.O. Box 1331, 70546. Tel: 337-824-3182; 824-3186. [CEM]
Catechesis/Religious Programs—Tel: 337-824-3703. D.R.E.: Harriet Lawdins; Maynell Guilbeaux.
Students 95.

Kinder, Allen Parish, St. Philip Neri (1937) (Acadian French), Rev. Carlos Garcia Cardona. In res., Rev. Austin Park, S.J.
Res., P.O. Box 146, 70648. Tel: 337-738-5612; Fax: 337-738-2728. [CEM]
Catechesis/Religious Programs—Nancy Burleigh, D.R.E.
Students 340.
Missions—Indian Village, Sacred Heart Parish, Sacred Heart, 70648. Tel: 337-328-8476; Reeves, Sacred Heart Parish, St. Maurice, HC 64 Box 142 A, 70634.

Lake Arthur, Jefferson Davis Parish, Our Lady of the Lake (1922), Rev. Maurice J. Martineau.
Res., P.O. Drawer P, 70549. Tel: 337-774-2614; Fax: 337-774-3793. [CEM][JC 3]
Catechesis/Religious Programs—203 Commercial St., 70549. Tel: 337-774-2675.
Students 375.
Missions—Thornwell, Jefferson Davis Parish, St. Francis of Assisi Chapel; Andrus Cove, Jefferson Davis Parish, St. Gertrude Chapel.

Oakdale, Allen Parish, Sacred Heart (1948), Rev. Fred F. Russi.
Mailing Address: P.O. Box 926, 71463-0926.
Res., 1208 E. Seventh Ave., 71463. Tel: 318-335-3780; Fax: 318-335-0708. [CEM]
Catechesis/Religious Programs—Students 138.
Mission—Elizabeth, Allen Parish, St. Frances, P.O. Box 926, 71463-0926.

Oberlin, Allen Parish, St. Joan of Arc (1920), Rev. Jude Brunnert, M.S.; Deacon Norris Chapman.
Res., 110 W. Fifth Ave., P.O. Box 479, 70655. Tel: 337-639-4399; 639-4798; Fax: 337-639-4799. [CEM]
Catechesis/Religious Programs—Sheryl Reed, D.R.E.
Students 273.
Mission—Soileau, Allen Parish, St. Joseph, P.O. Box 479, 70655.

Raymond, Jefferson Davis Parish, St. Lawrence (1957), Rev. Eappen Joseph.
Res., 5505 Pine Island Hwy., Jennings, 70546. Tel: 337-584-2700.
Catechesis/Religious Programs—Students 270.

Sulphur, Calcasieu Parish,

1—IMMACULATE CONCEPTION OF THE B.V.M., (1959), Rev. Msgr. Vincent Sedita.
Res., 2700 Maplewood Dr., 70663. Tel: 337-625-3364; Fax: 337-625-9547.
Catechesis/Religious Programs—Paula Hunter, D.R.E.
Students 333.

2—OUR LADY OF LASALETTE, (1961), Rev. Lawrence A. Kohler, M.S.; Deacons Johnny Mounce; Maurice Serice. In res., Rev. Joseph A. Decoteau.
Res., 602 N. Claiborne St., 70663. Tel: 337-527-6722; Fax: 337-527-0909.
Catechesis/Religious Programs—Tel: 337-527-8307. Stella Barkate, D.R.E.
Students 407.

3—OUR LADY OF PROMPT SUCCOR, (1919), Revs. Charles A. Gendron, M.S.; William O'Brien, M.S.; Henry Lenz, M.S.; Bro. Donald V. Smith, M.S.
Res., 1109 Cypress St., 70663. Tel: 337-527-5261; Fax: 337-528-2991.
School—Tel: 337-527-7828; Fax: 337-528-3778. Mrs. Sharon Tolin, Prin.
Lay Teachers 23; Students 295.
Catechesis/Religious Programs—1029 Lasalette Dr., 70663. Tel: 337-527-9964. D.R.E.: Theresa Cooper; Terry Sittig.
Students 367.
Mission—Sulphur, Calcasieu Parish, St. Peter Claver, 465 Maple St., 70663. Tel: 337-527-5987.

4—ST. THERESA, (1971), Rev. Francis Fitzsimmons, M.S.; Mary Little, Admin.
Res., 4822 Carlyss Dr., 70665. Tel: 337-583-4800; Fax: 337-583-4818.
Catechesis/Religious Programs—Tel: 337-583-4010. Charlotte Giese, D.R.E.
Students 352.

Vinton, Calcasieu Parish, St. Joseph (1920), Rev. Keith A. Pellerin.
Res., 1502 Industrial, 70668. Tel: 337-589-7358; Fax: 337-589-7843.
Catechesis/Religious Programs—Tel: 337-589-2982.
Students 300.
Missions—Edgerly, St. John Evangelist; Starks, St. Michael.

Welsh, Jefferson Davis Parish, Our Lady of the Seven Dolors (1904), Rev. Herbert May.
Res., P.O. Box 515, 70591. Tel: 337-734-3446; Fax: 337-734-3697. [CEM][JC]
Catechesis/Religious Programs—Tel: 337-734-3848. Betty LaBouve, D.R.E.
Students 312.
St. Joseph (1941) (African American), Rev. William D. Hogan, S.S.J.
Res., P.O. Box 607, 70591. Tel: 337-734-3673. [JC]
Mission—Iowa, Calcasieu Parish, St. Peter Claver, 400 W. 2nd St., 70547.

Westlake, Calcasieu Parish, St. John Bosco (1955), Rev. Peter Revel; Deacons Fred Reed, Jr.; Garrett Caraway, Jr. In res., Rev. Cyprian Eze.
Res., P.O. Box 66, 70669. Tel: 337-433-2467; Fax: 337-436-7766.
Catechesis/Religious Programs—Tel: 337-439-6585; Fax: 337-436-9766. D.R.E.: Fred Reed; Judy Reed.
Students 450.

Chaplains of Public Institutions

LAKE CHARLES. *Lake Charles Memorial Hospital.* Rev. Scott DesOrmeaux.

DEQUINCY. *Phelps Correctional Center.* Rev. John Vianney Ijeoma, Chap.

SULPHUR. *West Clacasieu Cameron Hospital.* Rev. William P. O'Brien, M.S., Chap.

On Special Assignment:
Reverend Fathers—
Harris, Whitney G., Dir. Ministry Relations, McNeese State University, Lake Charles, LA 70605. Tel: 318-475-5426

On Duty Outside the Diocese:
Reverend Monsignors—
Melancon, Louis J., 1074 Hwy. 748, Washington, LA 70589
Reverend Fathers—
Miles, James, 115 Gladys Ave., Lansdowne, MD 21227
Mullen, Thomas, 70 Nutwell Ct., Lothian, MD 20711

Retired:
Reverend Monsignors—
Bourque, Joseph A., 2960 Lake St., Apt.142, Lake Charles, LA 70601
DeBlanc, Irving A., 1505 Jeff Ln., Lake Charles, LA 70605
Vincent, Amos J., 943 Tamela Dr., Lake Charles, LA 706
Reverend Fathers—
Herlong, Theophilus L., 5635 B Welcome Rd., Lake Charles, LA 70611
Smit, Gerard C., 105 Justice Way, Elkton, MD 21921
Soileau, Charles, 1017 Rose Ann St., Opelousas, LA 70570

Permanent Deacons:
Bonnaffee, Vic, St. Margaret, Lake Charles
Broussard, Gordon, St. Raphael, IA
Caraway, Julius G., Jr., St. John Bosco Church, Westlake
Chapman, Norris, St. Joan of Arc, Oberlin
Dronet, Manny, Immaculate Conception, Maplewood
Eaves, John, St. Paul, Elton
Granger, James R., St. Henry, Lake Charles
Hebert, Malone, St. Theresa, Carlyss
Hinchee, Richard, Our Lady of Seven Dolors, Welsh
Kohlhund, Sumner, St. Joseph's, De Ridder
Landry, Dan, St. Margaret, Lake Charles
LaPoint, Frederick, St. Philip Neri, Kinder
Lavine, Edward, Sacred Heart, Lake Charles
Mathews, Michael, Supt. of Schools, Diocese of Lake Charles
McNally, Ed, Immaculate Conception, Jennings
Mounce, Johnny, Our Lady of LaSalette, Sulphur
Reed, Frederick, St. John Bosco, Westlake
Reynolds, Jack J., St. Theodore's, Lake Charles
Serice, Maurice, Our Lady of LaSalette, Sulphur
Stearns, George, Our Lady of Good Counsel, Lake Charles
Thompson, Paul, Holy City Community, Lake Charles
Viau, Glenn, Our Lady of Good Counsel, Lake Charles
Wagner, Harry E., Jr., Immaculate Conception Cathedral, Lake Charles
White, Milton, Immaculate Conception Cathedral, Lake Charles

INSTITUTIONS LOCATED IN THE DIOCESE

[A] HIGH SCHOOLS, INTERPAROCHIAL

LAKE CHARLES. *St. Louis High School*, 1620 Bank St., 70601. Tel: 337-436-7275. Vic Bonnaffee, Prin. Lay Teachers 42; Students 593.
For Catholic Studies: 920 Seventh St. Tel: 337-439-7432.

[B] GENERAL HOSPITALS

LAKE CHARLES. *CHRISTUS St. Patrick Hospital of Lake Charles*, 524 S. Ryan St., 70601. Tel: 337-436-2511; Fax: 337-430-4300
For a complete listing, refer to the Hospitals section.

[C] RETREAT HOUSES

LAKE CHARLES. *Holy City Community*, 5611 Welcome Rd., 70611. Tel: 337-855-2871. Deacon Ed McNally, Moderator & Admin.; Rev. Oris Broussard, Chap.

MOSS BLUFF. *St. Charles Center*, 2151 Sam Houston Jones Pkwy., 70611. Tel: 337-855-1232; Fax: 337-855-9062. Rev. Don Piraro, Dir.

[D] MONASTERIES AND RESIDENCES OF PRIESTS AND BROTHERS

ELTON.
Herald of Good News, Inc., P.O. Box 789, 70532. Tel: 337-584-2038. Rev. Jose Vattakunnel.

[E] SPECIAL RESIDENCES

LAKE CHARLES. *Our Lady Queen of Heaven Manor*, Villa Maria, 3905 Kingston St., 70605. Tel: 337-478-4780; Fax: 337-474-8822. Rev. Msgr. Irving A. DeBlanc, Pres. Units 62.

[F] NEWMAN CENTERS

LAKE CHARLES. *Catholic Student Center*, McNeese State University, 221 Aqua Dr., 70605. Tel: 337-477-1434; Fax: 337-479-2129. Rev. Jace Eskind; Sr. Shirley Gobert, S.E.C., Campus Min.; Kerry Berryhill, Campus Min.

[G] SOCIAL SERVICE CENTERS

LAKE CHARLES. *Catholic Service Center*, 2333 E. Broad St., 70601. Tel: 337-439-7436, Ext. 11; Fax: 337-439-7435. Deacon Edward Lavine, Dir.

[H] MISCELLANEOUS

LAKE CHARLES. *School Food Services of Lake Charles, Inc.*, 411 Iris St., 70601. Tel: 337-439-7426, Ext. 24; Fax: 337-439-7428.

RELIGIOUS INSTITUTES OF MEN REPRESENTED IN THE DIOCESE

For further details refer to the corresponding bracketed number in the Religious Institutes of Men or Women section.

[0275]—*Carmelites of Mary Immaculate.*—C.M.I.
[]—*Heralds of Good News.*
[0690]—*Jesuit Fathers and Brothers.*—S.J.
[0720]—*The Missionaries of Our Lady of La Salette.* (Prov. of Mary Queen).—M.S.
[0700]—*St. Joseph's Society of the Sacred Heart.*—S.S.J.

RELIGIOUS INSTITUTES OF WOMEN REPRESENTED IN THE DIOCESE

[1010]—*Congregation of Divine Providence of San Antonio, Texas.*—C.D.P.
[0470]—*Congregation of the Sisters of Charity of the Incarnate Word, Houston, Texas.*—C.C.V.I.
[]—*Daughters of Mary, Mother of Mercy.*
[1140]—*Eucharistic Missionaries of St. Dominic.*—O.P.
[]—*Sisters of Emanuel.*—S.E.
[3830-16]—*Sisters of St. Joseph.*—S.S.J.
[]—*Sisters of the Eucharistic Covenant.*—S.E.C.

NECROLOGY

† Bernard, Rev. Msgr. Murphy J., (Retired).—Died Sept. 4, 2000.
† Vidrine, Rev. Msgr. Curtis S., (Retired).—Died Oct. 23, 2000.

Diocese of Lansing

(Dioecesis Lansingensis)

Most Reverend

CARL F. MENGELING, D.D., S.T.D.

Bishop of Lansing; ordained May 25, 1957; appointed Bishop of Lansing November 7, 1995; consecrated and installed January 25, 1996. *Address all communications to Chancery: 300 W. Ottawa St., Lansing, MI, 48933.* Tel.: 517-342-2452; Fax: 517-342-2505.

Most Reverend

KENNETH J. POVISH, D.D.

Retired Bishop of Lansing; ordained June 3, 1950; appointed Bishop of Crookston July 28, 1970; consecrated September 29, 1970; appointed Bishop of Lansing October 8, 1975; installed December 11, 1975; retired November 7, 1995. *Res., 401-A E. Madison, DeWitt, MI, 48820.*

ESTABLISHED MAY 22, 1937.

CANONICALLY ERECTED AUGUST 4, 1937.

Square Miles 6,218.

Comprises the Counties of Clinton, Eaton, Genesee, Hillsdale, Ingham, Jackson, Lenawee, Livingston, Shiawassee and Washtenaw, in the State of Michigan.

For legal titles of parishes and diocesan institutions, consult the Chancery Office.

Chancery: 300 W. Ottawa, Lansing, MI, 48933. Tel.: 517-342-2440; Fax: 517-342-2515.

Web site address: www.dioceseoflansing.org

E-mail address: chancery@dioceseoflansing.org

STATISTICAL OVERVIEW

Personnel	
Bishop	1
Retired Bishops	1
Priests: Diocesan Active in Diocese	101
Priests: Active Outside Diocese	11
Priests: Retired, Sick or Absent	31
Number of Diocesan Priests	143
Religious Priests in Diocese	32
Extern Priests in Diocese	27
Ordinations:	
Diocesan Priests	3
Religious Priests	1
Transitional Deacons	6
Permanent Deacons	20
Permanent Deacons in Diocese	73
Total Brothers	12
Total Sisters	484
Parishes	
Parishes	95
With Resident Pastor:	
Resident Diocesan Priests	76
Resident Religious Priests	8
Without Resident Pastor:	
Administered by Priests	2
Administered by Professed Men Religious	1
Administered by Women Religious	6
Administered by Lay People	2
Pastoral Centers	2
Professional Ministry Personnel:	
Brothers	3
Sisters	35
Lay Ministers	156
Welfare	
Catholic Hospitals	4
Total Assisted	1,388,260
Health Care Centers	3
Total Assisted	7,102
Homes for the Aged	2
Total Assisted	400
Day Care and Extended Day Care Centers	1
Total Assisted	100
Specialized Homes	4
Total Assisted	287
Special Centers for Social Services	13
Total Assisted	165,899
Residential Care of Disabled	1
Total Assisted	70
Educational	
Diocesan Students in Other Seminaries	27
Total Seminarians	27
Colleges and Universities	2
Total Students	3,877
High Schools, Diocesan and Parish	4
Total Students	2,483
High Schools, Private	2
Total Students	176
Elementary Schools, Diocesan and Parish	37
Total Students	9,809
Elementary Schools, Private	5
Total Students	710
Catechesis/Religious Education:	
High School Students	3,100
Elementary Students	21,700
Total Students Under Catholic Instruction	41,882
Teachers in the Diocese:	
Priests	6
Brothers	1
Sisters	18
Lay Teachers	636
Vital Statistics	
Receptions into the Church:	
Infant Baptism Totals	4,041
Adult Baptism Totals	695
Received into Full Communion	1,344
First Communions	4,829
Confirmations	3,778
Marriages:	
Catholic	892
Interfaith	629
Total Marriages	1,521
Deaths	2,045
Total Catholic Population	224,166
Total Population	1,722,146

Former Bishops—Most Rev. JOSEPH H. ALBERS, D.D., J.C.D., appt. Titular Bishop of Lunda and Auxiliary to the Archbishop of Cincinnati, Dec. 16, 1929; cons. Dec. 27, 1929; appt. first Bishop of Lansing, Aug. 4, 1937; died Dec. 1, 1965.—Most Rev. ALEXANDER M. ZALESKI, D.D., S.S.L., appt. Titular Bishop of Lyrbe and Auxiliary of Detroit, March 28, 1950; cons. May 23, 1950; transferred to Lansing Oct. 7, 1964; acceded See Dec. 1, 1965; died May 16, 1975.—Most Rev. KENNETH J. POVISH, D.D., appt. Bishop of Crookston, July 28, 1970; cons. Sept. 29, 1970; appt. Bishop of Lansing, Oct. 8, 1975; installed Dec. 11, 1975; retired Nov. 7, 1995.

Chancery—300 W. Ottawa St., Lansing, 48933. Tel: 517-342-2440; Fax: 517-342-2519. (see Diocesan Departments for additional Fax numbers). Office Hours: Mon.-Fri. 8-12; 1-4:30. Address all communications to this office.

Bishop's Office—300 W. Ottawa St., Lansing, 48933. Tel: 517-342-2452; Fax: 517-342-2505. Rev. Msgr. ROBERT D. LUNSFORD, Chancellor and Administrative Asst. to the Bishop. Tel: 517-342-2454. Rev. Msgr. MICHAEL D. MURPHY, Moderator of the Curia. Tel: 517-342-2450. Rev. GEORGE C. MICHALEK, Vice Chancellor. Tel: 517-485-9902.

Vicar General—Rev. Msgr. RICHARD GROSHEK, *St. Pius X Church, G-3139 Hogarth Ave., Flint, 48532.* Tel: 810-235-8574; Fax: 810-235-8580.

Regional Vicars—Rev. MATTHEW FEDEWA, Lansing; Rev. VINCENT DELORENZO, Genesee/Owosso; Rev. JAMES SHAVER, Jackson; Rev. DANIEL WHEELER, Lenawee; Rev. DAVID HOWELL, Livingston; Rev. THOMAS FIRESTONE, Washtenaw.

College of Consultors—Rev. Msgr. SYLVESTER FEDEWA; Revs. THOMAS BUTLER; PAUL GREHL; MARK INGLOT; ROBERT KERR; JOHN KLEIN; DAN MCKEAN; ROGER PROKOP; DARIN ROBERT; DONALD RUSCH.

Vicar for Charismatic Communities—Rev. WILLIAM ASHBAUGH, *St. Joseph Church, 440 E. Washington, Howell, 48843.* Tel: 517-546-0090.

Vicar for Religious—Rev. Msgr. MICHAEL D. MURPHY, *Chancery Office, 300 W. Ottawa St., Lansing, 48933.* Tel: 517-342-2450; Fax: 517-342-2505.

Ecumenical Officer—Rev. ROBERT T. KERR, *St. Joseph Church, 9425 Whittaker Rd., Ypsilanti, 48197.* Tel: 734-461-6555; Fax: 734-461-1444.

Commissions and Councils—
Pastoral Council—SALLY ELLIS, Exec. Sec., *300 W. Ottawa St., Lansing, 48933.* Tel: 517-342-2517; Fax: 517-342-2468.
Presbyteral Council—Rev. ROGER PROKOP, Chm., *St. Thomas the Apostle, 520 Elizabeth St., Ann Arbor, 48104.* Tel: 734-761-8606; Fax: 734-997-8432.
Board of Education and Catechesis—RICHARD SPANKE, Pres., *2733 Eason, Howell, 48843.* Tel: 517-373-1358.
Building Commission—Rev. GILBERT O. RAHRIG.
Cursillo Movement—Rev. Msgr. SYLVESTER L. FEDEWA, Spiritual Dir., *120 N. Willow St., Box 412, Westphalia, 48894.* Tel: 517-587-4379.
Conciliation/Arbitration—WILLIAM D. PARSLEY, *232 S. Capitol, Ste. 1000, Lansing, 48933.* Tel: 517-482-2400.
Finance Council—Rev. FRANCIS WILLIAMS, *401 B E. Madison, DeWitt, 48820.* Tel: 517-669-7127.
Priest's Assignment Commission—Vacant.

Diocesan Offices And Departments

Moderator of the Curia—Rev. Msgr. MICHAEL D. MURPHY. Tel: 517-342-2450; Fax: 517-342-2505.
Cemeteries—PAUL GARRIEPY, Dir. Tel: 517-342-2534.
Diocesan Archivist—Rev. GEORGE C. MICHALEK, *300 W. Ottawa St., Lansing, 48933.* Tel: 517-485-9902; Fax: 517-484-8880.
Diocesan Mission Office—(Includes Propagation of the Faith, Holy Childhood Assoc., Inter-Parish Sharing) Rev. TIMOTHY KRZYZANIAK, Dir., *109 Linden St., St. Johns, 48879.* Tel: 517-227-8774; Fax: 517-227-8565.
Legal Advisor—HARRY IWASKO. Tel: 517-342-2456; Fax: 517-342-2505.
Diocesan Tribunal—
Judicial Vicar—Rev. Msgr. RAYMOND J. GOEHRING, J.C.L., *300 W. Ottawa St., Lansing, 48933.* Tel: 517-484-8870; Fax: 517-484-9080. (Address all rogatory commissions to the Diocesan Tribunal.).
Tribunal Judges—Rev. JEFFREY KASSIAN, J.C.L.; Rev. Msgr. SYLVESTER L. FEDEWA, S.T.L.; EILEEN JARAMILLO, J.C.L.
Defender of the Bond—Rev. BENNETT P. CONSTANTINE, J.C.D.; JOHN CAMERON.
Promoter of Justice—Rev. CHARLES IRVIN.
Auditor/Assessor—JOHN CAMERON; Rev. WILLIAM THOMAS.
Court Expert—RICHARD G. STRIFE, Ph.D.
Notaries—VIRGINIA A. DELUCA; WANDA D. MILLER.
Office of Pastoral Planning—Sr. RITA WENZLICK, O.P., Dir. Tel: 517-342-2502; Fax: 517-342-2468.
Christian Initiation Steering Committee—Sr. RITA WENZLICK, O.P., Chm. Tel: 517-342-2502.
Faith Magazine—PATRICK O'BRIEN, Editor. Tel: 517-342-2595.
Department of Catholic Charities—ROBERT J. SMITH, A.C.S.W., Chm. Tel: 517-342-2562; Fax: 517-342-2446.
Aging Ministry—ELLEN MCKAY, A.C.S.W., Dir. Tel: 517-342-2467.
Bishop's Council on Alcoholism-Chemical Dependency—ROBERT LAPRAD, Dir. Tel: 517-342-2513.
Campaign for Human Development—Vacant.
Catholic Relief Services—Vacant.
Family Life Ministry—SANDRA MILLAR. Tel: 517-342-2471.
Natural Family Planning—SANDRA MILLAR. Tel: 517-342-2471.
Peace and Justice Ministry—C. MICHAEL LIBERATO, Dir. Tel: 517-342-2466.
Respect Life Ministry—C. MICHAEL LIBERATO, Dir. Tel: 517-342-2466.
Project Rachel (Post-Abortion Counseling)—TONI ROSSI, Dir., *1500 E. Saginaw, Lansing, 48906.* Tel: 517-484-4449; Fax: 517-484-8880.
Diocesan Council on Womens Concerns—JOHANNA VANDEN BERG. Tel: 517-342-2465.
Department of Communication—MICHAEL DIEBOLD, Chm. Tel: 517-342-2475; Fax: 517-342-2519.
Department of Diocesan Ministries—Dr. RICHARD STRIFE, Ph.D., Chm. Tel: 517-342-2500; Fax: 517-342-2468.
Black Catholic Ministry—RONALD LANDFAIR, Dir. Tel: 517-342-2496.
Campus Ministries—Rev. THOMAS FIRESTONE, *St. Mary Student Parish, 331 Thompson St., Ann Arbor, 48104.* Tel: 734-663-0557; Fax: 734-663-2756.
Ministry with Persons with Disabilities/Deaf Ministry/Catholic Inquiry for the Blind—RICHARD STRIFE, Ph.D., Dir. Tel: 517-342-2500. Sr. MARLENE TAYLOR, A.D., Outreach Worker. Tel: 517-342-2500. Rev. MICHAEL DEPCIK, O.S.F.S. Tel: 810-233-6992 (TTY); 800-649-3777 (Voice).
Hispanic/Migrant Ministry—SERAPIO C. HERNANDEZ, Dir. Tel: 517-342-2498.
Worship Office—Rev. DAVID HARVEY, Dir. RITA THIRON, Assoc. Dir. Tel: 517-342-2480.
Worship Commission—Rev. WILLIAM WEGHER. Tel: 810-238-2679.
Music Consultant—Dr. TIMOTHY FLYNN. Tel: 517-342-2473.
Young Adult Ministry/Criminal Justice Ministry—GARY ASHBY, Dir. Tel: 517-342-2495.
Department of Education and Catechesis—Sr. DORITA WOTISKA, O.P., Ph.D., Chm. Tel: 517-342-2481; Fax: 517-342-2515.
Superintendent of Schools—Sr. DORITA WOTISKA, O.P. Tel: 517-342-2481.
Instructional Programs PreK-12—MARY OLIVE DION, Dir. Tel: 517-342-2483.
Catechesis—PETER RIES, Dir. Tel: 517-342-2486.
Youth Ministry—JAMES CORDER, Dir. Tel: 517-342-2485.
Department of Finance—THOMAS PASTULA, Chm. & Finance Officer. Tel: 517-342-2442; Fax: 517-342-2519.
Development—JAY JOHNSON, Dir. Tel: 517-342-2503.
Real Estate/Environmental Issues—CHARLES BAKER. Tel: 517-342-2443.
Technology Administrator—SHARON BYERS. Tel: 517-342-2538; Fax: 517-342-2515.
Department of Formation and Lay Ministry—Rev. J. THOMAS MUNLEY, Chm. Tel: 517-342-2507; Fax: 517-342-2515.
Assistant Director of Seminarians—Rev. KARL PUNG. Tel: 517-342-2507.
Joseph H. Albers Trust Fund for Diocesan Vocations—Rev. J. THOMAS MUNLEY. Tel: 517-342-2507.
Lay Ministry—MARY TARDIF, Dir. Tel: 517-342-2512.
Permanent Diaconate—Rev. WILLIAM ASHBAUGH, Dir. Tel: 517-342-2509. WILLIAM SIRL, Asst. Dir. Tel: 517-342-2451.
Priestly Life and Ministry—Rev. LARRY DELANEY, Dir. Tel: 517-669-8321; 669-8279; Fax: 517-669-2708.
Vocation Services—Sr. CARLA MOEGGENBORG, O.P., Dir. Tel: 517-342-2506.
Discernment Houses—
Emmaus House—Rev. J. THOMAS MUNLEY, Dir., *320 M.A.C. Ave., East Lansing, 48823.* Tel: 517-351-1543.
CHI RHO—Rev. ROGER PROKOP, Dir., *St. Thomas the Apostle Church, 520 E. Elizabeth St., Ann Arbor, 48104.* Tel: 734-761-8606.

CLERGY, PARISHES, MISSIONS AND PAROCHIAL SCHOOLS

CITY OF LANSING
(Ingham County)

1—ST. MARY CATHEDRAL (1866), Rev. Msgr. Michael D. Murphy; Rev. Michael A. Petroski. In res., Rev. Msgr. Robert D. Lunsford.
Res., 219 Seymour, 48933. Tel: 517-484-5331; Fax: 517-484-0475.

2—ST. CASIMIR (1921), Rev. William Lugger.
Res., 815 Sparrow Ave., 48910-8003. Tel: 517-482-1347; Fax: 517-482-1313.
Catechesis/Religious Programs—Tel: 517-482-1346.
Students 118.

3—HOLY CROSS (1924), Rev. Pius Poff, O.F.M.Conv. In res., Revs. Bonaventure Crowley, O.F.M.Conv.; Timothy Byrnes.
Res., 1611 Oakland Ave., 48915. Tel: 517-484-7768; Fax: 517-484-5741.
School—1514 W. Saginaw St., 48915. Tel: 517-487-6079; Fax: 517-487-6695. Jeanne Gratz, Prin.
Lay Teachers 5; Students 80.
Catechesis/Religious Programs—Students 60.

4—IMMACULATE HEART OF MARY (1949), Revs. John Byers; Joseph Mundadan; Deacons William Fudge, III; John Cameron; Oliver G. Washington. In res., Rev. Gildasio Dos Santos, S.D.B. (Brazil).
Office: 3815 S. Cedar, 48910. Tel: 517-393-3030; Fax: 517-393-0855.
School—Tel: 517-882-6631.
Lay Teachers 17; Students 343.
Catechesis/Religious Programs—Tel: 517-393-3033.
Students 346.

5—RESURRECTION (1922), Rev. William J. Koenigsknecht.
Res., 1531 E. Michigan Ave., 48912. Tel: 517-482-4749; Fax: 517-484-4740.
School—Tel: 517-487-0439; Fax: 517-487-3198.
Lay Teachers 14; Students 234.
Catechesis/Religious Programs—1527 E. Michigan Ave., 48912. Tel: 517-482-2605.
Students 110.

6—ST. ANDREW DUNG-LAC (1998) (Vietnamese), Rev. Joseph Tran.
5430 S. Washington Ave., 48911. Tel: 517-882-8205; Fax: 517-882-8209.
Catechesis/Religious Programs—3220 Boston Blvd., 48910. Tel: 517-887-9308. Trang Van Le, D.R.E.
Students 38.

7—ST. GERARD (Delta Township, Eaton Co.) (1958), Revs. John P. Klein; Timothy MacDonald; Deacons Edwin Schneider; Robert McPhilamy; Richard Savage.
Res., 4437 W. Willow, 48917. Tel: 517-323-2379; Fax: 517-886-1394. [JC]
School—4433 W. Willow, 48917. Tel: 517-321-6126; Fax: 517-323-8046.
Lay Teachers 28; Students 524.
Catechesis/Religious Programs—Tel: 517-321-4179.
Students 423.

8—ST. THERESE (1949), Rev. Michael W. Kuchar; Sr. Margaret Ann Roggenbuck, O.P., Pastoral Min.; Deacon David Borzenski.
Res., 102 W. Randolph St., 48906. Tel: 517-487-3749; Fax: 517-487-3755. [CEM]
School—2620 N. Turner St., 48906. Tel: 517-482-1634. Mrs. Jan Nurenberg, Prin.
Lay Teachers 10; Students 96.
Catechesis/Religious Programs—Tel: 517-487-3730. Mary Langguth, D.R.E.
Students 108.

9—CRISTO REY (1961) (Hispanic), Rev. Frederick L. Thelen; Deacon Rogelio Alfaro.
Office: 201 W. Miller Rd., 48911. Tel: 517-394-4639; Fax: 517-394-8090.
Res., 6121 Rosedale Rd., 48911. Tel: 517-394-0676.
Catechesis/Religious Programs—Students 120.

OUTSIDE THE CITY OF LANSING

Adrian, Lenawee Co., St. Joseph (1864), Rev. Michael J. Williams.
Res., 415 Ormsby St., 49221. Tel: 517-265-8938; Fax: 517-265-1987. [CEM]
Catechesis/Religious Programs—Students 190.
Convent—404 Finch St., 49221. Tel: 517-263-1973.
St. Mary of Good Counsel (1853), Rev. Thomas J. Helfrich, O.S.F.S.; Deacons Richard Bayes, Jr.; Calistro Torres; Sr. Regina Albers, C.P.P.S. In res., Revs. Joseph M. Baraniewicz, O.S.F.S.; Louis A. Komorowski, O.S.F.S.
Office: 305 Division St., 49221. Tel: 517-263-4681; Fax: 517-263-4682.
Res., 320 Division St., 49221. Tel: 517-265-6543. [CEM]
Catechesis/Religious Programs—Tel: 517-265-4160; Fax: 517-263-4682.
Students 349.

Ann Arbor

1—CHRIST THE KING (1981), Rev. Edward O. Fride (LAN); Deacons Daniel R. Foley; Gerald P. Holowicki; Louis J. Russello. In res., Rev. Liam M. Barr (LIN).
4000 Ave Maria Dr., 48105. Tel: 734-665-5040; Fax: 734-663-3735.
Catechesis/Religious Programs—Tel: 734-663-3873.
Students 355.

2—ST. FRANCIS OF ASSISI, Washtenaw Co., (1950), Revs. James G. McDougall; Jay Joseph Kersten.
Res., 2150 Frieze Ave., 48104. Tel: 734-769-2550; Fax: 734-821-2102. [CEM]
School—(Grades K-8). Tel: 734-821-2203; Fax: 734-821-2202.
Lay Teachers 28; Students 525.
Catechesis/Religious Programs—Tel: 734-821-2130.
Students 860.

3—ST. PATRICK, Washtenaw Co., (1831), Rev. Terrence J. Dumas.
Res., 5671 Whitmore Lake Rd., 48105. Tel: 734-662-8141; 663-1851; Fax: 734-994-9136. [CEM]
Catechesis/Religious Programs—Students 230.

4—ST. THOMAS THE APOSTLE, Washtenaw Co., (1835), Revs. Roger Prokop; Gerald L. Vincke; Sr. Diane Meuller, Business Mgr.; Deacons James Miles; Warren Hecht.
517 Elizabeth St., 48104. Tel: 734-761-8606; Fax: 734-997-8432. [CEM]
School—Tel: 734-769-0911; Fax: 734-769-9078.
Sisters 1; Lay Teachers 17; Students 287.
Catechesis/Religious Programs—Tel: 734-761-8606. Elizabeth Martin, D.R.E.
Students 430.

5—ST. MARY STUDENT PARISH, Washtenaw Co., (1915), Revs. Thomas M. Firestone; Dennis T. Glasgow, S.J.; Nicole J. Smith, Campus Min.; Grace M. Girvan, Business Mgr.; Susan L. Waters, Devel. Dir. Pastoral Assocs.: Anita M. Bohn; Patrick J. Waters.

Office: 331 Thompson St., 48104-2295. Tel: 734-663-0557; 0558; Fax: 734-663-2756. (Serving students, faculty, and staff at the University of Michigan.).

Bellevue, Eaton Co., St. Ann (1923). (Quasi Parish). Rev. Msgr. Raymond Goehring, Admin.
Res., 312 S. Main St., 49021. Tel: 616-763-9372; Fax: 616-763-0067.

Blissfield, Lenawee Co., St. Peter the Apostle (1910), Rev. Vincent H. Van Doan; Deacon James Martinez.
Res., 309 S. Lane St., 49228. Tel: 517-486-2156; Fax: 517-486-2157.
Catechesis/Religious Programs—Students 143.

Brighton, Livingston Co., St. Mary Magdalen Church (1993),
Res., 2201 Old U.S. 23, 48114. Tel: 810-229-8624; Fax: 810-229-6471. Rev. David Howell; Deacon H. David Scharf.
Catechesis/Religious Programs—Students 645.

St. Patrick (1832) (Irish), Revs. Dan J. McKean; Bob Pienta; Deacon Patrick A. McDonald. Pastoral Ministers: Sr. Theresa M. Fifer, O.S.F.; Margaret Mullally-Henne; Mary Ann Helie; Robert Wolf; Martha Goode; H. William Smeal. In res., Rev. William J. Carolin Tel: 810-229-8646.
Res., 711 Rickett Rd., 48116. Tel: 810-229-9863; Fax: 810-220-0730. [CEM]
School—710 Rickett Rd., 48116. Tel: 810-229-7946; Fax: 810-229-6206. Judy McCusker, Prin.
Lay Teachers 16; Students 266.
Catechesis/Religious Programs—Tel: 810-229-4221; Fax: 810-229-6206. Sr. Theresa M. Fifer, O.S.F., D.R.E.
Students 1,154.

Brooklyn, Lenawee Co., St. Joseph's Shrine (Irish Hills) (1845), Rev. Carl A. Simon.
Res., 8743 U.S. 12, 49230. Tel: 517-467-2183; Fax: 517-467-4285. [CEM]
Catechesis/Religious Programs—Tel: 517-467-2106.
Students 181.

Burton, Genesee Co., Blessed Sacrament (1957) (Hungarian), Rev. Joseph S. Kim; John Griffith, Pastoral Assoc.; Deacon Ronald Rowe.
Res., 6340 Roberta, 48509. Tel: 810-742-3151; Fax: 810-742-1409.
Catechesis/Religious Programs—Paul Schlegelmilch, D.R.E.
Students 134.

Holy Redeemer 1940, Revs. Vincent DeLorenzo; Timothy Nelson; Earl Matte, Pastoral Min.
Res., 1227 E. Bristol Rd., 48529. Tel: 810-743-3050; Fax: 810-743-4381.
School—3468 S. Grand Traverse, 48529. Tel: 810-743-2520; Fax: 810-743-9102. Carol Olson, Prin.
Lay Teachers 20; Students 229.
Catechesis/Religious Programs—Tel: 810-742-9460. Susan Kachel, D.R.E.
Students 330.

Charlotte, Eaton Co., St. Mary (1868), Rev. Denis R. Spitzley.
Res., 812 St. Mary Blvd., 48813. Tel: 517-543-4319; Fax: 517-543-9078.
School—905 St. Mary Blvd., 48813. Tel: 517-543-3460.
Lay Teachers 6; Students 104.
Catechesis/Religious Programs—Tel: 517-543-3460.
Students 257.

Chelsea, Washtenaw Co., St. Mary (1845), Rev. William J. Turner; Deacons Richard Shaneyfelt; Thomas Franklin.
Res., 14200 Old U.S. 12, 48118. Tel: 313-475-7561; Fax: 313-475-3207. [CEM][JC]
Catechesis/Religious Programs—Tel: 313-475-8164; Fax: 313-475-3250.
Students 470.

Clarklake, Jackson Co., St. Rita (1916), Rev. Lehr Barkenquest, O.S.F.S.; Deacon Louis Weitzel.
Res., 10720 Hayes Rd., 49234. Tel: 517-592-5470; Fax: 517-592-4098.
Catechesis/Religious Programs—Tel: 517-592-5718.
Students 143.

Clinton, Lenawee Co., St. Dominic's (1853), Rev. Donald P. Rusch.
Res., 220 Brown St., 49236. Tel: 517-456-4559; Fax: 517-456-4559. [CEM]
Catechesis/Religious Programs—Students 82.

Clio, Genesee Co., SS. Charles and Helena (1953), Rev. Gerald J. Ploof.
Res., 230 E. Vienna St., 48420-1423. Tel: 810-686-9861; Fax: 810-686-8070.
Catechesis/Religious Programs—Tel: 810-686-6720.
Students 280.

Concord, Jackson Co., St. Catherine Laboure (1953), Joyce Rochow, Pastoral Coord.
Res., 211 Harmon Ave., P.O. Box 188, 49237. Tel: 517-524-7578; Fax: 517-524-7518.
Catechesis/Religious Programs—Students 127.

Davison, Genesee Co., St. John (1871), Rev. Andrew A. Czajkowski; Deacons Dan Fairweather; Neil Huiskens. In res., Rev. Leroy E. White.
Res., 404 N. Dayton St., 48423-1397. Tel: 810-653-2377; 653-8015; 658-4776 (Voice Mail); Fax: 810-658-1123. [CEM]
Catechesis/Religious Programs—425 N. Genesee, 48423. Tel: 810-653-4056. D.R.E.: Elaine Davis; Marianne Muehmel.
Students 724.

Deerfield, Lenawee Co., St. Alphonsus (1864), Rev. John Loughran, O.S.F.S.
Church Office: 222 Carey St., 49238. Tel: 517-447-3500; Fax: 517-447-3210; 447-3766 (Rectory). [CEM]
Catechesis/Religious Programs—Students 103.

De Witt, Clinton Co., St. Jude (1971), Rev. Dwight M. Ezop.
Res., 409 Wilson, P.O. Box 280, 48820. Tel: 517-669-8335; Fax: 517-669-8343.
Catechesis/Religious Programs—Tel: 517-669-8341.
Students 539.

Dexter, Washtenaw Co., St. Joseph (1840), Rev. Brendan J. Walsh; Deacon Romolo Leone.
Res., 3430 Dover St., 48130. Tel: 734-426-8483; Fax: 734-426-6451. [CEM]
Catechesis/Religious Programs—Tel: 734-426-2674; Fax: 734-426-6451.
Students 500.

Durand, Shiawassee Co., St. Mary (1900), Rev. Joseph Aubin.
Res., 700 Columbia Dr., 48429. Tel: 517-288-6704.
Catechesis/Religious Programs—Tel: 512-288-6704.
Students 145.

East Lansing, Ingham Co., St. John the Evangelist, Student Parish (1958), Rev. Mark Inglot. Campus Ministers: Sr. Mary Ann Warner, H.M.; Kathleen Kurta; Liz Schweitzer; Al Weilbaecher.
Res., 327 MAC, 48823. Tel: 517-337-9778; Fax: 517-337-8358.

St. Thomas Aquinas (1940), Revs. David J. Speicher; Dominic Tirkey (India); Deacon Stephen Hilker. In res., Rev. Joseph J. Krupp.
Res., 955 Alton Rd., 48823. Tel: 517-351-7215; Fax: 517-351-7271.
School—915 Alton Rd., 48823. Tel: 517-332-0813; Fax: 517-332-9490.
Lay Teachers 23; Religious 1; Students 472.
Catechesis/Religious Programs—Tel: 517-351-5460.
Students 437.

Eaton Rapids, Eaton Co., St. Peter (1891), Rev. Bennett Constantine.
Res., 515 E. Knight St., 48827. Tel: 517-663-4735; Fax: 517-663-7110.
Catechesis/Religious Programs—Tel: 517-665-2088. Nick Kostopoulos, D.R.E.
Students 127.

Fenton, Genesee Co., St. John (1843), Revs. David W. Harvey; Bernard Tyler.
Res., 600 N. Adelaide St., 48430. Tel: 810-629-2251; Fax: 810-629-2302. [CEM 2]
School—514 Lincoln St., 48430. Tel: 810-629-6551; Fax: 810-629-2213. Sr. Patricia Fischer, O.P., Prin.
Lay Teachers 17; Students 324.
Catechesis/Religious Programs—512 N. Adelaide St., 48430. Tel: 810-629-1850. D.R.E.: Elaine Schilling; Ronald Kenney.
Students 836.

Flint, Genesee Co.,

1—St. Agnes, (1928), Rev. James F. Eisele.
Res., 500 W. Pierson Rd., 48505. Tel: 810-785-3483; Fax: 810-785-4983.
Catechesis/Religious Programs—Students 18.

2—All Saints, (1910) (Polish), Rev. Anthony P. Majchrowski.
Res., G-4063 W. Pierson Rd., 48504. Tel: 810-787-0491. [CEM]
Catechesis/Religious Programs—Students 29.

3—Christ the King, (1929) (African American), Rev. John Aduba; Sr. Joanne Fedewa, S.L.W., Pastoral Coord.
Res., 1832 Seymour St., 48503. Tel: 810-233-0402; Fax: 810-233-0402.
Catechesis/Religious Programs—3202 Forest Hill, 48503. Tel: 810-239-5851; Fax: 810-239-9864.
Students 5.

4—St. Francis of Assisi. Closed. For inquiries for parish records contact the Chancery.

5—Holy Rosary, (1951), Rev. Paul Schwermer.
Res., 5199 Richfield Rd., 48506. Tel: 810-736-4040; Fax: 810-736-9129.
School—5191 Richfield Rd., 48506. Tel: 810-736-4220; Fax: 810-736-9129.
Lay Teachers 10; Students 188.
Catechesis/Religious Programs—Students 210.

6—Our Lady of Guadalupe, (1957) (Spanish), Rev. Eduardo Lorenzo.
Res., G-2316 W. Coldwater Rd., 48505. Tel: 810-787-5701; Fax: 810-787-3198.
Catechesis/Religious Programs—Tel: 810-789-7970.
Students 140.

7—St. John Vianney, (1941), Rev. Douglas Osborn.
Res., 2415 Bagley St., 48504. Tel: 810-235-1812; Fax: 810-235-4911.
School—2319 Bagley St., 48504. Tel: 810-235-5687; Fax: 810-235-2811. Mrs. Kathleen Slattery, Prin.
Sisters 2; Lay Teachers 18; Total Staff 20; Students 369.
Catechesis/Religious Programs—Students 369.

8—St. Leo the Great, (1957), Rev. James B. Bettendorf.
Res., 3632 Wyoming Ave., 48506. Tel: 810-736-2150; Fax: 810-736-0122.
Catechesis/Religious Programs—Tel: 810-736-7200.
Students 78.

9—St. Luke, (1950), Rev. Gary McInnis; Sr. Judith A. Blake, S.S.J., Pastoral Coord.
Res., 3202 Forest Hill, 48504. Tel: 810-239-5851; Fax: 810-239-9864.
Catechesis/Religious Programs—Tel: 810-232-1015.
Students 29.

10—St. Mary, (1919), Rev. Francis Faraci.
Res., 2500 N. Franklin Ave., 48506. Tel: 810-232-4012; Fax: 810-232-3889.
Catechesis/Religious Programs—Students 27.

11—St. Matthew, (1911), Rev. Frederick H. Taggart, O.S.A.
Res., 706 Beach St., 48502. Tel: 810-232-0880; Fax: 810-232-4148.
Catechesis/Religious Programs—Tel: 810-627-4123.
Students 18.

12—St. Michael, (1843), Rev. William F. Wegher; Sue Meissner, Pastoral Assoc.
Res., 609 E. Fifth Ave., 48503. Tel: 810-238-2679; Fax: 810-232-6820.
Catechesis/Religious Programs—Tel: 810-238-7931; Fax: 810-232-6820.
Students 120.

13—St. Pius X, (1955), Rev. Msgr. Richard J. Groshek; Revs. Cecilio Reyna; Michael Depcik, O.S.F.S.
Res., G-3139 Hogarth Ave., 48532. Tel: 810-235-8574; Fax: 810-235-8580.
School—Tel: 810-235-8572; Fax: 810-235-2675.
Sisters 1; Lay Teachers 12; Students 220.
Catechesis/Religious Programs—Tel: 810-235-8573.
Students 194.

14—Sacred Heart, (1928), Rev. Philip Schmitter; Dr. Connie McClanahan, Pastoral Coord.; Deacon Anthony Verdun.
Res., 719 E. Moore St., 48505. Tel: 810-789-8579. [CEM]
Catechesis/Religious Programs—Students 20.

Flushing, Genesee Co., St. Robert (1875), Revs. Steven F. Makranyi; Nicholas Ritter, O.S.A.; Deacon Michael Lynch.
Res., 310 N. Cherry St., 48433. Tel: 810-659-2501; Fax: 810-659-2564. [CEM]
School—Tel: 810-659-2503; Fax: 810-659-4002.
Lay Teachers 21; Students 443.
Catechesis/Religious Programs—Tel: 810-659-8556.
Students 490.

Fowler, Clinton Co., Most Holy Trinity (1881) (German), Revs. Raymond M. Rademacher; Vincent Ferrer, P.V.; Deacons Mark Simmon; Michael Barrett.
Res., Box 349, 48835. Tel: 517-593-2162; Fax: 517-593-2171. [CEM]
School—11144 Kent St., 48835. Tel: 517-593-2616.
Lay Teachers 7; Students 125.
Catechesis/Religious Programs—Tel: 517-593-3174; Fax: 517-593-2801.
Students 323.

Fowlerville, Livingston Co., St. Agnes (1891) (Irish-German-Polish), Rev. Karl L. Pung; Deacon Peter Guditas.
Res., 855 E. Grand River Ave., 48836. Tel: 517-223-8684; Fax: 517-223-0813. [CEM]
Catechesis/Religious Programs—Tel: 517-223-8684.
Students 400.

Gaines, Genessee Co., St. Joseph (1871), Rev. Robert McKeon; Sr. Ann Marie Petri, O.P., Pastoral Coord.; Deacon Currie Cormier.
Res., 118 E. Lord St., 48436. Tel: 517-271-8434; Fax: 517-271-3017. [CEM]
Catechesis/Religious Programs—Tel: 517-271-8434.
Students 128.

Goodrich, Genesee Co., St. Mark the Evangelist (1978), Sr. Joan M. May, S.S.J., Pastoral Coord.; Rev. Mark Dehetre.
Church—7296 Gale Rd., P.O. Box 131, 48438. Tel: 810-636-2216; Fax: 810-636-7319.
Catechesis/Religious Programs—Students 194.

Grand Blanc, Genesee Co., Holy Family (1946), Revs. James R. Swiat; Randall J. Miller.
Res., 11824 S. Saginaw, 48439. Tel: 810-694-4891; Fax: 810-694-1583.
School—(Grades PreK-8) 215 Orchard St., 48439. Tel: 810-694-9072; Fax: 810-694-9405.
Lay Teachers 31; Students 746.
Catechesis/Religious Programs—Tel: 810-694-9072, Ext. 28.
Students 416.

Grand Ledge, Eaton Co., St. Michael (1901), Rev. Robert H. McGraw.
Res., 345 Edwards, 48837. Tel: 517-627-8493; 627-8494; Fax: 517-627-1289.
School—Tel: 517-627-2167.
Lay Teachers 10; Students 197.
Catechesis/Religious Programs—Students 305.

Hamburg, Livingston Co., Holy Spirit (1979), Rev. William Thomas.
Res., P.O. Box 610, 48139. Tel: 810-231-9199; Fax: 810-231-6129.
Catechesis/Religious Programs—Tel: 810-231-6780.
Students 350.

Hartland, Livingston Co., St. John The Baptist (1843), Rev. Francis M. George; Deacons Francis Wines; David Piggot.
Res., 2099 Hacker Rd., Howell, 48843. Tel: 517-546-7200; Fax: 517-546-0403. [CEM]
Catechesis/Religious Programs—Tel: 517-548-2540; Fax: 517-546-0403.
Students 567.

Hillsdale, Hillsdale Co., St. Anthony (1858), Rev. Thomas W. Butler; Deacon Michael Nunez.
Res., 11 N. Broad St., 49242. Tel: 517-437-3305; Fax: 517-437-0034. [CEM]
Catechesis/Religious Programs—Tel: 517-437-2777.
Students 275.

Howell, Livingston Co., St. Augustine (1843). (Quasi Parish). Rev. Gregg A. Pleiness.
Church—6481 Fausset Rd., 48843. Tel: 517-546-9807. [CEM]
Res., 8011 Faussett Rd., Fenton, 48430.
Parish House: Tel: 810-750-0354.
Catechesis/Religious Programs—Students 155.

St. Joseph (1900), Rev. William A. Ashbaugh; Deacon Endre Doran.
Res., 440 E. Washington, 48843. Tel: 517-546-0090; Fax: 517-546-0090. [CEM]
School—425 E. Washington, 48843. Tel: 517-546-1380; Fax: 517-546-8939.
Lay Teachers 18; Students 350.
Catechesis/Religious Programs—Tel: 517-546-3171.
Students 661.

Hudson, Lenawee Co., Sacred Heart (1846), Rev. H. Paul Ruddy, O.S.F.S.
Res., 207 S. Market St., 49247. Tel: 517-448-3811; Fax: 517-448-3811. [CEM]
School—Tel: 517-448-6405.
Lay Teachers 7; Students 106.
Catechesis/Religious Programs—Students 118.

Jackson, Jackson Co.,

1—St. John the Evangelist, (1856), Revs. James R. Shaver; George Puthenpeedika; Deacon Joseph A. Kratofil. Pastoral Assocs.: Sr. Eileen Souva, O.P.; Patricia Willson.
Res., 711 Cooper St., 49201. Tel: 517-784-0553; Fax: 517-788-5381. [CEM][JC]
School—405 E. North St., 49202. Tel: 517-784-1714; Fax: 517-788-5382.
Lay Teachers 17; Students 341.
Catechesis/Religious Programs—Tel: 517-784-5746.
Students 275.

2—St. Joseph, (1902) (Polish-Lithuanian), Rev. Marian J. Lesniak.
Res., 705 N. Waterloo Ave., 49202. Tel: 517-784-9716; Fax: 517-784-5411. [JC]
School—717 N. Waterloo Ave., 49202. Tel: 517-784-4660; Fax: 517-784-3536.
Felician Sisters 2; Lay Teachers 8; Students 147.
Catechesis/Religious Programs—Students 20.

3—St. Mary, Star of the Sea, (1881), Rev. Bernard Reilly; Deacons William Everett; Vincent C. Genco.
Res., 120 E. Wesley St., 49201. Tel: 517-784-7184; Fax: 517-783-2571.
School—116 E. Wesley St., 49201. Tel: 517-784-8811; Fax: 517-788-3425.
Lay Teachers 11; Students 171.
Catechesis/Religious Programs—Tel: 517-788-6153.
Students 125.

4—Queen of the Miraculous Medal, (1934), Revs. Thomas D. Nenneau; Robert F. Copeland; Deacons David Barrett; Kenneth Spaulding; Jack Kowalski.
Res., 606 S. Wisner, 49203. Tel: 517-783-2748; Fax: 517-788-4528.
School—811 S. Wisner, 49203. Tel: 517-782-2664; Fax: 517-782-3570.
Lay Teachers 17; Students 442.
Catechesis/Religious Programs—Tel: 517-782-3609.
Students 239.

5—St. Stanislaus Kostka, (1920) (Polish), Rev. Canon Darius W. Wyszynski; Sr. Maristella Nowakowski, C.S.S.F., Pastoral Assoc., Tel: 517-782-5958.
Res., 608 S. Elm Ave., 49203. Tel: 517-784-0551; Fax: 517-784-2639. [CEM]
School—St. Stanislaus Kostka School Cooperative Interparish Venture with St. Mary's 614 S. Elm Ave., 49203. Tel: 517-784-0551; Fax: 517-784-2639. Julia Hurlburt, Prin.
Students 24.
Catechesis/Religious Programs—116 E. Wesley, 49203. Tel: 517-788-6153; Fax: 517-783-2571.
Students 31.

Laingsburg, Shiawassee Co., St. Isidore (1902), Rev. Duaine H. Pamment.
Res., 310 Crum St., 48848. Tel: 517-651-6617; 651-6722 (Office); Fax: 517-651-6722. [CEM]
Catechesis/Religious Programs—Tel: 517-651-6722.
Students 180.

Leslie, Ingham Co., SS. Cornelius and Cyprian (Bunker Hill) (1863), Rev. Eugene J. Beiter.
Res., 1320 Catholic Church Rd., 49251. Tel: 517-589-8492. [CEM]
Catechesis/Religious Programs—Students 98.

Manitou Beach, Lenawee Co., St. Mary on the Lake (1959), Sr. Helen Walling, I.H.M., Pastoral Coord.; Rev. Paul F. Grehl, O.S.F.S.
Res., 450 Manitou Rd., 49253. Tel: 517-547-7496; Fax: 517-547-7496.

Manchester, Washtenaw Co., St. Mary (1871), Rev. Charles E. Irvin.
Res., 210 W. Main St., P.O. Box 249, 48158. Tel: 734-428-8811; Fax: 734-428-1393. [CEM]
Catechesis/Religious Programs—Students 199.

Mason, Ingham Co., St. James (1942), Rev. Alan J. Wakefield; Deacon Thomas Feiten, Pastoral Assoc.
Office: 1010 S. Lansing St., 48854. Tel: 517-676-9111; Fax: 517-676-1343.
Catechesis/Religious Programs—Rose Robertson, D.R.E.
Students 365.

Michigan Center, Jackson Co., Our Lady of Fatima (1954), Revs. Andrew J. Dunne, O.S.F.S.; Thomas J. Smith, O.S.F.S.
Res., 913 Napoleon Rd., 49254. Tel: 517-764-2088; 764-2112; Fax: 517-764-0461.
School—911 Napoleon Rd., 49254. Tel: 517-764-2563.
Lay Teachers 10; Students 148.
Catechesis/Religious Programs—Tel: 517-764-1321.
Students 170.

Milan, Washtenaw Co., Immaculate Conception (1854), Rev. John M. Bosco.
Church—420 North St., 48160. Tel: 734-439-2667; Fax: 734-439-2030.
Catechesis/Religious Programs—Tel: 734-439-2030.
Students 198.

Montrose, Genesee Co., Good Shepherd (1979), Sr. Josephine McNamara, Pastoral Coord.; Revs. Eoin Murphy (Ireland); Gildasio Dos Santos, S.D.B. (Brazil).
Res., 400 N. Saginaw, P.O. Box 3274, 48457-0974. Tel: 810-639-7600; Fax: 810-639-7600.
Catechesis/Religious Programs—Tel: 810-639-3245.
Students 156.

Morrice, Shiawassee Co., St. Mary (1892), Rev. Matthew J. Fedewa; Deacon Gary Edington.
Res., 509 N. Main St., P.O. Box K, 48857. Tel: 517-625-4260; Fax: 517-625-3050. [CEM]
Catechesis/Religious Programs—Tel: 517-625-6140.
Students 211.

Mount Morris, Genesee Co., St. Mary (1867), Rev. Raymond J. Urbanek.
Res., 11110 Saginaw St., 48458. Tel: 810-686-3920; Fax: 810-686-0759. [CEM]
School—Tel: 810-686-4790; Fax: 810-686-4749.
Sisters of the Immaculate Heart of Mary 2; Lay Teachers 12; Students 199.
Catechesis/Religious Programs—Students 151.

Okemos, Ingham Co., St. Martha (1988), Rev. Jonathan Wehrle; Deacons Thomas Quasarano; Vince Guarnaccia.
Church—1100 W. Grand River, 48864. Tel: 517-349-1763; Fax: 517-349-7602.
School—Tel: 517-349-3322.
Sisters of Charity 4; Lay Teachers 8; Students 125.
Catechesis/Religious Programs—Students 688.

Otisville, Genesee Co., St. Francis Xavier (1947), Rev. Eoin Murphy (Ireland); Deacon Richard Soucy.
212 Center St., 48463. Tel: 810-631-6305; Fax: 810-631-4412. [JC]
Catechesis/Religious Programs—Students 110.

Ovid, Shiawassee Co., Holy Family (1966). (Mission). Rev. Paul J. Cummings.
Res., 620 N. Mabbitt Rd., P.O. Box 612, 48866. Tel: 517-834-5855; Fax: 517-834-1208.
Catechesis/Religious Programs—Tel: 517-834-2138.
Students 114.

Owosso, Shiawassee Co., St. Paul (1871), Rev. Robert D. Kolenski; Deacon Tom Moore.
Res., 111 N. Howell St., 48867. Tel: 517-723-4277; Fax: 517-723-9503. [CEM 2]
School—738 W. Main St., 48867. Tel: 517-725-7766.
Lay Teachers 11; Students 189.
Catechesis/Religious Programs—718 W. Main St., 48867. Tel: 517-723-1400.
Students 173.

St. Joseph (1923) (Slavic), Rev. David E. Fisher; Mary Ann Dunn, Pastoral Min.
Res., 915 E. Oliver St., 48867. Tel: 517-725-5215; Fax: 517-725-1519.
School—811 E. Oliver St., 48867. Tel: 517-725-8067; Fax: 517-725-1802.
Students 69.
St. Joseph Child Care Services—Tel: 517-723-2030. Child Care 119.
Catechesis/Religious Programs—811 E. Oliver St., 48867. Tel: 517-723-4765.
Students 156.

Pinckney, Livingston Co., St. Mary (1857), Rev. Kenneth F. Coughlin.
Res., 551 E. Hamburg St., 48169. Tel: 734-878-3161; Fax: 734-878-2383. [CEM]
School—Tel: 734-878-5616.
Lay Teachers 12; Students 211.
Catechesis/Religious Programs—Tel: 734-878-2217.
Students 440.

St. Johns, Clinton Co., St. Joseph (1874), Rev. Timothy D. Krzyzaniak; Deacon Marvin Robertson.
Res., 109 Linden St., 48879. Tel: 517-224-8994; Fax: 517-224-3475.
School—Tel: 517-224-2421; Fax: 517-224-1900.
Lay Teachers 11; Students 298.
Catechesis/Religious Programs—Tel: 517-224-8537.
Students 337.

Saline, Washtenaw Co., St. Andrew (1968), Rev. William J. Stevenson; Deacon Paul Ellis.
Res., 910 Austin Dr., 48176. Tel: 734-429-5210; Fax: 734-429-0680.
Catechesis/Religious Programs—Tel: 734-429-7776.
Students 1,001.

Swartz Creek, Genesee Co., St. Mary (1912) (Czechoslovakian), Rev. Amos H. Wischmeyer.
Res., 7563 Mary St., 48473. Tel: 810-635-3240; Fax: 810-635-0688. [CEM]
School—4413 Morrish Rd., 48473. Tel: 810-635-4985.
Lay Teachers 8; Students 138; Kindergarten 24; PreK 32.
Catechesis/Religious Programs—Tel: 810-635-3989.
Students 224.

Tecumseh, Lenawee Co., St. Elizabeth (1947), Rev. Daniel Wheeler; Deacons James Nicholson; Ray Pizana.
Res., 506 N. Union St., 49286. Tel: 517-423-2447; Fax: 517-424-7706.
Catechesis/Religious Programs—512 N. Union St., 49286. Tel: 517-423-4501; Fax: 517-423-4501.
Students 367.

Westphalia, Clinton Co., St. Mary (1836) (German). Unassigned.
Res., 201 N. Westphalia St., P.O. Box 267, 48894. Tel: 517-587-4201; Fax: 517-587-3838. [CEM]
School—Tel: 517-587-3702; Fax: 517-587-3706.
Lay Teachers 14; Students 228.

Catechesis/Religious Programs—Tel: 517-587-4201.
Students 199.

Williamston, Ingham Co., St. Mary (1869), Rev. Thomas W. Thompson.
Res., 157 High St., 48895. Tel: 517-655-2620; Fax: 517-655-3933. [CEM]
School—220 Cedar St., 48895. Tel: 517-655-4038; Fax: 517-655-3855. Katherine White, Prin.
Sisters 1; Lay Teachers 5; Students 138.
Catechesis/Religious Programs—Tel: 517-655-2520. Bernadette Moline, D.R.E.
Students 203.

Ypsilanti, Washentaw Co.,

1—St. Alexis. Closed. For inquiries for parish records contact Transfiguraton Catholic Church.

2—St. John, Washtenaw Co., (1858), Rev. Edmond L. Ertzbischoff; Deacons Wayne Charlton; Robert Chadwick.
Res., 410 W. Cross St., 48197. Tel: 734-483-3360; Fax: 734-483-0712. [CEM]
Catechesis/Religious Programs—Tel: 734-483-6378.
Students 189.
Convent—411 Florence St., 48197. Tel: 734-483-0742.

3—St. Joseph, Washtenaw Co., (1889), Rev. Robert T. Kerr.
Res., 9425 Whittaker Rd., 48197. Tel: 313-461-6555; Fax: 313-461-1444. [CEM]
Catechesis/Religious Programs—Tel: 313-461-6321.
Students 180.

4—St. Ursula, Washtenaw Co. Closed. For inquiries for parish records contact Transfiguration Catholic Church.

5—Holy Trinity Student Chapel, Washtenaw Co., (1965), Rev. Louis Madey.
Res., 511 W. Forest, 48197. Tel: 734-482-1400; 734-487-9756 (Rectory); Fax: 734-482-0542.
Catechesis/Religious Programs—Students 150.

6—Transfiguration Catholic Church, Washtenaw Co., (1994), Rev. David Franco, O.S.F.S.
Res., 1705 E. Forest Ave., 48198-4160. Tel: 734-482-6240; Fax: 734-482-1547.
Catechesis/Religious Programs—Students 47.

Chaplains of Public Institutions

Hospitals

Lansing. *Michigan Capital Medical Center, Sparrow Hospital*. Alice Hill, Chap., Tel: 517-646-6850.

Ann Arbor. *University of Michigan Hospitals/Pastoral Care Dept.* Revs. Darin Robert Tel: 734-936-4041; Ben Werner; Deacon Wayne Charlton.
Veterans' Hospital. Rev. Emeka L. Odor, J.C.L., Chap.

Prisons

Jackson. *Southern Michigan Prison*. Vacant.

Milan. *Federal Correctional Institution*. Rev. Howard Stunek, O.F.M., Chap., Tel: 734-439-2298.

Special Assignment:
Reverend Fathers—
Dougherty, C. Peter, P.O. Box 14062, Lansing, MI 48901
Schmitter, Philip, 2381 E. Carpenter, Flint, MI 48505

On Duty Outside the Diocese:
Reverend Monsignors—
Raica, Steven J.
Reverend Fathers—
Bui, Vincent, Theological College, 401 Michigan Ave., N.E., Washington, D.C. 20017
Crowley, Timothy
Gerl, Robert, P.O. Box 19225, Kalamazoo, MI 49019
Irish, Robert
Kropf, Richard, Star Rte. 1, P.O. Box 629, Johannesburg, MI 49751
Sessions, Phillip D., Diocese of San Diego
Taylor, Jon, The College of Great Falls, 1301-20th St. S., Great Falls, MT 59405
Thomsen, Stephen

Retired:
Reverend Monsignors—
Fedewa, Sylvester L., 120 N. Willow St, Box 412, Westphalia, MI 48894
Howard, Vincent, 1849 Pierce Rd., Chelsea, MI 48118
Reverend Fathers—
Bednarski, Mitchell J., Marywood Nursing Care Center, 36975 5 Mile Rd., Livonia, MI 48154
Bottazzo, Alex, Senior Clergy Village, 14455 D Levan St., Livonia, MI 48154
Brakora, Anthony, 2705 Ridgecliff Dr., Flint, MI 48532
Brennan, Thomas, 468 Lancaster Ct., Saline, MI 48176
Bush, John H., 9787 Burning Tree Dr., Grand Blanc, MI 48439
Carolin, William J., Angela Hospice Home Care, 1400 Newburgh Rd., Livonia, MI 48154
Cornelli, Neil, 1501 Via Del Ray, Fernandina Beach, FL 32034
Cummings, Paul, Holy Family Parish, 620 N. Mabbitt Rd., Ovid, MI 48866
Dupuis, Philip, 13280 Friendly Dr., Wolverine, MI 49799
Eder, Donald, 6290 Oak Creek Dr., Swartz Creek, MI 48473
Foglio, John, P.O. Box 4098, East Lansing, MI 48826
Immel, Joseph, 1971 Watkins Lake Rd., Waterford, MI 48328
Koenigsknecht, William J., Independence Village, 11525 Hartel Rd., Grand Ledge, MI 48837
Ledwidge, Brendan K., 432 Pearl St., Pinckney, MI 48169-9101
Martin, Francis T., St. Gerard Church, 4437 W. Willow, Lansing, MI 48917
McDevitt, Thomas, St. Francis Retreat Center, 703 E. Main St., DeWitt, MI 48820
McDonald, Kenneth, 401-D E. Madison, DeWitt, MI 48820
McKeon, Robert, 10018 Lehring Rd., P.O. Box 132, Byron, MI 48418-0132. Tel: 810-266-5674
Murray, Francis J., 2642 Walden Woods, Jackson, MI 49201. Tel: 517-768-9483
Novak, James, 16269 W. Starry Sky Dr., Surprise, AZ 85374
O'Grady, Edward F., Countryside Manor, 3637 McCain Rd., Apt. 17, Jackson, MI 49203
Rademacher, William, 3842 Azalea Dr., Las Cruces, NM 88005-1027
Rahrig, Gilbert
Ramer, Leo, 235 Quebec St., Goderich, ON N7A 2H2 Canada
Schmitt, James, J., 215 Banberry N., Lansing, MI 48906
Srebernak, Francis, R.R. 1, Rural Box 82B, Hancock, MI 49930-9705
Stockwell, C. Robert, 335 Walnut St., Mount Morris, MI 48458-1948
Williams, Francis, 401 B E. Madison, DeWitt, MI 48820

Permanent Deacons:
Alfaro, Rogelio R., Cristo Rey, Lansing
Amon, Rodney, St. Michael, Flint
Barrett, David P., Queen of the Miraculous Medal, Jackson
Barrett, Michael, Most Holy Trinity, Fowler
Bayes, Richard B., Jr., St. Mary of Good Counsel, Adrian
Borzenski, David J., St. Therese, Lansing
Brown, James S., St. Mary, Mt. Morris
Cameron, John, Tribunal and Immaculate Heart of Mary, Lansing
Ceballos, Santos R., Sr., Diocese of Lansing, Hispanic Office
Chadwick, Robert, St. John the Baptist, Ypsilanti
Charlton, Wayne, St. John the Baptist, Ypsilanti
Corder, James, Holy Redeemer, Burton
Cormier, Currie, St. Joseph, Gaines
Daunt, Jack, Holy Family, Grand Blanc
Doran, Endre, St. Joseph, Howell
Eddington, Gary, St. Mary, Morrice
Ellis, Paul, St. Andrew, Saline
Everett, William, St. Mary of the Sea, Jackson
Fairweather, Daniel, St. John the Evangelist, Davison
Feiten, Thomas, St. James, Mason
Foley, Daniel R. (BGP), Christ the King, Ann Arbor
Franklin, Thomas, St. Mary, Chelsea
Franssen, Carol, St. John the Evangelist, Jackson
Fudge, William H., III, Immaculate Heart of Mary, Lansing
Gallagher, Gary, St. Pius X, Flint
Genco, Vincent, Star of the Sea, Jackson
Giesige, Richard, St. Joseph, Ypsilanti
Guarnaccia, Vincent, St. Martha, Okemos
Gudaitis, Peter, St. Agnes, Fowlerville
Hausmann, Eugene, St. Joseph Shrine, Brooklyn
Hecht, Warren Jay, St. Thomas the Apostle, Ann Arbor
Heutsche, Edward, Community of St. Jude, Dewitt
Hilker, Stephen, St. Thomas Aquinas, East Lansing
Holowicki, Gerry, Christ the King, Ann Arbor
Huiskens, Neil F., St. John the Evangelist, Davison
Igoe, James Gerard, Criminal Justice Ministry, Lansing
Kowalski, John, Queen of the Miraculous Medal, Jackson
Kratofil, Joseph A., St. John the Evangelist, Jackson
Krieger, Albert, St. Joseph, Jackson
Lennon, Joseph, Holy Spirit, Hamburg
Leone, Romolo Joseph, St. Joseph, Dexter
Lynch, Michael T., St. Robert, Flushing
Martinez, James N., Diocese of Lansing, Hispanic Office
Mc Philamy, Robert E., St. Gerard, Lansing
McCarthy, John L., St. Michael, Grand Ledge
McDonald, Patrick A., St. Patrick Church, Brighton
Miles, James J., St. Thomas the Apostle, Ann Arbor
Moore, Thomas, St. Paul, Owosso
Nicholson, James R., St. Elizabeth, Tecumseh
Novak, Edwin, Diocese of Lansing, Criminal Justice Ministry
Nunez, Michael, St. Anthony, Hillsdale
Piggot, David, St. John the Baptist, Hartland
Pigott, David J., Jr., SS. Charles & Helena, Clio
Pizana, Eulalio (Ray), St. Elizabeth, Tecumseh
Pohl, Bernard J., St. Mary's, Westphalia
Robertson, Marvin, St. Joseph, St. Johns
Rowe, Ronald, Blessed Sacrament, Burton
Russello, Lou, Christ the King, Ann Arbor
Savage, Richard, St. Gerard, Lansing
Scharf, H. David, St. Mary Magdalene, Brighton
Schneider, Edwin J., St. Gerard, Lansing
Shaneyfelt, Richard, St. Mary, Chelsea
Simmon, Mark C., Most Holy Trinity, Fowler
Sirl, William, St. Michael, Flint
Soucy, Richard, St. Francis Xavier, Otisville
Spaulding, Kenneth R., Queen of the Miraculous Medal, Jackson
Sundwick, John, St. John Vianney, Flint
Tardif, Joseph A., St. Michael, Grand Ledge
Torres, Calistro, St. Mary of Good Counsel, Adrian
Verdun, Anthony W., Sacred Heart, Flint
Washington, Oliver G., Immaculate Heart, Lansing
Weitzel, Louis U., St. Rita, Clarklake
Wines, Deacon Frank, St. John the Baptist, Hartland

INSTITUTIONS LOCATED IN THE DIOCESE

[A] COLLEGES AND UNIVERSITIES

Adrian. *Siena Heights University*, 1247 E. Siena Heights Dr., 49221-1796. Tel: 517-263-0731; Fax: 517-264-7702.
Web site: www.sienahts.edu
For a complete listing, refer to the Colleges and Universities section.

Ann Arbor. *Ave Maria School of Law*, 3475 Plymouth Rd., 48105-2550. Tel: 734-930-4408.
E-mail: avemarialaw.edu
For a complete listing, refer to the Colleges and Universities section.

Ypsilanti. *Ave Maria College*, 300 W. Forest Ave., 48197. Tel: 734-482-4180; 1-877-285-9072 (Toll Free); Fax: 734-482-2140.
E-mail: admissions@avemaria.edu
Web site: www.avemaria.edu
For a complete listing, refer to the Colleges and Universities section.

[B] HIGH SCHOOLS, DIOCESAN

Lansing. *Lansing Catholic Central High School*, 501 N. Marshall St., 48912. Tel: 517-267-2100; Fax: 517-267-2135.
E-mail: draminsk@mail.lcchs.pvt.k12.mi.us
James B. Olin, Prin. Lansing Catholic Central Board of Education. Priests 1; Lay Teachers 31; Students 585.

Ann Arbor. *Father Gabriel Richard High School*, 530 Elizabeth St., 48104. Tel: 734-662-0496; Fax: 734-662-4133.
E-mail: rbayhan@fgrhsaa.org
Web site: www.fgrhsaa.org
Mr. Richard Bayhan, Prin. Gabriel Richard Board of Education. Priests 1; Lay Teachers 22; Students 310.

Flint. *Luke M. Powers Catholic High School*, G-2040 W. Carpenter Rd., 48505. Tel: 810-591-4741; Fax: 810-591-0383.
E-mail: powers@kode.net
Web site: kode.net/~powers/front.html
Mr. Joseph Forlenza, Prin. Powers Catholic Board of Education. Priests 1; Sisters 1; Lay Teachers 42; Students 871; Total Staff 51.

JACKSON. *Lumen Christi High School*, 3483 Spring Arbor Rd., 49203. Tel: 517-787-0630; Fax: 517-787-1066. Oblates of St. Francis de Sales. Revs. Thomas W. Rieden, O.S.F.S., Prin.; Richard L. McLernan, O.S.F.S.; James Bradley, O.S.F.S.; Paul F. Grehl, O.S.F.S.; John W. Bailey, O.S.F.S. Priests 4; Sisters 2; Lay Teachers 35; Students 606.

[C] ELEMENTARY & MIDDLE SCHOOLS, DIOCESAN

FLINT. *Dukette Catholic School*, 530 W. Pierson Rd., 48505. Tel: 810-785-4743; Fax: 810-785-7184.
E-mail: dukettecs@aol.com
Gail Schneider-Negrinelli, Prin. Lay Teachers 17; Total Staff 27; Students 180.

JACKSON. *Jackson Catholic Middle School*, 915 Cooper, 49202. Tel: 517-784-3385; Fax: 517-782-7883.
E-mail: jcms@dmci.net
Mr. Ronald E. Niedzwiecki, Prin. Lay Teachers 16; Students 310.

[D] SCHOOLS, PRIVATE

ADRIAN. *St. Joseph Academy Montessori Children's House*. (Grades PreK-8), 1267 E. Siena Heights, 49221. Tel: 517-263-4898; Fax: 517-265-6470. Sisters of St. Dominic, Congregation of the Most Holy Rosary (Adrian, MI). Mrs. Deborah Keller, Prin. Lay Teachers 40; Total Staff 46; Students 340.

ANN ARBOR. *Spiritus Sanctus Academy*. (Grades K-8), 4101 E. Joy Rd., 48105. Tel: 734-996-3855; Fax: 734-996-4270.
Web site: www.spiritussanctus.org
Sr. John Dominic, Prin. Lay Teachers 6; Students 90; Staff 12.

Spiritus Sanctus Academy. (Grades K-8), 2600 Via Sacra, 48105. Tel: 734-995-4770; Fax: 734-930-9885.
E-mail: srmarysamuel@rc.net
Web site: www.spiritussanctus.org
Sr. Mary Samuel, Prin. Priests 1; Sisters 2; Lay Teachers 12; Students 103; Staff 15.

BURTON. *St. Thomas More Academy*. (Grades K-12), 6456 E. Bristol Rd., 48519. Tel: 810-742-24111; Fax: 810-742-4803. Mr. Rick C. Manns, Prin. Priests 1; Lay Teachers 13; Students 126.

CLINTON. *St. Thomas More High-Boysville*, 8744 Clinton-Macon Rd., 49236. Tel: 517-423-7451; Fax: 517-423-5214.
Web site: www.boysville.org
Mr. Carl LaGore, Prin. Brothers 1; Total Staff 24; Students 146.

PLYMOUTH. *Spiritus Sanctus Academy*, 10450 Joy Rd., 48197. Tel: 734-995-4449. Irene Wottreng, Prin.

YPSILANTI. *Spiritus Sanctus Academy*. (Grades K-8), 3875 Golfside Dr., 48197. Tel: 734-528-3980; Fax: 734-528-3983.
E-mail: rouellette@rc.net
Robert W. Oullette, Prin. Staff 8; Students 75.

[E] SPECIALIZED CHILD CARE FACILITIES & SCHOOLS

LANSING. *Boysville of Michigan, Inc.*, Grants Management Office, 4601 W. Saginaw Hwy., Ste. A, 48917. Tel: 517-327-0892; Fax: 517-327-0895. Bro. Francis Boylan, C.S.C., Exec. Dir.; Adolf Armbruster, Grants Mgr.

CHELSEA. *St. Louis Center for Exceptional Children & Adults*, 16195 Old U.S. 12, 48118. Tel: 734-475-8430; Fax: 734-475-0310.
E-mail: stlouiscty@aol.com
Web site: www.stlouiscenter.org
Revs. Joseph Rinaldo, S.C., Prov. Admin.; Fortunato Turati, S.C.; Matthew Weber, S.C.; Cecilio Silgvero. Operated by the Servants of Charity. Priests 4; Staff 45; Students 70.

CLINTON. *Boysville of Michigan, Inc.*, 8744 Clinton-Macon Rd., 49236. Tel: 517-423-7451; Fax: 517-423-5442.
Web site: www.boysville.org
Bro. Francis Boylan, C.S.C., Exec. Dir.; Mr. Eugene Hausmann, Pastoral Min.; Bro. Chester Freel, C.S.C., Regl. Dir. Brothers 7; Boys 148; Total Staff 186. Residential and community based treatment programs for troubled youth and families with facilities located throughout the state of Michigan and one in the state of Ohio under the auspices of the Brothers of Holy Cross & Notre Dame.

Boysville's Family & Community Support Program, 8744 Clinton-Macon Rd., 49236. Tel: 517-423-7451, Ext. 532.
Web site: www.boysville.org
Bros. Francis Boylan, C.S.C., Exec. Dir.; Chester Freel, C.S.C., Reg. Dir. Specialized Foster Care Treatment and Supervised Independent Living.

Supervised Independent Living Office. Boysville of Michigan, 2310 Packard, Ste. 3, Ypsilanti, 48197. Tel: 734-528-3960; Fax: 734-528-4237. Total Staff 6; Total Assisted 70.

JACKSON. *St. Joseph Home for Children, Inc.*, 1000 E. Porter, 49202. Tel: 517-787-3320. Sr. Mary Presentine Ugorowski, C.S.S.F.; Rev. Patrick Cwik, Chap. Felician Sisters (C.S.S.F.). Day Care Center-Retreat-Conference Center and Kindergarten (ages 2 months-5 years). Children 100.

MOUNT MORRIS. *Corcoran House/Boysville of Michigan, Inc.*, 8212 N. Jennings Rd., 48458. Tel: 810-687-5100; Fax: 810-687-5020. Bro. Francis Boylan, C.S.C., Exec. Dir.; Mr. Rick Boone, Regional Dir. A day treatment program for 12 boys and girls. Total Assisted 33; Total Staff 27; Total in Residence 6.

[F] CATHOLIC CHARITIES & SERVICE AGENCIES

LANSING. *Catholic Social Services - St. Vincent Home*, 913 W. Holmes Rd., Ste. 290, 48910. Tel: 517-272-1524, Ext. 102; Fax: 517-272-1562.
E-mail: csssvn@aol.com
Sharon Hall Solomon, Pres.

Family Mental Health Clinic, 913 W. Holmes Rd., Ste. 179, 48910. Tel: 517-887-8580; Fax: 517-887-9105.

Foster Grandparent Program, 6545 Mercantile Way, Ste. 2B1, 48911. Tel: 517-272-9119; Fax: 517-272-9264.

Refugee Services, 2722 E. Michigan Ave., Ste. 100-B, 48912. Tel: 517-484-1010; Fax: 517-484-2560. St. Vincent Home for Children, 2800 W. Willow St., 48917. Tel: 517-323-4734; Fax: 517-323-0257. In Residence 36.

Senior Companion Program, 5815 Wise Rd., 48911. Tel: 517-882-8777; Fax: 517-325-6344.

Intergenerational Community Center, 13060 U.S. 27, Dewitt, 48820. Tel: 517-669-1551; Fax: 517-668-0034.

Child Welfare Programs. (Includes Shield, Foster Care, Intensive Foster Care and Adoption), 2800 W. Willow St., 48917. Tel: 517-323-4734; Fax: 517-323-0257.

Ballentine Stepping Stones, 825 N. Pennsylvania Ave., 48906. Tel: 517-485-4644; Fax: 517-485-4644.

Capital Area Interfaith Respite, 6545 S. Mercantile Dr., Ste. 1-A, 48911. Tel: 517-393-8520; Fax: 517-394-5256.

Health Care and Social Ministry, 6545 Mercantile Way, Ste. 1A, 48911. Tel: 517-394-4435; Fax: 517-394-5256.

Retired and Senior Volunteer Program, 6545 Mercantile Way, 1A-1, 48911. Tel: 517-887-6116; Fax: 517-887-7313.

Homemaker, 825 N. Pennsylvania Ave., 48906. Tel: 517-485-4644; Fax: 517-485-4644. Total Assisted 7,725; Total Staff 249.

Cristo Rey Community Center, 1717 N. High St., 48906. Tel: 517-372-4700; Fax: 517-372-8499.
E-mail: cristorey@earthlink.net
Tony Benavides, Dir. Total Assisted 59,916; Total Staff 54.

Migrant Clinic-Cristo Rey Community Center, 1717 N. High St., 48906. Tel: 517-372-4700; Fax: 517-372-8499.
E-mail: cristorey@earthlink.net
Tomasa Velasquez, Coord.; Dr. Peter Cooke, Medical Dir. Total Assisted 420; Total Staff 1.

ADRIAN. *Catholic Social Services of Lenawee County*, 307 E. Church St., 49221. Tel: 517-263-2191; Fax: 517-264-6080.
E-mail: css@dmci.net
Web site: www.catholicservices.org
Luanne Reaume, Dir. Total Assisted 1,073; Total Staff 24.

ANN ARBOR. *C.S.S. of Washtenaw County*, 4925 Packard Rd., 48108. Tel: 734-971-9781; Fax: 734-971-2730.
E-mail: jwisniew@csswashtenaw.org
Lawrence J. Voight, A.C.S.W. Total Assisted 5,600; Total Staff 70.

DAVISON. *Outreach East*, 425 N. Genesee St., P.O. Box 61, 48423. Tel: 810-653-7711. Rita Berby, S.S.J., Dir. Total Assisted 1,500; Total Staff 1.

FLINT. *Catholic Outreach*, 509 N. Grand Traverse, P.O. Box 815, 48501. Tel: 810-234-4693; Fax: 810-234-9428. Sr. Claudia Burke, S.F.P., Dir. Total Assisted 2,456; Total Staff 20.

Catholic Social Services - North End Soup Kitchen, 901 Chippewa St., 48503. Tel: 810-232-9950; Fax: 810-232-7599.
E-mail: dmccormack@cssflint.org
Deborah J. McCormack, A.C.S.W., Pres. Total Assisted Daily 750; Total Staff 9.

Catholic Social Services of Flint, 901 Chippewa St., 48503. Tel: 810-232-9950; Fax: 810-232-7599.
E-mail: cssflint@9ix.net
Web site: dmccormack@cssflint.org
Deborah J. McCormack, A.C.S.W., Pres. Total Assisted 75,388; Total Staff 52.

Shelter of Flint, Inc., 432 N. Saginaw St., Ste. 902, 48502. Tel: 810-238-4711; Fax: 810-238-6001.
E-mail: amartin_sofine@tir.com
Web site: www.tir.com~sofinc
Patricia A. Motter, CEO.

Emergency Shelter for Women, 1917 Delaware St., 48506. Tel: 810-233-0689; Fax: 810-233-0850. Allan Martin, COO. Total Assisted 1,500.

HOWELL. *Livingston County Catholic Social Services*, 2020 E. Grand River Ave., Ste. 103, 48843. Tel: 517-545-5944; Fax: 517-545-7390.
E-mail: lccss@voyager.net
Cynthia Irimescu, Dir. Total Assisted 1,900; Total Staff 15.

JACKSON. *Catholic Social Services of Jackson*, 407 S. Mechanic St., 49201. Tel: 517-782-2551; Fax: 517-783-1986. Mr. Keith Krusky, Dir. Total Assisted 7,300; Total Staff 12.

OWOSSO. *Catholic Social Services of Shiawassee County*, 120 W. Exchange, Ste. 204, 48867. Tel: 517-723-8239; Fax: 517-723-8230.
E-mail: dmccormack@cssflint.org
Total Assisted 371; Total Staff 6.

[G] SOCIETY OF ST. VINCENT DE PAUL

LANSING. *St. Vincent de Paul Society*, St. Vincent de Paul Store & Referral Office, 1020 S. Washington Ave., 48910. Tel: 517-484-5395; 517-484-4228; Fax: 517-484-2426. John Fiero, Pres.; Rhett Johnston, Dir. Total Staff 14.

ANN ARBOR. *Society of St. Vincent de Paul - St. Thomas Conference*, 517 Elizabeth St., 48104. Tel: 734-761-1400. Barbara Norman, Pres.

FLINT. *Particular Council of Flint*, Society of St. Vincent DePaul Store, 1912 N. Franklin, 48506. Tel: 810-234-5381; Fax: 810-234-1697. Gene R. Myers, Pres.; Richard Twomley, Store Dir.

JACKSON. *Society of St. Vincent de Paul*, St. Vincent de Paul Store, 1509 E. Michigan, 49202. Tel: 517-784-0609. Particular Council of Jackson. O.J. Pierce, Particular Council Pres.

Society of St. Vincent de Paul, 1812 Spring Arbor Rd., 49203. Tel: 517-784-0721.

[H] GENERAL HOSPITALS

ANN ARBOR. *Ascension Health Great Lakes Division*, 455 E. Eisenhower, Ste. 300, 48108. Tel: 734-741-1700; Fax: 734-623-7240.
E-mail: jnusbaum@ascensionhealth.org
For a complete listing, refer to the Hospitals section.

Catherine McAuley Health Services Corporation, 5305 E. Huron River Dr., P.O. Box 992, 48106. Tel: 734-712-3791; Fax: 734-712-5459
For a complete listing, refer to the Hospitals section.

St. Joseph Mercy Health System, 5305 E. Huron River Dr., Box 992, 48106. Tel: 734-734-4986; Fax: 734-712-5459
For a complete listing, refer to the Hospitals section.

St. Joseph Mercy Hospital, 5301 E. Huron River Dr., P.O. Box 995, 48106. Tel: 734-712-3791; Fax: 734-712-5459
For a complete listing, refer to the Hospitals section.

FLINT. *Center for Gerontology*, 3919 Beecher Rd., 48532. Tel: 810-762-4550; Fax: 810-762-4576.
E-mail: ssstevens@genesys.org
For a complete listing, refer to the Hospitals section.

Genesys Ambulatory Health Services, Inc., 3935 Beecher Rd., 48532. Tel: 810-762-4340; Fax: 810-762-4283.
E-mail: dcaudle@genesys.org
For a complete listing, refer to the Hospitals section.

Genesys Home Health & Hospice, 3933 Beecher Rd., 48532. Tel: 810-762-4600; Fax: 810-762-0027
For a complete listing, refer to the Hospitals section.

GOODRICH. *Genesys Hospice*, 7280 S. State Rd., 48438. Tel: 810-636-5000; Fax: 810-636-5019.
E-mail: lmccombs@coenesys.org
For a complete listing, refer to the Hospitals section.

GRAND BLANC. *Genesys Health System*, One Genesys Pkwy., 48439. Tel: 810-606-6600; Fax: 810-606-6605.
E-mail: atucker@genesys.org
For a complete listing, refer to the Hospitals section.

Genesys Regional Medical Center, One Genesys Pkwy., 48439. Tel: 810-606-6600; Fax: 810-606-6605.
E-mail: atucker@genesys.org
For a complete listing, refer to the Hospitals section.

HOWELL. *McPherson Hospital*, 620 Bryon Rd., 48843-1093. Tel: 517-545-6000; Fax: 517-545-6192
For a complete listing, refer to the Hospitals section.

SALINE. *Saline Community Hospital*, 400 W. Russell, 48176. Tel: 734-429-1600; Fax: 734-429-4662
For a complete listing, refer to the Hospitals section.

[I] HOMES FOR THE AGED & CONVALESCENT

DIMONDALE. *Dimondale Nursing Center*, 4000 N. Michigan Rd. (M-99), 48821-9744. Tel: 517-646-6258; Fax: 517-646-0405
For a complete listing, refer to the Special Care Facilities section.

GRAND BLANC. *Genesys Convalescent Center, Grand Blanc, Inc.*, 8481 Holly Rd., 48439-1899. Tel: 810-694-1711; Fax: 810-694-9717.
E-mail: r.stevens@genesys.org
For a complete listing, refer to the Special Care Facilities section.

[J] CONVENTS AND RESIDENCES FOR SISTERS

LANSING. *Mexican Passionate Sisters*, St. Therese Covent, 109 E. Randolph, 48906.

ADRIAN. *Adrian Dominican Office of Development*, 1257 E. Siena Heights. Dr., 49221-1793. Tel: 517-266-3417; Fax: 517-266-3545.
E-mail: devoffad@aol.com
Web site: www.op.org/adrian
Adrian Dominican Sisters.
Dominican Sisters of Adrian, MI, Inc., 1257 E. Siena Heights Dr., 49221. Tel: 517-266-3570. Sr. Janet Capone, O.P., Pres.
Motherhouse of the Sisters of St. Dominic.
Congregation of the Most Holy Rosary, 1257 Siena Heights Dr., 49221-1793. Tel: 517-266-3400; Fax: 517-266-3545. Sr. Janet Capone, O.P., Prioress. Chaplains: Revs. Roland Calvert, O.S.F.S.; George Ssebadduka. Total Congregation 1,070.
Motherhouse Mission Chapter, 1257 Siena Heights Dr., 49221-1793. Tel: 517-266-4107; Fax: 517-266-3545. Sr. Celestine Dunne, O.P., Chap. Prioress.
Rosa de Lima Mission Chapter. (located in the Dominican Republic), c/o 1257 Siena Heights Dr., 49221-1793. Tel: 809-533-0272; Fax: 809-534-8017. Sr. Rose Ann Schlitt, O.P., Chapter Prioress.
Dominican Life Center, 1277 Siena Heights Dr., 49221-1755. Tel: 517-266-3650; Fax: 517-266-3656. Sr. Rosemary Abramovich, O.P., Admin.

ANN ARBOR. *Benedictine Nuns of Corpus Christi Monastery*, 4485 Earhart Rd., 48105-9710. Tel: 734-995-3876. Mother Regina Mary Kust, O.S.B., Prioress.
Servants of God's Love, 4399 Ford Rd., 48105. Tel: 734-663-6128.
E-mail: sg/ravenwood@juno.com
Sr. Ann Shields, Supvr.
Sisters of Mary, Mother of the Eucharist, 4597 Warren Rd., 48105. Tel: 313-994-7437; Fax: 313-994-7438.
E-mail: sjab@rc.net
Web site: www.sistersofmary.org
Mother M. Assumption Long, Prioress.

DE WITT. *St. Albert the Great House of Studies*, 217 Schavey Rd., P.O. Box 309, 48820. Tel: 517-669-2277; Fax: 517-669-8123. Religious Sisters of Mercy, Alma Michigan 2.

[K] PASTORAL CENTERS

FLUSHING. *Mt. Zion Pastoral Center*, 8228 McKinley Rd., 48433. Tel: 810-639-7175; Fax: 810-639-5262. Rev. Dennis Howard, Chap.

JACKSON. *Sacred Heart Chapel*, 1501 E. Michigan, 49202. Tel: 517-783-2772. Sr. Paz de Guadalupe Bucio, C.F.P., Pastoral Assoc.; Rudy Flores, Pres. Parish Pastoral Council; Angela Medina, Treas.

[L] RETREAT CENTERS

ADRIAN. *Weber Retreat Center*, 1257 Siena Heights Dr., 49221-1793. Tel: 517-266-4000; Fax: 517-266-4004.
E-mail: webercenter@admc-op.org
Web site: www.op.org/adrian/weber
Sr. Kathleen Schanz, O.P., Dir.

BROOKLYN. *Lake Vineyard Camps, Inc., (De Sales Center)*, 1124 Ventura, 49230-9078. Tel: 517-592-8218; Fax: 517-592-8218.
E-mail: mckenna@desales.org
Web site: www.desales.org
Rev. Kenneth N. McKenna, O.S.F.S., Contact Person. De Sales Center is a Catholic Retreat Center operated by Lake Vineyard Camps, Inc. for the Oblates of St. Francis de Sales, Inc. Also on the property is the Novitiate House for the Toledo-Detroit Province of the Oblates of St. Francis de Sales. Total in Residence 5; Total Staff 3.

DE WITT. *St. Francis Retreat Center*, 703 E. Main St., 48820. Tel: 517-669-8321; 866-669-8321 (Toll Free); Fax: 517-669-2708.
E-mail: stfrancis@voyager.net
Revs. Lawrence Delaney, Dir.; Thomas McDevitt; Sr. Suzanne Eichhorn, O.P., Assoc. Dir.
Bethany House (Spiritual Life Center for Youth), St. Francis Retreat Center, 703 E. Main St., DeWitt, 48820. Tel: 517-669-8321. Rev. Gerald Vincke, Dir. Total in Residence 2; Total Staff 25.

[M] CAMPUS MINISTRY

ADRIAN. *Siena Heights University.* Campus Ministry. 1247 E. Siena Heights Dr., 49221. Tel: 517-264-7192; Fax: 517-264-7656.
E-mail: tpuszcze@sienahts.edu
Tom Puszczewicz, Dir. Campus Ministry.

ANN ARBOR. *St. Mary Student Parish*, 331 Thompson St., 48104-2295. Tel: 734-663-0557; Fax: 734-663-2756.
E-mail: stmarys@umich.edu
Web site: www.umich.edu/~stmarys
Rev. Thomas M. Firestone. Serving the University of Michigan.
(Refer to the parish section for complete campus ministry staff). Total Staff 12.

BELLEVUE. *St. Ann.* Serving Olivet College. (Refer to parish section for complete ministry staff.), 312 S. Main St., 49021. Tel: 616-763-9372; Fax: 616-763-0067.

EAST LANSING. *St. John Student Parish.* Serving Michigan State University, 327 M.A.C. Ave., 48823-4388. Tel: 517-337-9778; Fax: 517-337-8358.
E-mail: stjohnsp@msu.edu
Web site: www.msu.edu/~stjohnsp/
(Refer to the parish section for complete campus ministry staff).

FLINT. *St. Leo the Great Church*, 3632 Wyoming Ave., 48506. Tel: 810-736-2150; Fax: 517-736-0122. Rev. James Bettendorf.

HILLSDALE. *St. Anthony Family Center.* (Serving Hillsdale College), 11 Broad St., 49242. Tel: 517-437-3305; Fax: 517-437-0034.
E-mail: stanthony@dmci.net
Total Assisted 300; Total Staff 1.

YPSILANTI. *Holy Trinity Student Chapel*, 511 W. Forest, 48197. Tel: 734-482-1400; Fax: 734-482-0542.
E-mail: htchapel@online.emich.edu
Web site: www.rc.net/lansing/holy_trinity
Rev. Louis Madey; Victoria Emch, D.R.E. Serving Eastern Michigan University and Washtenaw Community College.

[N] ENDOWMENTS AND TRUSTS

LANSING. *Chancery Office*, 300 W. Ottawa, 48933. Tel: 517-342-2440.
Camilla Madden Charitable Trust (Adrian).
Church of the Resurrection Educational Trust Fund (Church of the Resurrection, Lansing). Tel: 517-482-4749; Fax: 517-484-4740.
Father Al Miller Educational Trust Fund (St. Mary Parish, Westphalia). Tel: 517-587-4201; Fax: 517-587-3838.
Father Gabriel Richard High School Trust Fund (Fr. Gabriel Richard H.S., Ann Harbor). Tel: 734-662-0496; Fax: 734-662-4133.
Greater Lansing Catholic Education Foundation (Lansing). Tel: 517-485-8333; Fax: 517-484-8880.
Immaculate Heart of Mary St. Casimir School Mary Goeddeke Educational Trust Fund. (IHM-St. Casimir School, Lansing). Tel: 517-882-6631.
Luke M. Powers Educational Trust Fund (Flint). Tel: 810-591-4741; Fax: 810-591-0383.
Lumen Christi High School Endowment Fund (Lumen Christi H.S., Jackson). Tel: 517-787-0630; Fax: 517-787-1066.
Most Holy Trinity Educational Trust Fund (Most Holy Trinity Church, Fowler). Tel: 517-593-2616; Fax: 517-593-2801.
Msgr. Lawrence H. Soest Educational Trust Fund (St. Mary Parish, Flint). Tel: 810-232-4012; Fax: 810-232-4013.
Rev. Joseph R. Robb Educational Trust Fund (Holy Rosary Parish, Flint). Tel: 810-736-4040; Fax: 810-736-9129.
Sacred Heart Educational Fund (Sacred Heart Parish, Hudson). Tel: 517-448-3811.
St. Francis of Assisi Educational Trust Fund (St. Francis of Assisi Parish, Ann Harbor). Tel: 734-821-2200; Fax: 734-821-2202.
St. John the Evangelist Parish Educational Trust Fund (St. John the Evangelist Parish, Jackson). Tel: 517-784-0553; Fax: 517-788-5381.
St John School Educational Foundation, Inc. (St. John Parish, Fenton). Tel: 810-629-2251; Fax: 810-629-2302.
St. John Vianney Educational Trust Fund (St. John Vianney Parish, Flint). Tel: 810-235-1812; Fax: 810-235-4911.
St. Joseph Church of Howell Trust Fund (St. Joseph Church, Howell). Tel: 517-546-0090.
St. Joseph Educational Trust Fund (St. Joseph Church, Owosso). Tel: 517-725-5215; Fax: 517-725-1519.
St. Joseph Educational Trust Fund (St. Joseph Church, St. Johns). Tel: 517-224-8994; Fax: 517-224-3475.
St. Louis Center for Exceptional Children & Adults Endowment Trust Agreement (St. Louis Center, Chelsea). Tel: 734-475-8430; Fax: 734-475-0310.
St. Mary Educational Trust Fund (St. Mary Parish, Mt. Morris). Tel: 810-686-3920; Fax: 810-686-0759.
St. Mary Parish Educational Trust Fund (St. Mary Parish, Charlotte). Tel: 517-543-4319; Fax: 517-543-9078.
St. Mary Star of the Sea Educational Trust Fund (St. Mary Star of the Sea Parish, Jackson). Tel: 517-784-7184; Fax: 517-783-2571.
St. Michael's School Endowment Fund Policy (St. Michael School, Grand Ledge). Tel: 517-627-2167.
St. Paul's School Education Trust Fund (St. Paul Parish, Owosso). Tel: 517-723-4277; Fax: 517-723-9503.
St. Pius X Church Educational Trust Fund (St. Pius X Church, Flint). Tel: 810-235-8574; Fax: 810-235-8580.
St. Robert Bellarmine/Fr. Charles Jacobs Educational Trust Fund (St, Robert Bellarmine Parish, Flushing). (St. Robert Bellarmine Parish, Flushing). Tel: 810-659-2501; Fax: 810-659-2564.
St. Therese Educational Trust Fund (St. Therese Parish, Lansing). Tel: 517-487-3749; Fax: 517-487-3755.
St. Thomas Aquinas Educational Foundation Trust (St. Thomas Aquinas Parish, East Lansing). Tel: 517-351-7215; Fax: 517-351-7271.
St. Thomas Grade School Trust Agreement (St. Thomas the Apostle Parish, Ann Arbor). Tel: 734-761-8606; Fax: 734-997-8432.
St. Patrick Parish Educational Trust Fund (St. Patrick Parish, Brighton). Tel: 810-229-9863; Fax: 810-220-0730.
St. Gerard Educational Trust Fund (St. Gerard Parish, Lansing). Tel: 517-323-2379; Fax: 517-886-1394.
Holy Redeemer Educational Trust Fund (Holy Redemer Parish, Burton). Tel: 810-743-3050; Fax: 810-743-4381.

[O] MISCELLANEOUS LISTINGS

LANSING. *Catholic Lawyers Guild*, 219 Seymour St., 48933. Tel: 517-484-5332; Fax: 517-484-0475.
Diocesan Service Committee. (Catholic Charismatic Renewal), 835 Maycroft Rd., 48917. Tel: 517-321-8661. Jack Karr, Chm.; Rev. William Ashbaugh, Bishop's Liaison, St. Mary Parish, Westphalia.
Liturgical Commission Publishings, 1500 E. Saginaw, Ste. #1, 48906. Tel: 517-484-4449; Fax: 517-484-8880.
E-mail: litcom@worldnet.att.net
Mary Jo Gillilland, Editor.
Michigan Catholic Conference, 505 N. Capitol Ave., 48933. Tel: 517-372-9310; Fax: 517-372-3940.
E-mail: srmonica@micatholicconference.org
Web site: www.micatholicconference.org
Sr. Monica Kostielney, R.S.M., Pres. & CEO.

ADRIAN. *Adrian Dominican Montessori Teacher Education Institute*, 1257 E. Siena Heights Dr., 49221. Tel: 517-266-3415, Ext. 619; Fax: 517-266-3545.
E-mail: admtei@tc3net.com
Web site: www.tc3net.com/admtei
Sr. Anthonita Porta, O.P., Dir.

ANN ARBOR. *Alma Redemptoris Mater*, 331 Thompson St., 48104-2295. Tel: 734-663-0557; Fax: 734-663-2756.
E-mail: tmf@umich.edu
Rev. Thomas M. Firestone, Contact Person.
Catholic Men's Movement, P.O. Box 466, 48106. Tel: 734-930-4524; Fax: 734-930-3101.
E-mail: cmmdesk@catholic-men.org
Web site: www.catholic-men.org
Rev. Patrick Egan, Chap. Tel: 734-930-3246.
The Marnee and John DeVine Foundation, 4925 Packard, 48108. Tel: 734-971-9781; Fax: 734-971-2730.
E-mail: jwisniew@csswashtenaw
Lawrence J. Voight, Contact Person. Total Assisted 1,312; Total Staff 1.
Renewal Ministries Inc., 230 Collingwood Blvd., Ste. 250, 48103. Tel: 734-662-1730; Fax: 734-662-4697.
E-mail: gseromik@renewalministries.net
Web site: www.renewalministries.net
Ralph Martin, Pres. Total Staff 13.

BROOKLYN. *Oblate Fathers of St. Francis De Sales, Inc.*, 1124 Ventura Dr., 49230. Tel: 517-592-8218; Fax: 517-592-8218.
E-mail: mckenna@desales.org
Web site: www.desales.org
Total in Residence 7.

GRASS LAKE. *The Pious Union of St. Joseph*, 971 E. Michigan Ave., 49240-9210. Tel: 517-522-8017 (Voice/TDD); Fax: 517-522-8387.
E-mail: piousunion@aol.com
Web site: members.aol.com/guanella/stjoseph.html
"Now and at the Hour" Magazine: Revs. Joseph Rinaldo, S.C., Admin. & Editor in Chief; Germano Pegoraro, S.C., Dir.; Estelle M. Humenay, Mng. Editor.

RELIGIOUS INSTITUTES OF MEN REPRESENTED IN THE DIOCESE

For further details refer to the corresponding bracketed number in the Religious Institutes of Men or Women section.

[0140]—*The Augustinians.*—O.S.A.
[0480]—*Conventual Franciscans.*—O.F.M.Conv.
[0920]—*Oblates of St. Francis de Sales.*—O.S.F.S.
[1220]—*Servants of Charity.*—S.C.

RELIGIOUS INSTITUTES OF WOMEN REPRESENTED IN THE DIOCESE

[1070-13]—*Dominican Sisters.*—O.P.

[1070-14]—*Dominican Sisters.* (Grand Rapids).—O.P.

[1170]—*Felician Sisters.*—C.S.S.F.

[1470]—*Franciscan Sisters of St. Joseph.*—F.S.S.J.

[1440]—*Franciscan Sisters of the Poor.*—S.F.P.

[2575]—*Institute of the Sisters of Mercy of the Americas.*—R.S.M.

[]—*Mexican Passionist Sisters.*—C.F.P.

[0440]—*Sisters of Charity of Cincinnati, Ohio.*—S.C.

[0660]—*Sisters of Christian Charity.*—S.C.C.

[1560]—*Sisters of St. Francis of the Holy Eucharist.*—O.S.F.

[3830-11]—*Sisters of St. Joseph.*—S.S.J.

[2110]—*Sisters of the Humility of Mary.*—H.M.

[2350]—*Sisters of the Living Word.*—S.L.W.

[3260]—*Sisters of the Precious Blood (Dayton, OH).*—C.PP.S.

[3320]—*Sisters of the Presentation of the Blessed Virgin Mary.*

[2150]—*Sisters Servants of the Immaculate Heart of Mary.*—I.H.M.

DIOCESAN CEMETERIES

LANSING. *St. Joseph.*

FLINT. *New Calvary.*

NECROLOGY

† King, William, (Unassigned). —Died May 26, 2000.

† Stotenbur, Rev. Msgr. David, East Lansing, MI St. Thomas Aquinas. —Died May 29, 2000.

† Wunderlich, Daniel, DeWitt, MI St. Jude. —Died Dec. 15, 1999.

Diocese of Laredo

Most Rev.

JAMES A. TAMAYO, D.D.

Bishop of Laredo; ordained June 11, 1976; appointed Titluar Bishop of Ita and Auxiliary Bishop of Galveston-Houston January 26, 1993; consecrated March 10, 1993; appointed first Bishop of Diocese of Laredo July 3, 2000; installed August 9, 2000. *Mailing Address: 1901 Corpus Christi St., P.O. Box 2247, Laredo, TX, 78044.* Tel.: 956-727-2140; Fax: 956-727-2777.

ESTABLISHED JULY 3, 2000.

Square Miles 10,905.

Comprises the Counties of Webb, Zapata, Jim Hogg, La Salle, Maverick, Zavala and Dimmitt.

STATISTICAL OVERVIEW

Personnel	
Bishop	1
Priests: Diocesan Active in Diocese	16
Number of Diocesan Priests	16
Religious Priests in Diocese	24
Extern Priests in Diocese	5
Ordinations:	
Permanent Deacons	1
Permanent Deacons in Diocese	23
Total Brothers	20
Total Sisters	83
Parishes	
Parishes	25
With Resident Pastor:	
Resident Diocesan Priests	15
Resident Religious Priests	10
Without Resident Pastor:	
Administered by Priests	1
Missions	26
Professional Ministry Personnel:	
Brothers	7
Sisters	15
Lay Ministers	6
Welfare	
Catholic Hospitals	1
Total Assisted	195,544
Residential Care of Children	1
Total Assisted	62
Specialized Homes	2
Total Assisted	1,895
Special Centers for Social Services	1
Total Assisted	576
Educational	
High Schools, Diocesan and Parish	1
Total Students	631
Elementary Schools, Diocesan and Parish	5
Total Students	1,064
Elementary Schools, Private	1
Total Students	721
Catechesis/Religious Education:	
High School Students	1,299
Elementary Students	5,232
Total Students Under Catholic Instruction	8,947
Teachers in the Diocese:	
Priests	1
Sisters	20
Lay Teachers	143
Vital Statistics	
Receptions into the Church:	
Infant Baptism Totals	3,416
Adult Baptism Totals	71
Received into Full Communion	249
First Communions	3,124
Confirmations	2,184
Marriages:	
Catholic	523
Interfaith	31
Total Marriages	554
Deaths	1,122
Total Catholic Population	217,707
Total Population	286,457

Chancery—1901 Corpus Christi St., Laredo, 78043. Tel: 956-727-2140; Fax: 956-727-2777., *Mailing Address: P.O. Box 2247, Laredo, 78044.*

Vicar General—Rev. Msgr. STANLEY A. SLIWIAK.

Chancellor—Rev. Msgr. ALEJANDRO SALAZAR, *P.O. Box 2247, Laredo, 78044-2247.*

Tribunal—Sr. MARY WALDEN, O.S.U., Dir., *1901 Corpus Christi, Laredo, 78043.* Tel: 956-717-9668.

Fiscal Officer—PATRICIA GUAJARDO.

Presbyteral Council—Rev. Msgr. STANLEY SLIWIAK; Rev. Msgr. THOMAS DAVIS; Rev. Msgr. JAMES E. HARRIS; Revs. JOSE M. GUEVARA; RICHARD GUERRA, O.M.I.; Rev. Msgr. ALEJANDRO SALAZAR; Revs. BENJAMIN OROZCO, O.F.M.; JOSE ROMERO, O.S.A.; P. NOLASCO HINOJOSA, JR.; DANIEL RAMIREZ PORTUGAL; FRANCISCO MUNOZ, S.D.B.; TORIBIO GUERRERO.

College of Consultors—Rev. Msgr. STANLEY SLIWIAK; Rev. Msgr. THOMAS DAVIS; Revs. JOSE M. GUEVARA; RICHARD GUERRA, O.M.I.; Rev. Msgr. ALEJANDRO SALAZAR; Rev. P. NOLASCO HINOJOSA, JR.

Diocesan Offices and Directors

Campus Ministry—Vacant, Brothers of St. John, Texas A&M International University; Laredo and Laredo Community College; *P34, Fort McIntosh, Laredo, 78040.* Tel: 956-722-2324.

Laredo Catholic Communications, Inc.—BENNETT MCBRIDE, Exec. Vice Pres. & Gen. Mgr. JOSE A. JIMENEZ, Chief Radio Operator/KHOY; MARIO SEPULVEDA, Part-time Radio Operator, *1901 Corpus Christi St., Laredo, 78043.* Tel: 956-722-4167; Fax: 956-722-4464.

Catholic Social Services of Laredo, Inc.—ROXANNA GUERRA, Exec. Dir. GRACIE SEPULVEDA, Sec., *1901 Corpus Christi, Laredo, 78043.* Tel: 956-722-2443; Fax: 956-725-2238.

Adoption—SARA THOMPSON. Tel: 956-722-2443.

Emergency Assistance Program—ELIDA GARCIA. Tel: 956-722-2443.

Immigration Services—ROXANNA GUERRA, Admin., *Servicios Para Inmigrantes, 1901 Corpus Christi St., Laredo, 78043.* Tel: 956-722-2443.

Catholic Cemetery—Deacon LUIS TREVINO, Dir. ROSA ALDAPE, Mgr., *3600 McPherson, P.O. Box 2366, Laredo, 78040.* Tel: 956-723-6811; Fax: 956-724-5720.

Charismatic Renewal—Rev. MICHAEL DELEON, Liaison. Tel: 956-726-0210.

Cursillo Movement—Rev. VLADIMIRO MANENTE, Spiritual Dir. for Western Vicariate. Tel: 956-723-3850.

Family Violence Program—Night Attendants: HILARIA DELEON; DIANA L. MIRANDA; ANGELA MICHELLE RODRIGUEZ, Child/Legal Advocate; CARMEN RENDON, Coord., *La Frontera, 1616 Callaghan, Laredo, 78040.* Tel: 956-722-7271; Fax: 956-727-7888.

Finance Committee—Mr. PAT HEARN; Mr. SABAS ZAPATA; Mr. ARMENGOL GUERRA; Rev. P. NOLASCO HINOJOSA, JR.; Rev. Msgr. ALEJANDRO SALAZAR.

Natural Family Planning—BERNICE SEPULVEDA, NFP Coord. Tel: 956-722-7017., *Mercy Center, 1611 Hendricks, Laredo, 78044.* Tel: 956-722-7017.

Understanding Sexuality—MARIA LOURDES "LULU" SANCHEZ, Instructor. Tel: 956-724-9776.

Pastoral Institute for Ministry & Christian Service—Sr. MARIA GUADALUPE HERRERA, R.S.M., Asst. Coord. YOLANDA MOLINA, Sec. Aide, *1901 Corpus Christi, Laredo, 78043.* Tel: 956-722-0959.

Persons with Disabilities—Rev. DAVID T. WALSH, Dir.; SANDRA MARTINEZ, Coord., *1901 Corpus Christi, Laredo, 78043.* Tel: 956-724-9924.

Priests' Personnel Board—Revs. NOEL DAVIS; DANIEL RAMIREZ-PORTUGAL; SALVADOR PEDROZA; JOSE LUIS BALDERAS; Rev. Msgr. ALEJANDRO SALAZAR.

Religious Education Office—Sr. MARIA GUADALUPE HERRERA, R.S.M., Dir. YOLANDA MOLINA, Sec. Aide, *1901 Corpus Christi, Laredo, 78043.* Tel: 956-724-0959.

Other Offices and Organizations

Birthright Counseling—ROXANNA GUERRA, Admin, *1901 Corpus Christi St., Laredo, 78043.*

Catholic Daughters of the Americas—BEA ALLEN, District 15: Laredo. Tel: 956-723-7276.

Legion of Mary—MANUEL GARCIA, Laredo Area Contact. Tel: 956-723-4333.

CLERGY, PARISHES, MISSIONS AND PAROCHIAL SCHOOLS

CITY OF LAREDO
(Webb County)

1—SAN AGUSTIN CATHEDRAL (1762), Rev. Msgr. James E. Harris; Deacon Miguel Vallarta.

200 San Agustin Ave., 78040. Tel: 956-722-1382; Fax: 956-722-0441.

2—BLESSED SACRAMENT (1950), Rev. Msgr. Stanley A. Sliwak, Ph.D.; Rev. Leszek Waclawik; Deacons David Vargas; Larry Sandlin.

2219 Galveston St., 78043. Tel: 956-722-1295; 722-1231; Fax: 956-722-2823.

3—CHRIST THE KING (1954), Rev. Daniel Ramirez-Portugal.

1105 Tilden Ave., 78040. Tel: 956-723-4267; Fax: 956-791-8034.

4—DIVINE MERCY (1998), Rev. Michael De Leon.

Res., 605 Sesame Ln., 78045. Tel: 956-726-0210; Fax: 956-726-1286.

5—HOLY FAMILY (1984), Rev. P. Nolasco Hinojosa, Jr.

2705 McPherson, 78044. Tel: 956-724-6881; Fax: 956-724-5581.

6—HOLY REDEEMER (1940), Rev. Jose Romero Z., O.S.A.

Mailing Address: P.O. Box 1087, 78040.

1602 Garcia St., 78040. Tel: 956-723-7171; Fax: 956-723-7194.

Mission—Laredo, Webb Co., Santa Cruz, 2002 Lee Ave., 78042.

7—OUR LADY OF GUADALUPE (1926), Revs. Edward Ward, O.M.I.; Edward Vrazel, O.M.I.

Mailing Address: P.O. Box 671, 78042.

1718 San Jorge Ave., 78042. Tel: 956-723-6954; Fax: 956-723-6047.

8—SAN FRANCISCO JAVIER INDEPENDENT MISSION (1966), Rev. Vladimiro Manente, O.M.I.; Deacon Jorge Garza.
Mailing Address: P.O. Box 1175, 78042-1175.
2502 Zaragoza St., 78042-1175. Tel: 956-723-3850; Fax: 956-725-6544.

9—SAN LUIS REY (1958), Revs. Juan Francisco Munoz, S.D.B.; Jose Sergio Abreu, S.D.B.; Deacon Jose Rodriguez.
Mailing Address: P.O. Box 2294, 78044-2294.
3502 Sanders Ave., 78044-2294. Tel: 956-723-6587; Fax: 956-723-6825.

10—SAN MARTIN DE PORRES (1979), Rev. Msgr. Alejandro Salazar; Rev. Ralph Anthony Mendoza.
Mailing Address: P.O. Box 2666, 78044-2294.
1702 Sandman, 78044-2666. Tel: 956-723-5215; Fax: 956-723-9443.

11—SANTA MARGARITA DE ESCOCIA INDEPENDENT MISSION, Rev. Francis Stodola; Deacon Leonel San Miguel.
320 Segovia Dr., 78043. Tel: 956-724-9669.
Mission—Ntra. Sra. Del Rosario (Colonia Los Obispos).

12—SANTO NINO INDEPENDENT MISSION, Rev. Noel Davis.
2717 Cross St., 78043. Tel: 956-724-6638; Fax: 956-712-8096.

13—ST. FRANCES CABRINI (1958), Rev. Jose Alfredo Gaytan, S.O.L.T.
3018 Davis Ave., 78040. Tel: 956-722-2919; Fax: 956-724-5232.

14—ST. JOHN NEUMANN (1979), Rev. Randy Cain; Deacon Gerardo Morales.
102 W. Hillside Rd., 78041. Tel: 956-726-9488; Fax: 956-726-0540.

15—ST. JOSEPH (1953), Rev. Alessandro Ditaddeo; Deacon Crispin O. Soto.
109 N. Meadow, 78040. Tel: 956-723-4172; Fax: 956-728-8824.

16—ST. JUDE (1984), Rev. Santiago Domingo.
Mailing Address: P.O. Box 440502, 78044-0502.
2031 Lowry Rd., 78044-0502. Tel: 956-722-2280; Fax: 956-726-8017.

17—ST. PATRICK (1970), Rev. Msgr. Thomas A. Davis; Rev. Richard Voigt.
555 E. Del Mar Blvd., 78041. Tel: 956-722-6215; Fax: 956-722-6266.
Mission—Apostolate Missions in Northern Mexico.

18—ST. PETER THE APOSTLE (1897), Rev. Wojciech Kosowicz, Ph.D.
Mailing Address: P.O. Box 26, 78040.
1502 Matamoros, 78040. Tel: 956-723-6301; Fax: 956-729-1229.

19—ST. VINCENT DE PAUL (1969), Revs. Pastor Martinez, O.S.A.; Alberto Palmeno, O.S.A.
2710 Boulanger St., 78043. Tel: 956-722-3034; Fax: 956-722-4829.

OUTSIDE THE CITY OF LAREDO

Asherton, Dimmit Co., Immaculate Conception (1918), Rev. Toribio C. Guerrero.
Mailing Address: P.O. Box 8, 78827. Tel: 830-468-3343; Fax: 830-468-3342.
Missions—Big Wells, St. Michael, P.O. Box 266, 78830-0266. Tel: 830-457-2093; Catarina, St. Henry, P.O. Box 15, 78836. Tel: 830-468-3343.

Carrizo Springs, Dimmit Co., Our Lady of Guadalupe (1881), Rev. Salvador Pedroza; Deacons Jose F. Perez; Genaro Ramon; Juan Sauceda.
1107 N. Eighth St., 78834. Tel: 830-876-2239; Fax: 830-876-2172.

Cotulla, La Salle Co., Sacred Heart (1917), Rev. John van Lare, C.M.; Deacon Jose Patterson.
Mailing Address: P.O. Box 560, 78014. Tel: 830-879-2658.

Crystal City, Zavala Co., Sacred Heart (1917), Rev. Msgr. Jose Maria Guevara; Deacons Jose L. Lopez; Jose Garza; Aurelio Medina.
115 E. Kinney St., 78839. Tel: 830-374-3148; Fax: 830-374-2211.

Eagle Pass, Maverick Co., Our Lady of Refuge (1859), Revs. Alfonso Giopatto, O.M.I.; Patricio Dominguez, O.M.I.; Deacons Efren Maldonado; Miguel Velez.
Mailing Address: P.O. Box 909, 78853-0909.
810 Ceylon St., 78853-0909. Tel: 830-773-8451 (Office); 830-773-8421 (Res.).
Missions—Seco Mines, Our Lady of Lourdes, 210-773-8288; Quemado, Our Lady of Guadalupe, Tel: 210-758-1888.
Sacred Heart (1966), Revs. Richard Guerra, O.M.I.; Richard Hall, O.M.I.
Mailing Address: 2055 Williams St., 78853-0806. Tel: 830-773-2451; Fax: 830-773-0643.
St. Joseph (1967), Rev. John McGrath, O.M.I.
Mailing Address: 800 Comal St., 78852-0246. Tel: 830-773-6114.

Encinal, La Salle Co., Immaculate Heart of Mary (1898), Rev. P. Nolasco Hinojosa, Jr.
Mailing Address: P.O. Box 5, 78019-0005.
400 Santa Fe St., 78019-0005. Tel: 956-948-5328; Fax: 956-948-5328.

Hebbronville, Jim Hogg Co., Our Lady of Guadalupe (1926), Revs. Benjamin Orozco, O.F.M.; Silvestre Rodriguez, O.F.M.; Rafael Garcia, O.F.M.
504 E. Santa Clara St., 78361. Tel: 512-527-3865; Fax: 512-527-5548.
Missions—Mirando City, Webb Co., Immaculate Conception; Oilton, Webb Co., St. Agnes; Bruni, Webb Co., St. Bridget; Realitos, Dual Co., Sacred Heart.

La Pryor, Zavala Co., St. Joseph (1917), Rev. Jose Luis Balderas; Deacons Gene Corrigan; Juan Gallegos.
Mailing Address: P.O. Box 436, 78872. Tel: 830-365-4107.
Mission—Batesville, St. Patrick, P.O. Box 83, 78829.

Rio Bravo, Santa Rita de Casia Independent Mission, Rev. Mariano Martinez.
1001 Espejo Molina, 78043. Tel: 956-725-7215.
Mission—Rio Bravo, Santa Monica Mission, 507 Morales (El Cenizo), 78043.

Zapata, Zapata Co., Our Lady of Lourdes (1940), Revs. Arturo Rodriguez; Arturo Rodriguez; Bro. Francis Delgadillo, O.S.B.
Mailing Address: P.O. Box 3213, 78076.
Res., 1609 Glenn St., 78076. Tel: 956-765-4216; Fax: 956-765-6188.
Missions—Zapata, Zapata Co., Ntra. Sra. Del Refugio, P.O. Box 3213, 78076.; San Ignacio, St. Ignatius; Lopeno, San Pedro; Falcon, Santa Ana.

Missions

Laredo, Webb Co., Missions, Deacon Gerardo Morales.
Mailing Address: c/o Chancery Office, 1901 Corpus Christi St., P.O. Box 2247, 78044. Tel: 956-727-2140; Fax: 956-727-2777. @ = Chaplains of Public Institutions

LAREDO, TX. *Mercy Health Center* 1700 E. Saunders Ave., 78401. Tel: 956-796-5000. Rev. Cyriacus Udegbulem, Chap.
Webb County Jail. Chaplaincy Apostolate to Refugees & Jail Ministry. 4402 Tilden Ave., 78041. Tel: 956-723-5029. Deacon Jose Rodriguez.

INSTITUTIONS LOCATED IN THE DIOCESE

[A] HIGH SCHOOLS

LAREDO. *St. Augustine.* (Diocesan), 1300 Galveston St., 78040. Tel: 956-724-8131; Fax: 956-725-9241.
E-mail: almarose@st-augustine.org
Sr. Alma Rose Booty, C.D.P., Prin. Lay Teachers 33; Students 631.

[B] JUNIOR HIGH AND ELEMENTARY SCHOOLS

LAREDO. *Blessed Sacrament*, 1501 N. Bartlett St., 78043. Tel: 956-722-1222; Fax: 956-722-5635.
E-mail: school@lmtonline.com
Sr. Patrice Floyd, I.W.B.S., Prin. Sisters 2; Lay Teachers 8; Students 131.
Mary Help of Christians. (Private), 10 E. Del Mar Blvd., 78045. Tel: 956-722-3966. Sr. Martina Ponce, F.M.A., Prin. Sisters 12; Lay Teachers 60; Students 721.
Our Lady of Guadalupe. (Parochial), 400 Callaghan St., 78040-3834. Tel: 956-722-3915; Fax: 956-727-2840.
E-mail: eperales@icsi.net
Mr. Eduardo Perales, Prin. Sisters 1; Lay Teachers 8; Students 136.
St. Augustine. (Diocesan), 1300 Galveston, 78040. Tel: 956-724-1176; Fax: 956-725-9891. Sr. Marie Elise van Dijk, Prin. Sisters 1; Lay Teachers 11; Students 223.
St. Peter Memorial. (Diocesan), 1519 Houston St., P.O. Box 520, 78040. Tel: 956-723-6302. Mrs. Olga Ayala, Prin. Sisters 1; Lay Teachers 9; Students 116.

EAGLE PASS. *Our Lady of Refuge*, 577 Washington, 78852. Tel: 830-773-3531; Fax: 830-773-7310.
E-mail: asacsoloreap@impressso.com
Sr. Mary Elizabeth Orr, S.S.N.D., Prin. Sisters 3; Lay Teachers 15; Students 395.

[C] GENERAL HOSPITALS

LAREDO. *Mercy Hospital of Laredo dba Mercy Health Center*, 1700 E. Saunders St., 78041. Tel: 956-796-5000; Fax: 956-793-3173.
Web site: www.mercylaredo.com
For a complete listing, refer to the Hospitals section.

[D] ORPHANAGES AND INFANT HOMES

LAREDO. *Sacred Heart Children's Home*, 3310 S. Zapata Hwy., 78046. Tel: 956-723-3343; Fax: 956-723-3409
For a complete listing, refer to the Special Care Facilities section.

[E] MONASTERIES AND RESIDENCES OF PRIESTS AND BROTHERS

LAREDO. *Marist Brothers*, 1511 E. Cherry Hill Dr., 78041. Tel: 956-724-2651; Fax: 956-724-1963.
E-mail: fmslaredo@prodigy.net
Bros. Philip R. Degagne, F.M.S., Dir.; Joseph E. Herrera, F.M.S.; Thomas W. Coyne, F.M.S.; John A. Allen, F.M.S.; Robert Warren, F.M.S. Marist Brothers 5.
St. John Priory, F.J. Congregation of St. John, 505 Century Dr., S., 78046. Tel: 956-722-2399; Fax: 956-722-3299. Revs. Dominique F. Peridans, F.J., Prior; Didier-Marie Dugas Viallis (France); Juan de Dios Saavedra (Spain); Marianus Hough (Canada); Bros. Louis-Mary Ketterhagen; John Victor Shoemaker; John Mary Ignatius Crawley, F.J.; Deacon John Therese Crews. Priests 3; Brothers in Formation 12; Total in Residence 20.

[F] CONVENTS AND RESIDENCES FOR SISTERS

LAREDO. *Eucharistic Missionary Soceity*, 1101 Cortez St., 78040. Tel: 956-726-4085.
Mary Help of Christians, 10 E. Del Mar Blvd., 78045. Tel: 956-722-3966; Fax: 956-722-1413.
E-mail: fmasuolr@icsi.net
Sr. Martina Ponce, F.M.A., Prin. & Supr. Daughters of Mary Help of Christians Salesian Sisters. Sisters 13; Total Staff 67.
Misioneras del Rosario de Fatima, 555 Del Mar Blvd., 78041. Tel: 956-722-6215.
Sacred Heart Children's Home Convent, 3310 S. Zapata Hwy., 78046. Tel: 956-723-3343; Fax: 956-723-3409. Sr. Maria Teresa Grajeda, S.S.H.J.P., Supr. Servants of the Sacred Heart of Jesus and of the Poor. Sisters 22.
Sisters of Divine Providence, 1501 Guerrero, 78040. Tel: 956-725-9951; Fax: 956-725-9241. 1414 Hendricks, 78040. Tel: 956-722-3245; Fax: 956-718-6904.
Sisters of Incarnate Word and Blessed Sacrament, 1414 Hendricks, 78040. Tel: 956-723-1364; Fax: 956-718-6904.
Sisters of Mercy Convent, 1414 Hendricks Ave., 78040. Tel: 956-723-1364.
E-mail: oobregon@lare.smhs.com
Sr. Olivia M. Obregon, Local Coord. Religious Sisters of Mercy. Mercy Hospital Convent. Tel: 956-723-1353. Su Casa, 2905 Monterrey Ave., 78046. Tel: 956-718-8762. Sisters 8; Total Staff 4.
Sisters of Our Lady of the Most Holy Trinity, 2454 Colonia Loop, 78046. Tel: 956-727-3965.
Sisters of St. John, 504 Century Dr., S., 78046. Tel: 956-727-1028; Fax: 956-727-1028. Sr. Marie-Abel Buisset, Local Supr. Total in Residence 6.
Ursuline Convent, 2302 Corpus Christi St., 78043. Tel: 956-723-9185; Fax: 956-723-4322.
E-mail: marmullen@juno.com
Sr. Marianne Mullen, O.S.U., Prioress, Roman Union Central Province of the U.S., 1415 Jarvis St., 78043. Tel: 956-723-8968. Sisters 8.

ASHERTON. *Misioneras Cordi-Marianas*, P.O. Box 8, 78827-0008. Tel: 830-468-3343.

BIG WELLS. *Carmelitas del Sagrado Corazon, O.C.D.*, P.O. Box 276, 78830. Tel: 830-457-2693. Sr. Maria Guadalupe Esparza, O.C.D., Supr. Sisters 3.

CARRIZO SPRINGS. *Hermanas Catequistas Guadalupanas*, 501 Easton St., 78834. Tel: 830-876-2239; 876-2217.

EAGLE PASS. *Congregation of Benedictine Sisters*, 779 Encinal Dr., 78852. Tel: 830-758-0812.
Congregation of the Sisters of the Incarnate Word, 577 Washinton St., 78852-4299. Tel: 830-773-8270; Fax: 830-773-7310.
Missionary Sisters of Our Lady of Perpetual Help, 859 Webster, 78852. Tel: 830-773-8915.
School Sisters of Notre Dame, 577 Washington St., 78852. Tel: 830-773-8270.

ZAPATA. *Misioneras del Rosario de Fatima*, P.O. Box 3213, 78076. Tel: 956-765-4216; Fax: 956-765-6188.

[G] RETREAT HOUSES

LAREDO. *Holy Spirit Retreat and Conference Center*, 501 S. Century Dr., 78046. Tel: 956-726-4352; Fax: 956-726-4363.
E-mail: stjohn@border.net
Web site: www.stjean.com/laredo/hsrc/holy.htm
Rev. Dominique Peridans, F.J., Prior; Bro. John Mary Ignatius Crawley, F.J., Guestmaster. Total in Residence 2; Postulants 6; Total Staff 4.

[H] MISCELLANEOUS

LAREDO. *Bethany House*, 819 Hidalgo St., 78040. Tel: 956-722-4152; Fax: 956-726-2349; 728-7471. Barbara Kazen, Pres.; Nanette Dion, Devel. Svcs.

Casa de Misericordia. Domestic Violence Shelter for Women and Children, P.O. Box 430175, 78044. Tel: 956-712-9590; 877-782-2722. Sr. Rosemany Welsh, R.S.M., Exec. Dir.

International Order of the Alhambras-Zahara Caravan No. 64, 1015 Eden Ln., 78045. Tel: 956-723-0065; Fax: 956-723-3633. Alberto P. Cardenas, Grand Commander.

La Frontera Halfway House, 1616 Callaghan, 78040. Tel: 956-722-7271. Roxanna Guerra, Admin.

St. Augustine School Endowment Fund, Inc., 1300 Galveston, 78040. Tel: 956-724-8131; Fax: 956-725-9241.
E-mail: almarose@st.augustine.org
Web site: www.st-augustine.org
Sr. Alma Rose Booty, Prin.

San Agustin Historical Preservation & Restoration Society, Inc., 200 San Agustin Ave., 78040. Tel: 956-722-1382; Fax: 956-722-0441. Rev. Msgr. James E. Harris, Contact Person.

[I] NECROLOGY

(No Deaths)

Diocese of Lexington

Most Reverend

JAMES KENDRICK WILLIAMS, D.D.

Bishop of Lexington; ordained May 25, 1963; appointed Titular Bishop of Catula and Auxiliary Bishop of Covington on April 15, 1984; consecrated June 19, 1984; transferred to Lexington March 2, 1988. *Res., 1310 W. Main St., Lexington, KY, 40508-2048.*

ESTABLISHED MARCH 2, 1988.

Square Miles 16,423.

Comprises the counties of Anderson, Bath, Bell, Bourbon, Boyd, Boyle, Breathitt, Carter, Clark, Clay, Elliott, Estill, Fayette, Floyd, Franklin, Garrard, Greenup, Harlan, Jackson, Jessamine, Johnson, Knott, Knox, Laurel, Lawrence, Lee, Leslie, Letcher, Lincoln, McCreary, Madison, Magoffin, Martin, Menifee, Mercer, Montgomery, Morgan, Nicholas, Owsley, Perry, Pike, Powell, Pulaski, Rockcastle, Rowan, Scott, Wayne, Whitley, Wolfe and Woodford.

For legal titles of parishes and diocesan institutions, consult the Chancellor.

The Catholic Center: 1310 W. Main St., Lexington, KY, 40508-2048. Tel.: 606-253-1993; Fax: 606-254-6284.

Web site address: www.cdlex.org

E-mail address: jguentert@cdlex.org

STATISTICAL OVERVIEW

Personnel	
Bishop	1
Priests: Diocesan Active in Diocese	36
Priests: Active Outside Diocese	2
Priests: Retired, Sick or Absent	10
Number of Diocesan Priests	48
Religious Priests in Diocese	19
Extern Priests in Diocese	3
Ordinations:	
Diocesan Priests	1
Transitional Deacons	4
Permanent Deacons	33
Permanent Deacons in Diocese	37
Total Brothers	4
Total Sisters	152
Parishes	
Parishes	60
With Resident Pastor:	
Resident Diocesan Priests	32
Resident Religious Priests	4
Without Resident Pastor:	
Administered by Priests	5
Administered by Deacons	1
Administered by Professed Men Religious	2
Administered by Women Religious	3
Administered by Lay People	3
Administered by Pastoral Teams, etc.	10
Missions	5
Professional Ministry Personnel:	
Brothers	1
Sisters	23
Lay Ministers	24
Welfare	
Catholic Hospitals	6
Total Assisted	929,666
Health Care Centers	4
Total Assisted	71,436
Homes for the Aged	1
Total Assisted	82
Day Care and Extended Day Care Centers	1
Total Assisted	80
Special Centers for Social Services	1
Total Assisted	8,200
Educational	
Diocesan Students in Other Seminaries	10
Total Seminarians	10
High Schools, Diocesan and Parish	1
Total Students	874
High Schools, Private	2
Total Students	80
Elementary Schools, Diocesan and Parish	14
Total Students	3,018
Elementary Schools, Private	1
Total Students	206
Catechesis/Religious Education:	
High School Students	740
Elementary Students	2,781
Total Students Under Catholic Instruction	7,709
Teachers in the Diocese:	
Priests	2
Sisters	16
Lay Teachers	246
Vital Statistics	
Receptions into the Church:	
Infant Baptism Totals	780
Adult Baptism Totals	119
Received into Full Communion	232
First Communions	806
Confirmations	803
Marriages:	
Catholic	105
Interfaith	162
Total Marriages	267
Deaths	248
Total Catholic Population	42,345
Total Population	1,421,558

The Catholic Center—1310 W. Main St., Lexington, 40508-2048. Tel: 859-253-1993; Fax: 859-254-6284. Office Hours: Mon.-Fri. 8:30-4:30.

Vicar General—Rev. ROBERT H. NIEBERDING.

Chancellor—Deacon JIM PARIS.

Vice Chancellor—JANE GUENTERT.

Executive Secretary To The Bishop—SHEILA STEWART.

Finances—Dr. STUART DUBA, Dir., *1310 W. Main St., Lexington, 40508-2048.*

Diocesan Consultors—Revs. ROBERT H. NIEBERDING, V.G.; JAY VON HANDORF; TERENCE HOPPENJANS; MICHAEL WEGLICKI; JOHN CURTIS; KENNETH WAIBEL; RICHARD EDELEN, *1310 W. Main St., Lexington, 40508-2048.*

Regional Councillors—Rev. JAY VON HANDORF, Fayette Region; Rev. MICHAEL WEGLICKI, Bluegrass West Region; Rev. KENNETH WAIBEL, Bluegrass East Region; Rev. JOHN CURTIS, Mt. West Region; Rev. RICHARD EDELEN, Mt. East Region; Rev. TERENCE HOPPENJANS, Big Sandy-Licking Region.

Diocesan Tribunal—1310 W. Main St., Lexington, 40508-2048. Tel: 859-253-1993. Rev. JAMES ZUSY, O.P., J.C.D., Dir.

Judicial Vicar—Rev. JOHN E. LIST, J.C.L.

Associate Judges—Revs. JAMES AARON, M.Div., M.Ed.; JOACHIM CULOTTA, O.P., J.C.D.; Sr. MARGARET STALLMEYER, C.D.P., J.C.L.; RENATA BABICZ, J.U.D., J.C.L.; Mrs. LAURA LE FAVE, M.A., J.L.L.

Defenders Of The Bond—Revs. THOMAS THAI, Ph.D.; MICHAEL WEGLICKI; MAURICE RAJKOVICH, J.D.; Sr. GAYLE BRABEC, B.V.M.; TOBY TOMAZIC.

Case Instructor—CAROLYN SNOWDEN.

Secretary—VILMA O'NEIL.

Promoter of Justice—Rev. PAUL PRABELL, M.S.

Notary—CAROLYN SNOWDEN.

Ministry Admissions Board—Most Rev. J. KENDRICK WILLIAMS.

Priests' Retirement Board—Revs. PATRICK STEWART; GREGORY SCHULER; JOSEPH SAULINO; WILLIAM FEDDERS; THOMAS V. THAI; Mr. JOHN D. PRICE; WILLIAM TOZER; JOB D. TURNER; STUART DUBA.

Diocesan Offices And Directors

Archives—JIM PARIS, Archivist, *1310 W. Main St., Lexington, 40508-2048.* Tel: 859-253-1993, Ext. 236.

Campus Ministry—Newman Center Dir., Contact The Catholic Center, *1310 W. Main St., Lexington, 40508-2048.* Tel: 859-253-1993.

Catholic Charismatic Prayer Groups—Rev. CHARLES HOWELL, Liaison.

Catholic Scouting—Rev. MICHAEL WEGLICKI, Diocesan Dir. Tel: 859-792-4009.

Catholic Social Service Bureau—Sr. FRANCES MOORE, C.D.P., Dir., Office: *1310 W. Main St., Lexington, 40508-2048.* Tel: 859-253-1993.

Communications—THOMAS SHAUGHNESSY, Interim Dir., *1310 W. Main St., Lexington, 40508-2048.* Tel: 859-253-1993.

Conciliation, Arbitration Board—CAROL JACKSON, Chm.

Continuing Formation of Priests—Rev. JOSEPH MUENCH.

Deaf Ministry—Coordinators: CARLENE BUSCHMAN; JOE BUSCHMAN; Rev. JOHN LIST, Chap., *1310 W. Main St., Lexington, 40508-2048.* Tel: 859-253-1993. Tel: TDD: 859-223-2135.

Development Office—J. GRANT CHAPLINE, *1310 W. Main St., Lexington, 40508-2048.* Tel: 859-253-1993, Ext. 230.

Ecumenical Liaison—Mr. ARDEN WOLTERMAN, *3 Lansdowne Estates, Lexington, 40508.* Tel: 859-253-1993, Ext. 221.

Education—

Secretary of Educational Ministries—Dr. MARGARET RALPH, *1310 W. Main St., Lexington, 40508-2048.* Tel: 859-253-1993, Ext. 220.

Director Of Instructional Services—Sr. BERNADETTE MCMANIGAL, B.V.M., *1310 W. Main St., Lexington, 40508-2048.* Tel: 859-253-1993, Ext. 219.

Director For Catechetical Services—Mr. PATRICK GUENTERT, *1310 W. Main St., Lexington, 40508-2048.* Tel: 859-253-1993, Ext. 221.

Director R.C.I.A., And Evangelization—Dr. MARGARET RALPH, *1310 W. Main St., Lexington, 40508-2048.* Tel: 859-253-1993, Ext. 220.

Disciples in Mission—Sr. CHRISTEN SHUKWIT, O.S.F., Dir., *1310 W. Main St., Lexington, 40508-2048.* Tel: 859-253-1993, Ext. 212.

Family Ministry—Ms. KATHLEEN TOMAZIC, Diocesan Coord., *1310 W. Main St., Lexington, 40508-2048.* Tel: 859-253-1993, Ext. 228.

Fayette Catholic Elementary Schools Campaign—DON FULFORD, Dir., *1310 W. Main St., Lexington, 40508-2048.* Tel: 859-253-1993.

Healthcare—Vacant, Diocesan Coord., *1310 W. Main St., Lexington, 40508-2048.* Tel: 859-253-1993.

Hispanic Ministry—Sr. SANDRA DELGADO, O.P., Diocesan Coord.; Rev. JOSEPH VON HANDORF, Sacramental Minister, *1310 W. Main St., Lexington, 40508-2048.* Tel: 859-253-1993.

HIV/AIDS Ministry—Rev. JOHN C. CURTIS, Diocesan Coord.

Justice and Peace—Rev. JOHN RAUSCH, G.H.M., Diocesan Coord.

Commission for African American Catholic Concerns—Vacant, Contact, *P.O. Box 13006, Lexington, 40583-3006.* Tel: 859-254-0030.

Rural Life—The Catholic Center, 1310 W. Main St., Lexington, 40508-2048. Tel: 859-253-1993, Ext. 244.

Liturgy—Sr. CLARA FEHRINGER, O.S.U., Dir., *1310 W. Main St., Lexington, 40508-2048.* Tel: 859-253-1993, Ext. 244.

Ministry Formation—Sr. IRIS ANN LEDDEN, S.S.N.D., Dir., *1310 W. Main St., Lexington, 40508-2048.* Tel: 859-253-1993, Ext. 248.

Mission Office, Propagation Of The Faith And The Holy Childhood—Sr. MICHAEL LEO MULLANEY, S.C.N., Diocesan Dir., *1310 W. Main St., Lexington, 40508-2048.* Tel: 859-253-1993, Ext. 245.

Newspaper "Cross Roads"—THOMAS F. SHAUGHNESSY, Editor, *1310 W. Main St., Lexington, 40508-2048.* Tel: 859-253-1993, Ext. 258; Fax: 859-259-0951.

Parish Leadership—Sr. ELIZABETH WENDELN, S.C.N., Dir., *1310 W. Main St., Lexington, 40508-2048.* Tel: 859-253-1993, Ext. 251.

Pastoral Services—Sr. HELEN MAHER GARVEY, B.V.M., Diocesan Dir., *1310 W. Main St., Lexington, 40508-2048.* Tel: 859-253-1993. 247.

Permanent Diaconate—Co-Directors: ARDEN WOLTERMAN; BETTY WOLTERMAN, *3 Lansdowne Estate, Lexington, 40502-3321.* Tel: 859-276-4123.

Persons with Disabilities—Mrs. MARY PETRY, *124 Rolling Hills, Danville, 40422.* Tel: 859-236-5017.

Presbyteral Council—Most Rev. J. KENDRICK WILLIAMS, Pres., Ex Officio; Revs. ROBERT H. NIEBERDING, V.G.; RICHARD EDELEN; JOHN CURTIS; TERENCE HOPPENJANS; KEN WAIBEL; JAY VON HANDORF; MICHAEL WEGLICKI.

Priests' Personnel—Rev. LAWRENCE HEHMAN, Dir., *1332 Viley Rd., Lexington, 40504.* Tel: 859-252-4259.

Prison Ministry—Rev. JOHN NOE, Diocesan Coord., *900 Winchester Ave., Ashland, 41101-7497.* Tel: 606-329-1607.

Religious—Sr. HELEN MAHER GARVEY, B.V.M., Dir., *1310 W. Main St., Lexington, 40508-2048.* Tel: 859-253-1993, Ext. 236.

Respect Life—JIM PARIS, Diocesan Coord.

Vocations—Revs. MARK DREVES, Dir. JOHN MORIARTY, Assoc. Dir.; Sr. AMINO BEJOS, S.C.N.; Sr. KATHLEEN WEIGAND, O.S.B., *1310 W. Main St., Lexington, 40508-2048.*

Youth and Young Adult Ministries—BARBARA MURRAY, Dir., *The Catholic Center, 1310 W. Main St., Lexington, 40508-2048.*

CLERGY, PARISHES, MISSIONS AND PAROCHIAL SCHOOLS

CITY OF LEXINGTON
(Fayette County)

1—CATHEDRAL OF CHRIST THE KING (1945), Revs. Gregory Schuler, Rector; Robert J. Murphy, S.J.; Charles W. Howell; Sr. Kathy Bilskie, O.S.B, Pastoral Assoc.; Deacon Arden Wolterman. In res., Deacons Michael Burns; Richard Watson.
Res., 299 Colony Blvd., 40502. Tel: 606-268-2861; Fax: 606-268-2861.
School—(Grades K-8) 412 Cochran Rd., 40502. Tel: 606-266-5641.
Lay Teachers 28; Students 530.

2—THE NEWMAN CENTER, HOLY SPIRIT (1963). Parish for Students, Faculty and Staff of the University of Kentucky. Revs. Thomas Farrell; Walter Bado, S.J.
Res., 320 Rose Ln., 40508. Tel: 859-255-8566; Fax: 859-255-8567.

3—MARY, QUEEN OF THE HOLY ROSARY (1960), Revs. Robert H. Nieberding; Linh Nguyen; Deacons Jeremiah Noe; Jim Paris.
Res., 601 Hill'N Dale Rd., 40503. Tel: 859-278-7432; Fax: 859-278-2453.
Church—2523 Clays Mill Rd., 40503.
School—Tel: 859-277-3030; Fax: 859-277-1784.
Lay Teachers 32; Students 575.

4—PAX CHRISTI CATHOLIC CHURCH (1994), Rev. Lawrence W. Hehman; Deacon Dennis O'Neil.
Res., P.O. Box 8348, 40533. Tel: 859-223-7960; Fax: 859-223-7960 (Call first).

5—ST. ELIZABETH ANN SETON (1980), Revs. Wilfred J. Fraenzle; Norman A. Fischer; Sr. Eileen Golby, O.S.F., Pastoral Assoc. In res., Rev. Joseph Saulino; Deacon Michael Rupinen.
Res., 1750 Summerhill Dr., 40515. Tel: 859-273-0134.
Parish Center: Tel: 859-273-1318; Fax: 859-272-6988.; Education Office: Tel: 859-273-2318.

6—ST. PAUL (1865), Revs. Daniel Noll; Gino Donatelli, S.J.; Deacon Louis Fister; Sr. Clara Fehringer, O.S.U., Pastoral Assoc. In res., Rev. James Zusy, O.P.
Res., 501 W. Short St., 40507-1254. Tel: 859-252-0738; Fax: 859-225-6127. [JC]
School—Inter-Parish Elementary - Sts. Peter and Paul School. See St. Peter for details.

7—ST. PETER (1812), Revs. Daniel Noll; Gino Donatelli, S.J.; Deacon Bill Wakefield; Lisa Boley, Pastoral Assoc. In res., Revs. Theodore Keller, (Retired); Henry Kenney, S.J.
Res., 153 Barr St., 40507. Tel: 859-252-7551; Fax: 859-252-1853. [JC]
School—Inter-Parish Elementary - Sts. Peter and Paul School, Tel: 859-254-9257; Fax: 859-254-9050.
Lay Teachers 24; Students 372.

8—ST. PETER CLAVER (1887), Rev. Norman A. Fischer; Sr. M. Lea Paolucci, S.N.D., Pastoral Dir.; Deacon Boyd Marshall.
Res., 410 Jefferson St., 40508-1319. Tel: 859-254-0030; Fax: 859-253-6740.

OUTSIDE THE CITY OF LEXINGTON

Ashland, Boyd Co., Holy Family (1860), Revs. John P. Noe; Thobias Sabariar, H.G.N. In res., Rev. John Dane.
Res., 900 Winchester Ave., 41101-7497. Tel: 606-329-1607; Fax: 606-329-1806. [CEM]
School—932 Winchester Ave., 41101. Tel: 606-324-7040.
Lay Teachers 16; Students 190.
Mission—Greenup, St. Lawrence.

Barbourville, Knox Co., St. Gregory (1910), Rev. Bernard Lutkenhoff, Admin.
Church—329 N. Sycamore Dr., 40906-1540. Tel: 606-546-4461; Fax: 606-546-4416.

Beattyville, Lee Co., Queen of All Saints (1965), Rev. Richard D. Edelen; Sr. Alice Retzner, O.S.F., Pastoral Assoc.
Mailing Address: P.O. Box 563, 41311-0563. Tel: 606-464-8695.
Res., 90 Railroad St., 41311. Tel: 606-464-3357.
Mission—Booneville, Owsley Co., Booneville Catholic Church of the Holy Family, (1984) R.R. 2, Box 221, Booneville, 41314. Tel: 606-593-6948. Pastoral Assocs.: Sr. Karen Lindenberger, O.S.F.; Sr. Beatrice Herman, O.S.F.
Missions—Campton, Wolfe Co., Catholic Church of the Good Shepherd, (1987) P.O. Box 742, Campton, 41301. Tel: 606-668-3731. Sr. Margie Zureick, C.PP.S., Pastoral Assoc.; Heidelberg, Lee Co., St. Therese, (1948) P.O.Box 563, Beattyville, KY 41311. Tel: 606-464-3357.

Berea, Madison Co., St. Clare (1950), Rev. John C. Curtis; Sr. Anne Regina Lannon, S.S.J., Pastoral Assoc.
Res., 622 Chestnut St., 40403. Tel: 859-986-4633.
Mission—McKee, Jackson Co., St. Paul, (1973) P.O. Box 189, McKee, 40447. Tel: 606-287-7601. Pastoral Assocs.: Sr. Elaine Betoncourt, C.S.J.; Sr. Mary Dormody, C.S.J.

Carlisle, Nicholas Co., Shrine of Our Lady of Guadalupe (1962), Rev. Thomas Vu Minh Thai.
Church—617 E. Main St., 40311. Tel: 859-289-5502.
Res., 1007 Main St., Paris, 40361-1709. Tel: 859-987-1571.

Corbin, Knox Co., Sacred Heart (1902), Rev. Robert Damron, Admin. In res., Rev. Thomas J. Imfeld, (Retired).
Res., 703 Masters St., P.O. Box 455, 40702. Tel: 606-528-5222; Fax: 606-523-9901.

Danville, Boyle Co., SS. Peter & Paul (1807), Rev. Paul Prabell; Deacon Michael Pope.
Res., 117 W. Main St., 40422. Tel: 859-236-2111; Fax: 859-236-2922.

Cumberland, Harlan Co., St. Stephen (1940), Rev. Edward H. Lammert, O.F.M.; Sr. Margaret Mary Mouch, S.N.D., Pastoral Assoc. In res., Rev. Maynard Tetreault, O.F.M.
Res., 304 Central St., 40823. Tel: 606-589-5616; Fax: 606-589-4549.

Frankfort, Franklin Co., Good Shepherd (1845), Rev. Michael Ramler; Deacons Joseph Alessio; Thomas Snyder.
Res., 310 Wapping St., 40601-2060. Tel: 502-227-4511; Fax: 502-875-9854.
School—(Grades K-8) 316 Wapping St., 40601. Tel: 502-223-5041; Fax: 502-223-2755.
Lay Teachers 21; Students 319.

Georgetown, Scott Co., St. John's (1869), Rev. John E. List; Deacon John Calandrella.
Res., 604 E. Main St., 40324. Tel: 502-863-3404; Fax: 502-863-3404. [CEM]
School—(Grades K-6) 106 Military St., 40324. Tel: 502-863-2607; Fax: 502-863-2259.
Religious 2; Lay Teachers 6; Students 142.
Mission—White Sulphur, Scott Co., St. Francis de Sales, (1794) 4086 Frankfort Pike, 40324. Tel: 502-863-4516.

Grayson, Carter Co., Ss. John & Elizabeth (1964), Sr. Maria Goretti Browne, O.P., Pastoral Dir.; Revs. Bruce C. Brylinski, Glmy.; Robert Dalton, Glmy.
Church—799 State Hwy. 1947, 41143. Tel: 606-474-9979; Fax: 606-474-9979.
Res., P.O. Box 841, 41143. Tel: 606-474-9897.

Harlan, Harlan Co., Holy Trinity (1948), Bro. Mark Ligett, O.F.M., Pastoral Dir.; Rev. Edward H. Lammert, O.F.M., Pastoral Coord.
Res., 2536 S. U.S. Hwy. 421, 40831-1798. Tel: 606-573-6311; Fax: 606-574-0093.
School—Tel: 606-573-3570.
Sisters of Notre Dame 3; Lay Teachers 4; Students 67.

Harrodsburg, Mercer Co., St. Andrew (1858), Rev. Joseph Muench.
Res., 334 S. Chiles, 40330. Tel: 606-734-4270; Fax: 606-733-9770. [CEM]
Mission—Perryville, Boyle Co., St. Mary, (1949).

Hazard, Perry Co., Mother of Good Counsel (1913), Rev. Michael Chowning, O.F.M.; Ms. Patricia Riestenberg, Pastoral Assoc.
Res., 329 Poplar St. & Cedar St., 41701. Tel: 606-436-2533; Fax: 606-435-0171.

Jackson, Breathitt Co., Holy Cross (1923), Bro. Jerome Beetz, O.F.M., Pastoral Dir.; Rev. Michael Chowning, O.F.M., Pastoral Coord.
Church—51 Brewers Dr., 41339-9616. Tel: 606-666-7871.

Jellico, Whitley Co., KY & Campbell Co., TN, St. Boniface (1886), Rev. Robert Damron; Frank Agnoli, Pastoral Assoc.
Res., 76 W. Sycamore St., Williamsburg, 40769. Tel: 606-549-2156. [CEM]

Jenkins, Letcher Co., St. George (1912), Rev. Edward L. Randall, O.M.I.
Res., P.O. Box 787, 41537. Tel: 606-832-2409.
Mission—McRoberts, Letcher Co., Holy Angels, (1960).

Lancaster, Garrard Co., St. William (1951), Rev. Michael Weglicki.
Res., 224 Lexington St., P.O. Box 269, 40444. Tel: 859-792-4009.

Lawrenceburg, Anderson Co., St. Lawrence (1873), Rev. Charles J. McDonald; Deacon Thomas Rohan.
Res., 105 Woodland Park Cir., 40342. Tel: 502-839-6381; Fax: 502-859-2419.

London, Laurel Co., St. William/St. Sylvester (1888), Rev. Jerome F. Stern.
Res., 525 W. 5th St., 40741. Tel: 606-864-7500; Fax: 606-864-8263. [CEM]

Louisa, Lawrence Co., St. Jude (1982), Rev. Msgr. Ralph Beiting; Rev. Siby Thomas, H.G.N. (India).
Res., P.O. Box 177, 41230. Tel: 606-638-0219; Fax: 606-638-0220.
Mission—Hode, Martin Co., St. John Neumann, (1980) Rte. 292, Hode 41223. Tel: 606-395-5947.

Lynch, Harlan Co., Church of the Resurrection (1917), Rev. Edward H. Lammert, O.F.M.; Sr. Margaret Mary Mouch, S.N.D., Pastoral Assoc.
Res., 304 Central St., Cumberland, 40823. Tel: 606-589-5616; Fax: 606-589-4549.

Manchester, Clay Co., St. Ann (1952), Bernadette McMasters, Pastoral Assoc.
Church and Res.: 222 Town Branch Rd., 40962. Tel: 606-599-0230 (Res.); 598-2718 (Church); Fax: 606-598-2718.

Middlesboro, Bell Co., St. Julian (1890), Rev. Lee Francis Trimbur, Admin.
Res., 118 E. Chester Ave., 40965-1256. Tel: 606-248-2068; Fax: 606-248-2068.
School—(Grades K-8) 116 E. Chester Ave., 40965. Tel: 606-248-8309; Fax: 606-248-8307.
Sisters 1; Lay Teachers 3; Students 76.
Mission—Pineville, Bell Co., St. Anthony, (1889) P.O. Box 628, Pineville 40977-0628. Tel: 606-337-2189.

Morehead, Rowan Co., Church of Jesus Our Savior (1961), Rev. William J. Fedders; Deacon William T. Buelterman.
Res., 315 Battson, Box 307, 40351. Tel: 606-784-4392; Fax: 606-783-0190.
Chapel—Morehead, St. Claire Medical Center, Tel: 606-783-6500.

Monticello, Wayne Co., St. Peter (1967), Deacon John Tohill, Pastoral Dir.; Rev. John L. Kieffer, S.J.
Office: P.O. Box 669, 42633. Tel: 606-348-9416.
Res., 109 Cooper Dr., Somerset, 42501. Tel: 606-678-4928.

Mt. Sterling, Montgomery Co., St. Patrick (1868), Rev. Kenneth Waibel; Joan Houk, M. Div., Pastoral Dir.
Res., 139 W. Main St., 40353. Tel: 859-498-0300. [CEM]

Mt. Vernon, Rockcastle Co., Our Lady of Mt. Vernon (1954), Rev. John C. Curtis; Rose Mullen, Pastoral Assoc.
Res., 622 Chestnut St., Berea, 40403. Tel: 606-256-4170.

Nicholasville, Jessamine Co., St. Luke (1867), Rev. William C. Bush.
Res., 304 S. Main St., 40356. Tel: 859-885-4892; Fax: 859-885-6762.

Ottenheim, Lincoln Co., St. Sylvester (1885), Rev. Michael Weglicki.
Res., 224 Lexington St., P.O. Box 269, Lancaster, 40444. Tel: 859-792-4009. [CEM]

Paintsville, Johnson Co., St. Michael Catholic Church (1941), Rev. Terence E. Hoppenjans; Deacon John M. Lewis.
Res., 720 Washington Ave., 41240. Tel: 606-789-4455; Fax: 606-789-4455.
School—Our Lady of the Mountains, 405 Third St., 41240. Tel: 606-789-3661; Fax: 606-789-3661.
Sisters 1; Lay Teachers 5; Students 61.

Paris, Bourbon Co., Annunciation of the Blessed Virgin Mary (1856), Rev. Thomas Vu Minh Thai.
Res., 1007 Main St., 40361. Tel: 859-987-1571; Fax: 859-987-7367. [CEM]
School—St. Mary, 1121 Main St., 40361. Tel: 859-987-3815; Fax: 859-987-3815.
Sisters of Charity of Nazareth 1; Lay Teachers 6; Students 78.

Pikeville, Pike Co., St. Francis of Assisi (1949), Rev. Stephen Gallenstein; Deacon Robert Boduch.
Res., 132 Bryan St. (Keel), 41501-1404. Tel: 606-437-6822; Fax: 606-437-4901.
Church—149 College St., 41501.
School—(Grades K-6) 147 Bryan St., 41501. Tel: 606-437-6117; Fax: 606-437-6192.
Sisters 1; Lay Teachers 4; Students 78.
Missions—Elkhorn City, Pike Co., St. Joseph the Worker, (1985) P.O. Box 55, Elkhorn City, 41522. Tel: 606-754-5225. Sr. Joan Shalapin A.S.C., Pastoral Min.; Phelps, Pike Co., Jesus of the Mountains Catholic Church, (1988) 38 Birch Ct., Phelps, 41553. Tel: 606-456-7907. Sr. Grace Pasquarello, S.S.J., Pastoral Min.

Prestonsburg, Floyd Co., St. Martha (1984), Rev. John P. Moriarty.
Res., 60 Martha Vineyard, 41653. Tel: 606-874-9526; Fax: 606-874-9526.
Chapel—Martin, Our Lady of the Way Hospital, Tel: 606-285-5181.

Ravenna, Estill Co., St. Elizabeth (1932), Rev. William G. Poole. Pastoral Assocs.: Sr. Marcella Francis Milhouse, O.S.F.; Sr. Francis Acton, O.S.F.
Res., 316 5th St., 40472. Tel: 606-723-4705.
Mission—Stanton, Powell Co., Our Lady of the Mountains, (1984) 1093 E. College, Stanton, 40380. Tel: 606-663-5919. Pastoral Assocs.: Sr. Kathleen McMullin, O.S.F.; Sr. Eileen Doherty, O.S.F.

Richmond, Madison Co., St. Mark (1867), Rev. Patrick F. Stewart; Deacon Richard Jackson; Elaine Caldwell, Pastoral Assoc.
Res., 608 W. Main St., 40475. Tel: 859-623-2989; Fax: 859-623-4652.
School—Tel: 859-623-9112; Fax: 859-623-9947.
Lay Teachers 9; Students 175.
Mission—Richmond, St. Stephen the Martyr, (1977). (Eastern Kentucky University, Newman Center). Tel: 859-623-9400.

Salyersville, Magoffin Co., St. Luke, Revs. John Moriarty; Stephen Gallenstein, Mod.; Sr. Mary Catherine Vukmanic, O.S.U., Pastoral Dir.
1221 Parkway Dr., 41465. Tel: 606-349-5320.

Somerset, Pulaski Co., St. Mildred (1887), Rev. Dennis D. Knight (OG); Deacons G. A. Weigel; Vincent E. Cheshire; Larry Cranfill; Carter Ross. 203 S. Central Ave., 42501. Tel: 606-678-5051.

Versailles, Woodford Co., St. Leo (1891), Rev. Frank C. Osburg.
Res., 213 D. Berry Ave., 40383. Tel: 859-879-8481; Fax: 859-873-1495.
Church—295 Huntertown Rd., 40383. Tel: 859-873-4573.
School—239 N. Main St., 40383. Tel: 606-873-4591.
Sisters of Notre Dame 1; Lay Teachers 12; Students 174.

West Liberty, Morgan Co., Prince of Peace (1963), Rev. Peter Richardson, Glmy.
Res., Pine Acres Dr., P.O. Box 393, 41472. Tel: 606-743-4817; Fax: 606-743-3266.
Mission—Owingsville, Bath Co., St. Julie Billiart, (1969) P.O. Box 382, 40360. Tel: 606-674-3261. Deacon William R. Grimes.

Williamsburg, Whitley Co., Our Lady of Perpetual Help (1963), Rev. Robert Damron; Frank Agnoli, Pastoral Assoc.
Res., 76 W. Sycamore St., 40769. Tel: 606-549-2156.

Winchester, Clark Co., St. Joseph (1872), Rev. Kenneth Waibel; Deacon Charles Kennedy.
Res., 254 S. Main St., 40391. Tel: 859-744-4917.
School—St. Agatha Academy, (Grades K-8). (Montessori) 244 S. Main St., 40391. Tel: 859-744-6484.
Sisters of Divine Providence of Kentucky 1; Lay Teachers 9; Students 181.

Whitley City, Mc Creaky Co., Good Shepherd Chapel (1974), Rev. Carroll Howlin (JOL) Admin.
Res., P.O. Box 427, 42653. Tel: 606-376-5815.

Chaplains of Public Institutions

LEXINGTON. *Federal Medical Center* 3301 Leestown Rd., 40507. Rev. Arturo Molina, Chap.; Deacon Thaddeus Harbowy.
Veterans Administration Hospital Leestown Pk., 40511. Tel: 859-233-4511. Rev. George C. Maynard, S.J (DET) Chap.

ASHLAND. *Federal Correctional Institution.* 900 Winchester Dr., Ashland, 41101-7497. Rev. John P. Noe, Chap.

Special Assignment:
Reverend Fathers—
Arnsparger, Roger, In service to Diocese of Charlotte, N.C., St. Barnabas Parish, P.O. Box 38, Arden, NC 28704. Tel: 828-684-6098
Dreves, Mark, Vocations Dir., 1310 W. Main St., Lexington, KY 40508
Johnson, Carl, Federal Bureau of Prisons, Beckley, WV
Kenney, Henry, S.J., Spiritual Dir., Lexington, KY
Sichko, James, Catholic High School, Lexington

Retired:
Reverend Monsignors—
Nienaber, Leonard B., Vianney Renewal Center, 6476 Eime Rd., Dittmer, MD 63023
Rolf, John J., 15 Lemans Dr., Naples, FL 34112
Reverend Fathers—
Blandford, James T., 101 Covington, Springfield, KY 40069-1107
Brinker, Maurice J., Taylor Manor, 300 Berry Ave., Versailles, KY 40383
Imfeld, Thomas J., P.O. Box 455, Corbin, KY 40702
Keller, Theodore, 153 Barr St., Lexington, KY 40507
Lutkenhof, Bernard (LFT), 8700 Highway 92-W, Williamsburg, KY 40769
Pilger, Joseph J., 260 Pleasant Point Dr., Lexington, KY 40517
Stratman, Raymond, 310 Wapping St., Frankfort, KY 40601. Tel: 502-227-4511

Permanent Deacons:
Alessio, Joseph J.
Arnold, Paul J., Jr.
Barton, James
Boduch, Robert
Buelterman, William
Burns, Michael
Calandrella, John
Cheshire, Vincent
Cox, James H.
Cranfill, Larry
Daukas, Michael R.
Fister, Louis
Flowers, Don K.
Grimes, William R.
Harbowy, Thaddeus
Horine, James
Jackson, Richard
Kennedy, Charles
Lewis, John M.
Marshall, Boyd
Mellenger, Karl
Noe, Jeremiah, H.
O'Neil, Dennis J.
Paris, Jim
Piasecki, Stanley
Pope, Michael
Rohan, Thomas
Ross, Carter, Jr.
Rupinen, Michael
Schueneman, Joseph T.
Snyder, Thomas
Tohill, John J.
Wakefield, Bill
Watson, Richard
Weigel, Gerard A.
Wolterman, Arden J.
Young, Melvin

PARISH PILGRIMAGE SHRINES

CARLISLE. *Our Lady of Guadalupe Shrine* 617 E. Main St., 40311.

INSTITUTIONS LOCATED IN THE DIOCESE

[A] HIGH SCHOOLS, DIOCESAN

LEXINGTON. *Lexington Catholic High School*, 2250 Clays Mill Rd., 40503. Tel: 859-277-7183; Fax: 859-276-5086.
Web site: lexingtoncatholic.com
Rev. James Sichko; Mrs. Sally Stevens, Prin. Priests 1; Sisters 1; Lay Teachers 59; Students 874.

[B] HIGH SCHOOLS, PRIVATE

LONDON. *All Saints High School*, 4934 S. Laurel, 40744. Tel: 606-878-8458; Fax: 606-864-8963.
E-mail: jturner@sun-spot.com
Mrs. Janine Turner, Prin. Lay Teachers 6; Students 40.

MARTIN. *The Piarist School.* (Grades 9-12), Rte. 80, P.O. Box 870, 41649. Tel: 606-285-3950; Fax: 606-285-3950.
E-mail: piarist@kih.net
College Prep High School. Rev. Thomas R. Carroll, Sch.P., Prin. Priests 1; Lay Teachers 7; Students 40.

[C] ELEMENTARY SCHOOLS, PRIVATE

CORBIN. *St. Camillus Academy.* (Grades PreK-8), 709 E. Center St., 40701. Tel: 606-528-5077; Fax: 606-526-0106.
E-mail: stcam@tenet.net
Coed Day School. Sisters of Divine Providence of KY. Sisters 4; Lay Teachers 14; Students 206.

[D] GENERAL HOSPITALS

LEXINGTON. *St. Joseph Health Care, Inc. dba St. Joseph East*, 150 N. Eagle Creek Dr., 40509. Tel: 859-268-3750
For a complete listing, refer to the Hospitals section.
St. Joseph Hospital, 1 St. Joseph Dr., 40504. Tel: 859-278-3436
For a complete listing, refer to the Hospitals section.

ASHLAND. *BS-OLBH, Inc.*, St. Christopher Dr., 41101. Tel: 606-833-3333
For a complete listing, refer to the Hospitals section.
Our Lady of Bellefonte Hospital, Inc., St. Christopher Dr., 41101. Tel: 606-833-3333; Fax: 606-833-3695.
E-mail: rmaker@olbh.com
Web site: www.olbh.com
For a complete listing, refer to the Hospitals section.

IRVINE. *Marcum and Wallace Memorial Hospital*, 60 Mercy Ct., 40336. Tel: 606-723-2115; Fax: 606-723-2951
For a complete listing, refer to the Hospitals section.

LONDON. *London, Marymount dba Marymount Medical Center*, 310 E. Ninth St., 40741. Tel: 606-878-6520; Fax: 606-877-3707.
E-mail: ljones@marymount.com
Web site: marymount.com
For a complete listing, refer to the Hospitals section.

MARTIN. *Our Lady of the Way Hospital, Inc.*, Box 910, 41649. Tel: 606-285-5181; Fax: 606-285-6422.
Web site: www.olwh.org
For a complete listing, refer to the Hospitals section.

MOREHEAD. *Saint Claire Medical Center*, 40351. Tel: 606-783-6500; Fax: 606-783-6503.
E-mail: mneff@st-claire.com
Web site: st-claire.com
For a complete listing, refer to the Hospitals section.

[E] PRIMARY HEALTH CARE SERVICES

FRENCHBURG. *Menifee Medical Center*, HCR 71, Box 220, Kentucky 36, 40322. Tel: 606-768-2191
For a complete listing, refer to the Hospitals section.

OLIVE HILL. *Carter County Medical Clinic*, P.O. Box 1268, 155 Bricklayer St., 41164. Tel: 606-286-4152; Fax: 606-286-2385
For a complete listing, refer to the Hospitals section.

OWINGSVILLE. *Bath County Medical Clinic*, 632 Slate Ave., 40360. Tel: 606-674-6386; Fax: 606-674-3096
For a complete listing, refer to the Hospitals section.

SANDY HOOK. *Elliot County Medical Clinic*, P.O. Box 748, 41171. Tel: 606-738-5155
For a complete listing, refer to the Hospitals section.

[F] NURSING HOMES

VERSAILLES. *Taylor Manor Nursing Home*, 300 Berry Ave., 40383. Tel: 606-873-4201
For a complete listing, refer to the Special Care Facilities section.

[G] RESIDENCES OF PRIESTS

PRESTONSBURG. *Piarist Fathers*, 99 Martha's Vineyard, 41653. Tel: 606-874-4261. Rev. Thomas R. Carroll, Sch.P. Priests 1.

[H] MONASTERIES FOR SISTERS

MARTIN. *Sisters of St. Benedict-The Dwelling Place Monastery*, 150 Mt. Tabor Rd., 41649. Tel: 606-886-9624; Fax: 606-886-9624.
E-mail: mtabor150@hotmail.com
Web site: www.geocities.com/atheus/9871
Sr. Judy Yunker, O.S.B., Supr. Total number in community perpetually professed 5; Resident Oblates 2.

[I] SECULAR INSTITUTES

LEXINGTON. *Society of St. Vincent de Paul*, 3900 Crosby Dr., #2524, 40517. Tel: 606-971-2219.
E-mail: bsdup0@pop.uky.edu
Bernadette Dupont, Pres. District Council of Lexington; Deacon James Barton, Spiritual Dir.

[J] SOCIAL SERVICES

MOUNT VERNON.
Appalachia Science in the Public Interest, 50 Lair St., 40456. Tel: 606-256-0077; Fax: 606-256-2779.
E-mail: aspi@kih.net
Web site: www.kih.net/aspi
Revs. Albert J. Fritsch, S.J.; John L. Kieffer, S.J.

[K] RENEWAL CENTERS

HAZARD. *Father Farrell Spiritual Life Center*, 329 Poplar at Cedar, 41701. Tel: 606-436-2533; Fax: 606-435-0171. Rev. Michael Chowning, O.F.M., Dir.; Pat Riestenberg, Assoc. Dir.

LANCASTER. *Cliffview Retreat Center*, 777 Bryants Camp Rd., 40444. Tel: 859-792-3333; 877-792-3330; Fax: 859-792-1223.
E-mail: cliffctr@searnet.com
Web site: www.cdlex.org
Co-Directors: Deacon Joseph Schueneman; Judy Schueneman.

MARTIN. *Sisters of St. Benedict, Mt. Tabor Retreat Center*, 150 Mt. Tabor Rd., 41649. Tel: 606-886-9624; Fax: 606-886-9624.
E-mail: mtabor150@hotmail.com
Web site: www.geocities.com/atheus/9871
Staff Sisters 5.

[L] NEWMAN CENTERS

LEXINGTON. *The Newman Center Holy Spirit Parish University of Kentucky*, 320 Rose Ln., 40508. Tel: 859-255-8566; Fax: 859-254-7519.
E-mail: timenewman@aol.com
Revs. Thomas Farrell; Walter Bado, S.J.

BARBOURVILLE. *St. Gregory Church-Union College*, 329 N. Sycamore St., 40906-1540. Tel: 606-546-4461; Fax: 606-546-4416.
E-mail: gregory@barbourville.com
Web site: http//barbourville.catholicweb.com
Rev. Bernard Lutkenhoff.

BEREA. *St. Clare Church-Berea College*, 622 Chestnut St., 40403. Tel: 859-986-4633.
E-mail: stclare@zeus.chapel1.com
Rev. John C. Curtis; Sr. Anne Regina Lannon, S.S.J.

MOREHEAD. *Catholic Student Center-Morehead State University*, P.O. Box 307, 40351. Tel: 606-784-4392; Fax: 606-783-0190.
E-mail: joscc@mis.net
Web site: www.cdlex.org/morehead
Rev. William J. Fedders, Campus Min.

RICHMOND. *St. Stephen Newman Center-St. Mark Church*, Eastern Kentucky University, 405 University Dr., 40475-2154. Tel: 859-623-9400 (Center).
E-mail: ekunewman@kih.net
Web site: http://stmark-richmond.org/newman
Rev. Patrick F. Stewart; Ms. Katherine A. Schmitt, Pastoral Assoc., Campus Min.

[M] MISCELLANEOUS

ASHLAND. *Bon Secours Health System, Inc.*, St. Christopher Dr., 41101. Tel: 606-833-3333; Fax: 606-833-3593.
Web site: www.olbh.com
Mr. Robert J. Maher, Pres.

RELIGIOUS INSTITUTES OF MEN REPRESENTED IN THE DIOCESE

For further details refer to the corresponding bracketed number in the Religious Institutes of Men or Women section.

[0520]—*Franciscan Friars*. (St. John Baptist Province).—O.F.M.
[0570]—*Glenmary Home Missioners*.—Glmy.
[]—*Heralds of Good News*. (India).—H.G.N.
[0690]—*Jesuit Fathers and Brothers*. (Chicago & Detroit Provs.).—S.J.
[0910]—*Oblates of Mary Immaculate*. (Eastern American Prov.).—O.M.I.
[0430]—*Order of Preachers*.—O.P.
[1040]—*Piarist Fathers*. (U.S. Prov.).—Sch.P.

RELIGIOUS INSTITUTES OF WOMEN REPRESENTED IN THE DIOCESE

[0100]—*Adorers of the Blood of Christ*. (Ruma, IL).—A.S.C.
[0230]—*Benedictine Sisters of Pontifical Jurisdiction*. (Pittsburgh, PA; Covington, KY; Martin, KY).—O.S.B.
[1810]—*Bernardine Sisters of the Third Order of St. Francis*.—O.S.F.
[2100]—*Congregation of Humility of Mary*.—C.H.M.
[2230]—*Congregation of the Infant Jesus*.—C.I.J.
[1920]—*Congregation of the Sisters of the Holy Cross*.—C.S.C.
[1730]—*Congregation of the Sisters of the Third Order of St. Francis*. (Oldenburg, IN).—O.S.F.
[1780]—*Congregation of the Sisters of the Third Order of St. Francis of Perpetual Adoration*. (Eastern Region).—F.S.P.A.
[1070-03]—*Dominican Sisters*. (Sinsinawa, WI).—O.P.
[1070-13]—*Dominican Sisters*. (Adrian, MI).—O.P.
[1070-14]—*Dominican Sisters*. (Grand Rapids, MI).—O.P.
[1230]—*Franciscan Sisters of Christian Charity*.—O.S.F.
[1415]—*Franciscan Sisters of Mary*.—F.S.M.
[1440]—*Franciscan Sisters of the Poor*.—S.F.P.
[2080]—*Home Mission Sisters of America (Glenmary)*.—G.H.M.S.
[2575]—*Institute of the Sisters of Mercy of the Americas*. (Charlotte, NC; Philadelphia, PA; West Hartford, CT).—R.S.M.
[2470]—*Maryknoll Sisters of St. Dominic*.—M.M.
[2710]—*Missionaries of Charity*.—M.C.
[2070]—*Religious of the Holy Union of the Sacred Hearts*.—S.U.S.C.
[2970]—*School Sisters of Notre Dame*. (Baltimore).—S.S.N.D.
[1680]—*School Sisters of St. Francis*.—O.S.F.
[3580]—*Servants of Mary*.—O.S.M.
[0430]—*Sisters of Charity of Blessed Virgin Mary*. (Dubuque, IA).—B.V.M.
[0440]—*Sisters of Charity of Cincinnati, OH*.—S.C.
[0500]—*Sisters of Charity of Nazareth*.—S.C.N.
[0580]—*Sisters of Charity of St. Augustine*. (Rienfield, OH).—C.S.A.
[1000]—*The Sisters of Divine Providence of Kentucky*.—C.D.P.
[]—*Sisters of Mercy*. (Ireland).—R.S.M.
[]—*Sisters of Mercy*. (South Africa).—R.S.M.
[2990]—*Sisters of Notre Dame*. (Covington Prov.).—S.N.D.
[3000]—*Sisters of Notre Dame de Namur*. (Cincinnati Prov.).—S.N.D.deN.
[3360]—*Sisters of Providence of St. Mary-of-the-Woods, Indiana*.—S.P.
[3893]—*Sisters of Saint Joseph of Chestnut Hill, Philadelphia*.—S.S.J.
[1540]—*Sisters of St Francis*. (Clinton, IA).—O.S.F.
[3750]—*Sisters of St. Chretienne*. (Wrentham, MA).—S.S.Ch.
[1650]—*The Sisters of St. Francis of Philadelphia*.—O.S.F.
[3830-05]—*Sisters of St. Joseph*. (Baden, PA; Brentwood, NY).—C.S.J.
[3830-05]—*Sisters of St. Joseph*. (Brentwood, NY).—C.S.J.
[3850]—*Sisters of St. Joseph of Chambery*.—C.S.J.
[3920]—*Sisters of St. Joseph the Worker*.—S.J.W.
[3260]—*Sisters of the Precious Blood (Dayton, Ohio)*.—C.PP.S.
[3320]—*Sisters of the Presentation of the B.V.M.* (Fargo, ND; Dubuque, IA).—P.B.V.M.
[1760]—*Sisters of the Third Order of St. Francis of Penance and Charity*. (Tiffin, OH).—O.S.F.
[1720]—*Sisters of the Third Order Regular of St. Francis of the Congregation of Our Lady of Lourdes*.—O.S.F.
[2150]—*Sisters, Servants of the Immaculate Heart of Mary*.—I.H.M.
[4120-03]—*Ursuline Sisters of the Immaculate Conception*. (Louisville, KY).—O.S.U.
[4170]—*Vincentian Sisters of Charity*. (Bedford, OH).—V.S.C.

DIOCESAN CEMETERIES

LEXINGTON. *Calvary*.
ASHLAND. *Calvary*.
MT. STERLING. *St. Thomas*.

NECROLOGY

† Spalding, William A., Danville, KY SS. Peter & Paul Church. —Died May 23, 2000.
† Wordeman, John J., Ashland, KY Holy Family Church. —Died May 3, 2000.

Diocese of Lincoln

(Dioecesis Lincolnensis)

Most Reverend

FABIAN W. BRUSKEWITZ, D.D., S.T.D.

Bishop of Lincoln; ordained July 17, 1960; appointed Bishop of Lincoln March 24, 1992; consecrated May 13, 1992. *Mailing Address: Address all communications to P.O. Box 80328, Lincoln, NE, 68501-0328.*

Erected August 2, 1887.

Square Miles 23,844.

Comprises that part of the State of Nebraska south of the Platte River.

Legal Title: "The Catholic Bishop of Lincoln".

For legal titles of parishes and diocesan institutions, consult the Chancery.

Chancery: P.O. Box 80328, Lincoln, NE, 68501-0328. Tel.: 402-488-0921; Fax: 402-488-3569.

STATISTICAL OVERVIEW

Personnel	
Bishop	1
Priests: Diocesan Active in Diocese	115
Priests: Active Outside Diocese	8
Priests: Diocesan in Foreign Missions	2
Priests: Retired, Sick or Absent	24
Number of Diocesan Priests	149
Religious Priests in Diocese	10
Extern Priests in Diocese	6
Ordinations:	
Diocesan Priests	4
Religious Priests	1
Transitional Deacons	1
Permanent Deacons in Diocese	2
Total Brothers	3
Total Sisters	127
Parishes	
Parishes	135
With Resident Pastor:	
Resident Diocesan Priests	85
Resident Religious Priests	2
Without Resident Pastor:	
Administered by Priests	48
Missions	1
Welfare	
Catholic Hospitals	3
Total Assisted	197,890
Homes for the Aged	3
Total Assisted	271
Day Care and Extended Day Care Centers	1
Total Assisted	4,923
Special Centers for Social Services	21
Total Assisted	14,294
Residential Care of Disabled	1
Total Assisted	18
Other Institutions	1
Total Assisted	5,913
Educational	
Seminaries, Diocesan	1
Students from This Diocese	18
Students from Other Diocese	1
Diocesan Students in Other Seminaries	12
Seminaries, Religious	1
Students Religious	62
Total Seminarians	92
High Schools, Diocesan and Parish	6
Total Students	1,590
Elementary Schools, Diocesan and Parish	25
Total Students	5,910
Non-residential Schools for the Disabled	1
Total Students	18
Catechesis/Religious Education:	
High School Students	2,375
Elementary Students	5,353
Total Students Under Catholic Instruction	15,338
Teachers in the Diocese:	
Priests	32
Sisters	36
Lay Teachers	398
Vital Statistics	
Receptions into the Church:	
Infant Baptism Totals	1,438
Adult Baptism Totals	180
Received into Full Communion	182
First Communions	1,576
Confirmations	1,247
Marriages:	
Catholic	272
Interfaith	201
Total Marriages	473
Deaths	677
Total Catholic Population	89,225
Total Population	538,527

Former Bishops—Most Rev. Thomas Bonacum, D.D., Bishop of Lincoln; cons. Nov. 20, 1887; died Feb. 4, 1911.—Most Rev. J. Henry Tihen, D.D., cons. Bishop of Lincoln, July 6, 1911; transferred to the See of Denver, Sept. 21, 1917; died Jan. 14, 1940.—Most Rev. Charles J. O'Reilly, D.D., cons. Bishop of Baker City, Aug. 24, 1903; transferred to the See of Lincoln, March 20, 1918; died Feb. 4, 1923.—Most Rev. Francis J. L. Beckman, S.T.D., cons. Bishop of Lincoln, May 1, 1924; elevated to the Metropolitan See of Dubuque, Jan. 17, 1930; died Oct. 17, 1948.—Most Rev. Louis B Kucera, D.D., cons. Bishop of Lincoln, Oct. 28, 1930; died May 9, 1957.—Most Rev. James V. Casey, D.D., J.C.D., appt. Auxiliary of Lincoln April 5, 1957; cons. April 24, 1957; appt. Bishop of Lincoln June 14, 1957; promoted to Archbishop of Denver, Feb. 22, 1967; died March 14, 1986.—Most Rev. Glennon P. Flavin, D.D., appt. Titular Bishop of Joannina and Auxiliary Bishop of St. Louis April 24, 1957; cons. May 30, 1957; promoted to See of Lincoln, May 29, 1967; retired March 24, 1992; died Aug. 27, 1995.

Chancery—3400 Sheridan Blvd., Lincoln, 68506., P.O. Box 80328, Lincoln, 68501-0328. Tel: 402-488-0921; Fax: 402-488-3569. Office Hours: 9-5.

Moderator of the Curia—Rev. Msgr. Timothy J. Thorburn, J.C.L.

Vicar General—Rev. Msgr. Timothy J. Thorburn, J.C.L.

Chancellor—Rev. Msgr. Mark D. Huber, J.C.L.

Diocesan Tribunal—3400 Sheridan Blvd., Lincoln, 68506., P.O. Box 80328, Lincoln, 68501-0328.

Officialis—Rev. Daniel J. Seiker, J.C.L.

Adjutant Judicial Vicars—Rev. Maurice H. Current, J.C.L.

Promoter Justitiae—Rev. Msgr. Timothy J. Thorburn, J.C.L.

Defensores Vinculi—Rev. Msgr. Timothy J. Thorburn, J.C.L.; Rev. Milton Thomas, J.C.L.

Judges—Revs. Garold L. Gabel, J.C.L.; Mark D. Huber, J.C.L.

Advocates—Revs. Thomas Y. Au; Michael K. Houlihan; James W. Cooper; Peter M. Mitchell; Daniel J. Rayer; Gary L. Coulter; David F. Bourek; Richard A. Gyhra; Andrew V. Menke; Scott M. Courtney; Ramon E. Decaen; Brian P. Kane; Matthew J. Vandewalle; Mr. David A. Battiato.

Notaries—Very Rev. John T. Folda; Rev. Christopher L. Barak; Sr. Collette Bruskewitz, O.S.F.

Diocesan Consultors—Rev. Msgr. Adrian Herbek; Rev. Msgr. Timothy J. Thorburn; Revs. Nicholas Baker; Gary Gross; Dennis Hunt; James Schrader; Daniel Seiker.

Presbyteral Council—Rev. Msgr. Timothy J. Thorburn; Rev. Msgr. Jerome Murray; Rev. Msgr. James Dawson; Revs. Gerald Vap; John Keefe; John J. Perkinton; David Hintz; Daniel Seiker; Gary Brethour; Lawrence Stoley; Mark D. Huber; Robert Mayta; K. William Holoubek; Chad Ripperger, F.S.S.P.; Thomas McGuire.

Vicars For Religious—Very Rev. John T. Folda; Rev. Daniel J. Seiker.

Deaneries and Deans—Rev. Msgr. Thomas L. Holoman, Crete; Rev. Msgr. Adrian F. Herbek, David City; Very Rev. Paul E. Sheehy, Fairbury; Very Rev. Robert A. Roh, Falls City; Very Rev. Gregory P. Pawloski, Grant; Very Rev. Lawrence J. Gyhra, Hastings; Rev. Msgr. Daniel J. Pohl, Indianola; Very Rev. Stanley F. Schieffer, Lawrence; Rev. Msgr. Myron J. Pleskac, Lincoln; Very Rev. James M. O'Connor, Orleans; Very Rev. Ronald E. Patterson, Plattsmouth; Very Rev. Rudolf F. Oborny, Wahoo; Rev. Msgr. Ivan F. Vap, York.

Diocesan Offices and Directors

Apostleship of Prayer—Revs. John W. Kelly, Dir. Jeremy L. Hazuka, Asst.

Apostolate to the Elderly—Rev. Edwin L. Stander.

Apostolate to the Spanish Speaking—Revs. Julius P. Tvrdy, Dir. Bernard A. Lorenz, Asst. Dir.

Apostolate of Suffering—Rev. Patrick F. Murphy, Dir.

Archivist—Sr. Loretta Gosen, C.PP.S.

Bishop's Lay Committee for Vocations—Rev. Robert A. Matya, Chap.

Bishop's Pastoral Plan for Pro-Life Activities—Greg Schleppenbach, State Dir., *215 Centennial Mall South, Ste. 410, Lincoln, 68508.*

Building Commission—Rev. John J. Perkinton, Chm.; Rev. Msgr. Raymond B. Hain; Rev. Msgr. Adrian F. Herbek; Rev. Msgr. Ivan F. Vap; Rev. Msgr. Timothy J. Thorburn; Rev. Peter J. Gadient; Very Rev. Stanley F. Schieffer; Rev. Mark D. Huber.

Catholic Relief Services—Rev. Mark D. Huber, Dir.

Cemeteries—Rev. David R. Hintz, Dir.

Censores Librorum—Rev. M. James Divis, S.T.L.; Very Rev. John T. Folda; Rev. Msgr. Timothy J. Thorburn.

Charities—Rev. Joseph M. Walsh, Dir. John Kopetzky, Vice Pres. Oper., *Catholic Social Services, 123 N. 25th St., Lincoln, 68503.* Tel: 402-474-1600., *Administrative Offices, 8101 "O" St., Ste. 111, Lincoln,*

68510. Tel: 402-489-1834., *Catholic Social Services, 515 W. 3rd St., Hastings, 68901.* Tel: 402-463-2112.

Clergy Relief Society—The Saint John Vianney Association—Rev. Msgr. TIMOTHY J. THORBURN, Sec. & Treas., *Mailing Address: P.O. Box 80328, Lincoln, 68501-0328.*

Commission on Alcohol and Drug Abuse—Rev. Msgr. CHARLES J. KEENAN, Dir., *3301 Sheridan Blvd., Lincoln, 68506.* Tel: 402-483-1941.

Commission for Sacred Liturgy and Sacred Music—Rev. WILLIAM D. GRANT, Chm.; Revs. CHRISTOPHER L. BARAK; ROBERT K. BARNHILL; MAURICE H. CURRENT; M. JAMES DIVIS; JOSEPH J. NEMEC; Sr. COLLETTE BRUSKEWITZ, O.S.F.

Catholic Planned Giving Office—Mr. MICHAEL L. HENKENIUS, Dir., *P.O. Box 80328, Lincoln, 68501-0328.* Tel: 402-488-2142.

Catholic Physicians Guild—Rev. JOHN FOLDA, Spiritual Dir., *1301 280th Rd., Seward, 68434-7541.* Tel: 402-643-4052.

Office of Religious Education (CCD)—Rev. CHRISTOPHER L. BARAK, Diocesan Dir. Tel: 402-488-2040. Diocesan Area CCD Directors: Revs. THOMAS Y. AU; THOMAS S. BROUILLETTE; JOHN A. COOPER; MAURICE H. CURRENT; WILLIAM D. GRANT; K. WILLIAM HOLOUBEK; DENNIS M. HUNT; LEO D. KOSCH; RANDALL L. LANGHORST; JAMES J. MEYSENBURG; MELVIN L. REMPE; TROY J. SCHWEIGER; MARK E. SEIKER; MICHAEL S. STEC; GERALD F. VAP.

Cursillo—Rev. MARK E. SEIKER, M.Div.

Deaf Ministry—Rev. ROBERT K. BARNHILL, Dir. Tel: 402-488-2040 (TTY); Rev. MICHAEL S. STEC, Asst. Dir.

Diocesan Council of Catholic Women—Mrs. JOANNE MESSING, Pres.; Rev. PETER J. GADIENT, Moderator; Rev. THOMAS J. LUX, Asst. Spiritual Dir., *P.O. Box 4, Bee, 68314.*

Diocesan Director of Liturgy—Rev. WILLIAM D. GRANT, *P.O. Box 406, Fairbury, 68352.*

Bishop Bruskewitz Charity and Stewardship Appeal (DDP)—Very Rev. JOHN C. ROONEY, Dir., *P.O. Box 80328, Lincoln, 68501-0328.*

Diocesan Finance Council—Most Rev. FABIAN W. BRUSKEWITZ, D.D., S.T.D.; Rev. Msgr. TIMOTHY J. THORBURN; Very Rev. JOHN C. ROONEY, Finance Officer. Members: Rev. Msgr. ADRIAN F. HERBEK; Very Rev. JOHN T. FOLDA; Rev. MICHAEL G. MCCABE.

Diocesan Health Ministries, Inc.—Most Rev. FABIAN W. BRUSKEWITZ, D.D., S.T.D., Pres.; Rev. Msgr. TIMOTHY J. THORBURN, Vice Pres.; Rev. JOHN T. FOLDA, Sec., *P.O. Box 80328, Lincoln, 68501-0328.* Tel: 402-488-0921; Fax: 402-488-3569.

Diocesan Housing Ministries, Inc.—Most Rev. FABIAN W. BRUSKEWITZ, D.D., S.T.D., Pres.; Rev. Msgr. TIMOTHY J. THORBURN; Very Rev. JOHN T. FOLDA; Very Rev. JOHN C. ROONEY; Rev. JOSEPH M. WALSH; Ms. HATON, *P.O. Box 80328, Lincoln, 68501-0328.* Tel: 402-488-0921.

Ecumenical Affairs, Commission for—Rev. M. JAMES DIVIS, Chm.; Rev. Msgr. DANIEL J. POHL; Revs. PAUL K. WITT; MAURICE H. CURRENT; MARK D. HUBER.

Engaged Encounter—Rev. MATTHEW F. EICKHOFF.

Evangelization Committee—Rev. PAUL K. WITT, Chm. Tel: 402-435-2125. Rev. Msgr. JAMES DAWSON; Rev. Msgr. MYRON J. PLESKAC; Rev. Msgr. TIMOTHY J. THORBURN; Revs. ROBERT K. BARNHILL; M. JAMES DIVIS; CHRISTOPHER L. BARAK; GAROLD L. GABEL; WILLIAM D. GRANT; Very Rev. LAWRENCE J. GYHRA; Rev. JOSEPH J. NEMEC.

Family Life Office—Revs. ROBERT K. BARNHILL, S.T.L., Dir. MATTHEW F. EICKHOFF, Asst. Dir. JOHN R. SULLIVAN, Asst. Dir., *P.O. Box 80328, Lincoln, 68501-0328.* Tel: 402-488-2040.

Holy Childhood, Pontifical Association—Rev. MATTHEW F. EICKHOFF, Dir., *P.O. Box 80328, Lincoln, 68501-0328.*

Health Care Facilities—Rev. PAUL J. RUTTEN, *5401 South St., Lincoln, 68506.*

Office of Information and Media—Rev. KENNETH A. BOROWIAK, Dir., *P.O. Box 80329, Lincoln, 68501.* Tel: 402-488-0090.

Insurance—Rev. Msgr. TIMOTHY J. THORBURN, Dir.; Mr. JAMES F. MCLAUGHLIN, *P.O. Box 80328, Lincoln, 68501-0328.*

Legion of Mary—Revs. PETER J. GADIENT, Spiritual Dir. PETER M. MITCHELL, Asst. Spiritual Dir. JEREMY L. HAZUKA, Asst. Spiritual Dir.; Mrs. JACKIE SCOTT, Pres.

Liturgical Ministries—Revs. MARK D. HUBER, Diocesan Dir.

Marriage Encounter—Rev. ROBERT K. BARNHILL, Dir.

Missionary Union of the Clergy—Rev. MATTHEW F. EICKHOFF.

Natural Family Planning—Rev. ROBERT K. BARNHILL, Diocesan Dir. MICHELLE KEUTEN, Diocesan Coord. Tel: 402-488-2040.

Nebraska Catholic Conference—JAMES R. CUNNINGHAM, Exec. Dir., *215 Centennial Mall South, Ste. 410, Lincoln, 68508.* Tel: 402-477-7517; Fax: 402-477-1503.

Newman Center University of Nebraska—Rev. ROBERT A. MATYA, Chap., *320 N. 16th St., Lincoln, 68508.* Tel: 402-474-7914.

Newspaper—"The Southern Nebraska Register"; Rev. KENNETH A. BOROWIAK, Editor, *3336 High St., Lincoln, 68508., Mailing Address: P.O. Box 80329, Lincoln, 68501.* Tel: 402-488-0090.

Office of Diocesan & Social Development—Very Rev. JOHN C. ROONEY, Delegate, *P.O. Box 80328, Lincoln, 68501.* Tel: 402-488-0921; Fax: 402-488-3569.

Permanent Deacon Continuing Education Committee—Revs. MARK D. HUBER, Dir. LEO V. SEIKER; DOUGLAS D. DIETRICH.

Pre Cana—Rev. MATTHEW F. EICKHOFF.

Priests' Continuing Education Committee—Rev. Msgr. JAMES D. DAWSON; Rev. Msgr. THOMAS L. HOLOMAN; Rev. Msgr. MYRON J. PLESKAC; Rev. Msgr. TIMOTHY J. THORBURN; Very Rev. JOHN T. FOLDA; Revs. CHRISTOPHER L. BARAK; MAURICE H. CURRENT; JOHN J. PERKINTON; DANIEL J. SEIKER; MARK D. HUBER; ROBERT A. MAYTA.

Pro Life—Rev. Msgr. THOMAS L. HOLOMAN.

Project Rachel—Catholic Social Services. Tel: 1-800-829-3477.

Propagation of the Faith—Rev. MATTHEW F. EICKHOFF, Dir., *P.O. Box 80328, Lincoln, 68501-0328.*

Retreat Program—Rev. Msgr. JOHN J. PERKINTON, Dir., *Our Lady of Good Counsel Retreat House.* Tel: 402-786-2705.

Rural Life Conference—Rev. DAVID F. BOUREK, *P.O. Box 80328, Lincoln, 68501-0328.* Tel: 402-488-0921.

Serra Club—Rev. ROBERT A. MATYA, Chap. & Spiritual Dir. Tel: 402-474-7914.

Schools—Rev. JOHN J. PERKINTON, M.Div., M.A., Supt.; Sr. COLLETTE, O.S.F., Asst. Supt., *3400 Sheridan Blvd., Lincoln, 68506., Mailing Address: P.O. Box 80328, Lincoln, 68501-0328.*

Scouting—Rev. ROBERT K. BARNHILL.

Society of St. Vincent de Paul - Lincoln Council—Rev. PAUL K. WITT, Spiritual Advisor; THOMAS SAFRANEK, M.D., Pres. JOYCE BURGESS, Council Sec. & Res. Agent, *Blessed Sacrament Conference, 1720 Lake St., Lincoln, 68502.* Tel: 402-474-4249.

Teens Encounter Christ (TEC)—Rev. JOHN R. SULLIVAN.

Tridentine Mass Apostolate—Rev. KARL PIKUS, F.S.S.P., *St. Francis of Assisi Church, 3400 S. 17th St., Lincoln, 68502.* Tel: 402-477-5145.

Vocations—Revs. ROBERT A. MATYA, Dir. THOMAS DUNAVAN, Asst., *St. Thomas Aquinas Church, 320 North 16th St., Lincoln, 68508.* Tel: 402-474-7914.

CLERGY, PARISHES, MISSIONS AND PAROCHIAL SCHOOLS

CITY OF LINCOLN
(Lancaster County)

1—CATHEDRAL OF THE RISEN CHRIST (1932), Revs. Robert G. Tucker; Jamie S. Hottovy. In res., Revs. Mark D. Huber; Robert K. Barnhill.
Res., 3500 Sheridan Blvd., 68506. Tel: 402-488-0948; Fax: 402-488-7895. [JC]
School—Tel: 402-489-9621.
Lay Teachers 25; Students 386.
Catechesis/Religious Programs—Students 266.

2—BLESSED SACRAMENT (1922), Revs. John R. Sullivan; Joseph P. Finn.
Res., 1720 Lake St., 68502. Tel: 402-474-4249; Fax: 402-474-4258. [JC]
School—Tel: 402-476-6202; Fax: 402-476-0232.
Priests 2; Sisters 2; Lay Teachers 14; Students 226.

3—IMMACULATE HEART OF MARY (1979) (Vietnamese), Rev. Mark Nguyen Thanh Huynh, C.M.C. (Vietnam).
Res., 2601 P St., 68503. Tel: 402-476-0133; Fax: 402-476-2041.
Catechesis/Religious Programs—Students 200.

4—NORTH AMERICAN MARTYRS (1993), Revs. Garold L. Gabel; Richard A. Gyhra.
Res., 931 W. Harvest Dr., 68521. Tel: 402-476-8088. [JC]
School—1101 Issac Dr., 402-476-7373.
Priests 2; Sisters 4; Lay Teachers 14; Students 423.
Catechesis/Religious Programs—Students 193.

5—SACRED HEART (1919), Rev. Thomas R. Walsh. In res., Revs. Edwin L. Stander; Julius Tvrdy.
Res., 3128 S St., 68503. Tel: 402-476-2610; Fax: 402-476-2610. [JC]
School—Tel: 402-476-1783; Fax: 402-476-3040.
Sisters 3; Lay Teachers 10; Students 144.
Catechesis/Religious Programs—Students 62.

6—ST. JOHN THE APOSTLE (1959), Revs. James F. Benton; Brian P. Kane. In res., Rev. Milton Thomas.
Res., 731 Sky Way Rd., 68505. Tel: 402-489-1946; Fax: 402-489-2048. [JC]
School—Tel: 402-486-1860; Fax: 402-486-4732.
Sisters 2; Lay Teachers 22; Students 380.
Catechesis/Religious Programs—Students 136.

7—ST. JOSEPH (1976), Rev. Msgr. Myron J. Pleskac; Rev. Andrew V. Menke.
Res., 7607 Trendwood Dr., 68506. Tel: 402-483-2288; Fax: 402-489-9729. [JC]
School—(Grades PreK-8). Tel: 402-489-0341; Fax: 402-489-3260.
Sisters 3; Lay Teachers 33; Students 533.
High School—Pius High School.
Students 173.
Catechesis/Religious Programs—Students 268.

8—ST. MARY (1867), Revs. Paul K. Witt; Daniel J. Rayer.
Res., 1420 K St., 68508. Tel: 402-435-2125. [JC]
School—Tel: 402-476-3987; Fax: 402-476-0838.
Sisters 1; Lay Teachers 10; Students 151.
Catechesis/Religious Programs—Students 25.

9—ST. PATRICK'S (1893), Revs. David R. Hintz; Gary L. Coulter.
Res., 6126 Morrill Ave., P.O. Box 29106, 68507. Tel: 402-466-2752; Fax: 402-466-3572. [JC]
School—Tel: 402-466-3710; Fax: 402-466-3752.
Marian Sisters (Waverly, NE) 2; Lay Teachers 12; Students 156.
Catechesis/Religious Programs—Students 151.

10—ST. PETER (1990), Revs. Michael R. Christensen; Peter M. Mitchell.
Res., 4500 Duxhall Dr., 68516. Tel: 402-423-1239; Fax: 402-421-6507. [JC]
School—Tel: 402-421-6299.
Priests 2; School Sisters of Christ the King 3; Lay Teachers 24; Students 530.
Catechesis/Religious Programs—Students 313.

11—ST. TERESA'S (1926), Revs. Joseph J. Nemec; Scott M. Courtney; Deacon Stephen T. Kuchar. In res., Rev. Joseph M. Walsh.
Res., 735 S. 36th St., 68510. Tel: 402-477-3979. [JC]
School—616 S. 36th St., 68510. Tel: 402-477-3358; Fax: 402-477-3361.
Sisters 3; Lay Teachers 13; Students 302.
Catechesis/Religious Programs—Students 85.

12—ST. THOMAS AQUINAS (1958), Revs. Robert A. Matya; Thomas Dunavan.
Res., 320 N. 16th St., 68508. Tel: 402-474-7914; Fax: 402-476-2620. [JC]

13—BISHOP BONACUM CHANCERY, Rev. Msgr. Timothy J. Thorburn, J.C.L., Moderator of the Curia.
Res., 3400 Sheridan Blvd., P.O. Box 80328, 68501. Tel: 402-488-0921; Fax: 402-488-3569.

OUTSIDE THE CITY OF LINCOLN

Alma, Harlan Co., St. Joseph's (1909), Rev. John B. Birkel.
Res., 810 4th, P.O. Box 764, 68920. Tel: 308-928-2575.
Catechesis/Religious Programs—Students 27.
Missions—Bloomington, Franklin Co., Sacred Heart; Naponee, Franklin Co., St. Mary.

Ashland, Saunders Co., St. Mary's (1900), Rev. Paul York.
Res., 1625 Adams St., 68003. Tel: 402-944-3554.
Catechesis/Religious Programs—Students 95.
Mission—Greenwood, Cass Co., St. Joseph's.

Auburn, Nemaha Co., St. Joseph's (1881), Rev. Philip J. Rauth.
Res., 1306 23rd St., P.O. Box 406, 68305. Tel: 402-274-3733. [CEM]
Catechesis/Religious Programs—Tel: 402-274-5364.
Students 142.
Mission—Peru, Nemaha Co., St. Clara.

Aurora, Hamilton Co., St. Mary's (1888), Rev. John J. Keefe.
Res., 1419 10th St., P.O. Box 291, 68818. Tel: 402-694-3427.
Catechesis/Religious Programs—Students 194.
Mission—Giltner, Hamilton Co., St. Joseph's. [CEM]

Beatrice, Gage Co., St. Joseph's (1869), Revs. Mark E. Seiker; Finnian Nwaozor.
Res., 612 High St., 68310. Tel: 402-223-2923; Fax: 402-228-0100. [CEM]
School—Tel: 402-223-5033.
Lay Teachers 9; Students 100.
Catechesis/Religious Programs—Students 119.

Beaver Crossing, Seward Co., Sacred Heart (1890), Rev. Maurice H. Current.
Res., 401 Dimery, P.O. Box 208, 68313. Tel: 402-532-2545.
Catechesis/Religious Programs—Students 81.

Mission—Utica, Seward Co., St. Patrick's. [CEM 2]

Bellwood, Butler Co., Presentation (1874), Rev. Leo D. Kosch.
Res., 1291 41 Rd., 68624. Tel: 402-367-3666. [JC]
Catechesis/Religious Programs—Students 33.
St. Peter's (1889), Rev. Jeremy L. Hazuka.
Res., 211 Esplanade St., 68624-2402. Tel: 402-538-3135. [JC]
Catechesis/Religious Programs—Students 103.
Mission—Bellwood, Butler Co., St. Joseph's.

Benkelman, Dundy Co., St. Joseph's (1911), Rev. Douglas D. Dietrich.
Res., 817 Cheyenne St., P.O. Box 447, 69021. Tel: 308-423-2329. [CEM]
Catechesis/Religious Programs—Students 54.
Mission—Stratton, Hitchcock Co., St. Joseph's.

Brainard, Butler Co., Holy Trinity (1888), Rev. Mathew F. Eickhoff.
Res., P.O. Box 39, 68626. Tel: 402-545-2691; Fax: 402-545-2691. [CEM]
Catechesis/Religious Programs—Students 104.

Bruno, Butler Co., St. Anthony (1899), Rev. Thomas J. Lux.
Res., 405 Pine St., 68014. Tel: 402-543-2233. [CEM]
Catechesis/Religious Programs—Tel: 402-543-2465.
Students 55.
Mission—Abie, Butler Co., SS. Peter and Paul. [CEM 2]

Cambridge, Furnas Co., St. John's (1880), Rev. Melvin L. Rempe.
Res., 815 Nelson, P.O. Box F, 69022. Tel: 308-697-3722. [CEM]
Catechesis/Religious Programs—Students 88.
Mission—Arapahoe, Furnas Co., St. Germanus.

Campbell, Franklin Co., St. Anne (1880), Rev. James C. Schrader, Jr.
Res., 518 S. Stewart, P.O. Box 156, 68932-0156. Tel: 402-756-8006. [CEM]
Catechesis/Religious Programs—Students 82.
Mission—Blue Hill, Webster Co., Holy Trinity.

Cheney, Lancaster Co., St. Michael (1909), Rev. Msgr. James D. Dawson.
Res., 9230 First St., 68526. Tel: 402-423-5078. [CEM]
Catechesis/Religious Programs—Students 107.

Colon, Saunders Co., St. Joseph's (1919), Rev. K. William Holoubek.
Res., 111 Cherry St., P.O. Box 58, 68018. Tel: 402-647-4901. [CEM]
Mission—Cedar Bluffs, Saunders Co., St. Mary. [CEM]

Cortland, Gage Co., St. James (1882), Rev. Michael J. Morin.
Res., 255 W. First, 68331. Tel: 402-798-7335; Fax: 402-798-7336. [CEM]
Catechesis/Religious Programs—Students 107.

Crete, Saline Co., Sacred Heart (1873), Rev. Nicholas J. Baker.
Res., 515 E. 14th St., 68333. Tel: 402-826-2044; Fax: 402-826-2318. [CEM]
School—(Grades K-6). Tel: 402-826-2318.
Sisters 2; Lay Teachers 6; Students 81.
Catechesis/Religious Programs—Students 252.

Curtis, Frontier Co., St. James (1914), Rev. Ferdinand Boehme.
Res., 313 E. 6th St., P.O. Box 144, 69025. Tel: 308-367-4280.
Catechesis/Religious Programs—Students 44.
Missions—Farnam, Dawson Co., St. Joseph's; Wellfleet, Lincoln Co., St. William's.

Davey, Lancaster Co., St. Mary's (1876), Rev. Kenneth F. Hoesing.
Res., 17630 N. 3rd St., P.O. Box 37, 68336. Tel: 402-785-3445. [CEM]
Catechesis/Religious Programs—Students 107.

David City, Butler Co., St. Mary's (1877), Rev. Msgr. Adrian F. Herbek, V.F.; Rev. Casey Porada, O.S.
Res., 580 I St., 68632. Tel: 402-367-3579. [CEM]
School—(Grades K-5). Tel: 402-367-3669.
Priests 1; Sisters 3; Lay Teachers 13; Students 225.
Catechesis/Religious Programs—Students 59.
Mission—David City, Butler Co., Assumption, (1878) 68632.
St. Francis (Center) (1878), Rev. Brian P. Connor.
Res., 3071 P Rd., 68632. Tel: 402-367-4202. [CEM]
Catechesis/Religious Programs—Students 46.

Dawson, Richardson Co., St. Mary's (1873), Rev. Troy J. Schweiger.
Res., 312 4th St., P.O. Box 96, 68337. Tel: 402-855-3595. [CEM]
Catechesis/Religious Programs—Students 57.
Mission—Shubert, Richardson Co., St. Anne's. [CEM 2]

Denton, Lancaster Co., St. Mary's (1906), Rev. Msgr. Thomas L. Holoman.
Res., 7105 Cass, P.O. Box 406, 68339. Tel: 402-797-2105.
Catechesis/Religious Programs—Students 32.

Doniphan, Hall Co., St. Ann's (1888), Rev. James J. Meysenberg.
Res., 301 W. 7th St., Hastings, 68901. Tel: 402-845-2707. [CEM]
Catechesis/Religious Programs—Students 65.

Dwight, Butler Co., Assumption (1899), Rev. Loras K. Grell.
Res., P.O. Box 70, 68635. Tel: 402-566-2765. [CEM]
Mission—Bee, Seward Co., St. Wenceslaus, 350 Elm St., Bee, 68314. [CEM]
In res., Rev. Peter Gadient.

Exeter, Fillmore Co., St. Stephen's (1871), Rev. Kenneth A. Borowiak.
Res., 207 N. Union Ave., P.O. Box 57, 68351. Tel: 402-266-5581; Fax: 402-266-5581. [JC]
Catechesis/Religious Programs—Students 86.

Fairbury, Jefferson Co., St. Michael's (1885), Rev. William David Grant.
Res., 807 F St., P.O. Box 406, 68352. Tel: 402-729-2058; Fax: 402-729-2058. [CEM]
School—(Grades PreK-6). Tel: 402-729-2151; Fax: 402-729-3027.
Lay Teachers 6; Students 75.
Catechesis/Religious Programs—Students 70.
Mission—Alexandria, Thayer Co., St. Mary's, 511 Amanda, Alexandria, 68303.

Falls City, Richardson Co., SS. Peter and Paul (1871), Very Rev. Robert A. Roh, V.F.
Res., 1820 Fulton St., 68355. Tel: 402-245-3002; Fax: 402-245-3002. [CEM 2]
School—(Grades PreK-12). Tel: 402-245-4151; Fax: 402-245-5217.
Lay Teachers 20; Students 282.
Catechesis/Religious Programs—Students 48.

Friend, Saline Co., St. Joseph's (1874), Revs. James W. Cooper; David F. Bourek, Admin.
Res., 405 S. Main St., 68359. Tel: 402-947-3651. [CEM]
Catechesis/Religious Programs—Tel: 402-947-3657.
Students 73.
Mission—Milligan, Fillmore Co., St. Wenceslaus, (1874).

Geneva, Fillmore Co., St. Joseph's (1898), Rev. Msgr. Ivan F. Vap.
Res., 831 E St., P.O. Box 383, 68361. Tel: 402-759-3225; Fax: 402-759-3225. [CEM 2]
Catechesis/Religious Programs—Students 99.
Mission—Shickley, Fillmore Co., St. Mary, Tel: 402-627-7395.

Grafton, Fillmore Co., St. Helena's (1877), Rev. Mark S. Pfeiffer.
Res., P.O. Box 65, 68365. Tel: 402-282-7255.
Catechesis/Religious Programs—Students 35.

Grant, Perkins Co., Mother of Sorrows (1928), Rev. Joseph S. Steele.
Res., 739 Garfield Ave., P.O. Box 536, 69140. Tel: 308-352-4803.
Catechesis/Religious Programs—Students 76.

Harvard, Clay Co., St. Joseph's (1878), Rev. Bernard A. Lorenz.
Res., 605 N. Kearney, P.O. Box 70, 68944. Tel: 402-772-3511.
Catechesis/Religious Programs—Students 47.

Hastings, Adams Co., St. Cecilia's (1878), Very Rev. Msgr. Lawrence J. Gyhra; Rev. Christopher K. Kubat. In res., Rev. James J. Meysenburg.
Res., 301 W. 7th St., 68901. Tel: 402-463-1336; Fax: 402-463-1336. [JC]
Catechesis/Religious Programs—Hastings Catholic Schools, Tel: 402-462-2105; Fax: 402-462-2106.
Students 735.
St. Michael's (1945), Revs. Michael K. Houlihan; Harlon D. Waskowiak.
Res., 715 Creighton Ave., P.O. Box 331, 68901. Tel: 402-463-1023.
Catechesis/Religious Programs—Hastings Catholic Schools, 721 Creighton Ave., 68901. Tel: 402-462-6310; Fax: 402-462-6035.
Students 357.

Hebron, Thayer Co., Sacred Heart (1878), Very Rev. Paul E. Sheehy.
Res., 436 N. 3rd St., 68370. Tel: 402-768-6293. [CEM]
Catechesis/Religious Programs—Students 101.

Holdrege, Phelps Co., All Saints (1902), Rev. Stephen A. Cooney.
Res., 1204 Logan St., 68949. Tel: 308-995-4590.
Catechesis/Religious Programs—Tel: 308-995-8931.
Students 197.
Mission—Smithfield, Gosper Co., St. John's.

Imperial, Chase Co., St. Patrick's (1903), Very Rev. Gregory P. Pawloski.
Res., 126 E. 7th St., P.O. Box 96, 69033. Tel: 308-882-4995; Fax: 308-882-3995.
Catechesis/Religious Programs—Students 129.
Mission—Wauneta, Chase Co., St. John's, Tel: 308-394-5440 (Church). [CEM]

Indianola, Red Willow Co., St. Catherine's (1888), Rev. Msgr. Daniel J. Pohl, V.F.
Res., 835 D St., P.O. Box 0, 69034. Tel: 308-364-2428. [CEM]
Catechesis/Religious Programs—Students 85.

Kenesaw, Adams Co., Sacred Heart (1908), Rev. James Meysenburg, Admin.
Res., 301 W. 7th, Hastings, 68901-4460. Tel: 402-463-1336 (Pastor).
Catechesis/Religious Programs—Tel: 402-752-8149.
Students 17.

Lawrence, Nuckolls Co., Sacred Heart (1893), Rev. Dennis Hunt.
Res., P.O. Box 247, 68957. Tel: 402-756-7393. [CEM 3]
School—(Grades 1-8). Tel: 402-756-7043.
Lay Teachers 4; Students 67.
Catechesis/Religious Programs—Students 130.
Missions—Deweese, Clay Co., Assumption, Tel: 402-756-7437; Lawrence, Nuckolls Co., St. Stephen's.
In res., Revs. Michael Okere, Dir. Owerri Archdiocesan Missions; Alexander Okoro.

Loma, St. Luke's Czech Catholic Shrine (1912) (Czech), Mailing Address: c/o Rev. Msgr. Myron J. Pleskac, 7607 Trendwood Dr., Lincoln, 68506. Tel: 402-483-2288; Fax: 402-489-9729. [CEM]

Manley, Cass Co., St. Patrick's (1881), Rev. Ronald Patterson.
Res., 101 N. Broadway, P.O. Box 27, 68403. Tel: 402-234-3595. [CEM]
Catechesis/Religious Programs—Students 168.
Mission—Elmwood, Cass Co., St. Mary's. [CEM]

McCook, Red Willow Co., St. Patrick (1886), Revs. Gary G. Brethour; Thomas R. Bush.
Res., 612 E. 4th St., P.O. Box 216, 69001. Tel: 308-345-6734. [CEM]
School—(Grades PreK-8) 401 E. F St., 69001. Tel: 308-345-4546; Fax: 308-345-5542.
Priests 2; Lay Teachers 11; Students 125.
Catechesis/Religious Programs—Students 217.
Missions—McCook, Red Willow Co., Sacred Heart; McCook, Red Willow Co., St. Ann's. [CEM]

McCool Junction, York Co., St. Patrick's, Rev. Mark S. Pfeiffer.
Res., P.O. Box 65, Grafton, 68365. Tel: 402-282-7255. [CEM]

Mead, Saunders Co., St. James (1882), Rev. Charles P. Townsend.
Res., 320 S. Cedar St., P.O. Box 91, 68041. Tel: 402-624-3555. [CEM 2]
Catechesis/Religious Programs—Students 49.

Minden, Kearney Co., St. John's (1882), Very Rev. James M. O'Connor, V.F.
Res., 624 N. Garber Ave., P.O. Box 245, 68959. Tel: 308-832-1245.
Catechesis/Religious Programs—Tel: 308-832-1626.
Students 90.
Mission—Heartwell, Kearney Co., Holy Family.

Morse Bluff, Saunders Co., St. George (1945), Rev. Bernard F. Kimminau.
Res., 260 Short St., P.O. Box 98, 68648. Tel: 402-666-5280.
Catechesis/Religious Programs—Students 42.
Mission—Cedar Hill, Saunders Co., Sacred Heart. [CEM]

Nebraska City, Otoe Co., St. Mary's (1869), Revs. Michael G. McCabe; Ramon E. Decaen.
Res., 218 N. 6th St., 68410. Tel: 402-873-3024. [CEM]
Catechesis/Religious Programs—Students 86.
St. Benedict's (1856), Rev. Mark A. Tasler.
Res., 411 5th Rue, 68410. Tel: 402-873-3047. [CEM]
School—(See Lourdes Catholic Schools). Tel: 402-873-6154.

North Platte, Lincoln Co, St. Elizabeth Ann Seton (1994), Rev. Thomas Brouillette.
Res., 3301 Echo Dr., P.O. Box 781, 69103. Tel: 308-534-5461; Fax: 308-534-0914.
Catechesis/Religious Programs—Students 43.

Orleans, Harlan Co., St. Mary's (1878), Rev. Gerald F. Vap.
Res., 109 W. Linn, P.O. Box 446, 68966. Tel: 308-473-3475. [CEM]
Catechesis/Religious Programs—Students 38.
Mission—Oxford, Furnas Co., St. Michael's.

Osceola, Polk Co., St. Vincent Ferrer (1946), Rev. Thomas D. McGuire.
Res., 751 S. Nance, P.O. Box 212, 68651. Tel: 402-747-3491; Fax: 402-747-3491.
Catechesis/Religious Programs—Students 77.
Mission—Osceola, Polk Co., St. Mary's, (1893).

Palmyra, Otoe Co., St. Leo's (1874), Rev. Christopher L. Barak.
Res., 330 W. 8th St., 68418-2537. Tel: 402-780-5535. [CEM 2]
Catechesis/Religious Programs—Students 40.
Mission—Douglas, Otoe Co., St. Martin's.

Paul, Otoe Co., St. Joseph's (1871), Rev. Sean P. Redmond.
Res., 5592 O Rd., Nebraska City, 68410. Tel: 402-873-4569. [CEM]
Mission—Julian, Nemaha Co., St. Bernard's. [CEM]

Plattsmouth, Cass Co., Church of the Holy Spirit (1862), Revs. Patrick J. O'Byrne; Matthew J. Vandewalle.
Res., 520 S. 18th St., P.O. Box C, 68048. Tel: 402-296-3139; Fax: 402-296-2408. [CEM]
School—(Grades K-8). Tel: 402-296-6230.
Lay Teachers 14; Students 226.
Catechesis/Religious Programs—Students 109.

Prague, Saunders Co., St. John's (1901), Rev. Ronald G. Homes.
Res., 122 Center St., P.O. Box 96, 68050. Tel: 402-663-4615. [CEM]
Catechesis/Religious Programs—Students 120.
Mission—Plasi, Saunders Co., SS. Cyril and Methodius. [CEM]

Red Cloud, Webster Co., Sacred Heart (1893), Rev. Stanley F. Schieffer.
Res., 413 N. Seward St., 68970. Tel: 402-746-3750. [CEM]
Catechesis/Religious Programs—Students 32.
Mission—Riverton, Franklin Co., St. Catherine's.

Roseland, Adams Co., Sacred Heart (1921), Rev. Thomas Y. Au.
Res., 11818 W. Alexander, P.O. Box 67, 68973. Tel: 402-756-6251.
Catechesis/Religious Programs—Students 66.
Mission—Juniata, Adams Co., Assumption. [CEM]

Rulo, Richardson Co., Immaculate Conception (1863), Rev. Lawrence J. Stoley.
Res., R.R. 1, Box 89C, 68431. Tel: 402-245-4731. [CEM]
Catechesis/Religious Programs—Students 32.
Mission—Arago, Richardson Co., St. Mary's.

Seward, Seward Co., St. Vincent de Paul (1878), Rev. Brad Zitek.
Res., 152 Pinewood, 68434. Tel: 402-643-3421; Fax: 402-643-2594.
Catechesis/Religious Programs—Tel: 402-643-3521.
Students 313.

Shelby, Polk Co., Sacred Heart, Rev. Robert McDermott, Admin.
Res., 200 S. Walnut St., P.O. Box 340, 68662. Tel: 402-527-5425. [CEM]
Catechesis/Religious Programs—Students 91.

Steinauer, Pawnee Co., St. Anthony (1882), Rev. Thomas L. Wiedel.
Res., P.O. Box 98, 68441. Tel: 402-869-2256. [CEM]
Mission—Burchard, Pawnee Co., Sacred Heart. [CEM]

Superior, Nuckolls Co., St. Joseph's (1934), Rev. John Copenhaver.
Res., 1415 California, 68978-1019. Tel: 402-879-3735; Fax: 402-879-4495. [CEM]
Catechesis/Religious Programs—Students 113.
Mission—Nelson, Nuckolls Co., Sacred Heart.

Sutton, Clay Co., St. Mary's, Rev. David J. Davis.
Res., 312 S. Saunders Ave., P.O. Box 406, 68979. Tel: 402-773-5346. [CEM]

Syracuse, Otoe Co., St. Paulinus (1906), Rev. Michael S. Stec.
Mailing Address: 863 5th St., 68446-9504. Tel: 402-269-3382.
Catechesis/Religious Programs—Students 122.
Mission—Avoca, Cass Co., Holy Trinity. [CEM]

Tecumseh, Johnson Co., St. Andrew's (1866), Rev. John A. Cooper.
Res., 186 N. 5th St., P.O. Box 656, 68450. Tel: 402-335-3742; Fax: 402-335-2234. [CEM]
School—(Grades K-8). Tel: 402-335-2234; Fax: 402-335-2234.
Marian Sisters 2; Lay Teachers 3; Students 46.
Catechesis/Religious Programs—Students 75.
Mission—St. Mary, Johnson Co., St. Mary's. [CEM]

Trenton, Hitchcock Co., St. James (1894), Rev. Philip L. Luther.
Res., 117 W. B St., P.O. Box 488, 69044. Tel: 308-334-5328. [CEM]
Catechesis/Religious Programs—Students 48.
Mission—Palisade, Hitchcock Co., Holy Family.

Ulysses, Butler Co., Immaculate Conception (1915), Rev. Valerian Bartek.
Res., 205 S. 6th St., P.O. Box 128, 68669. Tel: 402-549-2437. [CEM]
Catechesis/Religious Programs—Students 37.

Valparaiso, Saunders Co., Sts. Mary and Joseph's, Rev. Thomas Kuffel.
Res., 631 S. Iver St., P.O. Box 248, 68065. Tel: 402-784-2511. [CEM]

Wahoo, Saunders Co., St. Wenceslaus (1877), Very Rev. Rudolf F. Oborny, V.F.; Rev. William A. Ryland. In res., Rev. Gary L. Gross.
Res., 214 E. 2nd St., 68066. Tel: 402-443-4235. [CEM 2]
School—(Grades K-6). Tel: 402-443-3336; Fax: 402-443-5551.
Sisters 2; Lay Teachers 13; Students 306.
Catechesis/Religious Programs—Students 41.

Wallace, Lincoln Co., St. Mary's, Rev. David C. Drewelow.
Res., 221 N. Commercial Ave., P.O. Box 191, 69169. Tel: 308-387-4441.
Catechesis/Religious Programs—Students 73.
Mission—Elsie, Perkins Co., Resurrection of Our Lord.

Weston, Saunders Co., St. John Nepomucene (1885), Rev. Randall L. Langhorst.
Res., 110 Front St., P.O. Box 10, 68070. Tel: 402-642-5245. [CEM 2]
School—(Grades K-6). Tel: 402-642-5234.
Notre Dame Sisters (Omaha, NE) 2; Lay Teachers 6; Students 122.
Mission—Touhy, Saunders Co., St. Vitus. [CEM]

Wilber, Saline Co., St. Wenceslaus (1878), Rev. Joel S. Panzer.
Res., 501 N. Wilson, P.O. Box 706, 68465. Tel: 402-821-2689.
Catechesis/Religious Programs—Students 95.
Mission—Tobias, Saline Co., St. Joseph's.

Wymore, Gage Co., St. Mary's (1881), Rev. Dennis W. Hotovy.
Res., 107 N. 11th St., P.O. Box 295, 68466. Tel: 402-645-3051. [CEM]
Catechesis/Religious Programs—Students 77.
Missions—Barneston, Gage Co., St. Joseph's; Odell, Gage Co., St. Mary's.

York, York Co., St. Joseph's (1878), Rev. Leo V. Seiker; Deacon David Dalton.
Res., 505 East Ave., 68467. Tel: 402-362-4595. [CEM]
School—(Grades K-8). Tel: 402-362-3021; Fax: 402-362-3021.
Franciscan Apostolic Sisters 3; Lay Teachers 11; Students 125.
Catechesis/Religious Programs—Students 162.

Shrines

Loma, St. Luke's Czech Catholic Shrine.

Chaplains of Public Institutions

LINCOLN. *Nebraska Penal Complex* 3128 S St., 68503. Tel: 402-435-0251. Rev. Edwin L. Stander, Chap.

DENTON. *U.S. Veterans' Hospital* 7105 Cass, P.O. Box 406, 68339. Tel: 402-797-2105. Rev. Msgr. Thomas L. Holoman, Chap.

On Duty Outside the Diocese:
Reverend Monsignors—
Jackels, Michael O., Villa Stritch, Via della Nocetta, 63, 00164 Rome, Italy
Reinert, James M., 143 E. 43rd St., New York, NY 10017
Reverend Fathers—
Barr, Liam M., Ave Maria Foundation, 2600 N. Earhart Pl., Ann Arbor, MI 48105
Fucinaro, Thomas J., Villa Stritch, Via della Nocetta, 63, 00164 Rome, Italy
Johnson, Lyle M., Apartado 407, Barquisimeto, Venezuela, S.A.
Kalin, William A., Our Lady of Angels, 565 Hermiston Ave., Hermiston, OR 97838
Major, Steven P., Apartado 407, Barquisimeto, Venezuela, S.A.

Graduate Studies:
Reverend Fathers—
Doty, Craig A., Casa Santa Maria, Via dell'Umilta 30, Roma, 00187 Italy
Eickhoff, Jeffrey R., Casa Santa Maria, Via dell'Umilta 30, Roma, 00187 Italy
Jansen, Raymond L., 4001 Yuma St., N.W., Washington, DC 20016 Italy

On Sick Leave:
Reverend Fathers—
Mika, John M., 5010 S. 41st Ave., Omaha, NE 68017

Retired:
Reverend Monsignors—
Hain, Raymond B., 142 E. St., David City, NE 68632
Kalin, Leonard I., Legacy Terrace, 5706 Freemont #329, Lincoln, NE 68507
Keenan, Charles J., Bonacum House, 3301 Sheridan Blvd., Lincoln, NE 68506
Murray, Jerome E., Bonacum House, 3301 Sheridan Blvd., Lincoln, NE 68506
Reisdorff, Clarence P., Bonacum House, 3301 Sheridan Blvd., Lincoln, NE 68506
Reverend Fathers—
Banach, Walter F., P.O. Box 324, Geneva, NE 68361
Danko, Michael S., 201 N. Gregg Rd., Nixa, MO 65714
Derwinski, Victor A., 806 13th St., P.O. Box 281, Aurora, NE 68818
Gadient, Peter J., 380 Elm St., P.O. Box 4, Bee, NE 68314
Gergen, Charles L., Mount Carmel Home, 412 W. 18th St., Kearney, NE 68847
Glaves, John J., Bonacum House, 3301 Sheridan Blvd., Lincoln, NE 68506
Halligan, James, Drumloeher, Moydow, Co. Longford, Republic of Ireland
Hebert, John M., St. Joseph Retirement Community, 320 E. Decatur, West Point, NE 68788
Kelly, John W., Bonacum House, 3301 Sheridan Blvd., Lincoln, NE 68506
Kotz, Anthony A., 28680 Aline Dr., Warren, MI 48093
Lyons, Patrick J., Bonacum House, 3301 Sheridan Blvd., Lincoln, NE 68506
Messman, Gerald C., Box 204, Duncan, NE 68634
Mroczkowski, Joseph A., P.O. Box 238, Cedar Creek, NE 68016
Murphy, Francis J., #1 West End, Millstreet, Co. Cork, Republic of Ireland
Redmerski, Stanley J., Madonna Rehab. Hospital, 5401 South St., Lincoln, NE 68506
Rydz, Zygmund S., 2981 Bluff Rd., Marianna, NE 68015
Schnoebelen, Kenneth F., Garnett Place, 208 35th St. Dr., #329, Cedar Rapids, IA 52403
Zastrow, John A., Bonacum House, 3301 Sheridan Blvd., Lincoln, NE 68506

INSTITUTIONS LOCATED IN THE DIOCESE

[A] SEMINARIES, RELIGIOUS OR SCHOLASTICATES

DENTON. *Our Lady of Guadalupe Seminary*, P.O. Box 147, 7700 W. Denton Rd., 68339. Tel: 402-797-7700; Fax: 402-797-7705. Very Rev. James Jackson, F.F.S.P., Rector; Revs. Charles Van Vliet, F.S.S.P., Procurator & Vice Rector; Calvin R. Goodwin, F.S.S.P.; James B. Buckley, F.S.S.P.

SEWARD. *St. Gregory the Great Seminary*, 1301 280th Rd., 68434. Tel: 402-643-4052; Fax: 402-643-6964. E-mail: st55511@alltel.net
Web site: www.stgregoryseminary.edu
Very Revs. John T. Folda, Rector; John C. Rooney, Procurator; Rev. M. James Divis, Spiritual Dir.; Dr. John D. Thornbrugh, Academic Dean; Rev. Chad A. Ripperger, F.S.S.P.

[B] ELEMENTARY SCHOOLS, INTERPAROCHIAL

HASTINGS. *St. Michael's Elementary, Hastings Catholic Schools*, 721 Creighton Ave., 68901. Tel: 402-462-6310; Fax: 402-462-6035.
E-mail: smb@esu9.k12.ne.us
Priests 6; Lay Teachers 21; Students 366.

NEBRASKA CITY. *Lourdes Elementary*. (Grades K-6), 412 2nd Ave., 68410. Tel: 402-873-6154. Ursuline Sisters (Maple Mount, KY) 1; Lay Teachers 9; Students 151.
Lourdes Primary. (Grades K-3), 411 5th Rue, 68410. Tel: 402-873-3739. Lay Teachers 4; Students 90.

[C] HIGH SCHOOLS, INTERPAROCHIAL

LINCOLN. *Pius X Central High School*, 6000 A St., 68510. Tel: 402-488-0931; Fax: 402-488-1061.
E-mail: webmaster@piusx.lincoln.ne.us

Web site: www.piusx.lincoln.ne.us
Rev. Michael J. Morin, Supt.; Mr. Thomas Seib, Prin.; Mr. Daniel Donahue, Asst. Prin.; Mr. Tom Korta, Asst. Prin.; Mrs. Jan Frayser, Dir. of Guidance; Mr. George O'Boyle, Dir. Activities..Priests 11; Sisters 4; Lay Teachers 52; Students 1021.

DAVID CITY. *Aquinas / St. Mary's Schools.* (Grades K-12), P.O. Box 149, 68632. Tel: 402-367-3175; Fax: 402-367-3176.
E-mail: bconnor@esu.7.org
Web site: www.esu7.org/~dcaweb/acquinas.html
Rev. Brian P. Connor, Supt.; Mr. David G. McMahon, Prin. (Aquinas High School); Mrs. JoAnn Havlovic, Prin. (St. Mary's); Rev. Thomas J. Lux, Guidance Dir..Priests 7; Sisters 4; Lay Teachers 33; Students 560.

FALLS CITY. *Sacred Heart School,* 1820 Fulton St., 68355. Tel: 402-245-4151; Fax: 402-245-5217.
E-mail: frlarry.stoley@piusx.lincoln.ne.us
Revs. Robert A. Roh, Supt.; Lawrence J. Stoley, Prin.; Troy J. Schweiger, Dir. Guidance.
High School. Priests 3; Lay Teachers 9; Students 97.
Elementary School. Priests 3; Lay Teachers 21; Students 165.

HASTINGS. *St. Cecilia's Middle School / High School.* (Grades 6-12), 521 N. Kansas, 68901. Tel: 402-462-2105; Fax: 402-462-2106.
E-mail: mbutler@esu9.k12.ne.us
Web site: www.esu9.k12.ne.us/nhas
Rev. James J. Meysenburg, Supt. Priests 4; Sisters 1; Lay Teachers 26; Students 380.

NEBRASKA CITY. *Lourdes Central Catholic Schools.* (Grades 7-12), 412 2nd Ave., 68410. Tel: 402-873-6154; Fax: 402-873-3154.
E-mail: nc606064@navix.net
Rev. Michael G. McCabe, Supt..Priests 5; Lay Teachers 9; Students 117.

WAHOO. *Bishop Neumann Jr.-Sr. High School,* 202 S. Linden, 68066. Tel: 402-443-4151; Fax: 402-443-5551. Revs. Gary L. Gross, Supt.; Charles P. Townsend, Prin. Priests 9; Sisters 1; Lay Teachers 21; Students 365.

[D] GENERAL HOSPITALS

LINCOLN. *St. Elizabeth Regional Medical Center,* 555 S. 70th St., 68510. Tel: 402-489-7181; Fax: 402-486-8973.
E-mail: blanik@stez.org
Web site: www.stez.org
For a complete listing, refer to the Hospitals section.

NEBRASKA CITY. *St. Mary's Hospital,* 1314 3rd Ave., 68410. Tel: 402-873-3321; 873-9033.
E-mail: dkelly@stez.org
For a complete listing, refer to the Hospitals section.

[E] HOMES FOR AGED

LINCOLN. *Bonacum House,* 3301 Sheridan Blvd., 68506. Tel: 402-483-0391
For a complete listing, refer to the Special Care Facilities section.
Madonna Rehabilitation Hospital, 5401 South St., 68506. Tel: 402-489-7102; Fax: 402-483-9460.
E-mail: feedback@madonna.org
Web site: www.madonna.org
For a complete listing, refer to the Special Care Facilities section.

DAVID CITY. *St. Joseph's Villa, Inc.,* 927 7th St., 68632. Tel: 402-367-3045; Fax: 402-367-3730.
E-mail: st33446@navix.net
For a complete listing, refer to the Special Care Facilities section.

[F] RETREAT HOUSES

WAVERLY. *Our Lady of Good Counsel Retreat House,* 7303 N. 112th St., R.R. No. 1, Box 110, 68462. Tel: 402-786-2705. Rev. John J. Perkinton, Dir. Private Rooms 50. In res. Revs. Peter E. Cops, S.S.S.; Daniel Polzer, L.C.

[G] MONASTERIES AND RESIDENCES OF PRIESTS AND BROTHERS

CRETE. *Our Lady of the Sacred Heart Cistercian Monastery,* 340 State Hwy. 103, P.O. Box 276, 68333. Rev. Leo Slatterie.

[H] CONVENTS AND RESIDENCES FOR SISTERS

LINCOLN. *Adoration Convent and Church of Christ the King,* 1040 S. Cotner Blvd., 68510. Tel: 402-489-0765; Fax: 402-489-0864.
E-mail: christkingchurch@navix.net
Sister Servants of the Holy Spirit of Perpetual Adoration. Sr. Mary Henrita, Supr.; Rev. Joseph J. Nemec, Chap. Professed Sisters 9.
Congregation of Missionary Sisters of the Blessed Virgin Mary, Queen of Mercy, Queen of Mercy Motherhouse, 6400 Nebraska Hwy. 2, 68516. Tel: 402-421-1704.
Daughters of the Holy Spirit, Nazareth of the Good Shepherd, Hispanic Apostolate, 110 W "E" St., 68508-3087. Tel: 402-477-7646.
E-mail: dhs24@juno.com
Sr. Margarita Iturbide, Supr.
Holy Family Sisters of the Needy - Holy Family Convent, 5720 A St., 68510. Tel: 402-486-3706. Sr. Claret Nze, Supr.
St. Agnes Convent, 3405 Sheridan Blvd., 68506. Tel: 402-484-7348. Sr. Collette Bruskewitz, Contact Person.
School Sisters of Christ the King, Villa Regina Motherhouse & Novitiate, 4100 S.W. 56th St., 68522-9201. Tel: 402-477-5232; Fax: 402-477-5232.
E-mail: villaregina@juno.com
Web site: www.rcnet/lincoln/schoolsisters
Mother Joan Paul, C.K., Supr. In res. Rev. Daniel J. Seiker. Tel: 402-477-1768.

NEBRASKA CITY. *The Franciscan Sisters of the Sorrowful Mother,* 1503 4th Corso, 68410. Tel: 402-873-3052.
E-mail: fs93813@alltel.net
Sr. Ana Maria Solis, O.S.F., Supr.

VALPARAISO. *Carmel of Jesus, Mary, and Joseph,* 9300 Agnew Rd., 68065. Mother Teresa of Jesus, O.C.D., Prioress.

WAVERLY. *Marian Sisters of the Diocese of Lincoln Motherhouse and Novitiate,* 6905 N. 112th St., 68462-9690. Mailing Address: Rte. 1, Box 108, 68462. Tel: 402-786-2750; Fax: 402-786-7256.
E-mail: adivis@inetnebr.com
Res., 6905 N. 112th St., 68462-9690. Sr. Bernadette Radek, M.S. Professed 36; Postulants 2.

[I] SPECIAL EDUCATION

LINCOLN. *Villa Marie School and Home for the Educable Mentally Handicapped,* P.O. Box 80328, 68501. Tel: 402-786-3625. Marian Sisters (Waverly, NE). Sr. Patricia Stoeckinger, M.S., Prin.; Rev. John J. Perkinton, Dir. Sisters 3; Students 18.

[J] NEWMAN CENTERS

LINCOLN. *University of Nebraska, Newman Club,* 320 N. 16th St., 68508. Tel: 402-474-7914; Fax: 402-476-2620.
E-mail: newmancenter@usa.net
Web site: members.tripod.com/newmancenter
See also: St. Thomas Aquinas, Lincoln, NE. Revs. Robert A. Matya, Vocation Dir.; Thomas Dunavan.

[K] FUNDS, FOUNDATIONS AND TRUSTS

LINCOLN. *Chancery,* P.O. Box 80328, 3400 Sheridan Blvd., 68501.
Seminary Burse Fund.
Mass Stipends.
Food for the Starving.
Latin America Fund.
Mission Office Fund.
Catholic Evangelization Fund.
St. Gregory the Great Seminary Fund.
The Catholic Foundation of the Diocese of Lincoln, P.O. Box 80328, 68501-0328. Tel: 402-488-0921; Fax: 402-488-3569. Rev. Msgr. Timothy J. Thorburn.

[L] CATHOLIC SOCIAL SERVICES

LINCOLN. *Catholic Social Services,* Administrative Offices, 8101 "O" St., S111, 68510. Tel: 402-489-1834; Fax: 402-489-2046.
E-mail: frjwalsh@csshope.org
Rev. Joseph M. Walsh, Dir.; John Kopetzky, Dir. Oper.
Other Addresses: 123 N. 25th St., 68503. Tel: 402-474-1600; Fax: 402-474-1612.
E-mail: jkopetzky@csshope.org
515 W. Third St., Hastings, 68901. Tel: 402-463-2112; Fax: 402-463-2322.
E-mail: tschik@csshope.org

[M] MISCELLANEOUS LISTINGS

LINCOLN. *Calvary Cemetery and Mausoleum,* 145 S. 40th St., 68510. Tel: 402-476-8787. Joint cemetery for Lincoln parishes. Rev. David R. Hintz, Dir.
Catholic Social Services, 8101 "O" St., S111, 68510. Tel: 402-489-1834; Fax: 402-489-2046.
E-mail: frjwalsh@csshope.org
St. Thomas Orphanage. Rev. Joseph M. Walsh, Dir.
Chancery Annex, 3325 Sheridan Blvd., 68506. Tel: 402-488-2040.
Cristo Rey Catholic Hispanic Center, 1335 N. 30th, 68503. Tel: 402-474-6201.
Holy Family Convent, 5720 A St., 68510.
Magnificat - Lincoln, 917 S. 33rd St., 68510. Tel: 402-476-1880.
E-mail: mharper@yahoo.com
Mary Harper, Pres.
Pius X Foundation and Pius X Endowment Fund, 6000 A St., 68510. Tel: 402-488-0931; Fax: 402-488-1061.
E-mail: angi.mcandrew@piusx.lincoln.ne.us
Web site: www.piusx.lincoln.ne.us
Rev. Michael J. Morin, Sec. & Treas.
St. Francis of Assisi Church, 3400 S 17th St., 68502. Tel: 402-328-0308; Fax: 402-328-0309. Rev. Karl A. Pikus, F.S.S.P., Chap.

DAVID CITY. *Aquinas High School Endowment Fund,* P.O. Box 149, 68632. Tel: 402-367-3175. Rev. Brian P. Connor, Sec. & Treas.

FALLS CITY. *Sacred Heart High School Endowment Fund,* 1820 Fulton St., 68355. Tel: 402-245-4151; Fax: 402-245-3002. Very Rev. Robert A. Roh, Sec. & Treas.

HASTINGS. *Crosier Monastery of Hastings,* P.O. Box 789, 68902-0789. Legal Title: *Crosier Fathers, A Nebraska Nonprofit Corporation.*
Registered Agent: Helmann & Sullivan, P.C., 747 N. Burlington, Ste. 305, 68901. Tel: 402-462-2119.
St. Cecilia High School Endowment Fund, 521 N. Kansas, 68901. Tel: 402-462-2105; Fax: 402-462-2106. Rev. James J. Meysenberg, Sec. & Treas.

NEBRASKA CITY. *Lourdes Central High School Endowment Fund,* 412 Second Ave., 68410. Tel: 402-873-6154; Fax: 402-873-3154. Rev. Michael G. McCabe, Sec. & Treas.

WAHOO. *Bishop Neumann High School Endowment Fund,* 202 S. Linden, 68066. Tel: 402-443-4151; Fax: 402-443-5551.
E-mail: mailiggross@bnewman.org
Rev. Gary L. Gross, Sec. & Treas.

RELIGIOUS INSTITUTES OF MEN REPRESENTED IN THE DIOCESE

For further details refer to the corresponding bracketed number in the Religious Institutes of Men or Women section.

[0220]—*Congregation of the Blessed Sacrament.*—S.S.S.

[]—*Congregation of the Mother Coredemptrix.* (Vietnamese).—C.M.C.

[]—*Oblates of Wisdom.*—O.S.

[0730]—*Legionaries of Christ.*—L.C.

[]—*Priestly Fraternity of St. Peter.*—F.S.S.P.

RELIGIOUS INSTITUTES OF WOMEN REPRESENTED IN THE DIOCESE

[0100]—*Adorers of the Blood of Christ.*—A.S.C.

[0230]—*Benedictine Sisters of Pontifical Jurisdiction.*—O.S.B.

[]—*Carmelite Monastery of Jeseu, Mary, and Joseph.*—O.C.D.

[]—*Congregation of Missionary Sisters of the Blessed Virgin Mary, Queen of Mercy.* (Vietnam).

[]—*Daughters of the Holy Spirit, Nazareth of the Good Shepherd.*—H.Sp.S.

[1070-01]—*Dominican Sisters.*—O.P.

[]—*Franciscan Apostolic Sisters.*—F.A.S.

[2575]—*Institute of the Sisters of Mercy of the Americas.*—R.S.M.

[2400]—*Marian Sisters of the Diocese of Lincoln.*—M.S.

[2960]—*Notre Dame Sisters.*—N.D.

[]—*Schoenstatt Sisters of Mary.*

[]—*School Sisters of Christ the King.*—C.K.

[1680]—*School Sisters of St. Francis.*—O.S.F.

[3540]—*Sister Servants of the Holy Spirit of Perpetual Adoration.*—S.Sp.S.deA.P.

[1600]—*Sisters of St. Francis of Martyr St. George.*—O.S.F.

[1640]—*Sisters of St. Francis of Perpetual Adoration.* (Prov. of St. Joseph).—O.S.F.

[3270]—*Sisters of the Most Precious Blood (O'Fallon, MO).*—C.PP.S.

[4120-05]—*Ursuline Nuns of the Congregation of Paris.*—O.S.U.

DIOCESAN CEMETERIES

LINCOLN. *Calvary,* 145 S. 40th St., 68510.

NECROLOGY

† Barry, Rev. Msgr. Denis L., (Retired). —Died Nov. 10, 2000.

† Machovec, Frank J., (Retired). —Died July 30, 2000.

† Sloup, Ernest O., (Retired). —Died Aug. 30, 2000.

Diocese of Little Rock

(Dioecesis Petriculana)

Most Reverend

JAMES PETER SARTAIN, D.D., S.T.L.

Bishop of Little Rock; ordained July 15, 1978; appointed Bishop of Little Rock January 4, 2000; consecrated and installed March 6, 2000. *Mailing Address: Diocese of Little Rock, 2500 N. Tyler St., P.O. Box 7565, Little Rock, AR, 72217.* Tel.: 501-664-0340; Fax: 501-664-9075.

Most Reverend

ANDREW J. McDONALD, D.D., J.C.D.

Bishop Emeritus of Little Rock; ordained May 8, 1948; appointed Bishop of Little Rock July 4, 1972; consecrated September 5, 1972; installed September 7, 1972. *Res., 30 Sherrill Rd., Little Rock, AR, 72202.* Tel.: 501-664-6738; 664-0340 (Office). *Mailing Address: Diocese of Little Rock, 2500 N. Tyler, P.O. Box 7565, Little Rock, AR, 72217; Fax: 501-664-9075.*

ESTABLISHED NOVEMBER 28, 1843.

Square Miles 53,104.

Comprises the State of Arkansas.

For legal titles of parishes and diocesan institutions, consult the Chancery Office.

Chancery: 2500 N. Tyler St., P.O. Box 7565, Little Rock, AR, 72217. Tel.: 501-664-0340.

STATISTICAL OVERVIEW

Personnel	
Bishop	1
Retired Bishops	1
Abbots	1
Retired Abbots	1
Priests: Diocesan Active in Diocese	59
Priests: Active Outside Diocese	1
Priests: Retired, Sick or Absent	20
Number of Diocesan Priests	80
Religious Priests in Diocese	57
Extern Priests in Diocese	20
Permanent Deacons in Diocese	76
Total Brothers	32
Total Sisters	298
Parishes	
Parishes	90
With Resident Pastor:	
Resident Diocesan Priests	49
Resident Religious Priests	24
Without Resident Pastor:	
Administered by Priests	12
Administered by Deacons	3
Administered by Women Religious	2
Missions	43
Professional Ministry Personnel:	
Brothers	1
Sisters	28
Lay Ministers	54
Welfare	
Catholic Hospitals	13
Total Assisted	1,171,195
Health Care Centers	6
Total Assisted	26,461
Homes for the Aged	25
Total Assisted	718
Day Care and Extended Day Care Centers	7
Total Assisted	417
Specialized Homes	9
Total Assisted	576
Special Centers for Social Services	1
Total Assisted	227
Other Institutions	8
Total Assisted	32,333
Educational	
Diocesan Students in Other Seminaries	10
Total Seminarians	10
High Schools, Diocesan and Parish	3
Total Students	984
High Schools, Private	2
Total Students	775
Elementary Schools, Diocesan and Parish	31
Total Students	6,432
Elementary Schools, Private	1
Total Students	75
Catechesis/Religious Education:	
High School Students	2,657
Elementary Students	5,737
Total Students Under Catholic Instruction	16,670
Teachers in the Diocese:	
Priests	6
Brothers	3
Sisters	45
Lay Teachers	597
Vital Statistics	
Receptions into the Church:	
Infant Baptism Totals	2,076
Adult Baptism Totals	319
Received into Full Communion	555
First Communions	1,855
Confirmations	1,515
Marriages:	
Catholic	314
Interfaith	323
Total Marriages	637
Deaths	945
Total Catholic Population	93,480
Total Population	2,551,373

Former Bishops—Rt. Rev. ANDREW BYRNE, D.D., cons. March 10, 1844; died in Helena, June 10, 1862.—Rt. Rev. EDWARD FITZGERALD, D.D., preconized June 22, 1866; cons. Feb. 3, 1867; died in Hot Springs, Feb. 21, 1907.—Most Rev. JOHN B. MORRIS, D.D., ord. June 11, 1892; cons. June 11, 1906; died in Little Rock, Oct. 22, 1946.—Most Rev. ALBERT L. FLETCHER, D.D., ord. June 4, 1920; cons. April 25, 1940; appt. Bishop of Little Rock Dec. 7, 1946; retired July 3, 1972; died Dec. 6, 1979.

Vicar General—Rev. Msgr. J. GASTON HEBERT, V.G.

Chancery—2500 N. Tyler St., P.O. Box 7565, Little Rock, 72217. Tel: 501-664-0340; Fax: 501-664-9075. Office Hours: Mon.-Fri. 8:30-5.

Chancellor for Canonical Affairs—Rev. Msgr. FRANCIS I. MALONE, J.C.L.

Chancellor for Administration—Mr. GREGORY WOLFE.

Vice Chancellor—Rev. Msgr. SCOTT L. MARCZUK, J.C.L.

Finance Officer—Vacant.

Diocesan Tribunal—2500 N. Tyler St., P.O. Box 7565, Little Rock, 72217. Tel: 501-664-0340; Fax: 501-664-9075.

Judicial Vicar—Rev. Msgr. SCOTT L. MARCZUK, J.C.L.

Judges—Revs. JOHN K. ANTONY, J.C.L.; JAMES M. DIXON, S.J.; GREGORY HART; GREGORY T. LUYET, J.C.L.; Rev. Msgr. FRANCIS I. MALONE, J.C.L.; Rev. Msgr. SCOTT L. MARCZUK, J.C.L.

Defenders of the Bond—Rev. Msgr. JOHN KORDSMEIER; Mrs. BARBARA ANHALT.

Notaries—Ms. DIANA GRISWOLD; Mrs. JEANNIE MOORE.

Minister to Men and Women Religious—Sr. MAXINE VOGAN, D.L.F., *621 S. Washington, Forrest City, 72335.* Tel: 870-633-1665; Fax: 870-633-6307.

Diocesan Consultors—Rev. Msgr. J. GASTON HEBERT, V.G.; Rev. Msgr. JOHN F. O'DONNELL, V.F.; Rev. Msgr. BERNARD G. MALONE, V.F.; Rev. Msgr. FRANCIS I. MALONE, J.C.L.; Rev. Msgr. SCOTT L. MARCZUK, J.C.L.; Rev. JACK D. Harris.

Deans—Very Rev. Msgr. BERNARD G. MALONE, V.F.; Very Rev. Msgr. JOHN F. O'DONNELL, V.F.; Very Rev. Msgr. LEO RIEDMUELLER, V.F.; Very Revs. ROBERT T. DIENERT, V.F.; ERNEST HARDESTY, V.F.; Very Rev. Msgr. RICHARD OSWALD, V.F.; Very Revs. JOSEPH L. PALLO; W. ANDREW SMITH, V.F.; THOMAS MARKS, V.F.; Rt. Rev. JEROME KODELL, O.S.B., V.F.

Diocesan Offices and Directors

Adoption Services, Inc.—Ms. ANTJE HARRIS, Dir., *2415 N. Tyler St., P.O. Box 7239, Little Rock, 72217.* Tel: 501-664-0340; Fax: 501-664-9186.

Diocesan Council for Black Catholics—Rev. WARREN HARVEY, *1516 Parker St., North Little Rock, 72114.* Tel: 501-374-7123; Fax: 501-372-2995.

Building Commission—Mr. JAMES DAVIS, Exec. Sec., *2500 N. Tyler St., P.O. Box 7565, Little Rock, 72217.* Tel: 501-664-0340; Fax: 501-664-9075.

Catholic Social Services—Mr. DENNIS LEE, Dir., *2415 N. Tyler St., P.O. Box 7239, Little Rock, 72217.* Tel: 501-664-0340; Fax: 501-664-9186. This office also handles: *Catholic Campaign for Human Development* and *Catholic Relief Services.*

Catholic Campus Ministries—Deacon PAUL CRONAN, Dir., *St. Thomas Aquinas University Parish, 603 Leverett Ave., Fayetteville, 72701.* Tel: 501-444-0223; Fax: 501-442-2633.

Catholic Immigration Services—Mrs. SHEILA GOMEZ, Dir., *2415 N. Tyler St., P.O. Box 7239, Little Rock, 72217.* Tel: 501-664-0340.

Catholic Immigration Services NW Arkansas Office—Mr. FRANK HEAD, Immigration Coord., *1677 W. Sunset Ave., Springdale, 72762.* Tel: 501-927-2979; 1996; Fax: 501-927-2979.

Catholic Women, Diocesan Council of—Rev. JAMES P. WEST, *589 W. Grand Ave., Hot Springs, 71901.* Tel: 501-623-6201.

Catholic Youth Ministries—Mr. JOHN HALL, Dir., *2500 N. Tyler St., P.O. Box 7565, Little Rock, 72217.* Tel: 501-664-0340; Fax: 501-664-9075. This office also handles: Scouting.

Cemetery, Greater Little Rock—Mr. JIM DAVIS, Dir., *2500 N. Tyler St., Little Rock, 72207.* Tel: 501-664-0340; Fax: 501-664-9075.

Charismatic Movement, Bishop's Liaison—Rev. JAMES E. MANCINI, *St. Michael's Church, 12 Micanopy Cir., P.O. Box 970, Cherokee Village, 72525.* Tel: 870-257-4456 (Rectory); 257-2850 (Office); Fax: 870-257-2200.

Clergy Welfare Board—Rev. Msgr. J. GASTON HEBERT, V.G., Chm., *2500 N. Tyler St., P.O. Box 7565, Little Rock, 72217.* Tel: 501-664-0340; Fax: 501-664-9075.

Communications Department—Vacant, Dir., *P.O. Box 7417, Little Rock, 72217.* Tel: 501-664-0340; Fax: 501-664-9075.

Continuing Education for the Clergy—Rev. Msgr. DAVID LESIEUR, Dir., *2500 N. Tyler St., P.O. Box 7565, Little Rock, 72217.* Tel: 501-664-0340; Fax: 501-664-9075.

Cursillo Movement—Rev. LESLIE FARLEY, Moderator; Mrs. DEBBIE ECKERT, Exec. Dir., *2500 N. Tyler St., P.O. Box 7565, Little Rock, 72217.* Tel: 501-664-0340; Fax: 501-664-9075.

Data Processing—Rev. THOMAS SEBAUGH, Dir., *2500 N. Tyler St., P.O. Box 7565, Little Rock, 72217.* Tel: 501-664-0340; Fax: 501-664-9075.

Development Office—Dr. JOHN HEIRD, Dir., *P.O. Box 7239, Little Rock, 72217.* Tel: 501-664-0340; Fax: 501-664-9075.

Diaconate Program—Deacon JOHN DUKE, Dir., *2500 N. Tyler St., P.O. Box 7565, Little Rock, 72217.* Tel: 501-664-0340; Fax: 501-664-9075.

Ecumenical and Inter-Religious Affairs Office—Deacon JOHN MARSCHEWSKI, Dir., *P.O. Box 7565, Little Rock, 72217.* Tel: 501-664-0340; Fax: 501-664-9075.

Family Life Office: (Beginning Experience, Pre-Cana, Marriage Encounter, Retrouvaille)—Ms. ELIZABETH REHA, Dir., *2500 N. Tyler St., P.O. Box 7565, Little Rock, 72217.* Tel: 501-664-0340; Fax: 501-664-9075.

Hispanic Ministry—This office also handles: Radio Hispano. Rev. SCOTT FRIEND, Dir., *P.O. Box 7565, Little Rock, 72217.* Tel: 501-664-0340; Fax: 501-664-9075.

Radio Hispano—Sr. BARBARA PHILIPPART, S.C., Program Mgr.

Hospitals—*2500 N. Tyler St., P.O. Box 7565, Little Rock, 72217.* Tel: 501-664-0340; Fax: 501-664-9075.

Lay Ministry and Parish Renewal—Deacon BO MCALLISTER, Dir., *2500 N. Tyler St., P.O. Box 7565, Little Rock, 72217.* Tel: 501-664-0340; Fax: 501-664-9075.

Liturgical Commission—Rev. Msgr. FRANCIS I. MALONE, J.C.L., Dir., *2500 N. Tyler St., P.O. Box 7565, Little Rock, 72217.* Tel: 501-664-0340; Fax: 501-664-9075.

Minister to Priests—Rev. Msgr. DAVID LESIEUR, *2500 N. Tyler St., P.O. Box 7565, Little Rock, 72217.* Tel: 501-664-0340; Fax: 501-664-9075.

Newspaper "Arkansas Catholic"—Mrs. MALEA HARGETT, Editor, *2500 N. Tyler St., P.O. Box 7565, Little Rock, 72217.* Tel: 501-664-0340; Fax: 501-664-9075.

Presbyteral Council—Rev. Msgr. J. GASTON HEBERT, V.G., Chm., *2500 N. Tyler St., P.O. Box 7565, Little Rock, 72217.* Tel: 501-664-0340; Fax: 501-664-9075.

Priests Personnel Board (Diocesan)—Rev. Msgr. J. GASTON HEBERT, V.G., Chm., *2500 N. Tyler St., P.O. Box 7565, Little Rock, 72217.* Tel: 501-664-0340; Fax: 501-664-9075.

Propagation of the Faith—Mr. DENNIS LEE, Dir., *2415 N. Tyler St., P.O. Box 7239, Little Rock, 72217.* Tel: 501-664-0340; Fax: 501-664-9186.

Refugee Resettlement Program—Col. DUTCH DORSCH, Dir., *2415 N. Tyler St., P.O. Box 7239, Little Rock, 72217.* Tel: 501-664-0340; Fax: 501-664-9075.

Religious Education Department/Christian Initiation—Sr. MARY GLYNN, S.J.C., Dir., *2500 N. Tyler St., P.O. Box 7565, Little Rock, 72217.* Tel: 501-664-0340; Fax: 501-664-9075.

Respect Life Office—This office also handles: Project Rachel. Mrs. ANNE DIERKS, Dir., *2415 N. Tyler St., P.O. Box 7239, Little Rock, 72217.* Tel: 501-664-0340; Fax: 501-664-9186. This office also handles: Project Rachel.

Rural Life Department—Vacant, *2500 N. Tyler St., P.O. Box 7565, Little Rock, 72217.* Tel: 501-664-0340; Fax: 501-664-9075.

St. John's Catholic Center—Mr. JOHN ROBINETTE, Mgr., *2500 N. Tyler St., P.O. Box 7565, Little Rock, 72217.* Tel: 501-664-0340; Fax: 501-664-9075.

Schools—Dr. MICHAEL ROCKERS, Supt., *2500 N. Tyler St., P.O. Box 7565, Little Rock, 72217.* Tel: 501-664-0340; Fax: 501-664-9075.

Little Rock Scripture Study—Ms. CACKIE UPCHURCH, Dir.; Ms. LILLY HESS, Assoc. Dir., *2500 N. Tyler St., P.O. Box 7565, Little Rock, 72217.* Tel: 501-664-0340; Fax: 501-664-9075.

Seminary Endowment Fund (The Msgr. James E. O'Connell Seminary Burse)—Rev. Msgr. JAMES E. O'CONNELL, Dir., *2500 N. Tyler St., P.O. Box 7565, Little Rock, 72217.* Tel: 501-664-0340; Fax: 501-664-9075.

Social Action Office—Sr. JOAN PYTLIK, D.C., Dir., *2415 N. Tyler St., P.O. Box 7239, Little Rock, 72217.* Tel: 501-664-0340; Fax: 501-664-9186. This office also handles: Parish Social Ministry.

Vocations—Rev. LESLIE FARLEY, Dir., *2500 N. Tyler St., P.O. Box 7565, Little Rock, 72217.* Tel: 501-664-0340; Fax: 501-664-9075. Also serves as Director of Seminarians.

Westside Free Medical Clinic—Mrs. KAREN DIPIPPA, Dir., *2415 North Tyler St., P.O. Box 7239, Little Rock, 72217.* Tel: 501-664-0340; Fax: 501-664-9186.

CLERGY, PARISHES, MISSIONS AND PAROCHIAL SCHOOLS

GREATER LITTLE ROCK
(Pulaski County)

1—CATHEDRAL OF ST. ANDREW (1845), Rev. Msgr. Scott L. Marczuk, J.C.L., Rector; Deacon Gary Dollar.
617 Louisiana St., 72201. Tel: 501-374-2794; Fax: 501-375-3292. [JC]

2—ST. ANNE (North Little Rock) (1935), Rev. Msgr. Francis I. Malone, J.C.L.; Rev. Thomas Allen Elliott; Mr. Ronald F. Stager, Pastoral Admin.
Mailing Address: 6150 Remount Rd., North Little Rock, 72118. Tel: 501-753-3977; Fax: 501-753-3991.
Res., 7000 John F. Kennedy Blvd., North Little Rock, 72116. Tel: 501-835-4323; Fax: 501-834-5598. [JC]

3—ST. AUGUSTINE (1929) (African American), Revs. L. Warren Harvey; Oliver Ochieze.
1421 E. Second, North Little Rock, 72114. Tel: 501-375-9617; Fax: 501-375-9617. [JC]

4—ST. BARTHOLOMEW'S (1911) (African American), Rev. Donald Murrin, S.V.D.; Deacon Kirke Herman.
1622 Marshall St., 72202. Tel: 501-372-4682.

5—CHRIST THE KING (1966), Rev. Msgr. J. Gaston Hebert, V.G.; Rev. Erik T. Pohlmeier; Deacons Bill Hartmann; Bo McAllister; Richard Patterson.
4000 N. Rodney Parham Rd., 72212. Tel: 501-225-6774; Fax: 501-225-7169. [JC]
School—Tel: 501-225-7883; Fax: 501-225-1315. Mrs. Kathy House, Prin.
Lay Teachers 35; Students 706.
Msgr. Hebert Endowment Fund—Tel: 501-225-7883; Fax: 501-225-1315.

6—ST. EDWARD (1884), Rev. John K. Antony, J.C.L.; Deacon Daniel Hennessey.
815 Sherman St., 72202. Tel: 501-374-5767; Fax: 501-374-5839. [JC]
School—E. Ninth & Ferry St., 72202. Tel: 501-374-9166. Vernell Bowen, Prin.
Lay Teachers 12; Students 178.
Educational Trust Fund for St. Edward School—.

7—IMMACULATE CONCEPTION (1948), Rev. Msgr. Francis I. Malone, J.C.L.; Rev. Thomas Allen Elliott; Deacons William Nolan; John Marschewski.
7000 John F. Kennedy Blvd., North Little Rock, 72116. Tel: 501-835-4323; Fax: 501-834-5598. [JC]
School—Tel: 501-835-0771; Fax: 501-834-8652. David Cox.
Lay Teachers 33; Students 441.
Immaculate Conception School Endowment Fund—Fax: 501-834-0165.

8—IMMACULATE HEART OF MARY (Marche) (1878) (Polish), Very Rev. Msgr. Bernard G. Malone, V.F.; Deacon Brunon Strozyk. In res., Rev. Leslie A. Farley.
7006 Jasna Gora Dr., North Little Rock, 72118. Tel: 501-851-2763; Fax: 501-851-4769. [CEM]
School—Tel: 501-851-2760; Fax: 501-851-4769. Mary Lensing, Interim Prin.
Lay Teachers 13; Students 187.
Immaculate Heart of Mary Educational Trust Fund for Immaculate Heart of Mary School—Tel: 501-851-4769.

9—ST. MARY (North Little Rock) (1897) (Polish), Revs. L. Warren Harvey; Oliver Ochieze.
1516 Parker St., North Little Rock, 72114. Tel: 501-374-7123; Fax: 501-372-2995.
School—1518 Parker St., North Little Rock, 72114. Tel: 501-374-5237; Fax: 501-374-5237. Denise Troutman, Prin.
Lay Teachers 16; Students 239.
St. Mary's School Endowment Fund—Tel: 501-758-2220; Fax: 501-753-6623.

10—OUR LADY OF GOOD COUNSEL (1894), Revs. Gregory T. Luyet, J.C.L.; Martin Osuji.
1321 S. Van Buren St., 72204. Tel: 501-666-5073; Fax: 501-664-1964.
School—1204 S. Jackson St., 72204. Tel: 501-663-7426; Fax: 501-666-2239. Kim McGeorge, Prin.
Lay Teachers 16; Students 194.
Msgr. Scheper Endowment Fund for Our Lady of Good Counsel Catholic School—Tel: 501-666-5073.

11—OUR LADY OF THE HOLY SOULS (1947), Rev. Msgr. David LeSieur; Rev. Norbert Frank Rappold; Deacons Larry Jegley; Bill Cranford; Warren Baldwin, Jr.
1003 N. Tyler St., 72205. Tel: 501-663-8632; Fax: 501-663-8699.
Mailing Address: P.O. Box 250202, 72225.
School—901 N. Tyler St., 72205. Tel: 501-663-4513; Fax: 501-663-1014. Beverly Gray, Prin.
Lay Teachers 35; Students 524.
Msgr. Allen Trust Fund for Holy Souls School—.

12—ST. PATRICK'S (1880), Revs. L. Warren Harvey; Oliver Ochieze; Deacons George Siebenmorgan; Peter Stubbs. In res., Rev. Do Duy Nho.
211 W. 19th St., North Little Rock, 72114. Tel: 501-758-1155; Fax: 501-753-8251. [JC]
School—1900 Orange St., North Little Rock, 72114. Tel: 501-758-1508; Fax: 501-758-4945. Jane Tillery, Prin.
Lay Teachers 16; Students 133.
St. Patrick's School Endowment Fund—.

13—ST. THERESA'S (1950), Rev. John M. Connell; Mrs. Mary Peck, Pastoral Admin.; Deacons Don Francis; Bill R. Wrape, II.
6219 Baseline Rd., 72209. Tel: 501-565-9198; Fax: 501-565-3949. [JC]
School—Tel: 501-565-3855; Fax: 501-565-9522. Patricia Baker, Prin.
Lay Teachers 22; Students 286.
St. Theresa's Catholic School Endowment Fund—Fax: 501-565-3855.

OUTSIDE THE CITY OF LITTLE ROCK

Adona, Conway Co., St. Elizabeth's (Oppelo) (1884) (German). Attended by St. Boniface Church, New Dixie. Rev. Richard P. Davis.
Mailing Address: 20 St. Boniface Dr., Bigelow, 72016. Tel: 501-354-0631. [CEM]

Altus, Franklin Co., St. Mary (1879), Rev. Hilary Filiatreau, O.S.B.; Deacon Matthew Post.
5118 St. Mary's Ln., 72821. Tel: 501-468-2585. [CEM]

Arkadelphia, Clark Co., St. Mary's (1971). Attended by St. John, Hot Springs. Rev. Linus Ukomadu; Sr. Teresa Daly, D.C., Admin.
Church—P.O. Box 26, 71923. Tel: 870-246-7575.

Atkins, Pope Co., Assumption B.V.M. (1878) (German), Rev. Vincent Flusche; Deacon Veo J. Condley.
P.O. Box 337, 72823. Tel: 501-641-7179; Fax: 501-641-7179. [CEM]
Mission—Dardanelle, Yell Co., St. Augustine, 1000 N. 2nd, Dardanelle, 72834. Tel: 501-229-3972.

Barling, Sebastian Co., Sacred Heart of Mary (1902), Rev. William Elser.
Res. and Office: 1301 Frank St., 72923. Tel: 501-452-1795; Fax: 501-452-1795. [CEM]

Batesville, Independence Co., St. Mary's (1978), Rev. Jon McDougal.
3800 Harrison St., 72501. Tel: 870-793-7717; 793-7464; Fax: 501-793-7717.
Missions—Mountain View, Stone Co., St. Mary's, Mabry St. & Luther St., Mountain View, 72560. Tel: 870-269-5194; Newport, Jackson Co., St. Cecilia, 2475 Galleria Dr., Newport, 72112. Tel: 870-523-6542.

Bella Vista, Benton Co., St. Bernard (1980), Rev. Joseph J. Enderlin.
1 St. Bernard Ln., 72715. Tel: 501-855-9060; 855-9069; Fax: 501-855-9067.

Benton, Saline Co., Our Lady of Fatima (1942), Rev. Michael E. Bass; Deacon John Duke.
900 W. Cross St., 72015. Tel: 501-315-5186 (Office); 315-1747 (Rectory); Fax: 501-315-1479.
School—Tel: 501-315-3398. Marguerite Olberts, Prin.
Lay Teachers 13; Students 130.
Our Lady of Fatima School Endowment Trust Fund—.
Station—Benton, Benton Services Center, Tel: 501-860-0500.

Bentonville, Benton Co., St. Stephen (1989), Rev. Michael D. Sinkler; Carol M. Patterson, Pastoral Admin.; Deacon Jerry Becker.
Mailing Address: 1300 N.E. J St., 72712. Tel: 501-273-1240; Fax: 501-464-0969.
Rectory: 1208 N.E. J St., 72712. Tel: 501-273-1240.

Berryville, Carroll Co., St. Anne (1958), Rev. James M. Fanrak.
614 S. Main, 72616.
Mailing Address: P.O. Box 605, 72616. Tel: 870-423-3927.
Res., 30 Crescent Dr., Eureka Springs, 72632. Tel: 501-253-9853.

Bigelow, Perry Co., St. Boniface's (1879) (German), Rev. Richard P. Davis.
20 St. Boniface Dr., 72016. Tel: 501-759-2371. [CEM]
Missions—Little Italy, Pulaski Co., St. Francis; Adona, Conway Co., St. Elizabeth's.

Blytheville, Mississippi Co., Immaculate Conception (1894), Very Rev. Joseph L. Pallo, V.F.; Deacon William G. Brandon.
1301 W. Main St., 72315. Tel: 870-762-2506; Fax: 870-762-2506.
School—Tel: 870-763-9444. Sharon Warren, Prin. Lay Teachers 8; Students 85.

Booneville, Logan Co., Church of Our Lady of the Assumption (1953), Rev. Eugene Luke, O.S.B.
Res. & Mailing Address: Subiaco Abbey, Subiaco, 72865. Tel: 501-934-1126.; E. 6th & Cherry St., 72927. Tel: 501-675-3371.

Brinkley, Monroe Co., St. John the Baptist (1875), Rev. Benedict Meyer, O.S.B.
203 W. Ash, 72021-3201. Tel: 870-734-1202. [CEM]

Camden, Ouachita Co., St. Louis (1923), Rev. Wilfred C. Okorochukwu.
Mailing Address: 202 Adams, N.W., 71701. Tel: 870-836-2426.
Res., 962 Ridgeview, 71701. Tel: 870-836-0036; Fax: 870-352-5037.
Missions—Fordyce, Dallas Co., Good Shepherd, 410 Oak St., P.O. Box 565, Fordyce, 71742. Tel: 870-352-2328; Fax: 870-352-5037; Sheridan, Grout Co., Holy Cross, 921 Vine St., P.O. Box 624, Sheridan, 72150-0624. Tel: 870-942-4532.

Carlisle, Lonoke Co., St. Rose of Lima Church (1895), Rev. Joseph A. Seiter, C.S.Sp.; Deacon William Cunningham, Jr.
603 E. Park, P.O. Box M, 72024. Tel: 870-552-3601.
Mission—England, Lonoke Co., Holy Trinity, 1240 Arkansas Hwy. 161 W., P.O. Box 243, England, 72046. Tel: 501-842-2460.

Center Ridge, Conway Co., St. Joseph's (1881) (Italian), Rev. Edward G. Marley, C.S.Sp.
Mailing Address: 44 Valley Rd., 72027. Tel: 501-893-2887; Fax: 501-354-2711; 893-2887.
Church—323 Catholic Point Rd., 72027. Tel: 501-893-2887; Fax: 501-354-2711. [CEM]

Charleston, Franklin Co., Sacred Heart (1879), Rev. Peter Sharum, O.S.B.
18 Prairie St., 72933-9403. Tel: 501-965-2432. [CEM]

Cherokee Village, Sharp Co., St. Michael's (1939), Rev. James E. Mancini; Deacons Michael Cumnock; Anthony Ludolph; Ray Siwek; Jim Thompson.
Mailing Address: P.O. Box 970, 72525. Tel: 870-257-2850; Fax: 870-257-2200.
Res., 12 Micanopy Circle, 72529. Tel: 870-257-4456.
St. Michael Memorial Garden (Columbarium)—Hwy. 62/167 S. Tekakwitha Dr., 72529. Tel: 870-257-2375.

Clarksville, Johnson Co., Holy Redeemer (1879), Rev. William Wewers, O.S.B.
103 E. Main St., 72830. Tel: 501-754-3610. [CEM]

Conway, Faulkner Co., St. Joseph's (1878), Revs. Anthony McKay, C.S.Sp.; Joseph Deniger, C.S.Sp.; John Yates, C.S.Sp.; Edward T. Crowley, C.S.Sp., (Retired); Deacons David Westmoreland; Richard Bemrich, (Retired).
1115 College Ave., 72032. Tel: 501-327-6568; Fax: 501-329-6305. [CEM]
Parish Business Office: 375 Harkrider, 72032. Tel: 501-327-5528; Fax: 501-327-6607.
School—(Grades K-6). Tel: 501-327-1204; Fax: 501-327-8350. Daniel Fields, Prin. (Elementary and High School).
Lay Teachers 27; Students 369.
High School—(Grades 7-12) 502 Front St., 72032. Tel: 501-329-5741; 329-5606; Fax: 501-327-8350.
Lay Teachers 17; Students 224.

Crossett, Ashley Co., Holy Cross (1954), Rev. Chet Artysiewicz, Glmy.; Neil Pezzulo, Glmy.
Box 1245, 71635. Tel: 870-364-4847; Fax: 870-364-4847. [JC]
Mission—Hamburg, Ashley Co., P.O. Box 188, Hamburg, 71646. Tel: 870-853-8991.

Dardanelle, Yell Co., St. Augustine (1925). A mission of the Assumption B.V.M., Atkins.

De Queen, Sevier Co., St. Barbara's (1911), Rev. John W. Kerr, Admin.
P.O. Box 86, 71832. Tel: 870-642-2256; Fax: 870-642-3426.
Mission—Nashville, Howard Co., St. Martin, 1011 W. Leslie St., Nashville, 71852. Tel: 870-845-1271.

El Dorado, Union Co., Holy Redeemer (1923) (Spanish), Rev. Pius A. Iwuchukwu.
433 W. Elm St., 71730-5757. Tel: 870-863-3620; Fax: 870-863-7537.
School—Ann Finch, Prin. Lay Teachers 14; Students 137.
El Dorado Holy Redeemer School Endowment Fund—1103 W. Cedar St., 71730. Tel: 870-863-8677; Fax: 870-863-7779.
Holy Redeemer Endowment Fund—.

Engelberg, Randolph Co., St. John the Baptist (Pocahontas P.O.) (1885) (German), Rev. Kevin Atunzu.
4650 Engelberg Rd., Pocahontas, 72455. Tel: 870-892-3780. [CEM]
Missions—Corning, Clay Co., St. Joseph, P.O. Box 385, Corning, 72422. Tel: 870-892-3780; Walnut Ridge, Lawrence Co., Immaculate Heart of Mary, 320 Free St., P.O. Box 70, Walnut Ridge, 72176. Tel: 870-886-2119.

Eureka Springs, Carroll Co., St. Elizabeth of Hungary (1909), Rev. James M. Fanrak; Deacons Samuel Hilburn; Bill Reuter.
Mailing Address: 232 Passion Play Rd., 72632. Tel: 501-253-9853; Fax: 501-253-6616.
Res., #30 Crescent Dr., 72632.
Mission—Berryville, Carroll Co., St. Anne, Hwy. 62, P.O. Box 305, Berryville, 72616. Tel: 870-423-3927. Rev. James M. Fanrak.

Fairfield Bay, Van Buren Co., St. Francis Assisi (1976), Rev. Francis D. Colavechio.
Res., 250 Woodlawn Dr., 72088. Tel: 501-884-3349; Fax: 775-923-7106.

Fayetteville, Washington Co., St. Joseph's (1844), Rev. Paul Worm; Deacons Paul Cronan; Chuck Marino.
Church and Office: 321 E. Lafayette St., 72701-4308. Tel: 501-442-0890; Fax: 501-973-0150. [CEM]
School—Tel: 501-442-4554; Fax: 501-442-7887. Paula Thiessen, Prin.
Lay Teachers 22; Students 285.
St. Joseph Endowment and Educational Trust Fund—313 E. Lafayette St., 72701. Tel: 501-442-4554.

St. Thomas Aquinas University Parish (1960), Revs. Paul Worm, Sacramental Min.; James Fischer, C.M.; Deacon Paul Cronan, Pastoral Admin.
603 N. Leverett Ave., 72701-3220. Tel: 501-444-0223; Fax: 501-444-2633.

Fordyce, Dallas Co., Good Shepherd (1977). A mission of St. Louis, Camden.

Forrest City, St. Francis Co., St. Francis of Assisi (1876), Very Rev. Thomas C. Marks, V.F.; Sr. Maxine Vogan, D.L.F., Pastoral Admin.
621 S. Washington St., P.O. Box 786, 72336-0786. Tel: 870-633-1665; Fax: 870-633-6307.

Fort Smith, Sebastian Co., Immaculate Conception 1849, Rev. Msgr. John F. O'Donnell, V.F.; Revs. Jose Tharakan; Aaron Fosado.
Mailing Address: P.O. Box 1866, 72902-1866.
Church—22 North 13th, 72901. Tel: 501-783-7963; Fax: 501-783-7865. [JC]
School—223 South 14th St., 72901. Tel: 501-783-6798; Fax: 501-783-0510. Sharon Blentlinger, Prin.
Sisters of Mercy 1; Lay Teachers 31; Students 354.
Mission—Hartford, Sebastian Co., St. Leo's, P.O. Box 1866, 72902.
Immaculate Conception School Educational Trust—.

St. Boniface (1886), Rev. William Elser; Deacon John Burns.
1820 North B St., 72901. Tel: 501-783-6711; Fax: 501-783-7423. [JC]
School—201 N. 19th St., 72901. Tel: 501-783-6601; Fax: 501-783-6605. Marc Soucy, Prin.
Benedictine Sisters 1; Lay Teachers 12; Students 165.
Catholic Education Endowment Trust of Fort Smith, Arkansas—.

Christ the King (1928), Rev. Msgr. Royce R. Thomas; Rev. Peter LeQuang.
2112 S. Greenwood Ave., 72901. Tel: 501-783-7745; Fax: 501-783-7075. [JC]
School—1918 S. Greenwood, 72901. Tel: 501-782-0614; Fax: 501-782-1098. Pam Byrd, Prin.
Lay Teachers 18; Students 221.
Christ the King Catholic School Trust and Endowment Fund—Tel: 501-783-1937.

Hamburg, Ashley Co., Holy Spirit Church (1987). Attended by Holy Cross, Crossett. Revs. Chet Artysiewicz, Glmy.; Neil Pezzulo, Glmy.
Mailing Address: c/o Holy Cross Church, P.O. Box 1245, Crossett, 71635. Tel: 870-853-4847.
Church—110 E. Franklin, 71646. Tel: 870-853-8991. [CEM]

Harrison, Boone Co., Mary, Mother of God (1919), Rev. Gregory G. Hart.
P.O. Box 2150, 72601. Tel: 870-741-5234.

Hartford, Sebastian Co., St. Leo's (1901). A mission of Immaculate Conception, Fort Smith.

Helena, Phillips Co., St. Mary's (1858), Rev. C. Edwin Graves, III.
123 Columbia St., 72342. Tel: 870-338-6990; Fax: 870-338-6990. [CEM]

Hope, Hempstead Co., Our Lady of Good Hope (1875), Rev. Msgr. Robert C. Rehkemper; Deacon Robert V. Regan, (Retired).
Office: P.O. Box 517, 71801. Tel: 870-777-3202.
Res., 325 S. Walker St., 71801. [CEM]

Horseshoe Bend, Izard Co., St. Mary of the Mount (1974), Rev. Fredrick Schneider, O.F.M.
4th & Church St., P.O. Box 4012, 72512. Tel: 870-670-5896. [CEM]

Hot Springs National Park, Garland Co., St. Mary's of the Springs (1869), Very Rev. Msgr. Leo A. Riedmueller, V.F.
100 Central Ave., 71901. Tel: 501-623-3233.

St. John the Baptist (1907), Revs. James P. West; Linus Ukomadu; Deacons David Briselden; Frank Sluppick, (Retired); John Connell; Patrick McCruden.
Res., 589 W. Grand Ave., 71901. Tel: 501-623-6201; Fax: 501-318-0328.
School—583 W. Grand Ave., 71901. Tel: 501-624-3141; Fax: 501-624-3141. Sr. Claudia Ward, Prin.
Sisters of Mercy 3; Lay Teachers 10; Students 190.
St. John's School Endowment—Tel: 501-624-3171.
Missions—Arkadelpia, Clark Co., St. Mary, P.O. Box 26, Arkadelphia, 71923. Tel: 870-246-7575. Sr. Teresa Daly, D.C., Pastoral Admin.; Malvern, Hot Spring Co., 1114 Pine Bluff St., P.O. Box 6, Malvern, 72104. Tel: 501-332-6244.

Hot Springs Village, Garland Co., Sacred Heart of Jesus (1979), Rev. Raymond R. Rossi; Deacons Bernard Bauer; Wallace Gieringer; Larry Lipsmeyer.
Rectory: 22 Descollar, 71909. Tel: 501-922-2062.
Church—295 Balearic, 71909. Fax: 501-922-4153.

Huntsville, Madison Co., St. John's (1963), Rev. Leo Michael, S.D.B.
Church and Mailing Address: (Attn. Anne Beer) Rte. 6, Box 99A, 72740. Tel: 501-738-2709.
Res., 1119 W. Poplar, Rogers, 72756. Tel: 501-636-0200. [JC]

Jacksonville, Pulaski Co., St. Jude the Apostle (1966), Revs. Thomas W. Keller; Thomas Arackal, I.M.S.
2403 McArthur Dr., 72076. Tel: 501-982-4891; Fax: 501-982-0821.

Jonesboro, Craighead Co., Blessed Sacrament (1885), Rev. Jack D. Harris; Deacon Victor Stepka. In res., Rev. James M. Dixon, S.J.
614 S. Church St., P.O. Box 1735, 72401. Tel: 870-932-2529; Fax: 870-935-4444. [CEM]
School—Tel: 870-932-3684. Lee Ann Graddy, Prin.
Olivetan Benedictine Sisters 2; Lay Teachers 10; Students 152.
Blessed Sacrament Educational Endowment Fund—.

Lake Village, Chicot Co., Our Lady of the Lake (1869) (Italian), Rev. Henry B. Mischkowiuski.
P.O. Box 272, 71653. Tel: 870-265-5439. [CEM 2]
School—Tel: 870-265-2921; Fax: 870-265-2921. Kelly Pironi, Prin.
Lay Teachers 9; Students 110.
St. Mary's Educational Trust Fund—.

McGehee, Desha Co., St. Mary (1906), Rev. Sylvano Pera, O.F.M.; Bro. Michel LeMier, O.F.M.
401 N. 3rd St., 71654. Tel: 870-222-3389; Fax: 870-222-4805.
Missions—Dumas, Desha Co., Holy Child, 807 E. Waterman, Dumas, 71639.; Dermott, Chicot Co., Nativity of the Blessed Virgin Mary, Gaines St., Dermott, 71638.

Magnolia, Columbia Co., Immaculate Heart of Mary (1946), Rev. Pius Iwuchukwu.
P.O. Box 365, 71754. Tel: 870-234-2710.

Malvern, Hot Spring Co., St. John the Baptist (1949). A mission of St. John the Baptist, Hot Springs.

Marianna, Lee Co., St. Andrew, Rev. Clarence Edwin Graves.
54 W. Tennessee St., P.O. Box 724, 72360. Tel: 870-338-6990; Fax: 870-338-6990.

Marked Tree, Poinsett Co., St. Norbert, Rev. Nicholas Fuhrmann.
Church—501 Normandy St., 72365. Tel: 870-972-4100.

Mena, Polk Co., St. Agnes (1896), Rev. Clayton Gould.
203 8th St., 71953. Tel: 501-394-1017. [CEM]
Missions—Waldron, Scott Co., St. Jude Thaddeus, P.O. Box 1688, Waldron, 72958. Tel: 501-637-2055; Mount Ida, Montgomery Co., All Saints, P.O. Box 724, Mount Ida, 71957. Tel: 870-326-4641.

Monticello, Drew Co., St. Mark (1975), Rev. Chet Artysiewicz, Glmy.
Rectory: 452 W. Jefferson, 71655. Tel: 870-367-5974.
Church—1016 N. Hyatt St., 71655. Tel: 870-367-2848.
Mission—Warren, Bradley Co., St. Luke, 508 W. Pine, Warren, 71671. Tel: 870-226-5284.

Morrilton, Conway Co., Sacred Heart (1879), Rev. Charles Thessing; Deacon Oscar Rohlman.
506 E. Broadway, 72110. Tel: 501-354-4181. [CEM]
School—Tel: 501-354-8113.
Lay Teachers 7; Students 150.
High School—106 N. St. Joseph, 72110. Sr. Rachel Auringer, Prin.
Lay Teachers 9; Students 84.
Sacred Heart School Endowment—.

Morrison Bluff, Logan Co., SS. Peter and Paul (1878), Rev. William Wewers, O.S.B.
Res. & Mailing Address: c/o Holy Redeemer Church, 103 E. Main St., Clarksville, 72830. Tel: 501-754-3610.

Mountain Home, Baxter Co., St. Peter the Fisherman (1959), Revs. Dennis Mark Wood; Stan Swiderski, S.D.S; Deacons Bob Daye; John Krug; Richard Linstad.
249 Dyer St., P.O. Box 298, 72654. Tel: 870-425-2832; Fax: 870-424-5172.
Mission—Yellville, Marion Co., St. Andrew's, (1980) P.O. Box 197, Yellville, 72687. Tel: 870-449-4850.

Newport, Jackson Co., St. Cecilia's, Rev. Jon McDougal, V.F.
Church—2475 Galeria Subdivision, 72112. Tel: 870-793-7464; 523-6542.
Res., St. Mary's Church, 3800 Harrison St., Batesville, 72501. Tel: 870-793-7717.

Osceola, Mississippi Co., St. Matthew's (1879). Attended by Immaculate Conception, Blytheville. Very Rev. Joseph L. Pallo, V.F.
Church—P.O. Box 583, 72370. Tel: 870-563-9991.
Res., 1301 W. Main St., Blytheville, 72315. Tel: 870-762-2506; Fax: 870-762-2506.

Paragould, Greene Co., St. Mary's (1883), Rev. John E. Marconi.
301 W. Highland St., P.O. Box 861, 72450. Tel: 870-236-2568. [CEM]
School—Tel: 870-236-3681; Fax: 870-236-1073. Inez Ray, Prin.
Lay Teachers 8; Students 97.
Missions—Rector, Clay Co., St. Henry's, 800 Ballard St., Rector, 72461.; Corning, Clay Co., St. Joseph, 1409 Harb St., Corning, 72422. Tel: 870-857-6607.
St. Mary Educational Trust Fund—.

Paris, Logan Co., St. Joseph's (1879) (German), Rev. Denis Soerries, O.S.B.
15 S. Spruce St., 72855. Tel: 501-963-2131. [CEM]
School—Tel: 501-963-2119; Fax: 501-963-8039. Sue Hewett, Prin.
Lay Teachers 6; Students 69.
St. Joseph Endowment Fund—.

Pine Bluff, Jefferson Co., St. Joseph's (1858), Very Rev. W. Andrew Smith, V.F.; Deacon Tim Massanelli.
412 W. 6th Ave., P.O. Box 7434, 71611. Tel: 870-534-4701; Fax: 870-534-4703. [CEM 5]
School—St. Joseph's Junior High School, 422 W. 6th, 71601. Tel: 870-534-7545; Fax: 870-535-4928. Sam Ameen, Prin.
Lay Teachers 20; Students 115.
Mission—Plum Bayou, Jefferson Co., St. Mary's, P.O. Box 7434, 71611.
St. Joseph's Education Fund—Tel: 870-879-4217. Gertrude Schimmel, Pres.
Junior High Trust Fund—.
Senior High Trust Fund—.

St. Peter's (1894) (African American), Rev. Bernard C. Keller, S.V.D.; Deacon Elton Harrison.
207 E. 16th Ave., 71601. Tel: 870-534-6418; Fax: 870-534-6418.
School—Tel: 870-535-4017; Fax: 870-535-4017. Sr. Mary Gottsponer, Prin.
Sisters of Notre Dame 3; Lay Teachers 7; Students 175.
Convent—Tel: 870-534-2316.
Mission—Pine Bluff, Jefferson Co., St. Raphael's, 71601.
St. Peter Catholic School Foundation—.

Pocahontas, Randolph Co., St. Paul the Apostle (1868), Rev. David E. Jacobs; Deacons George Edwards; Roy Goetz.
1002 Convent St., 72455. Tel: 870-892-3319; Fax: 870-892-5199. [CEM]
School—Tel: 870-892-5639. Karla Thielemier, Prin.
Olivetan Benedictine Sisters 2; Lay Teachers 8; Students 122.

Ratcliff, Logan Co., St. Anthony (1879) (German), Rev. Harold Heiman, O.S.B.
Res., Subiaco Abbey, Subiaco, 72865. Tel: 501-934-1000; Fax: 501-934-4328. [CEM]

Rogers, Benton Co., St. Vincent de Paul (1941), Rev. Msgr. Richard S. Oswald, V.F.; Deacon Bill Cook.
Church—1305 W. Cypress St., 72758-4118. Tel: 501-636-4020; Fax: 501-631-2548. [CEM]
School—1315 W. Cypress St., 72758. Tel: 501-636-4421; Fax: 501-631-2548. Ann Morrison, Prin.
Lay Teachers 16; Students 262.
St. Vincent de Paul Endowment Fund—Tel: 501-621-1723; Fax: 501-621-1723. Rob Brothers.

Russellville, Pope Co., St. John's (1950), Very Rev. Ernest L. Hardesty, V.F.
1900 W. Main St., P.O. Box 308, 72801. Tel: 501-967-3699; Fax: 501-967-6215.
School—Tel: 501-967-4644; Fax: 501-967-4644. Paula Gallagher, Prin.
Benedictine Sisters 3; Lay Teachers 11; Students 99.
St. John's Educational Trust—1912 W. Main St., 72801.

St. Vincent, Conway Co., St. Mary (1880), Rev. Arthur B. Chiasson, M.Afr.
11 Kaufman Ln., Hattieville, 72063. Tel: 501-354-3206; Fax: 501-354-4132. [CEM]

Scranton, Logan Co., St. Ignatius (1913) (German), Rev. Placidus Eckart, O.S.B.
Church—P.O. Box 87, 72863. Tel: 501-938-2821. [CEM]
Mission—Prairie View, Logan Co., St. Meinrad, c/o P.O. Box 87, Scranton, 72863.

Searcy, White Co., St. James (1915), Very Rev. Robert T. Dienert, V.F.
1102 Pioneer Rd., P.O. Box 172, 72143. Tel: 501-268-2418 (Rectory); 268-5252 (Office); Fax: 501-268-2418.
Missions—Heber Springs, Cleburne Co., St. Albert, 21 Park Rd., Heber Springs, 72543. Tel: 501-362-2914. Deacon Robert Morris.; Bald Knob, White Co., St. Richard.

Sheridan, Grant Co., Holy Cross (1949). A mission of St. Louis, Camden.

Shoal Creek, Logan Co., St. Scholastica's (New Blaine) (1878) (German), Rev. Raphael DeSalvo, O.S.B.
288 St. Scholastica Rd., New Blaine, 72851. Tel: 501-938-7566.

Siloam Springs, Benton Co., St. Mary's (1963), Rev. Richard M. Strock.
P.O. Box 118, 72761. Tel: 501-524-8526; Fax: 501-524-5677.

Slovak, Prairie Co., SS. Cyril and Methodius. Attended by Holy Rosary, Stuttgart. Rev. John A. Janesko.
Rte. 1, Box 117, Stuttgart, 72160. Tel: 870-241-3359. [CEM]

Springdale, Washington Co., St. Raphael's (1949), Rev. Joseph M. Correnti; Deacon Clarence A. Leis, Pastoral Admin.
Church—1386 S.West End, 72764. Tel: 501-756-6711; Fax: 501-756-8818.
Rectory: P.O. Box 39, Tontitown, 72770. Tel: 501-361-2612.

Stamps, Lafayette Co., St. Vincent de Paul. Closed. For inquiries for parish records contact the Chancery.

Star City, Lincoln Co., St. Justin's (1986). Unassigned. Sr. Kathleen Miles, D.C., Admin.
Mission—Grady, Lincoln Co., Blessed Sacrament, 1207 S. Main, Grady, 71644.

Stuttgart, Arkansas Co., Holy Rosary (1887), Rev. John A. Janesko.
1815 S. Prairie St., 72160. Tel: 870-673-8351; Fax: 870-673-6701. [CEM]
School—Tel: 870-673-3211. Kathy Lorince, Prin.
Benedictine Sisters 1; Lay Teachers 5; Students 82.

Subiaco, Logan Co., St. Benedict (1878), Rev. Victor Gillespie, O.S.B.
Res., 81 W. Parish Dr., 72865. Tel: 501-934-4321. [CEM]

Texarkana, Miller Co., St. Edward's (1903), Rev. Phillip A. Reaves; Vincent Ogbuji; Deacons Joe Bruick; Al Calzada.
Mailing Address: Office, P.O. Box 1186, 75504.
410 Beech St., 71854. Tel: 870-772-1115; Fax: 870-773-2890.; Rectory: 407 Beech St., P.O. Box 1186, 75504. Tel: 870-772-1115; Fax: 870-773-2890. [CEM]
Missions—Ashdown, Little River Co., St. Elizabeth Ann Seton, P.O. Box 966, Ashdown, 71822. Tel: 870-898-8529; Foreman, Little River Co., Sacred Heart, P.O. Box 43, Foreman, 71836.

Tontitown, Washington Co., St. Joseph's (1898) (Italian), Rev. Joseph M. Correnti.
P.O. Box 39, 72770. Tel: 501-361-2612. [CEM]

Van Buren, Crawford Co., St. Michael's (1872), Rev. Ralph Esposito; Deacons Al Genna; Joe Kramer.
1019 Pointer Tr. E., 72956. Tel: 501-474-4595; Fax: 501-471-1219.
Catechesis/Religious Programs—Students 220.
Mission—Jenny Lind, Sebastian Co., Sts. Sabina and Mary's Church.

Walnut Ridge, Lawrence Co., Immaculate Heart of Mary (1925). Attended by St. John the Baptist, Engelberg. Rev. Kevin Atunzu; Deacon Marlyn Tate.
320 Free St., P.O. Box 70, 72476. Tel: 870-886-2119.

Weiner, Poinsett Co., St. Anthony's (1902), Rev. James M. Dixon, S.J.
Mailing Address: P.O. Box 76, 72479. Tel: 870-684-2656; Fax: 870-684-7506.
415 Kings Hwy., 72479. Fax: 870-931-3337. [CEM]

West Memphis, Crittenden Co., St. Michael's (1914), Rev. William F. Thomas.
Res., 208 W. Cooper Ave., 72301. Tel: 870-733-1114.
Church—411 Missouri, P.O. Box 899, 72303. Tel: 870-733-1212; 735-7983; Fax: 870-732-4808.
School—405 Missouri, P.O. Box 899, 72303. Tel: 870-735-1730. Sr. Georgia Felderhoff, Prin.
Olivetan Benedictine Sisters 3; Lay Teachers 8; Students 100.
St. Michael's School Endowment and Charitable Trust—.
Missions—Crawfordsville, Crittenden Co., Sacred Heart, Main St., Crawfordsville, 72327.; Horseshoe Lake, Crittenden Co., St. Mary's of the Lake, Hwy. 131, Horseshoe Lake, 72348.

Winslow, Crawford Co., Our Lady of the Ozarks Shrine (1946), Deacon Dan Daily.
Mailing Address: 22741 N. Hwy. 71, 72959. Tel: 501-634-2181. [CEM]

Wynne, Cross Co., St. Peter's (1921), Very Rev. Thomas C. Marks, V.F.
Mailing Address: P.O. Box 517, 72396. Tel: 870-238-2613; Fax: 870-238-3496.
Mission—McCrory, Woodruff Co., St. Mary's, Hwy. 64, McCrory, 72101. Tel: 870-731-0048.

Chaplains of Public Institutions

LITTLE ROCK. *U.S. Veterans Administration Hospital* 4300 W. 7th St., 72205. Tel: 501-257-1000. Rev. Victor E. Bertrand, C.S.V., Chap.

FAYETTEVILLE. *U.S. Veterans Administration Hospital.* Attended from St. Joseph Church.

NORTH LITTLE ROCK. *U.S. Veterans Administration Hospital* North Little Rock Division, 72114. Tel: 501-257-1000. Rev. Victor E. Bertrand, C.S.V., Chap.

On Duty Outside the Diocese:
Reverend Fathers—
Gunti, Frederick W., Springhill College, Mobile, AL 33608. Tel: 205-460-2169

Retired:
Reverend Monsignors—
De Clerk, Rainer J., St. John Manor, 2414 N. Tyler, Apt. 309, Little Rock, AR 72205. Tel: 501-660-4251
Kordsmeier, John, St. John's Manor, 2414 N. Tyler, Apt. 306, Little Rock, AR 72207. Tel: 501-614-8975
Maus, Rudolph E., 210 N. Vancouver, Russellville, AR 72801
Reverend Fathers—
Barnes, John E., St. John Manor, 2414 N. Tyler St., Apt. 308, Little Rock, AR 72207. Tel: 501-663-3887
Bauer, Ralph, P.O. Box 1172, Hot Springs, AR 71902. Tel: 501-525-2548
Booth, Earl J., St. John Manor, 2414 N. Tyler St., Apt. 202, Little Rock, AR 72207. Tel: 501-614-9135
Cheney, Jesse C., St. John Manor, Apt. #201, 2414 N. Tyler St., Little Rock, AR 72207. Tel: 501-663-7846
Donahue, Thomas J., St. John Manor, 2414 N. Tyler, Apt. 305, Little Rock, AR 72207. Tel: 501-664-6486
Hlavacek, John F., St. John Manor, Apt. #307, 2414 N. Tyler St., Little Rock, AR 72207. Tel: 501-664-0120
Janesko, Francis J., 1604 W. Oak St., Rogers, AR 72758-4135. Tel: 501-636-0387
Kepple, Robert, 107 Palm, Hot Springs, AR 71901. Tel: 501-624-1183
Lange, Milton R., P.O. Box 6037, Springdale, AR 72766
McGinnis, N. Charles, 101 2nd St., Apt. 302, Hot Springs, AR 71913-3446. Tel: 501-624-0927
Oswald, John, St. John Manor, 2414 N. Tyler, Apt. 304, Little Rock, AR 72207. Tel: 501-663-7472
Preske, Venantius, P.O. Box 4018, Horseshoe Bend, AR 72512. Tel: 870-670-4771
Savary, James, 6720 Brentwood Rd., Little Rock, AR 72205. Tel: 501-664-7616
Strassle, Paul, P.O. Box 1545, Fairfield Bay, AR 72088
Torres, Robert A., 630 Brierly Dr., North Little Rock, AR 72120-5002. Tel: 501-961-9958
Turner, George F., 10631 Gulf Beach Hwy., Pensacola, FL 32507. Tel: 904-492-5741
Walters, James, 2505 S. 17th St., Paragould, AR 72450

INSTITUTIONS LOCATED IN THE DIOCESE

[A] SEMINARIES, RELIGIOUS OR SCHOLASTICATES

LITTLE ROCK. *Marylake - Carmelite Novitiate,* 5151 Marylake Dr., 72206. Tel: 501-888-3052. Discalced Carmelite Friars of the Province of St. Therese, Little Rock. Revs. Stephen Sanchez, O.C.D., Supr.; Raphael Kitz, O.C.D., Novice Master; Evarist V. Foix, O.C.D.; Felix Da Prato, O.C.D.; Bonaventure Sauer, O.C.D., Prov.; Henry Bordeaux, O.C.D. Priests 6; Brothers 2; Novices 1.

SUBIACO. *Subiaco Monastery,* 72865. Tel: 501-934-4295; Fax: 501-934-1000.
E-mail: abbey@CSWNet.com
Rt. Rev. Jerome Kodell, O.S.B., Abbot; Revs. David Bellinghausen, O.S.B., Prior; Hugh Assenmacher, O.S.B.; Aaron Pirrera, O.S.B.; Andrew Wewer; Brendan Miller; Camillus Cooney; David McKillin; Felix Fredeman; Harold Heiman; Herbert Vogelpohl; Leonard Wangler, Novice Master, Formation Dir.; Mark Stengel; Meinrad Marbaugh; Paul Hoedebeck; Timothy Donnelly, O.S.B.; Eugene Luke, O.S.B. Abbots 1; Monks 60.

[B] HIGH SCHOOLS, DIOCESAN

LITTLE ROCK. *Catholic High School,* 6300 Lee St., 72205. Tel: 501-664-3939; Fax: 501-664-6549.
E-mail: chs@lrchs.org
Rev. Msgr. George W. Tribou, Rector; Rev. Lawrence A. Frederick. Priests 2; Brothers 1; Lay Teachers 32; Students 676. Legal Title: *Catholic High School of Little Rock, AR.*
Catholic High School Foundation, Inc. Tel: 501-664-3939; Fax: 501-664-6549.

CONWAY. *St. Joseph High School,* 502 Front St., 72032-5408. Tel: 501-329-5741; Fax: 501-513-6804. Daniel Fields, Prin.; Rita Strause, Asst. Prin. Lay Teachers 16; Students 224.

FORT SMITH. *Trinity Junior High,* 1205 S. Albert Pike, 72903. Tel: 501-782-2451; Fax: 501-782-7263.
E-mail: trinityjh@earthlink.net
Web site: www.angelfire.com/yt/trinityjh
Rev. Msgr. Royce R. Thomas, J.C.L., Pastor Rep.; Mrs. Connie Gibson, Prin. Lay Teachers 17; Students 246.
Trinity Educational Trust Fund. Tel: 501-782-2451; Fax: 501-782-7263.

MORRILTON. *Sacred Heart Catholic School,* 106 N. St. Joseph St., 72110. Tel: 501-354-8113; Fax: 501-354-2001.
E-mail: shcs@mev.net
Sr. Rachel Auringer, O.S.U., Prin.; Katherine Etris, Asst. Prin. Ursuline Sisters 1; Lay Teachers 18; Students 103.

[C] HIGH SCHOOLS, PRIVATE

LITTLE ROCK. *Mount St. Mary Academy.* (Girls), 3224 Kavanaugh Blvd., 72205. Tel: 501-664-8006; Fax: 501-666-4382.
E-mail: pgustafson@mtstmary.edu
Web site: www.mtstmary.edu
Sr. Deborah Raye Troillett, R.S.M., Pres.; Jeffrey T. Corrigan, Prin.; Carolyn Chalmers, Asst. Prin., Student Life. Priests 2; Sisters of Mercy 8; Lay Teachers 37; Students 580.
Mount St. Mary Academy Endowment and Scholarship Fund. Tel: 501-664-8009; Fax: 501-666-4267.

SUBIACO. *Subiaco Academy.* (Boys), 72865. Tel: 501-934-1000; Fax: 501-934-1033.
E-mail: pweaver@subi.org
Web site: www.subi.org
Rt. Rev. Jerome Kodell, O.S.B., Pres.; Mr. Hans Broekman, Headmaster. Priests 2; Brothers 2; Lay Teachers 18; Students 195.

[D] DAY CARE CENTERS

LITTLE ROCK. *Little Angel Day Care,* 9111 Auxer Rd., 72209. Tel: 501-568-0694. Sr. Philippa Wavrick, Dir. Olivetan Benedictine Sisters 2; Students 20.

[E] GENERAL HOSPITALS

LITTLE ROCK. *St. Vincent Doctors Hospital,* 6101 St. Vincent Cir., 72205. Tel: 501-660-3564.
E-mail: Kellyv@exchange.svimc.com
For a complete listing, refer to the Hospitals section.
St. Vincent Infirmary Medical Center, No. 2 St. Vincent Circle, 72205. Tel: 501-660-3571; Fax: 501-671-4014.
E-mail: coleenh@exchange.SVIMC.com
For a complete listing, refer to the Hospitals section.

FORT SMITH. *Northside Community Health Center,* 3202 North 6th, 72904. Tel: 501-782-1456; Fax: 501-782-1462
For a complete listing, refer to the Hospitals section.
St. Edward Mercy Medical Center, 7301 Rogers Ave., 72917. Tel: 501-484-6000; Fax: 501-452-1770.
Web site: www.StEdwardMercy.com
For a complete listing, refer to the Hospitals section.
St. Edward Mercy Medical Center, dba Harbor View Mercy Hospital and Counseling Center, 10301 Mayo Rd., P.O. Box 17000, 72917-7000. Tel: 501-484-5550.
Web site: www.StEdwardMercy.com
For a complete listing, refer to the Hospitals section.

HOT SPRINGS NATIONAL PARK. *St. Joseph's Regional Health Center,* P.O. Box 29001, 71903-9001. Tel: 501-622-1000; Fax: 501-622-1199.
E-mail: tmcvey@htsp.smhs.com
Web site: www.saintjosephs.com
For a complete listing, refer to the Hospitals section.

JONESBORO. *St. Bernard's Regional Medical Center,* 224 E. Matthews St., 72401. Tel: 870-972-4100; Fax: 870-974-5112.
E-mail: Idalford@sbrmc.org
Web site: SBRMC.com
For a complete listing, refer to the Hospitals section.
St. Bernards Behavioral Health Servies, Inc., 2712 E. Johnson Ave., 72401. Tel: 870-932-2800
For a complete listing, refer to the Hospitals section.

MORRILTON. *St. Anthony's Hospital Association,* #4 Hospital Dr., 72110-4510. Tel: 501-977-2300; Fax: 501-354-2830.
E-mail: ceosmith@swbell.net
For a complete listing, refer to the Hospitals section.

OZARK. *St. Edward Health Facilities of Franklin County, dba Mercy Hospital / Turner Memorial,* 801 W. River St., 72949. Tel: 501-667-4138; Fax: 501-667-4751; 667-9778 (Admin.).
E-mail: jmaddox@ftsm.smhs.com
For a complete listing, refer to the Hospitals section.

PARIS. *St. Edward Health Facilities of Logan Co., dba North Logan Mercy Hospital,* 500 E. Academy, 72855. Tel: 501-963-6101; Fax: 501-963-6155
For a complete listing, refer to the Hospitals section.

ROGERS. *St. Mary-Rogers Memorial Hospital,* 72756. Tel: 501-636-0200, Ext. 705; Fax: 501-936-2906.
Web site: www.mercyhealthnwa.smhs.com
For a complete listing, refer to the Hospitals section.

SHERWOOD. *St. Vincent Medical Center / Sherwood,* 2215 Wildwood Ave., 72120. Tel: 501-660-3564.
E-mail: Kellyv@exchange.svimc.com
For a complete listing, refer to the Hospitals section.

WALDRON. *St. Edward Health Facilities of Scott County dba Mercy Hospital,* Hwy. 71 & 80, Box 2230, 72958. Tel: 501-637-4135; Fax: 501-637-3523
For a complete listing, refer to the Hospitals section.

WYNNE. *St. Bernards Community Hospital Corporation dba Crossridge Community Hospital,* 310 S. Falls Blvd., 72396. Tel: 870-238-3300
For a complete listing, refer to the Hospitals section.

[F] PROTECTIVE INSTITUTIONS

LITTLE ROCK. *ABBA House, Missionaries of Charity,* 1014 S. Oak St., 72204. Tel: 501-666-9718
For a complete listing, refer to the Special Care Facilities section.

HOT SPRINGS NATIONAL PARK. *Monastery of Our Lady of Charity of Refuge (Good Shepherd),* 1125 Malvern Ave., 71901. Tel: 501-623-9651; Fax: 501-623-1509
For a complete listing, refer to the Special Care Facilities section.
St. Michael's School, 1125 Malvern Ave., 71901. Tel: 501-623-9651; Fax: 501-623-1509.
E-mail: smichael@ipa.net
Web site: www.LightofMary.org
For a complete listing, refer to the Special Care Facilities section.

[G] HOMES FOR AGED

BARLING. *Mercy Crest of Arkansas, Inc.,* 1300 Strozier Ln., 72923. Tel: 501-478-3000; Fax: 501-452-8382.
E-mail: jarnold@ftsm. smns.com
Web site: www.mercycrest.com
For a complete listing, refer to the Special Care Facilities section.

[H] RESIDENCES FOR PRIESTS

LITTLE ROCK. *St. John Manor,* 2414 N. Tyler St., 72207. Rev. Msgr. Rainer DeClerk. Tel: 501-660-4251; Revs. Jesse C. Cheney. Tel: 501-663-7846; John F. Hlavacek. Tel: 501-664-0120; John E. Barnes. Tel: 501-663-3887; Thomas J. Donahue. Tel: 501-664-6486; Earl J. Booth. Tel: 501-614-9135; John Oswald. Tel: 501-663-7472; Rev. Msgr. John Kordsmeier. Tel: 501-614-8975. Priests 8.

[I] CONVENTS AND RESIDENCES FOR SISTERS

LITTLE ROCK. *Discalced Carmelite Nuns,* 7201 W. 32nd St., 72204-4716. Tel: 501-565-5121; Fax: 501-565-3877.
E-mail: lrcarmel@juno.com
Sr. Joan Monkhouse, Prioress. Legal Title: *Discalced Carmelite Nuns of Little Rock.* Sisters 12; Nuns with Solemn Vows 12.
Attended from Catholic High School, Little Rock & Our Lady of Holy Souls, Little Rock.
Mt. St. Mary's Convent, 3508 Kavanaugh Blvd., 72205. Tel: 501-664-5977; Fax: 501-666-4382.
E-mail: srbelmer@mtstmary.edu
Sisters 8.

BARLING. *McAuley Convent and Retirement Residence,* 1300 Strozier Ln., 72923. Tel: 501-478-3002; Fax: 501-478-3006.
E-mail: DAllenadm@aol.com; mjcareyrsm@juno.com
Sisters of Mercy 15; Bed Capacity 30; Number of Persons Served 21.

FORT SMITH. *St. Scholastica Monastery-Motherhouse,* 1301 S. Albert Pike, P.O. Box 3489, 72913. Tel: 501-783-4147; Fax: 501-782-4352.
E-mail: monast@ipa.net
Web site: www.catholic-church.org/scholastica/
Sr. Elise Forst, Prioress; Sr. Catherine Markey, Archivist; Rev. Juanito C. Santos de Dios, Chap. Benedictine Professed Sisters 105; Novices 1.
Sisters of Mercy of St. Edward, 2700 S. 74th St., 72903. Tel: 501-484-6098; Fax: 501-484-1760.
E-mail: srsjm@yahoo.com
Sr. Judith Marie Keith, R.S.M., Sec. Sisters of Mercy 7.

HOT SPRINGS. *Monastery of Our Lady of Charity of Refuge (Good Shepherd),* 1125 Malvern Ave., 71901. Tel: 501-623-9651; Fax: 501-623-1509. Sr. Mary Theresa Dionne, Supr.; Rev. Benoit Picard, O.F.F., Chap. Sisters 14.

JONESBORO. *Holy Angels Convent-Motherhouse,* 72403-0130. Tel: 870-935-5810; Fax: 870-935-4210.
E-mail: olivben@olivben.org
Web site: www.olivben.org
Olivetan Benedictine Sisters. Sr. Eileen Schneider, O.S.B., Prioress; Rev. Gregory Pilcher, O.S.B. Sisters 49.

WALDRON. *Waldron Convent of Mercy,* 435 E. 8th St., 72958. Tel: 501-637-2287. Sisters of Mercy.

[J] NEWMAN CENTERS

FAYETTEVILLE. *Catholic Campus Ministries,* 603 N. Leverett, 72701. Tel: 501-444-0223; Fax: 501-442-2633.
E-mail: ccm@comp.uark.edil
Web site: ccm@comp.uark.edu
Deacon Paul Cronan, Dir.
Univ. of Arkansas at Little Rock Campus Ministry, 7413 Henderson, Little Rock, 72210. Tel: 501-455-1412; Fax: 501-664-1964.
E-mail: RHanley644@aol.com
Mrs. Diane Hanley, Campus Min.
Henderson State Teachers College and Ouchita Baptist University Campus Ministry. (Arkadelphia), P.O. Box 26, Arkadelphia, 71329. Tel: 870-246-7575.
E-mail: teresa@hsnp.com
Sr. Teresa Daly, D.C., Campus Min.
University of Central Arkansas & Hendrix College Campus Ministry. (Conway), 2204 Bruce, Conway, 72032. Tel: 501-336-9091.
E-mail: Catholic@cyberback.com
Deacon Richard Papini, Campus Min.
University of Arkansas, St. Thomas Aquinas University Parish. (Fayetteville), 603 N. Leverett, 72701. Tel: 501-444-0223; Fax: 501-442-2633.
E-mail: ccm@comp.uark.edu
Deacon Paul Cronan, Pastoral Admin.; Revs. Paul Worm, Sacramental Min.; James Fischer, C.M., Sacramental Min.; Lela Nelson, Assoc. Campus Min. & Admin. Asst.; T.C. Long, Assoc. Campus Min.; Vera Langanke, Asst. Campus Min.
Harding University (Searcy) Campus Ministry, 109 Campbell Dr., Beebe, 72012. Tel: 501-882-6299; Fax: 501-882-5465.
E-mail: flofitch@hotmail.com
Flo Fitch, Campus Min.
University of Ozarks Campus Ministry (Clarksville), Rte. 1, Box 302, Hartman, 72840. Tel: 501-979-1434.
E-mail: mstickl@mail.ozarks.edu
Campus Ministers: Melodye Stickley.

JONESBORO. *Blessed John Newman University Parish,* 3800 E. Johnson Ave., 72401. Tel: 870-972-1888. Rev. Jack D. Harris; Mary Ruth Staudt, Dir.; Constance Akin, Campus Min.

RUSSELLVILLE. *St. Leo the Great University Parish,* 509 W. L St., 72801. Tel: 501-968-8249. Very Rev. Ernest L. Hardesty, V.F., Pastor; Mrs. Pat Buford, Dir. Campus Ministry.

[K] RETREAT CENTERS

BERRYVILLE. *Brothers and Sisters of Charity at Little Portion Hermitage.* (Integrated Monastery), 350 CR 248, 72616-8505. Tel: 501-253-7710; Fax: 501-253-6640.
E-mail: Hermitage@Arkansas.net
Web site: www.BrothersandSisters.org
Legal Title: *Brothers and Sisters of Charity at Little Portion, Inc.* John Michael Talbot, B.S.C., Gen. Min.; Viola Talbot, B.S.C., Vicar Gen. Min.

Little Flower Clinic for the Poor. Tel: 501-253-7710; Fax: 501-253-6640.

EUREKA SPRINGS. *Little Portion Retreat and Training Center at More Mt.*, 171 Hummingbird Ln., 72632. Tel: 501-253-7379; Fax: 501-253-2640. John Michael Talbot, Exec. Dir.; Tom Fink, Admin. Dir.; Deacon Samuel Hilburn, Spiritual Dir. Catholic Staff 4.

FORT SMITH. *St. Scholastica Center*, 1205 S. Albert Pike, P.O. Box 3489, 72913. Tel: 501-783-1135; Fax: 501-782-4352.
E-mail: scholast@ipa.net
Web site: www.catholic-church.org.scholastica/
Sr. Cabrini Schmitz, O.S.B., Dir. Center & Program Coord.; Sr. Gertrude Grabber, O.S.B., Dir. Maintenance and Hospitality; Sr. Macrina Wiederkehr, O.S.B., Retreats/Spiritual Dir. Conducted by Benedictine Sisters 5.

SHOAL CREEK. *Hesychia House of Prayer.* Tel: 501-938-7375. 204 St. Scholastica Rd., New Blaine, 72851. Sr. Louise Sharum, O.S.B., Dir. Benedictine Sisters 4. Attended from New Subiaco Abbey, Subiaco, AR. Rev. Raphael DeSalvo, O.S.B.

[L] MISCELLANEOUS LISTINGS

LITTLE ROCK. *The "Arkansas Catholic".* Published by Arkansas Catholic, Inc. of the Diocese of Little Rock. 2500 N. Tyler St., P.O. Box 7417, 72217. Tel: 501-664-0340; 664-0125; Fax: 501-664-9075. Mrs. Malea Hargett, Editor.

Christopher Homes of Arkansas, Inc., 2417 N. Tyler St., 72207. Tel: 501-664-1881; Fax: 501-664-1631.
E-mail: CHRHOMES@aol.com
James T. Davis, Exec. Dir. Total in Residence 550.

Christopher Homes of Augusta, Inc. Tel: 870-347-2388; Fax: 870-347-2388.

Christopher Homes of Brinkley, Inc. Tel: 870-734-2201; Fax: 870-734-2201.

Christopher Homes of Camden, Inc. Tel: 870-837-1911; Fax: 870-837-1911.

Christopher Homes of Clarendon, Inc. Tel: 870-747-5441; Fax: 870-747-5441.

Christopher Homes of DeQueen, Inc. Tel: 870-642-6211; Fax: 870-642-6211.

Christopher Homes of DeValls Bluff, Inc. Tel: 870-998-7280; Fax: 870-998-7280.

Christopher Homes of Elaine, Inc. Tel: 870-827-3705; Fax: 870-827-3705.

Christopher Homes of El Dorado, Inc. Tel: 870-862-9711; Fax: 870-862-9711.

Christopher Homes of Forrest City, Inc. Tel: 870-633-4804; Fax: 870-633-4804.

Christopher Homes of Horatio, Inc. Tel: 870-832-4014; Fax: 870-832-4014.

Christopher Homes of Hot Springs, Inc. Tel: 501-318-1317; Fax: 501-318-1317.

Christopher Homes of Jonesboro, Inc. Tel: 870-931-9575; Fax: 870-931-9575.

Christopher Homes of Marianna, Inc. Tel: 870-295-6345; Fax: 870-295-6345.

Christopher Homes of Monette, Inc. Tel: 870-486-2748; Fax: 870-486-2748.

Christopher Homes of North Little Rock, Inc. Tel: 501-758-8582; Fax: 501-758-8582.

Christopher Homes of Palestine, Inc. Tel: 870-581-2023; Fax: 870-581-2023.

Christopher Homes of Paragould, Inc. Tel: 870-239-8609; Fax: 870-239-8609.

Christopher Homes of Parkin, Inc. Tel: 870-755-2939; Fax: 870-755-2939.

Christopher Homes of Searcy, Inc. Tel: 501-268-7804; Fax: 501-268-7804.

Christopher Homes of Strong, Inc. Tel: 870-797-7525; Fax: 870-797-7525.

Christopher Homes of West Helena, Inc. Tel: 870-572-9433; Fax: 870-572-9433.

Christopher Homes of Wynne, Inc. Tel: 870-238-3388; Fax: 870-238-3388.

The Guadalupe Prenatal Clinic, 801 Sherman St., 72202. Tel: 501-374-5767; Fax: 501-374-5839. Rev. John K. Antony, J.C.L.

John Gazzola Trust Estate, P.O. Box 7239, 72217. Tel: 501-664-0340; Fax: 501-664-9186. Mr. William Hartmann, Trustee; Mr. Charles Baker, Trustee; Mr. Paul Hiegel, Trustee.

Little Rock Scripture Study, 2500 N. Tyler St., P.O. Box 2500, 72217. Tel: 501-664-0340; Fax: 501-664-9075.
E-mail: littlerockscripturestudy@dolr.org
Web site: www.littlerockscripture.org
Ms. Cackie Upchurch, Dir.; Ms. Lilly Hess, Assoc. Dir.

St. John's Seminary, Inc., Endowment Fund, P.O. Box 7565, 72217. Tel: 501-664-0340, Ext. 331; Fax: 501-664-9075.

St. Thomas More Society of Arkansas, Inc., 111 Center St., 22nd Fl., 72201. Tel: 501-372-6453.
E-mail: dmenz@williamsanderson.com
David F. Menz, Chm.

Sophia's Center, 1016 N. Harrison St., 72205-1820. Tel: 501-280-2955; Fax: 501-280-1899.
E-mail: lamrsm1016@msn.com
Sr. Lee Ann McNally, R.S.M., Dir.

BERRYVILLE. *St. Vincent de Paul Thrift Shop*, 204 S. Main, 72616. Tel: 870-423-3572. Ms. Margaret Duran, Pres. Patients assisted annually 60.

BLYTHEVILLE. *Immaculate Conception Trust Fund*, 1301 W. Main St., 72315. Tel: 870-762-2506; Fax: 870-762-2506. Very Rev. Joseph L. Pallo, V.F.

CONWAY. *St. Joseph Parish Catholic School, Conway, Endowment Fund*, 502 Front St., 72032-5408. Tel: 501-327-5528; Fax: 501-327-5528.
E-mail: StJoseph@Cyperback.com
Joseph G. Koch, Sec. & Treas.

DUMAS. *Daughter of Charity Services*, 145 W. Waterman, P.O. Box 158, 71639. Tel: 870-382-4878; Fax: 870-382-4895.
E-mail: sferrero@DCARK.org
Sr. Seraphine Ferrero, D.C., Exec. Dir.
Clinics:

St. Elizabeth Health Center, P.O. Drawer 370, Gould, 71643. Tel: 870-263-4317; Fax: 870-263-4782.

DePaul Health Center, P.O. Box 158, 71639. Tel: 870-382-4878; Fax: 870-382-4895.

Wellness Center, Hwy. 65 S., P.O. Box 473, Gould, 71643. Tel: 870-263-4748; Fax: 870-263-4233. Patients assisted annually 22,131.

EUREKA SPRINGS. *Heart of Mercy Solitude, Inc.*, P.O. Box 255, 72632. Tel: 501-253-5557. Sr. Judith A. Ayers, Dir.

St. Vincent de Paul Society, 1471 CR222, 72631. Tel: 501-253-8292.
E-mail: Jimbev@aol.com
Ms. Beverly Anne Wright, Pres. Patients assisted annually 91.

JONESBORO. *Catholic Hispanic Center*, 308 W. Monroe, 72401. Tel: 870-931-8853; Fax: 870-931-1884.
E-mail: ewillett@fastclata.net
Rev. James M. Dixon, S.J. Tel: 870-931-3337, P.O. Box 1735, 72403-1735. Tel: 870-931-3337; Fax: 870-935-4444. Sr. M. Elaine Willett, O.S.B. Tel: 870-930-1177 (Pager), P.O. Box 130, 72403. Tel: 870-930-1177 (Pager); Fax: 870-930-4444. Sponsored by Blessed Sacrament Church, Jonesboro, AR. Patients assisted annually 1,000.

Jonesboro Real Estate Holding Company, Inc., 224 E. Matthews, 72401. Tel: 870-972-4326. James P. Stanzell, Legal Counsel.

St. Bernard's Village, Inc. (Affiliated with Olivetan Benedictine Sisters, Inc., Jonesboro, AR), 1606 Heern Dr., 72401. Tel: 870-932-8141; Fax: 870-933-5563.
Web site: www.sbrmc.com
Mr. Kevin Hodges, Exec. Dir. & Contact Person; Mr. Raymond Heern, Pres. Patients assisted annually 100.

LONSDALE. *Annunzitta, Inc.*, P.O. Box 63, 72087. Tel: 501-939-2060. Ms. Janice Sehgal, Dir.

NORTH LITTLE ROCK. *Priestly Fraternity of St. Peter*, 1418 W. 20th St., 72114. Tel: 501-812-9155; Fax: 501-812-9225. Revs. Evaristus Eshiowu, F.S.S.P.; Joseph Portzer, F.S.S.P., Chap.

STUTTGART. *Holy Rosary Catholic School "Vision 2000" Educational Trust Fund*, 1815 S. Prairie St., 72160. Tel: 870-673-8351; Fax: 870-673-6701.
E-mail: HolyRos@IPA.net
Rev. John A. Janesko.

RELIGIOUS INSTITUTES OF MEN REPRESENTED IN THE DIOCESE

For further details refer to the corresponding bracketed number in the Religious Institutes of Men or Women section.

[0200]—*Benedictine Monks.* (New Subiaco Abbey).—O.S.B.
[0460]—*Brothers of the Poor of St. Francis.*—C.F.P.
[1320]—*Clerics of St. Viator.*—C.S.V.
[1330]—*Congregation of the Mission.*—C.M.
[0260]—*Discalced Carmelite Friars.* (St. Therese Prov.).—O.C.D.
[0520]—*Franciscan Friars.* (Prov. of the Sacred Heart).—O.F.M.
[0570]—*Glenmary Home Missioners.*—Glmy.
[0650]—*Holy Ghost Fathers.* (Western Vice Prov.).—C.S.Sp.
[0690]—*Jesuit Fathers and Brothers.*—S.J.
[0850]—*Missionaries of Africa.* (Prov. of Quebec, Canada).—M.Afr.
[1065]—*Priestly Fraternity of St. Peter.*—F.S.S.P.
[]—*Public Association of the Faithful - Celibate Brotherhood of the Brothers and Sisters of Charity.*—B.S.C.
[0420]—*Society of the Divine Word.* (Techny, IL).—S.V.D.

RELIGIOUS INSTITUTES OF WOMEN REPRESENTED IN THE DIOCESE

[0230]—*Benedictine Sisters of Pontifical Jurisdiction.* (Fort Smith, AR).—O.S.B.
[0470]—*Congregation of the Sisters of Charity of the Incarnate Word, Houston, Texas.*—C.C.V.I.
[0760]—*Daughters of Charity of St. Vincent de Paul.* (West Central Prov.).—D.C.
[]—*Daughters of Mary of the Cross.*—D.M.C.
[]—*Daughters of Our Lady of Fatima.*—D.L.F.
[0420]—*Discalced Carmelite Nuns.* (Little Rock, AR).—O.C.D.
[1070-10]—*Dominican Sisters.*—O.P.
[2575]—*Institute of the Sisters of Mercy of the Americas.* (St. Louis, MO).—R.S.M.
[2710]—*Missionaries of Charity.*—M.C.
[0390]—*Missionary Carmelites of St. Teresa.*—C.M.S.T.
[2690]—*Missionary Catechists of Divine Providence.* (San Antonio, TX).—M.C.D.P.
[1360]—*Missionary Franciscan Sisters of the Immaculate Conception.*—O.S.F.
[2860]—*Missionary Sisters of the Sacred Heart.*—M.S.C.
[]—
Missioneras Catequestas de los Pobres.—M.C.P.
[3070]—*North American Union Sisters of Our Lady of Charity.* (Hot Springs, AR).—N.A.U.-O.L.C.
[0240]—*Olivetan Benedictine Sisters.* (Jonesboro, AR).—O.S.B.
[]—*Public Association of the Faithful - Celibate Sisterhood of the Brothers and Sisters of Charity.*—B.S.C.
[2940]—*School Sisters of Notre Dame.* (Prov. of Dallas).—S.S.N.D.
[0440]—*Sisters of Charity of Cincinnati, OH.*—S.C.
[0500]—*Sisters of Charity of Nazareth.*—S.C.N.
[3860]—*Sisters of St. Joseph of Cluny.*—S.J.C.
[0970]—*Sisters of the Divine Compassion.*—R.D.C.
[4100]—*Sisters of the Sorrowful Mother of the Third Order of St. Francis.*—S.S.M.
[4120-03]—*Ursuline Nuns of the Congregation of Paris.*—O.S.U.
[4160]—*Vincentian Sisters of Charity.*—V.S.C.

CEMETERIES

LITTLE ROCK. *Calvary.*
FORT SMITH. *Calvary.*

NECROLOGY

† Freyaldenhoven, George P., (Retired). —Died June 5, 2000.

† Stemac, Rev. Msgr. Louis Vincent, (Retired). —Died Oct. 8, 2000.

Archdiocese of Los Angeles

(Archidioecesis Angelorum in California)

His Eminence

ROGER CARDINAL MAHONY, D.D.

Archbishop of Los Angeles; ordained May 1, 1962; appointed Titular Bishop of Tamascani and Auxiliary Bishop of Fresno January 7, 1975; consecrated March 19, 1975; appointed Bishop of Stockton February 26, 1980; installed as the third Bishop of Stockton April 17, 1980; appointed Archbishop of Los Angeles July 16, 1985; installed as the fourth Archbishop of Los Angeles September 5, 1985; Created Cardinal June 28, 1991. *Res., 555 W. Temple St., Los Angeles, CA, 90012. Office: 3424 Wilshire Blvd., Los Angeles, CA, 90010-2241.* Tel.: 213-637-7261; Fax: 213-637-6510.

Archdiocesan Catholic Center Office: 3424 Wilshire Blvd., Los Angeles, CA, 90010-2241. Tel.: 213-637-7000; Fax: 213-637-6607.

Web site address: www.LA-Archdiocese.org

Most Reverend

JOHN J. WARD, D.D., J.C.L., V.G.

Auxiliary Bishop and Vicar General; ordained May 4, 1946; appointed Titular Bishop of Bria and Auxiliary October 16, 1963; consecrated December 12, 1963; Assigned Titular Bishop of California, June 15, 1996; retired July 1, 1996. *Office: 3424 Wilshire Blvd., Los Angeles, CA, 90010-2248.*

Most Reverend

JUAN A. ARZUBE, D.D.

Retired Auxiliary Bishop and Vicar General; ordained May 5, 1954; appointed Titular Bishop of Civitate and Auxiliary February 9, 1971; consecrated March 25, 1971; retired June 1, 1993. *Res., c/o Sacred Heart Church, 2889 N. Lincoln Ave., Altadena, CA, 91001-4598.*

Most Reverend

THOMAS J. CURRY, D.D., PH.D.

Auxiliary Bishop and Vicar General; ordained June 18, 1967; appointed Titular Bishop of Ceanannus Mor February 8, 1994; ordained Bishop March 19, 1994. *Office: Santa Barbara Pastoral Region, 3240 Calle Pinon, Santa Barbara, CA, 93105.*

Most Reverend

JOSEPH M. SARTORIS, D.D., V.G.

Auxiliary Bishop and Vicar General; ordained May 30, 1953; appointed Titular Bishop of Oliva and Auxiliary Bishop of Los Angeles February 8, 1994; ordained a Bishop March 19, 1994. *Office: San Pedro Pastoral Region, 3555 St. Pancratius Pl., Lakewood, CA, 90712-1416.*

Most Reverend

GABINO ZAVALA, D.D., J.C.L., V.G.

Auxiliary Bishop and Vicar General; ordained May 28, 1977; appointed Titular Bishop of Tamascani and Auxiliary Bishop of Los Angeles February 8, 1994; ordained Bishop March 19, 1994. *Office: San Gabriel Pastoral Region, 16009 E. Cypress Ave., Irwindale, CA, 91706.*

Most Reverend

GERALD E. WILKERSON, D.D.

Auxiliary Bishop and Vicar General; ordained May 1, 1965; appointed Titular Bishop of Vincennes and Auxiliary Bishop of Los Angeles November 5, 1997; ordained Bishop January 21, 1998. *Office: San Fernando Pastoral Region, 15101 San Fernando Mission Blvd., Mission Hills, CA, 91345-1109.*

Most Reverend

EDWARD W. CLARK

Auxiliary Bishop; ordained May 9, 1972; appointed Titular Bishop of Gardar and Auxiliary Bishop of Los Angeles January 16, 2001; ordained Bishop March 26, 2001.

DIOCESE ESTABLISHED 1840; AN ARCHBISHOPRIC JULY 11, 1936.

Square Miles 8,762.

Comprises the Counties of Los Angeles, Santa Barbara and Ventura in the State of California.

PATRONESS OF THE DIOCESE: ST. VIBIANA.

Legal Titles:

The Roman Catholic Archbishop of Los Angeles, a Corporation Sole.

Archdiocese of Los Angeles Education and Welfare Corporation.

Our Lady Queen of Angels Seminary.

St. John's Seminary College.

St. John's Seminary in California.

The Cardinal McIntyre Fund for Charity.

Catholic Charities of Los Angeles, Inc.

Catholic Charities Community Development Corporation.

The Tidings.

Vida Nueva.

For legal titles of parishes and archdiocesan institutions, consult the Chancery Office.

STATISTICAL OVERVIEW

Personnel	
Cardinal	1
Auxiliary Bishops	5
Retired Bishops	2
Abbots	1
Priests: Diocesan Active in Diocese	418
Priests: Active Outside Diocese	11
Priests: Diocesan in Foreign Missions	1
Priests: Retired, Sick or Absent	152
Number of Diocesan Priests	582
Religious Priests in Diocese	580
Extern Priests in Diocese	150
Ordinations:	
Diocesan Priests	7
Religious Priests	7
Permanent Deacons	14
Permanent Deacons in Diocese	188
Total Brothers	173
Total Sisters	1,878
Parishes	
Parishes	287
With Resident Pastor:	
Resident Diocesan Priests	225
Resident Religious Priests	62
Without Resident Pastor:	
Administered by Priests	22
Administered by Women Religious	1
Administered by Pastoral Teams, etc.	20
Missions	7
Pastoral Centers	1
Professional Ministry Personnel:	
Brothers	8
Sisters	181
Lay Ministers	619
Welfare	
Catholic Hospitals	19
Total Assisted	1,569,850
Health Care Centers	5
Total Assisted	15,422
Homes for the Aged	7
Total Assisted	3,406
Residential Care of Children	2
Total Assisted	604
Day Care and Extended Day Care Centers	82
Total Assisted	5,264
Specialized Homes	11
Total Assisted	1,809
Special Centers for Social Services	80
Total Assisted	352,006
Residential Care of Disabled	2
Total Assisted	225
Other Institutions	40
Total Assisted	120
Educational	
Seminaries, Diocesan	2
Students from This Diocese	62
Students from Other Diocese	81

Diocesan Students in Other Seminaries	11
Seminaries, Religious	12
Students Religious	96
Total Seminarians	169
Colleges and Universities	5
Total Students	10,484
High Schools, Diocesan and Parish	29
Total Students	16,652
High Schools, Private	22
Total Students	13,658
Elementary Schools, Diocesan and Parish	218
Total Students	66,754
Elementary Schools, Private	9
Total Students	2,644
Catechesis/Religious Education:	
High School Students	30,000
Elementary Students	230,200
Total Students Under Catholic Instruction	370,561
Teachers in the Diocese:	
Priests	109
Scholastics	1
Brothers	28
Sisters	357
Lay Teachers	4,185
Vital Statistics	
Receptions into the Church:	
Infant Baptism Totals	82,869
Adult Baptism Totals	2,340
Received into Full Communion	4,703
First Communions	56,422
Confirmations	18,013
Marriages:	
Catholic	10,276
Interfaith	2,130
Total Marriages	12,406
Deaths	13,268
Total Catholic Population	4,148,720
Total Population	11,055,000

Former Bishops—Rt. Rev. FRANCIS GARCIA DIEGO Y MORENO, O.F.M., D.D., cons. Oct. 4, 1840; Bishop of both Californias; died at Santa Barbara, April 30, 1846.—Rt. Rev. JOSEPH SADOC ALEMANY, O.P., D.D., cons. June 30, 1850; Bishop of Monterey; transferred to San Francisco, July 29, 1853; died in Valencia, Spain, April 14, 1888.—Rt. Rev. THADDEUS AMAT, C.M., D.D., cons. March 12, 1854; died May 12, 1878.—Rt. Rev. FRANCIS MORA, D.D., cons. Titular Bishop of Mosynopolis and Coadjutor to Bishop Amat, Aug. 3, 1873; resigned May 6, 1896; died Aug. 3, 1905 in Sarria, Barcelona, Spain.—Rt. Rev. GEORGE MONTGOMERY, D.D., cons. April 8, 1894, Bishop of Tmul and Coadjutor-Bishop of Monterey and Los Angeles *cum jure successionis* succeeded to May 6, 1896; appt. Coadjutor-Archbishop of San Francisco, Jan. 1, 1903; died in San Francisco, Jan. 10, 1907.—Rt. Rev. THOMAS JAMES CONATY, D.D., cons. Nov. 24, 1901, Titular-Bishop of Samos; appt. Bishop of Monterey and Los Angeles, March 27, 1903; died at Coronado, CA, Sept. 18, 1915.—Most Rev. JOHN J. CANTWELL, D.D., LL.D., appt. Bishop of Monterey-Los Angeles, Sept. 21, 1917; cons. Dec. 5, 1917; appt. Assistant to the Pontifical Throne, Sept. 30, 1929; transferred to Los Angeles, June 1, 1922; elevated to Archepiscopal dignity, July 11, 1936; installed Dec. 3, 1936; died Oct. 30, 1947, at Los Angeles, CA.—His Eminence JAMES FRANCIS CARDINAL MCINTYRE, D.D., appt. Auxiliary Bishop of New York, Nov. 16, 1940; cons. Jan. 8, 1941; promoted to Coadjutor Archbishop, July 20, 1946; appt. Archbishop of Los Angeles, Feb. 7, 1948; installed March 19, 1948; created Cardinal Priest, Jan. 12, 1953; resigned Jan. 21, 1970; died July 16, 1979.—His Eminence TIMOTHY CARDINAL MANNING, D.D., J.C.D., appt. Titular Bishop of Lesvi and Auxiliary Bishop of Los Angeles, Aug. 3, 1946; cons. Oct. 15, 1946; installed as first Bishop of Fresno, Dec. 15, 1967; appt. Titular Bishop of Capri and Coadjutor Archbishop of Los Angeles, May 26, 1969; appt. Archbishop of Los Angeles, Jan. 21, 1970; created a Cardinal Priest, March 5, 1973; retired Sept. 4, 1985; died June 23, 1989 at Los Angeles, CA.

Archdiocesan Catholic Center Office—3424 Wilshire Blvd., Los Angeles, 90010-2241. Tel: 213-637-7000; Fax: 213-637-6607.

Office of the Cardinal—His Eminence ROGER CARDINAL MAHONY, D.D., *3424 Wilshire Blvd., Los Angeles, 90010-2241.* Tel: 213-637-7288; Fax: 213-637-6510.

Priest Secretary/Master of Ceremonies—Rev. PAUL M. ALBEE. Tel: 213-637-7261.

Master of Ceremonies for Stational Liturgies—Rev. Msgr. KEVIN KOSTELNIK. Tel: 213-637-7264.

Executive Coordinator—Mrs. EILEEN BONADUCE. Tel: 213-637-7298.

Cardinal's Theologian—Dr. MICHAEL DOWNEY. Tel: 213-637-7447.

Director of Special Services—Sr. MARY JEAN MEIER, R.S.M. Tel: 213-637-7520.

General Counsel—Sr. JUDY MURPHY, C.S.J. Tel: 213-637-7511.

Vicar for Canonical Services/Vice Chancellor—Rev. MODESTO LEWIS PEREZ, J.C.D. Tel: 213-637-7888.

Auxiliary Bishops-Vicars General—Most Rev. JOHN J. WARD, V.G., (Retired), *3424 Wilshire Blvd., Los Angeles, 90010-2241.* Tel: 213-637-7265; Fax: 213-637-6265. Most Rev. JUAN A. ARZUBE, (Retired), *Sacred Heart Church, 2889 N. Lincoln Ave., Altadena, 91001-4598.* Tel: 626-794-2046; Fax: 626-794-2046. Most Rev. THOMAS J. CURRY, Santa Barbara Region, *3240 Calle Pinon, Santa Barbara, 93105-2760.* Tel: 805-682-0442; Fax: 805-682-7509. Most Rev. JOSEPH M. SARTORIS, San Pedro Region, Office: *3555 Pancratius Pl., Lakewood, 90712-1416.* Tel: 562-634-0456; Fax: 562-531-4783. Most Rev. GABINO ZAVALA, San Gabriel Region, Office: *16009 E. Cypress Ave., Irwindale, 91706-2122.* Tel: 626-960-9344; Fax: 626-962-0455. Most Rev. GERALD E. WILKERSON, San Fernando Regional Office, *15101 San Fernando Mission Blvd., San Fernando, 91341-1109.* Tel: 818-361-6009; Fax: 818-361-6270.

Episcopal Vicar—Rev. Msgr. LLOYD A. TORGERSON, *Our Lady of the Angels Pastoral Region, 2636 S. Mansfield Ave., Los Angeles, 90016.* Tel: 323-936-2588; Fax: 323-938-1190.

Moderator of the Curia-Vicar General—Rev. Msgr. TERRANCE L. FLEMING, V.G., S.T.D. Tel: 213-637-7255.

Chancellor—Sr. CECILIA LOUISE MOORE, C.S.J. Tel: 213-637-7605.

Office for the Synod—Sr. MARILYN VOLLMER, S.S.M. Tel: 213-637-7474.

Secretariat for Administrative Services—Bro. THOMAS FAHY, O.S.F., Dir. Tel: 213-637-7608.

ACC Operations—Tel: 213-637-7000.

Archival Center—Tel: 818-365-1501.

Catholic Cemeteries—Tel: 213-637-7801.

Development—Tel: 213-637-7617.

Human Resources/Insurance—Tel: 213-637-7596.

Information Services Computer Department—Tel: 213-637-7271.

Media Relations—Tel: 213-637-7215.

Purchasing/Mail Center—Tel: 213-637-7535.

Real Estate—Tel: 213-637-7270.

Telecommunications—Tel: 213-637-7312.

The Tidings/Vida Nueva—Tel: 213-637-7599.

Secretariat for Church Ministerial Services—Rev. Msgr. RICHARD LOOMIS, Dir. Tel: 213-637-7890.

Cardinal Timothy Manning House of Prayer for Priests—Tel: 323-662-0092.

Diaconate Formation—Tel: 213-637-7282.

Office of Vicar for Clergy—Tel: 213-637-7284.

Office of Vicar for Women Religious—Tel: 213-637-7592.

Office of Vocations—Tel: 213-637-7248.

Pastoral Associate Program—Tel: 213-637-7533.

Pastoral Councils—Tel: 213-637-7430.

Religious Brothers—Tel: 213-637-7330.

Tribunal—Tel: 213-637-7245.

Secretariat for Educational and Formational Service—Sr. BERNADETTE MURPHY, S.S.L., Dir. Tel: 213-637-7416.

Department of Catholic Schools—Tel: 213-637-7300.

Ministry with Persons with Disabilities—Tel: 213-637-7252.

Mission Office—Tel: 213-637-7223.

Office for Campus Ministry—Tel: 213-637-7527.

Office of Family Life—Tel: 213-637-7228.

Office of Religious Education—Tel: 213-637-7335.

Office for Worship—Tel: 213-637-7262.

Spirituality Center—Tel: 213-747-6508.

Secretariat for Pastoral and Community Services—Mr. THOMAS A. CHABOLLA, Dir. Tel: 213-637-7610.

A.C.C.W.—Tel: 213-637-7394.

African American Ministry and Evangelization—Tel: 213-637-7435.

Cardinal McIntyre Fund for Charity—Tel: 213-637-7438.

Catholic HIV/AIDS Ministry—Tel: 213-637-7448.

Detention Ministries—Tel: 213-637-7648.

Ethnic Groups Ministries—Tel: 213-637-7540.

Filipino Ministry—Tel: 213-637-7480.

Health Affairs—Tel: 213-637-7531.

Hispanic Ministries—Tel: 213-637-7287.

Lay Organizations—

Apostleship of Prayer—Tel: 213-466-2406.

Catholic Daughters—Tel: 209-358-9666.

Charismatic Renewal/SCRC—Tel: 818-771-1361.

Council of Catholic Women—Tel: 213-637-7394.

Cursillo—Tel: 213-637-7268.

Holy Name Union—Tel: 310-673-8977.

Ladies of Charity—Tel: 213-382-3659.

Marriage Encounter Worldwide—Tel: 805-882-1942.

Office of Ecumenical/Interreligious Affairs—Tel: 213-637-7556.

Office of Justice and Peace/CHD/CRS—Tel: 213-637-7690.

Office of Respect Life—Tel: 213-637-7621.

Pastoral Ministry with Lesbian and Gay Catholics—Tel: 213-637-7658.

Chief Financial Officer—Mr. JOSE A. DEBASA. Tel: 213-637-7285.

Accounting—Tel: 213-637-7292.

Budget—Tel: 213-637-7623.

Financial Services—Tel: 213-637-7218.

Internal Audit—Tel: 213-637-7622.

Investments—Tel: 213-637-7292.

Payroll—Tel: 213-637-7594.

Pension Plan for Laity—Tel: 213-637-7286.

Archdiocesan Pastoral Regions

Santa Barbara Region—Most Rev. THOMAS J. CURRY, *3240 Calle Pinon, Santa Barbara, 93105-2760.* Tel: 805-682-0442; Fax: 805-682-7509.

Deanery 1—Rev. Msgr. JOHN G. FITZGERALD, V.F. Tel: 805-733-2735.

Deanery 2—Rev. Msgr. STEPHEN DOWNES, V.F. Tel: 805-967-5641.

Deanery 3—Rev. Msgr. PETER D. NUGENT, V.F. Tel: 805-487-3891.

Deanery 4—Rev. Msgr. MICHAEL BUNNY, V.F. Tel: 805-498-3602.

San Fernando Region—Most Rev. GERALD E. WILKERSON, *P.O. Box 7608, Mission Hills, 91346-7608. 15101 San Fernando Mission Blvd., Mission Hills, 91345-2526.* Tel: 818-361-6009; Fax: 818-361-6270.

Deanery 5—Rev. Msgr. JAMES C. GEHL, V.F. Tel: 818-341-6634.

Deanery 6—Rev. JOSEPH P. SHEA, V.F. Tel: 818-247-2222.

Deanery 7—Rev. JOHN H. KEESE, V.F. Tel: 818-894-1176.

Deanery 8—Rev. Msgr. EDMOND M. RENEHAN, V.F. Tel: 661-252-3353.

San Gabriel Region—Most Rev. GABINO ZAVALA, *16009 E. Cypress Ave., Irwindale, 91706-2122.* Tel: 626-960-9344; Fax: 626-962-0455.

Deanery 9—Rev. RICHARD SIEBENAND, V.F. Tel: 323-526-3800.

Deanery 10—Rev. FRANCIS R. COLBORN, V.F. Tel: 626-792-4183.

Deanery 11—Rev. Msgr. NORMAN F. PRIEBE, V.F. Tel: 626-447-1671.

Deanery 12—Rev. Msgr. JAMES J. LOUGHNANE, V.F. Tel: 909-861-7106.

Our Lady of the Angels Pastoral Region—Rev. Msgr. LLOYD A. TORGERSON, V.F., Episcopal Vicar, *2636 S. Mansfield Ave., Los Angeles, 90016.* Tel: 323-936-2588; Fax: 323-938-1190.

Deanery 13—Rev. Msgr. LLOYD A. TORGERSON, V.F. Tel: 310-393-9287.

Deanery 14—Rev. ALEX SALAZAR, V.F. Tel: 323-664-8426.

Deanery 15—Rev. JARLATH CUNNANE, V.F. Tel: 323-737-3325.

Deanery 16—Rev. Msgr. TIMOTHY J. DYER, V.F. Tel: 323-759-1562.

San Pedro Region—Most Rev. JOSEPH M. SARTORIS, *3555 St. Pancratius Pl., Lakewood, 90712-1416.* Tel: 562-634-0456; Fax: 562-531-4783.

Deanery 17—Rev. Msgr. HENRY GOMEZ, V.F. Tel: 562-867-2337.

Deanery 18—Rev. JOHN WOOLWAY, V.F. Tel: 562-692-3758.

Deanery 19—Rev. Msgr. MICHAEL F. LENIHAN, V.F. Tel: 310-540-0329.

Deanery 20—Rev. Msgr. DOUGLAS W. SAUNDERS, V.F. Tel: 562-594-4657.

Archdiocesan Catholic Center Offices

Unless otherwise listed, all ACC offices are located at 3424 Wilshire Blvd., Los Angeles, CA 90010-2241. Tel: 213-637-7000; Fax: 213-637-6607

Accounting Department—Managers: ELISITA LANDRY. Tel: 213-637-7291. Mr. HENRY NIERODZIK. Tel: 213-637-7297.

African-American Ministry and Evangelization—Rev. CHARLES ANDRUS, S.S.J., Dir. Tel: 213-637-7435.

AIDS/HIV Ministry—Rev. CHRIS PONNET, Liaison, *1911 Zonal Ave., Los Angeles, 90033.* Tel: 213-637-7HIV; 323-223-9047.

Alcohol and Substance Abuse—Rev. Msgr. T. TERRENCE RICHEY, Dir. Tel: 213-637-7644.

Annual Catholic Appeal—Mr. JOSEPH HINDLEY, Dir. Tel: 213-637-7673; Fax: 213-637-6434.

Apostleship of Prayer—Rev. FRANCIS PARRISH, S.J., Dir., *5322 Franklin Ave., Los Angeles, 90027.* Tel: 323-466-2406.

Apostleship of the Sea—Rev. Msgr. PATRICK GALLAGHER, Port Chap.; Rev. SYLVESTER THOMAS, Maritime Chap., *870 W. Eighth St., San Pedro, 90731-3091.* Tel: 310-833-3541.

Archives—Rev. Msgr. FRANCIS J. WEBER, Archivist, *15151 San Fernando Mission Blvd., Mission Hills, 91345-2617.* Rev. KEVIN FEENEY, Adjunct Archivist. Tel: 818-365-1501; Fax: 818-361-3276.

Audit Services—(See Internal Audit).

Brothers Council, Religious—Bro. TIMOTHY MAYWORM, F.S.C., Chm. Tel: 213-637-7289.

Budget—Mrs. JEANNE ZEIND. Tel: 213-637-7623.

Campaign for Human Development—THOMAS A. CHABOLLA, Diocesan Dir. Tel: 213-637-7610. MARIA ELENA PERALES, Prog. Admin. Tel: 213-637-7560.

Campus Ministry (Newman Apostolate)—Mrs. LAURIE W. OESTER, Ph.D., Dir. Tel: 213-637-7527; Fax: 213-637-6527.

Canonical Services, Episcopal Vicar for—Rev. MODESTO LEWIS PEREZ, J.C.D. Tel: 213-637-7888; Fax: 213-637-6888.

Canonical Services Coordinator—Rev. NELSON TRINIDAD. Tel: 213-637-7201.

Cardinal Manning House of Prayer for Priests—Rev. JOHN D. MCANULTY, S.J., Dir. Tel: 323-662-0044. Rev. JOHN CLARK, S.J., Assoc. Dir. Tel: 323-662-7966., *3441 Waverly Dr., Los Angeles, 90027-2597;* Fax: 323-953-4802. Staffed by: Little Brothers of the Good Shepherd; Bro. MALACHY CORBETT, B.G.S., Superior; Bro. MARK HARMUELLER, B.G.S.; GERALD SULLIVAN, B.G.S. Tel: 323-662-0092., Staff Residence: *3445 Waverly Dr., Los Angeles, 90027-2597.* Tel: 323-662-3620.

Cardinal McIntyre Fund for Charity—SUSAN V. WEIGHT, Dir. Tel: 213-637-7438; Fax: 213-637-6438.

Catholic Charities of Los Angeles—*1531 James M. Wood Blvd., Los Angeles, 90015-1194.* Tel: 213-251-3400; Fax: 213-380-4603.

Executive Director—Rev. Msgr. GREGORY A. COX, M.S.W., M.B.A. Tel: 213-251-3464.

Chief Administrative Officer—RONALD G. LOPEZ, M.S.W. Tel: 213-251-3412.

Chief Financial Officer—JAMES E. BATHKER. Tel: 213-251-3410.

Department of Human Resources—MARILYN KAMERER, Dir. Tel: 213-251-3414.

Department of Resource Development—ALEXANDRIA "SANDI" ARNOLD, Dir. Tel: 213-251-3495.

Adeste—Child Development Services—ARMINE LALAIAN-SANJAR, Dir. Tel: 213-251-3468.

C.Y.O. Athletics—TOM DAVIDSON, Prog. Dir. Tel: 213-251-3562.

Immigration and Refugee Services—LOC NAM NGUYEN, Quality Assurance Dir. Tel: 213-251-3489.

Refugee Resettlement—JO MARCEL, Asst. Prog. Dir. Tel: 213-251-3470.

Psychological Services—Dr. EDWARD NELSON, Quality Assurance Dir. Tel: 213-251-3459.

Regional Offices—JACKIE LAZARUS, Regl. Dir., Our Lady of the Angels: Metro. Tel: 323-662-1462. JAMES STRATTON, Regl. Dir., Our Lady of the Angels, Western. Tel: 310-392-8701. MOEED KHAN, Regl. Dir., San Fernando Pastoral Region. Tel: 818-883-6015. MARY ROMERO, Regl. Dir., San Gabriel Pastoral Region. Tel: 323-266-3130. LUPE U. MACKER, Regl. Dir., San Pedro Pastoral Region. Tel: 562-591-1641.

Santa Barbara County—DAVIDA WILLIS, Regl. Dir. Tel: 805-965-7045.

Ventura County—ROBERT BAGDAZIAN, L.C.S.W., Regl. Dir. Tel: 805-643-4694.

Catholic Charities Community Development Corporation, Inc.—Rev. Msgr. GREGORY A. COX, M.S.W., M.B.A., CEO, *Central Office, 1531 James M. Wood Blvd., P.O. Box 15095, Los Angeles, 90015.* Tel: 213-251-3477.

Catholic Relief Services—THOMAS A. CHABOLLA, Diocesan Dir. Tel: 213-637-7610. MARIA ELENA PERALES, Prog. Admin. Tel: 213-637-7560.

Cemeteries, Catholic—Tel: 213-637-7801; Fax: 213-637-6800. JAMES M. TIXIER, Dir. & Gen. Mgr. Tel: 213-637-7808. Deacon SAM FRIAS, Pastoral Rels. Dir. Tel: 213-637-7807. MARY ANN MCADAMS, Operations Dir. Tel: 213-637-7805. GEORGE HARSCH, Dir. Property Devel. Tel: 213-637-7817. BRIAN MCMAHON, Dir. Information Svcs. Tel: 213-637-7815.

Censores Librorum—Coordinators: Rev. Msgr. CRAIG A. COX, J.C.D. Tel: 213-637-7284. Sr. MARY BRIGID FITZPATRICK, C.S.J., Ph.D. Tel: 213-637-7523.

Clergy, Vicar for—Rev. Msgr. CRAIG A. COX, J.C.D. Tel: 213-637-7284.

Personnel Board—Rev. Msgr. JAMES J. LOUGHNANE, V.F., Chm.; Revs. ALBERT BAHHUTH; RODEL BALAGTAS; Rev. Msgr. HENRY GOMEZ, V.F.; Rev. JOHN KEESE, V.F.; Rev. Msgr. PETER D. NUGENT, V.F.; Revs. ALLAN ROBERTS; ALEXANDER SALAZAR, V.F.

Conciliation/Arbitration—Rev. Msgr. TERRANCE L. FLEMING, V.G., S.T.D. Tel: 213-637-7255.

Continuing Formation for Clergy—Rev. BRIAN DORAN, Dir. Tel: 213-637-7571.

Construction—Bro. HILARION O'CONNOR, O.S.F., Dir. Tel: 213-637-7852. JAVIER H. RODRIGUEZ, Construction Mgr. Tel: 213-637-7853. THOMAS FITZPATRICK, Construction Project Supvr.-Cemeteries. Tel: 213-637-7861. Construction Project Supvrs.: RICHARD VILLACORTA, JR. Tel: 213-637-7860. CECILIA URIBE. Tel: 213-637-7855. RUSS PITTELKAU, Cathedral Project. Tel: 213-637-7859.

Council of Catholic Women—ANNE-MARIE ROBERTSON, Pres. Tel: 213-637-7394.

Council of Priests—Rev. RICHARD VEGA, Chm. Tel: 213-637-7289.

Cursillo Movement—Revs. MODESTO LEWIS PEREZ, J.C.D., Cursillo Board Dir. Tel: 213-637-7888. Rev. GUSTAVO RAMON, Spanish-Speaking Dir. Tel: 213-637-7482. Rev. GAEL SULLIVAN, English Speaking Dir. Tel: 562-920-7796.

Deacons—Deacon JOSEPH ORTH, Dir. Deacons. Tel: 213-637-7734.

Detention Ministry—Sr. SUZANNE JABRO, C.S.J., Dir. Tel: 213-637-7648.

Development—KEVIN T. O'CONNOR, Chief Devel. Officer. Tel: 213-637-7617.

Annual Appeal—JOSEPH HINDLEY, Dir. Tel: 213-637-7673.

Cathedral Development—AMANDA MANSOUR, Dir. Tel: 213-637-7432. CAROLYN L. CANNING, Assoc. Dir. Tel: 213-637-7465. MAUREEN PADILLA, Donor Svcs. Tel: 213-637-7460.

Cathedral Lay Leadership Office—BILL CLOSE; PHYLLIS HENNIGAN; GRETCHEN WILLISON; BILL WARDLAW. Tel: 213-637-7426.

Corporations & Foundations Programs/UCLA Campaign—ALEXANDRIA H. LUSTGARTEN, Dir. Tel: 213-637-7365.

Development Information Services—FERDINAND NAVALTA, Admin. Tel: 213-637-7393.

Offertory Increase Program—KEVIN T. O'CONNOR. Tel: 213-637-7617.

Seminaries Development—Tel: 805-482-2755.

Trust and Estates Programs—H. RICHARD CLOSSON, Dir. Tel: 213-637-7472.

Education Foundation—HUGH RALSTON, Exec. Dir. Tel: 213-637-7576.

Education Foundation/Development Programs—MARGOT JENSEN, Dir. Tel: 213-637-7443.

Diaconate, Formation Office—Sr. CHRIS MACHADO, S.S.S., Acting Dir. Tel: 213-637-7747; Fax: 213-637-6383. Assoc. Directors: Rev. FRANK FERRANTE, C.M.F. Tel: 213-637-7536. Deacon CRIS VEGA. Tel: 213-637-7738. VICTOR STAFORELLI. Tel: 213-637-7755. Deacons CHARLES DENISAC, JR. Tel: 213-637-7282. VALENTIN SAUCEDO. Tel: 213-637-7754.

Ecumenical and Interreligious Affairs—Rev. ALEXEI R. SMITH. Tel: 213-637-7556; Fax: 213-637-6555.

Ethnic Groups Ministry—IRMA ISIP, Dir. Tel: 213-637-7540.

Family Life Office—JOAN T. VIENNA, Dir. Tel: 213-637-7227; Fax: 213-637-6681.

Coordinator, Marriage Preparation and Natural Family Planning, English Speaking—CANDY METOYER. Tel: 213-637-7250.

Coordinator, Marriage Preparation and Natural Family Planning, Spanish Speaking—GLORIA REYNOSA. Tel: 213-637-7561.

Leadership Training and Project Coordinator—JOHN PEREZ. Tel: 213-637-7582 (English). GRACIELA VILLALOBOS. Tel: 213-637-7214 (Spanish).

Parent Education, Coordinator—GILDA SILVER. Tel: 213-637-7396 (English). MICAELA REGALADO. Tel: 213-637-7504 (Spanish).

Divorce Recovery Ministry—Tel: 213-637-7227.

Widowed Ministry—Tel: 213-637-7227.

Filipino Ministry—Sr. MARY CHRISTINA SEVILLA, R.G.S., Dir. Tel: 213-637-7480.

Financial Services—RANDY E. STEINER, Dir. Tel: 213-637-7218.

Financial Services Information Desk—Tel: 213-637-7500.

Gay and Lesbian Catholics, Ministry with—Rev. PETER LUIZZI, O.Carm., Dir. Tel: 213-637-7658.

Government Funded Programs—*1543 W. Olympic Blvd., Ste. 424, Los Angeles, 90015-3821;* Fax: 213-383-1529. LOU CASEY, Dir. Tel: 213-383-0199.

Pre-School Dir.—ETHEL ANTOINE. Tel: 213-388-1291.

Youth Employment Programs Dir.—ROBERT GUTIERREZ, *3250 Wilshire Blvd., #1010, Los Angeles, 90010.* Tel: 213-736-5456.

Health Affairs—Sr. M. CAROLITA HART, C.S.C., Dir. Tel: 213-637-7531.

Hispanic Ministry—Mr. LOUIS VELASQUEZ, Dir. Tel: 213-637-7280. HUMBERTO RAMOS, Assoc. Dir. Tel: 213-637-7276.

Pastoral Coordinator, Queen of Angels Region—Sr. ANTONIETA M. ZAPATA, M.G.Sp.S. Tel: 323-932-0998.

Pastoral Coordinator, San Fernando Region—MARCO ANTONIO RAMIREZ. Tel: 818-361-9418.

Pastoral Coordinator, San Gabriel Region—LUCY BOUTTE. Tel: 818-960-2805.

Pastoral Coordinator, San Pedro Region—HERIBERTO CAYETANO. Tel: 562-531-8155.

Pastoral Coordinator, Santa Barbara Region—JORGE A. RODRIGUEZ. Tel: 805-687-5422.

Holy Childhood Association—(See Mission Office).

Holy Name Union, Archdiocesan Union of Societies—*546 E. Florence Ave., Inglewood, 90301-1402.* JOHN SHEA, Pres. Tel: 310-673-8977.

Moderator—Rev. Msgr. PAUL MONTOYA. Tel: 661-259-2276.

House of Prayer for Priests—(See Cardinal Manning House of Prayer for Priests).

Human Resources/Insurance—WILLIAM HEINEN, Dir. Tel: 213-637-7596; Fax: 213-637-6116. MARGARET M. ANTCZAK, ACC Human Resources Mgr. Tel: 213-637-7625. SOFIA SANDRU, H.R. Assoc. Dir. Cemeteries. Tel: 213-637-7812. LEVONTINE TOMACAN, Assoc. Dir. Insurance. Tel: 213-637-7279. STEPHEN VAN BUREN, Risk Mgr. Tel: 213-637-7629. HOURIG H. DAKESSIAN, Benefits Admin. Tel: 213-637-7671. Sr. ANNA MARY MEYER, C.S.J., Medical Benefits Consultant. Tel: 213-637-7680.

Information—*ACC Switchboard.* Tel: 213-637-7000.

Information Services for Computers—JAMES R. CELONI, Dir. Tel: 213-637-7271.

Internal Audit—SANDRA SMITH, C.P.A., Dir. Tel: 213-637-7622.

Investments—EDNA CRISTOBAL, C.P.A., Dir. Tel: 213-637-7292.

Justice and Peace—THOMAS A. CHABOLLA, Exec. Dir. Tel: 213-637-7610. JEFF BONINO-BRITSCH, Assoc. Dir. Tel: 213-637-7690. MARIA ELENA PERALES, Prog. Admin. Tel: 213-637-7560.

Knights of Columbus-California State Council Office—*10604 Trademark Pkwy. N., Ste. 307, Rancho Cucamonga, 91730.* Tel: 909-466-3964; Fax: 909-466-5609.

State Deputy—JOSEPH P. SCHULTZ. Tel: 760-726-5340.

Chaplain—Rev. CHARLES HOFSCHULTE, C.J. Tel: 805-730-1113.

Ladies of Charity of St. Vincent de Paul—*2131 W. Third St., Seton Hall, Los Angeles, 90057-0992.* Tel: 213-413-3688.

Lay Mission Helpers—(See Mission Office).

Marriage Encounter—Rev. JAMES GALVIN, C.M., *1964 Las Canoas Rd., Santa Barbara, 93105.* Tel: 805-882-1942.

Media Relations—Mr. TOD TAMBERG, Dir. Tel: 213-637-7215; Fax: 213-385-6586.

Ministry with Persons with Disabilities—VERONICA GRAY, Dir. Tel: 213-637-7236; 637-7252.

Mission Office—Rev. DAVID JOHN AYOTTE, Dir. Tel: 213-637-7223; Fax: 213-637-6223.

Holy Childhood Association—Tel: 213-637-7223.

Lay Mission Helpers—Tel: 213-637-7222.

Mission Circles—Tel: 213-637-7223.

Mission Doctors Assoc.—Dr. TIMOTHY LEFEVRE, Pres. Tel: 213-637-7222.

Propagation of the Faith—Tel: 213-637-7223.

Operations—EILEEN O'BRIEN. Tel: 213-637-7618.

Pastoral Associate Program—Sr. MARY GENINO, R.S.H.M., Coord. Tel: 213-637-7533.

Pastoral Councils—MARIA ELENA URIBE, Coord. Tel: 213-637-7430; Fax: 213-637-6430.

Payroll—ROSA PADILLA. Tel: 213-637-7544.

Pension Plan for Laity—SANDRA PULIDO LENZ. Tel: 213-637-7286.

Priest Pension Plan—LUPE A. GARIBAY. Tel: 213-637-7320.

Project Rachel—LICIA NICASSIO, Dir. Tel: 213-637-7621. Sr. RITA CALLAHAN, I.H.M. Tel: 213-637-7362.

Purchasing/Mail Center—SANDY B. VILLAREAL, Purchasing Agent. Tel: 213-637-7535.

Real Estate—MICHAEL DAVITT, Dir. Tel: 213-637-7273; Fax: 213-637-6675.

Religious Education—Tel: 213-637-7335; Fax: 213-637-6574. Sr. EDITH PRENDERGAST, R.S.C., Dir. Tel: 213-637-7309. Assoc. Dirs.: MONICA HUGHES. Tel: 213-637-7350. MARUJA SEDANO. Tel: 213-637-7345. GAIL KRAUSE, Office Coord. Tel: 213-637-7342.

Adult Education—Rev. JAMES J. CLARKE. Tel: 213-637-7654. Dr. ANNE DUNN, I.H.M., Santa Barbara. Tel: 805-569-2779. MARY LOU MCGEE. Tel: 213-637-7704; 818-361-4133.

Spanish—MARUJA SEDANO. Tel: 213-637-7345. MARIA EMILIA MAIRENA. Tel: 213-637-7355.

Advanced Cathechetical Ministries and Formation—MONICA HUGHES. Tel: 213-637-7350.

Spanish—LOURDES GONZALES-RUBIO. Tel: 213-637-7344.

Asian-Pacific Perspective—Vacant. Tel: 213-637-7669.

Catechesis in a Black Perspective—SHERYL LANGE. Tel: 213-637-7354.

Confirmation, Junior High and Youth Ministry—MIKE NORMAN. Tel: 213-637-7674. VIKKI KRAETZER. Tel: 213-637-7616. DENNIS SANTOS. Tel: 805-682-5500.

Spanish—JUSTINA PIMENTEL. Tel: 213-637-7343.

Early Childhood—JAN PEDROZA. Tel: 213-637-7352.
Elementary—STEVEN ELLAIR, Spanish. Tel: 213-637-7410. THELMA DELGADO. Tel: 213-637-7351.
Media—YOLANDA ARANDA. Tel: 213-637-7340.
Religious Education Congress—ADRIAN WHITAKER. Tel: 213-637-7332.
Regional Offices—Our Lady of the Angels Region: LANETT REID, *2636 S. Mansfield Ave., Los Angeles, 90016-3512.* Tel: 323-931-2875; Fax: 323-938-1190. San Fernando Region: LYNN LANG, *15101 San Fernando Mission Blvd., Mission Hills, 91345.* Tel: 818-365-5123; Fax: 818-361-4133., *P.O. Box 7608, Mission Hills, 91341.* San Gabriel Region: EILEEN GATELEY, *San Gabriel Region Pastoral Center, 16009 E. Cypress Ave., Irwindale, 91706.* Tel: 626-962-7707; Fax: 626-962-0455. San Pedro Region: PATRICIA O'BRIEN, *San Pedro Regional Center, 3555 St. Pancratius Pl., Lakewood, 90712.* Tel: 562-630-6272; Fax: 562-531-4783. Santa Barbara Region: PEGGI RANSOM, *Bishop Garcia Diego Center, 4032 La Colina Rd., Santa Barbara, 93110.* Tel: 805-569-1135; Fax: 805-569-2746.
Young Adult Ministry (18-35)—LEILANI GOECKNER. Tel: 213-637-7498. MARTHA NUNEZ, Spanish. Tel: 213-637-7705.
Religious, Vicar for Women—Sr. MARY FAITH CLARKE, S.N.J.M. Tel: 213-637-7592.
Respect Life Office and Project Rachel—Mrs. LICIA NICASSIO, Dir. Tel: 213-637-7621.
Schools, Dept. of Catholic—Tel: 213-637-7300; Fax: 213-637-6140.
President of Schools—Vacant. Tel: 213-637-7313.
Superintendent Elementary Schools—Sr. MARY ELIZABETH GALT, B.V.M. Tel: 213-637-7315.
Associate Superintendents of Elementary Schools—Sr. JOAN FARAONE, R.J.M. Tel: 213-637-7584. PATRICIA LIVINGSTON. Tel: 213-637-7322.
Superintendent Secondary Schools—Ms. NANCY J. COONIS. Tel: 213-637-7381.
Associate Superintendent of Secondary Schools—DOROTHY PITTELKAU. Tel: 213-637-7325.
Elementary School Supervisors—Sr. MONICA QUIGLEY, S.S.L. Tel: 213-637-7318. Sr. JOAN FARAONE, R.J.M. Tel: 213-637-7584. FRANK MONTEJANO. Tel: 213-637-7317. SANDRA BROSNAHAN. Tel: 213-637-7319. KATHLEEN DAMISCH. Tel: 213-637-7333. PATRICIA LIVINGSTON. Tel: 213-637-7322.
Director of Elementary School Finances—KATHLEEN DAMISCH. Tel: 213-637-7333.
Director of Elementary Personnel—MARION FALCHI. Tel: 213-637-7314.
Director of Professional Resources—SANDRA BROSNAHAN. Tel: 213-637-7319.
Secondary School Supervisors—ROBERT GEBAUER. Tel: 213-637-7485. DOROTHY PITTELKAU. Tel: 213-637-7325.
Secondary School Finance Director—LOURDES SANTA MARIA. Tel: 213-637-7368.
Coordinator of Religious Formation and Instruction: Secondary Schools—Sr. ANGELA HALLAHAN, C.H.F. Tel: 213-637-7538.
School Accreditation/Assessment—PATRICIA LIVINGSTON, Elementary. Tel: 213-637-7322. DOROTHY PITTELKAU, Secondary. Tel: 213-637-7325.
Curriculum Director—Mrs. RINA NGO. Tel: 213-637-7311.
Director for Federal and State Programs—Sr. PATRICIA SUPPLE, C.S.J. Tel: 213-637-7537.
Director of Educational Technology—GRACE WALKER. Tel: 213-637-7329.
Administrative Coordinator—GUING A. RAMOS. Tel: 213-637-7331.
Scouting and Camp Fire Ministry—EILEEN GALLAGHER, Admin. Asst., *P.O. Box 91764, Long Beach, 90809-1764.* Tel: 562-427-2149.
Seminaries' Development—
Alumni Relations—Rev. WILLIAM PILETIC, C.M. Tel: 805-482-2755, Ext. 2021.
Sisters' Council—Tel: 213-637-7559.
Society of St. Vincent de Paul—HILMAR ROSENAT, Pres., *210 N. Ave. 21, Los Angeles, 90031-1713.* Tel: 323-224-6287. JOSE J. ROSSIER, Exec. Dir. Tel: 800-974-3571.
Spirituality Center, Archdiocesan—Sr. THOMAS BERNARD MACCONNELL, C.S.J., Dir., *2 Chester Pl., Los Angeles, 90007.* Tel: 213-747-7508.
Telecommunications—DAVE MOORE, Dir. Tel: 213-637-7312. Rev. ANTHONY SCANNELL, O.F.M.Cap. Tel: 213-637-7431.
Technical Staff—DAVID SCHMITT, Chief Engineer. Tel: 213-637-7526.
Studio Technician—FERNANDO DIAZ. Tel: 213-637-7399.
Theological Commission—Rev. Msgr. CRAIG A. COX, J.C.D., Chm. Tel: 213-637-7289. Sr. KAREN WILHELMY, C.S.J., Sec. Tel: 805-486-7301.
"The Tidings" (Archdiocesan Newspaper)—Tel: 213-637-7360; Fax: 213-637-6360. DENNIS W. HEANEY, Exec. Publisher. Tel: 213-637-7599. Vacant, Editor. Tel: 213-637-7493. MARY TRUDEAU-MOTTOLA, Circulation Mgr. Tel: 213-637-7477. JOSE VELASQUEZ, Production Mgr. Tel: 213-637-7380. HERMINE LEES, Directory. Tel: 213-637-7392. COA LEUTERIO, Finance Officer. Tel: 213-637-7391. IRMA CROW, Office Mgr. Tel: 213-637-7251.
Tribunal—Main Office: *3424 Wilshire Blvd., Los Angeles, 90010-2241.* Tel: 213-637-7245; Fax: 213-637-6245., Santa Barbara/Ventura Branch: *P.O. Box 2215, Oxnard, 93034.* Tel: 805-486-6553; Fax: 805-486-3884.
Judicial Vicar—Rev. THOMAS C. ANSLOW, C.M., J.C.L. Tel: 213-637-7204.
Adjutant Judicial Vicar—Rev. GERALD B. FESSARD, J.C.L. Tel: 213-637-7397.
Canonical Staff—Revs. ROBERT V. BIROSCHAK, J.C.L. Tel: 213-637-7220. ROBERT W. GAVOTTO, O.S.A., J.C.D. Tel: 213-637-7202. Sr. ANNE GIBLIN, R.S.C., J.C.L. Tel: 213-637-7211. ADELA-MARIE KIM, J.C.L. Tel: 213-637-7275. Sr. MARGARET ANN MCCAULEY, O.P., J.C.L. Tel: 213-637-7205. Rev. PETER T. NGO, J.C.L. Tel: 213-637-7211. Deacon HAROLD A. PARISH, J.C.D. Tel: 805-486-6553. CARLOS VENEGAS, J.C.L. Tel: 213-637-7275. Sr. MARY ANNE WITTMAN, S.H.F., J.C.L. Tel: 805-486-6553.
Judges—Revs. THOMAS C. ANSLOW, C.M., J.C.L.; ROBERT V. BIROSCHAK, J.C.L.; MICHAEL CARCERANO, J.C.L.; CHARLES J. CHAFFMAN, J.C.L.; JARLATH DOLAN; GERALD B. FESSARD, J.C.L.; Rev. Msgr. TERRANCE L. FLEMING, V.G., S.T.D.; Sr. ANNE GIBLIN, R.S.C., J.C.L.; ADELA-MARIE KIM, J.C.L.; Rev. Msgr. WILLIAM LESER, C.B., S.T.B.; Rev. Msgr. JAMES J. LOUGHNANE; Sr. MARGARET ANN MCCAULEY, O.P., J.C.L.; Rev. Msgr. AUGUST MORETTI, J.C.D.; Rev. Msgr. DONAL MULCAHY; Rev. PETER C. NGO, J.C.L.; Deacon HAROLD A. PARISH, J.C.D.; Revs. MODESTO L. PEREZ, J.C.D.; LAURENCE J. SPITERI, J.C.L.; Mr. CARLOS VENEGAS, J.C.L.; Sr. MARY ANN WITTMAN, S.H.F., J.C.L.; Rev. WILLIAM P. WOLFE, J.C.L.
Promoters of Justice—Rev. Msgr. HELMUT A. HEFNER, J.C.L.; Rev. Msgr. FRANCIS T. WALLACE, J.C.L.
Defenders of the Bond—Rev. Msgr. ARNOLD BIEDERMANN; Rev. JEROME A. BOUSKA, M.A.; Rev. Msgr. HELMUT A. HEFNER, J.C.L.; Revs. RAUL PLUTH, O.S.B., J.C.L.; JAMES SHIFFER, S.S.C., J.C.L.; NELSON TRINIDAD, J.C.L.; Rev. Msgr. FRANCIS T. WALLACE, J.C.L.
Advocates and Auditors—MARIA AUEN; CESAR CASTRO; D. ANN CLABBY; FERNANDO ENGEL; Rev. ROBERT W. GAVOTTO, O.S.A., J.C.D.; Deacon JAMES HENRY; Rev. PATRICK J. HILL; MARTHA ESTER LUNA; Sr. MARY ANN MARTIN, C.S.J.; Deacon JON C. MCPHEETERS; JOAN SUTHERLAND; Sr. KAREN WILHELMY, C.S.J.
Notaries and Other Officials—LETICIA ASCENCIO; LICIA BAROCIO; RUTH GOMEZ; ALBA GUTIERREZ; BOBBIE LOPEZ; LILIA MONROY; ANNA PARISH; TERESITA POSTIGO; MERCED SALCEDO.
Trust and Estate Programs—H. RICHARD CLOSSON, Dir. Tel: 213-637-7472.
Vicar for Clergy—Rev. Msgr CRAIG A. COX, J.C.D. Tel: 213-637-7284. Rev. BRIAN DORAN, Continuing Formation Dir. Tel: 213-637-7571. Rev. Msgr. T. TERRENCE RICHEY, Alcohol/Substance Abuse Ministry Dir. Tel: 213-637-7644. Dr. THOMAS OLONA, Staff Consultant. Tel: 213-637-7668. Rev. Msgr. HELMUT HEFNER, Ministry to Newly Ordained Priests. Tel: 805-482-2755. Sr. ANNA MARY MEYER, C.S.J., Ministry to Retired and Ill Priests. Tel: 213-637-7680. Deacon JOSEPH ORTH, Dir., Deacons. Tel: 213-637-7734. LUCILLE MILLER, Exec. Asst. Tel: 213-637-7304; Fax: 213-637-6289.
"Vida Nueva" (Archdiocesan Spanish Newspaper)—Tel: 213-637-7360; Fax: 213-637-6360. DENNIS W. HEANEY, Exec. Publisher. Tel: 213-637-7599. VICTOR ALEMAN, Editor. Tel: 213-637-7310. EDUARDO ALVAREZ, Advertising Dir. Tel: 213-637-7232. MARY TRUDEAU-MOTTOLA, Circulation Mgr. Tel: 213-637-7477. JOSE VELASQUEZ, Production Dir. Tel: 213-637-7380.
Vocations—Tel: 213-637-7248. Rev. RICHARD MARTINI, Dir., Sr. KATHLEEN BRYANT, R.S.C., Sister Dir., Rev. ROBERT JUAREZ, Dir. Hispanic Vocations.
Vocations in Progress—Rev. MICHAEL UME, Dir. Tel: 213-637-7356. Sr. KAREN COLLIER, S.S.L., Dir. Tel: 213-637-7356.
Worship—Tel: 213-637-7262. KATHY LINDELL, Dir. Tel: 213-637-7265.
Rite of Christian Initiation for Adults, (RCIA)—Sr. ROSEANNE BELPEDIO, C.S.J., Coord. Tel: 213-637-7591.
Hispanic Liturgy—Deacon ARTURO BARRAGAN, Coord. Tel: 213-637-7588.
Music—FRANK BROWNSTEAD, Coord. Tel: 213-637-7587.
Certification—MARIA MARTINEZ, Coord. Tel: 213-637-7586.
Women, Archdiocesan Council of Catholic—(See Council of Catholic Women).
Young Adult Ministry—(See Religious Education).

Archdiocesan Advisory Boards

Archdiocesan Finance Council—JOSE A. DEBASA, CFO. Tel: 213-637-7285. Members: His Eminence ROGER CARDINAL MAHONY, D.D.; KAREN JUAREZ BOYD, Pres., Lumen Financial, Inc. AVIS CHEUNG, Occidental Petroleum Co.; Rev. Msgr. STEPHEN DOWNES, Regl. Dean, Pastor, St. Raphael Church, Santa Barbara; ROBERT F. ERBURU, Retired Chm. Bd., Times Mirror Co. MARGARET MARY GRAF, Attorney-at-Law, Brand, Farrar & Burnbaum; MARK S. GRANICH, CEO, Granich & Stromme; Deacon WILLIAM D. HAWKINS, Pres., Hawkins Co. STEVEN HILTON, Conrad N. Hilton Foundation; JOSEPH KEARNS, Retired CEO, J. Paul Getty Trust; THOMAS LARKIN, Pres. & CEO, Trust Co. of the West; Rev. Msgr. MICHAEL LENIHAN, Regl. Dean, Pastor, St. Lawrence Martyr Church, Redondo Beach; JOHN MCMAHON, Retired Mng. Dir., Johnson & Higgins/Marsh & McLennan Inc. KENNETH OLSEN, Retired Pres. & CEO, Vons Grocery Co.; Rev. Msgr. NORMAN PRIEBE, Regl. Dean, Pastor, Holy Angels Church, Arcadia; Rev. Msgr. EDMOND RENEHAN, Regl. Dean, Pastor, St. Clare Church, Santa Clarita; ROLAND SEIDLER, JR., Chm. & CEO, The Seidler Companies, Inc. WILLIAM E. SIART, Pres. & CEO, EXED, LLP; Rev. Msgr. LLOYD A. TORGERSON, Episcopal Vicar, Our Lady of the Angels Region, Regl. Dean, Pastor, St. Monica Church, Santa Monica; JOHN T. WHOLIHAN, Dean, College of Business Admin., Loyola Marymount University.
Archdiocesan Commission for Catholic Life Issues—Rev. Msgr. TIMOTHY O'CONNELL, Chm. Tel: 310-261-1145. Mrs. LICIA NICASSIO, Dir. Respect Life. Tel: 213-637-7621. Sr. PAULA VANDEGAER, S.S.S., Chm. Tel: 213-382-2156. Commission Members: PADDY JIM BAGGOT, M.D.; ANDREA BURMAN; MARIAN BURMAN; THOMAS CHABOLLA; Revs. THOMAS CUSACK, S.S.C.; LUKE DYSINGER, O.S.B., M.D.; VINCENT FORTANASCE, M.D.; Rev. MARCOS GONZALEZ; MARCELLA MELENDEZ; GLORIA MILLER, R.N.; BETTY ODELLO, R.N., M.S.N.; Rev. SAL PILATO; ERNEST SANCHEZ, Esq.; KATHERINE DOWLING SCHLAERTH, M.D.; MARY SHERIDAN; ALAN SHEWMON, M.D.; Sr. PAULA VANDEGAER, S.S.S., L.C.S.W.; ENRIQUETA VILLAREAL, M.D.; KATHRYN WATSON, M.D.; Rev. STEPHEN WATSON, O.C.D.; GERMAINE WENSLEY, R.N.; Ms. MARLENE WILSON, M.S.W., L.C.S.W.; Rev. JOHN WOOLWAY. Advisory Members: Rev. Msgr. GEORGE PARNASSUS, Ex Officio Chm. DAVID M. FRELINGER, M.D.; T. MURPHY GOODWIN, M.D.; GLORIA GRIFFIN; Sr. CAROLITA HART, C.S.C.; Rev. Msgr. JEREMIAH MCCARTHY; Rev. Msgr. JOHN MORETTA; MAGGIE STAPP; LOUIS VELASQUEZ.
Project Rachel—Sr. RITA CALLAHAN, I.H.M. Tel: 213-637-7362.
Archdiocesan Commission for Ecumenical and Interreligious Affairs—Tel: 213-637-7556. Members: Rev. Msgr. WILLIAM BARRY; MARY CASS; THOMAS CHABOLLA; Sr. MOLUA CONHEADY, S.S.L.; Sr. ANNE FIELD, S.S.S.; Sr. LAURA GORMLEY, S.S.L.; MONICA HUGHES; Sr. EMILE ANN PALLADINO, S.N.D.; Rev. THOMAS RAUSCH, S.J.; KATHERINE ROUSSEAU; Revs. ALEXEI SMITH; EARL WALKER.
Archdiocesan Justice and Peace Commission—PAM RECTOR, Chm. BERNARDO PEREZ, Vice Chm.; Mr. THOMAS A. CHABOLLA, Exec. Dir. Tel: 213-637-7610. Members: Rev. GREG CHISHOLM, S.J.; REBECCA CIRIACO; Sr. PATRICIA CONNOR, R.S.H.M.; GREGORY FLYNN; TIM JOHNSTON; FERNANDO MORENO; MARIE ALEXIS NAVARRO; Rev. Msgr. DAVE O'CONNELL; ROSA MARIA SANCHEZ; CAMBRIA SMITH; CONSUELO VALDEZ; RAFAEL VEGA.
Archdiocesan Catholic School Board—JOHN GUTIERREZ; MARGARET HERNANDEZ; DELIA JOHNSON; Rev. Msgr. ANTHONY LEUER; TERRI MENDOZA, Ph.D.; RICHAR L. MORA; MARGARET M. MORRIS; JOHN QUIGLEY, M.D.; RICCI J. RUFFINELLI; JAMES P. SARNI; Rev. JOSEPH SHEA; JULIE TIEMPO-LIBATIQUE; RALPH VALENTE; TINA R. WHELAN; VICTOR M. ZEPEDA. Ex Officio: Sr. BERNADETTE MURPHY, S.S.L.; NANCY COONIS; Sr. MARY ELIZABETH GALT, B.V.M.
Cardinal McIntyre Fund for Charity—His Eminence ROGER CARDINAL MAHONY, Chm.; Rev. Msgr. TERRANCE L. FLEMING, V.G., S.T.D., Pres.; Rev. FISHER ROBINSON, S.V.D., Vice Pres.; Sr. MARY BRIGID FITZPATRICK, C.S.J., Sec. THOMAS A. CHABOLLA, Treas. SUSAN VALERIE WEIGHT, Dir. Tel: 213-637-7438; Fax: 213-637-6438. Board of Directors: Rev. Msgr. TERRANCE L. FLEMING, V.G., S.T.D.; Rev. STANLEY BOSCH, S.T.; THOMAS A. CHABOLLA; Rev. KENNETH DEASY; Sr. MARY BRIGID FITZPATRICK, C.S.J.; Sr. CECILIA LOUISE MOORE, C.S.J.; Revs. FISHER ROBINSON, S.V.D.; JOSEPH P. SHEA.
College of Consultors—Most Rev. THOMAS J. CURRY; Most Rev. JOSEPH M. SARTORIS; Most Rev. GERALD E. WILKERSON; Most Rev. GABINO ZAVALA; Rev. Msgr. LLOYD A. TORGERSON; Rev. Msgr. TERRANCE L. FLEMING, V.G., S.T.D.; Rev. Msgr. CRAIG A. COX; Rev.

Msgr. CHARLES E. HILL; Rev. Msgr. RICHARD A. LOOMIS; Revs. MICHAEL JENNETT; ALEXANDER SALAZAR; WILLIAM BONNER, S.V.D.

Council of Priests—His Eminence ROGER CARDINAL MAHONY, D.D., Pres.; Rev. RICHARD VEGA, Chm. Tel: 213-637-7330. Revs. ALEXEI R. SMITH, Vice Chm. WILLIAM J. BONNER, S.V.D., Sec. LORENZO MIRANDA, Treas.

Exec. Committee Members at Large—Rev. Msgr. MICHAEL W. MEYER; Revs. PHILLIP M. KAVANAUGH; MARK A. WARNSTEDT.

Recording Secretary—Rev. JASON A. SOUZA.

Appointees—Revs. WILLIAM BONNER, S.V.D.; MARK D. CHOI; ANTHONY J. GOMEZ; ROBERTO F. JARANILLA; ALBERT VASQUEZ, C.M.F.; MARK A. WARNSTEDT.

Deanery Reps.—Revs. RICHARD VEGA; JEREMIAH P. HELFRICH, S.J.; MICHAEL J. JENNETT; WILLIAM R. PILECTIC, C.M.; ROBERT J. MCNAMARA; KEVIN L. NOLAN; NORMAN SUPANCHECK; JESSE C. GALAZ; MICHAEL P. GLEESON; PEDRO J. LOPEZ; WILLIAM T. EASTERLING; JAMES H. BARNES; PHILIP M. KAVANAUGH; RAYMOND J. TINTLE, O.F.M.; Rev. Msgr. DAVID O'CONNELL; Revs. EDWARD J. DOBER; MARK MARTINEZ; ALEXEI R. SMITH; Rev. Msgr. MICHAEL W. MEYER.

Representative at Large—Rev. Msgr. CHARLES E. HILL.

Ex Officios—Most Rev. JOHN J. WARD; Most Rev. JUAN ARZUBE; Most Rev. THOMAS J. CURRY; Most Rev. JOSEPH M. SARTORIS; Most Rev. GERALD E. WILKERSON; Most Rev. GABINO ZAVALA; Rev. Msgr. LLOYD A. TORGERSON; Rev. Msgr. TERRANCE L. FLEMING, V.G.; Rev. Msgr. JEREMIAH J. MCCARTHY; Rev. Msgr. CRAIG COX; Sr. MARY FAITH CLARKE, S.N.J.M.

Consultants and Liaisons—Rev. BRIAN D. DORAN; Brother JOSEPH ESPARZA, C.S.C.; Rev. JESSE E. GALAZ; Rev. Msgr. CHARLES E. HILL; Rev. Msgr. RICHARD A. LOOMIS; Sr. ANN MCMULLEN, C.S.J.; Sr. JUDITH VALLIMONT, S.Sp.S.; Rev. MARK WARNSTEDT, Representative to RECOPS.

Sisters' Council—Tel: 213-637-7559.

Vicar for Women Religious—Sr. M. FAITH CLARKE, S.N.J.M.

Members—Sr. SEBASTIAN ADZA, C.S.C.; Sr. DOROTHY MARIE AHERN, S.P.; Sr. PATRICIA ARNOLD, C.S.J.; Sr. PILAR BEDOYA, S.M.; Sr. PHILOMENE BREEMANS, I.C.M.; Sr. LEONA BRUNNER, S.S.F.; Sr. VIRGINIA BUCHHOLZ, S.C.R.H.; Sr. RITA CAMPOS, O.S.F.; Sr. NOELLA CHANCE, O.C.D.; Sr. MARY ROSE CHINN, J.M.J.; Sr. PAUL CHOI, S.K.M.; Sr. MARGARET CLARE, P.S.N.; Sr. ANTOINETTE CLAY, O.S.F.; Sr. CHRISTINA MARIE CONROY, C.S.S.F.; Sr. ANNE JOSEPH CROOKSTON, S.S.J.-T.O.S.F.; Sr. LUCILLE DEAN, S.P.; Sr. ALBA DE LA ROSA, H.C.J.S.; Sr. FRANCES MARIE DINARDO, S.N.D.; Sr. CARMEL DONOHUE, S.S.L.; Sr. BARBARA DUGAN, C.S.J.; Sr. MARIE CELINE ENRIGHT, S.B.S.; Sr. GEMMA EUM, I.H.M.M.; Sr. JOAN MARIE FARAONE, R.J.M.; Sr. LORETTA FLOOD, C.S.J.; Sr. MARTHA GARCIA, D.C.; Sr. MARY GENINO, R.S.H.M.; Sr. MARY BRIDE GORMLEY, O.S.B.; Sr. FELICITAS HONG, C.S.T.; Sr. BARBARINE HOUDEK, O.S.F.; Sr. BENIGNA HWANG, O.S.B.; Sr. MARY JENSCH, D.M.J.; Sr. MARY BRENDA JOHNSON, I.H.M.; Sr. CRISTINA JUAREZ, S.M.; Sr. ANNE KELLEY, R.G.S.; Sr. CAROL KENNING, S.N.D.deN.; Sr. PACOIMA KIM, O.S.B.; Sr. JOSEPH ANN KOSTKA, O.L.V.M.; Sr. RENE LANGENECKER, O.S.F.; Sr. ANNA MARIA LAW, R.S.M.; Sr. ANNE LENNON, C.H.F.; Sr. NICHOLAUS MAENG, S.L.J.; Sr. M. DIANE MARTIN, O.S.F.; Sr. MILAGROS MARTIN, R.A.D.; Sr. MARGARET MCCAULEY, O.P.; Sr. MARY MCCLUSKEY, C.C.V.I.; Sr. UNA MCMAHON, R.S.C.; Sr. ANNE MCMULLEN, C.S.J.; Sr. HENRIETTA MEANS, O.S.F.; Sr. MARY NAAB, M.M.; Sr. RITA O'DEA, S.S.C.; Sr. JEANNINE PERCY, O.S.M.; Sr. CESIRA PIEROTTI, F.M.A.; Sr. MARIE ANNE REAGEN, L.S.P.; Sr. PATRICIA REINHART, P.B.V.M.; Sr. ELVIRA RIOS, O.D.N.; Sr. MARY ERNEST ROTHE, B.V.M.; Sr. TERESITA SAAVEDRA, S.S.S.; Sr. FLORELIA SALAZAR, C.V.D.; Sr. IRENE SAN ROMAN, O.S.F.; Sr. AMANDA SANTOS, F.S.P.; Sr. MARY SCHLEHUBER, O.P.; Sr. SARAH MARIE SCHMITT, C.S.C.; Sr. ROSE SERAPHIM, E.F.M.S.; Sr. DONNA SHANAHAN, C.S.J.; Sr. ELIZABETH ANNE SHEEHEY, C.S.J.P.; Sr. MARJORIE SHELVY, D.C.; Sr. DOROTHY SIMPSON, S.N.J.M.; Sr. MARY ELIZABETH STRECKER, S.C.L.; Sr. MIRIAM JOSEPH TERESI, O.S.F.; Sr. ANN LAN THI TRAN, L.H.C.; Sr. MARY TOMASELLA, S.D.S.H.; Sr. ANN LANH TRAM, L.H.C.; Sr. EMMA LUZ TRESLER, O.C.D.; Sr. GUADALUPE VALDEZ, S.S.N.D.; Sr. JUDITH VALLIMONT, S.Sp.S; Sr. ROSE MARIE WILSON, O.S.F.; Sr. MARY ANNE WITTMAN, S.H.F.; Sr. KATHLEEN WOOD, O.S.F.; Sr. GIULLI ZOBELEIN, O.P.

Spirituality Commission—Rev. JAMES CLARKE, Chm. Tel: 213-637-7654. Members: Dr. MICHAEL DOWNEY; STEVEN ELLAIR; Sr. LAURA GORMLEY, S.S.L.; IRMA ISIP; Sr. THOMAS BERNARD MACCONNELL, C.S.J. Tel: 213-747-6508. Rev. KENNETH MCGUIRE, C.S.P.

Theological Commission—Rev. Msgr. CRAIG A. COX, J.C.D., Dir. Tel: 213-637-7204. Sr. KAREN WILHELMY, C.S.J., M.A., Sec. Tel: 805-486-7301.

Members—Revs. RICHARD B. BENSON, C.M., S.T.D.; JOHN P. BRENNAN, S.M.A., D.D.; DOUGLAS BURTON-CHRISTIE, Ph.D.; Rev. Msgr. EDWARD WILLIAM CLARK, S.T.D.; Revs. FRANCIS R. COLBORN, S.T.D.; Dr. MICHAEL DOWNEY; ELIZABETH ANNE DUNN, Ph.D.; Rev. LUKE DYSINGER, O.S.B., M.D.; PAUL F. FORD, Ph.D.; Rev. Msgr. JEREMIAH MCCARTHY, Ph.D.; JOHN R. POPIDEN, Ph.D.; Revs. THOMAS P. RAUSCH, S.J., Ph.D.; GILBERT ROMERO, Ph.D.

CLERGY, PARISHES, MISSIONS AND PAROCHIAL SCHOOLS

CITY OF LOS ANGELES
(Los Angeles County)

1—CATHEDRAL RESIDENCE (1876). The Cathedral of Our Lady of the Angels is currently under construction. Please direct inquiries to: Rev. Msgr. Kevin Kostelnik, 555 W. Temple St., Los Angeles, CA 90012. Tel: 213-637-7264. His Eminence Cardinal Roger Mahony; Rev. Msgr. Kevin J. Kostelnik; Rev. Msgr. Terrance L. Fleming; Revs. Carl M. Sutphin; Paul M. Albee.
555 W. Temple St., 90012.

2—CATHEDRAL OF OUR LADY OF THE ANGELS (1876). Closed. For inquiries for Sacramental Records contact 55 W. Temple St., Los Angeles, CA 90012.

3—ALL SAINTS (1926) (Hispanic), Revs. Jose L. Vega, O.M.; Gino Vanzillotta, O.M.; Deacon Pedro Rojas.
Rectory—3431 Portola Ave., 90032-2215. Tel: 323-223-1101; Fax: 323-223-9592.
School—3420 Portola Ave., 90032. Tel: 323-225-7264; Fax: 323-225-1240.
Sisters 1; Lay Teachers 9; Students 281.
Catechesis/Religious Programs—Tel: 323-225-5193.
Students 505.

4—ASCENSION (1923) (Hispanic-African American), Revs. David O'Connell, Mod.; Paul E. Vigil, Admin.
Res., 517 W. 112th St., 90044. Tel: 323-754-2978; Fax: 323-754-3905.
School—500 W. 111th Pl., 90044. Tel: 323-756-4064; Fax: 323-756-1060. Mr. Neil Quinly, Prin.
Lay Teachers 9; Students 284.
Catechesis/Religious Programs—Tel: 323-777-6356.
Students 300.

5—ASSUMPTION (1926) (Hispanic), Rev. Gustavo J. Ramon (Cuba). In res., Rev. Modesto Perez.
Res., 2832 Blanchard St., 90033. Tel: 323-269-8171; Fax: 323-269-0106.
School—3016 Winter St., 90063. Tel: 323-269-4319; Fax: 323-269-2434. Ms. Lydia Ortega, Prin.
Lay Teachers 10; Students 220.
Catechesis/Religious Programs—Tel: 213-269-5920.
Students 224.
Mission—Los Angeles, Old Co., Assumption, 414 N. Fresno St., 90063. Tel: 213-264-6363.

6—BLESSED SACRAMENT (1924), Revs. Michael J. Mandala, S.J.; John J. Brennan, S.J.; James A. Rude, S.J.; James R. Gallas, S.J.; John LeVecke, S.J.; Deacon Richard Morgan; Bro. James C. Siwicki, S.J., Dir. of Social Svc.
Res., 6657 Sunset Blvd., 90028. Tel: 323-462-6311; Fax: 323-462-0113.
School—6641 Sunset Blvd., 90028. Tel: 323-467-4177; Fax: 323-467-6099.
Lay Teachers 9; Students 295.
Catechesis/Religious Programs—Tel: 323-463-9820. Sr. Maricarlos Valdez, E.I.N., D.R.E.
Students 420.

7—CATHEDRAL CHAPEL (1927), Revs. Earl G. Walker, Pastor Emeritus; Charles L. Schwehr.
Church—927 S. La Brea Ave., 90036.
Res., 922 S. Detroit St., 90036. Tel: 323-935-1128; Fax: 323-935-7308.
School—755 S. Cochran Ave., 90036. Tel: 323-938-9976; Fax: 323-938-9930.
Lay Teachers 11; Students 255.
Catechesis/Religious Programs—Students 42.

8—CHRIST THE KING (1926), Revs. Antonio Cacciapuoti; Elias Rodrigues.
Res., 624 N. Rossmore Ave., 90004. Tel: 323-465-7605; Fax: 323-463-4895.
School—617 N. Arden Blvd., 90004. Tel: 323-462-4753; Fax: 323-462-8475.
Lay Teachers 9; Students 249.
Catechesis/Religious Programs—Tel: 323-465-7084; Fax: 323-463-4895.
Students 357.

9—CRISTO REY (1954) (Hispanic), Revs. Domingos A. Machado, O.A.R.; Juan J. Orobiourritia, O.A.R. In res., Rev. Anthony Iroz, O.A.R.
Res., 4343 Perlita Ave., 90039. Tel: 323-245-4585; Fax: 818-247-8831. [CEM]
Catechesis/Religious Programs—Students 300.

10—DIVINE SAVIOUR (1907) (Hispanic), Revs. Thomas Boudreau; Miguel Plascencia.
Res., 610 Cypress Ave., 90065. Tel: 323-225-9181; Fax: 323-225-1099.
School—Tel: 213-222-6077; Fax: 213-225-1099.
Lay Teachers 9; Students 277.
Catechesis/Religious Programs—Alice Perez, D.R.E.
Students 1,500.

11—DOLORES MISSION (1945) (Hispanic), Revs. Michael E. Kennedy, S.J.; Theodore Gabrielli, S.J.; Mr. Eddy Martinez, Admin. In res., Revs. Robert Dolan, S.J.; Gregory Boyle, S.J.
Res., 171 S. Gless St., 90033. Tel: 323-881-0039 (Church); Fax: 323-881-0034.
School—Tel: 323-881-0001. Sr. Pat Reinhart, P.B.V.M., Prin.
Lay Teachers 9; Students 253.
Catechesis/Religious Programs—Sr. Giulil Zobelein, O.P., D.R.E.
Students 155.

12—HOLY CROSS (1906) (African American-Hispanic), Revs. Xavier Colleoni, M.C.C.J. (Italy); Bartholomew Battirossi, M.C.C.J. (Italy); Peter McGinley, M.C.C.J. (United Kingdom); Paul O'Donnell, M.C.C.J.; Bro. Robert Strabla, M.C.C.J. (Italy).
Res., 4705 S. Main St., 90037. Tel: 323-234-5984; Fax: 323-234-0130.
Catechesis/Religious Programs—Students 950.

13—HOLY NAME OF JESUS (1921) (African American), Revs. Gregory C. Chisholm, S.J.; Jose Corrall, S.J.; Deacon John Gaudin.
Res., 2190 W. 31st St., 90018. Tel: 213-734-8888; Fax: 213-734-8430.
School—Tel: 213-731-2255; Fax: 323-730-0321. Mrs. Marva Belisle, Prin.
Lay Teachers 9; Students 299.
Catechesis/Religious Programs—Tel: 323-731-5448.
Students 115.

14—HOLY SPIRIT (1926), Rev. Paul A. Sustayta.
Res., 1421 S. Dunsmuir Ave., 90019-4031. Tel: 323-935-1333; Fax: 323-935-7741.
School—(Grades K-4) 1418 S. Burnside Ave., 90019. Tel: 323-933-7775; Fax: 323-933-7453.
Sisters of the Holy Faith 2; Lay Teachers 4; Students 138.
Catechesis/Religious Programs—Tel: 323-935-4591.
Students 280.

15—HOLY TRINITY (1925) (Filipino-Hispanic), Revs. James E. McElroy; John Daly, Pastor Emeritus; Thomas Peacha; Theodore Jang.
Res., 3722 Boyce Ave., 90039. Tel: 323-664-4723; Fax: 323-664-2581.
School—3716 Boyce Ave., 90039. Tel: 323-663-2064; Fax: 323-663-0732.
Lay Teachers 11; Students 288.
Catechesis/Religious Programs—Tel: 323-793-2901.
Students 155.

16—IMMACULATE CONCEPTION (1908) (Hispanic), Revs. Pedro E. Amezcua (Mexico); Jose Trinidad Rodriguez (Mexico); Ariel Munoz (Mexico); Rafael Ochoa (Mexico).
Res., 1433 W. Ninth St., 90015. Tel: 213-384-1019; Fax: 213-384-0437.
School—830 Green St., 90017. Tel: 213-382-5931; Fax: 213-382-4563. Ms. Mary Ann Murphy, Prin.
Lay Teachers 9; Students 310.
Catechesis/Religious Programs—832 Green Ave., 90017. Tel: 213-389-7277.
Students 525.

17—IMMACULATE HEART OF MARY (1910), Revs. Henry L. Hernando; Mateo Hicarte; Deacon George Asmar. In res., Rev. Michael Wempe.
Res., 4954 Santa Monica Blvd., 90029. Tel: 323-660-0034; 662-0564; Fax: 323-660-0047.
School—1055 N. Alexandria Ave., 90029. Tel: 323-663-4611; Fax: 323-663-6216.
Sisters 1; Lay Teachers 11; Students 319.
Catechesis/Religious Programs—4954 W. Santa Monica Blvd., 90029. Tel: 323-667-2675.
Students 290.

18—MOTHER OF GOOD COUNSEL (1925), Revs. Christopher J. Drennan, O.S.A.; Gary C. Rye, O.S.A. In res., Rev. Robert W. Gavotto, O.S.A.
Res., 2060 N. Vermont Ave., 90027. Tel: 323-664-2111; Fax: 323-664-0556.
School—4622 Ambrose Ave., 90027. Tel: 323-664-2131; Fax: 323-664-1906. Miss Tina Katherine Kipp, Prin.
Sisters 1; Lay Teachers 9; Students 312.
Catechesis/Religious Programs—Students 315.

19—MOTHER OF SORROWS (1923) (Hispanic-African American), Rev. R. Dario Miranda, Admin.
Res., 114 W. 87th St., 90003. Tel: 323-758-7697; Fax: 323-758-7853.
School—Tel: 323-758-6204; Fax: 323-758-6203. Sr. Martha Garcia, D.C., Prin.
Lay Teachers 10; Students 228.
Catechesis/Religious Programs—Tel: 323-789-6316.
Students 459.

20—NATIVITY (1920) (Hispanic-African American), Rev. Msgr. Timothy J. Dyer; Rev. Mario Torres.
Res., 953 W. 57th St., 90037. Tel: 323-759-1562; Fax: 323-759-7716.
School—Tel: 323-752-0720; Fax: 323-752-1945.
Lay Teachers 8; Students 320.
Catechesis/Religious Programs—Tel: 213-752-1770.
Students 1,080.
Loretto Literary & Benevolent Institution—.

21—NATIVITY OF BLESSED VIRGIN MARY (1947) (Ukrainian-Byzantine), Rev. Oleh Romanenko.
Res., 5154 De Longpre Ave., 90027. Tel: 323-663-6307; Fax: 323-663-0369.

22—OUR LADY OF SOLITUDE (1925) (Hispanic), Revs. Gilberto Torres, M.S.P.; Genaro Zavala, M.S.P.; Deacon Fernando Aranda, Jr.
Res., 4561 Cesar Chavez Ave., 90022. Tel: 323-269-7248; Fax: 323-269-3600.
School—4545 Dozier St., 90022. Tel: 323-261-1083; Fax: 323-261-5300. Victoria Riveros, Prin.
Lay Teachers 10; Students 225.
Catechesis/Religious Programs—Tel: 323-269-7248, Ext. 22.
Students 448.

23—OUR LADY HELP OF CHRISTIANS (MARIA AUXILIADORA) (1923) (Hispanic), Revs. Ramon Farre, Sch.P.; Miguel Campos, Sch.P.; Romualdo Gonzalez, Sch.P.
Res., 512 S. Ave. 20, 90031. Tel: 323-223-4153; Fax: 323-223-1427.
School—2024 Darwin Ave., 90031. Tel: 323-222-3913; Fax: 323-222-2561. Sr. Celia Martinez, M.C., Prin.
Poor Clare Missionary Sisters 4; Lay Teachers 7; Students 288.
Catechesis/Religious Programs—Tel: 323-225-2846.
Students 200.

24—OUR LADY OF THE BRIGHT MOUNT (1925) (Polish), Rev. Edward Mroczynski, S.Chr. (Poland). In res., Rev. Wojciech M. Kania, S.Chr.
Res., 3424 W. Adams Blvd., 90018. Tel: 323-734-5249; Fax: 323-734-0046.
Catechesis/Religious Programs—Students 160.
Convent—Tel: 323-734-6754.
Missionary Sisters of Christ the King (Polonia) 3.

25—OUR LADY OF GUADALUPE (1923) (Hispanic), Revs. Robert Juarez; Porfirio Alvarez.
Res., 4018 Hammel St., 90063. Tel: 323-261-8051; Fax: 323-261-1259.
School—436 Hazard Ave., 90063. Tel: 323-269-4998; Fax: 323-780-7001.
Lay Teachers 12; Students 275.
Catechesis/Religious Programs—Tel: 213-262-7957.
Students 469.
Mission—Los Angeles, Los Angeles Co., San Felipe, 738 N. Geraghty Ave., 90063. Tel: 213-266-1433; Fax: 323-261-1259.

26—OUR LADY OF GUADALUPE (Rosehill) (1928) (Hispanic), Revs. Thomas E. Baker; Gustavo Lara; Stephen C. Hernandez, (Retired); Deacon Miguel Arroyo.
Res., 4509 Mercury Ave., 90032. Tel: 323-225-4201; Fax: 323-225-3668.
School—4504 Browne Ave., 90032. Tel: 323-221-8187.
Missionary Sisters of the Immaculate Heart of Mary 2; Lay Teachers 8; Students 280.
Catechesis/Religious Programs—Tel: 323-223-1777.
Students 425.

27—OUR LADY OF GUADALUPE SANCTUARY (1929) (Hispanic), Rev. Leslie N. Delgado (Panama).
Res., 4100 E. Second St., 90063. Tel: 323-261-4365; Fax: 323-261-2735.
Catechesis/Religious Programs—Students 313.

28—OUR LADY OF LORETTO (1905), Revs. Walter Miller, S.V.D.; Gerard O'Doherty, S.V.D. (Ireland); Dominic Hoan Nguyen, C.M., Vietnamese Ministry; Richard Casillas, S.V.D.; Deacon Pedro Torres.
Res., 250 N. Union Ave., 90026. Tel: 213-483-3013; Fax: 213-483-3017.
School—258 N. Union Ave., 90026. Tel: 213-483-5251; Fax: 213-463-6709.
Lay Teachers 9; Students 339.
Catechesis/Religious Programs—Tel: 213-483-8137.
Students 410.

29—OUR LADY OF LOURDES (1910), Revs. Richard Siebenand; William E. Ruther; Deacon Jose Lopez.
Res., 3772 E. Third St., 90063-2408. Tel: 323-526-3800; Fax: 323-526-3807.
School—315 S. Eastman Ave., 90063. Tel: 323-526-3813; Fax: 323-526-3814.
Lay Teachers 9; Students 264.
Catechesis/Religious Programs—Tel: 323-526-3804.
Students 673.

30—OUR LADY OF VICTORY (1966) (Spanish), Revs. Francisco Gomez, S.T.; Carlos Zacarias, S.T. In res., Rev. Norbert Sharon, S.T.
Res., 1316 S. Herbert Ave., 90023. Tel: 323-268-9502; Fax: 323-780-1719.
Catechesis/Religious Programs—1317 S. Herbert Ave., 90023. Tel: 323-262-2101.
Students 650.

31—OUR LADY QUEEN OF THE ANGELS (1781) (Spanish), Revs. Albert M. Vazquez, C.M.F.; Theo Fuentes, C.M.F.; Domingo Zuniga, C.M.F.; Albert Domingo, C.M.F.
Res., 535 N. Main St., 90012. Tel: 213-629-3101; Fax: 213-629-1951.
Catechesis/Religious Programs—Students 770.

32—OUR LADY OF THE ROSARY OF TALPA (1928) (Spanish), Revs. Francisco Mateos, C.M.; Venancio Goyeneche; Helios del Cerro, C.M. In res., Rev. Felix Sarachaga, C.M.
Res., 2914 E. Fourth St., 90033. Tel: 323-268-9176; Fax: 323-268-4026.
School—411 S. Evergreen Ave., 90033. Tel: 323-261-0583; Fax: 323-261-0352.
Daughters of Charity of St. Vincent de Paul 1; Lay Teachers 9; Students 280.
Catechesis/Religious Programs—Tel: 323-264-3345.
Students 470.
Convent—427 S. Evergreen St., 90033. Tel: 323-268-7731.
Mission—Los Angeles, Los Angeles Co., La Purisima Chapel, 3236 Inez St., 90023.

33—OUR LADY QUEEN OF MARTYRS (Armenian), Revs. Raphael Minassian, P.I.A.; Antoine Panossian, P.I.A.
Res., 1327 Pleasant Ave., 90033. Tel: 323-261-9898; Fax: 323-261-0522.

34—OUR SAVIOUR CATHOLIC CENTER (1957), Rev. William Messenger.
Res., 3207 University Ave., 90007. Tel: 213-749-5341; Fax: 213-749-3475.

35—PRECIOUS BLOOD (1923), Rev. Philip M. Kavanaugh. In res., Rev. Don R. Kribs.
Res., 435 S. Occidental Blvd., 90057. Tel: 213-389-8439; Fax: 213-389-1951.
School—307 S. Occidental Blvd., 90057. Tel: 213-382-3345; Fax: 213-382-2078.
Lay Teachers 11; Students 246.
Catechesis/Religious Programs—Tel: 213-382-3906.
Students 235.

36—PRESENTATION OF THE MARY (1925) (Hispanic), Rev. Benigno A. Rodriguez.
Res., 6406 Parmelee Ave., 90001. Tel: 323-585-0570; Fax: 323-585-8148.
Catechesis/Religious Programs—Students 624.

37—RESURRECTION (1923) (Mexican), Rev. Msgr. John T. Moretta; Rev. Rafael Casillas; Deacons Richard Fajardo; Hernando Rodriguez.
Res., 3324 E. Opal St., 90023. Tel: 323-268-1141; Fax: 323-268-1143.
School—3360 E. Opal St., 90023. Tel: 323-261-5750. Angelica Figueroa, Prin.
Franciscan Sisters of Mary Immaculate 2; Lay Teachers 10; Students 300.
Catechesis/Religious Programs—Tel: 323-264-1963.
Students 1,073.

38—SACRED HEART (1887) (Hispanic), Revs. Gabriel Gonzales; Robert Victoria; Mr. Fred Flores, Admin. In res., Rev. George Horan.
Res., 2210 Sichel St., 90031. Tel: 323-221-3179; Fax: 323-221-3613.
School—2109 Sichel St., 90031. Tel: 323-225-4177; Fax: 323-225-2615.
Dominican Sisters of Mission San Jose 3; Lay Teachers 18; Students 320.
Catechesis/Religious Programs—Tel: 323-223-7571.
Students 500.
Convent—2108 Sichel St., 90031. Tel: 323-222-5157.

39—ST. AGATHA (1923), Rev. Ken Deasy; Deacon Hosea Alexander.
Res., 2646 S. Mansfield Ave., 90016. Tel: 323-935-8127; Fax: 323-939-3547.
Catechesis/Religious Programs—Tel: 323-933-0963.
Students 400.

40—ST. AGNES (1903) (Hispanic-Korean), Revs. William Delaney, C.PP.S.; James Franck, C.PP.S.; Peter Kim, S.J.
Res., 2625 S. Vermont Ave., 90007. Tel: 323-731-2464; Fax: 323-731-6186.
School—Tel: 323-734-6441.
Lay Teachers 10; Students 335.
Catechesis/Religious Programs—Tel: 323-731-0014. Mrs. Miriam Oliva, D.R.E.
Students 550.

41—ST. ALOYSIUS GONZAGA (1908) (Hispanic), Revs. George Aguilera; Ubaldo Chueca (Peru).
Res., 7814 Crocket Blvd., 90001. Tel: 323-585-4485; Fax: 323-589-8485. [CEM]
School—Tel: 213-582-4965. Sr. Anna Marie Law, S.M., Prin.
Lay Teachers 9; Students 236.
Catechesis/Religious Programs—2023 E. Nadeau St., Tel: 323-582-7990.
Students 770.

42—ST. ALPHONSUS (1935) (Hispanic), Revs. Jesse C. Galaz; Brian T. Castaneda; Hugo R. Neyra.
Res., 5223 Hastings St., 90022-2625. Tel: 323-264-3353; Fax: 323-264-4858.
School—Tel: 323-268-5165; Fax: 323-268-7784.
Lay Teachers 12; Students 275.
Catechesis/Religious Programs—552 South Amalia Ave., 90022. Tel: 323-266-0855.
Students 570.

43—ST. ANASTASIA (1953), Rev. Msgr. Royale M. Vadakin. In res., Rev. Msgr. Gregory A. Cox.
Res., 7390 W. Manchester Ave., 90045. Tel: 310-670-2243; Fax: 310-670-5052.
School—8631 S. Stanmoor Dr., 90045. Tel: 310-645-8816; Fax: 310-645-6923. Mrs. Rosemary Connolly, Prin.
Lay Teachers 20; Students 303.
Catechesis/Religious Programs—Tel: 310-215-9806.
Students 260.

44—ST. ANN (1937), Rev. Hugh Crowe; Rev. Msgr. John R. Brosnan, Pastor Emeritus.
Office: 1365 Blake Ave., 90031. Tel: 323-221-6368.
Res., 2302 Riverdale Ave., 90031. Fax: 323-276-9351.
Catechesis/Religious Programs—Tel: 323-222-9749. Ramona Lopez, D.R.E.
Students 183.

45—ST. ANSELM (1924), Rev. Lawrence Shelton.
Res., 2222 W. 70th St., 90043. Tel: 323-758-6729; Fax: 323-758-8455.
School—7019 S. Van Ness Ave., 90043. Tel: 323-759-9371; Fax: 323-759-1131.
Lay Teachers 9; Students 280.
Catechesis/Religious Programs—Students 57.

46—ST. ANTHONY (1910) (Croatian), Revs. John Segaric, Pastor Emeritus; Mate Bizaca, Admin.; Milenko Majic; Rev. Msgr. Felix S. Diomartich, Pastor Emeritus.
Res., 712 N. Grand Ave., 90012. Tel: 213-628-2938; Fax: 213-628-1635. [CEM]

47—SAN ANTONIO DE PADUA (1926) (Hispanic), Rev. Msgr. Joseph W. Herres.
Res., 555 N. Fairview Ave., 90033. Tel: 323-225-1301; Fax: 323-225-2534.
School—1500 Bridge St., 90033. Tel: 323-221-6970; Fax: 323-343-9183.
Sisters of the Company of Mary 3; Lay Teachers 9; Students 230.
Catechesis/Religious Programs—Tel: 323-225-1086.
Students 140.

48—ST. BASIL'S (1920), Rev. Msgr. Charles Hill; Revs. Martin Minaberry; Phillip Pak (Korea). In res., Rev. Msgr. Terrence Richey.
Res., 637 S. Kingsley Dr., 90005. Tel: 213-381-6191; Fax: 213-382-5883. [CEM]
Catechesis/Religious Programs—Students 130.

49—ST. BERNADETTE (1947) (African American), Revs. Patrick J. Gorman, Pastor Emeritus; Thomas F. King; Deacon Emile Adams.
Res., 3825 Don Felipe Dr., 90008. Tel: 323-293-4877; Fax: 323-293-2838.
School—4196 Marlton Ave., 90008. Tel: 323-291-4284; Fax: 323-291-0839. Sr. Joan Mary O'Dwyer, C.S.J., Prin.
Sisters 5; Lay Teachers 9; Students 260.
Catechesis/Religious Programs—Students 67.

50—ST. BERNARD (1924), Rev. Gerald McSorley; Rev. Msgr. Patrick McNulty, Pastor Emeritus. In res., Rev. Patrick Hill.
Res., 2500 W. Ave. 33, 90065. Tel: 323-255-6142; Fax: 323-255-2351.
School—Tel: 323-256-4989; Fax: 323-256-4963.
Sisters of Charity of the Blessed Virgin Mary 2; Lay Teachers 9; Students 288.
Catechesis/Religious Programs—2515 W. Ave. 33, 90065. Tel: 323-256-6242.
Students 350.

51—ST. BRENDAN (1915), Rev. Charles W. Gard.
Res., 310 S. Van Ness Ave., 90020. Tel: 323-936-4656; Fax: 323-936-9058.
School—238 S. Manhatten Pl., 90004. Tel: 323-382-7401; Fax: 323-382-8918.
Sisters 3; Lay Teachers 17; Students 315.
Catechesis/Religious Programs—Students 120.

52—ST. BRIGID'S (1920) (African American-Hispanic), Revs. John G. Harfmann, S.S.J.; Fernando Arizti, S.J.; Deacons Gilbert Lanoix; William Hawkins, Jr.; John Turner. In res., Very Rev. Charles Andrus, S.S.J.
Res., 5214 S. Western Ave., 90062. Tel: 323-292-0781; Fax: 323-290-1254.

53—ST. BRIDGET'S CHINESE CATHOLIC CENTER (1940) (Chinese), Rev. Joseph Cheng, S.D.B., (China) Admin.
Res., 445 1/2 Cottage Home St., 90012. Tel: 323-222-5518; Fax: 323-222-0814.
Catechesis/Religious Programs—Students 63.
Church—510 Cottage Home, 90012-1418. [JC]

54—ST. CAMILLUS DE LELLIS (1952). (Center for Pastoral Care). Chaplains: Revs. Christopher D. Ponnet, Dir.; Gustavo Lara; Robert J. Jones, C.M.; Kurt Schweiss; Sr. Dora Hauchecorne, I.C.M.; Sr. Nancy Bartasavich, S.P.; Sr. Matilde Ortiz; Sr. Mary Jean Ferry, B.V.M.; Sr. Patricia Walsh, O.P.; Sr. Angela Pacheco, C.S.J.; Deacon James Dillon.
Res., 1911 Zonal Ave., 90033-1032. Tel: 323-225-4461; Fax: 323-225-9096.

55—ST. CASIMIR (1946) (Lithuanian), Rev. Msgr. Algirdas Olsaukas; Rev. Msgr. John A. Kucingis; Rev. Stanislovas Anuzis.
Res., 2718 St. George St., 90027. Tel: 323-664-4660; Fax: 323-664-4660.
School—2716 St. George St., 90027. Tel: 323-661-9200; Fax: 323-668-1440.
Lay Teachers 9; Students 255.
Catechesis/Religious Programs—Tel: 818-248-4046.
Students 125.

56—ST. CECILIA (1909) (African American-Hispanic), Revs. Luigi Zanotto, M.C.C.J.; Gerardo De Tomasi, M.C.C.J. In res., Revs. Francis Abel Modi, M.C.C.J. (Sudan); Peter McGinley, M.C.C.J. (Scotland).
Res., 4230 S. Normandie Ave., 90037. Tel: 323-294-6628; Fax: 323-294-3310.
School—4224 S. Normandie Ave., 90037. Tel: 323-293-4266; Fax: 323-293-5556.
Lay Teachers 9; Students 305.
Catechesis/Religious Programs—Students 400.

57—ST. COLUMBAN (1945) (Filipino), Rev. Colm Rafferty, S.S.C., Admin.; Deacon Felix Dumlao. In res., Rev. Sean John McGrath, S.S.C.
Res., 125 S. Loma Dr., 90026. Tel: 213-250-8818; Fax: 213-250-8818.

58—ST. COLUMBKILLE (1921) (Hispanic-African American), Revs. Timothy J. Dyer; Mario Torres.
Res., 6315 S. Main St., 90003. Tel: 323-758-5540; Fax: 323-758-8108.
School—145 W. 64th St., 90003. Tel: 323-758-2284; Fax: 323-750-7141.
Sisters 3; Lay Teachers 8; Students 159.
Catechesis/Religious Programs—Tel: 323-789-3344.
Students 487.

59—SAN CONRADO MISSION (1966). (See St. Peter, Los Angeles for details.).

60—ST. DOMINIC (1921), Very Rev. Anthony M. Patalano, O.P.; Revs. Carl Schlichte, O.P.; Roberto Reyes, O.P.; Bro. Frederick Narberes, O.P. In res., Rev. Donald Bramble, O.P.
Res., 2002 Merton Ave., 90041. Tel: 323-254-2519; Fax: 323-255-3067.
School—Tel: 323-255-5803; Fax: 323-255-2817.
Dominican Sisters of San Rafael 1; Lay Teachers 23; Students 497.
Catechesis/Religious Programs—Tel: 323-255-6373.
Students 193.

61—ST. EUGENE (1942), Rev. Patrick J. Walsh. In res., Rev. Michael Ume.
Res., 9505 Haas Ave., 90047. Tel: 323-757-3121; Fax: 323-757-8872.
School—9521 Haas Ave., 90047. Tel: 323-754-9536; Fax: 323-754-0913.
Lay Teachers 12; Students 300.

62—ST. FRANCES XAVIER CABRINI (1946) (African American-Latino), Revs. David O'Connell; Anthony Gonzalez, Pastoral Admin.; Sr. Teresita Carrillo, R.S.H.M., Pastoral Assoc.
Res., 1440 W. Imperial Hwy., 90047. Tel: 323-757-0271; Fax: 323-757-9267.
School—1428 W. Imperial Hwy., 90047. Tel: 323-756-1354; Fax: 323-756-1157. Sr. Celeste Botello, O.P., Prin.
Dominican Sisters 2; Lay Teachers 9; Students 300.
Catechesis/Religious Programs—Tel: 323-756-8111.
Students 451.

63—SAN FRANCISCO CHURCH (1982) (Mexican), Rev. Severiano Castaneda; Deacon Benjamin Torres.
Res., 4800 E. Olympic Blvd., 90022. Tel: 323-262-4253; Fax: 323-268-8246. [CEM][JC]
Catechesis/Religious Programs—Tel: 323-261-2447.
Students 496.

64—MARYKNOLL JAPANESE CATHOLIC CENTER (1921) (Japanese), Rev. David L. Doerner, S.A., Admin.
Res., 222 S. Hewitt St., 90012. Tel: 213-626-2279; Fax: 213-628-1757.
Catechesis/Religious Programs—Students 60.
Chapel—St. Francis Xavier.

65—ST. FRANCIS OF ASSISI (1920), Revs. Charles R. Lueras, C.R.I.C.; James G. Garceau, C.R.I.C.; Sergio E. Garcia, C.R.I.C.
Res., 1523 Golden Gate Ave., 90026. Tel: 323-664-1305; Fax: 323-664-4975.
School—1550 Maltman Ave., 90026. Tel: 323-665-3601; Fax: 323-665-4143.
Sisters of Notre Dame 2; Lay Teachers 8; Students 266.
Catechesis/Religious Programs—Tel: 323-664-9033.
Students 255.

66—ST. GERARD MAJELLA (1952), Revs. William J. Connor; Gerhart Habison (Austria); Deacons Tony Bravo; Ricardo Flores. In res., Rev. Pius Itodo (Nigeria).
Res., 4439 Inglewood Blvd., 90066. Tel: 310-390-5034; Fax: 310-397-0964. [CEM]
School—Tel: 310-397-9489; Fax: 310-398-2081.
Sisters 1; Lay Teachers 10; Students 273.
Catechesis/Religious Programs—Tel: 310-391-9637.
Students 600.

67—ST. GREGORY NAZIANZEN (1923), Revs. Edward J. Johnson; Noel Ryan; Paul White, S.S.C.
Res., 900 S. Bronson Ave., 90019. Tel: 323-935-4224; Fax: 323-934-0016.
School—Tel: 323-936-2542; Fax: 323-936-1690. Zulay Chavez, Prin.
Religious 1; Lay Teachers 9; Students 271.
Catechesis/Religious Programs—Tel: 213-935-4701. Irene Rodriguez, D.R.E.
Students 246.

68—ST. IGNATIUS OF LOYOLA (1911), Rev. Arturo Velasco.
Res., 322 N. Ave. 61, 90042. Tel: 323-256-3041; Fax: 323-256-0105.
School—6025 Monte Vista St., 90042. Tel: 323-255-6456; Fax: 323-255-0959.
Dominican Sisters, San Jose Mission 4; Lay Teachers 9; Students 316.
Catechesis/Religious Programs—Tel: 323-254-9073; Fax: 323-254-9073.
Students 635.

69—SANTA ISABEL (1948) (Mexican), Rev. Bernard Gatlin, Admin.
Res., 918 S. Soto St., 90023. Tel: 213-268-4065; Fax: 213-268-4180.
School—2424 Whittier Blvd., 90023. Tel: 213-263-3716.
School Sisters of Notre Dame 2; Lay Teachers 7; Students 301.
Catechesis/Religious Programs—Tel: 213-268-3019.
Students 337.
Convent—943 S. Soto St., 90023. Tel: 213-262-1711; 264-6556; Fax: 213-526-1655.
Misioneras Eucaristicas Franciscanas 8.

70—ST. JEROME (1949), Rev. James F. Kavanagh. In res., Rev. Peter Burns, S.J.
Res., 5550 Thornburn St., 90045. Tel: 310-348-8212; Fax: 310-417-3577.
School—Tel: 310-670-1678; Fax: 310-670-1678.
Sisters of St. Joseph of Carondelet 3; Lay Teachers 9; Students 312.
Catechesis/Religious Programs—Tel: 310-645-8318.
Students 253.
Convent—5570 Thornburn St., 90045. Tel: 310-670-8838.

71—ST. JOAN OF ARC (1943) (Spanish), Revs. James H. Barnes; John F. Cunningham, Pastor Emeritus; Rev. Msgr. Robert F. Condon, Pastor Emeritus; Rev. Frederick Byaruhanga (Uganda).
Res., 11534 Gateway Blvd., 90064. Tel: 310-479-5111; Fax: 310-479-2513.
School—11561 Gateway Blvd., 90064. Tel: 310-479-3607; Fax: 310-478-1398.
Lay Teachers 9; Students 245.
Catechesis/Religious Programs—Tel: 310-479-1490.
Students 226.

72—ST. JOHN, THE EVANGELIST (1909) (Hispanic-African American), Revs. Melvin P. James, S.V.D.; Efrain Flores, S.V.D.; Deacon Willard Hall. In res., Rev. Fisher Robinson, S.V.D.; Bro. Richard Morrill, S.V.D.
Res., 6028 Victoria Ave., 90043. Tel: 323-758-9161; Fax: 323-758-0112.
School—Tel: 323-751-8545; Fax: 323-751-1651. Carla Cotton, Prin.
Lay Teachers 9; Students 294.
Catechesis/Religious Programs—Students 230.

73—ST. JOSEPH (1888) (Hispanic), Revs. Raymond Tintle, O.F.M.; Armando Lopez, O.F.M.; Alan McCoy, O.F.M.; Martial Luebke, O.F.M.; Enrique Parisi, O.F.M.; Eugene David Burnett, O.F.M.; Angus C. Cooper, O.F.M.; William Brand, O.F.M.; Emil Kyranon, O.F.M.; Kurt Schweiss, O.F.M.
Res., 218 E. 12th St., 90015. Tel: 213-748-5394; Fax: 213-748-4793.
School—Tel: 213-749-8894; Fax: 213-749-0424. Sr. Jean Marie Chavez, O.S.F., Prin.
Sisters 2; Lay Teachers 10; Students 280.
Catechesis/Religious Programs—Students 250.
Mission—Los Angeles, Los Angeles Co., St. Turibius, 1524 Essex, 90021. Tel: 213-749-8894; Fax: 213-749-0424.

74—ST. KEVIN (1923) (Hispanic-Filipino), Rev. Leo E. Steinbock. In res., Rev. Ramon R. Andreu, S.J. (Spain).
Res., 4072 Beverly Blvd., 90004. Tel: 213-383-8206; Fax: 213-386-4390.
Catechesis/Religious Programs—Students 174.

75—ST. LAWRENCE OF BRINDISI (1908) (African American-Hispanic). Capuchin Franciscan Friary. Revs. Peter Banks, O.F.M.Cap.; James L. Cleary, O.F.M.Cap.; Jesus Vela, O.F.M.Cap.
Res., 10122 Compton Ave., 90002. Tel: 323-567-1439; Fax: 323-564-4050.
School—10044 Compton Ave., 90002. Tel: 323-564-3051.
Sisters of Notre Dame 4; Lay Teachers 7; Students 302.
Catechesis/Religious Programs—Tel: 213-567-4698.
Students 506.

76—ST. LUCY (1970) (Hispanic), Revs. Vicente Casaus, Sch.P.; Frank Boronat, Sch.P.
Res., 1419 N. Hazard Ave., 90063. Tel: 323-266-0451; Fax: 323-266-4907. [CEM]
Catechesis/Religious Programs—Tel: 323-266-0456.
Students 189.

77—ST. MALACHY (1926) (Hispanic), Revs. William J. Bonner, S.V.D.; Enrique Huerta, S.V.D.
Res., 1221 E. 82nd St., 90001. Tel: 323-585-1437; Fax: 323-583-5391.
School—1220 E. 81st St., 90001. Tel: 323-582-3112; Fax: 213-582-9340.
Lay Teachers 8; Students 237.
Catechesis/Religious Programs—Tel: 323-582-0203; Fax: 323-582-2826. Sr. Magnolia, D.R.E.
Students 675.
Convent—St. Malachy Convent, 1228 E. 81st St., 90001. Tel: 323-582-0203. Missionaries of Jesus Crucified
Sisters 5.

78—ST. MARCELLINUS (1957), Rev. Jules A. Mayer.
Res., 2349 Strong Ave., 90040. Tel: 323-269-2733.
Catechesis/Religious Programs—Tel: 323-266-4938.
Students 221.

79—ST. MARTIN OF TOURS (1946), Rev. Msgr. Lawrence O'Leary; Rev. Donal Keohane (Ireland).
Res., 11967 Sunset Blvd., 90049. Tel: 310-476-7403.
Church—11967 Sunset Blvd., 90049. Fax: 310-476-0290.
School—Tel: 310-472-7419; Fax: 310-440-2298.
Sisters 2; Lay Teachers 14; Students 275.
Catechesis/Religious Programs—Tel: 310-472-1757.
Students 60.

80—ST. MARY (1886), Revs. James Nieblas, S.D.B.; Avelino Lorenzo, S.D.B.; Hugo Santucci, S.D.B.; Lucian B. Lomello, S.D.B., Hospital Chap.
Res., 407 S. Chicago St., 90033. Tel: 323-268-7432; Fax: 323-268-8076.
School—(Grades K-8). Tel: 323-262-3395; Fax: 323-262-4738.
Daughters of Mary Help of Christians 2; Lay Teachers 12; Students 320.
Catechesis/Religious Programs—Tel: 323-268-2351.
Students 510.

81—ST. MARY MAGDALEN (1930), Revs. Patrick H. Sullivan; Samuel Aririatu; Josephat Ddungu.
Res., 1241 Corning St., LA, 90035. Tel: 310-652-2444.
School—Tel: 310-652-4723.
Sisters of the Holy Faith 1; Lay Teachers 6; Students 141.

Catechesis/Religious Programs—Students 45.

82—St. Michael (1907) (Hispanic-African American), Rev. Bruce Correio. In res., Revs. Donatus Ekanachi (Nigeria); Nelson Trinidad (El Salvador).
Res., 1016 W. Manchester Ave., 90044. Tel: 323-753-2696; Fax: 323-753-3475.
School—(Grades K-8) 1027 W. 87th St., 90044. Tel: 323-752-6101.
Dominican Sisters of Mission San Jose 2; Lay Teachers 8; Students 250.
Catechesis/Religious Programs—Tel: 323-753-2976.
Students 300.

83—San Miguel (1927) (Hispanic), Rev. Raul Silva.
Res., 2214 E. 108th St., 90059. Tel: 323-569-5951; Fax: 323-567-1850.
School—2270 E. 108th St., 90059. Tel: 323-567-6892; Fax: 323-567-4065.
Lay Teachers 8; Students 208.
Catechesis/Religious Programs—Students 235.

84—St. Odilia (1926) (Hispanic-African American), Revs. Wilfred Tyrrell, S.A.; Henry Mair, S.A.
Res., 5222 Hooper Ave., 90011-4807. Tel: 323-232-8677; Fax: 323-231-9714.
School—5300 S. Hooper Ave., 90011. Tel: 323-232-5449; Fax: 323-233-6154. Ms. Sharon E. Oliver, Prin.
Lay Teachers 8; Students 255.
Catechesis/Religious Programs—Tel: 323-233-2651.
Students 550.
Mission—Los Angeles, Los Angeles Co., St. John Bosco, 5516 Duarte St., 90058. Tel: 323-581-3345.

85—St. Patrick (1904) (Hispanic), Rev. Francisco X. Ramirez.
Res., 1046 E. 34th St., 90011. Tel: 323-234-5963; Fax: 323-234-6725.
Catechesis/Religious Programs—Tel: 323-232-5460.
Students 500.

86—St. Paul (1917), Revs. Eugenio Romo, M.G.; Antonio Moreno, M.G.
Office: 1920 S. Bronson Ave., 90018. Tel: 323-730-9490; Fax: 323-734-5266.
Res., 4112 W. Washington Blvd., 90018. Tel: 323-730-9491.
School—1908 S. Bronson Ave., 90018. Tel: 213-734-4022; Fax: 323-734-4022. Mrs. Iris Trouillier, Prin.
Lay Teachers 8; Students 293.
Catechesis/Religious Programs—Tel: 323-734-1784.
Students 342.

87—St. Paul the Apostle (1928), Revs. Tom Jones, C.S.P., Supr.; William T. Kenney, C.S.P.; Harold J. Powers, C.S.P.; Paul A. Lannan; Theodore A. Vierra; Edward D. Wrobleski, C.S.P.; Jeremiah Sullivan, C.S.P.; James McNulty; Edward Donovan, C.S.P.; Frank Desiderio C.S.P.; Brad Schoeberle, C.S.P.
Res., 10750 Ohio Ave., 90024. Tel: 310-474-1527; Fax: 310-474-2897.
School—Tel: 310-474-1588; Fax: 310-474-4272.
Daughters of Mary and Joseph 2; Lay Teachers 27; Students 537.
Catechesis/Religious Programs—Tel: 310-474-1527, Ext. 104.
Students 220.

88—St. Peter (1904) (Italian), Rev. Giovanni Bizzotto, C.S. In res., Rev. Guillermo Diaz, C.S.
Res. & Mailing Address: 1039 N. Broadway, 90012-1429. Tel: 323-225-8119; Fax: 323-225-0085.
Mission—Los Angeles, Los Angeles Co., San Conrado, 1820 Bouett St., 90012. Tel: 323-223-6581.
Scalabrini House of Discernment (Seminary)—Tel: 323-225-4436.
Scalabrini Vocation Center—Tel: 323-225-8027.

89—St. Raphael (1924) (Hispanic-African American), Revs. Tracy O'Sullivan, O.Carm.; Vicente O. Lopez, O.Carm.; Deacon Hernan Ramirez; Sr. Brigida Riveros, C.M.S.T., Dir. Hispanic Ministry; Sr. Soledad Arellano, C.M.S.T.; Mr. Harry Wiley, Dir. African American Ministry.
Res., 942 W. 70th St., 90044. Tel: 323-758-7100; Fax: 323-758-7134.
School—924 W. 70th St., 90044. Tel: 323-751-2774; Fax: 323-751-1244. Mrs. Barbara Curtis, Prin.
Lay Teachers 10; Students 286.
Catechesis/Religious Programs—Tel: 213-752-5965.
Students 330.

90—St. Sebastian (1924), Rev. Gilbert Martinez, C.S.P.
Res., 1453 Federal Ave., 90025-2301. Tel: 310-478-0136; Fax: 310-479-5121.
Parish Center—11607 Ohio Ave., 90025.
School—1430 Federal Ave. W., 90025. Tel: 310-473-3337; Fax: 310-473-3178.
Lay Teachers 12; Students 250.
Catechesis/Religious Programs—Students 245.

91—St. Stephen (1928) (Hungarian-German), Rev. Hermann-Joseph K. Rettig, O.Praem.
Res., 3705 Woodlawn Ave., 90011. Tel: 323-234-9246; Fax: 323-234-2455.
Catechesis/Religious Programs—Students 195.

92—St. Teresa of Avila (1921), Revs. Alexander Salazar; Charles Carolan, S.S.C.; Thomas W. McLaughlin, Pastor Emeritus.
Res., 2216 Fargo St., 90039. Tel: 323-664-8426; Fax: 323-665-3115.
School—(Grades K-8) 2215 Fargo St., 90039. Tel: 323-662-3777; Fax: 323-662-3420.
Lay Teachers 9; Students 305.
Catechesis/Religious Programs—Tel: 323-664-8426.
Students 260.
Convent—2223 Fargo St., 90039. Tel: 323-661-4284.

93—Santa Teresita (1923) (Hispanic), Rev. Raymond Farre, Sch.P.
Res., 2645 Zonal Ave., 90033. Tel: 323-221-2446; Fax: 323-221-2216.
School—(Grades K-8) 2646 Zonal Ave., 90033. Tel: 323-221-1129; Fax: 323-221-6339.
Dominican Sisters 3; Lay Teachers 8; Students 261.
Catechesis/Religious Programs—Tel: 213-221-2511.
Students 493.

94—St. Thomas the Apostle (1903) (Hispanic), Revs. Jarlath Cunnane; J. Rigoberto Rodriguez; Antonio Garcia.
Res., 1321 S. Mariposa Ave., 90006. Tel: 323-737-3325; Fax: 323-737-2665.
School—Tel: 323-737-4730; Fax: 323-737-6348.
Lay Teachers 10; Students 320.
Catechesis/Religious Programs—Tel: 323-737-5624.
Students 1,400.

95—St. Timothy (1943), Rev. William J. Brelsford.
Res., 10425 W. Pico Blvd., 90064. Tel: 310-474-1216; Fax: 310-475-6047.
School—Tel: 310-474-1811; Fax: 310-470-1391. Sr. Francis Marie DiNardo, S.N.D., Prin.
Lay Teachers 14; Students 225.
Catechesis/Religious Programs—Students 255.

96—St. Vincent De Paul (1887), Revs. Antonio Ruiz, C.M.; Michael F. Walsh, C.M.; Bro. Anthony B. Wiedemer, C.M., Admin. In res., Rev. Joseph L. Brennan, C.M.
Res., 621 W. Adams Blvd., 90007. Tel: 213-749-8950; Fax: 213-749-9137.
School—2333 S. Figueroa St., 90007. Tel: 213-748-5367; Fax: 213-748-5347.
Sisters 5; Lay Teachers 6; Students 309.
Catechesis/Religious Programs—Tel: 213-741-9347.
Students 450.
Mission—Los Angeles, Los Angeles Co., Santo Nino, 601 E. 23rd St., 90011. Tel: 213-748-5246.

97—Transfiguration (1923) (African American), Rev. Msgr. Robert E. Howard. In res., Rev. Michael. McCullough.
Res., 2515 W. Martin Luther King Blvd., 90008-2728. Tel: 323-291-1136; Fax: 323-291-8216.
School—4020 Roxton Ave., 90008. Tel: 323-292-3011; Fax: 323-292-1527.
Lay Teachers 12; Students 287.
Catechesis/Religious Programs—Students 80.

98—Visitation (1943), Rev. Msgr. Timothy O'Connell; Rev. James F. O'Grady, Pastor Emeritus.
Res., 6561 W. 88th St., 90045. Tel: 310-216-1145; Fax: 310-216-1002.
School—8740 Emerson Ave., 90045. Tel: 310-645-6620; Fax: 310-645-4407.
Sisters 2; Lay Teachers 20; Students 286.
Catechesis/Religious Programs—Tel: 310-568-9085.
Students 173.

OUTSIDE THE CITY OF LOS ANGELES

Alhambra, Los Angeles Co., All Souls (1912), Rev. Msgr. William P. O'Toole; Revs. Christopher E. Troxell; Benjamin Le.
Res., 17 S. Electric Ave., 91801. Tel: 626-281-0466; Fax: 626-281-2163.
Catechesis/Religious Programs—29 S. Electric Ave., 91801. Tel: 626-284-7835.
Students 345.

St. Therese (1924). (Little Flower). Revs. Matthew Williams, O.C.D.; William Fenton, O.C.D.; Jerome Lantry, O.C.D.
Res., 510 N. El Molino St., 91801. Tel: 626-282-2744; Fax: 626-282-7560.
School—Tel: 626-289-3364; Fax: 626-284-6700.
Lay Teachers 18; Students 315.
Catechesis/Religious Programs—Tel: 626-284-0020.
Students 100.

St. Thomas More (1948), Revs. Paul F. Menke; Jeremiah O'Neill, Pastor Emeritus; Robert E. Butler, S.J.
Res., 2510 S. Fremont Ave., 91803. Tel: 626-284-8333; Fax: 626-282-4459.
School—Tel: 626-284-5778; Fax: 626-284-3303.
Lay Teachers 12; Students 286.
Catechesis/Religious Programs—Tel: 626-457-5302.
Students 230.

Altadena, Los Angeles Co., St. Elizabeth of Hungary (1918), Revs. Edwin C. Duyshart; Humberto Bernabe; Bernard J. Jennings, (Retired).
Office: 1879 N. Lake Ave., 91001.
Res., 1849 N. Lake Ave., 91001. Tel: 626-797-1167; Fax: 626-797-9245.
School—Tel: 626-797-7727; Fax: 626-797-6541.
Lay Teachers 15; Students 300.
Catechesis/Religious Programs—Students 280.

Sacred Heart (1935), Rev. Jerome L. Schmit.
Church—2889 N. Lincoln Ave., 91001. Tel: 626-794-2046; Fax: 626-794-8315.
Catechesis/Religious Programs—Tel: 626-798-6961.
Students 550.

Arcadia, Los Angeles Co., Annunciation (1948), Rev. Eugene Herbert; Deacon Gilbert Chavez. In res., Rev. Msgr. Roland G. Zimmerman, (Retired), Pastor Emeritus; Revs. Ramon Marti, Sch.P.; Michael Callahan, M.M., (Retired).
Church Office & Mailing Address—2701 S. Peck Rd., Monrovia, 91016. Tel: 626-447-6202; Fax: 626-447-9834.
Res., 1307 E. Longden Ave., 91006.
School—(Grades K-8). Tel: 626-447-8262; Fax: 626-447-3841.
Lay Teachers 14; Students 285.
Catechesis/Religious Programs—Tel: 626-446-1625. Mrs. Patricia Taylor, D.R.E.
Students 179.

Holy Angels (1935), Rev. Msgr. Norman F. Priebe; Rev. Msgr. Robert Walsh, Pastor Emeritus; Rev. Olin W. Mayfield; Deacon Arnaldo Lopez.
Res., 370 Campus Dr., 91007. Tel: 626-447-1671; Fax: 626-447-7617.
School—360 Campus Dr., 91007. Tel: 626-447-6312; Fax: 626-447-2843.
Lay Teachers 16; Students 318.
Catechesis/Religious Programs—Tel: 626-445-2967.
Students 400.

Artesia, Los Angeles Co., Holy Family (1931), Rev. Msgr. Loreto Gonzales; Rev. Rolly P. Jardiniano; Deacon Guadalupe Mejia.
Res., 18708 S. Clarkdale Ave., 90701. Tel: 562-865-2185; Fax: 562-860-0718.
School—Our Lady of Fatima, 18626 S. Clarkdale Ave., 90701. Tel: 562-865-1621; Fax: 562-860-1091.
Lay Teachers 13; Students 290.
Catechesis/Religious Programs—Tel: 310-860-5973.
Students 1,029.

Avalon, Los Angeles Co., St. Catherine of Alexandria (1902), Rev. Paul Alcuin Siebenand.
Res., Box 735, 90704. Tel: 310-510-0192; Fax: 310-510-8360.
Catechesis/Religious Programs—Students 135.

Azusa, Los Angeles Co., St. Frances of Rome (1908) (Hispanic), Revs. David F. Granadino; Michael Sears; Rogue Fernandes.
Res., 501 E. Foothill Blvd., P.O. Box 637, 91702. Tel: 626-969-1829; Fax: 626-815-2755. [CEM]
School—734 N. Pasadena Ave., 91702. Tel: 626-334-2018; Fax: 626-815-2760.
Lay Teachers 10; Students 285.
Catechesis/Religious Programs—508 N. Soldano, 91702. Tel: 626-334-3500.
Students 1,035.

Baldwin Park, Los Angeles Co., St. John the Baptist (1946) (Hispanic-Filipino), Revs. James R. Forsen; Mario De La Torre (Mexico); Miguel Java (Philippines); Jose A. Ortiz (Salvador).
Res., 3848 Stewart Ave., 91706. Tel: 626-960-2795; Fax: 626-960-5085.
School—3870 Stewart Ave., 91706. Tel: 626-337-1421; Fax: 626-337-3733.
Sisters of the Love of God 4; Lay Teachers 14; Students 559.
Catechesis/Religious Programs—Tel: 626-962-1004.
Students 827.
Convent—3963 Baldwin Park Blvd., 91706. Tel: 626-337-0527.

Bellflower, Los Angeles Co., St. Bernard (1923), Revs. Thomas F. Feltz; Philip J. McGrath, Pastor Emeritus; Daniel Fox.
Res., 9647 E. Beach St., Box 576, 90706. Tel: 310-867-2337; Fax: 310-867-4863.
School—9626 Park St., 90706. Tel: 310-867-9410; Fax: 310-866-2310. Mrs. Claudia Roach, Prin.
Lay Teachers 11; Students 299.

Catechesis/Religious Programs—Tel: 310-925-9886.
Students 442.

St. Dominic Savio (1954), Revs. Gael Sullivan, S.D.B.; Ramon Zarati, S.D.B.
Res., 9720 Foster Rd., 90706. Tel: 562-920-7796; Fax: 562-920-0149.
School—9750 Foster Rd., 90706. Tel: 562-866-3617; Fax: 562-804-6738.
Salesian Sisters of St. John Bosco 4; Lay Teachers 10; Students 391.
Catechesis/Religious Programs—Tel: 562-920-7796, Ext. 317.
Students 951.

Bell Gardens, Los Angeles Co., St. Gertrude (1938) (Hispanic), Rev. Msgr. Henry Gomez; Rev. Jose Luis Ruiz (Guadalajara). In res., Deacon Chris Vega.
Res., 7025 Garfield Ave., 90201. Tel: 562-927-4495; Fax: 562-927-5826.
School—6824 Toler Ave., 90201. Tel: 562-927-1216.
Salesian Sisters of St. John Bosco 3; Lay Teachers 9; Students 304.
Catechesis/Religious Programs—Tel: 562-927-3185.
Students 1,390.

Beverly Hills, Los Angeles Co., Good Shepherd (1924), Rev. Colm O'Ryan. In res., Rev. George O'Brien.
Res., 505 N. Bedford Dr., 90210. Tel: 310-285-5425; Fax: 310-285-5433.
School—Tel: 310-275-8601; Fax: 310-275-0366. Sr. Mary Elena Lopez, C.S.J., Prin.
Sisters 1; Lay Teachers 9; Students 257.
Catechesis/Religious Programs—Students 72.

Burbank, Los Angeles Co., St. Robert Bellarmine (1907), Rev. Msgr. Patrick Reilly; Rev. Msgr. Peter C. Healy; Rev. David Whorton.
Res., 133 N. Fifth St., 91501. Tel: 818-846-3443; Fax: 818-954-9441.
Church—Fifth St. and E. Orange Grove Ave., 91501.
School—154 N. Fifth St., 91501. Tel: 818-842-5033; Fax: 818-842-9789.
Sisters of Charity of the Blessed Virgin Mary 1; Lay Teachers 10; Students 333.
Catechesis/Religious Programs—Tel: 818-845-3521; Fax: 818-842-3246.
Students 435.

St. Finbar (1938), Revs. Jose R. Holguin; Thomas Cook; John Hoa Nguyen.
Res., 2010 W. Olive Ave., 91506. Tel: 818-846-6251; Fax: 818-846-1703.
School—2120 W. Olive Ave., 91506. Tel: 818-848-0191; Fax: 818-848-4315.
Lay Teachers 15; Students 275.
Catechesis/Religious Programs—Tel: 818-846-8715.
Students 939.

St. Francis Xavier (1954), Rev. Richard Albarano. In res., Rev. John Murray.
Res., 3801 Scott Rd., 91504. Tel: 818-767-2445; Fax: 818-767-5096.
School—Tel: 818-767-2071, Ext. Z; Fax: 818-767-2661.
Lay Teachers 12; Students 314.
Catechesis/Religious Programs—Tel: 818-767-7000. Lee Jolly, D.R.E.
Students 160.

Camarillo, Ventura Co., Blessed Junipero Serra (1988). Liturgies celebrated at: Padre Serra Parish, 5205 Upland Rd., Camarilla, CA 93012. Rev. Jarlath Dolan; Deacons John Picard; Ludger Gueringer; John Mecozzi.
Office and Mailing Address: 5205 Upland Rd., 93012. Tel: 805-482-6417; Fax: 805-987-8100.
Res., 5104 Hillridge Dr., 93012.
Catechesis/Religious Programs—Students 548.

St. Mary Magdalen (1940), Rev. James Stehly; Rev. Msgr. John C. Hughes, Pastor Emeritus; Rev. Steven Guitron; Deacons George Bednar; Johnnie Hammonds; Larry Modugno.
Res., 2532 Ventura Blvd., 93010. Tel: 805-484-0532; Fax: 805-987-2941.
School—2534 Ventura Blvd., 93010. Tel: 805-482-2611; Fax: 805-987-8211.
Lay Teachers 15; Students 300.
Catechesis/Religious Programs—Tel: 805-987-2941.
Students 650.

Canoga Park, Los Angeles Co., Our Lady of the Valley (1921), Revs. Alden J. Sison; Samuel Rendon; Sr. Estela del Bando, M.I.C. (Canada).
Pastoral Center—22021 Gault St., 91303-1804. Tel: 818-592-2880; Fax: 818-592-0299.
School—Tel: 818-592-2894; Fax: 818-592-2896.
Lay Teachers 9; Students 282.
Catechesis/Religious Programs—Tel: 818-592-2892.
Students 550.

St. Joseph the Worker (1956) (Hispanic-Vietnamese), Revs. James C. Gehl; Rodel Balagtas; Huy Nguyen; Raymonde Bennett, Admin.
Res., 19850 Cantlay St., 91306. Tel: 818-341-6634; Fax: 818-341-3875.
Parish Center—19808 Cantlay St., 91306.
School—19812 Cantlay St., 91306. Tel: 818-341-6616. Sr. Eva Bryan, R.S.C., Prin.
Lay Teachers 15; Students 342.
Catechesis/Religious Programs—Tel: 818-998-4166. Elizabeth Mattera Hise, D.R.E.
Students 696.

Carpinteria, Santa Barbara Co., St. Joseph (1933), Rev. Jose Blanco; Rev. Msgr. Joseph V. Kearney, Pastor Emeritus. In res., Rev. Melchor B. Bernal, S.V.D.
Mailing Address: 5084 El Carro Lane, 93013. Tel: 805-684-2181; Fax: 805-684-0534.
Catechesis/Religious Programs—Tel: 805-684-2210.
Students 305.

Carson, Los Angeles Co., St. Philomena (1956) (Philipino), Revs. Demetrio Bugayong; Owen de Souza; Joseph Dass. In res., Rev. Cesar Raffo (Peru).
Res., 21900 S. Main St., 90745. Tel: 310-835-7161; Fax: 310-830-5494. [CEM]
School—Tel: 310-835-4827; Fax: 310-835-1655.
Carmelite Sisters 7; Lay Teachers 16; Students 314.
Catechesis/Religious Programs—Tel: 310-830-6180; Fax: 310-830-6287.
Students 1,386.
Convent—21832 1/2 S. Main St., 90745. Tel: 310-834-9180.

Chatsworth, Los Angeles Co., St. John Eudes (1963), Rev. Robert J. McNamara; Deacon Chet Holly, Admin.
Res., 10001 Mason Ave., 91311.
Church—9901 Mason Ave., 91311. Tel: 818-341-3680; Fax: 818-882-4326.
School—Tel: 818-341-1454; Fax: 818-341-3093.
Sisters of the Pious Schools 3; Lay Teachers 12; Students 336.
Catechesis/Religious Programs—9925 Mason Ave., Chatsworth, 91311. Tel: 818-700-5142; Fax: 818-700-5142.
Students 763.

Claremont, Los Angeles Co., Our Lady of the Assumption (1947), Revs. Thomas Welbers; John Nghi Tran; Anthony Sangwook Lee; Christopher Offor (Nigeria).
Res., 435 Berkeley Ave., 91711. Tel: 909-626-3596; Fax: 909-624-3680.
School—Tel: 909-626-7135; Fax: 909-398-1395.
Lay Teachers 21; Students 495.
Catechesis/Religious Programs—Tel: 909-624-1360.
Students 990.

Compton, Los Angeles Co., Our Lady of Victory (1920) (Hispanic-African American), Revs. Stan Bosch, S.T.; Jose Luis Reyes, S.T.; Kent Weidie, S.T.
Res., 519 E. Palmer Ave., 90221. Tel: 310-631-3233; Fax: 310-886-5681.
School—Tel: 310-631-1320; Fax: 310-631-4280.
Catechesis/Religious Programs—Tel: 310-631-1831.
Students 595.

Sagrado Corazon, Sacred Heart (1956) (Hispanic), Revs. Stan Bosch, S.T.; Jose Luis Reyes, S.T.; Kent Weidie, S.T.
Res., 1720 North Culver Ave., 90222. Tel: 310-635-5436; Fax: 310-635-2121.
Catechesis/Religious Programs—Tel: 310-635-8483.
Students 600.

St. Albert the Great (1949) (Hispanic-African American), Revs. Richard Hoynes; Tulio Maya; Deacons Joseph H. Ledoux; Frank Millholland.
Res., 804 E. Compton Blvd., 90220. Tel: 323-321-0240; 310-329-7548; Fax: 310-329-8462.
School—Tel: 325-770-0984; 310-323-4559; Fax: 310-323-4825.
Sisters of the Holy Family 3; Lay Teachers 17; Students 650.
Catechesis/Religious Programs—Tel: 310-327-4199. Arturo Gallardo, D.R.E.
Students 385.

Covina, Los Angeles Co., Sacred Heart (1927), Revs. Brian Cavanagh; Mario Pacheco; Deacon Ralph Fry.
Res., 314 W. Workman St., 91723. Tel: 626-332-3570; Fax: 626-967-4884.
School—360 W. Workman St., 91723. Tel: 626-332-7222; Fax: 626-967-8836.
Religious 1; Lay Teachers 12; Students 315.
Catechesis/Religious Programs—Tel: 626-331-7914.
Students 665.

St. Louise de Marillac (1963), Rev. Msgr. Robert T. Pierce; Rev. Dennis Marrell. In res., Rev. Mark Yina, M.S.P.
Mailing Address: 1720 E. Covina Blvd., 91724.
Res., 1770 E. Covina Blvd., 91724. Tel: 626-915-7873; Fax: 626-332-4431.
School—Tel: 626-966-2317.
Lay Teachers 11; Students 309.
Catechesis/Religious Programs—Tel: 626-332-5822.
Students 590.

Cudahy, Sagrado Corazon y Santa Maria de Guadalupe (1991) (Hispanic), Revs. Salvador M. Villarruel, M.S.C.; Jorge Luis de la Torre, M.S.C.
4235 Clara St., 90201. Tel: 323-562-3356.
Catechesis/Religious Programs—Students 550.

Culver City, Los Angeles Co., St. Augustine (1919), Rev. Alfred S. Burnham; Rev. Msgr. Ian E. Holland, Pastor Emeritus; Revs. Anthony J. Gomez; Martin Slaughter; Deacon Rafael Victorin. In res., Rev. Charles Ufomadu (Nigeria).
Res., 3850 Jasmine Ave., 90232. Tel: 310-838-2477; Fax: 310-838-3070.
School—Tel: 310-838-3144; Fax: 310-838-7479.
Daughters of Mary and Joseph 1; Lay Teachers 16; Students 322.
Catechesis/Religious Programs—Tel: 310-836-6561.
Students 836.

Diamond Bar, Los Angeles Co., St. Denis (1971), Rev. Msgr. James J. Loughnane; Revs. James J. Kelly; Ikechukuu "I.K." Ikeocha (Nigeria); Deacon Tom Le Donne. In res., Rev. Donald W. Potthoff, Pastor Emeritus.
Res., 2151 S. Diamond Bar Blvd., 91765-2981. Tel: 909-861-7106; Fax: 909-861-2697.
Catechesis/Religious Programs—Tel: 909-861-8018.
Students 1,200.

Downey, Los Angeles Co., Our Lady of Perpetual Help (1911), Rev. John Moloney; Deacons Charles Denisac; Richard Medina; Carlos Origel.
Res., 10727 S. Downey Ave., P.O. Box 280, 90241. Tel: 562-923-3246; Fax: 562-862-7020.
School—10441 S. Downey Ave., 90241. Tel: 562-869-9969; Fax: 562-923-0659.
Lay Teachers 13; Students 274.
Catechesis/Religious Programs—Tel: 562-862-7268. Theresa Nicholas, D.R.E.
Students 580.

St. Raymond (1956), Revs. Thomas O'Hanlon; Roberto Jaranilla, Jr.; Deacon Ralph Riera. In res., Rev. Msgr. John A. Fosselman.
Res., 12348 Paramount Blvd., 90242. Tel: 562-923-4509; Fax: 562-869-3359.
School—Tel: 562-862-3210; Fax: 562-862-6328.
Sisters of Holy Faith 4; Lay Teachers 10; Students 333.
Catechesis/Religious Programs—Tel: 562-862-6959. Sr. Nancy Hale, C.H.F., D.R.E.
Students 399.
Missions—Downey, Los Angeles Co., Rancho Los Amigos Hospital, 7601 Imperial Hwy., 90242. Tel: 562-401-7111; Downey, Los Angeles Co., Los Padrinos Juvenile Hall, 7285 Quill Dr., 90242. Tel: 562-940-8711.

El Monte, Los Angeles Co., Nativity (1923), Revs. Pedro J. Lopez; Leo W. Alberg; John K. Vo (Vietnam).
Res., 3743 N. Tyler Ave., 91731. Tel: 626-444-2511; Fax: 626-443-1417.
School—10907 St. Louis Dr., 91731. Tel: 626-448-2414; Fax: 626-448-2763.
Sisters of St. Louis 5; Lay Teachers 8; Students 274.
Catechesis/Religious Programs—Tel: 626-448-8895.
Students 557.

Our Lady of Guadalupe (1973) (Hispanic), Revs. Francisco Vitela; Jesus Castrillo, C.M.F. (Spain).
Res., 11359 Coffield Ave., 91731. Tel: 626-448-1795; Fax: 626-448-7137.
Catechesis/Religious Programs—Tel: 626-448-7131; Fax: 626-448-9507.
Students 700.

El Segundo, Los Angeles Co., St. Anthony (1925), Rev. James F. O'Grady; Deacon Theodore A. Goodreau. In res., Revs. Manuel J. Magallanes, O.S.B.; Gregory V. Nguyen.
Res., 710 E. Grand Ave., 90245. Tel: 310-322-4392; Fax: 310-322-0797.
School—233 Lomita St., 90245. Tel: 310-322-4218; Fax: 310-322-2659.
Sisters 2; Lay Teachers 10; Students 270.
Catechesis/Religious Programs—Tel: 310-615-0766.
Students 261.

St. Andrew (1936) (Russian-Greek Catholic), Rev. Alexei R. Smith.
Res., 538 Concord St., 90245. Tel: 310-322-1892; Fax: 310-322-1919.
Catechesis/Religious Programs—Students 4.

Encino, Los Angeles Co., Our Lady of Grace (1945), Revs. Austin C. Doran; John M. Kyebasuuta. In res., Rev. Msgr. Francis M. Osborne, Pastor Emeritus; Rev. Msgr. Craig A. Cox.
Res., 5011 White Oak Ave., 91316. Tel: 818-342-4686; Fax: 818-342-6579.
School—Tel: 818-344-4126; Fax: 818-344-1736.

Sisters 5; Lay Teachers 12; Students 323.
Catechesis/Religious Programs—Tel: 818-342-4505.
Students 313.

St. Cyril (1949), Rev. Msgr. Carl F. Bell; Rev. Msgr. Cyril Navin, Pastor Emeritus.
Res., 4601 Firmament Ave., 91436. Tel: 818-986-8234; Fax: 818-986-3310.
School—4548 Haskell Ave., 91436. Tel: 818-501-4155; Fax: 818-501-8480.
Lay Teachers 12; Students 311.
Catechesis/Religious Programs—Tel: 818-789-5947.
Students 77.

Fillmore, Ventura Co., St. Francis of Assisi (1926), Revs. Joseph Hernandez; George J. Punchekunnel (India).
Church—1048 West Ventura St., P.O. Box 757, 93016. Tel: 805-524-1306; Fax: 805-524-0784. [JC]
Catechesis/Religious Programs—Tel: 805-524-2865.
Students 550.
Mission—Piru, Ventura Co., San Salvador, 4039 E. Center St., P.O. Box 508, Piru, 93040. Tel: 805-521-1077; Fax: 805-521-1077.

Gardena, Los Angeles Co., St. Anthony of Padua (1910), Revs. Samuel Orellana; Honesto Bismonte.
Res., 1050 W. 163rd St., 90247. Tel: 310-327-5830; Fax: 310-327-6440.
School—1003 W. 163rd St., 90247. Tel: 310-329-7170; Fax: 310-329-9843.
Sisters of Providence of St. Mary-of-the-Woods 3; Lay Teachers 16; Students 254.
Catechesis/Religious Programs—Tel: 310-323-0860; Fax: 310-323-0860.
Students 675.
Convent—St. Gardena, 1050 W. 161 St., 90247. Tel: 213-321-3820.

Maria Regina (1956), Rev. Thomas M. Acton; Deacon Phuoc Van Nguyen. In res., Rev. Theodore C. Ley, S.M.
Res., 2150 W. 135th St., 90249. Tel: 310-323-0030; Fax: 310-323-8081. [CEM]
School—Tel: 310-327-9133; Fax: 310-327-2636.
Lay Teachers 9; Students 310.
Catechesis/Religious Programs—13510 S. VanNess Ave., 90249. Tel: 310-327-4999.
Students 415.

Glendale, Los Angeles Co., Holy Family (1907) (Hispanic-Filipino), Rev. Joseph Shea; Rev. Msgr. Arthur J. Lirette, P.A., Pastor Emeritus; Revs. Glenn N. Sequeira; Albert Bahhuth; Deacons Fred Pelletier; John Steele.
Res., 209 E. Lomita Ave., 91205. Tel: 818-247-2222; Fax: 818-247-4780.
School—(Grades K-8). Tel: 818-243-9239; Fax: 818-243-0976.
Sisters 1; Lay Teachers 9; Students 323.
High School—(Girls) 400 E. Lomita Ave., 91205. Tel: 818-241-3178; Fax: 818-241-7753.
Sisters 2; Lay Teachers 16; Students 280.
Catechesis/Religious Programs—400 S. Louise, 91205. Tel: 818-240-6551.
Students 475.

Church of the Incarnation (1927), Rev. Paul Hruby; Rev. Msgr. Eugene P. Frilot, Pastor Emeritus; Rev. Thomas Schweitzer; William Shaules, Pastoral Assoc.; Deacon Restie Noriega.
Res., 1001 N. Brand Blvd., 91202. Tel: 818-242-2579; Fax: 818-507-4976.
School—Tel: 818-241-2269.
Lay Teachers 9; Students 302.
Catechesis/Religious Programs—Tel: 818-241-7045.
Students 241.

Glendora, Los Angeles Co., St. Dorothy (1958), Rev. Msgr. John A. Acton, Pastor Emeritus; Rev. Msgr. Michael Meyers; Revs. Allan Roberts; Ikechukwu "I.K." Ikeocha.
Res., 241 S. Valley Center, 91741. Tel: 626-914-3941; Fax: 626-335-0059.
School—215 S. Valley Center, 91741. Tel: 626-335-0772.
Sisters 1; Lay Teachers 15; Students 306.
Catechesis/Religious Programs—Tel: 626-335-2811.
Students 800.

Goleta, Santa Barbara Co., St. Mark University Parish (1966), Revs. Edward C. Nowak, C.S.P.; Paul Respond, C.S.P.
Res., 6550 Picasso Rd., 93117. Tel: 805-968-1078; Fax: 805-968-3965.

Granada Hills, Los Angeles Co., St. John Baptist de la Salle (1953), Rev. Robert Milbauer; Rev. Msgr. Emmanuel G. Manahan; Rev. Msgr. Peter O'Sullivan, Pastor Emeritus; Deacon Samuel Frias.
Res., 10738 Hayvenhurst Ave., 91344. Tel: 818-363-2535; Fax: 818-360-7407.
School—Tel: 818-363-2270; Fax: 818-832-8950.
Lay Teachers 22; Students 602.
Catechesis/Religious Programs—Tel: 818-368-1514.
Students 665.

St. Euphrasia (1963), Revs. Michael Wakefield; Raymond Saplis, Pastor Emeritus; Deacon Joseph Orth.
Res., 11766 Shoshone Ave., 91344. Tel: 818-360-4611; Fax: 818-360-2755.
School—Tel: 818-363-5515; Fax: 818-832-6678.
Lay Teachers 10; Students 300.
Catechesis/Religious Programs—Tel: 818-368-4512.
Students 126.

Guadalupe, Santa Barbara Co., Our Lady of Guadalupe (1867) (Hispanic), Rev. Abel Suquilvide.
Res., 1164 Obispo St., P.O. Box 897, 93434. Tel: 805-343-2181; Fax: 805-343-6642. [JC]
Catechesis/Religious Programs—Tel: 805-343-4404.
Students 269.

Hacienda Heights, Los Angeles Co., St. John Vianney (1965), Rev. Msgr. John T. Kane; Revs. Myles Roban, S.S.C.; Lloyd Ukaegbu; Rev. Msgr. James A. O'Callaghan, Pastor Emeritus; Deacons Eduardo Delgado; Jesse Martinez; Richard Noon. In res., Rev. Dave Gallardo.
Res., 1345 Turnbull Canyon Rd., 91745. Tel: 626-330-2269; Fax: 626-330-0220.
Catechesis/Religious Programs—Students 800.

Hawaiian Gardens, Los Angeles Co., St. Peter Chanel (1986) (Mexican-Filipino), Revs. Lawrence T. Darnell, O.M.V.; Edward Broom, O.M.V.; Gregory Staab, O.M.V.; John Lyons, O.M.V.
Res., 21611 Juan Ave., 90716-1117. Tel: 562-924-7591; Fax: 562-402-9411.
Church—12001 E. 214 St., 90716-1117.
Catechesis/Religious Programs—Tel: 562-860-3637.
Students 1,510.

Hawthorne, Los Angeles Co., St. Joseph (1915), Revs. Perry D. Leiker; Eugene Buhr; Enrique de los Rios; Raymond Perez.
Res., 11901 Acacia Ave., 90250. Tel: 310-679-1139; Fax: 310-679-3034.
School—11886 Acacia Ave., 90250. Tel: 310-679-1014; Fax: 310-679-1310.
Lay Teachers 20; Students 556.
Catechesis/Religious Programs—Tel: 310-679-1139, Ext. 113.
Students 1,071.

Hermosa Beach, Los Angeles Co., Our Lady of Guadalupe (1927), Revs. Gary Klauer, O.F.M.Conv.; Emil Robu, O.F.M.; Arthur Gamboa, O.F.M.Conv.
Res., 320 Massey Ave., 90254. Tel: 310-372-7077; Fax: 310-798-4051.
School—340 Massey Ave., 90254. Tel: 310-372-7486. Mrs. Cheryl Hunt, Prin.
Lay Teachers 15; Students 250.
Catechesis/Religious Programs—Tel: 310-374-4649.
Students 127.

Huntington Park, Los Angeles Co., St. Martha (1913) (Hispanic), Revs. Ricardo de Alba, M.Sp.S.; Celso Marquez, M.Sp.S.; Roberto Saldivar, M.Sp.S.; Bro. Santos Mendoza, M.Sp.S.
Res., 6019 Stafford Ave., 90255. Tel: 323-585-5776; Fax: 323-585-4560.
Catechesis/Religious Programs—Tel: 323-583-3678; 323-585-4941 (Confirmation).
Students 950.

St. Matthias (1913) (Latino), Revs. Abelardo Bailon; Jorge I. Vasquez. In res., Revs. Samuel C. Villegas; Rody I. Gorman.
Res., 7125 Mission Pl., 90255. Tel: 323-588-2134; Fax: 323-588-4519.
School—Tel: 323-588-7253; Fax: 323-588-1136.
Sisters 2; Lay Teachers 10; Students 328.
Catechesis/Religious Programs—7105 Mission Pl., 90255. Tel: 323-277-1188; Fax: 323-277-1192.
Students 1,390.

Inglewood, Los Angeles Co., St. John Chrysostom (1923) (Hispanic), Revs. Stephen Woodland; Javier Altuna, S.J.; Luciano Kamienski, S.D.B.; Deacon Roberto Vasquez.
Res., 546 E. Florence Ave., 90301. Tel: 310-677-2736; Fax: 310-677-0584.
School—Tel: 310-677-5868; Fax: 310-677-3429.
Sisters of St. Joseph of Carondelet 6; Lay Teachers 9; Students 277.
Catechesis/Religious Programs—Tel: 310-674-3733.
Students 650.

Irwindale, Los Angeles Co., Our Lady of Guadalupe (1964), Rev. Joseph Canna.
Res., 16025 Cypress St., 91706. Tel: 626-962-3649; Fax: 626-337-3318.
Catechesis/Religious Programs—Tel: 626-960-1310.
Students 723.

La Canada Flintridge, Los Angeles Co., St. Bede the Venerable (1951), Rev. Msgr. Francis T. Wallace; Rev. Msgr. Leland J. Boyer, Pastor Emeritus; Rev. Lawrence Signey; Sr. Kathleen McDonough, S.N.J.M, Pastoral Assoc.
Res., 215 Foothill Blvd., 91011. Tel: 818-790-5155; Fax: 818-790-9520.
School—(Grades K-8) 217 Foothill Blvd., 91011. Tel: 818-790-7884; Fax: 818-790-7887.
Lay Teachers 16; Students 281.
Catechesis/Religious Programs—Tel: 818-790-5094. D.R.E.: Sr. Margaret Marso, B.V.M.; Marian Macho.
Students 490.

La Crescenta, Los Angeles Co., St. James the Less (1955), Rev. Msgr. Robert W. Gipson; Rev. Robert Maechler; Deacon Joe Hegenbart.
Res., 4625 Dunsmore Ave., 91214. Tel: 818-248-3442; Fax: 818-248-9332.
School—4635 Dunsmore Ave., 91214. Tel: 818-248-7778; Fax: 818-248-5242.
Sisters 1; Lay Teachers 12; Students 270.
Catechesis/Religious Programs—Tel: 818-541-1750.
Students 200.

La Mirada, Los Angeles Co., Beatitudes of Our Lord (1964), Revs. Anthony J. Page; Emile Belletty.
Res., 13013 S. Santa Gertrudes Ave., 90638. Tel: 562-943-1521; Fax: 562-902-7627.
School—Tel: 562-943-3218.
Lay Teachers 12; Students 300.
Catechesis/Religious Programs—Tel: 562-943-5678; Fax: 562-943-9419.
Students 485.

St. Paul of the Cross (1956), Revs. Patrick J. Gannon; Emile Belletty; Deacon Arthur Fitzpatrick.
Res., 14020 Foster Rd., 90638. Tel: 562-921-2914; Fax: 562-926-1514.
School—14030 Foster Rd., 90638. Tel: 562-921-2118; Fax: 562-802-2048.
Lay Teachers 14; Students 295.
Catechesis/Religious Programs—Tel: 562-921-4911.
Students 360.

La Puente, Los Angeles Co., St. Joseph (1919), Rev. Msgr. Patrick J. Staunton; Rev. Matthew T. Cumberland; Deacon Ruben Guerra. In res., Rev. Eric A. Lewis.
Res., 550 N. Glendora Ave., 91744. Tel: 626-336-2001; Fax: 626-336-6010.
School—551 N. Glendora Ave., 91744. Tel: 626-336-2821; Fax: 626-369-8921.
Carmelite Sisters 6; Lay Teachers 6; Students 261.
Catechesis/Religious Programs—15650 E. Temple Ave., 91744. Tel: 626-336-1191.
Students 470.

St. Louis of France (1955), Revs. Lorenzo Miranda; Cesar A. Fernandez; Deacon Oscar Valeriano, Jr. In res., Rev. Msgr. James R. Mulcahy, Pastor Emeritus.
Res., 13935 E. Temple, 91746-2098. Tel: 626-918-8314; Fax: 626-917-8413.
School—Tel: 626-918-6210; Fax: 626-918-9549.
Sisters of St. Louis 1; Lay Teachers 13; Students 315.
Catechesis/Religious Programs—Tel: 626-918-7002.
Students 1,203.

Lakewood, St. Pancratius (1953), Rev. Msgr. Ronald E. Royer; Rev. Mark A. Warnstedt.
Res., 3519 St. Pancratius Pl., 90712. Tel: 562-634-6111; Fax: 562-634-7817.
School—3601 St. Pancratius Pl., 90712. Tel: 562-634-6310; Fax: 562-633-0731.
Lay Teachers 9; Students 304.
Catechesis/Religious Programs—Tel: 562-634-1611; Fax: 562-634-2524.
Students 350.

Lancaster, Los Angeles Co., Blessed Junipero Serra (Quartz Hill) (1987), Rev. Ernest Candelaria, C.S.J. In res., Revs. Mariano Biasio, C.S.J.; Joseph Scalco, C.S.J.; Mark Withers, C.S.J.; Deacon Edward Caputo.
Res., 6122 W. Azalea Dr., 93536-3767. Tel: 666-943-4933; Fax: 661-943-6863.
Office: 42121 60th St. W., 93536-3767. Tel: 805-943-9314; Fax: 805-943-6863.
Catechesis/Religious Programs—Tel: 661-943-9314.
Students 780.
Mission—Lancaster, Los Angeles Co., St. Elizabeth, P.O. Box 3307, 93586-0307.

Sacred Heart (1886), Revs. John J. Vogel; Maurice D. Harrigan.
Res., 45007 N. Cedar Ave., 93534. Tel: 661-942-7122; Fax: 661-945-4255.
School—45002 N. Date Ave., 93534. Tel: 661-948-3613; Fax: 661-945-4235.
Lay Teachers 14; Students 324.
Catechesis/Religious Programs—45027 N. Cedar Ave., 93534. Tel: 661-948-3011; Fax: 661-948-2697.
Students 693.

Lomita, Los Angeles Co., St. Margaret Mary Alacoque (1937), Rev. Msgr. Patrick Thompson; Revs. Gerard O'Brien; Marco T. Solis; Deacons Dick Corwin; Craig Siegman.
Res., 25429 Eshelman Ave., 90717. Tel: 310-326-3364; Fax: 310-539-1570.
Parish Center—25511 Eshelman Ave., 90717.
Church—25505 Eshelman Ave., 90717.
School—(Grades K-8) 25515 Eshelman Ave., 90717. Tel: 310-326-9494.
Lay Teachers 12; Students 318.
Catechesis/Religious Programs—Tel: 310-326-3364, Ext. 11.
Students 870.

Lompoc, Santa Barbara Co., La Purisima Concepcion (1787), Rev. Msgr. Andrew McGrath, Pastor Emeritus; Rev. Richard Vega; Deacons John Burke; Charles Hays; Don Francisco Lopez; Darrell Meter.
Res., 213 W. Olive Ave., 93436. Tel: 805-735-3068; Fax: 805-735-7649.
School—219 W. Olive Ave., 93436. Tel: 805-736-6210; Fax: 805-735-7649.
Lay Teachers 9; Students 250.
Catechesis/Religious Programs—Tel: 805-735-3068.
Students 550.

Our Lady Queen of Angels (1972), Rev. John G. Fitzgerald.
Res., 3495 Rucker Rd., 93436. Tel: 805-733-2735; Fax: 805-733-1235.
Catechesis/Religious Programs—Tel: 805-733-3155.
Students 310.

Long Beach, Los Angeles Co.,

1—St. Anthony, (1902), Rev. Richard Krekelberg; Rev. Msgr. Ernest J. Gualderon, Pastor Emeritus; Rev. Freddie Chua.
Mailing Address: 600 Olive Ave., 90802.
Res., 540 Olive Ave., 90802. Tel: 562-590-9229; Fax: 562-590-9048.
School—855 E. 5th St., 90802. Tel: 562-432-5946; Fax: 562-435-8606.
Students 298.
High School—620 Olive Ave., 90802. Tel: 562-432-4496; Fax: 562-437-3055.
Sisters 4; Lay Teachers 12; Students 338.
Catechesis/Religious Programs—Tel: 562-590-9229, Ext. 34.
Students 455.
Mission—Long Beach, Los Angeles Co., Our Lady of Mt. Carmel Cambodian Catholic Center, 1851 Cerritos Ave., 90806. Tel: 562-591-8477; Fax: 562-591-5367.

2—St. Athanasius, (1933), Revs. William McLean; John C. Gutting, Pastor Emeritus.
Res., 5390 Linden Ave., 90805. Tel: 562-423-7986; Fax: 562-422-0306.
School—5369 Linden Ave., 90805. Tel: 562-428-7422.
St. Francis Mission Community 4; Lay Teachers 7; Students 245.
Catechesis/Religious Programs—Tel: 562-428-3494.
Students 850.

3—St. Barnabas, (1939), Rev. Msgr. John P. Twomey; Rev. Lawrence Seyer; Rev. Msgr. Christopher J. Kennedy, Pastor Emeritus; Sr. Bernice Jordan, C.S.J., Pastoral Assoc.; Deacon Alden Bohlig.
Res., 3955 Orange Ave., 90807. Tel: 562-424-8595; Fax: 562-595-7875.
School—(Grades K-8). Tel: 562-424-7476; Fax: 562-981-3351.
Lay Teachers 13; Students 285.
Catechesis/Religious Programs—Tel: 562-988-6855; Fax: 562-981-8792.
Students 460.

4—St. Bartholomew, (1937), Revs. Jerome C. Elder; Edward G. Fremgen. In res., Rev. Msgr. Peter C. Caslin, Pastor Emeritus.
Res., 252 Granada Ave., 90803. Tel: 562-438-3826; Fax: 562-438-2227.
Catechesis/Religious Programs—Tel: 562-439-1802.
Students 257.

5—St. Cornelius, (1951), Rev. Michael Reardon; Rev. Msgr. John Folliard, Pastor Emeritus; Deacon Alexander Lipski.
Res., 5500 Wardlow Rd., 90808. Tel: 562-421-8966; Fax: 562-421-5096.
School—3330 Bellflower Blvd., 90808. Tel: 562-425-7813; Fax: 562-425-2743.
Lay Teachers 9; Students 332.
Catechesis/Religious Programs—Tel: 562-420-7613; Fax: 562-420-7613.
Students 254.

6—St. Cyprian, (1945), Rev. Peter Foran.
Res., 4714 Clark Ave., 90808. Tel: 562-421-9487; Fax: 562-496-1024.
School—5133 Arbor Rd., 90808. Tel: 562-425-7341.
Sisters of St. Louis (Monaghan) 1; Lay Teachers 9; Students 301.
Catechesis/Religious Programs—Tel: 562-420-6885.
Students 542.

7—Holy Innocents, (1923) (Spanish-Asian), Revs. Antonio P. Astudillo; Moises Apolinar.
Res., 425 E. 20th St., 90806. Tel: 562-591-6924; Fax: 562-591-2164.
School—2500 Pacific Ave., 90806. Tel: 562-424-1018; Fax: 562-424-4126.
Carmelite Sisters of the Most Sacred Heart 3; Lay Teachers 7; Students 324.
Catechesis/Religious Programs—Tel: 562-427-8449; Fax: 562-424-3270.
Students 817.

8—St. Joseph, (1955), Rev. Michael W. Meyer. In res., Rev. Harold L. Ford.
Res., 6220 E. Willow St., 90815. Tel: 562-594-4657; Fax: 562-431-7424.
School—6200 E. Willow St., 90815. Tel: 562-596-6115; Fax: 562-596-6725.
Lay Teachers 14; Students 301.
Catechesis/Religious Programs—Tel: 562-598-0519.
Students 262.

9—St. Lucy, (1944), Revs. Michael Roebert; Francis T. Bui; Deacon Carlito de los Reyes.
Res., 2344 Cota Ave., 90810. Tel: 562-424-9051; Fax: 562-988-0376.
School—2320 Cota Ave., 90810. Tel: 562-424-9062; Fax: 562-424-8572.
Lay Teachers 13; Students 300.
Catechesis/Religious Programs—Tel: 562-997-0511.
Students 280.

10—St. Maria Goretti, (1955), Rev. Msgr. Douglas Wm. Saunders, V.F. In res., Rev. Anslem Deehr, S.T.
Res., 3954 Palo Verde Ave., 90808-2298. Tel: 562-425-7459; Fax: 562-421-0475.
School—Tel: 562-425-5112; Fax: 562-425-5672.
Lay Teachers 14; Students 300.
Catechesis/Religious Programs—3950 Palo Verde Ave., 90808-2298. Tel: 562-420-1321.
Students 161.

11—St. Matthew, (1920), Revs. Gerald Meisel; Guillermo Rodriguez (El Salvador).
Res., 672 Temple Ave., 90814. Tel: 562-439-0931; Fax: 562-434-7621.
Catechesis/Religious Programs—Tel: 562-434-6402; Fax: 562-434-7621.
Students 500.

12—Our Lady of Refuge, (1948), Rev. Msgr. William J. O'Keeffe. In res., Revs. Alfonso Scott; Ernest Montoya; Deacon Witold Engel.
Res., 5195 Stearns St., 90815. Tel: 562-498-6641; Fax: 562-498-3344.
School—5210 Los Coyotes Diagonal, 90815. Tel: 562-597-0819; Fax: 562-597-1419.
Lay Teachers 12; Students 266.
Catechesis/Religious Programs—Tel: 562-597-3102; Fax: 562-494-4381.
Students 283.

Los Nietos, Los Angeles Co., Our Lady of Perpetual Help (1958), Revs. John S. Woolway; Josef Draugialis.
Res., 8545 S. Norwalk Blvd., 90606. Tel: 562-692-3758; Fax: 562-695-4068.
Catechesis/Religious Programs—Tel: 562-463-3389.
Students 1,150.

Lynwood, Los Angeles Co., St. Emydius (1924), Rev. Msgr. Dennis O'Neil; Revs. David Ochoa (Mexico); Luis Garcia (Mexico); John C. O'Connor.
Res., 10900 California Ave., P.O. Box 100, 90262-2094. Tel: 310-637-7095; Fax: 310-637-3319.
School—10990 California Ave., 90262. Tel: 310-635-7184; Fax: 310-605-3041.
Sisters of the Holy Faith 3; Lay Teachers 21; Students 610.
Catechesis/Religious Programs—Tel: 310-639-1249.
Students 2,640.
Convent—10950 California Ave., 90262. Tel: 310-635-3264.
Missionaries of Charity 6.

St. Philip Neri (1948) (Hispanic), Rev. Joseph G. Sanchez; Deacon Joe T. Battle Tel: 310-632-4745.
Res., 4311 Olanda St., 90262. Tel: 310-632-7179; Fax: 310-632-5119.
Pastoral Center—12435 Cookacre Ave., 90262.
School—12522 Stoneacre Ave., 90262. Tel: 310-638-0341; Fax: 310-638-9805.
Lay Teachers 9; Students 322.
Catechesis/Religious Programs—Tel: 310-632-3698.
Students 958.

Malibu, Los Angeles Co., Our Lady of Malibu (1946), Rev. William F. Kerze; Rev. Msgr. John V. Sheridan, Pastor Emeritus.
Res., 3625 Winter Canyon Rd., 90265. Tel: 310-456-2361; Fax: 310-456-3942.
School—Tel: 310-456-8071; Fax: 310-456-7767.
Sisters of St. Louis 1; Lay Teachers 12; Students 195.
Catechesis/Religious Programs—Tel: 310-456-8813.
Students 210.

Manhattan Beach, Los Angeles Co., American Martyrs (1930), Rev. Msgr. John F. Barry; Rev. Michael J. Evans; Deacon Fred Rose.
Res., 624 15th St., P.O. Box 3639, 90266. Tel: 310-545-5651; Fax: 310-546-9209.
School—Tel: 310-545-8559; Fax: 310-546-7219.
Sisters 1; Lay Teachers 17; Students 486.
Catechesis/Religious Programs—1701 Laurel Ave., 90266. Tel: 310-546-4734.
Students 1,042.

Maywood, Los Angeles Co., St. Rose of Lima (1922) (Hispanic), Rev. Msgr. George Duran; Revs. Pedro Antonio Esteban; Edward Soto.
Res., 4450 E. 60th St., 90270. Tel: 213-560-2381; Fax: 213-560-8537.
School—4422 E. 60th St., 90270. Tel: 213-560-3376.
Sisters of Notre Dame 1; Lay Teachers 8; Students 250.
Catechesis/Religious Programs—Tel: 213-560-0187.
Students 1,187.

Mission Hills, Los Angeles Co., San Fernando Rey Mission (1797), Rev. Msgr. Francis J. Weber, Admin.; Deacon Heriberto Vega.
Res., 15151 San Fernando Mission Blvd., 91345. Tel: 818-361-0186; Fax: 818-361-3276.

Monrovia, Los Angeles Co., Immaculate Conception (1904), Revs. Charles J. Ramirez; Francis Cassidy; Deacon Fred Conrey.
Res., 740 S. Shamrock Ave., 91016. Tel: 626-358-1166; Fax: 626-358-6466.
School—726 S. Shamrock Ave., 91016. Tel: 626-358-5129; Fax: 626-358-3933.
Religious 1; Lay Teachers 10; Students 258.
Catechesis/Religious Programs—Tel: 626-357-3010; Fax: 626-357-5299.
Students 1,130.

Montebello, Los Angeles Co., St. Benedict (1906), Revs. Anthony Z. Palos, O.A.R.; James D. McGuire, O.A.R.; Ruben Rocha, O.A.R.; Bro. Anthony J. Torretti, O.A.R.; Deacons James Dillon; David J. Estrada.
Res., 1022 W. Cleveland Ave., 90640. Tel: 323-721-1184; Fax: 323-721-5075.
School—Tel: 323-721-3348; Fax: 323-721-8698. Ms. Patricia Cuesta, Prin.
Lay Teachers 21; Students 456.
Catechesis/Religious Programs—1009 W. Madison Ave., 90640. Tel: 323-722-6020, Ext. 10; Fax: 323-722-6006. Mrs. Helen Arvayo, D.R.E.
Students 650.

Our Lady of the Miraculous Medal (1950), Rev. Msgr. Juan Matas; Rev. John T. Collins; Deacons Joseph Spada; Fred Rios. In res., Rev. Brian Delaney.
Res., 820 N. Garfield Ave., 90640. Tel: 323-722-5866; Fax: 323-722-2654.
School—Tel: 323-728-5435; Fax: 323-728-8038.
Daughters of Charity of St. Vincent de Paul 3; Lay Teachers 21; Aides 6; Students 596.
Catechesis/Religious Programs—Tel: 213-725-6962; Fax: 323-722-2654. Carol Lazar, D.R.E.
Students 390.
Convent—840 N. Garfield Ave., 90640. Tel: 323-721-4321.

Montecito, Santa Barbara Co., Our Lady of Mount Carmel (1856), Rev. Maurice O'Mahony; Rev. Msgr. Sylvester O'Byrne, Pastor Emeritus; Rev. Carrol O'Sullivan, (Retired).
Res., 1300 E. Valley Rd., Santa Barbara, 93108. Tel: 805-969-6868; Fax: 805-565-5959.
School—530 Hot Springs Rd., 93108. Tel: 805-969-5965; Fax: 805-565-9841.
Lay Teachers 15; Students 240.
Catechesis/Religious Programs—Tel: 805-969-4868.
Students 166.

Monterey Park, Los Angeles Co., St. Stephen (1921), Rev. Lawrence E. Estrada. In res., Rev. Jose' J. Velasco, S.J.
Res., 320 W. Garvey Ave., 91754. Tel: 626-573-0427; Fax: 626-288-0260.
School—Tel: 626-573-1716; Fax: 626-573-3251.
Lay Teachers 20; Students 435.
Catechesis/Religious Programs—Tel: 626-573-4517.
Students 298.

St. Thomas Aquinas (1960) (Chinese), Revs. Edward R. Dover; Gabriel Lui.
Res., 1501 S. Atlantic Blvd., 91754. Tel: 323-264-4447; Fax: 323-264-2524.
Catechesis/Religious Programs—Tel: 323-264-1338.
Students 75.

Montrose, Los Angeles Co., Holy Redeemer (1925), Revs. John K. Foley; Gordon Chang.
Res., 2411 Montrose Ave., 91020. Tel: 818-249-2008; Fax: 818-249-5642.
School—2361 Del Mar Rd., 91020. Tel: 818-541-9005; Fax: 818-541-9006.
Lay Teachers 15; Students 249.
Catechesis/Religious Programs—Tel: 818-249-8026.
Students 201.

Moorpark, Ventura Co., Holy Cross (1982), Rev. Msgr. Joseph Cosgrove; Rev. Michael Sezzi.
Res., 13955 Peach Hill, 93021. Tel: 805-529-1397; Fax: 805-529-3939.
Parish Church & Administration Bldg.: 13955 Peach Hill Rd., 93021.
Catechesis/Religious Programs—Tel: 805-529-0283; Fax: 805-529-3939.
Students 834.

Newbury Park, Ventura Co., St. Julie Billiart (1969), Rev. Msgr. Michael Bunny; Rev. Cornelius Phelan; Deacon Louis Henschel.
Church—2475 Borchard Rd., 91320. Tel: 805-498-3602; Fax: 805-376-2332.
Catechesis/Religious Programs—Tel: 805-499-0979.
Students 331.

New Cuyama, Santa Barbara Co., Immaculate Conception (1969), Sr. Mary D. Quinn, C.S.J., Parish Dir.
Res., 4793 Cebrian St., P.O. Box 257, 93254. Tel: 661-766-2741; Fax: 661-766-2919.
Catechesis/Religious Programs—Students 35.

North Hollywood, Los Angeles Co.,

1—Sacred Heart Syriac Catholic Parish, (1996). (Jesus Sacred Heart Antiochene Syrian Catholic Mission, Antiochean Syriac Rite). Rev. Hay Tham Zillo.
10837 Collins St., 91601. Tel: 818-766-7001; Fax: 818-766-7254.

2—St. Charles Borromeo, (1921), Rev. Robert J. Gallagher; Rev. Msgr. Thomas Kiefer, Pastor Emeritus; Revs. Vaughn Winters; H. Francis Dang. In res., Rev. Msgr. Richard Loomis; Deacon Walter Hanson.
Res., 10828 Moorpark St., 91602. Tel: 818-766-3838; Fax: 818-766-2855.
Parish Center—10834 Moorpark St., 91602. Fax: 818-766-5711.
School—10850 Moorpark St., 91602. Tel: 818-508-5359; Fax: 818-508-4511.
Sisters 1; Lay Teachers 14; Students 293.
Catechesis/Religious Programs—Tel: 818-980-1826.
Students 480.

3—St. Jane Frances de Chantal, (1948), Revs. Michael Higgins, O.Carm.; Ferdinand Lansang, O.Carm.
Res., 13001 Victory Blvd., 91606. Tel: 818-985-8600; Fax: 818-985-0606.
School—Tel: 818-766-1714. Mr. Joseph Brown, Prin.
Lay Teachers 10; Students 325.
Catechesis/Religious Programs—Tel: 818-985-8272.
Students 365.

4—St. Patrick, (1948), Rev. Gregory C. King; Deacon Bob Seidler.
Res. & Office: 6153 Cahuenga Blvd., 91606-5117. Tel: 818-752-3240; Fax: 818-769-6174.
School—10626 Erwin St., 91606. Tel: 818-761-7363; Fax: 818-761-6349.
Lay Teachers 15; Students 305.
Catechesis/Religious Programs—Tel: 818-769-0263.
Students 786.

5—St. Paul Assyrian-Chaldean (1980) (Assyrian-Chaldean), Revs. Noel Gorgis; Poles Ghouzran.
Res., 13050 Vanowen St., 91605. Tel: 818-765-3665; Fax: 818-765-0493.
Mission—Placentia, Orange Co., St. George, 451 W. Madison, Placentia, 92670.

Northridge, Los Angeles Co., Our Lady of Lourdes (1958), Rev. Msgr. Peter C. Moran; Rev. Andrew Diviney, S.J.; Deacon Juan Galido.
Church—18405 Superior St., 91325. Tel: 818-349-1500; Fax: 818-349-2516.
Res., 9800 Canby Ave., 91325.
School—Tel: 818-349-0245; Fax: 818-349-4156.
Sisters 2; Lay Teachers 9; Students 310.
Catechesis/Religious Programs—Tel: 818-349-1285.
Students 440.

Norwalk, Los Angeles Co., St. John of God (1950), Rev. Msgr. Bernard M. Leheny; Revs. Alex Aclan; Jason A. Souza.
Res., 13819 S. Pioneer Blvd., 90650. Tel: 562-863-5721; Fax: 562-406-3927.
School—13817 S. Pioneer Blvd., 90650. Tel: 562-863-5721, Ext. 228.
Sisters of the Holy Faith 2; Lay Teachers 22; Students 303.
Catechesis/Religious Programs—Tel: 562-863-5721, Ext. 231.
Students 863.

St. Linus (1961), Revs. Joseph V. Brennan; Mark M. Martinez; Deacon Chuck Baker. In res., Rev. John Montejano.
Res., 13915 Shoemaker Ave., 90650. Tel: 310-921-6649; Fax: 310-921-5150.
School—Tel: 310-921-0336; Fax: 310-921-1666.
Sisters of the Holy Faith 1; Lay Teachers 15; Students 324.
Catechesis/Religious Programs—Tel: 310-921-5179.
Students 446.

Ojai, Ventura Co., St. Thomas Aquinas (1919), Revs. Patrick J. Keane, O.S.A.; William V. Olivas, O.S.A.; Michael J. McFadden, O.S.A.; Deacon Allan Doane. In res., Rev. Gary E. Sanders, O.S.A.
Res., 185 St. Thomas Dr., 93023. Tel: 805-646-4338; Fax: 805-646-5928.
Catechesis/Religious Programs—Tel: 805-646-0307.
Students 319.

Oxnard, Ventura Co.,

1—St. Anthony, (1959), Rev. George Sullivan; Rev. Msgr. Michael J. Condon, Pastor Emeritus; Revs. Angel Sagardoy; John Neiman; Deacons James Henry; Jon McPheeters; Oscar Duke.
Res., 2511 S. C St., P.O. Box 2215, 93034. Tel: 805-486-7301; Fax: 805-486-3142.
School—Tel: 805-487-5317; Fax: 805-486-1537.
Sisters 1; Lay Teachers 9; Students 300.
Catechesis/Religious Programs—2421 S. C St., 93033. Tel: 805-486-0784.
Students 1,050.

2—Santa Clara, (1904), Rev. Msgr. Peter D. Nugent; Rev. Msgr. Charles F. O'Gorman, Senior Priest; Revs. Joaquin Haefeli; Marco A. Ortiz; Deacons Milton Rosenberg; John G. Castorena.
Res., 323 S. E St., 93030. Tel: 805-487-3891; Fax: 805-483-1734.
School—324 S. E St., 93030. Tel: 805-483-6935; Fax: 805-487-6686.
Lay Teachers 11; Students 312.
Catechesis/Religious Programs—Tel: 805-487-6742.
Students 1,180.
Mission—El Rio, Ventura Co., Santa Clara Chapel, 1333 Ventura Blvd., El Rio, 93030. Tel: 805-485-7335; Fax: 805-981-1183.

3—Our Lady of Guadalupe Parish, (1958) (Hispanic), Revs. Enrique Espinosa Ramirez, M.Sp.S.; Conrado Aquino, M.Sp.S.; Jose de Jesus Sanchez, M.Sp.S.; Deacon Ricardo Barragan. In res., Rev. Francisco Altamira, M.Sp.S.
Res., 500 N. Juanita Ave., P.O. Box 1091, 93030. Tel: 805-483-0987; 483-1481; Fax: 805-486-2434.
School—530 N. Juanita Ave., 93030. Tel: 805-483-5116; Fax: 805-385-7242.
Lay Teachers 9; Students 315.
Catechesis/Religious Programs—Tel: 805-487-4737; Fax: 805-486-2434.
Students 900.
Mission—Oxnard, Ventura Co., Christ the King, 535 Cooper Rd., 93030. Tel: 805-483-3499.

4—Mary Star of the Sea, (1963) (Filipino-Mexican), Revs. Euben Capacillo, O.A.R.; Etelvino Igelsias, O.A.R.; Deacons Harold A. Parish; Fidel Ramirez; Ben Perez.
Res., 463 W. Pleasant Valley Rd., 93033. Tel: 805-486-6133; Fax: 805-483-6913.
Catechesis/Religious Programs—Tel: 805-483-9313.
Students 1,042.
Convent—4924 S. "F" St., 93033. Tel: 805-487-8008.

Pacific Palisades, Los Angeles Co., Corpus Christi (1950), Rev. Msgr. Liam J. Kidney; Rev. G. Neville Rucker, Pastor Emeritus; Deacon John P. Allen. In res., Rev. Richard M. Martini.
Res., 887 Toyopa Dr., 90272. Tel: 310-454-1328; Fax: 310-573-5021.
School—Tel: 310-454-9411; Fax: 310-454-3776.
Sisters of St. Louis (Monaghan) 2; Lay Teachers 15; Students 291.
Convent—875 Toyopa Dr., 90272. Tel: 310-454-6262.

Pacoima, Los Angeles Co., Guardian Angel (1956), Rev. Juan Enriquez. In res., Rev. Alberto Villalobos.
Res., 10886 Lehigh Ave., 91331. Tel: 818-899-2345; Fax: 818-899-2537.
School—Tel: 818-896-1113.
Religious of Jesus and Mary 4; Lay Teachers 6; Students 309.
Catechesis/Religious Programs—Tel: 818-899-8907.
Students 315.

Mary Immaculate (1957) (Spanish), Revs. James M. Fee, O.M.I.; Edgar Garcia, O.M.I. (Peru); Patrick Thompson, O.M.
Res., 10390 Remick Ave., 91331. Tel: 818-899-0278; Fax: 818-890-9878.
School—Tel: 818-834-8551; Fax: 818-896-7996.
Lay Teachers 13; Students 308.
Catechesis/Religious Programs—Tel: 818-899-2111.
Students 1,060.

Palmdale, Los Angeles Co., St. Mary (1890), Revs. Robert Rankin; Cyprian Carlo; Leonel Vargas (El Salvador); Joseph Visperas (Philippines); Deacon Paul Schwerdt. In res., Rev. Thomas White.
Res., 1600 E. Ave., R-4, 93550. Tel: 661-947-3306; Fax: 661-947-8687.
School—Tel: 805-273-5555; Fax: 661-273-3845.
Salesian Sisters of St. John Bosco 3; Lay Teachers 11; Students 333.
Catechesis/Religious Programs—Tel: 661-273-5554.
Students 1,950.

Panorama City, Los Angeles Co., St. Genevieve (1950), Rev. Msgr. Christian M. Van Liefde; Revs. Jeff J. Deikel; Doan T. Pham; Marcial Juan.
Res., 14061 Roscoe Blvd., 91402. Tel: 818-894-2261; Fax: 818-893-4284.
School—Tel: 818-892-3802; Fax: 818-893-8143.
Sisters 3; Lay Teachers 21; Students 670.
High School—13967 Roscoe Blvd., 91402. Tel: 818-894-6417; Fax: 818-892-9853.
Sisters 1; Lay Teachers 24; Students 355.
Catechesis/Religious Programs—Tel: 818-892-7177.
Students 569.

Paramount, Los Angeles Co., Our Lady of the Rosary (1913) (Hispanic-Tongan), Rev. Edward J. Dober; Rev. Msgr. Bernard O'Reilly, (Retired); Revs. Idelfonso Madrigal; Brian G. Chung.
Res., 14815 S. Paramount Blvd., 90723. Tel: 562-633-1126; Fax: 562-633-3192.
School—Tel: 562-633-6360; Fax: 562-633-2641.
Sisters of the Daughters of Mary and Joseph 4; Lay Teachers 6; Students 301.
Catechesis/Religious Programs—Tel: 562-602-0086.
Students 1,450.
Mission—Paramount, Los Angeles Co., Catholic Korean Community of St. Raphael. (Downey Ave. & Alondra Blvd.) 15946 Downey Ave., 90723. Tel: 562-630-6168. Rev. Mark Choi.

Pasadena, Los Angeles Co., St. Andrew (1886) (Hispanic), Rev. Francis Colborn; Rev. Msgr. Tobias P. English, Pastor Emeritus; Revs. Truc Nguyen; Marcos J. Gonzalez; Truc N. Quang.
Res., 311 N. Raymond Ave., 91103. Tel: 626-792-4183; Fax: 626-792-4456.
School—(Grades K-8). Tel: 626-796-7697; Fax: 626-796-1931.
Sisters of the Holy Names of Jesus and Mary 3; Lay Teachers 8; Students 288.
Catechesis/Religious Programs—42 Chestnut St., 91103. Tel: 626-577-1770.
Students 613.

Assumption of the Blessed Virgin Mary (1950), Rev. Msgr. August Moretti; Rev. Walter Fernando; Deacon James J. Crowley.
Res., 2640 E. Orange Grove Blvd., 91107. Tel: 626-792-1343.
School—2660 E. Orange Grove Blvd., 91107. Tel: 626-793-2089; Fax: 626-793-4070. Lou Anne Insprucker, Prin.
Lay Teachers 18; Students 300.
Catechesis/Religious Programs—Tel: 626-792-6844. Elly Dunbar, D.R.E.
Students 231.

St. Philip the Apostle (1921), Revs. Joseph V. Moniz; Marc V. Trudeau; Robert V. Biroschak; Deacon William Landa.
Res., 151 S. Hill Ave., 91106. Tel: 626-793-0693; Fax: 626-793-0733.
School—161 S. Hill Ave., 91106. Tel: 626-795-9691; Fax: 626-795-9946.
Lay Teachers 19; Students 414.
Catechesis/Religious Programs—Students 350.

Pico Rivera, Los Angeles Co., St. Hilary (1950), Revs. Joshua Peter Lee; Alex Chung; Pedro Valdes.
Res., 5465 Citronell Ave., 90660. Tel: 562-942-7300; Fax: 562-948-3760.
School—Tel: 562-942-7361; Fax: 562-801-9131.
School Sisters of Notre Dame 3; Lay Teachers 21; Students 365.
Catechesis/Religious Programs—5401 S. Citronell Ave., 90660. Tel: 562-942-7018.
Students 731.
Convent—5333 S. Citronell Ave., 90660. Tel: 562-942-7151.

St. Mariana de Paredes (1951) (Hispanic), Revs. Fernando Iglesias; Richard Carey; Augustine Abayomi.
Res., 7922 S. Passons Blvd., 90660. Tel: 562-949-8240; Fax: 562-942-2405.

School—7911 Buhman Ave., 90660. Tel: 562-949-1234; Fax: 562-948-3855. Sr. Francis Rose Rivers, S.S.N.D.
School Sisters of Notre Dame 1; Lay Teachers 10; Students 300.
Catechesis/Religious Programs—Tel: 562-949-5653; Fax: 562-949-9277.
Students 450.

St. Francis Xavier (1939) (Hispanic), Revs. Jorge Penaloza; Jose Antonio Medina, C.SS.R.; Deacon Ben Torres.
Res., 4245 S. Acacia Ave., 90660. Tel: 562-699-7517; Fax: 562-699-5331.
Catechesis/Religious Programs—Tel: 562-699-8527.
Students 450.

Pomona, Los Angeles Co., St. Joseph (1886), Rev. Vlatko Poljicak. In res., Rev. Hisham Dabaen.
Res., 1150 W. Holt Ave., 91768. Tel: 909-629-4101; Fax: 909-623-0265.
School—Tel: 909-622-3365; Fax: 909-469-5146.
Felician Sisters 3; Lay Teachers 8; Students 301.
Catechesis/Religious Programs—1200 W. Holt Ave., 91768. Tel: 909-629-1404; Fax: 909-469-5146.
Students 1,080.

Sacred Heart (1935), Revs. Juan Silva; Wayne Noble. In res., Rev. Msgr. Manuel O. Sanchez, Pastor Emeritus (Retired).
Res., 1215 S. Hamilton Blvd., 91766. Tel: 909-622-4553; Fax: 909-623-0841.
Catechesis/Religious Programs—Ruth Ibarra, D.R.E.
Students 1,500.

St. Madeleine (1963), Rev. Msgr. Andrew Tseu.
Res., 931 E. Kingsley Ave., 91767. Tel: 909-629-9495; Fax: 909-623-7148.
Catechesis/Religious Programs—Tel: 909-620-1300; Fax: 909-623-7148.
Students 268.

Rancho Palos Verdes, Los Angeles Co., St. John Fisher (1961), Rev. Msgr. David A. Sork; Rev. Msgr. Eugene A. Gilb, Pastor Emeritus; Rev. Michael Rocha.
Res., 5448 Crest Rd., 90275. Tel: 310-377-5571; Fax: 310-377-6303.
School—Tel: 310-377-2800; Fax: 310-377-3863.
Lay Teachers 9; Students 265.
Catechesis/Religious Programs—5400 Crest Rd., 90275. Tel: 310-377-4573. Eileen Loughran, D.R.E.
Students 851.

Redondo Beach, Los Angeles Co., St. James (1892), Revs. Timothy Nichols; Hung Tran; Brendan Kearney, S.J.; Deacons Richard Shinkle; Bob Miller. In res., Rev. Jim Clarke.
Mailing Address: and Res.: 415 Vincent St., 90277.; Parish Office: 124 N. Pacific Coast Hwy., 90277. Tel: 310-372-5228; Fax: 310-379-5552.
School—4625 Garnet St., Torrance, 90503. Tel: 310-371-0416; Fax: 310-371-8377.
Sisters of St. Joseph of Carondelet 4; Lay Teachers 12; Students 309.
Catechesis/Religious Programs—Tel: 310-379-3221. Diana Holly, D.R.E.
Students 360.

St. Lawrence Martyr (1955), Rev. Msgr. Michael Lenihan, V.F.; Revs. Christopher Cunningham; Leonard Goswitz; Deacon Frank Dieter.
Res., 1900 S. Prospect Ave., 90277-6099. Tel: 310-540-0329; Fax: 310-540-8999.
School—1950 Prospect Ave., 90277-6003. Tel: 310-540-3049; Fax: 310-316-0888.
Sisters of St. Joseph of Carondelet 1; Lay Teachers 22; Students 320.
Catechesis/Religious Programs—Tel: 310-316-4460.
Students 1,500.

Reseda, Los Angeles Co., St. Catherine of Siena (1949), Rev. Msgr. Sean B. Flanagan; Rev. Raul Cortes; Deacon Pedro Lira.
Res., 18115 Sherman Way, 91335. Tel: 818-343-2110; Fax: 818-343-1018.
School—7311 Lindley Ave., 91335. Tel: 818-343-9880; Fax: 818-343-6851.
Lay Teachers 11; Students 300.
Catechesis/Religious Programs—Tel: 818-996-4588; Fax: 818-996-4588.
Students 685.

Rowland Heights, Los Angeles Co., St. Elizabeth Ann Seton (1981), Rev. Msgr. Michael F. Killeen; Deacons Steven V. Hillman; Eduardo Delgado; Peter K. Chu.
Church—1835 Larkvane Rd., 91748.
Res., 18090 Via Amorosa, 91748. Tel: 626-964-3629; Fax: 626-913-2209.
Catechesis/Religious Programs—Tel: 626-965-5792.
Students 873.

San Dimas, Los Angeles Co., Holy Name of Mary (1957), Revs. Thomas J. Mullen, SS.CC.; John Roche, SS.CC.; Sr. Philomena Cassidy, S.S.L., Pastoral Assoc.; Deacons Jack Clinton; Marv Estey.
Res., 724 E. Bonita Ave., 91773. Tel: 909-599-1243; Fax: 909-599-4230.
School—Tel: 909-599-1234, Ext. 24.
Sisters 1; Lay Teachers 18; Students 315.
Catechesis/Religious Programs—Tel: 909-599-1243, Ext. 32.
Students 860.

San Fernando, Los Angeles Co., St. Ferdinand (1902), Revs. Paul Nourie, O.M.I.; Erhard Schmitt, O.M.I. Office: 1109 Coronel St., 91340. Tel: 818-365-3967; Fax: 818-365-0067.
School—1012 Coronel St., 91340. Tel: 818-361-3264; Fax: 818-361-5894.
Sisters of St. Joseph of Carondelet 2; Lay Teachers 10; Students 303.
Catechesis/Religious Programs—Tel: 818-361-1813.
Students 312.

Santa Rosa (1927) (Hispanic), Revs. Paul W. Wilhelm, O.M.I.; Rufino Nava; Donald Bernard, O.M.I.
Res., 668 S. Workman St., 91340. Tel: 818-361-4617; Fax: 818-365-8599.
School—1309 Mott St., 91340. Tel: 818-361-5096; Fax: 818-361-2259.
Franciscan Missionary Sisters of the Immaculate Conception 9; Lay Teachers 4; Students 278.
Catechesis/Religious Programs—Tel: 818-365-5161.
Students 501.

San Gabriel, Los Angeles Co., San Gabriel (1771). (Old Mission). Revs. Dennis G. Gallo, C.M.F.; Jose Sanchez, C.M.F.; Arnold Gonzalez, C.M.F.; Binh Nguyen, C.M., Vietnamese Ministry. In res., Rev. John Gregory Hencier, C.M.F.
Church and Res.: 428 S. Mission Dr., 91776. Tel: 626-457-3035; Fax: 626-282-5308. [CEM]
School—416 S. W. Mission Dr., 91776. Tel: 626-281-2454; Fax: 626-281-4817.
Dominican Sisters 2; Lay Teachers 10; Students 290.
High School—254 S. Santa Anita St., 91776. Tel: 626-282-3181; Fax: 626-282-4209.
Sisters 6; Lay Teachers 21; Girls 365.
Catechesis/Religious Programs—Tel: 626-457-3041.
Students 667.
Convent—412 S. Mission Dr., 91776. Tel: 626-284-9585.

St. Anthony (1945), Revs. Michael Gleeson (Ireland); Finbarr Divine.
Res., 1901 S. San Gabriel Blvd., 91776. Tel: 626-288-8912; Fax: 626-288-3730.
School—1905 S. San Gabriel Blvd., 91776. Tel: 626-280-7255; Fax: 626-280-3870. Ann Bouvet, Prin.
Sisters of the Holy Names of Jesus and Mary 2; Lay Teachers 30; Students 630.
Catechesis/Religious Programs—Tel: 626-288-5511. Stephanie Ramos, D.R.E.
Students 1,200.
Convent—626 E. Marshall St., 91726. Tel: 626-288-2200.

San Marino, Los Angeles Co., Saints Felicitas and Perpetua (1938), Rev. Msgr. Lawrence J. Gibson.
Res., 1190 Palomar Rd., 91108. Tel: 626-796-0432; Fax: 626-796-0363.
School—2955 Huntington Dr., 91108. Tel: 626-796-8223.
Sisters 5; Lay Teachers 11; Students 290.
Catechesis/Religious Programs—Students 139.

San Pedro, Los Angeles Co., Mary, Star of the Sea (1889), Rev. Msgr. Patrick J. Gallagher; Revs. Lorenzo De Dominici, (Retired); Gilbert Cruz; Christopher Lawrence; Deacons Nino Crisafulli; William Garcia.
Res., 870 W. 8th St., 90731. Tel: 310-833-3541; Fax: 310-833-9254.
School—Tel: 310-831-0875; Fax: 310-831-0877.
Priests 1; Lay Teachers 11; Students 294.
High School—Tel: 310-547-1138; Fax: 310-547-1827.
Priests 7; Lay Teachers 25; Students 454.
Catechesis/Religious Programs—717 S. Cabrillo Ave., 90731. Tel: 310-833-3933.
Students 610.

Holy Trinity (1924), Revs. Thomas J. Glynn; Joseph J. Kammerer; Francis J. Hicks.
Parish Center: 209 N. Hanford Ave., 90732. Tel: 310-548-6535; Fax: 310-833-1134.
Church—1292 W. Santa Cruz St., 90732.
School—1226 W. Santa Cruz St., 90732. Tel: 310-833-0703; Fax: 310-833-5219.
Lay Teachers 26; Students 606.
Catechesis/Religious Programs—Tel: 310-833-3500.
Students 567.

St. Peter (1965) (Hispanic), Revs. Claudio De Agostini, C.S.J.; Bruno De Santi, C.S.J.; Sylvan Schiavo, C.S.J. In res., Rev. John Trimaglio, C.S.J.
Res., 338 N. Grand Ave., 90731-2006. Tel: 310-831-5360; Fax: 310-831-0415.
Catechesis/Religious Programs—Tel: 310-832-6731.
Students 650.

Santa Barbara, Santa Barbara Co.,

1—HOLY CROSS, (1973), Revs. Ludo DeClippel, C.J. (Belgium); J. Walter Munton, C.J. (United Kingdom); Deacons Nicholas Curran; David Huff; Rick Sanchez.
Res., 1740 Cliff Dr., 93109. Tel: 805-962-0411; Fax: 805-564-6921.
Catechesis/Religious Programs—Tel: 805-962-7311.
Students 208.

2—OLD MISSION SANTA BARBARA, (1786), Revs. Vincent Mesi, O.F.M.; Howard Hall, O.F.M.; Bro. Daniel Barica, O.F.M.; Deacons Jim Bret; Jack Ryan.
Res., 2201 Laguna St., 93105. Tel: 805-682-4713; Fax: 805-687-7841. [CEM]
Catechesis/Religious Programs—Students 70.

3—OUR LADY OF SORROWS, (1856), Revs. P. Jeremiah Helfrich, S.J.; Martin L. Brewer, S.J.; Thomas P. Delaney, S.J.; Luis H. Quihuis, S.J.; Deacon William Sangster.
Res., 21 E. Sola St., 93101. Tel: 805-963-1734; Fax: 805-965-6461.
School—Notre Dame, 33 E. Micheltorena St., 93101. Tel: 805-965-1033. Carol Hoffer, Prin.
Lay Teachers 12; Students 245.
Catechesis/Religious Programs—Tel: 805-966-4941.
Students 370.

4—OUR LADY OF GUADALUPE, (1928) (Hispanic), Rev. Guillermo C. Garcia, C.J. In res., Rev. Charles Hofschulte, C.J.
Res., 801 Jennings Ave., 93103. Tel: 805-965-4060; Fax: 805-965-3386.
Catechesis/Religious Programs—Tel: 805-962-4441.
Students 695.

5—ST. RAPHAEL, (1896), Rev. Msgr. Stephen N. Downes; Revs. Alberto Ledesma; Sabas Mallya, A.L.C.P.
Res., 5444 Hollister Ave., 93111. Tel: 805-967-5641; Fax: 805-964-2988.
School—160 St. Joseph St., 93111. Tel: 805-967-2115; Fax: 805-683-9765. Ellen Manning, Prin.
Lay Teachers 10; Students 324.
Catechesis/Religious Programs—Tel: 805-967-1641.
Students 761.

6—SAN ROQUE, (1953), Rev. James M. Ford.
Res., 325 Argonne Cir., 93105. Tel: 805-687-5215; Fax: 805-682-9778. [JC]
School—3214 Calle Cedro, 93105. Tel: 805-687-3717; Fax: 805-687-0510. Dorothy C. Reed, Prin.
Lay Teachers 13; Aides 4; Students 254.
Catechesis/Religious Programs—Tel: 805-682-1097.
Students 160.

Santa Clarita, Los Angeles Co., Blessed Kateri Tekakwitha (1997), Revs. Michael J. Slattery; Blaise Brockman.
Mailing Address: P.O. Box 802200, 91380-2200.
Res., 22508 Copper Hill Dr., 91350. Tel: 661-296-3180; Fax: 661-296-7854.
Catechesis/Religious Programs—Tel: 661-296-6945; Fax: 661-296-3723.
Students 1,505.

Our Lady of Perpetual Help (1944), Rev. Msgr. Paul M. Montoya; Revs. Patrick A. Power, Pastor Emeritus; Malcolm Ambrose; Norm Supancheck; Sr. M. Jane Mast, S.H.F., Pastoral Min.; Deacon Richard Karl.
Res., 23233 Lyons Ave., 91321-2632. Tel: 661-259-2276; Fax: 661-259-1873.
School—Tel: 661-259-1141; Fax: 661-259-8254.
Franciscan Sisters of the Immaculate Conception 6; Lay Teachers 6; Students 325.
Catechesis/Religious Programs—Tel: 661-259-4266.
Students 1,500.
Convent—23719 Rotunda Rd., 91355. Tel: 661-259-5591.

St. Clare (1977), Rev. Msgr. Edmond M. Renehan; Revs. William B. Ustaski, C.R.I.C.; Valentine Zdilla.
Res., 27341 Camp Plenty Rd., 91351. Tel: 661-252-3353; Fax: 661-252-1539.
Catechesis/Religious Programs—Tel: 661-252-6950; Fax: 661-299-6594. Peggy Pigors, D.R.E.
Students 120.

Santa Fe Springs, Los Angeles Co., St. Pius X (1954) (Hispanic), Revs. John McHugh; Jose Luis Ochoa, M.G.; Peter Ha Son Le (Vietnamese).
Res., 10827 S. Pioneer Blvd., 90670. Tel: 562-863-8734; Fax: 562-868-0051.
School—Tel: 562-864-4818; Fax: 562-864-7120.
Lay Teachers 12; Students 349.
Catechesis/Religious Programs—Tel: 562-868-2389.
Students 840.

Santa Maria, Santa Barbara Co., St. Mary of the Assumption (1905), Rev. Msgr. James P. Colberg, Pastor Emeritus; Revs. John M. Vianney (India); Riz Carranza.
Res., 414 E. Church St., 93454. Tel: 805-922-5826; Fax: 805-922-1986. [JC]
School—424 E. Cyprus St., 93454. Tel: 805-925-6713; Fax: 805-925-3815.
Sisters 1; Lay Teachers 8; Students 238.
Preschool—209 S. School St., 93454. Tel: 805-346-6541; Fax: 805-347-7658.
Teachers 6; Students 32.
Catechesis/Religious Programs—Tel: 805-925-1334; Fax: 805-928-4964.
Students 263.

St. Louis de Montfort (Santa Barbara) (1963), Revs. Mark L. Newman, C.J.; Campion W. Aspinall, C.J.; John A. Mayhew, C.J.; L. Bede Johnson, C.J., (Retired); Deacons Richard Carmody; Douglas Halvorsen; Robert Maciel; Trino Andrade.
Res., 5075 Harp Rd., 93455. Tel: 805-937-4555; Fax: 805-934-2805. [JC]
School—Tel: 805-937-5571; Fax: 805-937-3181.
Sisters 2; Lay Teachers 9; Students 280.
Catechesis/Religious Programs—Tel: 805-937-8363.
Students 860.
Mission—Los Alamos, Santa Barbara Co., St. Anthony's Church, 260 Helena St., Los Alamos, 93440. Tel: 805-344-1604.

St. John Neumann (Santa Barbara) (1986) (Hispanic), Revs. Emigdio Herrera; Delfino Lara; Deacons Manuel Liendo; Ricardo Berumen; Lyle Goodspeed, (Retired); Sr. Margaret Bannan, O.S.F., Pastoral Asst.
Res., 966 W. Orchard, 93458-2063. Tel: 805-922-7099; Fax: 805-346-1747.
Catechesis/Religious Programs—Tel: 805-922-5288.
Students 780.

Santa Monica, Los Angeles Co., St. Monica (1886), Rev. Msgr. Lloyd A. Torgerson; Rev. Paul K. Fitzpatrick; Deacon Gene McNamara. In res., Revs. Bernard O'Connor, C.M.F.; Robert A. Dowd, C.S.C (FTW).
Church—725 California Ave., 90403. Tel: 310-393-9287; Fax: 310-319-9758.
School—1039 Seventh St., 90403. Tel: 310-451-9801; Fax: 310-394-6001.
Lay Teachers 12; Students 294.
High School—1030 Lincoln Blvd., 90403. Tel: 310-394-3701; Fax: 310-458-1353.
Sisters 4; Lay Teachers 42; Students 600.
Catechesis/Religious Programs—Tel: 310-395-8903.
Students 850.

St. Anne (1951) (Hispanic), Rev. Michael D. Gutierrez.
Res., 2011 Colorado Ave., 90404. Tel: 310-829-4411; Fax: 310-829-9006.
School—2017 Colorado Ave., 90404. Tel: 310-829-2775; Fax: 310-829-3945.
Lay Teachers 9; Students 213.
Catechesis/Religious Programs—Tel: 310-829-4040.
Students 345.

St. Clement (1904), Rev. Juan Romero. In res., Rev. Hilary Nwadei (Nigeria).
Res., 3102 Third St., 90405. Tel: 310-396-2679; Fax: 310-396-4239.
Catechesis/Religious Programs—204 Hampton Dr., Venice, 90291. Tel: 310-392-5769.
Students 98.

Santa Paula, Ventura Co., St. Sebastian (1896), Rev. Pasquale Vuoso, C.R.I.C.
Res., 235 N. Ninth St., 93060. Tel: 805-525-2149; Fax: 805-933-5520.
School—325 E. Santa Barbara St., 93060. Tel: 805-525-1575; Fax: 805-525-1576.
Lay Teachers 8; Students 180; Pre-School 34.
Catechesis/Religious Programs—Students 190.

Our Lady of Guadalupe (1929) (Hispanic), Rev. Pasquale Vuoso, C.R.I.C.
Res., 427 N. Oak St., 93060. Tel: 805-525-3716; Fax: 805-525-3788. [CEM]
Catechesis/Religious Programs—423 N. Oak St., 93060. Tel: 805-525-2225.
Students 753.
Convent—432 N. Oak St., 93060. Tel: 805-525-9207.

Sepulveda, Los Angeles Co., Our Lady of Peace (1944), Revs. John Keese, Admin.; Sang V. Tran; Jose Magana; Gladys Rodriguez, Pastoral Assoc.
Res., 15444 Nordhoff St., North Hills, 91343. Tel: 818-894-1176; Fax: 818-894-3838.
School—9022 Langdon Ave., North Hills, 91343. Tel: 818-894-4059.
Lay Teachers 9; Students 286.
Catechesis/Religious Programs—Tel: 818-891-3578; Fax: 818-894-5498.
Students 776.

Sherman Oaks, Los Angeles Co., St. Francis de Sales (1938), Revs. Kevin J. Larkin; James J. Maher; Deacon John Coplen. In res., Rev. Jerome O'Mahony, M.S.C.
Res., 13360 Valleyheart Dr., 91423. Tel: 818-784-0105; Fax: 818-784-4807.
Church—Moorpark St. at Dixie Canyon Ave., 91423.
School—13368 Valleyheart Dr., 91423. Tel: 818-784-9573; Fax: 818-784-9649. Sr. Ellen Marie McGovern, Prin.
Sisters 2; Lay Teachers 18; Students 310.
Catechesis/Religious Programs—Tel: 818-784-2940.
Students 313.

Sierra Madre, Los Angeles Co., St. Rita (1908), Rev. Msgr. Joseph J. Cokus; Deacon Ernest Nosari.
Res., 50 E. Alegria Ave., 91024. Tel: 626-355-1292; Fax: 818-355-2290.
School—Tel: 626-355-6114; Fax: 626-355-0713.
Lay Teachers 20; Students 304.
Catechesis/Religious Programs—Tel: 626-355-3841.
Students 215.

Simi Valley, Ventura Co., St. Peter Claver (1972), Rev. Msgr. Gary P. Bauler; Rev. Rock Janowski.
Res., 5649 Pittman St., 93063. Tel: 805-526-6499; Fax: 805-526-7233.
Catechesis/Religious Programs—Tel: 805-526-0680; 526-3685; Fax: 805-526-3658.
Students 578.

St. Rose of Lima (1921), Revs. Michael J. Carcerano; Laurence J. Spiteri, J.C.L.; Michael S. Grieco; Deacon Peter Wilson.
Res., 1305 Royal Ave., 93065. Tel: 805-526-1732; Fax: 805-526-0067.
School—1325 Royal Ave., 93065. Tel: 805-526-5304; Fax: 805-526-0939.
Lay Teachers 19; Students 286.
Catechesis/Religious Programs—Tel: 805-526-5513; Fax: 805-526-5516.
Students 1,045.

Solvang, Santa Barbara Co., Old Mission Santa Ines (1804) (Spanish), Revs. Robert Barbato, O.F.M.Cap; Daniel Kabat, O.F.M.Cap.; Bro. Steve Tetreault, O.F.M.Cap. In res., Revs. Cyril Kelleher, O.F.M.Cap.; Timothy O'Sullivan, O.F.M.Cap.
Res., 1760 Mission Dr., P.O. Box 408, 93464. Tel: 805-688-4815; Fax: 805-686-4468.
Catechesis/Religious Programs—Tel: 805-688-4138.
Students 456.

South El Monte, Los Angeles Co., Epiphany (1956), Revs. Tomas A. Elis, Admin.; Benito Armenta.
Res., 10911 Michael Hunt Dr., 91733. Tel: 626-442-6262; Fax: 626-575-1738.
School—10915 Michael Hunt Dr., 91733. Tel: 626-442-6264; Fax: 626-442-6074.
Religious 1; Lay Teachers 10; Students 276.
Catechesis/Religious Programs—Tel: 626-448-3636.
Students 1,301.

South Gate, Los Angeles Co., St. Helen (1931), Revs. John F. Provenza; William Van Gastel, M.H.M.; Victor Ruvalcaba.
Res., 8912 South Gate Ave., 90280. Tel: 323-563-3522; Fax: 323-563-0161.
School—Tel: 323-566-5491; Fax: 323-566-2810.
Sisters of Notre Dame 2; Lay Teachers 10; Students 370.
Catechesis/Religious Programs—Tel: 323-563-3536.
Students 689.

South Pasadena, Los Angeles Co., Holy Family (1910), Rev. Msgr. Clement J. Connolly; Revs. Roger Labonte; Niall O'Leary, Dir. of Spirituality.
Pastoral Center—1527 Fremont Ave., 91030. Tel: 626-799-8908; Fax: 626-799-0423.
School—1301 Fremont Ave., 91030. Tel: 626-799-4354; Fax: 626-799-4530. Mrs. Evelyn Ortiz, Prin.
Lay Teachers 16; Students 318.
Catechesis/Religious Programs—Tel: 626-403-5118; Fax: 626-403-6118.
Students 700.

Sun Valley, Los Angeles Co., Our Lady of the Holy Rosary (1937), Revs. Livio Stella, C.S. (Italy); Pedro Nel Lopez (Colombia); Deacon Elie Calonge (Philippines).
Res., 7800 Vineland Ave., 91352. Tel: 818-765-3350; Fax: 818-765-3170.
School—7802 Vineland Ave., 91352. Tel: 818-765-4897; Fax: 818-765-5791.
Servant Sisters of the Blessed Sacrament 7; Lay Teachers 6; Students 295.
Catechesis/Religious Programs—Tel: 818-982-4248. Dina Calonge, D.R.E.
Students 1,416.
Convent—7757 Cleon St., 91352. Tel: 818-764-9857.
Mission—North Hollywood, Los Angeles Co., Our Lady of Zapopan, 7824 Lankershim Blvd., North Hollywood, 91605. Tel: 818-503-8920.

Sylmar, Los Angeles Co., St. Didacus (1957), Rev. Msgr. Peter L. Amy; Rev. Julio Roman (Panama).
Res., 14339 Astoria St., 91342. Tel: 818-367-6181; Fax: 818-367-0604.
School—14325 Astoria St., 91342. Tel: 818-367-5886.
Lay Teachers 9; Students 320.
Catechesis/Religious Programs—Tel: 818-367-4155.
Students 800.

Temple City, Los Angeles Co., St. Luke the Evangelist (1946), Revs. Donald F. Grasha; Stephen V. Davoren; Joseph Barita (Africa).
Parish Administrative Center—5605 Cloverly Ave., 91780.
Res., 9451 E. Broadway, P.O. Box 798, 91780. Tel: 626-291-5900; Fax: 626-287-2332.
School—Tel: 626-291-5959; Fax: 626-285-5367.
Lay Teachers 9; Students 275.
Catechesis/Religious Programs—Tel: 626-291-5925; Fax: 626-291-5925.
Students 431.

Thousand Oaks, Ventura Co., St. Paschal Baylon (1960), Rev. Msgr. Joseph S. George; Revs. Larry Neumeier; Joseph Gaffney; Deacon James Robinson.
Res., 155 E. Janss Rd., 91360. Tel: 805-496-0222; Fax: 805-379-2506.
School—Tel: 805-495-9340; Fax: 805-778-1509.
Lay Teachers 22; Students 324.
Catechesis/Religious Programs—Tel: 805-496-0222, Ext. 115.
Students 719.

Torrance, Los Angeles Co., Nativity (1924), Revs. Alfred Hernandez, Admin.; John P. Fahey; Alfonso Borgen-Reithel, O.F.M.Conv.; Patrick J. McHugh, Pastor Emeritus.
Res., 1447 Engracia Ave., 90501-3234. Tel: 310-328-2776; Fax: 310-328-0508.
School—2371 Carson, 90501. Tel: 310-328-5387; Fax: 310-328-5365.
Lay Teachers 12; Students 294.
Catechesis/Religious Programs—Tel: 310-320-6673.
Students 353.

St. Catherine Laboure (1949), Revs. John O'Byrne; Tovia Lui; J. Kim-Dang Nguyen; Deacon Matilde Magana; Margaret Plummer, Admin. In res., Rev. Sabato Pilato.
Res., 3846 Redondo Beach Blvd., 90504. Tel: 310-323-8900; Fax: 323-321-0486.
School—Tel: 310-324-8732; Fax: 310-324-2471. Mrs. Kathleen Gorze, Prin.
Lay Teachers 20; Students 554.
Catechesis/Religious Programs—16831 Ainsworth, 90504. Tel: 310-515-6033. Elaine O'Keefe, D.R.E.
Students 640.

Tujunga, Los Angeles Co., Our Lady of Lourdes (1920), Revs. Mark A. Strader; Damian Fernando; Deacon Paul Chacon.
Res., 10321 Tujunga Canyon Blvd., 91042. Tel: 818-352-3218; Fax: 818-352-2738.
School—Tel: 818-353-1106; Fax: 818-951-4276.
Sisters of Charity of the Blessed Virgin Mary 1; Lay Teachers 10; Students 272.
Catechesis/Religious Programs—Tel: 818-353-3053.
Students 430.

Valinda, Los Angeles Co., St. Martha (1958) (Hispanic-Filipino), Revs. William T. Easterling; Daniel G. Perez; Mauricio O. Goloran (Philippines); Deacon Jacob Favela. In res., Rev. Msgr. Aidan M. Carroll.
Res., 444 N. Azusa Ave., 91744-4299. Tel: 626-964-4313; Fax: 626-913-2953.
School—Tel: 626-964-1093; Fax: 626-912-2014.
Sisters of the Love of God 4; Lay Teachers 5; Students 254.
Catechesis/Religious Programs—Tel: 626-912-2581.
Students 926.

Van Nuys, Los Angeles Co., St. Elisabeth (1919) (Hispanic), Revs. Kevin Nolan; Jose A. Bautista; John Brady; Deacons Wesley Balbuena; Salvador Espana.
Res., 6635 Tobias Ave., 91405. Tel: 818-779-1756; Fax: 818-785-4492.
School—Tel: 818-779-1766; Fax: 818-779-1768.
Lay Teachers 11; Students 321.
Catechesis/Religious Programs—Tel: 818-779-1772.
Students 905.

St. Bridget of Sweden (1955), Rev. Raymond Morales; Deacon Ramon Rivera. In res., Rev. James Anguiano.
Res., 16711 Gault St., 91406. Tel: 818-782-7180; Fax: 818-782-7184.
School—7120 Whitaker, 91406. Tel: 818-785-4422; Fax: 818-785-0490.
Lay Teachers 11; Students 313.

Catechesis/Religious Programs—Tel: 818-782-7711. Jacinta O'Connor, D.R.E.
Students 216.
Convent—16707 Gault St., 91406. Tel: 818-786-1401.

Venice, Los Angeles Co., St. Mark (1923), Revs. Roderic M. Guerrini; Jon F. Majarucon.
Res., 940 Coeur d'Alene Ave., 90291. Tel: 310-821-5058; Fax: 310-821-7031.
School—912 Coeur d'Alene Ave., 90291. Tel: 310-821-6612; Fax: 310-822-6101.
Lay Teachers 9; Students 295.
Catechesis/Religious Programs—Tel: 310-822-1201.
Students 230.

Ventura, Ventura Co., San Buenaventura Mission (1782) (Hispanic), Rev. Msgr. Patrick J. O'Brien; Rev. David Velazquez, M.Sp.S.; Rev. Msgr. Michael Hughes, (Retired).
Res., 211 E. Main St., 93001. Tel: 805-643-4318; Fax: 805-643-7831.
School—183 E. Main St., 93001. Tel: 805-643-1500.
Lay Teachers 11; Students 187.
Catechesis/Religious Programs—Students 647.

Our Lady of the Assumption (1954), Revs. Michael Jennett; Lawrence J. Dowdel, Jr.; George L. Reynolds, II; Deacons James M. Farley; Rodger Adams.
Res., 3175 Telegraph Rd., 93003-3283. Tel: 805-642-7966; Fax: 805-642-7635.
School—3169 Telegraph Rd., 93003-3282. Tel: 805-642-7198; Fax: 805-642-7110.
Sisters 2; Lay Teachers 11; Students 308.
Catechesis/Religious Programs—Tel: 805-642-0568.
Students 565.

Sacred Heart (1966), Revs. Daniel O'Sullivan; John Higgins; Rev. Msgr. Arnold Biedermann, Pastor Emeritus.
Res., 10800 Henderson Rd., 93004. Tel: 805-647-3235; Fax: 805-647-8087.
School—(Grades K-8). Tel: 805-647-6174; Fax: 805-647-2291.
Lay Teachers 12; Students 310.
Catechesis/Religious Programs—Tel: 805-647-6260.
Students 450.

Vernon, Los Angeles Co., Holy Angels Parish of the Deaf (1987), Rev. Tom Schweitzer.
Res., 4433 Santa Fe Ave., 90058. Tel: 323-587-0397 (TDD); 587-2096; Fax: 323-587-7193.
Catechesis/Religious Programs—Students 60.

Walnut, Los Angeles Co., St. Lorenzo Ruiz (1991), Rev. Michael J. Carroll.
Res., 747 Meadowpass Rd., 91789. Tel: 909-595-9545; Fax: 909-594-3940.
Catechesis/Religious Programs—Tel: 909-595-3400.
Students 495.

West Covina, Los Angeles Co., St. Christopher (1954), Rev. Donal O'Connor; Rev. Msgr. John P. Won; Rev. Robert A. Folbrecht, Admin.; Deacons Douglas Moloney; Loc Nguyen.
Res., 629 S. Glendora Ave., 91790. Tel: 626-960-1805; Fax: 626-851-0595.
School—900 W. Christopher St., 91790. Tel: 626-960-3079; Fax: 626-338-7910. Mrs. Adela Solis, Prin.
Lay Teachers 9; Students 325.
Catechesis/Religious Programs—Tel: 626-338-2937. Dolores Zavala, D.R.E.
Students 700.
Convent—840 W. Christopher St., 91790. Tel: 818-338-6056.
Mission—West Covina, Los Angeles Co., St. Christopher Korean Catholic Community, 833-835 W. Christopher St., 91790. Tel: 626-960-5647.

West Hollywood, Los Angeles Co., St. Ambrose (1922), Rev. William P. Wolfe. In res., Rev. Brian Doran.
Res., 1281 N. Fairfax Ave., 90046. Tel: 323-656-4433; Fax: 323-656-6634.
Catechesis/Religious Programs—Students 27.

St. Victor (1906), Rev. Msgr. George J. Parnassus; Rev. Msgr. Jeremiah Murphy.
Res., 8634 Holloway Dr., 90069. Tel: 310-652-6477; Fax: 310-652-6478.
Catechesis/Religious Programs—Students 10.

Westlake Village, Los Angeles Co., St. Jude (1970), Rev. Msgr. William J. Leser, C.B.; Rev. Daniel C. White; Deacon Dick Dornan.
Res., 32032 W. Lindero Canyon Rd., 91361-4270. Tel: 818-889-1279; Fax: 818-889-3405.
School—32036 W. Lindero Canyon Rd., 91361-4270. Tel: 818-889-9483.
Lay Teachers 13; Students 230.
Catechesis/Religious Programs—32034 W. Lindero Canyon Rd., 91361-4270. Tel: 818-889-0612.
Students 535.

St. Maximilian Kolbe, Ventura Co., (1992), Rev. Msgr. Peter A. O'Reilly.
Res., 5801 Kanan Rd., 91362. Tel: 818-991-3915; Fax: 818-991-7152.
Catechesis/Religious Programs—Tel: 818-991-5604.
Students 517.

Whittier, Los Angeles Co., St. Mary of the Assumption (1803), Revs. Arturo Uribe, C.SS.R.; Tuan Pham, C.SS.R.; Joseph Tobin, C.SS.R.; Joseph Morin, C.SS.R.; Deacon James Fitzgerald, M.D. In res., Revs. Joseph Elliott, C.SS.R.; Donald Liberty, C.SS.R.; George Dawson, C.SS.R.; Arthur Frost, C.SS.R.; William Adams, C.SS.R.; Bro. Don E. O'Mara, C.SS.R.
Res., 7215 S. Newlin Ave., 90602. Tel: 562-698-0107; Fax: 562-696-1617.
School—Tel: 562-698-0253; Fax: 562-698-0206.
Lay Teachers 24; Students 578.
Catechesis/Religious Programs—Tel: 310-693-3764.
Students 704.

St. Bruno (1955), Revs. Patrick O'Dwyer; James Bradley, S.D.S.; Deacon P. Michael Freeman. In res., Rev. Frank Mannion, S.S.C.
Res., 15740 Citrustree Rd., 90603. Tel: 310-947-5637; Fax: 310-943-3193.
School—15700 Citrustree Rd., 90603. Tel: 310-943-8812; Fax: 310-943-2172.
Lay Teachers 14; Students 315.
Catechesis/Religious Programs—Tel: 310-943-2510.
Students 505.
Convent—10734 S. Widener Ave., 90603. Tel: 310-947-1177. Sr. Miriam Vu, L.H.C., Supr.

St. Gregory the Great (1951), Revs. John S. Schiavonne; Nestor Rebong; Jerald Thompson; Deacons Servando Patlan; Bruce Sago.
Res., 13935 Telegraph Rd., 90604. Tel: 562-941-0115; Fax: 562-941-3785.
School—13925 Telegraph Rd., 90604. Tel: 562-941-0750; Fax: 562-903-7325.
Lay Teachers 10; Students 311.
Catechesis/Religious Programs—Tel: 562-944-8311.
Students 1,010.

Wilmington, Los Angeles Co., SS. Peter and Paul's (1866), Revs. Peter Irving; Roberto Pirrone.
Res., 515 W. Opp St., 90744. Tel: 310-834-5215; Fax: 310-834-4685.
School—706 Bayview Ave., 90744. Tel: 310-834-5574; Fax: 310-518-6100.
Sisters 3; Lay Teachers 8; Students 279.
Catechesis/Religious Programs—Tel: 310-549-2048.
Students 880.

Holy Family (1929) (Hispanic), Rev. Msgr. Joseph F. Greeley; Revs. Esteban Marquez; Ramona G. Palomera.
Res., 1220 N. Sanford Ave., P.O. Box 416, 90748. Tel: 310-834-6333; Fax: 310-834-9038.
School—1122 E. Robidoux St., 90748. Tel: 310-518-1440; Fax: 310-518-1257. Mrs. Carmen A.O. Hart, Prin.
Lay Teachers 10; Students 230.
Catechesis/Religious Programs—Tel: 310-549-0011.
Students 596.

Woodland Hills, Los Angeles Co., St. Mel (1955), Rev. Msgr. Padraic Loftus; Rev. Msgr. John T. Naughton, Pastor Emeritus; Rev. Msgr. Michael J. O'Connor, Pastor Emeritus; Rev. Ramon Valera.
Res., 20870 Ventura Blvd., 91364. Tel: 818-340-6020; Fax: 818-340-0261.
School—20874 Ventura Blvd., 91364. Tel: 818-340-1924; Fax: 818-347-4426.
Sisters of St. Louis 2; Lay Teachers 33; Students 586.
Catechesis/Religious Programs—Tel: 818-340-6250.
Students 315.

St. Bernardine of Siena (1962), Rev. Msgr. Paul T. Dotson; Rev. Msgr. Richard H. Murray, Pastor Emeritus; Rev. Paul Brogan; Deacons Jerry Cellner; Dan McHugh; Dale Taufer.
Res., 24410 Calvert St., 91367. Tel: 818-888-8200; Fax: 818-888-5046.
School—Tel: 818-340-2130; Fax: 818-340-3417.
Lay Teachers 15; Students 325.
Catechesis/Religious Programs—6061 Valley Circle Blvd., 91367. Tel: 818-340-1440.
Students 427.

Chaplains of Public Institutions

Non-Catholic Hospitals/Institutions

LOS ANGELES. *Cedar Sinai Medical Center.* Rev. Michael Wempe, Chap., 8700 Beverly Blvd., Rm. 2508, 90048. Tel: 310-855-5550; Fax: 310-967-0643.

Immigration and Naturalization Service Tel: 213-251-3509. Rev. Robert W. McChesney, Coord.; Alice Linsmeier, Juvenile Coord., Tel: 213-251-3533; Rev. Peter G. Neeley, S.J. Tel: 310-241-2347.

L.A. City Fire Dept. Rev. Msgr. Christian M. Van Liefde, Chap., Tel: 818-894-2261.

L.A. County Fire Dept. Rev. Robert A. Folbrecht, Chap., Tel: 626-960-1136.

L.A. County/University of Southern California Hospital. Norris Cancer and USC University Hospital, St. Camillus Center for Pastoral Care, 1911 Zonal Ave., 90033. Tel: 323-225-4461; 213-223-9047 (AIDS Center); Fax: 323-225-9096. Chaplains: Revs. Christopher D. Ponnet; Michael Baker; Robert J. Jones; Gustavo Lara; Deacon James Dillon; Sr. Dora Hauchecorne, I.C.M.; Sr. Mary Jean Ferry, B.V.M.; Sr. Matilda Ortiz, C.M.S.T.; Sr. Angela Pacheco, C.S.J.; Sr. Nancy Bartasavich, S.P.; Sr. Pat Walsh, O.P.

L.A. Police Department. Rev. Michael P. McCullough, Chap., Employee Assistance Unit, 150 N. Los Angeles St., 90012. Tel: 213-485-0703.

Martin Luther King, Jr., Drew Medical Center 12021 Wilmington Ave., 90059-3019. Rev. Don R. Kribs, Chap., 435 S. Occidental, 90057-1598. Tel: 213-388-3742 (Precious Blood Church).

Metropolitan Detention Center. (Federal Institution) 535 N. Alameda St., 90012. Tel: 213-253-9575. Rev. Mark Santo, Chap.

CAMARILLO. *Camarillo State Hospital-Development Center.* Rev. Hippolyte L. Goossens, C.J., Chap., Tel: 805-484-3661 Ext. 4459, P.O. Box 6022-250, 93011. Tel: 805-484-3661, Ext. 4459.

Youth Correctional Facility, California Youth Authority 3100 Wright Rd., 93010-8307. Rev. Leo John Celano, O.Praem. Tel: 805-278-3846.

DOWNEY. *Rancho Los Amigos Medical Center* 7601 E. Imperial Hwy., 90242. Rev. Msgr. John A. Fosselman Tel: 562-940-7257.

DUARTE. *City of Hope Medical Center.* Rev. Ramon Marti, Sch.P., Chap., 1500 E. Duarte Rd., 91010. Tel: 626-359-8911.

LANCASTER. *Immigration and Naturalization Service* Mira Loma Facility, 45100 N. 60th St., W., 93536. Tel: 661-949-3811. Rev. John Galvan, S.J., Chap., Tel: 661-949-3848.

LOMPOC. *Lompoc Federal Correctional Institution.* Federal Intensive Confinement Center 3600 Guard Rd., 93436-2705. Tel: 805-736-4154, Ext. 725 & 450. Chaplains: Rev. Michael D. Kirkness, Supvr.; Deacon John Burke.

US Penitentiary 3901 Klein Rd., 93436. Tel: 805-735-2771, Ext. 450 & 345. Chaplains: Rev. Michael D. Kirkness; Deacon John Burke.

Vandenberg Air Force Base. Rev. David J. Ivey, Chap., Tel: 805-606-5773, 30SW/HC, 587 Utah St., Bldg. 16200, Vandenberg AFB, 93437-6309.

LONG BEACH. *Veterans Affairs Medical Center.* Rev. Leo M. Miller, O.M.I., Chap.; Rev. Msgr. Joseph F. Brennan, (Retired), USN; Rev. Anselm Deehr, S.T., 5901 E. 7th St., 90822. Tel: 562-494-5418.

NORWALK. *California Youth Authority.* Rev. Tom Moletteire, Chap., Southern Youth Correction Reception, 13200 S. Bloomfield Ave., 90650. Tel: 562-868-9979, Ext. 2467.

Metropolitan State Hospital. Rev. Jerome Stack, C.PP.S., Chap., Tel: 310-863-7011, 11400 S. Norwalk Blvd., 90650. Tel: 562-651-4311.

POINT MUGU. *Naval Air Station.* Rev. Adrian R. Gervacio, LCDR, CHC, USNR, Bldg. 121, Code NASCG, 93042. Tel: 805-989-7967.

POMONA. *Frank D. Lanterman Development Center* 3035 W. Pomona Blvd., 91768. Tel: 909-595-1221, Ext. 7162. Mailing Address:Mailing Address: P.O. Box 100, 91769. Sr. Nuala Ryan, S.S.L., Chap., Tel: 909-869-1181.

PORT HUENEME. *Naval Construction Battalion Center.* Rev. Adrian R. Gervacio, NCBC Code CBCHP, 1000 23rd Ave. Tel: 805-982-4358.

SAN PEDRO. *Fort MacArthur Annex.* Rev. Michael J. DiRenzo, 61-ABG/HC, Chaplain's Office, 325 Challenger Way, Ste. 1901, LAAFB, El Segundo, 90245-5677. Tel: 310-363-1956.

Immigration and Naturalization Service San Pedro Service Processing Center, 2001 Seaside Ave., 90731. Tel: 310-241-2347. Rev. Peter G. Neeley, S.J.

SEPULVEDA. *Veterans Administration Medical Center.* Rev. Patrick O'Hagan, SS.CC. Tel: 818-895-9322, 16111 Plummer St., 91343-2099.

TERMINAL ISLAND. *Federal Correctional Institution.* Rev. Henry L. Hernanco, Contract Chap., 1299 Seaside Ave., San Pedro, 90731-0207. Tel: 626-918-8314.

TORRANCE. *L.A. County-Harbor-U.C.L.A. Medical Center* 1000 W. Carson, 90509. Tel: 310-222-2345; 222-2167 (Catholic Chap. Office). Rev. Cesar Raffo-Rivasplata, 21900 S. Main St., Carson, 90745. Tel: 310-835-7161 (St. Philomena Parish).

WEST LOS ANGELES. *Veterans Administration Wadsworth Hospital Center.* Rev. Francis Kelly Tel: 310-824-4312, Chaplain Service, 11301 Wilshire Blvd. 691/125, 90099-5786. Tel: 310-268-3391.

Detention Ministries

LOS ANGELES. *L.A. Juvenile Detention Facilities* Central Juvenile Hall, 1605 Eastlake Ave., 90033. Tel: 323-226-8530. Javier E. Stauring, Chap.,

MacLaren Hall.

Dorothy Kirby Center, Sr. Claudia L. Romero, O.D.N., Chap., Tel: 213-637-7615.

Los Angeles County Jails in the City of Los Angeles, Adult Facilities Biscailuz Center, 1060 N. Eastern Ave., Tel: 323-881-3636. Deacon Thomas E. Brandlin, Chap., Tel: 213-353-6509 (Pager),

L.A. Men's Central Jail, 441 Bauchet St., 90012. Tel: 213-974-8081. Chaplains: Rev. George Horan; Deacon Paulino R. Jaurez; Bro. Lawrence J. Moen, C.M.F. Tel: 213-974-8081; Catherine Conneally-Salazar,

Sybil Brand Institute, 4500 E. City Terrace Dr., 90063. Tel: 213-267-2809. Mrs. Karen E. Brudney; Sr. Mary Leo Grijalva, S.N.J.M.; Sr. Rose Waldron, D.M.J.

Metropolitan Detention Center. (Federal Institution) 535 N. Alameda St., 90053. Tel: 213-253-9575. Rev. Mark Santo.

Office of Detention Ministry 3424 Wilshire Blvd., 90010-2241. Tel: 213-637-7648; Fax: 213-637-6161. Sr. Suzanne Jabro, C.S.J., Dir.

Twin Towers Correctional Facility I. (Men). 450 Bauchet St., 90063. Tel: 213-893-5241; Fax: 213-830-0907. Gerardo F. Gomez, Chap.

Twin Towers Correctional Facility II. (Women) 450 Bauchet St., 90063. Sr. Catherine Marie Bazar, O.P. Tel: 213-893-5152; Fax: 213-830-0907.

CAMARILLO. *Youth Correctional Facility* 3100 Wright Rd., 93010. Tel: 805-278-3746. Rev. Leo John Celano, O.Praem.

DOWNEY. *Los Padrinos Juvenile Hall* 7285 Quill Dr., 90242. Tel: 562-940-8711; 8712. Sr. Teresa Doherty, R.S.C.

LANCASTER. *California State Prison, L.A. County* 44750 60th St. W., 93536-7620. Tel: 805-729-2000, Ext. 6129. Rev. Tomas White, Chap.

Challenger Youth Memorial Center. (Vacant) 5300 West Ave. I, 93536. Tel: 805-940-4165; 4166.

LYNWOOD. *Century Regional Detention Facility* 11705 S. Alameda St., 90262. Tel: 323-357-5114. Teddy B. Harder, Chap.

NORWALK. *Southern Youth Correctional Reception* 13200 S. Bloomfield Ave., 90650. Tel: 562-868-9979, Ext. 2467. Tom Moletteire, Chap.

OJAI. *Ojai Men's Honor Farm* 370 W. Baldwin Rd., 93023. Tel: 805-649-6020. Margaret Oberon, Chap., Tel: 805-654-5087.

Ojai Women's Jail Farm 370 W. Baldwin Rd., 93023. Tel: 805-649-3020. Margaret Oberon, Chap., Tel: 805-654-5087.

SANTA BARBARA. *Los Prietos Boy's Camp* Star Route, 93105-9722. Tel: 805-681-5334. Eduardo Arnouil, Chap.

Santa Barbara County Jail 4436A Calle Real, 93110. Eduardo Arnouil, Chap., Tel: 805-681-5334.

Santa Barbara Juvenile Hall 4500 Hollister Avenue, 93111. Tel: 805-692-4800. Eduardo Arnouil, Chap.

SANTA MARIA. *Juvenile Hall* 812-B W. Foster Rd., 93454. Tel: 805-681-5334. Eduardo Arnouil, Chap.

SANTA PAULA. *Santa Paula Jail* 600 S. Todd Rd., 93060. Tel: 805-933-8564. Margaret Oberon, Chap., Tel: 805-654-5087.

SAUGUS. *North County Correctional Facility* 29340 The Old Road, 91350. Tel: 661-295-7800, Ext. 5217. William B. McKinley, Chap.

Pitchess Detention Center 29300 The Old Road, 91350. Medium South, Rev. John D. Murray Tel: 661-257-8853 Ext. 3020, Medium North, Gonzalo De Vivero Tel: 661-257-8840 Ext. 3445, Maximum East, Patricia R. Bartlett, Chap., Tel: 661-257-8815 Ext. 3337.

SYLMAR. *Barry J. Nidorf Juvenile Hall* 16350 Filbert St., 91342. Tel: 818-364-2021. Marciano Avilla, Chap.

THOUSAND OAKS. *East County Jail* 2101 E. Olsen Rd., 93162. Tel: 805-933-8564. Margaret Oberon, Chap., Tel: 805-654-5087.

VENTURA. *Colston Treatment Center* 315 N. Hillmont Ave., 93003. Tel: 805-652-5721. Margaret Oberon, Chap.

Ventura County Jail 800 S. Victoria Ave., 93009. Margaret Oberon, Chap., Tel: 805-654-5087.

Ventura Juvenile Hall-Clifton Tatum Center. Vacant. 380 N. Hillmont Ave., 93003. Tel: 805-652-5727. Margaret Oberon, Chap.

Ventura Juvenile Restitution Project. Vacant. 381 Hospital Rd., 93003. Tel: 805-652-6594. Margaret Oberon, Chap.

WHITTIER. *Fred C. Nelles Correctional Facility.* (Vacant) 11850 E. Whittier Blvd., 90601.

Camps

LOS ANGELES. *Juvenile Probation Camps.*

Camp C.B. Afflerbaugh, 6331 N. Stephens Ranch Rd., La Verne, 91750. Tel: 909-596-0686. Connie Arambula, Chap.

Camp Dorothy Kirby Center, 1500 S. McDonnell Ave., 90022. Tel: 213-637-7615. Sr. Claudia L. Romero, Chap.,

Camp David Gonzales, 1301 N. Las Virgines Rd., Calabasas, 91302. Tel: 310-821-4126. Bob Strickland, Chap.,

Camp Holton, 12653 N. Little Tujunga Canyon Rd., San Fernando, 91342. Tel: 213-637-7632. Tom Molttierre, Chap.,

Camp Kilpatrick, 427 S. Encinal Canyon Rd., Malibu, 90265. Tel: 818-991-7878. Jim Graham, Chap.,

Camp McLaren Children's Center, 4024 Durfee Rd., El Monte, 91732. Tel: 310-393-7460; 213-637-7615. Sr. Claudia L. Romero, O.D.N., Chap.,

Camp Mendenhall, 42230 Lake Hughes Rd., Lake Hughes, 93532. Tel: 661-942-1370. Alfred Miller, Chap.,

Camp Miller, 433 S. Encinal Canyon Rd., Malibu, 90265. Tel: 310-820-2191. Jerry P. Vogler, Chap.,

Camp John Munz, 42220 Lake Hughes Rd., Lake Hughes, 93532. Tel: 805-942-1370. Alfred E. Miller, Chap.,

Camp Paige, 6601 N. Stephens Ranch Rd., La Verne, 91750. Tel: 909-593-7056. Chaplains: Frank Cunningham; Cindy Cunningham,

Camp Rockey, 1900 N. Sycamore Canyon Rd., San Dimas, 91773. Tel: 909-592-3132. Jim Drolet, Chap.,

Camp Routh, 12500 Big Tujunga Rd., Tujunga, 91042. Tel: 213-663-1142. Bro. Kevin Cunniff, Chap.,

Camp Scott, (Girls) 28700 N. Bouquet Canyon Rd., Saugus, 91350. Tel: 805-527-2408. Deacon Pete Wilson, Chap.,

Camp Kenyon J. Scudder, 28750 N. Bouquet Canyon Rd., Saugus, 91350. Tel: 805-268-1564. Maria La Monica, Chap.

Sierra Conservation Camps, California Department of Correction.

#4 Fransciquito, Vacant. 35100 N. San Francisquito Canyon Rd., Saugus, 91350. Tel: 661-296-4409.

#11 Acton, Vacant. 8800 Soledad Canyon Rd., Acton, 93510. Tel: 661-268-0113.

#13 Malibu, Vacant. 1250 S. Encinal Canyon Rd., Malibu, 90265. Tel: 310-457-2253.

#16 Mount Gleason, Vacant. 26650 N. Angeles Forest Hwy., Palmdale. Tel: 661-947-7784.

#19 Julius Klein, Vacant. 22550 E. Fork Rd., Azusa, 91702. Tel: 818-910-1213.

On Duty Outside the Archdiocese:
Reverend Fathers—
Beck, Lawrence J.
Collins, John M.
Cummins, Charles T.
Joy, Laurence
Miskella, Richard
O'Shea, Patrick
Palacios, Joseph M., S.J.
Tucker, James S.
Young, Gerald A.
Zak, Steven B.

Military and VA Chaplains:
Reverend Fathers—
Kelly, Francis
Llanos, Philip S.
Marrell, Dennis P.
McNulty, Gerard J.

Graduate Studies:
Reverend Fathers—
Chaffman, Charles J.
Hill, Patrick J.
Lima, Vivian B.
Love, John W.
Wolkovits, Paul

On Sick Leave:
Reverend Fathers—
Cavanaugh, James
Griffin, Noel
Higson, John P.
LaNier, Michael L.
Lee, Joseph P.
McDonnell, Anthony
Nuanez, Anthony
Warren, Thomas

Retired:
Most Rev.—
Arzube, Juan A., Sacred Heart Church, 2889 N. Lincoln Ave., Altadena, CA 91001-4598
Ward, John J., 3424 Wilshire Blvd., Los Angeles, CA 90010-2241
Reverend Monsignors—
Acton, John A., St. Dorothy Church, 241 S. Valley Center Ave., Glendora, CA 91740-3899
Atwill, William H., Nazareth House, 3333 Manning Ave., Los Angeles, CA 90064-4804
Biedermann, Arnold, Sacred Heart, 10800 Henderson Rd., Ventura, CA 93004-1895
Boyer, Leland J., St. Bede the Venerable, 215 Foothill Blvd., LaCanada, Flintridge, CA 91011-3754
Brennan, Joseph F., 800 E. Ocean Blvd., Apt. #1205, Long Beach, CA 90802-5455
Brosnan, John R., St. Ann Church, 2302 Riverdale Ave., Los Angeles, CA 90031-1133
Caslin, Peter C., St. Bartholomew, 252 Granada Ave., Long Beach, CA 91011-0809
Clark, Laurence E., 15322 Roselle Ave., Lawndale, CA 90260
Clyne, James B., Nazareth House, 3333 Manning Ave., Los Angeles, CA 90064-4804
Colberg, James P., 208 Miller St., Santa Maria, CA 93454
Collins, Fachtna P., P.O. Box 535, Montrose, CA 91020
Condon, Michael J., St. Anthony, 2511 S. C St., P.O. Box 2215, Oxnard, CA 93034-2215
Condon, Robert F., Nazareth House, 3333 Manning Ave., Los Angeles, CA 90064-4804
Dessert, James A., Nazareth House, 3333 Manning Ave., Los Angeles, CA 90064-4804
Diomartich, Felix S., St. Anthony, 712 N. Grand Ave., Los Angeles, CA 90012-2299
Doherty, John B., Nazareth House, 3333 Manning Ave., Los Angeles, CA 90064
Donnelly, Lawrence E., 1065 W. Lomita Blvd., Space 411, Harbor City, CA 90710
Doyle, Thomas, 3618 Valihi Way, Glendale, CA 91208
English, Tobias P., St. Andrew, 311 N. Raymond Ave., Pasdena, CA 91103-3896
Escutin, Ciriaco E., 16151 Elgenia St., Covina, CA 91722
Folliard, John P., St. Cornelius Church, 5500 E. Wardlow Rd., Long Beach, CA 90808-3698
Fosselman, John A., St. Raymond, 12348 Paramount Blvd., P.O. Box 2085, Downey, CA 90242-0285
Frilot, Eugene P., Incarnation Church, 1001 N. Brand, Glendale, CA 91202-2979
George, Alexander C., P.O. Box 208, Blue Jay, CA 92317
Gilb, Eugene A., St. John the Fisher, 5448 Crest Rd., Rancho Palos Verdes, CA 90275-5097
Grill, Philip L., Nazareth House, 3333 Manning Ave., Los Angeles, CA 90064-4804
Gualderon, Ernest J., St. Anthony, 540 Olive Ave., Long Beach, CA 90802-2651
Hayes, Thomas G., Nazareth House, 3333 Manning Ave., Los Angeles, CA 90064-4804
Healy, Peter C., St. Robert Bellarmine, 133 N. Fifth St., Burbank, CA 91501-2178
Hernandez, Alfred, P.O. Box 777, Cedar Glen, CA 92321
Holland, Ian E., P.O. Box 11475, Marina Del Rey, CA 90295
Hughes, John C., St. Mary Magdelen, 2532 Ventura Blvd., Camarillo, CA 93010-6649
Kearney, Joseph V., St. Joseph, 5048 El Carro Ln., Carpinteria, CA 93013-1450
Kelly, Matthew H., Pinyon Crest, P.O. Box 253, Mountain Center, CA 92361
Kennedy, Christopher J., 3938 Cerritos Ave., Long Beach, CA 90807-3799
Kiefer, Thomas A., St. Charles Borremeo, 10828 Moorpark St., North Hollywood, CA 91602
Kucingis, John A., St. Casimir, 2718 St. George St., Los Angeles, CA 90027
McCabe, Vincent, P.O. Box 30471, Santa Barbara, CA 93105
McGovern, Thomas, 564 Bellflower Blvd. #309, Long Beach, CA 90814
McGrath, Andrew, 101 South U St. #5, Lompoc, CA 93436-7299
McNulty, Patrick, 2501 West Avenue 33, Los Angeles, CA 90065-2892
Mihan, John A., Maria Prima Retirement Residence, 1501 Selby Ave., Los Angeles, CA 90024
Mulcahy, Donal, Our Lady of the Assumption, 3175 Telegraph Rd., Ventura, CA 93003-3283
Mulcahy, James R., St. Louis of France, 13935 E. Temple Ave., La Puente, CA 91746
Murray, Richard H., St. Bernardine of Siena, 24410 Calvert St., Woodland Hills, CA 91367-1099
Naughton, John T., St. Mel Church, 20870 Ventura Blvd., Woodland Hills, CA 91364-2396
Navin, Cyril, St. Cyril of Jerusalem Church, 4601 Firmament Ave., Encino, CA 91436-3108
O'Brien, Kenneth R., St. John of God Nursing Home, 2035 W. Adams Blvd., Los Angeles, CA 90018
O'Byrne, Sylvester, Our Lady of Mt. Carmel, 1300 E. Valley Rd., Santa Barbara, CA 93108-1294
O'Callaghan, James A., St. John Vianney Church, 1345 Turnbull Canyon Rd., Hacienda Heights, CA 91745-2699

O'Connor, Michael J., St. John of God Hospital and Nursing Home, 2035 W. Adams Blvd., Los Angeles, CA 90018
O'Reilly, Bernard, 15360 Virginia Ave., Paramount, CA 90723
O'Sullivan, Peter, St. John Baptist de la Salle, 10738 Hayvenhurst St., Granada Hills, CA 91344
Osborne, Francis M., Our Lady of Grace, 5011 White Oak Ave., Encino, CA 91316-3799
Ravlic, Cornelius C., Nazareth House, 3333 Manning Ave., Los Angeles, CA 90064-4804
Rawden, John A., St. Francis Hospital, 601 E. Micheltorena, Santa Barbara, CA 93103
Sanchez, Manuel, Plaza de los Lobos #1, Piso 5A, Granada, Spain
Segaric, John, St. Anthony, 712 N. Grand Ave., Los Angeles, CA 90012-2299
Sheridan, John V., Our Lady of Malibu, 3625 S. Winter Canyon Rd., Malibu, CA 90265
Valle, Fernando, 2nda Avenida A3-44, Zona #1, Guatemala 001, Guatemala
Von Son, Henry A., 11075 S.W. Muirwood, Portland, OR 97225
Walsh, Michael, Monea, Ardmore, Youghal, County Cork, Ireland
Walsh, Robert, Holy Angels, 370 Campus Dr., Arcadia, CA 91006-6917
Young, John M., 4142 Los Padres Dr., Fallbrook, CA 92028
Zimmerman, Roland G., Annunciation, 1307 E. Longden Ave., Arcadia, CA 91006-5597

Reverend Fathers—
Amengual, Miguel, Nativity, 1447 Engracia Ave., Torrance, CA 90501-3234
Barry, William J., Proto Notary Apostolic, 68 Balboa Coves, Newport Beach, CA 92663
Bebek, Dominic L.
Bradley, Robert M., 108 Courtside Dr., Butler, PA 16001-2466
Buckley, Michael, St. John of God Nursing Home, 2035 W. Adams Blvd., Los Angeles, CA 90018
Byrne, Robert P., Nazareth House, 3333 Manning Ave., Los Angeles, CA 90064-4804
Ciordia, Pedro M., Concejo de Egues #20, 2B, 31016 Mendillorri-Pamplona, Navarro
Combs, Regis V., Ventura Marina Park #74, 1215 Anchor Way, Ventura, CA 93001
Cooley, John E., 31402 Paseo del Mar, Laguna Niguel, CA 92677-2745
Coronado, Genero, 2505 W. Foothill Blvd., #145, San Bernardino, CA 92410
Cotter, Patrick John, 1854 Hanscom Dr., South Pasadena, CA 91030
Cullen, Francis J., 211 S. Beach Blvd., Space 75, Anaheim, CA 92804-1838
Cunningham, John F., 20053 S.W. Rock Bluff Cir., Bend, OR 97702
Daly, John, Holy Trinity, 3722 Boyce Ave., Los Angeles, CA 90039-1810
Dao, Nhuong V., 5571 Angelus Ave., San Gabriel, CA 91776
DeDominici, Lorenzo, Mary Star of the Sea, 870 W. 8th St., San Pedro, CA 90731-3091
Delaney, Matthew S., P.O. Box 2007, Seal Beach, CA 90740-2998
Duffy, Eugene J., Bridge St., Louisburgh, County Mayo, Ireland
Feeney, John J., Nazareth House, 3333 Manning, Los Angeles, CA 90064-4804
Ferrer, Peter C., 11544 Henry St., Carlsbad, CA 92009-3946
Fitzgerald, John B., 951 Laurelwood St., Carlsbad, CA 92009-3946
Ford, Harold L., St. Joseph, 6220 E. Willow St., Long Beach, CA 90815-2295
Gabriel, Vicente S., 3045 N. Gold Star Dr., Long Beach, CA 90810-2708
Gaffney, James T., Nazareth House, 3333 Manning Ave., Los Angeles, CA 90064
George, Alexander C., P.O. Box 2208, Blue Jay, CA 92317
Gorman, Patrick J., St. Bernadette, 3825 Don Felipe Dr., Los Angeles, CA 90008-4299
Gorman, Rody I., St. Matthias, 7125 Mission Pl., Huntington Park, CA 90255-5299
Gutting, John C., St. Athanasius, 5390 Linden Ave., Long Beach, CA 90805-6062
Halloran, John J., 5255 Stevens Creek, Santa Clara, CA 95051-6664
Han, Andrew
Hanly, John J., Nazareth House, 3333 Manning Ave., Los Angeles, CA 90064-4804
Harman, Charles W., 261 South Rodeo Dr., Beverly Hills, CA 90212
Hernandez, Stephen C., Our Lady of Guadalupe, 4509 Mercury Ave., Los Angeles, CA 90032-1931
Hughes, Patrick M., 2020 Via Mariposa E., Laguna Woods, CA 92653
Hunter, William R., St. John of God Hospital, 2035 W. Adams Blvd., Los Angeles, CA 90018
Infuhr, Frank J., St. John of God Nursing Home, 2035 W. Adams, Los Angeles, CA 90018
Jennings, Bernard J., St. Elizabeth, 1849 N. Lake Ave., Altadena, CA 91001-3097
Johnson, Henry J., 1211 N. Gardsen, Covina, CA 91724
Kass, George P., Nazareth House, 3333 Manning Ave., Los Angeles, CA 90064-4804
Kelly, Paul M.
Kennedy, John A., c/o The Presbytery, Grove Hill, Cornwall, TR2 5BJ England
Landreau, Edward J., St. Frances of Rome, 501 E. Foothill Blvd., P.O. Box 637, Azusa, CA 91702-0637
Lee, Peter, 605 S. Sefton Ave., Monterey Park, CA 91754-1698
Lirette, Arthur J., Proto Notary Apostolic, Holy Family, 209 E. Lomita Ave., Glendale, CA 91205-1689
Luck, Robert O., 388 Thornhill Circle, Henderson, NV 89014
Luistro, Abelardo R., 4263 W. Ave. 40, Los Angeles, CA 90065
Maechler, Edmund F., 613 California St., Huntington Beach, CA 92648
Maechler, Gerald T., 18401 Delaware Ave., Huntington Beach, CA 92648
Martin, Diodado, Assumption, 2832 Blanchard St., Los Angeles, CA 90033-2699
McGee, Peter J., 848 Lois Lane, Fullerton, CA 92632
McGrath, Philip J., St. Bernard, 9627 E. Beach St., Bellflower, CA 90706-0576
McHugh, Patrick J., Nativity Church, 1447 Engracia Ave., Torrance, CA 90501-3234
McLaughlin, Thomas W., St. John of God, 2035 W. Blvd., Los Angeles, CA 90018
Merino, Santiago, 959 LaDeney Dr., Ontario, CA 91762
Meskill, Patrick A., 63 Ilex Dr., Newbury Park, CA 91320
Miller, George M.
Murphy, Denis J., Our Lady of the Assumption, 3175 Telegraph Rd., Ventura, CA 93003-3283
Nagy, Joseph
Nocero, Pascal F., P.O. Box 279, Oak View, CA 93022
O'Grady, James F., Visitation Church, 6561 W. 88th St., Los Angeles, CA 90045-3716
O'Leary, Neil F.
O'Neill, Jeremiah, St. Thomas More, 2510 S. Fremont Ave., Alhambra, CA 91803-4398
O'Shea, Michael, 9919 Ramona St., Apt. 403, Bellflower, CA 90706
O'Sullivan, Thomas C., Our Lady of Mt. Carmel Church, 1300 E. Valley Rd., Santa Barbara, CA 93108-1294
Pisano, Andrew, 6938 Grange Ave., Bell Gardens, CA 90201
Potthoff, Donald W., St. Denis Church, 2151 Diamond Bar Blvd., P.O. Box 4096, Diamond Bar, CA 91765-2860
Power, Patrick A., Our Lady of Perpetual Help, 23233 W. Lyons Ave., Santa Clarita, CA 91321-2632
Raymundo, Gregorio G., 1948 Frank St., Unit 1, Santa Monica, CA 90404-4935
Rodriguez, Lawrence, Soto y Amio, Santovenio de San Marcos, C.P. 24125, (Leon) Spain
Rothe, James A., P.O. Box 962, Bridgeport, CA 93517-0692
Rucker, Neville, Corpus Christi Church, 887 Toyopa Dr., P.O. Box 887, Pacific Palisades, CA 90272-0887
Sanchez, Eliseo, 13308 E. Loumont, North Whittier, CA 90601
Saplis, Raymond A., Mother Gertrude Balcazar Home, 11320 Laurel Canyon Blvd., San Fernando, CA 91340
Segaric, John, St. Anthony, 712 N. Grand Ave., Los Angeles, CA 90012-2299
Seymour, Francis J., St. John of God Nursing Home, 2035 W. Adams Blvd., Los Angeles, CA 90018
Stehly, Thomas J., 9432 S. Bloomfield Ave., Cypress, CA 90630
Thomas, Sylvester J., Mary Star of the Sea, 870 W. Eighth St., San Pedro, CA 90731-3091
Thompson, Jerome H., 6123 Centralia St., Lakewood, CA 90713
Torralba, Antolin B., Sapalicio St., Polangui, Albay, Philippines
Tsang, Peter, St. Elizabeth Ann Seton, 1835 Larkvane Rd., Rowland Hgts., CA 91748-2501
Vecsey, Stephen N., 1120 Northwood Rd., 186D, Seal Beach, CA 90740
Vellucci, Dennis C., Sacred Heart Retreat Center, 410 Granada Ave., Alhambra, CA 91801
Villa, Nemorio, Calle Durango 1208, Sec. Hildalgo, Guadalajara, Jalisco, CP442-60 Mexico
Villacis, Jose H., 10814 Dalerose Ave., Lennox, CA 90304-2230
Villegas, Samuel C., St. Matthias, 7125 Mission Pl., Huntington Park, CA 90255-5299
Walker, Earl G., Cathedral Chapel, 922 S. Detroit St., Los Angeles, CA 90036-4812
Walker, Gerald B., 2020 Via Mariposa E., Laguna Hills, CA 92653
Weible, Thomas C., 9 Highview Dr., Sandwich, MA 02563
Wishard, John W., 4830 Sanchez Dr., Guadalupe, CA 93434

Permanent Deacons:
Acquaviva, Dick, St. Clare, Canyon Country
Adams, Emile, Jr., St. Bernadette, Los Angeles
Adams, J. Rodger, Our Lady of the Assumption Church, Ventura
Adams, James V., Chaminade College Preparatory, West Hills
Aguirre, Eduardo, St. Emydius, Lynwood
Alexander, Hosea, Sr., St. Agatha, Los Angeles
Allen, John P., Corpus Christi, Pacific Palisades
Andrade, Trinidad, St. Louis de Montfort, Santa Maria
Aranda, Fernando, Jr., Our Lady of Solitude, Los Angeles
Arroyo, Miguel, Our Lady of Guadalupe, Los Angeles
Auela, Uikirifi, Samoan Catholic Community
Baker, Charles, St. Linus, Norwalk
Balbuena, Wesley M., Jr., St. Elisabeth, Van Nuys
Barragan, Arturo, St. Hilary, Pico Rivera
Battle, Joe T., St. Philip Neri, Lynwood
Bautista, Rolando, Holy Trinity, Los Angeles
Bednar, George T., St. Mary Magdalen, Camarillo
Berumen, Ricardo, St. John Neumann
Bohlig, Alden W., St. Barnabas, Long Beach
Brandlin, Thomas E., Century Regional Detention Facility, Lynwood
Bravo, Anthony, St. Gerard Majela, Los Angeles
Bret, James, Santa Barbara Mission, Santa Barbara
Burke, John, La Purisma Concepcion, Lompoc
Calonge, Ellie, Our Lady of the Holy Rosary, Sun Valley
Caputo, Edward E., Blessed Junipero Serra, Lancaster
Carmody, Richard, St. Louis de Montford, Santa Maria
Caro, Jose, St. Cecilia, Los Angeles
Castorena, John G., Santa Clara, Oxnard
Cellner, Jerry, St. Bernardine of Siena, Woodland Hills
Chacon, Paul, Our Lady of Lourdes, Tujunga
Charters, John, Sacred Heart, Lancaster
Chavez, Gilbert M., Annunciation, Monrovia
Chu, Peter, St. Elizabeth Ann Ston, Rowland Heights
Clements, Brian, St. Peter Claver, Simi Valley
Clinton, Jack, Holy Name of Mary, San Dimas
Conrey, Fred, Immaculate Conception, Monrovia
Coplen, John L., St. Francis de Sales, Sherman Oaks
Corcios, Oscar, Our Lady of the Rosary, Paramount
Corwin, Richard, St. Margaret Mary Alacoque, Lomita
Crisafulli, Nino D., Mary Star of the Sea, San Pedro
Crowley, James, Assumption, Pasadena
Cuevas, Frank, St. Madeleine, Pomona
Curran, Nicholas P., Holy Cross, Santa Barbara
De Los Reyes, Carlito, St. Lucy, Long Beach
Delgado, Eduardo T., St. John Vianney, Hacienda Heights
Denisac, Charles M., Jr., Our Lady of Perpetual Help, Downey
Dieter, Frank, St. Lawrence Martyr, Redondo Beach
Dillon, James, St. Benedict, Montebello
Doane, Allan E., St. Thomas Aquinas, Ojai
Dornan, Richard, St. Jude, Westlake Village
Duke, Oscar M., St. Anthony, Oxnard
Dumlao, Felix, St. Anthony of Padua, Gardena
Edmonds, Tom, Queen of Angels, Lompoc
Engel, Witold, Our Lady of Refuge, Long Beach
Escovedo, Arthur, Our Lady of the Assumption, Claremont
Espana, Salvador, St. Elisabeth, Van Nuys
Estey, Marvin, Holy Name of Mary, San Dimas
Estrada, David, St. Benedict, Montebello
Fajardo, Richard, Resurrection, Los Angeles
Farley, James, Our Lady of the Assumption, Ventura
Favela, Jacobo M., Jr., St. Martha, Valinda
FitzGerald, Gerald M., St. Francis of Assisi, Fillmore
Fitzgerald, James, St. Mary of the Assumption, Whittier
Fitzpatrick, Arthur J., St. Paul of the Cross, La Mirada

Freeman, P. Michael, St. Bruno, Whittier
Frias, Sam, St. John the Baptist de la Salle, Granada Hills
Fry, Ralph M., Sacred Heart, Covina
Galido, Juan, Jr., Our Lady of Lourdes, Northridge
Garcia, Armando R., Holy Spirit, Los Angeles
Garcia, William J., Mary Star of the Sea, San Pedro
Gaudin, John, Holy Name of Jesus, Los Angeles
Goodreau, Theodore, St. Anthony, El Segundo
Goodspeed, Lyle, St. John Neumann, Santa Maria
Gueringer, Ludger A., Blessed Junipero Serra, Camarillo
Guerra, Ruben, St. Joseph, La Puente
Gutierrez, Eliseo, Unassigned
Hall, Willard J., Sr., St. John the Evangelist, Los Angeles
Halley, James, St. Matthew, Long Beach
Halvorsen, Douglas A., St. Louis de Montfort, Santa Maria
Hammonds, Johnnie, Jr., St. Mary Magdalen, Camarillo
Hanson, Walter, St. Charles Borromeo, North Hollywood
Harrison, Russell J., SS Peter and Paul, Wilmington
Hawkins, Bill, St. Brigid, Los Angeles
Hays, Charles D., La Purisima Concepcion, Lompoc
Hegenbart, Joseph, St. James the Less, La Crescenta
Henry, James J., St. Anthony, Oxnard
Henschel, Louis E., St. Julie Billiart, Newbury Park
Hillman, Steven V., St. Elizabeth Ann Seton, Rowland Heights
Holly, Chester N., St. John Eudes, Chatsworth
Huff, David W., Holy Cross, Santa Barbara
Juarez-Ramirez, Paulino, St. Theresa of Avila, Los Angeles
Karl, Richard J., Our Lady of Perpetual Help, Santa Clarita
Lacy, William S., St. Joseph the Worker, Canoga Park
Lambey, Alvin S., Mother of Sorrows, Los Angeles
Landa, William, St. Philip the Apostle, Pasadena
Lanoix, Gilbert, St. Brigid, Los Angeles
Ledonne, Tom, St. Denis, Diamond Bar
Ledoux, Joseph, St. Albert the Great, Compton
Lee, Paul D., St. Bruno, Whittier
Liendo, Manuel, St. John Neumann, Santa Maria
Lim, James, Korean Catholic Center, Canoga Park
Lipski, Alexander, St. Cornelius, Long Beach
Lira, Pedro, St. Catherine of Siena, Reseda
Lopez, Arnaldo, Holy Angels, Arcadia
Lopez, Francisco, La Purisima Concepcion, Lompoc
Lopez, Jose R., Our Lady of Lourdes, Los Angeles
Macial, Robert, Sr., St. Louis de Montfort, Santa Maria
Madrigal, Carlos, Sacred Heart, Pomona
Magana, Matilde, St. Catherine Laboure, Torrance
Manion, Joseph, Sr., St. Jude, Westlake Village
Martinez, Jesse, St. John Vianney, Hacienda Heights
Martinez, Manuel J., Our Lady of Guadalupe, Santa Barbara
Martinez, Randolph M., Santa Clara, Oxnard
McHugh, Daniel J., St. Bernardine of Siena, Woodland Hills
McKinley, Braden, Sacred Heart, Ventura
McNamara, Eugene, St. Monica, Santa Monica
McPheeters, Jon C., St. Anthony, Oxnard
Mecozzi, John, Blessed Junipero Serra, Camarillo
Medina, Richard J., Our Lady of Perpetual Help, Downey
Mejia, J. Guadalupe, Holy Family, Artesia
Messer, John, St. Anthony, San Gabriel
Meter, Darrell, La Purisima Concepcion, Lompoc
Miller, Robert, St. James, Redondo Beach
Millholland, Frank O., St. Albert the Great, Compton
Mimiaga, Guillermo R., St. Raphael, Los Angeles
Mizerski, Joseph R., St. Theresa, Alhambra
Modugno, Larry L., St. Mary Magdalen, Camarillo
Moloney, Douglas, St. Christopher, West Covina
Morgan, Richard, Blessed Sacrament, Los Angeles
Moske, Thomas, St. Joseph, Hawthorne
Nawrocik, Zenon L., St. Mary and Marian Medical Center, Santa Maria
Nguyen, Loc, St. Christopher, West Covina
Nguyen, Matthew Van, Maria Regina, Gardena
Noon, Richard, St. John Vianney, Hacienda Heights
Noriega, Restie T., Incarnation, Glendale
Nosari, Ernest, St. Rita, Sierra Madre
Orcutt, Mark A., St. Paul of the Cross, La Mirada
Origel, Carlos, Our Lady of Perpetual Help, Downey
Orth, Joseph, St. Euphrasia, Granada Hills
Palmer, William, Our Lady of Guadalupe, Hermosa Beach
Parish, Harold A., J.C.D., Mary Star of the Sea, Oxnard
Patian, Servando, Sr., St. Gregory the Great, Whittier
Patterson, Gary R., Our Lady of Guadalupe, Irwindale
Pelletier, Frederick H., Holy Family, Glendale
Pepe, Joseph, Office of the Catholic Chaplain, NCB, Oxnard
Perez, Buenaventura, Mary Star of the Sea, Oxnard
Picard, John B., Blessed Junipero Serra, Camarillo
Pruitt, Richard A., Little Company of Mary Hospital, Torrance
Ramirez, Fidel M., Mary Star of the Sea, Oxnard
Ramirez-Chavez, Hernan, St. Raphael, Los Angeles
Rascati, Wayne, St. Raphael, Goleta
Riera, Ralph, Holy Innocents, Long Beach
Rios, Fred, Our Lady of the Miraculous Medal, Montebello
Rivera, Ramon, St. Bridget of Sweden, Van Nuys
Rivet, Joseph A., St. Louise de Marillac, Covina
Roberto, Timothy, St. Paul of the Cross, La Mirada
Robinson, James M., St. Paschal Baylon, Thousand Oaks
Rodriguez, Hernando, Resurrection, Los Angeles
Rojas, Pedro, All Saints, Los Angeles
Rose, Frederick, American Martyrs, Manhattan Beach
Rosenberg, Milton, Santa Clara, Oxnard
Ryan, Jack, Santa Barbara Mission, Santa Barbara
Ryan, Joseph M., St. Raymond, Downey
Sago, Bruce, St. Gregory the Great, Whittier
Sanchez, Enrique R., Our Lady of Sorrows, Santa Barbara
Sangster, William B., Our Lady of Sorrows, Santa Barbara
Saucedo, Valentin, St. Helen, South Gate
Schwerdt, Paul, St. Mary, Palmdale
Sebenius, Wayland, "Gus", St. Therese, Alhambra
Seidler, Robert, St. Patrick, North Hollywood
Sevilla, Rodolfo, Our Lady Queen of Angels, (La Placita) Los Angeles
Shea, Clarke, St. Raphael, Goleta
Shinkle, Richard D., St. James, Redondo Beach
Shinn, John, Korean Catholic Center, Canoga Park
Siegman, Craig A., St. Margaret Mary, Lomita
Skupnik, Raymond P., St. Cyprian, Long Beach
Soto, Antonio P., St. Hilary, Pico Rivera
Spada, Joseph D., Our Lady of the Miraculous Medal, Montebello
Steele, John, Holy Family, Glendale
Suh, Ignatius Jin, St. Mary's Korean Catholic Center, Rowland Heights
Taufer, Wm. Dale., St. Bernardine of Siena, Woodland Hills
Torres, Antonio B., San Franciso, Los Angeles
Torres, Pedro M., Our Lady of Loretto, Los Angeles
Turner, John, Jr., St. Brigid, Los Angeles
Ulibarri, Ralph J., Holy Family, Wilmington
Valeriano, Oscar J., Jr., St. Louis of France, La Puente
Vazquez, Roberto L., St. John Chrysostom, Inglewood
Vega, Cris T., St. Gertrude, Bell Gardens
Vega, Heriberto (Ed), San Fernando Mission, Mission Hills
Victorin, Rafael, St. Augustine Church, Culver City
Wauthy, Guy, St. Rose of Lima, Simi Valley
Wilson, Peter, St. Rose of Lima, Simi Valley
Wu, Jay, St. John Vianney, Hacienda Heights

INSTITUTIONS LOCATED IN THE ARCHDIOCESE

[A] SEMINARIES, ARCHDIOCESAN

CAMARILLO. *St. John's Seminary*, 5012 Seminary Rd., 93012-2598. Tel: 805-482-2755; Fax: 805-484-4074.
E-mail: JMcCarthy@SJS-SC.ORG
Major Seminary of the Archdiocese of Los Angeles. Rev. Msgr. Jeremiah J. McCarthy, Rector & Pres.; Revs. Richard Benson, C.M., Vice Rector; Richard Prindle, Spiritual Dir.; David Heney, Dir. Dev.; Kevin Collins, Student Dir.; Sr. Jennifer Gaeta, S.S.S., Dir. Psych. Svcs.; Dr. Jean Liddell, Field Education Dir.; Revs. Leon Hutton, Spiritual Formation Dir.; John D. Stoeger, Assoc. Dir. Spiritual Formation; Ms. Jacquelein Rotter, Dir. Fin.; Mr. Greg Julius, Facilities Mgr.; Dr. Mark F. Fischer, Ph.D., Dir. Admissions; Dr. Patricia Lyons Basu, M.L.S., Libraries Dir.; Ms. Esme Takahashi, Registrar; Revs. Richard Benson, C.M.; John P. Brennan, S.M.A.; Eugenio Cardenas, M.Sp.S.; Roberto Gomez, C.M.; Daniel E. Harris, C.M.; Rev. Msgr. Helmut Hefger; Revs. Leon Hutton; Kevin McCracken, C.M.; Charles E. Miller, C.M.; Patrick Mullen; Edward Owens, O.SS.T.; John D. Stoeger; Binh Nguyen, C.M. Priests 16; Sisters 1; Lay Teachers 8; Students 106.

St. John's Seminary College of the Archdiocese of Los Angeles, 5118 Seminary Rd., 93012-2599. Tel: 805-482-2755; Fax: 805-987-5097.
E-mail: sjsc@west.net
Web site: http://www.west.net/sjsc
Staffed by Archdiocesan, Religious Priests and Sisters. Rev. Msgr. Edward Wm. Clark, President & Rector; Rev. Kenneth J. Rudnick, S.J., Vice Rector, Dean Formation; Dr. Lawrence Ryan, Vice Pres. & Academic Dean; Revs. David Heney, Dir. Devel.; Joel Henson, Dir. Students; Lawrence Herrera, S.J., Dir. of Spiritual Formation; William Piletic, C.M., Dir. of Recruitment, Alumni Relations & Liturgy; Gary S. Landry, C.M., Dir. Admissions; Richard MacDonough, S.S.; Joseph Duc-Minh; Jesus Olivares, C.S.; Manuel Sanahuja, Sch.P.; Sr. Patrice Benson, S.S.L.; Sr. Catherine Foley, S.S.L., Dir. of Apostolic Work Program; Sr. Tracey Sharp, S.C.R.H. Priests 11; Sisters 3; Lay Teachers 8; Students 94.

[B] SEMINARIES, RELIGIOUS OR SCHOLASTICATES

LOS ANGELES. *Canons Regular of the Immaculate Conception-Novitiate*, 1523 Golden Gate Ave., 90026. Tel: 323-664-1305; Fax: 323-664-4975. Revs. Charles R. Lueras, C.R.I.C.; James G. Garceau, C.R.I.C., Supr.; Sergio E. Garcia, C.R.I.C., St. Clare's, 27341 Camp Plenty Rd., Santa Clarita, 91351. Tel: 661-252-3353; Fax: 661-252-1539. Rev. William B. Ustaski, C.R.I.C. Priests 6.

St. Joseph's Novitiate, 2035 W. Adams Blvd., 90018; Fax: 213-731-5987. Hospitaller Brothers of St. John of God. Bros. Edward Francis McEnroe, O.H., Prov.; Stephen de la Rosa, O.H., Formation Dir. Brothers 2; Scholastics 1; Novice 1.

Scalabrini House of Discernment (Seminary). Tel: 323-225-4436.

Scalabrini Vocation Center. Tel: 323-225-8027.

ARLETA. *Carmel West Community*, 13600 Wingo St., 91331. Tel: 818-890-6630; Fax: 818-890-6630.
E-mail: thetopwopp@cs.com
Revs. Dominic Savino, O.Carm.; Peter J. Liuzzi, O.Carm..Priests 2.

SANTA MARIA. *St. Joseph Seminary (Josephite Fathers' Novitiate)*, 180 Patterson Rd., 93455. Tel: 805-937-5378; Fax: 805-937-5759. Revs. Thomas J. Elewaut, C.J.; Timothy R. Lane, C.J.; Bede L. Johnson, C.J.; Anthony Runtz, C.J.; John A. Mayhew, C.J.; Bro. Thaddeus Haynes, C.J. Priests 5; Brothers 1.

SANTA YNEZ. *San Lorenzo Novitiate and Seminary*, 1802 Sky Dr., P.O. Box 247, 93460. Tel: 805-688-5630; Fax: 805-686-0775.
E-mail: frchris@sanlorenzo.org
Capuchin Fransiscan Friars. Revs. Christopher Kearney, O.F.M.Cap., Guardian; Evangelist Kelly, O.F.M.Cap.; Sebastian Ward, O.F.M.Cap., Chap.; Fintan Whelan, O.F.M.Cap.; Bros. Pius Higgins, O.F.M.Cap., Vicar; Joseph Slominski, O.F.M.Cap.; Alex Escalera, Postulant. Prayer Center: Priests 4; Brothers 2; Postulants 1.

[C] COLLEGES AND UNIVERSITIES

LOS ANGELES. *Loyola Marymount University*, 7900 Loyola Blvd., 90045-2699. Tel: 310-338-2700.
Web site: www.lmu.edu
For a complete listing, refer to the Colleges and Universities section.

Mount St. Mary's College. Tel: 310-954-4010; Fax: 310-954-4019.
E-mail: jpdoud@msmc.la.edu
Web site: www.msmc.la.edu
Chalon Campus, 12001 Chalon Rd., 90049-1599. Tel: 310-954-4000; Fax: 310-954-4019.
For a complete listing, refer to the Colleges and Universities section.

RANCHO PALOS VERDES. *Marymount College, Palos Verdes, California*, 30800 Palos Verdes Dr., E., 90275-6299. Tel: 310-377-5501; Fax: 310-265-0642.
E-mail: shart@marymountpv.edu
Web site: www.marymountpv.edu
For a complete listing, refer to the Colleges and Universities section.

ROSEMEAD. *Don Bosco Technical Institute*, 1151 San Gabriel Blvd., 91770-4299. Tel: 626-307-6500; Fax: 626-280-9316.
E-mail: malvarez@netdbti.boscotech.tec.ca.us
Web site: www.boscotech.tec.ca.us
For a complete listing, refer to the Colleges and Universities section.

SANTA PAULA. *Thomas Aquinas College*, 10000 N. Ojai Rd., 93060. Tel: 805-525-4417; Fax: 805-525-0620.
E-mail: admissions@thomasaquinas.edu
Web site: www.thomasaquinas.edu
For a complete listing, refer to the Colleges and Universities section.

[D] HIGH SCHOOLS, ARCHDIOCESAN

LOS ANGELES. *Bishop Conaty-Our Lady of Loretto High School.* (Girls), 2900 W. Pico Blvd., 90006-3802. Tel: 323-737-0012; Fax: 323-737-1749.
E-mail: bclhs@earthlink.net
Sisters 5; Lay Teachers 20; Students 444.

Bishop Mora Salesian High School. (Boys), 960 S. Soto St., 90023. Tel: 213-261-7124; Fax: 213-261-9474. Salesians of Don Bosco. Mr. Manuel Villarreal, Prin.; Mr. Mark Johnson, Vice Prin.; Rev. Cresencio Rosales, S.D.B., Dir.; Bro. Robert Hennings, S.D.B. Priests 12; Brothers 2; Sisters 1; Lay Teachers 18; Students 400.

Daniel Murphy Catholic High School. (Boys), 241 S. Detroit St., 90036. Tel: 323-935-1161; Fax: 323-935-1621.
E-mail: dmhs@danielmurphyhs.org
Web site: www.danielmurphyhs.org
Jeffrey Guzman, Prin. Lay Teachers 20; Students 358.

Sacred Heart High School. (Girls), 2111 N. Griffin Ave., 90031. Tel: 323-225-2209; Fax: 323-225-5046.
E-mail: shhsprin@msjdominicans.org
Sr. S. Mary Diane Scott, O.P., Prin. Sisters 2; Lay Teachers 20; Students 345.

Verbum Dei High School. (Boys), 11100 S. Central Ave., 90059-1199. Tel: 323-564-6651; Fax: 323-564-9009.
E-mail: verbumdei@n2education.com
Conducted by the Archdiocese of Los Angeles. Dr. Charlie Haynes, Prin.; Bro. Richard Morrill, S.V.D. Priests 2; Brothers 5; Lay Teachers 9; Students 180.

BURBANK. *Bellarmine Jefferson High School.* (Coed), 465 E. Olive Ave., 91501. Tel: 818-972-1400 (Main Office); 972-1401 (Athletic); 972-1402 (Attendance); Fax: 818-559-6387.
Web site: www.bell-jefp.net
Sr. Cheryl Milner, Prin. Sisters 2; Brothers 1; Lay Teachers 24; Students 368.

COMPTON. *Queen of Angels Academy.* (Girls), 823 E. Compton Blvd., 90220. Tel: 310-515-3891; Fax: 310-515-3894.
E-mail: la968H@impresso
Conducted by the Archdiocese of Los Angeles. Staffed by the Sisters of the Holy Family. Sr. Henrietta Lazare, S.S.F., Prin. Sisters 4; Lay Teachers 8; Students 200.

DOWNEY. *St. Matthias High School,* 7851 E. Gardendale St., 90242. Tel: 562-861-2271; Fax: 562-869-8652.
E-mail: mryan@stmatthiashs.org
Web site: www.stmatthiashs.org
Sisters 2; Lay Teachers 30; Students 500.

GARDENA. *Junipero Serra High School,* 14830 S. Van Ness Ave., 90249. Tel: 310-324-6675; Fax: 310-352-4953.
E-mail: SPilato@SerraHighSchool.com
Web site: www.SerraHighSchool.com
Rev. Sabato Pilato, Prin.; Mrs. Margaret Shoukry, Vice Prin. Priests 1; Sisters 2; Lay Teachers 22; Students 463.

LA PUENTE. *Bishop Amat Memorial High School.* (Coed), 14301 Fairgrove Ave., 91746. Tel: 626-962-2495; Fax: 626-960-0994.
E-mail: Principal@BishopAmat.org
Web site: www.bishopamat.org
Conducted by the Archdiocese of Los Angeles. Rev. Msgr. Aidan M. Carroll, Prin.; Mrs. Kathleen Wiard, Vice Prin. Asst. Principals: Ms. Deborah Oswald; Ms. Maria Gover; Ms. Patricia Tereschuk. Priests 2; Sisters 4; Lay Teachers 69; Students 1,476.

LA VERNE. *Damien High School,* 2280 Damien Ave., 91750. Tel: 909-596-1946; Fax: 909-596-1946.
E-mail: dhstravers@hotmail.com
Web site: www.damien-hs.edu
Conducted by the Archdiocese of Los Angeles. Revs. Patrick Travers, SS.CC., Prin.; Peadar Cronin, SS.CC., Vice Prin.; Mr. Kenneth Kowalewski, Asst. Prin. & Campus Minister; Mr. Bob Baiz, Asst. Prin. Academic Affairs; Mr. Sam Pearsall, Asst. Prin. Summer Program; Rev. Donal McCarthy, SS.CC., Asst. Prin. Guidance; Mr. Thomas Carroll, Asst. Prin. Athletic Activities. Legal Title: *Congregation of the Sacred Hearts, Inc.* Faculty Res., 2150 Damien Ave., 91750. Priests 3; Brothers 1; Sisters 1; Lay Teachers 53; Students 1,100.

LAKEWOOD. *Saint Joseph High School.* (Girls), 5825 N. Woodruff Ave., 90713. Tel: 562-925-5073; Fax: 562-925-3315.
E-mail: @sj-jester.org
Web site: www.sj-jester.org
Conducted by Archdiocese of Los Angeles. Terri Mendoza, Ph.D., Prin.; Revs. Alfonso Scott; James Henry, S.V.D. Priests 2; Sisters 7; Lay Teachers 44; Students 835.

LANCASTER. *Paraclete High School.* (Coed), 42145 N. 30th St., W., 93536. Tel: 805-943-3255; Fax: 805-722-9455.
E-mail: mserrano@paraclete.pvt.k12.ca.us
Web site: www.paraclete.pvt.k12.ca.us
Conducted by Archdiocese of Los Angeles. Martha Izabal-Serrano, M.A., M.Ed., Prin.; Revs. Joseph Scalco, C.S.J.; Mark Withers, C.S.J. Priests 2; Lay Teachers 43; Students 700.

MISSION HILLS. *Alemany High School,* 15101 San Fernando Mission Blvd., 91345. Tel: 818-365-3925; Fax: 818-365-2064.
E-mail: principal@alemany.pvt.k12.ca.us
Web site: www.alemany.pvt.k12.ca.us
Revs. James Anguiano; Alberto Villalobos; Patrick Argue, SS.CC. (Ireland). Priests 3; Brothers 3; Sisters 4; Lay Teachers 75; Students 1,581.

MONTEBELLO. *Cantwell Sacred Heart of Mary High School.* (Coed), 329 N. Garfield Ave., 90640. Tel: 323-887-2066; Fax: 213-724-4332.
E-mail: cshm@cshm.org
Web site: www.cshm.org
Archdiocesan Institution. David Chambers, Prin. Sisters 2; Lay Teachers 26; Students 504.

OXNARD. *Santa Clara High School,* 2121 Saviers Rd., 93033. Tel: 805-483-9502; Fax: 805-483-1588.
E-mail: schs@westnet
Mr. Keith Murphy, Prin.; Mrs. Helen Scovell, Vice Prin. and Dean of Studies; Mrs. Kay Brisslinger, Asst. Prin. & Dean of Discipline; Mr. Anthony G. Foley, Campus Minister; Mr. Matthew Crow, Dir. of Activities; Bro. Edward Gresnigt, C.F.M.M. Brothers 2; Lay Teachers 15; Students 243.

PLAYA DEL REY. *St. Bernard High School.* (Coed), 9100 Falmouth Ave., 90293. Tel: 310-823-4651; Fax: 310-827-3365.
E-mail: mclunejim@hotmail.com
Web site: www.stbernardhs.com
Conducted by Archdiocese of Los Angeles. Priests 1; Brothers 2; Sisters 3; Lay Teachers 32; Total Staff 40; Students 605.

POMONA. *Pomona Catholic High School.* (Girls), 533 W. Holt Ave., 91768. Tel: 909-623-5297; Fax: 909-620-6057.
E-mail: paganucc@gte.net
Web site: www.pomonacatholic.org
Mrs. Patricia Paganucci, Prin.; Mrs. Ann Hardman, Dean of Students. Sisters 4; Lay Teachers 18; Students 330.

ROSEMEAD. *Don Bosco Technical Institute.* (Boys), 1151 San Gabriel Blvd., 91770-4299. Tel: 626-307-6500; Fax: 626-280-9316.
E-mail: malvarez@netdbti.boscotech.tec.ca.us
Web site: www.boscotech.tec.ca.us
Secondary Section.
Staffed by Salesians of St. John Bosco. Rev. Carmine Vairo, S.D.B., Pres.; Mr. Michael Alvarez, Prin.; Revs. Zbigniew Baran, S.D.B.; Michael Gergen, S.D.B. Priests 4; Brothers 6; Lay Teachers 73; Students 1,122.

SANTA BARBARA. *Bishop Garcia Diego High School.* (Coed), 4000 La Colina Rd., 93110. Tel: 805-967-1266; Fax: 805-964-3178.
E-mail: bishop@bishopdiego.org
Web site: www.bishopdiego.org
Revs. Charles Hofschulte, C.J.; Alfred Verstreken, C.J. Priests 3; Sisters 1; Lay Teachers 24; Students 350.

SANTA FE SPRINGS. *St. Paul High School,* 9635 S. Greenleaf Ave., 90670. Tel: 562-698-6246; Fax: 562-696-8396.
E-mail: sphsprincipal@netscape.net
Conducted by Archdiocese of Los Angeles. Rev. Robert J. Gallagher, Prin. Priests 1; Brothers 2; Sisters 1; Lay Teachers 45; Students 856.

SANTA MARIA. *St. Joseph High School.* (Coed), 4120 Bradley Rd., 93455. Tel: 805-937-2038; Fax: 805-937-4248.
E-mail: sjhs@sjhsknights.com
Web site: www.sjhsknights.com
Conducted by Archdiocese of Los Angeles. Revs. Timothy R. Lane, C.J.; Thomas J. Elewaut, C.J., 180 Patterson Rd., 93455. Tel: 805-937-5378; Fax: 805-937-5759. Priests 2; Sisters 1; Lay Teachers 36; Students 658.

TORRANCE. *Bishop Montgomery High School.* (Coed), 5430 Torrance Blvd., 90503. Tel: 310-540-2021; Fax: 310-543-5102.
E-mail: r_libbon@bmhs.com
Conducted by the Archdiocese of Los Angeles. Rosemary Libbon, Prin. Priests 2; Lay Teachers 78; Students 1,250.

VENTURA. *St. Bonaventure High School.* (Coed), 3167 Telegraph Rd., 93003-3281. Tel: 805-648-6836; Fax: 805-648-4903.
E-mail: office@saintbonaventure.com
Web site: www.saintbonaventure.com
Conducted by Archdiocese of Los Angeles. Bro. Paulinus Horkan, O.S.F., Prin. Sisters 1; Brothers 1; Lay Teachers 33; Students 725.

[E] HIGH SCHOOLS, PAROCHIAL

LOS ANGELES. High Schools are maintained in the following parishes (for particulars refer to the individual parishes): Glendale: Holy Family; Long Beach: St. Anthony; San Gabriel: San Gabriel Mission; San Pedro: Mary Star of the Sea; Santa Monica: St. Monica; Van Nuys: St. Genevieve.

[F] HIGH SCHOOLS, PRIVATE

LOS ANGELES. *Cathedral High School of Los Angeles, Incorporated.* (Boys), 1253 Bishops Rd., 90012. Tel: 323-225-2438; Fax: 323-225-7223.
Web site: cathedralphantoms.org
Conducted by the Brothers of the Christian Schools. Bros. James Meegan, F.S.C., Pres.; John Montgomery, F.S.C., Prin. Brothers 5; Sisters 1; Lay Teachers 31; Students 575.

Immaculate Heart High School. (Girls), 5515 Franklin Ave., 90028. Tel: 323-461-3651; Fax: 323-462-0610.
E-mail: ihhs1@aol.com
Web site: www.immaculateheart.org
Conducted by the Immaculate Heart Community. Lay Teachers 47; Students 515.

Loyola High School of Los Angeles, 1901 Venice Blvd., 90006. Tel: 213-381-5121; Fax: 213-368-1758.
E-mail: rwalsh@loyolahs.edu
Web site: loyolahs.edu
Jesuit Fathers. Revs. Robert T. Walsh, S.J., Pres.; Eugene R. Growney, S.J., Rector; Stephen Barber, S.J.; J. Philip Conneally, S.J.; Lawrence B. Murphy, S.J.; Louis A. Peinado, S.J.; Kevin A. Leidich, S.J., Min.; John Francis Vu, S.J.; John I. Geiszel, S.J.; Thomas J. Reilley, S.J.; James V. Schaukowitch, S.J.; John D. Murphy, S.J.; Bros. Robert McDermott, S.J.; William Sessing, S.J. Scholastics: Robert Balleeca, S.J.; Jerry Hayes, S.J.; Mark Magennis, S.J. Priests 12; Brothers 2; Scholastics 3; Lay Teachers 69; Students 1,180.

Marymount High School. (Girls), 10643 Sunset Blvd., 90077. Tel: 310-472-1205; Fax: 310-476-0910.
E-mail: alumnae@marymounths.com
Web site: www.marymount-la.org
Religious of the Sacred Heart of Mary. Dr. Mary Ellen Gozdecki, Head. Sisters 4; Lay Teachers 46; Students 393.

Notre Dame Academy. (Girls), 2851 Overland Ave., 90064. Tel: 310-839-5289; Fax: 310-839-7957.
E-mail: Ndamp@aol.com
Web site: www.ndala.com
Sr. Marie Paul, S.N.D., Prin. Sisters of Notre Dame of Los Angeles 4; Sisters of Providence 2; Sisters of Holy Cross 1; Lay Teachers 34; Students 485.

ALHAMBRA. *Ramona Convent Secondary School, Ramona Convent of the Holy Names.* (Girls Grades 7-12), 1701 W. Ramona Rd., 91803-3099. Tel: 626-282-4151; Fax: 626-281-0797.
E-mail: ramona@ramona.pvt.k12.ca.us
Ms. Kathleen Pillon, Prin.; Sr. Kathleen Callaway, S.N.J.M., Pres. Sisters of Holy Names of Jesus and Mary 8; Lay Teachers 55; Total Staff 63; Students 552.

BELLFLOWER. *St. John Bosco High School.* (Boys), 13640 S. Bellflower Blvd., 90706. Tel: 562-920-1734; Fax: 562-867-5322.
E-mail: jitzaina@bosco.org
Web site: www.bosco.org
Revs. John Itzaina, S.D.B., Pres.; Mel Trinidad, S.D.B.; Mario Mich, S.D.B.; Joseph Ahn Le, S.D.B.; Bros. Frank Bracchi, S.D.B.; Barney Hagus, S.D.B.; John McLinden, S.D.B.; Chinh Nguyen, S.D.B.; Gerardo Rodriguez, S.D.B.; Noel Degruton, S.D.B. Priests 2; Brothers 3; Lay Teachers 62; Students 1,124.

BURBANK. *Providence High School.* (Coed), 511 S. Buena Vista St., 91505. Tel: 818-846-8141; Fax: 818-843-8421.
E-mail: lucille@providencehigh.org
Web site: www.providencehigh.org
Sr. Lucille Dean, S.P., Prin.; Joanie Fenstermaker, Dir. Campus Ministry; Sr. Mary Hawkins, S.P., Academic Vice Prin.; C. Victor LeBreton, Vice Prin. Discipline & Student Activities; Sr. Mary Hawkins, S.P., Vice Prin. Academics. Sisters 3; Lay Teachers 34; Students 540.

CHATSWORTH. *Chaminade College Preparatory,* Office of the President, 10210 Oakdale Ave., 91311-3533. Tel: 818-360-4211; Fax: 818-363-0127.
E-mail: jadams@chaminade.org
Web site: www.chaminade.org
James V. Adams, Pres., 19800 Devonshire St., 91311. Tel: 818-363-8127; Fax: 818-363-1219. (Coed Grades 6-8). Ms. Christine Hunter, Prin. Chatsworth, 7500 Chaminade Ave., West Hills, 91304. Tel: 818-347-8300; Fax: 818-348-8374. (Coed Grades 9-12). Gary E. Murphy, Prin. West Hills. Legal Title: *Chaminade College Preparatory.* Priests 3; Sisters 5; Brothers 2; Lay Teachers 110; Students 1,719.

Marianist Community. Tel: 818-347-8043; Fax: 818-347-2788. Revs. Edwin Johnson, S.M., Dir.; Lawrence Mann, S.M.; Thomas Hogan, S.M. Priests 3; Brothers 5.

ENCINO. *Crespi Carmelite High School*, 5031 Alonzo Ave., 91316. Tel: 818-345-1672; Fax: 818-345-6468.
E-mail: jmkocarm@juno.com
Web site: www.crespi.org
Rev. John Knoernschild, O.Carm., Pres.; Mr. David Doyle, Prin.; Mr. Jeff Thornton, Vice Prin. & Dean of Men; Ms. Margie Moreno, Treas.; Mr. Daniel Flaherty, Dir. Dev.; Ms. Catherine Scheibe, Academic Vice Prin.; Mr. Richard Fong, Athletic Dir.; Mr. Joseph Schnelldorfer, Campus Min.; Ms. Donna Long, Dir. of Student Activities; Revs. Dominic Savino, O.Carm.; Joseph Fitzgerald, O.Carm., Alumni Relations Dir.; Bro. John Sprissler, O.Carm. In res. Revs. Augustine W. Carter, O.Carm.; John Coleman, O.Carm.; Kevin McBrien, O.Carm., Prior; Mathias Ewing, O.Carm.; William Heery, O.Carm. Priests 3; Brothers 1; Lay Teachers 37; Students 465.

GLENDORA. *St. Lucy's Priory High School*. (Girls), 655 W. Sierra Madre Ave., 91741. Tel: 626-335-3322; Fax: 626-335-4373.
E-mail: slphs@aol.com
Conducted by the Benedictine Sisters. Sr. Monica Collins, O.S.B., Prin. Priests 1; Sisters 2; Lay Teachers 41; Students 890.

INGLEWOOD. *St. Mary's Academy*. (Girls), 701 Grace Ave., 90301. Tel: 310-674-8470; Fax: 310-674-6255.
E-mail: faycsj@aol.com
Sr. Fay Hagen, C.S.J., Prin. Sisters of St. Joseph of Carondelet 7; Lay Teachers 18; Students 312.

LA CANADA FLINTRIDGE. *Flintridge Sacred Heart Academy*. (Girls), 440 St. Katherine Dr., 91011. Tel: 626-685-8500; Fax: 626-685-8555.
E-mail: fsha.org
Web site: www.fsha.org
Legal Title: *Flintridge Sacred Heart Academy, A Corporation*. Sr. Ramona Bascom, O.P., Prin. Dominican Sisters of Mission San Jose 7; Lay Teachers 36; Students 424.

St. Francis High School. (Boys), 200 Foothill Blvd., 91011. Tel: 818-790-0325; Fax: 818-790-5542.
Web site: sfhs.net
Legal Title: *The Capuchin Franciscan Order of the Western American Province*. Revs. Matthew Elshoff, O.F.M.Cap., Pres. St. Francis High School; Cris Thiel, O.F.M.Cap.; Anthony Scannel, O.F.M.Cap.; Tony Marti; Harold Snider, O.F.M.Cap., Chap., Campus Ministry; Bros. Robert Edwards, O.F.M.Cap.; Bernard McAllister, O.F.M.Cap.; Steven Tetreault, O.F.M.Cap., Dir. Campus Ministry; Sr. Barbarine Houdek, O.S.F. Priests 5; Brothers 2; Sisters 1; Lay Teachers 39; Total Teachers 44; Students 600.

OJAI. *Villanova Preparatory School*, 12096 Ventura Ave., 93023-3999. Tel: 805-646-1464; Fax: 805-646-4430.
E-mail: info@villanovaprep.org
Web site: www.villanovaprep.org
Legal Title: *Villanova Preparatory School of California*. Revs. John P. Pejza, O.S.A., Pres.; John F. Glynn, O.S.A.; Gary E. Sanders, O.S.A. Conducted by Augustinian Fathers (Order of St. Augustine). Priests 3; Sisters 1; Lay Teachers 29; Students 240.

PASADENA. *La Salle High School*, 3880 E. Sierra Madre Blvd., 91107. Tel: 626-351-8951; Fax: 626-351-0275.
E-mail: principal@lasallehs.org
Web site: lasallehs.org
Mr. Patrick Bonacci, Prin. Brothers 2; Lay Teachers 49; Students 761.

Mayfield Senior School of the Holy Child Jesus, 5000 Bellefontaine St., 91105-2439. Tel: 626-799-9121; Fax: 626-799-8576.
E-mail: jeanne.register@mayfieldsenior.org
Web site: http://www.mayfieldsenior.org
Mrs. Jeanne G. Registrar; Mr. Raymond Valtierra, Business Mgr. Sisters 1; Lay Teachers 34; Students 273.

SHERMAN OAKS. *Notre Dame High School*, 13645 Riverside Dr., 91423. Tel: 818-993-3600; Fax: 818-501-0507.
E-mail: connelly@ndhs.org
Web site: www.ndhs.org
Bro. William C. Nick, C.S.C., Pres.; Mrs. Stephanie Connelly, Prin. Brothers 1; Lay Teachers 67; Students 1,128.

SIERRA MADRE. *Alverno High School*. (Girls), 200 N. Michillinda Ave., 91024. Tel: 626-355-3463; Fax: 626-355-3153.
Web site: Alverno-hs.org
Ann M. Gillick, M.S., Prin. Lay Teachers 20; Students 230.

THOUSAND OAKS. *La Reina High School*. (Girls Grades 7-12), 106 W. Janss Rd., 91360. Tel: 805-495-6494; Fax: 805-494-4966.
E-mail: lareina@adnetsol.com
Web site: www.lareina.com
Sr. Antoinette Marie Moon, S.N.D., Prin. Sisters of Notre Dame 3; Lay Teachers 39; Total Staff 56; Students 586.

WOODLAND HILLS. *Louisville High School*. (Girls), 22300 Mulholland Dr., 91364. Tel: 818-346-8812; Fax: 818-346-9483.
E-mail: mmcpartland@louisvillehs.org
Web site: louisvillehs.org
Sr. Myra McPartland, S.S.L., Prin. Sisters 6; Lay Teachers 34; Students 497.

[G] ELEMENTARY SCHOOLS, PRIVATE

LOS ANGELES. *Notre Dame Academy (Elementary)*, 2911 Overland Ave., 90064. Tel: 310-287-3895; Fax: 310-838-8983. Sr. Mary LaReina Kelly, S.N.D., Prin. Sisters of Notre Dame of Los Angeles 2; Lay Teachers 10; Students 309.

PASADENA. *Mayfield Junior School*, 405 S. Euclid Ave., 91101. Tel: 626-796-2774; Fax: 626-796-5753. Sisters of the Society of the Holy Child Jesus 1; Lay Teachers 41; Students 420.

SANTA BARBARA. *Marymount Academy*. (Grades K-8). (Coed), 2130 Mission Ridge Rd., 93103. Tel: 805-569-1811; Fax: 805-682-6892.
E-mail: mmountsbar@hotmail.com
Web site: marymountsb.org
Lay Teachers 19; Students 240.

[H] ORPHANAGES AND INFANT HOMES

ROSEMEAD. *Maryvale*, P.O. Box 1039, 91770-1003. Tel: 626-280-6510; 323-283-9311; Fax: 626-288-8903.
E-mail: maryvalel/@aol.com
For a complete listing, refer to the Special Care Facilities section.

[I] DAY NURSERIES

LOS ANGELES. *Divine Providence Pre-school and Kindergarten*, 2620 Monmouth St., 90007. Tel: 213-747-3074; Fax: 213-747-3074. Sr. M. Peter Pedroza, Dir. Sisters of the Company of Mary 6; Lay Teachers 11; Children 140.

St. Jeanne de Lestonnac Kindergarten and Day Nursery, 4001 Venice Blvd., 90019. Tel: 213-737-1217; Fax: 323-737-3672. (Formerly Little Flower Kindergarten & Day Nursery). Sr. Charlotte Turritta, Supervisor. Sisters 1; Lay Teachers 12; Children 205.

GARDENA. *St. Anthony's Day Nursery*, 1044 W. 163rd St., 90247. Tel: 310-329-8654. Sr. Rosa Lilia Arreola, M.C., Dir. Sisters 11; Children 90.

SAN FERNANDO. *Poverello of Assisi School*, 1519 Woodworth St., 91340. Tel: 818-361-5864. Franciscan Missionary Sisters of the Immaculate Conception. Sr. Irene San Roman. Sisters 7; Children 185.

[J] GENERAL HOSPITALS

LOS ANGELES. *St. Vincent Medical Center*, 2131 W. 3rd St., 90057. Tel: 213-484-7111
For a complete listing, refer to the Hospitals section.

Santa Marta Hospital, 319 N. Humphreys Ave., 90022. Tel: 323-266-6500; Fax: 213-260-8641 (Admin.).
Web site: www.santamarta.org
For a complete listing, refer to the Hospitals section.

BURBANK. *Providence Health System*, 501 S. Buena Vista St., 91505. Tel: 818-843-5111; Fax: 818-843-0641.
Web site: www.providence.org
For a complete listing, refer to the Hospitals section.

Providence Saint Joseph Medical Center, 501 S. Buena Vista, 91505. Tel: 818-843-5111; Fax: 818-843-0641
For a complete listing, refer to the Hospitals section.

DUARTE. *Santa Teresita Hospital*, 819 Buena Vista St., 91010. Tel: 626-359-3243; Fax: 626-357-7166.
E-mail: sth@santa-teresita.org
Web site: www.santa-teresita.org
For a complete listing, refer to the Hospitals section.

HAWTHORNE. *Hawthorne Community Hospital, Inc. dba Robert F. Kennedy Medical Center*, 4500 W. 116th St., 90250
For a complete listing, refer to the Hospitals section.

Robert F. Kennedy Medical Center, 4500 W. 166th St., 90250. Tel: 310-973-1711
For a complete listing, refer to the Hospitals section.

INGLEWOOD. *Daniel Freeman Memorial Hospital*, 333 N. Prairie Ave., 90301. Tel: 310-674-7050; 678-0361; Fax: 310-419-8273.
Web site: www.danielfreeman.org
For a complete listing, refer to the Hospitals section.

LONG BEACH. *St. Mary Medical Center*, 1050 Linden Ave., 90813. Tel: 562-491-9000
For a complete listing, refer to the Hospitals section.

St. Mary Medical Center Foundation, P.O. Box 887, 90801. Tel: 562-491-9225; Fax: 562-491-9888
For a complete listing, refer to the Hospitals section.

St. Mary Professional Building, Inc., 1045 Atlantic Ave., 90813
For a complete listing, refer to the Hospitals section.

LYNWOOD. *St. Francis Medical Center*, 3630 E. Imperial Hwy., 90262. Tel: 310-603-6000
For a complete listing, refer to the Hospitals section.

MARINA DEL REY. *Daniel Freeman Marina Hospital*, 4650 Lincoln Blvd., 90292. Tel: 310-823-8911; Fax: 310-574-7854.
Web site: www.danielfreeman.org
For a complete listing, refer to the Hospitals section.

OXNARD. *St. John's Regional Medical Center*, 1600 N. Rose Ave., 93030. Tel: 805-988-2500; Fax: 805-981-4440.
Web site: www.stjohnshealth.com
For a complete listing, refer to the Hospitals section.

PASADENA. *Catholic Healthcare West Southern California*, Regional Office, 251 S. Lake Ave., 8th Fl., 91101-4842. Tel: 626-744-2300.
Web site: www.chwsocalregion.org
For a complete listing, refer to the Hospitals section.

SAN PEDRO. *San Pedro Peninsula Hospital*, 1700 W. Seventh St., 90732. Tel: 310-832-3311; Fax: 310-514-5314.
E-mail: smbabcock@lcmhs.org
For a complete listing, refer to the Hospitals section.

SANTA BARBARA. *St. Francis Medical Center of Santa Barbara*, 601 E. Micheltorena St., 93102. Tel: 805-962-7661; Fax: 805-568-5704.
E-mail: cbowman@chw.edu
Web site: www.saintfrancis.org
For a complete listing, refer to the Hospitals section.

SANTA MARIA. *Marian Medical Center*, 1400 E. Church St., 93454. Tel: 805-739-3000
For a complete listing, refer to the Hospitals section.

SANTA MONICA. *Saint John's Health Center*, 1328 22nd St., 90404. Tel: 310-829-5511; Fax: 310-315-6134
For a complete listing, refer to the Hospitals section.

TORRANCE. *Little Company of Mary Hospital*, 4101 W. Torrance Blvd., 90503. Tel: 310-540-7676; Fax: 310-540-7659
For a complete listing, refer to the Hospitals section.

WEST COVINA. *Citrus Valley Health Partners, Queen of the Valley Campus*, 1115 S. Sunset Ave., P.O. Box 1980, 91790. Tel: 818-962-4011; Fax: 818-814-2482.
E-mail: vip.pm@cvhp.org
Web site: cvhp.com
For a complete listing, refer to the Hospitals section.

[K] SPECIAL HOSPITALS AND SANATORIA FOR INVALIDS

LOS ANGELES. *Franciscan Health Center*, 2859 Glassell St., 90026. Tel: 213-413-1050
For a complete listing, refer to the Special Care Facilities section.

Knights of Malta Free Clinic, Inc., 2222 W. Ocean View #112, 90057. Tel: 213-384-4323; Fax: 213-384-4097.
E-mail: freemed112@aol
For a complete listing, refer to the Special Care Facilities section.

CULVER CITY. *Marycrest Manor, Convalescent Home*, 10664 St. James Dr., 90230-5498. Tel: 310-838-2778; Fax: 310-838-9647
For a complete listing, refer to the Special Care Facilities section.

NEWBURY PARK. *Mary Health of the Sick Convalescent and Nursing Hospital*, 2929 Theresa Dr., 91320. Tel: 805-498-3644; Fax: 805-498-5112.
E-mail: health@ftel.net
For a complete listing, refer to the Special Care Facilities section.

OJAI. *St. Joseph's Health and Retirement Center*, 2464 E. Ojai Ave., P.O. Box 760, 93024. Tel: 805-646-1466; Fax: 805-646-1013
For a complete listing, refer to the Special Care Facilities section.

[L] HANDICAPPED

LOS ANGELES. *Ministry with Persons with Disabilities*, 3424 Wilshire Blvd., Second Floor, 90010. Tel: 213-637-7236; Fax: 213-637-6161.
E-mail: vjgray@la-archdiocese.org
Web site: www.la-archdiocese.org
Veronica Gray, Dir., Marian Homes for the Developmentally and Physically Disabled, Inc., Office of the Admin., 3424 Wilshire Blvd., 2nd Fl., 90010-2241. Tel: 213-637-7243; Fax: 213-637-6161. Linda Payne, Prog. Dir.

SANTA MONICA. *Saint John's Child Study Center, Saint John's Hospital & Health Center*, 1339 20th St., 90404. Tel: 310-829-8921; Fax: 310-829-8455. Conducted by Sisters of Charity of Leavenworth. Affiliated with Saint John's Hospital. Rebecca Refuerza, L.C.S.W., Dir. Children Treated Annually 1,800.

SUNLAND. *Tierra del Sol Foundation*, 9919 Sunland Blvd., 91040. Tel: 818-352-1419; Fax: 818-353-0777. Community Program Supportive Employment for Adults with Disabilities. Stephen J. Miller, Exec. Dir.; Nancy Bissonette-Andrew, Assoc. Dir. Licensed Capacity 304.

VAN NUYS. *Tierra Del Sol West*, 14547 Gilmore St., 91411. Tel: 818-904-9164. Behavior Management Community Program for Adults with Developmental Disabilities. Stephen J. Miller, Exec. Dir.; Karen Alitz-Pelga, Program Dir. Capacity 50.

[M] CHILD ADOPTION SERVICES

PASADENA. *Holy Family Services, Adoption & Foster Care*, 402 S. Marengo Ave., 91101-3113. Tel: 626-578-1156; Fax: 626-578-7321.
E-mail: hfsadopt@aol.com
Web site: http://www.hfs.org
Branch Offices: 1403 South Main St., Santa Ana, 92707-1790. Tel: 714-835-5551; Fax: 714-973-4971. 80 E. Hillcrest Ave., Thousand Oaks, 91360-4219. Tel: 805-374-6797; Fax: 805-379-3088. 1441 N. D St. #201, San Bernardino, 92405-4738. Tel: 909-885-4882; Fax: 909-888-7065.
Holy Family Adoption Foundation, Inc. Tel: 626-578-1156; Fax: 626-578-7321.
Auxiliaries of Holy Family Services: Holy Family's Adoptive Parents Organization, Inc., Adoption Guild of Southern Orange County, Angelique Guild, The 200 Associates. Birthparent unplanned pregnancy counseling 408; Foster care families recruited 11; Children placed in adoptive homes 89.

[N] VISITING NURSE SERVICES

LOS ANGELES. *Sisters Servants of Mary, Ministers of the Sick*, 2131 W. 27th St., 90018-3018. Tel: 213-731-5747; Fax: 323-731-4251. Sr. Esther Fonseca, S.M., Supr. Sisters 17; Total Assisted 92; Total Staff 7.

[O] PROTECTIVE INSTITUTIONS

LOS ANGELES. *Convent of the Good Shepherd-Good Shepherd Shelter*, 2561 Venice Blvd., 90019. Tel: 323-737-6111; Fax: 323-737-6113.
E-mail: rgslai@aol.com
For a complete listing, refer to the Special Care Facilities section.
Little Flower Missionary House, 2434 Gates St., 90031-2824. Tel: 323-221-9248; Fax: 323-221-9831.
E-mail: littleflowercarmel@netzero.net
Web site: www.geocities.com/athens/acropolis/7053
For a complete listing, refer to the Special Care Facilities section.
Missionary Brothers of Charity, 1345 Alvarado Ter., 90006. Tel: 213-251-9707
For a complete listing, refer to the Special Care Facilities section.
St. Anne's, 155 N. Occidental Blvd., 90026. Tel: 213-381-2931; Fax: 213-381-7804.
E-mail: stannes@stannes.org
Web site: www.stannes.org
For a complete listing, refer to the Special Care Facilities section.

CHATSWORTH. *Rancho San Antonio*, 21000 Plummer St., 91311. Tel: 818-882-6400; Fax: 818-882-6404
For a complete listing, refer to the Special Care Facilities section.

SANTA BARBARA. *St. Vincent Residence*, 4200 Calle Real, P.O. Box 669, 93102-0669. Tel: 805-683-6381; Fax: 805-967-7508
For a complete listing, refer to the Special Care Facilities section.

[P] HOMES FOR AGED

LOS ANGELES. *Nazareth House*, 3333 Manning Ave., 90064. Tel: 310-839-2361; Fax: 310-839-4204.
E-mail: naz-la@pacbell.net
Web site: www.nazarethouse.org
For a complete listing, refer to the Special Care Facilities section.
St. John of God Retirement and Care Center, 2035 W. Adams Blvd., 90018. Tel: 323-731-0641; Fax: 323-731-1452
For a complete listing, refer to the Special Care Facilities section.

SAN FERNANDO. *Mother Gertrude Home for Senior Citizens*, 11320 Laurel Canyon Blvd., 91340. Tel: 818-898-1546; Fax: 818-365-3159
For a complete listing, refer to the Special Care Facilities section.

SAN PEDRO. *Little Sisters of the Poor*, Jeanne Jugan Residence, 2100 S. Western Ave., 90732. Tel: 310-548-0625; Fax: 310-548-4504
For a complete listing, refer to the Special Care Facilities section.

SANTA MARIA. *Marian Residence*, 124 S. College Dr., 93454. Tel: 805-922-7731; Fax: 805-922-9834
For a complete listing, refer to the Special Care Facilities section.

SUN VALLEY. *Villa Scalabrini*, 10631 Vinedale St., 91352. Tel: 818-768-6500; Fax: 818-768-0684.
E-mail: nazzani@aol.com
For a complete listing, refer to the Special Care Facilities section.

[Q] MONASTERIES AND RESIDENCES OF PRIESTS AND BROTHERS

LOS ANGELES. *Atonement Friars*, 222 S. Hewitt St., 90012. Tel: 213-626-2279; Fax: 213-628-1757. Rev. David L. Doerner, S.A.

Brothers of John of God, Inc., The, 2425 S. Western Ave., 90018-2608. Tel: 323-734-0233; Fax: 323-731-5987.
E-mail: efmcenroe@msn.com
Web site: www.hospitallers.org
Bro. Edward Francis McEnroe, O.H., Prov.
Women's League of St. John of God, Inc. Tel: 323-731-7141; Fax: 323-731-5717.
Helper's Club, Inc. Tel: 323-731-7141; Fax: 323-731-5717.
St. John of God Retirement and Care Center. Tel: 323-731-0641; Fax: 323-737-1452.
St. Joseph's Health and Retirement Center. Tel: 805-646-1466; Fax: 805-646-1013.
Hospitaller Foundation of California, Inc. Tel: 323-731-7141; Fax: 323-731-5717.
Women's League of St. Joseph's Health and Retirement Center. Tel: 805-646-1466; Fax: 805-643-1013.
Grande Apartments-Los Angeles. Tel: 323-730-4100; Fax: 323-737-1452.
Hospitaller Brothers Healthcare, Inc. Tel: 323-734-6624; Fax: 323-731-5987.
St. John of God Health Care Services. Tel: 760-241-4917; Fax: 760-241-8911.

Brothers of Our Lady, Mother of Mercy Inc., 7140 Ramsgate Ave., 90045. Tel: 310-649-3370. Bro. John H. Grever, C.F.M.M., Community Rep. Brothers 3.

Brothers of the Good Shepherd, Inc. of California, 3445 Waverly Dr., 90027. Tel: 323-662-3620; 323-662-0092; Fax: 323-662-3619. Bro. Malachy Corbett, B.G.S.

Canons Regular of the Immaculate Conception, 1523 Golden Gate Ave., 90026. Tel: 323-664-1305; Fax: 323-664-4975. Revs. James G. Garceau, C.R.I.C., Pastor; Charles R. Lueras, C.R.I.C.; Pasquale Vuoso, C.R.I.C.; Sergio E. Garcia, C.R.I.C.; Thomas Dome, C.R.I.C. Priests 5.

Casa Guadalupe, Divine Word Missionaries, 807 N. Fresno St., 90063; Fax: 323-263-1221. Revs. Lukas Bao Teluma, S.V.D. Tel: 323-263-1253; Raymundus Bhia Wea, S.V.D. Tel: 323-267-1121.

Claretian Retreat Center Community, 1119 Westchester Pl., 90019. Tel: 323-731-9329; Fax: 323-733-6201. Very Rev. Ralph Berg, C.M.F., Provincial Superior; Revs. Roland Lozano, C.M.F., Supr.; Frank J. Ferrante, C.M.F., Dir.; Bro. Rene LePage, C.M.F., Admin.; Revs. Carlos C. Castillo, C.M.F.; George Whedbee, C.M.F.; John Hampsch, C.M.F.; Roland Lozano, C.M.F.; John Raab, C.M.F.; Bro. Larry Moen, C.M.F.

Columban Fathers, Procure House, 2600 N. Vermont Ave., 90027-1245. Tel: 323-665-4289; Fax: 323-664-7160.
E-mail: orourkecj@aol.com
Revs. Charles L. O'Rourke, S.S.C., Supr.; Thomas Cusack, S.S.C.; Seamus Leddy, S.S.C.; Anthony Mortell, S.S.C.; Dan McGinn, S.S.C.; Gerard P., Dunne, S.S.C.; Jim Shiffer, S.S.C.

Columbiere House. Formerly Connolly House. 5322 Franklin Ave., 90027. Tel: 323-466-3723; Fax: 323-466-3826. Jesuit Fathers. Revs. Francis J. Parrish, S.J.; John D. McAnulty, S.J.; Grant S. Garinger, S.J.; Charles Prussing, S.J.; Peter Chu, S.J.; George R. Sullivan, S.J. (Wisconsin); Patrick Connolly, S.J. (Wisconsin); Frederick J. Heney, S.J. (Japan); Felix A. Maiza, S.J.; Robert E. Griffin, S.J.; William K. Delaney, S.J.; Manuel M. Flores, S.J. (Phillippines); Philip D. Kraus, S.J.; John W. Clark, S.J. Priests 14.

Congregation of St. Joseph Casa Nazareth, 2702 Abrigo Ave., 90031. Tel: 213-221-4809. Revs. Giampietro Gasparin, C.S.J.; John Trimaglio, C.S.J., Supr.

Dominic Savio Salesian Residence, 920 S. Soto St., 90023-1396. Tel: 323-266-1977; Fax: 323-266-0486.
E-mail: SDBinELA@aol.com
Web site: www.donboscowest.org
In res. Revs. Hugo Santucci, S.D.B., St. Mary's; James Nieblas, S.D.B., Vicar for the Community, St. Mary's; Marc Rougeau, S.D.B., Supr. of the Community, Salesian High School; Avelino Lorenzo, S.D.B., St. Mary's; William Schafer, S.D.B., Executive Director, Salesian Boys' & Girls' Club, Salesian Family Youth Center; Ted Montemayor, S.D.B., Vocation Dir.; Bros. Rudy Bertagnolli, S.D.B.; Robert Hennings, S.D.B., Community Treas., Salesian High, Salesian Clubs.
Salesians in Community but not in res.: Revs. Joseph Cheng, S.D.B., St. Bridget's Chinese Catholic Center; Lucian B. Lomello, S.D.B., Chap., Hospital.

Franciscan Brothers of the Third Order Regular, 4552 Gainsborough Ave., 90027-1227. Tel: 323-644-2740; Fax: 323-644-2977. Bro. Hilarion O'Connor, O.S.F., Regl. Supr. Brothers 11.

Guadalupe Missioners Procure, 4714 W. 8th St., 90005. Tel: 323-937-2780; Fax: 323-937-2782. Revs. Santiago G. Lara, M.G., Local Supr.; Abraham R. Garcia, M.G., Asst.

Hospitaller Brothers of St. John of God, 2035 W. Adams Blvd., 90018. Tel: 323-731-0641; Fax: 323-731-5987.
E-mail: efmcenroe@msn.com
Web site: www.hospitallers.org
Peter Gelfer, O.H., Prior. Brothers 14.

Maryknoll Fathers and Brothers. (Catholic Foreign Mission Society of America), 745 W. Adams Blvd., 90007. Tel: 213-747-9676; Fax: 213-747-8923.
Web site: www.maryknoll.org
Revs. Roberto Rodriguez, M.M.; Robert A. Hurteau, M.M.; Robert W. Golish, M.M.; Michael G. Callahan, M.M.; William M. Boteler, M.M., 255 S. Grand Ave., #413, 90012-3017. Tel: 213-625-5702. Rev. James P. Colligan, M.M. Priests 6.

Mill Hill Missionaries Procure. (St. Joseph Society for Foreign Missions), 1841 Camino Palmero, 90046. Tel: 323-876-0505; Fax: 323-876-0508. Revs. Theo M. Feldbrugge, M.H.M.; Henk Riesthuis, M.H.M. Priests 2.

Minim Fathers, 3431 Portola Ave., 90032. Tel: 323-223-1101; Fax: 323-223-9592.
E-mail: jvega@earthlink.net
Web site: home.earthlink.net/~jvega/
Revs. Constantino Mandarino, O.M., Supr.; Gino Vanzillotta, O.M., Supr.; Jose L. Vega, O.M. Priests 3.

Missionaries of Charity Brothers.
Casa Teresa. Regional Office, 1316 S. Westlake Ave., 90006. Tel: 213-380-5225. Hospitality for men. Temporary shelter for sick homeless men.
House of Formation, 1325 S. Westlake Ave., 90006. Tel: 213-384-6116. Brothers 7.
Nuestro Hogar, 1345 Alvarado Terr., 90006. Tel: 213-251-9707. Daycenter for young adults. Total Assisted 60; Total Staff 5.

Missionary Sons of the Immaculate Heart of Mary. (Claretian Priests and Brothers). Tel: 323-734-1824; Fax: 323-737-0301. Prov. Headquarters of the Western Prov. of the USA, 1119 Westchecter Place, 90019. Tel: 323-734-1824; Fax: 323-737-0301. Legal Title: *Claretian Missionaries - Western Province, Inc.* Very Rev. Ralph Berg, C.M.F., Prov. Supr.; Rev. Roland Lozano, C.M.F., Prov. Treas.
Claretian Tape Ministry, Inc. Tel: 323-734-1234; Fax: 323-734-0973.
Dominguez Seminary, Inc., Compton. Tel: 310-631-5981; Fax: 310-631-3518.
Claretian Educational and Renewal Center, Inc. Tel: 323-737-8464; Fax: 323-733-6201. This is a non-profit corporation under the laws of the State of California having as its purpose the support of any Roman Catholic benevolent, charitable, educational or missionary undertakings of the Claretian Missionaries - Western Province, Inc.

Mount Carmel Priory, Carmelite Fathers and Brothers, 801 W. 70th St., 90044. Tel: 213-752-3972. Legal Title: *Fathers of the Order of Mount Carmel, Corporation.* Revs. Augustine W. Carter, O.Carm.; Matt J. Ewing, O.Carm., Prior; Bernard Kangley, O.Carm.; Bro. Stephen Diekemper, O.Carm. Priests 3.

Piarist Fathers, 512 S. Avenue 20, 90031. Tel: 213-223-4153. Revs. Raul Palma, Sch.P.; Francis Boronat, Sch.P., Rector of the Community; Juan Trenchs, Sch.P.; Miguel Campos, Sch.P. Priests 4.

St. John of God Retirement and Care Center, 2035 W. Adams Blvd., 90018. Tel: 323-731-0641; Fax: 323-737-1452. Bros. Edward F. McEnroe, O.H., Prov. & Chm.; Stephen de la Rosa, O.H., Novice Master; Peter Gelfer, O.H., Local Supr. Brothers 14.

Society of St. Paul. (Mexican Province), 112 Herbert St., 90063. Tel: 213-269-9814. Revs. Gilberto Martinez, S.S.P., Supr.; Tomas Martinez, S.S.P., Vice Supr.; Valeriano Giachino, S.S.P.

Society of the Divine Word Missionaries, Western Province, Provincial Offices, 2181 W. 25th St., 90007. Tel: 323-735-8130 (Provincial Office); 731-9982 (Community Phone); Fax: 323-735-8122 (Provincial Office). Mailing Address: Office of the Provincial, P.O. Box 7195, 90007. Revs. Eamonn Donnelly, S.V.D., Prov. Supr.; Gerard O'Doherty, S.V.D., Prov. Treas.; Francis L. Shigo, S.V.D., 1255 7th St., #4, San Pedro, 90731. Tel: 310-514-9360.

Western Province (1964) Province of St. Therese of the Child Jesus, 2181 W. 25th St., P.O. Box 7195, 90007. Tel: 323-735-8130; Fax: 323-735-8122. Very Rev. Eamonn Donnelly, S.V.D., Prov.; Revs. Melvin P. James, S.V.D., Vice Prov.; Gerard O'Doherty, S.V.D., Prov. Treas.

AZUSA. *Casa Comboni Mission Seminary*, 525 N. Pasadena Ave., 91702. Tel: 626-334-3531; Fax: 626-969-8681.
E-mail: pep44@earthlink.net
Rev. Jose Luis Cuevas (Mexico), Supr., Vocation Dir. In res. Rev. Mario Merino, Formation Dir. Priests 2; Students 4.

BALDWIN PARK. *Vietnamese Redemptorist Mission*, 3452 N. Big Dalton Ave., 91706. Tel: 626-337-7735; Fax: 626-851-1280. Revs. Vu Minh Nghiem, C.Ss.R.; Ngo Dinh Thoa, C.Ss.R.; Dinh Ngoc Que, C.Ss.R.; Nguyen

Thanh Son, C.Ss.R.; Tran Quoc Bao, C.Ss.R.; Pham Quoc Hung, C.Ss.R.; Bros. John M. Viet Hien, C.Ss.R.; Martin Nguyen Van Moi, C.Ss.R.
In Residence Elsewhere: 8800 E. 22nd St., Tuscon, AZ, 85710. Tel: 602-751-2060. Rev. Tran Ngoc Bich, C.Ss.R., 22 Stone St., Salinas, 93901. Tel: 408-772-8227. Rev. Tran Dinh Phuc, C.Ss.R., 2458 Atlantic Ave., Long Beach, 90806. Tel: 562-424-2041; Fax: 562-424-2152. Revs. Nguyen Duc Mau, C.Ss.R.; Phan Phat Huon, C.Ss.R.; Ngo Van Dao, C.Ss.R.; Bui quang Tuan, C.Ss.R.; Nguyen Tat Hai, C.SS.R.; Nguyen Truong Luan; Bro. Vo Thanh Ha, C.Ss.R., 1907 E. Grauwyler Rd., Irving, TX, 75061. Tel: 972-438-4082. Revs. Nguyen Duc Thong, C.Ss.R.; Dinh Minh Hai, C.Ss.R.; Nguyen Duc Thanh, C.Ss.R.; Chau Xuan Bau, C.SS.R., 3417 W. Little York Rd., Houston, TX, 77091. Tel: 214-321-9493; Fax: 713-868-4589. Revs. Le Quang Phung, C.Ss.R.; Le Huy Bang, C.Ss.R., 1011 Farm Rd., P.O. Box 1060, Rockport, TX, 78381. Tel: 361-729-3008. Rev. Nguyen Van Phan, C.Ss.R. Priests 23; Brothers 3; Student Clerics 25.

CAMARILLO. *Rogationist Fathers*, 2530 E. Ventura Blvd., 93010. Tel: 805-389-9910; Fax: 805-384-0189.
E-mail: RogVoc@aol.com
Revs. F. Antonio Carlucci, R.C.J., Supr., Dean of Studies; Loji Pilones, R.C.J., Treas., Vocation Dir., Vice Supr.

CULVER CITY. *Ignatius House, The Novitiate of the California Province, Society of Jesus*, P.O. Box 5166, 90231-5166. Tel: 310-815-0166; Fax: 310-815-0170. 10775 Deshire Pl., 90230-5017. Tel: 310-815-0166 (Staff); 815-0185 (Novices); Fax: 310-815-0170. Revs. Robert A. Fambrini, S.J., Supr. & Dir. of Novices; James W. Reites, S.J., Asst. Dir. Novices; Leo J. Hombach, S.J., Treas. & Min. In res. Revs. Mark D. McGregor, S.J.; Michel Marcil, S.J., Dir. Inter Friendship House Assoc.

LA VERNE. *Congregation of the Sacred Hearts of Jesus and Mary*, 2150 Damien Ave., 91750-5114. Tel: 909-593-5441(Provinical Office); Fax: 909-593-3971.
E-mail: ssccw@tstonramp.com
Revs. Michael W. Barry, SS.CC., Prov.; Peter K. Dennis, SS.CC.; Donal McCarthy, SS.CC.; Patrick Travers, SS.CC.; Peadar Cronin, SS.CC.; Martin P. O'Loghlen, SS.CC.; Bro. Brian V. Guerrini, S.S.C.C. Priests 6; Brothers 1.

MISSION HILLS. *Congregation of the Sacred Hearts*, Alemany High School, 15201 Rinaldi St., 91345. Tel: 818-365-3925; Fax: 818-365-2064. Rev. Patrick Argue, SS.CC. Tel: 818-365-3925; 3927. Priests 1.

MONTEBELLO. *Vincentian Fathers & Brothers*, 420 Date St., 90640. Tel: 213-747-1227; Fax: 213-749-4504.
E-mail: AMATHOUSE@aol.com
Very Rev. Bernard J. Quinn, Prov. & Supr.; Revs. Jeffrey H. Harvey, C.M.; Hoan N. Nguyen. Priests 3.
De Paul Center, 1105 Bluff Rd., 90640-6198. Tel: 323-721-6060; Fax: 323-887-1765. Revs. Patrick J. Mullin, Supr.; Andrew E. Bellisario, Dir.; John J. Casey; Peter J. Diliberto; Robert J. Jones; Thomas J. McIntyre, C.M.; Jacques J. Nouws; Victor J. Sarrazin; Philip A. Van Linden; Bro. Edward D. Graham. Priests 9; Brothers 1.
St. Mary's Center, 1964 Las Canoas Rd., Santa Barbara, 93105-2351. Tel: 805-966-4829; Fax: 805-966-7819. Revs. Walter L. Housey, Supr.; James F. McOwen; Roy A. Persich, Dir.; James M. Galvin; Gregory J. Schlarb. Priests 5.
Vincent House. House of Studies, 252 F St., Oxnard, 93030. Tel: 805-240-1012; Fax: 805-483-8340. Revs. Binh Van A. Nguyen, Supr.; Gary S. Landry, C.M. Priests 2.
Vincentian Residence, 641 W. Adams Blvd., Los Angeles, 90007-2546. Tel: 213-748-9829; Fax: 213-748-9829. Revs. Pedro Villarroya, Supr.; Edward F. Danagher; Francis David Pansini; Stafford Poole. Priests 4.
Vincentian Fathers and Brothers. Province of the West, 420 Date St., 90640. Tel: 323-721-5486; Fax: 323-721-5499.
E-mail: cmwestusa@att.net
Web site: www.vincentiansca.org
Legal Titles: *Congregation of the Mission in California, a Corporation.*; *Vincentian Community Charitable Trust.*; *Vincentian Foreign Mission Society.*; *DePaul Center Corporation.* Revs. Bernard J. Quinn, Prov.; Andrew E. Bellisario, Prov. Treas.; Francis David Pansini, Assoc. Treas.; Stafford Poole, Archivist; Jeffery H. Harvey, Vocation Dir. Priests 5.

NORTH HILLS. *Rogationist Fathers*, 9815 Columbus Ave., 91343. Tel: 818-893-4526; Fax: 818-895-8934.
E-mail: rogdevoff@aol.com
Revs. Vincenzo Buccheri, R.C.J.; John Bruno, R.C.J.; Sal Ciranni, R.C.J. Legal Title: *Congregation of Rogationists, Inc.*

OXNARD. *Brothers of Our Lady, Mother of Mercy*, Mother of Mercy Novitiate, 2336 S. C St., 93033. Tel: 805-486-3692; Fax: 805-487-4155.
E-mail: cwgresnigt@juno.com
Web site: web.inter:nl.net/users/gbcmm/indexe.html
Conducted by the Brothers of Our Lady, Mother of Mercy. Bros. Edward Gresnigt, Reg. Supr.; Edward Gresnigt, C.F.M.M., Local Supr. Brothers 6.
St. Augustine Priory, St. Augustine Priory, 400 Sherwood Way, 93033. Tel: 805-486-7433. Prepostulancy & Postulancy Vocation Center. Total in Residence 16.
St. Augustine Priory O.A.R., 400 Sherwood Way, 93033-7510. Tel: 805-486-7433; 486-9651 (Vocations); Fax: 805-487-2805.
E-mail: augustineofhippo@saintly.com
Web site: augustinianrecollects.org
Prepostulancy and Postulancy Augustinian Recollects & Vocation Center. Revs. Francis Cregan, O.A.R., Prior; Fidel Hernandez, O.A.R., Prefect of Students; Jose Luis Martinez, O.A.R., Subprior. In res. Revs. Albert Polt, O.A.R., (Retired); Robert Huse, O.A.R.; Placid Lanz, O.A.R.; Bros. Raymond Fabrin, O.A.R.; Eric Crelencia, O.A.R. Students 6.

PASADENA. *Legionaries of Christ*, 1453 E. California Blvd., 91106. Tel: 626-792-0447; Fax: 626-792-0475.
E-mail: amulcahey@familink.com
Web site: http://www.legionaries.org
In res. Revs. Andrew Mulcahey, L.C.; Juan Rivas, L.C.; Patrick Langan, L.C.; Thomas Maher, L.C.; Bros. Jason Smith, L.C.; Joseph Freymann, L.C.; Kenneth Pullis, L.C. Priests 4; Brothers 3.
Passionist Community, 651 N. Sierra Madre Blvd., 91107. Tel: 626-564-1099; Fax: 626-564-1930.
E-mail: office.manager@worldnet.att.net
Passionist Retreat House, 700 N. Sunnyside Ave., Sierra Madre, 91024. Tel: 626-355-7188; Fax: 626-355-0485. Passionist Residence, 651 N. Sierra Madre Blvd., 91107. Tel: 626-564-1099; Fax: 626-564-1930. Congregation of the Passion, Mater Dolorosa Community. Very Rev. Alfred Pooler, C.P., Local Supr.; Revs. Damian McHale, C.P.; Patrick Brennan, C.P., Retreat Dir.; Godfrey Poage, C.P.; Alan Phillip, C.P., Asst. Supr.; George Stanfield, C.P.; Bros. John Rockenbach, C.P., Retreat House; Kurt Wernert, C.P., Retreat House. Priests 6; Brothers 2.

RANCHO DOMINGUEZ. *Dominguez Seminary Inc.*, 18127 S. Alameda St., 90220. Tel: 213-636-6030; 310-631-5981; 631-8484; Fax: 310-631-3518. Retirement Center, Ministries Community. Congregation of Missionaries, Sons of the Immaculate Heart of Mary (Claretian Missionaries). Revs. Robert Bishop, C.M.F., Supr.; Diego Barrios, C.M.F., Vicar Supr.; Donald Lavelle, C.M.F., Econome; Patrick McPolin, C.M.F.; John Corominas, C.M.F.; Albert Connors, C.M.F.; Basil Frison, C.M.F.; Francis X. Hogan, C.M.F.; Celestino de la Iglesia, C.M.F.; Isidor Garcia, C.M.F.; Raymond Martinez, C.M.F.; Flavian Willathgamuwa, C.M.F.; Salvatore Bonano, C.M.F., Vicar; Joseph Daries, C.M.F.; Bros. Paul Roy, C.M.F.; Franklin Stanford, C.M.F. Priests 14; Brothers 2.

SAN GABRIEL. *Claretian Missionaries (Missionary Sons of the Immaculate Heart of Mary)*, 428 S. Mission Dr., 91776. Tel: 626-457-3035; Fax: 626-282-5308.
E-mail: sgm@sangabrielmission.org
Web site: sangabrielmission.org
Claretians Old Mission. Revs. Dennis G. Gallo, C.M.F.; Jose Sanchez, C.M.F.; John Gregory Hencier, C.M.F.; Arnold J. Gonzalez, C.M.F.; Deacon Darrin Merlino, C.M.F. Priests 4.

SANTA BARBARA. *Franciscan Friary, Order of Friars Minor (Old Mission)*, 2201 Laguna St., 93105. Tel: 805-682-4713. Revs. Alberic Smith, O.F.M., Guardian; Virgil Cordano, O.F.M., Theological Institute; Gordon Urbine, O.F.M.; Nevin Ford, O.F.M.; Felipe Baldonado, O.F.M.; Benvenute Bavero, O.F.M.; Virgilio Biasiol, O.F.M.; Maurus Kelly, O.F.M., Chap.; Vincent Mesi, O.F.M., St. Barbara's; Howard Hall, O.F.M.; Leo Sprietsma, O.F.M.; Bartholomew Welsh; Ralph Weishaar; Kieran McCarty, O.F.M.; Dan Barica, O.F.M., St. Barbara's; Bros. Timothy Arthur, O.F.M., Prov. Archivist; Ernest Duplessis, O.F.M.; Adrian Furman, O.F.M.; Wenceslaus Farlow, O.F.M.; Joachim Grant, O.F.M.; Conrado Duran, O.F.M.; Augustine Hootka, O.F.M.; Philip Morales, O.F.M.; Peter Raferty, O.F.M.; Jan Honchosky, O.F.M.; Ernest LuVisi, O.F.M. Priests 15; Brothers 11.
St. Anthony's Seminary, 2300 Garden St., 93105-3696. Tel: 805-682-4720; Fax: 805-682-2870.
E-mail: stanthonys@home.com
Web site: sbfranciscans.org
Rev. Leo Sprietsma, O.F.M., Dir. In res. Rev. Nevin Ford, O.F.M.; Bros. Timothy Arthur, O.F.M.; Jan Honchosky, O.F.M. Priests 2; Brothers 2.

TORRANCE. *Franciscan Friars, St. Bonaventure Friary*, 5432 Torrance Blvd., 90503. Tel: 310-540-1452.
E-mail: JHOCONNOR@yahoo.com
Conventual Franciscan Friars (St. Joseph Cupertino Province). Legal Title: *Conventual Franciscans of California, Inc.* Revs. Alexander J. Lewis, O.F.M.Conv., Supr.; Gary Klauer, O.F.M.Conv. In res. Revs. Ceaser Inserra, O.F.M.Conv.; Francisco Nahoe, O.F.M.Conv.; Bros. Casimir Roland, O.F.M.Conv.; Patrick Lytell, O.F.M.Conv.; Paul Gawlowski, O.F.M.Conv.; Anthony Tuyen Pham, O.F.M.Conv.

VALYERMO. *St. Andrew's Abbey*, 31001 N. Valyermo Rd., P.O. Box 40, 93563-0040. Tel: 661-944-2178; Fax: 661-944-1076.
E-mail: monks@valyermo.com
Web site: www.valyermo.com
Benedictine Monks. Rt. Rev. Francis Benedict, O.S.B., Abbot; Very Rev. Simon O'Donnell, O.S.B., Prior; Revs. John Bosco Stoner, O.S.B., Subprior; Eleutherius Winance, O.S.B.; Werner Papeians de Morchoven, O.S.B.; Bro. Peter Zhou Bang-jiu, O.S.B.; Rev. Philip Edwards, O.S.B.; Bro. Dominic Guillen, O.S.B.; Rev. Gregory Elmer, O.S.B.; Bros. Benedict Dull, O.S.B.; Joseph Iarrobino, O.S.B.; Very Rev. Luke Dysinger, O.S.B.; Revs. Martin Yslas, O.S.B.; Isaac Kalina, O.S.B.; Paul Pluth, O.S.B.; Bros. Anselmo Taborda, O.S.B.; Andrew Hayes, O.S.B.; Rev. Joseph (Dennis) Brennan, O.S.B.; Bros. Michael Weeks, O.S.B.; Thomas Babusis, O.S.B.; Carlos Lopez, O.S.B.; James Brennan, O.S.B.; Damien Toilolo, O.S.B.; John Donaldson, O.S.B. Priests 12; Brothers 12.

WHITTIER. *Redemptorist Fathers Mission House*, 7215 Newlin Ave., 90602-1266. Tel: 562-698-0107; Fax: 562-696-1617. Revs. Joseph Morin, C.SS.R., Supr.; Arturo Uribe, C.SS.R.; Joseph Elliott, C.SS.R.; Joseph Tobin, C.SS.R.; Donald Liberty, C.SS.R.; Tuan Pham, C.SS.R.; George Dawson, C.SS.R.; Arthur Frost, C.SS.R.; William Adams, C.SS.R.; Bro. Don E. O'Mara, C.SS.R.; Deacon Richard Fischer, C.SS.R. Priests 9; Brothers 1; Deacons 1.

[R] CONVENTS AND RESIDENCES FOR SISTERS

LOS ANGELES. *California Institute of the Sisters of the Blessed Virgin Mary, I.H.M.*, Motherhouse, Novitiate, Retreat House: 3431 Waverly Dr., 90027. Tel: 323-664-1124; Fax: 323-664-2215. Legal Title: *California Institute of the Sisters of the Most Holy and Immaculate Heart of the Blessed Virgin Mary.* Sr. Mary Rita Stukey, I.H.M., Supr. Gen. Sisters 21.
Congregation of the Poor Sisters of Nazareth Motherhouse, U.S.A. and Novitiate, 3333 Manning Ave., 90064. Tel: 310-839-2361; 2362; Fax: 310-839-0648. Sr. John Berchmans, Reg. Supr. Sisters 9.
Eucharistic Franciscan Missionary Sisters, Motherhouse: 943 S. Soto St., 90023. Tel: 213-264-6556; Fax: 213-526-1655.
E-mail: efms@earthlink.net
Rev. Mother Rose Seraphim, E.F.M.S., Supr. Gen. Sisters 25.
Eucharistic Franciscan Missionary Sisters of Los Angeles, Nativity Convent: 1421 Cota Ave., Torrance, 90501. Tel: 310-328-6725; Fax: 310-328-5248.
Formation Community, Religious of the Sacred Heart of Mary, 2833 Sichel St., 90031. Tel: 323-225-5486; Fax: 323-887-8952.
E-mail: rshmwap@earthlink.net
Web site: www.rshm.org
Sisters 3.
Guadalupanas Missionaries of the Holy Spirit. Novitiate. 758 S. Dunsmuir Ave., 90036. Tel: 213-936-0135.
Guadalupanas Missionaries of the Holy Spirit, 5467 W. 8th St., 90036. Tel: 323-936-6565; Fax: 323-930-0394.
E-mail: mgspscala@aol.com
Apostolate House. Sisters 6.
Lovers of the Holy Cross Sisters, 90249. Tel: 310-516-0271; Fax: 310-352-6435.
E-mail: lhcmh@aol.com
Mother House & Novitiate, 14700 S. Van Ness Ave., Gardena, 90249. Tel: 310-768-1906; 516-0271; Fax: 310-352-6435. Good Shepherd Center, 267 N. Belmont Ave., 90026. Tel: 213-250-5241; Fax: 213-482-0567. St. Bruno's Convent, 10734 S. Widener Ave., Whittier, 90603. Tel: 562-947-1177; Fax: 562-947-1177. Total Sisters & Novices 57.
Missionary Servants of the Most Blessed Trinity Ascension Missionary Cenacle, 518 W. 111th Pl., 90044. Tel: 213-754-0020.
Missionary Sisters of Christ the King (Poland), 3424 W. Adams Blvd., 90018. Tel: 323-734-6754; Fax: 323-734-0046.
E-mail: plchurchla@earthlink.net
Sisters working in Archdiocese of Los Angeles 3. Sr. Gertruda I. Szymanska, Local Supr.; Sr. Zofia Turczyn, Sacristan Work; Sr. Bozena Blad, Sec. (Parish Office).
Monastery of the Angels (Contemplative), 1977 Carmen Ave., 90068. Tel: 323-466-2186; Fax: 323-466-6645. Sr. Mary Raymond, O.P., Prioress; Rev. Armando Ibanez, O.P., Chap. Tel: 323-463-6488. Nuns of the Order of Preachers. Professed Cloistered Nuns 23; Professed Extern Sisters 2.
Pious Disciples of the Divine Master, 215 S. Los Angeles St., 90012. Tel: 213-680-9271; Fax: 213-680-3466. Sr. Trinity Taricco. Sisters 6.

Provincial House of the Sisters of St. Joseph of Carondelet. (St. Mary's Provincialate, Carondelet Center), 11999 Chalon Rd., 90049-1524. Tel: 310-889-2100; Fax: 310-476-8735.
E-mail: lacsj@aol.com
Web site: www.csjla.org
Sr. Maureen O'Connor, Prov. Supr.; Sr. Kathleen Kelly, Asst. Prov. Supr.; Sr. Claire Marie Williams, Asst. Prov. Supr. Sisters 87.

Sisters of St. Joseph in California. Tel: 310-889-2154; Fax: 310-472-5982.

Sisters of St. Joseph Ministerial Services. Tel: 310-889-2155; Fax: 310-472-5982.

Sisters of St. Joseph in Arizona. Tel: 310-889-2142; Fax: 310-476-8735.

Sisters of Our Lady of Perpetual Help, S.O.L.P.H., St. Brendan Convent, 220 S. Manhattan Pl., 90004. Tel: 213-389-6398.

Sisters of Social Service of Los Angeles, General Motherhouse, 2303 S. Figueroa Way, 90007. Tel: 213-746-2117; Fax: 213-747-4499.
E-mail: ssocialser@aol.com
Web site: www.socialservicesisters.org
Legal Titles: *Sisters of Social Service of Los Angeles, Inc.; Sisters of Social Service Support Trust Fund.* Sr. Michele Walsh, Gen. Dir. Sisters 100.
Sisters of Social Service, Formation, 2303 S. Figeroa Way, 90007. Tel: 213-746-2117; Fax: 213-747-4499. Sr. Martha Vega, S.S.S., Team Chair. In Formation 4.

Sisters of St. Joseph of Orange, 8000 Regis Way, 90045. Tel: 310-645-2514; 645-0718. Sisters 3.

Sisters of the Company of Mary, 2634 Monmouth Ave., 90007. Tel: 213-747-3542; 737-3672. Sr. Teresa Zapata, O.D.N., Supr. Sisters 6.

Sisters of the Good Shepherd, 2561 Venice Blvd., 90019. Tel: 323-737-6111; Fax: 323-737-6113.
E-mail: rgslai@aol.com
Sisters 12.

Sisters of the Guardian Angel, 4529 New York St., 90022. Tel: 323-266-4431; Fax: 323-981-0187.

Sisters of the Immaculate Heart of Mary at Mirinae, I.H.M., P.O. Box 75867, 90075. Tel: 213-381-2481. Total in Residence 6.

Sisters of the Society Devoted to the Sacred Heart, Local Convent: 628 S. Irving Blvd., 90005. Tel: 323-936-8647; Fax: 323-931-8875. Sr. Lucia Tu, S.D.S.H., Supr. Sisters 5.

Sisters of the Society Devoted to the Sacred Heart, 869 S. Rimpau Blvd., 90005. Tel: 323-935-2372; Fax: 323-935-5943. Sisters 3.

ALHAMBRA. *Carmel of St. Teresa*, 215 E. Alhambra Rd., 91801. Tel: 626-282-2387; Fax: 626-282-2053.
E-mail: momaria@aol.com
Discalced Nuns of the Order of Our Blessed Lady of Mt. Carmel. Mother Maria, Prioress. Sisters 16.

Carmelite Sisters of the Most Sacred Heart of Los Angeles, Generalate Motherhouse, Novitiate and Retreat House: 920 E. Alhambra Rd., 91801. Tel: 626-289-1353; Fax: 626-308-1913.
E-mail: decor-carmeli@CatholicFamilies.net
Web site: carmelitegeneralate.homestead.com
Mother Regina Marie Gorman, O.C.D., Supr. General; Sr. Mary Colombiere Welch, O.C.D., Vicar Gen. Total Professed Sisters 141.

Carmelite Sisters of the Most Sacred Heart of Los Angeles. Tel: 626-289-1353; Fax: 626-308-1913.

ALTADENA. *Franciscan Sisters of the Sacred Heart*, 579 W. Mariposa St., 91001. Tel: 626-791-4359.
E-mail: ruthagee@juno.com
Sisters 6.

BONITA. *Sisters Servants of the Blessed Sacrament*, U.S. Provincial House, 3173 Winnetka Dr., 91902. Tel: 619-267-0720; Fax: 619-267-0920.
E-mail: joramosil@msn.com
Sisters in the Vice Province 62.

CULVER CITY. *Daughters of St. Paul*, 3908 Sepulveda Blvd., 90230. Tel: 310-390-4699; Fax: 310-397-8366.
E-mail: fspla@aol.com
Web site: pauline.org
Sr. Armanda Santos, F.S.P., Supr. Sisters 9.

Religious Sisters of Charity, 10664 St. James Dr., 90230. Tel: 310-559-0176; Fax: 310-559-3530. Sisters 9.

DOWNEY. *Sisters of the Holy Faith in California*, 12322 S. Paramount Blvd., 90242. Tel: 562-869-6092; Fax: 562-869-4609.
E-mail: shfaith@aol.com
Sisters 39.

ENCINO. *Sisters of St. Louis*, 5001 White Oak Ave., 91316. Tel: 818-344-7825. Sisters 5. St. Joseph of Carondolet. Ursuline Sisters. Presentation Sisters.

GARDENA. *Poor Clare Missionary Sisters, Inc.*, 1103 W. 164th St., 90247. Tel: 310-323-9942. Sr. Maria S. Miranda, M.C., Supr. Sisters 12.

GLENDORA. *St. Lucy's Priory*, 19045 E. Sierra Madre Ave., 91741. Tel: 626-335-1682; Fax: 626-914-9398.
E-mail: stlucysebrown@aol.com
Sr. Elizabeth Brown, Prioress. Legal Title: *St. Lucy's Priory of Glendora California, Inc.* Sisters 24.

LOMITA. *[*]Sisters of the Korean Martyrs, S.K.M.*, 2263 W. 255th St., 90717. Tel: 310-325-2540; Fax: 310-325-2540.
E-mail: koreanmartyrs@yahoo.com

MONROVIA. *Convent of the Maryknoll Sisters of St. Dominic*, 340 Norumbega Dr., 91016-2445. Tel: 626-358-1825; Fax: 626-358-1227.
E-mail: ktbyrne@juno.com
Rev. Gerald B. Fessard, J.C.L., Chap.; Sr. Katherine Byrne, M.M., Coord. Sisters 42.

MONTEBELLO. *Religious of the Sacred Heart of Mary*, Provincial Center, 441 N. Garfield Ave., 90640-2901. Tel: 323-887-8821; Fax: 323-887-8952.
E-mail: rshmwap@earthlink.net
Web site: www.rshm.org

NORTHRIDGE. *Mother of Mercy Convent*, 9329 Crebs Ave., 91324. Tel: 818-882-4095. Sister of Mercy Burlingame.

Sisters of the Society Devoted to the Sacred Heart, Motherhouse: 9814 Sylvia Ave., 91324. Tel: 818-772-9961; Fax: 818-772-2742. Sr. Lucia Tu, S.D.S.H., Supr. Gen. Sisters 3.

OJAI. *Sisters of Mary Mother of the Church*, 431 Montanna Cir., 93023. Tel: 805-640-1798; Fax: 805-640-1798.
E-mail: SRSMMC@aol.com

OXNARD. *Sisters Servants of Mary*, 428 S. F St., 93030. Tel: 805-486-5502; Fax: 805-486-0663. Sr. Felisa Ripa, S.M., Mistress of Novices. Professed Sisters 15; Novices 10.

PASADENA. *Convent of the Holy Child.* Corporate Title: Society of the Holy Child Jesus, American Province, Inc. 1833 E. Orange Grove Ave., 91104-4805. Tel: 626-345-1633.
E-mail: shcj1833@aol.com
Web site: www.shcj.org

RANCHO PALOS VERDES. *Daughters of Mary & Joseph, D.M.J.*, Provincial House: 5300 Crest Rd., 90275-5004. Tel: 213-377-9968; 541-0784; Fax: 310-544-0387.
E-mail: dmjca@earthlink.net
Web site: home.earthlink.net/~dmjca.
Sisters 67.

Sisters of Charity of Rolling Hills, 28600 Palos Verdes Dr. E., 90275. Tel: 310-831-4104.
E-mail: svbuchholz@aol.com
Sr. Virginia Buchholz, S.C.R.H., Supr. Gen. Sisters 9.

SAN FERNANDO. *Franciscan Sisters of the Immaculate Conception*, 11320 Laurel Canyon Blvd., 91340. Tel: 818-365-2582; Fax: 818-365-3159.
E-mail: sisters.franciscan@gte.net
Legal Title: *Franciscan Missionary Sisters of the Immaculate Conception.* Sisters 111; Novices 5; Postulants 8.

Religious Sisters of Charity, 1608 Eighth St., 91340. Tel: 818-365-7926; Fax: 818-898-3382. Sisters 2.

SAN PEDRO. *Little Sisters of the Poor*, 2100 S. Western Ave., 90732. Tel: 310-548-0625; Fax: 310-548-4504. Sr. Marie Anne, Supr. Sisters 11.

SANTA BARBARA. *Monastery of Poor Clares*, Cloistered Contemplative Monastery, 215 E. Los Olivos St., 93105. Tel: 805-682-7670; Fax: 805-682-8041. Mother Mary Clare of Jesus, Abbess. Professed 14. Attended by Franciscan Fathers of the Old Mission.

St. Francis Convent, 601 E. Micheltorena St., 93103. Tel: 805-962-7661; Fax: 805-568-5822.
E-mail: cbowman@chw.edu
Web site: http://www.saintfrancis.org
Sr. Christine Bowman, O.S.F., Local Leader. Sisters 6.

SOLVANG. *Sisters of the Society Devoted to the Sacred Heart*, 1762 Mission Dr., 93463. Tel: 805-688-6158; Fax: 805-688-9247.
E-mail: sdshsol@juno.com
Sr. Elizabeth Normanly, S.D.S.H., Supr. Sisters 5.

SYLMAR. *Poor Clare Missionary Sisters*, P.O. Box 922046, 91392. Tel: 818-361-0591. Sr. Beatriz Aguilar, M.C., Supr. Sisters 5.

THOUSAND OAKS. *Sisters of Notre Dame*, Provincial House, Provincialate, 1776 Hendrix Ave., 91360. Tel: 805-496-3243; Fax: 805-379-3616.
E-mail: manningm@vcss.k12.ca.us
Web site: http://www.sndca.org/ca.html
Sr. Mary Amy, S.N.D., Supr. Sisters 43.

TORRANCE. *Little Company of Mary Convent*, 20552 Mansel Ave., 90503. Tel: 310-214-3190; 514-5230 (Office); Fax: 310-514-5314.
E-mail: smbabcock@lemhs.org
Sr. Mary Babcock, L.C.M. Sisters 4. 20562 Mansel Ave., 90503. Tel: 310-370-3992, 310-540-7676 (Office). Sr. Terrence, Landini, L.C.M. Sisters 2.

VENTURA. *Handmaids of the Sacred Heart of Jesus, Mary and Joseph*, P.O. Box 2957, 93002. Tel: 805-653-2379; Fax: 805-653-1383.
E-mail: jmj@anacapa.net
Web site: http://www.anacapa.net/~handmaids/

Sisters of the Holy Cross, 342 Cedar St., 93001. Tel: 805-641-2906.
E-mail: patrice25@juno.com
Legal Title: *Sisters of the Holy Cross.* Sisters 4.

Sisters of the Holy Cross, Saint Catherine-by-the-Sea, 1931 Poli St., 93001. Tel: 805-652-1700; Fax: 805-653-1354. Residence for Retired Sisters. Legal Title: *Sisters of the Holy Cross of California.* Rev. William Olivas, O.S.A.; Sr. Patricia Ann Thompson, C.S.C., Supr. Sisters 38.

WHITTIER. *Sisters of the Sacred Heart of Jesus, H.C.J.S.*, 11506 Walnut St., 90606. Tel: 310-908-0618; Fax: 760-723-2271.
E-mail: hcjsfbrk@aol.com

WOODLAND HILLS. *Sisters of St. Louis, Louisville Convent*, 22300 Mulholland Dr., 91364. Tel: 818-883-1678; Fax: 818-346-6109.
E-mail: sslca4@worldnet.att.net
Sr. Donna Hansen, S.S.L., Reg. Supr. Sisters 14.

[S] SECULAR INSTITUTES

LOS ANGELES. *Society of Our Lady of the Way*, 2339 N. Catalina St., 90027. Tel: 323-665-0333.
E-mail: jllaca27@aol.com
Web site: www.execpc.com/uscsi/index.html.
Legal Title: *Society of Our Lady of the Way of Southern California, Inc.*

WEST COVINA. *Fr. Kolbe Missionaries of the Immaculata*, 531 E. Merced Ave., 91790. Tel: 626-917-0040; Fax: 626-917-0900.
E-mail: FkMinCAL@aol.com
Web site: www.kolbemission.org

[T] ASSOCIATIONS OF THE FAITHFUL

OJAI. *Trinitas*, P.O. Box 1477, 93024-1477. Tel: 805-659-4158 (English); 646-4579 (Spanish).

TUJUNGA. *Community of the Holy Spirit, C.H.S.*, 10358 Las Lunitas Ave., 91042-1812. Tel: 818-951-6002.

VENTURA. *Handmaids of the Sacred Heart of Jesus, Mary, and Joseph, J.M.J.*, P.O. Box 2957, 93002-2957. Tel: 805-653-2379; Fax: 805-653-1383.
E-mail: jmj@anacapa.net

[U] RESIDENCES FOR WOMEN

LOS ANGELES. *Bethany House*, 850 N. Hobart Blvd., 90029. Tel: 323-665-6937; Fax: 323-664-0754. Sisters 7; Residents 22.

Estrella del Mar, Inc. dba Regis House, 2303 S. Figueroa Way, 90025. Tel: 310-477-8168. Sr. Georgina Cahill, S.S.S., Dir.; Sr. Jennifer Gaeta, S.S.S., Dir. Sisters of Social Service 2.

Good Shepherd Center for Homeless Women, Languille Emergency Shelter, 267 N. Belmont Ave., 90026. Tel: 213-250-5241; Fax: 213-250-5073.
E-mail: srjuliamary@mail.com
Web site: www.thegoodshepherdcenter.com
(A Division of Catholic Charities). Women in Residence 30; Women Assisted Annually 2,444.

Mother-Child Transitional Residence Administrative Site, 267 N. Belmont Ave., 90026. Tel: 213-469-6540; Fax: 213-469-0370. Mother-Children in Residence 30; Mother-Children Sheltered Annually 150.

Hawkes Residence / Women's Village, 1640 Rockwood St., 90026. Tel: 213-482-0281; Fax: 213-482-0299. Women Sheltered Annually 150.

St. Anne's. For further details refer to listing in Special Care Facilities section. 155 N. Occidental Blvd., 90026. Tel: 213-381-2931; Fax: 213-381-7804.
E-mail: stannes@stannes.org
Web site: www.stannes.org
Group Home for pregnant, parenting teens and their babies.

St. Joseph's Residence, 1124 W. Adams Blvd., 90007. Tel: 213-749-9577; Fax: 213-747-6468.
E-mail: odnadams@earthlink.net
Sisters of the Company of Mary. Women 62. Mailing Address, 16791 E. Main St., Tustin, 92780-4034.

[V] RESIDENCES FOR MEN

LOS ANGELES. *"Casa Teresa," Missionaries of Charity Brothers*, 1316 S. Westlake Ave., 90006. Tel: 213-380-5225. Temporary shelter for sick homeless men. Brothers 6; Postulants 1.

"Nuestra Hogar" Missionaries of Charity Brothers, 1345 Alvarado Ter., 90006. Tel: 214-251-9707.

Catholic Kolping House, 1225 S. Union Ave., 90015. Tel: 213-388-9438. Rev. Richard J. Russell, Spiritual Dir.; Ruby Payne, Mgr. Capacity 60.

The Little Brothers of the Good Shepherd, B.G.S., 3445 Waverly Dr., 90027. Tel: 213-662-0092 (Office); 662-3620 (Res.); Fax: 323-662-3619. Staff for Cardinal Manning House of Prayer.

Missionaries of Charity Brothers, House of Formation, 325 S. Westlake Blvd., 90006. Tel: 213-384-6116.

[W] RETREAT HOUSES

LOS ANGELES. *Claretian Retreat Center (All Groups)*, 1119 Westchester Pl., 90019. Tel: 323-737-8464; Fax: 323-733-6201. Revs. Roland Lozano, C.M.F., Supr.; Frank J. Ferrante, C.M.F., Dir.; Bro. Rene Lepage, C.M.F., Admin.

Immaculate Heart Retreat Center. (Days of Recollection Only), 3431 Waverly Dr., 90027. Tel: 323-664-1126; Fax: 323-664-2215. Conducted by the Sisters of the Immaculate Heart. Sr. Margaret Mary, I.H.M., Dir. Capacity 48; Sisters 10.

ALHAMBRA. *Retreat House of the Sacred Heart*, 920 E. Alhambra Rd., 91801. Tel: 626-289-1353; Fax: 626-281-3546.
E-mail: shrhrd@pacbell.com
Carmelite Sisters of the Most Sacred Heart of Los Angeles. Sr. Marisa, O.C.D., Contact Person. Capacity 89; Sisters 16; Novices 6; Postulants 3.
(See Convents).

ENCINO. *Holy Spirit Retreat Center*, 4316 Lanai Rd., 91436. Tel: 818-784-4515; Fax: 818-784-0409.
E-mail: hsrcenter@earthlink.net
Web site: www.hsrcenter.com
Sisters of Social Service.

MALIBU. *Serra Retreat*, 3401 Serra Rd., P.O. Box 127, 90265. Tel: 310-456-6631; Fax: 310-456-6051.
E-mail: warrenr480@aol.com
Web site: sbfranciscans.org
Franciscan Friars. Revs. Warren Rouse, O.F.M., Dir.; Michael Doherty, O.F.M., Vicar; Alex Manville, O.F.M., Guardian; Bros. Samuel Cabot, O.F.M.; Pierre Despres, O.F.M. Priests 3; Brothers 2.

MONTEBELLO. *DePaul Center*, 1105 Bluff Rd., 90640-6198. Tel: 323-721-6060; Fax: 323-887-0765.
E-mail: DePaulCenter@att.net
(Formerly St. Vincent's Seminary). Congregation of the Mission (Vincentians). Retreat and Evangelization Center. Revs. Andrew E. Bellisario, C.M., Dir.; Patrick J. Mullin, C.M., Superior; Victor J. Sarrazin, C.M.; Philip A. Van Linden, C.M. In res. Revs. John J. Casey, C.M., (Retired); Peter J. Diliberto, C.M., (Retired); Robert J. Jones, C.M.; Thomas J. McIntyre, C.M., (Retired); James J. Nouws, C.M., (Retired); James V. Connors, C.M., (Retired); Bro. Edward D. Graham, C.M.

RANCHO PALOS VERDES. *Mary and Joseph Retreat Center*, 5300 Crest Rd., 90275-5004. Tel: 310-377-4867; Fax: 310-541-1176.
E-mail: registrar@maryjoseph.org
Web site: www.maryjoseph.org
Daughters of Mary and Joseph. Retreat Center Capacity 67; Sisters 3.

ROSEMEAD. *St. Joseph's Salesian Youth Renewal Center*. (Boys and Girls), 8301 Arroyo Dr., P.O. Box 1639, 91770. Tel: 626-280-8622; Fax: 626-280-0545.
E-mail: stjosephrc@aol.com
Conducted by Salesians of St. John Bosco. Revs. Paul M. Caporalli, S.D.B.; Bill Bolton, S.D.B., Dir. Retreat Center; Mirko Flak, S.D.B., (Retired); Bros. George Ghiselli, S.D.B., Treas.; Phil Mandile, S.D.B.; Larry King, S.D.B.; Bruno DePretto, S.D.B. Priests 3; Brothers 4.

SAN FERNANDO. *Poverello of Assisi Retreat House*, 1519 Woodworth St., 91340. Tel: 818-365-1071; Fax: 818-361-2751. For men and women. Marriage Encounter in Korean and Spanish. Engaged Encounter in English, Vietnamese and Spanish couples. Other Denominations workshops seminars, staff meetings. Priests and Sisters retreats, assemblies and chapters. Franciscan Missionary Sisters of the Immaculate Conception. Sr. Mary Jesus, O.S.F., Dir. Capacity 112.

SANTA BARBARA. *St. Mary's Seminary Center*, 1964 Las Canoas Rd., 93105. Tel: 805-966-4829; Fax: 805-966-7819.
E-mail: schlarb@aol.com
Web site: home.catholicweb.com/stmaryseminary retreatcenter
Revs. James F. McOwen, C.M.; Roy A. Persich, C.M., Dir.; James M. Galvin, C.M.; Walter Housey, C.M.; Gregory J. Schlarb, C.M. Priests 5.

SIERRA MADRE. *Mater Dolorosa Retreat Center*, 700 N. Sunnyside Ave., Box 68, 91025. Tel: 626-355-7188; Fax: 626-355-0485.
E-mail: Materdolorosa@compuserve.com
Web site: www.passionist.org
Conducted by the Passionist Community. Lay Retreat League for men and women. Specialized Retreats.
Retreat Team: Revs. Patrick Brennan, C.P., Retreat Dir.; Alfred Pooler, C.P.; George Stanfield, C.P.; Sr. Judy Rinek, S.N.J.M.; Bros. John Rockenbach, C.P.; Kurt Wernert, C.P.; Mrs. Mary Lou Butler, Business Admin. Priests 3; Brothers 2.

VALYERMO. *St. Andrew's Abbey Retreat House (All Groups)*, 31001 N. Valyermo Rd., P.O. Box 40, 93563. Tel: 661-944-2178, Ext. 0; Fax: 661-944-1076.
Web site: www.valyermo.com
Conducted by the Benedictine Monks. Revs. Francis Benedict, O.S.B., Retreat Dir. & Abbot. Tel: 661-944-2178; Philip Edwards, O.S.B., Guestmaster. Tel: 661-944-2178 Ext. 0; Bro. Benedict Dull, O.S.B., Guestmaster; Rita Jones, Youth Center Contact Person. Tel: 661-944-2734.

[X] PERSONAL PRELATURES

LOS ANGELES. *Prelature of the Holy Cross and Opus Dei*. Tilden Study Center, 655 Levering Ave., 90024. Tel: 310-208-0941. Revs. Rene J. Schatteman; John R. Waiss.

[Y] CATHOLIC CHARITIES OF CALIFORNIA

LOS ANGELES. *Catholic Charities of Los Angeles, Inc.* Tel: 213-251-3400; Fax: 213-380-4603. His Eminence Roger Cardinal Mahony, D.D.; Rev. Msgr. Gregory A. Cox, M.S.W., Exec. Dir. Tel: 213-251-3464.

Central Administrative Offices, 1531 James M. Wood Blvd., P.O. Box 15095, 90015-0095. Tel: 213-251-3400; Fax: 213-380-4603. Rev. Msgr. Gregory A. Cox, M.S.W., Exec. Dir. Tel: 213-251-3464; Ronald G. Lopez, M.S.W., Chief Admin. Officer. Tel: 213-251-3412; James E. Bathker, CFO. Tel: 213-251-3410; Marilyn Kamerer, Dir. Dept. Human Resources. Tel: 213-251-3414; Alexandria "Sandi" Arnold, Dir. Dept. Resource Devel. Tel: 213-251-3495.

ADESTE Child Care Services. Tel: 213-251-3468; Fax: 213-251-3510. Armine Lalaian-Sanjar, Quality Assurance Dir. Tel: 213-251-3468.

CYO Athletics. Tel: 213-251-3562; Fax: 213-251-3510. Tom Davidson, Prog. Dir. Tel: 213-251-3562.

Commission on Aging, 123 E. 14th St., Long Beach, 90813. Tel: 562-591-1641; Fax: 562-591-2481.

Immigration & Refugee Services. Tel: 213-251-3489; Fax: 213-251-3444. Loc Nam Nguyen, Quality Assurance. Tel: 213-251-3489; Jo Marcel, Asst. Dir. Tel: 213-251-3470.

Immigration Reception. Tel: 213-251-3411; 251-3471; Fax: 213-251-3444.

Refugee Resettlement. Tel: 213-251-3470.

Central Intake Project. Tel: 213-251-3445; Fax: 213-251-3580. Joe Dinh Le, Quality Assurance. Tel: 213-251-3445.

Psychological Services Department. Tel: 213-251-3459; Fax: 213-251-3563. Edward Nelson, Ph.D., Dir. Tel: 213-251-3459.

(see pastoral regions for other locations).
Regional Offices and Community Centers:

Welfare to Work, 1531 James M. Wood Blvd., 90015-0095. Tel: 213-251-3417; Fax: 213-380-4603. John Russell, Quality Assurance Monitor.

Tobacco Control Program, 1530 James M. Wood Blvd., 90015. Tel: 213-251-3524; Fax: 213-251-3526. Leticia Arriola, Prog. Coord.

OUR LADY OF THE ANGELS METRO REGION. (Los Angeles Inner City), 4665 Willowbrook Ave., 90029. Tel: 323-662-1462; Fax: 323-662-3627. Jackie Lazarus, Regional Dir. Tel: 323-662-1462.

ADESTE Child Care, 4665 Willowbrook Ave., 90029. Tel: 323-662-8860; Fax: 323-662-3627.

Central Intake Unit, 1530 James M. Wood Blvd., 90015. Tel: 213-251-3514; Fax: 213-251-3580.
Community Service Centers: St. Mary's Center, 4665 Willowbrook Ave., 90029. Tel: 323-662-4391; Fax: 323-662-3627. St. Catherine of Alexandria Center, 1039 W. 87th St., 90044. Tel: 323-752-3786; Fax: 323-752-9763. El Santo Nino Center, 601 E. 23rd St., 90011. Tel: 213-748-5246; Fax: 213-748-9006.

Education & Training, 1530 James M. Wood Blvd., 90015. Tel: 213-251-3570; Fax: 213-251-3554. Richard Cadena, Prog. Dir.

Immigration & Refugee Services, 1530 James M. Wood Blvd., 90015. Tel: 213-251-3514; Fax: 213-251-3580.

Psychological Services, 1530 James M. Wood Blvd., 90015. Tel: 213-251-3572; Fax: 213-251-3563.
Shelters & Housing Services: Angels Flight - Runaway/Homeless Youth Shelter, 357 S. Westlake Ave., 90057. Tel: 213-413-2311; 800-833-2499 (Hotline); Fax: 213-413-5690. Outreach, 4665 Willowbrook Ave., 90029. Tel: 323-660-1942; Fax: 323-660-6392. Good Shepherd Center for Homeless Women, 267 N. Belmont Ave., 90026. Tel: 213-250-5241; Fax: 213-250-5073. Sr. Julia Mary Farley, C.S.J., Prog. Dir., Good Shepherd Mother & Child Center, 1719 N. Taft Ave., 90028. Tel: 323-469-6540; Fax: 323-469-0376. Good Shepherd Hawkes Transitional Residence, Women's Village, 1650 Rockwood St., 90026. Tel: 213-482-0281; Fax: 213-482-0299. Hayward Hotel Social Services, 206 W. Sixth St., 90014. Tel: 213-622-0224; Fax: 213-913-2626. Community United for Meals at Home, 1039 W. 87th St., 90044. Tel: 323-752-3786.

OUR LADY OF THE ANGELS WESTERN REGION. (Inglewood, Crenshaw District, Korea Town, West Los Angeles, Malibu & Los Angeles Airport region), 211 Third Ave., Venice, 90291. Tel: 310-392-8701; Fax: 310-399-4097. Jim Stratton, Regl. Dir.

ADESTE Child Care, 211 Third Ave., Venice, 90291. Tel: 310-392-8701; Fax: 310-399-4097.
Community Service Centers: St. Margaret's Center, 10505 Hawthorne Blvd., Lennox, 90304. Tel: 310-672-2208; Fax: 310-672-1841. St. Peter Claver Center, 4202 W. Jefferson Blvd., 90016. Tel: 323-737-6036; Fax: 323-737-3649. St. Robert's Center, 211 Third Ave., Venice, 90291. Tel: 310-392-8701; Fax: 310-399-4097.

Immigration & Refugee Services, St. Margaret's Center, 10505 Hawthorne Blvd., Lennox, 90304. Tel: 310-672-2208.

Psychological Services, 211 Third Ave., Venice, 90291. Tel: 310-399-1451; Fax: 310-399-4097.

SAN FERNANDO REGION. (Burbank, Glendale, Eagle Rock, Verdugo Hills, Antelope Valley, San Fernando Valley), 21600 Hart St., Canoga Park, 91303. Tel: 818-883-6015; Fax: 818-883-4122. Moeed Khan, Regl. Dir.

ADESTE Child Care, 511 Kalisher St., San Fernando, 91340. Tel: 818-361-5686.

Central Intake Unit, 217 E. Alameda Ave., #211, Burbank, 91502. Tel: 818-841-2430.
Community Service Centers: Glendale Community Services Center, 4322 San Fernando Rd., Glendale, 91204. Tel: 818-409-3080; Fax: 818-244-7579. Guadalupe Community Center, 21600 Hart St., Canoga Park, 91303. Tel: 818-340-2050. Loaves and Fishes I, 4322 San Fernando Rd., Glendale, 91204. Tel: 818-409-3080. Loaves and Fishes II, 14640 Keswick St., Van Nuys, 91405. Tel: 818-997-0943; Fax: 818-497-6980. Loaves and Fishes III, 511 Kalisher St., San Fernando, 91340. Tel: 818-365-3195. Loaves and Fishes IV, 21600 Hart St., Canoga Park, 91303. Tel: 818-340-2050. Santa Rosa Center, 511 Kalisher St., San Fernando, 91340. Tel: 818-365-3194; Fax: 818-365-4645.

Immigration & Refugee Services, 511 Kalisher St., San Fernando, 91340. Tel: 818-365-3194; 3195.

Immigration & Refugee Services, 4322 San Fernando Rd., Glendale, 91204. Tel: 818-409-3080.

Psychological Services, 7120 Hayvenhurst Ave., #200, Van Nuys, 91406. Tel: 818-988-2850; Fax: 818-988-0685.

Residential Youth Services, Rancho San Antonio, 21000 Plummer St., Chatsworth, 91311. Tel: 818-882-6400; Fax: 818-882-3838. Bro. John Crowe, C.S.C., Dir.
Shelter/Housing Services: Lancaster Community Shelter, 44611 Yucca Ave., Lancaster, 93534. Tel: 805-945-7524; Fax: 805-949-6804.

SAN GABRIEL REGION. (San Gabriel Valley, Mt. Baldy, Pomona Valley, East Los Angeles), 1307 Warren St., 90033. Tel: 323-266-3130; Fax: 323-266-3269. Mary Romero, Regl. Dir.

ADESTE Child Care, 1307 Warren Ave., 90033. Tel: 323-264-4981; Fax: 323-266-3269.

Central Intake Unit, 11100 Valley Blvd., Ste. 100, El Monte, 91731. Tel: 626-582-8074; Fax: 626-582-8434.
Community Service Centers: Brownson House Community Center, 1307 Warren Ave., 90033. Tel: 323-264-8700; Fax: 323-266-3269. Brother Miguel Center, 315 North Park Ave., Pomona, 91768. Tel: 909-622-3466; Fax: 909-622-4621. El Monte Center, 3017 Tyler Ave., #9, El Monte, 91733. Tel: 626-575-7652; Fax: 626-575-1072. El Monte Multi-Service Center, 11411 E. Valley Blvd., El Monte, 91731. Tel: 626-401-9636; Fax: 626-401-9447. West Covina Community Services, 420 S. Glendora Ave., West Corvina, 91790. Tel: 626-918-2005.

Immigration & Refugee Services, 3017 Tyler Ave., El Monte, 91731. Tel: 626-575-7633.

San Gabriel Outreach, Irwindale Community Services, 16009 E. Cypress Ave., Irwindale, 91706. Tel: 626-338-5057.

Tobacco Control Program, 11100 Valley Blvd., Ste. 103, El Monte, 91737. Tel: 626-582-8073.

SAN PEDRO REGION. (Long Beach, South Bay, Compton, Rio Hondo, Vernon, Huntington Park, Whittier, Pico Rivera), 123 E. 14th St., Long Beach, 90813. Tel: 562-591-1641; Fax: 562-591-2481. Lupe U. Macker, Regl. Dir.

ADESTE Child Care, 123 E. 14th St., Long Beach, 90813. Tel: 562-591-1351.

Central Intake Unit, 944 Pacific Ave., Ste. 2, Long Beach, 90813. Tel: 562-437-1399.
Community Service Centers: Long Beach Community Services, 123 E. 14th St., Long Beach, 90813. Tel: 562-591-1351; Fax: 562-591-2481. Mahar House Center, 1115 Mahar Ave., Wilmington, 90744. Tel: 310-834-7265; Fax: 310-834-8813. Pico Rivera Food Pantry, 4522 Rosemead Blvd., Pico Rivera, 90660.

Tel: 562-463-6127. Pico Rivera Community Services, 4522 Rosemead Blvd., Pico Rivera, 90660. Tel: 562-463-6127.

Family Shelter for the Homeless, 123 E. 14th St., Long Beach, 90813. Tel: 562-591-1351.

Psychological Services, 6505 Rosemead Blvd., Ste. 108, Pico Rivera, 90660. Tel: 562-949-2496; Fax: 562-949-1697.

TASC (Teens Assisting Seniors), 9200 Mines, P.O. Box 1016, Pico Rivera, 90660. Tel: 562-948-2554.

SANTA BARBARA REGION. (Lompoc, Santa Maria, Santa Barbara, Carpinteria), 609 E. Haley St., Santa Barbara, 93103. Tel: 805-965-7045; Fax: 805-963-2978. Davida Willis, Regl. Dir.

ADESTE Child Care, 609 E. Haley St., Santa Barbara, 93103. Tel: 805-965-7045.
Community Service Centers: Santa Barbara Community Services, 609 E. Haley St., Santa Barbara, 93103. Tel: 805-965-7045. Carpenteria Community Services, 941 Walnut St., Carpenteria, 93013. Tel: 805-684-8621; Fax: 805-684-9771. Lompoc Community Services, 118 N. G, St., Ste. B, P.O. Box 665, Lompoc, 93436. Tel: 805-736-6226; Fax: 805-763-7499. Santa Maria Community Services, 607 W. Main, Santa Maria, 93454. Tel: 805-922-2059; Fax: 805-925-1979.

Guadalupe Community Services, 4681-11th St., Guadalupe, 93434. Tel: 805-343-1194.

New Cuyama Community Services, 4711 Hwy. 166, New Cuyama, 93254. Tel: 661-766-2469.
Thrift Stores: Lompoc Thrift Store, 1015 N. A St., Lompoc, 93436. Tel: 805-735-5236. St. Vincent de Paul/Catholic Charities Thrift Store, 609 E. Haley St., Santa Barbara, 93103. Tel: 805-966-9659. Santa Maria Thrift Store, 607 W. Main St., Santa Maria, 93454. Tel: 805-925-8372.

Immigration Services, 609 E. Haley St., Santa Barbara, 93103. Tel: 805-965-7045. Oasis, 4033 La Colina Rd. #8, Santa Barbara, 93110. Tel: 805-569-5368.

Psychological Services. 609 E. Haley St., Santa Barbara, 93103. Tel: 805-965-7045; Fax: 805-963-2978. 215 E. Fesler St., Santa Maria, 93454. Tel: 805-348-1627; Fax: 805-348-1629.

VENTURA COUNTY REGION. (Camarillo, Moorpark, Oxnard, Thousand Oaks, Simi Valley, Ventura, Conejo Valley), 303 N. Ventura Ave., Ste. A, Ventura, 93001. Tel: 805-643-4694; Fax: 805-643-4781. Robert Bagdazian, L.C.S.W., Regl. Dir.

ADESTE Child Care, 303 N. Ventura Ave., Ste. A, Ventura, 93001. Tel: 805-643-4760.
Community Service Centers: Ventura Community Services, 303 N. Ventura Ave., Ste. C, Ventura, 93001. Tel: 805-643-4694. Oxnard Community Services, 401 N. A St., Oxnard, 93030. Tel: 805-486-2900. Moorpark Community Services, 30 Flory Ave., Moorpark, 93021. Tel: 805-529-0720. Thousand Oaks Community Services, 80 E. Hillcrest Dr., #216, Thousand Oaks, 91360. Tel: 805-496-1113.
Handicapables. Tel: 805-527-7806; 482-4050.
OASIS - Older Adult Services. 2532 Ventura Blvd., Camarillo, 93010. Tel: 805-987-2083; Fax: 805-383-1318. 5649 Pittman St., Simi Valley, 93063. Tel: 805-526-3009; Fax: 805-526-4231.

Psychological Services, 303 N. Ventura Ave., Ste. A, Ventura, 93001. Tel: 805-643-4780; Fax: 805-643-4781. Conejo Valley Clinical Services, 80 E. Hillcrest, #216, Thousand Oaks, 91360. Tel: 805-373-1256.

[Z] SUMMER CAMPS

LOS ANGELES. *Scouting and Camp Fire Ministry/ Catholic Youth Camps.* P.O. Box 91764, Long Beach, 90809-1764. Eileen Gallagher, Contact Person. Tel: 652-427-2149; William Leahy, Chm. ACCS. Tel: 661-949-2355; Sharon Shellman, Chm. ACCGS. Tel: 626-792-2076; Rev. James J. Maher, Boy Scout Chap.; Sr. Lucille Coulihan, I.H.M., Girl Scout Chap. Tel: 213-664-1124.

St. Vincent dePaul Ranch Camp. (Boys -Ages: 7-13), 210 N. Ave. 21st, 90031. Tel: 213-221-9886; Fax: 213-224-6213. Capacity 100.
Sponsored by St. Vincent de Paul Society.

Camp Mariastella. (Girls). Coed Program for Developmentally Disabled, Ages 7-Adult. 1120 Manchester Pl., 90019. Tel: 213-733-1208.
Owned & Operated by Sisters of Social Service. Capacity 140.
Located in Wrightwood.

Sacred Heart Retreat Camp. Girls & Boys Sessions, Ages 8-17 years. 869 S. Rimpau Blvd., 90005. Tel: 213-935-2372. Camp Office, P.O. Box 1795, Big Bear Lake, 92315. Tel: 909-866-5696; Fax: 909-866-5650.
Owned and operated by the Sisters of the Society Devoted to the Sacred Heart. Capacity 150.
Located at Big Bear Lake.

Lions Camp at Teresita Pines. (Girls), Ages 7-15 years. P.O. Box 98, Wrightwood, 92397; Fax: 760-249-1063.
E-mail: teresitapines@snowline.net
Web site: www.lionswildcamp.com
Owned & Operated by Lions. Capacity 125.
Located in Big Pines Area near Wrightwood.

St. Nicholas Camp, 1170 Frontier Rd., Frazier Park, 93225. Tel: 805-245-3571; Fax: 805-245-0710.
Available for year round camps & rates.

[AA] ST. VINCENT DE PAUL SOCIETY

LOS ANGELES. *St. Vincent de Paul Society*, 210 N. Avenue 21, 90031. Tel: 323-224-6288; Fax: 323-225-4997.
Web site: www.svdpla.org
Jose J. Rossier, Exec. Dir.

St. Vincent de Paul Ranch Camp & Retreat Center, 210 N. Avenue 21, 90031. Tel: 323-224-6213; Fax: 323-225-4997. Ricardo Garcia, Dir.

St. Vincent's Cardinal Manning Center, 231 Winston St., 90013. Tel: 213-229-9963; Fax: 213-620-9141. Joan Sotiros, Dir.

St. Vincent de Paul Stores, 210 N. Avenue 21, 90031. Tel: 323-224-6280; Fax: 323-225-4997.
For Pick Up: 323-224-6280; 800-974-3571. Anthony Terrazas, Store Dir.

[BB] NEWMAN CENTERS

LOS ANGELES. *Archdiocesan Office for Campus Ministry*, 3424 Wilshire Blvd., 90010-2241. Tel: 213-637-7527; Fax: 213-637-6527.
E-mail: drlwoester@la-archdiocese.org
Web site: www.la-archdiocese.org
Laurie W. Oester, Ph.D., Archdiocesan Dir.
California State University, Los Angeles. Tel: 323-343-2571; Fax: 323-343-6407. Mr. Robert Warren, Dir., 5300 Paseo Rancho Castilla, 90032-8731. Tel: 323-343-2571; Fax: 323-343-6407.

Loyola Law School, 919 S. Albany St., P.O. Box 15019, 90015. Tel: 213-736-1084; Fax: 213-380-3769. Robert Scholla, S.J., Dir.

Loyola Marymount University, 7900 Loyola Blvd., 90045. Tel: 310-338-2860; Fax: 310-338-1845. Mr. Fernando Moreno, Dir.; Revs. John Boyle, S.J.; Thomas P. Higgins, S.J.; Tri M. Dinh, S.J.; Sr. Cecilia Magladry, C.S.J.; Sr. Carol Quinlivan, C.S.J.; Rev. Fernando Arizti, S.J.; Mr. John Flaherty; Rabbi Arthur Gross-Schaeffer.
Mount St. Mary College, Chalon Campus, 12001 Chalon Rd., 90049. Tel: 310-954-4126; Fax: 310-954-4119. Ms. Gail Gresser, Dir.
Mount St. Mary College, Doheny Campus, 10 Chester Pl., 90007-2598. Tel: 213-477-2672, Ext. 2672; Fax: 213-477-2669.
Occidental College, Catholic Campus Ministry, 1600 Campus Rd., 90041. Tel: 323-259-2500, Ext. 3426; Fax: 323-255-3067. Carl Schlichte, Dir.
University of California, Los Angeles, University Catholic Center, 633 Gayley Ave., 90024. Tel: 310-208-5015; Fax: 310-208-6077. Revs. Bob Sadowski, C.S.P., Dir.; Jim Moran, C.S.P.; Ms. Cindy Yoshitomi, University of Southern California, Our Saviour University Parish, 3207 University Ave., 90007. Tel: 213-749-5341; Fax: 213-749-3475. Rev. William Messenger, O.S.M., Dir.
University of Southern California, Health Sciences Campus, Catholic Campus Ministry, MCH 160, 1333 San Pablo St., 90033. Tel: 323-442-3311; Fax: 626-792-0475. California Institute of Technology, I-88, Pasadena, 91125. Tel: 626-395-6212; Fax: 626-792-0475. Rev. Andrew Mulcahey, L.C., Dir.
Claremont Colleges, McAllister Religious Center, 919 N. Columbia, Claremont, 91711. Tel: 909-621-8825, Ext. 2937; Fax: 909-621-8304. Rev. Wayne Maro, C.P.P.S., Dir.
University of California Santa Barbara. St. Mark University Parish, 6550 Picasso Rd., Goleta, 93117. Tel: 805-968-1078; Fax: 805-968-3965. Revs. Paul Rospond, C.S.P.; Edward C. Nowak, C.S.P., Dir.
University of La Verne (La Verne). Catholic Campus Ministry, 1950 Third St., 91750. Tel: 909-593-3511, Ext. 4322; Fax: 909-392-2753. Sr. Margaret Devlin, S.S.C., Dir.
California State University - Long Beach. University Interfaith Center, 1250 Bellflower Blvd., USU-103, 90840. Tel: 562-985-7629; Fax: 562-985-5367. Ms. Carol Clason, Dir.
California State University - Northridge. CSUN/ CNM, 1811 Nordhoff St., Northridge, 91330. Tel: 818-677-4850; Fax: 818-677-5815. Sr. Patricia Boroughs, S.N.J.M., Dir.
California State Polytechnic University (Pomona). Union Plaza Interfaith Center, 3801 West Temple Ave., 91768. Tel: 909-869-3608; Fax: 909-869-3611. David C. Miank, Ph.D., Dir.
Marymount College (Rancho Palos Verdes). Campus Ministry, 30800 Palos Verdes Dr. E., 90274. Tel: 310-377-4240; Fax: 310-377-6223. Rev. Msgr. Tony Lever.

Don Bosco Technical Institute (Rosemead). Campus Ministry, 1151 San Gabriel Blvd., 91770. Tel: 626-307-6551; Fax: 626-280-9316. Rudy Herrera, Dir.

[CC] MISCELLANEOUS LISTINGS

LOS ANGELES. *Archdiocesan Spirituality Center*, 2 Chester Pl., 90007. Tel: 213-747-6508; Fax: 213-477-2649.
E-mail: tbernard@msmc.la.edu
Web site: spirituality.la-archdiocese.org
Sr. Thomas Bernard, C.S.J., Dir.

Catholic Big Brothers, Inc., 3300 W. Temple St., 90026. Tel: 213-251-9800; TTY: 213-251-7760; Fax: 213-251-9855.
E-mail: cbbhip@aol.com
Web site: www.catholicbigbrothers.org
Ken Martinet, Exec. Dir.; His Eminence Roger Cardinal Mahony, Honorary Chm.
Five branch offices in Los Angeles.
A mentoring organization that matches adult volunteers with fatherless children between the ages of 7 and 14. Volunteer mentors provide role modeling and friendship to the children in one-to-one relationships, group mentoring, community-based & school-based programs. The agency also has a program for deaf and hard-of-hearing children and volunteers.

Catholic Charities Community Development Corporation, Inc., 1531 James M. Wood Blvd., P.O. Box 15095, 90015-0095. Tel: 213-251-3477; Fax: 213-380-4603.

Charisma in Missions, La Porciuncula, 1059 S. Gage Ave., 90023; Fax: 213-260-7221. Catholic Center of Evangelization and renewal ministries. A service for hispanic people through ongoing affirmation and growth seminars and courses; Catholic evangelizers' formation courses; direct evangelization missions; social service programs; prayer hot-line services; television and radio ministries; and a bookstore providing Catholic books, audio and video cassettes.

Collaborative Project for Aging Religious, 2035 W. Adams Blvd., 90018. Tel: 323-735-3625; Fax: 323-737-6320.
E-mail: linkages@cpar.org
Web site: www.cpar.org

Conrad N. Hilton Fund for Sisters, 10100 Santa Monica Blvd. #1000, 90067. Tel: 310-785-0746; Fax: 310-785-0166.
E-mail: hltnsister@aol.com
Web site: members.aol.com/hltnsister
Sr. Joyce Meyer, P.B.V.M.

Filipino Pastoral Ministry (Artesia), 18708 S. Clarkdale Ave., 90701. Tel: 562-402-9226; Fax: 310-860-0178.
E-mail: mac3exodus@aol.com
Rev. Msgr. Loreto Gonzales, Dir.

The Focolare Movement, Men's Branch (California) (Work of Mary), 8016 Cowan Ave., 90045-1405. Tel: 310-670-6736; Fax: 310-670-8036.
E-mail: focolare-mla@att.net
Web site: www.focolare.org
Formation in the Spirituality of Unity. Mr. Fritz Zuger, Dir. West Coast.

The Focolare Movement, Women's Branch (California) (Work of Mary), 3138 Glendon Ave., 90034-3404. Tel: 310-470-8505.

Friends of John Paul II Foundation of Southern California, 3424 W. Adams Blvd., 90018. Tel: 626-281-0516; Fax: 626-293-8196.
E-mail: kcybulski@earthlink.net
Stanislaw K. Cybulski, Pres.

Guadalupe Center, Inc., 1531 James M. Wood Blvd., P.O. Box 15095, 90015-0095. Tel: 213-251-3464. Rev. Msgr. Gregory A. Cox, Exec. Dir.

Hospitaller Foundation of California, Inc., The, 2035 W. Adams Blvd., 90018. Tel: 323-731-7141; Fax: 323-731-5717.
E-mail: Hospitaller-Foundation@worldnet.att.net
Bro. Patrick Corr, O.H., Pres., Dir. & Moderator. (Fundraising for St. John of God Retirement and Care Center).
Women's League of St. John of God. Tel: 323-731-7141; Fax: 323-731-5717.
Helpers Club of St. John of God. Tel: 323-731-7141; Fax: 323-731-5717.

Korean Catholic Renewal Movement of Southern California, 3422 W. 8th St., 90005.

Luz De Cristo USA. Member of Lumen 2000. 5953 W. 86th Pl., 90045. Tel: 310-641-2000; Fax: 310-641-1127.
E-mail: luzcristo@aol.com
Web site: www.luz-de-cristo.org
Non-profit corporation. Spanish evangelism through modern means of communication.

National Catholic Council for Hispanic Ministry, Inc. (NCCHM), 2025 Chickasaw Ave., 90041. Tel: 213-344-9153; Fax: 213-344-9526.
E-mail: NCCHM@aol.com

Perpetual Eucharistic Adoration, Inc., 660 Club View Dr., 90024. Tel: 310-273-3856. L. Owen Traynor, Contact Person.

Rosary Hour Inc., The, 809 S. Flower St., 90017. Tel: 213-627-6863; Fax: 213-627-6864.
E-mail: RosaryHour@aol.com
Web site: therosaryhour.com
Rev. James L. Kolling, Dir.

St. Francis Center, 1835 S. Hope St., 90015. Tel: 213-747-5347; Fax: 213-765-8915.
E-mail: stfrasisi@aol.com
His Eminence Roger M. Mahony, Honorary Pres.; Rev. Finian McGinn, O.F.M.Prov.

Provincial Definitors of the Province of Saint Barbara. Tel: 213-765-8915. Legal Title: *Provincial Definitors of the Province of Saint Barbara Franciscan Friars of California*. Sr. Patricia Krommer, C.S.J., Exec.Dir.

St. Peter Claver Center, 4202 W. Jefferson Blvd., 90016-4113. Tel: 323-737-6036; Fax: 323-737-3649.

St. Vincent Senior Citizen Nutrition Program, Inc., 2131 W. Third St., 90057. Tel: 213-484-7778; Fax: 213-484-7276. Meals served daily 2,400.

Salesian Boys & Girls Club of Los Angeles, 3218 Wabash Ave., 90063. Tel: 323-263-7519; Fax: 323-263-8558.
E-mail: Clubinfo@Salesianclubs-la.org
Web site: www.salesianclubs-la.org

Santa Marta Hospital Foundation, 319 N. Humphreys Ave., 90022-1422. Tel: 323-260-8686; Fax: 323-260-8687.
E-mail: srkreta@santamarta.org
Web site: www.santamarta.org
Mr. Roger Hughes, Chm.; Mr. David M. Walsh, Vice Chm.; Sr. Catherine Marie Kreta, C.S.J., Exec. Dir.; Mr. Sal Varela, Treas.

Serra Ancillary Care, 3424 Wilshire Blvd., 90010. Tel: 213-637-7531; Fax: 213-637-6531. Sr. M. Carolita Hart, C.S.C., Pres.

Serra Institute, 2060 N. Vermont, 90027. Tel: 323-664-9292.
E-mail: gcrye@aol.com

Servants of the Immaculate Child Mary, 5135 Dartsmouth Ave., 90032. Tel: 323-225-3279; Fax: 323-225-3279.
E-mail: ImmaculateAL@.com
Sr. Enedina Cuevas, Contact Person.

South Central Los Angeles Ministry Project (LAMP), 104 W. 47th Pl., 90037. Tel: 323-234-1471; Fax: 323-234-1472.
E-mail: SouthCentralLAMP@juno.com
Sr. Mary Hoffman, S.P.

Vincentians Province of the West, Support Trust Fund. 3663 Martin Luther King Blvd., Lynwood, 90262. Tel: 310-603-6007; Fax: 310-638-0075. Mr. Robert Issai, Contact Person.

AGOURA HILLS. *Veritas Communications, Inc.*, 29963 Mulholland Hwy., 91301. Tel: 818-991-1813; Fax: 818-991-2024.
E-mail: youmag@earthlink.net
Web site: www.youmagazine.com

ALHAMBRA.

Carmelite Educational Centers, Inc., 920 E. Alhambra Rd., 91801. Tel: 626-289-1353; Fax: 626-308-1913.
E-mail: decor-carmeli@CatholicFamilies.net
Web site: carmelitegeneralate.homestead.com
Mother Regina Marie Gorman, O.C.D., Dir..Sisters 141.

Little Flower Center, 920 E. Alhambra Rd., 91801. Tel: 626-289-1353; Fax: 626-308-1913.

BALDWIN PARK. *The Redemptorist Vietnamese Mission Corporation*, 3452 N. Big Dalton Ave., 91706. Tel: 626-337-7735; Fax: 626-851-1280. Rev. Vu Minh Nghiem, C.SS.R., Pres.

BELLFLOWER. *St. John Bosco High School Alumni*, 13640 S. Bellflower Blvd., 90706. Tel: 562-920-1734; Fax: 562-867-5322.
E-mail: kdusserr@bosco.org
Web site: www.Bosco.org
Rev. John Itzaina, S.D.B.

World Apostolate of Fatima, Blue Army, USA, Los Angeles Division, 15550 Bellflower Blvd., 90706-3819. Tel: 562-867-8661; Fax: 562-867-8661.

BURBANK. *SCRC (Southern California Renewal Communities)*, 9795 Cabrini Dr., Ste. 105, 91504-1739. Tel: 818-771-1361; Fax: 818-771-1379.
E-mail: spirit@fea.net
Web site: www.scrc.org
Dominic Berardino, Pres.; Rev. William Delaney, S.J., Pastoral Coord.
Serving Catholic Charismatic Renewal through annual summer convention, pastoral teaching events, healing masses, retreats, book & tape ministry and a bi-monthly publication.

COVINA. *Comboni Missionaries*, 645 S. Aldenville Ave., 91723. Tel: 626-339-1914; Fax: 626-974-4238.
E-mail: combonicovin@earthlink.net

CULVER CITY. *Pauline Book and Media*, 3908 Sepulveda Blvd., 90230. Tel: 310-397-8676; Fax: 310-397-8366.
E-mail: fspla@aol.com
Web site: pauline.org
Sr. Armanda Santos, Supr.

EL MONTE. *Hombre Nuevo*, 12036 Ramona Blvd., 91732. Tel: 626-444-4442; Fax: 626-444-1435.
E-mail: hn@catolico.com
Web site: www.catolico.com
Rev. Juan Rivas, L.C.

FILLMORE. *Servants and Handmaids of the Sacred Heart of Jesus, Mary and Joseph.* Mailing Address: P.O. Box 547, 93016-0547. House of Prayer, 411 First St., 93016. Tel: 805-524-5890; Fax: 805-524-7729.
E-mail: info@theServantsandHandmaids.net
Web site: TheServantsandHandmaids.net

LA VERNE. *Picpus Charitable Trust*, 2150 Damien Ave., 91750. Tel: 909-596-1946; Fax: 909-596-6112.
E-mail: dhstravers@hotmail.com

LANCASTER. *Our Lady of Charity, Inc.*, P.O. Box 412. Tel: 805-942-3222. Ellen Butera. Tel: 805-948-8044.

LONG BEACH. *St. Mary Catholic Housing Corp.*, 1050 Linden Ave., P.O. Box 887, 90801.

St. Mary Medical Center Foundation. (Catholic Healthcare West), 1050 Linden Ave., P.O. Box 887, 90801. Tel: 562-491-9225; Fax: 562-491-9888. John T. Wagner, Pres.

LYNWOOD. *Daughters of Charity Ministry Services Corp.*, 3663 Martin Luther King Jr. Blvd., 90262. Tel: 310-603-6007; Fax: 310-638-0075.

Hotel Dieu, 3663 Martin Luther King Jr. Blvd., 90262. Tel: 310-603-6156. Robert Issai, Chief Fin. Officer.

Rosalie Rendu, Inc., 3663 Martin Luther King Jr. Blvd., 90262. Tel: 310-603-6156. Robert Issai, Chief Fin. Officer.

MONTEREY PARK. *Congregation of St. John the Baptist*, 220 S. Ynez Ave., 91754. Tel: 626-280-3430; Fax: 626-280-1590.
E-mail: csjb@gus.net
Web site: www2.gus.net/home/c/csjb
Very Rev. Stanislaus Su, C.S.J.B., Contact Person.

Theresian Sisters, 901 W. El Repetto Dr., 91754. Tel: 323-780-1965; Fax: 323-780-1965. Sr. Felicitas M. Hong, C.S.T., Contact Person.

United Chinese Apostolate Council, 300 Garfield Ave., Ste. 208, 91754. Tel: 626-280-7721.

OJAI.

St. Joseph's Health and Retirement Center Foundation, P.O. Box 760, 2464 E. Ojai Ave., 93024-0760. Tel: 805-646-1466; Fax: 805-646-0806.
E-mail: stjosfnd@pacbell.net
Ms. Rita Smith, Contact Person.

PACIFIC PALISADES. *Paulist Pictures*, P.O. Box 1057, 90272. Tel: 310-454-0688; Fax: 310-459-6549.
E-mail: Paulistpic@aol.com
Web site: http://www/paulistproductions.org

Paulist Productions, (Insight) 17575 Pacific Coast Hwy., 90272. Tel: 310-454-0688; Fax: 310-459-6549.
E-mail: Paulistpro@aol.com
Web site: paulistproductions.org
Rev. Frank Desiderio, C.S.P., Pres.; Enid Sevilla, Gen. Mgr.

PASADENA.

Journey House, Inc., 1232 N. Los Robles Ave., 91104-2814. Tel: 626-798-9478; Fax: 626-358-2766.
E-mail: tmayworm@earthlink.net
Bro. Timothy Mayworm, F.S.C., Contact Person.
Six bed group home for wards of the court helping young people finish high school. Clients have little or no family support. Clients have the opportunity to attend Catholic high schools. After-care support is provided for graduates who attend college.

Ramona Blvd., Inc., 1453 E. California Blvd., 91106. Territorial Administrative Office, P.O. Box 162, Thornwood, NY, 10594. Tel: 914-773-1368; Fax: 914-773-1438. Bro. Juan Sabadell, Sec. & Treas.

PASADINA. *Franciscan Communications*, P.O. Box 463, 90602-0463. Tel: 213-251-9880, Ext. 202. Kenneth E. Martinet, Pres. & CEO.
(St. Francis Theatre: Winston Press, TeleKETICS, AudioSPOTS, TeleSPOTS).

SAN FERNANDO. *Valley Family Center*, 302 S. Brand Blvd., 91340. Tel: 818-365-8588; Fax: 818-898-3382. Religious Sisters of Charity. Sr. Una Connolly, R.S.C., Exec. Dir.; Sr. Carmel Somers, R.S.C., Dir. of Learning Center. All Services are in English and Spanish. Counseling is available for individual, marriage, family, children/teen, chemical dependency, victims of sexual and physical abuse, and adults molested as children (AMAC). Special Programs include School Counseling; Parent Education; anger management; violence prevention; victims and perpatrators of domestic violence; at risk youth. Learning Center Programs include tutorials; basic skill building for children and adults, and opportunities for gifted students.

SAN PEDRO. *Apostleship of the Sea, Catholic Maritime Ministry*, Mary, Star of the Sea Parish, 870 W. 8th St., 90731. Tel: 310-833-3541; Fax: 310-833-9254.
E-mail: marystar2@aol.com
Rev. Msgr. Patrick J. Gallagher, Port Chap.; Rev. Sylvester J. Thomas, Dir. of Chap. Svcs., Center: Berth 93A, World Cruise Center, Port of Los Angeles, 90731. Tel: 310-521-1041; Fax: 310-521-1046.

SANTA BARBARA.

The Cause of Blessed Junipero Serra, 2201 Laguna St., Santa Barbara Old Mission, 93101-1817. Tel: 805-682-4713; Fax: 805-682-6067.
E-mail: FriarTim@aol.com
Bro. Timothy Arthur, O.F.M., Contact Person.

The Franciscan Sisters of the Sacred Heart in CA. (A California non-profit corp.), 601 E. Micheltorena, 93103. Tel: 805-962-7661; Fax: 805-568-3822.
E-mail: cbowman@chw.edu
Web site: http://www.saintfrancis.org
Franciscan Sisters of the Sacred Heart, (Frankfort, IL). Sr. Mary Elizabeth Imler, Gen. Supr.; Mr. Ron Biscaro, Admin.; Sr. Christine Bowman, Local Community Leader.

World Wide Marriage Encounter, 1964 Las Canoas Rd., 93105-2351. Tel: 805-882-1942; Fax: 805-882-1942.
E-mail: galcmwwme@aol.com
Web site: www.ccwwme.org
Rev. James M. Galvin, C.M.

STUDIO CITY. *Association of Christian Therapists*, 3709 Laurel Canyon Blvd., 91604. Tel: 818-762-3329.

VENICE. *St. Joseph Center*, 204 Hampton Dr., 90219. Tel: 310-396-6468; Fax: 310-392-8402.
E-mail: stjosephctr@earthlink.net
Web site: home.earthlink.net/~stjosephctr
Sr. Mary Allen, Contact Person.

VENTURA. *CAREGIVERS: Volunteers Assisting the Elderly*, 2021 Sperry Ave., Ste. 47, 93003. Tel: 805-658-8530; Fax: 805-658-8537.
E-mail: caregivers@vcnet.com
126 N. 8th St., Santa Paula, 93060. Tel: 805-525-5006.

VISTA. *Equestrian Order of the Holy Sepulcher of Jerusalem*, 1802 Key Largo Rd., 92083-7002. Tel: 760-727-5711; Fax: 760-598-5256. H.E. Sir James F. McGlone, K.G.C.H.S., Lieutenant, 3424 Wilshire Blvd., Los Angeles, 90012-2241. His Eminence Roger Cardinal Mahony, K.G.C.H.S., Grand Prior.

WEST COVINA. *Federation of Filipino Rosary Groups, Inc.*, 2809 Elena Ave., 91792. Eddie B. De Sagun, Contact. Purpose: To provide evangelization of people, particularly the Filipinos, and to aid in building communities of faith through the propagation of the devotion to the Holy Rosary.

WESTLAKE VILLAGE. *West San Fernando Valley Magnificat Chapter Ministry to Catholic Women*, 32149 Lakemeadow Ln., 91361. Tel: 818-889-8515.

[DD] LEGAL TITLES

LOS ANGELES. *Chancery Office*, 3424 Wilshire Blvd., 90010-2241. Tel: 213-637-7000; Fax: 213-637-6000.
E-mail: webmaster@la-archdiocese.org
Web site: www.la-archdiocese.org
For further information contact the Chancery. Also see Miscellaneous for additional listings.

Recollect Augustinian Fathers & Brothers, Province of St. Augustine, Inc. Tel: 805-486-7433; Fax: 805-487-2805.

Missionary Oblates of Mary Immaculate, Western Province, Inc. Tel: 818-891-0579; Fax: 818-893-9819.

School Sisters of Notre Dame de Namur of the California Province, Inc. Tel: 314-544-0455; Fax: 314-544-6754.

Congregation of the Sacred Heart of Jesus & Mary and of Perpetual Adoration, Inc. Tel: 909-593-5441; Fax: 909-593-3971.

Sisters of St. Louis Monaghan, Inc. Tel: 818-883-1678; Fax: 818-346-6109.

Ursulines of the Western Province, Inc. Tel: 707-545-6811; Fax: 707-579-8571.

RELIGIOUS INSTITUTES OF MEN REPRESENTED IN THE ARCHDIOCESE

For further details refer to the corresponding bracketed number in the Religious Institutes of Men or Women section.

[0140]—*The Augustinians.*—O.S.A.

[0200]—*Benedictine Monks (Congregation of the Annunciation).*—O.S.B.

[0980]—*Brothers of Our Lady Mother of Mercy.*—C.F.M.M.

[1350]—*Brothers of St. Francis Xavier.*—C.F.X.

[1160]—*Brothers of St. Patrick.*—F.S.P.

[0330]—*Brothers of the Christian Schools.*—F.S.C.

[]—*Canons Regular of the Immaculate Conception.*—C.R.I.C.

[0470]—*The Capuchin Friars (St. Patrick's Custody).*—O.F.M.Cap.

[0270]—*Carmelite Fathers & Brothers.* (Prov. of the Most Pure Heart of Mary).—O.Carm.
[0360]—*Claretian Missionaries.* (Western Prov.).—C.M.F.
[0380]—*Comboni Missionaries of the Heart of Jesus.* (Verona).—M.C.C.J.
[0310]—*Congregation of Christian Brothers.*—C.F.C.
[]—*Congregation of St. John the Baptist.*—C.S.J.B.
[1150]—*Congregation of St. Joseph.*—C.S.J.
[1330]—*Congregation of the Mission.* (Prov. of the West).—C.M.
[1210]—*Congregation of the Missionaries of St. Charles.*—C.S.
[1000]—*Congregation of the Passion.* (Western Prov.).—C.P.
[1140]—*Congregation of the Sacred Hearts of Jesus and Mary.*—SS.CC.
[0480]—*Conventual Franciscans.* (St. Joseph Cupertino Prov.).—O.F.M.Conv.
[0520]—*Franciscan Friars.* (St. Barbara Prov.).—O.F.M.
[0530]—*Franciscan Friars of the Atonement.*—S.A.
[]—*Guadalupe Missioners.* (Mexico).—M.G.
[0650]—*Holy Ghost Fathers.*—C.S.Sp.
[0670]—*Hospitaller Brothers of St. John of God.*—O.H.
[0690]—*Jesuit Fathers and Brothers.* (Calif. Prov.).—S.J.
[0710]—*Josephite Fathers.*—C.J.
[0730]—*Legionaries of Christ.*—L.C.
[0580]—*Little Brothers of the Good Shepherd.*—B.G.S.
[0780]—*Marist Fathers.*—S.M.
[0800]—*Maryknoll.*—M.M.
[0830]—*Mill Hill Missionaries.*—M.H.M.
[]—*Missionaries of Charity Brothers.*—M.C.
[0660]—*Missionaries of the Holy Spirit.*—M.Sp.S.
[1110]—*Missionaries of the Sacred Heart.*—M.S.C.
[0840]—*Missionary Servants of the Most Holy Trinity.*—S.T.
[0910]—*Oblates of Mary Immaculate.* (Western Prov.).—O.M.I.
[0930]—*Oblates of St. Joseph.*—O.S.J.
[0940]—*Oblates of the Virgin Mary.*—O.M.V.
[]—*Operarios del Reino de Cristo.*—O.R.C.
[0835]—*Order of Minims.*—O.M.
[0430]—*Order of Preachers-Dominicans.* (Western Prov.).—O.P.
[0150]—*Order of the Augustinian Recollects.*—O.A.R.
[1020]—*Pauline Fathers and Brothers, Society of St. Paul.*—S.S.P.
[1030]—*Paulist Fathers.*—C.S.P.
[1040]—*Piarist Fathers.*—Sch.P.
[1050]—*Pontifical Institute for Foreign Missions.*—P.I.M.E.
[0610]—*Priests of the Congregation of Holy Cross.*—C.S.C.
[1070]—*Redemptorist Fathers.* (Oakland Prov.).—C.SS.R.
[1090]—*Rogationist Fathers.*—R.C.J.
[0700]—*St. Joseph's Society of the Sacred Heart.*—S.S.J.
[1190]—*Salesians of Don Bosco.*—S.D.B.
[1240]—*Servites.*—O.S.M.
[0110]—*Society of African Missions.*—S.M.A.
[1260]—*Society of Christ.*—S.Ch.
[0760]—*Society of Mary.*—S.M.
[0850]—*Society of Missionaries of Africa.*—M.Afr.
[0370]—*Society of St. Columban.*—S.S.C.
[0420]—*Society of the Divine Word.*—S.V.D.
[1060]—*Society of the Precious Blood.*—C.PP.S.
[1290]—*Society of the Priests of St. Sulpice.*—S.S.

RELIGIOUS INSTITUTES OF WOMEN REPRESENTED IN THE ARCHDIOCESE

[]—*Armenian Sisters of the Immaculate Conception.*—C.I.C.
[0230]—*Benedictine Sisters of Pontifical Jurisdiction.*—O.S.B.
[1810]—*Bernardine Sisters of the Third Order of St. Francis.*—O.S.F.
[2930]—*California Institute of the Sisters of the Most Holy and Immaculate Heart of the Blessed Virgin Mary.*—I.H.M.
[]—*Caritas Sisters of Miyazaki.*
[0370]—*Carmelite Sisters of the Most Sacred Heart of Los Angeles.*—O.C.D.
[]—*Congregation of Kkottongnae Sisters of Jesus.*—C.K.S.J.
[2100]—*Congregation of the Humility of Mary.*—C.H.M.
[]—*Congregation of the Immaculate Heart of Mary Reparatrix.*—I.H.M.R.
[0470]—*Congregation of the Sisters of Charity for the Incarnate Word.*—C.C.V.I.
[3935]—*Congregation of the Sisters of St. Louis, Juilly Monaghan.*—S.S.L.
[1920]—*Congregation of the Sisters of the Holy Cross.*—C.S.C.
[1940]—*Congregation of the Sisters of the Holy Faith.*—C.H.F.
[1950]—*Congregation of the Sisters of the Holy Family.*—S.S.F.
[0760]—*Daughters of Charity of St. Vincent de Paul.* (Prov. of the West).—D.C.
[0880]—*Daughters of Mary and Joseph.*—D.M.J.
[0850]—*Daughters of Mary Help of Christians.*—F.M.A.
[]—*Daughters of Mary, Mother of Mercy.*—D.M.M.M.
[0420]—*Discalced Carmelite Nuns.*—O.C.D.
[1050]—*Dominican Comtemplative Nuns (Cloistered).*—O.P.
[1070-03]—*Dominican Sisters.*—O.P.
[1070-04]—*Dominican Sisters.*—O.P.
[1070-12]—*Dominican Sisters.*—O.P.
[1070-13]—*Dominican Sisters.*—O.P.
[1070-19]—*Dominican Sisters.*—O.P.
[1070-21]—*Dominican Sisters.*—O.P.
[]—*Dominican Sisters of Adrian (Pacific West Chapter).*—O.P.
[]—*Dominican Sisters of Adrian (Southwest Mission Chapter).*—O.P.
[1150]—*Eucharistic Franciscan Missionary Sisters.*—E.F.M.S.
[]—*Evangelizadores Eucaristicas de los Pobres.*—E.E.P.
[1170]—*Felician Sisters.*—C.S.S.F.
[1350]—*Franciscan Missionary Sisters of the Immaculate Conception.*—O.S.F.
[1230]—*Franciscan Sisters of Christian Charity.*—O.S.F.
[1310]—*Franciscan Sisters of Little Falls.*—O.S.F.
[1500]—*Franciscan Sisters of Mary Immaculate of the Third Order of St. Francis of Assisi.*—F.M.I.
[1780]—*Franciscan Sisters of Perpetual Adoration.*—O.S.F.
[1450]—*Franciscan Sisters of the Sacred Heart.*—O.S.F.
[1845]—*Guadalupan Missionaries of the Holy Spirit.*—M.G.Sp.S.
[]—*Handmaids of the Sacred Heart of Jesus, Mary & Joseph.*—J.M.J.
[]—*Hermanas Misioneras Servidoras de la Palabra.*—H.M.S.P.
[2575]—*Institute of the Sisters of Mercy of the Americas.* (Burlingame, CA).—R.S.M.
[2340]—*Little Sisters of the Poor.*—L.S.P.
[2390]—*Lovers of the Holy Cross Sisters.*—L.H.C.
[2470]—*Maryknoll Sisters of St. Dominic.*—M.M.
[2500]—*Medical Sisters of St. Joseph.*—M.S.J.
[]—*Misioneras Eucaristicas De Maria Immaculada.*—M.E.M.I.
[2710]—*Missionaries of Charity.*—M.C.
[]—*Missionaries of Jesus Crucified.*—M.J.C.
[0210]—*Missionary Benedictine Sisters.*—O.S.B.
[0390]—*Missionary Carmelites of St. Theresa.*—C.M.S.T.
[2715]—*Missionary Sisters of Christ the King.*—M.Chr.
[2880]—*Missionary Sisters of St. Columban.*—S.S.C.
[2750]—*Missionary Sisters of the Immaculate Heart of Mary.*—I.C.M.
[3530]—*Missionary Sisters Servants of the Holy Spirit.*—S.Sp.S.
[]—*Missionary Sisters, Oblates of the Holy Family.*—O.H.F.
[0240]—*Olivetan Benedictine Sisters.*—O.S.B.
[3760]—*Order of St. Clare.*—P.C.C.
[3130]—*Our Lady of Victory Missionary Sisters.*—O.L.V.M.
[0980]—*Pious Disciples of the Divine Master.*—P.D.D.M.
[0950]—*Pious Society Daughters of St. Paul.*—F.S.P.
[2840]—*Poor Clare Missionary Sisters.*—M.C.
[3242]—*Poor Sisters of Nazareth.*—P.S.N.
[0930]—*Religious Daughters of St. Joseph.*—F.S.J.
[1145]—*Religious Missionaries of St. Dominic.*—O.P.
[3450]—*Religious of Jesus-Mary.*—R.J.M.
[3465]—*Religious of the Sacred Heart of Mary.*—R.S.H.M.
[3400]—*Religious Sisters of Charity.*—R.S.C.
[1505]—*St. Francis Mission Community.*—O.S.F.
[2970]—*School Sisters of Notre Dame.*—S.S.N.D.
[1680]—*School Sisters of St. Francis.*—O.S.F.
[3580]—*Servants of Mary (Servite Order).*—O.S.M.
[3499]—*Servants of the Blessed Sacrament.*—S.J.S.
[]—*Servants of the Immaculate Child Mary.*—E.I.N.
[0250]—*Sisters of Bethany.*—C.V.D.
[0480]—*Sisters of Charity of Leavenworth, Kansas.*—S.C.L.
[]—*Sisters of Charity of Rolling Hills.*—S.C.R.H.
[0570]—*Sisters of Charity of Seton Hill, Greensburg, Pennsylvania.*—S.C.
[0430]—*Sisters of Charity of the Blessed Virgin Mary.*—B.V.M.
[]—*Sisters of Little Jesus.*
[2360]—*Sisters of Loretto At the Foot of the Cross.* (Southern Prov.).—S.L.
[]—*Sisters of Mary, Mother of the Church.*—M.M.C.
[2575]—*Sisters of Mercy.* (New York).—R.S.M.
[2990]—*Sisters of Notre Dame.* (Prov. of Los Angeles).—S.N.D.
[3000]—*Sisters of Notre Dame de Namur.*—S.N.D.deN.
[]—*Sisters of Our Lady of Perpetual Help.*—S.O.L.P.H.
[3350]—*Sisters of Providence.*—S.P.
[3360]—*Sisters of Providence of Saint Mary-Of-The-Woods, Indiana.*—S.P.
[4080]—*Sisters of Social Service of Los Angeles, Inc..*—S.S.S.
[1705]—*Sisters of St. Francis of Assisi.*—O.S.F.
[1710]—*Sisters of St. Francis of Joliet.*—O.S.F.
[1620]—*Sisters of St. Francis of Millvale, Pennsylvania.*—O.S.F.
[1760]—*Sisters of St. Francis of Oldenburg.*—O.S.F.
[1630]—*Sisters of St. Francis of Penance and Christian Charity.*—O.S.F.
[1650]—*The Sisters of St. Francis of Philadelphia.*—O.S.F.
[1530]—*Sisters of St. Francis of Sylvania.*—O.S.F.
[1730]—*Sisters of St. Francis of Tiffin.*—O.S.F.
[3830-03]—*Sisters of St. Joseph.*—C.S.J.
[3830-18]—*Sisters of St. Joseph.*—C.S.J.
[3840]—*Sisters of St. Joseph of Carondelet.*—C.S.J.
[3860]—*Sisters of St. Joseph of Cluny.*—S.J.C.
[3830-11]—*Sisters of St. Joseph of Nazareth.*—S.S.J.
[3830]—*Sisters of St. Joseph of Orange.*—C.S.J.
[3890]—*Sisters of St. Joseph of Peace.*—C.S.J.P.
[3930]—*Sisters of St. Joseph to the Third Order of St. Francis.*—S.S.J.-T.O.S.F.
[3960]—*Sisters of St. Mary of Oregon.*—S.S.M.O.
[0260]—*Sisters of the Blessed Sacrament for Indians and Colored People.*—S.B.S.
[0700]—*Sisters of the Company of Mary Our Lady.*—O.D.N.
[3180]—*Sisters of the Cross and Passion.*—C.P.
[1830]—*Sisters of the Good Shepherd.*—R.G.S.
[1850]—*Sisters of the Guardian Angel.*—S.A.C.
[]—*Sisters of the Heart of Jesus in the Blessed Sacrament.*—H.C.J.S.
[1960]—*Sisters of the Holy Family.*—S.H.F.
[1990]—*Sisters of the Holy Names of Jesus and Mary.*—S.N.J.M.
[]—*Sisters of the Immaculate Heart of Mary at Mirinae.*—I.H.M.M.
[]—*Sisters of the Korean Martyrs.*—S.K.M.
[2270]—*Sisters of the Little Company of Mary.*—L.C.M.
[]—*Sisters of the Love of God.*—R.A.D.
[3200]—*Sisters of the Pious Schools.*—Sch.P.
[]—*Sisters of the Poor of St. Catherine.*—S.D.P.
[3260]—*Sisters of the Precious Blood (Dayton, Ohio).*—C.PP.S.
[3320]—*Sisters of the Presentation of the B.V.M..* (San Francisco, CA).—P.B.V.M.
[]—*Sisters of the Sacred Heart of Mary.*—C.S.C.M.
[4050]—*Sisters of the Society Devoted to the Sacred Heart.*—S.D.S.H.
[1490]—*Sisters of the Third Franciscan Order.*—O.S.F.
[3600]—*Sisters Servants of Mary.*—S.M.
[4060]—*Society of the Holy Child Jesus.*—S.H.C.J.
[]—*Theresian Sisters.*—C.S.T.
[3330]—*Union of Sisters of Presentation of the B.B.M..*—P.B.V.M.
[4110]—*Ursuline Nuns (Roman Union).*—O.S.U.
[]—*Verbum Dei Missionary Fraternity.*—V.D.M.F.

ARCHDIOCESAN CEMETERIES

LOS ANGELES. *Calvary Cemetery and Mausoleum.* Tel: 323-261-3106. Maria Orozco, Mgr.
CULVER CITY. *Holy Cross Cemetery & Mausoleum & Columbarium.* Tel: 310-776-1855.
LANCASTER. *Good Shepherd Cemetery & Mausoleum.* Tel: 661-722-0887. Daniel Rejniak, Mgr.
LONG BEACH. *All Souls Cemetery and Mausoleum.* Tel: 562-424-8601. Jesus Castillo, Mgr.
MISSION HILLS. *San Fernando Mission Cemetery & Mausoleum.* Tel: 818-361-7387. Rosalie Castillo, Mgr.
MONTEBELLO. *Resurrection Cemetery & Mausoleum.* Tel: 323-887-2024. Margaret Hunter, Mgr.
OXNARD. *Santa Clara Cemetery & Mausoleum.* Tel: 805-485-5757. Elizabeth Welsh, Mgr.
POMONA. *Holy Cross Cemetery.* Tel: 909-627-3602. Lupe Ramirez, Mgr.
ROWLAND HEIGHTS. *Queen of Heaven Cemetery.* Tel: 626-964-1291. Norberta Orta, Mgr.

SANTA BARBARA. *Calvary Cemetery & Mausoleum.* Tel: 805-687-8811. Gwen Hueston, Mgr.

SIMI. *Assumption Cemetery.* Tel: 805-583-5825. Elizabeth Welsh, Mgr.

NECROLOGY

† Antoci, Mario J., Downey, CA Our Lady of Perpetual Help. —Died Jan. 1, 2000.

† Bellavista, Jose B., Los Angeles, CA St. Aloysius Gonzaga. —Died March 11, 2000.

† Gara, Rev. Msgr. Robert, Sierra Madre, CA St. Rita. —Died June 10, 2000.

† Hanley, John J., Los Angeles, CA Nazareth House. —Died Sept. 29, 2000.

† Herrera, David S., Carpinteria, CA St. Joseph. —Died Jan. 15, 2000.

† Konoske, Rev. Msgr. Paul M., (Retired). —Died March 11, 2000.

† Ruddy, Rev. Msgr. Donald J., Whittier, CA St. Gregory the Great. —Died Sept. 27, 2000.

† Stephan, George J., Los Angeles, CA St. John the Evangelist. —Died Jan. 2, 2000.

† Wilson, Leland P., Pomona, CA Sacred Heart. —Died Aug. 25, 2000.

Archdiocese of Louisville

(Archidioecesis Ludovicopolitana)

Most Reverend

THOMAS C. KELLY, O.P., D.D., J.C.D.

Archbishop of Louisville; ordained June 5, 1958; appointed Titular Bishop of Tusuro July 12, 1977; promoted Archbishop of Louisville December 29, 1981. *Office: 212 E. College St., P.O. Box 1073, Louisville, KY, 40201.*

Most Reverend

CHARLES G. MALONEY, D.D.

Auxiliary Bishop Emeritus of the Archdiocese of Louisville; born September 9, 1912; ordained December 8, 1937; appointed Auxiliary December 30, 1954; consecrated February 2, 1955; appointed Titular Bishop of Bardstown February 2, 1995. *Res., 212 E. College St., P.O. Box 1073, Louisville, KY, 40201.*

ESTABLISHED AT BARDSTOWN APRIL 8, 1808.; TRANSFERRED TO LOUISVILLE FEB. 13, 1841; CREATED AN ARCHDIOCESE DEC. 10, 1937.

Square Miles 8,124.

Comprises the following twenty-four Counties in central Kentucky: Adair, Barren, Bullitt, Casey, Clinton, Cumberland, Green, Hardin, Hart, Henry, Jefferson, Larue, Marion, Meade, Metcalfe, Monroe, Nelson, Oldham, Russell, Shelby, Spencer, Taylor, Trimble and Washington.

For legal titles of parishes and archdiocesan institutions, consult the Chancery.

Chancery: 212 E. College St., P.O. Box 1073, Louisville, KY, 40201. Tel.: 502-585-3291.

Web site address: www.archlou.org

E-mail address: chancery@archlou.org

STATISTICAL OVERVIEW

Personnel	
Archbishop	1
Retired Bishops	1
Abbots	1
Retired Abbots	1
Priests: Diocesan Active in Diocese	118
Priests: Active Outside Diocese	7
Priests: Diocesan in Foreign Missions	2
Priests: Retired, Sick or Absent	59
Number of Diocesan Priests	186
Religious Priests in Diocese	65
Ordinations:	
Diocesan Priests	6
Permanent Deacons in Diocese	107
Total Brothers	83
Total Sisters	987
Parishes	
Parishes	112
With Resident Pastor:	
Resident Diocesan Priests	77
Resident Religious Priests	11
Without Resident Pastor:	
Administered by Priests	15
Administered by Deacons	5
Administered by Women Religious	3
Administered by Lay People	1
Missions	12
Pastoral Centers	3
Professional Ministry Personnel:	
Sisters	28
Lay Ministers	148
Welfare	
Catholic Hospitals	2
Total Assisted	185,428
Health Care Centers	1
Total Assisted	2,400
Homes for the Aged	5
Total Assisted	677
Residential Care of Children	2
Total Assisted	100
Day Care and Extended Day Care Centers	1
Total Assisted	150
Specialized Homes	1
Total Assisted	200
Special Centers for Social Services	8
Total Assisted	30,000
Educational	
Diocesan Students in Other Seminaries	10
Total Seminarians	10
Colleges and Universities	3
Total Students	4,290
High Schools, Diocesan and Parish	4
Total Students	2,153
High Schools, Private	6
Total Students	4,220
Elementary Schools, Diocesan and Parish	57
Total Students	17,764
Elementary Schools, Private	2
Total Students	498
Non-residential Schools for the Disabled	1
Total Students	48
Catechesis/Religious Education:	
High School Students	1,117
Elementary Students	6,391
Total Students Under Catholic Instruction	36,491
Teachers in the Diocese:	
Priests	9
Brothers	8
Sisters	29
Lay Teachers	1,745
Vital Statistics	
Receptions into the Church:	
Infant Baptism Totals	3,107
Adult Baptism Totals	483
Received into Full Communion	555
First Communions	3,065
Confirmations	2,695
Marriages:	
Catholic	667
Interfaith	465
Total Marriages	1,132
Deaths	1,919
Total Catholic Population	196,910
Total Population	1,215,069

Former Bishops—Rt. Rev. BENEDICT JOSEPH FLAGET, S.S., D.D., cons. Bishop of Bardstown, Nov. 4, 1810; died Feb. 11, 1850.—Rt. Rev. JOHN B. DAVID, S.S., D.D., Coadjutor; cons. Aug. 15, 1819; died July 12, 1841.—Rt. Rev. GUY IGNATIUS CHABRAT, S.S., D.D., Coadjutor; cons. July 20, 1834; died Nov. 21, 1868.—Rt. Rev. MARTIN JOHN SPALDING, D.D., Coadjutor with right of succession; cons. Sept. 10, 1848; transferred to Baltimore, May 6, 1864; died Feb. 7, 1872.—Rt. Rev. PETER JOSEPH LAVIALLE, D.D., cons. Sept. 24, 1865; died May 11, 1867.—Rt. Rev. WILLIAM GEORGE MCCLOSKEY, D.D., cons. May 24, 1868; died Sept. 17, 1909.—Rt. Rev. DENIS O'DONAGHUE, D.D., ord. Sept. 6, 1874; cons. Titular Bishop of Pomario and Auxiliary of Indianapolis on April 25, 1900; transferred to Louisville, Feb. 7, 1910; transferred to the Titular See of Lebedus, July 26, 1924; died Nov. 7, 1925.—Most Rev. JOHN A. FLOERSH, D.D., ord. June 10, 1911; appt. Titular Bishop of Lycopolis and Coadjutor Bishop of Louisville with right of succession, Feb. 6, 1923; cons. April 8, 1923; succeeded to See July 26, 1924; elevated to Archiepiscopal dignity Dec. 10, 1937; resigned and named to Titular See of Sistroniana, March 1, 1967; died June 11, 1968.—Most Rev. THOMAS J. MCDONOUGH, D.D., transferred Louisville, May 2, 1967; resigned Sept. 29, 1981; died Aug. 4, 1998.

Vicars General—Very Rev. BERNARD J. BREEN; Most Rev. CHARLES G. MALONEY, D.D.

Chancery—212 E. College St., P.O. Box 1073, Louisville, 40201. Tel: 502-585-3291. Office Hours: 8:30-4:30 All applications for dispensations are to be sent to this office.

Archivist - Chancellor—Rev. ROBERT DALE CIESLIK.

Vice Chancellor—NORMA L. MERRICK.

Secretary to Archbishop—NORMA L. MERRICK.

Chief Administrative Officer—BRIAN B. REYNOLDS.

Chief Financial Officers—JEROME J. PAKENHAM; PATRICIA J. MEYER.

Diocesan Tribunal—212 E. College St., P.O. Box 1073, Louisville, 40201. Tel: 502-585-3291.

Judicial Vicar and Director—Very Rev. J. MARK SPALDING, J.C.L.

Adjutant Judicial Vicar—Rev. PHILIP L. ERICKSON, J.C.L.

Assistant Director and Tribunal Judge—Ms. JACQUELINE RAPP, J.D., J.C.L.

Promoter of Justice—Rev. JOHN W. HANRAHAN.

Defenders of the Bond—Revs. DONALD R. GOETZ; JOHN J. STOLTZ; ROBERT E. OSBORNE; ANTHONY L.

CHANDLER; PATRICK J. DOLAN; Deacon WALTON JONES; Dr. ROBERT L. STENGER; DONALD M. SWIFT.

Associate Judges—Revs. CHARLES C. THOMPSON, J.C.L.; KENNETH R. FORTENER; THOMAS A. HOMMRICH; THOMAS P. CREAGH; T. MICHAEL TOBIN.

Assessor and Tribunal Administrator—PATRICIA A. NORRIS.

Assessor—JO ANN KALB.

Notaries—SHARON A. ARCHER; LINDA D. THOMAN; ANN TUMBLIN.

College of Consultors—Most Rev. CHARLES G. MALONEY; Very Rev. BERNARD J. BREEN; Revs. WILLIAM D. HAMMER; TIMOTHY A. HOGAN; THOMAS ANTHONY SMITH; G. NICHOLAS RICE; CHARLES C. THOMPSON; WILLIAM F. MEDLEY.

Deans—Rev. WILLIAM F. MEDLEY, Bardstown Deanery; Rev. CHARLES C. THOMPSON, Lebanon Deanery; Rev. J. RICHARD SULLIVAN, Elizabethtown Deanery.

Clergy Personnel Commission—Revs. ROY E. DENTINGER; JOHN R. BURKE; THOMAS L. BOLAND; GARY T. PADGETT; VINCENT J. SCHWEIZER; Deacon WALTON JONES, Dir.

Priests' Council—Most Rev. THOMAS C. KELLY, O.P., Presider; Revs. G. NICHOLAS RICE, Pres., *508 Breckenridge Lane, Louisville, 40207.* Mrs. ROSEMARIE BAUER, Sec. Ex Officio: Most Rev. CHARLES G. MALONEY; Very Rev. BERNARD J. BREEN; Very Rev. J. MARK SPALDING; Revs. JOSEPH H. VOOR; ROBERT E. OSBORNE; DONALD W. SPRINGMAN; JAMES W. GRAF; JOSEPH T. GRAFFIS; WILLIAM F. MEDLEY; JOHN W. BIRK; HARRY J. GELTHAUS; JOSEPH M. RANKIN; CHRISTOPHER M. SCALISE; FREDERICK W. KLOTTER; JOSEPH M. FOWLER; GERALD L.TIMMEL; WILLIAM M. BOWLING; TRUMIE C. ELLIOTT; FRANK J. EIMER; LAWRENCE J. GELTHAUS; MAURICE HAYES, O.F.M.Conv.; RICHARD PARKS, C.P.

Archdiocesan Examiners—Revs. JOHN HANRAHAN; VINCENT SCHWEIZER; WILLIAM WAGNER.

Archdiocesan Offices and Directors

Archdiocesan Communications Center—CECELIA PRICE, Chief Communications Officer, *Maloney Center, 1200 S. Shelby St., Louisville, 40203.* Tel: 502-636-0296; Fax: 502-636-2379.

Byzantine Rite Faithful—Rev. JOHN W. BIRK, Chap., *2914 S. Third St., Louisville, 40208.* Tel: 502-637-2058.

Catholic Cemeteries Office—JAVIER FAJARDO, Exec. Dir. KENNETH POPP, Dir. Operations, *1600 Newburg Rd., P.O. Box 4096, Louisville, 40204.* Tel: 502-451-7710; Fax: 502-456-9270.

Catholic Deaf Office—Rev. J. RANDALL HUBBARD, Dir., *Maloney Center, 1200 S. Shelby St., Louisville, 40203.* Tel: 502-636-0296; 634-8947 (TTY).

Catholic Charities—Mr. STEVEN E. BOGUS, Exec. Dir., *2911 S. 4th St., Louisville, 40208.* Tel: 502-637-9786; Fax: 502-637-9780.

Office of Migration and Refugee Services—Ms. BECKY JORDAN.

Office of Parish Social Ministry—DAVID J. DUTSCHKE.

Respect Life—HELEN ROTHGERBER.

Clergy Personnel Office—Deacon WALTON G. JONES, Dir., *P.O. Box 1073, Louisville, 40201.* Tel: 502-585-3291; Fax: 502-585-2466.

Clerical Aid Society—*212 E. College St., P.O. Box 1073, Louisville, 40201.* Tel: 502-585-3291.

Continuing Education for Clergy-Ministry to Priests—Rev. WILLIAM S. GRINER, Dir., *P.O. Box 1073, Louisville, 40201.* Tel: 502-585-3291.

Cursillo Movement—Rev. AL WILSON, Spiritual Advisor, *Flaget Center, 1935 Lewiston Pl., Louisville, 40216.* Tel: 502-448-8581.

Due Process Board—JOHN LAUN, Chm., *Kentucky Home Life Building, 239 S. 5th St., Louisville, 40202.* Tel: 502-587-0330.

Ecumenism, Office of—Rev. JUDE WEISENBECK, S.D.S., Dir., *Maloney Center, 1200 S. Shelby St., Louisville, 40203.* Tel: 502-636-0296.

Family Ministries, Center for—BARBARA MACDONALD, Dir. THOMAS D. ROBBINS, Ph.D., Clinical Dir., *Maloney Center, 1200 S. Shelby St., Louisville, 40203.* Tel: 502-636-0296; Fax: 502-636-2379.

Holy Childhood Association—Rev. JAMES E. HARGADON, Dir., *212 E. College St., Box 1073, Louisville, 40201.* Tel: 502-585-3291.

Holy Name Society—MICHAEL HEEB, Pres., *2302 Bradford Dr., Louisville, 40218.* Tel: 502-454-7151.

L.A.M.P.—(Louisville Archdiocesan Mission Promoters), Most Rev. THOMAS C. KELLY, O.P.; Most Rev. CHARLES G. MALONEY; Very Rev. BERNARD J. BREEN, *212 E. College St., P.O. Box 1073, Louisville, 40201.* Tel: 502-585-3291.

Mass of the Air—*508 Breckenridge Ln., Louisville, 40207.* Tel: 502-893-5120; Fax: 502-895-4535.

Office of the Diaconate—Deacon BRIAN KARLEY, C.R., Dir., *Maloney Center, 1200 S. Shelby St., Louisville, 40203.* Tel: 502-636-0296; Fax: 502-636-2379.

Office of Lifelong Formation and Education—MATTHEW J. HAYES, Exec. Dir., *Flaget Center, 1935 Lewiston Pl., Louisville, 40216.* Tel: 502-448-8581; Fax: 502-448-5518.

Superintendent of Schools—LEISA SPEER.

Director of Youth Ministry—CAROLE GOODWIN.

Director of Catechesis—SUE GRENOUGH.

Office of Ministry and Spirituality—MARTI JEWELL, Dir., *Maloney Center, 1200 S. Shelby St., Louisville, 40203.* Tel: 502-636-0296.

Office of Multicultural Ministry—M. ANNETTE TURNER, Dir., *Maloney Center, 1200 S. Shelby St., Louisville, 40203.* Tel: 502-636-0296.

Office of Pastoral Care—Rev. PAUL A. SCAGLIONE, Dir., *Maloney Center, 1200 S. Shelby St., Louisville, 40203.* Tel: 502-636-0296; Fax: 502-636-2379.

Office of Worship—JUDY BULLOCK, Dir., *Maloney Center, 1200 S. Shelby St., Louisville, 40203.* Tel: 502-636-0296; Fax: 502-636-2379.

Opportunities for Life—LYNDIE RUSCHELL, Dir., *1042 Burlington Lane, Frankfort, 40601.* Tel: 502-223-5330; 800-822-5824; Fax: 502-875-2841.

Personnel and Planning—BRIAN B. REYNOLDS, Dir., *212 E. College, P.O. Box 1073, Louisville, 40201.* Tel: 502-585-3291.

Propagation of the Faith—(Missions Office), Rev. JAMES E. HARGADON, Dir., *P.O. Box 1073, Louisville, 40201.* Tel: 502-585-3291.

Sacred Heart Enthronement Center—Rev. LAWRENCE H. LINDLE, Dir., *8191 New Haven Rd., New Haven, 40051.* Tel: 502-549-3751.

Stewardship and Development Office—ROSEMARY BISIG SMITH, Dir., *212 E. College St., P.O. Box 1073, Louisville, 40201.* Tel: 502-585-3291; Fax: 502-585-2466.

Vicar for Clergy—Rev. KENNETH L. KAMBER, *4029 Busath Ave., Louisville, 40218.* Tel: 502-491-1323.

Vocations—Rev. J. RONALD KNOTT, Dir., *Maloney Center, 1200 S. Shelby St., Louisville, 40203.* Tel: 502-636-0296.

CLERGY, PARISHES, MISSIONS AND PAROCHIAL SCHOOLS

CITY OF LOUISVILLE
(Jefferson County)

1—CATHEDRAL OF THE ASSUMPTION, Very Rev. William L. Fichteman; Revs. Bryan T. Lamberson; H. Anthony Olges; Deacon Joseph P. Wright. In res., Most Rev. Thomas C. Kelly, O.P.
Res., 443 S. 5th St., 40202. Tel: 502-582-2971; Fax: 502-582-3919.

2—ST. AGNES, Revs. John Baptist Ormechea, C.P.; Albert Schwer, C.P.
Res., 1920 Newburg Rd., 40205. Tel: 502-451-2220; Fax: 502-454-8483.
School—1800 Newburg Rd., 40205. Tel: 502-458-2850; Fax: 502-459-5215. Beverly McAuliffe, Prin. Sisters of Charity of Nazareth 1; Lay Teachers 26; Students 442.

3—ST. ALBERT THE GREAT, Revs. Donald M. Hill; Theodore R. Sans; Deacons Kenneth M. Ward; Vincent (Jim) G. Stanley.
Res., 1395 Girard Dr., 40222. Tel: 502-425-3940; Fax: 502-394-9896.
School—Tel: 502-425-1804. Jeanne Flowers, Prin.
Lay Teachers 36; Students 580.

4—ST. ALOYSIUS. Closed. For inquiries for parish records contact the Chancery.

5—ST. ANN. Merged with St. George, Louisville, to form St. Andrew, Louisville. For inquires for parish records contact the Chancery.

6—ST. ANDREW. Closed. For inquiries for parish records contact the Chancery.

7—ST. ANTHONY, Rev. Leo Kennedy, O.F.M.Conv. In res., Rev. James Cantwell, O.F.M.Conv.; Bro. John Maurer, O.F.M.Conv.
Res., 2222 W. Market St., P.O. Box 11219, 40212. Tel: 502-778-7413; Fax: 502-776-3599.

8—ASCENSION OF OUR LORD, Rev. John B. Helm; Deacon Michael Edwards.
Res., 4600 Lynnbrook Dr., 40220. Tel: 502-451-3860; Fax: 502-459-9782.
School—Tel: 502-451-2535; Fax: 502-451-2535. Maureen Clerkin, Prin.
Lay Teachers 36; Students 478.

9—ST. ATHANASIUS, Rev. Terry L. Bradshaw. In res., Revs. Robert L. Huber; James E. Wafzig.
Res., 5915 Outer Loop Dr., 40219. Tel: 502-969-3332; Fax: 502-966-8948.
School—(Grades K-8). Tel: 502-969-2345; Fax: 502-969-8974. Diane Arrow, Prin.
Lay Teachers 25; Students 417.

10—ST. AUGUSTINE, Rev. Joseph T. Graffis; Deacon John Churchill.
Res., 1310 W. Broadway, 40203. Tel: 502-584-4602; Fax: 502-581-0893.
Hines Center—Tel: 502-584-5463.
Station—Blanton House, Tel: 502-587-1259.

11—ST. BARNABAS, Revs. Wayne Jenkins; John A. Barker; Deacons James R. Plummer; Robert C. Bryant.
Parish Office: 3042 Hikes Ln., 40220. Tel: 502-459-4251; Fax: 502-459-9815.
Res., 3054 Hikes Ln., 40220. Tel: 502-451-0333.
School—3044 Hikes Ln., 40220. Tel: 502-458-4038; Fax: 502-452-1117. Mary Helen Thompson, Prin.
Lay Teachers 26; Students 416.

12—ST. BARTHOLOMEW, Revs. Anthony L. Chandler; R. Joseph Hemmerle; Bertrand J. Rapp; Deacon Thomas E. Box; Mrs. Becky Box, Pastoral Assoc.
Parish Office: 2042 Buechel Bank Rd., 40218. Tel: 502-499-0883; Fax: 502-499-0887.
Res., 2040 Buechel Bank Rd., 40218. Tel: 502-499-0876.
School—2036 Buechel Bank Rd., 40218. Tel: 502-499-0421; Fax: 502-499-0421. Doris Swenson, Prin.
Lay Teachers 14; Students 200.

13—ST. BASIL. Merged with St. Denis, Louisville.

14—ST. BENEDICT. Consolidated with St. Charles Borromeo, Louisville, and Holy Cross, Louisville, to form St. Martin de Porres, Louisville.

15—ST. BERNARD, Rev. Joseph E. Vest; Deacon Phillip Hettich.
Res., 7500 Tangelo Dr., 40228. Tel: 502-239-5178; Fax: 502-239-9025.
School—7501 Tangelo Dr., 40228. Tel: 502-239-5178; Fax: 532-239-9025. Donald Matlock, Prin.
Lay Teachers 24; Students 399.

16—ST. BONIFACE, Rev. Timothy A. Hogan.
Parish Office: 531 E. Liberty St., 40202-1107. Tel: 502-584-4279; Fax: 502-584-8659.

17—ST. BRIGID, Revs. Donald R. Goetz; Joseph H. Voor; Sr. Helen McCarthy, O.P., Pastoral Assoc.
Res., 1520 Hepburn Ave., 40204. Tel: 502-584-5565; Fax: 502-584-1328.

18—ST. CECILIA, Rev. Joseph Scollard, C.R.; Deacons Paul Bissig; Philip Tremblay, C.R.
Res., 338 N. 25th St., 40212. Tel: 502-772-3694; Fax: 502-772-3695.
School—Community Catholic, 2530 Slevin St., 40211. Tel: 502-778-1941; Fax: 502-778-9935. Mrs. Olga Golub, Prin.
Lay Teachers 8; Students 122.

19—ST. CHARLES BORROMEO. Consolidated with St. Benedict, Louisville, and Holy Cross, Louisville, to form St. Martin de Porres, Louisville.

20—CHRIST THE KING, Rev. John R. Burke; Deacon Richard Dawson.
Res., 718 S. 44th St., 40211. Tel: 502-778-5055; Fax: 502-776-5120 (Call first).

21—ST. COLUMBA. Closed. For inquiries for parish records contact the Chancery.

22—ST. DENIS, Rev. James P. Hendricks; Deacon Robert M. Kampschaefer.
Res., 4205 Cane Run Rd., 40216. Tel: 502-448-2961; Fax: 502-448-3656.
School—4209 Cane Run Rd., 40216. Tel: 502-447-5832. Ann Montgomery, Prin.
Lay Teachers 10; Students 189.

23—ST. ELIZABETH ANN SETON, Rev. Thomas A. Hommrich; Deacon James C. Olrich; Sr. Alice Casper, S.C.N., Pastoral Assoc.
Res., 11501 Maple Way, 40229. Tel: 502-966-3164; 966-0661; Fax: 502-969-0004 (call first).

24—ST. ELIZABETH OF HUNGARY, Revs. J. Roy Stiles; Robert B. Gray; Herman J. Naber.
Res., 1020 E. Burnett Ave., 40217. Tel: 502-636-3706; Fax: 502-636-3707.
School—St. Rose Catholic School, (Grades PreK-8) 1016 E. Burnett Ave., 40217. Tel: 502-634-1831; Fax: 502-634-0422. Anthony Riegling, Prin.
Lay Teachers 11; Aides 2; Students 135.

25—EPIPHANY, Rev. William S. Griner; Sr. Josette Gocella, S.S.J., Pastoral Assoc.; Deacon Gary E. Becker.
Res., 914 Old Harrods Creek Rd., 40223. Tel: 502-245-9733; Fax: 502-245-7658.

26—ST. FRANCES OF ROME, Rev. John G. Eifler; Sr. Carmelita Dunn, S.C.N., Pastoral Assoc.; Deacon William Mullins.
Res., 2119 Payne St., 40206. Tel: 502-896-8401; Fax: 502-895-0310.

27—St. Francis of Assisi, Rev. Joseph M. Rankin. In res., Rev. Joseph T. Merkt; Deacon Walton G. Jones.
Res., 1960 Bardstown Rd., 40205-1572. Tel: 502-456-6394; Fax: 502-456-9462.
School—1938 Alfresco Pl., 40205-1876. Tel: 502-459-3088. Katherine Schloemer, Prin.
Lay Teachers 15; Students 260.

28—St. Gabriel the Archangel, Revs. William D. Hammer; John R. Tran; Deacon William Skeeters.
Res., 5505 Bardstown Rd., 40291. Tel: 502-239-5481; Fax: 502-239-7717.
School—5503 Bardstown Rd., 40291. Tel: 502-239-5535; Fax: 502-231-1404. Margaret Bowen, Prin.
Lay Teachers 34; Students 795.

29—St. George. Merged with St. Ann, Louisville, to form St. Andrew, Louisville. For inquires for parish records contact the Chancery.

30—Guardian Angels, Rev. Joseph Palubeski, C.R.; Deacon Cletus A. Ratterman.
Res., 6000 Preston Hwy., 40219. Tel: 502-968-5421; Fax: 502-962-1080.
School—Thomas Merton Academy, Tel: 502-969-5462. Larry Winegarden, Prin.
Lay Teachers 13; Students 178.

31—St. Helen, Revs. Thomas E. Gentile; Charles J. Bindner; Sr. Darlene Denton, O.S.U., Pastoral Assoc.
Res., 4005 Dixie Hwy., 40216. Tel: 502-448-4008; Fax: 502-448-4045 (Call first).
School—4007 Dixie Hwy., 40216. Tel: 502-447-9671. Diane Smith, Prin.
Lay Teachers 12; Students 179.

32—Holy Cross. Consolidated with St. Benedict, Louisville, and St. Charles Borromeo, Louisville, to form St. Martin de Porres, Louisville.

33—Holy Family, Rev. Thomas P. Creagh; Deacon Lamar Fante.
Res., 3926 Poplar Level Rd., 40213. Tel: 502-459-6066; Fax: 502-459-6066 (Call first).
School—3934 Poplar Level Rd., 40213. Tel: 502-458-4531; Fax: 502-456-9188. Diana Oechsli, Prin.
Lay Teachers 11; Students 180.

34—Holy Name, Rev. John W. Birk.
Res., 2914 S. 3rd St., 40208. Tel: 502-637-2058; Fax: 502-634-0819.

35—Holy Spirit, Revs. Thomas L. Boland; Gary T. Padgett; Frank B. Grauel.
Res., 3345 Lexington Rd., 40206. Tel: 502-893-3982; Fax: 502-893-8287.
School—322 Cannons Ln., 40206. Tel: 502-893-7700; Fax: 502-893-8078. Bernadette Ritchey, Prin.
Lay Teachers 24; Students 450.

36—Holy Trinity, Rev. Joseph M. Fowler.
Pastoral Center—501 Cherrywood Rd., 40207. Tel: 502-897-5207; Fax: 502-897-0962.
School—423 Cherrywood Rd., 40207. Tel: 502-897-2785; Fax: 502-896-0990. Mrs. Mary Alice Zettel, Prin.
Lay Teachers 34; Students 625.

37—St. Ignatius, Rev. James R. Schook; Deacon James R. Young.
Res., 1816 Rangeland Rd., 40219. Tel: 502-964-5904; Fax: 502-964-5905.
Thomas Merton Child Development Center—1818 Rangeland Rd., 40219. Tel: 502-969-2336. Ms. Mona Wilkerson, Dir.
Lay Teachers 18; Students 86.

38—Immaculate Heart of Mary, Rev. Louis J. Meiman.
Office: 1545 S. 34th St., 40211. Tel: 502-774-5772; Fax: 502-774-5899.

39—Incarnation, Rev. Ronald Bohl, O.F.M. Conv.; Deacon Robert Markert.
Res., 2229 Lower Hunters Trace Rd., 40216. Tel: 502-447-2013; Fax: 502-448-3821.

40—St. James, Revs. Donald R. Goetz; Joseph H. Voor; Deacon Jerome Fargen.
Res., 1826 Edenside Ave., 40204. Tel: 502-451-1420; Fax: 502-451-1429.
School—1818 Edenside Ave., 40204. Tel: 502-454-0330. Colette Dumstorf, Prin.
Lay Teachers 5; Students 120.

41—St. John. Closed. For inquiries for parish records contact the Chancery.

42—St. John Vianney, Revs. Robert E. Ray; Anthony Chinh N'go (CHI); Deacons John T. Kromer; Tom Morton, Pastoral Assoc.
Res., 4839 Southside Dr., 40214. Tel: 502-366-5517; Fax: 502-366-3544.
School—4841 Southside Dr., 40214. Tel: 502-366-1266; Fax: 502-366-3257. Mrs. Dean Haueter, Prin.
Sisters 2; Lay Teachers 7; Students 165.

43—St. Joseph, Revs. Melvin Holtel, O.F.M.; Joachim Lux, O.F.M.; Bro. Luke Simon, O.F.M.
Res., 1406 E. Washington St., 40206. Tel: 502-583-7401; Fax: 502-589-7465.
School—1420 E. Washington St., 40206. Tel: 502-583-0892; Fax: 502-583-4607. Tom Watson, Prin.
Lay Teachers 8; Students 92.

44—St. Lawrence, Rev. Robert L. Stuempel; Sr. Ann Marie Howard, O.S.B., Pastoral Assoc.; Deacons James H. Abell; David Dalton.
Res., 1925 Lewiston Dr., 40216. Tel: 502-448-2122; Fax: 502-448-2163.
School—1927 Lewiston Dr., 40216. Tel: 502-447-3155. Bernice Scherr, Prin.
Religious 1; Lay Teachers 22; Students 402.

45—St. Leo the Great. Closed. For inquiries for parish records contact St. John Vianney, Louisville.

46—St. Leonard, Rev. Joseph T. Herp; Mr. Robert G. Dever, Pastoral Assoc.
Res., 440 Zorn Ave., 40206. Tel: 502-897-2595; Fax: 502-896-8259.
School—Tel: 502-897-5265. Tom Schmitt, Prin.
Lay Teachers 13; Students 166.

47—St. Louis Bertrand, Revs. Charles H. O'Brien, O.P.; George G. Christian, O.P.; Robert R. Blais, O.P.; Carl Louis Mason, O.P.; J. Peter Gerhard, O.P.; Joseph C. Burns, O.P.
Res., 1104 S. 6th St., 40203. Tel: 502-583-4448; Fax: 502-583-6874.
Shrine—Lourdes Rosary Shrine, Inc., Tel: 502-583-1950; Fax: 502-589-0056.

48—St. Luke, Rev. Richard P. Berding.
Res., 4211 Jim Hawkins Dr., 40229. Tel: 502-969-3291; Fax: 502-969-1718.

49—St. Margaret Mary, Very Rev. Bernard J. Breen; Revs. Jeffrey D. Gatlin; William J. Brennan; Deacon John L. Simpson.
Res., 7813 Shelbyville Rd., 40222. Tel: 502-426-1588; Fax: 502-426-1503.
School—Tel: 502-426-2635; Fax: 502-426-1304. Ann Kalmey, Prin.
Lay Teachers 34; Students 560.

50—St. Martha, Rev. John D. Deatrick; Deacons Raymond G. Kramer, Pastoral Assoc.; John P. Maher.
Res., 2825 Klondike Ln., 40218. Tel: 502-491-8535; Fax: 502-491-8536.
School—Tel: 502-491-3171; Fax: 502-495-6107. Sharon Dutton, Prin.
Lay Teachers 28; Students 549.

51—St. Martin, Rev. Dennis Cousens; Deacons Jarvis Jackson; Michael Murphy.
Res., 639 S. Shelby St., 40202. Tel: 502-582-2827; Fax: 502-582-1780.

52—St. Martin de Porres. Consolidated with St. Benedict, Louisville, St. Charles Borromeo, Louisville, and Holy Cross, Louisville, parishes. Rev. R. Dale Cieslik; Deacon James Turner, Pastoral Admin.; Sr. Dorothy Jackson, S.C.N., Pastoral Assoc.
Mailing Address: 3112 W. Broadway, 40211. Tel: 502-778-1118.

53—St. Mary (Bullitt Co.), Revs. Thomas A. Hommrich; Kenneth R. Fortener; Deacons Paul J. George; Kenneth J. Mitchell.
Res., 299 Crestwood Ln., 40229. Tel: 502-957-3385; Fax: 502-957-2059.

54—St. Mary Magdalen. See separate listing under Oratories.

55—St. Matthias, Gene Scheich; Sr. Joan Riedley, O.S.U., Pastoral Assoc.
Res., 2208 Dixie Hwy., 40210. Tel: 502-776-3250.

56—Most Blessed Sacrament, Rev. John U. Caskey; Deacons Harry Prestwood; John Simmons.
Res., 3509 Taylor Blvd., 40215. Tel: 502-361-0149; Fax: 502-375-1076.
School—1128 Berry Blvd., 40215. Tel: 502-361-7103; Fax: 502-367-1513. Fred J. Klausing, III, Prin.
Lay Teachers 13; Students 213.

57—Mother of Good Counsel, Rev. John T. Judie; Deacons Patrick Harris; Charles Voll; Joseph Raibert.
Res., 8509 Westport Rd., 40242. Tel: 502-425-2210; Fax: 502-425-0941.
School—Tel: 502-425-2637; Fax: 502-425-2699. Elizabeth Lueke, Prin.
Lay Teachers 26; Students 409.

58—Our Lady, Rev. Robert E. Reilly; Deacon William Klump.
Res., 3511 Rudd Ave., 40212. Tel: 502-776-4666; Fax: 502-776-7746.

59—Our Lady of Lourdes, Revs. G. Nicholas Rice; William Miller; Deacon Norbert Miller. In res., Rev. Robert Dale Cieslik.
Res., 508 Breckenridge Ln., 40207. Tel: 502-896-0241; Fax: 502-895-5435.
School—510 Breckenridge Ln., 40207. Tel: 502-895-5122; Fax: 502-893-5051. Laura Glaser, Prin.
Lay Teachers 24; Students 462.

60—Our Lady of Mount Carmel, Revs. Niles J. Gillen, O.Carm.; Cecil Pickert, O.Carm.
Res., 5505 New Cut Rd., 40214. Tel: 502-366-5651; Fax: 502-368-9972.
School—5501 New Cut Rd., 40214. Tel: 502-368-8506. Carol Nord, Prin.
Lay Teachers 25; Students 521.

61—Our Mother of Sorrows, Rev. Terry L. Langford; Deacon Richard E. Steinmetz.
Res., 747 Harrison Ave., 40217. Tel: 502-637-7442; Fax: 502-637-3794.
School—(Grades PreK-8) 770 Eastern Pkwy., 40217. Tel: 502-637-7814; Fax: 502-636-0260. Sr. Sharon Marie Blank, O.S.F., Prin.
Lay Teachers 12; Students (Grades K-8) 208; Students (Preschool) 15.

62—St. Patrick, Revs. John L. Schindler; James E. Hargadon; Deacon Jack Conrad.
Res., 1000 N. Beckley Station Rd., 40245-4550. Tel: 502-244-6083; Fax: 502-244-6083 (Call first).
School—Tel: 502-244-7083. Mary Beth Bowling, Prin.
Lay Teachers 31; Students 578.

63—St. Paul. Closed. For inquiries for parish records contact the Chancery.

64—St. Peter Claver, Rev. Patrick D. Delahanty, Admin.
Res., 526 Lampton St., 40203. Tel: 502-585-3910.

65—St. Philip Neri. Closed. For inquiries for parish records contact St. Elizabeth of Hungary, Louisville.

66—St. Pius X, Revs. Charles D. Walker; T. Michael Tobin; Sr. Mary Elaine Zehnder, S.C.N., Pastoral Assoc.
Res., 3521 Goldsmith Ln., 40220. Tel: 502-451-4124; Fax: 502-458-7109.
School—3525 Goldsmith Ln., 40220. Tel: 502-452-1712; Fax: 502-451-2462. Carolyn Zierer, Prin.
Lay Teachers 25; Students 412.

67—St. Raphael the Archangel, Revs. James F. Hackett; J. Randall Hubbard; John A. Dalton; Deacon Jim Sturgeon.
Res., 2141 Lancashire Ave., 40205. Tel: 502-451-2864.
Parish Offices: 2121 Lancashire Ave, 40205. Tel: 502-458-2500; Fax: 502-458-8049.
School—2131 Lancashire Ave., 40205. Tel: 502-456-1541. Paul DeZarn, Prin.
Lay Teachers 40; Students 642.

68—Resurrection D.N.J.C. Closed. For inquiries for parish records please see Guardian Angels, Louisville.

69—St. Rita, Revs. William J. Martin; Gladstone H. Stevens; Deacon Charles "Mack" Nevitt, Pastoral Assoc.
Res., 8709 Preston Hwy., 40219. Tel: 502-969-4579; Fax: 502-969-3679.
School—Tel: 502-969-7067; Fax: 502-968-0510 (Call first). Mary Lee Lanning, Prin.
Lay Teachers 22; Students 425.

70—SS. Simon and Jude, Rev. William F. Wagner; Sr. Ann Carol Mann, S.C.N., Pastoral Assoc.
Res., 4335 Hazelwood Ave., 40215. Tel: 502-368-4887; Fax: 502-375-1988.
School—4333 Hazelwood Ave., 40215. Tel: 502-366-2424. Michelle Duvall, Prin.
Lay Teachers 14; Students 232.

71—St. Stephen, Martyr, Rev. James J. Lichtefeld; Deacon Sylvester Nitzken.
Res., 1000 English Ave., 40217. Tel: 502-635-5813; Fax: 502-635-5888.
School—2931 Pindell, 40217. Tel: 502-635-7141.
Lay Teachers 21; Students 391.

72—St. Therese, Revs. J. Roy Stiles; Robert B. Gray; Herman J. Naber.
Res., 1010 Schiller Ave., 40204. Tel: 502-634-3671; Fax: 502-634-3672.

73—St. Thomas More, Rev. James Wayne Murphy; Deacon Michael A. Tolbert.
Res., 6105 S. Third St., 40214. Tel: 502-366-1463; Fax: 502-366-1464.
School—226 Inverness Ave., 40214. Tel: 502-363-3719. Mrs. Donna Sansone, Prin.
Lay Teachers 10; Students 242.

74—St. Vincent de Paul. See separate listing under Oratories.

75—St. William, Rev. Joseph H. Stoltz; Sharan A. Benton, Pastoral Admin.
Res., 1226 W. Oak St., 40210. Tel: 502-635-6307.

OUTSIDE THE CITY OF LOUISVILLE

Albany, Clinton Co., Emmanuel Catholic, Rev. Lawrence J. Gelthaus.
Res., Hwy. 127 N., P.O. Box 126, 42602. Tel: 606-387-7251.
Mission—Burkesville, Cumberland Co., Holy Cross Catholic, 264 Glasgow Rd., P.O. Box 197, Burkesville, 42717. Tel: 270-864-4107.

Bardstown, Nelson Co., St. Joseph, Revs. William F. Medley; David W. Naylor; Deacons Richard J. Walsh; John Hamilton. In res., Revs. Vincent Lopez, O.P.; C. Joseph Batcheldor.
Res., P.O. Box 548, 310 W. Stephen Foster Ave., 40004. Tel: 502-348-3126; Fax: 502-349-0941. [CEM]
School—320 W. Stephen Foster Ave., 40004. Tel: 502-348-5994; Fax: 502-348-4694. Mary Spalding, Prin.
Sisters of Charity of Nazareth 2; Lay Teachers 21; Students 453.
High School—Bethlehem High School, 309 W. Stephen Foster Ave., 40004. Tel: 502-348-8594; Fax: 502-349-1247.
Sisters of Charity 3; Lay Teachers 25; Students 324.

St. Monica, Rev. Stephen A. Pohl; Deacon Samuel R. Filiatreau, Pastoral Admin.
Res., 407 S. Third St., 40004. Tel: 502-348-5250; Fax: 502-348-3635.

Brandenburg, Meade Co., St. John the Apostle, Rev. Philip L. Erickson; Sr. Justina Heneghan, R.S.M., Pastoral Admin.; Deacon J. Michael Jones.
Res., 491 E. Broadway, 40108. Tel: 270-422-2196; Fax: 270-422-2471. [CEM]
School—513 E. Broadway, 40108. Tel: 270-422-2088; Fax: 270-422-5716. Sr. Lucilla Mangion, Prin.
Augustinian Sisters, Servants of Jesus and Mary 4; Lay Teachers 4; Students 153.

Calvary, Marion Co., Holy Name of Mary, Rev. Joseph I. Dawson.
Res., 3265 Hwy. 208, Lebanon, 40033. Tel: 270-692-2298; Fax: 270-692-5708. [CEM]
Missions—Phillipsburg, Marion Co., Our Lady of Fatima; Spurlington, Taylor Co., St. Frances de Sales. [CEM 2]
Station—Lebanon, Parish Center, Tel: 270-692-6491.

Campbellsville, Taylor Co., Our Lady of Perpetual Help, Rev. Jeffrey P. Leger; Deacon Joseph Ohnemus.
Office: 425 N. Central Ave., 42719. Tel: 270-465-4282; Fax: 270-789-9669. [CEM]

Cecilia, Hardin Co., St. Ambrose, Rev. Stanley L. Osborne, Admin.
Res., c/o 657 St. John Church Rd., Elizabethtown, 42701. Tel: 270-862-9816.

Clementsville, Casey Co., St. Bernard, Rev. Joseph S. Hall.
Res., 5075 Ky 551, Liberty, 42539. Tel: 606-787-7570.
Mission—Liberty, Casey Co., Sacred Heart, Tel: 606-787-7324.

Culvertown, Nelson Co., Immaculate Conception, Rev. Lawrence H. Lindle; Deacon William A. Downs.
Res., 8191 New Haven Rd., New Haven, 40051-6030. Tel: 502-549-3757; Fax: 502-549-7258.
Mission—Bardstown, Nelson Co., St. Mark. Closed. For information contact Immaculate Conception, Culvertown.

Edmonton, Metcalfe Co., Christ the Healer, Rev. John J. Stoltz.
Res., 1610 W. Stockton St., 42129. Tel: 270-432-5024.
Mission—Tompkinsville, Monroe Co., Christ the King, P.O. Box 548, Tompkinsville, 42167. Tel: 270-487-8881.

Elizabethtown, Hardin Co., St. James, Revs. J. Richard Sullivan; Christopher M. Scalise; Deacons Jay Jenkins; Joseph Chathaparampil; William Clark.
Res., 307 W. Dixie Ave., 42701. Tel: 270-765-6268; Fax: 270-737-5661. [CEM]
School—114 N. Miles St., 42701. Tel: 270-765-7011; Fax: 270-769-5745. Sr. Michael Marie Friedman, Prin.
Religious Teachers 1; Lay Teachers 20; Students 414.

Fairdale, Jefferson Co., St. Jerome, Revs. Isaac McDaniel, O.S.B.; Robert E. Ray; Anthony Chinh N'go (CHI); Deacon Charles Walther.
Res., 903 Fairdale Rd., 40118. Tel: 502-363-9929; Fax: 502-363-9960.

Fairfield, Nelson Co., St. Michael, Revs. Donald L. Ryan; Albert J. Hartlage.
Res., P.O. Box 27, 40020. Tel: 502-252-8308. [CEM]
Mission—Taylorsville, Spencer Co., All Saints Church, 410 W. Main St., P.O. Box 531, 40071. Tel: 502-477-6676. [CEM]
Rev. Donald L. Ryan, Admin.; Deacon Martin J. Brown.

Finley, Taylor Co., Our Lady of the Hills, Rev. Jeffrey P. Leger.
Office: 425 N. Central Ave., Campbellsville, 42718. Tel: 270-465-4282; Fax: 270-789-9669. [CEM]

Flaherty, Meade Co., St. Martin of Tours, Revs. Thomas A. Smith; Robert N. Mills; Deacons John R. Whelan; Robert Hall.
Res., 440 Saint Martin Rd., Vine Grove, 40175. Tel: 270-828-2552; Fax: 270-828-2562. [CEM]

Glasgow, Barren Co., St. Helen, Revs. Peter R. Stryker, C.P.M.; Joel C. Rogers, C.P.M.; Deacon Lee Bidwell. In res., Rev. John J. Molloy, C.P.M.
Res., 103 W. Brown St., 42141. Tel: 270-651-5263.
Mission—Horse Cave, Hart Co., Our Lady of the Caves Church, Rte. 31 W., Horse Cave, 42749. Tel: 270-786-1188.

Goshen, Oldham Co., Transfiguration of Our Lord, Rev. Herbert L. Lattis; Deacon Joseph F. Stuber.
Res., 1620 S. Hwy. 1793, 40026. Tel: 502-228-8665; Fax: 502-228-0355.

Greensburg, Green Co., Holy Redeemer, Rev. Jeffrey P. Leger; Deacon Joseph Ohnemus.
Office: 425 N. Central Ave., Campbellsville, 42718-0484. Tel: 270-465-4282.
Church—110 Industrial Rd., 42743.

Hodgenville, Larue Co., Our Lady of Mercy, Rev. James T. Mudd.
Res., 208 Walters Ave., 42748. Tel: 270-358-4697. [CEM]

Holy Cross, Marion Co., Holy Cross, Rev. Frederick W. Klotter, 96; Sr. Mary Ellen Curl, R.S.M., Pastoral Admin.
Res., 3560 N. Saint Francis Rd., Loretto, 40037. Tel: 270-865-2521; Fax: 270-865-2071. [CEM]

Howardstown, Nelson Co., St. Ann, Rev. James T. Mudd, Admin. In res., Rev. Robert A. Brown.
Res., 7490 Howardstown Rd., 40051. Tel: 502-549-3285. [CEM]
School—(Grades 1-8). Tel: 502-549-7310. Lois Cecil, Prin.
Lay Teachers 4; Students 58.

Jamestown, Russell Co., Holy Spirit, Rev. Daniel L. Lincoln; Sr. Karen Freund, O.P., Pastoral Assoc.; Deacon Jerry Antle.
Res., 406 N. Main St., P.O. Box 247, 42629. Tel: 270-343-3346.
Mission—Columbia, Adair Co., Good Shepherd, P.O. Box 354, Columbia, 42728. Tel: 270-384-4528. Sr. Judith A. Prindiville, C.S.C., Pastoral Assoc.

Jeffersontown, Jefferson Co., St. Edward, Rev. Frank J. Eimer; Mrs. Betty Deerwester, Pastoral Assoc.
Res., 9608 Sue Helen Dr., 40299. Tel: 502-267-7494; Fax: 502-267-7495. [CEM]
School—9610 Sue Helen Dr., Jefferstown, 40299. Tel: 502-267-6633. Susan Jones, Prin.
Lay Teachers 30; Students 618.

St. Michael, Revs. Gary G. Davis; Kenneth L. Kamber; Agnes Tompkins, Pastoral Assoc.
Res., 12707 Taylorsville Rd., 40299. Tel: 502-266-5611; Fax: 502-267-4272.
School—(Grades (PreK-4)). Tel: 502-267-6155; Fax: 502-267-4272. Sheila Marstiller, Prin.
Lay Teachers 18; Students 282.

LaGrange, Oldham Co., Immaculate Conception, Very Rev. J. Mark Spalding; Deacon Kenneth Carter.
Res., 502 N. Fifth St., 40031. Tel: 502-222-0255; Fax: 502-225-9844.
School—Tel: 502-222-0671. Gayle Bauch, Prin.
Lay Teachers 9; Students 136.
Mission—Bedford, Trimble Co., St. Matthew, Rte. 2, Bedford, 40006.
Stations—LaGrange, Luther Luckett Correctional Center, Tel: 502-222-0363; Kentucky State Reformatory, Tel: 502-222-9441; Roederer Farm Prison, Tel: 502-222-0173; Cedar Lake Lodge, Tel: 502-222-7157; Tri-County Community Hospital, Tel: 502-222-5388.

Lebanon, Marion Co., St. Augustine, Revs. Charles C. Thompson; John A. Schwartzlose; Deacon Tom Mattingly. In res., Rev. Frederick W. Klotter.
Res., 235 S. Spalding Ave., 40033. Tel: 270-692-3019; Fax: 270-692-5532. [CEM]
School—(Grades 1-8). Tel: 270-692-2063; Fax: 270-692-6597. Mary Gardner, Prin.
Lay Teachers 13; Students 236.

Lebanon Junction, Bullitt Co., St. Benedict, Revs. Gerald L. Bell; Ivo E. Cecil; James W. Graf.
Res., 139 N. Brook St., 40150. Tel: 502-833-4886; Fax: 502-833-4886 (Call first).
School—227 W. Oak St., 40150. Tel: 502-833-4926. Iris Whitney, Prin.
Lay Teachers 4; Students 67.
Mission—St. Clare. See separate listing under Oratories. [CEM]

Mount Washington, Bullitt Co., St. Francis Xavier, Rev. Scott J. Wimsett; Cathy Blanford, Pastoral Assoc.; Deacon Martin J. Brown.
Res., 155 Stringer Ln., 40047. Tel: 502-538-4933; Fax: 502-955-5366. [CEM]

New Haven, Nelson Co., St. Catherine, Rev. Clarence J. Howard; Deacons George B. Clark; Irvine Marshall.
Res., 174 N. Main St., P.O. Box 88, 40051. Tel: 502-549-3152; Fax: 502-549-5410. [CEM]
School—413 First St., P.O. Box 88, 40051. Tel: 502-549-3680. Carolyn Edelen, Prin.
Sisters 1; Lay Teachers 12; Students 256.

New Hope, Nelson Co., St. Vincent de Paul, Rev. Clarence J. Howard, Admin.; Deacon Edward J. Hutchins.
Mailing Address: 174 N. Main St., P.O. Box 88, New Haven, 40051.
Res., 101 Church St., 40052. Tel: 502-549-3152; Fax: 502-549-5410. [CEM]

Payneville, Meade Co., St. Mary Magdalen of Pazzi, Rev. Robert M. Abel; Deacon Joseph Padgett.
Res., P.O. Box 110, Hwy. 376, 40157. Tel: 270-496-4333; Fax: 270-496-4790. [CEM]

Pewee Valley, Oldham Co., St. Aloysius, Revs. Vincent J. Schweizer; John W. Dickman; John A. Caldwell; Deacon Francis E. Klosterman, (Retired).
Res., 202 Mount Mercy Dr., P.O. Box 468, 40056. Tel: 502-241-8452; Fax: 502-243-1740. [CEM]
School—208 Mt. Mercy Dr., 40056. Tel: 502-241-8516; Fax: 502-243-2241. Rita Yates, Prin.
Lay Teachers 21; Students 464.
Stations—Pewee Valley, Kentucky Correctional Institute for Women, Tel: 502-241-8454; Pewee Valley, Friendship Manor Nursing Home, Tel: 502-241-8821.

Pleasure Ridge Park, Jefferson Co., St. Paul, Rev. Maurice Hayes, O.F.M.Conv. In res., Revs. James Kent, O.F.M.Conv.; John Elmer, O.F.M. Conv.
Res., 6901 Dixie Hwy., 40258. Tel: 502-935-1223; Fax: 502-933-7747.
School—Tel: 502-935-5511; Fax: 502-935-5596. Kathleen Blanton, Prin.
Lay Teachers 12; Students 223.

St. Polycarp, Rev. William P. Burks; Deacons Jon Hosch; Tony Hasson.
Res., 7718 Columbine Dr., 40258. Tel: 502-935-4578; Fax: 502-933-1093.
School—7724 Columbine Dr., Louisville, 40258. Tel: 502-935-2022. Liz Kenobbie, Prin.
Lay Teachers 22; Students 427.

Radcliff, Hardin Co., St. Christopher, Rev. Patrick J. Dolan; Deacon Robert Imel.
Res., 1225 S. Wilson Rd., 40160. Tel: 270-351-3706. [CEM]
School—1181 S. Wilson Rd., 40160. Tel: 270-351-3150; Fax: 270-351-3934. Wayne Muscar, Prin.
Lay Teachers 11; Students 158.

Raywick, Marion Co., St. Francis Xavier Church, Rev. Frederick W. Klotter; Deacon Joseph R. Dant, Pastoral Admin.
Res., 108 Main St., 40060. Tel: 270-692-2245; Fax: 270-692-3515. [CEM]

Rhodelia, Meade Co., St. Theresa, Revs. Robert M. Abel; Albert L. Wilson, Pastor Emeritus.
Res., 9245 Rhodelia Rd., Payneville, 40157. Tel: 270-496-4343; Fax: 270-496-4416. [CEM]
Convent—Tel: 270-496-4314. Sisters of Charity of Nazareth

St. Francis, Marion Co., St. Francis of Assisi, Rev. Frederick W. Klotter; Sr. Mary Ellen Curl, R.S.M., Pastoral Admin.
Res., 6785 Hwy. 52, 40062. Tel: 270-865-2521; Fax: 270-865-2071. [CEM]

St. John, Hardin Co., St. John the Baptist, Rev. Stanley L. Osborne; Deacon Michael Vessels.
Res., 657 St. John Church Rd., Elizabethtown, 42701. Tel: 270-862-9816. [CEM]

St. Joseph, Marion Co., St. Joseph. Closed. For inquiries for parish records contact St. Francis Xavier, Raywick.

St. Mary, Marion Co., St. Charles, Rev. Gary Young, C.R.; Deacon Joseph R. Dant, Pastoral Admin.
Res., 675 Hwy. 327, Lebanon, 40033. Tel: 270-692-4513; Fax: 270-692-6204. [CEM]

St. Thomas, Nelson Co., St. Thomas, Revs. Stephen A. Pohl; J. Irvin Mouser.
Res., 870 Saint Thomas Ln., Bardstown, 40004. Tel: 502-348-3717; Fax: 502-348-1905.

Samuels, Nelson Co., St. Gregory, Rev. Trumie Culpepper Elliott; Deacons Joseph E. Livers; Joseph H. Filiatreau.
Parish Office: 330 Samuels Loop, Cox's Creek, 40013. Tel: 502-348-6337; Fax: 502-348-5784. [CEM]
School—350 Samuel's Loop, Cox's Creek, 40013. Tel: 502-348-9583. Sue Clements, Prin.
Lay Teachers 11; Students 199.

Shelbyville, Shelby Co., Annunciation of the Blessed Virgin Mary, Rev. William S. Bowling; Sr. Lelia Mattingly, M.M., Pastoral Assoc.; Deacons John Shoulta; Brendan Kinsella; Charles Brown.
Res., 105 W. Main St., 40065. Tel: 502-633-1547; Fax: 502-633-1547 (Call first).
Mission—Eminence, Henry Co., St. John Chrysostom, 122 Penn St., Eminence, 40019.

Shepherdsville, Bullitt Co., St. Aloysius, Revs. Gerald L. Bell; Ivo E. Cecil; James W. Graf.
Res., 187 Plum St., 40165. Tel: 502-543-5918; 955-6370; Fax: 502-955-6370.
School—197 Plum St., 40165. Tel: 502-543-6721; Fax: 502-955-1490. Iris Whitney, Prin.
Lay Teachers 9; Students 213.

Springfield, Washington Co.,

1—St. Dominic, Rev. Leon C. Spalding.
Res., 303 W. Main St., 40069. Tel: 859-336-3569; Fax: 859-336-3549. [CEM]
School—309 W. Main St., 40069. Tel: 859-336-7165; Fax: 859-336-7169. Milton Wheeler, Prin.
Lay Teachers 8; Students 212.

2—Holy Rosary, Rev. Charles E. Reteneller; Deacon Ernest Cooper, Pastoral Admin.
Mailing Address: Box 146, 40069. Tel: 859-336-3898; Fax: 859-336-3898 (Call first).

3—Holy Trinity, Rev. John Christopher Allegra.
Res., 306 Fredericktown Rd., 40069. Tel: 859-284-5242. [CEM]
Mission—Manton, Washington Co., Holy Rosary, 306 Fredericktown Rd., 40069. [CEM]

4—St. Rose, Revs. Thomas Bernard Smith, O.P.; James Stephen Murray, O.P. In res., Revs. Gerard Arthur Lessard, O.P.; William Brandon Tarrier, O.P.
Res., Hwy. 152, P.O. Box 71, 40069. Tel: 859-336-3121; Fax: 859-336-3841. [CEM]

Valley Station, Jefferson Co.,

1—St. Clement, Revs. Harry J. Gelthaus; Thomas E. Donohue; Deacon David McGinty.
Res., 5431 Johnsontown Rd., 40272-3400. Tel: 502-937-5920; Fax: 502-937-5927.
School—5437 Johnsontown Rd., 40272. Tel: 502-937-1616; Fax: 502-995-3227. Cecile Chandler, Prin.
Lay Teachers 16; Students 220.

2—Our Lady Help of Christians, Rev. Thomas R. Clark, Admin.; Deacon Robert L. Burns, Pastoral Assoc.
Res., 13512 Dixie Hwy., 40272. Tel: 502-937-1818.
Mission—West Point, Hardin Co., St. Patrick Church, 1216 Main St., West Point, 40177.

3—Our Lady of Consolation, Rev. Donald W. Springman; Deacons Wayne Thieneman; Charles Beckmann.
Res., 10801 Deering Rd., 40272. Tel: 502-937-2100; Fax: 502-937-2160.
School—10803 Deering Rd., 40272. Tel: 502-937-7400; Fax: 502-937-6588. Patricia Leonard, Prin.
Lay Teachers 16; Students 205.

4—St. Timothy, Rev. Thomas R. Clark.
Res., 10300 Lower River Rd., 40272. Tel: 502-937-1238.

Vine Grove, Hardin Co., St. Brigid, Rev. Thomas A. Smith, Admin.; Deacons James Benton; Robert Caspar.
Res., 306 E. Main St., 40175. Tel: 270-877-2461; Fax: 270-877-2523. [CEM]
School—310 E. Main St., 40175. Tel: 270-877-2451; Fax: 270-877-6864. Don Lynch, Prin.
Lay Teachers 8; Students 133.

White Mills, Hardin Co., St. Ignatius, Revs. J. Richard Sullivan; Christopher M. Scalise; Deacon Jay Jenkins.
Mailing Address: P.O. Box 67, 42788. Tel: 270-369-6279.
Res., 307 W. Dixie Ave., Elizabethtown, 42701. Tel: 270-765-6268; Fax: 270-737-5661. [CEM]

Oratories

1—St. Mary Magdalen, Jefferson Co. Closed. For inquiries for parish records contact the Chancery.

2—St. Vincent de Paul, Jefferson Co. Closed. For inquiries for parish records contact St. Elizabeth of Hungary, Louisville.

3—St. Clare, Hardin Co. Closed. For inquiries for parish records contact St. Benedict, Lebanon Junction.

Chaplains of Public Institutions

Louisville. *Alliant Medical Pavillion.*
Baptist Hospital East. Attended by Our Lady of Lourdes. Rev. G. Nicholas Rice.
Caritas Medical Center. Rev. Joseph H. Stoltz.
Central State Hospital Lakeland Rd., 40223. Tel: 502-245-4121. Rev. James W. Graf, Chap.
Jewish Hospital.
Kosair-Children's Hospital.
Norton Hospital. Deacon Wheatley, Chap.
Southwest Hospital. Attended by Our Lady of Consolation.
Suburban Hospital. Attended by Ascension.
University Hospital. Rev. James E. Wafzig.
Vencor Hospital. Rev. Joseph H. Voor.

On Special Assignment:
Reverend Fathers—
Bryan, Kevin J., The Blessing Pl., P.O. Box 30, Lacombe, LA 70445
Clark, Daniel C., Passionist Community, 1924 Newburg Rd., Louisville, KY 40205
Covert, James A., 1027 S. Fourth St., Louisville, KY 40203
Linebach, Martin A., 5630 N. Sheridan Rd., Apt. 1230, Chicago, IL 60660
Spalding, Francis Larry, 3316 Pinehurst Dr., Holiday, FL 34691
Volpert, Robert C., 3004 Aspenwood Way, Louisville, KY 40241

On Duty Outside the Archdiocese:
Reverend Fathers—
Branch, Edward B., Office of Campus Ministry, Catholic Center at Atlanta University Complex, 809 Beckwith St., S.W., Atlanta, GA 30314. Tel: 404-755-2646
Brown, James J., St. Margaret Church, 122 W. Hawk Ave., Pharr, TX 78577. Tel: 956-787-8563
Dittmeier, Charles R., Maryknoll, P.O.Box 632, Phnom Penh, Cambodia
Hayden, Joseph F., Parroquia Santa Rosa De Lima, Apartado 159, Chimbote, Peru. Tel: 011-51-44-322713

Graduate Studies:
Reverend Fathers—
Hamilton, Mark M., North American College, Rome

Military Chaplains:
Reverend Fathers—
Brown, Benedict J., U.S. Navy
Nicolas, Jeffrey S., U.S. Navy

Retired:
Reverend Monsignors—
Horrigan, Alfred F., Christopher East Health Care Facility, 4200 Browns Ln., Louisville, KY 40220
O'Bryan, J. A., Rte. 1, Box 111, McDaniels, KY 40152
Reverend Fathers—
Batcheldor, C. Joseph, St. Joseph Church, P.O.Box 548, Bardstown, KY 40004
Birkel, Robert C., 7496 Stiles Rd., Howardstown, KY 40051
Boehmicke, Roger A., Nazareth Village, P.O. Box 1000, Nazareth, KY 40048
Bowling, George K., 15 Audubon Plaza Dr., Louisville, KY 40217
Brennan, William J., St. Margaret Mary Church, 7813 Shelbyville Rd., Louisville, KY 40222
Brian, Bertrand J., Nazareth Village II, P.O. Box 2000, #22, Nazareth, KY 40048
Brown, Robert A., St. Ann Church, 7490 Howardstown Rd., Howardstown, KY 40051
Butler, John J., 3115 Lexington Rd., Louisville, KY 40206
Caldwell, William T., 3320 Bardstown Rd., No. 82, Louisville, KY 40218
Cecil, Ivo E., 1080 Optimist Rd., Lebanon Junction, KY 40150
Craycroft, Bernard L., 388 University Dr., Radcliff, KY 40160
Craycroft, George P., 229 N. Main St., New Haven, KY 40051
Creed, C. Patrick, 1500 Hurricane Hills-A3, Boston, KY 40107
Dalton, John A., 2141 Lancashire, Louisville, KY 40205
Dentinger, Roy E., 3030 Breckenridge Ln., Bldg. 1, Apt. 501, Louisville, KY 40220
Dentinger, Vincent Paul, Nazareth Village, #223, P.O. Box 2000, Nazareth, KY 40048
Dickman, John W., 202 Mount Mercy Dr., Pewee Valley, KY 40056
Diersen, William M., 1695 County Line Rd., N.E., Palmyra, IN 47164
Dollinger, Robert J., P.O. Box 75, Georgetown, PEI C0A 1L0 Canada
Donohue, Thomas E., 9104 Mahoney Dr., Louisville, KY 40258
Flynn, James E., P.O.Box 262, Heber City, UT 84032-0262
Gephart, John B., Bishop David Apartments, 5146 Dixie Hwy., Louisville, KY 40216
Grauel, Frank B., Holy Spirit Church, 3345 Lexington Rd., Louisville, KY 40206
Gray, Robert B., St. Elizabeth, 1020 E. Burnett, Louisville, KY 40217
Hamilton, Joseph K., 4208 Browns Ln., #206, Louisville, KY 40220
Hannifin, Francis M., 1730 N. Stillwell Rd., Boston, KY 40107
Hanrahan, John W., 1170 Castlevale Dr., #3, Louisville, KY 40217
Hargadon, James E., P.O. Box 4205, Louisville, KY 40204
Hartlage, William C., Bishop David Apartments, 5146 Dixie Hwy., Louisville, KY 40216
Hogan, William E., 3320 Bardstown Rd., Apt. 52, Louisville, KY 40218
Howard, Anthony, 6304 Southside Dr., Louisville, KY 40214
Huber, Robert L., 5915 Outer Loop Dr., Louisville, KY 40219
Jones, John E., 1697 Taylor Wood Rd., Simpsonville, KY 40067
Kamber, Kenneth L., 4029 Busath Ave., Louisville, KY 40218
Lenahan, John B., 3931 S. Third St., Louisville, KY 40214
Lyon, Joseph A., Doe Valley Park, 228 Pine Ridge Pk., Brandenburg, KY 40108
Magel, John E., Bishop David Apartments, 5146 Dixie Hwy., Louisville, KY 40216
Mills, Robert N., 5500 Hwy. 111, S.E., Elizabeth, IN 47117
Nord, Clarence C., 2820 Flora Ave., #15, Louisville, KY 40220
Osborne, Robert E., 3910 Village Green Dr., Louisville, KY 40299
Oyler, George F., 7004 Upper River Rd., Prospect, KY 40059
Pank, Julian F., 2832 Pomeroy Dr., Louisville, KY 40218
Rapp, Bertrand J., 2040 Buechel Bank Rd., Louisville, KY 40218
Scherzer, Edwin J., Bishop David Apartments, 5146 Dixie Hwy., Louisville, KY 40216
Smith, F. Harold, P.O. Box 15, Versailles, OH 45380
Stuecker, Henry C., Bishop David Apts., 5146 Dixie Hwy., Louisville, KY 40216
Thompson, James W., Bishop David Apartments, 5146 Dixie Hwy., Louisville, KY 40216
Timmel, Gerald L., 1816 Rangeland Rd., Louisville, KY 40219
Voor, Joseph H., St. James Church, 1826 Edenside Ave., Louisville, KY 40204
Wafzig, James E., 5915 Outer Loop, Louisville, KY 40219
Weyhing, John, 340 Causeway Blvd., #116, Dunedin, FL 34698-1781
Wilson, Albert L., 980 Ray Rd., Payneville, KY 40157
Zahner, William, Twinnbrook Nursing Home, 3526 Dutchmans Ln., Louisville, KY 40205

Permanent Deacons:
Abell, James H., St. Lawrence and Vencor, Louisville
Antle, Jerry L., Holy Spirit, Jamestown; Good Shepherd, Columbia
Becker, Gary E., Epiphany
Beckmann, Charles, Our Lady of Consolation, Louisville
Bell, Kenneth, Immaculate Heart of Mary, Louisville
Benton, James L., St. Brigid, Vine Grove
Bidwell, Lee G., St. Helen, Glasgow
Bishop, Joseph C., St. Dominic/Holy Rosary, Springfield
Bissig, Paul F., St. Cecilia Church
Box, Thomas E., Jr., St. Bartholomew, Louisville
Brown, Charles K., Annunciation, Shelbyville
Brown, Martin J., St. Francis Xavier, Mt. Washington
Bryant, Robert C., St. Barnabas, Louisville; Jefferson County Jail
Burns, Robert L., Our Lady Help of Christians, Valley Station
Carney, Edward P., Unassigned
Carter, Kenneth, Immaculate Conception, La Grange
Caspar, Robert J., St. Brigid, Vine Grove
Chathaparampil, Joseph, St. James Church, Elizabethtown
Churchill, John R., St. Augustine, Louisville
Clark, George B., St. Catherine, New Haven
Clark, William V., Family Ministries, St. James, Elizabethtown
Collard, Paul J., (Retired)
Conrad, Jack, St. Patrick, St. Paul-Minneapolis
Cooper, Ernest A., Holy Rosary, Springfield
Dalton, David L., Dismas Charities, St. Patrick, St. Lawrence
Dant, Joseph R., St. Charles, St. Mary; St. Francis Xavier, Raywick
Dawson, Richard L., (Retired), Christ the King, Louisville
Dever, Robert Glen, St. Leonard
Dew, Joseph M., Military Parish of St. Patrick, Fort Knox
Downs, William A., Immaculate Conception, Culvertown
Edwards, Michael, Ascension, Louisville

Fante, Lamar W., Holy Family, Louisville; Vicar for Senior Deacons
Fargen, J. Jerome, (Retired), St. James Church, Louisville
Filiatreau, Joseph H., St. Gregory, Samuels
Filiatreau, Samuel R., St. Monica, Bardstown
Flowers, Donald K. (Lexington), St. Dominic, Springfield
George, Paul J., St. Mary, Louisville
Hall, Robert, St. Martin of Tours, Flaherty
Hamilton, John (Mobile), St. Joseph, Bardstown
Harris, Patrick D., Mother of Good Counsel, Louisville
Hasson, Anthony P., St. Polycarp, Pleasure Ridge Park
Hettich, Philip, St. Bernard, Louisville
Higgins, Frederick, (Retired), St. Martin de Porres, Louisville
Hosch, Jon E., St. Polycarp, Pleasure Ridge Park
Houck, Peter L., Chap., Kentucky State Reformatory
Hutchins, Joseph E., St. Vincent De Paul, New Hope
Imel, Robert, St. Christopher, Radcliff
Ishmael, Raymond L., Veterans Hospital
Jackson, Jarvis, St. Martin of Tours, Louisville
Jenkins, Jay R., St. James, Elizabethtown
Jones, J. Michael, St. John the Apostle, Brandenburg
Jones, Walton G., Dir., Office of Clergy Personnel, St. Francis of Assisi, Louisville
Kampschaefer, Robert M., St. Denis, Louisville
Karley, Brian, Dir., Diaconate Office
Kinsella, Brendan, Annunciation, Shelbyville
Klosterman, Francis E., (Retired), St. Aloysius Church, Pewee Valley
Klump, William R., Church of Our Lady, Louisville
Kramer, Raymond G., St. Martha, Louisville
Kromer, John T., St. John Vianney, Louisville
Lincoln, James Bruce, Spiritual Advisor Cursillo; St. Barnabas, Louisville
Livers, Joseph E., St. Gregory, Samuels
Maher, John P., St. Martha, Louisville
Markert, Clarence Robert, Incarnation, Louisville
Marshall, Irvine (Chicago), St. Catherine, New Haven
Masterson, Donald E., Jefferson County Youth Facility
Mattingly, Thomas, (Retired), St. Augustine, Lebannon
McCulloch, Thomas B., (Retired)
McGinty, David L., St. Clement, Valley Station
Miller, Norbert F., Our Lady of Lourdes, Louisville
Mitchell, Kenneth J., St. Mary, Louisville
Mullins, William L., St. Francis of Rome, Louisville
Murphy, Michael, St. Martin of Tours, Louisville
Nevitt, Charles, St. Rita, Louisville
Nitzken, Syl J., St. Stephen Martyr, Louisville
Ohnemus, Joseph, Our Lady of Perpetual Help, Campbellsville
Olrich, James Charles, St. Elizabeth Ann Seton Church, Louisville
Osborne, Kenneth F., On Leave
Padgett, Joseph E., St. Mary Magdalen of Pazzi, Payneville; St. Theresa, Rhodelia
Patterson, Daniel Eugene, Leave of Absence
Plummer, James R., St. Barnabas, Louisville
Prestwood, Harry, Most Blessed Sacrament, Louisville
Raibert, Joseph A., Mother of Good Counsel, Louisville
Ratterman, Cletus A., Guardian Angels, Louisville
Ronald, Edward R., (Retired), Jefferson County Department of Corrections, Louisville
Ryan, Thomas, Catholic Deaf Office
Shoulta, John, Annunciation, Shelbyville
Shutts, John F., (Retired), Caritas Medical Center, Louisville
Simmons, John, Most Blessed Sacrament, Louisville
Simpson, John L., Holy Trinity & St. Margaret Mary, Louisville
Skeeters, William L., St. Gabriel, Louisville
Stanley, Vincent G., St. Albert, Louisville; Catholic Charities
Steinmetz, Richard Earl, Our Mother of Sorrows, Louisville
Stuber, Joseph F., Transfiguration, Goshen
Sturgeon, James C., Sr., St. Raphael, Louisville
Thieneman, C. Wayne, Our Lady of Consolation, Valley Station
Thomas, William A., (Retired)
Tolbert, Michael A., St. Thomas More, Louisville
Tomes, David R., St. Boniface, Louisville
Tremblay, Philip, St. Cecilia, Louisville
Turner, James R., St. Martin de Porres, Louisville
Vessels, Michael, St. John the Baptist, Rineyville
Voll, Charles Joseph, Mother of Good Counsel, Louisville
Walsh, Richard J., St. Joseph, Bardstown
Walther, Charles F., St. Jerome, Fairdale
Ward, Kenneth M., St. Albert the Great, Louisville
Wheatley, Joseph P., Norton Hospital & Kosair Children's Hospital, Louisville
Whelan, John R., St. Martin of Tours, Flaherty
Wright, J. Patrick, Cathedral of the Assumption, Louisville
Young, R. James, St. Ignatius Martyr, Louisville

INSTITUTIONS LOCATED IN THE ARCHDIOCESE

[A] COLLEGES AND UNIVERSITIES

LOUISVILLE. *Bellarmine University*, 2001 Newburg Rd., 40205-0671. Tel: 502-452-8211; Fax: 502-452-8033.
Web site: www.bellarmine,edu
For a complete listing, refer to the Colleges and Universities section.

Spalding University, 851 S. 4th St., 40203. Tel: 502-585-9911; Fax: 502-585-7158.
Web site: www.spalding.edu
For a complete listing, refer to the Colleges and Universities section.

ST. CATHARINE. *St. Catharine College*, 2735 Bardstown Rd., 40061. Tel: 606-336-5082; Fax: 606-336-5031.
Web site: www.scky.edu
For a complete listing, refer to the Colleges and Universities section.

[B] HIGH SCHOOLS, DIOCESAN

LOUISVILLE. *Holy Cross High School*, 5144 Dixie Hwy., 40216. Tel: 502-447-4363; Fax: 502-448-1062.
E-mail: holycross@ntr.net
Dr. Penney Sanders, Exec. Dir.; Mr. Kevin Brever, Dir. of Advancement; Sr. Maryann Tarquinio, Dir. of Academics. Sisters 1; Lay Teachers 28; Students 359.

St. Francis DeSales High School, 425 Kenwood Dr., 40214. Tel: 502-368-6519; Fax: 502-366-6172.
E-mail: dhs@ntr.net
Web site: www.ntr.net/~dhs
Dr. Penney Sanders, Exec. Dir.; Mr. Frank DeSensi, Dir. of Academics. Lay Teachers 25; Students 343.

The Carmelite Community of The St. Francis De-Sales Priory. Tel: 502-368-6553; Fax: 502-366-6172. Rev. Kyrin Caggiano, O.Carm., Faculty, DeSales High School.

Trinity High School, 4011 Shelbyville Rd., 40207. Tel: 502-895-9427; Fax: 502-895-6837.
E-mail: trinity@thsrock.net
Web site: www.thsrock.net
Mr. Robert J. Mullen, Pres.; Mr. David Winkler, Prin.; Revs. Ronald J. Domhoff; R. Joseph Hemmerle; David H. Zettel. Priests 3; Lay Teachers 76; Students 1,127.

BARDSTOWN. *Bethlehem High School*, 40004. Tel: 502-348-8594; Fax: 502-349-1247.
E-mail: BHS@bethlehemhigh.org
Web site: www.bethlehemhigh.org
Sisters of Charity of Nazareth. Vincent Lopez, O.P., Prin. Sisters 3; Lay Teachers 26; Students 324.

[C] HIGH SCHOOLS, PRIVATE

LOUISVILLE. *Academy of Our Lady of Mercy*, 1176 E. Broadway, 40204. Tel: 502-584-4273; Fax: 502-584-9651.
E-mail: mikejohnson@mercyacademy.com
Web site: www.win.net/mercy
Mr. Michael C. Johnson, Prin.; Melinda C. Ernstberger, Asst. Prin. Sisters of Mercy 1; Lay Teachers 28; Students 388.

Assumption High School, 2170 Tyler Ln., 40205. Tel: 502-458-9551; Fax: 502-454-8411.
E-mail: ahs@iglou.com
Web site: www.ashrockets.org
Sisters of Mercy. Mary Lee McCoy, Prin. Lay Teachers 84; Students 948.

Holy Rosary Academy. Owned by Spalding University. 4801 Southside Dr., 40214. Tel: 502-366-4561; Fax: 502-368-4734.
E-mail: hra4801@aol.com
Web site: holyrosaryacademy.org
Dr. Karen M. Juliano, Prin. Sisters of St. Dominic (St. Catharine, KY) 1; Ursuline Sisters 1; Lay Teachers 17; Students 181.

Presentation Academy, 861 S. 4th St., 40203. Tel: 502-583-5935; Fax: 502-583-1342.
E-mail: psamuels@spalding.edu
Web site: www.spalding.edu/pres/prespage
Spalding University. Leslie Gayle Kaster, Prin. Sisters 2; Lay Teachers 35; Students 416.

Sacred Heart Academy, 3175 Lexington Rd., 40206. Tel: 502-897-6097; Fax: 502-896-3935.
E-mail: sacredheartacad@ka.net
Web site: www.sacredheartacad.com
Ursuline Sisters. Sr. Paula Kleine-Kracht, O.S.U., Prin. Sisters 3; Lay Teachers 50; Students 702.

St. Xavier High School, Xaverian Brothers, 1609 Poplar Level Rd., 40217. Tel: 502-637-4712; Fax: 502-634-2171.
E-mail: admin@saintx.com
Web site: www.saintx.com
Bro. James M. Kelly, C.F.X., Pres.; Dr. Perry E. Sangalli, Prin. Priests 2; Brothers 6; Lay Teachers 111; Students 1,585.

[D] CONSOLIDATED SCHOOLS

LOUISVILLE. *Community Catholic School*, 2530 Slevin St., 40212. Tel: 502-778-1941; Fax: 502-778-9935. Olga G. Golub, Prin. Lay Teachers 8; Students 122. Children from St. Cecilia and Our Lady attend this school.

[E] ELEMENTARY SCHOOLS, PRIVATE

LOUISVILLE. *Holy Angels Academy, Inc.*, 1408 S. Second St., 40208. Tel: 502-634-3223. Principals: Joseph M. Norton, (Head of Academy and Grade School); Marilyn G. Malone, (High School). Sisters 2; Lay Teachers 15; Students 132.

Mercy Montessori School, Inc., 2181 Tyler Ln., 40205. Tel: 502-459-6545. Sr. Mary Alicia McGinty, R.S.M., Dir. Students 70.

Sacred Heart Model School, 3107 Lexington Rd., 40206. Tel: 502-896-3931; Fax: 502-896-3932.
E-mail: wannemuehl@aol.com
Web site: ucschools.com/shms
Dr. Sarah Wannemuehler, Prin. Sisters 1; Lay Teachers 40; Students 366.

Thomas Merton Academy, 6010 Preston Hwy., 40219. Tel: 502-969-5462; Fax: 502-966-4371.
E-mail: thomasmertonacademy@yahoo.com
Rev. Joseph Palubeski, C.R.; Larry Winegarden, Prin. Lay Teachers 12; Students 178.

Ursuline Montessori School, 3105 Lexington Rd., 40206. Tel: 502-895-7798; Fax: 502-896-3943.
Web site: www.ucschools.com
Linda Otto, Dir. Lay Teachers 11; Students 150. Montessori School.

NAZARETH. *Nazareth Montessori Children's Center*, P.O. Box 44, 40048. Tel: 502-348-1540; Fax: 502-331-4050.
E-mail: nmcc@bardstown.com
Web site: scnazarethky.org/montessori
Sr. Patricia Marie Hill, S.C.N., Dir.; Teri Bishop, Asst. Adm. Sisters 1; Lay Teachers 6; Students 75.

[F] SPECIAL SCHOOLS

LOUISVILLE. *Pitt Academy*, 4605 Poplar Level Rd., 40213. Tel: 502-966-6979; Fax: 502-962-8878.
E-mail: pitt@aye.net
Web site: www.pitt.com
Mr. Tom Jones, Prin. Lay Teachers 6; Students 48.

St. Joseph Child Development Center, 2823 Frankfort Ave., 40206. Tel: 502-893-0241; Fax: 502-896-2394.
E-mail: sjkids@aol.com
Web site: www.sjkids.org
Linda Compton, Admin. Students 160.

Ursuline School of Music and Drama, 3105 Lexington Rd., 40206. Tel: 502-897-1816; Fax: 502-896-3927.
Web site: www.ucschools.com/usmd
Anna Jo Paul, Dir. Students 450.

[G] ORPHANAGES AND INFANT HOMES

LOUISVILLE. *St. Joseph Catholic Orphan Society*, 2823 Frankfort Ave., 40206. Tel: 502-893-0241; Fax: 502-896-2394.
E-mail: sjkid@aol.com
Web site: www.sjkids.org
For a complete listing, refer to the Special Care Facilities section.

St. Joseph Children's Home, 2823 Frankfort Ave., 40206. Tel: 502-893-0241; Fax: 502-896-2394.
E-mail: sjkids@aol.com
Web site: www.sjkids.org
For a complete listing, refer to the Special Care Facilities section.

St. Thomas Orphan Society, Inc., P.O. Box 1073, 40201
For a complete listing, refer to the Special Care Facilities section.

St. Vincent's Orphan Society, Inc., P.O. Box 1073, 40201
For a complete listing, refer to the Special Care Facilities section.

[H] GENERAL HOSPITALS

LOUISVILLE. *Caritas Medical Center*, 1850 Bluegrass Ave., 40215. Tel: 502-361-6000; Fax: 502-361-6799.
Web site: www.caritas.com
For a complete listing, refer to the Hospitals section.

BARDSTOWN. *Flaget Memorial Hospital*, 201 Cathedral Manor, 40004. Tel: 502-348-3923, Ext. 4641; Fax: 502-349-4643
For a complete listing, refer to the Hospitals section.

[I] SPECIAL HOSPITALS

LOUISVILLE. *Caritas Peace Center*, 2020 Newburg Rd., 40205. Tel: 502-451-3330; Fax: 502-473-1797.
Web site: www.caritas.com
For a complete listing, refer to the Special Care Facilities section.

[J] PROTECTIVE INSTITUTIONS

LOUISVILLE. *Boys' Haven*, 2301 Goldsmith Ln., 40205. Tel: 502-458-1171; Fax: 502-451-2161.
E-mail: boyshaven@win.net
Web site: www.boyshaven.org
For a complete listing, refer to the Special Care Facilities section.

[K] NURSING HOMES

LOUISVILLE. *Franciscan Health Care Center*, 3625 Fern Valley Rd., 40219. Tel: 502-964-3381; Fax: 502-964-3395
For a complete listing, refer to the Special Care Facilities section.

Marian Home, 3105 Lexington Rd., 40206. Tel: 502-893-0121; Fax: 502-896-3925
For a complete listing, refer to the Special Care Facilities section.

Nazareth Home, 2000 Newburg Rd., 40205. Tel: 502-459-9681; Fax: 502-456-9077.
E-mail: Jdencz@Nazhome.org
Web site: Nazhome.org
For a complete listing, refer to the Special Care Facilities section.

St. Joseph Home for the Aged, 15 Audubon Plaza Dr., 40217. Tel: 502-636-2300; Fax: 502-636-2239
For a complete listing, refer to the Special Care Facilities section.

[L] MONASTERIES AND RESIDENCES OF PRIESTS AND BROTHERS

LOUISVILLE. *Bishop David Apartments*, 5146 Dixie Hwy., 40216. Tel: 502-447-8617. Revs. William C. Hartlage, Dir.; John E. Magel; Edmund R. Moore, O.F.M.; James W. Thompson; John B. Gephart; Edwin J. Scherzer; James P. Hendricks; Henry C. Stuecker. Priests 8; Sisters 2.

Sacred Heart Retreat. (Corporate Title: Congregation of the Passion, Sacred Heart Community), 1924 Newburg Rd., 40205. Tel: 502-451-2330; Fax: 502-451-0192.
E-mail: passky@iglou.com
Web site: www.passionist.org
Very Rev. Richard L. Parks, C.P., Supr. In res. Revs. Francis W. Cusack, C.P.; Joachim Gemperline, C.P.; Forrest Macken, C.P.; Germain Legere, C.P. (Nova Scotia); Howard Ralenkotter, C.P.; John Anthony Parenza, C.P.; Emmet Linden; Walter Kaelin, C.P.; James DeManuele, C.P.; John Baptist Ormechea, C.P.; Albert Schwer, C.P.; Bro. Jerome Milazzo, C.P. Priests 12.

St. Francis Friary, 2229 Lower Hunters Trace, 40216. Tel: 502-447-2013. Revs. Ronald Bohl, O.F.M. Conv.; Christian Moore, O.F.M. Conv.; Thomas Smith, O.F.M. Conv.

Villa Pacis, Resurrectionist Retirement Home, 4607 Poplar Level Rd., 40213. Tel: 502-968-8010; Fax: 502-969-6375.
E-mail: crvillapacis@gateway.net
In res. Revs. Raymond Hofmann, C.R.; John Miles, C.R.; Charles Schoenbaechler, C.R.; John Lesousky, C.R.

TRAPPIST. *Abbey of Our Lady of Gethsemani, of the Order of Cistercians of the Strict Observance*, 3642 Monks Rd., 40051. Tel: 502-549-3117; Fax: 502-549-8281.
E-mail: getabbot@iglou.com
Rt. Revs. Damien Thompson, O.C.S.O., Abbot; Timothy Kelly, O.C.S.O., Abbot (Retired); Bernard Murray, O.C.S.O. (Chile); Roman Ginn, O.C.S.O.; James Conner, O.C.S.O.; Paschal Phillips, O.C.S.O.; Chrysogonus Waddell, O.C.S.O.; Bede Kok, O.C.S.O.; Hilarion Schmock, O.C.S.O.; Alan Gilmore, O.C.S.O.; Matthew Kelty, O.C.S.O.; Michael Casagram, O.C.S.O.; Carlos Rodriguez, O.C.S.O.; Peter Tong, O.C.S.O. Priests 14; Brothers 55.

[M] CONVENTS AND RESIDENCES FOR SISTERS

LOUISVILLE. *Monastery of the Discalced Carmelite Nuns*, 1740 Newburg Rd., 40205. Sr. Francis of the Mother of God, O.C.D., Prioress. Professed Nuns 10; Novices 1; Postulants 1.

St. Catherine Convent, 1172 E. Broadway, 40204. Tel: 502-583-7641; Fax: 502-584-2752.
E-mail: scathcvt@bellsouth.net
Sr. Mary Quentin Barth, R.S.M., Local Coord. Sisters of Mercy in residence 32.

Sisters of the Good Shepherd, 1013 Dorsey Ln., 40223. Tel: 502-245-1679; Fax: 502-245-4737.
E-mail: rglouky@aol.com
Sisters 2.

Ursuline Motherhouse of the Immaculate Conception, 3115 Lexington Rd., 40206. Tel: 502-893-0125; Fax: 502-896-3914.
E-mail: webmaster@ursulineslov.org
Web site: www.ursulineslov.org
Sr. Sarah Stauble, O.S.U., Pres.; Sr. Mary Aidan Hogan, O.S.U., Coord.; Rev. John J. Butler, Chap. Sisters in Motherhouse 51; Total in Congregation 193.

Ursuline Sisters. (Mount St. Joseph), 1731 Edenside Ave., 40204-1595. Tel: 502-451-8685.
E-mail: eamunsterman@juno.com
Sr. Amanda Rose Mahoney, Coord. Sisters 8. Attended from St. James.

BARDSTOWN. *Bethlehem Convent*, 40004. Tel: 502-348-3514. Sisters of Charity of Nazareth 4.

COLUMBIA. *Sisters of the Holy Cross*, 1221 Greensburg St., 42728. Tel: 270-384-4528.

GAMALIEL. *Sisters of the Holy Cross*, P.O. Box 207, 42140. Tel: 270-457-2157. Sr. Mary Eliza Martin, C.S.C., Gen. Treas. Sisters 2.

NAZARETH. *Generalate, Motherhouse and Novitiate of the Sisters of Charity of Nazareth*, P.O. Box 172, 40048. Tel: 502-348-1555 (SCN Center & Generalate); 348-1500 (Motherhouse); Fax: 502-348-1502.
E-mail: scnpres@scnazarethky.org
Web site: www.scnazarethky.org
Rev. Gary Young, C.R., Chap., Motherhouse. Sisters at Motherhouse 91; Sisters at Russell Hall 31; Sisters at David Hall 28; Sisters at SCN Center 2; Sisters at Guest House 3; NativityHall 3; Nazareth Village 7.

NERINX. *Motherhouse and Novitiate of the Sisters of Loretto at the Foot of the Cross*, 515 Nerinx Rd., 40049. Tel: 270-865-5811; Fax: 270-865-2200.
E-mail: maryswain@juno.com
Web site: www.lorettocommunity.org
Sr. Mary Catherine Rabbit, S.L., Pres.; Rev. J. Irvin Mouser, Chap. Sisters in the Motherhouse 119; Total in Congregation 370.

ST. CATHARINE. *St. Catharine of Siena Convent*, 2645 Bardstown Rd., 40061. Tel: 859-336-9303; Fax: 859-336-9306.
E-mail: rmccarthyo@aol.com
Sr. Joan Scanlon, O.P., Pres.; Rev. Charles E. Reteneller, Chap. Motherhouse of Dominican Sisters. Sisters in Motherhouse 29; Total in Congregation 262.

Sansbury Care Center, 2625 Bardstown Rd., 40061. Tel: 859-336-3974; Fax: 859-336-1068. Sr. Susan Morris, O.P., Admin.; Revs. Charles E. Reteneller, Chap.; Thomas Bernard Smith, O.P.; John Christopher Allegra; Roger A. Boehmicke; Bertrand J. Brian. Sisters in Infirmary 52.

[N] HOMES FOR MEN AND WOMEN

LOUISVILLE. *Sacred Heart Village, Inc.*, 2120 Payne St., 40206. Tel: 502-895-9888; 895-9425; Fax: 502-894-9619
For a complete listing, refer to the Special Care Facilities section.

[O] RETREAT HOUSES

LOUISVILLE. *Catholic Charismatic Renewal*, Maloney Center, 1200 S. Shelby St., 40203. Tel: 502-636-0296; Fax: 502-636-2379. Marti Jewell, Contact Person; Rev. James E. Wafzig, Spiritual Advisor.

Flaget Center, 1935 Lewiston Dr., 40216. Tel: 502-448-8581; Fax: 502-448-5518.
E-mail: dmc@archlou.org
Donna M. McHugh, Admin.

CRESTWOOD. *Lake St. Joseph Center*, 5800 Old LaGrange Rd., 40014. Tel: 502-241-4469.

NAZARETH. *Catherine Spalding Retreat and Conference Center*, P.O. Box 24, 40048. Tel: 502-348-1516; Fax: 502-348-1518.
E-mail: ruthann@scnazarethky.org
Web site: www.scnazarethky.org
Sr. Ruthann Williams, O.P., Dir. Staff Sisters 3; Lay Persons 5.

NERINX. *Knobs Haven*, 515 Nerinx Rd., 40049. Tel: 270-865-2621. Sr. Elaine Prevallet, S.L., Dir.

NEW HAVEN. *Bethany Spring*, 115 Dee Head Rd., 40051. Tel: 502-549-8277. Sr. Danielle Witt, S.S.N.D., Dir.

[P] ST. VINCENT DE PAUL SOCIETY

LOUISVILLE. *Society of St. Vincent de Paul, Council of Louisville*, P.O. Box 17126, 40217-0126. Tel: 502-584-2480; Fax: 502-587-1977.
Web site: www.svdplou.org
John K. Cecil, Exec. Dir.; J. Thomas Nelson, Trustee & Bd. Chm.

De Paul Apartments. (Transitional Shelter for Homeless Single Parent Families). Tel: 502-589-7837; Fax: 502-587-1977.

De Paul Thrift Stores. 1029 S. Preston St., 40203. Tel: 502-589-7844; Fax: 502-587-1977. 248 E. Market St., 40202. Tel: 502-583-1370; Fax: 502-587-1977.

Open Hand Kitchen and Community Center, 1026 S. Jackson St., 40203. Tel: 502-584-2480; Fax: 502-587-1977.

Ozanam Inn. (Men's Emergency & Transitional Shelter). Tel: 502-584-2480; Fax: 502-587-1977.

Parish Conferences. Tel: 502-584-2480; Fax: 502-587-1977.

Roberts Hall. (Women's Housing). Tel: 502-636-3549.

St. Jude Women's Recovery Center. (Women's Recovery). Tel: 502-589-6024; Fax: 502-587-1977.

Simon Hall. (Men's Recovery). Tel: 502-584-2480; Fax: 502-587-1977.

Tranquil House. Tel: 502-584-2480; Fax: 502-587-1977. (Housing for Mentally Ill).

[Q] MISCELLANEOUS LISTINGS

LOUISVILLE. *Camp Tall Trees*, 2321 Carolina Ave., 40205. Tel: 502-454-0088.

Cathedral Heritage Foundation, Inc., 429 W. Muhammad Ali Blvd. #100, 40202-2334. Tel: 502-583-3100; Fax: 502-583-8524.
Web site: www.cathedral-heritage.org
Michelle Staggs Doninger, Exec. Dir.

Catholic Health Initiatives, 2120 Newburg Rd., Ste. 300, 40205. Tel: 502-458-0045; Fax: 502-549-7947.
Web site: www.catholichealthinit.org
Kevin E. Lofton, Group Pres.

Franciscan Shelter House, 748 S. Preston St., 40203. Tel: 502-589-0140.

Mass of the Air, 508 Breckenridge Ln., 40207. Tel: 502-893-5120; Fax: 502-895-4535.

Our Lady's Rosary Makers, 4611 Poplar Level Rd., P.O. Box 37080, 40233. Tel: 502-968-1434. Michael Ford, Gen. Mgr.; Rev. Edwin J. Scherzer, Chap.

Perpetual Eucharistic Adoration, P.O. Box 39191, 40233-9191. Tel: 502-637-5309; 549-3757; Fax: 502-549-7258. Rev. Lawrence H. Lindle, Spiritual Dir.

PROJECT AIMM, 1850 Bluegrass Ave., 40215. Tel: 502-361-5475; Fax: 502-361-5475.
E-mail: lsiers6720@aol.com
Sr. Lucianne Siers, O.P., Exec. Dir.

Publication: "The Record", Maloney Center, 1200 S. Shelby St., 40203-2600. Tel: 502-636-0296; Fax: 502-636-2379.
E-mail: record@archlou.org
Official newspaper of the Archdiocese of Louisville (Weekly).
Office: Archdiocesan Communications Center. Joseph E. Duerr, Editor & Gen. Mgr.

St. Patrick School Foundation, Inc., 1000 N. Beckley Station Rd., 40245. Tel: 502-244-7083. Daniel Ash, Chm.

Ursuline Campus Schools, Inc., 3105 Lexington Rd., 40206. Tel: 502-896-3910; Fax: 502-895-0989.
E-mail: ucs@ucschools.com
Web site: www.ucschools.com
Sponsored by Ursuline Sisters.

Ursuline Society and Academy of Education, 3105 Lexington Rd., 40206. Tel: 502-897-1811; Fax: 502-896-3913.
E-mail: webmaster@ursulineslou.org
Web site: www.ursulineslou.org

BARDSTOWN. *Flaget Healthcare, Inc.*, 201 Cathedral Manor, 40004. Tel: 502-348-3923; Fax: 502-349-4643.
E-mail: flaget.com
Bruce Klockars, Interim Pres. & CEO.

LEBANON. *The Laura*, 1995 Sam Browning Rd., 40033. Tel: 270-692-1790.
E-mail: thelaura@kyol.net

LORETTO. *Holy Cross Cemetery Trust, Inc.*, 7945 Loretto Rd., 40037. Tel: 502-348-5404.

NAZARETH. *Nazareth Arts For Life, Inc.*, O'Connell Hall, P.O. Box 14, 40048. Tel: 502-348-1554; Fax: 502-348-1527.
E-mail: nazarts@scnazarethky.org
Web site: www.nazarethky.org/nazarts

Office of Congregational Advancement, P.O. Box 9, 40048. Tel: 502-348-1578; Fax: 502-348-1587.
E-mail: gatzscn@scnazarethky.org
Web site: www.scnazarethky.org
Sisters of Charity of Nazareth.

NERINX. *Sisters of Loretto Charitable Trust*, 515 Nerinx Rd., 40049-9999. Tel: 270-865-3414; Fax: 270-865-2200.
E-mail: maryswain@juno.com
Sr. Mary Swain, S.L., Treas.

NEW HAVEN. *Archdiocesan Marian Committee*, 8191 New Haven Rd., 40051-6030. Tel: 502-549-3757; Fax: 502-549-7258.
E-mail: icmary@couriernet.infi.net
Rev. Lawrence H. Lindle, Dir.

World Apostolate of Fatima (Blue Army), 8191 New Haven Rd., 40051-6030. Tel: 502-549-3757; Fax: 502-549-7258.
E-mail: icmary@couriernet.infi.net
Rev. Lawrence H. Lindle, Spiritual Dir.

Sacred Heart Apostolate, 8191 New Haven Rd., 40051-6030. Tel: 502-549-3757; Fax: 502-549-7258.
Rev. Lawrence H. Lindle, Dir.

NEW HOPE. *St. Martin De Porres Lay Dominican Community*, 40052. Tel: 270-325-3061; Fax: 270-325-3091. Rev. Ernest Schumacher, C.R., Chap.; Hugh Pimentel, T.O.P., Prior.

PLEASURE RIDGE PARK. *The Franciscan Foundation, Inc.*, 6901 Dixie Hwy., 40258.

RELIGIOUS INSTITUTES OF MEN REPRESENTED IN THE ARCHDIOCESE

For further details refer to the corresponding bracketed number in the Religious Institutes of Men or Women section.

[0200]—*Benedictine Monks.* (St. Meinrad Archabbey).—O.S.B.

[1350]—*Brothers of St. Francis Xavier.* (American Central Prov.).—C.F.X.

[0600]—*Brothers of the Congregation of Holy Cross.* (Midwest Prov.).—C.S.C.

[0270]—*Carmelite Fathers & Brothers.* (Pure Heart of Mary Prov.).—O.Carm.

[0350]—*Cistercians Order of the Strict Observance-Trappists.*—O.C.S.O.

[0820]—*Congregation of the Fathers of Mercy.*—C.P.M.

[1000]—*Congregation of the Passion.* (Holy Cross Prov.).—C.P.

[1080]—*Congregation of the Resurrection.* (Rome, Italy).—C.R.

[0480]—*Conventual Franciscans.* (Prov. of Our Lady of Consolation).—O.F.M.Conv.

[0520]—*Franciscan Friars.* (St. John the Baptist Prov.).—O.F.M.

[0690]—*Jesuit Fathers and Brothers.*—S.J.

[0430]—*Order of Preachers-Dominicans.* (St. Joseph Prov.).—O.P.

[0430]—*Orders of Preachers-Dominicans.* (Prov. of the Holy Name).—O.P.

[1200]—*Society of the Divine Savior.*—S.D.S.

[1060]—*Society of the Precious Blood.*—C.PP.S.

RELIGIOUS INSTITUTES OF WOMEN REPRESENTED IN THE ARCHDIOCESE

[0230]—*Benedictine Sisters of Pontifical Jurisdiction.*—O.S.B.

[2145]—*Congregation of Augustinian Sisters Servants of Jesus and Mary.*—O.S.A.

[3830-10]—*Congregation of Sisters of St. Joseph of Tipton.*—C.S.J.

[1920]—*Congregation of the Sisters of the Holy Cross.*—C.S.C.

[0420]—*Discalced Carmelite Nuns.*—O.C.D.

[1070-01]—*Dominican Sisters.*—O.P.

[1070-13]—*Dominican Sisters.*—O.P.

[1070-10]—*Dominican Sisters.*—O.P.

[1070-14]—*Dominican Sisters.*—O.P.

[2575]—*Institute of the Sisters of Mercy of the Americas.*—R.S.M.

[2340]—*Little Sisters of the Poor.*—L.S.P.

[2470]—*Maryknoll Sisters of St. Dominic.*—M.M.

[2490]—*Medical Mission Sisters.*—M.M.S.

[0670]—*Order of Trappistines.*—O.C.S.O.

[3130]—*Our Lady of Victory Missionary Sisters.*—O.L.V.M.

[2970]—*School Sisters of Notre Dame.*—S.S.N.D.

[3580]—*Servants of Mary.*—O.S.M.

[0440]—*Sisters of Charity of Cincinnati, OH.*—S.C.

[0500]—*Sisters of Charity of Nazareth.*—S.C.N.

[2360]—*Sisters of Loretto At the Foot of the Cross.*—S.L.

[3000]—*Sisters of Notre Dame de Namur.*—S.N.D.deN.

[3360]—*Sisters of Providence of Saint Mary-of-the-Woods, IN.* (St. Gabriel Prov.).—S.P.

[1540]—*Sisters of St. Francis.* (Clinton, IA).—O.S.F.

[1630]—*Sisters of St. Francis of Penance and Christian Charity.*—O.S.F.

[3830-13]—*Sisters of St. Joseph of Northwest Pennsylvania.*—S.S.J.

[1830]—*Sisters of the Good Shepherd.*—R.G.S.

[1960]—*Sisters of the Holy Family.*

[2150]—*Sisters, Servants of the Immaculate Heart of Mary.*—I.H.M.

[4120-03]—*Ursuline Nuns, of the Congregation of Paris.*—O.S.U.

[4120-05]—*Ursuline Sisters of Mt. St. Joseph.*—O.S.U.

ARCHDIOCESAN CEMETERIES

Offices for all cemeteries: 1600 Newburg Rd., Louisville, KY 40205; Mailing Address: P.O. Box 4096, Louisville, KY 40204. Tel: 502-451-7710; Fax: 502-456-9270.

LOUISVILLE. *Calvary*, 1600 Newburg Rd., 40205.
St. John, 2601 Duncan St., 40212.
St. Louis, 1215 Barret Ave., 40204.
St. Michael, 1153 Charles St., 40204.

NECROLOGY

† Clark, C. Thomas, (Retired). —Died May 21, 2000.
† Kelty, Charles J., (Retired). —Died Jan. 18, 2000.
† Meder, James R., (Retired). —Died July 23, 2000.
† Riede, Clifford A., (Retired). —Died June 18, 2000.
† Russell, Paul M., (Retired). —Died Jan. 30, 2000.

Diocese of Lubbock

Most Reverend

PLACIDO RODRIGUEZ, C.M.F.

Bishop of Lubbock; ordained May 23, 1968; consecrated December 13, 1983; installed Auxiliary Bishop of Chicago; appointed Second Bishop of Lubbock April 5, 1994; installed June 1, 1994. *Res., Catholic Center, P.O. Box 98700, Lubbock, TX, 79499-8700; Fax: 806-792-2953. E-mail address: prodriguez@catholiclubbock.org.*

Legal Title: Roman Catholic Diocese of Lubbock.

ESTABLISHED AND CREATED A DIOCESE, JUNE 17, 1983.

Square Miles 23,382.

Comprises the Counties of Bailey, Lamb, Hale, Floyd, Motley, Cottle, Cochran, Hockley, Lubbock, Crosby, Dickens, King, Yoakum, Terry, Lynn, Garza, Kent, Stonewall, Haskell, Gaines, Dawson, Borden, Scurry, Fisher and Jones.

The Catholic Center: P.O. Box 98700, Lubbock, TX, 79499-8700. Tel.: 806-792-3943; Fax: 806-792-8109.

Web site address: www.catholiclubbock.org

E-mail address: ooc@catholiclubbock.org

STATISTICAL OVERVIEW

Personnel	
Bishop	1
Priests: Diocesan Active in Diocese	28
Priests: Active Outside Diocese	2
Priests: Retired, Sick or Absent	6
Number of Diocesan Priests	36
Religious Priests in Diocese	9
Extern Priests in Diocese	5
Permanent Deacons in Diocese	49
Total Sisters	30
Parishes	
Parishes	34
With Resident Pastor:	
Resident Diocesan Priests	29
Resident Religious Priests	5
Missions	28
Pastoral Centers	1
Professional Ministry Personnel:	
Sisters	8
Lay Ministers	4
Welfare	
Catholic Hospitals	1
Total Assisted	223,400
Health Care Centers	35
Total Assisted	451,000
Other Institutions	1
Total Assisted	37,000
Educational	
Diocesan Students in Other Seminaries	12
Total Seminarians	12
Elementary Schools, Diocesan and Parish	2
Total Students	411
Catechesis/Religious Education:	
High School Students	5,768
Elementary Students	3,607
Total Students Under Catholic Instruction	9,798
Teachers in the Diocese:	
Lay Teachers	33
Vital Statistics	
Receptions into the Church:	
Infant Baptism Totals	2,064
Adult Baptism Totals	284
Received into Full Communion	142
First Communions	1,573
Confirmations	993
Marriages:	
Catholic	375
Interfaith	78
Total Marriages	453
Deaths	438
Total Catholic Population	55,701
Total Population	451,995

Former Bishops—Most Rev. MICHAEL J. SHEEHAN, S.T.L., J.C.D., ord. July 12, 1964; cons. and installed as the first Bishop of Lubbock, June 17, 1983; appt. Apostolic Administrator of Santa Fe, April 6, 1993; installed as the 11th Archbishop of Santa Fe, Sept. 21, 1993.

The Catholic Center—4620 Fourth, Lubbock, 79416., Mailing Address: P.O. Box 98700, Lubbock, 79499-8700. Tel: 806-792-3943; Fax: 806-792-8109; 792-2953 (Bishop's Office). Office Hours: Mon.-Fri. 8-5.

Chancellor—Rev. NICOLAS RENDON.

Moderator of the Curia—Rev. NICOLAS RENDON.

Bishop's Secretary—JUDY LEOS RODRIGUEZ.

Diocesan Tribunal—P.O. Box 98700, Lubbock, 79499-8700. Tel: 806-792-3943.

Officialis—Rev. Msgr. JOHN P. BELL, J.C.L.

Administrative Secretary—RITA ORTIZ.

Promoter of Justice—Rev. Msgr. ROLAND BUXKEMPER.

Defender of the Bond—Rev. EUGENE J. DRISCOLL.

Defender of the Bond-Appeal—Rev. EUGENE J. DRISCOLL.

Notaries—RITA ORTIZ; JUDY LEOS RODRIGUEZ; DORA FIERRO.

Presbyteral Council—Very Rev. BEN KASTEEL, V.G.; Rev. NICOLAS RENDON; Rev. Msgr. CURTIS T. HALFMANN; Revs. DAVID R. CRUZ; JAMES MCCARTNEY; MICHAEL MELCHER; REY SORGON, O.S.A.; GLENN ROSENDALE; MICHAEL O'DWYER, S.A.C.

College of Consultors—Very Rev. BEN KASTEEL, V.G.; Revs. NICOLAS RENDON; JAMES MCCARTNEY; DAVID R. CRUZ; MICHAEL MELCHER; REY SORGORN, O.S.A.; GLENN ROSENDALE; Rev. Msgr. CURTIS T. HALFMANN; Revs. JOHN CASEY, S.A.C.; MICHAEL O'DWYER, S.A.C.

Priests Personnel Board—Rev. NICOLAS RENDON; Most Rev. PLACIDO RODRIGUEZ, C.M.F.; Very Rev. BEN KASTEEL, V.G.; Rev. Msgr. CURTIS T. HALFMANN; Revs. ELBERT FADALLAN; GEORGE RONEY; Deacon CLARKE COCHRAN.

Vicars Forane—Vacant, Plainview Deanery; Vacant, Brownfield Deanery; Rev. MICHAEL J. MELCHER, Snyder Deanery, *St. Ann's Church, 104 New Braunfels St., Stamford, 79553.* Tel: 915-773-2659. Vacant, Lubbock Deanery.

Superintendent of Schools—ROBERTA MEYER, *P.O. Box 98700, Lubbock, 79499.* Mrs. CHRISTINE WANJURA, Prin., *Christ the King Elementary/Middle School, 4011 54th St., Lubbock, 79413.* Mrs. LYNNE WHITE-BROWN, Prin., *St. Joseph Elementary School, 20th & W. Division St., Slaton, 79364.*

Director of Youth—PAUL FLOREZ, *P.O. Box 98700, Lubbock, 79499.*

Campus Ministry, Texas Tech University—Sr. DIANA AKROUSH, O.S.F., *2305 Main St., Lubbock, 79401.* Tel: 806-762-5225.

Director of Scouting—Rev. THOMAS DIEBEL, *P.O. Box 10753, Lubbock, 79408.* Tel: 806-792-3943.

Priests' Retirement Board—Most Rev. PLACIDO RODRIGUEZ, C.M.F.; Rev. NICOLAS RENDON; Rev. Msgr. CURTIS HALFMANN; Rev. JOHN OHLIG; Ms. CELIDA HERNANDEZ; Revs. GERARD KENNEY; JAMES MCCARTNEY; LAWRENCE HEMP; Mr. SONNY GARZA; Mr. MARK WAGNON; Mr. DON MCCULLOUGH.

Diocesan Building Commission—Rev. BEN KASTEEL, V.G.; Mr. MARK CHAPMAN; JOHN CONNORS; PAUL MEYER; MAX GARZA; BOB PAIKOWSKI; Rev. Msgr. ROLAND BUXKEMPER; Mr. LYLE FETTERLY; Ms. CELIDA HERNANDEZ; Mr. PAUL MEYER; Mr. MARK ROBERTI; Mr. BILL HOGGE; Mr. JOSEPH RAPIER.

Diocesan Liturgical Commission—Mrs. GLENDA SHAMBURGER, Chm.; Most Rev. PLACIDO RODRIGUEZ, C.M.F., *P.O. Box 98700, Lubbock, 79499.* Tel: 806-792-3943. Very Rev. BEN KASTEEL, V.G., *4011 54th St., Lubbock, 79413.* Tel: 806-792-6168. STEPHEN JOHNS, Sec., *128 Bowie Lane, Levelland, 79336.* Tel: 806-894-9611, Ext. 2210. GLENDA SHAMBURGER, Chm., *P.O. Box 1350, Levelland, 79336.* Tel: 806-894-9611, Ext. 2239. Sr. CELINE THAMES, O.S.F., *St. Alice Convent, 1114 Houston, Plainview, 79072-5344.* Tel: 806-296-5426. Deacon JOE MARTINEZ, *1308 49th St., Lubbock, 79412.* Tel: 806-744-8817. Rev. MICHAEL O'DWYER, S.A.C., *St. Joseph's Church, 102 N. Ave. P, Lubbock, 79401.* Tel: 806-765-9935. Rev. MARTIN PINA, *P.O. Box 599, Lamesa, 79331.* Tel: 806-872-7100.

Office of Christian Formation—Ms. ALICIA ALVAREZ, *P.O. Box 98700, Lubbock, 79499.* Tel: 806-792-3943.

Delegate of Religious—Sr. MARY JANE ALANIZ, O.S.F., Pres., *St. Francis Convent, 4305 54th St., Lubbock, 79413.*

Catholic Family Service, Inc.—JEFF MALPIEDE, Dir., *102 Ave. J, Lubbock, 79401.* Tel: 806-765-8475.

Director of Hispanic Affairs—Catholic Center, P.O. Box 98700, Lubbock, 79499-8700. Tel: 806-792-3943.

Ecumenical Affairs—Vacant.

Diocesan Council of Catholic Women—Rev. GERARD KENNEY, Chap. MARCY DEMEL, Pres., *Rte. 1, Box 144, Sudan, 79371.*

Director of Vocations—Revs. RAYMUNDO MANRIQUEZ; REYNALDO REYES, Seminarian Recruitment; Rev. DAVID R. CRUZ, Seminarian Formation. Tel: 806-792-3943. Rev. GLENN ROSENDALE, Continuing Education for Priests, *P.O. Box 98700, Lubbock, 79499.* Tel: 806-792-3943.

Diocesan Attorney—MADISON SOWDER, *1703 Ave. K, Lubbock, 79401.* Tel: 806-763-0409.

Diocesan Health Coordinator—Vacant.

Propagation of the Faith—Rev. NICOLAS RENDON, *P.O. Box 98700, Lubbock, 79499-8100.* Tel: 806-792-3943.

Office of Peace & Justice—Vacant.

Catholic Campaign for Human Development—Deacon DARIO RENDON, *Catholic Family Service, Inc., 102 Ave. J, Lubbock, 79401.* Tel: 806-765-8475.

Director of the Permanent Diaconate—Deacon CLARKE E. COCHRAN, *P.O. Box 98700, Lubbock, 79499.* Tel: 806-792-3943.

Cursillo Movement—Vacant.

Newspaper—"South Plains Catholic"; Deacon LEROY BEHNKE, Exec. Dir., *P.O. Box 98700, Lubbock, 79499.* Tel: 806-792-3943.

Director of Communications—Deacon LEROY BEHNKE.

Office of Evangelization—Mr. PAUL KEY, *P.O. Box 98700, Lubbock, 79499.* Tel: 806-792-1105.

Director of Family Life—Deacon JESSIE ESQUIVEL, *P.O. Box 98700, Lubbock, 79499.* Tel: 806-792-3943.

Respect Life Office—LAWRENCE D'SOUZA, *P.O. Box 98700, Lubbock, 79499.* Tel: 806-792-3943.

Diocesan Rural Life Office—Deacon DARRIS LINDER, *1225 Division St., Slaton, 79364.*

CLERGY, PARISHES, MISSIONS AND PAROCHIAL SCHOOLS

CITY OF LUBBOCK
(Lubbock County)

1—CATHEDRAL CHRIST THE KING (1958), Very Rev. Ben Kasteel, V.G.; Rev. Raymundo Manriquez.
Res., 4011 54th St., 79413-4699. Tel: 806-792-6168; Fax: 806-792-1417.
School—Tel: 806-795-8283; Fax: 806-795-9715. Mrs. Christine Wanjura, Prin.
Lay Teachers 19; Students 259.
Middle School—Tel: 806-795-6477.
Lay Teachers 8; Students 58.
Catechesis/Religious Programs—Tel: 806-795-8283. Mrs. Roberta Meyer, D.R.E.
Students 344.

2—HOLY SPIRIT (1998), Rev. Eugene J. Driscoll.
Mailing Address: P.O. Box 53959, 79453. Tel: 806-698-6400.
Res., 98th St. & Frankford Ave., 79453. Tel: 806-698-6464.
Catechesis/Religious Programs—Students 120.

3—OUR LADY OF GRACE (1960) (Hispanic), Rev. Msgr. Antonio Gonzalez; Rev. Rudolf Crasta; Deacons Jesse Guerrero; Ernest Hernandez.
Res., 3111 Erskine St., 79415-1623. Tel: 806-763-4156; Fax: 806-763-2521.
Catechesis/Religious Programs—Tel: 806-763-8727. Sr. Vianney Martinez, O.S.F., D.R.E.
Students 463.

4—OUR LADY OF GUADALUPE (1980) (Mexican), Rev. James O'Connor.
Res., 52nd & Ave. L, P.O. Box 3947, 79452-3947. Tel: 806-763-0710; Fax: 806-741-1915. [CEM]
Catechesis/Religious Programs—Tel: 806-763-0732. Sr. Mechtilde Gogel, O.L.V.M., D.R.E.
Students 583.

5—ST. ELIZABETH UNIVERSITY PARISH (1935), Rev. Msgr. Timothy Schwertner; Rev. Jesse Cruz; Sr. Diana Akroush, O.S.F., Campus Ministry, Tel: 806-762-1672; Deacon Sid Little.
Res., 2305 Main St., 79401-2924. Tel: 806-762-5225; Fax: 806-741-1962.
Catechesis/Religious Programs—Tel: 806-747-2230. Pat Key, D.R.E.
Students 275.

6—ST. JOHN NEUMANN (1979), Rev. Msgr. Curtis T. Halfmann; Rev. Peter D'Sousa; Deacons Thomas F. McCarthy; Richard Wood; Kyle Broderson; Clarke Cochran.
Res., 5802 22nd, 79407-1721. Tel: 806-799-2649; Fax: 806-799-0037.
Catechesis/Religious Programs—Students 417.

7—ST. JOSEPH'S (1924) (Hispanic), Revs. Michael O'Dwyer, S.A.C.; Brendan J. Walsh, S.A.C.
Res., 102 N. Ave. P, 79401-1199. Tel: 806-765-9935; Fax: 806-740-0032.
Catechesis/Religious Programs—Tel: 806-763-9695. Sr. Martha Molohon, O.L.V.M., D.R.E.
Students 555.

8—ST. PATRICK (1960) (Spanish), Rev. Cornelio C. Ramirez, S.A.C.
Res., 1603 Cherry Ave., 79403-6099. Tel: 806-765-5123.
Catechesis/Religious Programs—Tel: 806-765-6979. D.R.E.: Dario Rendon; Stephanie Rendon.
Students 235.
Mission—New Deal, Lubbock Co., Our Lady Queen of Apostles, Main St. N., 79403. Tel: 806-765-5123. Deacon Daniel Castro.

9—ST. THERESA'S (1961) (Mexican American), Rev. Nicolas A. Rendon.
Res., 2202 Upland, Rte. 5, Box 285, 79407-9545. Tel: 806-795-2249.
Catechesis/Religious Programs—Nancy Sanchez, D.R.E.
Students 75.

OUTSIDE THE CITY OF LUBBOCK

Anson, Jones Co., St. Michael's (1960) (Mexican), Rev. John Cherolikal.
Res., 2010 County Rd. 477, 79501. Tel: 915-823-2777.
Catechesis/Religious Programs—D.R.E.: Mrs. Andrea Ramirez; Mrs. Sylvia Ruiz.
Students 144.
Mission—Hamlin, Jones Co., Holy Trinity, Hwy. 83, 79520.

Brownfield, Terry Co., St. Anthony's (1952) (Hispanic), Rev. Reynaldo Reyes.
Res., P.O. Box 671, 79316-0671. Tel: 806-637-6626; Fax: 806-637-6626.
Catechesis/Religious Programs—Jimmy Garza, D.R.E.
Students 284.
Mission—Ropesville, Hockley Co., San Francisco de Asis, P.O. Box 92, Ropesville, 79358.

Denver City, Yoakum Co., St. William (1955) (Hispanic), Rev. Andres Mendoza.
Res., 401 Mustang Ave., 79323-2749. Tel: 806-592-2063; Fax: 806-592-2239.
Catechesis/Religious Programs—D.R.E.: Lidia Ramirez; Alice Espinoza; Alice Gomez.
Students 520.
Mission—Plains, Yoakum Co., Sacred Heart, 1305 11th St., Plains, 79355. Tel: 806-456-7002; Fax: 806-592-3943.

Floydada, Floyd Co., St. Mary Magdalen (1928) (Hispanic), Rev. John Ohlig.
Res., 809 W. Ross, 79235. Tel: 806-983-5878; Fax: 806-983-2601. [JC]
Catechesis/Religious Programs—D.R.E.: Elida Garza; Ester Caballero.
Students 95.
Missions—Matador, Motley Co., Our Lady of Guadalupe, 701 Bundy St., Matador, 79244.; Paducah, Cottle Co., St. Elizabeth, Second St. & Clare St., Paducah, 79348. Tel: 806-492-3053.

Hale Center, Hale Co., St. Theresa's (1944) (Hispanic), Rev. David R. Cruz.
P.O. Box 528, 79041-0528. Tel: 806-839-2310; Fax: 806-285-2140.
Catechesis/Religious Programs—Tel: 806-839-9938.
Students 90.
Mission—Olton, Lamb Co., St. Peter, Apostle, (1958) P.O. Box 655, Olton, 79064. Tel: 806-285-2140; Fax: 806-285-2140.

Idalou, Lubbock Co., St. Philip Benizi (1979) (Spanish), Rev. Msgr. Roland Buxkemper; Deacon Urbano Rodriguez.
Res., Box 1337, 79329-1337. Tel: 806-892-2743.
Catechesis/Religious Programs—Students 236.
Mission—Lorenzo, Crosby Co., San Lorenzo. Jackson & Monroe.

Lamesa, Dawson Co., St. Margaret Mary (1929) (Hispanic),
Res., 908 S. 2nd St, P.O. Box 599, 79331-6104. Tel: 806-872-7100; Fax: 806-872-3630. [CEM]
Catechesis/Religious Programs—Tel: 806-872-7455. Miss Delfina Luna, D.R.E.
Students 485.
Mission—Lamesa, Dawson Co., Our Lady of Guadalupe, P.O.Box 599, 79331.

Levelland, Hockley Co., St. Michael's (1956), Rev. Glenn Rosendale.
Res., 316 E. Washington St., 79336-2611. Tel: 806-894-2268; Fax: 806-894-9348.
Catechesis/Religious Programs—Tel: 806-894-9880. Sr. Mildred Warminski, C.C.V.I., D.R.E.
Students 507.
Mission—Sundown, Hockley Co., San Isidro, 1306 S. Slaughter, P.O. Box 764, Sundown, 79372-0764.

Littlefield, Lamb Co., Sacred Heart (1921), Rev. Patrick Maher.
Res., Eighth & Sunset, P.O. Box 1347, 79339-4234. Tel: 806-385-6043. [CEM]
Catechesis/Religious Programs—Mary Jane Aguirre, D.R.E.
Students 190.

Morton, Cochran Co., St. Ann (1955), Rev. Ricardito P. Salditos (Philippines).
Res., 105 N.E. Eighth St., 79346-2719. Tel: 806-266-8693. [CEM]
Catechesis/Religious Programs—Tel: 806-266-5410. Alfred Franco, D.R.E.
Students 115.
Mission—Pep, Hockley Co., St. Philip Neri, Fm. Rd., #303, P.O. Box 395, Pep, 79353. Tel: 806-933-4355.

Muleshoe, Bailey Co., Immaculate Conception (1956), Rev. Joseph Augustine Chorikavunkal (India).
Res., R.R. 3, Box 247, 79347-2460. Tel: 806-272-4384; Fax: 806-272-4384. [CEM 2][JC]
Catechesis/Religious Programs—Tel: 806-272-4167. Andy Martinez, D.R.E.
Students 175.
Mission—Earth, Lamb Co., St. Mary Magdalen, c/o R.R.3 P.O. Box 247, Muleshoe, 79347.
Catechesis/Religious Programs—Irma Olvera, D.R.E.
Students 35.

O'Donnell, Lynn Co., St. Pius X (1959) (Hispanic), Rev. Rey N. Sorgon (Philippines).
Res., Rt. 1, Box 41-A, 79351. Tel: 806-428-3490; Fax: 806-428-3490. [CEM]
Catechesis/Religious Programs—Students 24.
Mission—Tahoka, Lynn Co., St. Jude, P.O. Box 128, Tahoka, 79373-0128. Tel: 806-998-4436.

Petersburg, Hale Co., Sacred Heart (1959), Rev. Louis R. Dussan, C.M.F. In res., Rev. Timothy E. Judd.
Mailing Address: P.O. Box 330, 79250-0330. Tel: 806-667-3763.
Res., R.R. 2, Box 159-A, Abernathy, 79311-6921. Tel: 806-298-4278.
Catechesis/Religious Programs—Tel: 806-667-3301. Mary Esther, D.R.E.
Students 80.
Mission—Abernathy, Hale Co., St. Isidore, 510 S. Ave. D, 79311. Deacon Juan Villanueva.
Mailing Address: RR 2, Box 159A, Abernathy, 79311.
Catechesis/Religious Programs—Tel: 806-298-4519. Connie Regna, D.R.E.
Students 123.

Plainview, Hale Co., St. Alice (1911), Rev. James McCartney.
Res., 1114 Houston St., 79072-7124. Tel: 806-293-1903.
Catechesis/Religious Programs—Tel: 806-293-2891. Sr. Lisa Taylor, O.S.F., D.R.E.
Students 200.
Mission—Lockney, Floyd Co., San Jose, 303 S.E. Fourth, Lockney, 79241. Tel: 806-652-2321. Sr. Sophie Bonelli, O.S.F., Pastoral Assoc.

Our Lady of Guadalupe (1946), Rev. Gerard J. Kenney.
Mailing Address: P.O. Box 1269, 79073-1269. Tel: 806-291-0195.
Church—211 W. Seventh St., 79072. Tel: 806-293-0085; Fax: 806-293-4507. [CEM]
Catechesis/Religious Programs—Tel: 806-293-0086. D.R.E.: Yolanda Gonzales, (Elementary); Armeldo Gonzales, (Junior High School & High School).
Students 520.

Sacred Heart (1964) (Hispanic), Rev. Elbert Fadallan.
Res. & Mailing Address—400 W. 29th St., 79072-2399. Tel: 806-296-2753; Fax: 806-296-6553.
Catechesis/Religious Programs—Tel: 806-296-6553.
Students 350.

Post, Garza Co., Holy Cross (1955), Rev. Malcolm Neyland, M.C.L., J.C.L.
Res., Box 190, 79356-0190. Tel: 806-495-2791. [JC]
Catechesis/Religious Programs—D.R.E.: Paula Valdez; Richard Flores.
Students 66.
Mission—Wilson, Lynn Co., Blessed Sacrament, P.O. Box 119, Wilson, 79381-0119.

Ralls, Crosby Co., St. Michael (1959) (Hispanic), Rev. Leonardo Pahamtang.
Mailing Address: P.O. Box 906, 79357-0906. Tel: 806-253-2008. [JC]
Catechesis/Religious Programs—Tel: 806-253-2242.
Students 98.
Mission—Crosbyton, Crosby Co., St. Joseph, P.O. Box 906, Ralls, 79357. Tel: 806-675-7017.

Rotan, Fisher Co., St. Joseph (1929), Rev. Johnrose H. Hayden; Deacon Saragosa DeLeon.
Res., 301 E. Lee, 79546-3011. Tel: 915-735-3285; Fax: 915-735-2181.
Catechesis/Religious Programs—Tel: 915-735-3051. D.R.E.: Rosemary Carrillo; Frances Zambrano.
Students 61.
Missions—Ranchito, Fisher Co., Sacred Heart. [CEM]
Aspermont, Stonewall Co., St. Mary.

Seminole, Gaines Co., St. James (1958), Rev. John Casey, S.A.C. (Ireland).
Res., P.O. Box 898, 79360-0898. Tel: 915-758-2371.
Catechesis/Religious Programs—D.R.E.: Maria Hernandez; Margie Martinez.
Students 233.

Mission—Seagraves, Gaines Co., St. Paul's, P.O. Box 1321, Seagraves, 79359-1321. Tel: 806-546-2950.

Shallowater, Lubbock Co., St. Phillip Benizi (1967) (Hispanic), Rev. Nicolas Rendon (Phillippines). Pastoral Assocs.: Deacons Nash Revilla; Leroy Behnke; Tommy Alvarado; Richard Flores.
Res., P.O. Box 39, 79363-0039. Tel: 806-832-5915; 832-4088. [JC]
Catechesis/Religious Programs—Tel: 806-832-5576; 997-5341. D.R.E.: Dora Garcia; Julia Escobedo.
Students 206.
Missions—Anton, Hockley Co., St. Anthony, (1966) P.O. Box 545, Anton, 79313. Tel: 806-997-5831; Carlisle, Lubbock Co., St. Theresa, Rte. 5, Box, Carlisle, 79407-9545. Tel: 806-795-2245. Rev. Aidan McGuire.

Slaton, Lubbock Co., Our Lady of Guadalupe (1952), Rev. Lawrence A. Hemp; Deacon Phillip Maldonado.
Res., 705 S. Fourth, 79363-5406. Tel: 806-828-5108 (Office). [JC]
Catechesis/Religious Programs—Tel: 806-828-4573. D.R.E.: Iris Garcia, (Elementary); David Martinez, (High School).
Students 162.

St. Joseph's (1912) (German), Rev. Lawrence A. Hemp.
Res., 205 S. 19th, 79364-3755. Tel: 806-828-3944; Fax: 806-828-3944. [JC]
School—20th W. Division, 79364. Tel: 806-828-6761; Fax: 806-828-5396. Lynne Brown, Prin.
Lay Teachers 14; Students 95.
Catechesis/Religious Programs—Students 41.

Snyder, Scurry Co., St. Elizabeth's (1952), Rev. Gerald Leatham.
Res., 3005 Ave. A, 79549-3909. Tel: 915-573-2590; Fax: 915-573-1553. [CEM]
Catechesis/Religious Programs—Tel: 915-573-8824. Chris Bane, D.R.E.
Students 75.
Mission—Hermeleigh, Scurry Co., St. John, Hwy. 84, 79549.

Our Lady of Guadalupe (1945) (Hispanic), Rev. Leo Moras.
Res., 1311 Ave. K, 79549-9533. Tel: 915-573-3866 (Office); 573-1569 (Res.). [CEM]
Catechesis/Religious Programs—Tel: 915-573-7142; Fax: 915-573-7142. D.R.E.: Maria Ramirez; Roberto Ramirez.
Students 170.

Spur, Dickens Co., St. Mary (1948), Rev. Joseph Ouseph Vazhupaclickal, S.A.C.
Res., Box 189, 79370-0189. Tel: 806—271-3161.
Mission—Jayton, Kent Co., Epiphany.

Stamford, Jones Co., St. Ann (1952), Rev. Michael Melcher.
Res., 104 New Braunfels, 79553-6415. Tel: 915-773-2659; Fax: 915-773-3622. [CEM]
Catechesis/Religious Programs—Students 140.
Mission—Haskell, Haskell Co., St. George, 901 N. 16th St., Haskell, 79521-3340. Tel: 817-864-3171.
Catechesis/Religious Programs—Students 95.

Wolfforth, St. Francis of Assisi Mission. See San Ramon, Woodrow for details.

Woodrow, Lubbock Co., San Ramon (1974), Rev. George Roney.
Church—15706 Loop 493, Lubbock, 79423. Tel: 806-863-2201.
Catechesis/Religious Programs—Tel: 806-863-3435.
Students 178.
Mission—Wolfforth, Lubbock Co., St. Francis of Assisi, P.O. Box 785, Wolfforth, 79382. Tel: 806-866-9007.

Special Assignment:
Reverend Fathers—
Diebel, Thomas, Dir. Scouting, P.O. Box 10753, Lubbock, TX 79408
Thekkedam, George, Pastoral Care, St. Mary's Hospital, 4000 24th St., Lubbock, TX 79410

On Duty Outside the Diocese:
Reverend Fathers—
Krisman, Ronald, Annunciation Catholic Church, P.O. Box 915887, Longwood, FL 32791-5887
Wanjura, Victor, St. Mark the Evangelist, 7501 Adelphi Rd., Hyattsville, MD 20783

Retired:
Reverend Monsignors—
Comiskey, James, 3815 50th, Ste. 70, Lubbock, TX 79413
Reverend Fathers—
Bach, James To Duc, c/o 7301 101 St. #207, Bloomington, MN 55438
Diebel, Thomas, Box 10753, Lubbock, TX 79408
Huber, Clarence, 5062 N. Franks Ln., Monticello, IN 47960
Judd, Timothy, Sacred Heart Mission, P.O. Box 530, Petersburg, TX 79250-0530
Vaze Parampil, Thomas, St. Thomas Priest Home, Desam P.O., Aluva-Kerala 683103, India

Permanent Deacons:
Acevedo, Miguel, (Retired), St. Mary Magdalen, Earth
Aguilar, Francisco, St. Jude, Tahoka
Almager, Ramon, St. James, Seminole
Alvarado, Tommy, St. Anthony, Anton
Barrera, Salome, Our Lady of Guadalupe, Snyder
Behnke, Leroy, St. Phillip Benizi, Shallowater
Brito, Benny, Our Lady of Grace, Lubbock
Broderson, Kyle, St. John Neumann, Lubbock
Bustamante, Juan, St. Ann, Stamford
Canale, Randy, Christ the King, Lubbock
Cantu, Agustin, Sacred Heart, Plainview
Castro, Daniel L., St. Patrick, Lubbock
Cavazos, Jesus Z., On Duty Outside the Diocese
Cochran, Clarke E., St. John Neumann, Lubbock
DeLeon, Saragosa, (Retired), St. Joseph, Rotan
Esquivel, Jessie, St. William, Denver City.
Estrada, Julian, St. George, Haskell
Flores, Antonio B., St. Michael's, Ralls
Flores, Richard, St. John Neumann, Lubbock
Franco, Alfredo, St. Ann, Morton
Garcia, Doroteo, Sacred Heart, Littlefield
Garcia, Pedro, St. Michael's, Ralls
Gracia, Pedro, St. Mary, Spur
Guerrero, Jesus, Our Lady of Grace, Lubbock
Hernandez, Ernesto, Our Lady of Grace, Lubbock
Jaime, Alfredo B., Our Lady of Grace, Lubbock
Juarez, Pedro, Sacred Heart, Littlefield
King, Edward, St. Michael, Levelland
Linder, Darris D., St. Joseph's, Slaton
Little, Sidney R., St. Elizabeth's, Lubbock
Maldonado, Phillip, Jr., Our Lady of Guadalupe, Slaton
Martinez, Joe, Our Lady of Guadalupe, Lubbock
Martinez, Nasario, (Retired), St. Mary's, Sudan
McCarthy, Thomas E., St. John Neumann, Lubbock
McDonald, Isaac, St. Michael, Levelland
Mireles, Ted, (Retired)
Ortegon, Frank, Our Lady of Guadalupe, Snyder
Peralez, Catarino, (Retired), St. Philip Benizi, Idalou
Ramirez, Robert, Our Lady of Guadalupe, Snyder
Rendon, Dario, (Retired), St. Patrick's, Lubbock
Revilla, Nash, St. Phillip Benizi, Shallowater
Richard, Joseph N., St. John Newmann, Lubbock
Rodriguez, Simon, Christ the King, Lubbock
Rodriguez, Urbano, Outside the Diocese
Serna, Ray, Sacred Heart, Littlefield
Thompson, Richard, Sacred Heart, Littlefield
Valenzuela, Daniel, St. Margaret Mary, Lamesa
Vasquez, Enrique, St. Mary Magdalen, Floydada
Villanueva, Juan, St. Isidore, Abernathy
Wood, Richard, St. John Neumann, Lubbock

INSTITUTIONS LOCATED IN THE DIOCESE

[A] CHRISTIAN RENEWAL CENTERS

LUBBOCK. *Christian Renewal Center*, P.O. Box 98296, 79499-8296. Tel: 806-792-1105; Fax: 806-792-5613. Paul Key, Exec. Dir.; Blanche Arreola, Asst. Dir. Total Staff 5.
Office of Evangelization, P.O. Box 98296, 79499-8296. Tel: 806-792-1105; Fax: 806-792-5613. Paul Key, Dir. Evangelization. Total Staff 3.
Office for Cursillo Movement (Vacant), P.O. Box 98296, 79499-8296. Tel: 806-792-4308.

[B] GENERAL HOSPITALS

LUBBOCK. *St. Mary of the Plains Hospital*, 4000 24th St., 79410-1894. Tel: 806-796-6000; Fax: 806-796-6081
For a complete listing, refer to the Hospitals section.

[C] RETREAT HOUSES

SLATON. *Our Lady of Mercy Retreat Center*, P.O. Box 744, 19th & Division, 79364-0744. Tel: 806-828-6428; Fax: 806-828-3856.
E-mail: mercy@door.net
Web site: www.door.net/mercycenter
Rev. Msgr. Joseph W. James, Dir. Total in Residence 4; Total Staff 12.

[D] CONVENTS AND RESIDENCES FOR SISTERS

LUBBOCK. *Casa de San Jose*, 3817 23rd St., 79410. Tel: 806-796-6000; Fax: 806-796-6081. St. Mary of the Plains Hospital Convent. Sisters of St. Joseph of Orange, C.S.J. 2.
Casa Merced, Sisters of Mercy of the Americas, 4104 68th, 79413-5912. Tel: 806-791-4692.
E-mail: merced413@aol.com
Sisters of Mercy of the Americas 4.
Our Lady of Grace Convent, 3101 Erskine, 79415. Tel: 806-747-7472. Missionary Catechists of the Sacred Hearts of Jesus and Mary 3.
St. Francis Mission Community Central House (1981), St. Francis Convent, 4305 54th St., 79413-4617. Tel: 806-793-9859; Fax: 806-799-0689.
E-mail: franciscans@door.net
St. Francis Mission Community 7.
St. Joseph Convent, 1602 First St., 79401. Tel: 806-763-9695. Missionary Sisters of Our Lady of Victory 2.
St. Mary Convent, 3820 24th St., 79410. Tel: 806-725-6000.
E-mail: colivier@covhs.org
St. Mary of the Plains Hospital Convent. Sisters of St. Joseph of Orange, C.S.J. 3.
Sisters of St. Francis, Millvale, PA, 2706 Genoa Ave., K1, 79407. Tel: 806-793-0331. Sisters 2.

LEVELLAND. *Sisters of Charity of the Incarnate Word*, 320 E. Washington, 79336. Tel: 806-894-3424; Fax: 806-894-9348.
E-mail: mwarminski@juno.com

PLAINVIEW. *St. Alice Convent*, 1114 Houston, 79072. Tel: 806-296-5426; Fax: 806-296-5426. St. Francis Mission Community Sisters 3; Novices 1; Postulants 1.

[E] MISCELLANEOUS LISTINGS

LUBBOCK. *Catholic Foundation of the Diocese of Lubbock, Inc.*, P.O. Box 98700, 79499-8700. Tel: 806-792-3943; Fax: 806-792-2953.
E-mail: mroberti@catholiclubbock.org
Web site: www.catholiclubbock.org
Christ the King Cathedral School Foundation, 4011 54th St., 79413. Tel: 806-795-6477; Fax: 806-795-9715.
E-mail: ccason@CTKCathederal.org
Web site: www.CTKCathederal.org
Art Chavez, Chm. Total Staff 16.

RELIGIOUS INSTITUTES OF WOMEN REPRESENTED IN THE DIOCESE

For further details refer to the corresponding bracketed number in the Religious Institutes of Men or Women section.

[0460]—*Congregation of the Sisters of Charity of the Incarnate Word.*—C.C.V.I.
[]—*Dominican Sisters.*—O.P.
[2700]—*Missionary Cathechists of the Sacred Hearts of Jesus and Mary.*—M.C.SS.CC.J.M.
[3130]—*Our Lady of Victory Missionary Sisters.*—O.L.V.M.
[]—*St. Francis Mission Community.* (Amarillo, TX).—O.S.F.
[2575]—*Sisters of Mercy of the Americas.*—R.S.M.
[1620]—*Sisters of Saint Francis of Millvale, PA.*—O.S.F.
[3830]—*Sisters of St. Joseph of Orange.*—C.S.J.

NECROLOGY

† Del Rio, Oscar, Anson, TX St. Michael. —Died Sept. 10, 2000.
† Furlong, James, Chap., Lubbock, TX St. Mary's Hospital. —Died Aug. 2, 2000.

Diocese of Madison

(Dioecesis Madisonensis)

Most Reverend

WILLIAM H. BULLOCK, D.D., ED.S.

Bishop of Madison; ordained June 7, 1952; appointed Auxiliary Bishop of St. Paul and Minneapolis and Titular Bishop of Natchez June 3, 1980; consecrated August 12, 1980; appointed Bishop of Des Moines February 10, 1987; installed April 2, 1987; appointed Bishop of Madison April 13, 1993; installed June 14, 1993.

Most Reverend

GEORGE O. WIRZ, D.D., S.T.L.

Auxiliary Bishop of Madison and Titular Bishop of Municipa; ordained May 31, 1952; appointed December 20, 1977; consecrated March 9, 1978. *Chancery: Bishop O'Connor Catholic Pastoral Center, 3577 High Point Rd., P.O. Box 44983, Madison, WI, 53744-4983.*

ESTABLISHED 1946.

Square Miles 8,070.

Corporate Title: "Roman Catholic Diocese of Madison."

Comprises the Counties of Columbia, Dane, Grant, Green, Green Lake, Iowa, Jefferson, Lafayette, Marquette, Rock and Sauk in the State of Wisconsin.

For legal titles of parishes and diocesan institutions, consult the Chancery.

Chancery: Bishop O'Connor Catholic Pastoral Center, 3577 High Point Rd., P.O. Box 44983, Madison, WI, 53744-4983. Tel.: 608-821-3000; Fax: 608-821-3013.

Web site address: www.madisondiocese.org

E-mail address: diocese@madisondiocese.org

STATISTICAL OVERVIEW

Personnel	
Bishop	1
Auxiliary Bishops	1
Priests: Diocesan Active in Diocese	108
Priests: Active Outside Diocese	3
Priests: Retired, Sick or Absent	40
Number of Diocesan Priests	151
Religious Priests in Diocese	13
Extern Priests in Diocese	6
Ordinations:	
Diocesan Priests	5
Transitional Deacons	3
Permanent Deacons in Diocese	5
Total Brothers	7
Total Sisters	321
Parishes	
Parishes	137
With Resident Pastor:	
Resident Diocesan Priests	97
Resident Religious Priests	2
Without Resident Pastor:	
Administered by Priests	38
Professional Ministry Personnel:	
Sisters	37
Lay Ministers	151
Welfare	
Catholic Hospitals	4
Total Assisted	288,750
Health Care Centers	2
Total Assisted	346
Homes for the Aged	5
Total Assisted	605
Day Care and Extended Day Care Centers	29
Total Assisted	2,685
Special Centers for Social Services	7
Total Assisted	30,250
Residential Care of Disabled	1
Total Assisted	425
Educational	
Diocesan Students in Other Seminaries	19
Total Seminarians	19
Colleges and Universities	1
Total Students	1,909
High Schools, Private	1
Total Students	639
Elementary Schools, Diocesan and Parish	44
Total Students	7,015
Elementary Schools, Private	1
Total Students	281
Catechesis/Religious Education:	
High School Students	8,961
Elementary Students	15,524
Total Students Under Catholic Instruction	34,348
Teachers in the Diocese:	
Brothers	2
Sisters	31
Lay Teachers	559
Vital Statistics	
Receptions into the Church:	
Infant Baptism Totals	3,359
Adult Baptism Totals	586
First Communions	3,035
Confirmations	2,642
Marriages:	
Catholic	746
Interfaith	467
Total Marriages	1,213
Deaths	1,707
Total Catholic Population	264,536
Total Population	903,212

Former Bishops—Most Rev. WILLIAM P. O'CONNOR, D.D., Ph.D., ord. March 10, 1912; appt. Bishop of Superior, Dec. 31, 1941; cons. March 7, 1942; transferred as first Bishop of Madison, Feb. 22, 1946; resigned Feb. 22, 1967; died July 13, 1973.—Most Rev. CLETUS F. O'DONNELL, D.D., J.C.D., ord. May 3, 1941; appt. Titular Bishop of Abrittum and Auxiliary of Chicago, Oct. 26, 1960; cons. Dec. 21, 1960; promoted to Bishop of Madison, Feb. 22, 1967; resigned April 18, 1992; died Aug. 31, 1992.

Vicar-General—Most Rev. GEORGE O. WIRZ, D.D., S.T.L.; Rev. Msgr. PAUL J. SWAIN, J.D.

Chancery—Bishop O'Connor Catholic Pastoral Center, 3577 High Point Rd., P.O. Box 44983, Madison, 53744-4983. Office Hours: Mon.-Fri. 8-4:30.

Moderator of the Curia—Rev. JOHN G. STILLMANK, S.T.L.

Chancellor—Rev. Msgr. JOSEPH P. HIGGINS, S.T.L.

Director of Finance—GREGORY J. KELLER. Tel: 608-821-3025.

Diocesan Tribunal—Bishop O'Connor Catholic Pastoral Center, 3577 High Point Rd., P.O. Box 44983, Madison, 53744-4983. Tel: 608-821-3060; Fax: 608-821-3067.

Judicial Vicar—Rev. MICHAEL E. HIPPEE, J.C.L.

Director of the Tribunal—Vacant.

Judges—Rev. JAMES W. HINNEN, J.C.L.; Rev. Msgr. MICHAEL E. HIPPEE, J.C.L.

Defender of the Bond—Vacant.

Auditor/Advocate—Vacant.

Notary—Rev. BERNARD H. DEITELHOFF; SUSAN STACK; HOWARD KMAK.

Diocesan Consultors—Most Rev. GEORGE O. WIRZ; Rev. Msgr. JOSEPH P. HIGGINS, Sec.; Rev. Msgr. PAUL J. SWAIN; Rev. Msgr. DANIEL T. GANSHERT; Rev. Msgr. JAMES L. GUNN; Revs. JOHN H. HEDRICK; DAVID H. RUNDE; JOHN G. STILLMANK.

Presbyteral Council—Most Rev. WILLIAM H. BULLOCK, Pres.; Most Rev. GEORGE O. WIRZ, Ex Officio. Elected: Revs. JOHN R. AUBY; ARTHUR R. KOTH; DAVID H. RUNDE; JOHN H. HEDRICK, Chm. KENNETH J. KLINK; THOMAS P. MARR; STEPHEN J. UMHOEFER; RONALD G. RANK; O. CHARLES SCHLUTER; GARY L. KRAHENBUHL; ROGER G. NILLES; DAVID W. TIMMERMAN; STANLEY DRONGOWSKI, O.P. Appointed: Rev. Msgr. RAYMOND E. KLAAS, P.A.; Rev. Msgr. MICHAEL L. BURKE; Rev. Msgr. DANIEL T. GANSHERT; Rev. Msgr. JOSEPH P. HIGGINS; Rev. THOMAS M. SEGERSON; Rev. Msgr. PAUL J. SWAIN; Rev. JOHN G. STILLMANK.

Personnel Board—Revs. JOHN M. MEINHOLZ; JOHN L. URBAN; THOMAS R. DOHENY; LAWRENCE M. BAKKE; DOUGLAS L. DUSHACK; Rev. Msgr. RAYMOND N. KERTZ; Rev. Msgr. PAUL J. SWAIN.

Vicars for Religious—Rev. DANIEL T. GANSHERT, *222 W. Main St., Madison, 53703-3197.* Tel: 608-257-5000. Sr. LUCILLE MARIE FROST, O.P., *1000 Edgewood College Dr., Madison, 53711.*

Deaneries—Rev. RAYMOND J. DISCHLER, Columbia Deanery; Rev. DAVID H. RUNDE, East Dane Deanery; Rev. Msgr. THOMAS F. BAXTER, Grant Deanery; Rev. HENRY N. KALSCHEUER, Iowa Deanery; Rev. THOMAS P. MARR, Jefferson Deanery; Rev. GEORGE M. HASTRICH, Lafayette Deanery; Rev. Msgr. KENNETH J. FIEDLER, Madison Deanery; Rev. DALE W. GRUBBA, Marquette-Green Lake Deanery; Rev. Msgr. RAYMOND N. KERTZ, Rock-Green Deanery; Rev. GERALD P. VOSEN, Sauk Deanery; Rev. Msgr. DELBERT L. SCHMELZER, West Dane Deanery.

Diocesan Offices and Directors

Apostleship of Prayer—Rev. JOSEPH L. HENRY, *432 Maxwell St., Baraboo, 53913.*

Apostolate to the Handicapped—Rev. THOMAS F. CAMPION, *P.O. Box 443, Monroe, 53566.* Tel: 608-324-1000.

Apostolate to the Deaf—PATRICIA DYRESON, *St. Joseph Church, 1905 Beltline Hwy., Madison, 53713.* Tel: 608-278-1980.

Archives—Rev. JOHN G. STILLMANK, Archivist; CARRIE BOHMAN, Asst. Archivist, *Bishop O'Connor Catholic Pastoral Center, 3577 High Point Rd., P.O. Box 44983, Madison, 53744-4983.* Tel: 608-821-3140; Fax: 608-821-3013.

Boy Scouts—Rev. BRUCE M. HENNINGTON, *1550 Farnham St., Columbus, 53925-1861.* Tel: 920-623-3753.

Building Commission—Rev. Msgr. DANIEL T. GANSHERT, Chm.; Rev. Msgr. MICHAEL E. HIPPEE; Rev. Msgr. RAYMOND N. KERTZ; Rev. Msgr. DUANE R. MOELLENBERNDT; Rev. Msgr. DELBERT L. SCHMELZER; Dr. PATRICK GORMAN; Mr. PAUL BROWN; Mr. ARTHUR MCCLURE; Mr. TONY PAWLOWSKY.

Camp Gray—PHILIP C. DELONG, Dir., *E10213 Shady Lane Rd., Reedsburg, 53959.* Tel: 608-356-8200.

Catholic Relief Services—Rev. Msgr. PAUL J. SWAIN.

Cemeteries—THOMAS B. HANLON, JR., Diocesan Dir., Central Office: *2705 Regent St., Madison, 53705.* Tel: 608-238-5561.

Charities—*Catholic Charities of the Diocese of Madison, Inc.*—*Bishop O'Connor Catholic Pastoral Center, 3577 High Point Rd., P.O. Box 46550, Madison, 53744-6550.* Tel: 608-821-3100. BRIAN CAIN, Dir., . Fax: 608-821-3125., *Madison District Office, 30 S. Franklin St., Madison, 53703.* Tel: 608-256-2358., *Beloit District Office, 3311 Prairie Ave., Beloit, 53511.* Tel: 608-365-3665., *Janesville District Office, 2020 E. Milwaukee St., Ste. 208, Janesville, 53545.* Tel: 608-752-4906.

Office for the Continuing Education of Priests—Most Rev. GEORGE O. WIRZ, *Bishop O'Connor Catholic Pastoral Center, 3577 High Point Rd., P.O. Box 44983, Madison, 53744-4983.* Tel: 608-821-3000.

Education—Mr. MICHAEL J. NACHMAN, Dir., Religious Educ., *Bishop O'Connor Catholic Pastoral Center, 3577 High Point Rd., P.O. Box 44983, Madison, 53744-4983.* Tel: 608-821-3160. JACK MCBRIDE, Assoc. Dir., Adult & Special Educ. BEN WIESSE, Assoc. Dir., Youth Ministries & Child Catechetics; JAMES R. SILVER, Supt., Schools. Tel: 608-821-3180. JUDY L. PEPPARD, Asst. Supt., *Bishop O'Connor Catholic Pastoral Center, 3577 High Point Rd., P.O. Box 44983, Madison, 53744-4983.*

Saint Raphael Society Clergy Retirement Plan—Rev. Msgr. PAUL J. SWAIN, *Bishop O'Connor Catholic Pastoral Center, 3577 High Point Rd., P.O. Box 44983, Madison, 53744-4983.* Tel: 608-821-3015.

Confraternity of the Blessed Sacrament—Rev. Msgr. JOSEPH HENRY, Dir., *1414 Jefferson St., Baraboo, 53913.* Tel: 608-356-4838.

Council of Catholic Women—Rev. DUANE R. MOELLENBERNDT, Moderator, *Sacred Hearts of Jesus & Mary, 221 Columbus St., Sun Prairie, 53590-2297.* Tel: 608-837-7381. Rev. LORIN M. BOWENS, Co-Moderator, *St. Boniface Parish, P.O. Box 60, Lime Ridge, 53942.* Tel: 608-986-2101.

Director of Communications—WILLIAM K. BROPHY. Tel: 608-821-3033.

Holy Childhood, Pontifical Association—Rev. Msgr. DELBERT L. SCHMELZER, Dir., *Bishop O'Connor Catholic Pastoral Center, 3577 High Point Rd., P.O. Box 44983, Madison, 53744-4983.* Tel: 608-821-3052.

Information—Rev. Msgr. PAUL J. SWAIN, Dir., *P.O. Box 44983, Madison, 53744-4983.*

Office of Worship—PATRICK GORMAN, Ph.D., *Bishop O'Connor Catholic Pastoral Center, 3577 High Point Rd., P.O. Box 44983, Madison, 53744-4983.* Tel: 608-821-3080.

Office of Family Ministry—Mr. MICHAEL NACHMAN, Dir. BEVERLY HARTBERG, Assoc. Dir., *Bishop O'Connor Catholic Pastoral Center, 3577 High Point Rd., P.O. Box 44983, Madison, 53744-4983.* Tel: 608-821-3168.

Office for Justice and Peace—J. MARK BRINKMOELLER, Dir., *Bishop O'Connor Catholic Pastoral Center, 3577 High Point Rd., P.O. Box 44983, Madison, 53744-4983.* Tel: 608-821-3086.

Newman Apostolate—Madison: Rev. STEVEN J. KORTENDICK, Dir., *St. Paul Univ. Catholic Center, 723 State St., Madison, 53703.* Tel: 608-258-3140. Platteville: Rev. JAMES H. MURPHY, *St. Augustine Newman Center, 135 S. Hickory St., Platteville, 53818.* Tel: 608-348-7530.

Newspaper—*"Catholic Herald, Madison Edition"*, MARY UHLER, Editor, *Bishop O'Connor Catholic Pastoral Center, 3577 High Point Rd., P.O. Box 44983, Madison, 53744-4983.* Tel: 608-821-3070.

Priests' Eucharistic League—Rev. Msgr. JOSEPH HENRY, Dir., *1414 Jefferson St., Baraboo, 53913.* Tel: 608-356-4838.

Office of Hispanic Ministry—Sr. TERESA ANN WOLF, O.S.B., Dir., *Bishop O'Connor Catholic Pastoral Center, 3577 High Point Rd., P.O. Box 44983, Madison, 53744-4983.* Tel: 608-821-3092.

Centro Pastoral Guadalupano—ROMILIA SCHLUETER, Coord., *1862 Beld St., Madison, 53725-9226.* Tel: 608-255-8471. *Our Lady of Guadalupe Migrant Center, Endeavor, and Queen of Americas Migrant Center, Cambria.*

Office of Pastoral Services—KATE WISKUS, Dir., *Bishop O'Connor Catholic Pastoral Center, 3577 High Point Rd., P.O. Box 44983, Madison, 53744-4983.* Tel: 608-821-3083.

Propagation of the Faith—Rev. Msgr. DELBERT L. SCHMELZER, Dir., *Bishop O'Connor Catholic Pastoral Center, 3577 High Point Rd., P.O. Box 44983, Madison, 53744-4983.* Tel: 608-821-3052.

St. Vincent de Paul Society—Rev. FRANCIS J. STEFFEN, *305 W. Main St., P.O. Box 429, Dickeyville, 53808-0429.* Tel: 608-568-7519.

Serra Clubs—Madison: Rev. NICHOLAS OKERE, Janesville: Rev. DELBERT D. KLINK, Beloit: Rev. GARY L. KRAHENBUHL.

Vigilance Council—The Very Rev. Deans.

Vocations—Rev. Msgr. PAUL J. SWAIN, Dir., *Bishop O'Connor Catholic Pastoral Center, 3577 High Point Rd., P.O. Box 44983, Madison, 53744-4983.* Tel: 608-821-3088.

Wisconsin Catholic Conference—JOHN HUEBSCHER, Exec. Sec., *131 W. Wilson St., Ste. 1105, Madison, 53703.* Tel: 608-257-0004.

Office of Human Resources—JOHN MILLER, Dir., *Bishop O'Connor Catholic Pastoral Center, 3577 High Point Rd., P.O. Box 44983, Madison, 53744-4983.* Tel: 608-821-3047.

CLERGY, PARISHES, MISSIONS AND PAROCHIAL SCHOOLS

CITY OF MADISON
(Dane County)

1—ST. RAPHAEL CATHEDRAL, Rev. Msgr. Daniel T. Ganshert. In res., Revs. Steven J. Kortendick; Robert Joseph Butz; Anthony Iheanacho.
Res., 222 W. Main St., 53703. Tel: 608-256-5614. [JC]

2—ST. BERNARD, Rev. Msgr. Michael E. Hippee.
Res., 2450 Atwood Ave., 53704. Tel: 608-249-9256; Fax: 608-244-3773. [JC]

3—BLESSED SACRAMENT, Revs. Stanley Drongowski, O.P.; Roman P. Shemayer, O.P. In res., Rev. Gregory J. Moore, O.P.
Res., 2131 Rowley Ave., 53705. Tel: 608-238-3471; Fax: 608-238-4220. [JC]
School—2112 Holister Ave., 53705. Tel: 608-233-6155.
Lay Teachers 19; Students 347.

4—HOLY REDEEMER, Rev. Lawrence M. Bakke.
Res., 120 W. Johnson St., 53703. Tel: 608-255-1658; Fax: 608-255-5386.

5—IMMACULATE HEART OF MARY, Rev. John M. Meinholz. In res., Rev. Thomas C. Manahan, S.J.
Res., 5101 Schofield Ave., 53716. Tel: 608-221-1521; Fax: 608-221-1794. [JC]
School—4913 Schofield Ave., 53716.
Lay Teachers 13; Students 164.

6—OUR LADY, QUEEN OF PEACE, Rev. Msgr. Kenneth J. Fiedler; Revs. Randy Timmerman; Todd Robert Van Natta; Sr. Susan M. Dubec, S.S.N.D., Pastoral Assoc.
Res. and Parish Center: 401 S. Owen Dr., 53711. Tel: 608-231-4600; Fax: 608-213-4606. [JC]
School—418 Holly Ave., 53711. Tel: 608-231-4580.
Lay Teachers 28; Students 481.

7—ST. DENNIS, Revs. Kent A. Schmitt; Jason Edward Hesseling.
Res., 313 Dempsey Rd., 53714. Tel: 608-246-5124; Fax: 608-246-5138. [JC]
School—Dominican Sisters Sinsinawa 4; Lay Teachers 14; Students 208.

8—ST. JAMES, Rev. Douglas L. Dushack.
Res., 1128 St. James Ct., 53715. Tel: 608-255-1656. [JC]
School—1204 St. James Ct., 53715. Tel: 608-256-3095; Fax: 608-256-6311.
Lay Teachers 17; Students 160.

9—SAINT JOSEPH, Rev. John R. Dowd.
Res., 1905 W. Beltline Hwy., 53713. Tel: 608-271-5771; Fax: 608-271-9366.

10—ST. MARIA GORETTI, Rev. Msgr. Michael L. Burke.
Res., 10 Maria Pl., 53711. Tel: 608-271-7421; Fax: 608-275-6621. [JC]
School—5405 Flad Ave., 53711. Tel: 608-271-7551; Fax: 608-271-7551.
Lay Teachers 12; Students 206.

11—ST. PATRICK, Rev. William J. Seipp.
Res., 404 E. Main St., 53703. Tel: 608-257-5000; Fax: 608-257-5565. [JC]

12—ST. PAUL UNIVERSITY PARISH, Revs. Steven J. Kortendick; Randy J. Timmerman; Faye A. Darnall, M.Div., Pastoral Assoc.; Steven W. Dressel, J.D., Dir. of Liturgical Ministries.
Office: 723 State St., 53703. Tel: 608-258-3140; Fax: 608-258-3141. [JC]

13—ST. PETER, Rev. Roger G. Nilles.
Res., 5001 N. Sherman Ave., 53704. Tel: 608-249-6651; Fax: 608-249-6651. [JC]

14—ST. THOMAS AQUINAS, Rev. Donald J. Murray; Sr. Georgeann Roudebush, C.S.A., Pastoral Assoc.
Res., 602 Everglade Dr., 53717. Tel: 608-833-2600; Fax: 608-833-1129. [JC]

OUTSIDE THE CITY OF MADISON

Albany, St. Patrick, Rev. Msgr. Elmer J. Dietzel.
Res., 1005 W. Second Ave., Brodhead, 53520. Tel: 608-897-2666. [CEM]

Argyle, Lafayette Co., St. Joseph, Rev. Msgr. George M. Hastrich; Rev. Bernard H. Deitelhoff.
Res., 313 N. Lafayette St., P.O. Box 76, 53504. Tel: 608-543-3631. [CEM]

Ashton, Dane Co., St. Peter's, Rev. Eugene F. Hollfelder.
Res., 7121 Co. Trunk K, Middleton, 53562. Tel: 608-831-4843. [CEM]
School—Tel: 608-831-4846.
Lay Teachers 4; Students 50.

Avoca, St. Joseph, Rev. Roger H. Taylor.
Res., 341 N. Wisonsin Ave., P.O. Box 35, Muscoda, 53573. Tel: 608-739-3391; Fax: 608-739-9195. [CEM]

Baraboo, Sauk Co., St. Joseph, Rev. Gerald P. Vosen.
Res., P.O. Box 70, 53913. Tel: 608-356-4773; Fax: 608-356-4024. [CEM]
School—Lay Teachers 11; Students 153.

Barneveld, Immaculate Conception, Rev. Donald F. Lange.
Res., 803 W. Main St., Ridgeway, 53582. Tel: 608-924-2441. [CEM]

Belleville, Dane Co., St. Mary of Lourdes, Rev. Kenneth J. Klink.
Res., 221 Frederick St., P.O. Box 349, 53508. Tel: 608-424-3681. [CEM]

Belmont, LaFayette Co., St. Philomena, Rev. Monte E. Robinson.
Res., 338 Chestnut St., Box 345, 53510. Tel: 608-762-5446.

Beloit, Rock Co.,

1—OUR LADY OF THE ASSUMPTION, Rev. Gary L. Krahenbuhl.
Res., 2222 Shopiere Rd., 53511. Tel: 608-362-9066; Fax: 608-368-2820. [JC]
School—Lay Teachers 15; Students 185.

2—ST. JUDE, Rev. William R. Connell.
Res., 747 Hackett St., 53511. Tel: 608-364-2820; Fax: 608-364-2822. [JC]
School—Brother Dutton School.
Lay Teachers 14; Students 161.

3—ST. PAUL. Closed 1988. For inquiries for parish records contact St. Thomas the Apostle, Beloit.

4—ST. THOMAS THE APOSTLE, Rev. Thomas R. Doheny.
Res., 822 E. Grand Ave., P.O. Box 933, 53512. Tel: 608-362-1034; Fax: 608-363-9931.

Benton, Lafayette Co., St. Patrick, Rev. Cyril O. Weisensel.
Res., P.O. Box 3, 53803. Tel: 608-759-2131. [CEM]

Berlin, Green Lake Co., St. Joseph, Rev. Jerome J. Maksvytis.
Res., 167 N. Wisconsin, 54923. Tel: 920-361-2354.
Church—246 E. Park Ave., 54923. Tel: 920-361-0453.
School—Consolidated School. See separate listing.

St. Michael, Rev. Jerome J. Maksvytis.
Res., 167 N. Wisconsin, 54923. Tel: 414-361-2354; Fax: 920-361-9781. [CEM]
School—Consolidated School. See separate listing.
St. Stanislaus, Rev. Jerome J. Maksvytis.
Res., 167 N. Wisconsin St., 54923. Tel: 920-361-2354; Fax: 920-361-9781. [CEM]
School—Consolidated School. See separate listing.

Blanchardville, Immaculate Conception, Rev. Randy J. Budnar.
Res., P.O. Box 37, Hollandale, 53544. Tel: 608-967-2344; Fax: 608-967-2344. [CEM]

Bloomington, Grant Co., St. Mary, Rev. Steven G. Steele.
Res., P.O. Box 35, 53804. Tel: 608-994-2526; Fax: 608-994-2530. [CEM 2]
School—Lay Teachers 6; Students 77.

Boscobel, Grant Co., Immaculate Conception, Rev. John L. Urban.
Res., 405 E. LeGrand St., 53805. Tel: 608-375-4257; Fax: 608-375-4256.

Briggsville, Marquette Co., St. Mary Help of Christians, Revs. John H. Hedrick; Donald Joseph Heiar, Jr.
Res., N565 Hwy. A, Box 127, 53920-0127. Tel: 608-981-2282.

Brodhead, Green Co., St. Rose, Rev. Msgr. Elmer J. Dietzel.
Res., 1005 W. Second Ave., 53520. Tel: 608-897-2666.

Buffalo, St. Andrew, Revs. John H. Hedrick; Donald Joseph Heiar, Jr.
Res., N565 Hwy. A, Box 127, Briggsville, 53920-0127. Tel: 608-981-2282.

Calamine, St. Michael, Rev. Monte E. Robinson.
Res., 338 Chestnut St., Box 345, Belmont, 53510. Tel: 608-762-5446. [CEM]

Cambridge, Dane Co., St. Pius X, Rev. William A. Nolan.
Res., 701 W. Water St., P.O. Box 110, 53523. Tel: 608-423-3015.

Cassville, Grant Co., St. Charles Borromeo, Rev. John Norder.
Res., 605 E. Dewey St., 53806. Tel: 608-725-5595; Fax: 608-725-2343. [CEM 2]
School—521 E. Dewey St., 53806. Tel: 608-725-5173; Fax: 608-725-5179.
School Sisters of St. Francis 1; Lay Teachers 8; Students 104.

Castle Rock, St. John Nepomucene, Rev. John L. Urban.
Res., 405 E. LeGrand St., Boscobel, 53805. Tel: 608-375-4257; Fax: 608-375-4256.

Clinton, Rock Co., St. Stephen, Rev. J. Thomas Fitzgerald.
Res., Box 399, 53525. Tel: 608-676-2241; Fax: 608-676-4981.

Clyde, St. Malachy, Rev. John R. Auby.
Res., P.O. Box 628, Spring Green, 53588. Tel: 608-588-2028. [CEM]
School—Lay Teachers 6; Students 67.

Columbus, Columbia Co., St. Jerome, Rev. Bruce M. Hennington.
Parish Office—1550 Farnham St., 53925. Tel: 920-623-3753; Fax: 920-623-1115.
Res., 329 Folsom St., 53925. Tel: 920-623-2720. [CEM]
School—Sisters 1; Lay Teachers 13; Students 154.

Cottage Grove, Dane Co., St. Patrick, Rev. David H. Runde.
Res., P.O. Box 400, 53527-0400. Tel: 608-251-7857; Fax: 608-839-3593.

Cross Plains, Dane Co., St. Francis Xavier, Rev. D. Stephen Smith.
Res., 2947 Thinnes St., P.O. Box 35, 53528. Tel: 608-798-3491; Fax: 608-798-2976.
School—Lay Teachers 14; Students 200.

Cuba City, Grant Co., St. Rose of Lima, Rev. David J. Flanagan.
Res., 519 W. Roosevelt, 53807. Tel: 608-744-2010; Fax: 608-744-3709. [CEM]
School—Dominican Sisters Sinsinawa, WI 1; Lay Teachers 9; Students 148.

Dane, Dane Co., St. Michael, Revs. Kevin D. Holmes; Basil C. Osuigwe (Nigeria).
Res., 53529. Tel: 608-849-5610; Fax: 608-850-5610. [CEM]
School—Lay Teachers 5; Students 36.

Darlington, Lafayette Co., Holy Rosary, Rev. Thomas L. Kelley.
Res., 104 E. Harriet St., P.O. Box 208, 53530. Tel: 608-776-2251. [CEM 2]
School—Lay Teachers 7; Students 60.

Dayton, St. James, Rev. Kenneth J. Klink.
Res., 221 Frederick St., P.O. Box 349, Belleville, 53508. Tel: 608-424-3681. [CEM]

De Forest, Dane Co., St. Olaf, Rev. Gary A. Wankerl.
Res., 623 Jefferson St., 53532. Tel: 608-846-3812.

Dickeyville, Grant Co., Holy Ghost, Rev. Francis J. Steffen.
Res., 305 W. Main St., 53808. Tel: 608-568-7519; Fax: 608-568-3872. [CEM]
School—Tel: 608-568-7790; Fax: 608-568-3872.
Lay Teachers 7; Students 129.

Dodgeville, Iowa Co., St. Joseph, Rev. Henry N. Kalscheuer.
Res., 310 S. Ellwood St., 53533-1799. Tel: 608-935-3392; Fax: 608-935-1722. [CEM 3]
School—305 E. Walnut St., 53533.
Lay Teachers 11; Students 201.

Doylestown, Columbia Co., St. Patrick, Rev. Donald J. Wiecki.
Res., N4085 Bruce St., P.O. Box 40, 53928. Tel: 920-992-3343; Fax: 920-992-3107. [CEM]

Durward's Glen, Columbia Co., St. Camillus, Rev. Louis Lussier, O.S.Cam.
Res., W. 11876 McLeish Rd., Baraboo, 53913. Tel: 608-356-8113. [CEM]

East Bristol, Dane Co., St. Joseph, Revs. Gary A. Wankerl, Admin.; Sebastian Igbokwe.
Res., 623 Jefferson St., DeForest, 53532. Tel: 608-846-3812. [CEM]

Edgerton, Rock Co., St. Joseph, Rev. William J. Hower.
Res., St. Joseph's Cir., P.O. Box 147, 53534. Tel: 608-884-3038; Fax: 608-884-3298. [CEM 2]

Elk Grove, St. Peter, Rev. James R. Lins.
Res., Rte. 1, Shullsburg, 53586. Tel: 608-776-2833. [CEM]

Evansville, Rock Co., St. Paul, Rev. Eric H. Nielsen.
Res., 35 Garfield Ave., 53536. Tel: 608-882-4138. [CEM]

Fennimore, Grant Co., St. Mary, Rev. George B. Horath.
Res., 930 Jefferson St., 53809. Tel: 608-822-6425. [CEM]

Footville, Rock Co., St. Augustine, Rev. Eric H. Nielsen.
Res., P.O. Box 325, 53537. Tel: 608-876-6251.

Fort Atkinson, Jefferson Co., St. Joseph, Rev. James G. Kuhn.
Res., 11 N. 3rd St., 53538. Tel: 920-563-3029; Fax: 920-563-3150. [CEM]
School—310 N. Main St., 53538. Mr. Leonard Bannon, Prin.
Lay Teachers 15; Students 110.

Glen Haven, St. Mary Help of Christians, Rev. John Norder.
Res., 605 E. Dewey St., Cassville, 53806. Tel: 608-725-5595; Fax: 608-725-2343. [CEM 2]
School—521 E. Dewey St., Cassville, 53806. Tel: 608-725-5173; Fax: 608-725-5179.
School Sisters of St. Francis 1; Lay Teachers 8; Students 104.

Gratiot, Lafayette Co., St. Joseph, Rev. Jerold F. Fitzpatrick.
Res., Box 37, 53541. Tel: 608-922-6456. [CEM]

Green Lake, Green Lake Co., Our Lady of the Lake, Rev. Philip J. Krogman.
Res., 530 Ruth St., P.O. Box 215, 54941. Tel: 920-294-6440; Fax: 920-294-6550.

Hazel Green, Grant Co., St. Francis de Sales, Rev. Cyril O. Weisensel.
Res., 2630 N. Main St., 53811-9681. Tel: 608-854-2392. [CEM]

Highland, Iowa Co., SS. Anthony and Philip, Rev. Kenneth J. Frisch.
Res., 726 Main St., P.O. Box 306, 53543. Tel: 608-929-7490; Fax: 608-929-7701. [CEM 2]

Hollandale, Iowa Co., St. Patrick, Rev. Randy J. Budnar.
Res., P.O. Box 37, 53544. Tel: 608-967-2344; Fax: 608-967-2344. [CEM]

Janesville, Rock Co.,

1—Nativity of St. Mary, Rev. Msgr. Raymond N. Kertz.
Res., 313 E. Wall St., 53545. Tel: 608-752-7861; Fax: 608-758-0720. [JC]
School—Sisters 1; Lay Teachers 12; Students 242.

2—St. John Vianney, Rev. Michael J. Doro.
Res., 1245 Clark St., 53545. Tel: 608-752-8708; Fax: 608-752-1970. [JC]
School—Lay Teachers 17; Students 240.

3—St. Patrick, Rev. J. Daryl Furlong.
Res., 315 Cherry St., 53545. Tel: 608-754-8193; Fax: 608-754-0357. [JC]
School—Lay Teachers 14; Students 118.

4—St. William, Rev. Delbert D. Klink.
Res., 1815 Ravine St., 53545. Tel: 608-755-5180; Fax: 608-755-5190. [JC]
School—1822 Ravine St., 53545.
Lay Teachers 9; Students 175.

Jefferson, Jefferson Co., St. John the Baptist, Rev. Terrence L. Connors.
Res., 214 N. Sanborn Ave., 53549. Tel: 920-674-2025; Fax: 920-674-2521. [CEM]
School—Lay Teachers 12; Students 129.
St. Lawrence, Rev. Thomas E. Gillespie.
Res., W. 4926 Hwy. 18, 53549. Tel: 920-674-3217. [CEM]

Johnson Creek, St. Mary Magdalene, Rev. John B. Walsh.
Res., 602 College St., P.O. Box 16, Lake Mills, 53551. Tel: 920-648-2468; Fax: 920-648-2468. [CEM]

Kieler, Grant Co., Immaculate Conception, Revs. Thomas J. Coyle; Casimir E. Chimeziri (Nigeria).
Res., Box 57, 53812. Tel: 608-568-7530. [CEM]
School—Lay Teachers 7; Students 79.

Kingston, St. Mary, Rev. Richard D. Lesniak.
Res., 45 St. Joseph St., P.O. Box 370, Markesan, 53946-0370. Tel: 414-398-3146. [CEM]

Lake Mills, Jefferson Co., St. Francis Xavier, Rev. John B. Walsh.
Res., 602 College St., P.O. Box 16, 53551. Tel: 920-648-2468; Fax: 920-648-2468.

Lancaster, Grant Co., St. Clement, Rev. Msgr. Thomas F. Baxter.
Res., 135 S. Washington St., 53813. Tel: 608-723-4990. [CEM 2]
School—Sisters 4; Lay Teachers 5; Students 103.

La Valle, Holy Family, Rev. Lorin M. Bowens.
Res., Lime Ridge, 53942. Tel: 608-986-2101. [CEM 2]

Lime Ridge, Sauk Co., St. Boniface, Rev. Lorin M. Bowens.
Res., 53942. Tel: 608-986-2101. [CEM 2]

Lodi, Columbia Co., St. Patrick, Rev. Kenneth E. Klubertanz.
Res., 515 Fair St., 53555. Tel: 608-592-4510; Fax: 608-592-2078. [CEM]

Loreto, St. Patrick, Rev. Michael A. Resop.
Res., 1240 Nachreiner Ave., Plain, 53577. Tel: 608-546-2482; Fax: 608-546-2616. [CEM 2]
School—Lay Teachers 9; Students 126.

McFarland, Dane Co., Christ the King, Rev. David W. Timmerman.
Res., 5211 Timber Ln., 53558-8609. Tel: 608-838-8776; Fax: 608-838-6449.

Markesan, Green Lake Co., St. Joseph, Rev. Richard D. Lesniak.
Res., 45 St. Joseph St., P.O. Box 370, 53946-0370. Tel: 414-398-3146.

Marshall, Dane Co., St. Mary's of the Nativity, Rev. Msgr. Raymond E. Klaas, P.A.
Res., P.O. Box 250, 53559-0250. Tel: 608-655-3708. [CEM]

Martinsville, Dane Co., St. Martin, Rev. Francis J. Schmidt.
Res., 5959 St. Martin Cir., Cross Plains, 53528-9312. Tel: 608-798-2815. [CEM]

Mazomanie, Dane Co., St. Barnabas, Rev. Kevin F. Dooley.
Res., 113 E. Division St., P.O. Box 68, 53560-0068. Tel: 608-795-2480. [CEM]

Merrimac, St. Mary, Health of the Sick, Rev. Louis Lussier, O.S.Cam.
Res., W. 11876 McLeish Rd., Baraboo, 53913. Tel: 608-356-8113. [CEM]

Middleton, Dane Co., St. Bernard, Rev. Msgr. Joseph P. Higgins. In res., Rev. Edward J. Erbe.
Res., 2015 Parmenter St., P.O. Box 620187, 53562-0187. Tel: 608-831-6531; Fax: 608-831-8101. [CEM]

Mill Creek, St. John the Baptist, Rev. Kevin F. Dooley.
Res., 113 E. Division St., P.O. Box 68, Mazomanie, 53560-0068. Tel: 608-795-2480. [CEM]

Milton, Rock Co., St. Mary, Rev. Msgr. James J. Uppena.
Res., 837 Parkview Dr., 53563. Tel: 608-868-3338; Fax: 608-868-3337. [CEM]

Mineral Point, Iowa Co., Congregation of St. Mary-St. Paul, Rev. James W. Hinnen.
Res., 224 Davis St., 53565. Tel: 608-987-2026. [JC 2]

Monroe, Green Co., St. Victor, Rev. Stephen J. Umhoefer.
Res., 1760 14th St., 53566. Tel: 608-325-9506; Fax: 608-325-3115. [CEM]
School—Lay Teachers 10; Students 79.

Montello, Marquette Co., St. John the Baptist, Rev. Richard M. Heilman.
Res., 277 E. Montello St., 53949. Tel: 608-297-2217; Fax: 608-297-8047. [CEM]

Montfort, Grant Co., St. Thomas, Rev. Kenneth J. Frisch.

Res., Box 68, 53569. Tel: 608-943-6944; Fax: 608-943-6944. [CEM]

Mount Hope, St. Lawrence O'Toole, Rev. George B. Horath.
Res., 930 Jefferson St., Fennimore, 53809. Tel: 608-822-6425. [CEM]

Mount Horeb, Dane Co., St. Ignatius, Rev. John G. Stillmank.
Res., 111 S. Sixth St., 53572. Tel: 608-437-5195; Fax: 608-437-7691. [CEM 2]

Muscoda, Grant Co., St. John the Baptist, Rev. Roger H. Taylor.
Res., 341 N. Wisconsin Ave., P.O. Box 35, 53573. Tel: 608-739-3391; Fax: 608-739-9195. [CEM]

Neshkoro, Marquette Co., St. James, Rev. Dale W. Grubba.
Res., 315 N. Main St., P.O. Box 48, 54960. Tel: 920-293-4211; Fax: 920-293-4370. [CEM]

Oregon, Dane Co., Holy Mother of Consolation, Rev. Anthony J. Schumacher.
Res., 651 N. Main St., 53575. Tel: 608-835-5763; Fax: 608-835-5764. [CEM]

Palmyra, Jefferson Co., St. Mary, Rev. Msgr. John H. Hebl.
Res., 919 W. Main St., P.O. Box P, 53156. Tel: 414-495-2395. [CEM]

Paoli, St. William, Rev. Msgr. Delbert L. Schmelzer.
Res., 301 W. Main St., Verona, 53593. Tel: 608-845-7323. [CEM]

Pardeeville, Columbia Co., St. Mary, Revs. John H. Hedrick; Donald Joseph Heiar, Jr.
Res., 318 S. Main St., 53954-0216. Tel: 608-429-3030. [CEM]
Education Center & Hall—Tel: 608-429-3129.

Patch Grove, St. John, Rev. Steven G. Steele.
Res., P.O. Box 35, Bloomington, 53804. Tel: 608-994-2526; Fax: 608-994-2530.
School—Lay Teachers 6; Students 77.

Perry, Holy Redeemer, Rev. John G. Stillmank.
Res., 111 S. Sixth St., Mount Horeb, 53572. Tel: 608-437-5195; Fax: 608-437-7691. [CEM 2]

Pine Bluff, Dane Co., St. Mary of Pine Bluff, Rev. Kevin W. Cassidy.
Res., 3673 Co. Trunk P, Cross Plains, 53528. Tel: 608-798-2111; Fax: 608-798-2112. [CEM]

Plain, Sauk Co., St. Luke, Rev. Michael A. Resop.
Res., 1240 Nachreiner Ave., 53577. Tel: 608-546-2482; Fax: 608-546-2616. [CEM 2]
School—Lay Teachers 9; Students 126.

Platteville, Grant Co., St. Mary, Rev. O. Charles Schluter.
Res., 130 W. Cedar St., 53818. Tel: 608-348-9735; Fax: 608-348-9920. [CEM]
School—Lay Teachers 9; Students 130.
St. Augustine University Parish, Rev. James H. Murphy.
Res., 135 S. Hickory St., 53818. Tel: 608-348-7530; Fax: 608-348-7530.

Portage, Columbia Co., St. Mary of the Immaculate Conception, Revs. John H. Hendrick; Donald Joseph Heiar, Jr.
Res., 307 W. Cook St., P.O. Box 216, 53901-0216. Tel: 608-742-6998; Fax: 608-747-1039. [CEM]
School—315 W. Cook St., 53901. Tel: 608-742-4998; Fax: 608-742-1039.
Lay Teachers 13; Students 153.

Poynette, Columbia Co., St. Thomas, Rev. Raymond J. Dischler.
Res., 655 S. Main, P.O. Box 310, 53955-0310. Tel: 608-635-4326; Fax: 608-635-8374.

Princeton, Green Lake Co., St. John the Baptist, Rev. Dale W. Grubba.
Res., 1211 W. Main, 54968. Tel: 920-295-6209; Fax: 920-295-0231. [CEM]
School—Lay Teachers 10; Students 91.

Reedsburg, Sauk Co., Sacred Heart, Rev. Thomas J. Monaghan.
Res., 624 N. Willow St., 53959. Tel: 608-524-2412; Fax: 608-524-3831. [CEM 3]
School—545 N. Oak St., 53959. Tel: 608-524-3611.
Lay Teachers 12; Students 210.

Ridgeway, Iowa Co., St. Bridget, Rev. Donald F. Lange.
Res., 803 W. Main, 53582. Tel: 608-924-2441. [CEM]

Rio, St. Joseph, Rev. Donald J. Wiecki.
Res., N4085 Bruce St., P.O. Box 40, Doylestown, 53928. Tel: 920-992-3343; Fax: 920-992-3107. [CEM]

Roxbury, Dane Co., St. Norbert, Rev. Laverne G. Meier.
Res., 8944 County Rd. Y, Sauk City, 53583-9510. Tel: 608-643-3661. [CEM]

Sauk City, Sauk Co., St. Aloysius, Revs. Kevin D. Holmes, Admin.; Basil C. Osuigwe (Nigeria).
Res., 115 Madison St., 53583. Tel: 608-643-2449; Fax: 608-643-2440. [CEM 2]
School—Tel: 608-643-6868.
Lay Teachers 8; Students 148.

Seymour, Lafayette Co., Our Lady of Hope, Rev. James R. Lins.
Res., Rte. 1, Shullsburg, 53586. Tel: 608-776-2833. [CEM]

Shullsburg, Lafayette Co., St. Matthew, Rev. James R. Lins.
Res., 344 Judgment St., 53586. Tel: 608-965-4518. [CEM 2]

Sinsinawa, Grant Co., St. Joseph, Revs. Thomas J. Coyle; Casimir E. Chimeziri.
Res., 780 Hwy. Z, Hazel Green, 53811. Tel: 608-748-4528. [CEM 2]
School—Lay Teachers 5; Students 69.

South Wayne, St. John, Rev. Jerold F. Fitzpatrick.
Res., Box 37, Gratiot, 53541. Tel: 608-922-6456. [CEM]

Spring Green, Sauk Co., St. John the Evangelist, Rev. John R. Auby.
Res., P.O. Box 628, 53588. Tel: 608-588-2028. [CEM]
School—Lay Teachers 6; Students 67.

Stoughton, Dane Co., St. Ann, Rev. Msgr. Gerard M. Healy; Sr. Mary Ann Schroedl, O.S.F., Pastoral Assoc.
Res., 320 N. Harrison St., 53589. Tel: 608-873-7633; Fax: 608-873-6425. [CEM]
School—Poor Sisters of Nazareth 2; Students 142.

Sullivan, Jefferson Co., St. Mary Help of Christians, Rev. Msgr. John H. Hebl.
Res., W. 856 Hwy. 18, 53178. Tel: 262-593-2250; Fax: 262-593-5450. [CEM]

Sun Prairie, Dane Co., Sacred Hearts of Jesus and Mary, Rev. Msgr. Duane R. Moellenberndt; Rev. Paul Ugochukwu Arinze; Sr. Anne Raymond Gasser, S.S.N.D., Pastoral Assoc.
Res., 221 Columbus St., 53590. Tel: 608-837-7381; Fax: 608-825-9585. [CEM]
School—Lay Teachers 28; Students 420.
St. Albert the Great, Rev. Michael C. Richel.
Res., 2420 St. Albert Dr., 53590. Tel: 608-837-3798; Fax: 608-837-8576.

Tennyson-Potosi, Grant Co., SS. Andrew and Thomas, Rev. Richard J. Leffler.
Res., 101 Church St., Potosi, 53820. Tel: 608-763-2671. [CEM 2]
School—100 Hwy. 61 N., P.O. Box 160, Potosi, 53820. Tel: 608-763-2120; Fax: 608-763-2120.
Lay Teachers 7; Students 81.

Truman, Immaculate Conception, Rev. Monte E. Robinson.
Res., 338 Chestnut St., Box 345, Belmont, 53510. Tel: 608-762-5446.

Verona, Dane Co., St. Andrew, Rev. Msgr. Delbert L. Schmelzer.
Res., 301 N. Main St., 53593. Tel: 608-845-7323.

Waterloo, Jefferson Co., St. Joseph, Rev. Ronald G. Rank.
Res., 205 W. Milwaukee Ave., 53594-1329. Tel: 920-478-2032. [CEM]
School—Lay Teachers 4; Students 85.

Watertown, Jefferson Co., St. Bernard, Rev. Thomas P. Marr.
Res., 114 S. Church St., 53094-4399. Tel: 920-261-5133; Fax: 920-261-8371. [CEM]
School—Sisters 2; Lay Teachers 14; Students 188.
St. Henry, Rev. Bernard E. Rott.
Res., 412 N. 4th St., 53094. Tel: 920-261-7273; Fax: 920-261-3681. [CEM]
School—300 Cady St., 53094. Tel: 920-261-2586.
Lay Teachers 10; Students 187.

Waunakee, Dane Co., St. John the Baptist, Revs. James L. Gunn; Eric Nielsen; Sanctus Kodilinye Ibe, Jr.
Res., 209 South St., 53597. Tel: 608-849-5121; Fax: 608-849-5866. [CEM]
School—Lay Teachers 18; Students 274.

Westfield, Westfield Co., Good Shepherd, Rev. Richard M. Heilman.
Res., 277 E. Montello St., Montello, 53949. Tel: 608-297-2217; Fax: 608-397-8047. [CEM]

Westport, Dane Co., St. Mary of the Lake, Rev. Daniel P. Finnane.
Res., 5460 Marylake Rd., Waunakee, 53597-9121. Tel: 608-849-4116. [CEM]

Wisconsin Dells, Columbia Co., St. Cecilia, Rev. Felix G. Oehrlein.
Res., 604 Oak St., P.O. Box 436, 53965. Tel: 608-254-8381; Fax: 608-254-8382. [CEM]

Yellowstone, St. Michael, Rev. Msgr. George M. Hastrich; Rev. Bernard H. Deitelhoff.
Res., 313 N. Lafayette St., P.O. Box 76, Argyle, 53504. Tel: 608-543-3631. [CEM]

Chaplains of Public Institutions

MADISON. *Columbia County Institution.* Attended from St. Mary's Church, Portage.
Dane County Institution. Attended from St. Andrew, Verona.
Grant County Institution. Attended from St. Clement Church, Lancaster.
Green County Institution. Attended from St. Victor Church, Monroe.
Iowa County Institution. Attended from St. Joseph Church, Dodgeville.
Madison-Meriter General Hospital. Vacant.
Mendota State Hospital. Vacant.
University Hospitals. Rev. Lawrence M. Bakke, Chap., 120 W. Johnson, 53703.

JANESVILLE. *Jefferson County Institution.* Attended from St. John the Baptist Church, Jefferson.
LaFayette County Institution. Attended from Holy Rosary Church, Darlington.
Mercy Hospital. Attended from Janesville Parishes, Janesville.
Rock County Institution. Attended from Janesville Parishes, Janesville.
Sauk County Institution. Attended from St. Boniface Church, Lime Ridge.
Wisconsin State School for the Blind. Attended from St. Patrick's Church, Janesville.

Military Chaplains:
Reverend Fathers—
Hughes, Robert W.
Klarer, Michael E.

Leave of Absence:
Reverend Fathers—
Clauder, J. Gibbs
Jiru, Richard A.

Absent on Sick Leave:
Reverend Fathers—
Adams, Archie H.
Doherty, Patrick J.
Dutchoff, C. Robert
Runde, Raymond E.
Sosinski, Thomas P.

Retired:
Reverend Monsignors—
DeBock, William A., Bishop O'Connor Catholic Pastoral Center, 3577 High Point Rd., P.O. Box 44983, Madison, WI 53744-4983
Doherty, Francis E., Rte. 3 W., 11031 Lakeview Dr., Lodi, WI 53555
Erbe, Edward J., 7419 Franklin Ave., Middleton, WI 53562
Henry, Joseph L., 1414 Jefferson St., Baraboo, WI 53913
Kramer, James G., Bishop O'Connor Catholic Pastoral Center, 3577 High Point Rd., P.O. Box 44983, Madison, WI 53744-4983
Niglis, Joseph C., 814 Jackson St., Stoughton, WI 53589
Stack, William E., 706 Jefferson, Sauk City, WI 53583
Reverend Fathers—
Bauhs, Eugene J., 6205 Mineral Point Rd., #216, Madison, WI 53705
Beck, Charles L., 636 Skyview Dr., Milton, WI 53563
Brechtl, Joseph A., 8301 Old Sauk Rd., Apt. 270, Middleton, WI 53562
Brickl, Joseph M., 6130 Century Ave., Apt. 103D, Middleton, WI 53562
Brophy, Robert J., P.O. Box 44342, Madison, WI 53744-4342
Browne, Vincent T., 19 Moygannon Ct., Warren Point, Ireland
Buenzil, August H., Bishop O'Connor Catholic Pastoral Center, 3577 High Point Rd., P.O. Box 44983, Madison, WI 53744-4983
Buholzer, Robert E., 300 Silverado Dr., Apt. 204, Stoughton, WI 53589-5472
Conlon, Philip J., 306 Michael Ave., P.O. Box 326, Hollister, MO 65672
Cox, Joseph C., 2515 Deerfield St., Portage, WI 53901-1081
Dominic, Francis J., 2029 Brennan Ct., Cuba City, WI 53807
Fox, George W., 1850 Beld St., Apt. 8, Madison, WI, 53713
Grasso, Philip A., 211 N. Lincoln, Cuba City, WI 53807
Heindl, Arthur W., N. 7157 Cottage Dr., Westboro, WI 54490
Kieffer, Lawrence J., 2500 Overlook Ter., Rm. B 1061, Madison, WI 53705-2286

Koth, Arthur R., 1626 Wheeler Rd., #103, Madison, WI 53704

Lenarz, Richard J., 2123 Highland Ave., Janesville, WI 53545

Marx, Lambert M., 1927 N. Pontiac, Janesville, WI 53545

Mattucci, James J., Bishop O'Connor Catholic Pastoral Center, 3577 High Point Rd., P.O. Box 44983, Madison, WI 53744-4983

McEnery, James G., 5001 N. Sherman Ave., Madison, WI 53704-1499

Pickarts, Bernard J., River House, Co Hwy Y- # 10126, Mazomanie, WI 53560

Pierick, Bernard E., Bishop O'Connor Catholic Pastoral Center, 3577 High Point Rd., P.O. Box 44983, Madison, WI 53744-4983

Reddington, Benjamin J., 201 Wallace Ave., Pottsville, PA 17901

Schubiger, Albert B., 10800 Henderson Rd., Ventura, CA 93004

Schuster, Wilfred J., Bishop O'Connor Catholic Pastoral Center, 3577 High Point Rd., P.O. Box 44983, Madison, WI 53744-4983

Segerson, Thomas M., Bishop O'Connor Catholic Pastoral Center, 3577 High Point Rd., P.O. Box 44983, Madison, WI 53744-4983

Turner, Jerome R., St. Mary's, Star of the Sea, 1010 Windsor Ln., Key West, FL 33040

Turner, Wayne A., 502 St. Lawrence Ave., Janesville, WI 53545

Young, Anthony J., 2411 Tawhee Dr., Apt. 104, Madison, WI 53711

INSTITUTIONS LOCATED IN THE DIOCESE

[A] SEMINARIES, RELIGIOUS OR SCHOLASTICATES

BARABOO. *St. Camillus Monastery and Retreat Center*, W 11876 McLeish Rd., 53913. Tel: 608-356-8113; Fax: 608-356-5530. Rev. Louis Lussier, O.S.Cam. Priests 1.

[B] COLLEGES

MADISON. *Edgewood College*, 1000 Edgewood College Dr., 53711. Tel: 608-663-4861; Fax: 608-663-6717
For a complete listing, refer to the Colleges and Universities section.

[C] HIGH SCHOOLS, PRIVATE

MADISON. *Edgewood High School*, 2219 Monroe St., 53711. Tel: 608-257-1023; Fax: 608-257-9133. Dominican Sisters, Sinsinawa. Mr. Thomas E. Shipley, Pres.; Mr. Robert Growney, Prin. Lay Teachers 48; Students 639.

[D] CONSOLIDATED ELEMENTARY SCHOOLS

BERLIN. *Berlin Catholic School*, 151 S. Grove St., 54923. Tel: 920-361-1781; Fax: 920-361-7379. Ronda Krystofiak, Prin. Consolidation of the following parishes: St. Joseph; St. Michael; and St. Stanislaus. Lay Teachers 11; Students 143.

[E] ELEMENTARY SCHOOLS, PRIVATE

MADISON. *Edgewood Campus Grade School*, 829 Edgewood College Dr., 53711. Tel: 608-663-4100; Fax: 608-663-4101. Dominican Sisters, Sinsinawa. Connie Irlbeck, Pres. & Prin. Sisters 1; Brothers 1; Lay Teachers 21; Students 281.

[F] GENERAL HOSPITALS

MADISON. *St. Marys Hospital Medical Center*, 707 S. Mills St., 53715. Tel: 608-251-6100; Fax: 608-258-6731
For a complete listing, refer to the Hospitals section.

BARABOO. *St. Clare Hospital and Health Services*, 707 14th St., 53913. Tel: 608-356-1400.
Web site: www.stclare.com
For a complete listing, refer to the Hospitals section.

MONROE. *The Monroe Clinic, Inc.*, 515 22nd Ave., 53566. Tel: 608-324-1000; Fax: 608-324-1471.
E-mail: Tom_Huber@themonroeclinic.org
Web site: www.themonroeclinic.org/
For a complete listing, refer to the Hospitals section.

PORTAGE. *Divine Savior Healthcare, Inc.*, 1015 W. Pleasant St., P.O. Box 387, 53901. Tel: 608-742-4131; Fax: 608-742-6098
For a complete listing, refer to the Hospitals section.

[G] HOMES FOR THE AGED

MADISON. *St. Marys Care Center*, 1347 Fish Hatchery Rd., 53715. Tel: 608-257-0781; Fax: 608-257-9420
For a complete listing, refer to the Special Care Facilities section.

BARABOO. *St. Clare Meadows Care Center*, 1414 Jefferson St., 53913. Tel: 608-356-5764; Fax: 608-356-5441
For a complete listing, refer to the Special Care Facilities section.

JANESVILLE. *St. Elizabeth Home*, 502 St. Lawrence Ave., 53545. Tel: 608-752-6709; Fax: 608-752-1724
For a complete listing, refer to the Special Care Facilities section.

PORTAGE. *Divine Savior Nursing Home*, 715 W. Pleasant St., 53901. Tel: 608-742-4131; Fax: 608-742-3463
For a complete listing, refer to the Special Care Facilities section.

STOUGHTON. *Nazareth House*, 814 Jackson St., 53589. Tel: 608-873-6448; Fax: 608-873-0829
For a complete listing, refer to the Special Care Facilities section.

[H] MONASTERIES AND RESIDENCES OF PRIESTS

MADISON. *Bishop O'Connor Catholic Pastoral Center*, 3577 High Point Rd., P. O. Box 44983, 53744-4983. Tel: 608-821-3000; Fax: 608-821-3013. In res. Most Rev. George O. Wirz; Rev. Msgr. Paul J. Swain; Rev. Msgr. William A. DeBock; Rev. Msgr. James G. Kramer; Rev. Msgr. Joseph C. Niglis; Revs. August H. Buenzli; Thomas M. Segerson; Wilfred J. Schuster; James J. Mattucci; Bernard J. Pierick; Nicholas Okere; Richard J. Lenarz; John C. Stillmark.

EDGERTON. *Legion of Christ, Inc.*, 432 Liguori Rd., 53534. Tel: 608-884-3425; Fax: 608-884-9231. Revs. Thomas Moylan, L.C., Supr.; Fergus O'Carroll, L.C., Chap.; Bros. Paul Lara, L.C.; Thang Bui, L.C.; Matthew Zeik, L.C.; Gregory Usselmann, L.C.; Chad Wahl, L.C.

[I] CONVENTS AND RESIDENCES FOR SISTERS

MADISON. *Franciscan Sisters of Mary*, 901 High St., 53715-1913. Tel: 608-255-1510; Fax: 608-258-6731. Sisters 2.

Monastery of Saint Benedict Center, P.O. Box 5070, 53705-0070. Tel: 608-836-1631; Fax: 608-836-5586. Monastery of the Sisters of Saint Benedict. Sr. Mary David Walgenbach, O.S.B., Prioress. Sisters 6.

Secular Institute of Schoenstatt Sisters of Mary, 5901 Cottage Grove Rd., 53718-1397. Tel: 608-222-7208; Fax: 608-222-0430. Rita-Marie Otto, Supr. Sisters 7.

BARABOO. *Community of Hope*, 1021 Ash St., 53913-2163. Tel: 608-356-8641. Sisters 3.

BELOIT. *Blessed Sacrament Convent*, 916 Bluff St., 53511. Tel: 608-362-3326.
Motherhouse of the Auxiliaries of the Blessed Sacrament. Sr. Pauline Labrecque, A.B.S., Supr. Gen. Sisters in Residence 4.

PRAIRIE DU SAC. *Valley of Our Lady Monastery*, 53578-9737. Tel: 608-643-3520; 643-7986 (Altar Breads); Fax: 608-643-0684.
E-mail: volocist@juno.com
Cistercian Nuns. Mother M. Paula Hannah, O.Cist., Prioress. Solemnly Professed 13; Simply Professed 1; Novice 1.

SINSINAWA. *Dominican Motherhouse*, 585 County Rd. Z, 53824-9700. Tel: 608-748-4411; Fax: 608-748-4491.
E-mail: toniharrisop@aol.com
Web site: www.sinsinawa.org
Sinsinawa Dominican Congregation of the Most Holy Rosary. Sr. Toni Harris, O.P., Prioress of the Congregation. Provincials: Sr. Mary Ellen Green, O.P., Eastern Prov.; Sr. Christa Cunningham, O.P., Southern Prov.; Sr. Mary Ann Nelson, O.P., Western Prov.; Sr. Helen Martin, O.P., Prioress of the Motherhouse; Revs. Matthias Walsh, O.P.; John C. Risley, O.P. Sisters in the Congregation 828; Sisters 175.
Dominican Novitiate: Novices 2.

[J] CHARITABLE INSTITUTIONS

MADISON. *Catholic Charities, Inc.* Diocese of Madison, Administrative Center, 3577 High Point Rd., P.O. Box 46550, 53744-6550. Tel: 608-821-3100; Fax: 608-821-3125.
E-mail: cathcharities@straphael.org
Web site: www.ccmdsn.org
Brian Cain, Dir.

Central City Counseling Services, 30 S. Franklin St., 53703. Tel: 608-256-2358; Fax: 608-256-2350.

Beloit District Office, 3311 Prairie Ave., Beloit, 53511. Tel: 608-365-3665; Fax: 608-365-1279.

Janesville District Office, 2020 E. Milwaukee St., Janesville, 53545. Tel: 608-752-4906; Fax: 608-752-9699.

Saint Martin House. (Interracial Center), 1862 Beld St., 53713. Tel: 608-255-1287; Fax: 608-255-8471.
E-mail: smmaurice@facstaff.wisc.edu
Rev. George M. Hastrich, Spiritual Dir. Volunteer Staff; Steve Maurice, Coord.

Society of St. Vincent de Paul. (District Council of Madison, Inc.), 1109 Jonathon Dr., 53713-3230. Tel: 608-278-2920; Fax: 608-278-2926.
E-mail: svdpmad@svdpmadison.org
Web site: www.svdpmadison.org
Mr. Jack W. Mussey, Council Pres.

JEFFERSON. *St. Coletta of Wisconsin, Inc.*, W4955 Hwy. 18, 53549. Tel: 920-674-4330; Fax: 920-674-4603.
Web site: www.msmicro.com/stcoletta
Sponsored by the Sisters of St. Francis of Assisi. Milwaukee. Rev. Thomas E. Gillespie, Chap.; Robert Stearns, Pres. & CEO. Sisters 13; Brothers 1; Residents 415; Lay Staff 504.

[K] RETREAT HOUSES

MADISON. *Saint Benedict Center, Ecumenical Retreat and Conference Center*, P.O. Box 5070, 53705-0070. Tel: 608-836-1631; Fax: 608-831-9312.
E-mail: mwalgenbach@sbcenter.org
Web site: www.sbcenter.org
Sr. Mary David Walgenbach, O.S.B. Sisters 6.

[L] MISCELLANEOUS

MADISON. *Catholic Health Association of Wisconsin, Inc.*, 5721 Odana Rd., Ste. 204, 53719-1222. Tel: 608-274-5588; Fax: 608-274-6872.
E-mail: chaw@execpc.com
Web site: www.execpc.com/~chaw
Sr. Rosemary Sabino, R.S.M., Pres. & CEO; Rosann Geiser, Chairperson of the Board.

Edgewood Incorporated, 1000 Edgewood College Dr., 53711. Tel: 608-663-4861; Fax: 608-663-6717.
E-mail: ebben@edgewood.edu
Web site: www.edgewood.edu
Dr. James A. Ebben, Pres. Sponsored by Sinsinawa Dominican Sisters of Sinsinawa, WI. Purpose: The education of individuals in such subjects as are usually taught in high schools, academies, and colleges.

Mid-America Catholic Colleges. (MACC), 3577 High Point Rd., P.O. Box 44983, 53744-4983. Membership consists of the following 9 colleges: Clarke College; College of St. Catherine; College of Saint Teresa; College of St. Thomas; Loras College; Mount Mercy College; Saint Mary's College; St. Norbert College; and Viterbo College.

San Damiano Friary, 4123 Monona Dr., 53716. Tel: 608-222-6238; Fax: 608-222-6766. Capuchin Order-Province of St. Joseph. House of Healing and Hospitality. Revs. Leo Petrimoulx, O.F.M.Cap., Local Min.; Rupert Dorn, O.F.M.Cap; Garrett Keegstra, O.F.M.Cap.; Bro. Edward Hagman, O.F.M.Cap.

SSM Health Care of Wisconsin, Inc., 707 S. Mills St., 53715. Tel: 608-258-6120. Bernard C. Huger, Contact Person. Sponsored by: Franciscan Sisters of Mary. Purpose: To provide either directly or in conjunction with other persons or organizations health care, health education and related facilities and services.

University of Wisconsin - Madison Roman Catholic Foundation Inc., 723 State St., 53703-1087. Tel: 808-258-3140; Fax: 608-258-3141. Rev. Steven J. Kortendick.

BARABOO. *Saint Vincent de Paul Society-Baraboo*, 100 S. Boulevard, P.O. Box 233, 53913. Tel: 608-356-4649; Fax: 608-356-4430. Tim Nolden, Contact Person. Sponsored by: Saint Vincent de Paul Society. Purpose: To help the poor and needy in a Vincentian spirit and manner.

EDGERTON. *Oaklawn Academy*, 432 Liguori Rd., 53534. Tel: 608-884-3425; Fax: 608-884-8175.
E-mail: oaklawnusa.com

Oaklawn Incorporated, 432 Liguori Rd., R.R., 53534. Tel: 608-884-3425; Fax: 608-884-9231.
E-mail: oaklawnusa@aol.com
Chaplains: Thomas Moylan, L.C.; Rev. Fergus O'Carroll, L.C.; Mr. Javier Valenzuela, Prin.

JEFFERSON. *Assisi Homes-Rockview, Inc* 121 E. Henry St., 53549. Susan Dillberg, Pres. Purpose: to provide housing projects for low income families. Sponsored by: Franciscan Sisters, Daughters of the Sacred Hearts of Jesus and Mary of Wheaton, IL.

PLATTEVILLE. *St. Augustine Newman Center*, 135 S. Hickory, 53818. Tel: 608-348-7530; Fax: 608-348-7530.
E-mail: newmanclub@uwplatt.edu
Web site: vms.www.uwplatt.edu/~newmanclub/
Please refer to St. Augustine University Parish, Platteville.

PRAIRIE DU SAC. *Society of Saint Vincent de Paul, Sauk-Prairie/Roxbury Area*, 815 19th St., 53578. Tel: 608-643-8905; Fax: 608-643-8905. Jim Vande Hey, Pres. Sponsored by: Saint Vincent de Paul Society. Purpose: To help the poor and needy in a Vincentian spirit and manner.

SINSINAWA. *Sinsinawa Dominican Community Support Trust.* Mother Samuel Coughlin Charitable Trust. 585 County Rd. Z, 53824-9700. Tel: 608-748-4411; Fax: 608-748-5501.
E-mail: toniharrisop@aol.com
Web site: www.sinsinawa.org
Sr. Antoinette Harris, O.P., Contact Person. Sponsored by: Sinsinawa Dominicans. Purpose: To provide financial support to the aged, infirm or diabled vowed members of the Sinsinawa Dominicans.

Sinsinawa Housing, Inc., 585 County Rd. Z, 53824-9700. Tel: 608-748-4411; Fax: 608-748-4491.
E-mail: tharris@sinsinawa.org
Web site: www.sinsinawa.org
Sr. Karen Krall, O.P., Contact Person. Sponsored by the Sinsinawa Dominicans. Purpose: To provide low-to moderate-income housing for senior residents of southwestern Wisconsin.

RELIGIOUS INSTITUTES OF MEN REPRESENTED IN THE DIOCESE

For further details refer to the corresponding bracketed number in the Religious Institutes of Men or Women section.

[0470]—*The Capuchin Fathers.*—O.F.M., Cap.
[0730]—*Legionaires of Christ.*—L.C.
[0430]—*Order of Preachers-Dominicans.* (Prov. of St. Albert the Great).—O.P.
[0240]—*Order of St. Camillus.*—O.S.Cam.

RELIGIOUS INSTITUTES OF WOMEN REPRESENTED IN THE DIOCESE

[]—*Auxiliaries of the Blessed Sacrament.*—A.B.S.
[0230]—*Benedictine Sisters of Pontifical Jurisdiction.* (Yorktown, Watertown, SD).—O.S.B.
[0680]—*Cistercian Nuns.*—O.Cist.
[]—*Congregation of the Handmaids of the Holy Child Jesus.* (Nigeria, Africa).—H.H.C.J.
[3710]—*Congregation of the Sisters of Saint Agnes.*—C.S.A.
[1070-03]—*Dominican Sisters.*—O.P.
[1070-09]—*Dominican Sisters.*—O.P.
[1230]—*Franciscan Sisters of Christian Charity.*—O.S.F.
[1310]—*Franciscan Sisters of Little Falls, MN.*—O.S.F.
[1415]—*Franciscan Sisters of Mary.*—F.S.M.
[2575]—*Institute of the Sisters of Mercy of the Americas.*—R.S.M.
[2970]—*School Sisters of Notre Dame.*—S.S.N.D.
[1680]—*School Sisters of St. Francis.*—O.S.F.
[]—*Secular Institute of Schoenstatt Sisters of Mary.*
[3020]—*Sisters Oblates to the Blessed Trinity.*
[0530]—*Sisters of Charity of Our Lady, Mother of the Church.*—S.C.M.C.
[3930]—*Sisters of St. Joseph of the Third Order of St. Francis.* (Prov. of St. Joseph).—S.S.J.-T.O.S.F.
[1030]—*Sisters of the Divine Savior.*—S.D.S.
[1705]—*Sisters of the Third Order of St. Francis of Assisi.*—O.S.F.

DIOCESAN CEMETERIES

MADISON. *Resurrection*, 2705 Regent St., 53705. Tel: 608-238-5561.

BELOIT. *Calvary.* 1827 N. Washington, Janesville, 53545. Tel: 608-754-3472.
Mount Thabor. 1827 N. Washington, Janesville, 53545. Tel: 608-754-3472.

DOYLESTOWN. *Rocky Run*, P.O. Box 40, 53928. Tel: 414-992-3343.

JANESVILLE. *Mount Olivet*, 1827 N. Washington St., 53545. Tel: 608-754-3472.

NECROLOGY

† Holzer, Rev. Msgr. Ambrose W., (Retired). —Died March 10, 2000.

Diocese of Manchester

(Dioecesis Manchesteriensis)

Most Reverend

JOHN B. McCORMACK, D.D., M.S.W.

Bishop of Manchester; ordained February 2, 1960; consecrated December 27, 1995; installed September 22, 1998. *Res., 657 N. River Rd., Manchester, NH, 03104.*

Most Reverend

ODORE J. GENDRON, D.D.

Retired Bishop of Manchester; ordained May 31, 1947; appointed December 12, 1974; consecrated February 3, 1975. *Res., St. Joseph Cathedral, 145 Lowell St., Manchester, NH, 03104-6135.*

Most Reverend

FRANCIS J. CHRISTIAN, PH.D.

Auxiliary Bishop of Manchester; ordained June 29, 1968; appointed April 2, 1996; consecrated May 14, 1996. *Res., St. Joseph Cathedral, 145 Lowell St., Manchester, NH, 03104-6135.*

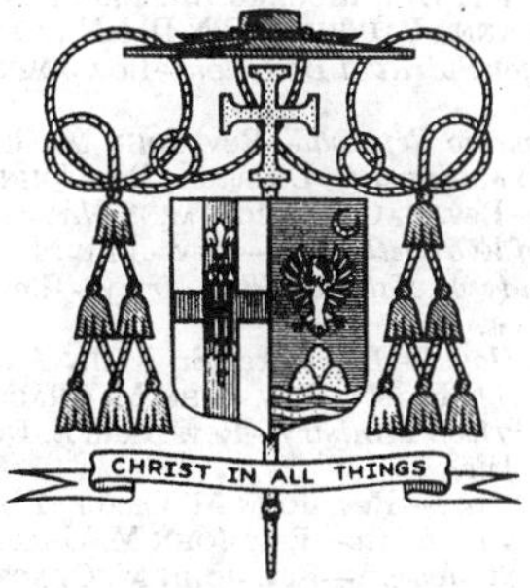

ESTABLISHED 1884.

Square Miles 9,305.

Comprises the State of New Hampshire.

For legal titles of parishes and diocesan institutions, consult the Chancery Office.

Chancery Office: 153 Ash St., P.O. Box 310, Manchester, NH, 03105. Tel.: 603-669-3100; Fax: 603-669-0377.

Web site address: www.catholicchurchnh.org

E-mail address: webmaster@rcbm.org

STATISTICAL OVERVIEW

Personnel	
Bishop	1
Auxiliary Bishops	1
Retired Bishops	1
Abbots	1
Priests: Diocesan Active in Diocese	149
Priests: Active Outside Diocese	9
Priests: Retired, Sick or Absent	77
Number of Diocesan Priests	235
Religious Priests in Diocese	85
Extern Priests in Diocese	3
Ordinations:	
Diocesan Priests	3
Transitional Deacons	3
Permanent Deacons in Diocese	25
Total Brothers	26
Total Sisters	688
Parishes	
Parishes	131
With Resident Pastor:	
Resident Diocesan Priests	105
Resident Religious Priests	12
Without Resident Pastor:	
Administered by Priests	14
Missions	38
Closed Parishes	3
Professional Ministry Personnel:	
Brothers	1
Sisters	29
Lay Ministers	85
Welfare	
Catholic Hospitals	2
Total Assisted	258,562
Homes for the Aged	9
Total Assisted	501
Residential Care of Children	2
Total Assisted	41
Educational	
Diocesan Students in Other Seminaries	16
Students Religious	2
Total Seminarians	18
Colleges and Universities	5
Total Students	5,533
High Schools, Diocesan and Parish	3
Total Students	1,590
High Schools, Private	2
Total Students	951
Elementary Schools, Diocesan and Parish	34
Total Students	6,939
Elementary Schools, Private	3
Total Students	929
Catechesis/Religious Education:	
High School Students	5,756
Elementary Students	29,456
Total Students Under Catholic Instruction	51,172
Teachers in the Diocese:	
Priests	1
Brothers	5
Sisters	62
Lay Teachers	766
Vital Statistics	
Receptions into the Church:	
Infant Baptism Totals	4,587
Adult Baptism Totals	191
First Communions	4,916
Confirmations	3,168
Marriages:	
Catholic	895
Interfaith	362
Total Marriages	1,257
Deaths	2,608
Total Catholic Population	325,674
Total Population	1,201,000

Former Bishops—Rt. Rev. DENIS M. BRADLEY, D.D., first Bishop of Manchester; cons. June 11, 1884; died Dec. 13, 1903.—Rt. Rev. JOHN B. DELANY, D.D., cons. Sept. 8, 1904; died June 11, 1906.—Most Rev. GEORGE ALBERT GUERTIN, D.D., cons. March 19, 1907; died Aug. 6, 1931.—Most Rev. JOHN B. PETERSON, D.D., cons. Auxiliary Bishop of Boston, Nov. 10, 1927; transferred to See, May 13, 1932; died March 15, 1944.—Most Rev. MATTHEW F. BRADY, D.D., cons. Oct. 26, 1938; transferred to See, Nov. 11, 1944; died Sept. 20, 1959.—Most Rev. ERNEST J. PRIMEAU, S.T.D., appt. Nov. 27, 1959; resigned Jan. 30, 1974; died June 15, 1989.—Most Rev. ODORE J. GENDRON, D.D., ord. May 31, 1947; appt. Dec. 12, 1974; cons. Feb. 3, 1975.—Most Rev. LEO E. O'NEIL, D.D., ord. June 4, 1955; appt. Coadjutor Oct. 17, 1989; succeeded to See June 12, 1990; died Nov. 30, 1997.

Vicar General—Most Rev. FRANCIS J. CHRISTIAN, D.D., Ph.D., *153 Ash St., P.O. Box 310, Manchester, 03105-0310.* Tel: 603-669-3100.

Vicar for Clergy—Most Rev. FRANCIS J. CHRISTIAN, D.D., Ph.D.

Vicars Forane—Very Rev. JAMES W. HALLER, V.F., Manchester East; Very Rev. Msgr. PAUL L. BOUCHARD, V.F., Manchester West; Very Rev. WILFRED H. DESCHAMPS, Berlin; Very Rev. C. PETER DUMONT, V.F., Concord; Very Rev. PAUL D. MONTMINY, V.F., Dover; Very Rev. ROGER BILODEAU, V.F., Franconia; Very Rev. THOMAS DUSTON, V.F., Keene; Very Rev. WILLIAM J. QUIRK, V.F., Laconia; Very Rev. RICHARD T. LOWER, V.F., Lebanon; Very Rev. ROBERT E. GORSKI, V.F., Nashua; Very Rev. DANIEL O. LAMOTHE, V.F., Salem.

Judicial Vicars and Diocesan Tribunal—153 Ash St., P.O. Box 310, Manchester, 03105-0310. Tel: 603-669-3101; Fax: 603-669-3102.

Judicial Vicar—Rev. JOHN J. MAHONEY, JR., J.C.L.

Associate Judicial Vicar—Rev. RICHARD P. TETU, J.C.L.

Promoter of Justice—Rev. Msgr. PAUL L. BOUCHARD, S.T.L., J.C.L.

Advocates—Revs. ROGER H. CROTEAU; KARL E. DOWD; MICHAEL E. GENDRON; MICHAEL KERPER.

Defenders of the Bond—Rev. Msgr. PAUL L. BOUCHARD, S.T.L., J.C.L.; Rev. Msgr. DONALD J. GILBERT, J.C.L.

Diocesan Judges—Revs. FRANCIS L. DEMERS, O.M.I., J.C.D.; JOHN J. MAHONEY, JR., J.C.L.; Sr. LOUISE TESSIER, P.M., J.C.L.; Rev. RICHARD P. TETU, J.C.L.

Notaries—SHEILA BODKIN; KATHLEEN MASSE; SHIRLEY PEDRICK.

Council of Priests—Most Rev. JOHN B. MCCORMACK, D.D., Pres.; Rev. C. PETER DUMONT, V.F., Chm.; Very Rev. ROBERT E. GORSKI, V.F., Vice Chm.; Rev. STEVEN G. MONTESANTI, Sec.; Most Rev. FRANCIS J. CHRISTIAN, D.D., Ph.D.; Rev. EDWARD J. ARSENAULT; Very Rev. WILFRED H. DESCHAMPS, V.F.; Very Rev. JAMES W. HALLER, V.F.; Rev. Msgr. JOHN E. MOLAN, P.A.; Rev. Msgr. JOHN P. QUINN; Very Rev. ROGER P. BILODEAU; Revs. ROLAND P. COTE; GILLES GENEST, M.S.; THOMAS HORAN, O.M.I.; AGAPIT H. JEAN, JR.; MICHAEL KERPER; GARY KOSMOWSKI; Very Rev. RICHARD T. LOWER, V.F.; Revs. FREDERICK J. PENNETT;

BENET C. PHILLIPS, O.S.B.; Rev. Msgr. FERNAND L. PICHETTE; Rev. Msgr. THOMAS J. HANNIGAN.

College of Consultors—Most Rev. FRANCIS J. CHRISTIAN, D.D., Ph.D.; Rev. EDWARD J. ARSENAULT; Very Revs. WILFRED H. DESCHAMPS, V.F.; C. PETER DUMONT, V.F.; ROBERT E. GORSKI, V.F.; Rev. Msgr. JOHN E. MOLAN, P.A.; Rev. Msgr. JOHN P. QUINN.

Diocesan Pastoral Council—Most Rev. JOHN B. MCCORMACK, D.D.; Most Rev. FRANCIS J. CHRISTIAN, D.D., Ph.D.; MIKE ANGIULO; DAVID GAMACHE; JANICE STEENBEKE; LAURIE LEWIS; SUSAN HOLDEN; IRENE DUVAL; JANET LEROUX; SUSAN SMITH; FRANCIS X. KUSHI; ALBERT CORMIER; RAMON ANDRADE; SHARON MARTIN; SHAWN MCDONOUGH; DE PHAM; IRENE PLOURDE; Sr. BONITA COTE, F.C.S.C.J.; Bro. PAUL CRAWFORD, O.F.M.Cap.; Sr. MARIE HENAULT, P.M.; Sr. RACHEL M. JETTE, C.S.C.; Sr. FELICIA MCKONE, R.S.M.; Sr. IRENE TURGEON, S.N.D.deN.; Sr. PATRICIA A. SULLIVAN, R.S.M.; Revs. ROLAND P. COTE; MICHAEL KERPER; JOHN R. POIRIER; Deacon W. CARL LAFLEUR, JR.

Diocesan Finance Council—Most Rev. JOHN B. MCCORMACK, D.D., Chm.; Rev. Msgr. JOHN P. QUINN, Sec. for Finance & Real Estate; HAROLD ACRES; FRANK O. BUHL; DORIS M. DESAUTEL; RUSSELL GRADY; Very Rev. JAMES W. HALLER, V.F.; MARC A. JOLICOEUR; STEPHEN J. KANEB; JOHN H. LYNCH; STEVEN R. MCMANIS; RONALD J. RIOUX; FRANK YANCO.

Clergy Personnel Board—Most Rev. JOHN B. MCCORMACK, D.D.; Most Rev. FRANCIS J. CHRISTIAN, D.D., Ph.D.; Very Rev. WILLIAM L. QUIRK, V.F.; Revs. EDWARD J. ARSENAULT; DENNIS AUDET; GERALD R. BELANGER; DONALD E. CLINTON; PAUL L. GREGOIRE; JOHN C. HORAN; DANIEL A. ST. LAURENT; RICHARD B. THOMPSON.

Masters of Ceremonies—Revs. JOSEPH M. COOPER; MARC F. GUILLEMETTE.

Secretary for Administration—Rev. EDWARD J. ARSENAULT, *153 Ash St., P.O. Box 310, Manchester, 03105-0310.* Tel: 603-669-3100.

Secretary for Christian Formation—Sr. PAULINE LEBEL, C.S.C., *153 Ash St., P.O. Box 310, Manchester, 03105-0310.* Tel: 603-669-3100.

Secretary for Finance & Real Estate—Rev. Msgr. JOHN P. QUINN, *153 Ash St., P.O. Box 310, Manchester, 03105-0310.* Tel: 603-669-3100.

Secretary for Human Services—Mr. RAYMOND MAILLOUX, *153 Ash St., P.O. Box 310, Manchester, 03105-0310.* Tel: 603-669-3100.

Secretary for Pastoral Services—Vacant.
- *Coordinator of Community Services*—Sr. MARGARET CROSBY, S.N.D.deN., Dir., *153 Ash St., P.O. Box 310, Manchester, 03105-0310.* Tel: 603-669-3100.
- *Coordinator of Pastoral Services*—Rev. MARC F. GUILLEMETTE, Dir., *153 Ash St., P.O. Box 310, Manchester, 03105-0310.* Tel: 603-669-3100.

Chancellor—Rev. EDWARD J. ARSENAULT, S.T.L., *153 Ash St., P.O. Box 310, Manchester, 03105-0310.* Tel: 603-669-3100.

Assistant to Bishop for Canonical Affairs—Very Rev. PAUL L. BOUCHARD, V.F.

Secretary to Bishop—FRANCEEN M. MORASSE.

Administration—
- *Communications Office*—Vacant, Dir. JOHN HAYWOOD, TIDINGS, Acting Editor.
- *Development Office*—Vacant, Dir.
- *Diocesan Museum*—KATHERINE STAUB, Dir., *140 Laurel St., Manchester, 03103.* Tel: 603-624-1729.
- *Legal Affairs Office*—Rev. EDWARD J. ARSENAULT, Sec.
- *Operations & Information Systems*—Sr. SHEILA GARVEY, R.S.M., Dir.
- *Risk Management and Insurance Office*—MARTHA KIPP, Dir.

Christian Formation—
- *Department of Catholic Schools*—Bro. KENNETH HOGAN, F.M.S., Supt.; JOAN L. DOBZANSKI, Assoc. Supt.; DAVID A. GABERT, Assoc. Supt.
- *Department of Faith Development*—Sr. BERNADETTE TURGEON S.N.D.deN., Dir.
  - *Office of Adult Education*—PATRICIA GABREE, Dir.
  - *Office of Catechetics*—PATRICIA GABREE, Dir.
  - *Office of the Catechumenate, Re-Membering Church and Small Church Communities*—Sr. MARY ELIZABETH WHALEN, S.N.D.deN., Dir.
- *Department of Spiritual Renewal Services*—Rev. JOHN M. GRACE, Dir.; RICHARD KIERNAN, Assoc. Dir.; Sr. MARY ANNE LAUGHLIN, S.N.D.deN., Assoc. Dir.
  - *Center for Spiritual Direction*—Rev. JOHN M. GRACE, Dir.
  - *Charismatic Renewal*—Rev. JOHN M. GRACE, Dir.
  - *Cursillo Movement*—Directors: Rev. JOHN M. GRACE; Very Rev. PAUL D. MONTMINY, V.F.
  - *Office of Evangelization*—Rev. JOHN M. GRACE, Dir.
  - *Our Lady of Fatima (Blue Army)*—Rev. JOHN M. GRACE, Dir.
  - *Joseph House*—Directors: Sr. MARY ANNE LAUGHLIN, S.N.D.deN.; Rev. JOHN M. GRACE.
  - *Kairos Prison Ministry*—Rev. KARL E. DOWD, Spiritual Dir.
  - *La Rencontre*—Rev. JOHN M. GRACE, Dir.
  - *Marian Apostolate*—Rev. JOHN M. GRACE, Dir.
  - *Men of St. Joseph*—Rev. JOHN M. GRACE, Spiritual Dir.; RICHARD KIERNAN, Spiritual Dir.
  - *Young Adult Ministry*—Rev. JOHN M. GRACE, Dir.
- *Youth Services*—
  - *Catholic Scouting Office*—Rev. RAYMOND A. BALL, Dir.
  - *Catholic Youth Organization Office*—THERESA ROOT, Dir.
  - *Diocesan Camps*—GUS PLANCHET, Dir., *P.O. Box 206, Gilmanton Iron Works, 03837-0206.* Tel: 603-364-5851; Fax: 603-364-5038.
  - *Youth Ministry Office*—Directors: Sr. BERNADETTE TURGEON, S.N.D.deN.; MATTHEW GOODY.

Finance and Real Estate—
- *Finance Officer*—Rev. Msgr. JOHN P. QUINN.
- *Controller*—MAURICE PRATTE, Controller.
- *Real Estate Office*—PAUL HARRINGTON, Dir. Facilities Mgmt. RAY CLEMENT, Asst. Dir.
- *Propagation of the Faith*—Rev. GERARD A. BOUCHER, Diocesan Dir.
- *Catholic Campaign for Human Development/Operation Rice Bowl*—Sr. MARGARET CROSBY, S.N.D.deN., Dir.
- *Catholic Relief Services*—Rev. Msgr. JOHN P. QUINN, Dir.
- *Manchester Mission*—CLARE AUCOIN, R.N., Dir.
- *Liaison for Religious Congregations*—Rev. Msgr. JOHN P. QUINN, Liaison.

Human Services—
- *New Hampshire Catholic Charities, Inc.*—*153 Ash St., P.O. Box 310, Manchester, 03105.* Tel: 603-669-3030; Fax: 603-626-1252.
  - *Family Services Office*—ROBERT P. CLOHOSEY, A.C.S.W., Dir.
  - *Elderly Services*—Sr. MARY ROSE ORLANDO, R.S.M., Social Worker.
  - *Adoption and Maternity Services*—ELAINE C. LANGTON, Social Worker.
  - *Project Rachel*—ROBERT P. CLOHOSEY, A.C.S.W., Coord.
  - *Our Place*—ROBERT P. CLOHOSEY, A.C.S.W., Program Dir.
- *Parish Social Ministry Office*—RICHARD J. SHANNON, Dir.
  - *Family Ministries Office*—JANE COSMO, Dir.
  - *Rainbows*—Directors: JANE COSMO; DENIS J. DAIGLE.
  - *Persons with Disabilities*—Rev. BERNARD J. CAMPBELL, O.F.M.Cap., Dir.
  - *Good Beginnings*—DENIS J. DAIGLE, Coord.
  - *Morehouse*—DENIS J. DAIGLE, Coord.
  - *Diocesan HIV/AIDS Ministry*—DICK SHANNON, Facilitator.
- *Immigration and Refugee Services*—Sr. MARGARET CROSBY, S.N.D.deN., Dir. LAN TRUONG, Refugee Svcs. Coord. KIMBERLY GEORGE, Immigration Attorney; MARIA FULLER, Immigration Svcs. Coord. Tel: 603-641-1259.
  - *New England Detention Project*—MARY HOWELL, Clinic Immigration Attorney.
- *Diocesan Bureau of Housing*—CAROL A. HAEBLER, Housing Coord., *323 Franklin St., Manchester, 03101.* Tel: 603-625-5422; Fax: 603-625-1014.

Community & Pastoral Services—
- *Diocesan Public Policy Committee*—Sr. MARGARET CROSBY, S.N.D.deN., Dir.
- *Institutional Ministries Office*—Sr. MARGARET CROSBY, S.N.D.deN., Dir.
- *Ecumenical and Inter-religious Affairs*—Rev. ROBERT G. BIRON, Dir., *St. Martin Parish, 120 Maple St. Ext., Somersworth, 03878-1999.* Tel: 603-692-5403.
- *Marriage Preparation Program*—JANE COSMO, Dir.
- *Multi-Cultural Ministries Office*—Sr. MARGARET CROSBY, S.N.D.deN., Dir.
  - *African Apostolate*—Rev. ANTHONY SUNDAY OGUNLEYE. Tel: 603-623-8809.
  - *Hispanic Apostolate*—Rev. JOHN GALLAGHER, O.F.M.Cap.; Sr. MARIA LUZ CERVANTES. Tel: 603-623-8809. Rev. MARCEL I. MARTEL. Tel: 603-881-8065. Rev. JORGE REYES, O.S.A. Tel: 603-898-1927. Rev. DANIEL A. ST. LAURENT. Tel: 603-868-2666.
  - *Korean Apostolate*—Very Rev. DANIEL O. LAMOTHE, V.F. Tel: 603-898-4933.
  - *Portuguese-Speaking Apostolate*—Rev. EUSEBIO F. SILVA. Tel: 603-882-4362.
  - *Vietnamese Apostolate*—*St. Anne Rectory, 231 Merrimack St., Manchester, 03103.* Tel: 603-623-8809.
- *NH Council of Catholic Women*—Sr. MARGARET CROSBY, S.N.D.deN., Moderator.
- *Office of Priestly Life and Ministry*—Rev. MICHAEL KERPER, Dir.
- *Office of the Permanent Diaconate*—Rev. MARC F. GUILLEMETTE, Dir.
- *Office of Worship*—Rev. JOSEPH M. COOPER, Dir.
- *Pastoral Ministries Office*—Sr. MARY ELIZABETH WHALEN, S.N.D.deN., Dir.
- *Respect Life Office*—JUDITH DELISLE, Dir.
- *Vocations Office*—Directors: Revs. MARC F. GUILLEMETTE; MARC R. MONTMINY.

Censor Librorum—Most Rev. FRANCIS J. CHRISTIAN, D.D., Ph.D.

Society of Saint Vincent de Paul—RAYMOND RIOUX, Pres., NH State Council, *8 Maplewood Ave., Manchester, 03102.* Tel: 603-622-1036.

CLERGY, PARISHES, MISSIONS AND PAROCHIAL SCHOOLS

CITY OF MANCHESTER
(Hillsborough County)

1—ST. JOSEPH CATHEDRAL (1869), Revs. Humbert M. Oliveira, Rector; Joseph M. Cooper; Joan Poro, Pastoral Assoc.; Deacon Lionel A. St. Laurent. In res., Most Revs. Francis J. Christian; Odore J. Gendron; Rev. Msgr. Laurence R. Gardner; Rev. Msgr. Charles E. Crosby; Rev. Msgr. Colin A. MacDonald.
Res., 145 Lowell St., 03104-6135. Tel: 603-622-6404; Fax: 603-626-4415. [CEM]
Chapels—St. Joseph Eucharistic.; Convent, Tel: 603-624-6897.
Catechesis/Religious Programs—Students 121.

2—ST. ANNE (1848), Revs. John M. Gallagher, O.F.M.Cap.; Patrick Sullivan, O.F.M.Cap.; Sr. Maria Luz Cervantes, M.S.C., Pastoral Assoc. In res., Revs. Bernard J. Campbell, O.F.M.Cap; Robert J. Densmore, (Retired).
Office & Mailing Address: 383 Beech St., 03103-5397.
Res., 231 Merrimack St., 03103. Tel: 603-623-8809; Fax: 603-626-1517.
Church—447 Union St.
Catechesis/Religious Programs—Tel: 603-623-8800.
Students 85.

3—ST. ANTHONY OF PADUA (1899) (French), Rev. Charles E. DesRuisseaux; Dr. Elise B. Tougas, Pastoral Assoc. In res., Revs. Normand A. Fillion, O.M.I.; Raymond H. Laferriere.
Res., 172 Belmont St., 03103-4452. Tel: 603-625-6409; Fax: 603-625-0099.
School—(Grades K-6) 148 Belmont St., 03103. Tel: 603-622-0414; Fax: 603-669-5212. Constance Bilodeau, Prin.
Catechesis/Religious Programs—Students 94.

4—ST. AUGUSTIN (1871) (French), Rev. John Gallagher, O.F.M.Cap. In res., Revs. John J. Mahoney, Jr.; Patrick Sullivan, O.F.M. Cap.
Office: 383 Beech St., 03103-5397. Tel: 603-625-5655; Fax: 603-626-1517. [CEM]
Res., St. Anne Rectory, 231 Merrimack St., 03103.
Catechesis/Religious Programs—251 Merrimack St., Tel: 603-623-8800.
Students 12.

5—BLESSED SACRAMENT (1907), Rev. Michael E. Sevigny, O.F.M.Cap. In res., Bro. Paul Crawford, O.F.M.Cap.; Rev. Gabriel Massaro, O.F.M.Cap.
Res., 14 Elm St., 03103-7297. Tel: 603-622-5445; Fax: 603-627-5983.
Catechesis/Religious Programs—Students 80.

6—ST. CATHERINE (1954), Very Rev. Msgr. Thomas J. Hannigan, V.F.; Rev. James P. Walsh. In res., Rev. Michael S. Taylor.
Res., 207 Hemlock St., 03104-3299. Tel: 603-622-4966; Fax: 603-622-0236.
School—(Grades K-6) 206 N. St., 03104. Tel: 603-622-1711; Fax: 603-624-4935. Sr. Janet Belcourt, C.S.C., Prin. & D.R.E.
Catechesis/Religious Programs—Tel: 603-622-2711; Fax: 603-622-0236.
Students 743.

7—ST. EDMUND (1914) (French), Very Rev. Msgr. Paul L. Bouchard, V.F.; Sr. Sally A. Howe, C.S.C., Pastoral Assoc. In res., Rev. William J. Hamilton, S.J.
Res., 55 Edmond St., 03102-3398. Tel: 603-625-6025; Fax: 603-625-4067.
Catechesis/Religious Programs—Tel: 603-623-6820. Anita H. Plourde, D.R.E.
Students 242.

8—ST. FRANCIS OF ASSISI (1953), Rev. Paul F. Ruzzo.
Parish Office: 9 St. Francis Way, Litchfield, 03052-8050. Tel: 603-424-3456; Fax: 603-424-8603.
School—(Grades K-6)., 03103. Tel: 603-424-3312; Fax: 603-424-9128.
Sisters of Mercy 1; Lay Teachers 9; Students 151.
Catechesis/Religious Programs—Tel: 603-424-9061.
Students 401.

9—ST. GEORGE (1890) (French), Rev. George A. Desjardins. In res., Revs. Roland O. Blais; Donald E. Lafond; Wilfred G. Demers.

Res., 517 Pine St., 03104-6013. Tel: 603-623-6434; Fax: 603-645-1857.
Catechesis/Religious Programs—Combined with St. Joseph Cathedral. Tel: 603-622-6404.
Students 17.

10—ST. HEDWIG, Rev. Msgr. Alfred Daniszewski.
Res., 147 Walnut St., 03104-4225. Tel: 603-623-4835. [CEM]
School—St. Casimir, (Grades K-8) 456 Union St., 03103. Tel: 603-623-6411. Sr. Mary Lawrence Lojko, C.S.S.F., Prin.
Felician Sisters 4; Students 231.

11—ST. JOHN THE BAPTIST (1914) (French), Revs. Leo A. LeBlanc; Raymond A. Ball. In res., Rev. Msgr. James J. Markham; Rev. Msgr. Roland Tancrede; Rev. Msgr. Wilfrid H. Paradis; Rev. Leonard R. Foisy.
Res., 107 Alsace St., 03102-3006. Tel: 603-623-4715; Fax: 603-623-4715.
Catechesis/Religious Programs—Tel: 603-622-0504; Fax: 603-623-4715.
Students 250.

12—ST. MARIE (1880), Revs. Marc R. Montminy, V.F.; Steven G. Montesanti; Deacon Frank Gallinaro. In res., Revs. John Grace; Richard P. Tetu.
Res., 378 Notre Dame Ave., 03102-3793. Tel: 603-622-4615; Fax: 603-666-4732. [CEM 2]
Chapels—Joseph House Chapel, 279 Cartier St., 03102. Tel: 603-627-9493; Chapel of North American Martyrs.; St. Joan of Arc.
Catechesis/Religious Programs—Tel: 603-668-5863. Mary Mosher, D.R.E.
Students 216.
Convent—133 Wayne St., 03102-3793. Tel: 603-623-0815. Sisters of the Presentation of Mary

13—OUR LADY OF PERPETUAL HELP (1911) (English), Rev. Marcel M. Allard. In res., Rev. Msgr. John F. Burke.
Res., 266 Cypress St., 03103-3700. Tel: 603-622-2535; Fax: 603-668-0356.
Catechesis/Religious Programs—870 Hayward St., 03103-3700. Tel: 603-668-3985.
Students 180.

14—ST. PATRICK (1898) (Irish), Rev. Nicholas P. Rogers; Deacon Harry Kram.
Res., 138 Coolidge Ave., 03102-3298. Tel: 603-624-4115; Fax: 603-621-9616. [CEM]
Catechesis/Religious Programs—100 Coolidge Ave., 03102. Tel: 603-624-0916.
Students 101.

15—ST. PIUS X (1955), Rev. Edward J. Arsenault.
Res., 575 Candia Rd., 03109-4708. Tel: 603-622-6510; Fax: 603-626-1323.
Catechesis/Religious Programs—Tel: 603-669-4547.
Students 490.

16—ST. RAPHAEL (1888), Rev. Bede G. Camera, O.S.B.
Res., 103 Walker St., 03102-4534. Tel: 603-623-2604; Fax: 603-623-2604 (call ahead). [CEM]
Catechesis/Religious Programs—Tel: 603-647-2283.
Students 137.

17—SACRED HEART OF JESUS (1911) (French), Revs. Marc R. Montminy; Steven G. Montesanti.
Mailing Address: & Office: 247 S. Main St., 03102-4890.
Res., St. Mary Rectory, 378 Notre Dame Ave., 03102-3793. Tel: 603-622-4615.
Church—265 S. Main St., 03102. Tel: 603-625-9525; Fax: 603-666-4732.

18—ST. THERESA, Rev. Jean Lemay.
Res., 140 Mitchell St., 03103-6599. Tel: 603-623-5055; Fax: 603-622-6138.

OUTSIDE THE CITY OF MANCHESTER

Alton, Belknap Co., St. Joan of Arc (1961), Rev. Richard H. Wegman.
Res., Mitchell Ave., P.O. Box 729, 03809-0729. Tel: 603-875-7191; Fax: 603-875-5747.
Catechesis/Religious Programs—Students 120.
Mission—Center Barnstead, Belknap Co., St. Paul, Maple St., Center Barnstead, 03225.

Ashland, Grafton Co., St. Agnes, Rev. Gerard W. Timmerman, S.M.
Res., 6 Hill St., P.O. Box 556, 03217-0556. Tel: 603-968-4433; Fax: 603-968-9870.

Auburn, Rockingham Co., St. Peter (1948), Very Rev. James W. Haller, V.F. In res., Rev. Msgr. John E. Molan.
Res., 567 Manchester Rd., 03032-3123. Tel: 603-623-5429; Fax: 603-669-5598.
Catechesis/Religious Programs—Tel: 603-669-5134.
Students 581.

Bedford, Hillsborough Co., St. Elizabeth Seton (1964), Rev. Msgr. John P. Quinn. In res., Rev. Andrew M. Meehan.
Res., 190 Meetinghouse Rd., 03110-6027. Tel: 603-669-7444; Fax: 603-644-5371.
Catechesis/Religious Programs—Tel: 603-647-1940. James Whittaker, D.R.E.
Students 1,310.

Belmont, Belknap Co., St. Joseph (1949), Rev. Albert J. Tremblay, Jr.
Res., 6 High St., P.O. Box 285, 03220-0285. Tel: 603-267-8174; Fax: 603-267-1170.
Catechesis/Religious Programs—Students 230.

Bennington, Hillsborough Co., St. Patrick (1936), Rev. Richard A. Smith.
Res., 10 Greenfield Rd., P.O. Box 147, 03442-0147. Tel: 603-588-2180; Fax: 603-588-4917. [CEM]
Catechesis/Religious Programs—Tel: 603-547-2670; Fax: 603-547-3623.
Students 196.

Berlin, Coos Co.,

1—ST. ANNE, (1885) (French). Consolidated. For inquiries for parish records contact Good Shepherd Parish, Berlin.

2—GOOD SHEPHERD, (2000), Revs. Richard A. Roberge; Michael Monette; Sr. Monique Therriault, R.S.M., Pastoral Assoc.; Deacon Merle Albert.
Res. & Mailing Address: 162 Madison Ave., P.O. Box 570, 03570-0570. Tel: 603-752-2880; Fax: 603-752-1855. [CEM 4]
Office: 151 Emery St., P.O. Box 570, 03570.
Catechesis/Religious Programs—Tel: 603-752-5443; Fax: 603-752-1743.
Students 457.

3—ST. JOSEPH, (1943) (French). Consolidated. For inquiries for parish records contact Good Shepherd Parish, Berlin.

4—ST. KIERAN, (1894). Consolidated. For inquiries for parish records contact Good Shepherd Parish, Berlin.

5—GUARDIAN ANGEL, (1917). Consolidated. For inquiries for parish records contact Good Shepherd Parish, Berlin.

Bristol, Grafton Co., St. Timothy (1900), Very Rev. William L. Quirk, V.F.
Res., 111 School St., P.O. Box 37, 03222-0037. Tel: 603-744-2700; Fax: 603-744-2700.
Catechesis/Religious Programs—Students 93.
Mission—Newfound Lake, Grafton Co., Our Lady of Grace, 2 W. Shore Rd., 03222.

Candia, Rockingham Co., St. Paul (1971), Rev. Michael Kerper.
Res., 54 Main St., P.O. Box 276, 03034-0276. Tel: 603-483-8481; Fax: 603-483-8481.
Catechesis/Religious Programs—Tel: 603-483-5516.
Students 145.
Station—Chester, St. Jerome.

Cascade, Coos Co., St. Benedict. Closed. For Sacramental records contact Good Shepherd, Berlin.

Center Ossipee, Carroll Co., St. Joseph (1965), Rev. Mark A. Rundzio; Deacon William Rich.
Res., 23 Moultonville Rd., P.O. Box 248, 03814-0248. Tel: 603-539-5036; Fax: 603-539-5036.
Catechesis/Religious Programs—Tel: 603-542-5993.
Students 218.
Mission—Chocorua, Carroll Co., Our Lady of Perpetual Help.

Charlestown, Sullivan Co., St. Catherine, Rev. Shawn M. Therrien.
Res., 285 Main St., Box 332, 03603-0332. Tel: 603-826-3359; Fax: 603-826-5875.

Claremont, Sullivan Co., St. Joseph (1922) (Polish), Rev. Stanley J. Piwowar.
Res., 58 Elm St., P.O. Box 824, 03743-0824. Tel: 603-542-5732; Fax: 603-543-3673.
Catechesis/Religious Programs—Tel: 603-542-5993.
Students 218.

St. Mary (1823), Rev. Michael J. Ciullo.
Res., 32 Pearl St., 03743-2552. Tel: 603-542-9518; Fax: 603-542-9614. [CEM]
School—(Grades PreK-8) 18 Central St., 03743. Tel: 603-542-6341; Fax: 603-542-5260. JoAnne Woodstock, Prin. (Grades K-8).
Lay Teachers 13; Students 171.
Catechesis/Religious Programs—Tel: 603-542-9518; Fax: 603-542-9614.
Students 58.
Mission—W. Claremont, Sullivan Co., Old St. Mary, Old Church Rd., W. Claremont.

Colebrook, Coos Co., St. Brendan (1953), Rev. Albert A. Bellefeuille.
Res., 28 Pleasant St., P.O. Box 65, 03576-0065. Tel: 603-237-4342. [CEM]
Catechesis/Religious Programs—Students 108.
Mission—Errol, Coos Co., St. Pius X, P.O. Box 65, 03576. [CEM]
Station—Dixville, St. William of York.

Concord, Merrimack Co.,

1—ST. JOHN THE EVANGELIST, (1886), Revs. Donald E. Clinton; Paul M. Gousse.
Res., 72 S. Main St., 03301-4887. Tel: 603-224-2328; Fax: 603-224-2625.
Catechesis/Religious Programs—Tel: 603-244-2062. Margaret Cotterly, D.R.E.
Students 779.

2—ST. PETER, (1946), Revs. Mitchell J. Wanat, C.M.; Bogdah Konarzewski, C.M.
Res., 135 N. State St., 03301. Tel: 603-225-2131; Fax: 603-228-4580.
Catechesis/Religious Programs—Students 258.

3—SACRED HEART, (1892) (French), Rev. Aime A. Boisselle.
Res., 52 Pleasant St., 03301-3925. Tel: 603-225-6942; Fax: 603-225-3526.
Catechesis/Religious Programs—Tel: 603-225-6942.
Students 182.

4—IMMACULATE HEART OF MARY, (1956), Rev. Florent R. Bilodeau.
Res., 180 Loudon Rd., 03301-6028. Tel: 603-224-4393; Fax: 603-224-6229.
Catechesis/Religious Programs—176 Loudon Rd., 03301. Tel: 603-225-2026.
Students 225.

Derry, Rockingham Co., Holy Cross (1989), Rev. Roger H. Croteau.
Church & Office: 187 Hampstead Rd., 03038-4835.
Res., 4 Belle Brook Ln., 03038. Tel: 603-437-9544; Fax: 603-537-1208.
Catechesis/Religious Programs—Tel: 603-437-7550.
Students 588.

St. Thomas Aquinas (1885), Revs. Joseph F. Lorenzo, O.F.M.; Marcellinus Borg, O.F.M.; Thomas Washburn, O.F.M.; Deacon George Long.
Res., 26 Crystal Ave., 03038-1799. Tel: 603-432-5000; Fax: 603-434-0518.
School—(Grades K-8) 3 Moody St., 03038. Tel: 603-432-2712; Fax: 603-432-2179. Sr. Jacqueline Brodeur, C.S.C., Prin.
Sisters 3; Lay Teachers 11; Students 304.
Catechesis/Religious Programs—16 Rollins Street, 03038. Tel: 603-432-7530. Dr. Jane Dwyer, D.R.E.
Students 1,000.

Dover, Strafford Co., St. Charles (1893) (French), Rev. Paul L. Gregoire.
Res., 577 Central Ave., 03820-3464. Tel: 603-742-1354; Fax: 603-743-3360. [CEM]
Catechesis/Religious Programs—150 Central Ave., Tel: 603-742-8838.
Students 78.

St. Joseph (1945), Revs. Robert F. Cole; John R. Poirier.
Res., 150 Central Ave., 03820-4090. Tel: 603-742-4837; Fax: 603-749-6779.
Catechesis/Religious Programs—Tel: 603-742-8868.
Students 606.
Mission—Barrington, Chapel of the Nativity, Rte. 9, P.O. Box 163, Barrington, 03825. Tel: 603-664-9336; Fax: 603-664-2310.

St. Mary (1833), Rev. Fritz J. Cerullo, O.S.A.
Res., 25 Third St., 03820-3385. Tel: 603-742-2619; Fax: 603-742-7166.
Catechesis/Religious Programs—Tel: 603-742-8868.
Students 84.

Durham, Strafford Co., St. Thomas More, Rev. Daniel A. St. Laurent.
Res., 6 Madbury Rd., Box 620, 03824-0620. Tel: 868-2666 (Office); Fax: 603-868-3765.
Catechesis/Religious Programs—Students 282.

Enfield, Grafton Co., St. Helena (1899), Rev. Paul Rainville, M.S.; Deacon John St. George.
Res., 36 Shaker Hill Rd., 03748-3524. Tel: 603-632-4263; Fax: 603-632-7874.
Catechesis/Religious Programs—Tel: 603-632-7874.
Students 150.
Mission—Canaan, Grafton Co., St. Mary, Rte. 4, Canaan, 03741. Tel: 603-523-9955 (Hall).

Epping, Rockingham Co., St. Joseph (1898), Rev. Ronald E. Corriveau.
Res., 14 Church St., P.O. Box 337, 03042-0337. Tel: 603-679-8805; Fax: 603-679-5192. [CEM]
Catechesis/Religious Programs—Tel: 603-679-5724.
Students 239.

Exeter, Rockingham Co., St. Michael (1859), Revs. Marc B. Drouin; Richard E. St. Louis, Jr.
Res., 9 Lincoln St., 03833-3297. Tel: 603-772-2494; Fax: 603-778-1629.
Catechesis/Religious Programs—Michael House, 11 Linden St., 03833. Tel: 603-772-3916. Catherine Smith, D.R.E.
Students 900.

Farmington, Strafford Co., St. Peter (1920), Rev. Eddy N. Bisson.
Res., 90 Central St., P.O. Box 565, 03835-0565. Tel: 603-755-2280; Fax: 603-755-9124.
Catechesis/Religious Programs—Tel: 603-755-3921.
Students 87.

Franklin, Merrimack Co., St. Paul (1884), Rev. William E. Babineau; George L. Desautel, Pastoral Assoc.
Res., 108 School St., P.O. Box 490, 03235-0490. Tel: 603-934-5013; Fax: 603-934-6694. [CEM]
Catechesis/Religious Programs—Students 115.

Goffstown, Hillsborough Co., St. Lawrence (1955), Rev. Donald F. Gauthier, Jr.
Res., 51 Main St., 03045-1644. Tel: 603-497-2651; Fax: 603-497-3668.
Catechesis/Religious Programs—Tel: 603-497-4093.
Students 360.

Gonic, Strafford Co., St. Leo (1892), Rev. Paul D. Montminy.
Res., 59 Main St., 03839-5220. Tel: 603-332-1624; Fax: 603-332-7623. [CEM]
Catechesis/Religious Programs—16 Bridge St., Rochester, 03867. Tel: 603-332-4803.
Students 61.

Gorham, Coos Co., Holy Family, Very Rev. Wilfred H. Deschamps, V.F.; Deacon Merle M. Albert.
Res., 5 Church St., 03581-1695. Tel: 603-466-2335; Fax: 603-466-3490. [CEM]

Greenville, Hillsborough Co., Sacred Heart (1888) (French), Rev. Anthony DiRusso.
Res., 15 High St., 03048-3121. Tel: 603-878-1121; Fax: 603-878-4657. [CEM]
Catechesis/Religious Programs—Tel: 603-878-2274.
Students 159.

Groveton, Coos Co., St. Francis Xavier (1899) (French), Rev. Daniel R. Deveau.
Res., 10 State St., Box 72, 03582-0072. Tel: 603-636-1047; Fax: 603-636-2549. [CEM]
Catechesis/Religious Programs—Students 96.

Hampstead, Rockingham Co., St. Anne, Rev. Frederick J. Pennett.
Res., 26 Emerson Ave., P.O. Box 339, 03841-0339. Tel: 603-329-5886; Fax: 603-329-4468.
Catechesis/Religious Programs—Students 1,272.

Hampton, Rockingham Co., Our Lady of the Miraculous Medal (1948), Revs. George E. Ham; John B. MacKenzie; Michael J. Griffin.
Res., 289 Lafayette Rd., 03842-2109. Tel: 603-926-2206; Fax: 603-926-8602.
School—Sacred Heart School, (Grades PreK-8). Tel: 603-926-3254; Fax: 603-929-1109. Sr. Mary Joan Walsh, O.L.L., Prin.
Sisters 4; Lay Teachers 21; Students 449.
Catechesis/Religious Programs—(Grades K-12). Tel: 603-926-5573.
Students 592.
Mission—Seabrook Beach, Rockingham Co., St. Elizabeth's, Rte. 1-A, Seabrook Beach, 03874. Tel: 603-474-3839.

Hampton Beach, Rockingham Co., St. Patrick. Closed. Attended from Chancery. For all records contact O.L.M.M. Parish, Hampton.

Hanover, Grafton Co., St. Denis (1907), Rev. A. Stephen Marcoux, III.
Res., 8 Sanborn Rd., 03755-2182. Tel: 603-643-2166; Fax: 603-643-9881.
Catechesis/Religious Programs—Fax: 603-643-9881.
Students 280.

Harrisville, Cheshire Co., St. Denis. Attended by Sacred Heart, Marlborough.
Mission—Dublin, Our Lady of the Snows. [CEM]

Henniker, Merrimack Co., St. Theresa (1945), Rev. Mark E. Dollard.
Res., 2 Rush Rd., P.O. Box 557, 03242-0557. Tel: 603-428-3325; Fax: 603-428-4479.
Mission—Contoocook, Merrimack Co., St. Mary, P.O. Box 557, Henniker, 03242.
Catechesis/Religious Programs—Students 240.

Hillsboro, Hillsborough Co., St. Mary (1892), Rev. Andre M. Thibodeau.
Res., 38 Church St., P.O. Box 907, 03244-0907. Tel: 603-464-5565; Fax: 603-464-5565. [CEM][JC]
Catechesis/Religious Programs—Students 128.
Parish Hall—Tel: 603-464-6021.

Hinsdale, Cheshire Co., St. Joseph (1884), Rev. Raymond J. Potvin.
Res., 12 Prospect St., P.O. Box 14, 03451-0014. Tel: 603-336-5414; Fax: 603-336-7314. [CEM]
Catechesis/Religious Programs—Students 156.

Hooksett, Merrimack Co., Holy Rosary, Rev. Fernand A. Croteau.
Res., 21 Main St., 03106-1630. Tel: 603-485-3523; Fax: 603-485-3523. [CEM]

Hudson, Hillsborough Co., St. John the Evangelist (1949), Rev. John C. Horan. In res., Rev. Msgr. Joseph E. Desmond; Rev. Norman J. Simoneau.
Res., 27 Library St., 03051-4239. Tel: 603-882-3603; Fax: 603-594-0813.
Catechesis/Religious Programs—23 Library St., 03051. Tel: 603-882-6541. Mrs. Kathleen Cox, D.R.E.
Students 597.

St. Kathryn (1968), Rev. Gary J. Belliveau; Deacon Robert J. Anderson, Jr.
Church & Mailing Address: 4 Dracut Rd., 03051-5006. Tel: 603-882-7793; Fax: 603-595-1465.
Catechesis/Religious Programs—D.R.E.: Susan Levesque; Marianne Hutchins.
Students 898.

Jaffrey, Cheshire Co., St. Patrick (1885), Very Rev. Richard J. Kelley; Deacon W. Carl Lefleur.
Res., 87 Main St., 03452-6139. Tel: 603-532-6634; Fax: 603-532-6633. [CEM]
School—(Grades K-8) 70 Main St., 03452. Tel: 603-532-7676; Fax: 603-532-7476. David L. O'Connell, Prin.
Sisters 3; Lay Teachers 11; Students 195.
Catechesis/Religious Programs—Tel: 603-532-8831.
Students 260.

Keene, Cheshire Co., St. Bernard (1862), Revs. W. Pierre Baker; John J. Hurley.
Res., 173 Main St., 03431-3790. Tel: 603-352-3525; Fax: 603-352-7472. [CEM]
Catechesis/Religious Programs—St. Joseph School, 92 Wilson St., 03431. Tel: 603-352-2720; Fax: 603-358-5465.
Students 143.

St. Margaret Mary (1955), Rev. Dennis A. Broussard.
Res., 35 Arch St., 03431-2297. Tel: 603-352-1311; Fax: 603-358-5250.
Catechesis/Religious Programs—Tel: 603-357-3781.
Students 194.
Mission—Chesterfield, Cheshire Co., Our Lady of the Lake, 754 B, Rte. 63, Chesterfield, 03443.

Laconia, Belknap Co., St. Joseph (1871), Rev. Gary J. Kosmowski.
Res., 30 Church St., 03246-3401. Tel: 603-524-1442; Fax: 603-527-3534. [CEM]
Catechesis/Religious Programs—Tel: 603-524-4196.
Students 172.

Sacred Heart (1891) (French-Canadian), Rev. Adrien R. Longchamps.
Res., 291 Union Ave., 03246-3122. Tel: 603-524-9609; Fax: 603-527-2617. [CEM]
Catechesis/Religious Programs—Tel: 603-524-4155.
Students 79.

Lakeport, Belknap Co., Our Lady of the Lakes, Rev. George J. Soberick.
Res., 50 Washington St., 03246-2339. Tel: 603-524-1357; Fax: 603-524-4524.
Catechesis/Religious Programs—Tel: 603-528-4225.
Students 209.
Mission—Weirs Beach, St. Helena.

Lancaster, Coos Co., All Saints (1856), Rev. John C. Mazzei.
Res., 163 Main St., 03584-1723. Tel: 603-788-2083; Fax: 603-788-5553. [CEM]
Catechesis/Religious Programs—Students 181.
Mission—Jefferson, Coos, St. Agnes, Rte. 2, 03583.

Lebanon, Grafton Co., Sacred Heart (1875) (French), Revs. Gilles Genest, M.S., Admin.; Gerald M. Baril, M.S. In res., Revs. John F. Mullin, S.J.; Richard Delisle, M.S.
Res., 2 Hough St., P.O. Box 482, 03766-0482. Tel: 603-448-1262; Fax: 603-448-3754.
Catechesis/Religious Programs—Tel: 603-448-1575.
Students 300.

Lincoln, Grafton Co., St. Joseph (1902), Very Rev. Roger P. Bilodeau, V.F.
Res., Church St., P.O. Box 128, 03251-0128. Tel: 603-745-2266; Fax: 603-745-2266.
Catechesis/Religious Programs—Students 72.

Lisbon, Grafton Co., St. Catherine of Siena (1957), Rev. Daniel J. Sinibaldi.
Res., c/o 21 Pine St., Woodsville, 03785-1215. Tel: 603-747-2038; Fax: 603-747-8071.
Church—28 Highland Ave.

Littleton, Grafton Co., St. Rose of Lima (1882), Rev. Joseph S. Klatka.
Res., 77 Clay St., 03561-1205. Tel: 603-444-2593; Fax: 603-444-3126. [CEM]
Catechesis/Religious Programs—Students 265.
Missions—Bethlehem, Grafton Co., Christ the King, Main St., Bethlehem, 03574.; Franconia, Grafton, Our Lady of the Snows, Main St., 03580.

Londonderry, Rockingham Co., St. Jude (1962), Rev. Robert Couto; Sr. Janice Rooney, S.N.D.deN., Pastoral Assoc.
Res., 435 Mammoth Rd., 03053-2304. Tel: 603-432-3333; Fax: 603-432-1639.
Catechesis/Religious Programs—Tel: 603-437-7026.
Students 821.

St. Mark the Evangelist (1981), Rev. Maurice R. Larochelle.
Res., One South Rd., 03053-3814. Tel: 603-432-8711; Fax: 603-434-6748.
Catechesis/Religious Programs—Tel: 603-434-5711.
Students 800.

Marlborough, Cheshire Co., Sacred Heart (1886), Very Rev. Thomas L. Duston, V.F.; Sr. Lucie E. Ducas, C.S.C., Pastoral Assoc.
Res., 9 Ling St., P.O. Box 517, 03455-0517. Tel: 603-876-3804; Fax: 603-876-4327. [CEM]

Meredith, Belknap Co., St. Charles (1946), Rev. Richard B. Thompson.
Res., 281A Daniel Webster Hwy., P.O. Box 237, 03253-0237. Tel: 603-279-4403; Fax: 603-279-9924. In res., Rev. Gerard A. Boucher.
Catechesis/Religious Programs—Tel: 603-279-8691.
Students 220.
Mission—Center Harbor, Belknap Co., Our Lady of Victory, Bean Rd., 03226.

Merrimack, Hillsborough Co., Our Lady of Mercy (1954), Rev. Dennis J. Audet; Christine Patterson, Pastoral Assoc. In res., Rev. Marc F. Guillemette.
Res., 16 Baboosic Lake Rd., 03054-3603. Tel: 603-424-3757; Fax: 603-424-1780.
Catechesis/Religious Programs—14 Baboosic Lake Rd., 03054. Tel: 603-424-4477. Elizabeth Lochman, D.R.E.
Students 834.

St. John Neumann (1982), Very Rev. Robert E. Gorski, V.F.; Deacon Richard A. Cloutier.
Res., 708 Milford Rd., 101-A, 03054-4612. Tel: 603-880-4689; Fax: 603-881-9668.
Catechesis/Religious Programs—Tel: 603-880-0825.
Students 900.

Milford, Hillsborough Co., St. Patrick (1895), Revs. Andrew W. Cryans; Donald Jacques.
Res., 34 Amherst St., P.O. Box 27, 03055-0027. Tel: 603-673-1311; Fax: 603-673-3687. [CEM]
Catechesis/Religious Programs—Tel: 603-673-4797.
Students 960.
Share Program—(A non-denominational outreach program for the local needy). Tel: 603-673-9898. Mrs. Mariette Facques, Dir.
Mission—Brookline, Hillsborough Co., Infant Jesus, P.O. Box 27, 03055.

Nashua, Hillsborough Co.,

1—St. Aloysius, (1871), Revs. Roland P. Cote; Eusebio F. Silva.
Res., 48 W. Hollis St., 03060-3286. Tel: 603-882-4362; Fax: 603-886-8923. [CEM]

2—St. Casimir, Rev. Francis M. Spencer, M.S.
Res., 119 Temple St., 03060-3582. Tel: 603-882-1313; Fax: 603-882-1313. [CEM]

3—St. Christopher, (1950), Revs. Richard J. Kelley; Norman A. Meiklejohn, A.A. In res., Rev. Bruce W. Collard.
Res., 62 Manchester St., 03064-6296. Tel: 603-882-0632; Fax: 603-881-8728.
School—(Grades K-6) 20 Cushing Ave., 03060. Tel: 603-882-7442; Fax: 603-594-9253. Sr. Joan Marie Messier, R.S.M., Prin.
Students 377.
Catechesis/Religious Programs—Tel: 603-883-2572. Mrs. Mary Roy, D.R.E.
Students 418.

4—St. Francis Xavier, (1885), Rev. Marcel I. Martel.
Res., 41 Chandler St., 03060-2888. Tel: 603-882-2333; Fax: 603-594-9648. [CEM]
Catechesis/Religious Programs—Students 155.

5—Immaculate Conception, (1968), Rev. Marc R. Gagne.
Res., 216 E. Dunstable Dr., 03062-2344. Tel: 603-888-0321; Fax: 603-888-8407.
Parish Hall: Tel: 603-888-0608.
Catechesis/Religious Programs—Tel: 603-888-0608.
Students 1,092.

6—Infant Jesus, (1909) (French), Rev. Raymond E. Gagnon. In res., Rev. Andre L. Bedard.
Res., 121 Allds St., 03060-6395. Tel: 603-882-2462; Fax: 603-882-7104.
School—(Grades K-6) 3 Crown St., 03060-6366. Tel: 603-889-2649; Fax: 603-594-9117. Sr. Marie Henault, P.M., Prin.

Catechesis/Religious Programs—Tel: 603-886-9725. Mr. Gerard Bergeron, D.R.E.
Students 214.

7—St. Joseph, (1955), Rev. Gerard R. Desmarais; Deacon Alfred A. LaBonte, Jr. In res., Rev. Karl E. Dowd.
Res., 265 Lake St., 03060-4189. Tel: 603-883-0757; Fax: 603-883-8057.
Catechesis/Religious Programs—Tel: 603-889-4372.
Students 478.

8—St. Patrick, (1855), Rev. Martin T. Kelly. In res., Rev. Msgr. T. Joseph McDonough; Revs. Alfred Bouchard; John E. Healey.
Res., 29 Spring St., 03060-3490. Tel: 603-882-2262; Fax: 603-577-9817. [CEM]
Catechesis/Religious Programs—27 Spring St., 03060. Tel: 603-882-5417.
Students 221.

9—Resurrection, (1970), Rev. Albion F. Bulger; Deacon E. Carl Hilston.
Pastoral Center: 449 Broad St., 03063-3412. Tel: 603-882-0925; Fax: 603-881-3561.
Catechesis/Religious Programs—Tel: 603-889-0012.
Students 542.

10—St. Stanislaus, (1908) (Polish), Revs. Richard J. Kelley; Norman A. Meiklejohn, A.A.
Res., c/o 62 Manchester St., 03064-6296. Tel: 603-882-0893; Fax: 603-881-7542. [CEM]
Church—5 Green St., 03060.

New London, Merrimack Co., Our Lady of Fatima (1952), Very Rev. Richard T. Lower, V.F.
Res., 75 Main St., 03257-4609. Tel: 603-526-4484; Fax: 603-526-8055.
Mission—Potter Place, Merrimack Co., Immaculate Conception, Church St., 03216. Tel: 603-735-5821.
Catechesis/Religious Programs—Students 198.

Newmarket, Rockingham Co., St. Mary (1878), Rev. John B. Finnigan. In res., Rev. Joseph E. Shields.
Res., 182 Main St., P.O. Box 337, 03857-0337. Tel: 603-659-3643; Fax: 603-659-8924. [CEM]
Catechesis/Religious Programs—Tel: 603-659-6474.
Students 157.
Mission—Newfields, Rockingham Co., Sacred Heart, 52 Main St., Newfields, 03856.

Newport, Sullivan Co., St. Patrick (1902), Rev. Richard H. Dion; Sr. Kathleen Haight, Pastoral Assoc.
Res., 32 Beech St., 03773-1416. Tel: 603-863-1422; Fax: 603-863-7898. [CEM]
Catechesis/Religious Programs—Tel: 603-863-4085.
Students 230.
Mission—Sunapee, Sullivan Co., St. Joachim, Rte. 11, Sunapee, 03782. Tel: 603-763-5940.

Newton, Rockingham Co., Mary, Mother of the Church (1967), Rev. Leo G. Gagnon.
Res., 12 Amesbury Rd., 03858-0322. Tel: 603-382-6566; Fax: 603-382-5102.
Catechesis/Religious Programs—1 New Boston Rd., Kingston, 03848. Tel: 603-642-8885; Fax: 603-642-7446.
Students 428.
Mission—Kingston, Rockingham Co., St. Frederick, 3 New Boston Rd., Kingston, 03848.

North Conway, Carroll Co., Our Lady of the Mountains (1904), Revs. Gerald R. Belanger; Louis A. Soucey.
Res., 15 Grove St., P.O. Box 189, 03860-0189. Tel: 603-356-2535 (Office); 356-7368 (Rectory); Fax: 603-356-2877. [CEM 2]
Catechesis/Religious Programs—P.O. Box 593, 03860. Tel: 603-356-3421.
Students 234.
Mission—Conway, Carroll Co., St. Charles Borromeo, P.O. Box 189, 03860. Tel: 603-356-2535; Fax: 603-356-2877.

North Stratford, Coos Co., Sacred Heart (1888) (French), Rev. Daniel R. Deveau. Pastoral Assocs.: Sr. Marie Mansfield, S.G.M.; Sr. Helene Georges, S.G.M.
Church—121 Main St., P.O. Box C, 03590-0227. Tel: 603-922-3360; Fax: 603-636-2549.
Res., St. Francis Xavier Rectory, Groveton, 03582. Tel: 603-636-1047. [CEM 2]
Catechesis/Religious Programs—Students 19.

North Walpole, Cheshire Co., St. Peter (1877), Rev. Shawn M. Therrien.
Church—38 Church St., 03609-1715. Tel: 603-445-5304; Fax: 603-445-2115. [CEM]
Res., St. Catherine of Siena Rectory, P.O. Box 332, Charlestown, 03603-0332. Tel: 603-826-3359.
Catechesis/Religious Programs—Students 81.
Mission—Walpole, Cheshire Co., St. Joseph, Elm St., 03608. Tel: 603-756-3444.

Pelham, Hillsborough Co., St. Patrick (1946), Rev. Edward D. Richard.
Res., 12 Main St., 03076-3724. Tel: 603-635-3525; Fax: 603-635-3919.
School—(Grades K-8) 16 Main St., 03076. Tel: 603-635-2941; Fax: 603-635-9800. Phyllis B. McCarthy, Prin.
Lay Teachers 13; Students 234.
Catechesis/Religious Programs—Tel: 603-635-1447.
Students 705.

Penacook, Merrimack Co., Immaculate Conception (1880), Rev. W. Timothy Thibeault.
Res., 9 Bonney St., 03303-1654. Tel: 603-753-4413; Fax: 603-753-4071. [CEM]
Catechesis/Religious Programs—Tel: 603-753-6702.
Students 150.

Peterborough, Hillsborough Co., St. Peter (1900), Rev. William J. Kelley.
Res., 18 Vine St., 03458-2403. Tel: 603-924-3819; 603-924-7647 (Office); Fax: 603-924-8365. [CEM]
Catechesis/Religious Programs—Students 185.

Pittsfield, Merrimack Co., Our Lady of Lourdes (1889), Rev. Georges F. de Laire.
Res., 20 River Rd., 03263-3314. Tel: 603-435-6242; Fax: 603-435-8840.
Catechesis/Religious Programs—25 Crescent St., 03263. Tel: 603-435-2433.
Students 275.
Mission—Northwood, Rockingham Co., St. Joseph, 20 River Rd., Pittsfield, 03263. [CEM]

Plaistow, Rockingham Co., Holy Angels (1892), Rev. Michael E. Gendron; Deacon George J. Borkush.
Res., 8 Atkinson Depot Rd., Rte. 121, 03865-3103. Tel: 603-382-8324; Fax: 603-382-1113. [CEM]
Catechesis/Religious Programs—Tel: 603-382-8824. Mrs. Beverly Fisher, D.R.E.
Students 531.

Plymouth, Grafton Co., St. Matthew (1916), Rev. Gerard W. Timmerman, S.M., Admin.
Res., 46 Langdon St., 03264-1438. Tel: 603-536-4700; Fax: 603-536-4709.
Catechesis/Religious Programs—Students 290.

Portsmouth, Rockingham Co., Immaculate Conception (1851), Rev. Edward J. Kelley; Deacon Charles Schladenhauffen. In res., Rev. Timothy R. O'Donnell.
Res., 98 Summer St., 03801-4398. Tel: 603-436-0048; Fax: 603-436-8848. [CEM 2]
Catechesis/Religious Programs—Students 135.

St. Catherine of Siena (1951), Rev. Msgr. Lawrence E. Burns.
Res., 845 Woodbury Ave., 03801-3294. Tel: 603-436-0344; Fax: 603-334-3393.
Catechesis/Religious Programs—Students 107.

St. James (1958), Rev. Agapit H. Jean, Jr.
Res., 2075 Lafayette Rd., 03801-5697. Tel: 603-436-4555; Fax: 603-433-4401. [JC]
Catechesis/Religious Programs—Students 220.

Rochester, Strafford Co., St. Mary (1868), Rev. Francis E. Kelso.
Res & Mailing Address: 38 Charles St., 03867-2994. Tel: 603-332-1869; Fax: 603-332-2040. [CEM]
Church—71 Lowell St.
Catechesis/Religious Programs—Students 300.

Holy Rosary (1883) (French), Very Rev. Paul D. Montminy, V.F.; Rev. Gerard L. Bertin.
Res., 189 N. Main St., 03867-1299. Tel: 603-332-1863; Fax: 603-330-0865. [CEM]
Catechesis/Religious Programs—16 Bridge St., 03867. Tel: 603-332-3026.
Students 100.

Rollinsford, Strafford Co., St. Mary (1856), Rev. Steven M. Kucharski.
Mailing Address: 421 Pleasant St., P.O. Box 250, 03869-0250.
Res., Holy Trinity Rectory, 404 High St., Somersworth, 03878. Tel: 603-692-4367; Fax: 603-692-4454. [CEM]
Catechesis/Religious Programs—Tel: 603-749-1666.
Students 53.

Rye Beach, Rockingham Co., St. Theresa (1979), Rev. Maurice D. Lavigne.
Res., 815 Central Rd., P.O. Box 482, 03871-0482. Tel: 603-964-6440; Fax: 603-964-4139.
Catechesis/Religious Programs—Tel: 603-964-9878.
Students 340.

Salem, Rockingham Co., Mary, Queen of Peace (1966), Rev. John W. Fleming; Deacon Leonard B. Albis.
Res., 200 Lawrence Rd., 03079-3978. Tel: 603-893-8661; Fax: 603-890-0292.
Catechesis/Religious Programs—Tel: 603-893-8662; Fax: 603-890-0292. Mrs. Marie Mullen, D.R.E.
Students 350.

St. Joseph (1910), Very Rev. Daniel O. Lamothe, V.F.; Rev. Ronald R. Goupil; Deacon David Costello. In res., Rev. Thomas J. Bresnahan, (Retired).
Res., 33 Main St., 03079-1922. Tel: 603-898-4933; Fax: 603-893-9236.
Catechesis/Religious Programs—40 Main St., 03079. Tel: 603-893-9692. Mary H. Nedder, D.R.E.
Students 665.

Sanbornville, Carroll Co., St. Anthony (1908), Rev. Edmund A. Babicz.
Res., 239 Meadow St., P.O. Box 490, 03872-0490. Tel: 603-522-3304; Fax: 603-522-8273. [CEM]
Catechesis/Religious Programs—Students 133.
Mission—Milton, Strafford Co., Sacred Heart, P.O. Box 647, Milton, 03851. Tel: 603-652-9034.

Seabrook, Rockingham Co., St. Elizabeth. Attended by Our Lady of the Miraculous Medal. For all records contact Our Lady of the Miraculous Medal Parish, Hampton.

Somersworth, Strafford Co., Holy Trinity (1857), Rev. Steven M. Kucharski.
Res., 404 High St., P.O. Box 350, 03878-0350. Tel: 603-692-4367; Fax: 603-692-4454. [CEM]
Catechesis/Religious Programs—Tel: 603-692-5403.
Students 185.

St. Martin (1882) (French), Rev. Robert G. Biron.
Res., 120 Maple St. Ext., 03878-1999. Tel: 603-692-2172; Fax: 603-692-2499. [CEM]
Catechesis/Religious Programs—Tel: 603-692-5878.
Students 190.

Suncook, Merrimack Co., St. John the Baptist (1873), Very Rev. C. Peter Dumont, V.F.; Deacon Thomas J. Cloutier.
Res., 10 School St., 03275-1917. Tel: 603-485-3113; Fax: 603-485-2113. [CEM 2]
Catechesis/Religious Programs—Tel: 603-485-3972.
Students 317.

Tilton, Belknap Co., St. Mary of the Assumption, Rev. Richard M. Giroux.
Res., 16 Chestnut St., 03276-5546. Tel: 603-286-4445; Fax: 603-286-4663. [CEM]
Catechesis/Religious Programs—Tel: 603-286-4554.
Students 132.

Troy, Cheshire Co., Immaculate Conception, Very Rev. Thomas L. Duston, V.F.; Sr. Lucie Ducas, C.S.C., Pastoral Assoc.
Office & Mailing Address: c/o Sacred Heart Rectory, 9 Ling St., P.O. Box 517, Marlborough, 03455-0517. Tel: 603-876-3804; Fax: 603-876-4327.; Rectory: 37 School St., 03465. Tel: 603-242-6415; Fax: 603-242-6415. [CEM]
Mission—Fitzwilliam, St. Joseph, 16 Church St., Fitzwilliam, 03465.

West Lebanon, Grafton Co., Holy Redeemer (1953), Rev. Donald P. Jeffrey, M.S.
Res., 8 Prospect St. W., Box 5484, 03784-5484. Tel: 603-298-8530; Fax: 603-298-8791.
Catechesis/Religious Programs—Tel: 603-298-5578.
Students 68.

West Stewartstown, Coos Co., St. Albert (1926), Rev. John B. Loughnane, Jr.
Mailing Address: P.O. Box 176, Beecher Falls, VT 05902-0176.
Res., 10 Church St., 03597. Tel: 603-246-8829; Fax: 603-246-7167. [CEM]
School—(Grades 1-8) P.O. Box 177, Beecher Falls, 05902. Tel: 603-246-8631.
Students 55.
Station—Coos County Institution.
Catechesis/Religious Programs—Students 71.

West Swanzey, Cheshire Co., St. Anthony, Revs. W. Pierre Baker; John Hurley.
Res., St. Bernard Rectory, 173 Main St., Keene, 03431-3790. Tel: 603-352-3525.
Office & Mailing Address: 50 S. Winchester St., Box 117, 03469-0117. Tel: 603-352-6246; Fax: 603-352-3770.
Catechesis/Religious Programs—Students 60.
Mission—North Swanzey, Cheshire Co., St. Stephen, Lake St., North Swanzey, 03431.

Whitefield, Coos Co., St. Matthew (1886), Rev. George Majka; Deacon Joseph A. Polcari.
Res., 9 Jefferson Rd., 03598-3101. Tel: 603-837-2558; Fax: 603-837-2558. [CEM 2]
Catechesis/Religious Programs—Students 60.
Mission—Carroll, Coos Co., St. Patrick, Rte. 3 & 302, Twin Mountain, 03595.
Shrine—Bretton Woods, Our Lady of the Mountains.

Wilton, Hillsborough Co., Sacred Heart, Rev. Anthony DiRusso.
Res. & Mailing Address—c/o Sacred Heart Rectory, 15 High St., Greenville, 03048-3121. Tel: 603-654-6554 (Parish); 878-1121 (Res.); Fax: 603-878-4657.
Church—49 Maple St., 03086. [CEM]
Catechesis/Religious Programs—Students 97.

Winchester, Cheshire Co., St. Stanislaus (1962) (Polish), Rev. Raymond J. Potvin.
Res. & Mailing Address: c/o St. Joseph Rectory, 12 Prospect St., P.O. Box 14, Hinsdale, 03451-0014.

Church—80 Richmond St., 03470. Tel: 603-336-5414; Fax: 603-336-7314.
Mission—Ashuelot, St. Michael.

Windham, Rockingham Co., St. Matthew (1962), Rev. Msgr. Donald J. Gilbert; Deacon Clarence R. Cummins.
Res., 2 Searles Rd., 03087-1298. Tel: 603-893-3336; Fax: 603-898-4008. [JC]
Catechesis/Religious Programs—Tel: 603-898-4818.
Students 936.

Wolfeboro, Carroll Co., St. Cecilia, Rev. George H. Robichaud.
Res., 205 S. Main St., P.O. Box 180, 03894-0180. Tel: 603-569-2548; Fax: 603-569-6659.

Woodsville, Grafton Co., St. Joseph (1896), Rev. Daniel J. Sinibaldi.
Res., 21 Pine St., 03785-1215. Tel: 603-747-2038; Fax: 603-747-8071. [CEM]
Catechesis/Religious Programs—15 Pine St. Students 88.
Mission—Warren, Grafton Co., St. John Vianney. On the Common.

Chaplains of Public Institutions

MANCHESTER. *Elliott Hospital*. Rev. Andrew M. Meehan.
Hillsborough County Jail. Revs. Steven G. Montesanti; Patrick Sullivan, O.F.M.Cap.
Veterans Administration Medical Center. Vacant.
Youth Development Center. Capuchin Friars, Blessed Sacrament.

BERLIN. *Androscoggin Valley Hospital*. Sr. Monique Theriault, R.S.M., Chap.

CONCORD. *N.H. State Hospital*. St. John and St. Peter, Concord.
N.H. State Prison. Vacant.

LEBANON. *Mary Hitchcock Memorial Hospital, Dartmouth-Hitchcock Medical Center*. Rev. John Mullin, S.J.

NASHUA. *Southern N.H. Regional Medical Center and Nursing Homes*. Chaplains: Sr. Doris Gagnon, P.M.; Rev. Norman J. Simoneau.

On Duty Outside the Diocese:
Reverend Monsignors—
Frontiero, Anthony R., Permanent Observer of the Holy See to the United Nations, St. Monica Rectory, 413 E. 79th St., New York, NY 10021. Tel: 212-288-6250
Reverend Fathers—
Coyne, Emmett A., 520 N St., S.W. #S318, Washington, D.C. 20024
Pfaff, Aaron J., St. Francis Xavier, 2321 Green St., Philadelphia, PA 19130. Tel: 215-765-4568
Polito, Victor V.J., St. Mary Rectory, 156 E. Main St., Amsterdam, NY 12010-4899. Tel: 518-842-4500

Military Chaplains:
Reverend Fathers—
Cody, Kevin W., CH, Cpt. USAF, 5265 Bunk House Ln., Colorado Springs, CO 80917-2245
Crowley, Edmund G., CH, Maj., USAF, 1558 Eglin Way #C, Bolling AFB, DC 20336-5242. Tel: 202-767-5900
Decker, James D., CH, Cpt., USAF, PSC 9, Box 4993, APO, AE 09123
Glasgow, Robert K., CH, Maj., USA, P.O. Box 637, Fort Campbell, KY 42223-0637. Tel: 502-798-2543
Lamy, Raymond J., CH, Maj., USAF, 377 ABW/HC, 1950 Second St., Kirkland AFB, NM 87117

Absent on Sick Leave:
Reverend Fathers—
LaForest, Conrad V.
Lord, Gary F.
Valliere, Romeo J.

Absent on Leave:
Rev.—
Connor, Kevin T.
Reverend Fathers—
Dion, Gerard J.
Fortier, Roger A.
MacRae, Gordon J.
Memolo, Rocco C.

Sabbatical:
Reverend Fathers—
Aube, Paul L., P.O. Box 4602, Manchester, NH 03108-4602

Retired:
Reverend Monsignors—
Blair, Raymond O., P.O. Box 998, Lincoln, NH 03251-0998
Burke, John F., Our Lady of Perpetual Help Rectory, 266 Cypress St., Manchester, NH 03103
Curran, Francis L., Bishop Peterson Residence, 221 Orange St., Manchester, NH 03104-4324
Desmond, Joseph E., St. John the Evangelist Rectory, 27 Library St., Hudson, NH 03051
Gardner, Laurence R., Cathedral Rectory, 145 Lowell St., Manchester, NH 03102. Tel: 603-622-6404
Kenney, Philip J., 5 Thorndike St., Concord, NH 03301-3629
MacDonald, Colin A., St. Francis of Assisi Rectory, 3221 Brown Ave., Manchester, NH 03103
Markham, James J., St. John the Baptist Rectory, 107 Alsace St., Manchester, NH 03102
McDonough, T. Joseph, Bishop Peterson Residence, 221 Orange St., Manchester, NH 03108-48240
Molan, John E., St. Peter Rectory, 567 Manchester Rd., Auburn, NH 03032-3123
Murphy, Eugene, Holy Angels, 8 Atkinson Depot Rd., Plaistow, NH 03865
Paradis, Wilfrid H., 107 Alsace St., Manchester, NH 03102
Pichette, Fernand L., 164 Boutwell St., Manchester, NH 03102
St. Pierre, Leo L., 165 Golfview Dr., Manchester, NH
Tancrede, Roland, St. John the Baptist Rectory, 107 Alsace St., Manchester, NH 03102
Watson, James P., 2 Overlook Tr., Concord, NH 03301-5245
Reverend Fathers—
Auger, Gerald E., 235 Alsace St., Manchester, NH 03102-3008
Baillargeon, Albert G., 12 Jacobs Dr., Rochester, NH 03867-2453
Bedard, Andre L., Infant Jesus, 121 Allds St., Nashua, NH 03060-6395. Tel: 603-882-3832
Blais, Roland O., St. George Rectory, 517 Pine St., Manchester, NH 03104-6013
Boisvert, Robert G., 6 Faith Ln., Center Barnstead, NH 03225
Boucher, Gerard A., St. Charles Rectory, 281A Daniel Webster Hwy., P.O. Box 237, Meredith, NH 03253-0237
Boulanger, Albert L., Delany Residence, 255 Coolidge Ave., P.O. Box 5633, Manchester, NH 03108-5633. Tel: 603-627-4154
Bracq, Edward E., 14 Oldfield Rd., Nashau, NH 03060-5067
Bresnahan, Thomas J., St. Joseph, 33 Main St., Salem, NH 03079-1922. Tel: 603-898-0044
Chalifour, Gerald F., P.O. Box 6272, Manchester, NH 03108-6272
Clifford, Francis M., 399 Pleasant St., South Weymouth, MA 02190-2647
Cote, Joseph A., 457 Norway St., P.O. Box 394, Berlin, NH 03570-0394. Tel: 603-752-5277
Demers, Raymond A., Stonecrest #1, 738 Weirs Beach Blvd., Laconia, NH 03246
Demers, Wilfred G., St. George Rectory, 517 Pine St., Manchester, NH 03104-6013
Densmore, Robert J., St. Anne, 231 Merrimack St., Manchester, NH 03103-5295. Tel: 603-668-0334
Desjardins, Raymond S., 51 Partridge Green, Rochester, NH 03867
Dowd, Karl E., St. Joseph, P.O. Box 3810, Nashua, NH 03061-3810. Tel: 603-883-0757
Dunn, Gerald R., P.O. Box 1390, Wolfelboro, NH 03894-1390. Tel: 603-569-5058
Foisy, Leonard R., St. John the Baptist Rectory, 107 Alsace St., Manchester, NH 03102-3006
Frechette, Leo L., P.O. Box 68, West Nottingham, NH 03291-0068
Gallant, Rodrigue J., P.O. Box 428, Belmont, NH 03220-0428
Goggin, Cornelius J., 96 River Rd., Manchester, NH 03104. Tel: 603-644-5150
Goodwin, Robert T., 4851 W. Gandy Blvd., #8-40, Tampa, FL 33611-3039
Griffin, Robert F., Bishop Peterson Residence, 221 Orange St., Manchester, NH 03104-4324
Horan, Denis F., 3 Oak Hill Ln., #309, Nashua, NH 03062-4639
Houde, Arthur O., 5626 Marshfield Dr., Port Orange, FL 32127-5326
Hughes, Lawrence J., 2601 N.E. 14th St. #536, Pompano Beach, FL 33062-8319
Irwin, Patrick F., P.O. Box 1974, Ogunquit, ME 03907
Keenan, Thomas E., 679 Lemoine Beach Rd., Lemoine, ME 04605
Kemmery, Robert J., 18 Gull Ln., Orleans, MA 02653-3003
Knott, Edward J., Bishop Peterson Residence, 221 Orange St., Manchester, NH 03104-4324
Lacroix, Maurice R., St. Marie Rectory, 378 Notre Dame Ave., Manchester, NH 03102-3793
Laferriere, Raymond H., St. Anthony of Padua Rectory, 172 Belmont St., Manchester, NH 03103-4452
Lampron, Maurice W., P.O. Box 717, Wolfeboro Falls, NH 03896-0717
Lefebvre, Leo P., Delany Residence, 3247 Brown Ave., Manchester, NH 03103
Marchand, Robert A., 419 Coolidge Ave., Manchester, NH 03102-3214
McHugh, Paul F., P.O. Box 3352, Concord, NH 03301-3352
Montplaisir, Roland A., 2950 Palm-Aire Dr., Apt. 502, Pompano Beach, FL 33069-3441
Reverend Fathers—
Moran, John V., 3202 Lafayette Rd., Portsmouth, NH 03801-6009
Reverend Fathers—
Nolin, John W., 4604 Edwin Mechem Ave. N.W., Albuquerque, NM 87114-5316
O'Connor, Francis J., 15 Pilgrim Cir., Apt. D, Methuen, MA 01844
O'Donnell, Timothy R., Immaculate Conception, 98 Summer St., Portsmouth, NH 03801-4398. Tel: 603-433-1819
Pelletier, Eugene J., Bishop Peterson Residence, 221 Orange St., Manchester, NH 03104-4324
Savage, Thomas J., P.O. Box 5531, Manchester, NH 03108
Shea, Leo A., P.O. Box 187, Danbury, NH 03230-0187
Shields, Joseph E., St. Mary Rectory, 182 Main St., P.O. Box 337, Newmarket, NH 03857-0337
Soucey, Louis A., 141 Lamplighters Park #16, North Conway, NH 03860-5174
Tremblay, Jean A., 110 Cilley Rd., Manchester, NH 03103-5638
Turgeon, Armand A., Winchester Arms, 53 New Rochester Rd. #12, Dover, NH 03820-2158
Vickery, Richard F., P.O. Box 984, Manchester, NH 03105-0984
Wright, John A., 1850 Front St. #1, Manchester, NH 03102

Permanent Deacons:
Albert, Merle M., Good Shepherd and Holy Family, Gorham
Albis, Leonard B., Mary, Queen of Peace, Salem
Anderson, Robert J., Jr., St. Kathryn, Hudson
Borkush, George J., Holy Angels, Plaistow
Cloutier, Richard A., St. John Neumann, Merrimack
Costello, David T., St. Joseph, Salem
Cummins, Clarence R., St. Matthew, Windham
Esposito, Robert, Epsom, NH
Fitzpatrick, T. Kelly, Piermont, NH
Ford, Thomas J., Waldoboro, ME
Gallinaro, Frank, St. Mary, Manchester
Hilston, Edmund C., Resurrection Parish, Nashua
Kayser, Charles Douglas, (On Leave of Absence)
Kram, Harry A., St. Patrick, Manchester
LaBonte, Alfred A., Jr., St. Joseph, Nashua
LaFleur, William Carl, Jr., St. Patrick, Jaffrey
Long, George H. (Gary), Jr., St. Thomas Aquinas, Derry
Martin, John J., St. Joseph Hospital, Nashua
Polcari, Joseph A., St. Matthew, Whitefield
Rich, William, St. Joseph, Center Ossipee
Schladenhauffen, Charles D., Immaculate Conception, Portsmouth
St. George, John H., St. Helena, Enfield
St. Laurent, Lionel A., St. Joseph Cathedral, Manchester
Testa, Paul E., (On Leave of Absence)
Tumulty, Peter J., Laconia, NH

INSTITUTIONS LOCATED IN THE DIOCESE

[A] SEMINARIES, RELIGIOUS OR SCHOLASTICATES

MANCHESTER. *St. Anselm Abbey Seminary*, 100 St. Anselm Dr., 03102. Tel: 603-641-7000; Fax: 603-641-7116.
E-mail: wsulliva@anselm.edu
Web site: www.anselm.edu
Order of St. Benedict. Rev. William J. Sullivan, O.S.B., Dir. Studies. Faculty 4; Students 3.

CENTER HARBOR. *Immaculate Conception Apostolic School*, Plymouth St., P.O. Box 936, 03226. Tel: 603-253-7728; Fax: 603-253-8740. Revs. David Steffy, L.C., Prin.; John Curran, L.C., Vice Prin.; Patrick Walsh, L.C.; Victor Franco, L.C.; Bros. Jacob Dumont, L.C.; Justin Kielhorn, L.C.; George Kim, L.C.; Thomas Vendetti, L.C. Priests 4; Brothers 4; Lay Teachers 6; Students 128.

[B] COLLEGES AND UNIVERSITIES

MANCHESTER. *Notre Dame College*, 2321 Elm St., 03104. Tel: 603-222-7100; Fax: 603-222-7101.

E-mail: info@notredame.edu
Web site: www.notredame.edu
For a complete listing, refer to the Colleges and Universities section.

Saint Anselm College, 03102. Tel: 603-641-7000; Fax: 603-641-7284.
E-mail: jdefelic@anselm.edu
Web site: www.anselm.edu
For a complete listing, refer to the Colleges and Universities section.

MERRIMACK. *The Thomas More College of Liberal Arts*, 6 Manchester St., 03054. Tel: 603-880-8308; Fax: 603-880-9280.
E-mail: thomaemorae@earthlink.com
Web site: www.thomasmorecollege.edu
For a complete listing, refer to the Colleges and Universities section.

NASHUA. *Rivier College*, 03060. Tel: 603-888-1311; Fax: 603-897-8883.
E-mail: poneil@rivier.edu
Web site: www.rivier.edu
For a complete listing, refer to the Colleges and Universities section.

WARNER. *Magdalen College*, 511 Kearsarge Mountain Rd., 03278-9206. Tel: 603-456-2656; Fax: 603-456-2660.
E-mail: admissions@magdalen.edu
Web site: www.magdalen.edu
For a complete listing, refer to the Colleges and Universities section.

[C] HIGH SCHOOLS, DIOCESAN

MANCHESTER. *Trinity High School*, 581 Bridge St., 03104-5395. Tel: 603-668-2910; Fax: 603-668-2913.
E-mail: trinity@hs.org
Web site: www.trinity.hs.org
Mr. Denis Mailloux, Prin.; Edward McMonagle, Asst. Prin.; Kathleen Lombard, Asst. Prin.; Rev. Raymond A. Ball, Chap.; Karen Courter, Camp. Min. Lay Teachers 28; Students 475.

CONCORD. *Bishop Brady High School*, 25 Columbus Ave., 03301. Tel: 603-224-7418; Fax: 603-228-6664.
E-mail: info@bishopbrady.edu
Web site: www.bishopbrady.edu
Jean Barker, Prin.; Joy Degnan, Asst. Prin. Sisters of Mercy. Sisters 2; Lay Teachers 36; Students 450.

DOVER. *St. Thomas Aquinas High School*, 197 Dover Point Rd., 03820. Tel: 603-742-3206; Fax: 603-749-7822.
E-mail: sta@stalux.org
Web site: www.stalux.org
Mr. Jeffrey A. Quinn, Prin.; Rev. George F. de Laire, Chap. Sisters 2; Lay Teachers 50; Students 690.

[D] HIGH SCHOOLS, PRIVATE

NASHUA. *Bishop Guertin High School*, 194 Lund Rd., 03060. Tel: 603-889-4107; Fax: 603-889-0701.
E-mail: lrl@bghs.org
Web site: www.bghs.org
Brothers of the Sacred Heart. (Coed). Bro. Leo Labbe, S.C., Pres.; Edward Quinn, Prin.; Bro. Paul Demers, S.C., Chap. Brothers 13; Lay Teachers 62; Students 830.

[E] REGIONAL ELEMENTARY SCHOOLS

MANCHESTER. *Mt. St. Mary Academy*. (Grades PreK-6), 147 Laurel St., 03103. Tel: 603-623-3155; Fax: 603-621-9254. Sr. Gloria Morin, R.S.M., Prin. Sisters 3; Lay Teachers 6; Students 120.

St. Anthony School. (Grades K-6), 148 Belmont St., 03103. Tel: 603-622-0414; Fax: 603-669-5212.
E-mail: school@holytony.org
Web site: wwww.holytony.org
Mrs. Constance A. Bilodeau, Prin. Sisters 1; Lay Teachers 24; Boys 205; Girls 229.

St. Casimir School. (Grades K-8), 456 Union St., 03103. Tel: 603-623-6411; Fax: 603-627-7745.
E-mail: stcasimirhn@mediaone.net
Web site: people.ne.mediaone.net/stcasimirnh
Sr. Mary Lawrence Lojko, C.S.S.F., Prin. Sisters 3; Lay Teachers 6; Students 187.

St. Catherine School. (Grades K-6), 206 North St., 03104. Tel: 603-622-1711; Fax: 603-624-4935.
E-mail: stcatherinenh@mediaone.net
Sr. Janet Belcourt, C.S.C., Prin. Sisters 3; Lay Teachers 23; Students 424.

St. Francis of Assisi School. 9 St. Francis Way, Litchfield, 03052-8050. Tel: 603-424-3312; Fax: 603-424-9128.
E-mail: sfschool@hotmail.com
Jude Chauvette, Prin. Sisters 1; Lay Teachers 7; Students 166.

St. Joseph Diocesan Regional Junior High Building. (Grades 7-8), 460 Pine St., 03104-6102. Tel: 603-624-4811; Fax: 603-624-6670.
E-mail: bmclean650@aol.com
Web site: members.aol.com/stjoesjrhs
Sr. Barbara McLean, R.S.M., Prin. Sisters 1; Lay Teachers 18; Students 319.

West Side Catholic Regional School. (Grades K-6), 85 Third St., 03102. Tel: 603-669-3932. Sr. Maria Rosa, P.M., Prin. Sisters 1; Lay Teachers 7; Students 178.

BERLIN. *St. Michael School*. (Berlin Regional Catholic School), 140 Blanchard St., 03570. Tel: 603-752-7413; Fax: 603-752-2746. Karen Wood, Prin. Lay Teachers 12; Students 138.

CLAREMONT. *St. Mary School*. (Grades K-8), 18 Central St., 03743. Tel: 603-542-6341; Fax: 603-542-5260. JoAnne Woodstock, Prin. Lay Teachers 9; Students 183.

CONCORD. *St. John Regional School*, 61 S. State St., 03301. Tel: 603-225-3222; Fax: 603-225-0195.
E-mail: fthrfoot@aol.com
Sr. Irene Turgeon, S.N.D., Prin. Sisters 3; Lay Teachers 9; Students 265.

DERRY. *St. Thomas Aquinas School*. (Grades K-8), 3 Moody St., 03038. Tel: 603-432-2712; Fax: 603-432-2179.
E-mail: staqderry@mediaone.net
Sr. Jacqueline Brodeur, C.S.C., Prin. Sisters 2; Lay Teachers 9; Students 300.

DOVER. *St. Mary Academy*, 222 Central Ave., 03820. Tel: 603-742-3299; Fax: 603-743-3483.
E-mail: stmarysdover@mediaone.net
Rosemary S. Reese, Prin. Sisters 1; Lay Teachers 19; Students 498.

HAMPTON. *Sacred Heart School*. (Grades PreK-8), 289 Lafayette Rd., 03842. Tel: 603-926-3254; Fax: 603-929-1109. Sr. Mary Joan Walsh, S.L.L., Prin. Sisters 2; Lay Teachers 22; Students 449.

JAFFREY. *St. Patrick School*. (Grades K-8), 70 Main St., 03452. Tel: 603-532-7676; Fax: 603-532-7476.
E-mail: faculty@stpats.mv.com
David L. O'Connell, Prin. Sisters 2; Lay Teachers 12; Students 186.

KEENE. *St. Joseph School*. (Grades PreK-8), 92 Wilson St., 03431. Tel: 603-352-2720; Fax: 603-358-5465. Carolyn O'Connell, Prin. Lay Teachers 14; Total Staff 25; Students 221.

LACONIA. *Holy Trinity*, 50 Church St., 03246. Tel: 603-524-3156.
E-mail: ccass@holytrinity.pvt.k12.nh.us
Web site: holytrinity.pvt.k12.nh.us
Mr. Jack Fortier, Prin. Lay Teachers 13; Total Staff 24; Students 200.

NASHUA. *Infant Jesus School*. (Grades K-6), 3 Crown St., 03060. Tel: 603-889-2649; Fax: 603-594-9117.
E-mail: school@infantjesus.mv.com
Web site: www.infantjesusparish.org/ijs
Sr. Marie Henault, P.M., Prin. Sisters 2; Lay Teachers 16; Students 363.

Nashua Catholic Regional Junior High. (Grades 7-9), 6 Bartlett Ave., 03064-1602. Tel: 603-883-6707; 882-7011; Fax: 603-594-8955. Mr. George R. LaVoice, Prin. Lay Teachers 20; Students 335.

St. Christopher School. (Grades K-6), 20 Cushing Ave., 03064. Tel: 603-882-7442; Fax: 603-594-9253. Sr. Joan Marie Messier, R.S.M., Prin. Sisters 1; Lay Teachers 15; Students 362.

PELHAM. *St. Patrick School*. (Grades K-8), 16 Main St., 03076. Tel: 603-635-2941; Fax: 603-635-9800.
E-mail: stpatsk8@aol.com
Web site: ultranet.com/~stpats
Phyllis B. McCarthy, Prin. Lay Teachers 10; Students 235.

PORTSMOUTH. *St. Patrick*. (Grades PreK-8), 125 Austin St., 03801. Tel: 604-436-0739; Fax: 604-436-1569. Janet DiNatale, Prin. Lay Teachers 14; Students 200.

ROCHESTER. *St. Elizabeth Seton School*. (Grades K-8), 16 Bridge St., 03867. Tel: 603-332-4803; Fax: 603-332-2915. Suzanne T. Boutin, Prin. Sisters 2; Lay Teachers 22; Students 325.

SALEM. *St. Joseph Regional School*. (Grades K-8), 40 Main St., 03079. Tel: 603-893-6811; Fax: 603-893-6811. Ms. Pauline A. Boulanger, Prin., Kindergarten. Rev. Daniel Lamonthe, Pastor. Lay Teachers 3; Students 72. Lay Teachers 23; Total Staff 38; Students 415.

WEST STEWARTSTOWN. *St. Albert School*. (Grades 1-8). P.O. Box 177, Beecher Falls, VT, 05902. Tel: 603-246-8631.
E-mail: stalbert@homestead.com
Web site: stalbert.homestead.com
Lay Teachers 4; Students 50.

[F] ELEMENTARY SCHOOLS, PRIVATE

MANCHESTER. *Holy Cross Kindergarten*, 357 Island Pond Rd., 03109-4811. Tel: 603-668-0510. Sr. Yvette M. Robert, C.S.C., Prin. & Admin. Sisters 3; Students 26.

St. Augustin Pre-School, 383 Beech St., 03103. Tel: 603-669-1864; Fax: 603-626-1517. Mrs. Mary Tremblay, Dir. Lay Teachers 6; Boys 20; Girls 27.

GOFFSTOWN. *Villa Augustina School*. (Grades K-8), 208 S. Mast St., 03045. Tel: 603-497-2361; Fax: 603-497-5981. Sr. Cecile Provost, C.S.C., Prin. Sisters 7; Lay Teachers 17; Students 332.

HUDSON. *Presentation of Mary Academy*. (Grades K-8), 182 Lowell Rd., 03051. Tel: 603-889-6054; Fax: 603-883-8054.
Web site: www.pmaschool.org
Sisters of the Presentation of Mary. Paul Raikey, Prin. Sisters 5; Lay Teachers 27; Students 502.

[G] CATHOLIC CHARITIES

MANCHESTER. *Catholic Charities Administration*, 215 Myrtle St., 03104. Tel: 603-669-3030; Fax: 603-626-1252.
Web site: catholiccharitiesnh.org
Mr. Raymond V. Mailloux, Diocesan Dir.; Mrs. Dominque Rust, Dir. Admin. Svcs.; Mr. Robert P. Clohosey, Dir. Family Svcs.; Ms. Kathleen A. Crane, Dir. Devel.; Sr. Peggy Crosby, S.N.D.deN., Dir. Immigration & Refugee Svcs.; Mr. Jeffrey J. Martin, Dir. Health Care Svcs.; Mr. Richard J. Shannon, Dir. Parish Social Ministry; Mrs. Kathy St. Onge, Dir. Supportive Svcs.
District Offices:
153 Grafton St., Berlin, 03570. Tel: 603-752-1325; Fax: 603-752-6174. Nicole Plourde, Admin. Mgr.
176 Loudon Rd., Concord, 03301. Tel: 603-228-1108; Fax: 603-228-1108. Sr. Rosemary Crowley, Admin. Mgr.
372 West St., Keene, 03431. Tel: 603-357-3093; Fax: 603-357-7810. Barnes Peterson, Admin. Mgr.
17 Gilford Ave, Laconia, 03246. Tel: 603-528-3035; Fax: 603-524-7153. Janet O'Connell, Admin. Mgr.
24 Hanover St., #8, Lebanon, 03766. Tel: 603-448-5151; Fax: 603-448-5155. Marc Cousineau, Admin. Mgr.
P.O. Box 323, Littleton, 03561. Tel: 603-444-7727; Fax: 603-444-7728. Anthony Poekert, Admin. Mgr.
325 Franklin St., 03101. Tel: 603-624-4717; Fax: 603-624-4736. Joseph Naff, Admin. Mgr.
261 Lake St., Nashua, 03060. Tel: 603-889-9431; Fax: 603-880-4643. Mary Kenison, Admin. Mgr.
23 Grant St., Rochester, 03867. Tel: 603-332-7701; Fax: 603-332-9629. Joseph Naff, Admin. Mgr.
23 Searles Rd., Windham, 03087. Tel: 603-893-1971; Fax: 603-898-8661. Mary Kenison, Admin. Mgr.
Other Programs:
Consultation Services for Church Ministers, 282 Concord St., 03104. Tel: 603-668-0014. Robert P. Clohosey, Dir.
Diocesan Bureau of Housing, 323 Franklin St., 03101. Tel: 603-625-5422; Fax: 603-625-1014.
E-mail: dbhinc@grolen.com
Carol A. Habler, Mgr.
Immigration and Refugee Services, 215 Myrtle St., 03104. Tel: 603-641-1259; Fax: 603-641-8476. Sr. Peggy Crosby, S.N.D.DeN., Dir. Legal and case management services for immigrants and refugees.
New Hampshire Food Bank, 62 W. Brook St., 03101. Tel: 603-669-9725; Fax: 603-669-0270. Albert J. Tremblay, Sr., Admin. Statewide food distribution to soup kitchens, food pantries and direct service programs.
Our Place, 323 Franklin St., 03101. Tel: 603-663-6376; Fax: 603-663-6536. Robert P. Clohosey, Dir. Family Svcs. Services for pregnant and parenting teens.
St. Charles Children's Home, 19 Grant St., Rochester, 03867. Tel: 603-332-4768.
E-mail: Stcharle@worldpath.net
Mother Paul Marie Santa Lucia, S.C.M.C., Admin. Residential services for children who have been removed from unsafe home environments. Total Staff 100; Total Assisted 35,000.

[H] CHILD CARE INSTITUTIONS

MANCHESTER. *St. Peter's Home*, 300 Kelley St., 03102-3093. Tel: 603-625-9313; Fax: 603-625-1910
For a complete listing, refer to the Special Care Facilities section.

ALLENSTOWN. *Pine Haven Boys Center*, River Rd., P.O. Suncook, 03275. Tel: 603-485-7141; Fax: 603-485-7142
For a complete listing, refer to the Special Care Facilities section.

ROCHESTER. *St. Charles Children's Home*, 19 Grant St., 03867-3099. Tel: 603-332-4768; Fax: 603-332-3948
For a complete listing, refer to the Special Care Facilities section.

[I] GENERAL HOSPITALS

MANCHESTER. *Catholic Medical Center of Manchester, NH, Inc.*, 100 McGregor St., 03102. Tel: 603-668-3545; Fax: 603-663-6850.
Web site: www.catholicmedicalcenter.org
For a complete listing, refer to the Hospitals section.

NASHUA. *St. Joseph Hospital*, 172 Kinsley St., 03061. Tel: 603-882-3000; Fax: 603-598-3344.
E-mail: cdescoteaux@sjh_nh.org
Web site: www.stjosephhospital.com
For a complete listing, refer to the Hospitals section.

[J] HEALTH CARE FACILITIES

MANCHESTER. *Carpenter Center, Inc.*, 323 Franklin St., 03101. Tel: 603-625-5422; Fax: 603-625-1014.
E-mail: dbhinc@grolen.com
For a complete listing, refer to the Special Care Facilities section.
Frances Warde House, Inc., 435 Union St., 03103
For a complete listing, refer to the Special Care Facilities section.
Mt. Carmel Nursing Home, 235 Myrtle St., 03104-4399. Tel: 603-627-3811; Fax: 603-626-4696
For a complete listing, refer to the Special Care Facilities section.
St. Teresa's Manor, 519 Bridge St., 03104-5396. Tel: 603-668-2373; Fax: 603-668-0059
For a complete listing, refer to the Special Care Facilities section.

BERLIN. *St. Vincent de Paul Nursing Home*, 29 Providence Ave., 03570-3199. Tel: 603-752-1820; Fax: 603-752-7149
For a complete listing, refer to the Special Care Facilities section.

DOVER. *St. Ann Home*, 195 Dover Point Rd., 03820-4693. Tel: 603-742-2612; Fax: 603-743-3055
For a complete listing, refer to the Special Care Facilities section.

JAFFREY. *Good Shepherd Nursing Home*, 20 Plantation Dr., 03452-1935. Tel: 603-532-8762; Fax: 603-532-6057
For a complete listing, refer to the Special Care Facilities section.

LACONIA. *Bishop Bradley Apartments*, 406 Court St., 03246
For a complete listing, refer to the Special Care Facilities section.
St. Francis Health Care Facility, 406 Court St., 03246-3000. Tel: 603-524-0466; Fax: 603-527-0884
For a complete listing, refer to the Special Care Facilities section.

NASHUA. *Marguerite's Place*, 87 Palm St., 03060. Tel: 603-598-1582; Fax: 603-598-7574.
E-mail: margplace@aol.com
For a complete listing, refer to the Special Care Facilities section.

WINDHAM. *Warde Health Center*, 21 Searles Rd., 03087-1297. Tel: 603-890-1290; Fax: 603-890-1293
For a complete listing, refer to the Special Care Facilities section.

[K] MONASTERIES AND RESIDENCES OF PRIESTS AND BROTHERS

MANCHESTER. *St. Anselm Abbey*, of the Order of St. Benedict and St. Anselm College, including Seminary and Formation Program. 100 St. Anselm Dr., 03102-1310. Tel: 603-641-7000; Fax: 603-641-7267.
E-mail: webmaster@anselm.edu
Web site: www.anselm.edu/abbey/index.html
Rt. Rev. Matthew K. Leavy, O.S.B., Abbot and Chancellor; Very Revs. William J. Sullivan, O.S.B., Prior; Peter J. Guerin, O.S.B., Subprior; Revs. Aquinas F. Cafarelli, O.S.B.; Bede G. Camera, O.S.B.; James G. Cassidy, O.S.B.; Mark A. Cooper, O.S.B.; David W. Cotter, O.S.B.; Michael H. Custer, O.S.B.; Jerome J. Day, O.S.B.; Jonathan P. DeFelice, O.S.B.; Daniel G. Dempski, O.S.B.; Cecil J. Donahue, O.S.B.; Brendan P. Donnelly, O.S.B.; Gerard J. Donnelly, O.S.B.; Mathias D. Durette, O.S.B.; Very Rev. John R. Fortin, O.S.B.; Revs. Jude J. Gray, O.S.B.; Benedict M. Guevin, O.S.B.; Augustine G. Kelly, O.S.B.; Iain G. MacLellan, O.S.B.; Finbar P. O'Mahony, O.S.B.; Benet C. Phillips, O.S.B.; Placidus H. Riley, O.S.B.; Lawrence Schlegel, O.S.B.; Patrick M. Sullivan, O.S.B. Priests 27; Brothers 8; Joan of Arc Sisters 9; Benedictine Sisters 2.

COLEBROOK. *Shrine of Our Lady of Grace*, 03576. Tel: 603-237-5511. Oblates of Mary Immaculate (United States Province). Revs. Robert G. Levesque, O.M.I., Supr.; Roland St. Pierre, O.M.I.; Roland M. Hamel, O.M.I.; Charles Moreau, O.M.I.; Bros. Onil Lauziere, O.M.I.; Maurice Violette, O.M.I.; Paul Ricard, O.M.I. Priests 4; Brothers 3.

ENFIELD. *Shrine of Our Lady of La Salette*, 410 NH Rte. 4A, P.O. Box 420, 03748-0420. Tel: 603-632-4301 (Gift Shop); 632-7087 (Business); Fax: 603-632-7648. Revs. Robert Campbell, M.S., Dir.; William Slight, M.S., Subprior. Chaplains: Revs. Leo Maxfield, M.S.; Joseph Ross, M.S.; Bros. Emile Morin, M.S.; Robert Roy, M.S.; Jean Denis Roy, M.S.; Claude Rheaume, M.S.; Deacon David Carignan, M.S. Priests 4; Brothers 4; Deacons 1; Total Staff 13.

LES CAYES, HAITI. *Paroisse Ste. Anne*, B.P. 14. Rev. George Brown, O.M.I., 33 Clark St., Framingham, MA, 01701-6407. Tel: 508-872-9142. Rev. Norman Comtois, O.M.I. 184 Highland Ave., Lowell, MA, 01851-3917. Tel: 978-452-9254. Rev. Wilfred Harvey, O.M.I. 184 Highland Ave., Lowell, MA, 01851-3917. Tel: 978-453-6265. Rev. John King, O.M.I., Monastery of Our Lady in Beatitude, Grooville Rd., Livingston Manor, NY, 12758. Tel: 914-439-4300. Rev. Maurice Lang, O.M.I., Genesis Farm, 41A Silver Lake Rd., Blairstown, NJ, 07825. Tel: 908-362-6735; Fax: 908-362-7486. Rev. Michael Lauze, O.M.I., 438 East Ave., Lewiston, ME, 04240. Tel: 207-784-5233. Rev. Michael O'Hara, O.M.I., Box 729, Peck Slip Station, New York, NY, 10272. Rev. Paul Ouellette, O.M.I., Ste. Jeanne d'Arc Parish, 129 Fourth Ave., Lowell, MA, 01854-2799. Tel: 978-458-6316; Fax: 978-970-2299. Rev. George Roy, O.M.I.

NASHUA. *Brothers of the Sacred Heart*, 28 Berkeley St., 03064. Tel: 603-595-2712. Bro. Raymond Hetu, S.C., Dir. Brothers 6. 194 Lund Rd., 03060. Tel: 603-883-3683. Bro. Roger Lemoyne, S.C., Dir. Brothers 8.

[L] CONVENTS AND RESIDENCES OF SISTERS

MANCHESTER. *Cathedral Rectory*, 145 Lowell St., 03101-6135. Tel: 603-622-6404; Fax: 603-626-4415. Little Sisters of the Holy Family in charge of domestic department. Sr. Lucille Brunette, P.S.S.F., Supr. Sisters 4.
Monastery of the Precious Blood, 700 Bridge St., 03104. Tel: 603-623-4264; Fax: 603-647-8385. Sisters Adorers of the Precious Blood. Sr. Mary Agnes, Supr.; Rev. Msgr. Albert W. Olkovikas, Chap. Sisters 30.
Regional Office of the Sisters of Holy Cross, 377 Island Pond Rd., 03109. Tel: 603-622-9504; Fax: 603-622-9782.
E-mail: sraandy99@yahoo.com
Sr. Louise Auclair, C.S.C., Regl. Rep. Total Staff 8.
St. Catherine Convent, 539 N. River Rd., 03104. Tel: 603-669-7854; Fax: 603-624-4935. Sisters of the Holy Cross 2.
St. George Manor, 357 Island Pond Rd., 03109. Tel: 603-624-4557. Sr. Lorraine Paille, C.S.C., Supr.; Rev. Andre J. Gagnon, Chap. (Non-residential). Sisters 82.
Sisters of Holy Cross, 326 Ash St., 03104-3205. Tel: 603-222-2080.
E-mail: lulucsc@aol.com
Sisters 2.
Sisters of Holy Cross, 2298 Elm St., 03104. Tel: 603-668-6143. Sisters 3.
Sisters of Holy Cross, 346 Coolidge Ave. M #2, 03102. Tel: 603-622-6818. Sisters 5. 971 Chestnut St., 03104. Sisters 4.
Sisters of Holy Cross, 2264 Elm St., 03104. Sisters 2.
Sisters of Holy Cross, 454 Island Pond Rd., 03109-4812. Sisters 3.
Sisters of Holy Cross, 136 Lynwood Ln., 03109. Tel: 603-622-6055. Sr. Louise Audette, C.S.C., Supr. Sisters 5.
Sisters of Holy Cross. Queen of Angels Convent, 113 Wedgewood Ln., 03109-4825. Sisters 4.
Sisters of the Presentation of Mary Provincial House, 495 Mammoth Rd., 03104-5494. Tel: 603-669-1080; Fax: 603-622-4953. Sr. Suzanne Bourret, P.M., Prov. Supr. Sisters in the Diocese 195; Sisters of the Presentation of Mary 210. St. Joseph Residence, 495 Mammoth Rd., 03104-5494. Tel: 603-627-5831; 668-6011. St. Marie Residence, 495 Mammoth Rd., 03104-5494. Tel: 603-623-0671. Bethany House, 25 Garmon St., 03104. Tel: 603-625-1957. St. Marie Convent, 133 Wayne St., 03102. Tel: 603-623-0815. St. Bernard Convent, 161 Main St., Keene, 03431. Tel: 603-357-4472. Rivier College, 420 Main St., Nashua, 03060. Tel: 603-888-1311, Ext. 8291; Fax: 603-897-8883. Presentation of Mary Academy, 182 Lowell Rd., Hudson, 03051-4987. Tel: 603-883-8192; 889-6362; Fax: 603-883-8054. Presentation of Mary Novitiate, 180 Lowell Rd., Hudson, 03051-4987. Tel: 603-880-8186; Fax: 603-880-0298. Trinity House, 186 Lowell Rd., Hudson, 03051-4908. Tel: 603-882-1347. Presentation of Mary Convent, 633 Third Ave., Berlin, 03570. Tel: 603-752-1176; Fax: 603-752-4115. Our Lady of Hope House of Prayer, 400 Temple Rd., New Ipswich, 03071. Tel: 603-878-2346; Fax: 603-878-4552. Holy Angels Convent, 6 Atkinson Depot Rd., Rte 121, Plaistow, 03865. Tel: 603-382-2744.

CONCORD. *Monastery of Discalced Carmelites*, 275 Pleasant St., 03301-2590. Tel: 603-225-5791. Sr. Emmanuel Sache, O.C.D., Prioress. Professed Sisters 10; Novices 1.

GOFFSTOWN. *Villa Augustina Convent*, 208 S. Mast Rd., 03045. Tel: 603-497-3636; 603-497-3445; Fax: 603-497-4080. Sr. Michelle Authier, R.J.M., Supr. Religious of Jesus and Mary 19.

LITTLETON. *Provincial House of Daughters of the Charity of the Sacred Heart of Jesus*, Mount Sacred Heart, Grove St., P.O. Box 642, 03561. Tel: 603-444-5346; Fax: 603-444-5348.
E-mail: sjrpro@landmarknet.net
Local Superiors: Sr. Lucille Grandpre; Sr. Yvette Beloin; Sr. Jeannette Roy, Prov. Supr. Sisters 37.

LONDONDERRY. *Sisters of Holy Cross*, Londonderry House, 68 Mammoth Rd., 03053.

NEW IPSWICH. *Our Lady of Hope, House of Prayer*, 400 Temple Rd., 03071. Tel: 603-878-2346; Fax: 603-878-4552.
E-mail: jleblanc@earthlink.net
Web site: presentationofmary.com
Sr. Jacqueline LeBlanc, P.M., Supr. & Dir. Sisters 5.

PITTSFIELD. *Berakah*. A Place for Blessing, 96 Fairview Rd., 03263-3817. Tel: 603-435-7271; Fax: 603-435-6670.
E-mail: berakah@aol.com
Sisters 6.

PORTSMOUTH. *Our Lady of Lourdes Convent*, 125 Austin St., #2, 03801. Tel: 603-436-6612; Fax: 603-436-7429.
E-mail: oll11@mediaone.net
Sisters of Our Lady of Lourdes (S.L.L.). Sr. Mary Joan Walsh, S.L.L., Supr. Sisters 2.

WINDHAM. *Sisters of Mercy of the Americas*. Tel: 603-893-6550; Fax: 603-893-2413.
E-mail: nhsistersofmercy@worldnet.att.net
Motherhouse of the Sisters of Mercy, Inc., Regional Community of New Hampshire, 21 Searles Rd., 03087-1297. Tel: 603-893-6550 (Admin. Office); Fax: 603-893-2413. Sisters of Mercy of New Hampshire. Sr. Patricia Sullivan, Regl. Community Pres. Sisters 45.
Mount Saint Mary Corporation of the Sisters of Mercy, Inc., Nashua. Tel: 603-883-7874; Fax: 603-594-4178.
Manchester Convent of the Sisters of Mercy, Manchester.
Warde Health Center, Inc. Tel: 603-890-1290; Fax: 603-890-1293.
Mount St. Mary Academy, Inc., Manchester. Tel: 603-623-3155; Fax: 603-621-9254.
Frances Warde House, Manchester.

[M] RETREAT HOUSES

MANCHESTER. *Emmaus House*, 286 Concord St., 03104. Tel: 603-624-1173. Sr. Bernadette Turgeon, S.N.D-.deN., Co-Dir.; Matthew Goody, Co-Dir. Total Staff 14.

ENFIELD. *La Salette Shrine and Center of Enfield*, 417 N.H. Rte. 4A, P.O. Box 420, 03748. Tel: 603-632-7087 (Business); 632-4301 (Gift Shop); Fax: 603-632-7648. Revs. William Slight, M.S., Supr.; Robert Campbell, M.S., Shrine Dir. Chaplains: Revs. Leo Maxfield, M.S.; Joseph Russ. Priests 4; Deacons 1; Brothers 4; Total Staff 13.

[N] CAMPUS MINISTRY AND NEWMAN CENTERS

MANCHESTER. *Campus Ministries*, Diocese of Manchester, 153 Ash St., P.O. Box 310, 03105, Ext. 8537. Bro. Paul R. Demers, S.C., Dartmouth College, Aquinas House, P.O. Box 147, Hanover, 03755. Tel: 603-643-2154; Fax: 603-643-9411. Revs. Brendan Buckley, O.F.M.Cap.; John P. McHugh, O.F.M.Cap., New Hampshire College, 2500 N. River Rd., 03104. Tel: 603-668-2211, Ext. 2139. Rev. Bruce W. Collard, Saint Anselm College, 100 St. Anselm Dr., 03102. Tel: 603-641-7130.
E-mail: cdonahue@anselm.edu
Rev. Cecil J. Donahue, O.S.B., Rivier College, 420 Main St., Nashua, 03060. Tel: 603-888-1311; 897-8537.
E-mail: gcouture@rivier.edu
Web site: www.rivier.com
Sr. Guyleane Couture, P.M.; Bro. Paul Demers, S.C. Tel: 603-897-8537, Plymouth State College, 46 Langdon St., Plymouth, 03264. Tel: 603-535-2673.
E-mail: mdougher@mail.plymouth.edu
University of New Hampshire, Catholic Student Center, P.O. Box 620, Durham, 03824. Tel: 603-862-1310; Fax: 603-868-3765.
E-mail: aehickey@kopper.unh.edu
Web site: www.pubpages.unh.edu/~bjs
Rev. Daniel St. Laurent.
Keene State College, Newman Center, 232 Main St., P.O. Box 491, Keene, 03431. Tel: 603-352-1909.
E-mail: mdamato@ksc.edu
Notre Dame College, 2321 Elm St., 03104. Tel: 603-669-4298, Ext. 100. Rev. James P. Walsh; Sr. Edie Daly, S.N.D.deN.

DURHAM. *St. Thomas More Catholic Student Center at the University of New Hampshire*, 6 Madbury Rd., P.O. Box 620, 03824-0620. Tel: 603-862-1310; Fax: 603-868-3765.
E-mail: stmdurham@aol.com
Rev. Daniel A. St. Laurent, Chap; Amy E. Hickey, Assoc. Chap.; Mary Beth Nazzaro, Assoc. Chap.

HANOVER. *The Catholic Student Center at Dartmouth, Aquinas House, Aquinas at Dartmouth, Inc.*, 2 Occom Ridge, P.O. Box 147, 03755. Tel: 603-643-2154; Fax: 603-643-9411.
Web site: http://www.dartmouth.edu/~aquinas
Revs. John P. McHugh, O.F.M.Cap., Dir.; Brendan

Buckley, O.F.M.Cap., Assoc. Chap.; Anna Mae Mayer, Assoc. Chap. Total Staff 4; Total in Residence 2.

HENNIKER. *New England College Newman Center*, St. Theresa Rectory, 03242. Tel: 603-428-3325. Rev. Andre M. Thibodeau, Chap.

KEENE. *Keene State College, Catholic Newman Center*, 232 Main St., P.O. Box 491, 03431. Tel: 603-352-7785; 358-2100.

NEW LONDON. *Colby-Sawyer College Newman Center*, Our Lady of Fatima Rectory, 03257. Tel: 603-526-4484. Rev. Richard T. Lower, Chap.

PLYMOUTH. *Plymouth State College Campus Ministry*, Plymouth State College, Ste. A6, 03264. Tel: 603-535-2673.
E-mail: mdougher@mail.plymouth.edu
Maura M. Dougherty, Catholic Campus Min. Tel: 603-535-2673.

RINDGE. *Franklin Pierce College Newman Center*, Keene State College, 232 Main St., P.O. Box 491, 03431. Tel: 603-352-7785. Mary Ann Damato, Chap.

[O] MISCELLANEOUS

MANCHESTER. *Alliance Ambulatory Services, Inc.*, 100 McGregor St., 03102. Tel: 603-668-3545. Alyson Pitman Giles, Pres. & CEO.
Alliance Resources Inc, 100 McGregor St., 03102. Tel: 603-668-3545. Alyson Pitman Giles, Pres. & CEO.
Catholic Medical Center Physician Practice Associates (CMCPPA), 100 McGregor St., 03102. Tel: 603-668-3545. Alyson Pitman Giles, Pres. & CEO.
Crown Ministries —New Hampshire, 25 Maybrook Ave., 03102. Tel: 603-627-8898.
Web site: www.crownnh.org
Geoff Ashman, Treas.
Diocesan Museum, 140 Laurel St., 03103. Tel: 603-624-1729; 623-8196. Judith Fosher, Coord.
Hillcrest Terrace Inc., 200 Alliance Way, 03102. Tel: 603-645-6500. Alyson Pitman Giles, Pres. & CEO.
Holy Cross Health Center, Inc., 357 Island Pond Rd., 03109-4811. Tel: 603-628-3550; Fax: 603-626-6270.
E-mail: hchcjudy@banet.net
Sr. Judith Langevin, C.S.C., N.H.A., Admin. Nursing home for women religious.
Sophia Institute Press, P.O. Box 5284, 03108. Tel: 603-641-9344; Fax: 603-641-8108.
E-mail: sipress@grolen.com
Web site: sophiainstitute.com
John L. Barger, Publisher.

CENTER HARBOR. *L.C. Center Harbor, Inc.*, Plymouth St., P.O. Box 936, 03226. Tel: 603-253-7728; Fax: 603-253-8740.

FRANKLIN. *Holy Cross Associates of U.S. Region*, 33 Holy Cross Rd., 03235. Tel: 603-934-4874; 837-2835. Jan Rondeau, H.C.A., Pres. & Exec. Dir.; Lorraine Richard, H.C.A., Vice Pres.; Betty Poliquin, H.C.A., Treas.; Fran Miller, H.C.A., Sec.

GILFORD. *The Missionary Servants of Pope John Paul I*, 22 Boyd Hill Rd., 03246. Tel: 603-524-4740; Fax: 603-524-4740. The Missionary Servants of Pope John Paul I is a lay missionary association founded to aid established missionaries. Help is mainly given to Mother Teresa's missions in Haiti; however, shipments have also been made to Honduras, the Sudan, British Columbia, areas of the U.S. and to the local poor.

[P] SPECIAL APOSTOLATE CENTERS

DURHAM. *Christian Life Center*, 6 Madbury Rd., P.O. Box 471, 03824. Tel: 603-868-5514. Sr. Claudette Carisse, S.A.S.V., Dir.

KEENE. *Christian Life Center*, P.O. Box 293, 03431. Tel: 603-352-7662; Fax: 603-352-7662.
E-mail: sisterjoan3@juno.com

LACONIA. *Christian Life Center*, Box 306, 03247. Tel: 603-524-7503. Janet Leroux, Coord.

NASHUA. *Nashua Deanery Toward Marriage Program*, P.O. Box 3403, 03061-3403. Tel: 603-889-0707.

SALEM. *Christian Life Center*, P.O. Box 314, 03079. Tel: 603-893-5878. Paul J. Ashton, Dir.

[Q] CAMPS AND COMMUNITY CENTERS

CENTER OSSIPEE. *Camp Marist*, Rte. 25 E., 03814. Tel: 603-539-4552; Fax: 603-539-8318.
E-mail: marist@ix.netcom.com
Web site: cmarist.org
Bro. Jim Halliday, Dir. Total Staff 100; Total Assisted 250.

GILMANTON IRON WORKS. *Camp Bernadette*. (Girls), Winter Business Office, P.O. Box 206, 03837-0206. Tel: 603-364-5851; Fax: 603-364-5038.
E-mail: diocamps@worldpath.net
Web site: www.diocamps.org
Summer Business Office, 83 Richards Rd., Wolfeboro, 03894. Tel: 603-569-1692. Mr. Gus Planchet, Dir. Total Staff 80; Total Assisted 1,080.
Camp Fatima. (Boys), Business Office, P.O. Box 206, 03837-0206. Tel: 603-364-5851; Fax: 603-364-5038.
E-mail: diocamps@worldpath.net
Web site: www.diocamps.org
Mr. Gus Planchet, Dir. Total Staff 80; Total Assisted 1,100.

RELIGIOUS INSTITUTES OF MEN REPRESENTED IN THE DIOCESE

For further details refer to the corresponding bracketed number in the Religious Institutes of Men or Women section.

[0190]—*Basilian Salvatorian Fathers*.—B.S.O.
[0200]—*Benedictine Monks*. (American Cassinese & Camaldolese Benedictine Congregations).—O.S.B.
[1100]—*Brothers of the Sacred Heart*. (New England Prov.).—S.C.
[0470]—*The Capuchin Friars*. (Prov. of St. Mary).—O.F.M.Cap.
[1320]—*Clerics of St. Viator*.—C.S.V.
[1330]—*Congregation of the Mission*. (New England Prov.).—C.M.
[0260]—*Discalced Carmelite Fathers*. (Prov. of Immaculate Heart of Mary).—O.C.D.
[0520]—*Franciscan Friars*. (Province of the Immaculate Conception).—O.F.M.
[0690]—*Jesuit Fathers and Brothers*. (Maryland & New England Provinces).—S.J.
[0730]—*Legionaries of Christ*.—L.C.
[0770]—*The Marist Brothers*.—F.M.S.
[0720]—*The Missionaries of Our Lady of La Salette*. (Immaculate Heart of Mary & Our Lady of Seven Dolors Provinces).—M.S.
[0720]—*Missionaries of Our Lady of LaSalette (Providence of Our Lady of Seven Dolors)*.—M.S.
[0910]—*Oblates of Mary Immaculate*. (Prov. of St. John the Baptist).—O.M.I.
[0430]—*Order of Preachers (Dominicans)*.—O.P.
[0610]—*Priests of the Congregation of Holy Cross*.—C.S.C.
[0690]—*The Society of Jesus (Korean Prov.)*.—S.J.
[0370]—*The Society of St. Columban*.—S.S.C.
[1250]—*Somascan Fathers*.—C.R.S.
[0410]—*Sons of Divine Providence (Bon Orione Fathers)*.—F.D.P.

RELIGIOUS INSTITUTES OF WOMEN REPRESENTED IN THE DIOCESE

[0200]—*Benedictine Sisters*.—O.S.B.
[0230]—*Benedictine Sisters of Pontifical Jurisdiction*. (from Kaunas, Lithuania).—O.S.B.
[2410]—*Congregation of the Marianites of Holy Cross*.—M.S.C.
[3815]—*Congregation of the Sisters of St. Joan of Arc*.—S.J.A.
[1150]—*Congregation of the Sisters of St. Joseph of Boston*.—C.S.J.
[0750]—*Daughters of the Charity of the Sacred Heart of Jesus*.—F.C.S.C.J.
[0420]—*Discalced Carmelites Nuns*.—O.C.D.
[]—*Dominican Sisters of Hope*.—O.P.
[1170]—*Felician Sisters*.—C.S.S.F.
[1310]—*Franciscan Sisters of Little Falls, MN*.—O.S.F.
[1190]—*Franciscan Sisters of the Atonement*.—S.A.
[1840]—*Grey Nuns of the Sacred Heart*.—G.N.S.H.
[2575]—*Institute of the Sisters of Mercy of the Americas*. (Manchester, NH).—R.S.M.
[2320]—*The Little Sisters of the Holy Family*.—P.S.S.F.
[2470]—*Maryknoll Sisters of St. Dominic*.—M.M.
[3450]—*Religious of Jesus and Mary*.—R.J.M.
[2970]—*School Sisters of Notre Dame*.—S.S.N.D.
[1680]—*School Sisters of St. Francis*.—O.S.F.
[3500]—*Servants of the Blessed Sacrament*.—S.S.S.
[0110]—*The Sisters Adorers of the Precious Blood*.—A.P.B.
[0490]—*Sisters of Charity of Montreal (Grey Nuns)*.—S.G.M.
[0530]—*Sisters of Charity of Our Lady, Mother of the Church*.—S.C.M.C.
[0610]—*Sisters of Charity of St. Hyacinthe (Grey Nuns)*.—S.C.S.H.
[0640]—*Sisters of Charity of St. Vincent De Paul, Halifax*.—S.C.
[1930]—*Sisters of Holy Cross*.—C.S.C.
[3000]—*Sisters of Notre Dame de Namur*.—S.N.D.deN.
[3080]—*Sisters of Our Lady of Christian Doctrine*.—R.C.D.
[]—*Sisters of Our Lady of Lourdes (Pius Association of the Faithful)*.—O.L.L.
[3350]—*Sisters of Providence*. (Montreal).—S.P.
[3360]—*Sisters of Providence of Saint Mary-of-the-Woods, IN*.—S.P.
[3718]—*Sisters of St. Ann*.—S.S.A.
[3750]—*Sisters of St. Chretienne*.—S.S.C.h.
[3840]—*Sisters of St. Joseph of Carondelet*. (Prov. of Albany).—C.S.J.
[0150]—*Sisters of the Assumption*.—S.A.S.V.
[1990]—*Sisters of the Holy Names of Jesus and Mary*.—S.N.J.M.
[3310]—*Sisters of the Presentation of Mary*.—P.M.
[3320]—*Sisters of the Presentation of the B.V.M.*—P.B.V.M.
[]—*Society of Sisters for the Church*.—S.S.C.

NECROLOGY

† Bolduc, Rev. Msgr. Norman P, Auburn, NH St. Peter. —Died Sept. 30, 2000.
† Bombardier, Wilfrid F., (Retired). —Died Sept. 16, 2000.
† Boucher, Nelson, (Retired). —Died June 21, 2000.
† Cameron, Albert S., (Retired). —Died Jan. 3, 2001.
† Nolan, Rev. Msgr. William L., (Retired). —Died May 1, 2000.
† Olkovikas, Rev. Msgr. Albert W., P.A, Manchester, NH NH Monastery of the Precious Blood. —Died May 13, 2000.

Diocese of Marquette

(Dioecesis Marquettensis)

Most Reverend

JAMES H. GARLAND, M.A., M.S.W., D.D.

Bishop of Marquette; ordained 1959; appointed Titular Bishop of Garriana and Auxiliary Bishop of Cincinnati June 2, 1984; consecrated July 25, 1984; appointed Bishop of Marquette October 6, 1992; installed November 11, 1992. *Res., 300 Rock St., P.O. Box 550, Marquette, MI, 49855.* Tel.: 906-225-1141.

Most Reverend

MARK F. SCHMITT, D.D.

Retired Bishop of Marquette; ordained May 22, 1948; appointed Titular Bishop of Kells and Auxiliary of Green Bay May 5, 1970; consecrated June 24, 1970; appointed to Marquette March 21, 1978; installed May 8, 1978; retired November 11, 1992. *Res., HCO1 Box 159, Marquette, MI, 49855.*

Chancery Office: 444 S. Fourth St., P.O. Box 550, Marquette, MI, 49855. Tel.: 906-225-1141; Fax: 906-225-0437.

E-mail address: asample@dioceseofmarquette.org

VICARIATE-APOSTOLIC JULY 29, 1853; DIOCESE 1857.

Square Miles 16,281.

Comprises the Upper Peninsula of the State of Michigan.

For legal titles of parishes and diocesan institutions, consult the Pastoral Office.

STATISTICAL OVERVIEW

Personnel	
Bishop	1
Retired Bishops	1
Priests: Diocesan Active in Diocese	56
Priests: Active Outside Diocese	5
Priests: Retired, Sick or Absent	39
Number of Diocesan Priests	100
Religious Priests in Diocese	13
Extern Priests in Diocese	8
Ordinations:	
Diocesan Priests	1
Permanent Deacons in Diocese	22
Total Sisters	59
Parishes	
Parishes	74
With Resident Pastor:	
Resident Diocesan Priests	53
Resident Religious Priests	8
Without Resident Pastor:	
Administered by Priests	10
Administered by Women Religious	3
Missions	23
Professional Ministry Personnel:	
Sisters	13
Lay Ministers	31
Welfare	
Catholic Hospitals	1
Total Assisted	80,043
Homes for the Aged	1
Total Assisted	123
Special Centers for Social Services	6
Total Assisted	2,083
Educational	
Diocesan Students in Other Seminaries	9
Total Seminarians	9
Elementary Schools, Diocesan and Parish	10
Total Students	1,669
Catechesis/Religious Education:	
High School Students	3,086
Elementary Students	5,998
Total Students Under Catholic Instruction	10,762
Teachers in the Diocese:	
Sisters	8
Lay Teachers	113
Vital Statistics	
Receptions into the Church:	
Infant Baptism Totals	990
Adult Baptism Totals	66
Received into Full Communion	127
First Communions	959
Confirmations	973
Marriages:	
Catholic	346
Interfaith	191
Total Marriages	537
Deaths	1,244
Total Catholic Population	70,237
Total Population	309,000

Former Bishops—Most Rev. FREDERIC BARAGA, D.D., first Bishop; cons. Nov. 1, 1853; died Jan. 19, 1868.—Most Rev. IGNATIUS MRAK, D.D., cons. Feb. 7, 1869; resigned 1878; transferred to Antinoe 1879; died Jan. 2, 1901.—Most Rev. JOHN VERTIN, D.D., cons. Sept. 14, 1879; died Feb. 26, 1899.—Most Rev. FREDERICK EIS, D.D., cons. Aug. 24, 1899 made Asst. at the Pontifical Throne July 13, 1922; resigned July 8, 1922; appt. Titular Bishop of Bita; died May 5, 1926.—Most Rev. PAUL JOSEPH NUSSBAUM, D.D., cons. Bishop of Corpus Christi May 20, 1913; resigned March 26, 1920; appt. Bishop of Marquette Nov. 14, 1922; died June 24, 1935.—Most Rev. JOSEPH CASIMIR PLAGENS, D.D., LL.D., cons. Sept. 30, 1924, Auxiliary Bishop of Detroit Titular Bishop of Rhodiopolis; appt. to See of Marquette Nov. 16, 1935; transferred to the See of Grand Rapids Dec. 16, 1940; died March 31, 1943.—Most Rev. FRANCIS J. MAGNER, D.D., appt. Dec. 21, 1940; cons. Feb. 24, 1941; died June 13, 1947.—Most Rev. THOMAS L. NOA, D.D., cons. March 19, 1946; Titular Bishop of Salona and Coadjutor Bishop of Sioux City; appt. Bishop of Marquette Aug. 20, 1947; retired March 25, 1968; died March 13, 1977.—Most Rev. CHARLES A. SALATKA, D.D., appt. Titular Bishop of Cariana and Auxiliary of Grand Rapids Dec. 9, 1961; cons. March 6, 1962; appt. Bishop of Marquette Jan. 10, 1968; installed March 25, 1968; appt. Archbishop of Oklahoma City Oct. 11, 1977.—Most. Rev. MARK F. SCHMITT, D.D., appt. Titular Bishop of Kells and Auxiliary of Green Bay May 5, 1970; cons. June 24, 1970; appt. Bishop of Marquette March 21, 1978; installed May 8, 1978; retired November 11, 1992.

Chancery Office—444 S. Fourth St., P.O. Box 550, Marquette, 49855. Tel: 906-225-1141; Fax: 906-225-0437. Office Hours: June-Aug. Mon.-Fri. 8-4; Sept.-May Mon.-Fri. 9-5.

Vicar General—Rev. JOHN E. PATRICK, V.G.

Chancellor—Rev. ALEXANDER K. SAMPLE, J.C.L.

Secretary to the Bishop—Mrs. PATRICIA A. PETERSON. Tel: 906-227-9115.

Diocesan Tribunal—444 S. Fourth St., P.O. Box 550, Marquette, 49855. Tel: 906-227-9111.

Judicial Vicar—Rev. Msgr. PETER OBERTO, J.C.L.

Adjutant Judicial Vicar—Rev. ALEX K. SAMPLE, J.C.L.

Diocesan Judges—Revs. ALEX K. SAMPLE, J.C.L.; JOSEPH NAGAROOR, J.C.D.

Defensore Vinculi—Rev. JOHN J. SHIVERSKI.

Advocates—Revs. FRANCIS J. DEGROOT; JOHN L. LONGBUCCO.

Notary—MARY C. JESKE.

Priests' Council—

Executive Board—Revs. MICHAEL A. WOEMPNER, Chm. RONALD J. SKUFCA, Vice Chm. MARK A. MCQUESTEN, Treas. GLENN J. THEORET, Sec.

Deans—Revs. JOHN J. SHIVERSKI, Marquette; CHRISTOPHER B. GARDINER, Escanaba; WAYNE E. MARCOTTE, Houghton; Rev. Msgr. JAMES A. KACZMAREK, Iron Mountain; Revs. DARRYL J. PEPIN, Ironwood; S. PATRICK WISNESKE, Menominee; FRANCIS J. DEGROOT, Sault Ste. Marie; OTTO J. SARTORELLI, Iron River; JOHN E. MARTIGNON, Manistique.

Consultors—Revs. CHRISTOPHER B. GARDINER; JOHN F. MCARDLE; RAYMOND J. ZEUGNER; NORMAN A. CLISCH; WAYNE E. MARCOTTE; Rev. Msgr. JOHN E. PATRICK; Rev. ALEXANDER K. SAMPLE.

Diocesan Offices and Directors

Administration & Finance, Dept. of—RICHARD R. SCHAEFER, C.P.A., Dir. CAROL J. PARKER, Accountant & Computer Information Coord., *444 S. Fourth St., P.O. Box 550, Marquette, 49855.* Tel: 906-227-9105; Fax: 906-225-0437.

Archives—Rev. ALEX K. SAMPLE, Chancellor; ELIZABETH DELENE, Archivist, *347 Rock St., Marquette, 49855.* Tel: 906-227-9117; Fax: 906-228-2469.

Development, Office of—TERRI GADZINSKI, Dir., *444 S. Fourth St., P.O. Box 550, Marquette, 49855.* Tel: 906-227-9138; Fax: 906-225-0437.

Catholic Social Services, Dept. of—LARRY ZIOMKOWSKI, Dir., *347 Rock St., Marquette, 49855.* Tel: 906-227-9119. Branch Offices: Houghton, Escanaba, Iron Mountain, Sault Ste., Marie, Ironwood.

Christian Education/Formation Services, Dept. of—Sr. JOYCE ROSE, O.S.F., Dir. CLIFFORD LUFT, Supt. of Schools; PAT NIKSICH, Pres., Board of Educ. ROBERT ST. LOUIS, Vice Pres., Board of Educ., *347 Rock St., P.O. Box 280, Marquette, 49855.* Tel: 906-227-9123; Fax: 906-228-1522.

Communication Services, Dept. of—LOREENE ZENO KOSKEY, Dir., *347 Rock St., P.O. Box 548, Marquette, 49855.* Tel: 906-227-9129; Fax: 906-226-6941.

Newspaper "The Upper Peninsula Catholic"—JOSEPH ZYBLE, Editor, *347 Rock St., P.O. Box 548, Marquette, 49855.* Tel: 906-227-9131; Fax: 906-226-6941.

Ministry Personnel Services, Dept. of—Rev. ALEXANDER K. SAMPLE, Dir., *444 S. Fourth St., P.O. Box 550, Marquette, 49855.* Tel: 906-227-9111; Fax: 906-225-0437.

Priests' Personnel, Office of—Rev. JAMES C. ZIMINSKI, Dir., *1200 Hebard Court, Marquette, 49855.* Tel: 906-228-0229; Fax: 906-228-0280.

Spiritual Development Services, Dept. of—JAMES HANSEN, Dir., *444 S. Fourth St., P.O. Box 550, Marquette, 49855.* Tel: 906-226-9884; Fax: 906-225-0437.

Apostleship of the Sea—Rev. TED BRODEUR, Chap., *Holy Name of Mary Parish, 377 Maple St., Sault Ste. Marie, 49783.* Tel: 906-632-3381.

Bishop Baraga Association Inc.—347 Rock St., P.O. Box 548, Marquette, 49855. Tel: 906-227-9117; Fax: 906-228-2469. An international organization to promote the Cause of the Beatification of the Most Rev. Frederic Baraga. Rev. ALEX K. SAMPLE, Exec. Dir., Treas. & Vice-Postulator; Rev. PAOLO LOMBARDO, O.F.M., Postulator; ELIZABETH J. DELENE, Archivist & Editor of the Baraga Bulletin.

Building Commission, Diocese of Marquette—RICHARD R. SCHAEFER, Sec., *P.O. Box 550, Marquette, 49855.* Tel: 906-227-9108.

Catholic Relief Services—Rev. LAWRENCE T. GAUTHIER, Dir., *P.O. Box 550, Marquette, 49855.*

Cemeteries—RICHARD R. SCHAEFER, Bishop's Rep. for Catholic Cemeteries, *444 S. Fourth St., Marquette, 49855.* Tel: 906-227-9102.

Charismatic Prayer Groups—Rev. RAYMOND J. ZEUGNER, Diocesan Liaison, *Guardian Angels Parish, Crystal Falls, 49920.* Tel: 906-875-3019.

Clergy Continuing Education—Rev. JAMES P. CHALLANCIN, Dir., *St. Joseph Parish, 1889 Prairie Ave., Ishpeming, 49849.* Tel: 906-485-4200.

Council of Catholic Women—Sr. ROSALIE HUGHES, S.P.C., *1300 County Rd. 492, Marquette, 49855.* Tel: 906-226-3932.

Cursillo—Rev. Msgr. TIMOTHY H. DESROCHERS, Diocesan Moderator, *Marygrove, P.O. Box 38, Garden, 49835.* Tel: 906-644-2771.

Ecumenical Officer—Vacant.

Family Life Ministry—ROSALYN GROVES, Coord., *221 S. 13th St., Escanaba, 49829.* Tel: 906-789-2604.

Holy Childhood Association—Rev. LAWRENCE T. GAUTHIER, Dir., *P.O. Box 550, Marquette, 49855.* Tel: 906-227-9106.

Knights of Columbus—Rev. ALEX K. SAMPLE, Diocesan Chap., *P.O. Box 550, Marquette, 49855.* Tel: 906-227-9111.

Office of Stewardship—Vacant.

Panama Mission Fund—Rev. PAUL G. MANDERFIELD, *444 S. Fourth St., Marquette, 49855.* Tel: 906-225-1141.

Permanent Diaconate Formation Program—Deacon SCOTT JAMIESON, Dir., *P.O. Box 550, Marquette, 49855.* Tel: 906-228-3302.

Planning, Office of—Deacon ROBERT LACOSSE, *444 S. Fourth St., P.O. Box 550, Marquette, 49855.* Tel: 906-227-9112; Fax: 906-225-0437.

Propagation of the Faith—Rev. LAWRENCE T. GAUTHIER, Diocesan Dir., *P.O. Box 550, Marquette, 49855.* Tel: 906-227-9106.

Retreats—Rev. Msgr. TIMOTHY H. DESROCHERS, Dir., *Marygrove Retreat Center, Garden, 49835.* Tel: 906-644-2771.

St. Joseph Association—An Association of the Priests of the Diocese to provide Retirement Benefits. Rev. C. MICHAEL RHOADES, Pres., *St. Ignatius Loyola Parish, 120 Church St., St. Ignace, 49781.* Tel: 906-643-7671.

U.P. Catholic Services Appeal—RICHARD R. SCHAEFER, Coord., *444 S. Fourth St., P.O. Box 796, Marquette, 49855.* Tel: 906-227-9101.

Vocation Office—Rev. JAMES C. ZIMINSKI, Dir., *1200 Hebard Court, Marquette, 49855.* Tel: 906-228-0229; Fax: 906-228-0280.

Women Religious—Sr. DYONNE FINN, S.S.N.D., *P.O. Box 550, Marquette, 49855.* Tel: 906-789-5680.

CLERGY, PARISHES, MISSIONS AND PAROCHIAL SCHOOLS

CITY OF MARQUETTE
(Marquette County)

1—ST. PETER CATHEDRAL, Revs. Louis C. Cappo; James M. Roetzer; Deacon Scott A. Jamieson. In res., Rev. Alexander K. Sample.
Res., 311 Baraga Ave., 49855. Tel: 906-226-6548; Fax: 906-226-8683.
School—Father Marquette Catholic Central Schools System. See Elementary Inter-Parochial Schools under Institutions Located in the Diocese.
Mission—Big Bay, Marquette Co., St. Mary.

2—ST. CHRISTOPHER, Rev. Alexander K. Sample; Sr. Colleen Sweeting, O.S.F., Pastoral Coord.
Res., 2372 Badger St., 49855. Tel: 906-226-2265; Fax: 906-226-8678.

3—ST. JOHN THE BAPTIST. Closed. 1986. For inquiries for parish records, contact St. Peter's Cathedral.

4—ST. LOUIS (Harvey), Rev. Guy S. Thoren; Deacon David P. Adler.
Res., 264 Silver Creek Rd., 49855. Tel: 906-249-1438; Fax: 906-249-3428.
School—Father Marquette Catholic Central Schools System. See Elementary Inter-Parochial Schools under Institutions Located in the Diocese.

5—ST. MICHAEL, Rev. John E. Patrick. In res., Rev. James C. Ziminski.
Res., 401 W. Kaye Ave., 49855. Tel: 906-228-8180; Fax: 906-228-5502.
School—Father Marquette Catholic Central Schools System. See Elementary Inter-Parochial Schools under Institutions Located in the Diocese.

OUTSIDE THE CITY OF MARQUETTE

Ahmeek, Keweenaw Co., Our Lady of Peace. (Keweenaw Catholic Missions). Rev. Miles Pfalzer, O.F.M.
Mailing Address: Box 517, Mohawk, 49950. Tel: 906-337-1966; Fax: 906-337-1966.
Missions—Eagle Harbor, Keweenaw Co., Holy Redeemer; Copper Harbor, Keweenaw Co., Our Lady of the Pines.

Alpha, Iron Co., St. Edward. Closed. For inquiries for parish records contact the Chancery.

Assinins, Baraga Co., The Most Holy Name of Jesus-Blessed Kateri Tekakwitha, Revs. George J. Kallarackal, M.C.B.S., (India) Co-Pastor; Gregory R. Heikkala, Co-Pastor.
Res., P.O. Box 460, Baraga, 49908. Tel: 906-353-6565; Fax: 906-353-6562.

Baraga, Baraga Co., St. Ann, Rev. George J. Kallarackal, M.C.B.S. (India).
Res., 318 Lyons St., P.O. Box 340, 49908. Tel: 906-353-6565; Fax: 906-353-6562.

Barbeau, Chippewa Co, Holy Family Mission, Rev. John S. Hascall, O.F.M.Cap.
Res., 1529 Marquette Ave., Sault Sainte Marie, 49783. Tel: 906-632-3213; Fax: 906-632-8490.

Bark River, Delta Co., St. Elizabeth Ann Seton. Formerly St. George, Bark River; Sacred Heart of Jesus, Schaffer; & St. Michael, Perronville. Rev. Christopher B. Gardiner.
Res., 1216 12th Rd., P.O. Box 187, 49807. Tel: 906-466-9938; Fax: 906-466-0194.

Bessemer, Gogebic Co., St. Sebastian, Rev. Joseph D. Carne.
Res., 210 E. Iron St., 49911. Tel: 906-667-0952.
School—Tel: 906-667-0322.
Lay Teachers 7; Students 62.

Brimley, Chippewa Co., St. Francis Xavier, Rev. Jeff G. Johnson; Deacon Joseph A. LaPlante.
Mailing Address: P.O. Box 429, 49715. Tel: 906-248-3443; Fax: 906-632-9084.
Mission—Bay Mills, Chippewa Co., Blessed Kateri Tekakwitha. (Formerly St. Catherine). Fax: 906-248-3443. Deacon Joseph LaPlante.

Calumet, Houghton Co., Sacred Heart, Rev. Marian Douglas, O.F.M.
Mailing Address: P.O. Box 546, 49913. Tel: 906-337-0810; Fax: 906-337-6424.

St. Paul the Apostle, Rev. Cyprian E. Berens, O.F.M.
Res., 301 Eighth St., 49913. Tel: 906-337-2044; Fax: 906-337-2058.

Caspian, Iron Co., St. Cecilia, Rev. Otto J. Sartorelli; Deacon Robert J. Kostka.
Mailing Address: P.O. Box 517, 49915. Tel: 906-265-3777; Fax: 906-265-3224.

Champion, Marquette Co., Sacred Heart, Rev. Gilles Brault. Pastoral Coordinators: Sr. Margey Schmelzle, O.S.F.; Sr. Lois Risch, O.S.F.
Mailing Address: 107 Kloman Ave., Republic, 49879. Tel: 906-376-8475; Fax: 906-376-8475.

Channing, Dickinson Co., St. Rose, Rev. George J. Kuppayil, M.S.T. (India).
Mailing Address: P.O. Box 235, 49815. Tel: 906-542-3215; Fax: 906-542-9084.
Mission—Foster City, Dickinson Co., St. Joseph, Tel: 906-246-3490.

Chassell, Houghton Co., St. Anne, Rev. Sebastian Ettolil, M.C.B.S. (India).
Mailing Address: P.O. Box 407, 49916. Tel: 906-523-4912; Fax: 906-523-4904.
Missions—Painesdale, Houghton Co., Sacred Heart. Closed. For inquiries for parish records contact Holy Family, South Range.; Donken, Houghton Co., Immaculate Heart of Mary. Closed. For inquiries for parish records contact Holy Family, South Range.

Cooks, Schoolcraft Co., St. Mary Magdalene, Rev. John E. Martignon.
Mailing Address: P.O. Box 68, Garden, 49835. Tel: 906-644-2626; Fax: 906-644-2626. [CEM]

Crystal Falls, Iron Co., Guardian Angels, Rev. Raymond J. Zeugner; Deacon Bernard Kut.
Res., 412 Crystal Ave., 49920. Tel: 906-875-3019; Fax: 906-875-1034.

Daggett, Menominee Co., St. Frederick. Closed. For inquiries for parish records contact Precious Blood Parish, Stephenson.

DeTour, Chippewa Co., Sacred Heart, Revs. Jacek S. Wtyklo; Jerome A. Nowacki.
Mailing Address: P.O. Box 8, 49725. Tel: 906-297-3781; Fax: 906-297-5108.
Mission—Drummond Island, Chippewa Co., St. Florence.

Engadine, Mackinac Co., Our Lady of Lourdes, Rev. Timothy W. Hruska.
Mailing Address: P.O. Box 123, 49827. Tel: 906-477-6223; Fax: 906-477-6731.
Missions—Naubinway, Mackinac Co., St. Stephen; Gulliver, Schoolcraft Co., Divine Infant of Prague. Deacon Gilbert G. Sablack.

Escanaba, Delta Co., St. Anne, Rev. Michael J. Steber; Deacon Lewis Vailliencourt.
Res., 817 S. Lincoln Rd., 49829. Tel: 906-786-1421; Fax: 906-786-9346.
School—Holy Name Central Grade School. See Elementary Inter-Parochial Schools under Institutions Located in the Diocese.

St. Joseph & St. Patrick. Merged (Formerly St. Joseph, Escanaba; Formerly St. Patrick, Escanaba). Revs. Joseph Nagaroor (India); Paul P. Karottekunnel, M.S.T. (India); Deacon Bill D. Hemes.
Res., 709 First Ave. S., 49829. Tel: 906-789-6244; Fax: 906-789-1213.
School—Holy Name Central Grade School. See Elementary Inter-Parochial Schools under Institutions Located in the Diocese.

St. Thomas the Apostle, Rev. Rick L. Courier.
Res., 1820 Ninth Ave. N., 49829. Tel: 906-786-4627; Fax: 906-789-5558.
School—Holy Name Central Grade School. See Elementary Inter-Parochial Schools under Institutions Located in the Diocese.

Ewen, Ontonagon Co., Sacred Heart, Rev. Thomas Valayathil (India).
Mailing Address: P.O. Box 169, 49925. Tel: 906-988-2310; Fax: 906-988-2631.
Mission—Sidnaw, Houghton Co., St. Francis Xavier.

Garden, Delta Co., St. John the Baptist, Rev. John E. Martignon.
Mailing Address: P.O. Box 68, 49835. Tel: 906-644-2626; Fax: 906-644-2626.

Gladstone, Delta Co., All Saints, Rev. Arnold J. Grambow.
Res., 715 Wisconsin Ave., P.O. Box 392, 49837. Tel: 906-428-3199; Fax: 906-428-2829.

Holy Family, Rev. Raymond C. Cotter.
Res., 4011 CO 416-20th Rd., 49837. Tel: 906-786-1209; Fax: 906-786-0846.

Goetzville, Chippewa Co., St. Stanislaus Kostka, Revs. Jerome A. Nowacki; Jacek S. Wtyklo.
Mailing Address: 12841 E. Traynor Rd., 49736. Tel: 906-297-5211; Fax: 906-297-5108. [CEM]
Mission—Hessel, Mackinac Co., Our Lady of the Snows, Tel: 906-484-3825; 484-2773 (Parish House).

Grand Marais, Alger Co., Holy Rosary Church, Rev. Glenn A. Theoret.
Mailing Address: P.O. Box 424, 49839. Tel: 906-494-2589; Fax: 906-494-2589. [CEM]
Missions—Germfask, Schoolcraft Co., St. Therese; Curtis, Mackinac Co., St. Timothy.

Gwinn, Marquette Co., St. Anthony, Rev. Ronald K. Timock.
Res., 320 Iron St., P.O. Box 1358, 49841. Tel: 906-346-5312; Fax: 906-346-3040.
Mission—Northland, Marquette Co., St. Joseph, Tel: 906-238-4444.

Hancock, Houghton Co., Resurrection, Rev. Wayne E. Marcotte.
Res., 900 Quincy St., 49930. Tel: 906-482-0215; Fax: 906-482-5268. [CEM]
Mission—Dollar Bay, Houghton Co., St. Francis of Assisi, Tel: 906-482-6489.

Hermansville, Menominee Co., St. John Neumann. (Formerly St. Mary, Hermansville; St. Francis Xavier, Spalding). Rev. Michael T. Vichich.
Res., P.O. Box 125, 49847. Tel: 906-498-7730; 497-5800 (Spalding); Fax: 906-497-5800.

Houghton, Houghton Co., St. Ignatius Loyola, Rev. Thomas L. Poisson.
Res., 305 Portage St., 49931. Tel: 906-482-0212; Fax: 906-482-8110.
Mission—Atlantic Mine, Houghton Co., St. Mary. Closed. For inquiries for parish records contact St. Ignatius Loyola, Houghton.
St. Albert the Great University Parish. (Michigan Technological University). Rev. Larry P. Van-Damme.
Res., 411 MacInnes Dr., 49931. Tel: 906-482-5530; Fax: 906-482-4828.

Hubbell, Houghton Co., St. Cecilia, Rev. Eric E. Olson.
Mailing Address: c/o 701 Calumet St., Lake Linden, 49945. Tel: 906-296-6851; Fax: 906-296-1190.

Iron Mountain, Dickinson Co., Immaculate Conception of the Blessed Virgin Mary, Rev. Msgr. James A. Kaczmarek; Deacon Donald R. Christy.
Res., 500 E. Blaine St., 49801-1840. Tel: 906-774-0511; Fax: 906-779-9953.
School—Dickinson Area Catholic School System. See Elementary Inter-Parochial Schools under Institutions Located in the Diocese.
St. Mary and St. Joseph, Rev. Daniel S. Zaloga.
Res., 411 W. B St., 49801. Tel: 906-774-2046; Fax: 906-774-6015.
School—Dickinson Area Catholic School System. See Elementary Inter-Parochial Schools under Institutions Located in the Diocese.

Iron River, Iron Co., St. Agnes, Rev. Norman A. Clisch.
Res., 702 N. Fourth St., 49935. Tel: 906-265-4557; Fax: 906-265-7155.

Ironwood, Gogebic Co., Our Lady of Peace. Merged Merger of the following three parishes: Holy Trinity, St. Ambrose & St. Michael, 1986. Revs. Darryl J. Pepin; Shaun A. Erno; Deacon Robert A. Hamen.
Res., 108 S. Marquette St., 49938. Tel: 906-932-0174; Fax: 906-932-1019.
School—Tel: 906-932-3200.
Lay Teachers 8; Students 116.
St. Ambrose. Consolidated with Holy Trinity & St. Michael to form Our Lady of Peace Parish, 1986.
St. Michael. Consolidated with St. Ambrose & Holy Trinity to form Our Lady of Peace Parish, 1986.

Ishpeming, Marquette Co., St. John the Evangelist, Rev. Msgr. Peter Oberto.
Res., 325 S. Pine, 49849. Tel: 906-486-6212; Fax: 906-486-4244.
Religious Education Center—335 S. Pine St., 49849. Tel: 906-486-9361. Betty Lou Bosio, Admin.
St. Joseph, Rev. James Challancin.
Office (All Mail): 1889 Prairie Avenue, 49849-1045.
Res., 1890 Prairie Ave., 49849-1044. Tel: 906-485-4200; Fax: 906-485-4185.
St. Pius X. Closed. For inquiries for parish records contact St. Joseph Church, 1889 Prairie Ave., Ishpeming, MI 49849.

Kingsford, Dickinson Co., American Martyrs, Rev. Joseph O. Gouin.
Res., 908 W. Sagola Ave., 49802. Tel: 906-774-0630; Fax: 906-774-4417.
St. Mary Queen of Peace, Rev. Paul J. Nomellini.
Res., 432 Edsel St., 49802. Tel: 906-774-6122; Fax: 906-774-2349.

Lake Linden, Houghton Co., St. Joseph, Rev. Eric E. Olson.
Res., 701 Calumet St., 49945. Tel: 906-296-6851; Fax: 906-296-1190.

L'Anse, Baraga Co., Sacred Heart, Rev. Gregory R. Heikkala.
Res., 16 S. Sixth St., 49946. Tel: 906-524-6424; Fax: 906-524-6422.
School—433 E. Baraga Ave., 49946. Tel: 906-524-5157; Fax: 906-524-5154.
Sisters 1; Lay Teachers 7; Students 91.

Mackinac Island, Mackinac Co., Ste. Anne de Michilimackinac (1695), Rev. James M. Williams.
Mailing Address: P.O. Box 537, 49757. Tel: 906-847-3507; Fax: 906-847-0361.

Manistique, Schoolcraft Co., St. Francis de Sales, Rev. Peter A. Minelli; Deacons Gilbert G. Sablack; Robert M. Cross.
Res., 330 Oak St., 49854. Tel: 906-341-5355; Fax: 906-341-3984.
School—Tel: 906-341-5512.
Sisters 6; Lay Teachers 7; Students 109.

Menominee, Menominee Co., Holy Redeemer (Birch Creek), Rev. Ronald J. Skufca; Deacon Roland Chaltry.
Res., W-5541 Birch Creek Rd. No. 6, 49858. Tel: 906-863-6920; Fax: 906-863-7303.
School—Menominee Catholic Central. See Elementary Inter-Parochial Schools under Institutions Located in the Diocese.
Holy Spirit, Rev. S. Patrick Wisneske.
Res., 1016 10th Ave., 49858. Tel: 906-863-5239; Fax: 906-863-2249.
School—Menominee Catholic Central. See Elementary Inter-Parochial Schools under Institutions Located in the Diocese.
Resurrection, Rev. Dino F. Silvestrini; Deacon Vincent W. Beckley.
Res., 2607 18th St., 49858. Tel: 906-863-3405; Fax: 906-863-9090.
School—Menominee Catholic Central. See Elementary Inter-Parochial Schools under Institutions Located in the Diocese.

Moran, Mackinac Co., Immaculate Conception, Rev. C. Michael Rhoades.
Res., 120 Church St., St. Ignace, 49781. Tel: 906-643-7671; Fax: 906-643-7755. [CEM]

Munising, Alger Co., Sacred Heart of Jesus, Rev. Dennis L. Borca; Deacon James E. Anderson.
Office: 110 W. Jewell St., P.O. Box 99, 49862. Tel: 906-387-4900; Fax: 906-387-4422.

Nadeau, Menominee Co., St. Bruno, Rev. Raymond J. Hoefgen.
Res., 49863. Tel: 906-639-2388; Fax: 906-639-3207.

Nahma, Delta Co., St. Andrew, Rev. John E. Martignon.
Mailing Address: P.O. Box 68, Garden, 49864. Tel: 906-644-2626; Fax: 906-644-2626.

Negaunee, Marquette Co., St. Paul, Rev. John J. Shiverski.
Res., 202 W. Case St., 49866. Tel: 906-475-9969; Fax: 906-475-9987.
Mission—Palmer, Marquette Co., Our Lady Perpetual Help, Tel: 906-475-4630.

Newberry, Luce Co., St. Gregory, Rev. George S. Maki.
Office: 212 W. Harrie St., 49868. Tel: 906-293-5511; Fax: 906-293-5575.
Res., 111 W. Harrie St., 49868. Tel: 906-293-5001.
Mission—Paradise, Chippewa Co., Our Lady of Victory.

Norway, Dickinson Co., St. Mary, Rev. Mark A. McQuesten.
Res., 401 Main St., 49870. Tel: 906-563-9845; Fax: 906-563-7623.
School—Holy Spirit Central Grade School. See Elementary Inter-Parochial Schools under Institutions Located in the Diocese.

Ontonagon, Ontonagon Co., Holy Family, Rev. John L. Longbucco.
Res., 515 Pine St., 49953. Tel: 906-884-2569; Fax: 906-884-6030. [CEM]

Perkins, Delta Co., St. Joseph, Rev. Emmett M. Norden.
Res., 5803 Hwy. M-35, P.O. Box 99, 49872. Tel: 906-359-4701; Fax: 906-359-4701.

Perronville, Menominee Co., St. Elizabeth Ann Seton. (Formerly St. Michael. See Bark River.).

Quinnesec, Dickinson Co., St. Mary. Closed. For inquiries for parish records contact St. Mary Parish, Norway, MI.

Ramsay, Gogebic Co., Christ the King. Closed. For inquiries for parish records contact St. Sebastian, Bessemer.

Rapid River, Delta Co., St. Charles Borromeo, Rev. David W. Sedlock; Deacon William Green.
Mailing Address: P.O. Box 247, 49878. Tel: 906-474-6606; Fax: 906-474-9087.

Republic, Marquette Co., St. Augustine, Rev. Gilles Brault (STA). Pastoral Coordinators: Sr. Margey Schmelzle, O.S.F.; Sr. Lois Risch, O.S.F.
Mailing Address: 107 Kloman Ave., 49879. Tel: 906-376-8475; Fax: 906-376-8475. [CEM]

Rockland, Ontonagon Co., St. Mary, Rev. John L. Longbucco; Deacon Karl L. Wadman.
Mailing Address: Holy Family Parish, 515 Pine St., Ontonagon, 49953. Tel: 906-884-2569; Fax: 906-884-6030.

Rudyard, Chippewa Co., St. Joseph, Rev. Francis J. DeGroot.
Mailing Address: P.O. Box 150, 49780. Tel: 906-478-4331.
Mission—Trout Lake, Chippewa Co., St. Mary.
Stations—Kinross Correctional Facility.; Chippewa Correctional Facility.; Chippewa Regional Facility.; Hiawatha Correctional Facility.

St. Ignace, Mackinac Co., St. Ignatius Loyola, Rev. C. Michael Rhoades; Deacon Donald F. Olmstead.
Res., 120 Church St., 49781. Tel: 906-643-7671; Fax: 906-643-7755. [CEM]

Sault Sainte Marie, Chippewa Co.,

1—HOLY NAME OF MARY, Revs. Theodore J. Brodeur; Sebastian Kavumkal, M.S.T. (India).
Res., 377 Maple St., 49783. Tel: 906-632-3381; Fax: 906-632-0741.
School—Tel: 906-635-6141.
Sisters 1; Lay Teachers 6; Students 147.
Mission—Sugar Island, Chippewa Co., Sacred Heart.

2—NATIVITY OF OUR LORD. Closed. For inquiries for parish records contact St. Joseph, Sault Sainte Marie.

3—ST. ISAAC JOGUES MISSION, Rev. John S. Hascall, O.F.M.Cap.
Res., 1529 Marquette Ave., 49783. Tel: 906-632-3213; Fax: 906-632-8490.

4—ST. JOSEPH, Rev. Pawel J. Mecwel; Deacon William J. Piche.
Res., 606 E. Fourth Ave., 49783. Tel: 906-632-9625; Fax: 906-632-9625, Ext. 18.

Schaffer, Delta Co., St. Elizabeth Ann Seton. (Formerly Sacred Heart of Jesus. See Bark River.).

South Range, Houghton Co., Holy Family, Rev. Sebastian Ettolil, M.C.B.S. (India); Deacon Paul D. Lucchesi.
Mailing Address: Box 369, 49963. Tel: 906-482-0684; Fax: 906-482-6824.

Spalding, Menominee Co., St. Francis Xavier. Merged with St. Mary, Hermansville to form St. John Neumann, Hermansville. P.O. Box 125, Hermansville, MI 49847.

Stephenson, Menominee Co., Precious Blood Church, Revs. Raymond J. Hoefgen; Peter Fosu.
Res., S304 Bluff St., 49887. Tel: 906-753-2562; Fax: 906-753-2811.

Trenary, Alger Co., St. Rita, Rev. Thomas J. Thekkel, M.S.T. (India).
Mailing Address: P.O. Box 207, 49891. Tel: 906-446-3350; Fax: 906-446-3523.
Mission—Autrain, Alger Co., St. Therese.

Vulcan, Dickinson Co., St. Barbara, Rev. William P. Callari; Deacon Donald Giesen.
Mailing Address: P.O. Box 493, 49892. Tel: 906-563-9834; Fax: 906-563-7664.
School—Holy Spirit Central Grade School, Norway. See Elementary Inter-Parochial Schools under Institutions Located in the Diocese.

Wakefield, Gogebic Co., Immaculate Conception of the Blessed Virgin Mary, Rev. Chacko D. Kakaniyil (India).
Res., 407 Ascherman St., 49968. Tel: 906-224-7851; Fax: 906-224-9118.
Mission—Marenisco, Gogebic Co., St. Catherine, Tel: 906-787-2353. In res., Rev. Raymond F. Moncher.

Watersmeet, Gogebic Co., Immaculate Conception, Rev. Thomas Valayathil (India). In res., Rev. Aloysius J. Hasenberg.
Mailing Address: E23933 D Ave., P.O. Box 398, 49969. Tel: 906-358-4607.

Wells, Delta Co., St. Anthony, Rev. Richard C. Schaeffer.
Mailing Address: 6576 N. Third St., 49894. Tel: 906-786-5002; Fax: 906-786-8992.
School—Holy Name Central Grade School, Escanaba. See Elementary Inter-Parochial Schools under Institutions Located in the Diocese.

White Pine, Ontonagon Co., St. Jude, Rev. Michael A. Woempner.
Mailing Address: P.O. Box 427, 49971. Tel: 906-885-5763; Fax: 906-885-5332.
Mission—Bergland, Ontonagon Co., St. Ann.

Zeba, Baraga Co., The Most Holy Name of Jesus-Blessed Kateri Tekakwitha. (See Assinins.).

Indian Missions

Assinins, Baraga Co., The Most Holy Name of Jesus-Blessed Kateri Tekakwitha. Indian Mission. Revs. George J. Kallarackal, M.C.B.S., (India) Co-Pastor; Gregory R. Heikkala, Co-Pastor.
Res., P.O. Box 469, Baraga, 49908.

Watersmeet, Gogebec Co., Lac Vieux Desert Reservation, Rev. Thomas Valayathil (India).
P.O. Box 78, 49969.

Zeba, Baraga Co., The Most Holy Name of Jesus-Blessed Kateri Tekakwitha. (See Assinins).

Bay Mills, Chippewa Co., Blessed Kateri Tekakwitha, Rev. Jeff G. Johnson.
P.O. Box 429, Brimley, 49715.

Sault Sainte Marie, Chippewa Co., St. Isaac Jogues, Rev. John S. Hascall, O.F.M.Cap.
1529 Marquette Ave., 49783.

Sugar Island, Chippewa Co., Sacred Heart. Indian Missionaries, East. Rev. Theodore J. Brodeur.
377 Maple St., Sault Sainte Marie, 49783.

Chaplains of Public Institutions

MARQUETTE. *Marquette General Hospital* Tel: 906-228-9440; 225-3404. Revs. Frank M. Lenz; Gilles Brault (STA) Assoc. Chap.

On Duty Outside the Diocese:
Reverend Fathers—
Dobrzenski, Francis G., Sacred Heart Major Seminary, 2701 Chicago Blvd., Detroit, MI 48206
Murphy, Patrick E., Dept. of Veterans Affairs Medical Center, 5500 Armstrong Rd. (118c), Battle Creek, MI 49016
Oniskiewicz, Mieczyslaw T., St. Mary Parish, P.O. Box 68, Kinde, MI 48455-0068
Wantland, Thomas, 21505 August Ave., No. 4, Port Charlotte, FL 33952

Special Assignment:
Reverend Fathers—
Paris, Benedetto, Edifice Deschatelets, 175 Main St., Ottawa, ON K1S 1C3 Canada
Sample, Alexander K., Chancellor; Dir., Dept. of Ministry Personnel Service
Schmied, Thomas, O.F.M.Cap., P.O. Box 368, Ahmeek, MI 49901
Ziminski, James C., Pastoral Office; Dir. of Vocations

Leave of Absence:
Reverend Fathers—
Craig, Richard T.
Kurtz, Jeffrey A.
Rupp, Daniel N.
Sheedlo, Walter J.

Retired:
Reverend Monsignors—
LaViolette, Matt H., P.O. Box 497, Escanaba, MI 49829
Spelgatti, David P., (Winter), 21362 Walling Ct., Port Charlotte, FL 33954
Reverend Fathers—
Andary, Thomas M., 18515 Caminito Pasadero, Apt. 345, San Diego, CA 92128
Beyer, Emil J., Bishop Noa Home, 2916 Third St. S., Apt. 12, Escanaba, MI 49829
Bracket, Louis P., 307 Eddy St., Wakefield, MI 49968
Brewer, Gervase, P.O. Box 158, Marquette, MI 49855
Dunleavy, Thomas P., Bishop Noa Home, 2900 Third Ave. S., Escanaba, MI 49829
Gauthier, Lawrence T., P.O. Box 550, Marquette, MI 49855
Goerner, Basil S., 29 High Bluff Villa 2005, Hilton Head, SC 29926
Gondek, Joseph A., P.O. Box 624, Caspian, MI 49915
Harris, David T., P.O. Box 88, Rockland, MI 49960
Hasenberg, Aloysius J., P.O. Box 396, Watersmeet, MI 49969
Hollenbach, Frank A., 9255 E. Pueblo A, Mesa, AZ 85208
Kichak, Joseph A., Keen Agers, 303 Brotherton St., Wakefield, MI 49968
LaCosse, Norbert R., 1534A W. Ridge St., Apt. 5, Marquette, MI 49855
Landreville, Norbert B., 131 Mackinac Hts. Dr., St. Ignance, MI 49781
LePine, Clement J., 2017 14th St., Menominee, MI 49858
Maloney, John, 917 Woodward Ave., Apt. 5, Kingsford, MI 49801
Manderfield, Geraldo R.P., Apartado 2810, Managua, Nicaragua
Mayotte, Allan J., 405 'C' St., Wakefield, MI 49968
McArdle, John F., 4305 Sixth St., Menominee, MI 49858
Menapace, James L., Rte. 1, Box 56, Gulliver, MI 49840
Moncher, Raymond F., P.O. Box 175, Marenisco, MI 49947
Neurohr, Gilbert N., 5719 Pine 0-25 St., Gladstone, MI 49837
Olivier, John H., S.S., St. Charles Villa, 603 Maiden Choice Ln., Baltimore, MD 21228
Parrotta, Arthur J., St. Francis Hospital, 3401 Ludington St., Escanaba, MI 49829
Polakowski, Joseph, 1869 E. Shore Dr., Green Bay, MI 54302
Ryan, John, 1600 N. 19th St., Escanaba, MI 49829
Schiska, Paul A., 1490 15.5 Rd., Bark River, MI 49807
Shiroda, Donald L., 807 W. 28th Ave., Apt. 4B, Sault Sainte Marie, MI 49783
Smith, Neil B., Box 451, Ramsay, MI 49959
Strelick, Charles J., 4420 Devonshire Ave., Spring Hill, FL 34609
Valerio, Raymond A., 831 E. Grant, Iron Mountain, MI 49801
Vanitvelt, Milton H., 1524 Seventh St., Menominee, MI 49858
Wenzel, Edward J., Rte. 1, Box 491, Baraga, MI 49908

Permanent Deacons:
Adler, David, St. Louis the King, Marquette
Anderson, James, Sacred Heart of Jesus, Munising
Beckley, Vincent W., Resurrection, Menominee
Chaltry, Roland, Holy Redeemer, Menominee
Christy, Donald R., Immaculate Conception, Iron Mountain
Cross, Robert M., St. Francis de Sales (Incardinated in Diocese of Sioux Falls, South Dakota)
Giesen, Donald, St. Barbara, Vulcan
Green, William, St. Charles Borromeo, Rapid River
Hamen, Robert, Our Lady of Peace, Ironwood
Hemes, Dr. Bill D., St. Joseph & St. Patrick, Escanaba
Hermann, Dean, St. Gregory, Newberry
Jamieson, Scott A., St. Peter Cathedral, Marquette
Kostka, Robert J., St. Cecilia, Caspian
Kut, Bernard, Guardian Angels, Crystal Falls (Incardinated in Diocese of Chicago, OH)
LaCosse, Robert, Chancery Office, Marquette (Incardinated in diocese of Chicago, IL)
LaPlante, Joseph A., St. Francis Xavier, Brimley & Mission of Blessed Kateri Tekakwitha, Bay Mills (Incardinated in diocese of Rockford, IL)
Lucchessi, Paul, Holy Family, South Range
Olmstead, Donald F., St. Ignatius Loyola, St. Ignace
Piche, William J., St. Joseph, Sault Ste. Marie
Sablack, Gilbert G., Engadine Cathloic Missions & St. Francis de Sales, Manistique
Vailliencourt, Lewis, St. Anne, Escanaba
Wadman, Karl L., St. Mary, Rockland

INSTITUTIONS LOCATED IN THE DIOCESE

[A] ELEMENTARY INTER-PAROCHIAL SCHOOLS

MARQUETTE. *Fr. Marquette Catholic Central Schools System*, 500 S. Fourth St., 49855. Tel: 906-225-1129; Fax: 906-225-1987. Judy Hanson, C.A.O. Serving the following parishes: St. Peter's Cathedral; St. Louis; St. Michael. Lay Teachers 27; Students 366.

ESCANABA. *Holy Name Central Grade School*, 409 S. 22nd St., 49829. Tel: 906-786-7550; Fax: 906-786-7582. Barbara Mead, Prin. Lay Teachers 19; Students 323.

IRON MOUNTAIN. *Dickinson Area Catholic School System*, 406 W. B St., 49801. Tel: 906-774-2277; Fax: 906-774-8704. Patricia Covitz, Prin. Lay Teachers 9; Students 164.

MENOMINEE. *Menominee Catholic Central*, 1406 10th Ave., 49858. Tel: 906-863-3190; Fax: 906-863-3990. Eric Weydt, Prin. Lay Teachers 12; Students 180.

NORWAY. *Holy Spirit Central School*, 201 Saginaw St., 49870. Tel: 906-563-8817; Fax: 906-563-8854. Barbara L. Heiser, Prin. Lay Teachers 11; Students 112.

[B] ENDOWMENT FUNDS

MARQUETTE. *Endowment Foundation of the Diocese of Marquette*, 444 S. Fourth St., P.O. Box 550, 49855. Tel: 906-225-1141. Mr. Richard R. Schaefer.
Marquette Area Catholic Education Fund, P.O. Box 550, 49855. Tel: 906-225-1141.
St. John's Memorial Scholarship Committee, 1300 Kimber, 49855. Tel: 906-225-1936. Joylyn Wahla, Pres.

BESSEMER. *St. Sebastian School Endowment Fund*, 210 E. Iron St., 49911. Tel: 906-667-0952.

ESCANABA. *Holy Name Central Endowment Fund, Inc.*, 409 S. 22nd St., 49829. Tel: 906-786-7550.
Holy Name Scholarship Foundation, 409 S. 22nd St., 49829. Tel: 906-786-7550.

IRON MOUNTAIN. *Dickinson Area Catholic School Education Foundation*, 406 W. B St., 49801. Tel: 906-774-2277.

IRONWOOD. *Our Lady of Peace School Educational Fund*, 106 S. Marquette St., 49938. Tel: 906-932-3200.

L'ANSE. *Sacred Heart School Endowment Fund*, 16 S. 6th St., 49946. Tel: 906-524-6424.

MANISTIQUE. *St. Francis de Sales Education Foundation, Inc.*, 330 Oak St., 49854. Tel: 906-341-5355.

MENOMINEE. *Menominee Catholic Education Fund*, 1406 Tenth Ave., 49858-2604. Tel: 906-863-2723. Carrie Warren-Wendke, Office Mgr.

NEGAUNEE. *Negaunee St. Paul Endowment Fund*, 202 W. Case St., 49866.

NORWAY. *Holy Spirit Central School Educational Fund*, 201 Saginaw, 49870. Tel: 906-563-8817.

SAULT SAINTE MARIE. *Holy Family School Endowment Fund, Inc.*, 377 Maple St., 49783. Tel: 906-632-3381.

[C] GENERAL HOSPITALS

ESCANABA. *O.S.F. St. Francis Hospital*, 49829. Tel: 906-786-3311; Fax: 906-786-4004
For a complete listing, refer to the Hospitals section.

[D] HOMES FOR THE AGED

ESCANABA. *Bishop Noa Home for Senior Citizens*, 2900 3rd Ave. S., 49829. Tel: 906-786-5810; Fax: 906-786-5372
For a complete listing, refer to the Special Care Facilities section.

[E] CONVENTS AND RESIDENCES OF SISTERS

MARQUETTE. *Provincialate of the Sisters of St. Paul de Chartres*, 1300 County Rd. 492, 49855. Tel: 906-226-3932; Fax: 906-226-8734. Sr. Mary Ann Laurin, District Supr. Sisters 18.

IRON MOUNTAIN. *Monastery of the Holy Cross*, N4028 Hwy. U.S. 2, P.O. Box 397, 49801. Tel: 906-774-0561. Discalced Carmelite Nuns. Mother Maria of Jesus, O.C.D., Prioress; Rev. Leonard Cornelius, O.F.M., Chap. Cloistered Nuns: Professed 13; Extern Professed Sisters 2; Temporary Professed Sister 2; Novices 1.

[F] RETREAT HOUSES

GARDEN. *Marygrove Retreat Center*, 49835. Tel: 906-644-2771. Rev. Msgr. Timothy H. Desrochers, Dir. Retreats and workshops for priests, religious and laity.

[G] NEWMAN CLUBS

MARQUETTE. *Catholic Campus Ministry-Northern Michigan University*, 1200 Hebard Ct., 49855. Tel: 906-228-3302; Fax: 906-228-0280. Rev. James C. Ziminski, Chap.; B. Kim Dolan, Dir.

HOUGHTON. *St. Albert the Great, University Parish*, 411 MacInnes Dr., 49931. Tel: 906-482-5530. Rev. Larry P. VanDamme, Dir.

SAULT SAINTE MARIE. *Lake Superior State University, Newman Center*, 517 W. Easterday, 49783. Tel: 906-635-5941. Kristy Kwarciany, Dir.

[H] MISCELLANEOUS

MARQUETTE. *St. Vincent De Paul Society*, 2118 Fitch Ave., Room #101, 49855. Tel: 906-226-2311.

MENOMINEE. *Missionaries of the Liturgy*, 2408-17th St., 49858. Tel: 906-863-3405. Sr. Maria Volp, Supr.

RELIGIOUS INSTITUTES OF MEN REPRESENTED IN THE DIOCESE

For further details refer to the corresponding bracketed number in the Religious Institutes of Men or Women section.

[0470]—*The Capuchin Friars.* (Detroit, MI).—O.F.M.Cap.

[0520]—*Franciscan Friars.* (Cincinnati, OH).—O.F.M.

RELIGIOUS INSTITUTES OF WOMEN REPRESENTED IN THE DIOCESE

[3710]—*Congregation of the Sisters of Saint Agnes.*—C.S.A.

[0420]—*Discalced Carmelite Nuns.*—O.C.D.

[1070-09]—*Dominican Sisters.*—O.P.

[1070-13]—*Dominican Sisters.*—O.P.

[1630]—*Franciscan Sisters of Christian Charity.*—O.S.F.

[2380]—*Institute of the Blessed Virgin Mary (Sisters of Loretto).*—I.B.V.M.

[2970]—*School Sisters of Notre Dame.*—S.S.N.D.

[3830-15]—*Sisters of St. Joseph.* (Concordia, Kansas).—C.S.J.

[3840]—*Sisters of St. Joseph of Carondelet.*—C.S.J.

[3980]—*Sisters of St. Paul of Chartres.*—S.P.C.

[2180]—*Sisters of the Immaculate Heart of Mary.*—I.H.M.

[3260]—*Sisters of the Precious Blood.*—C.PP.S.

[1770]—*Sisters of the Third Order of St. Francis.* (Peoria, Illinois).—O.S.F.

[2760]—*Misssionary Sisters of the Immaculate Conception.*

DIOCESAN CEMETERIES

MARQUETTE. *Holy Cross.*

ESCANABA. *Holy Cross.*

NECROLOGY

† Franczek, Walter J., (Retired). —Died Dec. 20, 1999.

† Hartman, Donald, (Retired). —Died Nov. 15, 1999.

† Hebein, James M., (Retired). —Died Jan. 19, 2000.

Diocese of Memphis

(Memphitana in Tennesia)

Most Reverend

J. TERRY STEIB, S.V.D., D.D.

Bishop of Memphis; ordained January 6, 1967; appointed Titular Bishop of Fallaba and Auxiliary Bishop of St. Louis December 6, 1983; consecrated February 10, 1984; appointed Bishop of Memphis March 23, 1993; installed May 5, 1993.

ESTABLISHED JANUARY 6, 1971.

Square Miles 10,682.

Comprises the Counties of Benton, Carroll, Chester, Crockett, Decatur, Dyer, Fayette, Gibson, Hardeman, Hardin, Haywood, Henderson, Henry, Lake, Lauderdale, McNairy, Madison, Obion, Shelby, Tipton and Weakley in the State of Tennessee.

For legal titles of parishes and diocesan institutions, consult the Chancery Office.

Catholic Center: P.O. Box 341669, Memphis, TN, 38184-1669. Tel.: 901-373-1200; Fax: 901-373-1269.

Web site address: www.cdom.org

STATISTICAL OVERVIEW

Personnel	
Bishop	1
Priests: Diocesan Active in Diocese	46
Priests: Active Outside Diocese	4
Priests: Retired, Sick or Absent	18
Number of Diocesan Priests	68
Religious Priests in Diocese	10
Extern Priests in Diocese	6
Ordinations:	
Diocesan Priests	5
Permanent Deacons	32
Permanent Deacons in Diocese	50
Total Brothers	49
Total Sisters	90
Parishes	
Parishes	42
With Resident Pastor:	
Resident Diocesan Priests	37
Resident Religious Priests	5
Without Resident Pastor:	
Administered by Women Religious	1
Missions	5
Pastoral Centers	1
Professional Ministry Personnel:	
Brothers	1
Sisters	11
Lay Ministers	36
Welfare	
Homes for the Aged	2
Total Assisted	480
Residential Care of Children	1
Total Assisted	350
Day Care and Extended Day Care Centers	8
Total Assisted	1,200
Specialized Homes	5
Total Assisted	600
Special Centers for Social Services	4
Total Assisted	3,200
Residential Care of Disabled	4
Total Assisted	200
Educational	
Diocesan Students in Other Seminaries	7
Total Seminarians	7
Colleges and Universities	1
Total Students	2,055
High Schools, Diocesan and Parish	4
Total Students	1,274
High Schools, Private	2
Total Students	1,208
Elementary Schools, Diocesan and Parish	15
Total Students	3,990
Elementary Schools, Private	2
Total Students	520
Non-residential Schools for the Disabled	1
Total Students	47
Catechesis/Religious Education:	
High School Students	280
Elementary Students	2,350
Total Students Under Catholic Instruction	11,731
Teachers in the Diocese:	
Brothers	10
Sisters	14
Lay Teachers	492
Vital Statistics	
Receptions into the Church:	
Infant Baptism Totals	1,183
Adult Baptism Totals	507
Received into Full Communion	295
First Communions	1,251
Confirmations	1,081
Marriages:	
Catholic	151
Interfaith	206
Total Marriages	357
Deaths	472
Total Catholic Population	65,939
Total Population	1,455,808

Former Bishops—Most Rev. CARROLL T. DOZIER, D.D., ord. March 19, 1937; appt. Nov. 17, 1970; cons. Jan. 6, 1971; retired July 27, 1982; died Dec. 7, 1985.—Most Rev. J. FRANCIS STAFFORD, D.D., ord. Dec. 15, 1957; cons. Bishop Feb. 29, 1976; appt. Nov. 16, 1982; appt. to Archdiocese of Denver, June 3, 1986.—Most Rev. DANIEL M. BUECHLEIN, O.S.B., D.D., ord. May 3, 1964; appt. Jan. 20, 1987; appt. to Archdiocese of Indianapolis, July 14, 1992.

Vicar General—Rev. Msgr. PETER P. BUCHIGNANI, *St. Francis of Assisi, 8151 Chimney Rock, Cordova, 38018.* Tel: 901-756-1213.

Catholic Center Offices—Mailing Address: P.O. Box 341669, Memphis, 38184-1669. Tel: 901-373-1200; Fax: 901-373-1269. Office Hours: Mon.-Fri. 7:45-4:45, *5825 Shelby Oaks Dr., Memphis, 38134.*

Chancery

Chancellor and Executive Director of the Catholic Center—Deacon CHARLES R. WELLS, *P.O. Box 341669, Memphis, 38184-1669.* Tel: 901-373-1200.

Notaries—MARIANNA RAMPERSAD; M. TERESA WILTCHER.

Catholic Public Policy Commission of Tennessee—P.O. Box 341669, Memphis, 38184-1669.

Office of Ecumenism—Vacant, Dir.; Rev. GREG SALATA, Assoc. Dir., *6529 Stage Rd., Memphis, 38134.* Tel: 901-373-6011.

Clergy Personnel Board—Revs. JOSEPH L. PAOLOZZI; MICHAEL L. STEWART; GREGORY SALATA; Rev. Msgr. PETER BUCHIGNANI; Rev. ROBERT D. PONTICELLO.

Continuing Education for the Clergy—Rev. BRYAN P. TIMBY, Dir., *4851 Park Ave., Memphis, 38117.* Tel: 901-767-6949.

College of Consultors—Rev. Msgr. PETER P. BUCHIGNANI; Rev. Msgr. EDWARD O. HEYMER; Revs. J. EDWIN CREARY; EDWARD E. EVERITT, O.P.; VICTOR P. CIARAMITARO; RICHARD M. GANTERT; STEPHEN K. KENNY; ALBERT E. KIRK; ROBERT D. PONTICELLO; GABRIEL DIFEDERICO, Dir. Diaconal Formation. Tel: 901-767-6949.

Permanent Deacons Community—Deacon JOHN T. OATES, Dir., *5825 Shelby Oaks Dr., Memphis, 38134.* Tel: 901-373-1216.

Dean of the Jackson Deanery—Rev. VICTOR CIARAMITARO, *Holy Cross Church, 1210 E. Wood St., Paris, 38242.* Tel: 901-642-4681.

Director of Seminarians—Rev. DAVID GRAHAM.

Director of Vocations—Rev. DAVID GRAHAM.

Tribunal

Judicial Vicar—Rev. JOSEPH L. TAGG, III, J.D., J.C.L.

Defender of the Bond—Rev. ROBERT D. PONTICELLO, J.C.L.

Promoter of Justice—Rev. ROBERT D. PONTICELLO, J.C.L.

Auditor—Rev. GABRIEL DIFEDERICO.

Notary—M. TERESA WILTCHER.

Department of Financial Administration

Secretary—JAMES A. KLEISER, JR., *P.O. Box 341669, Memphis, 38184-1669.* Tel: 901-373-1200.

Calvary Cemeteries and All Saints Cemetery—RICHARD B. SMITH, Supt., *1663 Elvis Presley Blvd., Memphis, 38106.* Tel: 901-948-1529.

Controller—EDDIE WALDRUP.

Data Processing—BETTY FURR.

Employee Benefits—KATHY OWINGS.

Facilities and Risk Management—WILLIAM F. HERBERS.

Maintenance—ROBERT PELT.

Department of Education

Secretary—Rev. ALBERT E. KIRK, *P.O. Box 341669, Memphis, 38184-1669.* Tel: 901-373-1200.

Office of Catechetical Ministry—Mr. MARLON DELATORRE, Dir.

Office of Catholic Schools—Dr. MARY MCDONALD, Supt. JANET M. DONATO, Asst. Supt. SALLY HERMSDORFER, Asst. Supt.; Sr. MARIE DEMONTFORT, Asst. Supt. SONDRA MORRIS, Dir. Diocesan Athletics; DAVE NIELSON, Dir. Diocesan Fine Arts; DEBRA SLOSSON, Dir. Food Service; CATHY BIRD, Dir. Inclusion & Special Needs.

Department Of Associated Catholic Charities

Secretary—BRIAN J. O'MALLEY, Exec. Dir., *1325 Jefferson Ave., P.O. Box 41705, Memphis, 38174-1705.* Tel: 901-722-4777.

Catholic Charities, Inc.—KEVIN HICKEY, Dir. CHANDRA TUGGLE, Communication Dir. JAMES ABERNATHY, Finance Dir.

Community Outreach Services—JOSEPH PFEIFFER, Dir. ALICE HARDY, Parish Liaison.

Parish Social Ministry—Vacant.
Ministry to the Sick and Elderly—Vacant.
Genesis House—GERALD BETTICE, Dir. Transitional shelter for homeless.
Refugee Resettlement Unit—CAROLYN TISDALE, Dir.
Day Care Services—VIRGINIA DAVENPORT, Dir.
Holy Names Center—LINDA STEED, Dir. TOMMIE HILL, Site Supvr.
St. Ann-Bartlett Extended Care Program—KAREN OTTS, Site Supvr.
St. Benedict at Auburndale Extended Care—PAMELA O'BRYAN, Site Supvr.
St. John Center—VELTEEN MCGHEE, Program Coord.
St. Louis Extended Care—LORI TUCKER, Site Supvr.
St. Peter Home Day Care Center—ANNE WOOD, Dir.
St. Michael Extended Care—REGINA BLAKEMORE, Site Supvr.
Extended Care Programs (After-School Care)—Vacant.
Diocese of Memphis Housing Corporation—DAVID FIELD, Exec. Dir.
St. Peter Villa Nursing Home—KAE WERK HOVEN, Admin.
St. Peter Home for Children—BRENT ADAMS, Admin.
St. Therese Little Flower Day Care Center—SHARON WEBB, Prog. Dir.
Mid South Caring, Inc.—BRIAN J. O'MALLEY, *1325 Jefferson Ave., P.O. Box 41705, Memphis, 38174-1705.*

Department for Worship and Spiritual Life

Secretary—Rev. R. BRUCE CINQUEGRANI, *P.O. Box 341669, Memphis, 38184-1669.* Tel: 901-373-1200.
Office of Worship—Vacant, Assoc. Dir.; Sr. MAUREEN GRINER, O.S.U., Diocesan Dir. of Music.
Commission for Initiation Ministries—PAUL GRAY, Chm.; Rev. R. BRUCE CINQUEGRANI, Liaison.
Cursillo Movement—Rev. GABRIEL J. DIFEDERICO, Spiritual Advisor. Assoc. Spiritual Advisors: Rev. CHARLES BAUER; Mr. ERNIE ALBONETTI, Lay Dir.
Charismatic Renewal—Rev. RICHARD MICKEY, Diocesan Liaison.

Department for Development and Communications

Secretary—Deacon CHARLES LIGHTCAP, *P.O. Box 341669, Memphis, 38184-1669.* Tel: 901-373-1200.
Planned Giving and Major Donors—LLOYD CROCKETT, Dir.
Communications—JOHN E. MORRIS, Dir.
Information Coordinator—PAIGE EMANUEL.
Newspaper—"West Tennessee Catholic", 5825 Shelby Oaks Dr., Memphis, 38134.

Department of Evangelization and Pastoral Services

Secretary—EILEEN C. HIVNER, *P.O. Box 341669, Memphis, 38184-1669.* Tel: 901-373-1200.
Resource Library—MARY BETH BOLTON.
Professional Ministry Enrichment Programs—EILEEN HIVNER.
Parish Pastoral Councils—EILEEN HIVNER.
Diocesan Ministries Training—EILEEN HIVNER.
Office of Family Ministries—PATRICIA PERRY, Dir.
Committee for Separated, Divorced, Widowed—PAT PERRY.
Marriage Encounter—DAVE D'EMARI; RITA D'EMARI.
Retrouvaille—Deacon JOHN HIVNER, Coord.
Natural Family Planning Center—MARY PAT VAN EPPS, Coord. Tel: 901-765-1757.
Programs for the Engaged—PAT PERRY.
Project Rachel—PAT PERRY.
Office of Youth and Young Adult Ministries—CATHERINE MENSI, Dir.
Search Program—Rev. J. DAVID GRAHAM, JR., Dir.
Scouting—Mrs. CATHERINE MENSI.
Campus Ministry—Memphis, Rev. DERRAN COMBS, O.F.M., Dir. Martin, Rev. JOSEPH PAOLOZZI, Dir. Christian Brothers University, Sr. DOLORES MONTINI, C.S.P., Dir.
Office of Multicultural & African American Catholic Ministries—Deacon CURTISS J. TALLEY, Dir.
Comunidad Hispana Catolica de Memphis—JUAN KINDELAN, Chm.; Rev. RICHARD CORTESE, Spiritual Advisor.
Council for African American Catholic Ministry—Mr. ROBERT ATKINS, Chm.
Native American Ministry—RUTH ALLEN, Coord.
Polish Catholic Mission—BARBARA WALKOWE.
Vietnamese Community—Rev. JOSEPH T.D. NGUYEN, Blessed Sacrament; Sr. MARY PHUC, O.P., Sacred Heart.
Filipino Catholic Ministry—Dr. FRED DONATO.
Korean Catholic Ministry—Coordinators: Mr. JOHN KANG; Mrs. JOHN KANG.

CLERGY, PARISHES, MISSIONS AND PAROCHIAL SCHOOLS

CITY OF MEMPHIS
(Shelby County)

1—CATHEDRAL OF THE IMMACULATE CONCEPTION (1921), Revs. Valentine N. Handwerker, Rector; J. Keith Stewart; Deacons Dick Powelson; James Miller.
Res., 1695 Central Ave., 38104. Tel: 901-725-2700; Fax: 901-725-2709.
School—1669 Central Ave., 38104. Tel: 901-725-2710; Fax: 901-725-2715. Gail Fox, Prin.
Priests 2; Lay Teachers 20; Students 357.
High School—See separate category.

2—ST. ANN (Bartlett) (1950), Revs. R. Bruce Cinquegrani; Joseph Thinh Duc Nguyen; Joel P. Schultz; Deacons Nick Bonaiuto; Chip Jones.
Res., 6529 Stage Rd., Bartlett, 38134. Tel: 901-373-6011; 386-3377; Fax: 901-373-9030.
School—Tel: 901-386-3328; Fax: 901-386-1030.
Sisters 1; Lay Teachers 42; Students 691.

3—ST. ANNE'S (1933), Rev. James L. Pugh; Deacons Jack Chitwood; Charles O'Bryan; Frank Williams.
Res., 706 S. Highland St., 38111. Tel: 901-323-3817; Fax: 901-323-3151.
School—670 S. Highland St., 38111. Tel: 901-323-1344.
Lay Teachers 18; Students 190.

4—CHURCH OF THE ASCENSION (1974), Rev. Richard L. Mickey; Deacons F. Joseph Mensi; John T. Oates; Harvey Stewart.
Res., 3680 RaMill Rd., 38128. Tel: 901-372-1364; Fax: 901-372-9411.

5—ST. AUGUSTINE (1937), Rev. Frank Coens, O.F.M.; Deacons Curtiss Talley; Robert Atkins; Andrew Terry.
Church—1169 Kerr Ave., 38106. Tel: 901-774-2297; Fax: 901-774-3067.

6—ST. BRIGID (1992), Rev. Michael L. Stewart.
Church—7801 Lowrance Rd., 38125-2825. Tel: 901-758-0128; Fax: 901-758-8862.
Res., 4200 Thunderstone Cir. W., 38125-3108. Tel: 901-759-9628.

7—BLESSED SACRAMENT (1912), Rev. Michael A. Morgera.
Church—2564 Hale Ave., 38112. Tel: 901-452-1543; Fax: 901-452-1592.

8—ST. FRANCIS OF ASSISI (1985), Rev. Msgr. Peter P. Buchignani, V.G.; Rev. Kevin W. Bravata; Deacons Max Saller; Bill Davis; Chuck Lightcap; Mick Hovanec.
Res., 8247 Chimneyrock Blvd., Cordova, 38018. Tel: 901-753-1494; Fax: 901-755-2168.
Church—8151 Chimneyrock Blvd., Cordova, 38018. Tel: 901-756-1213.

9—HOLY NAMES OF JESUS AND MARY (1939), Rev. Milton J. Guthrie; Deacon Fred Brunner.
Res., 697 Keel Ave., 38107-2599. Tel: 901-525-9870; Fax: 901-527-7436.

10—HOLY ROSARY (1955), Revs. Bryan P. Timby; Gabriel DiFederico.
Res., 954 Ivy, 38117.
Church and Office: 4851 Park Ave., 38117. Tel: 901-767-6949; Fax: 901-767-8504.
School—4841 Park Ave., 38117. Tel: 901-685-1231; Fax: 901-818-0335.
Sisters 1; Lay Teachers 36; Students 567.

11—HOLY SPIRIT (1975), Revs. Albert E. Kirk; Richard D. Coy; Deacons Ned Turner; Richard Griffith; Bill Nourse; Werner Rose.
Res., 2315 Hickory Crest, 38119.
Church—2300 Hickory Crest, 38119. Tel: 901-754-7146; Fax: 901-754-0102.

12—INCARNATION (1978), Revs. William R. Kantner; Robert W. Marshall; Deacons Charles R. Wells, Chancellor; Miles Merwin.
Res., 360 Bray Station Rd., Collierville, 38017. Tel: 901-853-7468; Fax: 901-854-0536.

13—ST. JAMES (1956), Rev. Patrick F. Heenan.
Res., 4180 LeRoy, 38108. Tel: 901-767-8672; Fax: 901-767-8672.

14—ST. JOHN'S (1947), Rev. Joseph L. Tagg, III.
Res., 2742 Lamar Ave., 38114. Tel: 901-743-4551; Fax: 901-743-5944.

15—ST. JOSEPH'S (1878), Rev. William F. Stelling.
Res., 3825 Neely Rd., 38109. Tel: 901-396-9996; Fax: 901-332-8691.

16—ST. LOUIS (1957), Revs. Richard Cortese; John B. McArthur; Wayne H. Arnold; Deacon Ralph Donati.
Office: 203 S. White Station Rd., 38117. Tel: 901-682-6606; Fax: 901-680-0571.
School—5192 Shady Grove Rd., 38117. Tel: 901-682-9692.
Lay Teachers 29; Aides 3; Students 506.

17—ST. MARY'S (1860), Rev. Bill Rooney, O.F.M.
Church and Office: 155 Market St., 38105. Tel: 901-522-9420; Fax: 901-522-8314.
Res., Franciscan Friary, 1254 S. Lauderdale, 38106. Tel: 901-774-8191.

18—ST. MICHAEL'S (1951), Revs. John V. Atkinson; Alfred Graham.
Office: 3848 Forrest Ave., 38122. Tel: 901-323-0896; 324-6411; Fax: 901-323-3557.
Res., 3867 Summer Ave., 38122. Tel: 901-454-1349; 452-6036.
School—3880 Forrest Ave., 38122. Tel: 901-323-2162; Fax: 901-323-3557.
Lay Teachers 13; Students 158.

19—CHURCH OF THE NATIVITY (1979), Rev. Robert D. Ponticello; Deacon Franklin O. Larker.
Res., 5955 St. Elmo, Barlett, 38135. Tel: 901-382-2504; Fax: 901-382-3644.

20—ST. PATRICK'S (1866), Revs. James F. Wiesner, C.S.P.; Bruce Nieli, C.S.P.; James F. Fisher, C.S.P., (Retired); Deacons James Calicott; Eugene Champion; Eddie Ramsey.
Res., 277 S. Fourth St., 38126. Tel: 901-527-2542; Fax: 901-525-1147.

21—ST. PAUL THE APOSTLE (1944), Rev. Richard M. Gantert; Deacon Richard H. Williams, Jr. In res., Rev. James B. Murray.
Res., 1425 E. Shelby Dr., 38116. Tel: 901-346-2380; Fax: 901-346-2385.
School—Tel: 901-346-0862; Fax: 901-348-2023.
Sisters 2; Lay Teachers 25; Students 325.

22—OUR LADY OF PERPETUAL HELP (1952), Revs. J. Edwin Creary; Marian Spadini; Deacons Paul Hamblen; William Herbers; John Kang; Walter Chandler, (Retired).
Res., 8151 Poplar, Germantown, 38138. Tel: 901-754-1204; Fax: 901-754-0969.

23—ST. PETER'S (1840), Revs. Edward E. Everitt, O.P.; Bertrand Ebben; Thomas M. Condon, O.P.
Res., 190 Adams Ave., 38103. Tel: 901-527-8282; Fax: 901-526-6882.

24—CHURCH OF THE RESURRECTION (1973), Rev. Ernie DeBlasio.
Res., 5475 Newberry, 38115-3629. Tel: 901-794-8970; Fax: 901-794-8806.

25—SACRED HEART (1899), Rev. David B. Knight.
Res., 1324 Jefferson Ave., 38104. Tel: 901-726-1891; Fax: 901-726-9272.

26—OUR LADY OF SORROWS (1926), Rev. James Martell; Deacon Don Bennis.
Res., 3700 Thomas St., 38127. Tel: 901-353-1530; Fax: 901-353-1052.
School—3690 Thomas St., 38127. Tel: 901-358-7431.
Lay Teachers 10; Students 178.

27—ST. THERESE OF THE INFANT JESUS (1930), Rev. David M. Foley; Deacons Lawrence Howell; Harold Yarbrough.
Res., 1644 Jackson Ave., 38107. Tel: 901-276-1412; Fax: 901-274-4476.

28—ST. WILLIAM (1951), Rev. William F. Burke; Deacons James P. Schmall; John W. Hivner.
Res., 4932 Easley Ave., Millington, 38053. Tel: 901-872-4099; 872-2279; Fax: 901-872-8920.

OUTSIDE SHELBY COUNTY

Brownsville, Haywood Co., St. John (1949), Rev. William J. Parham.
Church—901 N. Washington Ave., Box 872, 38012. Tel: 901-772-3514.

Bolivar, Hardeman Co., St. Mary (1950), Rev. Carl J. Hood.
Res., 223 Mecklinberg Dr., 38008-1736. Tel: 901-658-4627; Fax: 901-658-4627.

Camden, Benton Co., St. Mary Church (1981), Rev. Stephen K. Kenny.
Res., 220 W. Main St., 38320. Tel: 901-584-6459; Fax: 901-584-6446.
Mission—Huntingdon, Carroll Co., Holy Family Church, 265 Cotham Dr., Huntingdon, 38344. Tel: 901-986-2817.

Covington, Tipton Co., St. Alphonsus (1952), Rev. William J. DeVries.
Res., 1512 Evergreen, 38019. Tel: 901-476-0374; Fax: 901-476-9650.
Church—1225 Hwy. 51 S., P.O. Box 430, 38019. Tel: 901-476-8140.
Mission—Ripley, Lauderdale Co., Ave Maria, 664 S. Washington, Ripley, 38063. Tel: 901-635-8800.

Dyersburg, Dyer Co., Holy Angels (1940), Rev. Elbert Callis.
Res., 526 Charles St., P.O. Box 1929, 38025-1929. Tel: 901-287-8000; Fax: 901-287-7632.

Humboldt, Gibson Co., Sacred Heart (1872), Rev. Charles A. Bauer.
Res., 2887 E. Main, 38343. Tel: 901-784-3904; Fax: 901-784-5048.
Mission—Crockett Co.

Jackson, Madison Co., St. Mary's (1867), Revs. William J. Parham; Herman J. Lattus; Deacons Dr. Bill Lafont; Jim Cooley.
Res., 1665 Hwy. 45 Byp., 38305. Tel: 901-668-2596; Fax: 901-668-9809.
School—Tel: 901-668-2525; Fax: 901-668-9809.
Sisters 3; Lay Teachers 25; Students 353.
Mission—Brownsville, Haywood Co., St. John Church, P.O. Box 872, Brownsville, 38012. Tel: 901-772-3514.

Lexington, Henderson Co., St. Andrew (1981), Rev. Edward J. Galvin, S.M.A.
Church—895 N. Broad St., 38351. Tel: 901-968-6393; Fax: 901-967-1228.
Res., 311 Elizabeth Circle, 38351. Tel: 901-968-7949; Fax: 901-967-1228.
Mission—Parsons, Decatur Co., St. Regina, 108 Skyline Ln., Parsons, 38361. Tel: 901-847-2054.

Martin, Weakley Co., St. Jude's (1968), Rev. Joseph L. Paolozzi.
Church and Mailing Address: 435 Moody St., 38237. Tel: 901-587-9777; Fax: 901-587-9778.
Res., 110 Hannings Ln., 38237.

Milan, Gibson Co., St. Matthew Mission (1977), Rev. Charles A. Bauer.
Mailing Address: c/o Sacred Heart Church, 2887 E. Main St., Humboldt, 38343. Tel: 901-784-3904; Fax: 901-784-5048.
Church—9060 Telecom Dr., 38358. Tel: 901-686-8686.

Paris, Henry Co., Holy Cross (1921), Rev. Victor P. Ciaramitaro; Deacons Michael Gore; Rodney Seyller.
Res., 1210 E. Wood St., 38242. Tel: 901-642-4681; Fax: 901-644-9668.

Savannah, Hardin Co., St. Mary's (1948), Rev. Thomas Kirk.
Res., 1107 Clifton Rd., 38372. Tel: 901-925-4852; Fax: 901-925-4852.
Mission—Pickwick, Our Lady of the Lake.

Selmer, McNairy Co., St. Jude (1982), Rev. Carl J. Hood; Deacons Jim Gray; Jim Tucker.
Res., P.O. Box 342, 38375. Tel: 901-645-4188.

Somerville, Fayette Co., St. Philip the Apostle (1981), Sr. Jeanne L. Dion, O.P., Pastoral Admin.
Church—11710 Hwy. 64, 38068. Tel: 901-465-8685; Fax: 901-466-1645.

Union City, Obion Co., Immaculate Conception (1891), Rev. Jim McCarver.
Res., 1303 E. Reelfoot Ave., 38261. Tel: 901-885-0963; Fax: 901-885-9960.

Chaplains of Public Institutions

MEMPHIS. *Federal Correctional Institute at Memphis.* Rev. Faustino Maramot, Chap.

On Duty Outside the Diocese:
Reverend Fathers—
Henkes, Donald E.
Kelly, Edward, St. Louis University, St. Louis, MO
Nobile, Angelo

Military Chaplains:
Reverend Fathers—
Danner, James L., COMNAVSURFPAC (N01G), 2841 Rendova Rd., San Diego, CA 92155-5490
Lamb, Gary E., Chap., U.S. Navy

Retired:
Reverend Monsignors—
Batson, John R., 2000 S. Ocean Dr. #508, Ft. Lauderdale, FL 33316. Tel: 954-467-1972
Davis, William F., 745 Loeb St., Memphis, TN 38111
Heymer, Edward D., 941 Ivy Rd., Memphis, TN 38117
Lynch, Patrick J., 214 W. Brow Rd., Lookout Mountain, TN 37350
Wiggs, Joel M., 4250 Main St., P.O. Box 306, Humboldt, TN 38343-0306. Tel: 901-784-3233
Reverend Fathers—
Cleary, Edward J., 4776 Childs Dr., Memphis, TN 38116. Tel: 901-397-5997
Elliott, Edward C., Our Lady of Perpetual Church, 8151 Poplar Ave., Germantown, TN 38138. Tel: 901-754-1204
Gaffney, James
Kelly, Edgar M., Ave Maria Home, 2805 Charles Bryan Rd., #209, Memphis, TN 38134
Murphy, James W., Ave Maria Home, 2805 Charles Bryan Rd., Memphis, TN 38134
Oglesby, J. Leonard, 76 Lakeside Rd., Pope, MS 38658
St. Charles, Paul W., 122 Tallwood Dr., Nashville, TN 37211-2711
Stritch, Morris G., Ave Maria Home, 2805 Charles Bryan Rd., #121, Memphis, TN 38134

Permanent Deacons:
Atkins, Robert
Bass, George
Bennis, Don
Bonaiuto, Nick
Brunner, Fred
Calicott, James
Champion, Eugene
Champion, James
Chandler, Walter
Chitwood, Jack
Cooley, Jim
Davis, Bill
Donati, Ralph
Finnegan, William
Gore, Michael
Gray, Jim
Griffith, Richard
Hamblen, Paul
Herbers, Bill
Hicks, Joseph
Hivner, John
Hovanec, Mick
Howell, Larry
Johnson, Eldon
Jones, Chip
Kang, John
Lafont, Bill
Larker, Frank
Lightcap, Charles
McCarver, Kenneth
Mensi, Joseph
Merwin, Miles
Miller, James
Nourse, Bill
O'Bryant, Charles
Oates, John
Powelson, Richard
Ramsey, Eddie
Rose, Werner
Saller, Max
Schmall, James
Seyller, Rod
Steele, Mike
Stewart, Harvey
Talley, Curtiss
Terry, Andrew, Jr.
Tucker, Jim
Turner, Ned
Wells, Charles
Williams, Frank
Williams, Richard
Yarbrough, Harold

INSTITUTIONS LOCATED IN THE DIOCESE

[A] COLLEGES AND UNIVERSITIES

MEMPHIS. *Christian Brothers University*, (1871) 650 E. Parkway S., 38104. Tel: 901-321-3000; Fax: 901-321-3494
For a complete listing, refer to the Colleges and Universities section.

[B] DIOCESAN SCHOOLS

MEMPHIS. *Bishop Byrne High School* (1965), 1475 E. Shelby Dr., 38116. Tel: 901-346-3060; Fax: 901-346-9488. Mr. Albert Langston, Jr., Prin. Sisters 2; Lay Teachers 23; Students 230.
Memphis Catholic High School and Middle School, 61 N. McLean Blvd., 38104. Tel: 901-276-1221; Fax: 901-725-1447.
E-mail: memmc@impresso.com
Mr. Donald Edwards, Prin. Sisters 1; Lay Teachers 33; Students 305.
St. Augustine School, 1169 Kerr Ave., 38106. Tel: 901-942-8002; Fax: 901-942-8002 (Call First). Mrs. Sally Hermsdorfer, Acting Prin. Sisters 1; Lay Teachers 1; Students 43.

CORDOVA. *St. Benedict at Auburndale School.* (Grades PreK-12), 2100 N. Germantown Pkwy., 38018. Tel: 901-388-7321; Fax: 901-388-8201. Special programs for gifted and learning disabled. Mr. George Valadie, Pres. of Campus; Prin. (Grades 9-12); Mr. Doug Workman, Prin. (Grades PreK-8); Mrs. Cathy Bird, Prin. (Plus Program). Lay Teachers 75; Students 1,022.

[C] HIGH SCHOOLS, PRIVATE AND PAROCHIAL

MEMPHIS.
Christian Brothers High School, 5900 Walnut Grove Rd., 38120-2174. Tel: 901-682-7801; Fax: 901-682-7815.
E-mail: info@cbhs.org
Web site: www.cbhs.org
Title of Incorporation: Christian Brothers (LaSalle) High School. Bros. Christopher Englert, F.S.C., Prin.; Michael Fugger, Co-Dir. Brothers' Community; Michael Livaudais, Co-Dir. Brothers' Community. Brothers 12; Lay Teachers 56; Students 869.
Immaculate Conception Cathedral Middle and High School (1950), 1725 Central Ave., 38104. Tel: 901-276-6341; Fax: 901-726-0141. Mrs. Cheri Kamler, Prin.; Rev. Valentine Handwerker. Lay Teachers 27; Students 280.
St. Agnes Academy (1851), 4830 Walnut Grove Rd., 38117. Tel: 901-767-1377; Fax: 901-682-8199.
E-mail: bdaush@saa-sds.org
Title of Incorporation: St. Agnes Academy-St. Dominic School, Inc. Sisters of St. Dominic (St. Catharine, KY). Barbara Daush, Pres.; Joy Maness, Dean of Upper School; Kathy Toes-Boccia, Dean of Lower School. Lay Teachers 75; Students 605.

[D] ELEMENTARY SCHOOLS, PRIVATE

MEMPHIS. *St. Agnes Academy.* (Grades PreK-12), 4830 Walnut Grove Rd., 38117. Tel: 901-767-1377; Fax: 901-682-8199.
E-mail: bdaush@SAA-sds.org
Web site: http://www.saa-sds.org
Sisters of St. Dominic. (St. Catharine, KY). Barbara Daush, Pres. Lay Teachers 45; Students 334.
St. Dominic Boys School, 30 Avon Rd., 38117. Tel: 901-682-3011; Fax: 901-682-8199. Sisters of St. Dominic. (St. Catharine, KY). Mrs. Barbara Daush, Pres.; Mr. John Murphy, Dean. Lay Teachers 43; Students 249.

[E] CHILD-CARING INSTITUTIONS

MEMPHIS. *St. Peter Home for Children*, (1852) 3060 Baskin St., 38127-7799. Tel: 901-354-6300; Fax: 901-354-6343
For a complete listing, refer to the Special Care Facilities section.

[F] DAYCARE CENTERS

MEMPHIS. *Holy Names Preschool & After School Center*, 709 Keel, 38107. Tel: 901-525-8443. Legal Title: *Holy Names Center.* Ms. Linda Steed, Coord. & Prog. Dir.; Mr. Tommie Hill, Site Supvr. Children 300.
St. Louis Extended, 5192 Shady Grove Rd., 38117. Tel: 901-682-9692. Ms. Lori Tucker, Site Supvr. Children 100.
St. Michael Extended, 3880 Forrest Ave., 38122. Tel: 901-324-6662. Ms. Regina Blakemore, Site Supvr. Children 100.
St. Therese Little Flower Day Care Center, 1666 Jackson Ave., 38107. Tel: 901-276-5111. Ms. Sharon Webb, Prog. Dir. Children 125.

CORDOVA. *St. Benedict at Auburndale Extended*, 2100 N. Germantown Rd., 38018. Tel: 901-388-7321; Fax: 901-381-2595. Ms. Pamela O'Bryan, Dir. Children 118.

[G] ADULT RESIDENCES & HOMES FOR AGED

MEMPHIS. *Diocese of Memphis Housing Corp.*, P.O. Box 41705, 38174-1705. Tel: 901-722-4761; 722-4772; Fax: 901-722-4791.
E-mail: davidf@cathchar.org; michelle@cathchar.org
Web site: www.cathchar.org
For a complete listing, refer to the Special Care Facilities section.
St. Peter Manor, 108 N. Auburndale, 38104. Tel: 901-278-8200; Fax: 901-278-8210.
E-mail: mtwig@mecca32.mecca.org
For a complete listing, refer to the Special Care Facilities section.
St. Peter Villa, 141 N. McLean, 38104-2644. Tel: 901-276-2021; Fax: 901-725-3564.
E-mail: kae@cathchar.org
For a complete listing, refer to the Special Care Facilities section.

DYERSBURG. *St. Joseph Manor*, 885 Hwy. 51, Byp. W., 38024. Tel: 901-285-8560; Fax: 901-285-8562.
E-mail: stjoseph@usit.net
For a complete listing, refer to the Special Care Facilities section.
St. Joseph Village, 885 Hwy. 51 Byp. W., Box 151, 38024. Tel: 901-285-8560; Fax: 901-285-8562.
E-mail: stjoseph@usit.net
For a complete listing, refer to the Special Care Facilities section.

HUMBOLDT. *St. Matthew Manor*, 2575 Viking Dr., 38343. Tel: 901-784-7229
For a complete listing, refer to the Special Care Facilities section.
St. Matthew Manor - West, 2575 Viking Dr., 38343. Tel: 901-824-3793
For a complete listing, refer to the Special Care Facilities section.

JACKSON. *St. Mary Manor,* 1771 Hwy. 45 By-Pass, 38305. Tel: 901-668-5633; Fax: 901-668-9252
For a complete listing, refer to the Special Care Facilities section.

MOSCOW. *St. Mark Village Apartments,* 85 St. Mark Cove, 38057. Tel: 901-877-3456
For a complete listing, refer to the Special Care Facilities section.

[H] CATHOLIC CHARITIES

MEMPHIS. *St. Ann-Bartlett Extended Care,* 6529 Stage Rd., 38134. Tel: 901-382-3370. Ms. Karen Otts, Site Supvr.

St. John Center, 2718 Lamar Ave., 38114. Tel: 901-743-5925. Ms. Velteen McGhee, Prog. Dir.

St. Peter Day Care, 125 N. McLean Blvd., 38104. Tel: 901-725-8263. Ms. Anne Wood, Prog. Dir.

[I] RESIDENCES OF PRIESTS AND BROTHERS

MEMPHIS. *Brothers Of The Christian Schools (Mid-West Prov.),* Christian Brothers University, 650 E. Parkway S., 38104. Tel: 901-321-3000; Fax: 901-321-3290.
Web site: www.cbu.edu
Christian Brothers High School, 5900 Walnut Grove Rd., 38119. Tel: 901-682-4704; Fax: 901-682-7815.
Web site: www.cbhs.org
Brothers 46.

The Dominican Friars of Memphis, Inc., 190 Adams Ave., 38103. Tel: 901-527-8282. Rev. Edward E. Everitt, O.P., Chm. & Pres.

Franciscan Friars (Sacred Heart Prov.) of Memphis, 1254 S. Lauderdale, 38106. Tel: 901-774-8191.
E-mail: friarfc@aol.com
Revs. Frank Coens, O.F.M.; J. Derran Combs, O.F.M.; William Rooney, O.F.M.; Bro. Roch Pfeifer, O.F.M. Priests 3; Brothers 1.

Order Of Preachers (Southern Dominican Prov.), 190 Adams Ave., 38103. Tel: 901-527-8282; Fax: 901-526-6882.
E-mail: edelms@mindspring.com
Revs. Bertrand E. Ebben, O.P.; Edward E. Everitt, O.P.; Thomas M. Condon.

Paulist Fathers (New York), St. Patrick Church, 277 S. Fourth St., 38126. Tel: 901-527-2542; Fax: 901-525-1147. Revs. James F. Wiesner, C.S.P., Pastor; Bruce Nieli, C.S.P., Assoc. Pastor; James F. Fisher, C.S.P., (Retired). Priests 3.

JACKSON. *Brothers of St. Francis Xavier (Xaverians),* 611 Burkett St., 38301. Tel: 901-424-5003; Fax: 901-668-9809.
E-mail: dobrien@mail.stmarys.tn.org
Bro. Dan O'Brien, C.F.X.

[J] CONVENTS AND RESIDENCES FOR SISTERS

MEMPHIS. *Dominican Sisters, Congregation of St. Cecila,* 1488 Maurine Dr., 38116. Tel: 901-346-0251; Fax: 901-346-0333. Legal Title: *Dominican Sisters, Congregation of St. Cecilia (Nashville, TN), St. Paul Convent.* Sisters 6.

The House of the Good Shepherd of Memphis, 3911 Mallard Point Dr., 38128. Tel: 901-387-1972; Fax: 901-379-0483. Sr. Michael Maguire, Supr. & Admin. Sisters 6.

Missionaries of Charity, 700 N. 7th St., 38107. Tel: 901-527-4947. Shelter. Tel: 901-526-5456. Sr. M. Zita, M.C., Superior. Sisters 4.

Missionary Sisters Of The Society Of Mary (Waltham, MA) S.M.S.M., 60 S. Auburndale, 38104. Tel: 901-272-2808; Fax: 901-272-2808. Sisters 7.

Monastery Of St. Clare O.S.C., 1310 Dellwood Ave., 38127. Tel: 901-357-6662; Fax: 901-353-3783.
E-mail: stclaire@socomm.net
Web site: www.poorclare.org/memphis
Sr. Mary Marguerite, O.S.C., Abbess. Sisters 7; Huehuetenango, Guatemala 3.

Sisters Of Charity Of The Blessed Virgin Mary (Dubuque, IA) B.V.M., 437 N. Dickinson, 38112. Tel: 901-274-9015; Fax: 901-774-3067.
E-mail: memphisbvm@aol.com
Sr. Mary Immacula DeVlieger, B.V.M., Community Rep. Sisters 3.

Sisters Of St. Joseph Of Pennsylvania (Erie, PA) S.S.J., 931 Ivy, 38117. Tel: 901-821-9907. Sr. Marilyn Terwilliger, S.S.J.

HUNTINGDON. *Franciscan Sisters of Little Falls (Little Falls, MN),* 257 Cotham Dr., 38344-4401. Tel: 901-986-2481; 986-4944; Fax: 901-986-4944. Sr. Jeanette E. Martell, O.S.F.; Sr. Clara Schroedl, O.S.F.; Sr. Ruth Nistler, O.S.F. Sisters 3.

[K] NEWMAN CENTERS

MEMPHIS. *Campus Ministry, University of Memphis, Rhodes College, UT - Memphis,* 3625 Mynders Ave., 38111. Tel: 901-323-3051; Fax: 901-323-0925.
E-mail: dcombs@cdom.org
Rev. J. Derran Combs, O.F.M.

MARTIN. *Cooperative Ministries Interfaith Center,* 312 Lovelace Ave., 38237. Tel: 901-587-2603. Rev. Joseph L. Paolozzi.

[L] MISCELLANEOUS

MEMPHIS. *Catholic Charities, Inc.,* 1325 Jefferson Ave., 38104-2097. Tel: 901-722-4758; Fax: 901-722-4791.
Web site: www.cathchar.org
P.O. Box 41705, 38174-1705.

Cenacle Retreat League, 5135 Tarrytown Dr., 38117. Tel: 901-685-7497. Mrs. Jane Antrobus, Pres.

Charismatic Prayer Groups. Tel: 901-774-8191. Rev. Cyril Wagner, O.F.M.

DeNeuville Learning Center, 840 Dickinson Ave., 38107. Tel: 901-726-5902; Fax: 901-726-0010. Sr. Lakshmie Napagoda, R.G.S., Prog. Dir. Operated by the House of the Good Shepherd of Memphis.

Diocesan Council of Catholic Women, 1811 Glenview Ave., 38114. Tel: 901-276-1456; Fax: 901-276-0463.
E-mail: gwirving@bellsouth.net
Oratory. Mrs. Hattie C. Irving.

House of the Good Shepherd of Memphis DeNeuville Learning Center, 840 Dickinson St., 38107. Tel: 901-726-5902; Fax: 901-726-0010. Sr. Lakshmie Napagoda, Dir.

House of the Good Shepherd of Memphis, Casa Maria, 4083 Remingway, 38128. Tel: 901-373-7456. Sr. M. Guadalup Ruiz, Dir.

Knights of St. Peter Claver (St. Benedict the Black Council No. 188) and Assembly 26 Bishop James P. Lyke, 5600 Santa Barbara, 38116. Tel: 901-396-8315. Mr. Joseph Randolph, Grand Knight & Faithful Comptroller.

Ladies of Charity of Memphis, P.O.Box 17699, 38187-0699. Tel: 901-948-5175. Mrs. Katherine Trippe, Pres.

Madonna Circle, Inc. (Catholic Women's Service Organization), P.O. Box 172174, 38187-2174. Tel: 901-842-6652. Patsy Barrow, Pres.

Marriage Preparation Program, The Catholic Center, 5825 Shelby Oaks Dr., 38134. Tel: 901-373-1235; Fax: 901-373-1269. Mrs. Patricia A. Perry, Coord.

St. Patrick's Center, 277 S. Fourth St., 38126. Tel: 901-527-2542; Fax: 901-525-1147. Rev. James F. Wiesner, C.S.P., Dir.

Society of St. Vincent DePaul, 3649 Winplace Rd., 38118. Tel: 901-365-4830, Ext. 312; Fax: 901-365-2796. Mr. Kenny Bowen, District Council Pres. Tel: 901-365-4830; Rev. Michael A. Morgera, Spiritual Advisor.

CAMDEN. *Good Samaritan Village,* 192A Post Oak Ave., 38320. Mrs. Francine Mabbett, Mgr. Tel: 901-584-1300 (Fax; 901-584-1344).

COLLIERVILLE. *Serra Club of Memphis,* 2760 Halle Pkwy., 38017. Tel: 901-861-6588. Deacon Charles Lightcap, Pres.; Rev. J. David Graham, Chap.

JACKSON. *Jonah Inc.,* P.O. Box 26, 38302. Tel: 901-427-1630; Fax: 901-427-2689. Mrs. Yvonne Williamson, Exec. Dir.

RELIGIOUS INSTITUTES OF MEN REPRESENTED IN THE DIOCESE

For further details refer to the corresponding bracketed number in the Religious Institutes of Men or Women section.

[1350]—*Brothers of St. Francis Xavier.*—C.F.X.
[0330]—*Brothers of the Christian Schools.* (St. Louis Prov.).—F.S.C.
[1130]—*Congregation of the Priests of the Sacred Heart.*—S.C.J.
[0520]—*Franciscan Friars.*—O.F.M.
[0430]—*Order of Preachers (Dominicans).*—O.P.
[1030]—*Paulist Fathers.*—C.S.P.

RELIGIOUS INSTITUTES OF WOMEN REPRESENTED IN THE DIOCESE

[0230]—*Benedictine Sisters of the Pontifical Jurisdiction.*—O.S.B.
[1070-01]—*Dominican Sisters.*—O.P.
[1070-03]—*Dominican Sisters.*—O.P.
[1070-07]—*Dominican Sisters.*—O.P.
[1070-13]—*Dominican Sisters.*—O.P.
[1310]—*Franciscan Sisters of Little Falls, Minnesota.*—O.S.F.
[2070]—*Holy Union Sisters.*—S.U.S.C.
[2420]—*Marist Missionary Sisters.*—S.M.S.M.
[2490]—*Medical Mission Sisters.*—S.C.M.M.
[2710]—*Missionaries of Charity.*—M.C.
[1360]—*Missionary Franciscan Sisters of the Immaculate Conception.*—O.S.F.
[3760]—*Order of St. Clare.* (Memphis, TN).—O.S.C.
[0440]—*Sisters of Charity of Cincinnati, Ohio.*—S.C.
[0500]—*Sisters of Charity of Nazareth.*—S.C.N.
[0430]—*Sisters of Charity of the Blessed Virgin Mary.*—B.V.M.
[1640]—*Sisters of St. Francis of Perpetual Adoration.* (Prov. of the Immaculate Heart of Mary).—O.S.F.
[3830-09]—*Sisters of St. Joseph.*—S.S.J.
[3830-13]—*Sisters of St. Joseph.*—C.S.J.
[1830]—*Sisters of the Good Shepherd.* (St. Louis Prov.).—R.G.S.

DIOCESAN CEMETERIES

MEMPHIS. *All Saints,* c/o Calvary Cemetery, 1663 Elvis Presley Blvd., 38106. Tel: 901-948-1529.

Calvary, 1663 Elvis Presley Blvd., 38106. Tel: 901-948-1529.

JACKSON. *Calvary.*

NECROLOGY

† Kleiser, Rev. Msgr. William J., (Retired). —Died June 5, 2000.

Diocese of Metuchen

Most Reverend

VINCENT DE PAUL BREEN, D.D.

Bishop of Metuchen; ordained July 15, 1962; appointed Third Bishop of Metuchen July 8, 1997; consecrated and installed September 8, 1997. *Res., 10 Library Pl., Metuchen, NJ, 08840.*

Most Reverend

EDWARD T. HUGHES, D.D.

Bishop Emeritus of Metuchen; ordained May 31, 1947; appointed Auxiliary to Archbishop of Philadelphia and Titular Bishop of Segia June 14, 1976; consecrated July 21, 1976; appointed Second Bishop of Metuchen December 16, 1986; installed February 5, 1987; retired September 8, 1997. *Res., Bethany Ridge, P.O. Box 241, Little York, NJ, 08834.*

The Diocesan Center: P.O. Box 191, Metuchen, NJ, 08840. Tel.: 732-283-3800; Fax: 732-283-2012.

Web site address: www.diometuchen.org

ESTABLISHED NOVEMBER 19, 1981.

Square Miles 1424.55.

Comprises the Counties of Warren, Hunterdon, Somerset and Middlesex in the State of New Jersey.

Legal Corporate Title: The Diocese of Metuchen.

STATISTICAL OVERVIEW

Personnel	
Bishop	1
Retired Bishops	1
Priests: Diocesan Active in Diocese	165
Priests: Active Outside Diocese	13
Priests: Diocesan in Foreign Missions	5
Priests: Retired, Sick or Absent	22
Number of Diocesan Priests	205
Religious Priests in Diocese	42
Extern Priests in Diocese	20
Ordinations:	
Diocesan Priests	3
Permanent Deacons in Diocese	102
Total Brothers	20
Total Sisters	418
Parishes	
Parishes	108
With Resident Pastor:	
Resident Diocesan Priests	98
Resident Religious Priests	5
Without Resident Pastor:	
Administered by Priests	5
Professional Ministry Personnel:	
Brothers	19
Sisters	269
Lay Ministers	122
Welfare	
Catholic Hospitals	1
Total Assisted	105,617
Health Care Centers	2
Total Assisted	6,525
Day Care and Extended Day Care Centers	6
Total Assisted	557
Specialized Homes	6
Total Assisted	227
Special Centers for Social Services	9
Total Assisted	20,366
Other Institutions	2
Total Assisted	38
Educational	
Diocesan Students in Other Seminaries	27
Total Seminarians	27
High Schools, Diocesan and Parish	4
Total Students	3,496
High Schools, Private	2
Total Students	1,080
Elementary Schools, Diocesan and Parish	43
Total Students	15,569
Elementary Schools, Private	1
Total Students	38
Catechesis/Religious Education:	
High School Students	2,221
Elementary Students	39,723
Total Students Under Catholic Instruction	62,154
Teachers in the Diocese:	
Brothers	2
Sisters	71
Lay Teachers	667
Vital Statistics	
Receptions into the Church:	
Infant Baptism Totals	7,168
Adult Baptism Totals	202
Received into Full Communion	364
First Communions	7,421
Confirmations	5,674
Marriages:	
Catholic	1,372
Interfaith	414
Total Marriages	1,786
Deaths	4,012
Total Catholic Population	522,719
Total Population	1,253,288

Former Bishops—Most Rev. THEODORE E. MCCARRICK, ord. May 31, 1958; appt. Titular Bishop of Rusibisir and Auxiliary to the Archbishop of New York, May 24, 1977; cons. June 29, 1977; appt. first Bishop of Metuchen, Nov. 19, 1981; installed Jan. 31, 1982; promoted to the Archdiocese of Newark, June 3, 1986; installed July 25, 1986.—Most Rev. EDWARD T. HUGHES, ord. May 31, 1947; appt. Titular Bishop of Segia and Auxiliary to the Archbishop of Philadelphia, June 14, 1976; cons. July 21, 1976; appt. second Bishop of Metuchen, Dec. 16, 1986; installed Feb. 5, 1987; retired Sept. 8, 1997.

The Diocesan Center—P.O. Box 191, Metuchen, 08840. Tel: 732-283-3800; Fax: 732-283-2012.

Vicar General—Rev. Msgr. JOHN B. SZYMANSKI.

Episcopal Vicars—Rev. Msgr. ANTHONY J. LUISINI; Very Rev. TERRANCE M. LAWLER; Rev. Msgr. J. NEVIN KENNEDY; Very Rev. GLENN J. COMANDINI.

Secretary to the Bishop—Rev. THOMAS J. SERAFIN.

The Diocesan Curia

Moderator—Rev. Msgr. JOHN B. SZYMANSKI, V.G.

The Chancery

Chancellor—Rev. CHARLES T. O'CONNOR, J.C.L.

The Center for Counseling and Consultation Svcs.—109 Lawrence Pkwy., Lawrence Harbor, 08879. Rev. JOSEPH B. SZULWACH, Dir.

Vice Chancellor for Community Affairs—EILEEN A. TABERT, Office of Parish Leadership Services.

The Tribunal

The Diocesan Center—P.O. Box 191, Metuchen, 08840. Tel: 732-283-3800; Fax: 732-283-2012.

Judicial Vicar—Rev. Msgr. WILLIAM BENWELL, J.C.L.

Associate Judicial Vicar—Rev. RICHARD J. LYONS, J.C.L.

Staff—

Judges—Revs. NEIL W. DAVIN, C.P., J.C.L.; ROBERT V. MEYERS, J.C.L.; GEORGE M. PISANELLO, J.C.L.

Defenders of the Bond—LORI BROWERS, J.C.L.; Rev. CHESTER H. CARINA, J.C.L.

Auditors—Sr. MARY A. KERWIN, R.S.M.; CAROL MACDERMOTT; BARBARA J. REAVEY.

Chancery Dispensations—CAROL MACDERMOTT.

Psychological Consultants—FRED J. MCDONALD, Ph.D.; MARY ANN SODROSKI.

Notaries—Sr. M. WILLIAM WASIELEWSKI, C.S.S.F.

Vicariate for Administration

Vicar for Administration—Rev. Msgr. JAMES P. MORAN.

Office of Finance—DAVID A. SMELKO, Dir.

Department of Insurance and Pensions—M. BARBARA FRANCFORT, Mgr.

Department of Cemeteries—RUSSELL B. DEMKOVITZ, Dir.; Very Rev. ANDREW L. SZAROLETA, Dir., Pastoral Care.

Department of Management Information Systems—MICHAEL L. GIRASOLI, Mgr.

Department of Property Management—ROGER A. STONE, Supvr., Building Maintenance.

Office of Stewardship—Rev. Msgr. MICHAEL J. CORONA, Dir. Development Officer, Bishop's Appeal & Diocesan Projects.

Office of the Missions—Rev. Msgr. RICHARD A. BEHL, Dir.

Office of Personnel Management—RUTH E. MELCHIORRE, Dir. CEBS.

Commission on Building—Rev. Msgr. JAMES P. MORAN, Chm.

Commission for Sites and Boundaries—Rev. STEPHEN H. CONGDON, Chm.

Vicariate for Education

Vicar for Education—Rev. Msgr. GEORGE M. BREMBOS, Ed.D.

Office of the Schools—Dr. THOMAS E. HART, Ph.D., Supt. Associate Superintendents: Bro. BRENDAN RAMOS; Sr. MARYANN JACOBS, S.C.C.; Sr. PATRICIA MCCLURE, S.S.J.

Office of Religious Education—MARY KAY CULLINAN, Dir. MARY MORRELL, Assoc. Dir. Rel. Educ.
Office of Youth and Young Adult Ministry—Rev. DAVID J. NICGORSKI, O.M.V., Dir.
"The Catholic Spirit"—RAYANNE DAMIANO, Editor-in-Chief.

Vicariate for Personnel in Ministry

Vicar for Personnel in Ministry—Rev. Msgr. SEAMUS F. BRENNAN.
Office of Ministry to Priests—Rev. CHARLES W. CICERALE, Dir.
Office of the Diaconate—Deacon JOEL R. LIVINGSTON, Dir.
Office for Religious—Sr. JULIA JAMINK, S.J.H.
Office of Shared/Collaborative Ministry—DOROTHY S. DEITZ, Dir.
Office of Vocations—Revs. ROBERT W. MEDLEY, Dir. JONATHAN TOBOROWSKY, Assoc. Dir., Elementary and High School Awareness; MICHAEL C. SAHARIC, Assoc. Dir., College Awareness.
Office of the Health Care Apostolate—Rev. JOSEPH L. DESMOND, Dir.
Commission for the Continuing Education of Priests—Rev. Msgr. ROBERT J. ZAMORSKI.
Board for Seminary Education—Rev. ROBERT W. MEDLEY.

Vicariate for Pastoral Life

Mailing Address: P.O. Box 6189, E. Brunswick, 08816. Tel: 732-651-8084
Vicar for Pastoral Life—Rev. Msgr. MICHAEL J. ALLIEGRO.
Office of Family Life Ministry—JUDITH A. PSOTA, Dir.
Commission for African-American Catholic Ministry—JOSEPH J. POWELL, Chm.
Commission for Ecumenical and Interreligious Affairs—Rev. JEROME A. JOHNSON, Chm.
Commission for the Filipino Apostolate—Rev. EDGARDO D. ABANO, Chm.
Commission for Hispanic Ministry—Very Rev. GLENN J. COMANDINI, Chm.
Chinese Apostolate—Rev. JOSEPH FU, Chap.
Korean Apostolate—Vacant.
Portuguese Apostolate—Rev. LAURO C. SEDLMAYER, Chap.
Commission for Pro-Life Action—Rev. Msgr. RICHARD A. BEHL, Chm.
Commission for Ministry with People with Disabilities—Rev. ROBERT W. MEDLEY, Chm.
Vietnamese Apostolate—Vacant.
Commission for Worship and Preaching—Rev. THOMAS J. SERAFIN, Chm.

Diocesan Organizations, Movements and Moderators

Campaign for Human Development—NEIL GRANSTRAND, Diocesan Liaison.
Catholic Lawyers Guild—Rev. Msgr. MICHAEL J. ALLIEGRO, Moderator.
Catholic Scouting Movement—Rev. Msgr. MICHAEL J. CORONA, Moderator.
Catholic League for Religious and Civil Rights—Rev. Msgr. JAMES P. MORAN, Diocesan Liaison.
Charismatic Movement—Co-Moderators: Rev. ROBERT L. SANTA BARBARA; DORIS BRENNAN.
Diocesan Council of Catholic Women—Rev. EDWARD M. O'NEILL, Moderator.
Diocesan Eucharistic League—Rev. JUAN A. ALBALADEJO, Dir.
Diocesan Holy Name Society—Rev. JOSEPH HOLUP, Moderator.
Diocesan Home School Association—Rev. Msgr. GEORGE M. BREMBOS, Moderator.
Legion of Mary—Rev. THOMAS F. RYAN, Moderator.
National Shrine of the Immaculate Conception—Vacant.
St. Vincent de Paul Societies—Mr. JOSEPH D. FLANNIGAN, Pres.

Vicariate For Charities and Social Ministry

Vicar for Charities and Social Ministry—Rev. Msgr. MICHAEL J. CASHMAN.
Catholic Charities—MARIANNE MAJEWSKI, L.C.S.W., Exec. Dir. MARY E. DAVEY, L.C.S.W., Asst. Exec. Dir.; (See category for Catholic Charities under Institutions Located in the Diocese for the full listing).

Consultative Bodies

College of Consultors—Rev. Msgr. JOHN B. SZYMANSKI, V.G.; Rev. Msgr. ANTHONY J. LUISINI; Rev. Msgr. JAMES P. MORAN; Rev. Msgr. WILLIAM BENWELL; Rev. Msgr. SEAMUS F. BRENNAN; Rev. Msgr. NEVIN KENNEDY; Rev. Msgr. GEORGE M. BREMBOS; Very Rev. GLENN J. COMANDINI; Very Rev. MICHAEL G. KRULL; Very Rev. TERRANCE M. LAWLER; Rev. CHARLES T. O'CONNOR, Sec.
Deans—Very Rev. SYLVESTER J. CRONIN, Cathedral Deanery; Very Rev. MICHAEL J. KRULL, Arthur Kill Deanery; Very Rev. ROBERT J. LYNAM, Forsgate Deanery; Very Rev. DAVID J. PEKOLA, Morris Canal Deanery; Very Rev. STANLEY G. GROMADZKI, Raritan Bay Deanery; Very Rev. RAYMOND L. COLE, County Seat Deanery; Very Rev. JOHN J. CASEY, Somerset Hills Deanery; Very Rev. JOHN J. BARBELLA, Round Valley Deanery; Very Rev. RAYMOND LEONARD, New Brunswick Deanery; Very Rev. GLENN J. COMANDINI, Perth Amboy Deanery.
Presbyteral Council—Most Rev. VINCENT D. BREEN, Pres.
Theological Commission—Very Rev. GLENN J. COMANDINI, S.T.D., Chm.
Administrative Council—Rev. Msgr. JOHN B. SZYMANSKI, V.G., Chm.; Rev. Msgr. MICHAEL J. ALLIEGRO; THOMAS E. HART, Ph.D.; Rev. Msgr. WILLIAM BENWELL; Rev. Msgr. GEORGE M. BREMBOS; Rev. Msgr. SEAMUS F. BRENNAN; Rev. Msgr. MICHAEL J. CASHMAN; Rev. Msgr. MICHAEL J. CORONA; Mrs. RAYANNE DAMIANO; MARIANNE MAJEWSKI; Rev. Msgr. JAMES P. MORAN; Revs. CHARLES T. O'CONNOR; THOMAS J. SERAFIN; Mr. DAVID A. SMELKO.
Diocesan Pastoral Council—Most Rev. VINCENT D. BREEN; Rev. Msgr. JOHN B. SZYMANSKI, V.G.; JULES BORSHADEL; Rev. Msgr. J. NEVIN KENNEDY; Mr. JOSEPH POWELL; Sr. JULIA JAMINK, S.J.H.; Bro. BRENDAN RAMOS, C.F.C.; WILLIAM GIBSON; LOUISE MCDYER; JOHN VITALI; ART STAINNER; HENRY PHILLIPS; LOUIS WILLIAMS; Dr. ISTVAN DEAK; LYNN YENCIK; DANIEL OSTROWSKI; BRUCE TEELING; KATHY SHOEMAKER; MICHAEL MYSZKA; BILL KENNEDY; TINA SALVEMINI; CATHARINE SUTLIFF; CHARLOTTE SNOW; EILEEN A. TABERT, Exec. Sec. RAYANNE DAMIANO.

CLERGY, PARISHES, MISSIONS AND PAROCHIAL SCHOOLS

BOROUGH OF METUCHEN (Middlesex County)

1—CATHEDRAL OF ST. FRANCIS (1871), Rev. Msgr. Richard A. Behl, Rector; Revs. Michael C. Saharic; Richard M. Rusk; Deacons Frank J. Cammarano; Cornelius S. Smoyak; Paul G. Licameli; Guido J. Brossoni.
Res., 32 Elm Ave., 08840. Tel: 732-548-0100; Fax: 732-549-1033.
School—45 Library Pl., 08840. Tel: 732-548-3107; Fax: 732-548-5760.
Sisters of Mercy 2; Lay Teachers 22; Students 433.

OUTSIDE THE BOROUGH OF METUCHEN

Alpha, Warren Co., St. Mary (1902), Rev. Msgr. Anthony J. Luisini; Rev. John J. Werner.
Res., 830 Fifth Ave., 08865. Tel: 908-454-0444; Fax: 908-454-7745.

Avenel, Middlesex Co., St. Andrew (1920), Revs. David B. Kosmoski, O.M.V.; Alan S. Hall, O.M.V. In res., Revs. David J. Nicgorski, O.M.V.; Mark Yavarone, O.M.V.
Res., 244 Avenel St., 07001. Tel: 732-634-4355; Fax: 732-750-5905.
Stations—Avenel, Woodbridge State School.; Avenel, Woodbridge Emergency Reception Center, Tel: 732-636-4261.

Baptistown, Hunterdon Co., Our Lady of Victories (1973), Revs. David I. Fulton; Edward J. Nester, Pastor Emeritus; Deacon John T. Monahan.
Res., P.O. Box 127, 08803. Tel: 908-996-2068; Fax: 908-996-3525.

Basking Ridge, Somerset Co., St. James (1864), Rev. Msgr. William J. Capik; Rev. Jonathan S. Toborowski; Deacons James S. Bell; Luke J. Hally.
Res., 184 S. Finley Ave., P.O. Box 310, 07920. Tel: 908-766-0888; Fax: 908-766-1815.
School—200 S. Finley Ave., P.O. Box 310, 07920. Tel: 908-766-4774; Fax: 908-766-4432.
Felician Sisters 3; Lay Teachers 18; Students 413.

Belvidere, Warren Co., St. Patrick (1892), Rev. Michael A. Driscoll; Deacon John F. Dumschat.
Res., 327 Greenwich St., 07823. Tel: 908-475-2559; Fax: 908-475-1943.

Bernardsville, Somerset Co., Our Lady of Perpetual Help (1898), Rev. Chester H. Carina; Rev. Msgr. John R. Torney, P.A., Pastor Emeritus; Rev. Daniel Gomez; Deacons Joseph E. O'Keefe; Joel R. Livingston; Benigno Ruiz-Diaz.
Res., 111 Claremont Rd., 07924. Tel: 908-766-0079; Fax: 908-766-1185. [CEM]
School—School of St. Elizabeth, Seney Dr., 07924. Tel: 908-766-0244; Fax: 908-766-5372.
Sisters of Christian Charity 1; Lay Teachers 10; Students 246.
Chapel—Bernardsville, Sacred Heart (Chapel of Convenience).

Blairstown, Warren Co., St. Jude (1945), Rev. William J. Smith.
Res., 7 Eisenhower Rd., P.O. Box N, 07825. Tel: 908-362-6444; Fax: 908-362-6862.

Bloomsbury, Hunterdon Co., Church of the Annunciation (1948), Rev. James W. Hagerman.
Res., 80 Main St., P.O. Box 136, 08804-0136. Tel: 908-479-4905.

Bound Brook, Somerset Co., St. Joseph (1876), Revs. Charles T. O'Connor; Randall J. Vashon; Deacon George D. Coleman.
Office: 124 E. Second St., P.O. Box 72, 08805. Tel: 732-356-0027; Fax: 732-356-8092.
Res., 304 John St., 08805. Tel: 732-356-8936. [CEM]
St. Mary of Czestochowa (1914) (Polish), Revs. Stanley J. Walega; Marian Drozd.
Res., 193 W. High St., 08805. Tel: 732-356-0358; Fax: 732-356-1338.

Bridgewater, Somerset Co., Holy Trinity (1948), Rev. John R. Pringle; Deacon Michael A. Forrestall.
Res., 60 Maple St., 08807. Tel: 908-526-2394; Fax: 908-526-5837.
St. Bernard (1843), Rev. Joseph G. Celano; Deacons Patrick J. Cline; Paul L. Anderson; Gerard C. Sims.
Office: Tel: 908-725-0552; Fax: 908-725-4524.
Res., 500 Rte. 22, 08807. Tel: 908-526-6859. [CEM]

Califon, Hunterdon Co., St. John Neumann (1982), Rev. J. William Mickiewicz; Deacon Thomas J. Gilheany.
Res., P.O. Box 455, 07830. Tel: 908-832-2513; Fax: 908-832-7618.

Carteret, Middlesex Co.,

1—ST. JOSEPH, (1893), Rev. Edward C. Puleo. In res., Rev. Msgr. Donald M. Endebrock.
Res., 7 Locust St., 07008. Tel: 732-541-8946; Fax: 732-969-2282.
School—865 Roosevelt Ave., 07008. Tel: 732-541-7111; Fax: 732-541-0676.
Lay Teachers 13; Students 241.

2—HOLY FAMILY, (1907) (Polish), Very Rev. Edmund J. Shallow.
Res., 213 Pershing Ave., 07008. Tel: 732-541-5768; Fax: 732-541-5871.
School—132 Emerson St., 07008. Tel: 732-541-2941; Fax: 732-541-5736.
Bernardine Sisters 1; Lay Teachers 9; Students 174.

3—SACRED HEART, (1910) (Slovak), Rev. Gerald Browne.
Res., 67 Fitch St., 07008. Tel: 732-541-5410.

4—ST. ELIZABETH OF HUNGARY, (1914) (Hungarian), Rev. Patrick H. Barrett.
Res., 119 Washington Ave., 07008. Tel: 732-541-5202.

Clinton, Hunterdon Co., Immaculate Conception (1864), Rev. Andrew L. Szaroleta; Deacon William R. Bauer.
Res., Rte. 633, Old Allerton Rd., P.O. Box 5400, 08809-0400. Tel: 908-735-7319; Fax: 908-735-4552. [CEM]
Stations—Edna Mahan Correctional Facility for Women, Tel: 908-735-7111; Fax: 908-735-5246; Hunterdon Developmental Center, Tel: 908-735-4031; Fax: 908-730-1311.

Colonia, Middlesex Co., St. John Vianney (1959), Revs. Edward M. O'Neill; John R. Butler (RIC); Deacon Joseph D. Ragucci. In res., Rev. John D. Murphy.
Res., 420 Inman Ave., 07067. Tel: 732-574-0150; Fax: 732-574-0050.
School—440 Inman Ave., 07067. Tel: 732-388-1662.
Bernardine Sisters 2; Lay Teachers 34; Students 832.

Cranbury, Middlesex Co., Nativity of Our Lord (1992), Rev. Stephen H. Congdon; Deacons Michel G. Morend; Gregory R. D'Angelo. In res., Rev. Msgr. William J. Haughney.
Res., 185 Applegarth Rd., Monroe Township, 08831. Tel: 609-371-0499.

Dunellen, Middlesex Co., St. John the Evangelist (1879), Rev. Richard J. Lyons. In res., Rev. James A. Kyrpczak.
Res., 317 First St., 08812. Tel: 732-968-2621; Fax: 732-968-2588.

East Brunswick, Middlesex Co., St. Bartholomew (1959), Rev. Msgr. Michael J. Alliegro; Revs. Thomas A. Odorizzi, C.O.; Joseph J. Kerrigan; Deacons John F. Kenny; Anthony J. Gostkowski.
Res., 460 Ryders Ln., 08816. Tel: 732-257-7722; Fax: 732-257-7723.
School—470 Ryders Ln., 08816. Tel: 732-254-7105.
Lay Teachers 26; Students 457.

East Millstone, Somerset Co., St. Joseph (1883), Rev. Raymond L. Cole; Deacons George D. LaPolice; Leo F. Clementi; Joseph C. Moscinski.
Res., P.O. Box 2129, Livingston Ave., 08875. Tel: 908-874-3141; Fax: 908-874-7040.

Edison, Middlesex Co., Guardian Angels (1959), Rev. R. Kevin Crowley.
Res., 37 Plainfield Ave., P.O. Box 1216, 08817-1216. Tel: 732-985-7565; Fax: 732-985-0970.
Mission—Bonhamtown, Middlesex Co., St. Margaret Mary Alacoque, Woodbridge Ave., 08817.
St. Helena (1965), Rev. Msgr. Armando J. Perini; Revs. L. Roger Labonte; Salvatore J. Rossetti, O.P.
Res., 950 Grove Ave., 08820. Tel: 732-494-3399; Fax: 732-494-2076.
School—930 Grove Ave., 08820. Tel: 732-549-6234.
Felician Sisters 3; Lay Teachers 23; Students 408.
Convent—882 Grove Ave., 08820. Tel: 732-321-1462.
St. Matthew (1952), Rev. Msgr. Seamus F. Brennan; Rev. George A. Farrell; Deacons Barry C. Demarest; Eric S. Massimei; Bernard A. Cribbin. In res., Revs. Neil W. Davin, C.P.; Thomas Myladil, O.C.D.
Res., 81 Seymour Ave., 08817. Tel: 732-985-5063; Fax: 732-985-9104.
School—Tel: 732-985-6633; Fax: 732-985-7748.
Sisters of Mercy 2; Lay Teachers 20; Students 376.

Far Hills, Somerset Co., St. Elizabeth (1906), Rev. Msgr. George M. Brembos, Ed.D.; Deacon Lawrence Duffy.
Res., Peapack Rd., Box 37, 07931. Tel: 908-234-0079; Fax: 908-234-2923.
Mission—Peapack, Somerset Co., St. Brigid, Main St., Peapack, 07977. Tel: 908-234-1265; Fax: 908-234-2923.

Flemington, Hunterdon Co., St. Magdalen de Pazzi (1864), Rev. John J. Barbella; Deacons John H. Purdy; Thaddeus Wislinski.
Res., 105 Mine St., 08822. Tel: 908-782-2922; Fax: 908-782-0952. [CEM]

Fords, Middlesex Co., Our Lady of Peace (1919), Rev. Msgr. Robert J. Zamorski; Revs. J. Philip Vadakkekara; Mark E. Kehoe; Deacons Joseph S. Petrovich; Salvatore J. Gagliano.
Res., 26 Maple Ave., P.O. Box 69, 08863. Tel: 732-738-7940; Fax: 732-738-3848.
School—Amboy Ave., 08863. Tel: 732-738-7464; Fax: 732-738-0026.
Dominican Sisters of Divine Providence 1; Lay Teachers 24; Students 385.

Great Meadows, Warren Co., SS. Peter and Paul (1921) (Polish), Very Rev. Ignatius H. Kuziemski.
Res., 360 Rt. 46, P.O. Box 156, 07838. Tel: 908-637-4269; Fax: 908-637-6896.

Hackettstown, Warren Co., Assumption of the Blessed Virgin Mary (1864), Very Rev. David J. Pekola; Rev. Msgr. Stephen A. Bielen, Pastor Emeritus.
Res., 305 High St., P.O. Box 547, 07840-0547. Tel: 908-852-3320; Fax: 908-852-3662.
School—Cook & Liberty Sts., 07840. Tel: 908-852-4791; Fax: 908-852-4180.
Sisters of Christian Charity 2; Lay Teachers 21; Students 336.

Hampton, Hunterdon Co., St. Ann (1859), Revs. William J. Hewitt; Garret J. Fitzgerald; Deacon Joseph J. Foldvary.
Res., 6 Church St., P.O. Box 405, 08827. Tel: 908-537-2221. [CEM]
Station—Glen Gardner, NJ State Hospital for Geriatrics.

Helmetta, Middlesex Co., Holy Trinity (1911) (Polish), Rev. Stanley Jarosz.
Res., 100 Main St., 08828. Tel: 732-521-0172; Fax: 732-521-0824. [CEM]

High Bridge, Hunterdon Co., St. Joseph (1880), Rev. Leonard F.A. Rusay; Deacon Charles A. Paolino.
Res., 59 Main St., 08829. Tel: 908-638-6211; Fax: 908-638-5802.

Highland Park, Middlesex Co., St. Paul the Apostle (1912), Rev. Sylvester J. Cronin. In res., Revs. Maurice T. Carlton; John Brundage.
Res., 502 Raritan Ave., 08904. Tel: 732-572-0977; Fax: 732-574-7497.
Convent—20 S. 6th Ave., 08904. Tel: 732-572-2485. Sisters of St. Joseph of Chesnut Hill, PA

Hillsborough, Somerset Co., Mary, Mother of God (1948), Revs. Liam A. Minogue; Joseph F. Hogan; Deacon Alfred C. Payne, Jr.
Res., 157 S. Triangle Rd., 08876. Tel: 908-874-8220; Fax: 908-874-4183.

Iselin, Middlesex Co., St. Cecelia (1923), Revs. Jerome A. Johnson; A. Gregory Uhrig; Ronald L. Jandernoa; Deacon Belardino A. Lupini.
Res., 45 Wilus Way, 08830. Tel: 732-283-2300; Fax: 732-283-3326.
School—Tel: 732-283-2824.
Religious Teachers Filippini 4; Lay Teachers 20; Students 370.
Stations—NJ State Home for Disabled Veterans.; Roosevelt Care Center.

Jamesburg, Middlesex Co., St. James the Less (1878), Revs. Louis F. Stingel; Charles P. Scillieri.
Res., 36 Lincoln Ave., 08831. Tel: 732-521-0100; Fax: 732-521-8287. [CEM]
Station—State Home for Boys, Tel: 732-521-0030.

Kendall Park, Middlesex Co., St. Augustine of Canterbury (1952), Revs. Robert G. Lynam; Robert V. Meyers; Deacon Richard McCarron.
Res., 51 Henderson Rd., 08824. Tel: 732-297-3000; Fax: 732-940-1746.
School—45 Henderson Rd., 08824. Tel: 732-297-6042.
Brothers of Sacred Heart 1; Lay Teachers 24; Students 353.

Lambertville, Hunterdon Co., St. John the Evangelist (1843), Revs. Leon J. Kasprzyk; John J. Szczepanik; Deacon Joseph J. Masterson.
Res., 44 Bridge St., 08530. Tel: 609-397-3350; Fax: 609-397-8713. [CEM]
Mission—Stockton, Hunterdon Co., St. Agnes, Main St., Stockton, 08559.

Laurence Harbor, Middlesex Co., St. Lawrence (1943), Rev. Joseph Szulwach; Deacon Stephen J. Gajewski.
Res., 109 Laurence Pkwy., 08879. Tel: 732-566-1093; Fax: 732-566-3252.

Manville, Somerset Co., Sacred Heart of Jesus (1919) (Polish), Revs. Boguslaw Augustyn, C.Ss.R.; Jan Kwiecien; Wladyslaw Wiktorek, C.Ss.R.
Res., 136 S. Main St., P.O. Box 924, 08835. Tel: 908-725-0072; Fax: 908-685-3029. [CEM]
Christ the King (1948), Rev. Daniel Sloan; Deacon Donald J. De Lorenzo.
Res., 211 Louis St., 08835. Tel: 908-231-1330; Fax: 908-231-1645.
School—99 N. 13th Ave., 08835. Tel: 908-526-1339; Fax: 908-526-3541.
Lay Teachers 18; Students 217.

Martinsville, Somerset Co., Blessed Sacrament (1968), Rev. Msgr. Eugene Prus; Rev. Manuel Morales; Deacon Martin Mulroy.
Res., 852 Newmans Ln., P.O. Box 563, 08836. Tel: 732-356-4442; Fax: 732-356-5172.

Middlesex, Middlesex Co., Our Lady of Mount Virgin (1943), Rev. Blaise R. Baran; Deacon John R. Tietjen.
Res., 650 Harris Ave., 08846. Tel: 732-356-2149; Fax: 732-356-1302.
School—410 Harris Ave., 08846. Tel: 732-356-6560; Fax: 732-356-7860.
Sisters Apostles of the Sacred Heart 4; Lay Teachers 13; Students 287.

Milford, Hunterdon Co., St. Edward the Confessor (1944), Rev. Michael E. Crummy; Deacon James W. Hendrix.
Res., 61 Mill St., P.O. Box 522, 08848. Tel: 908-995-4723; Fax: 908-995-9353.

Milltown, Middlesex Co., Our Lady of Lourdes (1921), Revs. Thomas V. Perunilam; Edward A. Czarcinski.
Res., 233 N. Main St., 08850. Tel: 732-828-0011; Fax: 732-828-3133.
School—43 Cleveland Ave., 08850. Tel: 732-828-1951; Fax: 732-828-7871.
Little Servant Sisters of the Immaculate Conception 4; Lay Teachers 8; Students 240.

Monmouth Junction, Middlesex Co., St. Cecilia (1904), Rev. Joseph L. Desmond; Deacon John P. McShane.
Office: 10 Kingston Ln., 08852. Tel: 732-329-2893; Fax: 732-329-4693 (call first).
Res., 46 Kingston Ln., 08852. Tel: 732-274-1761.

New Brunswick, Middlesex Co.,

1—St. Peter Apostle, (1829), Rev. James McLaughlin; Deacon Thaddeus C. Raczkowski. In res., Rev. Richard Palumbo.
Res., 94 Somerset St., 08901. Tel: 732-545-6820; Fax: 732-545-4069. [CEM]
School—165 Somerset St., 08901. Tel: 732-545-1473; Fax: 732-545-2508.
Sisters 1; Lay Teachers 28; Students 289.
High School—175 Somerset St., 08901. Tel: 732-846-8046; Fax: 732-220-9560.
Lay Teachers 28; Students 140.

2—St. John the Baptist, (1867) (German-Spanish), Rev. Marco A. Caceres, C.Ss.R., Admin.; Deacon Luis F. Moral.
Res., 29 Abeel St., 08901. Tel: 732-545-5267; Fax: 732-545-0446. [CEM]
Church—Neilson and Carman Sts., 08901.

3—Our Lady of Mt. Carmel, (1977) (Hispanic), Revs. Raymond L. Nacarino; Antonio M. Alvarez.
Res., 86 New St., 08901. Tel: 732-846-5873; Fax: 732-846-5397.
Church—75 Morris St., 08901. Tel: 732-246-9826.

4—St. Joseph, (1924) (Polish), Rev. Norbert M Karava, O.F.M.Cap. In res., Revs. John F. Salwowski, O.F.M.Cap.; Joseph M. Kubiak, O.F.M.Cap.
Res., 15 Maple St., 08901. Tel: 732-545-2195.

5—Sacred Heart, (1883), Rev. Raymond Leonard; Deacon Richard R. Kaseta.
Res., 56 Throop Ave., 08901. Tel: 732-545-1681; Fax: 732-545-5059.

6—St. Ladislaus, (1904) (Hungarian), Revs. Capistran L. Polgar, O.F.M.; Stephen L. Galambos, O.F.M.
Res., 215 Somerset St., 08901. Tel: 732-545-1427; Fax: 732-545-8501.

7—St. Mary of Mount Virgin, (1905) (Italian), Rev. Robert L. Santa Barbara.
Res., 190 Sandford St., 08901. Tel: 732-545-5090; Fax: 732-937-9290.
School—192 Sandford St., 08901. Tel: 732-249-7753.
Sisters 2; Lay Teachers 7; Students 162.
Mission—Edison, Middlesex Co., St. Therese of the Infant Jesus, Fox Rd., Edison, 08817.

North Brunswick, Middlesex Co., Our Lady of Peace (1969), Rev. John V. Polyak.
Res., 277 Washington Pl., 08902. Tel: 732-297-9680; Fax: 732-297-1024.

North Plainfield, Somerset Co., St. Joseph (1882), Rev. John J. Casey.
Res., 41 Manning Ave., 07060. Tel: 908-756-3383; Fax: 908-756-1155.
School—101 Westervelt Ave., 07060. Tel: 908-756-9539.
Sisters of Mercy 3; Lay Teachers 12; Students 192.
St. Luke (1965), Rev. John C. Giordano; Deacons Albert C. Parenti; Dann C. Rossi.
Res., 300 Clinton Ave., 07063. Tel: 908-754-8811; Fax: 908-754-0120.

Old Bridge, Middlesex Co., St. Ambrose (1961), Revs. Charles F. Kelly; Virgilio Tolentino; Frank W. Fellrath; Deacons Charles J. Damian; Andrew J. Strus.
Res., 96 Throckmorton Ln., 08857. Tel: 732-679-5666; Fax: 732-679-0853.
School—Tel: 732-679-4700; Fax: 732-679-6062.
Sisters of St. Joseph (Chestnut Hill) 2; Lay Teachers 34; Students 449.
Convent—94 Throckmorton Ln., 08857. Tel: 732-679-5509.
St. Thomas the Apostle (1921), Rev. Msgr. John B. Szymanski, V.G.; Revs. Michael A. Makara; Kevin M. Casey, C.P.; Deacons John J. Fitzsimmons; Paul E. Featherman; Robert Bonfante, Sr.; Frank C. D'Auguste.
Res., One St. Thomas Plaza, 08857. Tel: 732-251-4000; Fax: 732-251-4946.
School—333 Hwy. 18, 08857. Tel: 732-251-4812.
Lay Teachers 22; Students 515.
Most Holy Redeemer (1983), Rev. Henry L. Hemmerling; Deacon Robert T. McGovern.
Res., 133 Amboy Rd., Old Bridge Township, Matawan, 07747. Tel: 732-566-9334; Fax: 732-566-2245.

Oxford, Warren Co., St. Rose of Lima (1864), Rev. Francis F. Vaz.
Res., Academy St., P.O. Box 88, 07863. Tel: 908-453-2034; Fax: 908-453-4425. [CEM]

Parlin, Middlesex Co., St. Bernadette (1956), Revs. Lawrence H.F. Smith; Edward R. Flanagan; Deacons Nicholas J. Thornton; Samuel Rutch.
Res., 20 Villanova Rd., 08859. Tel: 732-721-2772; Fax: 732-727-5188.

Perth Amboy, Middlesex Co.,

1—St. Mary, (1845), Rev. Michael P. Scott; Deacons Basilio D. Perez; Antonio Bezares.
Res., 104 Center St., 08861. Tel: 732-442-0039; Fax: 732-324-4383.

2—St. Stephen, (1892) (Polish), Revs. John Stec; Jaroslaw Kucharczyk.
Res., 490 State St., 08861. Tel: 732-826-1395; Fax: 732-826-4217. [CEM]

3—Holy Trinity, (1899) (Slovak-Hispanic), Rev. Thomas F. Ryan; Deacon Jose M. Martinez.
Res., 474 Penn St., 08861. Tel: 732-826-0439; Fax: 732-826-2758. [CEM]

4—Our Lady of Fatima, (1960) (Hispanic), Revs. Jesse Carrero, C.M.F.; George Morgan, C.M.R.; Benjamin Martinez, C.M.F.; Bro. Richard Paquette C.M.F.; Deacons Angel P. Perez; Herminio Rivera; Pablo Bencosme; Ramon L. Torres.
Res., 380 Smith St., 08861. Tel: 732-442-6634; Fax: 732-826-0958.

5—Our Lady of Hungary, (1902) (Hungarian), Rev. Thomas F. Ryan, Admin.
Res., 697 Cortlandt St., 08861. Tel: 732-442-0512; Fax: 732-442-3037. [CEM]

6—Our Lady of the Most Holy Rosary, (1904) (Italian), Very Rev. Glenn J. Comandini; Deacon Edward Holowienka.
Res., 625 Florida Grove Rd., 08861. Tel: 732-826-2771; Fax: 732-826-0320.

7—Holy Spirit, (1944), Rev. Robert G. Gorman; Deacon Sam Costantino. In res., Rev. Sean Winters.
Res., 580 Hazel Ave., 08861. Tel: 732-826-4859; Fax: 732-697-9380.

8—LA ASUNCION, (1981) (Hispanic), Rev. John B. Gordon, Admin.; Deacons Corpus V. Perez; Noe Cortez.
Mailing Address: 777 Cortlandt St., P.O. Box 1335, 08862. Tel: 732-826-4991; Fax: 732-826-6951.

9—OUR LADY OF THE ROSARY OF FATIMA, (1981) (Portuguese), Rev. Lauro C. Sedlmayer (Brazil) Admin.
Res., 188 Wayne St., 08861. Tel: 732-826-4350.

Phillipsburg, Warren Co., St. Philip & St. James (1860), Rev. Msgr. Michael J. Corona; Revs. Vincent P. Chen (Taiwan); Guy W. Selvester; Deacons John F. Flynn; Enock Berluche, Sr.
Res., 430 S. Main St., 08865-3094. Tel: 908-454-0112; Fax: 908-454-0125. [CEM]
Mission—New Village, Warren Co., St. Christopher.
SS. Peter and Paul (1913) (Slovak). Closed. Records at St. Philip & St. James, Phillipsburg.

Piscataway, Middlesex Co., Our Lady of Fatima (1948), Revs. Herbert J. Stab; Paul daSilva; Roberto D. Coruna (Philippines); Deacons Stanley J. Lorenc; Lawrence P. Reilly.
Res., 501 New Market Rd., 08854. Tel: 732-968-5555; Fax: 732-968-5959.
School—499 New Market Rd., 08854. Tel: 732-968-5017; Fax: 732-968-9259.
Sisters 1; Lay Teachers 17; Students 233.
Convent—50 Van Winkle Pl., 08854. Tel: 732-968-6136. Franciscan Sisters of Allegany
St. Frances Cabrini (1961), Revs. Edgardo D. Abano; Francis E. Grabowski, Pastor Emeritus; Deacon James O'Neill.
Res., 208 Bound Brook Ave., 08854-4097. Tel: 732-885-5313; Fax: 732-885-9031.
School—2300 Cooper St., 08854. Tel: 732-885-1066; Fax: 732-885-5252.
Sisters of Mercy 1; Lay Teachers 13; Students 234.

Pittstown, Hunterdon Co., St. Catherine of Siena (1992), Rev. Peter Suhaka; Deacon Dennis K. Webster.
Res., P.O. Box 245, 08867-0245. Tel: 908-735-4024; Fax: 908-735-0355.
Catechesis/Religious Programs—Students 400.

Plainsboro, Middlesex Co., Queenship of Mary (1982), Rev. Edward J. Struzik; Deacon James A. Long.
Res., P.O. Box 759, 08536. Tel: 609-799-7511; Fax: 609-799-8904.

Port Murray, Warren Co., St. Theodore (1983), Rev. Albert L. Roca.
Res., P.O. Box 146, 07865. Tel: 908-689-8318.

Port Reading, Middlesex Co., St. Anthony of Padua (1906), Rev. Michael G. Krull; Deacon Joseph V. Szoke.
Res., 436 Port Reading Ave., 07064. Tel: 732-634-1403; Fax: 732-602-0119.

Raritan, Somerset Co., St. Ann (1903) (Italian), Revs. Anthony Dandry; Kenneth D. Brighenti; Kenneth R. Kolibas; Deacon John R. Pacifico.
Res., 45 Anderson St., 08869. Tel: 908-725-1008; Fax: 908-707-1915.
School—29 Second Ave., 08869. Tel: 908-725-7787.
Religious Teachers Filippini 2; Lay Teachers 13; Students 300.
St. Joseph (1912) (Slovak), Rev. Kevin A. Kaminski; Deacon James Hewitt, III. In res., Rev. Charles W. Cicerale Tel: 908-253-0630.
Res., 16 E. Somerset St., 08869. Tel: 908-725-5775.

Sayreville, Middlesex Co., Our Lady of Victories (1885), Very Rev. Terrance M. Lawler; Revs. Wayne Haddad; Jeffrey R. Willingham.
Mailing Address: 42 Main St., 08872.
Res., 24 Main St., 08872. Tel: 732-257-0077; Fax: 732-651-1898.
School—36 Main St., 08872. Tel: 732-254-1676; Fax: 732-254-5066.
Sisters of Mercy 1; Lay Teachers 19; Students 479.
St. Stanislaus Kostka (1914) (Polish), Rev. Kenneth R. Murphy.
Res., 225 MacArthur Ave., 08872. Tel: 732-254-0212; Fax: 732-390-2989. [CEM]
School—MacArthur Ave., 08872. Tel: 732-254-5819; Fax: 732-257-2903.
Lay Teachers 15; Students 185.

Skillman, Somerset Co., St. Charles Borromeo (1982), Rev. Gregory E. S. Malovetz; Deacon Thomas J. Giacobbe.
Res., 376 Burnt Hill Rd., 08558. Tel: 609-466-0300; Fax: 609-466-0602.

Somerset, Somerset Co., St. Matthias (1962), Rev. Douglas J. Haefner; Deacons Stephen J. Holzinger, II; Ronald J. Caimi; John M. Radvanski.
Mailing Address: 168 J.F. Kennedy Blvd., 08873. Tel: 732-828-1400; Fax: 732-828-0866.
Res., 166 J.F. Kennedy Blvd., 08873.
School—170 J.F. Kennedy Blvd., 08873.
Sisters 3; Lay Teachers 28; Students 592.

Somerville, Somerset Co., Immaculate Conception (1882), Rev. Msgr. J. Nevin Kennedy; Revs. Alexander J. Carles; Sean W. Kenney; Deacons John B. Ivers; Arnold J. De Marco; Frank J. Quinn.
Res., 35 Mountain Ave., 08876. Tel: 908-725-1112; Fax: 908-725-6269. [CEM]
School—Tel: 908-725-6516; Fax: 908-725-3172.
Sisters 4; Lay Teachers 23; Preschool 24; Students 536.
High School—Tel: 908-722-0200; Fax: 908-218-7765.
Sisters 13; Lay Teachers 67; Students 888.
Convent—230 Mountain Ave., 08876. Tel: 908-722-6894. Sisters, Servants of the Immaculate Heart of Mary

South Amboy, Middlesex Co., St. Mary (1864), Rev. Dennis R. Weezorak; Deacon Stephen N. Laikowski.
Res., 256 Augusta St., 08879. Tel: 732-721-0179; Fax: 732-721-0360. [CEM]
School—Second St., 08879. Tel: 732-721-1514; Fax: 732-721-9666.
Lay Teachers 13; Students 175.
Sacred Heart (1895) (Polish), Revs. Joseph V. Romanoski; Joseph A. Krajewski; Deacon Robert J. Klein.
Res., 224 N. Feltus St., 08879. Tel: 732-721-0040; Fax: 732-721-4448. [CEM]
School—Tel: 732-721-0834; 721-1446 (Preschool); Fax: 732-316-0326.
Felician Sisters 1; Lay Teachers 16; Students 259.

South Bound Brook, Somerset Co., Our Lady of Mercy (1949), Rev. Daniel J. Herlihy.
Res., 122 High St., 08880. Tel: 732-356-1037; Fax: 732-356-1318.

South Plainfield, Middlesex Co., Sacred Heart (1906), Revs. John Paul Alvarado; John Primich; Thomas P. Ganley; Deacon Joseph J. Stanczak.
Res., 149 S. Plainfield Ave., 07080. Tel: 908-756-0633; Fax: 908-757-5655. [CEM]
School—Tel: 908-756-0632.
Sisters 2; Lay Teachers 24; Students 378.
Our Lady of Czestochowa (1943) (Polish), Rev. John M. Skwara.
Mailing Address: P.O. Box 141, South Plainfield, 07080.
Res., 807 Hamilton Blvd., 07080. Tel: 908-756-1333.

South River, Middlesex Co., St. Mary of Ostrabrama (1903) (Polish), Very Rev. Stanely G. Gromadzki.
Res., 30 Jackson St., 08882. Tel: 732-254-2220; Fax: 732-651-8182. [CEM]
School—22 Holmes Ave., 08882. Tel: 732-254-2417.
Bernardine Sisters 1; Lay Teachers 10; Students 156.
St. Stephen Protomartyr (1907) (Hungarian), Rev. J. Maciej Melaniuk.
Res., 20 William St., 08882. Tel: 732-257-0100; Fax: 732-257-4646.
Corpus Christi (1944), Rev. Kevin P. Duggan.
Res., 100 James St., 08882. Tel: 732-254-1800; Fax: 732-254-8063.
School—80 David St., 08882. Tel: 732-257-5200; Fax: 732-257-6390.
Lay Teachers 11; Students 158.

Spotswood, Middlesex Co., Immaculate Conception (1946), Revs. Harold L. Hirsch; James W. McGuffy; Leon S. Aniszczyk; Deacon John H. McGuire.
Res., 18 South St., 08884. Tel: 732-251-3110; Fax: 732-251-2407.
School—23 Manalapan Rd., 08884. Tel: 732-251-3090; Fax: 732-251-8270.
Felician Sisters 4; Lay Teachers 20; Students 329.
Convent—Tel: 732-251-3446.

Three Bridges, Hunterdon Co., St. Elizabeth Ann Seton (1984), Rev. Msgr. James P. Moran; Rev. Anthony J. Sirianni.
Mailing Address: 105 Summer Road, 08887.
Res., 7 Forest Hill Dr., 08887. Tel: 908-782-1475; Fax: 908-782-6230.

Warren, Somerset Co., Our Lady of the Mount (1911), Rev. Msgr. William Benwell; Deacons Walter S. Maksimik; Thomas Sicola. In res., Rev. Robert W. Medley.
Res., 167 Mount Bethel Rd., 07059. Tel: 908-647-1075; Fax: 908-647-7885.

Washington, Warren Co., St. Joseph (1872), Rev. Robert J. Ascolese.
Res., 200 Carlton Ave., 07882. Tel: 908-689-0058; Fax: 908-689-3436. [CEM]

Watchung, Somerset Co., St. Mary-Stony Hill (1847), Rev. Brian J. Nolan, Admin.; Deacons Henry F. Albert; Arthur J. Wise.
Res., 225 Mountain Blvd., 07069. Tel: 908-756-6524; Fax: 908-756-2111. [CEM]

Whitehouse Station, Hunterdon Co., Our Lady of Lourdes (1923), Rev. Florian J. Gall; Deacons Samuel J. Damiano; John H. Hanna.
Res., 390 Country Rd. 523, 08889. Tel: 908-534-2319; Fax: 908-534-5670.

Woodbridge, Middlesex Co., St. James (1860), Rev. Msgr. Michael J. Cashman; Rev. John C. Grimes; Deacon Carl E. Psota. In res., Rev. Sebastian D. Kaithackal, C.M.I.
Res., 145 Grove St., 07095. Tel: 732-634-0500; Fax: 732-602-1487. [CEM]
School—341 Amboy Ave., 07095. Tel: 732-634-2090.
Bernadine Franciscan Sisters 1; Lay Teachers 15; Students 370.
Convent—Tel: 732-634-0176.
Our Lady of Mount Carmel (1921) (Hungarian), Revs. Vincent C. Cornejo; Michael M. Vincze, Pastor Emeritus.
Res., 267 Smith St., 07095. Tel: 732-634-1438; Fax: 732-634-5368.

Chaplains of Public Institutions

ANNANDALE. *Mountainview Youth Correctional Facility* 08801. Tel: 732-741-6208. Rev. Robert G. Hoffman, Chap.

AVENEL. *Woodbridge State School*. Attended by St. Andrew the Apostle.

BELLE MEAD. *Carrier Clinic*. Rev. Norman R. St. John, S.V.D.

BELVIDERE. *Warren Correctional Center*. Attended by St. Patrick, Belvidere.

CLINTON. *Edna Mahan Correctional Facility for Women*. Attended by Immaculate Conception, Clinton. Tel: 908-735-7319.
Hunterdon State School. Attended by Immaculate Conception, Clinton. Rev. Andrew L. Szaroleta, Chap.

EDISON. *John F. Kennedy Medical Center*. Revs. John D. Murphy, Chap.; Pauly Thekkan, C.M.I.

FLEMINGTON. *Hunterdon Medical Center*. Attended by St. Magdalen de Pazzi.

GLEN GARDNER. *N.J. State Hospital for Geriatrics*. Attended by St. Ann, Hampton.

HACKETTSTOWN. *Hackettstown Community Hospital*. Attended by Assumption of the Blessed Virgin Mary.

JAMESBURG. *N.J. State Training School for Boys*. Attended by St. James the Less.

LYONS. *U.S. Veterans Medical Center*. Revs. George F. Kelly, C.Ss.R.; William Warman (BAL); Joseph C. Chacko.

MENLO PARK. *Roosevelt State Hospital*. Attended by St. Cecelia, Iselin.

NEW BRUNSWICK. *Robert Wood Johnson University Hospital*. Rev. Joseph M. Kubiak, O.F.M.Cap.

NORTH BRUNSWICK. *Middlesex County Adult Detention Center*. Attended by Our Lady of Peace.

OLD BRIDGE. *Old Bridge Regional Hospital*. Attended by St. Ambrose.

PERTH AMBOY. *Raritan Bay Medical Center* Tel: 732-826-2771. Revs. Sean Winters; Sebastian D. Kaithackal, C.M.I.

PHILLIPSBURG. *Warren Hospital* Tel: 908-454-0112. Rev. Vincent P. Chen (Taiwan).

RAHWAY. *East Jersey State Prison*. Attended from St. Andrew the Apostle Church, Avenel. Tel: 732-634-4355.

SKILLMAN. *NJ State Neuropsychiatric Institute*. Attended by St. Charles Borromeo.

SOMERVILLE. *Somerset Medical Center* Tel: 908-526-2394. Rev. Wladyslaw Wiktorek, C.Ss.R.

SOUTH AMBOY. *South Amboy Memorial Hospital*. Attended by St. Mary and Sacred Heart.

On Duty Outside the Diocese:
Reverend Fathers—
Carpena, Octavio R., Society of Jesus Christ the Priest, Murcia, Spain
Escribano, Peter E., Society of Jesus Christ the Priest, Murcia, Spain
Fell, John N., Rome, Italy
Kottar, Michael T., Diocese of Charlotte, NC
Littleton, Gregory J., Diocese of Charlotte, NC
Marin, John L., Society of Jesus Christ the Priest, Guayaquil, Ecuador
McCord, Kent G., Bremerton, MA
Moya, Peter O., Society of Jesus Christ the Priest Murcia, Spain
Muccilli, Sebastian L., 618 Third St., Lake Park, FL 33403
Oterino, Francis L., Society of Jesus Christ the Priest, Guayaquil, Ecuador
Pepel, Clement, Diocese of Phoenix, AZ
Prats, Charles R., Society of Jesus Christ, Murcia, Spain
Ruiz, Faustino C., Society of Jesus Christ the Priest, Chile
Scarcella, Philip J., 6300 Woodbend Dr., Apt. N, Charlotte, NC 28212-2039
Shaner, Edward G., Pauline Fathers, Doylestown, PA
Venditti, J. Michael, Eparchy of Passaic, NJ

Retired:
Reverend Monsignors—
Bielen, Stephen A.

Endebrock, Donald M.
Haughney, William J.
Krysztofik, Joseph M.
Torney, John R., P.A.

Reverend Fathers—
Abramowicz, Richard B.
Avery, Raymond
Cashioli, Lawrence J.
Egierd, Henry A.
Ewing, Richard A.
Grabowski, Francis E.
Kearns, Edward A.
Nebus, Vincent J.
Nester, Edward J.
Przechacki, Casimir J.
Roos, William A.
Szulecki, Raymond L.
Thul, Joseph T.
Vielgus, Thaddeus A.
Vincze, Michael A.

Permanent Deacons:
Albert, Henry F.
Alexander, Russell C., (Retired)
Anderson, Paul L.
Bauer, William R.
Bell, James S.
Bencosme, Pablo
Berluche, Enock, Sr.
Bezares, Antonio
Bolash, George L.
Bonfante, Robert, Sr.
Brossoni, Guido J.
Caimi, Ronald J.
Cammarano, Frank J.
Clementi, Leo F.
Cline, Patrick J., Brooklyn
Coleman, George D.
Cortez, Noe
Costantino, Samuel J.
Cribbin, Bernard A.
Czekaj, John R.
D'Auguste, Frank C.
Daley, James M., (Retired)
Damian, Charles J.
Damiano, Samuel J.
De Blasio, Anthony A., On Leave
De Frange, David A.
De Lorenzo, Donald J.
De Marco, Arnold J.
Demarest, Barry C.
Dominiecki, Thomas F.
Duffy, Lawrence J.
Dumschat, John F.
Featherman, Paul E.
Fitzsimmons, John J.
Flynn, John T.
Foldvary, Joseph J.
Forrestall, Michael J.
Gagliano, Salvatore J.
Gajewski, Stephen J., Sr.
Gellentien, Robert P.
Gilheany, Thomas J., Newark
Gleason, Michael P.
Gostkowski, Anthony J.
Hally, Luke J.
Hanna, John H.
Heissenbuttel, Thomas A., On Leave
Hendrix, James W.
Hewitt, James, III
Holowienka, Edward
Holzinger, Stephen J., II
Ivers, John B.
Janthor, William G.
Kaseta, Richard R.
Kenny, John F.
Klein, Robert J.
Koy, Martin L.
La Police, George D.
Laikowski, Stephen N.
Licameli, Paul G.
Livingston, Joel R.
Long, James A.
Lorenc, Stanley J.
Lupini, Belardino A., M.D.
Maksimik, Walter S.
Marano, Francis J., (Retired)
Martinez, Jose M.
Massimei, Eric S.
Masterson, Joseph J.
Maurer, Joseph S., (Retired)
McCarron, Richard
McGovern, Robert T.
McGrath, James G., On Leave
McGreevy, Robert A., On Leave
McGuire, John H.
McShane, John P.
Monahan, John T.
Moral, Luis S.
Morend, Michel G., Newark
Moscinski, Joseph C.
Mulroy, Martin B., Brooklyn
Murtha, Michael P., On Leave
Nardi, Samuel, On Leave
Nemeth, Stephen F.
O'Keefe, Joseph E.
Pacifico, John R.
Page, Warren C., Syracuse
Paolino, Charles
Parenti, Albert C.
Payne, Alfred C.
Perez, Angel P.
Perez, Basilio A., Dominican Republic
Perez, Corpus V.
Petrovich, Joseph S.
Psota, Carl E.
Purdy, John H., II
Quinn, Frank J.
Raczkowski, Thaddeus C.
Radvanski, John M.
Ragucci, Joseph D.
Reilly, Lawrence P.
Rivera, Herminio
Rossi, Dann P.
Ruiz-Diaz, Benigno I.
Rutch, Samuel
Sheridan, John T.
Sicola, Thomas
Sims, Gerard C.
Smoyak, Cornelius S.
Stanczak, Joseph J.
Strus, Andrew J.
Suswal, Carl S., (Retired)
Szoke, Joseph V.
Thornton, Nicholas J.
Tietjen, John R.
Torres, Ramon L.
Vanzino, William C.
Vivona, Joseph A.
Webster, Dennis K.
Wise, Arthur J.
Wislinski, Thaddeus

INSTITUTIONS LOCATED IN THE DIOCESE

[A] HIGH SCHOOLS, DIOCESAN

EDISON. *Bishop Ahr High School*, One Tingley Ln., 08820. Tel: 732-549-1108; Fax: 732-494-2229.
E-mail: 5BGAED@Diometuchen.org
Web site: www.bgahs.com
Sr. Donna Marie Trukowski, C.S.S.F., Prin.; Rev. James A. Kyrpczak, Chap. Felician Sisters 3; Lay Teachers 59; Students 925.

SOUTH AMBOY. *St. Mary Regional High School*, 310 Augusta St., 08879. Tel: 732-721-0748; Fax: 732-727-7018. Frank J. Ianniruberto, Prin. Chaplains: Revs. Wayne Haddad; Jeffrey R. Willingham. Sisters 7; Lay Teachers 20; Students 456.

[B] HIGH SCHOOLS, PRIVATE

METUCHEN. *St. Joseph High School*, 145 Plainfield Ave., 08840-1099. Tel: 732-549-7600; Fax: 732-549-0664.
E-mail: SJALUMNI@CASTLE.NET
Web site: STJOES.ORG
Bros. Joseph Holthaus, S.C., Pres.; Dennis Wermert, S.C., Dean of Pastoral Life; Matthew Scanlon, S.C., D.R.E.; Peter Murphy, S.C., Chap.; Mr. Lawrence N. Walsh, Prin. Brothers of the Sacred Heart 11; Sisters of St. Joseph (Philadelphia) 2; Lay Teachers 54; Boys 776.

RARITAN. *Shoreless Lake School*, 52 W. Somerset St., 08901. Tel: 908-725-4879; Fax: 908-526-6232. Rev. Lope D. Pascual (Spain), Headmaster. Priests 5; Lay Teachers 8; Students 21.

WATCHUNG. *Mount St. Mary Academy*, 07060. Tel: 908-757-0108; Fax: 908-756-7528.
E-mail: lgambacorto@mountsaintmary.org
Web site: members.aol.com/msmalion
Sr. Lisa D. Gambacorto, R.S.M., E.D.S.; Rev. William T. Morris (NEW), Chap. Day school for girls. College preparatory only. Sisters of Mercy 19; Lay Teachers 32; Girls 320.

[C] INTER-PAROCHIAL ELEMENTARY SCHOOLS

BOUND BROOK. *Holy Family Academy*, St. Joseph Campus, 120 E. Second St., 08805. Tel: 732-356-1151; Fax: 732-356-6884. Mrs. Donna Kanowitz, Prin.
St. Mary Campus, 08805. Sr. Maryann Ronneburger, O.P., Prin., 333 W. Second St., 08805. Tel: 732-469-0055. Sisters 3; Students 401.

PERTH AMBOY. *Perth Amboy Catholic Elementary School*. (Grades K-5), 500 State St., 08861. Tel: 732-826-1598; Fax: 732-826-7063.
E-mail: rpiatek@diometuchen.org
Perth Amboy Catholic Elementary School. (Grades PreK-5), Brace & Carlock Aves., 08861. Tel: 732-826-5747. Lay Teachers 10.
Perth Amboy Catholic School, 583 McKeon St., 08862. Tel: 732-442-9533. Sr. Jeanette DeSena, M.P.F., Admin. Sisters 9; Students 478.
Perth Amboy Middle School. (Grades 6-8), 680 Catherine St., 08861. Tel: 732-442-1713. Sisters 2; Lay Teachers 5.

PHILLIPSBURG. *Saints Philip & James School*, 137 Roseberry St., 08865. Tel: 908-859-1244; Fax: 908-859-1202.
E-mail: isena@diometuchen.org
Web site: www.catholic-church.org/sspj/
Mrs. Irene D. Sena, Prin. Sisters 3; Lay Teachers 19; Students 438.

[D] SPECIAL SCHOOLS, PRIVATE

WATCHUNG. *McAuley School for Exceptional Children*, 1633 U.S. Hwy. 22, 07069. Tel: 908-754-4114; Fax: 908-754-3312.
E-mail: mcaschool@aol.com
Sr. Lee Ann Amico, R.S.M., Dir. Students 46.

[E] CATHOLIC CHARITIES

BRIDGEWATER. *Family Service Office*, 540-550 U.S. Rte. 22, 08807. Tel: 908-722-1881; Fax: 908-704-0215.
Web site: ccdom.org
Mary Grace Billek, M.S.W., Prog. Dir.
Somerset County Services, 540-550 U.S. Rte. 22, 08807. Tel: 908-722-1881. Area Directors: Suzanne Silverio; Sominic Romero.

EAST BRUNSWICK. *Mental Health Center*, 288 Rues Ln., 08816. Tel: 732-257-6100; Fax: 732-257-6929.
Web site: CCDOM.ORG
Mary Grace Billek, M.S.W., Admin.

EDISON. *Family Service Office*, 26 Safran Ave., 08863. Tel: 732-738-1323.
Web site: CCDOM.ORG
Nelida Aranciba, Multi-Prog. Dir.
Middlesex County Office, 26 Safran Ave., 08837. Tel: 732-738-1323; Fax: 732-738-3896.
Web site: CCDOM.ORG
Jean Beil, L.C.S.W., Area Dir., Shelter & Homeless Svcs.

FLEMINGTON. *Hunterdon County Services*, 6 Park Ave., 08822. Tel: 908-782-7905. Douglas A. Reichert, M.S., C.A.S., Dir.

MANVILLE. *Child Care Service Center*, 210 W. Camplain Rd., 08835. Tel: 908-725-1912. Kandyss Stuphen, Prog. Dir.

MILFORD. *Family Service Office*, 69 Water St., 08848. Tel: 908-782-7905. Douglas A. Reichert, M.S., C.A.S., Multi-Prog. Dir.

PERTH AMBOY. *Catholic Charities Central Office*, 319 Maple St., 08861. Tel: 732-324-8200; Fax: 732-826-3549. Mary E. Davey, L.C.S.W., Asst. Exec. Dir.; Marianne Majewski, L.C.S.W., Exec. Dir.; Vanessa M. Wilson, J.D., Human Resources Dir.
Trinity Health & Community Services Center Catholic Charities, 271 Smith St., 08861. Tel: 732-826-9160; Fax: 732-826-8342.
E-mail: ngranstrand@ccdom.org
Ernest Revoir, Area Dir.; Neil Granstrand, Area Dir.

PHILLIPSBURG. *Family Service Office*, 700 Sayre Ave., 08865. Tel: 908-454-2074; Fax: 908-454-9871.
Web site: CCDOM.ORG
Connie Citro.
Social Service Center, 309 S. Main St., 08865. Tel: 908-454-7986. Program Directors: Sr. M. Michaelita Popovice, R.S.M.; Joan Lorah.
Warren County Office, 700 Sayre Ave., 08865. Tel: 908-454-2074; Fax: 908-454-9871.
E-mail: jlorah@ccdom.org
Web site: CCDOM.ORG
Joan Lorah, Service Area Dir.

[F] GENERAL HOSPITALS

NEW BRUNSWICK. *St. Peter's University Hospital*, 254 Easton Ave., P.O. Box 591, 08903-0591. Tel: 732-745-8600; Fax: 732-247-9888.
E-mail: inforasaintpetersuh.com
Web site: www.saintpetersuh.com
For a complete listing, refer to the Hospitals section.

[G] HOMES FOR AGED

NORTH PLAINFIELD. *Villa Maria Sanitarium*, 641 Somerset St., 07060-4909. Tel: 908-757-3050; Fax: 908-754-4939.
E-mail: www.villamariahome.com
For a complete listing, refer to the Special Care Facilities section.

SOMERSET. *McCarrick Care Center*, 15 Dellwood Ln., 08873. Tel: 732-545-4200
For a complete listing, refer to the Special Care Facilities section.

WOODBRIDGE. *St. Joseph Assisted Living Residence*, One St. Joseph Terr., 07095. Tel: 732-634-0004; Fax: 732-634-4586
For a complete listing, refer to the Special Care Facilities section.

[H] MONASTERIES AND RESIDENCES FOR PRIESTS AND BROTHERS

METUCHEN. *Brothers of the Sacred Heart*, 145 Plainfield Ave., 08840. Tel: 732-548-2292. Bro. Paul Joseph, S.C., Supr. Brothers 12.

ASBURY. *Lanteri House*, 668 Mountain View Rd., 08802. Tel: 908-689-5242. Rev. Robert L. Weil.

NEW BRUNSWICK. *De Porres House*, 29 Mine St., 08901-1111. Tel: 732-545-6663; Fax: 732-545-3495.
E-mail: fergusop@rci.rutgers.edu
Web site: www.catholic-center.rutgers.edu
Revs. Ronald A. Stanley, O.P.; Kieran Fergus, O.P.

NEW VILLAGE. *Society of Jesus Christ the Priest*, 70 Edison Rd., 08886. Tel: 908-213-1447. Rev. Lope D. Pascual, Dir.

PLAINSBORO. *Vincentian Residence*, 65 Mapleton Rd., Box 807, 08536-0807. Tel: 609-452-2144. Revs. Joseph A. Morris, C.M., Supr. & Dir.; Charles F. Krieg, C.M.; Joseph P. McClain, C.M.; John G. Nugent, C.M.; Hydo Emerick, C.M.; John T. Maher, C.M.; Bro. Frank Mallaghan, C.M.

RARITAN. *Clairvaux House*, 52 W. Somerset St., 08869. Tel: 908-526-6232. Revs. Lope D. Pascual; Juan A. Albaladejo.

SOMERSET. *Consolata Society for Foreign Missions*, Provincial Headquarters, 2301 Rt. 27, P.O. Box 5550, 08875. Tel: 732-297-9191; Fax: 732-940-3121.
E-mail: supreus@ismico.org
Web site: www.consolata.org
Very Rev. Leonard DePasquale, I.M.C., Prov. Supr.; Revs. Robert Rezac, I.M.C.; Charles Bonelli, I.M.C.; Joseph Sesana, I.M.C.; John Peter Nyaga, I.M.C.; Aventino Oliveira, I.M.C.; George J. Hickey, I.M.C.; Alphonsus Mwariri Kariuki, I.M.C.; Bro. Mario Petrino, I.M.C.

Maria Regina Residence, 5 Dellwood Ln., 08873. Tel: 732-828-6800. Rev. Msgr. John R. Torney, P.A.; Rev. Msgr. Joseph M. Krysztofik; Rev. Msgr. Stephen A. Bielen; Revs. Raymond Avery; Edward J. Nester; Francis E. Grabowski; Joseph T. Thul; Raymond Szulecki; Joseph M. Holup. Retirement home for Diocesan priests.

The Metuchen Oratory, Congregation of the Oratory of St. Philip Neri, 2301 Hwy. 27, P.O. Box 6078, 08875. Tel: 732-297-6401; Fax: 732-297-6403.
E-mail: Oratorymet@aol.com
Very Rev. Peter R. Cebulka, C.O., Provost; Revs. Thomas J. Walsh, C.O., Vicar; Thomas A. Odorizzi, C.O., Treas.; Bro. Kevin P. Kelly, C.O..Priests 3; Brothers 1.

SOUTH RIVER. *Passionist Provincial Office*, 80 David St., 08882. Tel: 732-257-7177; Fax: 732-257-0042. Very Rev. Terence Kristofak, C.P.
Consultors: Revs. Gerald Laba, C.P.; Joseph Jones, C.P.; Melvin Shorter, C.P.; Francis Finnigan, C.P. Priests 5. USAF, PSC Box 826, Randolph Air Force Base, TX, 78148. Tel: 210-565-2889; Fax: 210-566-3614. Revs. James Schiffer, C.P., CH-COL; Stephen Dunn, C.P.; John M. Lee, C.P., St. Gabriel's Monastery, 650 Sheppard Ave. E., Willowdale, Ontario, Canada, M2K 1B7. Tel: 416-221-8866; Fax: 416-221-8893. Revs. Paul Cusack, C.P.; John M. Lee, C.P.; Luigi Malorzo, C.P., 10 Red Maple Ct., Willowdale, Ontario, Canada, M2K 2T3. Tel: 416-225-2660; Fax: 416-222-5445.
Religious of the Province in Residences Not Listed Elsewhere: Rev. Michael Brennan, C.P., Mercy Medical Center, P.O. Box 6009, Redding, CA, 90099. Tel: 530-225-6000. Rev. Kevin Casey, C.P., St. Thomas the Apostle, One St. Thomas Plaza, Old Bridge, 08857. Tel: 732-251-4000; Fax: 732-251-4946. Rev. Neil W. Davin, C.P., St. Mathew's Rectory, 81 Seymour Ave., Edison, 08817. Tel: 732-985-5063; 283-3800 (Office). Rev. Norman Demeck, C.P., Georgian Institution, 391-D Picardy Court, Lakewood, 08701. Tel: 732-367-4543. Rev. Gerald Hynes, C.P., St. Ursula Rectory, 8801 Harford Rd., Baltimore, MD, 21234. Tel: 410-665-2111; Fax: 410-665-0758. Bro. Augustine Paul Lowe, C.P. (ORL), P.O. Box 1800, Orlando, FL, 32802-1800. Tel: 407-246-4800; Fax: 407-246-4941. Rev. Gerard A. Orlando, C.P., St. Patrick Home, 66 Van Cortlandt Park, Bronx, NY, 10463. Tel: 718-519-2800; Fax: 718-519-2817. Rev. Theodore Vitali, C.P., 5859 Nottingham St., Saint Louis, MO, 63109. Tel: 314-977-3149; Fax: 314-377-3696. 204 N. Church St., Dublin, GA, 31021. Rev. Thomas Bonacci, C.P., P.O. Box 2605, Greenville, NC, 27836. Tel: 252-757-3760; Fax: 252-757-3125. Rev. Conan Conaboy, C.P., St. Joseph's Parish, 312 Davis St., Scranton, PA, 18505. Tel: 570-344-1724; Fax: 570-344-1787. Rev. Carrol Thorne, C.P., 316 N. 6th St., Apt. 101, Leavenworth, KS, 66048. Tel: 913-651-2647. Rev. Thomas Berry, C.P., 4301-A Four Farms Rd., Greensboro, NC, 27410. Tel: 336-282-8236; Fax: 336-252-3164. Rev. John Cashman, C.P., St. Ann's Parish, 407-439 Ninth Ave. S., Naples, FL, 34102. Tel: 941-262-4256; Fax: 941-262-4296. Rev. James (Jim) O'Shea, C.P., Our Lady of Monserrate, 134 Vernon Ave., Brooklyn, NY, 11206. Tel: 718-388-5196; Fax: 718-388-5153. Rev. Dominic Papa, C.P., Curia Generalizia Dei Passionisti, Piazza SS Giovanni E Paolo 13, Rome, Italy, 00184. Tel: 39-060-772-711; Fax: 39—06-700-8454. Rev. Neil Tiedemann, C.P., Visitation of the B.V.M. Parish, 98 Richards St., Brooklyn, NY, 11231. Tel: 718-624-1572; Fax: 718-722-7748. Rev. Paul Zilonka, C.P. Oratory. St. Mary's Seminary, 5400 Roland Ave., Baltimore, MD, 21210-1994. Tel: 410-864-4279; Fax: 410-864-4278.

[I] CONVENTS AND RESIDENCES FOR SISTERS

BOUND BROOK. *Sisters of Jesus Our Hope*, 514 Church St., 08805. Tel: 732-271-5777; Fax: 732-271-8067.
E-mail: sjh@injersey.com
Web site: http://nj5/~sjh
Sr. Julia Jamink..Sisters 6.

CARTERET. *Sisters of Jesus Our Hope*, 55 High St., 07008. Tel: 732-541-4678. Sr. Carlotta LaRocca, S.J.H. Sisters 4.

EAST BRUNSWICK. *DePaul House*, 528 Ryders Ln., 08816. Tel: 732-238-3638; Fax: 732-238-0194.
E-mail: dceb@bellatlantic.net
Web site: www.do-northeast.org
Sr. Margaret Palmer, D.C., Local Supr. Sisters 4.

EDISON. *St. Thomas Aquinas Convent*, 15 Wren Ct., 08820. Tel: 732-321-0137.
E-mail: aquinasis@aol.com
Sr. Donna Marie, C.S.S.F., Local Min. Sisters 4.

FLEMINGTON. *The Carmel of Mary Immaculate and St. Mary Magdalen*, 26 Harmony School Rd., 08822. Mother Anne of Christ, O.C.D.; Rev. A. David Chalakal, C.M.I., Chap. Nuns professed with solemn vows 12; Novices 2.

HACKETTSTOWN. *Villa Madonna*. Retirement Home, 1686 Rte. 517, 07840. Tel: 908-852-4551; Fax: 908-852-7403. Daughters of Divine Charity. Sisters 25.

HAMPTON. *Sisters of Jesus Our Hope*, 32 Main St., 08827. Tel: 908-537-6583. Sr. Claire Marie Lessard, S.J.H. Sisters 5.

NEW BRUNSWICK. *Sisters of St. Joseph of Peace*, 61 Jefferson Ave., 08901. Tel: 732-249-5644. Sr. Joanne Rusch, C.S.J.P. Sisters 2.

NORTH PLAINFIELD. *St. Francis Convent*, 450 Grove St., 07060-3606. Tel: 908-769-6498; 757-3050; Fax: 908-754-9190. Sr. Dominic Ritter, O.S.F., Regl. Supr. Sisters 3.

Servants of the Holy Child Jesus Regional House, 641 Somerset St., 07060-4909. Tel: 908-757-3050; Fax: 908-754-9190.
E-mail: adominicl@aol.com
Regional House for Congregation of the Servants of the Holy Child of Jesus. Sr. M. Dominic Ritter, O.S.F., Regl. Supr.; Rev. Severin Dietrich, O.F.M.Conv., Chap.; Tel: 908-756-4186; 757-3050; Fax: 908-754-9190. Sisters 31.

PISCATAWAY. *Divine Providence Convent*, 137 Metlars Ln., 08854. Tel: 732-572-3138; Fax: 732-572-2353. Sr. Maria Michele Armato, O.P., Supr. Sisters 3.

SKILLMAN. *Religious of the Sacred Heart*, 54 Robin Dr., 08558. Tel: 609-924-0180. Sr. Barbara Cooper, R.S.C.J.

SOMERSET. *St. Elizabeth Convent*, 13 Renfro Rd., 08873. Tel: 732-247-3697. Sr. M. Jacoba Fifelski, O.S.F., Supr. Sisters 3.

SOUTH AMBOY. *Sacred Heart Convent*, P.O. Box 3005, 08879-3005. Tel: 732-727-2094. Sr. M. Anastasia Maher, O.S.F., Supr. Sisters 4.

WATCHUNG. *McAuley Hall Inc.*, Health Care Center, 1633 U.S. Hwy 22, 07060. Tel: 908-754-3663; Fax: 908-754-3502. Sr. Irene Gormley, R.S.M.; Rev. Otto Fouser, O.F.M.Conv. Retired Sisters 60.

Mount St. Mary, 1645 U.S. Hwy. 22 W., 07069-6587. Tel: 908-756-0994, Ext. 4025; Fax: 908-754-0164.
E-mail: arcives@newjerseymercy.org
Web site: www.newjerseymercy.org
Sisters of Mercy of the Americas, Regional Community of New Jersey. Sr. Diane Szubrowski, R.S.M., Pres., Regl. Com.; Rev. Edward M. Edwards, O.S.M., Chap. Professed Sisters 297.

Mt. St. Mary House of Prayer, 1651 U.S. Hwy. 22, 07069-6587. Tel: 908-753-2091; Fax: 908-754-0164.
E-mail: msmhope@juno.com
Web site: www.msmhope.com
Sr. Theresina Flannery, R.S.M., Supr. Sisters 3.

WOODBRIDGE. *St. Joseph Convent*, 184 Amboy Ave., 07095. Tel: 732-634-0807; Fax: 732-634-7888.
E-mail: lucylsic@aol.com
Sr. Mary Lucy, L.S.I.C., Supr. Sisters 7.

[J] RETREAT HOUSES

BELVIDERE. *Sacred Heart Renewal Center*, P.O. Box 68, 07823. Tel: 908-475-4694. Bro. Eric Gougen, S.C., Dir. Brothers 5.

FLEMINGTON. *Our Lady of Providence*, 31 Britton Dr., 08822. Tel: 908-782-4495. Little Sisters of the Poor. Sr. Jean of St. Peter, L.S.P., Dir.

HIGHLAND PARK. *Cenacle Retreat House*, (Attn. Cenacle) 411 River Rd., 08904-1999. Tel: 732-249-8100; Fax: 732-249-7888.
E-mail: cenaclehp@erols.com
Web site: www.cenacle.sisters.org
Sr. Barbara Whittemore, R.C. Sisters 5.

LITTLE YORK. *Bethany Ridge*, P.O. Box 241, 08834. Tel: 908-995-9758; Fax: 908-995-7299. Spirituality Center for Priests.

PERTH AMBOY. *Emmaus House*, 101 Center St., 08861. Tel: 732-442-7688; Fax: 732-442-5510. Sr. Susan McGrath, S.M.G., Dir. Sisters 2.

PLAINSBORO. *Vincentian Renewal Center*, 75 Mapleton Rd., P.O. Box 757, 08536. Tel: 609-520-9626; Fax: 609-520-0593.
E-mail: MorrisJ@Vincetianfamilycenter.com
Web site: www.Vincentianfamilycenter.com
Rev. Joseph A. Morrison, C.M., Dir.; Sr. Mary Francis Martin, D.C., Asst. Dir.

[K] SHRINES AND PUBLIC ORATORIES

BERNARDSVILLE. *Sacred Heart Chapel*. (Chapel of Convenience), 111 Claremont Rd., 07924; Fax: 908-766-1185. Rev. Chester H. Carina, Pastor.

RARITAN. *Shrine Chapel of the Blessed Sacrament*, 50 W. Somerset St., 08869. Tel: 908-722-1489. Rev. Juan A. Albaladejo, Rector.

WASHINGTON. *Blue Army Shrine of the Immaculate Heart of Mary*, 674-675 Mountainview Rd., P.O. Box 976, 07882. Tel: 908-213-2223; Fax: 908-213-2263.
E-mail: bluearmy@ix.netcom.com
Web site: www.bluearmy.com

[L] PUBLIC ASSOCIATIONS OF THE FAITHFUL

BOUND BROOK. *Sisters of Jesus Our Hope*, 514 Church St., 08805. Tel: 732-271-5777; Fax: 732-271-8067.
E-mail: sjh@infi.net
Web site: www.sistersofjesusourhope.org
Sr. Julia Jamink, S.J.H., Community Sister Servant. Sisters 17.

PHILLIPSBURG. *The Anawim Community*, 156 Broad St., 08865. Tel: 908-859-2049; Fax: 908-213-9032.
E-mail: anawimpburg@enter.net
Web site: www.anawim.com
Revs. Francis J. Marino, S.M., Dir.; Charles A. Sabella, Vocation Dir.; Richard M. Rusk, Admin.; Richard W. Palumbo.

PISCATAWAY. *Dominican Sisters of Divine Providence*. Tel: 732-572-3138; Fax: 732-572-2353. Sr. Maria Michele Armato, O.P., Supr. Sisters 3.

WASHINGTON. *Handmaids of Mary Immaculate*, Holy House Convent, Mountain View Rd., 07882. Tel: 908-689-7330; Fax: 908-689-0972.
E-mail: smami1@juno.com
Sr. Mary Joseph Brech, A.M.I., Supr. Sisters 10.

[M] CAMPUS MINISTRY

NEW BRUNSWICK. *Catholic Center at Rutgers University*, 17 Mine St., 08901-1111. Tel: 732-545-6663; Fax: 732-545-3495.
E-mail: fergusop@rci.rutgers.edu
Web site: www.catholic-center.rutgers.edu
Chaplains: Revs. Ronald A. Stanley, O.P.; Kieran Fergus, O.P.; Thomas Walsh, C.O.; Sr. Patricia Wormann, O.P., Pastoral Assoc.; Sr. Jeanne Goyette, O.P., Coord. of Community Service.

[N] MISCELLANEOUS LISTINGS

METUCHEN. *The Catholic Lawyers Guild of the Diocese of Metuchen, Inc.*, P.O.Box 191, 08840. Rev. Msgr. Michael J. Alliegro, Moderator.

The Foundation for Catholic Education, P.O. Box 191, 08840. Most Rev. Vincent D. Breen, D.D., Pres.

The Fund for the Future, Inc., P.O. Box 191, 08840. Most Rev. Vincent D. Breen, Pres.

The Priestly Education Fund, Inc., P.O. Box 191, 08840. Most Rev. Vincent D. Breen, Pres.

EDISON. *The Ozanam Shelter for Families and Single Women*, 89 Truman Dr., 08817. Tel: 732-985-0327; Fax: 732-985-2449. Carmen Fernandez, Admin.

Pauline Books and Media, Wick Plaza, 561 Rte. 1 S., 08817. Tel: 732-572-1200; Fax: 732-572-5427.
E-mail: edison@pauline.org

JACKSON. *Nicholas House*, 384 Vath St., 08527. Tel: 732-408-0298. Alex & Millie Paen, Contact Persons. Residential Services.

LAMBERTVILLE. *The Jesus School*, (Church of St. John the Evangelist), 44 Bridge St., 08530. Tel: 609-397-0593; Fax: 609-397-8713. Sr. Marie Conaughton, Dir. Students 45.

NEW BRUNSWICK. *Catholic Charities Ozanam Men's Shelter*, 20-22 Abeel St., 08901. Tel: 732-729-0850; Fax: 732-729-0794.
E-mail: wsmoore@usa.net
Wesley R. Moore, Prog. Dir.
St. John of God Community Health Center, 24 Abeel St., 08901. Tel: 732-745-9800. Steven J. Levin, M.D., Medical Dir.; Sharon Oshatz, M.T. (A.S.C.P.), Dir.

PEAPACK. *Msgr. George E. Everitt Academy*, Main St., P.O. Box 33, 07977. Tel: 908-234-1524; Fax: 908-234-9435. Rev. Msgr. George M. Brembos; Sr. Madeline Sarli, S.S.J., Prin.

PERTH AMBOY. *Community House at St. Thomas*, 319 Maple St., 08861. Tel: 732-324-8200; Fax: 732-826-3549.
E-mail: mdavey@ccdom.org
Mary E. Davey.
Metuchen Community Services Corporation, 319 Maple St., 08861. Tel: 732-826-5142; Fax: 732-826-3549. Michael Sikora, M.B.A.
Nazareth House, 156 Wayne St., 08861. Tel: 732-324-0437. Dominic Romero, Program Dir.

PHILLIPSBURG. *St. Peter and Paul House*, 702 Sayre Ave., 08865. Tel: 908-454-0912. Lori Crago, Prog. Dir.

SOMERSET. *Mission International, Inc.*, 2301 Hwy. 27, 08873. Tel: 732-297-9191; Fax: 732-940-3121. Rev. Leonard DePasquale, I.M.C., Chm.

SOMERVILLE. *The Center for Great Expectations, Inc.*, 88 West End Ave., 08876. Tel: 908-218-0570; Fax: 908-218-1772. Mrs. Peg Wright, Exec. Dir. Residence and comprehensive program for homeless pregnant women and adolescents.

WASHINGTON. *Blue Army of Our Lady of Fatima, U.S.A., Inc.*, P.O. Box 976, 07882. Tel: 908-213-2223; Fax: 908-213-2263.
E-mail: bluearmy@ix.net.com
Web site: www.bluearmy.com

WATCHUNG. *McAuley Hall Foundation, Inc.*, 1633 U.S. Hwy. 22, 07069.

WOODBRIDGE. *Mt. Carmel Home Nursing Service*, 184 Amboy Ave., 07095. Tel: 732-634-0807. Sr. M. Lucy Szczepek, L.S.I.C., Dir.

RELIGIOUS INSTITUTES OF MEN REPRESENTED IN THE DIOCESE

For further details refer to the corresponding bracketed number in the Religious Institutes of Men or Women section.

[1100]—*Brothers of the Sacred Heart*.—S.C.
[0470]—*The Capuchin Friars*.—O.F.M.Cap.
[0275]—*Carmelites of Mary Immaculate*.—C.M.I.
[0360]—*Claretian Missionaries*. (Eastern Prov.).—C.M.F.
[0310]—*Congregation of Christian Brothers*.—C.F.C.
[1330]—*Congregation of the Mission*.—C.M.
[1000]—*Congregation of the Passion*.—C.P.
[0390]—*Consolata Missionaries*.—I.M.C.
[0520]—*Franciscan Friars*. (Custody of St. John Capistran).—O.F.M.
[0940]—*Oblates of the Virgin Mary*.—O.M.V.
[0950]—*Oratorians*.—C.O.
[0480]—*Order Friars Minor Conventual*.—O.F.M. Conv.
[0430]—*Order of Preachers (Dominicans)*. (Prov. of St. Joseph).—O.P.
[1070]—*Redemptorist Fathers*.—C.SS.R.

RELIGIOUS INSTITUTES OF WOMEN REPRESENTED IN THE DIOCESE

[0130]—*Apostles of the Sacred Heart of Jesus*.—A.S.C.J.
[1810]—*Bernardine Sisters of the Third Order of St. Francis*.—O.S.F.
[3110]—*Congregation of Our Lady of the Retreat in the Cenacle*.—R.C.
[0760]—*Daughters of Charity of St. Vincent De Paul*. (Albany Prov.).—D.C.
[0790]—*Daughters of Divine Charity*. (Prov. of St. Joseph).—F.D.C.
[0420]—*Discalced Carmelite Nuns*.—O.C.D.
[1070-18]—*Dominican Sisters*. (Caldwell).—O.P.
[1070-11]—*Dominican Sisters*. (Sparkill, N.Y.).—O.P.
[1070-15]—*Dominican Sisters*. (Blauvelt, N.Y.).—O.P.
[1070-06]—*Dominican Sisters of Hope*. (Ossining, N.Y.).—O.P.
[1170]—*Felician Sisters*. (Immaculate Conception Prov.).—C.S.S.F.
[1180]—*Franciscan Sisters of Allegany, New York*.—O.S.F.
[2575]—*Institute of the Sisters of Mercy of the Americas*. (New Jersey).—R.S.M.
[2300]—*Little Servant Sisters of the Immaculate Conception*.—L.S.I.C.
[2340]—*Little Sisters of the Poor*. (Brooklyn Prov.).—L.S.P.
[2700]—*Missionary Catechists of the Sacred Hearts of Jesus and Mary*.—M.C.
[2790]—*Missionary Servants of the Most Blessed Trinity*.—M.S.B.T.
[2810]—*Missionary Sisters of the Mother of God*. (Byzantine-Ukrainian).—M.S.M.G.
[0950]—*Pious Society Daughters of St. Paul*.—F.S.P.
[3640]—*Poor Servants of the Mother of God*.—S.M.G.
[3320]—*Presentation of the Blessed Virgin Mary*. (New Windsor, NY).—P.B.V.M.
[]—*Religious of the Blessed Virgin Mary*.—R.V.M.
[]—*Religious of the Virgin Mary*.—R.V.M.
[3430]—*Religious Teachers Filippini*. (St. Lucy Prov.).—M.P.F.
[1700]—*School Sisters of the Third Order of St. Francis*.—O.S.F.
[3580]—*Servants of Mary*. (American Prov.).—O.S.M.
[1980]—*Servants of the Holy Child of Jesus*.—O.S.F.
[3630]—*Servants of the Most Sacred Heart of Jesus*.—S.S.C.J.
[0590]—*Sisters of Charity of Saint Elizabeth, Convent Station*.—S.C.
[0660]—*Sisters of Christian Charity*. (North American Eastern Prov.).—S.C.C.
[2970]—*Sisters of Notre Dame*. (Baltimore, MD).—S.N.D.
[3893]—*Sisters of Saint Joseph of Chestnut Hill, Philadelphia*.—S.S.J.
[1650]—*Sisters of St. Francis of Philadelphia*.—O.S.F.
[1600]—*Sisters of St. Francis of the Martyr St. George*.—O.S.F.
[3890]—*Sisters of St. Joseph of Peace*.—C.S.J.P.
[1190]—*Sisters of the Atonement*. (Graymoor).—S.A.
[2170]—*Sisters Servants of the Immaculate Heart of Mary*.—I.H.M.
[4070]—*Society of the Sacred Heart*.—R.S.C.J.

DIOCESAN CEMETERIES

JAMESBURG. *Holy Cross Burial Park*, 840 Cranbury Rd., 08816. Tel: 800-943-8400.

PISCATAWAY. *Resurrection Burial Park*, 899 Lincoln Ave., P.O. Box 189, 08854. Tel: 732-463-1424.

NECROLOGY

† Banach, Joseph S., (Retired). —Died June 26, 2000.
† Dzurenda, Thomas J., Watchung, NJ St. Mary-Stony Hill. —Died Feb. 29, 2000.
† Gerety, Rev. Msgr. John L., South Amboy, NJ St. Mary . —Died Jan. 25, 2000.
† Kelly, Rev. Msgr. J. Morgan, East Brunswick, NJ St. Bartholomew. —Died Aug. 3, 2000.
† McGuire, Michael A., South Plainfield, NJ Sacred Heart. —Died March 10, 2000.
† Neumann, August, (Retired). —Died Dec. 29, 1998.

Archdiocese of Miami

(Archidioecesis Miamiensis)

Most Reverend

JOHN C. FAVALORA, D.D.

Archbishop of Miami; ordained December 20, 1961; appointed Bishop of Alexandria June 16, 1986; ordained and installed July 29, 1986; appointed Third Bishop of St. Petersburg March 7, 1989; installed May 16, 1989; appointed Third Bishop of St. Petersburg November 3, 1994; installed December 20, 1994. *Office: 9401 Biscayne Blvd., Miami, FL, 33138.*

Most Reverend

AGUSTIN A. ROMAN, D.D., V.G.

Auxiliary Bishop of Miami; ordained July 5, 1959; appointed Titular Bishop of Sertei and Auxiliary of Miami February 6, 1979; consecrated March 24, 1979. *Res., 3605 S. Miami Ave., Miami, FL, 33133.*

Most Reverend

GILBERTO FERNANDEZ, D.D., V.G.

Auxiliary Bishop of Miami; ordained May 17, 1959; appointed Titular Bishop of Irina and Auxiliary of Miami June 24, 1997; consecrated September 3, 1997. *Office: 9401 Biscayne Blvd., Miami Shores, FL, 33138.*

Most Reverend

THOMAS G. WENSKI, D.D, V.G.

Auxiliary Bishop of Miami; ordained May 15, 1976; appointed Titular Bishop of Kearney and Auxiliary of Miami June 24, 1997; consecrated September 3, 1997. *Office: 9401 Biscayne Blvd., Miami Shores, FL, 33138.*

Pastoral Center: 9401 Biscayne Blvd., Miami Shores, FL, 33138. Tel.: 305-757-6241; Fax: 305-754-1897 (Chancery); 758-0356 (Communications Office).

Web site address: www.archdioceseofmiami.org

E-mail address: miaarch@miamiarch.org

Most Reverend

EDWARD A. McCARTHY, D.D., S.T.D., J.C.D.

Retired Archbishop of Miami; ordained May 29, 1943; appointed Titular Bishop of Tamascani and Auxiliary of Cincinnati April 21, 1965; transferred to Phoenix August 25, 1969; installed December 2, 1969; appointed Coadjutor Archbishop of Miami *"cum jure successionis" September 17, 1976; Archbishop of Miami July 26, 1977; retired November 3, 1994. Office: 9401 Biscayne Blvd., Miami Shores, FL, 33138.*

ESTABLISHED AUGUST 13, 1958

CREATED AN ARCHBISHOPRIC, JUNE 13, 1968.

Square Miles 4,958.

Comprises the Counties in the southern part of the State of Florida, namely, Broward, Miami-Dade and Monroe.

For legal titles of Parishes and Archdiocesan institutions, consult the Pastoral Center.

STATISTICAL OVERVIEW

Personnel	
Archbishop	1
Retired Archbishops	1
Auxiliary Bishops	3
Priests: Diocesan Active in Diocese	193
Priests: Active Outside Diocese	7
Priests: Diocesan in Foreign Missions	1
Priests: Retired, Sick or Absent	57
Number of Diocesan Priests	258
Religious Priests in Diocese	109
Extern Priests in Diocese	23
Ordinations:	
Diocesan Priests	2
Religious Priests	1
Transitional Deacons	3
Permanent Deacons	8
Permanent Deacons in Diocese	140
Total Brothers	54
Total Sisters	316
Parishes	
Parishes	108
With Resident Pastor:	
Resident Diocesan Priests	98
Resident Religious Priests	10
Missions	7
Pastoral Centers	1
Professional Ministry Personnel:	
Brothers	3
Sisters	56
Lay Ministers	141
Welfare	
Catholic Hospitals	2
Total Assisted	679,886
Health Care Centers	3
Total Assisted	19,175
Homes for the Aged	5
Total Assisted	3,919
Residential Care of Children	2
Total Assisted	417
Day Care and Extended Day Care Centers	7
Total Assisted	3,862
Specialized Homes	9
Total Assisted	16,316
Special Centers for Social Services	64
Total Assisted	938,420
Residential Care of Disabled	1
Total Assisted	128
Other Institutions	11
Total Assisted	2,520
Educational	
Seminaries, Diocesan	1
Students from This Diocese	33
Students from Other Diocese	25
Diocesan Students in Other Seminaries	31
Students Religious	5
Total Seminarians	69
Colleges and Universities	2
Total Students	11,639
High Schools, Diocesan and Parish	9
Total Students	8,518
High Schools, Private	4
Total Students	2,954
Elementary Schools, Diocesan and Parish	55
Total Students	24,385
Elementary Schools, Private	2
Total Students	888
Non-residential Schools for the Disabled	2
Total Students	11,648
Catechesis/Religious Education:	
High School Students	5,090
Elementary Students	29,957
Total Students Under Catholic Instruction	95,148
Teachers in the Diocese:	
Priests	18
Brothers	25
Sisters	52
Lay Teachers	2,350
Vital Statistics	
Receptions into the Church:	
Infant Baptism Totals	17,544
Adult Baptism Totals	1,228
Received into Full Communion	1,282
First Communions	14,581
Confirmations	8,733
Marriages:	
Catholic	2,868
Interfaith	451
Total Marriages	3,319
Deaths	4,542
Total Catholic Population	816,207
Total Population	3,791,043

Former Archbishops—Most Rev. COLEMAN F. CARROLL, D.D., ord. June 15, 1930; appt. Titular Bishop of Pitanae and Auxiliary of Pittsburgh, Aug. 25, 1953; cons. Nov. 10, 1953; appt. first Bishop of Miami, Aug. 13, 1958; installed Oct. 7, 1958; appt. Archbishop of Miami, March 13, 1968; died July 26, 1977.—Most Rev. EDWARD A. MCCARTHY, D.D., S.T.D., J.C.D., ord. May 29, 1943; appt. Coadjutor Archbishop of Miami "cum jure successionis," Sept. 17, 1976; appt. Archbishop of Miami, July 26, 1977; retired Nov. 3, 1994.

Pastoral Center—9401 Biscayne Blvd., Miami Shores, 33138. Tel: 305-757-6241; Fax: 305-754-1897 (Chancery Office); 754-1797 (Communications Office).

Vicars General—Most Rev. AGUSTIN A. ROMAN, V.G.; Most Rev. GILBERTO FERNANDEZ, V.G.; Most Rev. THOMAS G. WENSKI, V.G.; Rev. Msgr. WILLIAM J. HENNESSEY, V.G.

Chancellor—Very Rev. TOMAS M. MARIN, J.C.L.

Moderator of the Curia—Rev. Msgr. WILLIAM J. HENNESSEY, V.G.

Secretary to the Archbishop—Rev. MICHAEL SOUCKAR.

Metropolitan Tribunal—Address all Rogatory commissions and matrimonial matters to the Tribunal, *9401 Biscayne Blvd., Miami Shores, 33138.* Tel: 305-762-1161; Fax: 305-762-1178.

Judicial Vicar and Administrator—Very Rev. ANDREW L. ANDERSON, J.C.D.

Adjutant Judicial Vicar—Rev. KENNETH SCHWANGER, J.C.D.

Judges—Very Rev. TOMAS MARIN, J.C.L.; Sr. JEANNE-MARGARET MCNALLY, J.C.L., Ph.D.; Revs. JOSE BIAIN, O.F.M.; ERNESTO MOLANO, J.C.L.; KENNETH SCHWANGER, J.C.D.; MICHAEL THOMAS, J.C.D.; GARY STEIBEL, J.C.L.; FERNANDO HERIA, J.C.L.;

ALVARO PINZON, J.C.L.; Sr. DEBORA CERVILL, J.C.L.; Dr. STEFANO BENIGNI, J.C.L.; MARIA PAZ RAMOS, J.C.L.

Promoter of Justice—Rev. CARL MORRISON, J.C.L.

Defenders of the Bond—Revs. CARL MORRISON, J.C.L.; RONALD PUSAK, J.C.L.

Notaries—Ms. KATIA ARRIAZA; LILLIAN HUMARA; CONCEPCION MONFORT; KATHLEEN CHERRIS, C.P.S.; VIRGINIA MARTIN; JOAN MATELIS; PAULETTE D'ANGELO VITALE.

Assessors—Rev. CHRISTOPHER MARINO; Sr. ISABEL MAZARREDO, O.P.; ROSARIO BERGOUIGNAN; Deacons ANTONIO MACEO; DEE DUGAN.

Counsel-Assistant to the Tribunal—J. PATRICK FITZGERALD, ESQ.

Consultors—Most Rev. AGUSTIN ROMAN, V.G.; Most Rev. GILBERTO FERNANDEZ, V.G.; Most Rev. THOMAS G. WENSKI, V.G.; Rev. Msgr. WILLIAM J. HENNESSEY, V.G.; Rev. Msgr. VINCENT T. KELLY; Very Rev. TOMAS M. MARIN; Revs. GUSTAVO MIYARES; ARTHUR DENNISON; ANTHONY MULDERRY.

Deans and Deaneries—Rev. Msgr. JOHN GLORIE, V.F., (Northeast Broward); Rev. Msgr. NOEL FOGARTY, P.A., V.F., (Northwest Broward); Very Rev. THOMAS O'DWYER, V.F., (South Broward); Very Rev. JOSE L. HERNANDO, V.F., (East Dade); Very Rev. SEAMUS DOYLE, V.F., (Northeast Dade); Very Rev. LUIS PEREZ, V.F., (Northwest Dade); Very Rev. JAMES FETSCHER, V.F., (South Dade); Rev. Msgr. XAVIER MORRAS, V.F., (West Dade); Very Rev. GERALD MCGRATH, V.F., (Monroe).

Incardination Committee—Most Rev. JOHN C. FAVALORA; Most Rev. AGUSTIN A. ROMAN, V.G.; Most Rev. GILBERTO FERNANDEZ, V.G.; Most Rev. THOMAS G. WENSKI, V.G.; Rev. Msgr. WILLIAM J. HENNESSEY, V.G.; Rev. Msgr. PABLO A. NAVARRO; Rev. Msgr. VINCENT T. KELLY; Very Rev. TOMAS M. MARIN; Revs. ARTHUR DENNISON; JAMES MURPHY.

Presbyteral Council—Most Rev. JOHN C. FAVALORA, Pres.; Revs. ARTHUR DENNISON, Vice Pres. MICHAEL HOYER, Sec.

Priests' Personnel Board—Rev. DANIEL KUBALA, Chm. Consultants: Most Rev. AGUSTIN ROMAN, V.G.; Most Rev. GILBERTO FERNANDEZ, V.G.; Most Rev. THOMAS G. WENSKI, V.G.; Rev. Msgr. WILLIAM J. HENNESSEY, V.G.; Very Rev. TOMAS M. MARIN. Members: Rev. ARTHUR DENNISON; JOSE LUIS HERNANDO; ANTHONY MULDERRY; THOMAS O'DWYER.

Ministry Of General Services

Executive Director—Very Rev. TOMAS M. MARIN.

Chancellor's Office—Very Rev. TOMAS M. MARIN, Chancellor; MARIA E. GALINDO, Ecclesiastical Notary.

Coordinator of Special Projects—Rev. PATRICK O'NEILL.

Legal Services—PATRICK FITZGERALD, *110 Merrick Way, Ste. 3-B, Coral Gables, 33134.* Tel: 305-443-9162; Fax: 305-443-6613.

Communications Dept.—MARY ROSS AGOSTA, Dir. OLGA VEGA, Coord. MIRIAM MIRANDA, Admin. Asst.

Public and Media Relations—MARY ROSS AGOSTA, Dir.

Community Information—MARY ROSS AGOSTA, Dir., Mailing Address: (for Communications, Public and Media Relations and Community Information): *9401 Biscayne Blvd., Miami, 33138.* Tel: 305-762-1043; 1045; Fax: 305-762-1048.

Television and Radio Center—MARY ROSS AGOSTA, Dir. ERNESTO GONZALEZ, Production Mgr. BETH LAGARON, Producer; Revs. JOSE P. NICKSE, Producer & TV Mass Coord. (Spanish); FRANCISCO SANTANA, Producer & TV Mass Coord. (Spanish); CHRISTOPHER MARINO, TV Mass Producer (English), Mailing Address: *9920 N.E. 2nd Ave., Miami, 33138.* Tel: 305-751-0990.

Newspapers—MARY ROSS AGOSTA, Dir., Mailing Address: for Newspapers: *9401 Biscayne Blvd., Miami, 33138.*

"The Florida Catholic"—ROBERT O'STEEN, Editor (English). Tel: 305-762-1131.

"La Voz Catolica"—Ms. ARACELI CANTERO, Exec. Editor (Spanish). Tel: 305-762-1125; Fax: 305-762-1130.

Pax Catholic Communications—Very Rev. JOSE LUIS HERNANDO, V.F., Pres.; Deacon RAFAEL DE LOS REYES, Exec. Vice Pres. & CFO; Dr. JUAN E. ROMAGOSA, Vice Pres. Intl. Advancement. Tel: 305-638-9729; Fax: 305-636-3280.

Radio Peace - WAXY, 790 AM—Rev. ALBERTO CUTIE, Dir., *20450 N.W. 2nd Ave., Miami, 33169.* Tel: 305-253-3101. SCOTT KALDAHL, Programming Coord.

Radio Paz - WACC, 830 AM—Rev. ALBERTO CUTIE, Dir., *1779 N.W. 28 St., N. Miami, 33142.* Tel: 305-638-9729; Fax: 305-636-3976. MARITE ALFONSO, Programming Coord.

Radio Ke Poze - WACC, 830 AM—Rev. ALBERTO CUTIE, Dir., *1779 N.W. 28 St., Miami, 33142.* Tel: 305-638-9729. HANS MARDY, Programming Coord.

PaxNet—1779 N.W. 28 St., Miami, 33142. Tel: 305-638-9100; Fax: 305-638-9944. GONZALO PENAGOS, Operations Dir.

Catholic Office for Inter-Faith Activities and Catholic-Jewish Relations Commission—Rev. Dr. PATRICK H. O'NEILL, Exec. Dir., *9401 Biscayne Blvd., Miami Shores, 33138.* Tel: 305-762-1254; Fax: 305-754-1897.

Christian Unity Commission—Rev. Dr. PATRICK H. O'NEILL, Ecumenical Officer, *9401 Biscayne Blvd., Miami Shores, 33138.* Tel: 305-762-1254; Fax: 305-754-1897.

Ministry Of Christian Formation

Executive Director—Rev. Msgr. VINCENT T. KELLY.

Department of Schools—Rev. Msgr. VINCENT T. KELLY, Vicar, Christian Formation; Bro. RICHARD DE MARIA, C.F.C., Supt. KRISTEN HUGHES; Sr. CORINNE GMUER, S.S.N.D.; RICHARD LYNN; JOSEPHINE KENNA; PATRICIA NORD; Bro. ANGELO PALMIERI, F.M.S.

Department of Religious Education—Sr. ROSA MONIQUE PENA, O.P., Dir. SILVIA DE LA PENA, Exec. Asst. NELSON BONET, Catechumenate Consultant. Consultants: FLORANGEL GONZALEZ; ELIZABETH LEVITZ; MARIA DOLORES PERNAS; ENMA PROANO.

Archdiocesan Media Center—Ms. GLORIA G. ALFONSO, Mgr.

Archdiocese of Miami Education Endowment Fund, Inc.—CHRISTOPHER SAILSBURY, Exec. Dir.

Catholic Charities, Inc

Archdiocesan Director and President—Most Rev. THOMAS G. WENSKI, D.D., Auxiliary Bishop; Rev. Msgr. BRYAN O. WALSH, P.A., Archdiocesan Dir. Emeritus; PETER D. COATS, Special Asst. & Admin., *9401 Biscayne Blvd., Miami Shores, 33138.* Tel: 305-754-2444; Fax: 305-754-6649.

Catholic Campaign for Human Development—9401 Biscayne Blvd., Miami Shores, 33138. Tel: 305-754-2444; Fax: 305-754-6649.

Catholic Charities Legal Services—RANDOLPH P. MCGRORTY, Supervising Attorney.

Miami Office—7101 Biscayne Blvd., Miami, 33138. Tel: 305-758-3301; Fax: 305-756-6435.

Hialeah Office—60 E. 3rd St., Ste. 206, Hialeah, 33010. Tel: 305-887-8333; Fax: 305-887-8813.

Catholic Commission for Social Advocacy—9401 Biscayne Blvd., Miami Shores, 33138. Tel: 305-754-2444; Fax: 305-754-6649.

Catholic Hospice, Inc.—TONY PALUMBO, CEO, *14100 Palmetto Frontage Rd., Miami Lakes, 33016.* Tel: 305-822-2380; Fax: 305-827-0221.

Catholic Relief Services—9401 Biscayne Blvd., Miami Shores, 33138. Tel: 305-754-2444; Fax: 305-754-6649.

Foreign Missions Board—9401 Biscayne Blvd., Miami Shores, 33138. Tel: 305-754-2444; Fax: 305-754-6649.

Genesis Programs, Inc.—Sr. EDITA ROJO, M.D., Dir.; Rev. BRENDAN SHANNON, Chap., *3675 S. Miami Ave., Miami, 33133.* Tel: 305-856-1043; Fax: 305-856-1633.

The Poverello Center, Inc.—Rev. WILLIAM COLLINS, O.F.M., Dir., *2292 Wilton Dr., Wilton Manors, 33305.* Tel: 954-561-3663; Fax: 954-566-7868.

Catholic Charities of the Archdiocese of Miami, Inc.—Most Rev. THOMAS G. WENSKI, Pres. RICHARD TURCOTTE, Ph.D., Exec. Dir., *9401 Biscayne Blvd., Miami Shores, 33138.* Tel: 305-754-2444; Fax: 305-754-6649. Rev. ROBERTO GARZA, Mission Effectiveness; RONALD A. HASSELL, Dir. Admin. ALBERT TRICOMI, A.C.S.W., Dir. Audit & Compliance; ALISON INGRAM, L.M.H.C., L.H.R.M., Assoc. Dir., Audit & Compliance; SONIA SANTANA, Human Resources Mgr. MARTIN TERRIS, Ph.D., Mgr. Grants; RICARDO RIESGO, Financial Accounting Mgr. ROSELYN DESROCHES, Budget Accounting Mgr. IANI MOYA, Information Systems Mgr. CARLOS BUSTABAD, Facilities Mgr. LLOYDINE MCGUINN, Exec. Asst.

Dade-Monroe Area Offices—

Division Office—Deacon THOMAS G. FRANKLIN, Dir., *9401 Biscayne Blvd., Miami Shores, 33138.* Tel: 305-762-1330; Fax: 305-754-6649.

Counseling Programs—GRACIELA PEREZ, L.C.S.W., Admin., *2711 Indian Mound Trail, Coral Gables, 33134.* Tel: 305-758-0024; Fax: 305-757-6287.

Emergency Services/Little Havana Office—ALICIA DEL TORO, M.S.W., Admin., *970 S.W. 1 St., Ste. 302, Miami, 33130.* Tel: 305-324-1104; Fax: 305-324-1083.

Resettlement and Employment Services—ELEANOR B. WILL, Admin., *60 E. 3rd St., Ste. 206, Hialeah, 33010.* Tel: 305-883-4555; Fax: 305-883-4498.

Services for the Elderly—MARY GREEN, Admin., *9900 N.E. 2nd Ave., Miami Shores, 33138.* Tel: 305-751-5203; Fax: 305-758-4972.

Pierre Toussaint Haitian Catholic Center, Human Services Division—EMILE VIARD, Exec. Dir., *110 NE 62 St., Miami, 33138.* Tel: 305-758-2462; Fax: 305-758-8216.

HIV/AIDS Ministry—1050 N.E. 129 St., North Miami, 33161. Tel: 305-899-0446; Fax: 305-899-7984.

Child Welfare Division—ANNE M. BRENNAN, A.C.S.W., Dir.

Foster Care, Maternity and Adoption Services—

Dade—DORA GUZMAN, L.C.S.W., Coord., *11400 S.W. 137 Ave., Miami, 33186.* Tel: 305-387-8322; Fax: 305-387-8344.

Broward—VICKY KAUFMAN, M.A., Dir., *1505 N.E. 26 St., Wilton Manors, 33305.* Tel: 954-630-9404; Fax: 954-566-6026.

Unaccompanied Minors Program—FRANCISCO BRIZUELA, M.Ed., Admin., *11400 S.W. 137 Ave., Miami, 33186.* Tel: 305-380-0141; Fax: 305-380-7756.

Catholic Home for Children—ANNE M. BRENNAN, A.C.S.W., Admin., *9615 Sterling Dr., Miami, 33157.* Tel: 305-238-2381; Fax: 305-232-5421.

Transitional Housing—OLGA GOLIK, Assoc. Div. Dir., *9401 Biscayne Blvd., Miami Shores, 33138.* Tel: 305-754-2444; Fax: 305-754-6649.

Providence Place—Shelter for Women and Children—ANITA GAWOR, Admin., *1299 E. Oakland Park Blvd., Oakland Park, 33305.* Tel: 954-630-9404, Ext. 213; Fax: 954-566-6026.

New Life Family Center—BETTINA GENSOLLEN, M.S.Ed., Admin., *3620 N.W. First Ave., Miami, 33127.* Tel: 305-573-3333; Fax: 305-576-5111.

Angelica House—ANITA GAWOR, Admin., *1077 S.E. 22 Ave., Pompano Beach, 33062.* Tel: 954-568-6610; Fax: 954-568-5075.

St. Luke's Apartments—Tel: 305-795-0077.

Substance Abuse Programs—

St. Luke's Addiction Recovery Programs (St. Luke Center, Inc.)—PATRICIA CARTER, Admin., *7707 N.W. 2 Ave., Miami, 33150.* Tel: 305-795-0077; Fax: 305-795-0030.

Outpatient Substance Abuse Counseling—1505 N.E. 26 St., Wilton Manors, 33305. Tel: 954-630-9404; Fax: 954-566-6026.

Miami DARE Substance Abuse Prevention Prog.—7707 N.W. 2nd Ave., Miami, 33150. Tel: 305-795-0077; Fax: 305-795-0030.

Child Care Division—LUCIA VICENCIO, Dir., *9401 Biscayne Blvd., Miami, 33138.* Tel: 305-754-2444; Fax: 305-754-6649.

Centro Hispano Catolico Child Care Center—FROILAN DOMINGUEZ, Admin., *144 N.W. 26 St., Miami, 33137.* Tel: 305-576-3461; Fax: 305-576-6446.

Centro Mater Child Care Center—LUIS RIVERA, Admin., *418 S.W. 4 Ave., Miami, 33130.* Tel: 305-545-6049; 545-7720; Fax: 305-324-6162.

Centro Mater West Child Care Center—MIRIAM ROMAN, M.S.W., Admin., *8298 N.W. 103 St., Miami, 33016.* Tel: 305-827-1050; Fax: 305-827-1079.

Good Shepherd Child Care Center—ALEIDA BARCENA-CAO, Admin., *18601 S.W. 97 Ave., Miami, 33157.* Tel: 305-235-1756; 235-1330; Fax: 305-255-2788.

Sagrada Familia Child Care Center—GLADYS PALACIOS, Admin., *970 S.W. 1 St., Room 205, Miami, 33130.* Tel: 305-324-5424;326-8212; Fax: 305-325-0642.

Notre Dame Child Care and Neighborhood Center—JOSEPH BATTJOL, Admin., *130 N.E. 62 St., Miami, 33138.* Tel: 305-751-6778; Fax: 305-751-6959.

South Dade Child Care Center—ROSE MARIE ISERNI, Admin., *28520 S.W. 148 Ave., Leisure City, 33033.* Tel: 305-245-0979; Fax: 305-242-8796.

Child Care Food Program—CHARIL FELDMAN, R.D., L.D., Admin., *9401 Biscayne Blvd., Miami Shores, 33138.* Tel: 305-754-2444; Fax: 305-754-6649.

Day Centers for the Elderly—MIRANDA SGOUROS, M.S.W., L.C.S.W., Assoc. Div. Dir.

Miami-Senior Center—MARY GREEN, Admin., *9900 N.E. 2 Ave., Miami Shores, 33138.* Tel: 305-751-5203; Fax: 305-758-4972.

Broward Catholic Adult Day Centers—MIRANDA SGOUROS, M.S.W., L.C.S.W., Dir., *1505 N.E. 26 St., Wilton Manors, 33305.* Tel: 954-630-9404; Fax: 954-566-6026.

Central West Senior Day Center—SUSAN LANDAIS, Coord., *4644 S.W. 64 Ave., Davie, 33314.* Tel: 954-583-6446; Fax: 954-583-6448.

St. Elizabeth Senior Day Center—JOHN CAVOTO, Coord., *801 N.E. 33 St., Pompano Beach, 33064.* Tel: 954-781-0461; Fax: 954-781-0596.

Wilton Manors Senior Day Center—KAY SWICORD, Coord., *1503 N.E. 26 St., Wilton Manors, 33305.* Tel: 954-630-9501; Fax: 954-566-6026.

Parish Social Ministry—

Parish Cluster Programs—

Dade—ELVIRA GONZALEZ, Coord., *9401 Biscayne Blvd., Miami Shores, 33138.* Tel: 305-762-1134; Fax: 305-754-6649.

Monroe—KEITH DOUGLAS, Coord., *c/o San Pedro Church, P.O. Box 456, Tavernier, 33070.* Tel: 305-852-5048; Fax: 305-852-3315.
Broward—MURIEL KROLL, Coord., *1505 N.E. 26 St., Wilton Manors, 33305.* Tel: 954-630-9404; Fax: 954-566-6026.
Archdiocesan Ministry to People with AIDS—Rev. DENNIS RAUSCH, Admin., *1881 N.E. 26 St., Ste. 238, Wilton Manors, 33305.* Tel: 954-565-7595; Fax: 954-537-2135.
Ascending Life—HUGH CLEAR, U.S. Rep., *7116 S.W. 110 Ave., Miami, 33173.* Tel: 305-279-8455; Fax: 305-279-2850.

Foundations and Trusts—
Catholic Health and Rehabilitation Services Foundation—Most Rev. THOMAS G. WENSKI, Exec. Dir., *9401 Biscayne Blvd., Miami, 33138.* Tel: 305-754-2444; Fax: 305-754-6649.
Catholic Family and Children's Services Trust of Broward County—WILLIAM CUTHBERTSON, Chm.; Most Rev. THOMAS G. WENSKI, Sec., *9401 Biscayne Blvd., Miami Shores, 33138.* Tel: 305-754-2444; 954-630-9404; Fax: 305-754-6649; 954-566-6026.
Catholic Child Welfare Trust—JOSEPH W. MYRTETUS, Chm.; Most Rev. THOMAS G. WENSKI, Sec., *9401 Biscayne Blvd., Miami Shores, 33138.* Tel: 305-754-2444; Fax: 305-754-6649.
Catholic Hospice Foundation, Inc.—*14100 Palmetto Frontage Rd., Miami Lakes, 33016.* Tel: 305-822-2380; Fax: 305-827-0221.

Ministry of Catholic Health Services

Catholic Health Services, Inc.—JOSEPH CATANIA, Pres. & CEO; MICHAEL A. CASCIATO, Chief Oper. Officer; BRENDA MCKENZIE, Dir., Health Care Svcs., *4790 N. State Rd. 7, Lauderdale Lakes, 33319.* Tel: 954-484-1515.
Catholic Housing for the Elderly and Handicapped, Inc.
Catholic Housing Management—TERE SPRING, Admin., *11440 N. Kendall Dr., Ste. E-209, Miami, 33176.* Tel: 305-757-2824.
Archbishop Carroll Manor—MARIO YANES, Mgr., *3667 S. Miami Ave., Miami, 33133.* Tel: 305-854-8953.
Archbishop Hurley Hall—LORETTA PALIS, Mgr., *632 N.W. 1st St., Hallandale, 33009.* Tel: 954-454-0855.
Marian Towers—FAUSTO FERNANDEZ, Mgr., *17505 N. Bay Rd., Miami Beach, 33160.* Tel: 305-932-1300.
Archbishop McCarthy Residence—ROSLYN WILLIAMS, Mgr., *13201 N.W. 28 Ave., Opa Locka, 33054.* Tel: 305-688-2700.
Palmer House—NOEMI DIAZ-MONTORO, Mgr., *1225 S.W. 107 Ave., Miami, 33174.* Tel: 305-221-9566.
St. Andrew Towers—CAROL NICHOLS, Mgr., *2700 N.W. 99 Ave., Coral Springs, 33065.* Tel: 954-752-3960.
St. Dominic Gardens—MARIO YANES, Mgr., *5849 N.W. 7th St., Miami, 33126.* Tel: 305-262-0962.
St. Elizabeth Gardens—JOHN CAMERON, Mgr., *801 N.E. 33rd St., Pompano Beach, 33064.* Tel: 954-941-4597.
St. Joseph Towers—DEBRA HAMELRATH, Mgr., *3475 N.W. 30th St., Lauderdale Lakes, 33311.* Tel: 954-485-5150.
St. Mary Towers—LORETA PALIS, Mgr., *7615 N.W. 2nd Ave., Miami, 33150.* Tel: 305-757-3190.
Stella Maris—ANN H. SMITH, Mgr., *8638 Harding Ave., Miami Beach, 33141.* Tel: 305-865-6841.
St. Anne's Gardens—*11800 Quail Roost Dr., Miami, 33177.* Tel: 305-757-2824.
St. Boniface Gardens—*4790 N. State Rd. 7, Lauderdale Lakes, 33319.* Tel: 305-757-2824.
Nursing and Retirement Centers—
BROWARD:
St. Joseph Residence, Inc.—LAVERNE KOONTZ, A.C.L.F., Admin., *3485 N.W. 30 St., Lauderdale Lakes, 33311.* Tel: 954-739-1483.
St. John's Rehabilitation Hospital and Nursing Center, Inc.—DIANE DUBE, Admin., *3075 N.W. 35 Ave., Lauderdale Lakes, 33311.* Tel: 954-739-6233.
Catholic Hospice of Broward, Inc.—*4740 N. State Rd. 7, Bldg. C, Ste. 100, Lauderdale Lakes, 33319.* Tel: 954-484-1515.
Catholic Home Health Medicare Services, Inc.—*4790 N. State Rd. 7, Lauderdale Lakes, 33319.* Tel: 954-484-1515.
Catholic Home Health Services, Inc.—*4790 N. State Rd. 7, Lauderdale Lakes, 33319.* Tel: 954-484-1515.
Catholic Home Health Services of Broward, Inc.—MARNI CARDILLO, Admin., *3075 N.W. 35 Ave., Lauderdale Lakes, 33311.* Tel: 954-486-3660.
DADE:
St. Anne's Nursing Center, St. Anne's Residence, Inc.—TIMOTHY REARDON, Admin., *11855 Quail Roost Dr., Miami, 33177.* Tel: 305-252-4000.
Miami-Dade Nursing Center, Inc.—*c/o 4790 N. State Rd. 7, Lauderdale Lakes, 33319.* Tel: 954-484-1515.
Villa Maria Nursing and Rehabilitation Center, Inc.—JAMES REISS, Admin., *1050 N.E. 125 St., North Miami, 33161.* Tel: 305-891-8850.
Villa Maria Health Care Services, Inc.—CAROL HYLTON, Admin., *1050 N.E. 125 St., N. Miami, 33161.* Tel: 305-899-0400.
Villa Maria Adult Day Care—GWEN DUNCAN, Dir., *20855 N.W. 9 Ct., Box R-2, North Miami, 33169.* Tel: 305-651-0034.
Villa Maria Foundation, Inc.—*1050 N.E. 125 St., N. Miami, 33161.* Tel: 305-891-8850, Ext. 5396.
Special Education—(Developmentally handicapped and mentally retarded) Marian Center Services. MARIA CONSUEGRA, Dir., *15701 N.W. 37 Ave., Opa Locka, 33054.* Tel: 305-625-8354; Fax: 305-625-0744.

Catholic Cemeteries of the Archdiocese of Miami, Inc.—PAUL JOHNSON, Admin. Cemeteries, *11411 N.W. 25th St., Miami, 33172.* Tel: 305-592-0521.
Archdiocesan Cemeteries—*Our Lady of Mercy Cemetery, 11411 N.W. 25th St., Miami, 33172.* Tel: 305-592-0521., *Our Lady Queen of Heaven Cemetery, 1500 S. State Rd. 7, N. Lauderdale, 33068.* Tel: 954-972-1234.
Catholic Elderly Services, Inc. dba Catholic Health Services Foundation—*4790 N. State Rd. 7, Lauderdale Lakes, 33319.* Tel: 954-484-1515.

Ministry of Pastoral Services

Ministry of Pastoral Services—Most Rev. GILBERTO FERNANDEZ, Exec. Dir.
Campus Ministry—PATRICIA STOCKTON, Dir. MARY PASETA, Admin. Asst., *9401 Biscayne Blvd., Miami, 33138.* Tel: 305-762-1096.
Barry University—Sr. ARLENE SCOTT, Dir.; Revs. SCOTT O'BRIEN, O.P., Assoc. Dir. JOHN LYDON, O.P., Assoc. Campus Min.; Sr. MARIE CAROL HURLEY, O.P., Min. Assoc.; Sr. JUDITH SHIELD, O.P., Mission Effectiveness; MICHELLE BROWN, Admin. Asst., *11300 N.E. 2nd Ave., Miami Shores, 33161.* Tel: 305-899-3650.
FIU-North Miami—Chaplains: Revs. FREDERICK ANDREW CHAN-A-SUE; ROBES CHARLES; SILVIA TARAFA, Campus Min., *3000 N.E. 151st St. & Biscayne Blvd., North Miami, 33181.* Tel: 305-919-5247.
FIU-University Park—Revs. FELIPE ESTEVEZ, Dir. VICTOR BABIN, S.S.C., Assoc. Dir.; Sr. SAGRARIO NUNEZ, *St. Agatha Church, 1111 S.W. 107th Ave., Miami, 33174.* Tel: 305-222-1506; 348-3900.
Miami Dade CC-South—Rev. MICHAEL KISH, Chap. CARMEN VILLAFANE, Campus Min., *7270 S.W. 120 St., Miami, 33156.* Tel: 305-238-7562.
Florida Memorial College—PATRICIA STOCKTON, Campus Min., *9401 Biscayne Blvd., Miami, 33138.* Tel: 305-762-1096.
St. Thomas University—Rev. EDWARD BLACKWELL, JR., Ed.D., Dir.; Rev. DANIEL KENT, Asst. Dir.; Rev. ANDREW ANDERSON, J.C.D., Law School Chap. TERRI WEIK, Grad. Asst. Community Devel.; Ms. ANA LUISA REZA, Grad. Asst.; Sr. MARY TINDELL, O.P., Music Coord. ANGELA SIMS, Admin. Asst., *16400 N.W. 32nd Ave., Miami, 33054.* Tel: 305-628-6525.
University of Miami—Rev. BERNARD KIRLIN, Pastor & Head Chap.; Rev. DAMIAN FLANAGAN, Assoc. Chap. VICTOR PIMENTEL, Dir. & Chap. JOHN KELLY, Assoc. Dir. PATRICIA BALESTRA, Assoc. Dir., *St. Augustine Church, 1400 Miller Rd., Coral Gables, 33146.* Tel: 305-661-1648.
Miami Dade CC-North—CARMEN VILLAFANE, Campus Min.
Miami Dade CC-Downtown Wolfson Campus—Rev. THOMAS MADDEN, S.J., Chap. CARMEN VILLAFANE, Campus Min. Faculty Advisors: Dr. ANGIE GONZALEZ; Dr. GERMAN MUNOZ; Dr. PAUL GEORGE, *Gesu Church, 118 N.E. 2 St., Miami, 33132.* Tel: 305-379-1424; 347-3000.
Broward CC-Central and NOVA University—SANDY BOUDEWYNS, Campus Min. MICHAEL FICARA, Assoc. Campus Min., *Pastoral Center, 9401 Biscayne Blvd., Miami, 33138.* Tel: 305-762-1013 (Dade). Tel: 305-525-5157, Ext. 1013 (Broward).
Catholic Daughters of America—Court 634, Regent: CARMELITA DE LOS TRINOS, Vice-Regent: VIOLET PITA, *St. Mary Star of the Sea Church, 1010 Windsor Ln., Key West, 33040.* Tel: 305-294-1018. Local Chaplain: Very Rev. GERALD MCGRATH, V.F.
Evangelization—Vacant, Dir.; Ms. ROSA MARIA MONTENEGRO, Coord., Evangelization for Hispanics, *9401 Biscayne Blvd., Miami, 33138.* Tel: 305-762-1094; 1093; Fax: 305-758-2027.
Family Life Ministry—DAWNE M. FLERI, Dir.; Vacant, Coord., Divorced & Separated; ELAINE M. SYFERT, Coord., Hispanic Ministry; GLADYS Z. GONZALEZ, Coord., Ministry to Engaged & Married Couples, *9401 Biscayne Blvd., Miami, 33138.* Tel: 305-762-1140; Fax: 305-762-1144.

Lay Apostolic Movements and Associations—
Agrupacion Catolica Universitaria (ACU)—Rev. AMANDO LLORENTE, S.J., Spiritual Dir., *720 N.E. 27 St., Miami, 33137.* Tel: 305-573-1418; 576-2748.
Archdiocesan Council of Catholic Women—Very Rev. ANDREW ANDERSON, Moderator, *9401 Biscayne Blvd., Miami Shores, 33138.* Tel: 305-762-1158. MARY WEBBER, Pres. Tel: 305-757-1587. Spiritual Moderators: Rev. GERALD MORRIS, (Monroe District); Rev. JOSEPH HUCK, (North Broward District); Rev. FRANCIS MCCARTHY, (South Broward District); Rev. MICHAEL GREER, (South Dade District); Rev. WILLIAM ELBERT, (North Dade District).
Camino (Spanish)—Deacon JORGE GONZALEZ, Dir., *P.O. Box 524160, Miami, 33152-4160.* Tel: 305-226-4664.
Catholic Charismatic Services—Archdiocese of Miami—Rev. Msgr. WILLIAM MCKEEVER, Archdiocesan Liaison, *3600 SW 32 Blvd., Hollywood, 33023.* Rev. DANIEL DOYLE, S.M., Assoc. Archdiocesan Liaison Charismatic Services: *P.O. Box 816128, Hollywood, 33081.* Tel: 954-961-1856. *Spanish:* Deacon RAFAEL DE LOS REYES, Spiritual Dir. CARLOS HERNANDEZ, Coord. *Centro Carismatico Catolico—500 N.W. 22 Ave., Miami, 33125.* Tel: 305-631-1007; Fax: 305-642-0006.
Christian Family Movement—Rev. JOSEPH CARNEY, Dir., *4020 Curtiss Pkwy., Miami Springs, 33166.* Tel: 305-871-5780. *Spanish:* Rev. ANGEL VILLARONGA, O.F.M., Spiritual Dir., *Casa Cana, 480 E. 8 St., Hialeah, 33010.* Tel: 305-888-4819.
Cofradia Nuestra Senora de la Caridad (Spanish)—Most Rev. AGUSTIN A. ROMAN, V.G., Dir., *3609 S. Miami Ave., Miami, 33133.* Tel: 305-854-2404; Fax: 305-854-8022.
Comunidad de Vida Cristiana (CVX) Regina Mundi—Rev. VICTOR HERNANDEZ, S.J., Ecclesiastical Asst., *Belen Jesuit Prep. School, 500 S.W. 127 Ave., Miami, 33184.* Tel: 305-223-8600.
Cursillo—Rev. DAVID SMITH, Spiritual Dir., *8670 S.W. 27 Ln., Miami, 33155.* Tel: 305-291-6611 (Beeper).; Deacon ROBERT BINDER, Assoc. Dir. *Spanish:* Rev. IGNACIO BLASCO, Dir., *Casa Emaus, 16250 S.W. 112 Ave., Miami, 33157.* Tel: 305-235-7160; 235-4215.
Encuentros Familiares (Spanish)—Rev. FLORENTINO AZCOITIA, S.J., Dir., *Casa Manresa, P.O. Box 651512, Miami, 33265.* Tel: 305-596-0001; Fax: 305-596-9655.
Encuentros Juveniles (Spanish)—Sr. ONDINA CORTES, R.M.I., Dir., *Youth Center, 3333 S. Miami Ave., Miami, 33133.* Tel: 305-856-3404; Fax: 305-854-8888.
Impacto (Spanish)—Deacon JORGE PRIETO, *P.O. Box 440973, Tamiami Station, Miami, 33144.* Tel: 305-571-7111.
Knights of Columbus (English and Spanish)—Rev. Msgr. XAVIER MORRAS, V.F., Archdiocesan Chap., *2711 Indian Mound Trail, Coral Gables, 33134.* Tel: 305-446-9950.
La Nueva Jerusalen - Comunidad de Alianza—WILLIAM F. BROWN, JR., Head Coord., *P.O. Box 65-1702, Miami, 33265-1702.* Tel: 305-385-5491; Fax: 305-382-6359.
Legion of Mary (English Speaking)—Rev. RICHARD SOULLIERE, Dir., *P.O. Box 221937, Hollywood, 33022.* Tel: 954-961-6740. (Spanish Speaking); ADOLFINA VAZQUEZ, Pres. Tel: 305-824-3060.
Marian Movements & Devotions—Rev. RICHARD SOULLIERE, Coord., *P.O. Box 221937, Hollywood, 33022.* Tel: 954-961-6740.

St. Martin de Porres Assoc.—LEONA COOPER, Pres., *Mailing Address: P.O. Box 330102, Miami, 33133.* Tel: 305-324-3128; 443-9466; Fax: 305-324-3222.
Ministry to Cultural Groups (Non-Hispanic Ethnicities)—Most Rev. THOMAS WENSKI, Dir.
African Apostolate—*St. Vincent de Paul Parish, 2000 N.W. 103 St., Miami, 33147.* Tel: 305-691-0771; Fax: 305-691-3352.
Brazilian and Portuguese Apostolate—
O.L. Aparecida Roman Catholic Mission—*1618 Polk St., Hollywood, 33020.* Tel: 954-920-1070; Fax: 954-920-0776. Rev. VILMAR ORSOLIN, C.S., Coord.
Chinese Apostolate—Deacon ALEX LAM, *7270 S.W. 120 St., Miami, 33156.* Tel: 350-238-7562.
Croatian Apostolate—Rev. ANTHONY PETRUSIC, *322 Virginia St., Hollywood, 33019.* Tel: 954-927-2092; Fax: 954-927-0950.
Filipino Apostolate—Ms. ROSA MARIA MONTENEGRO, *Evangelization Office, 9401 Biscayne Blvd., Miami Shores, 33138.* Tel: 305-762-1094, Ext. 1094.
French-Canadians—Rev. LEO DIONNE, O.M.I., Coord., *Holy Redeemer Parish, 1301 N.W. 71 St., Miami, 33147.* Tel: 305-691-1701; Fax: 305-691-7074.
Haitians—Most Rev. THOMAS WENSKI, Apostolate Dir., *Haitian Apostolate, 9401 Biscayne Blvd.,*

Miami, 33138. Tel: 305-762-1323; Fax: 305-762-1344. *Notre Dame d'Haiti Mission,* Rev. Msgr. GERARD DARBOUZE, *110 N.E. 62 St., Miami, 33138.* Tel: 305-751-6289. *St. Joseph Haitian Catholic Mission;* Rev. MARY KIDNEY ST. JEAN, *1210 N.W. 6th Ave., Pompano Beach, 33060.* Tel: 954-941-3095. Divine Mercy Haitian Catholic Mission; Rev. FRANKY JEAN, *1105 N.W. 6th Ave., Ft. Lauderdale, 33311.* Tel: 954-764-8519.

Hispanic—Most Rev. GILBERTO FERNANDEZ, V.G., Dir.

Indians—Rev. JAMES PARAPPALLY, (India), Chap., *St. Gabriel Church, 731 N. Ocean St., Pompano Beach, 33062.* Tel: 954-943-3684; Fax: 954-943-3656.

Jamaican—Mrs. JUNE CHIN, *11534 SW 127 Ct., Miami, 33186.* Tel: 305-387-0442; Fax: 305-382-8466.

Native Americans—Most Rev. THOMAS WENSKI, V.G., Dir.

Korean—Rev. DANIEL YANG, *15125 N.W. 8th St., Pembroke Pines, 33026.* Tel: 954-433-1824. KEVIN KIM, Asst. Tel: 954-355-0909.

Polish - (Our Lady of Czestochowa)—Rev. JAN FIEDUREK, S.Ch., Dir., *2400 N.E. 12 St., Pompano Beach, 33062.* Tel: 954-946-6347; Fax: 954-946-0512.

Vietnamese—Rev. ISIDORE BAKY, Coord., *St. Helen Church, 3033 N.W. 33 Ave., Ft. Lauderdale, 33311.* Tel: 954-714-9860; Fax: 954-739-9632.

Ministry to the Deaf and Disabled—Rev. JAMES VITUCCI, Pastoral Dir. JACK GREEN, Exec. Dir. IAN ROBERTSON, Asst. Exec. Dir.; Sr. CONLETH BRANNAN, C.S.J., Co-Dir. NERY RODRIGUEZ, Pastoral Worker & Interpreter, *Schott Memorial Center, 6591 S.W. 124 Ave., Fort Lauderdale, 33330.* Tel: 954-434-3306; Fax: 954-434-3307.

Apostleship of the Sea—(serving Seafarers); Rev. JOSE M. PAZ, Archdiocesan Dir. & Chap., Port of Miami; Rev. NICANOR SANTA MARIA, S.D.B., Asst. Dir.; Ms. ANGELA GREGORIO, Dir., *Stella Maris Seamen's Center, 1275 S. America Way, Miami, 33132.* Tel: 305-371-6272. Rev. ARMANDO PEREZ, Chap., *Stella Maris Seamen's Center, 2550 Eisenhower Blvd., Amman Bldg. No. 7, Port Everglades, 33316.* Tel: 954-527-0467.

Prison Ministry—SAMUEL DIAZ, Dir. MYRIAM NIEVES, Assoc. Dir., *9401 Biscayne Blvd., Miami, 33138.* Tel: 305-762-1109; 762-1108.

Respect Life Office—Rev. JORDI RIVERO, Dir. JOAN CROWN, Assoc. Dir., *18340 N.W. 12 Ave., Miami, 33169.* Tel: 305-653-2921; Fax: 305-653-1001.

Respect Life Branch Offices-Emergency Pregnancy Services—

—N. Dade Central Office, 18340 N.W. 12 Ave., Miami, 33169. Tel: 305-653-2921.

—North Broward Office, 5115 Coconut Creek Pkwy., Margate, 33063. Tel: 954-977-7769.

—Hialeah Office, 2024 E. 4th Ave., Hialeah, 33011. Tel: 305-883-2229.

—Hollywood Office (S. Broward), 6151 Washington St., Hollywood, 33023. Tel: 954-963-2229.

—Ft. Lauderdale Office, 2907 N. Andrews Ave., Wilton Manors, 33311. Tel: 954-565-8506.

—Sunset Office, 9642 Sunset Dr., Miami, 33173. Tel: 305-273-8507.

Rural Life Ministry—Rev. PEDRO GARCIA, Dir.

Everglades Community Assoc.—Everglades Villas, 19200 S.W. 380th St., Florida City, 33030., South Dade Ctr., 31248 S.W. 134 Ave., Homestead, 33033., Redlands Camp, US 1 & 298 St., Homestead, 33030., Royal Colonial, 14850 S.W. 280 St., Homestead, 33030.

St. Ann Mission—

Naranja and Migrant Ministry—13875 SW 264 St., Naranja, 33032., Mailing Address: P.O. Box 322278, Naranja, 33032. Tel: 305-258-3968; 258-9682; Fax: 305-258-3591.

Youth and Young Adult Ministry—Sr. ONDINA CORTES, R.M.I., Dir., *Pastoral Center, 9401 Biscayne Blvd., Miami Shores, 33138.* Tel: 305-762-1101.

Scouting—Sr. ONDINA CORTES, R.M.I., Dir.; Deacon THOMAS FRANKLIN, Chap., *9401 Biscayne Blvd., Miami, 33138.*

Ministry of Temporalities

Executive Director—Rev. Msgr. JOHN J. VAUGHAN.

Office of Temporalities—Rev. Msgr. JOHN J. VAUGHAN, Archdiocesan Finance Admin.

Management—Rev. Msgr. JOHN J. VAUGHAN, Archdiocesan Finance Admin.

Business Office—JOSEPH CATANIA, Treas.

Data Processing—CARLOS FERNANDEZ.

Building Commission—Most Rev. JOHN C. FAVALORA; ROBERT A. BROWN, Dir.; Rev. Msgr. JOHN J. VAUGHAN; Revs. FREDERICK J. BRICE; GABRIEL O'REILLY; EDMOND WHYTE; Rev. Msgr. XAVIER MORRAS; Rev. EMILIO MARTIN; Very Rev. GUSTAVO MIYARES; JAMES DETRICK.

Archdiocesan Fund-Raising & Assessments Committee—Rev. Msgr. WILLIAM J. HENNESSEY; Rev. Msgr. JOHN J. VAUGHAN; Very Rev. TERENCE HOGAN; Revs. GABRIEL O'REILLY; GUSTAVO MIYARES; FELIPE ESTEVEZ; RONALD PUSAK; EDWARD OLSZEWSKI; ARNALDO LOPEZ; WILLIAM CONROY; JOSEPH CATANIA.

Finance Council—Rev. Msgr. JOHN J. VAUGHAN; Revs. JOSE NICKSE; ANTHONY MULDERRY; Mr. J. PATRICK FITZGERALD; RAUL MASVIDAL; THOMAS PENNEKAMP; FRANK BUTTACAVOLI; MIRIAM LOPEZ; PEDRO GARCIA; JOSEPH CATANIA.

Lay Personnel—ETHEL MARINELLI.

Health and Welfare—Very Rev. TOMAS M. MARIN.

Pension—Most Rev. JOHN C. FAVALORA, Chm.; Rev. Msgr. NOEL FOGARTY, Vice Chm.

Real Estate Board—Rev. Msgr. JOHN J. VAUGHAN, Dir.; Revs. FREDERICK J. BRICE; ANTHONY MULDERRY; Mr. FRANK MCDONOUGH; HENRY BEZOLD.

Society for the Propagation of the Faith—Rev. FREDERICK J. BRICE.

Plant Operations—JOSE M. GARCIA.

Ministry Of Worship And Spiritual Life

Executive Director—Rev. JUAN J. SOSA. Assoc. Directors: MICHAEL DERRICK; ROGELIO ZELADA.

Worship & Spiritual Life Commission—Chms.: Rev. MICHAEL GREER; MYRNA GALLAGHER.

Celebration and Rite Committee—Rev. JUAN J. SOSA, Chm.

Spiritual Life Committee—BARBARA RIETBERG.

Sacred Art & Architecture—Rev. PAUL V. VUTURO.

Liturgical Music—MICHAEL DERRICK.

Committee on Popular Piety—Most Rev. AGUSTIN A. ROMAN, V.G.; Rev. JUAN J. SOSA, Chm.; Mr. ROGELIO ZELADA.

Ministry of Persons

Ministry of Persons—Most Rev. AGUSTIN ROMAN, Exec. Dir.

Vocations—Rev. PEDRO M. CORCES, Dir., *9401 Biscayne Blvd., Miami, 33138.* Tel: 305-762-1137.

Archdiocesan Vocations Review Board—Very Rev. JOHN NOONAN, Rector, St. John Vianney College Seminary, Miami; Rev. GUSTAVO MIYARES; Very Revs. JOSE LUIS HERNANDO, V.F.; THOMAS O'DWYER, V.F.; Revs. JAMES MURPHY; PEDRO CORCES; JAMES VITUCCI; MICHAEL CARRUTHERS; JUAN SOSA; KENNETH SCHWANGER; JEAN PIERRE; Sr. ONDINA CORTES, R.M.I.; Sr. ANN MCDERMOT, O.S.F.; Ms. PAT STOCKTON; Dr. BOB MORGAN.

Office for Religious—Rev. JOHN R. MADIGAN, O.M.I., Dir. MARIA CANO, Sec.

Priestly Life and Ministry—Rev. ARTHUR DENNISON, Dir., *9401 Biscayne Blvd., Miami, 33138.* Tel: 305-762-1139.

Permanent Diaconate—Most Rev. JOHN C. FAVALORA, Dir.; Deacons IAN TAYLOR, Exec. Dir. CARL CARIERI, Dir. Formation.

Lay Ministry—Sr. ANN E. MCDERMOTT, O.S.F., Dir. ADELE GONZALEZ, D.Min., Asst. Dir.; Sr. CLAUDIA STEGER, O.S.F., English Prog. Coord. FRANK VILLARONGA, D.Min. (Cand.), Educator; MARIA CANTON, Hispanic Ministry Outreach. Admin. Assistants: MAYRA ROSSELL; MARIA HORTENSIA SAN PELAYO.

Continuing Education for the Clergy—Rev. ARTHUR DENNISON, Dir., *9401 Biscayne Blvd., Miami, 33138.* Tel: 954-752-3950.

Priests' Sabbaticals—Rev. ARTHUR DENNISON, Chm.

Retired Priests' Committee—Rev. SEAMUS DOYLE, Chm.; Rev. Msgr. JOHN J. VAUGHAN; Rev. Msgr. BRYAN WALSH; Rev. Msgr. VINCENT T. KELLY; Revs. MICHAEL HOYER; MARTIN CASSIDY; PATRICK FITZGERALD, (Legal).

Ministry to Professional Groups—

Catholic Educators' Guild—Rev. Msgr. WILLIAM MCKEEVER, Chap.

Catholic Funeral Directors' Guild—Very Rev. ANDREW ANDERSON, Chap.

Catholic Lawyers' Guild—Very Rev. ANDREW ANDERSON, Chap.

Catholic Physicians' and Dentists' Guild—Very Rev. TOMAS M. MARIN, Chap., DADE; Vacant, Chap., BROWARD.

Catholic Law Enforcement Ministry—Police Chaplains: Rev. PAUL EDWARDS, Coord. (Metro-Dade Police); Rev. Msgr. JOHN J. VAUGHAN, (Miami Beach Police); Rev. MICHAEL KISH, (City of Miami Police); Vacant, (Florida Highway Patrol, Troop K); Vacant, (FBI, Broward Co., City of Coral Springs).

Catholic Fire Service Ministry—Fire Chaplains: Revs. THOMAS ENGBERS, Coord. (City of Miami; Metro Dade); MICHAEL LYNCH, (City of Coral Gables, Margate).

Special Apostolates

Amor En Accion—(Love in Action)—P.O. Box 141523, Coral Gables, 33114. Tel: 305-971-1535. ALICIA MARRILL; TERESITA GONZALEZ.

Archbishop Hurley Scholarship Fund—Rev. Msgr. VINCENT T. KELLY, Vicar, Christian Formation, *9401 Biscayne Blvd., Miami, 33138.* Tel: 305-762-1076.

Catholic Alumni Club of South Florida—Vacant.

Downtown Senior Citizens' Community Center at Gesu Church—Sr. LUCILA RESTREPO, O.P., *118 N.E. 2nd St., Miami, 33132.* Tel: 305-374-6099.

Food for the Poor, Inc.—ROBIN G. MAHFOOD, *550 S.W. 12 Ave., Deerfield Beach, 33442.* Tel: 954-427-2222 (Broward), Ext. 6419.

Holy Childhood Association—Rev. FREDERICK BRICE, Dir.

Pilgrimages—Rev. RICHARD SOULLIERE, Archdiocesan Dir., Natl. Shrine of the Immaculate Conception, Washington, DC.

Priests' Purgatorial Society—Rev. FREDERICK BRICE.

Serra Club—Mrs. PATRICIA GRANESE, Pres., *16178 S.W. 11 St., Pembroke Pines, 33027.* Tel: 954-436-8948. Chaplains—Dade County: Rev. PEDRO CORCES. N. Broward Co.: Rev. Msgr. FRANCIS FAZZALARO.

The St. Vincent De Paul Society of Miami, Inc.—Revs. WILLIAM ELBERT, Dade Co. Chap. FREDERICK BRICE, Broward County Chap.

CLERGY, PARISHES, MISSIONS AND PAROCHIAL SCHOOLS

CITY OF MIAMI
(Dade County)

1—ST. MARY'S CATHEDRAL (1930), Very Rev. Terence Hogan, Rector; Rev. Robes C. Charles, Assoc. Rector. In res., Very Rev. Tomas M. Marin; Revs. Marc Presume; Alvaro Pinzon.

Res., 7525 N.W. 2nd Ave., 33150. Tel: 305-759-4531; 4532; Fax: 305-757-7456.

School—Tel: 305-757-1993; Fax: 305-757-3050. Sr. Jane Stoecker, S.S.J., Prin.

Sisters of St. Joseph of St. Augustine 5; Lay Teachers 15; Students 357.

Catechesis/Religious Programs—Tel: 305-757-6870; Fax: 305-757-6870.

Students 230.

2—CHRIST THE KING (1961), Revs. James Joseph Flavin, O.M.I.; Raymond Crowe, O.M.I. In res., Revs. Paul Frank, O.M.I.; Charles Clements.

Res., 16000 S.W. 112th Ave., 33157. Tel: 305-238-2485; Fax: 305-254-0330.

Catechesis/Religious Programs—Tel: 305-235-0293.

Students 149.

3—CORPUS CHRISTI (1941), Revs. Jose L. Menendez; Roberto Garza; Jose Maria Herreras, S.J.

Res., 3220 N.W. 7th Ave., 33127. Tel: 305-635-1331; Fax: 305-635-2031.

School—Tel: 305-635-8571; Fax: 305-636-4421. Sr. Delores Aviles, S.T.J., Prin.

Sisters 3; Lay Teachers 14; Students 233.

Catechesis/Religious Programs—Sr. Carmen Alvarez, M.R.I. Tel: 305-633-5824.

Students 680.

Missions—Miami, San Francisco y Santa Clara, 402 N.E. 29 St., 33137.; Miami, San Juan Bautista, 3116 N.W. 2nd Ave., 33127.; Miami, Nuestra Senora de Altagracia, 1779 N.W. 28th St., 33142.; Miami, La Milagrosa, 1860 N.W. 18th Ter., 33125.

4—EPIPHANY (1951), Rev. Msgr. Jude O'Doherty; Rev. Jesus Arias.

Res., 8081 S.W. 54 Ct., 33143. Tel: 305-667-4911; Fax: 305-667-8067.

School—Tel: 305-667-5251; Fax: 305-667-6828. Sr. Mary Henrich, I.H.M., Prin.

Sisters Servants of the Immaculate Heart of Mary 4; Lay Teachers 62; Students 1,059.

Catechesis/Religious Programs—Tel: 305-665-0037.

Students 314.

5—GESU (1896), Revs. Thomas J. Madden, S.J.; Sergio Figueredo, S.J.; Fernando Lopez, S.J.; Thomas A. Griffin, S.J.; William Kidwell, S.J.; Salvator J. San Marco, S.J.; Thomas J. Hidding, S.J.

Res., 118 N.E. 2nd St., 33132. Tel: 305-379-1424; Fax: 305-372-9544.

Catechesis/Religious Programs—Students 45.

6—GOOD SHEPHERD (1977), Revs. Michael Greer; Eduardo Jimenez. In res., Rev. Michael Davis.

Res., 6804 S.W. 139th Pl., 33183. Tel: 305-386-1580.

Church—14187 S.W. 72nd St., 33183. Tel: 305-385-4320; Fax: 305-386-2407.

School—(Grades PreK-6). Tel: 305-385-7002; Fax: 305-385-7026. Maria Elena Lopez, Prin.

Lay Teachers 16; Students 170.

Catechesis/Religious Programs—Tel: 305-388-9877; Fax: 305-388-5272. D.R.E.: Maria Changsut, D.R.E.; Sr. Rosa Garcia, O.P.
Students 999.

7—HOLY REDEEMER (1950), Rev. Richard Sudlik, O.M.I.
Church—1301 N.W. 71st St., 33147. Tel: 305-691-1701; Fax: 305-691-7074.
Catechesis/Religious Programs—Students 56.

8—MOTHER OF CHRIST (1983), Revs. Raul Angulo; Joaquin Perez-Pupo (Cuba).
Rectory: 2390 S.W. 139th Pl., 33175. Tel: 305-551-7046 (Office); Fax: 305-551-7047.
Church—14141 S.W. 26th St., 33175. Tel: 305-559-6111; Fax: 305-551-7047.
Catechesis/Religious Programs—Tel: 305-559-0163.
Students 942.

9—MOTHER OF OUR REDEEMER (1988), Rev. Fernando Compaired (Spain).
Res., 18928 N.W. 80th Ct., 33015.
Church—8445 N.W. 186 St., 33015. Tel: 305-829-6141; Fax: 305-829-3059.
Catechesis/Religious Programs—Students 755.

10—NOTRE DAME D'HAITI (1981), Revs. Gerard Darbouze; Lesly Jean (Haiti).
Res., 110 N.E. 62nd St., 33138. Tel: 305-751-6289; Fax: 305-756-6470.
Catechesis/Religious Programs—Tel: 305-758-5560.
Students 400.

11—OUR LADY OF DIVINE PROVIDENCE (1973), Revs. Luis Rivera; Fermin Solana (Cuba).
Church and Mailing Address—10205 W. Flagler St., 33174. Tel: 305-551-8113; 8114; Fax: 305-220-3164.
Res., 10420 S.W. 4th St., 33174. Tel: 305-226-5058.
Catechesis/Religious Programs—Tel: 305-552-7974, Ext. 18.
Students 139.

12—OUR LADY OF THE HOLY ROSARY (1959), Revs. Sean J. Hyland; Adam F.X. Stromski; Luis Perez.
Res., 9500 S.W. 184th St., 33157. Tel: 305-235-5135; Fax: 305-254-9045.
School—Tel: 305-235-5442; Fax: 305-235-5670. Mariano Leone, Prin.
Lay Teachers 30; Students 515.
Catechesis/Religious Programs—Tel: 305-235-5135, Ext. 137.
Students 515.

13—OUR LADY OF LOURDES (1985), Revs. Anthony Massi; Enrique Estrada.
Res., 10452 S.W. 134 Pl., 33186. Tel: 305-380-8474.
Church—11291 S.W. 142 Ave., 33186. Tel: 305-386-4121; Fax: 305-386-6881.
School—Tel: 305-386-8446; Fax: 305-386-6694. Dr. Maria Avellar-Fleming, Prin.; Marilyn Bimonte, Asst. Prin.
Lay Teachers 31; Students 432.
Catechesis/Religious Programs—Tel: 305-386-4894. Mrs. Sandi Pardon, D.R.E.
Students 1,088.

14—PRINCE OF PEACE (1987), Revs. Francisco G. Diaz; Pedro Corces.
Res., 275 N.W. 130 Ave., 33182. Tel: 305-559-3171; Fax: 305-559-3172.
Church—12800 N.W. Sixth St., 33182.
Catechesis/Religious Programs—Students 398.

15—ST. AGATHA (1971), Revs. Felipe Estevez; Victor Babin; Samuel Muodiaju, C.S.Sp.
Res., 1111 S.W. 107th Ave., 33174. Tel: 305-222-1500; Fax: 305-222-1505.
School—Tel: 305-222-1500, Ext. 1040; Fax: 305-222-1517. Dr. Carlota Morales, Ed.D., Prin.; Maria Munoz-Bustamante, Asst. Prin.
Sisters 2; Lay Teachers 32; Students 744.
Catechesis/Religious Programs—Tel: 305-222-1500, Ext. 1030; Fax: 305-222-8078. Mrs. Matilde Menendez, D.R.E.; Mrs. Marie Gonzalez, Asst. D.R.E.
Students 877.

16—ST. BRENDAN (1954), Revs. Jose P. Nickse; Raul Soutuyo; Francisco Calderon; Charles Peterman.
Res., 8725 S.W. 32 St., 33165. Tel: 305-221-0881; Fax: 305-226-6249.
School—Tel: 305-221-2722; Fax: 305-554-6726. Mrs. Emma A. Ventura.
Lay Teachers 34; Students 648.
Catechesis/Religious Programs—Tel: 305-226-2628; 221-2861. D.R.E.: Sr. Bertha Penabad; Esperanza Ginoris; Rosmery Ortega.
Students 754.

17—ST. CATHERINE OF SIENA (1968), Revs. Juan J. Sosa; Rafael Cos (Cuba); Joseph Kottayil.
Res., 9200 S.W. 107 Ave., 33176. Tel: 305-274-6333; Fax: 305-274-6337.
Catechesis/Religious Programs—Tel: 305-270-0830. Lydia Mayorga, D.R.E.
Students 585.

18—ST. DOMINIC (1962), Revs. Jorge Presmanes, O.P.; Restituto Perez, O.P.; Desiderio Eguino, O.P.; Martin Gleeson, O.P. In res., Revs. Mark Wedig, O.P.; Henry B. Groover, O.P.; Scott O'Brien, O.P.; John E. Lydon, O.P.
Res., 5909 N.W. 7th St., 33126. Tel: 305-264-0181; Fax: 305-262-4685.
Catechesis/Religious Programs—Tel: 305-264-3372.
Students 523.

19—ST. FRANCIS XAVIER (1927), Rev. Gordon Orsino, O.M.I.
Mailing Address: P.O. Box 01-1901, 33101-1901.
Res., 1698 N.W. 4th Ave., 33136. Tel: 305-576-2957; Fax: 305-576-3120.
School—Tel: 305-573-8532; Fax: 305-573-0263.
Lay Teachers 14; Students 163.
Catechesis/Religious Programs—Students 63.

20—ST. JAMES (1952), Rev. Jean Pierre. In res., Rev. Patrick Obinabu.
Res., 540 N.W. 132nd St., 33168. Tel: 305-681-7428; Fax: 305-685-0631.
School—Tel: 305-681-3822; Fax: 305-681-6435.
Religious 3; Lay Teachers 12; Students 275.
Catechesis/Religious Programs—Tel: 305-681-2676.
Students 288.

21—ST. JOACHIM (1972), In res., Rev. Ignacio Blasco.
Res., 11711 S.W. 193rd St., 33177. Tel: 305-233-1278; Fax: 305-233-2573.
Church—19150 S.W. 117th Ave., 33177.
Catechesis/Religious Programs—Students 685.

22—ST. JOHN BOSCO (1962), Rev. Msgr. Emilio Vallina; Revs. Jorge I. Perales; Miguel Gil (Puerto Rico). In res., Rev. Msgr. Angel Gaztelu (Cuba); Rev. Msgr. William F. McKeever.
Mailing Address: P.O. Box 993, 33125.
Res., 1301 W. Flagler St., 33135. Tel: 305-649-5464; 5465; Fax: 305-541-0988.
Catechesis/Religious Programs—Tel: 305-649-5466; Fax: 305-649-5466. Angela Esparraguera, D.R.E.
Students 773.

23—ST. JOHN NEUMANN (1982), Revs. David Russell; Albert Lahens.
Res., 12125 S.W. 107th Ave., 33176. Tel: 305-255-6642; Fax: 305-233-3742.
School—Tel: 305-255-7315; 7316; Fax: 305-255-7316. Mrs. Maria M. Fernandez, Prin.
Lay Teachers 16; Aides 5; Students 350.
Catechesis/Religious Programs—Tel: 305-253-3081. Myrna E. Gallagher, D.R.E.
Students 1,450.

24—ST. KEVIN (1963), Revs. Jesus Saldana; Jose Garcia (Cuba); Ernest Biriruka (Burundi) (Ngozi).
Res., 12525 S.W. 42 St., 33175. Tel: 305-223-0633; Fax: 305-554-9950.
School—4001 S.W. 127 Ave., 33175. Tel: 305-223-4015; Fax: 305-220-9048. Mrs. Yolanda Minagorri, Prin.
Lay Teachers 30; Students 669.
Catechesis/Religious Programs—Tel: 305-223-2469. Mrs. Maggie Enjamio, D.R.E.
Students 1,201.

25—ST. KIERAN (1967), Revs. Donald Zarkoski, S.D.B.; John Grinsell, S.D.B.; Albino Simonetti, S.D.B.; Gumersindo Diaz, S.D.B. In res., Revs. Emil Fardelone, S.D.B.; Nicanor Santa Maria, S.D.B.
Res., 3605 S. Miami Ave., 33133. Tel: 305-854-1521; Fax: 305-854-5986.
Catechesis/Religious Programs—Tel: 305-854-8223.
Students 120.
Mission—Miami, La Purisima, 901 S.W. 3rd Ave., #6, 33130.

26—ST. LOUIS (1963), Revs. James F. Fetscher; Michael A. Kish; Wallace A. McGowan; John Peloso.
Res., 7270 S.W. 120 St., 33156. Tel: 305-238-7562; Fax: 305-238-6844.
Catechesis/Religious Programs—Tel: 305-238-7461. Peggy Santella, D.R.E.
Students 1,240.

27—ST. MICHAEL THE ARCHANGEL (1947), Revs. Jose M. Paz; Eduardo Pastor; Ronald Noguera.
Res., 2987 W. Flagler St., 33135. Tel: 305-649-1811; Fax: 305-642-6815.
School—300 N.W. 28 Ave., 33125. Tel: 305-642-6732. Sr. Florinda Bermudez, R.A., Prin.
Sisters 7; Lay Teachers 32; Students 580.
Catechesis/Religious Programs—Tel: 305-643-4661; Fax: 305-642-8574. George Briz, D.R.E.
Students 580.

28—SS. PETER AND PAUL (1938), Revs. Juan M. Lopez; Francisco Hernandez; Jose Berciano (Spain).
Res., 900 S.W. 26th Rd., 33129. Tel: 305-858-2621; Fax: 305-858-8073.
School—Tel: 305-858-3722; Fax: 305-856-4322.
Sisters of St. Joseph of St. Augustine 1; Lay Teachers 35; Students 633.
Catechesis/Religious Programs—Students 378.

29—ST. RAYMOND (1969), Rev. Msgr. Armando Balado; Rev. Sergio Cabrera.
Res., 3475 S.W. 17 St., 33145. Tel: 305-446-2427; Fax: 305-445-0472.
Catechesis/Religious Programs—Tel: 305-446-5108; Fax: 305-445-0472.
Students 191.

30—ST. RICHARD (1969), Revs. Ronald Pusak; Carlos Miyares.
Res., 7500 S.W. 152 St., 33157. Tel: 305-233-8711; Fax: 305-254-2756.
Catechesis/Religious Programs—Tel: 305-233-8755.
Students 712.

31—ST. ROBERT BELLARMINE (1968), Rev. Omar A. Huesca.
Res., 3405 N.W. 27th Ave., 33142. Tel: 305-633-6009; Fax: 305-638-9480.
Catechesis/Religious Programs—Sr. Flor Maria Matamoros, O.P., D.R.E.
Students 338.

32—ST. THOMAS THE APOSTLE (1959), Rev. Daniel I. Kubala.
Res., 7377 S.W. 64 St., 33143. Tel: 305-665-5600; Fax: 305-662-9034.
School—Tel: 305-661-8591; Fax: 305-661-7468. Nuria S. Baldor, Prin.
Lay Teachers 62; Students 700.
Catechesis/Religious Programs—Tel: 305-665-6862.
Students 268.

33—ST. TIMOTHY (1960), Rev. Msgr. Pablo A. Navarro; Revs. Paul Kane; Marcos Somarriba. In res., Rev. Armando Alonso.
Office: 5300 S.W. 102 Ave., 33165. Tel: 305-274-8224; Fax: 305-598-1159.
School—Tel: 305-274-8229; Fax: 305-598-7107. Mrs. Jo-Ann Leskanic, Prin.
Lay Teachers 37; Students 669.
Catechesis/Religious Programs—Tel: 305-274-8225. Sr. Mary Carolyn Meehan, O.P., D.R.E.
Students 852.

34—ST. VINCENT DE PAUL (1962), Rev. Hector Gonzalez-Abreu.
Res., 2000 N.W. 103rd St., 33147. Tel: 305-691-0771, 693-0529; Fax: 305-691-3352.
Catechesis/Religious Programs—Tel: 305-266-6485.
Students 100.

35—VISITATION (1956), Rev. Joseph Angelini.
Res., 19100 N. Miami Ave., 33169. Tel: 305-652-3624; Fax: 305-652-5207.
Catechesis/Religious Programs—100 N.E. 141 St., 33179. Tel: 305-651-7044.
Students 185.

METROPOLITAN DADE COUNTY

Coconut Grove, St. Hugh (1959), Revs. George Garcia; Fernando Heria. In res., Rev. Brendon Shannon.
Res., 3460 Royal Rd., 33133. Tel: 305-444-8363; Fax: 305-444-4312.
School—Tel: 305-448-5602. Sr. Kathleen Donnelly, O.P., Prin.
Sisters 3; Lay Teachers 17; Students 321.
Catechesis/Religious Programs—Students 110.

Coral Gables, Little Flower (1926), Rev. Msgr. Xavier Morras; Rev. Anthony O'Brien. In res., Revs. Sean O'Sullivan; Hernando Villegas.
Office: 2711 Indian Mound Tr., 33134. Tel: 305-446-9950; Fax: 305-446-7624.
Res., 1270 Anastasia Ave., 33134. Tel: 305-529-5475.
School—2701 Indian Mound Tr., 33134. Tel: 305-446-1738; Fax: 305-446-2877.
Sisters 4; Lay Teachers 44; Students 961.
Catechesis/Religious Programs—Tel: 305-446-5540.
Students 502.

St. Augustine (1969), Revs. Bernard Kirlin; Damian Flanagan.
Res., 1400 Miller Rd., 33146. Tel: 305-661-1648; Fax: 305-661-6392.
Catechesis/Religious Programs—Fax: 305-661-6293.
Students 385.

Hialeah

1—IMMACULATE CONCEPTION (1954), Revs. Gustavo J. Miyares; Michael Carruthers.
Res., 4497 W. First Ave., 33012. Tel: 305-822-2011; Fax: 305-821-3481.
School—Tel: 305-822-6461; Fax: 305-822-0289. Mr. Eddy Garcia, Prin.
Lay Teachers 49; Students 1,046.
Catechesis/Religious Programs—Tel: 305-823-9563. Nubia Stanley, D.R.E.
Students 890.

2—San Lazaro (1982), Revs. Pedro Luis Perez; Carlos Perez (Cuba).
Res., 4400 W. 18th Ave., 33012. Tel: 305-556-1717; Fax: 305-556-8918.
Catechesis/Religious Programs—Tel: 305-558-4078. Sr. Gloria Plasencia, D.R.E.
Students 700.

3—St. Benedict (1973), Revs. Jose L. Paniagua (Spain); John M. Paszko; Jose Bardino (Cuba).
Res., 650 W. 80th St., 33014. Tel: 305-556-3278; Fax: 305-558-3705.
Church—701 W. 77th St., 33014. Tel: 305-558-2150.
Catechesis/Religious Programs—Tel: 305-557-2511. Maria de la Fe, D.R.E.
Students 582.

4—St. Cecilia (1971), Rev. Msgr. Emiliano Ordax; Rev. Isidro Perez.
Res., 1040 W. 29th St., P.O. Box 2931, 33012. Tel: 305-885-4614; 4615; Fax: 305-885-2327.
Catechesis/Religious Programs—Tel: 305-885-5504.
Students 280.

5—St. John the Apostle (1945), Revs. Emilio Martin; Anibal Morales. In res., Revs. George Cardona, (Retired); Ignacio Morras, (Retired); Luis Casabon.
Res., 475 E. 4th St., 33010. Tel: 305-888-9769; Fax: 305-888-9341.
School—Tel: 305-888-6819; Fax: 305-887-1256. Ms. Elizabeth Furmanick, Prin.
Lay Teachers 28; Students 557.
Catechesis/Religious Programs—Students 625.

Hialeah Gardens, Santa Barbara (1987), Revs. Miguel Gomez; Rolando Medina.
Mailing Address: 6801 W. 30 Ave., Hialeah, 33018.
Res., 3004 W. 68 Pl., Hialeah, 33018. Tel: 305-556-4442; Fax: 305-827-1110.
Catechesis/Religious Programs—Students 460.

Homestead, Sacred Heart (1929), Revs. James McCreanor; Jose Lopez; Andre Tanguay, O.M.I.
Mailing Address: P.O. Box 901248, 33090-1248.
Church & Res.: 106 S.E. 1st Dr., 33030. Tel: 305-247-4405; Fax: 305-245-3002.
School—300 S.E. 1st Dr., 33030. Tel: 305-245-2678; Fax: 305-247-6317. Mary Preston, Prin.
Lay Teachers 14; Students 216.
Catechesis/Religious Programs—Tel: 305-247-0760.
Students 437.

Key Biscayne, St. Agnes (1954), Revs. Jose L. Hernando; Fernando Isern.
Res., 100 Harbor Dr., 33149. Tel: 305-361-2351; 361-2451; Fax: 305-361-8514.
School—122 Harbor Dr., 33149. Tel: 305-361-3245; Fax: 305-361-6329. Mrs. Sheila Cruse, Prin.
Lay Teachers 26; Students 293.
Catechesis/Religious Programs—Tel: 305-361-1378. Nery Quintela, D.R.E.
Students 405.

Leisure City, St. Martin de Porres Church (1990), Rev. Rolando Garcia.
Church & Mailing: 14881 S.W. 288 St., 33033. Tel: 305-248-5355; Fax: 305-245-3047.
Res., 28514 S.W. 147 Pl., 33033.
Catechesis/Religious Programs—Students 210.

Miami Beach

1—St. Francis de Sales (1964), Revs. Alvaro Guichard; Luis Efrain Mojica (Columbia).
Res., 621 Alton Rd., 33139. Tel: 305-672-0093; Fax: 305-673-8559.
Catechesis/Religious Programs—Students 100.

2—St. Joseph (1942), Revs. Noel I. Bennett; Oscar Sarmiento.
Res., 8670 Byron Ave., 33141. Tel: 305-866-6567; Fax: 305-864-1069.
School—Tel: 305-866-1471; Fax: 305-866-3175. Mrs. Jill Bishop, Prin.
Lay Teachers 20; Students 248.
Catechesis/Religious Programs—Fax: 305-864-1049.
Students 270.

3—St. Mary Magdalen (1955), Rev. Thomas G. Honold.
Res., 17775 N. Bay Rd., 33160. Tel: 305-931-0600; Fax: 305-931-0601.
Catechesis/Religious Programs—Students 46.

4—St. Patrick (1926), Rev. Msgr. John J. Vaughan; Revs. Albert Cutie; George Puthusseril.
Office: 3716 Garden Ave., 33140. Tel: 305-531-1124; Fax: 305-538-3203.
Res., 3700 Meridian Ave., 33140. Tel: 305-531-1124; Fax: 305-538-3203.
School—Tel: 503-534-4616; Fax: 305-538-5463. Bertha Moro, Prin.
Lay Teachers 25; Students 220.
Catechesis/Religious Programs—Students 112.

Miami Lakes, Our Lady of the Lakes (1967), Revs. James Murphy; Juan Carlos Paguaga. In res., Rev. Oscar Brantome.
Res., 15801 N.W. 67 Ave., 33014. Tel: 305-558-2202; Fax: 305-558-2631.
School—6600 Miami Lakeway N., 33014. Tel: 305-362-5315. Shelly Sweeney, Prin.
Lay Teachers 36; Students 605.
Catechesis/Religious Programs—Students 750.
D.R.E.: Mary T. Tate; Diane Leahy.

Miami Shores, St. Martha (1970), Rev. Thomas J. Engbers. In res., Rev. Carl T. Morrison.
Res., 9301 Biscayne Blvd., 33138. Tel: 305-751-0005; Fax: 305-754-6930.
Catechesis/Religious Programs—Tel: 305-751-8759.
Students 115.

St. Rose of Lima (1946), Very Rev. Seamus Doyle, V.F.; Rev. Carlos Vega.
Res., 415 N.E. 105 St., 33138. Tel: 305-758-0539; Fax: 305-751-8398.
School—Tel: 305-751-4257; Fax: 305-751-5034. Sr. Nancy Kindelan, I.H.M., Prin.
Sisters 6; Lay Teachers 39; Students 611.
Catechesis/Religious Programs—Tel: 305-757-6434.
Students 151.

Miami Springs, Blessed Trinity (1952), Revs. Joseph T. Carney; Anthony Mercieca (Malta); Joaquin Rodriguez (Cuba).
Res., 4020 Curtiss Pkwy., 33166. Tel: 305-871-5780; Fax: 305-871-5781.
School—Tel: 305-871-5766. Mr. Pio Tei, Prin.
Lay Teachers 20; Students 282.
Catechesis/Religious Programs—Tel: 305-876-1753.
Students 270.

Naranja, St. Ann Mission (1960), Rev. Pedro Garcia.
Res., 13875 S.W. 264 St., P.O. Box 322278, 33032-1505. Tel: 305-258-3968; 258-9682; Fax: 305-258-3591.
Catechesis/Religious Programs—Tel: 305-248-3735; Fax: 305-247-0755.
Students 700.

North Miami, Holy Family (1950), Revs. Jordi S. Rivero; Ferry Brutus; Andrew Chan-A-Sue.
Res., 14500 N.E. 11 Ave., 33161. Tel: 305-947-5043; 947-1471; Fax: 305-949-5591.
School—Tel: 305-947-6535; Fax: 305-947-1826. Mr. James Stiber, Prin.
Lay Teachers 13; Students 208.
Catechesis/Religious Programs—Tel: 305-947-7739.
Students 342.

North Miami Beach, St. Lawrence (1956), Revs. William Elbert; Sergio Garcia-Miro.
Res., 2200 N.E. 191 St., 33180. Tel: 305-932-3560; Fax: 305-936-8050.
School—Tel: 305-932-4912; Fax: 305-932-7898. Mrs. Dian Lopez Hyatt, Prin.
Lay Teachers 12; Students 220.
Catechesis/Religious Programs—Tel: 305-931-6650.
Students 250.

Opa Locka, Our Lady of Perpetual Help Church (1954), Rev. Oscar Castaneda. In res., Rev. Jorge Noda.
Church & Res.: 13401 N.W. 28 Ave., 33054. Tel: 305-688-9663; 688-9664; 688-1688 (Res.); Fax: 305-685-8031.
Catechesis/Religious Programs—Tel: 305-685-5354.
Students 250.

St. Monica (1959), Revs. Alejandro Roque, O.M.I.; Philip Wagner, O.M.I.
Res., 3490 N.W. 191 St., 33056. Tel: 305-621-9846; Fax: 305-621-5608.
School—Tel: 305-621-2356.
Lay Teachers 21; Students 315.
Catechesis/Religious Programs—Students 152.

St. Philip (1953), Rev. John Madigan, O.M.I.
Res., 15700 N.W. 20 Ave. Rd., 33054. Tel: 305-624-6641; Fax: 305-624-8119.
Catechesis/Religious Programs—Students 71.

OUTSIDE METROPOLITAN DADE COUNTY

Big Pine Key, Monroe Co., St. Peter (1962), Rev. Thomas Mullane.
Res., P.O. Box 430657, 31300 Overseas Hwy., 33043-0657. Tel: 305-872-2537; Fax: 305-872-0122.
Catechesis/Religious Programs—Students 110.
Mission—Sugarloaf Shores, Sugarloaf Firehouse, Sugarloaf Shores, 33042.

Coconut Creek, Broward Co., St. Luke (1985), Rev. Stephen Hilley.
Res., 2370 Hammock Blvd., 33063. Tel: 954-977-0427; Fax: 954-978-1902.
Catechesis/Religious Programs—Tel: 954-974-1863.
Students 185.

Coral Springs, Broward Co., St. Andrew (1969), Revs. Arthur Dennison; Gabriel Vigues; Jeffrey McCormick; Manuel Costa-Soler.
Res., 9950 N.W. 29 St., 33065. Tel: 954-752-3950; Fax: 954-752-3986.
School—Tel: 954-753-1280; Fax: 954-753-1933. Mrs. Sonia Rodriguez, Prin.
Lay Teachers 65; Students 739.
Catechesis/Religious Programs—Tel: 954-752-3988. Deborah Andra, D.R.E.
Students 1,462.

St. Elizabeth Ann Seton (1985), Rev. Edward M. Kelly.
Res., 1401 Coral Ridge Dr., 33071. Tel: 954-753-3330; Fax: 954-753-8442.
Catechesis/Religious Programs—Tel: 954-345-7071.
Students 1,350.

Dania, Broward Co., Church of the Resurrection (1958), Revs. Anthony Tomasulo, O.S.A.; James G. Glennon, O.S.A.
Res., 441 N.E. Second St., 33004. Tel: 954-923-2806; Fax: 954-923-1018.
Catechesis/Religious Programs—Students 29.

Davie, Broward Co., St. David (1974), Revs. Gabriel O'Reilly; Patrick J. Naughton (Scranton).
Res., 3900 S. University Dr., 33328. Tel: 954-475-8046; Fax: 954-370-0819.
School—Tel: 954-472-7086; Fax: 954-452-8243. Mrs. Mariann Kiar, Prin.
Lay Teachers 28; Students 680.
Catechesis/Religious Programs—Tel: 954-475-1521. Pam McMillan, D.R.E.
Students 650.

Deerfield Beach, Broward Co., Our Lady of Mercy (1974), Rev. Michael Sullivan.
Parish Center and Office: 5201 N. Military Trail, Pompano Beach, 33064. Tel: 954-421-3246; Fax: 954-421-1973.
Catechesis/Religious Programs—Tel: 954-426-3197.
Students 45.

St. Ambrose (1962), Revs. John Bryan Dalton; James Connaughton, Pastor Emeritus; Kenneth Whittaker; John L. McCullen (TOL).
Res., 353 S.E. 12 Ave., P.O. Box 999, 33441. Tel: 954-427-2225; Fax: 954-421-1638.
School—Tel: 954-427-2226; Fax: 954-427-4293. Ms. Anita Gentile, Prin.
Lay Teachers 25; Students 405.
Catechesis/Religious Programs—Students 243.

Fort Lauderdale, Broward Co.,

1—Blessed Sacrament, (1961), Rev. John P. McLaughlin.
Res., 1701 E. Oakland Park Blvd., 33334. Tel: 954-564-1010; Fax: 954-566-0301.
Catechesis/Religious Programs—Students 88.

2—Divine Mercy Mission, Rev. Franky Jean, Admin. 1105 N.W. 6th Ave., 33311. Tel: 954-764-8519; Fax: 954-764-8583.

3—Our Lady Queen of Martyrs, (1956), Revs. Michael Hoyer; Armando Perez; Roman J. Schaefer (NU).
Res., 2731 S.W. 11 Ct., 33312. Tel: 954-583-8725; Fax: 954-583-9315.
School—Tel: 954-583-8112; Fax: 954-797-4984. Mrs. Althea Mossop, Prin.
Lay Teachers 25; Students 425.
Catechesis/Religious Programs—Tel: 954-583-3307.
Students 310.

4—St. Anthony, (1921), Revs. Timothy G. Hannon; John C. Baker (Providence, RI).
Res., 901 N.E. 2nd St., 33301. Tel: 954-463-4614; Fax: 954-527-5411.
School—820 N.E. Third St., 33301. Tel: 954-467-7747; Fax: 954-467-9908. Mrs. Elaine L. Patterson, Prin.
Lay Teachers 19; Students 337.
Catechesis/Religious Programs—Tel: 954-467-7749.
Students 225.

5—St. Bonaventure, (1985), Rev. Edmond Prendergast.
Res., 1301 S.W. 136th Ave., Davie, 33325-4300. Tel: 954-424-9504; 9505; Fax: 954-424-9505.
Catechesis/Religious Programs—Tel: 954-476-5204; Fax: 954-476-5203. Mariela Brink, D.R.E.
Students 1,872.

6—St. Clement, (1954), Rev. Msgr. Michael Conway (PAT); Revs. Peter Lambert; Abel Barajas; Henry Mullin, C.S.Sp. In res., Rev. Dennis Rausch.
Res., 2975 N. Andrews Ave., 33311. Tel: 954-563-1183; Fax: 954-564-6628.
School—Tel: 954-563-5608; Fax: 954-563-1355. Ms. Mary Ellen McKinney, Prin.
Lay Teachers 15; Students 240.
Catechesis/Religious Programs—Tel: 954-561-4641. Sr. Colette O'Rourke, D.R.E.
Students 350.

7—St. George, (1964), Rev. Robert F. Tywoniak.
Res., 3640 N.W. 8th St., 33311. Tel: 954-583-5892; Fax: 954-583-0725.
Catechesis/Religious Programs—Students 62.

8—St. Helen, (1968), Rev. Msgr. William Dever; Revs. Joseph Kalariparampil; Isidore Baky; Rev. Dr. William Muniz.
Res., 3033 N.W. 33rd Ave., 33311. Tel: 954-731-7314; Fax: 954-739-9632.
School—Tel: 954-739-7094; Fax: 954-739-0797. Ms. Antonia Ruiberriz, Prin.
Lay Teachers 17; Students 225.
Catechesis/Religious Programs—Tel: 954-484-3036.
Students 220.

9—St. Jerome, (1960), Rev. Paul Edwards. In res., Rev. Francis X. McCarthy, (Retired).
Res., 2533 S.W. 9th Ave., 33315. Tel: 954-525-4133; Fax: 954-525-0964.
School—Tel: 954-524-1990; Fax: 954-524-7439. Sr. Vivian Gomez, R.F., Prin.
Sisters of St. Philip Neri 4; Lay Teachers 19; Students 306.
Catechesis/Religious Programs—2601 S.W. 9th Ave., Ft. Lauderdale, 33315.
Students 65.

10—St. John the Baptist, (1969), Rev. Msgr. Vincent T. Kelly; Revs. James F. Daly, C.S.Sp.; Paul Frank, O.M.I.
Res., 4595 Bayview Dr., 33308. Tel: 954-771-8950; Fax: 954-771-4178.
Catechesis/Religious Programs—Students 189.

11—St. Mark, (1985), Revs. Edmond F. Whyte; Jaime H. Acevedo; Thomas Mannix Stack.
Res., 5601 S. Flamingo Rd., 33330. Tel: 954-434-3777; Fax: 954-434-3125.
School—Shirley Sandusky, Prin. Students 668.
Catechesis/Religious Programs—Tel: 954-252-9899. Susan Mikluscak, D.R.E.
Students 1,362.

12—St. Maurice, (1970), Rev. Roger Holoubek.
Res., 2851 Stirling Rd., 33312. Tel: 954-961-7777; Fax: 954-961-4358. [CEM]
Catechesis/Religious Programs—Tel: 954-961-4358.
Students 236.

13—St. Pius X, (1959), Revs. Patrick C. Slevin; Harry Ringenberger.
Res., 2500 N.E. 33rd Ave., 33305. Tel: 954-564-1763; Fax: 954-568-2212.
Church—2511 N. Ocean Blvd. (A1A), 33308.
Catechesis/Religious Programs—Students 36.

14—St. Sebastian, (1959), Rev. Msgr. Patrick McDonnell; Rev. William F. Mylchreest.
Res., 2518 Barbara Dr., 33316. Tel: 954-524-9344; Fax: 954-524-9347.
Catechesis/Religious Programs—Students 26.

Hallandale, Broward Co., St. Charles Borromeo (1968), Rev. Sean Mulcahy.
Res., 123 N.W. 6 Ave., 33009. Tel: 954-458-1914.
Catechesis/Religious Programs—Students 40.
St. Matthew (1959), Rev. James A. Quinn.
Res., 542 Blue Heron Dr., 33009. Tel: 954-458-1590; Fax: 954-458-0612.

Hollywood, Broward Co.,

1—Little Flower, (1924), Very Rev. Thomas O'Dwyer, V.F.; Revs. Thomas Hanly; Albert Lahens; Patrick O'Shea.
Res., 1805 Pierce St., 33020. Tel: 954-922-3517; Fax: 954-922-6634.
School—Tel: 954-922-1217; Fax: 954-927-8962. Mrs. Janet Gendusa, Prin.
Lay Teachers 17; Students 286.
Catechesis/Religious Programs—Tel: 954-923-7634.
Students 115.

2—Nativity, (1960), Very Rev. Patrick J. Murnane; Revs. Enrique Delgado; Abraham Joseph Pallivathuckal (India).
Res., 5220 Johnson St., 33021. Tel: 954-987-3300; Fax: 954-987-3044.
School—Mrs. Elena Ortiz, Prin.; Ms. Judy Skehan, Vice Prin. Sisters Servants of Immaculate Heart of Mary 1; Lay Teachers 35; Students 820.
Catechesis/Religious Programs—Students 454.

3—Our Lady Aparecida Mission, Rev. Vilmar Orsolin, C.S.
1618 Polk St., 33020. Tel: 954-920-1070; Fax: 954-920-0776.
Catechesis/Religious Programs—Students 140.

4—St. Bernadette, (1959), Rev. Brendan Dalton; Rev. Msgr. Robert J. Yates, (Retired).
Res., 7450 Stirling Rd., 33024. Tel: 954-432-5313; Fax: 954-432-5344.
School—Tel: 954-432-7022; Fax: 954-443-8030. Mrs. Mary Ellen Letvinchuk, Prin.
Lay Teachers 21; Students 367.
Catechesis/Religious Programs—Tel: 954-432-6300.
Students 324.

Key Largo, Monroe Co., St. Justin Martyr (1973), Rev. Edward Olszewski.
Res., 105500 Overseas Hwy., 33037. Tel: 305-451-1316; Fax: 305-451-4633.
School—St. Justin Marine Academy.
Catechesis/Religious Programs—Tel: 305-451-3031.
Students 175.

Key West, Monroe Co., St. Mary, Star of the Sea (1846), Rev. Gerald F. McGrath.
Res., 1010 Windsor Ln., 33040. Tel: 305-294-1018; Fax: 305-292-8096.
School—Tel: 305-294-1031; Fax: 305-294-2095.
Sisters 2; Brothers 1; Deacons 2; Lay Teachers 18; Students 214.
Catechesis/Religious Programs—Tel: 305-295-0306.
Students 214.

Lighthouse Point, Broward Co., St. Paul the Apostle (1968), Rev. Frederick J. Brice.
Res., 2700 N.E. 36th St., 33064. Tel: 954-943-9154; 9155; Fax: 954-943-9155.
Catechesis/Religious Programs—Students 149.

Marathon, Monroe Co., San Pablo (1958), Rev. Gerald R. Morris.
Res., 550 122nd St. Ocean, 33050. Tel: 305-289-0636; Fax: 305-743-8192.
Catechesis/Religious Programs—Students 60.

Margate, Broward Co., St. Vincent (1960), Revs. Neil Doherty; Michael Lynch.
Res., 6350 N.W. 18th St., 33063. Tel: 954-972-0434; Fax: 954-971-9411.
Catechesis/Religious Programs—Tel: 954-972-7708.
Students 155.

Miramar, Broward Co., St. Bartholomew (1962), Revs. Paul Vuturo; Yves Jocelyn (Les Cayes, Haiti); Gary Steibel.
Res., 8005 Miramar Pkwy., 33025. Tel: 954-431-3600; Fax: 954-435-9591.
School—Tel: 954-431-5253; Fax: 954-431-3385. Maria Glass, Prin.
Lay Teachers 19; Students 334.
Catechesis/Religious Programs—Students 550.
St. Stephen (1956), Revs. Stephen Conserva, O.M.I.; James Allen, O.M.I.; Paul M. Ouellette, O.M.I.
Res., 6044 S.W. 19th St., 33023. Tel: 954-987-1100; Fax: 954-966-9881.
School—Tel: 954-983-2636; Fax: 954-986-8557.
Sisters of St. Joseph of St. Augustine 2; Lay Teachers 24; Students 234.
Catechesis/Religious Programs—Tel: 954-962-2112.
Students 650.

North Lauderdale, Broward Co., Our Lady Queen of Heaven (1974), Rev. Joseph Huck.
Res., 6771 Kimberly Blvd., 33068.
Church—1400 South St., Rd. 7, 33068. Tel: 954-971-5400; Fax: 954-972-4008.
Catechesis/Religious Programs—Tel: 954-973-3406.
Students 376.

Parkland, Mary Help of Christians Church (1989), Rev. Thomas Wisniewski.
Church—5980 University Dr., 33067. Tel: 954-340-6462; Fax: 954-340-6838.
Catechesis/Religious Programs—Tel: 954-340-2872.
Students 659.

Pembroke Pines, Broward Co., St. Boniface (1971), Rev. Antonio R. Silio. In res., Rev. Kris Bartos.
Res., 8330 Johnson St., 33024. Tel: 954-432-2750; Fax: 954-432-2756.
Catechesis/Religious Programs—Students 403.
St. Edward (1995), Rev. Msgr. Michael Eivers.
Res., 1101 N.W. 184 Ter., 33029. Tel: 954-436-7944; Fax: 954-436-7506.
Church—19000 Pines Blvd., 33029.
Catechesis/Religious Programs—Tel: 954-430-4107.
Students 541.
St. Maximilian Kolbe (1983), Revs. James Vitucci; Joseph Maroor (India); Luis Garcia.
Res., 11051 N.W. 16th St., 33026. Tel: 954-432-8289.
Church—701 N. Hiatus Rd., 33026. Tel: 954-432-0206; Fax: 954-432-0775.
Catechesis/Religious Programs—Tel: 954-435-3000.
Students 994.

Plantation, Broward Co., St. Gregory (1959), Rev. Msgr. Noel Fogarty, P.A.; Revs. George Duffy; David A. Dueppen.
Res., 200 N. University Dr., 33324. Tel: 954-473-6261; Fax: 954-473-4599.
School—Tel: 954-473-8169; Fax: 954-472-1638. Ms. Barbara Rosini, Prin.; Mrs. Margaret Sternefeld, Asst. Prin.
Sisters 1; Lay Teachers 39; Students 883.
Catechesis/Religious Programs—Tel: 954-473-8321.
Students 330.

Pompano Beach, Broward Co.,

1—Assumption, (1951), Revs. Martin J. Cassidy; John Handrahan, S.J.
Res., 2001 S. Ocean Blvd., 33062. Tel: 954-941-7647; Fax: 954-941-9620.
Catechesis/Religious Programs—Students 72.

2—Our Lady of Czestochowa Mission, (Polish), Rev. Jan Fiedurek, S.Chr.
2400 N.E. 12th St., 33062. Tel: 954-946-6347; Fax: 954-946-0512.
Catechesis/Religious Programs—Students 86.

3—San Isidro, (1970), Revs. Ricardo C. Castellanos; Augustine C. Odilo, C.S.Sp.; William Chacon (Costa Rica).
Res., 2310 Martin Luther King Blvd., 33069-1591. Tel: 954-971-8780; 954-940-8719 (Dade); Fax: 954-972-3607.
Catechesis/Religious Programs—Students 450.

4—St. Coleman, (1959), Revs. Thomas F. Foudy; Pedro Lleo; James E. Quinn, (Retired).
Res., 1200 S. Federal Hwy., 33062. Tel: 954-942-3533; Fax: 954-942-7869.
School—Tel: 954-942-3500; Fax: 954-785-0603.
Lay Teachers 39; Aides 5; Students 633.
Catechesis/Religious Programs—1285 S.E. 22nd Ave., 33062. Tel: 954-782-1461.
Students 375.

5—St. Elizabeth of Hungary Catholic Church, (1959), Rev. Msgr. John W. Glorie; Revs. Julio Solano; Gary Wiesmann.
Res., 3331 N.E. 10 Ter., 33064-5298. Tel: 954-941-8117; Fax: 954-941-0999.
School—901 N.E. 33rd. St., 33064. Tel: 954-942-2161; Fax: 954-942-7551. Mrs. Rita A. O'Leary, Prin.
Sisters 1; Lay Teachers 26; Students 495.
Catechesis/Religious Programs—Tel: 954-943-6801.
Students 214.

6—St. Gabriel, (1967), Rev. Msgr. Francis J. Fazzalaro; Rev. James Parappally.
Res., 731 N. Ocean Blvd., P.O. Box 3044, 33062. Tel: 954-943-3684; Fax: 954-943-3656.

7—St. Henry, (1969), Rev. Msgr. Arthur T. Geoghegan; Rev. Msgr. James B. Reynolds; Rev. Francis Akwue, C.S.Sp.
Res., 1500 S. Andrews Ave., 33069. Tel: 954-785-2450; Fax: 954-785-6958.
Catechesis/Religious Programs—Students 67.

8—St. Joseph Mission, Rev. M. Kidney St. Jean, Admin.
1210 N.W. 6th Ave., 33060. Tel: 954-941-3095; Fax: 954-941-3115.
Catechesis/Religious Programs—Students 98.

Sunrise, Broward Co., All Saints (1982), Rev. Anthony J. Mulderry. In res., Rev. Guy Fenger.
Office: 10900 W. Oakland Park Blvd., 33351. Tel: 954-742-2666; Fax: 954-741-7238.
School—Tel: 954-742-4842. Mrs. Antoinette McNamara, Prin.
Students 240.
Catechesis/Religious Programs—Tel: 954-742-7742.
Students 1,096.
St. Bernard (1971), Very Rev. Michael Hourigan, V.F.
Res., 8279 Sunset Strip, 33322. Tel: 954-741-7800; Fax: 954-742-4558.
Catechesis/Religious Programs—Tel: 954-741-0275.
Students 170.

Tamarac, Broward Co., St. Malachy (1973), Revs. Dominick O'Dwyer; Daniel Cernauskas (Nassau).
Res., 6200 John Horan Terr., 33321. Tel: 954-726-1237; Fax: 954-726-0822.
Catechesis/Religious Programs—Tel: 954-721-5337. Concetta Sobkowski, D.R.E.
Students 200.

Tavernier, Monroe Co., San Pedro (1954), Rev. John D. McGrath.
Res., Overseas Hwy., Plantation Key, P.O. Box 456, 33070. Tel: 305-852-5372; Fax: 305-852-3315.
Catechesis/Religious Programs—Students 144.

West Hollywood, Broward Co., Annunciation (1959), Rev. Michael Quilligan.
Res., 3781 S.W. 39th St., 33023. Tel: 954-989-0606; Fax: 954-989-0660.
School—Tel: 954-989-8287. Sr. Josephine Sherry, R.S.M., Prin.
Sisters 2; Lay Teachers 17; Students 307.
Catechesis/Religious Programs—Students 141.

Special Assignment:
Reverend Fathers—
Clements, Charles, Baptist Hospital & South Miami Hospital, Miami

Doyle, Dan F., S.M., 4921 Lincoln St., Hollywood, FL 33021. Tel: 954-964-1026
Fink, John, Broward General Hospital
Fishwick, Joseph, Baptist Hospital & South Miami Hospital, Miami
O'Neill, Patrick H., Coord. Spec. Projects, Ministry of General Services
Smith, David, Jackson Memorial Hospital

On Duty Outside the Archdiocese:
Reverend Fathers—
O'Hala, Stephen, Boynton Beach (St. Vincent de Paul Seminary) (West Palm Beach)
O'Leary, John, Peru
Rios, Juan Carlos, Boynton Beach (St. Vincent de Paul Regional Seminary)
Scheiding, Philip, Mexico

Military Chaplains:
Reverend Fathers—
Gubbins, John

Higher Studies:
Reverend Fathers—
Cioffi, Alfred, Boston, MA
Powers, Charles J., Ottawa, Ontario, Canada
Quijano, Jose Juan, Rome, Italy

Sabbatical:
Reverend Monsignors—
Delaney, John
Reverend Fathers—
Capdepon, Federico
Sullivan, Michael

Absent on Sick Leave:
Reverend Fathers—
Brantome, Oscar
Montoya, Juan
Puerta, Jorge
Reiser, John

Absent on Leave:
Reverend Fathers—
Christman, Robert
Cinesi, Joseph
Fernandez, Fausto
Grogan, Brendan
Hayes, Joseph
Keener, Michael
Kiddy, Curtis
Kudlo, Frank
Piano, Timothy
Reyes, Jose L.
Sanchez, Juan Luis
Velie, Richard

Retired:
Most Rev.—
McCarthy, Edward A.
Reverend Monsignors—
McKeever, William F.
Walsh, Bryan O.
Reverend Fathers—
Boned, Enrique
Brohammer, Ronald
Cahill, Frank
Carbajales, Ignacio
Cardona, George
Carrilllo, Sergio
Connaughton, James
Conway, Laurence
Coucelo, Andres
Dunleavy, Francis J.
Escala, Rafael
Fernandez, Miguel A.
Fernandez, Nelson
Gunther, William
Hampton, James
Hanly, Thomas
Hudak, Cyril
Ireland, Donald
Lucking, Aloysius
Lyons, Francis
Lyons, Lawrence
McCarthy, Francis X.
Melley, James J.
Mitchell, Walter
Molano, Ernesto
Morras, Ignacio
O'Sullivan, Sean
Pedroso, Rafael
Planas, Salvador
Puisis, Leonard
Quinlan, Eugene
Quinn, James E.
Rivas, Romeo
Scherer, Richard
Shannon, Brendan
Soulliere, Richard
Valoret, Joseph
Vann, John C.
Villegas, Hernando

Permanent Deacons:
Abdallah, Mitchell C.
Aguayo, Orlando
Aguilu, Thomas
Alfonso, Manuel
Alonso, Jose P.
Asselin, Allen
Avery, John, On Duty Outside the Archdiocese.
Baez, Rodolfo
Batty, Peter
Bautista, Andres
Bechily, Antonio
Benavides, Luis, (PT)
Bestard, Fernando
Binder, Robert
Blaha, Daniel C.
Blanco, Eduardo
Bloom, David
Bouker, Richard
Brancheau, Paul
Brizuela, Humberto
Buigas, Manuel
Calvo, Pedro P.
Camacho, Vidal, (NY)
Canovaca, Manuel
Carieri, Carl
Carrion, Jose
Carroll, Dr. Norman
Chavez, Diego
Chinelly, John, Sr.
Colastin, Max
Coniglio, Philip, On Duty Outside the Archdiocese
Costea, Nicholas
Crawford, Jr. Frederick, On Duty Outside the Archdiocese
Cresswell, William H.
Cronin, Donald
Cuesta, Angel L.
Currier, Roger
Dauson, Thomas
DeGuzman, Abelardo
DeLuca, Arnold J.
DeNunzio, Arthur
Diehl, William, On Duty Outside the Archdiocese
Dinsmore, Robert B.
Donates, Rafael (CHI)
Draughon, Woodworth R.
Dugan, Richard
Eberling, Vincent, Jr.
Estrada, Francisco
Fallon, Martin
Farinato, Vincent
Fathauer, Ronald, On Duty Outside the Archdiocese
Fernandez, Pablo A.
Fiore, Charles, On Duty Outside the Archdiocese
Franklin, Thomas
Friel, John
Fuentes, Rafael
Galard, John, On Duty Outside the Archdiocese
Galvez, Rene
Gazitua, Ralph
Gervasi, Angelo
Gibson, George
Gonzalez, Blas
Gonzalez, Henri
Gonzalez, Jorge G.
Gonzalez, Luis
Gonzalez, Miguel
Gouthro, Ronald
Green, John F.
Hanlon, Thomas F.
Harris, Willie
Hubbell, Carl, On Duty Outside the Archdiocese
Irizarri, Jose
Jordan, Dennis E.
Karrenberg, William H.
Knox, Terrence, On Duty Outside the Archdiocese
Kroll, John
Lam, Alex S.
Lang, Irving
Lannon, Billy, Jr.
Leon, Michael
Livingstone, Donald
Llaneza, Oscar, (NEW)
Llorens, Julke
Lopez, Mario
Lopez, Pedro
Lopez, Victor
Lorenzo, John
Loyola, Benito
Maceo, Antonio J.
Martinez, Jose
McClain, Kirby
McInerney, Vincent
Mickwee, George, On Duty Outside the Archdiocese
Mieyal, Denis
Mindel, Albert
Moreno, Vicente, On Duty Outside of the Archdiocese
Moretti, Daniel
Morillo, Felix
Munter, Paul H.
Murphy, Charles
Murray, Paul, On Duty Outside the Archdiocese
Musselman, Randall O.
Nerys, Jose A., (SJN)
O'Malley, Robert F., Jr.
Ochoa, Roberto
Onelien, Montas
Ortega, Ray
Padron, Rodolfo
Panellas, Eduardo
Parlade, Miguel
Pearce, Joseph M.
Peremenis, John
Perez, Manuel
Perron, Charles
Phang Sang, Louis
Pintado, Angel
Pita, Bernardo
Plummer, Joseph
Plummer, Michael
Polcari, Joseph A., On Duty Outside the Archdiocese
Prieto, Jorge
Raymond, Donald, On Duty Outside the Archdiocese
Renuart, Albert, On Duty Outside the Archdiocese
Reyes, Rafael de los
Rodriguez, Ernesto
Rodriguez, Jorge, On Duty Outside the Archdiocese
Rodriguez, Santos
Romero, Alberto
Ruiz, Angel
Ruiz-Castaneda, Norman
Saavedra, Manuel
Scherrer, Thomas
Shaw, Roger M.
Sierra, Feliciano
Sierra, Luis
Smith, David
Solorzano, Jose
Sommovigo, Joseph
Soucy, Joseph O.
Starzinski, Louis
Sutcavage, George P.
Taylor, Ian
Taylor, Timm
Teolis, Matthew (CHI)
Thesing, John
Tola, Vincent
Tomonto, James R.
Tosco, Jesus
Ulloa, Lazaro
Velez, Gregorio, On Duty Outside the Archdiocese
Venezia, Richard (PMB)
Vitale, Perry
Waldman, Gerald
Watkins, William A.
Yglesias, Robert
Zayas, Julio
Zayas, Luis, On Duty Outside the Archdiocese

INSTITUTIONS LOCATED IN THE ARCHDIOCESE

[A] SEMINARIES, ARCHDIOCESAN

MIAMI. *St. John Vianney College Seminary*, 2900 S.W. 87th Ave., 33165. Tel: 305-223-4561; 4562; Fax: 305-223-0650.
E-mail: sjvc@gate.net
Very Rev. John Noonan, Rector; Bro. Edward Van Merrienboer, O.P., Academic Dean; Maria Rodriguez, Librarian; Revs. Oscar Mendez, S.J., Spiritual Dir.; Rolando Castillo, Vice Rector, Dean of Students & Dir. Pre-Theology Programs; Robert Vallee. In res. Rev. Liam Quinn. Priests 4; Brothers 1; Lay Teachers 5; Total Staff 20; Students 66.

[B] COLLEGES AND UNIVERSITIES

MIAMI. *Barry University*, 11300 N.E. 2nd Ave., 33161. Tel: 305-899-3000; Fax: 305-899-3018.
E-mail: jolaughlin@mail.barry.edu
Web site: www.barry.edu
For a complete listing, refer to the Colleges and Universities section.

OPA LOCKA. *St. Thomas University*, 16400 N.W. 32nd Ave., 33054. Tel: 305-625-6000; Fax: 305-628-6511.
Web site: www.stu.edu
For a complete listing, refer to the Colleges and Universities section.

[C] HIGH SCHOOLS, ARCHDIOCESAN

MIAMI. *Archbishop Coleman Carroll High School*, 10300 S.W. 167 Ave., 33196. Tel: 305-388-6700; Fax: 305-388-4371.
E-mail: carrollhigh@juno.com
Rev. Msgr. Pablo A. Navarro, Supervising Prin.; Rev. Michael Davis, Asst. Supervising Prin.; Richard Fenchak, Prin..Lay Teachers 23; Total Staff 36; Students 473.

Archbishop Curley-Notre Dame High School, 4949 N.E. 2nd Ave., 33137-3199. Tel: 305-751-8367; Fax: 305-751-3517.
E-mail: ACAVET@curley.pvt.k12.fl.us
Web site: http://www.curley.pvt.k12.fl.us
Bro. Anthony K. Cavet, C.F.C., Prin.; Ms. Beatriz Rodriguez, Asst. Prin.; Rev. Christopher Marino, Chap..Priests 1; Brothers 4; Lay Teachers 27; Students 472.

La Salle High School, 3601 S. Miami Ave., 33133. Tel: 305-854-2334; Fax: 305-858-5971.
E-mail: lashsmd@mailcity.com
Web site: www.lasallehighschool.com
Sr. Shermane Delgado, F.M.A., Prin.; Mr. Eric Shane, Asst. Prin. for Student Affairs; Ms. Luisa Torres, Asst. Prin. for Curriculum; Sr. Maryann Schaefer, F.M.A., Fin. Admin.; Mr. Christopher Crotty, Athletic Dir..Priests 1; Brothers 1; Sisters 4; Lay Teachers 44; Students 630.

Msgr. Edward Pace High School, 15600 Spartan Blvd., N.W. 32 Ave., 33054. Tel: 305-624-8534; Fax: 305-521-0185.
E-mail: pace@msgr-pace.com
Web site: www.msgr-pace.com
Bro. Anthony M. Iazzetti, F.M.S., Prin.; Revs. Gustavo J. Miyares, Supervising Prin.; Cyril J. Smith, O.S.A., Academic Dean; Mr. Les Brown, Asst. Prin. for Academics; Mrs. Ana Garcia, Asst. Prin. Curriculum Instruction; Bro. Ken Ward, Dean of Students (Grades 11-12); Mr. Samuel Lilly, Dean of Students (Grades 9-10)..Priests 2; Brothers 4; Lay Teachers 55; Students 1,150.

Our Lady of Lourdes Academy, 5525 S.W. 84th St., 33143. Tel: 305-667-1623; Fax: 305-663-3121.
E-mail: principal@olla.org
Web site: www.olla.org
Sr. Susan Marie Kuk, I.H.M., Prin..Servants of the Immaculate Heart of Mary 4; Lay Teachers 52; Students 842.

St. Brendan High School, 2950 S.W. 87 Ave., 33165. Tel: 305-223-5181; Fax: 305-220-7434.
E-mail: sabres@worldnet.att.net
Web site: stbs.org
Rev. Jose P. Nickse, Supervising Prin.; Bro. Felix A. Elardo, F.M.S., Prin.; Dr. Carmen Castello, Asst. Prin.; Ms. Barbara Behnke, Dean of Students; Ms. Gloria Ramos, Dean Curriculum..Priests 1; Brothers 3; Lay Teachers 66; Counselors 5; Students 1,207.

FORT LAUDERDALE. *Archbishop Edward A. McCarthy High School*, 5451 S. Flamingo Rd., 33330. Tel: 954-434-2280; Fax: 954-680-4835.
E-mail: mccarthyhigh@juno.com
Rev. Edmond F. Whyte, Supervising Prin.; Dr. Richard Perhla, Prin..Priests 2; Lay Teachers 36; Students 731.

Cardinal Gibbons High School, 2900 N.E. 47th St., 33308. Tel: 954-491-2900; Fax: 954-772-1025.
E-mail: cg-admin@ix.netcom.com
Web site: http://www.info-access.com/cardinalgibbons/
Very Rev. Joseph J. Kershner, Sch.P., Prin.; Sr. Marie Schramko, O.S.F., Asst. Prin.; Mr. Paul D. Ott, Asst. Prin.; Revs. Francis Pala, Sch.P., Asst. Prin.; Oscar Alonso, Sch.P.; Charles Newburn, Sch.P.; John Callan; Bro. Grant R. Ferris, O.S.F.S..Priests 5; Brothers 1; Sisters of St. Francis 2; Lay Teachers 59; Students 1,123.

St. Thomas Aquinas High School, 2801 S.W. 12 St., 33312. Tel: 954-581-2127; 581-0700.
E-mail: stahs@safari.net
Web site: http://www.safari.net/~stahs
Rev. Vincent T. Kelly, Supervising Prin.; Mr. William M. Heller, Prin.; Mrs. Tina Jones-Atkins, Asst. Prin.; Rev. Michael Grady, Asst. Prin.; Sr. Peggy Manning, O.P., Campus Min.; Mr. Paul Gomulinski, Dean of Students; Rev. Guy Fenger (OG-)..Priests 1; Sisters 1; Lay Teachers 95; Students 1,948.

[D] HIGH SCHOOLS, PRIVATE

MIAMI. *Belen Jesuit Preparatory School*, 500 S.W. 127 Ave., 33184. Tel: 305-223-8600; Fax: 305-227-2565.
E-mail: webmaster@belenjesuit.org
Web site: www.belenjesuit.org
Revs. Marcelino Garcia, S.J., Pres, Prin., Contact; Jorge Sardina, S.J.; Jose R. Tey, S.J.; Juan Manuel Dorta, S.J.; Eduardo Alvarez, S.J.; Jorge Munguia, S.J.; Francisco Perez-Lerena, S.J.; Victor M. Hernandez, S.J., Supr.; Fulgencio Mayorga, S.J.; Guillermo Garcia-Tunon, S.J.; Bros. Pedro Estevez, S.J.; Frank Permuy, S.J. Our Lady of Belen Jesuit Foundation, Inc. Priests 10; Brothers 2; Sisters 1; Lay Teachers 67; Students 1,030.

Carrollton School of the Sacred Heart, 3747 Main Hwy., 33133. Tel: 305-446-5673; Fax: 305-446-4160.
E-mail: scooke@carrolton.org
Web site: www.carrolton.org
Sr. Suzanne Cooke, R.S.C.J., Headmistress..Religious of the Sacred Heart 5; Lay Teachers 72; Students 654.

Christopher Columbus High School, 3000 S.W. 87 Ave., 33165. Tel: 305-223-5650; Fax: 305-559-4306.
E-mail: mia_cchs@msn.com
Web site: www.columbushs.com
Campus Ministers: Bros. Angelo Palmieri, F.M.S., Prin.; Edmund Sheehan, F.M.S., Asst. Prin. (Scheduling); Michael Brady, F.M.S., Svc. Coord.; Mrs. Patricia Call, Asst. Prin. (Grades & Academic Credit); Mr. Christopher McKeon, Asst. Prin. (Discipline). Marist Brothers 14; Lay Teachers 65; Students 1,390.

HOLLYWOOD. *Chaminade-Madonna College Preparatory*, 500 Chaminade Dr., 33021-5800. Tel: 954-989-5150; Fax: 954-983-4663.
E-mail: info@cmlions.com
Web site: www.chaminade-madonna.org
Bro. John Campbell, S.M., Pres.; Patrick W. Snay, Prin..Marianist Priest 1; Marianist Brothers 5; Lay Teachers 61; Students 887.

[E] ELEMENTARY SCHOOLS, PRIVATE

KEY WEST. *Mary Immaculate Star of the Sea*, 700 Truman Ave., 33040. Tel: 305-294-1031; Fax: 305-294-2095.
E-mail: seastar@key4ez.com
Brothers 1; Sisters 2; Deacons 1; Lay Teachers 18; Students 214.

[F] SHELTERS

MIAMI. *Camillus House, Inc.*, P.O. Box 11829, 33101-1829.
Web site: camillus.org
For a complete listing, refer to the Special Care Facilities section.

Gift of Hope, Missionaries of Charity, 724 N.W. 17 St., 33136. Tel: 305-326-0032
For a complete listing, refer to the Special Care Facilities section.

[G] GENERAL HOSPITALS

MIAMI. *Mercy Hospital*, 3663 S. Miami Ave., 33133. Tel: 305-854-4400; Fax: 305-285-2114.
E-mail: sisterliz@mercymiami.org
Web site: www.mercymiami.com
For a complete listing, refer to the Hospitals section.

FORT LAUDERDALE. *Holy Cross Hospital*, 4725 N. Federal Hwy., 33308. Tel: 954-771-8000; Fax: 954-351-5947.
E-mail: john.johnson@holy-cross.com
Web site: holy-cross.com
For a complete listing, refer to the Hospitals section.

[H] MONASTERIES AND RESIDENCES OF PRIESTS AND BROTHERS

MIAMI. *Casa San Lorenzo*, 16400 N.W. 32 Ave., 33054. Tel: 305-624-0775; Fax: 305-625-4529. Augustinian Fathers. Revs. Cyril J. Smith, O.S.A.; James L. MacDougall, O.S.A., Prior, Contact; Raymond E. Geisser, O.S.A.; John J. Kelly, O.S.A.; Thomas R. Cook, O.S.A.; Edward Doherty, O.S.A. Total in Residence 6.

Dominican Fathers of Miami, Inc., 5909 N.W. 7th St., 33126-3199. Tel: 305-264-0181, Ext. 24; Fax: 305-262-4685.
Web site: www.opsouth.org
Revs. Restituto Perez, O.P.; Desiderio Eguino, O.P.; Mark Wedig, O.P.; Henry B. Groover, O.P.; John E. Lydon, O.P.; Scott O'Brien, O.P.; Jorge Presmanes, O.P.; Martin Gleason, O.P., Southern Dominican Provice Vocations Office, P.O. Box 431283, 33423. Tel: 305-264-0181, Ext. 24. House of Religious Men 1; Total in Residence 8.

Franciscan Fathers' Residence, 2044 S.W. 22nd Ter., 33145. Tel: 305-856-5257. Revs. Jose Biain, O.F.M.; Angel Villaronga, O.F.M.

Marist Brothers Residences, 8230 S.W. 136th St., 33156. Tel: 305-251-6484; Fax: 305-378-2081. Bros. Charles Filiatraut, F.M.S., Contact; Damian Galligan, F.M.S.; Lawrence Poirier, F.M.S.; Peter Arel, F.M.S.; Fabian Mayor, F.M.S.; Simeon Ouellet, F.M.S.; Robert Ryan, F.M.S., 2790 S.W. 89 Ave., 33165. Tel: 305-223-5570. Bros. Bernard Nolan, F.M.S.; Michael Brady, F.M.S.; Cornelius Russell, F.M.S.

Villa Arrieta. Belen Jesuit Fathers, Inc. 2928 S.W. 10 St., 33135. Tel: 305-541-6221; Fax: 305-541-1278.
E-mail: omarti4334@aol.com
Revs. Pedro A. Suarez, S.J., (Superior) Contact; Juan Manuel Dorta, S.J.; Gerardo Freire, S.J.; Tomas Macho, S.J.; Otto Martinez, S.J.; Jorge Munguia, S.J.

Belen Jesuit Alumni Association, 6262 Bird Rd., 33155. Tel: 305-661-6180; Fax: 305-661-9639. Rev. Juan Manuel Dorta, S.J., Moderator.

Villa Javier. Belen Jesuit Fathers, Inc. 13339 S.W. 9 Ter., 33184. Tel: 305-559-9066; Fax: 305-222-1256.
E-mail: villajavier@att.net & belensj@aol.com
Revs. Eduardo Alvarez, S.J.; Guillermo Arias, S.J.; Florentino Azcoitia, S.J.; Marcelino Garcia, S.J.; Guillermo Garcia-Tunon, S.J.; Victor M. Hernandez, S.J., Supr., Contact; Francisco Lemus, S.J.; Fulgencio Mayorga, S.J.; Francisco Perez-Lerena, S.J.; Jose R. Tey, S.J.; Jorge Sardina, S.J.; Bro. Pedro Estevez, S.J.; Emilio Nunez, S.J., Seminarian; Francisco J. Permuy, S.J., Seminarian.

BAL HARBOUR. *Dominican Friars Residence*, The Plaza, No. 201, 10185 Collins Ave., 33154-1606. Tel: 305-864-6593; Fax: 305-899-3385.
E-mail: dmadden@mail.barry.edu
Web site: www.barry.edu/artsci/theology/madden/danspg96.htm
Rev. Daniel P. Madden, O.P.

[I] CONVENTS AND RESIDENCES FOR SISTERS

MIAMI. *Congregation of the French-Cuban Dominican Sisters of Holy Rosary, Inc.*, 8900 S.W. 19 St., 33165. Tel: 305-554-1710.
E-mail: maria56k@excite.com
Sr. Olga Martinez, Contact; Sr. Mary Cecilia Alonso, Pres. & Treas. Houses of Religious Women 1; Total in Residence 5.

Daughters of Charity of St. Vincent de Paul. (Santurce, P.R.), Mision San Vicente de Paul. 500 N.W. 63rd Ave., 33126. Tel: 305-266-6485; Fax: 305-265-9671.
E-mail: caridad@gate.net
Web site: www.gate.net/~caridad
Ermita Nacionalde Nuestra Senora de la Caridad, 3609 S. Miami Ave., P.O. Box 330555, 33133. Tel: 305-854-2404; Fax: 305-854-8022.
Asociacion Hijas de la Caridad de San Vicente de Paul del Estado de la Florida, Inc. Sr. Eva Perez-Puelles, Contact.

Daughters of St. Paul Convent, 11117 S.W. 2nd St., 33174. Tel: 305-554-0175; Fax: 305-220-1639.
E-mail: miami@pauline.org
Web site: www.pauline.org
Sr. Irene Mary Martineau, F.S.P., Supr., Contact. Houses of Religious Women 1; Total in Residence 6.

Guadalupan Missionaries of the Holy Spirit, 2483 S.W. 4 St., 33135-2907. Tel: 305-642-9544; Fax: 305-649-2422.
E-mail: mgspsus@aol.com
U.S. Delegation Headquarters. In Residence 8. Other Addresses: 869 S.W. Third St., Florida City, 33034-4605. Tel: 305-248-3735; Fax: 305-247-0755. In Residence 3. Legal Title: *Missionary Guadalupanas of the Holy Spirit, Inc.* Sr. Regina Vieyra, M.G.Sp.S. House of Religious Women 2; Total in Residence 12.

Handmaids of the Sacred Heart of Jesus A.C.J. St. Rafaela's Faith Community, 1615 N.E. 108 St., 33161. Tel: 305-891-9161; Fax: 305-891-8791.
E-mail: acjmiami@dc.seflin.org
Web site: www.acjusa.org
Sisters 4.

Missionaries of Charity, 727 N.W. 17th St., 33136. Tel: 305-545-5699. Sr. M. Veronica, M.C., Supr. (Contact). Houses of Religious Women 1; Total in Residence 6; Total Assisted 2,612.

MIAMI SHORES. *Franciscan Sisters of Allegany*. 138 N.E. 111 St., 33161. Tel: 305-751-3093. Total in Residence 4. St. Francis Convent, 99 N.W. 115 St., Miami, 33168. Tel: 305-751-1544. Total in Residence 3.
St. Francis Medical and Health Care Services, Inc.
St. Francis Hospital, Inc. (dba Franciscan Sisters of Allegany Ministries).
St. Francis Medical and Health Care Foundation, Inc.

[J] RETREAT HOUSES

MIAMI. *Dominican Retreat House, Mary Queen of Apostles*, 7275 S.W. 124 St., 33156. Tel: 305-238-2711; Fax: 305-238-2717. Dominican Sisters of St. Catherine de Ricci (Motherhouse-Elkins Park, PA). Sr. June Fitzgerald, O.P., Contact. Sisters 5; Capacity for Overnight Retreat Programs 60; Retreat Center 1; Total in Residence 4; Staff 11.

John Paul II Retreat House, 720 N.E. 27th St., 33137-4697. Tel: 305-576-2748; 573-1418; Fax: 305-576-2748.
E-mail: webmaster@acu-adsum.org
Web site: http://www.acu-adsum.org
Rev. Amando Llorente, S.J., Spiritual Dir., Contact. Total in Residence 2; Total Staff 8.
Agrupacion Catolica Universitaria, Inc.
Jesuit Fathers of the Province of the Antilles, Inc.

[K] CENTERS

MIAMI. *Family Life Ministry*. 9401 Biscayne Blvd., Miami Shores, 33138. Tel: 305-762-1140; Fax: 305-762-1144. Mrs. Dawn M. Fleri.

National Shrine of Our Lady of Charity, 3609 S. Miami Ave., P.O. Box 330555, 33133. Tel: 305-854-2404; Fax: 305-854-8022. Most Rev. Agustin Roman, V.G., Rector. Associate Rectors: Rev. Francisco Santana. In res. Rev. Romeo Rivas, (Retired). Sisters 2; Houses of Religious Women 1; Total in Residence 4.

Pauline Book & Media Center, 145 S.W. 107th Ave., 33174. Tel: 305-559-6715; 6716; Fax: 305-559-6717.
E-mail: miami@pauline.org
Web site: ww.pauline.org
Sr. Irene Mary Martineau, F.S.P., Supr. Daughters of St. Paul 6; Houses of Religious Women 1; Total in Residence 6; Pauline Book & Media Center 1; Staff 12.

Respect Life Office, 18340 N.W. 12 Ave., 33169. Tel: 305-653-2921; Fax: 305-653-1001.
E-mail: ilovlife@bellsouth.net
Rev. Jordi S. Rivero, Dir.; Ms. Joan Crown, Contact. Special Centers for Social Services 6; Total Assisted 7,261; Staff 7.

Southeast Pastoral Institute, 7700 S.W. 56th St., 33155. Tel: 305-279-2333; Fax: 305-279-0925.
E-mail: sepimiami@aol.com
Web site: socrates.barry.edu/lib-poneill/sepi.htm
Rev. Mario B. Vizcaino, Sch.P., Dir., Contact.

Res. *Southeast Regional Office for Hispanic Ministry, Inc.*, 7700 S.W. 56th St., 33155. Tel: 305-279-2333; Fax: 305-279-0925.
E-mail: sepimiami@aol.com
Web site: socrates.barry.edu/lib-poneill/sepi.htm
Rev. Mario B. Vizcaino, Sch.P., Regl. Dir. & Contact.

[L] MISCELLANEOUS LISTINGS

MIAMI. *Alumni Association of the Apostolate of Cuba (in Exile), Inc.*, P.O. Box 650721, 33265-0721. Tel: 305-271-4151. Maria Antonia Pena, Treas. Tel: 305-271-4151.

Alumni of Apostolate Charity Foundation, Inc., P.O. Box 650721, 33265-0721. Ramona Rodriguez de Rodriguez, Pres. Tel: 813-286-8149; Maria Antonia D. Pena, Treas., Contact. Tel: 305-271-4151.

Asociacion Nacional de Diaconos Hispanos, Inc., 7700 S.W. 56 St., 33155. Tel: 305-485-0949; Fax: 305-485-8704. Deacons Enrique Alonso, Pres.; Pedro Calvo, Vice Pres.; Luis Gonzalez, Treas.; Alfredo Vasquez, Sec.

Claretian Missions, Inc., 7080 S.W. 99 Ave., 33173. Tel: 305-274-6148; Fax: 305-274-5695.
E-mail: rmi@claretiansisters.org
Web site: www.claretiansisters.org
Sr. Ondina Cortes, Superior (Contact). Sisters 5; Houses of Religious Women 3; Total in Residence 10.

Discalced Carmelite Friars of Miami, Inc. Our Lady of Mt. Carmel Spiritual Life Center. 18330 N.W. 12 Ave., 33169. Tel: 305-654-9760; Fax: 305-654-9345.
E-mail: eusebio@gate.net
Web site: www.geocities.com/~eusebio
Revs. Eusebio Gomez, O.C.D., Pres., Contact; Lucio del Burgo, O.C.D., Vice Pres.; Denis William Read, O.C.D. Retreat Center 1; Total in Residence 3; Staff 6.

Foundation of the Cuban Association of the S.M.O. of Malta, Inc., Grand Bay Plaza, Ste. 200, 2665 S. Bayshore Dr., 33133. Tel: 305-285-0800; Fax: 305-285-0837.
E-mail: jon@abogados.com
Fernando Garcia-Chacon, Pres.; Juan T. O'Naghten, Vice Pres.; Manuel Menendez, Treas.; Lodovico Blanc, Dir.

Peruvian Mission, Inc. (A Florida Not-for-Profit Corporation), P.O. Box 432745, 33143. Tel: 305-596-6738; Fax: 305-596-6738.
E-mail: perumision@aol.com
Most Revs. Miguel Irizar, C.P., Bishop of Callao, Pres.; Luis Bambaren, S.J., Bishop of Chimbote, Vice Pres.; Maria Delia Salazar, Dir. & Sec.; Contact Person.

St. Luke's Center, Inc., 7707 N.W. 2nd Ave., 33150. Tel: 305-795-0077; Fax: 305-795-0030; 795-2022.
E-mail: stlukes@catholiccharitiesadm.org
Web site: catholiccharitiesadm.org/stluke
Patricia Carter, Program Dir. (Contact).

Addiction Recovery Center. Total in Residence 45; Total Staff 25.

SEPI Evangelization and Education Foundation, Inc., 7700 S.W. 56th St., 33155. Tel: 305-279-2333; Fax: 305-279-0925.
E-mail: sepimiami@aol.com
Rev. Mario B. Vizcaino, Sch.P., Exec. Dir., Sec., Contact.

Teresian Institute, Inc. (Rome, Italy), Teresian Institute of Florida, Inc., 3400 S.W. 99 Ave., 33165. Tel: 305-553-8567; 226-3317; Fax: 305-553-8567.
E-mail: delpoveda@earthlink.net
Web site: www.institucion-teresiana.org
An International Association of the Faithful. Dolores Gracian, Contact. Total in Residence 3; Total Staff 5.

Center of Activities, National Headquarters.

Theatine Sisters of the Immaculate Conception, Co. aka Religiosas Teatinas de la Immaculada Concepcion, 12261 S.W. 6th St., 33184. Tel: 305-223-2512; Fax: 305-227-6951.
E-mail: ncastillo@msn.com
Sr. Nilsa Castillo, Supr.

COCONUT CREEK. *Ministerio Catolico Verbo y Vida, Inc.*, 3730 Coconut Creek Pkwy., Ste. 190, 33066. Tel: 954-969-7809; Fax: 954-969-7879.
E-mail: ctm@vidatv.org
Web site: www.verboyvida.org
Rev. Ricardo C. Castellanos, Pres.; Karin Van Roo, Exec. Dir.; Alex Sanchez, Production Dir.; Gerardo Caro, Lay Min.

Word & Life Catholic Ministry, Inc., 3730 Coconut Creek Pkwy., Ste. 190, 33066. Tel: 954-970-7766; Fax: 954-969-7879.
E-mail: infor@wordandlife.org
Web site: www.wordandlife.org
P.O. Box 93-5150, Margate, 33066. Rev. Ricardo C. Castellanos, Pres.; Karin Van Roo, Exec. Dir.; Alex Sanchez, Production Dir.

CORAL GABLES. *Bahamas Mission of Florida, Inc.*, c/o J. Patrick Fitzgerald, Esq., 110 Merrick Way, Ste. 3-B, 33134. Tel: 305-443-9162; Fax: 305-443-6613.
E-mail: jpfitz@bellsouth.net

House of the Divine Will, Inc. dba Casa de la Divina Voluntad, 5900 Leonardo St., 33146-3332. Tel: 305-667-5714; Fax: 305-667-7173.
E-mail: fiatmio17@aol.com
Rev. Carlos Antonio Massieu Avila, Pres. & Chm.; Marianela Perez, Treas. & Contact Person.

Magnificat, Inc., 5031 Maggiore St., 33146. Tel: 305-661-9833; Fax: 305-663-0629. Board of Directors: Cristina Beato; Valli Leoni; Rory Lombana; Maria Vadia.

FORT LAUDERDALE. *Schott Memorial Center Foundation, Inc* (A Florida Not-for-Profit Corporation), 6591 S.W. 124th Ave., 33330. Tel: 954-434-3306; 434-7437; Fax: 954-434-3307.
E-mail: jrgschott@aol.com
John R. Green, Exec. Dir., Contact. Special Centers for Social Services & Assistance 1; Total Assisted 11,520; Total Staff 6.

HIALEAH. *Dominicas de la Inmaculada Concepcion*, 571 W. 33 Pl., 33012. Tel: 305-823-3282. Sr. Enith Montero, Supr. Houses of Religous Women 1; Total in Residence 2.

HOLLYWOOD. *Catholic Charismatic Services of the Archdiocese of Miami, Inc.*, 3600 S.W. 32 Blvd., 33023. Tel: 954-961-1856; Fax: 954-961-3662. P.O. Box 816128, 33023. Emery Horvath, Pres.; Mary Horvath, Sec.

KEY LARGO. *1-800-Mass-Times Trust*, 67 N. Bounty Lne, 33037. Tel: 305-852-4530; Fax: 305-852-1582.
E-mail: masstimes@aol.com
Web site: www.masstimes.org
Robert A. Hummel, Trustee; Phyliss H. Hummel, Sec. Governing Board: Jerry Early, Trustee; Rev. Jose P. Nickse, Trustee. Toll-free telephone listing of local Catholic Churches with Mass times to assist travelers in finding Mass schedules.

MIAMI SHORES. *Archdiocese of Miami Millennium Appeal, Inc.*, 9401 Biscayne Blvd., 33138. Tel: 305-757-6241; Fax: 305-758-5261. Most Rev. John C. Favalora, Pres.; Rev. Msgr. William J. Hennessey, Vice Pres.; Rev. Msgr. John J. Vaughan, Treas.; Very Rev. Tomas M. Marin, Sec.

Archdiocese of Miami, Inc., 9401 Biscayne Blvd., 33138. Tel: 305-757-6241; Fax: 305-758-5261. Most Rev. John C. Favalora, Pres.; Rev. Msgr. William J. Hennessey, Vice. Pres.; Rev. Msgr. John J. Vaughan, Treas.; Very Rev. Tomas M. Marin, Sec.

Catholic Community Foundation, Inc., 9401 Biscayne Blvd., 33138. Tel: 305-757-6241; Fax: 305-758-5261. Michael Bienes, Pres.; Roger Shay, Vice Pres.; Rev. Msgr. Vincent Kelly, Sec. & Treas.

DOM, Inc., 9401 Biscayne Blvd., 33138. Tel: 305-757-6241; Fax: 305-758-5261.

Francis Realty Corporation, 9401 Biscayne Blvd., 33138. Tel: 305-757-6241; Fax: 305-758-5261.

Marbella Condominium 207 Association, Inc., 9401 Biscayne Blvd., 33138. Tel: 305-757-6241; Fax: 305-758-5261.

P.O.M., Inc., 9401 Biscayne Blvd., 33138. Tel: 305-757-6241; Fax: 305-758-5261.

Pooled Income Trust Fund, 9401 Biscayne Blvd., 33138. Tel: 305-757-6241; Fax: 305-758-5261.

Provincial Realty Associates, Inc. (A Florida Not-for-Profit Corporation), 9401 Biscayne Blvd., 33138. Tel: 305-757-6241; Fax: 305-758-5261.
Land Holding Corporation.

POMPANO BEACH. *Indian Catholic Association of Florida, Inc.*, 731 N. Ocean Blvd., 33062. Tel: 954-943-3684; Fax: 954-943-3656. Rev. James Parappally, Chap.

RELIGIOUS INSTITUTES OF MEN REPRESENTED IN THE ARCHDIOCESE

For further details refer to the corresponding bracketed number in the Religious Institutes of Men or Women section.

[0140]—*The Augustinians.* (St. Thomas of Villanova Prov.).—O.S.A.
[0600]—*Brothers of the Congregation of Holy Cross.*—C.S.C.
[0580]—*Brothers of the Good Shepherd.*—B.G.S.
[0270]—*Carmelite Fathers & Brothers.*—O.Carm.
[0310]—*Congregation of Christian Brothers.* (Eastern Prov.).—C.F.C.
[1330]—*Congregation of the Mission.*—C.M.
[1080]—*Congregation of the Resurrection.*—C.R.
[1140]—*Congregation of the Sacred Hearts of Jesus and Mary.*—SS.CC.
[0260]—*Discalced Carmelite Friars.*—O.C.D.
[0520]—*Franciscan Friars.* (Most Holy Name & San Sebastion Provs.).—O.F.M.
[0650]—*Holy Ghost Fathers.*—C.S.Sp.
[0690]—*Jesuit Fathers and Brothers.* (Antilles, New Orleans and New England Provs.).—S.J.
[0770]—*The Marist Brothers.* (Esopus & Poughkeepsie Provs.).—F.M.S.
[1210]—*Missionaries of St. Charles-Scalabrinians.*—C.S.
[0910]—*Oblates of Mary Immaculate.*—O.M.I.
[0920]—*Oblates of St. Francis de Sales.*—O.S.F.S.
[0430]—*Order of Preachers (Dominican).* (St. Joseph & Southern Provs.).—O.P.
[1020]—*Pauline Fathers & Brothers.*—S.S.P.
[1040]—*Piarist Fathers.*—Sch.P. [0610]—*Priests of the Congregation of the Holy Cross.*—C.S.C.
[1190]—*Salesians of Don Bosco.*—S.D.B.
[1260]—*Society of Christ.*—S.Ch.
[0760]—*Society of Mary (Marianists).*—S.M.
[0370]—*Society of St. Columban*S.S.C.
[1060]—*Society of the Precious Blood.*—C.PP.S.

RELIGIOUS INSTITUTES OF WOMEN REPRESENTED IN THE ARCHDIOCESE

[0370]—*Carmelite Sisters of the Most Sacred Heart of Los Angeles.*—O.C.D.
[0670]—*Cistercian Nuns of the Strict Observance.*—O.C.S.O.
[0685]—*Claretian Missionary Sisters.*—R.M.I.
[0270]—*Congregation of Bon Secours.*—C.B.S.
[1710]—*Congregation of the Third Order of St. Francis of Mary Immaculate, Joliet, IL.*—O.S.F.
[0760]—*Daughters of Charity of St. Vincent de Paul.*—D.C.
[0790]—*Daughters of Divine Charity.*—F.D.C.
[0850]—*Daughters of Mary Help of Christians.*—F.M.A.
[]—*Daughters of Mary, Mother of Mercy (Nigeria).*—D.M.M.M.
[1070-13]—*Dominican Sisters (Adrian).*—O.P.
[1070-17]—*Dominican Sisters (Elkins Park).*—O.P.
[1070-06]—*Dominican Sisters (Newburgh).*—O.P.
[1070-03]—*Dominican Sisters (Sinsinawa).*—O.P.
[]—*Dominican Sisters of Our Lady of the Most Holy Rosary (Colombia).*—O.P.
[]—*Dominicas de la Inmaculada Concepcion (Ecuador).*
[1340]—*Franciscan Missionary Sisters of the Divine Child.*—F.M.D.C.
[1180]—*Franciscan Sisters of Allegany, New York.*—O.S.F.
[1845]—*Guadalupan Missionaries of the Holy Spirit.* (Mexico).—M.G.Sp.S.
[]—*Handmaids of the Holy Child of Jesus.* (Nigeria).—H.H.C.J.
[1870]—*Handmaids of the Sacred Heart of Jesus.*—A.C.J.
[2575]—*Institute of the Sisters of Mercy of the Americas.* (Pittsburgh, PA; Rochester, NY; Merion, PA; Clogher, Ireland; Newfoundland, Canada).—R.S.M.
[]—*Marianitas.* (Santa Mariana de Jesus Institute, Inc.).—R.M.
[2710]—*Missionaries of Charity.*—M.C.
[3040]—*Oblate Sisters of Providence.*—O.S.P.
[]—*Oblates of the Sacred Heart of Jesus (El Salvador).*—O.C.J.
[3130]—*Our Lady of Victory Missionary Sisters.*—O.L.V.M.
[0950]—*Pious Society Daughters of St. Paul.*—F.S.P.
[3380]—*Religious of the Apostolate of the Sacred Heart.*—R.A.
[3390]—*Religious of the Assumption.*—R.A.
[2970]—*School Sisters of Notre Dame.* (Baltimore, MD; Chicago, IL).—S.S.N.D.
[0430]—*Sisters of Charity of the Blessed Virgin Mary.* (Davenport, IA).—B.V.M.
[]—*Sisters of Jesus the Saviour.* (Nigeria).—S.J.S.

[2540]—*Sisters of Mercy.* (Clogher, Northern Ireland).—R.S.M.

[3000]—*Sisters of Notre Dame de Namur (Baltimore, MA).*—S.N.D.deN.

[3350]—*Sisters of Providence.*—S.P.

[4090]—*Sisters of Social Service.*—S.S.S.

[3740]—*Sisters of St. Casimir.*—S.S.C.

[1620]—*Sisters of St. Francis of Millvale, Pennsylvania.*—O.S.F.

[1630]—*Sisters of St. Francis of Penance and Christian Charity.*—O.S.F.

[3830-13]—*Sisters of St. Joseph (Baden, PA).*—C.S.J.

[3830-09]—*Sisters of St. Joseph (Erie, PA).*—S.S.J.

[]—*Sisters of St. Joseph Benedict Cottolengo.*—S.S.J.C.

[3840]—*Sisters of St. Joseph of Carondelet.* (St. Louis, MO).—C.S.J.

[3850]—*Sisters of St. Joseph of Chambery.* (Hartford, CT)C.S.J.

[3900]—*Sisters of St. Joseph of St. Augustine, Florida.*—S.S.J.

[]—*Sisters of St. Philip Neri Missionary Teachers.*—R.F.

[1970]—*Sisters of the Holy Family of Nazareth.*—C.S.F.N.

[2180]—*Sisters of the Immaculate Heart of Mary.*—I.H.M.

[1490]—*Sisters of the Third Franciscan Order.*—O.S.F.

[2150]—*Sisters, Servants of the Immaculate Heart of Mary.* (Monroe, MI).—I.H.M.

[2160]—*Sisters, Servants of the Immaculate Heart of Mary.* (Scranton, PA).—I.H.M.

[2170]—*Sisters, Servants of the Immaculate Heart of Mary.* (Immaculata, PA).—I.H.M.

[2180]—*Sisters, Servants of the Immaculate Heart of Mary.* (Clewiston, FL)I.H.M.

[2460]—*Society of Mary Reparatrix.*—S.M.R.

[4020]—*Society of St. Teresa of Jesus.*—S.T.J.

[4070]—*Society of the Sacred Heart.*—R.S.C.J.

[]—*Theatine Sisters of the Immaculate Conception (Religiosas Teatinas de la Inmaculada Concepcion).*—R.T.

NECROLOGY

† Fernandez, Rev. Msgr. Orlando, (Retired). —Died Jan. 13, 2000.

† LaCerra, Rev. Msgr. Gerard T., Miami, FL St. Timothy. —Died July 25, 2000.

Archdiocese for the Military Services, U.S.A.

Military Ordinariate

Most Reverend

EDWIN F. O'BRIEN, S.T.D.

Archbishop for the Military Services; ordained May 29, 1965; appointed Titular Bishop of Tizica and Auxiliary Bishop of New York March 25, 1996; appointed Coadjutor April 8, 1997; succeeded as Ordinary to the Military Services August 12, 1997.

Chancery: P.O. Box 4469, Washington, DC, 20017-0469. Tel.: 202-269-9100; Fax: 202-269-9022.

Web site address: www.milarch.org

E-mail address: info@milarch.org

Most Reverend

JOHN J. KAISING, D.D.

Auxiliary Bishop; ordained December 22, 1962; appointed Titular Bishop for Orrea Celia and Auxiliary Bishop of the Archdiocese of the Military Services February 21, 2000; ordained Bishop April 11, 2000.

Most Reverend

JOSEPH T. DIMINO, D.D.

Former Archbishop for the Military Services; ordained June 4, 1949; appointed Titular Bishop of Carini and Auxiliary Bishop to the Military Vicar March 29, 1983; consecrated May 10, 1983; appointed Ordinary to the Military Services May 13, 1991; resigned August 12, 1997.

Most Reverend

FRANCIS X. ROQUE, D.D.

Auxiliary Bishop; ordained September 19, 1953; appointed Titular Bishop of Bagai and Auxiliary Bishop to the Military Vicar March 29, 1983; consecrated May 10, 1983.

Most Reverend

JOSEPH J. MADERA, M.SP.S., D.D.

Auxiliary Bishop; ordained June 15, 1957; appointed Coadjutor Bishop of Fresno with the right of succession December 18, 1979; consecrated March 4, 1980; succeeded to See July 1, 1980; appointed Titular Bishop of Orte and Auxiliary Bishop of the Archdiocese of the Military Services May 28, 1991.

Most Reverend

JOHN J. GLYNN, D.D.

Auxiliary Bishop; ordained April 11, 1951; appointed Titular Bishop of Monteverde and Auxiliary Bishop of the Archdiocese for the Military Services December 10, 1991; ordained Bishop January 6, 1992.

ESTABLISHED AS MILITARY VICARIATE OF THE UNITED STATES SEPTEMBER 8, 1957.; CREATED ARCHDIOCESE FOR THE MILITARY SERVICES, U.S.A. (ORDINARIATUS CASTRENSIS) MARCH 25, 1985.

Serving U.S. Catholics of the Army, Navy, Air Force, Marine Corps, Coast Guard, Department of Veterans Affairs and those in Government Service overseas.

STATISTICAL OVERVIEW

Personnel

Archbishop	1
Retired Archbishops	1
Auxiliary Bishops	4

Priest Chaplains are on loan from their diocese or religious community.
Deacons who assist at chapels are volunteers from the local diocese.

Educational

Catechesis/Religious Education:

High School Students	21,000
Elementary Students	44,200
Total Students Under Catholic Instruction	65,200

Religious Education Teachers:

Sisters	12
Lay Teachers	220
Total	232

Vital Statistics

Receptions into the Church:

Infant Baptism Totals	10,399
Adult Baptism Totals	1,304
Received into Full Communion	493
First Communions	7,478
Confirmations	5,098

Marriages:

Catholic	870
Interfaith	700
Total Marriages	1,570
Catholics, Active Duty Military	375,000
Family Members	520,000
Reserve/Guard Catholic Personnel	204,000
Catholic residents, VA facilities	29,000
Civilian Catholics overseas	66,000
Total	1,194,000

Former Military Vicars—His Eminence PATRICK CARDINAL HAYES, cons. Titular Bishop of Tagaste, Oct. 28, 1914; appt. "Bishop Ordinary of U.S. Army and Navy Chaplains," Nov. 24, 1917; appt. Archbishop of New York, March 10, 1919; created Cardinal, March 24, 1924; died Sept. 4, 1938.—His Eminence FRANCIS CARDINAL SPELLMAN, cons. Auxiliary Bishop of Boston, Sept. 8, 1932; appt. Archbishop of New York, April 15, 1939; appt. "Military Vicar for the Armed Forces of U.S.," Dec. 11, 1939; created Cardinal, Feb. 18, 1946; died Dec. 2, 1967.—His Eminence TERENCE CARDINAL COOKE, cons. Auxiliary Bishop of New York, Dec. 13, 1965; appt. Archbishop of New York, March 2, 1968; appt. "Military Vicar of U.S. Armed Forces," April 4, 1968; created Cardinal, April 28, 1969; died Oct. 6, 1983.—Most Rev. JOSEPH T. RYAN, appt. first Archbishop of Anchorage, Feb. 7, 1966; cons. March 25, 1966; appt. Titular Archbishop of Gabi and Coadjutor Archbishop of the Military Vicar, Oct. 24, 1975; installed first Ordinary of the Archdiocese for the Military Services March, 25, 1985; retired May 13, 1991; died Oct. 9, 2000.—Most Rev. JOSEPH T. DIMINO, appt. Auxiliary Bishop of Military Vicar, March 29, 1983; cons. May 10, 1983; appt. Titular Bishop of Carini; appt. second Ordinary for the Military Services, May 13, 1991; retired Aug. 12, 1997.

Vicar General—Rev. Msgr. ALOYSIUS R. CALLAGHAN, S.T.L., J.C.D.

Archdiocese Offices

Chancery—415 Michigan Ave., N.E., Ste. 300, Washington, DC, 20017. Tel: 202-269-9100; Fax: 202-269-9022.

Moderator of the Curia / Chancellor—Rev. Msgr. ALOYSIUS R. CALLAGHAN, S.T.L, J.C.D.

Vice Chancellor—Rev. Msgr. GEORGE E. DOBES, J.C.L.

Vice Chancellor / Office for Management Information Systems—Rev. RONALD NEWLAND.

Vice Chancellor / Office for Legal Services—THOMAS CONNELLY, Esq.

Office of Chaplain Personnel—

Vicar for Chaplains and Seminarians—Most Rev. JOHN J. GLYNN, D.D.

Director—Mrs. MARGARET SCUDERI.

Pastoral Support, Community Concerns and Vocations—Most Rev. JOSEPH J. MADERA, M.Sp.S., D.D.

Veterans Concerns—Most Rev. FRANCIS X. ROQUE, D.D.

Priestly Development and Vocations—Most Rev. JOHN J. KAISING, D.D.

Assistant to the Archbishop—Ms. CHRISTINA ASHER.

Director of Administration—Mrs. JO ANN REDMOND.

Director of Sacramental Records—Mr. FRANK CALANDRA.

Director of Development—Mr. DAVID LEVITE.

Archivist—Mrs. PATRICIA THACKER.

Tribunal—

Judicial Vicar—Rev. Msgr. GEORGE E. DOBES, J.C.L.

Judges—Rev. Msgr. ALOYSIUS R. CALLAGHAN, J.C.D.; Rev. Msgr. GEORGE E. DOBES, J.C.L.; Rev. Msgr. JAMES MCGRATH, J.C.L.; Revs. GEORGE BRUBAKER, J.C.L.; EMMETT J. GAVIN, J.C.L.; G. PAUL HERBERT, J.C.L.; EDMUND PRENDEVILLE, J.C.L.; JOHN T. PUTMAN, J.C.L.; JOHN L. SULLIVAN, J.C.L.; MARK TUCKER, C.SS.R., J.C.L.

Defenders of the Bond—Revs. DAVID F. O'CONNOR, S.T., J.C.D.; MICHAEL LAWRENCE, J.C.L.

Procurator-Advocates—Most Rev. JOHN J. GLYNN, D.D.; Most Rev. FRANCIS X. ROQUE, D.D.; Ms. SARA MORELLA, J.C.L.

Notary—Mrs. MAY TOEPFER.

Presbyteral Council—Most Rev. EDWIN F. O'BRIEN, D.D.; Most Rev. JOHN J. GLYNN, D.D.; Most Rev. FRANCIS X. ROQUE, D.D.; Most Rev. JOSEPH J. MADERA, M.SP.S., D.D.; Rev. Msgr. ALOYSIUS R. CALLAGHAN, Exec. Sec.; Rev. Msgr. GEORGE E. DOBES; Rev. Msgr. PHILIP HILL, (U.S.A.); Revs. DAVID KENEHAN,

(U.S.A.); LOUIS IASIELLO, (U.S.N.); STEVE LINEHAN, (U.S.N.); JAMES DIXON, (U.S.A.F.); Rev. Msgr. WILLIAM J. DENDINGER, (U.S.A.F.); Revs. JONATHAN LAO, (V.A.); RONALD LAWSON, (V.A.).

Military Council of Catholic Women—Most Rev. JOSEPH J. MADERA, M.Sp.S., Episcopal Moderator.

Areas of Service

Armed Forces, Active Duty

The Archdiocese for the Military Services is responsible for the pastoral care of the Catholic men and women who serve on active duty in the five branches of the U.S. Armed Forces. It is also responsible for the dependents of these persons. Included also are the cadets and resident personnel of the three military academies (West Point—the U.S. Military Academy, the U.S. Air Force Academy at Colorado Springs, the U.S. Naval Academy at Annapolis) and the U.S. Coast Guard Academy at New London as well as the U.S. Merchant Marine Academy at Kings Point, NY. Pastoral care is provided by priest chaplains on loan from their dioceses or religious communities to serve as chaplains for the Military and Department of Veterans Affairs. Members of the Marines and Coast Guard are served by Navy Chaplains.

Armed Forces, Reserves, National Guard

In addition to the personnel on active duty in the Armed Forces, there is a considerable reserve component. Some of these personnel serve a number of days each year on active duty with a branch of the service; some serve on extended tours of active duty; all are subject to recall to active duty in a national emergency. In addition to the reserve components of the Army, Air Force, Navy and Coast Guard, there are also the Air National Guard and the Army National Guard, which are organized on a state-by-state basis.

Department of Veterans Affairs

The Archdiocese for the Military Services is responsible for the spiritual care of Catholics at V.A. medical facilities. Chaplaincy services are provided by full- and part-time priests, many of whom are retired military chaplains.

U.S. Government Civilian Employees Abroad

U.S. citizens in government service abroad (and their family members living with them) are subjects of the Archdiocese for the Military Services.

There are only two full-time Catholic chaplains conducting pastoral programs for embassies: in Moscow and Bonn. The Embassy in Moscow has a program conducted by the Augustinians of the Assumption and is separate from the Archdiocese; it serves Catholics in the Foreign Service of other countries as well as Americans.

Civil Air Patrol

The Civil Air Patrol, as an auxiliary of the Air Force, is under the jurisdiction of the Archdiocese for the Military Services. The jurisdiction applies to its chaplains and members only when participating in exercises on a military installation.

UNITED STATES ARMY CHAPLAINS

REGULAR ARMY CHAPLAINS

Reverends

Amezcua, Mario M., *l.c.*
Arnoldt, David L. (WIN)
Blickhan, Donald (SFD)
Bluett, James K. (PT)
Bolton, Paul (PRO)
Bomba, Paul (WOR)
Briganti, Phillip (PAT)
Burns, Vincent deP. (PH)
Carey, William F. (BGP)
Chilen, Michael D. (CC)
Coindreau, James M., *l.c.*
D'Emma, Gregory J. (NEW)
Deponai, Joseph (NY)
DiGregorio, Joseph (PH)
D'Silva, Joseph R. (India)
Ehrhart, Charles (RVC)
Glasgow, Robert K. (MAN)
Habarek, Jerome (PRO)
Herron, John (FAR)
Hill, Philip (NY)
Himmelsbach, James R. (STP)
Inghilterra, Vincent J. (TR)
Jones, James, *o.f.m.cap.*
Kenehan, David A., *o.s.f.s.*
Marceaux, Sidney (BEA)
Mauricio, Clemente B., *m.s.c.*
Minch, Richard (SAV)
Mullen, Owen J. (WIL)
Mulvaney, Andrew (OG)
Niemeier, Dennis A. (CIN)
O'Keeffe, Joseph L. (ALB)
O'Grady, John F. (PAT)
Prendergast, John (PEO)
Rodriguez, Aloysius M. (BR)
Roetzel, Robert E., *c.s.c.*
Rutherford, Donald (ALB)
Sanner, James E. (E)
Sheil, James E. (CLV)
Stahl, Allen M. (ORL)
Spiegel, Robert H. (DAV)
Sykes, Gregory (OG)
Tellez, Jairo, (SAT)
Travaglione, Michael, *o.f.m.*
Whalen, Frank J. (CIN)
Wilk, Mitchell S. (SPC)
Willett, William (OWN)
Wydeven, John L. (OAK)

ARMY RESERVE ON ACTIVE DUTY

Reverends

Albertson, Eric (ARL)
Angotti, Joseph A. (GAR)
Bendorf, Richard, *o.f.m*
Bleboo, Lawrence (Africa)
Borkowski, Frank J. (NY)
Borycz, Edmund S. (DET)
Buckon, Neal J. (CLV)
Carlson, Steven V. (RAL)
Cerrone, Michael J. (SAV)
Czech, Edward M. (CLV)
Denig, Philip (DEN)
Dynek, Wieslaw A. (Poland)
Fleury, Joseph, *s.m.*
Flores, Jose (ARE)
Fuller, Orlando (Philippines)
Goudreau, Joseph L. (PRT)
Hannon, Joseph, *s.d.b.*
Hightower, Oliver L. (HEL)
Hill, Donald W. (BIS)
Honor, Michael (Philippines)
Hurley, Paul K. (BO)
Jagielski, James J. (DET)
Kelley, Edward (PRO)
Kirk, David R. (TOL)
Kopec, Krzysztof (WIL)
Kopec, Rajmond (NEW)
Lagasse, Ronald (OAK)
Lanuevo, Victor (HON)
Lee, Sang Yi (AUS)
Livingston, Morson, *s.a.c.*
Madden, James J., *o.praem.*
Madu, Ferdinand E. (Nigeria)
Majkut, Tadeusz (Paraguay)
Martin, Edward C., *ss.cc.*
McLain, John J., *s.j.*
Passamonti, Paul (WDC)
Patton, Patrick G. (HEL)
Pawlikowski, Matthew (NEW)
Pfeiffer, Carl, *o.ss.t.*
Ratigan, Patrick (OG)
Reyes, Armando (Philippines)
Rzasowski, Jerzy (Poland)
Saltysiak, Paul (WDC)
Santry, Robert (HON)
Serban, Ronald (SR)
Spencer, Richard (BAL)
Stevenson, R. Francis (SAC)
Studnewski, Gary (WDC)
Tadeo, Victor (Philippines)
Torm, Agustin (CHR)
Vakoc, Timothy (STP)
VanAlstyne, Donald J., *m.i.c.*

UNITED STATES AIR FORCE CHAPLAINS

REGULAR AIR FORCE

Reverends

Angelo, Thomas (NOR)
Bailey, James L. (SEA)
Barlow, James P. (SAT)
Beck, R. Patrick (BEA)
Berthlette, Ernest (PRO)
Biewind, Michael, *c.j.*
Booth, Stephen, *m.m.*
Bruno, Robert, *o.f.m.*
Burnet, Donald T., *o.m.i.*
Cote, David P. (PRT)
Crowley, Edmund G. (MAN)
Cusack, John J. (PAT)
Dendinger, William J. (OM)
Diab, Thomas P. (SAN)
Dillon, James P. (BRK)
Diphe, Juan (HEL)
Di Renzo, Michael J. (STU)
Dixon, James R. (NO)
Dunn, Richard B. (SY)
Fey, Thomas (ALX)
Flood, Peter J. (TR)
Gallagher, Robert (STU)
Gosselin, Lawrence (NTN)
Guico, Manuel R. (Philippines)
Hall, Douglas (OM)
Hanley, Dennis (HRT)
Hanrahan, William P. (NEW)
Higginbotham, Robert (BLX)
Higgins, Richard B. (SAC)
Ippolito, Robert, *m.s.*
Kinney, John (LAF)
Koser, Rudolph J. (GBG)
Kovalcin, John (STL)
Kuan, Joseph (Philippines)
Lambert, Peter S. (DUL)
Lamy, Raymond (MAN)
Leurck, Raymond J. (CIN)
Lim, Joseph (Philippines)
Ludwikoski, James E. (KCK)
McCahon, Joseph (SP)
McKenna, Timothy (SEA)
McManus, Gerald (PH)
Malinsky, Gregory J. (PIT)
Mikalofsky, Hilarion (MIL)
Montecalvo, Carlo F. (PRO)
Moran, Edward C. (RIC)
Moreno, Antonio, *o.f.m.conv.*
Mueller, Jerome, *o.f.m.*
Mulnix, Gabriel R., *c.p.*
Munsell, Richard (GF)
Nguyen, Phillip D. (GR)
Nolan, John J. (SFD)
Novotny, Richard (RC)
Olszyk, Thomas P. (MIL)
O'Neill, Michael F. (NO)
Revello, James P. (DEN)
Ryan, Patrick J., *m.m.*
Saluta, Froilan (Philippines)
Schiffer, James A., *c.p.*
Schnipke, Eugene, *c.pp.s.*
Schueller, LaVerne L. (DUB)
Srode, John S., *c.pp.s.*
Thomas, James (ALN)
Toledo, Nelson (Philippines)
Volmi, Dennis G. (WIL)
Wagner, Joseph (SFS)
Wallroth, Joseph R., *o.carm.*
Zinzer, Walter W. (STL)

AIR FORCE RESERVE ON ACTIVE DUTY

Reverends

Abbott, Kerry, *o.f.m.cap.*
Adversario, Efren F. (AGN)
Bartoul, William (SAM)
Beale, Kenneth (NEW)
Bell, Brian T. (TUC)
Blair, Stephen (East Anglia)
Blazek, Eugene E. (HON)
Borkowski, Wladyslaw (Poland)
Breig, Gary (STL)
Brosk, Steven (NEW)
Butler, Timothy (BO)
Charbonneau, William (HRT)
Clegg, Timothy (LAF)
Cody, Kevin N. (MAN)
Czartorynski, David F. (ALN)
Decker, James D. (MAN)
Doyle, Thomas, *o.p.*
Deichert, Joseph (BIS)
Erickson, Richard (BO)
Fitzgerald, R. Martin (R)
Fitz-Patrick, David (WDC)
Fletcher, Patrick (PCE)
George, George C. (AUS)
Gonia, Raymond (SUP)
Hamel, James A. (NEW)
Harbour, Linn (MOB)
Hochreiter, Robert S. (SCR)
King, Martin L. (P)
Linsky, Gary S.(CHR)
Llanos, Philip (LA)
Lowe, Francis (SB)
Motsay, Joseph R. (SCR)
Omana, Max B.T. (Philippines)
Pieczara, Stanislaw, *s.d.s.*
Plate, Brian (NEW)
Raux, Redmond (BO)
Reeson, David (OM)
Roberts, Randall, *o.f.m.*
Sanchez, Albert M. (AGN)
Sanchez, Raul N. (GAL)
Sirianni, Klaus W. J. (WDC)
Swetnam, R. William (STL)
Torres, Ivan (SJN)
Torres, R. William (STL)
Tran, Joseph (RIC)
Underwood, Gary (TUC)
Voelker, David (BEL)
Voyt, Stephen (PT)
Vu, Joseph Minh (TLS)
Weber, Michael J., *o.praem.*
Zeller, Leonard H. (BAL)
Zygadlo, Mitchell (ROC)

UNITED STATES NAVY CHAPLAINS

REGULAR NAVY CHAPLAINS

Reverends

Barrett, Miles (SC)
Brzek, Jon (PIT)
Buchmiller, Ronald J. (SD)
Buenaventura, Cesar V. (Philippines)
Caiazzo, Gregory G., (RIC)
Ceriello, Joseph A. (BRK)
Coyle, Patrick, *ss.cc.*
Danner, James L. (MEM)
Dansak, Thomas E. (PIT)
Delis, Robert D., *s.d.b.*
Diaz, Michael, (SD)
Dillon, Jerome (OM)
Dillon, William P., *s.a.*
Dory, Michael (GB)
Elkin, Frederic F. (SY)
Estabrook, Joseph W. (ALB)
Falkenthal, Thomas W. (CHI)
Fix, Donald (PIT)
Fryer, Patrick L. (WH)
Gomulka, Eugene T. (ALT)
Gubbins, John M. (MIA)
Gwudz, John S., Jr. (NOR)
Hall, Thomas P., *c.s.p.*
Holloway, David (KC)
Iasiello, Louis V., *o.f.m.*
Ignacio, Simon G. (Philippines)
Jennings, Tommie Lee (SD)
Joslyn, James W. (CHI)
Kaul, John L. (DET)
Keane, Robert L., *s.j.*
Kelly, Brian (SCR)
Kennedy, William M. (BO)
Klarer, Michael (MAD)
Klepacki, Micahel S. (CHI)
Lamonde, Joseph (PIT)
Leibold, James C. (BRK)
Lesak, William (NEW)
McCord, Kent (MET)
McCormack, Patrick J. (ATL)
McKenzie, John H., *o.s.b.*
McLaughlin, Paul (VEN)
Malene, Robert (E)
Mandato, Kieran (NY)
Melley, James F. (MIA)
Mueller, Michael G. (ORL)
Murphy, Thomas E. (WDC)
NGuyen, Joseph (Vietnam)
Parisi, Michael J. (PAT)
Pucciarelli, George W. (BO)
Remy, David P. (DUB)
Rodes, Kenneth, *s.d.b.*
Shuley, Keith J. (CC)
Soto, Charles, *o.f.m.*
Targonski, Conrad, *o.f.m.*
Trapani, Anthony (RVC)
Valko, Robert A. (PIT)
Vanden Boogard, Steven, *o.praem.*
Yagesh, Richard C. (PIT)
Young, David (CI)
Zuffoletto, Michael (BUF)

NAVY RESERVE CHAPLAINS ON ACTIVE DUTY

Reverends

Aguilera, Salvador (ELP)
Berchmanz, Antony (NEW)
Biala, Romeo (Philippines)
Bjorklund, Brian (DET)
Bochnak, Zenon A. (MET)
Borzych, Alexander (GI)
Boucher, Roger R. (WOR)
Bower, Alan Eugene (STA)
Boyle, Dennis (PH)
Brown, Benedict (L)
Brown, Lewis (ROC)
Brown, Shaun S. (NTN)
Cain, Robert (TLS)
Carlos, Joseph, *o.f.m.*
Concha, Alfonso (PH)
Connolly, James (ALN)
Coyle, Robert J. (RVC)
Creider, Philip B. (OKL)
Cuddy, William (BO)
Cunha, Egionor (NEW)
Cunningham, Gerard M. (WDC)
Cusick, Kevin (WDC)
Dang, Chin Van (RIC)
Deeley, Kevin J. (BO)
Devine, William (BO)
Donohue, Stephen (BO)
D'Souza, Matthew (LUB)
Erestain, Alfonso (Philippines)
Evers, Paul (HON)
Ferretti, Sam (SCR)
Finley, James F. (BRK)
Foley, Francis P. (PH)
Fry, James Q. (ORG)
Gardocki, Patrick, *o.f.m.*
Garvey, Michael P. (Y)
Gay, James (BGP)
Geinzer, John A. (PIT)
Gergel, Stephen (ALT)
Gervacio, Adrian R. (HON)
Hellwig, Lee (HRT)
Hicks, Stephen (SAN)
Hickman, Stephen (RIC)
Hogan, Timothy (DET)
Hoog, Eric, *c.ss.r.*
Hughes, Robert W. (MAD)
Janning, Timothy (CIN)
Johnson, Lawrence P. (DUL)
Kalinowski, Joseph J. (E)
Kanicki, Phillip (RIC)
Kawczynski, Ronald (FAR)
Kienzle, Jerome (MIL)
Kloak, David G. (CHI)
Koch, Joseph (India)
Koester, Timothy (BUF)
Kurilec, Robert E., (SB)
Kuss, Allen (BIS)
Lamb, Gary (MEM)
Lee, Matthew (WDC)
Leslie, Lawrence (COV)
Lindblad, Karl A. (NY)
Linehan, Stephen J. (BO)
Logan, Aidan, *OCso*
Lopes, Richard, *o.f.m.cap*
Lott, Lawrence (MOB)
McClanahan, Robert (PT)
McGeory, Peter (NY)
MacNew, James. J., *o.s.f.s.*
Madej, Paul (SY)
Maxwell, Bruce, *o.s.c.*
Mensah, Gabriel (VIC)
Mikstay, Michael (Y)
Milewski, Robert F. (E)
Morris, John J. (NEW)
Moss, Donald (AUS)
Mudd, David A. (WDC)
Muhm, William J. (NY)
Mulkerin, Terrence (BRK)
Neis, William P. (LC)
Nicolas, Jeffrey (L)
Ohm, Edward U. (PEO)
Panek, Robert M. (NY)
Petruska, William (SCR)
Pugliese, Frank (NY)
Quinn, John T. (SD)
Rock, Stephen B. (BO)
Russo, Lawrence J., Jr. (BO)
Salamoni, Vincent, *m.s.a.*
Scordo, Joseph, *o.p.*
Shaughnessy, Paul J., *s.j.*
Shimotsu, John M. (ORG)
Shuppert, William T. (TUC)
Simpson, Brian L. (CHI)
Smith, Stewart D., *c.s.c.*
Spangenberg, George, *c.s.sp.*
Stake, Ronald P. (CHI)
Steed, Donald, *m.m.*
St. George, Peter (CIN)
Sweeney, Kevin (ORG)
Tran, Philip (NY)
Tran, Quang Minh (SAV)
Travers, Alan F. (NY)
Vidrine, Richard (LAF)
Walsh, Francis (SPR)
Wegierski, Anthony J., *o.f.m.conv.*
Welch, Bernard (PRT)
Wheatley, R. Carroll (OWN)

AUXILIARY CHAPLAINS

Reverends

Ahern, John J. (CHI)
Amateis, Jacques (Saudi Arabia)
Arminio, Alfonse (NEW)
Ashe, Michael B. (CC)
Ashkar, Dominic (SAM)
Balizan, Daniel M. (SFE)
Bauer, John J., *c.s.s.r.*
Betowski, E. Paul, *s.j.*
Boyle, Patrick J., *s.j.*
Bracken, John (BRK)
Buckley, Charles, *o.s.b.*
Butler, Michael (COS)
Carlin, Bernard, *c.ss.r.*
Casus-Ferrer, Guillermo, *t.c.*
Cavanaugh, Michael, *o.s.f.s.*
Chai, John (Taipei)
Chong, Young-Ku (Korea)
Cleary, William J., *o.s.a.*
Connolly, Leo L. (COL)
Crandall, Thomas A. (PT)
Creary, James (MEM)
Cuneo, James J.
de Verteuil, Jack (FBK)
Dillman, Alan (ATL)
Diniz, Felicio (Saudi Arabia)
Doody, Patrick, *c.s.sp.*
Dorney, James J. (NY)
Drury, Michael, *c.o.*
Dunham, Larry C., *o.f.m.*
Dunn, Stephen (SD)
Edwards, R. Dale (FWT)
Effing, Myron (Agana)
Evanstock, Philip, *c.s.sp.*
Farias, Joseph (PAT)
Ferrer, Gonzalo, *t.o.r.*
Fewell, Michael, *c.m.f.*
Flannery, Michael (NY)
Fosselman, David, *c.s.c.*
Frank, Lawrence J., *o.m.i.*
Freeman, James (TUC)
Gagliardo, Anthony F. (BUF)
Gillespie, Paul G., *o.s.f.s.*
Gitzen, Blase, *o.f.m.cap.*
Gnall, Joseph, *o.s.b.*
Goellen, Richard (FAR)
Gribbon, Joseph, *c.ss.r.*
Grothjan, James K. *c.pp.s.*
Habenight, James F., *m.m.*
Hacker, Louis, *o.s.b.*
Hamilton, Thomas M., *s.m.*
Hartgen, William, *s.s.*
Healy, Patrick, *o.m.i.*
Hickey, Dennis W., *c.s.p.*
Hillyard, Matthew J., *o.s.f.s.*
Hoffman, Louis, *s.f.*
Intranuovo, Ralph, *s.c.j.*
Jacobi, Joseph (OKL)
Kearney, Thomas L., *o.p.*
Kelley, Thomas W., *o.s.f.s.*
Kelley, William J., *s.v.d.*
Kelly, James C., *o.s.b.*
Keutzer, Walter (STL)
Kiczuk, Casimir, *c.m.*
Kieffer, Thomas, *c.o.*
Kita, Edward, *m.s.*
Kneip, Paschal, *o.s.b.*
Kobza, John, *m.i.c.*
Kohler, Joseph (STL)
Kroker, Wolfgang (Germany)
Kucera, Edward J., *o.s.b.*
Kuchar, Matthew, *o.s.b.*
Kukucka, Joseph (PBL)
Kyzysteczko, Gothard, *c.m.*
Labo, Timothy (ORL)
Lamendola, Salvatore (GBG)
Langston, Micheas, *o.s.b.*
Lenihan, Michael (CC)
Leveille, Andre (Japan)
Limon, Lidio, *c.o.*
Listecki, Jerome E. (CHI)
Loftus, Conrad, *o.f.m.*
Loth, Alan J. (OKL)
McCormick, Thomas, *s.j.*
McGrath, John (BLX)
McGrath, Thomas, *s.j.*
McHale, Damian, *c.p.*
McNally, Stephen (RIC)
McSwigan, William, *c.s.sp.*
Macalintal, Dionisio R. (SD)
Madden, Paul J., *o.praem.*
Mages, Mark, *o.s.b.*
Majerus, Daniel (SCL)
Malnar, Matthew (MIL)
Marsh, John, *c.ss.r.*
Martin, Michael, *o.s.b.*
Martire, Leonardo (Argentina)
Martinez, Anthony L. (SFE)
Martinez-Navarro, Modesto, *t.c.*
Massoth, Charles, *o.s.b.*
Merfeld, Vincent (DUB)
McLeod, David H. (PAT)
Messaro, Michael, *m.ss.cc.*
Metsy, Norman (PRO)
Metzbower, Francis X., *s.j.*
Middendorf, Cyril, *s.m.*
Mooney, Msgr. Robert M. (PRO)
Morley, John (NEW)
Mulhern, Joseph P., *o.p.*
Murphy, Dennis F., *s.a.*
Murphy, Msgr. Terrence J. (STP)
Nakireru, Omoviekobwa A. (Nigeria)
Nguyen, Huong Xuan (NO)
O'Donnell, Brian, *s.j.*
O'Keeffe, Msgr. Richard W. (TUC)
O'Loughlin, Michael, *s.s.c.*
O'Meara, Henry R., *c.ss.r.*
O'Neill, Joseph, *m.m.*
Olson, Benedict, *o.p.*
Ondo, Michael A., (LAF)
Perumpilly, Marcel (Bahrain)
Phillips, Christopher (SA)
Phillips, Randall (DET)
Picard, Norman, *c.i.c.m.*
Piskura, Joseph (CLV)
Potter, Gerald L. (FAR)
Power, Bernard, *c.ss.r.*
Quinlivan, Francis L., *c.s.c.*
Regan, John J. (BO)
Richardson, Edward, *s.m.a.*
Rimmele, Leo, *o.s.b.*
Roberson, Ronald G., *c.p.*
Rokusek, Robert (DET)
St. Pierre, Romeo A. (PRT)
Sanders, Peter, *c.o.*
Saucci, Robert R., *m.m.*
Scheller, John (OKL)
Schmidt, Raymond (BRK)
Schreiber, Gerard, c.ss.r.
Sego, Msgr. Arthur (LFT)
Shay, Michael, *s.d.s.*
Shay, Robert M., *s.t.*
Simonelli, Bruno, *o.f.m.cap.*
Smith, Ignatius E., *o.f.m.*
Smith, Msgr. Thomas (HBG)
Sousa, Peter, *c.ss.r.*
Spiteri, Joseph (Panama)
Stadmueller, Roman, *s.d.s.*
Stodola, Francis (CC)
Succi, Vincento, *o.f.m.cap.*
Sueper, Alban A., *s.s.c.*
Sullivan, Alan, *o.f.m.*
Thelen, Robert (BRK)
Thomas, Donald (HON)
Thorne, Carrol W., *c.p.*
Tomas, Francisco (Azores)
Valenti, Palmo, *s.f.*
Vaz, Rock I., *s.j.*
Waite, Patrick (SC)
Walljasper, Mark A. (LC)
Wood, Michael (SA)
Woster, Michael B. (RC)

DEPARTMENT OF VETERANS AFFAIRS HOSPITALS AND CHAPLAINS

Rev. **Ronald Lawson (Montreal), Associate Dir.**

ALABAMA

Birmingham
Vacant

Montgomery
Rev. David J. Tokarz (MOB)

Tuscaloosa
Vacant

Tuskegee
Vacant

ARIZONA

Phoenix
Rev. Kenneth R. Kleiber (CHI)

Prescott
Rev. Gerald J. Caffrey, *c.m.f.*

Tucson
Rev. David H. Reinders, (TUC)

ARKANSAS

Fayetteville
Vacant

North Little Rock
Rev. Victor E. Bertrand, *c.s.v.*

CALIFORNIA

Fresno
Revs. Richard F. Bevenour (DAV)
David LaPierre, *o.f.m.cap.*

Loma Linda
Rev. Msgr. Adolph Chavez (SB)
Rev. Aquinas J. Smith (SD)

Long Beach
Rev. Anselm T. Deehr, *s.t.*

Palo Alto
Revs. John Kenneth Coleman (SFR)
Augustine Koilparampil (India)

San Diego
Revs. Patrick J. Durkin, *c.s.v.*
Charles R. Eis (SPK)
Theodore Gryga (SY)
Jerry Hamperzonian (PSC)

San Francisco
Rev. Francis P. Filice (SFR)

Sepulveda
Rev. Patrick J. O'Hagan, *ss.cc.*

West Los Angeles
Rev. Francis Kelly (LA)

COLORADO

Denver
Rev. Thomas J. Woerth (DEN)

Fort Lyon
Rev. George S. Reynolds, *o.p.*

Grand Junction
Vacant

CONNECTICUT

Newington
Vacant

West Haven
Rev. Daniel Scott, *m.s.*

DELAWARE
Wilmington
Revs. Sean P. Connery, *o.s.f.s.*
William J. Dougherty, *o.s.f.s*

DISTRICT OF COLUMBIA
Rev. Jonathan D. Lao (Philippines)

FLORIDA
Bay Pines
Revs. Arthur D. Murray, *o.f.m.*
E. Matthew Turk, *s.j.*
Gainesville
Rev. Francisco Revilla (STA)
Lake City
Revs. Anthony Sebra (STA)
Patrick L. Murphy, *s.j.*
Miami
Revs. Rinaldo Damian (WOR)
J. Luis Fernandez (NO)
Tampa
Rev. Robert Schindler (Mexico)
West Palm Beach
Rev. Joseph B. Westfall (LFT)

GEORGIA
Augusta
Revs. P. James Costigan (SAV)
Miguel Grave de Peralta (NTN)
Thomas J. Peyton (SAV)
Decatur
Vacant
Dublin
Vacant

IDAHO
Boise
Rev. Simeon VanDeVoord, *o.s.b.*

ILLINOIS
Chicago—Lakeside
Rev. Robert J. Borre (MAD)
Chicago—West Side
Vacant
Danville
Rev. John Schultz (LFT)
Hines
Revs. James Burnett (DAV)
Max E.M. Saldua (Philippines)
Marion
Vacant
North Chicago
Revs. Paul B. McDermott (PEO)
William Vander Heyden (GB)

INDIANA
Fort Wayne
Rev. Daniel R. Leeuw (FTW)
Indianapolis
Revs. Joseph Kiene, *o.f.m.conv.*
Gordon P. Wagoner (LFT)
Marion
Rev. Joseph W. Grace (FTW)

IOWA
Des Moines
Rev. Paul S. Holt (WDC)
Iowa City
Revs. Andrew E. Kelly (DAV)
Louis J. Leonhart (DAV)
Brian J. Shepley (DAV)
Knoxville
Rev. Sylvester A. Conrad (DAV)

KANSAS
Leavenworth
Rev. Carrol W. Thorne, *c.p.*
Topeka
Rev. James E. Moster, *o.f.m.cap.*
Wichita
Rev. H. Patrick Malone (WCH)

KENTUCKY
Lexington
Revs. Wilton Henry Kenney, *s.j.*
George Maynard, *s.j.*
Louisville
Vacant

LOUISIANA
Alexandria
Revs. Stephen J. Brandow (ALX)
Christudas A. Nayak (India)
New Orleans
Revs. Lawrence A. DeMaria (NO)
Joseph Laboon (PIT)
Shreveport
Rev. Philip Michiels (ALX)

MAINE
Togus
Rev. Raymond R. Lagace, *o.f.m.*

MARYLAND
Baltimore
Revs. Paul J. Henry (BAL)
Edward T. Hill (BAL)
Stephen E. Jeselnick (E)
Fort Howard
Rev. Conan H. Timoney, *c.p.*
Perry Point
Revs. John J. Abrahams (BAL)
Paul J. Henry (BAL)
Jeffrie S. Reynolds (BIR)

MASSACHUSETTS
Bedford
Revs. Philip Cabasino, *c.ss.r.*
Joseph P. Robinson (BO)
Boston
Revs. Philip Salois (FR)
Roger A. Sinclair (GBG)
Brockton
Revs. Avelino R. Garcia (SP)
Henry Nichols (BO)
Northampton
Rev. Lionel E. Bonneville (SPR)

MICHIGAN
Ann Arbor
Revs. Luke U. Odor (ABA)
Vincent VanDoan (LAN)
Battle Creek
Rev. Patrick E. Murphy (MAR)
Detroit
Rev. Joseph Duc Vu (Vietnam)
Iron Mountain
Vacant
Saginaw
Revs. Richard E. Jozwiak (SAG)
Joseph A. Schabel (SAG)

MINNESOTA
Minneapolis
Rev. Joseph N. Safraniec (STU)
St. Cloud
Rev. Alfred E. Stangl (SCL)

MISSISSIPPI
Biloxi
Revs. Joseph A. Dilettuso (BLX)
Anthony E. Menz, *o.c.s.o.*
Jackson
Rev. Daniel N. Gallagher (JKS)

MISSOURI
Columbia
Rev. Edwin J. Cole (JC)
Kansas City
Rev. Ambrose Karels (KC)
Poplar Bluff
Rev. Michael V. McDevitt (SPC)
St. Louis
Revs. George P. Brennan (STL)
Patrick J. Christopher (STL)
John H. Schneider (STL)

MONTANA
Fort Harrison
Vacant
Miles City
Vacant

NEBRASKA
Grand Island
Revs. Donald O'Brien (GI)
Walter M. Phelan (GI)
David L. Rykwalder (GI)
Omaha
Rev. Richard Wolbach (OM)

NEVADA
Las Vegas
Rev. Gerard J. McNulty (LA)
Reno
Vacant

NEW HAMPSHIRE
Manchester
Revs. William J. Hamilton, *s.j.*
Francis A. Talbot (MAN)

NEW JERSEY
East Orange
Rev. Thomas J. Davis, *o.f.m.cap.*
Lyons
Revs. Joseph C. Chacko (India)
George F. Kelly, *c.ss.r.*
William Warman (BAL)

NEW MEXICO
Albuquerque
Revs. David O. Klein, *c.s.b.*
Julian M. Rousseau, *s.s.s.*

NEW YORK
Albany
Revs. John Minkler (ALB)
Dominick Ntsiful-Amissah (ALB)
Charles S. San Fratello, *o.f.m.*
Batavia
Revs. Donald W. Becker (BUF)
Ivan R. Trujillo (BUF)
Bath
Rev. David L. Carson (NY)
Bronx
Revs. Roland P. LaFontant (France)
Michael A. Lipareli (NY)
Gregory Lyttle (NY)
Rev. Msgr. Joseph J. Zammit (NY)
Brooklyn
Revs. Luke M. Karpil (Philippines)
Thomas J. Mullin (NY)
Vito Tiboni (NEW)
Buffalo
Rev. Francis Chmielewski (BUF)
Canandaigua
Revs. Miecislaus Curzydlo, *s.a.c.*
Francis Vogt (ROC)
Castle Point
Revs. Robert J. Brennan (NY)
Uldarico De la Pena (Philippines)
Raymond A. Pavlick (PAT)
Montrose
Revs. Joseph W. Hickey (NY)
Robert D. Tracy, *o.carm.*
New York City
Rev. Pasquale V. Laghezza, *ss.cc.*
Northport
Revs. John S. Malone, *c.s.sp.*
Lazar David Mani (India)
Augustine Sheehan (RVC)

Syracuse
Revs. Wilfred F. Evans (SY)
David J. James (SY)
Gregory C. LeStrange (SY)

NORTH CAROLINA
Asheville
Rev. Andrew J. Latsko (CHL)
Durham
Vacant
Fayetteville
Rev. Alexander O. Nakireru (Nigeria)
Salisbury
Rev. Thomas P. Clements (CHL)

NORTH DAKOTA
Fargo
Vacant

OHIO
Chillicothe
Revs. Jose C. Bengco (Philippines)
Richard F. Engle (COL)
Cincinnati
Revs. Matthias J. Crehan, *o.f.m.*
Warren Zeisler, *o.f.m.*
Cleveland
Revs. John Bolan, *c.pp.s.*
James N. Drucker (PSC)
Thomas J. Gallagher (CLV)
Dayton
Revs. John J. Butler (HON)
Edward P. Walsh (BIR)

OKLAHOMA
Muskogee
Vacant
Oklahoma City
Vacant

OREGON
Portland
Rev. William Wickham, *c.s.c.*
Roseburg
Vacant
White City
Revs. Donald H. Salisbury, *o.p.*
Joseph Shirey, *s.j.*

PENNSYLVANIA
Altoona
Rev. Edward Dabcosky (ALT)
Butler
Revs. Henry Preneta (GBG)
William J. Ritzert (PIT)
Coatesville
Revs. Joseph S. Hasieber (ALX)
McKinley E. Williams (RIC)
Erie
Revs. Robert G. Craig (E)
Thomas M. Fialkowski (E)
Lebanon
Revs. Joseph S. Hasieber (ALX)
Dennis M. Young (STA)
Philadelphia
Revs. Edward V. Griffin, *o.s.a.*
Gerald F. (Damien) Schill (FAR)
Pittsburgh—Highland Drive
Revs. Robert N. Craig, *o.f.m.cap.*
Frank A. Mitolo (PIT)
Emett J. Schuler, *o.f.m.cap.*
Pittsburgh—University Drive
Revs. Mark W. Glasgow (PIT)
Ralph Zehe, *o.f.m.cap.*
Wilkes-Barre
Rev. Benjamin Foerch, *o.f.m.*

RHODE ISLAND
Providence
Revs. Francis J. Crowley (BO)
Dennis P. Murphy (RIC)

SOUTH CAROLINA
Charleston
Rev. William C. Burn (CHR)
Columbia
Vacant

SOUTH DAKOTA
Fort Meade
Rev. Paul Dahms (RC)
Hot Springs
Rev. Thomas Tierney, *s.j.*
Sioux Falls
Rev. Kenneth J. Koster (SFS)

TENNESSEE
Memphis
Vacant
Mountain Home
Vacant
Murfreesboro
Vacant
Nashville
Rev. James Norman Miller (NSH)

TEXAS
Amarillo
Rev. George Thekkedam (LUB)
Big Spring
Rev. Jeremiah McCarthy, *m.s.c.*
Bonham
Rev. Felix F. Vistal (DAL)
Dallas
Rev. Timothy Gollob (DAL)
Houston
Revs. Peter Girardin (BO)
Clarito Z. Rara (Philippines)
Kerrville
Rev. Michael J. Boulette (SAT)
Marlin
Vacant
San Antonio
Rev. Harry Martin (SAT)
Temple
Rev. Richard J. Beyer (DAV)
Waco
Rev. Thomas Niemira (JKS)

UTAH
Salt Lake City
Revs. Gebran Bou-Merhi (SAM)
Reyes Garcis Rodriguez (SLC)

VERMONT
White River Junction
Revs. Adrien Pelletier, *s.m.*
Ronald Saunders, *s.m.*

VIRGINIA
Hampton
Revs. Donald Cavey (RIC)
Lloyd F. Stephenson (RIC)
Richmond
Rev. Lou Ruoff (RIC)
Salem
Rev. Thomas E. Mattingly (RIC)

WASHINGTON
Seattle
Rev. Thomas R. Park, *o.s.b.*
Spokane
Rev. Theodore F. X. Bradley (SPK)
Tacoma
Rev. Leo R. Rimmele, *o.s.b.*
Walla Walla
Rev. Otto Koltzenburg (SPK)

WEST VIRGINIA
Beckley
Vacant
Clarksburg
Rev. Peter A. Giannamore (WH)
Huntington
Rev. Andrew G. Kranyc (WH)
Martinsburg
Revs. William E. Coen, *s.t.*
T. Matthew Rowgh (WH)

WISCONSIN
Madison
Vacant
Milwaukee
Revs. Edward E. Lisowski (MIL)
Norman Oswald (MIL)
Tomah
Revs. Timothy E. Svea (LC)
Sebastian A. Ugochukwu (Nigeria)

WYOMING
Cheyenne
Vacant
Sheridan
Revs. John B. Norton, *o.p.*
Eugene P. Sullivan (CHY)

PUERTO RICO
San Juan
Revs. Hector Diaz (SJN)
Luis A. Lopez-Alvarado (CGS)

RESERVE CHAPLAINS

Reverends
Albrecht, Louis (BAK)
Alexander, Marc R. (HON)
Almendras, Joel (MRY)
Ameling, Richard H. (GRY)
Amora, Edito (Philippines)
Anderson, Ronald C. (BWN)
Arens, John F. (BO)
Arroyo, Brigido (Guam)
Augustyn, Boguslaw (Poland)
Austin, Walter (NO)
Baggetta, Joseph J. (BO)
Bailey, Douglas, *s.d.s.*
Bain, John K. (RNO)
Baratelli, David (NEW)
Barber, Michael, *s.j.*
Barch, Howard C., Jr., (PEO)
Barnhill, Robert K. (LIN)
Barry, Robert L., *o.p.*
Becker, Donald W. (BUF)
Beers, Michael (ALN)
Belanger, Gerald R.
Bendorf, Richard D., *o.f.m.*
Berberich, Thomas E. (HRT)
Bergbower, Daniel J. (SPC)
Betts, David A. (SCR)
Betz, James F. (CAM)
Beyer, Richard J. (DAV)
Bill, Ronald C. (SY)
Borlang, Stephen M. (Iceland)
Bowe, John F. (PH)
Bower, Lawrence (BAK)
Brando, Joseph (KNX)
Bratko, Kenneth R., *c.r.*
Brennan, Eugene P. (STL)
Brinkmann, Frederick C., *c.ss.r.*

RESERVE CHAPLAINS ***(Cont.)***

Brubaker, George (WIL)
Bucon, Raymond H. (DET)
Budnar, Randy J. (MAD)
Burns, Malcolm (GAL)
Butler, Michael (STL)
Butler, William L. (BO)
Calderone, Joseph D., *o.s.a.*
Camarda, Ronald A. (STA)
Campos, George C. (STO)
Canez, Jorge A. (PHX)
Cannon, Richard (BO)
Cannon, Robert (VEN)
Caputo, Louis, *s.d.v.*
Carmody, James F. (WOR)
Caron, David (BO)
Carrington, Richard J. (NEW)
Carter, Eli K., Jr. (HON)
Casaleggio, David (RNO)
Castillejo-Llusia, Jorge (SJN)
Chavez, Johnny Lee (SFE)
Cheney, James W. (FAR)
Chimiak, Karl A. (WDC)
Cienik, Kenneth, *s.a.*
Clark, John S., *s.s.s.*
Clark, Robert J., *o.s.b.*
Clarke, Thomas J., *c.s.c.*
Coe, Austin J. (Korea)
Coffey, Joseph (PH)
Collogan, Robert E. (JOL)
Condon, William G., *c.s.c.*
Condron, Patrick (WH)
Connelly, Christian T. (ARL)
Connolly, Leo L. (COL)
Congro, Basil (CHR)
Connor, Kevin (MAN)
Coogan, Roch A., *o.f.m.*
Cordery, Robert (BO)
Corneille, Cecil C. (STV)
Coulthard, Gregory, *s.d.s.*
Coyle, Edward J. (ALN)
Crews, John S. (SR)
Cronin, Daniel (CGS)
Crosby, Msgr. Charles E. (MAN)
Crotty, Desmond (NO)
Cuevas, Randy M. (BR)
Curcio, Ralph V. (NY)
Curley, Thomas J. (NY)
Dare, Glenn O. (PRT)
Darling, William G. (ROC)
D'Aurora, Joseph (RIC)
Dean, James N. (MOB)
Decker, Douglas A. (OG)
DeGuzman, Dennis (OM)
Denemark, Emil J., *s.j.*
DePorter, Arnold (WDC)
DeSanctis, Peter A. (BRK)
DeSocia, John (ROC)
Diacetis, Anthony (ALB)
Diegel, Ronald (FRS)
Diesta, Arwyn N. (Philippines)
DiLella, Mario (ATL)
Dinello, John E. (PIT)
Dolbec, Jacques D. (CC)
Donahue, Brian G. (FAR)
Donohoe, Richard (BIR)
Donohue, Michael T. (NOR)
Doran, John E. (WOR)
Dowling, Joseph K. (NSH)
Doyle, Michael J. (BO)
Drotar, Kent F. (DEN)
Duesterhaus, Michael (ARL)
Dura, Eduardo A. (SFR)
Duzza, Donald (ALT)
Dziedzic, Gerald H. (HRT)
Echert, John Paul (STP)
Echevia, Les Suberi (Philippines)
Emechete, Innocent A. (Nigeria)
Engelbrecht, Henry (NO)
Esquibel, Msgr. John L. (SFE)
Ethen, Jeffrey (SCL)
Evans, James L. (AUS)
Everett, Willis E. (COL)
Farana, Mario P. (SFR)
Farley, Daniel (LC)
Fawcett, Msgr. Henry F. (SD)
Fehn, Jerome W. (STP)
Feltz, John G. (BUR)
Fernandes, Stephen (FR)
Fialkowski, Thomas M. (E)
Fischer, Richard O. (BAK)
Fitzgibbons, Peter (CHL)
Fitzpatrick, Robert M. (OM)
Flanigan, Thomas P. (PH)
Folsom, Paul (SCL)
Foote, John, *o.s.b.*
Forry, Thomas P. (BO)
Fredericks, Michael (SB)
Fronk, Christopher, *s.j.*
Fukes, Gary (SY)
Gaeta, Bernard N. (Y)
Gaglione, John R. (BUF)
Gallagher, John P. (DAV)
Gallagher, William (BUF)
Garcia, Millan J., *s.f.*
Gayton, John, *m.i.c.*
Gegotek, Tadeusz J. (BEL)
Gerres, Daniel (WIL)
Giese, Samuel (WDC)
Gills, Thomas (BAL)
Giordani, Mark J. (PAT)
Girardin, Peter T. (BO)
Glasgow, Thomas (NO)
Glassmire, David R. (BUF)
Granadino, David F. (LA)
Greig, Harry D. (LAF)
Grice, Edward M. (NO)
Griffin, Thomas E., *o.s.a.*
Gross, Gary L. (LIN)
Gutierrez, Jose M. (CC)
Haddad, Wayne (MET)
Hamaday, Ronald A., *o.s.a.*
Hannigan, John (CHI)
Hart, John B. (SLC)
Healy, Stephen M. (BOS)
Hebert, Donald J. (SY)
Hendel, Lawrence M. (SJ)
Henke, Donald E. (STL)
Henke, James T. (SA)
Heninger, Michael B. (ATL)
Henson, Jerome M., *o.p.*
Herbert, G. Paul (WDC)
Herzog, Ronald P. (BLX)
Hewes, Robert (RVC)
Hirten, Timothy (BRK)
Hoak, Jack W., *o.f.m.*
Hoedl, Daniel (FAR)
Hoffman, Christopher (ORL)
Hogan, Michael J. (CHI)
Holzhauser, John J. (SF)
Honan, Eugene D. (SPR)
Hower, William (MAD)
Hubbs, Timothy (SCR)
Hudak, Thomas R. (SCR)
Hughes, Donald R. (BUF)
Humenay, Robert L. (E)
Ianucci, Thomas (RIC)
Isopo, Dominic (ALB)
Jackson, James (WCH)
Jackson, Robert (CLV)
Jacques, Roger N. (BO)
Jaeger, James (ROC)
Jankowski, Daniel (CHI)
Janecek, James E. (CC)
Jaramillo, Peter (AMA)
Jeselnick, Stephen E. (E)
Johnson, James B. (SP)
Johnson, Patrick *c.s.p.*
Jones, Michael (WDC)
Judge, Timothy M. (PH)
Kadera, Thomas (CHY)
Kahlich, Daniel (SA)
Kane, Edward R. (BRK)
Kantor, Robert (VEN)
Kasprzyk, James (BUF)
Kaszcak, Ivan (STF)
Kayatta, Francis P. (PRO)
Keenan, Patrick J. (NY)
Kehoe, James P. (CHI)
Keller, Robert J. (DET)
Keller, Thomas W. (LR)
Kiene, Joseph L., *o.f.m.conv.*
Kilian, Waldemar (CHI)
Kilmurray, Finton (BLX)
Kinnane, James F. (HRT)
Kinney, Thomas E. (NO)
Kiselica, John J., *s.m.*
Koster, Kenneth J. (SF)
Kowalik, Jacek (VEN)
Kozen, Bert S. (SCR)
Krische, James (BR)
Krough, Jack Lee (WIN)
Kruse, David B. (BAL)
Kuczborski, Joseph (PEO)
Kukucka, Joseph (PBL)
Kurzak, John F. (SC)
Kusmirek, Mark C. (TYL)
Labo, Timothy (ORL)
Ladniak, Lawrence J. (CHI)
Laible, Jeffrey (PEO)
LaMorte, Joseph P. (NY)
Lane, Frank (COL)
Lang, James P. (Y)
Langan, William J.P. (SCR)
Larche, James (OG)
Laroche, Christopher (PRT)
Lavastida, Jose I. (NO)
Lawrence, Andrew (DUB)
Legaspi, Alex (SFR)
Leone, William B. (ROC)
Lioi, Phillip J. (ROC)
Listecki, Jerome E. (CHI)
Lomax, Mark (NO)
Lordemann, Francis W. (OM)
Ludwig, Thomas (KC)
Lyle, John W., *o.s.f.s.*
McCabe, Kenneth O., *ss.cc.*
McCarthy, James C. (HEL)
McConville, James P. (STP)
McDonald, G. Malcolm (PIT)
McGinnis, James J. (PH)
McGrade, Kevin (BO)
McGuill, Martin F. (ARL)
McGuine, Peter (SD)
McInnis, Francis L. (GF)
McLaughlin, Peter A. (CAM)
McLaughlin, Richard P. (BO)
McNalis, John P. (CHI)
McNamara, Brian J. (RVC)
McSchane, James J. (BUR)
Macek, Joseph S., *s.s.j.*
Mack, John (BUF)
Madus, Peter P. (SCR)
Maguire, Stephen (NY)
Mahalic, Philip A. (LAF)
Maikowski, Thomas R. (GLP)
Malloy, Francis X. (MIL)
Manzo, Louis A., *c.s.c.*
Marcinano, Robert (PRO)
Martinez, Michael (TUC)
Matheny, William K. (WH)
Mathis, Raymond P. (SY)
Matienzo, Ariel R. (Arecibo)
Maughan, Richard N. (NO)
Mazziotta, Richard, *c.s.c.*
Medairos, Anthony (BO)
Meier, Denis E. (SFS)
Merrell, Arthur (PIT)
Mescher, Michael (DUB)
Messier, Joseph H. (BUR)
Metzdorf, William C. (WDC)
Midura, Francis S. (RVC)
Minder, Kevin W. (YAK)
Mink, John (WIL)
Mitolo, Frank A. (PIT)
Mizeur, Thomas R. (PEO)
Mockler, Patrick (BLX)
Molloy, Msgr. Thomas E. (RVC)
Monagle, Robert J. (BO)
Monekedick, Leo (SCL)
Moore, William (STO)
Moran, Michael (MIL)
Morris, Michael P. (NY)
Moss, Robert D. (BUF)
Motta, Anthony (ALB)
Mullin, Thomas (NY)
Murphy, David F. (WIL)
Murray, Gerald (NY)

RESERVE CHAPLAINS ***(Cont.)***

Musni, Eduardo (Philippines)
Myers, Christopher (CC)
Naughton, William M. (PAT)
Neitzke, Ron (JOL)
Nenneau, Thomas D. (LAN)
Neuman, Eugene C. (MIL)
Nguyen, Van T. (NO)
Nishigaya, Raymond J. (HON)
Nolan, Kevin L. (LA)
Noone, Charles J. (PH)
O'Brien, Sean (SY)
O'Connell, Terry (P)
O'Connor, John L. (ROC)
O'Donoghue, John J. (SA)
O'Hara, Daniel (SY)
O'Hear, Daniel J. (SPR)
O'Leary, David M. (BO)
O'Malley, John J., *o.p.*
Oberts, David P. (SUP)
Oge, Raymond J. (STL)
Orlandi, Joseph (PAT)
Padazinski, Michael (SFR)
Pagan, Alberto, *o.p.*
Parenti, Thomas M. (SFR)
Parker, Paul R. (BO)
Parker, Forrest Todd (RVC)
Pelletier, George C. (PRT)
Peoples, Joseph E. (HEL)
Perez, John C. (SJN)
Perez-Torro, Carlos (SJN)
Piekarczyk, Marian, *s.d.s.*
Piontkowski, Richard (GI)
Plaushin, Mark F., *o.s.f.s.*
Pleiness, Gregg A. (LAN)
Polk, Thomas T. (BAL)
Posey, Thaddeus J., *o.f.m.cap.*
Prez, Daniel J. (E)
Prinz, Gerald (HT)
Quinn, James A. (MIA)
Randall, Kevn S. (NOR)
Reamer, Mark, *o.f.m.*
Reilly, David F. (CIN)
Reyes, Marco (LA)
Richtsteig, Eric J. (SLC)
Rigdon, Vincent J. (WDC)
Rimassa, Paul (TR)
Rivera-Saez, Adalin (PCE)
Robbins, Thomas (COV)
Roberson, Henry (OKL)
Robert, Darin Thomass (LAN)
Robichaud, Paul G., *c.s.p.*
Rodriguez, Rafael A. (CGS)
Rogers, Francis J. (WIL)
Rogers, Patrick W. (COL)
Rowan, Mark (RVC)
Rowe, William (SAC)
Russo, Richardo, *o.f.m.*
Sable, Robert (DET)
Sacus, Samuel S. (WH)
St. Martin, Robert J. (HRT)
Santana, Edward (CGS)
Santiago-Burgess, Felipe (SJN)
Sanchez, Angel (Ponce)
Sanchez-Munoz, Alejandro (STV)
Scalone, Jonathan (FWT)
Schaff, Tyrone J. (SP)
Schaub, Gregory P., *o.s.b.*
Schindler, Carl A., *c.ss.r.*
Seminack, Richard S. (PH)
Sera, Enrique J. (ORG)
Sewell, Jack K. (ORG)
Shannon, Richard (CHI)
Shea, Michael J. (SFE)
Sheehan, Joseph P. (PH)
Sickler, Robert, *m.ss.a.*
Silva, Caesar (HT)
Sippel, Bernard S. (MIL)
Sirianni, Richard D. (P)
Skufca, Ronald (MAR)
Slowinski, Thomas (DET)
Smith, Francis J. (ELP)
Smith, Gabriel (CHR)
Smith, Lawrence C., *s.j.*
Smith, Lawrence H. (BRK)
Sousa, Peter S., *c.ss.r.*
Spellman, John, *o.s.f.s.*
Spencer, Robert (CHR)
Spiegel, Thomas J. (DAV)
Spring, Mark S. (DAV)
Stakem, Ward G., *o.f.m.cap.*
Stang, William, *c.pp.s.*
Sta.Maria, Nicanor (SJN)
Staszewski, Joseph P. (E)
Staszewski, Robert M. (PIT)
Stefula, Salvatore M., *t.o.r.*
Steiner, John W. (LC)
Stenson, Patrick J., *m.s.c.*
Stephenson, Alfonse (PAT)
Stevens, David, (SFS)
Stewart, Paul (PT)
Sticco, Peter, *s.a.c.*
Stites, John F. (TOL)
Strittmatter, Lawrence R. (CIN)
Stodola, Francis (CC)
Sturn, Michael L. (SB)
Suellentrop, Anthony (DOD)
Sullivan, Robert J. (BIR)
Sutton, Stephen R. (BAL)
Sweeney, Daniel, *s.j.*
Szczesniak, Harry F. (BUF)
Tamalis, John J. (SCR)
Taylor, Samuel J. (NY)
Taylor, Thomas (LAN)
Tejada, Denis J. (LC)
Tero, Richard D. (ANC)
Tetreault, Raymond A. (PRO)
Theroux, Paul D. (PRO)
Thomas, Royce R. (LR)
Thompson, Richard B. (MAN)
Thorne, Thomas P. (BGP)
Tirado, Ramon O. (SJN)
Toner, Patrick A. (COL)
Trabold, George R. (NEW)
Tracy, Robert D., *o.carm.*
Tran, Duy Kim N. (NEW)
Tran, Luan Quach (P)
Travers, Patrick (JUN)
Troha, Michel J. (CLV)
Troutman, Richard E. (TUC)
Tuite, Thomas (RVC)
Tykhovych, Ivan (STF)
Tyrrell, Robert D. (BO)
Ugwuanya, Valentine C. (NEW)
Uhde, Peter M. (NEW)
Urnick, Charles B. (NEW)
Valenzano, Joseph A. (BRK)
Valko, George J. (ALT)
Vavarek, Hayden (CHR)
Ventura, John J. (BIR)
Verbrugghe, Albert E. (TUC)
Vialpando, Kenneth L. (SLC)
Vigil, Michael (GLP)
Vigilanti, John A. (NY)
Vu, Joseph Duc (Vietnam)
Vucinovich, Albert P. (SFR)
Wagner, William C. (CIN)
Waibel, Philip, *o.s.b.*
Wallace, Richard J. (P)
Weber, Joseph A. (STL)
Wedeking, Patrick (GLP)
Welton, Arthur T. (NY)
Wendel, Alfred W. (CHY)
Wielunski, Gregory C. (BRK)
Willette, Donald (DEN)
Williams, John L. (HRT)
Williams, Ronald R. (DET)
Wilz, John C. (PH)
Worster, John (B)
Wulinski, Stanley (BRK)
Zeck, George F. (DUL)
Zerwas, Richard D. (SFE)
Ziemkiewicz, Frank, *o.s.b.*
Zientek, Benedict J. (SAN)

CIVIL AIR PATROL CHAPLAINS

Reverends

Allen, Joseph P. (CHI)
Ausperk, Michael D. (CLV)
Berean, Christopher H. (NY)
Birk, John G. (SPK)
Booth, Edward N. (STA)
Borkowski, Thomas (KC)
Brown, John T. (OWN)
Cameron, Albert S. (MAN)
Cantlow, Cronan (BAL)
Carney, John J. (BAL)
Caron, Eduardo J., *c.ss.p.*
Churchill, Raymond (HON)
DeCrans, Joseph J. (CR)
DeMure, Salvatore Patrick (HRT)
Devaney, Michael, *o.m.i.*
Diener, John E. (CIN)
Dupuis, George H. (BUR)
Duran, Alphonsus M., *m.j.*
Ebner, Frank H. (SCL)
Elliott, Edward C. (MEM)
Emala, Walter (MEM)
Farland, David M. (SPR)
Fitzgerald, John P. (PIT)
Friederick, John J. (DUB)
Goeser, Peter J., *o.s.b.*
Greer, Michael G. (COV)
Guischard, John A. (BUR)
Hayden, Joseph M. (CAM)
Hennington, Bruce M. (MAD)
Hoffmaster, Harry E. (DET)
Hurley, Most Rev. Francis T. (ANC)
Kaszczak, Ivan (STF)
Kelley, James F. (FR)
Kelly, George F., *c.ss.r.*
King, James E. (NTN)
Kost, Harold J. (SCL)
Kovarik, James, *o.s.cam.* (MIL)
Kremeier, James (GI)
LaBuda, David E., *m.m.*
Lamitie, Robert O. (OG)
LaPlante, Jean Paul (BUR)
LaPorte, Paul (PRO)
Lopez, Humberto, (MGZ)
McGuire, Richard J. (E)
McQuillen, Thomas J. (TOL)
Maag, Ronald (BAK)
Maskell, Anthony J. (BAL)
Merrill, Arthur R. (PIT)
Michalski, Thaddeus (CLV)
Miller, Bruce (ALX)
Nevins, Albert J., *m.m.*
Nollette, Neal P. (GI)
O'Connell, Msgr. James E. (LR)
Ondik, Michael J. (CLV)
Orlando, Vincent, *s.j.*
Parker, James (CHR)
Phillips, George M. (OG)
Quinn, Richard M., *c.ss.r.*
Ratchford, Robert J., *s.j.*
Reiter, James (E)
Scanlan, Cornelius J. (JUN)
Scanlan, Francis G. (CHI)
Schaefer, Roman J. (MIA)
Sevigny, Robert, *o.m.i.*
Shamsher, Paul (HRT)
Shortt, David J. (PBR)
Smalley, William R. (NEW)
Smith, Lawrence C., *s.j.*

CIVIL AIR PATROL CHAPLAINS (Cont.)

Sommer, Allan J. (MIL)
Strachota, Dennis J. (BAL)
Smith, Lawrence C., *s.j.*
Therrien, Shawn M. (MAN)
Van Sickler, Robert (BAK)
Vaughan, Richard F. (AMA)
Vogel, Walter J. (MIL)
Voity, Maurice J. (SAN)
Walters, James L. (LR)
Weber, Gabriel M., *o.s.m.*
Williams, John L. (HRT)
Wolesky, John A. (SAL)

PERMANENT DEACONS SERVING IN THE ARCHDIOCESE FOR THE MILITARY SERVICES

AMS Chancery
Deacon
Crowley, Ronald C.

Air Force
Deacons
Bonanno, Frederick R.
Ellis, Billy Joe
Henn, Dr. Thomas W.
Jachimowicz, John J.
Kwon, Peter H.
McAtee, Ralph H., Jr.
Neville, Richard F.
Perry, Robert W.
Pfleger, James W.
Pinto, Richard A.
Prentiss, Richard C.
Richardson, Walter H.
Scarbo, David B.
Sekinger, Eugene E.
Shields, Floyd M.
Sliger, Douglas R.
Stoll, F. Michael
Yarawsky, William S.

Air National Guard
Deacons
Salchert, Dr. John J.
Sloan, Joseph S.

Army
Deacons
Adam, Klaus M.
Barnard Robert P.
Dew, Joseph M.
Foster, George H.
Jones, Frederick B., Jr.
Kelly, James A.
Miller, Larry L.
Plowman, Kent M.
Rienzi, Thomas M.
Rowland, Robert D.
Schoebel, James G.
Shuffer, George M.

Army National Guard
Deacon
Salchert, Dr. John J.

Army Reserve
Deacon
Haddad, Victor (USAR)

Navy
Deacons
Gubatan, Nemsy, Jr.
Krebs, Brian J.
Ladouceur, Gerald J.
McGlade, Henry D.
Nartowicz, Edward C.
Pellosie, Dr. John C.
Pepe, Joseph A.
Rauen, Michael J.
Ryan, Richard R.
Wurm, Eugene L.

Marines
Deacon
Hernandez, Nieves J.

State Department
Deacon
Perez, Julio T.

Veterans Administration
Deacons
Abler, Donald J.
Dixon, Louis C.
Hare, Martin J.
Luft, Dennis M.
Martino, Anthony
Mills, Hugh, H., Jr.
Moseley, Cyrus P.
Rinkus, Louis P.
Salchert, Dr. John J.
Stenbeck, John H.
Watson, John W.

Civil Air Patrol
Deacon
Schaible, John A.

DIOCESES WITH PRIESTS SERVING IN THE ARCHDIOCESE FOR THE MILITARY SERVICES

Albany
Alexandria
Allentown
Altoona-Johnstown
Arlington
Atlanta
Austin
Baltimore
Baton Rouge
Beaumont
Belleville
Biloxi
Birmingham
Bismarck
Boston
Bridgeport
Brooklyn
Buffalo
Burlington
Caguas, Puerto Rico
Camden
Canton (Romanian Catholic Diocese of St. George)
Caroline Islands
Charleston
Charlotte
Cheyenne
Chicago
Cincinnati
Cleveland
Columbus
Corpus Christi
Covington
Dallas
Davenport
Denver
Detroit
Dubuque
Duluth
El Paso
Erie
Fargo
Fort Wayne-South Bend
Fresno
Gallup
Galveston-Houston
Grand Island
Grand Rapids
Great Falls-Billings
Green Bay
Greensburg
Hartford
Helena
Honolulu
Jackson
Jefferson City
Joliet
Kansas City
Kansas City-St. Joseph
LaCrosse
Lafayette, IN
Lafayette, LA
Lansing
Los Angeles
Louisville
Lubbock
Madison
Manchester
Marquette
Memphis
Metuchen
Miami
Milwaukee
Mobile
Nashville
Newark
New Orleans
Newton (Melkite Rite)
New York
Norwich
Oakland
Ogdensburg
Oklahoma City
Omaha
Orange
Orlando
Owensboro
Passaic (Byzantine)
Paterson
Pensacola-Tallahassee
Peoria

Philadelphia
Pittsburgh
Ponce, Puerto Rico
Portland, ME
Portland, OR
Providence
Raleigh
Rapid City
Richmond
Rochester
Rockville Centre
Sacramento
Saginaw
St. Augustine
St. Cloud
St. Louis
St. Maron
St. Paul-Minneapolis
St. Petersburg
Salt Lake City
San Angelo
San Antonio
San Bernardino
San Diego
San Francisco
San Juan, Puerto Rico
Santa Rosa
Savannah
Scranton
Seattle
Sioux City
Sioux Falls
Spokane
Springfield-Cape Girardeau
Springfield, IL
Springfield, MA
Steubenville
Superior
Syracuse
Toledo
Trenton
Tucson
Tulsa
Venice
Victoria
Washington, DC
Wheeling-Charleston
Wichita
Wilmington
Winona
Worcester
Youngstown

COUNTRIES WITH PRIESTS SERVING IN THE ARCHDIOCESE FOR THE MILITARY SERVICES

Africa
Canada
Colombia
Czechoslovakia
Ecuador
France
Ghana
India
Mexico
Nigeria
Pakistan
Paraguay
Peru
Philippines
Poland
Spain
Taiwan
United Kingdom
Vietnam

RELIGIOUS INSTITUTES WITH PRIESTS SERVING IN THE ARCHDIOCESE FOR MILITARY SERVICES

A.A.	Assumptionists
C.J.	Josephite Fathers
C.M.	Vincentian Fathers
C.M.F.	Claretian Missionaries
C.P.	Congregation of the Passion
C.PP.S.	Society of the Precious Blood
C.S.B.	Basilian Fathers
C.S.C.	Congregation of the Holy Cross
C.S.P.	Paulist Fathers
C.S.Sp.	Holy Ghost Fathers
C.SS.R.	Redemptorist Fathers
C.S.V.	Viatorian Fathers
L.C.	Legionaries of Christ
M.I.C.	Congregation of Marians of the Immaculate Conception
M.M.	Maryknoll Missioners
M.S.	Missionaries of Our Lady of LaSalette
M.S.C.	Missionaries of the Sacred Heart
M.Ss.A.	Missionaries of the Holy Apostles
O. Carm.	Carmelite Fathers
O.C.S.O.	Cistercians of the Strict Observance
O.F.M.	Franciscan Fathers
O.F.M.	Cap. Capuchins
O.F.M.	Conv. Conventual Franciscans
O.M.I.	Oblates of Mary Immaculate
O.P.	Order of Preachers
O.Praem.	Premonstratensian Fathers
O.S.A.	The Augustinians
O.S.B.	Benedictine Fathers
O.S.C.	Crozier Fathers
O.S.Cam.	Order of St. Camillus
O.S.F.S.	Oblates of St. Francis de Sales
O.SS.T.	Trinitarian Fathers
S.A.	Atonement Fathers
S.A.C.	Society of the Catholic Apostolate
S.D.B.	Salesian Fathers
S.D.S.	Society of Divine Savior
S.F.	Sons of the Holy Family
S.J.	Jesuit Fathers
S.M.	Marist Fathers
S.O.L.T.	Society of Our Lady of the Most Holy Trinity
SS.CC.	Fathers of the Sacred Hearts
S.S.J.	St. Joseph's Society of the Sacred Heart
S.S.S.	Congregation of the Blessed Sacrament
S.T.	Missionary Servants of the Most Holy Trinity

ASSOCIATIONS SUPPORTING THE MISSION OF THE ARCHDIOCESE

The Centurions
The Chaplains Aid Association

Archdiocese of Milwaukee

(Archidioecesis Milvauchiensis)

Most Reverend

REMBERT G. WEAKLAND, O.S.B., D.D.

Archbishop of Milwaukee; ordained June 24, 1951; appointed Archbishop of Milwaukee September 20, 1977; consecrated and installed as Ninth Archbishop November 8, 1977. *Res., 3303 S. Lake Dr., St. Francis, WI, 53235-3703. All official communications to the Most Rev. Archbishop should be addressed to: Archbishop Cousins Catholic Center, 3501 S. Lake Dr., P.O. Box 07912, Milwaukee, WI, 53207-0912.*

Most Reverend

RICHARD J. SKLBA, D.D.

Auxiliary Bishop of Milwaukee; ordained December 20, 1959; appointed Titular Bishop of Castro November 6, 1979; consecrated December 19, 1979. *Res., 2491 N. Murray Ave., Milwaukee, WI, 53211.* Tel.: 414-962-3941.

ESTABLISHED NOVEMBER 28, 1843; CREATED ARCHBISHOPRIC FEBRUARY 12, 1875.

Square Miles 4,758.

Corporate Title: *"Archdiocese of Milwaukee."*

Comprises the Counties of Dodge, Fond du Lac, Kenosha, Milwaukee, Ozaukee, Racine, Sheboygan, Walworth, Washington and Waukesha in the State of Wisconsin.

For legal titles of parishes and archdiocesan institutions, consult the Chancery Office.

Chancery Office: Archbishop Cousins Catholic Center, 3501 S. Lake Dr., P.O. Box 07912, Milwaukee, WI, 53207-0912. Tel.: 414-769-3340; Fax: 414-769-3408.

Web site address: www.archmil.org

E-mail address: archmil@execpc.com

STATISTICAL OVERVIEW

Personnel	
Archbishop	1
Auxiliary Bishops	1
Retired Abbots	2
Priests: Diocesan Active in Diocese	255
Priests: Active Outside Diocese	16
Priests: Diocesan in Foreign Missions	2
Priests: Retired, Sick or Absent	172
Number of Diocesan Priests	445
Religious Priests in Diocese	293
Extern Priests in Diocese	23
Ordinations:	
Diocesan Priests	1
Religious Priests	1
Transitional Deacons	3
Permanent Deacons	9
Permanent Deacons in Diocese	163
Total Brothers	68
Total Sisters	2,764
Parishes	
Parishes	234
With Resident Pastor:	
Resident Diocesan Priests	176
Resident Religious Priests	20
Without Resident Pastor:	
Administered by Priests	32
Administered by Women Religious	2
Administered by Lay People	4
Pastoral Centers	17
New Parishes Created	8
Closed Parishes	24
Professional Ministry Personnel:	
Brothers	3
Sisters	68
Lay Ministers	407
Welfare	
Catholic Hospitals	11
Total Assisted	2,322,939
Health Care Centers	1
Total Assisted	13,800
Homes for the Aged	27
Total Assisted	6,267
Day Care and Extended Day Care Centers	5
Total Assisted	538
Specialized Homes	5
Total Assisted	4,010
Special Centers for Social Services	40
Total Assisted	241,181
Residential Care of Disabled	4
Total Assisted	164
Educational	
Seminaries, Diocesan	1
Students from This Diocese	25
Seminaries, Religious	1
Students Religious	2
Total Seminarians	27
Colleges and Universities	5
Total Students	27,065
High Schools, Diocesan and Parish	7
Total Students	4,565
High Schools, Private	6
Total Students	3,075
Elementary Schools, Diocesan and Parish	133
Total Students	30,881
Elementary Schools, Private	2
Total Students	112
Non-residential Schools for the Disabled	2
Total Students	11
Catechesis/Religious Education:	
High School Students	13,840
Elementary Students	31,205
Total Students Under Catholic Instruction	110,781
Teachers in the Diocese:	
Priests	19
Scholastics	1
Brothers	8
Sisters	96
Lay Teachers	2,422
Vital Statistics	
Receptions into the Church:	
Infant Baptism Totals	9,156
Adult Baptism Totals	358
Received into Full Communion	712
First Communions	8,943
Confirmations	6,312
Marriages:	
Catholic	2,187
Interfaith	966
Total Marriages	3,153
Deaths	5,503
Total Catholic Population	685,004
Total Population	2,222,364

Former Bishops—Most Rev. JOHN MARTIN HENNI, D.D., cons. March 19, 1844; created Archbishop, Feb. 11, 1875; died Sept. 7, 1881.—Most Rev. MICHAEL HEISS, D.D., cons. Bishop of La Crosse, Sept. 6, 1868; appt. Coadjutor of Milwaukee and Titular Archbishop of Adrianople, March 14, 1880; succeeded to Archbishop Henni in 1881; died March 26, 1890.—Most Rev. FREDERICK XAVIER KATZER, D.D., cons. Sept. 21, 1886; Bishop of Green Bay; transferred to Milwaukee and raised to the Archiepiscopal Dignity, Jan. 30, 1891; died July 20, 1903.—Most Rev. SEBASTIAN GEBHARD MESSMER, D.D., D.C.L., ord. July 23, 1871; cons. March 27, 1892; Bishop of Green Bay; transferred to Milwaukee and raised to the Archiepiscopal dignity Dec. 10, 1903 made assistant at the Pontifical Throne, Nov. 16, 1906; died Aug. 4, 1930.—His Eminence SAMUEL ALPHONSUS STRITCH, D.D., ord. May 21, 1910; cons. Nov. 30, 1921; Bishop of Toledo; transferred to Milwaukee and raised to the Archiepiscopal dignity, Aug. 26, 1930; transferred to Chicago, Dec. 27, 1939; created Cardinal, Feb. 18, 1946; died May 27, 1958.—Most Rev. MOSES E. KILEY, S.T.D., appt. Bishop of Trenton, Feb. 10, 1934; cons. March 17, 1934; appt. Archbishop of Milwaukee, Jan. 1, 1940; died April 15, 1953.—His Eminence ALBERT G. MEYER, S.T.D., S.S.L., ord. July 11, 1926; cons. Bishop of Superior, April 11. 1946; appt. Archbishop of Milwaukee, July 21, 1953; transferred to Chicago, Sept. 24, 1958; created Cardinal, Dec. 14, 1959; died Apr. 9,

1965.—Most Rev. WILLIAM E. COUSINS, D.D., ord. April 23, 1927; appt. Titular Bishop of Forma and Auxiliary Bishop of Chicago Dec. 17, 1948; cons. March 7, 1949; appt. Bishop of Peoria, May 19, 1952; installed July 2, 1952; appt. Archbishop of Milwaukee, Dec. 18, 1958; installed Jan. 27, 1959; retired Sept. 20, 1977; died Sept. 14, 1988.

Archbishop Cousins Catholic Center—3501 S. Lake Dr., P.O. Box 070912, Milwaukee, 53207-0912. Tel: 414-769-3300; Fax: 414-769-3408. All Archdiocesan Offices are located at this address unless otherwise noted.

Vicars General—Most Rev. RICHARD J. SKLBA, S.S.L., S.T.D.; Very Rev. JOSEPH F. HORNACEK.

Deans—Very Revs. KENNETH J. METZ, District 1; PAUL M. ESSER, District 2; DAVID H. REITH, District 3; JEROME M. HUDZIAK, District 4; ROBERT D. GOSMA, District 5; GERALD W. BRITTAIN, District 6; CHARLES H. WESTER, District 7; PATRICK E. HEPPE, District 8; RICHARD J. CERPICH, District 9; Very Rev. Msgr. T. GEORGE GAJDOS, District 10; Very Revs. KENNETH P. KNIPPEL, District 11; DENNIS R. ACKERET, District 12; DENNIS J. LEWIS, District 13; JAMES L. DAMMEIR, District 14; THOMAS P. EICHENBERGER, District 15; KENNETH E. OMERNICK, District 16.

Chancery—Tel: 414-769-3340.

Chancellor—BARBARA ANNE CUSACK, J.C.D. Tel: 414-769-3341.

Vice Chancellor—Rev. JAMES C. CONNELL, J.C.D. Tel: 414-769-3338.

Archivist—TIMOTHY D. CARY. Tel: 414-769-3407.

Secretary to Archbishop—Rev. LEONARD S. VAN VLAENDEREN. Tel: 414-769-3496; Fax: 414-769-3430.

Metropolitan Tribunal Archbishop Cousins Catholic Center—3501 S. Lake Dr., P.O. Box 070912, Milwaukee, 53207-0912. Tel: 414-769-3300; Fax: 414-769-3310. Please direct all Rogatory Commissions to: Rev. JOHN D. AIELLO, Defender of the Bond.

Judicial Vicar—Rev. THOMAS T. BRUNDAGE, M.Div., J.C.L.

Adjutant Judicial Vicar—Rev. PAUL B.R. HARTMANN, M.Div., J.C.L.

Executive Secretary—MAURICE C. THOMPSON.

Judges for First Instance—Revs. THOMAS T. BRUNDAGE, M.Div., J.C.L.; PAUL B.R. HARTMANN, M.Div., J.C.L.; JACK HOPKA, J.C.L.; Mr. EDUARDO HUERTA, J.C.L.

Judges for Second Instance—Revs. FRANK ARESTA, S.C.J., J.C.L.; THOMAS T. BRUNDAGE, M.Div., J.C.L.; JAMES E. CONNELL, J.C.D.; BARBARA ANNE CUSACK, J.C.D.; Revs. CURT J. FREDERICK, J.C.L.; PAUL B.R. HARTMANN, M.Div., J.C.L.; JACK HOPKA, J.C.L.; JAMES J. JARUMBO, J.C.L.; JOSEPH A. JANICKI, J.C.L.; MICHAEL T. NEWMAN, J.C.L.; BERNARD S. SIPPEL, M.Div.; PHILIP D. REIFENBERG, J.C.L.; Mr. EDUARDO HUERTA, J.C.L.

Defender of the Bond Second Instance—Rev. JOHN D. AIELLO, M.Div.

Psychological Expert—THOMAS R. BUDDE, M.S.

Procurator Advocates—ZABRINA DECKER, M.R.E.; Sr. ELLEN SINCLAIR, S.D.S, J.D.; ANDREW VAUGHN, M.A.

Promoters of Justice—Revs. ROBERT G. SAMPON, S.T.L., J.C.D.; PHILIP D. REIFENBERG, J.C.L.

Assessor/Due Process Coordinator—JOHN CARINI, J.D.

Notaries—Rev. JOHN D. AIELLO, M.Div.; MAURICE C. THOMPSON; MARY CHRIS ELLISON; JOYCE HRYNIEWICKI; ALICE PRIER.

Office for Marital Reconciliation-Separation—Rev. PAUL B.R. HARTMANN, M.Div., J.C.L., Delegate.

Archdiocesan Court of Equity—Revs. THOMAS T. BRUNDAGE, M.Div., J.C.L.; PAUL B.R. HARTMANN, M.Div., J.C.L.; Mr. JOHN CARINI, J.D.; Sr. ELLEN SINCLAIR, S.D.S., J.D.

Archdiocesan Consultors—Most Rev. RICHARD J. SKLBA, S.S.L., S.T.D.; Very Rev. RICHARD J. CERPICH; Rev. LEONARD R. COPELAND, O.C.D.; Very Rev. Msgr. T. GEORGE GAJDOS; Revs. ROLLAND T. GLASS; RALPH C. GROSS; JEFFREY R. HAINES; JOHN P. HANLEY; Very Rev. JOSEPH F. HORNACEK; Rev. DANIEL J. SANDERS.

Archdiocesan Council of Priests—Very Rev. DAVID H. REITH, Moderator. Tel: 414-769-3498.

Archdiocesan Pastoral Council—Tel: 414-769-3499.

Department for Ministerial Formation

Saint Francis Seminary—Very Rev. ANDREW L. NELSON, S.T.L., Ph.D., Rector, *3257 S. Lake Dr., St. Francis, 53235.* Tel: 414-747-6400; Fax: 414-747-6442.

Continuing Formation of Clergy—Rev. STEPHEN V. DELEERS, Dir. Tel: 414-747-6417; Fax: 414-747-6442.

Vocations Office—Rev. ROBERT X. STIEFVATER, Dir., *3257 S. Lake Dr., St. Francis, 53235.* Tel: 414-747-6442.

College Program—Rev. JOSEPH JUKNIALIS, Dir., *2479 N. Murray Ave., Milwaukee, 53211.* Tel: 414-964-6970; Fax: 414-962-8183.

Department for Clergy

Department for Clergy—Tel: 414-769-3484.

Vicar for Clergy—Very Rev. JOSEPH F. HORNACEK. Tel: 414-769-3490.

Associate Vicar for Clergy—Rev. WILLIAM E. KOHLER. Tel: 414-769-3458.

Services for Senior Priests—Rev. THOMAS J. WALKER. Tel: 414-769-3345.

Deacon Services—Deacon DAVID L. ZIMPRICH, Coord. Tel: 414-769-3409.

Department for Communication

Department for Communication—Tel: 414-769-3453.

Archbishop's Delegate for Communication—JERRY TOPCZEWSKI. Tel: 414-769-3517.

Associate Director for Communication—JEAN MULLOOLY. Tel: 414-769-3461.

Communication Coordinator—KATHLEEN HOHL. Tel: 414-769-3494.

Coordinator of Publications—MARY CONARCHY. Tel: 414-769-3460.

"Catholic Herald"—Newspaper—P.O. Box 070913, Milwaukee, 53207-0913. Tel: 414-769-3500; Fax: 414-769-3468. Most Rev. REMBERT G. WEAKLAND, O.S.B., Publisher; ETHEL M. GINTOFT, Assoc. Publisher & Exec. Editor. Tel: 414-769-3478.

Department for Community Services

Department for Community Services—Tel: 414-769-3425.

Archbishop's Delegate for Community Services—CELIA JACKSON. Tel: 414-769-3389.

Ecumenical and Interfaith Concerns—JUDITH A. LONGDIN, Dir. Tel: 414-769-3389.

Social Concerns Office—CELIA JACKSON, Dir. Tel: 414-769-3389. MARJORIE MORGAN, Assoc. Dir. Tel: 414-769-3402.

Campaign for Human Development—DAVID FIELDS. Tel: 414-769-3424.

Office for World Mission—Sr. FRANCIS CUNNINGHAM, O.S.F., Dir. Tel: 414-769-3404. ROSEMARY HUDDLESTON, International Mission Coord. Tel: 414-769-3405.

Rural Life Office—MARJORIE MORGAN, Co-Dir., *118 W. Main St., Waupun, 53963.* Tel: 920-324-5400. Deacon BERNARD WENDT, Co-Dir., *202 E. Washington St., Slinger, 53086.* Tel: 262-644-8083.

Catholic Charities—DIANE KNIGHT, Acting Exec. Dir. Tel: 414-769-3417; Fax: 414-769-3428. (Legal Title: *Catholic Charities of the Archdiocese of Milwaukee, Inc.);* DIANE KNIGHT, Dir. Prog. Svc. Tel: 414-769-3417; Fax: 414-769-3428. CHRISTINE JOHNSON, Dir. Devel. & Comm. Tel: 414-769-3524; Fax: 414-769-3524. RUTH ANNE ALEXANDER, Dir. Human Resource. Tel: 414-769-3351; Fax: 414-769-3428. JACK SCHICKERT, Dir. Finance. Tel: 414-769-3413; Fax: 414-769-3428.

Catholic Charities Residential Programs for Developmentally Disabled—RONALD J. SPITZ, Dir. Tel: 414-769-3401; Fax: 414-769-3428.

Catholic Charities Ministry on Aging—WILLIAM LEON, Dir. Tel: 414-769-3412; Fax: 414-769-3428.

Department for Development

Department for Development—Tel: 414-769-3457; Fax: 414-769-3388.

Archbishop's Delegate for Development—JOAN FEIEREISEN. Tel: 414-769-3320.

Catholic Stewardship Appeal—DEBRA LETHLEAN, Dir. Tel: 414-769-3322.

Parish Stewardship and School Development—PAMELA MUELLER, Dir. Tel: 414-769-3485. JOHN JARACZEWSKI, Assoc. Dir. Tel: 414-769-3331.

Planned Giving Consultant—MARY ELLEN MARKOWSKI. Tel: 414-769-3451.

Department for Finance and Administration

Department for Archdiocesan Finance and Administration—Tel: 414-769-3326.

Archbishop's Delegate for Archdiocesan Finance and Administration—WAYNE A. SCHNEIDER. Tel: 414-769-3319.

Consultant for Legal Counsel—WAYNE A. SCHNEIDER. Tel: 414-769-3319.

Office for Archdiocesan Finance and Administrative Services—WAYNE A. SCHNEIDER, Dir. & Controller; JANE NIKOLAI, Assoc. Dir. Tel: 414-769-3347.

Office for Information Services—JERRY SCHULZ, Dir. Tel: 414-769-3530.

Webmaster/Coordinator Electronic Communication—MARK BARTHEL. Tel: 414-769-3454.

Office for Parish Finances—DAVID LAUER, Dir. Tel: 414-769-3377.

Office for Cemeteries and Mausoleums—GREGG F. APOSTOLOFF, Dir., *7301 W. Nash St., Milwaukee, 53216.* Tel: 414-438-4430.

Office for Cousins Center Building Services—WILLIAM KREITZER, Dir. Tel: 414-769-3491.

Office for Printing Services—THOMAS WAL, Dir. Tel: 414-769-3487.

Department for Human Resources

Department for Human Resources—Tel: 414-769-3329.

Archbishop's Delegate for Human Resources—RICHARD J. TANK. Tel: 414-769-3370.

Office for Human Resources, Central Offices and Agencies—JUDITH A. MYERS, Dir. Tel: 414-769-3328.

Office for Parish and School Personnel—RICHARD J. TANK, Dir. MAUREEN SIWULA, Assoc. Dir. Tel: 414-769-3370.

Office for Religious—Rev. ALAN D. VEIK, O.F.M.Cap., Dir. Tel: 414-769-3375.

Archdiocesan Office for Women—THELMA WALKER, Dir. Tel: 414-769-3434.

Sexual Abuse Response Coordinator—ELIZABETH C. PIASECKI, Psy.D. Tel: 414-769-3436.

Department for Parishes

Department for Parishes—Tel: 414-769-3449.

Archbishop's Delegate for Parishes—MAUREEN GALLAGHER, Ph.D. Tel: 414-769-3450.

Office for Multi-Cultural Concerns—SCHAUNEILLE ALLEN, Multi-Cultural Consultant & Dir. African-American Ministry. Tel: 414-769-3411. PEDRO MARTINEZ, Multi-Cultural Consultant & Dir. Hispanic Ministry. Tel: 414-769-3393. Rev. PAUL FLISS, Multi-Cultural Consultant, Asian Ministry. Tel: 414-769-3376.

Parish Consultants—Tel: 414-769-3539. Districts 1, 2, 3: VALERIE KELLER,Districts 4, 5, 7, 8: SHAWN COLBERG,Districts 6, 15, 16: JENNIFER JACKMAN,Districts 9, 10, 11, 12, 13: EVA J. DIAZ; CATHERINE O'NEILL,District 14 (Milwaukee Near Southside and Parishes of the Archdiocese with Hispanic Ministry): ROBERTO CORTES.

Parish Council Leadership Formation—NOREEN WELTE, Dir. Tel: 414-769-3378.

Office for Human Concerns/Respect Life—PEG FLAHIVE, Dir. Tel: 414-769-3426.

Office for Planning & Collaboration—MARK MITCHELL, Dir. Tel: 414-769-3379. ROBERT MELCHER, Assoc. Dir. Tel: 414-769-3381.

Office for Prayer and Worship—MICHAEL NOVAK, Dir. Tel: 414-769-3350. DEAN DANIELS, Assoc. Dir. Tel: 414-769-3348.

Office for Adult and Family Ministry—THERESA JOHANEK, Dir. Tel: 414-769-3439.

Marriage and Family Ministry—RANDY NOHL, Assoc. Dir. Tel: 414-769-3440.

Bereavement Ministry—POLLY HORKY, Assoc. Dir. Tel: 414-769-3456.

Engaged Programs—MARIE GREVSMUEHL, Coord. Tel: 414-769-3441.

Campus Ministry—Milwaukee: CONSTANCE M. POPP; Rev. ROBERT J. LOTZ. Tel: 414-964-6640. Kenosha/Racine: EDITH PADGETT. Tel: 262-654-3630. Whitewater: BRIAN ZANIN. Tel: 262-473-5555.

Special Needs—THERESA JOHANEK. Tel: 414-769-3439.

Ministry to the Hearing Impaired—KATEY COLLINS, Assoc. Dir.; Rev. SCOTT LEANNAH, Pastoral Min. Tel: 414-769-3455 (V/TTY).

Office for Schools, Child and Youth Ministries—Tel: 414-769-3366.

Director of Catholic Education—MAUREEN GALLAGHER, Ph.D. Tel: 414-769-3450.

Administrative Services—JOHN T. NORRIS, Ph.D., Dir. Tel: 414-769-3366.

Student Activities & Services—W. SCOTT WEYDA, Assoc. Dir. Tel: 414-769-3359.

Curriculum & Instruction—DAVID PROTHERO, Assoc. Dir. Tel: 414-769-3357.

Youth & Young Adult Ministry—ANN MARIE ECKERT, Assoc. Dir. Tel: 414-769-3361.

Catechetics to Children—JEAN MARIE WEBER, Assoc. Dir. Tel: 414-769-3373.

Early Adolescent Ministry—LISA MARIE CALDERONE-STEWART, Assoc. Dir. Tel: 414-769-3360.

Technology and Communication—Contracted services.

CLERGY, PARISHES, MISSIONS AND PAROCHIAL SCHOOLS

CITY OF MILWAUKEE
(Milwaukee County)

1—St. John Cathedral (1847), Very Revs. John H. Endejan, Rector; Carl A. Last, Vice Rector.
Res., 802 N. Jackson St., 53202. Tel: 414-276-9814; Fax: 414-276-8285.
Catechesis/Religious Programs—Tel: 414-263-8230.
Students 11.

2—St. Adalbert (1908) (Polish-Hispanic), Rev. Luis Pancheco-Sanchez.
Office: 1854 W. Windlake, 53215. Tel: 414-645-4773; Fax: 414-645-5622.
School—1913 W. Becher St., 53215-2688. Tel: 414-645-5450; Fax: 414-645-5510. Ms. Julia Hutchinson, Prin.
Lay Teachers 15; Students 262.

3—St. Agnes. Closed. For sacramental records contact Archdiocese of Milwaukee Archives Office. Tel.: 414-769-3407.

4—St. Albert. Closed. For sacramental records contact Archdiocese of Milwaukee Archives Office. Tel.: 414-769-3407.

5—St. Alexander (1926) (Polish), Rev. Robert W. Nawrocki.
Res., 3373 S. 15th Pl., 53215. Tel: 414-645-9820.
School—3344 S. 16th St., 53215. Tel: 414-383-3453; Fax: 414-672-2645. Sr. Elmerine Acker, S.S.S.F., Prin.
Sisters 3; Lay Teachers 4; Students 127.
Catechesis/Religious Programs—St. John Kanty, 2840 S. 10th St., Tel: 414-483-1906.
Students 31.

6—All Saints (1994) (African American), Rev. Dennis A. Dirkx; Deacon Edward Blaze.
Office: 4060 N. 26th St., 53209-6695. Tel: 414-444-5610; Fax: 414-444-5709.
Catechesis/Religious Programs—Students 110.
Mission—Milwaukee, Milwaukee Co., St. John's Chapel, 3717 W. Keefe, 53216.

7—St Anne. Closed. For sacramental records contact Archdiocese of Milwaukee Archives Office. Tel.: 414-769-3407.

8—St. Anthony (1872), Rev. Lawrence V. Dulek. In res., Revs. John B. Thanh Hung; Robert F. Mueller; Eleazar Perez (Mexico).
Res., 1711 S. 9th St., 53204. Tel: 414-645-1455; Fax: 414-645-1456.
School—1747 S. 9th St., 53204. Tel: 414-384-1730; Fax: 414-384-1733. Richard Mason, Prin.
Sisters 5; Lay Teachers 10; Students 400.
Catechesis/Religious Programs—Tel: 414-347-4465. Dennis Hondel, D.R.E.
Students 350.

9—St. Anthony of Padua (1923). Closed. For sacramental records contact St. Vincent Pallotti, Milwaukee. Tel.: 414-453-4225.

10—St. Augustine (1888) (German), Rev. Thomas F. Wittliff; Ms. Chiara Sainer, Pastoral Assoc.; Scott W. Eakins, Dir. of Worship.
Res., 2530 S. Howell Ave., 53207. Tel: 414-744-0808; Fax: 414-744-1231.
School—St. Elizabeth Ann Seton Academy, 1051 E. Russell Ave., 53207. Tel: 414-769-2485; Fax: 414-747-9219. Sr. Katherine D. Strandall, Prin.
Lay Teachers 14; Students 230.
Catechesis/Religious Programs—Students 125.

11—St. Barbara. Closed. For sacramental records, contact St. Rafael the Archangel, Milwaukee. Tel.: 414-645-9172.

12—St. Benedict the Moor (1908), Rev. John Celichowski, O.F.M.Cap.; Deacon John Champagne. In res., Rev. Michael Crosby, O.F.M.Cap.; Bros. Larry Ampe, O.F.M.Cap.; Kent Bauer, O.F.M.Cap.; Jerome Smith, O.F.M.Cap.; David Schwab, O.F.M.Cap.
Res., 1015 N. 9th St., 53233. Tel: 414-271-0135; Fax: 414-271-0637.
Catechesis/Religious Programs—Students 27.

13—St. Bernadette (1958), Rev. William H. Whalen; Deacon John A. Ebel.
Res., 8200 W. Denver Ave., 53223. Tel: 414-358-4600; Fax: 414-358-1478.
School—8202 W. Denver Ave., 53223. Tel: 414-358-4603; Fax: 414-760-1037. Mary Lorusso, Prin.
Lay Teachers 10; Students 208.
Catechesis/Religious Programs—Students 95.

14—Blessed Sacrament (1927) (Polish), Revs. James N. Jablonowski; Robert D. Turner; Deacon Richard Flynn.
Res., 3100 S. 41st St., 53215. Tel: 414-649-4720; Fax: 414-649-4727.
Church—S. 41st St. and W. Oklahoma Ave., 53215.
School—3126 S. 41st St., 53215. Tel: 414-649-4730; Fax: 414-649-4726. Sr. Rene Kuban, S.F.C.C., Prin.
Lay Teachers 12; Students 213.
Catechesis/Religious Programs—Tel: 414-649-4735.
Students 138.

15—Congregation of the Blessed Trinity (1991), Rev. Michael G. Savio; Deacon Peter Gust, (Retired).
Pastoral Offices—4717 N. 38th St., 53209. Tel: 414-463-6921; Fax: 414-463-0349.
Catechesis/Religious Programs—Students 41.

16—Blessed Virgin of Pompei. Closed. For sacramental records contact Three Holy Women, Milwaukee. Tel.: 414-271-2165.

17—St. Boniface. Closed. For sacramental records contact Archdiocese of Milwaukee Archives Office, 414-769-3407.

18—St. Casimir (1894) (Polish-Spanish), Rev. James M. Flynt, Adm.; Patricia Beirne, Pastoral Assoc.
Mailing Address: 924 E. Clarke St., 53212-3009. Tel: 414-263-8220; Fax: 414-263-8233.
Res., 3055 N. Fratney St., 53212. Tel: 414-264-9814; 263-8228 (Office); Fax: 414-264-8233.
School—Catholic East Consolidated. See All Saints Catholic East School System, Inc., Listing in the Consolidated Elementary Schools section. Tel: 414-964-1770.
Catechesis/Religious Programs—East Side Child & Youth Ministry, Tel: 414-263-8230; Fax: 414-263-8222. Ralph Stewart, D.R.E.
Students 96.

19—St. Catherine (1922), Rev. David J. Meinholz; Deacon Ralph W. Kornburger, Jr.; Darryl Olszewski, Parish Dir. In res., Rev. Wilson Paul Antony (India).
Res., 5101 W. Center St., 53210. Tel: 414-445-5115; Fax: 414-445-5198.
School—2647 N. 51st St., 53210. Tel: 414-445-2846; Fax: 414-445-0448. Deborah Zabinski, Prin.
Lay Teachers 15; Students 211.
Catechesis/Religious Programs—Students 71.

20—St. Catherine (Granville) (1855), Rev. Jeffery A. Prasser.
Office:—Tel: 414-365-2020; Fax: 414-365-2021.
Res., 8661 N. 76th Pl., 53223. Tel: 414-365-2039. [CEM]
School—8660 N. 76th Pl., 53223. Tel: 414-365-2030; Fax: 414-365-2021. Mr. Michael Howell, Prin.
Sisters 1; Lay Teachers 13; Students 190.
Catechesis/Religious Programs—Tel: 414-365-2025. Judith Kowalski, Ph.D., D.R.E.
Students 151.

21—St. Charles Borromeo (1960), Rev. Anthony J. Zimmer.
Res., 5571 S. Marilyn Ave., 53221. Tel: 414-281-8115; Fax: 414-281-8150.
School—3100 W. Parnell Ave., 53221. Tel: 414-282-0767; Fax: 414-817-9605.
Lay Teachers 15; Students 207.
Catechesis/Religious Programs—Tel: 414-282-5630.
Students 150.

22—Corpus Christi (1958), Rev. Michael D. Strachota; Deacons James L. Aschenbrener; Steven Przedpelski; Judith Adrian, Pastoral Assoc.
Parish Center: 8607 W. Villard Ave., 53225. Tel: 414-464-5033; Fax: 414-464-0079.
School—8545 W. Villard Ave., 53225. Tel: 414-464-5775; Fax: 414-464-5775. Kagey Burdick, Prin.
Lay Teachers 14; Students 150.
Catechesis/Religious Programs—Students 112.

23—SS. Cyril and Methodius (1893),
Office: c/o 1854 W. Windlake Ave., 53215. Tel: 414-645-4773; Fax: 414-645-5622.

24—St. Elizabeth. Closed. For sacramental records contact Archdiocese of Milwaukee Archives Office, 414-769-3407.

25—St. Emeric (1919) (Hungarian). Closed. For sacramental records, contact Sacred Heart, Milwaukee. Tel: 414-774-9418.

26—St. Florian (1911) (German-Austrian), Revs. Leonard R. Copeland, O.C.D.; Timothy McGough, O.C.D. In res., Revs. Dominic T. Scheerer, O.C.D.; William Healy, O.C.D.; Philip Thomas, O.C.D.; Jude Peters, O.C.D.; Ralph Elias-Haddix, O.C.D.; Bro. Bonaventure Potter, O.C.D.
Res., 1233 S. 45th St., 53214. Tel: 414-383-3565; Fax: 414-383-2708.
School—1215 S. 45th St., 53214. Tel: 414-383-4204; Fax: 414-383-4281.
Sisters 1; Lay Teachers 9; Students 110.
Catechesis/Religious Programs—Students 81.

27—St. Francis of Assisi (1871) (Hispanic-African American), Rev. Paul Koenig, O.F.M.Cap. In res., Revs. Ulric Buening, O.F.M.Cap.; Joseph Smetana, O.F.M.Cap.; Michael Zuelke, O.F.M.Cap.; Robert Kose, O.F.M.Cap.; Bro. Isidore Herriges, O.F.M.Cap.
Res., 327 W. Brown St., 53212. Tel: 414-374-5750; Fax: 414-374-5553.

28—St. Gabriel (1913) (Lithuanian). Closed. For sacramental records contact Archdiocese of Milwaukee Archives Office. Tel.: 414-769-3407.

29—St. Gall. Closed. For sacramental records contact Archdiocese of Milwaukee Archives Office. Tel.: 414-769-3407.

30—St. Gerard (1925). Closed. For sacramental records contact Archdiocese of Milwaukee Archives Office. Tel.: 414-769-3407.

31—Gesu Parish (1893), Revs. George E. Winzenburg, S.J., Supr.; John D. Campbell, S.J.; James E. Grummer, S.J.; David J. Haschka, S.J.; Kenneth J. Herian, S.J.; D. Edward Mathie, S.J.; Patrick E. Walsh, S.J.
Res., 1210 W. Michigan St., P.O. Box 495, 53201-0495. Tel: 414-288-7101; Fax: 414-288-5339.
Catechesis/Religious Programs—Students 158.

32—Congregation of the Great Spirit (1989) (Native American), Rev. Edward J. Cook.
Res. & Mailing Address: 1050 W. Lapham St., 53204. Tel: 414-672-6989.

33—St. Gregory the Great (1955), Very Rev. Kenneth E. Omernick; Rev. Patrick James O'Loughlin.
Office: 3160 S. 63rd St., 53219. Tel: 414-543-8292; Fax: 414-328-3881.
Res., 3129 S. 63rd St., 53219.
School—3132 S. 63rd St., 53219. Tel: 414-321-1350.
Lay Teachers 20; Students 473.
Catechesis/Religious Programs—Tel: 414-543-8292.
Students 200.

34—St. Hedwig (1871) (Polish). Closed. For sacramental records contact Three Holy Women, Tel.: 414-271-2165.

35—St. Helen (1925) (Polish), Rev. Michael A. Ignaszak; Sr. Helen Bronner, S.S.N.D., Pastoral Assoc.
Res., 3307 S. 10th St., 53215. Tel: 414-744-3695; 744-8292; Fax: 414-744-2874.
School—3329 S. 10th St., 53215. Tel: 414-744-7188. Sr. Kathleen Sowinski, S.S.S.F., Prin.
Sisters 4; Lay Teachers 5; Students 123.
Catechesis/Religious Programs—Clustered with St. John Kanty and St. Alexander. 2480 S. 10th St., Tel: 414-483-1906.
Students 58.

36—Holy Angels. Closed. For sacramental records contact Archdiocese of Milwaukee Archives Office. Tel.: 414-769-3407.

37—Holy Cross (1879). Closed. For sacramental records contact St. Vincent Pallotti, Milwaukee. Tel.: 414-453-4225.

38—Holy Redeemer. Closed. For sacramental records contact Archdiocese of Milwaukee Archives Office. Tel.: 414-769-3407.

39—Holy Rosary (1885) (Irish). Closed. For sacramental records contact Three Holy Women, Milwaukee. Tel: 414-271-2165.

40—Holy Spirit (1902) (German). Closed. For sacramental records, contact St. Rafael the Archangel, Milwaukee, 414-645-9172.

41—Holy Trinity-Our Lady of Guadalupe (1849) (Hispanic). Closed. For sacramental records contact, Our Lady of Guadalupe, Milwaukee. Tel.: 414-271-6181.

42—St. Hyacinth (1883) (Polish-Hispanic), Rev. Ronald E. Kotecki.
Res., 1414 W. Becher St., 53215. Tel: 414-383-4010; Fax: 414-383-3252.
Catechesis/Religious Programs—Students 121.

43—St. Ignatius Loyola. Closed. For sacramental records contact Archdiocese of Milwaukee Archives Office. Tel.: 414-769-3407.

44—Immaculate Conception (1870), Rev. Dennis M. Witz; Deacon John Wargin.
Res., 1023 E. Russell Ave., 53207. Tel: 414-769-2480.
School—St. Elizabeth Ann Seton Academy. Consolidated School. Parish Sponsors: Immaculate Conception and St. Augustine. 1051 E. Russell Ave., 53207. Tel: 414-769-2485; Fax: 414-747-9219.
Lay Teachers 15; Students 222.
Catechesis/Religious Programs—Tel: 414-769-2488.
Students 37.

45—St. John de Nepomuc. Closed. For sacramental records contact Archdiocese of Milwaukee Archives Office. Tel.: 414-769-3407.

46—St. John Kanty (1907) (Polish), Rev. Carl M. Kazmierczak.
Res., 966 W. Dakota St., 53215. Tel: 414-744-5885; Fax: 414-744-1393.
School—2840 S. 10th St., 53215. Tel: 414-483-8780; 744-1846. Lois Maczuzak, Prin.
School Sisters of Notre Dame 1; Lay Teachers 10; Students 163.

Catechesis/Religious Programs—Tel: 414-483-1906.
Students 34.

47—BASILICA OF ST. JOSAPHAT (1888) (Polish), Revs. William P. Callahan, O.F.M.Conv., Rector; Robert Joseph Switanowski, O.F.M.Conv., Vicar; Michael Glastetter, O.F.M.Conv., Vicar.
Res., 2333 S. 6th St., 53215. Tel: 414-645-5623; Fax: 414-645-0912.
School—801 W. Lincoln Ave., 53215. Tel: 414-645-4378; Fax: 414-645-1978. Mrs. Carolyn Trawitzki.
Lay Teachers 11; Students 180; School Sisters of St. Francis 1.
Catechesis/Religious Programs—Parish Center, 2322 S. 7th St., Tel: 414-671-3938.
Students 34.

48—ST. JOSEPH. Closed. For sacramental records contact St. Joseph, Wauwatosa. Tel.: 414-771-4626.

49—ST. LAWRENCE (1888). Closed. For sacramental records, contact Archdiocese of Milwaukee Archives Office, 414-769-3407.

50—ST. LEO. Closed. For sacramental records contact Archdiocese of Milwaukee Archives Office. Tel.: 414-769-3407.

51—ST. MARGARET MARY (1955), Revs. Ralph C. Gross Tel: 414-536-8720; Allen Bratkowski Tel: 414-616-3192; Deacon Michael R. Rooney.
Rectory Office: 3930 N. 92nd St., 53222-2588. Tel: 414-461-6073; Fax: 414-463-2373.
School—3950 N. 92nd St., 53222-2587. Tel: 414-463-8760; Fax: 414-463-2373. Susan Nelson, Prin.
Sisters of St. Agnes 1; Lay Teachers 25; Students 453.
Catechesis/Religious Programs—Tel: 414-462-9660.
Students 249.

52—ST. MARTIN DE PORRES (1994) (African American), Rev. Brian Braun, O.F.M.Cap.
Office: 128 W. Burleigh St., 53212-2046. Tel: 414-372-3090; Fax: 414-372-0356.
Catechesis/Religious Programs—Students 45.

53—OLD ST. MARY (1846) (Bavarian/German), Rev. George M. Rebatzki.
Res., 836 N. Broadway, 53202. Tel: 414-271-6180; Fax: 414-271-7782.
Catechesis/Religious Programs—Students 40.

54—ST. MARY OF CZESTOCHOWA (1907) (Polish), Rev. James M. Flynt.
Res., 3055 N. Fratney St., 53212. Tel: 414-264-0049; Fax: 414-264-7177.
School—All Saints Catholic Elementary. See All Saints Catholic East School System, Inc., Listing in the Consolidated Elementary Schools section. Tel: 414-964-1770.
Catechesis/Religious Programs—Tel: 414-264-8230; Fax: 414-264-8222. Ralph Stewart, D.R.E.
Students 4.

55—ST. MARY MAGDALEN (1925) (Polish), Rev. Luis Pancheco-Sanchez.
Res., 1854 W. Windlake Ave., 53215. Tel: 414-645-4773; Fax: 414-645-5622.

56—ST. MATTHEW (1892). Closed. For sacramental records, contact Archdiocese of Milwaukee Archives Office, 414-769-3407.

57—ST. MATTHIAS (1851), Revs. David E. Cooper; Scott R. Leannah; Joseph A. Aufdermauer.
9306 W. Beloit Rd., 53227. Tel: 414-321-0893; Fax: 414-321-1330. [CEM]
School—Tel: 414-321-0894; Fax: 414-321-9228.
Sisters 2; Lay Teachers 26; Students 535.
Catechesis/Religious Programs—Students 336.

58—ST. MICHAEL (1883), Very Rev. Dennis J. Lewis, Admin. Pastoral Assocs.: Sr. Alice Thephouthay, Laotian Pastoral Ministry; Sr. Maria Herlinda, Hispanic Pastoral Ministry; Deacon Blong Yang, Hmong Pastoral Ministry; Shanedra Johnson, Youth Director.
Res., 1445 N. 24th St., 53205. Tel: 414-933-3143; Fax: 414-933-1915.
Catechesis/Religious Programs—Tel: 414-259-0441.
Students 303.

59—MOTHER OF GOOD COUNSEL (1925), Rev. Carey T. Lahrs, S.D.S.; Deacons Dean J. Collins; Andrew Meuler.
Church—6924 W. Lisbon Ave., 53210-1259. Tel: 414-442-7600; Fax: 414-444-0408.
School—3001 N. 68th St., 53210. Fax: 414-442-0664. Regina Shaw, Prin.
Sisters 1; Lay Teachers 27; Students 458.
Catechesis/Religious Programs—Students 59.

60—MOTHER OF PERPETUAL HELP (1941), Rev. Richard J. Robinson; Deacon Thomas J. Schimmels.
Res., 5409 W. Villard Ave., 53218. Tel: 414-438-0669; Fax: 414-438-9265.
School—Resurrection Catholic Academy, 5140 N. 55th St., 53218. Tel: 414-438-4783; Fax: 414-463-8721. Barbara O'Donnell, Prin.
Lay Teachers 17; Students 227.
Catechesis/Religious Programs—Students 51.

61—ST. NICHOLAS. Closed. For sacramental records contact Archdiocese of Milwaukee Archives Office. Tel.: 414-769-3407.

62—OUR LADY OF GOOD HOPE (1952), Revs. Donald Hying; Joseph A. Wolf; Deacons Michael Cesarec; Joseph H. Kastenholz; Robert M. Schieffer. In res., Rev. John R. Kolanko.
Office: 7152 N. 41st St., 53209. Tel: 414-352-1148; Fax: 414-352-3042.
School—7140 N. 41st St., 53209. Tel: 414-352-7980. Michael Taylor, Prin.
Lay Teachers 12; Students 189.
Catechesis/Religious Programs—Tel: 414-352-8140. Barbara Krieger, D.R.E.
Students 164.

63—OUR LADY OF GUADALUPE PARISH (2000), Rev. Vincent Kobida; Deacons Jose H. Gutierrez; Juan A. Molina, Sr.
Res., 613 S. 4th St., 53204. Tel: 414-271-6181; Fax: 414-278-6090.
Catechesis/Religious Programs—Students 129.

64—OUR LADY OF LOURDES (1958), Rev. Thomas M. Suriano; Deacon John Monday; Mrs. Judith Bialk, Pastoral Assoc.
Office: 3722 S. 58th St., 53220. Tel: 414-545-4316; Fax: 414-541-2251.
Catechesis/Religious Programs—Tel: 414-541-9470.
Students 265.

65—OUR LADY, QUEEN OF PEACE (1948), Rev. Leonard Van Vlaenderen, Admin.
Res., 3222 S. 29th St., 53215. Tel: 414-672-0313; Fax: 414-672-0441.
School—2733 W. Euclid Ave., 53215. Tel: 414-672-6660; Fax: 414-672-2739. Janet Orlowski, Prin.
Sisters 2; Lay Teachers 13; Students 210.
Catechesis/Religious Programs—Students 6.

66—OUR LADY OF SORROWS (1955), Rev. Gregory A. Chycinski.
Res., 4063 N. 64th St., 53216. Tel: 414-463-3180; Fax: 414-463-3668.
School—4059 N. 64th St., 53216. Tel: 414-463-3878; Fax: 414-463-3878. Miss Patricia Wilkum, Prin.
Lay Teachers 11; Students 172.
Catechesis/Religious Programs—Students 16.

67—ST. PATRICK (1876) (Hispanic), Revs. Joseph G. Spieler, S.J.; David M. Shields, S.J.; William Buennon, S.J.
Res., 723 W. Washington St., 53204. Tel: 414-645-7624; Fax: 414-645-3733.
Catechesis/Religious Programs—Tel: 414-645-7624.
Students 185.

68—ST. PAUL (1920), Revs. James Winiarski, M.S.; Francis Kula, M.S.
Res., 1720 E. Norwich Ave., 53207. Tel: 414-482-3510; Fax: 414-482-1031.
School—3945 S. Kansas Ave., 53207. Tel: 414-482-4790; Fax: 414-482-2983.
Lay Teachers 9; Students 144.
Catechesis/Religious Programs—Tel: 414-482-3911.
Students 131.

69—SS. PETER AND PAUL (1889) (German), Revs. Thomas D. DeVries; Joseph J. Juknialis. Pastoral Assocs.: Jane Ore; Monica Meagher; Thomas Koester Tel: 414-962-8103. In res., Most Rev. Richard J. Sklba.
Res., 2491 N. Murray Ave., 53211. Tel: 414-962-2443; Fax: 414-962-8183.
School—Catholic East Elementary, Tel: 414-964-1770; Fax: 414-964-4656.
See Catholic East School, Inc. listing in the Consolidated Elementary Schools section.
Day Care Center—2480 N. Cramer St., 53211. Tel: 414-964-6638; Fax: 414-964-8360.
Children 100.
Catechesis/Religious Programs—East Side Child & Youth Ministry. Consolidated from the following parishes: SS. Peter & Paul, St. Casimir, St. Mary Czestochowa, Cathedral of St. John the Evangelist, and Three Holy Women. 924 E. Clarke St., 53212. Tel: 414-263-8230; Fax: 414-962-2443.
Students 45.

70—ST. PHILIP NERI (1956), Rev. Melvin P. Breit, Admin.
Res., 5566 N. 69th St., 53218. Tel: 414-464-6721; Fax: 414-464-8504.
School—5501 N. 68th St., 53218. Tel: 414-466-0470; Fax: 414-466-3740. Mr. Michael Brown, Prin.
Lay Teachers 11; Students 189.
Catechesis/Religious Programs—Tel: 414-466-3816. Ms. Mary Teeters, D.R.E.
Students 34.

71—PRINCE OF PEACE/PRINCIPE DE PAZ (1999), Very Rev. James L. Dammeir. In res., Rev. Marti Colom.
Res., 1138 S. 25th St., 53204-1940. Tel: 414-645-8786; Fax: 414-645-8918.
Schools—(25th St. Campus), 1114 S. 25th St., 53204. Tel: 414-383-2157; Fax: 414-645-8918.; (Layton Blvd. Campus), 1646 S. 22nd St., 53204. Tel: 414-645-4922. Ms. Donna Schmidt, Prin.; Mr. Norbert Smurawa, Assoc. Prin.
Religious 2; Lay Teachers 18; Students 319.
Catechesis/Religious Programs—Students 420.

72—ST. RAFAEL THE ARCHANGEL (1999) (Polish-German), Rev. James Kimla, Mod.
Res., 2059 S. 33rd St., 53215. Tel: 414-645-9172; Fax: 414-645-4732.
Catechesis/Religious Programs—Students 157.

73—ST. RITA (1936) (Italian). Closed. For sacramental records contact Three Holy Women, Milwaukee. Tel.: 414-271-2165.

74—ST. ROBERT (1912), Revs. John J. Pulice; Michael J. Erwin; Deacon Dan Zozakiewicz; Sr. Ruth Brings, Pastoral Assoc.; Eileen Ambrose Steckbauer, Pastoral Min.
Res., 4019 N. Farwell Ave., 53211. Tel: 414-332-1164; Fax: 414-332-2599.
School—2200 E. Capital Dr., 53211. Tel: 414-332-1164, Ext. 3018; Fax: 414-332-7355. Mary Miller, Prin.
Sisters 1; Lay Teachers 25; Students 356.
Catechesis/Religious Programs—Tel: 414-332-1164, Ext. 3012.
Students 329.

75—ST. ROMAN (1956) (Polish), Revs. William C. Burkert; Larry Sepich.
Res., 1710 W. Bolivar Ave., 53221. Tel: 414-282-9063; Fax: 414-282-6464.
School—1810 W. Bolivar Ave., 53221. Tel: 414-282-7970; Fax: 414-282-5140.
Lay Teachers 21; Students 438.
Catechesis/Religious Programs—Students 256.

76—ST. ROSE (1888), Very Rev. Dennis J. Lewis; Deacon Julio Lopez.
Res., 528 N. 31st St., 53208. Tel: 414-342-1778; Fax: 414-342-7510.
School—See Elementary Schools, Archdiocesan, Catholic Urban Academies. Tel: 414-933-6070; Fax: 414-933-6071.

77—SACRED HEART (1917) (Croatian), Rev. Paul Maslach, O.F.M. (Croatia).
Res., 917 N. 49th St., 53208. Tel: 414-774-9418; Fax: 414-774-7406.
Catechesis/Religious Programs—Students 10.

78—ST. SEBASTIAN (1911), Revs. Charles H. Schramm; David J. Meinholz; Deacons James J. Peterson; Warren D. Braun.
Res., 5400 W. Washington Blvd., 53208. Tel: 414-453-1061; Fax: 414-453-9449.
School—1747 N. 54th St., 53208. Tel: 414-453-5830.
Sisters 1; Lay Teachers 25; Students 451.
Catechesis/Religious Programs—Tel: 414-453-7150.
Students 244.

79—ST. STANISLAUS (1866) (Polish-Hispanic). Unassigned.
Res., 524 W. Mitchell St., 53204. Tel: 414-645-8170; Fax: 414-645-8170.
Catechesis/Religious Programs—Tel: 414-383-4010; Fax: 414-383-3252.
Students 1.

80—ST. STEPHEN (Airport) (1847) (German), Rev. Richard A. Liska; Anita H. Kowalski, Pastoral Assoc.
Office: 5880 S. Howell Ave., 53207. Tel: 414-483-2685; Fax: 414-483-3160. [CEM 2]
Catechesis/Religious Programs—Tel: 414-483-2658.
Lay Teachers 10; Students 198.

81—ST. STEPHEN, MARTYR (1907) (Slovak), Rev. Richard J. Robinson; Karen A., Abler, Pastoral Assoc.
Res., 5409 W. Villard Ave., 53218. Tel: 414-438-4780; Fax: 414-438-9265.
School—Resurrection Catholic Academy, 5140 N. 55th St., 53218. Tel: 414-438-4783; Fax: 414-463-8721. Barbara O'Donnell, Prin.
Lay Teachers 16; Students 239.
Catechesis/Religious Programs—Students 6.

82—ST. THERESE (1954), Rev. Philip D. Reifenberg, Admin.
Res., 9525 W. Bluemound Rd., 53226. Tel: 414-771-2500; Fax: 414-771-2410.
Catechesis/Religious Programs—Tel: 414-476-5580. Jim Beuscher, D.R.E.
Students 207.

83—ST. THOMAS AQUINAS. Closed. For sacramental records contact Archdiocese of Milwaukee Archives Office. Tel.: 414-769-3407.

84—THREE HOLY WOMEN (2000), Rev. Timothy L. Kitzke.
Res., 1716 N. Humboldt Ave., 53202. Tel: 414-271-2165; Fax: 414-271-7988. [CEM]

85—ST. VERONICA (1926), Very Rev. Thomas Eichenberger; Rev. Ronald Engel; Deacons John R. Burns; John Dziennik.
Mailing Address: 353 E. Norwich St., 53207. Tel: 414-482-2920.
School—341 E. Norwich St., 53207. Tel: 414-744-1214; Fax: 414-482-3025. Sr. Marie Estelle Kuczynski, Prin.
Sisters 2; Lay Teachers 21; Students 416.
Catechesis/Religious Programs—Tel: 414-481-0777.
Students 196.

86—ST. VINCENT PALLOTTI (1998), Rev. Greg Serwa, S.A.C., Temporary Admin.
Res., 7622 W. Stevenson St., 53213. Tel: 414-453-5344; Fax: 414-453-4225.
Schools—West Site, 7632 W. Stevenson St., 53213. Tel: 414-258-4165; 414-258-0687; Fax: 414-453-4225.; East Site, 5510 W. Bluemound Rd., 53208. Sr. Janet Neureuther, Prin.
Sisters 1; Lay Teachers 13; Students 185.
Catechesis/Religious Programs—Students 58.

87—ST. VINCENT DE PAUL (1888) (Polish), Rev. Vincent F. Kobia; Deacon Jorge Benavente.
Res., 2114 W. Michell St., 53204. Tel: 414-645-3400; Fax: 414-645-3450.

88—ST. WENCESLAUS (1883) (Hispanic). Closed. for sacramental records contact Our Lady of Guadalupe, Milwaukee. Tel.: 414-271-6181.

OUTSIDE THE CITY OF MILWAUKEE

Adell, Sheboygan Co., St. Patrick (1853) (Irish). Closed. For sacramental records contact Our Lady of the Lakes, Random Lake. Tel.: 920-994-4380.

Allenton, Washington Co., Resurrection (1997). Consolidation of Sacred Heart, Allenton; St. Anthony, Allenton; and Ss. Peter and Paul, Nenno. Rev. Richard C. Breitbach; Sr. Mary Arnold Franz, S.S.N.D., Pastoral Assoc.
Parish Office:—215 Main St., P.O. Box 96, 53002. Tel: 262-629-5240.
Church—209 Main St., 53002. [CEM 3]
Catechesis/Religious Programs—Tel: 262-629-1500.
Students 207.
Convent—632 Church St., P.O. Box 356, 53002. Tel: 262-629-5342. School Sisters of Notre Dame
Sacred Heart (1917). Closed. For sacramental records contact Resurrection, Allenton. Tel.: 262-629-5240.
St. Anthony (1851). Closed. For sacramental records contact Resurrection, Allenton. Tel: 262-629-5240.

Armstrong, Fond du Lac Co., Good Shepherd, Rev. Kevin J. Wester; Deacon Donald Wright, Pastoral Assoc.
Res., W762 Armstrong Rd., Campbellsport, 53010-1400. Tel: 920-477-3201; Fax: 920-477-3030. [CEM 3]
School—W771 Armstrong Rd., Campbellsport, 53010. Tel: 920-477-2081. Roselyn Baker, Prin.
Lay Teachers 5; Students 51.
Catechesis/Religious Programs—303 E. Main St., Eden, 53019. Tel: 920-477-3741; Fax: 920-477-7211.
Students 250.
Mission—Mitchell, Sheboygan Co., St. Michael Chapel, Scenic Dr., Cascade, 53011.
Our Lady of Angels (1856) (Irish). Merged with St. Michael, Dotyville and St. Mary, Eden to form Good Shepherd, Armstrong.

Ashford, Fond du Lac Co., St. Martin (1847). Also serves St. Kilian, St. Kilian. Rev. Francis X. Malloy. In res., Rev. Wayne J. Barta.
Mailing Address: P.O. Box 740, Campbellsport, 53010. Tel: 920-533-4441; Fax: 920-533-5280. [CEM]

Auburn, Fond du Lac Co., St. Matthias (1863) (German). Closed. For sacramental records contact Holy Trinity, Kewaskum. Tel.: 262-626-2860.

Beaver Dam, Dodge Co., St. Michael (1893), Revs. William W. Key; Daniel J. Massie; Deacon Randal S. Wells.
835 Madison St., 53916. Tel: 920-887-2082.; Res. & Mailing Address: 131 W. Maple Ave., 53916. Fax: 920-885-7602. [CEM]
Catechesis/Religious Programs—Students 117.
St. Patrick (1860), Revs. William W. Key; Daniel J. Massie; Deacon Robert A. Truttschel.
Res., 131 W. Maple Ave., 53916. Tel: 920-887-2082; Fax: 920-885-7602. [CEM]
School—Unified Catholic Parish Schools of Beaver Dam. See St. Peter. Tel: 920-885-5558; Fax: 920-885-7610.
Catechesis/Religious Programs—Students 98.
St. Peter (1855), Revs. William W. Key; Daniel J. Massie.
Mailing Address: 131 W. Maple Ave., 53916. Tel: 920-887-2082.
Res., 101 E. South St., 53916-2599. Tel: 920-885-5525; Fax: 920-885-7602. [CEM]
School—Consolidated with St. Patrick and St. Michael to form Unified Catholic Parish Schools of Beaver Dam. 503 S. Spring St., 53916-2598. Tel: 920-885-5558; Fax: 920-885-7610.
Lay Teachers 23; Students 175.
Catechesis/Religious Programs—Christian Formation, 503 S. Spring St., 53196-2598. Tel: 920-885-6023.
Students 345.

Belgium, Ozaukee Co., St. Mary (1848) (German-Luxembourg), Rev. Donald A. Schmidt.
Res., 6092 Lake Church Rd., 53004. Tel: 262-285-3040; Fax: 262-285-4104. [CEM]
School—Tel: 262-285-3532; Fax: 262-285-3532. Norita Barrett, Prin.
Lay Teachers 5; Students 74.

Big Bend, Waukesha Co., St. Joseph (1920), Rev. Robert F. Surges.
Res., S89 W22650 Milwaukee Ave., 53103. Tel: 262-662-2832; Fax: 262-662-0783.
School—W227 S8930 St. Joseph Dr., 53103. Tel: 262-662-2737. Susan Holman, Prin.
Lay Teachers 11; Students 244.
Catechesis/Religious Programs—Tel: 262-662-3317. D.R.E.: Mary L. Kozlik; Barb Gawlik.
Students 428.

Brandon, Fond Du Lac Co., St. Brendan (1921) (German). Also serves St. Joseph, Waupun and St. Mary, Springvale. Rev. Michael F. Moran.
Mailing Address: 118 W. Main St., Waupun, 53963. Tel: 920-324-5400; Fax: 920-324-1040. [JC]

Brighton, Kenosha Co., St. Francis Xavier (1838) (German), Rev. James T. Volkert; Cheryl Theigs, Pastoral Assoc.
Res., 1704 240th Ave., Kansasville, 53139. Tel: 262-878-2267; Fax: 262-878-3683. [CEM]
School—Providence Catholic School. Consolidated with St. John the Baptist, 1481-172 N. Ave., Paris, Union Grove, WI 53182, Tel.: 414-859-2007. 1714 240th Ave., Kansasville, 53139. Tel: 414-878-2713. Dr. Kimberly Strike, Prin.
Sisters 2; Lay Teachers 8; Students 132.
Catechesis/Religious Programs—Students 40.

Bristol, Kenosha Co., St. Scholastica (1945), Rev. Andrew V. Garber, O.S.B.
Res., 18700 116th St., 53104. Tel: 414-857-2068. [CEM]
Catechesis/Religious Programs—Tel: 414-857-9032.
Students 161.

Brookfield, Waukesha Co., St. Dominic (1866), Rev. Curt J. Frederick; Deacons John Libecki; Larry LaFond; Patrick J. Russell, Ph.D., Pastoral Assoc.
Res., 18255 W. Capitol Dr., 53045-1422. Tel: 262-781-3480; Fax: 262-781-3283. [CEM]
School—18105 W. Capitol Dr., 53045-1425. Tel: 262-783-7565. Ms. Joyce Steffan, Prin.
Lay Teachers 22; Students 483.
Catechesis/Religious Programs—D.R.E.: Kathleen Beuscher; Debbie Olla.
Students 865.
St. John Vianney (1956), Rev. Dennis M. Andrews; Gerald J. Dominiak.
Office: 1755 N. Calhoun Rd., 53005-5036. Tel: 262-796-3940; Fax: 262-796-3958.
School—17500 W. Gebhardt Rd., 53045-5096. Tel: 262-796-3942; Fax: 262-796-3953. Colleen Terry, Prin.
Lay Teachers 26; Students 486.
Catechesis/Religious Programs—Tel: 262-796-3944.
Students 1,044.
St. Luke (1956), Rev. Harvey W. Brahm.
Res., 1300 San Lucas Dr., 53045. Tel: 262-782-0032; Fax: 262-782-6057.
School—Tel: 262-782-4892. Mary Laidlaw-Otto, Prin.
Lay Teachers 17; Students 256.
Catechesis/Religious Programs—Tel: 262-782-0892. Sr. Virgena Clark, R.S.M., D.R.E.
Students 239.
Convent—1305 Davidson Rd., 53045. Tel: 262-782-8148.

Burlington, Racine Co., Immaculate Conception (1838), Revs. David H. Reith; Joseph E. Debski.
Res., 108 McHenry St., 53105. Tel: 262-763-1500; Fax: 262-763-1680. [CEM]
School—225 W. State St., 53105. Tel: 262-763-1515; Fax: 262-763-1508.
Priests 2; Lay Teachers 27; Students 411.
Catechesis/Religious Programs—Tel: 262-763-1505. Mary Spiegelhoff, D.R.E.
Students 227.
Chapel—Powers Lake, St. Theresa.
St. Charles (1908), Rev. Jan M. Kieliszewski.
Res., 456 Kendall St., 53105. Tel: 262-763-2260; Fax: 262-763-9171. [CEM]
School—449 Conkey St., 53105. Tel: 262-763-2848; 762-2637 (Grade School); Fax: 262-763-3818. Sr. Margaret Pietsch, Prin.
Lay Teachers 16; Students 270.
Catechesis/Religious Programs—Tel: 262-763-1505; Fax: 262-763-4229.
Students 214.

Butler, Waukesha Co., St. Agnes (1915), Rev. Timothy C. Bickel; Deacon Raymond Waitrovich.
Office:—12801 W. Fairmount Ave., 53007. Tel: 262-781-9521; Fax: 262-781-3512.
School—Tel: 262-781-4996. Mr. Aaron Hilts, Prin.
Sisters 1; Lay Teachers 17; Students 248.
Catechesis/Religious Programs—Tel: 262-781-6998. Robert Thibault, II, D.R.E.
Students 151.

Byron, Fond du Lac Co., Sons of Zebedee: Saints James and John (2000), Rev. James B. Posanski.
Mailing Address: W5882 Church Rd., Fond du Lac, 54937-8602. Tel: 920-922-1167; Fax: 920-922-1924. [CEM]
Catechesis/Religious Programs—Students 181.
St. John (1847). Closed. For sacramental records contact Sons of Zebedee: Saints James and John, Byron. Tel.: 920-922-1167.

Caledonia, Racine Co., St. Louis (1846), Rev. Gerald J. Hessel.
Parish Office: 13207 Hwy. G, 53108. Tel: 262-835-4533; Fax: 262-835-0421. [CEM]
School—13125 Hwy. G, 53108. Tel: 262-835-2166. Mrs. Beth Eichman, Prin.
Lay Teachers 10; Students 80.
Catechesis/Religious Programs—Students 145.

Campbellsport, Fond du Lac Co., St. Matthew (1864), Rev. Francis X. Malloy; Deacon Robert Fazen.
Parish Center: 419 Mill St., P.O. Box 740, 53010. Tel: 920-533-4441; Fax: 920-533-5280. [CEM]
School—Tel: 920-533-4103. Joan M. Wuest, Prin.
Lay Teachers 13; Students 158.
Catechesis/Religious Programs—Students 297.

Cascade, Sheboygan Co., St. Mary- Cascade (1852). Closed. For sacramental records contact Our Lady of the Lakes, Random Lake. Tel.: 920-994-4380.

Cedarburg, Ozaukee Co., Divine Word (1970), Very Rev. Msgr. Thomas Gajdos.
Res., 1375 Covered Bridge Rd., 53012. Tel: 262-377-1070; Fax: 262-377-6898.
Catechesis/Religious Programs—Tel: 262-377-7371.
Students 584.
St. Francis Borgia (1844) (Irish-German), Rev. Edward J. Wawrzyniakowski.
Res., N44 W6055 Hamilton Rd., 53012. Tel: 262-377-1968; Fax: 262-377-6704. [CEM]
School—N43 W6005 Hamilton Rd., 53012. Tel: 262-377-2050; Fax: 262-377-4099. Sue Brandley, Prin.
Lay Teachers 32; Students 412.
Catechesis/Religious Programs—Tel: 262-377-4891. D.R.E.: Linda Burgan; Helen Jackson.
Students 206.

Clyman, Dodge Co., St. John (1900) (German-Irish). Also serves Holy Family, Reeseville & St. Columbkille, Elba. Rev. John L. Simon.
Mailing Address: P.O. Box 277, Reeseville, 53579-0277. Tel: 920-696-3430; 920-927-3102; Fax: 920-927-3127. [CEM 2] [JC 2]
Catechesis/Religious Programs—Students 55.

Cudahy, Milwaukee Co.,

1—ST. FREDERICK, (1896). Closed. For sacramental records, contact Nativity of the Lord, Cudahy. Tel.: 414-744-6622.

2—NATIVITY OF THE LORD PARISH, (2000), Revs. Terrance J. Huebner; Thomas Walker.
Res., 4611 S. Kirkwood Ave., 53110. Tel: 414-744-6622; Fax: 414-744-6694. [JC]

3—HOLY FAMILY, (1900). Closed. For sacramental records contact Nativity of the Lord, Cudahy. Tel.: 414-744-6622.

4—ST. JOSEPH, (1909) (Slovak-Moravian). Closed. For sacramental records contact Nativity of the Lord, Cudahy. Tel.: 414-744-6622.

Dacada, Sheboygan Co., St. Nicholas (1848) (Luxembourg). Closed. For sacramental records contact Our Lady of the Lakes, Random Lake. Tel.: 920-994-4380.

Delafield, Waukesha Co., St. Joan of Arc (1923), Rev. James P. Loehr.
Res., 120 Nashotah Rd., Nashotah, 53058. Tel: 262-646-8078; Fax: 262-646-8079. [CEM]
School—N50 W34835 Wisconsin Ave., P.O. Box 116, Okauchee, 53069. Tel: 414-567-5775; Fax: 414-567-5786. Dan Hanrahan, Prin.
Lay Teachers 6; Students 59.

Catechesis/Religious Programs—Tel: 262-646-8078; Fax: 262-646-8079.
Students 274.

Delavan, Walworth Co., St. Andrew (1848), Rev. Charles J. Wheatly, Temporary Admin.
Res., 714 E. Walworth Ave., 53115. Tel: 262-728-5922; Fax: 262-728-5878. [CEM]
School—Tel: 262-728-6211; Fax: 262-728-3683. Julie Supernaw, Prin.
Lay Teachers 13; Students 219.
Catechesis/Religious Programs—Tel: 262-728-2792. Mrs. Kathy Zambito, D.R.E.
Students 184.

Dotyville, Fond du Lac Co., St. Michael (1853) (German). Merged with Our Lady of Angels, Armstrong, and St. Mary, Eden to form Good Shepherd, Armstrong.

Dousman, Waukesha Co., St. Bruno (1850), Rev. John P. Schreiter; Deacons Tom Filipiak; Gordon Snyder.
Res., 266 W. Ottawa Ave., 53118. Tel: 262-965-2332; Fax: 262-965-4749. [CEM]
School—Tel: 262-965-2291; Fax: 262-965-2249. David Lesczynski, Prin.
Lay Teachers 10; Students 125.
Catechesis/Religious Programs—Tel: 262-965-4200.
Students 312.

Eagle, Waukesha Co., St. Theresa (1852) (German), Rev. Michael G. Krejci.
Office: 136 W. Waukesha Rd., 53119-2026. Tel: 262-594-5200; Fax: 262-594-5201. [CEM]
Catechesis/Religious Programs—Tel: 262-594-5201; Fax: 262-594-5201.
Students 192.

East Troy, Walworth Co., St. Peter (1854) (Irish-German), Rev. Louis Luljak; Deacon Donald Kuban.
Res., 1975 Beulah Ave., 53120. Tel: 262-642-7225; Fax: 262-642-7228. [CEM]
School—3001 Elm St., 53120. Tel: 262-642-5533; Fax: 262-642-5633. Dr. Siri J. Voskuil, Prin.
Lay Teachers 10; Students 140.
Catechesis/Religious Programs—Tel: 262-642-3634.
Students 248.

Eden, Fond du Lac Co., St. Mary (1888) (Irish). Merged with Our Lady of Angels, Armstrong, and St. Michael, Dotyville to form Good Shepherd, Armstrong.

Elba, Dodge Co., St. Columbkille (1843) (Irish). Also serves Holy Family, Reeseville and St. John the Baptist, Clyman. Rev. John L. Simon.
Mailing Address: P.O. Box 277, Reeseville, 53579-0277. Tel: 920-623-3989; 920-927-3102; Fax: 920-927-3127. [CEM]
Catechesis/Religious Programs—Students 7.

Eldorado, Fond Du Lac Co., St. Mary. Closed. For sacramental records contact Our Risen Savior, Eldorado. Tel.: 920-922-2412.
Our Risen Savior (1998), Rev. Roger A. Savage.
W8272 Forest Avenue Rd., 54932-9801. Tel: 920-922-2412. [CEM 2]
Catechesis/Religious Programs—Students 155.

Elkhart Lake, Sheboygan Co., St. George (1896). Also serves St. Fridolin, Glenbeulah. Rev. Daniel J. Lasecki.
Res., 94 N. Lincoln, 53020-0396. Tel: 920-876-2457. [CEM]
Catechesis/Religious Programs—Theresa Koenig, D.R.E.
Students 198.

Elkhorn, Walworth Co., St. Patrick (1878) (Irish-German), Rev. Michael Benham; Sr. Mary Lou Fischbach, Pastoral Assoc.
Res., 107 W. Walworth St., 53121. Tel: 262-723-5565; Fax: 262-723-7856. [CEM]
School—534 Sunset Dr., 53121. Tel: 262-734-4258; Fax: 262-723-8793. Mrs. Mary Ann Jandura, Prin.
Lay Teachers 18; Students 159.
Catechesis/Religious Programs—Students 295.

Elm Grove, Waukesha Co., St. Mary (1848), Revs. Daniel J. Pakenham; Steven Dunn; Deacons Charles J. Kustner; Richard Piontek; Richard Niggemann.
Res., 1260 Church St., 53122. Tel: 262-782-4575; Fax: 262-782-0677. [CEM]
School—Tel: 262-782-7057; Fax: 262-782-3035. Larry Patterson, Prin.
Sisters 2; Lay Teachers 23; Students 485.
Catechesis/Religious Programs—Tel: 262-782-9470.
Students 295.

Farmington, Washington Co., St. John of God (1859) (Irish). Closed. For sacramental records contact St. Michael Parish, St. Michaels. Tel.: 262-334-5270.

Fond du Lac, Fond du Lac Co.,

1—Holy Family, (2000), Very Rev. Patrick E. Heppe, Team Mod.; Revs. Dennis G. Budka; Victor R. Capriolo; John J. Radetski; Jerome A. Wagner.
26 W. Follett St., 54935. Tel: 920-921-0580; Fax: 920-921-6708.
Catechesis/Religious Programs—Fax: 920-922-4866.
Students 974.

2—St. Joseph, (1871). Closed. For sacramental records through June 12, 1967, contact Archdiocese of Milwaukee Archives Office. Tel.: 414-769-3407; for records after June 12, 1967, contact Holy Family, Fond du Lac. Tel.: 920-921-0580.

3—St. Louis, (1847) (French). Closed. For sacramental records through September 19, 1959, contact Archdiocese of Milwaukee Archives Office. Tel.: 414-769-3407; for records after September 19, 1959 contact Holy Family, Fond du Lac. Tel.: 920-921-0580.

4—St. Mary, (1866) (German). Closed. For sacramental records through 1975, contact Archdiocese of Milwaukee Archives Office. Tel.: 414-769-3407; for records after 1975 contact Holy Family, Fond du Lac. Tel.: 920-921-0580.

5—St. Patrick, (1855). Closed. For sacramental records through September 18, 1960, contact Archdiocese of Milwaukee Archives Office. Tel.: 414-769-3407; for records after September 18, 1960, contact Holy Family, Fond du Lac. Tel.: 920-921-0580.

6—Sacred Heart, (1957) (German). Closed. For sacramental records through November 1970, contact Archdiocese of Milwaukee Archives Office. Tel.: 414-769-3407; for records after November 1970, contact Holy Family, Fond du Lac. Tel.: 920-921-0580.

Fontana, Walworth Co., St. Benedict (1912), Rev. Daniel J. Sanders.
Res., 137 Dewey Ave., 53125. Tel: 262-275-2480; Fax: 262-275-6426. [JC]
Catechesis/Religious Programs—Tel: 414-275-2993. D.R.E.: Patricia J. Donovan; Edward Konieczka, (Grades 7-11).
Students 155.

Fox Lake, Dodge Co., Annunciation (1998), Rev. Michael L. Wild.
Res., 305 W. Green St., P.O. Box 85, 53933-0085. Tel: 920-928-3513; Fax: 920-928-6334. [CEM 3]
Catechesis/Religious Programs—Tel: 920-928-6022. D.R.E.: Barbara Bath; Linda Lentz.
Students 125.
St. Mary (1850) (Irish). Closed. For sacramental records contact Annunciation, Fox Lake. Tel.: 920-928-3513.

Fox Point, Milwaukee Co., St. Eugene (1957), Very Rev. Kenneth P. Knippel; Sr. Mary Rose Accetturo, F.S.S.C., Pastoral Assoc.
Res., 7600 N. Port Washington Rd., 53217. Tel: 414-918-1100; Fax: 414-918-1111.
School—Tel: 414-918-1120; Fax: 414-918-1122. Mrs. Janice Stauske, Prin.
Lay Teachers 19; Students 272.
Catechesis/Religious Programs—Tel: 414-918-1130. D.R.E.: Ms. Barbara Malueg, (Child Ministry); Ms. Patrice Van Hyle, (Youth Ministry).
Students 383.

Franklin, Milwaukee Co., St. James (1857), Rev. Kenneth J. Augustine.
Office: 7219 S. 27th St., 53132. Tel: 414-761-0480; Fax: 414-761-2208. [CEM]
Catechesis/Religious Programs—Students 199.
St. Martin of Tours (1998), Rev. Anthony P. Russo, S.C.J.; Mrs. Bonnie Jachowicz, Pastoral Assoc. In res., Rev. John Nitzki, S.C.J.
Res., 7963 S. 116th St., 53132. Tel: 414-425-1114; 427-8469 (Rectory); Fax: 414-425-2527. [CEM]
School—7933 S. 116th St., 53132. Tel: 414-425-9200. Jeanne Johnson, Prin.
Lay Teachers 14; Students 188.
Catechesis/Religious Programs—Students 400.
Sacred Hearts of Jesus and Mary (1858). Closed. For sacramental records, contact St. Martin of Tours, Franklin, 414-425-1114.

Fredonia, Ozaukee Co., St. Rose of Lima (1909). Also serves Mother of Sorrows, Little Kohler & Holy Cross, Holy Cross. Rev. Neil G. Zinthefer; Deacon Gerald Malueg.
Res., 305 Fredonia Ave., P.O. Box 250, 53021. Tel: 262-692-9994; Fax: 262-692-3085. [CEM]
School—Rosemary Catholic, 53021. Tel: 262-692-2141; Fax: 262-692-3085.
Lay Teachers 7; Students 89.
Catechesis/Religious Programs—Students 78.

Genesee Depot, Waukesha Co., St. Paul (1863), Very Rev. Robert D. Gosma; Deacon Larry Normann; Len Grassman, Pastoral Assoc.
Mailing Address: P.O. Box 95, 53127.
Res., 53127. Tel: 262-968-3865; Fax: 262-968-5546. [CEM]
School—Tel: 262-968-3175; Fax: 262-968-3867. Linda Cooney, Prin.
Lay Teachers 11; Students 206.
Catechesis/Religious Programs—Tel: 262-968-2276. D.R.E.: Janet Shanahan, (Grades K-5); Gary Newman, (Grades 6-12); Marion Lopina, (Adult).
Students 490.

Germantown, Washington Co., St. Boniface (1845), Very Rev. Bernard S. Sippel.
Res., W204 N11940 Goldendale Rd., 53022. Tel: 262-628-2040; Fax: 262-628-2076. [CEM]
School—W204 N11968 Goldendale Rd., 53022. Tel: 262-628-1955; Fax: 262-628-1689.
Lay Teachers 19; Students 268.
Catechesis/Religious Programs—Tel: 262-628-8143.
Students 420.

Glenbeulah, Sheboygan Co., St. Fridolin (1878). Also serves St. George, Elkhart Lake. Rev. Daniel J. Lasecki.
Mailing Address: Box T, Elkhart Lake, 53020. Tel: 920-876-2437. [CEM]

Grafton, Ozaukee Co., St. Joseph (1849), Rev. Michael G. Barrett; Deacons Richard J. Govek; Donald F. Kabara.
Pastoral Center: 1619 Washington St., 53024. Tel: 262-375-6500; Fax: 262-375-6509. [CEM]
School—1206 16th Ave., 53024. Tel: 262-375-6505.
Lay Teachers 18; Students 182.
Catechesis/Religious Programs—Tel: 262-375-6510.
Students 519.

Greendale, Milwaukee Co., St. Alphonsus (1938), Revs. Richard J. Aiken; Walter J. Vogel; Deacon Theodore A. Gurzynski.
Res., 5960 W. Loomis Rd., 53129. Tel: 414-421-2442; Fax: 414-421-8744.
School—6000 W. Loomis Rd., 53129. Tel: 414-421-1760. Margaret Roushar, Prin.
Sisters 1; Lay Teachers 29; Students 464.
Catechesis/Religious Programs—Tel: 414-421-0690.
Students 691.

Greenfield, Milwaukee Co., St. John the Evangelist (1916), Revs. Richard J. Talaska; Richard R. Verberg; Deacon Peter L. LoCoco.
Res., 8500 W. Cold Spring Rd., 53228. Tel: 414-321-1965; Fax: 414-321-4407.
School—53228. Tel: 414-321-8540. Maria Schram, Prin.
Lay Teachers 12; Students 220.
Catechesis/Religious Programs—Tel: 414-321-8922. Debbie Melian, D.R.E., Tel: 414-321-4450.
Students 275.

Hales Corners, Milwaukee Co., St. Mary (1842), Revs. Arthur G. Heinze; Gary D. Nowicki; Mary Matestic, Pastoral Assoc.
Res., 9520 W. Forest Home Ave., 53130. Tel: 414-425-2174; Fax: 414-425-9432. [CEM]
School—9553 W. Edgerton Ave., 53130. Tel: 414-425-3100; Fax: 414-425-6270. Mary Ann Rudella, Prin.
Lay Teachers 28; Students 432.
Catechesis/Religious Programs—Tel: 414-425-3101; Fax: 414-425-9432. D.R.E.: Barbara Searing, (Children); Timothy Winters, (Young Adult).
Students 708.

Hartford, Washington Co., St. Kilian (1863), Rev. Michael J. Petrie Tel: 262-673-4831 Ext. 401; Sr. Helen Hurley, Pastoral Assoc., Tel: 262-673-4831 Ext. 402.
Res., 264 W. State St., 53027. Tel: 262-673-4831; Fax: 262-673-4872. [CEM 4]
School—245 High St., 53027. Tel: 262-673-3081; Fax: 262-673-0412. Beverly Miller, Prin., Tel: 262-673-3081 Ext. 116.
Lay Teachers 19; Students 263.
Catechesis/Religious Programs—Tel: 262-673-3746. June Strobel, D.R.E., Tel: 262-673-4831 Ext. 406.
Students 390.

Hartland, Waukesha Co., St. Charles (1906), Revs. Thomas P. Demse; Romanus Nwaru.
Office: 313 Circle Dr., 53029-1899. Tel: 262-367-0800; Fax: 262-367-6960.
Res., 521 Renson Rd., 53029. Tel: 262-367-9936. [CEM]
School—Tel: 262-367-2040. Sr. Rosemary Rombalski, S.S.S.F., Prin.
Lay Teachers 10; Students 227.
Catechesis/Religious Programs—Tel: 262-367-3277.
Students 936.

Holy Cross, Ozaukee Co., Holy Cross (1845) (Luxembourg). Also serves St. Rose of Lima, Fredonia & Mother of Sorrows, Little Kohler. Rev. Neil G. Zinthefer.
Mailing Address: 305 Fredonia Ave., P.O. Box 250, Fredonia, 53021.
Res., Tel: 262-692-9994; Fax: 262-692-3085. [CEM]

Holy Hill, Washington Co., St. Mary of the Hill (1860) (German-Irish), Rev. Fred Alexander, O.C.D.
Res., 1515 Carmel Rd., Hubertus, 53033. Tel: 262-628-3606; 673-7505; Fax: 262-673-7568. [CEM][JC]

Catechesis/Religious Programs—Christine Day, D.R.E.
Students 175.

Horicon, Dodge Co., St. Malachy (1856), Rev. M. Eugene Kinney.
Mailing Address: Parish Center, 113 Valley St., 53032. Tel: 920-485-2427; Fax: 920-485-2427.
Res., 319 N. Main St., Juneau, 53039. Tel: 920-386-4964. [CEM]
Catechesis/Religious Programs—Tel: 920-485-2708. D.R.E.: Lora Benway, Grades 6-10; Danelle Kegley, Grades PreK-5.
Students 187.

Hubertus, Washington Co., St. Hubert (1846), Rev. Charles T. Hanel.
Res., 3727 Hubertus Rd., 53033. Tel: 262-628-1141; Fax: 262-628-1911. [CEM]
School—3733 Hubertus Rd., 53033. Tel: 262-628-1711; Fax: 262-628-0280.
Lay Teachers 12; Students 195.
Catechesis/Religious Programs—Tel: 262-628-2840.
Students 200.

Johnsburg, Fond du Lac Co., St. John the Baptist (1840), Rev. Joseph H. Coerber.
Res., N9288 County W, Fond du Lac, 54935. Tel: 920-795-4316. [CEM]
Schools—(Grades 3-6). Tel: 920-795-4222. Sharon Allen, Coord.; Consolidated Parochial Elementary School. See Holy Cross, Mount Calvary. Tel: 920-753-4811.
Catechesis/Religious Programs—Students 94.

Juneau, Dodge Co., Immaculate Conception (1875). Also serves St. Malachy, Horicon. Rev. M. Eugene Kinney.
Res., 319 N. Main St., 53039. Tel: 920-386-4964; Fax: 920-485-2427. [CEM]
Catechesis/Religious Programs—Tel: 414-386-4964. Pat Porten, D.R.E.
Students 167.

Kansasville, Racine Co., St. Mary-Dover (1869), Rev. James B. Cera.
Mailing Address: P.O. Box 126, 53139.
Res., 23211 Church Rd., 53139. Tel: 262-878-1762. [CEM]
Catechesis/Religious Programs—Students 92.

Kenosha, Kenosha Co.,

1—St. Anthony, (1910) (Slovak), Rev. Paul L. Raczynski.
Mailing Address: 2223 51st St., 53140. Tel: 262-652-1844; Fax: 262-605-8262. [JC]
Catechesis/Religious Programs—Students 5.

2—St. Casimir, (1901). Closed. For sacramental records, contact Archdiocese of Milwaukee Archives Office. Tel.: 414-769-3407.

3—St. Elizabeth, (2000), Rev. Roman Stikel.
Res., 4804 7th Ave., 53140-3397. Tel: 262-657-6875. [CEM]
Catechesis/Religious Programs—Students 30.

4—St. George, (1851) (German). Closed. For sacramental records, contact Archdiocese of Milwaukee Archives Office. Tel.: 414-769-3407.

5—St. James, (1845) (Irish), Rev. Frederick A. Heuser.
Res., 5804 Sheridan Rd., 53140. Tel: 262-658-8071; Fax: 262-658-2490. [CEM]
Catechesis/Religious Programs—Students 55.

6—St. Mark, (1924), Very Rev. Kenneth J. Metz; Rev. James P. Vojtik; Deacons Patrick H. Frye; Gregorio M. Lebron; Roberto Salazar; Alvaro Dominguez; Charles Short, Business Mgr.; Karen Metallo, Pastoral Assoc.
Res., 7117 14th Ave., 53143. Tel: 262-656-7373; 656-7374; Fax: 262-656-7375.
School—7202 14th Ave., 53143. Tel: 262-656-7360. Miss Shirley A. Boss, Prin.
School Sisters of St. Francis 1; Lay Teachers 15; Students 267.
Junior Academy—(Preschool). Tel: 262-656-7363.
Lay Teachers 12; Students 136.
Catechesis/Religious Programs—Tel: 262-656-7362. Colleen A. Reddy, D.R.E.
Students 415.
Latin American Center—1320 73rd St., 53143-5459. Tel: 262-656-7370.

7—St. Mary, (1929), Revs. Michael T. Newman; Mark J. Danczyk; Deacons Ronald F. Lesjak; James S. Francois; Wilson Shierk.
Res., 7307 40th Ave., 53142. Tel: 262-694-6018; Fax: 262-694-6048.
School—7400 39th Ave., 53142. Tel: 262-694-6650; Fax: 262-694-6740. Sandra Wiercinski, Prin.
Lay Teachers 23; Students 401.
Catechesis/Religious Programs—Tel: 262-694-5474. D.R.E.: Jane Delfield; Sandy Slivon.
Students 788.

8—Our Lady of Mount Carmel, (1904) (Italian), Rev. John J. Richetta.
Res., 1919 54th St., 53140. Tel: 414-652-7660; 652-7683; Fax: 262-652-2542.
School—5400 19th Ave., 53140. Tel: 414-652-7660. Paul Cera, Prin.
Lay Teachers 8; Students 140.
Catechesis/Religious Programs—Tel: 414-652-5057.
Students 211.

9—Our Lady of the Holy Rosary, (1904) (Italian), Revs. John J. Molnar, O.S.A.; Henry B. Maibusch, O.S.A.; Bro. Robert Schurman, O.S.A.
Res., 2224 45th St., 53140. Tel: 262-652-2771; Fax: 262-652-0183.
School—4400 22nd Ave., 53140. Tel: 262-652-5950. Sr. M. Bertina, F.S.S.J., Prin.
Franciscan Sisters of St. Joseph (Hamburg, NY) 7; Lay Teachers 16; Students 397.
Catechesis/Religious Programs—Mrs. Emily Selovich, D.R.E.
Students 214.

10—St. Peter, (1903), Revs. Dan Cambra, M.I.C.; Pete Cibulskis, M.I.C.; Deacon Terrance A. Maack.
Res., 2224 30th Ave., 53144. Tel: 262-551-9004; Fax: 262-552-7004.
School—Tel: 262-551-8383; Fax: 262-551-9833. Mr. Sigmund Kolano, Prin.
Lay Teachers 7; Students 116.
Catechesis/Religious Programs—Tel: 262-897-2602.
Students 275.

11—St. Therese, (1953), Rev. Brian T. Holbus.
Res., 9005 22nd Ave., 53143-6699. Tel: 262-694-4695; Fax: 262-694-7284.
School—2020 91st St., 53143. Tel: 262-694-8080. Mrs. Jean Kuklenski, Prin.
Lay Teachers 10; Students 135.
Catechesis/Religious Programs—Tel: 262-694-0118.
Students 217.

12—St. Thomas Aquinas, (1911). Closed. For sacramental records contact St. Mary, Kenosha. Tel.: 262-694-6018.

Kewaskum, Washington Co., Holy Trinity (1861), Rev. Mark R. Jones.
Res., 331 Main St., P.O. Box 461, 53040. Tel: 262-626-2860; Fax: 262-626-2301. [CEM 2][JC 3]
School—305 Main St., 53040. Tel: 262-626-2603; Fax: 262-626-8863. Mrs. June Gauvin, Prin.
Lay Teachers 14; Students 165.
Catechesis/Religious Programs—Tel: 262-334-4195. Sr. Eileen Curran, S.S.N.D., D.R.E.
Students 248.

Kohler, Sheboygan Co., St. John Evangelist (1927), Rev. Louis J. Wilimek.
Res., 600 Green Tree Rd., 53044. Tel: 920-452-9623; Fax: 920-452-9633.
Catechesis/Religious Programs—Tel: 920-458-9931.
Students 200.

Lake Five, Washington Co., St. Columba (1843), Rev. Charles Hanel.
Mailing Address: 106 Hwy.164, Colgate, 53017. Tel: 262-628-9089; Fax: 262-628-2350. [CEM]
Catechesis/Religious Programs—Students 112.

Lake Geneva, Walworth Co., St. Francis de Sales (1842), Revs. David J. Braun; Julio Mirables Drago.
Res., 148 W. Main St., 53147. Tel: 262-248-8524; Fax: 262-248-5302. [CEM]
School—130 Main St., 53147. Tel: 262-248-2778; Fax: 262-248-7860.
Lay Teachers 9; Students 225.
Catechesis/Religious Programs—Tel: 262-248-8526. Sr. Evelyn Trapp, S.S.S.F., D.R.E.
Students 327.

Le Roy, Dodge Co., St. Andrew (1849). Also serves St. Mary, Mayville. Very Rev. Charles H. Wester.
Res., W3081 County Tr. Y, Lomira, 53048. Tel: 920-583-4125; 387-2470; Fax: 920-387-1121. [CEM]
Catechesis/Religious Programs—Fax: 920-387-0312.
Students 52.

Lima, Sheboygan Co., St. Rose (1860). Also serves St. George, St. George. Rev. Eugene D. Winkler; Deacon William T. Jens.
Mailing Address: N3589 County Rd., A.E., Sheboygan Falls, 53085. Tel: 920-467-4576; Fax: 920-467-4586. [CEM]

Little Kohler, Ozaukee Co., Mother of Sorrows. Also serves St. Rose of Lima, Fredonia and Holy Cross, Holy Cross. Rev. Neil G. Zinthefer.
Mailing Address: 305 Fredonia Ave., P.O. Box 250, Fredonia, 53021. Tel: 262-692-9994; Fax: 262-692-3085. [CEM]

Lomira, Dodge Co., St. Mary (1870), Rev. Vincent B. Holubowicz; David C. Gilles, Pastoral Assoc.
Res., 645 Milwaukee St., 53048. Tel: 920-269-4429; Fax: 920-269-7359. [CEM]
School—(Grades 4-8) 705 Milwaukee, 53048. Tel: 920-269-4326. Sr. Rosemary Herriges, O.S.F., Prin.
Sisters 1; Lay Teachers 13; Students 109. Consolidated with St. Theresa to form Consolidated Catholic School of Lomira-Theresa. Tel: 920-488-4543.
Catechesis/Religious Programs—Tel: 920-269-7273.
Students 169.

Lost Lake, Dodge Co., St. Mary (1893). Closed. For sacramental records contact Annunciation, Fox Lake. Tel.: 920-928-3513.

Lyons, Walworth Co., St. Joseph (1870) (German), Daniel L. Hull, Parish Dir.
Res., 1540 Mill St., Box 60, 53148-0060. Tel: 262-763-2050; Fax: 262-763-9377. [CEM 2]
Catechesis/Religious Programs—Students 60.
St. Kilian, Walworth N Co. Closed. For sacramental records contact St. Joseph, Lyons. Tel.: 262-763-2050.

Mapleton, Waukesha Co., St. Catherine (1847) (Irish), Rev. David A. Verhasselt.
Res., W359 N8512 Brown St., Oconomowoc, 53066. Tel: 920-474-7000; 877-871-8489 (Toll free); Fax: 920-474-4661. [CEM]
Catechesis/Religious Programs—Students 160.

Marytown, Fond du Lac Co., St. Mary (1849), Rev. Joseph H. Coerber.
Res., N10232 Hwy. 149, New Holstein, 53061. Tel: 920-898-4040; Fax: 920-898-9002. [CEM]
School—See Holy Cross, Mt. Calvary for details. Tel: 920-753-4811.
Catechesis/Religious Programs—Students 50.

Mayville, Dodge Co., St. Mary (1856). Also serves St. Andrew, LeRoy. Very Rev. Charles H. Wester.
Res., 112 S. German St., P.O. Box 22, 53050-0022. Tel: 920-387-2470; 387-3130 (Parish Center); Fax: 920-387-1121. [CEM]
Schools—(Grades PreK-2) W. 3018 City Hwy. Y, Lomira, 53048. Tel: 920-583-4286.; (Grades 3-8) 28 Naber St., 53050. Tel: 920-387-2920.
Lay Teachers 12; Students 116.
Catechesis/Religious Programs—Fax: 920-387-0312.
Students 285.

Menomonee Falls, Waukesha Co.,

1—St. Anthony, (1846), Revs. Jerry Repenshek; Robert S. Kroeger; Deacon Robert Wodushek.
Res., N74 W13604 Appleton Ave., 53051. Tel: 414-251-5910; Fax: 414-251-6564. [CEM]
School—N74 W13646 Appleton Ave., 53051. Tel: 414-251-4390; Fax: 414-251-2412. Anne Schramka, Prin.
Lay Teachers 11; Students 215.
Catechesis/Religious Programs—Tel: 414-251-8868. D.R.E.: Rita Capriolo; Chris Meier.
Students 562.

2—Good Shepherd, (1957), Rev. Kenneth A. Mich; Deacon Gene Christensen; Joseph Strazishar, Dir. of Admin. Svcs.
Church & Office: N88 W17658 Christman Rd., 53051-2630. Tel: 262-255-2035; Fax: 262-255-2020.
Catechesis/Religious Programs—D.R.E.: Matthew Hakes; Jean Newman; Richard Harter.
Students 645.

3—St. James, (1847), Rev. Eugene J. Doda, Jr.; Patricia Knuth, Pastoral Assoc.
Res., W 220-N 6588 Town Line Rd., 53051. Tel: 262-251-3944; Fax: 262-250-2679. [CEM]
Catechesis/Religious Programs—D.R.E.: Sr. Carol Ann Jaeger, (Adult Min.); Vicki Lopez-Kaley, (Child Min.).
Students 727.

4—St. Mary, (1905), Rev. Gregory J. Greiten; Sr. Jane Mary Lorbiecki, S.S.N.D., Pastoral Assoc.; Deacons Robert H. Buth; Thomas H. Wuchterl; Thomas Monday.
Res., N89W 16297 Cleveland Ave., 53051. Tel: 262-251-0220; Fax: 262-251-6948. [CEM]
School—N. 89 W. 16215 Cleveland Ave., 53051. Tel: 262-251-1050; Fax: 262-502-1671. Susan Perzewski, Prin.
Lay Teachers 25; Students 412.
Catechesis/Religious Programs—Tel: 262-251-1154. Leonard Pacaia, D.R.E.
Students 443.

Mequon, Ozaukee Co., St. James (1851) (German), Revs. Gregory M. Spitz Tel: 262-242-4198; Kevin Kowalske Tel: 262-242-7978. In res., Rev. William H. Wallaik Tel: 262-242-3750; Deacon Clif Perryman Tel: 262-242-7967.
Res., 11300 N. St. James Ln., 28W, 53092. Tel: 262-242-7967; Fax: 262-242-7970. [CEM]
School—SS. Cecilia and James, (Grades PreK-8). Tel: 262-242-7960; Fax: 262-512-8986. Mr. Richard Goeden, Prin.
Lay Teachers 39; Students 570. Consolidated with

St. Cecilia, Thiensville to form SS. Cecilia and James.
Catechesis/Religious Programs—Tel: 262-512-8983; Fax: 262-242-7970. D.R.E.: Sr. Dorothy Land, S.S.N.D., (Adult Min.); Ms. Pat Roehrig, (Child Min.); Deborah Gannon, (Youth Min.).
Students 391.

Mitchell, Sheboygan Co., St. Michael (1852). Closed. For sacramental records, contact Our Lady of Angels, Campbellsport. Tel.: 920-477-3201.

Monches, Waukesha Co., St. John (1843), Rev. Anthony T. McCarthy.
c/o St. Clare, P.O. Box 68, North Lake, 53064. Tel: 262-966-2191; Fax: 262-966-1829. [CEM]
Catechesis/Religious Programs—Clustered with St. Clare, North Lake. Tel: 262-966-7010.
Students 44.

Mount Calvary, Fond du Lac Co., Holy Cross (1849), Rev. Peter P. Kutch, O.F.M.Cap.
Res., P.O. Box 176, 53057. Tel: 920-753-3311; Fax: 920-753-2130. [CEM]
School—(Grades 1-8) 100 Notre Dame St., 53057. Tel: 920-753-4811; Fax: 753-2411.
Lay Teachers 13; Students 44. Consolidated Parochial Elementary School of Mount Calvary (CPES): St. John the Baptist, Johnsburg; St. Mary, Marytown; Holy Cross, Mount Calvary; St. Cloud, St. Cloud.
Catechesis/Religious Programs—Students 134.

Mukwonago, Waukesha Co., St. James (1896), Rev. Robert J. Drutowski.
Res., 830 Hwy. NN East, 53149. Tel: 262-363-7615; Fax: 262-363-2416.
School—Tel: 262-363-8152. Betty Hafemeister, Prin.
Lay Teachers 11; Students 173.
Catechesis/Religious Programs—Tel: 262-363-5529.
Students 575.

Muskego, Waukesha Co., St. Leonard Congregation (1957), Rev. Jerome A. Rinzel; Deacon Ralph Wisniewski; Carlene S. Larson, Pastoral Assoc.
Res., W173 S7743 Westwood Dr., 53150. Tel: 262-679-1773; Fax: 262-679-4210.
School—Tel: 262-679-0451; Fax: 262-679-8519. Sharon Warsh, Prin.
Lay Teachers 16; Students 260.
Catechesis/Religious Programs—Tel: 262-679-0880. Judee Weber, D.R.E.
Students 978.

Nabob, Washington Co., St. Matthias (1848). Closed. For sacramental records, contact St. Lawrence Parish, St. Lawrence, 262-644-5701.

Nenno, Washington Co., St. Anthony. Closed. For sacramental records contact Resurrection, Allenton. Tel.: 262-629-5240.

SS. Peter and Paul (1848). Closed. For sacramental records contact Resurrection, Allenton. Tel.: 262-629-5240.

Neosho, Dodge Co., St. Matthew (1857) (German). Also serves St. Mary, Woodland & St. John, Rubicon. Rev. Russell J. Stommel.
Res., 148 W. Lehman St., P.O. Box 45, 53059. Tel: 920-625-3144; Fax: 920-625-2143. [CEM]
Catechesis/Religious Programs—Tel: 920-625-3092.
Students 139.
Mission—Woodland, Dodge Co., St. Mary.

New Berlin, Waukesha Co., Holy Apostles (1855), Revs. David C. Filut; Joseph G. Anderson.
Res., 16000 W. National Ave., 53151. Tel: 262-786-7330; Fax: 262-786-0425. [CEM]
School—Tel: 262-786-7331. Brenda Sue White, Prin.
Sisters 2; Lay Teachers 23; Students 495.
Catechesis/Religious Programs—Tel: 262-786-2035.
Students 626.

St. Elizabeth Ann Seton (1981), Rev. Steven J. Amann; Deacons Eugene Brah; John D'Alessio; Marni Geissler, Pastoral Assoc.
Church & Office—12700 W. Howard Ave., 53151. Tel: 262-782-6760; Fax: 262-782-4763.
Catechesis/Religious Programs—Tel: 262-782-8982. Joanne Prei, D.R.E.
Students 658.

Newburg, Washington Co., Holy Trinity (1859) (German), Rev. Robert G. Sampon.
Res., Box 16, 53060-0016. Tel: 262-675-6256. [CEM 3]
Catechesis/Religious Programs—Students 90.
Stations—Trenton, St. Augustine, (1857).; Farmington, St. Peter, (1855).

New Munster, Kenosha Co., St. Alphonsus (1849) (German), Rev. Thomas E. Biersack.
Res., 6301 344th Ave., P.O. Box 767, 53152. Tel: 262-537-4370; Fax: 262-537-4370. [CEM]
School—Tel: 262-537-4379; Fax: 262-537-3527.
Lay Teachers 6; Students 87.
Catechesis/Religious Programs—Tel: 262-537-4359.
Students 209.

North Fond du Lac, Fond du Lac Co., Presentation of the Blessed Virgin (1902), Rev. John A. O'Brien, Ph.D.; Deacon Paul S. Monzel.
Res., 705 Michigan Ave., 54937. Tel: 920-921-9383; Fax: 920-921-1309. [JC]
Catechesis/Religious Programs—Tel: 920-921-5873. Jean Sheely, D.R.E.
Students 336.

North Lake, Waukesha Co., St. Clare (1916), Rev. Anthony T. McCarthy.
Res., P.O. Box 68, 53064. Tel: 262-966-2191; Fax: 262-966-1829. [CEM]
Catechesis/Religious Programs—Tel: 262-966-7010.
Students 416.

Oak Creek, Milwaukee Co., St. Matthew (1841), Rev. William L. Stanfield; Alice Hatzenbeller, Pastoral Assoc.
Res., 9303 S. Chicago Rd., 53154. Tel: 414-762-4200; Fax: 414-571-9973. [CEM]
School—9329 S. Chicago Rd., 53154. Tel: 414-762-6820; Fax: 414-762-3686.
Lay Teachers 12; Students 221.
Catechesis/Religious Programs—Tel: 414-762-6847.
Students 417.

Oakfield, Fond Du Lac Co., St. James (1909). Closed. For sacramental records, contact Sons of Zebedee: Saints James and John, Byron. Tel.: 920-583-4376.

Oconomowoc, Waukesha Co., St. Jerome (1860), Rev. John G. Yockey.
Res., 211 S. Main St., 53066. Tel: 262-569-3020; Fax: 262-569-3022. [CEM]
School—110 Third St., 53066. Tel: 262-569-3030; Fax: 262-569-3023.
Third Order Schoenstatt 1; Lay Teachers 25; Students 286.
Catechesis/Religious Programs—Tel: 262-569-3025.
Students 464.

Paris, Kenosha Co., St. John the Baptist (1859), Rev. James T. Volkert; Cheryl Theigs, Pastoral Assoc.
Parish Office: 1501 172nd Ave., Union Grove, 53182. Tel: 262-859-2484; Fax: 262-859-2684. [CEM]
School—Providence Catholic School. Consolidated with St. Francis Xavier, Brighton. 1481 172nd Ave., Union Grove, 53182. Tel: 262-859-2007; 878-2713; Fax: 262-859-2604. Dr. Kimberly Strike, Prin.
Religious 2; Lay Teachers 8; Students 122.
Catechesis/Religious Programs—Students 40.

Pell Lake, Walworth Co., St. Mary (1928), Rev. Dennis D. Callahan; Deacon Anthony Martino; Marilyn Kingston, Parish Coord.
Res., Box 34, 53157. Tel: 262-279-6295. [JC]

Pewaukee, Waukesha Co.,

1—Queen of Apostles, (1997). Consolidation of St. Mary's, Pewaukee and Ss. Peter and Paul, Pewaukee. Rev. R. Michael Grellinger. In res., Rev. Carl P. Alberte.
Mailing Address: P.O. Box 220, 53072. Tel: 262-691-1535; Fax: 262-691-9219. [CEM 2]
School—449 W. Wisconsin Ave., Tel: 262-691-2120; Fax: 262-691-8606. Pamela Kalaczynski, Prin., Tel: 262-691-2120.
Lay Teachers 9; Students 176.
Catechesis/Religious Programs—Tel: 262-691-2878. D.R.E.: Lynn Famularo; Bill Eder.
Students 298.

2—St. Anthony, (1918), Rev. R. Thomas Venne; Deacon Dennis Anderson.
Res., W 280 N 2101 Hwy. SS., 53072. Tel: 262-691-2326; Fax: 262-691-7376.
School—Tel: 262-691-0460; 691-1173 (Parish Center); Fax: 262-691-2063.
Lay Teachers 13; Students 165.
Catechesis/Religious Programs—Tel: 262-691-1640. Kathleen Amidei, D.R.E.
Students 682.

3—St. Mary, (1858). Closed. For sacramental records contact Queen of Apostles, Pewaukee. Tel.: 262-691-1535.

4—SS. Peter and Paul, (1848). Closed. For sacramental records contact Queen of Apostles, Pewaukee. Tel.: 262-691-1535.

Pleasant Prairie, St. Anne (1998), Rev. Donald H. Thimm; Pat Quinn-Casper, Pastoral Assoc.
Mailing Address: 8550 88th Ave., 53158-2016. Tel: 262-942-8300; Fax: 262-942-8472.
Catechesis/Religious Programs—Students 122.

Plymouth, Sheboygan Co., St. John the Baptist (1861), Rev. Dennis E. Van Beek.
Res., 115 Plymouth St., 53073. Tel: 920-892-4006; Fax: 920-893-8444. [CEM]
School—116 Pleasant St., 53073. Tel: 920-893-5961. Mary Jo Sizonen, Prin.
Lay Teachers 15; Students 296.
Catechesis/Religious Programs—Tel: 920-892-6015.
Students 393.

Port Washington, Ozaukee Co., St. Mary (1853), Rev. Allan J. Sommer.
Office: 430 N. Johnson St., 53074. Tel: 262-284-5771; Fax: 262-284-4112. [CEM]
School—Consolidated with St. Peter of Alcantara to form Port Washington Catholic School, Inc. 1802 N. Wisconsin St., 53074. Tel: 262-284-2441 (K-4); 284-2682 (5-8); Fax: 262-284-4216.
School Sisters of Notre Dame 1; Lay Teachers 20; Students 298.
Catechesis/Religious Programs—Consolidated with St. Peter of Alcantara. Tel: 262-284-6472. D.R.E.: Sr. Mary Hornung, C.S.A., (Grades K-6); Jeffrey Montoya, (Grades 7-11), Tel: 262-284-2102.
Students 462.

St. Peter of Alcantara (1966), Rev. Joseph H. Haas; Deacon Thomas J. Surges.
Res., 1800 N. Wisconsin St., 53074. Tel: 262-284-4266; Fax: 262-284-4216.
School—Port Washington Catholic School. See St. Mary for details. Tel: 262-284-2682.
Catechesis/Religious Programs—Clustered with St. Mary, Port Washington. Tel: 262-284-6472; Fax: 262-284-2102. D.R.E.: Sr. Mary Hornung, C.S.A., (Grades K-6); Jeffrey S. Montoya, (Grades 7-12).
Students 462.

Racine, Racine Co.,

1—St. Casimir, (1913) (Lithuanian). Closed. For sacramental records, contact Archdiocese of Milwaukee Archives Office. Tel.: 414-769-3407.

2—Cristo Rey, (1980) (Hispanic), Rev. Robert J. McGlinn (CHI) Admin.
Res., 800 Wisconsin Ave., 53403. Tel: 262-632-3151; Fax: 262-632-6167.
Catechesis/Religious Programs—Students 190.

3—Holy Trinity, (1914). Closed. For sacramental records contact Archdiocese of Milwaukee Archives Office. Tel.: 414-769-3407.

4—St. Edward, (1919), Rev. Richard J. Molter.
Office: 1430 Grove Ave., 53405. Tel: 262-636-8040; Fax: 262-636-8052.
Res., 1401 Grove Ave., 53405. Tel: 262-636-8049.
School—1435 Grove Ave., 53405. Tel: 262-636-8044. Joseph Majowski, Prin.
Dominican Sisters (Racine) 1; Lay Teachers 22; Students 395.
Catechesis/Religious Programs—Tel: 262-636-8042.
Students 210.

5—Holy Name. Closed. For sacramental records contact Archdiocese of Milwaukee Archives Office. Tel.: 417-769-3407.

6—St. John Nepomuk, (1896), Rev. Thomas F. Lijewski.
Res., 700 English St., 53402. Tel: 262-634-5647; Fax: 262-637-1436. [JC]
School—1923 Green St., 53402. Tel: 262-637-9349; Fax: 262-637-0711.
School Sisters of St. Francis 2; Lay Teachers 13; Students 135.
Catechesis/Religious Programs—Tel: 262-634-0703.
Students 50.

7—St. Joseph, (1875) (German), Rev. Richard J. Stoffel.
Office: 1532 N. Wisconsin St., 53402. Tel: 262-633-8284; Fax: 262-633-8285.
Res., 1712 Chatham St., 53402. Tel: 262-632-6487. [JC 4]
School—1525 Erie St., 53402. Tel: 262-633-2403. Charles T. Cooper, Prin.
Lay Teachers 16; Students 251.
Catechesis/Religious Programs—Tel: 262-633-9005. Susan Gehrig, D.R.E.
Students 196.

8—St. Lucy, (1958), Rev. Jeffrey M. Thielen.
Res., 3101 Drexel Ave., 53403. Tel: 262-554-1801; Fax: 262-554-2009.
School—3035 Drexel, 53403. Fax: 262-554-7618.
Lay Teachers 13; Students 276.
Catechesis/Religious Programs—Tel: 262-554-1801. Sandra Gottfredsen, D.R.E.
Students 337.

9—St. Mary by the Lake, (1852), Rev. Stephen J. Stradinger, Admin.; Deacon James Devona.
Mailing Address: P.O. Box 044200, 53404-7004. Tel: 262-639-3616; Fax: 262-639-1999.
Church—7605 Lakeshore Dr., 53402.
Catechesis/Religious Programs—Tel: 262-639-4493.
Students 151.

10—ST. PATRICK, (1856) (Hispanic), Sr. Carol Kottewitz, R.C., Parish Dir.; Deacon Emilio Coca.
Res., 1100 Erie St., 53402. Tel: 262-632-8808; Fax: 262-637-1536. [JC 4]
Catechesis/Religious Programs—Students 50.

11—ST. PAUL THE APOSTLE, (1965), Rev. Paul M. Esser; Deacon Willard Widmar.
Res., 5700 Washington Ave., 53406-4082. Tel: 262-886-0530; Fax: 262-886-0737. [JC]
Catechesis/Religious Programs—Tel: 262-886-0531. D.R.E.: Carol Badzinski; Pat Jorgenson.
Students 200.

12—HOLY NAME, (1884) (German). Closed. For sacramental records, contact Archdiocese of Milwaukee Archives Office. Tel.: 414-769-3407.

13—ST. RICHARD OF CHICHESTER, (1998), Revs. John R. Kern, Co-Pastor; Russell G. Roetzer, Co-Pastor; Deacons Russell A. Missureli; Howard J. Wirtz.
Res., 1509 Grand Ave., 53403. Tel: 262-637-8374; Fax: 262-637-4230.
School—1510 Villa St., 53403. Tel: 262-637-7673; Fax: 262-637-6364. Charles Leonard, Prin.
Lay Teachers 12; Students 235.
Catechesis/Religious Programs—Students 168.

14—ST. RITA, (1925), Revs. Joseph G. Stobba, O.S.A.; John T. Shirley, O.S.A. In res., Revs. Eugene DelConte, O.S.A.; Alvin Metzger, O.S.A.; Raymond R. Ryan, O.S.A.
Res., 4339 Douglas Ave., 53402. Tel: 262-639-3223; Fax: 262-639-3602. [CEM]
School—Tel: 262-639-3333.
Lay Teachers 15; Students 243.
Catechesis/Religious Programs—Tel: 262-639-6280. Barbara Kratz, D.R.E.
Students 206.

15—ST. ROSE, (1886). Closed. For sacramental records contact Archdiocese of Milwaukee Archives Office. Tel.: 414-769-3407.

16—SACRED HEART, (1916), Rev. Ronald O. Crewe.
Res., 2201 Northwestern Ave., 53404. Tel: 262-634-5526; Fax: 262-634-5767. [JC]
School—2023 Northwestern Ave., 53404. Tel: 262-637-2012; Fax: 262-637-5130. Mr. Robert Hesse, Prin.
Lay Teachers 10; Students 253.
Catechesis/Religious Programs—Tel: 262-634-3607. Mrs. Donna Joas, D.R.E.
Students 210.

17—ST. STANISLAUS, (1904) (Polish). Closed. For sacramental records contact Archdiocese of Milwaukee Archives Office. Tel.: 414-769-3407.

Randolph, Columbia Co., St. Gabriel. Closed. For sacramental records contact Annunciation, Fox Lake. Tel.: 920-928-3513.

Random Lake, Sheboygan Co., St. Mary- Random Lake (1855). Closed. For sacramental records contact Our Lady of the Lakes, Random Lake. Tel.: 920-944-4380.

Our Lady of the Lakes (1998), Very Rev. Richard J. Cerpich.
Mailing Address: 230 Butler St., 53075-1710. Tel: 920-994-4380; Fax: 920-994-2605. [CEM 4]
School—306 Butler St., 53075-1712. Tel: 920-994-9962; Fax: 920-994-2499. Mayron J. Zaydel, Prin.
Lay Teachers 9; Students 152.
Catechesis/Religious Programs—Tel: 920-994-8033. Claire Anderson, D.R.E.
Students 239.
Chapels—St. Mary, 230 Butler St.; St. Nicholas, W4274 Hwy. K.; St. Patrick, W4690 Hwy. A, Adell.; St. Mary, 111 Madison Ave., Cascade.

Reeseville, Dodge Co., Holy Family (1901) (German). Also serves St. Columbkille, Elba and St. John the Baptist, Clyman. Rev. John L. Simon.
Res., 302 Prairie St., P.O. Box 277, 53579-0277. Tel: 920-927-3102; Fax: 920-927-3127. [CEM 2]
Catechesis/Religious Programs—Students 46.

Richfield, Washington Co., St. Mary (1854) (German), Rev. Charles T. Hanel.
Res., 2414 Hillside Rd., 53076. Tel: 414-628-3533. [CEM]
Catechesis/Religious Programs—Students 72.

Ripon, Fond du Lac Co., St. Patrick (1858), Rev. John A. Schmitz.
Res., 218 Blossom St., 54971-1560. Tel: 920-748-2345. [CEM]
School—222 Blossom St., 54971. Tel: 920-748-3760. Dorothy Tessmann, Prin.
Lay Teachers 6; Students 63.
Catechesis/Religious Programs—Students 174.

St. Wenceslaus (1896) (Polish), Rev. Robert A. Fictum.
Res., 411 E. Fond du Lac St., 54971-1591. Tel: 920-748-2325; Fax: 920-748-8218. [JC]
Catechesis/Religious Programs—Tel: 920-748-3826.
Students 155.

Rubicon, Dodge Co., St. John (1870) (German). Also serves St. Matthew, Neosho and St. Mary, Woodland. Rev. Russell J. Stommel.
Mailing Address: W1170 Rome Rd., 53078. Tel: 262-673-3380; Fax: 920-625-2143.
Res., 148 W. Lehman, Neosho, 53059. Tel: 920-625-3144. [CEM][JC]
Church—W1170 Rome Rd., P.O. Box 17, 53078. Tel: 262-673-3380.
Catechesis/Religious Programs—Tel: 262-673-4397.
Students 14.

St. Cloud, Fond du Lac Co., St. Cloud (1870) (German), Rev. Peter P. Kutch, O.F.M.Cap.
Res., 924 Main St., P.O. Box 138, 53079. Tel: 920-999-2011; Fax: 920-753-2130. [CEM]
School—(Grades 6-8) 920 Main St., Box 89, 53079-0138. Tel: 920-999-2411. Mrs. Jeanette Jankowski, Bldg. Coord. Consolidated Parochial Elementary School. See Holy Cross, Mount Calvary.
Catechesis/Religious Programs—Students 54.

St. Francis, Milwaukee Co., Sacred Heart of Jesus (1868), Dr. Alexandra Guliano, Parish Dir.
Office: 3635 S. Kinnickinnic Ave., 53235. Tel: 414-481-2330; Fax: 414-744-7222. [CEM]
School—Tel: 414-744-2483. Sr. Rita Jean Schmitz, S.S.S.F., Prin.
Sisters 1; Lay Teachers 8; Students 55.
Catechesis/Religious Programs—Tel: 414-486-3945.
Students 68.

St. George, Sheboygan Co., St. George (1860). Also serves St. Rose, Lima. Rev. Eugene D. Winkler; Deacon William T. Jens.
Res., N3589 County Rd. A E., Sheboygan Falls, 53085. Tel: 920-467-4576; Fax: 920-467-4586. [CEM]
Catechesis/Religious Programs—Students 90.

St. Joe, Fond du Lac Co., St. Joseph (1858) (German), Rev. Peter P. Kutch, O.F.M.Cap.
Res., W620 County G, P.O. Box 138, St. Cloud, 53079-0138. Tel: 920-999-3131; Fax: 920-753-2130. [CEM]
Catechesis/Religious Programs—Students 63.

St. Kilian, Fond du Lac Co., St. Kilian (1848), Rev. Francis X. Malloy. In res., Rev. Victor A. Kemmer.
Res., 419 Mill St., P.O. Box 470, Campbellsport, 53010. Tel: 920-533-4441; Fax: 920-533-5280. [CEM]

St. Lawrence, Washington Co., St. Lawrence (1846) (German), Rev. Alois R. Van Beek.
Res., 4886 Hwy. 175, Hartford, 53027. Tel: 262-644-5701. [CEM]
Catechesis/Religious Programs—Clustered with St. Matthias. Tel: 262-644-0011.
Students 270. Also serves St. Matthias, Nabob.

St. Martin, Milwaukee Co., Holy Assumption. Closed. For sacramental records through 1990 contact St. Mary, Hales Corners. Tel.: 414-425-2174. For sacramental records after 1990 contact St. Martin of Tours, Franklin. Tel.: 414-425-1114.

St. Michael, Washington Co., St. Michael (1846) (German), Rev. Robert J. Artmann.
Res., 8877 Forestview Rd., Kewaskum, 53040. Tel: 262-334-5270. [CEM][JC 2]
Catechesis/Religious Programs—Tel: 262-334-4195. Sr. Eileen Curran, S.S.N.D., D.R.E.
Students 98.

St. Peter, Fond du Lac Co., St. Peter (1867) (German). Closed. For sacramental records through 1952, contact Archdiocese of Milwaukee Archives Office. Tel.: 414-769-3407; for records after 1952, contact Holy Family, Fond du Lac. Tel.: 920-921-0580.

Saukville, Ozaukee Co., Immaculate Conception (1858), Rev. Karl H. Acker.
Res., 145 W. Church St., 53080. Tel: 262-284-0276; Fax: 262-284-3090. [CEM]
Catechesis/Religious Programs—Tel: 262-284-0277.
Students 149.

Sharon, Walworth Co., St. Catherine (1854), Rev. Richard R. Dolezal; Thomas McKenna, Parish Dir.
Mailing Address: P.O.Box 502, 53585. Tel: 262-736-4615.
Res., Tel: 815-569-2530. [CEM]
Catechesis/Religious Programs—Students 22.

Sheboygan, Sheboygan Co.,

1—ST. CLEMENT, (1914), Revs. James E. Connell; Edward F. Monroe, C.SS.R.; Deacon Baleriano Gonzales.
Res., 522 New York Ave., 53081. Tel: 920-457-4629; Fax: 920-452-2417. [JC]
Catechesis/Religious Programs—High School collaborated with St. Dominic. Tel: 920-452-5256.
Students 170.

2—SS. CYRIL AND METHODIUS, (1910) (Slovenian), Rev. Richard J. Fleischman; Deacon Michael Burch, Pastoral Assoc.
Res., 822 New Jersey Ave., 53081. Tel: 920-457-7110; Fax: 920-457-4001. [CEM]
Catechesis/Religious Programs—Tel: 920-457-8422.
Students 78.

3—ST. DOMINIC, (1927) (German-Dutch), Rev. James J. Jarumbo; Deacon Donald J. Lydolph.
Res., 2133 N. 22nd St., 53081. Tel: 920-458-8787; Fax: 920-458-3280. [JC]
School—2108 N. 21st St., 53081. Tel: 920-452-8747. Peggy Henseler, Prin.
Lay Teachers 14; Students 181.
Catechesis/Religious Programs—Tel: 920-458-5390. D.R.E.: Elizabeth Thompson; Jean Puls; Sharon Pentek, (Preschool).
Students 438.

4—HOLY NAME, (1845) (German), Rev. James E. Connell.
Res., 807 Superior Ave., 53081. Tel: 920-458-7721; Fax: 920-459-9108. [CEM]
School—814 Superior Ave., 53081. Tel: 920-452-1571; Fax: 920-208-4371. Kay Miller, Prin.
Lay Teachers 17; Students 206.
Catechesis/Religious Programs—Tel: 920-452-0129. D.R.E.: Mary Ann Zoch; Sue Seymour.
Students 285.

5—IMMACULATE CONCEPTION, (1903) (Lithuanian), Rev. Glenn E. Powers.
Res., 2705 S. 14 St., 53081. Tel: 920-457-3967; Fax: 920-457-5885. [CEM]
School—Christ Child Academy.
(Grades K-5): 1449 S. 12th St., 53081. Tel: 920-459-2663.; (Grades 6-8): 2722 Henry St., 53081. Tel: 920-459-2660. Carol Makholm, Prin.
Lay Teachers 16; Students 178.
Catechesis/Religious Programs—Tel: 920-208-7922. Sally Schenk, D.R.E.
Students 165.

6—ST. PETER CLAVER, (1888) (German), Rev. Brian J. Szyszko; Sr. Marilyn Brodd, O.S.F., Pastoral Assoc.
Res., 1444 S. Eleventh St., 53081. Tel: 920-457-9408; Fax: 920-457-5290. [CEM]
School—Christ Child Academy, (Grades PreK-5). See Immaculate Conception for Details. Tel: 920-459-2663.
Catechesis/Religious Programs—Tel: 920-452-2759. D.R.E.: Judy Stalter; Barbara Leonhardt.
Students 270.

Sheboygan Falls, Sheboygan Co., St. Mary (1896) (German), Rev. Eugene Neuman.
Rectory: 327 Giddings Ave., 53085. Tel: 920-467-4616; Fax: 920-467-4290. [CEM]
School—Tel: 920-467-6291. Mr. James P. O'Brien, Prin.
Lay Teachers 13; Students 138.
Catechesis/Religious Programs—Tel: 920-467-6282. Marsha Roecker, D.R.E., Tel: 920-467-6282.
Students 460.

Slinger, Washington Co., St. Peter (1856) (German), Rev. Robert J. Bales; Deacon Bernard J. Wendt; Bill Thimm, Pastoral Assoc.
Res., 202 E. Washington St., 53086. Tel: 262-644-8083; Fax: 262-644-7951. [CEM 2][JC]
School—Tel: 262-644-8325; Fax: 262-644-5203. Virginia Miller, Prin.
Lay Teachers 12; Students 128.
Catechesis/Religious Programs—Tel: 262-644-7333; Fax: 262-644-0160. Jennifer Funk, D.R.E.
Students 603.

South Milwaukee, Milwaukee Co.,

1—ST. ADALBERT, (1898) (Polish), Rev. Herbert B. Schubert.
Res., 1611 Manitoba Ave., 53172. Tel: 414-762-0291; Fax: 414-762-2482. [JC]
School—1800 16th Ave., 53172. Tel: 414-762-0064. Felician Sisters 2; Lay Teachers 8; Students 209.
Catechesis/Religious Programs—Students 181.
Convent—1610 Minnesota Ave., 53172. Tel: 414-762-2885.

2—ST. JOHN, (1893) (Irish), Rev. Robert L. Betz.
Res., 800 Marquette Ave., 53172. Tel: 414-762-2440; Fax: 414-762-8600. [JC]
Catechesis/Religious Programs—Tel: 414-762-6810; Fax: 414-762-8326. D.R.E.: Elaine Tessmer; Bob Steckbauer.
Students 183.

3—ST. MARY, (1893), Rev. Robert L. Betz, Admin.
Res., 1304 Manitoba Ave., 53172. Tel: 414-762-6810; Fax: 414-762-8326. [JC]
TOTS Christian Preschool/Childcare—1314 Manitoba Ave., 53172. Tel: 414-764-0283.
Catechesis/Religious Programs—805 Marquette Ave., 53172.
Students 184.

4—ST. SYLVESTER, (1962) (Polish-Irish), Rev. Ronald J. Gramza; Deacon A. James Leggett.
Res., 675 College Ave., 53172. Tel: 414-762-6800; Fax: 414-762-5803. [JC]
School—695 College Ave., 53172. Tel: 414-764-4360; Fax: 414-764-6740.
Lay Teachers 14; Students 211.

Catechesis/Religious Programs—Tel: 414-764-5488. Michelle Heeren, D.R.E.
Students 200.

Springvale, St. Mary (1858) (Irish). Also serves St. Joseph, Waupun and St. Brendan, Brandon. Rev. Michael F. Moran.
Mailing Address: 118 W. Main St., Waupun, 53963-1453. Tel: 920-324-5400; Fax: 920-324-1040. [CEM]

Sturtevant, Racine Co., St. Sebastian (1906), Rev. James Kendzierski, O.F.M.; Deacon DeSales Wisniewski, O.F.M., Pastoral Assoc.
Res., 3126 95th St., 53177. Tel: 262-886-4398; Fax: 262-886-2055.
School—3030 95th St., 53177. Tel: 262-886-2806. Diane Davis, Prin.
Lay Teachers 10; Students 190.
Catechesis/Religious Programs—Tel: 262-886-4420.
Students 128.

Theresa, Dodge Co., St. Theresa (1849), Rev. Vincent B. Holubowicz, Admin.; David C. Gilles, Pastoral Assoc.
102 Church St., 53091. Tel: 920-269-4429; Fax: 920-269-7359.
Mailing Address: 645 Milwaukee St., Lomira, 53045. Tel: 920-269-4429. [CEM]
School—Consolidated Catholic School of Lomira-Theresa, (Grades K-3) 105 W. Rock River St., 53091. Tel: 920-488-4543. Sr. Rosemary Herriges, S.S.S.F., Prin., Tel: 920-488-4543.
Catechesis/Religious Programs—Students 49.

Thiensville, Ozaukee Co., St. Cecilia (1919), Rev. Joseph A. Janicki; Deacon Joseph P. Wenzler.
Parish Office: 138 W. Buntrock Ave., 53092. Tel: 262-512-8980; Fax: 262-242-7977.
Res., 101 Ellenbecker Rd., 53092.
School—(Grades PreK-3). Consolidated with St. James, Mequon to form SS. Cecilia and James. 116 N. Orchard, 53092. Tel: 262-242-7965; Fax: 262-242-7976. Mr. Richard Goeden, Prin.
Lay Teachers 21; Students 309.
Catechesis/Religious Programs—Program consolidated with St. James, Mequon. Tel: 262-512-8984. Patricia Roehrig, D.R.E.
Students 660.

Thompson, Washington Co., St. Patrick (Tn. Erin) (1855) (Irish). Closed. For sacramental records, contact St. Kilian, Hartford, 262-673-4831.

Twin Lakes, Kenosha Co., St. John (1932), Rev. Ronald C. Kowalski; Deacon Stanley Cebrzynski.
Res., 701 N. Lake Ave., 53181. Tel: 262-877-2557; Fax: 262-877-2431. [CEM]
Catechesis/Religious Programs—Tel: 262-877-3033. Dianne Baltazar, D.R.E.
Students 101.

Union Grove, Racine Co., St. Robert Bellarmine (1965), Rev. Howard G. Haase.
Res., 3320 S. Colony Ave., P.O. Box 107, 53182-0107. Tel: 262-878-3476; Fax: 262-878-0194. [JC]
Catechesis/Religious Programs—Tel: 262-878-2009. Ms. Lisa Marin, D.R.E.
Students 331.

Waterford, Racine Co., St. Thomas Aquinas (1851), Rev. Edwin M. Kornath; Deacons Carl A. Mahnke; Joseph Hying.
Res., 305 First St., 53185. Tel: 414-534-2255; Fax: 414-534-2929. [CEM]
School—Tel: 414-534-2265.
Lay Teachers 15; Students 263.
Catechesis/Religious Programs—Students 456.

Waukesha, Waukesha Co.,

1—St. John Neumann, (1981), Rev. Glen G. Graczyk; Deacon Thomas McGuine.
Mailing Address: 2400 W. State Hwy. 59, 53189-6323. Tel: 262-549-0223; 549-0898; Fax: 262-549-0444.
School—Waukesha Catholic School System, (Grades PreK-8). Tel: 262-547-3020; Fax: 262-896-2925.
Students 151.
Catechesis/Religious Programs—D.R.E.: Sr. Dolores Pertzborn, (Grades K-6); Sr. Virginia Azqueta, (Grades 7-12); June Wessa, Pastoral Assoc.
Students 632.

2—St. Joseph, (1844) (Hispanic), Revs. Michael F. Michalski; Aurelio Perez; Deacons Gene Kempka; Jorge Benavente.
Parish Office: 818 N. East Ave., 53186. Tel: 262-542-2589; Fax: 262-542-2570.
Res., 822 N. East Ave., 53186. Tel: 262-542-5487.
School—Waukesha Catholic School System, (Grades 6-8) 841 Martin St., 53186. Tel: 262-896-2930; Fax: 262-896-2935. Mrs. Kathy Rempe, Prin.
Catechesis/Religious Programs—D.R.E.: Ruth Weiss; Marian Lamoureux.
Students 381.

3—St. Mary, (1950), Rev. Brian G. Mason.
Res., 225 S. Hartwell Ave., 53186-6400. Tel: 262-547-6555; Fax: 262-547-6714.
School—School is a campus of the Waukesha Catholic School System. Tel: 262-896-2932; Fax: 262-896-2931. Mrs. Carolynn Caruso, Prin.
Sisters 3; Lay Teachers 15; Students 388.
Catechesis/Religious Programs—Tel: 262-547-6326. Phyllis Hamann, D.R.E.
Students 375.

4—St. William, (1957), Revs. Leonard M. Barbian; Mark Payne, O.Praem. Tel: 262-970-0740.
Res., 440 N. Moreland Blvd., 53188. Tel: 262-542-0456; Fax: 262-547-3616. [JC]
School—Waukesha Catholic School System, (Grades PreK-5) 444 N. Moreland Blvd., 53188. Tel: 262-896-2920; Fax: 262-896-2925. Robert Radomski, Campus Prin.
Students 200.
Catechesis/Religious Programs—D.R.E.: Kay Curty Tel: 262-547-3216; Joseph Schmidt Tel: 262-547-3375; Joe Nettesheim Tel: 262-547-0614.
Students 742.

Waupun, Fond du Lac Co., St. Joseph (1866) (Irish). Also serves St. Brendan, Brandon & St. Mary, Springvale. Rev. Michael F. Moran.
Office: 118 W. Main St., 53963. Tel: 920-324-5400; Fax: 920-324-1040. [CEM]
Catechesis/Religious Programs—Tel: 920-324-3891; Fax: 920-324-3891. D.R.E.: Karen Schmidt.
Students 200.

Wauwatosa, Milwaukee Co.,

1—St. Bernard, (1911) (Irish), Rev. Peter C. Drenzek.
Res., 1500 Wauwatosa Ave., 53213. Tel: 414-258-4320; Fax: 414-258-9972.
School—7440 Harwood Ave., 53213. Tel: 414-258-9977. Mary Kopp, Prin.
Religious 1; Lay Teachers 15; Students 199.
Catechesis/Religious Programs—Tel: 414-476-5968.
Students 187.

2—Christ King, (1939), Very Rev. Dennis R. Ackeret; Rev. Michael E. Nowak; Deacon Arthur C. Dallman.
Res., 2604 Swan Blvd., 53226. Tel: 414-258-2604; Fax: 414-258-1993.
School—2646 N. Swan Blvd., 53226. Tel: 414-258-4160. Greg Dehli-Young, Prin.
Lay Teachers 25; Students 430.
Catechesis/Religious Programs—Tel: 414-258-0916. Barbara Schveidler, D.R.E.
Students 225.

3—St. Joseph Congregation, (1855), Rev. Jerome M. Hudziak; Deacon Jose Gonzales.
Mailing Address: Office, 12130 W. Center St., 53222-4096. Tel: 414-771-4626; Fax: 414-771-4311.
Res., 12130 W. Hadley St., 53222-4097. Tel: 414-771-4627.
School—2750 N. 122nd St., 53222. Fax: 414-771-9826. Jane Uebelher, Prin.
Lay Teachers 17; Students 278.
Catechesis/Religious Programs—Students 365.

4—St. Jude the Apostle, (1928), Rev. Peter P. Carek; Sr. Mary La Von Lauer, O.S.F., Pastoral Assoc.; Deacon Donald Borkowski; Gary Heun, Pastoral Assoc. In res., Revs. Emmanuel Udo (Nigeria); Joseph Uko (Nigeria).
Res., 734 Glenview Ave., 53213. Tel: 414-258-8821; Fax: 414-258-7371.
School—8042 St. Jude Ct., 53213. Tel: 414-771-1520; Fax: 414-771-3748. Roger Baehr, Prin.
Sisters 2; Lay Teachers 26; Students 470.
Catechesis/Religious Programs—Tel: 414-259-0950. D.R.E.: Gary Heun; Dave Baudry.
Students 220.

5—St. Pius X, (1952), Rev. Michael J. Bigley, S.D.S.
Res., 2506 Wauwatosa Ave., 53213. Tel: 414-453-3875; Fax: 414-453-7570.
School—2520 Wauwatosa Ave., 53213. Tel: 414-778-0880.
Lay Teachers 11; Students 117.
Catechesis/Religious Programs—Tel: 414-453-1153. Mary Jane Duffey, D.R.E.
Students 142.

Wayne, Washington Co., St. Bridget. Closed. For sacramental records contact Holy Trinity, Kewaskum. Tel.: 262-626-2860.

West Allis, Milwaukee Co.,

1—St. Aloysius, (1920), Revs. John H. Baumgartner; Robert E. Massey.
Res., 1414 S. 93rd St., 53214. Tel: 414-476-3803; Fax: 414-774-7727.
School—1435 S. 92nd St., 53214. Tel: 414-476-0751; Fax: 414-259-9285. Richard Bagemihl, Prin.
Lay Teachers 13; Students 191.
Catechesis/Religious Programs—Tel: 414-257-3088. Martha Van Duser, D.R.E.
Students 155.

2—St. Augustine, (1928) (Croatian), Rev. Robert Galinac, O.F.M.
Res., 6762 W. Rogers St., 53219. Tel: 414-541-5207; Fax: 414-541-0273.
School—6763 W. Rogers St., 53219. Tel: 414-545-2120.
Sisters 1; Lay Teachers 8; Students 144.

3—Holy Assumption, (1902), Rev. Charles E. Conley; Deacons George P. Sherman; Claude Kennedy.
Res., 1525 S. 71st St., 53214. Tel: 414-774-3010; Fax: 414-774-3735.
School—1532 S. 72nd St., 53214. Tel: 414-476-0508. Barbara A. Nehrbass, Prin.
School Sisters of Notre Dame 1; Lay Teachers 13; Students 141.
Catechesis/Religious Programs—Students 80.

4—Immaculate Heart of Mary, (1948), Rev. Karl J. Schneider; Deacons Dennis E. Fietz; Walter Henry.
Res., 1121 S. 116th St., 53214. Tel: 414-453-5192; Fax: 414-453-0137.
Catechesis/Religious Programs—Tel: 414-453-0300.
Students 129.

5—St. Joseph, (1909) (Polish). Closed. For sacramental records, contact Archdiocese of Milwaukee Archives Office, 414-769-3407.

6—Mary, Queen of Heaven, (1958), Rev. Michael F. Merkt.
Office: 2322 S. 106th St., 53227. Tel: 414-328-5566; Fax: 414-328-5561.
School—2360 S. 106th St., 53227. Tel: 414-328-5577; Fax: 414-328-5573. Mrs. Marilyn Marzolf, Prin.
Lay Teachers 12; Students 158.
Catechesis/Religious Programs—Tel: 414-328-5570. Nicholas Balducci, D.R.E.
Students 314.

7—St. Mary, Help of Christians, (1907) (Slovenian), Rev. Denis P. Weis.
Res., 1210 S. 61st St., 53214. Tel: 414-771-8313. [CEM]
Catechesis/Religious Programs—Students 26.

8—Our Lady of Mt. Carmel, (1938) (Italian). Closed. For sacramental records contact Archdiocese of Milwaukee Archives Office. Tel.: 414-769-3407.

9—St. Rita, (1924), Revs. Richard E. Mirsberger; Robert Katorski; Deacon Richard Brown.
Res., 2318 S. 61st St., 53219. Tel: 414-541-7515; Fax: 414-541-7568.
School—6021 W. Lincoln Ave., 53219. Tel: 414-327-5020; Fax: 414-327-7308. Sr. Joyce Wagner, S.S.S.F., Prin.
Sisters 4; Lay Teachers 15; Students 252.
Catechesis/Religious Programs—Tel: 414-541-7515. Sr. Mary Theiss, S.S.S.F., D.R.E.
Students 186.

West Bend, Washington Co., Holy Angels (1852), Revs. Gerald W. Brittain; John Wutscheck; Deacon Joseph Gates.
Res., 138 N. 8th Ave., 53095. Tel: 262-334-3038; Fax: 262-334-3088. [CEM]
School—230 N. 8th Ave., 53095. Tel: 262-338-1148; Fax: 262-334-1334. Mike Sternig, Prin.
Lay Teachers 21; Students 450.
Catechesis/Religious Programs—Tel: 414-334-9393. Nan Jacoby, D.R.E.
Students 399.

Immaculate Conception (1857), Rev. Patrick R. Wendt.
Res., 406 Jefferson St., 53090. Tel: 262-338-5600; Fax: 262-335-2475. [CEM]
School—Tel: 414-338-5602.
Lay Teachers 14; Students 151.
Catechesis/Religious Programs—Tel: 262-338-5605. D.R.E.: Mary Abel; Marge Schinker.
Students 362.

St. Frances Cabrini (1955), Revs. Jeffrey R. Haines; Michael Petersen; Deacon Michael Koebel; Mike Sepersky, Dir. of Admin. Svcs.
Parish Office: 1025 S. 7th Ave., 53095. Tel: 262-338-2366; Fax: 262-338-2348.
School—529 Hawthorn Dr., 53095. Tel: 262-334-7142; Fax: 262-334-8168. Janice Stauske, Prin.
Lay Teachers 30; Students 422.
Catechesis/Religious Programs—Tel: 262-334-9511. Judy Schroeder, D.R.E.
Students 538.

Whitefish Bay, Milwaukee Co., Holy Family (1949), Rev. Laurin J. Wenig.
Office: 4825 N. Wildwood Ave., 53217. Tel: 414-332-9220; Fax: 414-961-7396.
School—4849 N. Wildwood Ave., 53217. Tel: 414-332-8175. Rebecca Jones, Prin.
Lay Teachers 19; Students 247.
Catechesis/Religious Programs—Tel: 414-332-8156. Barbara O'Neil, D.R.E.
Students 491.

St. Monica (1923), Rev. Alan F. Jurkus; Deacon Eugene Van Garsse. In res., Rev. John R. Paczesny.
Res., 160 E. Silver Spring Dr., 53217. Tel: 414-332-1576; 332-1577; Fax: 414-332-2462.
School—Tel: 414-332-3660; Fax: 414-332-8649. Dr. Maureen Polczynski, Prin.
Lay Teachers 30; Students 457.

Catechesis/Religious Programs—Tel: 414-964-8780; Fax: 414-964-2493. Bridget Flad, D.R.E. Students 263.

Whitewater, Walworth Co., St. Patrick (1853), Rev. James M. Godin.
Office: 1225 W. Main St., 53190-1620. Tel: 262-473-3143; Fax: 262-473-3052.
Res., 126 S. Elizabeth St., 53190-1628. [CEM]
Catechesis/Religious Programs—Tel: 262-473-8834. Sr. Therese Rekowski, S.S.N.D., D.R.E. Students 238.

Wilmot, Kenosha Co., Holy Name of Jesus (1856), Sr. Kathleen Hurley, O.S.F., Parish Dir.
Res., P.O. Box 188, 53192. Tel: 262-862-6466; Fax: 262-862-7244. [CEM]
Catechesis/Religious Programs—Tel: 262-862-2361. Students 200.

Wind Lake, Racine Co., St. Clare (1965), Rev. John D. Hemsing; Deacon Richard E. Milbauer.
Res. & Mailing Address: Parish Office, 7616 Fritz St., 53185. Tel: 262-895-2729; Fax: 262-895-3601.
Catechesis/Religious Programs—Mrs. Millie Luhmann, D.R.E. Students 298.

Woodhull, Fond du Lac Co., St. John the Baptist. Closed. For sacramental records contact Our Risen Savior, Eldorado. Tel.: 920-922-2412.

Woodland, Dodge N Co., St. Mary (German). Also serves St. Matthew, Neosho & St. John, Rubicon. Rev. Russell J. Stommel.
Mailing Address: 148 W. Lehman St, P.O. Box 45, Neosho, 53059. Tel: 920-625-3144; Fax: 920-625-2143. [CEM]
Catechesis/Religious Programs—Students 46.

Chaplains of Public Institutions

MILWAUKEE. *Milwaukee County House of Correction.* Attended by St. James, Franklin.
Milwaukee County Jail. Bro. Jerome Smith, O.F.M.Cap., Chap.
St. Luke's Medical Center Box 21677, 53221. Rev. Donald E. Sass, Chap.

JUNEAU. *Dodge County Center.* Attended by Immaculate Conception.

KENOSHA. *Kenosha Hospital and Medical Center.* Vacant. 6308 8th Ave., 53143-5082.

WALES. *Ethan Allen School for Boys* P.O. Box 900, 53183-0900. Tel: 414-646-3341. Rev. Mark L. Molling, Chap.

WAUWATOSA. *Froedtert Memorial Lutheran Hospital.* Rev. Robert J. Gloudeman, Chap., 9200 W. Wisconsin Ave., Milwaukee, 53226.

WEST ALLIS. *West Allis Memorial Hospital* 8901 W. Lincoln Ave., 53227. Tel: 414-328-6000. Rev. Charles G. Zabler, Chap.

WOOD. *Veterans Administration Medical Center* P.O., 53193. Tel: 414-384-2000. Chaplains: Revs. James Kovarik, O.S.Cam.; Edward E. Lisowski; Norman R. Oswald, Chief, Chap. Svc.

Special Assignment:
Most Rev.—
Sklba, Richard J., Auxiliary Bishop, 3501 S. Lake Dr., P.O. Box 07912, Milwaukee, WI 53207-0912
Reverend Fathers—
Aiello, John D., Metropolitan Tribunal, 3501 S. Lake Dr., P.O. Box 07912, Milwaukee, WI 53207-0912
Avella, Steven M., Marquette University Faculty, 422 E. Fremont Pl., Milwaukee, WI 53207
Bandle, Ronald J., Nursing Home Ministry, 5937 N. 35th St., #2, Milwaukee, WI 53209
Beno, Brian M., Coord. Min., Health Care Facilities, 3827 N. 66th St., Milwaukee, WI 53216
Brundage, Thomas T., Judicial Vicar, Metropolitan Tribunal, 3501 S. Lake Dr., P.O. Box 07912, Milwaukee, WI 53207-0912. Tel: 414-769-3300
Connell, James E., Vice Chancellor, Archdiocese of Milwaukee, 3501 S. Lake Dr., P.O. Box 07912, Milwaukee, WI 53207-0912
Duffy, James H., Madonna House, Combermere, Ontario KOJ 1LO Canada
Hammer, Michael J., Coord. Catholic AIDS Ministry, 802 N. Jackson St., Milwaukee, WI 53202-3879
Knoebel, Thomas L., Sacred Heart School of Theology Faculty, P.O. Box 429, Hales Corner, WI 53130-0429
Kohler, William E., Assoc. Vicar, Clergy, Priests' Placement Board, 3501 S. Lake Dr., P.O. Box 07912, Milwaukee, WI 53207-0912. Tel: 414-769-3458
Lazarski, Marvin I., Arch. Cemetery System, 7301 W. Nash St., Milwaukee, WI 533216. Tel: 414-438-4430
O'Brien, Timothy J., Faculty, Marquette University, 8521 Kenyon Ave., Wauwatosa, WI 53226
Stiefvater, Robert X., Dir. Office of Vocations, 3257 S. Lake Dr., St. Francis, WI 53235. Tel: 414-747-6437
Sturm, Michael O., Coord., Detention Ministries, Dismas Ministries, W192 N16330 Lea Fon Cir., Jackson, WI 53037. Tel: 262-677-8390
Van Vlaenderen, Leonard S., Sec. to the Archbishop, 3501 S. Lake Dr., P.O. Box 07912, Milwaukee, WI 53207-0912
Walker, Thomas J., Coord. Services for Senior Priests, 3501 S. Lake Dr., P.O. Box 07912, Milwaukee, WI 53207-0912. Tel: 414-769-3345
Very Rev.—
Hornacek, Joseph F., Vicar Gen. & Vicar for Clergy Personnel, 3501 S. Lake Dr., P.O. Box 07912, Milwaukee, WI 53207-0912. Tel: 414-769-3490

On Duty Outside the Archdiocese:
Reverend Monsignors—
Malloy, David J., Residenca Santa Marta, 00120, Vatican City State, Europe
Reverend Fathers—
Briske, Larry F., 12818 Pinefield Rd., Poway, CA 92064
Brophy, John L., 445 Broad St. North, Regina, Saskatchewan S4R 243 Canada
Clapp, Kenneth A., Holy Family Parish, Apartado 53, Azua, Dominican Republic
Dolezal, Richard R., 5053 N. Ridgeway, Chicago, IL 60625-6021
Knighton, Marvin T., St. Mary High School, 2525 N. 3rd St., Phoenix, AZ 85004
Konkel, Eugene J., S.S., Vatican II Institute, 320 Middlefield Rd., Menlo Park, CA 94025
Lamb, Matthew L., Faculty, Boston College, Horizon East 411, 125 Coolidge Ave., Watertown, MA 02172
Marek, Dean V., Chap., Rochester Methodist Hospital, Box 1332, Rochester, MN 55903-1332
McDermott, Robert T., St. Joseph, 7607 Trendwood Dr., Lincoln, NE 68506-6544
Santo, Mark, Federal Prison Chap., 13934 Lemoel Ave., Hawthorne, CA 90250
Shmauz, Donald A., Mendota Mental Health Center, 5570 Woodland Dr., Waunakee, WI 53597
Thompson, Jerome F., La Sagrada Familia, Apartado 53, Azua, Dominican Republic. Tel: 809-521-0525
Tino, Robert F., Western State Hospital, 9601 Steilacoom Blvd., S.W., Tacoma, WA 98498-7213
Van Abel, John W., W5431 Hwy 106 E., R.R. #2, Fort Atkinson, WI 53538-9616

Military Chaplains:
Reverend Fathers—
Kienzle, Jerome C.
Mikalofsky, Hilarion A.
Olszyk, Thomas P.
Richter, Robert J.

Graduate Studies:
Reverend Fathers—
Lee, Roy A.
Stanosz, Paul A.

On Leave:
Reverend Fathers—
Arciszewski, Gilbert G., 9151 S. Aspen Dr. #9, Oak Creek, WI 53154
Becker, Franklyn W.
Bittner, Wayne W.
Broach, Richard
Collova, S. Joseph
Conley, Charles
De Vries, Thomas
Fait, Thomas G.
Lampe, Stephen
Neuberger, Michael T.
O'Brien, John
Sosa, Carlos
Wagner, John C.
Wells, Robert

Awaiting Assignment:
Reverend Fathers—
Gaberle, Jiri P.
Gurath, Guy G.

Retired:
Reverend Monsignors—
Donovan, John T., Cousins Center, P.O. Box 070912, Milwaukee, WI 53207-0912
Gass, Sylvester F., Cousins Center, P.O. Box 070912, Milwaukee, WI 532007-0912
Kapalczynski, Eugene J., Cousins Center, P.O. Box 070912, Milwaukee, WI 53207-0912
Murphy, John F., 5510 N. Lake Dr., Oconomowoc, WI 53066
Schmit, Ralph R., Alexian Village, 7979 W. Glenbrook Rd. #5012, Milwaukee, WI 53223
Reverend Fathers—
Adamsky, Raymond J., 3253 S. Lake Dr., St. Francis, WI 53235
Alberte, Carl P., P.O. Box 220, Pewaukee, WI 53072
Amrhein, Peter T., St. Camillus Health Center, 10101 W. Wisconsin Ave. #104A, Wauwatosa, WI 53226
Andre, Leonard J., 11926 W. Mill Rd., #1, Milwaukee, WI 53225
Badem, Wendel J., 3253 S. Lake Dr., #206, St. Francis, WI 53235
Baran, Joseph L., 2022 N. 86th St., Wauwatosa, WI 53226-2745
Baranowski, Stanley A., W782 County Rd. A, Randolph, WI 53956
Barta, Wayne J., N1271 Minnie Lane, Campbellsport, WI 53010
Beck, Richard P., 5606 Cynthia Ln., Sarasota, FL 34235
Beitzinger, George J., 4139 Los Altos Ct., Naples, FL 34109
Belda, Leo W., Camillus Court East #321, 10100 W. Bluemound Rd., Wauwatosa, WI 53226
Berghammer, Robert J., 201 A-J Ct., Theresa, WI 53091
Bistricky, Frederick J., 5171 N. 64th St., Milwaukee, WI 53218
Brady, James J., Cousins Center, P.O. Box 070912, Milwaukee, WI 53207-0912
Braun, Donald B., 108 Lakeshore Terr., Beaver Dam, WI 53916
Braun, Edgar F., W6895 Lost Lake Rd., Pearson, WI 54462-8009
Brey, Lawrence S., 1625 County Rd. 137, W. St. Cloud, MN 56387
Bryl, Thaddeus J., 3965 Lakewood Rd., Harshaw, WI 54529
Budzynski, Daniel A., 3253 S. Lake Dr., #305, St. Francis, WI 53235
Carroll, Edward E., 15000 W. Cleveland Ave., #226, New Berlin, WI 53151-3766
Clark, Gerard J., 3508 5th Ave., South Milwaukee, WI 53172
Cox, William E., 4816 Westway Ave., Racine, WI 53406-3634
Cunningham, Joseph L., W 369 S10450 Shearer Rd., Eagle, WI 53119
Daniels, Paul A., 1216 N. Sunnyslope Dr., #103, Racine, WI 53406
Darnieder, Donald A., Meyer Hall #201, 3253 S. Lake Dr., St. Francis, WI 53235
Derfus, Kenneth J., 3501 S.Lake Dr., St. Francis, WI 53235
Dineen, Michael P., 435 N. Ave., Sheboygan, WI 53083
Dionne, Earl J., Cousins Center, P.O. Box 070912, Milwaukee, WI 53207-0912
Dreher, Ernest O., 310 E. 11th St., Fond du Lac, WI 54935
Enders, Robert F., 238 S. Hartwell Ave., Waukesha, WI 53186-6403
Ernster, James M., 570 Hwy. D, Belgium, WI 53004
Eschweiler, Edward R., Cousins Center, P.O. Box 070912, Milwaukee, WI 53207-0912
Etzel, George A., 365 Gillett St., Fond du Lac, WI 54935
Fetterer, Raymond A., 930 N. 6th St., Sheboygan, WI 53081-4162
Fleischmann, George R., Cousins Center, P.O. Box 070912, Milwaukee, WI 53207-0912
Frederick, Joseph B., 237 Southtowne Pl., #BB212, S. Milwaukee, WI 53172
Gehl, Walter N., Rte. 2, Box 250, Hiles, WI 54511
Glass, Rolland T., St. Francis Home, 365 Gillett St. #7, Fond du Lac, WI 54935
Goebel, Nicholas L., N9628 Winnebago Park Rd., Fond du Lac, WI 54935
Grebasch, Richard L., E6118 Snowtrasse, Bessemer, MI 49911
Hanauska, Joseph F., 31068 Timber Lane, Burlington, WI 53105-9738
Hanley, John P., Camillus Court East #317, 10100 W. Bluemound Rd., Wauwatosa, WI 53226
Hauser, Gerald B., Cousins Center, P.O. Box 070912, Milwaukee, WI 53207-0912
Heck, Roger C., 172 N. Brookfield Rd., Brookfield, WI 53045
Heffron, William M., Meyer Hall, 3253 S. Lake Dr., St. Francis, WI 53235
Hentzner, John T., 3501 S. Lake Dr., St. Francis, WI 53235
Herkowski, Arthur M., 1299 Flora Glen Dr., Sparks, NV 89434-0742
Hess, James W., 1607A N. 8th St., Sheboygan, WI 53081-2733
Hickey, Thomas D., 3253 S. Lake Dr., #303, St. Francis, WI 53235
Hmircik, Donald A., 104 St. Franciscus St., P.O. Box 64, Mount Calvary, WI 53057-0064
Hopf, George S., 80 W. Northwest Hwy., Palatine, IL 60067

Huber, George L., 3253 S. Lake Dr., St. Francis, WI 53235
Hussli, Edward J., HCR1, Box 81, Clam Lake, WI 54517
Ide, Harold J., Cousins Center, P.O. Box 070912, Milwaukee, WI 53207-0912
Janette, Paul, 929 N. Astor St. #203, Milwaukee, WI 53202-3435
Jautz, Martin L., Camillus Health Center #155, 10101 W. Wisconsin Ave., Wauwatosa, WI 53226
Johnson, Howard J., W6332 Lake Ellen Dr., Cascade, WI 53011
Jordan, Francis W., 2527 Ole Davidson Rd., Racine, WI 53405-1442
Kasten, Edward F., 7979 W. Glenbrook Rd., #6002, Milwaukee, WI 53223
Kemmer, Victor A., 188 Hwy. W S., Rte. 4, Campbellsport, WI 53010
Klauck, Stanley B., 12621 E. Laurel Ln., Scottsdale, AZ 85259
Klemme, Dennis C., W267 N2517 Meadowbrook Rd., Pewaukee, WI 53072
Klink, Anthony G., P.O. Box 93, Berlin, WI 54923
Knotek, John T., 5116 22nd Ave., Kenosha, WI 53140-5925
Kolanda, George A., 10101 W. Wisconsin Ave. #101B, Wauwatosa, WI 53226
Kolanko, John R., 7164 N. 42nd St., #2, Milwaukee, WI 53209
Kowalski, Leo S., 3441 S. 10th St., Milwaukee, WI 53215-5117
Kreuzer, Eugene T., 21618 Plank Rd., Kansasville, WI 53139
Kurkiewicz, Raymond J., Cousins Center, P.O. Box 070912, Milwaukee, WI 53207-0912
Lambert, Leo M., Cousins Center, P.O. Box 070912, Milwaukee, WI 53207-0912
Lanser, Jerome E., 4232 N. 90th Ct., Milwaukee, WI 53222
Le Mieux, Thomas A., 1732 N. Prospect Ave. #601, P.O. Box 510306, Milwaukee, WI 53203-0051
Leack, Lawrence J., 1845 N. 60th St., Milwaukee, WI 53208-1637
Lippert, Paul R., Box 238, Plainfield, WI 54966-0238
Loehr, Charles D., W1452 Hwy. T, Mount Calvary, WI 53057
Lukaszewicz, John C., 3257 S. Lake Dr., St. Francis, WI 53235
Lyons, Mark J., Camillus Health Center #108A, 10101 W. Wisconsin Ave., Wauwatosa, WI 53226
Mackin, William H., Cousins Center, P.O. Box 070912, Milwaukee, WI 53207-0912
Macoskie, Melvin H., Cousins Center, P.O. Box 070912, Milwaukee, WI 53207-0912
Maney, Robert L., Camillus Court East #319, 10100 W. Bluemound Rd., Wauwatosa, WI 53226
Matt, Erwin H., 3253 S. Lake Dr., St. Francis, WI 53235
McCormick, Robert J., 11274 Pineapple Rd., Punta Gorda, FL 33955-1238
McLaughlin, Owen F., 400 Sunnyslope Dr., Apt. 119, Hartland, WI 53029-1416
Mogilka, Erwin E., 4321 Marine Dr., Burlington, WI 53105
Morgan, Walter N., 523 W. 11th St., Fond du Lac, WI 54935
Mueller, Joseph J., 10100 W. Bluemound Rd., Wauwatosa, WI 53226
Mueller, Robert F., 1711 S. 9th St., Milwaukee, WI 53204-3586
Murphy, John M., Cousins Center, P.O. Box 070912, Milwaukee, WI 53207-0912
Murray, William F., 3253 S. Lake Dr., St. Francis, WI 53235-3705
Musinski, Donald T., Camillus Court East #309, 10100 W. Bluemound, Wauwatosa, WI 53226
Myszel, George G., 26503 Angelica Rd., Punta Gorda, FL 33955-1408
Nickolai, Arthur A., 6100 Hwy. 73N., Rte. 2, Marshall, WI 53559-9423
Novotny, Robert J., 3253 S. Lake Dr., St. Francis, WI 53235
O'Brien, Eugene C., 1193 Masterpiece Dr., Oceanside, CA 92057
Okopinski, Louis S., 3253 S. Lake Dr., St. Francis, WI 53235
Orzechowski, Walter B., N8180 Lakeview Rd., Fond du Lac, WI 54935
Palermo, Albert A., 1524 Arthur Ave., Racine, WI 53405
Parr, Raymond A., 4031 E. Van Norman Ave., Cudahy, WI 53110-1231
Peters, Donald R., P.O. Box 91245, Lakeland, FL 33804-1245
Piechowski, Leonard E., 5761 Lakeview Dr., Greendale, WI 53129
Podolak, William S., Cousins Center, P.O. Box 070912, Milwaukee, WI 53207-0912
Quartana, Donald F., 8500 W. Coldspring Rd., Greenfield, WI 53228
Rausch, John W., Box 475, Eagle, WI 53119
Rodriguez, Robert, 502 Amber Horizon St., Henderson, NV 89015
Roensch, Frederick J., P.O. Box 210, Nashotah, WI 53058
Roscioli, Dominic J., 5412 23rd Ave., Kenosha, WI 53140-3505
Rykowski, Valerian J., 1411 Winfield, Swartz Creek, MI 48473
Safiejko, Edward M., 10420 Plum Tree Cir., Hales Corners, WI 53130
Sanfelippo, Frank J., P.O. Box 1504, Milwaukee, WI 53201-1504
Schaefer, Verne B., 412 Oak Lodge Rd., Waterford, WI 53185
Scheuerell, Charles A., P.O. Box 211, Nashotah, WI 53058
Schlenker, Richard J., Cousins Center, P.O. Box 070912, Milwaukee, WI 53207-0912
Schmelzer, Linus L., Cousins Center, P.O. Box 070912, Milwaukee, WI 53207-0912
Schmitt, Warren J., 9115 S. Cactus Ln., Sun Lakes, AZ 85248-6903
Schmitz, Gerald T., 365 Gillett St., Fond Du Lac, WI 54935
Schneider, Leon J., 1440 Main St. #7, Racine, WI 53403
Schuster, Valery P., 199 Vine St., Sun Prairie, WI 53590
Schwinn, Joseph F., Camillus Court, 10100 W. Bluemound Rd., Wauwatosa, WI 53226
Seramur, Leo J., 3253 S. Lake Dr., St. Francis, WI 53235
Sippel, Edward F., 519 W. 11th St., Fond du Lac, WI 54935
Skeris, Robert A., 722 Dillingham Ave., Sheboygan, WI 53081
Sowinski, Albin F., St. Camillus Health Center #226, 10101 W. Wisconsin Ave., Wauwatosa, WI 53226
Stangel, Mark J., Cousins Center, P.O. Box 070912, Milwaukee, WI 53207-0912
Strenski, Joseph A., Cousins Center, P.O. Box 070912, Milwaukee, WI 53207-0912
Strupp, James A., 580 S. 18th Ave., West Bend, WI 53095-3755
Sukup, Joseph G., 1104 Park Ave. #4, S. Milwaukee, WI 53172
Thanh Hung, John B., 1711 S. 9th. St., Milwaukee, WI 53204
Theisen, John J., 536 Lake Dr., Random Lake, WI 53075
Trenier, Anthony S., 1154 N. 45th St., Milwaukee, WI 53208-2733
Twomey, John E., 2885 Klovar Ln., #3, East Troy, WI 53120
Uhen, Cletus V., 1100 Fountain Dr. #208A, Racine, WI 53406-3767
Van Beck, Alfred F., 2009 Elevada St., Oceanside, CA 92054
Verhalen, Charles J., 3253 S. Lake Dr., St. Francis, WI 53235
Wallaik, William H., 11300 N. St. James Ln., 28W, Mequon, WI 53092-3047
Walter, Charles W., 2205 S. Cypress Bend Dr., #804, Pompano Beach, FL 33069
Walter, John F., 10100 W. Bluemound Rd., Wauwatosa, WI 53226
Wawiorka, Ray W., P.O. Box 578, Kenosha, WI 53141
Weber, Donald N., Brookfield Highlands #1006, 20950 George Hunt Cir., Waukesha, WI 53186
Weber, Gordon A., Brookfield Highlands #1006, 20950 George Hunt Cir., Waukesha, WI 53186
Weishar, Paul M., N110 W16973 Ashbury Cir., #6, Germantown, WI 53022
Wieland, Edward R., Cousins Center, P.O. Box 070912, Milwaukee, WI 53207-0912
Witkowski, Raymond A., 3939 S. 92nd St., Greenfield, WI 53228
Witon, Russell F., 11200 W. Morgan #3, Milwaukee, WI 53228
Wittemann, Paul J., 104 St. Franciscus St., Mount Calvary, WI 53057
Wolf, Robert J., Cousins Center, P.O. Box 070912, Milwaukee, WI 53207-0912
Yaniak, Frank J., 3501 S. Lake Dr., St. Francis, WI 53235
Zeihen, Joseph N., Cousins Center, P.O. Box 070912, Milwaukee, WI 53207-0912
Zens, Roger A., 2620 S. 30th St., Milwaukee, WI 53215
Zerkel, Donald F., W15519 McKinley Ln., Athelstane, WI 54104
Zwaska, Victor L., 1201 Hughitt Ave., Box 969, Superior, WI 54880

Permanent Deacons:
Acosta, Carlos R., (Retired)
Anderberg, Russell F. (CHI), St. Benedict, Fontana
Anderson, Dennis D., St. Anthony, Pewaukee
Aschenbrener, James L., Corpus Christi, Milwaukee
Banach, William A., Holy Spirit, Milwaukee
Benavente, Jorge, St. Joseph, Waukesha
Blas, Franciso, Cristo Rey, Racine
Blaze, Edward, All Saints, Milwaukee
Borkowski, Donald A., St. Jude the Apostle, Wauwatosa
Brah, Eugene D., St. Elizabeth Ann Seton, New Berlin
Braun, Warren D., St. Sebastian, Milwaukee
Brousseau, Gerald A., Out of Archdiocese
Brown, Richard J., St. Rita, West Allis
Burch, Michael F., SS. Cyril & Methodius, Sheboygan
Burns, John R., St. Veronica, Milwaukee
Buth, Robert H., St. Mary's, Menomonee Falls
Buyck, Gerald W., Out of Archdiocese
Castaneda, Claudio C., Leave of Absence
Cebrzynski, Stanly J., (Retired)
Cesarec, Michael E., Our Lady of Good Hope, Milwaukee
Champagne, John I., St. Benedict the Moor, Milwaukee
Chrisien, James, St. Boniface, Germantown
Christensen, Eugene M., Good Shepherd, Menomonee Falls
Coca, Emilio, St. Patrick, Racine
Cody, Edward F., St. Patrick, Beaver Dam
Colainni, Arthur R., Awaiting Assignment
Collins, Dean J., Mother of Good Counsel, Milwaukee
Connors, Joseph, Cong. of the Great Spirit, Milwaukee
Cornejo, Carlos, St. Anthony, Milwaukee
Corsten, Dale, Leave of Absence
D'Alessio, John, St. Elizabeth Ann Seton, New Berlin
Dahlen, Clarence J., (Retired)
Dallman, Arthur C., Christ King, Wauwatosa
Devona, James E., St. Mary, Racine
Doerr, George J., Out of Archdiocese
Dominquez, Alvaro, St. Mark, Kenosha
Dziennik, John R., St. Veronica, Milwaukee
Ebel, John A., St. Bernadette, Milwaukee
Fazen, Robert J., St. Matthew, Campbellsport
Ference, Dennis H., Mother of God Counsel, Milwaukee
Fietz, Dennis E., Immaculate Heart of Mary, West Allis
Filipiak, Thomas P., St. Bruno, Dousman
Finley, Michael J., St. John Neumann, Waukesha
Flynn, Richard M., Blessed Sacrament, Milwaukee
Francois, James S., St. Mary, Kenosha
Fricano, John A., St. Aloysius, West Allis
Frye, Patrick H., St. Mark, Kenosha
Gamez, Antonio U., Leave of Absence
Gates, Joseph, Holy Angels, West Bend
Gliniecki, Harry F., (Retired)
Gonzales, Jose U., St. Joseph, Wauwatosa
Gonzalez, Baleriano O., Sick Leave
Goodman, Robert E., Three Holy Women, Milwaukee
Govek, Richard J., St. Joseph, Grafton
Gramza, Richard G., (Retired)
Griffiths, Joseph J., Out of Archdiocese
Grimyser, Peter G., Leave of Absence
Gurzynski, Theodore A., St. Alphonsus, Greendale
Gust, Peter L., (Retired)
Guttierrez, Jose H., Holy Trinity-Guadalupe, Milwaukee
Guzman, Armindo, Out of Archdiocese
Henry, Walter, Immaculate Heart of Mary, West Allis
Hiller, Richard D., (Retired)
Horner, Ralph E., St. Michael, St. Michael; St. John of God, Farmington
Huber, Paul, Divine Word, Cedarburg
Hughes, Larry L., St. Joseph, Fond du Lac
Hughes, Wayne W., Leave of Absence
Hunt, Thomas N., SS. Peter & Paul, Milwaukee
Hying, Joseph H., Personal Leave
Janasik, Ralph R., Personal Leave
Jens, William T., St. George, St. George; St. Rose of Lima, Lima
Kabara, Donald F., St. Joseph, Grafton
Kaczmarek, Raymond J., Sick Leave
Kastenholz, Joseph H., Our Lady of Good Hope, Milwaukee
Kehrer, Daniel F., St. Casimir, Kenosha
Kempka, Eugene A., St. Joseph, Waukesha
Kennedy, Claude V., Personal Leave
Kennedy, David L., Out of Archdiocese
Klinkhammer, Phillip H., (Retired)
Koebel, Michael S., St. Frances Cabrini, West Bend
Kornburger, Ralph W., Jr., St. Catherine, Milwaukee
Kuban, Donald J. (PHX), St. Peter, East Troy
Kustner, Charles J., St. Mary, Elm Grove
La Fond, M. Larry, Jr., St. Dominic, Brookfield
Lauer, David A., Sacred Heart, Racine

Lazaga, Alfred C., Out of Archdiocese
Lebron, Gregorio, Latin Amerian Center, Kenosha and St. Mark
Leggett, A. James, St. Sylvester, South Milwaukee
Lesjak, Ronald F., St. Mary, Kenosha
Libecki, John K., (Retired)
Lo Coco, Peter L., St. John the Evangelist, Greenfield
Lopez, Julio, Sts. Rose, Michael and Francis of Assisi, Milwaukee
Losiniecki, Thomas, Leave of Absence
Lowe, Stanley, St. Charles Borromeo, Milwaukee
Lukacevich, William J., (Retired)
Lupo, Samuel J., St. Rita, West Allis
Lydolph, Donald J., St. Dominic, Sheboygan
Maack, Terrance A., St. Peter, Kenosha
Macias, Rogelio, St. Patrick, Milwaukee
Mahnke, Carl A., St. Thomas Aquinas, Waterford
Maier, Louis A., Jr., Out of Archdiocese
Majewski, Edward H., (Retired)
Malischke, Carl J., Leave of Absence
Malueg, Gerald D., St. Rose of Lima, Fredonia; St. Mary, Little Kohler
Mandujano, J. Eufemio, Leave of Absence
Martinez, John S., St. Vincent de Paul, Milwaukee
Martino, Anthony, St. Mary, Pell Lake
McGuine, Thomas W., St. John Neumann, Waukesha
Mensah, Anthony J., St. Martin de Porres, Milwaukee
Merten, Arthur H., (Retired)
Meuler, Andrew, Mother of Good Counsel, Milwaukee
Milbauer, Richard E., St. Clare, Wind Lake
Miller, Kenneth J., Sick Leave
Missureli, Russell A., St. Richard, Racine
Moczydlowski, Chester A., (Retired)
Molina, Juan A., St. Rose of Lime, St. Michael, St. Francis of Assisi, Milwaukee
Monday, John P., Our Lady of Lourdes, Milwaukee
Monday, Thomas C., St. Mary, Menomonee Falls
Monzel, Paul S., Presentation, North Fond du Lac
Moser, Arnet L., (Retired)
Munoz, Ricardo, St. Louis, Fond du Lac
Nawrocik, Zenon L., Out of Archdiocese
Nguyen, Bruno Long H., St. Anthony, Milwaukee
Nicholas, Keith P., Leave of Absence
Niggemann, Richard D., St. Mary, Elm Grove
Normann, Larry E., St. Paul, Genesee Depot
Nowicki, Edward J., (Retired)
Ode, LeRoy, Sacred Heart of Jesus, St. Francis
Oelke, Gordon R., Leave of Absence
Pemper, Frank, Out of Archdiocese
Perryman, Clifton, St. James, Mequon
Peterson, James J., St. Sebastian, Milwaukee
Pettey, Lawrence C., (Retired)
Piontek, Richard T., St. Mary, Elm Grove
Pollak, David R., Holy Spirit, Milwaukee
Ponec, Gerald R., Holy Family, Cudahy
Poulin, Edwin D., Leave of Absence
Przedpelski, Steven J., St. Francis Cabrini, West Bend
Regan, Sylvester R., (Retired)
Rick, Wayne W., Leave of Absence
Rodriguez, Virgilio, Out of Archdiocese
Rooney, Michael R., St. Margaret Mary, Milwaukee
Rosado, Salvador, Sts. Francis of Assisi, Michael, Rose, Milwaukee
Salazar, Roberto, St. Mark, Kenosha
Schieffer, Robert M., Our Lady of Good Hope, Milwaukee
Schimmels, Thomas J., Mother of Perpetual Help, Milwaukee
Schopper, Eugene E., Out of Archdiocese
Sherman, George, Holy Assumption, West Allis
Shierk, Wilson A., St. Mary, Kenosha
Snyder, Gordon J., St. Bruno, Dousman
Sommers, David W., St. Matthias, Milwaukee
Spoke, Chester R., (Retired)
Surges, Thomas J., St. Peter of Alcantara, Port Washington
Thoresen, Norman, Out of Archdiocese
Treichel, Robert B., Out of Archdiocese
Truttschel, Robert A., St. Patrick, Beaver Dam
Van Garsse, Eugene E., St. Monica, Whitefish Bay
Vernon, Kenneth L., (Retired)
Waitrovich, Raymond, St. Agnes, Butler
Wargin, John R., Immaculate Conception, Milwaukee
Weber, C. Edward, St. Eugene, Fox Point
Wells, Randal S., St. Michael, Beaver Dam
Wendt, Bernard J., St. Peter, Slinger
Wenzel, Donald P., Personal Leave
Wenzler, Joseph P., St. Cecilia, Thiensville
Widmar, Willard M., St. Paul the Apostle, Racine
Wirtz, Howard
Wisniewski, DeSales, O.F.M., St. Sebastian, Sturtevant
Wisniewski, Ralph, St. Leonard, Muskego
Wodushek, Robert A., St. Anthony, Menomonee Falls
Wolf, Kenneth W., (Retired)
Wright, Donald J., Good Shepherd, Armstrong
Wuchterl, Thomas H., St. Mary, Menomonee Falls
Yang, Blong P., St. Michael (Hmong Community), Milwaukee
Zalewski, Leon J., St. Adalbert, South Milwaukee
Zimprich, David L., St. Anthony, Menomonee Falls
Zozakiewicz, Daniel T., Holy Family, Whitefish Bay

Reverend Fathers—
Niggeman, Richard D., St. Mary, Elm Grove

INSTITUTIONS LOCATED IN THE ARCHDIOCESE

[A] SEMINARIES, ARCHDIOCESAN

ST. FRANCIS. *Saint Francis Seminary*, 3257 S. Lake Dr., 53235. Tel: 414-747-6400; Fax: 414-747-6442.
E-mail: bjanczak@sfs.edu
Web site: www.sfs.edu
Very Rev. Andrew L. Nelson, S.T.L., Ph.D., Rector; Rev. Michael G. Witczak, M.Div., S.L.L., S.L.D., Vice Rector; Dr. David A. Stosur, Ph.D., Academic Dean; Ms. Susan Petersen, MAPS, Registrar; Rev. James T. Schuerman, Mag. Theol., D.Min. (Cand.), Spiritual Dir.; Mr. Gary Pokorny, M.Div., D.Min. (Cand.), Dir. Lay Formation; Dr. Nancy A. Sell, M.T.S., D.Min., Dir. Pastoral Formation; Rev. Stephen E. Malkiewicz, O.F.M., M.A., Dir. Worship; Sr. Mary Ellen Collins, O.S.F., M.A., Assoc. Dir. Worship for Music; Ms. Colleen O.Connor, M.Div., Dir. Salzmann Library; Ms. Mary E. Carian, M.A., M.S., Technical/Public Service Librarian; Mr. Timothy Charek, M.Div., Dir. Certificate Division; Dr. Barbara V. Schauer, M.T.S., D.Min., Assoc. Dir. Certificate Division; Ms. Maria Borda-Wiesner, M.A.P.S., C.N.A., Coord., Spanish-Speaking Certificate Formation Programs; Rev. Niles J. Kauffman, O.F.M.Cap., Coord., Pastoral Form. Certificate Programs; Ms. Sarita Herrera, Information System Admin.; Mr. Kevin Dean, Educ. Technology Specialist; Ms. Patricia Young, M.A.P.S., Advancement Dir.; Revs. Joseph J. Juknialis, M.A., Dir. Preaching Institute; Stephen V. DeLeers, M.Div., M.A., D.Min; Bryan N. Massingale, M.Div., S.T.L., S.T.D.; Melvin E. Michalski, M.Ph., Ph.L., D.Theo.; Ross A. Shecterle, M.Div., S.T.L., M.S., Ph.D.; Dr. Daniel J. Scholz, Ph.D.; Dr. Jane E. Linahan, Ph.D.; Dr. Dennis D. Sylva, Ph.D.; Dr. Barbara G. Turner, Ph.D.; Ms. Sharon Huizenga, M.A., Coord. ESL. Administration & Faculty 28; Priests 10; Sisters 1; Lay Staff 17; Seminarians 25; Lay Graduate Students 79; Certificate Lay Students 23; Certificate Deacon Students 7; Certificate Spanish Students 14.

College Formation Program, SS. Peter and Paul Residence, 2479 N. Murray Ave., Milwaukee, 53211. Tel: 414-964-6982; Fax: 414-962-8183. Rev. Joseph J. Juknialis, Dir. Tel: 414-964-6970. Priests 1; Students 8.

Casa San Antonio, 1711 S. 9th St., Milwaukee, 53204-3519. Tel: 414-645-1455; Fax: 414-645-1456. Rev. Lawrence V. Dulek, Dir. Casa Program. Priests 1; Students 4.

[B] SEMINARIES, RELIGIOUS OR SCHOLASTICATES

FRANKLIN. *Xaverian Missionary Fathers College Seminary*, 4500 Xavier Dr., 53132. Tel: 414-421-0831; Fax: 414-421-9108.
E-mail: xavmissionswi@hotmail.com
Web site: www.sigmaweb.net/xavmissions/
Very Rev. Vasco J. Milani, S.X.; Revs. Lawrence Crosara, S.X.; Alfredo Turco, S.X. (Italy); Dominic Caldognetto, S.X. (Italy). Priests 4.

HALES CORNERS. *Sacred Heart School of Theology*, 7335 S. Highway 100, P.O. Box 429, 53130-0429. Tel: 414-425-8300; Fax: 414-529-6999.
E-mail: shst@msn.com
Web site: www.shst.edu
Very Rev. James D. Brackin, S.C.J., M.Div., J.D., Pres.-Rector; Revs. Otto N. Bucher, O.F.M.Cap., S.T.L., S.S.L., Vice Rector, Dir. Recruitment; Thomas L. Knoebel, Ph.D., Academic Dean & Dir. M.A. Program & Admissions; Robert W. Schiavone, M.A., Dir. Field Education; Martin Barnum, M.A., M.Div., Dir. Spiritual Formation; Ms. Margaret E. Boyles, M.E.P.D., Dir. Public Rels.; Mr. Michael Erato, Dir. Plant Operations; Ms. Kathleen M. Harty, M.R., M.A.L.S., Dir. Library; Ms. Rose Stinefast, M.A., Dir. Continuing Educ.; Ms. Sally Smits, M.B.A., Vice Pres. Finance/Personnel; Mr. Robert Gotcher, Ph.D. Cand., Registrar & Asst. to Academic Dean; Revs. Matthias P. Cremer, S.C.J., S.T.L., Professor Emeritus; John T. O'Connor, S.C.J., J.C.L., S.T.D., Professor Emeritus; Joseph Gole, S.T.D. (Slovenia), Professor Emeritus; Sr. Martine Hundelt, S.S.S.F., Ph.D., Professor Emerita; Sr. Agnese Jasko, P.H.J.C., M.A.L.S., Professor Emerita.
Full-Time Faculty: Revs. Hugh G. Birdsall, S.D.S., M.A., M.S.; Jan de Jong, S.C.J., S.T.D., S.T.L.; Raul Gomez, S.D.S., M.Div., M.P.A., Ph.D. can; Paul Grizzelle-Reid, S.C.J., M.S., M.Div.; Jerome Higgins, O.F.M.Cap., M.Ed., M.A.S., D.Min.; Paul Kelly, S.C.J., M.Div., M.A.; Donald Krebs, M.A.; Thomas Michael McLernon, M.Ed.; Vincent McNally, Ph.D. (Canada); Andre Papineau, S.D.S., M.A.; Bro. Michael Fette, S.C.J., B.A.; Sr. Mary C. Carroll, S.S.S.F., M.A.; Sr. Marilyn Cowser, O.S.F., M.A.; Sr. Elizabeth M. Hoell, S.S.N.D., M.M., M.Chr.Sp.; Sr. Joan Koehler, S.S.S.F., M.Ed., M.A.; Sr. Roseann Wagner, S.S.S.F., B.M., M.T.S.; Dr. John Gallam, Ph.D.; Dr. Anthony LoPresti, Ph.D.; Dr. Richard Lux, Ph.D.; Dr. Bruce Malchow, Ph.D.; Dr. Steven Shippee, Ph.D.; Mr. C. Christian Rich, B.A., M.M.; Dr. M. Esther Warren, Psy.D.; Ms. Jean Garrity, M.Ed., M.S., ESL; Ms. Allegra Troiano, M.A., ESL.
Part-Time Faculty: Revs. Charles Brown, S.C.J., Ph.D.; Thomas T. Brundage, J.C.L.; Stephen DeLeers, M.A., M.Div., D.Min; Paul Hartmann, J.C.L.; Brian McCullough, S.C.J., M.Div.; Michael Van Der Peet, S.C.J., M.A.; John G. Yockey, Ph.D.; Ze'ev Harari, M.A., M.H.L., Rabbi; Ms. Mary DeSantis, B.A.; Ms. Eva Diaz, M.A.P.S.; Ms. Rosemarie Fisher, M.S.W.; Ms. Glenna Gustin, B.A., M.F.A.; Ms. Brigid O'Donnell, M.A.; Ms. Barbara Scherrer, B.A., M.S.T.; Mr. Joseph Schneider, M.S. Priests 25; Brothers 1; Sisters 7; Lay Faculty 17; Lay Staff 21; Non-Catholic Clergymen 1; Rabbis 1; Religious Candidates 2; Diocesan Candidates 117; M.A. Candidates 24; Students 143; Total Staff 71.

MOUNT CALVARY. *St. Felix Friary*, W1754 State Hwy. 149, 53057. Tel: 920-753-3111; Fax: 920-753-3111.
E-mail: harmoniken@juno.com
Novitiate House of the Capuchin Province of St. Joseph and St. Mary. Revs. Oliver Bambenek, O.F.M.Cap.; Kenneth R. Casper, O.F.M.Cap., Local Min., Novitiate Team; Simeon Keogh, O.F.M.Cap.; Bro. John Shento, O.F.M.Cap., Novice Dir. Priests 3.

St. Lawrence Seminary, 53057. Tel: 920-753-3911; Fax: 920-753-2907.
Web site: stlawrence.edu
High School Seminary and Ministry Program. Revs. Dennis Druggan, O.F.M.Cap., Rector & Pres.; Edwin F. Dziedziejko, O.F.M.Cap., Dean of Students; Kenan Siegel, O.F.M.Cap.; Campion Baer, O.F.M.Cap.; Oliver Bambenek, O.F.M.Cap.; Gary Wegner, O.F.M.Cap.; Keith Clark, O.F.M.Cap., Local Min.; Elroy Pesch, O.F.M.Cap.; Bros. Douglas Bode, O.F.M.Cap.; Dismas Seward, O.F.M.Cap.; Neal Plale, O.F.M.Cap.; John Willger, O.F.M.Cap.; Larry Groeschel, O.F.M.Cap.; Jerome Campbell, O.F.M.Cap.; John Scherer, O.F.M.Cap.; Mr. David Bartel, Academic Dean; Mr. Harlan Swift, Business Mgr. Priests 8; Brothers 7; Sisters 1; Lay Teachers 13; Non-teaching Lay Staff 43; Students 230; Total Staff 72.

[C] COLLEGES AND UNIVERSITIES

MILWAUKEE. *Alverno College*, 3400 S. 43rd St., P.O. Box 343922, 53234-3922. Tel: 414-382-6000; Fax: 414-362-6354.
Web site: www.alverno.edu
For a complete listing, refer to the Colleges and Universities section.

Cardinal Stritch University, 6801 N. Yates Rd., 53217. Tel: 414-410-4000; Fax: 414-410-4239.
Web site: www.stritch.edu
For a complete listing, refer to the Colleges and Universities section.

Marquette University, P.O. Box 1881, 53201-1881. Tel: 414-288-7250.
Web site: www.marquette.edu
For a complete listing, refer to the Colleges and Universities section.

Mount Mary College, 2900 N. Menomonee River Pkwy., 53222-4545. Tel: 414-258-4810; Fax: 414-256-1224.
Web site: www.mtmary.edu
For a complete listing, refer to the Colleges and Universities section.

FOND DU LAC. *Marian College of Fond du Lac*, 45 S. National Ave., 54935. Tel: 920-923-7600; Fax: 920-923-8087.
E-mail: admissions@mariancollege.edu
Web site: www.mariancollege.edu
For a complete listing, refer to the Colleges and Universities section.

[D] HIGH SCHOOLS, ARCHDIOCESAN AND PAROCHIAL

MILWAUKEE. *Messmer High School*, 742 W. Capitol Dr., 53206. Tel: 414-264-5440; Fax: 414-264-5120.
E-mail: brbob1211@aol.com
Web site: messmerhigh.com
Bro. Bob Smith, Pres.; Jeff Monday, Prin. Sisters 2; Lay Teachers 29; Students 515.

Pius XI High School, 135 N. 76th St., 53213. Tel: 414-290-7000; Fax: 414-290-7001.
E-mail: piusxi@piusxi.org.
Web site: www.piusxi.org
Revs. Robert V. Carney, S.A.C.; Richard J. Gunderman, S.A.C. School Sisters of St. Francis 5; Sisters of Mercy 1; Lay Teachers 99; Students 1,455.

Thomas More High School, 2601 E. Morgan Ave., 53207. Tel: 414-481-8370; Fax: 414-481-3382.
E-mail: lynumn@execpc.com
Web site: www.thomasmorehighschool.com
(Coed). Mr. Joel Eul, Prin. Sisters 1; Lay Teachers 42; Students 725; Total Staff 47.

BURLINGTON. *Catholic Central High School*, 148 McHenry St., 53105. Tel: 262-763-1510; Fax: 262-763-1509.
E-mail: LeoneJo@cchsnet.org
Web site: www.cchsnet.org
Mr. John T. Leone, Prin.; Rev. Lawrence J. Chapman, Chap. Priests 1; Lay Teachers 22; Students 230.

FOND DU LAC. *St. Mary's Springs High School*, 255 County Rd. K, 54935. Tel: 920-921-4870; Fax: 920-921-2786.
E-mail: tborek@springs.k12.wi.us
Thomas J. Borek, Pres. Sisters 1; Lay Teachers 22; Students 370; Total Staff 23.

KENOSHA. *St. Joseph High School*, 2401 69th St., 53143. Tel: 262-654-8651; Fax: 262-654-1615.
E-mail: sjhs@exelpc.com
Web site: stjosephhs.com
Mr. Robert Freund, Prin. Priests 1; Sisters 2; Lay Teachers 23; Students 308; Total Staff 26.

WAUKESHA. *Catholic Memorial High School*, 601 E. College Ave., 53186-5598. Tel: 262-542-7101; Fax: 262-542-1633.
E-mail: bvandeun@cathmem.org
Web site: www.cathmem.org
Bryan J. Van Deun, Ed.D., Pres.; Kathleen A. Cepelka, Ph.D., Prin.; J. Patrick Farrell, Asst. to the Pres. for Student Life; Michael J. George, Dir. of Advancement; Beth Dolan, Assoc. Dir. of Advancement. Franciscan Sisters of Christian Charity 4; Lay Teachers 85; Students 983; Total Staff 89.

[E] HIGH SCHOOLS, PRIVATE

MILWAUKEE. *Divine Savior Holy Angels High School, Inc.* (Girls). 4257 N. 100th St., 53222. Tel: 414-462-3742; Fax: 414-466-0590.
E-mail: dsha@dsha.k12.wi.us
Web site: www.dsha.k12.wi.us
Sponsored by the Sisters of the Divine Savior. Ellen Bartel, Pres.; Sr. Virginia Honish, S.D.S., Prin.; Rev. Jerome G. Herda. Priests 1; Sisters 4; Lay Teachers 45; Students 568; Total Staff 74.

Marquette University High School. (Boys). 3401 W. Wisconsin Ave., 53208. Tel: 414-933-7220; Fax: 414-937-8588.
Web site: www.muhs.edu
(See separate listing for resident information). Revs. Douglas J. Leonhardt, S.J., Pres.; Robert J. Kroll, S.J.; Terrence M. Brennan, S.J.; Thomas M. Doyle, S.J.; Michael R. Kolb, S.J.; Charles L. Stang, S.J.; Edward G. Witt, S.J. Priests 7; Scholastics 1; Lay Teachers 65; Students 979; Total Staff 72. Priests 7; Scholastics 1; Lay Teachers 65; Students 979; Total Staff 72.

St. Joan Antida High School, Inc (Girls). 1341 N. Cass St., 53202. Tel: 414-272-8423; Fax: 414-272-3135.
E-mail: sjahs@archmil.org
Web site: www.sja.edu
Sr. Monica Fumo, S.C.S.J.A., Pres.; Lynn Ann Reeseman, Prin. Sisters of Charity of St. Joan Antida 8; Lay Teachers 48; Students 390; Total Staff 56.

RACINE. *St. Catherine's High School*, 1200 Park Ave., 53403. Tel: 262-632-2785; Fax: 262-632-5144.
E-mail: dsisler@stcatherines.k12.wi.us
Web site: stcatherines.k12.wi.us
Ms. Marilyn J. McGoldrick, Pres.; Mr. Donald Sisler, Prin.; Sr. Jane Weiss, Asst. Prin. Dominican Sisters (Racine) 4; Lay Teachers 37; Students 503.

WHITEFISH BAY. *Dominican High School*, 120 E. Silver Spring Dr., 53217. Tel: 414-332-1170; Fax: 414-332-4101.
E-mail: dhs@dominicanhighschool.com
Web site: dominicanhighschool.com
Sponsored by Sinsinawa Dominicans. Paul M. McInerny, Ph.D., Pres.; James G. Piatt, Prin.; Judy Down, Assoc. Prin.; Michael Heimbach, Chm. Religion Dept. Dominican Sisters of the Congregation of the Most Holy Rosary, Sinsinawa, WI 1; Admin. 4; Lay Teachers 35; Students 405.

[F] ELEMENTARY SCHOOLS, ARCHDIOCESAN

MILWAUKEE. *St. Leo Catholic Urban Academy*, 2458 W. Locust St., 53209. Tel: 414-442-1100; Fax: 414-873-0119.
E-mail: birlemj@archmil.org
Sponsored and accredited by the Archdiocese of Milwaukee. Lay Teachers 16; Students 245; Total Staff 30.

St. Rose Catholic Urban Academy, 514 N. 31st St., 53208. Tel: 414-933-6070; Fax: 414-933-3071.
E-mail: prinlee@execpc.com
Web site: www.archmil.org/schools
Sponsored and accredited by the Archdiocese of Milwaukee. Lay Teachers 12; Students 225; Total Staff 15.

[G] ELEMENTARY SCHOOLS, PRIVATE

MILWAUKEE. *Nativity Jesuit Middle School, Inc.* (Boys). 1115 S. Seventh St., 53204. Tel: 414-645-1060; Fax: 414-645-0505.
E-mail: nativity@njms.org
Web site: www.njms.org
Wisconsin Province of the Society of Jesus. Rev. William T. Johnson, S.J., Pres.; Mr. Michael A. Frontier, Prin. Priests 2; Sisters 1; Lay Teachers 8; Students 50; Total Staff 10.

Notre Dame Middle School, Inc., 1420 W. Scott St., 53204. Tel: 414-671-3000; Fax: 414-671-3170.
E-mail: ndmswi@aol.com
Alvaro Garcia-Velez, Pres.; Marcia Roth, Prin. Sisters 3; Lay Teachers 7; Volunteers 3; Students 62. Sponsored by: School Sisters of Notre Dame. Purpose: To educate at-risk girls for college preparatory high schools and for community service and leadership.

St. Coletta Day School of Milwaukee, 1740 N. 55th St., 53208. Tel: 414-453-1850. For Exceptional Children. William A. Koehn, Prin. & Admin. Lay Teachers 2; Students 8.

[H] CONSOLIDATED ELEMENTARY SCHOOLS

MILWAUKEE. *All Saints Catholic East School System, Inc.*, 1716 N. Humboldt Ave., 53202. Tel: 414-276-9814; Fax: 414-964-4656.
E-mail: catheast@execpc.com
Sponsored by the following Milwaukee parishes: Cathedral of St. John the Evangelist; St. Casimir; Old St. Mary's; St. Mary Czestochowa; Ss. Peter and Paul; Three Holy Women Catholic Parish. Rev. James M. Flynt, Chm., Pastor Liaison. Sisters 1; Lay Teachers 12; Students 171.

Catholic East Elementary. (Grades K-8), 2461 N. Murray Ave., 53211. Tel: 414-964-1770; Fax: 414-964-6578.
E-mail: catheast@execpc.com
Members: SS. Peter and Paul, St. Mary of Czestochowa, Old St. Mary, St. Casimir, Cathedral of St. John the Evangelist, Three Holy Women. Mr. Christopher Montezon, Prin. Sisters 1; Lay Teachers 10; Students 174.

Resurrection Catholic Academy, 5140 N. 55th St., 53218. Tel: 414-438-2745; Fax: 414-438-9330. Barbara O'Donnell, Prin. Sisters 1; Lay Teachers 15; Students 227. Members: St. Stephen Martyr and Mother of Perpetual Help, Milwaukee.

St. Elizabeth Ann Seton Academy, Ltd., 1051 E. Russell Ave., 53207. Tel: 414-769-2485; Fax: 414-747-9219.
E-mail: seton@execpc.com
Sr. Sue Felice, Prin. Students 221. School sponsored by Immaculate Conception and St. Augustine parishes, Milwaukee.

BEAVER DAM. *Unified Catholic Parish Schools of Beaver Dam*, 503 S. Spring St., 53916-2598. Tel: 920-885-5558; Fax: 920-885-7610.
E-mail: ucps@powercom.net
Barbara M. Haase, Prin. Lay Teachers 21; Students 364. Members: St. Michael, St. Patrick, St. Peter.

FOND DU LAC. *Fond du Lac Area Catholic Education System (FACES)*, 26 W. Follett St., P.O. Box 2138, 54936-2138. Tel: 920-924-0993; Fax: 920-922-7849.
E-mail: facesl@faces.k12.wi.us
Members: Holy Family; Presentation of the Blessed Virgin; North Fond du Lac; St. Peter's Malone. Sr. Deborah Golias, C.S.A., Ph.D., System Admin.

Faces Primary Campus, 95 E. Second St., 54935. Tel: 920-921-5300; Fax: 920-921-5908. Sr. Colleen Walsh, Prin. Lay Teachers 14; Students 280.

Faces Middle School Campus, 63 E. Merrill St., 54935. Tel: 920-921-9610; Fax: 920-921-0457. Mrs. Susan Zacherl, Prin. Lay Teachers 14; Students 220.

Faces Intermediate Campus, 37 E. Follett St., 54935. Tel: 920-921-6710; Fax: 920-921-9610. Mrs. Jennifer Ryan, Prin. Lay Teachers 10; Students 190.

LOMIRA. *Consolidated Catholic School, Lomira-Theresa*, 705 Milwaukee St., 53048-9520. Tel: 920-269-4326.
E-mail: cclt@dotnet.com
Sr. Rosemary Herriges, O.S.F., Prin. Sisters 1; Lay Teachers 11; Students 108. Members: St. Mary, Lomira; St. Theresa, Theresa.

MEQUON. *Ss. Cecilia and James School*, 11300 N. St. James Ln., #28 W, 53092. Tel: 262-242-7960; Fax: 262-242-7976.
E-mail: rlg@stscj.org
Web site: www.stscj.org
Mr. Richard Goeden, Prin., St. Cecilia Campus: (Grades K-3), 116 W. Orchard St., Thiensville, 53092. Tel: 262-242-7965; Fax: 262-242-7976. St. James Campus: (Grades 4-8), 11300 N. St. James Ln., 53092. Tel: 262-242-7960; Fax: 262-512-8986. Members: St. Cecilia, Thiensville; St. James, Mequon. Lay Teachers 32; Students 570.

MOUNT CALVARY. *Consolidated Parochial Elementary School*, 100 Notre Dame St., 53057. Tel: 920-753-4811; Fax: 920-753-2411.
E-mail: cpesmtca@dotnet.com
Mary Beth Leonard, Prin./Admin. Sisters 1; Lay Teachers 16; Students 209. Members: St. John the Baptist, Johnsburg; St. Mary, Marytown; Holy Cross, Mount Calvary; St. Cloud, St. Cloud.

WAUKESHA. *Waukesha Catholic School System, Inc.*, 440 N. Moreland Blvd., 53188. Tel: 262-896-2920; Fax: 262-896-2925. Rev. Glen G. Graczyk, Pastor Liaison. Tel: 414-549-0223. Members: St. Joseph, St. Mary, St. John Neumann, St. William.

St. Joseph Campus, 818 N. East Ave., 53186. Tel: 262-896-2930; Fax: 262-896-2935. Mrs. Kathleen Rempe, Prin. Sisters 1; Lay Teachers 15; Students 259.

St. Mary Campus, 520 N. Newhall Ave., 53186. Tel: 262-896-2932; Fax: 262-896-2931. Mrs. Carolyn Caruso, Prin. Sisters 3; Lay Teachers 17; Students 388.

St. William Campus, 444 N. Moreland Blvd., 53188. Tel: 262-896-2920; Fax: 262-896-2925. Mr. Robert Radomski, Prin. Sisters 1; Lay Teachers 14; Students 191.

[I] SPECIAL SCHOOLS

WEST ALLIS. *Holy Assumption School for the Blind*, 1526 S. 72nd St., 53214. Tel: 414-774-8783; Fax: 414-774-3735.
E-mail: job@execpc.com
Sr. Melmarie Stoll, S.S.N.D., Dir. School Sisters of Notre Dame 1; Lay Teachers 1; Students 3.

[J] CHILD CARE CENTERS

MILWAUKEE. *Child Development Center of St. Joseph*, 1600 W. Oklahoma Ave., 53215. Tel: 414-645-5337; Fax: 414-645-5329.
Web site: www.childdevctr-stjoes.org
Sr. M. Ramona Dombrowski, Pres. Felician Sisters 10; Lay Teachers 27; Children 220; Total Staff 42.

Guardian Angel Learning Center, Inc., 1540 N. Jefferson, 53202. Tel: 414-277-9474; Fax: 414-277-9482.
E-mail: angels@mixcom.com
Sisters of Charity of St. Joan Antida. Sr. Marie Louise Balistrieri, S.C.S.J.A., Admin. Sisters of Charity of St. Joan Antida 3; Lay Teachers 18; Students 85. The center is licensed for ages 6 weeks to 11 years with a school age program.

St. Joan Antida Day Care Center, Inc., 8560 N. 76th Pl., 53223. Tel: 414-354-9233; Fax: 414-355-6463.

Seton Children's School, Inc., 8677 N. Port Washington Rd., 53217. Tel: 414-352-6115. Operated by the Ascension Health System. A licensed center for comprehensive early childhood educational programs and day care. Lay Teachers 10; Children 89. Other Locations: 2330 N. Prospect Ave., 53211. Tel: 414-220-8494. Lay Teachers 7; Children 56. 13133 N. Port Washington Rd., Mequon, 53097. Tel: 414-243-7318. Lay Teachers 2; Children 32.

SOUTH MILWAUKEE. *Franciscan Villa Child Day Care Center*, 3601 S. Chicago Ave., 53172. Tel: 414-764-4100; Fax: 414-764-0706.
Web site: www.franciscanvilla.com
Rachel Stolpe, Dir. Lay Teachers 10; Children 56. Affiliate of Catholic Health Initiatives.

WAUWATOSA. *Carmelite Home, Inc.*, 1214 Kavanaugh Pl., 53213. Tel: 414-258-4791; Fax: 414-258-8464. Residential Treatment Center for Adolescent Boys. Sr. M. Regina, Admin.; James E. Lewis, Treatment Dir. Residents 40; Lay Teachers 4.

[K] GENERAL HOSPITALS

MILWAUKEE. *Ministry Health Care, Inc.*, 11925 W. Lake Park Dr., 53224. Tel: 414-359-1060; Fax: 414-359-1656.
Web site: www.ministryhealth.org
For a complete listing, refer to the Hospitals section.

St. Francis Hospital, 3237 S. 16th St., 53215. Tel: 414-647-5000; Fax: 414-647-5565.
E-mail: mworley@covhealth.org
For a complete listing, refer to the Hospitals section.

St. Joseph's Hospital of Franciscan Sisters, Milwaukee, Inc., 5000 W. Chambers St., 53210. Tel: 414-447-2000; Fax: 414-874-4393.
Web site: www.covhealth.org
For a complete listing, refer to the Hospitals section.

St. Mary's Hospital of Milwaukee, 2323 N. Lake Dr., P.O. Box 503, 53201-0503. Tel: 414-291-1000; Fax: 414-291-1444
For a complete listing, refer to the Hospitals section.

St. Michael Hospital of Franciscan Sisters of Milwaukee, Inc., 2400 W. Villard Ave., 53209. Tel: 414-527-8000; Fax: 414-527-8461
For a complete listing, refer to the Hospitals section.

BROOKFIELD. *Elmbrook Memorial Hospital, Inc.*, 19333 W. North Ave., 53045. Tel: 262-785-2000; Fax: 262-785-2444
For a complete listing, refer to the Hospitals section.

FOND DU LAC. *Agnesian HealthCare, Inc.*, 430 E. Division St., 54935. Tel: 920-929-2300; Fax: 920-926-4866.
E-mail: fale@agnesian.com
For a complete listing, refer to the Hospitals section.

KENOSHA. *St. Catherine's Hospital*, 3556 Seventh Ave., 53140. Tel: 414-656-3011; Fax: 414-656-3804
For a complete listing, refer to the Hospitals section.

MEQUON. *St. Mary's Hospital Ozaukee, Inc.*, 13111 N. Port Washington Rd., 53097. Tel: 414-243-7300; 800-848-2844; Fax: 414-243-7416
For a complete listing, refer to the Hospitals section.

RACINE. *St. Mary's Medical Center, Inc.*, 3801 Spring St., 53405. Tel: 262-687-4011; Fax: 262-687-8039.
E-mail: kbuser@allsaintshealthcare.org
Web site: allsaintshealth.com
For a complete listing, refer to the Hospitals section.

SHEBOYGAN. *St. Nicholas Hospital*, 1601 N. Taylor Dr., 53081. Tel: 920-459-8300; Fax: 920-452-8336.
E-mail: al4425@stnicholashospital.org
Web site: www.stnicholashospital.org
For a complete listing, refer to the Hospitals section.

WAUPUN. *Waupun Memorial Hospital*, 53963. Tel: 920-324-5581; Fax: 920-324-2085
For a complete listing, refer to the Hospitals section.

[L] SPECIAL HOSPITALS AND SANATORIA

MILWAUKEE. *Sacred Heart Rehabilitation Institute, Inc.*, 2350 N. Lake Dr., 53211. Tel: 414-298-6700; Fax: 414-298-6712
For a complete listing, refer to the Special Care Facilities section.

[M] PROTECTIVE INSTITUTIONS

MILWAUKEE. *Daystar, Inc.*, P.O. Box 2130, 53201-2130. Tel: 414-385-0334; Fax: 414-385-0336
For a complete listing, refer to the Special Care Facilities section.

Rosalie Manor Community & Family Services, Inc., 4803 W. Burleigh St., 53210. Tel: 414-449-2868; Fax: 414-449-2870.
E-mail: rosaliemanor@aeronet
For a complete listing, refer to the Special Care Facilities section.

St. Charles Youth and Family Services, Inc., 151 S. 84th St., P.O. Box 14005, 53214. Tel: 414-476-3710; Fax: 414-778-5985.
E-mail: mstaz@execpc.com
Web site: www.st-charle.org
For a complete listing, refer to the Special Care Facilities section.

MOUNT CALVARY. *Cristo Rey Ranch, Inc.*, N8102 Calvary St., 53057. Tel: 920-753-2026; 753-3211; Fax: 920-753-3100.
E-mail: villasisters@netscape.net
For a complete listing, refer to the Special Care Facilities section.

[N] HOMES FOR AGED AND NURSING HOMES

MILWAUKEE. *Alexian Village of Milwaukee, Inc.*, 9301 N. 76th St., 53223. Tel: 414-355-9300; Fax: 414-357-5106.
E-mail: marketing@alexianvillage.org
Web site: www.alexianvillage.org
For a complete listing, refer to the Special Care Facilities section.

Catholic Charities Adult Day Services and Resource Center, 1919 N. 60th St., 53208. Tel: 414-771-5026, Ext. 162; Fax: 414-771-9115.
E-mail: catholiccharities@ccmke.org
Web site: www.ccmke.org
For a complete listing, refer to the Special Care Facilities section.

Hope Nursing Home, Inc., 8560 N. 76th Pl., 53223. Tel: 414-354-9233; Fax: 414-355-6463
For a complete listing, refer to the Special Care Facilities section.

Marian Franciscan Center, Inc., 9632 W. Appleton Ave., 53225. Tel: 414-461-8850; Fax: 414-461-9570
For a complete listing, refer to the Special Care Facilities section.

MCC Liquidation Corp., 9632 W. Appleton Ave., 53225. Tel: 414-461-8850; Fax: 414-461-9570
For a complete listing, refer to the Special Care Facilities section.

Milwaukee Catholic Home, 2462 N. Prospect Ave., 53211-4462. Tel: 414-224-9700; Fax: 414-224-1666.
E-mail: info@milwaukeecatholichome.org
Web site: milwaukeecatholichome.org
For a complete listing, refer to the Special Care Facilities section.

Mount Carmel Health and Rehabilitation Center (Mount Carmel, LLC), 5700 W. Layton Ave., 53220. Tel: 414-281-7200; Fax: 414-281-0744.
E-mail: lathomson@bhshealth.org
For a complete listing, refer to the Special Care Facilities section.

St. Ann Center for Intergenerational Care, Inc., 2801 E. Morgan Ave., 53207. Tel: 414-977-5000; Fax: 414-977-5050
For a complete listing, refer to the Special Care Facilities section.

St. Ann Rest Home, 2020 S. Muskego Ave., 53204-3522. Tel: 414-383-2642; Fax: 414-383-2642.
E-mail: stann2@execpc.com
For a complete listing, refer to the Special Care Facilities section.

St. Anne's Home for the Elderly, 3800 N. 92nd St., 53222. Tel: 414-463-7570; Fax: 414-463-2311.
E-mail: mah@execpc.com
Web site: www.wahsa.org/st.anne/index.html
For a complete listing, refer to the Special Care Facilities section.

St. Joan Antida Home, Inc., 8560 N. 76th Pl., 53223. Tel: 414-354-9233; Fax: 414-355-6463
For a complete listing, refer to the Special Care Facilities section.

St. Mary's Nursing Home, 3515 W. Hadley St., 53210. Tel: 414-873-9250; Fax: 414-873-6876
For a complete listing, refer to the Special Care Facilities section.

The Terrace at St. Francis, Inc., 3200 S. 20th St., 53215. Tel: 414-389-3200; Fax: 414-389-3300
For a complete listing, refer to the Special Care Facilities section.

Villa St. Francis, Inc., 1910 W. Ohio Ave., 53215. Tel: 414-649-2888; Fax: 414-649-2880
For a complete listing, refer to the Special Care Facilities section.

FOND DU LAC. *Nazareth Center-Nazareth Court*, 375 Gillett St., 54935. Tel: 920-923-7993; Fax: 920-907-6800.
E-mail: lccsa@vbe.com
For a complete listing, refer to the Special Care Facilities section.

St. Francis Home for Aged, 33 Everett St., 54935. Tel: 920-923-7980; Fax: 920-923-7995.
E-mail: stfran@vbe.com
For a complete listing, refer to the Special Care Facilities section.

GREENFIELD. *Clement Manor Health Center*, 3939 S. 92nd St., 53228. Tel: 414-321-1800; Fax: 414-546-7333
For a complete listing, refer to the Special Care Facilities section.

Clement Manor Retirement Community, 9339 W. Howard, 53228. Tel: 414-546-7374; Fax: 414-546-7357
For a complete listing, refer to the Special Care Facilities section.

KENOSHA. *St. Joseph's Adult Day Care Center, Inc.*, 9244 29th Ave., 53144. Tel: 414-694-6000; Fax: 414-694-0148.
E-mail: sjoseph@net
Web site: www.stjoseph.com
For a complete listing, refer to the Special Care Facilities section.

St. Joseph's Home for the Aged, 9244 29th Ave., 53143. Tel: 262-694-0080; Fax: 262-694-7325.
E-mail: sjoseph@acronet.net
Web site: www.sjosephs.com
For a complete listing, refer to the Special Care Facilities section.

MOUNT CALVARY. *Villa Loretto Nursing Home*, N8114 Calvary St., 53057. Tel: 920-753-3211; Fax: 920-753-3100.
E-mail: villasisters@netscape.net
For a complete listing, refer to the Special Care Facilities section.

RACINE. *Marian Housing Center, Inc*, 4105 Spring St., 53405. Tel: 262-633-5807
For a complete listing, refer to the Special Care Facilities section.

St. Monica's Senior Citizens Home, Inc., 3920 N. Green Bay Rd., 53404. Tel: 262-639-5050; Fax: 262-639-5673
For a complete listing, refer to the Special Care Facilities section.

ST. FRANCIS. *Canticle Court, Inc.*, 3201 S. Lake Dr., 53235. Tel: 414-744-9959; Fax: 414-744-7636.
E-mail: jcpres@seii.com
For a complete listing, refer to the Special Care Facilities section.

Juniper Court, Inc., 3209 S. Lake Dr., 53235-3702. Tel: 414-744-5878; Fax: 414-744-7636.
E-mail: jcpres@seii.com
For a complete listing, refer to the Special Care Facilities section.

SOUTH MILWAUKEE. *Franciscan Villa of South Milwaukee, Inc.*, 3601 S. Chicago Ave., 53172. Tel: 414-764-4100; Fax: 414-764-0706.
Web site: www.franciscanvilla.org
For a complete listing, refer to the Special Care Facilities section.

WAUWATOSA. *St. Camillus Health Center, Inc.*, 10101 W. Wisconsin Ave., 53226. Tel: 414-258-1814
For a complete listing, refer to the Special Care Facilities section.

San Camillo, Inc., 10200 W. Blue Mound Rd., 53226. Tel: 414-259-6300
For a complete listing, refer to the Special Care Facilities section.

[O] PERSONAL PRELATURES

BROOKFIELD. *Prelature of the Holy Cross and Opus Dei.*, 12900 W. North Ave., 53005. Tel: 414-784-1523.
E-mail: info@opusdei.org
Layton Study Center for men. Revs. Gregory Coyne; John C. Kubeck.

[P] MONASTERIES AND RESIDENCES FOR PRIESTS AND BROTHERS

MILWAUKEE. *Alexian Brothers Community.* Immaculate Conception Province, 7979 W. Glenbrook Rd., 53223. Tel: 414-355-9300; Fax: 414-357-5106. Bros. Robert Petersen, C.F.A., Supr.; Theodore Loucks, C.F.A.; John Howard, C.F.A.; Exequiel Mapa, C.F.A.; Richard Remetch, C.F.A.; Wendelin Brong, C.F.A. Brothers 6.

Arrupe House Jesuit Community, 831 N. 13th St., 53233-1706. Tel: 414-288-5855; Fax: 414-288-5852. Society of Jesus, Wisconsin Prov. Revs. Philip J. Rossi, S.J., Supr.; Thomas N. Brennan, S.J.; Michael A. Fahey, S.J.; D. Thomas Hughson, S.J.; Lawrence D. Kelly, S.J.; Michael R. Kolb, S.J.; Daniel C. McDonald, S.J.; Eugene F. Merz, S.J.; Charles L. Stang, S.J.; John L. Treloar, S.J. Priests 10.

Francis and Clare House, 1648 S. 37th St., 53215-1724. Tel: 414-383-7934; Fax: 414-383-0335. Revs. John Wojtowicz, O.F.M.; John Cella, O.F.M.; Stephen Malkiewicz, O.F.M.; Jerome Zawada, O.F.M.; Roch Niemier, O.F.M.; Bro. Ted Tokarz, O.F.M. Priests 5; Brothers 1.

Jesuit Community at Marquette University, 1404 W. Wisconsin Ave., 53233. Tel: 414-288-5000; Fax: 414-288-1758. Marquette Jesuit Associates, Inc. Very Rev. G. Thomas Krettek, S.J.; Revs. Robert W. Leiweke, S.J., Asst. Rector; James J. Gladstone, S.J., Min.; Philip Abraham, S.J. (Kohima); Richard H. Ahler, S.J.; Emmanuel Arockiam, S.J. (Madurai); Charles R. Baumann, S.J.; Ronald R. Bieganowski, S.J.; Harold C. Bradley, S.J.; Thaddeus J. Burch, S.J.; Peter N. Bwanal, S.J. (Zambia); Michael D. Class, S.J.; Paul Coelho, S.J. (Kohima); Keith D'Souza, S.J. (Bombay); John P. Donnelly, S.J.; Patrick J. Dorsey, S.J.; James E. Fitzgerald, S.J.; Matthew T. Gamber, S.J.; Raymond T. Gawronski, S.J.; Todd W. Harrison, S.J.; Gregorius Heliarko, S.J. (Indonesia); Robert J. Joda, S.J.; Michael T. Kelly, S.J. (Ireland); William J. Kelly, S.J.; William J. Kidd, S.J.; Eugene C. Kollasch, S.J.; William S. Kurz, S.J.; Robert W. Lambeck, S.J.; Timothy R. Lannon, S.J.; John D. Laurance, S.J.; Frank A. Majka, S.J.; Albert William Manuel (Madurai); Donald R. Matthys, S.J.; Richard A. McGarrity, S.J.; Charles J. Mehok, S.J.; Jose Moreno, S.J. (Mexico); Joseph G. Mueller, S.J.; Charles C. Murphy, S.J.; John E. Naus, S.J.; Petrus Pramudyarkara, S.J. (Indonesia); William F. Prospero, S.J.; Francis Paul Prucha, S.J.; Eugene F. Shaw, S.J.; Richard F. Sherburne, S.J.; Thomas D. Stegman, S.J.; Paul B. Steinmetz, S.J.; Walter J. Stohrer, S.J.; Roland J. Teske, S.J.; Andrew J. Thon, S.J.; Ranjit Tigga, S.J. (Madhya-Pradesh); Norbert J. Tracy, S.J.; Francis Xavier Baskara Tulus Wardaya, S.J. (Indonesia); Robert A. Wild, S.J.; Bro. Thomas R. Williams, S.J.; Revs. Frederick P. Zagone, S.J.; Michael J. Zeps, S.J. Priests 60.

Jesuit Provincial Office, Wisconsin Province, P.O. Box 080288, 53208-0288. Tel: 414-937-6949; Fax: 414-937-6950.
E-mail: wisprov@marquette.edu
Web site: www.jesuitswisprov.org
Very Rev. D. Edward Mathie, S.J., Prov. and Coord. for Higher Education; Revs. James E. Grummer, S.J., Asst. for Secondary Education, Coord. Province Planning & Communication; Richard P. Abert, S.J., Asst. Formation & Cross-Cultural Ministries; Eugene M. Dutkiewicz, S.J., Asst. for Finance; David J. Haschka, S.J., Asst. for Pastoral & Retreat Min., Asst. for Social & Intl. Min.; Richard A. McGarrity, S.J., Dir. of Devel. Priests 6.
Corporate Title: Wisconsin Province of the Society of Jesus.
Priests of the Province Serving Abroad: Rev. Nicholas F. Pope, S.J., Curia of the Society of Jesus, C.P. 6139, 00195 Rome, Italy. Tel: 3906-689-77-433; Fax: 3906-686-8214. Rev. Frederick E. Brenk, S.J., Pontifical Biblical Institute, Via della Pilotta 25, 00187 Rome, Italy. Tel: 3906-695-26-6119; Fax: 3906-695-26-6151. Rev. John D. Mace, S.J., Arrupe International Residence, P.O. Box 216, U.P. Post

Office, 1144 Quezon City, Philippines. Tel: 632-426-5911; Fax: 632-426-5964. Rev. Robert L. Faricy, S.J., Pontifical Gregorian University, Piazza della Pilotta 4, 00187 Rome, Italy. Rev. Thomas S. Anderson, S.J., Collegio S Roberto Bellarmino, Via del Seminario 120, 00186 Rome, Italy. Rev. Philip E. Pick, S.J., Casa Cural, Yoro, Honduras, 23101. Tel: 504-67-2154. Rev. Nicholas E. Schiel, S.J., Centro Loyola, Barrio Palmira, Apdo 676, Tegucigalpa, Honduras. Tel: 504-32-5467. Rev. John R. Schak, S.J., Iglesia San Jose Obrero, Juan Larrea 1161, 4400 Salta, Argentina. Tel: 54387 423-5519. Rev. Robert P. Raszkowski, S.J., Melhado Hall Jesuit Residence, P.O. Box 548, Belize City, Belize. Tel: 5012-33732; Fax: 5012-32752. Rev. Albert J. Dillio, S.J., P.O. Box 30105, Addis Ababa, Ethiopia. Rev. Anthony J. Wach, S.J., P.O. Box 7300, Kampala, Uganda. Tel: 25641-267-614; Fax: 25641-200-357. Rev. Robert W. Dundon, S.J., P.O. Box MP 320, Harrare, Zimbabwe. Tel: 2634-745-306; Fax: 2634-745-904. Rev. Daniel J. Kenney, S.J., P.O. Box 21399, Nairobi, Kenya. Tel: 2542-565-371; Fax: 2542-566-873. Rev. James A. Egan, S.J., Xavier House, P.O. Box 7300, Kampala, Uganda. Tel: 25641-267-614; Fax: 25641-200-357.

Priests of the Province Not Otherwise Listed: Rev. Joseph A. Brown, S.J., Southern Illinois University, Black American Studies Dept., Mail Code 4529, Carbondale, IL, 62901-4529. Tel: 618-453-7147. Rev. James F. Hanley, S.J., 1870 0. 75th St., Omaha, NE, 68124-1799. Rev. William R. Duffey, S.J., 9455 Watertown Plank Rd., 53226. Rev. Frederic A. Maples, S.J., 1420 Terrace Dr. Apt. 111, Roseville, MN, 55113-1753. Tel: 651-633-0317. Rev. Oscar L. Benzinger, S.J., Presentation Heights, 1500 N. Main, Aberdeen, SD, 57401-1299. Tel: 605-229-8402. Rev. George A. Maloney, S.J., 13338 Del Monte Dr., #3-K, Seal Beach, CA, 90740-5411. Tel: 562-430-7801; Fax: 562-493-0922. Rev. Cletus H. Pfab, S.J., 1325 N. Jefferson, #814, 53202-2614. Tel: 414-272-0143. Rev. William J. Ellos, S.J., 7626 Callaghan, Apt. 2201, San Antonio, TX, 78229-2722. Tel: 210-308-8742. Rev. James E. Mauel, S.J., St. Joseph's Convent, 1501 S. Layton Blvd., 53215-1924. Tel: 414-384-2120. Rev. James M. Radde, S.J., Georgetown Court, #211, 5820 E. River Rd., Minneapolis, MN, 55432-5338. Tel: 612-571-5955. Rev. John A. Mazzitello, S.J., 2560 Kenzie Terrace #215, Minneapolis, MN, 55418. Tel: 612-788-1468. Rev. Neil Cahill, S.J., 1870 S. 75th St., Omaha, NE, 68124-1799. Tel: 402-343-8767. Rev. James J. O'Leary, S.J., 5998 Alcala Park Unit 7181, San Diego, CA, 92110-2486. Tel: 619-260-2955. Rev. Thomas A. Halley, S.J., 1870 S. 75th St., Omaha, NE, 68124-1799. Tel: 402-343-8812. Rev. Timothy J. Howard, S.J., 5808 N. Placita Esplendora, Tucson, AZ, 85717-4523. Tel: 520-298-7930. Rev. J. Roger Lucey, S.J., 3431 Foothill Blvd., Oakland, CA, 94601. Tel: 510-532-0464. Rev. Robert H. Fitzgerald, S.J., 10980 Hillside Dr., Anchorage, AK, 99516-1100. Tel: 907-346-2343.

Priests of the Province Engaged in Higher Studies: Rev. James M. Pribek, S.J., Loyola House, 87 Eglinton Rd., Dublin 4, Ireland.

La Salette Fathers. Missionaries of Our Lady of La Salette, 1607 E. Howard Ave., 53207. Tel: 414-769-7113; Fax: 414-769-1057. Revs. Francis Kula, M.S.; James Winiarski, M.S.; Bro. Gerald Buraczewski, M.S. Priests 2; Brothers 1; Total in Residence 3.

Pallotti House, 5424 W. Bluemound Rd., 53208. Tel: 414-258-0653 (Provincial Offices); Fax: 414-258-9314.
E-mail: mdprov@dias.net
Web site: www.dias.net/~pallotti
Residence of Fathers and Brothers and Offices of Mother of God Province of the Society of the Catholic Apostolate also, Formation House: Novitiate. Very Rev. Robert V. Carney, S.A.C., Prov. Supr.; Revs. Jerome A. Hapka, S.A.C.; Leon J. Martin, S.A.C.; William E. Lemanski, S.A.C.; Robert J. Albers, S.A.C.; Gregory P. Serwa, S.A.C., Supr., Pallotti House; Bruce J. Schute, S.A.C.; Bro. James Scarpace. Priests 6; Brothers 1; Novices 2.

Pere Marquette House Jesuit Community, 726 N. 34th. St., 53208-3301. Tel: 414-342-7503; Fax: 414-937-8588. Society of Jesus, Wisconsin Province. Revs. Edward G. Witt, S.J., Supr.; Terrence M. Brennan, S.J.; Thomas M. Doyle, S.J.; Robert J. Kroll, S.J.; Douglas J. Leonhardt, S.J.; Warren J. Sazama, S.J.; Mr. Mark A. Carr, S.J. Priests 6; Scholastics 1.

Provincial Offices - Discalced Carmelites, 1233 S. 45th St., 53214-3693. Tel: 414-672-7212; Fax: 414-672-3138.
E-mail: juderj@juno.com
Very Rev. Jude Peters, O.C.D., Prov.; Sr. Beth Lyman, S.S.S.F., Prov. Admin. Asst.
Serving abroad: Revs. Thomas Martin, O.C.D., Philippines; Alan J. Rieger, O.C.D., Philippines; Ignacio Read, O.C.D., Philippines; Arnold Boehme, O.C.D., Philippines; Reginald Foster, O.C.D., Rome; Lawrence Daniels, O.C.D. (Nairobi); Dennis Geng, O.C.D. (Nairobi); Stephen Payne, O.C.D. (Nairobi); Eugene C. Wehner, O.C.D. (Nairobi); George Mangiaracina, O.C.D (Rome).
Priests of the Province not otherwise listed: Revs. Guy Lofy, O.C.D.; Daniel McCauley, O.C.D.; William McNamara, O.C.D. Total in Residence 23; Total Staff 8.

St. Conrad Friary, 3138 N. 2nd St., 53212. Tel: 414-372-3620; Fax: 414-372-119. Capuchin Friars, Province of St. Joseph. Revs. Brian Braun, O.F.M.Cap; Otto N. Bucher, O.F.M.Cap.; Richard Hart, O.F.M.Cap.; Jerome Higgins, O.F.M.Cap.; Adrian Staehler, O.F.M.Cap.; Niles J. Kauffman, O.F.M.Cap.; Timon W. Costello; Bro. Robert Smith, O.F.M.Cap. Priests 7; Brothers 1; Total in Residence 8.

St. Joseph House of Formation, 937 N. 37th St., 53208. Tel: 414-344-0710; Fax: 414-937-6665. Priests of the Sacred Heart. Revs. Charles Brown, S.C.J., Supr.; Michael Burke, S.C.J.; Paul Kelly, S.C.J., Supr.; John Klingler, S.C.J.; Jack Kurps, S.C.J.; Bros. Michael Fette, S.C.J.; Benedict Humpfer, S.C.J. Priests 5; Brothers 2.

St. Vincent Community, 145 S. 76th St., 53214. Tel: 414-476-3211. Very Rev. Robert V. Carney, S.A.C., Prov.; Revs. Richard J. Gunderman, S.A.C.; Francis Hueller, S.A.C., Rector; Harold J. Liebl, S.A.C.; Eugene H. Jarosch, S.A.C.; Richard J. Lorenz, S.A.C.

Salvatorian Provincial Residence, 1735 Hi-Mount Blvd., 53208-1720. Tel: 414-258-1735; Fax: 414-258-1934.
E-mail: salvatorians@sdsusa.org
Web site: salvatorians.com
Society of the Divine Savior.
USA Provincial Council: Revs. Peter Schuessler, S.D.S., Provincial; Joseph Rodrigues, S.D.S., Vicar Prov. & Dir. Initial Formation; John Gorman, S.D.S., Dir. Personnel; Bro. Sean McLaughlin, S.D.S., 9 Serpentine Ct., Silver Spring, MD, 20904-5336.
1735 Hi-Mount Blvd.: Revs. Michael Hoffman, S.D.S., Dir. Communications; Bruce Brentrup, S.D.S.; Michael Henseler, S.D.S.; Robert Marsicek, S.D.S.; Patrick Ritter, S.D.S.; Neil Durham, S.D.S.; Raphael Birringer, S.D.S. Tel: 414-476-9261, 7811 W. Center St., 53209-3051. Bro. Fidelis Rausch, S.D.S.
Priests at Residences Not Listed Elsewhere: Revs. Joseph Lubrano, S.D.S., Dir. Vocations; Keith Brennan, S.D.S., Dir. Planning & Ongoing Formation; Michael Kendall, S.D.S., 846 S. Second Ave., Tucson, AZ. Rev. Jude Weisenbeck, S.D.S., 1903 Lynn Lea Rd., Louisville, KY, 40216-2836. Tel: 502-448-4359; Fax: 502-636-2379. Rev. Bruce Clanton, S.D.S., P.O. Box 574, Racine, 53401-0574. Tel: 262-633-4032. Rev. Cyril Dickrell, S.D.S., W2754 St. Charles Rd., Chilton, 53014-9625. Tel: 920-849-4175. Rev. Paul Schulze, S.D.S. (GB), 1426 N. Alvin St., Appleton, 54911-3510. Tel: 920-733-8856. Rev. Joseph G. Wambach, S.D.S., 995 E. Baseline Rd. #1086, Tempe, AZ, 85283-1333. Tel: 480-777-7686.
Priests and Brothers of the USA Province Serving at the Generalate in Rome, Italy: Very Rev. Dennis D. Thiessen, S.D.S., Generalate; Revs. Thomas Novak, S.D.S.; Joseph Henn, S.D.S.

Salvatorians - Jordan Hall, 3800 N. 92nd St., 53222-2504. Tel: 414-463-6733.
E-mail: hchonney@aol.com
Fathers & Brothers of the Society of the Divine Savior. Bro. John Hauenstein, S.D.S., Local Coord.; Revs. Claude Klotz, S.D.S.; Eric Middlecamp, S.D.S.; Bros. George Armstrong, S.D.S.; Maurers Ellery, S.D.S.; Joseph Kreutzer, S.D.S.; Nilus Taddy, S.D.S.; Alex Peserik, S.D.S.; Cornelius Pope, S.D.S. Priests 2; Brothers 7.

St. Mary's Home for the Aged, 2005 Division St., Manitowoc, 54220-5699. Tel: 920-686-1132. Revs. Edward De Bruin, S.D.S.; Reginald Schrimpf, S.D.S.; James McKenna, S.D.S.; Donald Verhagen, S.D.S.

St. Anne's Home for the Elderly, 3800 N. 92 St., 53222-2589. Tel: 414-463-7570. Bros. Ladislaus Markoski, S.D.S.; Arthur Studt, S.D.S.

BENET LAKE. *St. Benedict's Abbey,* 12605 224th Ave., 53102. Tel: 262-396-4311; Fax: 262-396-4365.
E-mail: info@BenetLake.org
Web site: www.BenetLake.org
Rt. Revs. Andrew V. Garber, O.S.B., Resigned Abbot; Robert C. Schoofs, O.S.B., Retired Abbott; Leo M. Ryska, O.S.B., Resigned Abbot; Very Revs. Edmund J. Boyce, O.S.B., Admin.; Henry V. Nurre, O.S.B., Prior; Revs. Francis C. Reedy, O.S.B.; Kevin J. Murphy, O.S.B.; Leonard J. van Ackeren, O.S.B.; Basil J. Anderson, O.S.B., 1280 Med Park Dr., Las Cruces, NM, 88005. Tel: 505-523-7577; Fax: 505-524-3874. Rev. Jaime Velasco Rivera, O.S.B., Monasterio Benedictino, Apdo Postal 6-143, 62131, Cuernavaca, Morelos, Mexico. Priests 10; Brothers 11.

BURLINGTON. *Queen of Peace Friary,* 523 S. Brown's Lake Dr., P.O. Box 40, 53104-0040. Tel: 262-763-3241; Fax: 262-763-3326. Franciscan Friars of the Assumption B.V.M. Province. Retirement Home for Franciscan Friars. Revs. Robert Konkol, O.F.M., Guardian; Albin Miklaszewski, O.F.M.; Basil Janasik, O.F.M.; Edmund Czech, O.F.M.; Herbert Silko, O.F.M.; Colman Majchrzak; James Verdick, O.F.M.; Edgar Smigiel; Peter Machesky; Reynold Jarecki, O.F.M.; Sante De Angelis, O.F.M.; Sereno Baiardi, O.F.M.; Paschal Grigus, O.F.M.; George Dubowski; Michael Lacienski; Anthony Chojnacki; Anthony Cirignani; Raymond Zsolczai; Bros. Brendan Kowalski, O.F.M.; Joseph Krymkowski, O.F.M.; Boniface Bozacki, O.F.M.; Adrian Kolanczyk, O.F.M.; Edward Makowiecki, O.F.M.; Gregory Havel, O.F.M.; Michael Kulan, O.F.M.; Sebastian Nocinski; Craig Wilkine. Priests 15; Brothers 9.

EAST TROY. *Divine Word Seminary,* Box 107, 53120. Tel: 262-642-3300; Fax: 262-642-7754. Society of the Divine Word. Revs. John F. Fincutter, S.V.D.; Bernard Fisher, S.V.D.; Lucien Gaudreault, S.V.D.; Thomas Lavin, S.V.D.; Raymond Weisenberger, S.V.D.; Ralph Wiltgen, S.V.D.; Jerome Ziliak, S.V.D.; Bros. Bernard Scherger, S.V.D.; Raymond Albers, S.V.D.; William Morgan, S.V.D. Priests 9; Brothers 3; Total in Residence 12.

FRANKLIN. *Dehon Study Center,* 10731 W. Rawson Ave., 53132. Tel: 414-425-3768; Fax: 414-425-8768.
E-mail: mcguirescj@aol.com
Priests of the Sacred Heart. Rev. Paul J. McGuire, S.C.J.

St. Francis Residence, 12001 W. Woods Rd., 53132. Tel: 414-529-0332; Fax: 414-529-8777. Provincial Residence, Priests of the Sacred Heart. Revs. John Czyzynski, S.C.J., Supr.; Jan de Jong, S.C.J.; Anthony P. Russo, S.C.J.; Edward Kilianski, S.C.J., P.O. Box 960, Occidental, CA, 95465. Tel: 707-874-1438; Fax: 707-874-1433. Rev. James Schroeder, S.C.J., 5375 Kenrick Parke Dr. N. #305, St. Louis, MO, 63119. Tel: 314-968-3765; Fax: 314-657-3688. Rev. John Nitzki, S.C.J.

St. Martin of Tours, 7963 S. 116th St., 53132. Tel: 414-425-1114; Fax: 414-425-2527. Rev. Paul J. McGuire, S.C.J., Dehon Study Center, 10731 W. Rawson Ave., 53132. Tel: 414-425-3768; Fax: 414-425-8768.
E-mail: mcguirescj@aol.com
Priests 7.

Villa Maria, 7330 S. Lovers Lane Rd., 53132. Tel: 414-425-5968; 425-5981. Revs. Jim Alexander, S.C.J.; George Balderrama, S.C.J.; Donald Barnd, S.C.J.; Patrick M. Cremer, S.C.J.; Edward Griesemer, S.C.J.; Thomas Hunt, S.C.J.; Michael Van Der Peet, S.C.J.; Steve Wiese, S.C.J.; Thomas Simcox, S.C.J.; Bros. Raymond Kozuch, S.C.J.; Steve Cyr, S.C.J.; Matthew Miles, S.C.J., Supr.; Frank Miller, S.C.J.; Deacon Marion Quagliariello, S.C.J.; Rev. Peter Miller, S.C.J., 10101 W. Wisconsin Ave., Wauwatosa, 53226. Tel: 414-259-7977. Priests 10; Brothers 4; Deacons 1.

GREENDALE. *Salvatorian Formation Community,* 7100 W. Old Loomis Rd., 53129-2761. Tel: 414-427-8352.
Web site: salvatorians.com
Society of the Divine Savior. Revs. Donald Loskot, S.D.S., Dir. Novices; Scott Wallenfelsz, S.D.S.; Hugh Birdsall, S.D.S.; Bro. Wayne Madala, S.D.S., Dir. Candidates. Priests 3; Brothers 1; Novices 1; Candidates 1.

HALES CORNERS. *Priests of the Sacred Heart,* 6871 S. Lovers Lane Rd., P.O. Box 289, 53130-0289. Tel: 414-425-6910; Fax: 414-425-2938.
E-mail: scjuspro@powerworx.net
Web site: www.scj.org
Rev. John Czyzynski, S.C.J., Prov. Supr.; Bro. Raymond Kozuch, S.C.J., Prov. Sec.; Revs. Jerome Schaad, S.C.J., Prov. Treas.; Charles Brown, S.C.J., Dir. Foreign Missions, Dir. Justice & Peace; Timothy Gray, S.C.J., Dir. Justice & Peace; Stephen Huffstetter, S.C.J., Dir. Formation; John Klingler, S.C.J., Dir. Apostolates; Jack Kurps, S.C.J., Dir. Vocations; Paul J. McGuire, S.C.J., Dir. of Planning; Anthony P. Russo, S.C.J., Dir. Admissions & Dir. Denonian Affiliates.
Priests of the Province Serving Abroad: Most Rev. Evert Baaij, S.C.J., 10 Park Ln., 6001 Port Elizabeth, Rep. of S. Africa. Tel: 27-41-373-4734.
Provincialate Residence: Priests of the Sacred Heart, 12001 W. Woods Rd., 53132. Tel: 414-529-0332; Fax: 414-529-8777. Revs. John Czyzynski, S.C.J., Prov. Supr.; Jan de Jong, S.C.J.; Anthony P. Russo, S.C.J.
Attached to the Province but Living Elsewhere: Rev. Bryan Benoit, S.C.J., 4061 S. 35th St. #14, Greenfield, 53221. Tel: 414-817-1606. Rev. Jerome Clifford, S.C.J., 5463 Dempsey, St. Louis, MO, 63110. Tel: 314-771-5867. Rev. David Emerick, S.C.J., 16802 Springhaven Ct., Humble, TX, 77396-1364. Rev. Pat Gonsorcik, S.C.J., Ontario, 130 Springhurst, #203, Ottawa, Canada, K1S OE5. Tel: 613-565-4124; Fax: 613-567-0967. Rev. Robert Hess, S.C.J., 11061 W. Cobb Ave., 53130. Rev. Terence Langley, S.C.J., St. Irene Rectory, 187 East St.,

Carlisle, MA, 01741. Tel: 978-369-3940. Rev. Robert Naglich, 2949 Willowcreek Rd., Portage, IN, 46368. Tel: 219-762-4848; Fax: 219-762-3094. Rev. Douglas Watson, S.C.J., 3207 Sable Crossing, San Antonio, TX, 78232. Bro. Bernard Taube, S.C.J., 2833 Moland St., #3, Madison, 53704. Rev. Andrew Tran, S.C.J., 12750 Briar Forest #814, Houston, TX, 77077.

Sacred Heart Monastery, 7335 S. Lovers Lane, P.O. Box 566, 53130. Tel: 414-425-8300; Fax: 414-529-6988.
E-mail: fr.preid@juno.com
Priests of the Sacred Heart, 7335 S. Lovers Ln., P.O. Box 566, 53130-0566. Tel: 414-425-5323; Fax: 414-529-6988. Revs. Frank Aresta, S.C.J.; Charles Bisgrove, S.C.J.; James D. Brackin, S.C.J.; Joseph Gole, S.T.D. (Ljubljana); Justin Guiltnane, S.C.J.; Wayne Jenkins, S.C.J.; Brian McCullough, S.C.J.; John T. O'Connor, S.C.J.; Paul Grizzelle-Reid, S.C.J., Supr.; Bernard Rosinski, S.C.J.; Jerome Schaad, S.C.J.; Bro. James Willis, S.C.J. Priests 10; Brothers 1.

HOLY HILL. *Discalced Carmelite Monastery*, 1525 Carmel Rd., Hubertus, 53033. Tel: 262-628-1838; 673-3540; Fax: 262-628-4294. Very Rev. Jude Peters, O.C.D., Prov. Supr.; Revs. Matthias Montgomery, O.C.D., Subprior; Daniel Chowning, O.C.D., Dir. Novices; Francis Xavier Cotter, O.C.D.; Patrick J. Farrel, O.C.D.; Joseph-Mary Flanery, O.C.D.; Michael Griffin, O.C.D.; Cyril Guise, O.C.D., Prior & Shrine Dir.; Ernest Unverdorben, O.C.D.; Redemptus Short, O.C.D.; Fred Alexander, O.C.D.; John Grennon, O.C.D.; Mark Develis, O.C.D.; Donald Brick, O.C.D.; Bros. Martin Murphy, O.C.D.; Michael Berry; Fred Hickey. Priests 14; Brothers 1; Temporary Professed 2; Novices 3.

Holy Hill National Shrine of Mary Help of Christians, 1525 Carmel Rd., Hubertus, 53033. Tel: 262-628-1838; Fax: 262-628-4294.

Retreat Center, 1525 Carmel Rd., Hubertus, 53033. Tel: 262-628-1838; Fax: 262-628-4294.

KENOSHA. *Order of Preachers, Province of St. Albert the Great*. Friends of God, A Dominican Ashram, 720 35th St., 53140. Tel: 262-658-1062.
E-mail: ashram@dominicans.org
Revs. Donald J. Goergen, O.P.; James Q. Barnett, O.P.; Giles R. Klapperich, O.P.

MOUNT CALVARY. *St. Lawrence Friary*, 301 Church St., 53057. Tel: 920-753-3911; Fax: 920-753-2907. Revs. Keith Clark, O.F.M.Cap., Supr.; Edwin F. Dziedziejko, O.F.M.Cap.; Gary Wegner, O.F.M.Cap.; Campion Baer, O.F.M.Cap.; Joachim Strupp, O.F.M.Cap.; Dennis Druggan, O.F.M.Cap.; Ronald Jansch, O.F.M.Cap.; Elroy Pesch, O.F.M.Cap.; Kenan Siegel, O.F.M.Cap.; Eugene Tuller, O.F.M.Cap.; Anthony Will, O.F.M.Cap.; Eugene Wolf, O.F.M.Cap.; Paul Yaroch, O.F.M.Cap.; Bros. Douglas Bode, O.F.M.Cap.; Jerry Campbell, O.F.M.Cap.; Larry Groeschel, O.F.M.Cap.; Neal Plale, O.F.M.Cap.; Mark Rehlinger, O.F.M.Cap.; Arnold Sauter, O.F.M.Cap.; John Scherer, O.F.M.Cap., Vicar; Dismas Seward, O.F.M.Cap.; John Willger, O.F.M.Cap. Priests 13; Brothers 9.

OCONOMOWOC. *Austin Hall*. Mailing Address: Tolentine Center, 20300 Governors Hwy., Olympia Fields, IL, 60461-1081. 954 Dousman Rd., Oconomowac, 53066. Tel: 262-965-4640. Augustinians/Province of Our Mother of Good Counsel, Olympia Fields, IL. Bro. Bruce A. Jendraszak, O.S.A., Contact Person.

RACINE. *Augustinian Novitiate*, 4335 Douglas Ave., 53402-2956. Tel: 262-681-3221; Fax: 262-681-0628.
E-mail: racineosa@juno.com
Revs. Eugene A. Del Conte, O.S.A., Prior; Raymond R. Ryan, O.S.A., Novice Dir.; Alvin P. Metzger, O.S.A., Treas. Priests 3; Novices 3.

ST. FRANCIS. *St. Camillus Formation Community*, 3661 S. Kinnickinnic Ave., 53235. Tel: 414-481-3696; Fax: 414-481-8044. Rev. Louis Lussier, O.S.Cam., Supr.; Bros. Mario Crivello, O.S.Cam.; Scott Binet; Stephen Killilea; Allan Gidley. Priests 1; Brothers 1; Novices 1; Students 3.

TWIN LAKES. *La Salette Missionaries Shrine*, Box 777, 53181. Tel: 262-877-3111; Fax: 262-877-4508.
E-mail: lasalette@techeadnet.com
Web site: www.members.techeadnet.com/lasalette
Revs. James Stajkowski, M.S., Prov.; Thaddeus Galuszka, M.S.; Gerald Lebanowski, M.S.; Henry Wojtunik, M.S.; Bros. Adam Mateja, M.S.; Anthony Sepanik, M.S. Priests 4; Brothers 2.

WAUWATOSA. *Jesuit Community at St. Camillus*, 10100 W. Bluemound Rd., 53226-4386. Tel: 414-259-3784 (Court East); 258-1814 (Skilled Care). Society of Jesus, Wisconsin Province. Revs. Eugene M. Dutkiewicz, S.J., Supr.; Anthony L. Dagelen, S.J., Asst. Supr.; Leon S. Rausch, S.J., Min; Francis A. Arcuri, S.J.; Raymond O. Burger, S.J.; James B. Corrigan, S.J.; William E. Dooley, S.J.; Robert M. Frommelt, S.J.; George J. Guenther, S.J.; Cletus J. Healy, S.J.; Norbert J. Lemke, S.J.; Jeffrey R. Loebl, S.J.; Bro. Gerald E. McKeever, S.J.; Revs. Robert G. North, S.J.; Robert C. Ostertag, S.J.; Richard L. Porter, S.J.; Bernard J. Portz, S.J.; Robert F. Purcell, S.J.; Jerome E. Rohrer, S.J.; Joseph D. Scallon, S.J.; Paul G. Stockhausen, S.J.; William A. Van Roo, S.J.; Kenneth T. Walleman, S.J. Priests 21; Brothers 2.

St. Camillus Community House, 10213 W. Wisconsin Ave., 53226. Tel: 414-774-5634.
E-mail: jimcamk@execpc.com
Revs. James Kovarik, O.S.Cam., Supr.; Richard Korzinek, O.S.Cam.; Joseph L. Bisoffi, O.S.Cam.; Carlo Notaro, O.S.Cam.; Bros. Nelson DeLoria, O.S-.Cam.; Herman Moellenhoff, O.S.Cam.; Roland Wild, O.S.Cam.; Albert Schemp, Novice. Priests 4; Brothers 3.

St. Camillus Provincialate, 10101 W. Wisconsin Ave., 53226. Tel: 414-481-3696; Fax: 414-481-3696.
E-mail: nov45@aol.com
Provincial offices for the North American Province of the Order of the Servants of the Sick (Order of Saint Camillus). Very Rev. William F. Cronin, O.S-.Cam., M.S.W., Prov. Prov. Counselors: Revs. Bernard Blasich; Stephen Braddock; William Burt. Priests 4.

[Q] CONVENTS AND RESIDENCES FOR SISTERS

MILWAUKEE. *Ancilla Convent*. Tel: 414-384-6535. Inter-Community living for religious women. 3601 S. 41st St., 53221. Tel: 414-384-6535. Sr. Barbarina Jantsch, Dir.; Rev. Patrick M. Cremer, S.C.J., Chap. Sisters 22.

Marian Hall, 2925 W. Orchard St., 53215. Tel: 414-384-0995; Fax: 414-385-5316. Retired School Sisters of St. Francis. Sr. Phyllis Vater, O.S.F., Admin. Sisters 37.

Mercedes Molina - Instituto Santa Mariana de Jesus, 1234 N. 24th Pl., 53205. Tel: 414-931-7163; Fax: 414-931-7887.
E-mail: GPGarzon@aol.com
Sr. Gloria Piedad Garzon, Supr. Sisters 4.
Corporate Title: Mercedes Molina, Inc.

Monastery of the Perpetual Rosary, 217 N. 68th St., 53213. Tel: 414-258-0579.
E-mail: frannl@aol.com
Web site: opvocdir@mindspring.com
Cloistered Dominican Sisters of the Perpetual Rosary. Mother Miriam Leonard, O.P., Prioress. Professed Sisters 13.

Sacred Heart Center, 1545 S. Layton Blvd., 53215. Tel: 414-383-9038; Fax: 414-647-4889. Home for retired and infirm School Sisters of St. Francis. S. Joann Riesterer, O.S.F., Coord. of Health & Housing Svcs.; Sr. Rosalia Zachman, O.S.F., Coord. Sisters Living Group; Sr. Mary Louise Reinke, O.S.F., Facility Dir. Sisters 57.

St. Clare Convent, 3276 S. 16th St., 53215. Tel: 414-647-5812; 647-2437. Felician Sisters. Sr. M. Samuel Holowacz, Local Min. Sisters 4.

St. Dominic Center, 1727 S. 9th St., 53204. Tel: 414-384-4873; Fax: 414-384-0246. Vietnamese Dominican Sisters. Sr. Clara Nguyen, O.P., Supr. Sisters 4; Postulants 20.

St. Felix Convent, 3159 S. 17th St., 53215. Tel: 414-389-9803. Felician Sisters. Sr. Lisa Marie Drover, C.S.S.F., Local Minister. Sisters 3.

St. Francis Convent, 3170 S. 17th St., 53215. Tel: 414-643-6387. Felician Sisters. Sr. M. Gemma Franczak, C.S.S.F., Local Min. Sisters 6.

St. Joseph Convent, General Motherhouse of the School Sisters of St. Francis, 1501 S. Layton Blvd., 53215. Tel: 414-384-4105; Fax: 414-645-7198.
E-mail: generalate@sssf.org
Web site: www.sssf.org
Sr. Joan Puls, O.S.F., Pres.; Sr. Alida Lopez, 1st Vice Pres.; Sr. Toni Anne Gradisnik, Vice Pres.; Sr. Anna Maria Tharakan, Vice Pres.; Sr. Therese Thoenen, Prov.; Rev. James E. Mauel, S.J., Chap. Sisters 57; Total in Congregation 1,415. Legal Title: *School Sisters of St. Francis, Inc.*

San Damiano Convent, 2008 E. Euclid Ave., 53207. Tel: 414-489-9195. Sr. Lisa Marie Drover, C.S.S.F., Local Min. Felician Sisters 3.

Sisters of Charity of St. Joan Antida. Tel: 414-276-5153.
E-mail: stritas@scsja.org
St. Rita Convent, 1621 N. Cass St., 53202. Tel: 414-276-5153. Sr. Monica Fumo, S.C.S.J.A., Supr. Sisters 5.

Sisters of Charity of St. Joan Antida Convent (Maranatha), 3044 N. 25th St., 53206. Tel: 414-444-3994.
E-mail: marana@scsja.org
Sr. Andrea Christine Peters, S.C.S.J.A., Supr. Sisters 2.

Sisters of Charity of St. Joan Antida Convent (Presentation), 1329 N. Cass St., 53202. Tel: 414-276-4173.
E-mail: present@scsja.org
Sr. Anne Marie Baemmert, S.C.S.J.A., Supr. Sisters 8.

Sisters of Charity of St. Joan Antida Convent (St. Camillus Community), 624 N. 103rd St., 53226. Tel: 414-453-2472.
E-mail: camillus@scsja.org
Sr. Alice Thepouthay, S.C.S.J.A., Supr. Sisters 4.

Sisters of Charity of St. Joan Antida Convent (St. Charles Community), 3214 W. Parnell Ave., 53221. Tel: 414-282-9627.
E-mail: stchas@scsja.org
Sr. Marie Grohall, S.C.S.J.A., Supr. Sisters 8.

Sisters of Charity of St. Joan Antida Regina Mundi Provincial House and Novitiate, 8560 N. 76th Pl., 53223. Tel: 414-354-9233; Fax: 414-355-6463.
E-mail: sisters@scsja.org
Web site: www.scsja.org
Sr. Jennifer L. Daul, S.C.S.J.A., Prov. Sisters 3; Total in Community 45.

Sisters of the Divine Savior, 4311 N. 100th St., 53222-1393. Tel: 414-466-0810; Fax: 414-466-4335.
E-mail: schoedlJ@dsha.k12.wi.us
Provincial Administration. Prov. Team: Sr. Sheila Novak, S.D.S., Prov. Leader; Sr. Mary Lee Grady, S.D.S., Vicaress; Sr. Jeanette Clarke, S.D.S., Treas.; Sr. Pauline Feiner, Vice Pres. Total Sisters in Province 125.
Corporate Title: Sisters of the Divine Savior.

Salvatorian Heights Assisted Living Unit, 2720 N. 36th St., 53210. Tel: 414-445-8485; Fax: 414-445-6153. Sr. Deanna Schroeder, S.D.S., Coord.; Patricia Smith, Health Care Coord. Sisters 25.

United States Province, 1515 S. Layton Blvd., 53215. Tel: 414-384-1515; Fax: 414-384-1950.
E-mail: info@sssf.org
Web site: www.schoolsistersstfrancis.org
School Sisters of St. Francis. Provincial Team: Sr. Therese Thoenen, O.S.F.; Sr. Adelia Milligan, O.S.F.; Sr. Kathleen Kunze, O.S.F. Total in U.S. Province 918.
Corporate title: The School Sisters of St. Francis of St. Joseph's Convent, Milwaukee, Wisconsin, Inc.
Corporate Title: Congregational Support Charitable Trust.

BROWN DEER. *Sisters of the Sorrowful Mother-Generalate, Inc.*, 9056 N. Deerbrook Tr., 53223. Tel: 414-357-8940; Fax: 414-357-8950.
E-mail: ssmintl@aol.com
Web site: ssmfranciscans.org
Sr. M. Helen Malolepsy, Gen. Supr.

CAMPBELLSPORT. *St. Joseph Convent*, 526 Mill St., 53010. Tel: 920-533-8351; Fax: 920-533-5394. School Sisters of St. Francis. Retirement Home/Health Care Center. Sr. Phyllis Wirtz, O.S.F., Facility Dir.; Sr. Dorothy McKeague, O.S.F., Living Group Coord.; Sr. Joanne Armatowski, S.N.N.D., Dir. Pastoral Svcs.; Rev. Nicholas L. Goebel, Chap. Sisters 186; Total Staff 147.

CEDAR GROVE. *Sacred Heart of the Lake Chalet*, Box 46A, 53013. Tel: 262-285-3084. Sr. Mary Carlotta Myszka, Contact Person, Mailing Address: St. Mary's Home, 2005 Division St., Manitowoc, 54220. Recreation Home for Sisters of St. Mary's Home for Aged, Manitowoc, WI & Felician Sisters of the Mother of Good Counsel Province.

DELAVAN. *Villa Celine*, 3127 S. Shore Dr., 53115. Tel: 773-792-6363; Fax: 773-792-9590. Summer Rest Home for Sisters of the Resurrection. Sr. M. Barbara Sniegowski, C.R., Prov. Supr. & Contact Person, Mailing Address: 7432 W. Talcott Ave., Chicago, IL, 60631.

ELM GROVE. *Notre Dame of Elm Grove*, 13105 Watertown Plank Rd., 53122-2291. Tel: 262-782-1450; Fax: 262-782-2349.
S.S.N.D. Assisted Care, Independent Living. The School Sisters of Notre Dame, Milwaukee Province, Inc. Total in Residence 144; Total Staff 101.

School Sisters of Notre Dame, Provincial Offices, 13105 Watertown Plank Rd., 53122-2291. Tel: 262-782-9850; Fax: 262-782-5725.
E-mail: mkesler@ssnd-milw.org
Sr. Marilyn Kesler, S.S.N.D., Prov. Leader. Total in Milwaukee Province 530; Total Staff 35. Legal Titles: *School Sisters of Notre Dame, Milwaukee Province, Inc.; School Sisters of Notre Dame at Milwaukee, Wisconsin, Inc. Charitable Trust.*

FOND DU LAC. *Convent of the Sisters of St. Agnes*. Motherhouse. 1755 E. Johnson St., 54935. Tel: 920-923-2121; Fax: 920-923-3194.
E-mail: csaadm@vbemail.net
Web site: www.csasisters.org
Legal Title: *Congregation of Sisters of St. Agnes of Fond du Lac, Wisconsin, Inc.* Sr. Mary Mollison, C.S.A., Gen. Supr.; Rev. Anthony Will, O.F.M.Cap., Chap. Sisters 21; Total in Community 377.

KENOSHA. *Kenosha Dominicans*, P.O. Box 1288, 53141-1288. Tel: 262-694-2067; Fax: 262-694-6542.
E-mail: kenoshaop@aol.com
Congregation of the Dominican Sisters of St. Catherine of Siena of Kenosha. Sr. Susan Anne Snyder, O.P., Prioress. Total Religious in Community 22.

MANITOWOC. *Sisters of Saint Elizabeth, Inc.*, 2005 Division St., 54220-5699. Tel: 920-684-7171 (St. Mary's Home), Ext. 268. Sisters of St. Elizabeth. Mother

Mary Rita Amrhein, S.S.E., Mother General. Sisters 5.

MEQUON. *Sisters of the Sorrowful Mother, Novitiate House*, 4823 Bonniwell Rd., 53097-2202. Tel: 262-242-5770; Fax: 262-357-8950.
E-mail: ssmintl@aol.com
Web site: ssmfranciscan.org
Sisters 4.

MOUNT CALVARY. *Loretto Convent*, N8114 Calvary St., 53057. Tel: 920-753-3211; Fax: 920-753-3100.
E-mail: villasisterss@netscape.net
General Motherhouse of Sister-Servants of Christ the King. Sr. Mary Rose, Supr. Sisters 9.
Corporate Title: Congregation of Sister Servants of Christ the King, Inc.

Our Lady of Mt. Carmel Convent, 53057. Tel: 920-753-2131; 753-2036; Fax: 920-753-2116. Leadership: Sr. Mary Ann Srnka, S.S.N.D.
Home for Retired Sisters. School Sisters of Notre Dame 40.

OCONOMOWOC. *Villa St. Joseph Summer Day Camp*, 2653 Mill Rd., 53066. Tel: 414-646-2185; Fax: 414-645-5329.
Web site: www.childdevctr-stjoes.org
Sponsored by the Congregation of the Sisters of St. Felix of Cantalice of the United States of America, Inc. Chicago Province. Sr. M. Ramona Dombrowski, Pres. Total Assisted 125; Total Staff 12.

PEWAUKEE. *Carmel of the Mother of God*, W267 N2517 Meadowbrook Rd., 53072. Tel: 262-691-0336. Discalced Carmelite Nuns. Sr. Mary Agnes Kramer, O.C.D., Prioress; Rev. Dennis C. Klemme, Chap. Professed Sisters 7; Novices 1.

RACINE. *Convent of St. Catherine of Siena*. Siena Center, 5635 Erie St., 53402. Tel: 262-639-4100; Fax: 262-639-9702.
E-mail: sienactr@execpc.com
Web site: www.racinedominicans.org
Motherhouse of the Sisters of St. Dominic (Congregation of St. Catherine of Siena). Sr. Jean Ackerman, O.P., Pres. Sisters 117; Total Religious in Community 236.
Corporate title: Sisters of St. Dominic.

ST. FRANCIS. *St. Francis Convent, Motherhouse of the Sisters of St. Francis of Assisi*, 3221 S. Lake Dr., 53235-3799. Tel: 414-744-1160; Fax: 414-744-7193.
Web site: www.lakeosfs.org
Sr. Marcia Lunz, O.S.F., Dir. of the Congregation. Assoc. Directors: Sr. Rose Sevenich, O.S.F.; Sr. Charlotte Roost, O.S.F. Total in Community 333.
Corporate Title: The Sisters of St. Francis of Assisi, Milwaukee, Wis. Legal Titles: *The Sisters of St. Francis of Assisi, Inc.*; *The Ongoing Community Support Trust of the Sisters of St. Francis of Assisi*.

SHEBOYGAN. *Hospital Sisters of the Third Order of St. Francis*. Mailing Address: St. Francis Convent- La-Verna Road, P.O. Box 19431, Springfield, IL, 62794-9431. 1907 N. 29th St., 53081. Tel: 920-459-8785. Hospital Sisters of the Third Order of St. Francis 2.

SLINGER. *Franciscan Sisters of Christian Charity (O.S.F.)*. Tel: 262-644-8916. San Damiano Convent, 4270 Cedar Creek Rd., 53086-9795. Tel: 262-644-8916. Sr. Maria Casetta, O.S.F., Supr. Sisters 23; Total Staff 9.

WAUWATOSA. *Provincial Motherhouse of the Carmelite Sisters of the Divine Heart of Jesus*, 1230 Kavanaugh Pl., 53213. Tel: 414-453-4040; Fax: 414-453-5603.
E-mail: carmelwau@aol.com
Sr. M. Immaculata, Prov. Supr. Sisters 5; Total Religious in Province 23; Total Assisted 185; Total Staff 93.
Corporate Title: Carmelite Sisters of the Divine Heart of Jesus, Milwaukee, Wisconsin.

WEST ALLIS. *Missionary Sisters of the Holy Family*. (Poland). 1665 S. 64th St., 53214. Tel: 414-327-4068.
E-mail: hofasi@wi.net
Sr. Maria Sarafin, M.S.F.; Sr. Danuta Kujalowicz, M.S.F., Supr. Sisters 7.

[R] HERMITAGES

CAMPBELLSPORT. *Carmelite Hermit of the Trinity, Mount Carmel Hermitage*, N3493 Chapel Heights, 53010-1804.
E-mail: carmelitenun@homestead.com
Web site: carmelitehermit.homestead.com
Sr. Joseph Marie, Carmelite Hermit of the Trinity (Solitary).

[S] RETREAT HOUSES

MILWAUKEE. *Archdiocesan Retreat Center at Archbishop Cousins Catholic Center*, 3501 S. Lake Dr., P.O. Box 070912, 53207-0912. Tel: 414-769-3491; Fax: 414-769-3408.
E-mail: kreitzerw@archmil.org
Web site: www.archmil.org
William Kreitzer, Dir. Bldg. Svcs. Total Staff 2.

The Dwelling Place, 1704 E. Norwich St., 53207. Tel: 414-489-9444.
E-mail: jskap@hotmail.com
Revs. Francis J. Dombrowski, O.F.M.Cap.; Jerome Schroeder, O.F.M.Cap.; Mary Klotz, Team Member. Priests 2; Total in Residence 3; Total Staff 3.

BURLINGTON. *Franciscan Retreat Center, Inc.*, 503 S. Browns Lake Dr., 53105. Tel: 262-763-3600; Fax: 262-763-4229.
E-mail: sanfran@genevaonline.com
Web site: www.sfran@015-inc.com
Rev. James Connell, Pres.; Ms. Eloise Samano-Williamson, Exec. Dir. Total in Residence 6; Total Staff 17.

ELKHORN. *St. Vincent Pallotti Center*. Pallotine Fathers, N. 6409 Bowers Rd., 53121. Tel: 262-723-2108; Fax: 262-723-8608.
E-mail: vpallelk@elknet.net
Web site: www.vpallelk@elknet.net
Retreat and Christian formation Center. Lay Staff 2.

OCONOMOWOC. *The Redemptorist Retreat Center*, 1800 N. Timber Trail Ln., 53066-4897. Tel: 262-567-6900; Fax: 262-567-0134.
E-mail: phrc@globaldialog.com
Web site: www.redemptoristretreat.org
Revs. Peter Connolly, C.Ss.R., Supr.; John A. Broker, C.Ss.R.; William Broker, C.Ss.R.; Edward Monroe, C.Ss.R.; James White, C.Ss.R.; Sr. Olga Neft, O.S.F. Priests 5; Total in Residence 6; Sisters 1.

RACINE. *Racine Dominican Ministries, Inc. - Racine Dominican Retreat Program*, 5635 Erie St., 53402-1900. Tel: 262-639-4100; Fax: 262-639-9702.
E-mail: rdrp@miliserv.net
Sr. Rita Lui, O.P., Dir.

WAUKESHA. *Schoenstatt Retreat Center*, W284 N698 Cherry Ln., 53188-9402. Tel: 262-547-7733; Fax: 262-547-7749.
E-mail: schoenstattwaukesha@execpc.com
Sr. M. Jessica Swedzinski, Supr. Sisters 10; Total Staff 2.

[T] SECULAR INSTITUTES

MILWAUKEE. *Secular Institute of the Schoenstatt Sisters of Mary*, 5310 W. Wisconsin Ave., 53208-3061. Tel: 414-774-0520; Fax: 414-774-2911. Sr. Maria-Iris Quinones, Supr. Sisters 8.

WAUKESHA. *Secular Institute of Schoenstatt Fathers*. Tel: 262-548-9061; Fax: 262-548-9593.
E-mail: Schtx@attglobal.net
Schoenstatt Fathers, W284 N746 Cherry Ln., 53188. Tel: 262-548-9061; Fax: 262-548-9593. Revs. Hector R. Vega, Supr.; Dietrich A. Haas; Jonathan J. Niehaus. Priests 6; Total in Residence 3.
Attached to the house but living elsewhere: Revs. Gerold M. Langsch, C.C.; Robert DeCock, C.C.; Christian Christensen, C.C.

Secular Institute of the Schoenstatt Sisters of Mary, W284 N404 Cherry Ln., 53188-9416. Tel: 262-542-4384; 542-1544; Fax: 262-542-5730.
E-mail: schoenstattsisters@schsrmary.org
Sr. M. Virginia Riedl, Prov. Supr.; Sr. M. Jacinta Brunner, Supr. Sisters 30.

[U] ASSOCIATIONS OF THE FAITHFUL

MILWAUKEE. *The Christian Sisters*, 1910 W. Ohio Ave., Apt. 303, 53215. Tel: 414-643-1188. Sr. M. Corona Kroes, C.S., Pres. Sisters 2.

BELOIT. *Franciscan Sisters of Our Lady*, 2110 Bootmaker Dr., 53511. Tel: 608-365-7257. Sr. Mary Timothy Geenen, F.S.O.L., Supr. Sisters 4.

FRANKLIN. *Franciscan Sisters of Saint Clare, Inc.*, 7732 S. 51st St., 53132. Tel: 414-421-8257; Fax: 414-421-7869.
E-mail: smcfssc@execpc.com
Non-Cloistered Contemplative Community. Sr. Mary Celine Stein, F.S.S.C., Supr. Gen. Professed Sisters 3; Associate Sisters 2; Lay Affiliates 54.

[V] MISSIONARY ACTIVITIES

MILWAUKEE. *Milwaukee Archdiocesan Office for World Mission*. (Formerly Latin American Office), 3501 S. Lake Dr., P.O. Box 070912, 53207-0912. Tel: 414-769-3406; Fax: 414-769-3408.
E-mail: wmo@archmil.org
Web site: archmil.org/dept/wmo
Sr. Frances Cunningham, O.S.F., Dir.; Rosemary Huddleston, O.P., International Mission Coord. Sends priests and supports laity in overseas mission. Educates and raises funds for worldwide mission. Promotes parish twinning between archdiocese and other countries.

Missionary Association of Catholic Women, 3501 S. Lake Dr., P.O. Box 070912, 53207-0912. Tel: 414-769-3406; Fax: 414-769-3408.
E-mail: wmo@archmil.org
Web site: archmil.org/dept/wmo
Sr. Frances Cunningham, O.S.F., Dir. Office for World Mission. Provides aid to home and foreign missions.

Our Blessed Lady of Victory Mission, Inc., 5430 W. Vliet St., 53208-2175. Tel: 414-774-3128. Rev. Lawrence J. Leack, Chap.; Agnes J. Ryan, Pres.

St. Boniface Mission League, Inc., 3501 S. Lake Dr., P.O. Box 070912, 53207-0912. Tel: 414-769-3406; Fax: 414-769-3408.
E-mail: wmo@archmil.org
Web site: archmil.org/dept/wmo
Sr. Frances Cunningham, O.S.F., Pres.
Partners in World Mission formerly known as St. Boniface Mission League, Inc. Furnishes aid to home and foreign missions since 1913, with a special focus on the archdiocesan sister parish in the Dominican Republic.

Society for the Propagation of the Faith, Holy Childhood Association. (Pontifical Mission Aid Societies). Tel: 414-769-3406; Fax: 414-769-3408.
E-mail: wmo@archmil.org
Web site: archmil.org/dept/wmo
3501 S. Lake Dr., P.O. Box 070912, 53207-0912. Tel: 414-769-3406; Fax: 414-769-3408. Sr. Frances Cunningham, O.S.F., Dir.; Rosemary Huddleston, O.P., International Mission Coord. Raises funds and educates for worldwide mission, under papal auspices.

ELM GROVE. *Family Unity International, Inc.*, 12750 Stephen Pl., 53122-1964. Tel: 414-784-7448; Fax: 414-769-3408.
E-mail: wmo@archmil.org
Web site: archmil.org/dept/wmo
Patricia J. Parks, Pres. Raises and distributes funds to the missions of the Working Boys' Center. Organization is under the supervision of the Director of the Milwaukee Archdiocesan Office for World Mission.

[W] SOCIETIES

MILWAUKEE. *Milwaukee Archdiocesan Council of Catholic Women*, 3501 South Lake Dr., P.O. Box 07912, 53207-0912. Tel: 920-922-2739. Connie Forester, Pres.; Rev. Ronald O. Crewe, Moderator.

Priests' Purgatorial Society, 3501 S. Lake Dr., P.O. Box 070912, 53207-0912. Tel: 414-769-3340. Barbara Anne Cusack, Sec.

St. Vincent de Paul Society, 9601 W. Silver Spring Dr., 53225. Tel: 414-462-7837; Fax: 414-462-5458.
E-mail: svdp@execpc.com
Web site: www.execpc.com/~svdp
Mr. Gerald H. Felsecker, Exec. Dir., Milwaukee Archdiocesan Council, Council of Racine, 926 La-Salle St., Racine, 53404. Tel: 262-633-6468; Fax: 262-633-6408. Council of Kenosha, 6201 14th Ave., Kenosha, 53143. Tel: 262-657-6366; Fax: 262-657-5790. Council of Fond du Lac, 401 N. Hickory, Fond du Lac, 54935. Tel: 920-922-3650. Council of Sheboygan, 4215 Hwy. 42 N., Sheboygan, 53083. Tel: 920-457-4844; Fax: 920-457-4750. Council of Waukesha, 305 E. Main St., Waukesha, 53186. Tel: 262-547-3281; Fax: 262-547-6848. Council of Beaver Dam, 316 S. Spring St., Beaver Dam, 53916. Tel: 920-885-6971. Council of Washington County, 420 River Rd., West Bend, 53095. Tel: 262-334-7291. Council of Ozaukee County, P.O. Box 59, Port Washington, 53074. Tel: 262-284-4637; Fax: 262-284-6703. Total Assisted 30,000; Total Staff 5,000.

HORICON. *Legion of Mary*, 113 Valley St., 53032. Tel: 920-485-2427; Fax: 920-485-2427.
E-mail: mekinneymalachy@ameritech.net
Rev. M. Eugene Kinney, Spiritual Dir.; Ms. Virginia Wojtanowski, Pres.

RACINE. *Cursillos in Christianity*, 5110 Charles St., 53402. Tel: 262-639-6576.
E-mail: clardweb@yahoo.com
Rev. William W. Key, Spiritual Dir.; Sr. Anne Mary Rischar, O.S.F., Dir. English Speaking Secretariat; Clarence Weber, Lay Dir. Tel: 262-639-6576. Total Staff 7.

WAUWATOSA. *Milwaukee Archdiocesan Holy Name Union*, 2431 N. 63rd St., 53213. Tel: 414-258-1310; Fax: 414-258-1310. Mr. John Lando, Pres.; Rev. Edward Griesemer, S.C.J.

[X] NEWMAN CENTERS

MILWAUKEE. *Marquette University Ministry*. Tel: 414-288-6873; Fax: 414-288-3696.
E-mail: niemis@marquette.edu
Web site: www.mu.edu
Alumni Memorial Union 236, P.O. Box 1881, 53201-1881. Tel: 414-288-6873; Fax: 414-288-3696. Dr. Susan Mountin, Acting Dir.; Dr. Frank Majka, S.J., Acting Assoc. Dir.

Milwaukee Archdiocesan Campus Ministry, P.O. Box 070912, 53207-0912. Tel: 414-769-3439; Fax: 414-769-3408.
E-mail: johanekt@archmil.org
Legal Title: *Campus Ministry of the Archdiocese of Milwaukee*.
University of Wisconsin - Milwaukee, Newman Center, 3001 N. Downer Ave., 53211. Tel: 414-964-6640; Fax: 414-964-3608.
E-mail: cmfp@csd.wum.edu
Constance M. Popp; Rev. Robert J. Lotz.

U.W. Parkside and Carthage College, 6203-54th. Ave., Kenosha, 53142. Tel: 414-654-7416; Fax: 414-694-6048.
E-mail: padgette@archmil.org
Edith Padgett.
Whitewater Campus Ministry (Whitewater), 344 N. Prairie St., Whitewater, 53190. Tel: 262-473-5555; Fax: 262-473-5855.
E-mail: bzanin@idcnet.com

[Y] MISCELLANEOUS

MILWAUKEE. *Agape Community Center of Milwaukee, Inc.* Mailing Address: 11925 W. Lake Park Dr., 53224. 6100 N. 42nd St., 53209. Tel: 414-464-4440; Fax: 414-464-9420.
E-mail: agape@ministryhealth.org
Corporate Sponsor: Ministry Health Care, Inc. (Milwaukee, WI); Sponsored by Sisters of the Sorrowful Mother. Jenni Sevenich, Exec. Dir.

Alternative Residential Arrangements, Inc., P.O. Box 070912, 53207-0912. Tel: 414-769-3400; Fax: 414-769-3428.
E-mail: catholiccharities@ccmke.org
Web site: www.ccmke.org.
Group Homes for Developmentally disabled adults. Other Locations: 6609 N. 53rd St., 53223. Tel: 414-358-0852; Fax: 414-358-0669. Ronald J. Spitz, Dir. Tel: 414-769-3401, 5255 S. 18th St., 53221. Tel: 414-282-6366; Fax: 414-282-3205. Sponsored by Catholic Charities of the Archdiocese of Milwaukee, Inc.

Apostleship of the Sea, 3501 S. Lake Dr., P.O. Box 070912, 53207-0912.

Archdiocesan Marian Shrine, 141 N. 68th St., 53213. Tel: 414-257-0155. Rev. Anthony S. Trenier, Dir.

Archdiocese of Milwaukee Supporting Fund, Inc., 125 S. 84th St., Ste. 110, 53214. Tel: 414-607-6040; Fax: 414-607-6045. Erica P. John, CEO.

Assisi Homes - Jefferson Court, Inc., 415 E. Knapp St., 53202. Tel: 414-271-5370; Fax: 414-271-5988.

Assisi Homes - Mabess Manor, Inc., 415 E. Knapp St., 53202. Tel: 414-271-5370.

Assisi Homes of Milwaukee, Inc., 3345 W. Highland St., 53210. Tel: 414-934-9958; Fax: 414-271-5988. Franciscan Sisters, Daughters of the Sacred Hearts of Jesus and Mary (Wheaton, IL). Purpose: To acquire, or develop and operate housing projects for low income families and elderly persons and to provide for human and other charitable services required by the residents.

Assisi Homes of Wisconsin, Inc., 3345 W. Highland St., 53210. Tel: 414-934-9958.

Association of Franciscan Colleges and Universities, Inc., 6801 N. Yates Rd., P.O. Box 334, 53217. Tel: 414-410-4109. Sr. Gabrielle Kowalski, Exec. Dir.

Capuchin Franciscan Tertiary Province of St. Joseph of Wisconsin, Inc., 327 W. Brown St., 53212. Tel: 414-374-5750. Rev. Ulric Buening, O.F.M.Cap., Prov. Asst.

Capuchin Franciscan Volunteer Corps, Inc., 1015 N. 9th St., 53233-1468. Tel: 414-271-0135; Fax: 414-271-0637.
E-mail: capcorps@juno.com
Web site: www.capuchinfranciscans.org/capcorps.htm
Purpose: To serve as a religious organization which recruits, places, and supports Christian volunteers in service to people in need. Bro. David Schwab, O.F.M.Cap., Dir. Total Assisted 10,000; Total Staff 2.

Casa Romero Renewal Center, Inc., 423 W. Bruce St., 53204. Tel: 414-224-7564. Rev. David Shields, S.J., Pres. & Contact Person.

Cathedral Preservation Foundation, Inc., 802 N. Jackson St., 53202. Tel: 414-276-9814; Fax: 414-276-8285.
E-mail: johnendejan@archmil.org
Rev. John H. Endejan, Pres.

The Catholic Charismatic Renewal Office of Southeastern Wisconsin, Inc., P.O. Box 07912, 53207-0912. Tel: 414-482-1727; Fax: 414-482-3616.
E-mail: ccrarchmil@aol.com
Deacon Robert E. Goodman, Liaison; Mary Goodman, Admin.

Catholic Charities Foundation, Inc., 3501 S. Lake Dr., P.O. Box 070912, 53207-0912. Tel: 414-769-3400; Fax: 414-769-3428.
E-mail: Catholiccharities@ccmke.org
Web site: www.ccmke.org
Diane M. Knight, Registered Agent.

Catholic Charities of the Archdiocese of Milwaukee, Inc., 3501 S. Lake Dr., P.O. Box 070912, 53207-0912. Tel: 414-769-3400; Fax: 414-769-3428.
E-mail: catholiccharities@ccmke.org
Web site: www.ccmke.org
Diane M. Knight, Acting Exec. Dir.
Regional Offices: 2021 N. 60th St., 53208. Tel: 414-771-2881; Fax: 414-771-1674. Rachelle Alioto, Dir., 2711 19th St., Racine, 53403. Tel: 262-637-8888; Fax: 262-637-0695. Les Higgenbottom, Dir., 503 Wisconsin Ave., Sheboygan, 53081. Tel: 920-458-5726; Fax: 920-458-5826. Gary Howley, Dir., 741 N. Grand Ave., Suite 210, Waukesha, 53186. Tel: 262-547-2463; Fax: 262-547-8002. John Nesseth, Dir.
Area Offices: 5820 3rd Ave., Kenosha, 53140. Tel: 262-658-2088; Fax: 262-658-0841. 191 S. Main St., Fond du Lac, 54935. Tel: 920-923-2550; Fax: 920-923-1777.
Other Offices: Beaver Dam, Brookfield, Burlington, Menomonee Falls, Milwaukee North, Milwaukee South, Milwaukee Southwest, North Lake, Port Washington, West Bend. Total Assisted Annually 28,000.

Clare Towers II, Inc. dba Clare Woods, 3576 S. 43rd St., 53220. Tel: 414-643-6501; Fax: 414-643-4474. Sponsored by School Sisters of St. Francis. Housing Facility for physically disabled to live independently. Apartments 32.

Clare Towers, Inc., 1546 S. 29th St., 53215. Tel: 414-643-6501; Fax: 414-643-4474. Sponsored by School Sisters of St. Francis. Housing facility for physically disabled to live independently. Apartments 25.

Convergence, Inc., 1501 S. Layton Blvd., 53215. Tel: 414-384-4105; Fax: 414-645-7198. Sr. Jeanne Schweickert, S.S.S.F., Pres. & Exec. Dir.; Sr. Anne Beitzinger, Vice Pres. Board Members: Sr. Charlita Foxhoven; Sr. Frances Brenner; Sr. Anne Beitzinger.

Covenant Healthcare System, Inc., 1126 S. 70th St., Ste. S306, P.O. Box 14970, 53214-0970. Tel: 414-456-2300; Fax: 414-456-2363. Paul Dell Uomo, Pres. & CEO. Franciscan Sisters, Daughters of the Sacred Hearts of Jesus and Mary, Wheaton, IL. Congregation of the Sisters of St. Felix of Cantalice (Felician Sisters), Chicago, IL.

Covenant Home Health and Hospice, Inc., 9688 W. Appleton Ave., 53225. Tel: 414-535-6900; Fax: 414-535-6902.
E-mail: spfeifer@covhealth.org
Franciscan Sisters, Daughters of the Sacred Hearts of Jesus and Mary, Wheaton, IL. Total Served 6,000; Total Staff 280.

Divine Savior Holy Angels High School Endowment Foundation, Inc., 4257 N. 100th St., 53222. Tel: 414-462-3742; Fax: 414-466-0590.
E-mail: dsha@dsha.k12.wi.us

Dominican Center for Women, Inc., 2470 W. Locust St., 53206-1134. Tel: 414-444-9930. Sr. Ann Halloran, O.P., Dir. & Contact Person.

Eastside Senior Services, 2717 E. Hampshire, 53211. Tel: 414-961-0661; Fax: 414-964-0112. Marylou Parthum, Dir.
Corporate Title: Eastside Senior Services, Inc. - an Interfaith Outreach Program. Sponsored by SS. Peter and Paul, Lake Park Lutheran Church, ELCA, Plymouth Church United Church of Christ, St. Casmir's, St. Mary Czestochowa, and Three Holy Women, Milwaukee. Total Assisted 475; Total Staff 3.

Franciscan Peacemakers, Inc., Milwaukee, 2470 W. Locust St., 53206. Tel: 414-873-5078; Fax: 414-973-5101.
E-mail: franpax@earthlink.net
Web site: www.franpax.org
Revs. Robert Wheelock, O.F.M.Cap., Team Member; Michael J. Sullivan, O.F.M.Cap., Exec. Dir. Total Assisted 25,000; Total Staff 2.

Franciscan Pilgrimage Programs, Inc., 1648 S. 37th St., 53215-1724. Tel: 414-383-9870; Fax: 414-383-0335.
E-mail: frroch@execpc.com
Web site: www.franciscanpilgrimages.com
Rev. Roch Niemier, O.F.M., Pres. Operate a Catholic Franciscan Pilgrimage Program for religious men and women, leaders in Franciscan based institutions, members of the Secular Franciscan Order and others who desire to deepen their Franciscan values and spirituality.

House of Peace, 1702 W. Walnut St., 53205-1616. Tel: 414-933-1300; Fax: 414-933-0395. Charles Holton, Dir.; Rev. Matthew Gottschalk, O.F.M.Cap., Spiritual Dir. In res. Rev. Al Veik, O.F.M.Cap.; Bro. Booker T. Ashe, O.F.M.Cap., Dir. Emeritus. Total Assisted 5,500; Total in Residence 2; Total Staff 6.

The Jesuit Partnership, P.O. Box 080287, 53208-0287. Tel: 414-937-6955; Fax: 414-937-6950. Revs. Eugene M. Dutkiewicz, S.J., Treas.; Richard A. McGarrity, S.J., Pres.; Robert M. Frommelt, S.J., Asst. to Pres.

Korean Catholic Community, 1842 W. Windlake Ave., 53215. Tel: 414-672-6416; Fax: 414-672-6416.
E-mail: sheencheon@yahoo.com
Rev. Immanuel Pyo.

LaFarge Lifelong Learning Institute, Inc., 1501 S. Layton Blvd., 53215. Tel: 414-383-2550; Fax: 414-385-6647.
E-mail: lafargemc@lafarge.org
Continuing Education Program for older adults. Marion K. Hook, Exec. Dir.; Sr. Celia Schulte, Admin. Asst.

MAREDA. Archdiocese of Milwaukee, Office for Schools, Child and Youth Ministry. OSCYM/Dept. Parishes. 3501 S. Lake Dr., P.O. Box 070912, 53207-0912. Tel: 262-547-3216; Fax: 414-769-3408.
E-mail: weberjm@archmil.org
Web site: www.archmil.org
Kay Curty, Treas.

Milwaukee Achiever Program, Inc., 1506 W. Pierce St., 53204. Tel: 414-643-5108; Fax: 414-643-8804.
Web site: www.milwaukeeachiever.org
Dennis J. Purtell, Esq., Legal Counsel. Sponsored by the School Sisters of St. Francis; Sisters of St. Francis of Assisi; School Sisters of Notre Dame.
Purpose: To provide adult literacy education to economically and educationally disadvantaged adults in the Greater Milwaukee area. Total Assisted Annually 560; Total Staff 23.

Milwaukee Archdiocesan Council of Deacons. Tel: 251-8500.
E-mail: zimprichd@archmil.org
P.O. Box 070912, 53207-0912. Tel: 414-769-3409. Advisory/Governing Board of Deacons. Deacon Michael Rooney, Pres.

Milwaukee Archdiocesan Elementary Principals' Association (MAEPA). Archdiocese of Milwaukee, Office for Schools, Child and Youth Ministry, P.O. Box 070912, 53207-0912. Tel: 414-769-3363; Fax: 414-769-3408. Mort Zaydel, Treas. Tel: 920-994-9962.

Milwaukee Archdiocesan Secondary Principals' Association (MASPA), 3501 S. Lake Dr., P.O. Box 070912, 53207-0912. Tel: 414-769-3385; Fax: 414-769-3408.
E-mail: scheeln@archmil.org
Joel Eul, Pres.; Bro. Nivard Scheel, C.F.X., Asst. to the Supt. of Schools & Contact Person.

Ministry Health Care, Inc., 11925 W. Lake Park Dr., 53224. Tel: 414-359-1060. Sr. M. Lois Bush, S.S.M., CEO; Nicholas Desien, Pres. & COO.

National Association of Catholic Chaplains, 3501 S. Lake Dr., P.O. Box 070473, 53207-0473. Tel: 414-483-4898; Fax: 414-483-6712.
E-mail: nacc@nacc.org
Web site: www.nacc.org
Rev. Joseph J. Driscoll (BO), Exec. Dir.

National Office of Post-Abortion Reconciliation and Healing, Inc., 3501 S. Lake Dr., P.O. Box 070477, 53207-0477. Tel: 414-483-4141; Fax: 414-483-7376.
E-mail: noparh@juno.com
Web site: www.marquette.edu/rachel
Victoria M. Thorn, Pres. Total Assisted 4,500; Total Staff 3.

O.S.F. Services, Inc., 1126 S. 70th St., Ste. S306, P.O. Box 14970, 53214-0970. Tel: 414-456-2300. John D. Oliverio, Pres. Sponsored by Franciscan Sisters, Daughters of the Sacred Hearts of Jesus and Mary, Wheaton, IL.

Pallottine Fathers and Brothers, Inc., Disability Trust, 5424 W. Bluemound Rd., 53208. Tel: 414-259-0688; Fax: 414-258-9314.
E-mail: mdprov@dias.net
Web site: www.dias.net/~pallotti
Very Rev. Robert V. Carney, S.A.C., Pres.; Rev. Richard J. Gunderman, S.A.C., Treas.

Pallottine Fathers and Brothers, Inc., Educational and Apostolic Ministry Trust, 5424 W. Bluemound Rd., 53208. Tel: 414-259-0688; Fax: 414-258-9314.
E-mail: mdprov@dias.net
Web site: www.dias.net/~pallotti
Very Rev. Robert V. Carney, S.A.C., Prov.; Rev. Richard J. Gunderman, S.A.C., Treas.

S.E.T. Ministry, Inc., 2977 N. 50th St., 53210. Tel: 414-449-2680; Fax: 414-442-1770. Sr. Lucina Halbur, C.S.A., Pres. & C.E.O. Wheaton Franciscan Services, Inc., Corporate Sponsor, Joint Sponsored by 18 Religious Congregations. Health and Human Services Outreach Programs. Total Assisted 3,800.

S.I.S. (Sisters Interacting with Seniors), 222 N. 33rd St., #913, 53208. Tel: 414-933-2270. Sr. Julius Voelz, R.S.M., Coord. Total Assisted 50; Total Staff 2.

St. Benedict Community Meal. (Province of St. Joseph of the Capuchin Order, Inc.). 1015 North 9th St., 53233. Tel: 414-271-0135; Fax: 414-271-0637.
E-mail: stbens@execpc.com
Mr. Tom Plakut, Dir. Provides a free evening meal Sunday through Friday to those in need. Total Assisted 122,510 Meals Served; Total Staff 4.

St. Catherine Residence, Inc., 1032 E. Knapp St., 53202. Tel: 414-272-8470. A board house serving women in transition, with onsite programs advocating self-sufficiency. Includes a Right Start Program for first-time, single, pregnant women over the age of 17. Supportive programming for women learning to live with physical disabilities, mental health disease or other recovery challenges as well as long term rental units. Lynne J. Oehlke, M.S.W., Exec. Dir. Sisters 2; Residents 150. Legal Title: *St. Catherine Residence, Inc.*

St. Clare Management, Inc., 1545 S. Layton Blvd., 53215. Tel: 414-643-6501; Fax: 414-643-4474. Philip Aggen, Pres. & CEO. Sponsored by the School Sisters of St. Francis.

St. Francis Foundation of Milwaukee, Inc., 3237 S. 16th St., 53215. Tel: 414-647-5515; Fax: 414-647-5565.
E-mail: jhodnik@covhealth.org
Sponsored by the Felician Sisters. Fund development for St. Francis Hospital, Villa St. Francis, The Terrace at St. Francis, Child Development Center of St. Joseph and Community Outreach Efforts of the Felician Sisters. Sr. Mary Clarette Stryzewski, C.S.S.F.

St. Josaphat Basilica Foundation, Inc., 569 W. Lincoln Ave., 53207. Tel: 414-385-3263; Fax: 414-385-3269.
E-mail: basilica@execpc.com
Web site: www.thebasilica.org
Mr. Michael J. Murry, Chm.; Mr. Richard C. Thomas, Exec. Dir.

St. Joseph's Hospital Community Foundation, Inc., 5000 W. Chambers St., 53210. Tel: 414-447-2844; Fax: 414-874-4399. Amy Johnson, Exec. Dir. Sponsored by Franciscan Sisters, Daughters of the Sacred Hearts of Jesus and Mary, Wheaton, IL.

St. Mary's Hospital, Milwaukee Foundation, Inc., 2320 N. Lake Dr., 53202. Tel: 414-291-1425; Fax: 414-291-1441. Margaret Demet, Chm.; Charles Lobeck, Pres. Sponsored by Ascension Health System.

St. Michael Hospital Community Foundation, Inc., 2400 W. Villard Ave., 53209. Tel: 414-527-8205; Fax: 414-527-8461.
E-mail: scallaha@covhealth.org
Web site: www.covhealth.org/afficiat/smh.html
John H. Kopmeier, Jr., Pres.; Sean G. Callahan, Exec. Dir. Franciscan Sisters, Daughters of the Sacred Hearts of Jesus and Mary, Wheaton, IL.

St. Stephen's League. (of the Archdiocesan Council of Deacons). P.O. Box 070912, 53207-0912. Tel: 414-769-3409.
E-mail: zimprichd@archmil.org
Deacon David Zimprich.

St. Thomas More Lawyers Society, 3501 S. Lake Dr., P.O. Box 07912, 53207-0912. Tel: 414-769-3338; Fax: 414-769-3408. Chaplains: Revs. Thomas T. Brundage; James Connell.

Santa Fe Communications, Inc. Heart of the Nation, 1126 S. 70th. St., Ste. S216A, 53214. Tel: 414-475-4444; Fax: 414-475-3621.
E-mail: Bruno1@aol.com
Dr. William Thorn, Pres.; Mr. Jon Pray, Treas. Total Staff 3.

The School Sisters of Saint Francis of St. Joseph's Convent Congregational Support Charitable Trust, 1515 S. Layton Blvd., 53215. Tel: 414-384-1515.
E-mail: info@sssf.org
Sr. Helen Butzler, O.S.F., Trustee. Corporate Title: Congregational Support Charitable Trust.

Seton Health Corporation of Wisconsin, 2320 N. Lake Dr., 53211. Robert Henkel, Chm. Operated by Ascension Health System.

Shade Tree Family Resource Center, Inc., 1938 N. 4th St., 53212. Tel: 414-562-7934; Fax: 414-562-7935. Jerry Schroeder, Pres. Sponsored by: School Sisters of Notre Dame. Operation of a community-based family center committed to the preservation of families and the prevention of violence; conducts programs, education, support groups and self awareness. Total Assisted 300; Total Staff 11.

Society of the Divine Savior Ongoing Community Support Trust, 1735 Hi Mount Blvd., 53208-1720. Tel: 414-258-1735; Fax: 414-258-1934.
E-mail: salvatorians@sdsusa.org
Web site: salvatorians.com

St. Joan Antida High School Foundation, Ltd., 1341 N. Cass St., 53202. Tel: 414-354-9233. Sr. Kathy Lundwall, S.C.S.J.A., Contact Person, Mailing Address: 8560 N. 76th Pl., 53223.

Telos, Inc. dba Clare Heights, Clare Meadows, Clare Lakes, Clare Court, Clare Place and Clare Central. Tel: 414-643-6501; Fax: 414-643-4474. 1545 S. Layton Blvd., 53215. Tel: 414-643-6501; Fax: 414-643-4474. Sponsored by the School Sisters of St. Francis. Housing for physically disabled to live independently. Sr. Regina Pacis, Pres. Apartments 107.

Theological Studies, Inc., Marquette University, 100 Coughlin Hall, P.O. Box 1881, 53201-1881. Tel: 414-288-3164; Fax: 414-288-1413.
E-mail: Michael.Fahey@Marquette.edu
Publisher of the quarterly Theological Studies. Revs. Michael A. Fahey, S.J., Editor; David Schultenover, S.J. (OM), Book Review Editor.

VISION Ministries, Inc., 1515 S. Layton Blvd., 53215. Tel: 414-384-1515; Fax: 414-384-1950.
E-mail: rmeserv@sssf.org
Web site: www.sssf.org
Sr. Regina Pacis Meservey, Exec. Dir. Sponsored by The School Sisters of St. Francis of St. Joseph's Convent, Milwaukee, WI, Inc.
Purpose: To further the mission of the congregation and to manage, promote support and engage in related ministries.

Wisconsin Association of Principals of Catholic Secondary Schools. Archdiocese of Milwaukee, Office for Schools, Child and Youth, P.O. Box 070912, 53207-0912. Tel: 414-769-3363; Fax: 414-769-3408. Joseph J. Behr, Exec. Sec. Tel: 414-352-1148.

Women and Children Project, Inc., 1938 N. 4th St., 53212. Tel: 414-562-9120; Fax: 414-562-7935.
E-mail: wcpnetwork@dellnet.com
Purpose: Strengthens nine independent network agencies through fund development and collaborated programming; provides assistance in bilingual referral program (Woman to Woman); advocates for systemic change with women in poverty (The Face of Poverty).

BRISTOL. *Mercy Retreat Center*, 12009 221st Ave., 53104. Tel: 262-862-6648. Sisters of Mercy of the Americas, Regional Community of Chicago. Sr. Lois Graver, R.S.M., Contact Person.

BROWN DEER. *Sisters of the Sorrowful Mother Charitable Trust*, 9056 N. Deerbrook Rd., 53223. Tel: 414-357-8940; Fax: 414-357-8950.
E-mail: ssmintl@aol.com
Web site: ssmfranciscans.org
Sr. M. Helen Malolepsy. Provides for the needs of the aged and infirm members of the Sisters of the Sorrowful Mother.

Sisters of the Sorrowful Mother International Finance, Inc., 9056 N. Deerbrook Terr., 53223. Tel: 414-357-8940; Fax: 414-357-8950.
E-mail: ssmintl@aol.com
Web site: ssmfranciscan.org
Sr. M. Helen Malolepsy.

ELM GROVE. *Mercy Alumnae Association*, 15355 Marilyn Dr., #4, 53122-1072. Tel: 262-786-0871.
E-mail: hmercyme@aol.com
Sr. Mariann Horning, R.S.M., Coord.

FOND DU LAC. *Hazotte Ministries, Inc.*, 1755 E. Johnson St., 54935. Tel: 920-923-2121; Fax: 920-923-3194. Sponsored by the Congregation of Sisters of St. Agnes. Sr. Hertha Longo, C.S.A., Pres.

St. Francis Home Foundation, Inc., 33 Everett St., 54935. Tel: 920-923-7980; Fax: 920-923-7995.
E-mail: stfran@vbe.com
Mary Weber, Pres. Sponsored by the Congregation of Sisters of St. Agnes.

FRANKLIN. *Congregation of the Priests of the Sacred Heart Support and Maintenance Trust*, 6871 S. Lovers Lane Rd., 53132. Tel: 414-425-6910; Fax: 414-425-2938. Trustees: Revs. Justin Guiltnane, S.C.J.; Bernard Rosinski, S.C.J.; Bro. Benedict Humpfer, S.C.J.

COURAGE Association, 6865 S. 68th St., #207, 53132. Tel: 414-427-0340.
E-mail: CourageMKE@excite.com
Peter Caprise, Dir.

Friends of Theophane, P.O. Box 320101, 53132. Tel: 414-481-6739; Fax: 414-481-6764.
E-mail: Rzeilinger@aol.com
Mr. Ronald Zeilinger, Contact Person. To collect information and promote knowledge of the reputation for holiness of the late Frater Theophane Prenderville, S.C.J.

GREENDALE. *Volunteer Missionary Movement (VMM)*, 5980 W. Loomis Rd., 53129. Tel: 414-423-8660; Fax: 414-423-8964.
E-mail: vmm@execpc.com
Web site: www.execpc.com/~vmm
Richard A. Kirsch, Dir. Recruits, trains and sends Christian men and women to areas of need in the world.

HALES CORNERS. *Development Office.* Sacred Heart Monastery-Priests of the Sacred Heart-Reign of the Sacred Heart, Inc. 6889 S. Lovers Lane Rd., P.O. Box 900, 53130. Tel: 414-425-3383; Fax: 414-425-5719. Mr. Patrick R. Thompson, Pres. U.S. Province of the Priests of the Sacred Heart.

KENOSHA. *Assisi Homes - Kenosha, Inc.*, 1860 27th Ave., 53140. Tel: 414-551-9821; Fax: 414-551-9843. Independent Housing for Low Income Elderly.

Assisi Homes - Saxony, Inc., 1876 22nd Ave., 53140. Tel: 414-551-9005. Independent Housing for Low Income Elderly.

Franciscan Seniors, Kenosha, Inc., 1920 27th Ave., 53140. Tel: 630-462-9271.

St. Mark Latin American Center, 1320 73rd St., 53143-5459. Tel: 262-656-7370; Fax: 262-656-7375.
E-mail: stmark@acronet.net
Web site: www.stmark-kenosha.org
Rev. James Vojtik; Deacons Gregorio Lebron; Roberto Salazar; Alvaro Dominquez; Betty Salazar, Coord. of Human Resources; Mary Medrano, Secretary. Total Assisted 2,500; Total Staff 6.

The Women's Health Center Foundation, Inc., 9916 75th St., 53142. Tel: 262-697-1900; Fax: 262-653-5554.
E-mail: stcath@acronet.net
Web site: www.acronet.net/~stcath
Lynn Johnson, Contact Person. Sponsored by the Wheaton Franciscan Services, Inc.

MANITOWOC. *Sisters of St. Elizabeth, Inc., Congregational Support Charitable Trust*, 2005 Division St., 54220-5699. Tel: 920-684-7171, Ext. 268; 303. Mother M. Rita Amrhein, S.S.E., Trustee.

MEQUON. *St. Mary's Foundation Ozaukee, Inc.*, 13133 N. Port Washington Rd., Ste. G01, 53097. Tel: 414-243-7472; Fax: 414-243-7416. Jay Wilcox, Chm. Sponsored by Ascension Health System.

RACINE. *All Saints Healthcare Foundation, Inc.*, 1320 Wisconsin Ave., 53403. Tel: 262-687-2293; Fax: 262-687-2674.
E-mail: kbuser@allsaintshealthcare.org
Web site: allsaintshealth.com
Kenneth R. Buser, Pres. Franciscan Sisters, Daughters of the Sacred Hearts of Jesus and Mary, Wheaton, IL.

All Saints Healthcare System, Inc., 3801 Spring St., 53405. Tel: 262-687-4011; Fax: 262-687-4540.
E-mail: kbuser@allsaintshealthcare.org
Web site: allsaintshealth.com
Kenneth R. Buser, Pres. & C.E.O. Franciscan Sisters, Daughters of the Sacred Hearts of Jesus and Mary, Wheaton, IL.

All Saints Related Services, Inc., 3807 Spring St., 53405. Tel: 262-687-4277; Fax: 262-687-8039.
E-mail: jbeck@allsaintshealthcare.org
Web site: allsaintshealth.com

Catherine Marian Housing, Inc., 5635 Erie St., 53402. Tel: 262-639-4100; Fax: 262-639-9702.
Web site: www.racinedominicans.org
Racine Dominican Ministries, Inc. and Franciscan Ministries, Inc.

Dominican College of Racine, Inc., 5635 Erie St., 53402. Tel: 262-639-4100; Fax: 262-639-9702. Sr. Jean Ackerman, O.P., Pres.

Missionary Community of St. Paul the Apostle and Mary, Mother of the Church, Inc., 2512 Westwood Dr., 53404. Tel: 262-634-2666; Fax: 262-635-1910.
E-mail: 0mcsp@aol.com
Revs. Pere Cane, Pres.; Marti Colom, Sec. An international Public Association of Christian Faithful, comprised of clergy and laity. It is present in Africa, Europe, North and South America. It fosters pastoral activities and human development initiatives, while promoting mission awareness internationally.

Racine Dominican Ministries, Inc- Racine Dominican Retreat Program, 5635 Erie St., 53402-1900. Tel: 262-639-4100. Sr. Rita Lui, O.P., Dir. & Contact Person.

Racine Dominican Ministries, Inc., 5635 Erie St., 53402. Tel: 262-639-4100; Fax: 262-639-9702.
Web site: www.racinedominicans.org
Sr. Jean Ackerman, O.P., Pres.

Racine Dominican Ministries, Inc. Senior Companion Program, 5635 Erie St., 53402. Tel: 262-639-4100; Fax: 262-639-9702.
Web site: www.racinedominicans.org
Sr. Brenda Walsh, O.P., Dir.

Racine Dominican Ministries, Inc.- Adult Learning Program, 5635 Erie St., 53402-1900. Tel: 262-639-4100; Fax: 262-639-9702.
E-mail: alpsc@miliserv.net
Sr. Joyce Quintana, O.P., Dir. & Contact Person.

St. Catherine's High School Corporation, 1200 Park Ave., 53403. Tel: 262-632-2785; Fax: 262-632-5144. Daniel Horton, Chpn.

St. Catherine's High School of Racine, Inc., 5635 Erie St, 53402. Tel: 262-639-4100; Fax: 262-639-9702. Sr. Jean Ackerman, O.P., Pres.

St. Catherine's Infirmary, Inc., 5635 Erie St., 53402. Tel: 262-639-4100; Fax: 262-639-9702. Sr. Jean Ackerman, O.P., Pres.

Villa St. Anna, Inc., 5737 Erie St., 53402. Tel: 262-639-9757. To provide assisted living for the elderly of low and moderated income. Residents 71.

ST. FRANCIS. *Foundation for Religious Retirement, Inc.*, 3221 S. Lake Dr., 53235. Tel: 414-483-9128; Fax: 414-744-7193.
E-mail: japrrot@lakeosfs.org
Jan Parrott, Exec. Dir. Raises funds to fulfill the needs of retired women religious in the Milwaukee Archdiocese.

SHEBOYGAN. *St. Thomas High School, Inc.*, 822 New Jersey Ave., 53081. Tel: 920-457-7110; Fax: 920-457-4001. Rev. Richard J. Fleischman, Sec. & Treas. A fund to provide youth and adult religious education programs within the county.

STONE BANK. *Tyme Out Youth Ministry Center, Inc.* Tel: 262-966-1800; Fax: 262-966-1815.
E-mail: tymeout@execpc.com
Mailing Address: W332 N6786 County Rd. C, Nashotah, 53058-9737. Tel: 262-966-1800. Sr. Kieran Sawyer, S.S.N.D., Dir. Total in Residence 3; Total Staff 16.

WATERFORD. *General Secretariat of the Franciscan Missions, Inc.*, P.O. Box 130, 53185. Tel: 262-534-5470; Fax: 262-534-4342.
E-mail: framis@wi.net
Web site: franciscanmissions.org

Revs. Sereno Baiardi, O.F.M., Dir.; Sante De Angelis, O.F.M., Assoc. Dir. General Secretariat of the Franciscan Missions, Inc. Missionaries 5,400.

WAUWATOSA. *Franciscan Shared Laboratory, Inc.*, 11020 W. Plank Ct., Ste. 100, 53226. Tel: 414-476-3400; Fax: 414-256-5566.
E-mail: jholling@covhealth.org
Web site: covhealth.org
Sponsored by Franciscan Sisters, Daughters of the Sacred Hearts of Jesus and Mary (Wheaton, IL). Jeanne Holling, Pres. Medical Laboratory Serving Healthcare Institutions.

Friends of Calvary Cemetery, Inc., 2515 N. 66th St., 53213. Tel: 414-778-1187. Mr. Keith Schultz, Pres. Purpose: To raise funds in connection with the restoration of Calvary Chapel located at Calvary Cemetery, 5503 West Bluemound Rd., Milwaukee, WI and overseeing such restoration.

Order of St. Camillus Foundation, Inc., 10200 W. Bluemound Rd., 53226. Tel: 414-259-8335; Fax: 414-259-4590. David Kremer, Exec. Dir. & Contact Person.

St. Camillus Communities, Inc., 10101 W. Wisconsin Ave., 53226. Tel: 414-259-4511. Rev. Louis Lussier, O.S.Cam., Pres. Total in Residence 21.

St. Camillus Health System, Inc., 10101 W. Wisconsin Ave., 53226. Revs. Louis Lussier, O.S.Cam., Pres.; James Kovarik, O.S.Cam., Vice Pres. & Treas.; Bro. Nelson Deloria, Vice Pres. Management Corporation. Order of the Servants of the Sick (Order of St. Camillus). Total Assisted 700.

St. Camillus Ministries, Inc., 10101 W. Wisconsin Ave., 53226. Tel: 414-258-1814. Rev. Louis Lussier, O.S.Cam., Pres. St. Camillus Ministries, Inc. operates under the auspices of the Order of St. Camillus and sponsors Durward's Glen Retreat and Conference Center and all social concerns ministry of the Order. Total Served 300; Total Staff 6.

WEST ALLIS. *Region 6 Development Association*, 6753 W. Rogers, 53219. Tel: 414-545-2120; Fax: 414-483-7387.
E-mail: Fayview@aol.com
Mailing Address: 5402 W. Parkview Dr., Meguon, 53092. Sr. Mary Coffelt, F.D.C., Vice Pres.
Purpose: To build a community of educators with new resiliency in Catholic education, emphasizing the critical importance of on-going professional development.

WEST BEND. *Visitation Rural Ministries, Inc.*, 7660 Townline Rd., 53090. Tel: 414-629-4154; Fax: 414-629-5034.
E-mail: mmbub@juno.com
Mary Bub, Co-Dir., CEO & Pres.; Sr. Bernita Marie Bittner, S.S.N.D., Co-Dir.

WHITEFISH BAY. *Association of Ladies of Charity of Milwaukee, Wisconsin*, 4825 N. Wildwood Ave., 53217. Tel: 414-962-2462.
E-mail: djscw550@aol.com
Rev. Matthew Gottschalk, Archdiocesan Spiritual Advisor.

[Z] CLOSED PARISHES

MILWAUKEE. *Blessed Virgin of Pompeii.* For sacramental records, contact Three Holy Women Parish, 1716 N. Humboldt Ave. Milwaukee, 53202-1623. Tel.: 414-271-2165; Fax: 414-271-7988.

Holy Angels. For sacramental records, contact Archives, Archdiocese of Milwaukee, P.O. Box 070912, Milwaukee, 53207-0912. Tel.: 414-769-3407; Fax: 414-769-3408.

Holy Cross. For sacramental records, contact St. Vincent Pallotti Parish, 7622 W. Stevenson St., Milwaukee. Tel.: 414-453-5344; Fax: 414-453-4225.

Holy Redeemer. For sacramental records, contact Archives, Archdiocese of Milwaukee, P.O. Box 070912, Milwaukee, 53207-0912. Tel.: 414-769-3407; Fax: 414-769-3408.

Holy Rosary. For sacramental records, contact Three Holy Women Parish, 1716 N.Humboldt Ave., Milwaukee. Tel.: 414-271-2165; Fax: 414-271-7988.

Holy Spirit. For sacramental records, contact St. Rafael the Archangel, 2509 S. 33rd St. Milwaukee, 53215. Tel: 414-645-9172.

Holy Trinity-Our Lady of Guadalupe. For sacramental records, contact Our Lady of Guadalupe Parish, 613 S. 4th St., Milwaukee, 53204. Tel.: 414-271-6181; Fax: 414-278-6090.

St. Agnes. For sacramental records, contact Archives, Archdiocese of Milwaukee, P.O. Box 070912, Milwaukee, 53207-0912. Tel.: 414-769-3407; Fax: 414-769-3408.

St. Albert. For sacramental records, contact Archives, Archdiocese of Milwaukee, P.O. Box 070912, Milwaukee, 53207-0912. Tel.: 414-769-3407; Fax: 414-769-3408.

St. Anne. For sacramental records, contact Archives, Archdiocese of Milwaukee, P.O. Box 070912, Milwaukee, 53207-0912. Tel.: 414-769-3407; Fax: 414-769-3408.

St. Anthony of Padua. For sacramental records, contact St. Vincent Pallotti Parish, 7622 W. Stevenson St., Milwaukee, 53223. Tel.: 414-453-5344; Fax: 414-453-4225.

St. Barbara. For sacramental records, contact St. Rafael the Archangel Parish, 2059 S. 33rd St., Milwaukee, 53215. Tel.: 414-645-9172.

St. Boniface. For sacramental records, contact Archives, Archdiocese of Milwaukee, P.O. Box 070912, Milwaukee, 53207-0912. Tel.: 414-769-3407; Fax: 414-769-3408.

St. Elizabeth. For sacramental records, contact Archives, Archdiocese of Milwaukee, P.O. Box 070912, Milwaukee, 53207-0912. Tel.: 414-769-3407; Fax: 414-769-3408.

St. Emeric. For sacramental records, contact Sacred Heart Parish, 917 N. 49th St., Milwaukee, 53208. Tel.:414-774-9418; Fax: 414-774-7406.

St. Gabriel. For sacramental records, contact Archives, Archdiocese of Milwaukee, P.O. Box 070912, Milwaukee, 53207-0912. Tel.: 414-769-3407; Fax: 414-769-3408.

St. Gall. For sacramental records, contact Archives, Archdiocese of Milwaukee, P.O. Box 070912, Milwaukee 53207-0912. Tel.: 414-769-3407; Fax: 414-769-3408.

St. Gerard. For sacramental records, contact Archives, Archdiocese of Milwaukee, P.O. Box 070912, Milwaukee, 53207-0912. Tel.: 414-769-3407; Fax: 414-769-3408.

St. Hedwig. For sacramental records contact Three Holy Women Parish, 1716 N. Humboldt Ave., Milwaukee, 53202-1623. Tel.: 414-271-2165; Fax: 414-271-7988.

St. Ignatius. For sacramental records, contact Archives, Archdiocese of Milwaukee, P.O.Box 070912, Milwaukee, 53207-0912. Tel.: 414-769-3407; Fax: 414-769-3408.

St. John de Nepomuc. For sacramental records, contact Archives, Archdiocese of Milwaukee, P.O. Box 070912, Milwaukee, 53207-0912. Tel.: 414-769-3407; Fax: 414-769-3408.

St. Joseph. For sacramental records, contact St. Joseph Parish, 12130 Center St., Wauwatosa, 53222-4096. Tel.: 414-771-4626; Fax: 414-771-4311.

St. Lawrence. For sacramental records, contact Archives, Archdiocese of Milwaukee, P.O. Box 070912, Milwaukee, 53207-0912. Tel.: 414-769-3407; Fax: 414-769-3408.

St. Leo. For sacramental records, contact Archives, Archdiocese of Milwaukee, P.O. Box 070912, Milwaukee, 53207-0912. Tel.: 414-769-3407; Fax: 414-769-3408.

St. Matthew. For sacramental records, contact Archives, Archdiocese of Milwaukee, P.O. Box 070912, Milwaukee, 53207-0912. Tel.: 414-769-3407; Fax: 414-769-3408.

St. Michael. For sacramental records, contact Good Shepherd Parish, W762 Armstrong Rd., Campbellsport, 53010-1400. Tel.: 920-477-3201 Fax: 920-477-3030.

St. Nicholas. For sacramental records, contact Archives, Archdiocese of Milwaukee, P.O. Box 070912, Milwaukee, 53207-0912. Tel.: 414-769-3407; Fax: 414-769-3408.

St. Rita. For sacramental records, contact Three Holy Women Parish, 1716 N. Humboldt Ave., Milwaukee, 53202-1623. Tel.: 414-271-2165; Fax: 414-271-7988.

St. Thomas Aquinas. For sacramental records, contact Archives, Archdiocese of Milwaukee, P.O.Box 070912, Milwaukee, 53207-0912. Tel.: 414-769-3407; Fax: 414-769-3408.

St. Wenceslaus. For sacramental records, contact Our Lady of Guadalupe Parish, 613 S. 4th St., Milwaukee, 53204. Tel.: 414-271-6181; Fax: 414-278-6090.

ADELL. *St. Patrick.* For sacramental records, contact Our Lady of the Lakes Parish, 230 Butler St., Random Lake, 53075-1710. Tel.: 920-994-4380; 920-994-2605.

ALLENTON. *Sacred Heart.* For sacramental records, contact Resurrection Parish, P.O. Box 96, Allenton 53002-0096. Tel.: 262-629-5240.

ARMSTRONG. *Our Lady of Angels.* For sacramental records, contact Good Shepherd Parish, W762 Armstrong Rd., Campbellsport, 53010-1400. Tel.:920-477-3201; Fax:920-477-3030.

AUBURN. *St. Matthias.* For sacramental records, contact Holy Trinity Parish, 331 Main St., P.O. Box 461, Kewaskum, 53040. Tel.: 262-626-2860; Fax: 262-626-2301.

BYRON. *St. John.* For sacramental records, contact Sons of Zebedee: Saints James and John Parish W5882 Church Rd., Fond du Lac, 54937-8602. Tel.: 920-922-1167.

CASCADE. *St. Mary.* For sacramental records, contact Our Lady of the Lakes Parish, 230 Butler St., Random Lake, 53075-1710. Tel.: 920-994-4380; Fax: 920-994-2605.

CUDAHY. *Holy Family.* For sacramental records, contact Nativity of the Lord Parish, 4611 S. Kirkwood Ave., Cudahy, 53110. Tel.: 414-744-6622.

St. Frederick. For sacramental records, contact Nativity of the Lord Parish, 4611 S. Kirkwood Ave., Cudahy, 53110. Tel.:414-744-6622.

St. Joseph. For sacramental records, contact Nativity of the Lord Parish, 4611 S. Kirkwood Ave., Cudahy, 53110. Tel.: 414-744-6622.

DACADA. *St. Nicholas.* For sacramental records, contact Our Lady of the Lakes Parish, 230 Butler St., Random Lake, 53075-1710. Tel.: 920-994-4380; Fax: 920-994-2605.

DOTYVILLE. *St. Michael.* For sacramental records, contact Good Shepherd Parish, W762 Armstrong Rd., Campbellsport, 53010-1400. Tel.: 920-477-3201; Fax: 920-477-3030.

EDEN. *St. Mary.* For sacramental records, contact Good Shepherd Parish, W762 Armstrong Rd., Campbellsport, 53010-1400. Tel.: 920-477-3201; Fax: 920-477-3030.

ELDORADO. *St. Mary.* For sacramental records, contact Our Risen Savior Parish, W8272 Forest Ave. Rd., Eldorado, 54932-9801. Tel.: 920-922-2412.

FARMINGTON. *St. John of God.* For sacramental records, contact St. Michael Parish, 8877 Forestview Rd., Kewaskum, 53040. Tel.: 262-334-5270; Fax: 262-334-5233.

FOND DU LAC. *Sacred Heart.* For sacramental records prior to December, 1970 contact Archdiocese of Milwaukee Archives, 414-769-3407; for records after November, 1970 contact Holy Family Parish, 26 W. Follett St., Fond du Lac, 54935. Tel: 920-921-0580.

St. Joseph. For sacramental records prior to June 12, 1967 contact Archdiocese of Milwaukee Archives, 414-769-3407; for records after June 12, 1967 contact Holy Family Parish, 26 W. Follett St., Fond du Lac, 54935. Tel 920-921-0580.

St. Louis. For sacramental records prior to Sept. 20, 1959, contact Archdiocese of Milwaukee Archives Tel.: 414-769-3407; for records after Sept. 20, 1959 contact Holy Family Parish, 26 W. Follett St., Fond du Lac, 54935. Tel: 920-921-0580.

St. Mary. For sacramental records through 1975 contact Archdiocese of Milwaukee Archives, Tel: 414-769-3407; for records after 1975 contact Holy Family Parish, 26 W. Follett St., Fond du Lac, 54935. Tel: 920-921-0580.

St. Patrick. For sacramental records prior to September 19, 1960 contact Archdiocese of Milwaukee Archives, 414-769-3407; for records after September 19, 1960 contact Holy Family Parish, 26 W. Follett St., Fond du Lac, 54935, 920-921-0580.

FOX LAKE. *St. Mary.* For sacramental records, contact Annunciation Parish, 305 Green St., P.O. Box 85, Fox Lake, 53933-0085. Tel.: 920-928-3513; Fax: 920-928-6334.

FRANKLIN. *Sacred Hearts of Jesus and Mary.* For sacramental records, contact St. Martin of Tours, 7963 S. 116th St., Franklin. Tel.: 414-425-1114; Fax: 414-425-2527.

KENOSHA. *St. Casmir.* For sacramental records contact the Archdiocese of Milwaukee Archives, 414-769-3407.

St. George. For sacramental records contact the Archdiocese of Milwaukee Archives, 414-769-3407.

St. Thomas Aquinas. For sacramental records contact St. Mary Parish, 7307 40th Ave., Kenosha, 53142-4325. Tel.: 262-694-6018 Fax: 262-694-6048.

LOST LAKE. *St. Mary.* For sacramental records, contact Annunciation Parish, 305 Green St., P.O. Box 85, Fox Lake, 53933-0085. Tel.: 920-928-3513; Fax: 920-928-6334.

LYONS. *St. Kilian.* For sacramental records, contact St. Joseph Parish, 1540 Mill St., P.O. Box 60, Lyons, 53148-0060. Tel.: 262-763-2050; Fax: 262-763-9377.

MITCHELL. *St. Michael.* For sacramental records, contact Our Lady of Angels Parish, W762 Armstrong Rd., Campbellsport, 53010-1400. Tel.: 920-477-3201; Fax: 920-477-3030.

NABOB. *St. Matthias.* For sacramental records, contact St. Lawrence Parish, 4886 Hwy. 175, Hartford, 53027. Tel: 262-644-5701.

NENNO. *St. Anthony.* For sacramental records, contact Resurrection Parish, P.O. Box 96, Allenton, 53002-0096. Tel.: 262-629-5240.

SS. Peter and Paul. For sacramental records, contact Resurrection Parish, P.O. Box 96, Allenton, 53002-0096. Tel.: 262-629-5240.

OAKFIELD. *St. James.* For sacramental records, contact Sons of Zebedee: Saints James and John Parish, W5882 Church Rd., Fond du Lac, 54937-8602. Tel.: 920-922-1167.

PEWAUKEE. *St. Mary.* For sacramental records, contact Queen of Apostles Parish, W280 N2101 Hwy. SS, Pewaukee, 53072. Tel.: 262-691-1535; Fax: 262-691-7376.

SS. Peter and Paul. For sacramental records, contact Queen of Apostles Parish, W280 N2101 Hwy. SS, Pewaukee. Tel.: 262-691-1535; Fax: 262-691-7376.

RACINE. *Holy Name.* For sacramental records, contact Archives, Archdiocese of Milwaukee, P.O. Box 070912, Milwaukee, 53207-0912. Tel.: 262-769-3407; Fax: 262-769-3408.

Holy Trinity. For sacramental records, contact Archives, Archdiocese of Milwaukee, P.O.Box 070912, Milwaukee, 53207-0912. Tel.: 262-769-3407; Fax: 262-769-3408.

St. Casimir. For sacramental records, contact Archives, Archdiocese of Milwaukee, P.O.Box 070912, Milwaukee, 53207-0912. Tel.: 262-769-3407; Fax: 262-769-3408.

St. Rose. For sacramental records, contact Archives, Archdiocese of Milwaukee, P.O.Box 070912, Milwaukee, 53207-0912. Tel.: 262-769-3407; Fax: 262-769-3408.

St. Stanislaus. For sacramental records, contact Archives, Archdiocese of Milwaukee, P.O. Box 070912, Milwaukee, 53207-0912. Tel.: 262-769-3407; Fax: 262-769-3408.

RANDOLPH. *St. Gabriel.* For sacramental records, contact Annunciation Parish, 305 Green St., P.O. Box 85, Fox Lake, 53933-0085. Tel.: 920-928-3513; Fax: 920-928-6334.

St. Mary. For sacramental records, contact Annunciation, 305 Green St., P.O. Box 85, Fox Lake 53933-0085. Tel.: 920-928-3513; Fax: 920-928-6334.

RANDOM LAKE. *St. Mary.* For sacramental records, contact Our Lady of the Lakes Parish, 230 Butler St., Random Lake, 53075-1710. Tel.: 920-994-4380; Fax: 920-994-2605.

ST. MARTIN. *Holy Assumption.* For sacramental records through 1990, contact St. Mary Parish, 9520 W. Forest Home Ave., Hales Corners, 53130. Tel.: 414-425-2174; Fax: 414-425-9432. For records after 1990, contact St. Martin of Tours Parish, 7963 S. 116th St., Fanklin, 53132. Tel.: 414-425-1114; Fax: 414-425-1114.

ST. PETER. *St. Peter.* For sacramental records prior to 1953, contact Archdiocese of Milwaukee Archives, 414-769-3407; for records after 1952 contact Holy Family Parish, 26 W. Follett St., Fond du Lac, 54935, 920-921-0580.

THOMPSON (ERIN). *St. Patrick.* For sacramental records contact, St. Kilian Parish, 264 W. State St., Hartford, 53027. Tel.: 262-673-4831.

WAYNE. *St. Bridget.* For sacramental records, contact Holy Trinity Parish, 331 Main St., P.O. Box 461, Kewaskum, 53040. Tel.: 262-626-2860; Fax: 262-626-2301.

WEST ALLIS. *Our Lady of Mount Carmel.* For sacramental records, contact Archives, Archdiocese of Milwaukee, P.O.Box 070912, Milwaukee, 53207-0912. Tel.: 414-769-3407; Fax: 414-769-3408.

St. Joseph. For sacramental records, contact Archives, Archdiocese of Milwaukee, P.O. Box 070912, Milwaukee, 53207-0912. Tel.: 414-769-3407; Fax: 414-769-3408.

WOODHULL. *St. John the Baptist.* For sacramental records, contact Our Risen Saviour Parish, W8272 Forest Ave. Rd., Eldorado, 54932-9801. Tel.: 920-922-2412.

RELIGIOUS INSTITUTES OF MEN REPRESENTED IN THE ARCHDIOCESE

For further details refer to the corresponding bracketed number in the Religious Institutes of Men or Women section.

[0120]—*Alexian Brothers.* (Immaculate Conception Prov.).—C.F.A.

[0140]—*The Augustinians.* (Mother of Good Counsel Prov.).—O.S.A.

[0200]—*Benedictine Monks.*—O.S.B.

[0600]—*Brothers of the Congregation of Holy Cross.* (Midwest Prov.).—C.S.C.

[0470]—*The Capuchin Friars.* (Prov. of St. Joseph).—O.F.M.Cap.

[0740]—*Congregation of Marians of the Immaculate Conception.*—M.I.C.

[1130]—*Congregation of the Priests of the Sacred Heart.*—S.C.J.

[0480]—*Conventual Franciscans.* (St. Bonaventure, Prov. of Our Lady of Consolation).—O.F.M.Conv.

[0260]—*Discalced Carmelite Friars.* (Prov. of the Immaculate Heart of Mary).—O.C.D.

[0520]—*Franciscan Friars.*—O.F.M.

[0690]—*Jesuit Fathers and Brothers.*—S.J.

[0720]—*The Missionaries of Our Lady of La Salette.* (Prov. of Mary, Queen of Peace).—M.S.

[0430]—*Order of Preachers.* (Province of St. Albert the Great).—O.P.

[0240]—*Order of St. Camillus-Camillian Fathers and Brothers.*—O.S.Cam.

[1070]—*Redemptorist Fathers.* (St. Louis Prov.).—C.SS.R.

[0990]—*Society of the Catholic Apostolate.* (Mater Dei Prov.).—S.A.C.

[1200]—*Society of the Divine Savior.* (American Prov.).—S.D.S.

[0420]—*Society of the Divine Word.* (Northern Prov.).—S.V.D.

[1360]—*Xaverian Missionary Fathers.*—S.X.

RELIGIOUS INSTITUTES OF WOMEN REPRESENTED IN THE ARCHDIOCESE

[0230]—*Benedictine Sisters of Pontifical Jurisdiction.* (Erie, PA).—O.S.B.

[0360]—*Carmelite Sisters of the Divine Heart of Jesus.*—Carmel.D.C.J.

[]—*The Christian Sisters (Pious Union).*—C.S.

[]—*Congregation of Institutio Santa Mariana de Jesus.*

[3710]—*Congregation of the Sisters of Saint Agnes.*—C.S.A.

[1780]—*Congregation of the Sisters of the Third Order of St. Francis of Perpetual Adoration.* (Eastern Region).—F.S.P.A.

[0760]—*Daughters of Charity of St. Vincent De Paul.*—D.C.

[0790]—*Daughters of Divine Charity.*—F.D.C.

[0420]—*Discalced Carmelite Nuns.*—O.C.D.

[1060]—*Dominican Contemplative Sisters.*—O.P.

[1070-03]—*Dominican Sisters.*—O.P.

[1070-09]—*Dominican Sisters.*—O.P.

[1070-25]—*Dominican Sisters.*—O.P.

[1070-27]—*Dominican Sisters.*—O.P.

[]—*Dominican Sisters.* (Vietnam).

[1170]—*Felician Sisters.*—C.S.S.F.

[1230]—*Franciscan Sisters of Christian Charity.*—O.S.F.

[1310]—*Franciscan Sisters of Little Falls, MN.*—O.S.F.

[1415]—*Franciscan Sisters of Mary.*—F.S.M.

[]—*Franciscan Sisters of Our Lady (Pious Union).*—F.S.O.L.

[1430]—*Franciscan Sisters of Our Lady of Perpetual Help.*—O.S.F.

[]—*Franciscan Sisters of St. Clare (Pious Union).*—F.S.S.C.

[1470]—*Franciscan Sisters of St. Joseph.*—F.S.S.J.

[1240]—*Franciscan Sisters, Daughters of the Sacred Hearts of Jesus and Mary.*—O.S.F.

[]—*Hermitage of the Trinity.*

[1820]—*Hospital Sisters of the Third Order of St. Francis.*—O.S.F.

[]—*Missionary Sisters of the Holy Family.*—M.S.F.

[3230]—*Poor Handmaids of Jesus Christ.*—P.H.J.C.

[2970]—*School Sisters of Notre Dame.*—S.S.N.D.

[1680]—*School Sisters of St. Francis.*—O.S.F.

[]—*Secular Institute of Schoenstatt Sisters of Mary.*—I.S.S.M.

[0600]—*Sisters of Charity of St. Joan Antida.*—S.C.S.J.A.

[0430]—*Sisters of Charity of the Blessed Virgin Mary.*—B.V.M.

[2575]—*Sisters of Mercy of the Americas.*—R.S.M.

[3800]—*Sisters of St. Elizabeth.*—S.S.E.

[1705]—*The Sisters of St. Francis of Assisi.*—O.S.F.

[1520]—*Sisters of St. Francis of Christ the King.*—O.S.F.

[3930]—*Sisters of St. Joseph of the Third Order of St. Francis.*—S.S.J.-T.O.S.F.

[4020]—*Sisters of St. Rita.*—O.S.A.

[1030]—*Sisters of the Divine Savior.*—S.D.S.

[4100]—*Sisters of the Sorrowful Mother (Third Order of St. Francis).*—S.S.M.

[3510]—*Sisters Servants of Christ the King.*—S.S.C.K.

ARCHDIOCESAN CEMETERIES

MILWAUKEE. *Calvary.*

Holy Cross.

Holy Trinity.

Mount Olivet.

St. Adalbert.

FRANKLIN. *All Souls.*

KENOSHA. *All Saints.*

MEQUON. *Resurrection.*

SOUTH MILWAUKEE. *Holy Sepulcher*, 675 College Ave., 53172-1252. Tel: 414-762-6800. Gregg F. Apostoloff, Archdiocesan Dir.

TAYCHEEDAH. *St. Charles Cemetery.* (See St. Patrick Parish, Fond du Lac). Tel: 920-921-0347.

WAUKESHA. *St. Joseph.*

NECROLOGY

† Emmenegger, Rev. Msgr. Joseph, (Retired). —Died Jan. 15, 2000.

† Schmidt, Frederick N., (Retired). —Died Feb. 3, 2000.

† Silvestri, Vincent A., (Retired). —Died July 17, 2000.

† Simon, Martin M., (Retired). —Died Sept.15, 2000.

† Vogel, Edward A., (Retired). —Died March 23, 2000.

Archdiocese of Mobile

(Archidioecesis Mobiliensis)

Most Reverend

OSCAR H. LIPSCOMB, D.D., PH.D.

Archbishop of Mobile; ordained July 15, 1956; appointed July 29, 1980; consecrated November 16, 1980. *Res., 400 Government St., P.O. Box 1966, Mobile, AL, 36633.* Tel.: 334-434-1585.

Chancery Office: 400 Government St., P.O. Box 1966, Mobile, AL, 36633. Tel.: 334-434-1585; Fax: 334-434-1588.

E-mail address: archdioceseofmobile@netscape.net

ESTABLISHED AS VICARIATE-APOSTOLIC OF ALABAMA AND THE FLORIDAS, 1825; DIOCESE OF MOBILE, MAY 15, 1829; NAME CHANGED TO DIOCESE OF MOBILE-BIRMINGHAM, JULY 9, 1954; REDESIGNATED, JUNE 28, 1969. RAISED TO RANK OF ARCHDIOCESE NOVEMBER 16, 1980.

Square Miles 22,969.

Comprises the lower 28 Counties of the State of Alabama, namely: Choctaw, Clarke, Wilcox, Dallas, Autauga, Elmore, Lee, Russell, Macon, Montgomery, Lowndes, Barbour, Bullock, Pike, Crenshaw, Butler, Monroe, Conecuh, Escambia, Covington, Coffee, Geneva, Dale, Henry, Houston, Washington, Baldwin and Mobile.

For legal titles of parishes and archdiocesan institutions consult the Chancery Office.

STATISTICAL OVERVIEW

Personnel	
Archbishop	1
Priests: Diocesan Active in Diocese	76
Priests: Active Outside Diocese	8
Priests: Diocesan in Foreign Missions	1
Priests: Retired, Sick or Absent	27
Number of Diocesan Priests	112
Religious Priests in Diocese	41
Extern Priests in Diocese	8
Ordinations:	
Diocesan Priests	6
Religious Priests	1
Transitional Deacons	2
Permanent Deacons in Diocese	37
Total Brothers	12
Total Sisters	181
Parishes	
Parishes	76
With Resident Pastor:	
Resident Diocesan Priests	57
Resident Religious Priests	19
Missions	14
Pastoral Centers	3
Professional Ministry Personnel:	
Sisters	13
Lay Ministers	18
Welfare	
Catholic Hospitals	1
Total Assisted	215,039
Health Care Centers	2
Total Assisted	4,762
Homes for the Aged	2
Total Assisted	300
Residential Care of Children	1
Total Assisted	200
Day Care and Extended Day Care Centers	4
Total Assisted	245
Specialized Homes	1
Total Assisted	65
Special Centers for Social Services	9
Total Assisted	62,432
Residential Care of Disabled	3
Total Assisted	470
Other Institutions	3
Total Assisted	456
Educational	
Diocesan Students in Other Seminaries	10
Total Seminarians	10
Colleges and Universities	1
Total Students	1,005
High Schools, Diocesan and Parish	3
Total Students	1,525
Elementary Schools, Diocesan and Parish	22
Total Students	5,973
Catechesis/Religious Education:	
High School Students	791
Elementary Students	3,585
Total Students Under Catholic Instruction	12,889
Teachers in the Diocese:	
Priests	1
Sisters	13
Lay Teachers	411
Vital Statistics	
Receptions into the Church:	
Infant Baptism Totals	1,136
Adult Baptism Totals	239
Received into Full Communion	409
First Communions	1,230
Confirmations	1,137
Marriages:	
Catholic	176
Interfaith	233
Total Marriages	409
Deaths	628
Total Catholic Population	66,325
Total Population	1,600,020

Former Prelates—Rt. Rev. MICHAEL PORTIER, D.D., First Bishop; cons. Nov. 5, 1826; died May 14, 1859.—Rt. Rev. JOHN QUINLAN, D.D., cons. Dec. 4, 1859; died March 9, 1883.—Rt. Rev. DOMINIC MANUCY, D.D., appt. Vicar Apostolic of Brownsville and cons. Bishop of Dulma Dec. 8, 1874; transferred to Mobile March 9, 1884, but resigned in the same year; died at Mobile, Dec. 4, 1885.—Rt. Rev. JEREMIAH O'SULLIVAN, D.D., cons. Sept. 20, 1885; died Aug. 10, 1896.—Rt. Rev. E. P. ALLEN, cons. May 16, 1897; died Oct. 21, 1926.—Most Rev. THOMAS J. TOOLEN, D.D., cons. May 4, 1927; appt. Archbishop "ad personam," May 27, 1954; resigned Oct. 8, 1969; died Dec. 4, 1976.—Most Rev. JOHN L. MAY, D.D., ord. May 3, 1947; appt. Titular Bishop of Tagarbala and Auxiliary Bishop of Chicago, June 21, 1967; cons. Aug. 24, 1967; transferred to Mobile, Oct. 8, 1969; installed Dec. 10, 1969; appt. to Saint Louis, Jan. 29, 1980; died March 24, 1994.

Vicar General—Very Rev. JOHN AHERNE, V.G., *Holy Name of Jesus Church, P.O. Box 557, Semmes, 36575.* Tel: 334-694-4794.

Regional Episcopal Vicars—Very Rev. F. CHARLES TRONCALE, *Holy Spirit Church, 8570 Vaughn Rd., Montgomery, 36117.* Tel: 334-277-5631. Rev. Msgr. TIMOTHY DEASY, *Christ the King Church, P.O. Box 549, Daphne, 36526.* Tel: 334-626-2343. Very Rev. PATRICK GALLAGHER, *St. Columba Church, 2700 W. Main St., Dothan, 36301.*

Archivist—BERNADETTE MATHEWS.

Chancery Office—400 Government St., P.O. Box 1966, Mobile, 36633. Tel: 334-434-1585; Fax: 334-434-1588.

Chancellor—Very Rev. MICHAEL L. FARMER, S.T.L.

Metropolitan Tribunal—14 S. Franklin St., P.O. Box 2405, Mobile, 36652. Tel: 334-432-4609. Please address all rogatory commissions and matrimonial matters to the Office of the Tribunal.

Judicial Vicar—Rev. Msgr. JOHN R. AMOS, J.C.D., S.T.L., M.Div.

Associate Judges—Rev. Msgr. ANTHONY MCDEVITT, J.C.D., S.T.L.; Rev. Msgr. KENNETH J. KLEPAC, J.C.L.; Ms. DAWN S. DAS NEVES, J.C.L.

Defender of the Bond—Sr. MARY ELIZABETH BUTLER, M.S.B.T., J.C.L.; Deacon HENRY F. O'BRIEN; Mrs. KATHARINE S. WEBER.

Promoter of Justice—Rev. ARTHUR C. SCHRENGER.

Advocate—VICTOR WHELAN.

Court Clerk—DANICE ENTREKIN.

Notary—DOROTHY BARRETT.

Archdiocesan Consultors—Very Rev. JOHN AHERNE, V.G.; Rev. Msgr. JOHN R. AMOS; Revs. PETER J. CUNNINGHAM; FRANCIS V. CUSACK; PATRICK MAHER; Rev. Msgr. PATRICK C. O'CONNOR; Revs. WILLIAM J. SKONEKI; G. WARREN WALL.

Vicars for Religious—Mobile District-Baldwin Escambia Deanery: Rev. ROBERT B. RIMES, S.J., *Spring Hill College, 4000 Dauphin St., Mobile, 36608.* Tel: 334-460-2175. Montgomery-Dothan Deaneries: Rev. Msgr. WILLIAM R. JAMES, *P.O. Drawer 1367, Robertsdale, 36567.* Tel: 334-947-5054.

Acting Vicar for Education—THOMAS L. DOYLE, Ph.D., *P.O. Box 129, Mobile, 36601.* Tel: 334-438-4611.

Vicar for Ministry to Persons with Disabilities and the Deaf—Rev. PATRICK J. MADDEN, *4350 Moffett Rd., Mobile, 36618.* Tel: 334-342-6449.

Vicar for Vietnamese Affairs—c/o Chancery, P.O. Box 1966, Mobile, 36633.

Archdiocesan Offices and Directors

Apostleship of Prayer—Rev. Msgr. J. EDWIN STUARDI, *Mercy Medical, P.O. Box 1090, Daphne, 36526.* Tel: 334-626-2694.

Apostleship of the Sea—Rev. PRIMITIVO MARAVILLA, Port Chap. JOSEPH V. CONNICK, III, Dir., *Catholic Maritime Club, 261 Dauphin St., Mobile, 36602.* Tel: 334-432-7339; Fax: 334-433-4618.

Apostolate for Aging—Rev. Msgr. GEORGE C. ROYER, *Res., Sacred Heart Residence, P.O. Box 6805, Mobile, 36660.*

Archdiocese of Mobile Cursillo Center—Rev. DAVID J. TOKARZ, Spiritual Dir., *St. Bede Catholic Church, 3870 Atlanta Hwy., Montgomery, 36109.* Tel: 334-272-3463; Fax: 334-272-3492. Mr. FRANK YANDRASITS, *8827 Pine Run, Daphne, 36527.* Tel: 334-626-0879; Fax: 334-666-3062.

Archdiocesan Council of Catholic Women (ACCW)—Mrs. BARBARA SMYTH, Pres.; Mrs. MARIE D. MARTIN, Pres., *Priests' Burse Club, 400 Government St., Mobile, 36602.*

Boy Scouts—Rev. STEVEN WILLIAMS, *Mailing Address: St. Mary Church, 106 Providence St., Mobile, 36604., St. Mary Church, 1453 Old Shell Rd., Mobile, 36604.* Tel: 334-432-8678.

Campaign for Human Development—Rev. WILLIAM J. SKONEKI, Dir. Funding Office for charitable and other works of Archdiocese, *356 Government St., P.O. Box 230, Mobile, 36601.* Tel: 334-438-9668; Fax: 334-434-1547.

Catholic Charities Appeal Office—Rev. PAUL G. ZOGHBY, Dir. Funding Office for charitable and other works of Archdiocese, *356 Government St., P.O. Box 230, Mobile, 36601.* Tel: 334-438-9668; Fax: 334-434-1547.

Catholic Housing of Mobile, Inc.—Most Rev. OSCAR H. LIPSCOMB, Pres.; Very Rev. MICHAEL L. FARMER, Vice Pres.; Rev. Msgr. JOHN R. AMOS, Sec. & Treas. Non-profit Corp. of the State of Alabama, *Office: P.O. Box 1966, Mobile, 36633.* Tel: 334-434-1585.

Queen's Court I Apartments—W. Clark Ave., Prichard, 36610.

Catholic Housing Authority of Montgomery, Inc.—Very Rev. F. CHARLES TRONCALE, Pres. BILL PEARSON, Vice Pres.

Catholic Publishing Co., Inc.—Publisher of the Archdiocesan Newspaper *"The Catholic Week"*; LARRY WAHL, Editor, *P.O. Box 349, Mobile, 36601.* Tel: 334-432-3529.

Catholic University, Friends of—Rev. RUSSELL BIVEN, *Our Savior Church, 1801 Cody Rd. S., Mobile, 36695.* Tel: 334-633-6762.

Catholic Youth Organization—PAUL CRANE, Exec. Dir., *P.O. Box 6955, Mobile, 36660.* Tel: 334-471-0062.

Catholic Youth Ministry—WARREN DUNGEN, Acting Dir., *Seton Center, 1413 Old Shell Rd., Mobile, 36604.* Tel: 334-433-4138.

Cemeteries—Very Rev. MICHAEL L. FARMER, *P.O. Box 1966, Mobile, 36633.* Tel: 334-434-1585. Deacon EDWARD G. CONNICK, Mgr., *1700 Dr. Martin Luther King Jr. Ave., Mobile, 36617.* Tel: 334-479-5305., *P.O. Box 230, Mobile, 36601.*

Censor Librorum—Rev. J. ALEX SHERLOCK, S.T.M., M.A., *St. Peter Church, P.O. Box 114, Montgomery, 36101.* Tel: 334-262-7304; Fax: 334-262-9735.

Charismatic Movement—Deacon JAMES LABADIE, *Our Lady Queen of Mercy, 4421 Narrow Lane Rd., Montgomery, 36116.* Tel: 334-288-2850; Fax: 334-281-7884.

Charities—(Listing under Catholic Social Services).

Clergy Retirement Association—Very Rev. JOHN AHERNE, Chm., *Holy Name of Jesus Church, P.O. Box 557, Semmes, 36575.* Tel: 334-649-4794.

Archdiocesan Coordinator of Health Affairs—Mr. CLARK P. CHRISTIANSON, Pres. & CEO, *Providence Hospital, 6801 Airport Blvd., P.O. Box 850429, Mobile, 36685.* Tel: 334-633-1000.

Ecumenical Commission—Very Rev. MICHAEL L. FARMER, Chm., *St. Pius X Church, 217 S. Sage Ave., Mobile, 36606.* Tel: 334-471-2449; Fax: 334-471-2441.

Family Life Director—Mr. TOM MCDONALD; Mrs. CAROLINE MCDONALD, *Catholic Social Services, P.O. Box 7591, Mobile, 36601.* Tel: 334-434-1550.

Handicapped, Apostolate to the—Rev. PATRICK MADDEN, Dir., *4350 Moffett Rd., Mobile, 36618.* Tel: 334-342-6449.

Hispanic Apostolate—Rev. CHRISTOPHER VISCARDI, S.J., Dir., *Spring Hill College, 4000 Dauphin St., Mobile, 36608.* Tel: 334-380-3085.

Hispanic Pastoral Ministry—Rev. CHRISTOPHER VISCARDI, S.J., *712 Dauphin Island Pkwy., Mobile, 36606.* Tel: 334-478-3737.

Holy Childhood Association—Rev. LEO BLANCHET, Dir., *St. Bridget Church, P.O. Box 13357, Whistler, 36612.* Tel: 334-452-3676.

Holy Name Society—Vacant.

Liturgical Commission—Very Rev. MICHAEL L. FARMER, Chm., *P.O. Box 1966, Mobile, 36633.*

McGill Institute, A Corporation—P.O. Box 1966, Mobile, 36633.

McGill-Toolen Foundation, The—Mrs. MONDE DONALDSON, Dir., Devel., *1501 Old Shell Rd., Mobile, 36604.* Tel: 334-432-0788, Ext. 48.

Office of Ministry to the Deaf—4350 Moffett Rd., Mobile, 36618. Tel: 334-342-6449.

Mobile Provincial Conference of Bishops and Priests' Councils—P.O. Box 1966, Mobile, 36633. Tel: 334-434-1585.

Newspaper "The Catholic Week"—LARRY WAHL, Editor, *356 Government St., P.O. Box 349, Mobile, 36601.* Tel: 334-432-3529; 432-3520.

Pastoral Council—GEORGE VELLA, Chm., *6657 Hounds Run N., Mobile, 36608.* Tel: 334-344-9839.

Permanent Diaconate Program—Co-Dirs.: Very Revs. JOHN AHERNE; MICHAEL L. FARMER; Rev. PAUL G. ZOGHBY, *Holy Name of Jesus Church, P.O. Box 557, Semmes, 36575.* Tel: 334-649-4794.

Planned Giving—Deacon WILLIAM R. DOLAN, Dir., *P.O. Box 230, Mobile, 36601.* Tel: 334-432-1369.

Priests' Council—Most Rev. OSCAR H. LIPSCOMB, Pres. Officers: Rev. G. WARREN WALL, Chm.; Very Rev. F. CHARLES TRONCALE, Vice Chm.; Revs. WILLIAM J. SKONEKI, Treas. JOHNNY S. SAVOIE, Record. Sec. ERNEST HYNDMAN, Corresponding Sec.

Ex Officio Members—Rev. Msgr. TIMOTHY DEASY, Baldwin Dean; Very Rev. F. CHARLES TRONCALE, Montgomery Dean; Very Rev. JOHN P. AHERNE, V.G. Consultors: Rev. Msgr. JOHN R. AMOS; Revs. G. WARREN WALL; PATRICK MAHER; PETER CUNNINGHAM; Very Rev. JOHN AHERNE; Rev. FRANCIS CUSACK; Rev. Msgr. PATRICK O'CONNOR; Rev. WILLIAM SKONEKI; Very Rev. MICHAEL L. FARMER.

Appointed Members & Consultors—Rev. Msgr. JOHN R. AMOS; Rev. G. WARREN WALL.

Elected Members—Group I: Rev. Msgr. TIMOTHY DEASY; Very Rev. JOHN AHERNE, V.G.; Rev. FRANK CUSACK. Group II: Very Rev. PATRICK GALLAGHER; Revs. F. CHARLES TRONCALE; JAMES ZOGHBY. Group III: Rev. G. WARREN WALL; Rev. Msgr. JOHN R. AMOS; Rev. JAMES E. DANE. Group IV: Revs. DAVID CARUCCI; PAUL ZOGHBY; ERNEST HYNDMAN.

Religious—Revs. FRANCIS LYNCH, C.M.; JOHN LA BRAKE, S.S.E.; DONALD HAWKINS, S.J.

Priests' Eucharistic League—Rev. Msgr. J. EDWIN STUARDI, *Mercy Medical, P.O. Box 1090, Daphne, 36526.* Tel: 334-626-2694.

Priests' Personnel Board—Rev. FRANCIS V. CUSACK, Chm., *Our Lady of Lourdes Church, 1621 Boykin Blvd., Mobile, 36605.* Tel: 334-479-9885.

Priests' Retirement Fund—Very Rev. JOHN AHERNE, Pres., *P.O. Box 1966, Mobile, 36633.* Tel: 334-434-1585.

Propagation of the Faith—Rev. LEO BLANCHET, *St. Bridget Church, P.O. Box 13357, Whistler, 36613.* Tel: 334-452-3676.

Radio and Television Communications—c/o Chancery Office, P.O. Box 1966, Mobile, 36633. Tel: 334-434-1585.

School Education Department—Miss GWEN BYRD, Supt., *P.O. Box 129, Mobile, 36601.* Tel: 334-438-4611.

Office of Religious Education—14 S. Franklin St., P.O. Box 2405, Mobile, 36652. Tel: 334-433-6991. Ms. LORIE CREPEAU, Dir., *533 S. Union St., Montgomery, 36104.* Tel: 334-269-2389. Sr. FRANCIS ASSISI PIELMEIER, C.S.A., Dir., *P.O. Box A, Ozark, 36360.* Tel: 334-774-3214. Sr. PENNY SMITH, O.P., Dir.

Serra Club of Mobile—Mr. BERNIE DIAMOND, Pres.

Serra Club of Montgomery—LAURENCE RUSSO.

Serra Club of Dothan—JIM LOFTIN.

Seton Haven Management Corporation—Deacon EUGENE WADAS, Pres., *3721 Wares Ferry Rd., Montgomery, 36193.* Tel: 334-272-4000.

Toolen Institute for Parish Services (TIPS)—Dr. AIDAN LICARI, Dir., *P.O. Box 2405, Mobile, 36652.* Tel: 334-438-6121.

Vocations—Rev. MARK I. NESKE, Dir., *Little Flower Church, 2053 Government St., Mobile, 36606.* Tel: 334-478-3381. Rev. ARTHUR SCHRENGER, Assoc. Dir.

CLERGY, PARISHES, MISSIONS AND PAROCHIAL SCHOOLS

CITY OF MOBILE
(Mobile County)

1—CATHEDRAL OF THE IMMACULATE CONCEPTION (1704), Most Rev. Oscar H. Lipscomb, D.D., Ph.D.; Rev. Msgr. James W. Oberkirch, Rector; Rev. Michael J. Sreboth. In res., Revs. James F. Dorrill; Arthur C. Schrenger.
Cathedral & Rectory—400 Government St., P.O. Box 1966, 36633. Tel: 334-434-1565; Fax: 334-434-1588.

2—ST. CATHERINE OF SIENA (1913), Rev. Edwin P. Beachum.
Res., 2605 Springhill Ave., 36607. Tel: 334-473-1415; 473-1427; Fax: 334-473-6307.
Catechesis/Religious Programs—Students 47.
Novitiate, Josephite Fathers: 2609 Spring Hill Ave., 36607. Tel: 334-473-5130.

3—CORPUS CHRISTI (1958), Revs. James F. Zoghby; John S. Boudreaux (LAF); Deacon Arthur W. Robbins.
Res., 6300 McKenna Dr., 36608. Tel: 334-342-1852; Fax: 334-342-6313.
School—Tel: 334-342-5474; Fax: 334-380-0325. Mrs. Carol DuPree, Prin.
Lay Teachers 26; Students 574; Aides 14.
Catechesis/Religious Programs—Students 90.

4—ST. DOMINIC (1958), Revs. William J. Skoneki; Johnny S. Savoie; Deacon Edward Connick. In res., Rev. Msgr. Francis C. Murphy (Ireland).
Res., 4156 Burma Rd., 36693. Tel: 334-661-5130; Fax: 334-661-0469.
School—4160 Burma Rd., 36693. Tel: 334-661-5226; Fax: 334-660-2242. Mrs. Ann Zimlich, Prin.
Sisters of Mercy 1; Lay Teachers 26; Students 570.
Catechesis/Religious Programs—Students 100.
Convent—Tel: 334-661-3229.

5—ST. FRANCIS XAVIER (1867) (African American), Rev. Anietie Akama Ukanide, M.S.P.; Deacon Alexander Moore, Pastoral Assoc.
Res., 2034 St. Stephens Rd., 36617. Tel: 334-473-4975; Fax: 334-473-4940.

6—HOLY FAMILY (1959), Rev. Ernest R. Hyndman; Deacon Patrick Kelly.
Res., 1304 Garland St., 36618. Tel: 334-344-0271; Fax: 334-344-0296.
School—Tel: 334-344-1781. Ms. Maureen Glavey Goodwin, Prin.
Lay Teachers 16; Students 220.

7—ST. IGNATIUS (Spring Hill) (1947), Revs. G. Warren Wall; Alejandro E. Valladares; W. Bry Shields; James Montini Coleman; John Holleman; Deacons Charles J. Fontana; Marvin C. Johns; Abraham Lopez.
Res., 3704 Spring Hill Ave., 36608. Tel: 334-342-9221; Fax: 334-341-1481.
School—Tel: 334-342-5442; Fax: 334-344-0944. Miss Janet Murray, Prin.
Lay Teachers 34; Students 656.
Child Care Programs—Jeannie Harris, Child Care, Mother's Day Out.
Preschool—Jan Murray, Dir.
Catechesis/Religious Programs—Tel: 334-342-0516.
Students 106.

8—ST. JOAN OF ARC (1920), Rev. Msgr. Kenneth J. Klepac.
Res., 1260 Elmira St., 36604. Tel: 334-432-3505.

9—ST. JOSEPH (1857), Rev. E. J. Jacques, S.J.
Res., 808 Springhill Ave., 36602. Tel: 334-432-4218.

10—ST. JOSEPH (Maysville) (1944) (African American), Rev. Jeremiah A. Brady, S.S.J.
Res., 1703 Dublin St., 36605. Tel: 334-473-3761.
Convent—1701 Dublin St., 36605. Tel: 334-478-3292.

11—LITTLE FLOWER (1928), Rev. Mark I. Neske; Rev. Msgr. Maurice L. Shields, Pastor Emeritus; Rev. Joseph Muda Van Kunnel (India); Deacons Wallace McKinney; Fenwick Walsh; Hank Pouliot.
Res., 2053 Government St., 36606. Tel: 334-478-3381; Fax: 334-478-3381.
School—2103 Government St., 36606. Tel: 334-479-5761; Fax: 334-476-4064. Sr. Mary Joyce Bringer, C.S.J., Prin.
Lay Teachers 14; Students 249; Aides 3.
Catechesis/Religious Programs—Students 34.
Convent—411 Little Flower Ave., 36606. Tel: 334-479-1198.

12—ST. MARY (1867), Rev. Peter J. Cunningham; Rev. Msgr. Cordell J. Lang; Rev. Paul G. Zoghby; Sr. M. Magdalena Langlois, C.S.A., Pastoral Assoc.; Deacons Ernest J. Johnson, Jr.; William Dolan. In res., Rev. Steven T. Williams.
Mailing Address: 106 Providence St., 36604.
Res., 1453 Old Shell Rd., 36604. Tel: 334-432-8678.
School—Tel: 344-433-9904. Mrs. Marie Pishko, Prin.
Lay Teachers 15; Students 206.
Catechesis/Religious Programs—Tel: 344-432-0929.
Students 47.

13—ST. MATTHEW (1904), Rev. Joseph M. Bolling.
Res., 906 Garrity St., 36605-4699. Tel: 334-432-4784.

14—ST. MONICA (1950), Rev. Cu Minh Duong; Deacon James C. Burns.
Res., 1131 Dauphin Island Pkwy., 36605. Tel: 334-479-7360.

15—MOST PURE HEART OF MARY (1899) (African American), Rev. John Tyne, S.S.J. In res., Rev. William McKenna, S.S.J.
Residence & Mailing Address: 304 Sengstak St., 36603. Tel: 334-432-3344; Fax: 334-432-1192.
School—Most Pure Heart of Mary, Tel: 334-432-5270; Fax: 334-432-5271. Sr. Nancy Crossen, O.S.F., Prin.
Catechesis/Religious Programs—Students 49.
Convent—310 Sengstak St., 36603. Tel: 334-433-6519.

16—OUR LADY OF LOURDES, Rev. Francis V. Cusack; Deacon Gordon Kenny.
Res., 1621 Boykin Blvd., 36605. Tel: 334-479-9885.
School—Tel: 334-479-4007; 479-2367. Mr. Edwin Benson, Prin.
Lay Teachers 12; Students 174.
Catechesis/Religious Programs—Students 44.

17—OUR SAVIOR, Rev. Louis Russell Biven.
Office: 1801 Cody Rd. S., 36695. Tel: 334-633-6762; Fax: 334-633-7790.
Catechesis/Religious Programs—Students 161.

18—PRINCE OF PEACE (1970) (African American), Rev. Jeremiah D. Brady, S.S.J.
Res., 454 Charleston St., 36603. Tel: 334-432-2364.
Catechesis/Religious Programs—Tel: 334-433-1494.
Students 60.

19—ST. PIUS X (1954), Revs. Matthew O'Connor; Paul A. Halladay; Very Rev. Michael L. Farmer; Deacons William L. Tew; Gerald F. Kingman.
Res., 217 S. Sage Ave., 36606. Tel: 334-471-2449; Fax: 334-471-2441.
School—Tel: 334-473-5004; Fax: 334-473-5008. Mrs. Lauren Alvarez, Prin.
Sisters 1; Lay Teachers 27; Students 491.
Catechesis/Religious Programs—Tel: 334-473-4381.
Students 42.

OUTSIDE THE CITY OF MOBILE

Andalusia, Covington Co., Christ the King, Revs. Robert W. Fulton; John L. Holleman, Admin.
Res., 504 Sanford Rd., P.O. Drawer 1546, 36420. Tel: 334-222-4808.
Catechesis/Religious Programs—Students 56.

Atmore, Escambia Co., St. Robert Bellarmine (1943), Rev. Cecil Spotswood, Admin.
Res., 600 S. Main St., 36502-2825. Tel: 334-368-3615; Fax: 334-368-3615.

Auburn, Lee Co., St. Michael (1965), Revs. James S. Kee, Admin.; Todd Kreitinger, Campus Min.
Res., 302 E. Magnolia Ave., 36830. Tel: 334-887-5540; 887-5573; Fax: 334-887-5572.
Catechesis/Religious Programs—Students 250.
Joyland Child Development Center—Tel: 334-821-7624; Fax: 334-821-5583.
Chaplaincy—Auburn University, Auburn University Chapel, Catholic Student's Association. Tel: 334-887-5380; Fax: 334-887-1889.

Bay Minette, Baldwin Co., St. Agatha Church, Rev. James E. Dane.
Church—1001 Hand Ave., 36507. Tel: 334-937-2026; 580-3194 (Res.).

Bayou LaBatre, Mobile Co., St. Margaret (1880), Revs. Patrick Madden; John Trung Nguyen.
Res., P.O. Box 365, 36509. Tel: 334-824-2415; Fax: 334-824-4114. [CEM]
Catechesis/Religious Programs—Students 94.

Belle Fontaine, Mobile Co., St. Philip Neri (1908), Rev. John R. La Brake, S.S.E.
Res., 9101 Dauphin Island Pkwy., 36582. Tel: 334-973-2096.

Brewton, Escambia Co., St. Maurice (1948), Rev. Adrian L. Cook.
Res., 202 E. Jackson St., P.O. Box 206, 36427-0206. Tel: 334-867-5189; Fax: 334-867-7973.

Butler, Choctaw Co., St. John The Evangelist (1958), Rev. Austin Conry.
Res., 401 E. Pushmataha St., P.O. Box 456, 36904. Tel: 205-459-3129.
Mission—Chatom, Washington Co., St. Paul.

Camden, Wilcox Co., St. Joseph, Rev. Timothy Evans, Admin.
Res., 300 Whiskey Run Rd., 36767.
Mission—Monroeville, Dallas Co., Mission of Annunciation Parish, P.O. Box 883, Monroeville, 36461. Tel: 334-575-2644.

Chastang, Mobile Co., St. Peter the Apostle (1860), Rev. James P. Fallon, S.S.J.
Mailing Address: P.O. Box 456, Mount Vernon, 36560. Tel: 334-829-5134; Fax: 334-829-6874. [CEM]
Catechesis/Religious Programs—Students 60.
Missions—West Mount Vernon, Mobile Co., St. Theresa; Fairford, Washington Co., Our Lady of Sorrows.

Chickasaw, Mobile Co., St. Thomas the Apostle, Rev. John Lynes; Sr. Anne Matisek, C.S.A., Pastoral Assoc.
Res., 251 N. Craft Hwy., P.O. Box 11061, 36611. Tel: 334-456-7931; Fax: 334-452-9837.
Parish Center—253 N. Craft Hwy., 36611. Tel: 334-452-9837.

Citronelle, Mobile Co., St. Thomas (1913), Rev. John Coghlan.
Res., 8025 State St., P.O. Box 61, 36522. Tel: 334-866-7505.

Daphne, Baldwin Co., Christ the King (1896), Rev. Msgr. Timothy Deasy; Rev. James F. Carlsen; Deacons Malcolm Zellner; Leo Ollinger; Sr. Joan O'Donovan, Pastoral Assoc.
Res., 715 College Ave., P.O. Box 549, 36526. Tel: 334-626-2343; 626-3740; Fax: 334-621-1640. [CEM]
School—Tel: 334-626-1692; Fax: 334-626-9976. Sr. Maureen Nolan, Prin.
Presentation Sisters 2; Lay Teachers 30; Students 500.
Catechesis/Religious Programs—Tel: 334-626-5963.
Students 210.
Convent—1500 Main St., P.O. Box 901, 36526. Tel: 334-626-2431.
Presentation Sisters 3.
Shrine of the Holy Cross (1900), Rev. Robert M. McCown, S.J.
Res., P.O. Box 1497, 36526. Tel: 334-626-1447; Fax: 334-621-0012.
Mission—Bromley, St. John.

Dauphin Island, Mobile Co., St. Edmund-by-the-Sea, Rev. William N. Gorman. In res., Rev. Louis Suffredini.
Res., P.O. Box 6, 36528. Tel: 334-861-2352. [CEM]
Church—Cadillac Ave.

Dothan, Houston Co., St. Columba, Very Rev. Patrick J. Gallagher; Rev. David M. Shoemaker, Hispanic Min.; Deacon W. Harold Grant.
Res., 2700 W. Main St., 36301. Tel: 334-793-5802; Fax: 334-792-2816. [JC]
Catechesis/Religious Programs—Tel: 334-792-3065.
Students 293.
Mission—Columbia, Houston Co., Good Shepherd, Columbia, 36319.

Elberta, Baldwin Co., St. Bartholomew (1911) (German), Rev. Howard R. Moussier, O.S.B.
Res., P.O. Drawer 280, 36530. Tel: 334-986-8142; Fax: 334-987-5251. [CEM]
School—St. Benedict's, Tel: 334-986-8143; Fax: 334-986-8144. Mrs. Claudia Adam, Prin.
Lay Teachers 15; Students 230; Aides 4.
Catechesis/Religious Programs—St. Benedict's School.
Students 175.

Enterprise, Coffee Co., St. John (1959), Rev. Joseph S. Wadas; Deacon Gary Rasponi.
Church—123 Heath St. P.O. Box 311066, 36331-1066. Tel: 334-347-6751.
Res., 614 Alberta, 36331. Tel: 334-347-7345.
Catechesis/Religious Programs—Students 208.
Mission—Geneva, Geneva Co., St. Mary, 100 S. Commerce, Geneva, 36340.

Eufaula, Barbour Co., Holy Redeemer (1859), Rev. J. Francis Sofie, Jr.
Res., 515 W. Broad St., 36027. Tel: 334-687-3716; Fax: 334-687-3766.
Catechesis/Religious Programs—Students 40.
Missions—Union Springs, Bullock Co., St. Pius X, 308 Kennon St., Union Springs, 36089.; Union Springs, Bullock Co., Bullock County Correctional Facility, P.O. Box 5107, Union Springs, 36089. Tel: 334-738-5625; Clayton, Barbour Co., Ventress Correctional Facility, P.O. Box 769, Clayton, 36016. Tel: 334-775-3331.

Fairhope, Baldwin Co., St. Lawrence (1961), Revs. Gordon Milsted; Primitivo Maravilla (Philippines).
Res., 370 S. Section St., 36532. Tel: 334-928-5931; Fax: 334-928-5938.
Catechesis/Religious Programs—Students 255.
Chapel—Battles Wharf, Baldwin Co., Sacred Heart.

Foley, Baldwin Co., St. Margaret (1951), Rev. Michael D. Kelly.
Res., 601 Laurel St., 36535. Tel: 334-943-4009. [CEM]

Grand Bay, Mobile Co., St. John Baptist (1924), Rev. Hugh Maguire.
Res., P.O. Box 417, 36541. Tel: 334-865-6902; Fax: 334-865-1412.

Greenville, Butler Co., St. Elizabeth (1894), Revs. Robert W. Fulton, Admin.; John L. Holleman.
Res., 407 E. Walnut St., 36037. Tel: 334-382-6203.

Grove Hill, Clarke Co., Sacred Heart (1944), Rev. James Havens. In res., Rev. Francis Messing.
Res., Hwy. 43 N., P.O. Box 70, 36451. Tel: 334-275-3665.
Missions—Jackson, Clarke Co., Visitation, 135 W. Clinton St., Jackson, 36545.; Thomasville, Clarke Co., St. Joseph, W. Front St., Thomasville, 36784.

Gulf Shores, Baldwin Co., Our Lady of the Gulf (1952), Revs. Robert W. Fulton; Lee O'Neil.
Res., 308 E. 22nd Ave., P.O. Box 515, 36547-0515. Tel: 334-968-7062.
Catechesis/Religious Programs—322 Magnolia Dr., 36542. Tel: 334-968-6092. Denise Myers, D.R.E.
Students 35.

Heron Bay, Mobile Co., St. Michael the Archangel (1880), Rev. Patrick Madden.
Mailing Address: 15872 Heron Bay Loop Rd. E., Coden, 36523. Tel: 334-873-4719.

Holy Trinity, Russell Co., St. Joseph, Rev. Robert M. Shay, S.T. In res., Revs. Maurice Haiss; Clement Kovacsik, S.T.; Bros. Christopher Ilg, S.T.; Boris Farrah, S.T.; Gregory Martin, S.T.; Daniel Rezmer, S.T.; Michael Lobo, S.T.
Church—1444 Hwy. 165, 36859. Tel: 334-855-3148; Fax: 334-855-3115.

Lillian, Baldwin Co., St. Joseph, Rev. Edward P. Markley, O.S.B.
Res., 34290 U.S. Hwy. 98, 36549. Tel: 334-962-2049; Fax: 334-962-3649. [JC]

Magnolia Springs, Baldwin Co., St. John the Baptist (1881), Rev. Msgr. Guido Calleja.
Res., 10797 St. John's Ln., P.O. Box 206, 36555. Tel: 334-965-7719. [CEM][JC 2]
Mission—Bon Secour, Baldwin Co., Our Lady of Bon Secour.

Millbrook, Elmore Co., St. Elizabeth Ann Seton (1978), Rev. Albert P. Kelly.
Mailing Address: P.O. Box 585, 36054.
Church—4831 Hwy. 14, 36054-0585. Tel: 334-285-7000.
Res., 109 Crossgate Dr., Elmore, 36025.
Mission—Wetumpka, Elmore Co., St. Mark's.

Mon Luis Island, Mobile Co., St. Rose of Lima (1853), Rev. Msgr. John R. Amos.
Res., 2951 Durette Ave. (Mon Luis Island), Coden, 36523. Tel: 334-973-2592. [CEM]

Monroeville, Monroe Co., Annunciation, Rev. Timothy Evans.
Res., Whetstone St., P.O. Box 883, 36460. Tel: 334-575-2644.
Catechesis/Religious Programs—Students 32.
Missions—Uriah, Monroe Co., Our Lady of Mount Carmel, Hwy. 21 N., Uriah, 36480.; Vredenburgh, Monroe Co., St. Martin de Porres, Beech St., Vredenburgh, 36481. Tel: 334-337-4671; Camden, Wilcox Co., St. Joseph, 300 Whiskey Run Rd., Camden, 36767.

Montgomery, Montgomery Co.,

1—ST. PETER, (1834), Rev. Alexander Sherlock.
Res., 219 Adams Ave., P.O. Box 114, 36101. Tel: 334-262-7304; Fax: 334-262-9735. [CEM]

2—ST. ANDREW, Rev. Wilbur Kissell.
Mailing Address: P.O. Box 241303, 36124.
Res., 433 Clayton St., 36124. Tel: 334-262-3241.

3—ST. BEDE, (1925), Revs. David J. Tokarz; Fergus Prendergast; Bieu Van Nguyen; Deacon Charles Gulley.
Office: 3870 Atlanta Hwy., 36109. Tel: 334-272-3463; Fax: 334-272-3492.
School—3850 Atlanta Hwy., 36109. Tel: 334-272-3033; Fax: 334-272-9394. Mrs. Eleanor McCormack, Prin.
Lay Teachers 26; Students 415.
Catechesis/Religious Programs—Students 120.
Children's Center—3840 Atlanta Hwy., 36109. Tel: 334-277-8551.

4—CHURCH OF THE HOLY SPIRIT, (1977), Very Rev. F. Charles Troncale; Deacon Eugene Wadas.
Res., 8570 Vaughn Rd., 36117. Tel: 334-277-5631; Fax: 334-272-1008.
Catechesis/Religious Programs—Tel: 334-277-1989.
Students 220.

5—ST. JOHN THE BAPTIST, (1908), Rev. William P. Folsom, Jr., Admin.
Res., 553 S. Union St., 36104. Tel: 334-264-6274; Fax: 334-262-3012.

6—ST. JUDE, (1934) (African American), Revs. James Holden; Matthew A. Sindik.
Res., 2048 W. Fairview Ave., St. Jude, 36108. Tel: 334-265-1390; Fax: 334-265-1399.
School—Tel: 334-263-6121; Fax: 334-265-8847. Mr. Leon Robinson, Prin.
Lay Teachers 11; Students 201.
High School—Tel: 334-264-5376; Fax: 334-264-6669. Sr. Mary Beth, D.C., Prin.
Lay Teachers 22; Students 143.
Catechesis/Religious Programs—Students 82.

7—OUR LADY, QUEEN OF MERCY, (1954), Revs. David P. Carucci, Admin.; Jose Paillacho; Deacon James R. Labadie.
Res., 4421 Narrow Lane Rd., 36116. Tel: 334-288-2850; Fax: 334-281-7884.
School—Tel: 334-288-5334; Fax: 334-288-5395. Mrs. Mary Kaye McCooey, Prin.
Lay Teachers 15; Students 168.
Catechesis/Religious Programs—Tel: 334-288-5342.
Students 44.
Child Development Center—Tel: 334-613-0340.

8—RESURRECTION CATHOLIC CHURCH, (1943), Rev. Manuel Williams, C.R. In res., Revs. Casimir J. Wilczynski, C.R.; Henryk Licznerski, C.R. (Poland).
Res., 2815 Forbes Rd., 36110. Tel: 334-269-1770; Fax: 334-265-8081.

School—Resurrection Catholic School, Tel: 334-265-4615; Fax: 334-265-4568. Sr. Rita Washington, S.F.C.C., Prin.
Religious 5; Lay Teachers 15; Students 150.
Mission—Montgomery, Montgomery Co., Resurrection Catholic Mission, 2815 Forbes Rd., 36110. Tel: 334-263-4221; Fax: 334-263-4999. Rev. Manuel Williams, C.R., Dir.

Mount Vernon, Mobile Co., St. Cecilia (1929), Rev. John Coghlan.
Res., 1315 Military Rd., P.O. Box 847, 36560. Tel: 334-829-9531. [CEM]

Opelika, Lee Co., St. Mary of the Mission (1910), Rev. John J. Buckley, C.M.; Deacon Donald Canonica.
Res., 1000 4th Ave., 36801. Tel: 334-749-8359; Fax: 334-749-6312.
Catechesis/Religious Programs—Tel: 334-745-3432.
Students 75.

Orange Beach, Baldwin Co., St. Thomas by the Sea, Rev. Patrick Maher; Deacon Raymond Basoco.
Mailing Address: P.O. Box 1190, 36561. Tel: 334-981-8132; Fax: 334-981-1981.

Orrville, Dallas Co., Immaculate Conception, Rev. Carroll W. Plourde, S.S.E.
Church—13663 Alabama Hwy. 22 W., 36767.
Res., P.O. Box 248, 36767. Tel: 334-874-8931.

Ozark, Dale Co., St. John (1963), Rev. Charles J. McCabe.
Res., 709 Camilla Ave., P.O. Box 1008, 36361-1008. Tel: 334-774-6826; Fax: 334-774-8675. [JC]
Catechesis/Religious Programs—Students 35.

Phenix City, Russell Co., St. Patrick (1911), Rev. Thomas D. Weise.
Res., 1502 Broad St., P.O. Box 147, 36868-0147. Tel: 334-298-9025; Fax: 334-298-9233.
School—3910 Lakewood Dr., 36868. Tel: 334-298-3408. Mrs. Christi Ham, Prin.
Catechesis/Religious Programs—Students 110.
Convent—St. Patrick's Missionary Cenacle, 2701 40th St., 36867. Tel: 334-298-0708.
Missionary Servants of the Most Blessed Trinity 6.

Mother Mary Parish (1940), Rev. Thomas D. Weise, Admin.
Res., 318 Seale Rd., 36869. Tel: 334-298-2343; Fax: 334-298-9233.
School—Tel: 334-298-6371; Fax: 334-298-7934. Sr. M. Cecelia Harrison, F.M.S., Prin.
Sisters 3; Lay Teachers 10; Students 180.
Catechesis/Religious Programs—Students 200.

Plateau, Mobile Co., Our Mother of Mercy (1926) (African American), Rev. Anietie Akama Ukanide, M.S.P.
Mailing Address: P.O. Box 10306, Prichard, 36610.
Res., 805 East St., 36610. Tel: 334-456-3551.

Prattville, Autauga Co., St. Joseph Church (1963), Rev. Philip McKenna; Deacon Samuel Shippen.
Res., 511 N. Memorial Dr., 36067-2133. Tel: 334-365-8680; Fax: 334-365-2267.
Catechesis/Religious Programs—Students 332.

Prichard, Mobile Co., Our Lady of Fatima (1949). Closed. For inquiries for parish records contact the Chancery.

St. James Major (1925) (African American), Rev. Henry E. Dickson, S.S.J.
Res., 714 S. College St., 36610. Tel: 334-456-6842; Fax: 334-456-6843.
School—Tel: 334-452-1883. Sr. Brenda Monahan, D.C., Prin.
Daughters of Charity 3; Lay Teachers 8; Students 168.
Catechesis/Religious Programs—Students 48.
Convent—927 W. Prichard Ave., 36610. Tel: 334-457-9396.

Robertsdale, Baldwin Co., St. Patrick (1974), Rev. Msgr. William R. James.
Res., P.O. Box 1367, 36567. Tel: 334-947-5054; Fax: 334-947-7395.
School—(Grades K-8) P.O. Drawer 609, 36567. Tel: 334-947-7395. Sr. Margaret Harte, P.B.V.M., Prin.
Presentation Sisters 1; Lay Teachers 13; Students 204.
Catechesis/Religious Programs—Students 70.
Convent—P.O. Box 609, 36567. Tel: 334-947-7396; Fax: 334-947-3860.

Selma, Dallas Co., Our Lady Queen of Peace (1850), Rev. Carroll W. Plourde, S.S.E.
Office: 309 Washington St., 36701. Tel: 334-874-8931 (Office & Res.); Fax: 334-874-8976.
Res., 2511 Summer Field Rd., 36701. Tel: 334-874-8475.
Catechesis/Religious Programs—Students 78.

Semmes, Mobile Co., Holy Name of Jesus (1977), Very Rev. John Aherne, V.G.
Res., 2275 Snow Rd., P.O. Box 557, 36575. Tel: 334-649-4794.
Catechesis/Religious Programs—Students 70.

Tallassee, Elmore Co., St. Vincent De Paul (1955), Rev. Francis A. Lynch, C.M.
Res., 620 Gilmer Ave., P.O. Box 780487, 36078-0487. Tel: 334-283-2169; Fax: 334-283-8500. [JC]

Tillman's Corner, Mobile Co., St. Vincent de Paul (1971), Rev. James Cink; Deacon Robert Nouwen.
Res., 5023 Camelot Dr., Mobile, 36619. Tel: 334-661-3908; Fax: 334-661-3908.
School—Tel: 334-666-8022; Fax: 334-666-8022. Kendall F. McKee, Prin.
Lay Teachers 10; Students 190.
Catechesis/Religious Programs—Tel: 334-666-4066.
Students 80.

Troy, Pike Co., St. Martin of Tours, Rev. James N. Dean.
Res., 725 Elba Hwy., 36079. Tel: 334-566-2630.
Catechesis/Religious Programs—Students 60.

Tuskegee Institute, Macon Co., St. Joseph (1940), Rev. Charles E. McNeice, S.S.E.
Res., 2007 Montgomery Rd., 36088. Tel: 334-727-2710.
School—(Grades K-8) 2009 Montgomery Rd., 36088. Tel: 334-727-0620; 727-0642. Sr. Geraldine O'Meara, O.P., Prin.
Sinsinawa Dominicans 2; Lay Teachers 8; Students 129.

Whistler, Mobile Co., St. Bridget (1864), Rev. Leo Blanchet; Deacon Raymond Vrazel.
Res., 3625 W. Main St., P.O. Box 13357, 36613. Tel: 334-452-3676.

Chaplains of Public Institutions

CLAYTON. *Ventress Correctional Institution* 36016. Rev. J. Francis Sofie, Jr.

UNION SPRINGS. *Bullock County Correctional Facility* 36089. Rev. J. Francis Sofie, Jr.

On Leave from the Archdiocese:
Reverend Monsignors—
Cullen, Thomas J.
Reverend Fathers—
Dahmen, Vernon
Dalton, Peadar
Fields, William
Harbour, Linn S.
Kieltyka, Robert
Lemming, Patrick W.
Lott, Lawrence
Martin, Stephen E.
McGuiness, David
Nicholson, Patrick
Phan, Vincent Huo
Reskey, George A.
Robinson, Jerome
Schrenger, Authur C.
Smith, Edward E.
Staff, Stephen M.
Stryjewski, John J.
Tipton, Paul S.
Trosch, David

Retired:
Reverend Monsignors—
Aucoin, Charles
Cullen, Thomas J.
Jennings, Joseph
McDevitt, Anthony J.
McGuinness, Michael
Murphy, Francis
Royer, George C.
Stuardi, J. Edwin
Reverend Fathers—
Becherer, David
Desmond, Barry
Hay, Theodore H., S.T.L.
Keller, Brendan
McDonnell, Vincent
Robinson, John C.
Suffredini, Louis

Permanent Deacons:
Basoco, Raymond
Burns, James C.
Canonica, Donald A.
Connick, Edward G.
Dolan, William R.
Fontana, Charles J.
Grant, Harold
Gulley, Charles
Hamilton, John B., On Leave
Hicks, George, (Retired)
Johns, Marvin C.
Johnson, Ernest
Kelly, Patrick
Kenny, Gordon
King, A. B., On Leave
Kingman, Gerald
Labadie, James
Lopez, Abraham
May, Frank J.
McGonagle, Joseph P.
McKinney, Wallace R.
McMeans, Leo
Moore, Alexander
Nouwen, Robert
O'Brien, Henry F.
Ollinger, H. Leo, Jr.
Pouliot, Henry
Pry, Jackie T., (Retired)
Rasponi, Gary A.
Robbins, Arthur
Sheldon, Paul
Shippen, Samuel
Tew, William L., Jr.
Vrazel, Raymond
Wadas, Eugene
Walsh, Fenwick
Zellner, Malcolm

INSTITUTIONS LOCATED IN THE ARCHDIOCESE

[A] COLLEGES AND UNIVERSITIES

MOBILE. *Spring Hill College*, (1830) 4000 Dauphin St., 36608. Tel: 334-380-4000; Fax: 334-460-2195.
Web site: www.shc.edu
For a complete listing, refer to the Colleges and Universities section.

[B] HIGH SCHOOLS, ARCHDIOCESAN

MOBILE. *McGill-Toolen Catholic High School*, 1501 Old Shell Rd., 36604. Tel: 334-432-0784; Fax: 334-433-8356.
E-mail: shieldsb@mcgill.pvt.k12.al.us
Revs. W. Bry Shields, Pres.; Steven T. Williams; Mr. O. William Lee, Prin. Priests 2; Brothers of the Sacred Heart 2; Lay Teachers 88; Students 1,112.

MONTGOMERY. *Montgomery Catholic High School*, 5350 Vaughn Rd., 36116. Tel: 334-272-7220; Fax: 334-272-2440.
E-mail: F_Weber@knights.pvt.k12.al.us
Web site: www.knights.pvt.k12.al.us
Mr. Faustin N. Weber, Prin. Lay Teachers 15; Students 249.

St. Jude High School, 2048 W. Fairview Ave., 36108. Tel: 334-264-5376; Fax: 334-264-6669.
E-mail: stjude@mindspring.com
Web site: www.saintjudeschool.com
Sr. Mary Beth Kubera, D.C., Prin. Lay Teachers 26; Students 179.

[C] CHILDREN'S HOMES

MOBILE. *St. Mary's Home*, 4350 Moffat Rd., 36618. Tel: 334-344-7733
For a complete listing, refer to the Special Care Facilities section.

[D] GENERAL HOSPITALS

MOBILE. *Providence Foundation*, 6701 Airport Blvd., B. 227, P.O. Box 850429, 36608. Tel: 334-639-2050; Fax: 334-639-2052
For a complete listing, refer to the Hospitals section.

Providence Healthcare Services, 6801 Airport Blvd., P.O. Box 850429, 36685. Tel: 334-633-1000; Fax: 334-633-1679
For a complete listing, refer to the Hospitals section.

Providence Hospital, 6801 Airport Blvd., P.O. Box 850429, 36608. Tel: 334-633-1000; Fax: 334-633-1679.
Web site: www.providencehospital.org
For a complete listing, refer to the Hospitals section.

Seton Health Corp. of South Alabama, 6801 Airport Blvd., P.O. Box 850429, 36608. Tel: 334-633-1660; Fax: 334-633-1679
For a complete listing, refer to the Hospitals section.

Seton Medical Management, Inc., 6701 Airport Blvd., Suite D-439, 36608. Tel: 334-639-2660; Fax: 334-639-2664
For a complete listing, refer to the Hospitals section.

[E] SPECIAL HOSPITALS, SCHOOLS AND HOMES FOR THE AGED

MOBILE. *Allen Memorial Home Skilled Nursing Facility*, 735 S. Washington Ave., 36603. Tel: 334-433-2642; Fax: 334-431-6044.
E-mail: allenmhome@aol.com
For a complete listing, refer to the Special Care Facilities section.

Little Sisters of the Poor, Home For the Aged, Inc., Sacred Heart Residence, 1655 McGill Ave., 36604.

Tel: 334-476-6335; Fax: 334-478-6519
For a complete listing, refer to the Special Care Facilities section.

DAPHNE. *Mercy Medical*, P.O. Box 1090, 36526. Tel: 334-626-2694; Fax: 334-626-0315.
E-mail: dennis@mercymedical.com
Web site: www.mercymedical.com
For a complete listing, refer to the Special Care Facilities section.

MARBURY. *Resurrection Catholic Nursing Home*, 165 County Rd. 20 E., P.O. Box 89, 36051-0089
For a complete listing, refer to the Special Care Facilities section.

MONTGOMERY. *City of St. Jude, Inc., The*, 2048 W. Fairview Ave., 36108. Tel: 334-265-6791; Fax: 334-269-1988
For a complete listing, refer to the Special Care Facilities section.

Father Purcell Memorial Exceptional Children Center, 2048 W. Fairview Ave., 36108. Tel: 334-834-5590; Fax: 334-834-5592
For a complete listing, refer to the Special Care Facilities section.

Father Walter Memorial Center for Handicapped Children, 2815 Forbes Dr., 36199. Tel: 334-262-6421; Fax: 334-262-2265
For a complete listing, refer to the Special Care Facilities section.

Resurrection Early Childhood Center, 2815 Forbes Dr., 36110. Tel: 334-265-4615; Fax: 334-265-4568
For a complete listing, refer to the Special Care Facilities section.

St. Bede's Children's Center, 3840 Atlanta Hwy., 36109.
E-mail: klangston@school.stbede.org
For a complete listing, refer to the Special Care Facilities section.

[F] HOUSING FOR THE ELDERLY

MOBILE. *Cathedral Place*, 351 Conti St., 36602. Tel: 334-434-1590; Fax: 334-434-1562.
E-mail: jscan41974@aol.com
For a complete listing, refer to the Special Care Facilities section.

MONTGOMERY. *Laboure Complex Foundation*, P.O. Box 3074, 36109. Tel: 334-277-5213; Fax: 334-272-1788.
E-mail: smcarol@aol.com
Web site: www.laboure.org
For a complete listing, refer to the Special Care Facilities section.

Seton Haven, 3721 Wares Ferry Rd., 36109. Tel: 334-272-4000; Fax: 334-272-1788.
E-mail: sh36109@aol.com
For a complete listing, refer to the Special Care Facilities section.

PRICHARD. *Queen's Court I Apartments* Mailing Address: c/o Archdiocese of Mobile, P.O. Box 1966 Mobile, 36633.
For a complete listing, refer to the Special Care Facilities section.

[G] MONASTERIES AND RESIDENCES OF PRIESTS AND BROTHERS

MOBILE. *Brothers of the Sacred Heart*, 60 N. Catherine St., 36604. Tel: 334-438-3812.
E-mail: leebarkersc@hotmail.com
Bros. Lee Barker, S.C., Dir.; Paul Mulligan, S.C., Sub. Dir.; Celestine Algero, S.C.; John Moore, S.C. Brothers 4.

SELMA. *Edmundite Fathers*, Edmundite Missions House, 1401 Broad St., 36701. Tel: 334-872-6221; Fax: 334-872-8123.
E-mail: RogerLac@aol.com
Web site: http://www.EdmunditeMissions.com
Legal Title: *Fathers of St. Edmund Southern Missions, Inc.* Revs. Carroll W. Plourde, S.S.E., Supr.; Roger J. LaCharite, S.S.E., Missions Dir.; Francis A. Donnellan, S.S.E.; Robert J. Sheehey, S.S.E.; James F. Ryan, S.S.E.; Paul I. Plouffe, S.S.E.; Bros. Peter J. Stanfield, S.S.E., Programs Dir.; Francis J. Hagerty, S.S.E. Priests 6; Brothers 2; Total Assisted 151,744; Total Staff 60.

[H] CONVENTS AND RESIDENCES OF SISTERS

MOBILE. *Blessed Trinity Missionary Cenacle*, 604 Barksdale Dr. W., 36606. Tel: 334-476-4803. Missionary Servants 5.

Convent of the Sisters of Mercy of the Americas Baltimore Regional Community, 101 Wimbledon Dr., W., 36608. Tel: 334-344-1377; Fax: 334-344-1617.
E-mail: coberkirch@aol.com
Web site: www.mercysistersbalt.com
Sr. Carolyn Oberkirch, R.S.M., Admin. Sisters 18; Total Staff 11.
Other Residences: 4301 Bit & Spur Rd., 36608. Tel: 334-343-3674. 606 Bay Bluff East, Daphne, 36526. Tel: 334-626-0130. 2902 Brierwood Dr., 36606. Tel: 334-476-4605. 172 N. Lafayette St., 36604. Tel: 334-432-3178. Portier Place, 4363 Old Shell Rd., 36608. Tel: 334-304-3150; Fax: 334-304-3143. Sr. Ruth Handren, Asst. Admin., Huntleigh Woods, Apt. N-205, 375 Hillcrest Rd., 36608. Tel: 334-344-9388. 3700 Whispering Pines, Apt. 47C, 36608-1149. Tel: 334-343-4435.

Convent of the Sisters of St. Agnes, 1701 Dublin St., 36605. Tel: 334-478-3292. Sisters 5.

Monastery of Discalced Carmelite Nuns, 716 Dauphin Island Pkwy., 36606. Rev. Mother Marie Therese, O.C.D., Prioress. Solemnly Professed 4.

Sisters of Loretto, 1408 Old Shell Rd., 36604-2244. Tel: 334-431-6735; Fax: 334-690-9367.
E-mail: ardoyns@mcgill.pvt.k12.al.us
Sr. Sandra Ardoyno, S.L.

Visitation Monastery and Retreat House, 2300 Spring Hill Ave., 36607. Tel: 334-473-2321; Fax: 334-476-9761. Mother Jane de Chantal Word, Supr. Sisters 7; Total Staff 3.

ALBERTA. *Alberta Health Center*, P.O. Box 97, 36720. Tel: 334-573-2493.

CAMDEN. *Sisters of St. Joseph*, 490 Whiskey Run Rd., 36726. Tel: 334-682-4144.
E-mail: rcookmd@juno.com
Sisters 1; Total Staff 6.

HOLY TRINITY. *Blessed Trinity Shrine Retreat and Cenacle*, 107 Holy Trinity Rd., 36859. Tel: 334-855-4474; Fax: 334-855-4525.
E-mail: btsr@juno.com
Sr. Theresa Mary Finan, M.S.B.T., Co-Dir.; Sr. Geraldine Whelan, M.S.B.T., Co-Dir. Missionary Servants of the Most Blessed Trinity 5; Retreat House Capacity 40.

MARBURY. *Dominican Monastery of St. Jude (St. Jude Monastery)*, P.O. Box 170, 36051. Mother Mary Aimee, O.P., Prioress. Cloistered Dominican Nuns of Perpetual Adoration and Rosary. Professed Sisters 7.

MONTGOMERY. *Daughters of Charity*, 577-579 Eastdale Rd. S., 36117. Tel: 334-272-3354; Fax: 334-272-6477. Sisters 5.

Mater Dei Missionary Cenacle, 784 Spring Valley Rd., 36116. Tel: 334-288-4544; Fax: 334-288-9322.
E-mail: msbt-pat-langan@netzero.net
Missionary Servants of the Most Blessed Trinity 3 Sisters.

OZARK. *Sinsinawa Dominican Sisters*, Rte. 3, Box 50, 36360. Tel: 334-299-6671; Fax: 334-299-0171.
E-mail: PSmith8037@aol.com
Sr. Penny Smith, O.P.

PHENIX CITY. *St. Patrick's Missionary Cenacle*, 2701 Fortieth St., 36867. Tel: 334-298-0708. Missionary Servants of the Most Blessed Trinity 4.

PINE APPLE. *Sisters of St. Joseph of Rochester*, 702 County Rd. 59, 36768. Tel: 334-746-2584.
E-mail: ssjpineapple@juno.com
Web site: www.ssjvolunteers.org
Sisters 3.

SELMA. *Sisters Residence*, 911 Mabry St., 36701. Tel: 334-874-6536. Sisters 3.

VREDENBURGH. *Emmanuel Community*, P.O. Box 365, 36481. Tel: 334-337-4484.

[I] ARCHDIOCESAN SOCIAL SERVICES

MOBILE. *Catholic Social Services, Archdiocese of Mobile*. Mailing Address: P.O. Box 759, 36601. 400 Government St., 36602. Tel: 334-434-1550; Fax: 334-434-1549. Sr. Frances Louise Sheridan, M.S.B.T., Archdiocesan Dir.; Marilyn Davis King, Dir.
Branch Offices: 4455 Narrow Lane Rd., Montgomery, 36116. Tel: 334-793-3601; Fax: 334-702-0825. Dr. James Carter, Ph.D., Dir., P.O. Box 870, Robertsdale, 36567. Tel: 334-947-2293. Mrs. Michele Prockup, Dir., P.O. Box 1105, Chatom, 36518. Tel: 334-847-2708. Mrs. Joyce Yocum, Dir., P.O. Box 6184, Dothan, 36302. Tel: 334-793-3601. Mrs. Martha Coaker, Dir., P.O. Box 85, Jackson, 36545. Tel: 334-246-0131. Martha Coaker, Dir.

Service Center of Catholic Social Services, 555 Dauphin St., 36602. Tel: 334-434-1500; Fax: 334-434-1509.
E-mail: jgrinten@mobilecan.org
Sr. Judith Vander Grinten, C.S.A., M.S.W., Dir. Total Assisted 23,559; Total Staff 29.

CHATOM. *Chatom Office of Catholic Social Services*, P.O. Box 1105, 36518. Tel: 334-847-2708; Fax: 334-847-2708. Joyce Yocum, Supvr. Total Assisted 6,899; Total Staff 2.

DOTHAN. *Dothan Office of Catholic Social Services*, P.O. Box 6184, 36302. Tel: 334-793-3601; Fax: 334-702-0825.

MONTGOMERY. *Catholic Social Services of Montgomery*, 4455 Narrow Lane Rd., 36116. Tel: 334-288-8890; Fax: 334-288-9322. James Carter, Ph.D., Dir. Total Assisted 10,400; Total Staff 12.

ROBERTSDALE. *Robertsdale Office of Catholic Social Services*, P.O. Box 870, 36567. Tel: 334-947-2293; Fax: 334-947-4058.
E-mail: cssbald@hotmailcom
Ms. Michele Prockup, Dir. Total Assisted 8,679; Total Staff 5.

[J] NEWMAN CENTERS

MOBILE. *Spring Hill College Campus Ministry*, 4000 Dauphin St., 36608-1791. Tel: 334-380-3495; Fax: 334-460-2174.
E-mail: dhawkins@shc.edu
Web site: www.shc.edu
Rev. Donald A. Hawkins, S.J.

University of South Alabama Newman Center, Catholic Student Center, 6051 Old Shell Rd., 36608. Tel: 334-343-3662.
E-mail: usacsc@minsdspring.com
Rev. James F. Dorrill, Ph.D., Chap.; Salvatore M. Ballacchino, S.T.L., Dir. & Asst. Campus Min.

AUBURN. *Auburn University Newman Center*, 302 E. Magnolia Ave., 36830. Tel: 334-887-5380.
Web site: http://www.auburn.edu/~stmcso1
Rev. Todd Kreitinger,.

DOTHAN. *George C. Wallace Jr. Community College Newman Center*, 2700 W. Main St., 36301. Tel: 334-793-5802; Fax: 334-792-2816.
E-mail: saintcolumba@ala.net
Very Rev. Patrick J. Gallagher.

MONROEVILLE. *Alabama Southern Community College Newman Center*, P.O. Box 883, 36460-0883. Tel: 334-575-2644.
E-mail: annuneat@frontiernet.net
Rev. Tim Evans, K.H.S.

MONTGOMERY. *Alabama State University Newman Center*, 553 S. Union St., 36104. Tel: 334-264-6274. Rev. William P. Folsom, Jr.

Huntington College Newman Center, 4421 Narrow Lane Rd., 36116. Tel: 334-288-2850; Fax: 334-281-7884.
E-mail: veritas@knoway.net
Web site: olqm.org
Rev. David P. Carucci.

SELMA. *Marion Institute Newman Center*, 309 Washington St., 36703. Tel: 334-874-8931; Fax: 334-874-8976. Rev. Carroll W. Plourde, S.S.E.

TROY. *Troy State University Newman Center*, 725 Elba Hwy., 36079. Tel: 334-566-2630. Rev. James N. Dean.

TUSKEGEE INSTITUTE. *Tuskegee University Newman Center*, 2007 Montgomery Rd., 36088. Tel: 334-727-2710. Rev. Charles E. McNeice, S.S.E. Total Staff 1.

[K] MISCELLANEOUS LISTINGS

MOBILE. *Catholic High Schools Alumni Association of Mobile*, 1501 Old Shell Rd., 36604. Tel: 334-441-0809; Fax: 334-433-8356.
E-mail: wattsm@mcgill.pvt.k12.al.us
Web site: www.mcgill.pvt.k12.al.us
Marian Watts, Alumni Dir.

L'Arche, 151 S. Ann St., 36604. Tel: 334-438-2094; Fax: 334-433-5835.
E-mail: larchmob@hotmail.com
Web site: www.2.acan.net/~/archmob/
Christian non-profit organization-community where handicapped and non-handicapped people live. Marty O'Malley, Dir. Handicapped People 19; Assistants 14.

Ladies of Charity, P.O. Box 6987, 36660-0987. Tel: 334-661-9448. Mrs. Mary Johnson, Pres.

Providence Building Corporation, P.O. Box 850429, 36685. 6801 Airport Blvd., 36608. Tel: 334-633-1000; Fax: 334-633-1679. Sr. Marilyn Moore, D.C., Chm.; Sr. Elise Boudreaux, D.C., Pres.; Sr. Betty Gunselman, D.C., Sec. & Treas.

St. Ignatius Child Care - Mobile, 3704 Springhill Ave., 36608. Tel: 334-342-3322; Fax: 334-342-3530. Mrs. Jeanne Harris, Admin.

Society of St. Vincent de Paul, 411 S. Broad St., 36603. Tel: 334-432-5173. Wendy Makin, Pres., 411 S. Broad St., 36603.

DAPHNE. *Apostleship of Prayer*, P.O. Box 1090, 36532. Tel: 334-626-2694. Rev. Msgr. J. Edwin Stuardi.

DOTHAN. *St. Columba Preschool*, 2700 W. Main St., 36301. Tel: 334-793-6742. Mrs. Cathy Dedmon, Dir.

HAYNEVILLE. *Lowndes County Catholic Center*, 404 Wall St., 36040-6209. Tel: 334-563-9139; Fax: 334-563-9093.

HURTSBORO. *John XXIII Center*, P.O. Box 117, 36860. Tel: 334-667-7770. Julie Viera, Admin.

MONTGOMERY. *The City of St. Jude, Inc.*, 2048 W. Fairview Ave., 36108. Tel: 334-265-6791; Fax: 334-269-0720. Rev. Matthew A. Sindik, Dir.; Mr. Michael G. McCormack, Exec. Dir.

St. John's Soup Kitchen, Inc., 543 S. Union St., 36104. Tel: 334-264-6204; Fax: 334-262-3012.
E-mail: jjjbaker@mindspring.com
P.O. Box 230512, 36123-0512. Tel: 334-264-6274. Rev. William P. Folsom, Jr.

St. Margaret's Foundation, 818 S. Perry St., Ste. 2, 36104. Tel: 334-262-0785; Fax: 334-262-0786.
E-mail: docsms@worldnet.att.net
Susan Meehan, Pres.; Dick Hodges, Chm.; Jack Galassini, Sec. & Treas.

St. Margaret's Services, 818 S. Perry St., Ste. 2, 36104. Tel: 334-262-0784; Fax: 334-262-0786.
E-mail: docsms@worldnet.att.net

Susan Meehan, Pres.; Sr. Almeda Golson, D.C., Chm.; Sr. Judy Dusellier, D.C., Vice Chm.; Harold Parrish, Sec. & Treas. Daughters of Charity of St. Vincent de Paul 5. Care for the poor, frail elderly and homebound disabled through Elderly Outreach and Interfaith Volunteer Caregivers.

SELMA. *Edmundite Guild.* Society of St. Edmund, Inc. P.O. Drawer 490, 36701. Tel: 888-540-7722; Fax: 334-875-8189.
E-mail: Rogerlac27@aol.com
Rev. Roger J. La charite, S.S.E., Exec. Dir. Priests 1; Lay Person 1.

RELIGIOUS INSTITUTES OF MEN REPRESENTED IN THE ARCHDIOCESE

For further details refer to the corresponding bracketed number in the Religious Institute of Men or Women section.

[0200]—*Benedictine Monks.*—O.S.B.
[1100]—*Brothers of the Sacred Heart.* (New Orleans Prov.).—S.C.
[1330]—*Congregation of the Mission.* (Eastern Prov.).—C.M.
[1080]—*Congregation of the Resurrection.* (Chicago Prov.).—C.R.
[0690]—*Jesuit Fathers and Brothers.* (New Orleans Prov.).—S.J.
[0840]—*Missionary Servants of the Most Holy Trinity.*—S.T.
[0700]—*St. Joseph's Society of the Sacred Heart.* (Baltimore, MD).—S.S.J.
[0440]—*Society of Saint Edmund.* (Selma, AL).—S.S.E.

RELIGIOUS INSTITUTES OF WOMEN REPRESENTED IN THE ARCHDIOCESE

[3710]—*Congregation of the Sisters of Saint Agnes.*—C.S.A.
[1780]—*Congregation of the Sisters of the Third Order of St. Francis of Perpetual Adoration.*—F.S.P.A.
[0760]—*Daughters of Charity of St. Vincent de Paul.*—D.C.
[]—*Daughters of Mary Mother of Mercy.*—D.M.M.M.
[0820]—*Daughters of the Holy Spirit.*—D.H.S.
[0960]—*Daughters of Wisdom.*—D.W.
[0420]—*Discalced Carmelite Nuns.*—O.C.D.
[1050]—*Dominican Contemplative Nuns.*—O.P.
[1070-03]—*Dominican Sisters.*—O.P.
[1070-13]—*Dominican Sisters.*—O.P.
[1070-18]—*Dominican Sisters.*—O.P.
[]—*Franciscan Missionary Sisters.* Jamaica.—F.M.S.
[2575]—*Institute of the Sisters of Mercy of the Americas.*—R.S.M.
[2340]—*Little Sisters of the Poor.*—L.S.P.
[2790]—*Missionary Servants of the Most Blessed Trinity.*—M.S.B.T.
[3040]—*Oblate Sisters of Providence.*—O.S.P.
[]—*Order of St. Benedict.*—O.S.B.
[]—*Sisters for Christian Community* .—S.F.C.C.
[0430]—*Sisters of Charity of the Blessed Virgin Mary.*—B.V.M.
[2360]—*Sisters of Loretto At the Foot of the Cross.*—S.L.
[2550]—*Sisters of Mercy.*—R.S.M.
[3360]—*Sisters of Providence of Saint Mary-of-the-Woods, Indiana.*—S.P.
[1650]—*Sisters of St. Francis of Philadelphia.*—O.S.F.
[3830-14]—*Sisters of St. Joseph.*—S.S.J.
[3830-15]—*Sisters of St. Joseph.*—C.S.J.
[3840]—*Sisters of St. Joseph of Carondelet.*—C.S.J.
[3850]—*Sisters of St. Joseph of Chambery.*—C.S.J.
[1970]—*Sisters of the Holy Family of Nazareth.*—C.S.F.N.
[3480]—*Sisters of the Resurrection.*—C.R.
[2150]—*Sisters, Servants of the Immaculate Heart of Mary.*—I.H.M.
[3330]—*Union of the Sisters of the Presentation of the Blessed Virgin Mary.*—P.B.V.M.
[4170]—*Vincentian Sisters of Charity.* (Perryville, PA).—V.S.C.
[4190]—*Visitation Nuns.*—V.H.M.

NECROLOGY

† McArdle, Rev. Msgr. Joseph G., (Retired). —Died Aug. 23, 2000.
† O'Connor, Rev. Msgr. Patrick C, Gulf Shores, AL Our Lady of the Gulf Church. —Died Nov. 29, 2000.
† Rogers, Furman, (Retired). —Died June 3, 2000.

Diocese of Monterey in California

(Montereyensis in California)

Most Reverend

SYLVESTER D. RYAN, D.D.

Bishop of Monterey; ordained May 3, 1957; appointed Auxiliary Bishop of Los Angeles and Titular Bishop of Remesiana February 17, 1990; ordained Bishop on May 31, 1990; appointed Bishop of Monterey January 28, 1992; installed March 19, 1992. *E-mail address: Bishop@dioceseofmonterey.org*

Most Reverend

HARRY ANSELM CLINCH, D.D.

Retired Bishop of Monterey; ordained June 6, 1936; appointed Titular Bishop of Badiae and Auxiliary to the Bishop of Monterey-Fresno December 5, 1956; consecrated February 27, 1957; installed as Third Bishop of Monterey in California December 14, 1967; retired January 19, 1982. *Res., 3400 Paul Sweet Rd., C-119, Santa Cruz, CA, 95065.* Tel.: 408-476-5847.

Pastoral Office: 631 Abrego St., Monterey, CA, 93940. Tel.: 831-373-4345; Fax: 831-373-1175. Mailing Address: P.O. Box 2048, Monterey, CA, 93942-2048.

Web site address: www.dioceseofmonterey.org

E-mail address: diocese@dioceseofmonterey.org

ESTABLISHED NOVEMBER 20, 1849. RE-ESTABLISHED DECEMBER 14, 1967. FORMERLY DIOCESE OF MONTEREY-FRESNO.

Square Miles 21,916.

Legal Titles:

Diocese of Monterey in California.

The Diocese of Monterey Education and Welfare Corporation.

The Roman Catholic Bishop of Monterey, California, a Corporation Sole.

The Bishop Harry A. Clinch Endowment Fund of the Diocese of Monterey.

Catholic Charities of the Diocese of Monterey (Corporation).

Villa Serra Corporation.

Ave Maria Convalescent Hospital, Inc.

St. Francis Central Coast Catholic High School, Inc.

Comprises the Counties of Monterey, San Benito, San Luis Obispo and Santa Cruz in the State of California.

For legal titles of parishes and diocesan institutions, consult the Pastoral Office.

STATISTICAL OVERVIEW

Personnel	
Bishop	1
Retired Bishops	2
Retired Abbots	1
Priests: Diocesan Active in Diocese	47
Priests: Active Outside Diocese	1
Priests: Retired, Sick or Absent	22
Number of Diocesan Priests	70
Religious Priests in Diocese	21
Extern Priests in Diocese	6
Permanent Deacons in Diocese	2
Total Brothers	34
Total Sisters	108
Parishes	
Parishes	46
With Resident Pastor:	
Resident Diocesan Priests	35
Resident Religious Priests	8
Without Resident Pastor:	
Administered by Priests	4
Missions	9
Welfare	
Catholic Hospitals	1
Total Assisted	1,000
Health Care Centers	3
Total Assisted	13,500
Homes for the Aged	3
Total Assisted	396
Residential Care of Disabled	1
Total Assisted	3,400
Educational	
Diocesan Students in Other Seminaries	11
Seminaries, Religious	1
Students Religious	2
Total Seminarians	13
High Schools, Diocesan and Parish	2
Total Students	646
High Schools, Private	2
Total Students	977
Elementary Schools, Diocesan and Parish	11
Total Students	3,360
Elementary Schools, Private	3
Total Students	765
Catechesis/Religious Education:	
High School Students	1,750
Elementary Students	14,012
Total Students Under Catholic Instruction	21,523
Teachers in the Diocese:	
Priests	1
Brothers	4
Sisters	19
Lay Teachers	303
Vital Statistics	
Receptions into the Church:	
Infant Baptism Totals	6,620
Adult Baptism Totals	191
Received into Full Communion	385
First Communions	3,944
Confirmations	1,202
Marriages:	
Catholic	868
Interfaith	200
Total Marriages	1,068
Deaths	1,094
Total Catholic Population	313,405
Total Population	949,300

Former Prelates of the Diocese of Monterey—Rt. Rev. FRANCISCO GARCIA DIEGO Y MORENO, O.F.M., cons. Bishop of Both Californias, Oct. 1840; died April 30, 1846.—Most Rev. JOSEPH SADOC ALEMANY, O.P., cons. Bishop of Monterey, June 30, 1850; appt. first Archbishop of San Francisco, July 29, 1853; resigned and appointed Titular Archbishop of Pelusium, Dec. 28, 1884; died April 14, 1888.—Rt. Rev. THADDEUS AMAT, C.M., cons. Bishop of Monterey March 12, 1854 became Bishop of Monterey-Los Angeles, 1859; died May 12, 1878.—Rt. Rev. FRANCIS MORA, cons. Titular Bishop of Mosynopolis and Coadjutor to Bishop Amat, Aug. 3, 1873 became Bishop of Monterey-Los Angeles, 1878; resigned May 6, 1896; named Titular Bishop Hierapolis; died Aug. 3, 1905.—Rt. Rev. GEORGE MONTGOMERY, D.D., cons. April 8, 1894; Bishop of Tmul and Coadjutor-Bishop of Monterey-Los Angeles (cum jure successionis); succeeded to May 6, 1896; appt. Coadjutor-Archbishop of San Francisco, Titular Bishop of Auxum, Jan. 1, 1903; died Jan. 10, 1907.—Rt. Rev. THOMAS JAMES CONATY, cons. Nov. 24, 1901; Titular Bishop of Samos; appt. Bishop of Monterey-Los Angeles, March 27, 1903; died Sept. 18, 1915.—Most Rev. JOHN J. CANTWELL, D.D., LL.D., appt. Bishop of Monterey-Los Angeles, Sept. 21, 1917; cons. Dec. 5, 1917 assumed the title Bishop of Los Angeles-San Diego June 1, 1922; appt. Assistant to the Pontifical Throne, Sept. 30, 1929; elevated to Archepiscopal Dignity, June 11, 1936; installed Dec. 3, 1936; died Oct. 30, 1947.—Most Rev. JOHN B. MACGINLEY, D.D., cons. May 10, 1910; Bishop of Nueva Caceres; transferred to Monterey-Fresno as first Bishop, March 24, 1924; resigned Sept. 30, 1932; named Titular Bishop of Croae; died Oct. 18, 1969.—Most Rev. PHILIP G. SCHER, D.D., ord. June 6, 1903; appt. April 28, 1933; cons. June 29, 1933; died Jan. 3, 1953.—Most Rev. ALOYSIUS J. WILLINGER, C.SS.R., ord. July 2, 1911; appt. Bishop of Ponce, March 8, 1919; cons. October 28, 1929; appt. Titular Bishop of Bida and Coadjutor of Monterey-Fresno (cum jure successionis), December 12, 1946; installed Bishop of Monterey-Fresno, Jan. 3, 1953; appt. Assistant to the Pontifical Throne, Nov. 13, 1953; resigned Oct. 25, 1967; died July 25, 1973.—Most Rev. HARRY ANSELM CLINCH, D.D., ord. June 6, 1936; appt. Titular Bishop of Badiae and Auxiliary to the Bishop of Monterey-Fresno, Dec. 5, 1956; cons. Feb. 27, 1957; installed as Third Bishop of Monterey in California, Dec. 14, 1967; retired Jan. 19, 1982.—Most Rev. THADDEUS SHUBSDA, D.D., Fourth Bishop of Monterey; ord. April 26, 1950; Titular Bishop of Trau and Auxiliary Bishop of Los Angeles; Episcopal Ordination; appt. Feb. 19, 1977; named Bishop of Monterey in California, June 1, 1982; installed as fourth Bishop of Monterey, July 1, 1982; died April 26, 1991.—Rev. Msgr. CHARLES G. FATOOH, appt. Administrator of the Diocese of Monterey, April 26, 1991 - March 19, 1992.

Moderator of the Curia / Chancellor—Rev. Msgr. CHARLES G. FATOOH, *631 Abrego St., Monterey, 93940., Mailing Address: P.O. Box 2048, Monterey, 93942-2048.* Tel: 831-373-4345; Fax: 831-373-1175.

Vice Chancellor—Bro. JOHN F. O'BRIEN, C.F.X., K.C.H.S., *485 Church St., Monterey, 93940.* Tel: 831-373-2127; Fax: 831-373-3534.

Vicar General—Rev. Msgr. D. DECLAN MURPHY, V.G., *Carmel Mission Basilica, P.O. Box 2235, Carmel, 93921-2235.* Tel: 831-624-1271; Fax: 831-624-8050.

Vicar for Clergy—Rev. JERRY MCCORMICK, *St. Angela's Church, 146 8th St., Pacific Grove, 93950.* Tel: 831-655-4160; Fax: 831-372-5026.

Assistant Vicar for Clergy and Mentor for Clergy 1-10 Years—Rev. RICHARD O'HALLORAN, *1335 Byron Dr., Salinas, 93901.* Tel: 831-758-6285.

Assistant Vicar for Retired Clergy—Rev. RON WIECEK, C.P.P.S., *235 Main St., Soledad, 93960.* Tel: 831-678-2731; Fax: 831-678-2968.

Vicar for Religious—Sr. GABRIELA COVI-MAFFEI, I.M., *15785 Alto Way, Salinas, 93907.* Tel: 831-663-3675; Fax: 831-663-3749.

Pastoral Office—Administrative Assistants: DONA LOGEMAN ACUFF; IRENE CASAS; PATRICIA GRAB; Sr. MAUREEN ROONEY, C.S.C., *631 Abrego St., Monterey, 93940., Mailing Address: P.O. Box 2048, Monterey, 93942-2048.* Tel: 831-373-4345; Fax: 831-373-1175.

Pastoral Office, Ecclesiastical Notaries—DONA LOGEMAN ACUFF; IRENE CASAS; PATRICIA GRAB; Sr. MAUREEN ROONEY; GINA M. RUIZ.

Deans—Very Rev. CARL M.D. FARIA, V.U., Monterey; Very Rev. JOHN GRIFFIN, V.F., Santa Cruz; Very Rev. LARRY KAMTITSCH, V.F., Salinas; Very Rev. JAMES HENRY, V.F., San Luis Obispo.

Diocesan Consultors—Rev. Msgr. D. DECLAN MURPHY, V.G.; Rev. Msgr. CHARLES G. FATOOH, Chancellor; Very Revs. CARL M.D. FARIA, V.U.; JOHN C. GRIFFIN, V.F.; LARRY KAMBITSCH, V.F.; JAMES HENRY, V.F.

Diocesan Departments, Directors and Offices

Archivist—Bro. JOHN F. O'BRIEN, C.F.X., K.C.H.S., *485 Church St., Monterey, 93940.* Tel: 831-373-2127; Fax: 831-373-3534.

Attorneys—RICHARD K. HARRAY, Esq., *80 Garden Ct., Ste. 260, Monterey, 93940.* Tel: 831-373-3101; Fax: 831-373-6712. ALBERT S. HAM, Esq., *485 Church St., Monterey, 93940., Mailing Address: P.O. Box 2048, Monterey, 93942-2048.* Tel: 831-373-4345; Fax: 831-373-5765. MOLLY MCDONALD, Esq., *631 Abrego St., Monterey, 93940., Mailing Address: P.O. Box 2048, Monterey, 93942-2048.* Tel: 831-373-4345; Fax: 831-373-5765.

Business Manager & Diocesan Finance Officer—THOMAS H. RIORDAN, *631 Abrego St., Monterey, 93940.* Tel: 831-373-4345; Fax: 831-373-1175., *Mailing Address: P.O. Box 2048, Monterey, 93942-2048.*

Communication—"The Observer"; Rev. EDWARD J. KAMINSKI, C.S.C., Dir.; Most Rev. SYLVESTER D. RYAN, Publisher, *485 Church St., Monterey, 93940., Mailing Address: P.O. Box 2079, Monterey, 93942-2079.* Tel: 831-373-2919; Fax: 831-373-4510.

Curator—Sir RICHARD MENN, K.C.S.G., K.H.S., K.M., *3080 Rio Rd., Carmel, 93923.* Tel: 831-624-3600; Fax: 831-624-0658.

Finance Office—WILLIAM J. COAKER, II, Controller & Chief Investment Officer; ANNE M. MCGUIRE, Computer Services/Parish Business Outreach, Technical Support and Web Site Mgr., *580 Fremont St., Monterey, 93940., Mailing Address: P.O. Box 2048, Monterey, 93942-2048.* Tel: 831-373-4666; Fax: 831-373-2831.

Health Care Coordinator—Sr. JEANNE BURNS, O.P., *Dominican Santa Cruz Hospital, 1555 Soquel Dr., Santa Cruz, 95060.* Tel: 831-462-7670; Fax: 831-462-7555.

Human Resources—MOLLY A. MCDONALD, Esq.; STEPHANIE OLSEN, Admin. Asst., *631 Abrego St., Monterey, 93940., Mailing Address: P.O. Box 2048, Monterey, 93942-2048.* Tel: 831-373-4345; Fax: 831-373-5765.

Campus Ministry Department—Sr. MARY CATHERINE EVANS, O.P., Diocesan Dir., *435 Church St., Monterey, 93940., Mailing Address: P.O. Box 350, Monterey, 93942-0350.* Tel: 831-373-1608; Fax: 831-373-0173. Rev. ROLAND BUNDA, S.M., Dir. Campus Ministry Santa Cruz, *California State University at Monterey Bay, 285 Meder St., Santa Cruz, 95060.* Tel: 831-423-9400; Fax: 831-423-8163. Sr. THERESA HARPIN, C.S.J., Dir. Campus Ministry San Luis Obispo, *1472 Foothill Blvd., San Luis Obispo, 93401.* Tel: 805-543-4105; Fax: 831-543-5671.

Catechetical Ministries Department—14 Stone St., Salinas, 93901. Tel: 831-424-4076, Ext. 23; Fax: 831-424-5221. Sr. LYDIA SCHNEIDER, I.M., Dir. OLGA FLORES, Admin. Asst. Tel: 831-424-4076; Fax: 831-754-2474. SALLY EQUINOA, Consultant, San Luis Obispo Deanery, *221 Daly Ave., San Luis Obispo, 93405.* Tel: 805-541-1441.

Catholic Schools Department—435 Church St., Monterey, 93940., Mailing Address: P.O. Box 350, Monterey, 93942-0350. Tel: 831-373-1608; Fax: 831-373-0173. Sr. MARY CATHERINE EVANS, O.P., Supt. MARY MARCHI, Assoc. Admin.; MIRIAM "MIMI" SCHWERTFEGER, Asst. Dir.

Cemeteries—CLANCY D'ANGELO, Dir. Cemeteries, *Administrative Office, 792 Fremont St., Monterey, 93940., Mailing Address: P.O. Box 2048, Monterey, 93942-2048.* Tel: 831-373-4345; Fax: 831-373-4510.

Diocesan Tribunal—485 Church St., Monterey, 93940., Mailing Address: P.O. Box 350, Monterey, 93942-0350. Tel: 831-373-1833; Fax: 831-373-6761.

Judicial Vicar—Rev. KENNETH J. LAVERONE, M.A.

Administrator—FRAYLNE SAN FILIPPO, Admin. IRENE CASAS, Admin. Asst.

Judges—Revs. KENNETH J. LAVERONE; DAVID SCHUYLER, S.M., J.C.D.

Defenders of the Bond—Sr. LILIANA BONELLO, I.M., J.C.L.; Revs. PATRICK DOOLING; THOMAS KIEFFER, Orat. PAUL R. VALDEZ.

Advocates—Revs. JOHN C. GRIFFIN; MICHAEL MARINI; EUGENIO ARAMBURO; HEIBAR CASTANDA.

Promoter of Justice—Rev. THOMAS KIEFFER, Orat.

Notaries—DONA LOGEMAN ACUFF; IRENE CASAS; PATRICIA GRAB; FRAYLNE SAN FILIPPO; Sr. MAUREEN ROONEY; GINA M. RUIZ.

Divine Worship Department—Sr. BARBARA ANN LONG, O.P., Dir. Administrative Assistants: ANN KREYCHE; KELLY ODRON, *126 High St., Santa Cruz, 95060.* Tel: 831-423-4793; Fax: 831-423-4793.

Hispanic Ministry Department—Sr. PATRICIA MURTAGH, I.M., Dir. JUANITA ZEPEDA, Exec. Sec. BEATRIZ MUNOZ, Sec., *14 Stone St., Salinas, 93901.* Tel: 831-424-4076; Fax: 831-424-5221.

Migrant Ministry Coord.—MARINA OCAMPO, *14 Stone St., Salinas, 93901.* Tel: 831-424-4076; Fax: 831-424-5221.

Priestly Life & Ministry—Rev. MARK STETZ, *St. Elizabeth Ann Seton Church, 2050 Palisades Ave., Los Osos, 93402.* Tel: 805-528-5319; Fax: 805-528-8893.

Parish Life Ministry / Small Christian Communities—Sr. MOLLY NEVILLE, S.N.J.M., Dir. MARIA ORAZCO, Admin. Asst., *14 Stone St., Salinas, 93901.* Tel: 831-424-4076; Fax: 831-754-2474.

Respect Life / Family Life Ministry—Rev. DEREK HUGHES, Dir., *642 Trigo Lane, Paso Robles, 93446.* Tel: 805-238-2218; Fax: 805-238-2762.

Safety Coordinator—KEVIN DRABINSKI, Diocesan Safety Coord., *Old Mission Church, 751 Palm St., San Luis Obispo, 93401.* Tel: 805-781-8220; Fax: 805-781-8214.

Stewardship—Sr. LAURA GOEDKEN, O.P., Dir., *631 Abrego St., Monterey, 93940., Mailing Address: P.O. Box 2048, Monterey, 93942-2048.* Tel: 831-373-4345; Fax: 831-373-0302.

Youth and Young Adult Ministry—Rev. ROBERT STEIN, S.D.B., Dir. MARIA OROZCO, Admin. Asst., *14 Stone St., Salinas, 93901.* Tel: 831-424-4076; Fax: 831-754-2474.

Scouting—Rev. CARL M.D. FARIA, Chap., *303 Hillcrest Ave., Marina, 93933.* Tel: 831-384-5434; Fax: 831-384-7011.

Vocations Director—Sr. MOLLY NEVILLE, S.N.J.M., Dir. MARIA ORAZCO, Admin. Asst., *14 Stone St., Salinas, 93901.* Tel: 831-424-4076, Ext. 14; Fax: 831-754-2474. Rev. ANTONIO SANCHEZ, Asst. Dir., *Our Lady of the Assumption Church, 100 Salinas Rd., Watsonville, 95076.* Tel: 831-722-1931; Fax: 831-722-1254. Rev. RON WIECEK, C.P.P.S., Asst. Dir., *Our Lady of Solitude Church, 235 Main St., Soledad, 93960.* Tel: 831-678-2731.

Charismatics—Rev. GERONIMO CUEVAS, Diocesan Dir., *St. Mary of the Nativity Church, 1702 Second Ave., Salinas, 93905.* Tel: 831-758-1699; Fax: 831-758-4715.

Cursillo—Rev. MIKE MILLER, Spiritual Dir., *Sacred Heart Church, 22 Stone St., Salinas, 93901.* Tel: 831-424-1959; Fax: 831-424-0788. Rev. MICHAEL L. VOLK, Spiritual Dir., *St. Theodore's Church, Drawer B, Gonzales, 93926.* Tel: 831-675-3648; Fax: 831-675-8360.

Ecumenism—Rev. SCOTT (CORNELIUS) MCCARTHY, Dir., *Our Lady of Mt. Carmel Church, P.O. Box 195, Carmel Valley, 93924.* Tel: 831-659-2224; Fax: 831-659-9186.

Holy Childhood Association—Mrs. PATRICIA GRAB, Coord., *Diocese of Monterey, 631 Abrego St., Monterey, 93940.* Tel: 831-373-4345; Fax: 831-373-1175., *P.O. Box 2048, Monterey, 93942-2048.*

Native American Ministry—Rev. SCOTT (CORNELIUS) MCCARTHY, Dir., *Our Lady of Mt. Carmel Church, P.O. Box 195, Carmel Valley, 93924.* Tel: 831-659-2224; Fax: 831-659-9186.

Propagation of the Faith—Mrs. PATRICIA GRAB, Coord., *Diocese of Monterey, 631 Abrego St., Monterey, 93940.* Tel: 831-373-4345; Fax: 831-373-1175., *P.O. Box 2048, Monterey, 93942-2048.*

St. Joseph's Archive and Conference Center—485 Church St., Monterey, 93940.

St. Vincent de Paul—Rev. RICHARD BONJEAN, Dir., *994 Newington St., Salinas, 93906.* Tel: 831-444-8902.

Catholic Charities of the Diocese of Monterey—

Central Office—MARTINA S. O'SULLIVAN, Exec. Dir. BARBARA PASCAL, Assoc. Dir., *580 Fremont St., Monterey, 93940.* Tel: 831-375-1577; Fax: 831-373-3416.

Counseling Program—Tel: 831-375-3165.

Direct Material Aid—Tel: 831-375-1577.

Salinas Office—Buckley Hall, St. Mary of the Nativity Church, 1702 2nd St., Salinas, 93905. Tel: 831-422-0602; Fax: 831-422-0759.

Counseling—Tel: 831-375-3165.

Direct Material Aid—Tel: 831-375-1577.

Immigration—Tel: 831-422-0602.

Watsonville Office—406 Main St., #308, Watsonville, 95076. Tel: 831-722-2675; Fax: 831-722-9921.

Direct Material Aid—Tel: 831-722-2675.

Counseling—Tel: 831-722-2791.

Immigration—Tel: 831-722-2675.

Campaign for Human Development—MARTINA S. O'SULLIVAN, Dir., *580 Fremont St., Monterey, 93940.* Tel: 831-375-1577; Fax: 831-375-3416.

Catholic Relief Service—MARTINA S. O'SULLIVAN, Dir., *580 Fremont St., Monterey, 93940.* Tel: 831-375-1577; Fax: 831-375-3416.

Boards, Commissions, Committees and Councils

Administrative Committee Priest's Pension Plan—Most Rev. SYLVESTER D. RYAN; Rev. Msgr. CHARLES G. FATOOH; Revs. EUGENIO ARAMBURO; PETER CRIVELLO; GREG SANDMAN; MICHAEL L. CROSS, Chm. PAUL R. VALDEZ.

Ave Maria Board—Sr. M. CONSTANCE PETRUCELLI, O.S.F., Pres.; Sr. M. ROSANNA PELTIER, O.S.F., Sec.; Rev. Msgr. CHARLES G. FATOOH, Vice Pres. THOMAS H. RIORDAN, Treas.; Most Rev. SYLVESTER D. RYAN, Chm.

Bishop Harry A. Clinch Endowment Fund, The Bishop Sylvester D. Ryan Continuing Education Fund, The Bishop Shubsda Memorial Seminary Endowment Burse and The Cemetery Endowment Burse—Most Rev. SYLVESTER D. RYAN; Rev. Msgr. CHARLES G. FATOOH; Rev. EDWARD FITZ-HENRY; ROBERT SEMAS; ELIZABETH HELFRICH; MICHAEL MORRIS, Chm. RONALD PASQUINELLI; LARRY SAGE; LEAH DUNCAN; JOHN WECKER; THOMAS H. RIORDAN, Ex Officio, Diocesan Business Mgr.; Sr. LAURA GOEDKEN, O.P., Dir. Stewardship.

Building Commission—Contact Persons: Rev. JOHN GRIFFIN, *Holy Eucharist Church, 527 Corralitos Rd., Corralitos, 95076.* Tel: 831-722-5490; Fax: 831-722-8157. THOMAS H. RIORDAN, *Diocese of Monterey, 631 Abrego St., P.O. Box 2048, Monterey, 93942-2048.* Tel: 831-373-4345; Fax: 831-373-1175.

Catholic Charities—DIANE SAIGN; ROBIN L. COURTNEY, Pres.; Rev. Msgr. CHARLES G. FATOOH; MADELINE WRIGHT; Very Rev. JERRY MCCORMICK, V.F.; CELIA ORGANISTA; Most Rev. SYLVESTER D. RYAN; LARRY SAGE; BILL SLEZAK; MARTINA O'SULLIVAN, Exec. Dir. THOMAS H. RIORDAN, Diocesan Business Mgr. DONA LOGEMAN ACUFF, Recording Sec.

Diocesan Consultors—Rev. Msgr. D. DECLAN MURPHY, V.G.; Rev. Msgr. CHARLES G. FATOOH, Chancellor; Very Revs. CARL M.D. FARIA, V.U.; JOHN C. GRIFFIN, V.F.; LARRY KAMBITSCH, V.F.; JAMES HENRY, V.F.

Ecumenical Commission—DICK GORMAN; Sr. MARY KELLY, S.A.; Revs. IGNATIUS MARTINEZ; SCOTT MCCARTHY, Chm.; Bro. TONY YOUNG.

Emergency Preparedness Task Force—VIC COLLINS; KEVIN DRABINSKI; Sr. MARY CATHERINE EVANS, O.P.; Rev. Msgr. CHARLES G. FATOOH; Chief JAMES GARDINER; MOLLY MCDONALD; JACK MCGILVRAY, Chm.; Chief TERRY MEDINA; MARTINA O'SULLIVAN; THOMAS H. RIORDAN; Most Rev. SYLVESTER D. RYAN; TOM TREANOR.

Finance Council—Rev. Msgr. CHARLES G. FATOOH; RICHARD FALGE; TOD SANCHEZ; GARY WEITZ; Sr. JOANNE WIMMER, O.P.; Rev. Msgr. D. DECLAN MURPHY; ED MUSSELWHITE; Sr. CARLOTTA O'DONNELL; RONALD PASQUINELLI; Most Rev. SYLVESTER D. RYAN; Rev. PAUL R. VALDEZ. Ex Officio: THOMAS H. RIORDAN, Diocesan Business Mgr. DONA LOGEMAN ACUFF, Recording Sec.

Historical Review Committee—Sir RICHARD MENN, K.C.S.G., K.H.S., K.M., Diocesan Curator; Bro. JOHN F. O'BRIEN, C.F.X., K.C.H.S., Diocesan Archivist; ELIZABETH HILLEARY; Sir LEWIS CHARLES SCOTT; Rev. Msgr. FRANCIS J. WEBER.

Insurance Committee—MICHAEL KELLY, Chm. MOLLY MCDONALD; THOMAS H. RIORDAN; Rev. PAUL R. VALDEZ.

Lay Employees Non-Qualified Pension Committee—Rev. Msgr. CHARLES G. FATOOH; Rev. Msgr. D. DECLAN MURPHY; THOMAS H. RIORDAN, Chm. Consultants: ALBERT S. HAM; RICK HARRAY; TONY KARACHALE; STEFANIE OLSEN, Recording Sec.

Lay Employee Pension Plan Committee—Rev. Msgr. CHARLES G. FATOOH; CLANCY D'ANGELO; RONALD PASQUINELLI; THOMAS H. RIORDAN, Chm. TOD D.

SANCHEZ. Consultants: ALBERT S. HAM; RICK HARRAY; TONY KARACHALE; STEFANIE OLSEN, Recording Sec.

Observer Advisory Board—ALBERT CROSS; Rev. CARL FARIA; Bro. JOHN F. O'BRIEN, C.F.X., Chm. TOM RIORDAN; Sr. LYDIA SCHNEIDER, I.M.; BUDD STUBBS; Sr. MARIE WIEDNER, O.P.; Rev. ED KAMINSKI, C.S.C., Dir. Communications; DONA LOGEMAN ACUFF, Recording Sec.

Presbyteral Council—Very Revs. CARL M.D. FARIA, V.U.; JAMES R. HENRY, V.F.; LARRY KAMBITSCH, V.F.; Revs. PATRICK DOOLING; JOSEPH BUTTERS; MIGUEL GRAJEDA; JAMES NISBET; RICHARD O'HALLORAN; MARK STETZ; Rev. Msgr. CHARLES G. FATOOH; Very Rev. JOHN GRIFFIN, V.F.; Revs. JERRY MAHER; JERRY MCCORMICK; Rev. Msgr. D. DECLAN MURPHY; Most Rev. SYLVESTER D. RYAN; PATRICIA GRAB, Recording Sec.

Priestly Life and Ministry—ANDY ANDERSON; Revs. SCOTT MCCARTHY; JERRY MCCORMICK; MICHAEL MILLER; Sr. MOLLY NEVILLE, S.N.J.M.; Most Rev. SYLVESTER D. RYAN; Revs. RON SHIRLEY; RON WIECEK, C.PP.S.; EUGENIO ARAMBURO; AGNES LEONARDICH; Rev. MARK STETZ, Chm. JONDELL DEVEAUX WRIGHT.

Priest's Personnel Board—Rev. Msgr. CHARLES G. FATOOH; Very Revs. JOHN GRIFFIN, V.F.; CARL M.D. FARIA, V.U.; JAMES HENRY, V.F.; LARRY KAMBITSCH, V.F.; Revs. MICHAEL A. MARINI; PETER CRIVELLO; RON SHIRLEY; Very Rev. JERRY MCCORMICK, V.U.; Most Rev. SYLVESTER D. RYAN; Rev. ANTONIO SANCHEZ.

Real Estate Committee—RICK KENNIFER; DAVID KENT, Chm. THOMAS H. RIORDAN; RICHARD SELDOW.

Parish Life Ministry (Small Christian Communities)—Advisory Committee: Rev. MICHAEL MILLER; Sr. MOLLY NEVILLE, S.N.J.M., Dir. JONDELL DEVEAUX WRIGHT; PATRICK CONWAY.

Stewardship Board—DON CHAPIN; BARBARA CHAPIN; PETER CONIGLIO; LEN DART; ARLETTE DART; TOM SHIVELY; NORINNE SHIVELY; Sr. JULIE HYER, O.P.; BEVERLY KORDSMEIER; ROGER MAIROSE; WENDY MAIROSE; BRUCE MANILDI; CAROLYN MANILDI; CLEM RICHARDSON; JOHN RONCA; TRACY RONCA; Most Rev. SYLVESTER D. RYAN; Rev. RON SHIRLEY; CHRISTOPHER SIMPSON; SUZANNE SIMPSON; Rev. MICHAEL VOLK. Ex Officios: Rev. Msgr. CHARLES G. FATOOH; Sr. LAURA GOEDKEN, O.P.; THOMAS H. RIORDAN.

Villa Serra Board—Rev. Msgr. CHARLES G. FATOOH, Pres. ROGER HITE; Sr. JULIE HYER, O.P.; MCKENZIE MOSS; THOMAS H. RIORDAN; Most Rev. SYLVESTER D. RYAN; MICHAEL WEATHERFORD.

Vocations Board—Revs. ROLAND BUNDA, S.M.; RON GREEN; IGNACIO MARTINEZ; Sr. SUZANNE MILLER, F.M.A.; Sr. MOLLY NEVILLE, S.N.J.M., Dir.; Sr. ROSEANGELA FILIPPINI, I.M.; Rev. JAMES NISBET; Most Rev. SYLVESTER D. RYAN; Revs. ANTONIO SANCHEZ, Asst. Dir. MICHAEL A. VOLK; RON WIECEK, C.PP.S., Asst. Dir. & Priest Mentor; JONDELL DEVEAUX WRIGHT; PATRICIA GRAB, Recording Sec.

Web Site Development Committee—MARIO FEDERICO; Rev. Msgr. CHARLES G. FATOOH; ANNE MCGUIRE; TOM RIORDAN; Revs. ED KAMINSKI, C.S.C.; JOSEPH L. OCCHIUTO.

CLERGY, PARISHES, MISSIONS AND PAROCHIAL SCHOOLS

CITY OF MONTEREY
(Monterey County)

1—CATHEDRAL OF SAN CARLOS BORROMEO (1770), Revs. Joseph L. Occhiuto, Rector; Paul P. Murphy (Ireland); Deacon Harold Miller, Pastoral Assoc. In res., Rev. Edward J. Kaminski, C.S.C.
Mailing Address: 500 Church St., 93940. Tel: 831-373-2628; Fax: 831-373-0518.
Res., 550 Church St., 93940.
Preschool—450 Church St., 93940. Tel: 831-375-1324; Fax: 831-375-9736. Sr. Mary Jane Clark, O.P., Prin.
Dominican Sisters (Adrian, MI) 1; Lay Teachers 17; Students 300.
Catechesis/Religious Programs—Tel: 831-373-4101; Fax: 831-373-0510.
Students 154.

OUTSIDE THE CITY OF MONTEREY

Aptos, Santa Cruz Co., Resurrection (1968), Rev. Peter A. Crivello.
Res., 7600 Soquel Dr., P.O. Box 87, 95001. Tel: 831-688-4300; Fax: 831-688-6921.
School—Good Shepherd School (Inter-Parish), (Grades PreK-8). See Star of the Sea Parish, Santa Cruz. Tel: 831-429-1018; Fax: 831-429-5832.
Catechesis/Religious Programs—Tel: 831-688-4300; Fax: 831-688-6921.
Students 120.

Arroyo Grande, San Luis Obispo Co., St. Patrick (1886), Revs. James Henry, Pastor; Joseph Butters.
Res., 501 Fair Oaks Ave., P.O. Box 860, 93421. Tel: 805-489-2680; Fax: 805-489-1316.
School—(Grades K-8) 900 W. Branch St., 93420. Tel: 805-489-1210; Fax: 805-489-7662. Kathy Tyree, Prin.
Sisters of Mercy 3; Lay Teachers 13; Students 335.
Catechesis/Religious Programs—Tel: 805-481-2990; Fax: 805-489-4365.
Students 335.
Mission—Oceano, San Luis Obispo Co., St. Francis of Assisi. 17th & Beach.
Shamrock Thrift Shop—924 Grand Ave., Grover City, 93433. Tel: 805-481-0612. Alana Owen.

Atascadero, San Luis Obispo Co., St. William's (1948), Very Rev. Joseph R. Hercek, V.F.
Mailing Address: P.O. Box 2230, 93423. Tel: 805-466-0849; Fax: 805-461-0743.
Res., 6410 Santa Lucia Rd., 93422.
Catechesis/Religious Programs—Students 325.

Boulder Creek, Santa Cruz Co., St. Michael (1921), Rev. Paul R. Valdez.
Res., 13005 Pine St., 95006. Tel: 831-338-6112; Fax: 831-338-7522.
Catechesis/Religious Programs—Students 65.

Cambria, San Luis Obispo Co., Santa Rosa (1961), Rev. Dennis Gilbert.
Res., 1174 Main St., 93428. Tel: 805-927-4816; Fax: 805-927-2880. [CEM]
Catechesis/Religious Programs—Tel: 805-924-1728.
Students 106.

Capitola, Santa Cruz Co., St. Joseph (1904), Rev. Patrick Dooling; Sr. Marie Wiedner, O.P., Pastoral Assoc.; Tom McNamara, Pastoral Assoc./Business Mgr.
Res., 435 Monterey Ave., 95010. Tel: 831-475-8211; Fax: 831-475-2601.
School—Good Shepherd School (Inter-Parish), (Grades K-8). See Star of the Sea Parish, Santa Cruz and Resurrection Church, Aptos. Tel: 831-476-4000; Fax: 831-476-0948.
Catechesis/Religious Programs—Tel: 831-475-9510; Fax: 831-475-2601.
Students 273.

Carmel, Monterey Co., San Carlos Borromeo Basilica (1771) (American). (Carmel Mission). Rev. Msgr. D. Declan Murphy. In res., Rev. Martin McDonald.
Res., Rio Rd. and Lasuen Dr., P.O. Box 2235, 93921. Tel: 831-624-1271; Fax: 831-624-8050.
School—Junipero Serra School, (Grades K-8) 2992 Lasuen Dr., 93923. Tel: 831-624-8322. Ruth Matz, Prin.
Lay Teachers 14; Students 226.
Catechesis/Religious Programs—Tel: 831-624-6846.
Students 150.
Mission—Big Sur, Monterey Co., St. Francis of the Redwoods, Hwy. 1, Big Sur, 93920.
Chapel—Blessed Sacrament.

Carmel Valley, Monterey Co., Our Lady of Mt. Carmel (1953), Rev. Cornelius Scott McCarthy.
Res., 9 El Caminito, P.O. Box 195, 93924. Tel: 831-659-2224; Fax: 831-659-9186.
Catechesis/Religious Programs—Students 60.

Castroville, Monterey Co., Our Lady of Refuge (1869), Rev. Rudy Ruiz.
Res., 11140 Preston St., 95012. Tel: 831-633-4015; Fax: 831-633-4653. [JC]
Catechesis/Religious Programs—Tel: 831-633-4016.
Students 480.

Cayucos, San Luis Obispo Co., St. Joseph (1905), Rev. Anthony Gurnell, Admin.
Res., 360 Park Ave., P.O. Box 437, 93430. Tel: 805-995-3243; Fax: 805-995-2838.
Catechesis/Religious Programs—Students 14.

Corralitos, Santa Cruz Co., Holy Eucharist (1969), Rev. John Cullen Griffin.
Res., 527 Corralitos Rd., 95076. Tel: 831-722-5490; Fax: 831-722-5421.
Catechesis/Religious Programs—Students 150.

Davenport, Santa Cruz Co., St. Vincent De Paul (1935), Rev. Siro Dal Degan, O.S.J.
Res., 544 W. Cliff Drive, Santa Cruz, 95060. Tel: 831-471-1702; 429-1426; Fax: 831-457-1317.
Catechesis/Religious Programs—123 Marine View Ave., 95017.
Students 11.

Felton, Santa Cruz Co., St. John's (1952), Rev. Michael L. Cross.
Res., Russell at Hwy. 9, P.O. Box M-1, 95018. Tel: 831-335-4657; Fax: 831-335-4648.
Catechesis/Religious Programs—Students 48.

Gonzales, Monterey Co., St. Theodore (1892), Rev. Michael Volk.
Office: 125 S. Center St., 93926.
Res., 120 First St., P.O. Drawer B, 93926. Tel: 831-675-3648; Fax: 831-675-8360. [JC]
Catechesis/Religious Programs—Tel: 408-675-2100; Fax: 408-675-2975.
Students 705.
Mission—Chualar, Monterey Co., Chualar Mission, Scott & Grant Streets, Chualar. Tel: 831-679-2981.

Greenfield, Monterey Co., Holy Trinity (1951) (Mexican-Swiss-Italian), Revs. Eugenio Aramburo; Alberto Cabrera.
Res., 803 Elm Ave., Box 276, 93927. Tel: 831-674-5428; Fax: 831-674-5285.
Catechesis/Religious Programs—Tel: 831-674-3695. Rosa Garcia, D.R.E.
Students 507.

Hollister, San Benito Co., Sacred Heart (1877). Merged with St. Benedict, Hollister to form Sacred Heart/St. Benedict, Hollister.

St. Benedict, San Benito Co. Merged with Sacred Heart, Hollister to form Sacred Heart/St. Benedict Catholic Community, Hollister.

Sacred Heart/St. Benedict Catholic Community (1877), Rev. Msgr. Charles Fatooh, Admin.; Revs. Miguel Grajeda; Richard Clark; Robert Stein. In res., Rev. Fabian Vela.
Res., 540 College St., P.O. Box 1040, 95024. Tel: 831-637-9212; Fax: 831-637-7299. [CEM]
Church—St. Benedict, 1200 Fairview Rd., 95023. Tel: 831-637-6600.
Pastoral Center—680 College St., P.O. Box 1040, 95023.
School—(Grades K-8) 670 College St., 95023. Tel: 831-637-4157; Fax: 831-637-4164. Mr. Ray Burnell, Prin.
Sisters 1; Lay Teachers 24; Students 505.
Catechesis/Religious Programs—Tel: 831-637-8291. Tish Scargill, D.R.E.
Students 710.
Chapel—Hollister, Sacred Heart.
Station—St. Benedict.

Jolon, Monterey Co., San Antonio Mission (1771), Rev. John E. Gini, O.F.M. In res., Bros. Chris Rogan, O.F.M.; Anthony F. Lavorin, O.F.M.
Res., Box 803, 93928. Tel: 831-385-4478; Fax: 831-386-9332.
Mission—Jolon, Monterey Co., South Shore of Lake San Antonio.
Catechesis/Religious Programs—Students 20.

King City, Monterey Co., St. John the Baptist (1891) (Hispanic), Rev. Lawrence J. Kambitsch.
Res., 504 N. Third St., 93930. Tel: 831-385-3377; Fax: 831-385-3317.
Catechesis/Religious Programs—Tel: 831-385-3464. Cyndy LaFont, D.R.E.
Students 330.
Mission—San Lucas, Monterey Co., St. Luke, Main St., 93954.

Los Gatos, Santa Cruz Co., Christ Child (1983), Rev. Marvin J. Steffes, C.PP.S.
Res., 23230 Summit Rd., 95033. Tel: 408-353-2210; Fax: 408-353-8680.
Catechesis/Religious Programs—Students 45.

Los Osos, San Luis Obispo Co., St. Elizabeth Ann Seton (1984), Rev. Mark Stetz.
Res., 2050 Palisades Ave., 93402. Tel: 805-528-5319; Fax: 805-528-8893.
Catechesis/Religious Programs—Tel: 805-528-4019.
Students 179.

Marina, Monterey Co., St. Jude Parish Community (1963) (Filipino-Korean), Rev. Carl M.D. Faria.
Res., 303 Hillcrest Ave., 93933-3599. Tel: 831-384-5434; Fax: 831-384-7011.
Catechesis/Religious Programs—Tel: 831-384-8268.
Students 203.

Morro Bay, San Luis Obispo Co., St. Timothy (1950), Rev. Edward J. Holterhoff; Rev. Msgr. Cornelius Sweeney, Pastor Emeritus.
Mailing Address: P.O. Box 1449, 93443-1449.
Res., 962 Piney Way, 93442. Tel: 805-772-2840; Fax: 805-772-3184.
Catechesis/Religious Programs—Tel: 805-772-9272. Toni Guerra, D.R.E.
Students 15.

Nipomo, San Luis Obispo Co., St. Joseph (1968), Revs. James J. Frerkes; Enrique Herrera.
Res., 298 S. Thompson, 93444. Tel: 805-929-1922; Fax: 805-929-2662.
Catechesis/Religious Programs—Tel: 805-929-3730.
Students 159.

Pacific Grove, Monterey Co., St. Angela (1928), Revs. Anthony Phuc, C.SS.R., Assoc. Pastor; Jerry McCormick.
Res., 161 Ninth St., 93950. Tel: 831-655-4160; Fax: 831-372-5026.
Office: 146 Eighth St., 93950.
Preschool—136 Eighth St., 93950. Tel: 831-372-3555; Fax: 831-372-3555. Virginia Ziomek, Prin.
Catechesis/Religious Programs—Tel: 831-373-6311.
Students 235.

Paso Robles, San Luis Obispo Co., St. Rose (1922), Revs. Derek Hughes (Ireland); Ignacio Martinez (Mexico); Sr. Maris Stella O'Loghlen, Pastoral Assoc.
Office: 642 Trigo Ln., P.O. Box 790, 93447. Tel: 805-238-2218; Fax: 805-238-2762.
Res., 820 Creston Rd., P.O. Box 790, 93447. Tel: 805-238-2218; Fax: 805-238-2762. [CEM][JC]
School—(Grades PreK-8) 900 Tucker Ave., 93446. Tel: 805-238-0304; Fax: 805-238-7393. James Brescia, Prin.
Lay Teachers 17; Students 331.
Catechesis/Religious Programs—Tel: 805-239-2412; Fax: 805-238-2762.
Students 374.

Pismo Beach, San Luis Obispo Co., St. Paul the Apostle (1930), Revs. Charles Kozanecki, O.F.M.Conv.; Thomas Czeck, O.F.M.Conv. In res., Rev. Peter Parchem, O.F.M.Conv., Pastor Emeritus.
Res., 800 Bello St., 93449. Tel: 805-773-2219; Fax: 805-773-8617. [JC]
Catechesis/Religious Programs—Students 50.

Salinas, Monterey Co.,

1—Christ the King, (1995) (Hispanic), Rev. Manuel Canal.
Res., 240 Calle Cebu, 93901. Tel: 831-422-6543; Fax: 831-422-7218.
Religious Education Office: Tel: 831-422-6722.
Catechesis/Religious Programs—Students 440.

2—Sacred Heart, (1877), Revs. Michael J. Miller; James L. Plastino; Antonio Cortes.
Res., 22 Stone St., 93901-2643. Tel: 831-424-1959; Fax: 831-424-0788.
School—(Grades K-8) 123 W. Market St., 93901. Tel: 831-771-1310; Fax: 831-771-1314. Sr. Paulette Tiefenbrunn, S.S.N.D., Prin.
Sisters 3; Lay Teachers 10; Students 296.
Catechesis/Religious Programs—Tel: 831-772-8232. D.R.E.: Carolyn Benoit; Alicia Cordova.
Students 600.

3—St. Mary of the Nativity, (1947), Revs. Geronimo E. Cuevas; Felix Caicedo. In res., Rev. Jose J. Montoya.
Res., 1702 Second Ave., 93905. Tel: 831-758-1669; Fax: 831-758-4715.
Catechesis/Religious Programs—Tel: 831-422-9964.
Students 730.

4—Madonna Del Sasso, (1960), Revs. Ronald R. Shirley; Walter Espinoza; Sr. Angela Milioto, R.S.H.M., Pastoral Assoc.
Res., 320 E. Laurel Dr., 93906. Tel: 831-422-5323; Fax: 831-422-0536.
School—(Grades K-8) 20 Santa Teresa Way, 93906. Tel: 831-424-7813; Fax: 831-424-3359.
Sisters of Notre Dame 1; Lay Teachers 11; Students 343.
Catechesis/Religious Programs—Tel: 831-425-5323.
Students 455.

San Juan Bautista, San Benito Co., San Juan Bautista (1797) (Hispanic). (Old Mission). Rev. Edward Fitz-Henry.
Res., 406 Second St., P.O. Box 400, 95045. Tel: 831-623-2127; Fax: 831-623-2433. [CEM]
Catechesis/Religious Programs—Tel: 831-623-4178.
Students 180.

San Luis Obispo, San Luis Obispo Co., San Luis Obispo (1772). (Old Mission). Revs. Jerry Maher; Charles J. Tilley, S.J.; Carlton Whitten, S.J.; John Arul.
Res., 751 Palm St., 93401. Tel: 805-781-8220; Fax: 805-781-8214.
Preschool—221 Daly Ave., 93401. Tel: 805-549-8819. Monica Fagan, Prin.
School—(Grades PreK-8) 761 Broad St., 93401. Tel: 805-543-6019; Fax: 805-543-6246. Monica Fagan, Prin.
Lay Teachers 22; Students 355.
Catechesis/Religious Programs—Students 222.
Nativity of Our Lady (1964), Rev. Michael Cicinato; Deacon David Leach; Merlene Doko, M.A., Pastoral Assoc.
Res., 221 Daly Ave., 93405-1099. Tel: 805-544-2357; Fax: 805-544-6756.
Catechesis/Religious Programs—Students 132.

San Miguel, San Luis Obispo Co., San Miguel (1797). (Old Mission). Rev. Christopher Tomatis, O.F.M. Pastoral Assocs.: Sr. Loretta Guevarra, S.A.; Sr. Maria Del Rey Perezchica, S.A.
Res., 775 Mission St., P.O. Box 69, 93451. [CEM]
Parish—Tel: 805-467-2131; Fax: 805-467-2141.
Catechesis/Religious Programs—Tel: 805-238-6499; Fax: 805-467-3448.
Students 97.
Missions—San Ardo, Monterey Co., Our Lady of Ransom; Bradley, Monterey Co., Our Lady of Guadalupe.
Station—Heritage Ranch.

Santa Cruz, Santa Cruz Co., Holy Cross (1791), Revs. Michael A. Marini; Sergio Valdivia.
Res., 126 High St., 95060. Tel: 831-423-4182; Fax: 831-423-1043. [CEM 3][JC 2]
School—(Grades K-8) 150 Emmet St., 95060. Tel: 831-423-4447; Fax: 831-423-0752. Sr. Jean Williams, Prin.
Lay Teachers 13; Students 235.
Catechesis/Religious Programs—Tel: 831-458-3041; Fax: 831-458-1043.
Students 305.
Star of the Sea (1947), Revs. Rene Iturbe, S.M.; Hector Cruz, S.M.
Res., 515 Frederick St., 95062. Tel: 831-429-1018; Fax: 831-429-5832.
Good Shepherd Preschool—(Inter-Parish) 2727 Mattison Ln., 95062. Tel: 831-476-4000; Fax: 831-476-0948. Celeste Kathleen O'Donnel, Prin.
Students 140.
Catechesis/Religious Programs—Luis Enrique Motta Amezquita, D.R.E.
Students 225.
Chapel—Villa Maria del Mar, Tel: 831-475-1236; Fax: 831-475-8867.

Santa Margarita, San Luis Obispo Co., Santa Margarita de Cortona (1934), Rev. Joseph Grech, Admin.
Res., 22515 H St., P.O. Box 350, 93453-0350. Tel: 805-438-5383; Fax: 805-438-4313. [JC]
Catechesis/Religious Programs—Students 49.
Mission—Carrissa Plains, San Luis Obispo Co., St. James Mission, P.O. Box 3055, 93453. Tel: 805-475-2222.

Scotts Valley, Santa Cruz Co., San Agustin (1969), Rev. Matthew Pennington.
Res., 257 Glenwood Dr., 95066. Tel: 831-438-3633; Fax: 831-438-0973.
Catechesis/Religious Programs—Students 255.

Seaside, Monterey Co., St. Francis Xavier (1950), Rev. Heibar Castaneda, Admin. In res., Rev. Msgr. Charles G. Fatooh.
Res., 1475 LaSalle Ave., P.O. Box 247, 93955. Tel: 831-394-8546; Fax: 831-394-5414.
Catechesis/Religious Programs—Students 305.

Soledad, Monterey Co., Our Lady of Solitude (1933) (Spanish), Rev. Ronald P. Wiecek, C.PP.S.
Res., 235 Main St., 93960. Tel: 831-678-2731; Fax: 831-678-2968. [JC]
Catechesis/Religious Programs—Tel: 831-678-1277. Sr. Rosangela Filippini, D.R.E.
Students 725.
Mission—Soledad, Monterey Co., Nuestra Senora de la Soledad, Rte. 1, Box 72, 93960. Tel: 408-678-2586.

Spreckels, Monterey Co., St. Joseph (1969), Rev. Jim Nisbet.
Res., One Railroad Ave., P.O. Box 7158, 93962. Tel: 831-455-2249; Fax: 831-455-9357.
Catechesis/Religious Programs—St. Joseph's Religion Center, 15 First St., P.O. Box 7158, 93962. Tel: 831-455-8720; Fax: 831-455-9357. Sr. Liliana Bonello, I.M., J.C.L., D.R.E.
Students 400.

Tres Pinos, San Benito Co., Immaculate Conception (1904), Rev. Larry Betrozoff.
Res., 7290 Airline Hwy., P.O. Box 247, 95075. Tel: 831-628-3216; 628-3060 (Hall); Fax: 831-628-3602.
Catechesis/Religious Programs—Alice Farnham, D.R.E.
Students 100.

Watsonville, Santa Cruz Co., Our Lady Help of Christians (1854) (Portuguese), Revs. Harold Danielson, S.D.B.; Justo Davila, S.D.B.; John Roche, S.D.B.
Res., 2401 E. Lake Ave., 95076. Tel: 831-722-2665; Fax: 831-722-8305.
St. Patrick (1861), Revs. Gregory Sandman; Jose Chavez; Ronald Green.
Res., 721 Main St., 95076. Tel: 831-724-1317; Fax: 831-724-1627.
Catechesis/Religious Programs—Tel: 831-724-2141. Gregoria Alvarez, D.R.E. (English & Spanish).
Students 890.
Our Lady of the Assumption (1953) (Hispanic), Rev. J. Antonio Sanchez.
Res., 100 Salinas Rd., Pajaro, 95076. Tel: 831-722-1104; Fax: 831-722-1931. [CEM]
Catechesis/Religious Programs—Tel: 831-722-9938. Cristofina Carrillo, D.R.E.
Students 601.

Shrines

Santa Cruz, Santa Cruz Co., Shrine of St. Joseph Guardian of the Redeemer (1952),
Res., 544 W. Cliff Dr., 95060-6147. Tel: 831-471-0442; Fax: 831-457-1317. Rev. Philip Massetti, O.S.J.
Guardian of the Redeemer Bookstore—Tel: 831-471-1700; Fax: 831-457-1317.

Chaplains of Public Institutions

Atascadero. *Atascadero State Hospital.* Rev. Richard Miskella.
Boulder Creek. *Ben Lomond Youth Conservation Camp.* Vacant.
Paso Robles. *El Paso de Robles School.* Dept. of the Youth Authority. Sr. Mary E. McKay, S.N.J.M.
San Luis Obispo. *California Men's Colony East.* Vacant.
California Men's Colony West. Rev. Michael T. Bell.
Soledad. *Correctional Training Facility.* Rev. Joel Almendras.
Salinas Valley State Prison. Rev. Michael A. Bethancourt.

On Duty Outside the Diocese:
Reverend Fathers—
Adams, Michael T., Archdiocese of Samoa, APIA, Fetuolemoana, P.O. Box 532 APIA, Western Samoa. Tel: 685-20-400 20-401
Cadera, James R., 601-C Washington, Coalinga, CA 93210. Tel: 209-934-1450

Special Assignment:
Reverend Monsignors—
Fatooh, Charles G., Chancellor & Moderator of the Curia, Diocese of Monterey, P.O. Box 2048, Monterey, CA 93940. Tel: 408-373-4345
Reverend Fathers—
Almendras, Joel, P.O. Box 873, Salinas, CA 93902
Bethancourt, Michael A., Salinas Valley State Prison, P.O. Box 1020, Soledad, CA 93960
Hill, Scott F., O.M.I., Catholic Chap., Dominican Santa Cruz Hospital, 1555 Soquel Ave., Santa Cruz, CA 95065. Tel: 408-462-7707; Fax: 408-462-7558
Laverone, Kenneth J., O.F.M., Judicial Vicar, St. Francis Church, 1066-26th St., Sacramento, CA 95816. Tel: 916-448-8924; 916-443-7335 (Fax)
Sanchez, Antonio, Asst. Dir. of Vocations, Our Lady of the Assumption, 100 Salinas Rd., Watsonville, CA 95076. Tel: 408-722-1104; Fax: 408-722-1254
Wiecek, Ronald P., C.PP.S., Asst. Dir. of Vocations & Vicar for Clergy, Our Lady of Solitude Church, 235 Main St., Soledad, CA 93960. Tel: 831-678-2731; (Fax 831-678-2968)

Retired:
Reverend Monsignors—
Kennedy, John, P.O. Box 4023, Felton, CA 95018. Tel: 408-335-3119
MacMahon, Eamon, 24631 Guadalupe St., Carmel, CA 93923. Tel: 408-624-2275
Marron, James, 246 Ridge Rd., Pismo Beach, CA 93449. Tel: 805-773-3549
Morgan, Thomas, 1118 Victoria St., Hollister, CA 95023. Tel: 408-637-1084
Stieger, Joseph, c/o 161 Broad St., San Luis Obispo, CA 93405. Tel: 805-543-3284
Sweeney, Cornelius, 962 Piney Way, Morro Bay, CA 93442
Reverend Fathers—
Bonjean, Richard, 994 Newington St., Salinas, CA 93906. Tel: 831-444-8902
Carvajal, Raul H.
Cowan, Vincent, P.O. Box 3186, Fremont, CA 94539-3186. Tel: 415-656-7175
Freiermuth, Harry, P.O. Box 6923, Salinas, CA 93912-6923. Tel: 408-757-6656
Hall, Henry, P.O. Box 462312, Escondido, CA 92046-2312. Tel: 760-737-9001
Keating, Douglas, P.O. Box 2284, Avila Beach, CA 93424. Tel: 805-595-9415
Leonard, Joseph, 18430 Vista Granada Way, Los Gatos, CA 95030
Matz, Leo, Mount Angel Towers, One Tower Ln., Mount Angel, OR 97362. Tel: 503-845-7568
McSweeney, John, 1320 Padre Dr., Salinas, CA 93901. Tel: 408-422-4584
Migliazzo, Felix, 1249 Josselyn Canyon Rd., P.O. Box 88, Monterey, CA 93942. Tel: 408-373-9120
Murphy, John, c/o St. Clare's Retreat, 2381 Laurel Glen Rd., Soquel, CA 95073. Tel: 408-423-8093
O'Halloran, Richard, 1335 Byron Dr., Salinas, CA 93901. Tel: 408-758-6285
O'Sullivan, Michael, 2247 Idylwild Pl., Arroyo Grande, CA 93420. Tel: 805-489-9160

Santamaria, Max, Cr. de Arizala 7, 31178 Abaruza, Navarra, Spain. Tel: 011-344-452-0021
Sanz, Eleuterio, 727 Almond Dr., Watsonville, CA 95076. Tel: 831-763-3912
Schwarz, Robert, Golden Oaks #4103, 30 Monte Vista Dr., Monterey, CA 93940. Tel: 408-372-8848
Soares, Bernaro Manuel, P.O. Box 211, San Juan Bautista, 95045
Sweeney, James, 194 Island St., Morro Bay, CA 93442. Tel: 805-773-4108
Thome, Frank, 3056 Cruise Circle, Paso Robles, CA 93446. Tel: 805-238-4582
Toan, Francis, 2034 N. Main St., Salinas, CA 93906. Tel: 408-449-0449
Vela, Fabian
Watt, Joseph, 2010 Pleasant Valley Rd., Aptos, CA 95001. Tel: 408-724-2829

Permanent Deacons:
Leach, David, Nativity of Our Lady, 221 Daly Ave., San Luis Obispo, CA 93401. Tel: 805-544-2357
Miller, Harold, 121 Robin Dr., Marina, CA 93933. Tel: 408-883-2601

INSTITUTIONS LOCATED IN THE DIOCESE

[A] HIGH SCHOOLS, PRIVATE

MONTEREY. *Santa Catalina Upper School.* (Girls), 1500 Mark Thomas Dr., 93940-5291. Tel: 831-655-9315; Fax: 831-649-3056.
E-mail: sister_claire@santacatalina.org
Web site: www.santacatalina.org
Sr. Carlotta, Head of School. Lay Teachers 42; Total Enrollment (Grades 9-12) 307.

SALINAS. *Christian Brothers Institute of California, Inc. dba Palma High School.* (Boys). Tel: 831-422-6391; Fax: 831-422-5065.
E-mail: dunne@palmahs.org
Web site: www.palmahs.org
(Grades 7-12), 919 Iverson St., 93901-1816. Tel: 831-422-6391; Fax: 831-422-5065.
E-mail: dunne@palmahs.org
Congregation of Christian Brothers. Bro. Patrick D. Dunne, C.F.C., Prin. Brothers 6; Lay Teachers 34; Boys (Jr. High) 160; Boys (Total) 669. Congregation of Christian Brothers Residence, 935 Iverson St., 93901-1898. Tel: 831-758-2127; Fax: 831-422-5065. Bro. Charles J. Avendano, C.F.C., Dir. Brothers 7.

[B] HIGH SCHOOLS, DIOCESAN

SALINAS. *Notre Dame High School*, 455 Palma Dr., 93901. Tel: 831-751-1850; Fax: 831-757-5749.
E-mail: info@nd-spirits.org
Web site: www.nd-spirits.org
Fabienne M. Esparza, Prin. Sisters 1; Lay Teachers 44; Girls 430.

SAN LUIS OBISPO. *Mission College Preparatory Catholic High School*, 682 Palm St., 93401. Tel: 805-543-2131; Fax: 805-543-4359.
E-mail: missionprepi@impresso.com
Web site: www.missionprep.org
Rev. Charles J. Tilley, S.J., Prin. Sisters 1; Lay Teachers 14; Students 229.

WATSONVILLE. *Moreland Notre Dame School*, 133 Brennan St., 95076. Tel: 831-728-2051.
E-mail: morelandwat@impresso.com
Sisters of Notre Dame de Namur. Tel: 831-728-2051; Fax: 831-728-9205.
E-mail: morelandwat@impresso.com
Christine Grul, Prin. Sisters 2; Lay Teachers 9; Students 300.

St. Francis Central Coast Catholic High School, 2400 E. Lake Ave., P.O. Box 2649, 95077. Tel: 831-724-5933; Fax: 831-722-3274. Joint High School between Diocese of Monterey and Salesians of St. John Bosco.

[C] ELEMENTARY SCHOOLS, PRIVATE

MONTEREY. *Santa Catalina Lower School.* (Grades PreK-8). (Coed), 1500 Mark Thomas Dr., 93940. Tel: 831-655-9324; Fax: 831-655-9303.
E-mail: w-admissions@santacatalina.org
Web site: www.santacatalina.org
Mr. David M. Wickham, Div. Head Middle School; Mrs. Linda Mutty, Div. Head, Grades 3-5; Christy Pollacci, Div. Head, PreK-2. Secretaries: Vicki Demayo; Kim King. Lay Teachers 23; Total Enrollment (Grades Pre-K-8) 267.

CORRALITOS. *Salesian Elementary & Jr. High School Center: Mary Help of Christians Youth Center.* (Grades K-8), 605 Enos Ln., 95076. Tel: 831- 728-5518; Fax: 831-728-0273.
E-mail: salesiansrss@impresso.com
Sr. Charlotte Greer, F.M.A. Sisters 1; Lay Teachers 9; Students 205.

WATSONVILLE. *St. Francis Youth Center*, P.O. Box 2670, 95077. Tel: 831-761-5368.
St. Francis Youth Center includes athletics and recreation, and a tattoo removal program.

[D] GENERAL HOSPITALS

SANTA CRUZ. *Dominican Santa Cruz Hospital*, 1555 Soquel Dr., 95065. Tel: 831-462-7700; Fax: 831-462-7555.
Web site: www.dominicanhospital.org
For a complete listing, refer to the Hospitals section.

[E] SPECIAL HOSPITALS AND SANATORIA ACUTE CARE HOSPITAL

MONTEREY. *Ave Maria Convalescent Hospital*, 1249 Joselyn Canyon Rd., 93940. Tel: 831-373-1216; Fax: 831-373-2238
For a complete listing, refer to the Special Care Facilities section.

[F] MONASTERIES AND RESIDENCES OF PRIESTS AND BROTHERS

MONTEREY. *Brothers of St. Francis Xavier*, 485 Church St., 93940. Tel: 831-373-2127; Fax: 831-373-3534.
E-mail: archives@dioceseofmonterey.org
Bro. John F. O'Brien, C.F.X.

Congregation of the Holy Cross. Indiana Prov. P.O. Box 2079, 93942-2079. Tel: 831-373-2919; Fax: 831-373-4510. Rev. Edward J. Kaminski, C.S.C.

Oratorian Community-Congregation of the Oratory of Pontifical Right, 302 High St., P.O. Box 1688, 93942-1688. Tel: 831-373-0476; Fax: 831-373-1718. Very Rev. Peter C. Sanders, C.O., Provost. Tel: 831-375-9769; Revs. Michael P. Drury, C.O., Vicar & Sec. Tel: 831-646-8278; Lidio Limon, C.O. Tel: 831-372-6094; Thomas A. Kieffer, C.O., Treas. Tel: 831-372-1325. Priests 3.

ARROYO GRANDE. *St. Joseph Cupertino Province, Provincial Center*, P.O. Box 820, 93421. Tel: 805-489-1012; Fax: 805-489-8303.
E-mail: allenram@aol.com
Revs. Allen A. Ramirez, O.F.M.Conv., Minister Prov.; Victor Abegg, O.F.M.Conv., Vicar Prov.; Bros. James Reiter, O.F.M.Conv., Province Sec.; Casimir Roland, O.F.M.Conv., Prov. Econom; George Cherrie, O.F.M.Conv., Prov. Exactor.
Attached to the Province but outside friaries: Rev. Kerry Abbott, O.F.M.Conv., Chap. Captain, (U.S.A.F.). Total in Residence 10.

St. Joseph's Cupertino Novitiate, 1352 Dale Ave., P.O. Box 820, 93421. Tel: 805-473-2256; Fax: 805-489-8303. Bro. James M. Reiter, O.F.M.Conv., Dir. Novices & Guardian; Rev. Roch Bartman, O.F.M.Conv., (Retired). Priests 1; Brothers 3; Novices 7.

BIG SUR. *New Camaldoli Hermitage*, 62475 Coast Hwy. # 1, 93920-9656. Tel: 831-667-2456; Fax: 831-667-0209.
E-mail: monks@contemplation.com
Web site: www.contemplation.com
Very Rev. Raniero Hoffman, O.S.B.Cam., Prior; Revs. Bruno Barnhardt, O.S.B.Cam.; Peter Damian Belisle, O.S.B. Cam.; Cyprian Consiglio, O.S.B.Cam.; Joseph Diemer, O.S.B.Cam.; Romuald Duscher, O.S-.B.Cam.; Michael Fish, C.SS.R.; Daniel Manger, O.S.B. Cam.; Bernard Massicotte, O.S.B.Cam.; Zacchaeus Maria Naegele, O.S.B.Cam.; Isaiah Teichert, O.S.B.Cam.; Joseph Wong, O.S.B.Cam.
On Special Assignment: Revs. Andrew Colnaghi, O.S.B.Cam., Prior, Incarnation; Arthur Poulin, O.S.B.Cam.; Robert Hale, O.S.B.Cam, Incarnation Monastery, 1369 La Loma Ave., Berkeley, 94708. Tel: 510-845-0601; Fax: 510-548-6439.
On Leave: Revs. Louis Coddaire, O.S.B.Cam.; Robert John Powell, O.S.B.Cam. Professed Monks (including 17 priests) 25; Brothers 10.

SALINAS. *Palma Community*, 935 Iverson St., 93901. Tel: 831-758-2127; Fax: 831-422-5065.
E-mail: ombuda@aol.com
Congregation of Christian Brothers. Bros. B. Sebastian Samp, C.F.C.; Patrick D. Dunne, C.F.C.; Anthony C. O'Grady, C.F.C.; Gerard F. Murray, C.F.C.; Dennis J. Peterson, C.F.C.; Daniel L. Oehrle, C.F.C.; Charles J. Avendano, C.F.C., C.L.; John J. Fagan, C.F.C. Brothers 8.

SAN JUAN. *Franciscan Friars*, P.O. Box 970, 95045. Tel: 831-623-4234; Fax: 831-623-9046.
E-mail: info@stfrancisretreat
Web site: www.stfrancisretreat.com

SAN LUIS OBISPO. *Monastery of the Risen Christ*, P.O. Box 3931, 93403. Tel: 805-544-1810; Fax: 805-544-1810.
E-mail: rohosb@aol.com
Men's Residence, 2308 O'Connor Way, 93405. Tel: 805-544-1810; Fax: 805-544-1810. Rt. Rev. David Geraets, O.S.B., Supr.; Revs. Raymond V. Roh, O.S.B.; Stephen Odenbrett, O.S.B.; Albert Meyer, O.S.B.; Bro. Steve Coffey, O.S.B.; Rev. Raymond Greco, O.S.B., (Retired). Total Staff 3; Total in Residence 6.

SAN MIGUEL. *Franciscan Friars, O.F.M.* (Province of St. Barbara, Old Mission), P.O. Box 69, 93451. Tel: 805-467-3256; Fax: 805-467-2248.
E-mail: johnvaugh@aol.com
Revs. John Vaughn, O.F.M., Vicar; Jerry Ahles, O.F.M.; Christopher Tomatis, O.F.M., Pastor; Thomas Messner, O.F.M.; Bros. Bill Short, O.F.M., Guardian; Bartholomew Mitchell, O.F.M.; Quentin Watson, O.F.M. Total Staff 3; Total in Residence 7.

Novitiate House for the Franciscan Friars, O.F.M. (Province of St. Barabara), P.O. Box 69, 93451. Tel: 805-467-2801; Fax: 805-467-2448.
E-mail: johnvaugh@aol.com
Revs. John Vaughn, O,F.M., Master of Novices; Thomas Messner, O.F.M.; Christopher Tomatis, O.F.M., Pastor; Bro. Bill Short, O.F.M., Guardian. Novices 2; Total in Residence 12.

SANTA CRUZ. *Oblates of St. Joseph Provincial House and Shrine*, 544 W. Cliff Dr., 95060; Fax: 831-457-1317.
E-mail: provincial@osjoseph.org
Web site: www.osjoseph.org
Religious Community. Tel: 831-471-1702; Fax: 831-457-1317.
Provincial. Tel: 831-457-1868; Fax: 831-457-1317.
Shrine of St. Joseph. Tel: 831-471-0442; Fax: 831-457-1317. Revs. Siro Dal Degan, O.S.J. (Italy); Aldo Grasso, O.S.J. (Italy); Bronius Kaunas, O.S.J. (Lithuania); Philip Massetti, O.S.J., Prov. Supr. & Rector; Thomas Russo, O.S.J.; Bro. Duain O'Mara, O.S.J. Priests 5; Brothers 1; Total in Residence 6.
Religious Community. Tel: 831-471-1702; Fax: 831-457-1317. Legal Title: *Oblates of St. Joseph, Provincial House and Shrine of St. Joseph, Guardian of the Redeemer.*

Society of Mary, Marianists, 285 Meder St., 95060. Tel: 831-423-9400; Fax: 831-423-8163.
E-mail: RolBunda@aol.com
Web site: www.newmanite.org
Rev. Roland Bunda, S.M., Dir.; Bro. Anthony Young, S.M. Total Staff 2; Total in Residence 2.

Society of Mary, Marists, Marist Community, 436 Effey St., 95062-2640. Tel: 831-425-5202; Fax: 831-429-5832. Revs. Rene Iturbe, S.M.; David Musso, S.M.; Hector Cruz, S.M. Total in Residence 3.

WATSONVILLE. *Salesians of St. John Bosco*, 2401 East Lake Ave., P.O. Box 2670, 95077. Tel: 805-763-4487; Fax: 831-722-3274. Friars John Roche, Dir. & Pres.; Harold Danielson, Vice Dir. & Pastor; Justo Davila; Bros. Michael Touchstone, Prin.; Joseph Lockwood, Treas.; Abel Zanella.

[G] CONVENTS AND RESIDENCES FOR SISTERS

MONTEREY. *Ave Maria Convent*, 1249 Josselyn Canyon Rd., P.O. Box 1977, 93942-1977. Tel: 831-373-1216; 831-375-8680. Motherhouse of the Franciscan Sisters of the Immaculate Conception and St. Joseph for the Dying. Sr. Constance, Supr.; Rev. Felix Migliazzo, Chap. Sisters 6.

Congregation of the Most Holy Rosary. Sinsinawa Dominican Sisters, O.P. c/o P.O. Box 2048, 93942-2048. Tel: 831-373-4345; Fax: 831-373-0302.
E-mail: lgdom@aol.com

APTOS. *St. Joseph's Monastery of the Poor Clares (Colettines)*, 1671 Pleasant Valley Rd., P.O. Box 160, 95001-0160. Tel: 831-761-9659; 761-9481; Fax: 831-761-9481. Mother Mary Clare, P.C.C., Abbess. Professed Sisters (Cloistered) 13; Extern 2. Poor Clares of California, Inc.

ARROYO GRANDE. *Sisters of Mercy*, 900 W. Branch St., 93420. Tel: 805-489-1438; Fax: 805-489-4367.

CARMEL. *Carmelite Monastery of Our Lady and St. Therese*, 27601 Hwy. 1, 93923-9612. Tel: 831-624-3043; Fax: 831-624-5495.
E-mail: carmelit@familink.com
Mother Mercedes of Mary Immaculate, O.C.D., Prioress. Professed Nuns 14.

Sisters of Notre Dame de Namur, 27951 Hwy. 1, 93921. Tel: 831-624-9416; Fax: 831-624-4865.
E-mail: carmelhop@aol.com

CORRALITOS. *Daughters of Mary Help of Christians*, 605 Enos Ln., 95076. Tel: 831-728-4700; Fax: 831-728-5802.
E-mail: fmasuocor@aol.com
Sr. Charlotte Greer, F.M.A., Supr. Sisters 7; Candidates in Formation 2.

GONZALES. *Sisters of Charity of the Infant Mary Capitanio Convent*, 512 Fairview Dr., Box 178, 93926. Tel: 831-675-2975; Fax: 831-675-2974.
E-mail: SisterLiliana@aol.com
Sr. Liliana Bonello, I.M., Supr. Residents 5.

MORRO BAY. *Sisters of Charity of the Infant Mary*, 465 Monterey #4, 93442. Tel: 805-772-8949.

PISMO BEACH. *Franciscan Sisters of the Atonement (Graymoor)*, 344 Pomeroy Ave., 93449. Tel: 805-773-3427.

SALINAS. *Bethany*, 15785 Alto Way, 93907. Tel: 831-663-3675; Fax: 831-663-3749. Sisters of Charity of the Infant Mary. Sr. Patricia Murtagh, Supr. Residents 4.

Holy Cross Convent, 322 Hayes St., Apt. B, 93906. Tel: 831-442-9766. Sisters 2.

Sisters of Notre Dame, 456 E. Laurel Dr., 93906. Tel: 831-424-4370.
E-mail: bmatasci@aol.com
Residents 2.

Sisters of St. Joseph Carondolet, 1335 Byron Dr., 93901. Tel: 831-754-0786; Fax: 831-758-1318.
E-mail: madonnacsj@juno.com
Web site: www.csjla.org
Rev. Richard O'Halloran, Chap. Sisters 4. Madonna Manor.

Sisters of the Holy Names of Jesus and Mary, c/o Sr. Molly Neville, 1330 Byron Dr., Apt. 10 I, 93901. Tel: 831-753-1567; Fax: 831-754-2474.
E-mail: mnevsnjm@aol.com
Web site: www.dioceseofmonterey.org

SAN JUAN BAUTISTA. *Franciscan Sisters of the Atonement*, P.O. Box 1094, 95045. Tel: 831-623-4267. Franciscan Sisters of Atonement 4.

SAN LUIS OBISPO. *Monastery of the Risen Christ*. (Women's Residence), P.O. Box 3931, 93403-3931. Tel: 805-544-7808. 2304 O'Connor Way, 93405. Tel: 805-544-7808. Marie DiSciullo, O.S.B., O.B.L.

Sisters of St. Joseph of Carondelet, 1750 Prefumo Canyon Rd. # 64, 93405-6134. Tel: 805-544-9020; Fax: 805-544-9020.
E-mail: mtlarkin@juno.com
Sr. Miriam Therese Larkin, C.S.J.; Sr. Janet Husung, C.S.J., 138-A Cerro Romouldo Ave., 93405. Tel: 805-782-9028. Sr. Theresa Harpin, C.S.J.

SAN MIGUEL. *Franciscan Sisters of the Atonement (Graymoor)*, P.O. Box 238, 93451. Tel: 805-467-0022.

SANTA CRUZ. *Adrian Dominican Sisters*, Pacific West Mission Chapter, P.O. Box 2235, 95063-2235. Tel: 831-457-7117; Fax: 831-457-7139.
E-mail: PacificADS@aol.com
Web site: http://www.op.org/adrian/
Sr. Jane Robert Stuckel, O.P., Chapter Prioress.

Daughters of Charity of St. Vincent de Paul, 441 Rodriguez St., 95062. Tel: 831-475-5699; Fax: 831-763-0702.
E-mail: sccasa@aol.com

Franciscan Hospitaller Sisters of the Immaculate Conception, 143 Swift St., 95060. Tel: 831-426-5035. Sr. Elisa Santos, F.H.I.C., Local Supr. Total Residents 3.

Immaculate Heart of Mary, Holy Cross Church, 126 High St., 95060. Tel: 831-423-4182; Fax: 831-423-1043.
E-mail: bpedrazzi@compuserve.com

Sisters of the Holy Names of Jesus and Mary, Villa Maria del Mar, 2-1918 East Cliff Dr., 95062. Tel: 831-475-1236; Fax: 831-475-8867.
E-mail: jmvillasc@impresso.com
Sisters 6.

SOQUEL. *St. Clare's Retreat*, 2381 Laurel Glen Rd., 95073. Tel: 831-423-8093; Fax: 831-423-1541.
E-mail: stclaresretreat@juno.com
Web site: www.infoteam.com/nonprofit/stclaresretreat/index.html
Sr. Mary Francis Coleman, O.S.F., Supr.; Rev. John Murphy, Chap. Total Staff 17; Total Residents 7.

WATSONVILLE. *Moreland Notre Dame Convent*, 656 Main St., 95076. Tel: 831-724-7696; 724-3670; Fax: 831-768-9828.
E-mail: watsonsnd@aol.com
Sisters of Notre Dame de Namur. Sr. Denis Marie Harney, S.N.D., Coord. Residents 6.

Sisters of the Holy Names of Jesus and Mary, Watsonville Community, 26 Kilburn St., 95076. Tel: 831-728-4063. Sisters 4.

[H] RETREAT HOUSES

APTOS. *Camp St. Francis*, 2320 Sumner Ave., 95003. Tel: 831-763-4486.
Conducted by Salesians of St. John Bosco. Summer Camp for Boys 8-17, Meeting Center for large groups, and Retreat Center for large groups of youth or adults.

BIG SUR. *New Camaldoli Hermitage*, 62475 Coast Hwy. #1, 93920-9656. Tel: 831-667-2456; Fax: 831-667-0209.
E-mail: monks@contemplation.com
Web site: www.contemplation.com
Very Rev. Raniero Hoffman, O.S.B.Cam., Prior. Camaldolese Hermitage and retreat house. Total in Residence 24.

SAN JUAN BAUTISTA. *St. Francis Retreat Center*, P.O. Box 970, 95045. Tel: 831-623-4234; Fax: 831-623-9046.
E-mail: stfranret@aol.com
Web site: www.sbfranciscans.org
Conducted by Franciscan Friars. Province of St. Barbara. Revs. Angelo Cardinalli, O.F.M.; Richard McManus, O.F.M., Dir. and Local Guardian; Fabian Walker, O.F.M.; Michael Weldom, O.F.M. Priests 2; Brothers 2; Total in Residence 10; Total Staff 18. Retreats for men, women, singles, married couples, A.A. and 12-step. Programs include Spiritual Growth, Ecumenical, Spanish.

SAN MIGUEL. *San Miguel Retreat House*, P.O. Box 69, 93451. Tel: 805-467-3256; Fax: 805-467-2448. Bro. Bill Short, O.F.M., Supr. Total Staff 2.

SANTA CRUZ. *Villa Maria del Mar*, 2-1918 E. Cliff Dr., 95062. Tel: 831-475-1236; Fax: 831-475-8867.
E-mail: 103006.627@compuserve.com
Sr. Patricia Doyle, S.N.J.M., Admin. Sisters of the Holy Names of Jesus and Mary; Total Staff 18.

SOQUEL. *St. Clare's Retreat House*, 2381 Laurel Glen Rd., 95073. Tel: 831-423-8093; Fax: 831-423-1541.
E-mail: stclaresretreat@juno.com
Web site: www.infoteam.com/nonprofit/stclaresretreat/index.html
Sr. Mary Francis Coleman, O.S.F., Retreat Dir.; Rev. Enda Heffernan, O.F.M.Cap., Retreat Master. Franciscan Missionary Sisters of Our Lady of Sorrows 7; Total Staff 17.

[I] NEWMAN CHAPLAINS AND CENTERS

MONTEREY. *Department of Campus Ministry*, 435 Church St., P.O. Box 350, 93942. Tel: 831-373-1608; Fax: 831-373-0173.
E-mail: schools@dioceseofmonterey.org
Web site: www.dioceseofmonterey.org
Sr. Mary Catherine Evans, O.P., Dir.; Miriam "Mimi" Schwertfeger, Asst. Dir. Total in Residence 2; Total Staff 15.

California State Polytechnic Institute / Cuesta College, Newman Catholic Center, 1472 Foothill Blvd., San Luis Obispo, 93405-1416. Tel: 805-543-4105; Fax: 805-543-5671.
E-mail: ncc@slonewman.org
Web site: www.slonewman.org
Sr. Theresa Harpin, C.S.J., Dir.; Sr. Mary Pat White, R.S.C.J., Assoc. Dir.; Linda Garcia-Inchausti, Dir. of Admin.; Vivien-Valentine Hidalgo, Campus Min.; Kathy Smith, Development Dir. Student Assistants: Chris Fesenmaier, Music Ministry Asst.; Erin Hanley, Admin. Intern; Tom Stieger, Admin. Intern.

Cabrillo College, Santa Cruz, 95064. Tel: 831-479-6100.
E-mail: ddmusso@aol.com
Revs. Roland Bunda, S.M., Dir. Campus Ministry, Newman Catholic Community, (Marianist); David Musso, S.M., Assoc. Dir., (Marist); Bro. Anthony Young, S.M., Outreach & Ecumenical Min., (Marianist); Ann Brown, Lay Volunteer, (Marist).

University of California at Santa Cruz, 285 Meder St., Santa Cruz, 95060. Tel: 831-423-9400; Fax: 831-423-8163.
Web site: www.newmanite.org
Revs. Roland Bunda, S.M., Chap. & Dir. Campus Ministry, Newman Catholic Community, (Marianist); David Musso, S.M., Assoc. Dir., (Marist); Bro. Anthony Young, S.M., Outreach & Ecumenical Min., (Marianist); Ann Brown, (Marist Lay Volunteer).

California State University of Monterey Bay. Revs. Roland Bunda, S.M., Dir. Campus Ministry, Newman Catholic Community, (Marianist); David Musso, S.M., Assoc. Dir., (Marist); Bro. Anthony Young, S.M., Outreach & Ecumenical Min., (Marianist); Ann Brown, (Marist Lay Volunteer), 285 Meder St., Santa Cruz, 95060. Tel: 831-423-9400; Fax: 831-423-8163.

[J] SENIOR RESIDENCES

SALINAS, CA. *Villa Serra Corporation*, 1320 Padre Dr., 93901. Tel: 831-754-5532; Fax: 831-754-5609.
E-mail: villa-serra@earthlink.net
Sponsored by the Diocese of Monterey and Dominican Santa Cruz Hospital. Total in Residence 149; Total Staff 65.

SANTA CRUZ, CA. *Dominican Oaks Corporation*, 3400 Paul Sweet Rd., 95065. Tel: 831-462-6257; Fax: 831-462-6742.
E-mail: kbowen@chw.edu
Web site: www.infopoint.com/sc/oaks
Sponsored by the Dominican Santa Cruz Hospital. Total Staff 73; Total Residents 222.

[K] MISCELLANEOUS

MONTEREY. *Newman Institute for Historical and Religious Studies*, Domus Patris Foundation, P.O. Box 748, 93942. Tel: 831-373-0477. Rev. Thomas A. Kieffer, Orat., Admin.

SALINAS. *Villa Serra Corporation*, 1320 Padre Dr., 93901. Tel: 831-754-5532; Fax: 831-754-5609.
E-mail: villaserragm@aol.com
Total in Residence 144; Total Staff 62.

WATSONVILLE. *Magnificat the Monterey Bay Chapter*, 120 Enos Ln., 95076. Tel: 831-724-6933. Maureen Roach, Coord.; Yvonne Finneg, Co-Coord.; Jennifer Silva, Treas.; Gayle Stenstrom, Sec.; Rev. Patrick Doaling, Spiritual Advisor. A Ministry to Catholic Women.

St. Francis Central Coast Catholic High School, Inc., 2400 East Lake Ave., P.O. Box 2649, 95076. Tel: 831-724-5933.
E-mail: jrochesdb@aol.com

St. Thomas More Society, c/o 262 E. Lake Ave., 95076. Tel: 831-722-2456; Fax: 831-722-0414. Raymond A. AmRhein, Pres.

RELIGIOUS INSTITUTES OF MEN REPRESENTED IN THE DIOCESE

For further details refer to the corresponding bracketed number in the Religious Institutes of Men or Women section.

[1350]—*Brothers of St. Francis Xavier*.—C.F.X.

[]—*Camaldolesi Hermits*.—O.S.B.Cam.

[0310]—*Congregation of Christian Brothers*. (Western U.S. Province, Joliet, IL).—C.F.C.

[]—*Congregation of Holy Cross (Indiana Province)*.—C.S.C.

[0480]—*Conventual Franciscans*.—O.F.M.Conv.

[0520]—*Franciscan Friars*. (Santa Barbara Prov.).—O.F.M.

[1060]—*Missionaries of the Precious Blood (Province of the Pacific)*.—C.PP.S.

[0910]—*Oblates of Mary Immaculate*.—O.M.I.

[0930]—*Oblates of St. Joseph*. (Asti, Italy).—O.S.J.

[0950]—*Oratorians*.—Orat.

[0200]—*Order of St. Benedict*. Monastery of the Risen Christ.—O.S.B.

[1070]—*Redemptorist Fathers*.—C.SS.R.

[1190]—*Salesians of Don Bosco (Turin, Italy)*.—S.D.B.

[0690]—*Society of Jesus*.—S.J.

[0760]—*Society of Mary, Marianists*.—S.M.

[]—*Society of Mary, Marist*.—S.M.

RELIGIOUS INSTITUTES OF WOMEN REPRESENTED IN THE DIOCESE

[1070-13]—*Congregation of the Most Holy Rosary-Adrian Dominican Sisters*.—O.P. [1070-03]—*Congregation of the Most Holy Rosary - Sinsinawa Dominican Sisters*.—O.P.

[1920]—*Congregation of the Sisters of the Holy Cross*. (Western Region).—C.S.C.

[0760]—*Daughters of Charity of St. Vincent de Paul*.—D.C.

[0880]—*Daughters of Mary & Joseph*.—D.M.J.

[0850]—*Daughters of Mary of Help of Christians*.—F.M.A.

[0420]—*Discalced Carmelite Nuns*.—O.C.D.

[1270]—*Franciscan Hospitaller Sisters of the Immaculate Conception*.—F.H.I.C.

[1390]—*Franciscan Missionary Sisters of Our Lady of Sorrows*.—O.S.F.

[1190]—*Franciscan Sisters of the Atonement*.—S.A.

[1300]—*Franciscan Sisters of the Immaculate Conception and St. Joseph for the Dying*.—O.S.F.

[]—*Immaculate Heart of Mary*.—I.H.M.

[2575]—*Institute of the Sisters of Mercy of the Americas*.—R.S.M.

[3760]—*Order of St. Clare*.—P.C.C. [3465]—*Religious of the Sacred Heart of Mary*.—R.S.H.M.

[2970]—*School Sisters of Notre Dame*.—S.S.N.D.

[]—*Sisters for Christian Community*.—S.F.C.C.

[]—*Sisters of Charity of the Infant Mary*.—I.M.

[3000]—*Sisters of Notre Dame de Namur*.—S.N.D.deN.

[]—*Sisters of St. Benedict*. Monastery of the Risen Christ.—O.S.B.

[]—*Sisters of St. Benedict*.—O.S.B.

[3840]—*Sisters of St. Joseph of Carondelet*.—C.S.J.

[1990]—*Sisters of the Holy Name of Jesus and Mary*.—S.N.J.M.

DIOCESAN CEMETERIES

MONTEREY. *Diocesan Cemeteries Office*. Mailing Address: P.O. Box 2048, 93942-2048. 792 Fremont St., 93940. Tel: 831-373-4345; Fax: 831-373-4510.
E-mail: cemeteries@dioceseofmonterey.org
Mr. Clancy D'Angelo, Dir.

San Carlos. Tel: 831-372-0327; Fax: 831-372-8726.

CAMBRIA. *Old Santa Rosa*. Tel: 805-541-0584; Fax: 805-541-2127.

HOLLISTER. *Sacred Heart / Calvary*. Tel: 831-637-0131; Fax: 831-637-2980.

SALINAS. *Queen of Heaven*. Tel: 831-449-5890; Fax: 831-449-6928.

SAN LUIS OBISPO. *Old Mission*. Tel: 805-541-0584; Fax: 805-541-2127.

SANTA CRUZ. *Holy Cross*. Tel: 831-475-3222; Fax: 831-475-6132.

NECROLOGY

† Lane, Rev. Msgr. William, (Retired). —Died Feb. 26, 2000.

† McEvoy, John, (Retired). —Died July 27, 2000.

Diocese of Nashville

(Dioecesis Nashvillensis)

Most Reverend

EDWARD U. KMIEC, D.D., S.T.L.

Bishop of Nashville; ordained December 20, 1961; appointed Titular Bishop of Simidicca and Auxiliary Bishop of Trenton August 26, 1982; consecrated November 3, 1982; appointed Bishop of Nashville October 13, 1992; installed December 3, 1992. *Office: The Catholic Center, 2400 21st Ave., S., Nashville, TN, 37212.* Tel.: 615-383-6393.

Most Reverend

JAMES D. NIEDERGESES, D.D.

Retired Bishop of Nashville; ordained May 20, 1944; appointed April 8, 1975; consecrated May 20, 1975; retired October 13, 1992. *Res., 239 Cana Cir., Nashville, TN, 37205.*

ESTABLISHED JULY 28, 1837.

Square Miles 16,302.

Comprises the Counties of Bedford, Cannon, Cheatham, Clay, Coffee, Davidson, DeKalb, Dickson, Franklin, Giles, Grundy, Hickman, Houston, Humphreys, Jackson, Lawrence, Lewis, Lincoln, Macon, Marshall, Maury, Montgomery, Moore, Overton, Perry, Putnam, Robertson, Rutherford, Smith, Stewart, Sumner, Trousdale, VanBuren, Warren, Wayne, White, Williamson and Wilson in the State of Tennessee.

For legal titles of parishes and diocesan institutions, consult the Chancery Office.

Chancery Office: 2400 21st Ave., S., Nashville, TN, 37212. Tel.: 615-383-6393; Fax: 615-292-8411.

Web site address: www.serve.com/DIOCNASH/

E-mail address: nashdio@aol.com

STATISTICAL OVERVIEW

Personnel	
Bishop	1
Retired Bishops	1
Priests: Diocesan Active in Diocese	37
Priests: Active Outside Diocese	3
Priests: Retired, Sick or Absent	10
Number of Diocesan Priests	50
Religious Priests in Diocese	22
Extern Priests in Diocese	4
Ordinations:	
Diocesan Priests	2
Permanent Deacons in Diocese	54
Total Brothers	4
Total Sisters	149
Parishes	
Parishes	50
With Resident Pastor:	
Resident Diocesan Priests	30
Resident Religious Priests	9
Without Resident Pastor:	
Administered by Priests	10
Administered by Lay People	1
Missions	4
Professional Ministry Personnel:	
Brothers	2
Sisters	8
Lay Ministers	26
Welfare	
Catholic Hospitals	1
Total Assisted	204,113
Homes for the Aged	2
Total Assisted	590
Day Care and Extended Day Care Centers	2
Total Assisted	241
Special Centers for Social Services	5
Total Assisted	59,210
Other Institutions	2
Total Assisted	730
Educational	
Diocesan Students in Other Seminaries	4
Total Seminarians	4
Colleges and Universities	1
Total Students	629
High Schools, Diocesan and Parish	1
Total Students	1,000
High Schools, Private	1
Total Students	236
Elementary Schools, Diocesan and Parish	14
Total Students	3,480
Elementary Schools, Private	2
Total Students	764
Catechesis/Religious Education:	
High School Students	1,205
Elementary Students	6,548
Total Students Under Catholic Instruction	13,866
Teachers in the Diocese:	
Priests	3
Sisters	38
Lay Teachers	412
Vital Statistics	
Receptions into the Church:	
Infant Baptism Totals	1,609
Adult Baptism Totals	290
Received into Full Communion	413
First Communions	1,460
Confirmations	1,182
Marriages:	
Catholic	231
Interfaith	229
Total Marriages	460
Deaths	431
Total Catholic Population	73,652
Total Population	1,985,023

Former Bishops—Rt. Rev. RICHARD PIUS MILES, O.P., D.D., cons. Sept. 16, 1838; died Feb. 21, 1860.—Rt. Rev. JAMES WHELAN, O.P., D.D., cons. May, 1859; resigned May, 1863; died Feb. 18, 1878.—Rt. Rev. P. A. FEEHAN, cons. Nov. 1, 1865; created first Archbishop of Chicago, Sept. 10, 1880; died July 12, 1902.—Rt. Rev. JOSEPH RADEMACHER, D.D., cons. June 24, 1883; transferred to Ft. Wayne, July 13, 1893; died Jan. 12, 1900.—Rt. Rev. THOMAS S. BYRNE, D.D., cons. July 25, 1894; died Sept. 4, 1923.—Most Rev. ALPHONSE J. SMITH, D.D., cons. March 25, 1924; died Dec. 16, 1935.—Most Rev. WILLIAM L. ADRIAN, D.D., cons. April 16, 1936; died Feb. 13, 1972.—Most Rev. JOSEPH A. DURICK, D.D., cons. March 24, 1955; retired April 8, 1975; died June 26, 1994.—Most Rev. JAMES D. NIEDERGESES, D.D., cons. May 20, 1975; retired Oct. 13, 1992.

Vicars General—Rev. J. PATRICK CONNOR, *3019 Cayce Ln., Columbia, 38401.* Rev. Msgr. GEORGE W. ROHLING, *237 Cana Cir., Nashville, 37205.*

Moderator of the Curia and Administrative Assistant to the Bishop—Rev. DAVID R. PERKIN, J.C.L.

Deans—Rev. W. BERNARD NIEDERGESES, Central Deanery; Rev. DAVID R. CHOBY, Northeast Deanery; Rev. CHARLEY GIACOSA, Northwest Deanery; Rev. JOHN L. KIRK, Southeast Deanery; Rev. RICHARD G. BUCHIGNANI, Southwest Deanery.

Vicar for Catholic Charities—Rev. PHILIP M. BREEN, *5101 Charlotte Ave., Nashville, 37209.*

Chancery Office—2400 21st Ave. S., Nashville, 37212. Tel: 615-383-6393; Fax: 615-292-8411. Office Hours: Mon.-Fri. 8-4:30 All Official business should be directed to this office.

Chancellor and Chancery Facility Manager—Deacon HANS M. TOECKER.

Assistant Chancellor—MARY MARGARET LAMBERT.

Accounting Systems—MICHAEL F. NOLAN, Chief Fin. Officer; ELAINE FLICK, Controller; RICHARD NEAL, Asst. Controller for Social Svcs. TERESA OSBORNE, Mgr., Central Accounting.

General Counsel—Rev. JAMES K. MALLETT.

Diocesan Tribunal—2400 21st Ave. S., Nashville, 37212. Tel: 615-383-6393; Fax: 615-292-8411.

Judicial Vicar—Rev. DEXTER S. BREWER, J.C.L.

Adjutant Judicial Vicar—Rev. DAVID R. PERKIN, J.C.L.

Defenders of the Bond—Most Rev. JAMES D. NIEDERGESES; Revs. JOHN C. HENRICK; JOHN SIMS BAKER.

Advocates—Deacon THEODORE B. WELSH; Mrs. PATRICIA BURNS; Mrs. JULIE CONNOLLY; Mrs. LINDA NELSON.

Judges—Revs. DEXTER S. BREWER; DAVID R. CHOBY; RICHARD G. BUCHIGNANI; WILLIAM S. BEVINGTON; JAMES K. MALLETT; DAVID R. PERKIN, J.C.L.

Assessors—Mrs. LINDA NELSON; Mrs. PATRICIA BURNS.

Formal Case Instructor—Mrs. JULIE CONNOLLY.

Documentary Case Instructor—Mrs. LINDA NELSON.
Auditors—All priests and deacons assigned in the Nashville and Knoxville dioceses.
Secretary-Notaries—Mrs. PATRICIA BURNS; Mrs. JULIE CONNOLLY; Mrs. LINDA NELSON; Mrs. ANN H. KANENGIETER.
Presbyteral Council and College of Consultors—Most Rev. EDWARD U. KMIEC; Revs. MARK BECKMAN, Chm. JAMES K. MALLETT, Vice Chm. MICHAEL O. JOHNSTON; DAVID R. CHOBY; JOHN SIMS BAKER; RICHARD G. BUCHIGNANI; CHARLEY GIACOSA; ERIC FOWLKES; STEPHEN J. WOLF; JAMES F.X. PRATT, S.J.; JOHN P. SAPPENFIELD; DAVID R. PERKIN, J.C.L.
The Diocesan Finance Board—Most Rev. EDWARD U. KMIEC; Revs. J. PATRICK CONNOR; STEPHEN A. KLASEK; JAMES K. MALLETT; DAVID R. PERKIN; DAVID R. CHOBY; Mr. MICHAEL F. NOLAN; Mr. STEVE FRIDRICH; Mr. L. GINO MARCHETTI; Mr. J. TERRY HUNTER; Ms. SANDY DURBIN; Mr. RALPH GLASSFORD; Mr. WILLIAM HILL; Ms. SHEILA JACKSON PRIEBEL; Mr. WILLIAM PURYEAR; Mr. RICHARD SEVIER; Mr. STEVE TISDALE; Mr. DON TURK; Dr. JAMES WILSON.
DIONASH—A Partnership acting as Nominee for marketable securities for the Diocese of Nashville.

Diocesan Offices and Directors

The following offices and agencies are located at the Chancery unless otherwise indicated

Archives and Records—Deacon HANS M. TOECKER.
Campaign for Human Development—Mr. WILLIAM P. SINCLAIR, Dir., *St. Mary Villa, 30 White Bridge Rd., Nashville, 37205.*
Campus Ministries—Rev. JAMES F.X. PRATT, S.J., Diocesan Coord.
Vanderbilt—Rev. JAMES F.X. PRATT, S.J., *Vanderbilt Catholic Community, Box 6311, Station B, Nashville, 37235.* Tel: 615-322-0104.
MTSU-Murfreesboro—Rev. WIATT A. FUNK, *St. Rose of Lima Church, 1601 N. Tennessee Blvd., Murfreesboro, 37130.* Tel: 615-893-1843.
Austin Peay-Clarksville—Rev. ERIC FOWLKES, *Immaculate Conception, 709 Franklin St., Clarksville, 37040.* Tel: 931-645-6275.
Tenn. Tech-Cookeville—Rev. THOMAS PERRIN, S.D.S., *St. Thomas Aquinas Church, 401 N. Washington Ave., Cookeville, 38501.* Tel: 931-565-2575.
Fisk-Meharry-Tennessee State University Campus Ministries—Rev. FERNAND CHERI, O.F.M., *St. Vincent de Paul Church, 1700 Heiman St., Nashville, 37208.* Tel: 615-329-8755.
Univ. of South-Sewanee—Rev. DEXTER S. BREWER, *Good Shepherd Church, 2021 Decherd Blvd., Decherd, 37324.* Tel: 931-967-0961.
Catholic Charismatic Renewal—Rev. JOHN KIRK, Bishop's Liaison; Mrs. TERESA SEIBERT, Assoc. Liaison.
Catholic Charities of Tennessee, Inc.—WILLIAM P. SINCLAIR, A.C.S.W., Dir., *St. Mary Villa, 30 White Bridge Rd., Nashville, 37205.* Tel: 615-352-3087; Fax: 615-352-8591.
Catholic Public Policy Commission of TN—Exec. Secretaries: JENNFIER MURPHY; MICHAEL MURPHY.
Catholic Social Services of Nashville—Ms. EILEEN BEEHAN, Dept. Dir., *St. Mary Villa, 30 White Bridge Rd., Nashville, 37205.* Tel: 615-352-3087.
Catholic Youth Office and Search Program—Rev. MARK BECKMAN, *2011 West End Ave., Nashville, 37203.* Tel: 615-327-0674.
Cemeteries—MICHAEL F. NOLAN, Dir.
Censor Librorum—Rev. JAMES K. MALLETT.
Clergy Benefit Foundation—Most Rev. EDWARD U. KMIEC, Pres.; Revs. EDWARD F. STEINER, Chm. CHARLEY GIACOSA; JOHN BALTZ; JOHN SAPPENFIELD; Rev. Msgr. JAMES HITCHCOCK; Revs. JOSEPH MCMAHON; STEVE WOLF; Mr. MICHAEL F. NOLAN, Admin.
Clergy Personnel Board—Most Rev. EDWARD U. KMIEC; Revs. MICHAEL O. JOHNSTON; STEPHEN A. KLASEK; MARK BECKMAN; DAVID R. PERKIN, J.C.L.
Continuing Education of Clergy—Rev. ERIC FOWLKES, Dir.
Cursillo—DAN HOLDEN, Lay Dir.; Deacon MARTIN DESCHENES, Assoc. Spiritual Advisor.
Permanent Diaconate Office—Rev. CHARLEY GIACOSA, Dir.
Diocesan Communications Coordinator—RICK MUSSACHIO.
Diocesan Planning—Rev. STEPHEN A. KLASEK, Dir.
Ecumenical and Interreligious Relations—Deacon WILLIAM J. DICKSON, Dir.
Hispanic Ministry—Revs. RICHARD GAGNON, Dir. JOSE RAMON AYALA, Mexico; Mrs. ANABELL C. TREVINO, Asst. Dir., *30 White Bridge Rd., Nashville, 37205.* Tel: 615-356-2708.
Holy Childhood Association—Mr. STEPHEN J. HAMMOND, Dir.
Human Resources—TERRY ROBINSON, Dir.
Lay Retirement Administrative Board—Rev. JOSEPH BRANDO; MICHAEL F. NOLAN; LARRY COOL; JACK SMITHWICK, Chm. ROBERT TRUE; BRIAN DOWLING; DANIEL LAGRAFF; JAN LAWRENCE; JUDY POLINSKY; TERRY ROBINSON.
Liturgical Life—Rev. EDWARD T. ALBERTS, Dir.
Ministry Formation Services—Ms. JOCELINE LEMAIRE, Interim Dir. Contact this office for the following concerns: Religious Education, Family Ministry, Youth Ministry, Pastoral Services, Liturgy, Parish Councils, Leadership Training, Lay Ministry, Rite of Christian Initiation of Adults, Pro-Life Education Evangelization, Peace & Justice.
Newspaper—*"The Tennessee Register"*, RICK MUSACCHIO, Editor.
Prison Ministry—TERRANCE HORGAN, Ph.D., Criminal Justice Advocacy.
Propagation of the Faith—Deacon HANS M. TOECKER, Dir.
Catholic Charities Refugee Resettlement Program—HOLLY JOHNSON, Dir., *10 S. 6th St., Nashville, 37206.* Tel: 615-259-3567; Fax: 615-259-2851.
Schools Office—STEPHEN J. HAMMOND, Supr., *214 25th Ave., N., Nashville, 37203.* Tel: 615-329-9690; Fax: 615-329-9599.
Stewardship and Development—ANDY GAERTNER, Dir.
Vietnamese Ministry—Rev. PETER DO QUANG CHOU, *P.O. Box 90567, Nashville, 37209.* Tel: 615-463-7846.
Vocations—Rev. PATRICK J. KIBBY, Dir., *2001 West End Ave., Nashville, 37203.* Tel: 615-327-2330.

CLERGY, PARISHES, MISSIONS AND PAROCHIAL SCHOOLS

CITY OF NASHVILLE
(Davidson County)

1—CATHEDRAL OF THE INCARNATION (1909), Revs. J. Patrick Kibby; James E. Armour. In res., Most Rev. Edward U. Kmiec; Revs. David R. Perkin; James F.X. Pratt, S.J.; Deacons Mark Faulkner; John G. Krenson.
Res., 2001 West End Ave., 37203. Tel: 615-327-2330; Fax: 615-320-5650.
Catechesis/Religious Programs—Tel: 615-327-0919. Barbara Dodd, D.R.E. Students 300.

2—ST. ANN (1921), Rev. Philip M. Breen; Deacons John P. Casey; William J. Dickson.
Res., 5101 Charlotte Ave., 37209. Tel: 615-298-1782; Fax: 615-297-4326.
School—Tel: 615-269-0568; Fax: 615-297-1383. Mr. Robert Casey, Prin.
Lay Teachers 13; Students 173.
Catechesis/Religious Programs—Students 78. D.R.E.: Martin Mulloy, (RCIA); Stephanie Keller.

3—ASSUMPTION (1859). Attended by St. Pius X Church, Nashville. Rev. W. Bernard Niedergeses.
Church—1227 Seventh Ave. N., 37208. Tel: 615-256-2729; Fax: 615-256-0987.

4—CHURCH OF CHRIST THE KING (1937), Rev. James K. Mallett; Deacons Andrew D. McKenzie; James E. Stanford; Robert H. True.
Res., 3001 Belmont Blvd., 37212. Tel: 615-292-2884; Fax: 615-383-0026.
School—Tel: 615-292-9465; Fax: 615-292-2477. Mrs. Alice Valiquette, Prin.
Lay Teachers 18; Students 242.
Catechesis/Religious Programs—Tel: 615-292-2884, Ext. 302. Christine Caron, D.R.E. Students 119.

5—ST. EDWARD'S (1952), Rev. Joseph P. Breen; Deacons Gary D. Altman; Brian Edwards; Milton Von Mann.
Res., 188 Thompson Ln., 37211. Tel: 615-833-5520; Fax: 615-833-3738.
School—Tel: 615-833-5770; Fax: 615-833-9739. Jerry B. Beckman, Prin.
Lay Teachers 26; Students 441.
Catechesis/Religious Programs—Sr. Louise Shoulta, R.S.M., D.R.E. Students 220.

6—ST. HENRY (1958), Revs. Michael O. Johnston; John P. Sappenfield; Deacons Jack Srouji; Martin Deschenes. In res., Rev. Joseph V. McMahon.
Res., 6401 Harding Rd., 37205. Tel: 615-352-2259; Fax: 615-356-6321.
School—Tel: 615-352-1328; Fax: 615-356-9293. Sr. Mary Anne Zuberbueler, O.P., Prin.
Dominican Sisters of St. Cecilia Congregation 3; Lay Teachers 42; Students 661.
Catechesis/Religious Programs—Tel: 615-353-0668. Sr. Suzanne Stalm, R.S.M., D.R.E. Students 290.

7—HOLY ROSARY (1954), Rev. Stephen A. Klasek; Deacons Jonathan P. Borgerding; Joseph Coen, Sr.; Gilbert P. Huhlein; Kenneth Steinbrecher; Wayne Gregory.
Res., 190 Graylynn Dr., 37214. Tel: 615-889-4065; Fax: 615-889-3421.
School—Tel: 615-883-1108; Fax: 615-885-5100. Peggy Walker, Prin.
Lay Teachers 31; Students 552.
Catechesis/Religious Programs—Students 104.

8—ST. MARY VILLA PARISH COMMUNITY (1982), Rev. Msgr. George W. Rohling; Deacon Frank A. Bauman.
Church—30 White Bridge Rd., 37205. Tel: 615-352-3087; Fax: 615-352-8591.
Res., 237 Cana Cir., 37205. Tel: 615-356-4966.

9—ST. MARY'S OF THE SEVEN SORROWS (1847), Rev. James Norman Miller.
Mailing Address: P.O. Box 190606, 37219.
Res., 2823 Hazelwood Dr., #4, 37212. Tel: 615-297-3310.
Church—330 Fifth Ave. N., 37219. Tel: 615-256-1704; Fax: 615-256-7307.

10—CHURCH OF THE MOST HOLY NAME (1857), Rev. Joseph A. Sanches (ATL) Admin.
Res., 521 Woodland St., 37206. Tel: 615-254-8847; Fax: 615-254-1106.
Catechesis/Religious Programs—Tom Cook, D.R.E. Students 44.

11—ST. PATRICK'S (1891), Rev. Joseph A. Sanches (ATL) Admin.
Res., 1219 2nd Ave. S., 37210. Tel: 615-256-6498; Fax: 615-256-6476.
Catechesis/Religious Programs—Andy Dunn, D.R.E. Students 29.

12—ST. PIUS X (1958), Rev. W. Bernard Niedergeses.
Res., 2800 Tucker Rd., 37218. Tel: 615-244-4093; Fax: 615-256-0987.
School—Tel: 615-255-2049. Sr. Robert Ann Britton, O.P., Prin.
Dominican Sisters of St. Cecilia Congregation 5; Lay Teachers 12; Students 152.
Catechesis/Religious Programs—Allison Bernhardt, D.R.E.
Students 2.

13—ST. VINCENT DE PAUL (1932), Revs. Fernand J. Cheri, III, O.F.M.; Pio Jackson, O.F.M.
Church—1700 Heiman St., 37208. Tel: 615-320-0695; Fax: 615-320-0698.
School—Tel: 615-320-1374; Fax: 615-320-0277. Sr. Joanne Cozzi, D.C., Prin.
Lay Teachers 13; Students 152.

OUTSIDE THE CITY OF NASHVILLE

Antioch, Davidson Co., St. Ignatius of Antioch (1976), Rev. John C. Henrick; Deacons Jack Nulty; P. J. Hoefler; Edwin Rodgers; Doug Shafer.
Res., 601 Bell Rd., 37013. Tel: 615-367-0085; Fax: 615-367-1712.
Catechesis/Religious Programs—Kathryn Skinner, D.R.E.
Students 197.

Ashland City, Cheatham Co., St. Martha (1975), Rev. Charley Giacosa; Deacons Frank Bainbridge; Ralph Randall.
Church—311 Bell St., 37015. Tel: 615-792-4255; Fax: 615-792-1618.
Catechesis/Religious Programs—Anita Wilson, D.R.E.
Students 49.

Brentwood, Williamson Co., Holy Family (1989), Rev. Edward T. Alberts.
Church & Mailing Address: 9100 Crockett Rd., 37027. Tel: 615-373-4696; Fax: 615-377-3823.
Catechesis/Religious Programs—Tel: 615-373-4351. Catherine Birdwell, D.R.E.
Students 1,100.

Centerville, Hickman Co., Christ the Redeemer (1983). Attended by Holy Trinity, Hohenwald. Rev. Joseph Kevin Dowling; Deacon Donald A. Laws.
Mailing Address: P.O. Box 323, 37033. Tel: 931-796-3738.
Church—1515 Woodland Dr., 37033. Tel: 931-729-4669.

Clarksville, Montgomery Co., Immaculate Conception (1845), Revs. Eric L. Fowlkes; Wieslaw Burakowski (Poland); Deacons Dominick Azzara; Robert Berberich; Timothy Winters.
Res., 709 Franklin St., 37040. Tel: 931-645-6275; Fax: 931-552-0331.

Columbia, Maury Co., St. Catherine (1843), Rev. J. Patrick Connor; Deacon Price Keller.
Church & Mailing Address: 3019 Cayce Ln., 38401. Tel: 931-388-3803; Fax: 931-381-8837.
Res., 5018 Hays Dr., 38401. Tel: 931-540-0056.
Catechesis/Religious Programs—Tel: 931-381-6784. Candice Barton, D.R.E.
Students 316.

Cookeville, Putnam Co., St. Thomas Aquinas (1951), Revs. Peter Coffey, S.D.S.; Thomas Perrin, S.D.S.
Res., 421 N. Washington Ave., 38501. Tel: 931-526-2575; Fax: 931-526-5869.
Catechesis/Religious Programs—Tel: 931-526-4411. Valerie Richardson, D.R.E.
Students 204.
Mission—Celina, Clay Co., Divine Savior.

Decherd, Franklin Co., Good Shepherd (1900), Rev. Dexter S. Brewer.
Res., 2021 Decherd Blvd., 37324. Tel: 931-967-0961; Fax: 931-967-3569.
School—2037 Decherd Blvd., 37324. Tel: 931-967-5673. Sue Miller, Prin.
Lay Teachers 15; Students 108.
Catechesis/Religious Programs—Tel: 931-967-1067. June Skidmore, D.R.E.
Students 61.
Mission—Alto, Franklin Co., St. Margaret Mary, 9458 Old Alto Hwy., Alto, 37324. Tel: 931-962-2144.

Dickson, Dickson Co., St. Christopher (1951), Rev. Stephen Gideon.
Res., 713 W. College St., 37055. Tel: 615-446-3927; Fax: 615-446-7339.
Catechesis/Religious Programs—Tel: 615-446-1969. D.R.E.: Diane Minneci; Peter Minneci.
Students 114.

Dover, Stewart Co., St. Francis of Assisi (1982), Rev. Thomas Maurer, S.D.S.
Mailing Address: P.O. Box 307, 37058-0307.
Church—417 Spring St., Tel: 931-232-6982.
Catechesis/Religious Programs—Michelle Steen, D.R.E.
Students 26.

Fayetteville, Lincoln Co., St. Anthony (1983), Rev. Thomas McElhinney, Glmy.
Res., 1900 Huntsville Hwy., 37334. Tel: 931-433-6525.
Catechesis/Religious Programs—Students 62.

Franklin, Williamson Co., St. Matthew (1979), Revs. Luzerne A. Schnupp; Andrew J. Abraham; Deacons James Walsh; James Henry; Harold McBrayer.
Res., 535 Sneed Rd., 37069. Tel: 615-646-0378; Fax: 615-646-5230.
Catechesis/Religious Programs—Tel: 615-646-0378, Ext. 13. Sr. Lauren Cole, R.S.M., D.R.E.
Students 214.

St. Philip (1843), Rev. Edward C. Arnold; Deacon Alphonse Toppeto (CHI).
Res., 113 2nd Ave. S., 37064. Tel: 615-794-4236; Fax: 615-794-3083.
Catechesis/Religious Programs—Tel: 615-794-8588. Kimberlie Leisinger, D.R.E.
Students 771.

Gallatin, Sumner Co., St. John Vianney (1929), Rev. David R. Choby.
Res., 449 N. Water St., 37066. Tel: 615-452-2977; Fax: 615-452-0323.
Catechesis/Religious Programs—Students 115.

Hendersonville, Sumner Co., Our Lady of the Lake (1969), Rev. William S. Bevington; Sr. Maria Edwards, R.S.M., Pastoral Assoc.; Deacon James F. Carr.
Mailing Address: Box 279, 37077.
Church—1739 Stop Thirty Road, 37075. Tel: 615-824-3276; Fax: 615-824-7989.
Catechesis/Religious Programs—William Margulies, D.R.E.
Students 435.

Hohenwald, Lewis Co., Holy Trinity (1983), Rev. Joseph Kevin Dowling.
Church—610 Kimmins St., 38462. Tel: 931-796-3738; Fax: 931-796-3738.
Catechesis/Religious Programs—Carol Sharp, D.R.E.
Students 35.

Joelton, Davidson Co., St. Lawrence's (1885), Rev. Msgr. James R. Hitchcock.
Church—5655 Clarksville Hwy., 37080. Tel: 615-876-2127; Fax: 615-876-7923. [CEM]

Lafayette, Macon Co., Holy Family (1982). Attended by St. Frances Cabrini, Lebanon. Rev. Zacharias Payikat, C.M.I.
Church—901 Vinson Rd., 37083. Tel: 615-666-6466; Fax: 615-444-3704.
Catechesis/Religious Programs—Students 20.

Lawrenceburg, Lawrence Co., Sacred Heart (1870), Rev. Richard G. Buchignani.
Res., 222 Berger St., P.O. Box 708, 38464. Tel: 931-762-3183; Fax: 931-762-5128. [CEM]
School—Tel: 931-762-6125; Fax: 931-762-6125. Mrs. Bonnie Thigpen, Prin.
Lay Teachers 9; Students 110.
Catechesis/Religious Programs—Connie Hollman, D.R.E.
Students 39.

Lebanon, Wilson Co., St. Frances Cabrini (1953), Rev. Zacharias Payikat, C.M.I., Admin.
Res., 300 S. Tarver Ave., 37087. Tel: 615-444-0524; Fax: 615-444-3704.
Catechesis/Religious Programs—D.R.E.: Roger Hutto; Chris Crombie.
Students 150.
Station—Smith & Trousdale counties.

Lewisburg, Marshall Co., St. John the Evangelist (1982). Attended by St. William, Shelbyville. Rev. Paul Portland, S.D.S.
Church—1061 S. Ellington, 37091. Tel: 931-359-5017; Fax: 931-359-9844.
Catechesis/Religious Programs—Lynnette Cole, D.R.E.
Students 42.

Loretto, Lawrence Co., Sacred Heart (1872), Rev. Joseph Mundakal, C.M.I.; Deacon Samuel Beckman.
Mailing Address: P.O. Box 86, 38469.
Res., 305 Church St., 38469. Tel: 931-853-4370; Fax: 931-853-4373. [CEM]
School—Tel: 931-853-4388. Mrs. Catherine N. Bradley, Prin.
Lay Teachers 5; Students 69.
Catechesis/Religious Programs—Students 27.

McEwen, Humphreys Co., St. Patrick (1855), Rev. John Sims Baker.
Res., 123 St. Patrick St., 37101. Tel: 931-582-3417; Fax: 931-582-6386. [CEM]
School—Tel: 931-582-3493. Sr. Theresa Joseph, O.P., Prin.
Dominican Sisters of St. Cecilia Congregation 3; Lay Teachers 7; Students 101.

McMinnville, Warren Co., St. Catherine (1958), Rev. James J. Bretl, S.D.S. In res., Rev. Barry Griffin, S.D.S.; Deacon Robert L. Graham.
Res., 1024 Faulkner Spring Rd., 37110. Tel: 931-473-4932; Fax: 931-473-0799.
Catechesis/Religious Programs—Tel: 931-473-2435.
Students 73.
Station—Van Buren Co.

Madison, Davidson Co., St. Joseph's (1953), Revs. Edward F. Steiner, III; Christopher A. Steele; Deacons Gordon W. McBride; Theodore B. Welsh.
Res., 1225 Gallatin Rd. S., 37115. Tel: 615-865-1071; Fax: 615-868-4900.
School—Tel: 615-865-1491; Fax: 615-612-0228. Sr. Mary Francis deSales, O.P., Prin.
Dominican Sisters of St. Cecilia Congregation 3; Lay Teachers 23; Students 435.
Catechesis/Religious Programs—Rose M. Nicholson, D.R.E.
Students 237.

Murfreesboro, Rutherford Co., St. Rose of Lima (1929), Rev. Wiatt A. Funk; Deacon Bernard J. Casey.
Mailing Address: P.O. Box 4169, 37133-4169.
Res., 1601 N. Tennessee Blvd., 37130. Tel: 615-893-1843; Fax: 615-895-9787.
School—Tel: 615-898-0555; Fax: 615-898-0497. Sr. Ann Marie O.P., Prin.
Students 127.
Catechesis/Religious Programs—Tel: 615-898-1150. Robert Carney, D.R.E.
Students 628.

Old Hickory, Wilson Co., St. Stephen (1952), Revs. Stephen J. Wolf; Andrew J. Abraham; Deacons Robert Montini; Gordon S. Rose; Hans Toecker.
Res., 14544 Lebanon Rd., 37138. Tel: 615-758-2424; 754-4454; Fax: 615-754-0043.
Catechesis/Religious Programs—Mary Craven, D.R.E.
Students 386.

Pulaski, Giles Co., Immaculate Conception (1941). Attended by St. Anthony, Fayetteville. Rev. Thomas McElhinney, Glmy.; Kathleen M. O'Brien, Parish Coord.
Mailing Address: Box 363, 38478.
Church—Elkton Hwy. South, Tel: 931-363-5776; Fax: 931-363-6953.
Catechesis/Religious Programs—Lola Whitaker, D.R.E.
Students 22.

Saint Joseph, Lawrence Co., St. Joseph (1872). Attended by Sacred Heart, Loretto. Rev. Joseph Mundakal, C.M.I.
Mailing Address: P.O. Box 86, Loretto, 38469. Tel: 931-853-4370; Fax: 931-853-4373.
Church—American Blvd., 38481.

Shelbyville, Bedford Co., St. William (1941), Rev. Paul J. Portland, S.D.S.
Res., 719 N. Main St., 37160. Tel: 931-684-8745; Fax: 931-684-6154.
Catechesis/Religious Programs—Bro. Van Todd, S.D.S., D.R.E.
Students 45.

Smithville, DeKalb Co., St. Gregory (1982). Attended by St. Catherine, McMinnville. Rev. James J. Bretl, S.D.S.
Mailing Address: P.O. Box 712, 37166.
Church—712 Main St., Tel: 931-473-4932; Fax: 931-473-0799.
Catechesis/Religious Programs—Olga Beddingfield, D.R.E.
Students 26.

Smyrna, Rutherford Co., St. Luke (1982), Revs. Richard Gagnon, S.D.S.; Augustine Lucca, S.D.S.; Deacons Ken Levinson; Simeon Panagatos.
Mailing Address: P.O. Box 907, 37167-0907.
Res., 10682 Nashville Hwy., 37167. Tel: 615-459-9672; 459-3046; Fax: 615-459-3989.
Catechesis/Religious Programs—Denise M. Leaver, D.R.E.
Students 247.

Sparta, White Co., St. Andrew (1982), Rev. Fred J. Schmit, S.D.S.
Church—829 Valley View Dr., 38583. Tel: 931-738-2140; Fax: 931-738-3335.
Catechesis/Religious Programs—Students 17.

Springfield, Robertson Co., Our Lady of Lourdes (1946), Rev. Mark Beckman; Deacon W. Michael Hume.
Res., 103 Golf Club Ln., 37172. Tel: 615-384-6200; Fax: 615-384-5837. [CEM]
Catechesis/Religious Programs—Carol Twork, D.R.E.
Students 123.
Mission—Cedar Hill, Robertson Co., St. Michael. [CEM]

Tennessee Ridge, Houston Co., St. Elizabeth Ann Seton (1977). Attended by St. Patrick, McEwen. Rev. John Sims Baker. Pastoral Assocs.: Sr. Marlene Huck, C.PP.S.; Sr. Darlene Huck, C.PP.S.
Res., Rte. 3, Box 161, Erin, 37061. Tel: 931-289-5401.
Mailing Address: P.O. Box 85, 37178. Tel: 931-721-3769.
Church—755 State Rte. 49, 37178.
Catechesis/Religious Programs—Kelly Wootten, D.R.E.
Students 24.

Tullahoma, Coffee Co., St. Paul the Apostle (1954), Rev. John L. Kirk.
Res., 304 W. Grizzard St., 37388. Tel: 931-455-3050; Fax: 931-455-8298.
School—Tel: 931-455-4221. Suzanne Miller, Prin.
Lay Teachers 12; Students 150.
Catechesis/Religious Programs—Tel: 931-455-3060.
Students 140.
Station—Manchester, Coffee Co.

Waynesboro, Wayne Co., St. Cecilia (1982). Attended by Holy Trinity, Hohenwald. Rev. Joseph Kevin Dowling.
Mailing Address: Holy Trinity Church, 610 Kimmins St., Hohenwald, 38462.
Church—526 Hwy. 64 E., 38485. Tel: 931-796-3738; Fax: 931-796-3738.
Catechesis/Religious Programs—Sandy Bell, D.R.E.
Students 13.

On Special or Other Diocesan Assignment:
Reverend Fathers—
Ayala, Jose Ramon (Mexico), Hispanic Ministry
Chau, Peter Do Quang, Vietnamese Ministry
Perkin, David R., Mod. of the Curia

On Duty Outside the Diocese:
Reverend Fathers—
Campion, Owen F., Our Sunday Visitor, 200 Noll Plaza, Huntington, IN 46750
Flaherty, Jay M., Holy Cross Church, 144 Wears Valley Rd., Pigeon Forge, TN 37863
McMurry, John E., S.S., St. Mary's Spiritual Center, 600 N. Paca St., Baltimore, MD 21201-1995
McMurry, Vincent deP., S.S., St. Mary's Seminary, 5400 Roland Ave., Baltimore, MD 21210
Ney, Charles, Dennehotso Health Clinic, Dennehotso, AZ 86535

Absent on Leave:
Reverend Fathers—
Strobel, Charles
White, Alan

Retired:
Reverend Fathers—
Baltz, John P., Jr., 2146 Oakland St., Nashville, TN 37210
Briscoe, Orville, 2314 N. Griffin Dr., Leesburg, FL 34748
Cain, John N., 305 Davidson Rd., Nashville, TN 37205
Clements, Daniel A., 924 Rose Petal Ln., Knoxville, TN 37938

Doyle, Thomas, S.S., 1248 Brentwood Pointe, Brentwood, TN 37027
Julius, Joseph W., St. Francis of Assisi, 7715 River Rd., Townsend, TN 37882
Murray, James B., St. Paul the Apostle, 1425 E. Shelby Dr., Memphis, TN 38116
Nolan, William N, 1706 Crystal Spring Ln., Hermitage, TN 37076
Rudisill, James A., 3216 S. Waynoka Cir., Memphis, TN 38111-3615
Siener, Albert L., Alive Hospice, 1710 Patterson St., Nashville, TN 37203

Permanent Deacons:
Altman, Gary D., St. Edward, Nashville
Azzara, Dominic D., Immaculate Conception, Clarksville
Bainbridge, Frank, Prison Ministry, Nashville; St. Christopher, Dickson
Batcheldor, James M., Jr., St. Stephen, Old Hickory
Bauman, Frank, St. Mary Villa Parish Community, Nashville
Beckman, Samuel C., Sacred Heart, Loretto
Berberich, Robert R., Immaculate Conception, Clarksville
Borgerding, Jonathan P., Holy Rosary, Nashville
Carr, James F., Our Lady of the Lake, Hendersonville
Carroll, John B., (Retired)
Casey, Bernard J., St. Rose of Lima, Murfreesboro
Casey, John P., St. Ann, Nashville
Climer, Donald E., St. Frances Cabrini, Lebanon
Coen, Joseph, Sr., Holy Rosary, Nashville
Deschenes, Martin, St. Henry, Cursillo, Nashville
Dickson, William J., St. Ann, Nashville; Diocesan Ecumenical Dir.
Edwards, Brian, St. Edward, Nashville
Faulkner, Mark C., Cathedral of the Incarnation, Nashville
Francescon, Samuel A., (Retired)
Graham, Robert L., St. Catherine, McMinnville
Gregory, L. Wayne, Holy Rosary, Nashville
Henry, James R., St. Matthew, Franklin
Hoefler, Paul J., St. Ignatius, Antioch
Hooper, Hugh C., (Retired)
Huhlein, Gilbert P., Holy Rosary, Nashville
Hume, W. Michael, Our Lady of Lourdes, Springfield
Keller, I. Price, St. Catherine, Nashville
Krenson, John G., Cathedral of the Incarnation, Nashville
Laws, Donald A., Christ the Redeemer, Centerville
Levinson, Ken, St. Luke, Smyrna
Mahoney, Robert L., Holy Name, Nashville
McBrayer, J. Harold, Jr., (Retired)
McBride, Gordon W., Sr., St. Joseph, Madison
McGinn, George P., Hospital Ministry, Nashville
McKenzie, Andrew D., Christ the King, Nashville
McKenzie, James W., Vanderbilt Catholic Community, Nashville
Montini, Robert A., St. Stephen, Old Hickory
Nulty, Jack, St. Ignatius, Antioch
Panagatos, Simeon W., St. Luke, Smyrna
Randall, Ralph, St. Christopher, Dickson
Rodgers, Edwin C., St. Ignatius of Antioch, Antioch
Rose, Gordon, St. Stephen, Old Hickory
Shafer, L. Douglas, St. Ignatius of Antioch, Antioch
Srouji, Jack, St. Henry, Nashville
Stanford, James E., Christ the King, Nashville
Steinbrecher, Kenneth, Holy Rosary, Nashville
Steltemeier, William, Jr., Unassigned
Toecker, Hans M., St. Stephen, Old Hickory
Toppeto, Alphonse A. (CHI), St. Philip, Franklin
True, Robert H., Christ the King, Nashville
Von Mann, Milton, Prison Ministry, St. Edward, Nashville
Walsh, James F., Jr., St. Matthew, Franklin
Welsh, Theodore B., St. Joseph, Madison
Winters, Timothy F., Immaculate Conception, Clarksville

INSTITUTIONS LOCATED IN THE DIOCESE

[A] COLLEGES

NASHVILLE. *Aquinas College*, 4210 Harding Rd., 37205. Tel: 615-297-7545; Fax: 615-297-7970.
Web site: www.aquinas-tn.edu
For a complete listing, refer to the Colleges and Universities section.

[B] HIGH SCHOOLS, DIOCESAN

NASHVILLE. *Father Ryan High School* (1925), 700 Norwood Dr., 37204. Tel: 615-383-4200; Fax: 615-383-9056.
E-mail: postmaster@FATHERRYAN.org
Web site: www.FATHERRYAN.org
Corporate Title: Father Ryan High School, Inc. Mr. John J. Lanston, Prin.; Revs. Joseph V. McMahon, Assoc. Prin. Pastoral Affairs; John P. Sappenfield; James E. Armour. Priests 3; Lay Teachers 77; Students 1,000.

Father Ryan Board of Trust, Devel. & Alumni Office, 770 Norwood Dr., 37204. Tel: 615-269-7926.

[C] HIGH SCHOOLS, PRIVATE

NASHVILLE. *St. Cecilia Academy* (1860), The Dominican Campus, 4210 Harding Rd., 37205. Tel: 615-298-4525; Fax: 615-783-0561.
E-mail: coteg@stcecilia.edu
Web site: www.stcecilia.edu/sca
Legal Title: *St. Cecilia Academy*. Conducted by the St. Cecilia Congregation of Dominican Sisters. Sr. Mary Elizabeth Sallese, O.P., Prin. Sisters 7; Lay Teachers 28; Students 236.

[D] ELEMENTARY SCHOOLS, PRIVATE

NASHVILLE. *Overbrook School*, 4210 Harding Rd., 37205. Tel: 615-292-5134; Fax: 615-783-0560.
Web site: www.overbrook.edu
The St. Cecilia Congregation of Dominican Sisters. Sr. Mary Rose Bingham, O.P., Prin. Sisters 5; Lay Teachers 29; Students 379.

St. Bernard Academy, 2020 24th Ave. S., 37212-4202. Tel: 615-385-0440; Fax: 615-783-0241.
E-mail: mhonick@stbernard.org
Web site: www.stbernard.org
Legal Title: *Saint Bernard Academy Corporation*. Dr. Margaret Isabell, Dir. Sisters 5; Lay Teachers 25; Students 385.

[E] CHILD-CARING INSTITUTIONS

NASHVILLE. *St. Mary Villa Child Development Center*, 30 White Bridge Rd., 37205. Tel: 615-356-6336; Fax: 615-356-6421.
E-mail: jchase@edge.net
For a complete listing, refer to the Special Care Facilities section.

St. Mary Villa, Inc., 30 White Bridge Rd., 37205. Tel: 615-356-6336; Fax: 615-356-6421
For a complete listing, refer to the Special Care Facilities section.

St. Bernard After School Program, 2020 24th Ave. S., 37212. Tel: 615-298-1298; Fax: 615-783-0241
For a complete listing, refer to the Special Care Facilities section.

[F] GENERAL HOSPITALS

NASHVILLE. *St. Thomas Hospital*, (1898) 4220 Harding Rd., 37205. Tel: 615-222-2111; Fax: 615-222-6502.
E-mail: nshlsthl.stthomas.org
Web site: saintthomas.org
For a complete listing, refer to the Hospitals section.

[G] HOMES FOR THE AGED

NASHVILLE. *Villa Maria Manor, Inc. dba Villa Maria Manor*, 32 White Bridge Rd., 37205. Tel: 615-352-3084; Fax: 615-352-0553.
E-mail: thevilla@bellsouth.net
For a complete listing, refer to the Special Care Facilities section.

[H] MONASTERIES AND RESIDENCES OF PRIESTS AND BROTHERS

NASHVILLE. *Franciscan Friars*, 1608 Tynewood Dr., 37215-4214. Tel: 615-665-7313; Fax: 615-320-0698.
E-mail: ferdofm@aol.com
Revs. Fernand J. Cheri, III, O.F.M.; Pio Jackson, O.F.M.; Albert Merz, O.F.M.

Glenmary Home Missioners, 1307 6th Ave. N., 37208. Tel: 615-242-1885.
E-mail: Bhare95@aol.com
Revs. Robert Hare; Wilfred Steinbacher; Robert Dalton; Bro. William D. Wright.

[I] CONVENTS AND RESIDENCES FOR SISTERS

NASHVILLE. *Mercy Convent*, 2629 Pennington Bend Rd., 37214. Tel: 615-885-1863; Fax: 615-885-4304. Legal Title: *Sisters of Mercy of Nashville, TN, Inc.* Sr. Mary Judith Coode, R.S.M., Dir.; Rev. Stephen Stolowski, Chap. Sisters 25.

St. Cecilia Convent, 801 Dominican Dr., 37228-1909. Tel: 615-256-5486; Fax: 615-726-1333. Motherhouse and Novitiate of St. Cecilia Congregation of Dominican Sisters. Mother Rose Marie Masserano, O.P., Prioress Gen.; Sr. Mary George Barrett, O.P., Prioress; Rev. Joseph Angers, O.P., Chap. Sisters in Residence 91; Novices 9; Postulants 20.

[J] CAMPS AND COMMUNITY CENTERS

FAIRVIEW. *Camp Marymount*, 1318 Fairview Blvd., 37062. Tel: 615-799-0410; Fax: 615-799-2261.
E-mail: marymount@telalink.net
Web site: www.campmarymount.com
Catholic summer camp for boys and girls. Tommy Hagey, Dir.

[K] RENEWAL CENTERS

LIBERTY. *Carmel Center of Spirituality*, 610 Bluff Rd., 37095. Tel: 615-536-5177; Fax: 615-536-5499. P.O. Box 117, 37095. Revs. Zachary Payikat, C.M.I., Dir.; Anthony S. Puthussery, C.M.I.; Joseph Mundakal, C.M.I.

[L] MISCELLANEOUS

NASHVILLE. *Catholic Foundation of Tennessee, Inc.*, 2400 21st Ave. S., 37212. Andy Gaertner, Dev. Dir.

Catholic Media Productions, 700 Harpeth Knoll Ct., 37221. Tel: 615-646-4041; Fax: 615-662-7454.
E-mail: cmp.inc@home.com
Web site: www.catholicmediapro.com
James F. Walsh, Jr., Pres.

Diocesan Council of Catholic Women, 2400 21st Ave. S., 37212.
E-mail: merve8371@aol.com
Rev. David R. Perkin, Dir.

Diocesan Properties, Inc. dba Marina Manor East Apartments, 2400 21st Ave. S., 37212. Tel: 615-383-6393; Fax: 615-298-3192. Rev. David R. Perkin, Dir.; Michael F. Nolan, Sec./Treas.

Dismas, Inc., 30 White Bridge Rd., 37205. Tel: 615-352-3162; Fax: 615-353-9702.
E-mail: info@dismas.org
Web site: dismas.org
Francis McCaffrey, Pres. Homes in which former prisoners and college students live. Mentoring women prisoners by volunteers.

Families First Partners, Inc., 10 S. 6th St., 37206. Tel: 615-383-6393. Mr. Michael F. Nolan, Sec./Treas.

Glenmary Department of Pastoral Services, 1312 5th Ave. N., 37208. Tel: 615-256-1900; Fax: 615-256-1902.
E-mail: dps@glenmary.org
Web site: glenmary.org/dps/
A national center serving parishes and other ministries staffed by Glenmary Home Missioners. Rev. Michael Langell, Dir. Pastoral Svcs.; Bro. William D. Wright.

Glenmary Co-Missioners, 1312 5th Ave. N., 37208. Tel: 615-248-6325. A Lay Missionary Association working in the rural South among struggling communities.

Glenmary Personnel Office, 1312 5th Ave. N., 37208. Tel: 615-259-1235. Resource for Glenmary Member's Personnel. Rev. Robert Hare, Personnel Dir.

Establishing Mission Churches with Lay Leaders, 1312 5th Ave. N., 37208. Tel: 615-256-4384. A project for establishing new missions with lay persons. Rev. Robert Dalton.

Glenmary Reserch Center, 1312 5th Ave., N., 37208. Tel: 615-256-1905; Fax: 615-251-1472. Dr. Ken Sanchagrin, Dir.; Jim Johnson, Office Admin. Applied research for the ecumenical and rural apostolate.

Growing in Faith for Tomorrow Capital Campaign Trust, Inc., 2400 21st Ave., S., 37212. Tel: 615-383-6393; Fax: 615-292-8411. Rev. Patrick J. Kibby, Pres.

Holy Name Loaves and Fishes Community Meal, 521 Woodland St., 37206. Tel: 615-256-7256; Fax: 615-256-4763. Henry Beach, Exec. Dir.

Ladies of Charity of Nashville, Inc., 2216 State St., 37203. Tel: 615-327-3453; 327-3430; Fax: 615-321-3312. Affiliated with the Ladies of Charity of the United States of America, LCUSA, and the Association of International Charities, AIC.

Ladies of Charity Welfare Agency, Inc., 2212 State St., 37203. Tel: 615-327-3430; Fax: 615-321-3312. Mrs. Terri Puma, Exec. Dir.; Rev. Msgr. George W. Rohling, V.G., Moderator.

Mary, Queen of Angels. Inc., 30 White Bridge Rd., 37205. Tel: 615-760-4424; Fax: 615-352-8591.
E-mail: dglascoe@edge.net
David Glascoe, Dir.

Mid-Tennessee Rural Outreach Association, 30 White Bridge Rd., 37205. Tel: 615-352-3087. Legal Title: *Mid-Tennessee Rural Outreach Association; Assumption-St. Vincent North Nashville Outreach Association.*

Parish Twinning Program of the Americas, 208 Leake Ave., 37205. Tel: 615-356-5999; Fax: 615-352-5114.
E-mail: parishprog@aol.com
Theresa Patterson, Exec. Dir.

Pope John Paul II High School, Inc., 2400 Twenty-first Ave. S., 37212. Tel: 615-661-7591. James Tuerff, Pres.

The Roman Catholic Diocese of Nashville Endowment for the Advancement of Catholic Schools Trust, 2400 21st Ave. S., 37212. Tel: 615-383-6393; Fax: 615-292-8411. Most Rev. Edward U. Kmiec, Trustee.

St. Henry Property Development, Inc. dba The Cloister, 30 White Bridge Rd., 37205. Tel: 615-760-4424; Fax: 615-352-8591.
E-mail: dglascoe@edge.net
David Glacoe, Exec. Dir.

HENDERSONVILLE. *Legion of Mary*. Tel: 615-824-3276; Fax: 615-824-7989.
E-mail: WSBev@aol.com
Web site: www.catholic-church.org/OLOL
Rev. William S. Bevington, Dir., Mailing Address: P.O. Box 279, 37077-0279.

Priests Eucharistic League. Tel: 615-824-3276; Fax: 615-824-7989.
E-mail: WSBev@aol.com
Web site: www.catholic-church.org/OLOL
Rev. William S. Bevington, Dir., Mailing Address: P.O. Box 279, Nashville, 37077-0729.

RELIGIOUS INSTITUTES OF MEN REPRESENTED IN THE DIOCESE

For further details refer to the corresponding bracketed number in the Religious Institutes of Men or Women section.

[0275]—*Carmelites of Mary Immaculate*.—C.M.I.
[0520]—*Franciscan Friars*. (Prov. of Sacred Heart).—O.F.M.
[0570]—*Glenmary Home Missioners*.—Glmy.
[0690]—*Jesuit Fathers and Brothers*.—S.J.
[0430]—*Order of Preachers-Dominicans*. (Southern Prov.).—O.P.
[1200]—*Society of the Divine Savior*. (Milwaukee, WI).—S.D.S.

RELIGIOUS INSTITUTES OF WOMEN REPRESENTED IN THE DIOCESE

[0760]—*Daughters of Charity of St. Vincent de Paul*. (East Central Prov., Evansville, IN).—D.C.
[1070-03]—*Dominican Sisters*.—O.P.
[1070-07]—*Dominican Sisters*.—O.P.
[1070-09]—*Dominican Sisters*.—O.P.
[2575]—*Institute of the Sisters of Mercy of the Americas*. (Baltimore, MD; Cincinnati, OH).—R.S.M.
[]—*Sacred Heart Congregation (India)*.—S.H.
[]—*Sacred Heart Congregation (Mexico)*.
[1680]—*School Sisters of St. Francis*.—S.S.S.F. - O.S.F.
[]—*Sisters for Christian Community*. (St. Louis).—S.F.C.C.
[0990]—*Sisters of Divine Providence*. (St. Louis Prov.).—C.D.P.
[3270]—*Sisters of the Most Precious Blood*.—C.PP.S.
[1705]—*Sisters of St. Francis of Assisi*.—O.S.F.

DIOCESAN CEMETERIES

NASHVILLE. *Calvary Cemetery*, 1001 Lebanon Rd., 37210.

NECROLOGY

† Williams, Rev. Msgr. Charles M., Vicar Gen. Emeritus. —Died Nov. 21, 1999.

Archdiocese of Newark

(Archidioecesis Novarcensis)

Most Reverend

PETER LEO GERETY, D.D.

Archbishop Emeritus of Newark; ordained June 29, 1939; appointed Coadjutor Bishop of Portland March 4, 1966; Episcopal ordination June 1, 1966; appointed Apostolic Administrator February 18, 1967; succeeded to See September 15, 1969; appointed Archbishop of Newark April 2, 1974; installed June 28, 1974; Pallium conferred December 12, 1974; retired June 1, 1986. *Res., 60 Home Ave., Rutherford, NJ, 07070.* Tel.: 201-460-1369; Fax: 201-842-0724.

Most Reverend

PAUL G. BOOTKOSKI, D.D., V.G.

Auxiliary Bishop of Newark; ordained May 28, 1966; appointed Titular Bishop of Zarna and Auxiliary Bishop of Newark July 8, 1997; Episcopal ordination September 5, 1997. *Res., Cathedral Basilica of the Sacred Heart, 89 Ridge St., Newark, NJ, 07104.* Tel.: 973-484-4600; Fax: 973-497-4018.

Most Reverend

ARTHUR J. SERRATELLI, S.S.L.

Auxiliary Bishop of Newark; ordained December 20, 1968; appointed Titular Bishop of Enera and Auxiliary Bishop of Newark July 3, 2000; Episcopal ordination September 8, 2000. *Res., Cathedral Basilica of the Sacred Heart, 89 Ridge St., Newark, NJ, 07104.* Tel.: 973-484-4600; Fax: 973-497-4555.

(Vacant See)

Archdiocesan Center: 171 Clifton Ave., P.O. Box 9500, Newark, NJ, 07104-9500. Tel.: 973-497-4000; Fax: 973-497-4033.

Web site address: www.rcan.org

E-mail address: webmaster@rcan.org

Most Reverend

DOMINIC A. MARCONI, D.D.

Auxiliary Bishop of Newark; ordained May 30, 1953; appointed Titular Bishop of Bure and Auxiliary Bishop of Newark May 3, 1976; Episcopal ordination June 25, 1976. *Res., 238 E. Blancke St., Linden, NJ, 07036.* Tel.: 908-486-1022; Fax: 908-486-7701.

Most Reverend

DAVID ARIAS, O.A.R., D.D.

Auxiliary Bishop of Newark; ordained May 31, 1952; appointed Titular Bishop of Badie and Auxiliary Bishop of Newark January 25, 1983; Episcopal ordination April 7, 1983. *Res., St. Joseph of the Palisades Rectory, 6401 Palisade Ave., West New York, NJ, 07093.* Tel.: 201-861-6644; Fax: 201-861-7799.

Most Reverend

CHARLES J. McDONNELL, D.D.

Auxiliary Bishop of Newark; ordained May 29, 1954; appointed Titular Bishop of Pocofelto and Auxiliary Bishop of Newark March 15, 1994; Episcopal ordination May 12, 1994. *Res., Holy Trinity Rectory, 34 Maple Ave., Hackensack, NJ, 07601.* Tel.: 201-343-5170; Fax: 201-343-5067.

DIOCESE ESTABLISHED, 1853; ERECTED AN ARCHDIOCESE, DECEMBER 10, 1937.

Square Miles 513.

Comprises Four Counties in the State of New Jersey, viz.: Bergen, Hudson, Essex and Union.

For legal titles of parishes and archdiocesan institutions, consult the Chancery Office.

STATISTICAL OVERVIEW

Personnel	
Retired Archbishops	1
Auxiliary Bishops	5
Abbots	1
Priests: Diocesan Active in Diocese	513
Priests: Active Outside Diocese	30
Priests: Diocesan in Foreign Missions	9
Priests: Retired, Sick or Absent	170
Number of Diocesan Priests	722
Religious Priests in Diocese	239
Extern Priests in Diocese	83
Ordinations:	
Diocesan Priests	11
Transitional Deacons	14
Permanent Deacons in Diocese	251
Total Brothers	96
Total Sisters	1,374
Parishes	
Parishes	235
With Resident Pastor:	
Resident Diocesan Priests	206
Resident Religious Priests	29
Without Resident Pastor:	
Administered by Priests	6
Pastoral Centers	172
Professional Ministry Personnel:	
Brothers	6
Sisters	148
Lay Ministers	251
Welfare	
Catholic Hospitals	8
Total Assisted	829,735
Health Care Centers	114
Total Assisted	21,247
Homes for the Aged	7
Total Assisted	642
Day Care and Extended Day Care Centers	145
Total Assisted	5,199
Specialized Homes	8
Total Assisted	229
Special Centers for Social Services	242
Total Assisted	130,232
Residential Care of Disabled	2
Total Assisted	31
Other Institutions	8
Total Assisted	15,537
Educational	
Seminaries, Diocesan	3
Students from This Diocese	117
Students from Other Diocese	22
Diocesan Students in Other Seminaries	2
Seminaries, Religious	1
Students Religious	21
Total Seminarians	140
Colleges and Universities	4
Total Students	16,629
High Schools, Diocesan and Parish	17
Total Students	8,264
High Schools, Private	20
Total Students	7,783
Elementary Schools, Diocesan and Parish	132
Total Students	40,474
Elementary Schools, Private	7
Total Students	1,618
Non-residential Schools for the Disabled	6
Total Students	397
Catechesis/Religious Education:	
High School Students	3,141
Elementary Students	69,004
Total Students Under Catholic Instruction	147,450
Teachers in the Diocese:	
Priests	164
Brothers	29
Sisters	245
Lay Teachers	4,321
Vital Statistics	
Receptions into the Church:	
Infant Baptism Totals	17,618
Adult Baptism Totals	436
Received into Full Communion	599
First Communions	14,782
Confirmations	10,826
Marriages:	
Catholic	4,134
Interfaith	670
Total Marriages	4,804
Deaths	11,743
Total Catholic Population	1,319,558
Total Population	2,655,985

Former Bishops—Most Rev. JAMES ROOSEVELT BAYLEY, D.D., cons. Oct. 30, 1853; promoted to the Archiepiscopal See of Baltimore, July 30, 1872; died Oct. 3, 1877.—Most Rev. MICHAEL AUGUSTINE CORRIGAN, D.D., cons. May 4, 1873; promoted to the Archiepiscopal See of Petra, Oct. 1, 1880; succeeded to the Archiepiscopal See of New York, Oct. 10, 1885; died May 5, 1902.—Most Rev. WINAND MICHAEL WIGGER, D.D., cons. Oct. 18, 1881; died Jan. 5, 1901.—Most Rev. JOHN JOSEPH O'CONNOR, D.D., ord. Dec. 22, 1877; cons. July 25, 1901; died May 20, 1927.—Most Rev. THOMAS J. WALSH, S.T.D., J.C.D., ord. Jan. 27, 1900; appt. Bishop of Trenton, May 10, 1918; cons. July 25, 1918 made Assistant at the Pontifical Throne March 13, 1922; transferred to the See of Newark, March 2, 1928; appt. Archbishop of Newark, Dec. 10, 1937 Pallium conferred, Dec. 18, 1937; installed April 27, 1938; died June 6, 1952.—Most Rev. THOMAS A. BOLAND, S.T.D., LL.D., ord. Dec. 23, 1922; appt. Titular Bishop of Hirina and Auxiliary to the Archbishop of Newark, May 21, 1940; cons. July 25, 1940; transferred to Paterson, June 21, 1947; appt. Archbishop of Newark, Nov. 15, 1952; installed Jan. 14, 1953 Assistant at the Pontifical Throne, May 6, 1965; retired April 2, 1974; died March 16, 1979.—Most Rev. PETER LEO GERETY, D.D., ord. June 29, 1939; appt. Coadjutor Bishop of Portland, March 4, 1966; cons. June 1, 1966; succeeded to See, Sept. 15, 1969; appt. Archbishop of Newark, April 2, 1974; installed June 28,

1974; retired June 1, 1986.—Most Rev. THEODORE E. MCCARRICK, Ph.D., ord. May 31, 1958; appt. Auxiliary Bishop of New York and Titular Bishop of Rusibisir, May 24, 1977; Episcopal ordination June 29, 1977; appt. First Bishop of Metuchen, Nov. 19, 1981; appt. Archbishop of Newark, May 30, 1986; Pallium conferred June 29, 1986; installed July 25, 1986; appt. to See of Washington, D.C., Nov. 21, 2000; installed Jan. 3, 2001.

Chancery—Archdiocesan Center, 171 Clifton Ave., P.O. Box 9500, Newark, 07104-0500. Tel: 973-497-4000; Fax: 973-497-4033. Open Mon.-Fri. 8:45-4:45. (Dispensation Requests or Questions regarding Canonical Matters can be directed to: Rev. Msgr. Frank G. Del Prete, J.C.D., Judical Vicar, at P.O. Box 9500, Newark, NJ 07104-0500. Tel: 973-497-4145; Fax 973-497-4138.).

Vicar General and Moderator of Curia—Most Rev. PAUL G. BOOTKOSKI, D.D., V.G. Tel: 973-497-4002; Fax: 973-497-4018.

Vicar General for Human Services—Rev. Msgr. JOSEPH T. SLINGER, Ph.D., V.G. Tel: 973-596-3835; Fax: 973-596-3836.

Vicar General for Planning and Public Affairs—Rev. Msgr. RONALD J. ROZNIAK, V.G. Tel: 973-497-4015; Fax: 973-497-4018.

Chancellor/Delegate for Religious—Sr. THOMAS MARY SALERNO, S.C., M.A. Tel: 973-497-4010; Fax: 973-497-4018.

Vice Chancellor for Archdiocesan Archives—Rev. Msgr. FRANCIS R. SEYMOUR, *Walsh Library, Seton Hall University, 400 South Orange Ave., South Orange, 07079.* Tel: 973-761-9476; Fax: 973-761-9550.

Secretary to the Archbishop—Rev. JAMES V. TETI. Tel: 973-497-4005; Fax: 973-497-4018.

Executive Assistant to the Archbishop—Ms. ROSEANN BIASI-VASQUEZ. Tel: 973-497-4006.

Secretrary for Development—Rev. JAMES S. CHOMA. Tel: 973-497-4134; Fax: 973-497-4031.

Judicial Vicar Archdiocesan Metropolitan Tribunal—Rev. Msgr. FRANK G. DELPRETE, J.C.D. Tel: 973-497-4149; Fax: 973-497-4138.

Vicar for Priests—Rev. Msgr. JAMES J. FINNERTY, *St. John Rectory, 22 Mulberry St., Newark, 07102.* Tel: 973-799-0201; Fax: 973-623-6804.

Executive Director for Priest Personnel—Rev. Msgr. WILLIAM J. FADROWSKI, M.Div. Tel: 973-497-4222; Fax: 973-497-4219.

Vicar for Permanent Deacons—Rev. Msgr. THOMAS M. O'LEARY, *700 Wyckoff Ave., Wyckoff, 07481.* Tel: 201-891-1122; Fax: 201-847-8518.

Director of Vocations—Rev. RICHARD J. KELLY. Tel: 973-497-4367; Fax: 973-497-4369.

Vicar for Ministries—Most Rev. ARTHUR J. SERRATELLI, S.T.D., S.S.L. Tel: 973-497-4318; Fax: 973-497-4555.

Secretary for Education—Sr. DOMINICA ROCCHIO, S.C., Ed.D. Tel: 973-497-4250; Fax: 973-497-4249.

Vicar for Evangelization—Rev. Msgr. WILLIAM J. KOPLIK. Tel: 973-497-4360; Fax: 973-497-4033.

Vicar for Pastoral Life—Rev. Msgr. LOUIS F. FIMIANI. Tel: 973-497-4322; Fax: 973-497-4317.

Chief Financial Officer—Ms. CAROL PURCELL. Tel: 973-497-4051; Fax: 973-497-4033.

Regional Bishops—Most Rev. CHARLES J. MCDONNELL, D.D., Regional Bishop - Bergen Co.; Most Rev. DAVID ARIAS, O.A.R., D.D., Regional Bishop, Hudson Co. & Vicar, Hispanic Affairs; Most Rev. ARTHUR J. SERRATELLI, S.T.D., Regional Bishop, Essex County & Vicar for Ministries; Most Rev. DOMINIC A. MARCONI, D.D., Regional Bishop, Union County.

Episcopal Vicars—

Bergen County—Northwest (Deaneries 1, 4):; Vacant; South Bergen (Deaneries 5, 7): Rev. Msgr. THOMAS G. MADDEN, V.E., *St. John Vianney Res., 60 Home Ave., Rutherford, 07070.* Tel: 201-933-5155. East Bergen (Deaneries 2, 3, 6): Rev. Msgr. ROBERT H. SLIPE, V.E., *St. Peter the Apostle, 445 Fifth Ave., River Edge, 07661.* Tel: 201-261-3366.

Hudson County—North Hudson (Deaneries 8, 9, 14): Rev. Msgr. MICHAEL J. DESMOND, V.E., *St. Stephen, 141 Washington Ave., Kearney, 07032.* Tel: 201-998-3314. South Hudson (Deaneries 10-13): Rev. Msgr. CHARLES G. STENGEL, V.E., P.A., *St. John the Baptist, 3026 J.F.K. Blvd., Jersey City, 07306.* Tel: 201-653-8814.

Essex County—West Essex (Deaneries 15-18): Rev. Msgr. CHARLES W. GUSMER, V.E., *St. Catherine of Siena, 339 Pompton Ave., Cedar Grove, 07009.* Tel: 973-239-7960. City of Newark: Rev. Msgr. PAUL D. SCHETELICK, V.E., *Sacred Heart, 481 Sanford Ave., Newark, 07106.* Tel: 973-373-9790.

Union County—North and Southwest (Deaneries 22, 23, 26):; Vacant; Southeast and Elizabeth (Deaneries 24, 25): Very Rev. RONALD J. MARCZEWSKI, V.E., *St. Adalbert, 250 E. Jersey St., Elizabeth, 07206.* Tel: 908-352-2791.

Deans—

BERGEN COUNTY—Northwest Bergen Region Deanery 1: Very Rev. JOHN R. O'CONNELL, V.F., *Nativity, 315 Prospect St., Midland Park, 07432.* Tel: 201-444-6362; Fax: 201-444-5056. Northeast Bergen Region Deanery 2: Very Rev. EUGENE J. HAZEWSKI, V.F., *Assumption, 29 Jefferson Ave., Emerson, 07630.* Tel: 201-262-1122; Fax: 201-262-7855. Central Bergen Region Deanery 3: Rev. Msgr. RICHARD J. ARNHOLS, V.F., *St. John the Evangelist, 29 N. Washington Ave., Bergenfield, 07621.* Tel: 201-384-0101; Fax: 201-384-2055. Southwest Bergen Region Deanery 4: Very Rev. ROBERT G. MCBRIDE, V.F., *St. Philip the Apostle, 488 Saddle River Rd., Saddlebrook, 07663.* Tel: 201-843-1888; Fax: 201-368-9161. South Central Bergen Deanery 5: Very Rev. JOSEPH C. DOYLE, V.F., *St. Francis Rectory, 114 Mt. Vernon St., Ridgefield Park, 07660.* Tel: 201-641-6464; Fax: 201-641-2282. Southeast Bergen Region Deanery 6: Very Rev. JAMES B. SULLIVAN, V.F., *Holy Trinity, 2367 Lemoine Ave., Fort Lee, 07024.* Tel: 201-947-1216; Fax: 201-947-1217. South Bergen Region Deanery 7: Very Rev. CHARLES J. MILLER, V.F., *Sacred Heart Rectory, 324 Ridge Rd., Lyndhurst, 07071.* Tel: 201-438-1137; Fax: 201-507-5861.

HUDSON COUNTY—North Hudson Deanery 8: Very Rev. CARLO FORTUNIO, V.F., *St. Mary's, Help of Christians, 6502 Jackson St., West New York, 07093.* Tel: 201-868-9444; Fax: 201-868-6451. Central Hudson Region Deanery 9: Very Rev. KENNETH J. HERBSTER, V.F., *Our Lady of Grace, 400 Willow Ave., Hoboken, 07030.* Tel: 201-659-0369; Fax: 201-659-5833. Jersey City North Region Deanery 10: Very Rev. KEVIN E. CARTER, V.F., *St. Nicholas Rectory, 122 Ferry St., Jersey City, 07037.* Tel: 201-659-5354; Fax: 201-798-6868. Jersey City Downtown Deanery 11: Very Rev. MICHAEL E. GUBERNAT, V.F., *St. Anthony's Rectory, 330 Sixth St., Jersey City, 07302-1801.* Tel: 201-653-0343; Fax: 201-653-0005. Jersey City South Deanery 12: Very Rev. JOHN J. CRYAN, V.F., *Our Lady of Mercy Rectory, 40 Sullivan Dr., Jersey City, 07305.* Tel: 201-434-7500; Fax: 201-432-2885. Bayonne Deanery 13: Very Rev. ANTHONY J. KULIG, V.F., *Our Lady of Mt. Carmel Rectory, 39 E. 22nd St., Bayonne, 07002.* Tel: 201-339-2070; Fax: 201-339-3676. West Hudson Region Deanery 14: Very Rev. RUDOLPH ZUBIK, V.F., *Our Lady of Czestochowa Rectory, 115 S. 3rd St., Harrison, 07029.* Tel: 201-483-2255; Fax: 201-483-4688.

ESSEX COUNTY—West Essex Deanery 15: Very Rev. ALBERT J. BERNER, V.F., *Monclair State University, 894 Valley Rd., Upper Montclair, 07043.* Tel: 973-746-2323; Fax: 973-783-3313. North Essex Deanery 16: Very Rev. JOSEPH D. GIRONE, V.F., *St. Peter Rectory, 155 William St., Belleville, 07109.* Tel: 973-751-2002; Fax: 973-751-6201. Central Essex Deanery 17: Very Rev. MICHAEL M. WALTERS, V.F., *Holy Spirit/Help of Christians, 17 N. Clinton St., East Orange, 07017.* Tel: 973-673-1077; Fax: 973-676-6494. South Essex Deanery 18: Very Rev. THOMAS M. CEMBOR, V.F., *St. Leo's Rectory, 103 Myrtle Ave., Irvington, 07111.* Tel: 973-372-1272; Fax: 973-416-8819. North Newark Essex Deanery 19:; Vacant; Central Newark Deanery 20: Rev. Msgr. PAUL D. SCHETELICK, V.F., *Sacred Heart (Vailsburg), 481 Sanford Ave., Newark, 07106.* Tel: 973-373-9790; Fax: 973-374-4047. Ironbound Deanery 21: Very Rev. RICHARD G. FRANCESCO, V.F., *St. Benedict, 65 Barbara St., Newark, 07105-3401.* Tel: 973-589-7930; Fax: 973-589-3665.

UNION COUNTY—Union Northwest Deanery 22: Rev. Msgr. ROBERT E. HARAHAN V.F., *St. Teresa's Rectory, 306 Morris Ave., Summit, 07901.* Tel: 908-277-3700; Fax: 908-273-5909. Union North Deanery 23: Very Rev. JOSPEH S. BEJGROWICZ, V.F., *St. Theresa Rectory, 541 Washington Ave., Kenilworth, 07033.* Tel: 908-272-4444; Fax: 908-272-2252. Union County Southeast Deanery 24: Very Rev. BENEDICT M. WORRY, O.S.B., V.F., *St. Elizabeth of Hungary, 179 Hussa St., Linden, 07036.* Tel: 908-486-2514; Fax: 908-486-1757. Elizabeth Deanery 25: Very Rev. ROBERT E. TEMPLETON, V.F., *Blessed Sacrament Rectory, 1096 North Ave., Elizabeth, 07201.* Tel: 908-352-0338; Fax: 908-352-4553. Union County Southwest Deanery 26: Rev. Msgr. JOSEPH P. MASIELLO, V.F., *Holy Trinity, 315 First St., Westfield, 07090.* Tel: 908-232-8137; Fax: 908-654-8780.

Advisory Bodies

College of Consultors—Vacant, Pres.; Rev. Msgr. RONALD J. ROZNIAK, V.G., Sec.; Most Rev. DAVID ARIAS, O.A.R.; Most Rev. PAUL G. BOOTKOSKI, D.D., V.G.; Most Rev. DOMINIC A. MARCONI, D.D.; Most Rev. CHARLES J. MCDONNELL, D.D.; Most Rev. ARTHUR J. SERRATELLI, S.T.D.; Rev. Msgr. EDWARD J. CIUBA; Rev. Msgr. LAWRENCE CULL; Rev. Msgr. EDWARD J. EILERT; Rev. Msgr. PETER A. CHEPLIC; Rev. Msgr. JOHN GILCHRIST; Very Rev. JOSEPH S. BEJGROWICZ, V.F.; Rev. PAUL BOCHICCHIO.

Presbyteral Council—Vacant, Pres.; Very Rev. KENNETH J. HERBSTER, V.F., Exec. Sec. Members: Most Rev. DAVID ARIAS, O.A.R., D.D.; Most Rev. PAUL G. BOOTKOSKI, D.D., V.G.; Most Rev. DOMINIC A. MARCONI, D.D.; Most Rev. CHARLES J. MCDONNELL, D.D.; Most Rev. ARTHUR J. SERRATELLI, S.T.D.; Rev. Msgr. EDWARD J. EILERT; Rev. Msgr. RAYMOND J. POLLARD; Rev. Msgr. RONALD J. ROZNIAK, V.G.; Rev. Msgr. PAUL D. SCHETELICK, V.F., V.E.; Rev. Msgr. PETER J. ZACCARDO; Revs. PAUL L. BOCHICCHIO; DENNIS COCOZZA; JOHN CONNOLLY, S.D.B.; JOHN J. CRYAN, V.F.; LAWRENCE J. FAMA; RENATO GRASELLI; GERALD GREAVES; FERNANDO GUILLEN; KEVIN HANBURY; JAN SASIN; MICHAEL J. SHEEHAN; WILLIAM SHERIDAN; PETER SMUTELOVIC.

Priest Personnel Policy Board—Rev. Msgr. JAMES BOUFFARD; Rev. Msgr. EDWARD G. PRICE; Rev. Msgr. ROBERT M. CHABAK; Rev. Msgr. DONALD E. GUENTHER; Revs. MICHAEL A. HANLY; EUGENE J. HAZEWSKI, V.F.; ROBERT B. STAGG; JOHN J. LAFERRERA, Archbishop's Delegate.

Diaconate Executive Committee—Deacons ROBERT V. THOMANN, Chm.; CHARLES F. KILEY, Vice Chm. Tel: 973-497-4223.

Archdiocesan Incardination Board—Most Rev. PAUL G. BOOTKOSKI, D.D., V.G.; Most Rev. CHARLES J. MCDONNELL, D.D.; Rev. Msgr. FRANK G. DEL PRETE, J.C.D.; Rev. Msgr. WILLIAM J. FADROWSKI; Rev. VENANTIUS FERNANDO.

Archdiocesan Stewardship Advisory Committee—Rev. Msgr. RONALD J. ROZNIAK, V.G., Chm. Tel: 973-497-4015. Rev. JAMES S. CHOMA; Rev. Msgr. THOMAS M. O'LEARY; Rev. TIMOTHY J. HORGAN; Very Rev. PAUL L. BOCHICCHIO, V.F.; Rev. LOUIS CAPUTO, S.D.V.; Rev. Msgr. EDWARD J. CIUBA, S.T.L., S.S.L.; Rev. Msgr. PAUL D. SCHETELICK, V.F.; Rev. ANTHONY J. KULIG; Very Rev. VICTOR P. KENNEDY, V.F.; Rev. CARLO FORTUNIO; Rev. Msgr. GEORGE R. TRABOLD; Rev. Msgr. JOHN S. ANTAO; Rev. Msgr. RICARDO GONZALEZ; Revs. JAN SASIN; GEORGE D. GILLEN; Rev. Msgr. JEREMIAS R. REBANAL, J.C.D., Ph.D.

Priestly Vocation Board—Rev. Msgr. THOMAS MADDEN, V.E., Chm.; Rev. Msgr. THOMAS O'LEARY; Rev. Msgr. WILLIAM J. DALY; Revs. MICHAEL A. ANDREANO; THOMAS M. CEMBOR; SEAN R. CUNNEEN; JOSEPH C. DOYLE; JOHN D. GABRIEL; RENATO GRASSELLI; ANTHONY J. KULIG; GERARD H. MCCARREN.

Archdiocesan Pro-Life Commission—DANIEL KRAFT, Chm. Members: Rev. Msgr. LOUIS F. FIMIANI; Rev. Msgr. RICHARD M. MCGUINNESS; TRAUDE BARBIERO; ESTELE FRESE; BONNIE LUDWIG; BRIAN LUDWIG; CESAR ORTEGA; THOMAS RUSSO; JUAN RYAN, Esq.; JAMES SONDY; Dr. LEONIE WATSON; Dr. RICHARD WATSON; Rev. Msgr. ALOYSIUS WELSH, Consultant.

Women & Men Religious Council—

Chairperson—Sr. THOMAS MARY SALERNO, S.C., Chancellor & Delegate for Religious. Members: Sr. MARIE GAGLIANO, M.P.F.; Revs. ASHLEY HARRINGTON, O.Carm.; EDWIN LEAHY, O.S.B.; Sr. MARILYN MINTER, C.S.S.F.

Archdiocesan Finance Council—JOHN W. CULLIGAN, Chm. Members: CHARLES C. CARELLA; LAWRENCE R. CODEY; DONALD M. DANIELS; ANNE EVANS ESTABROOK; ADRIAN M. FOLEY, JR.; ALBERT R. GAMPER, JR.; LESLIE A. HYNES; ARTHUR E. IMPERATORE; BRIAN D. MCAULEY; W. PETER MCBRIDE; JOSEPH L. MUSCARELLE, JR.; EDWARD F. RYAN; GARRY J. SCHEURING; ANTHONY R. TERRACIANO; JOSEPH A. UNANUE.

Archdiocesan Women's Commission—Sr. THOMAS MARY SALERNO, S.C., Chm. Members: ANN BURGMEYER; MARTA CABRERA; MARY ELAINE CONNELL; JOANNE DEPASQUALE PARENT; LINDA ENGLISH; Dr. ZENI FOX; ANNA GROVES; ANA LOPO; Sr. MARGARET T. MCGOVERN, O.P.; PAULA METZGER; SHARON MUSCARELLE; LOIS PAGNOZZI.

Archdiocesan Theological Commission—Rev. Msgr. ROBERT E. HARAHAN, S.T.D., Chm.; Revs. JAMES M. CAFONE, S.T.D.; JOHN CHADWICK; LAWRENCE FRIZZELL, D.Phil.; Dr. JOHN M. GRONDELSKI, Ph.D.; Revs. THOMAS G. GUARINO, S.T.D.; PAUL HOLMES, S.T.D.; Rev. Msgr. THOMAS MCCARTHY; Rev. LAWRENCE PORTER, Ph.D.; Sr. MARGARET THOMAS MCGOVERN, O.P.; Rev. C. ANTHONY ZICCARDI, S.S.L.

Archdiocesan Pastoral Council—BLANCHE BISHOP, Chm.; OTTO PAYONZECK, Vice Chm.; GEORGEANNA CAMERON, Sec.; Sr. VIRGINIA STANTON, S.S.J., Staff. Tel: 973-497-4350.

Archdiocesan Commission for Christain Unity—Rev. Msgr. PHILIP D. MORRIS, S.T.D., Chm.; Rev. PHILIP F.A. LATRONICO, Exec. Sec., *69 Valley St., P.O. Box 308, Hillsdale, 07642.* Tel: 973-497-4321.

Archdiocesan Commission for Interreligious Affairs—Rev. Msgr. JOHN GILCHRIST, Chm.; Rev. PHILIP F.A. LATRONICO, Exec. Sec. Tel: 973-497-4321.

Archdiocesan Liturgical Commission—Rev. ROBERT LAFERRERA, Chm. Tel: 973-497-4345. ANITA FOLEY, Sec.

Metropolitan Tribunal of the Archdiocese of Newark

Metropolitan Tribunal of the Archdiocese of Newark—Archdiocesan Center, 171 Clifton Ave., P.O. Box 9500, Newark, 07104-0500. Tel: 973-497-4145; Fax: 973-497-4138.

Judicial Vicar—Rev. Msgr. FRANK G. DEL PRETE, J.C.D.

Associate Judicial Vicar—Rev. Msgr. JAMES P. MCMENEMIE, S.T.L.

Full-time Staff—Sr. CATHERINE MARY RAYMOND, J.C.L.; Rev. JOHN F. CONNOR, S.T.B.

Archdiocesan Judges—Rev. Msgr. VINCENT P. COBURN, J.C.D.; Revs. JOHN J. CRYAN, M.Div.; ROBERT E. EMERY, J.C.L.; RICHARD G. FRANCESCO, J.C.L.; Rev. Msgr. ROBERT J. HARRINGTON, M.Div.; Revs. NORBERT F. LASKOWSKI, B.A.; ROBERT G. MCBRIDE, J.C.L.; BERNARD N. MOHAN, B.S.; JOHN S. OLSZEWSKI, S.T.L.; Rev. Msgr. GEORGE R. TRABOLD, J.C.L.; Rev. MICHAEL M. WALTERS, J.C.L.

Part-time Staff—Rev. Msgr. FRANCIS HOUGHTON; Revs. JOSEPH D'AMICO; STANLEY GOMES; GERALD GEAVES; THOMAS KENNA; JEREMIAH MCGINLEY, O.F.M.; WILLIAM A. MAHON; Deacon VINCENT E. MESSINA; Sr. RUTHE MORGAN, R.S.M.; Rev. JAMES M. SHEEHAN.

Promoter of Justice—Rev. Msgr. ROBERT F. COLEMAN, J.C.D.

Defenders of the Bond—Rev. Msgr. VINCENT J. DOYLE, J.C.D.; Rev. ROBERT S. MEYER, J.C.L.

Notaries—MARGARET RUSSO; SANDRA PERRINI; CATHERINE LOBRUNO; JOHN WALSH.

Vicar General for Planning and Public Affairs

Vicar General for Planning and Public Affairs—Rev. Msgr. RONALD J. ROZNIAK, V.G. Tel: 973-497-4015; Fax: 973-497-4031.

Office of Development—Rev. JAMES S. CHOMA, Sec. for Devel. Tel: 973-497-4135; Fax: 973-497-4031.

Executive Director for Development—JOHN F. WALSH. Tel: 973-497-4124.

Special Events Office—Tel: 973-497-4130.

Planned Giving Program—BARBARA WARNER, Dir. Tel: 973-497-4125.

Office of Research and Planning—JOSEPH A. VANCIO, M.A., Dir. Tel: 973-497-4025; Fax: 973-497-4028.

Office of Stewardship—JOSEPH DWYER, Dir. Tel: 973-497-4128; Fax: 973-497-4031.

Coordinating Committee for Parish Renewal—171 Clifton Ave., P.O. Box 9500, Newark, 07104-0500. Tel: 973-497-4013; Fax: 973-497-4555.

Office of Parish Renewal—JOSEPH A. VANCIO, M.A., Acting Coord. Tel: 973-497-4013; Fax: 973-497-4555.

Vicar General and Moderator of the Curia

Vicar General and Moderator of the Curia—Most Rev. PAUL G. BOOTKOSKI, D.D., V.G., *Archdiocesan Center, 171 Clifton Ave., Newark, 07104.* Tel: 973-497-4002; Fax: 973-497-4018. All Offices are at the Archdiocesan Center unless otherwise noted.

Office of Counsel—WILLIAM A. CAMBRIA, ESQ. Tel: 973-497-4302; Fax: 973-497-4310.

Office of Communications and Public Relations—JAMES GOODNESS, Dir. Tel: 973-497-4190; Fax: 973-497-4185.

Chancellor/Delegate for Religious—Sr. THOMAS MARY SALERNO, S.C., M.A. Tel: 973-497-4010; Fax: 973-497-4018.

Vice Chancellor for Archives—Rev. Msgr. FRANCIS R. SEYMOUR. Tel: 973-761-9476; Fax: 973-761-9550.

Health Care Personnel—Sr. THOMAS MARY SALERNO, S.C., M.A. Tel: 973-497-4009; Fax: 973-497-4018.

Pastoral Associates—Sr. THOMAS MARY SALERNO, S.C., M.A. Tel: 973-497-4009; Fax: 973-497-4018.

St. John Vianney Priests' Residence—Rev. Msgr. EDWARD F. KAVIN, Dir. CAROL HUBBA, Admin., *60 Home Ave., Rutherford, 07070.* Tel: 201-933-5155.

Propagation of the Faith—Rev. Msgr. ROBERT J. FUHRMAN, Dir. Tel: 973-497-4375; Fax: 973-497-4371.

Holy Childhood Association—Sr. ARLINE ZURICH, O.S.B., Mission Coord. Tel: 973-497-4376; Fax: 973-497-4371.

Vocations Office—Rev. RICHARD J. KELLY, Dir. Tel: 973-497-4365; Fax: 973-497-4369.

Office of Clergy Personnel—Rev. Msgr. WILLIAM J. FADROWSKI, Exec. Dir. Tel: 973-497-4222; Fax: 973-497-4219.

Diocesan Priest Personnel—Rev. Msgr. WILLIAM J. FADROWSKI, Dir.; Ms. JOSEPHINE CHOKRAN, Admin. Asst. Tel: 973-497-4222; Fax: 973-497-4219.

Adjunct Clergy Personnel—Rev. VENANTIUS FERNANDO, Dir.; Ms. FRANCES DOWNING, Admin. Asst. Tel: 973-497-4222.

Ministry to Retired Priest—Rev. Msgr. EDWARD F. KAVIN, Dir. Tel: 973-497-4224.

Continuing Education of Priests—Rev. Msgr. THOMAS A. MCCARTHY, Dir. Tel: 973-497-4221.

Continuing Formation of Priests—Rev. Msgr. OWEN HENDRY, Dir. Tel: 973-497-4225.

Permanent Diaconate—Deacon EDWARD W. PORTER, Dir. Tel: 973-497-4223. Deacon DANIEL RAVELO, Coord. of Spanish-Speaking.

Secretary For Temporal Administration—CAROL PURCELL, CFO. Tel: 973-497-4051; Fax: 973-497-4031.

Risk Management/Insurance Services—JOSEPH A. FRANK, Dir. Tel: 973-497-4040; Fax: 973-497-4031.

Office of Finance—GEORGE PERALTA, Dir. Tel: 973-497-4055; Fax: 973-497-4031.

Office of Banking and Investments—GEORGE PERALTA, Dir. MATTHEW J. PHELAN, Mgr. Tel: 973-497-4070; Fax: 973-497-4031.

Office Services/Mailroom—RAYMOND QUINTANA, Oper. Mgr. Tel: 973-497-4035; Fax: 973-497-4033.

Computing Services—ROBERT J. KENNELLY, Dir. Tel: 973-497-4160.

Office of Plant Services—THEODORE DEC, Dir. Tel: 973-497-4110; Fax: 973-497-4033.

Office of Catholic Cemeteries—Rev. Msgr. WILLIAM NAEDELE, Dir.; Mr. JAMES T. FAHEY, Exec. Dir., *340 Ridge Rd., North Arlington, 07032.* Tel: 201-991-7404; Fax: 201-997-9560.

Office of Parish Services—ROBERT KENNA, Dir. Tel: 973-497-4080; Fax: 973-497-4033.

Office of Parish Internal Audit—NANCY F. LYSTASH, Dir. Tel: 973-497-4074; Fax: 973-497-4031.

Office of Human Resources—WILLIAM E. MULLIS, III, Dir. Tel: 973-497-4104; Fax: 973-497-4103.

Cooperative Supply Services—STEPHEN MICHALEK, JR., Dir. Tel: 973-497-4170; Fax: 973-497-4174. ERICA PHINN, Customer Svc. Rep. Tel: 973-497-4166.

Vicar General and Moderator of the Curia is the Archbishop's liaison to the following:

Archdiocesan Commission for Christian Unity—Rev. Msgr. PHILIP D. MORRIS, S.T.D., Chm.; Rev. PHILIP F.A. LATRONICO, Exec. Sec. Tel: 973-497-4338.

Archdiocesan Commission for Interreligious Affairs—Rev. Msgr. JOHN J. GILCHRIST, M.A., Chm.; Rev. PHILIP LATRONICO, Exec. Sec. Tel: 973-497-4338.

Archdiocesan Commission on Justice and Peace—Dr. WILLIAM TOTH, Chm. Tel: 973-497-4257.

Archdiocesan Liturgical Commission—Rev. ROBERT G. LAFERRERA, Chm. Tel: 973-497-4347.

Archdiocesan Pro-Life Commission—DANIEL KRAFT, Chm., *1805 Penbrook Ter., Union, 07036.* Tel: 908-925-6442.

RENEW International, Office of—Directors: Rev. Msgr. THOMAS A. KLEISSLER; Mr. MICHAEL BROUGH, *1232 George St., Plainfield, 07062-1717.* Tel: 908-769-5400; Fax: 908-769-5660. Sr. CHERYL ERB, R.S.M., Coord. International RENEW; Sr. PAT CROWLEY, O.P., Coord. North American RENEW; Sr. MARY MCGUINNESS, O.P., Coord. Small Christian Community Resources; MICHAEL FABIAN, Coord. Small Christian Community Svcs.; Sr. MARIA IGLESIAS, S.C., Coord. Hispanic RENEW. RENEW International Service Team: Sr. LOUISE ALFF, F.M.D.C.; KATHERINE ANDREWS; DOLLY BANDURA; Sr. MARGARITA CASTANEDA, C.N.D.; Dr. IRMA CHAVEZ; Sr. MAUREEN COLLEARY, F.S.P.; SUSAN SELTENRIGHT DEFERRARI; Rev. JACK FARLEY, S.V.D.; JERRY HERAUF; Dr. ROBERT HOWLETT; GREG KREMER; Rev. Msgr. JACK MCDERMOTT; WILLIAM REILLY; MARTIN ROMERO; Sr. BETH TAYLOR, C.S.J.P; Sr. DOT URBAN, S.S.J.; SUSAN WINCHELL; ANTHONY VISOCCHI; Sr. ALICE YOHE, S.S.J., Admin. Asst. SUSAN OLSZEWSKI, Fin. Controller; DEBI DONNELLY, Office Mgr.

Vicar for Ministries—Most Rev. ARTHUR J. SERATELLI, S.T.D., S.S.L., *Archdiocesan Center, 171 Clifton Ave., P.O. Box 9500, Newark, 07104-0500.* Tel: 973-497-4319; Fax: 973-497-4555. All Offices are at the Archdiocesan Center unless otherwise noted.

The Vicar for Ministries is the Vicar General/Moderator of the Curia's liaison to the following:

"The Catholic Advocate", Archdiocesan Newspaper—Mr. ROBERT DYLAK, Publisher. Tel: 973-497-4200; Fax: 973-497-4192.

Secretariat for Education—Sr. DOMINICA ROCCHIO, S.C., Ed.D., Admin. Asst.; Sr. CATHERINE ROCHE, S.S.J. Tel: 973-497-4260; Fax: 973-497-4249.

Catechetical Office—Mr. RONALD L. PIHOKKER, M.A., Dir. Tel: 973-497-4294. JOAN M. ROVERE, M.A., Deputy Dir. Tel: 973-497-4286. ANITA HERNANDEZ, M.A., Catechesis for Hispanics. Tel: 973-497-4290. CLAIRE OHALEK, M.A., Assoc. Dir. Parish Catechetics for Essex and Union. Tel: 973-497-4296. Sr. DELPHINE CROFT, O.P., M.A., Assoc. Dir. Parish Catechetics for Bergen and Hudson; ALICE HUGH BROWN, M.A., Assoc. Dir. Adult Catechesis. Tel: 973-497-4295. Sr. FRANCES CORDIS, S.C., M.A., Assoc. Dir. Catechist Certification and Enrichment. Tel: 973-497-4288. Mrs. CAROL HENDERSON, Inforamtion Technologies. Tel: 973-497-4292. JANET SANTELLO, Catechesis with Families. Tel: 973-497-4297.

Scholarship Fund for Inner City Children—KEVIN P. MORIARTY, Exec. Dir. Tel: 973-497-4281; Fax: 973-497-4279.

Office of the Superintendent of Schools—Sr. DOMINICA ROCCHIO, S.C., Ed.D., Supt. Tel: 973-497-4260. Bro. RALPH DARMENTO, F.S.C., Deputy Supt. Schools; Sr. CATHERINE ROCHE, S.S.J., M.A., Admin. Asst. Assoc. Superintendents: Rev. JOHN CONNOLLY, S.D.B., Education Technology; Sr. PATRICIA BUTLER, S.C., M.A., Elementary Schools; Mr. JOHN O'NEIL, M.A., Regl. High Schools; Sr. ELIZABETH SCULLY, C.N.D., M.A., Christian Formation. Asst. Superintendents for Elementary Schools: Sr. MURIEL SMITHWICK, C.S.J., M.A., Cluster 2; Sr. MARIE GAGLIANO, M.P.F., M.A., Cluster 3; Sr. JOAN AMELIA FERRUGGIARO, S.S.J., M.A., Cluster 1; Sr. LOUISE CABABE, O.P., Ph.D., Curriculum & Testing. Directors: Mrs. ESTELLE FRESE, M.A., Personnel & Events Mgr.; Mrs. GRACE PIETROPINTO, B.S., Finance for Regl. High Schools; PATRICIA BRAUN, B.A., Marketing; GLORIA CASTUCCI, M.A., Early Childhood Education; Mrs. ANN MCNIERNEY, M.S., Govt. Programs; Sr. LORETTA HOGAN, S.S.J., M.A., Elementary School Finance; MARVIN N. BROWN, B.S., Data Systems Operator & Technician.

Vicar for Evangelization—Rev. Msgr. WILLIAM J. KOPLIK, *199 Walnut St., Northvale, 07647.* Tel: 201-768-1177; Fax: 201-768-2522.

Vicar for Pastoral Life—Rev. Msgr. LOUIS F. FIMIANI. Tel: 973-497-4322; Fax: 973-497-4555.

Office of Leadership Development—WILLIAM J. TOTH, Ph.D., Dir. Tel: 973-497-4257; Fax: 973-497-4249.

Renew 2000—Rev. Msgr. LOUIS F. FIMIANI, Coord. Tel: 973-497-4358; Fax: 973-497-4555.

Hispanic Apostolate—Mrs. MARICELA QUINTANA. Tel: 201-497-4335. Centro Guadalupe: Rev. FERNANDO GOMEZ, O.A.R., Dir., *545 35 St., Union City, 07087.* Tel: 201-348-8400; Fax: 201-348-1809.

Office of Black Catholic Affairs—Mr. TRACEY BATTLES, Dir. Tel: 973-497-4340; Fax: 973-497-4317.

African-American and African Ethnic Apostolate Ministry—Tel: 973-497-4340.

Council for Multi-Cultural Concerns—Rev. Msgr. LOUIS F. FIMIANI, Chm. Tel: 973-497-4321.

Brazilian Apostolate—Rev. GEORGE C. LUTZ, Coord., *143 Madison St., Newark, 07105.* Tel: 973-344-8322.

Chinese Apostolate—Rev. Msgr. JOSEPH CHIANG, Coord., *Holy Rosary Rectory, 344 6th St., Jersey City, 07302.* Tel: 973-795-0210.

Indian Apostolate—Rev. THOMAS THOTTUNGAL, Coord., *691 West Side Ave., Jersey City, 07304.* Tel: 201-433-6365.

Filipino Apostolate—Rev. Msgr. JEREMIAS REBANAL, Coord., *800 Bergen Ave., Jersey City, 07306.* Tel: 201-433-6800.

Haitian Apostolate—Vacant, Coord.

Liaison to the Irish Community—Rev. Msgr. MICHAEL E. KELLY, *120 Northfield Ave., W. Orange, 07052.* Tel: 973-325-6624.

Italian Apostolate—Rev. JOSEPH F. AMBROSIO, Coord., *Our Lady of Mt. Carmel, 259 Oliver St., Newark, 07105.* Tel: 973-589-2090.

Korean Apostolate—Rev. Msgr. AUGUSTIN PARK, Coord., *St. Andrew Kim Parish, 257 Central Ave., Orange, 07050.* Tel: 973-673-1366.

Polish Apostolate—Rev. THADDEUS STASIK, Coord., *St. Ann, 291 St. Paul Ave., Jersey City, 07306.* Tel: 201-656-4018.

Portugese Apostolate—Rev. Msgr. JOHN S. ANTAO, Coord., *403 Spring St., Elizabeth, 07201.* Tel: 908-355-3810.

Vietnamese Apostolate—Rev. JOSEPH TRI MINH NGUYEN, Coord., *St. Michael, 252 Ninth St., Jersey City, 07302.* Tel: 201-434-8500.

Chaplain to the India Catholic Association (Syro-Malabar Rite)—Rev. SEBASTIAN KUNNATH, Coord., *Our Lady of the Visitation, 234 Fairview Ave., Paramus, 07652.* Tel: 201-444-0272.

Department of Human Concerns—KAY FURLANI, Dir. Tel: 973-497-4341; Fax: 973-497-4317.

Department of Shared Responsibility—Sr. REGINA SUPLICK, S.C., Dir. Tel: 973-497-4353; Fax: 973-497-4317.

Ministerial Development Center—Sr. VIRGINIA STANTON, S.S.J., Dir. Tel: 973-497-4350.

Worship Office—Sr. SANDRA DE MASI, S.S.J., Dir. Tel: 973-497-4345; Fax: 973-497-4348. Rev. MICHAEL J. SHEEHAN, Dir. RCIA; Rev. THOMAS B. IWANOWSKI, Assoc Dir. for Parish Life; Rev. THOMAS A. DENTE, Assoc. Dir. of Liturgical Formation; Rev. Msgr. RICHARD F. GRONCKI, Archdiocesan Ceremonies; Rev. Msgr. CHARLES W. GUSMER, S.T.D., Consultant for Liturgy; Rev. CHARLES PINYAN, Word on Worship.

Respect Life Office—Rev. Msgr. RICHARD M. MCGUINNESS, S.T.L., Ph.D., *1805 Penbrook Ter., Linden, 07036.* Tel: 732-388-8211.

Campus Ministry—Rev. JOHN B. BARON, Ph.D., Dir. DIANA ORSINI, Assoc. Dir., *Newman Center, 45 Bleeker St., Newark, 07112.* Tel: 973-642-1613; Fax: 973-642-1613.

Family Life Ministries—Ms. JUDITH MILLER, M.A., Dir. BARBARA KATULKA, Admin. Asst. Tel: 973-497-4325.

Family Life Center—256 Franklin Ave., Maplewood, 07040. Tel: 201-763-7659.

Pre-Cana Reservations—NANCY DELLISANTI. Tel: 973-497-4328.

Ministry with Separated, Divorced and Widowed Catholics—JANET MCCORMICK, Assoc. Dir.; Revs. ROBERT EMERY, Chap., Separated and Divorced; THOMAS ARMINIO, Chap., Widows and Widowers. Tel: 201-497-4327.

Hispanic Family Life Ministries—REINA BASUALDO, Assoc. Dir. Tel: 201-497-4326.

Catholic One Parent Organization—Rev. JOSEPH M. DOYLE, Chap. Tel: 201-433-0950.

Couples for Christ—Rev. PAUL J. LEHMAN, Chap. Tel: 973-623-0258. DANNY RODRIGUEZ, Coord., *26 Golf Rd., East Brunswick, 08816.* Tel: 732-562-2636.

Families for Nazareth—WALTER J. BOROWSKI, M.D., Contact Person, *812 N. Wood Ave., Ste. 101, Linden, 07036.* Tel: 908-486-3366; Fax: 908-486-0398.

Focolare Movement (East Coast Regional Directors)—HORTENSIA LOPEZ, *2615 Schurz Ave., Bronx, NY, 10465.* Tel: 718-828-1969; Fax: 718-892-0419. GARY BRANDI, *167 Commonwealth Ave., Mt. Vernon, NY, 10552.* Tel: 914-667-5916; Fax: 914-667-5939. Local Coordinators: JIM MILWAY; MARY JANE MILWAY. Tel: 973-275-1188.

Engaged Encounter—Rev. PETER K. FUNESTI, Chap., *60 Byrd Ave., Bloomfield, 07003.* Tel: 201-338-9190.

Marriage Encounter Resources—Rev. Msgr. FRANCIS J. HOUGHTON, Priest Coord. Tel: 732-899-1507. Area Coordinators: MICHAEL MUCCIA; PENNY MUCCIA, *248 Manning Ave., River Edge, 07661.* Tel: 201-265-0915; Fax: 201-265-1298. Registration/Information: STEPHANIE MURTHA; TOM MURTHA. Tel: 800-823-LOVE.

Pastoral & Matrimonial Renewal Center—Rev. CHARLES GALLAGHER, Dir., *67 Prince St., Elizabeth, 07209.* Tel: 908-353-8640.

Natural Family Planning—Rev. THOMAS NYDEGGER, Chap. & Coord. Chaircouple: KAREN DOYLE; KEVIN DOYLE, *31 Hill St., Haworth, 07641.* Tel: 201-384-9458.

Remarriage Ministry—Rev. RICHARD G. FRANCESCO, Chap. Coordinators: CAROLE MAZZUCCO; THOMAS MAZZUCCO, *28 Sherwood Downs, Park Ridge, 07656.* Tel: 201-391-1331.

CYO Youth and Young Adult Ministries—Rev. RICHARD R. CORBETT, Acting Exec. Dir. Tel: 973-497-4500; Fax: 973-497-4505. JUAN PAVLOWSKI, Acctg. Mgr. JOANNE DEPASQUALE PARENT, Dir. Young Adult Ministry. Tel: 973-497-4502. Directors Youth Ministry: ALBERT FORSYTHE. Tel: 973-497-4516. CAROLINE GAMBALE. Tel: 973-497-4504.

CYO Retreat Center—499 Belgrove Dr., Kearny, 07032. GLORIA WIERZALIS, Dir. Tel: 201-998-0088, Ext. 811. GLORIA O'NEIL, Facility Coord. Tel: 201-998-0088, Ext. 814. KEVIN EARLY, Dir. Retreats, , Ext. 826. REBECCA PACE, Dir. Food Svcs. Tel: 201-998-9607, Ext. 810.

Boy Scouts of America/Catholic Committee on Scouting—499 Belgrove Dr., Kearny, 07032. GABRIEL FELTZ, Dir. Tel: 201-998-0088, Ext. 135. Rev. VICTOR P. KENNEDY, Chap. Tel: 201-656-2490. Rev. MICHAEL M. WALTERS, Asst. Chap. Tel: 973-673-1077. Rev. EUGENE J. FIELD, Area Chap. Tel: 201-641-6464. Rev. KEVIN A. GUGLIOTTA, Area Chap. Tel: 973-379-3912. Rev. DONALD HUMMEL, NCCA Assoc. Chap. Tel: 908-322-5192. KEVIN O'BOYLE, Committee Chm. Tel: 201-385-2265. Bergen Council: KEVIN O'BOYLE. Tel: 201-385-2265. JIM TARANTO. Tel: 201-288-0785. Essex Council: ROSE MARIE MOSCHETTA. Tel: 908-273-6076. E. SCOTT GAIPA. Tel: 973-731-8998. Hudson: JUDY VERHEYEN; RON VERHEYEN. Tel: 201-433-0128. Watchung Area: JOSEPH A. MANCINI, *Immaculate Conception Seminary, Seton Hall University, South Orange, 07079.* Tel: 973-763-5204. FRANK BRUNO. Tel: 908-688-2893.

Archdiocesan Girl Scouts of America—171 Clifton Ave., P.O. Box 9500, Newark, 07104-0500. MAUREEN COLEMAN, Archdiocesan Coord. Tel: 973-497-4512. Rev. DONALD K. HUMMEL, Chap.

The Vicar for Ministries is the Vicar General and Moderator of the Curia's liaison to the following apostolates:

Archdiocesan Council of Catholic Women—ADELAIDE JACKSON, Pres.; Rev. DANIEL DANIK, Moderator, *171 Clifton Ave., Newark, 07104.* Tel: 973-497-4356. District Moderators: Bergen-Paramus: Vacant Bergen-Hackensack: Deacon NICHOLAS SIMONELLI-,North Hudson: Vacant South Hudson: Rev. HENRY M. NADDEO,Essex-Suburban: Vacant Essex-Montclair: Vacant Union-Westfield: Rev. DANIEL A. DANIK,Union-Elizabeth: Sr. MARITA FUNKE, O.S.B.

Charismatic Renewal—Rev. PHILIP J. ROTUNNO, Coord., *5808 Kennedy Blvd., West New York, 07093.* Tel: 201-867-5535.

The Community of God's Love—70 W. Passaic Ave., Rutherford, 07070. Tel: 201-935-0344. LEE WILLIAMS, Dir.; Rev. PHILIP LATRONICO, Chap.

Cursillo Movement—Rev. JOHN F. GORDON, Spiritual Dir. of the English Cursillo. Tel: 908-352-2791; Fax: 908-354-2828. Rev. JOSE M. JUANGO, O.A.R., Spiritual Dir. of the Spanish Cursillo. Tel: 201-867-6535. CATHY DRAKE, Cursillo Sec. Tel: 908-245-5500. PEG MANDELLO, Lay Dir.

Sacred Heart Institute—P.O. Box 985, West Caldwell, 07007-0985. Tel: 973-226-7077; Fax: 973-226-0818. Rev. GERALD P. RUANE, Dir.

Commission for Men's Apostolate—Rev. Msgr. WILLIAM C. HATCHER, Chm., *60 Byrd Ave., Bloomfield, 07003.* Tel: 973-338-9190.

Bukas-Loob Sa Diyos Community(B.L.D.) (Open to the Spirit)—NORBY GOMEZ; WAY GOMEZ, Sec.; Rev. PAUL J. LEHMAN, Chap., *321 Millburn Ave., Ste. 2, Millburn, 07041.* Tel: 973-376-4880; Fax: 973-912-9331.

Vicar General for Human Services

Vicar General—Rev. Msgr. JOSEPH T. SLINGER, Ph.D., V.G., Vicar, *1160 Raymond Blvd., Newark, 07102.* Tel: 973-596-3835; Fax: 973-596-3836.

Catholic Community Services—Tel: 973-596-4100. Affiliated Agencies: Associated Catholic Charities, Mt. Carmel Guild, New Jersey Boystown, The Guild Social Service Center. Rev. Msgr. DENNIS J. MAHON, Ph.D., Exec. Dir., *494 Broad St., Newark, 07102.* Tel: 973-596-4050; Fax: 973-621-9528. Bro. BENEDICT LO BALBO, Dir. Bd. Affairs. Tel: 973-596-4180; Fax: 973-623-2415., *Mt. Carmel Guild Special Hospital, 1160 Raymond Blvd., Newark, 07102.* RONALD A. FINCH, Ed.D., Dir. Healthcare. Tel: 973-639-5026; Fax: 973-596-4105.

Administration—JOSEPH A. DICKSON, ESQ., *494 Broad St., Newark, 07102.* Tel: 973-596-4120; Fax: 973-623-2876.

Finance Office—JOHN CARDILLO, CFO. Tel: 973-596-3945; Fax: 973-596-3949. JOHN WESTERVELT, Controller. Tel: 973-596-3984. CHERYL NASIF, M.P.A., Dir. Payor Svcs. Tel: 973-596-3702.

Human Resources—JOSEPH M. TURCO, S.P.H.R., Dir. Tel: 973-596-4071; Fax: 973-596-3822.

General Services—ROGER DEL RUSSO, Admin. Tel: 973-596-6592; Fax: 973-596-1746.

Plant Services—ANTHONY BIUNNO, Dir. Tel: 973-596-4092; Fax: 973-596-6436.

Information Systems—DONALD GAROFALO, M.B.A., Dir., *494 Broad St., Newark, 07102.* Tel: 973-596-5135; Fax: 973-639-9711.

Internal Auditor—EDWARD SNYDER. Tel: 973-596-5026; Fax: 973-242-0791.

Risk Management—MARISSA FELDMAN, Dir. Tel: 973-639-6500; Fax: 973-643-1261.

Development—REGINA ADESANYA, Psy.D., Dir., *494 Broad St., Newark, 07102.* Tel: 973-596-4067; Fax: 973-623-1267.

Fund Development—MICHELLE PIGNATELLO, Dir. Tel: 973-596-4060; Fax: 973-643-1267.

Public Affairs—DANIEL DEAN, J.D., Dir. Tel: 973-596-4046.

Office of Communications—CHRISTINA CROVETTA, Dir. Tel: 973-596-4086.

Special Events—DANIEL A. CORDASCO, Dir. Tel: 973-596-4064.

Planning—ROSEMARIE PRATT, L.C.S.W., Dir., *494 Broad St., Newark, 07102.* Tel: 973-596-4137; Fax: 973-824-5498.

Program Evaluation & Review—ELAINE V. COHEN, Ph.D., Dir. Tel: 973-596-4057.

MT. CARMEL GUILD BEHAVIORAL HEALTHCARE SYSTEM—RONALD FINCH, Ed.D., Dir. Healthcare, *1160 Raymond Blvd., Newark, 07102.* Tel: 973-639-5026; Fax: 973-596-4105. RENUKA TANK, M.D., Medical Dir. Tel: 973-596-3857; Fax: 973-596-3701. C. HENRY ENGLEKA, Chief of Staff. Tel: 973-596-3852; Fax: 973-596-4105. SEAN HEALY, Dir. Operations Support. Tel: 973-639-6508; Fax: 973-596-4105. MARLENE RIORDAN, Dir. Quality Assurance. Tel: 973-596-4140; Fax: 973-596-4105. DANIEL LACOVARA, Dir. Admin. Change Mgmt. Tel: 973-596-4147; Fax: 973-596-4105. RONALD PASSALACQUA, Special Asst. Admin. Tel: 973-596-4117; Fax: 973-596-4105. DAVID CRANDALL, Dir. Outcomes Mgmt. Tel: 973-596-4068; Fax: 973-594-4105. ED MARTIN, Coord. Clinical Training. Tel: 973-596-3959; Fax: 973-596-4105. MANNY GUANTEZ, Ph.D., Dir. Clinical Change Mgmt. Tel: 973-596-4179. ESTELLE PISANI, Dir. Clinical Svcs. Tel: 973-596-4083; Fax: 973-596-4105. BARBARA GEORGE MILLETTE, R.N., Patient Care Coord., *Mt. Carmel Guild Hospital.* Tel: 973-596-4084; Fax: 973-643-4996. LAUREN BALKAN, L.C.S.W., *ACCESS Center (Admissions).* Fax: 973-639-6501.

Behavioral Healthcare Counseling Centers—

Paramus Center—MICHAEL ZAVADA, L.C.S.W., Regl. Dir., *425 Paramus Rd., Paramus, 07652.* Tel: 201-689-6208; Fax: 201-444-3172. JAMES D. HUVAL, L.C.S.W. Tel: 201-689-6208.

Kearny Center—MARGERY GRIMM, L.C.S.W., M.A., Acting Regl. Dir., *499 Belgrove Dr., Kearny, 07032.* Tel: 201-246-7377; Fax: 201-991-7306. JANIS ORLOFSKY, L.C.S.W. Tel: 201-246-7387.

Behavioral Healthcare - Essex County—JULIE WILLIS, L.C.S.W., Regl. Dir., *1160 Raymond Blvd., Newark, 07102.* Tel: 973-596-4099; Fax: 973-642-0830.

Children's Case Management—Tel: 973-693-6517.

Outpatient Department—Tel: 973-596-4114; 596-3701; Fax: 201-596-4105.

Addictions Treatment Services—Tel: 973-596-3858.

Project Free—Tel: 973-639-5000.

Ambulatory Detox—Tel: 973-596-4059; Fax: 973-642-1598.

Day Treatment Center—Tel: 973-596-3800.

Patient Support Services—Tel: 973-596-4089.

MICA/Spanish MICA—NUZHAT IQBAL, M.A. Tel: 973-596-3971; Fax: 973-623-5473.

Medical Records—PAULINE CHANDLER. Tel: 973-596-4106.

Integrated Case Management (ICMS)—ROMAN Z. MYKYTA, L.C.S.W., *273 Oliver St., Newark, 07105.* Tel: 973-522-2100; Fax: 973-522-0437.

PACT Program—THOMAS PATITUCCI, M.S.W. Tel: 973-466-1348. Tel: 888-MCG-PACT., *269 Oliver St., Newark, 07105.* Tel: 973-466-1300., *37 Evergreen Pl., East Orange, 07017.* Tel: 973-395-2550.

Behavioral Healthcare - Union County—MARGERY GRIMM, L.C.S.W., M.A., Acting Regl. Dir., *108 Alden St., Cranford, 07016.* Tel: 908-497-3968; Fax: 908-272-9268.

Addiction Treatment Services—COLLEEN RUSHSZEFINSKI, M.A., CADC, *505 South Ave. E., Cranford, 07016.* Tel: 908-497-3904; Fax: 908-709-9612.

Outpatient Department—ELLEN J. GROSS, L.C.S.W., *505 South Ave. E., Cranford, 07016.* Tel: 908-497-3904; Fax: 908-709-9612.

Community Mental Health Center—108 Alden St., Cranford, 07016. Tel: 908-497-3968; Fax: 908-272-9268.

Day Treatment Center, Extended Day Treatment Center, Project Care 450 Program—MARGERY GRIMM, M.A. Tel: 908-497-3975.

Integrated Case Management (ICMS)—WILLIAM MERRITT, L.C.S.W., *654 E. Jersey St., Elizabeth, 07206.* Tel: 908-436-2200; Fax: 908-355-3940., *1038 Edgewood Ave., Plainfield, 07062.* Tel: 908-490-1000; Fax: 908-490-1005.

Behavioral Healthcare - Hudson County—MICHAEL ZAVADA, L.C.S.W., Regl. Dir., *249 Virginia Ave., Jersey City, 07304.* Tel: 201-395-5400; Fax: 201-434-4386.

Residential Programs—Project Home, 249 Virginia Ave., Jersey City, 07304. Tel: 201-395-5400; Fax: 201-434-4386. SANDRA POWELL, L.C.S.W., *Project Hudson House, 3201 Central Ave., Union City, 07087.* REGINA DEMARCO, M.A. Tel: 201-864-0270; Fax: 201-864-1899.

Day Treatment Center—CHRISTINE MUSCADIN, M.A., *249 Virginia Ave., Jersey City, 07304.* Tel: 201-395-5400; Fax: 201-434-4386., *285 Magnolia Ave., Jersey City, 07306.* Tel: 201-395-4800; Fax: 201-435-9580., *3201 Central Ave., Union City, 07087.* Tel: 201-864-0270; Fax: 201-864-1899.

MICA (Mentally ILL Chemical Abusers)—285 Magnolia Ave., Jersey City, 07306. Tel: 201-395-4800; Fax: 201-435-9580.

Addictions Treatment Services—249 Virginia Ave., Jersey City, 07304. Tel: 201-395-5400; Fax: 201-434-4386.

Supported Employment—HARRY FRAZIER, M.S., *1009 Kennedy Blvd., North Bergen, 07047.* Tel: 201-271-2758; Fax: 201-864-1522.

Outpatient Department—Admissions, 249 Virginia Ave., Jersey City, 07304. Tel: 201-395-5400; Fax: 201-434-4386. JAMES D. HUVAL, L.C.S.W., *400 38th St., Union City, 07087.* Tel: 201-553-8500; Fax: 201-601-0453.

Operations—MARY C. MCGREAL, J.D., Dir., *494 Broad St., Newark, 07102.* Tel: 973-596-3948; Fax: 973-623-2679.

BERGEN COUNTY Division—MICHAEL MATTHEWS, A.C.S.W., Div. Dir., *425 Paramus Rd., Paramus, 07652.* Tel: 201-689-6207; Fax: 201-444-3172.

Older Adult Case Management—DIANE MCTIGUE. Tel: 201-689-6213.

Parish Access Center—JANE SCERBO. Tel: 201-689-6209.

Telephone Conference & Cash Preference Programs—WILLIAM JOZWIAK. Tel: 201-689-6216.

Welfare to Work Program—KERI OGGERO. Tel: 201-689-6210.
Project Intercept—RENES CRUZ. Tel: 201-678-1471.
Kid-Care—Tel: 201-689-6200.
Outreach/case Management for HIV Hispanics (Ryan White)—SIDSEL VENGEL, L.C.S.W., *77 Essex St., Hackensack, 07601.* Tel: 201-678-1471; Fax: 201-678-1473.
ESSEX COUNTY Division—ELIZABETH MCCLENDON, L.C.S.W., Div. Dir., *494 Broad St., Newark, 07102.* Tel: 973-596-5110; Fax: 973-424-9556.
AmeriCorps Volunteer Program—DESARAY BRUNSON. Tel: 973-596-5114; Fax: 973-424-9556.
Parish Access Center—Sr. DOLORES PROCASSINI, M.A., *160 E. Passaic St., Bloomfield, 07003.* Tel: 973-743-5304; Fax: 973-743-5289.
Sunrise House—TRACY LLOYD, *185 Parkhurst Ave., Newark, 07105.* Tel: 973-642-9478.
St. Bridget's Residence Aids/HIV Support/Outreach Center—Bro. JOSEPH MCALISTER, M.A., *404 University Ave., Newark, 07102.* Tel: 973-799-0484; Fax: 973-799-0486.
Catholic School Social Service Program—NANCY MARNELLOS, M.S.W., *494 Broad St., Newark, 07102.* Tel: 973-297-4788; Fax: 973-424-9556.
Quest Essex Youth Services—JOYCE SMITH CARTER, *St. Charles Center, 85 Custer Ave., Newark, 07112.* Tel: 973-926-9895; Fax: 973-926-0448.
Mt. Carmel Guild Children's Center (Day Care)—PAULA JOHNSON, *39 Bleeker St., Newark, 07102.* Tel: 973-624-7890.
CCS Child Development Center (Day Care)—MIRNA LARUE, *87 Park Ave., Newark, 07104.* Tel: 973-483-9387; Fax: 973-268-2359.
Senior Day Care for the Frail Elderly & Visually Impaired Program—PAMELA LUKE, *494 Broad St., Newark, 07102.* Tel: 973-297-1567; Fax: 973-639-1371.
Department of Special Education—Vacant, *494 Broad St., Newark, 07102.* Tel: 973-848-3499; Fax: 973-424-9556.
Mt. Carmel Guild School—JOHN KOBUS, *60 Kingsland Ave., Kearny, 07032.* Tel: 201-955-3280; Fax: 201-991-7776.
Mt. Carmel Guild Pre-School—KATHARINE THORNTON, M.P.A., Prin., *10 Commerce Ct., Newark, 07102.* Tel: 973-639-6622; Fax: 973-639-6626.
St. Anthony's School—Sr. ANNE ROSALIE, M.A., Prin., *25 N. 7th St., Belleville, 07109.* Tel: 973-844-3700; Fax: 973-751-5725.
St. Patrick's Special Education School—BOB BAROSKA, *72 Central Ave., Newark, 07102.* Tel: 973-643-6772; Fax: 973-643-7625.
St. Patrick's Annex at St. Leo's—ANNE BOYD-HINTON, M.A., *100 Linden Ave., Irvington, 07111.* Tel: 973-373-1694.
Independence High School—RICHARD WILLIAMS, M.A., *100 Linden Ave., Irvington, 07111.* Tel: 973-372-5601.
The Guild Social Service Center—
Halfway House for Alcoholic Men—ROBERT ROBINSON, *56 Freeman St., Newark, 07105.* Tel: 973-344-0067; Fax: 973-344-6750.
St. Ann's Family Emergency Residence (SAFER)—TREVA POONG, *368 7th St., Newark, 07103.* Tel: 973-286-4175; Fax: 973-242-4854.
St. Rocco's Family Residence (Women & Children)—TREVA YOUNG, *368 S. 7th St., Newark, 07103.* Tel: 973-286-4175; Fax: 973-242-4854.
St. Rocco's Outreach Center (Men)—JOHN NJKOU, *712 Springfield Ave., Newark, 07103.* Tel: 973-371-5266; Fax: 973-371-5850.
Queen's Angels Program—DONNA SMITH, *28 Irving Turner Blvd., Newark, 07102.* Tel: 973-848-2381; Fax: 973-623-8790.
HUDSON COUNTY Division—LESLEY MOORE, L.C.S.W., Div. Dir., *3040 Kennedy Blvd., Jersey City, 07306.* Tel: 201-798-9957; Fax: 201-656-6216.
Coming Home Hospice—ELIZABETH PATTERSON, B.S.N., J.D., *3040 Kennedy Blvd., Jersey City, 07306.* Tel: 201-798-9923; Fax: 201-656-1707.
Parish Access Center—CARMEL GALASSO, M.A., *3040 Kennedy Blvd., Jersey City, 07306.* Tel: 201-798-9960; Fax: 201-659-6216.
New Jersey Boystown—*499 Belgrove Dr., Kearny, 07032.* Tel: 201-991-3770; Fax: 201-991-7306.
Family and Adoption Services—PATRICIA CHIARELLO, M.S.W. Tel: 201-991-3770.
Foster Grandparent Program—MELINDA ACEVEDO, *3040 Kennedy Blvd., Jersey City, 07306.* Tel: 201-798-9900; Fax: 201-656-1707.
Edna McLaughlin Residence at Carmel House—Sr. BRIDGET KAPIN, *162 Bidwell Ave., Jersey City, 07305.* Tel: 201-413-1556; Fax: 201-413-0825.
MICA Outreach—*308 Academy St., Jersey City, 07306.* Tel: 201-217-9665; Fax: 201-219-1902.
Intensive Family Support Services—*3040 Kennedy Blvd., Jersey City, 07306.* Tel: 201-798-9924; Fax: 201-656-1707.
Mt. Carmel Guild Family Resource Centers—MIGDALIA FIGUEROA, *3040 Kennedy Blvd., Jersey City, 07306.* Tel: 201-798-9900; Fax: 201-656-1707.
Intensive Family Counseling Program—BARBARA KAIRYS, *3040 Kennedy Blvd., Jersey City, 07306.* Tel: 201-798-9900; Fax: 201-656-1707.
Family Crisis Intervention—DOLORES WESTBROOKS, M.A., *114 Clifton Pl., Jersey City, 07305.* Tel: 201-915-1202; Fax: 201-985-2343.
St. Lucy's Homeless Programs—CHRISTIAN CARROLL, L.C.S.W.,Programs: Counseling and Outreach; Single Residence (Men & Women); Neuville Family Residence; Project Link. CHRISTIAN CARROLL, L.C.S.W. Tel: 201-656-7973; Fax: 201-656-0412., *619 Grove St., Jersey City, 07310.* Tel: 201-656-7201; Fax: 201-656-0412.
Franciska House (HIV/AIDS)—JANE NASH, L.S.W., *615 Grove St., Jersey City, 07310.* Tel: 201-653-5395.
Hope House (Women & Children)—NANCY PINEDA, *246 2nd St., Jersey City, 07302.* Tel: 201-420-1070; Fax: 201-420-1825.
Hudson County Prison Project, PAYBACC Program, Providence Malta Prep—RENEE CRUZ, *75 Greenville Ave., Jersey City, 07305.* Tel: 201-369-5580; Fax: 201-451-5198.
PRIDE Mentoring Program—GILMA GARCIA, *3040 Kennedy Blvd., Jersey City, 07306.* Tel: 201-798-9920; Fax: 201-798-2644.
Juvenile Justice and Corrections Development—THOMAS LYNCH, L.C.S.W., *75 Greenville Ave., Jersey City, 07305.* Tel: 201-369-5580; Fax: 201-451-5198.
Family & Adoption Services—PATRICIA CHIARELLO, M.S.W., *499 Belgrove Dr., Kearny, 07032.* Tel: 201-246-7378; Fax: 201-991-7306.
UNION COUNTY Division—CLARE ELTON, L.S.W., Div. Dir. Tel: 908-497-3938; Fax: 908-709-9580., *505 South Ave. E., Cranford, 07016.*
Family Resource Center—*505 South Ave. E., Cranford, 07016.* Tel: 908-497-3900; Fax: 908-709-9580.
In-Home Hispanic Family Service—ELAINE DILL, *505 South Ave. E., Cranford, 07016.* Tel: 908-497-3900; Fax: 908-709-9580.
Child Protective Services—ELAINE DILL, *505 South Ave. E., Cranford, 07016.* Tel: 908-497-3900; Fax: 908-709-9580.
Employee Assistance Program (CARE)—DAVID BENCIVERGO, *505 South Ave. E., Cranford, 07016.* Tel: 908-497-3954.
Workforce Development Resource Center—JANICE STUBBS, *103-110 Third St., Elizabeth, 07206.* Tel: 908-282-4600; Fax: 908-527-9168.
Education & Training—KRISTIN RETLIN, M.S. Tel: 973-242-1999.
Transportation Program—*505 South Ave. E., Cranford, 07016.* Tel: 908-497-3900; Fax: 908-709-9583.
Workforce Development—KRISTIN RETLIN, M.S. Tel: 973-242-1999.
Parish Access Center—GABRIELA CAMPBELL, *1096 North Ave., Elizabeth, 07201.* Tel: 908-352-0338; Fax: 908-352-4553.
Early Childhood Education Program—ELIZABETH DRISCOLL, *103-110 Third St., Elizabeth, 07206.* Tel: 908-282-4600; Fax: 908-352-4794.
Adult Protective Services—SUSAN CRONK, L.C.S.W., *505 South Ave. E., Cranford, 07016.* Tel: 908-497-3900; Fax: 908-709-9583.
The Engel Center (Adult Day Care)—HAZEL GARLIC, *505 South Ave. E., Cranford, 07016.* Tel: 908-497-3900; Fax: 908-709-9583.
Hispanic Seniors Services - New Jersey EASE—SILVANIA MUELLER, *505 South Ave. E, Cranford, 07016.* Tel: 908-497-3900; Fax: 908-709-9583.
Visually Impaired Seniors Program—ADDY NUNES, *505 South Ave. E., Cranford, 07016.* Tel: 908-497-3900; Fax: 908-709-9583.
Restorative Justice, Union County Correctional Program Juvenile Justice—*505 South Ave. E., Cranford, 07016.* Tel: 908-497-3900; Fax: 908-709-9583.
Faith Based Initiative Services—CHARLES ROBINSON, *St. Mary's Social Services Center, 516 W. 6th St., Plainfield, 07060.* Tel: 908-755-5940.
Refugee Resettlement and Immigration Assistance Division—*976 Broad St., Newark, 07102.* Tel: 973-733-3516; Fax: 973-623-7725.
Refugee Resettlement & Employment Services—Vacant.
Project Haven—SAWSON SORIAL. Tel: 973-242-1999.
Immigration Assistance—*976 Broad St., Newark, 07102.* Tel: 973-733-3516; Fax: 973-733-9631.
Immigration Assistance Citizenship—LOUISE FRANCIOSA, *505 South Ave. E., Cranford, 07016.* Tel: 908-497-3917; Fax: 908-709-9583. MARTA SAN MARTIN, M.A., *533 35th St., Union City, 07087.* Tel: 201-866-3208; Fax: 201-866-5854., *380 Monmouth St., Jersey City, 07302.* Tel: 201-653-6515; Fax: 201-653-1301.
Haitian Outreach Center—PIERRE MOREAU, *37 Evergreen Pl., East Orange, 07017.* Tel: 973-672-6607; Fax: 973-672-2032.
Workforce Development Division—JOSEPH P. BORDO, L.C.S.W., Div. Dir., *494 Broad St., Newark, 07102.* Tel: 973-848-3457; Fax: 973-242-3789.
Hispanic Women's Resource Center—*533 35th St., Union City, 07087.* Tel: 201-866-3208; Fax: 201-866-5854. Immigration Assistance - Citizenship; Refugee Resettlement; Drug/Alcohol Counseling and Education; Employment Services. MARTA SAN MARTIN, M.A.
Education & Training—*1501-9 Bergenline Ave., Union City, 07087.* Tel: 201-770-3520; Fax: 201-770-3529.
Office of Migration—*380 Monmouth St., Jersey City, 07302.* Tel: 201-653-6515; Fax: 201-653-1301. Employment Services; Education & Training; Immigration Assistance - Citizenship; Italian Social Service Center.
Vocational Rehabilitation Services—MICHAEL MYERS, M.A., *494 Broad St., Newark, 07102.* Tel: 973-848-3450; Fax: 973-242-3455. Skills Training, Sheltered Workshop, Counseling Services.
Vocational Evaluation & Assessment—ISKRA GOMEZ, *494 Broad St., Newark, 07102.* Tel: 973-242-1999; Fax: 973-242-3755.
Programs Managed by CCS—
SHARE NJ—LAVAUGHN DILLINGS, *56 Columbia, East Orange, 07017.* Tel: 973-344-2400; Fax: 973-344-3532.
Archdiocesan Housing Office (Domus Corporation)—CHRIS GARLIN, *494 Broad St., Newark, 07102.* Tel: 973-297-1425; Fax: 973-424-9559.
Programs Operated in Support of CCS—
New Jersey Boystown—Rev. Msgr. DENNIS J. MAHON, Ph.D., *499 Belgrove Dr., Kearny, 07032.* Tel: 201-246-7378; Fax: 201-991-7306.
New Ark of Hope Foundation—GEORGE PIEGARO, M.A., *494 Broad St., Newark, 07102.* Tel: 973-639-6598; Fax: 973-623-2098.
Special Assitant for Vicariate Services—CATHERINE L'INSALATA, M.S., C.S.W., *494 Broad St., Newark, 07102.* Tel: 973-297-0792; Fax: 973-824-5602.
Apostolate with the Developmentally Disabled—Sr. EILEEN BYRNE, O.P., M.A., *494 Broad St., Newark, 07102.* Tel: 973-297-0529.
Apostolate with the Deaf—Sr. JOAN WALTERS, S.C. Ed.D., *494 Broad St., Newark, 07102.* Tel: 973-348-0527; TTY: 596-3893.
Ministry with the Deaf—THOMAS SMITH, C.S.W., *494 Broad St., Newark, 07102.* Tel: 973-297-0476; TTY: 596-3893.
New Day Community—VINCENT MCMAHON, M.A., *494 Broad St., Newark, 07102.* Tel: 973-297-0491; Fax: 973-763-6430.
Emergency Food & Nutrition Network—SHARON REILLY-TOBIN, *494 Broad St., Newark, 07102.* Tel: 973-297-0538; Fax: 973-824-5602.
Prison Ministry—Tel: 973-297-0792.
HIV/AIDS Ministry—ROBERT HANSON, *494 Broad St., Newark, 07102.* Tel: 973-297-0528.
Bergen County—Rev. JOHN MCCRONE, Coord., *W. 50 Midland Ave., Paramus, 07652.* Tel: 201-967-4177.
Hudson County—Sr. RENEE ZINCIUK, Coord. Tel: 201-792-6161.
Essex County—Rev. JOHN P. NICKAS, Coord., *56 Elmwood Ave., Montclair, 07042.* Tel: 973-783-4852.
Union County—Rev. DOMINIC G. FUCCILE, Coord., *280 Parker Ave., Maplewood, 07040.* Tel: 973-763-5019.
Hispanic Community—Rev. Msgr. THOMAS W. HECK, Coord., *3900 New York Ave., Union City, 07087.* Tel: 201-863-5116.
AIDS Support Center—(See Catholic Community Services Essex).
Franciska House—(See Catholic Community Services Hudson).
Ministry to the People on the Move—
Apostleship of the Air—Rev. DAVID J. BARATELLI, Dir., *Newark International Airport Chaplaincy, P.O. Box 2220, Newark, 07114.* Tel: 973-961-0260.
Apostleship of the Sea—Rev. SALVATORE MALANGA, *Newark International Seaport Chaplaincy - Stella Maris Chapel, 114 Corbin St., Port Newark, 07101.* Tel: 973-483-0356.
Office of the Consultant for Health Affairs—Bro. BENEDICT LO BALBO, *494 Broad St., Newark, 07102.* Tel: 973-596-4180; Fax: 973-623-2415.
Catholic Campaign for Human Development—Sr. CATHERINE DALY, O.P., M.S., C.S.W., *494 Broad St., Newark, 07102.* Tel: 973-297-1426; Fax: 973-424-9559.
Office of Volunteer Services—CATHERINE L'INSALATA, M.S., C.S.W., *494 Broad St., Newark, 07102.* Tel: 973-297-0792; Fax: 973-824-5602. The Vicar for Human Services is the Archbishop's Liaison to and General Secretary for Archdiocesan Housing Commission.

Miscellaneous

Affirmative Action Council—WILLIAM A. CAMBRIA, Officer,*Archdiocesan Center, 171 Clifton Ave., Newark, 07104.* Tel: 973-497-4302.

Apostleship of Prayer—Rev. Msgr. ROBERT J. FUHRMAN, Dir., *171 Clifton Ave., P.O. Box 9500, Newark, 07104-0500.* Tel: 973-497-4375; Fax: 973-497-4033.

Association of St. Philomena's Helpers to the Suffering and the Poor—Rev. GEORGE KEATING, Dir., *P.O. Box 393, Union, 07083-0393.* Tel: 908-687-7205.

Blue Army—Vacant. Tel: 973-497-4011.

Catholic Relief Services—171 Clifton Ave., Newark, 07104. Tel: 973-497-4000.

Censores Librorum—Most Rev. ARTHUR J. SERRATELLI, S.T.D., S.S.L.; Rev. Msgr. EDWARD J. CIUBA, S.T.L., S.S.L.; Rev. Msgr. JOSEPH F. FLUSK, Music; Rev. Msgr. CARL D. HINRICHSEN, S.T.L., Ph.D.; Rev. Msgr. THOMAS P. IVORY, S.T.D.; Rev. Msgr. JOHN H. KOENIG, S.T.L.; Rev. Msgr. RICHARD M. LIDDY, S.T.D.; Rev. JAMES M. CAFONE, S.T.D.; Rev. Msgr. FRANCIS A. DEDOMENICO, S.T.L.; Rev. Msgr. CHARLES W. GUSMER, S.T.D.; Revs. GEORGE M. KEATING; FRANK MCNULTY, S.T.D.; JOHN RUSSELL, O.Carm.; JAMES B. SULLIVAN, S.T.L., Ph.D.

Archdiocesan School Advisory Board—Mr. FRANCIS X. FALCICCHIO, Pres.; Mrs. KATHLEEN MASKER, Vice Pres.; Mrs. MARY D. BAIER, Sec.; JOANNE ANDERSON; Mrs. DONNA J. BABOULIS; Mr. JOHN FIGUEIREDO; Ms. KAY GRUSENSKI; Mr. DAVID KIENAST; Mrs. BRENDA LEAHY; ELIZABETH MADARA; MARIA SADOWSKI; Sr. LILLIAN SHARROCK, S.C.; Bro. RALPH DARMENTO, School Office Liaison. Tel: 973-497-4260.

Scholarship Fund for Inner-City Children—DIEGO R. VISCEGLIA, ESQ., Pres., Board of Trustees; JOHN C. WALCOTT, Sec.; RONALD J. MOUNT, Treas.; KEVIN P. MORIARTY, Exec. Dir., *Archdiocesan Center, 171 Clifton Ave., Newark, 07104.* Tel: 973-497-4279.

The New Jersey Alliance of Catholic School Families & Supporters—Bro. RALPH DARMENTO, Coord. Tel: 973-497-4260.

Holy Name Federation—Rev. Msgr. RICHARD M. MCGUINNESS, Archdiocesan Dir. County Dirs.: Revs. JOHN LAFERRARA, Essex-West Hudson; RICHARD J. CARRINGTON, Hudson; MARTIN J. SILVER, Bergen; JOSEPH G. SHEEHAN, Union, *1805 Penbrook Ter., Linden, 07036.* Tel: 908-486-6363.

Legion of Mary—Newark Comitum: Rev. CHARLES H. MCTAGUE, Dir., *16 Church Square, Harrison, 07029.* Tel: 973-484-5678. Bergen County Curia: Rev. RINO LAVARONI, Dir., *2 Fremont Ave., Park Ridge, 07656.* Tel: 201-391-5315. Maria Immaculata of Hudson County: Rev. JAMES W. MCFARLAND, Dir., *21 Skillman Ave., Jersey City, 07306.* Tel: 201-963-7640. Hispanic Curia of Hudson County: Rev. FELIPE LOPEZ, Dir., *3900 New York Ave., Union City, 07087.* Tel: 201-863-0233. Hispanic Curia of Essex and Union: Rev. MICHAEL A. FUINO, Dir., *60 Home Ave., Rutherford, 07070.* Tel: 973-804-2750. Korean/Our Lady Mother of God Curia: Rev. Msgr. AUGUSTIN PARK, *595 Saddle River Rd., Saddle River, 07663.* Tel: 201-703-0080. Korean/Mary Most Humble Curia: Rev. DOMINIC ANN, *280 County Rd., Demarest, 07627.* Tel: 201-767-1954. Our Lady, Gate of Heaven Curia (Korean): Rev. Msgr. AUGUSTIN PARK, Dir., *257 Central Ave., Orange, 07050.* Tel: 973-672-6650.

Seton Hall University Archives—JOANN COTZ, Assoc. Dir.; Rev. Msgr. FRANCIS R. SEYMOUR, Archdiocesan Vice Chancellor for Archives, *Seton Hall University, Walsh Library, 400 South Orange Ave., South Orange, 07079.* Tel: 973-761-9476.

New Jersey Catholic Historical Records Commission—Most Rev. DOMINIC A. MARCONI, D.D., Chm.; JOSEPH F. MAHONEY, Ph.D., Dir., *Seton Hall University, Fahy Hall, 400 South Orange Ave., South Orange, 07079.* Tel: 973-275-2773.

Our Lady of Fatima First Saturday Club—Rev. PAUL BOCHICCHIO, Chap., *188 MacArthur Ave., Garfield, 07026.* Tel: 201-772-2295. Rev. KEVIN E. CARTER, Chap., *122 Ferry St., Jersey City, 07307.* Tel: 201-659-5354.

Propagation of the Faith; Society of St. Peter the Apostle Missionary Union of Priests/Religious—Rev. Msgr. ROBERT J. FUHRMAN, Dir., *Archdiocesan Center, 171 Clifton Ave., Newark, 07104.* Tel: 973-497-4375.

Priests' Eucharistic League—Rev. Msgr. WALTER G. JARVAIS, *60 Home Ave., Rutherford, 07070.* Tel: 201-939-8138.

Serra Clubs—Dr. AGNES M. MORSE, L.H.S., Regl. Representative (NJ, PA & DEL), *137 Bergen Court, Ridgewood, 07450-4603.* Tel: 201-444-0710. ALFRED G. MORSE, K.H.S., Deputy Regl. Representative, *137 Bergen Court, Ridgewood, 07450-4603.* Tel: 201-444-0710. RICHARD R. MARGERM, Governor-District 22, *71 Dale Dr., Summit, 07901.* Tel: 908-522-1496. Rev. GEORGE M. REILLY, Serra Club of Bergen County East, Chap., *105 Harrison St., New Milford, 07646.* Tel: 201-261-0148. Rev. JOSEPH M. QUINLAN, Serra Club of Bergen County South, Chap., *786 Kearny Ave., Kearny, 07032.* Tel: 201-998-6056. Rev. Msgr. CARL HINRICHSEN, Serra Club of Bergen County West, Chap., *137 Bergen Ct., Ridgewood, 07450-4603.* Tel: 201-444-0710. Vacant, Serra Club of the Oranges, Chap., *Seton Hall University, South Orange, 07079.* Tel: 973-761-9126. Rev. JOSEPH DERBYSHIRE, Serra Club of Union County West, *325 2nd Ave., Garwood, 07027.* Tel: 908-789-0280. Rev. DANIEL A. DANIK, Serra Club of West Essex, Chap., *2046 Ingalls Ave., Linden, 07036.* Tel: 908-486-9155.

Ministry for Young Adults—

BERAKAH-Gathering—Sacred Heart Church—HELEN LATRELLA, Contract, Office: *15 Forest Pl., Rochelle Park, 07662.* Tel: 973-368-3883.

Mothers of Priests Apostolate of Prayer—Mrs. FRANCES MONACO, Contact, Archdiocese of Newark Chapter, *522 William St., Maywood, 07607.* Tel: 201-843-8321.

CLERGY, PARISHES, MISSIONS AND PAROCHIAL SCHOOLS

CITY OF NEWARK

1—CATHEDRAL BASILICA OF THE SACRED HEART (1889), Rev. Msgr. Richard Groncki, Rector; Revs. Sean Manson; James V. Teti; Luis O. Gonzalez. In res., Most Revs. Paul G. Bootkoski, D.D.; Arthur J. Serratelli, S.S.L., S.T.D.
Res., 89 Ridge St., 07104. Tel: 973-484-4600; Fax: 973-483-8253.

2—ST. PATRICK'S PRO-CATHEDRAL (1848), Rev. Msgr. Neil J. Mahoney. In res., Revs. Guillermo Arias (Colombia); Joseph Khai Vu.
Res., 91 Washington St., 07102. Tel: 973-623-0497; Fax: 973-623-2030.

3—BLESSED SACRAMENT/ST. CHARLES BORROMEO (1905) (African American), Revs. Kenneth E. Jennings, Admin.; Valentine Ugwuanya; Ruth King, Pastoral Assoc.
Res., 15 Van Ness Pl., 07108. Tel: 973-824-6548; Fax: 973-624-6030.
School—600 Clinton Ave., 07108. Tel: 973-824-5859; Fax: 973-824-2304.
Sisters of St. Joseph 1; Lay Teachers 20; Students 425.
Catechesis/Religious Programs—Students 45.
Convent—Tel: 201-824-8475.

4—ST. ALOYSIUS (1877) (Hispanic), Rev. Javier Losarcos.
Res., 66 Fleming Ave., 07105. Tel: 973-344-4736; Fax: 973-522-1169.
Catechesis/Religious Programs—Students 105.

5—ST. ANTONINUS (1875), Revs. William J. Halbing; Eustace Edomobi (Nigeria).
Res., 337 South Orange Ave., 07103. Tel: 973-623-0258; Fax: 973-623-0694.
Catechesis/Religious Programs—Students 46.

6—ST. ANN (1886), Rev. Paul Lehman, Admin.; Deacon Cesar A. Ortega Escobar.
Church Office: 337 South Orange Ave., 07103.
Res., Tel: 973-642-4217; Fax: 973-623-0694.

7—ST. AUGUSTINE'S (1874) (German), Revs. Neil J. Mahoney, Admin.; Guillermo Arias; Deacons Vicente Rodriquez; Daniel Mendez.
Church Office: P.O. Box 1390, 07101-1390.
Res., Tel: 973-482-1817; Fax: 973-482-5475.
Convent—168 Sussex Ave., 07103. Tel: 973-483-0165. Sisters Missionaries of Charity
Women's Shelter Queen of Peace—170 Sussex Ave., 07103. Tel: 973-481-9056.

8—ST. BENEDICT'S (1854), Revs. Richard G. Francesco; Rene Lima. Pastoral Assocs.: Sr. Philomena McCartney, O.P.; Sr. Ann Jerome Kociolek, O.P.
Res., 65 Barbara St., 07105. Tel: 973-589-7930; Fax: 973-589-3665.
School—124 Niagara St., 07105. Tel: 973-589-7295; Fax: 973-589-2968. Mrs. Elaine Morehead, Prin.
Lay Teachers 23; Students 285.
Catechesis/Religious Programs—Students 244.

9—ST. BRIDGET'S (1887). Merged with St. Patrick's Pro-Cathedral. Records located at St. Patrick's, Newark. Tel: 973-623-0497.

10—ST. CASIMIR'S (1908) (Polish), Revs. Joseph Urban; Stanley Kostrzomb.
Res., 164 Nichols St., 07105-2596. Tel: 973-344-2743; Fax: 973-344-8182.
School—(1910), 366 E. Kinney St., 07105. Tel: 973-589-0108; Fax: 973-589-0239. Mrs. Lorraine Novak, Prin.
Lay Teachers 11; Students 256.
Catechesis/Religious Programs—Tel: 973-596-4500, Ext. 3674.
Students 50.
Convent—.

11—ST. CHARLES BORROMEO'S (1910). Merged with Blessed Sacrament. Records located at Blessed Sacrament, Newark, NJ 07108, Tel. No. 973-824-6548.

12—ST. COLUMBA'S (1869) (Hispanic), Revs. Yves-Michel Touzin, C.S. (Italy); Vincenzo Ronchi, C.S.
Res., 25 Thomas St., 07114. Tel: 973-622-7712; Fax: 973-621-2021.
School—(1882), 25 Pennsylvania Ave., 07114. Tel: 973-623-8859.
Lay Teachers 17; Students 340.
Catechesis/Religious Programs—Students 215.
Convent—Tel: 973-622-7325.

13—EPIPHANY (1992) (Portuguese), Rev. Peter M. Uhde, Admin.
Res., Holy Trinity Rectory, 207 Adams St., 07105. Tel: 973-491-9761; Fax: 973-344-5641.

14—QUEEN OF ANGELS (1930) (African American), Rev. James J. McConnell, S.M.A.; Deacons Robert Botts, (Retired); Edward Botts, (Retired); Tracey G. Battley, Pastoral Assoc.
Res., 44 Irvine Turner Blvd., 07103. Tel: 973-642-1610; Fax: 973-642-0755.
School—40 Irvine Turner Blvd., 07103. Tel: 973-642-1531; Fax: 973-622-0472. Mrs. Everlyn V. Hay, Prin.; Mrs. Sharon Massey, Vice Prin.
Lay Teachers 11; Students 266.
Catechesis/Religious Programs—Tel: 973-372-4992.
Students 266.

15—ST. FRANCIS XAVIER (1914), Revs. Jan Sasin; Frederick A. Pfeifer; Roberto Santamaria; Giovanni Rizzo; Sr. Rose Chuckerel, M.P.F., Pastoral Assoc.; Deacon Paul R. Daniele, J.D.
Res., 243 Abington Ave., 07107-2598. Tel: 973-482-8410; Fax: 973-485-7471.
School—(1924), 594 N. Seventh St., 07107. Tel: 973-482-9410; Fax: 973-482-2466.
Maestre Pie Filippini (Religious Teachers Filippini) 3; Lay Teachers 10; Students 247.
Catechesis/Religious Programs—D.R.E. Sr. Griselda Rodriguez, H.M.C.J., (Spanish); Sr. Clare Ricciardelli, M.P.F., (English).
Students 325.
Convent—Tel: 973-484-5200.

16—HOLY TRINITY (1901) (Lithuanian), Rev. Peter M. Uhde, Admin. In res., Rev. Zygmunt Pikula, (Retired).
Res., 207 Adams St., 07105. Tel: 973-344-6847; Fax: 973-344-5641.

17—ST. JAMES (1854) (Brazilian-Portuguese), Rev. George Lutz. In res., Rev. Raymond T. McKeon.
Res., 143 Madison St., 07105. Tel: 973-344-8322; Fax: 973-344-6158.
Catechesis/Religious Programs—Students 75.

18—ST. JOHN'S (1826), Rev. Msgr. James J. Finnerty.
Res., 22 Mulberry St., 07102. Tel: 973-623-0822; Fax: 973-623-6804.

19—ST. JOSEPH'S (1850). Closed. Records located at Seton Hall University Archives, South Orange, 07079. Tel: 973-761-9476; Fax: 973-761-9550.

20—IMMACULATE HEART OF MARY (1926) (Spanish), Revs. Gregorio Mateu, T.O.R., (Spain) Local Supr.; John Riera, T.O.R. (Spain); Deacons Escolastico Mejias; Miguel Loperena.
Res., 114 Prospect St., 07105. Tel: 973-589-8249; Fax: 973-589-1858.
Catechesis/Religious Programs—Tel: 973-589-5794; Fax: 973-589-0154.
Students 388.
Convent—121 Congress St., 07105.
Missionary Sisters of the Blessed Sacrament and Mary Immaculate 4.

21—IMMACULATE CONCEPTION (1925) (Italian), Rev. Anthony J. Lionelli. In res., Rev. John F. O'Connor, S.T.B.
Res., 390 Woodside Ave., 07104. Tel: 973-482-0619; Fax: 973-482-9456.

22—ST. LUCY'S (1891) (Italian), Rev. Msgr. Joseph J. Granato; Revs. Joseph S. Nativo; Anthony Forte.
Res., 118 Seventh Ave., 07104. Tel: 973-482-6663; Fax: 973-482-6575.
School—(1904), 12 Amity Pl., 07104. Tel: 973-482-4756; Fax: 973-482-7992.
Sisters 4; Lay Teachers 7; Students 232.
Catechesis/Religious Programs—Students 312.
Convent—Tel: 973-482-5750.

23—ST. MARY'S, Essex Co., (1842). (Newark Abbey Church). Revs. Philip J. Waters, O.S.B.; Linus V. Edogwo (Nigeria); Sr. Linda Klaiss, S.S.J., Pastoral Assoc.

Res., 528 Martin Luther King, Jr. Blvd., 07102. Tel: 973-792-5793, Ext. 202; Fax: 973-643-6922.
School—(1842), Tel: 973-792-5799; Fax: 973-792-5797.
Sisters of St. Joseph of Chestnut Hill 3; Lay Teachers 15; Students 260.
Catechesis/Religious Programs—Students 60.
Convent—Tel: 973-824-8475.

24—ST. MARY MAGDALENE (1893). Closed. Records located at Seton Hall University Archives, South Orange, 07079. Tel: 973-761-9476; Fax: 973-761-9550.

25—ST. MICHAEL'S (1878), Revs. Edgar Da Cunha, S.D.V.; Angelito Rosales, S.D.V.; Giosue Scotto DiCesare, S.D.V.; Lorenzo Gomez, S.D.V.; Deacons Alberto Gomez; Daniel Ravelo; Restituto Quintana.
Res., 25 Crittenden St., 07104. Tel: 973-484-7100; Fax: 973-482-7209.
School—(1881), 27 Crittenden St., 07104. Tel: 973-482-7400; Fax: 973-482-1833.
Sisters of St. Martha 2; Sisters of Charity of Ottawa 3; Lay Teachers 23; Students 644.
Perpetual Help Day Nursery—170 Broad St., 07104. Tel: 973-484-3535; Fax: 973-484-2526.
Vocationist Sisters 6; Lay Teachers 8; Children 194.
Catechesis/Religious Programs—Students 410.
Convent—Tel: 973-484-5261.

26—OUR LADY OF FATIMA (1956) (Portuguese), Revs. Mario Nunes, Admin.; Anthony Bico.
Res., 82 Congress St., 07105. Tel: 973-589-8433; Fax: 973-589-2611.
Day Nursery—79 Jefferson St., 07105. Tel: 973-589-1639.
Catechesis/Religious Programs—Students 1,080.

27—OUR LADY OF GOOD COUNSEL (1902), Rev. Msgr. Joseph P. Plunkett; Rev. Pawel Moleski (Poland); Deacons Ramon Villeda; Oscar Rivera; Carlos Valentin.
Res., 654 Summer Ave., 07104. Tel: 973-482-1274; Fax: 973-482-8257.
School—(1913), 239 Woodside Ave., 07104. Tel: 973-482-1241; Fax: 973-482-8257.
Sisters of Charity 1; Lay Teachers 14; Students 257.
High School—(1922), Tel: 973-482-1209.
Sisters of St. Joseph, Chestnut Hill 3; Lay Teachers 17; Students 283.
Catechesis/Religious Programs—Students 201.
Convent—Tel: 973-483-4256.

28—OUR LADY OF MT. CARMEL (1889) (Italian), Rev. Joseph Ambrosio, Admin. In res., Rev. Eugene Bernas (Philippines).
Res., 259 Oliver St., 07105. Tel: 973-589-2090; Fax: 973-589-2662.

29—OUR LADY OF THE ROSARY (1918) (Italian). Closed. For inquiries for parish records contact Our Lady of Mt. Carmel, Newark. Tel: 973-589-2090.

30—ST. PETER'S (1864). Closed. For inquiries for parish records contact Seton Hall University Archives, South Orange. Tel: 973-761-9476; Fax 973-761-9550.

31—ST. PHILIP NERI (1887). Closed. For inquiries for parish records contact Seton Hall University Archives, South Orange. Tel: 973-761-9476; 973-761-9550.

32—ST. ROCCO'S (1899). (National Historic Landmark). Rev. Josephat Kato Kalema, O.C.S.O., (Uganda) Admin.
Res., 208 Hunterdon St., 07103. Tel: 973-824-1652; Fax: 973-824-4944.
School—21 Ashland St., 07103. Tel: 201-622-0428. Sr. Eileen Jude Wust, S.S.J., Prin.
Lay Teachers 18; Students 453.

33—ST. ROSE OF LIMA (1888), Rev. Msgr. William J. Linder; Rev. Robert Cormier.
Res., 11 Gray St., 07107. Tel: 973-482-0682; Fax: 973-482-2137.
School—(1892), 540 Orange St., 07107. Tel: 973-481-5582; Fax: 973-481-3398. Arthur L. Wilson, Prin.
Sisters 2; Lay Teachers 12; Students 279.
Convent—Tel: 973-481-6566.

34—SACRED HEART (Vailsburg) (1892), Very Rev. Paul D. Schetelick, V.E., V.F.; Rev. John B. Martin.
Res., 481 Sandford Ave., 07106. Tel: 973-373-9790; Fax: 973-374-4047.
School—(Grades PreK-8) 24 Hazelwood Ave., 07106. Tel: 973-372-4441; Fax: 973-372-4157. Bro. Patrick Byrne, O.A.R., Prin.
Religious 22; Lay Teachers 53; Students 800.
Catechesis/Religious Programs—Students 750.
Convent—Tel: 973-374-2730; Fax: 973-374-4656.

35—ST. STANISLAUS (1889) (Polish), Rev. Bogumil Chrusciel.
Res., 146 Irvine Turner Blvd., 07103. Tel: 973-642-7961; Fax: 973-642-2295.

36—ST. STEPHEN'S (1902). Closed. For inquiries for parish records contact Seton Hall University Archives, South Orange. Tel: 973-761-9476; Fax: 973-761-9550.

37—ST. THOMAS AQUINAS (1957) (Hispanic), Revs. Raul E.L. Comesanas; Miguel A. Loredo, O.F.M., Weekend Asst.; Deacons Jose A. Rodriguez; Mario Eschavarria.
Res., 40 Ludlow St., 07114. Tel: 973-242-6703; Fax: 973-242-7143.
Catechesis/Religious Programs—Students 65.

OUTSIDE THE CITY OF NEWARK

Allendale, Bergen Co., Guardian Angel (1954), Rev. Gerald F. Greaves.
Res., 320 Franklin Turnpike, 07401. Tel: 201-327-4359; Fax: 201-327-6478.
School—St. Thomas More Interparochial School. See Nativity Parish, Midland Park for details. Tel: 201-447-3088.
Catechesis/Religious Programs—Tel: 201-327-0352; Fax: 201-327-6478.
Students 385.

Bayonne, Hudson Co.,

1—ST. MARY STAR OF THE SEA, (1861), Revs. Lawrence J. Miller; Thomas P. Conheeney; Paul Passant; Sr. Jane Veronica Walsh, S.S.J., Pastoral Assoc.
Res., 326 Avenue C, 07002. Tel: 201-437-4090; Fax: 201-437-0388.
School—(1879), 19 W. 13th St., 07002. Tel: 201-437-2888; Fax: 201-437-6084.
Lay Teachers 17; Students 320.
Catechesis/Religious Programs—Tel: 201-437-0010.
Students 250.
Convent—Tel: 201-436-0870.

2—ST. ANDREW'S, (1914), Rev. John R. Doherty; Rev. Msgr. Edward F. Wojtycha, Pastor Emeritus; Revs. Michael O'Grady; Gary Ward; Deacon Raymond Sanderson. In res., Rev. Thomas M. Foye.
Res., 125 Broadway, 07002. Tel: 201-437-0833; Fax: 201-858-3477.
School—124 Broadway, 07002. Tel: 973-437-0139.
Sisters of St. Joseph 1; Lay Teachers 9; Students 200.
Catechesis/Religious Programs—Tel: 201-437-9062.
Students 400.

3—ST. HENRY'S, (1889), Rev. Msgr. Edward J. Hajduk, S.T.L., M.S.S.; Rev. Paul A. Cannariato.
Res., 82 W. 29th St., 07002. Tel: 201-436-0857; Fax: 201-823-4611.
Catechesis/Religious Programs—Avenue C & 28 St., 07002. Tel: 201-339-0319. Miss Marie Pope.
Students 432.

4—ST. JOSEPH'S, (1888) (Slovak), Rev. Msgr. Edward M. Matash.
Res., 317 Ave. E, 07002. Tel: 201-339-1122; Fax: 201-339-1009.
Catechesis/Religious Programs—Students 50.

5—ST. VINCENT DE PAUL, (1894), Revs. Peter P. Galdon; Camilo Lopez. In res., Revs. Carl Arico; Joseph Murray, (Retired); Deacon Ralph Savo, Business Mgr.
Res., 979 Ave. C, 07002. Tel: 201-436-2222; Fax: 201-437-5235.
School—(1920), 80 W. 47th St., 07002. Tel: 201-339-4438; Fax: 201-339-3058.
Lay Teachers 12; Students 235.
Catechesis/Religious Programs—Tel: 201-823-0184. Kathleen DiMartino, D.R.E.
Students 364.

6—MT. CARMEL, (1898) (Polish), Very Rev. Anthony J. Kulig, V.F.; Rev. Msgr. Joseph A. Marjanczyk, Pastor Emeritus; Revs. Kazimierz Kuczynski; Robert A. Pachana; Jaroslaw Zaniewski (Poland).
Res., 39 E. 22nd St., 07002. Tel: 201-339-2070; Fax: 201-339-3676.
School—(1902), 19 E. 22nd St., 07002. Tel: 201-339-1839; Fax: 201-339-2268.
Lay Teachers 22; Students 301.
Catechesis/Religious Programs—Ms. Cathy-Lynn Hansen, D.R.E.
Students 140.

7—OUR LADY OF THE ASSUMPTION, (1902) (Italian), Rev. Joseph F. Barbone; Deacon William Giordano.
Res., 531 Ave. C, 07002. Tel: 201-436-8160; Fax: 201-436-4135.
Church—91 W. 23rd St., 07002.
Catechesis/Religious Programs—Tel: 201-437-1867; Fax: 201-339-8280. Sr. Helen Rado, M.P.F.
Students 300.
Convent—95 W. 23rd St., 07002. Tel: 201-858-0202.

8—ST. MICHAEL'S, (1907) (Lithuanian), Rev. John J. Gibbons, M.Div. In res., Rev. J. M. Patricius, Hospital Chap.
Res., 15 E. 23rd St., 07002. Tel: 201-436-1412; Fax: 201-436-5979.
Catechesis/Religious Programs—Students 50.

Belleville, Essex Co., St. Anthony's (1901) (Italian), Revs. Ray A. Francis; Joseph J. Cestaro, Pastor Emeritus; Neil J. Collins; Salvatore T. Malanga.
Res., 750 N. Seventh St., Newark, 07107. Tel: 973-481-1991; Fax: 973-481-1993.
Church—63 Franklin Ave., 07109.

St. Peter's (1837), Revs. Joseph D. Girone; Leo J. Butler; Mark A. O'Connell; Deacons William Valladares; Julio Roig.
Res., 155 William St., 07109. Tel: 973-751-2002; Fax: 973-751-6201. [CEM]
School—(1854), 152 William St., 07109. Tel: 973-759-3143; Fax: 973-759-4160.
Sisters of Charity 3; Lay Teachers 15; Students 252.
Catechesis/Religious Programs—Tel: 973-751-4290.
Students 200.
Convent—Tel: 973-759-2432.

Bergenfield, Bergen Co., St. John the Evangelist (1905), Rev. Msgr. Richard J. Arnhols; Rev. Msgr. Joseph J. Donovan, Pastor Emeritus, (Retired); Revs. Ernesto Tibay; Raymond R. Filipski; Jose E. Marquez; Jacek Marchewka; Deacon Patrick Miney.
Res., 29 N. Washington Ave., 07621. Tel: 201-384-0101; Fax: 201-384-2055.
School—(1921), 10 Bradley Ave., 07621. Tel: 201-384-3627.
Sisters 4; Lay Teachers 22; Students 400.
Catechesis/Religious Programs—35 N. William St., 07621. Tel: 201-384-3601; Fax: 201-384-9306.
Students 845.
Convent—Tel: 201-384-2675.

Berkeley Heights, Union Co., Church of the Little Flower (1955), Revs. Stephen S. Feehan; Alfred J. Burke; Charles Pinyan.
Res., 110 Roosevelt Ave., 07922. Fax: 908-464-6342.
Church—310 Plainfield Ave., 07922. Tel: 908-464-1585.
Catechesis/Religious Programs—Tel: 908-464-7444.
Students 606.

Bloomfield, Essex Co., Sacred Heart (1878), Revs. Richard P. Kwiatkowski; Daniel A. Danik, Pastor Emeritus; David Milliken.
Res., 76 Broad St., 07003. Tel: 973-748-1800; Fax: 973-748-2028. [CEM]
School—(1879), 683 Bloomfield Ave., 07003. Tel: 973-743-4015; Fax: 973-743-0723.
Sisters 2; Lay Teachers 17; Students 375.
Convent—Tel: 973-743-0838; Fax: 973-743-4167.
Catechesis/Religious Programs—Tel: 973-743-4061.
Students 212.

St. Valentine (1899) (Polish), Rev. Msgr. Robert M. Chabak; Rev. Juancho G. DeLeon. In res., Revs. Alan Guglielmo; John J. Donohue.
Res., 125 N. Spring St., 07003. Tel: 973-743-0220; Fax: 973-743-2041.
Catechesis/Religious Programs—Tel: 973-743-6122. Mrs. Patricia Hope, D.R.E.
Students 170.

Church of St. Thomas the Apostle (1939), Rev. Msgr. William C. Hatcher; Rev. Peter K. Funesti; Rev. Msgr. Vincent P. Coburn, Pastor Emeritus; Rev. Owen F. Ince. Pastoral Assocs.: Sr. Mary McGrath, S.S.J.; Sr. Anita Sibilia, M.P.F.; Mr. Kevin Bumpus. In res., Rev. John Connolly, S.D.B.
Res., 60 Byrd Ave., 07003. Tel: 973-338-9190; Fax: 973-338-4224.
School—(1939), 50 Byrd Ave., 07003. Tel: 973-338-8505; Fax: 973-338-9565.
Sisters 7; Lay Teachers 23; Students 440 (PreK-8).
Catechesis/Religious Programs—Tel: 973-338-7400.
Students 860.
Convent—Tel: 973-338-9118; Fax: 973-338-6495.

Bogota, Bergen Co., St. Joseph's (1929), Revs. Paul Schweizer, O.Carm.; James Mueller, O.Carm.; Sr. Catherine McDermott, C.N.D., Pastoral Assoc.; Deacons Walter Lynn; Michael Fitzgerald. In res., Rev. Gregory Battafarano, O. Carm.
Res., 115 E. Fort Lee Rd., 07603. Tel: 201-342-6300; Fax: 201-883-9392.
School—(1925), 131 E. Fort Lee Rd., 07603. Tel: 201-487-8641; Fax: 201-487-7405. Sr. Regina Miriam, F.S.P., Prin.
Franciscan Sisters of Peace 2; Lay Teachers 9; Students 261.
Catechesis/Religious Programs—Tel: 201-343-4316.
Students 445.
Convent—Tel: 201-342-4684.

Caldwell, Essex Co., St. Aloysius (1892), Revs. John J. Laferrera; Robert D. Jacunski; Mark Francis O'Malley; Deacon William J. McDermott. In res., Rev. Lester A. McGuinness, (Retired); Rev. Msgr. Benjamin A. Piazza, (Retired).
Res., 219 Bloomfield Ave., 07006. Tel: 973-226-0221; Fax: 973-226-2204.

School—(1991). (Co-Sponsored) Trinity Academy 235 Bloomfield Ave., 07006. Tel: 973-226-3386; Fax: 973-226-6548.
Sisters 6; Lay Teachers 30; (PreK-8) 564.
Catechesis/Religious Programs—Tel: 973-226-0209; Fax: 973-226-0923.
Students 768.

Cedar Grove, Essex Co., St. Catherine of Siena (1949), Rev. Msgr. Charles W. Gusmer, V.E.; Revs. James Redstone; John Chadwick.
Res., 339 Pompton Ave., 07009. Tel: 973-239-7960; Fax: 973-239-1008.
School—(1958), 39 E. Bradford Ave., 07009. Tel: 973-239-6968.
Sisters of St. Dominic 1; Lay Teachers 19; Students 276; Franciscan Sister of Peace 1.
Catechesis/Religious Programs—Tel: 973-239-3332.
Students 400.
Convent—Tel: 973-239-3362.

Clark, Union Co., St. Agnes (1961), Revs. James A. Choma; Dominic G. Ciriaco. In res., Rev. Leonard Dembow.
Res., 332 Madison Hill Rd., 07066. Tel: 732-388-7852; Fax: 732-388-7064.
School—(1963), 342 Madison Hill Rd., 07066. Tel: 732-381-0850.
Lay Teachers 11; Students 161.
Catechesis/Religious Programs—Students 510.

Cliffside Park, Bergen Co., Epiphany (1916), Revs. Donald J. Di Pasquale; Robert P. Cozzini; Joseph A. Scarangella.
Res., 247 Knox Ave., 07010. Tel: 201-943-7320; Fax: 201-943-1779.
School—(1930), 263 Lafayette Ave., 07010. Tel: 201-945-1194; Fax: 201-224-8721.
Lay Teachers 9; Students 278; Religious 3.
Catechesis/Religious Programs—Tel: 201-945-1164; Fax: 201-943-2255.
Students 250.
Convent—228 Knox Ave., 07010. Tel: 201-943-2660.

Closter, Bergen Co., St. Mary (1912), Rev. James T. McKenna. In res., Rev. Gerald Bajek.
Res., 20 Legion Pl., 07624. Tel: 201-768-7565; Fax: 201-784-5814.
School—300 High St., 07624. Tel: 201-768-2627; Fax: 201-768-6660.
Sisters 5; Lay Teachers 13; Students 140.
Catechesis/Religious Programs—Tel: 201-767-8247.
Students 186.

Cranford, Union Co., St. Michael's (1872), Revs. James J. Weiner; Krzysztof Maslowski; Sr. Arleen D. Crimmins, O.P., Pastoral Assoc.; Deacon Daniel Wilverding; Robert Jennings, Business Mgr.
Res., 40 Alden St., 07016. Tel: 908-276-0360; Fax: 908-272-0273.
School—(1929), Alden and Miln Sts., 07016. Tel: 908-276-9425; Fax: 908-276-4391.
Lay Teachers 31; Students 418.
Catechesis/Religious Programs—100 Alden St., 07016. Tel: 908-276-2050. Lynda Furey, D.R.E.
Students 1,131.

Cresskill, Bergen Co., St. Therese of Lisieux (1924), Revs. Joseph R. Atcher, O.Carm.; Samuel Citero, O.Carm.; Gerard Power, O.Carm.; Sr. Rosalie O'Connor, O.S.F., Pastoral Assoc. In res., Rev. Paul T. Hoban, O.Carm.
Res., 120 Monroe Ave., 07626. Tel: 201-567-2528; Fax: 201-567-6759.
School—220 Jefferson Ave., 07626. Tel: 201-568-4296; Fax: 201-568-3179.
Lay Teachers 15; Students 221.
Catechesis/Religious Programs—200 Jefferson Ave., 07627. Tel: 201-567-4781; Fax: 201-541-1269.
Students 578.

Demarest, Bergen Co., St. Joseph's (1931), Revs. William O'Malley, O.Carm.; Eugene Bettinger, O.Carm.
Res., 280 County Rd., 07627. Tel: 201-768-2371; Fax: 201-768-2466.
School—St. Joseph, Sacred Heart Interparochial School, 573 Piermont Rd., 07627. Tel: 201-768-5534; Fax: 201-768-2620.
Lay Teachers 13; Students 186.
Catechesis/Religious Programs—Tel: 201-768-6886; Fax: 201-768-4128.
Students 265.
St. Joseph (Korean), Rev. Dominic G. An.
Res., 274 County Rd., 07627. Tel: 201-767-1954; Fax: 201-767-1854.

Dumont, Bergen Co., St. Mary's (1914), Revs. Robert G. Laferrera; Edward C. Thompson; Donald McLaughlin; Sr. Elizabeth Mullen, C.S.J., Pastoral Assoc. In res., Revs. Mathew Chandrankunnel (India); Theodore A. Szelest, (Retired).
Res., 280 Washington Ave., 07628. Tel: 201-384-0557; Fax: 201-384-4986.
School—(1951), 21-31 New Milford Ave., 07628. Tel: 201-384-0512; Fax: 201-384-0819.
Sisters 2; Lay Teachers 15; Students 320.
Catechesis/Religious Programs—Tel: 201-384-3062.
Students 795.

East Newark, Hudson Co., St. Anthony's (1901) (Italian), Rev. Anthony F. Granato. In res., Rev. Francis T. Maione.
Res., 409 N. Second St., 07029. Tel: 973-483-4680; Fax: 973-483-2396.
Catechesis/Religious Programs—Students 122.

East Orange, Essex Co.,

1—Holy Name of Jesus, (1910), Revs. Robert J. Rischmann; Jerome S. Arthasseril (India); Edward J. Heavey, S.J.; Deacons Leo Woodruff; Thomas J. Bulgia. In res., Rev. Joseph L. Affanoso.
Res., 184 Midland Ave., 07017.
Parish Center—200 Midland Ave., P.O. Box 5244, 07017-1855. Tel: 973-675-4444; Fax: 973-674-1767.

2—Holy Spirit-Our Lady Help of Christians, (1882) (African American-Haitian), Very Rev. Michael M. Walters; Deacon Sidney Huff. In res., Rev. George Kelly, C.SS.R.
Res., 17 N. Clinton St., 07017. Tel: 973-673-1077; Fax: 973-676-6494.
School—(1883), 23 N. Clinton St., 07017. Tel: 973-677-1546; Fax: 973-677-3939.
Lay Teachers 17; Students 529.
Catechesis/Religious Programs—Students 100.

3—St. Joseph's, (1916), Rev. William A. Mahon, Admin.; Deacons Joseph Fiore, (Retired); Alonzo C. Jackson.
Res., 110 Telford St., 07018. Tel: 973-678-4030; Fax: 973-677-7875.
School—115 Telford St., 07018. Tel: 973-674-2326; Fax: 973-674-7718.
Religious Teachers Filippini 3; Lay Teachers 16; Students 380.
Catechesis/Religious Programs—Students 380.
Convent—Tel: 201-677-0812.

4—Our Lady of All Souls, (1914). Closed. For inquiries for parish records contact Seton Hall University Archives, South Orange. Tel: 973-761-9476; Fax: 973-761-9550.

5—Our Lady of the Most Blessed Sacrament, (1916). Closed. For inquiries for parish records contact Seton Hall University Archives, South Orange. Tel: 973-761-9476; Fax: 973-761-9550.

East Rutherford, Bergen Co., St. Joseph's (1872), Revs. Richard S. Husted, O.F.M.; Edward J. Donohue, O.F.M.; Paul Sinnema, O.F.M.; Sr. Agnes Morrissey, S.C., Pastoral Min., Tel: 201-507-8842; Edward J. Chaudron, Business Mgr.
Res., 120 Hoboken Rd., 07073. Tel: 201-939-0457; Fax: 201-939-4196. [CEM]
School—(1879), 20 Hackensack St., 07073. Tel: 201-939-3193; Fax: 201-939-1913. Mrs. Frances Alberta, Prin.
Lay Teachers 13; Students 206.
Catechesis/Religious Programs—Tel: 201-939-3441. Sr. Marigene Kennedy, O.S.F., D.R.E.
Students 471.
Convent—Tel: 201-460-4961.

Edgewater, Bergen Co., Holy Rosary (1906), Rev. George Ruane; Deacons Robert E. Thomson; Michael A. Lydon. In res., Rev. William M. Giblin, (Retired).
Res., 365 Undercliff Ave., 07020. Tel: 201-945-6329 (Parish Center); Fax: 201-945-6599.
Catechesis/Religious Programs—Students 97.

Elizabeth, Union Co.,

1—St. Mary of the Assumption, (1844), Rev. Msgr. Robert J. Harrington; Revs. William Crum; Hadmels R. DeFrias; Deacon Vincent Accardi. Pastoral Assocs.: Sr. Ruth Morgan, R.S.M.; Sr. Elaine Maguire, F.S.P.; Maria Castillo. In res., Rev. Edward Haber.
Res., 155 Washington Ave., 07202. Tel: 908-352-5154; Fax: 908-352-0350. [CEM]
School—(1868), 237 S. Broad St., 07202. Tel: 908-352-0717.
Lay Teachers 10; Students 251.
High School—Tel: 908-352-4350; Fax: 908-352-2359.
Sisters 1; Lay Teachers 25; Students 325.
Child Care Center—Tel: 908-355-8723.
Students 68.
Catechesis/Religious Programs—Tel: 908-352-0296.
Students 400.
Convent—Tel: 908-352-1455.

2—St. Adalbert's, (1905) (Polish), Revs. Ronald J. Marczewski; Krzysztof Szczotka, S.D.S. (Poland); John Gordon; Deacon Joseph J. Lubas.
Res., 250 E. Jersey St., 07206. Tel: 908-352-2791; Fax: 908-354-2828. [CEM]

3—St. Anthony's, (1895) (Italian), Revs. Donald Delaney, S.D.B.; Vincent Paczkowski, S.D.B.; Thomas Valukaran, S.D.B.; Joseph Santa-Bibiana, S.D.B.; Bro. David Iovacchini, S.D.B.
Res., 853 Third Ave., 07202. Tel: 908-351-3300; Fax: 908-351-3609.
School—227 Centre St., 07202. Tel: 908-352-7419.
Sisters of Charity of Convent Station 5; Lay Teachers 12; Students 400.
Catechesis/Religious Programs—Students 400.
Convent—Tel: 908-354-0825.

4—Blessed Sacrament, (1922), Very Rev. Robert Templeton, V.F.; Deacon Jose R. Fernandez; Cristina Pardo, Pastoral Assoc. In res., Rev. Anselm Nwaorgu.
Res., 1096 North Ave., 07201. Tel: 908-352-0338; Fax: 908-352-4553.
School—(1926), 1086 North Ave., 07201. Tel: 908-352-8629; Fax: 908-352-7934.
Lay Teachers 9; Students 245.
Catechesis/Religious Programs—Students 211.

5—Immaculate Conception, (1907), Revs. Jorge Chacon; Aurelio Yanez (Colombia).
Res., 425 Union Ave., 07208. Tel: 908-352-6662; Fax: 908-352-8484.
Catechesis/Religious Programs—417 Union Ave., Tel: 908-351-4242.
Students 206.
Convent—424 Westminister Ave., 07208. Tel: 908-282-9094.

6—St. Genevieve's, (1920), Rev. Msgr. Hugh A. O'Donnell; Rev. Msgr. Edward G. Price, Pastor Emeritus; Revs. Roy James DeLeo; John G. Netta.
Res., 200 Monmouth Rd., 07208. Tel: 908-351-4444; Fax: 908-351-5454.
School—(1929), 209 Princeton Rd., 07208. Tel: 908-355-3355; Fax: 908-355-1460.
Benedictine Sisters 3; Lay Teachers 20; Students 455.
Catechesis/Religious Programs—Tel: 908-355-1584.
Students 351.
Convent—Tel: 908-353-0736.

7—St. Hedwig's, (1926) (Polish). Unassigned. Revs. Henry P. Marciniak; Thomas J. Lewczak; Wladyslaw Govak (Poland).
Res., 716 Clarkson Ave., 07202. Tel: 908-352-1448; Fax: 908-352-8389.
School—(1928), Clarkson Ave. and Myrtle St., 07202. Tel: 908-354-5653; Fax: 908-354-6961.
Little Servant Sisters of the Immaculate Conception 3; Lay Teachers 12; Students 220.
Catechesis/Religious Programs—Students 278.
Convent—717 Polonia Ave., 07202. Tel: 908-355-8409.

8—St. Joseph's, (1911) (Slovak). Closed. Records at Holy Family, Linden. Tel: 908-862-1060.

9—Our Lady of Most Holy Rosary/St. Michael, (1886/1852), Revs. John E. Wassell, Admin.; Max Osias (Haiti); Jose M. De La Pena. In res., Rev. William C. Reed.
Res., 52 Smith St., 07201. Tel: 908-354-2454; Fax: 908-354-3207. [JC]

10—St. Patrick's, (1858) (Hispanic), Very Rev. Ronald J. Marczewski, V.E., Admin.; Deacon Nestor Charriez.
Res., 215 Court St., 07206. Tel: 908-354-0023; Fax: 908-355-0926. [CEM]
School—(1863). See Elizabethport Catholic School. 227 Court St., 07206. Tel: 908-351-2188; Fax: 908-351-6086.
High School—(1863), 221 Court St., 07206. Tel: 908-353-5220; Fax: 908-629-1123.
Brothers 1; Sisters 1; Lay Teachers 15; Students 233.

11—Sacred Heart, (1871). Merged Records at Our Lady of Fatima Parish, Elizabeth. Tel: 908-355-3810.

12—Holy Rosary, (1886). Merged Records at Our Lady of Most Holy Rosary/St. Michael, Elizabeth. Tel: 908-354-2454; Fax: 908-354-3207.

13—SS. Peter and Paul's, (1895) (Lithuanian), Revs. Alfred Zemeikis; Peter M. Aquino; Deacon Henry Keturwitis.
Res., 211 Ripley Pl., 07206. Tel: 908-352-2271; Fax: 908-353-2851.

14—Immaculate Heart of Mary, (1947) (Spanish), Rev. Francisco Dols, T.O.R. (Spain).
Res., 205 E. Jersey St., 07206. Tel: 908-355-0807; Fax: 908-355-0526.
Catechesis/Religious Programs—Tel: 908-354-8388; Fax: 908-354-8288.
Students 167.
Convent—Tel: 908-354-8388.

15—Our Lady of Fatima, (1973) (Portuguese), Rev. Msgr. John S. Antao; Rev. Jose Manuel Fernandes (Portugal).
Res., 403 Spring St., 07201. Tel: 908-355-3810; Fax: 908-355-4791.
Catechesis/Religious Programs—Students 750.

Elmwood Park, Bergen Co., St. Leo's (1912), Revs. Kevin J. Mullen, O.F.M.; Richard P. Biasiatto, O.F.M.; Theodore F. Lehr, O.F.M.; Robert J. Norton, O.F.M.

Res., 324 Market St., 07407. Tel: 201-796-3521; Fax: 201-703-8408.
School—(1912), 300 Market St., 07407. Tel: 201-796-5156.
Franciscan Sisters of Peace 3; Lay Teachers 15; Students 417.
Catechesis/Religious Programs—Students 200.
Convent—Tel: 201-797-6993.

Emerson, Bergen Co., Church of the Assumption (1947), Rev. Eugene J. Hazewski; Rev. Msgr. Caesar G. Orrico, (Retired), Pastor Emeritus; Revs. Michael Hansen; Bryan F.J. Adamcik.
Res., 29 Jefferson Ave., 07630. Tel: 201-262-1122; Fax: 201-262-7855.
School—35 Jefferson Ave., 07630. Tel: 201-262-0300; Fax: 201-262-5910.
Sisters 3; Lay Teachers 19; Students 310.
Catechesis/Religious Programs—Tel: 201-986-0970.
Students 320.

Englewood, Bergen Co., St. Cecilia's (1866), Revs. Robert A. Wolfe, O.Carm.; Robert Boley, O.Carm.; Bro. David McGinnis, O.Carm., Pastoral Assoc. In res., Rev. Noel Ahrens, O.Carm.; Very Rev. Timothy Moore, O.Carm.; Revs. Ellis Reinert, O.Carm.; Anthony Palo, O.Carm.; Carl Pfister, O.Carm.
Res., 55 Demarest Ave., 07631. Tel: 201-568-0364; Fax: 201-568-0654. [JC]
School—St. Cecilia Interparochial School, (1874), 85 W. Demarest Ave., 07631. Tel: 201-568-2615; Fax: 201-768-7734.
Lay Teachers 12; Students 155.
Catechesis/Religious Programs—Students 162.

Fairfield, Essex Co., St. Thomas More (1962), Revs. John D. Gabriel; Eugene Gniewyk; Sr. Agnes Bernard, O.P., Pastoral Assoc.; Sr. Catherine Reilly.
Res., 210 Horseneck Rd., 07004. Tel: 973-227-0055; Fax: 973-227-2495.
Catechesis/Religious Programs—(Grades 1-8) 12 Hollywood Ave., 07004. Tel: 973-227-3607; Fax: 973-808-9032. Cabrina Kinslow, D.R.E.
Students 406.

Fair Lawn, Bergen Co., St. Anne's (1909), Revs. Ronald J. Pecci, O.F.M.; Jeremiah V. McGinley, O.F.M.; Evan Banks, O.F.M.; Bernadine C. Kessing, O.F.M.; Deacon Richard McGarry. In res., Revs. Anthony R. Fedello, O.F.M.; Felican Foy, O.F.M.
Res., 15-05 Saint Anne St., 07410. Tel: 201-791-1616; Fax: 201-791-1871.
School—(1950), 1-30 Summit Ave., 07410. Tel: 201-796-3353; Fax: 201-796-9058.
Sisters of St. Joseph of Peace 2; Lay Teachers 17; Students 300.
Catechesis/Religious Programs—Tel: 201-791-2331.
Students 799.
Convent—Tel: 201-796-1899.

Fairview, Bergen Co., St. John the Baptist (1873), Revs. Eugene P. Heyndricks; James J. Carroll; Giordano Belanich; Deacon Anton Tarabokija.
Res., 239 Anderson Ave., 07022. Tel: 201-945-4865; Fax: 201-945-8171.
School—St. Elizabeth Seton Interparochial School, (1991). Co-Sponsored. Fourth & Walker, 07022. Tel: 201-945-2212; Fax: 201-945-6742.
Lay Teachers 10; Students 220.
Catechesis/Religious Programs—Students 170.

Our Lady of Grace (1922) (Italian), Revs. Peter T. Sticco, S.A.C.; Pompeo Luciani, S.A.C.
Res., 395 Delano Pl., 07022. Tel: 201-943-0904; Fax: 201-313-5616. Rev. Francis M. Gaetano, S.A.C.
School—400 Kamena St., 07022. Tel: 201-945-8300.
Lay Teachers 15; Students 342.
Catechesis/Religious Programs—Tel: 201-945-1201.
Students 225.

Fort Lee, Bergen Co., Holy Trinity (1906), Revs. James B. Sullivan; Nerva W. Dugue.
Res., 2367 Lemoine Ave., 07024-6269. Tel: 201-947-1216; Fax: 201-947-1217.
School—Christ the Teacher Interparochial School. Co-Sponsored. (See Madonna Parish, Fort Lee). Tel: 201-944-0421; Fax: 201-947-1217.
Catechesis/Religious Programs—Tel: 201-585-0381.
Students 185.
Convent—Tel: 201-944-2911.

Madonna (1858), Revs. John P. Ryan; Stanley Lobo; Ulysses L. Ubalde. In res., Rev. John M. Shih, (Retired).
Res., 340 Main St., 07024. Tel: 201-944-2727; Fax: 201-944-5986. [CEM]
School—(1991). Christ the Teacher Interparochial School 359 Whiteman St., 07024. Tel: 201-944-0421.
Sisters 3; Lay Teachers 19; Students 260.
Catechesis/Religious Programs—Madonna Religious Education Center, Tel: 201-944-4266.
Students 195.

Franklin Lakes, Bergen Co., Most Blessed Sacrament (1961), Rev. Msgr. Thomas J. McDade; Rev. Peter J. Palmisano.
Res., 787 Franklin Lake Rd., 07417. Tel: 201-891-4200; Fax: 201-891-4243.
School—(1963), 785 Franklin Lake Rd., 07417. Tel: 201-891-4250; Fax: 201-847-9227.
Sisters of St. Joseph of Chestnut Hill 1; Lay Teachers 24; Students 270.
Catechesis/Religious Programs—Tel: 201-891-8390.
Students 713.
Convent—Tel: 201-891-4292.

Garfield, Bergen Co.,

1—OUR LADY OF MT. VIRGIN, (1901) (Italian), Revs. Paul L. Bochicchio; Alfonso Picone (Italy); Deacon Dominic Riccio.
Res., 188 MacArthur Ave., 07026. Tel: 973-772-2295; Fax: 973-478-4389.
School—Garfield Catholic Academy, (1951) (Grades PreK-8). (Mt. Virgin Campus) 200 MacArthur Ave., 07026. Tel: 973-772-0416; Fax: 973-772-3301. Sr. Mary Lou Shulas, M.P.F., Prin.
Religious Teachers Filippini 2; Lay Teachers 10.
Catechesis/Religious Programs—Tel: 973-253-1399. Sr. Jo Ann Jankowski, M.P.F., D.R.E.
Students 175.
Convent—410 Maywood Ave., Maywood, 07607. Tel: 201-845-9568.

2—HOLY NAME, (1911), Rev. Msgr. William J. Reilly.
Res., 99 Marsellus Pl., 07026. Tel: 973-340-0032; Fax: 973-340-1618.
School—Garfield Catholic Academy, (Grades PreK-8) 200 MacArthur Ave., 07026. Tel: 973-772-0416.

3—CHURCH OF OUR LADY OF SORROWS, (1917), Revs. John K. Gurski; Michael Guba.
Res., 69 Market St., 07026. Tel: 973-772-7889; Fax: 973-772-7806.
Schools—Garfield Catholic Academy, (Grades PreK-8) 200 MacArthur Ave., 07026. Tel: 973-772-0416; Fax: 973-772-3301.; (Grades K-8) 208 Lanza Ave., 07026.
Catechesis/Religious Programs—Students 80.

4—ST. STANISLAUS KOSTKA, (1917) (Polish), Revs. Edward P. Szpiech; Marian Spanier; Marek Wiorkiewicz, S.D.S.
Res., 184 Ray St., 07026. Tel: 973-772-7922; Fax: 973-772-4178.
School—Garfield Catholic Academy, (1919) (Grades K-8). (St. Stanislaus Kostka Campus) 210 Lanza Ave., 07026. Tel: 973-772-0345; Fax: 973-772-8393.
Felician Sisters 1; Lay Teachers 9; Students 285.
Catechesis/Religious Programs—Tel: 201-794-0620.
Students 285.
Convent—Tel: 973-772-4644.

Garwood, Union Co., Church of St. Anne (1925), Rev. Msgr. John Philip O'Connor. In res., Rev. Eugene Marcone.
Res., 325 Second Ave., 07027. Tel: 908-789-0280; Fax: 908-789-3099.
Catechesis/Religious Programs—Tel: 908-789-4745.
Students 325.

Glen Rock, Bergen Co., St. Catharine (1953), Rev. Dennis J. Cohan; Rev. Msgr. Richard J. Holmes, Pastor Emeritus; Rev. Dominick J. Lenoci. Pastoral Assocs.: Jeannine Pond; Kathleen McCann; Virginia Bailey; Roberta Maguire; Vicki Peluse; Deacons Leonard A. Minichino; Paul Schneider; James Mueller. In res., Rev. Richard U. Odoemela.
Res., 905 S. Maple Ave., 07452. Tel: 201-445-3703; Fax: 201-670-7149.
School—Academy of Our Lady, 180 Rodney St., 07452. Tel: 201-445-0622; Fax: 201-445-8345. Mrs. Patricia Keenaghan, Prin.
Lay Teachers 28; Students 456.
Catechesis/Religious Programs—Tel: 201-444-5690.
Students 825.

Guttenberg, Hudson Co., St. John Nepomucene (1910) (Slovak), Revs. John F. Renard; David S. McLaughlin.
Res., 7007 Polk St., 07093. Tel: 201-869-6834; Fax: 201-869-2408.
School—7111 Polk St., North Bergen, 07047. Tel: 201-869-5404.
School Sisters of St. Francis 2; Lay Teachers 15; Students 260.
Catechesis/Religious Programs—Students 55.
Convent—Tel: 201-869-2099.

Hackensack, Bergen Co.,

1—HOLY TRINITY, (1861), Most Rev. Charles J. McDonnell, D.D.; Revs. Patrick W. Donohue; J. Orlando Rengifo; Robert M. Hoatson; Deacon Vincent Messina; Sr. Emily Marie Walsh, Parish Min.
Res., 34 Maple Ave., 07601. Tel: 201-343-5170; Fax: 201-343-5067. [CEM]
School—(1869), 43 Maple Ave., 07601. Tel: 201-489-6870; Fax: 201-489-2981.
Sisters of Charity 5; Lay Teachers 20; Students 280.
Catechesis/Religious Programs—Mrs. Carol Thee, D.R.E.
Students 350.
Convent—Tel: 201-342-1996; Fax: 201-968-0035.

2—IMMACULATE CONCEPTION, (1891), Rev. Gerard J. Graziano.
Res., 49 Vreeland Ave., 07601. Tel: 201-440-2798; Fax: 201-440-6756.
Catechesis/Religious Programs—Students 86.

3—ST. JOSEPH'S, (1909) (Polish), Rev. Martin J. Silver.
Res., 460 Hudson St., 07601. Tel: 201-440-3224; Fax: 201-440-3224.

4—CHURCH OF ST. FRANCIS OF ASSISI, (1917), Revs. Brian Tomlinson, O.F.M. Cap.; Paschal Caccavalle, O.F.M. Cap.; Eduardo Alapide, O.P.; Bro. Cory Moody, O.F.M. Cap.; Deacon Joseph Vrindten.
Res., 50 Lodi St., 07601. Tel: 201-343-6243; Fax: 201-343-0854.
School—100 S. Main St., 07601. Tel: 201-488-8862; Fax: 201-525-0498.
Lay Teachers 16; Students 273.
Catechesis/Religious Programs—Tel: 201-488-2614.
Students 225.

Harrington Park, Bergen Co., Our Lady of Victories (1910), Rev. Edward V. Duffy. In res., Rev. Msgr. Roger A. Reynolds, (Retired).
Res., 81 Lynn St., 07640-1831. Tel: 201-768-1706; Fax: 201-768-3962.
School—Holy Family Interparochial School, Norwood. (See Immaculate Conception, Norwood. Tel: 201-768-1605). Fax: 201-768-0796.
Catechesis/Religious Programs—(Grades K-8) 155 The Parkway, 07640-1820. Tel: 201-768-1400. Miss Elizabeth Foer, D.R.E.
Students 327.
Convent—145 The Parkway, 07640-1820. Tel: 201-768-1705.

Harrison, Hudson Co., Holy Cross (1865), Rev. Msgr. John J. Gilchrist; Rev. Paulo Frade. In res., Revs. Charles McTague, (Retired); James J. Reilly; Sr. Doris DeLotto, S.S.C., Pastoral Assoc.; Sr. Barbara Graziadei, S.S.C.
Res., 16 Church Sq., 07029. Tel: 973-484-5678; Fax: 973-484-0906.
School—(1871), 14 S. F.E. Rodgers Blvd., 07029. Tel: 973-485-0340; Fax: 973-481-0488.
Lay Teachers 10; Students 201.
Catechesis/Religious Programs—Students 201.
Convent—Tel: 973-485-2632. Holy Cross Convent

Our Lady of Czestochowa (1908) (Polish), Revs. Rudolf Zubik; John Borowik.
Res., 115 S. Third St., 07029. Tel: 973-483-2255; Fax: 973-483-4688.

Hasbrouck Heights, Bergen Co., Corpus Christi (1897), Rev. Msgr. Francis A. DeDomenico; Revs. Raymond M. Holmes; Andrew Zmerlicki.
Parish Offices & Center: 218 Washington Pl., 07604. Tel: 201-288-4844; Fax: 201-288-0237.
School—(1928), 215 Kipp Ave., 07604. Tel: 201-288-0614; Fax: 201-288-5956.
Lay Teachers 27; Students 290.
Catechesis/Religious Programs—Tel: 201-288-5133; Fax: 201-288-0137.
Students 585.

Haworth, Bergen Co., Sacred Heart (1914), Rev. Msgr. James F. Bouffard; Rev. Joseph W. Nealon, Pastor Emeritus.
Res., 123 Maple St., P.O. Box S, 07641. Tel: 201-387-0080; Fax: 201-439-1395.
School—St. Joseph's Interparochial School. (See St. Joseph, Demarest. Tel: 201-768-5534).
Catechesis/Religious Programs—400 St. Nicholas Ave., 07641. Tel: 201-384-6454.
Students 200.

Hillsdale, Bergen Co., St. John the Baptist (1925), Rev. Msgr. Philip D. Morris, S.T.D.; Revs. Michael J. Moran, M.Div.; Thomas A. Dente. Pastoral Assocs.: Sr. Kathryn A. Malone, S.S.J., M.A.; Sr. Thomas Therese, S.S.J.
Res., 69 Valley St., 07642. Tel: 201-664-3131; Fax: 201-664-0772.
School—St. John's Academy, (1955), 460 Hillsdale Ave., 07642. Tel: 201-664-6364; Fax: 201-664-8096.
Sisters of St. Joseph, Chestnut Hill, PA 2; Lay Teachers 24; Students 358.
Catechesis/Religious Programs—Faith Formation Center, Tel: 201-666-2707.
Students 513.
Convent—Tel: 201-664-3800.

Hillside, Union Co., St. Catherine of Siena (1912), Rev. Richard A. Villanova; Sr. Margaret A. Scarpone, R.S.M., Pastoral Assoc.; Deacon Osiris Molina.
Res., 19 King St., 07205. Tel: 908-351-1515; Fax: 908-351-2139.

School—(1920), 1003 N. Broad St., Elizabeth, 07205. Tel: 908-352-8029; Fax: 908-352-3677.
Lay Teachers 15; Students 240.
Catechesis/Religious Programs—Elizabeth, Tel: 908-352-8068.
Students 170.

Christ the King (1948), Revs. Venantius M. Fernando; William C. Cook.
Res., 411 Rutgers Ave., 07205. Tel: 908-686-0722; Fax: 908-686-2504.
School—(1953), 397 Columbia Ave., 07205. Tel: 908-686-6740; Fax: 908-686-3819.
Sisters 1; Lay Teachers 17; Students 225.
Catechesis/Religious Programs—Tel: 908-686-0234.
Students 80.

Hoboken, Hudson Co.,

1—OUR LADY OF GRACE, (1851), Very Rev. Kenneth J. Herbster, V.F.; Rev. Fernando E. Guillen. In res., Rev. Frederick M. Eid.
Res., 400 Willow Ave., 07030. Tel: 201-659-0369; Fax: 201-659-5833.
School—Hoboken Catholic Academy, (1999), 410 Hudson St., 07030. Tel: 201-659-7158; Fax: 201-659-8135.
Lay Teachers 23; Students 346.
Catechesis/Religious Programs—Students 115.

2—ST. JOSEPH'S, (1871), Very Rev. Kenneth J. Herbster, V.F.; Deacon Luis Montanez.
Res., c/o Our Lady of Grace, 400 Willow Ave., 07030. Tel: 201-659-0369; Fax: 201-659-5833.
School—Hoboken Catholic Academy, Tel: 201-963-7158.

3—ST. FRANCIS, (1888) (Italian), Rev. Michael V. Guglielmelli.
Res., 308 Jefferson St., 07030. Tel: 201-659-1772; Fax: 201-222-7975.
School—Hoboken Catholic Academy, Tel: 201-963-9535.
Catechesis/Religious Programs—Students 62.

4—SS. PETER AND PAUL'S, (1889), Rev. Msgr. Frank G. Del Prete, J.C.D.; Rev. Joseph D'Amico; Deacon Primitivo Cruz; Debra Sheridan, Pastoral Assoc.
Res., 404 Hudson St., 07030. Tel: 201-659-2276; Fax: 201-659-5062.
School—Hoboken Catholic Academy, 410 Hudson St., 07030. Tel: 201-659-7158; Fax: 201-656-8135.
Lay Teachers 9; Students 400.
Catechesis/Religious Programs—Students 60.
Convent—.

5—ST. ANN'S, (1900) (Italian), Revs. Francis Sariego, O.F.M.Cap.; Joseph Mezzanote, O.F.M.Cap.
Res., 704 Jefferson St., 07030. Tel: 201-659-1114; Fax: 201-659-1416.
School—Hoboken Catholic Academy, (1955), 555 Seventh St., 07030. Tel: 201-963-9535 (Madison Campus); 201-659-7158 (Hudson Campus).
Sisters 3; Lay Teachers 23; Students 435.
Catechesis/Religious Programs—Students 40.

Hohokus, Bergen Co., St. Luke's (1864), Revs. William J. Dowd; MinHyun Cho. In res., Rev. Msgr. Richard J. Holmes, Pastor Emeritus.
Res., 340 N. Franklin Tpke., 07423. Tel: 201-444-0272; Fax: 201-652-7044. [CEM]
School—St. Thomas More Interparochial School. Serving the Parish Communities of St. Luke's, Nativity and Guardian Angel. (See Nativity Parish, Midland Park).
Catechesis/Religious Programs—Tel: 201-447-2779. Miss Bridget Sarkowicz, D.R.E.
Students 598.

Irvington, Essex Co.,

1—ASSUMPTION OF THE BLESSED VIRGIN MARY, (1907) (Hungarian). Closed. For inquiries for parish records contact Seton Hall University Archives, South Orange. Tel: 973-596-9476.

2—ST. LEO'S, (1878), Revs. Thomas M. Cembor; Dennis R. McKenna, Pastor Emeritus; Deacon Victor Reyes.
Res., 103 Myrtle Ave., 07111. Tel: 973-372-1272; Fax: 973-416-8819.
School—(1892), 123 Myrtle Ave., 07111. Tel: 973-372-7555. Mr. Paulo Sociedade, Prin.
Lay Teachers 16; Students 236.
Catechesis/Religious Programs—Students 80.
Convent—Tel: 973-374-6397.

3—SACRED HEART OF JESUS, (1925) (Polish), Revs. Tadeusz Trela; Jordan Mysliwiec, S.D.S.
Res., 537 Grove St., 07111. Tel: 973-373-2232; Fax: 973-373-5935.
School—(1929), 15 Smalley Ter., 07111. Tel: 973-372-6372.
Felician Sisters 1; Lay Teachers 9; Students 190.
Catechesis/Religious Programs—Students 82.
Convent—Tel: 973-372-6528.

4—ST. PAUL THE APOSTLE, (1948), Revs. William R. Smalley, Pastor Emeritus; Theodore W. Osbahr; Robert Cio.
Res., 954 Stuyvesant Ave., 07111. Tel: 973-375-8568; Fax: 973-375-7040.
School—(1950), 285 Nesbit Ter., 07111. Tel: 973-375-0659; Fax: 973-373-4882.
Sisters of St. Dominic 3; Lay Teachers 10; Students 210.
Catechesis/Religious Programs—Tel: 973-375-2688.
Students 210.
Convent—972 Stuyvesant Ave., 07111. Tel: 973-374-2277.

Jersey City, Hudson Co.,

1—ST. AEDAN'S, (1912), Rev. Msgr. Jeremias R. Rebanal, J.C.D., Ph.D.; Revs. Edito Gamallo, S.T.B.; Henry M. Naddeo. In res., Rev. Romeo Panes (Philippines).
Res., 800 Bergen Ave., 07306. Tel: 201-433-6800; Fax: 201-433-1222.
School—(1913), 41 Tuers Ave., 07306. Tel: 201-435-6528; Fax: 201-985-8975.
Sisters 4; Lay Teachers 18; Students 325.
Convent—Tel: 201-451-8109.

2—ST. ALOYSIUS, (1897), Rev. Msgr. Peter A. Cheplic; Rev. Msgr. Martin Kelly; Revs. Thomas Thottungal; Manuel D. Rios; Deacons Stephen Liptak; Eliut Casanova. In res., Rev. Edward S. Malkiewicz, (Retired).
Res., 691 West Side Ave., 07304. Tel: 201-433-6365; Fax: 201-451-6438.
School—(1897), 721 West Side Ave., 07306. Tel: 201-433-4270; Fax: 201-433-6916.
Sisters of Charity 2; Lay Teachers 29; Students 550.
High School—Tel: 201-435-9240; Fax: 201-435-2115.
Lay Teachers 22; Students 340.
Catechesis/Religious Programs—Students 232.
Convent—Tel: 201-433-5759.

3—ST. ANNE'S, (1903), Revs. Victor P. Kennedy; Julio I. Roman. In res., Revs. Jose M. Parcon (Philippines); Kevin P. Ashe.
Res., 3545 J.F. Kennedy Blvd., 07307. Tel: 201-656-2490; Fax: 201-795-3817.
School—(1904), 255 Congress St., 07307. Tel: 201-659-0450. Mrs. Marlene Bartram, Prin.
Lay Teachers 18; Students 338.
Catechesis/Religious Programs—Tel: 201-659-1794. Sr. Alberta Manzo, F.S.R., D.R.E.
Students 175.
Convent—Tel: 201-963-0998.

4—ST. ANN'S, (1910) (Lithuanian). Closed. For inquiries for parish records contact Seton Hall University Archives, South Orange. Tel: 201-761-9476, Fax: 201-761-9550.

5—ST. ANN'S, (1911) (Polish), Revs. Thaddeus Stasik; George Idzik.
Res., 291 St. Paul's Ave., 07306-5008. Tel: 201-656-4018; Fax: 201-656-0741.
Catechesis/Religious Programs—Students 27.

6—ST. ANTHONY OF PADUA, (1884) (Polish), Very Rev. Michael E. Gubernat, V.F., Admin.; Rev. Andrzej Ostaszewski; Sr. Reginald Zajac, Pastoral Assoc. In res., Rev. Brendan Quinn.
Res., 330 Sixth St., 07302. Tel: 201-653-0343; Fax: 201-653-0005.
Catechesis/Religious Programs—Students 5.

7—ASSUMPTION/ALL SAINTS, (1896), Revs. Eugene P. Squeo, J.D.; Rony Fabien (Haiti); Francis E. Schiller; Deacons Joseph Del Monte; Jesus Reyes.
Res., 492 Bramhall Ave., 07304. Tel: 201-333-1971; Fax: 201-324-3919.
School—301 Whiton St., 07304. Tel: 201-433-6087.
Sisters of Charity 5; Lay Teachers 21; Students 220.
Catechesis/Religious Programs—Fax: 201-216-1600. Anne Marie Padillo, D.R.E.
Students 75.
Convent—Tel: 201-451-2765.

8—ST. BONIFACE'S, (1863). Merged with St. Bridget, St. Mary, St. Michael and St. Peter to form Parish of the Resurrection, June 1997. For inquiries for parish records call Tel: 201-434-8500.

9—ST. BRIDGET'S, (1869). Merged with St. Boniface, St. Mary, St. Michael and St. Peter to form Parish of the Resurrection, June 1997. For inquiries for parish records call Tel: 201-434-8500.

10—CHRIST, THE KING, (1930) (African American), Rev. John Edmunds, S.T.; Deacons Leon Johnson; Keith McKnight.
Res., 768 Ocean Ave., 07304. Tel: 201-333-4862; Fax: 201-433-6352.
Catechesis/Religious Programs—Students 62.

11—HOLY ROSARY, (1885) (Italian), Rev. Msgr. Joseph Chiang; Rev. Msgr. Gerard M. Santora, Pastor Emeritus; Deacon Aart Morkenstein. In res., Revs. Joseph Fu, (Retired) (China); Gerard J. Sudol.
Res., 344 Sixth St., 07302. Tel: 201-795-0120; Fax: 201-610-1389.
School—189 Brunswick St., 07302. Tel: 201-653-1699; Fax: 201-418-9019.
Religious Teachers Filippini 4; Lay Teachers 11; Students 166.
Catechesis/Religious Programs—Tel: 201-792-7959. Sr. Jean Raspolich, Prin.
Students 23.
Convent—Tel: 201-653-0697.

12—ST. JOHN THE BAPTIST, (1884), Rev. Msgr. Charles G. Stengel; Rev. Msgr. Joseph A. Beggans, Pastor Emeritus; Revs. Stanley J. Gomes; Boban Zachariah (India).
Res., 3026 John F. Kennedy Blvd., 07306. Tel: 201-653-8814; Fax: 201-653-3771.
School—(1886) (Grades PreK-8). Co-Sponsored. Saints John and Ann School. 3044 John F. Kennedy Blvd., 07306. Tel: 201-653-4416; Fax: 201-653-7452.
Lay Teachers 12; Students 319.
Catechesis/Religious Programs—Students 30.

13—ST. JOSEPH'S, (1856), Revs. James V. Pagnotta; Francisco Ponce.
Res., 511 Pavonia Ave., 07306. Tel: 201-653-0392; Fax: 201-222-6481.
Church—Baldwin Ave., 07306. Fax: 201-222-6481.
School—(1876), 509 Pavonia Ave., 07306. Tel: 201-653-0128; Fax: 201-222-5324.
Sisters of Charity 1; Lay Teachers 10; Students 200.
Convent—Tel: 201-963-1428.
Catechesis/Religious Programs—Tel: 201-659-5929.
Students 162.

14—ST. LUCY'S, (1884). Closed. For inquiries for parish records contact Parish of the Resurrection. Tel: 201-434-8500.

15—ST. MARY'S, (1854) (Hispanic-Filipino). Merged with St. Boniface, St. Bridget, St. Michael, and St. Peter, to form Parish of the Resurrection, June 1997. For inquiries for parish records call Tel: 201-434-8500.

16—ST. MICHAEL'S, (1867). Merged with St. Boniface, St. Bridget, St. Mary and St. Peter to form Parish of the Resurrection, June 1997. For inquiries for parish records call Tel: 201-434-8500.

17—OUR LADY OF MT. CARMEL, (1905) (Italian), Revs. Michael C. Santoro; Marcos Sequeira. In res., Rev. Walter L. Genzlinger.
Res., 99 Broadway, 07306. Tel: 201-435-7080; Fax: 201-432-4476.
School—(1955), 95 Broadway, 07306. Tel: 201-435-0209; Fax: 201-435-0298. JoAnne Oziemblo, Prin. & D.R.E.
Lay Teachers 14; Students 199.
Catechesis/Religious Programs—Students 20.

18—ST. NICHOLAS, (1886) (German), Rev. Kevin E. Carter; Rev. Msgr. Joseph C. Manz, Pastor Emeritus; Rev. Jose Saltarin. In res., Rev. Christopher Anyanwu (Nigeria); Deacon Robert A. Baker, Sr.
Res., 122 Ferry St., 07307. Tel: 201-659-5354; Fax: 201-798-6868.
School—(1884), 118 Ferry St., 07307. Tel: 201-659-5948.
Sisters of Christian Charity 6; Lay Teachers 14; Students 333.
Catechesis/Religious Programs—Tel: 201-659-5354, Ext. 127.
Students 95.
Convent—Tel: 201-659-5644.

19—OUR LADY OF CZESTOCHOWA, (1911) (Polish), Rev. Thomas B. Iwanowski. In res., Rev. Alexander M. Santora.
Res., 120 Sussex St., 07302. Tel: 201-434-0798; Fax: 201-985-0918.
School—(1911), Marin Blvd. & York St., 07302. Tel: 201-434-2405; Fax: 201-434-6068.
Lay Teachers 12; Students 180.
Catechesis/Religious Programs—Students 30.
Sisters Residence: Tel: 201-333-0410.

20—OUR LADY OF MERCY, (1963), Revs. John J. Cryan; Bartley P. Baker; Deacon Nicholas Fargo.
Res., 40 Sullivan Dr., 07305. Tel: 201-434-7500; Fax: 201-432-2885.
School—254 Bartholdi Ave., 07305. Tel: 201-434-4091; Fax: 201-434-8405.
Lay Teachers 30; Students 646.
Convent—Tel: 201-451-4615.
Catechesis/Religious Programs—Students 156.

21—CHURCH OF OUR LADY OF SORROWS, (1914), Rev. John Cryan, V.F., Admin.; Sr. Alice McCoy, O.P., Pastoral Assoc.
Res., 93-95 Clerk St., 07305. Tel: 201-433-0626; Fax: 201-433-2928.
Catechesis/Religious Programs—Students 48.

22—OUR LADY OF VICTORIES, (1917), Revs. Victor E. Paloma; Walter J.F. Swenson, Pastor Emeritus; William Yabao (Philippines). In res., Rev. James Tortora, Ph.D.
Res., 2217 John F. Kennedy Blvd., 07304-1497. Tel: 201-433-4152; Fax: 201-433-0705.

School—(1930), Tel: 201-434-4040; Fax: 201-434-5356.
Lay Teachers 21; Students 411.
Catechesis/Religious Programs—Students 350.

23—ST. PATRICK'S, (1869), Revs. Eugene P. Squeo, J.D.; Francis E. Schiller, J.D.; Rony Fabien (Haiti); Bro. Christopher Isinta. In res., Rev. Edward J. Kearney, (Retired).
Res., 492 Bramhall Ave., 07304. Tel: 201-332-8600; Fax: 201-324-3919.
School—(1909), Tel: 201-433-4664.
Sisters of Charity of St. Elizabeth 4; Lay Teachers 32; Students 525.
Catechesis/Religious Programs—Fax: 201-216-1600.
Students 56.
Convent—345 Pacific Ave., 07304. Tel: 201-451-2765.

24—PARISH OF THE RESURRECTION, (1997). (Formerly Parishes of St. Boniface, St. Bridget, St. Mary, St. Michael and St. Peter). Very Rev. Gregory J. Studerus, V.F.; Revs. Fabio R. De Jesus Brenes-Chaves; Richard J. Caplice, S.J.; John Martin; Vincent B. Sullivan, S.J.; Bro. Louis N. Mauro, S.J.; Deacons Pedro Gonzalez; Jaime Ortiz; Leopoldo Polanco. Pastoral Assocs.: Sr. Grace Reape, S.C.; Sr. Mercedes Salinas, S.C.; Sr. Jean Young, S.C.; Ms. Elizabeth Hopf.
Mailing Address: & Parish Office: 370 Montgomery St., 07302. Tel: 201-434-8500; Fax: 201-333-1816.
Churches—St. Boniface, 262 First St., 07302. Tel: 201-792-2504; Fax: 201-656-1070; St. Bridget, 372 Montgomery St., 07302. Tel: 201-434-5082; St. Michael. (Shrine of St. Jude Perpetual Novena) 252 Ninth St., 07302. Tel: 201-653-2147; Fax: 201-653-2247; St. Mary, 219 Third St., 07302. Tel: 201-653-2217; Fax: 201-653-1943; St. Peter, 144 Grand Street, 07302. Tel: 201-434-4900.
Schools—Resurrection, St. Bridget Campus, (1873), 372 Montgomery St., 07302. Tel: 201-432-3588; Fax: 201-432-7978.; Resurrection, St. Mary Campus, (1868), 209 Third St., 07302. Tel: 201-653-3333; Fax: 201-653-4518.; Resurrection, St. Peter's Campus, (1864), 153 York St., 07302. Tel: 201-434-8154; Fax: 201-434-1613.
High School—St. Mary, 209 Third St., 07302. Tel: 201-656-8008; Fax: 201-653-4518.
Catechesis/Religious Programs—Clustered with St. Bridget, Jersey City. Tel: 201-795-3426 (St. Mary). Students 415.

25—ST. PAUL OF THE CROSS, (1868), Revs. Andres J. Reyes, Admin.; Gerardo Gallo (Colombia).
Res., 156 Hancock Ave., 07307. Tel: 201-798-7900; Fax: 201-798-7902.
School—(1869), 211 Sherman Ave., 07307. Tel: 201-659-6919.
Sisters of Charity 2; Lay Teachers 9; Students 235.
Catechesis/Religious Programs—Students 190.
Convent—Tel: 201-659-1414.

26—ST. PAUL'S, (1861), Revs. Robert Antczak; Jose Gamba; John F. Bauman. In res., Rev. John F. Corbett.
Res., 14 Greenville Ave., 07305. Tel: 201-433-8500; Fax: 201-433-9886.
School—(1872), 193 Old Bergen Rd., 07305. Tel: 201-435-8204; Fax: 210-435-3048.
Sisters of St. Dominic 3; Lay Teachers 18; Students 283.
Catechesis/Religious Programs—Tel: 201-433-1054.
Students 155.
Convent—Tel: 201-434-2962.

27—ST. PETER'S, (1831) (Hispanic). Merged with St. Boniface, St. Bridget, St. Mary and St. Michael to form Parish of the Resurrection, June 1997. For parish inquiries call Tel: 201-434-8500.

28—SACRED HEART, (1905), Revs. Charles T. Quinn, O.P., Pastor; David C. Adiletta, O.P.; Sr. Elaine Keenan, O.P., Pastoral Assoc.
Res., 183 Bayview Ave., 07305. Tel: 201-332-6771 (Parish); 332-6773 (Priory); Fax: 201-332-5831 (Parish).
School—(1913), Tel: 201-332-7111; Fax: 201-332-7160. Sr. Frances Salemi, S.C., Prin.
Sisters of Charity 5; Sisters of St. Joseph of Peace 2; Lay Teachers 16; Students 375.
Sacred Heart Priory—Tel: 201-332-8667; Fax: 201-332-8375. Revs. Gerard Maley, O.P., Prior; Hugh D. Burns, O.P.; Ralph V. Townsend, O.P.; Henry Camacho, O.P.; Val La France, O.P.; Bro. John Jude Locchetto, O.P.

Kearny, Hudson Co., St. Cecilia's (1893), Revs. Norbert Laskowski; Michael Ward; Alphonse De Condorpusa. In res., Rev. Msgr. Francis R. Seymour; Rev. Msgr. Jose Agan.
Res., 120 Kearny Ave., 07032. Tel: 201-991-1116; Fax: 201-998-4437.
School—(1896), 114 Chestnut St., 07032. Tel: 201-991-9142.
Lay Teachers 11; Students 220.
Catechesis/Religious Programs—Students 310.

Our Lady of Sorrows (1915) (Lithuanian), Rev. Michael J. O'Brien; Rev. Msgr. Dominick A. Pocus, Pastor Emeritus; Rev. Patrick R.C. Wilhelm; Deacon Leonard J. Mackesy.
Res., 136 Davis Ave., 07032. Tel: 201-998-4616; Fax: 201-997-8659.
Catechesis/Religious Programs—Students 125.
Convent—Tel: 201-991-7983.

St. Stephen's (1904), Rev. Msgr. Michael J. Desmond, V.E.; Rev. Scott F. Attanasio; Deacon Herbert R. Gimbel. In res., Rev. Richard J. Kelly.
Res., 141 Washington Ave., 07032. Tel: 201-998-3314; Fax: 201-998-4924.
School—(1904), 131 Midland Ave., 07032. Tel: 201-991-3217; Fax: 201-998-4924. Madeline O'Sullivan, Prin.
Lay Teachers 15; Students 307.
Catechesis/Religious Programs—Tel: 201-991-0236. Sr. Rita Kearney, S.S.J., D.R.E.
Students 580.

Kenilworth, Union Co., St. Theresa's (1949), Rev. Joseph S. Bejgrowicz. In res., Rev. Msgr. Oscar Leano (Philippines); Revs. George M. Keating; Al Kowalski, (Retired); Jose Erlito Ebron.
Res., 541 Washington Ave., 07033. Tel: 908-272-4444; Fax: 908-272-2252.
School—540 Washington Ave., 07033. Tel: 908-276-7220; Fax: 908-709-1103. Sr. Marisa De Rose, F.M.A.
Salesian Sisters 4; Lay Teachers 14; Students 286.
Catechesis/Religious Programs—Tel: 908-276-4881. Maureen Madden, D.R.E.
Students 550.
Convent—Tel: 908-276-5028.

Leonia, Bergen Co., St. John the Evangelist's (1912), Revs. Robert Traudt, O.Carm.; Ronald Gray, O.Carm.; John Lord, O.Carm.; Sr. Patricia McDermott, F.S.P., Pastoral Assoc.; Deacon Joseph Yandoli, Business Mgr. In res., Revs. James Boyce, O.Carm.; John Lord, O.Carm.
Res., 235 Harrison St., 07605. Tel: 201-947-4545; Fax: 201-947-3891.
School—260 Harrison St., 07605. Tel: 201-944-4361; Fax: 201-944-2195.
School Sisters of Notre Dame 1; Lay Teachers 12; Students 210.
Catechesis/Religious Programs—Tel: 201-944-4346. Marlene Bergeen, D.R.E.
Students 302.
Convent—Tel: 201-944-4362.

Linden, Union Co.,

1—ST. ELIZABETH'S, (1909), Very Rev. Benedict Michael Worry, O.S.B., V.F.; Revs. Donal R. Fox, O.S.B.; Damian Breen, O.S.B.
Res., 179 Hussa St., 07036. Tel: 908-486-2514; Fax: 908-486-1757.
School—(1927), 170 Hussa St., 07036. Tel: 908-486-2507; Fax: 908-486-1757.
Dominican Sisters of Caldwell 6; Lay Teachers 20; Students 500.
Convent—Tel: 908-486-2737.
Catechesis/Religious Programs—170 Hussa St., Tel: 908-486-2509.
Students 500.

2—HOLY FAMILY, (Tremley Point) (1955) (Slovak), Rev. Eugene Diurczak; Rev. Msgr. Michael A. Komar, Pastor Emeritus.
Res., 210 Monroe St., 07036. Tel: 908-862-1060; Fax: 908-862-1060. [CEM]
Church—2709 Parkway Ave., 07036. Fax: 908-862-1060.

3—ST. JOHN THE APOSTLE, (1948), Rev. Msgr. Richard M. McGuinness; Revs. Brian McFadden; Joseph A. Meagher; Deacons Guy Paredes, (Retired); George Ross; Edward Campanella. In res., Rev. Joseph G. Sheehan, (Retired).
Res., 1805 Penbrook Ter., 07036. Tel: 908-486-6363; Fax: 908-486-5345.
School—(1950), Valley Rd., Clark, 07066. Tel: 732-388-1360; Fax: 732-388-0775.
Sister of St. Dominic 2; Lay Teachers 22; Students 451.
Catechesis/Religious Programs—Tel: 732-388-1253. Sr. Cynthia Johnson, D.R.E.
Students 600.
Convent—1731 Valley Rd., 07036. Tel: 908-486-3701.

4—ST. THERESA OF THE CHILD JESUS, (1925) (Polish), Rev. Msgr. Bronislaw Wielgus; Revs. Marek Chachlowski (Poland); Jan Christopher Lebdowicz; Sr. Mary Rita Karvetski, C.S.S.F., Pastoral Assoc.; Deacon Alexander Czerepka.
Res., 122 Liberty St., 07036. Tel: 908-862-1116; Fax: 908-862-2930.
Church—131 E. Edgar Rd., 07036.
School—(1930), 705 Clinton St., 07036. Tel: 908-862-7551; Fax: 908-862-5982.
Lay Teachers 10; Students 197.
Catechesis/Religious Programs—Tel: 908-862-1388.
Students 392.
Convent—18 Liberty Ave., 07036. Tel: 908-862-4820.

Little Ferry, Bergen Co., St. Margaret of Cortona (1941), Revs. Arthur Frank Humphrey, S.T.M., M.A.; William A. Lusik.
Res., 31 Chamberlain Ave., 07643-1898. Tel: 201-641-2988; Fax: 201-641-0664.
Catechesis/Religious Programs—Tel: 201-641-3937. Sr. Dorothy A. Donovan, S.S.J., D.R.E.
Students 329.

Livingston, Essex Co., St. Philomena (1927), Rev. Msgr. Edward J. Eilert; Rev. Msgr. William J. Daly, Pastor Emeritus; Revs. Stephen A. Kopacz; Timothy G. Graff; Deacon Joseph Francione; Anita Foley, Pastoral Assoc. In res., Rev. Msgr. Robert T. Lennon.
Res., 386 S. Livingston Ave., 07039. Tel: 973-992-0994; Fax: 973-992-0970.
Schools—Aquinas Academy, (1952), 388 S. Livingston Ave., 07039. Tel: 973-992-1587; Fax: 973-992-1742. Sr. Patricia Tavis, Prin.
Dominican Sisters of Caldwell 1; Lay Teachers 27; Students 285; Early Childhood Center, Tel: 973-992-5181; Fax: 973-992-2652.
Lay Teachers 13; Students 118.
Catechesis/Religious Programs—Tel: 973-992-4466.
Students 436.
Convent—Tel: 973-992-1581.

St. Raphael (1961), Rev. Msgr. G. Thomas Burns; Rev. Andrew Prachar. In res., Rev. John E. O'Brien.
Res., 346 E. Mt. Pleasant Ave., 07039. Tel: 973-992-9490; Fax: 973-740-0236.
Catechesis/Religious Programs—Students 550.

Lodi, Bergen Co., St. Francis de Sales (1854), Revs. Charles F. Theobald; Jesus A. Enciso (Philippines); Yesudasan Choondassery (India); Sr. Martine M. Pijanowski, C.S.S.F., R.N. In res., Rev. John B. Baron.
Res., 125 Union St., 07644. Tel: 973-779-4330; Fax: 973-779-8842. [CEM]
School—Mother Cabrini Interparochial, (1991), 123 Union St., 07644. Tel: 973-777-4635; Fax: 973-779-2352.
Lay Teachers 10; Students 196.
Catechesis/Religious Programs—Tel: 973-779-3949.
Students 145.
Convent—Tel: 973-773-4366.

St. Joseph's (1913) (Italian), Revs. Hector DiNardo, C.R.M.; Americo Salvi, C.R.M., Pastoral Assoc. In res., Rev. Gabriel M. Lucarelli, C.R.M.
Res., 40 Spring St., 07644. Tel: 973-779-0643; Fax: 973-447-1442.
School—Mother Cabrini Interparochial School, (1991), 123 Union St., 07644. Tel: 973-777-4635; Fax: 973-779-2352.
Lay Teachers 12; Students 196.
Catechesis/Religious Programs—Tel: 973-779-8275.
Students 310.

Lyndhurst, Bergen Co., Sacred Heart (1905), Very Rev. Charles J. Miller, V.F.; Rev. Raymond Rodriguez; Deacon Brett Moore.
Res., 324 Ridge Rd., 07071. Tel: 201-438-1147; Fax: 201-507-5861. [CEM]
School—620 Valley Brook Ave., 07071. Tel: 201-939-4277.
Sisters 1; Lay Teachers 28; Students 561.
Catechesis/Religious Programs—Tel: 201-935-3094.
Students 355.

Our Lady of Mount Carmel (1966) (Italian), Revs. Nazareno Orandi; Thomas J. Kenna.
Res., 197 Kingsland Ave., 07071. Tel: 201-935-1177; Fax: 201-935-5675.
Catechesis/Religious Programs—146 Copeland Ave., 07071. Tel: 201-935-5467.
Students 263.

St. Michael's (1912) (Polish), Revs. Richard S. Czachorowski; Joseph Szklarski; Deacon Vincent Serzan. In res., Rev. Msgr. James Mc Menemie.
Res., 624 Page Ave., 07071. Tel: 201-939-1161; Fax: 201-939-7571.
School—(1951), Tel: 201-939-0350; Fax: 201-438-6189.
Lay Teachers 11; Students 200.
Catechesis/Religious Programs—Students 125.
Convent—Tel: 201-438-1882.

Mahwah, Bergen Co., Immaculate Heart of Mary (1915) (Polish), Revs. John Masiello, S.D.B.; David Moreno, S.D.B.; Joseph S. Bajorek, S.D.B.
Res., 47 Island Rd., 07430. Tel: 201-529-3517; Fax: 201-529-4401.
School—St. Paul's Interparochial School, (1991). (See St. Paul's, Ramsey. Tel: 201-327-1108; Fax: 201-327-6197).

Sisters of Charity 2; Lay Teachers 12; Students 255.
Immaculate Conception (1929), Rev. M. Christen Beirne; S. Geraldine Muller, Pastoral Assoc. In res., Rev. James R. White.
Res., 900 Darlington Ave., 07430. Tel: 201-327-1276; Fax: 201-327-0185.
School—St. Paul's Interparochial School, Tel: 201-327-1108; Fax: 201-327-6197.
Catechesis/Religious Programs—Tel: 201-825-0333. Mrs. Roberta Medalis, D.R.E.
Students 268.

Maplewood, Essex Co., Immaculate Heart of Mary (1955), Revs. Dominic G. Fuccile; Frank J. Rocchi.
Res., 280 Parker Ave., 07040. Tel: 973-763-5019; Fax: 973-763-3622.
School—(1957), 276 Parker Ave., 07040. Tel: 973-763-0031.
Lay Teachers 14; Students 168.
Catechesis/Religious Programs—Students 100.
St. Joseph's (1914), Revs. Thomas Wisniewski; Joseph Ferraro; John T. Browne, O.S.B.
Res., 767 Prospect St., 07040. Tel: 973-761-5933; Fax: 973-761-6705.
School—(1930), 240 Franklin Ave., 07040. Tel: 973-761-4033.
Lay Teachers 20; Students 270.
Catechesis/Religious Programs—Students 205.

Maywood, Bergen Co., Our Lady Queen of Peace (1950), Revs. Joseph P. Pietropinto; Stephen J. Cinque; Neil X. O'Donoghue; Sr. Louise DelCarpine, Pastoral Assoc.; Deacon Anthony Balistieri.
Res., 400 Maywood Ave., 07607. Tel: 201-845-9566; Fax: 201-845-3742.
Catechesis/Religious Programs—Tel: 201-845-9545.
Students 346.
Convent—Tel: 201-845-9568.

Midland Park, Bergen Co., Nativity (1955), Very Rev. John R. O'Connell; Rev. James P. Whelan. In res., Rev. John T. Michalczak.
Res., 315 Prospect St., 07432. Tel: 201-444-6362; Fax: 201-444-5056.
School—St. Thomas More Interparochial School, 321 Prospect St., 07432. Tel: 201-447-3088; Fax: 201-447-4145.
Lay Teachers 16; Students 240.
Catechesis/Religious Programs—Tel: 201-447-1776.
Students 414.

Montclair, Essex Co., Immaculate Conception (1864), Rev. Msgr. Timothy J. Shugrue; Revs. Frank J. Burla; Donald P. Gleeson. Pastoral Assocs.: Sr. Margaret Tierney, S.C.; Sr. Cora Marie McGuire, M.S.B.T. In res., Rev. Louis M. Pambello.
Res., 30 N. Fullerton Ave., 07042. Tel: 973-744-5650; Fax: 973-744-7936. [CEM]
Parish Center: 1 Munn St., 07042. Tel: 973-509-1111.
Pre-School—(1997), Tegakwita Academy, 1 Munn St., 07042.
Lay Teachers 2; Students 19.
High School—(1919), 33 Cottage Pl., 07042. Tel: 973-744-7445; Fax: 973-744-3926.
Sisters 5; Lay Teachers 29; Students 296.
Catechesis/Religious Programs—Students 290.
Our Lady of Mt. Carmel (1907) (Italian), Revs. Thomas J. Petrillo; Donald Cialone. In res., Rev. Thomas C. Roberts.
Res., 94 Pine St., 07042. Tel: 973-744-1074; Fax: 973-744-0205.
Catechesis/Religious Programs—Students 115.
St. Peter Claver (1932), Rev. John P. Nickas; Deacons John Coffey; Wilfred Leconte.
Res., 56 Elmwood Ave., 07042. Tel: 973-783-4852; Fax: 973-783-3261.

Moonachie, Bergen Co., St. Anthony (1931). Closed. For inquiries for parish records contact Seton Hall University Archives: South Orange. Tel.: 973-761-9476; Fax: 973-761-9550.

Mountainside, Union Co., Our Lady of Lourdes (1958), Revs. Patrick J. Leonard, Admin.; Piotr Michota; Paul J. Prevosto; Rev. Msgr. Raymond J. Pollard, (Retired).
Res., 300 Central Ave., 07092. Tel: 908-232-1162; Fax: 908-232-0776.
School—Holy Trinity Interparochial School, (1991). (See Holy Trinity, Westfield. Tel: 908-233-0484).
Lay Teachers 15; Students 312.
Catechesis/Religious Programs—Tel: 908-233-1777. Mrs. Nancy Everett, D.R.E.
Students 300.

New Milford, Bergen Co., Ascension (1953), Revs. John P. McGovern; James Brown; Arcadio Munoz (Philippines); Deacons Harold Bates; Paul Kliauga.
Res., 256 Azalea Dr., 07646. Tel: 201-836-8961; Fax: 201-836-5896.
School—1092 Carnation Dr., 07646. Tel: 201-836-7074.
Sisters of St. Dominic 3; Students 184.
Catechesis/Religious Programs—Tel: 201-836-3085.
Students 335.

New Providence, Union Co., Our Lady of Peace (1942), Rev. Sean Cunneen; Rev. Msgr. Paul J. Hayes, Pastor Emeritus; Rev. Francis A. Heinen. In res., Rev. Thomas Hart.
Res., 111 South St., 07974. Tel: 908-464-7600; Fax: 908-508-1845.
School—99 South St., 07974. Tel: 908-464-8657; Fax: 908-464-3377.
Lay Teachers 18; Students 225.
Catechesis/Religious Programs—Tel: 908-464-8156.
Students 497.
Convent—Tel: 908-464-8223.

North Arlington, Bergen Co., Queen of Peace (1922), Rev. Msgr. William J. Fadrowski; Rev. Msgr. Thomas G. Madden, Pastor Emeritus; Revs. Peter Smutelovic; Stephen D. D'Andrea; Walter D. Lucey; Deacons William R. Benedetto; William H. Myers.
Res., 10 Franklin Pl., 07031. Tel: 201-997-0700; Fax: 201-997-6214.
School—(1925), 21 Church Pl., 07031. Tel: 201-998-8222; Fax: 201-997-7930.
Sisters of St. Joseph of Chestnut Hill 3; Lay Teachers 19; Students 440.
High School—(1930), 191 Rutherford Pl., 07031. Tel: 201-998-8227; Fax: 201-998-3040.
Brothers of the Christian School 3; Sisters 6; Lay Teachers 43; Students 680.
Catechesis/Religious Programs—Tel: 201-998-0901.
Students 500.
Convent—Tel: 201-997-2141.

North Bergen, Hudson Co., Sacred Heart (1917) (Polish), Rev. Anthony G. Robak.
Mailing Address: Box 9007, 07047.
Res., 246 Hudson Pl., Cliffside Park, 07010. Tel: 201-943-0305; Fax: 201-943-2676.
School—St. Elizabeth Seton Interparochial School, (1991). Co-Sponsored. (See St. John's Parish, Fairview. Tel: 201-945-2212).
Catechesis/Religious Programs—Students 40.
St. Brigid (1900), Rev. Robert E. Tooman; Deacon Edgar Caceres.
Res., 4501 Liberty Ave., 07047. Tel: 201-863-0160; Fax: 201-863-3877.
Catechesis/Religious Programs—Students 70.
Our Lady of Fatima (1963), Revs. John J. Korbelak; Edgar Devina (Philippines).
Res., 8016 Kennedy Blvd., 07047. Tel: 201-869-7244; Fax: 201-869-0940.

North Caldwell, Essex Co., Notre Dame (1962), Rev. Msgr. Edward J. Ciuba; Rev. Anthony J. Randazzo; Sr. Carol Jaruszewski, R.S.M., Pastoral Assoc.
Res., 358 Central Ave., 07006. Tel: 973-226-0979; Fax: 973-226-4118.
Catechesis/Religious Programs—Tel: 973-228-3338.
Students 580.

Northvale, Bergen Co., St. Anthony's (1890) (Italian), Rev. Msgr. William J. Koplik; Rev. Robert J. Halliwell. In res., Revs. Benedict P. Militello, (Retired); Thomas Norton.
Res., 199 Walnut St., 07647. Tel: 201-768-1177; Fax: 201-768-2522.
School—Holy Family School. (See Immaculate Conception, Norwood). Tel: 201-768-1605; Fax: 201-768-8006.
Catechesis/Religious Programs—Tel: 201-768-5945.
Students 288.

Norwood, Bergen Co., Immaculate Conception (1921), Rev. Charles B. Urnick; Deacons James Puliatte; Albert McLaughlin.
Res., 211 Summit St., 07648. Tel: 201-768-1600; Fax: 201-768-8006.
School—Holy Family Interparochial School, (1991), 200 Summit St., 07648. Tel: 201-768-1605; Fax: 201-768-0796. Miss Patricia Bliss., Prin.
Sisters 2; Lay Teachers 25; Students 450.
Catechesis/Religious Programs—Tel: 201-768-1771. Sr. Susanne Reynolds, S.S.J.
Students 300.

Nutley, Essex Co., St. Mary's (1876), Revs. David C. Hubba; Matthew Kunnath; George Sharp; Gerard W. Walsh, (Retired); Sr. Alicia Cavanaugh, C.S.J.P., Pastoral Assoc.
Res., 17 Msgr. Owens Pl., 07110. Tel: 973-235-1100; Fax: 973-661-0233.
School—Good Shepherd Academy. (See Holy Family, Nutley. Tel: 973-667-2049). Tel: 973-667-0026; Fax: 973-661-1714.
Catechesis/Religious Programs—Tel: 973-667-8239; Fax: 973-661-0233. Brian Lynch, D.R.E.
Students 600.
Holy Family (1909) (Italian), Rev. Msgr. Peter J. Zaccardo; Revs. Richard E. Cabezas; Anthony R. Lipari; Sr. Eileen Hubbert, S.S.J., Pastoral Assoc. In res., Rev. Alex Barbieto (Philippines).
Res., 28 Brookline Ave., 07110. Tel: 973-667-0026; Fax: 973-661-1714.
School—Good Shepherd Academy, (1992). Cosponsored by 3 area churches. 24 Brookline Ave., 07110. Tel: 973-667-2049; Fax: 973-661-9259.
Religious Teachers Filippini 4; Lay Teachers 21; Students 462.
Catechesis/Religious Programs—Tel: 973-667-6018. Sr. Angelina DelVecchio, M.P.F., D.R.E.
Students 782.
Convent—Tel: 973-667-2050.
Our Lady of Mount Carmel (1925) (Polish), Thomas J. Ciba, M.P.A.; Rev. Emmanuel A. Soriso (Philippines); Sr. Arlene Oswald, O.P. In res., Rev. William Gyure.
Res., 120 Prospect St., 07110. Tel: 973-667-2580; Fax: 973-667-0648.
School—Good Shepherd Academy. (See Holy Family, Nutley). Tel: 973-667-2049.
Catechesis/Religious Programs—Students 194.

Oakland, Bergen Co., Our Lady of Perpetual Help (1960), Rev. Thomas Lipnicki.
25 Purdue Ave., 07436. Tel: 201-337-7596; Fax: 201-337-7810.
Catechesis/Religious Programs—Tel: 201-337-5537, Ext. 21.
Students 610.
Convent—Tel: 201-337-5364.

Old Tappan, Bergen Co., St. Pius X (1954), Rev. Patrick M. Mulewski; Deacon Richard G. Hodges.
Res., 268 Old Tappan Rd., 07675. Tel: 201-664-0913; Fax: 201-664-1013.
School—Holy Family Interparochial School. (See Immaculate Conception, Norwood. Tel: 201-768-1605). Fax: 201-768-0796.
Catechesis/Religious Programs—Tel: 201-664-0927.
Students 400.

Oradell, Bergen Co., St. Joseph's (1903), Revs. George M. Reilly; Peter G. Wehrle; Richard J. Mroz; Joseph F. Coda, Weekend Asst.
Res., 105 Harrison St., New Milford, 07646. Tel: 201-261-0148; Fax: 201-261-0369.
School—(1939), 305 Elm St., 07649. Tel: 201-261-2388; Fax: 201-261-0830.
Sisters 3; Lay Teachers 23; Students 525.
Catechesis/Religious Programs—300 Elm St., 07649. Tel: 201-265-8880; Fax: 201-634-0640. Annette Ziegler, D.R.E.
Students 820.

Orange, Essex Co.,
1—St. John's, (1851) (Hispanic), Rev. Msgr. Ricardo Gonzalez; Rev. George Faour.
Res., 94 Ridge St., 07050. Tel: 973-674-0110. [CEM]
School—(1855), 455 White St., 07050. Tel: 973-674-8951; Fax: 973-674-6126.
Sisters of Charity 4; Lay Teachers 11; Students 387.
Convent—Tel: 973-673-1263.
2—Our Lady of the Valley, (1873), Rev. Floyd Rotunno; Deacon Marshall Andrews.
Res., 510 Valley St., 07050. Tel: 973-674-7500; Fax: 973-672-8341.
Catechesis/Religious Programs—Students 94.
3—St. Venantius, (1886). Merged For inquiries for parish records contact St. Andrew Kim Parish, Orange. Tel: 973-673-1366.
4—Mt. Carmel, (1896) (Italian), Rev. Achilles Cassiere, O.F.M.Cap. In res., Rev. Alexander Davis, O.F.M.Cap.
Res., 103 S. Center St., 07050. Tel: 973-674-2052; Fax: 973-675-1342.
School—(1939), 268 Capuchin Way, 07050. Tel: 973-673-5933; Fax: 973-677-2166. Ms. Rose Tomanelli, Prin.
Lay Teachers 11; Students 162.
Catechesis/Religious Programs—Students 31.
Center: 264 Capuchin Way, 07050.
5—Holy Spirit, (1931). Merged For inquiries for parish records contact Holy Spirit-Our Lady Help of Christians, East Orange. Tel: 201-673-1077.
6—St. Andrew Kim, (1972) (Korean), Rev. Msgr. Augustin C. Park. In res., Revs. Luis Kim (Korea); Thaddeus Park (Korea); Sae Wan Oh (Korea).
Res., 257 Central Ave., 07050. Tel: 973-673-1366; 672-6650; Fax: 973-673-2030.
Catechesis/Religious Programs—Students 245.
Convent—Tel: 973-674-1618.

Palisades Park, Bergen Co., St. Michael's (1912), Revs. James F. Reilly; Vincent J. Quinn, Pastor Emeritus; Michael T. Mickelson; Deacon Martin Hemberger, Pastoral Assoc.
Res., 19 Central Blvd. E., 07650. Tel: 201-944-1061; Fax: 201-947-1798.
Schools—Notre Dame Interparochial, Elementary Division, (1991) (Grades 2-8) 312 First St., 07650.

Tel: 201-947-5262; Fax: 201-945-3796.; Primary Division, (1991) (Grades PreK-1) 555 Prospect Ave., Ridgefield, 07657. Tel: 201-943-5757; Fax: 201-947-8319. Sr. Ellen McMahon, Prin.
Catechesis/Religious Programs—324 First St., 07650. Tel: 201-944-0070; Fax: 201-947-1798. Margaret M. Manley, D.R.E.
Students 180.

St. Nicholas (1923) (Italian-Brazilian), Revs. Antonio L. da Silva, S.D.V. (Brazil); Vernon Kohlmann, S.D.V.; Armando Palmieri, S.D.V.
Res., 442 Brinkerhoff Ave., 07650. Tel: 201-944-1154; Fax: 201-944-9510.
School—Notre Dame Interparochial School, (1991). (See St. Matthew, Ridgefield for Primary Division. Tel: 201-943-5757) (See St. Michael Palisades Park for Elementary Division. Tel: 201-947-5262).
Catechesis/Religious Programs—Students 120.

Paramus, Bergen Co., Our Lady of the Visitation (1952), Rev. Msgr. Joseph T. Slinger; Revs. Jose Montes De Oca; Sebastian Kunnath; Michael Saporito.
Res., 234 Farview Ave., 07652. Tel: 201-261-6080; Fax: 201-261-2995.
School—Visitation Academy, (1991). Co-Sponsored. 222 Farview Ave., 07652. Tel: 201-262-6067; Fax: 201-261-4613. Sr. Rene Donohue, S.C., Prin.
Sisters 3; Lay Teachers 19; Students 391.
Catechesis/Religious Programs—Tel: 201-265-3812. Mrs. Barbara D'Arrigo, D.R.E.
Students 560.

Annunciation (1953), Revs. Michael J. Sheehan; John M. McCrone; Deacons Joseph Niland; William D. Joyce.
Res., 50 W. Midland Ave., 07652. Tel: 201-261-6322; Fax: 201-261-6227.
Parish Center: 49 Demarest Rd., 07652.
School—(1991). (See Visitation Academy, Our Lady of the Visitation Parish, Paramus). Tel: 201-262-6067; Fax: 201-261-4613.
Catechesis/Religious Programs—Sr. Rita Dermody, S.C., D.R.E.
Students 461.

Carmelite Chapel of St. Therese (1970), Revs. Brice E. Riordan, O.Carm., Dir.; Zachary Monet, O.Carm.; Daniel Smith, O.Carm.
Res., 135 Gertrude St., 07652. Tel: 201-845-6392.
Church—Bergen Mall, 07652. Tel: 201-845-6115.

Park Ridge, Bergen Co., Our Lady of Mercy (1902), Revs. Charles P. Granstrand; Robert T. Ulak; Rev. Msgr. James C. Turro, S.T.L., S.S.L., M.A., Weekend Asst. In res., Rev. Msgr. Carl D. Hinrichsen.
Res., 2 Fremont Ave., 07656. Tel: 201-391-5315; Fax: 201-391-5614.
School—Our Lady of Mercy Interparochial School, (1950), 25 Fremont Ave., 07656. Tel: 201-391-3838; Fax: 201-391-3838.
Lay Teachers 30; Students 429.
Catechesis/Religious Programs—50 Pascack Rd., 07656. Tel: 201-391-3590; Fax: 201-802-1771.
Students 625.

Plainfield, Union Co., St. Mary (1851), Revs. Kenneth Jones; Sean Manson; Deacon Martin P. Macaluso, S.F.O. In res., Revs. Aloysius S. Carney; Ken St. Amand.
Res., 516 W. Sixth St., 07060. Tel: 908-756-0085; Fax: 908-756-1658. [CEM]
Catechesis/Religious Programs—Tel: 908-561-7143.
Students 306.
Convent—513 Liberty St., 07060. Tel: 908-754-1978. Missionaries of Charity, (Contemplative)
Sisters 21.

St. Bernard's (1921), Rev. Frank Rose; Deacon Raymundo Ranulfo. In res., Rev. Minh Hai Nguyen.
Catechesis/Religious Programs—
Office: 368 Sumner Ave., P.O. Box 2844, 07062. Tel: 908-756-3393; Fax: 908-756-3059.
Rectory—1235 George St., 07062.
Catechesis/Religious Programs—Students 150.

St. Stanislaus Kostka (1919), Rev. Frank Rose, Admin.
Mailing Address: 368 Sumner Ave., P.O. Box 2844, 07062. Tel: 908-756-3393; Fax: 908-756-3059.
Church—1020 W. Seventh St., 07063. (For Churches in North and South Plainfield see Diocese of Metuchen).

Rahway, Union Co., St. Mary's (1854), Rev. Michael J. Feketie; Deacon J. William Courtney.
Res., 232 Central Ave., 07065. Tel: 732-388-0082. [CEM]
School—(1873), 244 Central Ave., 07065. Tel: 732-382-0011; Fax: 732-382-4784.
Lay Teachers 18; Students 267.
Catechesis/Religious Programs—Tel: 201-382-0004.
Students 308.

St. Mark's (1871) (German), Rev. William T. Morris, Admin. In res., Rev. John S. Olszewski, (Retired).
Res., 287 Hamilton St., 07065. Tel: 732-499-9230; Fax: 732-388-7036.
Catechesis/Religious Programs—Tel: 732-388-7036.
Students 100.

Ramsey, Bergen Co., St. Paul (1904), Rev. Msgr. Lawrence W. Cull; Revs. James R. O'Neill, Pastor Emeritus; S. David Lee.
Res., 200 Wyckoff Ave., 07446. Tel: 201-327-0976; Fax: 201-327-6197.
School—St. Paul's Interparochial School, 187 Wyckoff Ave., 07446. Tel: 201-327-1108; Fax: 201-236-1318.
Dominican Sisters of Sparkill 1; Lay Teachers 26; Students 327.
Catechesis/Religious Programs—Tel: 201-327-8010; Fax: 201-327-6197.
Students 1,195.

Ridgefield, Bergen Co., St. Matthew's (1899), Revs. Donald P. Sheehan; Steven Conner, S.D.V.; Deacon Drew Dickson. In res., Rev. Msgr. James Johnson, (Retired); Rev. John E. Komar.
Res., 555 Prospect Ave., 07657. Tel: 201-945-3500; Fax: 201-945-3796.
School—Notre Dame Interparochial Primary Division, (1991) (Grades PreK-1) Edgewater Ave., 07657. Tel: 201-943-5757; Fax: 201-943-4209; 947-8319.
Sisters 2; Lay Teachers 12; Students 235.
Catechesis/Religious Programs—Students 357.

Ridgefield Park, Bergen Co., St. Francis of Assisi (1890), Revs. Joseph C. Doyle; Eugene J. Field; Deacon Nicholas Simonelli; Margaret Slattery, Pastoral Assoc.
Res., 114 Mt. Vernon St., 07660. Tel: 201-641-6464; Fax: 201-641-2282.
School—(1915), 110 Mt. Vernon St., 07660. Tel: 201-641-9159; Fax: 201-641-4091. Sr. Patricia Meidhof, Prin.
Sisters 1; Lay Teachers 16; Students 295.
Catechesis/Religious Programs—Students 373.

Ridgewood, Bergen Co., Our Lady of Mount Carmel (1889), Rev. Msgr. Ronald J. Rozniak, V.G.; Revs. Robert G. Gibney, Pastor Emeritus; Ivan Sciberras (Malta); Gerard M. Lombardo; Michael A. Andreano; Deacon Robert V. Thomann. Pastoral Assocs.: Sr. Rose Vincent, S.C.; Mrs. Linda English. In res., Rev. Mert Cordero.
Res., 1 Passaic St., 07450-4309. Tel: 201-444-2000; Fax: 201-444-2002.
School—Academy of Our Lady, Tel: 201-445-0622.
Catechesis/Religious Programs—Tel: 201-444-0211; Fax: 201-444-4421. D.R.E.: Sr. Bernard Mary Herlihy, M.S.B.T.; Paula Metzger.
Students 1,336.
Convent—Tel: 201-445-2077.

River Edge, Bergen Co., St. Peter the Apostle (1948), Rev. Robert H. Slipe; Rev. Msgr. David J. Casazza, Pastor Emeritus; Revs. Michael J. German; Christoph Lintz; Deacon Edward Bowen.
Res., 445 Fifth Ave., 07661. Tel: 201-261-3366; Fax: 201-261-0117.
School—St. Peter Academy, (1952), 431 Fifth Ave., 07661. Tel: 201-261-3468; Fax: 201-261-4316.
Sisters 2; Lay Teachers 18; Students 257.
Catechesis/Religious Programs—Tel: 201-265-6019.
Students 570.
Convent—Tel: 201-845-9568.

Rochelle Park, Bergen Co., Sacred Heart (1917), Very Rev. Lewis V. Papera, V.F.; Rev. William O'Brien.
Res., 12 Terrace Ave., 07662. Tel: 201-843-1722; Fax: 201-843-3542.
School—(1991). Co-Sponsored. (See Visitation Academy, Our Lady of Visitation Parish, Paramus). Tel: 201-262-6067.
Catechesis/Religious Programs—Tel: 201-843-1077. Angela Connelly, D.R.E.
Students 305.

Roseland, Essex Co., Our Lady of the Blessed Sacrament (1955), Rev. Msgr. Louis F. Fimiani; Revs. Stephen A. Carey; Calin Ciona. Pastoral Assocs.: Sr. Rie Crowley, S.S.J., (Sick and Homebound Parish Outreach); Sr. Regina Suplick, S.C., (Baptismal Ministry); Joseph Wozniak, (Liturgical Music).
Res., 28 Livingston Ave., 07068. Tel: 973-226-7288; Fax: 973-226-4893.
Catechesis/Religious Programs—Tel: 973-226-5251; Fax: 973-403-8871. Maurica Twaddell, D.R.E.
Students 561.

Roselle, Union Co., Church of St. Joseph the Carpenter (1895), Revs. George D. Gillen; John Spino; Deacon Vincent Belluscio.
Res., 157 E. Fourth Ave., 07203. Tel: 908-241-1250; Fax: 908-241-6311.
School—(1913), 150 E. Third Ave., 07203. Tel: 908-245-6560.
Sisters 1; Lay Teachers 24; Students 390.
Catechesis/Religious Programs—Students 60.
Convent—135 E. Fourth Ave., 07203. Tel: 908-245-1594. Sisters of St. Joseph, Chestnut Hill.

Roselle Park, Union Co., The Assumption (1907) (Italian), Revs. Dennis E. Cocozza; Armand Mantia. In res., Rev. Msgr. Edward G. Price, (Retired).
Res., 113 Chiego Pl., 07204. Tel: 908-245-1107; Fax: 908-245-2789.
Catechesis/Religious Programs—110 Chiego Pl., 07204. Tel: 908-245-6572.
Students 541.

Rutherford, Bergen Co., St. Mary's (1908), Revs. Michael J. Kreder; Charles W. Hartling.
Res., 91 Home Ave., 07070. Tel: 201-438-2200; Fax: 201-438-1098.
School—(1916), 72 Chestnut St., 07070. Tel: 201-933-8410; Fax: 201-531-9020.
Lay Teachers 23; Students 352.
High School—(1928), 64 Chestnut St., 07070. Tel: 201-933-5220; Fax: 201-933-0834.
Lay Teachers 27; Students 363.
Catechesis/Religious Programs—Tel: 201-438-2476.
Students 560.
Convent—Tel: 201-933-2910.

Saddle Brook, Bergen Co., St. Philip the Apostle (1953), Revs. Robert G. McBride; Matthew Fonseka; Richard D. Carlson; Deacon Philip Salerno.
Res., 488 Saddle River Rd., 07663. Tel: 201-843-1888; Fax: 201-368-9161.
School—492 Saddle River Rd., 07663-4634. Tel: 201-843-2240; Fax: 201-843-3150.
Sisters 3; Lay Teachers 10; Students 200.
Catechesis/Religious Programs—Students 520.

Korean Martyrs (1998) (Korean), Rev. John Hee Dong Park (Korea).
Res., 585 Saddle River Rd., 07663. Tel: 201-703-0002; Fax: 201-703-7111.

Saddle River Borough, Bergen Co., St. Gabriel the Archangel (1952), Rev. Msgr. Robert J. Fuhrman; Revs. John J. O'Brien, S.J., (Retired); Samuel Monaco.
Res., 3 W. Church Rd., 07458. Tel: 201-327-5663; Fax: 201-327-7063.
School—St. John's Academy. (See St. John's Parish, Hillsdale). Tel: 201-664-6364; Fax: 201-664-8096.
Catechesis/Religious Programs—Tel: 201-825-0275.
Students 270.

Scotch Plains, Union Co., St. Bartholomew (1948), Revs. Donald K. Hummel; John J. Lester; Antonio Kuizon (Philippines); Joy Alookaran (India). In res., Rev. John Paladino.
Res., 2032 Westfield Ave., 07076. Tel: 908-322-5192; Fax: 908-322-2598.
School—St. Bartholomew Interparochial, (1950), Tel: 908-322-4265; Fax: 908-322-2598.
Religious Teachers Filippini 4; Lay Teachers 15; Students 239.
Catechesis/Religious Programs—Tel: 908-322-2359.
Students 450.
Convent—Tel: 908-322-5619.

Immaculate Heart of Mary (1964), Very Rev. John F. Kennedy, V.F.; Revs. Charles Alookaran (India); Michael Patete; Robert Patterson. In res., Rev. John Farley, S.V.D.
Res., 1571 S. Martine Ave., 07076. Tel: 908-889-2100; Fax: 908-889-9477.
Catechesis/Religious Programs—Jeanne Fox, D.R.E.
Students 790.

Secaucus, Hudson Co., Immaculate Conception (1908), Rev. Msgr. Donald E. Guenther; Revs. Raymond T. Lukenda; Jose M. Abalon.
Res., 1219 Paterson Plank Rd., 07094. Tel: 201-863-4840; Fax: 201-863-3537.
School—(1949), 760 Post Pl., 07094. Tel: 201-864-9346.
School Sisters of Notre Dame 5; Lay Teachers 6; Students 230.
Catechesis/Religious Programs—Tel: 201-863-4840, Ext. 28.
Students 600.
Convent—Tel: 201-866-4752.

Short Hills, Essex Co., St. Rose of Lima (1852), Rev. Msgr. George R. Trabold; Revs. Edmund G. Bernauer; Kevin A. Gugliotta; Deacons Joseph M. Persinger; Daniel G. McCarren. In res., Rev. Msgr. Vincent P. Coburn, (Retired).
Res., 50 Short Hills Ave., 07078. Tel: 973-379-3912; Fax: 973-379-6157. [CEM]
School—(1869), 52 Short Hills Ave., 07078. Tel: 973-379-3973; Fax: 973-379-3722.
Lay Teachers 35; Students 331.
Catechesis/Religious Programs—52 Short Hills Ave., 07078. Tel: 973-376-1960; Fax: 973-376-3818.
Students 722.

South Orange, Essex Co., Our Lady of Sorrows (1887), Rev. Msgr. John E. Doran; Revs. Marc A. Vicari; John A. Palasits.
Res., 217 Prospect St., 07079. Tel: 973-763-5454; Fax: 973-763-9506.

School—(1890), 172 Academy St., 07079. Tel: 973-763-5169; Fax: 973-378-9781.
Lay Teachers 27; Religious 3; Students 410.
Catechesis/Religious Programs—Students 320.

Springfield, Union Co., St. James (1923), Revs. Robert B. Stagg; Robert J. Piatkowski; Anthony J. Nardo; Sr. Roseann M. Treston, S.S.J., Pastoral Assoc.; Deacons John M. Baltus; Jerry Bongiovanni.
Res., 45 S. Springfield Ave., 07081. Tel: 973-376-3044; Fax: 973-376-0560.
School—41 S. Springfield Ave., 07081. Tel: 973-376-5194. Sr. Mary Elizabeth Guyer, S.S.J., Prin.
Sisters of St. Joseph 2; Lay Teachers 10; Students 210.
Catechesis/Religious Programs—Tel: 973-376-2061. Ms. Diane McGee, D.R.E.
Students 420.

Summit, Union Co., St. Teresa's (1863), Rev. Msgr. Robert E. Harahan; Revs. Thomas F. Blind; Patrick R. Flannery. Pastoral Assocs.: Sr. Margaret Regan, S.S.N.J.; Sr. Winifred Tormey, S.S.J.; Mr. David O'Brien; Deacons Charles Cederroth; Frank Gisoldi; Joseph Wall; Alcides Vega. In res., Rev. Msgr. John H. Koenig; Rev. Frank McNulty.
Res., 306 Morris Ave., 07901. Tel: 908-277-3700; Fax: 908-273-5909. [CEM]
Catechesis/Religious Programs—Tel: 908-273-6975; Fax: 908-273-1770.
Students 1,075.

Teaneck, Bergen Co., St. Anastasia's (1908), Revs. Hilary Milton, O.Carm.; Peter McGarry, O.Carm.; Deacon Roland Bianchi. In res., Rev. Edward Ward, O.Carm.
Res., 1095 Teaneck Rd., 07666. Tel: 201-837-3354; Fax: 201-837-3360.
School—St. Cecilia's Interparochial School. (See St. Cecilia, Englewood. Tel: 201-568-2615).
Catechesis/Religious Programs—Tel: 201-837-3356. Sr. Adrienne Bradley, S.S.J., D.R.E.
Students 225.
Convent—Tel: 201-837-3153.

Korean Catholic Community of Teaneck. Closed. For inquiries for parish records contact the Chancery.

Tenafly, Bergen Co., Our Lady of Mount Carmel (1873), Revs. Ashley Harrington, O.Carm.; Peter Byrth, O.Carm.
Res., 10 County Rd., 07670. Tel: 201-568-0545; Fax: 201-568-3215.
School—(1879), Tel: 201-567-6491.
Lay Teachers 16; Students 252.
Catechesis/Religious Programs—Tel: 201-871-4662.
Students 405.

Union, Union Co., St. Michael's (1928), Revs. Matthias T. Conva; Charles B. McDermott; Christopher M. Ciccarino; Gerard W. Sogliuzzo; Sr. Ann Dominic, O.P., Pastoral Assoc. for Social Concerns; Joan Conlon, Business Mgr.
Res., 1212 Kelly St., 07083. Tel: 908-688-1232; Fax: 908-810-1076.
School—(1931), 1211 Orange Ave., 07083. Tel: 908-688-1063; Fax: 908-687-7927. Sr. Margaret Williams, Prin.
Sisters of St. Dominic 1; Lay Teachers 24; Students 300.
Catechesis/Religious Programs—Tel: 908-964-0965. Carol Skrocki, D.R.E.
Students 650.
Convent—Tel: 908-686-3839.

Holy Spirit (1963), Rev. Msgr. Vincent J. Doyle; Rev. Msgr. John H. Koenig, Pastor Emeritus; Revs. Edward G. Furrevig; James M. Manos; John M. Ballweg, Weekend Asst.
Res., 971 Suburban Rd., 07083. Tel: 908-687-3327; Fax: 908-687-1312.
School—Morris Ave. & Suburban Rd., 07083. Tel: 908-687-8415.
Lay Teachers 14; Students 218.
Catechesis/Religious Programs—984 Suburban Rd., 07083. Tel: 908-964-7533.
Students 665.

Union City, Hudson Co.,

1—Holy Family, (1857), Rev. Antonio Lasheras, O.A.R. (Spain). In res., Revs. Jose Maria Juango, O.A.R. (Spain); Jose Antonio Rodrigalvarez, O.A.R. (Spain); Fernando Gomez, O.A.R. (Spain).
Res., 530 35th St., 07087. Tel: 201-867-6535; Fax: 201-867-1357.

2—St. Augustine's, (1886), Rev. Msgr. Thomas W. Heck; Revs. Pedro Navarro; Felipe Lopez; Deacons John McCarthy; Edwardo Pons. In res., Rev. Paul J. Nolan.
Res., 3900 New York Ave., 07087. Tel: 201-863-0233.
School—(1891), 3920 New York Ave., 07087. Tel: 201-865-5319; Fax: 201-865-2567.
Sisters of Charity 5; Lay Teachers 16; Students 470.
Catechesis/Religious Programs—Students 1,000.
Convent—312 39th St., 07083. Tel: 201-348-0527.

3—Sts. Joseph and Michael, (1887; 1851), Revs. Fernando Carranza; Attilio Morelli; Deacons Thomas Barrett; Thomas De Benedictis; Asterio Velasco; Ricardo Flores.
Res., 1314 Central Ave., 07087. Tel: 201-865-2325; Fax: 201-348-4412.
School—Mother Seton Grammar School, 1501 New York Ave., 07087. Tel: 201-863-8433; Fax: 201-863-8145.
Lay Teachers 15; Students 300.
Catechesis/Religious Programs—Tel: 201-863-8145.
Students 350.

4—St. Anthony of Padua, (1899) (Italian), Rev. Ilario Crepaz (Italy).
Res., 615 Eighth St., 07087. Tel: 201-867-3818; Fax: 201-867-8859.
School—700 Central Ave., 07087. Tel: 201-864-5605; Fax: 201-223-1101.
Religious Teachers Filippini 1; Lay Teachers 13; Students 260.
Catechesis/Religious Programs—Students 200.

5—St. Rocco's, (1912) (Italian), Rev. Robert E. Tooman.
Res., 4206 Kennedy Blvd., 07087. Tel: 201-863-1427; Fax: 201-863-3877.
Catechesis/Religious Programs—Students 88.
Mission House—4214 Kennedy Blvd., 07087. Tel: 201-863-5727.

Upper Montclair, Essex Co., St. Cassian (1896), Revs. John G. Judge; Robert M. Brennan; Deacon Thomas J. Nilan.
Res., 187 Bellevue Ave., 07043. Tel: 973-744-2850; Fax: 973-744-6187.
School—190 Lorraine Ave., 07043. Tel: 973-746-1636; Fax: 973-746-3271.
Lay Teachers 15; Students 238.
Catechesis/Religious Programs—Students 400.

Upper Saddle River, Bergen Co., Church of the Presentation (1961), Rev. Msgr. Thomas Ivory.
Office: 271 W. Saddle River Rd., 07458. Tel: 201-327-1313; Fax: 201-818-0722.
Res., 41 Riverview Ter., 07458.
School—St. Paul's Interparochial School, (1990). (See St. Paul, Ramsey). Tel: 201-327-1108.
Catechesis/Religious Programs—Tel: 201-327-3055.
Students 1,400.

Verona, Essex Co., Our Lady of the Lake (1923), Revs. Michael A. Hanly; Robert Wolfee; Deacons Pat Vuolo; David Garcia; Michael Maione.
Res., 32 Lakeside Ave., 07044. Tel: 973-239-5696; Fax: 973-239-7190.
School—(1924), 22 Lakeside Ave., 07044. Tel: 973-239-1160; Fax: 973-239-6496. Sr. Mary Agnes Sullivan, O.P., Prin.
Sisters 1; Lay Teachers 13; Students 267.
Catechesis/Religious Programs—Tel: 973-239-7643.
Students 891.

Wallington, Bergen Co., Most Sacred Heart of Jesus (1942) (Polish), Very Rev. Felix R. Marciniak; Revs. Mark B. Wysocki; Marek Roman Bokota.
Res., 127 Paterson Ave., 07057. Tel: 973-778-7405; Fax: 973-778-7750.
School—(1943), 6 Bond St., 07057. Tel: 973-777-4817; Fax: 973-777-4982.
Sisters 4; Lay Teachers 10; Students 167.
Catechesis/Religious Programs—Tel: 973-777-9505.
Students 352.

Washington Township, Bergen Co., Our Lady of Good Counsel (1959), Rev. Msgr. Thomas A. McCarthy; Rev. Stephen J. Duffe; Sr. Joseph Miriam Blackwell, M.S.B.T., Pastoral Assoc.
Res., 668 Ridgewood Rd., Township of Washington, 07676. Tel: 201-664-6624; Fax: 201-664-0095.
School—Our Lady of Mercy Interparochial School. (See Our Lady of Mercy, Park Ridge. Tel: 201-391-3838; Fax: 201-391-5614).
Catechesis/Religious Programs—Tel: 201-664-1679. Catherine Russo, D.R.E.
Students 363.

Weehawken, Hudson Co., St. Lawrence's (1887), Rev. Robert E. Emery.
Res., 22 Hackensack Ave., 07087. Tel: 201-863-6464; Fax: 201-863-6656.
School—Hoboken Catholic Academy, Tel: 201-659-7158.
Catechesis/Religious Programs—Students 125.

Westfield, Union Co., St. Helen (1968), Rev. Msgr. William C. Harms; Revs. Richard R. Corbett; Lawrence J. Fama.
Res., 1600 Rahway Ave., 07090. Tel: 908-232-1214; Fax: 908-317-5459.
School—Holy Trinity Interparochial School, (1991). Co-Sponsored. (See Holy Trinity Parish, Westfield). Tel: 908-233-0484; Fax: 908-233-6204.
Catechesis/Religious Programs—Tel: 908-233-8757.
Students 2,055.

Holy Trinity (1872), Rev. Msgr. Joseph P. Masiello; Rev. James E. Starasinich; Sr. Eleanor McNichol, S.S.J., Pastoral Assoc.; Deacons Charles F. Kiley; Thomas A. Pluta.
Res., 315 First St., 07090. Tel: 908-232-8137; Fax: 908-654-8780.
School—(1991) (Grades PreK-8). Co-Sponsored, Holy Trinity Interparochial School. 336 First St., 07090. Tel: 908-233-0484; Fax: 908-233-6204.
Lay Teachers 21; Students 353.
Catechesis/Religious Programs—Tel: 908-233-7455. Sr. Kathleen J. Burton, S.S.J., D.R.E.
Students 683.

West New York, Hudson Co., St. Mary Help of Christians (1895), Rev. Carlo Fortunio, O.P., (Italy) Admin.
Res., 6502 Jackson St., 07093. Tel: 201-868-9444; Fax: 201-868-6451.
Catechesis/Religious Programs—Students 200.

St. Joseph of the Palisades (1875), Most Rev. David Arias, O.A.R., D.D.; Revs. Richard J. Carrington, Admin.; Agustin Pedrosa, S.M. (Spain); Minh Hai Nguyen; Siffredus B. Rwechungura; Carlos Viego.
Res., 6401 Palisade Ave., 07093. Tel: 201-854-7006; Fax: 201-861-7799.
School—(1872), 6408 Palisade Ave., 07093. Tel: 201-861-3227; Fax: 201-861-5744.
Franciscan Missionary Sisters of the Sacred Heart 5; Lay Teachers 20; Students 510.
High School—5400 Broadway, 07093. Tel: 201-864-9700.
Priests 2; Sisters 5; Lay Teachers 13; Students 220.
Catechesis/Religious Programs—Students 905.
Chapels—North Bergen, Immaculate Heart of Mary.; Cor Jesu.
Convent—Tel: 201-861-3337.

Our Lady of Libera (1902) (Italian), Rev. Philip J. Rotunno; Deacon Rosendo Abreu.
Res., 5808 John F. Kennedy Memorial Blvd., 07093. Tel: 201-867-2642.
School—5800 John F. Kennedy Memorial Blvd., 07093. Tel: 201-864-5557.
Sisters 3; Lay Teachers 14; Students 385.
Convent—Tel: 201-868-6113. Religious Teachers Filippini
Catechesis/Religious Programs—Students 150.

West Orange, Essex Co., Our Lady of Lourdes (1914), Revs. Joseph A. Petrillo; James N. Chern.
Res., 1 Eagle Rock Ave., 07052. Tel: 973-325-0110; Fax: 973-325-9105.
School—(1925), 100 Valley Way, 07052. Tel: 973-325-0555; Fax: 973-243-1480. Mary Cassels, Prin.
Sisters of Charity 1; Lay Teachers 20; Students 314.
Catechesis/Religious Programs—Tel: 973-325-0029. Sr. Ann Sweeney, O.P., D.R.E.
Students 110.
Convent—Tel: 973-325-0318; Fax: 973-325-0691.

St. Joseph's (1932), Revs. Bernard N. Mohan; Kevin J. Schott; Deacon Luis Velo. In res., Rev. Msgr. William J. Daly; Rev. John D. Sweeney.
Res., 44 Benvenue Ave., 07052. Tel: 973-669-3221; Fax: 973-669-0385.
School—(1956), 8 St. Cloud Pl., 07052. Tel: 973-731-3503.
Lay Teachers 11; Students 250.
Catechesis/Religious Programs—Students 330.

Westwood, Bergen Co., St. Andrew's (1889), Revs. Ward P. Moore; Gerald T. Hahn; Deacon Joseph J. Paulillo. Pastoral Assocs.: Mary Jean Conroy, Child Catechesis; Barbara Stewart, Parish Ministries; Alan Pitman, Teens.
Res., 120 Washington Ave., 07675. Tel: 201-666-1100; Fax: 201-722-1432. [CEM]
School—St. John's Academy. (See St. John the Baptist, Hillsdale. Tel: 201-664-6364; Fax: 201-664-8096).
Catechesis/Religious Programs—Tel: 201-664-6777.
Students 522.

Woodcliff Lake, Bergen Co., Our Lady Mother of the Church (1967), Rev. Msgr. Cajetan P. Salemi; Rev. Thomas G. Arminio, Pastor Emeritus; Sr. Frances Schier, O.P., Pastoral Assoc. In res., Rev. Msgr. Joseph C. Manz.
Church—209 Woodcliff Ave., 07675. Tel: 201-391-2826; Fax: 201-391-7101.
Rectory: 130 Apple Ridge, 07675.
School—St. John the Baptist Interparochial School. (See St. John the Baptist, Hillsdale). Tel: 201-664-3131; Fax: 201-664-0772.
Catechesis/Religious Programs—Tel: 201-391-7400.
Students 250.

Wood-Ridge, Bergen Co., Our Lady of the Assumption (1926), Revs. James W. Czerwinski, O.F.M.; Paul Sinnema, O.F.M.; Thomas Kelly, O.F.M.
Res., 143 First St., 07075. Tel: 201-438-5555; Fax: 201-438-6747.

School—151 First St., 07075. Tel: 201-933-0239; Fax: 201-438-6408.
Lay Teachers 20; Students 290.
Catechesis/Religious Programs—Hayes Center, 142 Second St., Tel: 201-933-6118.
Students 480.
Convent—Tel: 201-939-4274.

Wyckoff, Bergen Co., St. Elizabeth (1902), Rev. Msgr. Thomas M. O'Leary; Revs. Miroslaw K. Krol; Michael C. Fugee; Deacons Robert Kratchman; Joseph De Maria; William J. Toth.
Res., 700 Wyckoff Ave., 07481. Tel: 201-891-1122; Fax: 201-847-8518.
School—Greenwood Ave., 07481. Tel: 201-891-1481; Fax: 201-891-3147.
Sisters of St. Joseph of Peace; Lay Teachers 15; Students 304.
Catechesis/Religious Programs—Tel: 201-891-3262; Fax: 201-891-3708. Marlene Malenda, D.R.E. Students 125. @ = Chaplains of Public Institutions

Hospital Chaplaincy

NEWARK. *Office of Health Care Personnel* 171 Clifton Ave., 07102. Tel: 973-497-4009. Sr. Thomas Mary Salerno, S.C., Chancellor.

Bergen County

ENGLEWOOD. *Englewood Hospital* 350 Engle St., 07631. Tel: 201-894-3000. Chaplains: Revs. Mathew Chandrankunnel; John E. Komar.

HACKENSACK. *Hackensack University Medical Center* 30 Prospect Ave., 07601. Tel: 201-996-2000; 996-2345. Chaplains: Revs. Alphonsus Ezecke; Bernard Fernando; Ruth Kennedy, Dir.

PARAMUS. *Bergen Regional Medical Center* E. Ridgewood Ave., 07652. Tel: 201-967-4177; Fax: 201-967-4277. Chaplains: Revs. Joseph Buzzerio; Richard U. Odoemela; Joseph P. Rice; Gerald Bajek; Joseph Kokeram; Deacon Victor Peterson.

RIDGEWOOD. *Valley Hospital* Linwood Ave. & N. Van Dien Ave., 07451. Tel: 201-447-8160. Chaplains: Revs. John T. Michalczak; Mert Cordero; Anne Devine, Dir.

TEANECK. *Holy Name Hospital* 718 Teaneck Rd., 07666. Tel: 201-833-3000; 833-3243 (Pastoral Care). Chaplains: Sr. Lois Jablonski, S.S.J., Dir.; Mary Ellen Doran; Constance Forcillo; Revs. Jose Puthenparambil; John E. Basil; Deacons Willy Malarcher; Martin Hemberger; Edward Caceres.

WESTWOOD. *Pascack Valley Hospital* Old Hook Rd., 07675. Tel: 201-358-3000. Chaplains: Revs. Thomas Norton; Mert Cordero.

Essex County

NEWARK. *Beth Israel Hospital* 201 Lyons Ave., 07112. Tel: 973-926-7000; 926-7178 (Pastoral Care). Rev. Thomas R. McLaughlin, Chap., Columbus Hospital, 495 N. 13th St., 07107. Tel: 201-268-1400. Sr. Beatriz Dugue, Chap.
St. James Hospital 155 Jefferson St., 07015. Tel: 973-589-1300. Chaplains: Rev. Kenneth Martin; Sr. Dolores Cervi.
St. Michael Medical Center 306 Martin Luther King Blvd., 07102. Tel: 973-877-5467. Chaplains: Rev. Msgr. Jose Agan; Revs. Manuel Cruz; Kenneth Martin; Deacons Edward McFadden; Rafael Vargas.
University of Medicine & Dentistry 100 Bergen St., 07103. Tel: 973-972-4300. Chaplains: Rev. Eustace Edomobi; Deacons Leo Montini; William Morris; Cesar Ortega-Escobar.

BELLEVILLE. *Clara Maass Hospital* I-A Franklin Ave., 07109. Tel: 973-450-2000. Chaplains: Revs. John Donahue; George Joseph; Sr. Angela Vilin.

CEDAR GROVE. *Essex County Hospital Center* 125 Fairview Ave., 07009. Tel: 973-228-8000. Rev. Peter Suvokeen, Chap.

EAST ORANGE. *East Orange Hospital* 300 Central Ave., 07019. Tel: 973-672-8400. Rev. Deo Bocad, Chap.
Veterans Administration Hospital Tremont Ave. & Center St., 07019. Tel: 973-676-1000; 972-5688 (Pastoral Care). Rev. Alexander Davis, O.F.M.Cap.

LIVINGSTON. *St. Barnabas Medical Center* 94 Old Short Hills Rd., 07039. Tel: 973-533-5015. Chaplains: Revs. Richard Chilmark; Peter Vinh Q. Nguyen; Sr. Adele Solari, S.S.J., Dir.

MONTCLAIR. *Montclair Hospital* 120 Harrison Ave., 07042. Rev. Louis Pambello, Chap.
Mountainside Hospital Bay Ave. & Highland Ave., 07042. Tel: 973-429-6000; 429-6047 (Pastoral Care). Revs. Alan Guglielmo, Chap.; William Gyure.
St. Vincent Nursing Home 45 Elm St., 07102. Tel: 973-746-4000. Sr. Elizabeth Ann Noonan, S.C., Chap.

ORANGE. *Hospital Center at Orange* 188 S. Essex St., 07051. Tel: 973-266-2000. Rev. Deo Bocad, Chap.
Pope John Paul II Pavilion at St. Mary's 135 S. Centre St., 07050. Tel: 973-266-3000. Rev. Eugene E. Geiger, Chap.

WEST ORANGE. *Kessler Institute for Rehabilitation* 1199 Pleasant Valley Way, 07052. Tel: 973-731-3600. Rev. Louis Pambello, Chap.

Hudson County

BAYONNE. *Bayonne Hospital* 29 E. 29th St., 07002. Tel: 201-858-5000. Rev. J. M. Patricius.

HOBOKEN. *St. Mary's Hospital* 308 Willow Ave., 07030. Tel: 201-418-1000. Revs. Wilfred Yeo; Gerard J. Sudol.

JERSEY CITY. *Christ Hospital* 176 Palisades Ave., 07304. Tel: 201-795-8200. Rev. Christopher Anyanwu; Sr. Nancy Krug.
Jersey City Medical Center 50 Baldwin Ave., 07304. Tel: 201-915-2000. Rev. Edmundo A. Surban.
Progressive Health Care 100 Clifton Pl., 07304. Tel: 201-434-5883. Rev. John Corbett.
St. Francis Community Health Center 25 McWilliams Pl., 07302. Tel: 201-418-1000. Revs. Wilfred Yeo; Gerard J. Sudol.

KEARNY. *West Hudson Hospital* 206 Bergen Ave., 07032. Tel: 201-955-7000. Rev. Joseph Khai Vu.

NORTH BERGEN. *Palisades General Hospital* 7600 River Rd., 07047. Tel: 201-854-5000. Rev. David S. McLaughlin.

Union County

BERKELEY HEIGHTS. *Runnells County Hospital* 07922. Tel: 908-771-5700. Rev. Charles Anemelu.

ELIZABETH. *Trinitas Hospital* 925 E. Jersey St., 07201. Revs. Edward Haber; Brendan Quinn; Paterno Gorospe.

LINDEN. *Center for Hope Hospice* 176 Hussa St., 07036. Tel: 908-386-0700. Deacon Cyril Massar.

PLAINFIELD. *Muhlenberg Medical Center* Park Ave. & Randolph Rd., 07061. Tel: 908-668-2007. Revs. Aloysius S. Carney; Joy Olookaran; Kai Minh Nguyen.

RAHWAY. *Rahway Hospital* 865 Stone St., 07065. Tel: 908-381-4200. Deacons J. William Courtney; James O'Neill; Rev. William Reed.

SUMMIT. *Overlook Hospital* 99 Beauvoir Ave., 07902. Tel: 908-522-2000; 522-2108. Revs. John Quill; John P. Holian; Sr. Patricia Murphy, S.S.J., Dir.

UNION. *Union Hospital* 1000 Galloping Hill Rd., 07083. Tel: 908-687-7205. Rev. George M. Keating.

Prison Chaplaincy

NEWARK. *Office of Prison Ministry* P.O. Box 9500, 07104. Tel: 973-497-4223; Fax: 973-497-4018. Deacon David Loman.

Bergen County

HACKENSACK. *Bergen County Jail* 160 S. River St., 07601. Tel: 201-488-1190, Ext. 407. Rev. Joseph Buzzerio.

PARAMUS. *Bergen County Juvenile Detention Center* Tel: 201-599-6185. Deacon Lex Ferraioula; Mr. Michael Cechony.

Essex County

NEWARK. *Cura (Community United to Rehabilitate Addicts)*. Revs. Anthony Bico; Robert Cormier; Bro. Thomas Corey.
Essex County Jail 60 Nelson Pl., 07102. Tel: 973-621-5154. Deacons Ceasear Ortega; Juan Suarez.
Essex County Juvenile Correctional Center 203 Sussex Ave., 07102. Tel: 973-497-4735. Rev. Anthony Bico.
Northern State Prison 168 Frontage Rd., 07114. Tel: 973-465-0068, Ext. 4505. Revs. Thomas C. Roberts; Paul Nolan; Robert Cormier; Deacons Sam Ventola; David Loman; Mr. Edward Boyle.

CALDWELL. *Essex County Jail Annex* P.O. Box 349, 07006. Tel: 973-364-5347. Rev. Paul J. Nolan.

Hudson County

SECAUCUS. *Hudson County Youth Juvenile Correctional Center* 635 County Ave., 07094. Promise/Outreach Ministry, Tel: 201-659-0229. Deacon David Loman.

SOUTH KEARNY. *Hudson County Correctional Center* 35 Hackensack Rd., 07032. Tel: 973-497-5500. Deacons Joseph Del Monte; Wilford Le Conte; Juan Suarez; Sam Ventola.
Talbot Hall Assessment Center Tel: 201-491-5500. Rev. Paul J. Nolan; Mr. Joseph Nestor.

Union County

ELIZABETH. *Elizabeth Detention Center* 07201. Tel: 908-352-3776. Rev. George Sharp; Deacon Juan Suarez.
Union County Jail 15 Elizabeth Town Plaza, 07207. Tel: 908-558-2636. Rev. William Gyure.

Special Assignment:
Reverend Monsignors—
Kleissler, Thomas A., Dir. Renew International
Reverend Fathers—
Ashe, Kevin P., Exec. Dir. Park Theatre Performing Arts Ctr., Inc.
Barrow, Joseph A., Neo-Catechumenate Communities
Randl, Ewald, Neo-Catechumenate Communities

On Duty Outside the Archdiocese:
Reverend Monsignors—
Casale, Franklyn M., St. Thomas University, 16400 N.W. 32nd Ave., Miami, FL 33054
Radano, John A., Villa Stritch, Via Della Nocetta 63, Rome, Italy 00164
Reverend Fathers—
Arata, Miguel A., Tartu P. Neitsi Maarja Kogudus, Veski TN 1-1A, EE2400, Tartu, Estonia
Arvay, Alfred S., 5128 Mentmore Ave., Spring Hill, FL 34606
Balance, Harvey, Parroquia Nuestra Senora de Carppus, 1648 Tigre, Larrea, Argentina 500
Baldacchino, Peter, Chancellor, R.C. Mission, Holy Cross, P.O. Box 70, Grand Turks Is., BWI
Basile, Gioacchino, Parroquia San Jose, Apartado 25, Penuelas, Puerto Rico 00624
Batista, George L., 2552 Palm Rd., West Palm Beach, FL 33406
Becerra, Robert L., Church of St. Luke, 2892 S. Congress Ave., Palm Springs, FL 33461
Carraro, Francesco, Parroquia San Jose, Apartado 25, Penuelas, Puerto Rico 00624
DiGiovanni, Alfonso, P-De Apostlite Peetruse JA, Pauluse Kogudus Tallinas, Vene TN 18, EE0001, Tallin, Estonia
Donini, Leone, St. Roseline, 409 Edouard Herriot Escallion, Toulon, 83200 France
Figueiredo, Anthony Jesus, Casa Santa Maria, Via dell'Ulmita, Rome, 30, 00187 Italy
Guillen, Randy A., Jesus the Lord, 120 Broad St., Keyport, NJ 07735
Hall, Warren R., St. Elizabeth, 809 S. Broom St., Wilmington, DE 19805
Kirchner, James A., Church of St. Joseph, 2011 Darling Ave., Waycross, GA 31501
Kowalski, Erich, Our Lady of Grace, 2205 W. Market St., Greensboro, NC 27403
Krozser, John J., C.M., Church of the Resurrection, 2815 Forbes Dr., Montgomery, AL 36110
Kukura, Joseph W., Center for Ethics & Ministry, 935 Allwood Rd., Clifton, NJ 07012
Kunze, Robert W., St. Andrew's, 120 United States Ave., Gibbsboro, NJ 08026
Labranche, Raymond, Rector, Redemptoris Mater Seminary, Archdiocese of Agana, 196 B Cuestra San Ramon, Agana, Guam, 96910
Larrea, Hector, Jesus the Lord, 120 Broad St., Keyport, NJ 07735
Leahy, Robert T., St Luke's, 1674 Old Freehold Rd., Toms River, NJ 08755
Livolsi, Sylvester J., Sanctuary of Mary, 252 Wantage Ave., Branchville, NJ 07826
Merdinger, Philip E., Brotherhood of Hope, 194 Summer Ave., Sumerville, MA 02143
Miller, Frederick L., St. Charles Borromeo Seminary, 1000 E. Wynnewood Rd., Wynnewood, PA 19096
Papalia, Pasquale A., St. James, 94 Broad St., Red Bank, NJ 07701
Perricone, John A., St. Agnes, 143 E. 43rd St., New York, NY 10017
Prindiville, Gerald T., Pastor, Holy Cross, R.C. Mission, P.O. Box 70, Grand Turks Is., BWI
Ransom, Donald B., St. Paul's, 286 Haledon Ave., Prospect Park, NJ 07500
Reinbold, Charles, Mt. St. Francis, 250 South St., Peekskill, NJ 10566
Russo, Michael A., St. Mary College, Box 5166, Moraga, CA 94575
Scaramella, Renzo L., Pastor, Our Lady of Providence, R.C. Mission, P.O. Box 158 Providenciales, Turks & Caicos Islands, BWI
Scheip, Michael A., Epiphany Cathedral, 310 Sarasota St., Venice, FL 34285
Schute, Arthur B., 1404 Corktree Cir., Port Charlotte, FL 33952
Vo, Peter Phong, St. Anthony of Padua, 436 Port Reading Ave., Port Reading, NJ 07064
Wegg, Mark R., Our Lady of the Springs, 4047 N.E. 21st St., Ocala, FL 34470
West, Peter, Priests for Life, 128 Targee St., Staten Island, NY 10304
Wilson, William P., Nativity of the Blessed Virgin Mary, 99 E. Tioga St., Tunkhannock, PA 18657

Military Chaplains:
Reverend Fathers—
Arminio, Alfonse M., Wharfside MNR Condo, Apt. 17, 172 Park Rd., Monmouth Beach, NJ 07750
Beale, Kenneth R., Capt., PSC2, P.O. Box 9137, APO AE, 09012
Berchmanz, Anthony, 3670 Surface Navy Blvd., #368016, San Diego, CA 92136
Brosk, Steven J., PSC 94, Box 967, APO AE, 09824
Cunha, Egionor, Lt., CHC USNR, Courtney Chapel, PSC 559, Box 5210, FPO, AP, 96377
D'Emma, Gregory J., U.S. Army War College, Carlisle Barracks, PA 17013
Hanrahan, William P., Chap., Postal Service Center Box 10136, Wright-Patterson AFB, OH 45433

Kopec, Rajmund, Capt., 4035 W. Meadow Dr., Colorado Springs, CO 80906
Lesak, William P., 2457 Northwoods Dr., Jacksonville, NC 28540
Morris, John J., CHC USNR, 5424 Keystone Pl., Virginia Beach, VA 23464
Newland, Ronald A., Archdiocese for Military Services, P.O. Box 4469, Washington, DC 20017
Pawlikowski, Matthew, Capt., 6208 Lakeway Dr., Fayetteville, NC 28306
Plate, Brian G., Capt.; Chap., 35 FW/HC, APO, AP, 96319
Tiboni, Vito, Veterans' Hospital, 800 Poly Pl., Apt. #15 W., Brooklyn, NY 11209

Higher Studies:
Reverend Fathers—
Figueiredo, Anthony Jesus, Casa Santa Maria, Via dell'Umilta, 30, Rome, 00187 Italy

Retired:
Reverend Monsignors—
Abramowicz, Sylvester, 7 Pine Tree Ln., Columbia, NJ 07832
Alba, Jose M., 24 J.M. Basa St., Iloilo City, 5000 Philippines
Beggans, Joseph A., Pope John Paul II Pavilion, 135 S. Center St., Orange, NJ 07050
Bonelli, Theodore V., 120-B Ironwood Plaza, Monroe Twp., NJ 08831
Burke, James A., Nativity Church, 315 Prospect St., Midland Park, NJ 07432
Capozzelli, Emmanuel M., Rev. Msgr. James F. Kelley Residence, 247 Bloomfield Ave., Caldwell, NJ 07006
Casazza, David J., 426 Jefferson Ave., Avon-by-the-Sea, NJ 07717
Coburn, Vincent P., 1802 Ravine Dr., Forked River, NJ 08731
Daly, William J., St. Joseph's Rectory, 44 Benvenue Ave., West Orange, NJ 07052
Devine, William P., 15 Lakeview Point Ave., Branchville, NJ 07826
Donovan, Joseph J., 21 Wellington Ln., Lakewood, NJ 08701
Duffy, Robert E., Allendale Community for Mature Living, 85 Harreton Rd., Allendale, NJ 07401
Eid, Frederick M., Our Lady of Grace, 400 Willow Ave., Hoboken, NJ 07030
Fleming, Edward J., Immaculate Conception Seminary, Seton Hall University, South Orange, NJ 07079
Flusk, Joseph F., P.O. Box 66, Beachwood, NJ 08722
Hayes, Paul J., 197 Riverside Dr. N., Bricktown, NJ 08724
Hinrichsen, Carl D., Our Lady of Mercy Rectory, 2 Fremont Ave., Park Ridge, NJ 07656
Holmes, Richard J., St. Luke, 430 N. Franklin Tpke., Ho-Ho-Kus, NJ 07423
Houghton, Francis J., 2316 Blue Jay Tr., Point Pleasant, NJ 08742
Hourihan, John P., 5 Johnson St., Monmouth Beach, NJ 07750
Jarvais, Walter G., 60 Home Ave., Rutherford, NJ 07070
Johnson, James, 555 Prospect Ave., Ridgefield, NJ 07657
Koenig, John H., St. Teresa of Avila, 306 Morris Ave., Summit, NJ 07901
Komar, Michael A., 188 W. 31st Street, Bayonne, NJ 07002
Lennon, Robert T., St. Cloud Healthcare Center, 5 Brookend Dr., West Orange, NJ 07052
LoBianco, Francis R., 32 Woodland Ave., Jamaica Plain, MA 02130
Madden, Thomas G., St. John Vianney Residence, 60 Home Ave., Rutherford, NJ 07070
Manz, Joseph C., Our Lady Mother of the Church, 209 Woodcliff Ave., Woodcliff Lake, NJ 07675
Marjanczyk, Joseph A., P.O. Box 456, Point Pleasant, NJ 08742
Murray, Harold A., 50 Willow Way, Manasquan, NJ 08736
Orrico, Caesar G., 20 Locust Ave., Emerson, NJ 07630
Piazza, Benjamin A., St. Aloysius, 219 Bloomfield Ave., Caldwell, NJ 07006
Pocus, Dominick A., Clara Maass Continuing Care Center, 195 Belgrove Dr., Kearny, NJ 07032
Pollard, Raymond J., 2316 Blue Jay Tr., Point Pleasant, NJ 08742
Price, Edward G., Church of the Assumption, 113 Chiego Pl., Roselle Park, NJ 07204
Reynolds, Roger A., Our Lady of Victories Rectory, 81 Lynn St., Harrington Park, NJ 07640
Santora, Gerard M., St. John Vianney Residence, 60 Home Ave., Rutherford, NJ 07070
Sullivan, Edwin V., Seton Hall University, South Orange Ave., South Orange, NJ 07079
Turro, James C., S.T.L., S.S.L., M.A., Immaculate Conception Seminary, Seton Hall University, South Orange, NJ 07079
Welsh, Aloysius J., The Rev. Msgr. James F. Kelley Residence for Retired Priests, 247 Bloomfield Ave., Caldwell, NJ 07006
Wojtycha, Edward F., 1800 S.E. St. Lucie Blvd., 2202, Stuart, FL 34996

Reverend Fathers—
Affanoso, Joseph L., St. Nicholas, 1790 79th St., Causeway Apt. 305B, Northbay, FL 33141
Anta, Antonio, c/o Maria Rodriguez, 716 Dennis Pl., Linden, NJ 07036
Arminio, Thomas, 1057 Trent Pl., Union, NJ 07083
Ballweg, John M., P.O.Box 202, Monmouth Beach, NJ 07750
Bergeur, John X., c/o Mrs. Kay Fantony, P.O. Box 614, Summit, NJ 07901
Byrne, W. Gordon, St. John Vianney Residence, 60 Home Ave., Rutherford, NJ 07070
Cassidy, Joseph L., St. John Vianney Annex, 64 Home Ave., Rutherford, NJ 07070
Celiano, Alfred V., Seton Hall University, 400 South Orange Ave., South Orange, NJ 07079
Cestaro, Joseph J., St. John Vianney Residence, 60 Home Ave., Rutherford, NJ 07070
Clyde, George A., 2121 Butternut Rd., Sea Girt, NJ 08750
Coda, Joseph F., 60 Home Ave., Rutherford, NJ 07070
Connors, Robert A., 330 Lincoln Ave., Avon by the Sea, NJ 07717
Cooper, Donald A., 3220 Keith Ln., P.O. Box 3, Lavallette, NJ 08735
Daly, Robert L., Immaculate Conception Rectory, 18 South St., Spotswood, NJ 08884
Danik, Daniel A., 2046 Ingalls Ave., Linden, NJ 07036
Debold, Walter A., Seton Hall University, 400 South Orange Ave., South Orange, NJ 07079
Derbyshire, Joseph V., St. John Vianney Residence, 60 Home Ave., Rutherford, NJ 07070
DiGirolamo, Dante, Eucharistic Shrine of the Adorable Face of Jesus, P.O. Box 455, Kearny, NJ 07032
DiPeri, Joseph B., Leisure Ridge, 303 Devon St., Lakehurst, NJ 08733
Doherty, George E., St. John Vianney Residence, 60 Home Ave., Rutherford, NJ 07070
Dowling, John C., c/o Mrs. H. Battles, 595 Bloomfield Ave., Apt. 35, West Caldwell, NJ 07006
Dowling, Michael J., 4 Brookline Ct., Middletown, NJ 07748
Doyle, Joseph M., 145 Pearsall Ave., Jersey City, NJ 07305
Drexler, George D., Box 316, Sea Girt, NJ 08750
Driscoll, James J., Atria Assisted Living, 44 Pine St., Tinton Falls, NJ 07753
Driscoll, William D., 51 Monterey Ave., Teaneck, NJ 07666
Fagan, Joseph P., P.O. Box 545, Spring Lake, NJ 07762
Farley, Leo O., Rev. Msgr. James F. Kelley Residence, 247 Bloomfield Ave., Caldwell, NJ 07006
Ferrazoli, Henry R., 149 Orlando Blvd., Toms River, NJ 08757
Finn, Francis J., 26 Kent Dr., Bricktown, NJ 08723
Fiorino, Joseph, 1006 Sailor Dr., Manahawkin, NJ 08050
Foye, Thomas M., St. Andrew, 125 Broadway, Bayonne, NJ 07002
Frank, Joseph A., Rev. Msgr. James F. Kelley Residence, 247 Bloomfield Ave., Caldwell, NJ 07006
French, Walter V., 26 Rogerene Way, Landing, NJ 07850
Fuino, Michael A., St. John Vianney Residence, 60 Home Ave., Rutherford, NJ 07070
Garoffolo, Vincent, Ashbrook Nursing Home, 1610 Raritan Rd., Scotch Plains, NJ 07076
Gavin, Francis T., Seton Hall University, 400 South Orange Ave., South Orange, NJ 07079
Geiger, Eugene E., Pope John Paul II Pavilion, 135 S. Center St., Orange, NJ 07050
Genzlinger, Walter L., Mt. Carmel, 99 Broadway, Jersey City, NJ 07306
Giblin, William M., Holy Rosary, 365 Undercliff Ave., Edgewater, NJ 07020
Gibney, Robert G., Msgr. James F. Kelley Residence, 247 Bloomfield Ave., Caldwell, NJ 07006
Hayes, Edward J., St. Joseph's Home, 140 Shepherd Ln., Totowa, NJ 07512
Hermanns, Harold T., St. John Vianney Residence, 60 Home Ave., Rutherford, NJ 07070
Herr, Charles W., St. John Vianney Residence, 60 Home Ave., Rutherford, NJ 07070
Horgan, Timothy J., 102 Barbuda St., P.O. Box 3453, Toms River, NJ 08756-3453
Kearney, Edward J., St. Patrick, 492 Bramhall Ave., Jersey City, NJ 07304
Kenny, Thomas A., 24 Chesapeake Ct., Barnegat, NJ 08005
Kern, Charles P., 183 Evergreen Rd., Apt. 7A, Edison, NJ 08817
Koerner, Frederick C., St. John Vianney Residence, 60 Home Ave., Rutherford, NJ 07070
Kowalski, Alfred J., St. Theresa, 541 Washington Ave., Kenilworth, NJ 07033
Langdon, Robert H., John Vianney Residence, 60 Home Ave., Rutherford, NJ 07070
Lehman, Paul J., P.O. Box 499, Branchville, NJ 07826
Lennon, Peter F., Seton Hall University, 400 South Orange Ave., South Orange, NJ 07079
Ligos, George A., St. Paul of the Cross Rectory, 156 Hancock Ave., Jersey City, NJ 07307
Looney, Mathew D., 3411 Seaview Rd., Lavallette, NJ 08735
Lynch, Thomas F., 3 Horizon Rd., Apt. 1027, Fort Lee, NJ 07024
Macho, George S., 1825 Buttonwood Ave., Toms River, NJ 08755
Madden, John J., 60 Home Ave., Rutherford, NJ 07070
Mader, George L., Msgr. James F. Kelley Residence, 247 Bloomfield Ave., Caldwell, NJ 07006
Mahoney, Daniel F., 7450 Dundee Way, Brooksville, FL 34613
Marchand, Gerald A., P.O. Box 3102, Point Pleasant, NJ 08742
Marotta, Robert G., St. Catherine of Siena, 19 King St., Hillside, NJ 07205
McFarland, James W., 21 Skillman Ave., Jersey City, NJ 07306
McGuinness, Lester A., St. Aloysius, 219 Bloomfield Ave., Caldwell, NJ 07006
McKenna, Dennis R., 149 Meisel Ave., Springfield, NJ 07081
McNulty, Francis J., St. Teresa's, 306 Morn's Ave., Summit, NJ 07901
McTague, Charles H., Holy Cross, 16 Church Sq., P.O. Box 73, Harrison, NJ 07029
Merzena, Carl J., 60 Home Ave., Rutherford, NJ 07070
Miller, Ferdinand B., P.O. Box 4330, Brick, NJ 08723-1530
Miodowski, Leonard A., St. John Vianney Residence, 60 Home Ave., Rutherford, NJ 07070
Morel, John J., 381 Park Ave., Apt. 2L, Scotch Plains, NJ 07076
Mukalel, Joseph V., 2 Amherst Ct., Maplewood, NJ 07040
Murphy, Joseph H., 175 Mount Nebo Rd, Milford, NJ 08848
Myers, J. Edward, 432 Bethel Village Circle, Lehigh Acres, FL 33936
Nardone, Richard M., Seton Hall University, 400 South Orange Ave., South Orange, NJ 07079
Nealon, Joseph W., 3360 Canoe Creek Ter., Palm City, FL 34990
O'Brien, John E., 346 Mt. Pleasant Ave., Livingston, NJ 07039
O'Connor, Charles P., St. John Vianney Residence, 60 Home Ave., Rutherford, NJ 07070
O'Leary, Robert A., 252 Genes Dr., Toms River, NJ 08753
O'Neill, James R., St. Paul's, 200 Wyckoff Ave., Ramsey, NJ 07446
Olson, Thomas F., 26 E. 3rd St., Bayonne, NJ 07002
Olszewski, John S., St. Mark's Rectory, 287 Hamilton St., Rahway, NJ 07065
Osorio, Rudolfo B., 2438 Fruit Ave., S.E., Port Lucie, FL 34952
Provinzano, Rocco, St. Andrew's, 124 Washington Ave., Westwood, NJ 07675
Quinlan, Joseph M., 18 Ellsworth Ct., Red Bank, NJ 07701
Quinn, Vincent J., Msgr. James F. Kelley Residence, 247 Bloomfield Ave., Caldwell, NJ 07006
Rischmann, Edward, 146 Skyline Drive, Brick, NJ 08724
Rock, John J., 200 Springfield Ave., Apt. 5023, Springfield, NJ 07081
Sapeta, Joseph S., St. Hedwig, 1062 Dewey Pl., Elizabeth, NJ 07202
Scanlan, Charles V., 60 Home Ave., Rutherford, NJ 07070
Scherer, Donald R., P.O. Box 764, Robert, LA 70455
Schulte, William P., Brester's Guest House, 477 Mt. Prospect Ave., Newark, NJ 07104
Sheehan, Joseph G., St. John the Apostle, 1805 Penbrook Ter., Linden, NJ 07036
Sheerin, James O., St. John Vianney Residence, 60 Home Ave., Rutherford, NJ 07070
Shih, John M., Madonna Church, 340 Main St., Fort Lee, NJ 07024
Simko, Michael S., 380 Ave. E, Bayonne, NJ 07002
Smalley, William R., 4436 N.E. Ocean Blvd., Bldg 100-D-1, Jensen Beach, FL 34957

Stulb, Joseph A., 100 Clinton St., #2C, Hoboken, NJ 07030-2574
Sweeney, John D., St. Joseph, 44 Benvenue Ave., West Orange, NJ 07052-3227
Swenson, Walter J.F., 72 Windsor Pl., Kenilworth, NJ 07033
Swierzbinski, Edward, P.O. Box 342, Normandy Beach, NJ 08739
Szelest, Theodore A., Church of St. Mary, 280 Washington Ave., Dumont, NJ 07628
Tracy, John A., Pope John Paul II Pavilion, 135 Center St., Orange, NJ 07050
Waldron, John R., Chelsea at Forsgate, 350 Forsgate Dr., Jamesburg, NJ 08831
Wightman, John H., 1215 Windlass Dr., Manahawkin, NJ 08050
Zuber, Thaddeus F., 60 Home Ave., Rutherford, NJ 07070

Permanent Deacons:
Paul Kliauga, Ascension, New Milford
Abreu, Rosendo, Our Lady of Liberia, West New York
Accardi, Vincent, St. Mary's, Elizabeth
Acocella, Louis, St. Anthony, Belleville
Allgaier, John, On Duty Outside the Archdiocese
Alsing, Edwin J., (Retired)
Alvarez, Juan, On Duty Outside the Archdiocese
Amaro, Claudino, On Duty Outside the Archdiocese
Anders, Joseph L., On Duty Outside the Archdiocese
Andrews, Marshall, Our Lady of the Valley, Orange
Araya, Alfonso, On Duty Outside the Archdiocese
Baker, Robert, St. Nicholas, Jersey City
Balestrieri, Anthony A., Our Lady of Peace, Maywood
Baltus, John M., St. James, Springfield
Barrett, Thomas J., St. Joseph's and St. Michael's, Union City
Basch, Peter J.
Bates, Harold L., Ascension, New Milford
Bellascio, Vincent, St. Joseph the Carpenter, Roselle
Benedetto, William R., Queen of Peace, North Arlington
Besida, Dennis J., St. Thomas, Bloomfield
Bond, Charles H., Leave of Absence
Bongiovanni, Jerome C., St. James, Springfield
Bonilla, Benjamin, On Duty Outside the Archdiocese
Botts, Edward, Leave of Absence
Botts, Robert, Leave of Absence
Bowen, Edmund, (Retired)
Bowen, Edward J., St. Peter the Apostle, River Edge
Brennan, Vishno H., On Duty Outside the Archdiocese
Bulgia, Thomas, Holy Name, East Orange
Byrnes, Richard, Our Lady of Good Counsel, Washington Township
Caceres, Edgar, St. Brigid, North Bergen
Campanella, Edward, St. John the Baptist, Linden
Campione, Frank J., St. Thomas More, Fairfield
Carr, Patrick V., Community Hospital, Montclair
Carrasquillo, Francisco, St. Rocco, Union City
Casanova, Eliot, St. Aloysius, Jersey City
Cata, David, Leave of Absence
Cauceglia, Arthur J., St. Francis of Assisi, Hackensack
Centenera, Leandro, Holy Trinity, Fort Lee
Charriez, Nestor, St. Patrick, Elizabeth
Coffey, John J., St. Peter Claver, Montclair
Collins, Thomas F., Bergen Pines Hospital
Colon, German, On Duty Outside the Archdiocese
Colon, Hector, On Duty Outside the Archdiocese
Concepcion, Asuncion, On Duty Outside the Archdiocese
Cook, William R., On Duty Outside the Archdiocese
Cordasco, Ralph J., On Duty Outside the Archdiocese
Courtney, J. William, St. Mary's, Rahway
Coyle, Thomas J., St. Thomas, Bloomfield
Cruz, Primitivo, Sts. Peter & Paul, Hoboken
Cullinane, John, On Duty Outside the Archdiocese
Cunningham, Joseph, St. Joseph, West Orange
Czerepka, Alexander J., St. Theresa, Linden
Daher, Paul D., Inactive
Daniele, Paul, St. Francis Xavier, Newark
Davignon, Paul M., On Duty Outside the Archdiocese
DeBenedictis, Thomas, SS. Joseph and Michael, Union City
Degnon, Robert F., On Duty Outside the Archdiocese
Del Monte, Joseph J., Assumption-All Saints, Jersey City
Delgado, Carlos, On Duty Outside the Archdiocese
DeLucca, Nicholas J., Our Lady, Mother of the Church, Woodcliff Lake
DeMaria, Joseph, Jr., St. Elizabeth, Wyckoff
Denick, Anthony F., On Duty Outside the Archdiocese
Diaz-Rojas, Andres, (Retired)
Dickson, Joseph A., St. Matthew, Ridgefield
Dove, Winston, On Duty Outside the Archdiocese
Echevarria, Mario, St. Thomas Aquinas, Newark
Fargo, Nicholas C., Our Lady of Mercy, Jersey City
Fencik, Robert, St. Mary, Rahway
Fernandez, Jose R., Blessed Sacrament, Elizabeth
Ferraiuola, Lex, Our Lady of Mt. Carmel, Tenafly
Fiore, Joseph, (Retired)
Fischer, Robert, On Duty Outside the Archdiocese
Fitzgerald, Michael J., St. Joseph, Bogota
Flores, Ricardo, SS. Joseph & Michael, Union City
Francione, Joseph, St. Philomena, Livingston
Freeman, Gerald, St. Paul, Irvington
Fuentes, Julio, Leave of Absence
Garcia, David, Our Lady of the Lake, Verona
Gimbel, Herbert, St. Stephen, Kearny
Giordano, William J., Our Lady of Assumption, Bayonne
Gisoldi, Frank A., St. Teresa of Avila, Summit
Glasner, Robert, Our Lady of Good Counsel, Washington Township
Glogoza, Theodore J., Sacred Heart, Bloomfield
Gomez, Alberto, St. Michael's, Newark
Gonzalez, Frank, St. Paul the Apostle, Jersey City
Gonzalez, Pedro, St. Boniface, Jersey City
Gorini, Joseph, On Duty Outside the Archdiocese
Gray, Brandon, On Duty Outside the Archdiocese
Grieder, Gustave, On Duty Outside the Archdiocese
Haas, Henry W., Our Lady of Mt. Carmel, Montclair
Hall, J. Bruce, On Duty Outside the Archdiocese
Heinrich, Joseph R., On Duty Outside the Archdiocese
Hemberger, Martin R., Holy Name Hospital, Teaneck; St. Michael, Palisades Park
Higgins, Leonard F., Our Lady of Mercy, Park Ridge
Hildebrandt, Edward J., Inactive
Hodges, Richard G., St. Pius X, Old Tappan
Hoefling, Edward J., On Duty Outside the Archdiocese
Huff, Sidney E., Holy Spirit-Help of Christians, East Orange
Inguaggiato, John M., Our Lady of Sorrows, South Orange
Jackson, Alonzo, St. Joseph, East Orange
Johnson, Leon, Christ the King, Jersey City
Joyce, William, Annunciation, Paramus
Jurjevic, Svetko, On Duty Outside the Archdiocese
Kautz, Frederick, Immaculate Conception, Mahwah
Kelly, Walter, On Duty Outside the Archdiocese
Keturwitis, Henry J., Sts. Peter & Paul, Elizabeth
Kiley, Charles F., Permanent Diaconate Office, Holy Trinity, Westfield
King, Aidan P., St. Thomas More, Fairfield
Kirkham, Donald F., On Duty Outside the Archdiocese
Kliauga, Paul, Ascension, New Milford
Kramer, Richard D., On Duty Outside the Archdiocese
Kratchman, Robert M., St. Elizabeth, Wyckoff
Langlois, Jose, St. Anthony of Padua, Union City
Lawless, Timothy, On Duty Outside the Archdiocese
Leary, Gerald, St. Mary, Closter
LeConte, Wilfrid, St. Peter Claver, Montclair
Liptak, Stephen J., St. Aloysius, Jersey City
Llaneza, Oscar, On Duty Outside the Archdiocese
Loman, David B., Northern State Prison, Newark
Loperena, Miguel A., Immaculate Heart of Mary, Newark
Lopez, George, On Duty Outside the Archdiocese
Lopez, Sixto, University Hospital, Newark
Lorenzo, Michael, Inactive
Lubas, Joseph, St. Adalbert, Elizabeth
Lydon, Michael A., Holy Rosary, Edgewater
Lynn, Walter, St. Joseph, Bogota
Macaluso, Martin P., St. Mary, Plainfield
Mackesy, Leonard J., Our Lady of Sorrows, Kearny
Mainero, Frank A., On Duty Outside the Archdiocese
Maione, Michael, Our Lady of the Lake, Verona
Malanga, Joseph J., St. Valentine, Bloomfield
Malarcher, Willy J., Holy Name Hospital, Teaneck
Marchese, Stephen, St. Joseph, Lodi
Markenstein, Aart, Holy Rosary, Jersey City
Maron, Edward, On Duty Outside the Archdiocese
Martinez, Jose, St. Columba, Newark
Massar, Cyril J., Leave of Absence
Matos, William, Jr., St. Columba, Newark
Matthews, Michael, St. Mary, Rutherford
McAulay, John R., Leave of Absence
McCarren, Daniel G., Jr., St. Rose of Lima, Short Hills
McCarthy, John T., St. Augustine's, Union City
McDermott, William, St. Aloysius, Caldwell
McFadden, Edward, St. Michael's Hospital, Newark
McGarry, Richard M. (SA), St. Anne's, Fairlawn
McKeon, John W., St. Luke, Ho-ho-kus
McKnight, Keith, Christ the King, Jersey City
McLaughlin, Albert, Immaculate Conception, Norwood
McNulty, James, On Duty Outside the Archdiocese
Mejias, Escolastico, On Duty Outside the Archdiocese
Mendez, Daniel, St. Augustine's, Newark
Messina, Dominic S., St. Thomas More, Fairfield
Messina, Vincent, Holy Trinity, Hackensack
Meyers, Vincent J., (Retired)
Miney, Patrick F., St. John's, Bergenfield
Minichino, Leonard A., St. Catharine's, Glen Rock
Mistretta, Alfonso G., Leave of Absence
Mohr, Richard, Our Lady of Perpetual Help, Oakland
Molina, Osiris, St. Catherine, Hillside
Montanez, Luis A., St. Joseph, Hoboken
Montemurro, Michael V., Little Flower, Berkeley Heights
Montini, Leo, On Duty Outside the Archdiocese
Moore, Brett O., Sacred Heart, Lyndhurst
Morend, Michel, On Duty Outside the Archdiocese
Mueller, James A., St. Catherine, Glen Rock
Myers, William, Queen of Peace, North Arlington
Nazzaro, Joseph J., On Duty Outside the Archdiocese
Negron, Victor, On Duty Outside the Archdiocese
Nilan, Thomas, St. Cassian's, Upper Montclair
Niland, Joseph, Annunciation, Paramus
Niles, Donald P., St. Elizabeth of Hungary, Linden
Noone, Thomas H., On Duty Outside the Archdiocese
Nunez, Guillermo, On Duty Outside the Archdiocese
O'Connell, Brian, On Duty Outside the Archdiocese
O'Neill, James, On Duty Outside the Archdiocese
Ortega, Cesar, St. Ann, Newark
Ortiz, Jaime, St. Michael's, Jersey City
Osborne, Charles E., St. Rocco, Newark
Paredes, Guy, (Retired)
Paulillo, Joseph J., St. Andrew's, Westwood
Perez, Buenaventura, On Duty Outside the Archdiocese
Perez, Prudencio, On Duty Outside the Archdiocese
Persinger, Joseph M., St. Rose of Lima, Short Hills
Peterson, Victor, Bergen County Institutions
Pimentel, Simon B., On Duty Outside the Archdiocese
Pluta, Thomas A, Holy Trinity, Westfield
Polanco, Leopoldo, St. Boniface, Jersey City
Pons, Eduardo, Our Lady of Liberia, West New York
Porter, Edward W., Jr., Cathedral Basilica of the Sacred Heart-Permanent Diaconate Office
Postadan, Romulo D., On Duty Outside the Archdiocese
Puglisi, Robert, On Duty Outside the Archdiocese
Puliatte, James, Immaculate Conception, Norwood
Quintana, Restituto, St. Michael's, Newark
Ramos-Villeda, Ramon, Our Lady of Good Counsel, Newark
Ravelo, Daniel, St. Michael's, Newark
Raymundo, Ranulfo, Sacred Heart, Bloomfield
Rehse, Jeremiah, St. Paul, Ramsey
Restivo, Louis, On Duty Outside the Archdiocese
Reyes, Jesus, Assumption/All Saints, Jersey City
Reyes, Jose, On Duty Outside the Archdiocese
Reyes, Modesto, On Duty Outside the Archdiocese
Reyes, Victor, St. Leo, Irvington
Riccio, Dominick, Our Lady of Mount Virgin, Garfield
Rice, George F., Our Lady of Mercy, Park Ridge
Rivera, Oscar, Our Lady of Good Counsel, Newark
Rivera, Pedro, Leave of Absence
Roccanova, Rocco, Inactive
Rodack, Stephen, Inactive
Rodriguez, Gustavo, On Duty Outside the Archdiocese
Rodriguez, Jose A., St. Thomas Aquinas, Newark
Rodriguez, Justo, St. Rocco, Newark
Rodriguez, Vicente, St. Augustine's, Newark
Roig, Julio, St. Peter, Belleville
Rolon, Cristobal, On Duty Outside the Archdiocese
Romero, Alberto, St. Joseph of the Palisades, West New York
Rosado, Jose F., Immaculate Conception, Elizabeth
Ross, George A., St. John the Apostle, Linden
Salerno, Philip, St. Philip, Saddle Brook
Sanderson, Raymond, St. Andrew's, Bayonne
Savo, Ralph, St. Vincent, Bayonne
Schneider, Paul, (Retired)
Serzan, Vincent C., St. Michael's, Lyndhurst
Shea, Raymond, On Duty Outside the Archdiocese
Shelhamer, William, On Duty Outside the Archdiocese
Simonelli, Nicholas, St. Francis, Ridgefield Park
Somma, Alfred P., On Duty Outside the Archdiocese
Soto, Anibal, Bergen County Jail, Hackensack

Stanecki, Walter J., On Duty Outside the Archdiocese
Stoehr, George, On Duty Outside the Archdiocese
Stumbar, James P., Little Flower, Berkeley Heights
Suarez, Ibrahim, On Duty Outside the Archdiocese
Suarez, Juan B., St. Cecilia, Kearny
Swider, Charles P., Inactive
Tarabokija, Anton, St. John's, Fairview
Taylor, Michael A., On Duty Outside the Archdiocese
Thomann, Robert V., Mt. Carmel, Ridgewood
Thomson, Robert E., Holy Rosary, Edgewater
Titmas, Richard C., On Duty Outside the Archdiocese
Tizzano, Albert H., St. Thomas, Bloomfield
Torres, Antonio, On Duty Outside the Archdiocese
Toth, William, St. Elizabeth, Wyckoff
Valentin, Carlos, Our Lady of Good Counsel, Newark
Valladares, Guillermo, St. Peter's, Belleville
Vargas, Rafael, St. Michael's Medical Center, Newark
Vega, Alcides, St. Teresa, Summit
Velasco, Asterio, SS. Joseph & Michael, Union City
Velo, Luis, St. Joseph, West Orange
Ventola, Samuel, Northern State Prison, Newark
Vitale, Incoronato M., (Retired)
Vrindten, Joseph G., Ramapo College, Mahwah
Vuolo, Pasquale, Our Lady of the Lake, Verona
Walker, George, On Duty Outside the Archdiocese
Wall, Joseph J., St. Teresa, Summit
Wicks, Ronald, On Duty Outside the Archdiocese
Wilverding, Daniel J., St. Michael, Cranford
Woodruff, Leo A., Holy Name, East Orange
Yandoli, Joseph, St. John, Leonia

INSTITUTIONS LOCATED IN THE ARCHDIOCESE

[A] SEMINARIES, ARCHDIOCESAN

KEARNY. *Redemptoris Mater.* Archdiocesan Missionary Seminary, 672 Passaic Ave., 07032. Tel: 201-997-3220; Fax: 201-997-5552. Revs. Jose Matias Diaz, Rector; Luis P. Gonzalez, Asst. to the Rector; Renato Grasselli, Asst. to the Rector. Priests 4; Students 72.

SOUTH ORANGE. *Immaculate Conception Seminary,* 400 South Orange Ave., 07079. Tel: 973-761-9575; Fax: 973-761-9577.
E-mail: theology@shu.edu
Web site: http://www.shu.edu
Officers of Admin.: Rev. Msgr. Robert T. Sheeran, S.T.D., Pres.; Rev. Msgr. Robert F. Coleman, J.C.D., Rector & Dean; Rev. C. Anthony Ziccardi, S.S.L., Assoc. Dean; Dr. Dianne Traflet, S.T.D., Asst. Dean; Rev. Thomas P. Nydegger, M.Div., Vice Rector & Business Mgr.; Rev. Msgr. Andrew T. Cusack, M.A., M.Div., Ph.D. (BGP), Dir. Formation; Rev. Msgr. James C. Turro, M.A.,S.T.L.,S.S.L.,Ph.D., Library Svcs. & Spiritual Dir.; Patricia Feoranz, Registrar; Dr. Zeni Fox, Ph.D., Dir. Lay Ministry. Full-Time Faculty: Revs. W. Jerome Bracken, C.P., Ph.D.; Joseph R. Chapel, S.T.D.; Anthony J. Figueiredo, S.T.D.; Rev. Msgr. John W. Flesey, S.T.D., (on sabbatical); David R. Foster, Ph.D.; Zeni V. Fox, Ph.D.; Revs. Thomas G. Guarino, S.T.L., S.T.D.; Lawrence B. Porter, S.T.B., S.T.L., M.A., Ph.D.; Boniface Ramsey, O.P., S.T.D., (on leave for service to the Church); John F. Russell, O.Carm., M.A., S.T.L., S.T.D., (on leave for service to the Church); William J. Toth, Ph.D.; Rev. Msgr. Robert J. Wister, S.T.B., S.T.M., D.Eccl.Hist.; Rev. Gerard H. McCarren, S.T.D.

Darlington Fund. Tel: 973-761-9552; Fax: 973761-9577. Development Agency for Immaculate Conception Seminary. Priests 13; Lay Teachers 3; Total Enrollment 205.

Seton Hall University College Seminary, St. Andrew Hall, 07079. Tel: 973-761-9420; Fax: 973-761-9421. Rev. Msgr. Robert T. Sheeran, Pres.; Revs. Martin F. O'Brien; William P. Sheridan, Spiritual Dir. Priests 2; Total Enrollment 27.

[B] COLLEGES AND UNIVERSITIES

CALDWELL. *Caldwell College,* 9 Ryerson Ave., 07006. Tel: 973-618-3000; Fax: 973-618-3600.
E-mail: admissions@caldwell.edu
Web site: www.caldwell.edu
For a complete listing, refer to the Colleges and Universities section.

JERSEY CITY. *Saint Peter's College,* 2641 Kennedy Blvd., 07306-5997. Tel: 201-915-9000; Fax: 201-451-0036.
E-mail: nieves_l@spcvxa.spc.edu
Web site: www.spc.edu
For a complete listing, refer to the Colleges and Universities section.

LODI. *Felician College.* Tel: 201-559-6000; Fax: 201-559-6188.
E-mail: admissions@inet.felician.edu
Web site: www.felician.edu
For a complete listing, refer to the Colleges and Universities section.

SOUTH ORANGE. *Seton Hall University,* (1856) 400 South Orange Ave., 07079. Tel: 973-761-9000; Fax: 973-275-2361.
Web site: shu.edu
For a complete listing, refer to the Colleges and Universities section.

[C] HIGH SCHOOLS, PRIVATE

NEWARK. *St. Benedict's Preparatory School.* (Grades 7-12), 520 Dr. Martin Luther King, Jr. Blvd., 07102-1314. Tel: 973-643-4800; Fax: 973-643-6922.
E-mail: nwkabbey@connectinc.com
Web site: www.sbp.org
Rev. Edwin D. Leahy, O.S.B., Headmaster. Benedictine Monks of Newark Abbey 15; Priests 13; Brothers 2; Sisters 1; Lay Teachers 40; Boys 557.

St. Vincent Academy. (Girls), 228 W. Market St., 07103. Tel: 973-622-1613; Fax: 973-622-1128.
E-mail: sisterjunefavata@ba.dsg.net
Web site: www.svanewark.org
Sr. June Favata, Admin. Dir. Sisters 6; Lay Teachers 23; Students 316.

BAYONNE. *Holy Family Academy,* 239 Ave. A, 07002. Tel: 201-339-7341; Fax: 201-339-9295.
E-mail: hfa@bayonne.net
Web site: www.hfa.bayonne.net
Sisters of St. Joseph of Chestnut Hill, Philadelphia, PA. Sr. Mary Ellen Ford, S.S.J., Prin. Sisters 10; Lay Teachers 19; Girls 245.

Marist High Schoool. (Coed), 1241 Kennedy Blvd., 07002. Tel: 201-437-4544; Fax: 201-437-6013. Marist Brothers. Bros. John Klein, F.M.S., Pres.; Steve Schlitte, F.M.S., Prin. Brothers 7; Sisters 2; Lay Teachers 24; Students 400.

CALDWELL. *Mount St. Dominic Academy.* (Girls), 3 Ryerson Ave., 07006-6196. Tel: 973-226-0660; Fax: 973-226-2693.
E-mail: msda@academy.org
Web site: www.msdacademy.org
Sisters of St. Dominic of Caldwell. Sr. Fran Sullivan, O.P., Prin. Sisters 11; Lay Teachers 32; Girls 278.

DEMAREST. *Academy of the Holy Angels.* (Girls), 315 Hillside Ave., 07627. Tel: 201-768-7822; Fax: 201-768-6933.
E-mail: arnew12100@impresso.com
Web site: www.holyangels.org
Conducted by School Sisters of Notre Dame. Sr. Claire Bonneau, S.S.N.D., Pres. Brothers 1; Sisters 8; Lay Teachers 46; Girls 522.

ELIZABETH. *Benedictine Academy,* 840 N. Broad St., 07208-2508. Tel: 908-352-0670; Fax: 908-352-0698. Benedictine Sisters of Elizabeth, NJ. Adele Kosinski, Prin. Sisters 2; Lay Teachers 19; Girls 175. College Preparatory High School (Girls).

HOBOKEN. *Academy of the Sacred Heart.* (Girls), 713 Washington St., 07030. Tel: 201-659-7139; Fax: 201-659-8027.
E-mail: arnew32102@connectinc.com
Sisters of Charity of St. Elizabeth. Sr. Mary Fallon, S.C., Prin. Sisters 5; Lay Teachers 15; Girls 157.

JERSEY CITY. *Academy of St. Aloysius.* (Girls: Grades 9-12), 2495 John F. Kennedy Memorial Blvd., 07304. Tel: 201-433-8877; Fax: 201-433-8839.
E-mail: arnew32103@connectinc.com
Sisters of Charity of St. Elizabeth. Mrs. Tara Brunt, Prin. Sisters 5; Lay Teachers 20; Students 165.

St. Anthony High School, 175 Eighth St., 07302. Tel: 201-653-5143; Fax: 201-653-8120.
E-mail: www.stanthonys.k12.nj.us
Conducted by Felician Sisters. Sr. Mary Felicia, C.S.S.F., Prin. Brothers 1; Sisters 3; Lay Teachers 24; Students 280.

St. Dominic Academy. (Girls), 2572 John F. Kennedy Memorial Blvd., 07304. Tel: 201-434-5938; Fax: 201-434-2603.
E-mail: stdominicacad@hotmail.com
Web site: www.stdominicacad.com
Dominican Sisters of Caldwell. Sr. Vivien Jennings, O.P., Ph.D. Sisters 9; Lay Teachers 39; Students 532.

St. Peter's Preparatory School, 144 Grand St., 07302. Tel: 201-434-4400; Fax: 201-547-6421.
Web site: www.stpetersprep.org
Revs. Vincent B. Sullivan, S.J., Rector; James F. Keenan, S.J., Pres.; Mr. John R. Raslowsky, Prin.; Mr. Patrick Reidy, Vice Prin.; Mr. James Horan, Vice Pres. External Affairs; Mr. James Collins, Dean of Students; Mr. John M. Corcoran, Treas.; Mr. Kenneth Dandorph, Asst. Prin., Student Affairs; Revs. Charles F.X. Dolan, S.J., Vice Pres. Alumni Affairs; Anthony J. Azzarto, S.J., Chap.; Raymond J. Balduf, S.J., College Admissions; Erwin G. Beck, S.J.; Bro. Ralph Cilia, S.J.; Revs. Robert G. Cregan, S.J.; Daniel A. Degnan, S.J.; James S. Foley, S.J.; Francis J. Hamill, S.J.; James J. Dinneen, S.J.; Francis X. McFarland, S.J.; Bro. Paul J. Harrison, S.J.; Revs. Michael R. Hoag, S.J.; Stephen Katsouros, S.J., Asst. to the Pres.; Thomas F. McManus, S.J.; Thomas V. O'Connor, S.J.; Harold J. Oppido, S.J.; Enrico Raulli, S.J., Res., 220 W. 98th St., Apt. 4E, New York, NY, 10025. In res. Revs. Michael E. Browne, S.J.; D. Michael Flynn, S.J.; Peter F. O'Brien, S.J.; John J. Rohr, S.J.; Bros. Edward P. Sheehy, S.J.; Louis N. Mauro, S.J.; Revs. Edward J. Snyder, S.J.; Joseph T. Watson, S.J.; Bro. Joseph J. Griffin, S.J. Priests 24; Brothers 5; Scholastics 1; Sisters 1; Lay Teachers 61; Students 822.

LODI. *Immaculate Conception High School,* 258 S. Main St., 07644. Tel: 973-773-2400; 2401; Fax: 973-614-0893.
E-mail: arnew12101@impresso.com
Web site: www.ichs.pvt.k12.nj.us
Sr. Annelle Velivis, Ph.D., Prin. Sisters 3; Lay Teachers 19; Girls 212.

ORADELL. *Bergen Catholic.* (Boys), 1040 Oradell Ave., 07649. Tel: 201-261-1844; Fax: 201-599-9507.
E-mail: brmurphy@bergencatholic.org
Web site: www.bergencatholic.org
Congregation of Christian Brothers. Rev. James R. White, Chap.; Bro. Lawrence T. Murphy, C.F.C., Pres.; Mr. Joseph S. Fusco, Prin. Priests 1; Brothers 7; Lay Teachers 46; Boys 801.

RAMSEY. *Don Bosco Preparatory High School for Boys,* 492 N. Franklin Tpke., 07446. Tel: 201-327-8003; Fax: 201-327-3397.
Web site: donboscoprep.org
Salesians of St. John Bosco. Revs. Stephen Shafran, S.D.B., Dir.; Steven Dumais, S.D.B., Coord. of Youth Ministry; John Talamo, S.D.B., Prin.; Brendan K. Kilroy, S.P.S., Guidance Dir.; Peter Sella, S.D.B.; Bros. Kevin Connolly, S.D.B.; Frank Tilton, S.D.B. Priests 5; Brothers 2; Sisters 1; Lay Teachers 48; Students 775.

SOUTH ORANGE. *Marylawn of the Oranges, High School for Girls,* 445 Scotland Rd., 07079. Tel: 973-762-9222.
E-mail: arnew22106@impresso.com
Sisters 4; Lay Teachers 13; Girls 183.

SUMMIT. *Oak Knoll School of the Holy Child Upper School.* (Grades 7-12). (Girls), 44 Blackburn Rd., 07901. Tel: 908-522-8100 (Main); 522-8130; Fax: 908-273-4616.
E-mail: tina.hummerstone@oakknoll.org
Web site: www.oakknoll.org
Conducted by the Sisters of the Holy Child Jesus. Mrs. Bettina Hummestone, Head of School; Mary Ellen Ryan, Prin. Sisters 1; Lay Teachers 39; Students 283.

UPPER MONTCLAIR. *Lacordaire Academy, Secondary Division,* 155 Lorraine Ave., 07043. Tel: 973-744-1156; Fax: 973-783-9521.
Web site: www.lacordaire.net
Sisters of St. Dominic. Sr. Suzanne McCaffrey, O.P. Priests 1; Sisters 5; Lay Teachers 19; Girls 125.

WEST ORANGE. *Seton Hall Preparatory School,* 120 Northfield Ave., 07052. Tel: 973-325-6624; Fax: 973-325-6652.
E-mail: mkelly@shp.org
Web site: www.shp.org
Rev. Msgr. Michael E. Kelly, M.A., Headmaster. Resident Faculty: Revs. Edward G. Bradley, S.T.L., M.A.; Bruce G. Janiga, M.A.; Stephen M. Kilcarr, B.A.; William J. Melillo, M.A., M.Div.; Joseph R. Reilly, S.T.B., S.T.L., B.A.; Joseph F. Wortmann, M.A., S.T.L. Priests 7; Lay Instructors 70; Students 830.

[D] HIGH SCHOOLS, DIOCESAN

CLARK. *Mother Seton (Girls) Regional High School,* Valley Rd., 07066. Tel: 732-382-1952; Fax: 732-382-4725.
E-mail: mseton@bellatlantic.net
Web site: www.motherseton.org
Sisters of Charity of St. Elizabeth. Sr. Regina Martin, S.C., Prin. Sisters 10; Lay Teachers 28; Girls 400.

EAST ORANGE. *Bishop Francis Catholic High School,* 135 Glenwood Ave., 07017. Tel: 973-674-4200; Fax: 973-674-9121.
E-mail: BFEC2@mindspring.com
Web site: bfec.org
Congregation of Christian Brothers. Bros. Howard McKenzie, C.F.C., Prin.; Spencer Tafuri, C.F.C.; James Timoney, C.F.C.; Michael Valdes, C.F.C.; Rev. Dennis Kaelin. Sisters 1; Brothers 4; Lay Teachers 36; Boys 300.

JERSEY CITY. *Hudson Catholic High School,* 790 Bergen Ave., 07306. Tel: 201-332-5970; Fax: 201-332-6373.
E-mail: hudsoncath@aol.com
Web site: http://members.aol.com/hudsoncath/ppl.htm

Brothers of Christian Schools. Bro. Tim Ahern, F.S.C., Prin. Brothers 9; Sisters 2; Lay Teachers 28; Boys 558.

MONTVALE. *St. Joseph Regional High School.* (Boys), 40 Chestnut Ridge Rd., 07645. Tel: 201-391-3300; Fax: 201-391-8073.
Web site: www.saintjosephregional.org
John R. Job, Prin. Brothers 3; Sisters 1; Lay Teachers 31; Boys 451.

PARAMUS. *Paramus Catholic High School.* (Coed), 425 Paramus Rd., 07652. Tel: 201-445-4466; Fax: 201-445-6440.
Web site: www.paramus-catholic.org
James P. Vail, Pres. & Prin. Sisters of Charity of St. Elizabeth. Priests 1; Sisters 2; Lay Teachers 71; Students 1,111.

ROSELLE. *Roselle Catholic High School.* (Coed), Raritan Rd., 07203. Tel: 908-245-2350; Fax: 908-241-3869.
E-mail: rchs3@injersey.com
Web site: www.rosellecatholichs.org
Marist Brothers. Bro. Vincent Damian, F.M.S., Prin. Brothers 7; Sisters 1; Lay Teachers 50; Students 815.

SCOTCH PLAINS. *Union Catholic Regional High School.* (Coed), 1600 Martine Ave., 07076. Tel: 908-889-1600; Fax: 908-889-7867.
E-mail: ucrhs@idt.net
Web site: www.unioncatholic.org
Sr. Percylee Hart, R.S.M., Prin. Priests 1; Sisters 5; Lay Teachers 41; Students 712.

SUMMIT. *The Oratory Catholic Preparatory School.* (Grades 7-12), 1 Beverly Rd., 07901. Tel: 908-273-1084; Fax: 908-273-5505.
E-mail: kmheadmaster@oratoryprep.org
Web site: oratoryprep.org
Revs. F. Kevin Murphy, Headmaster; Nicholas G. Figurelli; John F. Johnston (BRK); Paul R. Manning, Res., 14 Bedford Rd. Tel: 908-273-7563. Priests 4; Lay Teachers 22; Students 219.

WASHINGTON TOWNSHIP. *Immaculate Heart Academy.* (Girls), 500 Van Emburgh Ave., 07676. Tel: 201-445-6800; Fax: 201-445-7416.
E-mail: teachername@ihahs.com
Web site: www.ihahs.com
Apostles of the Sacred Heart. Sr. Ellen Cronan, A.S.C.J., Prin. Sisters 2; Lay Teachers 51; Girls 758.

[E] ELEMENTARY SCHOOLS, PRIVATE

NEWARK. *Link Community School, Inc.*, 139 Livingston St., 07103. Tel: 201-642-0529; 642-8510; Fax: 973-642-1978.
E-mail: linkcs@bellatlantic.net
Dominican Sisters of Caldwell. William Kurtz, Prin. Sisters 1; Lay Teachers 13; Jesuit Volunteer 1; Students 120.

St. Lucy Filippini Academy, 142 Jefferson St., 07105. Tel: 973-344-4806; Fax: 973-344-8424.
E-mail: arnew21118@connectinc.com
Sr. Carolyn Houck, M.P.F., Prin. Sisters 3; Lay Teachers 24; Students 337.

ELIZABETH. *Bender Memorial Academy*, 416 Linden Ave., 07202. Tel: 908-352-4406; Fax: 908-352-7308.
E-mail: sister416@aol.com
Sisters of St. Benedict. Sr. Marie Therese Hayes, O.S.B., Prin. Sisters 2; Lay Teachers 9; Students 200.

Elizabethport Catholic School, 227 Court St., 07206. Tel: 908-351-2188; Fax: 908-353-3878. Students 182.

Lower Campus. (Grades K-5), 261 Fulton St., 07206. Tel: 908-353-3160; Fax: 908-352-3878.

Upper Campus. (Grades 6-8), 227 Court St., 07206. Tel: 908-351-2188; Fax: 908-351-6086. Students 125. Students 125.

JERSEY CITY. *St. Joseph's School for the Blind*, 253 Baldwin Ave., 07306. Tel: 201-653-0578; Fax: 201-653-4087. Mr. Herbert Miller, Admin.; Dennis Cruz, Prin. School for visually impaired, multi-disabled children; non-graded; Early Intervention Program, 5-day Residential Program, Outreach Services. Lay Teachers 10; Students 80.

KEARNY. *Sacred Heart School*, 22 Wilson Ave., 07032. Tel: 201-991-0628; Fax: 201-991-0226. Sisters of the Catholic Apostolate. Sr. M. Leonore Parlati, C.S.A.C., Prin. Sisters 2; Lay Teachers 17; Students 319.

Day Care Center. Tel: 201-991-6600. Mrs. Marjorie Flores, Head Teacher. Lay Teachers 4; Students 47.

LODI. *The Felician School for Exceptional Children*, 260 S. Main St., P.O. Box 530, 07644. Tel: 973-777-5355; Fax: 973-777-0725.
E-mail: FSECINLODI@aol.com
Web site: fsec.org
Sr. Mary Ramona, C.S.S.F., Dir.

Day Program. Capacity 150. Sisters 5; Lay Teachers 21; Children 145.

SUMMIT. *Oak Knoll School of The Holy Child, Lower School.* (Grades K-6). (Coed), 44 Blackburn Rd., 07901. Tel: 908-522-8120; 522-8100 (Main); Fax: 908-598-9757.
E-mail: tina.hummerstone@oakknoll.org
Web site: www.oakknoll.org
Mrs. Bettina Hummerstone, Head of School; Mrs. Joanne L. Ainsworth, Prin.; Mrs. Elizabeth Barclay, Guidance Counselor. Lay Teachers 27; Students 240.

UNION CITY. *Holy Rosary Academy*, 501 15th St., 07087. Tel: 201-864-0332; Fax: 201-864-5586. Sr. M. Gertrude Schiavone, C.S.A.C., Prin. Sisters of the Catholic Apostolate (Pallottine) 6; Lay Teachers 7; Students 230.

St. Francis Academy, 1601 Central Ave., 07087. Tel: 201-863-4112. Missionary Franciscan Sisters of the Immaculate Conception. Sr. Dora Sartino, O.S.F., Prin. Sisters 1; Lay Teachers 8; Students 238.

UPPER MONTCLAIR. *Lacordaire Academy-Elementary Division*, 153 Lorraine Ave., 07043. Tel: 973-746-2660; Fax: 973-783-6804.
E-mail: lacordaire
Web site: www.lacordaireacademy.net
Dominican Sisters of Caldwell. Mrs. Mary Anne Ford, Prin. Lay Teachers 10; Students 135.

[F] CATHEDRAL HEALTHCARE SYSTEM OF ARCHDIOCESE OF NEWARK

NEWARK. *Cathedral Healthcare System, Inc.*, 219 Chestnut St., 07105. Tel: 973-690-3600; Fax: 973-690-3601. Mr. Frank L. Fumai, Pres. & CEO.

Cathedral Health Services, Inc. Tel: 973-690-3600; Fax: 973-690-3601.

St. Michael's Medical Center Division, Newark. Tel: 973-877-5411; Fax: 973-877-5672.

St. James Hospital Division, Newark. Tel: 973-465-2707; Fax: 973-465-2861.

St. Mary's Life Center Inc.-Pope John Paul II Pavilion. Tel: 973-266-3200; Fax: 973-266-3302.

Columbus Hospital - Newark. Tel: 973-268-1475; Fax: 973-268-1523.

Cathedral / Columbus Group, 219 Chestnut St., 07105-1558. Tel: 973-268-1475; Fax: 973-268-1523. Anita Holland, Vice Pres. & Corp. Sec.

[G] GENERAL HOSPITALS

NEWARK. *Cathedral Affiliated Group at Montclair, Inc.*, 219 Chestnut St., 07105-1558
For a complete listing, refer to the Hospitals section.

Cathedral Affiliated Group at Orange, Inc., 219 Chestnut St., 07105-1558
For a complete listing, refer to the Hospitals section.

Catholic Community Services (C.C.S.) Mt. Carmel Guild Hospital, 1160 Raymond Blvd., 07102. Tel: 973-596-4084
For a complete listing, refer to the Hospitals section.

St. James Hospital, 155 Jefferson St., 07105. Tel: 973-589-1300; Fax: 973-465-2861.
E-mail: stjames@cathedralhealthcare.org
For a complete listing, refer to the Hospitals section.

Saint Michael's Medical Center, 268 Dr. Martin Luther King. Jr. Blvd., 07102-9880. Tel: 973-877-5411; Fax: 973-877-5672
For a complete listing, refer to the Hospitals section.

ELIZABETH. *Trinitas Hospital*, Jersey Street Campus, 925 E. Jersey St., 07201. Tel: 908-629-8065; Fax: 908-629-8073.
Web site: www.trinitashospital.com
For a complete listing, refer to the Hospitals section.

MONTCLAIR. *Montclair Community Hospital*, 120 Harrison Ave., 07042
For a complete listing, refer to the Hospitals section.

ORANGE. *Orange Mountain Healthcare, Inc.*, 188 S. Essex Ave., 07050
For a complete listing, refer to the Hospitals section.

Saint Mary Life Center, Inc. - Pope John Paul II Pavilion, 135 S. Center St., 07050. Tel: 973-266-3000; Fax: 973-266-3094
For a complete listing, refer to the Hospitals section.

The Hospital Center at Orange, 188 S. Essex Ave., 07050
For a complete listing, refer to the Hospitals section.

TEANECK. *Holy Name Hospital*, 718 Teaneck Rd., 07666. Tel: 201-833-3000; Fax: 201-833-3230
For a complete listing, refer to the Hospitals section.

[H] HOMES FOR AGED

CALDWELL. *St. Catherine of Siena*, 7 Ryerson Ave., 07006. Tel: 973-226-1577; Fax: 973-226-3977
For a complete listing, refer to the Special Care Facilities section.

CEDAR GROVE. *St. Vincent's Nursing Home*, 315 E. Lindsley Rd., 07009. Tel: 973-754-4800; Fax: 973-746-2362.
E-mail: pintod@sjhmc.org
For a complete listing, refer to the Special Care Facilities section.

JERSEY CITY. *St. Ann's Home for the Aged*, 198 Old Bergen Rd., 07305. Tel: 201-433-0950; Fax: 201-433-6554.
E-mail: paix2@aol.com
For a complete listing, refer to the Special Care Facilities section.

MONTCLAIR. *Mother Seton Residence*, 51 Washington St., 07042. Tel: 973-783-1400; Fax: 973-783-1402
For a complete listing, refer to the Special Care Facilities section.

PARAMUS. *Mount St. Andrew Villa*, 55 W. Midland Ave., 07652. Tel: 201-261-5950
For a complete listing, refer to the Special Care Facilities section.

SADDLE RIVER. *Villa Marie Claire*, 12 W. Saddle River Rd., 07458. Tel: 201-327-1325; Fax: 201-327-6647.
E-mail: vcmoshea@aol.com
For a complete listing, refer to the Special Care Facilities section.

[I] HOMES FOR THE BLIND

JERSEY CITY. *St. Joseph's Home for the Blind*, 537 Pavonia Ave., 07306. Tel: 201-653-8300; Fax: 201-653-7705.
E-mail: sjhb@compuserv.com
For a complete listing, refer to the Special Care Facilities section.

[J] DAY NURSERIES

NEWARK. *Our Lady of Perpetual Help Day Nursery*, 170 Broad St., 07104. Tel: 973-484-3535; Fax: 973-497-2700. Vocationist Sisters. Sisters 5; Lay Teachers 12; Total Staff 18; Children 194.

ELIZABETH. *Immaculate Heart of Mary Nursery, School & Kindergarten*, 205 E. Jersey St., 07206. Tel: 201-354-8388. Sr. Marianna Perrella, M.P.F., Prin. Religious Teachers Filippini 4; Children 111.

JERSEY CITY. *St. Elizabeth's Child Care Center*, 129 Garrison Ave., 07306. Tel: 201-795-1443; Fax: 201-795-4121. Franciscan Sisters of St. Elizabeth. Mother Rose Cosenza, Supr. Sisters 13; Total Staff 32; Children 270.

NUTLEY. *Holy Family Day Nursery and Convent*, 174 Franklin Ave., 07110. Tel: 201-235-1170; Fax: 201-235-1940. Franciscan Sisters of St. Elizabeth. Mother Romilda Chiga, F.S.S.E., Supr. Sisters 8; Children 80.

RAMSEY. *St. Joseph Pre-School*, 372 Wyckoff Ave., 07430. Tel: 201-825-8386. Franciscan Sisters of St. Elizabeth. Sr. Liberina De Pari, Supr. Sisters 4; Children 25.

[K] PROTECTIVE INSTITUTIONS

NEWARK. *Queen of Peace*, 60 Jay St., 07103. Tel: 973-481-9056
For a complete listing, refer to the Special Care Facilities section.

HOBOKEN. *Good Counsel, Inc. (St. Francis Home)*, 303 Madison St., 07030. Tel: 201-798-9059; 795-0637; 800-723-8331 (Hotline); Fax: 201-795-0809.
E-mail: cxbell@aol.com
For a complete listing, refer to the Special Care Facilities section.

JERSEY CITY. *St. Joseph's Home*, 81 York St., 07302. Tel: 201-413-9280
For a complete listing, refer to the Special Care Facilities section.

KEARNY. *New Jersey Boystown*, 499 Belgrove Dr., 07032. Tel: 201-991-3770
For a complete listing, refer to the Special Care Facilities section.

[L] HOMES FOR WOMEN

JERSEY CITY. *St. Mary's Residence for Business and Professional Women*, 240 Washington St., 07302. Tel: 201-432-6289; Fax: 201-451-0952
For a complete listing, refer to the Special Care Facilities section.

[M] PERSONAL PRELATURES

SOUTH ORANGE. *Opus Dei.* Prelature of the Holy Cross and Opus Dei, 170 Montrose Ave., 07079. Tel: 973-763-8397; Fax: 973-762-1794.
Web site: www.opusdei.org
Revs. James W. Albrecht; Thomas J. Lamb.

[N] MONASTERIES AND RESIDENCES OF PRIESTS AND BROTHERS

NEWARK. *Newark Abbey*, 528 Dr. Martin Luther King, Jr. Blvd., 07102. Tel: 973-792-5800; Fax: 973-643-6922.
E-mail: newarkabbey@sbp.org
Web site: www.newarkabbey.org
Rt. Rev. Melvin J. Valvano, O.S.B., Abbot & Pres. American Cassinese Congregation, O.S.B.; Very Rev. Mark M. Payne, O.S.B., Prior; Revs. Matthew S. Wotelko, O.S.B., Supr.; Albert T. Holtz, O.S.B., Novice Master; John T. Browne, O.S.B.; Bro. Maximillian Buonocore, O.S.B.; Revs. Declan J. Cunniff,

O.S.B.; Augustine J. Curley, O.S.B.; Lucien R. Donnelly, O.S.B.; Luke A. Edelen, O.S.B.; Francis Flood, O.S.B.; Theodore J. Howarth, O.S.B.; Edwin D. Leahy, O.S.B.; Bro. Thomas R. Lee, O.S.B.; Revs. Malachy M. McPadden, O.S.B.; Emilian Muschette, O.S.B.; Maynard G. Nagengast, O.S.B.; Bro. Gereon J. Reuter, O.S.B.; Revs. Boniface J. Treanor, O.S.B.; Philip J. Waters, O.S.B.; Bro. Francis M. Woodruff, O.S.B., St. Maur Priory, 4615 N. Michigan Rd., Indianapolis, IN, 46208. Tel: 317-925-9095. Very Rev. Charles W. Henry, O.S.B., Prior; Rev. Bernardin J. Patterson, O.S.B.; Bros. Francis Dachs, O.S.B.; Mark Hayden, O.S.B.; Jerome Rice, O.S.B.; Anthony Streit, O.S.B. Priests 20; Non-Clerical Brothers 7.

BAYONNE. *Marist Brothers*, Champagnat Residence, 1241 Kennedy Blvd., 07002. Tel: 201-437-4115. Bro. John Dunning, F.M.S., Dir. Brothers 6.

CALDWELL. *The Rev. Msgr. James F. Kelley Residence for Retired Priests*, 247 Bloomfield Ave., 07006. Tel: 973-364-1121; Fax: 973-364-9873.
E-mail: rcan445@intac.com
Mrs. Joan Stevens, Admin.; Rev. Msgr. Emmanuel M. Capozzelli; Rev. Msgr. Aloysius J. Welsh; Revs. Matthew Ayamanthil; Leo O. Farley; Joseph A. Frank; Robert G. Gibney; George L. Mader, Dir.; Vincent J. Quinn.

CLIFFSIDE PARK. *St. Patrick's Missionary Society*, 70 Edgewater Rd., 07010. Tel: 201-943-6575; Fax: 201-943-2946.
E-mail: mission@stpatrickfathers.org
Web site: www.stpatrickfathers.org
Revs. James Barry; Brendan K. Kilroy, S.P.S.; Michael Morris; John McLaughlin. Total Staff 4; Total in Residence 4.

EAST ORANGE. *Congregation of Christian Brothers*, Bishop Francis Essex Catholic H.S., 125 Glenwood Ave., 07017. Tel: 973-676-3334. In res. Bros. D. F. McCulloch, Local Leader; H. A. McKenzie; M. B. Ramos; J. C. Timoney; C. M. Valdes. Brothers 5.

EAST RUTHERFORD. *Sacred Heart Friary*, 4 Jersey St., 07073. Tel: 973-778-1915.
E-mail: WGFOFM3@aol.com
Bro. William G. Fitzgerald, O.F.M., Dir. in res. Rev. Brian Linehan, O.F.M. AIDS Residential Ministry of Holy Name Province, Franciscan Friars. Housing for six men with HIV/AIDS.

HOBOKEN. *F.A.I.T.H. Services.*, 307 Willow Ave., 07030. Tel: 201-792-6161; (Brothers Residence) 420-1554. Brothers of the Poor of St. Francis (C.F.P.). Bro. Robert J. Reinke, C.F.P. Total Staff 22; Total Assisted 2,298.

HOHOKUS. *St. Anthony of Padua*, 67 Arbor Dr., P.O. Box 40, 07423. Tel: 201-612-9763; Fax: 201-612-9869. Revs. Daniel Lanahan, O.F.M., Guardian; Brennan Connelly, O.F.M.; Kevin Cronin, O.F.M.; John Kelleher, O.F.M.; Emmet Murphy, O.F.M.

JERSEY CITY. *Brothers of the Christian Schools.* Hudson Catholic Brothers' Residence, 790 Bergen Ave., 07306-4535. Tel: 201-332-0971; Fax: 201-332-6373.
E-mail: hudsoncath@aol.com
Web site: members.aol.com/hudsoncath/pp1.htm
Bro. Raymond Murphy, F.S.C. Brothers 10.

Jesuits of Saint Peter's College, Inc., 50 Glenwood Ave., 07306-4606. Tel: 201-432-6288; Fax: 201-432-7397.
E-mail: novak_j@spc.edu
Revs. Joseph A. Novak, S.J., Rector; Thomas C. Blessin, S.J.; Edward W. Brande, S.J.; John M. Buckley, S.J.; Laurence L. Cassidy, S.J.; James A. Catalano, S.J.; Mark T. DeStephano, S.J.; J. Juan Diaz Vilar, S.J. (Spain); James F. Dolan, S.J.; Martin Doyle, S.J.; Bro. Patrick T. Flanagan, S.J.; Revs. Charles A. Gallagher, S.J.; Edward J. Heavey, S.J.; Robert E. Kennedy, S.J.; James N. Loughran, S.J.; Joseph W. Lux, S.J.; T. Patrick Lynch, S.J.; Donal T. MacVeigh, S.J.; Oscar G. Magnan, S.J.; William F.X. Maher, S.J.; Edmund W. Majewski, S.J.; Robert E. McCarty, S.J.; William A. McKenna, S.J.; Aidan C. McMullen, S.J.; John J. O'Brien, S.J.; John P. Ruane, S.J.; John P. St. George, S.J.; Patrick H. Samway, S.J.; Raymond A. Schroth, S.J.; Thomas L. Sheridan, S.J.; David X. Stump, S.J.; John F. Wrynn, S.J. Total Staff 32; Total in Residence 32.

MONTCLAIR. *Comboni Missionaries of the Heart of Jesus (Verona Fathers)*, 88 High St., P.O. Box 138, 07042-0138. Tel: 973-744-8080; Fax: 973-744-8919.
E-mail: comboninj@igc.apc.org
Revs. Pasquino Panato, M.C.C.J., Supr.; Paul Ewers, M.C.C.J., Bursar; J.M. Carillo, M.C.C.J. Total Staff 5; Total in Residence 3.

MONTVALE. *Xaverian Brothers*, Xaverian Brothers' Residence, 40 Chestnut Ridge Rd., 07645. Tel: 201-391-8071; Fax: 201-391-8073. Brothers 2.

NORTH ARLINGTON. *DeLaSalle Brothers of the Christian Schools*, Christian Brothers' Residence, 200 Ridge Rd., 07031. Tel: 973-991-0235.
E-mail: arnew12103@connectinc.com
Web site: www.qphs.org
Brothers 12.

ORADELL. *Congregation of Christian Brothers*, Bergen Catholic Brothers' Residence, 1040 Oradell Ave., 07649. Tel: 201-261-1816. Brothers 12.

ORANGE. *The Salesian Community*, Don Bosco Residence, 518-B Valley St., 07050. Tel: 973-674-2400; Fax: 973-674-7051.
E-mail: jheusersdb@aol.com
Revs. James Heuser, S.D.B., Dir. & Vice Prov. Tel: 973-674-7055; James Berning, S.D.B., Fin. Admin., Coord Youth Min., Vice Dir.; Clement Cardillo, S.D.B.; Francis Klauder, S.D.B.; Frank Nugent, S.D.B.; Bros. Jorge Barraza, S.D.B.; Donald Caldwell, S.D.B.; Quesnel Delvard, S.D.B.; Thomas DiDomenico, S.D.B.; Sebastin Francis, S.D.B.; Chinh Nguyen, S.D.B.; Tri Duc Nguyen, S.D.B.; Dominic Tran, S.D.B.; Johann Uriate, S.D.B. Total in Residence 20; Candidates 6.

ROSELLE. *Marist Brothers Residence*, Roselle Catholic High School, 1 Raritan Rd., 07203. Tel: 908-245-3574; Fax: 908-620-9507. Brothers 11.

RUTHERFORD. *St. John Vianney Residence for Priests*, 60 Home Ave., 07070. Tel: 201-933-5155; Fax: 201-933-4467. Miss Carol Hubba, Admin.; Rev. Msgr. Edward F. Kavin, Dir. In res. Most Rev. Peter L. Gerety, Archbishop Emeritus; Rev. Msgr. Walter G. Jarvais, P.A.; Rev. Msgr. Thomas G. Madden; Rev. Msgr. Gerard M. Santora; Revs. W. Gordon Byrne; Joseph L. Cassidy; Joseph J. Cestaro; Joseph F. Coda; Joseph Derbyshire; George E. Doherty; Michael Fuino; Charles W.A. Herk; Harold T. Hermanns; Frederick C. Koerner; Robert H. Langdon; John Madden; Carl J. Merzena; Leonard Midowski; Charles O'Connor; Maurice L. O'Keefe; Charles V. Scanlan; Thaddeus F. Zuber. Resident Priests 1; Total in Residence 24; Total Staff 15.

TENAFLY. *Society of African Missions, Provincialate, S.M.A. Fathers*, 23 Bliss Ave., 07670. Tel: 201-567-0450; Fax: 201-541-1280.
E-mail: SMAUSA-C@smafathers.org
Web site: http://www.smafathers.org
Very Rev. Ulick Bourke, S.M.A., Prov. Supr. Tel: 201-567-9085 (Prov. Office); 567-7156 (Fax); Revs. Brendan Darcy, S.M.A., Local Supr.; Daniel Cullen, S.M.A.; Francis Gilfether, S.M.A.; James C. Hickey, S.M.A.; George Landry, S.M.A.; John Francis Murray, S.M.A.; Kevin Scanlan, S.M.A.; James J. McConnell, S.M.A.; James H. Sullivan, S.M.A.; Thomas Wright, S.M.A.; M. Clark Yates, S.M.A.

UNION CITY. *Augustinian Recollects.* Prov. of St. Nicholas of Tolentine. 530 35th St., 07087. Tel: 201-867-6535. Rev. Antonio Lasheras, O.A.R., Supr.

Capuchin Friars - Province of the Sacred Stigmata of St. Francis, P.O. Box 809, 07087. Tel: 201-865-0611; Fax: 201-866-7035.
E-mail: VFortucap@aol.com
Very Rev. Vincent Fortunato, O.F.M.Cap., Prov. Min.; Bro. Kellen Mears, O.F.M.Cap., Vicar Prov.; Very Revs. John Aurilia, O.F.M.Cap., Councillor; Jude Duffy, O.F.M.Cap., Councillor; Prov. Sec.; John LoSasso, O.F.M.Cap., Councillor; Revs. Vincent Fortunato, Dir. Missionary Activity; Paul Daleo, O.F.M.Cap., Dir. Devel.; Margaret Milizzo, Sec.

Congregation of the Passion (Passionists)-St. Michael's Residence, 526 Monastery Pl., 07087. Tel: 201-864-0018; Fax: 201-867-8651.
E-mail: hoaglan@mail.idt.com
Web site: www.cptryon.org
Rev. Sebastian Kolinovsky, C.P., Mission Procurator.

Development Office. Tel: 201-867-6400; Fax: 201-867-7596. John DeGraaf, Dir.

Special Gifts & Special Events. Tel: 201-867-0235; Fax: 201-867-8857. Rev. Paul Wierichs, C.P.; Monica Sharp, Dir. Mgr.

Passionist Press, Inc. Tel: 201-867-6400; Fax: 201-867-8651.
E-mail: crossplace@cpprov.org

"Compassion" Magazine. Tel: 201-867-6400; Fax: 201-864-1337. Revs. Victor Hoagland, C.P., Dir., Editor & Supr. Dir. Tel: 201-864-0018; Xavier Vitacolonna, C.P. Tel: 201-864-0018; Mr. James Fitzgerald, Lay Assoc. Tel: 201-864-0018.

Financial Office. Tel: 201-867-7479; Fax: 201-867-0357. Sr. Mary Ann Tierney, S.C., CFO. Tel: 201-867-6400.

Passionist Archives. Tel: 201-867-6400; Fax: 201-617-7011. Miss Anita Lewis, Archivist. Tel: 201-867-6400.

VERONA. *The Salvatorian Fathers.* (Polish Mission House), 23 Crestmont Rd., 07044. Tel: 973-746-8770; Fax: 973-857-7789.
E-mail: salvatorianfathers@home.com
Web site: www.salvatorianie.pl or www.sds.org
Revs. Majcher Tadeusz, S.D.S., Supr.; Wlodzimierz R. Las, S.D.S., Vice Supr.; Palka Bogdan, S.D.S.; Emil Jarco, S.D.S.; Andrzej Kielkowski, S.D.S.; John L. Kozuch, S.D.S.; Jan J. Mysliwiec, S.D.S.; Grzegorz Szewczyk, S.D.S.; Edward A. Toman, S.D.S.; Andrzej Waszczenko, S.D.S.; Strzadala Wieslaw, S.D.S.; Marek Wiorkiewicz, S.D.S.; Bro. Damian Marek, S.D.S.

WEST ORANGE. *Augustinian Recollects.* Prov. Res., Monastery of St. Cloud, 29 Ridgeway Ave., 07052. Tel: 973-731-0616; Fax: 973-731-1033.
Web site: augustinianrecollects.org
Very Rev. John A. Gruben, O.A.R., Prior Prov.; Revs. Jose Arias, O.A.R. (Mexico); Charles Huse, O.A.R.; Galo Espinoza, O.A.R. (Mexico); Bro. Paul Rodriguez, O.A.R. Priests 4; Brothers 1.

[O] CONVENTS AND RESIDENCES FOR SISTERS

NEWARK. *Hermanas Misioneras del Corazon de Jesus (HMCJ).* Parish Ministry. Sacred Heart Convent, 109 Parker St., 07104. Tel: 973-484-1516; Fax: 973-484-9701. Sr. Josefina Rosario, Supr. Sisters 4.

Missionary Sisters of the Most Blessed Sacrament and Mary Immaculate. Day Care Center. 121 Congress St., 07105. Tel: 973-589-5794; Fax: 973-589-0154. Sr. Guadalupe Grande, Supr. Sisters 5.

Monastery of St. Dominic, 375 13th Ave., 07103-2124. Tel: 973-622-6622; Fax: 973-624-8998. Dominican Nuns of the Order of Preachers (Cloistered). Sisters 15.

St. Michael's Convent, 182 Broadway, 07104. Tel: 978-497-0614 (Convent); 482-7400 (School); Fax: 978-497-0486 (Convent); 482-1433 (School, Ext.).
E-mail: stfnewark@sigmaweb.net
Confraternity School of Religion; Lay Apostolate; Home Visiting; Elementary Teachers. Sisters of Charity of Ottawa 3; Sisters of St. Martha 2.

Sister Servants of the Merciful Redeemer, 5 Reynolds Pl., 07106. Tel: 973-761-9570. Sr. Andrea D'Angiolillo.

Sisters of Our Lady of Mercy. Mercederian Missionaries from Barcelona (Spain), 16 Longfellow Ave., 07106. Tel: 201-399-7322. Sisters of Our Lady of Mercy.

Sisters of St. Joseph of Chestnut Hill, Thea House, 39 Bleeker St., 07102. Tel: 201-622-7056. Total in Residence 4.

Vocationist Sisters, 172 Broad St., 07104. Tel: 973-484-3535; Fax: 973-484-2526. (Our Lady of Perpetual Help Center). Perpetual Help Day Nursery. Sisters 6; Total Assisted 194; Total Staff 21.

CALDWELL. *Motherhouse and Novitiate of Sisters of St. Dominic*, 1 Ryerson Ave., 07006. Tel: 973-403-3331; Fax: 973-228-9611.
E-mail: foloky@hotmail.com
Web site: www.caldwellop.org
Sr. Joan Doyle, Prioress. Sisters in Community 203; Sisters in Diocese 164.

ELIZABETH. *Little Servant Sisters of the Immaculate Conception (L.S.I.C.)*, St. Hedwig's School, 717 Polonia Ave., 07202. Tel: 908-355-8409. Sisters 4.

St. Walburga Monastery, 851 N. Broad St., 07208-2593. Tel: 908-352-4278; Fax: 908-352-6331.
E-mail: Bensisnj@aol.com
Web site: www.catholic-forum.com/bensisnj
Benedictine Sisters of Elizabeth, NJ. Sr. Louise Garley, O.S.B., Prioress. Sisters In Archdiocese 57; Professed Sisters 66.

ENGLEWOOD CLIFFS. *St. Joseph Province Shalom Center*, 399 Hudson Terrace, 07632. Tel: 201-568-6348; Fax: 201-568-3764.
Web site: www.csjp.org/sjp
Congregation of Sisters of St. Joseph of Peace. Sr. Mary Rattigan, C.S.J.P., Prov. Leader; Sr. Nora Molyneux, C.S.J.P., Asst. Province Leader; Sr. Theresette Hunting, C.S.J.P., Archivist. Sisters in Community 150. Provincial Office for St. Joseph's Province of the Sisters of St. Joseph of Peace.

St. Ann's Home for the Aged. Tel: 201-433-0950; Fax: 201-433-6554. Total Staff 183; Total in Residence 116.

St. Ann Day Care. Tel: 201-433-0950; Fax: 201-985-9638. Staff 9; Adults 50.

St. Joseph Home for the Blind. Tel: 201-653-8300; Fax: 201-963-4346. Total Staff 95; Total in Residence 129.

St. Joseph School for the Blind. Tel: 201-653-0578; Fax: 201-653-4087. Total Staff 99; Total in Residence 50.

St. Joseph Home. Tel: 201-413-9280. Total Staff 13; Total in Residence 64.

St. Mary's Residence. Tel: 201-432-6289. Total Staff 7; Total in Residence 38.

Villa Marie Claire. Tel: 201-327-1325; Fax: 201-327-6647. Total Staff 10; Total in Residence 29.

Nurturing Place Day Care. Child Development Center. Tel: 201-413-1982. Staff 15; Children 78.

St. Michael Villa, 399 Hudson Ter., 07632. Tel: 201-871-1620; Fax: 201-871-7313. Sisters of St. Joseph of Peace. Sr. Cecilia King, C.S.J.P., Admin.; Rev. Walter Cron, Chap. Sisters 44; Total Staff 48; Total in Residence 44. Senior Sisters Residence and Infirmary for St. Joseph Province.

FORT LEE. *Holy Trinity Convent*, 199 Myrtle Ave., 07024. Tel: 201-944-2911. Sisters 24.

IRVINGTON. *Immaculate Conception Convent*, 121 Myrtie Ave., 07111. Tel: 201-374-6397. Augustinian Recollect Sisters (Cloistered) 10.

JERSEY CITY. *Holy Rosary Convent*, 189 Brunswick St., 07302. Religious Teachers of St. Lucy Filippini 9.

Religious Institute of Our Lady of Mercy of Barcelona (Spain), 320 Whiton St., 07304. Tel: 201-451-0453. Sr. Maria Luz Palomino, R.M.M.

St. Nicholas Convent, 115 Ferry St., 07307. Tel: 201-659-5644. Sr. Mary Mark Smith, S.C.C., Supr.

Servants of the Gospel of Life, S.G.L., 19 Gautier Ave., 07306. Tel: 201-333-2443. Sr. Diane Carollo.

Sisters of St. Joseph of Peace, 25 Reservoir Ave., 07307. Tel: 201-656-7928.

KEARNY. *Our Lady of Sorrows Convent*, 55 Ivy St., 07032. Tel: 973-991-7983. Sisters of St. Francis of the Providence of God. Sr. Alma Pukel, O.S.F. Total in Residence 3.

LODI. *Immaculate Conception Convent*, 260 S. Main St., 07644-2196. Tel: 973-473-7447; Fax: 973-473-7126.
E-mail: CSSF@inet.felician.edu
Web site: http://www.felician.edu/CSSF.htm
Sr. Mary Antonelle Chunka, C.S.S.F. Chaplains: Revs. Sebastian Kus, O.F.M.; Damian Colicchio. Sisters in Community 223; Professed Sisters 223. Provincial House, Novitiate and Infirmary of the Felician Sisters.

PLAINFIELD. *Contemplative Convent of the Missionaries of Charity*, 513 Liberty St., 07060. Tel: 908-754-1978. Total in Residence 13.

SCOTCH PLAINS. *Union Catholic Convent*, 1600 Martine Ave., 07076. Tel: 908-889-5813. Sisters of Mercy of New Jersey (R.S.M.) and Sisters of St. Joseph (S.S.J.). Total in Residence 7.

SOUTH ORANGE. *Marylawn of the Oranges Convent*, 425 Scotland Rd., 07079. Tel: 973-762-7218; Fax: 973-762-6513. Sisters 10.

SPRINGFIELD. *St. James Convent*, 35 S. Springfield Ave., 07081. Tel: 973-376-7596. Sisters of St. Joseph, Chestnut Hill, Philadelphia. Total in Residence 9.

SUMMIT. *Monastery of Our Lady of the Rosary*, Morris Ave. & Springfield Ave., 07901. Tel: 908-273-1228; Fax: 908-273-6511.
E-mail: nunsopsummit@att.net
Web site: www.op.org/nunsopsummit
Sr. Mary Joseph Fox, O.P., Vicaress. Legal Title: *Monastery of Our Lady of the Rosary, Dominican Nuns of the Perpetual Adoration and Perpetual Rosary*. Professed Sisters 18.

TENAFLY. *Convent of Our Lady of the Angels*, 253 Knickerbocker Rd., 07670. Tel: 201-568-2171; Fax: 201-568-2352.
E-mail: OLAMarion@aol.com
Missionary Franciscan Sisters of the Immaculate Conception. Sr. Marion Morrissey, M.F.I.C., Supr. Sisters 63.
Attended by Carmelite Fathers from Tenafly.

UNION CITY. *Holy Rosary Convent*, 1514 Central Ave., 07087. Tel: 201-617-4638; Fax: 201-617-4366. Sisters of the Catholic Apostolate (Pallotines). Sr. Patricia Gatti, C.S.A.C. Sisters 7.

Monastery of the Dominican Nuns of the Perpetual Rosary. (Contemplative), 14th St. and West St., 07087-3199. Mother Mary Clare, O.O., Prioress. Professed Sisters 8; Aspirants 2; Total Staff 2; Total in Residence 10.

[P] RETREAT HOUSES

MAHWAH. *Carmel Retreat House*, 1071 Ramapo Valley Rd., 07430. Tel: 201-327-7090; Fax: 201-327-9133. Carmelite Community and House of Prayer. Retreats (groups, directed, private), Days of prayer, recollection for priests, religious and laity. Revs. David Simpson, O.Carm., Dir.; Kurt Holderied, O.Carm.; Michael Wastag, O.Carm., Prior. Priests 3; Sisters 1; Total Staff 9; Total in Residence 3.

[Q] CAMPUS MINISTRY

NEWARK. *Archdiocesan Campus Ministry*, 45 Bleeker St., 07102. Tel: 973-642-1613; Fax: 973-642-2601.
E-mail: newmanctr@aol.com
Web site: www.catholiccampusministry.org
Rev. John B. Baron, Ph.D., Dir. Total Staff 2.

Essex County College, Rutgers University/Newark, NJIT, 45 Bleeker St., 07102. Tel: 973-642-1613; Fax: 973-642-2601.
E-mail: newmanctr@aol.com
Web site: www.catholiccampusministry.org
Rev. John D. Dennehy, Campus Min. & Chap. Legal Title: *Essex County College, Rutgers University/Newark Campus, New Jersey Institute of Technology*. Total Staff 3.

BLOOMFIELD. *Bloomfield College*, 12 Austin Pl., 07003. Tel: 201-748-9000; 973-484-5678 (Rectory). Rev. James J. Reilly, Chap. & Campus Min.

CRANFORD. *Union County College*, 1033 Springfield Ave., 07016. Tel: 908-709-7092. Rev. James J. Reilly, Campus Min., Res. Holy Cross, 16 Church Sq., Harrison, 07029.

HOBOKEN. *Stevens Institute of Technology*, Castle Point on the Hudson, 07030. Tel: 201-963-4324; Fax: 201-659-5062. Rev. Kenneth J. Herbster, Campus Min. & Chap.; Debra Sheridan, Campus Min. Total Staff 1.

JERSEY CITY. *Jersey City State College*, 2039 Kennedy Blvd., 07305. Tel: 201-963-4324.

MAHWAH. *Ramapo College*, 505 Ramapo Valley Rd., Room SC207, 07430. Tel: 201-825-9693. Rev. Donald E. Blumenfeld, Chap. & Campus Min.; Deacon Joseph Vrindten, Campus Min. Total Staff 2; Students 4,700.

TEANECK. *Fairleigh Dickinson Univ.-Teaneck Campus*, 1000 River Rd., 07666. Tel: 201-692-2406; Fax: 201-799-8842. Rev. John B. Baron, Ph.D., Campus Min. Total Staff 1.

UNION. *Kean University*, Catholic Campus Ministry, Green Ln., 1000 Morris Ave., 07083-7131. Tel: 908-629-7106; Fax: 201-985-0918.
E-mail: padrealex@yahoo.com
Rev. Alexander M. Santora, Campus Min.

UPPER MONTCLAIR. *Montclair State University*, Newman Catholic Center, 894 Valley Rd., 07043-2116. Tel: 973-746-2323; Fax: 973-783-3313.
E-mail: berner@mail.montclair.edu or vingesm@mail.montclair.edu
Rev. Albert J. Berner, B.A., S.T.B., M.A., Campus Min. & Chap.; Mrs. Mary Lou Vinges, Admin. Asst. Total Staff 2.

[R] SHRINES

KEARNY. *Eucharistic Shrine of the Adorable Face of Jesus*, 672 Passaic Ave., 07032-1305. Tel: 201-997-6173; Fax: 201-997-1270.

[S] MISCELLANEOUS LISTINGS

NEWARK. *CatholiCare, Inc.*, 171 Clifton Ave., P.O. Box 9500, 07104-0500. Tel: 973-497-4002; Fax: 973-497-4018. Most Rev. Paul G. Bootkoski, D.D.

Deacon St. Lawrence Welfare Fund, Office of Permanent Diaconate, 171 Clifton Ave., P.O. Box 9500, 07104-9500. Tel: 973-497-4223; Fax: 973-497-4219.
E-mail: portered@rcan.org

Diaconate Executive Committee, Archdiocesan Center, 171 Clifton Ave., P.O. Box 9500, 07104-9500. Tel: 973-497-4223; Fax: 973-497-4219.
E-mail: portered@rcan.org
Deacon Edward Porter.

New Ark of Hope Foundation, Inc., 1160 Raymond Blvd., 07102. Tel: 973-596-4180. Bro. Benedict Lo-Balbo, Sec.

New Jersey Caritas Corporation, Inc., 171 Clifton Ave., P.O. Box 9500, 07104-0500. Tel: 973-497-4002; Fax: 973-497-4018. Most Rev. Paul G. Bootkoski, D.D.

CCS Holding Corporation, Inc. Catholic Community Services (See Curia Section, Vicariate for Human Services). Tel: 973-596-3835; Fax: 973-596-3836.

Domus Corporation, Inc., 494 Broad St., 07102. Tel: 973-297-1425; Fax: 973-424-9596.

Canaan House, Inc., 1160 Raymond Blvd., 07102. Tel: 973-596-4121; Fax: 973-242-0791.

Sunrise House, 494 Broad St., 07102. Tel: 973-297-1425; Fax: 973-424-9596.

Carmel House of Jersey City, Inc., 494 Broad St., 07102. Tel: 973-297-1425; Fax: 973-424-9596.

BAYONNE. *Marist Brothers Support Trust*, 1241 Kennedy Blvd., 07002. Tel: 201-823-1115; Fax: 201-823-2232. Bros. Stephen Martin, F.M.S.; Benedict Lo Balbo, F.M.S. Congregation of the Marist Brothers, Province of Esopus.

ELIZABETH. *Alexian Brothers of Elizabeth, Inc.*, 655 E. Jersey St., 07206. Tel: 201-351-9000. Congregation of Alexian Brothers, Immaculate Conception Province. Bruce Fisher, Pres. & CEO.

Alexian Brothers of New Jersey, Inc., 655 E. Jersey St., 07206. Parent Corporation of Alexian Brothers of Elizabeth, Inc.

St. Joseph's Social Service Center, 118 Division St., 07201. Tel: 908-352-2989; 352-2966; Fax: 908-354-1433. Sr. Jacinta Fernandes, O.S.B., Dir. Total Staff 5; Total Assisted 4,550.

HOBOKEN. *F.A.I.T.H. Services Inc.*, 307 Willow Ave., 07030. Tel: 201-792-6161. Bro. Robert J. Reinke, C.F.P., Admin.; Sr. Renee Zinciuk, C.S.W., L.C.S.W., Dir. Clinical Svcs. & Referrals for Svcs. Total Staff 22; Total Assisted 2,188. Extends the religious apostolate of charitable services of the Franciscan Sisters of the Poor, a religious congregation of the Roman Catholic Church by fulfilling the specific purposes set forth as follows: To provide community-based case management, education, counseling and other social support services for HIV/AIDS persons, their significant others and caregivers.

JERSEY CITY. *Bon Secours New Jersey Health System*, 25 McWilliams Pl., 07302. Tel: 201-418-1000; Fax: 201-418-2011. Joan Quigley, Vice Pres. External Affairs & Contact Person.

St. Francis Hospital, 25 McWilliams Pl., 07302. Tel: 201-418-1000; Fax: 201-418-2011. Robert S. Chaloner, Pres.; Richard Evans, Vice Pres., Mission; Sr. Mansueta Dolalas, R.V.M., Off. Mgr. Pastoral Care. Chaplains: Revs. Gerard J. Sudol; Wilfred Yeo; Janet Harney, Dir. Pastoral Care. Franciscan Sisters of the Poor 2; Bed Capacity 238; Patients assisted annually 52,000.

St. Mary Hospital. (Franciscan Health System of New Jersey, Inc.), 308 Willow Ave., Hoboken, 07030. Tel: 201-418-1000; Fax: 201-418-1011. Robert S. Chaloner, Pres.; Richard Evans, Vice Pres., Mission; Sr. Mansueta Dolalas, R.V.M., Off. Mgr. Pastoral Care. Chaplains: Rev. Wilfred Yeo; Janet Harney, Dir. Pastoral Care. Franciscan Sisters of the Poor 3; Bed Capacity 328; Patients assisted annually 105,000.

St. Patrick's Housing Corp., 492 Bramhall Ave., 07304. Tel: 201-332-8600. Christopher Garlin, Dir.

KEARNY. *The Family of Nazareth, Inc.*, 672 Passaic Ave., 07032. Tel: 201-997-3220; Fax: 201-997-5552. Fred Canlas, Pres. A foundation to support the work of the Redemptoris Mater Missionary Seminary and for the new evangelization.

LODI.

The Promise Outreach, Inc., 260 S. Main St., 07644. Tel: 201-638-2944.
E-mail: promiseoutreach@yahoo.com
We visit, correspond with, and provide opportunity to teens in programs, institutions and centers for spirituality and other basic needs. Total Staff 15.

MAHWAH. *Paulist Press*, 997 MacArthur Blvd., 07430. Tel: 201-825-7300; Fax: 201-825-8345.
E-mail: paulistp@pipeline.com
Web site: www.paulistpress.com
Revs. Kevin A. Lynch, C.S.P.; Lawrence Boadt, C.S.P.; Joseph J. Scott, C.S.P.; Michael Hunt, C.S.P. Total Staff 80.

ORANGE. *Mee Joo Catholic Digest, Inc.*, 18 Cleveland St., 07050. Tel: 973-672-6650. Rev. Augustin Chang D. Park.

Salesians of Don Bosco, S.D.B., Don Bosco Residence, 518-B Valley St., 07050. Tel: 973-674-2400; Fax: 973-674-7051.
E-mail: salres@aol.com
Very Rev. James Heuser, S.D.B., Vice Prov.; Revs. James Berning, S.D.B.; Francis Klauder, S.D.B.; Frank Nugent, S.D.B.; Mario Balbi, S.D.B.; Bros. Jorge Barraza, S.D.B.; Donald Caldwell, S.D.B.; Dominic Danh Tran, S.D.B.; Jean Quesnal Delvard, S.D.B.; Tom DiDomenico, S.D.B.; Sebastian Francis, S.D.B.; Chinh Nguyen, S.D.B.; Tri Duc Nguyen, S.D.B.; Johann Uriarte, S.D.B. Total in Residence 20.

PLAINFIELD. *RENEW International*, 1232 George St., 07062-1717. Tel: 908-769-5400; Fax: 908-769-5660. Rev. Msgr. Thomas A. Kleissler, Dir. Coordinators: Sr. Cheryl Erb, R.S.M., Worldwide RENEW; Sr. Paticia Crowley, O.P., N. American Renew; Sr. Mary McGuinness, O.P., Small Community Resources; Sr. Margarita Castaneda, C.N.D.; Sr. Maria Iglesias, S.C., Hispanic Renew.
RENEW International Service Team: Sr. Louise Alff, F.M.D.C.; Sr. Katherine Andrews; Dr. Irma Chavez; Sr. Maureen Colleary, F.S.P.; Rev. Jack Farley, S.V.D.; Jerome Herauf; Dr. Robert Howlett; Greg Kremer; Rev. Msgr. John F. McDermott; C. William Reilly; Sr. Beth Taylor, C.S.J.P.; Sr. Dot Urban, S.S.J.; Sr. Alice Yohe, S.S.J., Administrative Asst.; Debi Donnelly, Office Mgr.

RUTHERFORD. *The Community of God's Love*, 70 W. Passaic Ave., 07070. Tel: 201-935-0344; Fax: 201-804-8279.
E-mail: theCGL@aol.com
Catholic Charismatic Community. Rev. P. Latronico, Chap.; Leslie T. Williams, Community Dir.

SOUTH ORANGE. *The Pallottines of South Orange, Inc.*, 204 Raymond Ave., 07079-2305. Tel: 973-763-5591. Bro. Francis Meo, S.A.C., Supr.

Salesians of Don Bosco, Salesians House, 315 Self Pl., 07079. Tel: 973-761-4475; Fax: 973-763-9330.
E-mail: salvoc@aol.com
Offices of Vocation and Youth Ministry. Tel: 973-761-0102; Fax: 973-763-9330.
E-mail: salvoc@aol.com
Bro. Emile Dube, S.D.B., Vocation Dir.; Prov. Councillor for Youth Ministry; Rev. Dennis Kelleher, S.D.B. Total in Residence 2.

U.S. Catholic China Bureau, Seton Hall University, 07079-2689. Tel: 973-763-1131; Fax: 973-763-1543.
E-mail: chinabur@shu.edu
Eugene Theroux, Esq., Chm., Bd. Directors; Sr. Janet Carroll, M.M., Exec. Dir. Exists to foster communication and friendship with the people of China through sharing the values of the Gospel of Jesus Christ. It promotes understanding among American Catholics about the Catholic Church and the sitution of CAtholic communities in China. It fosters re-engagement of the U.S. Catholic Church in a new missionary partnership with the Chatholic Church in China. USCCB publishes the "China Church Quarterly", sponsors National Catholic China Conference, religious study tours to China and other activities to sustain a shared commitment to mission with the Catholic Church in China. Total Staff 2.

TEANECK. *Holy Name Health Care Foundation,* 718 Teaneck Rd., 07666. Tel: 201-833-3187; Fax: 201-227-6230.
Web site: www.holyname.org
Sisters of St. Joseph of Peace. Michael Maron, Pres.

UNION. *The Association of St. Philomena's Helpers to the Suffering & Poor,* P.O. Box 393, 07083-0393. Tel: 908-851-7205; Fax: 908-687-4209. Rev. George M. Keating, Spiritual Mod.

UNION CITY. *Park Performing Arts, Inc.* (Home of America's oldest Passion Play), 560 32nd St., 07087. Tel: 201-865-6980; Fax: 201-865-5339.
E-mail: passnplay@aol.com
Web site: www.passionplayusa.org
Rev. Kevin P. Ashe, Exec. Dir. Total Staff 7.

WATCHUNG. *Ministry Resource Center for Women Religious,* 1645 Hwy. 22, 07060-6587. Tel: 908-756-0994, Ext. 4016; Fax: 908-754-0164.
E-mail: ministrc@webspan.net
Web site: www.ministryconnect.org
Sr. Bernadette Dougherty, S.S.J., Dir. Total Staff 1; Total Assisted 240.

RELIGIOUS INSTITUTES OF MEN REPRESENTED IN THE ARCHDIOCESE

For further details refer to the corresponding bracketed number in the Religious Institutes of Men or Women section.

[0100]—*Adorno Fathers.*—C.R.M.
[0200]—*Benedictine Monks.* (Newark Abbey; St. Mary Abbey).—O.S.B.
[0330]—*Brothers of Christian Schools.* (Baltimore Prov.; New York Prov.).—F.S.C.
[1350]—*Brothers of St. Francis Xavier.*—C.F.X.
[0460]—*Brothers of the Poor of St. Francis.*—C.F.P.
[0470]—*The Capuchin Friars.* (Prov. of the Stigmata; Prov. of St. Mary).—O.F.M.Cap.
[0270]—*Carmelite Fathers & Brothers.* (American Prov.).—O.Carm.
[0380]—*Comboni Missionaries of the Heart of Jesus (Verona).*—M.C.C.J.
[0310]—*Congregation of Christian Brothers.*—C.F.C.
[1000]—*Congregation of the Passion.* (Eastern Prov.).—C.P.
[0480]—*Conventual Franciscans.*—O.F.M.Conv.
[0520]—*Franciscan Friars.* (Prov. of Most Holy Name; Prov. of the Assumption).—O.F.M.
[0530]—*Franciscan Friars of the Atonement.*—S.A.
[0690]—*Jesuit Fathers and Brothers.* (Prov. of New York).—S.J.
[0770]—*The Marist Brothers.*—F.M.S.
[1210]—*Missionaries of St. Charles (Scalabrinians).*—C.S.
[0840]—*Missionary Servants of the Most Holy Trinity.*—S.T.
[0150]—*Oder of the Augustinian Recollects.* (Prov. of St. Nicholas of Tolentine).—O.A.R.
[0430]—*Order of Preachers-Dominicans.* (Prov. of St. Joseph, Eastern Dominican Prov.).—O.P.
[0150]—*Order of the Augustinian Recollects(Prov. of St. Augustine).*—O.A.R.
[1030]—*Paulist Fathers.*—C.S.P.
[]—*Province of the Immaculate Conception.*
[1070]—*Redemptorist Fathers*(Byzantine Ukrainians).—C.Ss.R.
[1170]—*St. Patrick Missionary Society.*—S.P.S.
[1190]—*Salesians of Don Bosco.*—S.D.B.
[0110]—*Society of African Missions.*—S.M.A.
[0990]—*Society of the Catholic Apostolate.* (Prov. of the Immaculate Conception).—S.A.C.
[1200]—*Society of the Divine Savior.*—S.D.S.
[0560]—*Third Order Regular of Saint Francis.* (U.S.A. Commissarate of the Spanish Prov.).—T.O.R.
[]—*Union Lumen Dei.*—L.D.
[1340]—*Vocationist Fathers.*—S.D.V.

RELIGIOUS INSTITUTES OF WOMEN REPRESENTED IN THE ARCHDIOCESE

[0100]—*Adorers of the Blood of Christ.*—A.S.C.
[0130]—*Apostles of the Sacred Heart of Jesus.*—A.S.C.J.
[]—*Augustinian Recollect Sisters.* Mexico.—O.A.R.
[0230]—*Benedictine Sisters of Pontifical Jurisdiction-Newark.* (Benedictine Sisters of Baltimore; Benedictine Sisters of Elizabeth).—O.S.B.
[0760]—*Daughters of Charity of St. Vincent de Paul.* (North East Prov.).—D.C.
[0790]—*Daughters of Divine Charity.*—F.D.C.
[0850]—*Daughters of Mary Help of Christians.*—F.M.A.
[]—*Daughters of Mary, Mothers of Mercy.* (Nigeria).—D.M.M.M.
[1050]—*Dominican Contemplative Nuns (Cloistered).*—O.P.
[1070-11]—*Dominican Sisters.* (Sparkill, NY).—O.P.
[1070-15]—*Dominican Sisters.* (Blauvelt, NY).—O.P.
[1070-18]—*Dominican Sisters.* (Caldwell, NJ).—O.P.
[1070-06]—*Dominican Sisters of Hope.* (Newburgh, NY).—O.P.
[1070-09]—*Dominican Sisters of St. Catherine of Siena (Philippines).*
[1170]—*Felician Sisters.*—C.S.S.F.
[1400]—*Franciscan Missionary Sister of the Sacred Heart.*—F.M.S.C.
[1180]—*Franciscan Sisters of Allegany, New York.*—O.S.F.
[1425]—*Franciscan Sisters of Peace.*—F.S.P.
[1420]—*Franciscan Sisters of Ringwood.*—F.S.R.
[1460]—*Franciscan Sisters of St. Elizabeth.*—F.S.S.E.
[1190]—*Franciscan Sisters of the Atonement.*—S.A.
[]—*Franciscan Sisters of the Immaculate Heart of Mary (India).*—F.I.H.M.
[1440]—*Franciscan Sisters of the Poor.*—S.F.P.
[1240]—*Grey Nuns of the Sacred Heart.*—G.N.S.H.
[]—*Hermanas Missionaras del Corazon de Jesus.* (Dominican Republic).—H.M.C.J.
[3790]—*Institute of the Sisters of St. Dorothy.*—S.S.D.
[2300]—*Little Servant Sisters of the Immaculate Conception.*—L.S.I.C.
[2470]—*Maryknoll Sisters of St. Dominic.*—M.M.
[]—*Mercedarian Sisters (Missionary Sisters of Our Lady of Mercy).*—R.M.M.
[2710]—*Missionaries of Charity.*—M.C.
[1360]—*Missionary Franciscan Sisters of the Immaculate Conception.*—M.F.I.C.
[2790]—*Missionary Servants of the Most Blessed Trinity.*—M.S.B.T.
[2760]—*Missionary Sisters of the Immaculate Conception of the Mother of God.*—S.M.I.C.
[2780]—*Missionary Sisters of the Most Blessed Sacrament and Mary Immaculate.*—M.SS.M.I.
[]—*Religious of the Virgin Mary (Philippines).*—R.V.M.
[3430]—*Religious Teachers Filippini.*—M.P.F.
[2970]—*School Sisters of Notre Dame.*—S.S.N.D.
[1700]—*School Sisters of the Third Order of St. Francis.* (Bethlehem, PA).—O.S.F.
[]—*Sister Servants of the Merciful Redeemer.*
[0540]—*Sisters of Charity of Ottawa.*—S.C.O.
[0590]—*Sisters of Charity of Saint Elizabeth, Convent Station.*—S.C.
[0660]—*Sisters of Christian Charity.*—S.C.C.
[2575]—*Sisters of Mercy of the Americas.* (New Jersey).—R.S.M.
[]—*Sisters of Our Lady of Perpetual Help (Korea).*—S.O.L.P.H.
[1620]—*Sisters of Saint Francis of Millvale, Pennsylvania.*—O.S.F.
[3893]—*Sisters of Saint Joseph of Chestnut Hill, Philadelphia.*—S.S.J.
[3730]—*Sisters of St. Basil the Great.*—O.S.B.M.
[1650]— *The Sisters of St. Francis of Philadelphia.*—O.S.F.
[3820]—*Sisters of St. John the Baptist.*—C.S.J.B.
[3890]—*Sisters of St. Joseph of Peace.*—C.S.J.P.
[3930]—*Sisters of St. Joseph of the Third Order of St. Francis.*—S.S.J.-T.O.S.F.
[3140]—*Sisters of the Catholic Apostolate (Pallottine).*—C.S.A.C.
[2980]—*Sisters of the Congregation of Notre Dame.*—C.N.D.
[1490]—*Sisters of the Third Franciscan Order.*—O.S.F.
[3610]—*Sisters Servants of Mary Immaculate.*—S.S.M.I.
[2160]—*Sisters, Servants of the Immaculate Heart of Mary (Scranton).*—I.H.M.
[4060]—*Society of the Holy Child Jesus.*—S.H.C.J.
[]—*Union Lumen Dei.*—L.D.
[4210]—*Vocationist Sisters.*—S.D.V.

ARCHDIOCESAN CEMETERIES

COLONIA. *St. Gertrude.*
DARLINGTON. *Maryrest.*
EAST HANOVER. *Gate of Heaven.*
EAST ORANGE. *Holy Sepulchre.*
St. Mary.
FRANKLIN LAKES. *Christ the King.*
JERSEY CITY. *Holy Name.*
Saint Peter.
NORTH ARLINGTON. *Holy Cross.*
RIVER VALE. *St. Andrew.*

PAROCHIAL CEMETERIES

NEWARK. *Mount Olivet.*
BELLEVILLE. *St. Peter's.*
BLOOMFIELD. *Mount Olivet.*
CLARK. *St. Mary's.*
FORT LEE. *Madonna.*
HACKENSACK. *St. Joseph's.*
HO-HO-KUS. *St. Luke's.*
LINDEN. *Mount Calvary.*
LYNDHURST. *St. Joseph's.*
ORANGE. *St. John's.*
PLAINFIELD. *St. Mary's.*
RIVER VALE. *St. Andrew's.*
SHORT HILLS. *St. Rose of Lima.*
SUMMIT. *St. Teresa's.*
TENAFLY. *Mount Carmel.*
UPPER MONTCLAIR. *Immaculate Conception.*

NECROLOGY

✠ Garner, Most Rev. Robert F., D.D., (Retired). —Died Dec. 25, 2000.
† Byrne, Pierce D., (Retired). —Died March 21, 2000.
† Chagas, Virgilio P., (Retired). —Died Jan. 15, 2000.
† Fahy, Rev. Msgr. John J., (Retired). —Died Nov. 18, 2000.
† Fanelli, Rev. Msgr. Eugene A., (Retired). —Died May 9, 2000.
† Field, Rev. Msgr. William N., South Orange, NJ Seton Hall Univ. —Died Dec. 3, 2000.
† Galdon, Richard M., (Retired). —Died June 26, 2000.
† Henry, Thomas J., (Retired). —Died Jan. 17, 2000.
† Hogan, Rev. Msgr. William F., (Retired). —Died May 19, 2000.
† Horgan, John J. —Died May 19, 2000.
† Kaminski, Henry T., (Retired). —Died Aug. 17, 2000.
† Matulis, Albert J., (Retired). —Died Jan. 16, 2000.
† Merlucci, Michael A, Scotch Plains, NJ St. Bartholow. —Died Feb. 5, 2000.
† Piatkowski, Robert J., Springfield, NJ St. James. —Died Nov. 20, 2000.
† Pinho, Antonio M., (Military Chaplain). —Died July 6, 2000.
† Prestera, Vincent, (Retired). —Died April 22, 2000.
† Salomon, Jean Francois, Union City, NJ St. Anthony. —Died Jan. 20, 2000.
† Walsh, Rev. Msgr. Gerard W., (Retired). —Died Nov. 14, 2000.

Archdiocese of New Orleans

(Archidioecesis Novae Aureliae)

Most Reverend

FRANCIS B. SCHULTE, D.D.

Archbishop of New Orleans; ordained May 10, 1952; appointed Titular Bishop of Afufenia and Auxiliary Bishop of Philadelphia June 27, 1981; ordained to the episcopacy August 12, 1981; appointed Sixth Bishop of Wheeling-Charleston June 4, 1985; promoted to Metropolitan See of New Orleans December 13, 1988; installed February 14, 1989. *Office: 7887 Walmsley Ave., New Orleans, LA, 70125-3496.* Tel.: 504-861-9521.

Archdiocesan Administration Building: 7887 Walmsley Ave., New Orleans, LA, 70125-3496. Tel.: 504-861-9521; Fax: 504-866-2906.

Web site address: www.catholic.org/neworleans/

Most Reverend

ALFRED C. HUGHES

Coadjutor Archbishop of New Orleans and Titular See of Massimiana de Bizacena; ordained December 15, 1957; appointed Auxiliary Bishop of Boston July 21, 1981; ordained Auxiliary Bishop of Boston September 14, 1981; appointed Bishop of Baton Rouge September 7, 1993; installed Bishop of Baton Rouge November 4, 1993; appointed Coadjutor Archbishop of New Orleans February 16, 2001.

Most Reverend

PHILIP M. HANNAN, D.D., J.C.D., S.T.L.

Former Archbishop of New Orleans; ordained December 8, 1939; appointed Titular Bishop of Hieropolis and Auxiliary Bishop of Washington June 16, 1956; consecrated August 28, 1956; promoted to Archbishop of New Orleans September 29, 1965; installed October 13, 1965; retired February 14, 1989. *Address correspondence to: 106 Metairie Lawn Dr., Metairie, LA, 70001.* Tel.: 504-840-9898.

Most Reverend

DOMINIC CARMON, S.V.D., D.D., V.G.

Auxiliary Bishop of New Orleans and Titular Bishop of Rusicade; ordained February 2, 1960; appointed December 16, 1992; consecrated February 11, 1993. *Office: P.O. Box 641000, Kenner, LA, 70064-1000.* Tel.: 504-468-1441; Fax: 504-468-3305.

Most Reverend

NICHOLAS D'ANTONIO, O.F.M., D.D.

Retired; ordained June 7, 1942; appointed Prelate Nullius, Ordinary of Olancho, Honduras, C.A. December 31, 1963; consecrated July 25, 1966; appointed Vicar for Spanish-Speaking, New Orleans August 22, 1977; retired July 10, 1991. *Res., 2820 Burdette St., New Orleans, LA, 70125-2596.* Tel.: 504-866-2741.

ESTABLISHED APRIL 25, 1793; ARCHDIOCESE JULY 19, 1850.

Square Miles 4,208.

Comprises the following Parishes of Louisiana: Orleans, St. Bernard, Plaquemines, Jefferson, St. Charles, St. John the Baptist, St. Tammany and Washington.

For legal titles of parishes and archdiocesan institutions, consult the Chancery Office.

STATISTICAL OVERVIEW

Personnel	
Archbishop	1
Retired Archbishops	1
Auxiliary Bishops	1
Retired Bishops	1
Abbots	1
Priests: Diocesan Active in Diocese	160
Priests: Active Outside Diocese	12
Priests: Retired, Sick or Absent	53
Number of Diocesan Priests	225
Religious Priests in Diocese	190
Extern Priests in Diocese	19
Ordinations:	
Diocesan Priests	1
Religious Priests	1
Transitional Deacons	7
Permanent Deacons in Diocese	192
Total Brothers	123
Total Sisters	834
Parishes	
Parishes	146
With Resident Pastor:	
Resident Diocesan Priests	108
Resident Religious Priests	33
Without Resident Pastor:	
Administered by Priests	5
Missions	8
Pastoral Centers	1
Welfare	
Health Care Centers	4
Total Assisted	120,037
Homes for the Aged	25
Total Assisted	3,145
Residential Care of Children	2
Total Assisted	116
Day Care and Extended Day Care Centers	17
Total Assisted	2,234
Specialized Homes	3
Total Assisted	2,362
Special Centers for Social Services	57
Total Assisted	92,643
Residential Care of Disabled	9
Total Assisted	93
Other Institutions	8
Total Assisted	1,320
Educational	
Seminaries, Diocesan	2
Students from This Diocese	31
Students from Other Diocese	194
Seminaries, Religious	3
Students Religious	23
Total Seminarians	54
Colleges and Universities	3
Total Students	10,420
High Schools, Diocesan and Parish	10
Total Students	6,541
High Schools, Private	13
Total Students	9,896
Elementary Schools, Diocesan and Parish	72
Total Students	32,925
Elementary Schools, Private	8
Total Students	1,677
Non-residential Schools for the Disabled	1
Total Students	211
Catechesis/Religious Education:	
High School Students	4,244
Elementary Students	18,275
Total Students Under Catholic Instruction	84,243
Teachers in the Diocese:	
Priests	48
Brothers	36
Sisters	127
Lay Teachers	3,521
Vital Statistics	
Receptions into the Church:	
Infant Baptism Totals	6,784
Adult Baptism Totals	395
Received into Full Communion	335
First Communions	6,125
Confirmations	5,679
Marriages:	
Catholic	1,690
Interfaith	570
Total Marriages	2,260
Deaths	4,332
Total Catholic Population	489,652
Total Population	1,331,561

Former Bishops and Archbishops—Rt. Rev. LUIS PENALVER Y CARDENAS, D.D., cons. in 1793; transferred to Guatemala, in 1801; resigned in 1806; retired to Havana, Cuba; died in Havana, July 17, 1810. Under the administration of the Archbishop of Baltimore from 1805-1815.—Rt. Rev. FRANCIS PORRO, Bishop-elect.—Rt. Rev. LOUIS WILLIAM DUBOURG, S.S., D.D., cons. Sept. 24, 1815; died Archbishop of Besancon, Dec. 1833.—Rt. Rev. JOSEPH ROSATI, D.D., C.M., cons. March 25, 1824; Bishop of Tanagre and coadjutor; transferred to St. Louis, March 20, 1827; died Sept. 25, 1843.—Rt. Rev. LEO DE NECKERE, C.M., D.D., cons. Aug. 4, 1829; died Sept. 4, 1833.—Most Rev. ANTOINE BLANC, first Archbishop; cons. Nov. 22, 1835; Archbishop, July 19, 1850; died June 20, 1860.—Most Rev. JEAN MARIE ODIN, C.M., D.D., cons. Bishop of Claudiopolis and Vicar-Apostolic of Texas, March 6, 1842; transferred to Galveston, 1847; promoted to New Orleans in 1861; died at Ambierle, France, May 25, 1870.—Most Rev. NAPOLEON J. PERCHE, cons. Bishop of Abdera and coadjutor, March 21, 1870; promoted to the See of New Orleans, May 25, 1870; died Dec. 1883.—Most Rev. F. X. LERAY, D.D., cons. Bishop of Natchitoches, April 22, 1877; appt. coadjutor of New Orleans, and Bishop of Janopolis, Oct. 23, 1879; promoted to the See of New Orleans, Dec., 1883; died at Chateaugiron, France, Sept. 23, 1887.—Most Rev. FRANCIS JANSSENS, D.D., cons. Bishop of Natchez, MS, May 1, 1881; promoted to the Archiepiscopal See of New Orleans, Aug. 7, 1888; died June 9, 1897.—Most Rev. PLACIDE LOUIS CHAPELLE, D.D., Apostolic Delegate Extraordinary for Cuba and Puerto Rico; Archbishop of New Orleans; appt. Bishop of Arabissus and Coadjutor of Santa Fe *cum jure successionis,* Aug. 21, 1891; cons. Nov. 1, 1891; promoted to the Titular Archiepiscopal See of Sebaste May 10, 1893; Archbishop of Santa Fe, Jan. 9, 1894; appt. to New Orleans, Dec. 1, 1897; died Aug. 9, 1905.—Most Rev. JAMES H. BLENK, S.M., D.D., appt. Bishop of Puerto Rico, June 12, 1899; cons. July 2, 1899; promoted to the See of New Orleans, April 20, 1906; died April 20, 1917.—Most Rev. JOHN W. SHAW, D.D., appt. Coadjutor Bishop of San Antonio, Feb. 7, 1910; cons. Titular Bishop of Castabala,

April 14, 1910; succeeded to the See of San Antonio, March 11, 1911 made assistant at the Pontifical Throne, Sept., 1916; promoted to the See of New Orleans, Jan. 25, 1918; died Nov. 2, 1934.—Most Rev. JOSEPH FRANCIS RUMMEL, D.D., ord. May 24, 1902; appt. Bishop of Omaha, March 30, 1928; cons. May 29, 1928; appt. Archbishop of New Orleans, Mar. 9, 1935; died Nov. 8, 1964.—His Eminence JOHN CARDINAL CODY, D.D., cons. July 2, 1947; promoted to Coadjutor *cum jure successionis* of New Orleans, Aug. 10, 1961; acceded See, Nov. 8, 1964; transferred to Chicago, June 16, 1965; created Cardinal, June 26, 1967; died April 25, 1982.—Most Rev. PHILIP M. HANNAN, D.D., Archbishop of New Orleans; ord. Dec. 8, 1939; appt. Titular Bishop of Hieropolis and Auxiliary Bishop of Washington, June 16, 1956; cons. Aug. 28, 1956; promoted to Archbishop of New Orleans, Sept. 29, 1965; retired Feb. 14, 1989.

Vicars General—Most Rev. DOMINIC CARMON, S.V.D., *P.O. Box 641000, Kenner, 70064-1000.* Tel: 504-468-1441; Fax: 504-468-3305. Rev. Msgr. THOMAS J. RODI, V.G., *7887 Walmsley Ave., New Orleans, 70118-3496.* Tel: 504-861-6262; Fax: 504-861-6312.

Chancellor and Moderator of the Curia—Rev. Msgr. THOMAS J. RODI, V.G. Tel: 504-861-6262; 861-9521; Fax: 504-861-6312.

Financial and Administrative Services—Mr. JOHN L. ECKHOLDT.

Archdiocesan Administration Building—7887 Walmsley Ave., New Orleans, 70125-3496. Office Hours: Mon.-Fri. 9-5. Tel: 504-861-9521; Fax: 504-866-2906.

Metropolitan Tribunal—7887 Walmsley Ave., New Orleans, 70125-3496. All rogatorial commissions should be sent to this address: c/o; Very Rev. VIEN THE NGUYEN, J.C.L.

Judicial Vicar—Very Rev. VIEN THE NGUYEN, J.C.L.

Adjutant Judicial Vicars—Rev. Msgr. CLINTON J. DOSKEY, J.C.L.; Rev. JOSEPH P. MULLIN, S.M., S.T.L.

Judges—Rev. Msgr. THOMAS J. RODI, V.G., J.D., J.C.L.; Rev. Msgr. L. EARL GAUTHREAUX, J.C.L.; Rev. Msgr. ANDREW TAORMINA, J.D.; Revs. THOMAS E. KINNEY, J.C.L.; GERARD LAPORTE, C.SS.R., J.C.L.; PETER O'GRADY.

Associate Judges—Mr. PETER E. DUFFY, J.D.; Mr. FRANS LABRANCHE, JR., J.D.; Mr. PAUL A. NALTY, J.D.; Mr. PETER C. RIZZO, J.D.

Defensores Vinculi—Very Rev. GERALD L. SEILER, J.C.L.; Revs. CHRISTOPHER H. NALTY, J.C.L.; WILLIAM J. O'DONNELL, J.C.L.; BENJAMIN PIOVAN, M.A.; LEE J. SALOY, M.Div.; Sr. WALDIA A. WARDEN, O.P., J.C.L.

Coordinator, Court of First Instance—Deacon A. DAVID WARRINER.

Coordinator, Court of Second Instance—Sr. WALDIA A. WARDEN, O.P., J.C.L.

Archdiocesan Consultors—Most Rev. DOMINIC CARMON, S.V.D., D.D., V.G.; Rev. Msgr. CLINTON J. DOSKEY; Rev. Msgr. RAY P. HEBERT; Rev. Msgr. CROSBY W. KERN; Very Rev. NEAL W. MCDERMOTT, O.P., V.F.; Rev. Msgr. JOHN P. REYNOLDS; Rev. Msgr. THOMAS J. RODI, V.G.

Deans—Very Rev. MICHAEL P. JACQUES, V.F., Cathedral Deanery I; Very Rev. JAMES A. TARANTINO, V.F., City Park-Gentilly Deanery II; Rev. Msgr. HENRY J. BUGLER, V.F., Uptown Deanery III; Very Rev. PERRY HENRY, C.M., V.F., Inner City Deanery IV; Rev. Msgr. CROSBY W. KERN, V.F., East Jefferson Deanery V; Rev. Msgr. JOHN NGUYEN PHUC, V.F., St. John-St. Charles Deanery VI; Very Rev. MICHAEL B. FRASER, V.F., West Bank Deanery VII; Rev. Msgr. ALLEN J. ROY, V.F., Algiers-Plaquemines Deanery VIII; Very Rev. WARREN L. COOPER, V.F., St. Bernard Deanery IX; Very Rev. ALAN R. WESEMAN, V.F., St. Tammany-Washington Deanery X; Rev. Msgr. T. GASPARD GLASGOW, V.F., New Orleans East Deanery XI.

Archdiocesan Administrative Council—Most Rev. FRANCIS B. SCHULTE, D.D., Chm.; Rev. Msgr. THOMAS J. RODI, V.G., Vice Chm.; Very Rev. GERALD L. SEILER, Sec. Members of the Board: Most Rev. DOMINIC CARMON, S.V.D., V.G.; Very Rev. NEAL W. MCDERMOTT, O.P.; Sr. SUELLEN TENNYSON, M.S.C.; Rev. Msgr. RAY P. HEBERT; Mr. JOHN L. ECKHOLDT; Rev. Msgr. ROGER P. MORIN.

Archdiocesan Pastoral Council—Mr. ALDEN HAGARDORN, Pres.

Priests Council—Most Rev. FRANCIS B. SCHULTE, D.D., Pres.; Rev. CYPRIAN DEVOLD, Chm.

Archdiocesan Finance Council—Most Rev. FRANCIS B. SCHULTE, Chm.; Rev. Msgr. THOMAS J. RODI, V.G., Vice Chm.

Censores Librorum—Very Rev. GERALD L. SEILER, Coord.

Louisiana Catholic Conference—Mr. KIRBY J. DUCOTE, Dir., *3423 Hundred Oaks Ave., Baton Rouge, 70808-1548.* Tel: 225-344-7120; Fax: 225-383-9591.

Office of the Vicar General and Moderator of the Curia

Vicar General and Moderator of the Curia—Rev. Msgr. THOMAS J. RODI, *7887 Walmsley Ave., New Orleans, 70125-3496.* Tel: 504-861-6262; Fax: 504-861-6312.

Archives (Archdiocesan)—Dr. CHARLES E. NOLAN, *1100 Chartres St., New Orleans, 70116-2596.* Tel: 504-529-2651; Fax: 504-529-3075.

Catholic Foundation for the Archdiocese of New Orleans, Inc.—Mr. JOSEPH L. LANGENDERFER, Exec. Dir., *1000 Howard Ave., Ste. 700, New Orleans, 70113-1903.* Tel: 504-596-3045; Fax: 504-596-3068.

Communications—Mr. PETER P. FINNEY, JR., Dir., *1000 Howard Ave., Ste. 400, New Orleans, 70113-1903.* Tel: 504-596-3023; Fax: 504-596-3020.

Development Office—Mr. JOSEPH L. LANGENDERFER, Exec. Dir., *1000 Howard Ave., Ste. 700, New Orleans, 70113-1903.* Tel: 504-596-3045; Fax: 504-596-3068.

Legal Services—Rev. Msgr. THOMAS J. RODI, V.G., Dir. THOMAS A. RAYER; CHARLES I. DENECHAUD, III; OTTO SCHOENFELD; EDWARD DENECHAUD; RICHARD BORDELON, *210 Baronne St., New Orleans, 70112-4100.* Tel: 504-522-4756; Fax: 504-568-0783.

Newspaper—"Clarion Herald", Newspaper of the Archdiocese of New Orleans. Published by Clarion Herald Publishing Co., Inc.; Rev. Msgr. CROSBY W. KERN, Moderator; PETER P. FINNEY, JR., Gen. Mgr. & Exec. Editor, *1000 Howard Ave., Ste. 400, New Orleans, 70113-1903.* Tel: 504-596-3035; Fax: 504-596-3020.

Old Ursuline Convent—Rev. Msgr. ALVIN J. O'REILLY, Admin., *1100 Chartres St., New Orleans, 70116-2596.* Tel: 504-529-3040; Fax: 504-529-2001.

Department of Christian Formation

Executive Director—Very Rev. NEAL W. MCDERMOTT, O.P., *7887 Walmsley Ave., New Orleans, 70125-3496.* Tel: 504-861-8228; Fax: 504-861-6260.

Campus Ministry—Very Rev. NEAL W. MCDERMOTT, O.P., *7887 Walmsley Ave., New Orleans, 70125-3496.* Tel: 504-861-6228; Fax: 504-861-6260.

Catholic Schools Office—Dr. J. RENE COMAN, Supt. Assoc. Superintendents: Mr. VINCENT SCOZZARI; Mr. JOSEPH R. ROSOLINO; Dr. THOMAS BECKER; Mrs. CAROLYN MORVANT; Sr. GRETA JUPITER, S.S.F.; Mr. THOMAS E. MCLAUGHLIN, Finances & Planning; Mr. JOSEPH R. ROSOLINO, Coord. Personnel Svcs.; Sr. MARY HILARY SIMPSON, O.P., Dir. Instrumental Music; Mrs. CAROLYN MORVANT, Dir. Spec. Educ., *7887 Walmsley Ave., New Orleans, 70125-3496.* Tel: 504-861-9521; Fax: 504-861-6260.

Catholic Youth Organization and Youth Ministry Office—MICHAEL PATIN, Dir., *1000 Howard Ave., Ste. 700, New Orleans, 70113-1955.* Tel: 504-525-2699; Fax: 504-525-2122.

Lay Retreats—Rev. H. WILLIAM REED, Coord., Adult Programs, *2545 Bayou Rd., New Orleans, 70119-2398.* Tel: 504-945-3591; Fax: 504-945-3216. Youth Retreats: Contact CYO-Youth Ministry Office, *1000 Howard Ave., Ste. 700, New Orleans, 70113-1955.* Tel: 504-525-2699; Fax: 504-525-2122.

Ministry of Evangelization & Spiritual Renewal—Rev. Msgr. ROBERT I. GUSTE, *1908 Short St., Kenner, 70062-7599.* Tel: 504-464-0361; Fax: 504-465-0930.

Religious Education—Bro. EDWARD KIEFER, S.M., Dir., *7887 Walmsley Ave., New Orleans, 70125-3496.* Tel: 504-861-6270; 861-9521; Fax: 504-866-2906.

Department of Clergy

Executive Director—Rev. Msgr. RAY P. HEBERT, *4401 7th St., Marrero, 70072-2099.* Tel: 504-341-9516; Fax: 504-341-9517.

Continuing Formation for Priests—Rev. JOSE I. LAVASTIDA, *2901 S. Carrollton Ave., New Orleans, 70118-4391.* Tel: 504-866-7426; Fax: 504-866-1301.

Permanent Diaconate—Deacon JAMES W. SWILER, Dir., *7887 Walmsley Ave., New Orleans, 70125-3496.* Tel: 504-861-6265; 861-9521; Fax: 504-866-2906.

Priest Personnel Office—Rev. Msgr. DOUGLAS A. DOUSSAN, Dir.; Rev. Msgr. HENRY H. ENGELBRECHT, Assoc. Dir., *7887 Walmsley Ave., New Orleans, 70125-3496.* Tel: 504-861-6268; Fax: 504-866-2906.

Retired Priests—Rev. Msgr. W. WENDELL SONTHEIMER, Coord., *2724 Whitney Pl., Apt. 331, Metairie, 70002.* Tel: 504-837-2960.

Vocation Office—Rev. Msgr. HENRY J. BUGLER, V.F., Dir., *7887 Walmsley Ave., New Orleans, 70125-3496.* Tel: 504-861-6298; 861-9521; Fax: 504-866-2906.

Liaison with Conference of Major Superiors of Men and Retired Priests—Vacant.

Department of Community Services

Executive Director—Rev. Msgr. ROGER P. MORIN, *1000 Howard Ave., Ste. 800, New Orleans, 70113-1900.* Tel: 504-596-3090; Fax: 504-596-3098.

Archdiocesan Alcoholism Counseling Ministry—Rev. ANTHONY J. WHITE, Dir., *724 Camp St., New Orleans, 70130-3757.* Tel: 504-528-9916; Fax: 504-568-1324.

Archdiocesan Federation of Christian Life Communities—2545 Bayou Rd., New Orleans, 70119.

Archconfraternity of St. Ann—4920 Loveland St., Metairie, 70006.

Confraternity of the Holy Face—1050 Robert Blvd., Slidell, 70458.

Apostleship of the Sea—Deacon GILBERT W. SMITH, JR., Port Chap. & Dir., *Stella Maris Maritime Center, 4219 Constance St., New Orleans, 70115-1440.* Tel: 501-891-6677; Fax: 504-891-1237.

Archbishop's Community Appeal (Philmat, Inc.)—Sr. ADELE LAMBERT, C.S.J., Dir., *1000 Howard Ave., Ste. 800, New Orleans, 70113-1900.* Tel: 504-596-3083; Fax: 504-596-3098.

Catholic Campaign for Human Development—Sr. ADELE LAMBERT, C.S.J., *1000 Howard Ave., Ste. 800, New Orleans, 70113-1900.* Tel: 504-596-3085; Fax: 504-596-3098.

Catholic Human Relations Committee—Rev. Msgr. ROGER P. MORIN, Dir., *1000 Howard Ave., Ste. 800, New Orleans, 70113-1900.* Tel: 504-596-3090; Fax: 504-596-3098.

Charities—Catholic Charities Archdiocese of New Orleans—Mrs. JANET DRESSEL, Pres. Bd. Advisors; Sr. ANTHONY BARCZYKOWSKI, D.C., CEO, *1000 Howard Ave., Ste. 1200, New Orleans, 70113-1916.* Tel: 504-523-3755; Fax: 504-523-2789. Mr. DAVID J. LOGSDON, Chief Financial Officer; Mr. ORVILLE DUGGAN, Chief Admin. Officer. Div. Directors: Ms. JANE BREWER; Ms. PASHENA CASIMIRE.

AIDS Housing / Shelter:—Ms. LOIS FALK.

AIDS Peer Counseling—Ms. ANITA TIRCUIT.

Beyond Shelter—Ms. VALLARIE BURRISS.

Bridges to Self Sufficiency—Ms. ETTA HAYWOOD.

Ciara Community Services—Ms. MONETTA CLARK, Ciara House, Ciara Independent Living Program.

Congregational Care Team Program—Ms. ANITA TIRCUIT.

Hope Haven Center—Mr. ROBERT GUASCO,Hope Haven-Madonna Manor; St. Elizabeth's; Independent Living Skills Program.

Padua Adult Residential Program—Ocean Avenue Community Home, St. Catherine of Siena, St. Jude the Apostle, Sts. Mary and Elizabeth, St. Peter the Fisherman, St. Rosalie, Supervised Apartments. Mr. LEROY HUGHES, Admin.

Padua Pediatric Residential Program—Ms. RONNA TRAGER.

Adult Day Health Care Centers—Ms. GLORIA CABRERA,Alpha House, New Directions, Greenwalt Center for Alzheimer's Day Care & Research.

Children's Day Care Centers—Ms. GLORIA CABRERA,El Yo Yo, Flint Goodridge, Florida Head Start, Leslie Center, Louise, St. Anthony Head Start.

Maternity and Adoption Services—Ms. JANE BREWER-,ACCESS Pregnancy/Referral Centers; Adoption Services; St. Vincent Maternity Clinic; Second Glance Resale Shoppe.

Immigration and Refugee Services—Ms. SUSAN WEISHAR,Refugee Health Screening; Legal/Resettlement Services; Social Services; Immigrant Domestic Violence Prevention/Outreach; ESL Program.

Social Adjustment—Ms. SHARON ALEXIS.

CARE Centers—Ms. CONNIE ANDRY,CARE Center; Jefferson CARE Center; Baronne Street Transitional Housing.

Clinical Counseling Programs—Ms. JANE BREWER, Metairie & New Orleans Office, *433 Metairie Rd., Ste. 119, Metairie, 70005-4324.* Tel: 504-835-5007.

St. Tammany Branch Office—Ms. SONYA PETERS, *1925-C Corporate Sq. Blvd., Slidell, 70458-3165.* Tel: 985-641-8120.

St. Charles Branch Office—Mr. PETER YUSLUM, *P.O. Box 60, Hahnville, 70057-6000.* Tel: 985-783-2906.

St. John Branch Office—Ms. ANDREA KENT STEIMKAMP, *1706 Cannes Dr., LaPlace, 70068-2407.* Tel: 985-652-4330.

St. Bernard Branch Office—Ms. BARBARA LAUGHLIN, *2626 Charles Dr., Chalmette, 70043-3773.* Tel: 504-279-7636.

Westbank Branch Office—Sr. DENISE LEJEUNE, O.P., *781 Berhman Hwy., Ste. 102, Gretna, 70056.* Tel: 504-391-0370.

Crescent House I and II—Ms. LYNN YOUNG.

Deaf Action Center of Greater New Orleans—Ms. SHARI BERNIUS.

Information and Referral—Ms. DALANIE BANKS.

Family Preservation—Ms. MAMIE HALL-LANDRY.

Job Search—Ms. NELLIE STOKES-PERRY.

Senior Citizens Groups—Mr. RAPHAEL FOLEY.

Project S.A.V.E. (Spouse Abuse Victim Empowerment)—Ms. JANE ROBSON.

Therapeutic Family Services—Mr. JEFFREY SWEATT.

Transportation Assistance Program—Vacant.

Foster Grandparents—Ms. DORIS LALA.

Volunteer Department—Ms. AUDREY FONTANA.

Christopher Homes, Inc.—Mr. THOMAS P. PERKINS, Exec. Dir., *1000 Howard Ave., Ste. 100, New Orleans, 70113-1903.* Tel: 504-596-3460; Fax: 504-596-3466.

Disaster Relief—Rev. Msgr. ROGER P. MORIN, Dir., *1000 Howard Ave., Ste. 800, New Orleans, 70113-1900.* Tel: 504-596-3090; Fax: 504-596-3098.

Social Apostolate Office (PHILMAT, Inc.)—Most Rev. FRANCIS B. SCHULTE, Pres.; Sr. ADELE LAMBERT, C.S.J., Dir. GORDON R. WADGE, Assoc. Dir., *1000 Howard Ave., Ste. 800, New Orleans, 70113-1900.* Tel: 504-596-3080; Fax: 504-596-3098.

Careers to Self-Sufficiency—Mr. LARRY STANSBERRY.

Dignity of Work—Mrs. CHENITA L. FLETCHER.

Food for Families/Food for Seniors—Mr. TIMOTHY ROBERTSON, Dir., *8326 Apricot St., New Orleans, 70118-3198.* Tel: 504-861-3555; Fax: 504-861-1435.

IMATT (Integrated Mobile Assessment and Treatment Team)—Mrs. FELICE K. SIMIEN-HILL.

[*]Second Harvesters Food Bank of Greater New Orleans, Inc.—Mr. S. BRIAN GREENE, Dir., *1201 Sams Ave., Harahan, 70123-2236.* Tel: 504-734-1322; Fax: 504-733-8336.

Summer Social Action Program (Witness)—*1000 Howard Ave., Ste. 800, New Orleans, 70113-1903.* Tel: 504-596-3086; Fax: 504-596-3098.

SOCIAL ACTION CENTERS:

Incarnate Word Center—Ms. SHIRLEY LACHMANN, Dir., *8326 Apricot St., New Orleans, 70118-3198.* Tel: 504-866-8918; Fax: 504-864-9922.

Our Lady of Lourdes Center—Mrs. JANET M. ROUSSO, Dir., *2401 Jena St., New Orleans, 70115-5998.* Tel: 504-895-0216; Fax: 504-895-0629.

St. John the Baptist—Sr. MARION BRETT, D.C., Dir., *1920 Clio St., New Orleans, 70113-1214.* Tel: 504-581-4987; Fax: 504-581-4991.

St. Louis Community Center—Mrs. JEAN-MARIE BUXTON, *1022 Barracks St., New Orleans, 70116-2526.* Tel: 504-524-7023; Fax: 504-524-2881.

St. Mary of the Angels—Mr. ERNEST COLBERT, III, Dir., *2301 Gallier St., New Orleans, 70117-5833.* Tel: 504-949-1506; Fax: 504-945-9115.

St. Philip Community Center—Mrs. DOMINIQUE BRIGHT-WHEELER, Dir., *3333 Clouet St., New Orleans, 70126-5700.* Tel: 504-944-8848; Fax: 504-945-4648.

Department of Financial and Administrative Services

Officers—Mr. JOHN L. ECKHOLDT, Chief Financial Officer;Mr. LEON W. MATHES, JR., Chief Admin. Officer, *7887 Walmsley Ave., New Orleans, 70125-3496.* Tel: 504-861-6252; 861-9521; Fax: 504-866-2906.

Accounting and Financial Review Office—Mrs. KIM O. RAMSEY, Controller, *7887 Walmsley Ave., New Orleans, 70125-3496.* Tel: 504-861-6236; 861-9521; Fax: 504-866-2906.

Building Office—Mr. AUGUST J. BARBIER, JR., Dir., *7887 Walmsley Ave., New Orleans, 70125-3496.* Tel: 504-861-6210; 861-9521; Fax: 504-866-2906.

Human Resources—Ms. BETH TINTO, Dir., *7887 Walmsley Ave., New Orleans, 70125-3496.* Tel: 504-861-6238; Fax: 504-866-2906.

Insurance Office—Claim Mgrs.: Ms. CHERYL HARPER; Mr. TRAVIS BOURGEOIS, *7887 Walmsley Ave., New Orleans, 70125-3496.* Tel: 504-861-6259; 861-9521; Fax: 504-866-2906.

Internal Audit Office—Mrs. WANDA BROOKS, Internal Auditor, *7887 Walmsley Ave., New Orleans, 70125-3496.* Tel: 504-861-6203; Fax: 504-866-2906.

Internet Services—Mr. KEN BEASLEY, Interim Dir., *1000 Howard Ave., Ste. 700, New Orleans, 70113-1903.* Tel: 504-596-6683; Fax: 504-596-3068.

Missions Office—Society for the Propagation of the Faith, Holy Childhood Pontifical Assn., Missionaries of St. Therese—Rev. Msgr. JOHN A. TOMASOVICH, Dir., *7887 Walmsley Ave., New Orleans, 70125-3496.* Tel: 504-866-7410; Fax: 504-866-7498.

New Orleans Archdiocesan Cemeteries and New Orleans Cemeteries Trust—Mr. MICHAEL D. BOUDREAUX, Dir., *1000 Howard Ave., Ste. 500, New Orleans, 70113-1903.* Tel: 504-596-3050; Fax: 504-596-3055.

Parish Sites & Boundaries Committee—Rev. Msgr. FRANK J. GIROIR, Chm.; Rev. Msgr. THOMAS J. RODI, V.G., Coord., *7887 Walmsley Ave., New Orleans, 70125-3496.* Tel: 504-861-6262; 861-9521; Fax: 504-861-6312.

Property Committee—Most Rev. FRANCIS B. SCHULTE, D.D., Pres.; Mr. JOHN L. ECKHOLDT, Chm., *7887 Walmsley Ave., New Orleans, 70125-3496.* Tel: 504-861-6252; Fax: 504-866-2906.

Property Records Office—Mrs. EMILY MORRIS, *7887 Walmsley Ave., New Orleans, 70125-3496.* Tel: 504-861-6323; Fax: 504-866-2906.

School Food Services—Mrs. PATRICIA H. FARRIS, Dir., *1000 Howard Ave., Ste. 300, New Orleans, 70113-1925.* Tel: 504-596-3434; Fax: 504-596-3459.

Department of Pastoral Services

Executive Director—Very Rev. GERALD L. SEILER, *7887 Walmsley Ave., New Orleans, 70125-3496.* Tel: 504-861-6294; 861-9521; Fax: 504-866-2906.

Black Catholics Ministries—Deacon DAN VINCENT, *7887 Walmsley Ave., New Orleans, 70125-3496.* Tel: 504-861-6207; 861-9521; Fax: 504-866-2906.

Canonical Permissions and Dispensations—Very Rev. GERALD L. SEILER; Rev. JOSEPH P. MULLIN, S.M., *7887 Walmsley Ave., New Orleans, 70125-3496.* Tel: 504-861-6294; 861-9521; Fax: 504-866-2906.

Charismatic Renewal—Liaisons: Mr. AL MANSFIELD; Mrs. PATTI MANSFIELD, *3000 26th St., Ste. 200, Metairie, 70002-6002.* Tel: 504-828-1368; Fax: 504-828-2133.

Ecumenical Officer—Very Rev. GERALD L. SEILER, Chm., *7887 Walmsley Ave., New Orleans, 70125-3496.* Tel: 504-861-6294; 861-9521; Fax: 504-866-2906.

Family Life Apostolate—Mrs. PAULA D'ALBOR STUCKART, Dir., *7887 Walmsley Ave., New Orleans, 70125-3496.* Tel: 504-861-6243; 861-9521; Fax: 504-866-2906.

Commission for Persons with Disabilities—Mrs. PAULA D'ALBOR STUCKART, *7887 Walmsley Ave., New Orleans, 70125-3496.* Tel: 504-861-6243; Fax: 504-866-2906.

Filipino Catholic Ministry—Rev. DANILO C. DIGAL, Coord., *700 Maple St., Harvey, 70058-4008.* Tel: 504-368-1397.

Hispanic Apostolate—Mr. MARTIN GUTIERREZ, Exec. Dir., *3368 Esplanade Ave., New Orleans, 70119-3132.* Tel: 504-486-1983; Fax: 504-486-3985.

Mensaje, Inc.—Rev. PEDRO NUNEZ, *3368 Esplanade Ave., New Orleans, 70119-3132.* Tel: 504-482-8803; Fax: 504-943-5501.

Holy Name Societies—Mr. BEN RAPHAEL, Exec. Sec., *7887 Walmsley Ave., New Orleans, 70125-3496.* Tel: 504-283-5427; Fax: 504-866-2906.

Pastoral Planning—Sr. MYRA BANQUER M.S.C., Coord., *7887 Walmsley Ave., New Orleans, 70125-3496.* Tel: 504-861-6222; Fax: 504-866-2906.

Prisons Apostolate—Deacon LOUIS STALL, Archdiocesan Dir., *P.O. Box 388, Gretna, 70054-0388.* Tel: 504-374-7700, Ext. 3109.

Renovacion Carismatica Catolica Hispana—Deacon RODOLFO J. MARTINEZ, *4401 Seventh St., Marrero, 70072-2099.* Tel: 504-341-9516; Fax: 504-341-9517. JESUS ALCANTARA; EDITH ALCANTARA, *3368 Esplanade Ave., New Orleans, 70119-3132.*

Vietnamese Catholics Office—Rev. Msgr. DOMINIC LUONG, Dir., *5069 Willowbrook Dr., New Orleans, 70129-0745.* Tel: 504-254-5660; Fax: 504-254-9250.

Worship Office—Deacon RONALD GUIDRY, Dir., *7887 Walmsley Ave., New Orleans, 70125-3496.* Tel: 504-861-6300; 861-9521; Fax: 504-866-2906.

Liturgical Committee—Deacon RONALD GUIDRY, Coord., *7887 Walmsley Ave., New Orleans, 70125-3496.* Tel: 504-861-6300; 861-9521; Fax: 504-866-2906.

Master of Ceremonies—Deacon RONALD GUIDRY, *7887 Walmsley Ave., New Orleans, 70125-3496.* Tel: 504-861-6300; 861-9521; Fax: 504-866-2906.

Department of Religious

Executive Director—Sr. SUELLEN TENNYSON, M.S.C., *7887 Walmsley Ave., New Orleans, 70125-3496.* Tel: 504-861-6281; 861-9521; Fax: 504-866-2906.

Liaison with Leadership Conference of Women Religious, Religious Institutes of Brothers and Sisters and Secular Institutes—

Archdiocesan Offices and Corporations

Bernard A. Grehan Trust—*7887 Walmsley Ave., New Orleans, 70125-3496.* Tel: 504-861-9521.

Catholic Charities Children's Day Care Centers Inc.—Registered Office: *1000 Howard Ave., Ste. 1200, New Orleans, 70113-1916.*

Mental Health Association Development Corporation—*7887 Walmsley Ave., New Orleans, 70125-3496.* Tel: 504-861-9521.

St. Elizabeth's Home Registered Office—*1000 Howard Ave., Ste. 1200, New Orleans, 70113-1916.*

St. Gertrude's Retirement Center—Most Rev. FRANCIS B. SCHULTE, D.D., Pres., *7887 Walmsley Ave., New Orleans, 70125-3496.*

St. Mary's Catholic Orphan Boys' Asylum Board—*1000 Howard Ave., Ste. 1200, New Orleans, 70113-1916.*

St. Vincent's Infant and Maternity Home Registered Office—*1000 Howard Ave., Ste. 1200, New Orleans, 70113-1916.*

Catholic Organizations

Apostles of Divine Mercy, New Orleans—Mrs. MARGARET BIESER, Dir., *6968 Gen. Diaz St., New Orleans, 70124-3436.* Tel: 504-283-3070.

Blessed Brother Andre Acadians Prayer Group—Deacon IRVING J. DAIGLE, Spiritual Moderator, *529 S. Telemachus St., New Orleans, 70119-7043.* Tel: 504-486-7190.

Blue Army of Our Lady of Fatima—Rev. DENZIL M. PERERA, Spiritual Dir., *1342 Moss St., New Orleans, 70119-2998.* Tel: 504-488-2659; Fax: 504-488-6741.

Catholic Charities Association Inc.—Mr. LEONARD S. DELBERT, Pres., *1000 Howard Ave., Ste. 1200, New Orleans, 70113-1916.* Tel: 504-581-BALL.

Catholic Knights of America—Rev. BENJAMIN PIOVAN, Spiritual Dir., *799 Fairway Dr., LaPlace, 70068-2007.* Tel: 504-652-2615; Fax: 504-652-7291.

Catholic Order of Foresters—Mr. EDWIN HADLEY, State Chief Ranger, *4701 Stephen Girard Ave., New Orleans, 70126-4757.* Tel: 504-282-5432.

Catholic Physicians Guild of New Orleans—Dr. BRIAN BARKEMEYER, Pres., *6075 Argonne Blvd., New Orleans, 70124.* Tel: 504-568-4421; Fax: 504-568-7532.

Chateau de Notre Dame Guild—Rev. JOSEPH J. LAWLOR, S.S.J., Spiritual Dir., *2832 Burdette St., New Orleans, 70125-2596.* Tel: 504-866-2741; Fax: 504-866-6769.

Closer Walk Ministries—Rev. HAROLD F. COHEN, S.J., Dir., *P.O. Box 50860, New Orleans, 70150-0860.* Tel: 504-834-4200; Fax: 504-834-4204.

Come, Lord Jesus Program of Prayer and Scripture—Mrs. PAT ROBBINS, Coord., *906 Eleonore St., New Orleans, 70115.* Tel: 504-895-6821.

Community of John the Evangelist—Mr. DAN DEMERS, Chm., *3342 Hyman Pl., New Orleans, 70131-7040.* Tel: 504-394-1795.

Council of Catholic Men—Mr. BEN RAPHAEL, Dir., *7887 Walmsley Ave., New Orleans, 70125-3496.* Tel: 504-283-5427.

Council of Catholic School Cooperative Clubs—Rev. H. WILLIAM REED, Spiritual Moderator, *2545 Bayou Rd., New Orleans, 70119-2398.* Tel: 504-945-3591; Fax: 504-945-3216.

Council of Catholic Women—Rev. H. WILLIAM REED, Spiritual Dir., *2545 Bayou Rd., New Orleans, 70119-2398.* Tel: 504-945-3591. Mrs. LOLITA M. ALSTON, Pres.

Courage (Catholic Ministry to Homosexual Persons)—*P.O. Box 8074, New Orleans, 70182-8074.*

Cursillo—Mrs. SUSAN MAY, Lay Dir., *22417 Level St., Abita Springs, 70420.* Tel: 985-867-4805.

Engaged Encounter—Dr. GARY LEVY; Mrs. CLAUDIA LEVY. Tel: 504-837-9121.

Eucharistic Adoration Society—Mrs. NOVA LACOMBE, Pres., *6232 Milne Blvd., New Orleans, 70124-2016.* Tel: 504-482-9632.

Jesus Caritas Fraternity of Priests—Rev. Msgr. ROBERT I. GUSTE, *1908 Short St., Kenner, 70062-7599.* Tel: 504-464-0361; Fax: 504-465-0930.

Junior Catholic Charities Association—Ms. TRISHA M. VOLTZ, Pres., *1000 Howard Ave., New Orleans, 70113-1916.* Tel: 504-523-3755.

Knights of Columbus—Rev. FRANCIS J. CARABELLO, Archdiocesan Chap., *610 6th St., Gretna, 70053-6098.* Tel: 504-368-1313; Fax: 504-368-6841.

Ladies of Charity of the Archdiocese—Rev. HAROLD DICHARRY, C.M., Spiritual Dir., *1025 Napoleon Ave., New Orleans, 70115-2898.* Tel: 504-899-1378; Fax: 504-899-0480.

Ladies of Madonna—Ms. SHIRLEY OSTER, Pres., *500 Papworth Ave., Metairie, 70005.* Tel: 504-828-3157.

Lay Carmelites of Our Lady of Mount Carmel—*420 Robert E. Lee Blvd., New Orleans, 70124-2596.* Tel: 504-288-8553.

Legion of Mary—Deacon J. VERNON INSLEY, Spiritual Dir., New Orleans Comitium, *315 Desoto Dr., Luling, 70070.* Tel: 985-785-8491.

Living Waters Program (Radio Ministry)—Rev. Msgr. ROBERT I. GUSTE, Dir., *1908 Short St., Kenner, 70062.* Tel: 504-464-0361; Fax: 504-465-0930.

Magnificat, Ministry to Catholic Women—Mrs. PETER QUIRK, Pres. Central Svc. Team, *1201 Beverly Garden Dr., Metairie, 70002.* Tel: 504-834-0057.

Marians of New Orleans—Mrs. YAYI LAMY, Pres., *5815 Canal Blvd., New Orleans, 70124.* Tel: 504-488-2582.

Marians of Metairie—Mrs. IRENE BRIEDE, Pres., *103 Bordeaux St., Metairie, 70005.* Tel: 504-835-9021.

Marriage Encounter—JON GLUECK; NANCY GLUECK. Tel: 504-835-8831.

Maryknoll Mission Education Center (Promotion of Missionary Work)—Mr. MATT ROUSSO, Dir., *7730 Walmsley Ave., New Orleans, 70125.* Tel: 504-866-8516.

Mary's Children—Mrs. NORA LAMBERT, Pres., *631 St. Charles Ave., New Orleans, 70130-3411.* Tel: 504-288-4408.

Mary's Helpers (Medjugorje Information)—Mrs. MARGARET TROSCLAIR, Dir., *P.O. Box 1853, Marrero, 70073-1853.* Tel: 504-348-7729.

Medjugorje Star—Rev. CHARLES SELLARS, O.M.I., Spiritual Dir. Dirs.: HUBIE MULE; KAY MULE, *2627 David Dr., Metairie, 70003-4599.* Tel: 504-889-1708; Fax: 504-889-1714.

MIR Group (Medjugorje Information Center)—Ms. JERILYN GRAVOIS, *1 Galleria Blvd., Ste. 744, Metairie, 70001-2081.* Tel: 504-849-2570; Fax: 504-849-2574.

Missionaries of St. Therese—Rev. Msgr. JOHN A. TOMASOVICH, Spiritual Moderator, *7887 Walmsley Ave., New Orleans, 70125-3496.* Tel: 504-866-7410; Fax: 504-866-7498.

Naim Conference—Ms. CAROLYN CONN, *1495 Gardena Dr., New Orleans, 70122.* Tel: 504-282-8764.

National Council of Catholic Men—Mr. BEN RAPHAEL, Dir., *7887 Walmsley Ave., New Orleans, 70125-3496.* Tel: 504-283-5427.

National Council of Catholic Women—Rev. H. WILLIAM REED, Spiritual Dir., *2545 Bayou Rd., New Orleans, 70119-2398.* Tel: 504-945-3591.

Pax Christi New Orleans—Co-Chm.: Mrs. JUDY YUSLUM; Ms. WENDY KING, *P.O. Box 50304, New Orleans, 70150-0304.* Tel: 504-522-3751.

Priests for Life—Rev. Msgr. ROGER A. SWENSON, Coord., *105 Bonnabel Blvd., Metairie, 70005-3798.* Tel: 504-835-9343; Fax: 504-835-1525.

Rosary Congress Committee—Very Rev. NEAL W. MCDERMOTT, O.P., V.F., Spiritual Dir., *775 Harrison Ave., New Orleans, 70124-3192.* Tel: 504-482-4156.

St. Elizabeth's Guild—Mrs. HOWARD H. MCGREGOR, Pres., *1101 Barataria Blvd., Marrero, 70072.*

St. Margaret's Daughters—Mrs. AUGUSTINE MOLL, Pres., *6220 Chartres St., New Orleans, 70117.* Tel: 504-279-4411.

St. Thomas More Catholic Lawyers Association—Rev. JOSEPH S. PALERMO, JR., *5500 Paris Ave., New Orleans, 70122-2699.* Tel: 504-288-4224; Fax: 504-288-2152.

St. Vincent de Paul Society—Mr. WILLIAM BRANDNER, Pres.; Ms. ANN LAICHE, Exec. Sec., *2601 Canal St., New Orleans, 70119-6498.* Tel: 504-822-9288; Fax: 504-822-1964.

St. Vincent Infant and Maternity Home Guild—*1000 Howard Ave., Ste. 1200, New Orleans, 70113-1916.* Tel: 504-523-3755.

Scouting—Deacon DANIEL FLYNN, Chap., Boy Scouts, *251 Halsey Dr., Harahan, 70123-4401.* Tel: 504-737-8370. Mrs. COLLEEN R. LAROCCA, Chm., Girl Scouts, *25 Brentwood Dr., Metairie, 70003-3831.* Tel: 504-734-8527.

Serra Clubs—Serra Club of New Orleans; Rev. Msgr. HENRY J. BUGLER, V.F., Chap., *7887 Walmsley Ave., New Orleans, 70125-3496.* Tel: 504-861-6298; Fax: 504-866-2906. Serra Club of Downtown New Orleans; Rev. Msgr. ANDREW C. TAORMINA, Chap., *448 Metairie Rd., Metairie, 70005-4371.* Tel: 504-834-0340. Serra Club of East Jefferson; Mr. PATRICK DORION, Pres. Tel: 504-454-8255. Serra Club of St. Bernard; Rev. WAYNE C. PAYSSE, Chap., *58203 Hwy. 433, Slidell, 70460-3121.* Tel: 985-643-3832; 800-641-6771.

The Theresians—Mrs. KATHERINE TALLUTO, Co-Pres., Theresians II, *200 Winchester Pl., New Orleans, 70131.* Tel: 504-394-6270. Mrs. CHARLOTTE TODD, Co-Pres., Theresians II, *401 Metairie Rd., #408, Metairie, 70005.* Tel: 504-833-4664. Mrs. SALLY DUPLANTIER, Co-Pres., Sequoia, *5601 Charlotte Dr., New Orleans, 70122.* Tel: 504-288-1897. Mrs. STELLA DEJOIE, Co-Pres., Sequoia, *4501 S. Johnson St., New Orleans, 70125.* Tel: 504-822-4849.

Victorious Missionaries—Deacon ALBERT LEVY, III, Chap., *621 Lebeau St., Arabi, 70032.* Tel: 504-277-5053.

CLERGY, PARISHES, MISSIONS AND PAROCHIAL SCHOOLS

CITY OF NEW ORLEANS
(Orleans Civil Parish)

1—ST. LOUIS CATHEDRAL (1720). (A Minor Basilica). Rev. Msgr. Kenneth J. Hedrick, Rector; Rev. Msgr. John C. Sax; Rev. Frank Montalbano, O.M.I.; Deacons Ron Guidry; Jose Sierra.
Res., 615 Pere Antoine Alley, 70116-3291. Tel: 504-525-9585; Fax: 504-525-9583.
School—820 Dauphine St., 70116-3089. Tel: 504-525-3860; Fax: 504-525-3193. Mrs. Rhonda Parenton, Prin.
Lay Teachers 11; Students 147.
Mission—New Orleans, Orleans Civil Parish, Our Lady of Guadalupe, Tel: 504-525-1551; Fax: 504-525-1827.
Shrine—International Shrine of St. Jude. Revs. Joseph Ferraioli, O.M.I.; Raymond A. Lebrun, O.M.I.; Michael Amesse, O.M.I.; Sr. Christopher Foy, S.S.F., Pastoral Assoc.
Res., 411 N. Rampart St., 70112-3594.
St. Jude Community Center—400 N. Rampart St., 70112-3594. Tel: 504-522-8290; Fax: 504-522-8830.

2—ALL SAINTS (1919), Rev. Joseph J. Campion, S.S.J.
Res., 1441 Teche St., 70114-5899. Tel: 504-361-8835; Fax: 504-361-9802.
School—1415 Teche St., 70114-5898.
Sisters of the Holy Family 4; Lay Teachers 12; Students 289.

3—ANNUNCIATION (1844), Very Rev. Michael P. Jacques, S.S.E., V.F. In res., Rev. Luis Emilio Henao.
Res., 1221 Mandeville St., 70117-8498. Tel: 504-943-5561; Fax: 504-943-5562.

4—BLESSED SACRAMENT (1915) (African American), Rev. Howard W. Byrd, S.S.J., Admin. In res., Rev. Joseph E. Okoro, C.M.F. (Nigeria).
Res., 5018 Constance St., 70115-1798. Tel: 504-897-0955; Fax: 504-897-0950.
Catechesis/Religious Programs—Students 6.

5—CORPUS CHRISTI (1916) (African American), Revs. Ray P. Bomberger, S.S.J.; Francis Schroeder, S.S.J.; Bro. Louis Tomasso, S.S.J.; Deacon Alfred D. White, Jr.
Res., 2022 St. Bernard Ave., 70116-1388. Tel: 504-945-8931; Fax: 504-947-5347.
School—Tel: 504-943-6131; Fax: 504-947-7736. Sr. Marie Antoinette Sylvester, S.S.F., Prin.
Sisters 7; Lay Teachers 41; Students 395.
Catechesis/Religious Programs—Students 125.

6—EPIPHANY (1948) (African American), Rev. Henry J. Davis, S.S.J.
Res., 1949 Duels St., 70119-1198. Tel: 504-944-2646; Fax: 504-945-5251.
Catechesis/Religious Programs—Students 100.

7—HOLY GHOST (1915) (African American), Rev. Michel Boutot, C.S.Sp. In res., Rev. O. Hugh Stout.
Res., 2015 Louisiana Ave., 70115-5294. Tel: 504-891-3172; Fax: 504-891-9284.
School—2035 Toledano St., 70115-5295. Tel: 504-899-6782; Fax: 504-899-6782. Sr. Angela Smith, S.S.F., Prin.
Sisters 4; Lay Teachers 6; Students 290.

8—HOLY NAME OF JESUS (1892), Revs. Paul Patin, S.J.; Paul Schott, S.J.; Deacon Philip De Verges. In res., Rev. Donald Pearce, S.J.
Res., 6220 LaSalle Pl., 70118-6236. Tel: 504-865-7430; Fax: 504-866-3391.
School—6325 Cromwell Pl., 70118-6299. Tel: 504-861-1466; Fax: 504-861-1480. Sr. Mary Nicholas Schiro, R.S.M., Prin.
Sisters of Mercy 5; Lay Teachers 50; Students 525.
Catechesis/Religious Programs—Tel: 504-572-2469.
Students 75.

9—HOLY NAME OF MARY (ALGIERS) (1848), Very Rev. Gerald L. Seiler, Jr.; Deacon Dean Herrick.
Res., 500 Eliza St., 70114-1098. Tel: 504-362-5511; Fax: 504-367-3504. [CEM 2][JC 2]
School—502 Olivier St., 70114-1099. Tel: 504-361-4004; Fax: 504-361-4044. Mrs. Betty J. Sierra, Prin.
Lay Teachers 14; Students 252.

10—HOLY SPIRIT (1972), Rev. Msgr. Allen J. Roy, V.F.; Deacon Raphael Duplechain, Jr.
Res., 6201 Stratford Pl., 70131-7397. Tel: 504-394-5492; Fax: 504-398-0901.
Catechesis/Religious Programs—Mark Doyer, D.R.E.
Students 78.

11—IMMACULATE CONCEPTION (1851), Revs. Harry W. Tompson, S.J.; James Herbert Mead, S.J.; Thomas Stakel, S.J.
Res., 130 Baronne St., 70112-2304. Tel: 504-529-1477; 1478; Fax: 504-524-0155.

12—IMMACULATE HEART OF MARY (1954), Rev. Joseph M. de Water.
Res., 6300 Pines Blvd., 70126-2697. Tel: 504-242-6900; Fax: 507-243-6655.
School—6360 Pines Blvd., 70126-2699. Tel: 504-242-6151; Fax: 504-242-6301. Dr. David Chimento, Prin.
Lay Teachers 12; Students 230.

13—INCARNATE WORD (1922), Rev. Msgr. Roger P. Morin; Rev. Francis Ferrie.
Res., 8316 Apricot St., 70118-3199. Tel: 504-866-3679; Fax: 504-866-0722.

14—MARY, QUEEN OF VIETNAM (1983) (Vietnamese), Rev. Msgr. Dominic Mai Thanh Luong; Rev. Michael Nam Hoang Nguyen; Deacon Joseph Hiep Pham. In res., Rev. Peter Neuman, I.C.
Res., 5069 Willowbrook Dr., P.O. Box 29745, 70129-1047. Tel: 504-254-5660; Fax: 504-254-9250. [JC]
Catechesis/Religious Programs—Tel: 504-254-5247.
Students 907.
Mission—New Orleans, Orleans Civil Parish, Our Lady of La Vang, 6054 Vermillion Blvd., 70122-4296. Tel: 504-283-0559; Fax: 504-286-1937. Rev. Dominic Huyen Duc Nguyen.
Chapel—Vietnamese Martyrs, 14400 Peltier Dr., New Orleans East, 70129-1713. Tel: 504-254-5660.

15—MATER DOLOROSA (1848), Rev. John T. Hinton; Deacons Louis Barrilleaux; Walter Beyer; Richard E. Deichmann. In res., Rev. David A. Boileau.
Res., 8128 Plum St., 70118-2012. Tel: 504-866-3669; Fax: 504-866-2349.
Catechesis/Religious Programs—Tel: 504-866-5641.
Students 120.

16—OUR LADY OF GOOD COUNSEL (1887), Revs. Patrick Collum; Martin J. Smullen; Deacon Ray Richardson.
Res., 1307 Louisiana Ave., 70115-2494. Tel: 504-891-1906; Fax: 504-895-5871.

17—OUR LADY OF GUADALUPE /INTERNATIONAL SHRINE OF ST. JUDE (1826) (African American). (Quasi Parish). Revs. Joseph Ferraioli, O.M.I.; Michael Amesse. In res., Rev. Raymond A. Labrun, O.M.I.
Res., 411 N. Rampart St., 70112. Tel: 504-525-1551; Fax: 504-525-1827.
Catechesis/Religious Programs—Tel: 504-522-8546.
Students 87.

18—OUR LADY OF LOURDES (1905) (African American), Revs. John Cisewski; Raphael Ezeh, M.S.P.; Deacons Everett Williams; Raymond Lewis; Michael H. Stohlman.
Res., 4423 La Salle St., 70115-5909. Tel: 504-891-4401; Fax: 504-891-4402.
School—2437 Jena St., 70115-5998. Tel: 504-897-0154; Fax: 504-897-0155.
Lay Teachers 12; Students 260.
Catechesis/Religious Programs—Students 29.

19—OUR LADY OF THE ROSARY (1907), Very Rev. James A. Tarantino, V.F.; Rev. Denzil M. Perera, (Retired); Very Rev. Vien The Nguyen; Sr. Janine Beniger, C.S.J., Pastoral Assoc.; Deacons Richard Gaiennie; John David Hamm; Henry Nuss.
1322 Moss St., 70119-2998. Tel: 504-488-2659; Fax: 504-488-6741.

20—OUR LADY STAR OF THE SEA (1911), Rev. Rodney A. Richard.
Res., 1835 St. Roch Ave., 70117-8199. Tel: 504-944-0166; Fax: 504-948-9555.
Catechesis/Religious Programs—Students 48.

21—THE RESURRECTION OF OUR LORD (1963), Rev. Cyprian Devold; Deacon William P. Curry, Jr.
Res., 9701 Hammond St., 70127-3519. Tel: 504-242-8669; Fax: 504-242-8767.
School—4861 Rosalia Dr., 70127-3598. Tel: 504-242-6222; Fax: 504-241-7363. Dr. Louise A. Olsen, Prin.
Lay Teachers 22; Students 361.
Catechesis/Religious Programs—Students 42.

22—SACRED HEART OF JESUS (1879), Revs. C. Richard Nowery, C.S.C.; Joseph M. Moyer, C.S.C.; Deacon Irving J. Daigle. In res., Rev. Thomas E. Chambers, C.S.C.; Bro. Richard Kelly, C.S.C.
Res., 139 S. Lopez St., 70119-6284. Tel: 504-827-1481; Fax: 504-821-5109. [CEM]
Catechesis/Religious Programs—Students 95.

23—ST. ALPHONSUS (1847) (Irish), Revs. Gerard B. LaPorte, C.SS.R.; Binh Thanh Ta, C.SS.R.; Luong Uong, C.SS.R.; Byron J. Miller, C.SS.R.; Sr. Jane Briseno, R.S.M., Pastoral Assoc.; Bro. Andrew Lawson, C.SS.R.; Deacon Maurice J. Hartson, III.
Res., 2030 Constance St., 70130-5099. Tel: 504-522-6748; Fax: 504-523-3734.
School—2001 Constance St., 70130-5094. Tel: 504-523-6594. Sr. Monica Ellerbusch, R.S.M., Prin.
Sisters 2; Lay Teachers 14; Students 258.

24—ST. ANDREW THE APOSTLE (1952), Revs. Paul S. Hart, Parochial Admin.; Raul Venust Lobo (India); Deacon Chris J. DiGrado.
Res., 3101 Eton St., 70131-5399. Tel: 504-393-2334; Fax: 504-392-0635.
School—Tel: 504-394-4171; Fax: 504-391-3627.
Sisters 3; Lay Teachers 44; Students 810.
Catechesis/Religious Programs—Tel: 504-393-0140; Fax: 504-393-0334.
Students 127.

25—ST. ANTHONY OF PADUA (1915), Rev. Donald T. Dvorak, O.P.; Very Rev. Alberto Rodriguez, O.P., Prov.; Rev. Carl B. Trutter, O.P.; Very Rev. Bryan J. Fontenot, O.P., Prior; Revs. John N. Morgenthaler, O.P.; John A. Powers, O.P.; Ronald Henery, O.P.; Wilmo Candanedo, O.P.; John J. Markey, O.P.; Bros. Timothy Wrinn, O.P.; Richard Bontempo, O.P.; Herman Johnson, O.P.; Angel Del Rio, O.P.; Sr. M. Aimee Haulard, O.P., Pastoral Min.; Sr. Diane McOsker, O.P., Pastoral Assoc.
Res., 4640 Canal St., 70119-5892. Tel: 504-488-2651; Fax: 504-488-1842.
School—4601 Cleveland Ave., 70119-5893. Tel: 504-488-4426; 482-3672; Fax: 504-488-5373. Sr. Ruth Angelette, O.P., Prin.
Sisters of St. Dominic 3; Lay Teachers 25; Students 391.
Catechesis/Religious Programs—Tel: 504-488-2651, Ext. 251.
Students 30.

26—ST. AUGUSTINE (1841) (African American), Rev. Jerome LeDoux, S.V.D.; Deacon Lloyd S. Glapion.
Res., 1210 Gov. Nicholls St., 70116-2324. Tel: 504-525-5934; Fax: 504-523-2473.

27—ST. BRIGID (1977), Rev. Msgr. T. Gaspard Glasgow.
Res., 13435 Granville St., P.O. Box 29626, 70129-1210. Tel: 504-254-3538; Fax: 504-254-3520.
Catechesis/Religious Programs—Tel: 504-254-5115. Mary Kittles, D.R.E.
Students 75.

28—ST. CECILIA (1897), Rev. Joseph A. Benson. In res., Rev. Maurice Shepherd, S.O.L.T.
Res., 1015 France St., 70117-5398. Tel: 504-945-1597; 945-6622; Fax: 504-945-0188.

29—ST. DAVID (1937) (African American), Rev. Patrick S. Healy; Deacon Irvin Williams.
Res., 5617 St. Claude Ave., 70117-2533. Tel: 504-947-2853; Fax: 504-948-7852.
School—Tel: 504-943-1523; Fax: 504-943-1533. Sr. Teresa Rooney, C.H.F., Prin.
Sisters 3; Lay Teachers 14; Students 265.
Catechesis/Religious Programs—Iris Labeaud, D.R.E.
Students 80.

30—ST. DOMINIC (1924), Very Rev. Neal McDermott, O.P., V.F.; Revs. Edward W. Conley, O.P., Prior; Victor Brown, O.P.; Val A. McInnes, O.P., Dir. Devel.; John I. Reardon, O.P., (Retired); John M. Pitzer, O.P.; Richard B. Williams, O.P.; Ian G. Bordenave, O.P.; Bro. Roger Shondel, O.P.; Deacon John Pippinger.
Res., 775 Harrison Ave., 70124-3192. Tel: 504-482-4156; Fax: 504-488-0906.
School—Tel: 504-482-4123; Fax: 504-486-3870.
Sisters 4; Lay Teachers 39; Students 680.
Catechesis/Religious Programs—Tel: 504-486-9731.
Students 145.

31—ST. FRANCES XAVIER CABRINI (1952), Revs. Paul H. Desrosiers; Joseph S. Palermo, Jr.; Deacons Gerald J. Martinez; Peter C. Rizzo; Charles B. Hauseknecht, Sr.
Res., 5500 Paris Ave., 70122-2699. Tel: 504-288-4224; Fax: 504-288-2152.
School—1500 Prentiss Ave., 70122-2098. Tel: 504-288-4249; Fax: 504-283-8161.
Lay Teachers 21; Students 341.
Catechesis/Religious Programs—Students 341.

32—ST. FRANCIS OF ASSISI (1890), Rev. Desmond G. Crotty.
Res., 631 State St., 70118-5899. Tel: 504-891-4479; Fax: 504-891-4470.

33—ST. FRANCIS DE SALES (1870) (African American), Rev. Victor H. Cohea.
Res., 2203 Second St., 70113-2545. Tel: 504-895-7749; Fax: 504-899-0434.
Catechesis/Religious Programs—Tel: 504-891-9544.
Students 40.

34—ST. GABRIEL THE ARCHANGEL (1954) (African American), Rev. Msgr. Douglas A. Doussan.
Office: 4700 Pineda St., 70126-3599. Tel: 504-282-0296; Fax: 504-288-8585.
Catechesis/Religious Programs—Tel: 504-288-7914.
Students 113.

35—ST. GERARD (1971), Rev. Pedro F. Nunez.
Res., 3037 Dauphine St., 70117-6724. Tel: 504-943-2456; Fax: 504-945-7200.

36—ST. HENRY (1856), Rev. Msgr. Henry H. Engelbrecht, V.F.; Deacon Henry A. Garon.
Res., 812 General Pershing St., 70115-2797. Tel: 504-891-6359; Fax: 504-895-0486.

37—HOLY TRINITY. Closed. For inquiries for parish records contact the Chancery.

38—ST. JAMES MAJOR (1920), Rev. Leo A. Meyer. In res., Rev. Douglas C. Brougher.
Res., 3736 Gentilly Blvd., 70122-6199. Tel: 504-945-2165; Fax: 504-945-9899.
Day Care Center—3800 Gentilly Blvd., 70122-6130. Mrs. Peggy Frey, Dir.
Staff 7; Students 52.
Catechesis/Religious Programs—Students 73.

39—ST. JOAN OF ARC (1909) (African American), Rev. Peter C. Weiss, S.S.J.; Deacon Irvin Stewart, Sr.
Res., 8321 Burthe St., 70118-1195. Tel: 504-866-7330; Fax: 504-866-1319.
School—Tel: 504-861-2887; Fax: 504-866-9588.
Sisters of Holy Family 3; Lay Teachers 11; Students 245.
Catechesis/Religious Programs—Students 75.

40—ST. JOHN THE BAPTIST (1851) (Irish), Rev. Matthias Moore, C.Ss.P.
Res., 1139 Oretha Castle Haley Blvd., 70113-1215. Tel: 504-525-1726; Fax: 504-524-4090.

41—ST. JOSEPH (1844). (Legal Title: St. Joseph Roman Catholic). Rev. Perry F. Henry, C.M.
Res., 1802 Tulane Ave., 70112-2246. Tel: 504-522-3186; Fax: 504-522-3171.
Catechesis/Religious Programs—Students 14.

42—ST. JULIAN EYMARD (1952), Rev. Salvador Galvez; Deacon Harold Vincent.
Res., 2701 Lawrence St., 70114-3099. Tel: 504-367-7730; Fax: 504-367-2603.

43—ST. LEO THE GREAT (1920), Rev. Rhenne A. Cervantes.
Res., 2916 Paris Ave., 70119-1840. Tel: 504-945-8750; Fax: 504-949-8899.
School—1501 Abundance St., 70119-2098. Tel: 504-943-1482; Fax: 504-944-5895.
Dominican Sisters (Cabra, Ireland) 1; Lay Teachers 25; Students 372.
Catechesis/Religious Programs—Tel: 504-945-8750; Fax: 504-949-8899.
Students 70.

44—ST. MARIA GORETTI (1965), Rev. Msgr. L. Earl Gauthreaux; Rev. Jaime G. Apolinares (Philippines); Deacons Peter E. Duffy; Ildefonso R. DeLeon; Terrel J. Broussard.
Mailing Address: 7300 Crowder Blvd., 70127-1599. Tel: 504-242-7554; Fax: 504-242-0755.
School—(Grades PreK). Tel: 504-242-1313; Fax: 504-242-4126.
Lay Teachers 2; Students 14.
Catechesis/Religious Programs—Students 308.

45—ST. MARY OF THE ANGELS (1925) (African American), Rev. Bart Pax, O.F.M. In res., Bros. Gordon Boykin, O.F.M.; Luis Aponte-Merced, O.F.M.; Martin Humphreys, O.F.M.
Res., 3501 N. Miro St., 70117-5899. Tel: 504-945-3186; Fax: 504-945-9115.
School—2225 Congress St., 70117-5898. Tel: 504-943-5687; Fax: 504-943-6673. Ms. Beatrice P. Stanley, Prin.
Lay Teachers 17; Students 286.

46—ST. MATTHIAS (1920) (African American), Rev. John Cisewski; Deacons Everett Williams; Raymond Lewis; Michael H. Stohlman.
Res., 4230 S. Broad St., 70125-3699. Tel: 504-822-3394; Fax: 504-822-3395.
Catechesis/Religious Programs—Students 33.

47—ST. MAURICE (1852), Rev. Adrian B. Hall; Deacon Elliot Arendt, Sr.
Res., 605 St. Maurice Ave., 70117-1598. Tel: 504-279-5231; Fax: 504-279-5232.
Catechesis/Religious Programs—Students 30.

48—ST. MONICA (1924) (African American), Rev. John Asare-Dankwah (Ghana); Deacon Herman Williams.
Res., 2327 S. Galvez St., 70125-3198. Tel: 504-821-9500; Fax: 504-821-9502.
School—2323 Galvez St., 70125-3199. Tel: 504-821-3321; Fax: 504-821-5631.
Catechesis/Religious Programs—Students 185.

49—ST. NICHOLAS OF MYRA (1971), Rev. Arthur J. Ginart.
Res., Rte. 6, Box 146-BE, 70129-9799. Tel: 504-662-5339; Fax: 504-662-5339. [CEM]
Catechesis/Religious Programs—Students 30.

50—ST. PATRICK (1833), Revs. Stanley P. Klores; Anthony J. White.
Res., 724 Camp St., 70130-3757. Tel: 504-525-4413; Fax: 504-568-1324.

51—ST. PAUL THE APOSTLE (1947) (African American), Rev. Bernard Kwame Assenyoh, S.V.D.; Deacon Daniel P. Vincent.
Res., 6828 Chef Menteur Hwy., 70126-5297. Tel: 504-242-7934; Fax: 504-242-1777. [CEM]
School—Tel: 504-242-5962; Fax: 504-242-0584.
Lay Teachers 12; Students 206.
Catechesis/Religious Programs—Students 95.

52—ST. PETER CLAVER (1920) (African American), Very Rev. Michael P. Jacques, S.S.E., V.F.; Deacon Rudolph Rayfield. Pastoral Assocs.: Sr. Mary Anne Hebert, C.S.J.; Deacon Allen Stevens; Pearl Dupart.
Office: 1923 St. Philip St., 70116-2199. Tel: 504-822-8059; Fax: 504-822-9251.
School—1020 N. Prieur St., 70116-2194. Tel: 504-822-8191. Mr. Don Boucree, Prin.
Lay Teachers 15; Students 282.
Catechesis/Religious Programs—Tel: 504-822-8176. Alena Boucree, D.R.E.
Students 200.

53—SS. PETER AND PAUL (1848), Rev. Dennis J. Hayes, III; Deacon Rodrigo Alonso Fonseca.
Res., 2317 Burgundy St., 70117-8587. Tel: 504-945-1531; Fax: 504-945-1537.
Catechesis/Religious Programs—Students 37.

54—ST. PHILIP THE APOSTLE (1949) (African American), Rev. Rodney Anthony Ricard; Deacon Allen Stevens.
Res., 3304 Metropolitan St., 70126-5799. Tel: 504-945-2122; Fax: 504-945-2128.
Catechesis/Religious Programs—Students 60.

55—ST. PIUS X (1953), Rev. Msgr. Clinton J. Doskey; Rev. William Maestri; Deacon William A. Glennon.
Res., 6666 Spanish Fort Blvd., 70124-4398. Tel: 504-282-3332; Fax: 504-283-8984.
School—Tel: 504-282-2811; Fax: 504-282-3043.
Lay Teachers 26; Students 467.
Catechesis/Religious Programs—Students 90.

56—ST. RAPHAEL THE ARCHANGEL (1947), Rev. Horace L. Brignac, Jr.; Deacon Norbert Gubert.
Catechesis/Religious Programs—Students 49.
Res., 2212 Prentiss Ave., 70122-5399. Tel: 504-282-6494; Fax: 504-282-2955.

57—ST. RAYMOND (1927), Revs. John E. O'Hallaran, S.S.J.; Emmanuel Nwosu; Deacons John B. Williams; Dwight Alexander.
Res., 3738 Paris Ave., 70122-2399. Tel: 504-288-1272; Fax: 504-283-3069.
School—Tel: 504-282-5563; Fax: 504-282-2344. Sr. Patricia Ann Williams, S.S.F., Prin.
Sisters of the Holy Family 4; Lay Teachers 12; Students 300.
Catechesis/Religious Programs—Students 90.

58—ST. RITA (1921), Rev. Msgr. Henry J. Bugler; Deacons Wilbur A. Toups; Paul Cimino. In res., Rev. Wilfred F. Meridier; Rev. Msgr. Ignatius M. Roppolo.
Res., 2729 Lowerline St., 70125-3599. Tel: 504-866-3621; Fax: 504-861-0338.
School—65 Fontainebleau Dr., 70125-3495. Tel: 504-866-1777; Fax: 504-861-8512.
Marianites of Holy Cross 8; Lay Teachers 10; Students 275.
Catechesis/Religious Programs—Students 16.

59—ST. ROSE OF LIMA (1857), Rev. H. William Reed.
Res., 2545 Bayou Rd., 70119-2398. Tel: 504-945-3591; Fax: 504-945-3216.
Catechesis/Religious Programs—Students 36.

60—ST. SIMON PETER (1986), Rev. Msgr. Thomas Gaspard Glasgavi, V.F.; Rev. Harry J. Adams; Deacons Jesse A. Watley; Terrel J. Broussard.
Office: 7600 Gannon Rd., 70128-1402. Tel: 504-243-9214; Fax: 504-243-9251.
School—Tel: 504-243-9241. Mrs. Camille Treaudo, Prin.
Catechesis/Religious Programs—Students 75.

61—ST. STEPHEN (1849), Revs. James Garcia Ward, C.M.; Harold E. Dicharry, C.M.; Deacons Charles J. Smith, Jr.; Bertrand Scalise, Jr. In res., Revs. Jacob Chennakadan, C.M.; Perry F. Henry, C.M.; Bro. James Steinbach, C.M.
Res., 1025 Napoleon St., 70115-2898. Tel: 504-899-1378; Fax: 504-899-0480.
School—1027 Napoleon Ave., 70115-2899. Tel: 504-891-1927; Fax: 504-891-1928. Sr. Juanita Chenevert, D.C., Prin.
Daughters of Charity of St. Vincent de Paul 2; Lay Teachers 14; Students 266.

62—ST. THERESA OF AVILA (1848), Revs. Teodoro Agudo, O.F.M.Cap. (Spain); Eutiquiano Miguel, O.F.M.Cap.; Deacon Francis J. Fleischer.
Res., 1404 Erato St., 70130-4387. Tel: 504-525-4226; Fax: 504-525-6014.
Catechesis/Religious Programs—Students 12.

63—ST. THERESA OF THE CHILD JESUS (1927) (African American), Rev. Quentin Moody.
Res., 3810 Leonidas St., 70118-4698. Tel: 504-482-1668; Fax: 504-486-8179.

64—ST. THOMAS THE APOSTLE. (University of New Orleans). Rev. Francis Berner; Deacon Eric Gamble.
Res., UNO Newman Center, 70148-0001. Tel: 504-288-6336; Fax: 504-288-6344.

65—ST. THOMAS MORE (1970). (The Community of St. Thomas More for Tulane Univ.). Rev. Richard B. Williams, O.P.; Deacon Joseph R. Rosato.
Res., 1037 Audubon St., 70118-5294. Tel: 504-866-0984; Fax: 504-865-1914.
Catechesis/Religious Programs—Students 105.

66—ST. VINCENT DE PAUL (1838), Rev. Pedro F. Nunez; Deacon Lawrence Keller.
Res., 3053 Dauphine St., 70117-6794. Tel: 504-943-5566; Fax: 504-943-5501.

OUTSIDE THE CITY OF NEW ORLEANS

Abita Springs, St. Tammany Parish, St. Jane de Chantal (1887), Rev. William J. MacCandless, O.S.B.; Deacons Frans Labranche, Jr.; Don Bourgeois.
Res., 22122 Main St., P.O. Box 187, 70420-0187. Tel: 985-892-1439; Fax: 985-871-9547. [JC]
Catechesis/Religious Programs—72049 Hickory St., 70420-3931. Tel: 985-893-3914.
Students 275.
Mission—Bush, St. Tammany Civil Parish, St. Michael the Archangel, Hwy. 41, 70431. Tel: 985-886-3868; Fax: 985-886-0687.

Ama, St. Charles Parish, St. Mark (1974), Rev. John M. Perino.
Res., P.O. Box 556, 70031-0556. Tel: 985-431-8505; Fax: 985-431-8506.
Catechesis/Religious Programs—Tel: 504-431-8507. Opal Kreamer, D.R.E.
Students 73.

Arabi, St. Bernard Parish, St. Louise De Marillac (1954), Rev. Philip G. Landry; Deacons Alvin C. Miester, Jr.; Alex J. Seruntine, Jr.; Douglas H. Strahan.
Res., 6800 Patricia St., 70032-1496. Tel: 504-271-4671; Fax: 504-271-7727.
School—Tel: 504-271-1678. Edward Kavanagh, Prin. Congregation of the Most Holy Sacrament Sister 1; Lay Teachers 13; Students 323.
Catechesis/Religious Programs—Students 104.

St. Robert Bellarmine (1964), Rev. Lich Van Nguyen; Deacon Curles P. Reeson.
Res., 408 Cougar Dr., 70032-2098. Tel: 504-279-8215; Fax: 504-277-7656.
School—815 Badger Dr., 70032-1996. Tel: 504-279-6466; Fax: 504-279-2259.
Lay Teachers 25; Students 518.
Catechesis/Religious Programs—Students 126.

Avondale, Jefferson Parish, St. Bonaventure (1965), Rev. Peter Nam Van Tran; Deacon J. Vernon Insley.
Res., 329 S. Jamie Blvd., 70094-2821. Tel: 504-436-1279; Fax: 504-436-1300.
Catechesis/Religious Programs—Tel: 504-436-0744. Maxine Authement, D.R.E.
Students 120.

Belle Chasse, Plaquemines Parish, Our Lady of Perpetual Help (1928), Rev. Michael J. Schneller; Deacon Leslie D. Vincent.
Res., 8968 Hwy. 23, 70037-2296. Tel: 504-394-0314; Fax: 504-394-0376. [CEM]
School—Tel: 504-394-0757; Fax: 504-394-1627. Sr. Elizabeth Hebert, S.L.W., Prin.
Sisters 2; Lay Teachers 17; Students 251.
Catechesis/Religious Programs—Nanette Carpenter, D.R.E.
Students 298.

Bogalusa, Washington Parish, Annunciation B.V.M. (1906), Rev. Lawrence J. Phelps, O.S.B.; Deacon Charles Hartman, III.
Res., 517 Avenue B, 70427-3723. Tel: 985-732-4280; Fax: 985-735-1042. [JC 3]
School—511 Avenue C, 70427-3797. Tel: 985-735-6643; Fax: 985-735-6119.
Lay Teachers 16; Students 253.
Catechesis/Religious Programs—Tel: 504-735-8167.
Students 66.

Bridge City, Jefferson Parish, Holy Guardian Angels (1963), Rev. Msgr. J. Anthony Luminais.
Res., 1701 Bridge City Ave., P.O. Box 9069, 70094-9069. Tel: 504-436-4712; Fax: 504-436-4070.
Catechesis/Religious Programs—Tel: 504-436-9376.
Students 157.

Buras, Plaquemines Parish, Our Lady of Good Harbor (1864), Rev. Msgr. Terry B. Becnel.
Mailing Address: 240 Buras River Rd., 70041-9188. Tel: 985-657-9873; Fax: 985-657-9878. [CEM][JC]
Catechesis/Religious Programs—Students 206.
Missions—Empire, Plaquemines Parish, St. Ann; Venice, Plaquemines Parish, St. Anthony.

Chalmette, St. Bernard Parish, Our Lady of Prompt Succor (1951), Very Rev. Warren L. Cooper, V.F.; Rev. Jose Roel Lungay; Deacons Henry A. Cassou, Jr.; Julius Zimmer.
Res., 2320 Paris Rd., 70043-5098. Tel: 504-271-3441; Fax: 504-271-2927.
School—2305 Fenelon St., 70043-4951. Tel: 504-271-2953; Fax: 504-271-1470. Evelyn Kingston, Prin.
School Sisters of Notre Dame 1; Lay Teachers 42; Students 715.
Catechesis/Religious Programs—Tel: 504-271-1217. Brenda Tromatore, D.R.E.
Students 402.

Prince of Peace (1977), Rev. Walter J. Austin; Deacon Frank W. Rhodes, Jr.
Res., 3700 Jean Lafitte Pkwy., 70043-1199. Tel: 504-271-1664; Fax: 504-279-8023.
Catechesis/Religious Programs—Tel: 504-277-6070; Fax: 504-277-7473. Yvette Caillouet, D.R.E.
Students 201.

St. Mark (1964), Revs. Mark Lomax; Nicholas P. Pericone; Deacons Raymond Rivere; Albert A. Levy, III; Kenneth Madere.
Res., 3024 Charles Dr., 70043-3798. Tel: 504-279-6073; Fax: 504-279-9403.
School—Tel: 504-271-1694; Fax: 504-277-7195. Sharon Coll, Prin.
Daughters of Divine Providence 2; Lay Teachers 31; Students 577.
Catechesis/Religious Programs—Tel: 504-277-2584. Sr. Pier Carla, F.D.P., D.R.E.
Students 525.
Convent—3100 Mumphrey Rd., 70043-3735. Tel: 504-279-4619; Fax: 504-279-4619. Daughters of Divine Providence

Covington, St. Tammany Parish, St. Peter (1843), Revs. William J. McGough; Herbert J. Kiff, Jr.; Deacons Charles Heine; Charles Read.
Res., 125 E. 19th St., 70433-3195. Tel: 985-892-2422; Fax: 985-898-1998.
School—Tel: 985-892-1831; Fax: 985-898-2185. Miss Lana O'Dwyer, Prin.
Lay Teachers 30; Students 596.
Catechesis/Religious Programs—Tel: 985-893-2446.
Students 415.

Crown Point, Jefferson Parish, St. Pius X (1971), Rev. Terence Hayden.
Res., 8151 Baratoria Blvd., 70072. Tel: 504-689-2381; Fax: 504-689-7417.
Catechesis/Religious Programs—Students 89.

Des Allemands, St. Charles Parish, St. Gertrude (1955), Rev. Benedict Joseph Quang; Deacon Landry Matherne.
Res., P.O. Box 767, 70030-0767. Tel: 985-758-7542; Fax: 985-758-7591. [CEM]
Catechesis/Religious Programs—Tel: 985-758-1332. Mrs. Nellie Matherne, D.R.E.
Students 126.

Destrehan, St. Charles Parish, St. Charles Borromeo (1723), Rev. Msgr. John Phuc, I.V.F.; Deacons Harry Schexnayder; Theodore Roussel. In res., Rev. Msgr. Lawrence A. Hecker; Rev. Donald Duffy.
Res., 13396 River Rd., P.O. Box 428, 70047-0428. Tel: 985-764-6383; Fax: 985-764-3948. [CEM]
School—Tel: 985-764-9232; Fax: 985-764-3726.
Lay Teachers 35; Students 468; Preschool Students 74.
Catechesis/Religious Programs—Students 672.

Diamond, Plaquemines Parish, St. Jude (1981), Rev. John C. Hegarty, C.S.Sp.
Res., P.O. Box 36, Port Sulphur, 70083-0036. Tel: 504-564-2182; Fax: 504-564-2077.
School—Tel: 504-564-3773. Mrs. Mary Ann Riley, Prin.
Sisters of St. Francis of Perpetual Adoration 1; Lay Teachers 8; Students 145.
Catechesis/Religious Programs—Students 11.

Edgard, St. John the Baptist Parish, St. John the Baptist (1770), Rev. Michael Roberson.
Res., 2361 Hwy. 18, 70049-9101. Tel: 985-497-3412; 497-8470; Fax: 985-497-3965. [CEM]
Catechesis/Religious Programs—Students 158.

Florissant, St. Bernard Parish, San Pedro Pescador (1966) (Islenos), Rev. John Patrick Grenham.
Res., 205 Florissant Hwy., St. Bernard, 70085-9703.
Church—P.O. Box 457, St. Bernard, 70085-0457. Tel: 504-676-3719; Fax: 504-676-9996.
Catechesis/Religious Programs—Tel: 504-676-3565. Ms. Yvette Miller, D.R.E.
Students 105.

Folsom, St. Tammany Parish, St. John the Baptist (1921), Rev. Jonathan M. DeFrange, O.S.B.; Deacon Clayton J. Guitterrez.
Res., 11345 St. John Church Rd., 70437-7155. Tel: 985-796-9214.
Office: Tel: 985-796-3806; Fax: 985-796-9554.
Catechesis/Religious Programs—Tel: 985-796-5507.
Students 150.

Franklinton, Washington Parish, Holy Family (1982), Rev. William H. Blank.
Res., 1213 14th Ave., 70438. Tel: 985-839-4040; Fax: 985-839-2429.

Garyville, St. John the Baptist Parish, St. Hubert, Rev. Charles J. Caluda.
Res., P.O. Box K, 70051-0851. Tel: 985-535-2828; Fax: 985-535-1849.

Gretna, Jefferson Parish, St. Anthony (1920), Revs. Patrick Gannon; Louis A. Persac, (Retired).
Res., 924 Monroe St., 70053-2299. Tel: 504-368-6161; Fax: 504-362-7811.
School—Tel: 504-367-0689; Fax: 504-361-0054. Mrs. Marie K. Cannon, Prin.
Sisters of the Living Word 2; Lay Teachers 9; Students 261.
Catechesis/Religious Programs—Students 39.

St. Cletus (1965), Revs. Eugene F. Jacques; John C. Arnone; Deacon Louis W. Stall.
Res., 3600 Claire Ave., 70053-7699. Tel: 504-367-7951; Fax: 504-367-7928.
School—Tel: 504-366-3538; Fax: 504-366-0011. Mrs. Joan Fischer, Prin.
Lay Teachers 40; Students 581.
Catechesis/Religious Programs—Tel: 504-361-4805.
Students 330.

St. Joseph (1857), Rev. Francis J. Carabello.
Res., 610 Sixth St., 70053-6098. Tel: 504-368-1313; Fax: 504-368-6841.
Catechesis/Religious Programs—Students 40.

Hahnville, St. Charles Parish, Our Lady of the Holy Rosary (1877), Rev. Bernard C. Francis.
Res., #1 Rectory Ln., 70057. Tel: 985-783-1199; Fax: 985-783-1974. [CEM]

Harahan, Jefferson Parish, St. Rita (1950), Rev. Msgr. Frank J. Giroir; Rev. Minh Cong Phan; Mr. Al Martin, Pastoral Assoc. & D.R.E.; Deacons Nolen J. LeBlanc; Nicholas L. Mistretta; Danny Flynn.
Res., 160 Imperial Woods Dr., 70123-4998. Tel: 504-737-2915; Fax: 504-737-2921.
School—194 Ravan Ave., 70123-4999. Tel: 504-737-0744; Fax: 504-738-2184. Mrs. Barbara Hollier, Prin.
Lay Teachers 28; Students 571.
Catechesis/Religious Programs—Students 150.

Harvey, Jefferson Parish,

1—Infant Jesus of Prague, (1969), Rev. Danilo C. Digal; Deacon Ferris Duet.
Res., 700 Maple St., 70058-4008. Tel: 504-368-1397; Fax: 504-368-0662.
Catechesis/Religious Programs—Students 97.

2—St. John Bosco, (1983), Rev. Sidney Figlia, S.D.B.; Deacon Milton G. Webre.
Res., 2114 Oakmere Dr., 70058-2275. Tel: 504-340-0444; Fax: 504-340-9521.
Catechesis/Religious Programs—Brenda C. Baker, D.R.E.
Students 80.

3—St. Martha, (1973), Rev. William O'Riordan; Deacon Gerard L. Labadot.
Res., 2555 Apollo Dr., 70058-5813. Tel: 504-366-1604; Fax: 504-366-1100.
Catechesis/Religious Programs—Tel: 504-366-4142.
Students 84.

4—St. Rosalie, (1949), Revs. Thomas E. Ruekert, S.D.B.; Jonathan Parks, S.D.B.
Parish Offices:—600 2nd Ave., 70058-2728. Tel: 504-340-1962; Fax: 504-340-1546.
Res., 608 1st Ave., 70058-2799. Tel: 504-341-5656.
School—617 Second Ave., 70058-2798. Tel: 504-341-4342; Fax: 504-347-0271.
Middle School—2115 Oakmere Dr., 70058-2276. Tel: 504-348-9330; Fax: 504-348-9331. Mary C. Wenzel, Prin.
Lay Teachers 50; Students 1,200.
Catechesis/Religious Programs—Students 28.

Jefferson, Jefferson Parish, St. Agnes (1931), Revs. Peter O'Grady; Robustiano D. Morgia (Philippines); Deacon Piero Caserta. In res., Rev. Msgr. Louis P. LeBourgeois.
Res., 3310 Jefferson Hwy., 70121-2699. Tel: 504-833-3366; Fax: 504-834-1532.
School—Lay Teachers 17; Students 286.

Kenner, Jefferson Parish,

1—Nativity of Our Lord, (1977), Rev. Dean L. Robins; Deacons John LeDoux; Eddy Beckendorf; Roberto Mendieta. In res., Rev. Lance J. Campo.
Office: 3325 Loyola Dr., 70065-2567. Tel: 504-466-5016; Fax: 504-467-8575.
Catechesis/Religious Programs—Tel: 504-464-9664. Mrs. Donna Schloegel, D.R.E.
Students 317.

2—Our Lady of Perpetual Help, (1869), Rev. Richard M. Miles; Rev. Msgr. Robert I. Guste Tel: 504-464-0413; Deacons Edgar P. Dragon; Greg A. Gross.
Res., 1908 Short St., 70062-7599. Tel: 504-464-0361; Fax: 504-465-0930.
School—Tel: 504-464-0531; Fax: 504-464-0725. Michael Orkus, Prin.
Sisters of Mercy 1; Lay Teachers 25; Students 433.

3—St. Elizabeth Ann Seton, (1981), Most Rev. Dominic Carmon, S.V.D., V.G.; Revs. Patrick B. Wattigny; Christopher Nalty; Deacons Andrea Capaci; Noel W. Martinsen; Garland Bourgeois.
Parish Office: 4121 St. Elizabeth Dr., P.O. Box 641000, 70064-1000. Tel: 504-468-1441; Fax: 504-468-3305.
School—Tel: 504-468-3524.
Lay Teachers 29; Students 537.
Catechesis/Religious Programs—Tel: 504-468-3233.
Students 160.

4—St. Jerome, (1963), Rev. Edward Grice; Deacons Daniel Cordes; Luis Campuzano, Sr.; Ernesto Morales. In res., Rev. Donald M. Byrnes, (Retired).
Res., 2400 33rd St., 70065-3899. Tel: 504-443-3174; Fax: 504-443-5499.
Catechesis/Religious Programs—Gail Bordelon, D.R.E.
Students 181.

Lacombe, St. Tammany Parish, Sacred Heart (1890), Rev. William J. O'Donnell; Deacon James Biales.
Res., P.O. Box 1080, 70445-1080. Tel: 985-882-5229; Fax: 985-882-9034.
Catechesis/Religious Programs—Students 120.

St. John of the Cross (1984), Rev. Randy P. Roux; Deacon Joseph LeRose.
Res., 61051 Brier Lake Dr., 70445-2911. Tel: 985-882-3779; Fax: 985-882-9282.
Catechesis/Religious Programs—Tel: 504-882-6225.
Students 90.

Lafitte, Jefferson Parish, St. Anthony (1936), Rev. John Ryan; Deacon Brian Joseph Klause.
Res., 2653 Jean Lafitte Blvd., 70067. Tel: 504-689-4101; Fax: 504-689-4102. [CEM]
Catechesis/Religious Programs—Tel: 504-689-2451. Mrs. Patricia Klause, D.R.E.
Students 320.

La Place, St. John the Baptist Parish, Ascension of Our Lord (1979), Rev. Benjamin Piovan; Deacon Arthur Sandman, Sr.
Res., 799 Fairway Dr., 70068-2007. Tel: 985-652-2615; Fax: 985-652-7291.
School—1809 Greenwood Dr., 70068-2098. Tel: 985-652-4532; Fax: 985-651-5151.
Lay Teachers 27; Students 405.
Catechesis/Religious Programs—Fax: 504-652-2791.
Students 170.

St. Joan of Arc (1947), Rev. Msgr. Robert G. Vincent; Rev. James Richard Day.
Res., P.O. Box 490, 70069-0490. Tel: 985-652-9100; Fax: 985-651-2920. [JC]
School—412 Fir St., 70068-4310. Tel: 985-652-6310; Fax: 985-652-6390. Mr. Larry J. Bourgeois, Prin.
Sisters of St. Dominic 2; Lay Teachers 39; Students 753.
Catechesis/Religious Programs—Tel: 985-651-0894. Mrs. Connie Cambre, D.R.E.
Students 339.

Luling, St. Charles Parish, Holy Family (1980), Rev. John P. Finn; Deacon Coy Landry.
Res., 155 Holy Family Ln., 70070-6103. Tel: 985-785-8585; Fax: 985-785-1167.
Catechesis/Religious Programs—Tel: 985-331-9100. D.R.E.: Diane Faucheux, (High School); Marlene Savoie.
Students 533.

St. Anthony of Padua (1961), Deacon Paul J. Donnaud. In res., Rev. Patrick J. R. Kennedy.
Res., 234 Angus Dr., 70070-4427. Tel: 985-785-8885; Fax: 985-785-8882.
Catechesis/Religious Programs—Tel: 504-785-0050.
Students 136.

Madisonville, St. Tammany Parish, St. Anselm (1962), Very Rev. Alan R. Weseman, V.F.; Deacon John Glover.
Res., P.O. Box 40, 70447-0040. Tel: 985-845-7342; Fax: 985-845-3076.
Catechesis/Religious Programs—Tel: 985-845-7912. Celie Clark, D.R.E.
Students 486.

Mandeville, St. Tammany Parish, Mary Queen of Peace (1988), Rev. Ronald L. Calkins; Deacon Anthony J. Ferretti.
Res., 1501 W. Causeway Approach, 70471-3047. Tel: 985-626-6977; Fax: 985-626-6971.
School—1515 W. Causeway Approach, 70471. Tel: 985-674-2466; Fax: 985-674-1441. Dr. Thomas J. Spranley, Prin.
Students 191.
Catechesis/Religious Programs—Tel: 504-674-9794.
Students 837.

Our Lady of the Lake (1850), Rev. Msgr. Joseph L. Chotin; Rev. Thomas M. McCann; Deacons Dwight Johnson; Joseph Lazo; Philip Baham; Louis N. Mire.
Res., 2115 Jefferson St., 70448-5820. Tel: 985-626-5671; Fax: 985-626-5422.
School—Tel: 985-626-5678; Fax: 985-626-4337.
Lay Teachers 43; Students 722. Co-principal: Janet B. Buras; Margeret "Peggy" J. LaBlanc.
Catechesis/Religious Programs—Tel: 985-626-7901. Richard Beben, D.R.E.
Students 703.

Marrero, Jefferson Parish,

1—IMMACULATE CONCEPTION, (1924) (Hispanic), Rev. Msgr. Ray P. Hebert; Revs. Tuan Anh Pham; Alberto Bermudez; Deacons Wilfred Robichaux, Jr.; Rodolfo Martinez. In res., Rev. Denver B. Pentecost.
Res., 4401 7th St., 70072-2099. Tel: 504-341-9516; Fax: 504-341-9517.
School—601 Avenue C, 70072-2098. Tel: 504-347-4409; Fax: 504-341-2766. Sr. Mary Terzo, F.M.A., Prin.
Salesian Sisters 2; Lay Teachers 41; Students 936.
High School—Immaculata, 537 Avenue D, 70072-2027. Tel: 504-341-6217; Fax: 504-341-6229. Sr. Mary Terzo, F.M.A., Prin.
Sisters 2; Lay Teachers 35; Students 491.
Catechesis/Religious Programs—Tel: 504-347-8449.
Students 129.

2—ST. AGNES LE THI THANH (1995) (Vietnamese). (Personal Parish for Southeast Asians). Rev. John Baptist Han Vu.
Mailing Address, Office and Rectory: 1000 Westwood Dr., 70072-2415. Tel: 504-347-4725; Fax: 504-340-2476.
Church—6851 8th St., 70072-2556. [JC]
Missions—Avondale, Jefferson Civil Parish, Assumption of Mary, 172 Noel Dr., Avondale, 70094-2900. Rev. Andrew Tran Cao Tuong, Admin.; New Orleans, Orleans Civil Parish, St. Joseph, 6450 Kathy Ct., New Orleans, 70131-7515. Rev. Joseph Pham Van Tue, Admin.
Catechesis/Religious Programs—Students 921.

3—ST. JOACHIM, (1985), Rev. Burnick J. Terrebonne.
Res., 5505 Barataria Blvd., 70072-6660. Tel: 504-341-9226; Fax: 504-340-8829.
Catechesis/Religious Programs—Tel: 504-371-8997. Mrs. Peggy Toyne, D.R.E.
Students 260.

4—ST. JOSEPH THE WORKER, (1955) (African American), Rev. Paul G. McQuillen, S.S.E.
Res., 455 Ames Blvd., 70072-1599. Tel: 504-347-8438; Fax: 504-340-9538.
School—Tel: 504-347-3704; Fax: 504-347-0852.
Lay Teachers 15; Students 272.
Catechesis/Religious Programs—Tel: 504-348-4784.
Students 149.

5—THE VISITATION OF OUR LADY, (1963), Very Rev. Michael B. Fraser, V.F.; Rev. David J. Robicheaux; Deacons Larry Murphy; Francis Minor.
Res., 3500 Ames Blvd., 70072-5699. Tel: 504-347-2203; Fax: 504-347-2223.
School—3520 Ames Blvd., 70072-5698. Tel: 504-347-3377; Fax: 504-341-5378. Mary Kitterman, Prin.
Lay Teachers 37; Students 806.
Catechesis/Religious Programs—Tel: 504-341-4499. Cheryl Tourelle, D.R.E.
Students 171.

Metairie, Jefferson Parish,

1—OUR LADY OF DIVINE PROVIDENCE, (1965), Rev. Msgr. Milton L. Reisch; Rev. John-Nhan Van Tran; Deacons Fred C. Memleb, Jr.; Barry Campeaux.
Res., 1000 N. Starrett Rd., 70003-5899. Tel: 504-466-4511; Fax: 504-466-4858.
School—917 N. Atlanta St., 70003-5898. Tel: 504-466-0591; Fax: 504-466-0671. Mrs. Shirley Bertucci, Prin.
Lay Teachers 34; Students 548.
Catechesis/Religious Programs—Mrs. Nancy Campeaux, D.R.E.
Students 289.

2—ST. ANGELA MERICI, (1964), Rev. Msgr. Crosby W. Kern, V.F.; Deacons Gilbert R. Schmidt; Nicholas Chetta.
Res., 901 Beverly Garden Dr., 70002-5085. Tel: 504-835-0324; Fax: 504-834-9709.
School—835 Melody Dr., 70002-5095. Tel: 504-835-8491; Fax: 504-835-4463. James Campbell, Prin.
Lay Teachers 29; Students 542.
Catechesis/Religious Programs—Tel: 504-837-9347.
Students 72.

3—ST. ANN CHURCH AND SHRINE, (1971), Rev. Msgr. Joseph E. Bourgeois; Rev. Joseph Man Tran; Deacons Phillip E. Doolen; Raymond J. Bertin.
Res., 4920 Loveland St., 70006-4099. Tel: 504-455-7071; Fax: 504-455-7076.
School—4921 Meadowdale St., 70006-4098. Tel: 504-455-8383; Fax: 504-455-9572.
Lay Teachers 54; Students 1,131.
Catechesis/Religious Programs—Tel: 504-455-7809, Ext. 125.
Students 981.

4—ST. BENILDE, (1964), Rev. Joseph Dau Van Nguyen; Deacons Biaggio DiGiovanni; Clifford S. Wright; Richard Brady.
Res., 1901 Division St., 70001-2798. Tel: 504-834-4980; Fax: 504-831-5810.
School—1801 Division St., 70001-2799. Tel: 504-833-9894; Fax: 504-834-4380. Ms. Marylyn Malone, Prin.
Lay Teachers 40; Students 668.
Catechesis/Religious Programs—Students 95.

5—ST. CATHERINE OF SIENA, (1921), Rev. Msgr. Roger A. Swenson; Rev. Mark S. Raphael; Deacons Michael Coney; Jere Crago; Don M. Richard. In res., Rev. Curtis R. Thomas.
Res., 105 Bonnabel Blvd., 70005-3798. Tel: 504-835-9343; 835-5491; Fax: 504-835-1525.
School—400 Codifer Blvd., 70005-3797. Tel: 504-831-1166; Fax: 504-833-8982. Sr. Imelda Moriarty, Prin.
Sisters of Charity of the Incarnate Word 4; Lay Teachers 63; Students 1,121.
Catechesis/Religious Programs—Students 52.

6—ST. CHRISTOPHER THE MARTYR, (1947), Revs. Kenneth Harney; James Nguyen Bach; Deacons Charles Duke; Rodney A. Trahan, Sr. In res., Rev. Charles L. Mueller.
Res., 309 Manson Ave., 70001-4898. Tel: 504-837-8214; Fax: 504-837-8303.
School—(Grades PreK-8) 3900 Derbigny St., 70001-4999. Tel: 504-837-6871; Fax: 504-834-0522. Ruth Meche, Prin.
Lay Teachers 41; Students: (PreK) 134; (1-8) 794.
Catechesis/Religious Programs—Tel: 504-831-7691. Doris Marse, D.R.E.
Students 65.

7—ST. CLEMENT OF ROME, (1965), Rev. Msgr. Ralph E. Carroll; Rev. David Dufour; Deacons Kenneth Boe; Ed Dorvin; Jeff Fariss.
Res., 4317 Richland Ave., 70002-3097. Tel: 504-887-7821; Fax: 504-454-3906.
School—3978 W. Esplanade Ave., 70002-3099. Tel: 504-888-0386; Fax: 504-885-8273. Susan Perry, Prin.
Lay Teachers 31; Students 541.
Catechesis/Religious Programs—Students 175.

8—ST. EDWARD THE CONFESSOR, (1964), Revs. Gilmer J. Martin; Joel P. Cantones (Philippines); Deacons A. David Warriner, Jr.; Gerard J. Fasullo, Sr.; August Mendel.
Parish Office: 4921 W. Metairie Ave., 70001-4466. Tel: 504-888-0703; Fax: 504-455-5443.
School—Tel: 504-888-6353; Fax: 504-456-0960. Sr. Mary de Lourdes Charbonnet, S.L.W., Prin. & D.R.E.
Sisters of the Living Word 2; Lay Teachers 26; Students 566.
Catechesis/Religious Programs—Students 65.

9—ST. FRANCIS XAVIER, (1924), Rev. Msgr. Andrew C. Taormina; Rev. Thomas Kinney; Deacons Paul Nalty; Charles E. Coudrain, Jr.
Res., 448 Metairie Rd., 70005-4371. Tel: 504-834-0340; 837-4733; Fax: 504-837-8735.
School—215 Betz Ave., 70005-4167. Tel: 504-833-1471; Fax: 504-833-1498. Stephen R. Labranche, Prin.
Lay Teachers 25; Students 430.
Catechesis/Religious Programs—444 Metairie Rd., 70005-4307. Tel: 504-834-0348.
Students 120.

10—ST. LAWRENCE THE MARTYR, (1958), Rev. Richard N. Maughan; Deacons Randall L. Engel; Sterling Ohlmeyer.
Res., 2525 Maine Ave., 70003-5446. Tel: 504-466-6236; Fax: 504-467-4945.
Catechesis/Religious Programs—Tel: 504-469-5262.
Students 40.

11—ST. LOUIS KING OF FRANCE, (1947), Rev. Msgr. Joseph O. Lorio; Rev. Ronald Braud; Deacon Wilbur Martinez.
Res., 1609 Carrollton Ave., 70005-1498. Tel: 504-834-9977; Fax: 504-834-9979.
School—1600 Lake Ave., 70005-1499. Tel: 504-833-8224; Fax: 504-838-9938.
Lay Teachers 32; Students 501.
Catechesis/Religious Programs—Students 27.

12—ST. MARY MAGDALEN, (1955), Rev. Msgr. Robert D. Massett; Rev. Joseph Thang Dinh Tran; Deacons Angeles Robin; Alfred Zeringue.
Res., 6425 W. Metairie Ave., 70003-4327. Tel: 504-733-0922; Fax: 504-733-0869.
School—6421 W. Metairie Ave., 70003-4395. Tel: 504-733-1433; Fax: 504-736-0727. Sr. Amelia Ibarra, Prin.
Teresians Sisters 3; Lay Teachers 28; Students 655.
Catechesis/Religious Programs—Students 275.

13—ST. PHILIP NERI, (1960), Revs. Lee John Saloy; Joseph Duc Dzien; Deacons Jerry L. Harrison; Thomas E. Caffery, Jr.; Edward R. Cannon.
Res., 6500 Kawanee Ave., 70003-3298. Tel: 504-887-5535; Fax: 504-885-6259.
School—6600 Kawanee Ave., 70003-3199. Tel: 504-887-5600; Fax: 504-456-6857.
Lay Teachers 33; Students 616.
Catechesis/Religious Programs—Tel: 504-889-0089. Mr. Howard J. Jenkins, D.R.E.
Students 352.

Norco, St. Charles Parish, Sacred Heart of Jesus (1959), Rev. John J. Marse.
Res., 401 Spruce St., P.O. Box 515, 70079-2197. Tel: 985-764-6503; Fax: 985-725-0512.
School—Tel: 985-764-9958; Fax: 985-764-0041. Colleen S. Remont, Prin.
Lay Teachers 14; Students 240.
Catechesis/Religious Programs—Students 210.

Paradis, St. Charles Parish, St. John the Baptist (1971), Rev. Msgr. James C. Moragne.
Res., P.O. Box 1498, 70080-1498. Tel: 985-758-2668; Fax: 985-758-2901.
Catechesis/Religious Programs—Students 197.

Pearl River, St. Tammany Parish, SS. Peter and Paul (1970), Rev. Bac-Hai Viet Tran; Deacons John F. Howard; John Patrick Downey; Francis W. Drake.
Res., 66192 St. Mary Dr., 70452-5705. Tel: 985-863-7935; Fax: 985-863-5431.
Catechesis/Religious Programs—Students 137.

Pointe a la Hache, Plaquemines Parish, St. Thomas (1844), Rev. Amaldoss.
Res., P.O. Box 98, 70082-0098. Tel: 985-333-4465; Fax: 985-333-9933. [CEM 2]
Mission—Braithwaite, Plaquemines Parish, Assumption of the Blessed Virgin, 6951 Hwy. 39, Braithwaite, 70040-0063. Tel: 985-682-5607; Fax: 985-682-5617.

Port Sulphur, Plaquemines Parish, St. Patrick (1956), Rev. Gerard P. Stapleton.
Res., 28698 Hwy. 23, 70083-9623. Tel: 985-564-3284; Fax: 985-564-3108. [CEM]
Catechesis/Religious Programs—Tel: 985-564-2803.
Students 97.
Mission—Potash, Plaquemines Parish, St. Joseph.

Reserve, St. John the Baptist Parish, Our Lady of Grace (1937) (African American), Rev. Joseph C. Rodney, Jr., S.S.J. In res., Rev. Andrew Dodo (Nigeria).
Mailing Address: P.O. Box 464, 70084-0464.
Res., 772 Hwy. 44, 70084-0464. Tel: 985-536-2613; Fax: 985-536-1819.
School—Tel: 985-536-4291; Fax: 985-536-4250.
Lay Teachers 9; Students 175.
Catechesis/Religious Programs—Tel: 985-536-2028. Myrtle Ann Lucas, D.R.E.
Students 139.

St. Peter (1864), Rev. Patrick B. Sanders; Deacons David W. Farinelli; Paul H. Dupuy, Jr.
Res., 1550 Hwy. 44, P.O. Box 435, 70084-0435. Tel: 985-536-2887; Fax: 985-536-7078. [CEM]
School—Tel: 985-536-4296. Sr. Mary Germaine, Prin.
Lay Teachers 16; Students 237.
Catechesis/Religious Programs—Tel: 985-536-2886.
Students 223.

River Ridge, Jefferson Parish, St. Matthew the Apostle (1959), Rev. Nghiem Van Nguyen; Deacons Russell LeBlanc; Dan Dorsey; Roland Bienvenu.
Res., 10021 Jefferson Hwy., 70123-2498. Tel: 504-737-4537; Fax: 504-737-4033.
School—Tel: 504-737-4604; Fax: 504-738-7985.
Lay Teachers 32; Students 585.
Catechesis/Religious Programs—Students 75.

St. Benedict, St. Tammany Parish, St. Benedict (1970), Rev. Marian E. Larmann, O.S.B.; Deacon Nelvin Luke.
Res., Smith-Stafford Rd., 70457-9999. Tel: 985-892-1216; Fax: 985-892-4211.
Catechesis/Religious Programs—Tel: 985-809-7752; Fax: 985-867-2270.
Students 186.

St. Bernard, St. Bernard Parish, St. Bernard (1787), Rev. John P. Grenham.
Mailing Address: P.O. Box 220, 70085-0220.
Res., 2805 Bayou Rd., 70085-9748. Tel: 504-682-5493; 682-3709; Fax: 504-682-8915. [CEM]

Slidell, St. Tammany Parish,

1—Our Lady of Lourdes, (1890), Rev. Msgr. Howard H. Hotard; Deacon Charles B. Faler, Jr.
Res., 3924 Berkley Ave., 70458-5198. Tel: 985-643-4137; Fax: 985-643-1675. [CEM]
School—345 Westchester Pl., 70458-5299. Tel: 985-643-3230; Fax: 985-645-0648. Mr. Robert V. Kiefer, Jr., Prin.
Sisters 1; Lay Teachers 27; Students 575.
Catechesis/Religious Programs—Tel: 985-643-1742. Mrs. Patricia S. Andrews, D.R.E.
Students 365.

2—St. Genevieve, (1968), Rev. Wayne C. Paysse; Deacons George Menges; Daniel Haggerty, Jr.
Res. and Mailing Address: 58203 Hwy. 433, 70460-3121. Tel: 985-643-3832; Fax: 985-649-5294.
Catechesis/Religious Programs—Tel: 985-641-5220; Fax: 985-641-5220. Phillip A. Bellinil, D.R.E.
Students 265.

3—St. Luke the Evangelist, (1982), Revs. Rodney P. Bourg; James J. Jeanfreau; Deacons Robert Binney; Harold J. Burke; Robert Trainor. In res., Rev. Gerard P. Kinane.
Office: 910 Cross Gates Blvd., 70461-8414. Tel: 985-641-6429; Fax: 985-847-0742.
Catechesis/Religious Programs—Tel: 985-641-2570.
Students 841.

4—St. Margaret Mary, (1965), Rev. Msgr. Lanaux J. Rareshide; Revs. Thomas Gallagher, S.P.S.; Ray Hymel; Deacons Richard W. Calkins; John C. Weber; George H. Frilot, II.
Res., 1050 Robert Blvd., 70458-2098. Tel: 985-643-6124; Fax: 985-643-6126.
School—Tel: 985-643-4612; Fax: 985-643-4659. Mr. Bobby Ohler, Prin.
Lay Teachers 40; Students 733.
Catechesis/Religious Programs—Tel: 985-649-3055.
Students 486.

Terrytown, Jefferson Parish, Christ the King (1963), Revs. Kenneth Borgesen, O.Ss.T.; Jose Ladra; Deacons Cornelius Armshaw; James Swiler; Robert G. Beaumont, Sr.; Jose D. Perez.
Res., 535 Deerfield Rd., 70056-2899. Tel: 504-361-1500; Fax: 504-361-0632.
School—Tel: 504-367-3601; Fax: 504-367-3679.
Lay Teachers 27; Students 491.

Violet, St. Bernard Parish, Our Lady of Lourdes (1916), Rev. Msgr. Frank J. Lipps; Rev. Raymond Joseph Guillot; Deacon William Chiappetta.
Res., 6305 E. St. Bernard Hwy., 70092-9506. Tel: 504-682-3046; Fax: 504-682-4470.
Church—2621 Colonial Blvd., 70092.
Catechesis/Religious Programs—6413 E. St. Bernard Hwy., 70092-9508. Tel: 504-682-0919.
Students 445.

Waggaman, Jefferson Parish, Our Lady of the Angels (1978), Rev. Paul Van Tung Nguyen; Deacon Gilbert Smith.
Res., 139 Herman St., 70094-2404. Tel: 504-436-4459; Fax: 504-436-4459. [CEM]
Catechesis/Religious Programs—Tel: 504-437-0514.
Students 162.

Westwego, Jefferson Parish, Our Lady of Prompt Succor (1920), Rev. Anthony M. Serio; Deacon Ernest F. Elfer, Jr.
Res., 146 Fourth St., 70094-4297. Tel: 504-341-9522; Fax: 504-341-5957. [CEM][JC]
School—531 Avenue A, 70094-4294. Tel: 504-341-9505; Fax: 504-341-9508. Sr. Rita Fantin, F.M.A., Prin. & Supr.
Sisters 3; Lay Teachers 16; Students 350.
Catechesis/Religious Programs—Students 210.

Non-Parochial Churches & Chapels

New Orleans, Orleans Parish,

1—Korean Catholic Chapel and Community Center, Rev. Myung-Hwan Kim (Korea).
Chapel—140 27th St., Kenner, 70062-4906. Tel: 504-469-3956.

2—National Shrine of Blessed Francis Xavier Seelos, (2000), Rev. Byron J. Miller, C.SS.R., Dir.
2030 Constance St., 70130-5099. Tel: 504-525-2495.

3—Our Lady of Prompt Succor National Shrine, (1926), Deacon Charles E. Coudrain, Jr.
Church—2635 State St., 70118-6399. Tel: 504-866-1472; Fax: 504-866-8300.

4—St. Joseph Chapel,
Mailing Address: 1000 Howard Ave, Ste 500, 70113-1903. Tel: 504-596-3050.
St. Joseph Cemetery, 2200 Washington Ave., 70113-2647. Tel: 504-895-2507.

5—St. Mary Church, (1845). (Shrine of St. Lazarus of Jerusalem). Rev. Msgr. Alvin J. O'Reilly, Rector.
Church—1116 Chartres St., 70116-2596. Tel: 504-529-3040; Fax: 504-529-2001.

6—St. Mary's Assumption, (1858) (German), Rev. Gerard B. LaPorte, C.Ss.R.
Church—2030 Constance St., 70130-5099. Tel: 504-522-6748; Fax: 504-523-3734.

7—St. Mary's Chapel, Rev. Gerard B. LaPorte, C.SS.R. 1516 Jackson Ave., 70130. Tel: 504-522-6748.

8—St. Roch Chapel,
St. Roch Cemetery, St. Roch Ave. & Music St., 70117-8223. Tel: 504-945-5961.

9—Chapel of the Vietnamese Martyrs, (1978) (Vietnamese), Rev. Msgr. Dominic Mai Thanh Luong.
Church—14400 Peltier Dr., 70129-1713. Tel: 504-254-5660; Fax: 504-254-9250.

Mandeville, St. Tammany Parish, St. Dymphna Catholic Center and Chapel, Rev. Raphael Barousse, O.S.B., Chap.
Southeast Louisiana Hospital, P.O. Box 3850, 70470-3850. Tel: 504-626-6317.

Pilgrimage Shrines

New Orleans, Orleans Parish, Our Lady of Prompt Succor National Shrine (1926), Deacon Charles E. Coudrain, Jr.
Res., 2635 State St., 70118-6399. Tel: 504-866-1472.

Shrine of St. Jude Thaddeus, Rev. Joseph Ferraioli, O.M.I., Dir.
411 N. Rampart St., 70112-3594. Tel: 504-525-1551; Fax: 504-525-1827.

Shrine of St. Lazarus of Jerusalem, Rev. Msgr. Alvin J. O'Reilly, Rector.
Church—1116 Chartres St., 70116-2596. Tel: 504-529-2651; Fax: 504-529-2001.

Metairie, Jefferson Parish, St. Ann National Shrine (1971), Rev. Joseph E. Bourgeois.
Church—4920 Loveland, 70002-4099. Tel: 504-455-7071; Fax: 504-455-7076.
Catechesis/Religious Programs—Tel: 504-455-7809.
Students 981.

Non-Parochial Community

New Orleans, Orleans Parish, Byzantine Catholic Mission (1978). Ruthenian Rite Jurisdiction. Rev. Ellis L. DePriest, S.M.
Church—2437 S. Carrollton Ave., 70118. Tel: 504-524-5192; Fax: 504-524-9796.

Chaplains of Public Institutions

Hospitals

New Orleans. *Charity Hospital* 1532 Tulane Ave., 70140-1015. Tel: 504-679-9204. Rev. Eutiquiano Miguel, O.F.M.Cap., Chap.

DePaul Hospital 1040 Calhoun St., 70118. Tel: 504-899-8282. Chaplains: Deacons Richard E. Deichmann; Charles B. Hauseknecht, Sr.

Jo Ellen Smith Nursing Facility 4502 General Meyer Ave., 70114-3531. Tel: 504-361-7923. Deacon Robert G. Beaumont, Sr.

Memorial Medical Center. Mercy Campus 301 N. Jefferson Davis Pkwy., 70119-5397. Tel: 504-483-5248. Rev. Thomas Sheehan, S.J., Chap.

Memorial Medical Center. Baptist Campus 2700 Napoleon Ave., 70115-6996. Tel: 504-899-9311. Rev. Joseph E. Okoro, C.M.F.

Methodist Hospital 5620 Read Rd., 70127-0103. Tel: 504-244-5719. Deacon Joseph R. Rosato.

Touro Infirmary 1401 Foucher St., 70115-3593. Tel: 504-897-7011. Revs. Douglas C. Brougher, Chap., Tel: 504-897-7011; 945-5878; Edmund Akordor Tel: 504-314-6949.

United Medical Center. Attended from St. Vincent de Paul Parish. 3419 St. Claude Ave., 70117-6198. Tel: 504-948-8200.

University Hospital 2021 Perdido St., 70112-1396. Tel: 504-588-3000. Rev. Vincent Bechamps, O.SS.T., Chap., Tel: 504-588-3175.

Vencor Hospital 3601 Coliseum St., 70115-3687. Tel: 504-899-1555; Fax: 504-899-1509. Chaplains: Deacons Richard E. Deichmann; William A. Glennon.

Veterans Affairs Medical Center 1601 Perdido St., 70146-2000. Tel: 504-568-0811. Chaplains: Revs. Joseph D. Laboon; Lawrence A. deMaria.

Chalmette. *Chalmette Medical Centers* 9001 Patricia St., 70043-1799. Tel: 504-277-8011. 801 Virtue St., 70043-1298. Tel: 504-277-7711. Chaplains: Deacons Alex Serantine; Douglas H. Strahan.

Covington. *Lakeview Regional Medical Center* 95 E. Fairway Dr., 70433. Tel: 504-867-3800. Deacon Louis N. Mire, Chap.

St. Tammany Hospital 1202 S. Tyler St., 70433. Tel: 504-898-4000. Deacon Joseph LeRose, Chap.

Gretna. *Meadowcrest Hospital* 2500 Belle Chasse Hwy., 70056-7127. Tel: 504-392-3131. Deacons Milton G. Webre, Chap.; Leslie D. Vincent, Dir. Pastoral Care.

Jefferson. *Elmwood Partners* 1221 S. Clearview Pkwy., 70121-1029. Tel: 504-734-1900. Rev. Lawrence Pandolfo, O.P., Chap.

Ochsner Foundation Hospital 1516 S. Clearview Pkwy., 70121-2484. Tel: 504-842-3000. Rev. Wilfred F. Meridier, Chap., Tel: 504-866-7713.

Mandeville. *Southeast Louisiana Hospital* P.O. Box 3850, 70470-3850. Tel: 504-626-6317; Fax: 504-626-6658. Rev. Raphael Barousse, O.S.B.; Deacon John Patrick Downey.

Marrero. *West Jefferson General Hospital* 4500 11th St., 70072-3191. Tel: 504-347-5511. Rev. Denver B. Pentecost, Chap.; Deacons Francis M. Minor; Milton G. Webre.

Wynhoven Health Care Center 1050 Medical Center Blvd., 70072-3170. Tel: 504-347-0777. Rev. Denver B. Pentecost, Chap.

Metairie. *Doctors Hospital of Jefferson* 4320 Houma Blvd., 70002-2973. Tel: 504-849-8684. Deacon Charles Duke, Chap.

East Jefferson General Hospital 4200 Houma Blvd., 70002-2970. Tel: 504-454-4000. Rev. Charles L. Mueller, Chap.; Deacon Raymond E. Heap, Assoc. Chap.

Lakeside Hospital 4700 S.1-10 Service Rd. West, 70001. Tel: 504-780-8282. Deacon August Mendel, Chap.

SLIDELL. *Greenbriar Nursing & Convalescent Home* 505 Robert Rd., 70458-1699. Tel: 985-643-6900. Chaplains: Rev. Msgr. Lanaux J. Rareshide Tel: 504-643-6124; Rev. Thomas Gallagher, S.P.S.

Greenery Neurologic Rehabilitation Center at Slidell 1400 W. Lindberg Dr., 70458-3193. Tel: 985-641-4985. Chaplains: Rev. Msgr. Lanaux J. Rareshide Tel: 985-643-6124; Rev. Thomas Gallagher, S.P.S.

Guest House of Slidell Nursing Home 1051 Robert Rd., 70458-2011. Tel: 985-643-5630. Chaplains: Rev. Msgr. Lanaux J. Rareshide Tel: 504-643-6124; Rev. Thomas Gallagher, S.P.S.

North Shore Living Center. Attended by St. Luke the Evangelist, Slidell. 106 Medical Center Dr., 70461-7833. Tel: 985-643-0307.

North Shore Regional Medical Center. Attended by St. Luke the Evangelist, Slidell. 100 Medical Center Dr., 70461-7833. Tel: 985-649-7070.

Slidell Memorial Hospital. Attended by St. Margaret Mary, Slidell. 1001 Gause Blvd., 70458-2987. Tel: 985-643-2200. Deacons Richard W. Calkins; Francis W. Drake.

Colleges and Universities

NEW ORLEANS. *Delgado College* 615 City Park Ave., 70119. Tel: 504-288-6336. Chaplains: Revs. Francis Berner; Ronald Henery, O.P.; Deacon Eric Gamble, Assoc. Chap.

Delgado Community College, School of Nursing 4133 Banks St., 70119-6883. Tel: 504-568-6411. Rev. Louis E. Meyers, S.J., Chap.

Louisiana State University Medical Center 4133 Banks St., 70119-6883. Tel: 504-568-6411. Rev. Louis E. Meyers, S.J., Chap.

Southern University in New Orleans UNO Newman Center, 70148-0001. Tel: 504-288-6336. Rev. Francis Berner, Chap.

Tulane-Newcomb 1037 Audubon St., 70118-5294. Tel: 504-866-0984. Rev. Richard B. Williams, O.P.

University of New Orleans UNO Newman Center, 70148-0001. Tel: 504-288-6336. Rev. Francis Berner, Chap.

Prisons

NEW ORLEANS. *Orleans Parish Correctional Center* 521 S. Broad St., 70119-7490. Tel: 504-822-8000. Chaplains: Rev. Theodore M. Kalamaja, S.J.; Deacons Randolph J. Crochet, Jr.; Jeffrey Fariss; Jose A. Sierra; Rodrigo Alonso Fonseca; George H. Frilot, II; Rodney A. Trahan, Sr.

Orleans Parish House of Detention 2735 Perdido St., 70119-7390. Tel: 504-822-8000. Pastoral Ministers: Sr. Lilianne Flavin, O.P.; Sr. Victor Allain, R.S.M.

ANGIE. *Washington Correctional Institute* 27268 Hwy. 21, 70426-3030. Tel: 985-848-5232. Deacon Charles Hartman, Chap.

ANGOLA. *Louisiana State Penitentiary.* Deacon Joseph Mamou, Chap., P.O. Box 169, Garyville, 70051-0169. Tel: 985-535-3682.

CHALMETTE. *St. Bernard Parish Prison* St. Bernard Courthouse, 70043-4793. Tel: 504-279-8823. Deacon Alex J. Seruntine, Jr., Chap.

GRETNA. *Jefferson Parish Correctional Center* P.O. Box 388, 70054-0388. Tel: 504-374-7700, Ext. 3109. Chaplains: Rev. Robert J. Ratchford, S.J.; Deacons Louis Stall; Ralph Fray; Brian J. Klause; Gerard L. Labadot.

HARVEY. *Rivarde Juvenile Detention Home* 1525 Manhattan Blvd., 70058-3405. Tel: 504-392-2097. Deacon Ralph Fray, Chap.

MANDEVILLE. *St. Tammany Parish Prison* Tel: 985-892-8324. Deacon Charles Read, Jr.

On Archdiocesan Assignment:
Reverend Monsignors—
Rodi, Thomas J., Vicar General

On Duty Outside the Archdiocese:
Reverend Monsignors—
Calkins, Arthur B., Villa Stritch, Via della Nocetta, 63, 00164, Rome, Italy
Reverend Fathers—
Calamari, Paul, St. Peter the Apostle, 35 E. Fifth St., New Castle, DE 19720
Cavalier, Robert C., Trappist Monastery, Moncks Corner, SC
Fernandez, Luis J., VA Medical Center, 6863 S.W. 16th St., Miami, FL 33155-1709
Highfill, H. Brian, 1271 Mound House St., Las Vegas, NV 89110-5900
Maestri, William, Visiting Prof., Pepperdine University School of Law, Malibu, CA
Picado, Rodrigo, 50 Vs E. Cortel, Curridabat, San Jose, Costa Rica, CA
Planea, John (Philippines), Cardinal Rosales Pastoral Center, Patria Bldg. J. Avelino St., Calbayog City, 6710 Philippines
Rabe, David L., P.O. Box 129, Easton, KS 66020

Military Chaplains:
Reverend Fathers—
Dixon, James R., U.S.A.F., Headquarters, USAF/HCX, 112 Luke Ave., Bolling AFB, DC 20332-9050
O'Neill, Michael F., U.S.A.F., 100 ARW/HC, Unit 4905, Box 230, APO-AE, 09459-5230

Unassigned:
Reverend Fathers—
Duffy, Stephen
Heffner, Carroll E.

On Leave:
Reverend Fathers—
Lohan, James
Sizelove, Michael Dennis

On Medical Leave of Absence:
Reverend Fathers—
Mongeon, Peter M.

Retired:
Most Rev.—
D'Antonio, Nicholas, O.F.M., D.D., Chateau de Notre Dame, New Orleans
Reverend Monsignors—
Bane, Raymond T., P.O. Box 1550, Paradis, LA 70080-1550
Boeshans, Francis G., P.O. Box 6328, Diamondhead, MS 39525-6000
Byrnes, Donald M., St. Jerome, 2400 33rd St., Kenner, LA 70065
Carroll, Richard L., 9811 Ana Hula, Bay, St. Louis, MS 39520
Duke, Charles J., 3513 Lemon St., Metairie, LA 70006
Iverson, Stanley J., 5501 Tullis Dr., Bldg. 13-108, New Orleans, LA 70131
Landry, Michael, 36405 Old Bayou Liberty Rd., Slidell, LA 70460
O'Reilly, Alvin J., 1116 Chartres St., New Orleans, LA 70116
Poche, Gerard W.
Reynolds, John P., Chateau de Notre Dame, New Orleans
Roeten, Winus, 9512 Kuepferle Ct., River Ridge, LA 70123
Schutten, Marion F., P.O. Box 3174, Covington, LA 70434
Sontheimer, W. Wendell, 2724 Whitney Pl. #331, Metairie, LA 70002
Tomasovich, John A., 69 Lake Lynn Dr., Harvey, LA 70058
Van der Werff, Martin, 3609 Lake des Allemands, Harvey, LA 70058
Woods, Earl C., Chateau de Notre Dame, 2820 Burdette St., New Orleans, LA 70125
Reverend Fathers—
Arbizu, Juventino, 41 Calle, 12-29 Villasol, Zona 12, Guatemala City, Guatemala
Barattini, John H., Casella Postale 79, 16043, Chiavari, Italy
Dabria, Jerry J., 401 S. Gatehouse Dr., Apt. G, Metairie, LA 70001-2039
De La Pinera, Fernando, Casa Sacerdotal, Plaza Bendicho, 9, Almeria, 14001 Spain
DeMaria, Lawrence A., 8 Mesa St., Kenner, LA 70065
Duffy, Donald, P.O. Box 428, Destrahan, LA 70047
Ernst, Albert C., P.O. Box 640400, Kenner, LA 70064-0400
Gonzales, Gabriel, 4011 Gen. Pershing St., New Orleans, LA 70125
Gracias, Urbano, 1208 Mehle Ave., Arabi, LA 70032
Grennan, Thomas J., Chateau de Notre Dame, 2820 Burdette St., New Orleans, LA 70125-2596
Kennedy, Patrick J. R., 234 Angus Dr., Luling, LA 70070
Mele, Rudolph, 2832 Burdette St., New Orleans, LA 70125
Mitchell, Royce, 1512 Gardena Dr., New Orleans, LA 70122
Monzillo, Oneil, 532 Indian Bluff, Las Vegas, NV 89128
Morgan, Brendan P., P.O. Box 73128, Metairie, LA 70033
Perera, Denzil M., 1342 Moss St., New Orleans, LA 70119-2998
Perkovic, Anton, 444 Adair St., Mandeville, LA 70448
Persac, Louis A., 924 Monroe St., Gretna, LA 70053
Pieris, Timothy, 6564 Fleur de Lis St., Apt. 9, New Orleans, LA 70124
Pijoan, L. Adrian M. Figuerola, St. Augustine Home, 2345 W. 86th St., Indianapolis, IN 46260
Qui, Vincent, 421 Pat Dr., Avondale, LA 70094
Schmaltz, Bernard, 500 Prentiss Rd., Pass Christian, MS 39571
Schott, James E., 4744 Marigny St., New Orleans, LA 70122
Texada, David Ker, 1923 Salem St., Alexandria, LA 71301-3840
Tranchina, Joseph, 2820 Burdette St., New Orleans, LA 70125
Trinchard, Paul, 446 Crystal St., New Orleans, LA 70124
Vitte, Jules, 38 Grande Rue, 25300, Les Fourges, France
Walsh, Laurence, Lyrattin, Ballinamult, Co. Waterford, Ireland
Young, Bernard L., 176 Dotted Dove Ln., Indialantie, FL 32903

Permanent Deacons:
Alexander, Dwight, St. Raymond, New Orleans
Arendt, Elliott, Sr., Maurice, New Orleans
Armshaw, Cornelius, St. Anthony, Gretna
Attaway, Charles, On Leave
Baham, Philip C., Our Lady of the Lake, Mandeville
Balderas, Robert, Sr., Diocese of Lafayette
Barrillieaux, Louis E., Assoc. Dir., Permanent Diaconate Office, Mater Dolorosa, New Orleans
Bastian, Herman, (Retired)
Beaumont, Robert G., Christ the King, Terrytown
Beckendorf, Edward, Nativity of Our Lord, Kenner
Bertin, Raymond J., St. Ann, Metairie
Bertucci, Chris, Chap., Southeast Louisiana State Hospital, Mandeville
Beyer, Walter L., (Retired), Mater Dolorosa, New Orleans
Bialas, James, Sacred Heart, Lacombe; Lazarus House, New Orleans
Bienvenu, Roland, St. Matthew the Apostle, River Ridge; Children's Hospital, New Orleans
Binney, Robert, St. Luke the Evangelist, Slidell
Blanchard, John, (On leave)
Boe, Kenneth, Chap. Jefferson Parish Sheriff's Office, St. Clement of Rome, Metairie
Bourgeois, Don, St. Jane de Chantal, Abita Springs
Bourgeois, Garland, St. Elizabeth Ann Seton, Kenner
Brady, Richard, St. Benilde, Metairie
Broussard, Terrel J., St. Maria Goretti, New Orleans
Burke, Harold J., St. Luke the Evangelist, Slidell
Caffery, Thomas E., Jr., Assoc. Dir. Permanent Dioconate; Assoc. Dir. Archdiocesan Spirituality Ctr., St. Philip Neri, Metairie
Calamia, S.J., (Retired)
Calkins, Richard W., Chap., Slidell Memorial Hospital, St. Margaret Mary, Slidell
Campeaux, Barry G., Our Lady of Divine Providence, Metairie
Campuzano, Luis A., St. Jerome, Kenner
Cannon, Edward, St. Philip Neri, Metairie
Capaci, Andrea, St. Elizabeth Ann Seton, Kenner; Assoc. Dir., Family Life Apostolate
Caserta, Piero, St. Agnes, Jefferson; Covenant House, New Orleans
Cassou, Henry A., Jr., Our Lady of Prompt Succor, Chalmette
Chetta, Nick, St. Angela Merici, Metairie
Chiappetta, William, Our Lady of Lourdes, Violet
Cimino, Paul, St. Rita, New Orleans
Coney, Michael, St. Catherine of Siena, Metairie
Cordes, Daniel J., St. Jerome, Kenner
Coudrain, Charles E., Jr., Our Lady of Prompt Succor Shrine, New Orleans; St. Francis Xavier, Metairie
Crago, Jere, St. Catherine of Siena, Metairie
Crochet, Randolph J., Orleans Parish Correctional Ctr. and Ozanam Inn, New Orleans
Curry, William P., Jr., Resurrection of Our Lord, New Orleans
Daigle, Irving J., Sacred Heart of Jesus, New Orleans
Daly, Edward, (Retired)
Deichmann, Richard, Mater Dolorosa, Vencor and DePaul Hospitals, New Orleans
DeLeon, Ildefonso R., St. Maria Goretti, New Orleans
DeVerges, Philip, Holy Name of Jesus, New Orleans
DiGiovanni, Biaggio, St. Benilde, Metairie
DiGrado, Chris, St. Andrew the Apostle, New Orleans
Donnaud, Paul J., St. Anthony of Padua, Luling
Doolen, Philip E., St. Ann, Metairie
Dorsey, Dan, St. Matthew the Apostle, River Ridge
Dorvin, Edwin, St. Clement of Rome, Metairie
Downey, John Patrick, Chap., Southeast Louisiana State Hospital, Mandeville, Ss. Peter and Paul, Pearl River
Dragon, Edgar P., Our Lady of Perpetual Help, Kenner
Drake, Francis W., Ss. Peter and Paul, Pearl River
Duet, Ferris J., Jr., Infant Jesus of Prague, Harvey
Duffy, Peter E., St. Maria Goretti, New Orleans
Duke, Charles, St. Christopher the Martyr, Metairie

Duplechain, Raphael, Jr., Assoc. Dir., Permanent Diaconate, Holy Spirit, New Orleans
Dupuy, Paul H., Jr., St. Peter, Reserve
Durbin, Oscar A., (Retired)
Elfer, Ernest C., Jr., Stella Maris Maritime Center, New Orleans; Our Lady of Prompt Succor, Westwego
Engel, Randall L., St. Lawrence the Martyr, Metairie
Faler, Charles B., Our Lady of Lourdes, Slidell
Fandal, Wendolen, Jr., (Retired)
Farinelli, David W., St. Peter, Reserve; Assoc. Dir., Family Life Apostolate
Fariss, Jeffrey, St. Clement of Rome, Metairie
Fasullo, Gerard, Sr., St. Edward the Confessor, Metairie
Ferretti, Anthony J., Mary Queen of Peace, Mandeville
Fleischer, Francis J., St. Theresa of Avila, New Orleans
Flynn, Dan, St. Rita, Harahan, Catholic Committee on Scouting
Fonseca, Rodrigo Alonso, Chap., Orleans Parish Correctional Center, Ss. Peter and Paul, New Orleans
Fray, Ralph, Jefferson Parish Correctional Ctr., Gretna; Rivarde Juvenile Detention Home, Harvey
Frilot, George H., II, Chap., Orleans Parish Correctional Center, St. Margaret Mary, Slidell
Gaiennie, Richard M., Our Lady of the Rosary, New Orleans
Gamble, Eric, St. Thomas the Apostle, UNO
Garon, Henry A., St. Henry & Ozanam Inn, New Orleans
Glapion, Lloyd St. Clair, (Retired)
Glennon, William A., Jr., St. Pius X & Vencor Hospital, New Orleans
Glover, John A., St. Anselm, Madisonville
Gross, Greg Andrew Nicholas, Our Lady of Perpetual Help, Kenner
Gubert, Norbert, St. Raphael the Archangel, New Orleans
Guidry, Ronald, Dir., Office of Worship;, St. Louis Cathedral, New Orleans
Guitterrez, Clayton J., St. John the Baptist, Folsom
Haggerty, Daniel, Jr., Chap., F.B.I. and Slidell Police Dept., St. Genevieve, Slidell
Hamm, John David, Our Lady of the Rosary, New Orleans
Harrison, Jerry, St. Philip Neri, Metairie
Hartman, Charles, Annunciation, Bogalusa; Washington Correctional Institute, Angie
Hartson, Maurice, III, St. Alphonsus & Project Lazarus, New Orleans
Hauseknecht, Charles B., St. Frances Xavier Cabrini, New Orleans
Heap, Raymond E., East Jefferson Hospital, Metairie
Heine, Charles, St. Peter, Covington
Herrick, Dean D., Holy Name of Mary, New Orleans
Hooper, Edward B., (Retired)
Howard, John, Sts. Peter & Paul, Pearl River
Insley, J. Vernon, St. Bonaventure, Avondale
Johnson, Dwight J., Our Lady of the Lake, Mandeville
Jones, Melvin C., Sr., On Leave
Keller, Lawrence, St. Vincent de Paul, New Orleans
Klause, Brian Joseph, Chap., Jefferson Parish Correctional Center;, St. Anthony, Lafitte
Labadot, Gerard L., Chap. Jefferson Parish Correctional Center;, St. Martha, Harvey
Labranche, Frans, Jr., St. Jane de Chantal, Abita Springs
Landry, Coy, Holy Family, Luling
Lazo, Joseph, Our Lady of the Lake, Mandeville
LeBlanc, Ames P., Jr., On Leave
LeBlanc, Nolen J., St. Rita, Harahan
LeBlanc, Russell T., (Retired), St. Matthew the Apostle, River Ridge
LeDoux, John, Nativity of Our Lord, Kenner
LeRose, Joseph R., St. John of the Cross, Lacombe
Levy, Albert A., III, St. Mark, Chalmette
Lewis, Raymond, St. Matthias and Our Lady of Lourdes, New Orleans
Luke, Nelvin, St. Benedict Church, St. Benedict
Madere, Kenneth P., St. Mark, Chalmette
Mallerich, Walton J., On Leave
Mamou, Joseph, Chap., Louisiana State Penitentiary
Martinez, Gerald J., St. Frances Xavier Cabrini and St. Leo the Great, New Orleans
Martinez, Rodolfo J., Assoc. Dir., Permanent Diaconate, Immaculate Conception, Marrero
Martinez, Wilbur, St. Louis King of France, Metairie
Martinsen, Noel W., St. Elizabeth Ann Seton, Kenner
Matherne, Landry, St. Gertrude, Des Allemands
Mathews, Michael Schmid, (Duty Outside)
Memleb, Fred C., Jr., Our Lady of Divine Providence, Metairie
Mendel, August B., St. Edward the Confessor; Chap., Columbia Lakeside Hospital, Metairie
Mendieta, Roberto, Nativity of Our Lord, Kenner
Menges, George, St. Genevieve, Slidell
Miester, Alvin C., Jr., St. Louise de Marillac, Arabi
Minor, Francis M., Visitation of Our Lady, Marrero
Mire, Louis N., Our Lady of the Lake, Mandeville
Mistretta, Nicholas L., St. Rita, Harahan
Moore, Charles R., (Duty Outside)
Moragas, Lucien, (Duty Outside)
Morales, G. Ernesto, St. Jerome, Kenner
Muhleisen, John P., (Retired)
Mumme, Paul, Sr.
Murphy, Larry, Visitation of Our Lady, Marrero
Nalty, Paul A., St. Francis Xavier, Metairie; Chap, Malta Park Assisted Living Residence, New Orleans
Nunez, Charles R., Sr., (Retired)
Nuss, Henry, Our Lady of the Rosary, New Orleans
Ohlmeyer, Sterling, St. Lawrence the Martyr, Metairie
Peres, Anthony W., (Retired)
Perez, Jose D., Christ the King, Terrytown
Pham, Joseph Hiep, Mary Queen of Vietnam, New Orleans
Pippenger, John, St. Dominic, New Orleans
Rayfield, Rudolph J., Sr., Assoc. Dir., Permanent Diaconate;, St. Peter Claver, New Orleans
Read, Charles, Jr., St. Peter, Covington; St. Tammany Prison, Mandeville
Reeson, Curles P., Jr., St. Robert Bellarmine, Arabi
Rhodes, Frank W., Jr., Prince of Peace, Chalmette
Richard, Don Michael, St. Catherine of Siena, Metairie
Richardson, Ray, Our Lady of Good Counsel, New Orleans
Rivere, Raymond H., St. Mark, Chalmette; Chap., Chalmette Medical Facility
Rizzo, Peter C., St. Frances Xavier Cabrini, New Orleans
Robicheaux, Wilfred, Jr., Immaculate Conception, Marrero
Robin, Angelas, St. Mary Magdalen, New Orleans
Rosato, Joseph R., St. Thomas More, Christ the Healer Prog., New Orleans
Rougelot, Sidney, (Retired)
Roussel, Theodore, St. Charles Borromeo, Destrehan
Sandman, Arthur, Sr., Ascension of Our Lord, LaPlace
Scalise Jr., Bertrand, St. Stephen, New Orleans
Schaubhut, Anthony L., On Leave
Schexnayder, Harry, St. Charles Borromeo, Destrehan
Schlette, Peter B., (Duty Outside)
Schmidt, Gilbert R., Assoc. Dir., Permanent Diaconate;, St. Angela Merici, Metairie
Schonacher, Ralph, (Retired)
Seruntine, Alex J., Jr., St. Louise de Marillac, Arabi
Shelly, Ceaser, On Leave
Sierra, Jose A., St. Louis Cathedral, New Orleans; Chap., Orleans Parish Correctional Center
Smith, Charles J., Children's Hospital and St. Stephen, New Orleans
Smith, Gilbert, Dir. and Port Chap., Stella Maris Center, New Orleans, Our Lady of Angels, Waggaman
Sorensen, George A., Jr., (Retired)
Stall, Louis W., St. Cletus; Prisons Apostolate; Dir. Jefferson Parish Correctional Ctr., Gretna
Stevens, Allen, St. Philip the Apostle, New Orleans
Stewart, Irvin, Sr., St. Joan of Arc, New Orleans
Stohlman, Michael H., St. Matthias and Our Lady of Lourdes, New Orleans
Strahan, Douglas H., St. Louise de Marillac, Arabi
Swiler, James W., Dir. Office of Permanent Diaconate, Christ the King, Terrytown
Toups, Wilbur A., St. Rita, New Orleans
Trahan Sr., Rodney A., Chap., Orleans Parish Correctional Center, St. Christopher the Martyr, Metairie
Trainor, Robert, St. Luke the Evangelist, Slidell
Vicknair, Percy, (Retired)
Vicroy, Clarence, (Retired)
Vincent, Dan, Dir., Black Catholics Office;, St. Paul the Apostle, New Orleans
Vincent, Harold, St. Julian Eymard, New Orleans
Vincent, Leslie D., Our Lady of Perpetual Help, Belle Chasse; Chap., Meadowcrest Hospital, Gretna
Walsh, Donald, (Retired)
Warriner, David A, St. Edward the Confessor, Metairie
Watley, Jesse A., Assoc. Dir., Permanent Diaconate, St. Simon Peter, New Orleans
Weber, John C., St. Margaret Mary, Slidell
Webre, Milton G., St. John Bosco, Harvey
White, Alfred, Corpus Christi, New Orleans
Williams, Everett, Our Lady of Lourdes & St. Matthias, New Orleans
Williams, Herman, St. Monica, New Orleans
Williams, Irvin, St. David, New Orleans
Williams, John B., St. Raymond, New Orleans
Wilson, Earl McMahon, Jr., On Leave
Wong, Peter, (Duty Outside)
Wright, Clifford S., St. Benilde, Metairie
Zeringue, Alfred, St. Mary Magdalen, Metairie
Zimmer, Julius T., Our Lady of Prompt Succor, Chalmette
Zornman, Raymond L., On Leave

INSTITUTIONS LOCATED IN THE ARCHDIOCESE

[A] SEMINARIES, ARCHDIOCESAN

NEW ORLEANS. *Notre Dame Seminary Graduate School of Theology* (1923), 2901 S. Carrollton Ave., 70118-4391. Tel: 504-866-7426; Fax: 504-866-3119. Administration: Very Rev. Patrick J. Williams, M.Div., M.S., Pres. & Rector; Revs. Jose I. Lavastida, M.A., S.T.D., S.T.L., Academic Dean; Clarence C. Menard, O.M.I., H.E.L., H.E.D., Spiritual Dir.; Michael J. Nguyen, M.Ed., S.T.L., S.T.D., Dir. Spiritual Formation; Sr. Barbara Dupuis, M.S.C., M.S.L.S., Dir. Library; Sr. Joycelin Staempfli, M.S.C., M.S.T., Dir. Finances; Rev. F. Hampton Davis, M.Div., Dir. Field Education; Mrs. Margaret Ann Breaux, B.A., Registrar; Dr. John A. Brun, Ph.D., Psychological Counselor. Faculty: Rev. Glenn D. LeCompte, M.Div., S.T.L.; Rev. Msgr. Ignatius M. Roppolo, M.Div.; Rev. Msgr. Terry T. Tekippe, M.A., S.T.L., Ph.D.; Revs. Gregory S. Ross, O.C.D., M.Div., S.T.L.; Vien The Nguyen, M.Div., J.C.L.; Gerald L. Seiler, Jr., M.Div., J.C.L.; Frank Montalbano, O.M.I., S.T.L., S.S.L.; Dennis J. Hayes, III, M.Div., S.T.L.; Dau Nguyen, M.Div., S.T.L.; Carl Davidson, M.Mus.; Stanley Klores, M.A; M.Div; S.T.L, S.T.D.; Donald Martin, S.J., M.A.; Sr. Elizabeth Willems, S.S.N.D., M.A., Ph.D.; Sr. Elizabeth Fitzpatrick, O.Carm., M.A.; Sr. Janet Bodin, M.S.C., M.A., Ph.D.; Dr. Charles Nolan, H.E.D., M.Ed.; Bro. Philip Murphy, F.S.C., M.Litt, M.Ed.; Sr. Noel Toomey, O.P., M.A.; Rev. Roger A. Swenson, M.A.Ed., M.Ed., M.A.; Mr. Drecey Montegut, M.Mus.; Mrs. Jean Meade, M.A.T.; M.A.; M.A.; Ph.D.; Mr. Anthony Millbank, M.S.; Rabbi Edward Cohn, M.A.H.L.; D.D.; D.Min.; Rev. William F. Maestri, M.Div., M.A.; Sr. Kateri Battaglia, M.S.C., M.Ed.; Rev. Gerald M. Fagin, S.J., M.A., M.Th, Ph.D. Priests 21; Laymen 4; Laywomen 2; Men Religious 1; Women Religious 6; Seminarians 150.

ST. BENEDICT. *St. Joseph's Seminary College* (1890), 70457-9999. Tel: 504-892-1800; Fax: 504-867-2270.
E-mail: rectorsec@stjosephabbey.org
Web site: www.stjosephabbey.org
Benedictine Monks. Conducted by Provinces of New Orleans and Mobile and Monks of St. Joseph's Abbey. Very Rev. Gregory M. Boquet, O.S.B., M.A., Rector & Pres.; Rev. Aelred Kavanagh, O.S.B., S.S.L., S.T.D., Vice Rector & Dean of Students; Patricia Oman, M.Ed., Dean of Institutional Affiars; Bro. Brian Harrington, O.S.B., Dean of Students; Rev. Sean B. Duggan, O.S.B., M.F.A., M.A., Dir. Spiritual Formation; Dr. Russ Pottle, Academic Dean; Dr. Chris Baglow, Dir. of Apostolic Services; Mr. Leslie R. Lavergne, Dir. Fin. Aid; Alyce Cazayoux, Business Officer. Faculty: Revs. Peter E. Hammett, O.S.B., Th.M., M.T.S., M.A.Th.; Jonathan M. DeFrange, O.S.B., Ph.D.; Augustine E. Foley, O.S.B., M.A., M.A.Th.; Thomas L. Gwozdz, S.B.D., Ph.D.; Rt. Rev. Patrick J. Regan, O.S.B., S.T.D.; John E. Hebert, Ph.D.; Ann K. Nauman, Ph.D.; Peter M. Emerson, Ph.D.; Carlo deMaco, Ph.D.; Bro. Bernard Boudreaux, O.S.B.; Aileen Mootoo, M.A.; Mr. Michael Greene, M.A.; Russell Pottle, Ph.D.; Mr. George Danskar, M.P.H., M.L.I.S.; Ms. Josette Beaulieu-Grace, M.A. Priests 12; Brothers 2; Sisters 1; Lay Teachers 14; Seminarians 80; Total Enrollment 211; Lay People 6.

[B] SEMINARIES, RELIGIOUS OR SCHOLASTICATES

NEW ORLEANS. *Josephite House of Studies*, 2000 St. Bernard Ave., 70116-1390. Tel: 504-945-1359; Fax: 504-948-3049. Rev. Thomas R. Frank, S.S.J., Dir. Priest Candidates 2.

St. John of the Cross, Discalced Carmelite House of Studies, 2925 S. Carrollton Ave., 70118-4301. Tel: 504-861-9102; Fax: 504-865-1751. Rev. Gregory S. Ross, O.C.D. Priests 1; Religious Seminarians 4.

METAIRIE. *Congregation of the Mother Coredemptrix Formation House*, 112 Lilac St., 70005-1817. Tel: 504-835-9746; Fax: 504-835-9746.
E-mail: hvanvienvonhiem@hotmail.com
Rev. Joseph M. Phan Nam, C.M.C., Dir. Priests 1; Brothers 9.

[C] COLLEGES AND UNIVERSITIES

NEW ORLEANS. *Loyola University New Orleans*, (1912) 6363 St. Charles Ave., 70118-6195. Tel: 504-865-2011; Fax: 504-865-3851.
E-mail: RAMAGOS@LOYNO.EDU
For a complete listing, refer to the Colleges and Universities section.

Our Lady of Holy Cross College, 4123 Woodland Dr., 70131-7399. Tel: 504-394-7744; Fax: 504-391-2421.
E-mail: lmelancon@olhcc.edu
Web site: www.olhcc.edu
For a complete listing, refer to the Colleges and Universities section.

Xavier University of Louisiana, One Drexel Dr., 70125-1098. Tel: 504-486-7411; Fax: 504-485-7904.
Web site: www.xula.edu
For a complete listing, refer to the Colleges and Universities section.

[D] HIGH SCHOOLS, ARCHDIOCESAN

NEW ORLEANS. *Redeemer-Seton High School*, 1453 Crescent Dr., 70122-2099. Tel: 504-288-1494; Fax: 504-288-1499.
E-mail: redeemerseton@archdiocese-no.org
Mr. Arthur L. Schmitt, Pres.; Joan G. Johnson, Prin. School Sisters of Notre Dame 1; Daughters of Charity 2; Lay Teachers 32; Students 381.

COVINGTON. *St. Scholastica Academy*, P.O. Box 1210, 70434-1210. Tel: 985-892-2540; Fax: 985-893-5256.
E-mail: mcelestin@ssacad.com
Web site: www.ssacad.com
Mrs. Marguerite S. Celestin, Prin. Sisters 2; Lay Teachers 38; Students 604.

GRETNA. *Archbishop Blenk High School*, 17 Gretna Blvd., 70053-4989. Tel: 504-367-2626; Fax: 504-367-7128.
E-mail: archblenk@blenkhs.org
Web site: www.gnofn.org/~blenk
Mr. David Pooley, Prin. Priests 1; Lay Teachers 46; Students 624.

LA PLACE. *St. Charles Catholic High School*, 100 Dominican Dr., 70068-3499. Tel: 985-652-3809; Fax: 985-652-2609.
E-mail: stcharlescath@archdiocese-no.org
Web site: www.scc-comets.com
Mr. Andrew C. Cupit, Prin. Lay Teachers 30; Students 446.

MARRERO. *Archbishop Shaw High School*, 1000 Barataria Blvd., 70072-3052. Tel: 504-340-6727; Fax: 504-347-9883.
E-mail: shawprn@archdiocese.org
Web site: www.archbishopshaw.org
Salesians of St. John Bosco. Revs. James Berning, S.D.B., Dir.; Richard Rosin, S.D.B., Prin.; Mr. John Corb, Financial Admin.; Revs. Paul Aronica, S.D.B.; Joseph Vien Hoang, S.D.B. Priests 4; Brothers 4; Lay Teachers 51; Boys 531.

MERAUX. *Archbishop Hannan High School*, 2501 Archbishop Philip M. Hannan Blvd., 70075-2630. Tel: 504-279-1921; Fax: 504-279-0200.
E-mail: archhannan@archdiocese-no.org
Mr. John Serio, Prin. Priests 2; Lay Teachers 42; Students 520.

METAIRIE. *Archbishop Chapelle High School*, 8800 Veterans Blvd., 70003-5235. Tel: 504-467-3105; Fax: 504-466-3191.
E-mail: archchapellehs@archdiocese-no.org
Web site: www.achs.chapelle.k12.la.us
Miss Beth Johnson, Pres.; Mrs. Susan Gutierrez, Prin.; Ms. Mary Beth Drez, Asst. Prin. Priests 1; Lay Teachers 75; Girls 1,020.

Archbishop Rummel High School, P.O. Box 663, 70004-0663. Tel: 504-834-5592; Fax: 504-832-4016.
E-mail: archrummel@archdiocese-no.org
Web site: www.rummel.idsno.com
1901 Severn Ave., 70001-2893. Mr. David J. Hardin, Prin. Brothers 1; Lay Teachers 94; Boys 1,375.
Rummel Alumni Association, Inc.

SLIDELL. *Pope John Paul II High School*, 1901 Jaguar Dr., 70461-9098. Tel: 985-649-0914; Fax: 985-649-5494.
E-mail: pjp@pjp.org
Web site: www.slidell.com/schools/pjp
Mr. Richard Berkowitz, Prin. Lay Teachers 26; Students 327.

[E] HIGH SCHOOLS, PAROCHIAL

MARRERO. *Immaculata High School*, 537 Avenue D, 70072-2027. Tel: 504-341-6217; Fax: 504-341-6229.
E-mail: immaculatehs@archdiocese-no.org
Web site: www.homework-central.com/schools/ihswebsite
Sr. Mary Terzo, F.M.A., Prin. Sisters 3; Lay Teachers 36; Girls 437.

[F] HIGH SCHOOLS, PRIVATE

NEW ORLEANS. *Academy of the Sacred Heart "The Rosary"* (1887). (Grades 9-12), 4521 St. Charles Ave., 70115-9990. Tel: 504-891-1943; Fax: 504-891-9744.
E-mail: sacredheart@ashrosary.org
Web site: http://www.ashrosary.org
Sr. Shirley Miller, R.S.C.J., Headmistress; Sr. Lynne Lieux, R.S.C.J., Prin. Religious of the Sacred Heart 2; Carmelite 1; Ursuline 1; Lay Teachers 27; Girls 272.

Brother Martin High School (1869). (Grades 8-12), 4401 Elysian Fields Ave., 70122-3898. Tel: 504-283-1561; Fax: 504-286-8462. Mr. John J. Devlin, III, Pres.; Mr. Gerald E. Tullier, Prin. Sisters 2; Brothers of the Sacred Heart 10; Lay Teachers 92; Boys 1,457.

Cabrini High School, 1400 Moss St., 70119-2997. Tel: 504-482-1193; Fax: 504-483-8671. Mrs. Frances Dee Tarantino, Pres. & Prin. Missionary Sisters of the Sacred Heart 4; Lay Teachers 34; Girls 430.
Cabrini High School, Inc.

De La Salle Senior High School (1949). (Grades 10-12), 5300 St. Charles Ave., 70115-4999. Tel: 504-895-5717; Fax: 504-895-1300.
E-mail: delasalle@delasallenola.com
Web site: www.gnofn.org/~dlsalle
(Coed). Mrs. Yvonne Gelpi, Pres.; Gina Hall, Prin. Brothers of the Christian Schools 4; Sisters 1; Lay Teachers 65; Students 880.

Holy Cross School (1879). (Grades 5 - 12), 4950 Dauphine St., 70117-4399. Tel: 504-942-3100; Fax: 504-943-7676.
E-mail: coatactus@holycrosstigers.com
Web site: http://www.HolyCrossTigers.com
Bro. Stephen Walsh, C.S.C., Headmaster. Brothers of the Congregation of Holy Cross, Southwest Province 6; Lay Teachers 54; Boys; 848.

Jesuit High School (1847), 4133 Banks St., 70119-6883. Tel: 504-486-6631; Fax: 504-483-3816.
E-mail: jesuit@archdiocese-no.org
Web site: www.jesuithigh.org
(Boys). Revs. Raymond R. Fitzgerald, S.J., Rector; Anthony F. McGinn, S.J., Pres.; Mr. Barry J. Neuberger, Prin.; Revs. Claude P. Boudreaux, S.J.; Richard T. Hermes, S.J.; Norman B. O'Neal, S.J.; Nicholas T. Schiro, S.J. In res. Revs. John J. Capelle, S.J.; Paul Deutsch, S.J.; Louis E. Meyers, S.J. Priests 6; Brothers 1; Lay Teachers 83; Boys 1,119.

Mount Carmel Academy, 7027 Milne Blvd., 70124-2395. Tel: 504-288-7626; Fax: 504-288-7629.
E-mail: mca@mcacubs.org
Web site: www.mtcarmelcubs.org
Congregation of Our Lady of Mount Carmel. Sr. Camille Anne Campbell, O.Carm., Pres. & Prin. Sisters 7; Lay Teachers 97; Girls 1,080.

St. Augustine High School (1951), 2600 A.P. Tureaud Ave., 70119-1299. Tel: 504-944-2424; Fax: 504-947-7712.
Web site: purpleknights.com
Josephite Community. Rev. Joseph M. Doyle, S.S.J., Pres.; Mr. Reginald Delecia, Prin.
(See Separate Listing for Residence.). Priests 7; Lay Teachers 40; Boys 788.

St. Mary's Academy of the Holy Family, 6905 Chef Menteur Hwy., 70126-5291. Tel: 504-245-0200; Fax: 504-245-8732.
E-mail: stmaryac@archdiocese-no.org
Web site: www.gnofn.org/~stmaryac
Sr. Richard Francis Daigle, S.S.F., Prin. Priests 1; Sisters of the Holy Family 16; Lay Teachers 27; Girls 473.

St. Mary's Dominican High School, 7701 Walmsley Ave., 70125-3494. Tel: 504-865-9401; Fax: 504-866-5958.
E-mail: principal@stmarysdominican.org
Ms. Cynthia A. Thomas, Pres.; Mrs. Melanie B. Verges, Prin. Sisters 3; Brothers 1; Lay Teachers 70; Students 1,017.

Ursuline Academy, 2635 State St., 70118-6399. Tel: 504-861-9150; Fax: 504-861-9159.
E-mail: ursulinehs@archdiocese-no.org
Web site: www.gnofn.org/~ursuline
Secondary Dept. Day School College Prep. Barbara E. Turner, Pres.; Nancy M. Hernandez, Prin. Sisters 3; Lay Teachers 34; Girls 408.

Xavier Prep School, 5116 Magazine St., 70115-1899. Tel: 504-899-6061; Fax: 504-891-8766.
E-mail: xavierprep@archdiocese-no.org
Web site: www.acadiacom.net/xavierprep
Mr. Alvarez A. Peychaud, Prin. Priests 1; Sisters 5; Lay Teachers 29; Girls 445.

COVINGTON. *The St. Paul's School* (1911). (Grades 8-12), P.O. Box 928, 70434-0928. Tel: 985-892-3200; Fax: 985-892-4048.
E-mail: stpauls@stpauls.com
Web site: www.stpauls.com
Bro. Raymond Bulliard, F.S.C., Prin. Boarding and Day School for Young Men. Brothers of the Christian Schools of the New Orleans-Santa Fe Province 6; Lay Teachers 50; Boys 700.

[G] ELEMENTARY SCHOOLS, ARCHDIOCESAN

NEW ORLEANS. *Marian Central Catholic Middle School*, 2221 Mendez St., 70122-5267. Tel: 504-288-1411; Fax: 504-286-0209.
E-mail: mariancentral@archdiocese-no.org
Web site: www.mariancentral.org
Sr. Maeve McMahon, O.P., Pres.; Sr. Jennie Jones, S.S.F., Prin. Sisters 6; Lay Teachers 23; Students 432.

St. Joseph Central Catholic Elementary School. (Grades PreK - 5), 3774 Gentilly Blvd., 70122. Tel: 504-945-1015; Fax: 504-954-1050. Dr. Geralyn Dell, Prin. Sisters 4; Lay Teachers 12; Students 260.

MARRERO. *Archbishop Shaw Junior High School*. (Grades 8-9), 1000 Barataria Blvd., 70072-3052. Tel: 504-340-6727; Fax: 504-347-9883.
E-mail: shawprn@archdiocese-no.org
Web site: www.archbishopshaw.org
Rev. James Berning, S.D.B., Prin. Priests 2; Lay Teachers 33; Students 239.

METAIRIE. *Archbishop Rummel Junior High School*. (Grades 8-9), 1901 Severn Ave., 70001-2893. Tel: 504-834-5592; Fax: 504-832-4016.
E-mail: dhardin1901@netscape.net
Web site: www.rummelraiders.com
Mr. Steven Barton, Asst. Prin. Lay Teachers 48; Boys 495.

[H] ELEMENTARY SCHOOLS, PRIVATE

NEW ORLEANS. *Academy of the Sacred Heart*. (Grades PreK-8), 4521 St. Charles Ave., 70115-9990. Tel: 504-891-1943; Fax: 504-891-9939.
E-mail: sacredheart@ashrosary.org
Sr. Shirley Miller, R.S.C.J., Headmistress. Religious of the Sacred Heart 2; Lay Teachers 58; Girls 539.

Brother Martin High School. (Grade 8), 4401 Elysian Fields Ave., 70122-3898. Tel: 504-283-1561; Fax: 504-286-8462. Mrs. Anne Rivera, Prin. Lay Teachers 29; Boys 249.

Cabrini High School. (Grades 8-12), 1400 Moss St., 70119-2997. Tel: 504-482-1193; Fax: 504-483-8671. Mrs. Frances Dee Tarantino, Pres. & Prin. Brothers 1; Sisters 1; Lay Teachers 28; Students 430.

Christian Brothers School. (Grades 5-7), City Park, #8 Frederichs Ave., 70124-4602. Tel: 504-486-6770; Fax: 504-486-1053.
E-mail: school@cbs-no.org
Web site: www.homework-central.com/schools/christian
Bro. Edward Scanlan, F.S.C., Pres.; Mr. Joey M. Scaffidi, Prin. Brothers 7; Lay Teachers 14; Boys 273.

De La Salle Junior High School. (Grades 8-9), 5300 St. Charles Ave., 70115-4999. Tel: 504-895-5717; Fax: 504-895-1300.
E-mail: delasale@delasalle.nola.com
Web site: www.gnofn.org/~dlsalle
(Coed). Mrs. Yvonne Gelpi, Pres.; Mr. Gary L. Blackburn, Prin. Brothers 1; Lay Teachers 24; Students 203.

Henriette Delille Middle School, Inc., 4700 Pineda St., 70126. Tel: 504-288-1644; Fax: 504-288-0224.
E-mail: hdelille@archdiocese-no.org
Sr. Carmen Marie Bertrand, S.S.F., Pres. Sisters 1; Lay Teachers 1; Students 10.

Holy Cross School. (Grades 5-8), 4950 Dauphine St., 70117-4399. Tel: 504-942-3100; Fax: 504-943-7676.
E-mail: contactus@holycrosstigers.com
Web site: http://www.HolyCrossTigers.com
Bro. Stephen Walsh, C.S.C., Headmaster. Brothers of the Congregation of Holy Cross 6; Lay Teachers 23; Boys 280.

House of the Holy Family School. (Grades 1 - 3), 7100 Chef Menteur Hwy., 70126-5220. Tel: 504-242-1810; Fax: 504-241-5082.
E-mail: househlyfam@archdiocese-no.org
Sr. Elizabeth Ann Holmes, S.S.F., Admin. Sisters 1; Lay Teachers 3; Children 60.

Jesuit High School. (Grades 8), 4133 Banks St., 70119-6883. Tel: 504-486-6631; Fax: 504-483-3816.
E-mail: principal@jesuitnola.org
Web site: www.jesuitnola.org
Rev. Anthony F. McGinn, S.J., Pres.; Mr. Barry J. Neuberger, Prin. Priests 2; Lay Teachers 21; Boys 242.

St. Augustine High School. (Grades 8), 2600 A.P. Tureaud Ave., 70119-1299. Tel: 504-944-2424; Fax: 504-947-7712.
Web site: purpleknights.com
Rev. Joseph M. Doyle, S.S.J., Pres.; Mr. Reginald Delecia, Prin. Priests 1; Lay Teachers 7; Boys 62.

St. Benedict the Moor School. (Grades PreK- Grad), 5010 Piety Dr., 70126. Tel: 504-288-2745; Fax: 504-282-9386.
E-mail: stbenmoor@archdiocese-no.org
Mary Kate Scully, Prin. Lay Teachers 4; Students 64.

St. Mary's Academy. (Grades 7-8), 6905 Chef Menteur Hwy., 70126-5291. Tel: 504-245-0200; Fax: 504-245-8732. Sr. Richard Francis Daigle, S.S.F., Prin. Priests 1; Sisters of the Holy Family 16; Lay Teachers 23; Girls 140.

St. Mary's Dominican High School, 7701 Walmsley Ave., 70125-3494. Tel: 504-865-9401; Fax: 504-866-5958.
E-mail: principal@stmarysdominican.org
Web site: www.stmarysdominican.org
Ms. Cynthia A. Thomas, Pres.; Mrs. Melanie B. Verges, Prin. Brothers 1; Sisters 3; Lay Teachers 69; Girls 1,029.

Ursuline Academy. (Grades Toddler-8), 2635 State St., 70118-6399. Tel: 504-866-5260; Fax: 504-866-5293.
E-mail: ursulineelem@archdiocese-no.org
Web site: www.gnofn.org/~ursuline
Barbara E. Turner, Pres.; Mary Eleen Palmisano, Prin. Sisters 2; Lay Teachers 39; Students 352.

COVINGTON. *The St. Paul's School.* (Grades 8-12), P.O. Box 928, 70434-0928. Tel: 985-892-3200; Fax: 985-892-4048.
E-mail: stpauls@stpauls.com
Web site: www.stpauls.com
Brothers of the Christian Schools. Bro. Raymond Bulliard, F.S.C., Prin.; John Morvant, Asst. Prin. Brothers 6; Lay Teachers 50; Boys 700.
(See St. Paul's School Under High Schools, Private).

[I] SPECIAL EDUCATION

NEW ORLEANS. *Archdiocesan Department of Special Education.* Tel: 504-524-7285; Fax: 504-524-5883.
E-mail: stmichspecial@archdiocese-no.org
St. Michael Special School, 1522 Chippewa St., 70130-4513. Tel: 504-524-7285; Fax: 504-524-5883. Sr. M. Dona Lally, S.S.N.D., Prin. Religious 3; Lay Teachers 21; Students 211.

Bishop Perry Middle School. (Grades 5-8), 1941 Dauphine St., 70116-1609. Tel: 504-943-3734; Fax: 504-943-1320.
E-mail: bpms@bpms.org
Web site: www.bpms.org
(Boys). Rev. David G. Cray, S.S.E., Pres.; Mr. Kenneth D. White, Prin. Society of St. Edmund 2; Priests 2; Lay Teachers 4; Boys 60.

Holy Rosary Academy, 3368 Esplanade Ave., 70119-3132. Tel: 504-482-7173; Fax: 504-482-7229.
E-mail: arnohlyros@impresso.com
Michael J. Binder, Prin. Sisters 3; Lay Teachers 8; Students 68.

St. Gerard Majella Alternative School, 5500 Paris Ave., 70122-2699. Tel: 504-288-2789; Fax: 504-288-2789.
E-mail: majellaalt@archdiocese-no.org
Sr. Rose Elaine Kessler, S.S.N.D., Prin. Sisters 1; Lay Teachers 5; Students 20.

MARRERO. *Hope Haven Center,* 1101 Barataria Blvd., 70072-3085. Tel: 504-347-5581; Fax: 504-340-2075. Mrs. Barbara Garland, M.Ed., Prin. Lay Teachers 15; Students 69.

[J] DAY CARE CENTERS, CAMPS AND PRESCHOOLS

NEW ORLEANS. *Carmel in the Business District (Carmelite Ministries, Inc.),* 246 Loyola Ave., 70112. Tel: 504-529-8856; Fax: 504-529-8861.
E-mail: sisursula@yahoo.com
Web site: http//mountcarmel.home.mindspring.com/cbd
Sr. Ursula Diasselellis, O.Carm., Exec. Dir.; Sr. Gwen Grillot, O.Carm., Prog. Dir.; Elizabeth Coe, Child Care & Preschool Dir.

Cub Corner (Carmelite Ministires, Inc.), 420 Robert E. Lee Blvd., 70124. Tel: 504-283-9499; Fax: 504-283-9483.
E-mail: cubcorn@bellsouth.net
Sr. Mary Ellen Wheelahan, O.Carm., Dir.

El Yo Yo Day Care Center, 735 Gen. Pershing St., 70115-1448. Tel: 504-899-6165; Fax: 504-899-5409. Ms. Gaynell Anderson, Prog. Dir. Total Assisted 100; Total Staff 14.

Flint-Goodridge Day Care Center, 3306 Freret St., 70115-6029. Tel: 504-895-3487; Fax: 504-895-9830. Ms. Susie Foucher, Prog. Dir.

Florida Head Start, 2631 Alvar St., 70117-3364. Tel: 504-945-8115; Fax: 504-943-6813. Eve Pleasant, Prog. Dir. Total Assisted 66; Total Staff 13.

Incarnate Word Preschool Program, 8326 Apricot St., 70118-3198. Tel: 504-866-2309; Fax: 504-861-1435. Ms. Doris Williams, Spvr.

Lafon Child Development Center, 7024 Chef Menteur Hwy., 70126-5295. Tel: 504-242-2431. Sr. Barbara Batiste, S.S.F., Admin. Sisters 3; Children (Daily Average) 135; Total Staff 24.

Leslie Day Care Center, 2126 Constance St., 70130-5044. Tel: 504-522-2725. Jocelyn Jagers-Williams, Prog. Dir. Total Staff 5.

Louise Day Care Center, 1205 Louisiana Ave., 70115-2488. Tel: 504-891-2871; Fax: 504-895-3129. Ms. Irma Cavalier, Prog. Dir.

Rosary Child Development Center, 5100 Willow Brook Dr., 70129-1047. Tel: 504-254-1528; Fax: 504-244-1528.
E-mail: hunguyen@loyno.edu
Sr. Theresa Huyen Nguyen, F.M.S.R., Dir. Staff 16; Children (Daily Average) 90.

St. Anthony Head Start, 5407 Dauphine St., 70117-3023. Tel: 504-943-6952; Fax: 504-943-6813. Ms. Melba Hart, Program Dir.

St. James Major Day Care Center, 3800 Gentilly Blvd., 70122-6130. Tel: 504-949-1680. Peggy Frey, Dir. Staff 9; Average Daily Enrollment 59.

St. John Berchmans Child Development Center, 2710 Gentilly Blvd., P.O. Box 8623, 70182-3098. Tel: 504-943-5060; Fax: 504-943-5063. P.O. Box 8623, 70182-8623. Tel: 504-943-5060; Fax: 504-943-5063. Sr. Mary Laurita Oliver, S.S.F., Admin. Sisters 2; Lay Staff 13; Children 130; Total Assisted 1,125.

St. John the Baptist Pre-School Program, 1920 Clio St., 70113-1214. Tel: 504-529-2557 (Preschool); 581-4987 (Center); Fax: 504-581-2028 (Center). Sr. Marion Brett, D.C., Dir. Lay Staff 11; Children 57.

St. Philip Preschool, 3333 Clouet St., 70126-5700. Tel: 504-944-2640; Fax: 504-944-4450. Mrs. Betty Lavigne, Supvr. Staff 14; Children (Daily Average) 94.

CHALMETTE. *Our Lady of Prompt Succor Child Care Center,* 2217 Fenelon St., 70043-4991. Tel: 504-271-3491. Mrs. Cynthia Dazet, Dir.

METAIRIE. *St. Mary Magdalen Early Childhood Development Center,* 1005 Airline Park Blvd., 70003-4395. Tel: 504-736-0863; Fax: 504-733-0869. Ms. Dina L. Castille, M.Ed., Dir. Staff 16; Children (Daily Average) 55.

ST. BENEDICT. *Abbey Youth Camp, Inc.,* St. Joseph Abbey, 70457. Tel: 985-892-3600; Fax: 985-867-2270. Rev. Matthew Clark, O.S.B., Dir.

[K] HOMES FOR CHILDREN AND YOUTH

NEW ORLEANS. *Boys Hope,* 4128 Baudin St., 70119-6815. Tel: 504-486-6030; Fax: 504-484-6120.
E-mail: rallanach@bhgh.org
Web site: www.boyshopegirlshope.org
For a complete listing, refer to the Special Care Facilities section.

Covenant House, 611 N. Rampart St., 70112-3540. Tel: 504-584-1111; 800-999-9999 (Hotline); Fax: 504-584-1171.
E-mail: khyrii@bellsouth.net
Web site: covenanthouseno.org
For a complete listing, refer to the Special Care Facilities section.

BELLE CHASSE. *Padua Pediatric Residential Program,* 200 Beta St., 70037-1499. Tel: 504-392-0502; Fax: 504-392-5411
For a complete listing, refer to the Special Care Facilities section.

MARRERO. *Hope Haven Center,* (1925) 1101 Barataria Blvd., 70072-3085. Tel: 504-347-5581; Fax: 504-340-2075
For a complete listing, refer to the Special Care Facilities section.

[L] RESIDENCES, ADULT

NEW ORLEANS. *CARE CENTER,* 4222 S. Broad St., 70125-3660. Tel: 504-822-3751; Fax: 504-822-3761. Mrs. Connie Andry, Admin.; Wanda Ballier, Prog. Dir. Temporary Residence for Homeless Women and their Children.

Baronne Street Transitional Housing, 2407 Baronne St., 70113-1621. Tel: 504-269-9311. Ms. Michelle Brown, Prog. Dir.; Connie Andry, Admin.

Ciara House, 1131 St. Andrew St., 70130-5124. Tel: 504-524-8394; Fax: 504-524-0224. Ms. Monetta Clark, Admin.

Crescent House I and II. Tel: 504-866-9554 (crisis line); Fax: 504-865-0050.
E-mail: llyoung@archdiocese-no.org
Office, 1000 Howard Ave., 70113-1916. Tel: 504-865-0057; Fax: 504-866-7931. Temporary residence for abused women and their children. Ms. Lynn Young, Admin. Total Staff 11; Total Assisted 438.

Ozanam Inn, 843 Camp St., 70130-3751. Tel: 504-523-1184; Fax: 504-523-1187. Sponsored by Society of St. Vincent de Paul. Shelter for Homeless Men. Roy R. Allain, Admin.

Project Lazarus, P.O. Box 3906, 70177-3906. Tel: 504-949-3609; Fax: 504-944-7944. Residential Program for Persons with AIDS. Ms. Susan Banks, Exec. Dir. Total in Residence 24; Total Staff 32.

GRETNA. *Ocean Avenue Community Home,* 361 Ocean Ave., 70053-4726. Tel: 504-361-0674; Fax: 504-367-6952. Leroy Hughes, Admin. Residential Facility for Developmentally Disabled Adults.

St. Jude the Apostle, 1430 Claire Ave., 70053-7436. Tel: 504-361-8457; Fax: 504-367-6952. Leroy Hughes, Admin. Residential Facility for Developmentally Disabled Adults.

St. Rosalie, 119 Kass St., 70053-3828. Tel: 504-361-8320; Fax: 504-367-6952. Leroy Hughes, Admin. Padua Adult Residential Program for Developmentally Disabled Adults.

Supervised Apartments, 1430 Claire Ave., 70053-7436. Tel: 504-367-1465; Fax: 504-367-6952. Leroy Hughes, Admin. Supervised Apartments for Developmentally Disabled Adults.

HARVEY. *St. Catherine of Siena Supervised Apartment,* 3021 Sienna Dr., 70058-2180. Tel: 504-347-6069; Fax: 504-367-6952. Leroy Hughes, Admin. Residential Program for Developmentally Disabled Adults.

MARRERO. *Jefferson CARE Center,* 1108 Barataria Blvd., 70072-3025. Tel: 504-347-0772; Fax: 504-371-8783. Ms. Earline Perique, Prog. Dir. Temporary Residence for Homeless Families.

METAIRIE. *Ss. Mary & Elizabeth,* 720 N. Elm St., 70003-6022. Tel: 504-738-6959; Fax: 504-738-8320. Leroy Hughes, Admin. Residential Facility for Developmentally Disabled Adults.

SLIDELL. *St. Peter the Fisherman,* 62269 Airport Rd., 70460-5242. Tel: 985-641-4914; Fax: 985-641-7575. Leroy Hughes, Admin. Residential Facility for Developmentally Disabled Adults.

[M] DAY CARE CENTERS (ADULT)

NEW ORLEANS. *New Directions Adult Day Health Care Center,* 1523 N. Dorgenois St., 70119-2419. Tel: 504-943-9418; Fax: 504-948-3633. Carolyn Prosper, Prog. Dir.

People Program, 1200 Mirabeau Ave., 70122-1886. Tel: 504-288-3171; Fax: 504-288-3503. Ms. Mary Catherine Lombard, Prog. Dir.; Ms. Barbara McCurdy, Devel. Dir.

COVINGTON. *Alpha House Adult Day Health Care Center,* 20127 Hwy. 36, 70433-8658. Tel: 985-892-7074; Fax: 985-893-1962.
E-mail: jbankston@archdiocese-no.org
Ms. Jane Bankston, Prog. Dir.

KENNER. *The Greenwalt Center for Alzheimer's Day Care and Research,* 1926 18th St., 70062-6208. Tel: 504-461-5889; Fax: 504-461-5795. Ms. Linda Greenwalt, Asst. Admin.

NORCO. *Norco Adult Day Care,* 425 Spruce St., 70079-8464. Tel: 504-764-9084; Fax: 504-764-0041. Ms. Kathleen Landry, R.N., Dir.

[N] HOMES AND RESIDENCES FOR FAMILIES AND SENIOR CITIZENS

NEW ORLEANS. *The 1540 House,* 1540 N. Johnson St., 70116-1721. Tel: 504-945-0253
For a complete listing, refer to the Special Care Facilities section.

Annunciation Inn, 1220 Spain St., 70117-8369. Tel: 504-944-0512; Fax: 504-944-0514
For a complete listing, refer to the Special Care Facilities section.

Chateau de Notre Dame, 2832 Burdette St., 70125-2596. Tel: 504-866-2741; Fax: 504-866-6769
For a complete listing, refer to the Special Care Facilities section.

Christopher Inn Apts., 2110 Royal St., 70116-1693. Tel: 504-949-0312; Fax: 504-945-2634
For a complete listing, refer to the Special Care Facilities section.

DeLille Inn, 6924 Chef Menteur Hwy., 70126-5260. Tel: 504-241-4877; Fax: 504-241-1828.
E-mail: srtekawitha@christopherhomesinc.org
For a complete listing, refer to the Special Care Facilities section.

Haydel Heights Apartments, 4402 Reynes St., 70126. Tel: 504-242-4438; Fax: 504-242-4061
For a complete listing, refer to the Special Care Facilities section.

Josephine Apartments, 1410 St. Andrew St., Apt. #4, 70130-5344. Tel: 504-522-5425; Fax: 504-522-5446
For a complete listing, refer to the Special Care Facilities section.

Lafon Nursing Home of the Holy Family, 6900 Chef Menteur Hwy., 70126-5296. Tel: 504-246-1100; Fax: 504-241-6672
For a complete listing, refer to the Special Care Facilities section.

Mary-Joseph Residence for the Elderly, (1868) 4201 Woodland Dr., 70131-7398. Tel: 504-394-2200; Fax: 504-391-3347
For a complete listing, refer to the Special Care Facilities section.

Nazareth II, 9640 Hayne Blvd., 70127-4725. Tel: 504-246-9640; Fax: 504-240-6686
For a complete listing, refer to the Special Care Facilities section.

Nazareth Inn, 9630 Hayne Blvd., 70127-1260. Tel: 504-241-9630; Fax: 504-241-9631
For a complete listing, refer to the Special Care Facilities section.

Our Lady of Wisdom Health Care Center, 5600 Gen. deGaulle Dr., 70131. Tel: 504-394-5991; Fax: 504-304-5421.
E-mail: ourladyofwisdom@netscape.net
For a complete listing, refer to the Special Care Facilities section.

St. John Berchmans Manor, 3400 St. Anthony St., 70122-3098. Tel: 504-943-9343; Fax: 504-947-6090
For a complete listing, refer to the Special Care Facilities section.

St. Margaret's Daughters' Home, 6220 Chartres St., 70117-1595. Tel: 504-279-6414; Fax: 504-277-1834.
E-mail: stmargaretsl.org
For a complete listing, refer to the Special Care Facilities section.

St. Martin Manor, 1501 N. Johnson St., 70116-1720. Tel: 504-945-7728; Fax: 504-945-7726
For a complete listing, refer to the Special Care Facilities section.

Villa St. Maurice, 500 St. Maurice Ave., 70117-1568. Tel: 504-277-8477; Fax: 504-277-8493
For a complete listing, refer to the Special Care Facilities section.

Villa St. Maurice II (Villa Additions), 6101 Douglas St., 70117-2100. Tel: 504-277-8731; Fax: 504-277-8493
For a complete listing, refer to the Special Care Facilities section.

LA PLACE. *Place Dubourg, Inc.*, 201 Rue Dubourg, 70068-2433. Tel: 985-652-1981; Fax: 985-651-6147.
E-mail: chpalmisano@christopherhomesinc.org
For a complete listing, refer to the Special Care Facilities section.

MANDEVILLE. *Rouquette Lodge*, 4300 Hwy. 22, 70448-2824. Tel: 985-626-5217; Fax: 985-626-9226
For a complete listing, refer to the Special Care Facilities section.

MARRERO. *Villa D'Ames Apartments*, 6305 Fourth St., 70072-1513. Tel: 504-347-0474; Fax: 504-347-0451
For a complete listing, refer to the Special Care Facilities section.

Wynhoven Apartments and Wynhoven II, 4600-10th St., 70072-3048. Tel: 504-347-8442; Fax: 504-340-6076
For a complete listing, refer to the Special Care Facilities section.

Wynhoven Health Care Center, 1050 Medical Center Blvd., 70072-3170. Tel: 504-347-0777; 347-3443 (Convent); Fax: 504-341-7240.
E-mail: wynhoven@msn.com
For a complete listing, refer to the Special Care Facilities section.

MERAUX. *St. Bernard Manor, St. Bernard II, and St. Bernard III*, 2400 Archbishop Hannan Blvd., 70075-2640. Tel: 504-277-2441; Fax: 504-277-6300
For a complete listing, refer to the Special Care Facilities section.

METAIRIE. *Metairie Manor, Metairie II, and Metairie III*, 4929 York St., 70001-1013. Tel: 504-456-1467; Fax: 504-887-3718
For a complete listing, refer to the Special Care Facilities section.

[O] CATHOLIC HEALTH SERVICES

NEW ORLEANS. *Daughters of Charity Services of New Orleans*, 3900 S. Carrollton Ave., 70118-4712. Tel: 504-482-2080; Fax: 504-483-6016.
E-mail: dward@dcsno.org
For a complete listing, refer to the Hospitals section.

METAIRIE. *Sisters of Mercy Ministries*, 4444 York St., Ste 101, 70001. Tel: 504-779-5500; Fax: 504-779-5505
For a complete listing, refer to the Hospitals section.

[P] MONASTERIES AND RESIDENCES OF PRIESTS AND BROTHERS

NEW ORLEANS. *Brothers of the Sacred Heart*. Tel: 504-282-5693; Fax: 504-288-9920.
E-mail: bilebianc@hotmail.com
Provincial Office, New Orleans Province, 4540 Elysian Fields Ave., 70122-3826. Tel: 504-282-5693; Fax: 504-288-9920. Bro. Ray Kuhn, S.C., Vocation Dir. Tel: 504-288-7467, Hospitality Center/ Volunteer Service Community, 4600 Elysian Fields Ave., 70122-3938. Tel: 504-282-5631. Bro. Henry Gaither, S.C., Dir., 4601 Elysian Fields Ave., 70122-3937. Tel: 504-288-8301. Bro. Carl Bouchereau, S.C., Dir., Novitiate House, 1156 City Park Ave., 70119-3736. Tel: 504-488-1353. Bro. Matthias Amos, S.C., Dir., 4671 Painters St., Pre-Novitiate, 70122-5001. Tel: 504-283-6448. Total Brothers 22. Ordained Brothers: Bro. Louis Couvillon, S.C., 1156 City Park Ave., 70119. Tel: 504-488-1353. Bro. Carl Evans, S.C., 175 St. Joseph St., Thibodaux, 70360. Tel: 504-447-4354. Bro. Albert Guarino, S.C., (Retired), 4540 Elysian Fields Ave., 70122-3937. Tel: 504-282-5693. Bro. Farrel Lorio, S.C., (Retired), 4540 Elysian Fields Ave., 70122. Tel: 504-282-5693. Bro. William McCue, S.C., 855 Hearthstone Dr., Baton Rouge, 70806. Tel: 225-383-7117. Bro. Ray Hebert, S.C., 4601 Elysian Fields Ave., 70122.

Dominican Friars, Southern Dominican Province of St. Martin de Porres. Tel: 504-837-2129; Fax: 504-837-6604.
Web site: www.opsouth.org
Provincial Headquarters, 1421 N. Causeway Blvd., Ste. 200, Metairie, 70001-4144. Tel: 504-837-2129; Fax: 504-837-6604.
E-mail: provincial@opsouth.org
Very Revs. Alberto Rodriguez, O.P., Prov.; Carl B. Trutter, O.P., Socius & Vicar Prov.; James A. McDonough, O.P. (AUS), Steward; Bruce B. Schultz, O.P. (San Antonio), Promoter of Permanent Formation and Community Life; Rev. Henry B. Groover, O.P. (MIA), Promoter of Vocations. Priests in the Archdiocese 23; Brothers in the Archdiocese 6.
Assigned but working elsewhere: Revs. Wayne A. Cavalier, O.P., On Studies in Boston; Paul D. Watkins, O.P., On Leave; Armando Ibanez, O.P., Producer Dir., CA; Bros. Michael Curtis, O.P., (On leave); Francis Dinet, O.P., N.O. LA.
Working Abroad: Rev. Emanuel M. Camilleri, O.P., Home for the Clergy, Fleur de Lys, Malta, BRK 09. Tel: (011-35-6)498-166. Rev. James Linus Dolan, O.P., Provincia Dominicana de San Juan Bautista del Peru, Apartado 4169, Lima 1, Peru. Tel: (011-51-1)427-7426; Fax: (011-51-1)427-6791. Rev. Raymond C. Finn, O.P., Curia Generalizia Domenicani, Convento Santa Sabina, Piazza Pietro d'Illiria, 1 (Aventino), Rome, Italy, 00153. Tel: (011-39-06)57-94-210; Fax: (011-39-06)579-41. Rev. Jesus de Vianney Guerra, O.P., Parroquia de Santiago Apostol, Av. Varsovia Malta-California Sur, Apdo. 76176, Caracas, Venezuela, 1070. Tel: (011-58-02)272-7254. Rev. Michael O'Rourke, O.P., Convento Santa Sabrina, Piazza Pietro d' Illiria, 1 (Aventino), Rome, Italy, 00153. Tel: (011-39-06)57-94-0546; Fax: (011-39-06)579-41. Rev. Raphael Proenza, O.P., Calle 19, #258, Vedado D.P. 104, La Habana, Cuba. Tel: 53-7327329. Revs. Luis Roberto Aguilar-leal, O.P.; Brian J. Pierce, O.P., Frailes Dominicos, APDO 2608, San Pedro Sula Honduras, C.A. Tel: (011)-504-557-5712; Fax: (011)504-557-2920. Rev. Alfred W. Wilder, O.P., Universita San Tommaso, Largo Angelicum 1, Rome, Italy, 00184. Tel: (011-39-06)670-2226; Fax: (001-39-06)679-0407.

Dominican Vocation Sponsors, 1421 N. Causeway Blvd., Ste. 200, Metairie, 70001-4144. Tel: (504)-837-2129; Fax: (504)-837-6604.

Southern Dominican Foundation, 1421 N. Causeway Blvd., Ste. 200, Metairie, 70001-4144. Tel: (504)-837-2129- Fax: (504)-837-6604. Revs. Alberto Rodriguez, O.P., Pres.; Carl B. Trutter, O.P., Vice Pres. & Sec.; James A. McDonough, O.P. (AUS), Treas.; John Markey, O.P., Promoter of Devel.; Nora P. Fine, Dir. of Devel.

Southern Dominican Global Missions, 1421 N. Causeway Blvd., Ste. 200, Metairie, 70001-4144. Tel: (210)738-6668; Fax: (210)-738-1755. Rev. John Raymond Corr, O.P. (SA), Dir., St. Martin de Porres Shrine, 1421 N. Causeway Blvd., Ste. 200, Metairie, 70001-4144. Tel: (504)-832-2129, Ext. 14; Fax: (504)-837-6604. Rev. Thomas Condow, O.P., Dir. Total in Residence 29.

Franciscan Fraternity. Tel: 504-529-3569.
E-mail: earam@aol.com
Tau House, 1029 Gov. Nicholls St., 70116-2432. Tel: 504-529-3569. Revs. Ralph R. Parthie, O.F.M.; Michael J. Jennrich, O.F.M., On Sabbatical; Bro. Edward-Marc Arambasich, O.F.M. Center for the Spiritual Empowerment of those infected with or affected by the HIV/AIDS. Total in Residence 3; Total Staff 5.

Ignatius Residence, 6321 Stratford Pl., 70131-7325. Tel: 504-394-2411; Fax: 504-433-2882.
E-mail: ratchfrd@loyno.edu
Revs. John H. Edwards, S.J., Supr.; Robert L. Anderson, S.J.; Eugene T. Bannin, S.J.; Joseph E. Browning, S.J.; Thomas D. Culley, S.J.; John P. Driscoll, S.J.; Richard G. Hartnett, S.J.; Earl Johnson, S.J.; Warren S. Martin, S.J.; Herve P. Racivitch, S.J.; Robert J. Ratchford, S.J.; S. Joseph Rivoire, S.J.; Sidney A. Tonsmiere, S.J.; Roy W. Vollenweider, S.J.; Bros. Lloyd A. Barry, S.J.; C. Robert Doherty, S.J.; H. Francis Hinze, S.J.; Dennis P. Lonergan, S.J. Priests 14; Brothers 4.

Jesuit Provincial Office. New Orleans Province, 500 S. Jefferson Davis Pkwy., 70119-7192. Tel: 504-821-0334; Fax: 504-822-5322.
E-mail: noprovsj@norprov.org
Legal Title: *Catholic Society of Religious and Literary Education*. Very Rev. James P. Bradley, S.J., Prov.; Revs. Thomas H. Stahel, S.J., Socius; Paul Deutsch, S.J., Prov. Asst. Secondary Ed. and Formation; James L. Lambert, S.J., Asst. for Pastoral and Retreat Min.; Bro. Lawrence J. Lundin, S.J., Treas. Priests 4; Brothers 1.
Priests of the Province Abroad: Rev. Charles B. Thibodeaux, S.J., Casa Parroquial, Santa Rosa (Misiones), Paraguay. Tel: 595-858-221. Rev. John F. Schroder, S.J., St. John's College, P.O. Box 548, Belize City, Belize. Tel: 501-2-32411; Fax: 501-2-32752. Rev. Edward J. Dougherty, S.J., Ave. Rio de Janiero 327, Campinas, SP, Brazil, 13031-340. Tel: 55-19-3871-3422; Fax: 55-19-3871-0164. Rev. Edward G. Benya, S.J., CP 421, Teresina, PI, Brazil, 64.001.970. Tel: 55-86-235-1872. Rev. A. Gerard Fineran, S.J., Villa Kostka C.P. 9, Indaiatuba, SP, Brazil, 13330-970. Tel: 55-198-750-055; Fax: 55198-759-966. Rev. David H. Romero, S.J., Rua Castelo Branco, 101 Bairro Vitoria Regia, Manaus-AM, Brazil, 69033-230. Tel: 011-55-92-625-3721; Fax: 011-55-92-625-3721. Rev. Mark Lewis, S.J., C.P. 6139 Prati, Rome, Italy, 00195. Tel: 39-06-689-77215; Fax: 39-06-686-8214. Rev. Patrick S. Madigan, S.J., POB MP 320, Mt. Pleasant, Harare, Zimbabwe. Tel: 2634-745-411; Fax: 263-4-745-904. Rev. Stephen C. Rowntree, S.J., POB MP 320, Mt. Pleasant, Harare, Zimbabwe. Tel: 2634-745-411; Fax: 2634-745-904. Rev. John R. Stacer, S.J., POB MP 320, Mt. Pleasant, Harare, Zimbabwe. Tel: 2634-745-411; Fax: 2634-745-904. Rev. Joseph A. Tetlow, S.J., Curia, Society of Jesus, CP 6139, Prati, Rome, Italy, 00195. Tel: 39-06-6897-7384; Fax: 39-06-687-9283. Rev. Joseph A. Carola, S.J., Collegio S. Roberto Bellarmino, Via del Seminario 120, Rome, Italy, 00186. Tel: 39-06-6701-6558; Fax: 39-06-6701-6562. Rev. Leo V. Leise, S.J., Didzioji 34, 2001 Vilnius, Lithuania. Tel: 370-86-61417; Fax: 370-52-222-1876. Rev. O. Kenneth Johnson, S.J., Mukasa Minor Seminary, P.O. Box 630195, Choma, Zambia. Tel: 260-32-20058. Rev. Roland J. Lesseps, S.J., P.O. Box 30652, Lusaka, Zambia. Tel: 260-1-230-585; Fax: 260-1-293-763. Rev. Michael S. Gallagher, S.J., Campion Hall, Oxford OX1 IQS, England. Rev. Donald G. Bahlinger, S.J., Apdo 01-34, San Salvador, El Salvador. Tel: 503-243-2178.

Jesuit Health Trust. Tel: (504)821-0334; Fax: (504)822-5322. Rev. Eugene M. Dutkiewicz, S.J., Chm.; Bro. Lawrence J. Lundin, S.J., Sec.

Josephite Fathers and Brothers. Tel: 504-943-6593. The Josephite Faculty House of St. Augustine High School, 1911 Law St., 70119-1397. Tel: 504-943-6593; Fax: 504-947-7712. Very Rev. Wilbur J. Atwood, S.S.J., Rector; Bro. Laurence E. Price, S.S.J., Vice Rector; Revs. Vincent Keenan, S.S.J.; Joseph McKinley, S.S.J.; Robert Bowen, S.S.J.; Very Rev. Joseph Doyle, S.S.J.
(See Separate Listing for School).

Marist Fathers, 1706 Jackson Ave., 70113. Tel: 504-524-5192; Fax: 504-524-9796. Revs. Peter R. Blanchard, S.M.; Ellis L. DePriest, S.M.; Edwin L. Keel, S.M.; Joseph P. Mullin, S.M.; Bro. Albert Thiffault, S.M.

Vincentian Fathers. Tel: 504-897-3976; Fax: 504-899-3603. DePaul Residence, 812 Constantinople St., 70115-2726. Tel: 504-897-3976; Fax: 504-899-7603. Very Rev. Robert E. Lamy, C.M., Supr.; Revs. Anthony D. Fassbender, C.M.; Jerome Galcagnon, C.M.; Bernard P. Degan, C.M.

ST. BENEDICT. *St. Joseph Abbey* (1890), 70457-9999. Tel: 504-892-1800; Fax: 504-867-2270.
Web site: www.stjosephabbey.org
Rt. Rev. Patrick Regan, O.S.B., Abbot; Revs. Raphael Barousse, O.S.B.; Hugh Baumann, O.S.B.; Adam Begnaud, O.S.B., M.S.; Gregory M. Boquet, O.S.B.; Dominic R. Braud, O.S.B.; Justin Brown, O.S.B.; Timothy J. Burnett, O.S.B.; Kevin Clark, O.S.B.; Matthew R. Clark, O.S.B.; Jonathan M. DeFrange, O.S.B.; Sean B. Duggan, O.S.B.; Augustine E. Foley, O.S.B.; Peter E. Hammett, O.S.B.; Michael Jung, O.S.B.; Aelred Kavanagh, O.S.B., S.S.L., S.T.D.; Marian E. Larmann, O.S.B.; David Leftwich, O.S.B.; William J. MacCandless, O.S.B.; Paul Miranne, O.S.B.; Stan Moseley, O.S.B.; Thomas E. Perrier, O.S.B.; Lawrence J. Phelps, O.S.B.; Francis Sander, O.S.B.; Albert Terrillion, O.S.B.; Scott J. Underwood, O.S.B.; Ambrose G. Wathen, O.S.B. Priests 29; Brothers 17; Novices 3.

[Q] CONVENTS AND RESIDENCES FOR SISTERS

NEW ORLEANS. *Congregation of Divine Providence, C.D.P.*, 504 Fern, 70118-3830. Tel: 504-861-0284. Total Sisters in Archdiocese 1.

Congregation of the Sisters of the Holy Faith, C.H.F., 2741 St. Anthony St., 70119-1298. Tel: 504-945-7743. Total Sisters in Archdiocese 4.

Daughters of Charity of St. Vincent de Paul, D.C. Sisters' Residence, 2718 Cambronne St., 70118-3140. Tel: 504-866-0968. Sr. Clare Kelly, D.C., Supr. Total Sisters in Archdiocese 40.

Daughters of Our Lady of the Holy Rosary Provincial House, F.M.S.R., 1492 Moss St., 70119-2904. Tel: 504-486-0039; Fax: 504-483-7910. Sr. M John Bosco Dinh Thi Kim Thanh, F.M.S.R., Prov. Supr. Total Sisters in Archdiocese 46.

Dominican Sisters (Cabra, Ireland) O.P., 1930 Robert E. Lee Blvd., 70122-3518. Tel: 504-283-2042; Fax: 504-288-1593.
E-mail: cabop@worldnet.att.net
Web site: www.cabraop.org
Sr. Maeve Mc Mahon, O.P., Prioress. Total Sisters in Archdiocese 9.

Eucharistic Missionaries of St. Dominic, O.P., 3801 Canal St., Ste. 400, 70119-6049. Tel: 504-486-1133; Fax: 504-486-6547.
E-mail: srdotop@aol.com
Web site: www.emdsisters.org
Total Sisters in Archdiocese 23.
Regina Coeli Retreat Center, 17225 Regina Coeli Rd., Covington, 70435-9156. Tel: 504-892-4110. Total in Residence 2; Total Staff 4.

Generalate of the Dominican Sisters, O.P., Congregation of St. Mary, 7300 St. Charles Ave., 70118-3809. Tel: 504-861-8183; Fax: 504-861-8184.
E-mail: Rosebdom@aol.com
Web site: www. dominican-sisters.net/stmarys/
Sr. M. Jordan Langenhennig, O.P., Prioress. Generalate Staff Sisters 5; Total Sisters in Archdiocese 55.

Little Sisters of the Poor, L.S.P., 4201 Woodland Dr., 70131-7398. Tel: 504-394-2200; Fax: 504-391-3347. Sisters 11.

Marianites of Holy Cross, M.S.C. (1841), 1011 Gallier St., 70117-6111. Tel: 504-945-1620; Fax: 504-944-0756.
E-mail: mscsec@marianites.org
Web site: www.marianites.org
Sr. Mary Kay Kinberger, Congregational Leader. Total Sisters in Archdiocese 98.

Missionary Sisters of the Sacred Heart (Cabrini) M.S.C., 3443 Esplanade Ave., 70119. Tel: 504-822-5553; Fax: 504-822-5559. Total Sisters in Archdiocese 3.

Presentation Sisters of the Blessed Virgin Mary, 1920 Robert E. Lee Blvd., 70122-3512. Tel: 504-283-3352; Fax: 504-283-3352.
E-mail: presis@gnofn.org
Web site: www.gnofn.org/~presis
Legal Title: *Union of Sisters of the Presentation of the Blessed Virgin Mary (United States Prov.)*. Total Sisters in Archdiocese 2.

Religious of the Good Shepherd, R.G.S., 4934 Hanck Dr., 70127. Tel: 504-244-0034; Fax: 504-244-3202. Total Sisters in Archdiocese 4.
Good Shepherd Services. After school program for girls and adult counseling.

Religious of the Sacred Heart, R.S.C.J., 1837 Milan St., 70115. Tel: 504-899-3037; Fax: 504-899-6210. Sisters 4. 4600 Carondelet St., 70115-4822. Tel: 504-891-0412. Sisters 3. Mailing Address: 1719 Napoleon Ave., 70115-4809. Tel: 504-899-6027; Fax: 504-899-6210. Sr. Anne Sturges, R.S.C.J., Dir. Sisters 6. Total Sisters in Archdiocese 13.

St. Clare's Monastery of the Blessed Sacrament, O.S.C. (1885), 720 Henry Clay Ave., 70118-5891. Tel: 504-895-2019; Fax: 504-899-6218.
E-mail: monclare@bellsouth.net
Web site: www.poorclarenuns.com
Nuns of the Order of St. Clare. Sr. Marianne L. Zadrozyn, O.S.C., Abbess. Solemn Professed Nuns 10.

School Sisters of Notre Dame (Dallas, TX), S.S.N.D., Redeemer Convent, 7010 Milne Blvd., 70124-2343. Tel: 504-288-5002. Total Sisters in Archdiocese 21.

Sinsinawa Dominican Congregation of the Most Holy Rosary, O.P., 6350 General Diaz, 70124.
Web site: www.sinsinawa.org
Sisters 3.

Sisters of Mercy of the Americas, R.S.M. (St. Louis Regional Community), 6024 Freret St., 70118. Tel: 504-891-4639; Fax: 504-482-6125. Total Sisters in Archdiocese 50.

Sisters of St. Joseph of Medaille, New Orleans, C.S.J., 1200 Mirabeau Ave., 70122-1997. Tel: 504-283-9493; Fax: 504-288-4044.
E-mail: gracelyncsj@juno.com
Web site: www.sistersofstjoseph.org
Sr. Gracelyn Soignet, C.S.J., Coord. of Complex. Total Sisters in Archdiocese 60.
People Program, Inc., 1200 Mirabeau Ave., 70122-1997. Tel: 504-288-3171; Fax: 504-288-3503. Sr. Carolyn Brady, C.S.J., Pres.; Mrs. Mary Catherine Lombard, Dir.

Sisters of the Blessed Sacrament, S.B.S., 947 S. Cortez St., 70125-1105. Tel: 504-488-5325. 5116 Magazine St., 70115. Tel: 504-897-0235. 5014 Howard Ave., 70125. Tel: 504-486-2474. Xavier University Convent, 3812 Pine St., 70125. Tel: 504-482-0917; Fax: 504-482-6219. Total Sisters in the Archdiocese 29.

Sisters of the Holy Family Motherhouse and Novitiate, S.S.F. (1842), 6901 Chef Menteur Hwy., 70126-5290. Tel: 504-242-8315; 504-241-5400; Fax: 504-241-3957.
E-mail: sylviathib@aol.com
Web site: www.sistersoftheholyfamily.org
Sr. Sylvia Thibodeaux, S.S.F., Supr. Gen. Total Sisters in Archdiocese 134.
Sisters of the Holy Family Development Office, 2710 Gentilly Blvd., 70122-3098. Tel: 504-949-4572; Fax: 504-949-4733.

Sisters, Servants of Mary, S.M., 5001 Perlita St., 70122-1999. Tel: 504-282-5549. Sr. Auxilio Corrales, S.M., Supr. Total Home Nursing Sisters in Archdiocese 16.

Ursuline Sisters of the Roman Union, O.S.U. (1727), 2734 Nashville Ave., 70115-7008. Tel: 504-866-1472. Sr. Esther Redmann, O.S.U., Prioress. Total Sisters in Archdiocese 17.

CHALMETTE. *Daughters of Divine Providence, F.D.P.*, 3100 Mumphrey Rd., 70043-3735. Tel: 504-279-4617; Fax: 504-279-3002.
E-mail: convent@bellsouth.net
Total Sisters in Archdiocese 3.

COVINGTON. *Carmelite Nuns, Discalced, O.C.D., Monastery of St. Joseph and St. Theresa* (1877), 73530 River Rd., 70435-2206. Tel: 504-898-0923; Fax: 504-871-9333.
E-mail: covingtoncarmel@aol.com
Web site: www.ettinger.net/carmelcov
Professed Nuns 8; Novices 3.
Teresian Sisters (Society of St. Teresa of Jesus), S.T.J., Provincial House, 18080 St. Joseph's Way, 70435-5623. Tel: 504-893-1470; Fax: 504-893-2476.
E-mail: teresians@aol.com
Web site: www.teresians.org
Sr. Maria Isabel Ordono, S.T.J., Prov. Sisters 18.
Formation House, 18158 St. Joseph's Way, 70435-5624. Tel: 504-893-1557. Sr. Carmen Gloria Plasencia, S.T.J., Superior.

GRETNA. *Sisters of the Living Word, S.L.W.*, 901 Hancock St., 70053-2227. Tel: 504-366-5358.
E-mail: slw@slw.org
Sisters 2; Total Sisters in Archdiocese 12.

LACOMBE. *Congregation of Our Lady of Mount Carmel, O.Carm.* (1833), Generalate P.O. Box 476, 70445-0476. Tel: 985-882-7577; 524-2398; Fax: 985-524-5011.
E-mail: mountcarmel@mindspring.com
Web site: mountcarmel.home.mindspring.com
Sr. Rose Marie Penouilh, O.Carm., Pres. Sisters 58. Mount Carmel Development Office, P.O. Box 1160, 70445-1160. Tel: 985-882-7577; 524-2398; Fax: 985-524-5011. Sr. Andree Marie Bindewald, O.Carm., Dir.
Holistic Spirituality Center. Tel: 985-882-7579; Fax: 985-882-3619. Total in Residence 22; Total Staff 5.
Child Care Center: Carmel in the Business District. Tel: 504-529-8856; 8933; Fax: 504-529-8861. Sr. Ursula Diasselliss, O.Carm., Dir. Total Staff 11; Total Enrolled 52.
Cub Corner. Tel: 504-283-9499; Fax: 504-283-9483. Sr. Mary Ellen, Wheelahan, O.Carm., Dir. Total Staff 18; Total Enrolled 90.

MANDEVILLE. *St. Gertrude's Convent, Benedictine Sisters*, c/o Prieto & Prieto, Attorneys, 2900 E. Causeway Approach, Ste. D, 70448-3597.

MARRERO. *Salesian Sisters (Daughters of Mary Help of Christians) F.M.A.*, Immaculate Conception Convent, 612 Avenue B, 70072-2016. Tel: 504-347-8449; Fax: 504-347-8440.
E-mail: fmamarrero@aol.com
Web site: www.immaculata.com
Sisters in Archdiocese 7.

METAIRIE. *Daughters of St. Paul Convent, F.S.P.*, Pauline Book & Media Center, 4403 Veterans Memorial Blvd., 70006-5321. Tel: 504-887-7631; Fax: 504-888-1357.
E-mail: neworleans@pauline.org
Total Sisters in Archdiocese 4.
Incarnate Word Sisters, C.C.V.I., 2904 Houma Blvd., Apt. D, 70006-1422. Tel: 504-888-1410. Total Sisters in Archdiocese 5.
Religious of Our Lady of the Retreat in the Cenacle, R.C., The Cenacle Retreat House, 5500 St. Mary St., P.O. Box 8115, 70011-8115. Tel: 504-887-1420; Fax: 504-887-6624.
E-mail: cenacle2@aol.com
Web site: www.cenaclesisters.org/metairie.htm
Sr. Barbara Ehrler, R.C., Supr. Sisters 8; Total Staff 30.
Sisters of the Most Holy Sacrament, M.H.S., 422 Bonnabel Blvd., 70005-3240. Tel: 504-832-0513. Total Sisters in Archdiocese 4.

[R] RETREAT HOUSES

NEW ORLEANS. *Archdiocesan Spirituality Center*, 2901 S. Carrollton Ave., 70118-4391. Tel: 504-861-3254. Sr. Noel Toomey, O.P., Dir.
Center of Jesus the Lord, 1236 N. Rampart St., 70116-2497. Tel: 504-529-1636; Fax: 504-529-5003.
E-mail: CCRCNO@aol.com
Web site: www.members.aol.com/CCRCNO
Total Assisted 314; Total Staff 4; Total in Residence 4.
Dominican Conference Center, 540 Broadway, 70118-3593. Tel: 504-861-8711; Fax: 504-861-8718.
E-mail: dcc15@juno.com
Ms. Charlotte Fenerty Ewing, Admin. Total in Residence 6; Total Staff 7.
Sophie Barat House, 1719 Napoleon Ave., 70115-4809. Tel: 504-899-6027; Fax: 504-899-6210.
E-mail: jmckinlay@rscj.org
Sr. Mary Blish, R.S.C.J.; Sr. Margaret Hoffman, R.S.C.J.; Sr. Jane McKinlay, R.S.C.J.; Sr. Rose Marie Quilter, R.S.C.J.; Sr. Anne Sturges, R.S.C.J. Total Staff 5; Total in Residence 6.

COVINGTON. *Regina Coeli Retreat Center*, 17225 Regina Coeli Rd., 70435-9156. Tel: 985-892-4110; Fax: 985-892-4110. Managers: Earl Magner; June Magner.

CROWN POINT. *Ave Maria Retreat House*, 8089 Barataria Blvd, 70072. Tel: 504-689-3837; Fax: 504-689-2785. Rev. Gerald J. Fogarty, O.M.I., Dir.; Bro. Danna J. Gauthreaux, O.M.I., Assoc. Dir. Total Staff 7; Total in Residence 2.

LACOMBE. *Blessing Place*, P.O. Box 130, 70445-130. Tel: 504-882-7579; Fax: 504-882-3619.
E-mail: barbara@blessingplace.org
Web site: blessingplace.org
Sr. Barbara Breaud, O.Carm., Dir. Personal growth and development community for women and men religious and clergy.

METAIRIE. *Cenacle Retreat House*, 5500 St. Mary St., P.O. Box 8115, 70011-8115. Tel: 504-887-1420; Fax: 504-887-6624.
E-mail: cenacle2@aol.com
Web site: www.cenaclesisters.org/metairie.htm
Sr. JoAnn Viviano, R.C., Retreat House Admin. Religious 8; Total Staff 30.

PONCHATOULA. *Magnificat Center of the Holy Spirit*, 23629 Faith Rd., 70454. Tel: 225-386-5815; 800-531-9710; Fax: 504-200-7771. Rev. Harry J. Adams, Jr., S.C., Dir. Total in Residence 90; Total Staff 4.

ST. BENEDICT. *Abbey Christian Life Center*, St. Joseph Abbey, 70457-9999. Tel: 985-892-3473; 892-1800; Fax: 985-892-3448. Conducted by Benedictine Monks. Rev. Thomas E. Perrier, O.S.B., Dir.

[S] MISCELLANEOUS

NEW ORLEANS. *Christian Brothers Foundation*, 8 Friederichs Ave., 70124-4602. Tel: 504-486-1053; Fax: 504-488-2802.
E-mail: cbfoundation@yahoo.com
Equestrian Order of the Holy Sepulchre. (of Jerusalem, Southeastern Lieutenancy of the U.S.), 5614 Marcia Ave., 70124-1006. Tel: 504-832-0892; Fax: 504-832-1929. Lt. George H. Toye, K.G.C.H.S.
Jesuit Program for Living and Learning of New Orleans, Inc., 2726 Esplanade Ave., 70119. Tel: 504-484-7744; Fax: 504-484-6120.
E-mail: rallanach@bhgh.org
Web site: www.boyshopegirlshope.org
Rev. Robert C. Allanach, O.M.I., Ph.D., Exec. Dir.
Jesuit Seminary and Mission Fund, 500 S. Jefferson Davis Pkwy., 70119-7192. Tel: 504-827-4043; Fax: 504-827-9931.
E-mail: jsmb@norprov.org
Mr. Brian P. Berrigan, Exec. Dir.
MCA Foundation, 420 Robert E. Lee Blvd., 70124-2596. Tel: 504-524-2398; Fax: 504-524-2398.
E-mail: mountcarmel@mindspring.com
Web site: mountcarmel.home.mindspring.com
Sr. Rose Marie Penouilh, O.Carm., Pres.
The Patrons of the Vatican Museums in the South, Inc., 775 Harrison Ave., 70124-3192. Tel: 504-482-4158; Fax: 504-485-0906. Very Rev. Val A. McInnes, O.P., Founder & Pres. Emeritus; Mr. John J. Kelly, Pres.
Pierre Toussaint Foundation of New Orleans, Inc., 2600 A.P. Tureaud Ave., 70119-1299. Tel: 504-949-3113; Fax: 504-945-4134.
E-mail: josmdoyle@netscape.net
Rev. Joseph M. Doyle, S.S.J., Pres.
Second Harvesters Food Bank of Greater New Orleans, 1201 Sams Ave., 70123-2236. Tel: 504-734-1322; Fax: 504-733-8336.
E-mail: bgreen@secondharvest.org
Stella Roman Foundation, Inc., 210 Baronne St. Suite 1207, 70112-4100. Tel: 504-522-4756; Fax: 504-568-0783. Rev. Msgr. John P. Reynolds, Pres.

METAIRIE.
Focus Syndicate, Inc., 106 Metairie Lawn Dr., 70001. Tel: 504-840-9898; Fax: 504-840-9818.
E-mail: focus@gs.verio.net
Web site: www.focuschristiantv.com
Most Rev. Philip M. Hannan, Pres. & Board of Trustees.
Southern Dominican Foundation, 1421 N. Causeway Blvd., Ste. 200, 70001-4144. Tel: 504-837-2129; Fax: 504-837-6604.
Web site: www.opsouth.org
Revs. Alberto Rodriguez, O.P., Pres.; Carl B. Trutter, O.P., Vice Pres. & Sec.; James A. McDonough, O.P., Treas.; John Markey, O.P., Promoter of Devel.; Nora P. Fine, Dir. Devel.

Southern Dominican Global Missions, 1421 N. Causeway Blvd., Ste. 200, 70001-4144. Tel: (210)738-6688; Fax: (210)738-1755. Rev. John Raymond Corr, O.P. (SA), Dir.

WLAE-TV, Educational Broadcasting Foundation, Inc., 3330 N. Causeway Blvd., Ste. 345, 70002. Tel: 504-866-7411; Fax: 504-840-9838.
E-mail: info@wlae.pbs.org
Web site: www.pbs.org/wlae
Most Rev. Philip M. Hannan, Pres., Bd. of Trustees.

SLIDELL.

S.A.V.E., Inc. (Suffering Abortion Victims Embraced), 770 Gause Blvd., 70458. Tel: 859-428-0901; Fax: 859-428-3090. Mrs. Linda Jefferson, Pres.

SECULAR INSTITUTES

NEW ORLEANS. *Society of Our Lady of the Way*, 6044 Louis XIV St., 70124-2919. Tel: 504-486-2506.

ABITA SPRINGS. *Caritas*, Administration Center, P.O. Box 308, 70420-0308. Tel: 985-892-4345.
Daraja House, P.O. Box 524, Covington, 70434. Tel: 985-893-2261.

RELIGIOUS INSTITUTES OF MEN REPRESENTED IN THE ARCHDIOCESE

For further details refer to the corresponding bracketed number in the Religious Institutes of Men or Women section.

[0200]—*Benedictine Monks.*—O.S.B.
[0330]—*Brothers of the Christian Schools.* (New Orleans Prov.).—F.S.C.
[0600]—*Brothers of the Congregation of Holy Cross.* (Midwest; Southwest Provs.).—C.S.C.
[0470]—*The Capuchin Friars.*—O.F.M.Cap.
[0220]—*Congregation of the Blessed Sacrament.*—S.S.S.
[1330]—*Congregation of the Mission of St. Vincent de Paul Fathers & Brothers.* (Southern Prov.).—C.M.
[]—*Congregation of the Mother Coredemptrix.*—C.M.C.
[0260]—*Discalced Carmelite Friars.*—O.C.D.
[0520]—*Franciscan Friars.*—O.F.M.
[0650]—*Holy Ghost Fathers.* (Western Vice Prov.; Ireland).—C.S.Sp.
[]—*Incarnational Consecration.*—I.C.
[0690]—*Jesuit Fathers and Brothers.* (New Orleans).—S.J.
[0780]—*Marist Fathers and Brothers.* (Washington Prov.).—S.M.
[0840]—*Missionary Servants of the Most Holy Trinity.*—S.T.
[]—*Missionary Society of St. Paul.*—M.S.P.
[0910]—*Oblates of Mary Immaculate.* (Southern American Prov.).—O.M.I.
[0430]—*Order of Preacher-Dominicans.* (Southern Prov.).—O.P.
[1310]—*Order of the Most Holy Trinity.*—O.SS.T.
[1100]—*Priests and Brothers of the Sacred Heart.* (Metuchen, NJ).—S.C.
[0610]—*Priests of the Congregation of Holy Cross.* (Southern Prov.; Indiana Prov.).—C.S.C.
[1070]—*Redemptorist Fathers and Brothers.* (New Orleans).—C.SS.R.
[0700]—*St. Joseph's Society of the Sacred Heart.* (Baltimore, MD).—S.S.J.
[1170]—*St. Patrick Missionary Society.*—S.P.S.
[1190]—*Salesians of Don Bosco.*—S.D.B.
[0760]—*Society of Mary.* St. Louis Province.—S.M.
[0440]—*Society of St. Edmund.*—S.S.E.
[0420]—*Society of the Divine Word.* (St. Augustine Prov.).—S.V.D.

RELIGIOUS INSTITUTES OF WOMEN REPRESENTED IN THE ARCHDIOCESE

[0230]—*Benedictine Sisters of Pontifical Jurisdiction.* (Colorado).—O.S.B.
[0400]—*Congregation of Our Lady of Mount Carmel.*—O.Carm.
[3110]—*Congregation of Our Lady of the Retreat in the Cenacle.*—R.C.
[1940]—*Congregation of Sisters of the Holy Faith.*—C.H.F.
[2410]—*Congregation of the Marianites of Holy Cross.*—M.S.C.
[0460]—*Congregation of the Sisters of Charity of the Incarnate Word.*—C.C.V.I.
[1950]—*Congregation of the Sisters of the Holy Family.*—S.S.F.
[0800]—*Daughters of Divine Providence.*—F.D.P.
[0850]—*Daughters of Mary Help of Christians.*—F.M.A.
[0895]—*Daughters of Our Lady of the Holy Rosary.*—F.M.S.R.
[0760]—*Daughters of St. Vincent de Paul.*—D.C.
[0420]—*Discalced Carmelite Nuns.*—O.C.D.
[1110]—*Dominican Sisters of Our Lady of the Rosary and of Saint Catherine of Siena, Cabra, Ireland.*—O.P.
[1070-08]—*Dominican Sisters, Congregation of St. Mary.*—O.P.
[1070-02]—*Dominican Sisters, Congregation of St. Mary of the Springs.*—O.P.
[1070-13]—*Dominican Sisters, Congregation of the Most Holy Rosary.*—O.P.
[1070-03]—*Dominican Sisters, Sinsinawa Dominican Congregation of the Most Holy Rosary.*—O.P.
[1140]—*Eucharistic Missionaries of St. Dominic.*—O.P.
[1430]—*Franciscan Sisters of Our Lady of Perpetual Help.*—O.S.F.
[]—*Handmaids of the Holy Child of Jesus.*—H.H.C.J.
[2340]—*Little Sisters of the Poor.*—L.S.P.
[]—*Lovers of the Holy Cross Sisters at Cho Quan.*—L.H.C.
[2860]—*Missionary Sisters of the Sacred Heart.*—M.S.C.
[0950]—*Pious Society Daughters of St. Paul.*—F.S.P.
[3760]—*Poor Clare Nuns, Order of St. Clare.*—O.S.C.
[2970]—*School Sisters of Notre Dame.* (Dallas & Mankato).—S.S.N.D.
[]—*Sisters for Christian Community.*—S.F.C.C.
[0440]—*Sisters of Charity of Cincinnati, Ohio.*—S.C.
[0660]—*Sisters of Christian Charity.* (Wilmette, IL).—S.C.C.
[1010]—*Sisters of Divine Providence of San Antonio, Texas.*—C.D.P.
[2575]—*Sisters of Mercy of the Americas.* (Brooklyn; St. Louis).—R.S.M.
[2630]—*Sisters of Mercy of the Holy Cross.*—S.C.S.C.
[1640]—*Sisters of St. Francis of Perpetual Adoration.*—O.S.F.
[]—*Sisters of St. Francis of Philadelphia.*—O.S.F.
[1670]—*Sisters of St. Francis of Savannah.*—O.S.F.
[1530]—*Sisters of St. Francis of the Congregation of Our Lady of Lourdes, Sylvania, Ohio.*—O.S.F.
[3840]—*Sisters of St. Joseph of Carondelet.*—C.S.J.
[3880]—*Sisters of St. Joseph of Medaille.*—C.S.J.
[3830-11]—*Sisters of St. Joseph, Kalamazoo.*—S.S.J.
[0260]—*Sisters of the Blessed Sacrament for Indians and Colored People.*—S.B.S.
[1830]—*Sisters of the Good Shepherd.*—R.G.S.
[2050]—*Sisters of the Holy Spirit and Mary Immaculate.*—S.H.Sp.
[2120]—*Sisters of the Immaculate Conception.*—C.I.C.
[2350]—*Sisters of the Living Word.*—S.L.W.
[2940]—*Sisters of the Most Holy Sacrament.*—M.H.S.
[3600]—*Sisters Servants of Mary.*—S.M.
[4020]—*Society of St. Teresa of Jesus.*—S.T.J.
[4060]—*Society of the Holy Child Jesus.*—S.H.C.J.
[4070]—*Society of the Sacred Heart.*—R.S.C.J.
[3330]—*Union of the Sisters of the Presentation of the Blessed Virgin Mary.*—P.B.V.M.
[4110]—*Ursuline Nuns.*—O.S.U.

NECROLOGY

† Aleman, Rev. Msgr. Vernon P., (Retired). —Died July 8, 2000.
† Cau, Leon, (Retired). —Died Sept. 29, 2000.
† Dowling, Rev. Msgr. Thomas C., (Retired). —Died Aug. 12, 2000.

Diocese of New Ulm

(Dioecesis Novae Ulmae)

(Vacant See)

Catholic Pastoral Center: 1400 6th St., N., New Ulm, MN, 56073-2099. Tel.: 507-359-2966; Fax: 507-354-3667.

Web site address: www.dnu.org

E-mail address: dnucomm@ic.new-ulm.mn.us

ESTABLISHED NOVEMBER 18, 1957.

Square Miles 9,863.

Comprises the Counties of Big Stone, Brown, Chippewa, Kandiyohi, Lac Qui Parle, Lincoln, Lyon, McLeod, Meeker, Nicollet, Redwood, Renville, Sibley, Swift and Yellow Medicine in the State of Minnesota.

For legal titles of parishes and diocesan institutions, consult the Catholic Pastoral Center.

STATISTICAL OVERVIEW

Personnel	
Priests: Diocesan Active in Diocese	49
Priests: Active Outside Diocese	6
Priests: Diocesan in Foreign Missions	2
Priests: Retired, Sick or Absent	26
Number of Diocesan Priests	83
Religious Priests in Diocese	1
Extern Priests in Diocese	3
Permanent Deacons in Diocese	1
Total Sisters	85
Parishes	
Parishes	80
With Resident Pastor:	
Resident Diocesan Priests	44
Without Resident Pastor:	
Administered by Priests	17
Administered by Women Religious	16
Administered by Lay People	3
Missions	2
Professional Ministry Personnel:	
Sisters	7
Lay Ministers	25
Welfare	
Catholic Hospitals	2
Total Assisted	13,619
Homes for the Aged	6
Total Assisted	356
Residential Care of Disabled	2
Total Assisted	5,280
Educational	
Diocesan Students in Other Seminaries	11
Total Seminarians	11
High Schools, Diocesan and Parish	3
Total Students	510
Elementary Schools, Diocesan and Parish	19
Total Students	2,641
Catechesis/Religious Education:	
High School Students	3,736
Elementary Students	7,330
Total Students Under Catholic Instruction	14,228
Teachers in the Diocese:	
Sisters	6
Lay Teachers	223
Vital Statistics	
Receptions into the Church:	
Infant Baptism Totals	1,038
Adult Baptism Totals	43
Received into Full Communion	142
First Communions	1,240
Confirmations	1,215
Marriages:	
Catholic	220
Interfaith	195
Total Marriages	415
Deaths	766
Total Catholic Population	70,835
Total Population	281,065

Former Bishop—Most Rev. ALPHONSE J. SCHLADWEILER, D.D., ord. June 9, 1929; appt. Nov. 28, 1957; cons. Jan. 29, 1958; retired Dec. 23, 1975; died April 3, 1996.

Diocesan Officials

Catholic Pastoral Center—Most Rev. RAYMOND A. LUCKER, S.T.D., *1400 6th St. N., New Ulm, 56073-2099.* Tel: 507-359-2966; Fax: 507-354-3667.

Vicar General—Rev. DENNIS C. LABAT, *Catholic Pastoral Center, 1400 6th St. N., New Ulm, 56073-2099.* Tel: 507-359-2966.

Chancellor—Rev. DOUGLAS L. GRAMS, *Catholic Pastoral Center, 1400 6th St. N., New Ulm, 56073-2099.* Tel: 507-359-2966.

Vice-Chancellor—Rev. JOHN G. BERGER, *Church of St. Paul, 411 5th St., Nicollet, 56074-0248.* Tel: 507-387-6501.

Diocesan Tribunal—

Moderator—Sr. KATHLEEN BIERNE, P.B.V.M., *Catholic Pastoral Center, 1400 6th St. N., New Ulm, 56073-2099.* Tel: 507-359-2966.

Judicial Vicar (Officialis)—Rev. JOHN G. BERGER, *Church of St. Paul, 411 5th St., Nicollet, 56074-0248.* Tel: 507-387-6501.

Associate Judges—Revs. EUGENE L. LOZINSKI; PAUL L. WOLF; DOUGLAS L. GRAMS.

Defender of the Bond—Rev. MARK S. MALLAK.

Notaries—JANELLE DREXLER; SHERI JOHNSON.

Diocesan Boards and Councils

Building Committee—Rev. STEVEN J. VERHELST, Chm., *Church of St. Francis, 412 12th St. N., Benson, 56215-1228.* Tel: 320-843-2342. Rev. EUGENE C. HACKERT; Mr. RICHARD GREENE; Ms. JANE BERNARD HANSON; Mr. JOE EIKMEIER; Mr. RAYMOND MARTIN.

College of Consultors—Revs. DENNIS C. LABAT; GEORGE V. SCHMIT; BRIAN L. MANDEL; FRANCIS J. GARVEY; STEVEN J. VERHELST; ROBERT J. WYFFELS; JOSEPH A. STEINBEISSER.

Committee on Parishes—Sr. KATHRYN SCHOOLMEESTERS, S.S.N.D., Chm.; Revs. WILLIAM A. SPRIGLER; DENNIS C. LABAT; JAMES E. MORAN; PAUL H. VAN DE CROMMERT; Mr. JOSEPH EIKMEIER; Sr. JEANETTE HOMAN, O.S.F.; DOLORES BERG; NANCY HANNA; RAYMOND TRAEN; JUNE BRUST; MARK C. KEMMETER, Staff.

Corporate Board—Most Rev. RAYMOND A. LUCKER; Rev. DENNIS C. LABAT; Mr. WILLIAM T. O'CONNOR; Mr. PAUL ZINS; Rev. DOUGLAS L. GRAMS.

Diocesan Pastoral Council—LARRY LOKEN, Chm., *167 5th Ave., Granite Falls, 56241.* Tel: 320-564-3251. MICHAEL MONNENS, Vice Chm. CHRISTIE FOX, Sec. Members: Sr. RUTH ANN TAKES, P.B.V.M.; DOLORES BERG; MARY BOLEK; DONNA SCHEIBEL; GAIL BROMENSCHENKEL; Sr. JEANETTE HOMAN, O.S.F.; RICHARD HESSE; PAULETTE SVOBODA; MARY ANN HESSE; DONALD STROBEL; BETTY STROBEL; WAYNE CARLSON; JOHN HASSINGER; PATTY MCCAULEY; Revs. GEORGE V. SCHMIT, JR.; BRIAN L. MANDEL, Alternate; ROSEMARY DITTRICH; LAURIE YACKLEY; MIKE BREDECK; HOWARD RADERMACHER; GERI WEBER; BRYAN LISNAK; MARK C. KEMMETER, Staff.

Finance Council—Rev. BERNARD J. STEINER; GERI BURESH; NANCY O'LEARY; DONNA SANDERS; DAVID LYNN.

Priests' Council—Rev. GEORGE V. SCHMIT, JR., Chm., *Cathedral of the Holy Trinity, 605 N. State St., New Ulm, 56073-1898.* Tel: 507-354-4158. Rev. STEVEN J. VERHELST, Vice Chm. ROBERT J. WYFFELS, Treas.; Revs. DENNIS C. LABAT; FRANCIS J. GARVEY; BRIAN L. MANDEL; JOSEPH A. STEINBEISSER.

Sisters' Council—Executive Committee: Sr. KATHRYN SCHOOLMEESTERS, S.S.N.D.; Sr. JOANNE BACKES, O.S.B.; Sr. GLADYS MEINDL, O.S.F.; Sr. BETTY LARSON, O.S.B., Staff Liaison.

Catholic Pastoral Center

Coordinator of Diocesan Staff—MARK C. KEMMETER, *Catholic Pastoral Center, 1400 6th St. N., New Ulm, 56073-2099.* Tel: 507-359-2966.

Office of Finance—Mr. DUANE J. KOBLE, Dir., *Catholic Pastoral Center, 1400 6th St. N., New Ulm, 56073-2099.* Tel: 507-359-2966.

Office of Development—Vacant, Dir., *Catholic Pastoral Center, 1400 6th St. N., New Ulm, 56073-2099.* Tel: 507-359-2966.

Evangelization and Catechesis—

Religious Education / Adult Religious Education—JOANN BORCHERT, Dir., *Catholic Pastoral Center, 1400 6th St. N., New Ulm, 56073-2099.* Tel: 507-359-2966.

Catholic Schools—Sr. BETTY LARSON, O.S.B., Dir., Schools, *Catholic Pastoral Center, 1400 6th St. N., New Ulm, 56073-2099.* Tel: 507-359-2966.

Youth & Young Adult Ministry—BILL CASEY, Dir., *Catholic Pastoral Center, 1400 6th St. N., New Ulm, 56073-2099.* Tel: 507-359-2966.

A-TEC (Adult / Teens Encounter Christ)—Rev. DENNIS C. LABAT, Coord., *Catholic Pastoral Center, 1400 6th St. N., New Ulm, 56073-2099.* Tel: 507-359-2966.

Communications—PAULA MARTI, Dir., *Catholic Pastoral Center, 1400 6th St. N., New Ulm, 56073-2099.* Tel: 507-359-2966; Fax: 507-354-3667.

"Prairie Catholic"—PAULA MARTI, Editor, *Catholic Pastoral Center, 1400 6th St. N., New Ulm, 56073-2099.* Tel: 507-359-2966.

Committee for Evangelization & Catechesis—PATTY MCCAULEY, Chm.; Rev. TODD J. PETERSEN; Sr. MARY WEIDNER, O.S.B.; Sr. SHARON NOHNER, O.S.B; Sr. LOUISE BAUER, O.S.B.; LYNN SCHUELLER; ROGER OSBORNE; DAWN SCHOLL; KAREN ECKSTEIN; MARIAN BACH; DON CLASEMANN.

Office of Worship and Spiritual Life—JANE BERNARD HANSON, Dir., *1400 6th St. N., New Ulm, 56073-2099.* Tel: 507-359-2966.

Worship Committee—JANE BERNARD HANSON, Staff, *1400 6th St. N., New Ulm, 56073-2099.* Tel: 507-359-2966. Members: Rev. JEFFREY P. HOREJSI, Chm.; Revs. GERALD S. MEIDL; RONALD V. HUBERTY; Sr. MONICA WAGNER, S.S.N.D.; JOANN BORCHERT; KATIE HENRICH; KAY OSBORNE; MARY BOLEK; TOM JOHNSON; BEV SULLIVAN; KEVIN KALKFOFF; NANCY ELLEFSON; Sr. DARLENE GUTENKAUF, P.B.V.M.; DELLA CONROY.

RCIA Network—JANE BERNARD HANSON, *1400 6th St. N., New Ulm, 56073-2099.* Tel: 507-359-2966.

Charismatic Renewal—JAN CROWE, Diocesan Liaison, *21907 705th Ave., Dassel, 55325.* Tel: 320-275-2424.

Renew 2000—JANE BERNARD HANSON, Dir., *1400 6th St. N., New Ulm, 56073-2099.* Tel: 507-359-2966.

Renew Core Committee—Rev. ANTHONY J. STUBEDA; JOANN BORCHERT; CHRISTOPHER A. LOETSCHER; BETTY MOHR; PAULA MARTI; Sr. SUE TORGERSEN, C.S.J.; MARK C. KEMMETER, Staff.

Liturgical Guidelines Committee—Revs. JEFFREY P. HOREJSI, Chm. GEORGE V. SCHMIT, JR.; Sr. MONICA WAGNER, S.S.N.D.; TOM CHRISTOFFER; JANE BERNARD HANSON, Staff; Rev. DENNIS C. LABAT, Staff.

Center for Spiritual Development—Sr. JANET MALLAK, S.S.N.D., Dir., *211 10th St., P.O. Box 538, Bird Island, 55310-0538.* Tel: 320-365-3644.

Ecumenical Director—TOM CHRISTOFFER, *209 N. Field St., P.O. Box 277, Comfrey, 56019-0277.* Tel: 507-877-2361.

Ecumenical Committee—Sr. CAROLYN PUCCIO, C.S.J.; Rev. ALLAN JOHNSON; JANE BERNARD HANSON.

Office of Social Concerns and Family Life—CHRISTOPHER A. LOETSCHER, Dir., *1400 6th St. N., New Ulm, 56073-2099.* Tel: 507-359-2966.

Social Concerns Committee—CHRISTOPHER A. LOETSCHER, Staff; Rev. JOHN A. NORDICK; KAY FINNEMAN; MIKE MONNENS; TOM JOHNSON; Sr. RAMONA FALLON, O.S.B.

Family Life—CHRISTOPHER A. LOETSCHER, Dir., *1400 6th St. N., New Ulm, 56073-2099.* Tel: 507-359-2966. Marriage Preparation, Natural Family Planning, Resources & Referral for Marriage & Family Concerns, Divorced/Separated.

Retrouvaille—WAYNE KASTNER; DIANE KASTNER, *48593 210th St., Sanborn, 56083.* Tel: 507-648-3456.

AIDS Ministry—Rev. PAUL A. SCHUMACHER, *Church of St. Peter, 307 W. 4th St., Canby, 56220-1211.* Tel: 507-233-7304.

Propagation of the Faith/Holy Childhood Association—Rev. WILLIAM H. BOWLES, *1400 6th St. N., New Ulm, 56073-2099.* Tel: 507-359-2966.

San Lucas Mission Office—Rev. Msgr. GREGORY T. SCHAFFER; KATHY HUEBERT, *1400 6th St. N., New Ulm, 56073-2099.* Tel: 507-359-2966.

Hispanic Ministry—Rev. ANTHONY J. STUBEDA, Dir., *1400 6th St. N., New Ulm, 56073-2099.* Tel: 507-359-2966.

Office of Personnel—

Priest Personnel—Rev. FRANCIS J. GARVEY, Dir., *1400 6th St. N., New Ulm, 56073-2099.* Tel: 507-359-2966.

Priest Personnel Board—Revs. FRANCIS J. GARVEY, Dir. DENNIS C. LABAT; EDWARD J. ARDOLF; MARK S. MALLAK; BRIAN W. OESTREICH; CELESTINE C. PISTULKA; MICHAEL M. DOYLE; JOHN A. RICHTER; EUGENE L. LOZINSKI.

Pastoral Administrators—Rev. DENNIS C. LABAT; Supvr., *1400 6th St. N., New Ulm, 56073-2099.* Tel: 507-359-2966.

Bishop's Delegate in Matters Pertaining to Sexual Misconduct—Rev. FRANCIS J. GARVEY.

New Ulm Diocesan Review Board on Sexual Misconduct—LILA SCHMIDT, Chm. STEVE SCHNEIDER, Vice Chm. MARY BOHLMANN; Rev. PAUL A. SCHUMACHER; MARY LINDSTROM.

Office of Conciliation—Sr. KATHLEEN BIERNE, P.B.V.M., Dir., *1400 6th St. N., New Ulm, 56073-2099.* Tel: 507-359-2966; 233-5322.

Vocations—Rev. BRIAN W. OESTREICH, Dir., *Church of Japanese Martyrs, 30881 County Rd. 24, Sleepy Eye, 56085-4361.* Tel: 507-794-6974; Fax: 507-794-6972. Sr. SUE TORGERSEN C.S.J., Assoc. Dir., *1400 6th St. N., New Ulm, 56073-2099.* Tel: 507-359-2966; 233-5328.

Continuing Education of Clergy—Sr. SUE TORGERSEN C.S.J., Dir., *1400 6th St. N., New Ulm, 56073-2099.* Tel: 507-359-2966; 233-5328.

Committee for Continuing Education of Clergy—Revs. PHILIP M. SCHOTZKO; RONALD V. HUBERTY; JOHN G. BERGER; JEFFREY P. HOREJSI; JOSEPH A. STEINBEISSER; Sr. SUE TORGERSEN, C.S.J.; Rev. PAUL L. WOLF; Sr. VIVIAN PETERSEN, O.S.B.; Sr. JOVANN IRRGANG, S.S.N.D.

Board of Trustees for Pension Plan for Priests—Revs. DENNIS C. LABAT; HARRY P. BEHAN; DONALD GUGGEMOS, JR.; JOHN BRESNAHAN. Staff: DUANE J. KOBLE; SHERRY KALOW; Revs. JOHN H. BRUNNER; MARK S. MALLAK.

Vicar for Retired Priests—Rev. MERLE W. MONNENS, *225 Lakeview Dr., Spicer, 56288.* Tel: 320-796-4541. Rev. Msgr. JOHN C. WARD, *Leo C. Byrne Residence, 60 S. Mississippi River Blvd., Apt. 225, St. Paul, 55105-1052.* Tel: 651-698-8175.

Organizations in the Diocese of New Ulm

Diocesan Council of Catholic Women—LILA SCHMIDT, Pres., *2834 County Rd. 5, Marshall, 56258.* Tel: 507-532-7564. Rev. EUGENE L. LOZINSKI, Diocesan Moderator.

Girl Scouts—MARY HAUSER, *1608 17th Ave., N.W., Willmar, 56201.* Tel: 320-235-3471.

Boy Scouts—Rev. ANDREW J. MICHELS, *Church of St. Anastasia, 460 Lake St., S.W., Hutchinson, 55350-2349.* Tel: 320-587-6507.

Marriage Encounter—WAYNE CARLSON; DEB CARLSON, *R.R.2, Box 22, Hanley Falls, 56245.* Tel: 507-423-6328.

Minnesota Pax Christi—Most Rev. RAYMOND A. LUCKER, Pres., *1400 6th St. N., New Ulm, 56073-2099.* Tel: 507-359-2966.

CLERGY, PARISHES, MISSIONS AND PAROCHIAL SCHOOLS

CITY OF NEW ULM
(Brown County)

1—CATHEDRAL OF THE HOLY TRINITY (1856). Clustered with Searles. Revs. George V. Schmit, Jr.; Todd J. Petersen; Rev. Msgr. Antony J. Leifeld, (Retired), Tel: 507-359-9848.
Res., 605 N. State St., 56073-1898. Tel: 507-354-4158; Fax: 507-354-2563. [CEM][JC]
School—New Ulm Area Catholic Schools. See separate listing under the Institutions for further explanation and statistics. Tel: 507-354-2719; Fax: 507-354-7071.
Catechesis/Religious Programs—Students 308.

2—ST. MARY (1911), Rev. Douglas L. Grams.
Res., 417 S. Minnesota St., 56073-2120. Tel: 507-233-9500; Fax: 507-354-8414. [JC]
School—New Ulm Area Catholic Schools. See separate listing under the Institutions for further explanation and statistics. Tel: 507-354-2719; Fax: 507-354-7071.
Catechesis/Religious Programs—Tel: 507-233-9505; Fax: 507-354-8414.
Students 380.

OUTSIDE THE CITY OF NEW ULM

Appleton, Swift Co., St. John (1880), Rev. Michael M. Doyle.
Mailing Address: 450 S. Gaulke St., 56208-1516.
Church Address: 350 S. Edquist St., 56208-1516. Tel: 320-289-1211; 289-1146; Fax: 320-289-1146. [CEM 2][JC 2]
Catechesis/Religious Programs—Tel: 320-289-1146.
Students 87.

Arlington, Sibley Co., St. Mary (1864), Rev. Jerry E. Paulson.
Res., 504 7th Ave., N.W., P.O. Box 392, 55307-0392. Tel: 507-964-5413; Fax: 507-964-5425. [CEM]
Catechesis/Religious Programs—Tel: 507-964-5425.
Students 156.

Barry, Big Stone Co., St. Barnabas. Closed. For sacramental records contact Holy Rosary, Graceville.

Beardsley, Big Stone Co., St. Mary (1884). Clustered with Graceville. Sr. Marlene Konrady, O.S.B., Pastoral Admin.
Res., 101 Church St., P.O. Box 299, 56211-0299. Tel: 320-265-6916 (Church); 265-6113 (Rectory). [CEM]
Catechesis/Religious Programs—Students 79.

Bechyn, Renville Co., St. Mary. Closed. For sacramental records contact St. Aloysius, Olivia.

Belgrade, Nicollet Co., St. Michael. Closed. For sacramental records contact St. Paul, Nicollet.

Benson, Swift Co., St. Francis (1881). Clustered with Clontarf, Danvers, De Graff Murdock & Clara City. Rev. Steven J. Verhelst Tel: 320-843-2342. Area Pastoral Leaders: Rev. Ronald V. Huberty, (Murdock), Tel: 320-875-2246; Sr. Clara M. Stang, O.S.F., Pastoral Admin. (Danvers & Clontarf), Tel: 320-567-2278; Sr. Darlene Gutenkauf, P.B.V.M., Pastoral Admin. (De Graff), Tel: 320-843-3883; Sr. Ruth Ann Takes, P.B.V.M., Pastoral Admin. (Clara City), Tel: 320-847-2256; Sr. Louise Bauer, O.S.F., Pastoral Admin. (Clontarf), Tel: 320-843-2026.
Area Office—Tel: 320-842-4271; Fax: 320-843-2264.
Church—508 13th St. N., 56215-1228. [CEM]
Catechesis/Religious Programs—Students 267.

Birch Coolie, Renville Co., St. Patrick. Closed. For sacramental records contact Sacred Heart, Franklin. Earlier records located at St. John, Morton.

Bird Island, Renville Co., St. Mary (1879). Clustered with Hector. Rev. Philip M. Schotzko.
Res., 220 S. 10th St., P.O. Box 500, 55310-0500. Tel: 320-365-3593; Fax: 320-365-3142. [CEM]
School—(Grades K-8) 140 S. 10th St., P.O. Box 500, 55310-0500. Tel: 320-365-3693. Sr. Patricia McCusker, S.S.N.D., Prin.
Sisters 1; Lay Teachers 12; Students 189.
Catechesis/Religious Programs—Students 93.

Canby, Yellow Medicine Co., St. Peter (1897). Clustered with St. Leo. Rev. Paul A. Schumacher.
Res., 307 W. 4th St., 56220-1211. Tel: 507-223-7304; Fax: 507-223-5776. [CEM]
School—(Grades K-6) 410 Ring Ave. N., 56220-1237. Tel: 507-223-7729. Ms. Marian Bach, Prin.
Lay Teachers 4; Students 54.
Catechesis/Religious Programs—(Grades K-12).
Students 220.

Clara City, Chippewa Co., St. Clara (1890). Clustered with Murdock, DeGraff, Benson, Danvers & Clontarf. Sr. Ruth Ann Takes, P.B.V.M., Pastoral Admin. Area Pastoral Leaders: Revs. Ronald U. Huberty, (Murdock), Tel: 320-875-2246; Steven J. Verhelst, (Benson), Tel: 320-567-2342; Sr. Darlene Gutenkauf, P.B.V.M., (DeGraff), Tel: 320-843-3883; Sr. Clara Stang, O.S.F., (Danvers & Clontarf), Tel: 320-567-2278; Sr. Louise Bauer, O.S.F., (Clontarf), Tel: 320-843-2026.
Church—414 N. Main St., P.O. Box 310, 56222-0310. Tel: 320-847-2256; Fax: 320-843-2264. [CEM 2]
Catechesis/Religious Programs—Tel: 320-847-2445.
Students 123.

Clarkfield, Yellow Medicine Co., St. Isidore. Closed. For sacramental records contact St. Joseph, Montevideo.

Clements, Redwood Co., St. Joseph (1902). Clustered with Morgan. Sr. Kathryn Schoolmeesters, S.S.N.D., Pastoral Admin.
120 Ash St., P.O. Box 56, 56224-0056. Tel: 507-692-2181. [CEM]
Catechesis/Religious Programs—Students 25.

Clontarf, Swift Co., St. Malachy (1878). Clustered with Benson, Danvers, De Graff, Murdock & Clara City. Sr. Clara Stang, O.S.F., Pastoral Admin., Tel: 320-567-2278. Area Pastoral Leaders: Revs. Ronald V. Huberty, (Murdock), Tel: 320-875-2246; Steven J. Verhelst, (Benson), Tel: 320-567-2342; Sr. Darlene Gutenkauf, P.B.V.M., (De Graff), Tel: 320-843-3883; Sr. Ruth Ann Takes, P.B.V.M., (Clara City), Tel: 320-847-2256; Sr. Louise Bauer, O.S.F., Pastoral Admin., Tel: 320-843-2026.
Area Office—Tel: 320-842-4271.
Mailing Office: P.O. Box 218, 56226-0218. Tel: 320-843-2026; 843-2514 (Parish Hall); Fax: 320-843-2264. [CEM]
Church Address: 300 Arnaah St. S.W.
Catechesis/Religious Programs—Tel: 320-843-2037.
Students 56.

Comfrey, Brown Co., St. Paul (1900). Clustered with Leavenworth. Thomas R. Christoffer, Pastoral Admin.
Res., 209 N. Field St., P.O. Box 277, 56019-0277. Tel: 507-877-2361; Fax: 507-877-2361. [CEM]
Catechesis/Religious Programs—Tel: 507-877-2500; 877-9800.
Students 90.

Cottonwood, Lyon Co., St. Mary (1902). Clustered with Green Valley. Rev. Paul J. Hadusek.
Res., 255 W. 4th St., P.O. Box 228, 56229-0228. Tel: 507-423-5220; Fax: 507-423-5275. [CEM]
Catechesis/Religious Programs—Fax: 507-423-5220.
Students 176.

Danvers, Swift Co., Church of the Visitation (1885). Clustered with Benson, Clontarf, De Graff, Murdock & Clara City. Sr. Clara M. Stang, O.S.F., Pastoral Admin., Tel: 320-567-2278. Area Pastoral Leaders: Revs. Ronald V. Huberty, (Murdock), Tel: 320-875-2246; Steven J. Verhelst, (Benson), Tel: 320-843-2342; Sr. Darlene Gutenhauf, P.B.V.M., (De Graff), Tel: 320-843-3883; Sr. Ruth Ann Takes, P.B.V.M., (Clara City), Tel: 320-847-2256; Sr. Louise Bauer, O.S.F., (Clontarf), Tel: 320-843-2026.

Church—201 County Rd. 14, P.O. Box 18, 56231-0018. Tel: 320-567-2278. [CEM]
Rectory: 201 Washington Ave., 56231.
Area Office—Tel: 320-842-4271; Fax: 320-843-2264.
Catechesis/Religious Programs—Students 44.

Darwin, Meeker Co., St. John (1861). Clustered with Forest City. Rev. Patrick L. Casey.
Res., 106 N. 4th St., 55324-6016. Tel: 320-693-6878; 275-2915. [CEM]
Catechesis/Religious Programs—Tel: 320-286-2800.
Students 210.

Dawson, Lac Qui Parle Co., St. James (1898). Clustered with Madison. Sr. Vivian Petersen, O.S.B., Pastoral Admin.
Res., 10th & Locust, P.O. Box 270, 56232-0270. Tel: 320-769-4465. [CEM]
Catechesis/Religious Programs—Students 104.

De Graff, Swift Co., St. Bridget (1876). Clustered with Benson, Clontarf, Danvers & Murdock. Sr. Darlene Gutenkauf, P.B.V.M., Pastoral Admin., Tel: 320-843-3883. Area Pastoral Leaders: Revs. Ronald V. Huberty, (Murdock), Tel: 320-875-2246; Steven J. Verhelst, (Benson), Tel: 320-843-2342; Sr. Clara M. Stang, O.S.F., Pastoral Admin. (Danvers & Clontarf)), Tel: 320-567-2278; Sr. Ruth Ann Takes, P.B.V.M., Pastoral Admin. (Clara City), Tel: 320-847-2256; Sr. Louise Bauer, O.S.F., (Clontarf).
Church—501 3rd St. S., 56271. Tel: 320-843-3883. [CEM]
Area Office—Tel: 320-842-4271; Fax: 320-843-2264.
Catechesis/Religious Programs—St. Bridget Activity Center, 405 5th St. S., DeGraff, 56233. Tel: 320-843-2005.
Students 33.

Eden Valley, Meeker Co., St. Peter (1903). Closed. For inquiries for parish records contact Assumption Church, Eden Valley, Diocese of St. Cloud.

Fairfax, Renville Co., St. Andrew (1871). Clustered with Franklin. Rev. John H. Brunner.
Res., 15 S.E. First St., P.O. Box C, 55332-0903. Tel: 507-426-7125; Fax: 507-426-7125. [CEM]
School—(Grades 1-6) 101 S.E. 1st Ave., Tel: 507-426-7739. Rev. John H. Brunner, Prin.
Lay Teachers 3; Students 23.
Catechesis/Religious Programs—Students 100.

Faxon Township, Sibley Co., St. John-Assumption (1859). Clustered with Green Isle, Henderson & Jessenland. Sr. Donna Wermus, S.S.N.D., Pastoral Admin., Tel: 612-873-4390.
Res., 26523 200th St., Belle Plaine, 56011-9302. Tel: 612-873-4390. [CEM 2]
Catechesis/Religious Programs—Tel: 952-873-4390.
Students 82.

Forest City, Meeker Co., St. Gertrude (1857). Clustered with Darwin. Thomas E. Johnson, Pastoral Admin.
Res., 31626 650th Ave., Litchfield, 55355-9998. Tel: 320-693-7801. [CEM]
Church—31608 650th Ave., Litchfield, 55355-9998.
Catechesis/Religious Programs—Students 60.

Franklin, Renville Co., Sacred Heart (1898) (Irish). Clustered with Fairfax. Rev. John H. Brunner, (Fairfax).
Res. & Mailing Address—15 S.E. First St., P.O. Box C, Fairfax, 55332-0903. Tel: 507-426-7125; Fax: 507-426-7125.
Church—E. Main St., 55333-0175. [CEM 2]
Catechesis/Religious Programs—Students 68.

Gaylord, Sibley Co., St. Michael (1882). Clustered with Winthrop. Rev. Richard G. Bonin.
Res., 361 4th St., P.O. Box 357, 55334-0357. Tel: 507-237-2851; Fax: 507-237-5300.
Catechesis/Religious Programs—P.O. Box 781, 55334. Tel: 507-237-2888. Sherri Kaufmann, D.R.E.
Students 113.

Ghent, Lyon Co., St. Eloi (1883). Clustered with Minneota & Taunton. Rev. Gerald A. Hillesheim Tel: 507-872-5263; Charles Pratt, Pastoral Admin. Intern.
Church—306 W. McQuestion, 56239-9750. Tel: 507-428-3285; Fax: 507-872-5263. [CEM]
Catechesis/Religious Programs—Fax: 507-428-3200.
Students 81.

Gibbon, Sibley Co., St. Willibrord (1886), Rev. Eugene C. Hackert.
Res., 1032 Ash Ave., P.O. Box 187, 55335-0187. Tel: 507-834-6461. [CEM]
Catechesis/Religious Programs—Tel: 507-834-6659.
Students 91.

Glencoe, McLeod Co., St. George. Closed. For sacramental records, contact St. Pius X, Glencoe.
Ss. Peter and Paul. Closed. For sacramental records, contact St. Pius X, Glencoe.
St. Pius X (1983), Rev. Eugene L. Lozinski.
Res., 1014 Knight Ave., 55336-2300. Tel: 320-864-5162; 864-2963 (Rectory). [CEM]
School—(Grades PreK-6) 1103 10th St. E., 55336-2399. Tel: 320-864-3214; Fax: 320-864-5163. Joanne Pohland, Prin.
Lay Teachers 5; Students 89.
Catechesis/Religious Programs—Tel: 320-864-5162.
Students 183.

Graceville, Big Stone Co., Holy Rosary (1878). Clustered with Beardsley. Rev. John A. Nordick; Deacon Art D. Abel Tel: 320-748-7573.
Res. & Mailing Address: 511 Studdart Ave., P.O. Box 7, 56240-0007. Tel: 320-748-7313. [JC]
Catechesis/Religious Programs—517 Studdart Ave., 56240. Tel: 320-748-7482.
Students 214.

Granite Falls, Yellow Medicine Co., St. Andrew (1885). Clustered with Montevideo. Rev. James Devorak.
Mailing Address: 1094 Granite St., 56241-1355. Tel: 320-564-2335; Fax: 320-564-2336.
Res., 512 Black Oak Ave., Montevideo, 56241. Tel: 320-269-8623; Fax: 320-269-7555. [CEM]
Catechesis/Religious Programs—1056 Fourth St., 56241. Tel: 320-564-2336.
Students 197.

Green Isle, Sibley Co., St. Brendan (1854). Clustered with Faxon Township, Henderson & Jessenland. Rev. Bernard J. Steiner.
Res., 221 McGrann St. S., P.O. Box 85, 55338-0085. Tel: 507-326-5111. [CEM]
Catechesis/Religious Programs—Students 53.

Green Valley, Lyon Co., St. Clotilde (1912). Clustered with Cottonwood. Rev. Paul J. Hadusek.
Res., 225 W. 4th St. S., P.O. Box 228, Cottonwood, 56229-0228. Tel: 507-423-5220; Fax: 507-423-5275. [CEM]
Church—R.R., Marshall, 56258-8903. Tel: 507-532-2841.
Catechesis/Religious Programs—Tel: 507-423-6496.
Students 68.

Greenleaf, Meeker Co., St. Columban. Closed. For inquiries for sacramental records contact St. Philip, Litchfield.

Hector, Renville Co., Church of St. John (1878). Clustered with Bird Island. Sr. Sharon F. Nohner, O.S.B., Pastoral Admin.
Church—301 Cedar Ave. E., P.O. Box 295, 55342-0295. Tel: 320-848-6437. [CEM]
Catechesis/Religious Programs—Students 96.

Hegbert, Swift Co., St. Agnes. Closed. For sacramental records, contact St. John, Appleton.

Henderson, Sibley Co., St. Joseph (1859). Clustered with Faxon Township, Green Isle & Jessenland. Sr. Jovann Irrgang, S.S.N.D., Pastoral Admin.
Res., 213 S. 6th St., P.O. Box 427, 56044-0427. Tel: 507-248-3550. [CEM]
Catechesis/Religious Programs—Students 82.
Mission—Jessenland, Sibley Co., St. Thomas.

Holloway, Swift Co., St. Joseph. Closed. For sacramental records, contact St. John, Appleton.

Hutchinson, McLeod Co., Church of St. Anastasia (1866). Clustered with Stewart. Revs. William A. Sprigler; Andrew J. Michels.
Res. & Mailing Address: 460 Lake St. S.W., 55350-2349. Tel: 320-587-6507; Fax: 320-234-6756.
Church—400 Lake St., S.W., 55350-2349. [CEM]
School—(Grades PreK-6). Tel: 320-587-2490. Karla Cross, Prin.
Lay Teachers 10; Students 165.
Catechesis/Religious Programs—Tel: 320-234-6129.
Students 457.

Ivanhoe, Lincoln Co., SS. Peter & Paul (1900). Clustered with Wilno. Rev. David L. Breu.
Res., 111 N. Sherwood, P.O. Box 49, 56142-0049. Tel: 507-694-1402; Fax: 507-694-1437. [CEM]
Catechesis/Religious Programs—RR. 1, Box 59, 56142. Tel: 507-694-1225; Fax: 507-694-1548. Sr. M. Ellen Hoemberg, I.S.S.M.
Students 91.

Jessenland, Sibley Co., St. Thomas (Mission) (1856). Clustered with Faxon Township, Green Isle, & Henderson. Sr. Jovann Irrgang, S.S.N.D., Pastoral Admin.
Res., 213 S. Sixth St., P.O. Box 427, Henderson, 56044-0427. Tel: 507-248-3550. [CEM]
Church—31624 Scenic Byway Rd., Henderson, 56044.

Kandiyohi, Kandiyohi Co., St. Patrick (1868). Clustered with Lake Lillian. Rev. William H. Bowles.
Res., 245 3rd St. E., P.O. Box 164, 56251-0164. Tel: 320-382-6424. [CEM]
Catechesis/Religious Programs—Students 136.

Lafayette, Nicollet Co., St. Gregory the Great (1942). Clustered with West Newton Township. Rev. James E. Moran.
Res., 440 6th St., P.O. Box 5, 56054-0005. Tel: 507-228-8298. [CEM]
Catechesis/Religious Programs—Students 110.

Lake Benton, Lincoln Co., St. Genevieve (1897). Clustered with Tyler. Rev. John A. Pearson, (Tyler), Tel: 507-247-3464.
Res. & Mailing Address: 213 Linwood St., P.O. 310, Tyler, 56178. Tel: 507-247-3464.
Church—119 S. Sherman St., 56149. [CEM]
Catechesis/Religious Programs—Fax: 507-247-3286.
Students 64.

Lake Lillian, Kandiyohi Co., St. Thomas More (1934). Clustered with Kandiyohi. Rev. William H. Bowles.
Res. & Mailing Address: 245 3rd St. E., P.O. Box 164, Kandiyohi, 56251-0164. Tel: 320-382-6424.
Church—840 Second St. E., P.O. Box 164, Kandiyohi, 56251-0164. Tel: 320-664-4810.
Catechesis/Religious Programs—Students 37.

Lamberton, Redwood Co., St. Joseph (1895). Clustered with Walnut Grove & Tracy. Sr. Marian Kemper, O.S.B., Pastoral Admin.
Res., 400 W. 2nd Ave., P.O. Box 458, 56152-0458. Tel: 507-752-7269; Fax: 507-629-4075. [CEM]
Catechesis/Religious Programs—Students 75.

Leavenworth, Brown Co., Church of the Japanese Martyrs (1867). Clustered with Comfrey. Rev. Brian W. Oestreich.
Res., 30881 County Rd. 24, Sleepy Eye, 56085-4361. Tel: 507-794-6974; Fax: 507-794-6972. [CEM]
Catechesis/Religious Programs—Tel: 507-794-6460.
Students 55.

Lester Prairie, McLeod Co., St. Conrad. Closed. Incorporated but never organized. No sacramental records.

Litchfield, Meeker Co., St. Philip (1859), Rev. Mark S. Mallak.
Res., 306 N. Holcombe Ave., 55355-2223. Tel: 320-693-3313; Fax: 320-693-2247. [CEM]
School—(Grades K-5) 225 E. 3rd St., 55355-2202. Tel: 320-693-6283. Teresa Hankins, Prin.
Lay Teachers 5; Students 62.
Catechesis/Religious Programs—225 E. Third St., 55355.
Students 306.

Lucan, Redwood Co., Our Lady of Victory (1889). Clustered with Wabasso, Seaforth and Wanda. Rev. John A. Richter; Sr. Michelle McGurran, O.S.B., Pastoral Admin. Intern.
Res., P.O. Box 96, 56255-0096. Tel: 507-747-2231. [CEM]
School—(Grades 1-6) 301 3rd St., 56255-0096. Tel: 507-747-2233; Fax: 507-747-2288. Mary Ann Kramer, Prin.
Lay Teachers 2; Students 14.
Catechesis/Religious Programs—Students 36.

Madison, Lac Qui Parle Co., St. Michael (1884). Clustered with Dawson. Rev. Jeffrey P. Horejsi.
Res., 412 3rd St., 56256-1494. Tel: 320-598-3690; Fax: 320-598-3690. [CEM]
Catechesis/Religious Programs—Students 126.

Manannah, Meeker Co., Church of Our Lady (1876), Rev. Francis J. Garvey.
Res., 57382 CSAH 3, Grove City, 56243-9786. Tel: 320-693-8900; 453-7526; Fax: 320-693-8900. [CEM]
Catechesis/Religious Programs—Students 88.

Marshall, Lyon Co., Holy Redeemer (1883). Clustered with Milroy. Revs. Gerald S. Meidl; Celestine C. Pistulka; Eugene M. Brown.
Res., 503 W. Lyon St., 56258-1390. Tel: 507-532-5711; Fax: 507-532-3262. [CEM][JC]
School—(Grades K-8) 501 S. Whitney, 56258-1995. Tel: 507-532-6642; Fax: 507-532-2636. Carol J. DeSmet, Prin.
Lay Teachers 24; Students 408.
Catechesis/Religious Programs—503 S. Whitney St., 56258. Tel: 507-532-3602. D.R.E.: Patti Watkins, (Grades K-6); Mary Beth Johnson, (Grades 7-12).
Students 488.

Middle Lake, Nicollet Co., St. Nicholas. Closed. For sacramental records, contact St. Paul's, Nicollet.

Milroy, Redwood Co., St. Michael (1904). Clustered with Marshall. Rev. Celestine C. Pistulka Tel: 507-532-5711; Sr. Rosine Kaminsk, O.S.F., Pastoral Admin. Intern.
Res., 400 Cedar St; P.O. Box 117, 56263-0117. Tel: 507-336-2505. [CEM]
Catechesis/Religious Programs—Students 133.

Minneota, Lyon Co., St. Edward (1880). Clustered with Ghent & Taunton. Rev. Gerald A. Hillesheim.
Church & Res.: 409 N. Adams St., 56264-9801. Tel: 507-872-6346; Fax: 507-872-5263. [CEM]
School—(Grades 1-8) 210 W. 4th St., 56264-9627. Tel: 507-872-6391. Kathleen Fjedheim, Prin.
Lay Teachers 9; Students 116.

Catechesis/Religious Programs—Tel: 507-428-3285.
Students 179.

Montevideo, Chippewa Co., St. Joseph (1882). Clustered with Granite Falls. Rev. James W. Devorak.
Res., 512 Eureka Ave., 56265-1874. Tel: 320-269-8623; Fax: 320-269-7555. [CEM]
Church—512 Black Oak Ave., 56265-1874. Tel: 320-269-5954.
Catechesis/Religious Programs—Students 234.

Morgan, Redwood Co., St. Michael (1890). Clustered with Clements. Rev. Robert J. Wyffels.
Res. & Mailing: 510 W. 3rd St., P.O. Box 459, 56266-0459. Tel: 507-249-3643; Fax: 507-249-2557.
Church—514 W. 3rd St. [CEM]
School—(Grades PreK-6) 612 W. 3rd St., P.O. Box 459, 56266-0459. Tel: 507-249-3192. Sr. Gladys Meindl, O.S.F., Prin.
Sisters 1; Lay Teachers 4; Students 76.
Catechesis/Religious Programs—Tel: 507-692-2181.
Students 98.

Morton, Renville Co., St. John (1873). Clustered with Redwood Falls. Sr. JoAnne Backes, O.S.B., Pastoral Admin.
Res., 341 W. 3rd St., P.O. Box 88, 56270-0088. Tel: 507-697-6120. [CEM]
Catechesis/Religious Programs—Students 49.

Murdock, Swift Co., Church of the Sacred Heart (1879). Clustered with Benson, Clontarf, Danvers, De Graff & Clara City. Rev. Ronald V. Huberty, (Murdock). Area Pastoral Leaders: Rev. Steven J. Verhelst, (Benson), Tel: 320-843-2342; Sr. Clara M. Stang, O.S.F., (Danvers), Tel: 320-567-2278; Sr. Darlene Gutenkauf, P.B.V.M., (De Graff), Tel: 320-843-3883; Sr. Ruth Ann Takes, P.B.V.M., (Clara City), Tel: 320-847-2256; Sr. Louise Bauer, O.S.F., (Clontarf), Tel: 320-843-2026.
Res. & Mailing Address: 201 Orleans, P.O. Box 9, 56271-0009. Tel: 320-875-2451; 842-4271 (Area Office); Fax: 320-843-2264. [CEM]
Catechesis/Religious Programs—Tel: 320-875-2451.
Students 120.

Nassau, Lac Qui Parle Co., St. James (1902). Clustered with Ortonville and Rosen. Rev. Robert P. Goblirsch, (Ortonville).
Res. & Mailing Address: 421 Madison Ave., P.O. Box 205, Ortonville, 56278-0205. Tel: 320-839-2772. [CEM]

Nicollet, Nicollet Co., St. Paul (1907), Rev. John Gerald Berger.
Res., 411 5th St., P.O. Box 248, 56074-0248. Tel: 507-232-3857. [CEM 4]
Catechesis/Religious Programs—Students 102.

Swan Lake, Nicollet Co., The Church of the Visitation. Closed. For sacramental records, contact St. Paul, Nicollet.

North Mankato, Nicollet Co., Holy Rosary (1924), Rev. Peter C. Nosbush.
Res., 525 Grant Ave., 56003-2939. Tel: 507-387-6501; Fax: 507-388-2017.
School—546 Grant Ave., 56003-2940. Tel: 507-345-6765. Tom Tacheny, Supt.
School is part of Mankato Area Catholic Schools, Diocese of Winona. Numbers are reported by Winona Diocese.
Catechesis/Religious Programs—Students 357.

Olivia, Renville Co., St. Aloysius (1888). Clustered with Renville. Rev. Paul van de Crommert.
Res., 302 S. 10th St., 56277-1288. Tel: 320-523-2030. [CEM 2]
Catechesis/Religious Programs—Tel: 320-523-2030.
Students 239.

Ortonville, Big Stone Co., St. John (1879). Clustered with Nassau & Rosen. Rev. Robert P. Goblirsch.
Res., P.O. Box 205, 421 Madison Ave., 56278-0205. Tel: 320-839-2772.
Catechesis/Religious Programs—Tel: 320-839-2873.
Students 174.

Raymond, Kandiyohi Co., Sacred Heart. Closed. For sacramental records, contact St. Clara, Clara City.

Redwood Falls, Redwood Co., St. Catherine (1870). Clustered with Morton. Rev. Germain P. Rademacher.
Church & Mailing Address: 900 E. Flynn St., P.O. Box 383, 56283-0383. Tel: 507-637-2278; Fax: 507-637-2643.
Res., 904 E. Flynn St., P.O. Box 383, 56283-0383. Tel: 507-637-8114.
Catechesis/Religious Programs—Students 323.

Regal, Kandiyohi Co., St. Anthony (Mission) (1933). Clustered with Spicer. Rev. Frederick T. Fink.
Res. & Mailing Address: 13722 Hwy. 23 N.E., Spicer, 56288-9659. Tel: 320-796-5664. [CEM]
Church—293rd Ave. & 145th St., Spicer, 56288.
Catechesis/Religious Programs—Tel: 320-243-3232.
Students 39.

Renville, Renville Co., Holy Redeemer (1891). Clustered with Olivia. Donald A. Clasemann, Pastoral Admin.
Church—106 S.E. 3rd St., P.O. Box 401, 56284-0401. Tel: 320-329-3884; Fax: 320-329-3884. [CEM]
Catechesis/Religious Programs—Tel: 320-329-8219.
Students 165.

Rosen, Lac Qui Parle Co., St. Joseph (1885). Clustered with Nassau & Ortonville. Rev. Robert P. Goblirsch, (Ortonville).
Mailing Address: 421 Madison Ave., P.O. Box 205, Ortonville, 56278-0205. Tel: 320-839-2772. [CEM]
Catechesis/Religious Programs—Tel: 320-839-2873; 568-2428.
Students 55.

St. Leo, Yellow Medicine Co., St. Leo (1881). Clustered with Canby. Rev. Paul A. Schumacher, (Canby), Tel: 507-223-7304.
Church—202 W. Church St., 56264. Tel: 507-224-2289. [CEM]
Catechesis/Religious Programs—Tel: 507-223-7729.
Students 11.

St. Peter, Nicollet Co., St. Peter (1856), Rev. Harry P. Behan. Pastoral Assocs: Sr. Ramona Fallon, O.S.B.; Kay Osborne.
Res., 1801 W. Broadway, P.O. Box 522, 56082-0522. Tel: 507-931-1628; Fax: 507-931-2977. [CEM]
School—John Ireland School, (Grades K-6). Tel: 507-931-2810; Fax: 507-931-9179. Mrs. Barbara Wood, Prin.
Lay Teachers 8; Students 116.
Catechesis/Religious Programs—Tel: 507-931-1628. Teresa Guillemette, D.R.E.
Students 433.
Immaculate Conception. Closed. For sacramental records, contact St. Peter's, St. Peter.

Sanborn, Redwood Co., St. Thomas (1902). Clustered with Springfield. Sr. Jeanette Homan, O.S.F., Pastoral Admin.
Res., 301 E. Winona St., P.O. Box 176, 56083-0176. Tel: 507-648-3754.
Catechesis/Religious Programs—Students 50.

Seaforth, Redwood Co., St. Mary (1880). Clustered with Wabasso, Lucan & Wanda. Rev. John A. Richter, (Wabasso).
Res. & Mailing Address: P.O. Box 239, Wabasso, 56293-0239. Tel: 507-342-5190 (Office); 984-5411 (Church); 342-5155 (Rectory). [CEM 2]
Catechesis/Religious Programs—Students 31.

Searles, Brown Co., St. John the Baptist (1905). Clustered with Cathedral, New Ulm. Sr. Monica Wagner, S.S.N.D., Pastoral Admin.
Res. & Mailing Address: 18241 First Ave. S., P.O. Box 113, 56084-0113. Tel: 507-359-4244; Fax: 507-359-4244. [CEM]
School—New Ulm Area Catholic Schools. See separate listing for details. Tel: 507-354-2719; Fax: 507-354-5711.
Catechesis/Religious Programs—Tel: 507-354-4158; Fax: 507-354-2563.
Students 36.

Silver Lake, McLeod Co., St. Adalbert. Closed. For sacramental records, contact Holy Family, Silver Lake.
St. Joseph. Closed. For sacramental records, contact Holy Family, Silver Lake.
Church of the Holy Family (1993), Rev. Robert J. Mraz.
Res., 720 W. Main St., P.O. Box 326, 55381-0326. Tel: 320-327-2261; Fax: 320-327-2261. [CEM 4][JC 4]
School—(Grades 1-6) 700 W. Main St., P.O. Box 346, 55381-0346. Tel: 320-327-2356; Fax: 320-327-2356. Rebecca Leicher, Prin.
Lay Teachers 8; Students 78.
Catechesis/Religious Programs—Tel: 320-327-2930; Fax: 320-327-2931.
Students 184.

Sleepy Eye, Brown Co., St. Mary (1876), Rev. Edward J. Ardoff.
Res., 636 First Ave. N., 56085-1004. Tel: 507-794-4171; Fax: 507-794-5871. [CEM]
School—(Grades PreK-6) 104 W. St. Mary St., 56085-1098. Tel: 507-794-6141; Fax: 507-794-4841. Mr. Wayne Pelzel, Prin.
Lay Teachers 17; Students 345.
High School—(Grades 7-12). Tel: 507-794-4121. Mr. Jerry Neubauer, Prin.
Lay Teachers 22; Students 194.
Catechesis/Religious Programs—Tel: 507-794-4067.
Students 146.

Spicer, Kandiyohi Co., Our Lady of the Lakes (1962). Clustered with Regal. Rev. Frederick T. Fink.
Res., 13722 Hwy. 23 N.E., 56288-9659. Tel: 320-796-5664. [CEM]
Catechesis/Religious Programs—Tel: 320-796-5968.
Students 334.
Mission—Regal, Kandiyohi Co., St. Anthony.

Springfield, Brown Co., St. Raphael (1874). Clustered with Sanborn. Rev. Dennis C. Labat.
Res., 112 W. Van Dusen St., 56087-1396. Tel: 507-723-4137(Office); 723-4141(Rectory). [CEM]
School—(Grades K-6) 20 W. VanDusen, 56087-1394. Tel: 507-723-4315; Fax: 507-723-5409. Sr. Therese Colison, S.S.N.D., Prin., Tel: 507-723-4136.
Sisters 3; Lay Teachers 5; Students 82.
Catechesis/Religious Programs—Tel: 507-723-4138.
Students 265.

Stewart, McLeod Co., Church of St. Boniface (1877). Clustered with Hutchinson. Sr. Idamarie Primus, O.S.B., Pastoral Admin.
Res., 551 Main St., P.O. Box 202, 55385-0202. Tel: 320-562-2344. [CEM]
Catechesis/Religious Programs—Students 87.

Swan Lake, Nicollet Co., Visitation. Closed. For sacramental records, contact St. Paul, Nicollet.

Taunton, Lyon Co., SS. Cyril and Methodius (1895). Clustered with Ghent & Minneota. Sr. Roselle Zollar, S.S.N.D., Pastoral Admin.
Res., Lincoln St., P.O. Box 368, 56291-0368. Tel: 507-872-5150. [CEM 2][JC 2]
Catechesis/Religious Programs—Students 26.

Tracy, Lyon Co., St. Mary (1880). Clustered with Walnut Grove & Lamberton. Rev. Brian L. Mandel.
Res., 249 6th St., 56175-1114. Tel: 507-629-3227; Fax: 507-629-3667. [CEM]
Church—285 6th St., 56175. Tel: 507-629-3841 (Church Hall).
School—(Grades K-6) 225 6th. St., Tel: 507-629-3270. Mrs. Lisa Schaar, Prin.
Lay Teachers 5; Students 65.
Catechesis/Religious Programs—Tel: 507-629-3667.
Students 145.

Tyler, Lincoln Co., St. Dionysius (1880). Clustered with Lake Benton. Rev. John A. Pearson.
Mailing Address: P.O. Box 310, 56178-0310.
Res., 513 E. Hughes St., P.O. Box 310, 56178-0310. Tel: 507-247-5167 (Res.); 247-3464 (Office); Fax: 507-247-3286. [CEM]
Church—203 Linwood St., 56178. Tel: 507-247-5807.
Catechesis/Religious Programs—Students 131.

Vesta, Redwood Co., Holy Name. Closed. For sacramental records, contact St. Catherine's, Redwood Falls.

Wabasso, Redwood Co., St. Anne (1900). Clustered with Seaforth, Lucan & Wanda. Rev. John A. Richter.
Res., 1052 Cedar St., P.O. Box 239, 56293-0239. Tel: 507-342-5155 (Rectory); 342-5190 (Office); Fax: 507-342-5156. [CEM]
School—(Grades K-6) 1054 Cedar St., Tel: 507-345-5389. Lisa Dudgeon, Prin.
Lay Teachers 9; Students 115.
Catechesis/Religious Programs—Tel: 507-342-5190.
Students 175.

Walnut Grove, Redwood Co., St. Paul (1902). Clustered with Tracy & Lamberton. Rev. Brian L. Mandel, (Tracy), Tel: 507-629-3227.
Res., 600 3rd St., P.O. Box 236, 56180-0236. Tel: 507-859-2164. [CEM]
Catechesis/Religious Programs—Students 37.

Wanda, Redwood Co., St. Mathias (1871). Clustered with Seaforth, Wabasso & Lucan. Rev. John A. Richter Tel: 507-342-5155.
Mailing Address: 308 St. Mathias Blvd., P.O. Box 308, 56294-0308. Tel: 507-342-5190; Fax: 507-342-5156. [CEM]
Catechesis/Religious Programs—Students 216.

Watkins, Meeker Co., Church of St. Anthony (1889), Rev. Richard C. Gross.
Res. & Mailing Address: 171 Central Ave. S., P.O. Box 439, 55389-0439. Tel: 320-764-2755; Fax: 320-764-2755. [CEM]
Church—151 Central Ave. S., 55389-0439.
Catechesis/Religious Programs—Students 216.

West Newton Township, Nicollet Co., St. George (1857). Clustered with Lafayette. Rev. James E. Moran, (Lafayette).
Res. & Mailing Address: 440 6th St., P.O. Box 5, Lafayette, 56054-0005. Tel: 507-228-8298; 359-9013.
Church—Hwy. 16 & County Rd. 5, Tel: 507-228-8298. [CEM]
Catechesis/Religious Programs—Students 6.

Willmar, Kandiyohi Co., St. Mary (1871), Rev. Joseph A. Steinbeisser.
Church—713 12th St., S.W., 56201-3099. Tel: 320-235-0118; Fax: 320-235-0153. [CEM]
Res., 56201-3025. Tel: 320-235-6365.
Catechesis/Religious Programs—Tel: 320-235-3982.
Students 694.

Wilno, Lincoln Co., St. John Cantius (1883). Clustered with Ivanhoe. Rev. David L. Breu, (Ivanhoe).
Res., R.R. 1, Box 59, Ivanhoe, 56142-9793. Tel: 507-694-1225; 694-1402; Fax: 507-694-1548. [CEM]
Catechesis/Religious Programs—Students 134.

Winsted, McLeod Co., Holy Trinity (1869), Rev. Paul L. Wolf.
Res., 111 Winsted Ave. W., P.O. Box 9, 55395-0009. Tel: 320-485-4421; Fax: 320-485-4283. [CEM 2]
School—(Grades PreK-6) 211 2nd St. N., P.O. Box 38, 55395-0038. Tel: 320-485-2314; Fax: 320-485-2167. Mrs. Ann Brown, Prin.
Lay Teachers 9; Students 200.
High School—(Grades 7-12). Tel: 320-485-2182. Rev. Paul L. Wolf, Prin. & Supt.
Lay Teachers 15; Students 111.
Catechesis/Religious Programs—Tel: 320-485-3752; Fax: 320-485-4283.
Students 160.

Winthrop, Sibley Co., St. Francis de Sales (1906). Clustered with St. Michael's, Gaylord. Rev. Richard G. Bonin.
Church & Mailing Address: N. Brown St., P.O. Box 447, 55396-0447. Tel: 507-647-5334.
Catechesis/Religious Programs—P.O. Box F, 55396. Tel: 507-647-5894; Fax: 507-647-7070. Pam Osborne, D.R.E.
Students 47.

Chaplains of Public Institutions

APPLETON. *Prarie Correctional Facility*. Rev. Michael M. Doyle, Chap.

IVANHOE. *Divine Providence Hospital & Home*. Rev. Marion G. Casey, Chap.

ST. PETER. *St. Peter Regional Treatment Center*. Rev. John G. Berger, Chap.

WILLMAR. *Regional Treatment Center*. Rev. Francis J. Garvey, Chap.

WINSTED. *St. Mary's Care Center*. Rev. Martin Rath, O.S.B., Chap.

On Special or Other Diocesan Assignment:
Reverend Fathers—
Labat, Dennis C.
Stubeda, Anthony J.

On Duty Outside the Diocese:
Reverend Monsignors—
Schaffer, Gregory T., Parroquia San Lucas Toliman, Depto. Solola 07013, Guatemala. Tel: 011-502-722-0112; Fax: 011-502-722-0112
Reverend Fathers—
Clark, Robert P., Jr., 548 Lafond Ave., St. Paul, MN 55103-1672. Tel: 651-293-1710
Goggin, John T., Parroquia San Lucas Toliman, Depto. Solola, 07013 Guatemala. Tel: 011-502-722-0112; Fax: 011-502-722-0112
Hansen, Lawrence H., Mercy Fitzgerald Hospital, 1500 Lansdowne Ave., Darby, PA 19023. Tel: 610-237-4000
Martinka, Stanley V., San Alfonso Mission, 1218 Lonewood, El Paso, TX 79925
Mead, Leland C., 22295 Lakewood Dr., Madison Lake, MN 56063-9706

Military Chaplains:
Reverend Fathers—
Wagener, John M., Lt. Col. (Retired), 117 E. Summit Ave., San Antonio, TX 78212-2953. Tel: 210-738-3481

Absent on Leave:
Reverend Fathers—
Thurn, Brian R., 7316 Cedar Lake Rd., Apt. 20, St. Louis Park, MN 55426. Tel: 952-593-6171

Retired:
Reverend Monsignors—
Berg, Arnold J., 107 W. Lincoln, Springfield, MN 56087-1302. Tel: 507-723-6316
Leifeld, Antony J., 605 N. State St., New Ulm, MN 56073-1898. Tel: 507-359-9848
Thomas, Arthur S., c/o Mrs. Charlotte Moore, 654 Circlewood, Venice, FL 34293. Tel: 941-493-5337
Ward, John C., Leo C. Byrne Residence, 60 S. Mississippi Blvd. Apt. 225, St. Paul, MN 55105-1052. Tel: 651-698-8175
Reverend Fathers—
Adrian, Stephen J., 10410 E. Twilight Dr., Sun Lakes, AZ 85248. Tel: 602-895-0465
Barry, James D., Raven Hill Apt., 109-13000 Harriet Ave., So., Burnsville, MN 55337. Tel: 952-846-0551
Becker, Dennis E., 11208 Co. Rd. 12 NW, Garfield, MN 56332. Tel: 320-834-2100
Brandes, John F. (STP), Parroquia San Lucas Toliman, Depto. Solola 07013, Guatemala. Tel: 011-502-722-0112; Fax: 011-502-722-0112
Casey, Marion G., Divine Providence Health Center, 312 E. George, Box 136, Ivanhoe, MN 56142-0136. Tel: 507-694-1414
Cepress, Adalbert J., Woodbury Health Care Center, 7012 Lake Rd., Woodbury, MN 55125-2499. Tel: 651-735-6000
Exley, Thomas G., 1128 Iowa Ave. W., St. Paul, MN 55108-2242. Tel: 651-489-3562
Fleming, John R., Gallery Towers Apt. 801, 26 W. 10th St., St. Paul, MN 55102-1038. Tel: 651-228-1717
Gorman, Paul J., P.O. Box 983, Winnebago, MN 56098-0983. Tel: 507-854-3103
Hayden, Ralph W., 259 Plum Run, Le Sueur, MN 56058-2176. Tel: 507-665-4143
Irrgang, Kenneth E., 740 14th St. S. Apt. 13, St. Cloud, MN 56301-5518. Tel: 320-654-1008
Jenniges, Leonard J. (STP), 18760 City Hwy. 17, Sanborn, MN 56083. Tel: 507-342-5134
Karels, Agdus S. (STP), 514 4th St. NW, Ortonville, MN 56278-1305. Tel: 320-839-3766
Kasel, Joseph M., 700 North Madison St., Apt. 227, Minneota, MN 56264. Tel: 507-872-5353
Krystosek, Robert H. (GI), P.O. Box 425, Clara City, MN 56222-0425. Tel: 320-847-2615
McGowan, Myles P., Leo C. Byrne Residence, 60 S. Mississippi River Blvd., Apt. 223, St. Paul, MN 55105-1052. Tel: 651-690-9002
Merth, Robert J., 19414 Cedar Island Ct., Richmond, MN 56368-8300. Tel: 320-597-3788
Monnens, Merle W., 225 Lakeview Dr., Spicer, MN 56288. Tel: 320-796-4541
Murphy, John M., 390 Cottage Ave. W., Apt. 33, St. Paul, MN 55117-4251. Tel: 651-487-9821
O'Connor, Michael F., Church of St. Joseph, 23945 Nicolai Ave. E., Hastings, MN 55033-9650. Tel: 651-437-3526
Plathe, Anthony H., 1805 Ryon Cove, Round Rock, TX 78681. Tel: 512-246-6557
Roney, David A., Parroquia San Lucas Toliman, Depto. Solola 07013, Guatemala. Tel: 011-502-722-0112; Fax: 011-502-722-0112
Schaefer, Roman J., Church of Our Lady Queen of Martyrs, 2731 S.W. 11th Ct., Ft. Lauderdale, FL 33312-2901. Tel: 305-583-8725
Schreiner, Bernard P., The Watkins House, 341 4th St. N., P.O. Box 246, Watkins, MN 55389-0246. Tel: 320-764-2894
Siebenand, Ambrose F., Benedict Village, 2000 15th Ave., S.E., Apt. 313, St. Cloud, MN 56304-2423. Tel: 320-253-2655
Siebenand, John N., Benedict Court, 1980 15th Ave., S.E., Apt. 5, St. Cloud, MN 56304. Tel: 320-253-2655
Wojtowicz, Edward L., Leo C. Byrne Residence, 60 S. Mississippi River Blvd., Apt. 310, St. Paul, MN 55105-1052. Tel: 651-698-6926

INSTITUTIONS LOCATED IN THE DIOCESE

[A] NEW ULM AREA CATHOLIC SCHOOLS

NEW ULM. *New Ulm Area Catholic Schools*, 515 N. State St., 56073-1897. Tel: 507-354-2719; Fax: 507-354-7071. David Schieffert, Supt. Consolidated: The three schools consolidated under the above title are as follows:
St. Anthony Elementary School. (Grades K-4), 514 N. Washington St., 56073. Tel: 507-354-2928; Fax: 507-359-7029. Sr. Sharon Waldoch, S.S.N.D., Prin., (Grades K-8).
Holy Trinity Middle School, 515 N. State St., 56073-1897. Tel: 507-354-4311; Fax: 507-354-7071. Sr. Sharon Waldoch, S.S.N.D., Elementary Prin., (Grades K-8).
Cathedral High School, 600 N. Washington St., 56073-1897. Tel: 507-354-4511; Fax: 507-354-5711. James Rogers, Prin.
High School: Sisters 1; Lay Teachers 18; Students 205.
Elementary: Sisters 1; Lay Teachers 32; Students 450.

[B] GENERAL HOSPITALS

GRACEVILLE. *Graceville Health Center dba Holy Trinity Hospital and Grace Home*, 115 W. 2nd St., 56240-0157. Tel: 320-748-7223; Fax: 320-748-7225.
E-mail: gracehc@info-link.net
For a complete listing, refer to the Hospitals section.

IVANHOE. *Divine Providence Health Center*, 312 E. George St., P.O. Box 136, 56142-0136. Tel: 507-694-1414; Fax: 507-694-1191
For a complete listing, refer to the Hospitals section.

[C] HOMES FOR AGED

CLINTON. *Graceville Health Center dba Clinton Providence Center*, Clinton Providence Center, 56225. Tel: 320-325-5414
For a complete listing, refer to the Special Care Facilities section.

GRACEVILLE. *Graceville Health Center dba Trinity Hospital and Grace Hospital*, 116 W. 2nd St., 56240-0157. Tel: 320-748-7261; Fax: 320-748-7225.
E-mail: gracehc@info-link.net
For a complete listing, refer to the Special Care Facilities section.

IVANHOE. *Divine Prividence Health Center*, 312 E. George St., P.O. Box G, 56142-0136. Tel: 507-694-1414; Fax: 507-694-1191
For a complete listing, refer to the Special Care Facilities section.

SLEEPY EYE. *Divine Providence Community Home & Lake Villa Maria Senior Apts.*, 700 3rd Ave. N.W., 56085-1099. Tel: 507-794-3011; 794-5333; Fax: 507-794-3020.
E-mail: divine@prairie.lake.com
For a complete listing, refer to the Special Care Facilities section.

WINSTED. *St. Mary's Care Center*, 551 4th St., N, P.O. Box 750, 55395-0750. Tel: 320-485-2151; Fax: 320-485-4241.
E-mail: jdhess@healthdimensions.com
Web site: www.bhshealth.org
For a complete listing, refer to the Special Care Facilities section.

[D] RETREAT HOUSES

BIRD ISLAND. *Center for Spiritual Development*, P.O. Box 538, 211 S. 10th St., 55310-0538. Tel: 320-365-3644; Fax: 320-365-4042.
E-mail: centerbi@willmar.com
Web site: www.centerbi.com
Sr. Janet Mallak, S.S.N.D., Dir. Total in Residence 4; Total Staff 5.

SLEEPY EYE. *Schoenstatt Sisters of Mary*, 27762 County Rd. 27, 56085-9801. Tel: 507-794-7727; 794-5622; Fax: 507-794-7727. Sr. M. Angela Macari, Supr.; Sr. Marie Day, Dir.; Sr. M. Alice Kunz, Librarian; Sr. M. Deanne Niehaus. Total Staff 4.

[E] YOUTH CENTERS

RENVILLE. *Center for Youth Ministry*. c/o Catholic Pastoral Center, 1400 6th St. N., New Ulm, 56073-2099. Tel: 507-359-2966. Bill Casey, Dir. Youth Ministry.

[F] MISCELLANEOUS

APPLETON. *Prairie Correctional Facility*, 445 S. Munsterman St., 56208. Tel: 320-289-2052. Rev. Michael M. Doyle, Chap. Patients assisted annually 210; Maximum Capacity 1,400.

ST. PETER. *St. Peter Regional Treatment Center*, 100 Freeman Dr., 56082-1599. Tel: 507-931-7100. Chaplains: Revs. John G. Berger, Chap.; Gordon Long, (Protestant) & Chap.
Developmental Disabilities Division: Patients assisted annually 4,380; Bed Capacity 612; Total Staff 900.

WILLMAR. *Willmar Regional Treatment Center*, 1550 Hwy. 71 N.E., 56201-1128. Tel: 320-231-5100; Fax: 320-231-5329. Sr. Cecile Schueller, S.S.N.D., Chap.; Rev. Francis J. Garvey, Chap. Patients assisted annually 900; Total Staff 350.

RELIGIOUS INSTITUTES OF MEN REPRESENTED IN THE DIOCESE

For further details refer to the corresponding bracketed number in the Religious Institutes of Men or Women Section.

[0200]—*Benedictine Monks*. (Collegeville, MN).—O.S.B.

RELIGIOUS INSTITUTES OF WOMEN REPRESENTED IN THE DIOCESE

[0230]—*Benedictine Sisters of Pontifical Jurisdiction*. (Federation of St. Benedict, St. Joseph, MN; Federation of St. Gertrude, Crookston, MN; Mother of God Monastery, Watertown, SD).—O.S.B.

[0940]—*Daughters of St. Mary of Providence*. (North American Province, Chicago, IL).—D.S.M.P.

[1310]—*Francisan Sisters of Little Falls, Minnesota.* (Little Falls, MN).—O.S.F.

[]—*Franciscan Sisters of Our Lady of Perpetual Help.* (St. Louis, MO).—O.S.F.

[0210]—*Missionary Benedictine Sisters of Pontifical Jurisdiction.* (Norfolk, NE).—O.S.B.

[]—*Schoenstatt Sisters of Mary.* (Waukesha, WI).

[2970]—*School Sisters of Notre Dame.* (Mankato Province, Mankato, MN; Milwaukee Province, Elm Grove, WI).—S.S.N.D.

[1680]—*School Sisters of St. Francis.* (Milwaukee, WI).—O.S.F.

[1710]—*Sisters of St. Francis of Mary Immaculate.* (Joliet, IL).—O.S.F.

[1570]—*Sisters of St. Francis of the Holy Family.* (Dubuque, IA).—O.S.F.

[3840]—*Sisters of St. Joseph of Carondelet.* (St. Paul, MN).—C.S.J.

[]—*Sisters of St. Joseph of La Grange.* (La Grange Park, IL).—C.S.J.

[3320]—*Sisters of the Presentation of the B.V.M.* (Aberdeen, SD; Dubuque, IA).—P.B.V.M.

[1720]—*Sisters of the Third Order Regular of St. Francis of the Congregation of Our Lady of Lourdes.* (Rochester, MN).—O.S.F.

[]—*Ursuline Sisters of Cleveland.* (Pepper Pike, OH).—O.S.U.

NECROLOGY

† Exley, Thomas G., (Retired). —Died Aug. 10, 2000.
† Fasching, Felix J., (Retired). —Died Aug. 28, 2000.
† Penzimas, Joseph A., (Retired). —Died June 21, 2000.

Archdiocese of New York

(Archidioecesis Neo-Eboracensis)

Most Reverend

PATRICK V. AHERN, D.D.

Auxiliary Bishop of New York; Titular Bishop of Najiera; ordained January 27, 1945; appointed February 3, 1970; consecrated March 19, 1970. *Res., St. Thomas More, 65 E. 89th St., New York, NY, 10128.*

Most Reverend

JAMES P. MAHONEY, D.D.

Retired Auxiliary Bishop of New York; Titular Bishop of Ipagro; ordained May 19, 1951; appointed July 25, 1972; consecrated September 15, 1972; retired December 1997. *Res., Assumption Parish, 131 Union Ave., Peekskill, NY, 10566.*

Most Reverend

ANTHONY F. MESTICE, D.D.

Auxiliary Bishop of New York; Titular Bishop of Villanova; ordained June 4, 1949; appointed March 5, 1973; consecrated April 27, 1973. *Res., Resurrection, 910 Boston Post Rd., Rye, NY, 10580.*

Most Reverend

FRANCISCO GARMENDIA, D.D.

Auxiliary Bishop of New York; Titular Bishop of Limisa; ordained June 28, 1947; appointed May 24, 1977; consecrated June 29, 1977. *Res., St. Thomas Aquinas, 1900 Crotona Pkwy., Bronx, NY, 10460.*

Most Reverend

JAMES F. McCARTHY, D.D.

Auxiliary Bishop of New York; Titular Bishop of Verrona; ordained June 1, 1969; appointed May 11, 1999; consecrated June 29, 1999. *Res., St. Elizabeth Ann Seton, 1377 N. Main St., Shrub Oak, NY, 10588.*

His Eminence

EDWARD CARDINAL EGAN, J.C.D., D.D.

Archbishop of New York; ordained December 15, 1957; appointed Titular Bishop of Allegheny and Auxiliary Bishop of New York April 1, 1985; consecrated May 22, 1985; appointed Bishop of Bridgeport November 8, 1988; installed December 14, 1988; appointed Archbishop of New York May 11, 2000; installed June 19, 2000. *Res., 452 Madison Ave., New York, NY, 10022.*

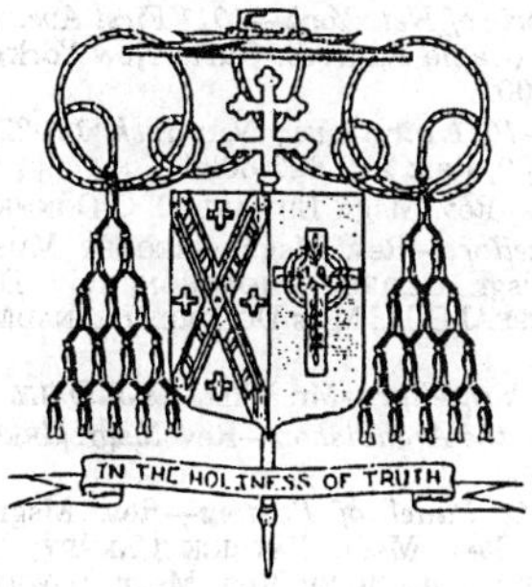

Chancery: 1011 First Ave., New York, NY, 10022. Tel.: 212-371-1000; Fax: 212-826-6020.

Web site address: www.ny-archdiocese.org

Most Reverend

WILLIAM J. McCORMACK, D.D.

Auxiliary Bishop of New York, Titular Bishop of Nicives; ordained February 21, 1959; appointed December 23, 1986; consecrated January 6, 1987. *Res., 142 E. 29th St., New York, NY, 10016.*

Most Reverend

PATRICK J. SHERIDAN, D.D.

Auxiliary Bishop of New York; Titular Bishop of Curzola; ordained March 1, 1947; appointed October 30, 1990; consecrated December 12, 1990. *Res., 452 Madison Ave., New York, NY, 10022.*

Most Reverend

ROBERT A. BRUCATO, D.D.

Auxiliary Bishop of New York; Titular Bishop of Temuniana; ordained June 1, 1957; appointed July 1, 1997; consecrated August 25, 1997. *Res., St. Joseph's Seminary, Yonkers, NY, 10704.*

SEE ERECTED APRIL 8, 1808.

CREATED AN ARCHDIOCESE JULY 19, 1850.

Square Miles 4,683.

(Legal Title: Archdiocese of New York).

Comprises the Boroughs of Manhattan, Bronx, and Richmond of the City of New York, and the Counties of Dutchess, Orange, Putnam, Rockland, Sullivan, Ulster and Westchester in the State of New York.

STATISTICAL OVERVIEW

Personnel	
Cardinal	1
Auxiliary Bishops	7
Retired Bishops	3
Priests: Diocesan Active in Diocese	561
Priests: Active Outside Diocese	46
Priests: Retired, Sick or Absent	231
Number of Diocesan Priests	838
Religious Priests in Diocese	911
Extern Priests in Diocese	251
Ordinations:	
Diocesan Priests	6
Religious Priests	4
Transitional Deacons	5
Permanent Deacons	10
Permanent Deacons in Diocese	343
Total Brothers	250
Total Sisters	3,490
Parishes	
Parishes	412
With Resident Pastor:	
Resident Diocesan Priests	310
Resident Religious Priests	77
Without Resident Pastor:	
Administered by Priests	25
Closed Parishes	1
Professional Ministry Personnel:	
Brothers	16
Sisters	182
Lay Ministers	1,169
Welfare	
Catholic Hospitals	17
Total Assisted	2,089,079
Health Care Centers	3
Total Assisted	166,890
Homes for the Aged	17
Total Assisted	21,852
Residential Care of Children	13
Total Assisted	4,500
Day Care and Extended Day Care Centers	15
Total Assisted	1,255
Specialized Homes	6
Total Assisted	1,298
Special Centers for Social Services	147
Total Assisted	322,850
Residential Care of Disabled	4
Total Assisted	500
Educational	
Seminaries, Diocesan	3
Students from This Diocese	118
Students from Other Diocese	22
Diocesan Students in Other Seminaries	1
Seminaries, Religious	3
Students Religious	100
Total Seminarians	219
Colleges and Universities	12
Total Students	44,904
High Schools, Diocesan and Parish	27
Total Students	15,654
High Schools, Private	28
Total Students	13,427
Elementary Schools, Diocesan and Parish	228
Total Students	76,763
Elementary Schools, Private	15
Total Students	4,165
Non-residential Schools for the Disabled	6
Total Students	222
Catechesis/Religious Education:	
High School Students	5,845
Elementary Students	103,438
Total Students Under Catholic Instruction	264,637
Teachers in the Diocese:	
Priests	54
Brothers	49
Sisters	105
Lay Teachers	3,539
Vital Statistics	
Receptions into the Church:	
Infant Baptism Totals	33,979
Adult Baptism Totals	983
Received into Full Communion	980
First Communions	28,037
Confirmations	20,527
Marriages:	
Catholic	5,684
Interfaith	1,300
Total Marriages	6,984
Deaths	15,944
Total Catholic Population	2,388,047
Total Population	5,276,900

Succession of Prelates—Rev. R. LUKE CONCANEN, O.P., D.D., first Bishop; cons. April 24, 1808; died June 19, 1810.—Rt. Rev. JOHN CONNOLLY, O.P., D.D., second Bishop; cons. Nov. 6, 1814; died Feb. 6, 1825.—Rt. Rev. JOHN DUBOIS, S.S., D.D., third Bishop; cons. Oct. 29, 1826; died Dec. 20, 1842.—Most Rev. JOHN HUGHES, D.D., cons. Titular Bishop of Basileopolis and coadjutor to the Bishop of New York, Jan. 7, 1838; succeeded to the See of New York, Dec. 20, 1842; created first Archbishop, July 19, 1850; died Jan. 3, 1864.—His Eminence JOHN CARDINAL McCLOSKEY, second Archbishop; cons.

Titular Bishop of Axiere, and coadjutor to the Bishop of New York, March 10, 1844 translated to the See of Albany, May 21, 1847; promoted to first U.S. Cardinal of New York, May 6, 1864; created Cardinal Priest of the Holy Roman Church, March 15, 1875 under the title of Sancta Maria Supra Minervam; died Oct. 10, 1885.—Most Rev. MICHAEL AUGUSTINE CORRIGAN, D.D., third Archbishop; cons. Bishop of Newark, NJ May 4, 1873; promoted to the Archiepiscopal See of Petra and made coadjutor to His Eminence CARDINAL MCCLOSKEY, Archbishop of New York, with the right of succession, Oct. 1, 1880; succeeded to the See of New York, Oct. 10, 1885 made Assistant at the Pontifical Throne, April 19, 1887; died May 5, 1902.—His Eminence JOHN CARDINAL FARLEY, fourth Archbishop of New York; ord. June 11, 1870; cons. Titular Bishop of Zeugma and Auxiliary to the Archbishop of New York, Dec. 21, 1895; promoted to this See, Sept. 15, 1902; preconized June 22, 1903 made Assistant at the Pontifical Throne, Dec. 4, 1904; created Cardinal Priest of the Holy Roman Church under the Title of Sancta Maria Supra Minervam, Nov. 27, 1911; died Sept. 17, 1918.—His Eminence PATRICK CARDINAL HAYES, fifth Archbishop of New York; ord. Sept. 8, 1892; appt. Auxiliary to the Archbishop of New York, July 3, 1914; cons. Titular Bishop of Tagaste, Oct. 28, 1914; appt. Bishop Ordinary of U.S. Army and Navy Chaplains by the Holy See, Nov. 24, 1917; promoted to the See of New York, March 10, 1919; created Cardinal Priest of the Holy Roman Church under the title of Sancta Maria in Via, March 24, 1924; died Sept. 4, 1938.—His Eminence FRANCIS CARDINAL SPELLMAN, sixth Archbishop of New York; ord. May 14, 1916; appt. Auxiliary Bishop of Boston, July 30, 1932; cons. Sept. 8, 1932; appt. to the See of New York, April 15, 1939; appt. Military Vicar for the Armed Forces of the United States, Dec. 11, 1939; created and proclaimed Cardinal Priest under the title of SS. John and Paul in the Consistory, Feb. 18, 1946; died Dec. 2, 1967.—His Eminence TERENCE CARDINAL COOKE, seventh Archbishop of New York; ord. Dec. 1, 1945; appt. Auxiliary Bishop of New York, Sept. 15, 1965; cons. Dec. 13, 1965; appt. to the See of New York, March 8, 1968; installed and appt. Military Vicar of the United States Armed Forces, April 4, 1968; created and proclaimed Cardinal Priest under the title of SS. John and Paul in the Consistory, April 28, 1969; died Oct. 6, 1983.—His Eminence JOHN CARDINAL O'CONNOR, eighth Archbishop of New York; ord. Dec. 15, 1945; appt. Titular Bishop of Curzola and Auxiliary Bishop to the Military Vicar, April 24, 1979; cons. May 27, 1979; appt. Bishop of Scranton, May 10, 1983; installed June 29, 1983; appt. Archbishop of New York, Jan. 31, 1984; installed March 19, 1984; created Cardinal Priest, May 25, 1985; died May 3, 2000.

Vicars General—Most Rev. PATRICK J. SHERIDAN, D.D., V.G.; Most Rev. ROBERT A. BRUCATO, D.D., V.G.

Assistant to the Vicars General—Rev. BRIAN T. MCSWEENEY.

Episcopal Vicars of the Archdiocese—

South Bronx—Most Rev. FRANCISCO GARMENDIA, D.D., *Church of St. Thomas Aquinas, 1900 Crotona Pkwy., Bronx, 10460.* Tel: 718-589-5235.

Central Westchester—Most Rev. ANTHONY F. MESTICE, D.D., *Church of the Resurrection, 910 Post Rd., Rye, 10508.* Tel: 914-967-0142.

Northern Westchester and Putnam—Most Rev. JAMES F. MCCARTHY, D.D., *Church of St. Elizabeth Ann Seton, 1377 N. Main St., Shrub Oak, 10588.* Tel: 914-528-3547.

Regional Coordinators of the Archdiocese—

Manhattan (West)—Rev. Msgr. THOMAS P. LEONARD, *Holy Trinity, 213 W. 82nd St., New York, 10024.* Tel: 212-787-0634.

Manhattan (North)—Rev. Msgr. GERALD T. WALSH, *St. Elizabeth, 268 Wadsworth Ave., New York, 10033.* Tel: 212-568-8803.

Manhattan (South)—Rev. Msgr. KEVIN P. O'BRIEN, *Immaculate Conception, 414 E. 14th St., New York, 10009.* Tel: 212-254-0200.

Manhattan (East)—Rev. Msgr. JOHN G. WOOLSEY, *St. John the Martyr, 259 E. 71st St., New York, 10021.* Tel: 212-744-4880. Rev. Msgr. THOMAS A. MODUGNO, *St. Monica, 413 E. 79th St., New York, 10021.* Tel: 212-288-6250.

Bronx (Northwest)—Rev. Msgr. PATRICK J. BOYLE, *St. Brendan's, 333 E. 206th St., Bronx, 10467.* Tel: 718-547-6655.

Bronx (Northeast)—Rev. Msgr. FRANCIS X. TONER, *St. Barnabas, 409 E. 241st St., Bronx, 10470.* Tel: 718-324-1478.

Bronx (East)—Rev. Msgr. CHARLES M. KAVANAGH, *St. Raymond, 1759 Castle Hill Ave., Bronx, 10462.* Tel: 718-792-4044.

Richmond—Rev. Msgr. JAMES J. DORNEY, *St. Peter's, 53 St. Mark's Pl., New Brighton, Staten Island, 10301.* Tel: 718-727-2672. Rev. Msgr. PETER G. FINN, *St. Joseph - St. Thomas, 6135 Amboy Rd., Pleasant Plains, Staten Island, 10309.* Tel: 718-984-4572.

Westchester (Yonkers)—Rev. Msgr. HUGH CORRIGAN, *Immaculate Conception, 103 S. Broadway, Yonkers, 10701.* Tel: 914-963-0156.

Westchester (South Shore)—Rev. Msgr. HOWARD W. CALKINS, *Sacred Heart, 115 Sharp Blvd., Mt. Vernon, 10550.* Tel: 914-668-7440.

Dutchess—Rev. Msgr. DOMINICK J. LAGONEGRO, *Church of St. Columbia, P.O. Box 428, Hopewell Junction, 12533.* Tel: 914-227-8380.

Orange—Rev. Msgr. GEORGE J. VALASTRO, *St. Joseph, 149 Cottage St., Middletown, 10940.* Tel: 914-343-6013.

Rockland—Rev. Msgr. WILLIAM J. BELFORD, *St. Catharine, 523 Western Hwy., Blauvelt, 10913.* Tel: 914-359-0542.

Ulster—Rev. Msgr. WILLIAM E. WILLIAMS, *St. John the Evangelist, 915 Rte. 212, Saugerties, 12754.* Tel: 914-246-9581.

Sullivan—Rev. EDWARD F. STRAUB, *St. Peter's, Liberty, 12748.* Tel: 914-292-4525.

Archbishopric of New York—1011 First Ave., New York, 10022. (Cable Address: Curia New York). Tel: 212-371-1000.

Chancery—1011 First Ave., New York, 10022. Tel: 212-371-1000; Fax: 212-826-6020.

Chancellor—Rev. Msgr. EDWARD D. O'DONNELL.

Vice-Chancellors—Rev. Msgr. GREGORY MUSTACIUOLO; Rev. Msgr. GEORGE THOMPSON; Rev. DOUGLAS J. MATHERS, J.C.D.; Miss DOLORES BERNADETTE GRIER, M.A.

Assistant Chancellor—Mr. WILLIAM J. DALY.

Secretary to the Archbishop—Rev. Msgr. GREGORY MUSTACIUOLO.

Canon 1742 Panel of Pastors—Rev. Msgr. EDWARD BARRY; Rev. Msgr. PATRICK CARNEY; Rev. Msgr. GERARDO COLACICCO; Rev. Msgr. LAWRENCE CONNAUGHTON; Rev. Msgr. JAMES DOYLE; Rev. Msgr. JOHN FARLEY; Rev. Msgr. RICHARD GUASTELLA; Rev. Msgr. LESLIE IVERS; Rev. Msgr. ROBERT LARKIN; Rev. Msgr. JOSEPH MARTIN; Rev. Msgr. DESMOND O'CONNOR; Rev. Msgr. ROBERT TRAINOR.

Metropolitan Tribunal—St. Joseph's Seminary, 1011 First Ave., New York, 10022. Tel: 212-371-1000.

Judicial Vicar—Rev. Msgr. DESMOND J. VELLA, J.C.D., S.T.L.

Vice Judicial Vicars—Revs. JOHN DELANEY, J.D.; JOHN VIGILANTI, J.C.L., Ph.D.

Judges—Revs. FRANCIS J. MULLER, O.F.M., J.C.D.; VINCENT GROGAN, O.F.M., J.C.D.; JOHN F. LAURI, J.C.L.; ALBERT DELUCA, M.S.; WILLIAM S. ELDER, J.C.D.; KENNETH SMITH, M.A., S.T.B.; GEORGE N. OONNOONNY, J.C.L.; Sr. AMADEUS MCKEVITT, O.S.U., J.C.L.

Defenders of the Bond—Revs. ROBERT J. HOSPODAR, J.C.L.; MAREK SUCKOCKI, J.C.L.

Promoter of Justice—Rev. JOHN A. VIGILANTI, J.C.L.

Canonical Consultants—Sr. DORIS HEINLEIN, S.C., M.S.; Mrs. ROSEMARY P. DOHERTY; Revs. RAFAEL CORNIEL; Mrs. INGRID PENA.

Mt. Kisco Office—Rev. JOHN VIGILANTI, J.C.L., Ph.D., *12 Green St., Mt. Kisco, 10549.* Tel: 914-666-2583.

Poughkeepsie Office—Rev. JOHN A. BIDA, J.C.L.; Rev. Msgr. GERARD J. COLACICCO, J.C.L.; Ms. JEAN RING, Canonical Consultant, *240 Church St., Poughkeepsie, 12601.* Tel: 914-452-1400.

Interdiocesan Tribunal of New York State—201 Seminary Ave., Yonkers, 10704. Tel: 914-968-4301.

Judicial Vicar—Rev. Msgr. WALTER F. KENNY, S.T.D.

Vicar for the Religious—Rev. BARTHOLOMEW DALY, M.H.M., *1011 First Ave., New York, 10022.* Tel: 212-371-1000, Ext. 2575. Sr. ANNE CONNELLY, O.P.

Archdiocesan Offices and Directors

Catholic Health Care Network in the Archdiocese of New York—MARY HEALEY-SEDUTTO, Ph.D., Exec. Dir., *1011 First Ave., New York, 10022.* Tel: 212-371-1000.

Providence Health Services Foundation, Inc.—Dr. MARY SEDUTTO, Pres. GERARD M. VILLUCCI, Vice Pres., *1011 First Ave., New York, 10022.* Tel: 212-752-2404.

Censors Librorum—Rev. Msgr. FRANCIS MCAREE; Rev. Msgr. WILLIAM SMITH; Rev. DONALD HAGGERTY.

Apostleship of Prayer—Vacant.

Apostleship of the Sea—Rev. KEVIN J. NELAN, Dir., *Stella Maris Maritime Center for Seamen, Pier 52, New York, 10019.* Tel: 212-265-5020.

Archdiocesan Consultors—Most Rev. ROBERT A. BRUCATO; Most Rev. PATRICK SHERIDAN; Rev. Msgr. THOMAS J. BERGIN; Rev. Msgr. DERMOT BRENNAN; Rev. Msgr. PETER FINN; Rev. Msgr. THOMAS GILLEECE; Rev. Msgr. LESLIE IVERS; Rev. Msgr. DOMINICK LAGONEGRO; Rev. Msgr. GREGORY MUSTACIUOLO; Rev. Msgr. EDWARD O'DONNELL; Rev. Msgr. GERALD WALSH; Rev. CARLOS RODRIGUEZ, *1011 First Ave., New York, 10022.* Tel: 212-371-1000.

Archbishop Hughes Archives & Heritage Center—LAURA M. CHMIELEWSKI, Dir.; Sr. MARGUERITA SMITH, Archivist, *St. Joseph's Seminary, 201 Seminary Ave., Yonkers, 10704.* Tel: 914-476-6333.

Bishops' Resettlement Committee for Refugees—Mr. PAUL MARTIN, Dir., *1011 First Ave., New York, 10022.* Tel: 212-371-1000.

Black Ministry, Office of—Bro. TYRONE DAVIS, C.F.C., Dir., *1011 First Ave., New York, 10022.* Tel: 212-371-1000.

Building Commission—St. Joseph's Seminary, Yonkers, 10704. Tel: 914-476-1058.

Director—Mr. WILLIAM J. O'CONNOR.

Business Manager—Mr. STEVEN BELLOISE.

Consultants—Mr. ANDREW J. CRYAN; HOWARD R. EVANS; DANIEL M. HARRIGAN; Deacon JOHN LARKIN; JOHN J. MASTRONARDI; LAURENCE J. RICE.

Archbishop's Archdiocesan Appeal—Ms. LINDA SPENCER, Dir., *1011 First Ave., New York, 10022.* Tel: 212-371-1000.

Cardinal's Committee of the Laity—Mr. JACK DUNNE, Dir., *1011 First Ave., New York, 10022.* Tel: 212-371-1000.

Catechetical Office—Sr. JOAN CURTIN, C.N.D. Tel: 212-371-1000, Ext. 2849.

Catechumenate, Office of—Rev. RUSSELL C. BECKER, O.F.M., Dir. Tel: 212-371-1000, Ext. 2690.

Catholic High School Association—1011 First Ave., New York, 10022.

Center for Catholic Lay Leadership Formation—Mr. RUDY VARGAS, IV, Exec. Dir., *1345 Grand Concourse, Bronx, 10452.* Tel: 718-588-4100.

Catholic New York—(See Ecclesiastical Communications Corp.), ANNE BUCKLEY, Editor; ARTHUR L. MCKENNA, Gen. Mgr., *1011 First Ave., New York, 10022.* Tel: 212-688-2399.

Cemeteries—(The Trustees of St. Patrick's Cathedral in the City of New York, Inc.); Mr. ANTHONY V. ROINA, Exec. Dir., *1011 First Ave., New York, 10022.* Tel: 212-753-4883.

Censors—Board of Diocesan Censors of Books, Rev. Msgr. DANIEL V. FLYNN, J.C.D., Chm., *215 Halsted Ave., Harrison, 10528.*

Center for Spiritual Development—ANN MARIE WALLACE, Ph.D., Dir.; Sr. MARY FRANCES MILLS, O.S.F., Assoc. Dir., *96 Milton Rd., Rye, 10580.* Tel: 914-967-7328.

Central Services—Archdiocese of New York, 1011 First Ave., New York, 10022. Tel: 212-371-1000.

Catholic Charities—Rev. Msgr. JAMES J. MURRAY; Rev. Msgr. WILLIAM J. TOOHY; Rev. Msgr. KEVIN SULLIVAN, *1011 First Ave., New York, 10022.* Tel: 212-371-1000. (Consult separate listing.).

Chinese Ministries—Rev. MICHAEL J. LYNCH, S.J., Co-ord., *Nativity Church, 44 Second Ave., New York, 10003.* Tel: 212-674-8590.

Commission on Church Music—Mr. BRIAN ZUAR, Dir., *St. Joseph's Seminary, 201 Seminary Ave., Yonkers, 10704.* Tel: 914-968-6200, Ext. 8109.

Committee on Housing—Mr. ROBERT PAUL, Coord., *1011 First Ave., New York, 10022.* Tel: 212-371-1000, Ext. 2536-2537.

Communications Office (Bureau of Information for the Media)—Mr. JOSEPH ZWILLING, Dir.; Rev. PAUL KEENAN, Asst. Dir., Radio Min.; Mrs. TANIA RIOS, Asst. Dir. Spanish Communications, *1011 First Ave., New York, 10022.* Tel: 212-371-1000, Ext. 2990.

Conciliation and Arbitration, Office of—Rev. Msgr. WILLIAM J. TOOHY, J.D., Dir., *1011 First Ave., New York, 10022.* Tel: 212-371-1000.

Coordinating Committee of Catholic Lay Organizations—Rev. Msgr. WILLIAM J. TOOHY, Moderator, *1011 First Ave., New York, 10022.* Tel: 212-371-1000.

Criminal Justice, Office of—Mr. KENNETH HOFFARTH, Dir., *1011 First Ave., New York, 10022.* Tel: 212-371-1000, Ext. 3166.

The Data Systems Center—Mr. ANDREW J. DONNELLY, Dir., *1011 First Ave., New York, 10022.* Tel: 212-371-1000.

Telecommunications Office—Mr. ANDREW J. DONNELLY, Dir.

Deaf, Catholic Center for—Rev. Msgr. PATRICK P. MCCAHILL, Dir., *1011 First Ave., New York, 10022.* Tel: 212-988-8563.

Development, Archdiocesan Office of—Rev. Msgr. CHARLES M. KAVANAGH, Vicar; HELEN T. LOWE, Exec. Dir., *1011 First Ave., New York, 10022.* Tel: 212-371-1000.

Disabilities, Office of Persons with—ANNE COGHLAN, Dir.

Ecclesiastical Assistance Corporation—1011 First Ave., New York, 10022. Tel: 212-371-1000.

Ecclesiastical Communications Corp.—1011 First Ave., New York, 10022. Tel: 212-371-1000.

Ecclesiastical Maintenance Services, Inc.—Mr. EDWARD WOODS, Gen. Mgr. Area Supvrs.: Mr. STEVEN MILISITS; Mr. FRANK ORTIZ; Mr. ROBERT SCULLY, *1011 First Ave., New York, 10022.* Tel: 212-371-1000.

Ecclesiastical Properties Corporation—1011 First Ave., New York, 10022.

Ecumenical and Interreligious Affairs, Commission on—Rev. Msgr. EDWARD D. O'DONNELL, Chm.; Rev. Msgr. FERDINANDO D. BERARDI, M.A., S.T.L., Vice Chm.; Rev. JAMES LOUGHRAN, S.A., Dir., *1011 First Ave., New York, 10022.*

Educational Services of the Archdiocese of New York, Inc.—1011 First Ave., New York, 10022.

Education, Dept. of, Archdiocese of New York—1011 First Ave., New York, 10022. Tel: 212-371-1000. (Consult separate listing.).

Education, Vicar for—Rev. Msgr. THOMAS J. BERGIN, Vicar; Sr. EILEEN CLIFFORD, O.P., Assoc. Vicar, *1011 First Ave., New York, 10022.* (Consult separate listing.).

Ethnic Affairs, Office of—Rev. BRIAN T. MCSWEENEY, Dir., *1011 First Ave., New York, 10022.* Tel: 212-371-1000.

Family Life/Respect Life Office—Rev. JOHN BONNICI S.T.D., Dir., *1011 First Ave., New York, 10022.* Tel: 212-371-1000. (Consult separate listing.).

Hispanic Affairs, Vicar—(Vicario, Asuntos Hispanos), Rev. Msgr. JOSU IRIONDO, C.R.L., *1011 First Ave., New York, 10022.* Tel: 212-371-1000, Ext. 2982.

Catholic Charismatic Center—(Centro Carismatico Catolico); Rev. Msgr. JOSU IRIONDO, C.R.L., Center Dir., *826 E. 166th St., Bronx, 10460.* Tel: 212-378-1734.

Hispanic Institute of Pastoral Formation—(Instituto Hispano de Formacion Pastoral); Deacon GUILLERMO ROMAGOSA, Dir.; Sr. MARIA TRANSITO SANCHEZ, Exec. Sec. Tel: 212-371-1000, Ext. 8270.

Human Resources, Office of—Deacon RANDY VELEZ, Dir.; Mrs. EILEEN F. EGAN, Dir. Personnel, *1011 First Ave., New York, 10022.* Tel: 212-371-1000, Ext. 3684.

Permanent Diaconate Formation Program—(Programa de Formacion para Diaconos); Deacon ANTHONY CASSANETO, Dir., *St. Joseph's Seminary, Dunwoodie, 10704.* Tel: 914-968-6200, Ext. 8269.

Intercultural Institute—Rev. Msgr. JOSU IRIONDO, C.R.L., Dir. ANGELA MARTINEZ, Sec. Tel: 212-371-1000, Ext. 2982.

Intercultural Council—Most Rev. PATRICK J. SHERIDAN, Chm.; Dr. RUTH DOYLE, Facilitator. Tel: 212-371-1000, Ext. 3250.

Language Institute—Class Schedule: Wed. 4-7 pm Cardinal Hayes High School. Mr. EDWARD CRESPO, Supvr., *1011 First Ave., New York, 10022.* Tel: 212-371-1000, Ext. 2982.

Lanubirt Psychological Services—Rev. GEORGE E. REINHEIMER, Ph.D., Dir., *1011 First Ave., New York, 10022.* Tel: 212-371-1000, Ext. 2719.

Light and Life Evangelization Program—(Luz y Vida), *St. Joseph's Cursillo Center, 523 W. 142nd St., New York, 10031.* Tel: 212-926-7433.

St. Joseph's Cursillo Center—Rev. FRANK PELUSO, O.A.R., Dir., *275 West 230th St., Bronx, 10463.* Tel: 718-796-4340.

Palante-Con-Cristo Evangelization and Prayer Movement—Rev. JOHN OLDFIELD, O.A.R., Spiritual Dir.; Deacon LUIS FONTANEZ, Asst. Spiritual Dir., *Tagaste Monastery, Suffern, 10901.* Tel: 914-357-0067. Deacon EDMUNDO RAMOS. Tel: 718-204-0816.

Mary Help of Christians Ev. Community—(Auxiliadora); Rev. KENNETH SMITH, Spiritual Dir.; Deacon LUIS FONTANEZ, Asst. Dir., *328 W. 14th St., New York, 10014.*

Holy Childhood, Pontifical Association—Rev. Msgr. FERDINANDO D. BERARDI, Dir.; Sr. PAULINE CHURCHIRILLO, P.B.V.M., Mission Educ. Dir., *1011 First Ave., New York, 10022.* Tel: 212-371-1000.

Holy Name Society Archdiocesan Union of New York—Rev. JAMES P. CONNOLLY, Dir.; Mr. ANTHONY J. MEROLLA, Exec. Sec., *1011 First Ave., New York, 10022.* Tel: 212-931-9239.

Hospital Apostolate—Rev. Msgr. MARC J. FILACCHIONE, *1011 First Ave., New York, 10022.* Tel: 212-371-1000.

Information, Bureau of and Radio-T.V. Communications—See Communications.

Inner City Scholarship Fund, Inc.—Mr. WILLIAM GOODLOE, Dir., *1011 First Ave., New York, 10022.* Tel: 212-371-1000.

Institutional Commodity Services Corporation—Mr. VINCENT HEINTZ, Gen. Mgr. Dept. Mgrs.: RICHARD HESSION; ROBERT MCGRATH; ROBERT SCHIAVI; NANETTE MELERA, Food Serv. Dir., *1011 First Ave., New York, 10022.* Tel: 212-371-1000.

Instructional T.V. Communications Center—Mr. MICHAEL LAVERY, Dir., *St. Joseph's Seminary, 201 Seminary Ave., Yonkers, 10704.* Tel: 914-968-7800.

Insurance Division—Vacant, *1011 First Ave., New York, 10022.* Tel: 212-371-1000, Ext. 3024.

Inter-Parish Financing, Commission for—Rev. Msgr. DENNIS P. KEANE, Chm.; Rev. Msgr. GEORGE F. BARDES, Exec. Sec., *1011 First Ave., New York, 10022.* Tel: 212-371-1000.

Italian Apostolate—Rev. Msgr. GEORGE J. CASCELLI, Dir., *1011 First Ave., New York, 10022.* Tel: 212-371-1000.

Justice and Peace, Archdiocesan Office of—1011 First Ave., New York, 10022. Tel: 212-371-1000.

Legal Affairs, Office of—Rev. Msgr. WILLIAM J. TOOHY, J.D. General Council: FRANK NAPOLITANO, J.D.; MARGARET M. MAHON, J.D., *1011 First Ave., New York, 10022.* Tel: 212-371-1000, Ext. 2440; Fax: 212-826-8795.

Legion of Mary—Rev. LAWRENCE M. PAOLICELLI, Dir., *1011 First Ave., New York, 10022.*

Liturgical Commission, Archdiocesan—Sr. JANET BAXENDALE, S.C., Exec. Sec., *Liturgical Resource Center, 1011 First Ave., New York, 10022.* Tel: 212-371-1000, Ext. 2692; 2685.

Office of Legal Affairs—Rev. Msgr. WILLIAM J. TOOHY, J.D.; FRANK NAPOLITANO, J.D., *1011 First Ave., New York, 10022.* Tel: 212-371-1000, Ext. 2440.

Parish Councils, Archdiocesan Office for—Rev. ROBERT J. AUFIERI, Dir., *1011 First Ave., New York, 10022.* Tel: 212-371-1000.

Parish Mission Team—Rev. EMILE FRISCHE, Dir., *586 McLean Ave., Yonkers, 10705.* Tel: 914-709-1300.

Pastoral Council, Archdiocesan—Ms. DOLORES RAMIREZ, Chm.; Rev. ROBERT J. AUFIERI, Exec. Sec.

Pastoral Life Conference—1011 First Ave., New York, 10022. Tel: 212-371-1000.

Pastoral Research and Planning Office—Dr. RUTH T. DOYLE, Dir., *1011 First Ave., New York, 10022.* Tel: 212-371-1000.

Pastoral Services, Archdiocese of New York—1011 First Ave., New York, 10022. Tel: 212-371-1000.

Pension Office, Archdiocesan—Mr. WILLIAM J. DALY, Exec. Sec., *1011 First Ave., New York, 10022.* Tel: 212-371-1000.

Personnel Board, Archdiocesan—Rev. Msgr. GEORGE THOMPSON, Dir. & Vice-Chancellor. Members of the Board: Rev. Msgr. FRANCIS BOYLE; Rev. FERNANDO HERNANDEZ; Rev. Msgr. DANIEL PEAKE; Rev. Msgr. RICHARD GUASTELLA; Rev. ANTHONY SORGIE, *1011 First Ave., New York, 10022.* Tel: 212-371-1000.

Preaching and Liturgy, Institute for—Vacant.

Priests Council of the Archdiocese of New York—Rev. Msgr. WALLACE A. HARRIS, Chm.; Rev. Msgr. DANIEL V. FLYNN, Vice Chm.; Rev. ANTHONY SORGIE, Sec. & Treas., *1011 First Ave., New York, 10022.* Tel: 212-371-1000.

Prison Apostolate—Rev. Msgr. LESLIE J. IVERS, Dir., *St. Frances de Chantal, 190 Hollywood Ave., Bronx, 10465.* Tel: 718-792-5500.

Propagation of the Faith—Archdiocesan Office, Rev. Msgr. FERDINAND O. BERARDI, Archdiocesan Dir.; Sr. PAULINE CHURCHIRILLO, P.B.V.M., Mission Educ. Coord., *1011 First Ave., New York, 10022.* Tel: 212-371-1000.

Propagation of the Faith—National Office, Most Rev. WILLIAM J. MCCORMACK, D.D., Natl. Dir., *366 Fifth Ave., New York, 10001.* Tel: 212-563-8700.

Real Estate Division—Mr. DAVID BROWN, Dir., *1011 First Ave., New York, 10022.* Tel: 212-371-1000.

Retirement Plan for Priests—Rev. Msgr. ROBERT A. FORD, Chm., *1011 First Ave., New York, 10022.* Tel: 212-371-1000, Ext. 2935.

Coordinator of Priest Retiree Affairs—Deacon DONALD QUIGLEY, *St. Joseph's Seminary, 201 Seminary Ave., Yonkers, 10704.* Tel: 914-968-6200, Ext. 8107.

Schools, Superintendent of—Dr. CATHERINE HICKEY, Supt., *1011 First Ave., New York, 10022.* Tel: 212-371-1000. (Consult separate listing.).

Sodalities, Federation—1011 First Ave., New York, 10022. Tel: 212-371-1000.

Spiritual Development, Office of—Rev. EUGENE J. FULTON, Dir., *One Pryer Manor Rd., Larchmont, 10538.* Tel: 914-235-6839.

Trustees of St. Patrick's Cathedral in the City of New York, Inc.—Rev. Msgr. JAMES K. VAUGHEY, Exec. Dir., Cemeteries; Mr. ANTHONY V. ROINA, Asst. Exec. Dir., Cemeteries.

University Apostolate—Rev. Msgr. MICHAEL CRIMMINS, Coord., *1011 First Ave., New York, 10022.* Tel: 212-371-1000.

Vocations—Revs. ROBERT MCKEON, Special Asst. to the Archbishop; MARK VAILLANCOURT, Asst., *St. Joseph's Seminary, Yonkers, 10704.* Tel: 914-968-1340. Sr. DEANNA SABETTA, Dir., Women's Vocations, *1011 First Ave., New York, 10022.* Tel: 212-371-1000.

Women Religious, Archdiocesan Council of—Sr. MARGARET KELLY, S.C., Pres., *1011 First Ave., New York, 10022.* Tel: 212-371-1000.

CLERGY, PARISHES, MISSIONS AND PAROCHIAL SCHOOLS

NEW YORK CITY
BOROUGH OF MANHATTAN

1—CATHEDRAL OF ST. PATRICK (Old, 1809; New, 1879), Rev. Msgr. Anthony Dalla Villa, Rector; Rev. Msgr. Thomas A. Nielson; Revs. Brian C. Brennan; Eugene G. Connolly; William A. Scafidi, M.Ss.A.; Marion Cascino, O.F.M.
Rectory: 460 Madison Ave., 10022. Tel: 212-753-2261; Fax: 212-755-4128.
Res., 452 Madison Ave., 10022. Most Revs. Patrick J. Sheridan; Henry Mansell; Rev. Msgr. Gregory Mustaciuolo; Rev. Msgr. James McCarthy.
Chapel—New York, Sts. Faith, Hope and Charity. Records at St. Patrick Cathedral.

2—ST. AGNES (1873), Rev. Msgr. Eugene V. Clark; Revs. William M. Shelley; Matthew Farrelly, C.S.Sp.; Venant LeLonde, O.F.M.; Kasimierz A. Kowalski. In res., Rev. Msgr. Carl J. Marucci (CAM); Rev. John A. Perricone; Rev. Msgr. James M. Reinert (LIN); Rev. George W. Rutler.
Res., 143 E. 43rd St., 10017. Tel: 212-682-5722; Fax: 212-370-5791.

3—ST. ALBERT (1916). Closed. Parochial records at Sacred Heart.

4—ALL SAINTS (1879) (African American), Rev. Theodore K. Parker, O.S.C.; Deacon Joseph Price. In res., Rev. Linus Iwuanyanwu.
Res., 47 E. 129th St., 10035. Tel: 212-534-3535; Fax: 212-987-1930.
School—(1900), 52 E. 130th St., 10037. Tel: 212-534-0558; Fax: 212-831-6343. Anthony Georges, Prin. Sisters of the Blessed Sacrament 4; Lay Teachers 12; Students 235.
Convent—14 E. 129 St., 10035. Tel: 212-410-3197.
Chapels—St. Benedict's Day Nursery, 34 W. 134th St., 10035. Tel: 212-283-3350; Rice High School Christian Brothers, 124 St. & Lenox Ave., 10035. Tel: 212-369-4100; Fax: 212-348-4631; Franciscan Handmaids of Mary Convent, 15 W. 124th St., 10035. Tel: 212-289-5655; Fax: 212-987-5447.
Catechesis/Religious Programs—Students 68.

5—ST. ALOYSIUS (1899), Revs. Kenneth J. Boller, S.J.; Thomas P. Green, S.J.; Edward J. Durkin, S.J. In res., Rev. Matthew J. Cassidy, S.J.
Res., 219 W. 132nd St., 10027. Tel: 212-234-2848; Fax: 212-234-4198.
School—(1940), 223 W. 132nd St., 10027. Tel: 212-283-0921. Ms. Laurel D. Senger, Prin.
Priests 2; Lay Teachers 20; Students 285.
Catechesis/Religious Programs—Students 40.

6—ST. ALPHONSUS (1847). Closed. Records at St. Anthony of Padua.

7—ST. AMBROSE (CHAPEL CENTRO MARIA) (1897). Closed. Records at Sacred Heart Church.

8—ST. ANDREW (1842). Blessed Sacrament Fathers and Brothers. Revs. Roger Pageot, S.S.S.; James Hayes, S.S.S.; Lionel Lavigne, S.S.S.; Thomas McKeon, S.S.S., New York Infirmary Beekman Downtown Hospital. In res., Bros. Stanley Kolwaski, S.S.S.; Thomas Mella, S.S.S.; Michael Perez, S.S.S., (Pace University).
Res., 20 Cardinal Hayes Pl., 10007. Tel: 212-962-3972; 3973; Fax: 212-962-1012.
Stations—New York Infirmary Beekman Downtown Hospital, 170 William St., 10007. Tel: 212-312-5000; St. Margaret's House, 49 Fulton St., 10007. Tel: 212-766-8122; Pace University, Pace Plaza, 10007. Tel: 212-346-1200.

9—ST. ANN'S ARMENIAN CATHOLIC CATHEDRAL (1983) (Armenian), Most Rev. Hovhannes Tertzakian.
Res., 110 E. 12th St., 10003. Tel: 212-477-2030; Fax: 212-477-2185.
Catechesis/Religious Programs—Students 4.

10—ST. ANN'S ROMAN CATHOLIC CHURCH (1852), Rev. Msgr. Kevin P. O'Brien, Admin.
Res., 110 E. 12th St., 10003. Tel: 212-254-0200; 477-2030; Fax: 212-477-2185.

11—ST. ANN (1911) (Spanish), Revs. Victor Muzzin, F.D.P. (Italy); Pasquale Ruggieri, F.D.P. (Italy).
Res., 312 E. 110th St., 10029. Tel: 212-534-3856; Fax: 212-534-3856.
School—(1926), 314-318 E. 110th St., 10029. Tel: 212-722-1295. Sr. Josephine Cioffi, Prin.
Priests 1; Sisters, Servants of the Immaculate Heart of Mary 4; Lay Teachers 12; Students 320.
Chapel—St. Ann's Convent, 319 E. 109 St., 10029. Tel: 212-534-8321.

12—ANNUNCIATION (1853), Revs. Felix Jimenez, Sch.P. (Spain); Jose M. Clavero, Sch.P. (Spain); Aroldo Guerra, Sch.P. (Cuba); Felix Ganuza, Sch.P. (Spain).
Res., 88 Convent Ave., 10027. Tel: 212-234-1919; Fax: 212-281-7205.
School—(1858), 461 W. 131st St., 10027. Tel: 212-281-7174. Peter Shyshka, Prin.
Lay Teachers 16; Students 350.
Catechesis/Religious Programs—Students 450.

13—ST. ANTHONY OF PADUA (Org. 1859; Re-org. 1866) (Italian), Revs. Daniel Morey, O.F.M.; Francis Hanudel, O.F.M.; Bro. Vincent Ciaravino.

Res. & Chapel—154 Sullivan St., 10012. Tel: 212-777-2755; Fax: 212-673-6684.
School—(1874), 60 MacDougal St., 10012. Tel: 212-477-1297; Fax: 212-529-2018.
Franciscan Sisters of Allegany 1; Lay Teachers 10; Students 240.
Catechesis/Religious Programs—Tel: 212-477-5792. Sr. Agenesine M.H.S.H., D.R.E.
Students 30.

14—ASCENSION (1895), Revs. John P. Duffell; Sixto Quezada (Dominican Republic); Sean McCaughley (Ireland); Deacon Constancio Soto.
Res., 221 W. 107th St., 10025. Tel: 212-222-0666; Fax: 212-961-1086.
School—(1912), 220 W. 108th St., 10025. Tel: 212-222-5161.
Lay Teachers 12; Students 247.
Catechesis/Religious Programs—Tel: 212-749-5938.
Students 449.
Chapels—C.Y.O. Grace Ministry, 218 W. 108th St., 10025. Tel: 212-666-6598; Riverside Study Center. (Opus Dei) 330 Riverside Dr., 10025. Tel: 212-222-3285; Fax: 212-316-3629.

15—ASSUMPTION (1858). Closed. Records at Sacred Heart Church.

16—ST. BENEDICT THE MOOR (1883) (Spanish). Attended by Sacred Heart of Jesus, 212-265-5020, 457 W. 51st St., New York, NY 10019. Rev. Kevin J. Nelan.
Res., 457 W. 51st St., 10019. Tel: 212-265-5020; Fax: 212-977-4116.

17—ST. BERNARD (1868), Revs. Kenneth J. Smith; George Carlin, S.O.L.T.; Jude Egbeji (Nigeria). In res., Rev. George Reinheimer.
Res., 328 W. 14th St., 10014. Tel: 212-243-0265; Fax: 212-255-8466.
School—(1916), 327 W. 13th St., 10014. Tel: 212-243-6368; Fax: 212-99-7363. Ms. Imelda David, Prin.
Lay Teachers 11; Students 235.
Catechesis/Religious Programs—Students 60.
Chapel—Crosier Fathers Priory, 326 W. 14th St., 10014. Tel: 212-255-5431.

18—BLESSED SACRAMENT (1887), Revs. Robert B. O'Connor; Alfredo Balinong, S.J. (Philippines); Alexis Bastidas (Venezuela). In res., Rev. Msgr. William J. Toohy.
Res., 152 W. 71st St., 10023. Tel: 212-877-3111; Fax: 212-799-6233.
School—(1902), 147-152 W. 70th St., 10023. Tel: 212-724-7561; Fax: 212-724-7561. Janice Desmond, Prin.
Lay Teachers 10; Students 265.
Catechesis/Religious Programs—Students 83.
Chapels—Convent of Blessed Sacrament, 133 W. 70th St., 10023. Tel: 212-877-8076; St. Agnes' Home, 237 W. 74th St., 10023. Tel: 212-874-9203; Archdiocese Teachers Residence, 22 W. 70th St., 10023.

19—ST. BONIFACE (1858). Closed. Records at Holy Family Church.

20—ST. BRIGID (1848; 1955), Revs. Michael J. Conway, O.SS.T., Admin.; Joseph C. Gidaro, O.SS.T.; Deacon Rafael Bello. In res., Rev. Aaron M. Dowdell, O.SS.T.
Res., 119 Avenue B, 10009. Tel: 212-228-5400; Fax: 212-254-0334.
School—185 E. Seventh St., 10009. Tel: 212-677-5210; Fax: 212-260-2262.
Sisters 1; Lay Teachers 15; Students 215.
Catechesis/Religious Programs—Students 125.

21—ST. CATHERINE OF GENOA (1887), Rev. David E. Nolan.
Res., 506 W. 153rd St., 10031. Tel: 212-862-6130; Fax: 212-491-6272.
School—(1910), 508-510 W. 153rd St., 10031. Tel: 212-926-0252.
Lay Teachers 10; Students 330.
Catechesis/Religious Programs—Students 460.

22—ST. CATHERINE OF SIENA (1897), Very Rev. Christopher Johnson, O.P., Prior; Revs. Vincent Ferrer McHenry, O.P., Sub-Prior; George Lawrence Concordia, O.P.; John Jerome Conroy, O.P.; Paul B. Fu, O.P.; Frank Bede Shipps, O.P.; Robert Philip Fitzsimmons, O.P.; John Thaddeus Murphy, O.P.; Robert Gregory Keeler, O.P.; David A. Butler, O.P.; Stephen Francis Carmody, O.P.
Res., 411 E. 68th St., 10021. Tel: 212-988-8300; Fax: 212-988-6918.

23—ST. CECILIA (1873), Revs. Francis G. Skelly, C.SS.R.; William Jacob, C.SS.R.; John K. Graham, C.SS.R.; Karl Krauser, C.SS.R.; Senen Javier, C.SS.R.; Blas Caceres, C.SS.R.; Leo Armada, C.SS.R.; Bro. Francis Alfone, C.SS.R.
Res., 125 E. 105th St., 10029. Tel: 212-534-1350; Fax: 212-410-6177.
Day Nursery—118 E. 106 St., 10029. Tel: 212-534-8423; Fax: 212-534-5757.
Catechesis/Religious Programs—Students 200. Sisters of the Atonement, Tel: 212-534-8423.

24—ST. CHARLES BORROMEO (1888) (African American), Rev. Msgr. Wallace A. Harris.
Res., 211 W. 141st St., 10030. Tel: 212-281-2100; Fax: 212-862-1881.
School—(1904), 214 W. 142 St., 10030. Tel: 212-368-6666. Sr. Marianne Poole, Prin.
Sisters of the Blessed Sacrament 7; Lay Teachers 17; Students 520.
Catechesis/Religious Programs—Students 517.

25—ST. CLARE (1903). Closed. Records at St. Raphael's Church.

26—ST. CLEMENS MARY (1909). Closed. Records at Holy Cross Church, Manhattan.

27—ST. COLUMBA (1845), Rev. Frank Scanlon, Admin. In res., Rev. Joseph Hien.
Res., 343 W. 25th St., 10001. Tel: 212-807-8876.
School—(1847), 331-333 W. 25th St., 10001.
Sisters of Congregation of Notre Dame 2; Lay Teachers 9; Students 243.
Chapel—Sisters of Congregation of Notre Dame, 329 W. 25th St., 10001.

28—CORPUS CHRISTI (1906), Rev. Raymond M. Rafferty; Rev. Msgr. Myles M. Bourke, Pastor Emeritus. In res., Rev. Msgr. Kevin L. Sullivan; Revs. Randall Renter, C.S.C.; James Blaettler, S.J.
Res., 529 W. 121st St., 10027. Tel: 212-666-9350; Fax: 212-531-2487.
School—(1907), 535 W. 121st St., 10027. Tel: 212-662-9344; Fax: 212-662-2725. Sr. Mary Tyler, O.P., Prin.
Lay Teachers 10; Students 229.
Catechesis/Religious Programs—Students 25.

29—SS. CYRIL AND METHODIUS - ST. RAPHAEL (1913; 1886) (Croatian), Revs. Slaven H. Mijatovic, O.F.M.; Roberto Jolic, O.F.M.
Res., 502 W. 41st St., 10036. Tel: 212-563-3395; Fax: 212-868-1203.

30—ST. CYRIL (1916) (Slovenian), Rev. Krizolog Cimerman, O.F.M.
Res., 62 St. Mark's Pl., 10003. Tel: 212-674-3442; Fax: 212-674-3442.

31—ST. ELIZABETH (1869), Rev. Msgr. Joachim B. Beaumont; Revs. Rudolph F. Gonzalez; Jose Serrano; Carlos Perez (Puerto Rico); Luis Saldana; Deacon Odalis R. Rosado.
Res., 268 Wadsworth Ave., 10033. Tel: 212-568-8803; Fax: 212-781-2754.
School—(1936), 612 W. 187th St., 10033. Tel: 212-568-7291; Fax: 212-928-2515.
Sisters 2; Lay Teachers 19; Students 696.
Catechesis/Religious Programs—Tel: 212-923-4900.
Students 600.
Chapels—Sisters Residence, 612 W. 187th St., 10033.; Cabrini Chapel, 701 Ft. Washington Ave., 10040.
Isabella Geriatric Center—515 Audubon Ave., 10040.

32—ST. ELIZABETH OF HUNGARY (1891) (Slovak), Rev. Msgr. Patrick P. McCahill.
Res., 211 E. 83rd St., 10028-2854. Tel: 212-734-5747; 988-1903 (TTY); Fax: 212-988-1903.
Catechesis/Religious Programs—Students 25.

33—ST. EMERIC (1949), Rev. Msgr. Joachim Beaumont. In res., Rev. Luis M. Dolan, C.P. (Argentina).
Res., 185 Avenue D, 10009. Tel: 212-228-4494; Fax: 212-375-1163.
Catechesis/Religious Programs—Students 222.

34—EPIPHANY (1868) (Irish), Rev. Msgr. Walter J. Niebrzydowski; Revs. Edmond J. Nixon, C.SS.R. (Australia); Dennis T. Williams; Sr. Doris Sayhonne, R.C.D., Pastoral Assoc.; Sr. Christine Gates, R.G.S., Social Worker. In res., Rev. Msgr. George J. Cascelli; Rev. John S. Bonnici.
Res., 239 E. 21st St., 10010. Tel: 212-475-1966; Fax: 212-477-0537.
School—(1869), 234 E. 22nd St., 10010. Tel: 212-473-4128; Fax: 212-473-4392.
141 E. 28th St., 10016. Tel: 212-473-4496; Fax: 212-473-4537.
Sisters 1; Lay Teachers 35; Students 540.
Catechesis/Religious Programs—Students 129.

35—ST. FRANCIS OF ASSISI (1844) (Franciscan), Revs. Ronald P. Stark, O.F.M., Guardian & Pastor; Thomas J. Walters, O.F.M., Vicar; Christian F. Camadella, O.F.M.; Gerald F. Carr, O.F.M.; Brian Carroll, O.F.M.; Bros. Denis Gordon Clark, O.F.M.; F. Edward Coughlin, O.F.M.; Revs. Alcuin Coyle, O.F.M.; Edward J. Dillon, O.F.M.; John M. Felice, O.F.M.; Brennan Fitzgerald, O.F.M.; Robert A. Gavin, O.F.M.; Bro. Charles Gilmartin, O.F.M.; Revs. Vincent B. Grogan, O.F.M.; Joseph M. Hertel, O.F.M.; Brian Jordan, O.F.M.; Michael Judge, O.F.M.; Joseph Juracek, O.F.M.; Francis de Paul Kealy, O.F.M.; Christopher Keenan, O.F.M.; Robert Kennedy, O.F.M.; Francis Kim, O.F.M.; Vincent A. Laviano, O.F.M.; Miguel A. Loredo, O.F.M.; Bro. William Mann, O.F.M.; Revs. Michael McDonnell, O.F.M.; Felix P. McGrath, O.F.M.; Cassian Miles, O.F.M.; Bro. Timothy Miskowski, O.F.M.; Revs. John J. McVean, O.F.M.; Francis J. Muller, O.F.M.; Bro. Nathanael Necaster, O.F.M.; Revs. Quintin A. Neyland, O.F.M.; James R. O'Connell, O.F.M.; Timothy J. Shreenan, O.F.M.; Bros. Daniel Sulmasy, O.F.M.; Sebastian Tobin, O.F.M.; Revs. Kevin Tortorelli, O.F.M.; Lambert F. Valentine, O.F.M.; Allan G. Von Kobs, O.F.M.; Rayner F. Williams, O.F.M.; Dennis M. Wilson, O.F.M. (For priests and brothers not listed here see St. Francis Monastery under Monasteries and Residences of Priests and Brothers.).
Res., 135 W. 31st St., 10001. Tel: 212-736-8500; Fax: 212-736-8545.

36—ST. FRANCIS DE SALES (1894), Rev. Robert V. Lott, S.T.M.; Rev. Msgr. Oscar Aquino, J.C.D.; William Ramos, Pastoral Assoc.
Res., 135 A E. 96th St., 10128. Tel: 212-289-0425; Fax: 212-996-2028.
School—St. Francis de Sales & St. Lucy Academy, (1993), 116-120 E. 97th St. & 340 E. 104th St., 10029. Tel: 212-289-0680; 534-4021; Fax: 212-534-4130. Bro. Terence M. Connolly, C.F.C., Prin.
Congregation of Christian Brothers 3; Lay Teachers 31; Students 651.
Catechesis/Religious Programs—Students 651.

37—ST. FRANCIS XAVIER (1847), Revs. Edward J. Coughlin, S.J.; John P. Bucki, S.J.; Mr. Thomas Kocherry, Business Mgr. Pastoral Assocs.: Ms. Lesley Ann Woo; Ms. Monica Maher.
Office: 55 W. 15th St., 10011. Tel: 212-627-2100; Fax: 212-675-6997.

38—ST. FRANCES XAVIER CABRINI (1973), Rev. Luke W. McCann.
Res., 555 Main St., Roosevelt Island, 10044. Tel: 212-751-4896; Fax: 212-826-9234.
Catechesis/Religious Programs—Students 90.

39—THE CHURCH OF ST. GABRIEL (1867). Closed. Records at Church of Sacred Hearts of Jesus and Mary.

40—ST. GREGORY (1907), Revs. Raymond M. Rafferty; Arturo Motolinia, O.S.A. (Mexico). In res., Rev. Msgr. Kevin L. Sullivan.
Res., 144 W. 90th St., 10024. Tel: 212-724-9766; 9767.
School—(1913), 138 W. 90th St., 10024. Ms. Deborah Hurd, Prin.
Lay Teachers 9; Students 210.

41—GOOD SHEPHERD (1912) (Dominican-Irish), Revs. Marcos Zamora, C.S.P.; J. Ernest Aguilar, C.S.P.; Lionel A. de Silva, C.S.P.; Kevin A. Devine, C.S.P.; Sr. Mary Gallagher, R.S.M.; Sr. Acela Rodriguez, H.C.C.S.; Deacon Rafael Then. In res., Revs. Lawrence E. Boadt, C.S.P.; Donald C. Campbell, C.S.P.; Thomas J. Clerkin, C.S.P.
Res., 608 Isham St., 10034. Tel: 212-567-1300; Fax: 212-567-1476.
School—(1925), Cooper St. & Isham St., 10034. Tel: 212-567-5800; Fax: 212-567-5839.
Sisters of Mercy of the Union 3; Lay Teachers 29; Students 600.
Catechesis/Religious Programs—Students 275.
Chapel—Convent of Sisters of Mercy. (Private) 630 Isham St., 10034. Tel: 212-567-1600.

42—GUARDIAN ANGEL (1888), Revs. Philip Phan; Richard Carbo, Admin.
Res., 193 Tenth Ave., 10011. Tel: 212-929-5966.
School—(1911), Tel: 212-989-8280. Maureen McElduff, Prin.
Sisters of St. Dominic 2; Lay Teachers 8; Students 225.
Chapel—Sisters of St. Dominic & Franciscan Sisters, 407 W. 21st St., 10011. Tel: 212-243-2266.

43—ST. HEDWIG (1934). Closed. Parochial records at St. Stanislaus Church.

44—HOLY AGONY (1930) (Spanish), Revs. Victor Elia, C.M.; Candido Arrizurieta, C.M.; Santiago Lluch, C.M.
Res., 1834 Third Ave., 10029. Tel: 212-289-5589; Fax: 212-289-8321.

45—HOLY CROSS (1852), Revs. Peter M. Colapietro; Gary G. Seibert, S.J.; Angel Cruces; Deacon Lawrence C. McNeill. In res., Rev. Thomas R. Kopfensteiner (STL).
Res., 329 W. 42nd St., 10036. Tel: 212-246-4732; Fax: 212-307-5033.
School—(1864), 332 W. 43rd St., 10036. Tel: 212-246-0923. Sr. Mary Theresa Dixon, O.P., Prin.
Sisters of St. Dominic of Blauvelt 1; Lay Teachers 15; Students 360.
Convent—460 W. 44th St., 10036. Tel: 212-246-9768. Dominican Convent
Chapels—St. Joseph's Home, 425 W. 44th St., 10036. Tel: 212-246-5363; Covenant House, 692 Eighth Ave., 10036. Tel: 212-613-0300.

46—HOLY FAMILY (1924), Revs. Robert J. Robbins; Cesar Ching Espineda, S.V.D.
Res., 315 E. 47th St., 10017-2318. Tel: 212-753-3401; Fax: 212-753-3428.

Catechesis/Religious Programs—Students 25.

47—HOLY INNOCENTS (1866), Rev. Msgr. Donald Sakano; Rev. William J. Delaney.
Res., 128 W. 37th St., 10018. Tel: 212-279-5861; Fax: 212-714-9313.

48—HOLY NAME OF JESUS (1868), Revs. Jerome Massimino, O.F.M.; Francis Gunn, O.F.M.; William Bried, O.F.M.; Richard Trezza, O.F.M.; Bros. Gerald Hudson, O.F.M.; William Margraf, O.F.M.
Res., 207 W. 96th St., 10025. Tel: 212-749-0276; Fax: 212-749-2045.
School—(1905), Amsterdam Ave. & 97th St., 10025. Tel: 212-749-1240; Fax: 212-663-1939. Bro. Richard Grieco, F.S.C., Prin.
Brothers 2; Lay Teachers 20; Students 632.
Catechesis/Religious Programs—Tel: 212-655-1888.
Students 240.

49—HOLY ROSARY (1884) (Augustinian), Revs. Angel Dulanto, O.S.A.; Abel Alvarez, O.S.A.; Juan Manuel Chaguaceda, O.S.A.
Res., 444 E. 119th St., 10035. Tel: 212-534-0740; Fax: 212-534-7572.
School—(1949), 371 Pleasant Ave., 10035. Tel: 212-876-7555; Fax: 212-876-0152.
Sisters 1; Lay Teachers 9; Students 224.
Catechesis/Religious Programs—Students 65.

50—HOLY TRINITY (1898), Rev. Msgr. Thomas P. Leonard; Rev. Mizael Roa (Venezuela). In res., Rev. Wilson Maina (Africa).
Res., 213 W. 82nd St., 10024. Tel: 212-787-0634; Fax: 212-787-4917.
Catechesis/Religious Programs—Students 89.
Chapel—Chinese Catholic Information Center, 86 Riverside Dr., 10024. Tel: 212-787-6969; Fax: 212-787-0351.

51—ST. IGNATIUS LOYOLA (1851), Revs. Walter F. Modrys, S.J.; William J. Bergen, S.J.; Mark C. Hallinan, S.J. Pastoral Assocs.: Ms. Mary Christine O'Connor, M.Div.; Ms. Joanne F. Cunneen, M.A., M.S.
Res., 980 Park Ave., 10028. Tel: 212-288-3588; Fax: 212-734-3671.
School—(1854), 50 E. 84th St., 10028. Tel: 212-861-3820; Fax: 212-879-8248.
Sisters of Charity of St. Vincent de Paul 3; Lay Teachers 21; Students 567.
Day Nursery—240 E. 84th St., 10028. Tel: 212-734-6427; Fax: 212-734-6972.
Lay Assistants 15; Capacity 107.
Catechesis/Religious Programs—Tel: 212-861-4764. Ms. Joanne Cunneen M.A., D.R.E.
Students 450.
Convent—Tel: 212-288-5544. St. Ignatius Loyola
High School—Regis High School, 55 E. 84th St., 10028. Tel: 212-288-1100; Fax: 212-794-1221.
Schools—Loyola School, Tel: 212-288-3522; Fax: 212-861-1021.; Marymount School, 1028 Fifth Ave., 10028. Tel: 212-744-4486; Fax: 212-744-0163.

52—IMMACULATE CONCEPTION (1855), Rev. Msgr. Kevin P. O'Brien; Revs. Francis X. Buu; John P. Moore; Richard J. Neuhaus; Misael Bacleon (Philippines). In res., Rev. Msgr. Desmond J. Vella; Revs. Edwin J. Conlin; John J. Delaney; Gabriel Anosike (Nigeria).
Res., 414 E. 14th St., 10009. Tel: 212-254-0200; Fax: 212-505-7610.
School—(1864), 419 E. 13th St., 10009. Tel: 212-475-2590; Fax: 212-475-7413.
Sisters 1; Lay Teachers 13; Students 370.
Catechesis/Religious Programs—Students 93.

53—INCARNATION (1908), Revs. Gabriel La Paz; John N. Paddack; Fernando Fernandez; Antonio Almonte; Aroldo Guerra.
Res., 1290 St. Nicholas Ave., 10033. Tel: 212-927-7474; Fax: 212-928-0315.
School—(1910), 568-570 W. 175th St., 10033. Tel: 212-795-1030; Fax: 212-795-1564.
Lay Teachers 22; Students 596.
Catechesis/Religious Programs—Sr. Teresa Sheehan, D.R.E.
Students 1,803.

54—ST. JAMES (1827), Revs. Robert J. Poveromo; Jesus P. Enojo; Joseph Chao.
Res., 23 Oliver St., 10038. Tel: 212-233-0161.
School—(1854), 37 St. James Place, 10038. Tel: 212-267-9289. Sr. Josefa Marie Curcio, C.S.J.B., Prin.
Sisters of St. John the Baptist 4; Lay Teachers 8; Students 210.
Chapel—St. James Convent, 21 Oliver St., 10038. Tel: 212-962-0840.

55—ST. JEAN BAPTISTE (1882), Revs. John Kamas, S.S.S.; Bernard J. Camire, S.S.S.; Mario Marzocchi, S.S.S.; Donald Brouillard, S.S.S. In res., Revs. Paul Bernier, S.S.S.; Eugene LaVerdiere, S.S.S.; William Dahms, S.S.S.
Res., 184 E. 76th St., 10021. Tel: 212-288-5082; Fax: 212-717-8397.
High School—173 E. 75th St., 10021. Tel: 212-288-1645; Fax: 212-288-6540.
Sisters of the Congregation of Notre Dame 6; Religious 2; Lay Teachers 36; Students 460.
Chapel—Sisters' Convent, Tel: 212-472-1230 (Apt. A); 472-8821 (Apt. B); Fax: 212-396-2025.

56—ST. JOACHIM (1888) (Italian). Closed. Parochial records are at Church of St. Joseph.

57—ST. JOHN THE BAPTIST (1840) (German). (Capuchin-Franciscan Friars). Revs. Francis Gasparik, O.F.M.Cap., Guardian & Pastor; Ramon Frias, O.F.M.Cap.; Gerard Mulvey, O.F.M.Cap.; Gavin Reilly, O.F.M.Cap. In res., Revs. Armand Dasseville, O.F.M.Cap., (Retired); Andrew Drew, O.F.M.Cap., Chap.; John Clermont, O.F.M.Cap.; Peter Kaseta, O.F.M.Cap., Dir. Devel. & Capuchin Mission Assn.; Thomas Houle, O.F.M.Cap., Chap.; Leonard Glavin, O.F.M.Cap., (Retired); Matthias Wesnofske, O.F.M.Cap., Spiritual Asst. of Secular Order of St. Francis; Bros. Luke Benbrook, O.F.M.Cap., Pastoral Assoc.; George McCloskey, O.F.M.Cap., Dir. Communications.
Res., 210 W. 31st St., 10001-2876. Tel: 212-564-9070; Fax: 212-564-3964.

58—ST. JOHN THE EVANGELIST (1840), Rev. Msgr. Michael J. Wrenn; Rev. James P. Connolly; Rev. Msgr. George A. Kelly; Rev. Msgr. Thomas J. Bergin.
Res., 348 E. 55th St., 10022. Tel: 212-753-8418; Fax: 212-826-1848. [CEM]

59—ST. JOHN NEPOMUCENE (1895) (Slovak), Revs. Martin Svitan; Jozef Krajnak.
Res., 411 E. 66th St., 10021. Tel: 212-734-4613; 734-4370; Fax: 212-734-2483.
Chapel—Sisters' Convent, 320 E. 66th St., 10021. Tel: 212-734-6640; Fax: 212-734-2483.

60—ST. JOHN THE MARTYR (1903), Rev. Msgr. John G. Woolsey; Rev. Joseph W. Baker. In res., Rev. Msgr. George P. Thompson.
Res., 259 E. 71st St., 10021-4596. Tel: 212-744-4880; 4881; Fax: 212-628-6662.
Catechesis/Religious Programs—Regional. See St. Ignatius Loyola, New York.

61—ST. JOSEPH (1829), Revs. Aldo J. Tos; Owen J. Lafferty; Michael K. Holleran; Sr. Anne Tahaney, O.P., Pastoral Assoc.; Deacon Thomas Johnson; Alvin Donius, Parish Mgr.
Res., 371 Sixth Ave., 10014. Tel: 212-741-1274; Fax: 212-741-2147.
School—111 Washington Pl., 10014. Tel: 212-929-5134; Fax: 212-929-5105.
Lay Teachers 10; Students 142.

62—ST. JOSEPH (1873) (German), Rev. Msgr. Lawrence M. Connaughton; Revs. Donald Partridge; Emmanuel Nartey. In res., Rev. William S. Elder.
Res., 404 E. 87th St., 10128. Tel: 212-289-6030; Fax: 212-348-8075.
School—(1880), 420 E. 87th St., 10128. Tel: 212-289-3057; Fax: 212-289-7239.
Sisters 1; Lay Teachers 13; Students 260.
Catechesis/Religious Programs—Regional. See St. Ignatius Loyola, New York. Tel: 212-861-4764; Fax: 212-734-3671.

63—ST. JOSEPH OF THE HOLY FAMILY (1860), Revs. Philip J. Kelly, Admin.; Victor Emuwen; Jose Mesa, S.J.; Deacon Domingo Lopez.
Res., 405 W. 125th St., 10027. Tel: 212-662-9125.
School—(1862), 168 Morningside Ave., 10027. Tel: 212-662-1736; Fax: 212-662-1490.
Daughters of Charity of St. Vincent de Paul 4; Lay Teachers 7; Students 250.
Catechesis/Religious Programs—Students 170.
Convent—400 W. 126th St., 10027. Tel: 212-678-0585.

64—ST. JOSEPH (1924) (Italian-Chinese), Revs. Ralph A. Bove, C.S.; Paul Dao (China) (Chinese Apostolate).
Res., 5 Monroe St., 10002. Tel: 212-267-8376; Fax: 212-267-4357.
School—(1926), One Monroe St., 10002. Tel: 212-233-5152.
Apostles of the Sacred Heart of Jesus 5; Lay Teachers 7; Students 258.
Convent—83 Madison St., 10002. Tel: 212-233-5670.
Apostles of the Sacred Heart of Jesus 6.

65—ST. JUDE (1949) (Spanish), Revs. Elias Isla; Rodrigo Ortega; Deacon Porfirio Rodriguez.
Res., 431 W. 204th St., 10034. Tel: 212-569-3000; Fax: 212-304-4545.
School—(1953), 433 W. 204th St., 10034. Tel: 212-569-3400; Fax: 212-304-4479.
Lay Teachers 16; Students 400.
Catechesis/Religious Programs—Tel: 212-569-3002.
Students 510.
Chapel—New York, St. Jude Convent.

66—ST. LEO (1880). Closed. Parochial records at St. Stephen's Church.

67—ST. LUCY (1900) (Hispanic), Revs. Robert V. Lott, Admin.; Esviardo Palomino, Pastor Emeritus; William Rivera, Pastoral Assoc.
Res., 344 E. 104th St., 10029. Tel: 212-534-1470.
School—(1942). Consolidated with St. Francis de Sales School to form St. Francis de Sales-St. Lucy Academy (1993). 340 E. 104th St., 10029. Tel: 212-534-4021; Fax: 212-354-4130. Bro. Paul Beaudin, C.F.C., Prin.

68—ST. MALACHY'S (1902). (The Actors' Chapel). Rev. Msgr. Michael C. Crimmins; Rev. Joseph A. Kelly, S.J.; Sr. Maureen Gibbons, O.P.
Res., 239 W. 49th St., 10019. Tel: 212-489-1340; Fax: 212-262-6224.
Encore Community Services—Tel: 212-581-2910; Fax: 212-757-0244. Sr. Elizabeth Hasselt, O.P., Exec. Dir.; Sr. Bernadette Gayor, S.H.C.J., Finance Dir.
Encore Community Center & Programs—Tel: 212-581-2910. Sr. Lillian McNamara, O.P., Dir.
Encore 49 Residence—Tel: 212-246-0880; 581-3490 (Social Svc.); Fax: 212-541-7697.
Catechesis/Religious Programs—Students 8.

69—ST. MARK THE EVANGELIST (1907) (African American), Revs. Thomas P. Tunney, C.S.Sp.; Daniel McCarthy, C.S.Sp.
Res., 65 W. 138th St., 10037. Tel: 212-281-4931; Fax: 212-491-6803.
School—(1912), 55 W. 138th St., 10037. Tel: 212-283-4848; Fax: 212-926-0419. Sr. Nora Gatto, D.C., Prin.
Daughters of Charity of St. Vincent de Paul 1; Lay Teachers 12; Students 281.
Catechesis/Religious Programs—Students 33.
Chapel—St. Mark's Convent, Tel: 212-283-4966.

70—ST. MARY (1826), Rev. Msgr. Neil A. Connolly; Revs. Peter Ma, (Chinese Apostolate); Robert J. O'Neil, M.H.M.
Res., 28 Attorney St., 10002. Tel: 212-674-3266.
Catechesis/Religious Programs—Students 310.

71—ST. MARY MAGDALEN (1873) (German). Closed. Parochial records at Immaculate Conception Church.

72—MARY HELP OF CHRISTIANS (1908) (Spanish), Revs. John P. Blanco, S.D.B.; Frank Santana. In res., Rev. James Heuser, S.D.B.; Bro. Gerald Warner, S.D.B.
Res., 440 E. 12th St., 10009. Tel: 212-254-0058; Fax: 212-505-3769.
School—435-437 E. 11th St., 10009. Tel: 212-254-3596; Fax: 212-505-5037.
Daughters of Mary Help of Christians 4; Lay Teachers 11; Students 210.
Catechesis/Religious Programs—Students 198.
Convent—429 E. 12 St., 10009. Tel: 212-254-2537.

73—ST. MATTHEW (1902). Closed. Parochial records at Blessed Sacrament Church.

74—ST. MICHAEL (1857), Rev. Msgr. Marc A. Filacchione; Rev. Brian T. McSweeney.
Res., 424 W. 34th St., 10001. Tel: 212-563-2575; Fax: 212-563-4087.
High School—(1866-1874), 425 W. 33rd St., 10001. Tel: 212-563-2547. Sr. Kathleen Cusak, P.B.V.M., Prin.
Sisters of the Presentation 7; Lay Teachers 28; Girls 445.
Catechesis/Religious Programs—Students 420.
Chapel—Sacred Heart, 419 W. 33rd St., 10001. Tel: 212-947-7668.

75—ST. MICHAEL CHAPEL (1936) (Russian), Rev. Juan Soles; Deacon Christopher LiGreci.
Res., 266 Mulberry St., 10012. Tel: 212-226-2644.
Catechesis/Religious Programs—Students 10.

76—ST. MONICA (1879), Rev. Msgr. Thomas A. Modugno; Revs. Joseph A. Francis, O.P.; Thomas M. Mulvanerty. In res., Rev. Msgr. Anthony R. Frontiero; Rev. Msgr. Ferdinando D. Berardi; Rev. Apolinari Ngirwa.
Res., 413 E. 79th St., 10021. Tel: 212-288-6250; Fax: 212-570-1562.
Chapel—St. Monica Convent, 404 E. 80th St., 10021. Tel: 212-288-1986.

77—MOST HOLY CRUCIFIX (1925) (Italian), Rev. Christopher Hartley, Admin.
Res., 378 Broome St., 10013. Tel: 212-226-2556.

78—MOST HOLY REDEEMER (1844), Revs. Joseph C. Tizio, C.SS.R.; Jerome Holland, C.SS.R. In res., Rev. Terrance Moran, C.SS.R.
Res., 173 E. Third St., 10009. Tel: 212-673-4224; Fax: 212-472-4097.
Catechesis/Religious Programs—Students 162.

79—MOST PRECIOUS BLOOD (1891) (Italian), Revs. Fabian Grifone, O.F.M.; Jose Tubianosa; Bro. James Welch, O.F.M.
Res., 109 Mulberry St., 10013. Tel: 212-226-6427; Fax: 212-226-1837.

80—NATIVITY (1842) (Hispanic). (Jesuit). Rev. Donald C. Gannon, S.J. In res., Revs. Michael J. Lynch, S.J.; George M. Anderson, S.J.; Robert E. Reiser, S.J.; John J. Podsiadlo, S.J.; Gerald J. Chojnacki,

S.J., Supr.; Bro. Christopher Derby, S.J.; Mr. Tomasz P. Nogaj.
Res., 44 Second Ave., 10003. Tel: 212-674-8590; Fax: 212-674-8789.
Nativity Mission Center—204 Forsyth St., 10002. Tel: 212-477-2472; Fax: 212-473-0538.

81—ST. NICHOLAS (1833) (German). Closed. Parochial records at Most Holy Redeemer Church.

82—NOTRE DAME (1910), Rev. Msgr. Christopher Maloney; Revs. Thomas J. Valenti (ROC); Daniel Ulloa, O.P. In res., Revs. Ngozi Osuji (Nigeria); Charles J. O'Byrne, S.J.
Res., 405 W. 114th St., 10025. Tel: 212-866-1500; Fax: 212-222-5704.
Catechesis/Religious Programs—Students 15.
Station—New York, St. Luke's Hospital Amsterdam House.

83—OUR LADY QUEEN OF ANGELS (1886) (German), Rev. Martin Curtin, O.F.M.Cap., Guardian & Pastoral Assoc.; Bros. Pius Blandino, O.F.M.Cap.; Christopher Varley, O.F.M.Cap.; George Tucker, O.F.M.Cap.; Deacon Luis Martinez.
Res., 226 E. 113th St., 10029. Tel: 212-369-9088.
School—(1886 and 1955), 229-231 E. 112th St., 10029. Tel: 212-722-9277. Bro. Louis J. Esposito, O.F.M.Cap., Prin. & Vicar.
Priests 1; Brothers 1; Sisters 1; Lay Teachers 18; Students 546.
Catechesis/Religious Programs—Bro. Carmine D.R.E.
Students 585.
Chapel—Parish Center, 232 E. 113th St., 10029. Tel: 212-860-7618; Fax: 212-828-0506.

84—OUR LADY OF ESPERANZA (1912) (Spanish), Rev. Msgr. Peter C. O'Donnell.
Res., 624 W. 156th St., 10032. Tel: 212-283-4340; Fax: 212-283-4388.
Catechesis/Religious Programs—Students 318.

85—OUR LADY OF GOOD COUNSEL (1886), Rev. Msgr. Dennis P. Keane, Ph.D.; Revs. Arthur Leone; Richard Terga.
Res., 230 E. 90th St., 10128. Tel: 212-289-1742; Fax: 212-427-5643.
School—(1904), 323-329 E. 91st St., 10128. Tel: 212-289-6730. Mr. Donald Kramer, Prin.
Lay Teachers 10; Students 230.

86—OUR LADY OF GRACE (Stanton St.) (1907). Closed. Parochial records at Church of the Nativity.

87—OUR LADY OF GUADALUPE (1902) (Spanish), Rev. Charles Murr; Deacon Rene Garcia.
Res., 229 W. 14th St., 10011. Tel: 212-243-5317; Fax: 212-675-0637. [CEM]

88—OUR LADY OF LORETO (1891) (Sicilian), Rev. Msgr. John B. Ahern; Rev. Patrick J. Carroll; Rev. Msgr. Philip J. Murnion.
Res., 309 Elizabeth St., 10012. Tel: 212-431-9840; Fax: 212-625-9096.
Holy Name Centre for Homeless Men—Tel: 212-226-5848.

89—OUR LADY OF LOURDES (1901), Revs. Joseph J. Tyrrell; Fabio E. Jaramillo (Quibdo); Deacon Pedro O'Brien. In res., Revs. Lawrence E. Lucas; Alphonsus Anumudu (Orlu).
Res., 472 W. 142nd St., 10031. Tel: 212-862-4380; Fax: 212-862-4126.
School—(1903), 462-468 W. 143rd St., 10031. Tel: 212-926-5820; Fax: 212-491-6034. Warren Switzler, Prin.
Lay Teachers 22; Students 640.
Catechesis/Religious Programs—Students 695.
Chapel—Convent of Our Lady of Lourdes, 463 W. 142nd St., 10031. Tel: 212-926-1150; Fax: 212-862-4126.

90—OUR LADY OF THE MIRACULOUS MEDAL (1926). Closed. Records at Holy Agony.

91—OUR LADY OF MT. CARMEL (1884) (Italian), Revs. Peter J. Rofrano, S.A.C.; Severino Dominicis, S.A.C.; Anthony Kelly, S.A.C.; Girolamo D'Ambrosi, S.A.C.; Chris Salvatori, S.A.C.
Res., 448 E. 116th St., 10029-0614. Tel: 212-534-0681; Fax: 212-534-0629.
School—Mt. Carmel-Holy Rosary, 371 Pleasant Ave., 10035. Tel: 212-876-7555; Fax: 212-876-0152.
Sisters 1; Lay Teachers 8; Students 230.
Catechesis/Religious Programs—Students 80.
Convent—456 E. 116th St., 10029-0614. Tel: 212-427-2381.
Sisters of Charity 10.

92—OUR LADY OF PERPETUAL HELP (1887). Closed. Sacramental records at Our Lady of Peace.

93—OUR LADY OF PEACE (1918) (Italian), Rev. Bartholomew Daly, M.H.M., Admin. In res., Rev. Paul A. Keenan.
Res., 237 E. 62nd St., 10021. Tel: 212-838-3189; Fax: 212-308-4819.

94—OUR LADY OF POMPEII (1892) (Italian), Revs. Joseph A. Cogo, C.S.; Bernabe Sison; Bro. Michael La Mantia, C.S.
Res., 25 Carmine St., 10014. Tel: 212-989-6805; Fax: 212-727-3139.
School—(1930), 240 Bleecker St., 10014. Tel: 212-242-4147; Fax: 212-691-2361.
Apostles of the Sacred Heart of Jesus 6; Lay Teachers 13; Students 240.
Catechesis/Religious Programs—Students 39.

95—OUR LADY QUEEN OF MARTYRS (1927), Revs. Daniel S. Kearney; Ambiorix Rodriguez; Manuel Hererra (Ecuador); Deacon Narciso Hernandez. In res., Rev. Donald Johnston, Chap., Columbia Presbyterian Hospital.
Res., 91 Arden St., 10040. Tel: 212-567-2637; Fax: 212-567-1305.
School—(1932), 71 Arden St., 10040. Tel: 212-567-3190; Fax: 212-304-8587. Andrew Woods, Prin.
Lay Teachers 18; Students 454.
Catechesis/Religious Programs—Students 700.

96—OUR LADY OF THE ROSARY (1883). Shrine of St. Elizabeth Ann Seton. Rev. Peter Meehan; Rev. Msgr. Timothy Collins, Pastor Emeritus; Revs. Joseph O'Meara; Martin Betances Torres. In res., Revs. Francis Valentino, S.J.; Vincent Euk.
Res., 7 State St., 10004. Tel: 212-269-6865; Fax: 212-849-6850.

97—OUR LADY OF THE SCAPULAR/ST. STEPHEN (1889; 1848) (Spanish), Revs. Matthew Faulkner, O.Carm.; John Canning, O.Carm. In res., Most Rev. William J. McCormack.
Res., 142 E. 29th St., 10016. Tel: 212-683-1675; 532-2232; Fax: 212-683-7921.
Catechesis/Religious Programs—Students 127.
Chapel—Bellevue Hospital, Chapel of Our Lady Helper of the Sick, Tel: 212-561-4440. Revs. John Logan, O.Carm.; Kenneth Murphy, O.Carm.; Philip Marani, O.Carm.

98—OUR LADY OF SORROWS (1867) (English-Spanish), Revs. Joseph Gurdak, O.F.M.Cap.; John Mellitt, O.F.M.Cap.; Bro. Robert Gerdin, O.F.M.Cap.; Deacon Eusebio Maldonado. In res., Rev. Thomas Faida, O.F.M.Cap., Guardian; Bros. James Wieland, O.F.M.Cap; Carlos Hernandez, O.F.M.Cap.; Thomas Franks, O.F.M.Cap.
Res., 213 Stanton St., 10002-1898. Tel: 212-673-0900; Fax: 212-982-0166.
Church—103 Pitt St., 10002.
School—(1867), 219 Stanton St., 10002. Tel: 212-473-0320; Fax: 212-420-0285.
Lay Teachers 13; Students 274.
Catechesis/Religious Programs—Students 226.

99—OUR LADY OF VICTORY (1944), Rev. Msgr. Edward J. Mitty, P.A.; Revs. John S. Kostek; Peter G. Philominraj, S.D.B. (India); Dominic Sequeira, S.D.B. (India); Krzysztof Kaczynski (Poland). In res., Rev. John E. Fanning.
Res., 60 William St., 10005. Tel: 212-422-5535; Fax: 212-509-5336.

100—OUR LADY OF VILNIUS (1905) (Lithuanian), Rev. Dr. Eugene A. Sawicki, R.N., J.C.L., Admin.
Res., 32 Dominick St., 10013. Tel: 212-255-2648; Fax: 212-924-6210.
Church—570 Broome St., 10013.

101—OUR SAVIOUR (1955), Rev. Msgr. Jeremiah P. O'Neill; Revs. Koshy George Chirayath (India); Patrick Ettampola (Sri Lanka). In res., Rev. Douglas J. Mathers.
Res., 59 Park Ave., 10016. Tel: 212-679-8166; Fax: 212-213-0352.

102—ST. PATRICK OLD CATHEDRAL (1809), Rev. Keith G. Fenness; Rev. Msgr. Nicholas Marinacci, Pastor Emeritus; Revs. Andrew Thi; Hector Mazabel.
Res., 263 Mulberry St., 10012. Tel: 212-226-8075; Fax: 212-226-8075.
School—Boys & Girls Depts., (1817), 233-239 Mott St., 10012. Tel: 212-226-3984; Fax: 212-226-4469. 32-38 Prince St., 10012. Tel: 212-226-4799.
Lay Teachers 18; Students 581.
Chapels—Immaculate Conception, 32 Prince St., 10012.; St. Michael, 266 Mulberry St., 10012. Tel: 212-226-2644; Fax: 212-226-1219.

103—ST. PAUL (1834), Revs. Walter D. Mallo, I.V.E.; Pablo Waldmann, I.V.E. (Argentina); Deacon Miguel Granda. In res., Rev. Jose Otero (Argentina).
Res., 113 E. 117th St., 10035. Tel: 212-534-4422; Fax: 212-996-5588.
School—(1870), 114-122 E. 118th St., 10035. Tel: 212-534-0619; Fax: 212-534-3990.
Lay Teachers 14; Students 267.
Catechesis/Religious Programs—Tel: 212-534-4481.
Students 230.
Convent—Exodus House, 149 E. 117th St., 10035.

104—ST. PAUL THE APOSTLE (1858), Revs. Michael E. Evernden, C.S.P., Supr.; Stephen J. Connor, C.S.P., Dir. Vocations; Thomas P. Ryan, C.S.P., Office of Ecumenism; Joseph F. Mahon, C.S.P., Missions; Rudolph T. Vorisek, C.S.P., Hospital Chap.; James F. McQuade, C.S.P., Hospital Chap.; Charles Kullmann, C.S.P.; James B. Lloyd, C.S.P.; John C. Reynolds, C.S.P.; Richard J. Walsh, C.S.P.; Joseph P. Flynn, C.S.P.; Francis X. Diskin, C.S.P.; John E. Collins, C.S.P., Missions; Donal F. Forrester, C.S.P.; Kevin A. Lynch, C.S.P.; Michael J. Hunt, C.S.P.; Timothy P. Tighe, C.S.P.; Patrick Traynor, C.S.P.; Robert A. O'Donnell, C.S.P.; Dennis W. Hickey, C.S.P.; Thomas A. Tavella, C.S.P., Missions; Joseph J. Scott, C.S.P., Paulist Press; Brett Hoover, C.S.P. Pastoral Assocs.: Revs. Ronald Franco, C.S.P.; Timothy F. Sullivan, C.S.P.
Mailing Address: 405 W. 59th, 10019. Tel: 212-265-3495; Fax: 212-262-9239.
Catechesis/Religious Programs—Students 152.
Chapel—Oblates of Jesus the Priest, Tel: 212-265-3209; Fax: 212-265-4154.

105—ST. PETER (1785), Rev. Msgr. Robert M. O'Connell; Revs. Michael B. Dibble; Donald T. Fussner; James J. Halligan.
Res., 16 Barclay St., 10007. Tel: 212-233-8355; Fax: 212-285-0497.
Chapel—St. Joseph's Chapel, 385 South End Ave., 10280. Tel: 212-466-0131. In res., Rev. Msgr. Joseph J. Zammit, Chap., N.Y.C. Police Dept.

106—ST. RAPHAEL (1886). See Sts. Cyril and Methodius.

107—RESURRECTION (1907) (African American-Hispanic), Revs. Michael P. Sepp, Admin.; Samuel Taylor; Deacon Kenneth Radcliff.
Res., 276 W. 151st St., 10039. Tel: 212-690-7555; Fax: 212-690-6590.
School—(1910), 282 W. 151 St., 10039. Tel: 212-690-7524; Fax: 212-690-6590.
Lay Teachers 9; Students 209.

108—ST. ROSE (1868). Closed. Parochial records at St. Mary Church.

109—ST. ROSE OF LIMA (1902), Revs. Manuel Machado; Eusebio Mana-Ay. In res., Rev. Frederick Carrigan.
Res., 510 W. 165th St., 10032. Tel: 212-568-0091.
School—(1924), 517 W. 164th St., 10032.
Sisters 2; Lay Teachers 10; Students 310.
Chapel—St. Rose of Lima Convent, 509 W. 164th St., 10032. Medical Centre.

110—SACRED HEART OF JESUS (1876), Rev. Kevin J. Nelan; Sr. Ana Ospina, Pastoral Assoc.; Rev. Jorge Jimenez. In res., Rev. Thomas Lynch.
Res., 457 W. 51st, 10019. Tel: 212-265-5020; Fax: 212-977-4116.
School—(1892), 456 52nd St., 10019. Tel: 212-246-3264.
Congregation of Christian Brothers 1; Lay Teachers 11; Students 280.
Chapels—Centro Maria, 539 W. 54th St., 10019.; Convent of Sacred Heart, 450 W. 51st St., 10019.
Catechesis/Religious Programs—Students 220.

111—SACRED HEARTS OF JESUS AND MARY (1914) (Italian), Rev. Albert J. DeLuca.
Res., 307 E. 33rd St., 10016. Tel: 212-889-2133; Fax: 212-481-2924.
Chapel—Convent of the Sacred Heart of Jesus and Mary, 325 E. 33rd St., 10016. Tel: 212-889-3886; Fax: 212-481-2924.
Station—N.Y.U. Rehabilitation Hospital, Tel: 212-889-3886.

112—ST. SEBASTIAN (1915). Closed. Parochial records at Epiphany Church.

113—ST. STANISLAUS (1872) (Polish), Revs. Christopher Wieliczko, O.S.P.; Bogdan Kolmaga, O.S.P.
Res., 101 E. Seventh St., 10009. Tel: 212-475-4576; Fax: 212-674-4894.

114—ST. STEPHEN (1848). Consolidated in 1990. See Our Lady of Scapular/St. Stephen for details.

115—ST. STEPHEN OF HUNGARY (1902) (Hungarian), Revs. Neil J. O'Connell, O.F.M., Guardian Franciscan Community; Dominic Csorba, O.F.M. (Hungary); Vianney M. Devlin, O.F.M.; Sr. Natalie M. Runfola, R.S.C.J., Pastoral Assoc. In res., Revs. Russell C. Becker, O.F.M.; Peter V. Brophy, O.F.M.; Anthony M. Carrozzo, O.F.M.; Leo Clifford, O.F.M.; Reginald A. Redlon, O.F.M.; Ronald P. Stark, O.F.M.; Bros. Gregory P. Day, O.F.M.; Glenn Humphrey, O.F.M.; John E. Quinn, O.F.M.
Res., 414 E. 82nd St., 10028. Tel: 212-861-8500; Fax: 212-535-9221.
School—(1918), 408 E. 82nd St., 10028. Tel: 212-288-1989; Fax: 212-517-5877. Carol O'Connor, Prin.
Religious Teachers 1; Lay Teachers 8; Students 185.
Cooke Center for Learning and Development—Tel: 212-472-7209; Fax: 212-280-4473.
Lay Teachers 7; Students 24.
Catechesis/Religious Programs—Interparish Religious Education Program, c/o St. Ignatius of Loyola, 980 Park Ave., 10028. Tel: 212-861-4764; Fax: 212-734-3671.
Students 15.
Dewitt Nursing Home—211 E. 79th St., 10021.

116—ST. TERESA (1863), Rev. Msgr. Dennis J. Sullivan; Revs. John B. Chiang (China); Alfredo Monteiro (India).

Res., 141 Henry St., 10002. Tel: 212-233-0233; Fax: 212-619-4538.
Church—16 & 18 Rutgers St., 10002. Tel: 212-233-0233; Fax: 212-619-4538.
Catechesis/Religious Programs—Students 164.

117—ST. THOMAS THE APOSTLE (1889) (African American), Revs. Paul Grauls, S.D.B.; George Hanna, S.D.B.; Bro. Anthony Ambrogio, S.D.B.
Res., 262 W. 118th St., 10026. Tel: 212-662-2693; Fax: 212-662-4560. [CEM]
Don Bosco Harlem Association, Inc.—262 W. 118th St., 10026. Tel: 212-662-9228.

118—ST. THOMAS MORE (1950), Revs. John A. Boehning; John E. Halborg; Stanley Moseley, O.S.B. In res., Most Rev. Patrick V. Ahern; Rev. Msgr. Thomas Shelley.
Res., 65 E. 89th St., 10128. Tel: 212-876-7718; Fax: 212-831-5756.
Catechesis/Religious Programs—Narnia Clubs, F.D.R. Station, P.O. Box 967, 10150. Tel: 212-697-3688; Fax: 212-697-3103.
Students 185.
Chapel—Convent of Sacred Heart and Academy, 1 E. 91st St., 10022. Tel: 212-722-4745; Fax: 212-996-1784.

119—TRANSFIGURATION (1827) (Chinese-English), Rev. Raymond J. Nobiletti, M.M.
Res., 29 Mott St., 10013. Tel: 212-962-5157; Fax: 212-962-5217.
School—(1853), Tel: 212-962-5265; Fax: 212-964-8965. Suzanne O'Reilly, Prin.
Lay Teachers 9; Students 278.

120—ST. VERONICA (1887), Rev. Kenneth J. Smith, Admin.
Res., 328 W. 14th St., 10014. Tel: 212-243-0265; Fax: 212-255-8466.
Church—149-155 Christopher St., 10014. Tel: 212-924-5628.
Mission—New York, New York Co., Gift of Love, 657 Washington St., 10014. Tel: 212-645-0587.

121—ST. VINCENT FERRER (1867), Very Rev. James Boniface Ramsey, O.P., Prior; Revs. Daniel Thaddeus Davies, O.P.; Kevin Anthony McGrath, O.P.; Bros. Christopher McCabe, O.P.; Damian McCarthy, O.P.
Res., 869 Lexington Ave., 10021-6680. Tel: 212-744-2080; Fax: 212-327-3011.
High School—151 E. 65th St., 10021. Tel: 212-535-4680; Fax: 212-988-3455. Ms. Margaret Quinn, Prin.
Sisters of St. Dominic, Columbus, OH 6; Lay Teachers 26; Girls 410.
Chapels—Sisters of St. Dominic, 152 E. 66th St., 10021. Tel: 212-744-2375; Dominican Academy, 44 E. 68th St., 10021. Tel: 212-744-0195; Fax: 212-744-0375; Grace Institute, 1233 Second Ave., 10021. Tel: 212-832-7605; Fax: 212-486-2869.

122—ST. VINCENT DE PAUL (1841) (French), Rev. Gerald E. Murray. In res., Revs. Robert J. Poveromo; John F. Harvey, O.S.F.S.; Harry Tiercelin, (Retired); Augustin Ohua Oguie (Cote d'Ivoire); Gerard Messier, A.A.; Matthew Ugwoji (Nigeria).
Res., 116 W. 24th St., 10011. Tel: 212-243-4727; Fax: 212-675-0528.
Church—123 W. 23rd St., 10011.
Catechesis/Religious Programs—Students 250.

BOROUGH OF BRONX

123—ST. ADALBERT (1898) (Polish). Closed. For inquiries for parish records contact the Chancery.

124—ST. ANGELA MERICI (1899), Revs. Peter Mushi, A.J.; Nestorio B.K. Agirembabazi, A.J.; Deacon Felipe Sin.
Res., 917 Morris Ave., 10451. Tel: 718-293-0984; Fax: 718-293-7325.
Church—E. 163rd St., 10451.
School—(1917), Morris Ave. & 163rd St., 10451. Tel: 718-293-3365; Fax: 718-293-6617. Patrick Kelly, Prin.
Lay Teachers 24; Students 625.
Catechesis/Religious Programs—Students 363.

125—ST. ANN (1927), Rev. Msgr. Robert M. Trainor; Rev. Michael Lipareli. In res., Revs. John Dam Tran; Edwin Emeli (Nigeria).
Res., 3519 Bainbridge Ave., 10467. Tel: 718-547-9350; Fax: 718-547-1718.
School—(1928), Bainbridge Ave. & Gun Hill Rd., 10467. Tel: 718-655-3449; Fax: 718-547-4020. Miss L. DiJusto, Prin.
Students 302.
Catechesis/Religious Programs—Tel: 718-655-3449; Fax: 718-547-2020.
Students 126.

126—ST. ANSELM (1892), Revs. Francisco J. Legarra, O.A.R.; Serafin Pineda, O.A.R.; Dionisio Gutierrez, O.A.R.
Res., 685 Tinton Ave., 10455. Tel: 718-585-8666; Fax: 718-401-6686.
School—(1908), Tel: 718-993-9464; Fax: 718-292-3496. Miss Theresa Lopes, Prin.
Sisters of St. Dominic of Blauvelt 2; Lay Teachers 22; Students 680.
Catechesis/Religious Programs—Tel: 718-585-8542.
Students 720.

127—ST. ANTHONY (1908) (Hispanic), Revs. Joseph J. Kelly; Michael N. Aggrey (Ghana). In res., Rev. Michael J. Allessandro.
Res., 1496 Commonwealth Ave., 10460. Tel: 718-931-4040; 4041; Fax: 718-792-4622.
School—(1931), St. Lawrence Ave. & Mansion St., 10460. Tel: 718-892-1244; Fax: 718-863-0202.
Sisters of Charity of St. Vincent de Paul of NY 1; Lay Teachers 9; Students 230.
Catechesis/Religious Programs—Students 219.
Chapel—Sisters of Charity, 1492 Commonwealth Ave., 10460. Tel: 718-823-1359.

128—ST. ANTHONY (1919) (Italian), Rev. Nicholas F. Milazzo.
Res., 4505 Richardson Ave., 10470. Tel: 718-324-8787; Fax: 718-324-6354.
School—(1953), 4520 Matilda Ave., 10470. Tel: 718-324-5104. Mrs. Roma Barone, Prin.
Lay Teachers 12; Students 202.
Convent—4500 Matilda Ave., 10470.

129—ST. ANTHONY OF PADUA (1903) (African American & Hispanic), Rev. Msgr. Josu Iriondo, Admin.; Rev. Francis Reginald John (St. Lucia).
Res., 832 E. 166th St., 10459. Tel: 718-542-7293; Fax: 718-378-1819. [CEM]
Catechesis/Religious Programs—Students 135.

130—ST. ATHANASIUS (1907), Rev. Msgr. William J. Smith; Rev. Pompilio Alvarez (Spain); Deacon Alejandro Rosado. In res., Rev. Louis R. Gigante.
Res., 878 Tiffany St., 10459. Tel: 718-328-2558; Fax: 718-328-3121.
School—(1913), 830 Southern Blvd., 10459. Tel: 718-542-5161; Fax: 718-542-7584. Marianne Kraft, Prin.
Sisters 2; Lay Teachers 12; Students 370.
Catechesis/Religious Programs—Students 400.

131—ST. AUGUSTINE (1849), Revs. S. Keith Outlaw; Carlos Alberto Zuluaga (Colombia). In res., Revs. Ruben Cammayo (PH); Edmund Okere (Nigeria).
Res., 1183 Franklin Ave., 10456. Tel: 718-893-0072; Fax: 718-861-3080.
Church—E. 167th St., 10456.
School—(1887), 1176 Franklin Ave., 10456. Tel: 718-542-3633; Fax: 718-542-7871. Yvonne Rhem-Tittle, Prin.
Lay Teachers 10; Students 300.

132—ST. BARNABAS (1910), Rev. Msgr. Francis X. Toner; Revs. Rees W. Doughty; Arul Rajan Peter (India); Deacons John Hennessy; Vincent Laurato; Cornelius Manning. In res., Revs. Thomas P. Flynn (Ireland); Cyprian I. Onyeihe (Nigeria).
Res., 409 E. 241st St., 10470. Tel: 718-324-1478; Fax: 718-324-1479.
School—(1912), 415 E. 241st St., 10470. Tel: 718-324-1088; Fax: 718-324-2397.
Lay Teachers 24; Students 757.
High School—High School for Girls, (1924), 425 E. 240th St., 10470. Tel: 718-325-8800; Fax: 718-325-8820.
Sisters 8; Lay Teachers 20; Students 290.
Catechesis/Religious Programs—Tel: 718-324-0865.
Students 250.
Chapel—Annunciation, 1033 McLean Ave., Yonkers, 10704.

133—ST. BENEDICT (1923), Revs. Anthony Sorgie; Thomas Kottoor; Rev. Msgr. Theophilus Nwalo; Rev. Andrew Bielak; Deacons John Simpson; Joseph Forte.
Res., 2969 Otis Ave., 10465-2198. Tel: 718-828-3403; Fax: 718-829-1304.
School—(1923), 1016 Edison Ave., 10465. Tel: 718-829-9557.
Sisters 2; Lay Teachers 24; Students 454.
Catechesis/Religious Programs—Tel: 718-829-1200. Sr. Anne Kelly, D.R.E.
Students 441.
Chapel—St. John, 1082 Edison Ave., 10465.

134—BLESSED SACRAMENT (1927), Rev. Msgr. James E. White; Rev. Juan Moscardo, O.F.M.; Deacon Epi Portalatin.
Res., 1170 Beach Ave., 10472. Tel: 718-892-3214; Fax: 718-892-3907.
School—(1929), 1160 Beach Ave. & 1141 Taylor Ave., 10472. Tel: 718-892-0433; Fax: 718-892-3337. Grace Chemi, Prin.
Lay Teachers 23; Students 504.
Catechesis/Religious Programs—Tel: 718-863-4620.
Students 188.

135—ST. BRENDAN (1908), Rev. Msgr. Patrick J. Boyle; Revs. Michael J. Morrow; Jose Soto, M.D.R. In res., Rev. Paul Hometowu (Ghana).
Res., 333 E. 206th St., 10467. Tel: 718-547-6655; Fax: 718-547-6579.
School—(1912), 268 E. 207th St., 10467. Tel: 718-653-2293. Mrs. Patricia Gatti, Prin.
Sisters of St. Dominic (Sparkill, NY) 1; Lay Teachers 20; Students 635.
Catechesis/Religious Programs—Tel: 718-654-4424.
Students 499.
Chapel—Dominican Sisters, 260 E. 207th St., 10467. Tel: 718-798-2460.

136—ST. CLARE OF ASSISI (1929) (Italian), Revs. Richard Guarnieri; John Voglio, S.D.B.; Deacon Bernie Moran.
Res., 1918 Paulding Ave., 10462. Tel: 718-863-8974; Fax: 718-931-6909.
Church—1027 Rhinelander Ave., 10462.
School—(1951), 1911 Hone Ave., 10461. Tel: 718-892-4080; Fax: 718-239-1007. Sr. Josephine Stabile, Prin.
Sisters 4; Lay Teachers 20; Students 620.
Catechesis/Religious Programs—Tel: 718-829-9624.
Students 180.
Chapel—Bronx, Morningside House Chapel, Tel: 718-409-8200.

137—CHRIST THE KING (1926) (Hispanic - African American), Revs. Fernando A. Hernandez; Aaron Gyamfi-Appiah, C.SS.P. In res.,
Res., 141 Marcy Pl., 10452. Tel: 718-538-5546; Fax: 718-538-3081.
School—Tel: 718-538-5959; Fax: 718-538-6369.
Lay Teachers 26; Students 584.
Catechesis/Religious Programs—Tel: 718-538-5959.
Students 616.

138—ST. DOMINIC (1924) (Italian), Revs. Thomas K. Dicks; S. Anthony Samy (India); Deacon Reynaldo Rosado.
Res., 1739 Unionport Rd., 10462. Tel: 718-828-2424; Fax: 718-823-4450.
School—(1953), 1684 White Plains Rd., 10462. Tel: 718-829-4837; Fax: 718-792-6912. Sr. Josefa Curcio, C.S.J.B., Prin.
Sisters of St. John Baptist 7; Lay Teachers 19; Students 570.
Convent—1710 Unionport Rd., 10462. Tel: 718-824-2580.
Sisters 11.

139—ST. FRANCIS OF ASSISI (1928), Rev. Carlos Lopez Acosta.
Mailing Address: P.O. Box 520013, 10452. Fax: 718-731-6841.
Res., 1544 Shakespeare Ave., 10452. Tel: 718-731-6840; 6841.
Catechesis/Religious Programs—Students 190.

140—ST. FRANCIS OF ASSISI (1949), Revs. Michael P. Morris; James P. Clark. In res., Rev. Thomas P. D'Angelo.
Res., 4343 Baychester Ave., 10466. Tel: 718-994-8736; Fax: 718-994-9460.
Church—4300 Baychester Ave., 10466.
School—Tel: 718-994-4650; Fax: 718-994-6990. Dr. Patrick Taharally, Prin.
Lay Teachers 12; Students 342.

141—ST. FRANCES DE CHANTAL (1927), Rev. Msgr. Leslie J. Ivers; Rev. Msgr. Joseph M. Devlin, Pastor Emeritus; Revs. Donald C. Baker; Epifanio Marcaida (Philippines); Deacon John Murphy.
Res., 190 Hollywood Ave., 10465. Tel: 718-792-5500; Fax: 718-792-1824.
School—(1929), 2962 Harding Ave., 10465. Tel: 718-892-5359; Fax: 718-892-6937. Marie McCarrick, Prin.
Lay Teachers 30; Students 820.
Catechesis/Religious Programs—Students 225.
Convent—198 Hollywood Ave., 10465. Tel: 718-863-2264. Convent of Sisters of Life
Chapel—House of the Holy Family, 2780 Schurz Ave., 10465. Tel: 718-863-9134.

142—ST. FRANCES OF ROME (1898), Revs. Francis J. Corry; John P. Sheehan; Sr. Ellen Hubflitz, O.P., Patoral Assoc. In res., Rev. Bernard Iheoha.
Res., 4307 Barnes Ave., 10466. Tel: 718-324-5340; 5341; Fax: 718-324-5373.
Church—Moore Plaza & E. 236 St., 10466.
School—(1926), 4321 Barnes Ave., 10466. Tel: 718-324-7360; Fax: 718-994-3694. Dina Monti, Prin.; Sr. M. Gregory West, D.B.V.M., D.R.E.
Sisters of the Presentation 2; Lay Teachers 12; Students 250.

143—ST. FRANCIS XAVIER (1928), Revs. Arthur T. Welton; Robert Holick; Sancho E. Garrote (Philippines); Peter D. Gibbons (Ireland); Allam Marreddy (India).
Res., 1703 Lurting Ave., 10461. Tel: 718-892-3330; Fax: 718-931-6890.
School—(1930), 1711 Haight Ave., 10461. Tel: 718-863-0531; Fax: 718-319-1152. Mrs. Angela Deegan, Prin.
Lay Teachers 25; Students 470.
Catechesis/Religious Programs—Students 83.

Chapel—St. Francis Xavier Convent, 1661 Haight Ave., 10461. Tel: 718-892-9466.

144—ST. GABRIEL (1939), Rev. Thomas R. Kelly; Rev. Msgr. Charles J. McManus, Senior Priest; Rev. Msgr. John T. Doherty, Pastor Emeritus; Rev. Myles P. Murphy; Deacon Eugene Burke.
Res., 3250 Arlington Ave., 10463. Tel: 718-548-4470; Fax: 718-548-6451.
Church—235th & Netherland Ave., 10463. Fax: 718-548-0444.
School—590 W. 235th St., 10463. Tel: 718-548-0444; Fax: 718796-2638. Sr. Claire Dandeneau, R.J.M., Prin.
Lay Teachers 11; Students 265.
Catechesis/Religious Programs—Tel: 718-548-6585. Mr. Glenn A. McCarthy, D.R.E.
Students 100.

145—ST. HELENA (1940), Rev. Msgr. Thomas B. Derivan; Revs. Joseph J. O'Shea; Edmundo Gomez; Albert P. Bartlett, S.J.; Joseph Ligory (Sri Lanka); Charles Szivos.
Res., 1315 Olmstead Ave., 10462. Tel: 718-892-3232; Fax: 718-892-3078.
School—(1941), 2050 Benedict Ave., 10462. Tel: 718-892-3234; Fax: 718-892-3924. Richard Meller, Prin.
Sisters of St. Dominic (Sparkill, NY) 2; Lay Teachers 22; Students 615.
High School—Msgr. Scanlan High School, (1949). (Coed) 915 Hutchinson River Pkwy., 10465. Tel: 718-430-0100; Fax: 718-892-8845.
Sisters of St. Dominic (Sparkill, NY) 12; Lay Teachers 32; Students 575.
School—Commercial School, St. Helena's, (1957). (Coed) 955 Hutchinson River Pkwy., 10465. Tel: 718-792-1395; Fax: 718-824-7392.
Sisters of St. Dominic (Sparkill, NY) 2; Lay Teachers 12; Students 235.
Catechesis/Religious Programs—Tel: 718-892-5557.
Students 105.

146—HOLY CROSS (1921), Revs. Aubrey McNeil, O.F.M.; Matthew A. Pravetz, O.F.M.; Thadeus M. Sapio, O.F.M.; Charles Miller, O.F.M., Formation Dir.; Bros. Daniel Murray, O.FM., Vicar; Peter Alheim, O.F.M.; Deacons Jaime A. Bello; Richard Bragg; Juan Rodriguez. In res., Rev. Joseph Kim (Korea).
Res., 600 Soundview Ave., 10473. Tel: 718-893-5550; Fax: 718-378-3655.
School—(1923 and 1955), Randall Ave. & Thieriot Ave., 10473. Tel: 718-842-4492; Fax: 718-842-4052.
Franciscan Sisters of Allegany, NY 4; Lay Teachers 30; Students 580.
Catechesis/Religious Programs—Tel: 718-328-1054.
Students 580.
Chapel—Franciscan Sisters of Allegany, 620 Thieriot Ave., 10473. Tel: 718-842-2615.

147—HOLY FAMILY (1896), Revs. James D. Flanagan; William Goldman, C.SS.R. (Australia); Deacon Dhoel Canals.
Res., 2158 Watson Ave., 10472. Tel: 718-863-9156; Fax: 718-597-5560.
School—(1913), 2169 Blackrock Ave., 10472. Tel: 718-863-7280; Fax: 718-931-8690.
Sisters of St. Agnes 1; Lay Teachers 32; Students 787.
Catechesis/Religious Programs—2169 Black Rock Ave., 10472. Tel: 718-822-8030.
Students 199.
Chapel—Sisters of St. Agnes, 2155 Blackrock Ave., 10472. Tel: 718-828-4488.

148—HOLY ROSARY (1925), Rev. Msgr. Lamont R. Hamilton; Rev. John J. Higgins; Deacon Joseph Solanto. In res., Rev. Gideon G. Wagay (Westminster, England).
Res., 1510 Adee Ave., 10469. Tel: 718-379-4432; 379-4654; Fax: 718-379-9028.
School—(1927; 1955), 1500 Arnow Ave., 10469. Tel: 718-652-1838; Fax: 718-515-9872. Sr. Cathleen Nahon, O.P., Prin.
Sisters 1; Lay Teachers 21; Students 650.
Chapel—Holy Rosary Convent, 2755 Woodhull Ave., 10469. Tel: 718-798-6435.

149—HOLY SPIRIT (1901) (Spanish), Revs. Pascual Cervera, Admin.; Joseph Vijayan (India).
Res., 1940 University Ave., 10453. Tel: 718-583-0120; Fax: 718-583-1444.
School—(1913), 1960 University Ave., 10453. Tel: 718-583-1570.
Lay Teachers 14; Students 357.
Catechesis/Religious Programs—Students 305.

150—IMMACULATE CONCEPTION (1853) (German), Very Rev. Bruce Lewandowski, C.Ss.R.; Revs. Thomas (Martin) Deely, C.Ss.R.; William Gaffney, C.Ss.R.; John McKenna, C.Ss.R.; Daniel Francis, C.Ss.R.; Francis Gargani, C.Ss.R.; Bro. Stephen Lendvay, C.Ss.R.; Deacon Cristobal Rodriguez. In res., Revs. Terrence Moran, C.Ss.R.; John Wirach Ammonpantana, C.Ss.R.; Joseph Maniyangatt, C.S.T.
Res., 389 E. 150th St., 10455. Tel: 718-292-6970; Fax: 718-292-4603.
Perpetual Help Center—294 E. 150th St., 10455. Tel: 718-585-3678; Fax: 718-993-5870.
School—(1854), 378 E. 151st St., 10455. Tel: 718-585-4843; Fax: 718-585-6846.
Sisters of Christian Charity 5; Lay Teachers 22; Students 620.
Catechesis/Religious Programs—Tel: 718-292-6780. Oscar Cruz, D.R.E.
Students 206.
Chapel—Sisters of Christian Charity, 371 E. 150th St., 10455. Tel: 718-585-8981.

151—IMMACULATE CONCEPTION (1903), Revs. John Lo Sasso, O.F.M.Cap.; Peter Napoli, O.F.M.Cap.; Eric Hall, O.F.M.Cap. Pastoral Associates: Bros. Jesu Perez, O.F.M.Cap.; Jose Hernandez, O.F.M.Cap.; Deacon Carlos Mercado.
Res., Capuchin Friary, 754 E. Gun Hill Rd., 10467. Tel: 718-653-2200; Fax: 718-882-0054.
School—Tel: 718-547-3346. Sr. Latecia Aviles, O.B.T., Prin.
Priests 5; Brothers 2; Oblates to the Blessed Trinity 3; Lay Teachers 13; Students 970.
Chapel—Immaculate Conception Convent, 3305 Wallace Ave., 10467.

152—ST. JEROME'S (1869), Revs. John Grange; Carmelo Amantegui, S.J.
Res., 230 Alexander Ave., 10454. Tel: 718-665-5533.
School—(1871), 222 Alexander Ave., 10454.
Lay Teachers 10; Students 267.
Catechesis/Religious Programs—D.R.E.: Sr. Josephin Stabile; Dina Monti.
Students 150.

153—ST. JOAN OF ARC (1949), Rev. Edward Bader; Deacon Ismael Camacho.
Res., 1372 Stratford Ave., 10472. Tel: 718-842-2233; Fax: 718-842-4720.
Catechesis/Religious Programs—Students 225.

154—ST. JOHN'S (1886), Revs. Gerard Cosgayon, O.A.R.; Edward J. Fagan, O.A.R.; Deacon Andrew Rivera. In res., Very Rev. Francis E. Peluso, O.A.R.; Bro. Mario Alvarez, O.A.R.
Res., 3021 Kingsbridge Ave., 10463. Tel: 718-548-1221; Fax: 718-548-7774.
School—(1903), 3143 Kingsbridge Ave., 10463. Tel: 718-548-0255; Fax: 718-548-0864. Sr. Patricia Brito, R.J.M., Prin.
Sisters 3; Lay Teachers 13; Students 350.
Catechesis/Religious Programs—Tel: 718-884-2627.
Students 250.
Convent—3029 Godwin Ter., 10463. Tel: 718-548-4902; 543-2454. Religious of Jesus and Mary

155—ST. JOHN CHRYSOSTOM'S (1899), Revs. Joseph P. O'Meara; John P. Sheehan; Deacon Victor Pino.
Res., 985 E. 167th St., 10459. Tel: 718-542-6164.
School—(1914), 1144 Hoe Ave., 10459. Tel: 718-328-7226; Fax: 718-378-5368. Sr. Mary Elizabeth Mooney, O.P., Prin.
Sisters of St. Dominic (Sparkill, NY) 13; Lay Teachers 18; Students 649.
Catechesis/Religious Programs—Tel: 718-328-3580.
Students 367.

156—ST JOHN NAM (1989) (Korean), Rev. Simon Nam.
Res., 3663 White Plains Rd., 10467. Tel: 718-231-2414; Fax: 718-405-0053.

157—ST. JOHN VIANNEY, CURE OF ARS (1960), Revs. Jesus M. Mena, O.A.R.; Blas Montenegro, O.A.R.; Deacons Al Leasiolagi; Andes Almanzar; Edwin Cruz.
Res., 715 Castle Hill Ave., 10473. Tel: 212-863-4411; Fax: 917-463-3837.
School—2141 Seward Ave., 10473. Tel: 718-892-4400.
Lay Teachers 9; Students 280.

158—ST. JOSEPH (1873) (Spanish & African American), Rev. Rufino Lecumberri.
Res., 1949 Bathgate Ave., 10457. Tel: 718-731-2504; Fax: 718-731-0478.
School—(1905), 1946 Bathgate Ave., 10457. Tel: 718-583-9432; Fax: 718-299-0780. Janine A. Duffy, Prin.
Lay Teachers 14; Students 347.
Catechesis/Religious Programs—Students 59.

159—ST. LUCY (1927), Revs. Robert J. Norris; Neil Kelly; Thomas B. Fenlon; Deacons Wilfredo Miranda; William Bebert. In res., Rev. Msgr. Frederick J. Becker; Rev. James C. Sheehan.
Church—833 Mace Ave., 10467. Tel: 718-882-0710; Fax: 718-882-8876.
School—(1955), 830 Mace Ave., 10467. Tel: 718-882-2203; Fax: 718-547-8351. Dr. Peter A. Mutarelli, Prin.
Lay Teachers 24; Students 621.
Catechesis/Religious Programs—Tel: 718-652-0295.
Students 259.

160—ST. LUKE (1897) (Hispanic-African American), Rev. Msgr. Gerald J. Ryan; Rev. Jose Aguilar (Colombia). Pastoral Assocs.: Mary Kay Louchart; Sharon Joslyn.
Res., 623 E. 138th St., 10454. Tel: 718-665-6677; Fax: 718-665-0898.
School—(1910), 608 E. 139th St., 10454. Tel: 718-585-0380.
Sisters of St. Dominic (Blauvelt) 2; Lay Teachers 16; Students 405.
Catechesis/Religious Programs—Tel: 718-665-8956.
Students 325.
Chapel—St. Luke Convent, 621 E. 138th St., 10454. Tel: 718-292-3016.

161—ST. MARGARET OF CORTONA (1887), Rev. Msgr. John J. Farley; Revs. Robert A. Quarato; Thomas Murphy, S.J. In res., Rev. Robert J. Aufieri.
Res., 6000 Riverdale Ave., 10471. Tel: 718-549-8053; Fax: 718-543-3432.
School—(1926), 452 W. 260th St., 10471. Tel: 718-549-8580; Fax: 718-549-3298. Sr. Dorothy DeYoung, Prin.
Sisters 1; Lay Teachers 14; Students 350.
Catechesis/Religious Programs—Tel: 718-884-9777. Sr. Theresa Sheehan, D.R.E.
Students 204.
Chapel—Bronx, Our Lady of Grace.

162—ST. MARGARET MARY (1923), Revs. Robert P. Arce; Alonso Escobar (Colombia). In res., Revs. Robert A. Jeffers; John Paul Opoku (Ghana).
Res., 1914 Morris Ave., 10453-5904. Tel: 718-299-4233; Fax: 718-583-3726.
School—(1923), 121 E. 177th St., 10453. Tel: 718-731-5905; Fax: 718-731-8924.
Sisters of Mercy of the Americas 3; Lay Teachers 11; Students 350.
Catechesis/Religious Programs—Students 600.

163—ST. MARTIN OF TOURS (1897), Revs. John C. Flynn; Benito Liriano; Deacons Frankie Vazques; Frankie Lopez.
Res., 664 Grote St., 10457. Tel: 718-295-0913.
School—(1926), E. 182nd St. & Crotona Ave., 10457. Tel: 718-733-0347. Sr. M. Cecilia, Prin.
Dominican Sisters (Sparkill, NY) 2; Lay Teachers 11; Students 250.
Catechesis/Religious Programs—Delia Mojica, D.R.E.
Students 350.
Chapel—Dominican Convent, 695 E. 182nd St., 10457.

164—ST. MARY (1866), Rev. John B. Sullivan. In res., Rev. James J. Cunningham.
Res., 650 E. 226th St., 10466. Tel: 718-547-8000; Fax: 718-547-8001.
Church—White Plains Rd., 10466.
School—(1950), 3956 Carpenter Ave., 10466. Tel: 718-547-0500; Fax: 718-547-0530.
Lay Teachers 14; Students 307.
Chapel—Convent, 3961 Carpenter Ave., 10466. Tel: 718-652-2873. School Chapel, E. 224th St., 10466.

165—ST. MARY STAR OF THE SEA (1887), Revs. Robert J. Moore; T. Augustine Badgley; Thomas Myladil, O.C.D. (India); Deacon William J. Mueller.
Res., 595 Minneford Ave., 10464-1118. Tel: 718-885-1440; Fax: 718-885-9498.
Church—600 City Island Ave., 10464.
School—(1931), 580 Minneford Ave., 10464. Tel: 718-885-1527; Fax: 718-885-1552.
Dominican Sisters of Blauvelt 2; Lay Teachers 9; Students 255.
Chapel—Dominican Sisters, 176 Kilroe St., 10464.

166—ST. MICHAEL (1969), Rev. William J. Luciano.
Res., 765 Co-Op City Boulevard, 10475-1601. Tel: 718-671-8050; Fax: 718-320-3776.
Catechesis/Religious Programs—Students 19.

167—NATIVITY OF OUR BLESSED LADY (1924), Rev. Jaime H. Duenas.
Res., Rectory, 1531 E. 233rd St., 10466. Tel: 718-324-3531; Fax: 718-798-0628.
School—(1953), 3893 Dyre Ave., 10466. Tel: 718-324-2188; Fax: 718-324-1128.
Lay Teachers 20; Students 326.
Convent—1534 E. 233rd St., 10466.

168—ST. NICHOLAS OF TOLENTINE (1906), Revs. John F. Dello Russo, O.S.A.; Joseph Tran; William Donnelly, O.S.A.; Mr. James McDonald, Pastoral Assoc. In res., Revs. William J. Wallace, O.S.A.; Russell Ortega, O.S.A.; Oanh Dang, S.V.D.; Bro. Michael Duffy, O.S.A.
Res., 2345 University Ave., 10468. Tel: 718-295-6800; Fax: 718-367-7411.
School—(1907), 2336 Andrews Ave., 10468. Tel: 718-364-5110; Fax: 718-561-3964.
Sisters of St. Dominic of Blauvelt 1; Dominican Sisters of Sparkhill 1; Lay Teachers 16; Students 500.
Catechesis/Religious Programs—Tel: 718-295-6770. Mrs. Gregoria Gomez, D.R.E.
Students 650.

Chapels—Convent of St. Nicholas of Tolentine, 2341 University Ave., 10468. Tel: 718-367-3102; St. Nicholas of Tolentine School Chapel, Tel: 718-364-5110.

169—OUR LADY OF ANGELS (1924), Revs. Robert T. Ritchie; Antonio Aldana (Mexico); Fabian Lopez; Deacon Luis Delgado. In res., Rev. Roland LaFontant (France).
Res., 2860 Webb Ave., 10468. Tel: 718-548-3005; Fax: 718-884-2450.
Church—2860 Sedgwick Ave., 10468.
School—(1928), 2865 Claflin Ave., 10468. Tel: 718-549-3503. Sr. Mary Ann Cleary, Prin.
Sisters of Charity of St. Vincent de Paul 2; Lay Teachers 18; Students 473.
Catechesis/Religious Programs—Students 340.

170—OUR LADY OF THE ASSUMPTION (1923), Revs. Donald M. Dwyer; Jarlath Quinn; Deacon Howard Banker. In res., Rev. Aloysius Thumma, S.T.D.
Res., 1634 Mahan Ave., 10461. Tel: 718-824-5454; Fax: 718-824-5456.
School—(1928), 1617 Parkview Ave., 10461. Tel: 718-829-1706. Barbara S. Kavanagh, Prin.
Sisters 1; Lay Teachers 20; Students 559.
Catechesis/Religious Programs—Tel: 718-904-8464. Patricia Gregory, D.R.E.
Students 439.
Chapel—Convent, 1639 Parkview Ave., 10461. Tel: 718-829-7980.

171—OUR LADY OF GOOD COUNSEL (1969) (Albanian), Revs. Peter Popovich, Admin.; Andrew Nargaj, O.F.M.
Res., Albanian Roman Catholic Center, 4221 Park Ave., 10457. Tel: 718-294-6981. [CEM]

172—OUR LADY OF GRACE (1924), Revs. Walter A. Birkle; Philip J. Caruso; Jose L. Soto, M.D.R. (Colombia).
Res., 3985 Bronxwood Ave., 10466. Tel: 718-652-4817; Fax: 718-652-2996.
School—Tel: 718-547-9918; Fax: 718-547-7602. Denise Rigano, Prin.
Lay Teachers 18; Students 430.

173—OUR LADY OF MERCY (Fordham) (1852-1892), Revs. Lawrence J. Quinn; John Rueda (Colombia); Pablo Rentino (Philippines); Deacon Rolando Nolasco.
Res., 2496 Marion Ave., 10458. Tel: 718-933-4400.
School—(1907), 2512 Marion Ave., 10458. Tel: 718-367-0237.
Lay Teachers 18; Students 310.
Catechesis/Religious Programs—Students 250.
Chapel—Convent, 2473 Valentine Ave., 10458. Tel: 718-367-5558.

174—OUR LADY OF MT. CARMEL (1906) (Italian), Rev. Msgr. John A. Ruvo; Rev. Msgr. Thomas F. Heneghan; Rev. Nikolin Pergjini. In res., Revs. Nicholas F. Basile; Anthony D'Antonio; Mario Bufalini, C.PP.S.
Res., 627 E. 187th St., 10458. Tel: 718-295-3770; Fax: 718-367-2240.
School—(1925), 189th St. & Bathgate Ave., 10458. Tel: 718-295-6080; Fax: 718-329-1269. Gail Davis, Acting Prin.
Lay Teachers 13; Students 288.
Catechesis/Religious Programs—Students 203.
Convent—2410 Hughes Ave., 10458. Tel: 718-329-0390. Suore Missionarie del Catechismo
Sisters 5.
Chapel—Brothers of Holy Cross, Tel: 718-733-8036.

175—OUR LADY OF PITY (1908) (Hispanic), Rev. Matthew Morreale, O.F.M., Guardian & Pastor; Friar Dominic Poirier, O.F.M.
Res., 276 E. 151st St., 10451. Tel: 718-665-3880.

176—OUR LADY OF REFUGE (1923), Rev. Msgr. John J. Jenik.
Res., 290 E. 196th St., 10458. Tel: 718-367-4690; Fax: 718-365-7644. [JC]
School—(1923), 2708 Briggs Ave., 10458. Tel: 718-367-3081; Fax: 718-367-0741.
Lay Teachers 11; Students 345.
Catechesis/Religious Programs—Tel: 718-367-3384.
Students 315.

177—OUR LADY OF SOLACE (1903), Revs. John M. Knapp; Francisco Imperial (Philippines); Thomas Seraphin Parambi, C.S.T. (India).
Res., 731 Morris Park Ave., 10462. Tel: 718-863-3282; Fax: 718-792-4950.
School—(1916), 1804 Holland Ave., 10462. Tel: 718-792-9947; Fax: 718-597-2482.
Religious of the Presentation 2; Lay Teachers 8; Students 324.
Catechesis/Religious Programs—Tel: 718-823-9044.
Students 327.

178—OUR LADY OF VICTORY (1909), Rev. Peter Gavigan.
Res., 1512 Webster Ave., 10457. Tel: 718-583-4044; Fax: 718-583-4764.
Catechesis/Religious Programs—Students 175.

179—OUR SAVIOUR (1912) (Hispanic), Revs. Jose Gabriel Piedrahita, M.X.Y.; Tulio Ramirez, M.X.Y.
Res., 2317 Washington Ave., 10458. Tel: 718-295-9600; Fax: 718-295-9601.

180—SANTA MARIA (1926) (Italian), Revs. Fernando Real, M.Id.; Antimo Fiorillo, Pastor Emeritus; Cristobal Martin, M.Id.
Res., 2352 St. Raymond Ave., 10462. Tel: 718-828-2380; Fax: 718-828-4296.
School—(1951), 1510 Zerega Ave., 10462. Tel: 718-823-3636; Fax: 718-823-7008. Sr. Ellen O,Connor, Prin.
Sisters Apostles of the Sacred Heart 3; Lay Teachers 9; Students 240.
Catechesis/Religious Programs—Students 135.
Chapel—Santa Maria Convent, 1460 Zerega Ave., 10462.

181—ST. PETER AND ST. PAUL (1897), Revs. Vincent A. Resta; Victor Pori; Martin Mejia Gomez.
Res., 833 St. Ann's Ave., 10456. Tel: 718-665-3924.
School—(1911), 838 Brook Ave., 10456. Tel: 718-665-2056.
Sisters 5; Lay Teachers 14; Students 485.
Chapel—Sisters of Charity, 839 St. Ann's Ave., 10456. Tel: 718-292-7057.

182—SS. PHILIP AND JAMES (1949), Rev. Pat F. Rossi, Ph.D.; Sr. Sharon Donohue, R.S.M., Pastoral Assoc.; Deacons Albert V. Welhous; Robert Santana. In res., Rev. Bededict Paul.
Res., 1160 E. 213th St., 10469. Tel: 718-547-2203; Fax: 718-231-8160.
School—(1953), 1160 E. 213th St., 10469. Tel: 718-882-4576; Fax: 718-653-6167.
Sisters of St. Dominic (Blauvelt) 1; Lay Teachers 9; Students 300.
Chapel—Dominican Sisters Convent, 1180 E. 214th St., 10469.

183—ST. PHILIP NERI (1898), Rev. Msgr. Kevin J. Colleran; Revs. Philip Ibasco; Carlos Mullins; Hyacinth Njoku. In res., Rev. Martin Onyebuchi (Nigeria).
Res., 3025 Grand Concourse, 10468. Tel: 718-733-3200; Fax: 718-733-4390.
School—(1913), 3031 Grand Concourse, 10468. Tel: 718-365-8806. Bro. John Casey.
Christian Brothers 1; Ursuline Sisters 2; Lay Teachers 23; Students 670.
Catechesis/Religious Programs—Students 240.
Chapels—Convent of Mount St. Ursula, Marion Ave. & 200th St., 10468. Tel: 718-365-7410; Kolping Residence, Kolping Society, 2916 Grand Concourse, 10468. Tel: 718-733-6119; Ursuline Residence, 2850 Marion Ave., 10468. Tel: 718-295-6094. St. Mary's Hall. (Ursuline) 323 E. 198th St., 10468. Tel: 718-933-9894.

184—ST. PIUS V (1907), Revs. Edward Russell; Adolfo Romero-Rios (Argentina); Deacons Raul Padron; Luis Torres.
Res., 420 E. 145th St., 10454. Tel: 718-665-6642; Fax: 718-665-4007.
School—(1913), 413 E. 144th St., 10454. Tel: 718-665-5075; Fax: 718-665-2987.
Lay Teachers 13; Students 340.
High School—500 Courtlandt Ave., 10454. Tel: 718-292-3636; Fax: 718-402-1704.
Lay Teachers 14; Students 210.
Catechesis/Religious Programs—Students 190.

185—ST. RAYMOND (1842), Rev. Msgr. Charles M. Kavanagh; Revs. George H. Hill; George R. Stewart; Eugene Cahoute, O.P.; Deacons Aldo Preti; Miguel Sepulveda. In res., Revs. Peter Abas; Michael Adeniji; Gideon Wagay.
Res., 1759 Castle Hill Ave., 10462. Tel: 718-792-4044; Fax: 718-863-8509. [CEM 2]
School—(1909), 2380 E. Tremont Ave., 10462. Tel: 718-597-3232; Fax: 718-892-4449. Ann Suydam, Prin.
Sisters 1; Lay Teachers 27; Students 629.
High Schools—(Boys) 2151 St. Raymond Ave., 10462. Tel: 718-824-5050; Fax: 718-863-8808. Bro. Frank Byrne, F.S.C., Prin.
Brothers of the Christian Schools 8; Lay Teachers 55; Students 850; (Girls). Tel: 718-824-4220; Fax: 718-829-3571. Sr. Mary Ann D'Antonio, Prin.
Sisters 3; Lay Teachers 19; Students 281.
Catechesis/Religious Programs—Tel: 718-792-4044, Ext. 238. Mrs. Ann O'Keefe, D.R.E.
Students 414.
Family Outreach Program—1720 Metropolitan Ave., 10462. Tel: 718-792-2087. Bro. Raymond Meagher, F.S.C., Dir.
Chapel—Brothers Residence, 1754 Castle Hill Ave., 10462. Tel: 718-829-1417; Fax: 718-863-8392.
Brothers of the Christian Schools 8.

186—ST. RITA OF CASCIA SHRINE CHURCH (1900) (Spanish), Revs. Antonio Morales; Jose Gregorio Gutierrez.
Res., 448 College Ave., 10451. Tel: 718-585-5900; Fax: 718-585-5901.

187—ST. ROCH (1899) (Spanish), Rev. Francisco Oviedo, O.A.R., Admin.
Res., 525 Wales Ave., 10455. Tel: 718-292-3834; Fax: 718-292-3834.

188—SACRED HEART (1875), Revs. Mark T. Cregan, C.S.C.; Pedro Foschiatti, S.D.B.; Javier Potes, A.A.; Ms. Yolanda Torres, Pastoral Assoc.
Res., 1253 Shakespeare Ave., 10452. Tel: 718-293-2766; Fax: 718-293-1581.
Schools—Primary Division, (1950), 95 W. 168th St., 10452. Tel: 718-293-4288; Fax: 718-293-4886. Joanne Walsh, Prin.
Lay Teachers 15; Students 440; Middle School, (1926), 1248 Nelson Ave., 10452. Tel: 718-293-6040. Bro. Stephen Milan, F.M.S., Prin.
Lay Teachers 16; Students 440.
Catechesis/Religious Programs—Sr. Christina Dougherty, P.B.V.M., D.R.E.
Students 340.
Chapel—St. Eugene, 979 Ogden Ave., 10452. Tel: 718-681-2222.

189—ST. SIMON STOCK (1919), Revs. Michael Kissane, O.Carm., Admin.; David Kearns, O.Carm.
Res., 2191 Valentine Ave., 10457. Tel: 718-367-1251; Fax: 718-933-8822.
Church—East 182nd St. & Ryer Ave., 10457.
School—182nd St. & Valentine Ave., 10457. Tel: 718-367-0453; Fax: 718-733-1441.
Lay Teachers 20; Students 640.
Catechesis/Religious Programs—Students 270.

190—ST. THERESA OF THE INFANT JESUS (1927) (Italian), Revs. Robert F. Grippo; Robert F. Ashman; Rev. Msgr. John L. Guido, Pastor Emeritus; Deacon Anthony P. Cassaneto; Christopher A. Buonocore, Parish Mgr. In res., Rev. Msgr. John G. Woolsey.
Res., 2855 St. Theresa Ave., 10461. Tel: 718-892-1900.
School—(1954), 2872 St. Theresa Ave., 10461. Tel: 718-792-3688; Fax: 718-892-9441. Mr. Malachy Cleary, Prin.
Lay Teachers 19; Students 387.

191—ST. THOMAS AQUINAS (1890), Most Rev. Francisco Garmendia, D.D.; Revs. Fortunato Romero; Lorenzo Ato.
Res., 1900 Crotona Pkwy., 10460. Tel: 718-589-5235; Fax: 718-893-0498.
School—(1907), 1909 Daly Ave., 10460. Tel: 718-893-7600; Fax: 718-378-5531.
Lay Teachers 23; Students 540.
Convent—1899 Daly Ave., 10460.

192—ST. VALENTINE (1891) (Polish), Rev. Msgr. Stanislaus Jablonski.
Res., 810 E. 221st St., 10467. Tel: 718-652-3197.

193—VISITATION (1928), Rev. Msgr. Robert W. Larkin; Rev. Michael Foody, C.S.Sp.; Deacon George McGowan. In res., Rev. Francis P. O'Malley.
Res., 160 Van Cortlandt Park S., 10463. Tel: 718-548-1455; Fax: 718-548-0289.
School—(1932), Putnam Ave. & W. 239th St., 10463. Tel: 718-543-2250; Fax: 718-543-3665.
Priests 2; Sisters 6; Lay Teachers 4; Students 275.
Catechesis/Religious Programs—Students 115.

BOROUGH OF RICHMOND STATEN ISLAND

194—ST. ADALBERT (Elm Park) (1901) (Polish), Rev. Eugene J. Carrella; Deacon Joseph J. Rentkowski.
Res., 337 Morningstar Rd., 10303. Tel: 718-442-8476; Fax: 718-727-1241.
School—(1905), 355 Morningstar Rd., Elm Park, 10303. Tel: 718-442-2020; Fax: 718-447-2012.
Priests 1; Lay Teachers 9; Students 370.
Catechesis/Religious Programs—Students 100.

195—ST. ANN (1914), Rev. Lawrence T. Quinn; Rev. Msgr. Vincent F. Clyne, Pastor Emeritus; Revs. Sylvester P. McGinn; Matthew Eraly (India); Terence O'Rourke, O.S.A.
Res., 101 Cromwell Ave., 10304. Tel: 718-351-0270; Fax: 718-980-4731.
School—(1955), 125 Cromwell Ave., 10304. Tel: 718-351-4343.
Presentation Nuns 1; Lay Teachers 12; Students 352.
Catechesis/Religious Programs—Michael Mazella, D.R.E.
Students 485.

196—ST. ANTHONY (1908), Rev. John J. Wroblewski.
Res., 24 Shelly Ave., 10314. Tel: 718-761-6660; Fax: 718-761-1029.
Church—Victory Blvd., 10314.
Catechesis/Religious Programs—Students 177.

197—ASSUMPTION (1922) (Italian), Rev. Canon John A. Pintabone, K.H.S.
Res., 15 Webster Ave., 10301. Tel: 718-727-4594.

198—ST. BENEDICTA (1925). Closed. For inquiries for parish records contact Our Lady of Mount Carmel.

199—BLESSED SACRAMENT (1910), Rev. Msgr. Francis V. Boyle; Revs. Stephen M. Ryan; Joseph Victor Arenas (Philippines); Michael R. Paradela (Philippines). In res., Rev. Francis A. Naccarato.

Res., 30 Manor Rd., 10310. Tel: 718-442-1581; Fax: 718-442-1398.
Church—Manor Rd. & Forest Ave., 10310.
School—(1917), 830 Delafield Ave., 10310. Tel: 718-442-3090; Fax: 718-442-9654. Sr. Ann McLaughlin, I.H.M., Prin.
Sisters, Servants of the Immaculate Heart of Mary 6; Lay Teachers 20; Students 698.
Catechesis/Religious Programs—Tel: 718-448-0378.
Students 333.

200—ST. CHARLES (1960), Rev. Msgr. Thomas J. Gaffney; Revs. Robert W. Dillon; Albin Roby; Deacons Vincent Brigande; Michael Calafiore.
Res., 644 Clawson St., 10306. Tel: 718-987-2670; Fax: 718-987-7950.
School—Tel: 718-987-0200.
Sisters of St. Dominic (Blauvelt) 1; Lay Teachers 24; Students 827.
Catechesis/Religious Programs—Tel: 718-979-6800.
Students 500.

201—ST. CHRISTOPHER (1926) (Italian-Irish), Rev. Msgr. Kenneth A. Gerathy; Rev. Michael A. Arputham.
Res., 130 Midland Ave., 10306. Tel: 718-351-2452; Fax: 718-351-1174.
School—(1930), 15 Lisbon Pl., 10306. Tel: 718-351-0902; Fax: 718-351-0975. Catherine Mizzi-Gili, Prin.
Lay Teachers 17; Students 335.
Catechesis/Religious Programs—Tel: 718-668-0048.
Students 209.

202—ST. CLARE (1921), Rev. Msgr. Joseph P. Murphy; Revs. Michael W. Cichon; Matthew J. Furey; Deacons Richard Mitchell; Nunzio Sorrentino.
Res., 110 Nelson Ave., 10308. Tel: 718-984-7873; Fax: 718-966-8420.
School—151 Lindenwood Rd., 10308. Tel: 718-984-7091. Sr. Rosemary Ward, Prin.
Sisters Religious of the Presentation 2; Lay Teachers 20; Students 703.
Catechesis/Religious Programs—Tel: 718-948-4829. Mrs. Virginia Tannacore, D.R.E.
Students 2,000.

203—ST. CLEMENT (1910), Rev. Msgr. Nicholas J. Soares; Revs. Manuel I. Rojas (Peru); John D'Cunha (India).
Res., 207 Harbor Rd., 10303. Tel: 718-442-1688; Fax: 718-442-4689.
Church—126 Van Pelt Ave., 10303.
Catechesis/Religious Programs—Tel: 718-727-6442.
Students 450.

204—HOLY CHILD (1966), Revs. Thomas P. Devery; Philip T. Persico; Emmanuel Nwogwugwu; Renato B. Cruz.
Res., 4747 Amboy Rd., 10312. Tel: 718-356-5890; Fax: 718-356-5995.
Preschool Office—4747 Amboy Rd., 10312. Tel: 718-356-5159; Fax: 718-356-1933.
School—School of Religion, Tel: 718-356-5277; Fax: 718-227-0898.
Lay Teachers 116; Students 1,200.

205—HOLY FAMILY (1966), Rev. John Hynes, Admin.; Rev. Msgr. Thomas Sandi; Revs. Patrick N. Nsionu; Henry Gentile, C.S.; Rev. Msgr. Francis J. Glynn, Pastor Emeritus; Rev. Msgr. Daniel J. Keehan, Pastor Emeritus.
Mailing Address: 366 Watchogue Rd., 10314. Tel: 718-761-6663; Fax: 718-982-0287. [JC]
School—School of Religion, (1967). (Elementary & High School) 330 Watchogue Rd., 10314. Tel: 718-761-1598.
Sisters 2; Lay Teachers 54; Students 540.
Catechesis/Religious Programs—Students 550.
Convent—85 Delmore St., 10314. Tel: 718-698-3118.

206—HOLY ROSARY (1927), Rev. Msgr. Richard J. Guastella; Revs. Albin Reddy Thumma; Stephen G. Challman; Deacon Rosario Tirella. In res., Rev. Percy Joseph Raj, O.F.M., Chap.
Res., 80 Jerome Ave., 10305. Tel: 718-727-3360; Fax: 718-876-6183.
School—(1955) (Grades PreK-8) 100 Jerome Ave., 10305. Tel: 718-447-1195; Fax: 718-815-5862. Diane R. Murphy, Prin.; Joanne DelGeorge, Asst. Prin.
Lay Teachers 23; Students 665.
Catechesis/Religious Programs—Tel: 718-273-6695. Sr. Catherine Shanahan, S.N.D.deN., D.R.E.
Students 436.

207—IMMACULATE CONCEPTION (1887), Rev. Peter J. Byrne. In res., Rev. Peter J. West.
Res., 128 Targee St., 10304. Tel: 718-447-2165; Fax: 718-447-4835.
School—(1908), 104 Gordon St., 10304. Tel: 718-447-7018; Fax: 718-447-7018. Ms. Kathleen Curatolo, Prin.
Sisters 2; Lay Staff 8; Students 220.
Catechesis/Religious Programs—Students 130.
Chapel—Bayley Seton Hospital, Bay St., 10304. Tel: 718-390-6000. Rev. Edward J. Datty, S.A.

208—ST. JOHN THE BAPTIST DE LA SALLE (1900), Rev. Peter J. Byrne, Admin.
Res., 128 Targee St., 10304. Tel: 718-447-2165; Fax: 718-447-4835.
Church—76 Jackson St., 10304.

209—ST. JOHN NEUMANN (1982), Revs. James Malley; Mario Ramirez, M.S.C.
Res., 1380 Arthur Kill Rd., 10312. Tel: 718-984-8535; Fax: 718-689-2498.
Catechesis/Religious Programs—Tel: 718-966-7327.
Students 468.

210—ST. JOSEPH (1902) (Italian), Rev. Msgr. John T. Servodidio.
Parish Office: 463 Tompkins Ave., 10305. Tel: 718-816-0047; Fax: 718-816-4529.
Res., 171 St. Mary's Ave., 10305.
Church—466 Tompkins Ave., 10305.
School—139 St. Mary's Ave., 10305. Tel: 718-447-7686. Linda Bilotti, Prin.
Lay Teachers 11; Students 278.
Catechesis/Religious Programs—Students 72.

211—ST. JOSEPH, ST. THOMAS (1848), Rev. Msgr. Peter G. Finn; Revs. Richard Veras; Evangelio R. Suaybaguio (Philippines); Francisco H. Lanzaderas (Philippines); Deacon Arthur Fama.
Res., 6135 Amboy Rd., 10309. Tel: 718-984-4572; Fax: 718-948-3885. [CEM]
School—Tel: 718-356-3344; Fax: 718-227-9531. Theresa Simmonds, Prin.
Lay Teachers 14; Students 350.
Catechesis/Religious Programs—Tel: 718-984-1156.
Students 1,326.

212—ST. MARGARET MARY (1926), Rev. Robert J. Navins. In res., Rev. Thomas M. Karikilate (India).
Res., 560 Lincoln Ave., 10306. Tel: 718-351-2612; Fax: 718-987-0446.
School—(1925), 556 Lincoln Ave., 10306. Tel: 718-351-4778; Fax: 718-351-3786. Sr. Barbara Helco, Prin.
Sisters, Religious of the Presentation 1; Lay Teachers 8; Students 232.
Catechesis/Religious Programs—Tel: 718-987-4388.
Students 141.

213—ST. MARY (1852), Revs. Victor J. Buebendorf; Peter Selvaraj.
Res., 1101 Bay St., 10305. Tel: 718-727-0671; Fax: 718-815-7393. [CEM]
School—(1853), 1124 Bay St., 10305. Tel: 718-447-1842; Fax: 718-447-0986. Virginia Savarese, Prin.
Lay Teachers 10; Students 260.
Catechesis/Religious Programs—Students 90.

214—ST. MARY OF THE ASSUMPTION (1853), Revs. William Harder, Admin.; Hilary Aidoo.
Res., 2230 Richmond Ter., 10302. Tel: 718-442-6372; Fax: 718-448-2159. [CEM]
Catechesis/Religious Programs—Students 96.
Mission—New York, Richmond Co., Christ the King, 182 Park Ave., 10302.

215—ST. MICHAEL (1922), Rev. Msgr. Nicholas J. Soares; Revs. Manuel I. Rojas (Peru); John D'Cunha (India).
Res., 207 Harbor Rd., 10303. Tel: 718-442-1688; Fax: 718-442-4689.
Church—211-213 Harbor Rd., 10303.
Catechesis/Religious Programs—Tel: 718-727-6442.
Students 450.

216—OUR LADY OF GOOD COUNSEL (1898), Revs. Stephen J. Baker, O.S.A., Pastor; Joseph F. Girone, O.S.A., Prior; Augustus C. Sandmann, O.S.A.; Robert F. Andrews, O.S.A.; John P. Hennessy, O.S.A.; Deacons Arthur W. Eccleston; Walter Sweeney. In res., Rev. Arthur D. Johnson, O.S.A.
Res., 10 Austin Pl., 10304. Tel: 718-447-1503; Fax: 718-447-7361.
School—(1923), 42 Austin Pl., 10304. Tel: 718-447-7260; Fax: 718-815-7262. Mrs. Frances Santangelo, Prin.
Lay Teachers 11; Students 285.
Catechesis/Religious Programs—Sr. Patricia Flattery, D.R.E.
Students 223.

217—OUR LADY HELP OF CHRISTIANS (1898), Revs. Edmund P. Connors; Abraham B. Dominic (Sri Lanka); Deacons Edward J. Wetherall; John Singler.
Res., 7396 Amboy Rd., 10307. Tel: 718-317-9772; Fax: 718-317-0038.
School—(1910 and 1955), 23 Summit St., 10307. Tel: 718-984-1360; Fax: 718-966-9356. Mrs. Nancy Lucas, Prin.
Lay Teachers 12; Students 287.
Catechesis/Religious Programs—Tel: 718-356-3888.
Students 700.

218—OUR LADY OF MT. CARMEL-ST. BENEDICTA (1913), Revs. Thomas N. Cerulo, O.SS.T.; Daniel Houde, O.SS.T. In res., Rev. Joseph F. Lupo, O.SS.T.
Res., 1265 Castleton Ave., 10310. Tel: 718-442-3411; Fax: 718-442-3997.
School—285 Clove Rd., 10310. Tel: 718-981-5131.
Catechesis/Religious Programs—Students 275.

219—OUR LADY, QUEEN OF PEACE (1922), Revs. Robert I. Gannon; John A. DeBellis; John J. Sheehan; Deacon Ross Calimano. In res., Rev. James Garisto.
Res., 90 Third St., 10306. Tel: 718-351-1093.
School—(1924), 22 Steele Ave., 10306. Tel: 718-351-0370. Sr. Mary Regina Gibbons, Prin.
Sisters of the Presentation 1; Lay Teachers 17; Students 600.
Catechesis/Religious Programs—Tel: 718-979-0989.
Students 570.
Mission—New Dorp Beach, Richmond Co., Our Lady of Lourdes, Cedar Grove Ave., 10306.
Chapel—St. Therese of the Child Jesus, 62 Cloister Pl., 10306. Tel: 718-351-0209.

220—OUR LADY OF PITY (1923) (Italian), Rev. Msgr. Philip J. Franceschini; Rev. John E. Mercer; Rev. Msgr. Robert R. Mazziotta, Pastor Emeritus.
Res., 1616 Richmond Ave., 10314. Tel: 718-761-5421; Fax: 718-983-6225.
Catechesis/Religious Programs—Tel: 718-477-5999.
Students 602.

221—OUR LADY STAR OF THE SEA (1916), Rev. Msgr. Jeffrey Conway; Revs. Eric Rapaglia; Angelo Palermo, S.A.C.; Dr. Patrick Del Zoppo, Pastoral Assoc.; Mrs. Debra Emigholz, Business Mgr.
Res., 5371 Amboy Rd., Huguenot Park, 10312. Tel: 718-984-0593; Fax: 718-984-5203.
School—(1958), 5411 Amboy Rd., 10312. Tel: 718-984-5750.
Sisters 1; Lay Teachers 27; Students 960.
Catechesis/Religious Programs—5411 Amboy Rd., 10312. Tel: 718-984-1885. Mrs. Cathy Alegre, D.R.E.
Students 1,225.

222—ST. PATRICK (1862), Rev. Msgr. John M. McCarthy; Rev. John C. Ablino; Deacon Joseph Hooghuis.
Parish Office: 3560 Richmond Rd., 10306. Tel: 718-979-4227; Fax: 718-979-7637.
Res., 53 St. Patrick's Pl., 10306. Tel: 718-351-0044; Fax: 718-351-0824.
School—(1919), 3560 Richmond Rd., 10306. Tel: 718-979-8815; Fax: 718-979-4984. Sr. Mary Ferro, S.S.D., Prin.
Sisters 3; Lay Teachers 22; Students 590.
Catechesis/Religious Programs—Tel: 718-979-1272.
Students 437.

223—ST. PAUL (1924), Rev. Vincent Bartley.
Res. & Mailing Address: 145 Clinton Ave., 10301. Tel: 718-447-6362; Fax: 718-720-0106.
School—(1954), 129 Clinton Ave., 10301. Tel: 718-447-5774; Fax: 718-447-5881. Ms. Mary Chiapperino, Prin.
Lay Teachers 9; Students 200.
Catechesis/Religious Programs—Students 210.
Christian Brothers Residence: 148 Cassidy Pl., 10301.

224—ST. PETER (1839), Rev. Msgr. James J. Dorney; Rev. John T. Thenen.
Res., 53 St. Mark's Pl., 10301. Tel: 718-727-2672; Fax: 718-720-9269. [CEM]
School—300 Richmond Ter., 10301. Tel: 718-447-1796; Fax: 718-447-4240. Mrs. Lisa Moudatsos, Prin.
Lay Teachers 14; Students 323.
High Schools—Boys High School, 200 Clinton Ave., 10301. Tel: 718-447-1676; Fax: 718-447-4027. Mr. John Fodera, Prin.; Bro. James Kelly, F.S.C., Pres.
Brothers of the Christian Schools 3; Lay Teachers 31; Students 700; Girls High School, Tel: 718-447-0304; Fax: 718-447-0832. Miss Florence Bricker, Prin.
Lay Teachers 12; Students 174. St. Joseph, Brothers' House, Tel: 718-447-2815.
Catechesis/Religious Programs—Students 32.

225—ST. RITA (1921), Revs. John F. Reardon; Austin E. Titus.
Res., 281 Bradley Ave., 10314. Tel: 718-698-3746; Fax: 718-698-3791.
School—(1922), 30 Wellbrook Ave., 10314. Tel: 718-961-2504.
Dominican Sisters 1; Lay Teachers 16; Students 560.
Catechesis/Religious Programs—Students 471.
Chapel—Dominican Sisters. (Roman Congregation of St. Dominic) 61 Wellbrook Ave., 10314. Tel: 718-761-1171.

226—St. Roch (1922), Revs. Alfred J. Pucci; John Boyle. In res., Rev. G. David Sears (SY).
Res., 602 Richmond Ave., 10302. Tel: 718-442-4755; Fax: 718-981-4455.
School—465 Villa Ave., 10302. Tel: 718-448-2424. Sr. Mary Patricia, Prin.
Sisters of St. John the Baptist 3; Lay Teachers 9; Students 297.
Catechesis/Religious Programs—Students 120.

227—Sacred Heart (1875), Rev. James E. Burke; Rev. Msgr. Andrew F. Quinn, Pastor Emeritus; Revs. Charles Oduro; Thomas Kallumady.
Res., 981 Castleton Ave., 10310. Tel: 718-442-0058; Fax: 718-816-8006.
School—(1875), 301 N. Burgher Ave., 10310. Tel: 718-442-0347; Fax: 718-440-6978. Mrs. Zoilita M. Herrera, Prin.
Lay Teachers 21; Students 548.
Catechesis/Religious Programs—Tel: 718-448-1536.
Students 285.

228—St. Stanislaus Kostka (1923) (Polish), Revs. Marek Suchocki, J.C.D., M.Th (Poland); Pawel Sochacki, M.Th (Poland).
Res., 109 York Ave., 10301. Tel: 718-447-3937; Fax: 718-815-5733.

229—St. Sylvester (1921) (Irish-Italian), Revs. Arthur A. Golino; Peter A. Miqueli.
Res., 854 Targee St., 10304-4517. Tel: 718-727-4639; Fax: 718-273-2950.
School—(1930), 884 Targee St., 10304. Tel: 718-442-4938; Fax: 718-442-8177. Nancy Bushman, Prin.
Lay Teachers 10; Students 290.
Catechesis/Religious Programs—Tel: 718-442-4949.
Students 240.

230—St. Teresa (1926), Revs. William J. Boldt; John J. O'Hara.
Res., 1634 Victory Blvd., 10314. Tel: 718-442-5412; Fax: 718-442-9041.
School—(1955), 1632 Victory Blvd., 10314. Tel: 718-448-9650.
Sisters of the Presentation 2; Lay Teachers 18; Students 600.
Catechesis/Religious Programs—Tel: 718-981-2632.
Students 425.
Mission—Staten Island, Staten Island Co., St. Nicholas, Northern Blvd., 10301.
Chapel—St. Nicholas, La Bau Ave. & Northern Blvd., 10314.

OUTSIDE THE CITY OF NEW YORK

Amenia, Dutchess Co., Immaculate Conception (1868), Rev. John L. Durkin; Deacon David Weinstein; Rev. Emeka Godfrey Amanchukwu (Nigeria).
Res., 4 Lavelle Rd., Box 109, 12501. Tel: 845-373-8193; Fax: 845-373-8194. [CEM]
Catechesis/Religious Programs—Students 193.
Mission—Millerton, Dutchess Co., St. Patrick, Church St., Millerton, 12546. [CEM]

Ardsley, Westchester Co., Our Lady of Perpetual Help (1929), Revs. Philip J. Gagliano; Robert J. Duane, Pastor Emeritus.
Res., One Cross Rd., 10502. Tel: 914-693-0030; Fax: 914-693-5332.
Catechesis/Religious Programs—Tel: 914-693-0037.
Students 373.

Armonk, Westchester Co., St. Patrick (1966), Rev. John F. Quinn; Rev. Msgr. Walter L. Schroeder, Pastor Emeritus.
Res., 29 Cox Ave., P.O. Box 6, 10504. Tel: 914-273-9724.
Catechesis/Religious Programs—Tel: 914-273-8226. Mrs. Ann O'Sullivan, D.R.E.
Students 420.

Bangall, Dutchess Co., Immaculate Conception (1919), Rev. Richard O'Gorman.
Res., Hunns Lake Rd., P.O. Box 623, 12506. Tel: 914-868-1923; Fax: 914-868-1593. [CEM]
Catechesis/Religious Programs—Students 28.
Mission—Clinton Corners, Dutchess Co., St. Joseph, (1883) Clinton Corners, 12514.

Barrytown, Dutchess Co., Sacred Heart. Closed. Parochial records at St. Christopher, Red Hook.

Beacon, Dutchess Co., St. Joachim (1853), Revs. Joseph F. Bisignano, Admin.; Thaddeus Obba (Nigeria).
Res., 61 Leonard St., 12508. Tel: 845-831-0377; Fax: 845-831-9504. [CEM 2]
Church—57 Leonard St., 12508.
School—St. Joachim/St. John, (Grades PreK-8) 60 Liberty St., 12508. Tel: 845-831-6550; Fax: 845-831-8845.
Lay Teachers 10; Students 221.
Catechesis/Religious Programs—Tel: 845-838-5376.
Students 102.

St. John Evangelist (1887), Revs. Joseph J. Bisignano; Nimal Mendis; Thomas Kallumady.
Res., 31 Willow St., P.O. Box 549, 12508. Tel: 845-831-0422; Fax: 845-831-1009.
School—Twinned with St. Joachim, Beacon.
Catechesis/Religious Programs—Tel: 914-831-3638; Fax: 914-831-1009.
Students 311.

Bedford, Westchester Co., St. Patrick (1928), Rev. Msgr. James T. Gorman; Rev. John B. Kauta (Uganda).
Res., 7 Pound Ridge Rd., 10506. Tel: 914-234-3668; Fax: 914-234-9126, Ext. 7.
School—(1956), State Rd., 10506. Tel: 914-234-7914. Mrs. Elizabeth Frangella, Prin.
Lay Teachers 11; Students 230.
Catechesis/Religious Programs—Tel: 914-234-3775.
Students 400.

Blauvelt, Rockland Co., St. Catharine (1868), Rev. Msgr. William J. Belford; Rev. Herbert P. Degaris; Deacon John C. Kelleher.
Res., 523 Western Hwy., 10913. Tel: 845-359-0542; Fax: 845-365-2387. [CEM]
School—(1957), 517 Western Hwy., 10913. Tel: 845-359-4330. Mr. Philip Gorrasi, Prin.
Sisters of St. Dominic of Blauvelt 1; Lay Teachers 10; Students 280.
Catechesis/Religious Programs—Tel: 914-359-4014. Sr. Marie Murphy, O.P., D.R.E.
Students 620.

Brewster, Putnam Co., St. Lawrence O'Toole (1878), Revs. Robert J. DeJulio; John A. Bida; Deacons Benjamin Wallace; Mark Shkreli; John Baffa.
Res., 31 Prospect St., 10509. Tel: 845-279-2021; Fax: 845-279-7441. [CEM]
School—(1928), Eastview Ave., 10509. Tel: 845-279-5164; Fax: 845-279-8165. Mrs. Sharyn O'Leary, Prin.
Lay Teachers 13; Students 300.
Catechesis/Religious Programs—Tel: 845-279-6098; Fax: 845-279-6098. Mrs. Nancy Breznicky, D.R.E.
Students 680.

Briarcliff Manor, Westchester Co., St. Theresa (1926), Rev. Msgr. James K. Vaughey; Rev. L. Praxid DeSilva (Sri Lanka).
Res., 1394 Pleasantville Rd., 10510. Tel: 914-941-1646; Fax: 914-944-9503.
School—Tel: 914-762-1050; Fax: 914-941-9483.
Sisters 2; Lay Teachers 8; Students 200.
Catechesis/Religious Programs—Tel: 914-923-3286.
Students 450.
Mission—Millwood, Westchester Co., Our Lady of the Wayside, Rte. 100, 10546.

Bronxville, Westchester Co., St. Joseph (1906), Rev. Msgr. James F. Doyle; Revs. William A. Kelleher; Carmine J. Rita. In res., Revs. Dawson Ambosta; Paul Vezhaparambil, C.M.I.
Res., 15 Cedar St., 10708. Tel: 914-337-1660; Fax: 914-337-1342.
School—(1951), 30 Meadow Ave., 10708. Tel: 914-337-0261; Fax: 914-395-1192. Nancy Langehennig, Prin.
Lay Teachers 28; Students 265.
Catechesis/Religious Programs—28 Meadow Ave., 10708. Tel: 914-337-6383; Fax: 914-337-1342.
Students 523.

Buchanan, Westchester Co., St. Christopher (1929), Rev. Msgr. Donald W. Hendricks; Rev. Leonard J. DiNola; Deacon Ronald J. Schlitt.
Res., 94 Albany Post Rd., 10511. Tel: 914-737-1046; Fax: 914-737-9320.
Catechesis/Religious Programs—Tel: 914-737-1437.
Students 244.

Callicoon, Sullivan Co., Holy Cross (1870), Rev. Ignatius E. Smith, O.F.M.
Res., 12723. Tel: 914-887-5450; Fax: 914-887-5873. [CEM][JC 2]
Catechesis/Religious Programs—Students 101.
Mission—Long Eddy, Sullivan Co., St. Patrick, c/o P.O. Box 246, 12723.
Chapel—Callicoon, Holy Cross Rectory.

Carmel, Putnam Co., St. James the Apostle (1913), Revs. Joseph J. Faraone; Vincent Howley; Godwin Nnamani; Joseph Xavier Arokiasamy; Deacons James Attridge; Charles T. Borsavage; Tony Guerio.
Res., 14 Gleneida Ave., 10512. Tel: 914-225-2079; Fax: 914-225-5566.
School—(1954), Tel: 914-225-9365; Fax: 914-228-2859.
Lay Teachers 15; Students 369.
Catechesis/Religious Programs—Tel: 914-225-6504.
Students 1,528.
Mission—Lake Carmel, Putnam Co., Our Lady of the Lake, Noonan Dr., 10512. Tel: 914-228-1235.

Centerville, Ulster Co., St. John the Evangelist (1886), Rev. Msgr. William E. Williams; Deacon Edwin R. Topple. In res., Rev. James W. Derrenbacher.
Res., 915 Rte. 212, Saugerties, 12477. Tel: 845-246-9581; Fax: 845-246-9582.
Office: Tel: 845-246-9581.
Catechesis/Religious Programs—Students 234.

Chappaqua, Westchester Co., St. John and St. Mary (1922), Rev. Msgr. Timothy A. McDonnell; Rev. Kenneth E. O'Toole, (Retired); Deacons Thomas Morrette; Louis Santore; Charles Devlin; Mrs. Joan Ferroni, Pastoral Assoc. In res., Rev. John A. Vigilanti.
Res., 15 St. John's Pl., 10514. Tel: 914-238-3274; Fax: 914-238-3354.
Catechesis/Religious Programs—30 Poillon Rd., 10514. Tel: 914-238-3696. Sr. Margaret Breslin, O.P., D.R.E.
Students 531.

Chester, Orange Co., St. Columba (1875), Revs. Thomas J. Curley; Salvatore Paterno; Joseph Doron; Waclaw Swierzbolek; Deacon Frank Carlino.
Res., 27 High St., 10918. Tel: 845-469-2108; Fax: 845-469-6165. [CEM]
Catechesis/Religious Programs—Tel: 914-469-9503.
Students 334.
Station—Greycourt, Camp La Guardia. (NYC Homeless Shelter). Tel: 914-469-6200.

Cold Spring-on-Hudson, Putnam Co., Our Lady of Loretto (1834), Rev. Frederick Sullivan; Deacon John O'Reilly.
Res., 24 Fair St., Cold Spring, 10516. Tel: 845-265-3718; Fax: 845-265-4309.
Catechesis/Religious Programs—Tel: 845-265-2594. Sr. Ann Teresa Nagy, S.A., D.R.E.
Students 281.
Mission—Garrison, Putnam Co., St. Joseph, Garrison, 10524.

Congers, Rockland Co., St. Paul (1896), Rev. Msgr. Thomas E. Gilleece; Rev. Mark T. Rossetti; Deacons Dominic Buonocore; John W. McSherry; James Gorman.
Res., 82 Lake Rd. W., 10920. Tel: 914-268-4464; Fax: 914-268-6790. [CEM]
School—365 Kings Hwy., Valley Cottage, 10989. Tel: 914-268-6506; Fax: 914-268-1809. Sr. Stephen Gerard, O.P., Prin.
Sisters 3; Lay Teachers 16; Students 408.
Catechesis/Religious Programs—Tel: 914-268-5442.
Students 734.
Chapel—Congers, Sisters' Convent and School.

Cornwall-on-Hudson, Orange Co., St. Thomas of Canterbury (1870), Revs. Bernard P. Heter; John P. McDonagh, P.V.
Res., 10 Second St., 12520. Tel: 914-534-2547; Fax: 914-534-1357. [CEM]
School—(1913), Hudson St., 12520. Tel: 914-534-2019. Sr. Ann Cecilia Regan, O.P., Prin.
Sisters 2; Lay Teachers 8; Students 253.
Catechesis/Religious Programs—Tel: 914-534-9393.
Students 520.
Chapel—St. Thomas' Convent, 336 Hudson St., 12520. Tel: 914-534-4215.

Cortlandt Manor, Westchester Co., St. Columbanus (Van Cortlandtville) (1950), Rev. Msgr. Patrick J. Keenan; Deacon John J. Coppola. In res., Rev. George Spiteri (Malta).
Res., 122 Oregon Rd., 10567. Tel: 914-737-4705; Fax: 914-736-7476.
School—122 Oregon Rd., 10567. Tel: 914-739-1200; Fax: 914-739-1109.
Sisters 1; Lay Teachers 9; Students 305.
Catechesis/Religious Programs—Tel: 914-739-2441.
Students 650.
Mission—Lake Peekskill, Putnam Co., North American Martyrs, 55 Oscawana Lake Rd., Putnam Valley, 10579. Tel: 914-528-6433.

Holy Spirit (1966), Rev. Thomas P. Kiely; Rev. Msgr. William J. McMahon, Ph.D., (Retired).
Res., 1969 Crompond Rd., 10567-4113. Tel: 914-737-2316; Fax: 914-737-6882.
Catechesis/Religious Programs—Tel: 914-734-9243.
Students 665.
Chapel—Cortlandt Manor.

Crestwood, Westchester Co., Church of the Annunciation (1931), Rev. Msgr. James R. Moore; Revs. William J. Damroth, III; Cyril Owambo (Kenya); Deacon Albert Conner.
Res., 470 Westchester Ave., 10707. Tel: 914-779-7345; 779-7542; Fax: 914-961-5688.

School—(1943), 465 Westchester Ave., 10707. Tel: 914-337-8760; Fax: 914-337-8878. Sr. Anne Massell, P.B.V.M., Prin.
Sisters 5; Lay Teachers 21; Students 480.
Catechesis/Religious Programs—Tel: 914-779-2374.
Students 70.

Croton Falls, Westchester Co., St. Joseph (1845), Revs. James E. Borstelmann; Jude Aquwa (Nigeria); Sr. Mary L. Mazza, C.N.D., Pastoral Assoc.; Maureen A. Lux, Business Mgr.
Res., 10 Croton Falls Rd., 10519. Tel: 914-277-3765; 277-3877; Fax: 914-277-1823.
School—(1949), Tel: 914-277-3783; Fax: 914-277-3238.
Lay Teachers 9; Students 145.
Catechesis/Religious Programs—14 Croton Falls Rd., 10519. Tel: 914-276-1067. Sr. Anne Egan, R.J.M., D.R.E.
Students 1,058.
Missions—Goldens Bridge, Westchester Co., St. Michael, Park Ave., Goldens Bridge, 10526.; North Salem, Westchester Co., St. John, Rte. 116, North Salem, 10560. [CEM]

Croton-on-Hudson, Westchester Co., Holy Name of Mary (1874), Revs. Kenneth A. Jesselli; Matthew Yatkauskas; Deacon Albert Mazza.
Res., 110 Grand St., 10520. Tel: 914-271-4797; Fax: 914-271-6841.
Catechesis/Religious Programs—114 Grand St., 10520. Tel: 914-271-4254.
Students 408.
Mission—Harmon, Westchester Co., Church of the Good Shepherd, Benedict Blvd. and Young Ave., 10520.

Dobbs Ferry, Westchester Co., Sacred Heart (1862), Sr. Connie Koch, O.P., Pastoral Assoc.; Deacons Patrick D. Troy; John J. Kollar.
Res., 18 Bellewood Ave., 10522. Tel: 914-693-0119; Fax: 914-693-3408.
Church—Broadway and Ashford Ave., 10522.
Catechesis/Religious Programs—Students 245.

Our Lady of Pompeii (1922) (Italian), Rev. Carmelo Glavina, Admin.; Deacon N. Anthony Barbieri.
Res., 95 Palisade St., 10522. Tel: 914-693-1839.

Dover Plains, Dutchess Co., St. Charles Borromeo (1859), Rev. Msgr. Edward Barry.
Res., P.O. Box 9, Mill St., 12522. Tel: 914-877-9934; Fax: 914-877-9936. [CEM]
Catechesis/Religious Programs—Tel: 914-832-6989.
Students 362.
Mission—Wingdale, Dutchess Co., Our Lady of Solace Mission.

East Kingston, Ulster Co., St. Colman (1904), Rev. John C. McGuire.
Res., 18 Brigham St., Kingston, 12401. Tel: 914-336-8237; Fax: 914-382-1488.

Ellenville, Ulster Co., St. Mary and St. Andrew (1850), Rev. Msgr. Robert P. Hickey.
Res., 137 S. Main St., 12428. Tel: 914-647-6080.
Mission—Kerhonkson, Ulster Co., Our Lady of Lourdes, Kerhonkson, 12446.

Elmsford, Westchester Co., Our Lady of Mt. Carmel (1904), Rev. Vincent A. Lancellotti; Deacon Peter E. Reynolds.
Res., 59 E. Main St., 10523. Tel: 914-592-6789; Fax: 914-592-7526.
School—(1929), E. Main St., 10523. Tel: 914-592-7575; Fax: 914-345-1591.
Sisters of Divine Compassion 4; Lay Teachers 7; Students 226.
Catechesis/Religious Programs—Tel: 914-592-4280.
Students 101.

Fishkill, Dutchess Co., Church of St. Mary, Mother of the Church (1953), Rev. Msgr. Joseph A. Martin; Revs. Kent Wilson; Rick De La Pena; Deacon Martin Kazimir.
Res., 103 Jackson St., P.O. Box L, 12524-0499. Tel: 914-896-6400; Fax: 914-896-4575.
School—(1955), Tel: 914-896-9561. Mrs. Elizabeth Carufe.
Lay Teachers 9; Students 260.
Catechesis/Religious Programs—Tel: 914-896-6430.
Students 950.

Florida, Orange Co., St. Joseph (1895) (Polish), Rev. Joseph Tokarczyk, Admin.
Res., 14 Glenmere Ave., 10921. Tel: 914-651-7792; Fax: 914-651-7793. [CEM]
School—(1915), 21 Glenmere Ave., 10921. Tel: 914-651-7792.
Sisters 1; Lay Teachers 10; Students 150.
Catechesis/Religious Programs—Students 125.
Mission—Pellets Island (New Hampton), Orange Co., St. Andrew Bobola, Maple Ave., Pellets Island, 10958.
Chapel—St. Joseph Convent, 19 Glenmere Ave., 10921. Tel: 914-651-4213.

Forestburgh, Sullivan Co., St. Thomas Aquinas (1900), Rev. Ivan L. Csete; Deacon Paul A. Rausch.
Res., One Forestburgh Rd., 12777. Tel: 914-791-7400; Fax: 914-791-7700. [CEM]

Gardiner, Ulster Co., St. Charles Borromeo (1883) (Irish-Italian), Rev. Eugene A. Kosnik; Deacon Harold N. Carroll.
Res., 12525. Tel: 914-255-1374; Fax: 914-256-9050. [CEM]
Catechesis/Religious Programs—Tel: 914-564-1153.
Students 215.

Garnerville, Rockland Co., St. Gregory Barbarigo (1961), Rev. John J. Backes; Deacons Augustine A. Pappalardo; Roland Dowen.
Res., 21 Cinder Rd., 10923. Tel: 845-947-1873; Fax: 845-947-8256.
School—Tel: 845-947-1330; Fax: 845-947-4392. Sr. Kathleen Gorres, O.P., Prin.
Sisters of St. Dominic (Sparkill) 2; Lay Teachers 9; Students 275.
Catechesis/Religious Programs—Tel: 845-429-2775. Marie Kiely, D.R.E.
Students 1,051.

Glasco, Ulster Co., St. Joseph (1921) (Italian-Irish), Rev. Charles F. Zanotti.
Res., Glasco Tpke., Box 208, 12432. Tel: 914-246-5453; Fax: 914-247-9343.
A-Villa St. Dominic—Rest House for Ladies. Dominican Sisters (Sparkill). Also Known as Corazon Center. Tel: 914-246-8941.
Catechesis/Religious Programs—Tel: 914-246-4598.
Students 150.

Goshen, Orange Co., St. John the Evangelist (1837), Revs. Richard T. Adams; Frank Bassett; Trevor Nicholls; Deacons Luis Baerga; James McGarry.
Res., 71 Murray Ave., 10924. Tel: 914-294-5328; Fax: 914-294-2577. [CEM]
School—77 Murray Ave., 10924. Tel: 914-294-6434; Fax: 914-284-7303. Sr. Barbara Werner, O.P., Prin.
Sisters 4; Lay Teachers 8; Students 234.
Catechesis/Religious Programs—Tel: 914-294-6847.
Students 730.
Chapels—Immaculate Conception Convent, 73 Murray Ave., 10924. Tel: 914-294-8620; Presentation Sisters Convent, Fletcher St., 10924.; John S. Burke H. S. Chapel; Our Lady of the Blessed Sacrament, Broadlea, 10924. Tel: 914-294-5481.
Stations—Orange County Home and Infirmary, Tel: 914-294-7971; Orange County Jail, Tel: 914-294-6166; Campbell Hall Nursing Facility, Tel: 914-294-8154; Arden Hill Life-Care Center, Tel: 914-294-9797.

Greenburgh, Westchester Co., Church of Our Lady of Shkodra (1989) (Albanian), Rev. Peter Popovich.
Res., 361 W. Hartsdale Ave., Hartsdale, 10530. Tel: 914-761-3523; Fax: 914-949-2690. [CEM]

Greenwood Lake, Orange Co., Holy Rosary (1954), Revs. Robert J. Sweeney; P. Joseph McAndrew; Deacon Ralph D. Longo.
Res., 41 Windermere Ave., 10925-2105. Tel: 914-477-8378; Fax: 914-477-7238.
Catechesis/Religious Programs—Tel: 918-477-0906.
Students 300.

Harriman, Orange Co., St. Anastasia (1899), Rev. Joseph F. Reynolds; Deacon Eugene E. Bormann. In res., Rev. Lawrence X. McCaffrey, S.J.
Res., 21 N. Main St., 10926. Tel: 914-783-3571; Fax: 914-783-0881. [CEM]
Catechesis/Religious Programs—Tel: 914-782-5099.
Students 410.

Harrison, Westchester Co., St. Gregory the Great (1911), Rev. Msgr. Daniel V. Flynn, J.C.D.; Rev. Msgr. Guy S. Vinci; Rev. Msgr. Joseph J. Raimondo, Senior Priest.
Res., 215 Halstead Ave., 10528. Tel: 914-835-0677; Fax: 914-835-5152.
School—(1953), 94 Broadway, 10528. Tel: 914-835-1278; Fax: 914-835-2070. Debra A. Trignani, Prin.
Lay Teachers 10; Students 142.
Catechesis/Religious Programs—189 Fremont St., 10528. Tel: 914-835-4291; Fax: 914-835-6080.
Students 670.

Hartsdale, Westchester Co., Sacred Heart (1926), Rev. Patrick J. Carney; Rev. Msgr. John V. Wilkinson, Pastor Emeritus; Rev. Divya Paul (India); Deacon Benjamin D'Arconte.
Res., 10 Lawton Ave., 10530. Tel: 914-949-0028; Fax: 914-289-0398.
School—(1953), 59 Wilson St., 10530. Tel: 914-946-7242; Fax: 914-946-7323. Mrs. Virginia Salamone, Prin.
Sisters 2; Lay Teachers 17; Students 286.
Catechesis/Religious Programs—Tel: 914-428-5043.
Students 170.
Convent—11 Lawton Ave., 10530. Tel: 914-946-2581.

Hastings-on-Hudson, Westchester Co., St. Matthew (1892), Rev. Msgr. Edward J. McCorry; Rev. James Smyth.
Res., 616 Warburton Ave., 10706. Tel: 914-478-2822; Fax: 914-478-3681.
School—(1911), Tel: 914-478-3343. Mrs. Tatianna Ferraro, Prin.
Lay Teachers 9; Students 160.
Catechesis/Religious Programs—Tel: 914-478-1092.
Students 270.
Mission—Hastings-on-Hudson, Westchester Co., Andrus Nursing Home.

St. Stanislaus Kostka (1912) (Polish), Rev. Msgr. Edward J. McCorry.
Res., 616 Warburton Ave., 10706. Tel: 914-478-2822; Fax: 914-478-3681.
Church—52 Main St., 10706.

Haverstraw, Rockland Co., St. Peter (1848), Rev. Msgr. Charles S. Kelly; Revs. Richard Smith; Miguel Castillo.
Res., 115 Broadway, 10927. Tel: 914-429-2196; Fax: 914-947-4564. [CEM][JC]
School—(1884), Ridge St., 10927. Tel: 914-429-5311. Miss Kathleen Dunn, Prin.
Lay Teachers 10; Students 230.
Catechesis/Religious Programs—21 Ridge St., 10927. Tel: 914-429-8824.
Students 580.
Stations—West Haverstraw, Helen Hayes Hospital, Tel: 914-947-3000; Walnut Hill, Senior Citizen Apts., Tel: 914-429-3033; Haverstraw, Green Hills Home, Tel: 914-429-8411; Haverstraw, Northern Riverview Health Care Center, Tel: 914-429-5381.

St. Mary (1899) (Slovak), Rev. Msgr. Robert J. McCabe, Admin.
Res., 46 Conklin Ave., 10927. Tel: 914-429-2245; Fax: 914-429-1350.

Hawthorne, Westchester Co., Holy Rosary (1901), Revs. Anthony J. Giuliano; Frank Dias, P.V.
Res., 170 Bradhurst, 10532. Tel: 914-769-0030; Fax: 914-769-3326.
School—(1955), 180 Bradhurst Ave., 10532. Tel: 914-769-4549; Fax: 914-769-2768.
Lay Teachers 10; Students 224.
Catechesis/Religious Programs—Tel: 914-769-3338. Sr. June Quinian, O.P., D.R.E.
Students 639.

Highland, Ulster Co., St. Augustine (1899), Revs. Eugene Keane; Thomas Lutz.
Res., 55 Main St., 12528. Tel: 845-691-7673; Fax: 845-691-6680.
School—(1958), Phillips Ave. and Elting Pl., 12528. Tel: 845-691-2338; Fax: 845-691-2338. Mrs. Laurette McKercher, Prin.
Lay Teachers 10; Students 211.
Catechesis/Religious Programs—Students 297.

Highland Falls, Orange Co., Sacred Heart of Jesus (1870). Unassigned. Rev. Michael P. McLoughlin.
Res., 353 Main St., 10928. Tel: 845-446-4609; Fax: 845-446-2343. [CEM]
School—(1930), 7 Cozzens Ave., 10928. Tel: 845-446-2674; Fax: 845-446-3713.
Lay Teachers 9; Students 250.
Catechesis/Religious Programs—Maryann Brigham, D.R.E.
Students 225.
Chapel—Fort Montgomery, Blessed Sacrament. Rev. Michael P. McLoughlin.

Highland Mills, Orange Co., St. Patrick (1957), Revs. Gerard P. Travers; Sebastian Pandarathikudiyil, V.C. (India); Deacon Paul Weireter.
Res., 26 Hunter St., 10930. Tel: 845-928-6027; Fax: 845-928-2982.
Catechesis/Religious Programs—Tel: 845-928-6688.
Students 600.

Hopewell Junction, Dutchess Co., St. Columba (1992), Rev. Msgr. Dominick J. Lagonegro; Revs. Andrew J. Walsh; Matthew M. Jelenek; Deacons William Alvarado; John Reilly; George Stewart; Warren Testa; Stanley Wyka.
Res., 835 Rte. 82, P.O. Box 428, 12533. Tel: 914-227-8380; Fax: 914-227-8390.
School—St. Denis-St. Columba, Tel: 914-227-7777. Sr. Ann Daniels, Prin.
Sisters 2; Lay Teachers 15; Students 506.
Catechesis/Religious Programs—P.O. Box 368, Hopewell Jct., 12533. Tel: 914-221-4900. Mrs. Joann Griffin, D.R.E.
Students 2,035.
Mission—LaGrangeville, Dutchess Co., Mission Church of Blessed Kateri Tekakwitha, Rte. 82, LaGrangeville, 12540.

St. Denis (1899), Rev. William B. Cosgrove; Deacons Walter Dauerer; Stanley Aviles.
Res. & Office: 602 Beekman Rd., P.O. Box 10, 12533. Tel: 914-227-8382; Fax: 914-227-3951. [CEM]
The Ark and The Dove Preschool:—Tel: 914-227-5232; Fax: 914-227-0435.
School—St. Denis-St. Columba. See St. Columba for details. Tel: 914-227-7777; Fax: 914-227-8390.
Catechesis/Religious Programs—P.O. Box 1139, 12533. Tel: 914-227-3949; Fax: 914-227-0435.
Students 1,000.

Hyde Park, Dutchess Co., Regina Coeli (1863), Revs. Michael L. Palazzo, Admin.; James Havane; Deacons William E. Biskup; Frank J. Gohl; Gerald Lindley. In res., Rev. James J. LeBar.
Res., 2 Harvey St., 12538. Tel: 845-229-2134; Fax: 845-229-1668.
School—(1955), Albany Post Rd., 12538. Tel: 845-229-8589.
Lay Teachers 16; Students 226.
Catechesis/Religious Programs—Tel: 845-229-9139.
Students 350.
Mission—Staatsburg, Dutchess Co., St. Paul, (1851) Mulford Ave., Staatsburg, 12580.

Irvington-on-the-Hudson, Westchester Co., Immaculate Conception (1873), Revs. Raymond J. Byrne; Abraham Kannampalackal, C.M.I.; Jacob Joseph, C.M.I.
Res., 16 N. Broadway, 10533. Tel: 914-591-7480; Fax: 914-591-7806.
School—(1908), Tel: 914-591-9330; Fax: 914-591-8639.
Lay Teachers 10; Students 173.
Catechesis/Religious Programs—Tel: 914-591-7740.
Students 320.

Jeffersonville, Sullivan Co., St. George (1963), Rev. Robert F. Nee, O.F.M.
Res., 12748. Tel: 914-482-4640; Fax: 914-482-3276. [CEM]

Katonah, Westchester Co., St. Mary of the Assumption (1908), Revs. William P. Dalton; Lawrence Paolicelli, Admin.
Res., 117 Valley Rd., 10536. Tel: 914-232-3356; Fax: 914-232-5736.
Catechesis/Religious Programs—99 Valley Rd., 10536. Tel: 914-232-4648.
Students 700.
Missions—Bedford Hills, Westchester Co., St. Matthias, (1909) Babbitt Rd., Bedford Hills, 10507.; South Salem, Westchester Co., South Salem Presbyterian Church, Spring St., South Salem, 10590.

Kingston, Ulster Co.,

1—Holy Name of Jesus, (1884). Closed.

2—Immaculate Conception, (1896) (Polish), Rev. John W. Borzuchowski (Poland).
Res., 467 Delaware Ave., 12401. Tel: 845-331-0846; Fax: 845-331-7647. [CEM]
Catechesis/Religious Programs—Tel: 847-331-7352.
Students 75.

3—St. Joseph, (1868), Revs. Frank J. Damis; Paul Thymootil, C.M.I.; Rick De La Pena; Deacons Donald Droulette; Richard Frohmiller; Robert Winrow; John Peters; Joseph Doherty. In res., Rev. Msgr. James V. Keating.
Res., 242 Wall St., 12401. Tel: 845-338-1554; Fax: 845-340-1961.
School—(1869), Wall & Pearl Sts., 12401. Tel: 845-339-4390; Fax: 845-339-7001.
Sisters, Society of St. Ursula 1; Lay Teachers 13; Students 380.
Catechesis/Religious Programs—Tel: 845-339-4391.
Students 252.
Chapel—St. Joseph Mission, Zandhoeck Rd., Hurley, 12443. Tel: 845-338-7121.

4—St. Mary, (1842), Rev. Edmund M. Burke.
Res., 160 Broadway, 12401. Tel: 845-331-0301; Fax: 845-339-6165. [CEM]
School—Kingston Catholic School, (1867), 159 Broadway, 12401. Tel: 914-331-9318; Fax: 914-331-2674. Jill Albert, Prin.
Lay Teachers 10; Students 223.
Catechesis/Religious Programs—Students 200.

5—St. Peter, (1858) (German), Rev. Msgr. William J. Collins.
Res., 93 Wurts St., 12401. Tel: 914-331-0436; Fax: 914-331-7149. [CEM]

Lake Katrine, Ulster Co., St. Catherine Laboure (1957), Rev. John T. Kearney; Deacon John M. Sullivan.
Res., Tuytenbridge Rd., P.O. Box 271, 12449. Tel: 914-382-1133; Fax: 914-382-1051.
Catechesis/Religious Programs—Students 163.

Larchmont, Westchester Co., St. Augustine (1892), Rev. Msgr. Walter F. Kenny; Rev. Michael Morris. In res., Rev. Joseph A. DeSanto.
Res., 18 Cherry Ave., 10538. Tel: 914-834-1220; Fax: 914-833-2130.
Catechesis/Religious Programs—Tel: 914-834-9523.
Students 340.

SS. John and Paul (1949), Revs. Joseph Boyd; Robert J. Verrigni; Deacon James Brown.
Res., 280 Weaver St., 10538. Tel: 914-834-5458; Fax: 914-833-5081.
School—(1952), Tel: 914-834-6332; Fax: 914-834-6332. Anne A. Menno, Prin.
Lay Teachers 16; Students 360.
Catechesis/Religious Programs—Tel: 914-834-4597; Fax: 914-834-7493.
Students 452.

Liberty, Sullivan Co., St. Peter (1894), Rev. Msgr. Edward F. Straub; Deacon John Riley.
Res., 264 N. Main St., 12754. Tel: 914-292-4525; Fax: 914-292-1627. [CEM]
Catechesis/Religious Programs—Students 210.

Livingston Manor, Sullivan Co., St. Aloysius (1899), Rev. Alfred M. Croke.
Res., Church St., Box 206, 12758. Tel: 914-439-5625; Fax: 914-439-5188. [CEM]
Missions—De Bruce, Sullivan Co., Sacred Heart, P.O. Box 206, 12758.; Roscoe, Sullivan Co., Gate of Heaven, Highland Ave., Roscoe, 12776.
Catechesis/Religious Programs—Students 70.

Mahopac, Putnam Co., St. John the Evangelist (1889), Revs. Brian C. Brennan; William F. Woodruff; Rayappan Arul Joseph (India); Juan Molina, O.SS.T.; Deacons John Armo; Robert Esposito; John Scarfi.
Res., 221 E. Lake Blvd., 10541. Tel: 845-628-2006; Fax: 845-628-5970.
School—(1955), Tel: 845-628-6464; Fax: 845-628-6469.
Religious of the Divine Compassion 2; Lay Teachers 9; Students 232.
Catechesis/Religious Programs—Students 1,796.
Chapel—Convent of Religious of the Divine Compassion, Tel: 914-628-6497.

Mamaroneck, Westchester Co., Holy Trinity (1874), Revs. Joseph F. Irwin; Gabriel Muteru (Kenya).
Res., 320 E. Post Rd., 10543. Tel: 914-698-5944; Fax: 914-698-5274.
Catechesis/Religious Programs—Tel: 914-698-1868.
Students 196.

St. Vito (1911) (Italian), Revs. James F. Healy; Edward O'Neil; C. Ambrose (India). Pastoral Assocs.: Sr. Catherine Duignan, O.P.; Sr. Loretta Florio, S.S.J.B.
Res., 816 Underhill Ave., 10543. Tel: 914-698-2648; Fax: 914-698-6081.
Catechesis/Religious Programs—826 Underhill Ave., Mamaronek, 10543. Tel: 914-698-2949.
Students 450.

Marlboro, Ulster Co., St. Mary (1900), Rev. Alfred R. Pizzuto. Pastoral Team: Tel: 845-236-4340. Sr. Mary O'Neill, P.B.V.M.; Deacons Vincent Porcelli; John T. Repke; Thomas Cornell.
Res., Bloom St., P.O. Box 730, 12542. Tel: 914-236-4340; Fax: 914-236-3183. [CEM]
Catechesis/Religious Programs—Tel: 845-236-7791. Sr. Joan Mary Gleason, P.B.V.M., D.R.E.
Students 450.
Mission—Roseton, Orange Co., Our Lady of Mercy, River Rd., 12550.

Maybrook, Orange Co., Assumption (1907), Revs. Daniel M. O'Hare; Andrew T. Magee, Pastor Emeritus; Deacon Edward M. Grosso.
Res., 211 Homestead Ave., 12543. Tel: 914-427-2046.
Catechesis/Religious Programs—Tel: 914-427-5318.
Students 243.

Middletown, Orange Co., Holy Cross (1999), Rev. Robert Porpora.
Res., 626 County Rte. 22, 10940. Tel: 845-355-4439; Fax: 845-355-4709.
Catechesis/Religious Programs—Tel: 845-355-6255.
Students 490.
Mission—Unionville, Orange Co., Our Lady of the Scapular, 125 Main St., Unionville, 10988. Tel: 845-726-3222.

St. Joseph (1865) Irish/Italian/Spanish, Rev. Msgr. George J. Valastro; Revs. Joseph P. Fallon; Rafael Leiton (Colombia); Ludovico Angella (Italy).
Res., 149 Cottage St., 10940. Tel: 914-343-6013; Fax: 914-344-4735. [CEM]
School—(1889), 113 Cottage St., 10940. Tel: 914-343-3139; Fax: 914-346-4647. Victor Presto, Prin.
Lay Teachers 14; Students 273.
Catechesis/Religious Programs—Tel: 914-343-4415.
Students 695.

Our Lady of Mt. Carmel (1912), Rev. Lucian W. Beltzner, O.Carm. Pastoral Assocs.: Revs. James Sidoti, O.Carm.; Raymond Bagdonis, O.Carm.; Patrick McGuigan, O.Carm.; Deacons Edward Woods; John Frohbose. In res., Revs. James Tamburrino, O.Carm.; Robert Greco, O.Carm.
Res., 90 Euclid Ave., 10940. Tel: 845-343-4121; Fax: 845-343-4433.
School—205 Wawayanda Ave., 10940. Tel: 845-343-8836; Fax: 845-342-1404.
Lay Teachers 15; Students 286.
Catechesis/Religious Programs—Tel: 845-342-1510.
Students 450.
Missions—Bloomingburgh, Sullivan Co., Our Lady of the Assumption, P.O. Box 216, Bloomingburgh, 12721. Tel: 845-733-1477; Fax: 845-733-6691; Bullville, Orange Co., St. Paul, Rte. 17K, Bullville, 10915. Tel: 845-361-3107; Fax: 845-361-4201.

Millbrook, Dutchess Co., St. Joseph (1890), Revs. James T. O'Connor; Vincent Michael Charles.
Res., North Ave., 12545. Tel: 845-677-3422; Fax: 845-677-3423. [CEM]
School—(1957), Tel: 845-677-3670.
Lay Teachers 10; Students 285.
Catechesis/Religious Programs—Tel: 845-677-3273.
Students 332.
Chapel—Millbrook, Cardinal Hayes Home for Children.
Station—Millbrook, Green Briar Home, Tel: 845-677-9997.

Milton, Ulster Co., St. James (1874) (Italian), Rev. Fred Kempfirl. In res., Rev. Eugene Daniels.
Res., State Rd., 12547. Tel: 914-795-2255; Fax: 914-795-1008.

Monroe, Orange Co., Sacred Heart Church (1957), Revs. Carl D. Johnson; George Pulparayil (India); Michael Martine; Deacons Peter Brockmann; James Burns; Richard McCarthy; Angelo Corsaro; Robert Duncan.
Res., 26 Still Rd., 10950. Tel: 914-782-8510; Fax: 914-782-3593.
School—(1965), Tel: 914-783-0365; Fax: 914-782-0354. Cynthia Reimer, Prin.
Sisters 1; Lay Teachers 11; Students 284.
Catechesis/Religious Programs—(Grades PreK-8). Tel: 914-782-7420. Sr. Rose O'Rourke, D.R.E.
Students 1,407.
Convent—Still Rd., 10950.
Chapel—Stage Rd., 10950.

Montgomery, Orange Co., Holy Name of Mary (1868), Rev. Joseph D. Sullivan.
Res., 89 Union St., 12549. Tel: 914-457-5276; Fax: 914-457-3072. [CEM]
Catechesis/Religious Programs—Tel: 914-457-1738. Sr. Grace Mary McGuire, D.R.E.
Students 330.

Monticello, Sullivan Co., St. Peter (1874), Revs. Robert J. Ginel; John Lynch. In res., Rev. Stanislaus Ogbonna, C.S.Sp. (Nigeria).
Res., 10 Liberty St., 12701. Tel: 914-794-5577; Fax: 914-791-1210. [CEM]
Catechesis/Religious Programs—Tel: 914-791-7172.
Students 420.
Missions—Mongaup Valley, Sullivan Co., St. Joseph; White Lake, Sullivan Co., St. Anne.

Mt. Kisco, Westchester Co., St. Francis of Assisi (1871), Rev. Ralph A. Villani; Rev. Msgr. George F. Bardes.
Res., 2 Green St., 10549. Tel: 914-666-5986; Fax: 914-666-3859. [CEM]
Catechesis/Religious Programs—Tel: 914-666-3161; Fax: 914-666-5474.
Students 375.

Mt. Vernon, Westchester Co.,

1—Sacred Heart, (1872), Rev. Msgr. Howard W. Calkins; Rev. Anthony P. Settle.
Res., 115 S. Fifth Ave., 10550. Tel: 914-668-7440; Fax: 914-668-1177.
School—(1895), Second St. & S. Fifth Ave., 10550. Tel: 914-667-1734; Fax: 914-667-1497.
Sisters of Mercy 1; Lay Teachers 9; Students 265.
Chapel—Sacred Heart Convent, 67 S. Fifth Ave., 10550. Tel: 914-668-5349.

2—Our Lady of Victory, (1871), Rev. John McDonagh.
Res., 28 W. Sidney Ave., 10550. Tel: 914-668-5861; Fax: 914-668-0161.
School—(1898), 38 N. Fifth Ave., 10550. Tel: 914-667-4063; Fax: 914-665-3135. Janet Heed, Prin.
Lay Teachers 12; Students 263.
Chapel—Dominican Convent, Tel: 914-667-2564.

3—St. Mary, (1894), Rev. John T. Meehan.
Res., 23 S. High St., 10550. Tel: 914-664-5855; Fax: 914-663-6097.
Catechesis/Religious Programs—Students 150.

4—Our Lady of Mount Carmel, (1897) (Italian), Revs. Octavio Jose Salinas, O.F.M.; James Villa, O.F.M.; Benedict J. D'Alessandro, O.F.M.; Bro. Dominic Poirier, O.F.M.; Deacon Vincent T. Piro.
Res., 10550. Tel: 914-668-3540; Fax: 914-668-4393.

5—SS. PETER AND PAUL, (1929) (Italian), Rev. Msgr. Patrick J. Barry; Deacon Robert F. Schimpf. In res., Rev. Msgr. Thomas F. Scanlon.
Res., 129 Birch St., 10552. Tel: 914-668-9815; Fax: 914-668-6052.
School—Tel: 914-664-1321; Fax: 914-664-2951.
Sisters 1; Lay Teachers 12; Students 240.
Catechesis/Religious Programs—Tel: 914-668-9880.
Students 150.

6—ST. URSULA, (1908), Revs. John T. McLoughlin; Sabbas J. Kilian, O.F.M.; Deacons Thomas J. Abbamont; Carl Degenhardt. In res., Rev. Patrick Okafor (Nigeria).
Res., 214 E. Lincoln Ave., 10552. Tel: 914-668-0085; Fax: 914-668-4228.
Saint Ursula's Learning Center For the Learning Disabled—183 Rich Ave., 10552. Tel: 914-664-6656; Fax: 914-668-0592.
Catechesis/Religious Programs—Tel: 914-699-7964. Sr. Margaret Hoban, C.R., D.R.E.
Students 315.

Nanuet, Rockland Co., St. Anthony (1897), Revs. William V. Reynolds; Thomas F. McDonald; Christopher Pliaplis; Deacon John Maloney. In res., Rev. Jos Kandathikudy.
Res., 36 West Nyack Rd., 10954. Tel: 914-623-2138; Fax: 914-623-5556. [CEM]
School—(1953), 32-34 West Nyack Rd., 10954. Tel: 914-623-2311; Fax: 914-623-2406. Barbara Casey, Prin.
Sisters 4; Lay Teachers 19; Students 552.
Catechesis/Religious Programs—Tel: 914-624-2230. Ms. Ann Malloy, D.R.E.
Students 820.

Narrowsburg, Sullivan Co., St. Francis Xavier (1862), Rev. Thomas Jones, O.F.M.
Res., 151 Bridge St., 12764. Tel: 845-252-6681; Fax: 845-252-6519. [CEM]
Catechesis/Religious Programs—Students 52.
Mission—Lake Huntington, Sullivan Co., Our Lady of the Lake, Rte. 52, Lake Huntington, 12752. Tel: 845-252-6681.

Newburgh, Orange Co.,

1—ST. PATRICK, (1836), Rev. Msgr. John J. Budwick; Revs. Louis Van Thanh; Alfonso Henao (Colombia); Deacons Fred Steup; Frank Russell; William Glover; Sr. Virginia Wilkinson, Adult Formation. Spanish Apostolates: Sr. Yliana Hernandez; Sr. Paula Cormier; Sr. Helen Raynor.
Res., 55 Grand St., 12550. Tel: 914-561-0885; Fax: 914-561-8629. [CEM 2]
Catechesis/Religious Programs—Tel: 914-561-6470. Ms. Mary Jane Newman, D.R.E.
Students 620.
Mission—Orange Lake, Orange Co., Our Lady of the Lake, Lakeside & Rte. 52, 12550. Tel: 914-561-9537.

2—ST. FRANCIS OF ASSISI, (1909) (Polish), Rev. John J. Vondras; Deacon Jack Seymour.
Res., 145 Benkard Ave., 12550. Tel: 914-561-1317; Fax: 914-561-1337. [CEM]
School—Now Sacred Heart-St. Francis of Assisi School. Merged in Sept. 1992. 24 S. Robinson Ave., 12550. Tel: 914-561-1433.
Catechesis/Religious Programs—Tel: 914-561-6697. Louise Pisano, D.R.E.
Students 443.
Chapel—St. Francis Convent, (1955), 153 Benkard Ave., 12550. Tel: 914-561-5914; Fax: 914-561-1123.

3—ST. MARY, (1875), Rev. William A. Scafidi, M.Ss.A.; Deacon John J. Buckley.
Res., 180 South St., 12550. Tel: 914-562-0862; Fax: 914-562-0876.

4—SACRED HEART, (1912) (Italian), Rev. Msgr. Gerardo J. Colacicco; Rev. Abraham Chacko (India); Deacons Dominick Casadone; Peter Haight; Lawrence Kawula. In res., Rev. Donald Timone.
Res., 301 Ann St., 12550. Tel: 914-561-2264; Fax: 914-562-7144.
School—(1951), 24 S. Robinson Ave., 12550. Tel: 914-561-1433; Fax: 914-561-4383.
Religious 2; Lay Teachers 11; Students 223.
Catechesis/Religious Programs—Tel: 914-561-2589.
Students 433.

New City, Rockland Co., St. Augustine (1957), Rev. Msgr. William J. Foley; Revs. Andrew M. O'Connor; Varghese I. Chethipuzha; Deacons Michael G. McCabe; Lawrence O'Toole.
Res., 140 Maple Ave., 10956. Tel: 845-634-3641; Fax: 845-639-6118.
School—Tel: 845-634-7060; Fax: 845-634-8725. Katharine Murphy, Prin.
Lay Teachers 15; Students 295.
Catechesis/Religious Programs—Tel: 845-634-8462.
Students 873.

New Paltz, Ulster Co., St. Joseph (1894), Revs. Maurice Moreau, O.F.M.Cap.; Barnabas Keck, O.F.M.Cap.; Raynold Thibodeau, O.F.M.Cap., Univ. Chap.; Bro. Timothy Jones, O.F.M.Cap., Regl. Facilities Chap. In res., Rev. Richard Donaldson, O.F.M.Cap.
Res., 34 S. Chestnut St., 12561. Tel: 914-255-5635; Fax: 914-255-5679.
Catechesis/Religious Programs—Tel: 914-255-0237; Fax: 914-256-0687.
Students 490.
Station—Lake Mohonk.

New Rochelle, Westchester Co.,

1—BLESSED SACRAMENT, (1848), Rev. Msgr. William J. Bradley; Revs. Charles Imokhai (Nigeria); Salagunla Xavier Amul; Lawrence Maria Singarayer (India); Deacons Charles Rizzo; Frank Orlando; Charles Wendelken.
Res., 15 Shea Pl., 10801. Tel: 914-632-3700; Fax: 914-632-0732. [CEM]
School—New Rochelle Catholic Elementary, (1866), 24 Maple Ave., 10801. Tel: 914-632-0511. Joan Woods, Prin.
Lay Teachers 16; Students 318.
High School—(Coed) 24 Shea Pl., 10801. Tel: 914-632-2595; Fax: 914-632-3321. Bro. Peter Zawot, C.F.C., Prin.
Congregation of Christian Brothers 3; Sisters 5; Lay Teachers 19; Students 260.
Catechesis/Religious Programs—Tel: 914-235-7311. Mrs. Judith Anastasio, D.R.E.
Students 445.

2—ST. GABRIEL, (1893) (Hispanic), Revs. Patrick V. McNamara; John Muscat, Chap.
Res., 120 Division St., 10801. Tel: 914-632-0211; Fax: 914-637-8991.

3—ST. JOSEPH, (1901) (Italian & Portuguese), Rev. Philip J. Caruso.
Res., 280 Washington Ave., 10801. Tel: 914-632-0675; Fax: 914-633-4264.
Catechesis/Religious Programs—Students 140.

4—HOLY FAMILY, (1913), Rev. Msgr. John Mescall; Rev. Gary Mead; Deacon Arthur Hull Hayes, Jr. In res., Rev. Lawrence McDonnell, C.S.P.
Res., 83 Clove Rd., 10801. Tel: 914-632-0673; Fax: 914-576-8556.
Church—Mayflower Ave. & Mt. Joy Pl., 10801.
School—(1921), Mayflower Ave., 10801. Tel: 914-632-3810; Fax: 914-636-6758.
Lay Teachers 9; Students 188.
Catechesis/Religious Programs—Tel: 914-636-6758.
Students 359.
Chapels—Ursuline Sisters, 1352 N. Ave., 10804. Tel: 914-636-3456; Fax: 914-576-2620; Iona Grammar and Preparatory Schools, 173 Stratton Rd., 10804. Tel: 914-633-7744; 632-2727; Fax: 914-235-6338; Iona College, 715 N. Ave., 10801. Tel: 914-633-2000; Fax: 800-633-2329; New Rochelle, St. Patrick Prov., 30 Montgomery Circle, 10801. Tel: 914-633-6851; Fax: 914-633-5579; New Rochelle, St. Joseph Chapel, Tel: 914-632-6592; Fax: 914-533-4264; Edmond Rice Hall, 33 Pryer Ter., 10804. Tel: 914-636-6194; Fax: 914-636-0021; Crosier Fathers, Holy Cross Priory, 326 W. 14th St., New York, 10014. Tel: 212-647-8534; Fax: 212-647-8182; Opus Dei, 99 Overlook Cir., 10804. Tel: 914-235-1201; Fax: 914-235-7805; Holy Cross Brothers Provincialate, 85 Overlook Cir., 10804. Tel: 914-632-1951; Fax: 914-632-2490.

5—HOLY NAME OF JESUS, (1929), Revs. Martin J. Biglin; John P. DeLora; Deacons Carmine DeMarco; Robert Gontcharuk.
Res., 75 Lispenard Ave., 10801. Tel: 914-636-4856; Fax: 914-636-8474.
Church—Petersville Rd. and Halligan St., 10801.
School—(1954), 70 Petersville Rd., 10801. Tel: 914-576-6672; Fax: 914-576-6676. Mr. Albert D'Angelo, Prin.
Sisters 1; Lay Teachers 9; Students 237.
Catechesis/Religious Programs—Tel: 914-576-6038.
Students 185.
Chapel—Sisters of Charity Convent, 78 Petersville Rd., 10801. Tel: 914-636-4354.

New Windsor, Orange Co., St. Joseph (1962), Rev. Robert G. Hilfiker; Deacons Joseph Lieby; Anthony Ferraiuolo.
Res., 4 St. Joseph Pl., 12553. Tel: 914-561-8467; Fax: 914-562-3269.
School—148 Windsor Hwy., 12553. Tel: 914-565-5110; Fax: 914-565-6321.
Sisters 1; Lay Teachers 9; Students 181.
Catechesis/Religious Programs—Tel: 914-561-8475.
Students 327.

North Tarrytown, Westchester Co., Holy Cross (1921) (Slovak-Polish), Rev. Francis P. Gorman; Rev. Msgr. Cyril J. Potocek.
Res., 118 Beekman Ave., 10591. Tel: 914-631-1493.

Nyack, Rockland Co., St. Ann (1869), Revs. Robert P. Henry; Emil Bettley; Cresus Fernando (Sri Lanka); Joseph Asuah (Ghana).
Res., 16 Jefferson St., 10960. Tel: 845-358-4707; Fax: 845-358-3246.
School—(1892), Tel: 845-358-0125; Fax: 845-358-7911. Mrs. Fatima deCarvalho Gianni, Prin.
Lay Teachers 7; Students 110.
Catechesis/Religious Programs—19 Jefferson St., 10960. Tel: 845-358-3758. Ms. Julie LePore, D.R.E.
Students 195.
Convent—150 Third Ave., 10960. Tel: 845-358-2697.

Obernburg, Sullivan Co., St. Mary (1854) (German), Rev. John M. Richardson, O.F.M.; Deacon Lawrence Knack.
Res., 12767. Tel: 914-482-5541; Fax: 914-482-9340. [CEM]

Ossining, Westchester Co., St. Augustine (1853), Rev. Msgr. Hilary Franco; Rev. Robert M. Dunn.
Res., Eagle Park Rte. 9, 10562. Tel: 914-941-0067; Fax: 914-944-0828. [CEM]
School—(1893), Tel: 914-941-3849; Fax: 914-941-4342. Sr. Mary Elizabeth Donoghue, Prin.
Priests 2; Sisters of St. Dominic (Columbus) 1; Lay Teachers 25; Students 555.

St. Ann (1927), Rev. Edward G. Byrne; Sr. Eileen Finnerty, Pastoral Assoc.; Deacon Jose DeJesus. In res., Rev. Gegorio Neri (Philippines).
Res., 25 Eastern Ave., 10562. Tel: 914-941-2556; Fax: 914-923-9239.
School—16 Elizabeth St., 10562. Tel: 914-941-0312; Fax: 914-941-3514. Mrs. Dorethea Muccigrosso, Prin.
Sisters 1; Lay Teachers 16; Students 365.
Catechesis/Religious Programs—Tel: 914-941-2420.
Students 360.
Convent—10 Elizabeth St., 10562.

Otisville, Orange Co., Holy Name (1969), Rev. Peter Tran Van Phat, Admin.
Res., P.O. Box 597, 10963. Tel: 914-386-1320; Fax: 914-386-6105. [CEM]
Catechesis/Religious Programs—Tel: 914-386-2327. Miss Penny-Jude Watkins, D.R.E.
Students 254.

Patterson, Putnam Co., Sacred Heart (1957), Revs. James P. Flynn, Pastor Emeritus; Ralph W. La Belle.
Res., 414 Haviland Dr., 12563. Tel: 845-279-4832; Fax: 845-278-0432.
Catechesis/Religious Programs—Mrs. Tee Vozzella, D.R.E.
Students 391.

Pawling, Dutchess Co., St. John the Evangelist (1848), Revs. John J. Duff; James J. Moriarty, Pastor Emeritus.
Res., 31 E. Main St., 12564. Tel: 845-855-5488; Fax: 845-855-1273. [CEM]
Catechesis/Religious Programs—Tel: 845-855-9408.
Students 420.

Pearl River, Rockland Co., St. Margaret (1923), Rev. Msgr. Rudolph Eisler; Revs. Leo Prince; Salvador Anonuevo (Philippines); Rev. Msgr. John Harrington; Deacons William Donovan; William Tobin.
Res., 115 W. Central Ave., 10965. Tel: 845-735-4746; Fax: 845-735-3511.
School—(1953), N. Magnolia St., 10965. Tel: 914-735-2855; Fax: 914-735-0131. Mrs. Patricia O'Connor, Prin.
Lay Teachers 13; Students 355.
Catechesis/Religious Programs—Tel: 914-735-5489. Mrs. Ellen Fanelli, D.R.E.
Students 690.

St. Aedan (1966), Rev. Msgr. Joseph P. Penna; Rev. Jacob Thumma (India); Deacon James F. Maher.
Res., 23 Reld Dr., 10965. Tel: 845-735-7405; Fax: 845-735-4125.
Catechesis/Religious Programs—Tel: 845-735-2531.
Students 799.

Peekskill, Westchester Co., Assumption (1859) (Indian-Hispanic), Rev. Msgr. Francis J. Ansbro; Revs. Arthur R. Leo; Steven E. Clark; Vernon P. Wickrematunge; Deacon James F. Roberts.
Res., 131 Union Ave., 10566. Tel: 914-737-2071; Fax: 914-737-1633. [CEM]
School—(1907), S. Division & First St., 10566. Tel: 914-737-0680; Fax: 914-737-1322.
Sisters 3; Lay Teachers 10; Students 269.
Catechesis/Religious Programs—Students 210.
Chapel—St. Joseph Home, Tel: 914-737-3373; Fax: 914-73-9614.

Pelham, Westchester Co., St. Catharine (1896), Rev. Peter F. Bannan.
Res., 25 Second Ave., 10803. Tel: 914-738-1491; Fax: 914-738-0398.
Catechesis/Religious Programs—Tel: 914-738-1332.
Students 270.

Pelham Manor, Westchester Co., Our Lady of Perpetual Help (1954), Rev. Msgr. Hugh D. Curran; Deacon Guy Pellegrini.
Res., 559 Pelham Manor Rd., 10803. Tel: 914-738-1449; Fax: 914-738-9454.
School—(1957), 575 Fowler Ave., 10803. Tel: 914-738-5158. Sr. Marie Morris, S.C., Prin.
Sisters 2; Lay Teachers 11; Students 229.
Catechesis/Religious Programs—Tel: 914-738-0670.
Students 530.

Phoenicia, Ulster Co., St. Francis de Sales (1902), Rev. Hector O. LaChapelle, M.S.
Res., Main St., P.O. Box 25, 12464. Tel: 845-688-5617; Fax: 845-688-5630. [CEM]
Catechesis/Religious Programs—Students 112.
Missions—Allaben, Ulster Co., Our Lady of Lourdes, Rte. 28, Allaben, 12480.; Boiceville, Ulster Co., Our Lady of La Salette, Rte. 28, Boiceville, 12412.

Piermont, Rockland Co., St. John (1852). Unassigned.
Res., 895 Piermont Ave., 10968. Tel: 914-359-0078; Fax: 914-359-2976.
Catechesis/Religious Programs—Tel: 845-359-7444.
Students 90.

Pine Bush, Orange Co., The Infant Saviour (1951), Rev. Alfred F. Gallant.
Res., 22 Holland Ave., 12566. Tel: 845-744-2391; Fax: 845-258-5526.
Catechesis/Religious Programs—Tel: 845-744-9944.
Students 570.
Mission—Walker Valley, Ulster Co., Our Lady of the Valley, Walker Valley, 12588.

Pine Island, Orange Co., St. Stanislaus (1912) (Polish), Rev. Joaquim J. Olendzki.
Res., 17 Pulaski Hwy., P.O. Box 248, 10969. Tel: 914-258-4426; Fax: 914-258-5526. [CEM]
Catechesis/Religious Programs—Students 200.

Pine Plains, Dutchess Co., St. Anthony (1958), Rev. William A. White; Deacons Salvatore P. Patricola; Jerome F. Stuetzle.
Res., 68 Poplar Ave., 12567-5531. Tel: 518-398-7115; Fax: 518-398-9146.
Catechesis/Religious Programs—Students 150.

Plattekill, Ulster Co., Our Lady of Fatima (1960), Rev. John Jaume, C.R.
Res., P.O. Box 77, 12568. Tel: 914-564-4972; Fax: 914-566-1954.
Catechesis/Religious Programs—Students 200.

Pleasant Valley, Dutchess Co., St. Stanislaus Kostka (1903), Rev. Charles P. Quinn.
Res., 1598 Main St., P.O. Box 558, 12569. Tel: 914-635-1700; Fax: 914-635-8675.
Catechesis/Religious Programs—Tel: 914-635-8611.
Students 509.

Pleasantville, Westchester Co., Holy Innocents (1894), Revs. Raymond Daley, O.P.; Daniel Davies, O.P.; Sean J. McConway, O.P.; Sr. Anne Marie Ryan, O.P., Pastoral Assoc. In res., Rev. Joseph Payne, O.P.
Res., 431 Bedford Rd., 10570. Tel: 914-769-0025; Fax: 914-747-2476. [CEM]
Catechesis/Religious Programs—Tel: 914-769-3297. Sr. Clare Kellener, F.S.P., D.R.E.
Students 650.
Mission—Pleasantville Park, Westchester Co., Our Lady of Pompeii, Saragota and Garrigan, 10570.

Port Chester, Westchester Co.,

1—Our Lady of Mercy, (1854), Rev. Ralph V. Curcio; Rev. Msgr. James T. Gorman; Revs. Joe Braganza; Longinus Nazareth; Sr. Lorraine Dougherty, P.B.V.M., Pastoral Assoc.; Deacons Raymond H. Daur; Robert A. Fien.
Res., 260 Westchester Ave., 10573. Tel: 914-939-0612; Fax: 914-939-2807. [CEM]
Catechesis/Religious Programs—Tel: 914-937-5288. Mrs. Kathleen McCarthy, D.R.E.
Students 220.
Chapel—Sister of Charity, 18 Spring St., 10573. Tel: 914-937-2440.

2—Corpus Christi, (1925) (Italian), Revs. James Marra, S.D.B.; Peter Granzotto, S.D.B.; Joseph Tyminski, S.D.B.; Armand Quinto, S.D.B.; Edward Frizzell, S.D.B.; Deacons John B. Munnick, Jr.; Dan Ciccone.
Res., 136 S. Regent St., 10573. Tel: 914-939-3169; Fax: 914-939-7249. [CEM]
School—135 S. Regent St., 10573. Tel: 914-937-4407; Fax: 914-937-6904.
Sisters, Daughters of Mary Help of Christians 4; Lay Teachers 16; Students 377.
Catechesis/Religious Programs—Students 200.

3—Our Lady of the Rosary, (1904) (Italian), Revs. Timothy C. Ploch, S.D.B.; John Murphy, S.D.B.; John Nedungatt, S.D.B. (India); Timothy Zak, S.D.B.; Deacons William Vaccaro; Frank Del Campo.
Church—22 Don Bosco Pl., 10573. Tel: 914-939-0547; Fax: 914-937-0692.
Res., 23 Nicola Pl., 10573. Tel: 914-937-5532.
School—(1945), Central Ave., 10573. Tel: 914-939-1021; Fax: 914-939-7127. Mr. Ray Hoblock, Prin.
Lay Teachers 7; Students 146.
Catechesis/Religious Programs—Students 146.
Chapel—Adoration Chapel, Tel: 914-939-4456.

4—Sacred Heart of Jesus, (1917), Rev. Henry G. d'Anjou.
Res., 229 Willett Ave., 10573. Tel: 914-939-1497.

Port Ewen, Ulster Co., Presentation of the Virgin Mary (1856), Rev. Paul A. Miller, C.SS.R.
Res., Fr. Kelley Dr., 12466. Tel: 914-331-0053.
Catechesis/Religious Programs—Students 200.
Mission—Esopus, Ulster Co., Sacred Heart, P.O. Box 219, Esopus, 12429. Tel: 914-384-6828. Rev. Eugene J. Grohe, C.SS.R.

Port Jervis, Orange Co., Immaculate Conception (1851), Rev. Denis M. Dinan; Mary Ellen Hubbard, Ph.D., Pastoral Assoc.; RoseMary Conklin, Office Admin.
Res., 46 Ball St., Box 712, 12771. Tel: 845-856-8212; Fax: 845-858-8375. [CEM]
Catechesis/Religious Programs—Students 213.

Most Sacred Heart (1899), Rev. David A. De Simonc.
Res., 12 McAllister St., 12771. Tel: 914-856-1331; Fax: 914-858-0687.

Poughkeepsie, Dutchess Co.,

1—St. Peter, (1837), Revs. James A. Garisto; Rozario Chinnappan; Deacons James R. Hayes; George F. Cacchione; Albert J. Klein.
Res., 6 Father Cody Plaza, Hyde Park, 12601. Tel: 914-452-8580; Fax: 914-483-0189. [CEM]
Church—147 Salt Point Rd., 12601.
School—(1853), Tel: 914-471-6600.
Sisters of Charity of St. Vincent de Paul 3; Lay Teachers 15; Students 230.
Catechesis/Religious Programs—Students 201.
Chapels—Poughkeepsie, Convent of St. Peter.; Poughkeepsie, Hudson River Psychiatric Center, Our Lady of the Holy Rosary, Tel: 914-471-2537.

2—St. Mary, (1873), Revs. John J. Brinn, M.A.; John J. Hunter, M.S.; Deacon Richard Dingee.
Res., 231 Church St., 12601-4114. Tel: 845-452-8250; Fax: 845-452-8266.
Catechesis/Religious Programs—Tel: 845-471-4747; Fax: 845-471-4747.
Students 122.

3—Holy Trinity, (1921), Revs. Joseph P. LaMorte; George T. M. Hafemann; Deacon Andrew J. Daubman. In res., Rev. Gamini E. Fernando (Sri Lanka) Chap., Green Haven Correctional Facility.
Res., 775 Main St., 12603. Tel: 845-452-1863; Fax: 845-485-7569.
School—(1952), 20 Springside Ave., 12603. Tel: 845-471-0520; Fax: 845-471-0520. Mrs. Mary Ann McGivney, Prin.
Sister Servants of the Immaculate Heart of Mary 3; Lay Teachers 8; Students 305.
Catechesis/Religious Programs—Tel: 845-471-5838. Sr. Maureen Davey, S.U., D.R.E.
Students 365.
Chapel—Holy Trinity Convent, 769 Main St., 12603. Tel: 914-454-2160.

4—St. John the Baptist, (1923) (Slovak), Rev. Peter J. Kihm, Admin.
Res., 1 Grand St., 12601. Tel: 914-454-0340.

5—St. Joseph, (1901) (Polish), Rev. Jan Jacmierski.
Res., 9 Lafayette Pl., 12601. Tel: 914-452-2333.
Chapels—Poughkeepsie, Rectory.; Cemetery Chapel, Evergreen Ave., 12601.

6—St. Martin de Porres, (1962), Revs. Brian E. McWeeney, D.Min.; Philip P. Tran; Kenneth M. Horst. Pastoral Assocs.: Deacons Robert Jarmick; Victor Salamone; Patrick Hogan.
Res., 40 Cedar Valley Rd., 12603. Tel: 914-473-4222; Fax: 914-473-4223. [CEM]
School—38 Cedar Valley Rd., 12603. Tel: 914-452-4428. Mrs. Mary Jane Daley, Prin.
Lay Teachers 11; Students 296.
Catechesis/Religious Programs—Tel: 914-471-8728. Eileen Andros, D.R.E.
Students 779.

7—Our Lady of Mt. Carmel, (1910), Rev. Peter J. Kihm.
Res., 11 Mt. Carmel Pl., 12601. Tel: 845-454-0340; Fax: 845-486-8154.
School—Tel: 845-471-2460; Fax: 845-471-2699. Mr. Gabriel F. Ponte, Prin.
Lay Teachers 11; Students 297.
Catechesis/Religious Programs—Students 202.

Red Hook, Dutchess Co., St. Christopher (1875), Revs. Charles P. Coen; Peter Kulandai.
Res., 7411 S. Broadway, 12571. Tel: 845-758-3732; Fax: 845-758-1214. [CEM]
Catechesis/Religious Programs—Tel: 845-758-5506; Fax: 845-758-5682.
Students 377.

Rhinebeck, Dutchess Co., The Good Shepherd (1901), Revs. George J. Kuhn; Lawrence Xavier.
Res., 3 Mulberry St., 12572. Tel: 914-876-4583; Fax: 914-876-7884. [CEM]
Catechesis/Religious Programs—Tel: 914-876-7298.
Students 300.
Mission—Rhinecliff, Dutchess Co., St. Joseph, Church St., Rhinecliff, 12574.
Chapel—Astor Home for Children, Tel: 914-876-4081; Fax: 914-876-2020.
Rhinebeck, Ferncliff Nursing Home: Tel: 914-876-2011; Fax: 914-876-4810.; Rhinebeck, Sisters of St. Ursula, Linwood Retreat House: Tel: 914-876-4178; Fax: 914-876-6544.

Rosendale, Ulster Co., St. Peter (1855), Revs. Paul Dmoch; Raphael Nwachukwu (Nigeria); Deacons John J. Larkin; John J. Liggan.
Res., 12472. Tel: 845-658-3117; Fax: 845-658-3540. [CEM]
School—(Old: 1890; New: 1965), Tel: 845-658-9209; Fax: 845-658-9827. Gerianne O'Rourke, Prin.
School Sisters of St. Francis (Milwaukee, WI) 1; Lay Teachers 10; Students 100.
Catechesis/Religious Programs—Tel: 845-658-8911. Debbie Ferry, D.R.E.
Students 345.
Mission—High Falls, Ulster Co., Our Lady Help of Christians, J.F.K. Ln., High Falls, 12440.

Rye, Westchester Co., Resurrection (1880), Most Rev. Anthony F. Mestice, D.D.; Revs. Jack Arlotta; Arthur Walsh; Zacharias Nadackal, C.M.I. (India).
Res., 910 Boston Post Rd., 10580. Tel: 914-967-0142; 967-0254; Fax: 914-967-6494.
School—(1906), 116 Milton Rd., 10580. Tel: 914-967-1218; Fax: 914-967-0295.
Lay Teachers 29; Students 417.
Catechesis/Religious Programs—Tel: 914-967-1270.
Students 980.
Chapel—Seton Hall Convent of the Sisters of Charity, Tel: 914-967-7085.

Saugerties, Ulster Co., St. Mary of the Snow (1833), Revs. Hugh R. Grace; Christopher H. Berean; Deacons Perry Bunyar; Donald Trees; Karl Pietkiewicz; Arnie Hyland; Hank Smith.
Res., 36 Cedar St., 12477. Tel: 914-246-4913; Fax: 914-246-4996. [CEM]
School—(1881), 25 Cedar St., 12477. Tel: 914-246-6381. Miss Christine M. Molinelli, Prin.
Lay Teachers 13; Students 176; Preschool 51.
Chapel—Saugerties, Parish Center.
Catechesis/Religious Programs—Tel: 914-246-7534.
Students 162.

Scarsdale, Westchester Co., Immaculate Heart of Mary (1912), Rev. Msgr. John J. Scanlon; Rev. Msgr. Edward M. Connors, Pastor Emeritus; Revs. Matthew F. Fernan; Richard Seagraves; Deacons Ernest F. Salomone; Robert di Targiani.
Res., 8 Carman Rd., 10583. Tel: 914-723-0276; Fax: 914-722-0628.
School—(1928), 201 Boulevard, 10583. Tel: 914-723-5608; Fax: 914-723-8004. Robert W. Billings, Prin.
Lay Teachers 19; Students 280.
Catechesis/Religious Programs—Tel: 914-723-7593; Fax: 914-723-7209.
Students 1,000.

Our Lady of Fatima (1948), Rev. Msgr. Hugh F. McManus; Rev. John W. Coppinger, S.A.; Deacons Francis Griffin; Michael J. Fox; John J. Kollar; Irene Ingham Kollar, Pastoral Assoc.
Res., 5 Strathmore Rd., 10583. Tel: 914-723-7421; Fax: 914-723-7229.
School—(1950), Tel: 914-723-0460. Mrs. Barbara Stofko, Prin.
Lay Teachers 10; Students 210.
Catechesis/Religious Programs—Students 158.

St. Pius X (1954), Rev. John P. O'Brien; Deacons Theodore A. Gaskin; William J. Hill.
Res., 91 Secor Rd., 10583. Tel: 914-725-2755; Fax: 914-725-2782.
School—(1957), 85 Palmer Ave., 10583. Tel: 914-725-0541.
Lay Teachers 9; Students 151.

Shrub Oak, Westchester Co., Saint Elizabeth Ann Seton (1963), Most Rev. James F. McCarthy; Revs. Matthew Grier, M.H.M.; S. Kulandairajan.
Res., Main St., 10588. Tel: 914-528-3547; Fax: 914-528-4216.
School—Tel: 914-528-3563; Fax: 914-528-0341. Sr. Gabriel Miriam, S.C., Prin.
Sisters 2; Lay Teachers 25; Students 568.
Catechesis/Religious Programs—Tel: 914-528-8553; Fax: 914-528-1047. Virginia McKeon, D.R.E.
Students 1,274.

Sleepy Hollow, Westchester Co., Immaculate Conception (1917) (Italian), Rev. Louis J. Mazza.
Res., 199 N. Broadway, 10591. Tel: 914-631-0446; Fax: 914-631-4157.

St. Teresa of Avila (1853) (Spanish-Portuguese), Revs. Francis P. Gorman; Joseph Walyaula.
Res., 130 Beekman Ave., 10591. Tel: 914-631-0720; Fax: 914-366-6459.
Catechesis/Religious Programs—Tel: 914-631-1831.
Students 249.

The Magdalene (1894), Rev. Joseph S. Dietz.
Res., 525 Bedford Rd., Pocantico Hills, 10591-1216. Tel: 914-631-0529; Fax: 914-331-7958.
Catechesis/Religious Programs—Students 150.

Sloatsburg, Rockland Co., St. Joan of Arc (1966), Rev. John P. Gallant.
Res., 32 Eagle Valley Rd., 10974. Tel: 914-753-5239.
Catechesis/Religious Programs—Tel: 914-753-5193.
Students 175.

Spring Valley, Rockland Co., St. Joseph (1894), Rev. Rudolph F. Gonzalez; Rev. Msgr. Carl Sansaricq; Rev. Armand Iavarone, O.SS.T. In res., Revs. Joseph Kazhuvidayil; Felix Kumai; Cletus Ogu.
Res., 333 Sneden Pl. W., 10977. Tel: 914-356-0311; Fax: 914-352-8126.
School—(1927), 245 N. Main St., 10977. Tel: 914-356-0054; Fax: 914-356-9654. Mrs. Dorothy Kelly, Prin.
Lay Teachers 11; Students 200.
Catechesis/Religious Programs—Tel: 914-356-9654; Fax: 914-352-5686.
Students 600.

Stony Point, Rockland Co., Immaculate Conception (1889), Revs. Robert J. Staar; Kevin Gallagher; Deacons Philip Marino; John Crapanzano.
Res., 26 John St., 10980. Tel: 845-786-2742; Fax: 845-942-2614.
School—(1902), Main St., 10980. Tel: 914-786-5245.
Lay Teachers 10; Students 211.
Catechesis/Religious Programs—Tel: 914-786-5298.
Students 650.

Suffern, Rockland Co., Sacred Heart (1868), Rev. Msgr. Joseph P. Meehan; Revs. Andrew P. Carrozza; John S. Odeyemi (Nigeria); Deacons John Baterbury; Robert J. Johnson, Business Mgr.; Joseph A. Witt.
Res., 125 Lafayette, 10901. Tel: 845-357-0035; Fax: 845-368-0393.
School—(1909), 60 Washington Ave., 10901. Tel: 845-357-1684; Fax: 845-357-0318. Sr. Rose Andrew, O.P., Prin.
Sisters 3; Lay Teachers 23; Students 528.
Catechesis/Religious Programs—Tel: 845-357-6044; Fax: 845-369-0625. Mary Ann von Doehren, D.R.E.
Students 643.
Chapels—Dominican Sisters Convent, Tel: 845-357-1544; Good Samaritan Hospital, Tel: 845-368-5000; Tagaste Monastery, Tel: 845-357-0067; Fax: 845-369-0625.

Tappan, Rockland Co., Our Lady of the Sacred Heart (1952), Rev. John F. Dwyer.
Res., 120 King's Hwy., 10983. Tel: 914-359-1230.
Catechesis/Religious Programs—Tel: 914-359-1410.
Students 300.

Tarrytown, Westchester Co., Transfiguration (1896), Revs. Alfred J. Isacsson, O.Carm.; Joseph Hickey. In res., Rev. Robert D. Tracy, O.Carm.
Res., 268 S. Broadway, 10591. Tel: 914-631-1672; Fax: 914-524-9352.
School—(1949), Prospect Ave., 10591. Tel: 914-631-3737; Fax: 914-631-6640. Mary Margaret Henshaw, Prin.
Lay Teachers 15; Students 246.
Catechesis/Religious Programs—Tel: 914-631-2380.
Students 240.

Tivoli, Dutchess Co., St. Sylvia (1890), Rev. H. Theriault, M.Div.
Res., 104 Broadway, P.O. Box 95, 12583-0095. Tel: 914-757-2442; Fax: 914-757-3533. [CEM]

Tuckahoe, Westchester Co., Immaculate Conception (1853), Rev. Msgr. Francis E. Oliverio; Revs. Patrick A. Walsh, S.M.A.; T. Augustine Badgley; Joseph Emmanuel (Sri Lanka); Deacon Anthony Viola.
Res., 53 Winterhill Rd., 10707. Tel: 914-961-3643; Fax: 914-961-0283. [CEM]
School—(1913), Tel: 914-961-3785; Fax: 914-961-6054. Dr. Elaine Farrell, Prin.
Sisters 2; Lay Teachers 25; Students 487.
Catechesis/Religious Programs—Tel: 914-961-1076. Lynn Callahan, D.R.E.
Students 780.
Chapel—Sisters Convent, Tel: 914-961-3970.

Assumption (1911) (Italian), Rev. Msgr. Francis E. Oliverio; Revs. Patrick A. Walsh, S.M.A.; T. Augustine Badgley; Joseph Emmanuel; Deacon Anthony Viola.
Res., 53 Winterhill Rd., 10707. Tel: 914-961-3643; Fax: 914-961-0283.
Church—100 Pleasant Ave., 10707.
Catechesis/Religious Programs—Clustered with Immaculate Conception, Tuckahoe.

Tuxedo, Orange Co., Our Lady of Mt. Carmel (1895), Rev. John F.X. Smith.
Res., Rte. 17, P.O. Box 697, 10987. Tel: 914-351-5284; Fax: 914-351-4866.
Catechesis/Religious Programs—Students 91.

Valhalla, Westchester Co., Holy Name of Jesus (1896), Revs. Joseph A. Blenkle; Michael J. O'Leary (Ireland).
Res., Two Broadway, 10595. Tel: 914-949-2323; Fax: 914-686-6325.
School—Tel: 914-948-1744; Fax: 914-686-1749. Judith Foster, Prin.
Lay Teachers 12; Students 151.
Catechesis/Religious Programs—Tel: 914-949-1422.
Students 499.

Verplanck, Westchester Co., St. Patrick (1843), Rev. Andrew E. Kurzyna.
Res., 240 11th St., 10596. Tel: 914-737-0635; Fax: 914-788-0584. [CEM]
Catechesis/Religious Programs—Tel: 914-737-1348.
Students 145.
Chapel—Convent, Seventh St., 10596. Tel: 914-737-1373.

Walden, Orange Co., Most Precious Blood (1894), Rev. Kenneth M. Loughman.
Res., 42 Walnut St., 12586. Tel: 914-778-5719; Fax: 914-778-5659.
School—Tel: 914-778-3028.
Sisters of St. Dominic (Sparkill) 2; Lay Teachers 8; Students 204.
Catechesis/Religious Programs—Tel: 914-778-7081.
Students 402.
Mission—Wallkill, Ulster Co., St. Benedict, Wallkill, 12589.

Wappingers Falls, Dutchess Co., St. Mary (1850), Rev. Msgr. Francis P. Bellew; Rev. Gnana Dhas.
Res., 11 Clinton St., 12590. Tel: 845-297-6261; 6262; Fax: 845-297-3227. [CEM]
School—(1890 and 1955), Convent Ave., 12590. Tel: 914-297-7500. Mrs. Mary Ellen LaRose, Prin.
Lay Teachers 13; Students 215.
Catechesis/Religious Programs—Tel: 914-297-7586. Patricia Manuli, D.R.E.
Students 667.
Chapel—Mt. Carmel, St. Mary Convent.

Warwick, Orange Co., St. Stephen (1865), Rev. Msgr. Desmond O'Connor; Rev. Msgr. Bernard J. Corrigan, Pastor Emeritus; Rev. Thomas Byrnes; Deacon Authur J. Cuccia.
Res., 75 Sanfordville Rd., 10990. Tel: 914-986-4028; Fax: 914-986-4109. [CEM]
School—Tel: 914-986-3533.
Lay Teachers 13; Students 342.
Catechesis/Religious Programs—Tel: 914-986-2231.
Students 1,292.
Mission—Florida, Orange Co., St. Edward, (1881) Main St., Florida, 10921.

Washingtonville, Orange Co., St. Mary (1902), Revs. John J. Keaveney; Andrew L. Florez; Deacon John Shepard.
Res., 2 Fr. Tierney Cir., 10992. Tel: 914-496-3730; Fax: 914-496-3159. [CEM]
Catechesis/Religious Programs—Tel: 845-496-4101.
Students 1,680.

Wesley Hills, Rockland Co., St. Boniface (1966), Rev. Robert D. Saccoman.
Res., 5 Willow Tree Rd., 10952. Tel: 914-354-7307; Fax: 914-354-9046.
Catechesis/Religious Programs—Students 437.

West Hurley-Woodstock, Ulster Co., St. John (Woodstock) (1860), Rev. George W. Hommel.
Res., 12 Holly Hills Dr., Woodstock, 12498. Tel: 914-679-7696; Fax: 914-679-8393.
Catechesis/Religious Programs—Tel: 914-679-2869.
Students 305.
Mission—West Shokan, Ulster Co., St. Augustine, Watson Hollow Rd., West Shokan, 12494. Tel: 914-657-2190.

West Nyack, Rockland Co., St. Francis of Assisi (1964), Rev. Edward J. Weber; Deacon Donald O'Brien. In res., Rev. Gerard F. Rafferty, S.S.L.
Res., 128 Parrott Rd., 10994. Tel: 845-634-4957; Fax: 845-639-6629.
Catechesis/Religious Programs—Tel: 845-638-4215.
Students 609.

West Point, Orange Co., Catholic Chapel of the Most Holy Trinity (1899). Most Holy Trinity is being served under the Archdiocese for Military Services. For inquiries for sacramental records before Jan. 1, 1999, please contact Sacred Heart, Highland Falls.

White Plains, Westchester Co.,

1—St. Anthony, (1952) (Italian), Revs. Lawrence C. Inzeo; Peter C. Scaramuzzo; Deacon Arthur Manzione.
Res., 85 Harrison St., West Harrison, 10604. Tel: 914-948-1480; Fax: 914-948-0488.
School—(1957), Gainsborg Ave., West Harrison, 10604. Tel: 914-949-6986; Fax: 914-328-1981.
Sisters of Divine Compassion 4; Students 200.
Catechesis/Religious Programs—Tel: 914-949-0212.
Students 500.

2—St. John the Evangelist, (1868), Rev. Msgr. Neil Graham; Rev. Msgr. William B. Delaney, Pastor Emeritus; Revs. Christopher H. Daly; Thomas J. Joyce; Donald V. O'Brien, S.J.; Thomas Kalarickal, C.M.I. (India).
Res., 148 Hamilton Ave., 10601. Tel: 914-949-0439; Fax: 914-421-1202. [CEM]
School—(1890), 146 Hamilton Ave., 10601. Tel: 914-949-4374.
Lay Teachers 12.
Catechesis/Religious Programs—Tel: 914-997-7137.
Students 270.

3—St. Bernard, (1926), Revs. Edward M. Roos; Jose Vilaplana, S.J. (Spain); George Spiteri (Malta); Benedict J. Kuolt, Chap.; Deacons Robert Whiteman; Daniel Pellegrin.
Res., 51 Prospect St., 10606. Tel: 914-949-2111; Fax: 914-949-6044.
Catechesis/Religious Programs—Students 511.

4—Our Lady of Mt. Carmel, (1902) (Italian), Rev. Albert Azrak, C.S.S. In res., Revs. Leonard Della-Badia, C.S.S.; Phillip Pornchoi, C.S.S.; Peter C. Pramote, C.S.S.
Res., 92 S. Lexington Ave., 10606. Tel: 914-948-5909; Fax: 914-428-2676.
Catechesis/Religious Programs—Tel: 914-428-2676.
Students 130.

5—Our Lady of Sorrows, (1929), Revs. Patrick J. Dunne; Ignatius Vu; Rev. Msgr. John K. Daly, Pastor Emeritus.
Res., 920 Mamaroneck Ave., 10605. Tel: 914-949-9819; Fax: 914-949-4148.
School—(1957), Tel: 914-761-0124; Fax: 914-761-0176. Sr. Marie Cecile, Prin.
Lay Teachers 14; Students 224.
Catechesis/Religious Programs—Tel: 914-761-5257.
Students 381.

Woodbourne, Sullivan Co., Immaculate Conception (1957), Rev. John J. Lynch.
Res., P.O. Box 66, 12788. Tel: 914-434-7643; Fax: 914-436-7370. [CEM]
Catechesis/Religious Programs—Tel: 914-436-7370.
Students 215.

Wurtsboro, Sullivan Co., St. Joseph (1880), Rev. Hugh A. Dardis.
Res., Sullivan St., P.O. Box 277, 12790. Tel: 914-888-4522. [CEM]

Yonkers, Westchester Co.,

1—St. Anthony, (Nepera Park) (1923), Revs. Karl A. Bauer; Robert Ashman.
Res., 10 Squire Ave., 10703. Tel: 914-965-2733; Fax: 914-963-2285.
Church—1405 Nepperhan Ave., 10703.
School—Tel: 914-476-8489; Fax: 914-965-7939. Mrs. Elizabeth Carney, Prin.
Lay Teachers 10; Students 212.
Catechesis/Religious Programs—Students 71.

2—St. Anthony, (Willow St.). Closed. For inquiries for parish records contact Our Lady of Mt. Carmel, Yonkers.

3—St. Ann, (1947), Revs. John A. De Bellis; John Carson.
Res., 854 Midland Ave., 10704. Tel: 914-965-1555; 965-5584; Fax: 914-965-0678.
School—40 Brewster Ave., 10704. Tel: 914-965-4333. Sr. Joanne Shortall, Prin.
Lay Teachers 14; Students 325.
Catechesis/Religious Programs—Students 320.

4—St. Bartholomew, (1911), Rev. Brian P. McCarthy; Rev. Msgr. Charles J. McManus, Pastor Emeritus; Deacons Robert A. Clemens; Anthony Mercandetti.
Res., 15 Palmer Rd., 10701. Tel: 914-965-0566; Fax: 914-965-9046.
School—(1958), 278 Saw Mill River Rd., 10701. Tel: 914-476-7949; Fax: 914-476-7957. Sr. Ann Marie McMahon, P.B.V.M., Prin.
Sisters 2; Lay Teachers 13; Students 300.
Catechesis/Religious Programs—Tel: 914-476-6676.
Students 150.

5—St. Casimir, (1899) (Polish), Revs. John Michalak, O.S.P.; Jerzy Maj, O.S.P.; Deacon John Radzilowicz.
Res., 239 Nepperhan Ave., 10701. Tel: 914-963-1254; Fax: 914-969-5204.

School—(1906), 259 Nepperhan Ave., 10701-3461. Tel: 914-965-2730; Fax: 914-965-3347. Mr. Paul Henshaw, Prin.
Lay Teachers 9; Students 180.

6—CHRIST THE KING, (1927), Rev. Msgr. A. Francis Burns; Rev. George C. Lodi. In res., Rev. Leo D. Lefebure (CHI).
Res., 740 N. Broadway, 10701. Tel: 914-963-7474; 963-7564; Fax: 914-963-7548.
School—(1955), 750 N. Broadway, 10701. Tel: 914-476-1711. Ms. Mary B. Augone, Prin.
Sisters 3; Lay Teachers 10; Students 286.
Catechesis/Religious Programs—Students 156.

7—ST. DENIS, (1910), Revs. Edward P. O'Halloran; Michael Chalinor. In res., Rev. Francis Susai-Marion.
Res., 470 Van Cortlandt Park Ave., 10705. Tel: 914-963-8468; Fax: 914-963-7354.
School—(1928), McLean Ave. & Lawrence St., 10705. Tel: 914-963-3438. Mrs. Dorothy O'Neill-Williams, Prin.
Lay Teachers 10; Students 250.
Catechesis/Religious Programs—Tel: 914-476-8077. Deacon Joseph Mulryan, D.R.E.
Students 100.

8—ST. EUGENE, (1949), Rev. Leonard F. Villa, Admin. In res., Revs. Richard Seagrams; P.J. Thawale; Deacon Donald M. Quigley, Pastoral Assoc.
Res., 32 Massitoa Rd., 10710. Tel: 914-779-5460; Fax: 914-793-8913.
School—(1951), 707 Tuckahoe Rd., 10710. Tel: 914-779-2956; Fax: 914-779-7668.
Sisters 3; Lay Teachers 20; Students 500.
Catechesis/Religious Programs—Tel: 914-793-2158; Fax: 914-337-9868.
Students 165.
Chapel—Yonkers, Franciscan Sisters Convent, Tel: 914-779-7379.

9—IMMACULATE CONCEPTION, (1848) (Spanish-Arabic), Rev. Msgr. Hugh J. Corrigan; Revs. Sami Totah (Jordan); Virgilio Compentente (Philippines).
Res., 103 S. Broadway, 10701. Tel: 914-963-0156; Fax: 914-963-1803. [CEM]
School—(1860), 15 St. Mary's St., 10701. Tel: 914-965-7048; Fax: 914-423-2826. Mr. Eugene T. Hewitt, Prin.
Sisters 3; Lay Teachers 10; Students 239.
Catechesis/Religious Programs—Students 216.
Chapel—Sisters of Charity, St. Mary Convent, 4 St. Mary's St., 10701. Tel: 914-963-1449.
Good Shepherd Arabic Community of St. Mary—Rev. Sami Totah (Jordan) Dir.

10—ST. JOSEPH, (1871), Rev. Msgr. John Plo, Temporary Admin.; Revs. Paul V. Sullivan, (Retired); Francis Susai Marian (India) Chap.; Deacon Abraham Santiago.
Res., 141 Ashburton Ave., 10701. Tel: 914-963-0730; 963-0780; Fax: 914-964-5833. [CEM]
Convent—Tel: 914-423-1351. Sisters of Charity
Sisters 7.

11—ST. JOHN THE BAPTIST, (1903) (Italian-Irish), Revs. John W. Lennon; Peter McKeown; Patrick Boyle; Gerard Critch; Deacon Martin J. Olivieri.
Res., 670 Yonkers Ave., 10704. Tel: 914-963-1486; Fax: 914-375-1115.
School—(1954), Tel: 914-965-2356.
Sisters 3; Lay Teachers 8; Students 360.
Catechesis/Religious Programs—Marian Caputo, D.R.E.
Students 175.
Chapel—Convent, 176 Sweetfield Circle, 10704. Tel: 914-965-1837.

12—ST. MARGARET OF HUNGARY, (1928), Rev. Gabriel Kiss, S.J., (Hungary) Admin.; Deacon Louis Juhasz.
Res., 76 Locust Hill Ave., 10701. Tel: 914-423-2211.

13—OUR LADY OF MT. CARMEL, (1913) (Italian), Revs. Terzo Vinci, S.A.C.; Barry Bossa, S.A.C.; Deacons Alfred R. Impallomeni; Nick A. Mazzei, Jr.
Res., 70 Park Hill Ave., 10701. Tel: 914-963-4766; Fax: 914-375-1069.
School—Mt. Carmel-St. Anthony, 85 Linden St., 10701. Tel: 914-476-8888; Fax: 914-375-1069. Mrs. Teresita Fajardo.
Lay Teachers 11; Students 178.
Catechesis/Religious Programs—Tel: 914-423-8848.
Students 300.

14—OUR LADY OF THE ROSARY, (1907) (Portuguese), Revs. Thomas Gumprecht, S.A.; George Ribeiro, S.A.; Bro. John Baptist Hildreth, S.A., Pastoral Min.; Deacon Joaquim Pereira.
Res., 226 Warburton Ave., 10701. Tel: 914-963-0806; Fax: 914-963-3958.
Catechesis/Religious Programs—Students 30.

15—ST. PAUL THE APOSTLE, (1923), Rev. Msgr. John A. Gallagher; Sr. Eileen Treanor, Parish Ministry; Deacon James Hamilton.
Res., 602 McLean Ave., 10705. Tel: 914-963-7330; Fax: 914-963-1952.
Church—Lincoln Park, 10705.
School—(1949), 77 Lee Ave., 10705. Tel: 914-965-2165; Fax: 914-965-5792. Grace Mallardi, Prin.
Lay Teachers 10; Students 317.
Catechesis/Religious Programs—Students 106.

16—ST. PETER, (1894), Rev. Edward J. Keehan; Deacons Pedro Irizarry; Randy Velez.
Res., 91 Ludlow St., 10705. Tel: 914-963-0822; Fax: 914-968-9305.
School—(1894 and 1955), 204 Hawthorne Ave., 10705. Tel: 914-963-2314; Fax: 914-966-8822.
Sisters 2; Lay Teachers 10; Students 278.
Catechesis/Religious Programs—Tel: 914-476-7946.
Students 529.

17—SACRED HEART, (1891), Revs. Edward Conway, O.F.M.Cap.; Christopher Dietrich, O.F.M.Cap.; James Gavin, O.F.M.Cap.; Thomas Murphy, O.F.M.Cap., Chap.; Peter McCall, O.F.M.Cap.; John B. Riordan, O.F.M.Cap., Guardian; Bros. Roger Deguire, O.F.M.Cap.; Walter Puhal, O.F.M.Cap.; Bernard Twomey, F.S.C.
Res., 110 Shonnard Pl., 10703. Tel: 914-963-4205; Fax: 914-476-4960.
School—(1893), Tel: 914-963-5318. Sr. Cecilia Reeves, S.C., Prin.
Sisters 2; Lay Teachers 14; Students 275.
High School—34 Convent Ave., 10703. Tel: 914-965-3114; Fax: 914-965-4510. Bro. Louis Esposito, O.F.M.Cap., Prin.
Lay Teachers 25; Students 300.
Sacred Heart Parish High School Foundation, Inc.—34 Convent Ave., 10703. Tel: 914-963-4205; Fax: 914-476-4960. Rev. John B. Riordan, O.F.M.Cap., Pres.
Catechesis/Religious Programs—Students 90.
Convent—27 Convent Ave., 10703. Tel: 914-476-4602.

18—MOST HOLY TRINITY, (1894) (Slovak), Rev. Anthony J. Pleho.
Res., 18 Trinity Pl., 10701. Tel: 914-963-0720; Fax: 914-709-0224.
Chapel—Franciscan Friars of the Renewal, 15 Trinity Pl., 10701. Tel: 914-476-7279; Fax: 914-476-5033. Rev. Glenn Sudano, C.F.R.

19—OUR LADY OF FATIMA, (1977) (Portuguese), Rev. Osvaldo Franklin, J.C.D., Admin.; Sr. Rosa dos Ajos, T.O.F., Pastoral Assoc.; William Farren, Business Mgr.
Res., Portuguese R.C. Center, 355 S. Broadway, P.O. Box 283, 10705. Tel: 914-423-9688; Fax: 914-423-8271.

Yorktown Heights, Westchester Co., St. Patrick (1898), Rev. Msgr. Dermot R. Brennan; Revs. Louis Jerome; Michael O'Looney, C.S.Sp.
Res., 137 Moseman Rd., 10598. Tel: 914-962-5050; 5051; Fax: 914-962-0595.
School—(1953), 117 Moseman Rd., 10598. Tel: 914-962-2211; Fax: 914-243-4814.
Sisters 2; Lay Teachers 22; Students 371.
Catechesis/Religious Programs—Tel: 914-962-5586; Fax: 914-962-3207.
Students 2,110.

Youngsville, Sullivan Co., St. Francis of Assisi (1963). Unassigned.
Res., Jeffersonville, 12748. Tel: 914-482-4640; Fax: 914-482-3276. [CEM]

Yulan, Sullivan Co., St. Anthony of Padua (1907) (Irish-German), Rev. Evan J. Greco, O.F.M.
Res., 12792. Tel: 845-557-8512; Fax: 845-557-3527. [CEM]
Catechesis/Religious Programs—Students 70.
Mission—Pond Eddy, Sullivan Co., Sacred Heart, Berme Church Rd., Pond Eddy, 12770.

Chaplains of Public Institutions

Military Installations

NEW YORK. *National Catholic Community Service.* (Cardinal Spellman Servicemen's Club) 487 Park Ave., 10022. Rev. Msgr. Richard Cahill, Dir.
New York City Veterans Administration Hospital 406 First Ave., 10022. Rev. Edmund McCaffrey, O.Carm.

BRONX. *Veterans Administration Hospital* 130 W. Kingsbridge Rd., 10460. Rev. Edward A. Kozlowski; Rev. Msgr. Charles P. Boccio.

MONTROSE. *Franklin D. Roosevelt Hospital.* Revs. Daniel F. Lynch, O.Carm.; Albert Daly, O.Carm.; William J. O'Donnell.

WEST POINT. *Stewart Field.* Rev. Nash P. Geany.
West Point. Vacant. U.S. Military Academy, 10966.

Societies

NEW YORK. *Marine and Aviation Department.* Vacant.
New York Fire Department. Rev. Msgr. Marc A. Filacchione.
New York Police Department. Rev. Msgr. Joseph J. Zammit.
New York Postal Service. Rev. John W. Lennon.
New York Sanitation Department. Revs. John W. Lennon; Peter M. Colapietro.

YONKERS. *Yonkers Fire Department.* Rev. John W. Lennon.
Yonkers Police Department. Rev. John W. Lennon.

Prisons

CITY. *Adolescent Remand & Detention Center.* Sr. Margaret McCabe; Rev. John H. Wilkinson, 11-11 Hazen St., East Elmhurst, 11370. Tel: 718-546-7223.
Anna M. Kross Center. Revs. George J. Dash, O.F.M.Cap.; Charles Keeney, 18-18 Hazen St., East Elmhurst, 11370. Tel: 718-546-3654.
Bronx House of Detention. Rev. Vincent P. McNamara; Deacon Kenneth Radcliff, 653 River Ave., Bronx, 10451. Tel: 718-579-4371.
Correctional Institution for Men. Sr. Mary O'Connor; Rev. Thomas Houle, O.F.M.Cap., 10-10 Hazen St., East Elmhurst, 11370. Tel: 718-546-5796.
George M. Motchan Detention Center. Revs. Joseph P. Kane, S.J.; Thomas Mestriparampil, 15-15 Hazen St., East Elmhurst, 11370. Tel: 718-546-4543.
George Vierno Center. Rev. Joseph P. Kane, S.J.; Sr. Marie Hermann, 09-09 Hazen St., East Elmhurst, 11370. Tel: 718-204-5079, Ext. 2254.
James A. Thomas Center. Sr. Simone Ponnet; Rev. Thomas Houle, O.F.M.Cap., 14-14 Hazen St., East Elmhurst, 11370. Tel: 718-546-5421.
Manhattan Detention Center. Rev. Reginald John, 125 White St., New York, 10013. Tel: 212-225-1367.
North Infirmary Command. Rev. Lawrence E. Lucas; Sr. Amy Henry, 15-00 Hazen St., East Elmhurst, 11370. Tel: 718-546-1256.
Otis Bantum Correctional Center. Revs. Lawrence E. Lucas; Thomas Mestriparampil, 16-00 Hazen St., East Elmhurst, 11370. Tel: 718-546-6617.
Rose M. Singer Center. Rev. Joseph P. Kane, S.J. Tel: 718-546-7498; Sr. Marion Defeis, 19-19 Hazen St., East Elmhurst, 11370.
Spofford Juvenile Center. Vacant. 1221 Spofford Ave., Bronx, 10474. Tel: 718-579-0100.
West Facility. Rev. Frank Passenant, 16-06 Hazen St., East Elmhurst, 11370. Tel: 718-546-4495.

COUNTY. *Dutchess County Jail.* Rev. Ernest D'Onofrio, O.F.M., Tel: 914-297-5706.
Orange County Jail. Attended from St. John, Goshen. Tel: 914-294-5328.
Putnam County Jail. Attended by St. James, Carmel. Tel: 914-225-2079.
Rockland County Jail. Attended by St. Augustine, New City. Tel: 914-634-3641.
Sullivan County Jail. Attended by St. Peter, Monticello. Tel: 914-794-5577.
Ulster County Jail. Attended by Church of St. Joseph, Kingston. Tel: 914-338-1554.
Westchester County Jail. Rev. Paul Tolve, O.F.M.Cap., Box 389, Valhalla, 10595. Tel: 914-347-6132.

FEDERAL. *Federal Correctional Institution.* Rev. Dennis Gabian, Otisville, 10963. Tel: 914-386-5855, Ext. 291.
Metropolitan Correctional Center. Revs. Juan Soles; Michael O'Hara, O.M.I., 150 Park Row, New York, 10007-1779. Tel: 212-240-9656, Ext. 6454.

STATE. *Arthur Kill Correctional Facility.* Rev. Frank Naccarato, 2911 Arthur Kill Rd., Staten Island, 10309-1197. Tel: 718-356-7333.
Bayview Correctional Facility. Rev. George J. Dash, O.F.M.Cap., 550 W. 20th St., New York, 10011-2878. Tel: 212-255-7590.
Beacon Correctional Facility. Rev. Richard Kulwiec, O.M.I.; Deacon John O'Reilly, Box 780, Beacon, 12508-0780. Tel: 914-831-4200.
Bedford Hills Correctional Facility. Rev. Michael O'Shea; Sr. Elaine Roulet, 247 Harris Rd., Bedford Hills, 10507-2499. Tel: 914-241-3100.
Downstate Correction Facility. Rev. Donald B. Licata; Deacon Anthony Gruerio, Box 445, Fishkill, 12524-0445. Tel: 914-831-6600.
Eastern Correctional Facility. Rev. Jose Mappilamattela; Deacon Franklyn Russell, Napanoch, 12458-0338. Tel: 914-647-7400.
Edgecombe Correctional Facility. Deacon Nicholas Mazzei, 611 Edgecombe Ave., New York, 10032-4398. Tel: 212-923-2575.
Fishkill Correctional Facility. Rev. Donald B. Licata, Box 307, Beacon, 12508. Tel: 914-831-4800.
Fulton Correctional Facility. Deacon Nicholas Mazzei, 1511 Fulton Ave., Bronx, 10457-8398. Tel: 718-583-8000.
Green Haven Correctional Facility. Rev. Gamini E. Fernando; Deacon David Weinstein, Stormville, 12582. Tel: 914-221-2711.
Lincoln Correctional Facility. Deacon Nicholas Mazzei, 31-33 W. 110 St., New York, 10026-4398. Tel: 212-860-9400.
Mid-Orange Correctional Facility. Deacon Ricardo Rosado; Rev. Augustine Graap, O.Carm., Warwick, 10990-0990. Tel: 914-986-2291.

Otisville Correctional Facility. Rev. Augustine Graap, O.Carm.; Deacon Eugene Bormann, Box 8, Otisville, 10963-0008. Tel: 914-386-1490.
Parkside Correctional Facility. Deacon Nicholas Mazzei, 10 Mt. Morris Park W., New York, 10027-6395. Tel: 212-860-6835.
Shawangunk Correctional Facility. Deacon Joseph Doherty, Box 750, Wallkill, 12589-0750. Tel: 914-895-2081.
Sing Sing Correctional Facility. Revs. Ronald J. Lemmert; George J. Dash; Sr. Antonia Maguire, 354 Hunter St., Ossining, 10562-5442. Tel: 914-941-0108.
Sullivan Correctional Facility. Rev. Stanislaus Ogbonna, P.O. Box AG, Fallsburg, 12733-0116. Tel: 914-434-2080.
Taconic Correctional Facility. Sr. Antonia Maguire; Rev. George J. Dash, O.F.M.Cap., 250 Harris Rd., Bedford Hills, 10507-2498. Tel: 914-241-3010.
Ulster Correctional Facility. Rev. Jose Mappilamattela; Deacon Joseph Doherty, Berme Rd., P.O. Box 800, Napanoch, 12458. Tel: 914-647-1670.
Wallkill Correctional Facility. Rev. Paul Thymoutil; Deacon Angelo Cosaro, Box G, Wallkill, 12589-0286. Tel: 914-895-2021.
Woodbourne Correctional Facility. Rev. Marcelo Blazquez Rodrigo, Pouch 1, Woodbourne, 12788. Tel: 914-434-7730.

Hospitals

BEACON. *Craig House Hospital*. Serviced by St. Joachim, Beacon. Tel: 914-831-1200.

BRONX. *Bronx Municipal Hospital Center, Abraham Jacobi Hospital, Nathan B. VanEtten Hospital*. Revs. Sancho G. Garrote; Robert Holick, M.H.M. Tel: 212-430-8771.
Bronx Psychiatric Center Tel: 212-931-0600. Rev. James J. Cunningham.
Bronx-Lebanon Hospital Center Tel: 212-590-1800; 518-5059. Revs. Robert A. Jeffers; Ruben Cammayo; Deacon Alfonso Ramos.
Calvary Hospital Tel: 212-518-2114. Ms. Mary Teresa O'Neill, Asst. Admin. Pastoral Ministries.
Lincoln Medical and Mental Health Center Tel: 212-579-5000; 579-5059. Rev. Abel Alvarez, O.S.U.
Montefiore Medical Center Tel: 212-920-4997. Revs. Thomas Aidoo, Dir. Pastoral Care; John Dam Tran.
North Central Bronx Hospital. Serviced by Jacobi Medical Chaplain. Tel: 212-519-5000.
Our Lady of Mercy Medical Center. Rev. Msgr. Frederick J. Becker, Vice Pres. Pastoral Svcs.; Revs. Thomas P. D'Angelo; Bernard Iheoha; Sr. Cathanne McVicar, S.M.; Sr. Joan Marie O'Leary, O.P.,
Pelham Bay Division, Serviced by priests and chaplains from Our Lady of Mercy Medical Center. Tel: 212-920-9086; 920-9000.
St. Barnabas Hospital Tel: 212-960-9000. Rev. Msgr. Thomas McGarry; Rev. Marcellius Uwando; Sr. Miriam Hanratty, O.P.; Deacon Victor Pino.
U.S.V.A. Medical Center. Rev. Msgr. Joseph J. Zammit; Revs. Roland LaFontant (France); Gregory Little; Eugene O'Hara; Stephen Shubiak, Tel: 212-584-9000, Ext. 1878.
Union Hospital. Serviced by St. Barnabas Hospital. Tel: 212-200-2020.
Westchester Square Hospital. Serviced by Santa Maria Parish. Tel: 718-828-2380.

BRONXVILLE. *Lawrence Hospital* Tel: 914-337-7300. Rev. Paul Vezhaparambil, C.M.I.; Sr. Agnes Regina Hughes, S.C.

CALLICOON. *Community General Hospital*. Serviced by St. Peter, Monticello Tel: 914-887-5530.

CARMEL. *Putnam Hospital Center*. Serviced by St. James the Apostle, Carmel. Tel: 914-279-5711. Rev. Robert J. Ginel.

CASTLE POINT. *Veterans Administration Medical Center* Tel: 914-831-2000, Ext. 5453. Revs. Donald Lynch, O'Carm.; Robert P. Tracy, O'Carm.

COLD SPRING. *Julia L. Butterfield Memorial Hospital*. Serviced by Our Lady of Loretto, Cold Spring. Tel: 914-265-3642.

CORNWALL. *The Cornwall Hospital*. Serviced by St. Thomas of Canterbury, Cornwall-on-Hudson. Tel: 914-534-7711.

DOBBS FERRY. *Community Hospital of Dobbs Ferry*. Serviced by Sacred Heart, Dobbs Ferry. Tel: 914-693-0700.
St. Cabrini Nursing Home Tel: 914-693-6800. Sr. Suzanne Poulin, C.N.D.; Rev. Edwin Robinson, O.F.M.

ELLENVILLE. *Ellenville Community Hospital*. Serviced by the Church of St. Mary & St. Andrew, Ellenville. Tel: 914-647-6080.

GOSHEN. *Arden Hill Hospital*. Serviced by St. John, Goshen. Tel: 914-294-5441.

HARRIS. *Community General Hospital of Sullivan County*. Serviced by St. Peter, Monticello. Tel: 914-292-4525.

HARRISON. *St. Vincent Hospital and Medical Center of New York*. Rev. Joseph F. Cavoto, S.A., Dir. Pastoral Care, Tel: 914-967-6500.

HAWTHORNE. *Rosary Hill Home* Tel: 914-769-0114. Rev. John Proppe, O.F.M.Cap.

KINGSTON. *Benedictine Hospital* Tel: 914-338-2500. Sr. M. Dorothy Huggard, O.S.B., Dir. Pastoral Care.; Revs. Louis Yoya; Lionel G. Trudel, M.M.
Kingston City Hospital Tel: 914-331-3131. Rev. Cornelius C. Woulfe, C.S.Sp.

MANHATTAN. *Beekman Downtown - New York Infirmary* Tel: 212-312-5000; 233-5300. Revs. Thomas McKeon, S.S.S.; Peter Ma.
Bellevue Hospital. Revs. John Logan, O.Carm.; Kenneth Murphy, O.Carm.; Philip Marani, O.Carm.
Beth Israel Medical Center Tel: 212-420-2000. Revs. Edmund O'Kere; Reynaldo Domagas.
Bird S. Coler Memorial Hospital and Home Tel: 212-838-8155. Revs. Harold F.X. O'Donnell, S.J.; Peter Murray, S.J.
Cabrini Medical Center Tel: 212-995-6056. Rev. Andrew Sioleti, O.F.M., Coord. Patient/Chaplaincy Svcs., Chaplains: Revs. Raymond G. Pierini, M.M.; Rafael R. Macaranas; Sr. Jean Cook, I.C.M.; Sr. Sofia Unneta Wood, R.S.C.J.; Sr. Stephanie Kabacinksi, M.S.C.; Sr. Consolata Demma, M.S.C.
Columbia Presbyterian Medical Center. Revs. Donald Johnson; Fred Carrigan,
Allen Pavilion, Rev. Thomas J. Clerkin, C.S.P.; Deacon Miguel Granda.
Goldwater Memorial Hospital Tel: 212-750-6800; 750-6674. Chaplains: Rev. Timothy A. Healey, S.J.; Mrs. Margaret Karwoski.
Gouverneur Hospital Tel: 212-374-4000. Rev. Dennis J. Sullivan; Sr. Clare Roche, P.B.V.M.
Gracie Square. Serviced by St. Jean Baptiste. Tel: 212-988-4400.
Harlem Hospital. Serviced by St. Mark. Tel: 212-491-8061.
Hospital for Special Surgery Tel: 212-606-1000. Sr. Margaret Oettinger, O.P.
Lenox Hill Hospital Tel: 212-439-2547. Rev. Edmund Slattery, S.S.S.; Bro. Michael Perez, S.S.S.
Manhattan Eye, Ear & Throat Hospital. Serviced by St. Vincent Ferrer. Tel: 212-838-9200.
Manhattan Psychiatric Center Tel: 212-369-0500, Ext. 2530. Rev. Andrew Cuu Nguyen.
Medical Arts Center Hospital. Serviced by St. Patrick Cathedral. Tel: 212-755-0200.
Memorial Sloan Kettering Cancer Center Tel: 212-639-5982. Rev. William Robert Gannon, O.P.
Metropolitan Hospital Tel: 212-230-6262. Rev. Michael J. Sala, S.J.; Sr. Kathleen Doyle, F.S.P., Coord. Pastoral Care.
Mount Sinai Medical Center. Revs. Apolinari J. Ngirwa; Philip Romano, O.F.M.Cap.; Sr. Mary Damian Glenane, S.A.
New York Eye & Ear Infirmary. Vacant. Tel: 212-673-3480.
New York Presbyterian Hospital Tel: 212-746-4690. Revs. Vincent McHenry, O.P.; David A. Butler, O.P.; Stephen Carmody, O.P.; Paul B. Fu, O.P.; Philip Fitzsimmons, O.P.; Sr. Margaret T. Oettinger, O.P.
New York University Medical Center Tel: 212-263-7300. Revs. Francisco Abaya; Gabriel Anosike,
Hospital for Joint Disease, Serviced by Mary Help of Christians, 212-254-0058.
North General Hospital. Serviced by All Saints. Rev. Lawrence E. Lucas, Tel: 212-650-4511.
Rockefeller University. Serviced by St. Catherine of Siena. Tel: 212-570-8000. Rev. George P. Carlin, O.P.
St. Clare's Hospital & Health Center Tel: 212-586-1500. Revs. John J. Donahue, C.S.C.; George Carlin; Sr. Pascal Conforti, O.S.U.
St. Luke's-Roosevelt Hospital Center Tel: 212-523-2016.
Roosevelt Site, Rev. James F. McQuade, C.S.P.
St. Vincent Hospital Tel: 212-790-7000. Revs. John Bickle, O.F.M., Dir. Pastoral Care; James O'Connell; Jefferson Hammer; Sr. Eileen Lambert, O.S.F.
Terence Cardinal Cooke Health Care Center Tel: 212-360-1000. Rev. Ronald Green; Sr. Joan Gannon, R.S.C.J.; Sr. Lorraine Cooper, S.C.; Sr. Maryanne Daly, S.C., Dir. Pastoral Care.
U.S.V.A. Medical Center Tel: 212-686-7500. Revs. Benedict D'Alessandro; Edmund McCaffrey, O.Carm.; Francis C. Morgan, SS.CC.

MIDDLETOWN. *Horton Memorial Hospital*. Serviced by St. Joseph, Middletown. Tel: 914-343-2424.
Middletown Psychiatric Center. Vacant. Tel: 914-342-5511.

MONTROSE. *FDR DVA Hospital*. Vacant.

MOUNT KISCO. *Northern Westchester Hospital*. Serviced by St. Francis, Mt. Kisco. Tel: 914-666-1200.

MOUNT VERNON. *Mount Vernon Hospital*. Rev. Isaac Aganbi, Tel: 914-664-8000.

NEW HAMPTON. *MID Hudson Psychiatric Center*. Rev. John Eyrrick, Senior Chap., Tel: 914-374-3171, Ext. 3601.

NEW ROCHELLE. *South Shore Medical Center*. Rev. John Muscat, Tel: 914-632-5000.

NEWBURGH. *St. Luke Hospital*. Serviced by St. Patrick, Newsburgh. Tel: 914-561-4400.

NORTH TARRYTOWN. *Phelps Memorial Hospital*. Serviced by St. Theresa's, Sleepy Hollow. Tel: 914-631-0720.

NYACK. *Nyack Hospital*. Serviced By St. Ann, Nyack. Shirley Blair, Dir. Pastoral Care, Tel: 914-358-6200.

ORANGEBURG. *Rockland Psychiatric Center*. Revs. Donald T. Driscoll; John Sullivan, O.P., Tel: 914-359-1000, Ext. 3589.

OSSINING. *Stony Lodge Hospital*. Serviced by St. Augustine, Ossining. Tel: 914-941-7400.

PEEKSKILL. *Hudson Valley Hospital Center*. Serviced by Holy Spirit, Cortlandt Manor. Tel: 914-737-9000.

POMONA. *Dr. Robert L. Yeager Health Center*. Susan Osborne, Pastoral Care, Tel: 914-354-0200, Ext. 2889.

PORT CHESTER. *United Hospital*. Serviced by Our Lady of Mercy, Port Chester. Tel: 914-939-0612.

PORT JERVIS. *Mercy Community Hospital* Tel: 914-856-5351. Sr. Margaret Costa, R.S.M., Dir. Pastoral Care; Rev. Bernard McDonald; Sr. M. Audrey Hallahan, R.S.M.; Deacon John Nash.

POUGHKEEPSIE. *Hudson River Psychiatric Center* Tel: 914-452-8000, Ext. 378. Rev. James J. LeBar; Deacon George Cacchone, Assoc. Chap.
St. Francis Hospital Tel: 914-471-2000. Pastoral Care Assocs.: Sr. Mary Ellen Smith, O.S.F.; Sr. Marie Colette, O.S.F.
Vassar Brothers Hospital Tel: 914-454-8500. Rev. Anthony S. Marian.

RHINEBECK. *Northern Dutchess Hospital*. Serviced by Good Shepherd, Rhinebeck. Tel: 914-876-4583.

RYE. *Rye Psychiatric Hospital Center*. Serviced by Church of the Resurrection, Rye. Tel: 914-967-4567.

STATEN ISLAND. *Bayley Seton Hospital* Tel: 718-390-6000. Rev. Edward J. Datty, S.A., Dir. Pastoral Care, Chaplains: Sr. Claire Marian Barton, S.C.; Bro. Kieran Cullen, S.A.
Doctor's Hospital of Staten Island. Serviced by St. Sylvester. Tel: 718-727-4639.
St. Vincent's Medical Center of Richmond Tel: 718-876-1234. Revs. Roger Vaughan, Dir. Pastoral Care; Ralph Dawis, Chap.; Peter Selvaj; Sr. Mary Alice Duggan, O.S.U.
Seaview Hospital and Home Tel: 718-371-3000, Ext. 3284. Rev. Blase B. Kardos, O.F.M.Conv.
Staten Island University Hospital North. Rev. Simon Savarimuthu; Sr. Francesca Cloutier; Deacon Rosario J. Tirella.
Staten Island University Hospital South Tel: 718-260-2000. Rev. Pius Ejifor.

SUFFERN. *Good Samaritan Hospital* Tel: 914-357-3300. Sr. Sheila Mullins, O.P.; Sr. Margaret Strouch, S.S.N.D., Dir. Pastoral Care; Rev. Gerardo DeFillippes; Sr. Anne Tonne, S.C.; Revs. George Mattioni, O.A.R.; Frank Cregon, O.A.R.

TUXEDO PARK. *Tuxedo Memorial Health Care Center*. Vacant. Tel: 914-351-4751.

VALHALLA. *Blythdale Children's Hospital*. Serviced by Holy Name of Jesus. Tel: 914-592-7555.
Westchester County Medical Center Tel: 914-347-7000. Revs. James Stewart, O.F.M.Cap.; Paul Tolve, O.F.M.Cap.

WARWICK. *St. Anthony Community Hospital* Tel: 914-986-2276. Rev. John Pierce, O.F.M.

WASSAIC. *Wassaic Development Center*. Serviced by Immaculate Conception Armenia. Rev. John Durkin.

WEST HAVERSTRAW. *Helen Hayes Hospital*. Rev. Anthony Louis, S.D.B.

WHITE PLAINS. *Burke Rehabilitation Center* Tel: 914-948-0050. Rev. Patrick J. Dunne, Pastor; Sr. Laura Morgan, F.M.S.C.
New York Hospital - Cornell Medical Center. Rev. Richard Liew, Dir. Pastoral Care & Education.
St. Agnes Hospital Tel: 914-681-4500. Sr. Mary Virginia Brady, R.D.C., Dir. Pastoral Care; Sr. Mary Vogl, Pastoral Assoc.; Rev. James Larkin, M.S.S.A., Chap.; Sr. Mary Lusk, P.B.V.M.
White Plains Hospital Tel: 914-681-0600. Rev. Benedict J. Kuolt.

YONKERS. *St. John Hospital*. (Night Call-Christ the King, Yonkers, 914-963-7474) Tel: 914-964-4444. Rev. Neal Kerrigan, O.F.M.Cap.
St. Joseph Hospital Tel: 914-378-7000. Sr. Carolyn Parker, R.S.M., Dir. Pastoral Care; Sr. Dolores Doyle, P.B.V.M., Pastoral Care Assoc.; Rev. Thomas Murphy, O.F.M.Cap.; Sr. Mary Spano, S.C.; Deacon John Treiling.
Yonkers General Hospital. See Archdiocesan Directory for Parishes that Service Nursing Homes and Homes for the Aged. Tel: 914-964-7399. Rev. Pedro Foschiatti.

On Duty Outside the Archdiocese:
Most Rev.—
McCormack, William J., Society for the Propagation of the Faith
Reverend Monsignors—
Balvo, Charles D., Apostolic Nunciatura, Prague, Czech Republic
Irwin, Kevin W., Catholic University of America, Washington, DC
Meier, John P., Notre Dame Univ., South Bend, IN
Murnion, Philip J., National Pastoral Life Conference
O'Brien, William B., Daytop Village, 54 W. 40th St., New York, NY 10018
White, William, St. Vincent de Paul Seminary, Boynton Beach, FL
Reverend Fathers—
Brown, Charles, Congregation Pro, Doctrina Fidei
Carden, Robert J., St. Joseph's, Pueblo, CO
Carson, David L., Dept. of Veterans Affairs, Bath, NY
Dillon, Richard J., Fordham University, Fordham Rd., Bronx, NY 10458
Hartmann, Edward J., Archdiocese of Fairbanks
Imbelli, Robert, Boston College
Kang, Paul, St. Andrew Kim, Orange, NJ
Kennedy, Robert T., Catholic University of America, Washington, DC
Komonchak, Joseph A., Catholic University of America, Washington, DC
LeBlanc, Paul, St. Mary's, P.O. Box 28, Church Point, Nova Scotia, Canada
Lonek, Stephen C., Diocese of Wilmington
Malcolm, Dennis E.
Marino, Umberto J.
Martin, William F., P.O. Box 65, Warren, VT 05674
McDonald, Thomas M., Fordham University, Lincoln Center, NY
O'Donnell, William J., V.A. Hospital, Montrose, NY
Rutler, George W., Legatus Apostolate
Serra, Dominic, St. Pauls Seminary, St. Paul, MN
Shelly, Thomas J., Fordham Univ.
Smarsh, Charles F., University of Maryland
Tou, John, Holy Family, Singapore
Whitson, Robley E., United Institute, Bethelem, CT
Young, William E., Archdiocese of Santa Fe, St. Anthony's Church, P.O. Box 200, Questa, NM 87556

Military Chaplains:
Reverend Monsignors—
Hill, Philip W., Office of the Chief of Chaplains, 2700 Army Pentagon, Washington, DC
Reverend Fathers—
Borkowski, Francis, U.S.A., 102 Honeysuckle Ct., Apt. 10, Radcliff, KY 40160
Deponai, Joseph J., U.S.A., Box 55, Black River, NY 13612
Keeley, Patrick P., (Retired), U.S.N.
Kelly, John R., 779 Galloway Dr., Fayetteville, NC 28303
Lindblad, Karl-Albert, U.S.N., Merchant Marine Academy, Kings Point, NY 11024
Mandato, Kieran, U.S.N., Fordham Univ.
McGeory, Peter, U.S.N., USS Carl Vinson, (CVN 70), FPO AP, 96306
Muhm, William M., Naval Air Facility Atsugi, PSC 477, Box 18, FPO AP, 96306
Mullin, Thomas
O'Reilly, Edward M., (Retired), U.S.A.
Panek, Robert M., U.S.N., Naval Odmin, Supv, SC 45, ASU Box 92, FPO AP, 09824
Pugliese, Francis A., 1854 Princeton Ct., Gurnee, IL 60031
Sandi, Thomas P., U.S.A.F., 2 Heritage Rd., Hanson AFB, Bedford, MA 01731
Tran, Philip P., Nctams West Pac, Guam PSC 488, Box 144, FPO AP, 96540
Travers, Alan, Box 2524, Havelock, NC 28532

On Special or Other (Arch)Diocesan Assignment:
Reverend Monsignors—
Barrett, Harry C., New York Medical College, Valhalla, NY 10595
Vaughey, James K., Exec. Dir., Cemeteries, The Trustees of St. Patrick's Cathedral in the City of New York, Inc.
Reverend Fathers—
Martin, William, Christian Foundation for Children & Aging, Woodstock, VT
O'Malley, Francis P., M.S. in Education, St. Clare's Hospital and Medical Center, 415 W. 51st St., New York, NY 10019
Quinn, John L., Christian Foundation for Children & Aging, Fort Lauderdale, FL

Graduate Studies:
Reverend Fathers—
Furey, Matthew, North America College
Kreiser, Thomas L.

Absent on Sick leave:
Reverend Monsignors—
Coyne, James F.
Reverend Fathers—
Altrui, Ronald
Coleman, John
Conlan, James S.
McKay, Frank
O'Connor, Maurice
Sandstrom, Philip J.
Slattery, Maurice C.

Absent on Leave:
Reverend Fathers—
Antony, Charles
Barjacoba, Peter
Beck, Steven Thomas
Bolger, James
Bowes, Bruce
Brogan, William
Calabrese, Daniel
Calhoun, C. John
Cassiero, Daniel
Ciaravolo, Ronald
Clark, Andrew
Doherty, John B.
Donahue, Joseph
Elmo, Francis E.
Eremito, Anthony
Geraghty, James
Gollinge, Donald
Hoehmann, George
Hoffay, Thomas
Kovach, Raymond J.
Malone, Donald
McGill, Joseph F.
McLucas, James
Mills, Henry
Mulloy, William
Peluso, Michael J.
Pipala, Edward A.
Quigley, Patrick
Quinn, James
Ross, Brenden
Surace, Robert J.

Retired:
Most Rev.—
Ahern, Patrick, St. Thomas More, 65 E. 89th St., New York, NY 10128
Mahoney, James P., Assumption, 131 Union Ave., Peekskill, NY 10566
Reverend Monsignors—
Alessandro, Michael J., 1496 Commonwealth Ave., Bronx, NY 10460
Arpie, Robert A., Marg Manning Walsh Home, 1339 York Ave, New York, NY 10021
Bardes, George F., Stephinac High School, 950 Mamaroneck Ave., White Plains, NY 10605
Bourke, Myles M., Portsmouth Abbey School, Portsmouth, RI
Byrne, Harry J., 222 E. 93rd St., Apt. 39E, New York, NY 10128
Clyne, Vincent F., 376 Baden Pl., Staten Island, NY 10306
Cohalan, Florence, St. Agnes, 143 E. 43rd St., New York, NY 10017
Connors, Edward M., Stepinac Archbishop Residence, 950 Mamaroneck Ave., White Plains, NY 10605
Corrigan, Bernard J., St. Stephen, 75 Sanfordville Rd., Warwick, NY 10990
Costello, Francis M., McKeen Residence, 311 Flager Dr., West Palm Beach, FL 33401
Curtin, Richard B., Lucas Ave., Cottekill, NY 12419
Daly, John, 14309 A Canalview Dr., Delray Beach, FL 33484
Delaney, William B., 43 W. Orland Rd., Milford, CT 06460
Devlin, Joseph M., 190 Hollywood Ave., Bronx, NY 10465
DiBlasi, Augustine J., Archbishop Stepinac Residence, 950 Mamaroneck, White Plains, NY 10605
Doherty, John T., Stepinac High School, 950 Mamaroneck Ave., White Plains, NY 10605
Duffy, Francis X., 1083 Washington Green, New Windsor, NY 12553
Dunne, Joseph A., 10777 Sample Rd., Coral Springs, FL 33065
Dwyer, Michael F., 3121 Ninth Ave. N., St. Petersburg, FL 33713
Fowler, Eugene A., Hearts Content Rd., Roxbury, CT 12474
Gallagher, Thomas V., Our Lady of Consolation, 3103 Arlington Ave., Bronx, NY 10463
Geissler, Robert, 196 Azalea Cir., Jackson, NY 08527
Gillen, John J., St. John Newmann Residence, 5655 Arlington Ave., Bronx, NY 10471
Glynn, Francis J., Holy Family, 366 Watchogue Rd., Staten Island, NY 10314
Goodwine, Joseph G., 960 Palm View Rd., Naples, FL 33942
Guido, William F., 121 Egbert Ave., Staten Island, NY
Hammer, Edmond, Bethel Nursing Home, Ossining, NY 10562
Hanlon, James J., 150 Riverside Dr., New York, NY 10024
Harrington, John M., St. Margaret, 115 W. Central Ave., Pearl River, NY 10965
Jablonski, Stanislaus, St. Valentine, 810 E. 221 St., Bronx, NY
Jeffers, Vincent W., Archbishop Stepinac Residence, 950 Mamaroneck Ave., White Plains, NY 10605
Keating, James V., St. Joseph, 242 Wall St., Kingston, NY 12401
Kelly, George A., 107-10 Shore Front Pkwy., Rockaway Beach, NY 11694
Keogh, Thomas J., 4 Dogwood Rd., Hampton Bays, NY 11946
Marbach, Joseph, 3410 Amalfi Dr., West Palm Beach, FL 33417
Marinacci, Nicholas, St. Patrick's Old Cathedral, 263 Mulberry St., New York, NY 10012
Mazziotta, Robert R., P.O. Box 705, Philmont, NY 12565
McCormack, Robert, 910 Boston Post Rd., Rye, NY 10580
McMahon, William J., Holy Spirit, 1969 Crompond Rd., Cortland Manor, NY 10566
McManus, Charles J., St. Gabriel, 3250 Arlington Ave., Bronx, NY 10461
Montano, Edward J., 4 Fiero Rd., P.O. Box 152, Malden-on-Hudson, NY 12453
Narkun, Peter P., Cardinal Hayes High School, 650 Grand Concourse, Bronx, NY 10451
Pavis, Victor C., Cardinal Hayes High School, 650 Grand Concourse, Bronx, NY 10451
Potocek, Cyril J., Holy Cross, 118 Beekman Ave. N., Sleepy Hollow, NY 10591
Quinn, Andrew F., Sacred Heart, 981 Castleton Ave., Staten Island, NY 10310
Quinn, John J., St. Joseph's Seminary, Yonkers, NY 10704
Quinn, Joseph J., John Paul II Residence, 603 First Ave., New York, NY 10016
Raimondo, Joseph J., St. Gregory the Great, 215 Halstead Ave., Harrison, NY 10528
Rigney, Raymond P., Archbishop Stepinac Residence, 950 Mamaroneck Ave., White Plains, NY 10605
Rooney, Hugh J., Our Lady of Consolation Residence, 3103 Arlington Ave., Bronx, NY 10463
Rossbach, George F., 45-315 Lilipuna Rd., B202, Kaneoke, HI 96744
Rosselli, Charles, 9765 B Tabebuia Tree Dr., Boynton Beach, FL 33436
Ryan, Gerald J., St. Luke's, Bronx, NY
Schroeder, Walter L., 525 Bedford Rd., North Tarrytown, NY 10591
Wilkinson, John, Archbishop Stepinac Residence, 950 Mamaroneck Ave., White Plains, NY 10605
Reverend Fathers—
Adamo, Joseph P., 136 Ridgewood Dr., Daphne, AL 36526
Arold, Richard J., 1851 Madison Rd., Brooklyn, NY 11229
Basile, Nicholas F., Our Lady of Mt. Carmel, 627 E. 187 St., Bronx, NY 10458
Brennan, Robert J., 35 Cerone Pl., Apt. 507, Newburgh, NY 12550
Buttinelli, Anthony, Via Valle della Storta 75, Rome, 00123 Italy
Cavanaugh, John L., Archbishop Stepinac Residence, 950 Mamaroneck Ave., White Plains, NY 10605
Chiang, John B.
Cholette, John B., 6606 Fairpines Rd., Chesterfield, VA 23832
Conlin, Edward, Immaculate Conception, 414 E. 14th St., New York, NY 10009
Conte, James W., 2555 Willow St., San Diego, CA 92106
Conti, John P., 537 Third St., Brooklyn, NY 11215
Crotty, John M., 660 Americana Dr., Annapolis, MD 21403
Cusma, Joseph S., 255 Bronx River Rd., Apt. 8N, Yonkers, NY 10704
d'Anjou, Henry G., Archbishop Stepinac Residence, 950 Mamaroneck Ave., White Plains, NY 10605
D'Antonio, Anthony, Our Lady of Mt. Carmel, 627 E. 187th St., Bronx, NY 10458
D'Auriol, Vincent, Sts. Peter & Paul Parish, 833 St. Ann Ave., Bronx, NY 10456
Darby, Thomas J., John Paul II Residence, 603 First Ave., New York, NY 10016
Derrenbacher, James W., St. John Evangelist, 915 Rte. 212, Woodstock Rd., Saugerties, NY 12477
DiSenso, Gerald, 8000 Shore Front Pkwy., Apt. 114, Rockaway Beach, NY 11693

Doersam, Carl G., Ferncliff Nursing Home
Doyle, Philip R., Box 1088, Carmel, NY 10512
Duane, Robert J., 8000 Shore Front Pkwy., Rockaway Beach, NY 11693
Dumpson, Roland J., 15 W. 124th St., New York, NY 10027
Dunn, Robert T., West Lake Springs, Rohnert Park, CA 94928
Fiorillo, Antimo, 2352 St. Raymond's Ave., Bronx, NY 10462
Fleming, John F., 1083 Washington Green, New Windsor, NY 12553
Flynn, James P., 1310 Stoneybrook Ave., Mamaronek, NY 10543
Fogarty, Daniel, 6333 Rancho Mission Rd., San Diego, CA 92108
Gallagher, Edward, S.A.
Gallagher, Eugene P., 40 W. Point Hwy., Highland Falls, NY 10928
Gilhooley, James, 112 Patchett Way, Montgomery, NY 12549
Griffin, James, 8440 - B Pebble Circle, Tampa, FL 33615
Gussoni, Lino, Via Rodini Tedeschi 19, Piacenza, 29100 Italy
Halpin, Leo F., 5 Tanglewylde Ave., Apt. 6H, Bronxville, NY 10708
Holihan, John W., 422 Ocean Blvd., Long Beach, NJ 07740
Jenko, Aloysius, Pope John Paul II Residence, New York, NY 10016
Kelleher, William A., St. Joseph's, 15 Cedar St., Bronxville, NY 10708
Kelly, William E., Our Lady of Consolation, 3103 Arlington Ave., Bronx, NY 10463
Kennedy, William J., John Paul II Residence, 603 First Ave., New York, NY 10016
Kuolt, Benedict J., St. Bernard, 51 Prospect St., White Plains, NY 10606
Larkin, John P., John Paul II Residence, 603 First Ave., New York, NY 10016
Magee, Andrew T., John Paul II Residence, 603 First Ave., New York, NY 10016
Maher, John J., 43 Hearth Dr., New Windsor, NY 10704
McCann, Vincent, 2 Somerset Dr., Belvidere, NJ 07823
McGann, Joseph F., P.O. Box 2593, Montauk, NY 11954
McHale, Charles P., 266 Near Rd., Red Hook, NY 12571
McKenna, John J., St. Joan of Arc, 32 Eagle Valley Rd., Sloatsburg, NY 10974
Meade, John F., 65 Wright Ave., Malverne, NY 11565
Miller, Frederick J., 56 Sprague Ave., Staten Island, NY 10307
Minielli, Anthony, Via Colombo 9, 70028 Sannicandro, Bari
Molony, Francis J., Our Lady of Consolation Residence, 3103 Arlington Ave., Bronx, NY 10463
Moran, Thomas J., Ferncliff Nursing Home, 52 River Rd., Rhinebeck, NY 12572
Moriarty, James J., St. John the Evangelist, Pawling, NY
Neilson, Richard J., P.O. Box 999, S. Orleans, MA 02662
O'Hara, Eugene R., Our Lady of Consolation Residence, 3103 Arlington Ave., Bronx, NY 10463
O'Keefe, Thomas E., Stepinac High School, 950 Mamaroneck Ave., White Plains, NY 10605
O'Shea, Joseph J., St. Helena, 1315 Olmstead Ave., Bronx, NY 10462
O'Toole, Kenneth E., 15 St. John's Pl., Chappaqua, NY 10514
Pane, Andrew, 9 Pasadena Rd., Bronxville, NY 10708
Parsons, Harold J., Our Lady of Consolation Geriatric Care Center, 111 Beach Dr., West Islip, NY 11795
Sheridan, Eugene, P.O. Box 653, Woodbourne, NY 12788
Smolinski, Joseph J., 11 Dale Ave., Apt. 21, Highland Falls, NY 10928
Smyth, James, 616 Warburton Ave., Hastings-on-Hudson, NY 10706
Sullivan, Paul V., St. Joseph, 141 Ashburton Ave., Yonkers, NY 10701
Thenen, James, St. Peter's, 53 St. Marks Pl., Staten Island, NY 10301
Tiercelin, Harry, Pope John Paul II Residence, 603 First Ave., New York, NY 10016
Tubridy, James J., 1214 Springdale Rd., Croton-on-Hudson, NY 10520
Vala, John B., John Paul II Residence, 605 First Ave., New York, NY 10016

Permanent Deacons:
Abbamont, Thomas J., St. Ursula, Mount Vernon
Aglietti, Richard, St. Mary's, Mt. Vernon
Almanzar, Andres A., St. John Vianney, Bronx
Alvarado, William, St. Columba, Hopewell Junction
Anderson, John J., St. Martha, Sarasota, FL
Armo, John, St. John Evangelist, Mahopac
Attridge, James C., St. James the Apostle, Carmel
Aviles, Stanley, St. Denis, Hopewell Junction
Baerga, Luis, St. John the Evangelist, Goshen
Baffa, John, St. Lawrence O'Toole, Brewster
Banker, Howard A., Our Lady of Assumption, Bronx
Barbieri, Nicola A., Our Lady of Pompeii, Dobbs Ferry
Baterbury, John J., Sacred Heart of Jesus, Suffern
Battersby, William L., St. Mary, Mount Vernon
Bellacicco, John A., St. Augustine, Highland
Bello, Rafael J., St. Brigid, Manhattan
Bernal, Enrique, Our Lady of Guadalupe, South Manhattan
Biasotti, John C.
Biskup, William E., Regina Coeli, Hyde Park
Blake, George W., Block Island, RI
Bonanno, Joseph M., Regina Coeli, Hyde Park
Bormann, Eugene, St. Anastasia, Harriman
Borsavage, Charles T., St. James the Apostle, Carmel
Bouwmans, Philip R., Immaculate Conception, Port Jervis
Bragg, Richard, Holy Cross, Bronx
Brigande, Vincent G., St. Charles, Staten Island
Brockmann, Peter, Sacred Heart, Monroe
Brown, James A., SS. John & Paul, Larchmont
Bruno, Gaspare F., St. Elizabeth Ann Seton, Shrub Oak
Buckley, John J., St. Mary, Newburgh
Bunyar, Perry A., St. Mary of the Snow, Saugerties
Buonocore, Dominc A., St. Paul, Congers
Burke, Eugene F., St. Gabriel, Bronx
Burnett, Robert V., St. John, Antigua, West Indies
Burns, James T., Sacred Heart, Monroe
Cacchione, George F., St. Peter, Poughkeepsie
Calafiore, Michael R., St. Charles, Staten Island
Calimano, Ross J., Our Lady Queen of Peace, Staten Island
Camacho, Ismael, Joan of Arc, Bronx
Camacho, Vidal J., St. Elizabeth of Hungary, Pompano Beach, FL
Canals, Dhoel M., Holy Family, Bronx
Carlino, Frank R., St. Columba, Chester
Carroll, Harold N., St. Charles Borromeo, Gardiner
Casadone, Dominic G., Sacred Heart, Newburgh
Cassaneto, Anthony P., St. Theresa of the Child Jesus, Bronx
Castellanos, Luis, Miami Beach, FL
Charlesworth, Myles J., Our Lady of Lourdes Parish, Raleigh, NC
Check, Raymond P., St. Gregory the Great, Virginia Beach, VA
Ciccone, Daniel J., Corpus Christi, Port Chester
Clemens, Robert A., St. Bartholomew, Yonkers
Collins, George J., St. Thomas More, Boynton Beach, FL
Colton, Thomas, St. Boniface, Wesley Hills
Conner, Albert C., Annunciation, Crestwood
Coppola, John J., St. Columbanus, Peekskill
Corsaro, Angelo, Sacred Heart, Monroe
Cosme, Felix, St. Michael, Gainesville, GA
Cotto, Angel L., Caguas, Puerto Rico
Cruz, Edwin J., St. John Vianney, Bronx
D'Aiello, Joseph, Our Lady of Grace, Bronx
D'Arconte, Benjamin, Sacred Heart, Hartsdale
Darlestin, Leones J., Holy Name of Jesus, Manhattan
Daubman, Andrew, Holy Trinity, Poughkeepsie
Dauerer, Walter P., St. Denis, Hopewell Junction
Daur, Raymond
De Jesus, Jose L., St. Ann, Ossining
De Los Santos, German, Incarnation, North Manhattan
De Maio, Donald J., Venice, FL
De Marco, Carmine J., Holy Name of Jesus, New Rochelle
De Meis, John, Our Lady of Grace, Staten Island
Degenhardt, Carl, St. Ursula, Mount Vernon
Del Campo, Francis, Our Lady Rosary, Port Chester
Delgado, Luis, Our Lady of Angels, Bronx
Deschler, Bernard M., St. Thomas More; St. Edmund, Rockaway Pt.
di Targiani, Robert, Immaculate Heart of Mary, Scarsdale
Dingee, Richard D., Ulster Correctional Facility, Napanoch
Doherty, Joseph, St. Joseph, Kingston
Donovan, William, St. Margaret, Pearl River
Dowen, Roland, St. Gregory, Garnerville
Dringus, William L., Holy Spirit, E. Greenbush
Droulette, Donald L., St. Joseph, Kingston
Duncan, Robert, Sacred Heart, Monroe
Duran, Nelson, St. Anthony of Padua, Bronx
Eccleston, Arthur W., Our Lady of Good Counsel, Staten Island
Edgerton, John M., St. Luke the Evangelist, Palm Harbor, FL
Esposito, Robert A., St. John the Evangelist, Mahopac
Estela, Jorge, St. Peter's, Haverstraw
Fama, Arthur, St. Joseph-St. Thomas, Staten Island
Feliciano, Ulises, Our Lady of Pillar, Santa Ana, CA
Fernandez, Roberto, St. Raymond, Bronx
Ferraiuolo, Anthony P., St. Joseph, New Windsor
Ferreira, Emetrio
Fien, Robert A., Our Lady of Mercy, Port Chester
Fontanez, Luis, Holy Cross, Bronx
Forte, Joseph, St. Benedict, Bronx
Fox, Michael J., Our Lady of Fatima, Scarsdale
Francis, James, Sts. Peter and Paul, Bronx
Frohbose, John M., Our Lady of Mt. Carmel, Middletown
Frohmiller, Richard J., St. Joseph, Kingston
Gallagher, Daniel J., Palm Beach, FL
Garcia, Rene, Our Lady of Guadalupe, New York
Gaskin, Theodore A., St. Pius X, Scarsdale
Gilbert, John, St. Paul, Leesburgh, FL
Glover, William, St. Patrick, Newburgh
Gohl, Frank, Regina Coeli, Hyde Park
Gontcharuk, Robert, Holy Name of Jesus, New Rochelle
Gonzalez, Faustino, Santiago de Compostella, Spain
Gonzalez, Ismael, Caguas, Puerto Rico
Gorman, James, St. Paul, Congers
Gorzka, Stephen S.
Graf, Joseph J., St. Margaret Mary, Staten Island
Granda, Miguel E., St. Paul, Manhattan
Griffin, Francis J., Our Lady of Fatima, Scarsdale
Grosso, Edward, Assumption, Maybrook
Gruerio, Anthony G., St. James, Carmel
Hafemann, Joseph R., St. Mary, Fishkill
Haight, Peter R., Sacred Heart, Newburgh
Hamilton, Eugene R., St. Peter, Haverstraw
Hamilton, James J., St. Paul the Apostle, Yonkers
Hanson, Lee, Conifer Park & Sanatoga Hospital Nursing Home, Albany
Hayes, James R., St. Peter, Poughkeepsie
Hennessy, John L., St. Barnabas, Bronx
Hernandez, Narcisco, Our Lady Queen of Martyrs, Manhattan
Hill, William J., St. Pius X, Scarsdale
Hodges, Raymond, Our Savior, Pine Bush
Hogan, Patrick J., St. Martin de Porres, Poughkeepsie
Hooghuis, Joseph, St. Patrick, Staten Island
Hopkins, Farrell J., St. Charles Borromeo, Dover Plains
Horvath, Robert J., St. Thomas More Parish, Sarasota, FL
Howley, Herbert, St. Joseph, Greenwich
Hudson, Alan A., St. Ann, Nyack
Hyland, Arnold, St. Mary of the Snow, Saugerties
Impallomeni, Alfred R., Our Lady of Mount Carmel, Yonkers
Irizarry, Pedro, St. Peter, Yonkers
Jarmick, Robert E., St. Martin de Porres, Poughkeepsie
Jean-Gilles, Gabriel
John, Scarfi, St. John the Evangelist, Mahopac
Johnson, Robert, Sacred Heart, Suffern
Johnson, Thomas R., St. Joseph, Greenwich Village
Juhasz, Lajos, St. Margaret of Hungary, Yonkers
Kawula, Lawrence, Sacred Heart, Newburgh
Kazimir, Martin, St. Mary, Fishkill
Kelleher, John C., St. Catharine, Blauvelt
Klein, Albert J., St. Peter, Poughkeepsie
Klein, John P., St. William, Ward, SC
Knack, Lawrence F., St. Mary, Obernberg
Knight, Charles C., Marysville, OH
Koch, George J., Our Lady of Lourdes, Sun City West, AZ
Kollar, John J., Our Lady of Fatima, Scarsdale
Lagotta, Anthony A., Our Lady of Mt. Carmel & St. Benedicta, Staten Island
Lambert, Pedro, Our Lady of Lourdes, Manhattan
Lamberty, Angel, Sts. Mary and Andrew, Ellenville
Larkin, John J., St. Peter, Rosendale
Laurato, Vincent I., St. Barnabas, Bronx
Le Blanc, Vincent F., Westchester Medical Center
Leasiolagi, Taulafoga, St. John Vianney, Bronx
Li Greci, Christopher, St. Michael Chapel, Manhattan
Lieby, Joseph, St. Joseph, New Windsor
Liegey, Gabriel, St. James, Carmel
Liggan, John J., St. Peter, Rosendale
Lindley, Gerard, Regina Coeli, Hyde Park
Longo, Ralph D., Holy Rosary, Greenwood Lake
Lopez, Domingo, St. Joseph of the Holy Family, Harlem
Lopez, Francisco, St. Martin of Tours, Bronx
Lugo, Alejandro, St. Cecilia, Manhattan
Maher, James, St. Aedans, Pearl River
Maldonado, Eusebio, Our Lady of Sorrows, Manhattan

Maloney, John R., St. Anthony, Nanuet
Manning, Cornelius J., St. Barnabas, Bronx
Manzione, Arthur, St. Anthony of Padua, West Harrison
Marino, Philip A., Immaculate Conception, Stony Point
Maroon, Phillip J., St. Rita, Staten Island
Martinez, Luis A., Our Lady Queen of Angels, Manhattan
Martinez, Rafael, Caguas, Puerto Rico
Mazza, Albert, Holy Name of Mary, Croton-on-Hudson
Mazzei, Nicholas A., Our Lady of Mt. Carmel, Yonkers
McCabe, Michael G., St. Augustine, New City
McCarthy, Richard, Sacred Heart, Monroe
McCormick, Daniel F., St. Mark, Virginia Beach, VA
McGarry, James, St. John the Evangelist, Goshen
McGowan, George J., Visitation B.V.M., Bronx
McNeill, Lawrence C., Holy Cross, Manhattan
McSherry, John W., St. Paul, Congers
Meier, Anthony C., St. Bernadette, Fuquay Varina, NC
Mercado, Carlos V., Immaculate Conception, Bronx
Mercandetti, Anthony, St. Bartholomew, Yonkers
Mirando, Wilfredo, St. Lucy, Bronx
Mitchell, Richard F., St. Clare, Staten Island
Monegro, Juan, Incarnation, Manhattan
Moran, Bernard, St. Clare's, Bronx
Morillo, Felix M., Holy Spirit, Bronx
Morrette, Thomas, SS. John & Mary, Chappaqua
Mueller, William J., St. Mary Star of the Sea, Bronx
Mulryan, W. Joseph, St. Denis, Yonkers
Munnick, John B., Corpus Christi, Port Chester
Munoz, Jose A., Prison Chap., Scranton, PA
Murphy, John G., St. Frances de Chantal, Bronx
Nash, John J., Mercy Hospital, Port Jervis
Nielsen, William, St. Thomas of Canterbury, Cornwall-on-Hudson
Nolasco, Rolando, Our Lady of Mercy, Bronx
Nunez, Acadio, Puerto Rico
O'Brien, Donald, St. Francis of Assisi, West Nyack
O'Brien, Henry F., St. Lawrence, Fairhope, AL
O'Connor, Gerard R., Albany County Nursing Home
O'Reilly, John F., Our Lady of Loretto, Cold Spring
O'Toole, Lawrence, St. Augustine, New York
Ocasio, Roberto, St. Catherine of Siena, Kissimmee, FL
Olivieri, Martin J., St. John the Baptist, Yonkers
Orlando, Francis B., Blessed Sacrament, New Rochelle
Ortiz, Louis, Ponce, Puerto Rico
Ortiz, Pablo, Puerto Rico
Ottaviano, Frank S., St. Augustine, Highland
Pacheco, Angel, St. Isaac Jogues Parish, Orlando, FL
Padron, Jose R., St. Pius V, Bronx
Palladino, Joseph, St. Joseph, New Paltz
Pappalardo, Augustine A., St. Gregory Barbarigo, Garnerville
Parchen, Raymond
Patricola, Salvatore P., St. Anthony's, Pine Plains
Pelella, John V., St. Thomas of Canterbury, Cornwall-on-Hudson
Pellegrin, Daniel, St. Bernard, White Plains
Pellegrini, Guy A., Our Lady Perpetual Help, Pelham
Pereira, Joaquim, Our Lady of the Rosary, Yonkers
Perez, Primitivo, Queen of Peace, Oscala, FL
Peters, John, St. Joseph, Kingston
Pietkiewicz, Karl J., St. Mary of the Snow, Saugerties
Pino, Victor M., St. John Chrysostom, Bronx
Pipher, Jesse E., Our Lady Queen of Martyrs, Sarasota, FL
Piro, Vincent T., Our Lady of Mt. Carmel, Mt. Vernon
Pollick, Donald F., Westchester Medical Center Hospital, Valhalla
Porcel, Carlos M.
Portalatin, Epimegnio, Blessed Sacrament, Bronx
Preti, Aldo, St. Raymond, Bronx
Price, Joseph E.
Quigley, Donald M., St. Eugene, Yonkers
Quinn, Thomas J., Holy Child, Staten Island
Radcliffe, Kenneth L., Resurrection, Central Harlem
Radzilowicz, John, St. Casimir, Yonkers
Ramos, Alfonso, Sacred Heart, Bronx
Ramos, Edmundo A., St. Patrick's Cathedral, Manhattan
Ramos, Epifanio, Altamonte Springs, FL
Ramos, Rafael, St. John Vianney, Bronx
Rausch, Paul A., St. Thomas Aquinas, Forestburg
Reilly, John P., St. Columba, Hopewell Junction
Rentkowski, Joseph, St. Adalbert, Staten Island
Repke, John W., St. Mary, Marlboro
Rescildo, Ralph J., St. Teresa, Woodbury, CT
Rettino, P. Robert
Reynolds, Peter E., Our Lady of Mt. Carmel, Elmsford
Riley, John M., St. Peter, Liberty
Rivera, Andrew A., St. John, Kingsbridge Ave., Bronx
Rivera, Jose A., Aquas Buenas, Puerto Rico
Rizzo, Charles A., Blessed Sacrament, New Rochelle
Roberts, James F., Our Lady of the Assumption, Peekskill
Rodriguez, Arnaldo, Nativity, Manhattan
Rodriguez, Cristobal, Immaculate Conception, Bronx
Rodriguez, Hector, St. Philip Neri, Bronx
Rodriguez, Jacinto, St. Anthony, Bronx
Rodriguez, Jesus, Guayanilla, Puerto Rico
Rodriguez, Juan J., Holy Cross, Bronx
Rodriguez, Porfirio, St. Jude, Manhattan
Romagosa, Guillermo P.
Rosado, Alejandro, St. Athanasius, Bronx
Rosado, Odalis R., St. Elizabeth, New York
Rosado, Reynaldo, St. Dominic, Bronx
Rosado, Ricardo, Mid-Orange Correctional Facility, Warwick
Rush, James J., Charleston, SC
Russell, Franklyn R., St. Patrick, Newburgh
Russo, Richard J., St. Jean Baptist, Manhattan
Salamone, Victor A., St. Martin de Porres, Poughkeepsie
Salomone, Ernest F., Immaculate Heart of Mary, Scarsdale
Sanchez, Oscar, Taujillo Alto, Puerto Rico
Santana, Richard, Albany, NY
Santana, Robert, SS. Philip & James, Bronx
Santiago, Abraham, St. Joseph, Yonkers
Santore, Louis, St. John & St. Mary, Chappaqua
Scarfi, John, St. John the Evangelist, Mahopac
Schimpf, Robert, Sts. Peter & Paul, Mt. Vernon
Schlitt, Ronald, St. Christopher, Buchanan
Sepulveda, Miguel A., St. Raymond, Bronx
Serrano, Jose I.
Seymour, John L., St. Francis of Assisi, Newburgh
Sheeley, Robert B., Holy Name of Jesus, Kingston
Shepard, John, St. Mary, Washingtonville
Shiel, Thomas P., Corpus Christi, Temple Terrace, FL
Shkreli, Marash, St. Lawrence O'Toole, Brewster
Simpson, John J., St. Benedict, Bronx
Sin-Garciga, Felipe, St. Angela Merici, Bronx
Singler, John A., Our Lady Help of Christians, Staten Island
Smith, Henry, St. Mary of the Snow, Saugerties
Smith, John A., St. Edmond, Rehoboth Beach, DE
Solanto, Joseph P., Holy Rosary, Bronx
Sorrentino, Nunzio, St. Clare, Staten Island
Soto, Constancio, Ascension, Manhattan
Stahlnecker, James J., St. Mary of the Assumption, Staten Island
Steup, Fredrick C., St. Patrick, Newburgh
Stewart, George, St. Columba, Hopewell Junction
Stuetzle, Jerome, St. Anthony, Pine Plains
Suarez, Israel, Guaynabo, Puerto Rico
Sullivan, John D., Holy Trinity, West Harwich, MA
Sullivan, John M., St. Mary, Kingston
Sweeney, Walter F., Our Lady of Good Counsel, Staten Island
Tayco, Renato, St. John the Baptist, Manhattan
Testa, Warren, St. Columba, Hopewell Junction
Then, Rafael, Good Shepherd, Manhattan
Thompson, Alfred
Tirella, Rosario J., Holy Rosary, Staten Island
Tobin, William D., St. Margaret, Pearl River
Tola, Vincente, Sunrise, FL
Topple, Edwin R., St. John the Evangelist, Centerville
Torres, Gilberto, St. Clare, Deltona, FL
Torres, Luis, Mayaguez, Puerto Rico
Torres, Luis A., St. Pius V., Bronx
Trapani, Richard
Trees, Donald F., St. Mary of the Snow, Saugerties
Treiling, John F., St. Joseph Home & Hospital, Yonkers
Troy, Patrick D., Sacred Heart, Dobbs Ferry
Vaccaro, William N., Our Lady of the Rosary, Port Chester
Vargas, Thomas A., Holy Trinity, Mamaroneck
Vazquez, Juan F., St. Martin of Tours, Bronx
Velez, Randy, St. Peter, Yonkers
Venezia, Ignatius, St. Joan of Arc, Sloatsburg
Verboys, Joseph, Our Lady of Peace, Hewitt
Viola, Anthony, Immaculate Conception, Tuckahoe
Wallace, Benjamin S., St. Lawrence O'Toole, Brewster
Weinstein, David, Immaculate Conception, Amenia
Weir, John E., Southberry, CT
Weireter, Paul J., St. Patrick, Highland Mills
Weiss, Robert W., St. Augustine, Highland
Welhous, Albert V., SS. Philip & James, Bronx
Wendelken, Charles L., Blessed Sacrament, New Rochelle
Wetherall, Edward J., Our Lady Help of Christians, Staten Island
Winrow, Robert P., St. Joseph, Kingston
Witt, Joseph A., Sacred Heart, Suffern
Woods, Edward J., Our Lady of Mt. Carmel, Middletown
Wyka, Stanley A., St. Columba, Hopewell Jct.
Zatarga, Michael, St. Thomas, Boynton Beach, FL

INSTITUTIONS LOCATED IN THE ARCHDIOCESE

[A] SEMINARIES, ARCHDIOCESAN

NEW YORK. *Cathedral Preparatory Seminary.* Tel: 914-968-6200; Fax: 914-966-1490.
E-mail: cathprep@aol.com
Web site: www.cathedralprep.com
Archdiocesan Preparatory Seminary, 201 Seminary Ave., Yonkers, 10704. Tel: 914-968-6200; Fax: 914-966-1490. Revs. Arthur Mastrolia, Formation Dir.; Mark G. Vaillancourt, Spiritual Dir. Priests 3; Students 24.

Bishop Ford Residence, St. Joseph's Seminary, Dunwoodie, Yonkers, 10704. Tel: 914-968-2916; Fax: 914-966-1490. In res. Revs. Arthur Mastrolia; Robert McKeon; Mark G. Vaillancourt. Students 10.

BRONX. *St. John Neumann Seminary Residence*, 5655 Arlington Ave., 10471. Tel: 718-549-4511; Fax: 718-796-5163. Rev. Msgr. Edmund J. Whalen, S.T.D., Rector; Revs. Eric P. Raaser, M.Div., Dean of Students - Procurator; Thomas F. Madden, M.S., Spiritual Dir.; Rev. Msgr. Daniel A. Peake, Asst. Spiritual Dir. In res. Rev. Msgr. John J. Gillen. Priests 8; Sisters 3; Lay Teachers 5.

YONKERS. *St. Joseph's Seminary*, Archdiocesan Major Seminary, 201 Seminary Ave., 10704-1896. Tel: 914-968-6200; Fax: 914-376-2019.
E-mail: dun1896@aol.com
Rev. Msgr. Francis J. McAree, S.T.D., Rector; Rev. Msgr. William B. Smith, S.T.D., Academic Dean & Dean of Institute of Religious Studies; Rev. Msgr. Lorenzo Albacete, S.T.D.; Rev. Msgr. John J. Quinn, M.A.; Revs. John Coughlin, O.F.M., J.C.D., Spiritual Dir.; Donald F. Haggerty, S.T.D., Spiritual Dir.; Joseph P. Tierney, M.Div., Dean of Students & Dir. Pastoral Formation; Peter John Cameron, O.P., M.F.A.; Michael F. Hull, S.T.D., (cand.), Faculty Sec.; Donald J. Keefe, S.J., S.T.D.; Thomas Lynch, Ph.D., (cand.); Joseph R. Giandurco, J.C.D., Dean of Admissions.
Non-Resident Faculty: Revs. Joseph T. Lienhard, S.J.; Kevin McMorrow, S.A., S.T.D.; Andrew D. Apostoli, C.F.R., M.S.; Benedict J. Groeschel, C.F.R., Ed.D.; Andrew R. King, S.T.L.; Rev. Msgr. Edmund J. Whalen, S.T.D.; Dr. Jose Aguilar, S.S.D.; Dr. Philip Cristantiello, Ph.D.; Mr. Brian Zuar, M.S.; Bros. Thomas Fox, L.C.; Alonso Aguilar, L.C.; Sr. Janet Baxendale, S.C., M.A.; Sr. Marie Pappas, C.R., M.A.; Dr. Christopher M. Bellitto, Ph.D.; Revs. Frederick L. Miller, S.T.D.; Gerard F. Rafferty, S.S.L.; Robert G. Kelly, S.J., M.A.T.; James B. Lloyd, C.S.P., Ph.D.; Robert McKeon, Vocation Dir.; Mark G. Vaillancourt, Asst. Vocation Dir.; Sr. Regina Anne Melican, O.P., M.S.L.S., Dir. Library Svcs.; Mrs. Deborah McCue, Registrar. Priests 28; Sisters 3; Lay Teachers 3; Students 54 (of Archdiocese 31); North American College 1.

[B] SEMINARIES, RELIGIOUS OR SCHOLASTICATES

NEW YORK. *Society of St. Paul*, 2187 Victory Blvd., 10314. Tel: 718-761-0047; Fax: 718-761-0057.
E-mail: sspsiny@aol.com
Web site: www.albahouse.org
Rev. Ignatius Staniszewski, S.S.P., Supr. & Dir. Alba House Publications; Bro. Peter C. Lyne, S.S.P., Vocations Dir. Book Stores Coordinators: Bros. Kevin J. Cahill, S.S.P.; Augustine Condon, S.S.P.; Lawrence H. Schubert, S.S.P., Bursar; Revs. Edmund C. Lane, S.S.P.; Ernesto Tigreros, S.S.P.; Victor L. Viberti, S.S.P.; Clarence A. Warren, S.S.P. Priests 5; Brothers 13.

BEACON. *St. Lawrence of Brindisi Friary*, Province of the Stigmata of St. Francis, 182 Sargent Ave., 12508-3993. Tel: 845-831-0394; 831-0451; 838-0759 (Infirmary); Fax: 845-831-0918; 838-1352 (Infirmary).
E-mail: beaconcap1@aol.com
(Friary and Infirmary). Bros. Kellen Mears, O.F.M.Cap., Guardian; Julius Tkaczyk, O.F.M.Cap., Vicar; Lawrence Emmert, O.F.M.Cap.; Douglas Soik, O.F.M.Cap.; Norbert G. Barron, O.S.F.; Francis Liermann, O.F.M.Cap.; Matthew Defamio, O.F.M.Cap.; Revs. Gerard De Leonardis, O.F.M.Cap.; Sylvester Catallo, O.F.M.Cap.; Joseph Mullen, O.F.M.Cap.;

Anthony Ciudice, O.F.M.Cap.; John Schug, O.F.M.Cap. Priests 5; Brothers 7; Lay Staff 11.

BRONX. *Ciszek Hall*, 2502 Belmont Ave., 10458-6282. Tel: 718-365-8752; Fax: 718-365-3166. Residence for Jesuit Scholastics engaged in Philosophy and Theology Studies at Fordham University. Revs. Thomas H. Feely, S.J., Rector; Edward F. Salmon, S.J., Spiritual Dir. Scholastics 23.

MARYKNOLL. *Center for Mission Research and Study at Maryknoll*, P.O. Box 305, 10545-0305. Tel: 914-941-7590; Fax: 914-941-5753.
E-mail: cmrsm@maryknoll.org
Web site: www.maryknoll.org/society/cmrsm
Thomas Bamat, Exec. Dir.; Rev. William D. McCarthy, M.M., Senior Researcher; Anne Reissner, Dir. of Study; Jean Paul Weist, Senior Researcher; Mary Ann Cejka, Assoc. Researcher; Donna Bonner, Asst. Researcher; Leonard Viggiano, Dir. Library.
Purpose: To investigate the contexts, trends and challenges of Christian Mission among Christians and peoples of other living faiths, and to foster reflection on the practical implications of these investigations. Priests 1; Lay Persons 6.

STATEN ISLAND. *St. Francis Friary*, 500 Todt Hill Rd., 10304. Tel: 718-981-3131; 981-3212.
E-mail: juniperjas@aol.com
Revs. Juniper Alwell, O.F.M.Conv., Guardian; Blase B. Kardos, O.F.M.Conv., Chap.; Edgar Holden, O.F.M.Conv., (Retired); Stephen Valenta, O.F.M.Conv., Preaching Min.; Shawn Nolan, O.F.M.Conv., Retreat Dir.; Philip Blaine, O.F.M.Conv., Spiritual Center Dir.; John Bickle, O.F.M.Conv., Chap.; Bro. Edward Handy, O.F.M.Conv., Social Svc.

Friars Minor Conventual Immaculate Conception Province Charitable Trust. Tel: 718-981-3131; Fax: 718-981-2742. Priests 6; Brothers 1.

SUFFERN. *Tagaste Monastery*, 220 Lafayette Ave., 10901. Tel: 914-357-0067; Fax: 914-369-0625.
E-mail: tagasteny@aol.com
Major Seminary of the Province of St. Augustine of the Augustinian Recollect Fathers & Brothers. Revs. Joseph J. Gallardo, O.A.R., Prior; Frank T. Wilder, O.A.R., Sub-Prior; George Mattioni, O.A.R.; Francis Moriones, O.A.R. (Spain); Marlon Beof, O.A.R., Prefect of Students; Bros. Ramiro Munoz, O.A.R.; Joseph Joly, O.A.R.; Gerardo DeFillippo, O.A.R. Priests 5; Brothers 3; Simple Professed 10; Solemn Professed Clerics 2.

[C] COLLEGES AND UNIVERSITIES

NEW YORK. *College of Mount Saint Vincent*, 6301 Riverdale Ave., 10471-1093. Tel: 718-405-3200; Fax: 718-549-2603.
E-mail: cfinegan@cmsv.edu
Web site: www.cmsv.edu
For a complete listing, refer to the Colleges and Universities section.

Marymount Manhattan College, 221 E. 71st St., 10021. Tel: 212-517-0400.
E-mail: vdorgan@mmm.edu
Web site: www.mmm.edu
For a complete listing, refer to the Colleges and Universities section.

BRONX. *Fordham University*, (1841) Fordham Rd., 10458 Fax: 718-817-4925.
Web site: www.fordham.edu
For a complete listing, refer to the Colleges and Universities section.

Manhattan College, Manhattan College Pkwy., 10471. Tel: 718-862-7200; 800-MC2-XCEL; Fax: 718-862-8019.
E-mail: admit@manhattan.edu
Web site: www.manhattan.edu
For a complete listing, refer to the Colleges and Universities section.

NEW ROCHELLE. *College of New Rochelle*, 29 Castle Pl., 10805. Tel: 914-654-5000; Fax: 914-654-5980.
E-mail: info@cnr.edu
Web site: www.cnr.edu
For a complete listing, refer to the Colleges and Universities section.

Iona College, 715 North Ave., 10801. Tel: 914-633-2000.
E-mail: webmaster@iona.edu
Web site: www.iona.edu
For a complete listing, refer to the Colleges and Universities section.

NEWBURGH. *Mt. St. Mary College*, (1954) Leslie Reggero, 12550. Tel: 914-561-0800; Fax: 914-562-6762.
E-mail: coyne@msmc.edu
Web site: www.msmc.edu
For a complete listing, refer to the Colleges and Universities section.

ORANGEBURG. *Dominican College*, 470 Western Hwy., 10962. Tel: 845-359-7800; Fax: 845-359-2313.
E-mail: admissions@dc.edu
Web site: www.dc.edu
For a complete listing, refer to the Colleges and Universities section.

POUGHKEEPSIE. *Marist College*, 12601-1328. Tel: 914-575-3000.
E-mail: hmaltmi@marista.marist.edu
Web site: www.marist.edu
For a complete listing, refer to the Colleges and Universities section.

SPARKILL. *St. Thomas Aquinas College*, 10976. Tel: 914-398-4000; Fax: 914-359-8136.
Web site: www.stac.edu
For a complete listing, refer to the Colleges and Universities section.

STATEN ISLAND. *St. John's University Staten Island Campus*, 300 Howard Ave., 10301. Tel: 718-390-4545; Fax: 718-816-4520
For a complete listing, refer to the Colleges and Universities section.

TARRYTOWN. *Marymount College*, 10591. Tel: 914-631-3200.
E-mail: admiss@mmt.marymt.edu
Web site: www.marymt.edu
For a complete listing, refer to the Colleges and Universities section.

THORNWOOD. *Legion of Christ College, Inc.*, 584 Columbus Ave., 10594
For a complete listing, refer to the Colleges and Universities section.

[D] DEPARTMENT OF EDUCATION

NEW YORK. *Department of Education*, 1011 First Ave., 10022. Tel: 212-371-1000; Fax: 212-758-3018.
E-mail: vicared@aol.com
Web site: www.ny-archdiocese.org
Rev. Msgr. Thomas J. Bergin, Vicar for Education; Sr. Eileen Clifford, O.P., Assoc. Vicar for Education; Rev. Msgr. Michael C. Crimmins, Assoc. Vicar for Higher Education.

Office of Finance. Tel: 212-371-1011, Ext. 2819; Fax: 212-371-1011, Ext. 1822. Mr. John D. Poling, Exec. Dir.; Mr. John Coyne, Exec. Dir.

Vocations Office. Tel: 212-371-1011, Ext. 2803; Fax: 212-758-3018. Sr. Deanna Sabetta, C.N.D., Vocations to Religious Life, 1011 First Ave., 10022.

Division of Elementary and Secondary Education, 1011 First Ave., 10022. Tel: 212-371-1000, Ext. 2870/2873; Fax: 212-371-1011, Ext. 3481. Dr. Catherine Hickey, Supt. of Schools; Dr. Paul Ward, Deputy Supt. Assoc. Supts.: Sr. Patricia Anastasio, P.V.B.M., Personnel; Sr. Dorothy Flanagan, C.N.D., Religious Education; Dr. Mary Jane Krebbs, Curriculum and Teachers Institute; Mr. James Mahoney, Publicly Assisted Programs; Bro. Thomas Schady, F.M.S., Secondary Education; Mr. James Simone, Special Education; Sr. Kathleen Sullivan, S.C., Teacher Recruitment. Asst. Supts.: Sr. Mary Kilmartin, S.C., Curriculum; Sr. Winifred Lyons, S.C., Pro-Life Coord., Parent Volunteer Program; Mrs. Catherine Mendrzycki, Teacher Staff Devel.; Mrs. Nora Murphy, Communications Mktg.; Sr. Marie Pappas, C.R., Catechist Formation. Directors: Sr. Breda Galavan, R.S.H.M., Writing to Read; Hugh Keenan, Admin.; Sr. Alice Kirk, O.P., Dir. Technology Staff Devel.; Sr. Lucy Sabatini, O.S.F., Early Childhood, 215 W. 15th St., 10011. Tel: 212-243-1881. Ms. Ann Maschin, Admin. Asst. District Supts.: Mr. Kevin Scanlon, Bronx; Mrs. Donna Carolan, Dutchess & Ulster; Mrs. Zoilita Herrera, Staten Island; Deacon Arthur Manzione, Westchester & Putnam; Sr. Helen Doychak, O.P., Rockland, Orange & Sullivan; Sr. June Clare Tracy, O.P., Manhattan.

Archdiocesan Drug Abuse Prevention Program. Tel: 718-904-1333; Fax: 718-823-2177. Mrs. Frances Maturo, Dir., 2789 Schurz Ave., Bronx, 10465. Tel: 718-904-1333.

Child Nutrition and School Management Service. Tel: 212-722-0111; Fax: 212-722-5252. Mr. Edward Albano, 323 E. 91st St., 10128.

Head Start Program. Mrs. Nora Feury, 1720 Metropolitan Ave., Bronx, 10462. Tel: 718-409-1277; Fax: 718-409-3219.

Cooke Center for Learning and Development. Tel: 212-280-4473; Fax: 212-280-4477. Dr. Michael Termini, 475 Riverside Dr., Ste. 730, 10115.

Seton Foundation for Learning. Tel: 718-447-1750; Fax: 718-447-8022. Ms. Patricia Cirbus, Ed. Dir., 104 Gordon St., 10304.

Bronx Alternative Special Education. Tel: 718-792-9669. James A. Simone, Assoc. Supt.; Mrs. Mary Carman, Admin. Asst., 1725 Castle Hill Ave., Bronx, 10462.

St. Ursula Learning Center. Tel: 914-664-6656; Fax: 914-663-7948. Mrs. Barbara Stefaniki, Educ. Dir., 183 Rich Ave., Mt. Vernon, 10550.

Joan Ann Kennedy Memorial Preschool. Tel: 718-876-0939; Fax: 718-816-6507. Dr. Kathryn Meyer, Educ. Dir., 26 Sharpe Ave., Staten Island, 10302.

Bishop Patrick V. Ahern High School. Tel: 718-982-5084; Fax: 718-982-5114. Ms. Diane Cunningham, Exec. Dir., 315 Arlene St., Staten Island, 10314.

Family Life/Respect Life Office, 1011 First Ave., 10022. Tel: 212-371-1000, Ext. 3186; Fax: 212-371-3382. Rev. John S. Bonnici, S.T.D., Dir.; Mr. Edward Mechmann, Asst. Dir. & Coord. of Marriage Preparation Programs; Dr. Charles Potter, Coord., Natural Family Planning; Vera V. Galeas, Coord., Respect Life & Spanish Programs; Dana Larson-Super, Coord., Wedding Anniversary Awards Ceremony; Mr. Stefano Galluzzo, Asst. Coord. Respect Life; Mrs. Nancy Rizzi, Coord. Marriage Enrichment; Mrs. Lisa Dunleavy-Jenning, Asst. Coord. Marriage Preparation Programs; Mrs. Eileen Murphy, Assoc. Dir., Educ. for Parenting; Mrs. Pat Hayes, Coord. Separated & Divorced Ministry; Mr. Mizraim Cordero, Asst. Coord. Sepatated & Divorced Ministry; Mrs. Mary Kay King, Coord. Bereavement Ministry; Mrs. Christine Gallagher, Coord. Project Rachel Ministry, Hudson River East, 12524. Tel: 914-896-0728. Mrs. Virginia Brown, Assoc. Dir., Educ. for Parenting, 103 Jackson St., Box L, Fishkill, 12524. Hudson River West. Tel: 914-342-0908. John & Laura Weidner, Coord. Couple, Engaged Encounter, 149 Cottage St., Middletown, 10940. Tel: 914-736-2590; Fax: 914-788-7278. Jim & Nancy Rizzi, Coord. Couple, Marriage Encounter, Tel: 718-966-0990; 317-5881.

Archdiocesan Catechetical Office, 1011 First Ave., 10022. Tel: 212-371-1000, Ext. 2849; Fax: 212-371-1011, Ext. 3482. Sr. Joan Curtin, C.N.D., Archdiocesan Dir. Tel: 212-371-1000, ext. 2849; Ms. Mary Burke, Asst. to Dir.; Sr. Mary Elizabeth Kelleher, O.P., Dir. Catechist Formation. Tel: 212-371-1000, ext. 2861; Sr. Teresita Morse, R.J.M., Dir. Formation of Directors/Coordinators. Tel: 212-371-1000, ext. 2858; Bro. Francis Zaglauer, F.M.S., Dir., Adult Catechesis. Tel: 212-371-1000, ext. 2851; Sr. Loretta DeDomenicis, F.M.A., Dir. Adolescent Catechesis. Tel: 212-371-1000, ext. 2864; Mrs. Linda Sgammato, Dir. Spec. Rel. Educ. Tel: 212-371-1000 ext.2852.

Catechetical Regional Offices.

Bronx. Tel: 718-367-0420; Fax: 718-367-7880. Sr. Catherine Ryan, F.S.P., Dir., c/o Mother Cabrini High School, 701 Fort Washington Ave., 10040.

Staten Island. Tel: 718-273-3833; Fax: 718-273-9602. Mrs. Frances DeFrange, Dir., 203 Sand Lane, Staten Island, 10305.

Dutchess & Ulster Counties. Tel: 845-471-5427; Fax: 845-471-5427. 26 S. Hamilton Ave., Poughkeepsie, 12601-2599.

Ulster County. Tel: 845-338-3222; Fax: 845-338-3222. Sr. Miriam Eugene Fenton, S.C., Dir., 157 Broadway, Kingston, 12401.

Central & Southern Westchester. Tel: 914-921-2678; Fax: 914-921-2678. Mrs. Linda DeMarkey, Dir., 910 Boston Post Rd., Rye, 10580.

Orange County. Tel: 845-294-6428; Fax: 845-294-6428. John S. Burke, Catholic High School, Fletcher St., P.O. Box 114, Goshen, 10924.

Rockland County. Tel: 914-627-1236. Mrs. Marilyn Hilpert, Dir., 798 Rte 304 & Germonds Rd., P.O. Box 9162, Bardonia, 10954-1694.

Orange & Sullivan County. Tel: 845-292-9100; Fax: 845-292-9100. Sr. Kevin John Shields, O.P., Dir., Blessed Kateri Tekakwitha Center, P.O. Box 1011, Liberty, 12754.

Center for Spiritual Development. Tel: 914-967-7328; Fax: 914-967-7387. Anne Marie Wallace, Ph.D., Dir., 96 Milton Rd., Rye, 10580.

Instructional Television. Tel: 914-968-7800; Fax: 914-968-2075. Mr. Michael Lavery, Admin. Dir., 215 Seminary Ave., Yonkers, 10704. Elementary School: Full-Time Sisters 265; Part-Time Sisters 75; Full-Time Brothers 21; Part-Time Brothers 24; Full-Time Order Priests 7; Part-Time Order Priests 9; Full-Time Lay Teachers 3,248; Part-Time Lay Teachers 722; Total Parish Enrollment 76,674; Total Inter-Parish Enrollment 1,105; Total Private Enrollment 4,165. High School: Full-Time Sisters 161; Part-Time Sisters 37; Full-Time Brothers 71; Part-Time Brothers 32; Full-Time Order Priests 46; Part-Time Order Priests 5; Full-Time Diocesan Priests 26; Full-Time Lay Teachers 1,877; Part-Time Lay Teachers 117; Total Diocesan Enrollment 10,543; Parish Enrollment 5,043; Private Enrollment 13,427.

[E] HIGH SCHOOLS, ARCHDIOCESAN

NEW YORK. *Cardinal Hayes High School*, 650 Grand Concourse, 10451. Tel: 718-292-6100; Fax: 718-292-5607.
E-mail: jgraham@cardinalhayes.org
Web site: www.cardinalhayes.org
(Boys). Rev. Msgr. John K. Graham, Prin.; Revs. James Byrnes, Dean of Studies; Harry Burke; Alfred D'Incecco; Jeffrey Galens; Robert Harrison; Rev. Msgr. Victor C. Pavis; Rev. Msgr. Harold Robertson. In res. Rev. Msgr. Peter P. Narkun. Priests 8; Brothers 3; Sisters 1; Lay Teachers 52; Students 1,000.

Cardinal Spellman High School. Tel: 718-881-8000; Fax: 718-515-6615.
E-mail: spellman@adnysch.org
Web site: www.cardinalspellman.org

One Cardinal Spellman Pl., Bronx, 10466. Tel: 718-881-8000; Fax: 718-515-6615. Rev. Msgr. James P. Sullivan, Pres.; Revs. John R. Kraljic; John T. Monaghan; James J. O'Shaughnessy; Peter R. Pilsner; Francis J. Principe. In res. Revs. Walter C. Adams; Richard F. Gorman. Priests 8; Sisters 3; Lay Teachers 79; Students 1,400.

Cathedral High School, 350 E. 56th St., 10022. Tel: 212-688-1545; Fax: 212-754-2024.
E-mail: egraham@cathedralhs.org
Web site: cathedralhs.org
(Girls). Rev. Msgr. Thomas J. Bergin, Pres.; Sr. Elizabeth Graham, O.P., Prin.; Revs. Robert J. Poveromo; John Scarangello. Priests 3; Sisters 10; Lay Teachers 51; Students 1,076.

Monsignor Farrell High School, 2900 Amboy Rd., 10306. Tel: 718-987-2900; Fax: 718-987-4241. Rev. Msgr. Emmet R. Nevin, Prin.; Revs. John P. Comiskey; Andrew R. King; Robert G. Macchietto; John Pedulla; John Lagiovane. Priests 6; Brothers 3; Sisters 3; Lay Teachers 70; Students 1,180.

Moore Catholic High School, 100 Merrill Ave., 10314. Tel: 212-761-9200; Fax: 718-982-7779. Revs. Robert I. Gannon; Edmund P. Connors. Priests 1; Sisters of the Presentation 1; Lay Teachers 48; Students 880.

GOSHEN. *John S. Burke Catholic High School*, 80 Fletcher St., 10924. Tel: 845-294-5481; Fax: 845-294-0817. Rev. Eugene Foley, O.Carm, Prin.; Miss Karen DeCrosta, Asst. Prin. Priests 1; Sisters 1; Lay Teachers 35; Students 585.

HARTSDALE. *Maria Regina High School*, 500 W. Hartsdale Ave., 10530. Tel: 914-761-3300; Fax: 914-761-0860.
E-mail: mariaregina@cloud9.net
Sisters of the Resurrection. Sr. Cecilia Mary Berdar, C.R., Supr.; Sr. Danielle M. Baran, C.R., Prin. Sisters 10; Lay Teachers 26; Students 500.

HURLEY. *John A. Coleman Catholic High School*, 430 Hurley Ave., 12443. Tel: 845-338-2750; Fax: 845-388-0250. Mrs. Ellen Jane Gonyea, Prin. Brothers 1; Sisters 2; Lay Teachers 18; Students 230.

POUGHKEEPSIE. *Our Lady of Lourdes High School*, 131 Boardman Rd., 12603. Tel: 845-471-0400; Fax: 845-463-0174.
E-mail: lourdes@adnysch.org
Web site: www.ladyoflourdes.org
Bros. Robert LeClerc, F.M.S.; Richard Sharpe, F.M.S., Prin.; Vincent Moriarty, F.M.S., Dean, Freshman Studies & Admissions; Larry Gordon, F.M.S., Asst. Prin., Academics; Henry Sawicki, F.M.S.; Gregory DelaNoy, F.M.S.; James Stevens, F.M.S.; Mr. James Lyons, Dean of Men; Mrs. Ellen Anderson, Dean of Women; Sr. Lois Dee, O.P., Asst. Prin., Faculty; Mrs. Gene Botsford, Dir., Inst. Advancement; Rev. Michael Keane, Campus Ministry. Priests 1; Brothers 7; Sisters 2; Lay Teachers 50; Students 927.

SOMERS. *John F. Kennedy High School*, 54 Rte. 138, 10589. Tel: 914-232-5061; Fax: 914-232-3416.
E-mail: jfkadmin@dbestweb.net
Sisters of Divine Compassion, Sisters of St. Francis. Rev. Msgr. Anthony D. Marchitelli, Prin.; Mr. Stephen Schmidt, Asst. Prin. & Academic Dean; Rev. James Teague; Sr. Barbara Heil, R.D.C., Treas.; Mr. Thomas Dolan, Dean of Students. Priests 2; Sisters 8; Lay Teachers 40; Students 614.

WHITE PLAINS. *Archbishop Stepinac High School*, 950 Mamaroneck Ave., 10605. Tel: 914-946-4800; Fax: 914-686-3615.
E-mail: stepinac50@aol.com
Web site: www.stepinac.org
Rev. Msgr. John J. O'Keefe, Pres.; Mr. Steven E. Murphy, Prin.; Deacon Al Impallomen, Jr., Admin. Asst. & Dean of Students; Rev. Thomas E. Collins, Assoc. Dean of Students. Staff of School: Revs. Patrick M. Carroll; Philip J. Quealy. In res. Rev. Msgr. George F. Bardes; Rev. Msgr. Edward M. Connors; Rev. Henry G. d'Anjou; Rev. Msgr. Augustine J. DiBlasi; Rev. Msgr. John T. Doherty; Rev. Thomas E. O'Keefe; Rev. Msgr. Raymond P. Rigney; Rev. Msgr. John Wilkinson. Priests 4; Sisters 3; Lay Teachers 42; Students 640.

[F] HIGH SCHOOLS, PRIVATE

NEW YORK. *Academy of Mount St. Ursula*, 330 Bedford Park Blvd., 10458. Tel: 718-364-5353; Fax: 718-364-2354.
E-mail: mread@amsu.org
Web site: www.amsu.org
(Girls). Ursuline Nuns. Sr. Mary Beth Read, O.S.U., Prin. Sisters 4; Lay Teachers 32; Students 450.

All Hallows Institute. (aka Hallows High School). 111 E. 164th St., 10452. Tel: 718-293-4545; Fax: 718-293-8634.
E-mail: alhallow@aol.com
(Boys). Mr. Sean J. Sullivan, Prin.; Bro. J. G. Sullo, C.F.C., Pres. Congregation of Christian Brothers 7; Lay Teachers 31; Students 46.

Aquinas High School. Tel: 718-367-2113; Fax: 718-295-5864.
E-mail: aqhs@aol.com
Web site: www.aquinashs.org
685 E. 182nd St., Bronx, 10457. Tel: 718-367-2113; Fax: 718-295-5864.
E-mail: aqhs@aol.com
Sisters 17; Lay Teachers 41; Students 787. (Girls). Sr. Margaret Ryan, O.P., Pres.; Sr. Catherine Rose Quigley, O.P., Prin.

Convent of the Sacred Heart, One E. 91st St., 10128-0654. Tel: 212-722-4745; Fax: 212-996-1784.
Web site: www.cshnyc.org
(Girls). Religious of the Sacred Heart. Sr. N. Salisbury, R.S.C.J., Headmistress. Sisters 3; Priests 1; Lay Teachers 75; Students 608.

Dominican Academy, 44 E. 68th St., 10021. Tel: 212-744-0195; Fax: 212-744-0375.
E-mail: danyc@mail.con2.com
Web site: www.dominicanacademy.org
(Girls). Sr. Martha Kunesh, O.P., Prin. Sisters 6; Lay Teachers 17; Students 230.

Fordham Preparatory School, E. Fordham Rd., 10458. Tel: 718-367-7500; Fax: 718-367-7598.
Web site: www.fordhamprep.com
(Boys). Mr. William J. Mulrow, Chm. Bd.; Rev. Joseph P. Parkes, S.J., Pres.; Mr. Robert J. Gomprecht, Prin.; Mr. Dennis M. Ahern, Asst. Prin.; Mr. Bruce G. Bott, Dean of Students; Revs. Mallick J. Fitzpatrick, S.J., Dir. Guidance; Matthew C. Flood, S.J.; John J. Leonard, S.J.; Stanley J. O'Konsky, S.J.; William J. O'Malley, S.J.; Charles D. Sullivan, S.J.; Raymond M. Sweitzer, S.J.; Thomas G. Benz; Michael P. Corcoran. Priests 10; Lay Teachers 65; Students 875.

La Salle Academy, 44 E. Second St., 10003. Tel: 212-475-8940; Fax: 212-529-3598. (Boys). Brothers of The Christian Schools. Bros. Carl Malacalza, F.S.C., Pres.; Joseph S. Wilkowski, F.S.C., Prin. Brothers 7; Sisters 1; Lay Teachers 34; Students 507.

Loyola School, 980 Park Ave., 10028. Tel: 212-288-3522; Fax: 212-861-1021.
Web site: www.loyola-nyc.org
(Coed). Society of Jesus. Mr. Francis Serbaroli, Chm. Bd.; Revs. Joseph J. Papaj, S.J., Pres. & Headmaster; James J. Curry, S.J.; Eugene J. Prior, S.J.; Thomas S. Prout, S.J.; Michael E. Sehler, S.J. Priests 5; Lay Teachers 27; Students 202.

Mother Cabrini High School. (Grades 9-12), 701 Ft. Washington Ave., 10040. Tel: 212-923-3540; Fax: 212-781-2051.
E-mail: info@cabrini.com
(Girls). Brian Donahue, Prin.; Noreen White, Asst. Prin.; Sr. Kathleen Clancy, I.H.M., Asst. Admin.; Sr. Sharon Casey, M.S.C., Campus Min.; Kathleen B. Muskopf, Devel. Dir. Sisters 3; Lay Teachers 30; Students 460.

Notre Dame Academy High School, 134 Howard Ave., 10301. Tel: 718-447-8878; Fax: 718-447-2926. Congregation of Notre Dame. Sr. Patricia Ells, C.N.D., Prin. Priests 1; Sisters 4; Lay Teachers 22; Girls 343.

Notre Dame School of Manhattan, 104 St. Mark Pl., 10009. Tel: 212-982-0740; Fax: 212-982-5441.
E-mail: ntdamehs@adnysch.org
(Girls). Mr. John Joven, Prin. Sisters 5; Lay Teachers 16; Students 215.

Preston High School, 2780 Schurz Ave., 10465. Tel: 718-863-9134; Fax: 718-863-6125. (Girls). Sr. Lucille Coldrick, R.D.C., Prin. Asst. Principals: Linda Youngren; Sr. Laura Donovan, R.D.C. Sisters of the Divine Compassion 7; Lay Teachers 38; Students 468.

Regis High School, 55 E. 84th St., 10028. Tel: 212-288-1100; Fax: 212-794-1221.
E-mail: vbiagi@regis-nyc.org
Web site: www.regis-nyc.org
(Boys). Society of Jesus. Revs. J. Thomas McClain, S.J., Pres.; Vincent L. Biagi, S.J., Prin.; Mr. James F. X. Lyness, Asst. Prin.; Mr. Daniel T. Dougherty, Dean of Students; Revs. Arthur C. Bender, S.J.; James R. Carney, S.J.; James J. DiGiacomo, S.J.; Stephen V. Duffy, S.J.; Kenneth J. Caufield, S.J. Priests 7; Lay Teachers 50; Students 523. Res., 53 E. 83rd St., 10028.

Rice High School, 74 W. 124th St., 10027. Tel: 212-369-4100; Fax: 212-348-4631.
E-mail: adnyricehs@connectinc.com
Web site: www.ricehighschool.com
(Boys). Congregation of Christian Brothers. Bro. John M. Walderman, C.F.C., Pres. Diocesan Priest 1; Brothers 4; Lay Teachers 30; Students 376.

St. Agnes Boys High School, 555 West End Ave., 10024-2795. Bro. Emil D. Denworth, Prin.

St. Catharine Academy, 2250 Williamsbridge Rd., 10469. Tel: 718-882-2882; Fax: 718-231-9099.
E-mail: awelchrsm@aol
(Girls). Sr. Ann M. Welch, R.S.M., Prin. Sisters 8; Lay Teachers 54; Students 750.

St. John Villa Academy High School, 26 Landis Ave., 10305. Tel: 718-442-6240; Fax: 718-447-6729.
E-mail: sjvilla@aol.com
Web site: sjva.org
Sr. Antonia Zuffante, C.S.J.B., Prin. Brothers 1; Sisters 11; Lay Teachers 28; Girls 635.

St. Joseph by the Sea, High School, 5150 Hylan Blvd., 10312. Tel: 718-984-6500; Fax: 718-984-6503; 227-6816.
E-mail: j.f.bolger@msn.com
(Coed). Rev. Msgr. Joseph C. Ansaldi, Prin.; Revs. John N. Paddack; Michael P. Reilly. Priests 3; Sisters 7; Lay Teachers 65; Students 1,300.

Xavier High School, 30 W. 16th St., 10011. Tel: 212-924-7900; Fax: 212-924-0303.
Web site: www.xavierhs.org
(Boys). Society of Jesus. Revs. Daniel J. Gatti, S.J., Pres.; David S. Ciancimino, S.J., Headmaster; Mr. John Burke, Asst. Headmaster; Mr. Kevin P. Cuddihy, Dean of Students; Miss Janet Bonica, Registrar; Revs. John Replogle, S.J.; Vincent E. Butler, S.J.; John F. Garvey, S.J.; William J. McGowan, S.J.; Robert V. O'Hare, S.J.; James Coughlin, S.J.; Vincent A. Taylor, S.J.; Joseph J. Walter, S.J.; David F. White, S.J.
(See listing for Xavier Jesuit Community for additional names of priests and brothers.). Priests 8; Scholastics 1; Lay Teachers 59; Students 908.

BARDONIA. *Albertus Magnus*, 798 Rte. 304, 10954. Tel: 914-623-8842; Fax: 914-623-0009.
E-mail: amadmin@albertusmagnus.org
Web site: http://www.lanline.com/~armadm
Sisters of St. Dominic (Sparkill) 6; Lay Teachers 31; Students 510.

BRONX. *Mount St. Michael Academy*, 4300 Murdock Ave., 10466. Tel: 718-515-6400; Fax: 718-994-7729.
Web site: www.mountstmichael.org
(Boys). Bros. John P. Bantz, F.M.S., Pres.; Michael J. Mullin, F.M.S., Prin. Brothers 11; Lay Teachers 50; Students 945.

Junior High School. Tel: 718-515-6400; Fax: 718-994-7729. Mrs. Lillian Dippolito, F.M.S., Prin. Lay Teachers 7; Students 155.

DOBBS FERRY. *Our Lady of Victory Academy High School*, 565 N. Broadway, 10522. Tel: 914-693-1633; Fax: 914-693-5250.
E-mail: olvamain@victoryhs.org
(Girls). Sisters of Mercy. Sr. Joan Agro, O.P., Prin. Sisters 8; Lay Teachers 26; Students 415.

NEW ROCHELLE. *Iona Preparatory School*, 255 Wilmot Rd., 10804. Tel: 914-632-0714; Fax: 914-632-9760.
E-mail: jjoc97@ionaprep.org
Web site: www.ionaprep.org
(Boys). Congregation of Christian Brothers. Bro. John J. O'Connor, C.F.C., Pres.; Mr. John R. Fogler, Asst. to the Pres.; Mr. James Clarkin, Acting Headmaster; Mr. Anthony R. Baxter, Asst. Headmaster; Mr. Daniel R. Poccia, Asst. Headmaster; Mr. Christopher J. Farrell, Vice Pres. for Advancement; Mr. Brian E. Terhune, Vice Pres. Finance; Bros. M. Austin Maus; J. John Adams; J. Anthony Brosnan; Gerard M. Gaffney; J. Richard Kelly; Carmine P. Pellegrino; J. Anthony Reynolds. Priests 1; Brothers 8; Sisters 2; Lay Teachers 48; Students 780.

Salesian High School, 148 Main St., 10801. Tel: 914-632-0248; Fax: 914-632-1362.
E-mail: salhsnr@aol.com
Web site: www.members.aol.com/salhsnr
Rev. John Nazzaro, S.D.B., Dir. & Pres.; Mr. John P. Flaherty, Prin.; Sr. Barbara Wright, O.P., Asst. Prin.; Mr. Robert Molinaro, Dean of Students; Rev. Richard Alejunas, Coord. of Youth Ministry; Mr. Donald Jordan, Business Mgr.; Mr. Louis Calvelli, Vice Pres. Inst. Advancement; Cary Jordan, Guidance; Bros. Kevin Connolly, S.D.B.; Michael Brinkman, S.D.B.; Joseph Lody, S.D.B. Reverend Fathers: Revs. James Mulloy, S.D.B.; Stephen Leake; Ernest Faggioni; Richard Alejunas. Priests 5; Sisters 1; Lay Teachers 30; Students 451.

Ursuline School. (Grades 6-12), 1354 North Ave., 10804. Tel: 914-636-3950; Fax: 914-636-3949.
E-mail: admin@ursuline.pvt.k12.ny.us
Web site: www.ursuline.pvt.k12.us
(Girls). Sr. Jean Baptiste Nicholson, O.S.U., Prin. Priests 1; Sisters 10; Lay Teachers 55; Students 750.

RYE. *School of the Holy Child*. (Grades 5-12), 2225 Westchester Ave., 10580. Tel: 914-967-5622; Fax: 914-967-6476.
E-mail: e.bracchitta@holychild.put.k12.ny.us
Web site: www.holychild.put.k12.ny.us
(Girls). Ann F. Sullivan, Headmistress; Anita L. Walsh, Admisssions Dir. Society of the Holy Child Jesus 1; Lay Teachers 40; Students 298.

STATEN ISLAND. *St. Joseph Hill Academy*, 850 Hylan Blvd., 10305-2095. Tel: 718-447-1374; Fax: 718-447-3041.
E-mail: joshill@adnysch.org
Web site: stjoephhill.org
(Girls). Daughters of Divine Charity. Sr. Marie Claire, F.D.C., Prin. Sisters 3; Lay Teachers 27; Students 364.

WHITE PLAINS. *Academy of Our Lady of Good Counsel*, 52 N. Broadway, 10603. Tel: 914-949-0178; Fax: 914-682-3531.
E-mail: olgdcoun@adny.org
Web site: www.goodcounsel.pvt.k12.ny.us
(Girls). Ms. Joan Close, Prin. Sisters of the Divine Compassion 7; Sisters of Charity 1; Lay Teachers 28; Students 355.

[G] SPECIAL SCHOOLS

NEW YORK. *Grace Institute*, 1233 Second Ave., 10021. Tel: 212-832-7605; Fax: 212-486-2869.
E-mail: graceinsti@rcn.com
Web site: www.graceinstitute.org
Sisters of Charity, Mt. St. Vincent. Sr. Mary Ellen O'Boyle, Admin. Sisters 1; Lay Teachers 3; Part Time Layteachers 10; Students 400.

Lavelle School for the Blind, 221st St. and Paulding Ave., 10469. Tel: 718-882-1212. Sisters of St. Dominic of Blauvelt. Sr. Louis Marie Baxter, O.P., Supt. Capacity 100.

Mount St. Ursula Speech Center. Tel: 718-584-7679; Fax: 718-584-7954. 2885 Marion Ave., Bronx, 10458. Tel: 718-584-7679; Fax: 718-584-7954. Ursuline Nuns. Sr. Bernadette Hannaway, O.S.U., Admin. Sisters 1; Lay Clinicians 8; Support Staff 5; Total Enrollment 140.

Seton Foundation for Learning, Inc. Tel: 718-982-5084; Fax: 718-982-5114.
E-mail: seton@adnysch.org
315 Arlene St., Staten Island, 10314. Tel: 718-982-5084; Fax: 718-982-5114. Rev. Msgr. James Dorney, Chm.; Rev. Msgr. Peter Finn, Co-Chm.; Diane Cunningham, Exec. Dir.; Mr. John Haugen, Pres. Lay Teachers 4; Assistants 5; Enrollment 43.

BRONX. *St. Joseph's School for the Deaf*, 1000 Hutchinson River Pkwy., 10465. Tel: 718-828-9000; 828-1671 (TDD); Fax: 718-792-6631.
E-mail: SJSDpmar@aol.com
(Birth to 14 years). Directed by Daughters of the Heart of Mary. Ms. Patricia Martin, Exec. Dir. Capacity 200; Enrollment 140.

MILLBROOK. *Cardinal Hayes School for Special Children*, St. Joseph Dr., P.O. Box CH, 12545-0140. Tel: 845-677-6363; Fax: 845-677-6691.
Web site: www.cardinalhayeshome.org
Fred Apers, Exec. Dir. Educational programs for multi-handicapped children. Lay Teachers 5; Capacity 35; Enrollment 29.

[H] ELEMENTARY SCHOOLS, PRIVATE

NEW YORK. *Academy of St. Dorothy*, 1305 Hylan Blvd., 10305. Tel: 718-351-0939; Fax: 718-351-0661.
E-mail: dorothy@adnysch.org
Sr. Sharon A. McCarthy, S.S.D., Prin. Sisters of St. Dorothy 5; Lay Teachers 8; Students 320.

Convent of the Sacred Heart, 1 E. 91st St., 10128. Tel: 212-722-4745; Fax: 212-996-1784.
Web site: cshnyc.org
(Girls). Dr. Mary Blake, Headmistress. Sisters 2; Lay Teachers 67; Students 625.

Marymount School. (Grades Nursery-12), 1026 Fifth Ave., 10028. Tel: 212-744-4486; Fax: 212-744-0163. Religious of the Sacred Heart of Mary. Sr. Kathleen Fagan, R.S.H.M., Headmistress. Sisters 6; Lay Teachers 49; Students 360.

Sacred Heart Private Elementary School, Inc., 1651 Zerega Ave., 10462. Tel: 718-863-5047; Fax: 718-828-1946.
E-mail: scrhrtps@adnysch.org
Web site: www.sacredheartprivate.org
Apostles of the Sacred Heart of Jesus. Sr. Mary Grace Walsh, A.S.C.J., Prin. Sisters 6; Lay Teachers 7; Students 155.

St. John Villa Academy Elementary School, Mailing Address: 57 Cleveland Pl., 10305. Sr. Rita Marie Carey, C.S.J.B., Prin. Sisters 9; Lay Teachers 10; Students 418.

St. Joseph Hill Academy Elementary, 850 Hylan Blvd., 10305. Tel: 718-981-1187; Fax: 718-448-7016.
E-mail: joshiles@adnysch.org
Mary Jane Truckenbrodt, Prin. Sisters 1; Lay Teachers 30; Students 558.

Villa Maria Academy, 3335 Country Club Rd., 10465. Tel: 718-824-3260.
E-mail: villa@adnysch.org
Congregation of Notre Dame. Sr. Teresa Barton, C.N.D., Prin. Sisters 2; Lay Teachers 24; Students 500.

NEW ROCHELLE. *Iona Grammar School*. (Grades PreK-8), 173 Stratton Rd., 10804. Tel: 914-633-7744; Fax: 914-235-6338. (Boys). Bro. John D. Dugan, C.F.C., Pres. & Headmaster. Brothers 2; Lay Teachers 36; Students 302.

NEWBURGH. *Bishop Dunn Memorial School*, 50 Gidney Ave., 12550. Sisters of St. Dominic. Mrs. Kathleen Mellon, Prin. Sisters 2; Lay Teachers 10; Students 212.

PORT JERVIS. *Trinity Catholic School*, 44 Ball St., 12771. Tel: 845-856-6868; Fax: 845-856-6869. Carol Doll, Prin. Lay Teachers 8; Enrollment 135.

STATEN ISLAND. *Notre Dame Academy-Elementary School*, 78 Howard Ave., 10301. Tel: 718-273-9096; Fax: 718-442-6919.
E-mail: ntdames@adnysch.org
Congregation of Notre Dame. Sr. Rose Mary Galligan, C.N.D., Prin. Lay Teachers 13; Students 330.

WHITE PLAINS. *Academy of Our Lady of Good Counsel*. (Elementary Dept.). Tel: 914-761-4423; Fax: 914-761-4427.
E-mail: gdounes@adrysch.org
52 N. Broadway, 10603. Sr. Clare Arenholz, R.D.C., Prin. Sisters 3; Lay Teachers 14; Students 190.

[I] THE CATHOLIC CHARITIES OF THE ARCHDIOCESE OF NEW YORK

NEW YORK. *The Catholic Charities of the Archdiocese of New York*, 1011 First Ave., 10022. Tel: 212-371-1000; Fax: 212-826-8795. Rev. Msgr. James J. Murray, Exec. Dir.; Rev. Msgr. William J. Toohy, Assoc. Exec. Dir. & Dir. Social Research; Rev. Msgr. Kevin L. Sullivan, Chief Oper. Officer; Mr. Kenneth Dempsey, Chief Financial Officer; Rev. Richard F. Gorman; Ms. Joanne Abruzzese, Dir. Personnel; Revs. Michael F. Gannon, Coord. Upstate Counties; Robert Pagliari, C.SS.R., Assoc. Dir./Dir. Behavioral Health Services.
Departments: Sr. Una McCormack, O.P., Dir. Child Care; Dr. Marjorie Stuckle, Interim Dir. Mental Health Svcs.; Mr. Mario Russell, Dir. Migration & Refugee Svcs.; Ms. Patricia Brennan, Dir. Parish & Community Outreach; Mr. George B. Horton, Dir. Social & Community Development; Mr. Joseph Panepinto, Exec. Dir. CYO/Youth Svcs.

The Ladies of Charity of the Catholic Charities of the Archdiocese of New York, 1011 First Ave., 10022. Tel: 212-371-1000, Ext. 2540; Fax: 212-319-8265. Ms. Joan M. Maguire, Pres.; Ms. Susan Grady, Exec. Dir. Spiritual Directors: Rev. Msgr. William J. Toohy; Rev. Msgr. Peter G. Finn.

Catholic Charities Community Services, Archdiocese of New York, 1011 First Ave., 10022. Tel: 212-371-1000; Fax: 212-826-8795. Rev. Msgr. Kevin L. Sullivan.

Roman Catholic Fund for Children and Other Purposes, 1011 First Ave., 10022. Tel: 212-371-1000; Fax: 212-826-8795. Rev. Msgr. James J. Murray.

Holy Name Centre for Homeless Men, Inc., 18 Bleeker St., 10012. Tel: 212-226-5848. Rev. Msgr. John B. Ahern, Dir.

Providence Health Services, 1249 Fifth Ave., 10029. Mary Healey-Sedutto, Ph.D., Pres.

[J] HOUSING

NEW YORK. *Catholic Charities Department of Housing, Housing Development Institute, Inc.*, 1011 First Ave., 10022. Tel: 212-371-1000, Ext. 2537; Fax: 212-753-7827. Robert E. Paul, Dir.

BRONX. *Angela House, Inc.*, 3323 Steuben Ave., 10467. Tel: 718-231-7592; Fax: 718-231-9487. Sr. M. Winifred Danwitz, O.S.U., Ph.D., Exec. Dir. A transitional residence for homeless women and their young children.

[K] MENTAL HEALTH SERVICES

NEW YORK. *Catholic Charities Department of Mental Health Services*, 1011 First Ave., 10022. Tel: 212-371-1000, Ext. 2040; Fax: 212-317-8719.
E-mail: robert.pagliari@archny.org
For a complete listing, refer to the Special Care Facilities section.

[L] MIGRATION SERVICES

NEW YORK. *Catholic Charities Department of Immigrant and Refugee Services*, 1011 First Ave. 12th Floor, 10022. Tel: 212-371-1000, Ext. 2260; Fax: 212-751-3197. Mr. C. Mario Russell, Dept. Dir.

Department of Immigrant and Refugee Services, 1011 First Ave., 12th Floor, 10022. Tel: 212-371-1000, Ext. 2260; Fax: 212-751-3197. Ms. Penni Bunyaviroch, Assoc.Dir. for Admin. Scvs.

Refugee Resettlement, 1011 First Ave., 12th Floor, 10022. Tel: 212-371-1000, Ext. 2485; Fax: 212-751-3197. Ms. Patricia O'Callaghan, Coord.; Mr. Dan R. Smulian, Assoc. Dir for Legal Svcs.

Project Irish Outreach, 1011 First Ave., 12th Floor, 10022. Tel: 212-371-1000, Ext. 2485; Fax: 212-751-3197. Ms. Patricia O'Callaghan, Coord.

[M] PARISH AND COMMUNITY OUTREACH

NEW YORK. *Catholic Charities Department of Parish and Community Outreach*, 1011 First Ave., 10022. Tel: 212-371-1000, Ext. 2004; Fax: 212-317-8719. Ms. Patricia Brennan, Dir.
Catholic Charities Centers: Central Harlem, 202 W. 141st St., 10030. Tel: 212-694-3939; Fax: 212-694-4242. Lower Manhattan, 530 Grand St., 10002. Tel: 212-777-3111; Fax: 212-677-9057. Central Manhattan, 1011 First Ave., 10022. Tel: 212-371-1000, Ext. 2031; Fax: 212-826-8377. Washington Hts., 652 W. 187 St., 10033. Tel: 212-795-6860; Fax: 212-928-4351. Bronx, 2380 Belmont Ave., Bronx, 10458. Tel: 718-364-7770; Fax: 718-364-1513. South Bronx, 402 E. 152nd St., Bronx, 10455. Tel: 718-292-9090; Fax: 718-993-6130. Staten Island, 120 Anderson Ave., Staten Island, 10302. Tel: 718-447-6330; Fax: 718-447-6060. Westchester County/Peekskill, 1045 Park Ave., Peekskill, 10566. Tel: 914-737-7338; Fax: 914-737-1050. Westchester County/Yonkers, 4 St. Mary's St., Yonkers, 10701. Tel: 914-476-2700; Fax: 914-965-4241. Dutchess County, 240 Church St., Poughkeepsie, 12601. Tel: 845-452-1400; Fax: 845-452-3336. Orange County, 185 Liberty Ave., P.O. Box 64, Newburgh, 10977. Tel: 845-561-3452; Fax: 845-561-2825. Rockland County, 78 Hudson Ave., Haverstraw, 10927. Tel: 845-942-5791; Fax: 845-429-2938. Sullivan County, North St. & Liberty St., P.O. Box 395, Monticello, 12701. Tel: 845-791-6023; Fax: 845-791-6104. Ulster County, 157 Broadway, Kingston, 12401. Tel: 845-340-9170; Fax: 845-340-9596.

Parish Social Ministry, 1011 First Ave., 10022. Tel: 212-371-1000, Ext. 2032; Fax: 212-826-8377. Mrs. Dorothy Meehan.

Ministry to Seniors, 1011 First Ave., 10022. Tel: 212-371-1000, Ext. 2003; Fax: 212-826-8377. Mrs. Eleanor Ramos.

Office for the Homeless and Hungry, 1011 First Ave., 10022. Tel: 212-371-1000, Ext. 2529; Fax: 212-319-0405. Ms. Maureen Sheehan.

[N] SOCIAL AND COMMUNITY DEVELOPMENT

NEW YORK. *Catholic Charities Department of Social and Community Development*, 1011 First Ave., Room 1180, 10022. Tel: 212-371-1000, Ext. 2480; Fax: 212-319-0405.
E-mail: g.b.horton@worldnet.att.net
Mr. George B. Horton, Dir.

Office for Justice and Peace, 1011 First Ave., Room 1180, 10022. Tel: 212-371-1000, Ext. 2480; Fax: 212-319-0405. Jeff Korgen, Coord.

Office of Criminal Justice, 1011 First Ave., Room 1180, 10022. Tel: 212-371-1000, Ext. 3166; Fax: 212-391-0405. Mr. Kenneth Hoffarth, Dir.

New York Institute for Human Development, Inc., 1011 First Ave., Room 1180, 10022. Tel: 212-371-1000, Ext. 2474; Fax: 212-319-0405. Ms. Lourdes Ferrer, Community Devel. Coord.

[O] SERVICES TO THE DISABLED

NEW YORK. *Catholic Guild for the Blind*, 1011 First Ave., 6th Floor, 10022. Tel: 212-371-1000, Ext. 2017; Fax: 212-826-8377
For a complete listing, refer to the Special Care Facilities section.

New York Catholic Deaf Center, 1011 First Ave., Room 670, 10022. Tel: 212-371-1000 Ext. 2011 (Voice); 212-758-3045 (TTY); Fax: 212-317-8719
For a complete listing, refer to the Special Care Facilities section.

Mental Health & Community Residences:

NEW YORK. *Beacon of Hope House*, Central Administrative Office, 116 E. 16th St., 5th Fl., 10003-2112. Tel: 212-982-3560; Fax: 212-982-2869. Alan H. Bernstein, Exec. Dir.; Joy Jasper, Dir. Personnel; Ravi Ramaswamy, C.P.A., Controller.

Supervised Units, 1400 Waters Pl., Bronx, 10461. Tel: 718-892-3494; Fax: 718-892-5507. Robert Franco, Prog. Mgr., Beacon I: Vadim Moldovan, Prog. Supvr. Tel: 718-931-0600 Ext. 3284, Beacon II: Theresa Duffy, Prog. Supvr. Tel: 718-931-0600 Ext. 2637, Beacon III: Jackie Rosario, Prog. Supvr. Tel: 718-931-0600 Ext. 3289.

Terence Cardinal Cooke Residence, 2467 Bathgate Ave., Bronx, 10458. Tel: 718-367-6990; 718-367-5405 (TTY); Fax: 718-365-2544. Hope Goshea, Prog. Supvr.; Gary Bernstein, Regl. Dir., Bronx Svcs.

Supervised Units, 777 Seaview Ave., Bldg. D, 2nd Fl., Staten Island, 10305. Tel: 718-980-1072; Fax: 718-980-1077. Dennis Scimone, Regl. Dir., Brooklyn & Staten Island Svcs.; Sharon Quattrachi, Admin. Sec., Beacon I: Barbara Ignatenko, Prog. Supvr. Tel: 718-980-0041, Beacon II: Marlene Rosenberg, Prog. Supvr. Tel: 718-980-1072.

Staten Island Apartment Programs. Sandy Mormile, Prog. Mgr., 90-92 Hancock St., Staten Island, 10305. Tel: 718-979-6241; Fax: 718-979-6941.

Highbridge Neighborhood Supported Housing Program, 1435 Ogden Ave., Bronx, 10452. Tel: 718-293-1009; Fax: 718-293-0939. Rick Downes, Prog. Supv.

Kingsborough Intensive Supported Apartment Program, 647 Vanderbilt Ave., Brooklyn, 11238. Tel: 718-398-4556; Fax: 718-398-4807. Tom Bove, Prog. Supv.

Services to the St. Anthony's Residence, 410 E. 156th St., Bronx, 10455. Tel: 718-993-5060; Fax: 718-993-4758. Rick Downes, Regl. Mgr.

East Bronx Supported Housing, 707 Brady Ave., Bronx, 10462. Tel: 718-829-7177; Fax: 718-829-7376. Nancy Santos, Prog. Mgr.

Barnes Avenue Program, 2758 Barnes Ave., Bronx, 10461. Tel: 718-654-4750; Fax: 718-654-4804. Nancy Santos, Prog. Mgr.

The Clubhouse, 512 Southern Blvd., Bronx, 10455. Tel: 718-993-1078; Fax: 718-993-0216. Kimberly Jones, Prog. Mgr.

BARRYVILLE. *New Hope Manor*, 35 Hillside Rd., 12719. Tel: 845-557-8353; Fax: 845-557-6603.
E-mail: newhopemnr@aol.com
Web site: www.newhopemanor.org
Nicholas A. Roes, Dir.
See Miscellaneous listing for further details. Board of Directors: Sr. Patricia Anne Reilly, O.P.; Sr. Nora Healey, O.P.; Sr. Joan Correra, O.F.M.; Bro. Charles Kinney, S.A. Staff: Rev. Aquinas Thomas, S.A., Dir., In-Service Training; Sr. Maureen Conway, O.P., Dir. of Educ., Housemother, Counselor & Teacher; Sr. Patricia Conway, O.P., Housemother, Counselor & Teacher; Sr. Rose Respol, O.P., Dir., Religious Ed.; Sr. Marie Cecelia Landis, S.C.C., Re-entry Co-director. An all-female substance abuse treatment center.

SPRING VALLEY. *Good Counsel / The Cardinal Cooke Residence*, 22 Linden Ave., 10977. Tel: 845-356-0517; 800-723-8331 (Info. & Referrals); Fax: 845-356-4175. Christopher Bell, Exec. Dir.; Dana Williams, House Mgr. A program of Good Counsel in Hoboken, NJ, helping pregnant and single mothers with children. For information and intake referral, call 800-723-8331.

Good Counsel / The Paraclete Foundation, 1157 Fulton Ave., Bronx, 10456. Tel: 718-328-8620; 800-723-8331 (Info. & Referrals); Fax: 718-378-0341. Christopher Bell, Exec. Dir.; Felicia Smith, House Mgr.

Good Counsel, 38 N. Clinton St., Poughkeepsie, 12601. Tel: 845-452-2944; 800-723-8331 (Info. & Referrals); Fax: 845-452-6390. Christopher Bell, Exec. Dir.; Kathy Aldrich, House Mgr.

Good Counsel, 38 Wiman Pl., Staten Island, 10305. Tel: 718-727-8266; 800-723-8266 (Info. & Referrals); Fax: 718-447-6625. Christopher Bell, Exec. Dir.; Ruthe Fox, House Mgr. Total Assisted 347; Total Staff 72.

[P] YOUTH SERVICES

NEW YORK. *Catholic Youth Organization of the Archdiocese of New York Inc.*, Executive Office, 1011 First Ave., 10022-4187. Tel: 212-371-1000; Fax: 212-826-3347. Mr. Henry Humphreys, Pres.; Mr. Joseph E. Panepinto, Exec. Dir.; Mrs. Judith Trancucci, Asst. Dir.; Sr. Judy Frasinetti, S.M.R., Consultant to Young Adult Ministry; Mrs. Antoinette Kerins, Dir. Teenage Federation & Blair Lodge; Mr. David Dennis, Dir. Outdoor Ministry.

Archdiocesan Committee on Scouting: Tel: 212-371-1000; Fax: 212-826-3347. Rev. Msgr. Anthony D. Marchitelli, Archdiocesan Boy Scout Chap.; Rev. Lawrence J. Quinn, Sea Cadet Chap.; Eugene Joconetti, Scouting Coord.

CYO Manhattan County and Bronx County: Tel: 212-371-1000; Fax: 212-826-3347. Mr. Anthony D'Angelo, Dir., 242 Bathgate Ave., Bronx, 10458. Tel: 718-367-7659; Fax: 718-904-1863.

Grace Youth Ministry Center: Tel: 212-666-6598; Fax: 212-665- 2271. Mr. Kinah Ventura, Dir., 218 W. 108th St., 10025. Tel: 212-666-6598; Fax: 212-665-2271.

Cardinal Spellman Center: Tel: 212-677-6600; Fax: 212-995-8537. Mr. Thomas Rosati, Dir., 137 E. Second St., 10009. Tel: 212-677-6600; Fax: 212-995-8537.

Lt. Joseph P. Kennedy, Jr., Memorial Center: Tel: 212-862-6401; Fax: 212-862-6421. Mr. David Dennis, Dir., 34 W. 134th St., 10037. Tel: 212-862-6401; Fax: 212-862-6421.

CYO Staten Island Office: Tel: 718-448-4949; Fax: 718-273-8361. Anthony Navarrino, Dir.
120 Anderson Ave., Staten Island, 10302. Tel: 718-448-4950; Fax: 718-448-0576.

Staten Island Center. Tel: 718-448-4949; Fax: 718-273-8361. Fran Mitilieri, Dir.; Laurie Maneski, Asst. Dir., 120 Anderson Ave., Staten Island, 10302. Tel: 718-448-4949; Fax: 718-273-8361.

CYO Westchester/Putnam Offices: Tel: 845-623-2785; Fax: 845-624-0889. Frank Magaletta, Dir., 9 Brookview Blvd., Chestnut Ridge, 10977. Tel: 845-623-2785; Fax: 845-624-0889. Blair Lodge Youth Ministry Center, Peekskill Rd., Putnam Valley, 10579. Tel: 845-528-5005; Fax: 845-528-6137. Mrs. Antoinette Kerins, Dir., 1011 First Ave., 10022. Tel: 845-783-1254; Fax: 212-826-3347.

CYO Orange Office: Tel: 845-783-1254; Fax: 212-826-3347. Ann Lawrence, Teen Federation Coord., 260 Carpenter, Newburgh, 12550. Tel: 845-561-6264; Fax: 212-826-3347. John Smith, Sports Coord., P.O. Box 234, Highland Mills, 10930. Tel: 845-534-7700; Fax: 212-826-3347.

CYO Rockland Office: Tel: 845-620-1662. Thomas F. Collins, 34 Granecy Ct., Pearl River, 10965. Tel: 845-620-1662; Fax: 845-452-3336.

CYO Dutchess Office: Tel: 845-452-1400; Fax: 845-452-3336. Mary Marshall, Dir., Catholic Center, 240 Church St., Poughkeepsie, 12601. Tel: 845-452-1400; Fax: 8454-452-3336.

CYO Ulster Office: Tel: 845-340-9170; Fax: 845-340-9596. Thomas Brinkmann, Dir., 157 Broadway, Kingston, 12401. Tel: 845-340-9170; Fax: 845-340-9596.

CYO Sullivan County: Tel: 845-292-9100. Sr. Kevin John Shields, Box 1011, Liberty, 12750. Tel: 845-292-9100.

[Q] SOCIETY OF ST. VINCENT DE PAUL

NEW YORK. *Society of St. Vincent De Paul, Archdiocesan Central Council of New York*, 1011 First Ave., 10022. Tel: 212-755-8615; Fax: 212-755-0151. Legal Title: *The Society of St. Vincent de Paul of the Archdiocese of New York, Inc.* Territory: Archdiocese of New York. Mr. Ramon Vidal, Pres.; Rev. Robert T. Ritchie, Spiritual Advisor.

District Council of Manhattan, 1011 First Ave., Ste. 607, 10022. Tel: 212-755-8615; Fax: 212-755-0151. Legal Title: *The Society of St. Vincent de Paul in the City of New York*. Territory: Manhattan. Mr. Edmund Keane, Pres.; Rev. Msgr. Wallace A. Harris, Spiritual Advisor; Mr. Vincent D. Reilly, Exec. Sec.

District Council of the Bronx, 402 E. 152nd St., Bronx, 10455. Tel: 718-292-9090; Fax: 718-993-6130. Dominick Galdieri, Pres.

District Council of Staten Island, 28 Bryson Ave., Staten Island, 10302. Tel: 718-727-3171. Carmen Malandro, Pres.

BRONX. *District Council of the Bronx*, 402 E. 152nd St., 10455. Tel: 718-292-9090; Fax: 718-993-6130. Legal Title: *The Society of St. Vincent de Paul, District Council of the Bronx, Inc.* Territory: Borough of The Bronx & Lower Westchester. Rev. Walter A. Birkle, Spiritual Dir.; Dominick Galdieri, Pres.

STATEN ISLAND. *Particular Council of Staten Island*. Tel: 718-727-3171. Carmen Malandro, Pres.; Deacon Joseph Graf, Spiritual Dir.

[R] INSTITUTIONS FOR DEPENDENT CHILDREN

NEW YORK. *Covenant House Under 21*, 460 W. 41st St., 10036. Tel: 212-613-0300; Fax: 212-629-3756
For a complete listing, refer to the Special Care Facilities section.

Vincent J. Fontana Center for Child Protection, 590 Ave. of the Americas, 10011. Tel: 212-633-9300; Fax: 212-886-4008.
E-mail: michaelg@nyfoundliving.org
For a complete listing, refer to the Special Care Facilities section.

BLAUVELT. *St. Dominic Home*, 10913. Tel: 914-359-3400; Fax: 914-359-4253.
Web site: www.st.dominichome.org
For a complete listing, refer to the Special Care Facilities section.

BRONX. *Pius XII Youth and Family Services, Inc.*, 188 W. 230th St., 10463
For a complete listing, refer to the Special Care Facilities section.

Saint Dominic's Home - Prevention Program (ASTAAN), 2345 University Ave., 10468. Tel: 718-584-4407
For a complete listing, refer to the Special Care Facilities section.

NANUET. *St. Agatha Home of the New York Foundling Hospital*, 135 Convent Rd., 10954. Tel: 914-623-3461
For a complete listing, refer to the Special Care Facilities section.

WEST PARK. *St. Cabrini Home*, 12493. Tel: 845-384-6500; Fax: 845-384-6001.
E-mail: cabrini@ulster.net
Web site: cabrinihome.com
For a complete listing, refer to the Special Care Facilities section.

WHITE PLAINS. *Cardinal McCloskey Services*, Two Holland Ave., 10603. Tel: 914-997-8000; Fax: 914-997-2166.
E-mail: mmcloughlin@cardinalmccloskey.org
For a complete listing, refer to the Special Care Facilities section.

[S] SPECIALIZED CHILD CARING HOMES

NEW YORK. *Good Shepherd Services*, 305 7th Ave., 9th Floor, 10001. Tel: 212-243-7070; Fax: 212-929-3412.
E-mail: plomonaco@goodshepherds.org
Web site: www.goodshepherds.org
For a complete listing, refer to the Special Care Facilities section.

Kennedy Child Study Center, 151 E. 67th St., 10021. Tel: 212-988-9500; Fax: 212-570-6690.
E-mail: k.c.s.c@worldnet.att.net
For a complete listing, refer to the Special Care Facilities section.

Mission of the Immaculate Virgin Mount Loretto Staten Island, 10309. Tel: 718-317-2600; Fax: 718-317-2830.
For a complete listing, refer to the Special Care Facilities section.

New York Foundling Charitable Corp., 590 Avenue of the Americas, 10011. Tel: 212-633-9300
For a complete listing, refer to the Special Care Facilities section.

New York Foundling Hospital for Pediatric, Medical and Rehabilitative Care, Inc., 590 Avenue of the Americas, 10011. Tel: 212-633-9300; Fax: 212-886-4091.
E-mail: carolb@nyfoundling.org
For a complete listing, refer to the Special Care Facilities section.

New York Foundling Hospital, The, 590 Avenue of the Americas, 10011. Tel: 212-633-9300; Fax: 212-741-7516.
E-mail: ritan@nyfoundling.org
For a complete listing, refer to the Special Care Facilities section.

MILLBROOK. *Cardinal Hayes Home for Children*, St. Joseph Dr., P.O. Box CH, 12545. Tel: 845-677-6363; Fax: 845-677-6691.
Web site: www.cardinalhayeshome.org
For a complete listing, refer to the Special Care Facilities section.

RHINEBECK. *Astor Home for Children, The*, 36 Mill St., P.O. Box 5005, 12572-5005. Tel: 845-876-4081; Fax: 845-876-2020.
E-mail: rlogan@ustorservices.org
Web site: www.ustorservices.org
For a complete listing, refer to the Special Care Facilities section.

Astor Learning Center, The, 36 Mill St., P.O. Box 5005, 12572-5005. Tel: 914-876-4081; Fax: 914-876-2020
For a complete listing, refer to the Special Care Facilities section.

[T] CHILDREN'S AGENCIES & PROTECTIVE INSTITUTIONS

NEW YORK. *Catholic Guardian Society*, 1011 First Ave., 10022. Tel: 212-371-1000
For a complete listing, refer to the Special Care Facilities section.

Catholic Home Bureau, 1011 First Ave., 10022. Tel: 212-371-1000; Fax: 212-755-4110.
E-mail: 6269xx@dfa.state.ny.us
For a complete listing, refer to the Special Care Facilities section.

Guild of the Infant Savior, 1011 First Ave., Room 1150, 10022. Tel: 212-371-1000, Ext. 2440
For a complete listing, refer to the Special Care Facilities section.

Pelletier School & Services, 147 W. 70th St., 10023
For a complete listing, refer to the Special Care Facilities section.

LINCOLNDALE. *Lincoln Hall*, P.O. Box 600, 10540. Tel: 914-248-7474; Fax: 914-248-8391.
E-mail: pt.lincolnhall@worldnet.att.net
For a complete listing, refer to the Special Care Facilities section.

[U] CATHOLIC CHARITIES - CHILD CARING AGENCIES

OSSINING. *The Cardinal McCloskey Emergency Residential School*, 155 N. Highland Ave., 10562. Tel: 914-762-5302; Fax: 914-762-7844.
E-mail: eesaunders@aol.com
For a complete listing, refer to the Special Care Facilities section.

THORNWOOD. *Catholic World Mission, Inc.*, 582 Columbus Ave., 10594. Tel: 914-749-3900; Fax: 914-749-3939
For a complete listing, refer to the Special Care Facilities section.

[V] DAY NURSERIES

NEW YORK. *Featherbed Lane Day Care Center*. 98108 Featherbed Ln., Bronx, 10452. Tel: 212-583-8970. Mrs. Joyce Thompson, Dir. Group Day Care Children 33; Family Day Care Children 76.

Nazareth Nursery, 214-216 W. 15th St., 10011-6501. Tel: 212-243-1881.
Web site: www.mindspring.com/~robisonp/nazareth.html
Montessori Day Care. Sr. Lucy Sabatini, O.S.F., Dir. & Admin. Sisters of St. Francis of the Mission of the Immaculate Virgin 2; Capacity 55 Children; Total Staff 14.

Providence Rest Child Day Care Center, Inc., 3310 Campbell Dr., 10465. Tel: 718-823-3588. Total Assisted 30/Day; Total Staff 5.

St. Benedict's Day Nursery, Day Care Center, 21 W. 124th St., 10027. Tel: 212-423-5715; Fax: 212-423-5917.
E-mail: stben124@aol.com
Sr. Rose Mary, Dir. Handmaids of the Most Pure Heart of Mary 4; Children 79.

St. Cecilia's Day Nursery, 118 E. 106th St., 10029. Tel: 212-534-8423. Sr. Frances Arduini, S.A., Dir. Franciscan Sisters of the Atonement 3; Capacity 30; Total Served 30.

San Jose Day Nursery, 432 W. 20th St., 10011. Tel: 212-929-0839; Fax: 212-924-0891. Sr. Guadalupe Sordo, Supr.; Sr. Trinidad Fernandez, Dir. Mothers of the Helpless 8; Children 57.

MILLBROOK. *Hayes Nursery School and Day Care Center*, St. Joseph Dr., P.O. Box CH, 12545. Tel: 8455-677-6363; Fax: 845-677-6691.
Web site: www.cardinalhayeshome.org
Fred Apers, Exec. Dir. Capacity 75.

YONKERS. *Queen's Daughters Day Care Center, Inc.*, 73 Buena Vista Ave., 10701. Tel: 914-969-4491; Fax: 914-969-4491. Barbara Berrios, Dir. Children 125; Total Staff 20.

[W] GENERAL HOSPITALS

NEW YORK. *Cabrini Medical Center (Cabrini Development Council, Inc.)*, 227 E. 19th St., 10003. Tel: 212-995-6000; Fax: 212-995-6568
For a complete listing, refer to the Hospitals section.

Our Lady of Mercy Medical Center. Tel: 718-920-9000; Fax: 718-920-9245.
Web site: www.ourladyofmercy.com
233rd St. Division, 600 E. 233 St. Bronx, 10466. Tel: 718-920-9000; Fax: 718-920-9245.
For a complete listing, refer to the Hospitals section.

St. Clare's Hospital and Health Center, 415 W. 51st St., 10019. Tel: 212-586-1500
For a complete listing, refer to the Hospitals section.

St. Vincents Catholic Medical Centers of New York, 153 West 11 St., 10011. Tel: 212-604-7554; 604-2300; Fax: 212-604-7533.
Web site: svcmc.org
For a complete listing, refer to the Hospitals section.

Sisters of Charity Health Care System Corp. Tel: 1-800-CARE-421.
Web site: www.schsi.org
75 Vanderbilt Ave. Staten Island, 10304. Tel: 718-354-5080.
For a complete listing, refer to the Hospitals section.

BEACON. *St. Francis Hospital*, 11 Hastings Dr., 12508. Tel: 914-831-3500; Fax: 904-831-8131
For a complete listing, refer to the Hospitals section.

KINGSTON. *Benedictine Hospital*, 105 Mary's Ave., 12401. Tel: 914-338-2500; Fax: 914-334-3149.
Web site: www.benedictine.org
For a complete listing, refer to the Hospitals section.

PORT JERVIS. *Mercy Community Hospital*, 160 E. Main St., 12771. Tel: 914-856-5351; Fax: 914-858-5402.
E-mail: mercycommunityhosp.org
For a complete listing, refer to the Hospitals section.

POUGHKEEPSIE. *St. Francis Hospital*, North Rd., 12601. Tel: 914-471-2000
For a complete listing, refer to the Hospitals section.

SUFFERN. *Good Samaritan Hospital of Suffern*, 10901. Tel: 914-368-5000
For a complete listing, refer to the Hospitals section.

WARWICK. *St. Anthony Community Hospital, Inc.*, 15-19 Maple Ave., 10990. Tel: 914-986-2276
For a complete listing, refer to the Hospitals section.

WHITE PLAINS. *St. Agnes Hospital and Children's Rehabilitation Center*, 305 North St., 10605. Tel: 914-681-4500; Fax: 914-681-4974.
Web site: www.saintagneshospital.com
For a complete listing, refer to the Hospitals section.

YONKERS. *St. Joseph's Medical Center*, 127 S. Broadway, 10701. Tel: 914-378-7000; Fax: 914-965-4838.
E-mail: SJMCgen@interactive.net
Web site: http://saintjosephs.org
For a complete listing, refer to the Hospitals section.

[X] SPECIAL HOSPITALS AND SANATORIA FOR INVALIDS

NEW YORK. *Calvary Hospital* 1740 Eastchester Rd. Bronx, 10461. Tel: 718-863-6900.
For a complete listing, refer to the Special Care Facilities section.

St. Rose's Home, 71 Jackson St., 10002. Tel: 212-677-8132; Fax: 212-982-3485
For a complete listing, refer to the Special Care Facilities section.

Terence Cardinal Cooke Health Care Center, 1249 Fifth Ave., 10029. Tel: 212-360-1000; Fax: 212-289-2739.
E-mail: tcchcc@chcsnet.org
Web site: www.catholichealthcaresystem.org/tcc
For a complete listing, refer to the Special Care Facilities section.

HARRISON. *St. Vincent's Hospital and Medical Center Westchester Branch*, 275 North St., 10528. Tel: 914-967-6500; Fax: 914-925-5157
For a complete listing, refer to the Special Care Facilities section.

HAWTHORNE. *Rosary Hill Home*, 10532. Tel: 914-769-0114; Fax: 914-769-3916
For a complete listing, refer to the Special Care Facilities section.

YONKERS. *St. Eleanora's Home for Convalescents*, 127 S. Broadway, 10471. Tel: 718-378-7000; 549-9200; Fax: 718-884-3013.
E-mail: scny@scny.org
For a complete listing, refer to the Special Care Facilities section.

[Y] ORDERS OF NURSING SISTERS

NEW YORK. *Convent of the Little Sisters of the Assumption*, 2604 Davidson Ave., 10468. Sr. Jean McCormack, Prov. Coord.; Sr. Mary Joseph, Local Coord. Sisters 6.

Family Health Service, Inc.; Little Sisters of the Assumption, 426 E. 119th St., 10035. Tel: 212-987-4422; Fax: 212-987-4430.
E-mail: lsafhs@mindspring.com
Web site: www.eastharlem.org/lsafhs/
Sr. Judith Garson, Exec. Dir.

BRONX. *Convent of the Sisters Servants of Mary S.M.*, 3305 Country Club Rd., 10465-1296. Tel: 718-829-0428; Fax: 718-829-2346. Mother Angeles Aizpurua. Mission: Private nursing in the homes. Sisters 22.

OSSINING. *Dominican Sisters Family Health Services, Inc. (Central Services / Administration)*, 299 N. Highland Ave., 10562. Tel: 914-941-1710; Fax: 914-941-0518.
E-mail: dsfhs.ceo@worldnet.att.net
Web site: www.dsfhs.org (OR) dominicansistersfamilyhealthservice.org
Community-based, certified, voluntary Home Health Agency and Long Term Home Health Care and AIDS Programs serving all of Westchester, Suffolk and the South Bronx. Sr. Virginia Hanrahan, O.P., B.S.N., M.S., Ph.D., Pres. & CEO; Sr. Margaret Flood, O.P., B.S.N., M.A., M.P.A., Chief Operating Officer (COO).

Bronx Office, 279 Alexander Ave., Bronx, 10454. Tel: 718-665-6557; Fax: 718-292-9113.
E-mail: dsfhs.sbronx@worldnet.att.net
Margaret Sweeney, B.S.N., M.S.N., Admin.

Westchester Office, 299 N. Highland Ave., 10562. Tel: 914-941-1654; Fax: 914-941-1556.
E-mail: dsfhs.mariandale@worldnet.att.net
Evelyn Bobb, B.S.N., Admin.

Suffolk County Offices (3 Offices in Suffolk), 103-6 W. Montauk Hwy., Box 209, Hampton Bays, 11946. Tel: 631-728-0181; Fax: 631-728-2943.
E-mail: dsfhs.hamptons@worldnet.att.net
Box 866, Amagansett, 11930. Tel: 631-267-1090; Fax: 631-728-2943.
E-mail: dsfhs.hamptons@worldnet.att.net

STATEN ISLAND. *Pax Christi Hospice*, 355 Bard Ave., 10310. Tel: 718-876-1022; Fax: 718-876-1803. Hospice and Home Care Services for the terminally ill. Sisters of Charity Health Care System.

[Z] NURSING HOMES

NEW YORK. *Cabrini Center for Nursing & Rehabilitation*, 542 E. 5th St., 10009. Tel: 212-358-3000; Fax: 212-358-6269.
E-mail: mdevlin@ccnr.cabrininy.org
For a complete listing, refer to the Special Care Facilities section.

Kateri Residence, 150 Riverside Dr., 10024-2201. Tel: 212-769-0744; Fax: 212-873-0658.
E-mail: 1bond@chcn.org
Web site: www.chcn.org/kateri
For a complete listing, refer to the Special Care Facilities section.

Mary Manning Walsh Home, 1339 York Ave., 10021. Tel: 212-628-2800; Fax: 212-861-4178.
E-mail: mmwhome@msn.com
For a complete listing, refer to the Special Care Facilities section.

Terence Cardinal Cooke Health Care Center, 1249 Fifth Ave., 10029. Tel: 212-360-1000; Fax: 212-289-2739
For a complete listing, refer to the Special Care Facilities section.

BRONX. *Bon Secours New York Health System, Inc.*, 2975 Independence Ave., 10463-4699. Tel: 718-548-1700; Fax: 718-601-3384.
E-mail: tbrooks@fhsny.org
Web site: scherviercares.org
For a complete listing, refer to the Special Care Facilities section.

Jeanne Jugan Residence, 142 Hollywood Ave., P.O. Box 1002, 10465. Tel: 718-464-1800; Fax: 718-464-0254
For a complete listing, refer to the Special Care Facilities section.

Medical Missionaries of Mary, 563 Minneford Ave., 10464-1118. Tel: 718-885-0945; Fax: 718-885-0010.
E-mail: mmmci@aol.com
Web site: www.mmmusa.org
For a complete listing, refer to the Special Care Facilities section.

Providence Rest, 3304 Waterbury Ave., 10465. Tel: 718-931-3000; Fax: 718-863-0185.
E-mail: providencerest@aol.com
Web site: www.chcn.org/providence
For a complete listing, refer to the Special Care Facilities section.

St. Patrick's Home for the Aged and Infirm, 66 Van Cortlandt Park S., 10463. Tel: 718-519-2800; Fax: 718-519-2817.
E-mail: stpatrickhome@aol.com
Web site: www.hometown.aol.com/stpatshome/stp/index.htm
For a complete listing, refer to the Special Care Facilities section.

St. Vincent de Paul Residence, 900 Intervale Ave., 10459. Tel: 718-589-6965; Fax: 718-589-7010.
E-mail: svdpres@chcn.org
Web site: www.svdpres.org
For a complete listing, refer to the Special Care Facilities section.

DOBBS FERRY. *St. Cabrini Nursing Home*, 115 Broadway, 10522. Tel: 914-693-6800; Fax: 914-693-1731
For a complete listing, refer to the Special Care Facilities section.

MIDDLETOWN. *St. Teresa's Nursing Home*, 120 Highland Ave., 10940. Tel: 914-342-1033; Fax: 914-344-5631
For a complete listing, refer to the Special Care Facilities section.

RHINEBECK. *Ferncliff Nursing Home*, 21 Ferncliff Dr., 12572. Tel: 845-876-2011; Fax: 845-876-4810
For a complete listing, refer to the Special Care Facilities section.

STATEN ISLAND. *Carmel Richmond Nursing Home, Inc.*, 88 Old Town Rd., 10304-4299. Tel: 718-979-5000; Fax: 718-979-8027
For a complete listing, refer to the Special Care Facilities section.

WARWICK. *Villa Frances at the Knolls*, 22 Van Duzer Pl., 10990. Tel: 914-987-5717; Fax: 914-986-1231
For a complete listing, refer to the Special Care Facilities section.

[AA] ADULT RESIDENCES

NEW YORK. *Centro Maria, Inc.*, 539 W. 54th St., 10019. Tel: 212-581-5273; Fax: 212-307-5687.
E-mail: cenmariany@mindspring.com
Web site: rmi.world.org
For a complete listing, refer to the Special Care Facilities section.

Cor Mariae, c/o 1011 First Ave., Rm. 1130, 10022. Tel: 212-371-1000, Ext. 2435
For a complete listing, refer to the Special Care Facilities section.

The Dwelling Place, 409 W. 40th St., 10018. Tel: 212-564-7887; Fax: 212-695-3642.
E-mail: thedwellingplace@juno.com
For a complete listing, refer to the Special Care Facilities section.

El Carmelo Residence, 249 W. 14th St., 10011. Tel: 212-242-8224
For a complete listing, refer to the Special Care Facilities section.

The Jeanne d'Arc Residence, 253 W. 24th St., 10011. Tel: 212-989-5952; Fax: 212-691-0257.
E-mail: jdr253@juno.com
For a complete listing, refer to the Special Care Facilities section.

Kolping Society of New York Men's Residence (Catholic Kolping Society New York, Inc.), 165 E. 88th St., 10128. Tel: 212-369-6647; Fax: 212-987-5652
For a complete listing, refer to the Special Care Facilities section.

Kolping-on-Concourse 2916 Grand Concourse Bronx, 10458. Tel: 718-733-6119.
For a complete listing, refer to the Special Care Facilities section.

The Leo House, 332 W. 23rd St., 10011. Tel: 212-929-1010; Fax: 212-366-6801
For a complete listing, refer to the Special Care Facilities section.

Padre Pio Shelter for Homeless Men 419 E. 155th St. Bronx, 10455. Tel: 718-292-3713.
For a complete listing, refer to the Special Care Facilities section.

Sacred Heart Residence, 432 W. 20th St., 10011. Tel: 212-929-5790; Fax: 212-924-0891
For a complete listing, refer to the Special Care Facilities section.

St. Agnes' Residence, 237 W. 74th St., 10023. Tel: 212-874-1361
For a complete listing, refer to the Special Care Facilities section.

St. Joseph's Immigrant Home, 425 W. 44th St., 10036-4402. Tel: 212-246-5363
For a complete listing, refer to the Special Care Facilities section.

St. Mary's Residence, 225 E. 72nd St., 10021. Tel: 212-249-6850; Fax: 212-249-4336
For a complete listing, refer to the Special Care Facilities section.

St. Zita's Home for Adults, 143 W. 14th St., 10011. Tel: 212-243-7200
For a complete listing, refer to the Special Care Facilities section.

Thorpe Family Residence, Inc., 2252 Crotona Ave., 10457. Tel: 718-933-7312; Fax: 718-933-7311.
E-mail: srbarbter@aol.com
For a complete listing, refer to the Special Care Facilities section.

GARRISON. *St. Christopher's Inn*, P.O. Box 150, 10524-0150. Tel: 914-424-3616; Fax: 914-424-3786.
Web site: atonementfrairs.org
For a complete listing, refer to the Special Care Facilities section.

MONTROSE. *Kolping-on-Hudson*, 95 Montrose Point Rd., 10548. Tel: 914-737-9547
For a complete listing, refer to the Special Care Facilities section.

[BB] CATHOLIC CAMPS

NEW YORK. *The Catholic Camp Association Inc.*, 1011 First Ave., Room 1287, 10022. Tel: 212-371-1000.
John V. Mara CYO Camps, Putnam Valley.
Hill Camp. Capacity 120.
Valley Camp. Capacity 120. Total Assisted 147; Total in Residence 271; Total Staff 48.

THORNWOOD. *Summertime Activities, Inc.*, 582 Columbus Ave., 10594. Tel: 914-749-3900; Fax: 914-749-3939. Bro. Michael Zirkle, L.C., Contact Person.

[CC] COMMUNITY CENTERS

NEW YORK. *Cardinal Spellman Center, Inc.*, 137 E. Second St., 10009. Tel: 212-677-6600; Fax: 212-995-8537. Mr. Thomas Rosati, Dir. All Centers are engaged in full time recreational and educational activities. Serves Lower East Side parishes and includes Cardinal Spellman Headstart. Total Staff 35; Total Assisted 1,550.

Casita Maria Inc.
E-mail: casita@gateway.net
Web site: www.casitamaria.org
928 Simpson St., Bronx, 10459. Tel: 718-589-2230; Fax: 718-842-4622. Gladys Padro-Soler; Mrs. Jacqueline Weld, Chm. Serves the Bronx and East Harlem. Casita Maria serves over 10,000 individuals each year through after school program, social services, senior citizens centers, homebound seniors and recreation programs.

Casita Maria-Carver Community Center, 55 E. 102nd St., 10029. Cristina Toosie, Exec. Dir.; Orlando Tomas Martinez, Dir. Serves Carver Houses and adjacent areas of East Harlem.

Drew-Hamilton CYO Center, 220 W. 143rd St., 10030. Serves Central Harlem.

Lieut. Joseph P. Kennedy, Jr. Memorial Community Center, 34 W. 134th St., 10037. Mr. Les Edwards, Exec. Dir. Serves Central Harlem. Serves 200 youth in afternoon and afterschool programs and 500 teenagers in evening programs.

Life Experience and Faith Sharing Association, 149 E. 117th St., 10035. Tel: 212-996-7303; Fax: 212-828-5904.
E-mail: lefslitera@aol.com
LEFS Team: James Addison; Timothy Dunnington; Sr. Dorothy Gallant, S.C.; Vaughn McLamb; Ann Quintano; Jimmie Robinson; Teresa H. Skehan, R.S.M.; Sr. Cecilia Palange, S.C.I.M.; Sr. Rosemary O'Donnell, S.C.; Ralph Thomas; Godfrey Xaba. Total Assisted 2,500.

Staten Island CYO Center. Tel: 718-420-1010. 120 Anderson Ave., Port Richmond, Staten Island, 10302; Fax: 718-273-8361. Frances M. Mitilieri, Dir. Serves residents of Port Richmond and surrounding areas.

NYACK. *Catholic Community Services of Rockland, Inc.*, 33 Jefferson St., 10960. Tel: 845-353-7540; 353-5562; Fax: 845-353-7360.
E-mail: rockcath@aol.com
Rev. Msgr. William J. Belford, Chm. Provides emergency services to those in need.

[DD] MONASTERIES AND RESIDENCES OF PRIESTS AND BROTHERS

NEW YORK. *"America;" Residence and publication office of the America Press*, 106 W. 56th St., 10019. Tel: 212-581-4640; Fax: 212-399-3596.
E-mail: jesuits@americapress.org
Web site: www.americapress.org
Revs. Robert A. Mitchell, S.J., Supr.; Thomas J. Reese, S.J., Editor-in-Chief; Robert C. Collins, S.J.; James J. DiGiacomo, S.J.; John W. Donohue, S.J.; Vincent J. Duminuco, S.J.; D. James French, S.J.; John J. Gallen, S.J.; Frank LaRocca, S.J.; Dennis Linehan, S.J.; John F. Long, S.J.; James J. Martin, S.J.; Eugene J. O'Brien, S.J.; Frederick J. O'Brien, S.J.; Vincent T. O'Keefe, S.J.; Michael E. Sehler, S.J.; Walter J. Smith, S.J.; James P. Stehr, S.J.; Charles M. Whelan, S.J.; Bro. Francis W. Turnbull, S.J. Priests 19; Brothers 1.

Apostolic Society of the Crusade of the Holy Spirit. Tel: 845-838-3793. c/o St. John's Rectory, 31 Willow St., P.O. Box 549, Beacon, 12508. Tel: 845-831-0422; Fax: 845-831-1009. Revs. Ignatius Peries, C.H.S. (Argentina), Dir. Gen., Argentina; Bernard Kelly, C.H.S. (U.K.), Vicar Gen., U.K.; Nimal Mendis, C.H.S. (U.S.A.), Asst. Gen., Sec. Gen. & Treas. Gen., U.S.A.

Atonement Friars, 138 Waverly Pl., 10014-3845. Tel: 212-243-4692. Rev. Elias D. Mallon, S.A., Dir. Graymoor Ecumenical & Interreligious Institute; Bro. William Martyn, S.A., Exec. Sec. Commission on Ecumenical & Interreligious Affairs, Archdiocese of NY; Revs. Joseph F. Cavoto, S.A., Vocation Dir.; James Loughran, S.A., Tel: 212-675-6389. Rev. James J. Gardiner, S.A., Natl. Pastoral Life Center, Tel: 212-255-6731. Rev. Charles Sharon, S.A., Admin.

Augustinian Recollects Provincial Residence, Province of St. Nicholas of Tolentine, 2800 Schurz Ave., 10465. Tel: 718-823-0460; Fax: 718-239-9554.
E-mail: snezequiel@aol.com
Legal Title: *The Province of St. Nicholas of Tolentine of the Augustinian Recollect Fathers.* Revs. Francisco Legarra, O.A.R., Delegate; Jesus Sobejano, O.A.R.

Brothers of the Christian Schools of Manhattan College, Inc. Tel: 718-884-0613; Fax: 718-884-3500. 4415 Post Rd., Bronx, 10471. Tel: 718-884-0613; Fax: 718-884-3500. Bros. Kenneth Fitzgerald, F.S.C., Dir.; Luke Salm, F.S.C., Sub-Dir.; Thomas Scanlan, F.S.C., Pres. In res. Revs. Anthony L. Rubsys, F.S.C.A.; Rinaldo Borzaga, F.S.C.A. Total Staff 9; Total in Residence 45.

Calasanzian Fathers (Piarists), 88 Convent Ave., 10027. Tel: 212-234-1919; Fax: 212-281-7205. Revs. Felix Jimenez, Sch.P.; Jose M. Clavero, Sch.P.; Felix Ganuza, Sch.P.

Crosier (Canons Regular of the Order of the Holy Cross), Holy Cross Priory, c/o All Saints Rectory, 47 E. 129th St., 10035. Tel: 646-489-4313.
E-mail: jjbreer@mail.com
Web site: crosier.org
Very Venerable Bro. Jeffrey J. Breer, O.S.C., Admin.; Revs. Roger Vaughn, O.S.C.; Theodore K. Parker, O.S.C.; Bros. Gregory Madigan, O.S.C.; Gabriel Guerrero, O.S.C.

Franciscan Friars, Order of Friars Minor, Holy Name Province, Holy Name Province Provincialate, 126 W. 32nd St., 10001-3202. Tel: 212-967-6300; Fax: 212-967-6344.
E-mail: hnp@hnp.org
Web site: www.hnp.org
Legal Title: *Franciscan Friars, Order of Friars Minor of the Province of the Most Holy Name.* Revs. John M. Felice, O.F.M., Prov. Minister; Charles J. Miller, O.F.M., Prov. Vicar.
Priests of the Province in Residences not listed elsewhere: Rev. David M. Bossman, O.F.M., Seton Hall University, South Orange, NJ, 07079-2696. Tel: 973-761-9660; Fax: 973-325-7136. Rev. Patrick C. Callaghan, O.F.M., Rte. 1, Spruce St., Saint Regis Falls, 12980-9712. Tel: 518-856-9729. Rev. Peter S. Chepaitis, O.F.M., Bethany Ministries, Box 420, Middleburgh, 12122-0420. Tel: 518-827-4699. Rev. Lawrence D. Ford, O.F.M., 3020 Royal Huntsman Ct., South Bend, IN, 46637. Tel: 219-631-7302; Fax: 219-631-3565. Rev. Russel Murray, O.F.M., St. James Frances de Chantal Friary, 2747 Jane St., Downview, Ontario M3L 3E8, Canada. Tel: 416-741-1463; Fax: 416-741-1469. Rev. Joseph Ganssle, O.F.M., 4165 Eaton St., Denver, CO, 80212-7306. Tel: 303-936-9738; Fax: 303-936-6250. Rev. Depaul A. Genska, O.F.M., Catholic Theological Union, 5401 S. Cornell Ave., Chicago, IL, 60615-5608. Tel: 773-324-8000; Fax: 773-324-4360. Rev. John Coughlin, O.F.M., St. Joseph's Seminary, Dunwoodie, Yonkers, 10704-1852. Tel: 914-968-6200; Fax: 914-375-5366. Rev. J. Patrick Kelly, O.F.M., FrancisCare, Elmwood Park Plaza, 475 Market St., Elmwood Park, NJ, 07407-3104. Tel: 201-791-1499; Fax: 201-791-3529. Rev. Venant Lalonde, O.F.M., St. Agnes Rectory, 143 E. 43 St., 10017-4065. Tel: 212-682-5722; Fax: 212-370-5791. Rev. Leonard Lencewicz, O.F.M., 8221 Tanglewood Ln., Tampa, FL, 33615. Tel: 813-885-7861; Fax: 813-886-3624. Rev. Declan Maddan, O.F.M., 3805 W. 26th Ave., Apt. 102, Denver, CO, 80211-4449. Tel: 303-433-6268; Fax: 303-455-5359. Rev. Rene F. Phillips, O.F.M., 850 Thomas Ln., Angola, 14006-9572. Tel: 716-549-7930. Rev. Lawrence Schulmeister, O.F.M., 612 Warner St., Baltimore, MD, 21230. Tel: 410-962-1233; Fax: 410-962-1233. Rev. Richard Mucowski, O.F.M., St. Mary College, 4100 S. 4th St., Leavenworth, KS, 66048-5082. Tel: 913-758-6102; Fax: 913-758-1158. Rev. Benedict M. Taylor, O.F.M., Create Inc., 73 Lenox Ave., 10026. Tel: 212-663-1975; Fax: 212-663-1293. Rev. Gerald M. Dolan, O.F.M., Chaplain's Residence, 20 Grand St., Warwick, 10990-1035. Tel: 914-986-4016; Fax: 914-986-3604. Rev. Edward C. Metzger, O.F.M., 770 West Ferry St., #10, Buffalo, 14222. Tel: 716-883-9411. Rev. Alfonso D. Guzman, O.F.M., Arzobispado de San Juan, P.O. Box 9021967, San Juan, PR, 00902-1967. Tel: 787-725-4975; Fax: 787-723-4040. Military Chaplains: Rev. Louis V. Iasiello, O.F.M., Deputy Chief of Chaplains, 2 Naval Annex (Code NO97B), Washington, DC, 20370-4000. Tel: 703-614-4043; Fax: 703-614-4725. Rev. Alan Sullivan, O.F.M., 3310 First Ave., Apt.7A, San Diego, CA, 92103-5659. Tel: 619-260-3640. Rev. Conrad W. Loftus, O.F.M., 2510 E. 104th Ave., G2-1, Denver, CO, 80233-4401. Tel: 303-450-6298; Fax: 303-452-7993. Rev. Carmel Lluria, O.F.M., Preakness Hospital, Box V, Unit 1, Paterson, NJ, 07509. Tel: 973-904-5000.
Priests Abroad: Rev. Giulio Basetti-Sani, O.F.M., Convento San Francesco Infermeria, Via S. Francesco, 13, Fiesole (Firenze), Italy, 50014. Tel: 011-39-05-559-9115; Fax: 011-39-05-559-7250. Rev. Pius Liu, O.F.M., 67 Chen-kund Rd., Sec. 3, Neihu Taipei, Taiwan, R.O.C., 11410. Tel: 011-886-2-2-790-0002; Fax: 011-886-2-2-790-9537. Rev. Alan Faddish, O.F.M., 188 S. Mansfield Ave., Margate, NJ, 08402. Tel: 609-822-9552; Fax: 609-822-0601. Rev. Howard O'Shea, 34, Rue Roux Alpheran, Aix-En-Provence 13100, France. Tel: 011-33-4-4226-7789; Fax: 011-33-4-4226-7789. Rev. Alexander DiZella, O.F.M., Catholic University, Curley Hall, Washington, DC, 20064-0001. Tel: 202-319-5867; Fax: 202-238-1657. For Information Regarding Vocations to the Brotherhood & Priesthood, write Franciscan Vocation Office, St. Francis Friary, 134 W. 32nd St., New York, NY 10001. Solemnly Professed Priests (including 3 Bishops) 359; Brothers 79; Temporary Vows: Brothers 6; Clerics 14; Novices 3; Permanant Deacons 3; Affiliates 8.

Franciscan Province of the Immaculate Conception, 125 Thompson St., 10012. Tel: 212-674-4388; Fax: 212-533-8034. Franciscan Province of the Immaculate Conception of New York City. Legal Title: *Friars Minor of the Order of St. Francis, Incorporated, New York, 1871.* Revs. Robert M. Campagna, O.F.M., Minister Prov.; Patrick Boyle, O.F.M., Vicar Prov.; Simeon Distefano, O.F.M., Prov. Sec.; Marion Cascino, O.F.M., Prov. Promoter of Missions.
Franciscan Mission Associates, 274-280 W. Lincoln Ave., Mt. Vernon, 10550. Tel: 914-664-5604; Fax: 914-664-3017. Ms. Madeline Bonnici, Exec. Dir.; Rev. Claude Scrima, O.F.M., Dir. of Secular Franciscans, St. Christopher Friary, 18 North Bennet St., Boston, MA, 02113. Tel: 617-742-4190; Fax: 617-725-0343. Pious League of Saint Anthony, 151 Thompson St., P.O. Box 489, 10013-0489. Tel: 212-674-4388; Fax: 212-533-8034.
Priests of the Province Abroad: Revs. Gilbert Silverio, O.F.M.; Richard Martignetti, O.F.M.; Antonio Nardoianni, O.F.M., Convento San Francesco, Via Nicolo V, 35, 00165 Rome, Italy. Tel: 011-39-06-393-88403; Fax: 011-39-06-393-80364.
Military Chaplains: Rev. Charles Soto, O.F.M., Chapel Center, P.O. Box 6, NAS, Jacksonville, FL, 32212-5000. Tel: 904-542-3058. Rev. Blaise Tranchida, O.F.M., Basilica of the Annunciation, P.O. Box 23, 16100 Nazareth, Israel.
Retired Military Chaplains: Rev. Edwin Bobrek, O.F.M., 1427 Ave. de las Adelsas, Encinatas, CA, 92024. Tel: 619-436-5355. Rev. Fidelis Travaglione, O.F.M., St. Francis Friary, 459 River Rd., Andover, MA, 01810. Tel: 978-851-3391; Fax: 978-858-0675.
Priests of the Province Residing Elsewhere: Rev. Sigmund Brambilla, O.F.M. 15A Park Ave., Northampton, MA, 01060. Rev. Albert McMahon, O.F.M., Holy Spirit Parish, 1000 Lantana Rd., P.O. Box 3978, Lantana, FL, 33465. Tel: 561-585-5970. Rev. Michael D. Ledoux, O.F.M., St. Felix Friary, 119 N. Jackson St., Wilmington, DE, 19805. Tel: 302-778-5910. Rev. Thaddeus Palmieri, O.F.M., Mary Help of the Christians Church, 6281 N.W. 66th Way, Parkland, FL, 33067. Tel: 305-752-2717. Rev. Clement Procopio, O.F.M., 306 S.18th St., Cottonwood, AZ, 86326. Tel: 520-634-3490. Revs. Victor Cesario, O.F.M.; John Bucchino, O.F.M., 14 Stuyvesant Oval #5D, 10009. Tel: 212-228-8798. Rev. Louis De Tommaso, O.F.M., St. Ignatius Rectory, P.O. Box 1306, Tarpon Springs, FL, 34688-1306. Tel: 813-937-4050. Rev. Ralph Di Pasquale, O.F.M., 2008 Crowberry Dr., Port St. Lucie, FL, 34983. Tel: 407-871-1588. On Sick Leave: Rev. Xavier Carnicelli, O.F.M., St. Cabrini Nursing Home, 115 Broadway, Dobbs Ferry, 10552. Tel: 914-693-0798. Rev. Matthew Kiss, O.F.M., Ferncliff Nursing Home, 29 Ferncliff Dr., 12572. Tel: 914-876-2011. Rev. Vincent Mele, O.F.M., Kateri Residence, 150 Riverside Dr., 10024. Tel: 212-769-0744. Rev. Cyril Morisco, O.F.M., St. Joseph Manor Nursing Care Facility, 1133 Washington Ave., Portland, ME, 04103. Tel: 207-797-0600.
Residing in Canada: Immaculate Conception Friary, 2 Richardson Ave., Toronto, Ont., M6M 3R4. Tel: 416-651-1787; Fax: 416-651-7881. Revs. Amadeo Nardone, O.F.M.; James Wells, O.F.M., St. Charles Borromeo Friary, 811 Lawrence Ave., Toronto, Ont., M6A 1C3. Tel: 416-787-0369; Fax: 416-256-4466. Revs. Primo Piscitello, O.F.M.; Gregory E. Imbroll, O.F.M.; Michael D'Cruz, O.F.M., St. Francis Friary, 72 Mansfield Ave., Toronto, Ont., M6J 2B2. Tel: 416-536-8195; Fax: 416-531-6883. Revs. Gregory Botte, O.F.M.; Isidoro di Miglio, O.F.M.; Frederick Mazzarella, O.F.M., St. Lawrence Friary, 2210

Lawrence Ave. E., Scarborough, Ont., M1P 2P9. Tel: 416-759-9359; Fax: 416-759-6725. Rev. Ralph Paonessa, O.F.M., St. Bonaventure, 56 Spadina Rd., Toronto, Ont., M5R 2T3. Tel: 416-925-1787; Fax: 416-925-0971. Revs. Celestine Pennisi, O.F.M.; Benedict Goveas, O.F.M., St. Jane Frances de Chantal Friary, 2747 Jane St., Downsview, Ont., M3L 2E8. Tel: 416-741-1463; Fax: 416-741-1469. Revs. Celestino Canzio, O.F.M.; Lawrence Parent, O.F.M.; Augustin Donini, O.F.M., St. Jude Friary, 3265 Weston Rd., Weston, Ont., M9M 2T9. Tel: 416-742-9072; Fax: 416-742-9081. Revs. Octavio Jose Salinas, O.F.M.; Nery Aguirre, O.F.M.

St. Francis Center for Religious, 208501 Hwy. #9, R.R. #8 (Mono Mills), Orangeville, Canada, L9W 3T5. Tel: 519-941-1747; Fax: 519-941-6961. Bro. Philip Adamo, O.F.M.; Rev. Michael Della Penna, O.F.M.

St. Peter Friary, 100 Bainbridge Ave., Woodbridge, Canada, L4L-3YL. Tel: 905-851-3600; Fax: 905-856-0171. Revs. Claudio Moser, O.F.M.; Edwin Paniagua, O.F.M. Priests 153; Brothers 31; Permanent Deacons 3; Bishops 3.

The Franciscan Vocation Ministry of Holy Name Province, 135 W. 31st St., 10001-3439. Tel: 212-629-5868; 800-677-7788; Fax: 212-629-4060.
E-mail: fribro@aol.com or NathanaelN@aol.com
Web site: www.vocation.org
Rev. Peter V. Brophy, O.F.M., Dir., HNP Vocation Ministry; Bro. Nathanael Necaster, O.F.M., Admin. Asst.

Immaculate Conception Friary, 754 E. Gun Hill Rd., 10467. Tel: 212-653-2200. Capuchin Friars of the Province of the Stigmata of St. Francis. Revs. Robert Grix, O.F.M.Cap.; Pius Caccavalle, O.F.M.Cap.; Robert Yurgel, O.F.M.Cap.; Eric Hall, O.F.M.Cap. Total Assisted 190; Total Staff 20; Priests 4; Brothers 2.

Jesuit Community at Fordham University, 441 E. Fordham Rd., 10458. Tel: 718-817-5322; Fax: 718-733-4456. Very Rev. Gerald R. Blaszczak, S.J., Rector, Jesuit Communities of Loyola Hall;Cardinal Spellman Hall & Kohlmann Hall, Loyola Hall, Jesuit Community. Tel: 718-817-5322; Fax: 718-733-4456. Revs. Edward F. Maloney, Supr.; David J. Casey, S.J., Min.; Joseph V. Dolan, S.J., Sub Min.; John D. Alexander, S.J.; Albert P. Bartlett, S.J.; Bro. Sebastian A. Boccabella, S.J.; Revs. John J. Conley, S.J.; Francis P. Canavan, S.J.; W. Norris Clarke, S.J.; T. Gerard Connolly, S.J.; Frederick J. Dillemuth, S.J.; G. Richard Dimler, S.J.; Robert R. Dobbins, S.J.; Edward T. Dowling, S.J.; Rev. Msgr. Charles J. Fahey, (S.Y.); Revs. Kizito S. Forbi, S.J.; Daniel J. Fitzpatrick, S.J.; Anthony E. Ciampietro, C.S.B.; C. Homer Giblin, S.J.; L. Augustine Grady, S.J.; Thomas C. Hennessy, S.J.; George B. Hoch, S.J.; William T. Hogan, S.J.; Bro. Frank W. Jensen, S.J.; Revs. J. Raymond Johnson; Robert G. Kelly, S.J.; John R. Keating, S.J.; Albert J. Loomie, S.J.; Edward F.X. Kennedy, S.J.; George J. McMahon, S.J.; George C. McCauley, S.J.; Gerald A. McCool, S.J.; Joseph Mitros, S.J. (Poland); Vincent M. Novak, S.J.; Ladislas Orsy, S.J.; Jung-Woo Park, S.J. (Korea); Louis B. Pascoe, S.J.; William L. Reilly, S.J.; James H. Reid, S.J.; Herbert W. Rogers, S.J.; Robert J. Roth, S.J.; James A. Sadowsky, S.J.; Bro. Gerard W. Schade, S.J.; Revs. Robert J. Sealy, S.J.; J. Francis Stroud, S.J.; Daniel J. Sullivan, S.J.; Patrick J. Sullivan, S.J.; Edward J. Sweeney, S.J., Jesuit Community, Kohlmann Hall. Tel: 718-584-1638; Fax: 718-584-0760. Revs. Raymond M. Sweitzer, S.J.; John J. Scully, S.J., Min.; John J. Leonard, S.J., Sub-Min.; Thomas G. Benz, S.J.; Michael P. Corcoran, S.J.; Mallick J. Fitzpatrick, S.J.; Matthew C. Flood, S.J.; Joseph P. Parkes, S.J.; Stanley J. O'Konsky, S.J.; William J. O'Malley, S.J.; Charles D. Sullivan, S.J., Cardinal Spellman Hall, Jesuit Community. Tel: 718-817-5330; Fax: 718-817-5717. Very Rev. Joseph A. O'Hare, S.J., Pres.; Revs. Daniel J. O'Brien, S.J., Min.; Robert Araujo, S.J.; Claudio Burgaleta, S.J.; Dean P. Bechard, S.J.; Robert D. Cloney, S.J.; Martin Chase, S.J.; Joseph A. Currie, S.J.; Brian Davies, O.P. (England); His Eminence Avery Dulles, S.J.; Revs. John T. Dzieglewicz, S.J.; Garrett J. Fitzgerald, S.J.; Robert R. Grimes, S.J.; Martin A. Hegyi, S.J. (Hungary); George Hunt, S.J.; Joseph W. Koterski, S.J.; Joseph T. Lienhard, S.J.; Nicholas D. Lombardi, S.J.; Mark S. Massa, S.J.; Donald C. Matthews, S.J.; Gerard Reedy, S.J.; Richard J. Regan, S.J.; Mr. Jose Luis Salazar, S.J.; Revs. Thomas J. Scirghi, S.J.; Michael F. Suarez, S.J.; Timothy Valentine, S.J.; Jeffrey P. von Arx, S.J. Priests 82; Brothers 3; Total in Residence 86.

Metro New York Christian Life Communities, Inc., Loyola Hall, Fordham University, Bronx. Tel: 718-817-5454.

Jesuit Provincial's Office, 39 E. 83rd St., 10028. Tel: 212-774-5500; Fax: 212-774-5510.
E-mail: nykprov@nysj.org
Very Rev. Kenneth J. Gavin, S.J., Prov.; Revs. James L. Dugan, S.J., Exec. Asst. to Prov.; Frederick J. O'Brien, S.J., Asst. for Secondary Education; D. James French, S.J., Asst. Pastoral Ministries & Asst. for Formation for New York Province; Bro. Gilbert J. Scott, S.J., Asst. to Prov.; Revs. J. Raymond Johnson, S.J., Prov. Treas., Auditor & American Rep. of the Missions of the Society of Jesus, Vatican City; Thomas E. Smith, S.J., Asst. to the Prov. for the Intl. Apostolate; Robert E. Reiser, S.J., Vocation Dir. for Maryland & New York Provinces; Edward J. Quinnan, S.J., Asst. for Retreat Houses & Ministry of Spiritual Exercises.
Priests of the Province Abroad: Rev. Vincent F. Blehl, S.J., Rabenkopfstr. 2, Apt. 229, Freiburg, Germany, 79102. Tel: 49-761-368-5229; Fax: 49-761-368-5107. Rev. James J. Bowes, S.J., C.P. 6139, 00195 Rome, Italy. Tel: 39-06-689-771; Fax: 39-06-686-8214. Rev. Michael P. Hilbert, S.J., Pontificia Universita Gregoriana, Piazza della Pilotta 4, 00187 Rome, Italy. Tel: 39-06-6701-1; Fax: 39-06-6701-5413. Rev. Henry J. Bertels, S.J., Pontifical Biblical Institute, via della Pilotta 25, 00187 Rome, Italy. Tel: 39-06-6701-6199; Fax: 39-06-6701-6151. Rev. Keith F. Pecklers, S.J., Coll Bellarmino, Via del Seminario 120, 00186 Rome, Italy. Tel: 39-06-579-1363; Fax: 39-06-574-8312. Rev. William L. Wizeman, S.J., Campion Hall, Oxford, England, 0X1 1QS. Tel: 44-1865-286100; Fax: 44-1865-286148. Rev. Charles H. Lohr, S.J., Raimundus-Lullus Institute der Universitat-Freiburg, Werthmann Platz, 3, D-79085 Freiburg i Br., Germany. Tel: 49-761-203-2082.
Priests of the Province in Residences Not Listed Elsewhere: Rev. Theodore V. Francois, S.J., 507 Macon St., Brooklyn, 11233. Tel: 718-452-0494. Rev. Gerard H. Ettlinger, S.J., 10-01 162nd St., Apt. 5-D, Whitestone, 11357. Tel: 718-767-5895; Fax: 718-990-1907. Rev. Edward J. Mally, S.J., 1S 150 Spring Rd., Apt. 2E, Oakbrook Terrace, IL, 60181. Tel: 630-833-0645; Fax: 708-756-6863. Rev. John J. Gerhard, S.J., 850 Hylan Blvd., Staten Island, 10305. Tel: 718-447-5639. Rev. Joseph P. Kane, S.J., 2674 Valentine Ave., Apt., 1A, Bronx, 10458. Tel: 718-430-4940; Fax: 718-365-8650. Rev. Gerard P. Bell, S.J., 15107 Interlachen Dr., Apt. 722, Silver Spring, MD, 20906. Tel: 301-438-3753. Rev. John H. Rainaldo, S.J., 3 Stephan Ave., New Hyde Park, 11040. Tel: 516-328-9777; Fax: 516-328-6039. Rev. George H. Belgarde, S.J., St. Regis Mission, P.O. Box 429, Hogansburg, 13655. Tel: 613-575-2066. Rev. Adelmo P. Dunghe, S.J., Regis, 567 Huron St., Toronto, Canada, M5R 2R6. Tel: 416-929-2801. Rev. Edward J. Snyder, S.J., 28 Marine Pl., Deal, NJ, 07723. Tel: 732-531-4795. Rev. Michael E. Donahue, S.J., c/o Provincial's Office, 39 E. 83rd St., 10028. Rev. Benedict Kim Sung-ho, S.J., 247 E. 39th St., Apt. 2C, 10016. Tel: 212-983-9079.

Jesuit Community, 860 Manida St., Bronx, 10474. Tel: 718-542-2283. Connected with Nativity Rectory. 44 Second Ave., 10003. Tel: 212-674-8590; Fax: 212-674-8789. In res. Rev. Joseph C. Towle, S.J.

The Little Brothers of the Gospel, 58 E. Fourth St., #10, 10003. Tel: 212-533-0530. Bro. Jay McGowan, Coord.

Maryknoll House, 121 E. 39th St., 10016. Tel: 212-697-4470; Fax: 212-697-4472.
E-mail: mklnyc@aol.com
Web site: www.maryknoll.org
Catholic Foreign Mission Society. Bro. Anthony Lopez, Dir.; Rev. Dennis W. Cleary.

Murray-Weigel Hall, 515 E. Fordham Rd., 10458-5004. Tel: 718-430-4900; Fax: 718-365-8650.
E-mail: stevepug2@aol.com
Revs. John J. McDonald, S.J.; Steven J. Pugliese, S.J., Min.; Joseph C. McKenna, S.J., Sub Min.; James J. Yannarell, S.J., Infirmarian; John D. Boyd, S.J.; John J. Barrett, S.J.; Robert W. Dahlke, S.J.; Francis X. Elsinghorst, S.J.; Thomas E. Brady, S.J.; Edwin Brooks, S.J.; William B. Cogan, S.J.; James F. Coleman, S.J.; Eugene K. Culhane, S.J.; Theodore J. Cunnion, S.J.; Timothy A. Curtin, S.J.; James A. Daly, S.J.; Roy A. Drake, S.J.; George F. Driscoll, S.J.; Richard P. English, S.J.; John K. Fahey, S.J.; John L. Farrand, S.J.; William J. Farrell, S.J.; James J. Fedigan, S.J.; James J. Finley, S.J.; Martin E. Feeney, S.J.; Joseph R. Frese, S.J.; Robert J. Haskins, S.J.; Alfred T. Hennelly, S.J.; Lawrence B. Hill, S.J.; James J. Hennesey, S.J.; Cornelius P. Hurley, S.J.; Joseph P. Kane, S.J.; Joseph V. Landy, S.J.; John McConnell, S.J.; James P. Jurich, S.J.; John A. Morrison, S.J.; Louis A. Mounteer, S.J.; John A. Nicholson, S.J.; Edward H. McGlinchy, S.J.; Richard J. Pendergast, S.J.; Francis V. Rooney, S.J.; Peter J. Roslovich, S.J.; Joseph D. Ryan, S.J.; Joseph B. Schuyler, S.J.; Edward J. Murphy, S.J.; Bernard E. Shannon, S.J.; Louis E. Soloman, S.J.; Francis J. Tierney, S.J.; Richard F. Timone, S.J.; Vincent T. O'Keefe, S.J.; James J. Wheeler, S.J.; Patrick T. Sullivan, S.J.; William T. Wood, S.J.; Robert H. Vogt, S.J. Scholastic: Mr. John S. Quigley; Bros. Stephen J. Andrews, S.J.; Theodore C. Bender, S.J.; Ignatius J. Fitzroy, S.J.; Daniel M. Hoey, S.J.; Raymond V. Whalen, S.J. Priests 53; Brothers 5; Scholastic 1.

Our Lady of Consolation Residence. Tel: 718-548-0888; Fax: 718-548-7824. 3103 Arlington Ave., Corner of W. 231st St., Bronx, 10463. Tel: 718-548-0889; Fax: 718-548-7824. Rev. Msgr. Charles R. Klein, Dir.; Rev. Msgr. Thomas V. Gallagher; Rev. Msgr. Hugh J. Rooney; Rev. Msgr. Vincent W. Jeffers; Revs. Joseph P. Adamo; Ronald P. Altrui; William E. Kelly; Francis J. Molony; Eugene P. O'Hara; Maurice C. Slattery; Thomas Tolentino.

Padua Friary, 151 Thompson St., 10012. Tel: 212-254-9553; Fax: 212-254-9644. Revs. John R. Scarangello, O.F.M., Guardian, Instructor (Cathedral High Sch.); John-Marie Cassese, O.F.M., Vicar, Prov. Archivist & Chronicler; Bro. Luke Storino, O.F.M., Prov. Bookkeeper; Revs. Marion Cascino, O.F.M., Secretariat for Missions & Evangelization; Emmanuel Faraone, O.F.M.; Sebastian Buccellato, O.F.M., FMU Prom.; Peter Walsh, O.F.M.; Stephen Caforio, O.F.M.; Louis Troiano, O.F.M.; Anthony Abate, O.F.M.

Pallottine Fathers, Society of the Catholic Apostolate, 448 E.116th St., 10029. Tel: 212-534-0681; Fax: 212-534-0629. Revs. Peter J. Rofrano, S.A.C.; Severino Dominicis, S.A.C., Mt. Carmel Society & Catholic Apostolate Assoc.; Girolamo D'Ambrosi, S.A.C.; Tony Kelly, S.A.C., Spanish Apostolate. Total Assisted 300; Total Staff 15.

Passionist Spiritual Center. Tel: 718-549-6500; Fax: 718-884-9732.
E-mail: pass.spirit.ctr.1@juno.com
Web site: www.passionist.org
5801 Palisade Ave., Riverdale, 10471. Very Rev. Malcolm Cornwell, C.P., Local Supr., Formation Dir.; Revs. Paul Fagan, C.P., Retreat Dir; Gregory Paul; Richard Scheiner, C.P.; Donald Ware, C.P., (Sabbatical); Gerard M. McGlone (SCR)); Bros. Damian Carroll, C.P.; James Johnson, C.P.; Terence Skorka, C.P.

Pope Paul VI Residence.
Frances Schervier Long Term Home Health Care. 2975 Independence Ave., Bronx, 10463. Rev. Albert Pellicane, C.P.

St. Catherine of Siena Priory, 411 E. 68th St., 10021. Tel: 212-988-8300; Fax: 212-988-6918. Very Rev. Christopher Johnson, O.P., Prior; Revs. Vincent Ferrer McHenry, O.P.; John Jerome Conroy, O.P.; David Aloysius Butler, O.P., Subprior; John Thaddeus Murphy, O.P.; Robert Philip Fitzsimmons, O.P.; Bartholomew Paul Fu, O.P.; George Lawrence Concordia, O.P.; Scott Matthew Erickson, O.P.

St. Clare Friary, 440 W. 36th St., 10018-6326. Tel: 212-594-4108; Fax: 212-563-0787.
E-mail: sground440@aol.com
Web site: www.solidgroundministry.com
Rev. James E. Goode, O.F.M., Ph.D., Guardian; Bro. Pius Abooki, Instructor, Cardinal Hayes High School; Harold Williams, Jr., Affiliate, Solid Ground Prog. Coord.; Carmela Rodriguez, Affiliate, Confraternity of Solid Ground; James P. Newson, Jr., Black Catholic Apostolate for Life Coord.

Shrine of Saint Josephine Bakhita. In the Holy Mother of God Chapel. Tel: 212-868-1847.

Solid Ground Ministry: A Franciscan Ministry with African American Families. Tel: 212-868-1847; Fax: 212-563-0787.

National Black Catholic Apostolate for Life. Tel: 212-594-4108.

St. Crispin Friary. Franciscan Friars of the Renewal, 420 E. 156th St., Bronx, 10455. Tel: 718-665-2441. Revs. Robert Lombardo, C.F.R., Community Vicar & Local Servant; Terry Messer, C.F.R., Vicar; Benedict J. Groeschel, C.F.R. Priests 3; Brothers 7.

St. Ignatius Loyola Residence, 53 E. 83rd St., 10028. Tel: 212-288-6200; Fax: 212-606-3460. Revs. Thomas E. Smith, S.J., Rector; Thomas F. Denny, S.J., Minister; Bro. Paul C. Acer, S.J.; Revs. William J. Bergen, S.J.; Vincent L. Biagi, S.J.; Gerard E. Braun, S.J.; Bro. John J. Campbell, S.J.; Revs. James R. Carney, S.J.; Kenneth J. Caufield, S.J.; James J. Curry, S.J.; Stephen V. Duffy, S.J.; James L. Dugan, S.J.; Kenneth J. Gavin, S.J.; Mark C. Hallinan, S.J.; Timothy A. Healey, S.J.; Anthony F. LaBau, S.J.; Joseph A. Latella, S.J.; J. Thomas McClain, S.J. (Detroit); Bro. Jerome P. Menkhaus, S.J.; Rev. Walter F. Modrys, S.J.; Most Rev. Martin J. Neylon, S.J.; Revs. Robert E. O'Brien, S.J.; Daniel G. O'Hare, S.J.; Joseph J. Papaj, S.J.; Eugene J. Prior, S.J.; Thomas S. Prout, S.J.; Michael J. Sala, S.J.; William J. Scanlon, S.J.; Bro. Gilbert J. Scott, S.J.; Revs. Paul J. Tabor, S.J. (BO); Damien Mugun Chong, S.J. (Korea); W.R. Suarez Villalobos, S.J. (Venezuela); Charles G. Wrightington, S.J.

St. Joseph's Friary. (Franciscan Friars of the Renewal), 523 W. 142nd St., 10031. Tel: 212-234-9089. Web site: www.ewtn.com/renewal
(Novitiate). Revs. Conrad Osterhout, C.F.R., Local Servant & Novice Dir.; Richard Roemer, C.F.R., Vocations Dir. Novices 9.

St. Vincent de Paul Residence, 900 Intervale Ave., 10459. Tel: 718-589-6965; Fax: 718-589-7010.
E-mail: svdpres@chcn.org
Web site: www.svdpres.org
Total Assisted 3,120; Total Staff 8.

St. Vincent Ferrer Priory, 869 Lexington Ave., 10021. Tel: 212-744-2080; Fax: 212-327-3011. Dominican Friars Provincial House (Province of St. Joseph). Very Revs. Norman Alfred Haddad, O.P., Prior Prov.; Kevin Dominic Robb, O.P., Vicar Prov. & Socius; James Boniface Ramsey, O.P., Prior; Revs. Albert Augustine Caprio, O.P., Prov. Treas.; John James Sullivan, O.P.; William Robert Gannon, O.P.; Bernard Lawrence Keitz, O.P.; Raymond Ferrer Halligan, O.P.; Kevin Anthony McGrath, O.P.; Deacon Edward Thomas Aquinas Dolan, O.P., Subprior; Bro. John Damian McCarthy, O.P.
Priests assigned but serving elsewhere: Revs. John Aedan McKeon, O.P.; Ralph Eugene Cahouet, O.P.; James Moneta Moyna, O.P.; Robert William Vaughn, O.P.; Ronald Henery, O.P.; Peter John Cameron, O.P.; Joseph Hugh Mulhern, O.P.; Robert Urban Sharkey, O.P.; Joseph Anthony Scordo, O.P.; John Patrick McGuire, O.P.; Bro. Christopher McCabe, O.P.; Revs. Edmund Augustine Ditton, O.P.; Joseph Edward Fox, O.P.; Jerome Joachim Haladus, O.P.; Kevin Palmer McCaffrey, O.P.; Athanasius Sulavik, O.P.; John Raymond Vandegrift, O.P.

Vincentian Fathers, 1834 Third Ave., 10029. Tel: 212-289-5589; Fax: 212-289-8321. Legal Title: *Padres Paules Community (Vincentians) Inc.* Revs. Victor Elia, C.M., Supr.; Candido Arrizurieta, C.M.; Santiago Lluch, C.M.

West Side Jesuit Community, 220 West 98th St., 10025. Tel: 212-663-4615; Fax: 212-866-3241.
E-mail: robjkeck@aol.com
Revs. Robert J. Keck, S.J., Supr.; Daniel J. Berrigan, S.J.; W. Alan Briceland, S.J.; Robert E. Carter, S.J.; Anthony Cowan; Owen W. Daley, S.J.; John Dear, S.J.; Theodore V. Francois, S.J.; G. Simon Harak, S.J.; Gerald T. Huyett, S.J.; Bro. Edward L. McCarthy, S.J.; Revs. John G. McSherry, S.J.; Donald J. Moore, S.J.; Peter Murray, S.J.; Enrico Raulli, S.J.; Bro. Joel Magallan Reyes, S.J.; Revs. Joseph Roccosalvo; Gary G. Seibert, S.J.; Robert Springer, S.J.; David S. Toolan, S.J.; Brian F. Zinnamon, S.J.; Edward G. Zogby, S.J.

Xavier Jesuit Community, 30 West 16th St., 10011. Tel: 212-924-7900; Fax: 212-337-7545.
E-mail: hzen@juno.com
Revs. Francis P. Golden, Rector; Alfred E. Caruana, S.J.; John J. Cecero, S.J.; Edward J. Coughlin, S.J.; George W. Drance, S.J.; James P. Flaherty, S.J.; Arthur C. Bender, S.J.; Vincent E. Butler, S.J.; Michael C. Lee, S.J.; Jose A. Mesa, S.J.; John A. Mullin, S.J.; James F. O'Brien, S.J.; Michael V. Tueth, S.J.; Harold F. O'Donnell, S.J.; Thomas H. O'Neill, S.J.; Joseph J. Walter, S.J.; David P. Marcotte, S.J.; Edward J. McMahon, S.J.; Henry J. Zenorini, S.J.

Jesuit Residence. Tel: 212-620-0537; Fax: 212-675-6997. 126 W. 17th St., 10011. Tel: 212-620-0537; Fax: 212-675-6997. Revs. William P. Cain, S.J.; John P. Bucki, S.J., Supr.
(For list of faculty see the high school listing for Xavier High School).

BRONX. *Idente Missionaries - Santa Maria Residence*, 2352 St. Raymond Ave., 10462. Tel: 718-828-2380; Fax: 718-828-4296. Revs. Fernando Real, M.Id., Prov. Supr.; Cristobal Martino, M.Id.; Bros. Francisco Sanchez, M.Id.; Norbert Schutte, M.Id; Jose Hanchi, M.Id.

Our Lady of the Angels Friary. (Franciscan Friars of the Renewal), 427 E. 155th St., 10455. Tel: 718-993-3405. (Postulant House). Revs. Bernard Murphy, C.F.R., Local Servant & Postulant Dir.; Stanley Fortuna, C.F.R.; Bros. Shaw O'Connor, C.F.R.; Francis Edkins, C.F.R.; Sharbel Alkhass, C.F.R.; Jacob Hausman, C.F.R.; Emmanuel Mansford, C.F.R. Postulants 9.

Passionist Residence, 5801 Palisade Ave. Tel: 718-548-1182; Fax: 718-548-2945. Revs. Robert Joerger, C.P.; Edward Beck, C.P.; Paul Ruttle, C.P.; Bros. Michael Moran, C.P.; Andre Mathieu, C.P. Total in Residence 5.

Yarumal Mission Society, Inc., Office of the Pres., 2317 Washington Ave., 10458. Tel: 718-561-8248; Fax: 718-562-2521.
E-mail: imeyusa@aol.com
Web site: www.hometown.aol.com/imeyusa/myhomepage/index.html
Revs. Tulio Ramirez, M.X.Y.; Gabriel Piedrahita, M.X.Y.; Rodrigo Velasquez.

CORNWALL. *Jogues Retreat*, Mailing Address: P.O. Box F, 12518. Tel: 914-534-7570; Fax: 914-534-3276.
E-mail: joguesret@aol.com
Revs. Herbert T. Kane, S.J., Supr. & Guest Master; Alfred L. Fiorino, S.J., Asst. Supr. & Treas.

ESOPUS. *Marist Brothers F.M.S. (Province of St. Joseph)*, Mailing Address: P.O. Box 197, 12429. Tel: 914-384-6625; Fax: 914-384-6277.
E-mail: brohent@aol.com
Bros. Henry J. Sawicki, F.M.S., Dir.; Thomas Simmons, F.M.S.; Francis Farrell, F.M.S.; Gregory De LaNoy, F.M.S.; Adolph Leo, F.M.S.; Leonard Voegtle, F.M.S. Brothers 6.

Redemptorist Priests and Brothers C.Ss.R. (Province of Baltimore), Mount Saint Alphonsus, Rte. 9W, P.O. Box 219, 12429. Tel: 845-384-8000; Fax: 845-384-8088.
Web site: www.msaretreat.com
Very Rev. John G. Kingsbury, C.Ss.R., Rector; Bro. Robert Skinner, C.Ss.R.; Revs. James Small, C.Ss.R.; Timothy Keating, C.Ss.R. In res. Revs. Eugene J. Grohe, C.Ss.R.; Raymond Weithman, C.Ss.R.; John Kennington, C.Ss.R.; Dennis Billy, C.Ss.R.; Bro. Charles Somers, C.Ss.R. Priests 8; Brothers 2.

GARRISON. *Franciscan Friars of the Atonement*, Graymoor, P.O. Box 300, 10524-0300. Tel: 845-424-3671; 3672; 3673; Fax: 845-424-2166.
E-mail: glucrezia@atonementfriars.org
Web site: www.atonementfriars.org
Revs. Fred Alvarez, S.A.; Norman Boyd, S.A.; Bro. Joseph Buettner, S.A.; Rev. Blase Burniston, S.A.; Bro. Raphael Colaciello, S.A.; Rev. Walter Gagne, S.A.; Bros. Francis Gutman, S.A.; Stephen Hanley, S.A.; John Joseph Bursis, S.A.; Revs. Simeon Heine, S.A.; Alexander Kelliher, S.A.; Thomas Orians, S.A.; Bros. Pius MacIsaac, S.A.; Joseph O'Gara, S.A.; Dominic McDonnell, S.A.; Revs. Kevin McMorrow, S.A.; Charles Murphy, S.A.; Owen Murphy, S.A.; William Murphy, S.A.; Bro. Theodore Novak, S.A.; Rev. Mark O'Connor, S.A.; Bro. Rocco Pace, S.A.; Revs. Normand Prevost, S.A.; George Ribeiro, S.A.; Bosco Schmidt, S.A.; Bros. Denis Sennett, S.A.; Edmund Sheridan, S.A.; Richard Skolinski, S.A.; Rev. Emmanuel Sullivan, S.A.; Bros. Robert Taylor, S.A.; Liam Young, S.A.; Joseph Marie Zakia, S.A.

St. Francis of Assisi Novitiate, Graymoor, P.O. Box 300, 10524-0300. Tel: 845-424-4055. Revs. Edward Boes, S.A., Novice Dir.; Emil Tomaskovic, S.A.; Bros. Raymond Saville, S.A.; William Weeks, S.A.; Leo Hall, S.A.; Peter Gannon, S.A.

St. Christopher's Inn, Graymoor, P.O. Box 150, 10524-0150. Tel: 845-424-3616; Fax: 845-424-3786. Rev. Bernard Palka, S.A., Pres/CEO; Bros. Thomas Banacki, S.A.; George Clay, S.A.; Charles Kenney, S.A.; Donald Perry, S.A.; Benedict Terasawa, S.A.; Revs. Robert Warren, S.A.; Charles Angell, S.A.

Graymoor Ecumenical and Interreligious Institute, 475 Riverside Dr., Room 1960, New York, 10115-1999. Tel: 212-870-2342; 870-2330; Fax: 212-870-2001. Rev. Elias D. Mallon, S.A., Dir.
Priests of the Province Serving Elsewhere: Revs. Gerald DiGiralamo, S.A., St. John of God Parish, Central Islip, NY.; David Fitzgerald, S.A., St. Andrew the Apostle, Apex, NC.; Aquinas Thomas, S.A., New Hope Manor, Barryville, NY.

Franciscan Friars of the Atonement, Minister General Office, Graymoor, P.O. Box 300, 10524-0300. Tel: 845-424-2113; Fax: 845-424-2166.
E-mail: ajohnson@atonementfriars.org
Web site: www.atonementfriars.org
Very Rev. Arthur M Johnson, S.A., Minister Gen.; Rev. Daniel O'Shea, S.A., Vicar General; Bro. Gregory Lucrezia, S.A., Sec. Gen.; Revs. Bernard Palka, S.A., Treas. Gen.; John Keane, S.A., 2nd General Councillor; Charles Sharon, S.A., 3rd General Councillor; Bro. Gregory Lucrezia, S.A., 4th General Councillor; Rev. Daniel O'Shea, S.A., Procurator General to the Holy See.
Friar-Priests serving in Japan, Diocese of Yokohama: Tel: 011-81-45-581-6374; Fax: 011-81-45-581-9068. Revs. Pacificus Von Essen, S.A.; Peter Katsuno, S.A.; Fidelis Fujihara, S.A. (Japan); Charles Brozat, S.A.; Joseph Hiramatsu, S.A. (Japan), Regl. Min.; Gabriel Shiraki, S.A. (Japan); Damian Sato, S.A.; Eric Tampe, S.A.; Bro. Ignatius Kobayashi, S.A. (Japan).
Friars on assignments or studies: Tel: 845-424-3671; Fax: 845-424-2166. Revs. Pius F. Keating, S.A.; Mark T; Joseph Scerbo, S.A.; Edward Gallagher, S.A.; Michael A. Daniel, S.A.; Frank Eldridge, S.A.
Friars stationed in England: Tel: 011-44-171-828-4163; Fax: 011-44-171-798-9090. Revs. Robert Mercer, S.A. (England); Michael Seed, S.A. (England); Peter Tarran, S.A.; Bros. Gerard Hand, S.A.; Daniel Houde, S.A.; Denis Bungelia, S.A.; Rev. Peter Taran, S.A.
Friars stationed in Canada, Archdiocese of Vancouver: Tel: 604-277-8353; Fax: 604-275-4034. Revs. William Linakis, S.A.; Dennis Polanco, S.A.; Bro. Timothy MacDonald, S.A.
Diocese of London, Ontario, Canada: Tel: 519-735-6023; Fax: 519-735-1174. Revs. Timothy MacDonald, S.A.; William Drobach, S.A.
Archdiocese of Toronto, Canada: Tel: 416-924-9945; Fax: 416-962-8531. Revs. John Kiesling, S.A., St. Joan of Arc Parish, Toronto. Tel: 416-762-1026 (Tel); 416-762-4194 (Fax); Damian MacPherson, S.A. (Canada); Paschal Breau, S.A. (Canada); Peter Tomaino, S.A.; Bede MacEachen, S.A. (Canada); Timothy Sullivan, S.A.; Bro. Guy Gartland, S.A.; Rev. Patrick Cogan, S.A.; Bros. Jonathan Wheat, S.A.; James Daly, S.A.
Archdiocese of Halifax, N.S. Canada: Revs. Arthur Gouthro, S.A. (Canada), 902-883-2427 (Tel); 902-883-7710 (Fax); David Poirier, S.A. Tel: 902-462-3569 (Tel); 902-434-5787 (Fax).
Friars in Military Service: Rev. William Dillon, S.A.
Friars residing in Italy: Tel: 011-39-06-687-9552; Fax: 011-39-06-683-3631. Rev. James Puglisi, S.A.; Bro. Alan LeMay, S.A.; Rev. Daniel Callahan, S.A.

St. Joseph's Rehabilitation Center, Inc., Saranac Lake. Tel: 518-891-3950.

Graymoor Ecumenical & Interreligious Institute. (G.E.I.I.), 475 Riverside Dr., Room 1960, New York, 10115-1999. Tel: 212-870-2330; Fax: 212-870-2001. Legal Titles: *Friars of the Atonement, Inc.*; *St. Christopher's Inn, Inc.*; *Union That Nothing Be Lost, Inc.*; *St. Joseph's Rehabilitation Center, Inc.*; *Paul Wattson Human Resources Fund, Inc.*

St. Christopher's Friary, Mailing Address: Box 150, 10524-0150. Tel: 845-424-3616; Fax: 845-424-3786.
Web site: www.atonementfriars.org
Revs. Charles Angell, S.A., Guardian; Robert Warren, S.A.; Bros. George Clay, S.A.; Donald Perry, S.A.; Benedict Terasawa, S.A.; Thomas Banacki, S.A.; Charles Kenny, S.A.

St. Francis Friary (Glenclyffe). Tel: 845-424-3488; Fax: 845-424-3548.
E-mail: robertjohna@juno.com
Web site: www.capuchins.org
Capuchin Franciscan Province of St. Mary, New York, New England. Mailing Address: Box 191, Garrison (Glenclyffe), 10524. Tel: 845-424-3488.
Web site: http://www.capuchins.org
Revs. Anthony Vetrano, O.F.M.Cap., Vicar & Vocation Ministry; Robert Abbatiello, O.F.M.Cap., Guardian & Youth & Family Ministries; Bro. Antonine Lizama, O.F.M.Cap.

HARTSDALE. *Mill Hill Fathers Residence*, 222 W. Hartsdale Ave., 10530-1667. Tel: 914-682-0645; Fax: 914-682-0862. Very Rev. Terence J. Lee, M.H.M., Regl. Rep.; Revs. James Brian Coffey, M.H.M.; Cornelius M. Snoeren, M.H.M.; Emile Frische, M.H.M.; Bro. Theodore Tolboom, M.H.M.

JAMAICA ESTATES. *Paulist Fathers Generalate*, 86-11 Midland Pkwy., 11432. Tel: 718-291-5995; Fax: 718-291-6646.
Web site: www.paulist.org
Very Rev. Francis P. DeSiano, C.S.P., Pres.; Revs. Michael J. Kallock, C.S.P.; Thomas W. Jones, C.S.P.; Edward D. Whitley, C.S.P.
Paulist Priests at Paulist Foundations outside the U.S.: Tel: 011-3906-482-7510. Via Venti Settembre 14, Rome, Italy, 00187. Tel: 011-3906-488-2748; Fax: 011-3906-474-0236. Revs. Paul G. Robichand, C.S.P.; Gregora Apparcel, C.S.P., 659 Markham St., Toronto, Ontario, Canada, M6G 2M1. Tel: 416-534-4219; Fax: 416-534-9644. Revs. Michael P. Kerrigan, C.S.P.; Philip W. Hart; Thomas R. Marshall, C.S.P.; Thomas P. Murphy, C.S.P.; James F. McCabe, C.S.P.; Deacon Richard J. Boudreau, C.S.P.
Military Chaplains: Rev. Thomas P. Hall, C.S.P.
On Special Assignment in the U.S. and Abroad: Tel: 011-39095-564-295. Revs. Justin J. McCormick, C.S.P.; Thomas A. Kane, C.S.P.; Joachim Lally, C.S.P.; Norman J. O'Connor, C.S.P.; Martin J. O'Looney, C.S.P.; Thomas F. Stransky, C.S.P.
Retired: Revs. Charles W. Albright, C.S.P.; Walter Anthony, C.S.P.; Robert W. Baer, C.S.P.; Edward R. Donovan, C.S.P.; Wilfred A. Brimley, C.S.P.; William J. Cantwell, C.S.P.; John A. Carr, C.S.P.; Phillip J. Cunningham, C.S.P.; Robert P. Curtis, C.S.P.; Wilfred Dewan, C.S.P.; Francis X. Diskin, C.S.P.; Charles A. Donovan, C.S.P.; Harry J. Dooley, C.S.P.; Thomas J. Dove; J. Aloysius Farrell, C.S.P.; James F. Fisher, C.S.P.; Joseph P. Flynn, C.S.P.; Donal F. Forrester, C.S.P.; Harold J. Foye, C.S.P.; Joseph T. Griffin, C.S.P.; Joseph M. Hanly, C.S.P.; George F. Helmich, C.S.P.; Donald E. Howard, C.S.P.; William J. Kenney, C.S.P.; James B. Lloyd, C.S.P.; Edward J. Lyons, C.S.P.; Stanley F. MacNevin, C.S.P.; Edward A. Maher, C.S.P.; Thomas J. Marley, C.S.P.; Edward J. McDonald, C.S.P.; Neil J. McEleney, C.S.P.; Kenneth H. McGuire, C.S.P.; Louis F. McKernan, C.S.P.; James F. McLean, C.S.P.; James D. McNulty, C.S.P.; Robert P. Michele, C.S.P.; Ernest C. Mort, C.S.P.; Thomas P. Murphy, C.S.P.; Robert A. O'Donnell, C.S.P.; Edward P. O'Hern, C.S.P.; Harold J. Powers, C.S.P.; Robert F. Quinn, C.S.P.; John C. Reynolds, C.S.P.; Vincent J.

Sampietro, C.S.P.; Warren H. Seedorf, C.S.P.; Joseph F. Troy, C.S.P.; Rudolph T. Vorisek, C.S.P.; Richard J. Walsh, C.S.P.; Charles S. White, C.S.P.; Edward D. Wroblewski, C.S.P.

On Leave: Revs. James Kolb, C.S.P.; Albert K.H. Kim, C.S.P.

MARYKNOLL. *M.M.A.F. Charitable Trust*, Treasury Office, P.O. Box 306, 10545-0306. Tel: 914-941-7590; Fax: 914-941-2411.
E-mail: rcallahan@maryknoll.org
Rev. Richard B. Callahan, M.M., Contact Person.

Maryknoll Fathers and Brothers, 10545-0303. Tel: 914-941-7590; Fax: 914-762-0316.
E-mail: mklcouncil@maryknoll.org
Web site: www.maryknoll.org
General Council: Revs. Raymond J. Finch, M.M., Supr. Gen.; Jeremiah R. Burr, M.M., Vicar Gen.; Thomas P. Henehan, M.M., Asst. Gen.; Michael J. Snyder, M.M., Asst. Gen.; Bro. Wayne J. Fitzpatrick, M.M., Asst. Gen.; Revs. Richard B. Callahan, M.M., Treas. Gen.; Norbert J. Rans, M.M., Asst. Treas.; Joseph P. LaMar, M.M., Asst. Treas.; Lawrence W. Flynn, M.M.; Donald L. Allen, M.M.; Jose A. Aramburu, M.M.; Joseph B. Arsenault, M.M.; Lionel A. Bouffard, M.M.; J. Ernest Brunelle, M.M.; Charles T. Huegelmeyer, M.M.; Leo R. Kennedy, M.M.; Dennis W. Cleary, M.M.; William J. Coy, M.M.; Wayman P. Deasy, M.M.; Robert A. Lilly, M.M.; Francis A. Diffley, M.M.; Donald J. Doherty, M.M.; Lionel G. Trudel, M.M.; Michael A. Duggan, M.M.; Arthur J. Dwyer, M.M.; George A. Egan, M.M.; Joseph L. Finan, M.M.; William B. Frazier, M.M.; Gorden N. Fritz, M.M.; Charles F. Girnius, M.M.; Fidelis C. Goodman, M.M.; Ronald L. Green, M.M.; J. Gerard Greene, M.M.; John K. Halbert, M.M.; Carroll B. Houle, M.M.; David J. Jones, M.M.; John M. Kaserow, M.M.; Thomas H. Keefe, M.M.; Martin P. Keegan, M.M.; John R. King, M.M.; Joseph P. LaMar, M.M.; James W. Lehr, M.M.; Peter M. Le Jacq, M.M.; Martin J. Lowery, M.M.; John J. McAuley, M.M.; William D. McCarthy, M.M.; Lawrence F. McCulloch, M.M.; Charles J. McPadden, M.M.; William T. Madden, M.M.; Philip W. Mares, M.M.; Thomas J. Marti, M.M.; Kenneth J. Moody, M.M.; John J. Moran, M.M.; Gerald J. Nagle, M.M.; George H. Ratermann, M.M.; Alan J. Ryan, M.M.; James M. Scanlon, M.M.; Steven Scherrer, M.M.; Leo B. Shea, M.M.; Michael A. Simone, M.M.; James P. Sinnott, M.M.; Richard P. Smith, M.M.; Raymond F. Sullivan, M.M.; William J. Tokus, M.M.; Joseph W. Towle, M.M.; Joseph R. Veneroso, M.M.; Edward F. Walck, M.M.; John J. Walsh, M.M.; Edward M. Wroblewski, M.M.; Juan M. Zuniga, M.M.

Maryknoll St. Teresa's Residence, 10545-0321. Tel: 914-941-4240; 941-4247; Fax: 914-923-3407. Staff: Revs. Thomas P. McDonnell, M.M., Dir.; John P. Hudert, M.M., Staff; Steven R. Wood, M.M. In res. Revs. Frederick J. Allen, M.M.; Louis I. Bayless, M.M.; Joseph E. Early, M.M.; Donat W. Chatigny, M.M.; William J. Coleman, M.M.; J. Gerard Greene, M.M.; Robert W. Greene, M.M.; William H. Moeschler, M.M.; Joseph R. English, M.M.; John F. Fay, M.M.; Henry J. Felsecker, M.M.; James B. Nagle, M.M.; Joseph J. O'Neill, M.M.; Thomas C. Higgins, M.M.; John P. Hudert, M.M.; James A. Jackson, M.M.; Roman A. Kasprzak, M.M.; Alfred V. Keane, M.M.; Walter T. Kelleher, M.M.; John J. McCabe, M.M.; Leo F. McCarthy, M.M.; J. Edmund McClear, M.M.; Thomas P. McDonnell, M.M.; Robert L. Mackesy, M.M.; Michael J. McKillop, M.M.; Stephen J. Maskell, M.M.; Joseph W. Matheis, M.M.; Leo F. Melancon, M.M.; George M. Mikolajczyk, M.M.; Carroll I. Quinn, M.M.; Joseph S. Smith, M.M.; Gervis J. Coxen, M.M.; Christopher W. Gibbons, M.M.; Most Rev. Richard J. Ham, M.M.; Revs. Francis S. Meccia, M.M.; John J. O'Brien, M.M.; Robert H. Winkels, M.M.
Special Assignments: Revs. Edward R. Arnold, M.M.; John P. Casey, M.M.; James P. Colligan, M.M.; Miguel F. d'Escoto, M.M.; Marvin F. Deutsch, M.M.; Patrick A. Bergin, M.M.; Stephen R. Booth, M.M.; Roy L. Bourgeois, M.M.; John T. Brinkman, M.M.; Patrick J. Donovan, M.M.; Curtis R. Cadorette, M.M.; George G. Cotter, M.M.; Joseph F. Croghan, M.M.; Francis J. Flynn, M.M.; Bernard R. Garritty, M.M.; Thomas F. Gibbons, M.M.; John E. Keegan, M.M.; Edward R. Killackey, M.M.; Joseph R. Lang, M.M.; Daniel A. Lanza, M.M.; Thomas J. Maney, M.M.; Joseph A. Farrell, M.M.; John J. Meaney, M.M.; W. Robert Golish, M.M.; Laurence T. Murphy, M.M.; Thomas S. Keane, M.M.; James P. Nieckarz, M.M.; Raymond J. Nobiletti, M.M.; Denis E. O'Brien, M.M.; Richard E. Paulissen, M.M.; Raymond G. Pierini, M.M.; Joseph S. Pulaski, M.M.; Robert R. Lefebvre, M.M.; Albert I. Reymann, M.M.; John A. Rich, M.M.; Patrick J. Ryan, M.M.; Alphonse A. Schiavone, M.M.; J. Daniel Schneider, M.M.; William E. McCarthy, M.M.; Daniel J. Sherman, M.M.; Donald R. Steed, M.M.; Francis J. Leong, M.M.; Wayne T. Weinlader, M.M.; Walter W. Winrich, M.M.; David J. Schwinghamer, M.M.; Francis J. Taney, M.M.; Donald J. Vittengl, M.M.; John F. Wymes, M.M.

The Maryknoll Fathers & Brothers Charitable Trust, 10545. Tel: 914-941-7540; Fax: 914-941-2411. Trustees: Revs. Richard B. Callahan, M.M.; Wayman P. Deasy, M.M.; Thomas H. Keefe, M.M.; William T. Madden, M.M.; Bro. Joseph Zeigler, M.M.

Maryknoll Fathers and Brothers. 586 McLean Ave., 10705. Tel: 914-963-0270. Revs. Alan J. Ryan, M.M.; Peter M. Le Jacq, M.M.

MIDDLETOWN. *Brandsma Priory*, Carmelite Interprovincial Novitiate, Carmelite Dr., P.O. Box 2127, 10940-0439. Tel: 845-343-2959; Fax: 845-344-1808. Carmelite Friars (North American Prov. of St. Elias and Most Pure Heart of Mary Province). Revs. John Russell, O.Carm., Novice Dir.; Paul Denault, O.Carm., Novice Dir.; Eugene Foley, O.Carm. Novices 7.

Carmelite Friars (North American Province of St. Elias). Tel: 914-344-2223; Fax: 914-344-2210.
E-mail: proelias@frontiernet.net
Web site: www.frontiernet.net/~ocarmvoc
Mailing Address: P.O. Box 3079, 10940-0890; Fax: 914-344-2210. Very Rev. Michael T. Driscoll, O.Carm., Prior Prov. Tel: 914-344-2223; Revs. Kenneth Murphy, O.Carm., Prov. Procurator. Tel: 914-344-2224; Michael Kissane, O.Carm., Vocation Dir. Tel: 914-344-2225.

St. Albert's Priory. Tel: 845-344-2220; Fax: 845-342-4412. Mailing Address: P.O. Box 868, Carmelite Dr., 10940-0868. Tel: 914-344-2220; Fax: 914-342-4412. Revs. Albert Daly, O.Carm.; Sean Reid, O.Carm.; Very Rev. Richard Nagle, O.Carm.; Revs. Richard Champigny, O.Carm., Prior; Augustine Graap, O.Carm.; Patrick McGuigan, O.Carm; Bro. James Andrews.

The National Shrine of Our Lady of Mount Carmel. Tel: 845-343-1879; Fax: 845-343-1912. Mailing Address: P.O. Box 868, Carmelite Dr., 10940-0868. Tel: 914-343-1879; Fax: 914-343-1912. Rev. Richard Champigny, O.Carm., Dir.; Bro. James Andrews, O.Carm. Donum Dei Missionary Family Members 2.

The Carmelite Development Office. Tel: 845-344-2220; Fax: 845-342-4412. Mailing Address: P.O. Box 868, Carmelite Dr., 10940-0868. Tel: 914-344-0876; Fax: 914-344-0093.

MOUNT VERNON. *Kolbe Friary*, 274-280 W. Lincoln Ave., 10550. Tel: 914-664-7169. Franciscan Friars, Province of the Immaculate Conception. Bro. Angelo Monti, O.F.M., Guardian.

St. Bernardine of Siena Friary, 25 Laurel Ave., 10552-1018. Tel: 914-699-1221. Franciscan Friars, Province of Immaculate Conception. In res. Revs. Alban V. Montella, O.F.M., Guardian; Benedict J. D'Alessandro, O.F.M. Priests 2.

NEW PALTZ. *St. Joseph Friary*, 34 S. Chestnut St., 12561. Tel: 914-255-5635; Fax: 914-255-5679.
E-mail: stjoenp@hvi.net
Capuchin Friars, Province of St. Mary. Bro. Timothy Jones, O.F.M.Cap., Supr.; Revs. Richard Donaldson, O.F.M.Cap.; Barnabas Keck, O.F.M.Cap.; Raynold Thibodeau, O.F.M.Cap.; Maurice Moreau, O.F.M.Cap.

NEW ROCHELLE. *Brothers of Holy Cross of the Eastern Province of the United States of America, Inc.*, 85 Overlook Cir., 10804-4501. Tel: 914-632-4468; 632-4469; Fax: 914-632-2490.
E-mail: gcscsc@aol.com
Web site: www.holycrossbrothers.org
Bros. George Schmitz, C.S.C., Prov.; William Zaydak, C.S.C., Asst. Prov. Councilors: Bros. Jerome Donnelly, C.S.C.; Joseph McDonnell, C.S.C.; Paul Bednarczyk, C.S.C. In res. Bros. George Schmitz, C.S.C.; William Farrell, C.S.C.; John Nicpon, C.S.C.; Robert Russo, C.S.C.; Paul Bednarczyk, C.S.C. Professed Brothers 7.

Holy Cross Brothers, Eastern Province, Charitable Trust, 85 Overlook Cir., 10804. Tel: 914-632-4468; Fax: 914-632-2490.
E-mail: gcscsc@aol.com
Web site: www.holycrossbrothers.org
Trustees: Bros. Peter Martin, C.S.C., Treas.; Renatus Foldenauer, C.S.C.; Richard Kiniry, C.S.C.; Stephen LaMendola, C.S.C.; George Schmitz, C.S.C.

Saint Joseph's Residence, Inc., 30 Montgomery Cir., 10804-4413. Tel: 914-633-6851; Fax: 914-633-5579.
E-mail: rroepke@atgnet.com
Congregation of Christian Brothers. Bros. James B. Moffett, C.F.C., Pres.; Robert J. Roepke, C.F.C., Vice Pres. Admin.; Thomas C. Higgins, Sec.; Thomas F. Feerick, Vice Pres. Finance. A facility of limited care for male religious. Total in Residence 13; Total Staff 5.

St. Patrick's Provincial House (Congregation of Christian Brothers), 21 Pryer Terr., 10804. Tel: 914-636-6194; Fax: 914-636-0021.
E-mail: alb@cbinstitute.org
Bros. James B. Moffett, C.F.C., Prov.; Brian M. Walsh, C.F.C., Deputy Prov. Consultors: Bros. Kevin G. Cawley, C.F.C.; V. Gregory McNally, C.F.C.; John P. Mostyn, C.F.C.; Vincent J. Dougherty, Prov. Treas.; James P. Hamilton, C.F.C., Dir. Vocations; John J. McCarthy, C.F.C., Direct Mail; Charles F. Miller, C.F.C., Dir. Mission Education; Robert D. Burke, C.F.C., Dir. Communications; A. Eugenio DeLorenzo, C.F.C., Dir. Archives; S. Anthony Ferro, C.F.C., Dir. Advancement; Lawrence A. Killelea, C.F.C., Dir. Educational Svcs.; Kevin Griffith, C.F.C., Dir. Formation, St. Joseph Residence, 30 Montgomery Cir., 10804. Tel: 914-633-6851; Fax: 914-633-5579.
Limited facility for male religious. Brothers Living in Community 6; Limited Care Center Total in Residence 15; Total Staff 7.

Salesian Cooperators of St. John Bosco, 148 Main St., 10802. Tel: 914-636-4225.
E-mail: cooperators@juno.com
Marlene Frederick, Prov. Coord.; Rev. John Puntino, S.D.B., Prov. Delegate.

Salesian Provincial House, 148 Main St., P.O. Box 639, 10802-0639. Tel: 914-636-4225; Fax: 914-636-0159.
E-mail: sdbsue@aol.com
Web site: www.salesians.org
Very Rev. Patrick Angelucci, S.D.B., Prov.; Revs. Richard Alejunas, S.D.B.; Javier Aracil, S.D.B., Prov. Sec.; Edward Cappelletti, S.D.B.; Patrick Diver, S.D.B.; Joseph Doran, S.D.B.; Attilio Klinger, S.D.B.; Stephen Leakei, S.D.B.; Peter Malloy, S.D.B.; James Mulloy, S.D.B.; John Nazarro, S.D.B.; Terrence O'Donnell, S.D.B.; Philip Pascucci, S.D.B., Archivist; Joseph Santa-Bibiana, S.D.B., Prov. Treas.; Robert Savage, S.D.B., Archives; Waclav Swierzbiolek, S.D.B.; Vincent Zuliani, S.D.B., Supr.; Bros. Andrew Lacombe, S.D.B.; Aldo Roman, S.D.B. Priests 17; Brothers 3.

PELHAM. *Marist Provincial Office*, 26 First Ave, 10803. Tel: 914-738-0740; Fax: 914-738-0915.
E-mail: pkpsepo@aol.com
Our Lady of Grace Residence, 850 E. 226th St., Bronx, 10466. Tel: 718-652-1848; Fax: 718-655-2614. Bros. John Byrd; Michael Mullin; Timothy Zorek.

Marist Brothers Champagnat Hall Community, 4300 Murdock Ave., Bronx, 10466. Tel: 718-994-4227; Fax: 718-994-0145. Bros. John Colbert, F.M.S.; Nicholas Caffrey; Denis Caverley; Valerian Doiron; James Gaffney; Simeon Gerald; Francis Hughes; George L. Mathews; Godfrey Robertson; Patrick Tyrrell; George Fontana; Thomas Kelly; James Devine, Dir.; Matthew Snowden; Sixtus Victor; Vincent Xavier.

Marist Residence, 272 West 91st St., New York, 10024. Tel: 212-769-4951; Fax: 212-769-0446. Bros. James Adams; James Kearney; George Kopper; Joseph Sacino; Antonio Ben Oliveira.

Marist Residence, 143 W. 87th St., New York, 10024. Tel: 212-362-4039. Bros. Gerald Doherty, Dir.; Emil Denworth; Thomas Schady; Albert Rivera.

Marist Provincial House, 26 First Ave., 10803. Tel: 914-738-1218; Fax: 914-738-0915. Bros. Patrick McNamara; Donnell Neary; Michael Flanigan, Asst. Prov.; Francis L. Zaglauer.

Marist Brothers, 40 S. Hamilton St., Poughkeepsie, 12601. Tel: 914-471-4077; Fax: 914-471-0205. Bros. Lawrence Gordon; Robert LeClerc; Vincent Moriarty; James Stevens.

Marist Brothers, 2 Eden Ter., Poughkeepsie, 12601-4803. Tel: 914-471-8354; Fax: 914-575-3299. Bros. John Nash; John Vianney Kim; Richard Sharpe; Michael Williams.

Marist Lay Volunteer Residence, 67 Sharpe Blvd. S., Mt. Vernon, 10550. Tel: 914-668-5349. Bros. Armand Lamagna, F.M.S., Dir.; Frederick Sambor; John Bantz, F.M.S., 2567 Tenbroeck Ave., Bronx, 10469. Tel: 718-547-6317.

PELHAM MANOR. *St. Vincent's Residence*, 190 Mt. Tom Rd., 10803-3309. Tel: 914-738-6138; Fax: 914-738-6138.
E-mail: cpstephen@aol.com
The Passionists. Revs. Stephen Haslach, C.P., Supr.; Paschal Smith, C.P.; Leo J. Gorman, C.P.; Vincent Youngberg, C.P.; James R. Gillette, C.P.

SCARBOROUGH. *Carmelite Fathers, NY Prov. of St. Elias*, Carmelite Priory, 3 Woodlea Ln., 10510. Tel: 914-762-3719.
E-mail: joachim@bestweb.net
Revs. Timothy C. Donohue, O.Carm.; Joachim J. Snyder, O.Carm.

STATEN ISLAND. *Scalabrinian Missionaries*, 209 Flagg Pl., 10304. Tel: 718-351-0232; Fax: 718-979-1241.
Web site: WWW.SCALABRINI.ORG
Scalabrinian Mission Center, The Center for Migration Studies; St. Charles Residence. Revs. Dominic Rodighiero, C.S., Supr. & Dir. Devel. Office; Lydio Tomasi, C.S., Dir. Center for Migration Studies. In res. Rev. Henry S. Gentile, C.S.; Bro. Louis Calisto, C.S.

TAPPAN. *St. Eliseus Priory.* (Carmelite Pre-Novitiate), P.O. Box 27, 10983-0027. Tel: 845-359-5299; Fax: 845-359-0856.
E-mail: steliseus @aol.com
Web site: http://frontiernet.net/~ocarmvoc
Very Rev. Mario Esposito, O.Carm., Dir. Students 14.

Office of Lay Carmelites. (Carmelite Third Order). Tel: 845-359-0535; Fax: 845-359-0856. Rev. Brocard Connors, O.Carm., Dir.

THORNWOOD. *Legionaries of Christ,* 582 Columbus Ave., 10594. Tel: 914-749-3900; Fax: 914-749-3939.

WEST PARK. *Congregation of Christian Brothers,* Santa Maria-on-Hudson, 12493. Tel: 845-384-6750. Bros. D. D. Crimmins, Community Leader; W. S. Barry; John F. Farrel, F.S.C. Total in Residence 3.

WHITE PLAINS. *St. Conrad Friary,* 30 Gedney Park Dr., 10605. Tel: 914-761-3008; Fax: 914-948-6429.
E-mail: NYNEPROV1@juno.com
Web site: www.capuchin.org
Legal Titles: *The Province of St. Mary of the Capuchin Order.; Capuchin Friars International, Inc.* Provincial Headquarters of the Province of St. Mary of the Capuchin Order. Development Office: 210 W. 31st St., New York, 10001. Tel: 212-564-0759; Fax: 212-563-5120. Very Rev. Bernard Smith, O.F.M.Cap., Min. Prov.; Revs. Michael Banks, O.F.M.Cap., Vice Prov.; Jerome McHugh, O.F.M.Cap., Sec. & Treas.; John Mahoney, O.F.M.Cap., Archivist; Bro. Joseph Yakimovich, O.F.M.Cap., Asst. Sec. & Treas.; Rev. Joel Daniels, O.F.M.Cap. Priests 4; Brothers 1. (Nature of Apostolate: Provincial Administration, Hospital, Prison, Preaching, Recruitment). Subject to the Provincial. Revs. Jose McCarthy, O.F.M.Cap., Puerto Rico; Gregory Reisert, O.F.M.Cap., Washington, DC; David Couturier, O.F.M.Cap., Beacon, NY; Paul Engel, O.F.M.Cap., New York, NY; Joseph Flynn, O.F.M.Cap., New Rochelle, NY; James Stewart, O.F.M.Cap., Amawalk, NY; John Rathschmidt, O.F.M.Cap., New Rochelle, NY; Paul Tolve, O.F.M.Cap., Amawalk, NY; Ephrem Karwowski, O.F.M.Cap., Fox Lake, IL; George J. Dash, O.F.M.Cap., Carmel, NY; Bro. Terence Taffe, O.F.M.Cap., Minneapolis, MN. Serving in the Military: Rev. James Jones, O.F.M.Cap., Chap., U.S.A. Total in Residence 58; Total Staff 11.

St. Francis of Assisi Foundation, c/o Capuchin Franciscans, St. Conrad Friary, 30 Gedney Park Dr., 10605. Tel: 914-761-3008, Ext. 21; Fax: 914-948-6429.

YONKERS. *Bishop Ford Residence,* St. Joseph's Seminary, Dunwoodie, 10704. Tel: 914-968-2916. Revs. Arthur Mastolia; Robert McKeon; Mark G. Vaillancourt. Students 10.

Cathedral Preparatory Seminary Residence, 201 Seminary Ave., 10704-1896. Revs. Arthur Mastriola; Mark G. Vaillancourt. Priests 2; Students 20.

Parish Mission Team Residence, 586 McLean Ave., 10705. Tel: 914-709-1300; Fax: 914-964-1728.
E-mail: pmteam@aol.com
Rev. Emile Frische, M.H.M.; Sr. Beth Ann Hermann, O.S.F.; Jaime Rickert; Brett Thoman; Nancy Sporbert.

St. Clare Friary, 110 Shonnard Pl., 10703. Tel: 914-423-2392. Capuchin Franciscan Friars, Province of St. Mary. Residence for Senior Friars. Revs. Senan Taylor, O.F.M.Cap., Guardian; Sylvan J. Conover, O.F.M.Cap.; Darius Devito, O.F.M.Cap.; Donatus Goetz, O.F.M.Cap.; Neal Kerrigan, O.F.M.Cap.; John Langweld, O.F.M.Cap.; James McIntyre, O.F.M.Cap.; Celsus Repole, O.F.M.Cap.; Charles Repole, O.F.M.Cap.; Owen Shelley, O.F.M.Cap.; Raymond Nard, O.F.M.Cap.; Bros. John Conway, O.F.M.Cap., Vicar; Bernard Frey, O.F.M.Cap.; Paul Murray, O.F.M.Cap.; Peter Reilly, O.F.M.Cap. Total in Residence 15; Total Staff 3.

St. Felix Friary. (Franciscan Friars of the Renewal), 15 Trinity Plaza, 10701. Tel: 914-476-7279; Fax: 914-476-5033. (House of Studies). Revs. Andrew D. Apostoli, C.F.R.; Robert Stanion, C.F.R.; Glenn Sudano, C.F.R., Gen. Community Servant; Bros. Thomas Francis Cacciola, C.F.R.; John Paul Ouellette, C.F.R.; Godfrey Joseph Godfrey, C.F.R.; Stephen Joseph Coleman, C.F.R.

St. Leopold's Friary. (Franciscan Friars of the Renewal), 259 Nepperhan Ave., 10701-3461. Tel: 914-965-8143.
Web site: www.ewtn.com/renewal
(House of Studies). Rev. Marius Casmir Koch, C.F.R., Local Servant; Bros. Fidelis Moscinski, C.F.R.; Angelus Marie Houle, C.F.R.; Godfrey Joseph Godfrey, C.F.R.; Sean Christopher McVeigh, C.F.R.; Leo Fisher, C.F.R.; John Anthony Boughton, C.F.R.; Sylvester Mary Mann, C.F.R.A; Joseph Mary Deane, C.F.R.; Anthony Marie Baetzold, C.F.R.; Luke Mary Fletcher, C.F.R.; Juniper Mary Sistare, C.F.R.; Elijah Mairi Ford, C.F.R.; Leopold Mariae Bokulich, C.F.R.

[EE] CONVENTS AND RESIDENCES OF SISTERS

NEW YORK. *Academy of St. Dorothy.* 1305 Hylan Blvd., Staten Island, 10305. Tel: 718-987-0677. Sisters of St. Dorothy. Sr. Mary Ann Keegan, S.S.D., Coord. Sisters 9.

Blessed Trinity Missionary Cenacle, 414 E. 14th St., 10009. Tel: 212-475-1450; Fax: 212-254-8565. Missionary Social Work and Parish Ministry. Family Division of Catholic Charities of New York, Campus Ministry N.Y.U. and Nazareth Housing. Missionary Servants of the Most Blessed Trinity 7; Total Assisted 4,240; Total Staff 7. Catholic Charities Family and Children's Services, 530 Grand St., 10002. Tel: 212-777-3111; Fax: 212-677-9057.

Carmelite Sisters Teresas of St. Joseph, Inc., 249 W. 14th St., 10011. Sr. Angela Perez, Supr.

Convent of Our Lady of the Presentation, 419 Woodrow Rd., 10312. Tel: 718-356-2121; Fax: 718-948-4115.
E-mail: srcathquinn@netzero.net
Motherhouse and Novitiate of the Sisters of the Presentation. Sr. Catherine Quinn. Sisters 26.

Convent of Sisters of the Congregation de Notre Dame, 76 Howard Ave., 10301. Tel: 718-447-0291; Fax: 718-273-0462. Sisters 6.

Corpus Christi Monastery, 1230 Lafayette Ave., 10474. Tel: 718-328-6996; Fax: 718-328-1974. Sr. Maria Pia, Prioress. Solemnly Professed 11; Perpetually Professed 2; Novices 4; Postulants 1.

Dalton Center for Mission and Peace. Sisters of the Holy Child Jesus, 325 E. 33rd St., 10016-9401. Tel: 212-689-3548; 889-3886; Fax: 212-545-7804.
E-mail: shcjapds@aol.com
Total in Residence 6; Total Staff 3.

The Dwelling Place of New York, Inc., 409 W. 40th St., 10018. Tel: 212-564-7887; Fax: 212-695-3642. Sr. Nancy Chiarello, Admin. Sisters 6.

Franciscan Handmaids of Mary Convent, 15 W. 124th St., 10027. Tel: 212-289-5655; Fax: 212-987-5447.
Web site: www.fhm.members.aol.com/fhm.nyc
Generalate of the Franciscan Handmaids of Mary. Sr. Maria Goretti Mannix, Congregation Min. Sisters 24; Total Assisted 300; Total Staff 20.
Other Convents: Camp St. Edward, 445 Woodvale Ave., Staten Island, 10309. Tel: 718-984-1625.

Handmaids of Mary Novitiate, 444 Woodvale Ave., Staten Island, 10309. Tel: 718-984-1625; Fax: 718-966-0814. Novitiate of the Franciscan Handmaids of the Most Pure Heart of Mary. Sr. Loretta Theresa Richards, Dir., Formation. Associates 1.

Franciscan Missionaries of Mary. Tel: 718-547-4604; Fax: 718-547-4607.
E-mail: fmmprov@aol.com
Web site: www.fmmusa.org
Provincialate, 3305 Wallace Ave., Bronx, 10467-6599. Tel: 718-547-4604; Fax: 718-547-4607.
E-mail: fmmprov@aol.com
Web site: www.fmm.org or www.fmmusa.org
Holy Name Convent, 204 W. 97th St., 10025-5620. Tel: 212-678-6901; Fax: 212-678-6865. Cardinal Hayes Home Convent, Box K, Millbrook, 12545. Tel: 845-677-6739; Fax: 845-677-6691.

Franciscan Sisters of Little Falls, MN., 20 Walden Ave., 10306-1345. Tel: 718-351-1328. Sisters 2.

Franciscan Sisters of the Poor Foundation, Inc., 708 Third Ave., Ste. 200, 10017. Tel: 212-818-1987; Fax: 212-808-0096.

Missionaries of Charity, Inc., 335 E. 145th St., 10451. Tel: 718-292-0019. Sr. M. Dominga, M.C., Reg. Supr.; Sr. M. Marina, M.C., Supr., 406 W. 127th St., 10027. Tel: 212-222-7229. Sr. M. Regis, M.C., Supr., 657 Washington St., 10014. Tel: 212-645-0587. Sr. M. Lisseria, M.C., Supr. Total Assisted 1,200; Total Staff (shared apostolates) 24.

Missionary Sisters of the Immaculate Heart of Mary. District House, 238 E. 15th St., Apt. 5, 10003-3901. Tel: 212-677-2959; Fax: 212-533-9124 (Emergencies only).
E-mail: icmusdist@juno.com
Sr. Alene Grothues, Supr. Sisters 3. St. Joseph Convent, 238 E. 15th St., 10003-3901. Tel: 212-254-0658; Fax: 212-533-9124 (Emergencies only). Sr. Jean Cook, Supr. Sisters 8.

Parish Visitors of Mary Immaculate. Tel: 718-823-0350. 2151 Watson Ave., Bronx, 10472. Tel: 718-823-0350. Sr. Maria Catherine Iannotti, P.V.M.I., Supr. Sisters 3.

Parish Visitors of Mary Immaculate. Tel: 845-783-2251; Fax: 845-783-2085. Marycrest, P.O. Box 658, Monroe, 10950-0658. Tel: 845-783-2251; Fax: 845-783-2085. Sr. Carole Marie Troskowski, Gen. Supr.; Sr. Rita Mairelenes, Juniorate Dir.; Sr. Dolores Marie, Novice Dir. Total in Community 68. A contemplative-missionary community serving the Church by person-to-person evangelization through visiting parish families on behalf of their priests; religious education for children and adults not connected with the Catholic schools, giving spiritual counsel and serving as a liaison for social service needs of family members.

St. Joseph Provincialate, 205 Major Ave., 10305. Tel: 718-720-4377; Fax: 718-442-9247.
E-mail: josiefdc@aol.com
Web site: godslovefdc.homestead.com/divinecharity-ns4.html
Provincialate of the Daughters of Divine Charity. Sisters 2; In Province 60.

Schoenstatt Sisters of Mary, Secular Institute, 337 Cary Ave., 10310. Tel: 718-727-8005. Sisters 7; Total Staff 4.

Shalom Convent, 714 W. 231st St., 10463. Tel: 718-884-1663.
E-mail: pauline_rita@compuserve.com
Franciscan Sisters of the Poor 4.

Sisters of Charity Center, Mount Saint Vincent, 6301 Riverdale Ave., 10471-9930. Tel: 718-549-9200; Fax: 718-884-3013.
E-mail: scny.org
Web site: www.scny.org
Sr. Elizabeth A. Vermaelen, Pres. Legal Titles: *The Sisters of Charity of Saint Vincent de Paul of New York.; Sisters of Charity Center.; Mount Saint Vincent on Hudson.; The Sisters of Charity of Saint Vincent de Paul of New York Pension Trust.* Total in Congregation 515; In Archdiocese 480.

The Elizabeth Seton Federation, Inc., Sisters of Charity Center, 6301 Riverdale Ave., Bronx, 10471. Tel: 718-549-9200; Fax: 718-884-3013. Sr. Mary Frances Hildenberger, D.C.

Sisters of the Good Shepherd, 337 E. 17th St., 10003-3804. Tel: 212-475-4245; Fax: 212-673-1240. Legal Title: *Sisters of the Good Shepherd-New York City.* Sisters 10.

Society of Helpers. Tel: 718-884-3100; Fax: 718-884-3101. 385 W. 263rd St., Bronx, 10471. Tel: 718-884-3100; Fax: 718-884-3101.
E-mail: nyhelper@claret.org
Web site: www.claret.org/~srmoore/goodc.html
Sr. Geraldine Finan, Supr. Sisters 6.

Society of the Sacred Heart, R.S.C.J., 515 E. 118th St., 10035. Tel: 212-578-2895.
E-mail: mlufkin@rscj.org
Other Residences: 436 W. 49th St., 10019. Tel: 212-581-3894. 222 E. 93rd St., 10128. Tel: 212-876-2276; Fax: 212-996-5277. 406 E. 80th St., 10021. Tel: 212-288-1986; 288-5116; Fax: 212-861-8851. 519 E. 118th St., 10035. Tel: 212-410-3465. 253 E. 110th St., #2, 10029. Tel: 212-410-4315.

Ursuline Bedford Park Convent, 2885 Marion Ave., 10458. Tel: 212-364-1289; 220-3387; Fax: 718-561-4896. Sr. Sheila Murphy, O.S.U., Supr. Sisters 31.

Ursuline Provincialate. 323 E. 198th St., Bronx, 10458. Tel: 718-365-7410; Fax: 718-733-4498.
E-mail: ursruepr@aol.com
Provincialate of the Ursulines of the Roman Union, Eastern Province. Sr. Marie-Celine Miranda, O.S.U., Prov. Sisters in Province 191.

Ursuline Sisters of Andrews Avenue, Inc., 323 E. 198th St., Bronx, 10458. Tel: 718-365-7410; Fax: 718-733-4498. Sr. Marie-Celine Miranda, O.S.U., Pres.

BEACON. *Carmelite Monastery,* 89 Hiddenbrooke Dr., 12508-3540. Tel: 845-831-5572; Fax: 845-831-5579.
E-mail: mafj55d@prodigy.com
Sr. Michael Ann Cladek, O.C.D., Prioress. Professed Nuns 27.

BLAUVELT. *Congregation of Sisters of St. Dominic of Blauvelt,* 496 Western Hwy., 10913. Tel: 845-359-5600; Fax: 845-359-5773.
E-mail: maryannop@aol.com
Web site: www.opblauvelt.org
Sr. Mary Ann Collins, O.P., Pres.; Sr. Rose Ellen Gorman, O.P., Asst. to the Pres. Sisters 215. Legal Title: *The Sisters of St. Dominic of Blauvelt, New York.*

BRONX. *Our Lady of Guadalupe Convent.* (Franciscan Sisters of the Renewal), 3537 Bainbridge Ave., 10467. Tel: 718-547-9840. (House of Formation). Sr. Lucille Cutrone, C.F.R., Community Servant. Sisters 7.

Sisters of Life, St. Francis Convent, 198 Hollywood, 10465. Tel: 212-397-1396; Fax: 212-397-1397. Mother Agnes Mary Donovan, S.V. Professed Sisters 31.

Sisters of St. John the Baptist, Provincial Residence, 3308 Campbell Dr., 10465-1358. Tel: 718-518-7820; Fax: 718-518-8930.
E-mail: usajohnag@aol.com
Web site: home.att.net/~baptistines
Sr. John Agnes Barone, C.S.JB., Prov. Supr. In Province 120; In Archdiocese 101.

Mt. St. John Convent. (Retired Sisters' Residence), 150 Anderson Hill Rd., Purchase, 10577. Tel: 914-761-7965; Fax: 914-761-2315. Sr. Theresa Ann D'Onafrio, C.S.JB., Supr. Sisters in residence 30.

Ursuline Communities, Inc., 323 E. 198 St., 10458. Tel: 718-365-7410; Fax: 718-733-4498.
E-mail: ursruepr@aol.com
Sr. Marie-Celine Miranda, O.S.U., Pres.

ESOPUS. *Mother of Perpetual Help Monastery*, 12429. Tel: 914-384-6533.
E-mail: rednuns@juno.com
Web site: www.catholic.org/macc/redemptoristine
Redemptoristine Nuns. Sr. Moira Quinn, O.SS.R., Prioress. Professed Sisters 10.

GARRISON. *Motherhouse and Novitiate of the Franciscan Sisters of the Atonement*, St. Francis Convent - Graymoor, 41 Old Highland Tpke., 10524-9716. Tel: 845-424-3623; Fax: 845-424-3298.
E-mail: dbernier@graymoor.org
Web site: www.graymoor.org
Legal Title: *Franciscan Sisters of the Atonement, Inc.* Sr. Diane Bernier, S.A., Congregation Minister. Co-Coordinators: Sr. Mary Kathleen Murray, S.A.; Sr. Paul Marie Gouthro, S.A. Sisters 75.

Our Lady's Guest and Retreat House, St. Francis Convent, 41 Old Highland Tpke., 10524. Tel: 914-424-3300; Fax: 914-424-3971.
E-mail: retreathouse@graymoor.org
Web site: www.graymoor.org
Franciscan Sisters of the Atonement. Sr. Josephine Dullaghan, S.A., Directress. Sisters 3.

GRAYMOOR. *Mother Lurana House*. 166 Old W. Point Rd., Garrison, 10524. Franciscan Sisters of the Atonement. Adult Social Day Care. Sr. Barbara Ohl, S.A., Directress.

HARRIMAN. *St. Patrick's Villa*, 10926. Provincial Retirement Home and Provincialate of the Sisters of the Catholic Apostolate (Pallottine). Sr. Theresa Martin, Supr.; Sr. Michele Ruggiero, Prov.; Rev. Lawrence X. McCaffrey, S.J., Chap. Sisters 35.

HARTSDALE. *Institute of the Sisters of Mercy of the Americas, Regional Community of New York*, 150 Ridge Rd., 10530-2205. Tel: 914-328-3200; Fax: 914-328-3761.
E-mail: Srsuee@aol.com
Sisters of Mercy. Sr. Patricia Wolf, R.S.M., Regl. Pres. Sisters of Mercy of the Americas 182. Legal Title: *The Sisters of Mercy, Inc.*

HASTINGS-ON-HUDSON. *Sisters of St. Francis*, 49 Jackson Ave., 10706-3217. Tel: 914-478-3932; Fax: 914-478-5470.
E-mail: hastingsosf@aol.com
Sisters of St. Francis, Hastings-on-Hudson. Motherhouse and Novitiate. Sr. Roberta Stark Smith, O.S.F., Gen. Minister; Rev. Gary W. Schwartzkopf, S.J., Chap. Sisters 76.

HAVERSTRAW. *Sisters of St. Francis of Peace*, Congregation Center, 20 Ridge St., 10927. Tel: 845-942-2527; Fax: 845-429-8141.
E-mail: congmin@aol.com
Web site: www.fspnet.org
Sr. Margaret Gaffikin, Congregation Min.

HAWTHORNE. *Motherhouse & Novitiate of the Sisters of St. Dominic, Congregation of St. Rose of Lima*, 10532. Tel: 914-769-0114; Fax: 914-769-3916.
Web site: www.hawthorne-dominicans.org
Mother Marie Edward, O.P., Mother Gen.; Rev. John Proppe, O.F.M.Cap., Chap. Legal Title: *Motherhouse and Novitiate of the Sisters of St. Dominic, Congregation of St. Rose of Lima.* Professed Sisters 24; Sisters in Community 80; In Archdiocese 34.

HIGHLAND MILLS. *Religious of Jesus and Mary*, 202 County Rd. 105, P.O. Box 1003, 10930-1003. Tel: 845-928-2213; Fax: 845-928-9437.
E-mail: thevenet@frontiernet.net
Web site: www.rcc.net/newyork/bethany
Sr. Margaret M. Quinn, R.J.M., Supr. In res. Rev. Thomas E. Clarke, S.J. Sisters 14.

HOPEWELL JUNCTION. *St. Aloysius Novitiate*, Beekman Rd., P.O. Box 98, 12533. Tel: 914-226-5671; Fax: 914-226-5671.
E-mail: jstab35097
Web site: www.staloysius.ny.org
Oblates to the Blessed Trinity. Mother Gloria Castro, Supr. Gen. Sisters 11; Postulants 2; Total in Residence 41; Total Staff 31.

LIBERTY. *Blessed Kateri Tekakwitha Religious Education Center*, Mailing Address: Box 1011, 12754. Tel: 914-292-9100. Dominican Sisters.

LIVINGSTON MANOR. *Monastic Sisters of Bethlehem and of the Assumption of the Virgin*, Grooville Rd., 12758. Tel: 914-639-6300; Fax: 914-439-3069. Sr. Amena Figeat, M.S.B.A.V., Supr. Total in Residence 14.

MARYKNOLL. *Maryknoll Community, Inc.*, 77 Ryder Rd., P.O. Box 306, 10545-3060.

Maryknoll Residential Care, Maryknoll Sisters Center, 10545-0311. Tel: 914-941-9230; Fax: 914-941-0213.
E-mail: mconnell@mksisters.org
Skilled Nursing home for the Maryknoll sisters only. Sr. Mary T. Connell, M.M., Admin. Beds 58; Sisters 54.

Maryknoll Sisters Charitable Trust, Treasury Office, P.O. Box 306, 10545-0306. Tel: 914-941-7590; Fax: 914-941-2411.
E-mail: reallahan@maryknoll.org
Rev. Richard B. Callahan, M.M., Trustee.

Maryknoll Sisters Contemplative Community, Mailing Address: P.O. Box 311, 10545-0311. Tel: 914-941-7575.
E-mail: mkcontemplativecom@juno.com
Contemplative Community of the Maryknoll Sisters of St. Dominic. Sr. Theresa Baldini, M.M., Coord. Sisters 11.

Maryknoll Sisters of St. Dominic Inc., P.O. Box 311, 10545-0311. Tel: 914-941-7575; Fax: 914-923-0733.
E-mail: chassey@mksisters.org
Web site: www.maryknoll.org
Sr. Carol Hassey, M.M., Center Coord. Professed Sisters 200; Total in Residence 203.

MILLBROOK. *Franciscan Missionaries of Mary*, Mailing Address: Box K, 12545. Tel: 845-677-6363; Fax: 845-677-6739.
E-mail: fmmch@aol.com
Sr. Anne Turbini, F.M.M., Local Coord. Sisters 5.

MONROE. *St. Joseph's Convent-Preschool*, 121 Harriman Heights Rd., 10950. Tel: 914-783-3006; Fax: 914-782-5645. Sr. M. Olivia Reginella, Coord. Sisters of the Catholic Apostolate (Pallottine) 6; Total Assisted 50; Total Staff 6.

MONSEY. *St. Zita's Villa*, 10952. Tel: 914-356-2011; Fax: 914-352-5209. Motherhouse and Novitiate of Sisters of Reparation of the Congregation of Mary. Sr. Maureen Francis, Supr. Sisters 11.

MONTICELLO. *St. Thomas Villa*, 12701. Sr. Agnes White, C.S.J., Admin. Summer residence for Sisters of St. Joseph, Brentwood. Please send all correspondence to:

NANUET. *St. Patrick Villa*, 2 Duryea Ln., 10954. Tel: 845-623-3371; Fax: 845-623-3371. Sisters of Charity of St. Vincent de Paul. Sr. Marita Regina Bronner, Admin. Sisters 20.

NEW ROCHELLE. *Monastery of St. Clare*, 86 Mayflower Ave., 10801-1615. Tel: 718-822-7271; Fax: 914-632-5227.
E-mail: claresnyeme@juno.com
Sr. Mary Bernadette Quinn, O.S.C., Abbess. Sisters 12.

Ursuline Convent of St. Teresa's, 39 Willow Dr., 10805. Tel: 914-632-1199; Fax: 914-633-5281. Legal Title: *Ursuline Convent of St. Teresa's, New York.* Sr. Alice Gallin, O.S.U., Supr. Sisters 43.

Ursuline Residence, Inc., 1338 North Ave., 10804. Tel: 914-636-3456; Fax: 914-576-2620.
E-mail: ursres@aol.com
Sr. Kathleen Mary Donohue, O.S.U., Supr. Sisters 30.

NEW WINDSOR. *Mt. St. Joseph*, 880 Jackson Ave., 12553. Tel: 914-564-6620; Fax: 914-567-0219.
E-mail: pbvmadmin@juno.com
Motherhouse of the Sisters of the Presentation of the Blessed Virgin Mary of New Winsor. Sr. Catherine Cleary, Pres.; Sr. Luke Mulraney, Community Archivist. Ministry in the field of academic education in parochial elementary and high schools; pastoral services; health care; social services. Sisters 182.

NEWBURGH. *Center of Hope Sisters' Residence*, 320 Powell Ave., 12550. Dominican Sisters of Hope. Sr. Maura Schefter, O.P., Admin.

Daughters of Mary Immaculate, 15 Stori Rd., 12550. Tel: 914-565-5034.
E-mail: 15storird.newb,ny
Italian Apostolate in Sacred Heart Church. Sr. Putorti, Admin. Total Assisted 235; Total Staff 2.

NYACK. *Sisters of Our Lady of Christian Doctrine aka Institute of Christian Doctrine.* Visitation House, 629 N. Midland Ave., 10960-1032. Tel: 845-358-7663; Fax: 845-358-7663.
E-mail: rcdpres@aol.com
Sr. Virginia Johnson, R.C.D., Pres. Sisters 35; Total in Residence 5; Total Staff 2.

Marydell Faith & Life Center, 640 N. Midland Ave., 10960. Tel: 914-358-5399; Fax: 914-358-1671.

OSSINING. *Dominican Sisters of Hope*, 299 N. Highland Ave., 10562. Tel: 914-941-4420; Fax: 914-941-1125.
E-mail: pmccartney@ophope.org
Web site: www.ophope.org
Sr. Philomena Marie McCartney, O.P., Prioress.

PEEKSKILL. *Mt. St. Francis, Motherhouse & Infirm of Franciscan Missionary Sisters of Sacred Heart*, 250 South St., 10566. Tel: 914-737-5409; Fax: 914-736-9614. Sr. Rose Cecilia Bozzo, F.M.S.C., Prov. Supr.; Sr. Mary Carmel Licameli, F.M.S.C., Supr. Legal Title: *Missionary Sisters of the Third Order of St. Francis.*
Canonical Name: Franciscan Missionary Sisters of the Sacred Heart.

Mt. St. Francis Infirmary, 250 South St., 10566. Tel: 914-737-3373; Fax: 914-736-9614.

Novitiate.

PURCHASE. *Society of the Sacred Heart*, Manhattanville College, 10577. Tel: 914-694-2200.
Web site: sofie.org/rscj/

RHINEBECK. *Linwood Spiritual Center*, 50 Minwood Rd., 12572-2507. Tel: 914-876-4178; Fax: 914-876-1920.
E-mail: linwood@ulster.net
Sisters of St. Ursula. Sr. Mary Isaac Koenig, S.U., Regl. Supr.; Sr. Maureen Steeley, S.U., Dir. Spiritual Center.

RYE. *Convent of the Holy Child*, 25 Convent Ln., 10580-1904. Tel: 914-967-5544; Fax: 914-925-2575.
E-mail: holychildd@aol.com
Sisters of the Holy Child Jesus 20; Sisters of Mercy (NY Region) 8.

SCARSDALE. *Blessed Sacrament Monastery*, 86 Dromore Rd., 10583-1706. Tel: 914-722-1657; Fax: 914-722-1665.
E-mail: obsny.com
Sacramentine Nuns. Sr. Mary Veronica Kiley, Prioress. Sisters 13.

SLOATSBURG. *St. Mary's Villa, Spiritual & Educational Center*, 150 Sisters Servants Ln., P.O. Box 6, 10974-0006. Tel: 914-753-5100; Fax: 914-753-5100.
E-mail: ssminy@aol.com
Sisters Servants of Mary Immaculate.

SPARKILL. *Dominican Convent of Our Lady of the Rosary*, 175 Rte. 340, 10976-1047. Tel: 914-359-6400; Fax: 914-359-6053.
E-mail: margaret.murphy@sparkill.org
Web site: www.sparkill.org
Motherhouse and General Novitiate of Dominican Sisters of Congregation of Our Lady of the Rosary. Sr. Kathleen Kane, O.P., Pres.; Rev. Rodolfo Ortiz, Chap. Sisters 120 in Residence in Dominican Convent; Sisters 453 in Congregation.

STATEN ISLAND. *Daughters of St. Paul, Pious Society*, 78 Fort Pl., 10301. Tel: 718-447-5071; Fax: 718-816-1332.
E-mail: fspny@aol.com
Web site: pauline.org
Missionary Sisters of the Communications Media. Sr. Patricia Mary Maresca, F.S.P., Supr. Sisters 11.

Pious Disciples of the Divine Master, Regional and Formation House, 60 Sunset Ave., 10314. Tel: 718-761-2323; 494-8597; Fax: 718-494-2123. Sr. M. Josephine Fallon, Regional Supr. Sisters 9.

TARRYTOWN. *Provincial Center, Religious Sacred Heart of Mary*, 50 Wilson Park Dr., 10591. Tel: 914-655-3440; 631-8872; Fax: 914-631-7803. Sr. Martina Crowley, Supr. Prov. Councillors: Sr. Letizia Pappalardo; Sr. Edna O'Connor; Sr. Frances Lane, Sec.; Sr. Marion Therese Shanahan, Treas.; Sr. Monica Walsh, Dir. Formation; Sr. Joanne Safian, Dir. Communications. Total in Residence 66; Total Staff 32.

WALDEN. *Convent of Most Precious Blood*, 100 Ulster Ave., 12586. Sisters 2.

Little Sisters of the Assumption, Provincial House, 100 Gladstone Ave., 12586. Tel: 914-778-0667; Fax: 914-778-0676.
E-mail: littlesrs@aol.com
Web site: www.littlesisters.org
Sr. Jean McCormack, Prov. Coord. Sisters 20; Sisters in Province 46; Total Assisted 3,000; Total Staff 35.
Other residences in New York: 218 E. 105th St., New York, 10029. Tel: 212-534-4932. 475 E. 115th St., New York, 10029. Tel: 212-369-2097. 310 E. 120th St., New York, 10035. Tel: 212-876-4661. 98 Gladstone Ave., P.O. Box 677, 12586-0677. Tel: 914-778-7252. 159-A Johnston St., Newburgh, 12550. Tel: 914-562-1757.

Little Sisters of the Assumption, P.O. Box 677, 12586-0677. Tel: 914-778-7252; Fax: 914-778-2457. Sr. Jean McCormack, Provincial; Sr. Joseph McCloat, Local Coord. Sisters 6.

WARWICK. *Mt. Alverno Center, Bon Secours Charity Health System*, 20 Grand St., 10990. Tel: 914-986-2267; Fax: 914-986-9269.
Web site: www.stanthonycommunityhosp.org
James Giordano, EVP, Warwick Campus; Mrs. Kathleen Deak, Admin., Mt. Alverno Center, Adult Home/Assisted Living Program; Sr. Maris Stella Footin, S.F.P.; Rev. Gerard Dolan, Chap. St. Francis Center at the Knolls, Villa Francis at the Knolls.

WHITE PLAINS. *Convent of Our Lady of Good Counsel*, 52 N. Broadway, 10603. Tel: 914-949-2950; Fax: 914-949-5169.
E-mail: alicefeeley@email.msn.com
Motherhouse of the Sisters of the Divine Compassion. Sr. Alice Feeley, R.D.C., Pres.

RDC Center for Counseling and Human Development, Inc., 52 N. Broadway, 10603. Tel: 914-949-0504; Fax: 914-997-1979. Sr. Lauren McLeod, R.D.C. To provide counseling services for laity, religious and clergy. Individual and group counseling are offered as well as marital and family therapy. Sisters 40.

YORKTOWN HEIGHTS. *Sisters of the Good Shepherd*, 2202 Mark Rd., 10567. Tel: 914-526-8587; Fax: 914-526-0291. Sisters of the Good Shepherd 4.

[FF] RETREAT HOUSES

NEW YORK. *Cardinal Spellman Retreat House*, Passionist Spiritual Center, 5801 Palisade Ave., 10471. Tel: 718-549-6500; Fax: 718-884-9732.
E-mail: preacherman@compuserve.com
Web site: www.passionists.org & www.preacherman.org
Rev. Paul R. Fagan, C.P., Dir.; Mr. William J. Gilberg, Admin.; Bro. James Johnson, C.P., Coord. of special events. Ministry Staff: Revs. Gregory Paul, C.P.; Malcolm Cornwell, C.P., Rector; Bro. Damian Carroll, C.P. Retreats for adults and youths and hosted non-profit groups.

BEDFORD VILLAGE. *Cenacle Retreat House*, Rte. 22, P.O. Box 467, 10506. Tel: 914-234-3344; Fax: 914-234-3344.
E-mail: srkobrien@msn.com
Sr. Thelma Hall, r.c.; Sr. Kathleen O'Brien. Directed retreats, Spiritual Direction, Days of prayer for individuals (religious or lay).

BRONX. *St. Joseph's Center.* (Spanish Cursillo Center), 275 W. 230th St., 10463. Tel: 718-796-4340. Revs. Francis E. Peluso, O.A.R., Dir.; Gregorio Arista, O.A.R. (Mexico); Domingos Machado, O.A.R. (Portugal); Bro. Mario Alvarez, O.A.R., Admin. Total in Residence 1; Total Staff 4.

ESOPUS. *Marist Brothers of Ulster County*, Mailing Address: P.O. Box 197, 12429. Tel: 914-384-6106; 384-6620; Fax: 914-384-6479.
E-mail: esopusdon1@aol.com
Mid Hudson Valley Camp - Summer camp for disadvantaged children. Bro. Donald Nugent, F.M.S., Dir. Total Staff 3.

Mount St. Alphonsus Redemptorist Retreat Center, 1001 Broadway, P.O. Box 219, 12429. Tel: 845-384-8000; Fax: 845-384-8088.
Web site: www.msaretreat.com
Redemptorist Fathers and Brothers. Very Rev. John G. Kingsbury, C.Ss.R., Rector; Bro. Robert Skinnner, C.Ss.R.; Revs. James Small, C.Ss.R.; Timothy Keating, C.Ss.R. Groups and individual retreats, conferences, workshops, and days of prayer. Available for Religious Chapters. Capacity 106 Rooms; Beds 161.

HIGHLAND MILLS. *Bethany Retreat House*, 202 County Rd. 105, P.O. Box 1003, 10930-1003. Tel: 845-928-2213; Fax: 845-928-9437.
E-mail: thevenet@frontiernet.net
Web site: www.rc.net/newyork/bethany
Religious of Jesus and Mary. Sr. Catherine McIntyre, R.J.M., Dir. In res. Rev. Thomas E. Clarke, S.J. Total in Residence 14.

LARCHMONT. *St. Francis Retreat, Inc.*, 1 Pryer Manor Rd., 10538. Tel: 914-235-6839; Fax: 914-576-6540. Rev. Benedict J. Groeschel, C.F.R. Tel: 914-632-3743.

Trinity Retreat, 1 Pryer Manor Rd., 10538. Tel: 914-235-6839. Revs. Eugene Fulton, Dir.; Benedict J. Groeschel, C.F.R., Assoc. Dir.

MIDDLETOWN. *National Shrine of Our Lady of Mount Carmel*, Carmelite Dr., P.O. Box 868, 10940-0868. Tel: 914-343-1879; Fax: 914-343-1912. Rev. Richard Champigny, O.Carm., Dir. Total Staff 10.

NEWBURGH. *Our Lady of Hope Center*, 532 River Rd., 12550. Tel: 914-568-0780; Fax: 914-561-7956. Conducted by the Oblates of Mary Immaculate of the U.S. Province. Revs. Richard Kulwiec, O.M.I., Supr.; Patrick Brady, O.M.I.; Michael O'Hara, O.M.I.; Robert Leising, O.M.I.; George M. White, O.M.I.; John King, O.M.I.

SLOATSBURG. *St. Mary's Villa*, 150 Sisters Servants Ln., P.O. Box 6, 10974-0006. Tel: 914-753-5100; Fax: 914-753-5100.
E-mail: ssminy@aol.com
Spiritual and Educational Center. (Retreats). Sisters Servants of Mary Immaculate. Total in Residence 9; Total Staff 4.

STATEN ISLAND. *Mount Manresa Jesuit Retreat House*, 239 Fingerboard Rd., 10305. Tel: 718-727-3844; Fax: 718-727-4881.
E-mail: skellym@idt.net
Web site: www.manresasi.org
Society of Jesus. Revs. John T. Ryan, S.J., Dir.; Joseph T. Browne, S.J., Supr.; Richard P. Grogan, S.J.; Robert E. Groenewold, S.J.; John J. King, S.J.; Joseph E. Moltesz, S.J.; Thomas J. Quinn, S.J.; Sr. Maureen Skelly; Ms. Christine Fiorillo, Youth Min.; Ms. Arlene Volsario, Admin. Total in Residence 8; Total Staff 8.

STONY POINT. *Don Bosco Retreat Center and Marian Shrine*, 174 Filors Ln., 10980. Tel: 914-947-2200; Fax: 914-947-2203.
E-mail: marianshrine@aol.com
Web site: www.mariancenter.org
Founded 1947. Bros. Mario Audero, S.D.B.; Jerome Cincotta, S.D.B.; Alfred Flatoff, S.D.B.; Richard Pasiak, S.D.B.; David Tierney, S.D.B., Vocations; Bernard Zdanowicz, S.D.B.; Revs. George Atok, S.D.B.; Paul Bedard, S.D.B.; William Burke, S.D.B., Retreats Coord.; James Chiosso, S.D.B., Dir.; Domenic DiGuardo, S.D.B.; John Divizia, S.D.B.; August Kita, S.D.B.; A. Joseph Louis, S.D.B.; Anthony Luzzi, S.D.B.; Paul Chuong Nguyen, S.D.B.; John Puntino, S.D.B., Dir.; Gennaro Sesto, S.D.B., Shrine Coord.; Kenneth Shaw, S.D.B.; Chester Szemborski, S.D.B.; Eugene Walter, S.D.B.; Frank Wolfram, S.D.B. Total in Residence 22; Total Staff 37.

Marian Shrine, 174 Filors Ln., 10980. Tel: 914-947-2200; Fax: 914-947-2203.
E-mail: marianshrine@aol.com
Web site: www.mariancenter.org
Revs. George Atok, S.D.B.; Paul Bedard, S.D.B.; William Burke, S.D.B., Retreats Coord.; James Chioso, S.D.B.; Domenic DiGuardo, S.D.B.; John Divizia, S.D.B.; August Kita, S.D.B.; A. Joseph Louis, S.D.B.; Anthony Luzzi, S.D.B.; Paul Choung Nguyen, S.D.B.; John Puntino, S.D.B., Dir.; Gennaro Sesto, S.D.B., Shrine Coord.; Kenneth Shaw, S.D.B.; Chester Szemborski, S.D.B.; Eugene Walter, S.D.B.; Frank Wolfram, S.D.B.; Bros. Mario Audero, S.S.D.; Jerome Cincotta, S.D.B.; Alfred Flatoff, S.D.B.; Richard Pasaik, S.D.B.; David Tierney, S.D.B.; Bernard Zdanowicz, S.D.B. Total in Residence 24; Total Staff 30.

WALDEN. *St. Andrew's Retreat House*, 257 St. Andrew's Rd., 12586. Tel: 914-778-5941; Fax: 304-242-8981. Sr. Rose Marie Levesque, Supr. North American Union Sisters of Our Lady of Charity.

WAPPINGERS FALLS. *Mt. Alvernia Retreat House*, 12590. Revs. Thomas More Nicastro, O.F.M.; Ernest D'Onofrio, O.F.M.; Adolph Giorda, O.F.M.; Armand Padula, O.F.M., Guardian; Brennan Egan, O.F.M.; Roch Ciandella, O.F.M., Dir. Retreats; Thomas Garone, O.F.M.; Bro. Joseph Messina, O.F.M.; Deacon Kenneth Ghastin, O.F.M.

WARWICK. *Franciscan Sisters of the Poor Convent*, 24 Grand St., 10990. Tel: 914-986-2267. Franciscan Sisters of the Poor. Miss Jean Wetstine, Exec. Dir.; Sr. Paula Adelman, Local Community Min.; Rev. Edward Sullivan, O.F.M., Chap.

YONKERS. *Sisters of Mary Reparatrix*, 287 Hayward St., 10704. Sr. Margaret Hoey, S.M.R., Prov. Supr. Sisters 4.

[GG] UNIVERSITY APOSTOLATES

NEW YORK. *University Apostolate*, 1011 First Ave., 10022. Tel: 212-371-1000, Ext. 2805; Fax: 212-758-3018. Rev. Msgr. Michael C. Crimmins, Coord.

Bard College, MSC-1227, P.O. Box 5000, Annondale-on-Hudson, 12504-5—. Tel: 914-758-7542.

Bronx Community College, Loew Hall - Room 422, University Ave. & W. 181 St., Bronx, 10453. Tel: 718-289-5954. Rev. James Sheehan.

City College of New York, NAC Bldg., Room 4102, 137 St. & Convent Ave., 10031. Tel: 212-650-5866. Mr. Gregory Pope.

Columbia University, 110 Earl Hall, 10027. Tel: 212-854-5110; 866-1500 (Notre Dame Rectory). Rev. Msgr. Christopher Maloney; Revs. Thomas J. Valenti (ROC); Daniel Ulloa, O.P.

Culinary Institute of America. Tel: 914-331-3459; Fax: 914-340-9596. Rev. Mark Oliver.

Dutchess Community College.

Vassar College, St. Mary's Convent, 157 Broadway, Kingston, 12401-6057. Tel: 914-331-3459; Fax: 914-340-9596.

Fashion Institute of Technology (SUNY), 227 W. 27th St., 10001. Tel: 212-564-9070, Ext. 232. Rev. Ray Frias, O.F.M.Cap.

Dominican College, 470 Western Hwy., Orangeburg, 10962. Tel: 914-359-7800, Ext. 255. Sr. Barbara McEneany, O.P.

Fordham University at Lincoln Center, 113 W. 60th St., (Lowenstein 217), 10023. Rev. Damian O'Connell, S.J. Tel: 212-636-6318; Ms. Joan Cavanagh. Tel: 212-636-6268.

Fordham University at Rosehill, Bronx, 10458. Tel: 718-817-4500 (C.M. Office); Fax: 718-817-4505. Revs. Joseph A. Currie, S.J.; Gerry Blaszczak, S.J.; Mr. Frank Rizzo; Sr. Regina DeVito, C.N.D.; Rev. John A. Mullin, S.J.; Mr. Robert Minotti.

Herbert H. Lehman College, Student Life Bldg. #222E, 220 Bedford Park Blvd. W., Bronx, 10468. Tel: 718-960-4979. Sr. Madeleine Smith, S.H.C.J.; Mrs. Kathryn Mastriaco.

Hostos Community College, 500 Grand Concourse, Room C371, Bronx, 10451. Tel: 718-518-4423 (message). Rev. James Sheehan.

Hunter/Baruch College, 695 Park Ave., Room 1317 E. Bldg., 10021. Tel: 212-772-4752 (Hunter); 802-6809 (Baruch).

Newman Catholic Center. Sr. Barbara Ann Mueller, O.P.

Iona College, New Rochelle, 10801. Tel: 914-633-2340; 633-2632; Fax: 914-633-2363. Rev. Jack Replogle, O.F.M.; Mr. Michael Hovey; Mr. Carl Procario-Foley; Bro. Jim Carroll, C.F.C.; Ms. Peggy Clark; Ms. Kate Maloney.

John Jay College, 445 W. 59 St., Rm. 1274, 10019-1128. Tel: 212-237-8281; Fax: 212-237-8465. Rev. Donald L. Allen, M.M.

Manhattan College, Bronx, 10471. Tel: 718-862-7972 (college). Rev. James Cerbone, S.D.B.; Bros. Dennis Lee, F.S.C. Tel: 914-862-7477; James Loxham, F.S.C.

Manhattanville College, 2900 Purchase St., Purchase, 10577. Tel: 914-323-5150, Ext. 447; Fax: 914-694-2496. Ms. Joanne Carrubba.

Marist College, Poughkeepsie, 12601. Tel: 914-575-3130; 914-575-3000 ext. 2275; Fax: 914-575-3299. Bros. Frank Kelly, F.M.S.; Michael Williams, F.M.S.

Marymount College, 100 Marymount Ave., Tarrytown, 10591. Tel: 914-332-8248. Mr. Terence McCorry.

Marymount Manhattan College, 221 E. 71st St., 10021. Tel: 212-517-0597. Sr. Virginia Dorgan.

Mt. St. Mary College, Campus Ministry Office, 330 Powell Ave., Newburg, 12550. Tel: 914-569-3517. Rev. Mark Connell.

College of Mt. St. Vincent, Riverdale, 10471. Tel: 718-405-3200; 405-3215; 3216. Rev. John A. Vigilanti; Mrs. Harriet Carew.

College of New Rochelle, 29 Castle Pl., New Rochelle, 10805. Tel: 914-654-5339; Fax: 914-654-5866. Rev. John Rathschmidt, O.S.M.; Mrs. Mary Naughton.

New York Maritime College, 6 Pennyfield Ave., Fort Schyler, Bronx, 10465-4198. Tel: 718-409-7200. Rev. Michael Moynihan.

New York Medical College, Valhalla, 10595. Tel: 914-993-4000. Deacon Lawrence O'Toole.

New York University, Catholic Center at NYU, 58 Washington Square South, 10012. Tel: 212-674-7236; 212-998-1065 (voice mail); Fax: 212-473-2971. Revs. John C. McGuire, O.P.; John Gregory Maturi, O.P.; Sr. Thomasmari Gore, M.S.B.T.

Pace University, 20 Cardinal Hayes Pl., 10007. Tel: 212-962-3972. Bro. Michael Perez, S.S.S.

Pace University-Westchester, SUNY, Purchase, Bedford Rd., Pleasantville, 10570. Tel: 914-723-0704. Mrs. Dorothy Lambert.

Rockland Community College, 145 College Rd., Suffern, 10901. Tel: 914-574-4531; Fax: 914-574-4134. Mr. Michael Ver'Schneider.

St. John's University, 300 Howard Ave., Staten Island, 10301. Tel: 718-390-4497; 390-4473; 390-4492; Fax: 718-390-4475. Rev. John Concagh, C.M.; Ms. Angela Pedi; Ms. Mary Reese.

St. Thomas Aquinas, 175 Rte. 340, Sparkill, 10976. Tel: 914-398-4197; Fax: 914-398-4061. Sr. Catherine Patrice Morgan, O.P.; Rev. Aquinas Stack, O.Carm.

SUNY/New Paltz, St. Joseph's Church, 34 S. Chestnut, New Paltz, 12561. Tel: 914-257-3024. Rev. Raynold Thibodeau, O.F.M.Cap.

Wagner College & the College of Staten Island, Kairos House, 631 Howard Ave., Staten Island, 10301. Tel: 718-390-3461. Sr. Elaine R. Schenk, M.ID.

[HH] MISCELLANEOUS

NEW YORK. *Alfred E. Smith Memorial Foundation, Inc., The*, 1011 First Ave., 10022-4134. Tel: 212-371-1000, Ext. 3315; Fax: 212-753-5980. Rev. Msgr. Charles M. Kavanagh, Exec. Vice Pres.

America Press, Inc., The Business & Editorial Offices, 106 W. 56th St., 10019. Tel: 212-581-4640; Fax: 212-399-3596.
E-mail: america@americapress.org
Web site: www.americapress.org
Revs. Thomas J. Reese, S.J., Pres.; Charles M. Whelan, S.J., Vice. Pres.; Robert C. Collins, S.J., Sec. & Treas.

American Committee on Italian Immigration, Inc., 352 W. 44th St., 10036-5419. Tel: 212-247-7373; Fax: 212-265-5793.
E-mail: ACIMNY@aol.com
Web site: www.acimny.com
Rev. Joseph Fugolo, C.S., Natl. Exec. Sec. Total Staff 3. To insure fair immigration policy favoring reunion of families and cultural integration of Italian Americans.

Apostolate for Family Consecration, Inc., Canonical Global Center, PMB #26N, 350 Fifth Ave., Ste. 3304, 10018-0069. Tel: 212-971-1370. Jerome Coniker, Pres.

Archdiocesan Council of Catholic Nurses. (Includes Manhattan), 1011 First Ave., 10022. Tel: 212-371-1000.

Brooklyn Prep Alumni Association, Loyola Hall, Fordham Univ., 10458. Tel: 718-817-5447; Fax: 718-733-4456.
E-mail: mborelli@interport.net
Web site: www.users.interport.net/~mborelli/bpaa.htm
Rev. John D. Alexander, S.J., Moderator. Membership 4,356.

Calvary Fund, Inc. 1740 Eastchester Rd., Bronx, 10461. Tel: 718-518-2077; Fax: 718-518-2477.
E-mail: webmaster@calvaryhospital.org
Web site: calvaryhospital.org
Frank A. Calamari, Pres.; Dennis E. Berberich, Chm.

Cardinal Cooke Guild, 1011 First Ave., 10022; Fax: 212-371-1011, Ext. 2478.
E-mail: abberykkmoy@aol.com
Web site: www.activo.com/ccg
Official organization for information on the cause of canonization of Cardinal Terence J. Cooke.

Cardinal Cooke Memorial Foundation, 1011 First Ave., Room 1940, 10022. Tel: 212-371-1000.

Cardinal's Fund for Children, 1011 First Ave., Room 1130, 10022.

Carmel Housing Development Fund Co., Inc., 1011 First Ave., 10022. Tel: 212-371-1000; Fax: 212-826-8795. Rev. Msgr. Kevin L. Sullivan, Pres.

Catholic Actors Guild of America, Inc., The, 1501 Broadway, Ste. 518, 10036; Fax: 212-398-1868. William O'Mally, Pres.; Rev. Thomas Donlan, Chap.

Catholic Alumni Club of the Archdiocese of New York, 83 Christopher St., 10014. Tel: 212-243-6513.
E-mail: nycacemail.@aol.com
Web site: www.caci.org/cac/newyorkcac.html
Mary Doherty, Pres.

Catholic Big Brothers of New York, Inc., 45 E. 20th St., 10003. Tel: 212-477-2250; Fax: 212-477-2739.
E-mail: cbb@aol.com
Web site: www.cbbnyc.org
Total Assisted 350; Total Staff 15.

The Catholic Big Sisters. Archdiocese of New York Family Outreach & Education Center, 220A East 4th St., 3rd Floor, 10009. Tel: 212-475-3291; Fax: 212-475-0280.
E-mail: director@catholicbigsisters.org
Web site: www.catholicbigsisters.org
Total Families Assisted 180; Total Staff 6.

Catholic Daughters of the Americas and Its Courts, 10 W. 71st St., 10023. Tel: 212-877-3041; Fax: 212-724-5923.
E-mail: cdofanatl@aol.com
Web site: www.catholicdaughters.org
Eunice Riles, National Regent; Mrs. Margaret O'Brien, Contact Person.

Catholic Family and Human Rights Institute, 866 United Nations Plaza, Ste. 4038, 10017. Tel: 212-754-5948; Fax: 212-754-9291.
E-mail: c-fam@c-fam.org
Web site: www.c-fam.org
Austin Ruse, Pres.

Catholic Foundation for the Dominican Republic, 1011 First Ave., Room 1150, 10022. Rev. Msgr. James P. Cassidy, Ph.D., Pres.; Oscar de la Renta, Chm.; Gerald Cunningham, Treas.; Richard Concannon, Sec.

Catholic Health Care Network, 155 East 56th St., 2nd Floor, 10022. Tel: 212-752-7300; Fax: 212-752-7547.
E-mail: ricka@chcn.org
Web site: www.chcn.org
Mary Healey-Sedutto, Ph.D., Pres. & CEO.

Catholic High School Association of New York, 1011 First Ave., Room 1856, 10022. Tel: 212-371-1000; Fax: 212-758-3018.
E-mail: vicared@aol.com
Web site: www.ny-archdiocese.org

Catholic High Schools' Athletic Association of the Archdiocese of New York, 650 Grand Concourse, 10451. Tel: 718-585-5556. 4300 Murdock Ave., Bronx, 10466. Tel: 718-325-6423. Mr. Richard Tricario, Pres.

Catholic Interracial Council of N.Y., The, 899 10th Ave., 10019. Tel: 212-237-8600. Gerard W. Lynch, Pres.

Catholic League for Religious and Civil Rights, 450 Seventh Ave., 10123. Tel: 212-371-3191; Fax: 212-371-3394.
E-mail: cl@catholicleague.org
Web site: www.catholicleague.org
Dr. William A. Donohue, Pres. Total Staff 13.

Catholic Medical Mission Board, Inc., National Headquarters, 10 W. 17th St., 10011-5765. Tel: 212-242-7757; Fax: 212-807-9161; 242-0930.
E-mail: info@cmmb.org
Web site: www.cmmb.org
Rev. Msgr. Ferdinando D. Berardi; Rev. Msgr. Robert J. Fuhrman; Rev. William J. Scanlon, S.J.; Most Rev. William S. Skylstad, D.D.; Sr. Marilyn Fischer, S.F.P.; Thomas Flynn, M.D.; Thomas P. Melady, Ambassador; Patricia Smith, M.D.; Terry Kirch, Pres. & CEO; James A. Cunningham, C.P.A.; Mr. Charles J. Casamento; Sr. Peggy Egan, O.S.F.

Catholic Near East Welfare Association (CNEWA), 1011 First Ave., 10022. Tel: 212-826-1480; Fax: 212-826-8979.
E-mail: cnewa@cnewa.org
Web site: www.cnewa.org
His Eminence Edward Cardinal Egan, Pres. & Treas.; His Eminence William H. Keeler, Vice Pres.; Rev. Msgr. Robert L. Stern, Sec. Gen.; Rev. Denis Madden, Assoc. Sec. Gen.

Catholic Social Policy Coalition of the Archdiocese of New York, The, 1011 First Ave., Room 1150, 10022. Agnes Kearns, Pres.

Catholic Women's Union. Tel: 718-352-4825; Fax: 718-352-7249. c/o Eunice Vasile, 15-25 Utopia Pkwy., Queens, 11357. Eunice Vasile, Pres.; Anna K. Weisz, Vice Pres.; Hilda McGlew, Treas.; Mary Sophie Ruedi, Sec.

The Center for Spirituality and Justice. Tel: 914-633-8667; Fax: 914-633-5281.
E-mail: miriamcosu@juno.com
323 E. 198th St., Bronx, 10458. Tel: 914-633-8667; Fax: 914-633-5281. Rev. Thomas F. Madden; Bro. Charles A. Reutemann, F.S.C., Vice Pres.; Sr. Miriam Cleary, O.S.U., Sec. Total Assisted 15; Total Staff 3.

Centro Carismatico Catolico Hispano De La Arquidiocesis De Nueva York. Tel: 718-378-1734; Fax: 718-378-1819.
Web site: centrocarismatico.com
826 E. 166th St., Bronx, 10459. Tel: 718-378-1734; Fax: 718-378-1819. Rev. Msgr. Josu Iriondo, Dir.

Chinese Catholic Information Center, 86 Riverside Dr., 10024. Tel: 212-787-6969; Fax: 212-787-0260. Rev. Paul Chan (Taiwan), Dir. Total in Residence 3; Total Staff 3.

Christ House, Inc. 432 E. 142nd St., Bronx, 10454. Tel: 718-665-8740; Fax: 718-665-1665.
E-mail: jhanney@christhouse-nyc.org
Shared Residence for Religious and Young Men Lacking Family Support. Rev. John Gilvey, O.S.F.S.; Bro. James V. Hanney, C.F.C., Dir.

The Christophers, 12 E. 48th St., 10017. Tel: 212-759-4050; Fax: 212-838-5073.
E-mail: tci@idt.net
Web site: www.christophers.org
Gerald M. Costello, Pres. & Admin. A multi-media organization reaching millions with the Gospel message. Total Staff 39.

Committee for Mission Responsibility Society, Inc. The Propagation of the Faith, 1011 First Ave., 10022. Tel: 212-371-1000, Ext. 2700; Fax: 212-371-7220.
E-mail: spofny@aol.com
Rev. Msgr. Ferdinando D. Berardi, Dir.

Community of St. Egidio, U.S.A., Inc., P.O. Box 250299, 10025-1534. Tel: 212-663-1483; Fax: 212-663-4178.
E-mail: ppiscitelli@hotmail.com
Web site: www.santegidio.org
Paola Piscitelli, Pres.

Cor Mariae Development Fund Corporation, 1011 First Ave., 10022. Rev. Msgr. Kevin L. Sullivan, Pres. & Contact Person.

Cor Mariae Housing Development Fund, Inc., 1101 First Ave., 10022. Tel: 212-371-1000, Ext. 2400. Rev. Kevin L. Sullivan, Pres.

Cornelia Connelly Center for Education, Holy Child Middle School, 220 E. 4th St., 10009. Tel: 212-982-2287; Fax: 212-982-0547.
E-mail: info@ccceholychild.org
Sr. Mary Claire Ryan, S.H.C.J., Dir.; Sr. Marcia Sichol, S.H.C.J., Contact Person.

Courage, Church of St. John the Baptist, 210 W. 31st St., 10001. Tel: 212-268-1010; Fax: 212-268-7150.
E-mail: NYcourage@aol.com
Web site: http://world.std.com/~courage
Rev. John F. Harvey, O.S.F.S., Dir. Total Staff 3.

CUSA - An Apostolate of the Sick or Disabled, Inc., 63 Wall St., Ste. 1802, 10005. Tel: 201-437-0412.
E-mail: ams4@juno.com
Web site: www.cusan.org
Mrs. Joan Donnelly, Pres.

Dominican Friars' Guilds, 141 E. 65th St., 10021. Tel: 212-744-2410; Fax: 212-737-3875.
E-mail: ferrerrev@aol.com

St. Jude Dominican Missions, 141 E. 65th St., 10021. Tel: 212-744-2410; Fax: 212-737-3875. Rev. Raymond Ferrer Halligan, O.P., Dir.

Dominican Rosary Apostolate, 141 E. 65th St., 10021. Tel: 212-744-2410; Fax: 212-737-3875.

Deserving Poor Boys Priesthood Association, 141 E. 65th St., 10021. Tel: 212-744-2410; Fax: 212-737-3875.

St. Martin de Porres Guild, 141 E. 65th St., 10021. Tel: 212-744-2410; Fax: 212-737-3875.

Dominican Shrine of St. Jude, Inc., St. Catherine of Siena Priory, 411 E. 68th St., 10021. Tel: 212-249-6067; 988-8300; Fax: 212-988-8920.
E-mail: concog@ prodigy.org
Web site: www.ophomily.org
Very Rev. Christopher Johnson, O.P.; Rev. George Lawrence Concordia, O.P., Admin. Dir.

Don Bosco Harlem Association, Inc., 147-159 St. Nicholas Ave., 10026. Tel: 212-662-2693. Rev. George Hanna, S.D.B., Contact Person.

Elizabeth Seton Women's Center, Inc., 133 W. 70th St., 10023. Tel: 212-579-3657; Fax: 212-579-3659.
E-mail: eswc@.aol.com

Felix Varela Foundation, Inc., The, 1011 First Ave., 10022. Rev. Msgr. Octavio Cisneros, Pres.

Foundation of the Order of Friars Minor Province of the Most Holy Name, 126 West 32nd St., 10001. Tel: 212-967-6300; Fax: 212-967-6344.
E-mail: hnpt@hnp.org
Web site: www.ofm.org
Rev. John M. Felice, O.F.M., Pres.

Franciscan Missionary Charities, Inc., 135 W. 31st St., 10001. Tel: 212-631-0852; Fax: 212-736-8545. Revs. Ronald P. Stark, O.F.M., Pres.; Francis Kim, O.F.M., Exec. Vice Pres.

Franciscan Missionary Union, Province of the Most Holy Name. Headquarters, St. Francis Friary, 135 W. 31st St., 10001-3439. Tel: 212-736-8500; Fax: 212-594-2769.
E-mail: gordonl35@aol.com
Bro. Denis Clark, O.F.M., Prov. Promoter.
Three schools in Brazil.

Franciscans International, Inc., 211 East 43rd St., Room 1100, 10017-4707. Tel: 212-490-4624.

Franciscans of Holy Name Province Benevolence Trust, Inc., 126 West 32nd St., 10001-3202. Tel: 212-967-6344; Fax: 212-967-6730.
E-mail: hnp@hnp.org
Web site: hnp.org
Rev. Dennis M. Wilson, O.F.M., Trustee.

Franciscans of the Holy Name Province Sick, Aged and Retired Trust, 126 W. 32nd St., 10001-3202. Tel: 212-967-6300; Fax: 212-967-6344.
E-mail: hnp@hnp.org
Web site: www.ofm.org

Franciscans of the Holy Name Province Education and Formation Trust. Tel: 212-967-6300; Fax: 212-967-6344.
E-mail: hnp@hnp.org

Friends of American Art in Religion, Inc., 143 E. 43rd St., 10017. Tel: 212-682-5722; Fax: 212-370-5791. His Eminence Edward Cardinal Egan, Pres.; Rev. Msgr. Eugene V. Clark, Sec. & Treas.

Friends of RADIO MARIA, Inc., 352 W. 44th St., 10036. Tel: 212-246-9620; Fax: 212-265-5793.
E-mail: radiomny@radiomaria.org
Web site: www.radiomaria.org
Rev. Joseph Fugolo, C.S., Dir.

Fundacion Guadalupe, Inc., 1011 First Ave., Ste. 1233, 10022. Mr. Mario Paredes, Contact Person.

Gregorian University Foundation, The, 106 W. 56th St., 10019. Tel: 212-582-5433; Fax: 212-956-2921.
E-mail: gregorian@mindspring.com
Web site: www.the-gregorian.com
Rev. Eugene J. O'Brien, S.J., Pres.

Guild of Catholic Lawyers, The. Mailing Address: c/o Kelly, Drye, & Warren, 101 Park Ave., 10178. Tel: 212-808-7847; Fax: 212-808-7898. 1011 First Ave., 10022. Rev. George W. Rutler, Spiritual Dir.; Gregory de Sousa, Pres., Emeritus, Exec. Dir.

Healing Through God Word Ministries, Inc., P.O. Box 080525, 10308-0007. Sr. Jean Marie Timko, O.P., Pres. Legal Title: *Healing Through God Word Ministries, Inc./Apostolate of Intercession Healing & Teaching the Word of God.* An evangelistic ministry of teaching the scriptures, intercession, and healing. Involves missions, retreats, days of renewal, healing services, and Bible studies.

Hispanic Catholic Charismatic Center of the Archdiocese of New York. Tel: 718-378-1734; Fax: 718-378-1819.
Web site: centrocarismatico.com
826 E. 166th St., Bronx, 10459. Tel: 718-378-1734; Fax: 718-378-1819. Rev. Msgr. Josu Iriondo, Dir.

House of Peace, Inc. Tel: 718-547-3230; Fax: 718-547-1765. 1291 Allerton Ave., P.O. Box 696, Bronx, 10469-0696. Tel: 718-547-3230; Fax: 718-547-1765. Rev. Peter McCall, O.F.M.Cap.; Maryanne Lacy. Healing Prayer Center for the Peace of Christ Prayer Ministry.

The Housing Fund of the Archdiocese of New York, 1011 First Ave., 10022. Tel: 212-371-1000. Rev. Msgr. James J. Murray, Pres.; Rev. Msgr. Kevin L. Sullivan, Vice. Pres.; Rev. Msgr. Donald Sakano, Sec. & Treas.

Hungarian Catholic League of America, Inc., 414 E. 82 St., 10016. Tel: 212-327-2959; Fax: 212-535-9221. Rev. Dominic L. Csorba, O.F.M., Pres.; Rev. Msgr. William I. Varsanyi, P.A., Chm. Bd.; A. Petrak, Sec.

Incarnation Children's Center Fund, Inc., 42 Audubon Ave., 10032. Tel: 212-371-1000, Ext. 2400. Rev. Msgr. James J. Murray, Exec. Dir. Capacity 18.

Institute of the Helpers. 385 W. 263rd St., Bronx, 10471. Sr. Teresa Cole, Pres.

Intercommunity Center for Justice & Peace, 20 Washington Square N., 10011. Tel: 212-475-6677; Fax: 212-475-6969.
E-mail: icjpny@aol.com
Sr. Arlene Flaherty, O.P., Exec. Dir. Peace and Justice Center is Sponsored by 42 religious congregations. The congregation assists its members in implementing values of peace and justice according to social teachings of the church. Total Staff 4.

International Catholic Child Bureau/North America, Inc., 595 West End Ave., #10C, 10024. Tel: 212-595-9180; Fax: 212-595-3917. Mr. David J. Sauer, Vice Pres., Admin. Svcs., The Catholic Health Association. An international convening agency for child care professionals interested in developing pilot projects, training seminars, research and advocacy for the physical, psychological, social, spiritual and religious well being of all children worldwide.

International Catholic Organizations Information Center, Inc., 323 E. 47 St., 10017. Tel: 212-355-5557; Fax: 212-355-9865. Mr. Josef Klee, Pres.

Jesuit Seminary and Mission Bureau, Inc., 39 E. 83rd St., 10028-0810. Tel: 212-734-1144; Fax: 212-794-1036.
E-mail: jsmb@nysj.org
Web site: www.nysj.org
Revs. William J. Scanlon, S.J., Dir.; Gerard E. Braun, S.J.; Anthony F. LaBau, S.J.; James F. O'Brien, S.J.; Bros. John J. Campbell, S.J.; Jerome P. Menkhaus, S.J.

John LaFarge Institute, The, c/o America Press, Inc., 106 W. 56th St., 10019. Tel: 212-581-4640; Fax: 212-399-3596. Rev. Vincent T. O'Keefe, S.J., Dir.

LAMP Ministries, Inc. 2704 Schurz Ave., Bronx, 10465. Tel: 718-409-5062; Fax: 718-904-0048.
E-mail: tscheuring@lampministries.org
Web site: www.lampministries.org
Co-Directors: Tom Scheuring, Ph.D.; Lyn Scheuring, Ph.D. Assoc. Directors: Marybeth Greene; Ed Greene.

LaSalle New York City, Inc., 44 E. 2nd St., 10003; Fax: 212-529-3598.
E-mail: lsawyc@pipeline.com
Bros. Michael Corry, F.S.C., Chm.; Carl Malacalza, F.S.C., Vice Chm. Total Assisted 530; Total Staff 52.

Legion of Mary, Office, 1011 First Ave., 10022. Tel: 212-752-7966.
E-mail: senatus@banet.net
Rev. Gerald Murray, J.C.D., Spiritual Dir.

Lower East Side Catholic Area Conference-Pastoral Center, 23 Oliver St., 10038. Tel: 212-962-1850; Fax: 212-571-4126.

Lumen Dei, 340 W. 53rd St., 10019. Tel: 212-586-4447; Fax: 212-586-1640.
E-mail: ld.prodein@att.net
Rev. Wilberto Reyes Garced, Reg. Supr. Priests of Lumen Dei 1; Sisters of Lumen Dei 5.

Manhattan North Community Services, Inc., 91 Arden St., 10040. Niki Montaluo, Pres.

Maria Droste Services, 386 Park Ave. S., Ste. 903, 10016-8804. Tel: 212-889-4042; Fax: 212-889-3936. Legal Title: *St. Germaine's Services*. Betsy Selman-Babinecz, Dir.

Monsignor Robert Fox Memorial Shelter Housing Development, Inc., Fox House, 111 E. 117th St., 10035. Tel: 212-534-6634; Fax: 212-427-8507.
E-mail: foxsheller@aol.com
Sr. Florence Speth, Exec. Dir. Total Assisted 400 families uniqueTotal Staff 17.

Narnia Catechetical & Cultural Centre, Inc., 20 Sutton Pl. S., 10022. Mrs. Charles Teetor, Pres.; Mr. George Sim Johnston, Sec.-Treas.

National Federation for Life, 1011 First Ave., Room 1417, 10022.

National Office of the Devotees of Padre Pio, Inc., 1154 1st Ave., 10021. Mr. Mario Bruscki, Dir.

Nativity Mission Center, Inc., 204 Forsyth St., 10002. Tel: 212-477-2472; Fax: 212-473-0538.
E-mail: jpodsiadlo@aol.com
Web site: www.nativitymission.org
Rev. John J. Podsiadlo, S.J., Dir. Students 48; Total Staff 13.

Nazareth Housing, Inc., 519 E. 11th St., 10009. Tel: 212-777-1010; Fax: 212-777-1867.
E-mail: nazareth@earthlink.net
Web site: www.nazarethhousing.com

New York Catholic Forum, c/o St. Thomas More Church, 65 E. 89th St., 10128. George Sim Johnston, Chm.

New York Society of the John Paul II Foundation, Inc., 101 East 7th St., 10009. Tel: 212-475-4576; Fax: 212-674-4894. Mr. Michael Pajak, Pres. Tel: 718-383-9587.

Nocturnal Adoration Society of the United States, 184 E. 76th St., 10021. Tel: 212-288-5082; Fax: 212-717-8397.
E-mail: mariomsss@aol.com
Web site: www.sjbrcc.org
Congregation of the Blessed Sacrament. Rev. Mario Marzocchi, S.S.S., Natl. Dir.

North American College of Rome, Alumni Assoc. of. Tel: 718-549-4511; Fax: 718-796-5163. Mailing Address: St. Joseph's Seminary, 201 Seminary Ave., Yonkers, 10704. Rev. Msgr. Edmund J. Whalen, S.T.D., St. John Neumann Residence, 5655 Arlington Ave., Riverdale, 10471. Tel: 718-549-4511; Fax: 718-796-5163.

Northeast Hispanic Catholic Center, 1011 First Ave., 10022. Tel: 212-751-7045. His Eminence John Cardinal O'Connor, Pres.; Mario J. Paredes, Exec. Dir.

Partnership for Quality Education, Inc., 1011 First Ave., 10022. Tel: 212-371-1011, Ext. 3356; Fax: 212-371-6461.
E-mail: eddev@adnysch.org
Web site: projectyess.org
Rev. Msgr. Charles M. Kavanagh, Vicar Devel. Partnership for quality education, assisting 148 inner-city schools, Operates Project YESS, an initiative for capital improvements or repairs in inner-city schools.

Patrons of the Arts in the Vatican Museums, 143 E. 43rd St., 10017. Tel: 212-682-5722; Fax: 212-370-5791. His Eminence Edward Cardinal Egan, Chm. of the Board; Rev. Msgr. Eugene V. Clark, Treas. & Sec. Total Staff 2.

Pauline Books & Media. 78 Fort Pl., Staten Island, 10301. Tel: 718-447-5071; 447-5086; Fax: 718-816-1332. Legal Title: *Pauline Books & Media.* Other location: 150 E. 52nd St., 10022. Tel: 212-754-1110; Fax: 212-754-2268. Total in Residence 11; Total Staff 16.

Pax Christi Metro New York, 135 W. Fourth St., 10012. Tel: 212-420-0250; Fax: 212-673-0826.
E-mail: nypaxchristi@igc.apc.org
Rosemarie Pace, Coord. We are a regional chapter of Pax Christi USA, the national Catholic movement for peace.

Perpetual Help Center. Tel: 718-585-3678; Fax: 718-993-5870.
E-mail: jcoralluzz
Web site: www.perpetualhelpcenter.org
Redemptorist Fathers of New York. 294 E. 150th St., Bronx, 10451. Tel: 718-585-3678; Fax: 718-993-5870. Bro. Stephen Lendvay, C.SS.R.

Pius XII Foundation, Inc., 570 Lexington Ave., 33rd Fl., 10022. Tel: 212-319-0464. Bro. Robert Fontaine, C.S.C., Pres.

Providence Health Services Foundation, Inc., 1011 First Ave., 10022. Tel: 212-752-4722; Fax: 212-752-7351.
E-mail: mcatalano@chcsnet.org
Web site: www.phsf.org
Gerard M. Villucci, Contact Person.

Regina Coeli Society, Mailing Address: P.O. Box 939, 10272-0604. Tel: 212-374-5060. First Friday Club for the Catholic Women of New York City Police Dept. Jacquelyn Fleming, Pres.

S.H.A.R.E. - New York, Inc. 1601 Bronxdale Ave., Bronx, 10462. Tel: 718-518-1513.
E-mail: SHARNYFood@aol.com
Ms. Elisa Perry, Exec. Dir.

St. Ansgar Scandinavian Catholic League, 28 W. 25 St. 7th Fl., 10010. Tel: 212-675-0400; Fax: 212-620-4687.
E-mail: viggorambusch@redconnect.com
Web site: www.saintansgars.org
Rev. Philip J Sandstrom, Spiritual Dir.; Dr. Astrid M. O'Brien, Pres.; Revs. Thomas A. Nielson, Chap.; John E. Halborg, Dir. Programs, Editor of the Bulletin; Mr. Viggo B. Rambusch, Chm.

St. Anthony Welfare Center, c/o Chancery Office, Room #1940, 1011 First Ave., 10022. Tel: 212-371-1000.

St. Francis Counseling Center, Inc., 135 W. 31st St., 10001. Tel: 212-736-8500; Fax: 212-736-8545. Rev. Ronald P. Stark, O.F.M., Pres.

St. Francis Monastery Breadline for the Poor, Inc., 135 W. 31st St., 10001-3439. Tel: 212-736-8500; Fax: 212-736-8545. Rev. Ronald P. Stark, O.F.M., Contact Person.

St. Joseph's Union of Staten Island, New York Inc. 108 Bedell St., Staten Island, 10309. Tel: 718-984-9296. Sr. Una McCormack, O.P., Treas.

St. Patrick's International Inc., c/o Cusack and Stiles LLP, 61 Broadway, Ste. 2100, 10006-2894. Tel: 212-480-0400; Fax: 212-943-8534.
E-mail: spsoff@iol.ie
Rev. Kieran Birmingham, Pres.

St. Paul's Guild, Inc., 1011 First Ave., Room 1940, 10022. Tel: 212-371-1000. Rev. Msgr. Francis X. Duffy, Exec. Sec.

St. Rose's Settlement, 1011 First Ave., Room 1940, 10022. Tel: 212-371-1000.

St. Thomas Aquinas Foundation. National Headquarters (Order of Preachers, St. Joseph Prov.), 141 E. 65th St., 10021-6618. Tel: 212-737-5757; Fax: 212-861-4216. Very Rev. Norman Alfred Haddad, O.P., Pres. Legal Title: *St. Thomas Aquinas Foundation of the Dominican Fathers of the United States (STAF).*

Scalabrini Pastoral Center, 352 W. 44th St., 10036-5419. Tel: 212-247-7373.
E-mail: jfugolo@aol.com
Web site: www.scalabrini.org
Directed by The Pius Society of the Missionaries of St. Charles Borromeo, Inc. (NY Prov.). Revs. Joseph Fugolo, C.S., Dir.; Vincenzo Ronchi, C.S., Asst. Dir. Total Staff 2.

American Committee on Italian Migration (A.C.I.M.). Tel: 212-247-7373; Fax: 212-265-5793.

Scalabrini Promotion Office & Press Office for Migration. Tel: 212-247-7374; Fax: 212-265-5793.

Shrine of St. Jude, Inc., St. Stephen of Hungary Parish, 414 E. 82nd St., 10028. Tel: 800-688-JUDE. Revs. John M. Felice, O.F.M., Pres.; Neil J. O'Connell, O.F.M., Spiritual Dir.; Sr. Natalie M. Runfola, R.S.C.J., Exec. Sec.

Sisters of Charity of New York Charitable Trust. Tel: 718-549-9200; Fax: 718-884-3013.
E-mail: scny.org
Web site: www.scny.org
Sisters of Charity Center, 6301 Riverdale Ave., Bronx, 10471-1093. Tel: 718-549-9200; Fax: 718-884-3013. Trustees: Sr. Elizabeth A. Vermaelen; Sr. Audrey Boylan; Sr. Mary Ellen Butler; Sr. Kathleen Hanrahan; Sr. Ann Marie Lafferty.

Sisters of the Holy Child Jesus-African Province Office, 325 E. 33rd St., 10016-9401. Tel: 212-696-5503; Fax: 212-545-7804.
E-mail: shcjapdo@aol.com
Sr. Margaret Rogers, S.H.C.J., Interim Dir. Legal Title: *Sisters of the Holy Child Jesus - African Province Office for the African Apostolates.*

Society for the Renewal of Christian Art, The, 217 E. 66th St., 10021. Tel: 212-288-8186. Rt. Rev. Alban W. Boultwood, O.S.B., Chm. of the Bd.; Emily J. Bouchard, Pres. Purpose: To work for the renaissance of Christian Art in our time and to foster a Christian dimension in the New York art world.

Contemporary Christian Art, Inc., 217 E. 66th St., 10021. Tel: 212-288-8186.
(Affiliated with the Society for the Renewal of Christian Art.). Emily Bouchard, Dir. Purpose: To work with artists in designing and producing Christian Art, art used in worship, presented in a contemporary manner. To bring the creators of Christian art and their works into contact with those who seek good art.

Society of Helpers. Tel: 718-884-3100; Fax: 718-884-3101. 385 W. 263rd St., Bronx, 10471. Tel: 718-884-3100; Fax: 718-884-3101.
E-mail: nyhelper_nyhelper@claret.org
Web site: www.claret.org/~srmoore/goodc.html
Sr. Geraldine Finan, Supr. Sisters 6.

St. Elizabeth Seton Women's Center, Inc., 133 W. 70th St., 10023. Tel: 212-579-3657; Fax: 212-579-3659.
E-mail: eswc@aol.com
Sr. Elizabeth A. Vermaelen, S.C., Pres. Total Staff 1.

The Elizabeth Seton Housing Development Fund Corporation, 1991 Lexington Ave., 10035. Tel: 212-348-1655; Fax: 212-348-1822. Sr. Elizabeth Vermaelen, Pres. Total Assisted 87; Total Staff 3.

Thorpe Family Residence, Inc. 2252 Crotona Ave., Bronx, 10457. Total Assisted Families 16; Total Staff 10.

Tri-State Coalition for Responsible Investment, 20 Washington Sq. N., 10011. Tel: 212-475-6677; Fax: 212-475-6969.
E-mail: tricri@mindspring.com
Sr. Patricia Daly, O.P., Exec. Dir.

Trust for the Center for Migration Studies in New York, 27 Carmine St., 10014-4423. Tel: 212-675-3993; Fax: 212-727-3139.
E-mail: scbprov@aol.com
Rev. Joseph Fugolo, C.S.

United States Catholic Historical Society, The, 1011 First Ave., Ste. 1940, 10022. Tel: 800-225-7999. Dr. Brian Butler, Pres. & Chm. of the Bd.; Mr. Charles J. James, Exec. Dir.

The United States Catholic Widows and Widowers Assoc., Inc., 1011 First Ave., Room 1940, 10022. Tel: 212-371-1000, Ext. 2900.

Xavier Society for the Blind, 154 E. 23rd St., 10010. Tel: 212-473-7800. Revs. Alfred E. Caruana, S.J., Exec. Dir.; James F. O'Brien, S.J.; Joseph A. Latella, S.J.

BARRYVILLE. *New Hope Manor*, 35 Hillside Rd., 12719. Tel: 914-557-8353; Fax: 914-557-6603.
E-mail: newhopemnr@aol.com
Nicholas A. Roes, Exec. Dir.; Sr. Patricia Conway, O.P., Counselor & House Mother; Barbara Skidmore, Program Dir.; Sr. Maureen Conway, O.P., Dir. Education; Sr. Rose Respil, O.P., Dir. Rel. Educ.; Rev. Aquinas Thomas, S.A., Dir. Inservice Training. Members of the Board: Revs. Daniel Egan, S.A.; Arte Johnson, S.A.; Sr. Cecelia LaPietra, O.P.; Sr. Rita Shea, O.P. Sparkill Dominican Sisters. A live-in therapeutic community for the substance abuse rehabilitation of women 13-40 years old.

BEACON. *Carmelite Communion, Inc.*, 89 Hidden brooke Dr., 12508-3540. Tel: 845-831-5572; Fax: 845-831-5579. Sr. Michael Ann Cladek, O.C.D., Contact Person.

BRONX. *Abraham House, Inc.*, 342 Willis Ave., 10452. Tel: 718-292-9321; Fax: 718-292-5925.
E-mail: abrahamhse@aol.com
Rev. Msgr. Howard W. Calkins, Pres. Total Assisted 800; Total Staff 6.

American St. Boniface Society, Incorporated, Mailing Address: P.O. Box 1352, 10466-1352. Tel: 718-994-0989; Fax: 718-994-6119. Rev. Joachim Von Kersenbrock, S.J., Prov.; Germainiae Septentrionalis, Exec. Dir.

Calvary Holding Company, Inc., 1740 Eastchester Rd., 10461. Tel: 718-518-2251; Fax: 718-518-2674. Frank A. Calamari, Pres.; Thomas J. Fahey, Jr., M.D., Chairman.

Foundation of Christ the Redeemer, Institute Id Misioneros y Misioneras Identes, 2352 St. Raymond Ave., 10462. Tel: 718-828-2380; Fax: 718-828-4296.

Marian Residence Fund, 323 E. 198th St., 10458. Tel: 718-365-7410; Fax: 718-733-4498.
E-mail: ursruepr@aol.com
Sr. Marie-Celine Miranda, O.S.U., Trustee.

Mercy Center, Inc., 413 E. 144th St., 10454. Tel: 718-993-2789; Fax: 718-402-1594.
E-mail: administration@mercycenterbronx.org
Web site: www.mercycenterbronx.org
Sr. Mary Ann Dirr, F.S.M., Exec. Dir.; Sr. Mary Galeone, R.S.M., Assoc. Dir. Parenting skills courses, business training, support groups.

O.S.U. Charitable Trust, 323 E. 198th St., 10458. Tel: 718-365-7410; Fax: 718-733-4498.
Web site: ursruepr@aol.com
Sr. Marie-Celine Miranda, O.S.U., Prov.

St. Benedict the Moor Center, 281/283 St. Ann's Ave., 10454. Tel: 718-665-9693; Fax: 718-402-9536.
E-mail: moorcenter@aol.com
Anthony R. Jordan, Dir. Oper. Total Staff 12.

St. Joseph's Center, 275 W. 230th St., 10463. Tel: 718-796-4340; Fax: 718-796-4340. Rev. Francis E. Peluso, O.A.R., Contact Person. For the development of Lay Leaders, Cursillo Center, Marriage Encounter. (Spanish). Total in Residence 2; Total Staff 4; Capacity 45.

St. Joseph's School for the Deaf Childrens Fund, Inc., 1000 Hutchinson River Pkwy., 10465. Tel: 718-792-8308; Fax: 718-792-2532.
E-mail: dorothydhm@aol.com
The Children's Fund assists St. Joseph's School for the Deaf in meeting the needs of the children and their educational experiences.

Saint Jutta Foundation, Inc., c/o Rev. John Adam, S.J., Fordham University, Loyola Hall, 10458. Tel: 718-817-3671; Fax: 718-817-5717.
E-mail: hegyi@fordham.edu
Rev. John Adam, S.J., Contact Person.

The Resource Center for Community Development, Inc., 1900 Crotona Pkwy., 10460. Tel: 718-893-0778. Most Rev. Francisco Garmedia, Pres. Total Assisted 15,000; Total Staff 6.

Tolentine-Zeiser Community Life Center, Inc., 2345 University Ave., 10468. Tel: 718-933-6935; Fax: 718-733-1653.
E-mail: smct2
Total Assisted 172; Total Staff 19.

Youth Ministries for Peace & Justice, Inc., 1384 Stratford Ave., 10472. Tel: 718-328-5622; Fax: 718-328-5630.
E-mail: ympj@yahoo.com
Alexie Torres-Fleming, Exec. Dir.

BRONXVILLE. *Polish Knights of Malta, Inc.*, 1 Stoneleigh Plaza, #5-K, 10708. Tel: 914-793-4596; Fax: 914-771-4034.
E-mail: wsulimirski@compuserve.com
Mr. Witold S. Sulimirski, Pres.

ELMSFORD. *Clarion Home Health Network, Inc.*, 5 W. Main St., 10523. Tel: 914-345-0242; Fax: 914-345-0249.
E-mail: dbaldssn@chcn.org
Web site: www.chcn.org/clarion
Donna Baldassin Light, Exec. Dir.

ESOPUS. *Holy Shroud Guild.* Tel: 716-394-2606; Fax: 716-394-9215.
E-mail: fcb@shroud.org
Web site: www.shroud.org
Mailing Address: P.O. Box 993, Canandaigua, 14424. Tel: 716-394-2606; Fax: 716-394-9215.
E-mail: fcbrink@aol.com
Web site: shroud.org
Material Distribution Center, 294 E. 150th St., Bronx, 10451. Tel: 718-585-3678. Executive Council: Very Rev. Frederick C. Brinkmann, C.SS.R., Pres.; Rev. John Kennington, C.Ss.R.

GARRISON. *House of Nazareth Life Institute Ltd. (Nazareth Life Center)*, Philipse Brook Rd., Box 242, 10524. Tel: 914-424-3116. Sr. Marita Paul, F.S.P., Dir. Total in Residence 8; Total Staff 2.

HARTSDALE. *Marian Woods, Inc.*, 150 Ridge Rd., 10530. Tel: 631-363-6544. Sr. Mary Paschal Hill, R.S.M., Pres.

HIGHLAND FALLS. *Ladycliff College Alumnae Association, Inc.*, P.O. Box 104, 10928. Tel: 914-446-2973; 446-5921.

HIGHLAND MILLS. *Thevenet Montessori School*, 202 Country Rte. 105, Box 1003, 10930-1003. Tel: 914-928-6981; Fax: 914-928-9437.
E-mail: thevenet@frontiernet.net
Religious of Jesus and Mary. PreK-1 Enrollment 120.

HYDE PARK. *Focolare Movement National Center.* (Women), 204 Cardinal Rd., 12538. Tel: 914-229-0230, Ext. 133; Fax: 914-229-1770.
Web site: rc.net/focolare
Miss Sharry Silvi, Dir. Tel: 914-229-0712 (Tel); 914-229-1770 (Fax). Founded in Trent, Italy in 1943. International Headquarters are in Rome, Italy.Movement was approved in March 1962 with the aim of working toward the fulfillment of Christ's prayer for unity, that all may be one. More than four million people, in all walks of life, married and single, are committed in or connected with the Movement. Centers in over fifty countries. Call for additional information. Focolare Women's Centers: Tel: 718-828-1969; Fax: 718-892-0419.
2615 Schurz Ave., Bronx, 10465. Hortensia Lopez.
1017 Calhoun Ave., Bronx, 10465. Tel: 718-904-1898. Clare Zanzucchi.
99-28 64 Rd., Rego Park, 11374. Tel: 718-275-2824. Lucia Compostella. Focolare Movement National Center. (Men), 196 Cardinal Rd., 12538. Tel: 914-229-0307; Fax: 914-229-0269.
Web site: rc.net/focolare
Mr. Julian Ciabattini, Dir. Founded in Trent, Italy in 1943. International Headquarters are in Rome, Italy. Movement was approved in March 1962 with the aim of working toward the fulfillment of Christ's prayer for unity, that all may be one. More than four million people, in all walks of life, married and single, are committed in or connected with the Movement. Centers in over fifty countries. Call for additional information. Focolare Men's Centers:
167 Commonwealth Ave., Mount Vernon, 10552. Tel: 914-667-5916; Fax: 914-268-2451. Carlos Bajo.
187 Union Tpke., #19A & B, Forest Hills, 11375. Tel: 718-268-2413. Patrick Markey.

JAMAICA. *The Fellowship of the Beloved Disciple*; Fax: 718-739-7370.
E-mail: lallycp@aol.com
Web site: www.john17.org
Mailing Address: Immaculate Conception Monastery, 86-45 Edgerton Blvd., 11432. Co-Directors: Rev. Owen Lally, C.P.; Yvonne Zeller.

LIVINGSTON MANOR. *The Monastic Family of Bethlehem*, Grooville Rd., 12758. Tel: 914-439-4300; Fax: 914-439-3069.

MARYKNOLL. *Asian Catholic Church Fund*, P.O. Box 306, 10545. Tel: 914-941-7590. Rev. Richard Callaham, M.M.

The Asian Catholic News Fund, P.O. Box 306, 10545. Tel: 914-941-7590. Rev. Richard Callahan, M.M., Contact Person.

Friends of St. Maria Goretti, U.S.A., Inc., P.O. Box 0043, 10545-0043. Tel: 914-941-6372; Fax: 914-945-0715.
E-mail: gzilli@maryknoll.org
Web site: www.mariagoretti.org
Bro. Goretti Zilli, Pres. Tel: 914-941-4240; 914-941-7590; Rev. William T. Madden, M.M., Treas.; Mrs. Marie Finn, Sec.

Maryknoll Mission Association of the Faithful, P.O. Box 307, 10545-0307. Tel: 914-762-6364; Fax: 914-762-7031.
E-mail: mmaf@mkl-mmaf.org
Web site: www.maryknoll.org
Association Leadership Team: Sheila Matthews; Patrick Capuano; Gerry G. Lee. Purpose: promoting and further developing a Catholic global mission effort which is open to Catholic lay, clerical, and religious mission vocations. The Association recruits and trains Catholic lay women, lay men, Priests, Brothers, and Sisters to conduct mission work. The Association sponsors Catholic lay men, lay women, Priests, Brothers, and Sisters in the performance of mission work and provides them with financial and other necessary support in the performance of mission work. Active in Bolivia, Brazil, Cambodia, Chile, El Salvador, Kenya, Mexico, Peru, Sudan, Tanzania, Thailand, United States, Venezuela, and Vietnam.

Maryknoll Mission Association of the Faithful, Inc., Philadelphia, PA. Tel: 215-724-2747; Fax: 215-724-7158.

Maryknoll Mission Association of the Faithful, Inc., El Paso, TX. Tel: 915-533-7708.

Maryknoll Mission Association of the Faithful, Inc., Castro Valley, CA. Tel: 510-889-1787; Fax: 510-889-7150.

MIDDLE VILLAGE. *National Italian Apostolate Conference*, 66-05 79th Pl., 11379. Tel: 718-326-1911; Fax: 718-326-1883.
E-mail: wazo2@aol.com
Rev. Msgr. William A. Varvaro, S.T.L., J.C.D., Exec. Dir.

MOUNT VERNON. *Franciscan Mission Associates*, 274-280 W. Lincoln Ave., P.O. Box 598, 10550. Tel: 914-664-5604; Fax: 914-664-3017. Province of the Immaculate Conception. Very Rev. Robert M. Campagna, O.F.M., Prov.; Madeline Bonnici, Exec. Dir.

St. Dymphna Devotion, 274-280 W. Lincoln Ave., P.O. Box 598, 10550. Tel: 914-664-5604; Fax: 914-664-3017. Province of the Immaculate Conception. Very Rev. Robert M. Campagna, O.F.M., Prov.; Madeline Bonnici, Exec. Dir.

NEW ROCHELLE. *Christian Brothers Foundation, Inc.*, 33 Pryer Ter., 10804. Tel: 914-636-5227. Vincent Dougherty, Contact Person.

Songcatchers, Inc., 44 Liberty Ave., 10801. Tel: (Day)914-654-1178; (Eve)914-576-6774; Fax: 914-636-4376.
E-mail: osuliberty@aol.com
Sr. Beth Dowd, O.S.U., Dir. Program activities for elementary school children, including Summer Choir Camp, Concert Choir, and an after-school music program.

Ursuline Social Outreach, Inc., 39 Willow Dr., 10805. Tel: 914-633-7298; Fax: 914-633-7393.
E-mail: osust@aol.com
Sr. Eileen Fane, O.S.U., Pres.

NEWBURGH.

Newburgh Ministry, 9 Johnston St., 12550. Tel: 845-561-0070; Fax: 845-561-5087. Sr. Margaret Gaffikin, F.S.P., Chairperson, Bd. of Dir.; Sr. Pat Chaffee, Coord.

Our Lady of Comfort Women's Center, 91 Ann St., 12550. Tel: 914-561-6267; Fax: 914-565-0572. Nina Faulkner, Treas. Shelter for Women & Children.

OSSINING. *Dominican Sisters of Hope Ministry Trust*, 299 N. Highland Ave., 10562. Tel: 914-941-4420; Fax: 914-941-1125.
E-mail: eshea@ophope.org
Web site: www.ophope.org

PEEKSKILL. *My Father's House, Inc.*, 143 Lafayette Pl., 10566. Tel: 914-737-8704.
E-mail: rdlxmfh@aol.com
Rev. Ronald D. Lemmert, Pres.

PELHAM. *Passionist Communications, Inc.*, Mailing Address: P.O. Box 440, 10803-0440. Tel: 914-738-3344; Fax: 914-738-7652.
E-mail: sundaymass@aol.com
Web site: www.thesundaymass.org
Rev. Leo J. Gorman, C.P., Exec. Producer. Assoc. Producers: Revs. Paschal Smith, C.P.; Stephen Haslach, C.P.

Passionist Communications Center, 19 Second Ave., 10803-1417. Tel: 914-738-3344; Fax: 914-738-7652.

RIVERDALE. *Holy Innocents Foundation*, 5272 Post Rd., 10471. Kevin T. O'Reilly, Pres.

RYE. *Catholic Women's Network, Inc.*, 815 Boston Post Rd., 10580. Tel: 203-795-2800; Fax: 203-281-6051. Rev. Anthony Bannon, L.C.

Center for Spiritual Development, 96 Milton Rd., 10580. Tel: 914-967-7328; Fax: 914-967-7387. Ann Marie Wallace, Ph.D., Dir.

Pastoral Support Services, Inc, 815 Boston Post Rd., 10580. Tel: 914-773-1368. Bro. Juan Sabadell, Sec.

SCARSDALE. *Catholic Charismatic Renewal Office*, 194 Gaylor Rd., 10583. Tel: 914-725-1773; Fax: 914-725-5227.
E-mail: charismny@aol.com
Co-Liaisons: Sr. Pauline Cinquini, S.C.; Rev. William B. Cosgrove, Tel: 914-227-8382; Fax: 914-227-3951.
E-mail: cosgrove@idsi.net

SLEEPY HOLLOW. *RSHM Life Center, Inc.*, 32-34 Beekman Ave. N., 10591. Tel: 914-366-9710; Fax: 914-366-9713.
E-mail: susanrshm@exario.net
Sacred Heart of Mary. Total Assisted 330; Adults 180; Children 150; Total Staff 4.

SLOATSBURG. *St. Mary's Villa, Inc.*, 150 Sisters Servants Ln., P.O. Box 6, 10974-0006. Tel: 914-753-5100; Fax: 914-753-5100.
E-mail: ssminy@aol.com
Sr. Michele Yakymovitch, S.S.M.I., Pres.; Sr. Bonaventure Kalowsky, S.S.M.I., Sec.

SPARKILL. *Hallel Institute*, 175 Rte. 340, 10976-1047. Tel: 914-365-2277; Fax: 914-365-2279.
E-mail: hallel@worldnet.att.net
Web site: hallelvision.org
Rev. George J. Torok, Pres. Total in Residence 37; Total Staff 9.

One to One Learning, Inc., 175 Rte. 340, 10976. Tel: 914-359-3171.

STATEN ISLAND. *Eastern Franciscan Common Novitiate, Inc.*, 444 Woodvale Ave., 10309. Tel: 718-966-4851; Fax: 718-966-0814.
E-mail: srkk@juno.com
Sr. Mary McCarrick, O.S.F., Pres.; Sr. Annette Lucchese, F.S.R., Sec.

Emmaus Ministries, Ltd., c/o Church of St. Clare, 110 Nelson Ave., 10308. Tel: 718-984-7873; Fax: 718-966-8420. Monica Brown, Pres.; Rev. Msgr. Joseph P. Murphy, Vice Pres. & Contact Person.

Indian Knanaya Catholic Community of Greater NY, Inc., 94 Wilcox St., 10303. Tel: 914-494-7571; Fax: 914-494-9183.
E-mail: ikcc@hotmail.com
Jose Chummar, Pres.

Priests for Life, P.O. Box 141172, 10314. Tel: 718-980-4400; Fax: 718-980-6515.
E-mail: mail@priestsforlife.org
Web site: www.priestsforlife.org
Rev. Frank A. Pavone, National Dir.; Anthony DeStefano, Exec. Dir.

SUFFERN. *Covenant Corporation of Suffern, NY*, c/o Good Samaritan Hospital, 255 Lafayette Ave., 10901. Tel: 914-368-5000; Fax: 914-368-5430. Sr. Barbara Conroy, Pres.
Good Samaritan Foundation for Better Health, Inc., 255 Lafayette Ave., 10901-4869. Tel: 914-368-5151; Fax: 914-368-5342. Sr. M. Angelica Doris, Pres.; Michael A. Divers, Exec. Dir. Fundraising arm of Good Samaritan Hospital, Suffern, NY.

TARRYTOWN. *Ladycliff College Alumnae Association*, 88 Wilson Park Dr.
Religious of the Sacred Heart of Mary Charitable Trust, 50 Wilson Park Dr., 10591. Tel: 914-631-2979; Fax: 914-332-4735. Sr. Bernadette Kenny, Contact Person.

THORNWOOD. *Alpha Omega Family Center, Inc.*, 582 Columbus Ave., 10594. Tel: 914-749-3900; Fax: 914-749-3939.
Catholic Kid's Network, Inc., 582 Columbus Ave., 10594. Tel: 914-749-3900; Fax: 914-749-3939. Bro. Scott Madgey, L.C., Contact Person.
Center for Family Life, Inc., 582 Columbus Ave., 10594. Tel: 914-749-3900; Fax: 914-749-3939. Rev. Emilio Diaz-Torre, L.C., Contact person.
Consolidated Catholic Administrative Services, Inc., 584 Columbus Ave., 10594. Tel: 914-773-1368; Fax: 914773-1438. Revs. Anthony Bannon, L.C.; Juan Sabadell, L.C., Contact Person.
Familia USA, Inc., 582 Columbus Ave., 10594. Tel: 914-749-3900; Fax: 914-749-3939. Bro. Scott Madgey, L.C., Contact Person.
Helping Hands Medical Missions, Inc., 582 Columbus Ave., 10594. Tel: 914-749-3900; Fax: 914-749-3939. Rev. Emilio Diaz Torre, L.C.
Legion of Christ, Incorporated, 582 Columbus Ave., 10594. Tel: 914-749-3900; Fax: 914-749-3939. Rev. Peter Hopkins, L.C., Contact Person.
Montessori Community, Inc., 118 Whittier Dr., 10594. Mary McElroy, Vice Pres.
Regina Apostolorum, Inc., 582 Columbus Ave., 10594. Tel: 914-749-3900; Fax: 914-749-3939. Rev. Juan Sabadell, L.C., Contact Person.
Youth and Family Encounter, Inc., 582 Columbus Ave., 10594. Tel: 914-749-3900; Fax: 914-749-3939. Bro. Scott Madgey, L.C., Contact Person.

WALDEN. *Contemplative Outreach, Ltd.*, 257 St. Andrews Rd., 12586. Tel: 973-838-3384; Fax: 973-492-5795.
E-mail: office@coutreach.org
Web site: www.contemplativeoutreach.org
Rt. Rev. Thomas Keating, O.C.S.O., Chairperson; Gail Fitzpatrick-Hopler, Pres. Total Staff 6.

WEST HEMPSTEAD. *La Casa Sollievo Della Sofferenza Opera Di Padre Pio.* (The Home for the Relief of Suffering), c/o St. Thomas the Apostle Church, 24 Westminster Rd., 11552. Tel: 516-538-7465, Ext. 236; Fax: 516-538-6991. Official United States Office. Rev. Armand Dasseville, O.F.M.Cap., Natl. Dir. & Coord.

WHITE PLAINS. *Company of St. Paul*, 52 Davis Ave., 10605. Tel: 914-946-1019. Rev. Stuart Sandberg, Pres.
Religious of Divine Compassion Charitable Trust, 52 N. Broadway, 10603.

YONKERS. *Leviticus 25:23 Alternative Fund, Inc.*, 928 McLean Ave., 10704-4103. Tel: 914-237-3306; Fax: 914-237-3916.
E-mail: info@leviticusfund.org
Web site: www.leviticusfund.org
David C. Raynor, Exec. Dir.; Sr. Patricia Russell, O.S.U., Loan Officer; Ms. Elizabeth Wighton, Credit Officer.

[II] PERSONAL PRELATURES

NEW YORK. *Prelature of the Holy Cross and Opus Dei*, 139 E. 34th St., 10016. Tel: 646-742-2700; Fax: 646-742-2747.
E-mail: newyork@opusdei.org
Web site: www.opusdei.org
Very Rev. Arne A. Panula, Regl. Vicar for the U.S.; Rev. Msgr. James A. Kelly, Ph.D.; Rev. Msgr. Javier Garcia de Cardenas; Revs. Robert A. Brisson; James W. Albrecht. Other priests residing in New York: Revs. Bradley K. Arturi, J.C.D.; Martin Heneghan.
Overlook Study Center. 99 Overlook Cir., New Rochelle, 10804. Tel: 914-235-6128. Rev. Malcolm M. Kennedy, 330 Riverside Dr., 10025. Tel: 212-222-3285.

RELIGIOUS INSTITUTES OF MEN REPRESENTED IN THE ARCHDIOCESE

For further details refer to the corresponding bracketed number in the Religious Institutes of Men or Women section.

[0130]—*Assumptionists.*—A.A.
[0140]—*The Augustinians.* (Prov. of St. Joseph).—O.S.A.
[0330]—*Brothers of the Christian Schools.* (New York Prov.).—F.S.C.
[0600]—*Brothers of the Congregation of Holy Cross.*—C.S.C.
[0400]—*Canons Regular of the Order of the Holy Cross.* (Prov. of St. Odilia, Minneapolis, MN).—O.S.C.
[0470]—*The Capuchin Friars.* (St. Mary Prov.).—O.F.M.Cap.
[0270]—*Carmelite Fathers & Brothers.* (St. Elias Prov.).—O.Carm.
[0310]—*Congregation of Christian Brothers.* (Eastern U.S.).—C.F.C.
[0220]—*Congregation of the Blessed Sacrament.*—S.S.S.
[1330]—*Congregation of the Mission.*—C.M.
[1210]—*Congregation of the Missionaries of St. Charles.*—C.S.
[1000]—*Congregation of the Passion.* (St. Paul Prov.).—C.P.
[0480]—*Conventual Franciscans.* (Immaculate Conception Prov.).—O.F.M.Conv.
[0520]—*Franciscan Friars.* (Provs. of Most Holy Name of Jesus, Immaculate Conception; Commissariats of Holy Cross, Holy Family).—O.F.M.
[0530]—*Franciscan Friars of the Atonement.*—S.A.
[0650]—*Holy Ghost Fathers.* (Eastern Prov.).—C.S.Sp.
[0690]—*Jesuit Fathers and Brothers.* (New York Prov.).—S.J.
[0730]—*Legionaries of Christ.*—L.C.
[]—*Little Brothers of the Gospel.*
[0770]—*The Marist Brothers.*—F.M.S.
[0780]—*Marist Fathers.* (Northeastern Prov.).—S.M.
[0800]—*Maryknoll.*—M.M.
[0830]—*Mill Hill Missionaries.*—M.H.M.
[0720]—*The Missionaries of Our Lady of La Salette.*—M.S.
[0910]—*Oblates of Mary Immaculate.* (Eastern Prov.).—O.M.I.
[0430]—*Order of Preachers-Dominicans.* (St. Joseph Prov.).—O.P.
[0150]—*Order of the Augustinian Recollects.*—O.A.R.
[1020]—*Pauline Fathers and Brother.*—S.S.P.
[1030]—*Paulist Fathers.*—C.S.P.
[1040]—*Piarist Fathers.*—Sch.P.
[1070]—*Redemptorist Fathers.* (Baltimore Prov.).—C.SS.R.
[1190]—*Salesians of Don Bosco.* (St. Philip Prov.).—S.D.B.
[0990]—*Society of the Catholic Apostolate.*—S.A.C.
[1280]—*Stigmatine Fathers and Brothers.*—C.S.S.
[1300]—*Theatine Fathers.*—C.R.
[0560]—*Third Order Regular of Saint Francis.*—T.O.R.

RELIGIOUS INSTITUTES OF WOMEN REPRESENTED IN THE ARCHDIOCESE

[0130]—*Apostles of the Sacred Heart of Jesus.*—A.S.C.J.
[0230]—*Benedictine Sisters of Pontifical Jurisdiction.*—O.S.B.
[0330]—*Carmelite Sisters for the Aged and Infirm.*—O.Carm.
[3110]—*Congregation of Our Lady of the Retreat in the Cenacle.*—R.C.
[2410]—*Congregation of the Marianites of Holy Cross.*—M.S.C.
[3710]—*Congregation of the Sisters of Saint Agnes.*—C.S.A.
[1920]—*Congregation of the Sisters of the Holy Cross.*—C.S.C.
[1710]—*Congregation of the Third Order of St. Francis of Mary Immaculate.*—O.S.F.
[0760]—*Daughters of Charity of St. Vincent de Paul.*—D.C.
[0790]—*Daughters of Divine Charity.* (St. Joseph Prov.).—F.D.C.
[0850]—*Daughters of Mary Help of Christians.*—F.M.A.
[0860]—*Daughters of Mary of the Immaculate Conception.*—D.M.
[0950]—*Daughters of St. Paul.*—F.S.P.
[0810]—*Daughters of the Heart of Mary.*—D.H.M.
[0420]—*Discalced Carmelite Nuns.*—O.C.D.
[1050]—*Dominican Contemplative Nuns.*—O.P.
[1070-02]—*Dominican Sisters.*—O.P.
[1070-03]—*Dominican Sisters.*—O.P.
[1070-05]—*Dominican Sisters.*—O.P.
[1070-06]—*Dominican Sisters.*—O.P.
[1070-11]—*Dominican Sisters.*—O.P.
[1070-13]—*Dominican Sisters.*—O.P.
[1070-15]—*Dominican Sisters.*—O.P.
[1070-16]—*Dominican Sisters.*—O.P.
[1070-23]—*Dominican Sisters.*—O.P.
[1120]—*Dominican Sisters of the Roman Congregation.*—O.P.
[1170]—*Felician Sisters.*—C.S.S.F.
[1260]—*Franciscan Handmaids of the Most Pure Heart of Mary.*—F.H.M.
[1370]—*Franciscan Missionaries of Mary.*—F.M.M.
[1400]—*Franciscan Missionary Sisters of the Sacred Heart.* (Peekskill, NY).—F.M.S.C.
[1180]—*Franciscan Sisters of Allegany, New York.*—O.S.F.
[1310]—*Franciscan Sisters of Little Falls, Minnesota.*—O.S.F.
[1425]—*Franciscan Sisters of Peace.*—F.S.P.
[1190]—*Franciscan Sisters of the Atonement.*—S.A.
[1440]—*Franciscan Sisters of the Poor.*—S.F.P.
[2070]—*Holy Union Sisters.*—S.U.S.C.
[3790]—*Institute of the Sisters of St. Dorothy.*—S.S.D.
[2310]—*Little Sisters of the Assumption.*—L.S.A.
[2340]—*Little Sisters of the Poor.*—L.S.P.
[2470]—*Maryknoll Sisters of St. Dominic.*—M.M.
[2480]—*Medical Missionaries of Mary.*—M.M.M.
[2680]—*Misericordia Sisters.*—S.M.
[2720]—*Mission Helpers of the Sacred Heart.*—M.H.S.H.
[2710]—*Missionaries of Charity.*—M.C.
[1360]—*Missionary Franciscan Sisters of the Immaculate Conception.*—O.S.F.
[2790]—*Missionary Servants of the Most Blessed Trinity.*—M.S.B.T.
[2900]—*Missionary Sisters of St. Charles Borromeo.*—M.S.S.C.B.
[2750]—*Missionary Sisters of the Immaculate Heart of Mary.*—I.C.M.
[2860]—*Missionary Sisters of the Sacred Heart.*—M.S.C.
[2920]—*Mothers of the Helpless.*—M.D.
[3030]—*Oblates of the Most Holy Redeemer.*—O.SS.R.
[3035]—*Oblates of the Mother of Orphans.*—O.M.O.
[3760]—*Order of St. Clare.*—O.S.C.
[2010]—*Order of the Most Holy Redeemer.*—O.SS.R.
[3160]—*Parish Visitors of Mary Immaculate.*—P.V.M.I.
[3450]—*Religious of Jesus-Mary.*—R.J.M.
[3460]—*Religious of Mary Immaculate.*—R.M.I.
[3465]—*Religious of the Sacred Heart of Mary.* (Eastern North American Prov.).—R.S.H.M.
[2519]—*Religious Sisters of Mercy, Alma, MI.*—R.S.M.
[3490]—*Sacramentine Nuns.*—O.S.S.
[2970]—*School Sisters of Notre Dame.*—S.S.N.D.
[1680]—*School Sisters of St. Francis.*—O.S.F.
[0980]—*Sister Disciples of the Divine Master.*—P.D.D.M.
[1830]—*Sister of the Good Shepherd.*—R.G.S.
[3020]—*Sisters Oblates of the Blessed Trinity.*—O.B.T.
[0590]—*Sisters of Charity of Saint Elizabeth, Convent Station.*—S.C.
[0650]—*Sisters of Charity of St. Vincent de Paul, New York.*—S.C.
[0660]—*Sisters of Christian Charity.*—S.C.C.
[2360]—*Sisters of Loretto.*—S.L.
[2575]—*Sisters of Mercy of the Americas.*—R.S.M.
[3000]—*Sisters of Notre Dame de Namur.*—S.N.D.deN.
[3080]—*Sisters of Our Lady of Christian Doctrine.*—R.C.D.
[3740]—*Sisters of St. Casimir.*—S.S.C.
[1510]—*Sisters of St. Francis of the Mission of the Immaculate Virgin.*—O.S.F.
[3820]—*Sisters of St. John the Baptist.*—C.S.J.B.
[3830-05]—*Sisters of St. Joseph.*—C.S.J.
[3890]—*Sisters of St. Joseph of Peace.*—C.S.J.P.
[0260]—*Sisters of the Blessed Sacrament for Indians and Colored People.*—S.B.S.
[3140]—*Sisters of the Catholic Apostolate (Pallottine).*—C.S.A.C.
[2980]—*Sisters of the Congregation de Notre Dame.*—C.N.D.
[0970]—*Sisters of the Divine Compassion.*—R.D.C.
[1000]—*Sisters of the Divine Providence of Kentucky.*—C.D.P.
[1990]—*Sisters of the Holy Names of Jesus & Mary.*—S.N.J.M.
[3320]—*Sisters of the Presentation of the B.V.M.* (Newburgh; Staten Island).—P.B.V.M.
[3320]—*Sisters of the Presentation of the B.V.M.* (Aberdeen, SD).—P.B.V.M.
[3470]—*Sisters of the Reparation of the Congregation of Mary.*—S.R.C.M.
[3480]—*Sisters of the Resurrection.*—C.R.
[1490]—*Sisters of the Third Franciscan Order (Syracuse).*
[3600]—*Sisters, Servants of Mary.*—S.M.
[2160]—*Sisters, Servants of the Immaculate Heart Of Mary.*—I.H.M.
[1890]—*Society of Helpers.*—H.H.S.
[2460]—*Society of Mary Repartrix.*—S.M.R.
[4040]—*Society of St. Ursula.*—S.U.
[4060]—*Society of the Holy Child Jesus.*—S.H.C.J.
[4070]—*Society of the Sacred Heart.*—R.S.C.J.
[4110]—*Ursuline Nuns.*—O.S.U.
[4130]—*Ursuline Sisters (Tildonk).*—O.S.U.

[4230]—*Xaverian Missionary Sisters.*—X.M.M.

ARCHDIOCESAN CEMETERIES

HAWTHORNE. *Cemetery of the Gate of Heaven.*
LONG ISLAND CITY. *Calvary.*
MONSEY. *Cemetery of the Ascension.*
STATEN ISLAND. *Cemetery of the Resurrection.*

NECROLOGY

✠ Vaughan, Most Rev. Austin B., (Retired). —Died June 25, 2000.
† Attridge, Rev. Msgr. Terence J, Dobbs Ferry, NY Sacred Heart Church. —Died April 20, 2000.
† Brady, Daniel J, Armonk, NY St. Patrick. —Died March 8, 2000.
† Breen, John P., (Retired). —Died Nov. 30, 2000.
† Clifford, David K, Valhalla, NY Holy Name of Jesus. —Died March 7, 2000.
† Conroy, Edward M, Bronx, NY St. Raymond. —Died Feb. 5, 2000.
† Considine, Rev. Msgr. John J, Bronx, NY St. Barnabas. —Died July 29, 2000.
† DeMunnik, Shawn, New York, NY St. Mary. —Died Sept. 28, 2000.
† Diersam, Carl G. —Died Jan. 10, 2001.
† Farrelly, Thomas J, Bronx, NY Blessed Sacrament. —Died Aug. 25, 2000.
† Flannery, Michael J., (Retired). —Died Jan. 16, 2000.
† Glancy, Alfred P, Kingston, NY St. Joseph Church. —Died Jan. 22, 2001.
† Hammer, Rev. Msgr. Edward, Haverstraw, NY St. Mary. —Died April 4, 2000.
† Jordan, Patrick J., (Sick Leave). —Died May 1, 2000.
† Laurenzano, Roch M., (Retired). —Died June 19, 2000.
† Loftus, Rev. Msgr. Robert B., (Retired). —Died Aug. 5, 2000.
† Madrid, Ramon, Rhinebeck, NY The Good Shepherd. —Died Feb. 2, 2000.
† Mahoney, Rev. Msgr. Francis X., (Retired). —Died Sept. 29, 2000.
† Marks, Kenneth L, Bronx, NY St. Benedict. —Died July 29, 2000.
† Murray, John J, Port Jervis, NY Immaculate Conception. —Died Nov. 30, 2000.
† O'Brien, Rev. Msgr. Cornelius M, Port Chester, NY Our Lady of Mercy. —Died Dec. 18, 2000.
† Pacacha, Joseph, (Retired). —Died May 8, 2000.
† Pakulniewicz, Rev. Msgr. Raphael F, Staten Island, NY St. Anthony. —Died May 8, 2000.
† Phillips, Thomas R., (Retired). —Died Nov. 30, 2000.
† Pisanelli, Humbert D., (Retired). —Died July 23, 2000.
† Quirk, Rev. Msgr. Edward J, Pearl River, NY St. Aedan. —Died Jan. 9, 2001.
† Rigney, Rev. Msgr. James F., (Retired). —Died Aug. 31, 2000.
† Rooney, William A, Monroe, NY Sacred Heart Church. —Died Nov. 13, 2000.
† Shevlin, Rev. Msgr. John G, Bangall, NY Immaculate Conception. —Died May 21, 2000.
† Sullivan, Rev. Msgr. Daniel L, Staten Island, NY Blessed Sacrament. —Died June 6, 2000.
† Thomas, Rev. Msgr. Gartland A., (Retired). —Died Jan. 8, 2000.
† Vier, Rev. Msgr. Henry J., (Retired). —Died Jan. 10, 2001.
† Warren, William, Bronx, NY St. Margaret of Cortona. —Died April 18, 2000.
† Welsh, David B., (Retired). —Died Sept. 6, 2000.

Diocese of Norwich

(Dioecesis Norvicensis)

Most Reverend

DANIEL A. HART, D.D.

Bishop of Norwich; ordained February 2, 1953; consecrated Auxiliary Bishop of Boston October 18, 1976; appointed September 12, 1995; installed as Bishop of Norwich November 1, 1995. *Res., 274 Broadway, Norwich, CT, 06360.*

Chancery: 201 Broadway, Norwich, CT, 06360.
Tel.: 860-887-9294; Fax: 860-886-1670.

Web site address: www.norwichdiocese.org

ESTABLISHED AUGUST 6, 1953.

Square Miles 1,978.

CORPORATE TITLE: *The Norwich Roman Catholic Diocesan Corporation.*

Comprises the Counties of Middlesex, New London, Tolland and Windham in the State of Connecticut and Fishers Island, a portion of Suffolk County in the State of New York.

For legal titles of parishes and diocesan institutions, consult the Chancery Office.

STATISTICAL OVERVIEW

Personnel	
Bishop	1
Priests: Diocesan Active in Diocese	92
Priests: Active Outside Diocese	10
Priests: Diocesan in Foreign Missions	1
Priests: Retired, Sick or Absent	36
Number of Diocesan Priests	139
Religious Priests in Diocese	64
Extern Priests in Diocese	7
Ordinations:	
Diocesan Priests	1
Religious Priests	2
Transitional Deacons	2
Permanent Deacons	48
Permanent Deacons in Diocese	48
Total Brothers	23
Total Sisters	269
Parishes	
Parishes	78
With Resident Pastor:	
Resident Diocesan Priests	65
Resident Religious Priests	12
Without Resident Pastor:	
Administered by Priests	1
Missions	10
Pastoral Centers	23
Professional Ministry Personnel:	
Brothers	2
Sisters	18
Lay Ministers	34
Welfare	
Homes for the Aged	3
Total Assisted	242
Special Centers for Social Services	1
Total Assisted	165
Educational	
Diocesan Students in Other Seminaries	12
Seminaries, Religious	1
Students Religious	30
Total Seminarians	42
High Schools, Diocesan and Parish	3
Total Students	1,013
High Schools, Private	3
Total Students	1,147
Elementary Schools, Diocesan and Parish	22
Total Students	4,543
Catechesis/Religious Education:	
High School Students	2,581
Elementary Students	17,466
Total Students Under Catholic Instruction	26,792
Teachers in the Diocese:	
Priests	8
Brothers	1
Sisters	19
Vital Statistics	
Receptions into the Church:	
Infant Baptism Totals	3,237
Adult Baptism Totals	153
Received into Full Communion	291
First Communions	2,979
Confirmations	2,245
Marriages:	
Catholic	675
Interfaith	233
Total Marriages	908
Deaths	2,289
Total Catholic Population	225,016
Total Population	633,722

Former Bishops—Most Rev. BERNARD J. FLANAGAN, D.D., J.C.D., ord. Dec. 8, 1931; cons. Nov. 30, 1953; installed Dec. 9, 1953; transferred to See of Worcester, Aug. 12, 1959; retired March 31, 1983; died Jan. 28, 1998.—Most Rev. VINCENT J. HINES, D.D., J.C.D., ord. May 2, 1937; appt. Nov. 27, 1959; cons. March 17, 1960; retired June 17, 1975; died April 23, 1990.—Most Rev. DANIEL P. REILLY, D.D., ord. May 30, 1953; appt. June 17, 1975; cons. Aug. 6, 1975; transferred to See of Worcester, Oct. 27, 1994; installed Dec. 8, 1994.

Office of the Bishop—Mrs. ALICE PUDVAH, Administrative Asst., Ext. 234. Mrs. REGINA WIEGERT, Sec., Ext. 246.

The Chancery

Chancery—201 Broadway, Norwich, 06360. Tel: 860-887-9294; Fax: 860-886-1670.

Vicar General—Rev. Msgr. THOMAS R. BRIDE, P.A., V.G., K.S.G., Ext. 231. Mrs. ANNA DEPTA, Sec., Ext. 235.

Chancellor—Rev. Msgr. ROBERT L. BROWN, Ext. 232. Mrs. SUSAN SULLIVAN, Sec., Ext. 236.

Diocesan Attorney—MICHAEL E. DRISCOLL, Esq., *22 Courthouse Sq., Norwich, 06360.* Tel: 860-889-3321.

Diocesan Attorney Emeritus—JAMES J. DUTTON, JR., Esq., K.S.G., *22 Courthouse Sq., Norwich, 06360.* Tel: 860-889-3321.

Diocesan Computer Center—Mrs. ANITA SINCLAIR, System Admin., Ext. 240.

Diocesan Finance Office—Mr. WILLIAM J. CONNELL, Diocesan Finance Officer; Mr. VICTOR WELTIG, Asst. Controller; MARY ANN WILLIAMS, Bookkeeper, Lay Pension; Ms. ROBIN HOLTSCLAW, Risk Mgr. (CMRS); Ms. JANET WEST, Accounts Receivable; Mrs. ANN MARIE OSOWSKI, Sec., Lay Pension.

College of Consultors—Rev. Msgr. THOMAS R. BRIDE, P.A., V.G., K.S.G.; Rev. Msgr. HENRY N. ARCHAMBAULT, P.A.; Rev. Msgr. ROBERT L. BROWN; Rev. Msgr. ANTHONY S. ROSAFORTE; Revs. RUSSELL L. BOISVERT; LAURENCE A.M. LAPOINTE; MARK O'DONNELL.

Presbyteral Council—Most Rev. DANIEL A. HART, D.D., Pres.; Revs. ROBERT CRONIN, Chm. RUSSELL L. BOISVERT, Vice Chm. ROLAND C. CLOUTIER, Sec. Members: Rev. Msgr. HENRY N. ARCHAMBAULT, P.A., J.C.D.; Rev. Msgr. THOMAS R. BRIDE, P.A., V.G., K.S.G.; Rev. Msgr. ROBERT L. BROWN; Rev. Msgr. RICHARD P. LAROCQUE; Rev. Msgr. ANTHONY S. ROSAFORTE; Very Revs. JOSEPH H. HANKS; LAURENCE A.M. LAPOINTE; ANTHONY P. GRUBER; JOHN WHITE; Revs. ARTHUR A. ARCHER; ROBERT W. BARNES; JAMES P. CARINI; LESZEK JANIK; JOHN W. MCWEENEY, M.S.; MARK D. O'DONNELL; MICHAEL PHILLIPPINO; RICHARD J. RICARD; MICHAEL SMITH; ROBERT WASHABAUGH; WILLIAM J. OLESIK.

Deans—Very Rev. ANTHONY GRUBER, Putnam; Very Rev. LAURENCE A.M. LAPOINTE, Willimantic; Very Rev. JOHN J. WHITE, Vernon; Rev. Msgr. HENRY N. ARCHAMBAULT, P.A., J.C.D., Norwich; Very Rev. THOMAS J. SMITH, New London; Very Rev. JOSEPH H. HANKS, Old Saybrook.

Diocesan Pastoral Council—Most Rev. DANIEL A. HART, D.D., Chm.; Rev. Msgr. THOMAS R. BRIDE, P.A., V.G., K.S.G.; Rev. Msgr. HENRY ARCHAMBAULT, P.A., J.C.D.; Rev. Msgr. ROBERT L. BROWN, Chancellor; Rev. Msgr. WILLIS W. WEST; Ms. DIANE BAKER; Rev. ROBERT W. BARNES; Ms. SARAH BECKER; Mrs. CAROL CONKLIN; Deacon AL R. FECTEAU; Mrs. NOREEN GRAVEL, R.N.; Bro. J. ROBERT HOULIHAN, C.F.X.; Mrs. AGNES KELLY; Sr. MARY ALICE KLINE, R.S.M.; Dr. ROBERT MILLER, Ph.D.; Dr. PETER MOORE, Ph.D.; Mrs. JUDITH PAPPAGALLO; Deacon ALEXANDER SAUNDERS; Mrs. FRANCES SCHOEN; Mr. JAMES SMART.

The Tribunal

Diocesan Tribunal—17 Otis St., Norwich, 06360. Tel: 860-887-9294.

Judicial Vicar—Rev. Msgr. HENRY N. ARCHAMBAULT, P.A., J.C.D., Ext. 250.

Adjutant Judicial Vicar—Revs. JOHN W. MCWEENEY, M.S., J.C.L.; LESZEK JANIK, J.C.L., Ext. 256.

Judges—Revs. J. CLIFFORD CURTIN; WILLIAM J. FLYNN; LESZEK JANIK, J.C.L.; FRANCIS J. O'KEEFE; Very Rev. JOHN J. WHITE; GEORGE J. RICHARDS, Ext. 263. Sr. SALLY TOLLES, D.H.S., J.D., J.C.L., Ext. 255.

Defenders of the Bond—Revs. ROGER J. LAMOUREUX, O.M.I., Ext. 253. JOSEPH CASTALDI, J.C.D.

Advocates—Revs. RUSSELL L. BOISVERT; MICHAEL T. DONOHUE; PAUL J. GAUMOND; PAUL L. HEBERT; WILLIAM J. FLYNN; RUSSELL F. KENNEDY; FRANCIS A. LISZEWSKI; ROBERT WASHABAUGH; LEO S. SUTULA; STANLEY J. SZCZAPA; Sr. BEATRICE THEROUX, D.H.S. Auditors: Deacons R. PHILIP HAYES; MELVIN NYGAARD.

Secretary of the Tribunal—Mrs. MARY J. SHEA, Ext. 254.

Notaries—Rev. Msgr. THOMAS R. BRIDE, P.A., V.G., K.S.G.; Rev. Msgr. ROBERT L. BROWN; Mrs. MARY J. SHEA.

Vicar for Clergy—Rev. Msgr. RICHARD P. LAROCQUE, Ext. 258. Mrs. SUSAN GARDINER, Sec., Ext. 261.

Diocesan Offices, Ministries, Societies

Annual Bishop's Appeal (ABA)—See Development, Diocesan Office.

Bishop's Liaison with Retired Clergy—Rev. Msgr. RICHARD P. LAROCQUE, *The Chancery, 201 Broadway, Norwich, 06360*. Tel: 860-887-9294, Ext. 258.

Bishop's Delegate to Hispanic Permanent Deacons—Mr. JESUS A. DIEZ CANSECO, *110 Pruett Pl., Oakdale, 06370*.

Diocesan Finance Council—Most Rev. DANIEL A. HART, D.D., Chm.; Rev. Msgr. THOMAS R. BRIDE, P.A., V.G., K.S.G.; Very Rev. THOMAS SMITH; Rev. KENNETH FLINT; Mr. JAMES CRONIN; Mr. PETER LAMALFA; Mrs. JOYCE PAGE; Mr. BERNARD PHANEUF; Mr. WILLIAM MCGURK; Mrs. DIANE KELLY; Mr. TERRENCE CAHILL; Mr. KENNETH PARZYCH; Mr. VINCENT ROEMMELE.

Diocesan Panel of Pastors, Canon 1742—Rev. Msgr. ANTHONY ROSAFORTE; Rev. RUSSELL L. BOISVERT; Very Revs. ANTHONY GRUBER; JOHN J. WHITE.

Diocesan Pastoral Council—See Chancery listing.

Board of Education—See School Office.

Building Commission—Rev. Msgr. WILLIS W. WEST; Very Rev. JOHN J. WHITE; Revs. MICHAEL T. DONOHUE; ROBERT A. MURPHY, M.S.A.; Mr. GERARD HALL.

Campaigns—

Campaign for Human Development—Rev. MICHAEL T. DONOHUE, Diocesan Dir., *St. Matthias Church, 317 Chesterfield Rd., P.O. Box 25, East Lyme, 06333-0025*. Tel: 860-739-5208; Fax: 860-739-0524.

Catholic Relief Services—Rev. Msgr. ROBERT L. BROWN, Dir.; Mrs. SUSAN SULLIVAN; Sec., *201 Broadway, Norwich, 06360-4328*. Tel: 860-887-9294.

Campus Ministry—Rev. LAURENCE A.M. LAPOINTE, Diocesan Dir., *Newman Hall, 290 Prospect St., Willimantic, 06226*. Tel: 860-423-0856; Fax: 860-456-8083. (See separate category under Institutions for details).

Middletown—Rev. LOUIS A. MANZO, C.S.C., *Wesleyan University - The University Chaplains, 171 Church St., Middletown, 06459-3625*. Tel: 860-685-2777, Ext. 2706; Fax: 860-685-2821.

New London—Rev. LAURENCE A.M. LAPOINTE, Chap., *Connecticut College, P.O. Box 5203, New London, 06320-5203*. Tel: 860-439-2452; Fax: 860-439-2463.

Storrs—Chaplains: Revs. RICHARD K. GROSS, S.J.; JAMES DRESSMAN, S.J.; PAUL D. HOLLAND, S.J.; Sr. ALBERTA SUROWIEC, F.S.S.J., *University of Connecticut - St. Thomas Aquinas Chapel, 46 N. Eagleville Rd., Storrs, 06268-1710*. Tel: 860-429-6436; Fax: 860-429-2809.

Catechetical Ministry, Office of Director—See Office for Faith Formation.

Catholic Charities-Catholic Family Services—

Diocesan Director—Mr. JOHN SMEY, L.C.S.W., Exec. Dir., *331 Main St., Norwich, 06360*. Tel: 860-889-8346; Fax: 860-889-2658.

Comprehensive Emergency Services—TONI GRIGG, M.A., Prog. Mgr.

District Offices—New London: *32 Huntington St., New London, 06320*. Tel: 860-443-5328; Fax: 860-443-6013. IRIS ORITZ, M.A., Supvr. DAWN WORKS, B.G.S., Social Worker; Norwich: *331 Main St., Norwich, 06360*. Tel: 860-889-8346; Fax: 860-889-2658. Sr. SUSANNE GEBRIAN, M.H.S.H., Supvr. Social Worker; ROSALINDA BAZINET, Program Coord.

Adolescent Substance Abuse Treatment—331 Main St., Norwich, 06360. Tel: 860-889-8346; Fax: 860-889-2658. LYNN WELCH, M.A., Prog. Coord.

Adoption Services—331 Main St., Norwich, 06360. Tel: 860-889-8346; Fax: 860-889-2658. MAREK KUKULKA, L.M.F.T., Prog. Mgr. CELIA ROBERT, L.C.S.W., Prog. Supvr. PATRICIA SHELBERG, M.S.W., Social Worker.

Behavioral Health Clinic—331 Main St., Norwich, 06360. Tel: 860-889-8346; Fax: 860-889-2658. MAREK KUKULKA, L.M.F.T., Prog. Mgr. BRIDGETTE JACKSON, Supvr.

Office of Family Life—331 Main St., Norwich, 06360. Tel: 860-889-8346; Fax: 860-889-2658. MAREK KUKULKA, L.M.F.T., Prog. Mgr. MICHAEL PETRIDES, M.S., Supvr.

Pregnancy Program—331 Main St., Norwich, 06360. Tel: 860-889-8346; Fax: 860-889-2658. TONI GRIGG, M.A., Prog. Mgr. ROSALINDA BASINET, Assoc. Prog. Coord.; Willimantic: *115 Ash St., Windham, 06280*. Tel: 860-423-7065; Fax: 860-456-1096. DIANE LAMBERT, M.P.H., Supvr.

Catholic Mutual Relief Society—Diocesan Insurance, Ms. ROBIN HOLTSCLAW, Claims/Risk Mgr. Office for all claims: *Catholic Mutual Group, 467 Bloomfield Ave., Bloomfield, 06002*. Tel: 800-331-2561; Fax: 860-726-9412. National Office, *Catholic Mutual Relief Society, 4223 Center St., Omaha, NE, 68105*. Tel: 1-800-228-6108.

Catholic Youth Organization (CYO)—See Faith Formation, Office for.

CCD—See Faith Formation, Office for.

Cemetery Corporation and Subsidiaries, Diocesan Cemeteries—Rev. Msgr. WILLIS W. WEST, Dir., *St. Joseph Rectory, 99 Jackson St., Willimantic, 06226-3077*. Tel: 860-423-8439. NICHOLAS W. MIGNONE, Mgr., Office: *815 Boswell Ave., Norwich, 06360-2536*. Tel: 860-887-1019; Fax: 860-889-4804. (For details on individual cemeteries see separate listing.) The following cemeteries are subsidiaries of the Norwich Diocesan Cemetery Corp. *815 Boswell Ave., Norwich, 06360-2536*. Tel: 860-887-1019.

New London—St. Mary Cemetery of New London Corp., 600 Jefferson Ave., New London, 06320-2412. Tel: 860-443-3465 (Office).

Norwich—St. Mary & St. Joseph Cemetery Corp., 815 Boswell Ave., Norwich, 06360-2536. Tel: 860-887-1019.

Taftville—Sacred Heart Cemetery Corp., Harland Rd., Taftville, 06380., Cemetery Office: *815 Boswell Ave., Norwich, 06360-2536*. Tel: 860-887-1019.

Uncasville—St. Patrick Cemetery, Depot Rd., Uncasville, 06382., Cemetery Office: *815 Boswell Ave., Norwich, 06360-2536*. Tel: 860-887-1019.

Westbrook—Resurrection Cemetery Corp., Rte. 145, Westbrook, 06498. Tel: 860-399-6503 (Cemetery Office).

Censor of Books—Rev. WILLIAM O'ROURKE, S.T.D., *St. Stephen Rectory, 130 Old Turnpike Rd., Box 222, Quinebaug, 06262-0222*. Tel: 860-935-5205. Rev. ROBERT W. CRONIN, *11 Middlefield Dr., West Hartford, 06107*. Tel: 860-232-1886. Very Rev. LAURENCE A.M. LAPOINTE, *Newman Hall, 290 Prospect St., Willimantic, 06226*. Tel: 860-423-0856.

Commission on Women—201 Broadway, Norwich, 06360-4328. Tel: 860-887-9294, Ext. 100. Mrs. SUSAN SEDENSKY, Chm.; Mrs. MARYELLEN GRACE; Ms. MARTHA KOWAC; Mrs. JANE LEGER; Ms. BEATRICE MACKENZIE; Mrs. JUDY PAPPAGALLO; Mrs. ANGELA MESICK; Mrs. LORRAINE CORTESE-COSTA; Mrs. MAUREEN BUTLER; Mrs. KAREN BOULEY; Ms. ELLEN BUXTON; Ms. SHERRY BASSI; Mrs. FLORENCE PARKER; Mrs. CONSTANCE STOLL; Mrs. PATRICIA LABONTE; Mrs. JOHANNA REILLY.

Office of Communications and Diocesan Teleconference Center—Miss JACQUELINE M. KELLER, Dir., Ext. 215. Mrs. HELEN M. ZANDER, Admin. Asst., *The Bishop Flanagan Ministry Center, 1595 Norwich-New London Tpke., Uncasville, 06382*. Tel: 860-848-2237.

Community Ministries—Sr. JOANNE CAMPANINI, I.H.M., Dir., *St. Vincent de Paul Place, 10 Railroad Place, Norwich, 06360*. Tel: 860-889-7374 (Office); 7375. Ms. CRYSTAL JUREIK, Meals Prog. Coord., *10 Railroad Place, Norwich, 06360*. Middletown: *St. Vincent de Paul Place, 617 Main St., P.O. Box 398, Middletown, 06457-0398*. Tel: 860-344-0097; Fax: 860-343-0023. Mr. PETER HARDING, Dir.; Miss ANGIE REALE, Meals Prog. Coord. TERRY CARBONE, Svc. Coord.

Connecticut Catholic Conference—Dr. MARIE HILLIARD, Exec. Dir., *134 Farmington Ave., Hartford, 06105-3784*. Tel: 860-524-7882; Fax: 860-525-0750.

Continuing Education and Formation Commission—Revs. MARK D. O'DONNELL, Chm. ROLAND C. CLOUTIER; WILLIAM OLESIK; DENNIS M. PERKINS; MICHAEL S. SMITH; PETER LISZEWSKI; RICHARD RICARD; Sr. MARYANNE GUERTIN, S.S.J.

Council of Catholic Nurses—Very Rev. THOMAS SMITH, Diocesan Moderator, *St. Mary Rectory, 10 Huntington St., New London, 06320-6198*. Tel: 860-437-1889; Fax: 860-437-1889.

Council of Catholic Women—Ms. DORIS BURY, Pres., *14 Windsor Ave., Apt. D-4, Plainfield, 06374*. Tel: 860-564-1559. Rev. EDWARD KONOPKA, Diocesan Moderator, *St. Peter Rectory, 30 St. Peter Ln., P.O. Box 707, Higganum, 06441-4236*. Tel: 860-345-8018. District Moderators: Rev. JOSEPH DECOSTA, New London Deanery; Rev. EUGENE PILATOWSKI, Norwich Deanery; Rev. Msgr. WILLIS W. WEST, Willimantic Deanery; Rev. JAMES P. CARINI, Rockville Deanery; Very Rev. JOSEPH HANKS, Shore Line Deanery; Rev. WILLIAM MCNULTY, Putnam Deanery; Rev. CHARLES LEBLANC, Middletown Deanery.

The Deaf, Ministry to—Sr. M. ESTHER COCKBURN, M.H.S.H., Dir., *31 Perkins Ave., Norwich, 06360*. Tel: 860-886-1281 (Voice & TTY).

Development, Diocesan Office of (DOD)—Mr. RICHARD COSTELLO, Exec. Dir., *197 Broadway, Norwich, 06360*. Tel: 860-886-1928; Fax: 860-886-2651.

Annual Bishop's Appeal—Mr. RICHARD COSTELLO, Dir., *197 Broadway, Norwich, 06360*. Tel: 860-886-1928; Fax: 860-886-2651.

Planned Giving Office—Mr. JOHN BUTLER, Dir., *197 Broadway, Norwich, 06360*. Tel: 860-886-1928.

Disabilities-People with—See His Able People, Ministry of.

Ecumenism—

Diocesan Commission for Ecumenical and Interreligious Affairs—Sr. MARYANNE GUERTIN, S.S.J., Ecumenical Officer; Revs. THEODORE J. KLEIN, Ph.D., Ex Officio, Emeritus; MARK D. O'DONNELL; MARTIN J. JONES; FRANCIS C. ROULEAU; Sr. JACQUELYN DONOHUE, I.H.M.; Mr. LEO BERNARD; Mrs. SANDRA CALABRO; Mrs. SHEILA ELLIOTT; Mr. CHUCK HENRY; Mrs. CAROL HANSEN; Ms. KATHLEEN BURTON; Mr. HENRY CAREY; Mr. SAMUEL MATOS; Deacon MELVIN NYGAARD; Dr. LORETTA ANDERSON; Mrs. JOANN HAY.

Ecumenical and Interreligious Affairs, Office of—Bishop Flanagan Ministry Center, 1595 Norwich-New London Tpke., Uncasville, 06382-1319. Tel: 860-848-2237, Ext. 204; Fax: 860-848-2816. Sr. MARYANNE GUERTIN, S.S.J., Dir.

Evangelization & Catechumenate (RCIA), Office of—SUSAN MYSHRALL, Dir., Ext. 317. Rev. STANLEY J. SZCZAPA; ERNEST GOLNIK; Sr. KATHERINE MCKENNA, P.B.V.M.; GAYLE MADDEN; THOMAS MADDEN; MILDRED STEARNS; SUSAN MYSHRALL, *The Bishop Flanagan Ministry Center, 1595 Norwich-New London Tpke., Uncasville, 06382-1319*. Tel: 860-848-2237.

Faith Formation, Office for—Bishop Flanagan Ministry Center, 1595 Norwich-New London Tpke., Uncasville, 06382-1319. Tel: 860-848-2237, Ext. 312; Fax: 860-848-2816. Sr. ELEANOR O'MALLEY, P.B.V.M., Dir.

Diocesan Media Center—Mrs. ROSEANN COFFEY, Assoc. Dir. MARJORIE VANNER, Admin. Asst.

Diocesan Scouting Committee—

Scout Chaplain—Rev. GREGORY P. GALVIN.

Chairmen—ISABEL GREENBAUGH; PAMELA PLASSE.

Consultants—JANET WALSH; Mrs. JANE O'FRIEL, Elementary Catechesis Consultant; Mrs. OLIVE GREEN, Youth Ministry Consultant, Ext. 313. Mrs. JANE O'FRIEL, Special Needs.

"Four County Catholic"—See Newspaper.

Haitian Ministries—EMILY SMACK, Dir., *Bishop Flanagan Ministry Center, 1595 Norwich-New London Tpke., Uncasville, 06382-1319*. Tel: 860-848-2237, Ext. 206. Haitian Ministries Board: Ms. NOREEN GIBSON; Mrs. EVELYN KIRBY; Very Rev. ANTHONY GRUBER; Deacon RONALD F. FREEDMAN; Ms. JANET MINELLA-DIDIER; Dr. THOMAS GORIN; Mrs. JUDITH SECORD; Mrs. MARIETTE STEVENS MCCOURT; Mr. GREG SECORD; Rev. GERALD KIRBY; Mr. WILLIAM MARSTON; Mrs. JOANNE WHITEHOUSE.

His Able People, Ministry of—Please refer all inquiries to the Chancery:Tel: 860-887-9294, Ext. 232.

Hispanic Ministry—Sr. MARY JUDE LAZARUS, S.C.M.C., Diocesan Dir., *Hispanic Apostolate, 61 Club Rd., Windham, 06280-1007*. Tel: 860-423-8617; Fax: 860-423-4157.

Clinton—

St. Mary of the Visitation Church - Spanish Apostolate—54 Grove St., Clinton, 06413-1999. Tel: 860-669-8512; Fax: 860-669-9052. Rev. MICHAEL SEQUIRA; Sr. MAIRENY SOTO ROJAS, R.O.D.A., Pastoral Assoc. Hispanic Ministry Board: Mrs. ELSIE SOLIS, Middletown; Mrs. CLARA DE LOS SANTOS, Middletown; Rev. ROBERT WASHABAUGH, Middletown; Mrs. JAVIER CRUZ, New London; Mr. JUAN D. HILARIO, New London; Sr. MARIE LOS BALLESTERO, R.O.D.A., New London; Mrs. ANTELMA CASAIEZ, Norwich; Mr. RAFAEL ORTIZ, Norwich; Sr. EDITH VILLALOBOS, R.O.D.A., Norwich; Miss LIZBETH HERNANDEZ, Willimantic; Mrs. VIRGINIA RODRIGUEZ, Willimantic; Mr. LISANDRO SUAREZ, Willimantic.

New London—

St. Mary Star of the Sea Church - Spanish Apostolate—Very Rev. THOMAS J. SMITH, Priest Dir., New London Area; Rev. MARTIN JONES; Rev. PHILIP A. PUSATERI, S.J., Parochial Vicar, *St. Mary Rectory, 10 Huntington St., New London, 06320-6198*. Tel: 860-447-1431; Fax: 860-437-1889. Deacon MARIANO RAMOS. Tel: 860-443-1986. Deacon JESUS A. DIEZ-CANSECO. Tel: 860-443-2364. Sr. MARIELOS BALLESTEROS, R.O.D.A., Pastoral Assoc., *Residence*. Tel: 860-886-6092., *Hispanic Apostolate Office, 60 Jay St., New London, 06320-5910*. Tel: 860-437-1285.

Windham—

Iglesia del Sagrado Corazon de Jesus - Spanish Apostolate—Rev. PAUL MURDOCK, Pastor, *Residence, 310 Elizabeth Lane, Stonegate Manor, North Windham, 06256*. Deacon FELIPE SILVA, *Residence*. Tel: 860-456-8725. Pastoral Associates: Sr. EDITH VILLALOBOS, R.O.D.A.; Mrs. VIRGINIA RODRIGUEZ, *Residence*. Tel: 860-886-6092., *La Iglesia del Sagrado Corazon de Jesus Office, 61 Club Rd., Windham, 06280-1007*. Tel: 860-423-8617; Fax: 860-423-4157.

Middletown—

St. Francis of Assisi Church - Spanish Apostolate—Revs. ROBERT WASHABAUGH, Pastor, *St. Francis of Assisi, 10 Elm St., Middletown, 06457-4426*. Sr. MAIRENY SOTO ROJAS, R.O.D.A., Pastoral Assoc. Tel: 860-347-4684; Fax: 860-347-7669.

Norwich—

St. Mary Church - Spanish Apostolate—Revs. ROBERT B. LYNCH, Pastor; RUSSELL KENNEDY,

Parochial Vicar; Sr. Edith Villalobos, R.O.D.A., Pastoral Assoc., *St. Mary Church, 70 Central Ave., Norwich, 06360-4794.* Tel: 860-887-2565.

Holy Childhood—See Pontifical Association of the Holy Childhood.

Holy Name Societies—Address all mail to: *Holy Name Societies, 201 Broadway, Norwich, 06360-4328.* Tel: 860-887-9294.

Internal Affairs Office of Sexual Misconduct Services and Information—201 Broadway, Norwich, 06360-4328. Tel: 800-624-7407.

Insurance—See Catholic Mutual Relief Society (C.M.R.S.).

Justice & Peace, Catholic Social Action for—Mr. Ray Mastronunzio, Dir., *The Bishop Flanagan Ministry Center, 1595 Norwich-New London Tpke., Uncasville, 06382-1319.* Tel: 860-848-2237. Advisory Council: Dr. Loretta Anderson; Mr. Maurice Bowen; Sr. M. John Baptist Donovan; Mr. Russell McDonough; Mr. James Vallario.

Lawyers, Guild of Catholic—Mailing Address: *The Chancery, 201 Broadway, Norwich, 06360-4328.* Tel: 860-887-9294. Michael E. Driscoll, Pres.; Mrs. Regina Wiegert, Sec., Ext. 246. Rev. Msgr. Henry Archambault, P.A., Chap.

Legion of Mary—Rev. Robert B. Lynch, Diocesan Spiritual Dir., *St. Mary Rectory, 70 Central Ave., Norwich, 06360-4794.* Tel: 860-887-2565.

Worship, Office of—Gerard T. Hall, Diocesan Dir., *Bishop Flanagan Ministry Center, 1595 Norwich, New London Turnpike, Uncasville, 06382-1319.* Tel: 860-848-2237, Ext. 209; Fax: 860-848-2816. Liturgical Commission: Mr. Gerard J. Hall; Rev. Mark Thomas Booth, O.F.M.Conv.; Mrs. Clara Burnside; Ms. Connie Butler; Mrs. Claire Kiritsis; Deacon Ron Kitlinski; Sr. Eleanor O'Malley, P.B.V.M.; Mrs. Yolanda Pereira; Mrs. Sandy Rusoo; Mrs. Millie Sterns; Rev. Stan Szczapa.

Marriage Encounter/Catholic Charities/Family Life Office—Mr. Marek Kulkulka, L.M.F.T., *331 Main St., Norwich, 06360.* Tel: 860-889-8346; Fax: 860-889-2658.

Mercy Xavier Development Corporation—Mr. James Joyce, Pres., *181 Randolph Rd., Middletown, 06457.* Tel: 860-347-2343; 346-7735.

Ministry Formation and Permanent Diaconate, Office of—The Bishop Flanagan Ministry Center, 1595 Norwich-New London Tpke., Uncasville, 06382-1319. Tel: 860-848-2237.

Newspaper—Official monthly newspaper of Diocese of Norwich—*"Four County Catholic"*; Mr. Peter L. Gill, Editor, Ext. 216. Mr. Bruce Avery, Advertising Mgr., Ext. 213., *Office of Communications, Bishop Flanagan Ministry Center, 1595 Norwich-New London Tpke., Uncasville, 06382-1319.* Tel: 860-889-0202; 848-2237 (Editor); 367-0130 (Advertising); Fax: 860-848-2816.

Nurses—See Council of Catholic Nurses.

Pastoral Planning, Office of—Sr. Mary Alice Kline, R.S.M., Coord., *Bishop Flanagan Ministry Center, 1595 Norwich-New London Tpke., Uncasville, 06382-1319.* Tel: 860-848-2237, Ext. 203; Fax: 860-848-2816.

People with Disability—See His Able People, Ministry of.

Permanent Deacon, Office of—Rev. Msgr. Richard P. LaRocque, Vicar for Clergy, Ext. 258. Mrs. Susan Gardiner, Sec., Ext. 261., *The Chancery, 201 Broadway, Norwich, 06360.* Tel: 860-887-9294; Fax: 860-886-1670.

Planned Giving Office—See Development, Diocesan Office of.

Pontifical Association of the Holy Childhood—Rev. William Olesik, *St. Maurice Church, 32 Hebron Rd., Bolton, 06043-7606.* Tel: 860-643-4466.

Pontifical Society for the Propagation of the Faith—Rev. William Olesik, Dir., *St. Maurice Church, 32 Hebron Rd., Bolton, 06043-7606.* Tel: 860-643-4466.

Prison Ministry for Diocese of Norwich—Bishop Flanagan Ministry Center, 1595 Norwich-New London Tpke., Uncasville, 06382. Tel: 860-848-2237. Ms. Sheree L. Antoch, Dir.; Deacon Dennis F. Dolan, *Bishop Flanagan Ministry Center, 2595 Norwich-New London Tpke., Uncasville, 06382.* Tel: 860-848-2237; Fax: 860-848-2816.

Brooklyn - Brooklyn Correctional Institution—59 Hartford Rd., Brooklyn, 06234. Tel: 860-779-4568. Chaplains: Deacon Robert Lambert; Rev. Louis Patruzo, *Immaculate Conception Rectory, P.O. Box 260610-0610, Station A, 574 Park St., Hartford, 06126-0610.* Tel: 860-525-1522.

Niantic - Gates Correctional Institution—131 N. Bridebrook Rd., Niantic, 06357. Tel: 860-691-4756. Sr. Patricia Cook, R.S.M., Chap., *149 Neck Rd., Madison, 06443-2728.* Tel: 203-245-4261.

York Correctional Institution—201 W. Main St., Niantic, 06357. Tel: 860-691-6544; 691-6673. Chaplains: Deacon Dennis F. Dolan, *452 Amston Rd., Colchester, 06415.* Tel: 860-537-1336. Rev. Russell Kennedy, *St. Mary Rectory, 70 Central Ave., Norwich, 06360-4794.* Tel: 860-887-2565.

Somers - Northern Correctional Institution—287 Bilton Rd., Somers, 06071. Tel: 860-763-8686. Rev. Robert Grant, Chap., *St. Gabriel Rectory, 379 Broad St., Windsor, 06095-3004.* Tel: 860-688-4905. Deacon Robert E. Bernd, Chap., *159 Brainard Rd., Apt. 23, Enfield, 06082.* Tel: 860-749-3563 (Home); 763-8691 (Work); Fax: 860-749-3563.

Osborn Correctional Institution—100 Bilton Rd., Somers, 06071. Tel: 860-749-8391, Ext. 5476. Chaplains: Deacon Robert P. Gale, *P.O. Box 826, Farmington, 06034.* Tel: 860-233-1089. Rev. Louis Patruzo, *Immaculate Conception Rectory, P.O. Box 260610-0610, Station A, 574 Park St., Hartford, 06126-0610.* Tel: 860-525-1522.

Somers-Enfield - Willard-Cybulski Correctional Institution—391 Shaker Rd., Enfield, 06082. Tel: 860-763-6106. Chaplains: Rev. Robert Grant; Deacon Robert Lambert, *St. Gabriel Rectory, 379 Broad St., Windsor, 06095-3004.* Tel: 860-688-4905.

Uncasville - Corrigan Correctional Institution—986 Norwich-New London Tpke., Uncasville, 06382. Tel: 860-848-5764. Rev. Justinian B. Rweyemamu, Chap., *St. Bernard Rectory, 25 St. Bernard Terr., Rockville, 06066-3258.* Tel: 860-875-0753.

Uncasville - Radgowski Correctional Institution—982 Norwich-New London Tpke., Uncasville, 06382. Tel: 860-848-5034. Rev. Russell L. Boisvert, Chap., *St. John the Evangelist Rectory, 22 Maple Ave., Uncasville, 06382.* Tel: 860-848-1257.

Pro-Life Activities—Mr. Joseph P. Collison, Dir., *201 Broadway, Norwich, 06360-4328.* Tel: 860-887-9294, Ext. 247; Fax: 860-886-1670.

Project Northeast—A program of Evangelization for the unchurched poor. Rev. Richard L. Archambault, Dir., *81 Church St., Putnam, 06260-1809.* Tel: 860-928-4078. Sr. Eleanor Baldoni, D.H.S., Assoc. Dir., *22 Pearl Ave., Putnam, 06260-1625.* Tel: 860-928-5965.

RCIA—See Evangelization & Catechumenate, Office of.

Religious—See Vicar for Religious.

Priests Retirement Board—Most Rev. Daniel A. Hart, D.D.; Revs. Brian Converse; Michael Gill; Very Rev. Anthony P. Gruber; Rev. Hugh J. Murphy; Mr. James Little; Ms. Mary Oliver.

Retirement—See Priests' Retirement Commission.

School Office, Diocesan—Dr. Howard B. Bennett, Supt.; Sr. Joan A. O'Conner, C.S.J., Assoc. Supt. Debra Jadofsky, Exec. Sec. to Supt., *43 Perkins Ave., Norwich, 06360-3698.* Tel: 860-887-4086; 887-9371; Fax: 860-887-9371.

Board of Education—Most Rev. Daniel A. Hart, D.D.; Sr. Joan O'Connor, C.S.J.; Dr. Howard Bennett; Ms. Linda Corona; Mr. Elmo Gianantoni, Chm.; Rev. Msgr. Anthony S. Rosaforte, School Pastor. Ex Officio: Rev. Msgr. Thomas R. Bride, P.A., V.G., K.S.G.; Rev. Charles LeBlanc; Mr. William F. O'Neil, Jr., K.S.G.; Rev. Robert Barnes.

Scouting—See Faith Formation, Office for.

Sick, Ministry to the—Sr. Rita Johnson, S.S.N.D., Dir., *W.W. Backus Hospital, 326 Washington St., Norwich, 06360-2742.* Tel: 860-889-8331., *Residence, 7 Otis St., Norwich, 06360.* Tel: 860-886-6948.

Soup Kitchen—See Community Ministries, Saint Vincent de Paul Place.

Spanish Speaking Apostolate—See Hispanic Ministry.

The Spiritual Renewal Services of the Diocese of Norwich—Co-Directors: Rev. Raymond D. Introvigne, *Residence, St. Mary Rectory, 1600 Main St., P.O. Box 250, Coventry, 06338-0250.* Tel: 860-742-0681; Fax: 860-887-0702. Mrs. Judith Hughes, *10 Bath St., P.O. Box 6, Norwich, 06360-5836.* Tel: 860-887-0702. Dial-A-Prayer. Tel: 860-887-7767.

Vicar for Religious—Rev. John W. McWeeney, M.S., J.C.L.; Sr. Sally J. Tolles, D.H.S., J.D., J.C.L., Assoc. Vicar, *The Tribunal, 17 Otis St., Norwich, 06360-4419.* Tel: 860-887-9294.

Vocations—Rev. Msgr. Thomas R. Bride, P.A., V.G., K.S.G., Diocesan Dir.; Revs. Michael L. Phillippino, Asst. Dir. Vocations; Mark D. O'Donnell, Diocesan Dir. for Promotion & Devel., *201 Broadway, Norwich, 06360-4328.* Tel: 860-887-9294. Mrs. Ann Depta, Sec., *Residence, St. John Rectory, 22 Maple Ave., Uncasville, 06382-2327.* Tel: 860-848-9335.

Vocation Review Committee, Diocesan—Rev. Msgr. Thomas R. Bride, P.A., V.G., K.S.G.; Rev. Msgr. Richard P. LaRocque; Rev. Msgr. Willis W. West; Revs. R. Thomas McConaghy; Mark D. O'Donnell; Michael L. Phillippino; Bro. William Ciganek, C.F.X.

Youth Ministry—See Faith Formation, Office of.

Youth Retreat Center—Alpha House West, Higganum. For details, contact Faith Formation Office; Sr. Eleanor O'Malley, P.B.V.M., *Bishop Flanagan Ministry Center, 1595 Norwich-New London Tpke., Uncasville, 06382-1319.* Tel: 860-848-2237, Ext. 209; Fax: 860-848-2816.

Women, Commission on—See Commission on Women.

Apostolate—Jewett City: *The World Apostolate of Fatima, Inc., Norwich Diocesan Div., 41 John Rd., Jewett City, 06351.* Tel: 860-376-1041; Fax: 860-376-1041. Denise Dudek, Pres.

CLERGY, PARISHES, MISSIONS AND PAROCHIAL SCHOOLS

CITY OF NORWICH
(New London County)

1—St. Patrick Cathedral (1879), Rev. Msgr. Anthony S. Rosaforte; Rev. David Choquette; Deacon Al R. Fecteau.

Res., 213 Broadway, 06360-4307. Tel: 860-889-8441; Fax: 860-889-2978.

School—211 Broadway, 06360. Tel: 860-889-4174; Fax: 860-889-4174. Sr. Mary Bernard Rivest, S.C.M.C., Prin.

Sisters of Charity of Our Lady Mother of the Church 1; Lay Teachers 10; Students 206.

Catechesis/Religious Programs—Agnes Carvel, D.R.E.

Students 308.

2—Sacred Heart (Norwichtown) (1902), Rev. R. Thomas McConaghy; Deacon Robert P. Hayes.

Res., 52 W. Town St., Norwichtown, 06360-2296. Tel: 860-887-1030; Fax: 860-887-6550.

Catechesis/Religious Programs—Tel: 860-887-1715. Susan Makowicki, D.R.E.

Students 158.

Mission—Fitchville, New London Co., St. John, 190 Fitchville Rd., Bozrah, 06334. Tel: 860-886-9151.

3—St. Joseph, New London Co., (1904) (Polish), Rev. Eugene Pilatowski.

Res., 120 Cliff St., 06360-5134. Tel: 860-887-1565.

School—Sr. M. Martin LeClair, S.C.M.C., Prin.

Catechesis/Religious Programs—Tel: 860-887-4565.

Students 215.

4—St. Mary (1845), Revs. Robert B. Lynch; Russell Kennedy; Sr. Edith Villalobos, Hispanic Min.; Deacon Dennis Doyle. In res., Rev. Joseph G. Finnerty.

Res., 70 Central Ave., 06360-4794. Tel: 860-887-2565; Fax: 860-892-1692.

Catechesis/Religious Programs—Students 48.

5—SS. Peter and Paul (1938), Revs. Ernest F. Passero, S.J.; John C. Monahan, S.J.; Barry C. Meehan, S.J.

Res., 181 Elizabeth St., 06360-6199. Tel: 860-887-9857; Fax: 860-886-4728. [CEM]

Catechesis/Religious Programs—Students 156.

OUTSIDE THE CITY OF NORWICH

Ashford, Windham Co., St. Philip (1937), Revs. Joseph D. Nguyen; Paul Ramen.

Res., 64 Pompey Hollow Rd., 06278-1540. Tel: 860-429-2860; Fax: 860-487-5703. [CEM 2]

Catechesis/Religious Programs—Tel: 860-429-1921; 450-1544; Fax: 860-487-5703. D.R.E. Anthony Lagroterria; John Doughty.

Students 109.

Ballouville, Windham Co., St. Anne (1882), Rev. Sylva P. LeCours.

Res., 227 Ballouville Rd., Box 125, 06233-0125. Tel: 860-774-6164.

Catechesis/Religious Programs—Tel: 860-774-4023.

Students 93.

Baltic, New London Co., St. Mary of the Immaculate Conception (1886), Rev. Joseph Tito.

Res., 70 W. Main St., 06330-1348. Tel: 860-822-6378. [CEM]

School—St. Joseph, 10 School Hill Rd., Tel: 860-822-6141; Fax: 860-822-6141. Sr. M. Elaine Moocroft, S.C.M.C., Prin.

Sisters of Charity of Our Lady Mother of the Church 6; Lay Teachers 4; Students 115.

Catechesis/Religious Programs—Students 172.

Bolton, Tolland Co., St. Maurice (1954), Rev. William J. Olesik.

Res., 32 Hebron Rd., 06043-7606. Tel: 860-643-4466.

Catechesis/Religious Programs—Tel: 860-643-8374. Mrs. Peg Rouleau, D.R.E.
Students 251.

Brooklyn, Windham Co., Our Lady of La Salette (1968), Rev. Brian D. Schloth, M.S.
Res., 06234-0211. Tel: 860-774-6275; Fax: 860-774-0679.
Catechesis/Religious Programs—Students 144.
Mission—Hampton, Windham Co., Our Lady of Lourdes, Cedar Swamp Rd., Hampton, 06247. Tel: 860-455-9897.

Canterbury, Windham Co., St. Augustine (1978), Rev. Frank W. McKenna.
Res., 144 Westminster Rd., 06331-1417. Tel: 860-546-6074.
Catechesis/Religious Programs—Tel: 860-546-6225.
Students 131.

Chester, Middlesex Co., St. Joseph (1885), Rev. Robert Murphy, M.Ss.A.
Res., 48 Middlesex Ave., 06412-1309. Tel: 860-526-5495; Fax: 860-526-7880. [CEM]
Catechesis/Religious Programs—Tel: 860-526-2139.
Students 210.

Clinton, Middlesex Co., St. Mary of the Visitation (1934), Rev. Michael Sequeira; Sr. Marieny Soto, R.O.D.A., Pastoral Assoc.; Deacon Paul Weber.
Res., 54 Grove St., 06413-1999. Tel: 860-669-8512; Fax: 860-669-9052. [CEM]
Catechesis/Religious Programs—Tel: 860-669-7375.
Students 413.

Colchester, New London Co., St. Andrew (1860), Rev. Michael C. Giannitelli; Deacons Robert Barlow; Dennis Dolan.
Res., 128 Norwich Ave., 06415-1269. Tel: 860-537-2355; Fax: 860-537-2356. [CEM 2][JC 2]
Catechesis/Religious Programs—Tel: 860-537-5415.
Students 850.

Columbia, Tolland Co., St. Columba (1960), Rev. Daniel C. Cronin.
Res., Rte. 66 at Rte. 87, P.O. Box 146, 06237-0146. Tel: 860-228-3735.
Catechesis/Religious Programs—Tel: 860-228-3727.
Students 207.

Coventry, Tolland Co., St. Mary (1877), Revs. Raymond D. Introvigne; J. Lawrence Ouimet.
Res., 1600 Main St., P.O. Box 250, 06238-0250. Tel: 860-742-0681; Fax: 860-742-1318. [CEM]
Catechesis/Religious Programs—Tel: 860-742-1092.
Students 352.
Mission—Eagleville, Tolland Co., St. Joseph.

Cromwell, Middlesex Co., St. John (1882), Revs. Raymond Borkowski, O.F.M.Conv.; Hilary Brzostowski, O.F.M.Conv.
Res., 5 St. John Ct., 06416-2118. Tel: 860-635-5590; Fax: 860-635-5591.
Catechesis/Religious Programs—Tel: 860-635-5156.
Students 589.

Danielson, Windham Co., St. James (1869) (French), Revs. John J. O'Neill, M.S.; John E. Welch, M.S.; Donald D. Simonds, M.S.; Thomas G. Sickler, M.S.
Res., 12 Franklin St., 06239. Tel: 860-774-3900; Fax: 860-774-4205. [CEM]
School—Tel: 860-774-3281; Fax: 860-779-2137. Ms. Marguerite Ouellette, Prin.
Lay Teachers 13; Students 282.
Catechesis/Religious Programs—Tel: 860-774-8459.
Students 298.
Mission—East Killingly, Windham Co., Our Lady of Peace, 06239.

Dayville, Windham Co., St. Joseph (1874), Rev. William J. McNulty.
Res., 350 Hartford Pke., Box 487, 06241-2109. Tel: 860-774-8656. [CEM]
Catechesis/Religious Programs—Tel: 860-774-2451. D.R.E.: Alyce Chartier; Norma Pokoski.
Students 104.
Convent—21 Williamsville Rd., Box 158, Rogers, 06263. Tel: 860-774-8154. Parish House Daughters of the Holy Spirit

Durham, Middlesex Co., Notre Dame (1953), Rev. Augustine Naduvilekoot.
Res., 272 Main St., 06422-1611. Tel: 860-349-3058; Fax: 860-349-8949.
Catechesis/Religious Programs—Students 384.

East Hampton, Middlesex Co., St. Patrick (1879) (Irish), Rev. Charles R. LeBlanc; Sr. Dominic Joseph Valla, A.S.C.J., Pastoral Assoc.; Deacon Warren J.F. Cyr.
Res., 47 W. High St., P.O. Box 177, 06424-0177. Tel: 860-267-6644; Fax: 860-267-7807. [CEM]
Catechesis/Religious Programs—Students 502.

East Lyme, New London Co., St. Matthias (Flannders) (1939), Rev. Michael T. Donohue; Sr. M. Rita Clare, R.S.M.; Deacon Steven Reed.
Res., 186 Chesterfield Rd. P.O. Box 25, 06333-0025. Fax: 860-739-0524.
Church Address: 317 Chesterfield Rd., P.O.Box 25, 06333-0025.
Catechesis/Religious Programs—Tel: 860-739-5208; Fax: 860-739-0524.
Students 340.

Ellington, Tolland Co., St. Luke (1961), Rev. Thomas Plathottam, C.S.T.
Rectory: 141 Maple St., P.O. Box 246, 06029-0246. Tel: 860-875-8552; Fax: 860-872-6548.
Church—141 Maple St., 06029.
Catechesis/Religious Programs—Tel: 860-875-4951.
Students 168.
Convent—8 Berr Ave., 06029-0246. St. Luke Convent

Essex, Middlesex Co., Our Lady of Sorrows (1926), Rev. Paul J. Ganmond.
Res., 14 Prospect St., 06426-1049. Tel: 860-767-1284.
Catechesis/Religious Programs—Tel: 860-767-2938.
Students 167.

Fishers Island, Suffolk Co., Our Lady of Grace (1902), Rev. Robert W. Barnes.
Res., Alpine Ave., Box 425, 06390-0425. Tel: 631-788-7353; Fax: 631-788-7353.
Catechesis/Religious Programs—Students 6.

Gales Ferry, New London Co., Our Lady of Lourdes (1960), Revs. Joseph F. DeCosta; Gregory C. Mullaney.
Res., 1650 Rte. 12, 06335-1534. Tel: 860-464-7251; Fax: 860-464-7252.
Catechesis/Religious Programs—Tel: 860-464-6676.
Students 521.

Groton, New London Co., Sacred Heart (1905), Revs. John J. Meagher, S.S.E.; Francis X. McMahon, S.S.E.
Res., 56 Sacred Heart Dr., 06340-4431. Tel: 860-445-2905; 445-6648; Fax: 860-445-6648.
School—(Grades PreK-8). Tel: 460-445-0611; Fax: 860-448-4999. Linda Corona, Prin.
Lay Teachers 22; Aides 5; Students 396.
Catechesis/Religious Programs—Tel: 860-445-2905.
Students 85.

St. Mary (1964), Rev. John C. Nash; Sr. Jacquelyn Donohue, I.H.M., Pastoral Assoc.; Deacon Peter H. Danesi, III.
Res., 69 Groton Long Point Rd., 06340. Tel: 860-445-1446; Fax: 860-448-7269.
Catechesis/Religious Programs—Tel: 860-448-0529. D.R.E. Mrs. Barbara Simoncini; Mrs. Theresa Seals.
Students 261.

Hebron, Tolland Co., The Church of the Holy Family (1987), Rev. Michael S. Smith.
Mailing Address: P.O. Box 146, 06248-0146. Tel: 860-228-0096; Fax: 860-228-1629.
Catechesis/Religious Programs—Lisa Furbush, D.R.E.
Students 450.

Higganum, Middlesex Co., St. Peter (1958), Rev. Edward M. Konopka.
Res., 30 St. Peter Ln., P.O. Box 707, 06441-0707. Tel: 860-345-8018; Fax: 860-345-4067.
Catechesis/Religious Programs—Tel: 860-345-4726.
Students 193.

Jewett City, New London Co., St. Mary (1870), Revs. Gerald Boulanger, M.S., Co-Pastor; Rene L. Parent, M.S., Co-Pastor; Deacon Paul R. Baillargeon.
Res., 34 N. Main St., 06351-2012. Tel: 860-376-2044; Fax: 860-376-2044. [CEM 2]
School—54 N. Main St., 06351. Tel: 860-376-0446; Fax: 860-376-4200. Freda Cale, Prin.
Lay Teachers 10; Students 160.
Catechesis/Religious Programs—Tel: 860-376-5150.
Students 383.

Killingworth, Middlesex Co., St. Lawrence (1978), Rev. Michael L. Phillippino; Deacon Raymond Gosselin.
Res., 7 Hemlock Dr., 06419-2227. Tel: 860-663-2576; Fax: 860-663-4238.
Catechesis/Religious Programs—Tel: 860-873-2956.
Students 306.

Lebanon, New London Co., St. Francis of Assisi (1980), Rev. Peter B. Liszewski; Deacon Albert Cote.
Res., 67 W. Town St., P.O. Box 172, 06249-0172. Tel: 860-642-6711.
Catechesis/Religious Programs—Students 176.

Middlefield, Middlesex Co., St. Colman (1890), Rev. Lester G. Morris.
Res., 145 Hubbard St., P.O. Box 457, 06455-0457. Tel: 860-349-3868.
Catechesis/Religious Programs—Tel: 860-347-1725. Barbara-Jean DiMauro, D.R.E.
Students 195.

Middletown, Middlesex Co.,

1—St. Francis, (1903), Rev. Robert Washabaugh.
Res., 10 Elm St., 06457-4426. Tel: 860-347-4684; Fax: 860-347-7669.
Catechesis/Religious Programs—Tel: 860-344-1098.
Students 131.

2—St. John, (1843), Rev. Joseph C. Ashe; Sr. Ann Mack, R.S.M., Pastoral Assoc.
Res., 19 John's Sq., 06457-2201. Tel: 860-347-5626; Fax: 860-638-3633. [CEM]
School—Tel: 860-347-3202; Fax: 860-347-3537.
Lay Teachers 15; Students 242.
Catechesis/Religious Programs—Students 45.

3—St. Mary of Czestochowa, (1903) (Polish), Revs. Aloysius J. Kisluk; Clement Jarnot, O.F.M.Conv.
Res., 79 S. Main St., 06457-3606. Tel: 860-347-2365; Fax: 860-347-2110. [CEM]
School—87 S. Main St., 06457. Tel: 860-347-2978; Fax: 860-347-7267. Mrs. Kathleen Dutil, Prin.; Rev. Clement Jarnot, Dir.
Lay Teachers 10; Students 270.
Catechesis/Religious Programs—Students 150.

4—St. Pius X, (1957), Revs. Frederick Nickle, O.F.M.Cap.; James Hammer, O.F.M.Cap.; Paul Steffan, O.F.M.Cap.; Bro. Eugene Sheehan, O.F.M.Cap. In res., Revs. Colman Boylan, O.F.M.Cap., (Retired); Cyprian Murray, O.F.M.Cap.; Bruce Quinn, O.F.M.Cap., Hospital Chap.; Walter O'Brien, O.F.M.Cap., (Retired); Bro. Richard Therrien, O.F.M.Cap., Vocation Office.
Res., 310 Westfield St., 06457-2047. Tel: 860-347-4441; 4442; Fax: 203-347-3001.
Catechesis/Religious Programs—Tel: 860-346-9100. Mary Ann Fagan, D.R.E.
Students 519.

5—St. Sebastian, (1930) (Italian), Revs. Daniel L. Schwebs, O.S.J.; Sebastian Perumbilly, O.S.J.; Deacons John P. Catalano; Nicholas J. Cannata.
Res., 155 Washington St., 06457-2819. Tel: 860-347-2638; Fax: 860-347-6736. [CEM]
School—61 Durant Ter., 06457-2819. Tel: 860-347-3438; Fax: 860-343-0543. Mrs. Joan Bennett, Prin.
Lay Teachers 11; Students 194.
Catechesis/Religious Programs—Students 181.

Montville, New London Co., St. John (1881), Rev. Russel L. Boisvert Tel: 860-848-1257; Deacon Melvin Nygaard. In res., Rev. Msgr. Robert L. Brown, Chancellor, Tel: 860-887-9294, Ext. 232 (Chancery); 848-3771 (Private); Rev. Mark D. O'Donnell, Dir. Vocations, Tel: 860-887-9294.
Res., 22 Maple Ave., Uncasville, 06382-2327. Tel: 860-848-9335; Fax: 860-848-1258. [CEM]
Catechesis/Religious Programs—Tel: 203-848-1409; Fax: 203-848-1258. Marc Cournoyer, D.R.E.
Students 236.

Moodus, Middlesex Co., St. Bridget (1914), Rev. Gregoire J. Fluet.
Res., 75 Moodus-Leesville Rd., P.O. Box 422, 06469-0422. Tel: 860-873-8623; Fax: 860-873-9407. [CEM]
Catechesis/Religious Programs—Students 238.

Moosup, Windham Co., All-Hallows (1859), Revs. Anthony Gruber; Walter M. Nagle.
Res., 130 Prospect St., 06354-1499. Tel: 860-564-2668; Fax: 860-564-3941. [CEM]
School—Plainfield Catholic, Tel: 860-564-3476; Fax: 860-564-3476.
Lay Teachers 12; Students 248.
Catechesis/Religious Programs—Tel: 860-230-0141. Anne Collelo, D.R.E.
Students 280.
Mission—Sterling, Windham Co., St. Joseph.

Mystic, New London Co., St. Patrick (1870), Rev. Charles A. McGrail.
Res., 32 E. Main St., P.O. Box 236, 06355-0236. Tel: 860-536-1800; Fax: 860-536-9635. [CEM]
Catechesis/Religious Programs—Tel: 860-536-6808. Susan Waters, D.R.E.
Students 242.

New London, New London Co., St. Joseph (1907), Revs. Joseph Castaldi; Stephen Gulino; Charles Rodrigo (Sri Lanka); Rev. Msgr. Paul J. St. Onge, (Retired); Bro. Robert Vozzo, Hospital Chap.; Deacon Gerard Gaynor, Jr.
Res., 17 Squire St., 06320-4891. Tel: 860-443-5393.
School—Tel: 860-442-1720.
Lay Teachers 10; Students 226.
Catechesis/Religious Programs—Students 240.

St. Mary, Star of the Sea (1870), Very Rev. Thomas J. Smith, V.F.; Revs. Martin J.W. Jones, Hispanic Min.; Philip A. Pusateri, S.J.; Stanley Grove,

M.S.A.; Deacons Mariano Ramos, Hispanic Min.; Jesus A. Diez Canseco, Hispanic Min. Pastoral Assocs.: Sr. Gemma Mancini, S.C.I.C.; Sr. Giuseppina Frontini, S.C.I.C.; Sr. Marielos Ballestero, R.O.D.A., Hispanic Min.
Res., 10 Huntington St., 06320-6198. Tel: 860-447-1431; Fax: 860-437-1889.
School—(1879), Tel: 860-443-7758; Fax: 860-444-2465. Sr. Angese Quarta, S.C.I.C., Prin.; Mrs. Paula Zeppieri, Vice Prin.
Priests 3; Sisters 3; Lay Teachers 6; Students 125.
Catechesis/Religious Programs—Tel: 860-443-5870; Fax: 860-443-8552. D.R.E. Sr. Immacolata DeCossio, S.C.I.C.; Mrs. Millie Ramos.
Students 265.
Convents—28 Huntington St., 06320. Tel: 860-443-5870; Fax: 860-443-8552. The Congregation of Sisters of Charity of the Immaculate Conception of Ivrea, Italy
Sisters 5; 28 River Ave., Norwich, 06360. Tel: 860-886-6092. Congregation of Oblate Sisters of Divine Love Sr. Brta Najela, R.O.D.A., Supr. The Oblate Sisters of Divine Love.
Hispanic Ministry—60 Jay St., 06320. Tel: 860-437-1285.

Niantic, New London Co., St. Agnes (1922), Rev. Arthur A. Archer; Deacons Roland J. LaCasse; Maurice J. Walsh.
Res., 22 Haigh Ave., 06357-3129. Tel: 860-739-9722; Fax: 860-691-2187.
Catechesis/Religious Programs—Tel: 860-739-9992.
Students 297.
Chapel—Crescent Beach, St. Francis Chapel (Summer).

North Grosvenordale, Windham Co., St. Joseph (1872), Rev. Richard J. Ricard, Admin.
Res., 12 Main St., P.O. Box 897, 06255-0897. Tel: 860-923-2361; Fax: 860-923-3396. [CEM]
School—Tel: 860-923-2090; Fax: 860-923-3609. Sharon Briere, Prin.
Lay Teachers 12; Students 125.
Catechesis/Religious Programs—Tel: 860-923-0155.
Students 270.
Mission—Mechanicsville, Sacred Heart, 15 Sacred Heart Dr., P.O. Box 897, Mechanicsville, 06255.

North Stonington, New London Co., St. Thomas More (1977), Rev. V. Antony Alaharasan, Admin.; Deacon Donald J. Donahue.
Res., 87 Mystic Rd., 06359. Tel: 860-535-1601; Fax: 860-535-2828.
Catechesis/Religious Programs—Tel: 860-535-3229.
Students 208.

Oakdale, New London Co., Our Lady of the Lakes (1966), Rev. Marek Masnicki.
Res., 752 Norwich, Salem Tpke., 06370. Tel: 860-859-1575; Fax: 860-859-3273.
Catechesis/Religious Programs—Students 225.

Occum, New London Co., St. Joseph (1878), Rev. Leszek T. Janik.
Res., 11 Baltic Rd., Box 256, Versailles, 06383-0256. Tel: 860-822-8020; Fax: 860-822-8007.
Catechesis/Religious Programs—Tel: 860-822-6963. Mrs. Monica Bernier, D.R.E.
Students 134.
Saint Society Church—(Corporate Title: St. Joseph Church Society of Occum, CT, Inc.).

Old Lyme, New London Co., Christ the King (1934), Rev. Msgr. Richard P. LaRocque; Sr. Katherine M. McKenna, P.B.V.M., Pastoral Assoc. In res., Rev. Thomas W. Ahern.
Office: 30 Lyme St., P.O. Box 443, 06371-0443. Tel: 860-434-1669; 860-434-1660 (Res.); Fax: 860-434-7140.
Catechesis/Religious Programs—Tel: 860-434-9873. Louise Young, D.R.E.
Students 381.
Chapel—Our Lady of Good Counsel at Sound View. (Summer Chapel) Shore Rd., 06371.

Old Saybrook, Middlesex Co., St. John (1884), Very Rev. Joseph H. Hanks; Rev. Dennis G. Carey; Deacon John R. Hancock.
Res., 161 Main St., 06475-2367. Tel: 860-388-3787; Fax: 860-388-6008. [CEM]
School—42 Maynard Rd., 06475. Tel: 860-388-0849; Fax: 860-388-6265. Sr. Marie Julie, S.C.M.C., Prin.
Sisters 4; Lay Teachers 15; Students 276.
Catechesis/Religious Programs—Tel: 203-388-6288. Sr. M. Christina S.C.M.C., D.R.E.
Students 236.

Pawcatuck, New London Co., St. Michael (1860), Revs. Dennis M. Perkins; Francis C. Rouleau.
Res., 60 Liberty St., 06379. Tel: 860-599-5580; Fax: 860-599-8079. [CEM 2]
School—Tel: 860-599-1084. Richard B. Woodworth, Prin.
Lay Teachers 9; Students 206.
Catechesis/Religious Programs—Tel: 860-599-0040. Mrs. Crystal F. Wilcox, D.R.E.
Students 260.

Plainfield, Windham Co., St. John the Apostle (1907), Rev. Michael J. Gill.
Res., 10 Railroad Ave., 06374-1215. Tel: 860-564-3313. [CEM]
School—Plainfield Catholic School, 12 Railroad Ave., 06374-1215. Tel: 860-564-3476. Sr. Marie Authur, S.C.M.C., Prin.
Catechesis/Religious Programs—12 Railroad Ave., 06374. Tel: 860-564-8380.
Students 155.

Pomfret, Windham Co., Most Holy Trinity (1886), Rev. Paul L. Hebert.
Res., 568 Pomfret St., P.O. Box 235, 06258-0235. Tel: 860-928-5830.
Catechesis/Religious Programs—Students 285.

Portland, Middlesex Co., St. Mary (1872), Rev. John F. Ashe; Sr. Mary Ida Dolan, R.S.M., Pastoral Assoc., Tel: 860-342-4913. In res., Rev. Mark Daniel Kirby, O.Cist., M.A., S.T.L.
Res., 51 Freestone Ave., P.O. Box 307, 06480-0307. Tel: 860-342-2328; Fax: 860-342-1433. [CEM]
Catechesis/Religious Programs—Tel: 860-342-2308.
Students 419.

Preston, New London Co., St. Catherine of Siena (1975), Rev. George J. Richards, Jr., Admin.
Res., 243 Rte. 164, 06365-8726. Tel: 860-887-9966; Fax: 860-889-7640.
Catechesis/Religious Programs—Students 162.

Putnam, Windham Co., St. Mary (1866), Revs. Rolamd C. Cloutier; Gregorsz Brozonowicz; Marcel G. Lachance; Sr. Rita St. Onge, Pastoral Assoc., Tel: 860-928-4507; Deacons Pierre M. Desilets; Bernard A. Phaneuf.
Res., 218 Providence St., 06260-1514. Tel: 860-928-6535; Fax: 860-928-7246. [CEM]
School—23 Marshall St., 06260. Tel: 860-928-7046; 928-1104; Fax: 860-928-9379. Miss Phyllis A. Hickey, Prin.
Catechesis/Religious Programs—15 Marshall St., 06260. Tel: 860-928-4507. Mrs. Priscilla Dowd, D.R.E.
Students 115.

Quaker Hill, New London Co., Our Lady of Perpetual Help (1904) (Polish), Rev. Msgr. Thomas R. Bride, P.A., KHS., V.G.; Deacon Ronald S. Kitlinski.
Res., 63 Old Norwich Rd., P.O. Box 329, 06375-0329. Tel: 860-443-1875; Fax: 860-437-1125.
Catechesis/Religious Programs—Sr. Michelle Sokol, S.S.J.-T.O.S.F., D.R.E.
Students 113.
Convent—59 Old Norwich Rd., 06375. Tel: 860-447-3550. Sisters of St. Joseph of Third Order of St. Francis

Quinebaug, Windham Co., St. Stephen (1955), Rev. William J. O'Rourke.
Res., 130 Old Turnpike Rd., 06262-0222. Tel: 860-935-5205; Fax: 860-935-5205.
Catechesis/Religious Programs—Students 78.

Rockville, Tolland Co., St. Bernard (1854), Very Rev. John J. White; Rev. Justinian B. Rweyemamu; Deacons Michael Berstene; Harry Grospitch; Alexander Saunders.
Res., 25 St. Bernard's Ter., 06066-3258. Tel: 860-875-0753; Fax: 860-871-7460. [CEM]
School—20 School St., 06066. Tel: 860-875-0475; Fax: 860-872-2444. Sr. Mary Gerald Creeden, R.S.M., Prin.
Sisters 1; Lay Teachers 9; Students 165.
Catechesis/Religious Programs—22 School St., 06066. Tel: 860-872-3828.
Students 554.
Convent—32 School St., 06066. Tel: 860-875-4016. Sisters of Mercy
Cemetery Office—Tel: 203-872-6601.

St. Joseph (1905) (Polish), Revs. Joseph M. Olczak, O.S.P.P.E.; Anselm Chalupka, O.S.P.P.E.
Res., 33 West St., 06066-6154. Tel: 860-871-1970; Fax: 860-872-0333.
School—41 West St., 06066. Tel: 860-875-4943. Sr. Theresa Mary Gonolek, C.S.S.F., Prin.
Felician Sisters 3; Lay Teachers 8; Students 128.
Catechesis/Religious Programs—Students 196.

Rogers, Windham Co., St. Ignatius (1939), Rev. William J. McNulty.
Res., 350 Hartford Pike, Box 487, Dayville, 06241. Tel: 860-774-8656.
Church—21 Williamsville Rd., Box 158, 06263.
Convent—17 Williamsville Rd., Box 158, 06263. Tel: 860-774-8154. St. Ignatius Parish House Daughters of the Holy Spirit
Catechesis/Religious Programs—Combined with St. Joseph, Dayville, CT.

Somersville, Tolland Co., All Saints (1915), Rev. Timothy C. Valliere; Deacons James J. Burgess; Lawrence W. Deraleau; John J. Abdalla.
Res., 25 School St., P.O. Box M, 06072-0913. Tel: 860-749-8625; Fax: 860-763-1890.
Catechesis/Religious Programs—Tel: 860-763-0348. Sandy E. Russo, D.R.E.
Students 506.

Stafford Springs, Tolland Co., St. Edward (1869), Revs. Richard-Jacob Forcier, O.F.M.Conv.; Mark-Thomas Booth, O.F.M.Conv.; Bro. Dennis Sokolowski, O.F.M.Conv.
Mailing Address: 6 Benton St., 06076-0433. Tel: 860-684-2705; Fax: 860-684-0757.
Res., 55 High St., 06076. [CEM]
School—(Grades PreK-8). Tel: 860-684-2600. Kathleen Walsh, Prin.
Lay Teachers 11; Students 180.
Catechesis/Religious Programs—Students 231.
Mission—Staffordville, Tolland Co., St. Joseph, 6 Benton St., 06076.

Stonington, New London Co., St. Mary (1850), Revs. Philip J. Geogan; Milroy Perera; Deacon Henry E. O'Reilly.
Res., 95 Main St., 06378-1219. Tel: 860-535-1700. [CEM]
Catechesis/Religious Programs—Tel: 860-535-4252. Matthew West, D.R.E.
Students 116.

Storrs, Tolland Co., St. Thomas Aquinas (1947), Revs. Paul D. Holland, S.J.; Richard K. Gross, S.J.; James J. Dressman, S.J.; Sr. Alberta Surowiec, F.S.S.J.
Res., 46 N. Eagleville Rd., 06268-1710. Tel: 860-429-6436; Fax: 860-429-2809.
Catechesis/Religious Programs—Tel: 860-429-6436. D.R.E. Bro. Edward J. Hall, C.P., D.R.E.; Susan Salesses; Tom O'Connell.
Students 247.

Taftville, New London Co., Sacred Heart (1883), Rev. Msgr. Henry N. Archambault, P.A.; J.C.D. In res., Rev. William J. Flynn.
Res., 156 Providence St., P.O. Box 208, 06380. Tel: 860-887-3072; Fax: 203-887-3072.
School—15 Hunters Ave., 063800208. Tel: 860-887-1757; Fax: 860-889-7276. Sr. Mary David, S.C.M.C., Prin.
Sisters of Charity of Our Lady Mother of the Church 4; Lay Teachers 6; Students 160.
Catechesis/Religious Programs—Tel: 860-887-4363; Fax: 860-889-7276.
Students 124.

Tolland, Tolland Co., St. Matthew (1964), Rev. James P. Carini; Deacon Ronald Freedman.
Mailing Address: P.O. Box 100, 06084-0100. Tel: 860-872-0200; Fax: 860-875-4413.
Catechesis/Religious Programs—Tel: 860-875-8663. Mrs. Nancy Rudek, (Grades K-8) D.R.E.
Students 851.

Vernon, Tolland Co., Sacred Heart (1958), Rev. Stanley J. Szczapa; Deacon Charles B. White; Rella Bernabucci, Pastoral Assoc.
Church—550 Hartford Tpke., 06066-5000. Tel: 860-875-4563; Fax: 860-872-2535.
Catechesis/Religious Programs—Students 103.

Voluntown, New London Co., St. Thomas Apostle (1892), Rev. James Joseph Sucholet.
Res., 61 Preston City Rd., P.O. Box 99, 06384-0099. Tel: 860-376-2293; Fax: 860-376-0287. [CEM]
Catechesis/Religious Programs—49 Preston City Rd., 06384. Tel: 860-376-8352.
Students 202.
Mission—Glasgo, New London Co., St. Anne, (1891) Rte. 201, Glasgo, 06384.

Waterford, New London Co., St. Paul (1960), Rev. Richard F. Roughan; Deacon Richard K. Walker.
Res., 170 Rope Ferry Rd., 06385-2609. Tel: 860-443-5587.
Catechesis/Religious Programs—Tel: 860-443-3375. Mrs. Roseann Ward, D.R.E.
Students 280.

Wauregan, Windham Co., Sacred Heart (1889) (French), Rev. Brian J. Converse.
Res., 620 Wauregan Rd., P.O. Box 468, 06387-0468. Tel: 860-774-6892. [CEM]
Catechesis/Religious Programs—Students 55.

West Willington, Tolland Co., St. Jude (1981), Rev. Thomas W. Sennik.
Res., 25 Old Farms Rd., P.O. Box 240, Willington, 06279-0240. Tel: 860-429-9655.
Catechesis/Religious Programs—Tel: 860-429-8604.
Students 132.

Westbrook, Middlesex Co., St. Mark (1962), Rev. Richard J. Albamonti.
Res., 222 McVeagh Rd., 06498-1515. Tel: 860-399-9207; Fax: 860-399-7751.
Catechesis/Religious Programs—Tel: 860-399-6208. Sr. Glorista Arackal, S.A.B.S., D.R.E.
Students 317.

Windham, Windham Co., Sagrado Corazon de Jesus (1991) (Hispanic), Rev. Paul J. Murdock; Deacon Felipe Silva. Pastoral Assocs.: Sr. Edith Villalobos, R.O.D.A.; Ms. Virginia Rodriguez.
Mailing Address: 61 Club Rd., 06280-1007. Tel: 860-423-8617; Fax: 860-423-4157.
Catechesis/Religious Programs—Students 137.

Willimantic, Windham Co., St. Joseph (1859), Rev. Msgr. Willis W. West; Revs. Luke A. Walaszek, O.P.; John Edward Lee; Deacon Lawrence Godwin. In res., Rev. Edward F. Frigault.
Res., 99 Jackson St., 06226-3077. Tel: 860-423-8439; Fax: 860-423-6825. [CEM]
School—St. Mary-St. Joseph, 35 Valley St., 06226. Tel: 860-423-8479; Fax: 860-423-8365. Frank Farino, Prin.
Catechesis/Religious Programs—Students 207.
Convent—88 Jackson St., 06226. Tel: 203-423-5122.
Mission—Scotland, Windham Co., St. Margaret, Rte. 14, Scotland, 06264. Tel: 203-423-1791.

St. Mary (1903) (French), Rev. Roger J. Lamoureux, O.M.I. In res., Rev. Edward Poulin.
Res., 80 Maple Ave., 06226-2733. Tel: 860-423-5835; Fax: 860-423-9933.
School—St. Mary-St. Joseph, 35 Valley St., 06226. Tel: 860-423-8479; Fax: 860-423-8365. Frank Farina, Prin.
Sisters 3; Lay Teachers 10; Students 219.
Catechesis/Religious Programs—Tel: 860-423-9700; Fax: 860-455-9407.
Students 130.
Convent—88 Jackson St., 06226. Tel: 860-423-5122. Sisters of Charity of Our Lady
Faith Formulation—Tel: 860-423-9700. Mrs. Tina Popeleski, Dir.

Chaplains of Public Institutions

NORWICH. *William W. Backus Hospital* 06360. Tel: 860-889-8331. Sr. Rita Johnson, S.S.N.D., Chaplaincy Svcs.

MIDDLETOWN. *Connecticut Valley Hospital* Eastern Dr., P.O. Box 351, 06457. Tel: 860-262-5900; Fax: 860-262-5900. Rev. Jose Rizal Dimapilis, O.P., Prin. Chap.
Long Lane School. Mailing Address:Mailing Address: P.O. Box 882, 06457. Tel: 860-344-2820. In res., (Mount St. John) 135 Kirtland St., Deep River, 06417-1817.
Middlesex Memorial Hospital 28 Crescent St., 06457-0822. Tel: 860-347-9471, Ext. 6725. Rev. Bruce Quinn, O.F.M.Cap.

NEW LONDON. *Lawrence and Memorial Hospitals* Montauk Ave., 06320. Tel: 860-442-0711, Ext. 2609. Bro. Robert Vozzo, C.S.C., Chap.; Deacon Roland J. LaCasse.
U.S. Coast Guard Memorial Chapel U.S. Coast Guard Academy, 15 Mohegan Ave., 06320-4195. Tel: 860-444-8418; Fax: 960-701-6729. Rev. William Dillon, S.A., Commander, C.H.C., U.S.N.R.

NIANTIC. *State Farm for Women*. Vacant.

On Special or Other Diocesan Assignment:
Reverend Monsignors—
Bride, Thomas R., P.A., Vicar Gen., The Chancery
Brown, Robert L., Chancellor, The Chancery

On Duty Outside the Diocese:
Reverend Fathers—
Angelo, Thomas M.
Bissonnette, Bernard
Boudreau, C. Paul
Byabato, Deus-Dedit
Caiazzo, Nicholas
Dudzik, Dariusz
Gwudz, John S.
Kirby, Gerald S., Diocesan Mission House, c/o Lynx Air, P.O. Box 407139, Ft. Lauderdale, FL 33340
Klimanskis, Adolfo, St. Casimir Rectory, 350 Smith St., Providence, RI 02908
Randall, Kevin, Pontifical Ecclesiastical Academy, Piazza della Minerva, 74, Rome, 00186 Italy
Shea, Thomas W.
Tumicki, Ted

Military Chaplains:
Reverend Fathers—
Angelo, Thomas M., Ch. Capt., 23 Wg/MC, Pope AFB, NC 28308
Gwudz, John S., Office of Chap., U.S.S. Independence, CV 62, FPO, AP 96618-2760

Absent on Leave:
Reverend Fathers—
Bolieau, Henry G.
Dempsey, Edward M., 75 Bushnell St., Hartford, CT 06114
Gaulin, Roger M.
Jean, Raymond J., 6 Foster Leigh Rd., Niantic, CT 06357
Liszewski, Francis A.
Surprenant, John L., 943 High St., Akron, PA 17501
Twomey, Thomas

Retired:
Reverend Monsignors—
Gadarowski, Bronislaw A., Winter, 357 Pineview Dr., Venice, FL 34293
Malanowski, Thaddeus F., 908 S. Prospect Ave., Clearwater, FL 34616
O'Brien, James J., St. Mary Home, 2021 Albany Ave., West Hartford, CT 06117
St. Onge, Paul J., 310 Montauk Ave., New London, CT 06320
Vytautas, Balciunas, Matulitis Nursing Home, 10 Thurber Rd., Putnam, CT 66260. Tel: 860-928-7976
Reverend Fathers—
Ahern, Thomas W.
Almendra, Leoncio T., Real St. Abuyog, Leyte, Philippines
Berube, Theodore E., Sacred Heart Rectory, W. Main St., P.O. Box 468, Wauregan, CT 06387. Tel: 860-774-6892
Bialkowski, Henry A., 162 Eddy Glover Blvd., New Britain, CT 06053. Tel: 203-223-4242
Cronin, Robert W., 11 Middlefield Dr., West Hartford, CT 06107
Curtin, Clifford J., 799 Prospect Ave. B-6, West Hartford, CT 06105. Tel: 860-236-2493
Davis, Edward J., 179 Train St., Dorchester, MA 02122. Tel: 617-282-0479
Drummond, Elsyn J.
Flint, Kenneth, Box 4, Charlestown, RI 02813. Tel: 401-364-1071
Frigault, Edward F., St. Joseph, 99 Jackson St., Willimantic, CT 06226
Giaquinto, Albert C., Theological College, 401 Michigan Ave., N.E., Washington, D.C. 20064
Kelley, J. Ralph, Heritage Commons, 38 Boston Rd., Middletown, CT 06457. Tel: 860-343-0164
Klein, Theodore J., Ph.D., 140 Greemanville Ave., Apt. 2, Mystic, CT 06355
Kozon, John A., 3780 Isherwood Cove, Memphis, TN 38125
Kuzdal, Anthony P., 1714 Beach Pkwy., A-2, Cape Coral, FL 33904. Tel: 813-542-9261
Liszewski, Francis A., 8 Hillcrest Dr., Tolland, CT 06084
Marciniak, John, 70 W. 18th Rd., Broad Channel, NY 11693
McGrath, Daniel F., 2433 Main St., Rocky Hill, CT 06067
McNulty, Robert E., 5 Holmes St., E-14, Mystic, CT 06355. Tel: 860-536-1758
Morrissette, Joseph H., 30 School Hill Rd., Baltic, CT 06330
Murphy, Hugh J., P.O. Box 261, Pomfret, CT 06258
Nichols, Joseph E., 810 Walnut St., Lebanon, PA 17042
Parker, George H., Human Life International, 4 Family Life, Front Royal, VA 22630. Tel: 540-635-7884
Poulin, Edward C., 13 Blissville Rd., Lisbon, CT 06351. Tel: 860-887-3689
Pupsys, Adam, P.O. Box 2163, Westerly, RI 02891
Ramen, Paul F., 350 Pond Hill Rd., Moosup, CT 06354. Tel: 860-887-2565
Ricard, Joseph M., 233 Spanish Moss Rd., Davenport, FL 33837
Smilga, Zenon A., Our Lady of Grace Rectory, Box 425, Fishers Island, NY 06390. Tel: 631-788-7353
Sutula, Leo S., 19 Maxwell Sr., Rocky Hill, CT 06067
Wisneski, Edward, S.T.D., Ph.D., 78 E. Ridge Rd., Middletown, CT 06457

Permanent Deacons:
Abdalla, John, All Saints, Somerville
Bachand, Francis J., St. Mary, Jewett City
Baillargeon, Paul R., St. Mary, Jewett City
Barlow, Robert C., St. Andrew, Colchester
Berstene, Michael C., St. Bernard, Rockville
Boucher, Richard A., St. Luke, Ellington
Burgess, James J., All Saints & Office of Evangelization, Somersville
Burke, John J., Jr., 15 Black Bear Tr., Hendersonville, NC 28739-9348
Cannata, Nicholas J., St. Sebastian, Middletown
Cartier, L. Robert
Catalano, John P., St. Sebastian, Middletown
Cote, Albert J., St. Francis, Lebanon
Coyne, Thomas
Cyr, Warren, St. Patrick, East Hampton
Danesi, Peter H., III, St. Mary, Groton
Deraleau, Lawrence W., All Saints, Somersville
Desilets, Pierre M., Project Northeast & St. Mary, Putnam
Diez Conseco, Jesus A., St. Mary, Hispanic Apostolate New London & Bishop's Delegate to Hispanic Permanent Deacons
Dogue, Eduardo, (Retired)
Dolan, Dennis F., Prison Ministry
Donahue, Donald J., St. Thomas More, North Stonington
Doyle, Dennis A., III, St. Mary, Norwich
Fecteau, Al R., Cathedral of St. Patrick, Norwich
Freedman, Ronald, St. Matthew, Tolland
Gaynor, Gerard J., Saint Joseph, New London
Goodwin, Lawrence, St. Margaret Mission, Scotland
Gosselin, Raymond P., St. Lawrence, Killingworth
Grospitch, Harry J., St. Bernard, Rockville
Hancock, John, St. John, Old Saybrook
Hayes, Robert P., St. John, Fitchville
Jolin, Joseph
Kitlinski, Ronald S., Our Lady Perpetual Help, Quaker Hill
LaCasse, Roland J., Chap. Asst., Lawrence & Memorial Hospitals; Asst., St. Agnes
LaPlante, Joseph A., Manset, ME
McMahon, James R., Sr., St. Michael, Pawcatuck
Melendez, Carlos
Midwood, Barry R.
Nygaard, Melvin G., St. John, Uncasville
O'Reilly, Henry E., St. Mary, Stonington
Osuba, Jose, Columbia
Phaneuf, Bernard A., St. Mary, Putnam
Ramos, Mariano, Hispanic Ministry, St. Mary, New London
Reed, Steven W., Our Lady of Lourdes, Gales Ferry
Saunders, Alexander, St. Bernard, Rockville
Silva, Felipe, St. Joseph, Willimantic
Walker, Richard K., St. Paul, Waterford
Walsh, Maurice, St. Agnes, Niantic
Weber, F. Paul, St. Mary of the Visitation, Clinton
White, Charles B., St. Luke, Ellington
Whittle, Joseph B.

INSTITUTIONS LOCATED IN THE DIOCESE

[A] SEMINARIES, RELIGIOUS OR SCHOLASTICATES

CROMWELL. *Holy Apostles College and Seminary*, 33 Prospect Hill Rd., 06416-2005. Tel: 860-632-3000; 632-3010 (Admissions); Fax: 860-632-3030.
E-mail: rector@holyapostles.edu
Web site: www.holyapostles.edu
Revs. Douglas L. Mosey, C.S.B., Ph.D., Pres. & Rector; Maurice Sheehan, O.F.M.Cap., Academic Dean; Michel Legault, M.S.A., Vice Rector; Raymond Halliwell, M.S.A.; Addison Hallock, M.S.A., Spiritual Dir.; Bradley Pierce, M.S.A.; Ronan P. Callahan, C.P.; Philip S. Kiley, S.J., Head Librarian; Benedict Klucinec, M.S.A.; Gerard Gibeault, M.S.A.; David Q. Liptak; Luis Luna, M.S.A.; Marc Daniel Kirby, O.Cist.; David Zercie, M.S.A.; Brian T. Mullady, O.P.; Joseph M. Olczak, O.S.P.P.E.; Robert Sickler, M.S.A.; John Hoover; John Hillier; Sr. Anne Linder, F.S.E., Dir. Field Education; Dr. Cynthia Toolin, Registrar; William J. Russell, P.C., Finance Officer. Priests 19; Brothers 2; Sisters 6; Lay Teachers 13; Seminarians 80; Seminary Division Lay Students 60; Total 140.

ENDERS ISLAND. *St. Edmund's Novitiate*, P.O. Box 399, 06355. Tel: 860-572-9538; Fax: 203-572-7655.
E-mail: endersisle@aol.com
Web site: www.sse.org
Society of St. Edmund. Revs. John Meagher; Thomas F.X. Hoar, S.S.E.; Paul Pinard, S.S.E.; Bros. Martin Slattery, S.S.E.; Francis McMahon, S.S.E.; Mr. Mark Gordon, Dir. Oper. Priests 2; Brothers 1.

[B] HIGH SCHOOLS, DIOCESAN

MIDDLETOWN. *Mercy High School*, 1740 Randolph Rd., 06457-5155. Tel: 860-346-6659; Fax: 860-344-9887.
E-mail: info@mercyhigh.com
Web site: www.mercyhigh.com
Sisters of Mercy. Sr. Mary A. McCarthy, R.S.M., Prin.; Sr. Patty Moriarty, R.S.M., Vice Prin. Student Life; Mr. Steven Brickey, Vice Prin. Academics; Sr. Peggy O'Neill, R.S.M., Vice Prin. & Registrar; Miss Ann Derbacher, Campus Min. Sisters 11; Lay Teachers 47; Students 629; Total Staff 69.
Xavier High School, 181 Randolph Rd., 06457-5635. Tel: 860-346-7735; Fax: 860-346-6859.
Web site: www.xavierhighschool.org
Brothers of St. Francis Xavier. Bro. William Ciganek, C.F.X., Prin.; Rev. Gregory Galvin, Chap.; Rorey Donaldson, Devel. Dir.; Bro. James Boyle, C.F.X., Community Dir. Asst. Principals. Mr. William Garrity; Mr. Thomas Aiello; Bro. Thomas Ryan, C.F.X. Brothers 12; Lay Teachers 50; Students 841.

UNCASVILLE. *St. Bernard High School*, 1593 Norwich-New London Tpke., 06382-1399. Tel: 860-848-1271;

Fax: 860-848-1274.
E-mail: sbhs@snet.net
Web site: www.saint-bernard.com
Rev. Santino Casimano, Chap.; Richard G. Arms, Jr., Prin.; James Venditto, Asst. Prin. Priests 1; Lay Teachers 24; Students 326.

St. Bernard Academy. (Grades 6-8). (Middle School), 1593 Norwich-New London Tpke., 06382-1399. Tel: 860-848-1271; Fax: 860-848-1274. Rev. Santino Casimano, Chap.; Ms. Mary C. Dillman, Prin.; Sr. Joan A. O'Connor, C.S.J., Asst. Prin. Lay Teachers 8; Students 126.

[C] HIGH SCHOOLS, PRIVATE

BALTIC. *Academy and Boarding-School of the Holy Family*, 54 W. Main St., P.O. Box 691, 06330-0691. Tel: 860-822-9272; Fax: 860-822-1318. Sisters of Charity of Our Lady Mother of the Church. Sr. Mary Patrick, S.C.M.C., Prin.; Rev. Michael Wood, Chap. Sisters 7; Lay Teachers 6; Students 75.

THOMPSON. *Marianapolis Preparatory School*, P.O. Box 368, 26 Chase Rd., 06277-0368. Tel: 860-923-9565; Fax: 860-923-3730.
E-mail: bromic1@aol.com
Web site: marianapolis.com
Marian Fathers. Revs. Timothy Roth, M.I.C., Headmaster; Albin Gurkis, M.I.C.; Bros. Donald Schaefer, M.I.C., Treas., Registrar & Dir. Devel.; Brian Manian, M.I.C., Asst. Resident Dir. & Supr. Priests 2; Brothers 1; Clerics 1; Lay Teachers 19; Students 263.

[D] PROTECTIVE INSTITUTIONS

DEEP RIVER. *Mount St. John*, 135 Kirtland St., 06417-1816. Tel: 860-526-5391; Fax: 860-526-1636.
E-mail: exdir@mountsaintjohn.org
Web site: mountsaintjohn.org
For a complete listing, refer to the Special Care Facilities section.

[E] HOMES FOR AGED

WILLIMANTIC. *Holy Family Home and Shelter, Inc.*, 88 Jackson St., P.O. Box 884, 06226-0884. Tel: 860-423-7719; Fax: 860-423-3770.
E-mail: holyfamily@neca.com
For a complete listing, refer to the Special Care Facilities section.

WINDHAM. *St. Joseph Living Center*, 14 Club Rd., 06280-1000. Tel: 860-456-1107; Fax: 860-450-7114
For a complete listing, refer to the Special Care Facilities section.

[F] MONASTERIES AND RESIDENCES OF PRIESTS AND BROTHERS

CROMWELL. *Society of the Missionaries of the Holy Apostles*, 24 Prospect Hill Rd., 06416-2005. Tel: 860-632-3039; Fax: 860-635-4823. Society of the Missionaries of the Holy Apostles. Very Rev. Raymond Halliwell, M.S.A., Prov. Animator; Revs. Maximo Asencios-Pablo, M.S.A.; Edward Doherty, M.S.A.; Stanley Grove, M.S.A.; Addison Hallock, M.S.A.; Daniel Karempelis, M.S.A.; Benedict Klucinec, M.S.A.; John Marcoux, M.S.A.; William McCarthy, M.S.A.; Robert McQueeney, M.S.A.; Ronald Mikasauskas, M.S.A.; Robert Murphy, M.S.A.; Bradley Pierce, M.S.A.; George Realmuto, M.S.A.; Robert Sickler, M.S.A.; Thomas Simon, M.S.A.; Richard Skarbek, M.S.A.; Pasquale Taliercio, M.S.A.; David Zercie, M.S.A.
Working Outside the Diocese: Revs. Humberto Almazan, M.S.A.; James Anderson, M.S.A.; J. Patrick Boyhan, M.S.A.; James J. Creedon, M.S.A.; Harold Dunn, M.S.A.; Francis Fajella, M.S.A.; Richard Hite, M.S.A.; Joseph Kenney, M.S.A.; Vincent Kilidjian, M.S.A.; James Larkin, M.S.A.; Marius Morin, M.S.A.; Michael Nofi, M.S.A.; Leo Ovian, M.S.A.; Gerard Petta, M.S.A.; Larry Preston, M.S.A.; Edward Przygocki, M.S.A.; Isaac Raney, M.S.A.; Martin Rooney, M.S.A.; Vincent Salamoni, M.S.A.; Jose Salazar, M.S.A.

GRISWOLD. *Marian Friary of Our Lady of Guadalupe*. 199 Colonel Brown Rd., Norwich, 06360-9011. Tel: 860-376-6840; Fax: 860-376-6848.
E-mail: ffi@connix.com
Web site: www.marymediatrix.com
Revs. Angelo Mary Geiger, Guardian & Novice Master; Bonaventure Maria Pio McGuire, Vicar; Peter Damian Mary Fehlner, Am. Supr. Priests 3; Novices 4.

MIDDLETOWN. *Congregation of the Brothers of St. Francis Xavier*, 181 Randolph Rd., 06457-5635. Tel: 860-346-8585; Fax: 860-346-6859. Bros. William Ciganek, C.F.X., Prin.; James Boyle, C.F.X., Dir.; D. Paschal Alford, C.F.C.; Eugene Behenna, C.F.X.; Labre Dillon, C.F.X.; Thomas Fahey, C.F.X.; J. Robert Houlihan, C.F.X.; Rev. Gregory Galvin, Chap.; Bros. John J. McDonald, C.F.X.; K. Paul McGlade, C.F.C.; H. Lawrence Nyhan, C.F.X.; Harold Pray, C.F.X.; Thomas Ryan, C.F.X. Total Staff 3; Total in Residence 13.

MYSTIC. *Society of St. Edmund*, P.O. Box 399, 06355-0399. Tel: 860-572-9538; Fax: 860-572-7655.
E-mail: endersisle@aol.com
Web site: www.sse.org
Revs. Thomas F.X. Hoar, S.S.E.; Paul Pinard, S.S.E.; Bro. Martin Slattery, S.S.E. Total in Residence 3.

THOMPSON. *Marian Fathers*, Marianapolis Prep School, 06277-0368. Tel: 860-923-9798; Fax: 860-923-3730.
E-mail: timothy.roth@snet.net
Web site: marianapolis.com
Revs. Timothy Roth, M.I.C., Headmaster, First Councillor, & Vice Provincial; Albin Gurkis, M.I.C.; Bros. Donald Schaefer, M.I.C., Provincial Treas. & Second Councillor; Brian Manian, M.I.C., Supr., Fourth Provincial Councillor; Donald Petraitis, M.I.C., Provincial. Total in Residence 4.

WILLIMANTIC. *Missionary Oblates of Mary Immaculate*, 289 Windham Rd., P.O. Box 55, 06226-0055. Tel: 860-423-8484; Fax: 860-423-5285.
E-mail: omict@ntplx.net
Web site: www.ntplx.net/~omict
Revs. Daniel Nassaney, O.M.I., Supr. & Dir.; Henri A. DeLisle, O.M.I.; Leroy Landry, O.M.I.; Lon Konold, O.M.I.; Bros. Donat Daigle, O.M.I.; Paul Ricard, O.M.I.; Rev. Olivier Renaud, O.M.I. Total in Residence 7; Total Staff 12.

[G] CONVENTS AND RESIDENCES FOR SISTERS

NORWICH. *School Sisters Notre Dame*, 7 Otis St., 06360. Tel: 860-886-6948.

BALTIC. *Holy Family Motherhouse*, 06330-0619. Tel: 860-822-8241; Fax: 860-822-9842. Rev. Michael Wood, Chap. Tel: 860-822-1561. Sisters of Charity of Our Lady, Mother of the Church. Mother M. Anthony, Supr. Gen. Professed 77; Junior Professed 5; Novices 1.

Sisters of the Holy Cross, 133 Main St., Box 199, 06330. Tel: 203-822-6794.

GALES FERRY. *Society of the Sisters for the Church*, 06335. Tel: 860-464-4023. Sr. Jeanette Serra, S.S.C., P.O. Box 295, 06335. Tel: 860-423-8484 (Work); 464-4023 (Home).

HIGGANUM. *Apostles of the Sacred Heart of Jesus*, Sacred Heart on the Lake, 529 Brainard Hill Rd., 06441-4010. Tel: 860-345-4653; Fax: 860-345-4469.
E-mail: sdjv@juno.com
Total in Residence 3.

MIDDLETOWN. *Mill Hill Sisters*, 6 Bluebird Rd., 06457. Total in Residence 3.

Sisters of Mercy, 251 Hunting Hill Ave., 06457. Tel: 860-343-1642.
E-mail: patmck@juno.com
Other Locations: 421 High St., 06457. Tel: 860-346-4906. 94 Warner Ave., 06457. Tel: 860-343-8533. 419 High St., 06457. Tel: 860-344-8569. 203 East St., Hebron, 06248. Tel: 860-228-0849. 56 Beaver Brook Rd., R.D. 3, Lyme, 06371-3201. Tel: 860-434-0724. 103 Golden St., #3, Norwich, 06360. Tel: 860-886-9196. 159 Otrobando Ave., Norwich, 06360. Tel: 860-887-5168. 32 School St., P.O. Box 177, Rockville, 06066. Tel: 860-875-4016. 28 Liberty St., Pawcatuck, 06379. Tel: 860-599-4816. 43 W. High St., East Hampton, 06424. Tel: 860-267-6112. 4 S. View Cir., Old Saybrook, 06475. Tel: 860-395-0913.

Sisters of Our Lady of the Garden, 67 Round Hill Rd., 06457-6119. Tel: 806-346-5765. Convent and Nursery School. Sr. Donna Beauregard, O.L.G., Supr. Total Assisted 82; Total Staff 9.

Sisters of St. Joseph, T.O.S.F., 46 Camp St., Apt. -2, 06457-2445. Tel: 860-347-8936.

MOODUS. *Sisters of St. Joseph of Chambery*, P.O. Box 22, 06469-0022. Tel: 860-873-1581; Fax: 860-873-2357.
E-mail: my-fathers-house@prodigy.net
Web site: www.myfathershouse.com
Mailing Address: P.O. Box 22, 06469-0022. Tel: 860-873-1581; Fax: 860-873-2357.

PUTNAM. *Holy Spirit Provincial House*, 72 Church St., 06260-1810. Tel: 860-928-0891. Daughters of the Holy Spirit. Sr. Bonnie Morrow, Prov.; Sr. Anita Paul, Coord.; Rev. Richard L. Archambault, Chap. Sisters 70.
Other Locations: Madonna Community, 207 Sabin St., Apt. 42, 06260. Tel: 860-928-2466. Notre Dame Community, 4 Ravine St., 06260. Tel: 860-928-6163; 928-9129. Daughters of the Holy Spirit, 26 Church St., 06260. Tel: 860-928-6869. 22 Pearl Ave., 06260. Tel: 860-928-5965. St. Ignatius Parish House Community, 17 Williamsville Rd., Rogers, 06263. Tel: 860-774-8154. 185 Farm Hill Rd., Middletown, 06457. Tel: 860-347-4382. Provincialate Community, 31 Ravine St., 06260. Tel: 860-928-7072; 928-3882. St. Mary Convent, 40 N. Main St., Jewett City, 06351. Tel: 860-376-4020. All Hallows Convent, 152 Prospect St., Moosup, 06354. Tel: 860-564-5409. 815B Boswell Ave., Norwich, 06360. Tel: 860-885-0419. 71 Pomfret St., 06260. Tel: 860-928-9649. 33 Pinecrest Ridge, Apt. E, Woodstock, 06281. Tel: 860-928-2099. DHS, 12 St. Regis Dr., Danielson, 06239. Tel: 860-779-0790. 14 Windsor Ave., E-20, Plainfield, 06374. Tel: 860-564-0617. 31 Lincoln Park Rd., B-4, Preston, 06365. Tel: 860-886-2993. New Roxbury Village, 60 Butts Rd., Apt. 16, Woodstock, 06281. Tel: 860-928-0777.

Immaculate Conception Convent, Spiritual Renewal Center and Novitiate, 600 Liberty Hwy., 06260-2503. Tel: 860-928-7955; Fax: 860-928-1930. Sr. M. Paul Savickas, Prov. Sisters of the Immaculate Conception of the Blessed Virgin Mary 13; Total in Residence 17; Total Staff 7.

Matulaitis Nursing Home Inc., 10 Thurber Rd., 06260-2522. Tel: 860-928-7976; Fax: 860-963-1920. Sisters of the Immaculate Conception of the Blessed Virgin Mary and the Congregation of the Sisters of St. Martha. Jane Logan, Admin.; Rev. Rapolas Krasauskas, Chap. Sisters 10; Residents 119.

Provincialate Community of the Daughters of the Holy Spirit. 31 Ravine St., 06260-1817; Fax: 860-928-6197.
E-mail: bmorrowdhs@juno.com
Sr. Bonnie Morrow, D.H.S., Prov. Tel: 860-928-7072; Sr. Linda Babineau, D.H.S., Prov. Councillor. Tel: 860-928-3882.

UNCASVILLE. *Emmaus Community*, 24 Maple Ave., 06382. Tel: 860-848-3379; Fax: 860-848-0755.
E-mail: emmausslc@aol.com
Total in Residence 3; Total Staff 3.

WILLIMANTIC. *Sisters of Charity of Our Lady, Mother of the Church*, St. Joseph Convent, 88 Jackson St., 06226. Tel: 860-423-5122.
E-mail: jackson881@earthlink.net
Total in Residence 7; Total Staff 7.

[H] PRIVATE ASSOCIATIONS OF THE FAITHFUL

ASHFORD, CT. *Benedictine Monastery*. Community of Our Lady of Mount Caritas Monastery, O.S.B.; Sisters of the Order of St. Benedict. Contemplative. Seckar Rd., 06278. Tel: 860-429-7457. Rev. Mother Mary Peter, O.S.B., Supr. Professed 2; Lay Oblates 6; Novices 1.

[I] RETREAT HOUSES

NORWICH. *Ministry of His Able People*. Tel: 860-887-9294.
Ave Maria Place.

MYSTIC. *St. Edmund's Retreat*, P.O. Box 399, 06355-0399. Tel: 860-536-0565; Fax: 860-572-7655.
E-mail: endersisle@aol.com
Web site: www.sse.org/enders
Rev. Thomas F.X. Hoar, S.S.E., Dir.; Mr. Mark Gordon, Dir. Operations; Mrs. Claire St. Clair, Coord. Svcs.; Dr. Thomas Richard, Programs Coord. Total in Residence 4; Total Staff 20.

WILLIMANTIC. *Immaculata Retreat House*, 289 Windham Rd., P.O. Box 55, 06226-0055. Tel: 860-423-8484; Fax: 860-423-5285.
E-mail: omict@ntplx.net
Web site: www.ntplx.net/~omict
Missionary Oblates of Mary Immaculate: U.S. Province. Revs. Daniel Nassaney, O.M.I., Supr. & Dir.; Henri A. Delisle, O.M.I., Treas.; Olivier Renaud, O.M.I.; Bro. Donat Daigle, O.M.I. Total in Residence 7; Total Statff 12.

[J] RENEWAL CENTERS

PORTLAND. *Affirmation Counseling Center*, 553 Portland Cobalt Rd., 06480-1968. Tel: 860-342-0760; Fax: 860-342-4226. John J. Smey, L.C.S.W., Exec. Dir.; Rev. Roland Cloutier, M.S.W., L.C.S.W., Consultant. Psychotherapists: James Lindsay, L.C.S.W.; Wendy A. Mauro, L.P.C., N.C.C., M.A.; Alice Nieto, M.S.W., L.C.S.W. Total Assisted 182; Total Staff 4.

UNCASVILLE. *Emmaus-Diocesan Spiritual Life Center*, 24 Maple Ave., 06382. Tel: 860-848-3427; Fax: 860-848-0755.
E-mail: emmausslc@aol.com
Sr. Mary Barbara Hobbs, P.B.V.M., Dir. Associate Directors: Sr. Mary Ann De Francesco, R.S.M.; Sr. Jane Higgins, R.S.M.; Rev. Joseph G. Finnerty, St. Mary Rectory, 70 Central Ave., 06360. Tel: 860-889-6657; 848-0555. Sisters 3; Total in Residence 3; Total Staff 4.

[K] CAMPUS MINISTRY

WILLIMANTIC. *Campus Ministry*. Eastern Connecticut State University, Newman Hall. 290 Prospect St., 06226. Tel: 860-423-0856; Fax: 860-456-8083.
E-mail: lapointel@easternct.edu
Web site: www.norichdiocese.org.htm/campus ministry
Rev. Laurence A.M. LaPointe, Diocesan Dir. Campus Ministry.

Wesleyan University-The University Ministry, Office of the University Chaplains, 171 Church St., Middletown, 06459-0029. Tel: 860-685-2277; Fax: 860-685-2286. Rev. Louis Manzo, C.S.C.

Connecticut College, Harkness Chapel, 270 Mohegan Ave., New London, 06320-4196. Tel: 860-439-2452; Fax: 860-439-2463. Rev. Laurence A.M. LaPointe, Catholic Chap.

University of Connecticut, St. Thomas Aquinas Chapel, 46 N. Eagleville Rd., Storrs, 06268-1710. Tel: 860-429-6436; Fax: 860-429-2809.
E-mail: stthomas@uconnvm.uconn.edu
Chaplains: Revs. James J. Dressman, S.J.; Richard K. Gross, S.J.; Paul D. Holland, S.J.; Sr. Alberta Surowiec, F.SS.J.

[L] MISCELLANEOUS

NORWICH. *The Annual Bishop's Appeal of the Diocese of Norwich, Inc.*, 197 Broadway, 06360. Tel: 860-886-1928; Fax: 860-886-2651.

The Catholic Foundation of the Diocese of Norwich, Inc., 201 Broadway, 06360. Tel: 860-887-9294.

The Donor Advised Funds of the Diocese of Norwich, Inc., 201 Broadway, 06360. Tel: 860-887-9294.

CROMWELL. *Basilian Fathers of Connecticut, Inc.*, 33 Prospect Hill Rd., 06416. Tel: 860-632-3010; Fax: 860-632-3030. Rev. Douglas L. Mosey, C.S.B., Pres. & Rector.

JEWETT CITY. *The World Apostolate of Fatima, Inc., Norwich Diocesan Division*, 41 John Rd., 06351. Tel: 860-376-1041; Fax: 860-376-1041.
E-mail: norwichwaf@hotmail.com
Denise Dudek, Pres.

MIDDLETOWN. *Diocese of Norwich Assisted Living Services, Inc.*, 10 Elm St., 06457. Tel: 860-347-4684; Fax: 860-347-7669.

Marian Housing Corporation, 10 Elm St., 06457. Tel: 860-347-4684; Fax: 860-347-7669.

Mercy Development Office, 1740 Randolph Rd., 06457. Tel: 860-347-8957; Fax: 860-344-9887.
E-mail: jhall@mercyhigh.com
Web site: www.mercyhigh.com
Janet Hall, Devel. Dir.

Mercy-Xavier Fund Corporation, 181 Randolph Rd., 06457. Tel: 860-346-7735; Fax: 860-346-6859.

Xavier Alumni & Development Office, 181 Randolph Rd., 06457. Tel: 860-347-6079; Fax: 860-346-6859. Mr. Rory Donaldson, Dir.; Mr. Joseph E. Lane, Asst. Devel. Office; Mrs. Kit La Rosa, Sec. Total in Residence 13; Total Staff 78.

PUTNAM. *The Daughters of the Holy Spirit Charitable Trust*, 72 Church St., 06260-1810. Tel: 860-928-0891. Sr. Bonnie Morrow, D.H.S., Trustee & Contact Person.

The Holy Spirit Health Care Center, Inc., 72 Church St., 06260. Tel: 860-928-0891; Fax: 860-928-1312. Sr. Bonnie Morrow, D.H.S., Prov. & Contact Person; Mrs. Annemarie Shiroka, Admin.

WILLIMANTIC. *Saint Joseph's Home for the Aged, Inc.*, 88 Jackson St., 06226.

WINDHAM. *Sagrado Corazon de Jesus, Inc. of Windham*, 61 Club Rd., 06280. Tel: 860-423-8617; Fax: 860-423-4157.
E-mail: aposthisano@juno.com

RELIGIOUS INSTITUTES OF MEN REPRESENTED IN THE DIOCESE

For further details refer to the corresponding bracketed number in the Religious Institutes of Men or Women section.

[0200]—*Benedictine Monks.*—O.S.B.
[1350]—*Brothers of St. Francis Xavier.* (St. Joseph Prov.).—C.F.X.
[0610]—*Brothers of the Congregation of Holy Cross.*—C.S.C.
[0470]—*The Capuchin Friars.* (Prov. of St. Mary).—O.F.M. Cap.
[0270]—*Carmelite Fathers and Brothers.*—O.Carm.
[0340]—*Cistercian Fathers.*—O.Cist.
[]—*Congregation of Christian Brothers.*—C.F.C.
[0480]—*Conventual Franciscans.*—O.F.M.Conv.
[0530]—*Franciscan Friars of Attonement.*—S.A.
[0533]—*Franciscan Friars of the Immaculate.*—F.F.I.
[0690]—*Jesuit Fathers and Brothers.*—S.J.
[]—*Little Flower Congregation.*—C.S.T.
[0740]—*Marian Fathers.*—M.I.C.
[0720]—*The Missionaries of Our Lady of La Salette.* (Prov. of Our Lady of the Americas).—M.S.
[0910]—*Oblates of Mary Immaculate.* (Missionary Oblates of Mary Immaculate, U.S. Prov.).—O.M.I.
[0930]—*Oblates of St. Joseph.* (Eastern Prov.).—O.S.J.
[0430]—*Order of Preachers (Dominicans).*—O.P.
[1010]—*Order of St. Paul.*—O.S.P.
[0440]—*Society of St. Edmund.*—S.S.E.
[0590]—*Society of the Missionaries of the Holy Apostles.*—M.S.A.
[1280]—*Stigmatine Fathers and Brothers.*—C.S.S.

RELIGIOUS INSTITUTES OF WOMEN REPRESENTED IN THE DIOCESE

[0130]—*Apostoles of the Sacred Heart of Jesus.*—A.S.C.J.
[1920]—*Congregation of Sisters of Holy Cross.*—C.S.C.
[]—*Contemplative Sisters of St. Benedict.*—O.S.P.
[0820]—*Daughters of the Holy Spirit.*—D.H.S.
[1170]—*Felician Sisters.*—C.S.S.F.
[]—*Franciscan Apostolic Sisters.*—F.A.S.
[1190]—*Franciscan Sisters of Atonement.*—S.A.
[2575]—*Institute of the Sisters of Mercy of the Americas.*—R.S.M.
[1410]—*Mill Hill Sisters.*—F.M.S.J.
[2720]—*Mission Helpers of the Sacred Heart.*—M.H.S.H.
[3465]—*Religious of the Sacred Heart of Mary.*—R.S.H.M.
[]—*Religious Teachers Fillippini.*—M.P.F.
[]—*Roncalli Sisters.*
[2970]—*School Sisters of Notre Dame.*—S.S.N.D.
[]—*Servants of Immaculate Heart of Mary.*—I.H.M.
[]—*Sisters Oblates to Divine Love.*—R.O.D.A.
[]—*Sisters of Charity of Immaculate Conception of Irrea, Italy.*—S.C.I.C.
[0530]—*Sisters of Charity of Our Lady, Mother of the Church.*—S.C.M.C.
[3000]—*Sisters of Notre Dame de Namur.* (Connecticut Prov.).—S.N.D.deN.
[]—*Sisters of Our Lady of the Garden.*—O.L.G.
[3720]—*Sisters of Saint Anne.*—S.S.A.
[3830]—*Sisters of St. Joseph.*—S.S.J.
[]—*Sisters of St. Joseph.*—C.S.J.
[3930]—*Sisters of St. Joseph of the Third Order of St. Francis.*—S.S.J.-T.O.S.F.
[3937]—*Sisters of St. Martha.*—C.S.M.
[3180]—*Sisters of the Cross of Passion.*—C.P.
[2140]—*Sisters of the Immaculate Conception of the Blessed Virgin Mary (Lithuanian).*
[3320]—*Sisters of the Presentation of the B.V.M.*—P.B.V.M.
[]—*Society of the Sisters for the Church.*—S.S.C.

NECROLOGY

† Dziadosz, Rev. Msgr. Henry J., Moodus, CT St. Bridget of Kildare. —Died May 28, 2000.
† Horan, F. Joseph, Versailles, CT St. Joseph. —Died Feb. 16, 2000.
† Murphy, Francis W., Essex, CT Our Lady of Sorrows. —Died Jan. 28, 2000.
† Sullivan, John J., Portland, CT St. Mary. —Died May 15, 2000.
† Wood, Robert J., Groton, CT Sacred Heart. —Died Jan. 6, 2000.

Diocese of Oakland

(Dioecesis Quercopolitana)

Most Reverend

JOHN S. CUMMINS, D.D.

Bishop of Oakland; ordained January 24, 1953; appointed Titular Bishop of Lambesi and Auxiliary Bishop of Sacramento February 26, 1974; consecrated May 16, 1974; appointed Bishop of Oakland May 3, 1977; installed June 30, 1977. *Res., 634 21st St., Oakland, CA, 94612.*

through christ our lord

ESTABLISHED JANUARY 13, 1962.

Square Miles 1,467.

Comprises two Counties in the State of California—viz., Alameda and Contra Costa.

Legal Title: The Roman Catholic Bishop of Oakland, a Corporation Sole.

For legal titles of parishes and diocesan institutions, consult the Chancery Office.

Chancery Office: 2900 Lakeshore Ave., Oakland, CA, 94610. Tel.: 510-893-4711; Fax: 510-893-0945.

E-mail address: chancellor@Oakdiocese.org

STATISTICAL OVERVIEW

Personnel	
Bishop	1
Priests: Diocesan Active in Diocese	108
Priests: Active Outside Diocese	2
Priests: Retired, Sick or Absent	47
Number of Diocesan Priests	157
Religious Priests in Diocese	110
Extern Priests in Diocese	25
Ordinations:	
Diocesan Priests	2
Permanent Deacons	24
Permanent Deacons in Diocese	99
Total Brothers	25
Total Sisters	340
Parishes	
Parishes	87
With Resident Pastor:	
Resident Diocesan Priests	61
Resident Religious Priests	15
Without Resident Pastor:	
Administered by Priests	8
Administered by Deacons	1
Administered by Women Religious	1
Administered by Lay People	1
Missions	2
Pastoral Centers	15
Closed Parishes	1
Professional Ministry Personnel:	
Brothers	1
Sisters	27
Lay Ministers	149
Welfare	
Catholic Hospitals	1
Total Assisted	80,000
Homes for the Aged	2
Total Assisted	2,000
Day Care and Extended Day Care Centers	5
Total Assisted	1,500
Specialized Homes	6
Total Assisted	24,000
Special Centers for Social Services	3
Total Assisted	26,500
Residential Care of Disabled	1
Total Assisted	900
Other Institutions	4
Total Assisted	22,000
Educational	
Diocesan Students in Other Seminaries	20
Students Religious	71
Total Seminarians	91
Colleges and Universities	3
Total Students	4,500
High Schools, Diocesan and Parish	3
Total Students	1,979
High Schools, Private	6
Total Students	4,518
Elementary Schools, Diocesan and Parish	51
Total Students	14,895
Catechesis/Religious Education:	
High School Students	2,000
Elementary Students	11,000
Total Students Under Catholic Instruction	38,983
Teachers in the Diocese:	
Brothers	18
Sisters	31
Lay Teachers	1,064
Vital Statistics	
Receptions into the Church:	
Infant Baptism Totals	9,964
Adult Baptism Totals	759
Received into Full Communion	1,217
First Communions	8,063
Confirmations	3,275
Marriages:	
Catholic	1,307
Interfaith	415
Total Marriages	1,722
Deaths	2,951
Total Catholic Population	429,477
Total Population	2,348,723

Former Bishops—Most Rev. FLOYD L. BEGIN, S.T.D., cons. May 1, 1947; appt. Bishop of Oakland on Feb. 21, 1962; died April 26, 1977.

Chancery Office—2900 Lakeshore Ave., Oakland, 94610-3697. Tel: 510-893-4711; Fax: 510-893-0945. Office Hours: 8:30-4:45.

Vicar General / Director of Pastoral Life—Rev. PAUL ROSS VASSAR.

Chancellor / Director Office of the Bishop—Sr. BARBARA FLANNERY, C.S.J.

Vicar of Temporalities—Rev. PATRICK GOODWIN.

Director of Services and Resources—Mr. KENNETH J. REGGIO.

Judicial Vicar—Rev. DONALD R. HUDSON, J.C.L.

Bishop's Representative for Eastern Rite Catholics—Rev. DAVID LINK.

Bishop's Representative for Permanent Deacons—Deacon DAVID REZENDES.

Bishop's Representative for Catholic Charismatics (English)—Mr. CHARLES PEISSNER.

Bishop's Representative for Catholic Charismatics (Spanish)—Mr. JESUS MACIAS.

Bishop's Representative for Italian Speaking Faithful—Rev. DANIEL E. CARDELLI.

The Roman Catholic Welfare Corporation of Oakland—2900 Lakeshore Ave., Oakland, 94610. Tel: 510-893-4711.

Consultors—Revs. DANIEL CARDELLI; FERNANDO CORTEZ; VINCENT COTTER; DANIEL DANIELSON; QUANG DONG; JAYSON LANDEZA; JOHN MAXWELL; GERARD MORAN; FRED RICCIO; LARRY SILVA; PAUL VASSAR.

Presbyteral Council—Revs. FRED RICCIO, Pres. DANIEL CARDELLI; LEO EDGERLY; DONALD HUDSON; JAYSON LANDEZA, Sec. JOHN MAXWELL; ROBERT MCCANN; SERGIO MORA; THUONG NGUYEN; RONALD SCHMIT; PAUL VASSAR; LARRY YOUNG; MARK WIESNER.

Diocesan Pastoral Council—Mr. ROBERT MALLON, Chm.; Region 1: Mr. RON FEDORE; Mr. JACK GREEN, Region 2: Mr. MICHAEL HENDERSHOT; Ms. GLORIA ASUNCION, Region 3: Mr. GREG TOMLIN; Mr. STEVE KONEFF KLATT; Ms. CATHY BROWN, Region 4: Ms. LINN BAUTISTA; Ms. MARIA HERNANDEZ, Region 5: Ms. ANN SNYDER; Ms. ELSA ZAVALA; Deacon CHARLES PALOMARES; Sr. MAUREEN THERESE MCGRODDY; Revs. THUONG NGUYEN; RAMIRO FLORES; JOSE LEON; JERROLD KENNEDY; PAUL ROSS VASSAR; Sr. BARBARA FLANNERY; Mr. CHUCK SIEBENAND.

Ecclesial Lay Ministers Council (ELMC)—KELLY O'LAGUE DULKA; Sr. BARBARA FLANNERY; NORAH HIPPOLYTE; DIANA KAULBACK; Rev. JAYSON LANDEZA; KAREN MILLER; STEVE MULLIN; GAIL MCGUIRE; FRANCES ROJEC; MARGARET RONCALLI; CHUCK SIEBENAND.

Diocesan Finance Committee—Mr. JOE TORT, Chm.; Mr. RICHARD CAMPBELL; Mr. MICHAEL CANIZZARO; Mr. GREG DUNN; Rev. PATRICK GOODWIN; Ms. JANICE MURPHY; Rev. JERROLD KENNEDY; Mr. VINCENT P. KUHN, JR.; Mr. MIKE NIEDERMEYER; Rev. FRED RICCIO; Mr. GREGORY THRONBURY; Mr. BILL UTIC; Mr. KIP WIXSON.

Pastoral Leadership Placement Board (PLPB)—Most Rev. JOHN S. CUMMINS; Ms. JOANN MASS; Revs. MICHAEL NORKETT; JOHN PROCHASKA; Mrs. BERNIE PURCELL; Sr. FELICIA SARATI; Revs. LARRY SILVA; PAUL SCHMIDT; Mr. BERNIE SUTTLE; Revs. BRIAN TIMONEY; ANTONIO VALDIVIA; PAUL VASSAR; RAY ZIELEZIENSKI.

Deans—Rev. DANIEL DANIELSON, Deanery #1; Rev. DAN CARDELLI, Deanery #2; Rev. JOHN MALLON, Deanery #3; Rev. JOHN KASPER, O.S.F.S., Deanery #4; Rev. BRIAN JOYCE, Deanery #5; Rev. VINCENT J. COTTER, Deanery #6; Rev. HELMUT RICHTER, Deanery #7; Rev. RICHARD MANGINI, Deanery #8; Rev. JEREMIAH HOLLAND, SS.CC., Deanery #9; Rev. SEAMUS GENOVESE, Deanery #10; Rev. JOSEPH SCOTT, S.V.D., Deanery #11; Rev. JAMES MATTHEWS, Deanery #12; Rev. PETER MCGRATH, S.J., Deanery #13; Rev. LARRY SILVA, Deanery #14; Rev. RAMON J. GOMEZ, Deanery #15; Vacant, Deanery #16; Rev. DAVID LINK, Deanery #17; Rev. KEVIN MULLINS, Deanery #18; Rev. JOHN PROCHASKA, Deanery #19; Rev. GEORGE MATANIC, O.P., Deanery #20; Rev. ANTONIO A. VALDIVIA, Deanery #21; Rev. JOHN F. MAXWELL, Deanery #22; Rev. DANA MICHAELS, Deanery #23.

Diocesan Departments

Apostleship of the Sea—Deacon STANLEY LEE, Port Chaplain, *Berth 40, Oakland, 94607.* Tel: 510-444-7885.

Archivist/Records Management—Ms. MARY C. BATIZA, *3014 Lakeshore Ave., Oakland, 94610.* Tel: 510-273-4980.

Campaign for Human Development—Mrs. BARBARA TERRAZAS, Dir., *433 Jefferson St., Oakland, 94607.*

Canon Law Department—

Adjutant Judicial Vicars and Canonical Consultant to the Bishop—Revs. ROBERT MCCANN, J.C.L.; GARY M. LUIZ, C.PP.S., J.C.L.

Defenders of the Bond—Revs. ANTHONY PHAN LAM, J.C.D.; DAVID K. O'ROURKE, O.P.

Pro Synodal Judges—Revs. RAYMOND BRETTON; DONALD HUDSON, J.C.L.; GARY LUIZ, C.PP.S., J.C.L.; ROBERT MCCANN, J.C.L.; SALVADOR MACIAS.

Notaries of the Tribunal—ALICE VIZCAINO; MARY O'SULLIVAN; JACQUELINE COMPTON; CAROL GAISER.

Promoter of Justice—Rev. RAYMOND BRETTON.

Auditors of the Tribunal—MERCEDES C. CORRAL; CAROL IZO; THERESA KOBAK; MELISA MATSUOKA; JOANNE MORGRET.

Catholic Charities—Mrs. BARBARA TERRAZAS, Dir. Legal Title: *Catholic Charities of the East Bay, Diocese of Oakland.*

Catholic Relief Services—Mrs. BARBARA TERRAZAS, Assoc. Dir.

Catholic Schools Office—ANN MEYERS MANCHESTER, Ed.D., Supt. Assistant Superintendent: Sr. BARBARA BRAY, S.N.J.M.; Mr. MARC DEMARCO, *3000 Lakeshore Ave., Oakland, 94610.* Tel: 510-273-4982.

FACE (Family Aid Catholic Education, tuition assistance)—Ms. ANNE RYNDERS, Dir., *3000 Lakeshore Ave., Oakland, 94610.* Tel: 510-273-4982.

Cemeteries and Mausoleums—Mr. ROBERT ROCHA, Dir., *1965 Reliez Valley Rd., P.O. Box 488, Lafayette, 94549.*

Directors—Most Rev. JOHN S. CUMMINS; Mr. MICHAEL CANIZZARO; Sr. BARBARA FLANNERY, C.S.J.; Rev. PATRICK GOODWIN,Oakland, Alameda County, St. Mary's Cemetery; Antioch, Contra Costa County, Holy Cross Cemetery; Hayward, Alameda County, Holy Sepulchre Cemetery and Mausoleum; Lafayette, Contra Costa County, Queen of Heaven Cemetery; Pleasanton, Alameda County, Christ the King Cemetery; San Pablo, Contra Costa County, St. Joseph's Cemetery and Mausoleum.

Censor—Rev. ROBERT MCCANN, *2900 Lakeshore Ave., Oakland, 94610.* Tel: 510-267-8375.

Christian Initiation—Mr. MARK GONZALEZ.

Clergy Services—Rev. MICHAEL NORKETT, Dir., *2900 Lakeshore Ave., Oakland, 94610.* Tel: 510-267-8366.

Office of Clergy Personnel—Rev. PAUL SCHMIDT, *2900 Lakeshore Ave., Oakland, 94610.* Tel: 510-267-8308.

Cursillo Movement—Vacant, Spiritual Dir.

Deaf and Hard of Hearing—ARDITH A. LYNCH, Dir., *St. Joseph's Center, 25580 Campus Dr., Hayward, 94542.* Tel: 510-489-9784 (Voice); 489-9786 (TTY).

Development/Stewardship—Ms. KATHERINE KING, Dir.

Episcopal Liturgies—Mrs. CARMEN VINELLA, Dir., *2900 Lakeshore Ave., Oakland, 94610.*

Ethnic Pastoral Centers—

Director of Ethnic & Cultural Services Division—Sr. FELICIA SARATI, C.S.J., *3014 Lakeshore Ave., Oakland, 94610.* Tel: 510-273-4998.

African American Pastoral Center—Dr. TOINETTE EUGENE, *3014 Lakeshore Ave., Oakland, 94610.* Tel: 510-273-4988.

Asian/Indian Pastoral Center—FILOMENA GIESE, *746 Peralta Ave., Berkeley, 94707.* Tel: 510-524-5802.

Chinese Pastoral Center—Rev. THOMAS NG, Dir., *176 Ridgeway Ave., Oakland, 94611.*

Filipino Catholic—Deacon STANLEY LEE, Dir., *3014 Lakeshore Ave., Oakland, 94610.* Tel: 510-273-4999.

Ge'ez Community—Rev. GEBRIEL WOLDAI, Bay Area Regl. Dir., *1640 Addison St., Berkeley, 94703.* Tel: 510-549-7529.

Haitian Pastoral Center—PIERRE LABOSSIERE, *55th Ave., Oakland, 94605.* Tel: 510-534-5149.

Indonesian Community—GRACE LIM, *25558 Crestfield Circle, Castro Valley, 94552.* Tel: 510-733-2011.

Khmmu/Laotian Pastoral Center—Rev. DON MACKINNON, C.SS.R., *2215 Rose St., Berkeley, 94709.* Tel: 510-582-8888.

Korean Pastoral Center—Rev. PAUL OH, Dir., *Mr. Andrew Kim Catholic Pastoral Center, 6226 Camden St., Oakland, 94605.* Tel: 510-562-3843.

Hispanic Pastoral Center—HECTOR MEDINA, Dir., *3014 Lakeshore Ave., Oakland, Ca, 94610.* Tel: 510-628-2180.

Polish Pastoral Center—Rev. LESZEK BARTOSZEWSKI, Dir., *2085 Miramar Ave., San Leandro, 94578.*

Portuguese Pastoral Center—Ms. MARIA ALCORTA, Dir., *5800 Thornton Ave., Newark, 94560.* Tel: 510-794-7910.

Tongan Pastoral Center—Ms. TENISIA FINAU, Bay Area Regl. Dir., *1515 Dolan Ave., San Mateo, 94401.* Tel: 415-342-2470.

Vietnamese Pastoral Center—Sr. ROSALINE NGUYEN, Dir., *3014 Lakeshore Ave., Oakland, 94610.* Tel: 510-273-4941.

Facilities, Planning and Services—Mr. ALEX HERNANDEZ, Dir.; Mr. JAMES H. MCCANN, Assoc. Dir.

Faith and Ministerial Formation—CARMEN DE LA VEGA NEAFSEY, Dir., *3014 Lakeshore Ave., Oakland, 94610.* Tel: 510-893-4711. Vacant, Assoc. Dir. In-Service Programming; Mr. CARLOS RIVA, Assoc. Dir. Spanish Programming.

Family Life Office—Mrs. RITA BILLECI, Dir. JUAN AMBRIZ, Assoc. Dir. SUE MEDINA, Coord. Divorced & Separated Catholics; Ms. MONIKA RODMAN, Respect Life, Women's Pregnancy Service and Bioethics Coord., *2350 Pacheco St., Concord, 94520.* Tel: 510-680-8510.

Services to Gays and Lesbians and Their Families—Mrs. RITA BILLECI.

Financial Services—Mr. MICHAEL CANIZZARO, Dir., *2900 Lakeshore Ave., Oakland, 94610.*

Holy Childhood—Ms. KATHERINE KING, Dir., *2900 Lakeshore Ave., Oakland, 94610.* Tel: 510-267-8357.

Hospital Ministry—Rev. JOHN RANALLO, Dir., *2900 Lakeshore Ave., Oakland, 94610.*

Human Resources—Dr. PENNY PENDOLA, Dir., *2900 Lakeshore Ave., Oakland, 94610.* Tel: 510-267-8359.

Newspaper: "The Catholic Voice"—Ms. MONICA CLARK, Editor, *3014 Lakeshore Ave., Oakland, 94610.* Tel: 510-893-5339.

Parish Resources—Mrs. NORA PETERSEN, Dir., *2900 Lakeshore Ave., Oakland, 94610.* Tel: 510-983-4711. Catechetics: Mr. MARC GONZALEZ, English; Ms. JESSY LIRA, Spanish.

Small Christian Communities—NORA PETERSEN, English; Vacant, Spanish.

Liturgy—LINDA KREHMEIER.

Pastoral Planning—Mr. CHUCK SIEBENAND, Dir., *2900 Lakeshore Ave., Oakland, 94610.* Tel: 510-267-8368.

Propagation of the Faith—Ms. KATHERINE KING, Dir. Legal Title: Oakland Society for the Propagation of the Faith.

St. Peter the Apostle Society—Ms. KATHERINE KING, Dir.

Special Religious Education Department (SPRED)—Sr. AURORA PEREZ, Dir., *3000 Lakeshore Ave., Oakland, 94610.* Tel: 510-273-4982.

Vicar for Religious—Sr. BARBARA FLANNERY, C.S.J., *2900 Lakeshore Ave., Oakland, 94610.* Tel: 510-893-4711.

Vocations—

Priestly and Religious & Director for Seminarians—Rev. JERROLD KENNEDY, *2900 Lakeshore Ave., Oakland, 94610.* Tel: 510-267-8345.

Youth and Young Adults—Mr. WILLIAM FORD, Dir., *3014 Lakeshore Ave., Oakland, 94610.* Tel: 510-893-4711. Mr. WILLIAM FORD, Dir. CYO Athletics & Catholic Scouting; Ms. EVELYN GONZALEZ, Dir. Youth and Young Adults Ministry; Vacant, Dir. Latino Ethnic Youth Ministry.

Organizations—

St. Vincent de Paul Society—JUDY YATES, Alameda County Exec. Dir., *9235 San Leandro St., Oakland, 94603.* Tel: 510-636-4246. RON COOPER, Contra Costa County Exec. Dir., *2210 Gladstone Dr., Pittsburg, 94565.* Tel: 925-439-5060, Ext. 19.

Diocesan Council of Catholic Women—Mrs. STEFANIE SILVIA, *5521 Columbia Ave., Richmond, 94804.*

CLERGY, PARISHES, MISSIONS AND PAROCHIAL SCHOOLS

CITY OF OAKLAND
(Alameda County)

1—CATHEDRAL OF ST. FRANCIS DE SALES (1886). Merged with St. Mary, Immaculate Conception to form St. Mary, Immaculate Conception-St. Francis de Sales.

2—ST. ANDREW-ST. JOSEPH (1965) (Latino-African American), Rev. Thomas Edwards; Sr. Marian Wright, S.N.J.M., Pastoral Life Coord.; Deacons Morris Soublet; Leo Edgerly; Eugene Stelly. In res., Rev. Ernest B. Brainard.
Res., 925 Brockhurst St., 94608. Tel: 510-653-7411; Fax: 510-652-5839.
Schools—St. Martin De Porres School.; St. Patrick Campus, (Grades 6-8). Tel: 510-832-1757; Fax: 510-832-6481.; Sacred Heart Campus, (Grades K-5). Tel: 510-652-2220; Fax: 510-652-2294.
Catechesis/Religious Programs—Students 80.

3—ST. ANTHONY'S (1871), Rev. Thuong Hoai Nguyen. In res., Revs. Joseph Son Nguyen; Jeff Acebo.
Res., 1535 16th Ave., 94606. Tel: 510-534-2117; Fax: 510-534-2119.
School—Tel: 510-534-3334; Fax: 510-534-3378.
Lay Teachers 9; Students 120.
Catechesis/Religious Programs—Tel: 510-534-4420.
Students 120.

4—ST. AUGUSTINE'S (1907), Revs. Ray Z; Paul Minihan.
Res., 400 Alcatraz Ave., 94609. Tel: 510-653-8631; Fax: 510-653-4256.
School—410 Alcatraz Ave., 94609. Tel: 510-652-6727; Fax: 510-652-4219.
Sisters 1; Lay Teachers 13; Students 183.
Catechesis/Religious Programs—Students 183.

5—ST. BENEDICT (1930), Rev. James Matthews. In res., Rev. Cuthbert Aronyu (Uganda).
Res., 2245 82nd Ave., 94605. Tel: 510-632-1847; Fax: 510-633-2092.
Catechesis/Religious Programs—Students 30.

6—ST. BERNARD'S (1912) (Hispanic-African American), Revs. Joseph Scott, S.V.D.; Roberto Flores, S.V.D., Pastoral Assoc.; Deacon Javier Fuentes. In res., Revs. Stephen Ernest, S.V.D.; Peter Sam Nguyen, S.V.D.
Res., 1620-62nd Ave., 94621. Tel: 510-632-3013; Fax: 510-633-1714.
School—1630-62nd Ave., 94621. Tel: 510-632-6323; Fax: 510-632-6110.
Lay Teachers 9; Students 226.
Catechesis/Religious Programs—Students 260.

7—ST. COLUMBA'S (1898) (African American), Rev. Jayson Landeza.
Res., 6401 San Pablo Ave., 94608. Tel: 510-654-7600; Fax: 510-654-7615.

8—ST. CYRIL (1926), Rev. John Fernandes, Parochial Admin. In res., Revs. Anthony Phan Lam; OH Young-min Paul; Ken Hamilton, S.V.D.
Res., 6226 Camden St., 94605. Tel: 510-638-1447; Fax: 510-638-5244.
School—3200 62nd Ave., 94605. Tel: 510-638-9445; Fax: 510-638-0744.
Lay Teachers 9; Students 320.
Catechesis/Religious Programs—Students 29.

9—ST. ELIZABETH'S (1892) (Hispanic), Revs. Marco Antonio Figueroa, O.F.M.; Tommy King, O.F.M.; Peter Krieg, O.F.M.; Damian Gamboa, O.F.M.; Deacon Noe Gonzalez. In res., Revs. Kenny Scott, O.F.M.; Gordon Urbine, O.F.M.
Res., 1500 34th Ave., 94601. Tel: 510-536-1266; Fax: 510-536-8560.
School—Tel: 510-532-7392; Fax: 510-532-0321.
Sisters 3; Lay Teachers 19; Students 499.
Catechesis/Religious Programs—Tel: 510-532-3766.
Students 702.
Mission—Oakland, Alameda Co., Mary Help of Christians, 2611 E. 9th St., 94601. Tel: 510-534-3501; Fax: 510-436-5157.

10—ST. JARLATH'S (1910), Rev. Salvador Macias.
Res., 2620 Pleasant St., 94602. Tel: 510-532-2068; Fax: 510-532-3745.
School—2634 Pleasant St., 94602. Tel: 510-532-4387; Fax: 510-532-1001.
Lay Teachers 9; Students 250.
Catechesis/Religious Programs—Students 37.

11—ST. LAWRENCE O'TOOLE (1916), Rev. Fernando J. Cortez.
Res., 3725 High St., 94619. Tel: 510-530-0761; Fax: 510-530-0974.
School—Tel: 510-530-0266; Fax: 510-530-7568.
Lay Teachers 15; Students 276.
Catechesis/Religious Programs—Students 110.

12—ST. LEO'S (1911), Rev. Timothy K. Johnson. In res., Revs. Thomas Ng; Daniel Melaba.
Res., 176 Ridgeway Ave., 94611-5122. Tel: 510-654-6177; Fax: 510-654-4203.
School—Tel: 510-654-7828; Fax: 510-654-4057.
Lay Teachers 10; Students 262.
Catechesis/Religious Programs—Students 16.

13—ST. LOUIS BERTRAND (1908) (Hispanic-African American), Rev. Stephan Kappler.
Res., 1410-100th Ave., 94603. Tel: 510-568-1080; Fax: 510-635-8618.
Catechesis/Religious Programs—Tel: 510-568-7038.
Students 1,000.

14—ST. MARGARET MARY (1922), Rev. Paul J. Schmidt, Admin.; Sr. Claude Marie Crinnion, S.H.F., Pastoral Assoc.
Res., 1219 Excelsior Ave., 94610. Tel: 510-482-0596; Fax: 510-482-2093.
Catechesis/Religious Programs—Students 16.

15—MARY HELP OF CHRISTIANS CHURCH (1915) (Spanish), Rev. Marco Antonio Figueroa, O.F.M.; Reyna Lupian, Admin.
Mailing Address: P.O. Box 7116, 94601.

Res., 2611 E. Ninth St., 94601. Tel: 510-534-3501.

16—St. Mary, Immaculate Conception. Merged with St. Francis de Sales to form St. Mary, Immaculate Conception-St. Francis de Sales.

17—St. Mary, Immaculate Conception-St. Francis de Sales (1993), Rev. Peter R. McGrath, S.J. In res., Revs. Jerrold F. Kennedy; Joseph Carroll, S.J.; Binh Quach, C.S.Sp.; Thai Trinh.
Res. & Office: St. Francis de Sales Rectory: 634 21st St., 94612. Tel: 510-832-5057; Fax: 510-832-0212.
Catechesis/Religious Programs—Students 150.

18—Our Lady of Lourdes (1921), Rev. Seamus D. Genovese; Sr. Mary Gallagher, S.H.J.M.
Res., 2808 Lakeshore Ave., 94610. Tel: 510-451-1790; Fax: 510-893-6443. [CEM]
Catechesis/Religious Programs—Students 25.

19—St. Paschal Baylon (1955), Revs. John Fernandes; Michael Galvan. In res., Rev. Michael Norkett.
Res., 3700 Dorisa Ave., 94605. Tel: 510-636-0335; Fax: 510-636-0287.
School—Tel: 510-635-7922; Fax: 510-635-4219.
Lay Teachers 12; Students 225.
Catechesis/Religious Programs—Students 35.

20—St. Patrick's (1879) (African American-Hispanic), Revs. Timothy S. Godfrey, S.J.; Sean O. Carroll, S.J. In res., Rev. William R. O'Neill, S.J.
Res., 1023 Peralta St., 94607. Tel: 510-444-1081; Fax: 510-444-1113.
School—1630 10th St., 94607. Tel: 510-832-1757; Fax: 510-832-6481.
Lay Teachers 11; Students 210.
Catechesis/Religious Programs—Students 24.

21—Sacred Heart (1876), Revs. Tom J. Edwards; Thomas Hayes, O.M.I.
Res., 4025 Martin Luther King Way, 94609-2317. Tel: 510-655-9209; Fax: 510-652-1958.
School—St. Martin De Porres, 675 41st St., 94609. Tel: 510-652-2220; Fax: 510-652-2294. Mrs. Sue Taylor, Prin.
Lay Teachers 5; Students 200.
Catechesis/Religious Programs—Special Religious Education Department (SPRED), Tel: 510-628-2157; Fax: 510-628-2174. Sr. Aurora Perez, S.H.F., D.R.E.
Students 16.

22—St. Theresa of the Infant Jesus (The Little Flower) (1925), Rev. Msgr. Bernard J. Moran. In res., Rev. John Bosco Ikemeh, O.P.
Res., 30 Mandalay Rd., 94618. Tel: 510-547-2777; Fax: 510-653-3575.
School—Tel: 510-547-3146; Fax: 510-547-3253.
Lay Teachers 20; Students 285.
Catechesis/Religious Programs—Students 125.

OUTSIDE THE CITY OF OAKLAND

Alameda, Alameda Co.,

1—St. Albert, (1976), Rev. James Cummings.
Res., 1022 Holly St., 94502. Tel: 510-522-2185; Fax: 510-522-1055. [CEM]
Catechesis/Religious Programs—Students 49.

2—St. Barnabas, (1925), Rev. Jeffrey R. Keyes, C.PP.S.
Res., 1427 Sixth St., 94501. Tel: 510-522-8933; Fax: 510-522-8380.
School—Tel: 510-521-0595; Fax: 510-521-3560.
Lay Teachers 10; Students 210.
Catechesis/Religious Programs—Tel: 510-337-8962; Fax: 510-521-3560.
Students 65.

3—St. Joseph Basilica, (1885), Revs. Jeremiah Holland, SS.CC.; Vincent Fallon, SS.CC.; Patrick J. Crowley, SS.CC.
Res., 1109 Chestnut St., 94501. Tel: 510-522-0181; Fax: 510-522-2864.
School—St. Joseph Elementary School, Tel: 510-522-4457; Fax: 510-522-2890.
Lay Teachers 18; Students 311.
High School—See separate category under High Schools, Parochial. Tel: 510-523-1526; Fax: 510-523-2181.
Catechesis/Religious Programs—Tel: 510-522-0445. Leia Rosales, D.R.E.
Students 852.

4—St. Philip Neri, (1925), Rev. James B. Pickett.
Res., 3108 Van Buren St., 94501. Tel: 510-522-2299; Fax: 510-522-1625.
School—1335 High St., 94501. Tel: 510-521-0787; Fax: 510-521-2418.
Lay Teachers 13; Students 298.
Catechesis/Religious Programs—Tel: 510-865-2626.
Students 130.

Antioch, Contra Costa Co., Holy Rosary (1874), Revs. Francisco Vicente; LaSalle Hallissey, O.P.; Francis Goode, O.P.; Deacons Jose Flores; Jerry Grigg; Mrs. Jackie Hooke, Pastoral Assoc.
Res., 1313 A St., 94509. Tel: 925-757-4020; Fax: 925-757-6828. [CEM][JC]
School—Tel: 925-757-1270; Fax: 925-757-9309.
Lay Teachers 35; Students 550.
Catechesis/Religious Programs—21 E. 15th St., 94059. Tel: 915-757-9515.
Students 900.

St. Ignatius (1979), Revs. Vince Cotter; Ramiro Flores; Sr. Ruth Anne Saunders, C.S.J., Pastoral Assoc.; Deacon Al Fleischer.
Res., 209 Tanganyika Ct., 94509. Tel: 925-778-0768; Fax: 925-778-0845. [CEM]
Catechesis/Religious Programs—3351 Contra Loma Blvd., 94509. Tel: 510-778-1314.
Students 522.

Bay Point, Contra Costa Co., Our Lady Queen of the World (1962), Revs. Richard J. Culver, Admin.; Joseph Duong Phan; Theo Palis, Pastor Emeritus.
Res., 3155 Winterbrook Dr., 94565. Tel: 925-458-4718; Fax: 925-458-3161.
Catechesis/Religious Programs—Tel: 925-458-4574.
Students 310.

Berkeley, Alameda Co.,

1—St. Ambrose, (1909), Revs. Andrews Amritharaj (India); George E. Crespin, Temp. Admin.
Res., 1145 Gilman St., 94706. Tel: 510-525-2620; Fax: 510-525-5399.
Catechesis/Religious Programs—Students 24.

2—Holy Spirit Parish/Newman Hall, (1967), Revs. Richard Sparks, C.S.P.; Albert Moser, C.S.P.; Peter Abdella, C.S.P.
Res., 2700 Dwight Way, 94704-3113. Tel: 510-848-7812; Fax: 510-848-0179.
Catechesis/Religious Programs—AnnMary Driscoll, D.R.E.
Students 150.

3—St. Joseph The Worker, (1879), Revs. George E. Crespin; William J. O'Donnell. In res., Revs. Thomas Martin (Australia); Thomas J. McElligott (SFR); Gerard E. Reid (Jamaica) (Montego Bay); Ghebriel Woldai (Eritrea).
Res., 1640 Addison St., 94703. Tel: 510-843-2244; Fax: 510-843-2730.
School—2125 Jefferson St., 94703. Tel: 510-845-6266; Fax: 510-845-6185.
Sisters 1; Lay Teachers 9; Students 162.
Catechesis/Religious Programs—Tel: 510-843-1588.
Students 277.

4—St. Mary Magdalen, (1923), Revs. George M. Matanic, O.P.; Bruno Gibson, O.P. In res., Revs. Mark O'Leary, O.P.; Hilary Martin, O.P.; Daniel Syverstad, O.P.; Jordan Bradshaw, O.P.
Res., 2005 Berryman St., 94709. Tel: 510-526-4811; Fax: 510-525-3638.
School—School of the Madeleine, 1225 Milvia St., 94709. Tel: 510-526-4744; Fax: 510-526-5152.
Lay Teachers 20; Students 305.
Catechesis/Religious Programs—Students 62.

Brentwood, Contra Costa Co., Immaculate Heart of Mary (1949) (English-Spanish), Rev. John G. Garcia; Deacon Frank Bustos.
Res., 813 First St., 94513. Tel: 925-634-4154; Fax: 925-516-9340.
Catechesis/Religious Programs—Students 460.

Byron, Contra Costa Co., St. Anne (1916), Rev. Ronald G. Schmit; Deacon Ron Horan.
Mailing Address: Camino DP.O. Box 476, 94514. Tel: 925-634-6625; Fax: 925-634-4194.
Catechesis/Religious Programs—Tel: 925-634-0605; Fax: 925-634-0605.
Students 149.

Castro Valley, Alameda Co., Our Lady of Grace (1947), Revs. Kevin C. Mullins, O.S.A.; Thomas W. Behan, O.S.A.; Deacon Robert Dowling.
Res., 3433 Somerset Ave., 94546-3398. Tel: 510-537-0806; Fax: 510-537-6281.
School—19920 Anita Ave., 94546-3398. Tel: 510-581-3155; Fax: 510-581-1059.
Lay Teachers 16; Students 292.
Catechesis/Religious Programs—Tel: 510-538-3464; 582-9266; 889-7017; Fax: 510-537-6281.
Students 390.

Transfiguration (1961), Rev. Mario L. Borges; Deacons Timothy L. Moore; Burt J. Rigley; Garry L. Evans. In res., Rev. John E. Ranallo, O.S.A.
Res., 4000 E. Castro Valley Blvd., 94552. Tel: 510-538-7941; Fax: 510-538-7983.
Catechesis/Religious Programs—Tel: 510-537-1502.
Students 388.

Concord, Contra Costa Co.,

1—St. Agnes, (1964), Rev. George E. Mockel.
Res., 3966 Chestnut Ave., 94519. Tel: 925-689-0838; Fax: 925-689-7899.
School—3886 Chestnut Ave., 94519. Tel: 925-689-3990; Fax: 925-689-3455.
Lay Teachers 13; Students 345.
Catechesis/Religious Programs—Tel: 925-689-3757.
Students 352.

2—St. Bonaventure, (1957), Revs. Richard A. Mangini; Herman Leong; David Lawrence, S.J.; Deacon William Gall.
Res., 5562 Clayton Rd., 94521. Tel: 925-672-5800; Fax: 925-672-4606.
Catechesis/Religious Programs—Tel: 925-672-5500.
Students 725.

3—St. Francis of Assisi, (1984). (Formerly Most Precious Blood, 1955). Revs. William V. Macchi; Nicholas Glisson; Deacon Charles Palomares.
Res., 860 Oak Grove Rd., 94518. Tel: 925-682-5447; Fax: 925-682-5491.
School—866 Oak Grove Rd., 94518. Tel: 925-682-5414; Fax: 925-682-5480.
Sisters 1; Lay Teachers 18; Students 331.
Catechesis/Religious Programs—Tel: 925-682-5422.
Students 251.

4—Queen of All Saints, (1923), Revs. Michael Cunningham; Joseph Welch; William Johnson. Pastoral Assocs.: Ellen L. Midgley; Deacon Robert Karp.
Res., 2390 Grant St., 94520. Tel: 925-825-0350; Fax: 925-825-6975. [CEM]
School—2391 Grant St., 94520. Tel: 925-685-8700; Fax: 925-685-2034.
Lay Teachers 19; Students 298.
Catechesis/Religious Programs—Tel: 925-685-8707.
Students 226.

Crockett, Contra Costa Co., St. Rose of Lima (1912), Rev. Ciarian Dillon, O.M.I.
Res., 555 Third Ave., 94525. Tel: 510-787-2052; Fax: 510-787-2163.
Catechesis/Religious Programs—Students 23.
Mission—Port Costa, Contra Costa Co., St. Patrick, c/o St. Rose, 94525.

Danville, Contra Costa Co., St. Isidore's (1910), Revs. Daniel E. Cardelli; Stan Zak; Augustine Joseph, S.D.B. In res., Revs. James E. Driscoll, (Retired); Frank L. Colacicco (SAN) (Retired).
Parish Office: 440 LaGonda Way, 94526. Fax: 925-362-1919.
Res., 445 LaGonda Way, 94526-2522. Tel: 925-837-2122; Fax: 925-837-3954.
School—Tel: 925-837-2977; Fax: 925-837-2407.
Lay Teachers 39; Students 625.
Catechesis/Religious Programs—Tel: 925-362-1900; Fax: 925-362-1099.
Students 830.

Dublin, Alameda Co., St. Raymond (1961), Revs. Patrick A. Goodwin; Michael Lacey.
Res., 11555 Shannon Ave., 94568. Tel: 925-828-2460; Fax: 925-828-8610.
School—Tel: 925-828-4064; Fax: 925-828-2454.
Lay Teachers 16; Students 306.
Catechesis/Religious Programs—Tel: 925-828-4033.
Students 625.

El Cerrito, Contra Costa Co., St. Jerome's (1941), Rev. E. Donald Osuna.
Res., 308 Carmel Ave., 94530. Tel: 510-525-0876; Fax: 510-526-2721.
School—310 San Carlos, 94530. Tel: 510-525-9484; Fax: 510-525-5227.
Lay Teachers 15; Students 300.
Catechesis/Religious Programs—Students 105.

St. John the Baptist (1925), Revs. John Maxwell; John Blaker. In res., Rev. Raymond Ogbemure.
Res., 11150 San Pablo Ave., 94530. Tel: 510-232-5659; Fax: 510-236-0960.
School—Tel: 510-234-2244; Fax: 510-234-3726.
Lay Teachers 16; Students 316.
Catechesis/Religious Programs—Students 92.

El Sobrante, Contra Costa Co., St. Callistus (1952), Rev. Dana Michaels.
Res., 3580 San Pablo Dam Rd., 94803. Tel: 510-223-1153; Fax: 510-223-1137.
Catechesis/Religious Programs—Tel: 510-222-0432.
Students 236.

Fremont, Alameda Co.,

1—Corpus Christi, (1914), Rev. Timothy Stier; Deacon Luis Trucios.
Res., 37891 Second St., 94536. Tel: 510-790-3207; Fax: 510-790-3227.
Catechesis/Religious Programs—Tel: 510-790-3226.
Students 225.

2—Holy Spirit, (1886), Revs. Gerard K. Moran; Terry Tomkins; Paulson Mundanmani; Deacons Rudolph Brazil; William Drobick; Richard Yee.
Res., 37588 Fremont Blvd., 94536. Tel: 510-797-1660; Fax: 510-797-7080. [CEM][JC]
School—Tel: 510-793-3553; Fax: 510-793-2694.
Lay Teachers 15; Students 318.

Catechesis/Religious Programs—Tel: 510-797-5395; Fax: 510-797-4400.
Students 752.

3—St. James The Apostle, (1972), Rev. Paul E. Cleu.
Res., P.O. Box 7084, 94537. Tel: 510-792-1962.
Catechesis/Religious Programs—Students 40.

4—St. Joseph Mission Church, (1797), Rev. Msgr. Manuel C. Simas; Rev. Leo Alban Asuncion.
Res., P.O. Box 3276, Mission San Jose, 94539. Tel: 510-656-2364; Fax: 510-656-2438. [CEM]
School—43222 Mission Blvd., 94539. Tel: 510-656-6525; Fax: 510-656-3608.
Dominican Sisters of San Jose 2; Lay Teachers 14; Students 285.
Catechesis/Religious Programs—Tel: 510-657-0905; Fax: 510-657-4165.
Students 518.

5—St. Leonard (1959). Merged with Santa Paula, Fremont to form St. Leonard-Santa Paula, Fremont.

6—Santa Paula (1965). Merged with St. Leonard, Fremont to form St. Leonard-Santa Paula, Fremont.

7—St.Leonard-Santa Paula, (2000), Revs. Larry Silva; James J. Thottapally; Lawrence C. D'Anjou; W. Scott Chavez; Deacons Ovide P. Guesnon; Steven Budnik, Sr.; Jorge Lara.
Office: 41933 Blacow Rd., 94538. Tel: 510-657-4043; Fax: 510-657-4055.
Res., 3600 St. Leonard's Way, 94538. Tel: 510-656-4921; Fax: 510-226-0714.
School—3635 St. Leonard's Way, 94538. Tel: 510-657-1674; Fax: 510-657-3659.
Sisters 3; Lay Teachers 9; Students 285.
Catechesis/Religious Programs—Tel: 510-651-4966 (St. Leonard's Campus); 657-3777 (Santa Paula Campus).
Students 650.

Hayward, Alameda Co.,

1—All Saints, (1898), Revs. Robert J. McCann; Theodore Lawson, C.SS.R.; Terrence O'Malley, S.C.J.; Deacon Nelson Gonsalves. In res., Rev. Luke Ssemakula (Uganda).
Church—22824 Second St., 94541. Tel: 510-581-2570; Fax: 510-581-9538. [CEM]
School—Tel: 510-582-1910; Fax: 510-582-0866.
Lay Teachers 9; Students 300.
Catechesis/Religious Programs—Tel: 510-538-2711; Fax: 510-581-3642.
Students 326.

2—St. Bede, (1955), Revs. Seamus J. Farrell; Filiberto Barrera; Deacon Denis Ryken.
Res., 26950 Patrick Ave., 94544. Tel: 510-782-2171; Fax: 510-782-9712.
School—26910 Patrick Ave., 94544. Tel: 510-782-3444; Fax: 510-782-2243.
Lay Teachers 11; Students 312.
Catechesis/Religious Programs—Tel: 510-782-4292.
Students 752.

3—St. Clement, (1951), Revs. Philip Sopke, C.S.C.; Thomas McNally, C.S.C.
Res., 738 Calhoun St., 94544. Tel: 510-582-7282; 582-7240; Fax: 510-582-1875.
School—790 Calhoun St., 94544. Tel: 510-538-5885. Mrs. Mary Pult, Prin.
Lay Teachers 12; Students 304.
Catechesis/Religious Programs—Students 532.

4—St. Joachim, (1951), Revs. Ray Zielezienski; Robert Matthews.
Res., 21250 Hesperian Blvd., 94541. Tel: 510-783-2766; Fax: 510-783-2760.
School—Tel: 510-783-3177; Fax: 510-783-2161.
Lay Teachers 14; Students 313.
Catechesis/Religious Programs—Tel: 510-785-1818.
Students 442.

Lafayette, Contra Costa Co., St. Perpetua (1952), Rev. John Kasper, O.S.F.S. In res., Rev. Francis J. Houdek, S.J.
Res., 3454 Hamlin Rd., 94549. Tel: 925-283-0272; Fax: 925-283-6534.
School—Tel: 925-284-1640; Fax: 925-284-5676.
Lay Teachers 17; Students 237.
Catechesis/Religious Programs—Students 373.

Livermore, Alameda Co., St. Charles Borromeo (1964), Rev. Richard McCafferty, S.J.
Res., 1315 Lomitas Ave., 94550. Tel: 925-447-4549; Fax: 925-373-7088. [JC]
Catechesis/Religious Programs—Tel: 925-449-0133.
Students 280.

St. Michael (1878), Rev. Raymond Sacca; Rev. Msgr. Robert Adams, Pastor Emeritus; Revs. Sergio Lopez; David E. Staal; Sr. Patricia Gastelum, O.P., Hispanic Min.; Sr. Lucia Orta, O.P., Hispanic Min.; Deacons David Rezendez; Bill Archer. In res., Revs. Augustine Koilparampil (India); Walter W. Mayer.
Res., 458 Maple St., 94550. Tel: 510-447-1585; Fax: 510-447-0520. [CEM]
School—Tel: 925-447-1888; Fax: 925-447-6720. Sr. Emmanuel Cardinale, O.P Prin.
Sisters 2; Lay Teachers 14; Students 350.
Catechesis/Religious Programs—Sr. Kathleen Kennedy, D.R.E.
Students 583.

Martinez, Contra Costa Co., St. Catherine of Siena (1873), Revs. Vincent R. Brylka; Carl H. Seewald, S.V.D.
Mailing Address: Parish Activity Center Office:, 1125 Ferry St., 94553.
Res., 1100 Estudillo St., 94553. Tel: 925-228-2230; Fax: 925-228-1318. [CEM]
School—Tel: 925-228-4140; Fax: 925-228-0697. Mrs. Nancy Libby, Prin.
Lay Teachers 9; Students 278.
Catechesis/Religious Programs—1125 Ferry St., 94553. Tel: 925-228-2230, Ext. 7.
Students 214.

Moraga, Contra Costa Co., St. Monica (1965), Mrs. Cath McGhee, Pastoral Admin.; Rev. Declan Deane; Deacon Jack Jordan. In res., Rev. Michael A. Russo (NEW).
Res., 1001 Camino Pablo, P.O. Box 128, 94556. Tel: 925-376-6900; Fax: 925-376-9796.
Catechesis/Religious Programs—Tel: 925-376-0500; Fax: 925-376-0558.
Students 430.

Newark, Alameda Co., St. Edward's (1920), Revs. Jeffrey Finley, C.PP.S.; Gene Wilson, C.PP.S.; Johnson C. Abraham; Sr. Jeanne Sullivan, S.N.D., Pastoral Assoc.; Deacons Ernest Perez; Nick Bruckner; Roger Wedl; Antonio Barreto; Alfonso Perez.
Res., 5788 Thornton Ave., 94560. Tel: 510-797-0241; Fax: 510-797-4557.
School—Tel: 510-793-7242; Fax: 510-793-3189.
Sisters 2; Lay Teachers 12; Students 315.
Catechesis/Religious Programs—Tel: 510-797-5588.
Students 979.

Oakley, Contra Costa Co., St. Anthony (1925) (English-Spanish-Portuguese), Rev. Bernardino Andrade; Joann Mass, Admin.; Deacons Joseph Tovar; Alan Layden.
Res., 971 O'Hara Ave., 94561. Tel: 925-625-2048; Fax: 925-625-4433. [JC]
Catechesis/Religious Programs—Tel: 925-625-2077.
Students 543.

Orinda, Contra Costa Co., Santa Maria (1947), Rev. J. Roger Lucey, S.J.
Res., 20 Santa Maria Way, 94563. Tel: 925-254-2426; Fax: 925-254-2468.
Catechesis/Religious Programs—Tel: 925-254-0554. D.R.E.: Dorothy Harrington, (Children); Mary Eaton, (Youth).
Students 333.

Piedmont, Alameda Co., Corpus Christi (1929), Rev. Leo J. Edgerly, Jr. In res., Rev. Basil DePinto.
Res., 322 St. James Dr., 94611. Tel: 510-530-4343; Fax: 510-530-6824.
School—One Estates Dr., 94611. Tel: 510-530-4056; Fax: 510-530-5926.
Lay Teachers 14; Students 279.
Catechesis/Religious Programs—Tel: 610-531-2576.
Students 110.

Pinole, Contra Costa Co., St. Joseph's (1947), Revs. Quang Minh Dong; Jan Rudzewicz; Geoffrey Baraan. In res., Rev. Richard Gagliardi, (Retired).
Parish Center, Office & Mailing Address: 2100 Pear St., 94564. Tel: 510-741-4900; Fax: 510-724-9185.
Church—837 Tennent Ave., 94564.
School—Tel: 510-724-0242; Fax: 510-724-9886.
Lay Teachers 25; Students 320.
Catechesis/Religious Programs—Students 780.

Pittsburg, Contra Costa Co., Good Shepherd (1965), Revs. Helmut W. Richter; Louis Dabovich, Pastor Emeritus; Deacon Ferris J. Anthony.
Res., 3200 Harbor St., 94565. Tel: 925-432-6404; Fax: 925-432-6748.
Catechesis/Religious Programs—Tel: 925-439-1091.
Students 663.

St. Peter Martyr of Verona (1914), Rev. Ricardo A. Chavez.
Res., 740 Black Diamond St., 94565. Tel: 925-432-4771; Fax: 925-432-3389.
School—Tel: 925-439-1014; Fax: 925-439-1506.
Lay Teachers 12; Students 331.
Catechesis/Religious Programs—Tel: 925-432-7200.
Students 433.

Pleasant Hill, Contra Costa Co., Christ the King (1951), Revs. Brian T. Joyce; Brian Timoney; Michael Dibble.
Res., 199 Brandon Rd., 94523. Tel: 925-682-2486; Fax: 925-682-5021.
School—Tel: 925-685-1109; Fax: 925-685-1289. Sr. Carmel Garcia, C.S.J., Prin.
Sisters of St. Joseph of Carondelet 3; Lay Teachers 12; Students 324.
Catechesis/Religious Programs—Tel: 925-686-1017.
Students 1,195.

Pleasanton, Alameda Co., The Catholic Community of Pleasanton, Revs. Daniel E. Danielson; Mark D. Weisner; Anthony Herrera; Padraig Greene; Deacons Richard Martin; Ernest Freeman.
Res., 3999 Bernal, P.O. Box 817, 94566. Tel: 925-846-4489; Fax: 925-426-5061. [CEM]
Catechesis/Religious Programs—Tel: 925-846-3531; Fax: 925-846-3543.
Students 1,768.

St. Augustine (1901). Merged with St. Elizabeth Seton, Pleasanton to form The Catholic Community of Pleasanton.

St. Elizabeth Seton (1991). Merged with St. Augustine, Pleasanton to form The Catholic Community of Pleasanton.

Point Richmond, Contra Costa Co., Our Lady of Mercy (1902), Rev. Msgr. Theodore W. Kraus, Admin.
Res., 301 W. Richmond Ave., 94801. Tel: 510-232-1843; Fax: 510-232-1805.

Richmond, Contra Costa Co., St. Cornelius (1952), Rev. Antonio A. Valdivia; Deacon Juan Beltran.
Res., 225-28th St., 94804. Tel: 510-233-5215; Fax: 510-233-7342. [CEM]
School—201-28th St., 94805. Tel: 510-232-3326; Fax: 510-232-4071.
Lay Teachers 11; Students 205.
Catechesis/Religious Programs—Students 200.

St. David of Wales (1952), Rev. Ronald E. Atwood.
Res., 5641 Esmond Ave., 94805. Tel: 510-237-1531; Fax: 510-237-3801.
School—871 Sonoma St., 94805. Tel: 510-232-2283; Fax: 510-231-0484. Mrs. Barbara Kringle-Fabiani, Prin.
Sisters 1; Lay Teachers 13; Students 328.
Catechesis/Religious Programs—5418 Esmond Ave., 94805.
Students 336.

St. Mark's (1912), Rev. Jose de Jesus Nieto-Ruiz, Admin.
Res., 159 Harbour Way, 94801. Tel: 510-234-5886; Fax: 510-236-5711.
Catechesis/Religious Programs—Students 164.

Rodeo, Contra Costa Co., St. Patrick's (1923), Rev. Larry E. Young.
Res., 825 Seventh St., 94572. Tel: 510-799-4406; Fax: 510-799-5681.
School—907 Seventh St., 94572. Tel: 510-799-2506; Fax: 510-799-6781.
Sisters of the Immaculate Heart of Mary 3; Lay Teachers 24; Students 285.
Catechesis/Religious Programs—Students 151.

San Leandro, Alameda Co.,

1—Assumption of the Blessed Virgin Mary, (1951), Rev. Msgr. Michael Lucid; Rev. Virendra Coutts (India).
Res., 1100 Fulton Ave., 94577. Tel: 510-352-1537; Fax: 510-352-9155.
School—Tel: 510-357-8772; Fax: 510-357-7018.
Lay Teachers 17; Students 292.
Catechesis/Religious Programs—Tel: 510-351-1235.
Students 170.

2—St. Alphonsus Liguori, (1955), Deacon George Peters.
Res., 2085 Miramar Ave., 94578. Tel: 510-276-3907; Fax: 510-276-3955. [CEM]
Catechesis/Religious Programs—Students 14.

3—St. Felicitas, (1952), Rev. Wayne Campbell; Deacon Jose Prado, (Retired). In res., Revs. Tran Thuc Dinh (Vietnam) (Retired); Joseph Fiedorowicz.
Res., 1662 Manor Blvd., 94579. Tel: 510-351-5244; Fax: 510-351-5730.
School—1650 Manor Blvd., 94579. Tel: 510-357-2530; Fax: 510-357-5358.
Sisters of St. Joseph of Wichita 2; Lay Teachers 10; Students 295.
Catechesis/Religious Programs—Tel: 510-483-4880.
Students 390.

4—St. Leander, (1864), Revs. John Prochaska; Robert A. Mendonca; Deacons Dennis Davis; Victor Silveira; Antonio Baptista. In res., Revs. Matthew R.D. Regan; Antonio Reis (Brazil).
Office: 474 W. Estudillo Ave., 94577. Tel: 510-895-5631; Fax: 510-352-3578.
School—Tel: 510-351-4144; Fax: 510-483-6060.
Lay Teachers 10; Students 319.
Catechesis/Religious Programs—Students 290.

5—Our Lady of Good Counsel, (1966) (Vietnamese), Rev. Thomas Duong Binh-Minh.
Res., 14112 Azores Pl., 94577. Tel: 510-895-1165; Fax: 510-483-7705.

Catechesis/Religious Programs—2500 Bermuda Ave., 94577. Tel: 510-483-2513.
Students 74.

San Lorenzo, Alameda Co., St. John the Baptist (1925), Revs. David Link; William J. Dunn; Deacon Leonard J. Bettencourt.
Res., 264 E. Lewelling Blvd., 94580. Tel: 510-351-5050; Fax: 510-276-0397.
School—Tel: 510-276-6632; Fax: 510-276-5645. Arlene Marseille, Prin.
Sisters 4; Lay Teachers 11; Students 306.
Catechesis/Religious Programs—Tel: 510-278-5080.
Students 250.

San Pablo, St. Paul (1864), Revs. Paul Fazio, O.F.M.Conv.; Ignatius Hinkle, O.F.M.Conv.; Dominic Castro, O.F.M.Conv.; Deacons Ysidro Madrigal; Isidoro R. Flores; Donaciano Perez.
Res., 1845 Church Ln., 94806. Tel: 510-232-5931; Fax: 510-232-1846.
School—Tel: 510-233-3080; Fax: 510-231-8777.
Lay Teachers 9; Students 298.
Catechesis/Religious Programs—1825 Church Ln., 94806.
Students 305.

San Ramon, Contra Costa Co., St. Joan of Arc (1979), Rev. Fred A. Riccio; Deacon Ruben Gomez.
Res., 2601 San Ramon Valley Blvd., 94583-1335. Tel: 925-830-0600; Fax: 925-830-5059.
Catechesis/Religious Programs—Tel: 925-830-4710.
Students 1,048.

Union City, Alameda Co., Our Lady of the Rosary (1951), Rev. Jose M. Leon; Deacons Federico Ceja, (Retired); Richard L. Folger; Gustaaf Roemers; Luis Trucios. In res., Rev. Roy V. Eco (Philippines).
Res., 703 C St., 94587. Tel: 510-471-2609; Fax: 510-471-4601.
School—Tel: 510-471-3765.
Lay Teachers 9; Students 214.
Catechesis/Religious Programs—Tel: 510-471-7419.
Students 426.

St. Anne (1973), Revs. Ramon J. Gomez; Marciano E. Santiago.
Res., 32223 Cabello St., P.O. Box 292, 94587. Tel: 510-471-7766; Fax: 510-487-6540.
Catechesis/Religious Programs—Tel: 510-489-2080.
Students 800.

Walnut Creek, Contra Costa Co.,

1—St. Anne, (1965), Rev. Msgr. John T. McCracken; Revs. Anthony S. Hannick (YAK); William M. Kegel, S.J.; Sr. Carole Pesce, S.H.F., Pastoral Assoc.
Res., 1600 Rossmoor Pkwy., 94595-2507. Tel: 925-932-2324; Fax: 925-932-4628.

2—St. John Vianney, (1965), Revs. Vincent J. Scott; Christopher Berbena; Deacon John Jee.
Res., 1650 Ygnacio Valley Rd., 94598. Tel: 925-939-7911; Fax: 925-939-0450.
Catechesis/Religious Programs—Tel: 925-939-9544.
Students 539.

3—St. Mary's, (1941) (Hispanic-Filipino), Revs. John J. Mallon; George Palamattathil. In res., Revs. Peter Charankat (India); Joseph Parekkatt, S.D.B.
Res., 1201 Alpine Rd., 94596. Tel: 510-934-2544; Fax: 510-934-1358. [JC]
School—Tel: 510-935-5054; Fax: 510-935-5063. Mrs. Mary Lou Curtis, Prin.
Lay Teachers 17; Students 284.
Catechesis/Religious Programs—2039 Mt. Diablo Blvd., 94596. Tel: 510-937-2414; Fax: 510-937-6487. Patricia Petromilli, D.R.E.
Students 320.

4—St. Stephen, (1966), Rev. Denis A. DesRosiers; Marlene Preuninger, Pastoral Assoc.; Deacon William Bothe.
Res., 525 Madonna Ln., 94596. Tel: 925-939-3826; Fax: 925-988-0417.
Catechesis/Religious Programs—Students 93.

Chaplains of Public Institutions

Hospitals

Oakland. *Children's Hospital*. Sr. Bernice Gotelli, P.B.V.M. Tel: 510-428-3325; 428-3000.
Highland Hospital. Sr. Maura O'Connor, S.N.J.M. Tel: 510-437-4800; Rev. Basil DePinto Tel: 510-425-2774.
Summit Medical Center, Pastoral Care. Attended by Sacred Heart. Tel: 510-835-4500.

Antioch. *Delta Memorial Hospital*. Attended by Holy Rosary.

Berkeley. *Alta Bates Hospital*. Sr. Kathleen Corbett, C.S.J. Tel: 510-204-4444; Rev. John O'Leary Tel: 510-204-6732.
Alta Bates-Herrick Hospital. Attended by St. Joseph the Worker, Berkeley.

Castro Valley. *Eden Hospital*. Rev. John E. Ranallo, O.S.A. Tel: 510-537-1234.

Concord. *Mount Diablo Hospital, Pastoral Care*. Attended by Queen of All Saints. Tel: 510-682-8200. Rev. William Johnson, Chap., Tel: 925-825-0350.

Fremont. *Washington Hospital*. Rev. Richard Peiris Tel: 510-505-0599; 797-1111; Sr. Jeanne Sullivan, S.N.D. Tel: 510-797-1111; Rev. Jeffrey Finley, C.PP.S. Tel: 510-797-1111.

Hayward. *Kaiser-Permanente Medical Center*. Attended by St. Bede.

Livermore. *Veterans Administration Hospital*. Rev. Augustine Koilparampil Tel: 510-447-2560; 447-1585.

Martinez. *Contra Costa Hospital*. Attended by St. CAtherine of Siena.
Kaiser-Permanente Medical Center. Sr. Moira MacPherson Tel: 510-372-1000; Rev. William Johnson Tel: 510-372-1000.

Pinole. *Doctor's Hospital*. Attended by St. Joseph, Pinole.

Pittsburg. *Los Medanos Hospital*. Attended by Good Shepherd.

Richmond. *East Bay Hospital*. Attended by St. Cornelius & St. Mark.
Kaiser-Permanente. Attended by St. Mark.

San Leandro. *Fairmont Hospital, Redemptorists* Tel: 510-667-3251. Deacon George Peters.
Humana Hospital. Attended by St. Leander.
Physicians Community Hospital. Attended by Assumption.

San Pablo. *Brookside-Hospital*. Attended by St. Paul. Tel: 510-235-7000.

San Ramon. *San Ramon Regional Medical Center*. Attended by St. Joan of Arc. Tel: 510-275-9200 (Hospital).

Walnut Creek. *John Muir Memorial Hospital, Pastoral Care*. Attended by St. John Vianney. Tel: 510-939-3000 (Hospital).
Kaiser-Permanente Medical Center. Rev. Peter Charankat Tel: 510-372-1000.
Walnut Creek Hospital. Attended by St. John Vianney.

Prisons and Jails

Oakland. *North County Jail*. Deacon Eugene Stelley Tel: 510-652-5453.
Victim Offender Reconciliation Program. (VORP). Rick Mockler, Dir., Tel: 510-834-5656.

Martinez. *Contra Costa County Jails*. Pat Conroy Tel: 510-672-7822.
Contra Costa County Juvenile Institution. Deacon Frank Beville Tel: 510-834-5656.

Pleasanton. *Alameda County Jail-Santa Rita Rehabilitation Center*. Deacon Frank Beville Tel: 510-834-5656; 828-5400, Ext. 261.
Federal Correctional Institution. Sr. Joan Campbell, P.B.V.M.; Rev. Efrin Casio Tel: 510-829-3522.
Valley Care Hospital. Sr. M. Cabrini Catania, J.H.F., St. Augustine Tel: 925-846-4489.
Victim Offender Reconciliation Program (VORP). Rick Mockler, Dir., Tel: 510-834-5656.

San Leandro. *Alameda County Juvenile Institutions*. Deacon Frank Beville, Coord., Tel: 510-834-5656.

On Special Assignment:
Reverend Fathers—
Vella, Francis, Chap., V.A. Medical Center, Alexandria, LA

Military Chaplains:
Reverend Monsignors—
Walsh, Martin E., Army Reserves
Reverend Fathers—
Hannick, Anthony S., Veterans Admin. Hospital, Martinez
Koilparampil, Augustine, U.S. Veterans Hospital, Livermore
Lagasse, Ronald J., Lt. Col., U.S. Army Reserves, Schofield Army Base, Hawaii
Wydeven, John

Graduate Studies:
Reverend Fathers—
Bretton, Ray
Minihan, Paul

Retired:
Reverend Monsignors—
Adams, Robert
Mullen, William J.
Walsh, Martin E.
Reverend Fathers—
Brainard, Ernest B.
Broderson, Donald
Cantillon, John Joseph
Clift, James C.
Cloutier, Edmond
Cooper, Hilary
Dabovich, Louis
Daly, George
Devine, Paul
Dinh, Tran Truc
Dollard, John J.
Driscoll, James E.
Dunn, William J.
Dybdal, Gerald
Eggerling, Milton
Ferraro, Joseph
Ferreira, Joseph A.
Gagliardi, Richard
Gallagher, Thomas B.
Haasl, Edgar
Hayburn, Edmund L.
Jaques, Domingos
Joyce, Michael
Keane, James
Kozina, Vladimir
Lanuevo, Tarcisio D.
Lester, Thomas
Lu, Matthias
Manning, John
Marshall, William
Mayer, Walter W.
McLeod, Daniel
Mifsud, Carmelo
Morgan, John
Mullen, William J.
Murray, Adrian
Palis, Theo
Ponciroli, Robert
Poon, Stanislaus
Ribero, Arthur
Ruffing, Norman
Russell, Kenneth
Schexnayder, James
Schwab, Joseph
Snyder, Alexander
Starbuck, James
Vella, Francis M.

Permanent Deacons:
Agustin, Benjamin, St. Joseph, Pinole
Anthony, Ferris J., Good Shepherd, Pittsburg
Archer, William, St. Michael, Livermore
Arteaga, William, St. Michael, Livermore
Baptista, Antonio, St. Leander, San Leandro
Barnes, Frank, On Duty Outside the Diocese
Barnes, James, (Retired)
Barreto, Antonio, St. Edward, Newark
Beltran, Juan, St. Cornelius, Richmond
Bettencourt, Leonard, St. John the Baptist Church, San Lorenzo
Beville, Frank, St. Stephen, Walnut Creek
Bothe, William, St. Francis of Assisi, Concord
Brazil, Rudolph, Holy Spirit, Fremont
Bruckner, Nick, St. Edward, Newark
Budnik, Steve, St. Leonard-Santa Paula, Fremont
Bustos, Frank, Immaculate Heart of Mary, Brentwood
Cabezas, Rigoberto, St. Joachim, Hayward
Cain, Jerry, Leave of Absence
Calub, Benigno, St. Ann, Union City
Cantlon, Michael, Holy Spirit, Fremont
Ceja, Federico, (Retired)
Chichon, Witold, Polis Pastoral Center, Martinez
Custodio, Maurice, St. Mary's, Walnut Creek
Davis, Dennis, St. Leander, San Leandro
Dowling, Robert, Our Lady of Grace, Castro Valley
Drobick, William, Holy Spirit, Fremont
Duhe, Gaston J., St. Columba, Oakland
Dulka, Matthew, Our Lady of Grace, Castro Valley
Durden, John, St. Charles, Livermore
Edgerly, Leo, Sr., St. Andrew-St. Joseph, Oakland
Ehling, Rex, St. Augustine, Oakland
Evans, Garry, Transfiguration, Castro Valley
Fleischer, Alfred, St. Ignatius, Antioch
Flores, Isidore, St. Paul, San Pablo
Flores, Jose, Most Holy Rosary, Antioch
Folger, Richard, Our Lady of the Rosary, Union City
Freeman, Ernest, St. Augustine, Pleasanton
Frumkin, Paul, St. Clement, Hayward
Fuentes, Javier, St. Bernard, Oakland
Gall, William, St. Bonaventure, Concord
Gilbert, John, (Retired)
Gomez, Ruben, St. Joan of Arc, San Ramon
Gonsalves, Nelson, All Saints, Hayward
Gonzalez, Noe, St. Louis Bertrand, Oakland
Grigg, Jerry, Most Holy Rosary, Antioch
Guesnon, Ovide, Santa Paula, Fremont
Hagenbach, Robert, On Duty Outside the Diocese
Hernandez, Gabriel, St. Bede, Hayward
Hoblitzell, Ross, (Retired)
Horan, Ronald, St. Anne, Byron
Jaramillo, Ernest, St. Joachim, Hayward
Jordan, Jack, St. Monica, Moraga
Karp, Robert, (Retired) Kenny, John
Kortuem, John, St. Anthony, Oakley

Lara, Jorge, St. Leonard, Stanta Paula, Fremont
Layden, Alan, St. Anthony, Oakley
Lee, Stanley, The Filipino Pastoral Center
Lewandowski, Daniel, On Duty Outside the Diocese
Macachor, Oscar, St. Joachim, Hayward
Madrigal, Ysidro, St. Paul, San Pablo
Marchese, Charles, Jr., On Duty Outside of Diocese
Martin, Richard, St. Augustine, Pleasanton
Mazibrook, John, St. John Vianney, Walnut Creek
McGowan, Thomas, St. John, El Cerrito
Miyashiro, Leslie, Korean Pastoral Center, Oakland
Moll, Herbert, On Duty Outside the Diocese
Molloy, Ernest, St. John the Baptist, San Lorenzo
Moore, Timothy, Transfiguration, Castro Valley
Oey, Hock Chuan, St. Joan of Arc, San Ramon
Palomares, Charles, St. Francis of Assisi, Concord
Perez, Alfonso, St. Edward, Newark
Perez, Donaciano, St. Paul, San Pablo
Perez, Ernest, St. Edward, Newark
Perry, Thomas, St. Augustine, Pleasanton
Peters, George, Queen of All Saints, Concord
Prado, Jose, (Retired)
Preza, Mariano, Concord Hispanic Community, Concord
Quigley, Edward, St. Augustine, Pleasanton
Rabuy, Carlos, St. Ann, Union City
Rezendes, David, St. Michael, Livermore
Rigley, Burton, Transfiguration, Castro Valley
Rivilla, Luis, On Duty Outside of Diocese
Romers, Gustaaf, Our Lady of the Rosary, Union City
Ryken, Dennis, St. Bede, Hayward
Silva, Richard, On Duty Outside the Diocese
Silveira, Victor, St. Leander, San Leandro
Silvernale, Charles, Holy Rosary, Antioch
Smith, Leo, (Retired)
Soublet, Morris, St. Andrew-St. Joseph, Oakland
Spano, Edward, St. Ann, Byron
Stelly, Eugene, St. Andrew-St. Joseph, Oakland
Taylor, Stephen, Holy Spirit, Fremont
Tovar, Joseph, St. Anthony, Oakley
Turcios, Luis, Corpus Christi, Fremont
Victoria, Hector, St. Raymond, Dublin
Walsh, Jerome, St. Bonaventure, Concord
Warren, William, Jr., On Duty Outside the Diocese
Wedl, Roger, St. Edward, Newark
Yee, Richard, Holy Spirit, Fremont

INSTITUTIONS LOCATED IN THE DIOCESE

[A] SEMINARIES, RELIGIOUS OR SCHOLASTICATES

OAKLAND. *Graduate School of Theology, School of Applied Theology*, 5890 Birch Ct., 94618. Tel: 510-652-1651; Fax: 510-420-0542.
E-mail: satgtu@aol.com
Web site: www.satgtu.org
An Affiliate of the Graduate Theological Union. Bro. Bernard LoCoco, F.S.C., Pres. & Dean; Sr. Therese McGroddy, R.S.H.M., Dir. Admissions. Trustees: Bro. Bernard LoCoca, F.S.C.; Claude Welch, Ph.D.; James A. Donahue, Ph.D.; Sr. Rosemary Chinnici, S.L.; Sr. Barbara Green, O.P.; Mr. James Jackson; Ms. Jennie Magid; Mr. James Penna, J.D.; Mrs. Sarah Seybold; Bro. Mel Anderson, F.S.C.; Revs. Eugene R. Zimmers, S.J.; Francis Buckley, S.J.; Francis J. Houdek, S.J. Sisters 2; Brothers 1; Lay Teachers 30; Students 49.

BERKELEY. *Brother Giles Franciscan Formation Community*. (Province of St. Barbara), 1920-7th St., 94710. Tel: 510-841-4102.
E-mail: Sevenstr@aol.com
Bro. John Kiesler, O.F.M., Guardian; Rev. Dan Lackie, O.F.M., Formation Dir.; Bros. Sebastian Sandoval, O.F.M.; Alvin Cachola, O.F.M.; William Minkel, O.F.M.; John Gutierrez, O.F.M.; Alberto Villafan, O.F.M.; Richard O'Lea, O.F.M.; Jose Alberto Barrera, O.F.M. Priests 1; Brothers 8.

Dominican School of Philosophy and Theology, 2401 Ridge Rd., 94709. Tel: 510-849-2030.
Web site: www.dspt.edu
(Dominican House of Studies at the Graduate Theological Union). Revs. Gregory Rocca, O.P., Pres. & Faculty (Regular); Eugene M. Ludwig, O.F.M.Cap., Academic Dean & Faculty; Mr. Scott Connolly, Registrar & Dean of Students; Susan McGinnis Hardie, Dir. Admissions & Recruitment; Mrs. Eleanor Westbrooke, Sec.
Faculty (Regular): Revs. Joseph Boenzi, S.D.B.; Luke D. Buckles, O.P.; Mr. Mark Delp; Rev. Michael Dodds, O.P.; Sr. Barbara Green, O.P.; Revs. Edward Krasevac, O.P.; Eugene M. Ludwig, O.F.M.Cap.; John Hilary Martin, O.P.; Michael Monshau, O.P.; Michael T. Morris, O.P.; Gregory Rocca, O.P.; Richard Schenk, O.P.; Gregory T. Tatum, O.P.
Faculty (Adjunct): Rev. Owen Carroll; Dr. Marilyn Anne Coffy; Revs. Arthur Lenti, S.D.B.; Stephen Ernest, S.V.D.; Sr. Mary Greenan, F.M.A. Priests 12; Sisters 1; Lay Teachers 2; Students 100.

Franciscan School of Theology, 1712 Euclid Ave., 94709. Tel: 510-848-5232; Fax: 510-549-9466.
E-mail: info@fst.edu
Web site: www.fst.edu
Revs. William M. Cieslak, O.F.M.Cap., Pres.; Joseph P. Chinnici, O.F.M., Academic Dean; Sr. Paschal Hocum, O.S.F., Dir. Spiritual Formation; Sr. Rita Dougherty, Registrar; Ernesto Zamora Gallardo, Recruitment Dir.
Faculty: Revs. Michael D. Guinan, O.F.M.; William M. Cieslak, O.F.M.Cap.; Rigoberto Caloca-Rivas, O.F.M.; Faustino Cruz, S.M.; Richard Gula, S.S.; Kenan B. Osborne, O.F.M.; Xavier J. Harris, O.F.M.; Joseph P. Chinnici, O.F.M.; Thomas West, O.F.M.; Sr. Mary McGann, R.S.C.J.; Sr. Eva Lumas, S.S.S.; Sr. Marion Moeser, O.S.F.; Bros. William J. Short, O.F.M.; John Kiesler, O.F.M. Priests 9; Brothers 2; Sisters 5; Lay Teachers 1; Total Enrollment 98.

The Jesuit School of Theology at Berkeley, 1735 LeRoy Ave., 94709. Tel: 510-841-8804; Fax: 510-841-8536.
E-mail: mmccanta@jstb.edu
A Pontifical Faculty of Theology. One of two theological centers of the U.S. Jesuit Conference, Society of Jesus. A Member of the Graduate Theological Union (GTU), Berkeley. Revs. Joseph P. Daoust, S.J., Pres.; George E. Griener, S.J., Academic Dean; George R. Murphy, S.J., Coord. Formation Programs; Ms. April M. Collier, Vice Pres. Institutional Advancement; Mr. Robert Lassalle-Klein, Dir. of Field Education; Mr. Bruce Lescher, Dir. Sabbatical Programs; Ms. Lorna Wallace McKeown, Asst. Academic Dean & In-House Registrar; Mrs. Karen Ripsom, Asst. Treas.; Ms. Linda A. Menes, Dir. of Admissions; C. M. McCanta, Bus. Mgr. & Treas.; Ms. Jill K. Marshall, Dean Students & Dir. Continuing Education.
Faculty (Emeriti): Rev. Donald L. Gelpi, S.J.
Faculty: Revs. James T. Bretzke, S.J.; Thomas E. Buckley, S.J.; Joseph P. Daoust, S.J.; John Donahue, S.J.; Sr. Mary Ann Donovan, S.C.; Rev. John C. Endres, S.J.; Dr. Alejandro Garcia-Rivera; Revs. Donald L. Gelpi, S.J.; George E. Griener, S.J.; Dr. Gina Hens-Piazza; Mr. Robert Lassalle-Klein; Revs. William R. O'Neill, S.J.; T. Howland Sanks, S.J.; Sr. Sandra M. Schneiders, I.H.M.; Rev. David J. Stagaman, S.J. Priests 11; Sisters 2; Lay Teachers 4; Full-time faculty 16; Students 170. (See listing for The Jesuit Community at The Jesuit School of Theology at Berkeley).

MORAGA. *Christian Brothers (F.S.C.) Vocation Office*, P.O. Box 5150, 94575. Tel: 925-631-4186; Fax: 925-631-9510.
E-mail: FSCinSF@earthlink.net
Web site: www.delasalle.org
Bros. James Joost, F.S.C.; Norman Cook, F.S.C.; Michael Avila, F.S.C. Brothers 3.

[B] COLLEGES AND UNIVERSITIES

OAKLAND. *Holy Names College*, (1868) 3500 Mountain Blvd., 94619. Tel: 510-436-1000; Fax: 510-436-1199.
Web site: www.hnc.edu
For a complete listing, refer to the Colleges and Universities section.

FREMONT. *Queen of the Holy Rosary College* Mailing Address: P.O. Box 3908 Mission San Jose, 94539. Tel: 510-657-2468; Fax: 510-657-1734.
For a complete listing, refer to the Colleges and Universities section.

MORAGA. *St. Mary's College*, 94575. Tel: 510-631-4000; Fax: 925-376-1847.
Web site: www.stmarys-ca.edu
For a complete listing, refer to the Colleges and Universities section.

[C] HIGH SCHOOLS, DIOCESAN

OAKLAND. *Bishop O'Dowd High School*, 9500 Stearns Ave., 94605. Tel: 510-577-9100; Fax: 510-638-3259.
E-mail: admin@odowd.pvt.k12.ca.us
Web site: odowd.pvt.K12.ca.us
Basilian Fathers (Congregation of St. Basil). Revs. John Huber, C.S.B.; Donald J. McLeod, C.S.B., Prin.; John B. Malo, C.S.B., Supr.; Robert H. Glass, C.S.B.; David Weise, C.S.B.; Benjamin Owens, C.SS.R.; Les F. Schaefer, C.S.B. Priests 7; Lay Teachers 64; Students 1,143.

St. Elizabeth High School, 1530-34th Ave., 94601. Tel: 510-532-8947. Sr. Mary Liam Brock, Prin. Sisters 3; Lay Teachers 23; Students 330.

[D] HIGH SCHOOLS, PAROCHIAL

ALAMEDA. *Saint Joseph Notre Dame High School*, 1011 Chestnut St., 94501. Tel: 510-523-1526; Fax: 510-523-2181.
Web site: www.sjnd.org
Mr. Anthony V. Aiello, Prin. Brothers 1; Lay Teachers 32; Total Staff 55; Students 540.

[E] HIGH SCHOOLS, PRIVATE

OAKLAND. *Holy Name High School*, 4660 Harbord Dr., 94618. Tel: 510-450-1110; Fax: 510-547-3111.
E-mail: aschenone@hnhs.k12.ca.us
Sisters of the Holy Names of Jesus and Mary. Laura M. Held, Pres.; Angela Schenone, Prin. Sisters 3; Lay Teachers 18; Students 316.

BERKELEY. *Saint Mary's College High School*, Peralta Park, 1294 Albina Ave., 94709. Tel: 510-526-9242; Fax: 510-559-6298. Brothers of the Christian Schools. Bro. Edmond Larouche, F.S.C., Pres.; Dr. Kathleen Rojan McGuire, Prin. Brothers 1; Lay Teachers 46; Students 630.

CONCORD. *Carondelet High School*, 1133 Winton Dr., 94518-3598. Tel: 510-686-5353; Fax: 510-671-9429.
E-mail: carondelet.pvt.k12.ca.us
Web site: www.carondelet.pvt.k12.ca.us
Sisters of St Joseph of Carondelet. Sr. Kathleen Lang, C.S.J., Prin. Brothers 1; Sisters 2; Lay Teachers 39; Students 825.

De La Salle High School of Concord, Inc. dba De La Salle High School. (Boys), 1130 Winton Dr., 94518. Tel: 925-686-3310; Fax: 925-686-3474.
Web site: www.dlshs.org
Brothers of the Christian Schools (De La Salle Christian Brothers). Mr. James Tschann, Pres.; Bro. Christopher Brady. Co-Asst. Principals: Mr. George Sabbagha; Mr. Rudy Schulze; Mr. Roger Hassett, Dir. of Campus Min. Priests 1; Brothers 3; Lay Teachers 55; Students 978.

HAYWARD. *Moreau Catholic High School*, 27170 Mission Blvd., 94544. Tel: 510-881-4300; Fax: 510-581-5669.
E-mail: tguevara@moreaucatholic.org
Web site: www.moreaucatholic.org
Brothers of Holy Cross. Patricia Geister, Prin.; Joseph Connell, Ph.D., Pres.; Margaret J. Walsh, Corp. Treas. Priests 1; Lay Teachers 51; Students 1,188.

RICHMOND. *Salesian High School*, 2851 Salesian Ave., 94804. Tel: 510-234-4433; Fax: 510-236-4636.
E-mail: info@salesian.com
Web site: www.salesian.com
Salesians of St. John Bosco. Rev. Christian H. Woerz, S.D.B., Dir. & Pres.; Mr. Timothy Chambers, Prin.; Bro. Ernest Martinez, S.D.B., Asst. Prin.; Revs. Gerald Wertz, S.D.B., Business Mgr.; Arthur Brainard, S.D.B., (Retired); Laurence Byrne, S.D.B., (Retired); Roger Luna, S.D.B.; Jesse Montes, S.D.B.; Bros. Jerry Weirich, S.D.B., Faculty; Armando Pacheco, S.D.B., Faculty; Thomas Mass, S.D.B., Faculty. Formation: Bros. Long Mai, S.D.B.; Tho Bui, S.D.B.; Thien Nguyen, S.D.B. Priests 5; Brothers 8; Lay Teachers 45; Students 560.

[F] EARLY CHILDHOOD EDUCATION CENTERS

MISSION SAN JOSE. *Dominican Kindergarten*, 43326 Mission Blvd., P.O. Box 3908, 94539. Tel: 510-651-7978; Fax: 510-657-1734.
E-mail: Kinderkate@aol.com
Web site: msjdominicans.org
Sr. Kathleen McAvoy, O.P., Dir. & Teacher. Sisters 1; Students 32.

[G] SUMMER SCHOOLS

OAKLAND. *Holy Names College*, 3500 Mountain Blvd., 94619. Tel: 510-436-1000; Fax: 510-436-1199.
Web site: www.hnc.edu
Sisters of the Holy Names of Jesus and Mary. Resident and Non-Resident Students. Total Enrollment 947.

MISSION SAN JOSE. *Queen of the Holy Rosary College*, 43326 Mission Blvd., P.O. Box 3908, 94539. Tel: 510-657-2468; Fax: 510-657-1734.
E-mail: msjdominicans.org
Web site: www.msjdominicans.org/college/html
Sisters of the Third Order of St. Dominic of the Congregation of the Queen of the Holy Rosary. Sisters 15; Lay Teachers 3; Students 196.

MORAGA. *St. Mary's College*, 94575. Tel: 925-631-4000; Fax: 925-376-1847.
Web site: www.stmarys-ca.us
Brothers of the Christian Schools, District of San Francisco. Priests 4; Brothers 12; Sisters 2; Lay Teachers 438.

[H] CATHOLIC CHARITIES OF THE DIOCESE OF OAKLAND

OAKLAND. *Catholic Charities of the Diocese of Oakland, Inc.*, 433 Jefferson St., 94607. Tel: 510-768-3100; Fax: 510-451-6998.
Web site: www.cceb.org

Legal Title: *Catholic Charities of the Diocese of Oakland, Inc., A Non-Profit Corporation.* Barbara S. Terrazas, Exec. Dir.; Marilyn Kihara, Controller; Marilyn Lovelace-Grant, Human Resources Dir.; Solomon Belette, Cluster Admin.

COMMUNITY AND PARISH SERVICES:

Counseling Services:

Alameda County Area Supervisor, 433 Jefferson St., 94607. Tel: 510-768-3100; Fax: 510-451-6998.

Chancery Annex, 3014 Lakeshore Ave., 94610. Tel: 510-763-0301; Fax: 510-893-6215. Regional Offices.

Alameda, 1109 Chestnut St., Alameda, 94501. Tel: 510-569-9307.

Antioch, 21 E. 15th St., Antioch, 94509. Tel: 510-778-7929.

Berkeley, 2700 Dwight Way, Berkeley. Tel: 510-834-5657, Ext. 4022.

East Oakland, 6226 Camden St., 94605. Tel: 510-569-9307; Fax: 510-569-9357.

Fremont Offices, 3767 Decoto Rd., Fremont, 94536. Tel: 510-792-2444; Fax: 510-792-2494. Fremont-Mission San Jose, 43148 Mission Blvd., Fremont, 94539. Tel: 510-490-5452.

Hayward, 22824 Second St., Hayward, 94541. Tel: 510-886-1331.

Hayward, 21250 Hesperian Blvd., Hayward, 94541. Tel: 510-886-1462.

Livermore, 458 Maple St., Livermore, 94550. Tel: 925-828-1462.

Concord, 2350 Pacheco St., Concord, 94521. Tel: 925-825-3099; Fax: 925-825-5503. Pat Spohn, Contra Costa County Area Supvr.

Pinole, 2150 Pear Ave., Pinole, 94564. Tel: 510-724-6263; Fax: 510-724-6057.

Pittsburg, 455 W. Fourth St., Pittsburg, 94565. Tel: 925-432-7363; Fax: 925-432-7337.

Richmond, 225 Civic Center St., Richmond, 94804. Tel: 510-232-1377; Fax: 510-232-2917.

San Ramon, 2601 San Ramon Valley Blvd., San Ramon, 94583. Tel: 925-828-1462.

Services to Parish Schools, 433 Jefferson St., 94607. Tel: 510-768-3100; Fax: 510-451-6998.

Department of Aging, 433 Jefferson St., 94607. Tel: 510-768-3100; Fax: 510-451-6998.

HIV/AIDS Services, 433 Jefferson St., 94607. Tel: 510-768-3100; Fax: 510-451-6998. Stephanie O'Louglin, Dir.

Victim Offender Reconciliation Program, 433 Jefferson St., 94607. Tel: 510-768-3100; Fax: 510-451-6998.

Detention Ministry, 433 Jefferson St., 94607. Tel: 510-768-3100; Fax: 510-451-6998. Frank Beville, Coord.

COMMUNITY SERVICES:

433 Jefferson St., 94607. Tel: 510-768-3100; Fax: 510-451-6998.

Emergency Services, 433 Jefferson St., 94607. Tel: 510-768-3100; Fax: 510-451-6998. Judy Moore, Dir.

English Action Center, 2369 Barrett Ave., Richmond, 94804. Tel: 510-234-5110; Fax: 510-237-6778. Solomon Belette, Dir.

English Action Center-Verde School, 2000 Giaramita, Room 17 & 18, Richmond, 94808. Tel: 510-234-5305.

English Action Center, 3200 Barrett Ave., Richmond, 94804. Tel: 510-234-2416; Fax: 510-234-2416.

Housing Services, 433 Jefferson Ave., 94607. Tel: 510-768-3100; Fax: 510-451-6998. Solomon Belette, Dir.

Refugee and Immigrant Services, 1232-33rd Ave., 94601. Tel: 510-261-1538; Fax: 510-532-3837. Raquel Aguirre, Dir.

Refugee Employment Assistance Center, 100 Hacienda Ave., P.O. Box 247, San Lorenzo, 94580. Tel: 510-481-0131; Fax: 510-481-0133. Vu Pham, Dir.

Refugee Employment Assistance Center, 707 Jefferson St., 94607. Tel: 510-465-0642; Fax: 510-465-4044.

Refugee Employment Assistance Center, 4700 Calaveras Ave., Fremont, 94538. Tel: 510-745-8731.

SPECIAL PROGRAMS:

Catholic Campaign for Human Development (CCHD), 433 Jefferson St., 94607. Tel: 510-768-3100; Fax: 510-451-6998.

Catholic Relief Services (CRS), 433 Jefferson St., 94607. Tel: 510-768-3100; Fax: 510-451-6998. Crystal Garland, Coord.

[I] SOCIETY OF ST. VINCENT DE PAUL

OAKLAND. *Society of St. Vincent de Paul of Alameda County*, 9235 San Leandro St., 94603. Tel: 510-638-7600; Fax: 510-638-8354.
E-mail: svdp@cwnet.com
Vaughn Donahue, Pres.

Society of St. Vincent de Paul of Alameda County. Free Dining Room, 675 23rd St., 94612. Tel: 510-451-7676; Fax: 510-451-0302.

PITTSBURG. *Society of St. Vincent de Paul of Contra Costa County*, 2210 Gladstone Dr., 94565. Tel: 510-439-5060. Marianne Hawkins, Pres.

[J] DAY NURSERIES

OAKLAND. *Saint Vincent's Day Home, Inc.*, 1086 Eighth St., 94607-2697. Tel: 510-832-8324; Fax: 510-832-5021.
E-mail: info@svdh.org
Web site: www.svdh.org
Legal Title: *Saint Vincent's Day Home, A Corporation.* Corinne M. Mohrmann, CEO. Religious 1; Lay Staff 35; Capacity 199; Total Assisted 300; Total Staff 39. Purpose: To provide quality child care services to those in greatest need while assisting parents in meeting their parental obligations.

[K] GENERAL HOSPITALS

HAYWARD. *St. Rose Hospital*, 1962 27200 Calaroga Ave., 94545-4383. Tel: 510-264-4000; Fax: 510-887-7421.
E-mail: smurray@strosehospital.org
Web site: www.strosehospital.org
For a complete listing, refer to the Hospitals section.

[L] ORGANIZATIONS FOR DEAF AND HARD OF HEARING

HAYWARD. *St. Joseph's Center for Deaf and Hard of Hearing*, 25580 Campus Drive, 94542. Tel: 510-881-2245 (Voice); 881-2248 (TDD); Fax: 510-489-2867.
E-mail: sjdeafctr@aol.com
Legal Title: *St. Joseph's Center for the Deaf and Hard of Hearing, A Corporation.* Ardith A. Lynch, Diocesan Dir.

[M] RETIREMENT AND CARE FACILITIES

OAKLAND. *Bishop Begin Villa*, 3418 E. 18th St., 94601. Tel: 510-536-0719; Fax: 510-536-3561
For a complete listing, refer to the Special Care Facilities section.

Mercy Retirement and Care Center, 3431 Foothill Blvd., 94601. Tel: 510-534-8540; Fax: 510-261-7551
For a complete listing, refer to the Special Care Facilities section.

[N] MONASTERIES AND RESIDENCES OF PRIESTS AND BROTHERS

OAKLAND. *Dominican Order (Western Province), St. Albert's Priory*, Dominican House of Formation, 5890 Birch Ct., 94618. Tel: 510-596-1800; Fax: 510-596-1860.
Web site: www.op.org/opwest/sap
Very Rev. Paul Scanlon, O.P., Prior; Revs. Anthony Rosevear, O.P., Novice Master; Christopher J. Renz, O.P., Master of Students; Richard Schenk, O.P., Regent of Studies; Luke D. Buckles, O.P.; Michael Dodds, O.P.; Finbarr Hayes, O.P.; Fabian Parmisano, O.P.; Antoninus Wall, O.P.; Janko Zagar, O.P.; Martin Walsh, O.P., Dir. Vocations; Bros. Robert Lavigne, O.P.; Jose Romero, O.P. In res. Revs. Basil B. Cole, O.P.; Jude Eli, O.P.; Sergius Probst, O.P. Brothers: Bros. Cyril Alvernaz, O.P.; Bernhard Blankenhorn, O.P.; Gary Cappleman, O.P.; Thomas Clark, O.P.; Jerome Cudden, O.P.; Dominic DeCana, O.P.; Raphael Domingo, O.P.; Aidan Floyd, O.P.; Anthony Garcias, O.P.; Maximilian Hallenius, O.P.; Michael Hurley, O.P.; Thomas Irish, O.P.; Vincent Kelber, O.P.; Robert King, O.P.; Francis Le, O.P.; Flannan McGrath, O.P.; Dominic Bao Nguyen, O.P.; Revs. David Orique, O.P.; Anselm Ramelow, O.P.; Bros. Peter Rogers, O.P.; James Thompson, O.P.; Carlo Verela, O.P.; Alphonsus Von Hazmburg. Novices 14; Total in Residence 53.

Dominican Order, Siena House, 5730 Presley Way, 94618. Tel: 510-654-8735. Revs. Emmerich Vogt, O.P., Supr. Mission Band; David O'Rourke, O.P.; Leo Tubbs, O.P.; Gregory Rocca, O.P., Pres., Dominican School of Philosophy and Theology; Michael Carey, O.P., Dir., Santa Fe Institute; Michael Morris, O.P., Prof., Dominican School of Philosophy and Theology. Priests 6.

Franciscan Friars, St. Elizabeth Friary, 1500 34th Ave., 94601. Tel: 510-536-1287; Fax: 510-536-3578, Ext. 35780.
Web site: www.sbfranciscans
Revs. Kenny Scott, O.F.M., Vicar; Rigoberto Caloca-Rivas, O.F.M.; Marco Antonio Figueroa, O.F.M., Pastor; Peter Krieg, O.F.M.; Melvin Stanley, O.F.M.; Thomas West, O.F.M.; Bros. Raul Alejos, O.F.M.; Rami Fodda, O.F.M.; Thomas More Ganmy, O.F.M.; Javier Garcia; David Gutierrez, O.F.M.; John Gutierrez, O.F.M., Guardian; Luis Alberto Guzman, O.F.M.; Marcos Hernandez, O.F.M.; Antonio Herrera, O.F.M.; Lawrence Abraham Kadaliyil, C.M.S.F.; James Locksman, O.F.M.; Sergio Mosqueda, O.F.M.; Tran Nguyen, O.F.M.; Balbino Rodriguez, O.F.M., Vicar; Cesar Rodriguez, O.F.M.; Ponchie Vasquez, O.F.M., Guardian.

Franciscan Friars Provincial Office, Province of St. Barbara, 1500-34th Ave., 94601. Tel: 510-536-3722; Fax: 510-536-3970.
E-mail: ofmcamain@aol.com
Web site: www.sbfranciscans.org
Revs. Finian McGinn, O.F.M., Prov.; Stephen Barnufsky, O.F.M., Vicar Prov.; Melvin A. Jurisich, O.F.M., Sec.; Ms. Guadalupe Aceves, Treas.; Rev. John S. Hardin, O.F.M., Assoc. Treas.; Bro. Franklin Fong, O.F.M., Vocation Coord. Priests 4; Total Staff 18.
On Duty Outside the Province: Revs. Rodrigo Ortiz, O.F.M., Assisi, Italy; Thomas Herbst, O.F.M., Oxford University, England; Michael Weldon, O.F.M., Catholic Theological Union, Chicago; Thomas King, O.F.M., Catholic Theological Union, Chicago; Bro. Jim Lockman, O.F.M., Penn State Univ, State College, PA.

Franciscan Friars, 1508 Arch St., Berkeley, 94708. Tel: 510-845-1124. Revs. John Hardin, O.F.M., Guardian; Joseph P. Chinnici, O.F.M.; Melvin A. Jurisich, O.F.M.; Stephen Barnufsky, O.F.M.; William M. Cieslak, O.F.M.Cap.

Murray Residence Community, 171 Santa Rosa Ave., 94610-1316. Tel: 510-655-8334. Revs. John A. Baumann, S.J., Supr.; Thomas C. Weston, S.J.; Joseph M. Palacios, S.J.; Michael Proterra, S.J.

Oblate Provincial House & Procure (1953), 290 Lenox Ave., 94610. Tel: 510-452-1550; Fax: 510-452-3421. Provincial Headquarters of the Oblates of Mary Immaculate, Western Prov. & Provincial Residence Pacific Area. Revs. Charles Banks, O.M.I., Dir. & Vice Pres.; Jose Arong, O.M.I., Dir. & Pacific Area Supr. In res. Revs. James P. McSorley, O.M.I.; Ruben Martinez, O.M.I.; Manuel Mesa, O.M.I.; Umberto Nespolo, O.M.I. Legal Title: *Oblate Fathers Western Province Inc.; Western Oblates Support Trust Fund.* Total in Residence 5; Total Staff 2.

Order of Preachers (Southern Province). De Porres House of Studies. 2215 Rose St., Berkeley, 94709. Tel: 510-644-8247; Fax: 510-644-8249. Revs. Jude Siciliano, O.P., Supr. & Prof., DSPT. Tel: 510-644-8247; John J. Markey, O.P., Assoc. Dir. Formation.

Redemptorists, 8945 Golf Links Rd., 94605. Tel: 510-562-9740; Fax: 510-562-1406.
E-mail: jtmcssr@aol.com
Web site: www.holyredeemercenter.org
Very Rev. Terrence McCloskey, C.Ss.R., Supr.; Revs. John Fahey, C.Ss.R.; Anthony Jude, C.Ss.R.; Patrick O'Brien, C.Ss.R.; Richard Ochiltree; Deacon Dennis Lee, C.Ss.R. Legal Title: *Redemptorist Society of California.*

Western Dominican Province, 5877 Birch Ct., 94618-1626. Tel: 510-658-8722; Fax: 510-658-1061.
E-mail: WDOMPROV@aol.com
Web site: www.op.org/opwest/
Province of the Holy Name of Jesus. Very Revs. Daniel Syverstad, O.P., Prior Prov.; Jordan C. Bradshaw, O.P., Vicar Prov. & Socius; Michael Dodds, O.P., Vicar Prov.; Revs. Donald J. Bramble, O.P., Dir. Dominican Mission Foundation; Nathan Castle, O.P., Promoter Campus Min.; Anthony Cordeiro, O.P., Treas.; Paul Duffner, O.P., Promoter Rosary Confraternity; Armando Ibanez, O.P., Promoter Media; Thomas Hayes, O.P., Promoter Holy Name Society; Jude Eli, O.P., Dir. Western Dominican Preaching; Patrick LaBelle, O.P., Promoter Preaching; John Morris, O.P., Promoter Social Justice; George M. Matanic, O.P., Promoter Dominican Laity; Christopher J. Renz, O.P., Student Master & Sec. Dominican Family; Anthony Rosevear, O.P., Novice Master; Richard Schenk, O.P., Regent Studies; Michael Sweeney, O.P., Promoter Parish Ministry & Dir. Catherine of Siena Institute; Jordan Vadja, O.P., Dir. Province Web Site; Martin Walsh, O.P., Dir. Vocations.
Serving in Latin America: Revs. David Bello, O.P.; Thomas Kraft, O.P.; Timothy Conlan, O.P.; Miguel delas Casas, O.P.; Bro. Raymond Bertheaux, O.P.
Serving in Kenya: Rev. Kieran J. Healy, O.P.
Serving in Vatican City: Rev. Allen Duston, O.P., Dir., Office of the Patrons of the Arts in the Vatican Museums.
Serving in Rome: Rev. Robert Christian, O.P., Prof. Pontificia Universita San Tommaso. Total in the Province 171.

BERKELEY. *Capuchin Franciscan Order, House of Studies*, 1534 Arch St., 94708. Tel: 510-841-2229; Fax: 510-849-0809. Saint Conrad Friary. Revs. Michael O'Shea, O.F.M.Cap.; James Johnson, O.F.M.Cap., Vicar & Asst. Student Dir.; Bros. Mark Mance, O.F.M.Cap., Guardian & Student Dir.; Lance Love, O.F.M.Cap. Friars in residence 10; Friars in formation 6; Total Staff 4.

Holy Cross Fathers-Holy Cross Center, 2597 Virginia St., 94709. Tel: 510-548-8515; Fax: 510-548-7903. Revs. E. Michael Alcoser, C.S.C., Religious Supr.; Daniel G. Groody, C.S.C.; William J. Dohar, C.S.C.; James P. Gunshinan, C.S.C.; Robert J. Loughery, C.S.C.

Jesuit Community at Jesuit School of Theology at Berkeley, 2621 Ridge Rd., 94709-1098. Tel: 510-841-2487; Fax: 510-549-1114. Rev. Charles L. Moutenot, S.J., Rector; Bro. Joseph M. Ritzman, S.J., Asst. Rector, Minister, & Treas.; Revs. Joseph M. Alminde, S.J. (Maryland); Steven A. Armstrong, S.J. (California); Kevin M. Bradt, S.J. (New York); James T. Bretzke, S.J. (Wisconsin); Thomas J. Buckley,

S.J. (California); Joseph P. Carroll, S.J. (California); Sean O. Carroll, S.J. (California); Michael T. Castori, S.J. (NY); Donald F. Crosby, S.J. (California); Joseph P. Daoust, S.J. (DET); John R. Donahue, S.J. (Maryland); Patrick F. Earl, S.J. (Maryland); John C. Endres, S.J. (Oregon); Peter J. Fennessy, S.J. (New England); Eduardo C. Fernandez, S.J. (NO); Donald L. Gelpi, S.J. (New Orleans); Timothy S. Godfrey, S.J. (Missouri); Jacek Granatowski, S.J. (North Poland); George E. Griener, S.J. (New Orleans); Michal Gutkowski, S.J. (North Poland); Simon J. Hendry, S.J. (New Orleans); Moses Kan, S.J. (Taiwan); Jean-Pierre Karegeye, S.J. (Rwanda); William M. Kegel, S.J. (Wisconsin); Denis Woo-Seon Kim, S.J. (Korea); Mark Chung-Mo Koo, S.J. (Korea); Clyde H. LeBlanc, S.J. (New Orleans); Lester E. Love, S.J. (Chicago); J. Roger Lucey, S.J. (Wisconsin); Robert R. Marsh, S.J. (Britain); Marco T. Martinez, S.J. (Central America); Francis X. McAloon, S.J. (Maryland); Peter R. McGrath, S.J. (New England); George R. Murphy, S.J. (New England); Robert J. Ochs, S.J. (Chicago); William R. O'Neill, S.J. (California); Deshi T.A. Ramadhani, S.J. (Indonesia); T. Howland Sanks, S.J. (Maryland); David J. Stagaman, S.J. (Chicago); Gaspar Sunhwa, S.J. (Tanzania); Osamu Takeuchi, S.J. (Japan); Kazadi Tshikolu, S.J. (Dem. Rep. Congo); Joseph F. Wagner, S.J. (CHI); Gregory Waldrop, S.J. (New Orleans). Total in Residence 93; Total Staff 2.

(See also listing for The Jesuit School of Theology at Berkeley).

Marist Fathers and Brothers, 2335 Warring St., 94704. Tel: 510-486-1232; 486-1276; Fax: 510-848-7204. Rev. Thomas M. Hamilton, S.M., Supr. & Formation Dir.; Bro. William Rowland, S.M., Formation Staff. Legal Title: *Marist Society Inc.*
Seminary Name: St. Peter Chanel Seminary - Marist Pre-novitate Program.

Salesian Community, Don Bosco Hall, 1831 Arch St., 94709. Tel: 510-204-0800; Fax: 510-843-4335.
E-mail: BoscoHall1@aol.com
Web site: www.donboscowest.org
Core Team: Revs. Joseph Boenzi, S.D.B., Dir.; Roy Shelly, S.D.B., Business Mgr.; Arthur Lenti, S.D.B., Counselor; Sr. Mary Greenan, F.M.A., Program Coord. Students In Residence: Revs. Luigi Brioni, S.X. (Sierra Leone); Peter Daniss, S.D.B. (Italy); Michael Hynes, S.D.B. (England); Paul Kim-Yong-Hwa (Korea); Joseph Nguyen-Thinh-Phuoc, S.D.B. (Vietnam); Joseph Nguyen-Van-Am, S.D.B. (Vietnam); Bernard Parkes, S.D.B. (England); Luis German Prato, S.D.B. (Venezuela); Vincent Rasquinha, S.D.B. (India); Bros. Timothy Nguyen, S.D.B.; Joseph Nguyen-Duc-Thinh, S.D.B.; Steve Way, S.D.B. Total in Residence 24; Total Staff 4.

Servite Community, Sarpi Priory. (United States of America Province), 2414 Virginia St., 94709-1206. Tel: 510-848-4086. Rev. Bruce J. Klikunas, O.S.M. Total in Residence 1.

Society of the Precious Blood, 2800 Milvia St., 94703-2209. Tel: 510-665-8434; Fax: 510-665-8437. Revs. Gary M. Luiz, C.PP.S., Dir.; James D. Sloan, C.PP.S.

MORAGA. *Dominican Community*, Siena Hall, St. Mary's College, P.O. Box 5185, 94575-5185. Tel: 510-631-4315; Fax: 510-631-4315. Dominican Order. Revs. John McDonough, O.P., Supr.; Michael Carey, O.P.; Michael T. Morris, O.P. Priests 3.

SAN LEANDRO. *Society of the Precious Blood*, 2337 W. Ave. 134th, 94577-4132. Tel: 510-357-4982; Fax: 510-357-4036.
E-mail: SLOANCPPS@aol.com
Web site: www.cin.org/gaspar
Province of the Pacific, Provincial Headquarters, Provincial Center. Very Rev. James D. Sloan, C.PP.S., Prov. Dir.; Revs. Joseph L. Brown, C.PP.S., Treas.; Jeffrey R. Keyes, C.PP.S., Prov. Sec. Total in Residence 1; Total Staff 1.

SAN PABLO. *Franciscans, Conventual of California*, St. Francis of Assisi Friary, Pre-Novitiate House of Studies, 1850 Church Ln., 94806-3706. Tel: 510-235-9119; Fax: 510-235-2045. Rev. Alexander J. Lewis, O.F.M.Conv., Supr. & Dir. Candidates. Total in Residence 10; Total Staff 1.

[O] CONVENTS AND RESIDENCES FOR SISTERS

OAKLAND. *Dominican Sisters of Mission San Jose*, St. Elizabeth Convent, 1555-34th Ave., P.O. Box 7465, 94601. Tel: 510-532-8344; Fax: 510-533-2365.
E-mail: patann@msjdominicans.org
Web site: www.msjdominicans.org
Sisters 16.

Dominican Sisters of Oakford, Bethany House, 919 Aileen St., 94608. Tel: 510-652-0986.
E-mail: bethany2@mindspring.com
Web site: oakford.op.org/
Sisters 2.

Franciscan Missionaries of Mary, 570 Boden Way, Apt. 2, 94610. Tel: 510-663-8983. Sisters 2.

Holy Names Sisters. Mailing Address: Provincial Administration, P.O. Box 907, Los Gatos, 95031. Tel: 408-395-5150; Fax: 408-354-8305.
E-mail: snjmcaasm@impresso.com
Holy Names College Sisters' Residence, 3500 Mountain Blvd., 94619. Tel: 510-436-1635.
E-mail: jmhnc@impresso.com
Sr. Margaret Spiller, S.N.J.M., Prov. Sisters 6. Sisters Reside In Numerous Residences; Holy Names High School, Elbert, St. Bede, St. Theresa, & San Antonio.

Presentation Sisters. Mailing Address: Sisters of the Presentastion, 2340 Turk Blvd, San Francisco, 94118. 11 Warren St., No. 7, 94611. Tel: 510-654-6407; Fax: 510-652-7270. 1725 Oxford St., #308, Berkeley, 94709. Tel: 510-548-6217; Fax: 510-644-9619. 1725 Oxford St., #104, Berkeley, 94709. Tel: 510-549-1256; Fax: 510-644-9472. 1055 47th St., #C, Emeryville, 94608. Tel: 510-655-8132; Fax: 510-655-9159. 1515 Lincoln St., Berkeley, 94703. Tel: 510-848-4851; Fax: 510-486-8247.

Providence Sisters, Summit South, 3100 Summit St., P.O. Box 23020, 94623-9966. Tel: 510-835-4500. Sisters 4.

St. Lawrence O'Toole Convent, 3693 High St., 94619-2105. Tel: 510-530-2621; Fax: 510-530-4120. Adrian Dominican Sisters 5; Grand Rapids Dominicans 1.

Sisters of Charity of Cincinnati, 809-42nd St., 94608. Tel: 510-658-7990. 529-41st St., No. 9, 94609. Tel: 510-654-7328.

Sisters of Mercy, Burlingame, Mercy Retirement and Care Center, 3431 Foothill Blvd., 94601. Tel: 510-534-8540. Sisters 4.

Sisters of Sacred Hearts of Jesus and Mary, 2150 Lake Shore Ave., 94606. Tel: 510-832-2935; Fax: 510-839-5256.
E-mail: lornashjm@jps.net
Sisters 4. St. Jerome Convent, 310 San Carlos Ave., El Cerrito, 94530. Tel: 510-525-6554; Fax: 510-559-3601. Sisters 7.

Sisters of St. Francis of Penance and Christian Charity, Casa Guadalupe/Novitiate House, 1815-33rd Ave., 94601. Tel: 510-534-4330; Fax: 510-436-5298. Sr. Maria Elena Martinez, OS.F., Dir.; Sr. Florence A. Koehler, O.S.F., Asst. Novice Dir. Sisters 3; Novices 2; Pre-Candidate 1. House of Hope, 2027 Nina Ct., Hayward, 94541. Tel: 510-537-1026; Fax: 510-655-3520. Sr. Lorraine Savage, O.S.F. Novices 1; Professed 2.

Sisters of St. Joseph of Carondelet. Carondelet Community, 1133 Winton Dr., Concord, 94518-3598. Tel: 925-686-9697; Fax: 925-671-9429. Sisters 6. Bay Area Crisis Nursery, Inc., 1506 Mendocino Dr., Concord, 94521. Tel: 925-685-8052; 685-9740; Fax: 925-689-5815. Concord Residential Club, 2141 California St., Concord, 94520-7800. Tel: 925-689-4939; Fax: 925-825-4423. Kwanza House Community, 529 Jean St., 94610-1906. Tel: 510-655-2382; Fax: 510-655-0249. Sisters 2. Christ the King Community, 3095 Diablo View Rd., Pleasant Hill, 94523-4535. Tel: 925-280-1562; Fax: 925-685-1289. Sisters 3. St. Anthony Community, 1520 E. 15th St., 94606-4422. Tel: 510-532-9455; Fax: 510-451-8920. Sisters 3.

Social Service Sisters, 4000 Waterhouse, 94602. 851 Trestle Glen Rd., 94610. Sisters 6.

BERKELEY, 1927 Haste, 94704. Tel: 510-631-4316.

Dominican Sisters of Mission San Jose, St. Mary Magdalen Community, 2004 Eunice St., 94709. Tel: 510-527-4817; Fax: 510-527-4817.
E-mail: berkeley@msjdominicans.org
Web site: www.msjdominicans.org
Sisters 4.

Franciscan Sisters of Little Falls, MN, 1418 A Fifth St., 94710. Tel: 510-526-2321; Fax: 510-526-2321.
E-mail: paulaosf@5pillars.res
Sisters 4.

Sisters of Charity, B.V.M., 1746 Addison St., 94703. Tel: 510-841-8791. 1708 Euclid Ave., No. 11, 94709. Tel: 510-843-0684. Sisters 2.

Sisters of Notre Dame de Namur, 1717 Oxford St., No. 101, 94709. Tel: 510-845-2113. 1717 Oxford St., No. 202, 94709. Tel: 510-540-6896. 1725 Oxford St., No. 210, 94709. Tel: 510-848-7439.

BRENTWOOD. *Religious Missionary Congregation of the Most Holy Sacrament and Mary Immaculate*, 636 - 3rd St., 94513. Tel: 925-513-8154.

CASTRO VALLEY. *Sisters of St. Joseph in the Third Order of St. Francis*, 22120 Center St., No. 523, 94546. Tel: 510-886-1170. 2063 Boniface St., Concord, 94520. Tel: 510-680-7396; Fax: 925-825-2439. Sr. Marygrace Puchac, 1412 Ninth St., Apt B, Alameda, 94501. Tel: 510-865-1326. Sr. Madeline Antoskiewicz; Sr. Marie Myers, 5427 Valley View Rd., El Sobrante, 94803. Tel: 510-222-0492; Fax: 707-644-3107. Sr. Philip Cservenyak, 141 Belleview Dr., Apt. 307, San Leandro, 94577. Tel: 510-632-0991. Sr. Rosita Wisniewski.

Sisters of the Holy Family, Holy Family Convent, 19697 Redwood Rd., 94546. Tel: 510-582-7314. Sr. M. John Bosco Crivello, Local Coord. Total in community 12.

CONCORD. *Quinhon Missionary Sisters of the Holy Cross*, Provincial House, 1685 Humphrey Dr., 94519-1810. Tel: 925-674-9639; Fax: 925-676-9320. Sr. Rosaline Lieu Nguyen, L.H.C., Prov., Aspirant House, 50 Santa Maria Way, Orinda, 94563. Tel: 925-253-0831.

Sisters of St. Joseph of the Third Order of St. Francis, 2301 Mt. Diablo St., 94520. Tel: 925-680-7396; 825-2091; Fax: 925-825-2439.

EL CERRITO. *Franciscan Sisters of Perpetual Adoration (FSPA)*, 1317 Liberty St., No. 17, 94530. Tel: 510-233-9797. 2629 34th Ave., Oakland, 94601. Tel: 510-536-1266.

Mercy Sisters, Ireland, St. John the Baptist Convent, 11154 San Pablo Ave., 94530. Tel: 510-233-6769. Sisters 4.

EL SOBRANTE. *Sisters of St. Joseph of the Third Order of St. Francis, S.S.J.-T.O.S.F.*, 5427 Valley View Rd., 94803. Tel: 510-222-0492.
E-mail: phil4389@aol.com
22120 Center St., #523, Castro Valley, 94546. Tel: 510-886-1170. 2063 Bonifacio St., Concord, 94520. Tel: 510-680-7396. Sisters 6.

HAYWARD. *Dominican Sisters of Adrian, MI*, 1128 D St., 94541. Tel: 510-582-2568.

Holy Names Sisters, St. Bede Convent, 26900 Patrick Ave., 94544. Tel: 510-782-6700.
E-mail: jmbede@impresso.com
Sisters 7.

Sisters of St. Joseph of Wichita, KS., 1626 Ashbury Ln., 94545. Tel: 510-782-5960.
E-mail: magirrens@strosehospital.org
Web site: www.feist.com/~wichitacsj
Sisters 5.

HERCULES. *Congregation of the Mother of Mount Carmel*, 142 Weiss St., 94547. Tel: 510-724-4178.

KENSINGTON. *Discalced Carmelite Nuns*, 68 Rincon Rd., 94707. Tel: 510-526-5050. Solemn Professed 6.

LIVERMORE. *Dominican Sisters of San Rafael*, St. Michael Convent, 375 Maple St., 94550. Tel: 925-443-1666; Fax: 925-447-6720.
E-mail: St-Michael@csdo.org
Sisters 2.

MISSION SAN JOSE. *Dominican Sisters of Mission San Jose*, 43326 Mission Blvd., P.O. Box 3908, 94539. Tel: 510-657-2468; Fax: 510-657-1734.
E-mail: evangela@msjdominicans.org
Web site: www.msjdominicans.org
Generalate Motherhouse and Novitiate of the Dominican Sisters of Mission San Jose, Congregation of The Queen of the Holy Rosary. Sr. Rose Marie Hennessy, Prioress Gen. Sisters 119 (In Oakland Diocese).

Queen of Peace Community. Tel: 510-657-2468; Fax: 510-657-1734. Sr. Sylvia Conant, O.P., Supr.

St. Joseph Priory. Tel: 510-657-2468; Fax: 510-657-1734. Sr. Mary Jarlath McGrath, O.P., Prioress.

St. Martin Infirmary. Tel: 510-657-2468; Fax: 510-657-1734. Sr. Mary Jarlath McGrath, O.P., Supr.

San Domenico Community. Tel: 510-657-2468; Fax: 510-657-1734. Sr. Rose Marie Hennessy, O.P., Supr. & Prioress Gen.

Siena House. Tel: 510-657-2468; Fax: 510-657-1734. Sr. Mary Mark Schonstein, O.P., Supr.

St. Edward Convent, 37088 Arden St., Newark, 94560-3702. Tel: 510-793-9447; Fax: 510-793-7242 (St. Edward School). Sr. Johnellen Turner, O.P., Supr.

St. Elizabeth Convent, 1555-34th Ave., P.O. Box 7465, Oakland, 94601-0465. Tel: 510-532-8344; Fax: 510-532-0321 (St. Elizabeth Elem. School, Ext.). Sr. Patricia Ann Smith, O.P., Supr.

St. Mary Magdalen Convent, 2004 Eunice St., Berkeley, 94709-1926. Tel: 510-527-4817; Fax: 510-527-4818. Sr. Mary Brennan, O.P., Supr.

Our Lady of Guadalupe Convent, 46752 Crawford St., Fremont, 94539-7164. Tel: 510-490-6902. Sr. Diane Claire Adams, O.P., Supr.

NEWARK. *Dominican Sisters of Mission San Jose*, St. Edward Convent, 37088 Arden St., 94560. Tel: 510-793-9447. Sisters 4.

PLEASANT HILL. *Holy Family Sisters*, Holy Family Center, 2059 Pleasant Hill Rd., 94523. Tel: 925-935-6151; Fax: 925-935-1394.
E-mail: holyfamcen@aol.com
Sisters 4; Total in Residence 4; Total Staff 4.

RODEO. *Sisters of Immaculate Heart of Mary*, St. Patrick Convent, 815 Seventh St., 94572. Tel: 510-799-6683.
E-mail: smc@stpatrickschool.rodeo.org
Web site: www.stpatrickschool/rodeo.org
Sisters 3.

SAN LEANDRO. *Dominican Sisters of Oakford*, Our Lady of Guadalupe House of Formation, 327 Woodland Park, 94577. Tel: 510-569-9189. Total in Residence 4; Total Staff 1; Sisters 4.

Marist Missionary Sisters, 1515 Boxwood Ave., 94579. Tel: 510-357-7876.
E-mail: smsmvoc@aol.com
Sr. Mary Jane Kenney, S.M.S.M. Sisters 3.

Marist Missionary Sisters-Vocation Ministry Office, 1515 Boxwood Ave., 94579. Tel: 510-357-7876.
E-mail: smsmvo@aol.com
Sr. AnnMarie Woeste, Vocation Ministry.

Sisters of St. Joseph of Wichita, St. Felicitas Convent, 1662 Manor Blvd., 94579. Tel: 510-351-5577; Fax: 510-351-5577. Sisters 2.

SAN LORENZO. *Presentation Sisters, Kildare, Ireland*, St. John the Baptist Convent, 16642 Ashland Ave., 94580. Tel: 510-278-7128; Fax: 510-278-5145. Sisters 6.

[P] PASTORAL CENTERS

OAKLAND. *Holy Redeemer Center, Redemptorist Retreat Center*, 8945 Golf Links Rd., P.O. Box 5427, 94605. Tel: 510-635-6341; Fax: 510-635-6342.
E-mail: hrcoakland@aol.com
Web site: www.holyredeemercenter.org
Retreat and spiritual hospitality center. Rev. Terrence McCloskey, C.Ss.R., Dir., Pastoral Ministry; Kevin Dwyer, Center Dir.

DANVILLE. *San Damiano Retreat*, Franciscan Retreat House, Mailing Address: Box 767, 94526. Tel: 925-837-9141; Fax: 925-837-0522.
E-mail: info@sandamiano.org
Web site: www.sandamiano.org
Retreat House for men, women and married couples. Rev. Raymond J. Bucher, O.F.M., Dir. In res. Revs. Barry Brunsman, O.F.M., Retreat Master & Guardian; Emmanuel Muessiggang, O.F.M.; Bro. Rufino Zaragoza, O.F.M. Total in Residence 5; Total Staff 25.

LAFAYETTE. *Diocesan Youth Retreat Center*, 1977 Reliez Valley Rd., 94549. Tel: 925-934-5802; 934-5801; Fax: 925-934-0642.
Web site: www.members.ad.com/~oakdiocythrtr
Total in Residence 2; Total Staff 2.

PLEASANT HILL. *Holy Family Center*, 2059 Pleasant Hill Rd., 94523. Tel: 925-935-6151; Fax: 925-935-1394.
E-mail: holyfamcen@aol.com
Ministries: Personal Growth Programs, Counseling, Spiritual Direction, Adult Faith Formation.

[Q] NEWMAN CENTERS

OAKLAND. *Holy Names College Campus Ministry*, 3500 Mountain Blvd., 94619. Tel: 510-436-1081; Fax: 510-436-1199.
E-mail: casey@hnc.edu
Web site: http://www.hnc.edu
Sr. Sharon Casey, O.P., Dir. Campus Min.

MORAGA. *St. Mary's College Campus Ministry*, Box 4777, 94575-4777. Tel: 510-631-4366; Fax: 510-631-4332.
Web site: www.stmarys-ca.edu
Rev. Tom McElligott; Sr. Ingrid Clemmensen, O.P., Dir. Campus Ministry; Mr. Christopher Fuller; Ms. Pamela Thomas; Ms. Diana Kaulback; Ms. Catherine Wazenski; Ms. Stephanie DeBenedetti-Emanuel.

[R] PERSONAL PRELATURES

BERKELEY. *Opus Dei*. Prelature of the Holy Cross and Opus Dei, Garber House, 2710 College Ave., 94705. Tel: 510-548-2819; Fax: 510-644-3898.
E-mail: padlan@mymailstation.com
Rev. Paul A. Donlan.

[S] MISCELLANEOUS LISTINGS

OAKLAND. *Adventus*, 2900 Lakeshore Ave., 94610. Tel: 510-893-4711; Fax: 510-893-0945. Rev. Patrick Goodwin. Purpose: To support the mission of the Roman Catholic Diocese of Oakland.

The Benilde Religious & Charitable Trust, c/o Plageman, Lund & Miller LLP, 1999 Harrison St., Ste. 2700, 94612. Tel: 510-273-8553; Fax: 510-273-8559.
E-mail: plageman@compuserve.com
Mr. William Plageman, Jr., Contact Person. Charitable trust fund to benefit the educational activities of the Brothers of the Christian Schools of San Francisco. Lasallian Education Opportunities.

Casa Vincentia, 3210 62nd Ave., 94605. Tel: 510-729-0316; Fax: 510-729-0319. Home for single pregnant women, 18-25 yrs. Barbara Jackson, Exec. Dir. Total in Residence 6; Total Staff 3.

Dominican Community Support Charitable Trust, 5877 Birch Ct., 94618. Tel: 510-655-0521; Fax: 510-658-1061. Anthony J. Cordeiro, O.P., Contact Person. Tel: 510-655-0521.

A Friendly Manor / A Friendly Place, 2298 San Pablo Ave., 94612. Tel: 510-451-8923; Fax: 510-451-8920. Sr. Maureen Lyons, C.S.J. Purpose: Daytime hospitality center for homeless women. Total Assisted 19,500; Total Staff 3.

Hesed Community, Benedictine Urban Community of Christian Meditation, 3745 Elston Ave., 94602. Tel: 510-482-5573; Fax: 510-482-8769.
E-mail: Hesedone@aol.com
Web site: hesedcommunity.org
Sr. Barbara Hazzard, O.S.B., Dir. Total in Residence 1; Total Staff 1.

Italian Catholic Federation, 675 Hegenberger Rd., Ste. 110, 94621. Tel: 510-633-9058; 888-ICF-1924; Fax: 510-633-9758.
E-mail: icf1924@earthlink.net
Web site: home.earthlink.net
Rev. Daniel E. Cardelli.

Marianist Commmunity, 3705 Dorissa Ave., 94605. Tel: 510-632-7429; Fax: 510-632-7467. Rev. John E. McEnhill, S.M.

Missionaries of the Kingship of Christ, 1500-34th Ave., 94601. Tel: 510-536-1266. A Franciscan Secular Institute for Women, Men, Priests. Rev. Guglielmo Lauriola, O.F.M., Contact Person. Tel: 510-647-2704.

Oakland Elizabeth House, 6423 Colby St., 94618. Tel: 510-601-1213; Fax: 510-658-1380.
E-mail: oakehouse.com
Courtenay Redis, Dir. Purpose: Transitional housing for low-income women and children.

Pacific Institute for Community Organization, 171 Santa Rosa Ave., 94610. Tel: 510-655-2801; Fax: 510-655-4816.
E-mail: BaumannPICO@aol.com
Web site: www.pico.rutgers.edu
Rev. John A. Baumann, S.J., Exec. Dir.; Mr. Robert Holstein, Jr., Chm.; Mr. Baxter Rice, Vice Chm.

Redemptorist Community Support Charitable Trust, 8945 Golf Links Rd., 94605. Tel: 510-562-9740.
E-mail: pobcssr@aol.com
Patrick O'Brien, Trustee.

St. Mary's Center, 635 22nd St., 94612. Tel: 510-893-4723; Fax: 510-893-0119.
E-mail: ed@stmaryscenter.org
Web site: www.stmaryscenter.org
Sr. Marilyn Medau, P.B.V.M., Dir. Food for all Ages Prog.; Sr. Veronica Lonergan, O.P., Co-Dir. Senior Outreach & Advocacy Prog.; Dorothy Green, Co-Dir. Senior Outreach & Advocacy Prog.; Georgia Barnes, Dir. Recovery 55 Prog.; Judith Deacon, Dir. Senior Homeless Case Mgt. Prog.; Corinne Lund, Dir. Pre-School Prog.; Sr. Joanna Bramble, C.S.J., Dir. Development; Carol Johnson, Exec. Dir. Total Assisted 1,900; Total Staff 22.

The Gamelin-California Association, Providence House, 540-23rd St., 94612-1718. Tel: 510-444-0839. Apartment building designed for disabled persons and persons with AIDS. Timothy Zaricznyj, Dir. Units 40.

Vietnamese Senior Care Center, 3014 Lakeshore Ave., 94610. Tel: 510-273-4986; Fax: 510-273-4982. Sr. Nicole Nguyen, D.C., Contact Person. Purpose: special outreach to the elder Vietnamese population. Total Staff 4; Total Assisted 155.

BERKELEY. *Academy of American Franciscan History*, 1712 Euclid Ave., 94709. Tel: 510-548-1755.
E-mail: AcadaFH@aol.com
Web site: www.aafa.org
Total Staff 1.

Franciscan Charities, Inc., 1712 Euclid Ave., 94709. Tel: 510-849-0234.
E-mail: ofmcafc@aol.com

Incarnation Monastery, Camaldolese Benedictines, 1369 La Loma Ave., 94708. Tel: 510-845-0601; Fax: 510-548-6439.
E-mail: monks@contemplation.com
Web site: www.contemplation.com
Rev. Andrew Colnaghi, Prior. In res. Revs. Robert Hale, O.S.B.Cam.; Arthur Poulin, O.S.B.Cam. Total in Residence 3.

Inter-Friendship House Association, Friendship Center, 1646 Addison St., 94703. Tel: 510-843-7675; Fax: 510-843-7675.
E-mail: ifha@jps.net
Web site: www.ifha-usa.org
Rev. Bernard M.C. Chu, S.J. (China), Dir. Total Staff 1.

Maria House, Redemptorist Asian Pacific Ministry Center, 2215 Rose St., 94709. Tel: 510-981-9005; Fax: 510-981-9004.
E-mail: kunpah@aol.com
Web site: www.kmhmu-catholic.org
Redemptorist Fathers: Revs. James Farrell; David Tobia; Caryle Blake; Anthony Nguyen; Donald MacKinson.

Multicultural Institute, 1712 Euclid Ave., 94709. Tel: 510-848-4075; Fax: 510-848-4095.
E-mail: rcaloca@pacbell.net
Web site: www.multiculturalinstitute.org
Board of Directors: Cass Candell; Rev. George E. Crespin; Eugene McCabe; Dr. Oscar Mendez, M.D.; Philip Murphy, B.A.; Rev. Kenan B. Osborne, O.F.M., Ph.D.; Alfredo Terrazas, J.D.; Barbara Terrazas, M.P.H. Administrative Staff: Rev. Rigoberto Caloca-Rivas, O.F.M., Exec. Dir.; Oscar Posada, Admin. Asst.; Anthony Nguyen, Admin. Asst.; Jose B. Rivera, Familias Unidas Program Dir.; Mercedes Rivera, Familias Unidas Program & Summer School Program Dir.; Hamerson Gil, MAS Program Dir.

CONCORD. *Carondelet High School Foundation*, 1133 Winton Dr., 94518. Tel: 925-686-5353; Fax: 925-671-9429.
Web site: www.carondelet.pvt.k12.ca.us
Sr. Kathleen Lang, C.S.J., Contact Person.

EL CERRITO. *Catholic Ladies' Aid Society, Grand Chaplain*, 11150 San Pablo Ave., 94530. Tel: 510-232-5659; Fax: 510-236-0960. Elizabeth Oishi.

EMERYVILLE. *Lasallain Educational Opportunities, Inc.*, 1266-61st St., 94608. Tel: 510-450-0555; Fax: 510-450-0554.
E-mail: leocenter@mindspring.com
Bro. Christopher Bassen, F.S.C., Prog. Dir. Total Assisted 210; Total Staff 7.

MISSION SAN JOSE. *Dominican Sisters of Mission San Jose Foundation (A Non-Profit Corp.)*, Mailing Address: P.O. Box 3908, 94539. Tel: 510-657-2468; Fax: 510-657-1734.
E-mail: dsmsjdev@infolane.com
Web site: www.msjdominicans.org/
Sr. Charlotte Shea, O.P., Exec. Vice Pres.; Kay Schultz, Pres.; Robert Lawrence, Sec. & Treas.

Pia Backes Support Trust, Dominican Sisters of Mission San Jose, 43326 Mission Blvd., P.O. Box 3908, 94539-0391. Tel: 510-657-2468; Fax: 510-683-0712. Sr. Diane Claire Adams, Trustee.

SAN LEANDRO. *Venerable Merlini Foundation*, 2337 W. Ave. 134th, 94577-4132. Tel: 510-357-4982. Jerome Stack, Pres.; Joseph L. Brown, Treas.

RELIGIOUS INSTITUTES OF MEN REPRESENTED IN THE DIOCESE

For further details refer to the corresponding bracketed number in the Religious Institutes of Men or Women section.

[0140]—*The Augustinians.*—O.S.A.
[0170]—*Basilian Fathers.*—C.S.B.
[0330]—*Brothers of the Christian Schools.* (Prov. of San Francisco).—F.S.C.
[0600]—*Brothers of the Congregation of Holy Cross.* (Southwest Prov.).—C.S.C.
[0200]—*Camaldolese Benedictines.*—O.S.B.Cam.
[0470]—*The Capuchin Friars.*—O.F.M.Cap.
[0480]—*Conventual Franciscans.*—O.F.M.Conv.
[0260]—*Discalced Carmelite Friars.*—O.C.D.
[1140]—*Fathers of the Sacred Hearts.*—SS.CC.
[0520]—*Franciscan Friars.* (Santa Barbara Prov.).—O.F.M.
[0530]—*Franciscan Friars of the Atonement.*—S.A.
[0690]—*Jesuit Fathers and Brothers.*—S.J.
[0770]—*The Marist Brothers.*—F.M.S.
[0910]—*Oblates of Mary Immaculate.* (Western Prov.).—O.M.I.
[0920]—*Oblates of St. Francis De Sales.*—O.S.F.S.
[0430]—*Order of Preachers-Dominicans.* (Prov. of Holy Name of Jesus).—O.P.
[1030]—*Paulist Fathers.*—C.S.P.
[0610]—*Priests of the Congregation of Holy Cross.*—C.S.C.
[1070]—*Redemptorist Fathers.* (Oakland Prov.).—C.SS.R.
[1190]—*Salesians of Don Bosco.* (Turin, Italy).—S.D.B.
[1240]—*Servites.* (Western Prov.).—O.S.M.
[0760]—*Society of Mary.*—S.M.
[0420]—*Society of the Divine Word.* (Techny, IL).—S.V.D.
[1060]—*Society of the Precious Blood.* (Prov. of the Pacific).—C.PP.S.

RELIGIOUS INSTITUTES OF WOMEN REPRESENTED IN THE DIOCESE

[0340]—*Carmelite Sisters of Charity.*—C.aCh.
[1780]—*Congregation of the Sisters of the Third Order of St. Francis of Perpetual Adoration.* (Spokane, WA).—F.S.P.A.
[0420]—*Discalced Carmelite Nuns.*—O.C.D.
[1070-03]—*Dominican Sisters.*—O.P.
[1070-04]—*Dominican Sisters.*—O.P.
[1070-12]—*Dominican Sisters.*—O.P.
[1070-13]—*Dominican Sisters.*—O.P.
[1070-30]—*Dominican Sisters.*—O.P.
[]—*Franciscan Sisters of Little Falls, Minnesota.*
[2420]—*Marist Missionary Sisters.*
[2470]—*Maryknoll Sisters of St. Dominic.*—M.M.
[]—*Quinhon Sisters of the Holy Cross.*
[]—*Sisters for Christian Community.*—S.F.C.C.
[0430]—*Sisters of Charity of the Blessed Virgin Mary.* (Mt. Carmel, Dubuque, IA).—B.V.M.
[2360]—*Sisters of Loretto at the Foot of the Cross.* (Nerink, KY).—S.L.
[2516]—*Sisters of Mercy.*—S.M.
[2570]—*Sisters of Mercy.* (Burlingame, CA).—S.M.
[3000]—*Sisters of Notre Dame de Namur.* (Prov. of California).—S.N.D.deN.
[3350]—*Sisters of Providence.* (Sacred Heart Prov.).—S.P.

[4080]—*Sisters of Social Service of Los Angeles, Inc.*—S.S.S.
[1630]—*Sisters of St. Francis of Penance and Christian Charity.*—O.S.F.
[1650]—*Sisters of St. Francis of Philadelphia.*—O.S.F.
[3840]—*Sisters of St. Joseph of Carondelet.* (Los Angeles Prov.).—C.S.J.
[3830-03]—*Sisters of St. Joseph of Orange.*—C.S.J.
[3930]—*Sisters of St. Joseph of the Third Order of St. Francis.* (Prov. of Our Lady of Czestochowa).—S.S.J.-T.O.S.F.
[3830-18]—*Sisters of St. Joseph of Wichita.*—C.S.J.
[]—*Sisters of the Congregation of the Mother of Mount Carmel.*
[1960]—*Sisters of the Holy Family.*—S.H.F.
[1990]—*Sisters of the Holy Names of Jesus and Mary.* (Prov. of Calif.).—S.N.J.M.
[3320]—*Sisters of the Presentation of the B.V.M.* (San Francisco, CA).—P.B.V.M.
[3680]—*Sisters of the Sacred Heart of Jesus and Mary.*—S.H.J.M.
[2150]—*Sisters, Servants of the Immaculate Heart of Mary.*—I.H.M.
[3330]—*Union of the Sisters of the Presentation of the Blessed Virgin Mary.*—P.B.V.M.

DIOCESAN CEMETERIES AND MAUSOLEUMS

OAKLAND. *The Roman Catholic Cemeteries of the Diocese of Oakland*, 2900 Lakeshore Ave., 94610. Tel: 510-893-4711; Fax: 510-893-0945. Directors: Most Rev. John S. Cummins; Revs. Albano Oliveira; David E. Staal; Sr. Barbara Flannery, C.S.J.
St. Mary's.
ANTIOCH. *Holy Cross.*
HAYWARD. *Holy Sepulchre Cemetery and Mausoleum.*
LAFAYETTE. *Queen of Heaven.*
PLEASANTON. *Christ the King.*
SAN PABLO. *St. Joseph's Cemetery and Mausoleum.*

NECROLOGY

† Hary, Melvin J., (Retired). —Died Nov. 5, 2000.
† Morrison, Harry B, Walnut Creek, CA St. Stephen Church. —Died April 10, 2000.
† Ribeiro, Arthur, (Retired). —Died Oct. 18, 2000.
† Ryan, Thomas J, Berkeley, CA St. Ambrose Church. —Died Jan. 25, 2000.
† Zitko, Rev. Msgr. Aloysius, (Retired). —Died June 15, 2000.

Diocese of Ogdensburg

(Dioecesis Ogdensburgensis)

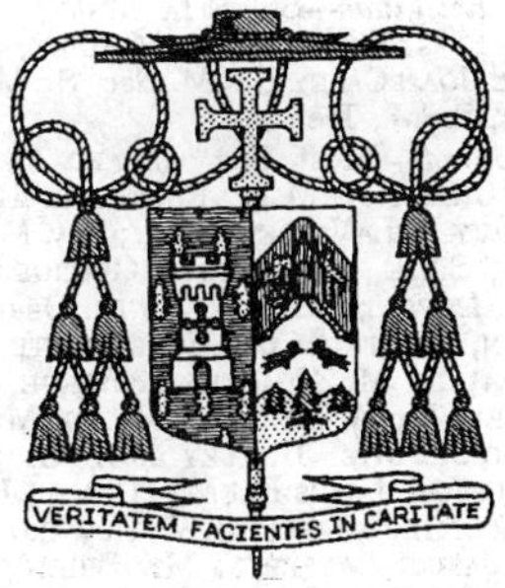

Most Reverend

GERALD M. BARBARITO, D.D, J.C.L.

Twelfth Bishop of Ogdensburg; ordained January 31, 1976; appointed Titular Bishop of Gisipa June 28, 1994; Episcopal ordination August 22, 1994; transferred Ogdensburg October 26, 1999; installed January 7, 2000. *Mailing Address: P.O. Box 369, Ogdensburg, NY, 13669.*

Chancery Office:. Mailing Address: P.O. Box 369, Ogdensburg, NY, 13669. Tel.: 315-393-2920; Fax: 315-394-7401.

E-mail address: Chancery@dioogdensburg.org

ERECTED BY HIS HOLINESS PIUS IX, FEBRUARY 16, 1872.

Square Miles 12,036.

Incorporated by a special act of the Legislature of the State of New York, April 10, 1945, with the title: The Roman Catholic Diocese of Ogdensburg, New York.

Comprises that part of Herkimer and Hamilton Counties north of the northern line of the townships of Ohio and Russia as existing in 1872 with the entire Counties of Lewis, Jefferson, St. Lawrence, Franklin, Clinton and Essex in the State of New York.

For legal titles of parishes and diocesan institutions, consult the Chancery Office.

STATISTICAL OVERVIEW

Personnel	
Bishop	1
Priests: Diocesan Active in Diocese	106
Priests: Active Outside Diocese	8
Priests: Diocesan in Foreign Missions	2
Priests: Retired, Sick or Absent	48
Number of Diocesan Priests	164
Religious Priests in Diocese	13
Extern Priests in Diocese	8
Ordinations:	
Diocesan Priests	3
Permanent Deacons in Diocese	56
Total Brothers	12
Total Sisters	171
Parishes	
Parishes	120
With Resident Pastor:	
Resident Diocesan Priests	83
Resident Religious Priests	5
Without Resident Pastor:	
Administered by Priests	30
Administered by Women Religious	2
Missions	25
Closed Parishes	1
Professional Ministry Personnel:	
Brothers	1
Sisters	34
Lay Ministers	404
Welfare	
Homes for the Aged	3
Total Assisted	424
Specialized Homes	1
Total Assisted	550
Special Centers for Social Services	6
Total Assisted	14,000
Educational	
Seminaries, Diocesan	1
Students from This Diocese	7
Students from Other Diocese	12
Diocesan Students in Other Seminaries	5
Total Seminarians	12
High Schools, Diocesan and Parish	2
Total Students	559
Elementary Schools, Diocesan and Parish	26
Total Students	3,996
Catechesis/Religious Education:	
High School Students	2,015
Elementary Students	9,985
Total Students Under Catholic Instruction	16,567
Teachers in the Diocese:	
Priests	2
Brothers	2
Sisters	25
Lay Teachers	266
Vital Statistics	
Receptions into the Church:	
Infant Baptism Totals	1,593
Adult Baptism Totals	196
Received into Full Communion	103
First Communions	1,795
Confirmations	1,502
Marriages:	
Catholic	473
Interfaith	271
Total Marriages	744
Deaths	1,878
Total Catholic Population	143,084
Total Population	450,982

Former Bishops—Rt. Rev. EDGAR P. WADHAMS, D.D., cons. May 5, 1872; died Dec. 5, 1891.—Rt. Rev. HENRY GABRIELS, D.D., cons. May 5, 1892; died April 23, 1921.—Most Rev. JOSEPH H. CONROY, D.D., LL.D., cons. May 1, 1912; succeeded to the See, Nov. 21, 1921; died March 20, 1939.—Most Rev. FRANCIS J. MONAGHAN, S.T.D., LL.D., cons. June 29, 1936; succeeded to the See, March 20, 1939; died Nov. 13, 1942.—Most Rev. BRYAN J. MCENTEGART, D.D., LL.D., cons. Aug. 3, 1943; transferred to Titular See of Aradi, Aug. 19, 1953; appt. June 26, 1953 to Rectorship of Catholic University of America, Washington, D.C., appt. Bishop of Brooklyn, April 16, 1957; installed June 13, 1957; appt. Archbishop, April 15, 1966; retired and appt. Titular Archbishop of Gabii, July 17, 1968; died Sept. 30, 1968.—Most Rev. WALTER P. KELLENBERG, D.D., cons. Oct. 5, 1953; appt. to Ogdensburg, Jan. 19, 1954; transferred to See of Rockville Centre, April 16, 1957; installed May 27, 1957; died Jan. 11, 1986.—Most Rev. JAMES J. NAVAGH, D.D., cons. Sept. 24, 1952; appt. to Ogdensburg, May 8, 1957; transferred to Paterson, Feb. 12, 1963; died in Rome, Oct. 2, 1965.—Most Rev. LEO R. SMITH, D.D., appt. Auxiliary Bishop of Buffalo, July 9, 1952; cons. Sept. 24, 1952; appt. Bishop of Ogdensburg, Feb. 12, 1963; died in Rome Oct. 9, 1963.—Most Rev. THOMAS A. DONNELLAN, D.D., appt. March 4, 1964; cons. April 9, 1964; appt. to Atlanta, May 29, 1968; transferred to Archdiocese of Atlanta, July 16, 1968; died in Atlanta, Oct. 15, 1987.—Most Rev. STANISLAUS J. BRZANA, S.T.D., LL.D, ord. June 7, 1941; appt. Titular Bishop of Cufruta and Auxiliary of Buffalo, May 24, 1964; cons. June 29, 1964; transferred to Ogdensburg, Oct. 22, 1968; retired Nov. 11, 1993; died March 1, 1997.—Most Rev. PAUL S. LOVERDE, D.D., S.T.L., J.C.L., ord. Dec. 18, 1965; appt. Titular Bishop of Ottabia and Auxiliary Bishop of Hartford, Feb. 3, 1988; cons. April 12, 1988; transferred Ogdensburg, Nov. 11, 1993; installed Jan. 17, 1994; appt. Bishop of Arlington, Jan. 25, 1999; installed March 25, 1999.

Diocesan Offices

Unless otherwise noted, all mail for the following offices to go to: *Spratt Memorial Bldg., 604 Washington St., P.O. Box 369, Ogdensburg, 13669.* Office Hours: Mon.-Fri. 8:15-4:30 (Sept.-June); Summer Hours: 8:45-4

Office of the Bishop—Most Rev. GERALD M. BARBARITO, D.D., J.C.L.

Secretary to the Bishop—Rev. DOUGLAS J. LUCIA, J.C.L.

Bishop's Office Secretary—Mrs. KATHY K. TAYLOR, Fax: 315-393-2150.

Fiscal Officer—Mr. JOHN J. GRAY, C.P.A., M.B.A., Fax: 315-393-5911.

Parish Administrative Services Coordinator—Mr. VINCE THOUIN.

Employee Benefits—Mrs. DEBRA L. MOUSAW.

Insurance Claims and Risk Management Department—Mr. HARRY A. GRANGER, Mgr. Tel: 315-393-0441; Fax: 315-393-1490.

Unless otherwise noted, all mail for the following offices to go to: *Bishop Stanislaus J. Brzana Diocesan Pastoral Center, 622 Washington St., P.O. Box 369, Ogdensburg, 13669.* Office Hours: Mon.-Fri. 8:15-4:30 (Sept.-June); Summer Hours: 8:45-4.

Vicar General—Rev. Msgr. ROBERT L. LAWLER, P.A., *St. Mary's Rectory, P.O. Box 187, Waddington, 13694.* Tel: 315-388-4466; Fax: 315-388-4722.

Moderator of the Curia and Episcopal Vicar for Pastoral Services—Rev. Msgr. JOHN R. MURPHY, S.T.L., M.A.

Chancellor and Episcopal Vicar for Diocesan Services—Rev. TERRY R. LAVALLEY, J.C.L.

Vice Chancellor—Rev. DOUGLAS J. LUCIA, J.C.L.

Matrimonial Tribunal and Office of Canonical Affairs—

Judicial Vicar and Vicar for Canonical Affairs—Rev. Msgr. HARRY K. SNOW, M.A., J.C.L.

Office Manager—Sr. MARY PATRICK MURPHY, S.S.J., M.S.

Adjutant Judicial Vicars—Revs. PHILIP T. ALLEN; TERRY R. LAVALLEY, J.C.L.; DOUGLAS J. LUCIA, J.C.L.

Promoter of Justice—Rev. Msgr. PETER R. RIANI, S.T.D., M.Ed.

Defenders of the Bond—Revs. LAWRENCE E. COTTER; RAYMOND J. MOREAU; JOSEPH MORGAN; ALAN D. SHNOB; J. LEE SNOW; JOHN R. YONKOVIG.

Pro-Synodal Judges—Rev. Msgr. BERNARD E. CHRISTMAN; Rev. Msgr. CLARENCE M. DEVAN; Rev. Msgr. ANTHONY A. MILIA; Rev. Msgr. FRANCIS A. WHITE; Revs. ROBERT L. COTTER; DANIEL T. KEEFE; CLYDE A. LEWIS; GILBERT B. MENARD; EARL W. NICHOLS.

Notary—Mrs. DIANNA L. SHAVER.

Advocates—Sr. MARY PATRICK MURPHY, S.S.J., M.S.; Rev. Msgr. DENNIS J. DUPREY; Rev. Msgr. JOHN R.

MURPHY, S.T.L., M.A.; Revs. FAY W. AGER; DOUGLAS A. DECKER; GARVIN J. DEMARAIS; GARRY B. GIROUX; ALBERT J. HAUSER; ALAN J. LAMICA; WILLIAM G. REAMER.

Co-Vicars for Religious—Rev. Msgr. DENNIS J. DUPREY; Sr. CATHERINE LIVERS, S.P.

Development Office—Mrs. JANICE SHOEN, Dir. Bishop's Fund Appeal; Planned Giving; Bishop's Heritage Circle.

Stewardship and Chairman of Bishop's Fund Committee—Rev. Msgr. GERALD H. SERVICE, Dir.

Evangelization—Sr. MARY ELLEN BRETT, S.S.J., Dir.

Formation for Ministry—Sr. JUDITH BAUMERT, S.S.J., Dir.

Mission Aid Societies—Rev. GEORGE F. MAROUN, Dir., Fax: 315-393-0981. Society for The Propagation of the Faith; Holy Childhood Association; Society of St. Peter the Apostle; Missionary Union of Clergy and Religious; Ogdensburg Peruvian Apostolate.

Office of Planning—Sr. JENNIFER VOTRAW, S.S.J., Dir.

Director of Priest and Pastoral Personnel—Rev. JOSEPH A. MORGAN.

Department of Worship—Rev. ALBERT J. HAUSER, Dir.

Unless otherwise noted, all mail for the following offices to go to: *Bishop Paul S. Loverde Center for Education and Formation, 100 Elizabeth St., P.O. Box 369, Ogdensburg, 13669;* Fax: 315-393-8977. Office Hours: Mon.-Fri. 8:15-4:30 (Sept.-June); Summer Hours: 8:45-4.

Department of Christian Formation—Rev. STEVEN M. MURRAY, Diocesan Dir.

Ogdensburg Regional Center—Sr. MARY RITA KEMPNEY, S.S.J., Dir.

Plattsburgh Regional Center—Sr. ELIZABETH MENARD, O.P., Dir., *114A Cornelia St., Plattsburgh, 12901.* Tel: 518-563-2022; Fax: 518-563-2138.

Watertown Regional Center—Mr. MICHAEL WAGNER, Dir., *866 Arsenal St., Watertown, 13601.* Tel: 315-782-3620; Fax: 315-782-2009.

Youth Ministry—Mr. DANIEL GIRARD, Dir.

Catholic Scouting—Sr. MARY RITA KEMPNEY, S.S.J., Diocesan Liaison.

Department of Education—Sr. KATHLEEN MURPHY, O.S.F., Supt.; Mrs. DOROTHY HOBBS, Asst. Supt.; Sr. MARY EAMON LYNG, S.S.J., Asst. Supt. of Faith Formation.

Family Life Department and Pre-Cana—Directors: Deacon GARY FRANK; Mrs. GAYLE FRANK.

Consultative Bodies

Deans—Rev. TIMOTHY J. SOUCY, Adirondack; Rev. DANIEL T. KEEFE, Clinton; Rev. Msgr. PETER R. RIANI, Essex; Rev. Msgr. DENNIS J. DUPREY, Franklin; Rev. LAWRENCE E. MARULLO, Hamilton-Herkimer; Rev. Msgr. ANTHONY A. MILIA, Jefferson; Rev. LEO A. WILEY, Lewis; Rev. ANDREW J. AMYOT, St. Lawrence.

Diocesan Consultors—Rev. Msgr. ROBERT L. LAWLER, P.A.; Rev. Msgr. WILLIAM J. ARGY; Rev. Msgr. PAUL WHITMORE; Revs. PIERRE AUBIN, M.S.C.; ARTHUR J. LABAFF; DONALD J. MANFRED; STEVEN M. MURRAY; KEVIN J. O'BRIEN; F. JAMES SHURTLEFF.

Council of Priests—Most Rev. GERALD M. BARBARITO, D.D., J.C.L., Chm.; Rev. Msgr. ROBERT L. LAWLER, P.A.; Rev. Msgr. WILLIAM J. ARGY; Rev. Msgr. ROBERT H. AUCOIN; Rev. Msgr. PAUL WHITMORE; Revs. PIERRE AUBIN, M.S.C.; JOHN M. DEMO; DONALD F. KRAMBERG; ARTHUR J. LABAFF; DONALD J. MANFRED; STEVEN M. MURRAY; KEVIN J. O'BRIEN; F. JAMES SHURTLEFF; JOSEPH P. WHEELOCK.

Council of Religious—Sr. RITA MARY MORRISSETTE, O.S.M., Pres.; Sr. CAROLYN MADDEN, R.S.M., Vice Pres.; Sr. JOAN CASEY, R.S.M., Sec.; Sr. MARY PATRICK MURPHY, S.S.J., Treas.

Pastoral Council—Most Rev. GERALD M. BARBARITO, D.D., J.C.L.; Rev. Msgr. ROBERT L. LAWLER, P.A.; Rev. TERRY R. LAVALLEY, J.C.L.; Rev. Msgr. JOHN R. MURPHY, S.T.L., M.A.; Revs. GEORGE F. MAROUN; JOHN L. DOWNS; JASON T. JONES; Deacon WILLIAM S. RAVEN; Sr. RITA MARY MORRISSETTE, O.S.M.; Mr. KEN KLAUCK; Mr. TIMOTHY LABARGE; Mrs. MARIE TROMBLEY; Mr. MARCEL CHARLAND; Mr. JOSEPH A. PROVONCHA; Mrs. HARLEY MCDIVITT; TERRY M. TRUDEAU; Mr. JAMES FEELEY; Deacon RONALD STE-MARIE; SOPHIA ROFFE; Mr. W. EDWARD WALLDROFF; Sheriff JAMES LAFFERTY; Mr. BRIEN TABOLT; Mr. MARC LARIBEE; Mr. FRANK BONDELLIO; CAROL DONOVAN; Mr. DANIEL BEHRENS; Mrs. KATHY B. LETTIERE; ANGELA BURKE; ALICIA GINGERICH; COREY ASHCRAFT; Sr. MARY PATRICK MURPHY, S.S.J.

Priest Personnel Board—Revs. JOSEPH A. MORGAN; RAYMOND J. MOREAU; DONALD A. ROBINSON; DANIEL T. KEEFE; F. JAMES SHURTLEFF; STEPHEN H. GRATTO.

Other Diocesan Offices and Directors

Diocesan Archivist—Rev. LAWRENCE E. COTTER, S.T.L., *P.O. Box 369, Ogdensburg, 13669.*

Apostleship of Prayer—Rev. ALBERT J. HAUSER, Dir., *P.O. Box 369, Ogdensburg, 13669.*

Building Commission—Rev. TERRY R. LAVALLEY, J.C.L., *P.O. Box 369, Ogdensburg, 13669.*

Campus Ministry—Rev. J. ROGER MCGUINNESS, Dir., *John XXIII College Community, 90 Broad St., Plattsburgh, 12901.* Tel: 518-561-7545; Fax: 518-561-1004. Revs. FRANCIS J. FLYNN; JOHN M. HUNT; EUGENE J. BEAUDET; Deacon WILLIAM S. RAVEN.

Catholic Charities—Sr. DONNA FRANKLIN, D.C., Dir., *P.O. Box 296, Ogdensburg, 13669.* Tel: 315-393-2255; Fax: 315-393-2402. Ogdensburg Office—MARTHA SHAVER, Dir., *P.O. Box 296, Ogdensburg, 13669.* Tel: 315-393-2660; Fax: 315-393-9362. Watertown Office—KATHLEEN MATTIS, Dir., *812 State St., Watertown, 13601.* Tel: 315-788-4330; Fax: 315-786-0539. Plattsburgh Office—PAMELA J. WILSON, M.S., Dir., *4914 S. Catherine St., Plattsburgh, 12901.* Tel: 315-561-0470; Fax: 315-561-0472. Malone Office— *63 E. Main St., P.O. Box 896, Malone, 12953.* Tel: 518-483-1460; Fax: 518-483-1460. Lowville Office— *7514 S. State St., Lowville, 13367.* Tel: 315-376-4141; Fax: 315-376-4141. Port Henry Office— *14 Park Pl., Port Henry, 12974.* Tel: 518-546-3565. Tupper Lake Office— *60 Park St., P.O. Box 701, Tupper Lake, 12986.* Tel: 518-359-7688.

Catholic Relief Services—Sr. DONNA FRANKLIN, D.C., *P.O. Box 296, Ogdensburg, 13669.* Tel: 315-393-2255; Fax: 315-393-2402.

Cemeteries—Rev. TERRY R. LAVALLEY, J.C.L., *P.O. Box 369, Ogdensburg, 13669.* Tel: 315-393-2920; Fax: 315-394-7401.

Censor Librorum—Rev. LAWRENCE E. COTTER, B.S., S.T.L., M.S., *P.O. Box 369, Ogdensburg, 13669.*

Charismatic Renewal—Rev. FRANCIS J. CORYER, Liaison, *St. Henry's Church, 3 Josephine St., Dekalb Junction, 13630.* Tel: 315-347-3540.

Department of Communications—Sr. JENNIFER VOTRAW, S.S.J., Dir., *P.O. Box 369, Ogdensburg, 13669.* Tel: 315-393-2920; Fax: 315-394-7401.

Bureau of Information—Rev. TERRY R. LAVALLEY, J.C.L., *P.O. Box 369, Ogdensburg, 13669.* Tel: 315-393-2920; Fax: 315-394-7401.

Newspaper—"The North Country Catholic"; Mrs. MARY LOU KILIAN, Editor; Mr. SCOTT A. WILSON, Circulation & Advertising, *P.O. Box 326, Ogdensburg, 13669.* Tel: 315-393-2540.

Bureau of Media—Mrs. LINDA J. KELLEY, *1900 State Hwy. 11B, Potsdam, 13617.* Tel: 315-268-0164; Fax: 315-268-7104.

Continuing Education of Clergy—Rev. J. ROGER MCGUINNESS, Dir., *90 Broad St., Plattsburgh, 12901.* Tel: 518-561-7545; Fax: 518-561-1004.

Ecumenical Commission—Rev. FAY W. AGER, Chm., *P.O. Box 908, Chateaugay, 12920.* Tel: 518-497-6673; Fax: 518-497-6165.

Legion of Mary—Vacant.

Natural Family Planning Services—Mr. ANGELO PIETROPAOLI; Mrs. ANGELO PIETROPAOLI, *36 First St., Malone, 12953.*

Permanent Diaconate Program—

Director of Deacon Formation—Rev. HOWARD J. VENETTE, *P.O. Box 315, Colton, 13625.*

Director of Ordained Deacons—Deacon FREDERICK A. BROUSSEAU, *32 Chestnut St., Potsdam, 13676.*

Priests' Eucharistic League—Rev. ALBERT J. HAUSER, Dir., *P.O. Box 369, Ogdensburg, 13669.* Tel: 315-393-2920; Fax: 315-394-7401.

Pro-Life Office—Rev. THOMAS E. KORNMEYER, Dir., *St. Therese Church, 5 Adams Lane, Newcomb, 12852.*

Director of Seminarians—Rev. JOSEPH A. MORGAN, *P.O. Box 369, Ogdensburg, 13669.* Tel: 315-393-2920; Fax: 315-394-7401.

St. Vincent de Paul Society—Vacant.

Vocations—Rev. TIMOTHY G. CANAAN, Dir., *Wadhams Hall Seminary College, 6866 State Hwy. 37, Ogdensburg, 13669.* Tel: 315-393-4231; Fax: 315-393-4249. Rev. CHRISTOPHER CARRARA, Assoc. Vocations Dir.

Young Adult Ministry—Rev. HARRY E. GIROUX, Dir., *St. Joseph's Church, P.O. Box 224, West Chazy, 12992.* Tel: 518-493-4521; Fax: 518-493-5880.

CLERGY, PARISHES, MISSIONS AND PAROCHIAL SCHOOLS

CITY OF OGDENSBURG
(St. Lawrence County)

1—ST. MARY'S CATHEDRAL (1748), Rev. Msgr. Harry K. Snow, Rector; Rev. Jason T. Jones; Rev. Msgr. William J. Argy; Rev. Sean M. Murray; Sr. Mary Theresa La Brake, G.N.S.H., Pastoral Assoc.; Deacons D. Thomas Sharrow; Richard E. Winter, Emeritus.
Res., 415 Hamilton St., 13669. Tel: 315-393-3930; Fax: 315-393-6680. [CEM]
Catechesis/Religious Programs—Tel: 315-393-1820; Fax: 315-393-1670. Mrs. Michele Rosteck, D.R.E.
Students 300.

2—NOTRE DAME (1859) (French), Rev. F. James Shurtleff; Deacons Victor Demers; Thomas Kilian; Mark A. LaLonde; Elizabeth J. Bernhard, Pastoral Assoc. In res., Rev. Joseph A. Morgan.
Res., 125 Ford Ave., P.O. Box 149, 13669. Tel: 315-393-5050; Fax: 315-393-5962. [CEM]
School—St. Marguerite D'Youville Academy, (Grades K-5) 315 Gates St., 13699. Tel: 315-393-0165; Fax: 315-394-0499. Mrs. Brenda Harder, Prin.
Lay Teachers 10; Students 124.
Catechesis/Religious Programs—Bishop Conroy Christian Formation Program, 214 Morris St., 13669. Tel: 315-393-1820.
Students 187.

OUTSIDE CITY OF OGDENSBURG

Adams, Jefferson Co., St. Cecilia (1870), Rev. Douglas Decker.
Res., 19 Grove St., 13605. Tel: 315-232-2392. [CEM]
Catechesis/Religious Programs—Students 230.

Alexandria Bay, Jefferson Co., St. Cyril of Alexandria (1000 Islands) (1885), Rev. Thomas F. Driscoll.
Res., Box 477, 13607. Tel: 315-482-2670; Fax: 315-482-4970. [CEM]
Catechesis/Religious Programs—Students 87.

Altona, Clinton Co., Holy Angels (1865) (Irish-French Canadian), Rev. Gilbert O. Boisvert.
Res., P.O. Box 113, 12910. Tel: 518-236-5848; Fax: 518-236-4249. [CEM]
Oratory—Jericho, St. Alexis.
Catechesis/Religious Programs—Tel: 518-594-3916. Mary Ellen Tomo, D.R.E.
Students 196.

Au Sable Forks, Clinton Co., Holy Name (1848), Rev. Bruce T. Favreau; Deacon John J. Ryan.
Res., 10 Church St., P.O. Box 719, 12912. Tel: 518-647-8225; Fax: 518-647-5394. [CEM]
School—(Grades PreK-6) 5 Pleasant St., 12912. Tel: 518-647-8444. Mrs. Susan Pulitzer, Prin.
Lay Teachers 8; Students 80.
Catechesis/Religious Programs—Students 101.

Black Brook, Clinton Co., St. Matthew (1848), Rev. Bruce T. Favreau; Deacon John J. Ryan.
Res., 10 Church St., P.O. Box 719, Au Sable Forks, 12912. Tel: 518-647-8225; Fax: 518-647-5394. [CEM]

Black River, Jefferson Co., St. Paul (1901), Rev. Theodore M. Gillette; Deacons Kenneth A. Seymour; William S. Raven.
Res., 208 LeRay St., 13612. Tel: 315-773-5672.
Church—210 LeRay St., 13612.
Catechesis/Religious Programs—Students 70.

Bloomingdale, Essex Co., St. Paul (1897), Rev. Francis J. Flynn.
Res., 50 Saranac Ave., P.O. Box 356, 12913. Tel: 518-891-0144; Fax: 518-891-5259. [CEM 2]
Mission—Gabriels, Franklin Co., Assumption of the B.V.M., Rte. 86, Gabriels, 12939.
Catechesis/Religious Programs—Tel: 518-891-3111. Kathy Gonyea, D.R.E., (Grades 1-12).
Students 105.

Bombay, Franklin Co., St. Joseph (1912), Rev. Kris C. Lauzon.
Res., P.O. Box 499, Fort Covington, 12937. Tel: 518-358-4471; Fax: 518-358-2500. [CEM]
Catechesis/Religious Programs—Tel: 518-358-2500.
Students 80.

Brasher Falls, St. Lawrence Co., St. Patrick (1830) (Irish-French), Revs. Clark S. White; Earl W. Nichols.
Res., P.O. Box 208, 13613. Tel: 315-389-5401; Fax: 315-389-4066.
Parish Center: Tel: 315-389-5191. [CEM]
Catechesis/Religious Programs—Helen Brown, D.R.E.
Students 165.

Brownville, Jefferson Co., Immaculate Conception of the B.V.M. (1874) (Irish-Italian), Rev. Joseph W. Elliott; Deacon David F. Moltz.
Res., 119 W. Main St., P.O. Box 99, 13615. Tel: 315-782-1143.
Catechesis/Religious Programs—Tel: 315-788-7240. Sr. M. Kateri Rose, S.S.J., D.R.E.
Students 197.
Mission—Dexter, Jefferson Co., St. Elizabeth Seton, P.O. Box 99, 13615. Tel: 315-639-3888.

Brushton, Franklin Co., St. Mary (1870), Rev. Alfred H. Fish.
Res., 12916. Tel: 518-529-7433. [CEM]
Catechesis/Religious Programs—Tel: 518-529-6580. Marian Roscoe, D.R.E.
Students 309.

Burke, Franklin Co., St. George (1874), Rev. Bill Edwards.
Res., 797 Depot St., P.O. Box 105, 12917. Tel: 518-483-5687; Fax: 518-483-5687, Ext. [*]51. [CEM]

Cadyville, Clinton Co., St. James Minor (1854), Rev. Msgr. Lawrence M. Deno.
Res., P.O. Box 117, 12918-0117. Tel: 518-293-7026; Fax: 518-293-8246. [CEM]
Catechesis/Religious Programs—Students 122.

Canton, St. Lawrence Co., St. Mary (1868), Rev. Msgr. Gerald H. Service.
Res., 66 Court St., P.O. Box 308, 13617. Tel: 315-386-2543; Fax: 315-386-2543. [CEM]
School—(Grades PreK-6) 2 Powers St., 13617. Tel: 315-386-3572. Mrs. Eleanor Beauvais, Prin.
Lay Teachers 9; Students 150.
Catechesis/Religious Programs—Mrs. Jeannine Ballard, D.R.E.
Students 196.

St. Thomas More (1959). (Campus Parish). Rev. John M. Hunt.
Res., 39 Court St., P.O. Box 424, 13617. Tel: 315-386-8425; Fax: 315-386-1200.
Catechesis/Religious Programs—St. Mary's.
Students 19.

Cape Vincent, Jefferson Co., St. Vincent of Paul (1851), Rev. E. John Silver.
Res., Box 288, 13618. Tel: 315-654-2662; Fax: 315-654-4721. [CEM]
Catechesis/Religious Programs—Students 40.

Carthage, Jefferson Co., St. James Minor (1818), Rev. Scott D. Fobare; Deacons Richard J. Staab, Pastoral Assoc.; James J. Gillen.
Res., 327 West St., 13619. Tel: 315-493-3224; Fax: 315-493-3280. [CEM 2]
School—Augustinian Academy, (Grades PreK-8) 317 West St., 13619. Tel: 315-493-1301; Fax: 315-493-0632. Sr. John Mary Brockway, S.S.J., Prin.; Sr. M. Victorine Brenon, S.S.J., Supr.
Sisters of St. Joseph 1; Lay Teachers 11; Students 189.
Catechesis/Religious Programs—Students 181.
Convent—Tel: 315-493-1672.

Champlain, Clinton Co., St. Mary (1861), Rev. Donald A. Robinson; Deacon Leonard Patrie.
Res., 86 Church St., P.O. Box 368, 12919. Tel: 518-298-8244; Fax: 518-298-2879. [CEM 2]
School—(Grades PreK-6). Tel: 518-298-3372; Fax: 518-298-3372. Karen M. Froehlich, Prin.
Daughters of Charity of the Sacred Heart of Jesus 2; Lay Teachers 8; Students 160.
Catechesis/Religious Programs—Students 140.

Chasm Falls, Franklin Co., St. Helen (1881), Rev. Msgr. Dennis J. Duprey; Sr. Sheila Moran, S.S.J., Admin.
Res. & Church Office: 753 County Rte. 41, Malone, 12953. Tel: 518-483-1515; Fax: 518-483-1515. [CEM]
Catechesis/Religious Programs—Students 62.
Missions—Lake Titus, Franklin Co., St. Mary, 12953.; Owl's Head, Franklin Co., St. Joseph, 12953.

Chateaugay, Franklin Co., St. Patrick (1848), Rev. Fay W. Ager; Sr. Mary Hallahan, O.S.U., Pastoral Assoc.
Res., 132 W. Main St., P.O. Box 908, 12920. Tel: 518-497-6673; Fax: 518-497-6165. [CEM]
Catechesis/Religious Programs—Tel: 518-497-6165.
Students 167.
Mission—Brainardsville, Franklin Co., St. Jude, 12920.

Chaumont, Jefferson Co., All Saints (1922), Rev. Pierre Aubin, M.S.C.
Res., P.O. Box 100, 13622. Tel: 315-649-2717; Fax: 315-649-5665.
Catechesis/Religious Programs—27396 Madison St.
Students 50.

Chazy, Clinton Co., Sacred Heart (1898), Rev. L. William Gordon; Deacon Robert J. LeClair.
Res., P.O. Box 459, 12921. Tel: 518-846-7650; Fax: 518-846-7655. [CEM 2]
Catechesis/Religious Programs—Tel: 518-846-7180.
Students 276.

Churubusco, Clinton Co., Immaculate Heart of Mary (1880), Rev. Howard McCasland, Admin.
Res., Rte. 189, 12923. Tel: 518-497-9956. [CEM 2]
Catechesis/Religious Programs—St. Edmund's Center, Ellenburg, Tel: 518-594-3907.
Students 49.

Clayton, Jefferson Co., St. Mary of Clayton (1838), Rev. Robert M. Shurtleff; Deacon Gary A. Frank.
Res., 521 James St., 13624. Tel: 315-686-3398 (Rectory); 686-2638 (Parish Office); Fax: 315-686-2639. [CEM 2]
Catechesis/Religious Programs—515 Mary St., 13624. Tel: 315-686-2638.
Students 92.

Colton, St. Lawrence Co., St. Patrick (1864), Revs. Howard J. Venette; Lawrence E. Cotter, Pastor Emeritus.
Res., P.O. Box 315, 13625. Tel: 315-262-2871; Fax: 315-262-2188. [CEM][JC]
Catechesis/Religious Programs—Students 45.
Missions—South Colton, St. Lawrence Co., St. Paul, 13625.; Parishville, St. Lawrence Co., St. Michael, 13625. Tel: 315-268-1733.

Constable, Franklin Co., St. Francis of Assisi (1872), Rev. Garry B. Giroux; Deacon Garry N. Burnell.
Res., 1197 State Rte. 122, P.O. Box 86, 12926. Tel: 518-483-2775 (Rectory); 483-0486 (Parish Office); Fax: 518-483-1618. [CEM]
Catechesis/Religious Programs—Students 97.
Mission—Westville, Franklin Co., Our Lady of Fatima, 4326 State Rte. 37, 12926.

Constableville, Lewis Co., St. Mary (1820), Rev. Paschal Rys, O.F.M.Conv.
Res., P.O. Box 382, 13325. Tel: 315-397-2556. [CEM][JC 2]
Catechesis/Religious Programs—Students 100.

Coopersville, Clinton Co., St. Joseph (1790), Rev. Normand C. Cote.
Res., 74 Mason Rd., Champlain, 12919-6201. Tel: 518-298-8619. [CEM]
Catechesis/Religious Programs—Tel: 518-846-7180.
Students 44.

Copenhagen, Lewis Co., St. Mary (1901) (Irish-French), Rev. Scott D. Fobare.
Res., 126 High St., P.O. Box 12, 13626-0012. Tel: 315-688-2683. [CEM]
Catechesis/Religious Programs—Students 47.

Croghan, Lewis Co., St. Stephen (1869), Rev. Leo A. Wiley.
Res., Main St., P.O. Box 38, 13327-0038. Tel: 315-346-6958; Fax: 315-346-1200. [CEM]
Catechesis/Religious Programs—Tel: 315-346-6963. Thomas Schneeberger, D.R.E.
Students 230.
Oratories—Belfort, St. Vincent de Paul; New Bremen, St. Peter. [CEM 3]

Crown Point, Essex Co., Sacred Heart Church (1874), Rev. William G. Muench; Sr. Carol Daul, S.A., Pastoral Assoc.; Deacon Elliott A. Shaw.
Church—12928. Tel: 518-597-3924. [CEM]
Catechesis/Religious Programs—Students 45.

Dannemora, Clinton Co., St. Joseph (1853), Rev. John J. Looby; Deacon Edward Mazuchowski. In res., Rev. Peter M. Berg.
Res., 179 Smith St., Box 418, 12929-0418. Tel: 518-492-7118; Fax: 518-492-7742. [CEM 2]
Catechesis/Religious Programs—Tel: 518-492-2524. Lynn Lynch, D.R.E.
Students 235.

Deferiet, Jefferson Co., St. Rita (1900), Rev. Theodore M. Gillette.
Mailing Address: 31 Riverside Dr., 13628.
Res., 208 Leray St., Black River, 13612. Tel: 315-773-5612.
Catechesis/Religious Programs—Students 8.

De Kalb Junction, St. Lawrence Co., St. Henry (1893), Rev. Francis J. Coryer.
Res., 3 Josephine St., 13630. Tel: 315-347-3540; Fax: 315-347-4925. [CEM]
Catechesis/Religious Programs—Students 63.
Mission—Russell, St. Lawrence Co., St. Rene Goupil, 24 Pestle St., Russell, 13684.

Edwards, St. Lawrence Co., Sacred Heart (1894), Rev. Francis J. Coryer; Deacon Peter J. Lawless.
Res., 3 Josephine St., De Kalb Junction, 13630. Tel: 315-347-3540; Fax: 315-347-4925.
Catechesis/Religious Programs—Students 37.

Elizabethtown, Essex Co., St. Elizabeth (1881), Rev. Msgr. Peter R. Riani.
Res., P.O. Box 368, 12932. Tel: 518-873-6760; Fax: 518-873-6530. [CEM]
Catechesis/Religious Programs—Students 45.

Ellenburg, Clinton Co., St. Edmund (1869), Rev. Joseph P. Trombley.
Res., 12933. Tel: 518-594-3907; Fax: 518-594-8843. [CEM 2]
Church—5528 Route 11, P.O. Box 119, 12933.
Catechesis/Religious Programs—Tel: 518-594-7774. D.R.E.: Marie Trombley; Betty Bulriss.
Students 281.

Essex, Essex Co., St. Joseph, Rev. James A. Delbel.
Res., P.O. Box 607, Willsboro, 12996. Tel: 518-963-4524; Fax: 518-963-7719. [CEM][JC]

Evans Mills, Jefferson Co., St. Mary (1847), Rev. Bernard Jakubco, M.S.C.
Res., 8408 S. Main St., P.O. Box 179, 13637. Tel: 315-629-4425. [CEM]
Catechesis/Religious Programs—Students 60.
Oratory—Antwerp, Jefferson Co., St. Michael, (1849) Antwerp, Tel: 315-659-8372. [CEM]
Rev. Bernard Jakubco, M.S.C.
Missions—Philadelphia, Jefferson Co., St. Joseph; Theresa, Jefferson Co., St. Theresa of Avila, Theresa, Tel: 315-628-4512.

Fort Covington, Franklin Co., St. Mary (1837), Rev. Kris C. Lauzon.
Res., P.O. Box 499, 12937. Tel: 518-358-4471; Fax: 518-358-2500. [CEM 2]
Catechesis/Religious Programs—Tel: 518-358-2500.
Students 185.

Glenfield, Lewis Co., St. Mary (1919), Revs. David Wisniewski; Sony G. Pulickal, C.M.F. In res., Rev. Robert L. Cotter.
Res., 5441 Shady Ave., Lowville, 13367. Tel: 315-376-6662; Fax: 315-376-6663. [CEM]
Catechesis/Religious Programs—Tel: 315-376-7570.
Students 84.
Mission—Greig, Lewis Co., St. Thomas, (1876). [CEM]

Gouverneur, St. Lawrence Co., St. James (1875), Rev. Daniel L. Chapin.
Res., 164 E. Main St., 13642. Tel: 315-287-0114; Fax: 315-287-0114. [CEM 2]
School—(Grades PreK-6) S. Gordon St., 13642. Tel: 315-287-0130. Sr. Ronald Marie Hax, S.S.J., Prin.
Sisters 2; Lay Teachers 7; Students 147.
Catechesis/Religious Programs—Elizabeth Bradford, D.R.E.
Students 109.

Hammond, St. Lawrence Co., St. Peter (1905) (French-Irish), Rev. Steven M. Murray.
Res., P.O. Box 218, 13646. Tel: 315-324-5718; Fax: 315-324-6338.
Catechesis/Religious Programs—Students 60.
Mission—Rossie, St. Lawrence Co., St. Patrick, P.O. Box 218, Hammond, 13646. [CEM]

Harrisville, Lewis Co., St. Francis Solanus (1879), Rev. John J. Cosmic, Admin.; Deacon Philip Looby.
Res., P.O. Box 208, 13648. Tel: 315-543-2421; Fax: 315-543-2421. [CEM]
Oratory—Lake Bonaparte, St. Rita.
Catechesis/Religious Programs—Students 60.
Mission—Natural Bridge, Jefferson Co., St. Henry, 13665.

Heuvelton, St. Lawrence Co., St. Raphael's (1880), Rev. Terry R. La Valley.
Res., 5 Clinton St., P.O. Box 377, 13654. Tel: 315-344-2383.
Catechesis/Religious Programs—Students 88.

Hogansburg, Franklin Co., St. Patrick (1834) (Irish), Rev. Kris C. Lauzon.
Res., 393 Church St., P.O. Box 427, 13655. Tel: 518-358-2557. [CEM][JC]
Catechesis/Religious Programs—Students 23.

Hopkinton, St. Lawrence Co., Church of the Holy Cross (1877), Rev. John M. Demo.
Res., P.O. Box 288, St. Regis Falls, 12980. Tel: 518-856-9456. [CEM]

Houseville, Lewis Co., St. Hedwig (1922) (Polish), Revs. David Wisniewski; Sony G. Pulickal, C.M.F.
Res., St. Peter's Church, 5441 Shady Ave., Lowville, 13367-1615. Tel: 315-376-6662; Fax: 315-376-6663.

Indian Lake, Hamilton Co., St. Mary's (1958), Rev. Rolland A. Hart; Deacon Gerard Gilner.
Res., Rte. No. 28, P.O. Box 332, 12842. Tel: 518-648-5422; Fax: 518-648-0323. [CEM]
Catechesis/Religious Programs—Students 32.
Mission—Blue Mountain Lake, Hamilton Co., St. Paul, P.O. Box 332, Indian Lake 12842.

Inlet, Hamilton Co., St. Anthony of Padua (1897), Rev. Lawrence Marullo, V.F.; Deacon Ronald Ste.-Marie.
Mailing Address: P.O. Box 236, Old Forge, 13420. Tel: 315-357-2811.
Catechesis/Religious Programs—Students 20.

Keene, Essex Co., St. Brendan (1868), Rev. Alan J. Lamica.
Res., P.O. Box 130, 12942-0130. Tel: 518-576-4434; Fax: 518-576-9318.
Mission—Wilmington, Essex Co., St. Margaret.

Keeseville, Clinton and Essex Cos., Church of the Immaculate Conception (1835) (Irish-French), Rev. Garvin J. Demarais.
Res., 1804 Main St., 12944-3745. Tel: 518-834-7100; Fax: 518-834-4612. [CEM]
Catechesis/Religious Programs—Twinned with St. John the Baptist, Keeseville.
Oratory—Clintonville, St. Catherine of Sienna. (Closed).

St. John the Baptist (1853) (French-Irish), Rev. Garvin J. Demarais.
Res., 1804 Main St., 12944-3745. Tel: 518-834-7100; Fax: 518-834-4612. [CEM]
Catechesis/Religious Programs—1806 Main St., 12944-3745. Tel: 518-834-6002.
Students 154.

Lafargeville, Jefferson Co., St. John the Evangelist (1898), Rev. Robert M. Shurtleff.
Res., 521 James St., Clayton, 13624. Tel: 315-686-3398; Fax: 315-686-2639.
Church—35923 Rte.180, P.O. Box 157, 13656. Tel: 315-658-2295 (Parish Center). [CEM]
Catechesis/Religious Programs—25923 Route 180. Students 41.

Lake Clear, Franklin Co., St. John in the Wilderness (1887), Revs. Timothy J. Soucy; Joseph P. Wheelock. Pastoral Assocs.: Sr. Cecilia Carey, O.P.; Sr. Ann Marie Conway, O.P.
Mailing Address: P.O. Box 260, 12945. Tel: 518-891-2286.
Res., 19 St. Bernard's St., Saranac Lake, 12983. Tel: 518-891-4616; Fax: 518-891-4619. [CEM][JC]
Catechesis/Religious Programs—Pius X Inter-Parish Religious Education Center, 32 River St., Saranac Lake, 12983. Tel: 518-891-3111.
Students 50.
Mission—Paul Smiths, Franklin Co., St. Gabriel, Pickett Hall #106, Paul Smiths, 12970. Tel: 518-327-6225.
Summer Station—Fish Creek, State Campsite.

Lake Placid, Essex, Co., St. Agnes (1896), Rev. J. Michael Gaffney.
Res., 6 Hillcrest Ave., 12946. Tel: 518-523-2200; Fax: 518-523-2203. [CEM]
School—(Grades PreK-6) 4 Hillcrest Ave., 12946. Tel: 518-523-3771. Paul Ruggeri, Prin.
Lay Teachers 10; Students 150.
Catechesis/Religious Programs—Tel: 518-523-3202. Mrs. Mary Lawrence, D.R.E.
Students 108.

Lake Pleasant, Hamilton Co., St. James Major (1924), Rev. Paul J. Kelly.
Res., P.O. Box 214, Speculator, 12164. Tel: 518-548-6275.
Catechesis/Religious Programs—Students 11.

Lisbon, St. Lawrence Co., SS. Philip and James (1872), Rev. Msgr. William J. Argy; Sr. Joan Marie Casey, R.S.M., Admin. Lay Ministers: Elaine Craig; David Sandburg.
Mailing Address: P.O. Box 175, 13658. Tel: 315-393-3796.
Catechesis/Religious Programs—Students 9.

Long Lake, Hamilton Co., St. Henry (1899), Rev. Thomas E. Kornmeyer.
Mailing Address: P.O. Box 455, 12847. Tel: 518-624-2541; Fax: 518-582-5483.
Res., 18 Adams Ln., Newcomb, 12852. Tel: 518-582-3671; Fax: 518-582-5483. [JC]
Catechesis/Religious Programs—Students 16.

Louisville, St. Lawrence Co., St. Lawrence (1930), Rev. Richard D. Demers; Sr. Mary Stephen Durant, O.S.M., Pastoral Assoc.
Res., 30 Willard Rd., Massena, 13662. Tel: 315-769-3120; Fax: 315-705-0070. [CEM]
Catechesis/Religious Programs—Tel: 315-764-0488.
Students 75.

Lowville, Lewis Co., St. Peter (1870), Revs. David Wisniewski; Sony G. Pulickal, C.M.F.; Deacon Ronald J. Pominville.
Res., 5441 Shady Ave., 13367. Tel: 315-376-6662; Fax: 315-376-6663.
School—(Grades PreK-6) 5445 Shady Ave., 13367. Tel: 315-376-2424; Fax: 315-376-2568.
Sisters of St. Joseph 1; Lay Teachers 8.
Catechesis/Religious Programs—Tel: 315-376-7570.
Students 142.

Lyon Mountain, Clinton Co., St. Bernard (1875), Rev. Msgr. Bernard E. Christman; Deacons Francis Siskavich; Reginald Merrill, (Retired).
Res., 10 Church Pond Rd., P.O. Box 23, 12952. Tel: 518-735-4357. [CEM]
Catechesis/Religious Programs—Students 83.
Mission—Standish, Clinton Co., St. Michael. [CEM 2]

Madrid, St. Lawrence Co., St. John the Baptist (1869), Rev. Richard D. Demers. In res., Rev. Lawrence E. Cotter.
Res., 30 Willard Rd., Massena, 13662. Tel: 315-769-3120. [CEM]
Church—3715 County Rte. 14, P.O. Box 68, 13660. Tel: 315-322-5661.
Catechesis/Religious Programs—Tel: 315-322-5661.
Students 42.

Malone, Franklin Co., Notre Dame (1868) (French-Canadian), Rev. Msgr. Dennis J. Duprey; Revs. Scott R. Seymour; Joseph W. Giroux; Sr. Maureen Welch, O.S.U., Pastoral Assoc.
Res., 11 Church Pl., P.O. Box 547, 12953. Tel: 518-483-4074; Fax: 518-483-4185. [CEM]
School—Holy Family, (Grades PreK-8). (Multi-Parish). Tel: 518-483-4443; Fax: 518-481-6762. Sr. Jeraldine Fritz, D.C., Prin.
Sisters 1; Lay Teachers 16; Students 205.
Catechesis/Religious Programs—Diana Grant, D.R.E. (Grades K-12).
Students 230.

St. John Bosco (1935), Rev. Thomas A. Moody; Sr. Helen Kelley, D.C., Pastoral Assoc.
Res., 57 Rennie St., 12953. Tel: 518-483-3642; Fax: 518-483-2595. [CEM]
Catechesis/Religious Programs—Students 170.

St. Joseph's (1849) (Irish), Rev. Msgr. C. John McAvoy; Tamra A. Murphy, Pastoral Assoc.; Deacon Richard D. Hart.
Res., 132 W. Main St., 12953. Tel: 518-483-1300; Fax: 518-483-1307. [CEM 2]
Catechesis/Religious Programs—Mrs. Tamra Murphy, D.R.E.
Students 193.

Massena, St. Lawrence Co., Sacred Heart (1874), Revs. Donald J. Manfred; Richard S. Williams; Sr. Juliana Fitzpatrick, O.S.M., Pastoral Assoc.; Deacon James J. Hotte.
Res., 212 Main St., P.O. Box 329, 13662. Tel: 315-769-2469; Fax: 315-769-6973. [CEM]
Catechesis/Religious Programs—Students 386.

St. Joseph (1947), Rev. John L. Downs.
Res., 72 Malby Ave., 13662. Tel: 315-769-3972 (Rectory); 769-9076 (Office/Religious Ed.); Fax: 315-764-5409. [JC]
Catechesis/Religious Programs—Students 127.

St. Mary (1913), Rev. Alan D. Shnob; Sr. Maureen Sweeney, S.S.J., Pastoral Assoc. In res., Rev. Msgr. Clarence M. Devan.
Res., 105 Cornell Ave., P.O. Box 609, 13662. Tel: 315-764-0239; Fax: 315-769-5526. [JC]
School—Trinity Catholic School, (Grades PreK-6) 188 Main St., 13662. Tel: 315-769-5911; Fax: 315-769-6973. Sr. Bernadette Marie Collins, S.S.J., Prin.
Sisters of Saint Joseph and Servants of Mary 4; Lay Teachers 14; Students 344.
Catechesis/Religious Programs—D.R.E.: Anne Borsellino, (Grades K-6); Sr. Maureen Sweeney, S.S.J., (Grades 7-12).
Students 212.

Mineville, Essex Co., The Church of All Saints (1872), Rev. Michael A. Toth.
Mailing Address: P.O. Box C, 12956. Tel: 518-942-5953.
Res., 17 St. Patrick's Pl., Port Henry, 12974. Tel: 518-546-7254; Fax: 518-546-3439. [CEM]
Catechesis/Religious Programs—Tel: 518-942-3326.
Students 95.

Mooers, Clinton Co., St. Joseph (1910) (French-Canadian), Rev. Gerald A. Cerank. In res., Rev. Cyril W. Rapin Tel: 518-236-7142.
Mailing Address: P.O. Box 98, Mooers Forks, 12959. Tel: 518-236-5632. [CEM]
P.O. Box 226, 12958.
Catechesis/Religious Programs—Tel: 518-236-4436.
Students 104.

Mooers Forks, Clinton Co., St. Ann (1860) (French-Canadian), Rev. Gerald A. Cerank; Deacon Tyrone A. Rabideau.
Res., 3062 Rte. 11, P.O. Box 98, 12959. Tel: 518-236-5632; Fax: 518-236-4446. [CEM]
Catechesis/Religious Programs—Tel: 518-236-4436.
Students 129.

Morrisonville, Clinton Co., St. Alexander (1897), Rev. Stephen H. Gratto; Mrs. Pamela J. Ballantine, Pastoral Assoc.
Res., Church St., P.O. Box 159, 12962. Tel: 518-561-5039; Fax: 518-561-1834. [CEM]
School—(Grades PreK). Tel: 518-563-5615.
Brothers of Christian Instruction 1; Lay Teachers 2.
Catechesis/Religious Programs—Tel: 518-563-7855.
Students 146.

Morristown, St. Lawrence Co., St. John the Evangelist (1941), Rev. Msgr. Leeward J. Poissant.
Res., P.O. Box 216, 13664. Tel: 315-375-6571; Fax: 315-375-4832.
Catechesis/Religious Programs—Students 117.
Mission—Brier Hill, St. Lawrence Co., Our Lady of Grace, 13664.

Newcomb, Essex Co., St. Therese (1902), Rev. Thomas E. Kornmeyer.
Res., 18 Adams Ln., 12852. Tel: 518-582-3671; Fax: 518-582-5483. [CEM]
Catechesis/Religious Programs—Students 8.

Norfolk, St. Lawrence Co., Visitation of the B.V.M. (1880), Rev. Andrew J. Amyot. In res., Rev. Msgr. Thomas J. Robillard.
Res., 3 Morris St., P.O. Box 637, 13667. Tel: 315-384-4242; Fax: 315-384-3575.
11 Hepburn St., P.O. Box 505, 13667. Tel: 315-384-3847. [CEM]
Catechesis/Religious Programs—Students 90.

North Bangor, Franklin Co., St. Augustine (1887), Rev. Raymond J. Moreau; Deacon John C. Dwyer.
Res., 2472 S.R. 11, P.O. Box 327, 12966. Tel: 518-483-6674; Fax: 518-481-6351. [CEM]
Catechesis/Religious Programs—Mary Cartier, D.R.E.
Students 119.
Mission—North Bangor, Franklin Co., St. Edward, 12966.

North Lawrence, St. Lawrence Co., St. Lawrence (1875) (Irish-French), Rev. Clark S. White.
Res., P.O. Box 208, Brasher Falls, 13613. Tel: 315-389-5401; Fax: 315-389-4066. [CEM]
Catechesis/Religious Programs—Clustered with St. Patrick, Brasher Falls.
Students 126.

Norwood, St. Lawrence Co., St. Andrew (1876), Rev. Paul F. Worczak.
Res., 2 Park Ave., 13668. Tel: 315-353-7303. [CEM]
Catechesis/Religious Programs—Tel: 315-353-2824.
Students 121.

Old Forge, Herkimer Co., St. Bartholomew (1897), Rev. Lawrence Marullo, V.F.
Res., P.O. Box 236, 13420. Tel: 315-369-3554; Fax: 315-369-3554.
Catechesis/Religious Programs—Students 12.

Olmstedville, Essex Co., St. Joseph (1871), Rev. Richard S. Sturtz. In res., Rev. Mark Traenkle, S.A.
Mailing Address: Box 368, Schroon Lake, 12870. Tel: 518-251-2565; 532-7100; Fax: 518-532-7461. [CEM 2]
Rectory: 639 Church Rd., P.O. Box 1, 12857.
Catechesis/Religious Programs—Students 28.

Peru, Clinton Co., St. Augustine (1883), Rev. Vicente F. Jazmines.
Res., 3035 Main St., P.O. Box 569, 12972. Tel: 518-643-2435; Fax: 518-643-0960.
School—Tel: 518-643-9505. Sr. Mary Helen Herman, S.S.J., Prin.
Sisters 2; Lay Teachers 7; Students 180.
Catechesis/Religious Programs—Tel: 518-643-0089; Fax: 518-643-2435.
Students 370.
Oratory—West Peru, Clinton Co., St. Patrick, 12972. [CEM 2]

Plattsburgh, Clinton Co.,

1—OUR LADY OF VICTORY, (1907) (French), Rev. Floyd J. Bleaux, Jr.; Mrs. Carol Pulsifer, Pastoral Assoc.
Res., 4919 S. Catherine St., 12901. Tel: 518-561-1842; Fax: 518-561-2269.
School—Our Lady of Victory Academy, 4917 S. Catherine St., 12901. Tel: 518-563-4262; Fax: 518-562-5403. Lorraine Laframboise, Prin.
Sisters 1; Lay Teachers 9; Students 152.
Catechesis/Religious Programs—Students 150.
Convent—4907 S. Catherine St., 12901. Tel: 518-563-7419; Fax: 518-563-0383. Sr. Louise Marceau, S.C.S.L., Supr.

2—ST. JOHN THE BAPTIST, (1837) (Irish), Rev. Kevin J. O'Brien; Bro. Louis St. Pierre, Pastoral Assoc.
Res., 7 Margaret St., 12901. Tel: 518-563-0730; Fax: 518-563-0754. [CEM]
School—(Grades PreK-8) 59 Broad St., 12901. Tel: 518-563-2260; Fax: 518-563-4553. John Fairchild, Prin.; Sr. Brian Marie Latour, R.S.M., Vice Prin.
Priests 1; Sisters 1; Lay Teachers 25; Students 289.
Catechesis/Religious Programs—Tel: 518-561-6694.
Students 110.

3—ST. JOSEPH, (Treadwells Mill) (1935), Rev. Stephen H. Gratto; Bro. Roland Gaudette, F.I.C., Pastoral Assoc.
Res. & Mailing Address—Church St., P.O. Box 159, Morrisonville, 12962. Tel: 518-563-6301.

4—ST. MARY OF THE LAKE, (Cumberland Head) (1965), Rev. Danel T. Keefe.
Res., 1202 Cumberland Head Road, P.O. Box 704, 12901. Tel: 518-561-2488; Fax: 518-561-3732. [CEM]
Catechesis/Religious Programs—Eunice Trombly, D.R.E.
Students 119.

5—ST. PETER, (1853), Rev. John R. Yonkovig; Deacons Robert King; Robert Diehl, Spiritual Life Dir. In res., Rev. Msgr. Morris L. Dwyer; Rev. Msgr. Joseph Aubin; Rev. Joseph A. Conti.
Res., 114 Cornelia St., 12901. Tel: 518-563-1692; Fax: 518-566-9420. [CEM]
School—(Grades PreK-8) St. Charles St., 12901. Tel: 518-561-7132; Fax: 518-561-7806. Mrs. Jean Mockry, Prin.
Sisters 2; Lay Teachers 19; Students 256.

Catechesis/Religious Programs—Tel: 518-563-3278. Sr. Ellen Donahue, S.A., D.R.E.
Students 309.

6—NEWMAN PARISH, JOHN XXIII COLLEGE COMMUNITY, (1970), Rev. J. Roger McGuinness; Sr. Bernadette Ducharme, S.C.S.L., Pastoral Assoc.; Mrs. Eileen Ward, Admin. Asst.
Res., 90 Broad St., 12901. Tel: 518-563-6852 (Res.); 561-7545 (Office); Fax: 518-561-1004.

Port Henry, Essex Co., St. Patrick (1854) (Irish), Rev. Michael A. Toth.
Res., 17 St. Patrick's Pl., 12974. Tel: 518-546-7254; Fax: 518-546-3439. [CEM]
Catechesis/Religious Programs—Tel: 518-546-3374.
Students 137.

Port Leyden, Lewis Co., St. Martin (1879), Rev. Msgr. Paul E. Whitmore; Sr. Gabriel Marie, S.S.J., Pastoral Assoc.
Res., P.O. Box 431, 13433. Tel: 315-348-6104; Fax: 315-348-6104. [CEM]
Catechesis/Religious Programs—Students 102.
Mission—Lyons Falls, Lewis Co., St. John.

Potsdam, St. Lawrence Co., St. Mary (1841), Revs. John P. Kennehan; Edward E. Papp; Deacons Frederick A. Brousseau; John A. Levison. In res., Rev. Euclid A. Marier.
Res., 17 Lawrence Ave., 13676. Tel: 315-265-9680; Fax: 315-268-1443. [CEM]
School—(Grades PreK-6). Tel: 315-265-3511; Fax: 315-265-5693.
Lay Teachers 7; Students 126.
Catechesis/Religious Programs—Tel: 315-265-6220.
Students 100.

St. Francis of Assisi Campus Parish (Newman Center) (1969), Rev. John M. Hunt.
Office: 41 Main St., 13676-2004. Tel: 315-265-9520; Fax: 315-268-1946.
Catechesis/Religious Programs—Students 51.

Raquette Lake, Hamilton Co., St. William, Rev. Lawrence Marullo, V.F.
Mailing Address: c/o P.O. Box 236, Old Forge, 13420. Tel: 315-369-3551.
Catechesis/Religious Programs—Students 3.

Raymondville, St. Lawrence Co., St. Raymond (1920), Rev. J. Everett Denesha.
Res., P.O. Box 178, 13678-0178. Tel: 315-384-3191. [CEM]
Catechesis/Religious Programs—Students 17.

Redford, Clinton Co., Assumption of the B.V.M. (1869), Rev. Philip T. Allen.
Res., 78 Clinton St., 12978. Tel: 518-293-6259. [CEM]
School—(Grades K-6). Tel: 518-293-6231. Mrs. Beth Newell, Prin.
Lay Teachers 6; Students 52.

Redwood, Jefferson Co., St. Francis Xavier (1848), Rev. Thomas F. Driscoll. In res., Rev. James L. Meehan, (Retired).
Mailing Address: P.O. Box 477, Alexandria Bay, 13607. Tel: 315-482-2670; Fax: 315-482-4970.
Res., P.O. Box 903, 13679. Tel: 315-482-6359. [CEM]
Catechesis/Religious Programs—Students 12.

Rosiere, Jefferson Co., St. Vincent de Paul (1871), Rev. E. John Silver. In res., Rev. Eugene A. Kelly, Pastor Emeritus.
Res., 31385 County Rte. 4, Cape Vincent, 13618. Tel: 315-654-2576; Fax: 315-654-4721. [CEM]

Rouses Point, Clinton Co., St. Patrick (1860), Rev. Wilfred L. DeRoche; Deacon Noel A. Hinerth.
Res., 138 Lake St., P.O. Box 217, 12979. Tel: 518-297-7361; Fax: 518-297-3181. [CEM][JC]
Catechesis/Religious Programs—Patricia Canning, D.R.E.
Students 111.

Sackets Harbor, Jefferson Co., St. Andrew (1886), Rev. Douglas G. Comstock.
Res., 110 E. Main St., Box 530, 13685. Tel: 315-646-3341; Fax: 315-646-3341.
Catechesis/Religious Programs—Students 116.
Mission—Henderson, Jefferson Co., Queen of Heaven, 13685.

Saint Regis Falls, Franklin Co., St. Ann (1883), Rev. John M. Demo.
Res., P.O. Box 288, 12980. Tel: 518-856-9456; Fax: 518-856-9456. [CEM]
Catechesis/Religious Programs—Students 59.
Oratory—Santa Clara, St. Peter.

Saranac Lake, Franklin Co., St. Bernard (1888), Revs. Timothy J. Soucy; Joseph P. Wheelock; Sr. Rita Mary Morrissette, O.S.M., Pastoral Assoc.; Deacons Frederick R. Oberst; Joseph Szwed.
Res., 19 St. Bernard St., 12983. Tel: 518-891-4616; Fax: 518-891-4619. [CEM][JC]
School—Tel: 518-891-2830. Rebecca P. Marlowe, Prin.
Lay Teachers 7; Students 150.
Catechesis/Religious Programs—Pius X Center, 32 River St., 12983. Tel: 518-891-3111. Mrs. Kathy Gonyea, D.R.E.
Students 230.

Schroon Lake, Essex Co., Our Lady of Lourdes (1883), Rev. Richard S. Sturtz.
Res., P.O. Box 368, 12870. Tel: 518-532-7100; Fax: 518-532-7461. [CEM]
Rectory: 1114 U.S. Rte. 9, 12870.
Catechesis/Religious Programs—Students 48.

Sciota, Clinton Co., St. Louis (1899) (French Canadian), Rev. Gilbert O. Boisvert.
Res., P.O. Box 113, Altona, 12910. Tel: 518-236-5848; Fax: 518-236-4249. [CEM]
Catechesis/Religious Programs—Students 118.

Star Lake, St. Lawrence Co., St. Hubert (1893), Rev. Eugene J. Beaudet; Deacon Philip F. Giardino.
Res., 1046 Oswegatchie Trail Rd., P.O. Box 9, 13690. Tel: 315-848-3612; Fax: 315-848-2510. [JC]
Catechesis/Religious Programs—Students 46.
Missions—Newton Falls, St. Lawrence Co., St. Anthony of Padua, P.O. Box 9, Star Lake, NY 13690 13666.; Fine, St. Lawrence Co., St. Michael, P.O. Box 9, Star Lake, NY 13690 13635-0008. [CEM]

Ticonderoga, Essex Co., St. Mary (1852), Rev. William G. Muench; Sr. Carol Daul, S.A., Pastoral Assoc.; Deacon Elliott A. Shaw.
Res., 12 Father Jogues Pl., 12883. Tel: 518-585-7144; Fax: 518-585-3632. [CEM]
School—(Grades K-8) 301 Amherst Ave., 12883. Tel: 518-585-7433; Fax: 518-585-3632. Sr. Sharon Anne Dalton, S.S.J., Prin.
Sisters 1; Lay Teachers 8; Students 193.
Catechesis/Religious Programs—Students 130.

Trout River, Franklin Co., St. Bridget (1865), Rev. Garry B. Giroux; Deacon Garry Burnell.
Res., 1197 State Rte. 122, P.O. Box 86, Constable, 12926. Tel: 518-483-2775 (Rectory); 483-0486 (Office); Fax: 518-483-1618. [CEM]

Tupper Lake, Franklin Co., Holy Name of Jesus (Faust) (1904), Rev. Christopher C. Carrara.
Res., 114 Main St., 12986. Tel: 518-359-9194; Fax: 518-359-9194. [CEM]
Catechesis/Religious Programs—Tel: 518-359-2551. Mrs. Claire Maroun, D.R.E.
Students 97.

St. Alphonsus (1890), Rev. Donald F. Kramberg; Sr. Barbara R. McCarthy, O.P., Pastoral Assoc.; Deacons James T. Ellis; Joseph H. Gilbert; Gerald H. Savage.
Res., 48 Wawbeek Ave., P.O. Box 1166, 12986. Tel: 518-359-3405; Fax: 518-359-2364. [CEM]
School—Holy Ghost Academy, (Grades PreK-6). Tel: 518-359-2203; Fax: 518-359-2203. Sr. Shirley Ann Brown, S.S.J., Prin.
Lay Teachers 7; Students 92.
Catechesis/Religious Programs—Tel: 518-359-2551.
Students 184.

Waddington, St. Lawrence Co., St. Mary (1826), Rev. Msgr. Robert L. Lawler, P.A., V.G.
Res., P.O. Box 187, 13694. Tel: 315-388-4466; Fax: 315-388-4722. [CEM 3]
Catechesis/Religious Programs—Msgr. Arquett Parish Center, Tel: 315-388-4423.
Students 80.

Watertown, Jefferson Co.,

1—HOLY FAMILY, (1895), Revs. Clyde A. Lewis; Theodore A. Crosby; Deacons Edward R. Miller; Douglas J. Marlow; Richard Gaebel; Michael J. Allan. In res., Rev. Mark R. Reilly.
Res., 129 Winthrop St., 13601. Tel: 315-782-2468; Fax: 315-782-4684.
School—(Grades N-8). Tel: 315-788-7011. Sr. Ellen Rose Coughlin, S.S.J., Prin.
Sisters of St. Joseph 3; Lay Teachers 17; Students 366.
Catechesis/Religious Programs—Holy Family Religious Education Office, Sterling Pl., 13601. Tel: 315-782-6750.
Students 236.

2—OUR LADY OF THE SACRED HEART, (1876), Rev. Andrew Torma, M.S.C.; Deacon David N. Henningan; Mrs. Joanne Lucidi, Business Mgr.
Parish Office: 664 Thompson St., 13601. Tel: 315-782-1474; Fax: 315-782-0473.
School—(1922) (Grades PreK-8) 320 W. Lynde St., Tel: 315-782-3060; Fax: 315-782-4939. Mrs. Jean Doell, Prin.
Sisters 2; Lay Teachers 14; Students 188.
Preschool and Day Care—Tel: 315-782-3060.
Catechesis/Religious Programs—Mrs. Patricia Cohen, D.R.E.
Students 98.

3—ST. ANTHONY, (1913) (Italian), Rev. Msgr. Anthony A. Milia, V.F.; Deacons Vincent J. Frattali; Richard C. Warner, Sr.
Res., 850 Arsenal St., 13601. Tel: 315-782-1190. [JC]
School—(Grades PreK-8). Tel: 315-788-1461; Fax: 315-779-1140. Mrs. Annette M. Connolly, Prin.
Lay Teachers 10; Students 165.
Catechesis/Religious Programs—Students 55.

4—ST. PATRICK, (1854), Rev. Arthur J. LaBaff; Deacon William G. Schmidt; Sr. Mary William Argy, S.S.J., Pastoral Assoc.
Res., 724 Ives St., 13601. Tel: 315-782-6086. [CEM]
School—(Grades K-8) 733 S. Massey St., 13601. Tel: 315-788-3935; Fax: 315-788-4447. Mrs. Gail Baker Graham, Prin.
Lay Teachers 10; Students 179.
Catechesis/Religious Programs—Mrs. Dorothy Neamand, D.R.E.
Students 117.

Wells, Hamilton Co., St. Ann (1890), Rev. Paul J. Kelly.
Mailing Address: P.O. Box 214, Speculator, 12164. Tel: 518-548-6275. [CEM]
Catechesis/Religious Programs—Students 13.

West Chazy, Clinton Co., St. Joseph (1884), Rev. Harry E. Giroux; Deacon Gerald Defayette.
Res., P.O. Box 224, 12992. Tel: 518-493-4521; Fax: 518-493-5880. [CEM]
Catechesis/Religious Programs—Students 183.

West Leyden, Lewis Co., St. Mary's Nativity (1900), Rev. Robert Cotter, Admin.
Res., P.O. Box 305, 13489. Tel: 315-942-2595. [CEM]
Catechesis/Religious Programs—Students 52.
Mission—Fish Creek, SS. Peter & Paul. [CEM]

Westport, Essex Co., St. Philip Neri (1879), Rev. Msgr. Peter R. Riani.
Res., P.O. Box 368, Elizabethtown, 12932. Tel: 518-873-6760; Fax: 518-873-6530. [CEM]
Catechesis/Religious Programs—Students 30.

Willsboro, Essex Co., St. Philip of Jesus (1909), Rev. James A. Delbel.
Res., P.O. Box 607, 12996. Tel: 518-963-4524; Fax: 518-963-7719. [CEM]
Catechesis/Religious Programs—Students 65.

Witherbee, Essex Co., St. Michael (1911). Closed. For inquiries for parish records contact the Chancery.

Chaplains of Public Institutions

Military and Medical

OGDENSBURG. *St. Lawrence Psychiatric Center* St. Vincent's Chapel, 13669. Tel: 315-393-3000, Ext. 3414; Fax: 315-393-4496. Sr. Kathryn Healey, G.N.S.H., Chap.; Rev. Jason T. Jones.

PLATTSBURGH. *Champlain Valley Physicians Hospital Medical Center* 75 Beekman St., 12901. Tel: 518-561-2000. Rev. William G. Reamer, Chap.

TUPPER LAKE, (SUNMOUNT). *Sunmount Developmental Center* 403 Park St., 12986. Tel: 518-359-3311; Fax: 518-359-4133. Deacon Joseph Szwed, Chap.

WATERTOWN. *Samaritan Medical Center* 830 Washington St., 13601. Tel: 315-785-4000. Jean Clark, Chap. and Coord.
U.S. Army Headquarters Fort Drum. Revs. James Bluett; David Dormer.

Prisons

OGDENSBURG. *Ogdensburg Correctional Facility* One Correction Way, 13669. Tel: 315-393-0281. Deacon Vincent E. Irvin, Jr.; Rev. Stephen R. Rocker.
Riverview Correctional Facility Box 158, 13669. Tel: 315-393-8400. Deacon D. Thomas Sharrow; Rev. Joseph A. Morgan.

ALTONA. *Altona Correctional Facility* P.O. Box 125, 12910. Tel: 518-236-7841; Fax: 518-236-6235. Rev. Joseph P. Trombley.

CAPE VINCENT. *Cape Vincent Correctional Facility* 13618. Tel: 315-654-4100, Ext. 548. Deacon Andrew Yarchuk; Rev. William Connor, M.S.C.

DANNEMORA. *Clinton Correctional Facility* P.O. Box 798, 12929-0798. Tel: 518-492-2511, Ext. 4800. Deacon Larry R. Debiec; Rev. Peter M. Berg Tel: 518-492-7118.

GABRIELS. *Gabriel's Correctional Facility* P.O. Box 100, 12939. Tel: 518-327-3111, Ext. 258. Rev. Francis J. Flynn, Chap.

GOUVERNEUR. *Gouverneur Correctional Facility* Scotch Settlement Rd., P.O. Box 370, 13642. Tel: 315-287-7351; Fax: 315-287-2533. Deacon Thomas F. Kilian; Rev. Daniel L. Chapin.

LYON MOUNTAIN. *Lyon Mountain Correctional Facility* P.O. Box 23, 12952. Tel: 518-735-4540. Rev. Bernard E. Christman.

MALONE. *Barehill Correctional Facility* Cady Rd., 12953. Tel: 518-483-8411, Ext. 409. Deacons James J. Hotte; Mark A. LaLonde; Rev. John M. Demo.
Franklin Correctional Facility P.O. Box 10, 12953-9720. Tel: 518-483-6040, Ext. 2402. Deacon Mark A. LaLonde; Rev. Bill Edwards.

Upstate Correctional Facility P.O. Box 2000, 12953. Tel: 518-483-6997. Deacon Richard D. Hart; Rev. Msgr. Dennis J. Duprey Tel: 518-483-6997.

MORIAH. *Moriah Shock Incarceration Correctional Facility*. Fisher Hill Rd., P.O. Box 999, Mineville, 12956-0999. Tel: 518-942-7561. Rev. James A. Delbel; Deacon Elliott Shaw.

RAY BROOK. *Adirondack Correctional Facility* Box 110, 12977-0110. Tel: 518-891-1343. Rev. Robert O. Lamitie, Res., Star Rte., Box 152, Saranac Lake, 12983. Tel: 518-891-6540, 891-1343.

Federal Correctional Institution P.O. Box 300, 12977. Tel: 518-891-5400.

WATERTOWN. *Watertown Correctional Facility* 13601. Tel: 315-782-7490, Ext. 445. Rev. William Connor, M.S.C., Chap., Res., Missionaries of the Sacred Heart, 668 Thompson St., 13601. Tel: 315-782-3480.

On Duty Outside the Diocese:
Reverend Fathers—
Decker, Robert L., San Martin de Porras, Casilla 105, Mollendo, Peru, S.A.
Ledermann, Paul F., Veterans Home, P.O. Box 7, Yountville, CA 94599
Leehy, Stephen G., 41701 Cambridge Ave., Bermuda Dunes, CA 92201
Mundy, Patrick W., San Martin de Porras, Casilla 105, Mollendo, Peru S.A.
Sestito, Joseph N., 114 Stanwood Ln., Manlius, NY 13104
Wertman, Raymond, 2292 Costa Rican Dr., Brahmin #56, Clearwater, FL 34623

Graduate Studies:
Reverend Fathers—
Fusco, Christopher J.
Giroux, Joseph W.
Seymour, James W.

Military Chaplains:
Reverend Fathers—
Mulvaney, Andrew R., LTC., Chap. U.S. Army, Box 6095, Fort Bliss, TX 79906
Ratigan, Patrick A., Maj., Chap. U.S. Army, 245 A Jasmine Pl., Honolulu, HI 96818
Sykes, Gregory, Chap. U.S. Army, 222 BSB, CMR 405, Box 1394, APO AE, 09034

Absent on Leave:
Reverend Fathers—
Andrews, Lawrence W.
Gonyo, Roland G.
Larche, James M.
Schudde, Derk M.

Absent on Sick Leave:
Reverend Fathers—
Helfrich, Peter G., P.O. Box 154, Saranac Lake, NY 12983
Lamore, Victor E., P.O. Box 369, Ogdensburg, NY 13669
Menard, Roland V., P.O. Box 369, Ogdensburg, NY 13669
O'Doherty, Liam, P.O. Box 369, Ogdensburg, NY 13669
Votraw, Thomas G., P.O. Box 369, Ogdensburg, NY 13669

Retired:
Reverend Monsignors—
Argy, William J., St. Mary's Cathedral Rectory, Ogdensburg, NY 13669. Tel: 315-393-3930
Aubin, Joseph G., 55, St. Peter's Rectory, 114A Cornelia St, Plattsburgh, NY 12901
Devan, Clarence M., St. Mary's Rectory, P.O. Box 609, Massena, NY 13662
Dwyer, Morris L., St. Peter's Rectory, 114 Cornelia St., Plattsburgh, NY 12901
Gefell, Gerard J., 2332 Humphrey Rd., Cape Vincent, NY 13618. Tel: 315-654-3504
Gefell, Joseph G., 2332 Humphrey Rd., Cape Vincent, NY 13618. Tel: 315-654-3504
Hannan, Herbert J., St. Joseph's Home, 420 Lafayette St., Ogdensburg, NY 13669
McCarthy, Robert J., 324 Pratt St., Watertown, NY 13601
Phillips, George M., Notre Dame Rectory, P.O. Box 149, Ogdensburg, NY 13669
Robillard, Thomas J., 11 Hepburn St., Norfolk, NY 13667
White, Francis A., St. Francis Neri Church, 66 Pleasant St., Box M, Westport, NY 12993

Reverend Fathers—
Beyette, Paul V., HC Box 218, Loon Lake, N.Y. 12989
Branche, John S., Two Fordham Hill Oval, #10C, Bronx, NY 10468
Callaghan, Patrick C., O.F.M., Spruce St., St. Regis Falls, NY 12980. Tel: 518-856-9729
Chase, Charles E., P.O. Box 2434, Duxbury, MA 02331
Cosmic, John J., 39 Anderson Ave., P.O. Box 117, Deferiet, NY 13628
Cotter, Charles B., Genesis Healthcare Center, 218 Stone St., Watertown, NY 13601
Cotter, Lawrence E., P.O. Box 606, Ogdensburg, NY 13669
Cotter, Robert L., St. Mary Rectory, P.O. Box 26, Glenfield, NY 13343
Crable, John M., 4 Edgewater Estates, Plattsburgh, NY 12901
Fallon, John J., Piux X Hall, 714 E. Brighton Ave., Syracuse, NY 13205
Franklin, Edward L., 12220 5th St., S.P. 105, Yucaipa, CA 92399
Igo, James P., 10 Daniel St., Arlington, MA 02174
Jarecki, Michael S., R.R. 1, Box 258, Constable, NY 12926
Jollet, Robert, M.S.C., Wadhams Hall Seminary, 6866 State Hwy. 37, Ogdensburg, NY 13669
Kelly, Eugene A., Regina Nursing Center, 230 North 65th St., Philadelphia, PA 19139
Ladden, Timothy M., 664 Thompson St., Watertown, NY 13601
LaLonde, Emile G., Cambry Court, 68 W. Main St., Apt. 2A4, Gouverneur, NY 13642
Lamitie, James F., 510 Lake Shore Dr., Apt. 27, Lake Park, FL 33403
Lyddy, Daniel F., 31 Sydney St., Lowell, MA 01852. Tel: 508-459-9448
Marier, Euclid A., St. Mary's Church, 17 Lawrence Ave., Potsdam, NY 13676
Martin, Roger, 54 W. Main St., P.O. Box 25, Baltic, CT 06330
McCasland, Howard, Immaculate Heart of Mary, Rt. 189-560, Churubusco, NY 12923
Meehan, James L., St. Francis Xavier, P.O. Box 185, Redwood, NY 13679
Menard, Francis A., 3860 State Rte. 11, Malone, NY 12953
Menard, Gilbert B., 2 Garrett Way, Schuyler Falls, NY 12985
Nichols, Earl W., 32 Church St., Apt. 15, Brasher Falls, NY 13613
Njeim, Elias, Colonial Manor, Apt. A9, Watertown, NY 13601
Patterson, Terrence R., Box 288, Potsdam, NY 13676. Tel: 315-265-2986
Poupore, Norman E., P.O. Box 824, Pierrepont Manor, NY 13674
Rapin, Cyril W., St. Joseph's Church, P.O. Box 226, Mooers, NY 12958-0288
Richard, Charles J., P.O. Box 389, Morristown, NY 13664
Rys, Paschal, O.F.M.Conv., St. Mary Church, Box 382, Constableville, NY 13325
Snow, J. Lee, P.O. Box 2864, Plattsburgh, NY 12901

Permanent Deacons:
Allen, Michael J., Holy Family, Watertown
Brousseau, Frederick A., St. Mary, Potsdam
Burnell, Garry N., St. Francis of Assisi, Constable
Debiec, Larry, St. Edmund, Ellenburg; Clinton Correctional Facility, Dannemora
Defayette, Gerald R., St. Joseph, West Chazy
Demers, Victor, Notre Dame, Ogdensburg
Diehl, Robert, St. Peter, Plattsburgh
Dwyer, John C., St. Augustine, North Bangor
Ellis, James T., St. Alphonsus, Tupper Lake
Frank, Gary A., St. Mary, Clayton
Frattali, Vincent J., St. Anthony, Watertown
Gaebel, Richard M., Holy Family, Watertown
Giardino, Philip F., St. Hubert, Star Lake
Gilbert, Joseph H., Holy Name, Ausable Forks
Gillen, James J., St. Francis Minor, Carthage
Gilner, Gerard, St. Mary, Indian Lake
Hart, Richard D., St. Joseph and Upstate Correctional Facility, Malone
Hennigan, David N., Our Lady of the Sacred Heart, Watertown
Hinerth, Noel A., St. Patrick, Rouses Point
Hotte, James J., Sacred Heart, Massena; Bare Hill and Franklin Correctional Facilities, Malone
Hunneyman, Norman L.
Irvin, Vincent E., Jr., Ogdensburg Correctional Facility, Ogdensburg
Keough, James R., St. Alphonsus, Tupper Lake
Kilian, Thomas F., Gouverneur Correctional Facility, Gouverneur; Notre Dame, Ogdensburg
King, Robert A., St. Peter, Plattsburgh
LaLonde, Mark A., Notre Dame, Ogdensburg; Barehill Correctional Facility and Franklin Correctional Facility, Malone
Lawless, Peter J., Sacred Heart, Edwards
LeClair, Robert J., Sacred Heart, Chazy
Levison, John A., St. Mary's, Potsdam
Looby, Phillip M., St. Francis, Solanus, Harrisville
Lyons, Patrick A.
Mader, Frederick J., St. Paul, Bloomingdale
Marlow, Douglas, Holy Family, Watertown
Mazuchowski, Edward, St. Joseph, Dannemora
Merrill, Reginald F., St. Bernard, Lyon Mountain
Miller, Edward R., Holy Family, Watertown
Moltz, David, St. Elizabeth Seton, Dexter
Oberst, Frederick R., St. Bernard, Saranac Lake
Patrie, Leonard L., St. Mary, Champlain
Pominville, Ronald J., St. Peter, Lowville
Rabideau, Tyrone, St. Ann, Mooers Forks
Raven, William S., St. Paul, Black River; Jefferson Community College, Watertown
Ruddy, Robert V., St. Theresa of Avila, Theresa
Ryan, John J., Holy Name, Ausable Forks
Savage, Gerald H., St. Alphonsus, Tupper Lake
Schmidt, William G., St. Patrick, Watertown
Seymour, Kenneth A., St. Paul, Black River
Sharrow, Thomas, St. Mary's Cathedral, Ogdensburg; Riverview Correctional Facility, Ogdensburg
Shaw, Elliott A., St. Mary's, Ticonderoga; Moriah Shock Incarceration Facility, Mineville
Siskavich, Francis, St. Bernard, Lyon Mountain
Staab, Richard J., St. James, Carthage
Ste.-Marie, Ronald, St. Anthony, Inlet
Szwed, Joseph, St. Bernard, Saranac Lake; Sunmount Developmental Center, Tupper Lake
Taylor, William M.
Trombly, John J., Bare Hill Correctional Facility, Malone
Warner, Richard C., Sr., St. Anthony, Watertown
Wight, Ed
Winter, Richard E., St. Mary's Cathedral, Ogdensburg
Yarchuk, Andrew, All Saints, Chaumont; Cape Vincent Correctional Facility, Cape Vincent

INSTITUTIONS LOCATED IN THE DIOCESE

[A] SEMINARIES, DIOCESAN

OGDENSBURG. *Wadhams Hall*, 6866 State Hwy. 37, 13669-4420. Tel: 315-393-4231; 393-3596 (Student); Fax: 315-393-4249.
E-mail: whsc@gisco.net
Web site: www.wadhams.edu
Open to candidates for the Diocesan and religious priesthood (and Christian Leadership Program). Four-year College and two-year Pre-Theology Program. Rev. Msgr. Robert H. Aucoin, S.T.L., M.Ed., Rector-Pres., Chm. & Asst. Prof. Languages; Rev. Msgr. Leeward J. Poissant, Ph.D., Prof. Philosophy; Revs. Albert J. Hauser, S.T.L., M.A., Asst. Prof. Latin, Religious Studies; George F. Maroun, B.A., M.A., Dir. Spiritual Formation, Asst. Prof. Religious Studies & Spanish, Dir. Social J; Edward J. Sheedy, M.A., M.S., Asst. Prof. Religious Studies; Stephen R. Rocker, Ph.D., Chm. & Prof. Philosophy, Dean of Students; Bro. Guy Roddy, F.I.C., B.A., M.A., M.S., D.Min., Chm. of Religious Studies, Dir. Special Prog., Assoc. Prof. of Social Sciences; Rev. Robert Jollet, M.S.C., M.S.L.S., Dir Library; Sr. Mary Christine Taylor, Ph.D., Academic Dean & Prof. Social Sciences; Mr. Daniel Victoor, B.M., Chair Fine Arts, Asst. Professor Music, Dir. Liturgical Music; Mrs. Diana C. Krisciunas, M.A., Chair. & Asst. Prof. English; Rev. Timothy G. Canaan, M.A., M.Div., Dir. Admissions; Rebecca Glover, Ph.D., Professor of Science; Sr. Constance Sylver, M.M.Ed., Instructor, Developmental Studies; Mr. Jeffrey Ward, A.A.S., Dir. Finance. Priests 8; Brothers 1; Sisters 2; Lay Teachers 3; Total Staff 16. Students 20.

[B] HIGH SCHOOLS, INTERPAROCHIAL

PLATTSBURGH. *Seton Catholic Central*, 5135 N. Catherine St., 12901. Tel: 518-561-4031; Fax: 518-563-1193. Sr. M. Cordata Kelly, S.S.J., Prin.; Rev. Joseph A. Conti, Chap. Priests 1; Sisters 3; Brothers 2; Lay Teachers 20; Students 287.

WATERTOWN. *Immaculate Heart Central High School*, 1316 Ives St., 13601. Tel: 315-788-4670; 788-8982 (Guidance); Fax: 315-788-4672.
E-mail: ihc@gisco.net
Web site: www.gisco.net/ihc
Mr. Pat A. Fontana, Prin.; Rev. Mark R. Reilly,

Spiritual Dir. Priests 1; Sisters 4; Lay Teachers 16; Students 282.

[C] RELIGIOUS EDUCATION

OGDENSBURG. *Bishop Conroy School of Religion*, 214 Morris St., 13669-1714. Tel: 315-393-1820; Fax: 315-393-1670.
E-mail: bcsr@gisco.net
Priests 3; Lay Teachers 34; Total Staff 39.

SARANAC LAKE. *Pius X Center*, 32 River St., 12983. Tel: 518-891-3111; Fax: 518-891-4619. Total Staff 42; Students 400.

WATERTOWN. *Watertown Catechetical Office*, Sterling Pl., 13601. Tel: 315-782-0030. Special Religious Education. Sr. Mary Maurice Black, S.S.J., Coord. Sisters 1; Students 220.

[D] SPECIAL HOSPITALS AND HOMES FOR INVALIDS AND AGED

OGDENSBURG. *St. Joseph's Home*, 420 Lafayette St., 13669. Tel: 315-393-3780; Fax: 315-393-3847.
E-mail: stjh@gisco.net
Web site: www.stjh.org
For a complete listing, refer to the Special Care Facilities section.

LAKE PLACID. *St. Margaret Convent*, 420 Old Military Rd., 12946. Tel: 518-523-2929; Fax: 518-523-1401
For a complete listing, refer to the Special Care Facilities section.
Uihlein Mercy Center, 420 Old Military Rd., 12946. Tel: 518-523-2464; Fax: 518-523-1401.
Web site: muhc.org
For a complete listing, refer to the Special Care Facilities section.

SARANAC LAKE. *St. Joseph's Rehabilitation Center, Inc.*, 99 Glenwood Estates, P.O. Box 470, 12983. Tel: 518-891-3950; 891-4135 (Admissions); Fax: 518-891-3986.
E-mail: stjoes@northnet.org
For a complete listing, refer to the Special Care Facilities section.

TUPPER LAKE. *Mercy Healthcare Center, Inc.*, 114 Wawbeek Ave., 12986. Tel: 518-359-3355; Fax: 518-359-9044.
E-mail: jpeters@muhc.org
Web site: muhc.org
For a complete listing, refer to the Special Care Facilities section.

[E] MONASTERIES AND RESIDENCES OF PRIESTS AND BROTHERS

SARANAC LAKE. *Atonement Friars*, 69 Franklin Ave., 12983. Tel: 518-891-2395.
E-mail: dancallahan@adelphia.net
Web site: graymoor.org
Revs. Daniel P. Callahan, S.A.; Carmen Guiliano, S.A. Total in Residence 2.
St. Joseph's Friary, P.O. Box 470, 12983. Tel: 518-891-3494. Bros. Alan Lemay, S.A.; Paschal Steen, T.S.A. Total in Residence 2.

WATERTOWN. *Missionaries of the Sacred Heart*, 668 Thompson St., 13601. Tel: 315-782-3480; Fax: 315-782-0473.
E-mail: shfound@gisco.net
Revs. Bernard Jakubco, M.S.C., Supr.; Benoit Dostie, M.S.C.; William Connor, M.S.C.; Robert Jollett, M.S.C.; Richard Huber, M.S.C.; Pierre Aubin, M.S.C.; Andrew Torma, M.S.C.; Bros. Peter Marceau, M.S.C.; Jean-Paul Paradis, M.S.C.

[F] CONVENTS AND RESIDENCES FOR SISTERS

OGDENSBURG. *St. Joseph's Convent, Grey Nuns of the Sacred Heart*, 709 Franklin St., 13669. Tel: 315-393-1763. Sr. Joan McElwain, G.N.S.H., Supr.
Sisters of St. Joseph, 5428 State Hwy. 37, 13669. Tel: 315-393-5965.

CARTHAGE. *St. James Convent, Sisters of St. Joseph*, 317 West St., 13619. Tel: 315-493-1672. Sr. Victorine Brenon, S.S.J., Supr. Total Staff 2; Total in Residence 2.

CHAMPLAIN. *St. Mary's Convent*, 1060 Main St., 12919. Tel: 518-298-3141.

CLAYTON. *Sisters of Holy Cross*, 415 John St, #1, 13624. Tel: 315-686-3640. Sr. Margaret Fleming, C.S.C. Sisters 2.

ELLENBURG CENTER. *Our Lady of the Adirondack's Inc. House of Prayer*, 7270 Star Rd., Rte. 190, 12934-2501. Tel: 518-594-3253; Fax: 518-594-7143. Franciscan Sisters of the Atonement. Sr. Jean T. Beyette, S.A., Dir. Our Lady of the Adirondacks Community. Rita S. Parrott, O.L.A.; Theresa M. Lindsey, O.L.A.; Rev. Joseph P. Trombley, Spiritual Dir.
Our Lady of the Adirondacks Prayer Association. Members 151.

GOUVERNEUR. *St. James' Convent, Sisters of St. Joseph*, 28 S. Gordon St., 13642. Tel: 315-287-0658. Sr. Jane Frances Cutting, S.S.J., Co-Supr.; Sr. Ronald Marie Hax, S.S.J., Co-Supr. Total Staff 2; Total in Residence 2.

MALONE. *Daughters of Charity*, 27 Webster St., 12953. Tel: 518-483-1203; Fax: 518-483-2595.
E-mail: naseau@northnet.org
Sr. Helen Kelley, D.C., Pastoral Assoc.-St. John Bosco; Sr. Jeraldine Fritz, D.C., Prin.-Holy Family.
St. Helen's, Sisters of St. Joseph, 753 Country Rte. 41, 12953. Tel: 518-483-1515; Fax: 518-483-1515.
St. Joseph's Ursuline Convent, Ursuline Nuns, 90 Elm St., 12953. Tel: 518-483-2880; Fax: 518-483-7091.
E-mail: ursulmal@slic.com
Sr. Ann Peterson, O.S.U., Supr. Sisters 9.
Ursuline Community, Ursuline Nuns, 104 Park St., 12953. Tel: 518-483-5356.
E-mail: mtwosu@slic.com
Sr. Maureen Welch, O.S.U., Coord.

MASSENA. *Sacred Heart Convent*, 188 Main St., P.O. Box 91, 13662. Tel: 315-769-6238. Total in Residence 3.
St. Joseph's Convent, Sisters of St. Joseph, 36 Alden St., 13662. Tel: 315-764-0379. Sr. Bernadette Marie Collins, S.S.J.; Sr. Mary Christine Taylor, S.S.J.; Sr. Maureen Sweeney, S.S.J. Total in Residence 3.

PERU. *St. Augustine's Convent*, 3012 N. Main St., Box 567, 12972. Tel: 518-643-6768.
E-mail: augustin@slic.com
Sisters of St. Joseph (S.S.J.), Dominican Sisters (O.P.). Total in Residence 3.

PLATTSBURGH. *Regina Maria Retreat House, Daughters of the Heart of Mary*, 77 Brinkerhoff St., 12901. Tel: 518-561-3421; Fax: 518-561-3816.
E-mail: reginamh@slic.com
Mary Curran, D.H.M.
St. John's Convent, 62-64 Court St., 12901. Tel: 518-561-9689; Fax: 518-563-4553.
E-mail: sisterb@northnet.com
Sisters of Mercy 5.
St. Peter's Convent, Dominican Sisters of Hope, 5240 N. Catherine, 12901. Tel: 518-563-4451.
E-mail: dshope2@juno.com
Sr. Mary Stephanie Frenette, O.P., Contact Person. Total in Residence 2.
Sisters of Charity of St. Louis, 4907 S. Catherine St., 12901. Tel: 518-563-7410; Fax: 518-563-0383.

SARANAC LAKE. *St. Bernard's Convent, Servants of Mary-Omaha*, 30 River St., 12983. Tel: 518-891-4363. Sr. Rita Mary Morrissette, O.S.M.
Sisters of Mercy of the Americas, Trudeau Rd., Rte. 1, Box 351, 12983. Tel: 518-891-3234. Sr. Carolyn Madden, R.S.M.

TICONDEROGA. *St. Mary's Convent, Sisters of St. Joseph*, 307 Lake George Ave., 12883. Tel: 518-585-6547; Fax: 518-585-7505.
E-mail: tistmary@capital.net
Sr. Sharon Anne Dalton, S.S.J. Total Staff 1; Total in Residence 1.

TUPPER LAKE. *Dominican Sisters of Hope, Ossining*, 37 Lake St., Apt. 2, 12986. Tel: 518-359-9632. Sr. Barbara McCarthy, O.P. Total in Residence 1.
Holy Spirit Convent, 48 High St., 12986. Tel: 518-359-3838. Daughters of the Holy Spirit 2.

WATERTOWN. *Precious Blood Monastery, Sister Adorers of the Precious Blood*, 400 Pratt St., 13601. Tel: 315-788-1669; Fax: 315-779-9046.
E-mail: swashb2252@aol.com
Web site: www.catholic.org/mace/sistersadorers.html
Sr. Martha Emery, A.P.B., Supr. Total Staff 7; Total in Residence 7.
Sisters of St. Joseph Motherhouse, 1425 Washington St., 13601-4533. Tel: 315-782-3460; Fax: 315-788-6574.
E-mail: ogdssjwa@impresso.com
Sr. Yvonne Therese Cusson, S.S.J., Supr.; Sr. Annunciata, S.S.J., Major Supr. Total Staff 15; Total in Residence 41.

[G] RETREAT HOUSES

PLATTSBURGH. *Regina Maria Retreat House*, 77 Brinkerhoff St., 12901. Tel: 518-561-3421; Fax: 518-561-3816.
E-mail: reginamh@slic.com
Mary A.E. Curran, D.H.M. Daughters of the Heart of Mary 4.

[H] INCORPORATED CEMETERIES

BRASHER FALLS. *St. Patrick's Cemetery Association of Brasher Falls, N.Y.*, Box 208, 13613. Tel: 315-389-5401; Fax: 315-389-4066.

CARTHAGE. *St. James Cemetery Corporation*, 327 West St., 13619. Tel: 315-493-3224; Fax: 518-493-3280.
E-mail: sjcarth@northnet.org

CROGHAN. *St. Stephen's Cemetery Association, Inc.*, Main St., Box 38, 13327. Tel: 315-346-6958; Fax: 315-346-1200.
E-mail: llwiley@gisco.net

MALONE. *Notre Dame Cemetery of Malone, N.Y., Inc.*, 11 Church Pl., P.O. Box 547, 12953. Tel: 518-483-4074; Fax: 518-483-4185.
E-mail: notrdame@slic.com
St. Joseph's Cemetery of Malone, N.Y., Inc., 132 W. Main St., 12953. Tel: 518-483-1300; Fax: 518-483-1307.
E-mail: stjoseph@northnet.org

PLATTSBURGH. *Mount Carmel Cemetery*, St. John the Baptist Church, 7 Margaret St., 12901. Tel: 518-563-0730; Fax: 518-563-0754.
E-mail: stjohnba@together.net

WATERTOWN. *Calvary Cemetery Association of Watertown, N.Y.*, Sacred Heart Church, 664 Thompson, 13601. Tel: 315-782-1474; Fax: 315-782-0473.
E-mail: sacredhrt@gisco.net
Web site: www.olshparish.org

[I] MISCELLANEOUS LISTINGS

OGDENSBURG. *St. Joseph's Foundation, Inc.*, 420 Lafayette St., 13669. Tel: 315-394-0463; Fax: 315-393-3847.

CHAUMONT. *Mission Project Service*, P.O. Box 100, 13622. Tel: 315-649-3716; Fax: 315-649-5665.
E-mail: misprojser@aol.com
Web site: www.missionprojectservice.org
Beverly Hennigan, Exec. Dir.; Rev. Pierre Aubin, M.S.C., Dir.

HOGANSBURG. *St. Regis Mission* (Akwesasne), Box 429, 13655. Tel: 613-575-2066. Reservation and parish on both sides of U.S.-Canadian border. Rev. George H. Belgarde, S.J., Pastor. Priests 1; Brothers 1.
Roman Catholic Community Center, Inc. (Kateri Tekakwitha Center). Mrs. Lucille Peters, Rel. Educ. Coord. Tel: 518-358-2931.

PLATTSBURGH. *Christ Child Day Nursery*, 5115 N. Catherine, 12901. Tel: 518-561-6451. Mrs. Nancy Fournier, Dir. Total Staff 5; Total Assisted 26.

SARANAC LAKE. *Guggenheim Center for Religious Programs*, P.O. Box 664, 12983. Tel: 518-891-0809 (Lodge); 891-3323 (Dorm). Mr. Ralph Bennett, Dir., Res., 15 Leona St., 12983. Tel: 518-891-2844.

WATERTOWN. *Sacred Heart Foundation*, 668 Thompson St., 13601. Tel: 315-782-3480; Fax: 315-782-0473.
E-mail: shfound@gisco.net
Web site: www.sacredheartfoundation.com
Rev. Pierre Aubin, M.S.C., Dir.

RELIGIOUS INSTITUTES OF MEN REPRESENTED IN THE DIOCESE

For further details refer to the corresponding bracketed number in the Religious Institutes of Men or Women section.

[0320]—*Brothers of Christian Instruction.* (Alfred, ME).—F.I.C.
[0360]—*Claretian Missionaries.*—C.M.F.
[0480]—*Conventual Franciscans.*—O.F.M.Conv.
[0530]—*Franciscan Friars of the Atonement.*—S.A.
[0690]—*Jesuit Fathers and Brothers.* (French Canadian Prov. of Montreal).—S.J.
[1110]—*Missionaries of the Sacred Heart.*—M.S.C.

RELIGIOUS INSTITUTES OF WOMEN REPRESENTED IN THE DIOCESE

[0760]—*Daughters of Charity of St. Vincent de Paul.*—D.C.
[0750]—*Daughters of the Charity of the Sacred Heart of Jesus.*—F.C.S.C.J.
[0810]—*Daughters of the Heart of Mary.*—D.H.M.
[0820]—*Daughters of the Holy Spirit.*—D.H.S.
[1070-03]—*Dominican Sisters.*—O.P.
[1070-22]—*Dominican Sisters.*—O.P.
[1105]—*Dominican Sisters of Hope.*—O.P.
[1190]—*Franciscan Sisters of the Atonement.*—S.A.
[1840]—*Grey Nuns of the Sacred Heart.*—G.N.S.H.
[2575]—*Institute of the Sisters of Mercy of the Americas.* (Burlington, VT; Providence, RI; New York, NY).—R.S.M.
[3580]—*Servants of Mary.* (Servite Sisters).—O.S.M.
[3360]—*Sister of Providence.*—S.P.
[0110]—*Sisters Adorers of the Precious Blood.*—A.P.B.
[0620]—*Sisters of Charity of St. Louis.*—S.C.S.L.
[1930]—*Sisters of Holy Cross.*—C.S.C.
[1800]—*Sisters of St. Francis of the Third Order Regular.*—O.S.F.
[3840]—*Sisters of St. Joseph of Carondelet.*—C.S.J.
[3830-12]—*Sisters of St. Joseph of Watertown.*—S.S.J.
[4110]—*Ursuline Nuns.*—O.S.U.

NECROLOGY

† Bailey, Rev. Msgr. Joseph G., (Retired). —Died April 17, 2000.
† Coffey, William H., (Retired). —Died Sept. 8, 2000.
† Dumas, Rev. Msgr. Edmund H., (Retired). —Died Aug. 7, 2000.
† Gardner, Louis C., (Retired). —Died Sept. 5, 2000.
† Giroux, Rev. Msgr. Robert J., (Retired). —Died Sept. 4, 2000.
† O'Neil, Maurice L., (On Duty Outside of the Diocese). —Died Nov. 27, 1999.
† Plante, Albert R., (Retired). —Died Aug. 31, 2000.

Archdiocese of Oklahoma City

(Archidioecesis Oklahomapolitana)

Most Reverend

EUSEBIUS J. BELTRAN, D.D.

Archbishop of Oklahoma City; ordained May 14, 1960; appointed Bishop of Tulsa February 28, 1978; installed April 20, 1978; appointed Archbishop of Oklahoma City November 24, 1992; installed January 22, 1993. *Res., P.O. Box 32180, Oklahoma City, OK, 73123.*

Catholic Pastoral Center: 7501 Northwest Expy., P.O. Box 32180, Oklahoma City, OK, 73123. Tel.: 405-721-5651; Fax: 405-721-5210.

Most Reverend

CHARLES A. SALATKA, D.D.

Retired Archbishop of Oklahoma City; ordained February 24, 1945; appointed Titular Bishop of Cariana and Auxiliary of Grand Rapids December 9, 1961; consecrated March 6, 1962; appointed Bishop of Marquette January 10, 1968; installed March 25, 1968; appointed Archbishop of Oklahoma City September 27, 1977; installed December 15, 1977; retired November 24, 1992. *Res., P.O. Box 32180, Oklahoma City, OK, 73123.*

ESTABLISHED FEBRUARY 6, 1973.

ERECTED INTO A VICARIATE APOSTOLIC BY BRIEF OF MAY 29, 1891. ERECTED INTO THE DIOCESE OF OKLAHOMA WITH THE SEE IN OKLAHOMA CITY BY A BRIEF OF POPE PIUS X, AUGUST 17, 1905. NAME CHANGED TO DIOCESE OF OKLAHOMA CITY AND TULSA BY BULL OF POPE PIUS XI, NOVEMBER 14, 1930. ERECTED INTO ARCHDIOCESE OF OKLAHOMA CITY BY A BULL OF POPE PAUL VI, DECEMBER 13, 1972. THE PROVINCE INCLUDES THE DIOCESES OF TULSA AND LITTLE ROCK.

Comprises the following 46 Counties: Alfalfa, Beaver, Beckham, Blaine, Caddo, Canadian, Carter, Cimarron, Cleveland, Comanche, Cotton, Custer, Dewey, Ellis, Garfield, Garvin, Grady, Grant, Greer, Harmon, Harper, Jackson, Jefferson, Johnston, Kay, Kingfisher, Kiowa, Lincoln, Logan, Love, McClain, Major, Marshall, Murray, Noble, Oklahoma, Pontotoc, Pottawatomie, Roger Mills, Seminole, Stephens, Texas, Tillman, Washita, Woods and Woodward.

Square Miles 42,470.

For legal titles of parishes and archdiocesan institutions, consult the Pastoral Office.

STATISTICAL OVERVIEW

Personnel	
Archbishop	1
Retired Archbishops	1
Abbots	1
Retired Abbots	3
Priests: Diocesan Active in Diocese	76
Priests: Active Outside Diocese	2
Priests: Diocesan in Foreign Missions	1
Priests: Retired, Sick or Absent	17
Number of Diocesan Priests	96
Religious Priests in Diocese	25
Extern Priests in Diocese	10
Ordinations:	
Diocesan Priests	2
Transitional Deacons	1
Permanent Deacons	3
Permanent Deacons in Diocese	61
Total Brothers	13
Total Sisters	154
Parishes	
Parishes	71
With Resident Pastor:	
Resident Diocesan Priests	65
Resident Religious Priests	6
Missions	43
Pastoral Centers	1
New Parishes Created	2
Closed Parishes	1
Professional Ministry Personnel:	
Brothers	2
Sisters	32
Lay Ministers	67
Welfare	
Catholic Hospitals	5
Total Assisted	641,916
Homes for the Aged	5
Total Assisted	571
Day Care and Extended Day Care Centers	2
Total Assisted	332
Special Centers for Social Services	1
Total Assisted	700
Residential Care of Disabled	1
Total Assisted	25
Educational	
Diocesan Students in Other Seminaries	12
Total Seminarians	12
Colleges and Universities	1
Total Students	755
High Schools, Diocesan and Parish	2
Total Students	942
Elementary Schools, Diocesan and Parish	17
Total Students	3,557
Elementary Schools, Private	2
Total Students	292
Catechesis/Religious Education:	
High School Students	3,037
Elementary Students	8,893
Total Students Under Catholic Instruction	17,488
Teachers in the Diocese:	
Sisters	7
Lay Teachers	252
Vital Statistics	
Receptions into the Church:	
Infant Baptism Totals	2,111
Adult Baptism Totals	349
Received into Full Communion	469
First Communions	2,102
Confirmations	1,555
Marriages:	
Catholic	366
Interfaith	311
Total Marriages	677
Deaths	868
Total Catholic Population	98,225
Total Population	2,224,000

Former Bishops—Rt. Rev. THEOPHILE MEERSCHAERT, D.D., ord. Dec. 23, 1871; appt. first Vicar-Apostolic of Indian Territory and Titular Bishop of Sidyma by Bulls of June 2, 1891; cons. in Natchez, Sept. 8, 1891; appt. first Bishop of Oklahoma, Aug. 23, 1905 made assistant at the pontifical throne, Nov. 30, 1916; died Feb. 21, 1924.—Most Rev. FRANCIS C. KELLEY, D.D., LL.D., Ph.D., Litt.D., Bishop of Oklahoma City & Tulsa; ord. Aug. 24, 1893; appt. Bishop of Oklahoma, June 25, 1924; cons. Holy Name Cathedral, Chicago, IL, Oct. 2, 1924; died Feb. 1, 1948.—Most Rev. EUGENE J. MCGUINNESS, D.D., Bishop of Oklahoma City & Tulsa; ord. May 22, 1915; cons. Bishop of Raleigh, Dec. 21, 1937; appt. Coadjutor, Oklahoma City and Tulsa *"cum jure successionis,"* Nov. 11, 1944; installed Jan. 10, 1945; succeeded to the See, Feb. 1, 1948; died Dec. 27, 1957.—Most Rev. VICTOR J. REED, D.D., Bishop of Oklahoma City & Tulsa; ord. Dec. 21, 1929; cons. March 5, 1958; died Sept. 8, 1971.—Most Rev. JOHN R. QUINN, D.D., ord. July 19, 1953; appt. Auxiliary Bishop of San Diego and Titular Bishop of Thisiduo, Oct. 21, 1967 Episcopal ordination, Dec. 12, 1967; transferred to Oklahoma City and Tulsa, Nov. 18, 1971; appt. as Archbishop of the Archdiocese of Oklahoma City, Dec. 13, 1972; installed as Archbishop of Oklahoma City, Feb. 6, 1973; transferred to Archbishop of San Francisco, April 26, 1977.

Vicars General—Revs. JAMES A. KASTNER, V.G.; EDWARD J. WEISENBURGER, V.G., M.A., J.C.L.

Regional Vicars Region I—Rev. THOMAS R. DOWDELL, *P.O. Box 60569, Oklahoma City, 73146. Region II,* Rev. LOWELL STIEFERMAN, *7336 W. Britton Rd., Oklahoma City, 73132. Region III,* Rev. RAY ACKERMAN, *P.O. Box 1585, Ada, 74821. Region IV,* Rev. JAMES D.M. STAFFORD, *P.O. Box 2546, Lawton, 73502. Region V,* Rev. JOSEPH JACOBI, *1500 Falcon Rd., Altus, 73521. Region VI,* Rev. THOMAS O'TOOLE, *P.O. Box 708, Woodward, 73802. Region VII,* Rev. JAMES J. MICKUS, *P.O. Box 3527, Enid, 73702. Region VIII,* Rev. JOHN MICHALICKA, *P.O. Box 1330, Ponca City, 74602. Region IX,* Rev. PHILIP DONOHOE, *208 S. Evans, El Reno, 73036.*

Catholic Pastoral Center—7501 Northwest Expy., P.O. Box 32180, Oklahoma City, 73123. Tel: 405-721-5651; Fax: 405-721-5210. Office Hours: Mon.-Fri. 8:30-4:30.

Chancellor—Rev. JOHN A. STEICHEN.

Vicar for Ministries—Rev. ANTHONY B. TAYLOR.

Archdiocesan Tribunal—7501 Northwest Expy., P.O. Box 32180, Oklahoma City, 73123. Tel: 405-721-5651.

Judicial Vicar—Rev. CHARLES H. SCHETTLER, S.T.L., J.C.D.

Adjutant Judicial Vicar—Rev. RICHARD STANSBERRY, M.A., J.C.L.

Pro-Synodal Judge—Revs. JOHN A. PETUSKEY, M.A.; EDWARD WEISENBURGER, V.G., M.A., J.C.L.; Mr. GEORGE RIGAZZI, J.C.L.

Defenders of the Bond—Revs. LOWELL STIEFERMAN; ALAN J. LOTH; JOHN W. FEEHILY.

Advocates—Rev. EDWARD MENASCO; Mrs. MONA CROSS; Mrs. WANDA J. LANE; Mrs. SUSAN LINDLEY; Mrs. JUDY REILLY.

Notaries—Mrs. MONA CROSS; Mrs. TONI NICHOLLS.

Interdiocesan Tribunal of Second Instance for the Province of Oklahoma City—P.O. Box 32180, Oklahoma City, 73123. Tel: 405-721-5651.

Judicial Vicar—Rev. ROBERTO QUANT, J.C.L.

Judges—Revs. JAMES A. KASTNER, V.G.; EDWARD WEISENBURGER, V.G., M.A., J.C.L.

Defenders of the Bond—Revs. PHILIP M. DONOHOE; ELMER C. SCHWARZ.

Consultors Archdiocesan—Revs. THOMAS BOYER; JAMES A. KASTNER, V.G.; BRUCE NATSUHARA; JOSEPH A. JACOBI; JOHN A. STEICHEN; EDWARD J. WEISENBURGER, V.G., M.A., J.C.L.; JOACHIM SPEXARTH, O.S.B.; RICHARD STANSBERRY.

Council of Priests Archdiocesan—Rev. THOMAS J. BOYER, Chm., *3214 North Lake, Oklahoma City, 73118.* Revs. RAYMOND K. ACKERMAN; JAMES A. KASTNER, V.G.; ALAN LOTH; RICHARD D. STANSBERRY; BRUCE NATSUHARA; TIMOTHY D. LUSCHEN; JOACHIM SPEXARTH, O.S.B.; JOHN A. STEICHEN; ANTHONY B. TAYLOR; EDWARD J. WEISENBURGER, V.G., M.A., J.C.L.; JOSEPH A. JACOBI.

Health Panel, Archdiocesan—Rev. WILLIAM B. ROSS, Chm., *P.O. Box 1280, Purcell, 73080.* Tel: 405-527-3077.

Personnel Committee—Revs. RAY ACKERMAN; JAMES A. KASTNER, V.G.; WILLIAM B. ROSS; LOWELL STIEFERMAN.

Archdiocesan Offices and Directors

Office of Stewardship and Development—Mr. JOSEPH H. COMBS, C.S.A., Dir., *P.O. Box 32180, Oklahoma City, 73123.* Tel: 405-721-5651.

Archdiocesan Development Fund—formerly *Diocesan Development Fund;* also formerly known as *Diocesan Fund, Bishop's Fund for Diocesan Development;* Mr. JOSEPH H. COMBS, C.S.A., Dir., *7501 N.W. Expy., P.O. Box 32180, Oklahoma City, 73123.* Tel: 405-721-5651.

Archdiocese of Oklahoma City Educational Trust Fund—Sr. CATHERINE POWERS, C.N.D., Dir., *7501 N.W. Expy., P.O. Box 32180, Oklahoma City, 73123.*

Associated Catholic Charities—Mr. TIMOTHY O'CONNOR, Dir., *1501 N. Classen Blvd., Oklahoma City, 73106.* Tel: 405-523-3000; Fax: 405-523-3030.

Archdiocesan Finance Council—Most Rev. EUSEBIUS J. BELTRAN, D.D.; Revs. JOHN A. STEICHEN; RICHARD D. STANSBERRY; ANTHONY B. TAYLOR; Mr. JOHN TORBETT; Mr. MICHAEL BLUBAUGH; Mr. WILLIAM BEAVERS; Mrs. ELLEN FLEMING; Mr. JOHN E. TORBETT; Mrs. SUSAN LOOSEN; Mr. MICHAEL MILLIGAN; Mr. HUGH D. RICE; Mr. MICHAEL R. STERKEL; Mr. DAVID JOHNSON, Business Mgr., *Business Office: P.O. Box 32180, Oklahoma City, 73123.* Tel: 405-721-5651.

Building Committee—Mr. DAVID JOHNSON, *P.O. Box 32180, Oklahoma City, 73123.* Tel: 405-721-5651.

Catholic Foundation of Oklahoma, Inc.—Mr. DAVID JOHNSON, Sec. & Treas.; Mr. JOSEPH H. COMBS, C.S.A., *7501 Northwest Expy., P.O. Box 32180, Oklahoma City, 73123.* Tel: 405-721-5651.

Catholic Lawyers Guild—Rev. RAYMOND K. ACKERMAN, Spiritual Moderator, *P.O. Box 1585, Ada, 74821.* Tel: 580-332-4811.

Catholic Physicians Guild—Rev. DANIEL MCCAFFREY, Chap., *P.O. Box 32180, Oklahoma City, 73123.*

Catholic Social Services—Mr. TIM O'CONNOR, *1501 N. Classen Blvd., Oklahoma City, 73106.* Tel: 405-523-3000; Fax: 405-523-3030.

Charismatic Renewal—Rev. MARVIN F. LEVEN, Episcopal Moderator, *P.O. Box 404, Okarche, 73762.* Tel: 405-263-7798.

Communications, Archdiocesan Department of—*P.O. Box 32180, Oklahoma City, 73123.* Tel: 405-721-1810; 721-5651.

Correction Related Ministry—Vacant.

Council of Catholic Women, Archdiocesan—Rev. JOSEPH C. KOLB.

Ecumenical and Interreligious Affairs, Office for Archdiocesan Dir.—Rev. JOHN A. PETUSKEY, *P.O. Box 510, Edmond, 73083.* Tel: 405-340-0691.

Education—Sr. CATHERINE POWERS, C.N.D., Archdiocesan Dir., *P.O. Box 32180, Oklahoma City, 73123.* Tel: 405-721-4202; 721-5651.

Catholic Schools, Office of—Sr. CATHERINE POWERS, C.N.D., Supt.; Ms. REBECCA JAMES, Assoc. Supt., *P.O. Box 32180, Oklahoma City, 73123.* Tel: 405-721-4202; 721-5651.

Religious Education, Office of—Ms. PATRICIA KOENIG, Dir.; Mr. MARCO OCANA, Assoc. Dir., Hispanic Religious Education, *P.O. Box 32180, Oklahoma City, 73123.* Tel: 405-721-1415; 721-5651.

Pastoral Ministry Office—Sr. M. DIANE KOORIE, R.S.M., Dir., *P.O. Box 32180, Oklahoma City, 73123.* Tel: 405-721-1415; 721-5651. Affiliated with Kansas Newman College, Wichita, KS and Aquinas Institute, St. Louis, MO.

Campus Ministry, Department of—Rev. C. JOSEPH MEINHART, *100 E. Stinson, Norman, 73072.* Tel: 405-321-0990.

Clergy Education, Department of—Rev. JAMES A. KASTNER, V.G., Dir., *P.O. Box 32180, Oklahoma City, 73123.* Tel: 405-721-5651.

Evangelization, Office of—Miss JOAN DARK, Dir., *P.O. Box 32180, Oklahoma City, 73123.* Tel: 405-728-3561; 721-5651, Ext. 150.

Family Life Department—Mr. GEORGE RIGAZZI, *P.O. Box 32180, Oklahoma City, 73123.* Tel: 405-721-8943; 721-5651.

Indian Ministries, Inc.—(Oklahoma), Rev. M. PRICE OSWALT, Liaison, *P.O. Box 628, Anadarko, 73005.* Tel: 405-247-5255.

Justice and Human Development, Commission for—Mrs. SHIRLEY COX, *1501 N. Classen Blvd., Oklahoma City, 73106.* Tel: 405-532-3000.

Legal Counsel—Mr. JACK R. LAWRENCE, *4900 Richmond Sq., Oklahoma City, 73118.* Tel: 405-841-6000.

Master of Ceremonies—Revs. ROBERT WOOD; TIMOTHY FULLER, Asst.

Ministry to Priests Program—Rev. ANTHONY B. TAYLOR, Dir., *P.O. Box 32180, Oklahoma City, 73123.* Tel: 405-721-5651.

Mission "Micatokla"—*Archdiocesan Mission of Santiago Atitlan, Guatemala*—Rev. JOHN A. STEICHEN, Archdiocesan Coord., *P.O. Box 32180, Oklahoma City, 73123.* Tel: 405-721-5651; Fax: 405-721-5210.

Newspaper—*"The Sooner Catholic";* Ms. JEANNE DEVLIN, Editor, *P.O. Box 32180, Oklahoma City, 73123.* Tel: 405-721-1810; 721-5651.

Pastoral Planning—Mr. JAMES WEINMANN, Dir., *7501 Northwest Expwy., P.O. Box 32180, Oklahoma City, 73123.* Tel: 405-721-5651.

Permanent Diaconate—Rev. EDWARD T. MENASCO, Dir., *P.O. Box 32180, Oklahoma City, 73123.* Tel: 405-721-5651. Deacon WALTER CULLINAN, Asst. to the Dir.

Priests' Medical Fund—formerly known as *Infirm Priest Fund.* Rev. JOHN A. STEICHEN, *P.O. Box 32180, Oklahoma City, 73123.* Tel: 405-721-5651.

Priests' Retirement Board—Most Rev. EUSEBIUS J. BELTRAN, D.D.; Revs. JOHN A. PETUSKEY; JOHN A. STEICHEN; ANTHONY B. TAYLOR, Chm., *Catholic Pastoral Center, P.O. Box 32180, Oklahoma City, 73123.* Tel: 405-721-5651.

Propagation of the Faith, Holy Childhood Assoc., Missionary Cooperation Plan—Rev. JOHN A. STEICHEN, *P.O. Box 32180, Oklahoma City, 73123.* Tel: 405-721-5651.

Rural Life—Rev. JAMES GREINER, Dir., *1100 N. Sara Road, P.O. Box 246, Mustang, 73064.* Tel: 405-376-9435.

Scouting—Rev. MICHAEL WHEELAHAN, *P.O. Box 360, Medford, 73759.* Tel: 580-395-2148.

St. Ann's Retirement Village—Mr. ROBERT O'CONNOR, Dir. Admin., *9400 St. Ann Dr., Oklahoma City, 73162.* Tel: 405-728-7888.

St. Francis de Sales Seminary (Legal Title)—Most Rev. EUSEBIUS J. BELTRAN, D.D., Pres.; Rev. JOHN A. STEICHEN, Sec. Trustees: Rev. DAVID F. MONAHAN; Mr. DAVID JOHNSON, Treas., *P.O. Box 32180, Oklahoma City, 73123.*

St. Vincent dePaul, Society of Oklahoma City District Council—Rev. JOHN A. PETUSKEY, Spiritual Moderator, *P.O. Box 510, Edmond, 73083.* Tel: 405-340-0691.

Vocations and Seminarians—Rev. LOWELL STIEFERMAN, Dir., *Catholic Pastoral Center, P.O. Box 32180, Oklahoma City, 73123.* Tel: 405-721-9351; 721-5651.

Worship and Spiritual Life, Office of—Rev. STEPHEN BIRD, Dir.; Sr. JOANNE YANKAUSKIS, O.S.B., Co-Dir., *P.O. Box 32180, Oklahoma City, 73123.* Tel: 405-721-5651.

Youth and Young Adult Ministry, Office of—Mrs. NANCY HOUSH, Dir.; Mrs. BECKY JAIME, Assoc. Dir., *P.O. Box 32180, Oklahoma City, 73123.* Tel: 405-721-9220; 721-5651.

CLERGY, PARISHES, MISSIONS AND PAROCHIAL SCHOOLS

OKLAHOMA CITY
(Oklahoma County)

1—CATHEDRAL OF OUR LADY OF PERPETUAL HELP (1919) (Vietnamese), Revs. Thomas J. Boyer, Rector; Thanh Van Nguyen; Deacon William Enos. In res., Rev. Paul Mollan.
Res., 3214 N. Lake Ave., 73118. Tel: 405-525-2349; Fax: 405-525-3628. [JC]
School—Bishop John Carroll, 1100 N.W. 32, 73118. Tel: 405-525-0956; Fax: 405-523-3053.
Lay Teachers 15; Students 176.
Catechesis/Religious Programs—Students 130.

2—ST. ANDREW DUNG-LAC (1994) (Vietnamese), Rev. Dominic Hung Hoang; Deacon San Nguyen.
Church—3000 S.W. 55th St., 73119. Tel: 405-681-2665; 681-6918; Fax: 405-681-7951. [JC]
Mailing Address: P.O. Box 891584, 73189.
Catechesis/Religious Programs—Students 148.

3—ST. CHARLES BORROMEO (1954), Revs. Paul H. Gallatin; Shane I. Tharp; Deacons John Pitt, (Retired); Marc LeWand; Walter Cullinan. In res., Rev. William L. Novak.
Res., 5024 N. Grove St., 73122. Tel: 405-789-2595; Fax: 405-789-4394. [JC]
School—5000 N. Grove St., 73122. Tel: 405-789-0224; Fax: 405-789-6292.
Lay Teachers 21; Students 263.
Catechesis/Religious Programs—Students 210.
Chapel—St. Michael Tridentine Chapel, 7501 N.W. Expwy., 73132. Tel: 405-720-2801. Rev. Anthony Tyrrell, F.S.S.P., Chap.

4—CHRIST THE KING (1949), Revs. Joseph R. Ross; James A. Kastner, V.G.; Deacon David Best.
Mailing Address: P.O. Box 20508, 73156.
Rectory: 1900 Elmhurst Ave., 73120. Tel: 405-842-1481; 841-6680; Fax: 405-843-0539. [JC]
Church—8005 Dorset Dr., 73120.
School—Tel: 405-843-3909; Fax: 504-843-6519. Leslie Bloomer, Prin.
Lay Teachers 22; Students 317.
Catechesis/Religious Programs—Tel: 405-843-4766.
Students 160.

5—CORPUS CHRISTI (1924) (African American), Rev. James A. Goin; Deacons James Barton; Dunn Cumby.
Res., 1005 N.E. 15th St., 73117. Tel: 405-236-4301; Fax: 405-235-0032. [JC]
Catechesis/Religious Programs—Students 50.
Mission—Jones, Oklahoma Co., St. Robert Bellarmine.

6—CHURCH OF THE EPIPHANY OF THE LORD (1976), Rev. Lowell L. Stieferman; Alveria Kopp, Pastoral Assoc.
Res., 7336 W. Britton Rd., 73132. Tel: 405-722-2110; Fax: 405-722-6719.
Catechesis/Religious Programs—Tel: 405-722-0051. Roxann Lackner, D.R.E.
Students 644.

7—ST. EUGENE'S (1958), Rev. Bill Pruett; Deacons Patrick Reynolds; Duane Descher.
Res., 2400 W. Hefner Rd., P.O. Box 20930, 73156. Tel: 405-751-7115; Fax: 405-751-8722. [JC]
School—Tel: 405-751-0067.
Lay Teachers 26; Students 373.
Catechesis/Religious Programs—Students 175.

8—ST. FRANCIS OF ASSISI (1925), Rev. Thomas R. Dowdell. In res., Rev. Charles H. Schettler.
Res., 1901 N.W. 18th St., P.O. Box 60569, 73146. Tel: 405-528-0485; Fax: 405-524-1260. [JC]
School—Rosary, 1910 N.W. 19th St., 73106. Tel: 405-525-9272. Dr. Harold A. Hayes, Prin.
Sisters 1; Lay Teachers 17; Students 214.
Catechesis/Religious Programs—Students 47.

9—ST. PAUL, APOSTLE (1956), Rev. Kenneth E. Kulinski; Deacons Philip LePage; Raymond LaChance.
Res., 3901 S. Sunnylane Rd., Del City, 73115. Tel: 405-677-4873; Fax: 405-619-0596. [JC]
Mission—Del City, Mission Co.
Catechesis/Religious Programs—Students 162.

10—HOLY ANGELS (1924) (Hispanic), Rev. Roberto Quant; Deacon Lucio Nieto.
Res., 317 N. Blackwelder St., 73106. Tel: 405-232-6572; Fax: 405-235-8334. [JC]
Convent—1522 N.W. Third St., 73106. Tel: 405-236-3407. Carmelite Missionaries of St. Teresa
Catechesis/Religious Programs—Students 311.

11—IMMACULATE CONCEPTION (1892), Rev. George Pupius; Deacons Agustin Hernandez; James Keene.
Res., 3901 S.W. 29th St., 73119. Tel: 405-685-4224; Fax: 405-685-4483. [CEM]
Catechesis/Religious Programs—Tel: 405-685-4806.
Students 155.

12—ST. JAMES (1954), Rev. Robert T. Wood; Deacon Marti Gulikers.
Res., 4308 S. Blackwelder St., 73119. Tel: 405-636-6800; Fax: 405-636-6848.
School—1224 S.W. 41st St., 73109. Tel: 405-636-6810; Fax: 405-636-6818.
Sisters 2; Lay Teachers 15; Students 193.
Convent—4212 S. Blackwelder, 73119. Tel: 405-636-6830. Sisters of Charity of Leavenworth
Catechesis/Religious Programs—Tel: 405-636-6840.
Students 188.

13—ST. JOSEPH (1889). (Old Cathedral). Rev. Bruce K. Natsuhara. In res., Rev. Larok Obwona Martin.
Res., 307 N.W. 4th St., 73102. Tel: 405-235-4565; Fax: 405-815-6644. [JC]
Mailing Address: P.O.Box 408, 73101.
Church—301 N.W. 4th St., 73102. Fax: 405-815-6644.

14—KOREAN MARTYRS (1996) (Korean),
Mailing Address: 3405 S. Wofford Ave., 73115. Tel: 405-672-4560; Fax: 405-672-4750.
Church—2600 S.W. 74th St., 73159. Tel: 405-681-6464. Rev. Anthony Ki-Hong Sung.

15—OUR LADY OF MOUNT CARMEL AND ST. THERESE LITTLE FLOWER (1921), Revs. Jenaro De La Cruz, O.C.D.; Ruben Garcia, O.C.D.; John Michael Payne, O.C.D.
Res., 1125 S. Walker Ave., Box 26127, 73126. Tel: 405-235-2037; Fax: 405-235-7023. [JC]
Mission—Packing Town, Oklahoma Co., Our Lady of Guadalupe, 2123 S.W. 11th St., Packing Town, 73108.
Catechesis/Religious Programs—Students 635.

16—ST. MICHAEL TRIDENTINE COMMUNITY (2000), Rev. Anthony Tyrrell, F.S.S.P. (Australia).
Mailing Address: P.O. Box 32180, 73123.
Church & Chapel: 7501 N.W. Expressway, 73132. Tel: 405-720-2801.

17—ST. PATRICK (1950), Rev. Stephen J. Bird; Deacon Dennis Frazier. In res., Rev. Donald C. Moore.
Res., 2121 N. Portland, P.O. Box 75835, 73147. Tel: 405-947-2275; 946-4441; Fax: 405-946-4894.
Catechesis/Religious Programs—Students 114.

18—ST. PHILIP NERI (Midwest City) (1946), Rev. Charles R. Murphy; Deacons Matthew Browne, (Retired); James G. Young, Pastoral Assoc.
Church & Mailing Address: 1107 Felix Pl., Midwest City, 73110. Tel: 405-737-4476; Fax: 405-741-0531. [JC]
Rectory: 301 Wilson Dr., Midwest City, 73110.
School—1121 Felix Pl., Midwest City, 73110. Tel: 405-737-4496; Fax: 405-732-7823.
Lay Teachers 27; Students 279.
Catechesis/Religious Programs—Tel: 405-737-4476, Ext. 108.
Students 178.

19—SACRED HEART (1911), Revs. Timothy D. Luschen; Salvador Ortiz; Deacons George Leal; Michael Rockey; Mariano Martinez.
Res., 2706 S. Shartel Ave., 73109. Tel: 405-634-2458; Fax: 405-634-2459. [JC]
School—2700 S. Shartel Ave., 73109. Tel: 405-634-5673. Sr. Jean Dworak, A.S.C., Prin.
Lay Teachers 11; Students 211.
Catechesis/Religious Programs—Tel: 405-634-6448.
Students 347.

OUTSIDE OKLAHOMA CITY

Ada, Pontotoc Co., St. Joseph (1902), Rev. Raymond K. Ackerman; Deacon Michael Radosevich.
Res., 1300 E. Beverly St., P.O. Box 1585, 74821. Tel: 580-332-4811; Fax: 580-436-1226.
Catechesis/Religious Programs—Students 80.

Altus, Jackson Co., Prince of Peace (1964), Rev. Joseph A. Jacobi.
Res., 1500 Falcon Rd., 73521. Tel: 580-482-3363; Fax: 580-482-6657.
Mission—Hollis, Harmon Co., Our Lady of Guadalupe, P.O. Box 107, Hollis, 73550. Tel: 580-688-2233; Fax: 580-688-9234.
Catechesis/Religious Programs—Students 237.

Alva, Woods Co., Sacred Heart (1897), Rev. David B. Imming.
Res., 627 12th St., 73717. Tel: 580-327-0339. [CEM]
Missions—Waynoka, Woods Co., Our Mother of Mercy, 210 S. Main St., Waynoka, 73860.; Cherokee, Alfalfa Co., St. Cornelius, (1895) 404 S. Massachusetts, Cherokee, 73728.
Catechesis/Religious Programs—Students 173.

Anadarko, Caddo Co., St. Patrick's (1892) (Native American), Rev. M. Price Oswalt; Deacon John Butler.
Res., 1115 W. Petree Rd., Box 628, 73005. Tel: 405-247-5255; Fax: 405-247-5249. [JC]
Missions—Binger, Binger Co., Our Lady of the Most Holy Rosary, Hwy. 152, Binger, 73009.; Carnegie, Caddo Co., St. Richard, Hwy. 9, Carnegie, 73015. Tel: 580-654-2177.
Catechesis/Religious Programs—Students 79.

Ardmore, Carter Co., St. Mary (1898), Revs. Louis J. Lamb; Juan Manuel Guerrero.
Res., 125 E St. S.W., 73401. Tel: 580-223-0231; Fax: 580-226-2129. [CEM]
Missions—Healdton, Carter Co., St. Cecilia, 300 E. Lincoln Ave., Healdton, 73438.; Marietta, Love Co., Good Shepherd, Broadway & N. 7th, Marietta, 73448.
Catechesis/Religious Programs—Students 255.

Bison, Garfield Co., St. Joseph's (1911) (Czech), Rev. Larry B. Gatlin.
Res., Box 117, 73720. Tel: 580-758-3558; Fax: 580-758-1219. [CEM]
Mission—Fairview, Major Co., St. Ann, 6th & Locust, Fairview, 73737. Tel: 580-227-2270.
Catechesis/Religious Programs—Students 34.

Blackwell, Kay Co., St. Joseph's (1901), Rev. Joseph W. Burger.
Res., 315 W. Blackwell Ave., P.O. Box 578, 74631. Tel: 580-363-2096; Fax: 580-363-2096.
Catechesis/Religious Programs—Tel: 580-363-0441.
Students 48.

Calumet, Canadian Co., Immaculate Heart of Mary (1940) (German-Irish), Rev. Omar Tabing.
Mailing Address: P.O. Box 99, 73014. Tel: 405-893-2336; Fax: 405-893-2715.
Church—239 Freehoma, 73014. Tel: 405-893-2336; Fax: 405-893-2715.

Chandler, Lincoln Co., Our Lady of Sorrows (1894), Rev. David M. Lafferty.
Res., 409 Price Ave., P.O. Box 543, 74834. Tel: 405-258-1239; Fax: 405-258-0010. [CEM]
Mission—Stroud, Lincoln Co., St. Louis, Hwy. 99 & Eighth Ave., Stroud, 74079. Tel: 918-968-2457.
Catechesis/Religious Programs—Students 90.

Cherokee, Alfalfa Co., St. Cornelius (1958). A mission of Sacred Heart, Alva.

Chickasha, Grady Co., Holy Name (1895), Rev. Elmer C. Schwarz.
Res., 210 S. Seventh St., Box 748, 73023. Tel: 405-224-7513; Fax: 405-224-4434. [CEM]
Catechesis/Religious Programs—Tel: 405-224-6068.
Students 121.

Clinton, Custer Co., St. Mary's (1944), Rev. Michael R. Vaught; Deacon Pedro Maldonado.
Res., 714 S. 12th St., 73601. Tel: 580-323-0309; Fax: 580-323-0345.
Mission—Cordell, Washita Co., St. Anne.
Catechesis/Religious Programs—1218 Knox Ave., P.O. Box 1295, 73601. Tel: 580-323-0345.
Students 145.

Duncan, Stephens Co., Assumption (1902), Revs. Donald J. Wolf; Oby J. Zunmas; Deacons Bernard T. O'Loughlin; James Conway.
Res., 711 Hickory Ave., 73533. Tel: 580-255-0590; Fax: 580-252-0866. [CEM]
Missions—Marlow, Stephens Co., Immaculate Conception, Fourth & Comanche, Marlow, 73055. Tel: 580-658-2365; Rush Springs, Grady Co., St. Francis of Assisi, Fifth & Choctaw, Rush Springs, 73082.; Ryan, Jefferson Co., San Jose, 1117 Lincoln Ave., Ryan, 73565. Tel: 580-757-2830.
Catechesis/Religious Programs—Mrs. Melissa Garcia, D.R.E.
Students 174.

Edmond, Oklahoma Co., St. John the Baptist (1889), Revs. John A. Petuskey; Louis VanderLey, O.S.B.; Stephen V. Hamilton; Deacons Bill Bawden; Bill Coyle; Lee Hunt.
Res., 900 S. Littler St., P.O. Box 510, 73083. Tel: 405-340-0691; Fax: 405-340-5715.
School—St. Elizabeth Ann Seton School, 925 South Blvd., 73083. Tel: 405-348-5364; Fax: 405-340-9627.
Lay Teachers 26; Students 498.
Catechesis/Religious Programs—Tel: 405-340-9871.
Students 821.

St. Monica (1993), Rev. Anthony B. Taylor.
Mailing Address: 2001 N. Western, 73003. Tel: 405-359-2700; Fax: 405-341-0023.
Res., 1121 N.W. 199th St., 73003. Tel: 405-330-2699. [CEM]
Catechesis/Religious Programs—Students 488.

Elgin, Comanche Co., St. Ann (1914), Rev. Joseph Kolb.
Res., 1005 Eighth St., P.O. Box 10, 73538. Tel: 580-492-5914; Fax: 580-492-5908.
Missions—Sterling, Comanche Co., Our Lady of Perpetual Help, 220 N. A St., Sterling, 73567.; Apache, Caddo Co., Mother of Sorrows, 521 E. Wallace, Apache, 73006.
Catechesis/Religious Programs—Students 65.

Elk City, Beckham Co., St. Matthew's (1970) (German), Rev. Timothy Fuller.
Mailing Address: 3001 E. Hwy. 66, 73648. Tel: 580-225-0066; Fax: 580-225-3522.
Res., 2900 E. Highway 66, 73648. Tel: 580-225-3980. [CEM][JC 3]
Mission—Sayre, Beckham Co., Queen of All Saints, 914 N. 5th St., Sayre, 73662. Tel: 580-928-5124.
Catechesis/Religious Programs—Students 190.

El Reno, Canadian Co., Sacred Heart (1890), Rev. Philip M. Donohoe.
Res., 208 S. Evans St., 73036. Tel: 405-262-1405; Fax: 405-262-2251. [CEM]
School—Sacred Heart School, 210 S. Evans, 73036. Tel: 405-262-2284. Adawnya Wiewel, Prin.
Teachers 8; Students 120.
Catechesis/Religious Programs—Tel: 405-262-2273.
Students 114.

Enid, Garfield Co., St. Francis Xavier (1893), Rev. James J. Mickus; Deacon Anthony Crispo.
Res., 110 N. Madison, Box 3527, 73702. Tel: 580-237-0812; Fax: 580-237-0909. [CEM][JC]
Catechesis/Religious Programs—Tel: 580-234-0152.
Students 331.

St. Gregory the Great (1971), Rev. Lawrence T. Kowalski.
Church—1924 W. Willow, 73703. Tel: 580-233-4589; Fax: 580-233-4590.
Res., 2045 Lantern Ln., 73703. Tel: 580-233-1845.
Mission—Goltry, Alfalfa Co., St. Michael, Main St., Goltry, 73739. [CEM]
Catechesis/Religious Programs—Students 310.

Frederick, Tillman Co., St. Helen (1927), Rev. Carl W. Janocha.
Res., 507 E. Highview Ave., 73542. Tel: 580-335-3298; Fax: 580-335-3953.
Catechesis/Religious Programs—Students 50.
Missions—Grandfield, Tillman Co., Our Lady of Perpetual Help, S. Main & 8th St., Grandfield, 73546.; Walters, Cotton Co., St. Patrick, 209 E. Iowa, Walters,; Waurika, Jefferson Co., St. Thomas Aquinas, 400 E. "D", Waurika.

Guthrie, Logan Co., St. Mary's (1889), Rev. Denis G. Hanrahan; Deacons Roy Ellison; Richard Washko.
Mailing Address: P.O. Box 1556, 7304.
Res., 411 N. Elm St., 73044. Tel: 405-282-4239; Fax: 405-282-5610. [CEM]
School—Tel: 405-282-2071; Fax: 405-282-2924.
Lay Teachers 7; Students 118.
Mission—Crescent, Logan Co., St. Margaret Mary, P.O. Box 632, Crescent, 73028. Tel: 405-969-2351.
Catechesis/Religious Programs—Students 68.

Guymon, Texas Co., St. Peter's (1906) (Hispanic), Revs. J. Carmen Flores; Scott Adams; Deacons Joe Cruz; Simon Guerra.
Res., 1220 N. Quinn St., P.O. Box 731, 73942. Tel: 580-338-7212; Fax: 580-338-5584. [CEM]
Missions—Hooker, Texas Co., Sacred Heart, 106 N. Albright, Hooker, 73945.; Boise City, Cimarron Co., Good Shepherd, S. Ellis at Second, Boise City, 73933. Tel: 580-544-3443.
Catechesis/Religious Programs—Tel: 405-454-9940.
Students 253.

Harrah, Oklahoma Co., St. Teresa of Avila (1907) (Polish), Rev. Alan J. Loth.
Res., 1576 Tim Holt Dr., Box 418, 73045. Tel: 405-454-2819; Fax: 405-454-0981. [CEM]
Catechesis/Religious Programs—Tel: 405-454-9940.
Students 185.

Hennessey, Kingfisher Co., St. Joseph's (1890), Rev. Mark E. Mason.
Res., 211 N. Cherokee St., 73742. Tel: 405-853-4425; Fax: 405-853-2166. [CEM]
Mission—Marshall, Logan Co., St. Camillus, Main St., Marshall, 73056.
Catechesis/Religious Programs—Tel: 405-853-2158.
Students 143.

Hitchcock, Blaine Co., Sacred Heart Mission. Closed. For inquiries for parish records contact St. Anthony of Padua Church, Okeene.

Jones, Oklahoma Co., St. Robert Bellarmine (1948). A mission of Corpus Christi, Oklahoma City.
Mission—Luther, Oklahoma Co., St. Theresa of the Infant Jesus. Closed. See Corpus Christi Church, Oklahoma City for records.

Kingfisher, Kingfisher Co., SS. Peter and Paul (1896), Rev. Richard D. Stansberry, Jr.
Res., 309 S. Main St., 73750. Tel: 405-375-4581; Fax: 405-375-3858. [CEM]
School—Tel: 405-375-4616.
Lay Teachers 8; Students 104.
Catechesis/Religious Programs—Students 105.

Konawa, Pottawatomie Co., Sacred Heart (1876), Rev. Matthew J. Brown, O.S.B.
Res., Rte. 1, Box 101, 74849. Tel: 580-925-2145; Fax: 580-925-2145. [CEM]
Missions—Wanette, Pottawatomie Co., St. Mary; Wewoka, Seminole Co., St. Joseph.
Catechesis/Religious Programs—Students 44.

Lawton, Comanche Co., Blessed Sacrament (1902), Rev. James D.M. Stafford; Deacon Bill Adamson.
Res., 12 S.W. Seventh St., Box 2546, 73502. Tel: 580-355-2054; Fax: 580-355-2055.
School—St. Mary's, 611 A Ave., 73501. Tel: 580-355-5288; Fax: 580-355-4336.
Sisters of Divine Providence 2; Lay Teachers 10; Students 155.
Catechesis/Religious Programs—Tel: 580-353-8182.
Students 123.

Holy Family (1959). (Formerly St. Barbara). Rev. Philip Seeton; Deacons Herman Lawrence; Leo Martinez, Jr.; Peter Dulcamara; Celine Benoit, Pastoral Assoc.
Res., 1010 N.W. 82nd St., P.O. Box 7948, 73506. Tel: 580-536-6351; Fax: 580-536-6352.
Catechesis/Religious Programs—Tel: 580-536-6355.
Students 270.

Lexington, St. John the Baptist. Closed. For parish records contact Our Lady of Victory, Purcell.

Loyal, Kingfisher Co., St. Joseph Mission. Closed. For inquiries for parish records contact Sts. Peter & Paul Church, Kingfisher.

Mangum, Greer Co., Sacred Heart (1896), Rev. Kevin J. Ratterman.
Res., 409 N. Byers, P.O. Box 310, 73554. Tel: 580-782-2657; Fax: 580-782-2457.
Mission—Hobart, Kiowa Co., Sts. Peter & Paul, 324 S. Randlett, P.O. Box 371, Hobart, 73651. Tel: 580-726-3925; Fax: 580-726-3925. [CEM]
Catechesis/Religious Programs—Students 88.

McLoud, Pottowatomie Co., St. Vincent de Paul (1903), Rev. Eugene C. Marshall, O.S.B.
Res., 122 S. 10th St., P.O. Box 585, 74851. Tel: 405-964-5606 (Res.); 878-5452; Fax: 405-878-5189.
Catechesis/Religious Programs—Students 65.

Medford, Grant Co., St. Mary's (1940), Rev. Michael Wheelahan.
Res., 214 W. Cherokee, Box 360, 73759. Tel: 580-395-2148; Fax: 580-395-2960. [CEM 3]
Missions—Wakita, Grant Co., St. Mary's Assumption, Main & Birch, Wakita, 73771. Tel: 580-594-2541; Pond Creek, Grant Co., St. Joseph's, S. Hwy. 81, Pond Creek, 73766.
Catechesis/Religious Programs—Tel: 580-395-2290.
Students 78.

Moore, Cleveland Co., St. Andrew's (1962), Rev. John W. Feehily; Deacon Angus Watford.
Res., 800 N.W. Fifth, 73153. Tel: 405-799-3334; Fax: 405-799-4880.
Catechesis/Religious Programs—Students 270.

Mustang, Canadian Co., Church of the Holy Spirit (1983), Rev. James A. Greiner.
Church—1100 N. Sara Rd., P.O. Box 246, 73064. Tel: 405-376-9435; 376-5218; Fax: 405-376-4929.
Catechesis/Religious Programs—Tel: 405-376-9162.
Students 103.

Newkirk, Kay Co., St. Francis of Assisi (1894), Rev. Richard J. Beckman.
Res., 610 W. Ninth St., P.O. Box 11, 74647. Tel: 580-362-3320; Fax: 580-362-3320.
Catechesis/Religious Programs—Students 75.

Nicoma Park, Oklahoma Co., Our Lady of Fatima (1949), Rev. Wilbur E. Moore.
Res., 2255 W. Meyer Cir., Box 368, 73066. Tel: 405-769-2490; Fax: 405-769-9113.
Catechesis/Religious Programs—Tel: 405-769-2655.
Students 105.

Norman, Cleveland Co., St. Joseph's (1896), Revs. Ernest A. Flusche; Edward J. Menasco; Deacons Larry Sousa; Patrick Gabrish; Jeff Willard.
Res., 425 E. Tonhawa, P.O. Box 1227, 73070. Tel: 405-321-8080; Fax: 405-321-4360. [CEM]
Catechesis/Religious Programs—Tel: 405-321-8084.
Students 254.

Church of St. Mark the Evangelist (1991), Rev. John Metzinger; Deacons Byron Jacobson; Lawrence Rossow.
Mailing Address: 3939 W. Tecumseh Rd., P.O. Box 722217, 73070. Tel: 405-366-7676; Fax: 405-447-0480.
Res., 3701 Castlerock Rd., 73072. Tel: 405-447-3085; Fax: 405-447-0480.
Catechesis/Religious Programs—Students 404.

St. Thomas More University Parish (1979), Rev. C. Joseph Meinhart; Judy Reilly, Pastoral Assoc.
Church—100 E. Stinson, 73072. Tel: 405-321-0990; Fax: 405-321-0964.
Res., 1501 Lincoln, 73072. Tel: 405-329-5319.
Catechesis/Religious Programs—Sr. Ursula Schones, A.S.C., D.R.E.
Students 117.

Okarche, Kingfisher Co., Holy Trinity (1893), Rev. Edward J. Weisenburger; Deacon Max Schwarz.
Res., 211 W. Missouri, Box 185, 73762. Tel: 405-263-7930; Fax: 405-263-9753. [CEM]
School—Box 485, 73762. Tel: 405-263-4422; Fax: 405-263-7475. Sr. Marita Rother, A.S.C., Prin.
Lay Teachers 8; Students 112.
Catechesis/Religious Programs—Tel: 405-263-4640.
Students 151.

Okeene, Blaine Co., St. Anthony's (1904), Rev. David A. Cowden.
Res., 211 S. Fifth St., Box 767, 73763. Tel: 580-822-3511; 822-3544; Fax: 580-822-3542. [CEM]
Missions—Seiling, Dewey Co., St. Thomas, 105 W. McAlister, Seiling, 73663. Tel: 580-922-4376; Watonga, Blaine Co., St. Rose of Lima, 900 N. Clarence Nash Blvd., Watonga, 73772. Tel: 580-623-7740.
Catechesis/Religious Programs—Students 48.

Pauls Valley, Garvin Co., St. Catherine of Siena (1949), Rev. David F. Monahan.
Res., 205 W. Bert St., 73075. Tel: 405-238-3741; Fax: 405-238-5325. [JC]
Mission—Lindsay, Garvin Co., St. Peter's, E. Second & Quapah, Lindsay, 73052.
Catechesis/Religious Programs—Students 100.

Perry, Noble Co., St. Rose of Lima (1893), Rev. Kevin Devlin.
Res., 421 Ninth St., 73077. Tel: 580-336-9300; Fax: 580-336-9795. [CEM]
Mission—Billings, Noble Co., Sacred Heart, Broadway & Lowe, Billings, 74630.
Catechesis/Religious Programs—Students 53.

Ponca City, Kay Co., Church of St. Mary (1893), Revs. John J. Michalicka; Babu Bathula (India); Deacons Richard Robinson; Jerry Rutherford.
Res., 707 E. Ponca St., Box 1330, 74602. Tel: 580-765-6031; Fax: 580-765-1327. [CEM][JC]
Schools—St. Mary, 415 S. 7th, 74601. Tel: 580-765-4387; Fax: 580-765-1352.; Sisters of St. Joseph of Wichita, 311 Fairview St., 74601. Tel: 580-765-0482; Fax: 580-765-0562. Sally Caughlin, Prin.
Lay Teachers 19; Students 234.
Catechesis/Religious Programs—Students 183.

Prague, Lincoln Co., St. Wenceslaus, National Shrine of the Infant Jesus of Prague (1899) (Czech), Rev. Adrian Vorderlandwehr, O.S.B.
Res., 304 Jim Thorpe Blvd., Box 488, 74864. Tel: 405-567-3404; Fax: 405-567-3404. [CEM]
Mission—Meeker, Lincoln Co., St. Michael, 217 S. Koonce, P.O. Box 684, Meeker, 74855.
Catechesis/Religious Programs—Students 67.

Purcell, McClain Co., Our Lady of Victory (1886) (Hispanic), Rev. William B. Ross.
Res., 316 W. Jefferson St., Box 1280, 73080. Tel: 405-527-3077; Fax: 405-527-3077. [CEM]
Catechesis/Religious Programs—Students 175.

Seminole, Seminole Co., Immaculate Conception (1927), Rev. Basil Keenan, O.S.B.
Mailing Address: P.O. Box 164, 74818-0164.
Res., 815 W. Boren Blvd., 74818-0164. Tel: 405-382-3602; Fax: 405-382-3602.
Mission—Maud, Seminole Co., St. Cecelia, Main St., Maud, 74854.
Catechesis/Religious Programs—Students 68.

Shawnee, Pottawatomie Co., St. Benedict (1895), Rev. Maurus P. Jaeb, O.S.B.; Deacon David Schrupp.
Res., 632 N. Kickapoo, 74801. Tel: 405-275-0001; Fax: 405-214-9181. [CEM]
Catechesis/Religious Programs—Students 175.

Sulphur, Murray Co., St. Francis Xavier (1974), Rev. Joseph H. Arledge.
Res., 1313 E. Seventh, 73086. Tel: 580-622-3070; Fax: 580-622-2863.
Church—700 E. Oklahoma Ave., 73086. Tel: 580-622-3780.
Missions—Madill, Marshall Co., Holy Cross, 14 W. Francis, Madill, 73446.; Tishomingo, Johnston Co., St. Anthony, 305 E. Wilson, Tishomingo, 73460.
Catechesis/Religious Programs—Students 139.

Tonkawa, Kay Co., St. Joseph's (1909), Rev. Joseph W. Burger.
Res., 320 W. North St., P.O. Box 525, 74653. Tel: 580-628-2416; Fax: 580-363-2096. [CEM]
Catechesis/Religious Programs—Students 49.

Union City, Canadian Co., St. Joseph's (1893), Rev. John A. Steichen.
Res., 404 N. Kate Boevers Ave., Box 100, 73090. Tel: 405-483-5329; Fax: 405-483-5329. [CEM]
Catechesis/Religious Programs—Tel: 405-381-2569.
Students 75.

Weatherford, Custer Co., St. Eugene's (1960), Rev. Michael L. Chapman; Deacon Joseph Dubey.
Res., 704 N. Bryan, Box 407, 73096. Tel: 580-772-3209; Fax: 580-772-3541. [CEM 3]
Missions—Thomas, Custer Co., Blessed Sacrament, 520 N. Oklahoma, Thomas, 73669.; Hinton, Caddo Co., Sacred Heart, 204 N. Clark Ave., Hinton, 73047.
Catechesis/Religious Programs—Students 75.

Woodward, Woodward Co., St. Peter's (1905) (German), Revs. Thomas O'Toole; Y. C. Irudayaraj (India).
Res., 2020 Oklahoma Ave., Box 708, 73802. Tel: 580-256-5305; Fax: 580-256-5840.
Missions—Mooreland, Woodward Co., Sacred Heart, 301 N. Main, Mooreland, 73852.; Shattuck, Ellis Co., Holy Name, 600 S. Main, Shattuck, 73858.; Beaver, Beaver Co., St. Frances Cabrini, 101 Ave. C, Beaver, 73932.; Buffalo, Harper Co., St. Joseph, 325 S.W. 2nd, Buffalo, 73834.
Catechesis/Religious Programs—Tel: 580-256-2966.
Students 256.

Yukon, Canadian Co., St. John Nepomuk (1889), Rev. Ben Zoeller; Deacon Jeffrey Kelly.
Mailing Address: P.O. Box 850249, 73085.
Church—600 S. Garth Brooks Blvd., 73099. Tel: 405-354-2743; Fax: 405-354-2770.
School—(Grades (K-8)). Tel: 405-354-2509. Sr. Laurentia Koehler, A.S.C., Prin.
Sisters 1; Lay Teachers 12; Students 190.
Catechesis/Religious Programs—Students 232.

Special Assignment:
Reverend Fathers—
Bash, Cletus, Chap. Mercy Health Center, 4300 W. Memorial Rd., Oklahoma City, OK 73120
Bird, Stephen J., Dir., Office of Worship & Spiritual Life, P.O. Box 32180, Oklahoma City, OK 73123. Tel: 405-721-5651
Leven, Marvin, Chap., Mercy Health Center, 4300 W. Memorial, Oklahoma City, OK 73120
McCaffrey, Daniel, Natural Family Planning Outreach, 3366 N.W. Expressway, Bldg. D, #630, Oklahoma City, OK 73112
McSherry, Thomas, Micatokla, Santiago-Atitlan, Departmento Solola, Guatemala
Menasco, Edward J., P.O. Box 32180, Oklahoma City, OK 73123
Mollan, Paul F., Chap., Deaconess and Baptist Hospitals, 3214 N. Lake, Oklahoma City, OK 73118
Moore, Donald C., St. Ann's Home, 9400 St. Ann's Dr., Oklahoma City, OK 73162
Novak, William, Chap., Bishop McGuinness High School, 901 N.W. 50th, Oklahoma City, OK 73118
Ratterman, Kevin, Chap., Mt. St. Mary High School, 2801 S. Shartel, Oklahoma City, OK 73109
Roberson, Henry, Chap., 2829 Williamsburg, Enid, OK 73702
Stieferman, Lowell, Seminarians & Vocations, P.O. Box 32180, Oklahoma City, OK 73123
Taylor, Anthony B., Vicar for Ministries, P.O. Box 32180, Oklahoma City, OK 73123. Tel: 405-721-5651
Vas, Joseph S., Chap. St. Anthony Hospital, 1000 N. Lee St., P.O. Box 205, Oklahoma City, OK 73101. Tel: 405-272-6263

Graduate Studies:
Reverend Fathers—
Nguyen, Hoa, Canon Law School, Catholic University of America, Washington, DC

Military Chaplains:
Reverend Fathers—
Creider, Philip B., Command Chap., U.S.S. Tarawa (LHA-1), FPD AP, 96622-1600

Absent on Leave:
Reverend Fathers—
Ashurst, Peter

Absent on Sick Leave:
Reverend Fathers—
Grimes, Price D., Jr., P.O. Box 32180, Oklahoma City, OK 73123. Tel: 405-720-9871
Parker, Rick, 26245 Ocean View Ave., Carmel, CA 93923
True, David

Retired:
Reverend Fathers—
Darnall, Thomas W., P.O. Box 32180, Oklahoma City, OK 73123. Tel: 405-720-9875
Flusche, Ernest A.
MacAulay, Gerard, 2000 E. Bay Dr., #161, Largo, FL 33771
Ross, James H., P.O. Box 32180, Oklahoma City, OK 73123. Tel: 405-720-9874
Scheller, John, P.O. Box 32180, Oklahoma City, OK 73123. Tel: 405-722-1902
Schwarz, Bernard F., Rte. 3, Box 203, Marlow, OK 73055
Talloen, Jerome G., P.O. Box 32180, Oklahoma City, OK 73123. Tel: 405-720-9873
VandeWalle, Victor, P.O. Box 32180, Oklahoma City, OK 73123. Tel: 405-720-9873
Vrana, John P.
Walch, John, P.O. Box 32180, Oklahoma City, OK 73123
Wrigley, Franklin, 10804 Greystone, Oklahoma City, OK 73120. Tel: 405-751-3185

Zagar, John T., 19000 N. County Line Rd, Piedmont, OK 73078. Tel: 405-341-1048

Permanent Deacons:
Adamson, Bill, Blessed Sacrament, Lawton
Amend, Carl, On Duty Outside the Archdiocese
Avila, Tomas, On Duty Outside the Archdiocese
Barton, James D., Corpus Christi, Oklahoma City
Bawden, William, St. John the Baptist Church, Edmond
Best, David, Church of Christ the King, Oklahoma City
Browne, Matthew, (Retired)
Butler, John, St. Patrick Church, Anadarko
Caplinger, Jerome, St. Andrew, Moore
Christophe, Norman, Retired
Collier, E. Charles, (Retired)
Coyle, Bill, Jr., St. John the Baptist, Edmond
Crispo, Anthony, St. Francis Xavier, Enid
Cruz, Joseph M., St. Peter, Guymon
Cullinan, Walter, St. Charles Borromeo Church, Oklahoma City
Cumby, Dunn, Corpus Christi Church, Oklahoma City
Descher, Duane, (Retired)
Dollins, Belvin G., (Retired)
Dubey, Joseph, St. Eugene, Weatherford
Dulcamara, Peter, Holy Family Church, Lawton
Ellison, Roy, St. Mary's, Guthrie
Enos, William, Cathedral of Our Lady of Perpetual Help, Oklahoma City
Forgue, Joseph, Chap., Federal Penitentiary, El Reno
Frazier, Dennis, St. Patrick Church, Oklahoma City
Gabrish, Patrick, St. Joseph Church, Norman
Guerra, Simon, St. Peter, Guymon
Gulikers, Marti, St. James, Oklahoma City
Guoladdle, Bobby, St. Richard Church, Carnegie
Hernandez, Agustin, Immaculate Conception, Oklahoma City
Huff, Louis, St. Robert Bellarmine Church, Jones
Hunt, Lee, St. John the Baptist, Edmond
Jacobsen, Byron, St. Mark Church, Norman
Jones, Bro. Justin, O.S.B., St. Gregory Abbey, Shawnee
Keene, James, Immaculate Conception Church, Oklahoma City
Kelly, Jeffrey, St. John Nepomuk Church, Yukon
Knipp, Stanley, Medical Leave
LaChance, Raymond, St. Joseph Church, Norman
Lawrence, Herman, Holy Family, Lawton
Leal, George, Sacred Heart Church, Oklahoma City
LePage, Philip, St. Paul Apostle, Del City
LeWand, Mark, St. Charles Borromeo, Oklahoma City
Maldonado, Pedro, St. Peter and Paul, Hobart
Martinez, Leopoldo, Holy Family Church, Lawton
Martinez, Mariano, Sacred Heart, Oklahoma City
Means, Gary, St. Cornelius, Cherokee
Neikirk, Dale, On Leave
Nguyen, San, St. Andrew Dung-Lac Church, Oklahoma City
Nieto, Lucio, Holy Angels, Oklahoma City
O'Loughlin, Bernard, Church of the Assumption, Duncan
Radosevich, Michael, St. Joseph, Ada
Reisinger, Conrad C.
Reynold, Patrick, St. Eugene, Oklahoma City
Robinson, Richard, Church of St. Mary, Ponca City
Rockey, Michael, Sacred Heart Church, Oklahoma City
Rossow, Lawrence, St. Mark, Norman
Rutherford, Gerard, Church of St. Mary, Ponca City
Schrupp, David, St. Benedict, Shawnee
Schwarz, Max, Holy Trinity, Okarche
Sousa, Lawrence, St. Joseph, Norman
Stoll, Michael, St. Francis, Tinker AFB
Vance, Herbert (Anchorage), Oklahoma Medical Complex, Oklahoma City
Warren, John, Our Lady of Victory Church, Purcell
Washko, Richard, St. Mary Church, Guthrie
Watford, Angus, St. Andrew, Moore
Willard, Jeff, St. Joseph, Norman
Young, James G., St. Philip Neri, Midwest City

INSTITUTIONS LOCATED IN THE ARCHDIOCESE

[A] COLLEGES AND UNIVERSITIES

SHAWNEE. *St. Gregory's University*, 74804. Tel: 405-878-5100; Fax: 405-878-5170.
E-mail: frlawrence@sgc.edu
Web site: www.sgc.edu/
For a complete listing, refer to the Colleges and Universities section.

[B] HIGH SCHOOLS, ARCHDIOCESAN

OKLAHOMA CITY. *Bishop McGuinness High School*. (Coed), 801 N.W. 50th St., 73118. Tel: 405-842-6638; Fax: 405-848-9363.
E-mail: pglorgio@ionet.net
Ms. Carolyn Henry, Pres. & Prin.; Rev. William Novak. Priests 1; Sisters 1; Lay Teachers 58; Students 683.

[C] HIGH SCHOOLS, PRIVATE

OKLAHOMA CITY. *Mount St. Mary High School*. (Coed), 2801 S. Shartel Ave., 73109. Tel: 405-631-8865; 8866; Fax: 405-631-9209.
E-mail: mountstmary.org
Sisters of Mercy of the Americas, Archdiocese of Oklahoma City. Rev. Kevin Ratterman, Chap.; Mrs. Mary Jane Wittrock, Prin.; Mr. Brian Boeckman, Chm., Rel. Studies Dept. Priests 1; Lay Teachers 28; Students 259.

[D] ELEMENTARY SCHOOLS, PRIVATE

OKLAHOMA CITY. *Villa Teresa*. (Grades N-4), 1216-1300 Classen Dr., 73103. Tel: 405-232-4286; Fax: 405-552-2658.
E-mail: admin@villateresa.com
Carmelite Sisters of St. Therese of the Infant Jesus. Mr. Todd Carel, Prin. Sisters 3; Lay Teachers 11; Students 191.

Villa Teresa Moore. (Grades N-K), 13501 S. Western Ave., 73170. Tel: 405-691-7737; Fax: 405-691-7981. Carmelite Sisters of St. Therese of the Infant Jesus. Mr. Todd Carel, Prin.; Sr. Sylvia Negrete, Dir. Sisters 1; Lay Teachers 6; Students 101.

NORMAN. *All Saints Catholic School*, 4001 36th Ave., N.W., 73072. Tel: 405-447-4600; Fax: 405-447-7227.
E-mail: gpeters@ascsn.org
Web site: www.ascsn.org
Dr. Glenda Peters, Prin. Lay Teachers 20; Pre-K Students 40; Students 391.

[E] GENERAL HOSPITALS

OKLAHOMA CITY. *Hillcrest Health Center, Inc.*, 2129 S.W. 59th St., 73119. Tel: 405-685-6671; Fax: 405-680-2817.
E-mail: ray_brazier@ssmhc.com
For a complete listing, refer to the Hospitals section.

Mercy Health Center, 4300 W. Memorial Rd., 73120. Tel: 405-755-1515; Fax: 405-752-3811.
E-mail: 1ryan@okla.smhs.com
For a complete listing, refer to the Hospitals section.

St. Anthony Hospital, 1000 N. Lee St., P.O. Box 205, 73101. Tel: 405-272-7000; Fax: 405-272-7075.
E-mail: valinda_rutledge@ssmhc.com
Web site: www.saintsok.com
For a complete listing, refer to the Hospitals section.

ARDMORE. *Mercy Memorial Health Center, Inc. (MMHC)*, 1011 14th Ave., N.W., 73401. Tel: 580-221-6611; Fax: 580-220-6580.
E-mail: BThompson@OKLA
For a complete listing, refer to the Hospitals section.

PONCA CITY. *St. Joseph Regional Medical Center*, 1900 N. 14th, 74602. Tel: 580-765-3321; Fax: 580-765-0341.
E-mail: susan_nolan@via-christi.org
Web site: sjrmcpc.com
For a complete listing, refer to the Hospitals section.

[F] SPECIAL CARE FACILITIES

OKLAHOMA CITY. *Bone and Joint Hospital*, 1111 North Dewey Ave., 73103. Tel: 405-272-9671; Fax: 405-551-9197.
E-mail: cathy_mckinney@ssmhc.com
Web site: www.boneandjoint.com
For a complete listing, refer to the Special Care Facilities section.

St. Ann's Home Inc., 9400 St. Ann's Dr., 73162. Tel: 405-728-7888; Fax: 405-728-1302.
E-mail: stann@swbell.net
For a complete listing, refer to the Special Care Facilities section.

[G] ECUMENICAL CENTERS

OKLAHOMA CITY. *Catholic Pastoral Center*, 7501 Northwest Expwy., P.O. Box 32180, 73123. Tel: 405-721-5651; Fax: 405-721-5210.
Web site: www.catharchdioceseokc.org
Mr. James Weinmann, Dir.; Mrs. Jeanine McFall, Events Coord. Used for Archdiocesan Chancery; ecumenical activities; retreat-meeting center for ecumenical and non-profit organizations; and retired priests' residence.

[H] HOMES FOR THE AGED

OKLAHOMA CITY. *St. Ann's Retirement Village, Inc.*, 7501 N.W. Expwy., P.O. Box 32180, 73123. Tel: 405-721-5651; Fax: 405-721-5210
For a complete listing, refer to the Special Care Facilities section.

Trinity Place Apartments, Catholic Charities, 3825 N.W. 19th St., 73107. Tel: 405-523-3000; Fax: 405-523-3030.
E-mail:toconnor@catholiccharitiesok.org
For a complete listing, refer to the Special Care Facilities section.

Villa Isenbart, Inc., c/o Catholic Charities, 1501 Classen Blvd., 73106. Tel: 405-523-3000; Fax: 405-523-3030.
E-mail:tooconnor@catholiccharitiesok.org
For a complete listing, refer to the Special Care Facilities section.

PONCA CITY. *St. Mary's Housing Foundation*, 408 S. 8th St., 74601. Tel: 580-765-7794; Fax: 580-765-1327.
E-mail: stmarys@poncacity.net
For a complete listing, refer to the Special Care Facilities section.

Westminster Village, Inc., 1601 Academy Rd., 74604. Tel: 580-762-0927; Fax: 580-762-0933
For a complete listing, refer to the Special Care Facilities section.

[I] MONASTERIES AND RESIDENCES OF PRIESTS AND BROTHERS

OKLAHOMA CITY. *Monastery of Our Lady of Mount Carmel and Little Flower*, 1125 S. Walker Ave., Box 26127, 73126. Tel: 405-235-2037. Order of Discalced Carmelites (Oklahoma Province).
Little Flower Clinic: Free medical service for the poor. Assisted annually 1,500.

SHAWNEE. *St. Gregory's Abbey*, 1900 W. MacArthur Dr., 74804. Tel: 405-878-5491; Fax: 405-878-5189.
E-mail: abbotmartin@sgc.edu
Web site: www.sgc.edu
Legal Title: *Benedictine Fathers of Sacred Heart Mission, Inc.* Order of St. Benedict, including University, Novitiate, and Mabee-Gerrer Museum of Art. Rt. Rev. Martin Lugo, O.S.B., Abbot; Revs. Patrick McCool, O.S.B., Prior; Joachim Spexarth, O.S.B., Subprior. Retired Abbots: Rt. Revs. Philip A. Berning, O.S.B.; Charles Massoth, O.S.B.; Adrian R. Vorderlandwehr, O.S.B.; Revs. Matthew J. Brown, O.S.B.; Charles Buckley, O.S.B., Dir.; Brendan Helbing, O.S.B.; Augustine S. Horn, O.S.B.; Maurus P. Jaeb, O.S.B.; Basil Keenan, O.S.B.; Manuel Magallanes, O.S.B.; Timothy Maloney, O.S.B.; Eugene C. Marshall, O.S.B.; James D. Murphy, O.S.B.; Victor W. Roberts, O.S.B.; Theodore T. Seneschal, O.S.B.; Lawrence R. Stasyszen, O.S.B.; Daniel M. Suellentrop, O.S.B.; Louis Vanderley, O.S.B.; Paul J. Zahler, O.S.B. Priests 22; Brothers 13; Deacons 2.

[J] CONVENTS AND RESIDENCES FOR SISTERS

OKLAHOMA CITY. *Carmelite Sisters of St. Therese of the Infant Jesus Motherhouse, Villa Teresa*, 1300 Classen Dr., 73103. Tel: 405-232-7926; Fax: 405-236-3170. Sr. Maria Francesca Forst, C.S.T., Supr. Sisters in Community 29; Resident Sisters 23.

Sisters of Mercy of the Americas, Mercy Health Center Convent, 4300 W. Memorial Rd., 73120. Tel: 405-755-1515; Fax: 405-936-5498.
E-mail: rpower@okla.smhs.com
Web site: www.mercyok.com
Retirement Center for Sisters of Mercy of Oklahoma. Sr. M. Rose Elizabeth Power, R.S.M., Coord. Sisters 15.

PIEDMONT. *Carmel of St. Joseph*, 20,000 N. County Line Rd., 73078. Tel: 405-348-3947; Fax: 405-348-4916. Discalced Carmelite Nuns (Cloistered). Sr. Monica Lotter, O.C.D., Prioress. Professed Sisters 11; Novices 1.

Sisters of Benedict Red Plains Monastery, 728 Richland Rd., SW, 73078-9324. Tel: 405-373-4565; 373-4569; Fax: 405-373-3392.
E-mail: osbokc@ionet.net
Web site: www.geocities.com/wellesley/6285
Sr. Marie Ballmann, O.S.B., Prioress. Sisters in Community 12; Scholastics 2.

[K] CAMPUS MINISTRY & NEWMAN CENTERS

NORMAN. *Campus Ministry for the Archdiocese of Oklahoma City*, 100 East Stinson, 73072. Tel: 405-321-0990; Fax: 405-321-0964.
Web site: stm-ou.org
Rev. C. Joseph Meinhart, Dir.

University of Oklahoma, 100 E. Stinson, 73072. Tel: 405-321-0990; Fax: 405-321-0964.
Web site: stm-ou.org
Rev. C. Joseph Meinhart.

Oklahoma City University, P.O. Box 60569, Oklahoma City, 73146. Tel: 405-528-0485; Fax: 405-524-1260. Rev. Thomas Dowdell.

East Central State University, P.O. Box 1585, Ada, 74820. Tel: 580-332-4811; Fax: 580-436-1226. Rev. Ray Ackerman.

Northwestern Oklahoma State College, 627 12th St., Alva, 73717. Tel: 580-327-0339; Fax: 580-327-0710. Rev. David B. Imming.

University of Science & Arts of Oklahoma, P.O. Box 748, Chickasha, 73023. Tel: 405-224-7513; Fax: 405-224-4434. Rev. Elmer C. Schwarz.

University of Central Oklahoma, 321 E. Clegern, Edmond, 73034. Tel: 405-340-6300; Fax: 405-340-5715. Rev. Louis Vanderley, O.S.B.

Oklahoma Panhandle State University, P.O. Box 277, Goodwell, 73942. Tel: 580-338-7212; Fax: 580-338-5584. Rev. Scott Adams.

Cameron University, P.O. Box 7948, Lawton, 73506. Tel: 580-536-6351. Rev. Philip Seeton.

Northern Oklahoma College, P.O. Box 525, Tonkawa, 74653. Tel: 580-628-2416; Fax: 580-531-2607. Rev. Joseph W. Burger.

Southwestern Oklahoma State University, P.O. Box 407, Weatherford, 73096. Tel: 580-772-3209; Fax: 580-772-3541. Rev. Michael L. Chapman; Deacon Joe Dubey.

[L] MISCELLANEOUS

OKLAHOMA CITY. *All Saints Catholic School.* (Catholic Pastoral Center), 7501 N.W. Expwy., P.O. Box 32180, 73123. Tel: 405-721-5651; Fax: 405-721-5210. Mr. David J. Johnson, Business Mgr.; Rev. Ernest A. Flusche, Pastor.

St. Anthony Hospital Foundation, Inc. Member of SSM Health Care, 826 N.W. 11, 73106. Tel: 405-272-7070; Fax: 405-270-7607.

SSM Health Care of Oklahoma, Inc. (For staff listings please see St. Anthony Hospital located under General Hospitals), 1000 N. Lee, P.O. Box 205, 73101. Tel: 405-272-7000.

CANTON. *Las Casas Ministry Among the Cheyenne and Arapaho.* Sponsored by the Dominican Leadership Conference. 524 W. Pine, 73724-9703. Tel: 580-886-3413.
E-mail: whiteearth@pldi.net
Web site: www.lascasasproject.org
The White Earth Center. Senior Citizens Nutrition Center. Tel: 580-886-3413. Children of the Plains Recreation Center. Youth Activities. Tel: 580-886-3413.

PIEDMONT. *Benedictine Spirituality Center.* Location at Red Plains Monastery, 728 Richland Rd., SW, 73078-9324. Tel: 405-373-4565; Fax: 405-373-3392.
E-mail: osbokc@ionet.net
Web site: www.geocities.com/wellesley/6285

PONCA CITY. *St. Joseph Medical Foundation, Inc.* (A subsidiary of Via Christi Health System, Inc.), 1900 N. 14th, P.O. Box 1270, 74602-1270. Tel: 580-763-0872; Fax: 580-765-0536.
E-mail: sgearhart@via-christi.org
Web site: www.sjrmcpc.com

PRAGUE. *National Shrine of the Infant Jesus of Prague.* Tel: 405-567-3080; Fax: 405-567-3404.
E-mail: shrine@chickasaw.com
Mailing Address: St. Wenceslaus Church, P.O. Box 488, 74864. 304 Jim Thorpe Blvd., 74864. Novena to the Infant Jesus of Prague takes place the 17th through 25th of each month. Pilgrimages take place on Sundays between the 17th and 25th of the month.

SHAWNEE. *Oklahoma Benedictine Institute on Mental Retardation, Inc.*, 1900 W. MacArthur, 74804. Tel: 405-878-5288; Fax: 405-878-5114.
Web site: www.nidd.org
Rev. Paul J. Zahler, O.S.B., Ph.D, Dir.

Oklahoma Benedictine Institute on Mental Retardation, Inc. Tel: 405-878-5289; Fax: 405-878-5114.

C. Harold and Connie Brand Early Child Development Center. Tel: 405-878-5289; Fax: 405-878-5114.

Home Start Program. Tel: 405-878-5289; Fax: 405-878-5114.

Lyle H. Boren Child Development Center. Tel: 405-878-5289; Fax: 405-878-5114.

Home Integration, Inc. Tel: 405-878-5289; Fax: 405-878-5114.

Community Integration Program. Tel: 405-878-5289; Fax: 405-878-5114.

Employment Integration Program. Tel: 405-878-5289; Fax: 405-878-5114.

St. Michael Foundation, Inc. Tel: 405-878-5289; Fax: 405-878-5114.

International Institute on Mental Retardation. Tel: 405-878-5289; Fax: 405-878-5114.

RELIGIOUS INSTITUTES OF MEN REPRESENTED IN THE ARCHDIOCESE

For further details refer to the corresponding bracketed number in the Religious Institutes of Men or Women section.

[0200]—*Benedictine Monks.*—O.S.B.
[0260]—*Discalced Carmelite Friars.* (Oklahoma Prov.).—O.C.D.
[0690]—*Jesuit Fathers.* (Missouri Prov.).—S.J.
[0920]—*Oblates of St. Francis De Sales.*—O.S.F.S.

RELIGIOUS INSTITUTES OF WOMEN REPRESENTED IN THE ARCHDIOCESE

[0100]—*Adorers of the Blood of Christ.*—A.S.C.
[0230]—*Benedictine Sisters of Pontifical Jurisdiction.*—O.S.B.
[0380]—*Carmelite Sisters of St. Therese of the Infant Jesus.*—C.S.T.
[0390]—*Congregation of Missionary Carmelites of St. Therese.* (Houston, TX).—C.M.S.T.
[0420]—*Discalced Carmelite Nuns.*—O.C.D.
[1070-13]—*Dominican Sisters.* (Adrian, MI).—O.P.
[1070-06]—*Dominican Sisters.* (Newburgh, NY).—O.P.
[1070-03]—*Dominican Sisters.* (Sinsinawa, WI).—O.P.
[1900]—*Eucharistic Missionaries of St. Theresa.* (Mexico).—M.E.S.T.
[1415]—*Franciscan Sisters of Mary.*—F.S.M.
[]—*Hermanas Catequistas Guadalupanas.*—H.C.G.
[1680]—*School Sisters of St. Francis.*—S.S.S.F.
[0480]—*Sisters of Charity of Leavenworth.*—S.C.L.
[2980]—*Sisters of Congregation de Notre Dame.*—C.N.D.
[1010]—*Sisters of Divine Providence of San Antonio, Texas.*—C.D.P.
[2575]—*Sisters of Mercy of the Americas.*—R.S.M.
[3360]—*Sisters of Providence of St. Mary-of-the-Woods.*—S.P.
[3840]—*Sisters of St. Joseph of Carondelet.*—C.S.J.
[2150]—*Sisters, Servants of the Immaculate Heart of Mary.*—I.H.M.

CEMETERIES

OKLAHOMA CITY. *Resurrection Memorial*, P.O. Box 32865, 73123. Tel: 405-721-4191.

NECROLOGY

(No Deaths)

Archdiocese of Omaha

(Archidioecesis Omahensis)

Most Reverend

ELDEN FRANCIS CURTISS

Archbishop of Omaha; ordained May 24, 1958; appointed Bishop of Helena March 4, 1976; consecrated April 28, 1976; appointed Archbishop of Omaha May 4, 1993; installed June 25, 1993. *Chancery Office: 100 N. 62nd St., Omaha, NE, 68132-2795.*

Chancery Office: 100 N. 62 St., Omaha, NE, 68132-2795. Tel.: 402-558-3100; Fax: 402-551-4212.

Web site address: www.oarch.org

E-mail address: 110377.1446@compuserve.com

ESTABLISHED AS A VICARIATE-APOSTOLIC JANUARY 6, 1857.

ERECTED A DIOCESE OCTOBER 2, 1885; ARCHDIOCESE AUGUST 7, 1945.

Square Miles 14,051.

Comprises the Counties of Boyd, Holt, Merrick, Nance, Boone, Antelope, Knox, Pierce, Madison, Platte, Colfax, Stanton, Wayne, Cedar, Dixon, Dakota, Thurston, Cuming, Dodge, Burt, Washington, Douglas and Sarpy in the State of Nebraska.

For legal titles of parishes and archdiocesan institutions, consult the Chancery Office.

STATISTICAL OVERVIEW

Personnel	
Archbishop	1
Retired Bishops	1
Abbots	1
Retired Abbots	1
Priests: Diocesan Active in Diocese	149
Priests: Active Outside Diocese	8
Priests: Retired, Sick or Absent	60
Number of Diocesan Priests	217
Religious Priests in Diocese	115
Extern Priests in Diocese	19
Ordinations:	
Diocesan Priests	3
Religious Priests	2
Transitional Deacons	4
Permanent Deacons	6
Permanent Deacons in Diocese	142
Total Brothers	21
Total Sisters	306
Parishes	
Parishes	138
With Resident Pastor:	
Resident Diocesan Priests	103
Resident Religious Priests	2
Without Resident Pastor:	
Administered by Priests	31
Administered by Deacons	1
Administered by Lay People	1
Missions	16
Pastoral Centers	2
Closed Parishes	3
Professional Ministry Personnel:	
Sisters	23
Lay Ministers	320
Welfare	
Catholic Hospitals	5
Total Assisted	349,495
Health Care Centers	1
Total Assisted	1,287
Homes for the Aged	4
Total Assisted	650
Day Care and Extended Day Care Centers	6
Total Assisted	5,500
Specialized Homes	1
Total Assisted	350
Special Centers for Social Services	14
Total Assisted	124,230
Other Institutions	2
Total Assisted	62,425
Educational	
Diocesan Students in Other Seminaries	34
Total Seminarians	34
Colleges and Universities	2
Total Students	7,218
High Schools, Diocesan and Parish	12
Total Students	3,557
High Schools, Private	5
Total Students	2,440
Elementary Schools, Diocesan and Parish	62
Total Students	16,097
Elementary Schools, Private	2
Total Students	195
Non-residential Schools for the Disabled	1
Total Students	40
Catechesis/Religious Education:	
High School Students	3,414
Elementary Students	16,708
Total Students Under Catholic Instruction	49,703
Teachers in the Diocese:	
Priests	34
Scholastics	2
Brothers	3
Sisters	46
Lay Teachers	2,588
Vital Statistics	
Receptions into the Church:	
Infant Baptism Totals	4,280
Adult Baptism Totals	444
Received into Full Communion	625
First Communions	4,610
Confirmations	4,247
Marriages:	
Catholic	958
Interfaith	595
Total Marriages	1,553
Deaths	1,935
Total Catholic Population	214,046
Total Population	830,522

Former Bishops—Rt. Rev. JAMES O'GORMAN, O.C.S.O., D.D., Vicar-Apostolic and Titular Bishop of Raphanea; cons. May 8, 1859; died July 4, 1874.—Rt. Rev. JAMES O'CONNOR, D.D., Vicar-Apostolic and Titular Bishop of Dibona; cons. Aug. 20, 1876; appt. first Bishop of Omaha, Oct. 2, 1885; died May 27, 1890.—Rt. Rev. RICHARD SCANNELL, D.D., cons. Bishop of Concordia, Nov. 30, 1887; transferred to Omaha, Jan. 30, 1891; died Jan. 8, 1916.—Most Rev. JEREMIAH J. HARTY, D.D., ord. April 28, 1878; cons. Archbishop of Manila, P.I., Aug. 15, 1903; transferred to Omaha, May 16, 1916; died Oct. 29, 1927.—Most Rev. FRANCIS J. BECKMAN, D.D., Bishop of Lincoln and Apostolic Administrator of Omaha from June 1, 1926 to July 4, 1928.—Most Rev. JOSEPH FRANCIS RUMMEL, D.D., Bishop of Omaha; appt. March 30, 1928; cons. May 29, 1928; installed July 4, 1928; transferred to the Archdiocese of New Orleans, March 9, 1935.—Most Rev. JAMES H. RYAN, D.D., appt. Titular Bishop of Modra, Aug. 15, 1933; cons. Oct. 25, 1933; transferred to See of Omaha, Aug. 3, 1935; installed Nov. 21, 1935 elected to Archiepiscopal dignity, Aug. 7, 1945; died Nov. 23, 1947.—Most Rev. GERALD T. BERGAN, D.D., ord. Oct. 28, 1915; appt. Bishop of Des Moines, March 24, 1934; cons. June 13, 1934; promoted to Omaha, Feb. 7, 1948; retired June 18, 1969 made Titular Archbishop of Tacarata; died July 12, 1972.—Most Rev. DANIEL E. SHEEHAN, D.D., J.C.D., ord. May 23, 1942; appt. Titular Bishop of Capsu and Auxiliary, Jan. 4, 1964; cons. March 19, 1964; succeeded to See, June 11, 1969; retired May 14, 1992; died Oct. 24, 2000.

Vicar General—Very Rev. MICHAEL W. GREWE.

Chancery Office—100 N. 62nd St., Omaha, 68132-2795. Tel: 402-558-3100; Fax: 402-551-4212. Office Hours: Mon.-Fri. 9-5.

Chancellor—Rev. MICHAEL F. GUTGSELL, J.C.L.

Moderator of the Curia—Rev. MICHAEL F. GUTGSELL, J.C.L.

Finance Director (canonical)—Rev. GERALD P. MELCHIOR, J.C.L.

Business and Finance Director—HERBERT L. KARRER.

Archdiocesan Tribunal—100 N. 62nd St., Omaha, 68132.

Judicial Vicar—Rev. PATRICK C. HARRISON, J.C.L.

Associate Judicial Vicars—Revs. MICHAEL F. GUTGSELL, J.C.L.; R. MICHAEL FITZPATRICK, J.C.L., S.T.L.

Judges—Rev. GERALD P. MELCHIOR, J.C.L.; Deacon JERRY OVERKAMP, J.C.L.

Promoter of Justice—Rev. JAMES R. CAIN, J.C.D.

Defenders of the Bond—Revs. JAMES R. CAIN, J.C.D.; VALENTINE J. PETER, S.T.D., J.C.D.

Advocates—Deacon JERRY OVERKAMP.

Attorneys—Appointed for each matrimonial case.

Appeal Court—The Tribunal of the Diocese of Lincoln, NE is the Appeal Court for Omaha.

Consultors—Revs. THOMAS J. ADAMS; HAROLD J. BUSE; JAMES R. CAIN; MICHAEL W. GREWE; CHARLES F. SWANSON; R. MICHAEL FITZPATRICK, J.C.L., S.T.L.

Deans—Rev. ROBERT F. PREISINGER, U.S.; Rev. CHARLES F. SWANSON, U.S.C.; Rev. JAMES E. GILG, U.S.E.; Rev. NORMAN F. HUNKE, U.N.E.; Rev. DANIEL KAMPSCHNEIDER, U.N.W.; Rev. FRANKLIN A. DVORAK, U.W.; Rev. STEPHEN J. GUTGSELL, R.S.W.; Rev. ROBERT K. ENGLISH, R.N.C.; Rev. DENNIS U. DEGUZMAN, R.S.E.; Rev. GERALD A. CONNEALY, R.C.; Rev. DOUGLAS P. SCHEINDST, R.N.W.; Rev. DAVID W. LAPLANTE, R.N.E.

Finance Council—Most Rev. ELDEN FRANCIS CURTISS; Revs. R. MICHAEL FITZPATRICK, J.C.L., S.T.L.; MICHAEL F. GUTGSELL; ROBERT H. NIENABER; RONALD S. WASIKOWSKI; GERALD P. MELCHIOR; Mr. HERBERT L. KARRER; Mr. MIKE KIRK; Ms. MARCIA KOORY; Mr. ROMAN UHING; Mr. HERMAN D. WEIST.

Archdiocesan Offices and Directors

Boy Scouts—Rev. DANIEL L. WITTROCK, Chap.

Building Commission—Rev. R. MICHAEL FITZPATRICK, J.C.L., S.T.L.; Mr. LEE KARRER, Contact Person; Rev. JAMES R. CAIN, J.C.D.; Mr. THOMAS L. FINLEY; Rev. ROBERT J. SMITH; Mr. DANIEL WITT; Bro. WILLIAM WOEGER, F.S.C.

Catholic University, Friends of—Rev. GERALD P. MELCHIOR, J.C.L.

Cemeteries—Rev. R. MICHAEL FITZPATRICK, J.C.L., S.T.L., Dir.

Censor Librorum—Rev. MICHAEL F. GUTGSELL, J.C.L.

Catholic Charities—SCOT L. ADAMS, Dir., *3300 N. 60th St., Omaha, 68104.*

Omaha Priests Retirement Plan and Trust, The—Revs. JAMES R. CAIN; ROBERT H. NIENABER; Mr. JAMES KINEEN; Mr. JOSEPH BEVERIDGE; Mr. DAVID DUREN; Mr. HERBERT L. KARRER.

Commission for Ecumenical Affairs—Rev. GERALD P. MELCHIOR.

Commission on Divine Worship—Bro. WILLIAM WOEGER, F.S.C., Coord., Environment & Art; Rev. RONALD NOECKER, Coord., Music.

Council of Catholic Women, Archdiocesan—Rev. EDGAR J. WORTMANN, Archdiocesan Moderator, *3020 Curtis, Omaha, 68111.*

Diaconate Program—Revs. THOMAS J. ADAMS, Urban Dir. Tel: 402-733-9327. PAUL ORTMEIER, Rural Dir. Tel: 402-986-1653.

Catholic School Office—Sr. MICHELLE FALTUS, S.F.C.C., Supt. Schools, *3212 N. 60th St., Omaha, 68104.* Tel: 402-554-8493.

Religious Formation, Office of—3212 N. 60th St., P.O. Box 4130, Omaha, 68104. Mr. JAMES CORR, Dir.; Sr. LEE AGNES HODAPP, Asst. Dir. Rural Rel. Education; MARTY KALKOWSKI, Asst. Dir. Young Adult Ministry; Ms. CAROLYN MEEKS, Asst. Dir. Adult Formation; Ms. RITA RAMOS, Asst. Dir., Youth; Ms. CATHI SNYDER, Asst. Dir. Elementary Catechesis; TERESA MONAGHEN, A.O., Campus Ministry. Tel: 402-554-8493; Fax: 402-554-8402.

Family Life—Sr. BARBARA MARKEY, N.D., Dir., *3214 N. 60th St., Omaha, 68104.* Tel: 402-551-9003.

Office for Formation and Education in Sexuality—DEBBIE SHEEHAN, Coord., *3218 N. 60th St., Omaha, 68104.* Tel: 402-556-8219.

Hispanic Ministry—Sr. ANGELA EREVIA, M.C.D.P., *3218 N. 60th St., Omaha, 68104.* Tel: 402-551-2255.

Holy Name Society—Rev. JOHN S. MICHALAK, Dir.

Hospitals—Rev. JAMES QUINN, S.J.

Legion of Mary—Rev. PETER F. DUNNE, Dir.

Natural Family Planning—Sr. BARBARA MARKEY, N.D., Dir., *3214 N. 60th St., Omaha, 68104.* Tel: 402-551-9003.

Newspaper—Mr. CHARLIE WIESER, Editor; Ms. JENNIFER WILHEMS, Assoc. Editor, *"The Catholic Voice", 6060 N.W. Radial Hwy., Omaha, 68104.* Tel: 402-558-6611; Fax: 402-558-6614.

Nocturnal Adoration Society—Vacant.

Office For Consecrated Life—Sr. JACQUELINE THORN, O.S.M., *100 N. 62nd St., Omaha, 68132.* Tel: 402-558-3100.

Pastoral Planning Office—MARY JO HUSTEN, Dir. Tel: 402-551-2255.

Priests' Eucharistic League—Rev. WILLIAM WHELAN.

Propagation of the Faith, Pontifical Association of Holy Childhood and Catholic Students Mission Crusade—Rev. GERALD P. MELCHIOR, J.C.L., Dir., *100 N. 62nd St., Omaha, 68132.*

Retreats, Laymen—Rev. ALBAN SUEPER, S.S.C., Dir.

Rural Life Conference—Rev. FRANK J. BAUMERT.

St. Vincent de Paul Society—Rev. JOHN L. PIETRAMALE, Spiritual Dir.; Mr. PATRICK McCARTHY, Pres., *2101 Leavenworth St., Omaha, 68102.*

St. Vincent de Paul Store, Inc.—2101 Leavenworth St., Omaha, 68102.

Priests' Council—

Officers—Revs. HARRY BUSE, Pres. ROBERT ENGLISH, Vice Pres. DAVID LAPLANTE, Sec. THOMAS WEISBECKER, Treas.

Age Groups—Revs. ROLAND PESCHEL; ROBERT A. SCHMITZ; JAMES KRAMPER; GARY L. OSTRANDER; OWEN W. KORTE; MICHAEL P. ECKLEY; DANIEL WITTROCK; THOMAS W. WEISBECKER.

Religious Orders—Revs. THOMAS SHANAHAN, S.J.; BERNARD SHEEHAN, O.S.B.; COLM STANLEY, S.S.C.

Deans—Revs. CHARLES F. SWANSON, (USC); JAMES E. GILG, (USE); ROBERT F. PREISINGER, (US); NORMAN HUNKE, (UNE); DANIEL KAMPSCHNEIDER, (UNW); FRANKLIN A. DVORAK, (UW); STEPHEN J. GUTGSELL, (RSW); ROBERT K. ENGLISH, (RNC); DOUGLAS P. SCHEINOST, (RNW); DENNIS U. DEGUZMAN, (RSE); DAVID W. LAPLANTE, (RNE); GERALD A. CONNEALY, (RC).

Archbishop's Appointees—Revs. GREGORY P. BAXTER, S.T.L.; MICHAEL F. GUTGSELL, J.C.L.; PATRICK C. HARRISON, J.C.L.

Ex Officio—Revs. MICHAEL W. GREWE, Vicar Gen. THOMAS J. ADAMS, Consultor; HAROLD J. BUSE; JAMES R. CAIN; CHARLES F. SWANSON; R. MICHAEL FITZPATRICK, J.C.L., S.T.L.

Social Ministry Commission—KELLY KELLER, *3300 N. 60th St., Omaha, 68104.* Tel: 402-554-0520; Fax: 402-554-0365.

Sodalities—Vacant.

Office for Spiritual Development for Lay Ministry—Rev. THOMAS A. GREISEN, Dir., *3218 N. 60th St., Omaha, 68104-3494.* Tel: 402-561-9274; Fax: 402-551-3050.

Catholic Charities, Inc.—SCOT L. ADAMS, Exec. Dir., *3300 N. 60th St., Omaha, 68104.* Tel: 402-554-0520.

Catholic Charities, Inc. Satellite Offices and Services—

The Shelter—Care for battered women, children, therapy for spouse abusers. CHRIS CARLSON, Contact Person, *P.O. Box 4346, Omaha, 68104.* Tel: 402-558-5700.

St. Martin de Porres Center—Social Justice education, counseling, food pantry, refugee program. A'JAMAL BYNDON, Emergency Svcs. VIOLA JACKSON, Vision of H.O.P.E., *2417 Burdette St., Omaha, 68111.* Tel: 402-341-4004.

Omaha. Archdiocesan Deposit and Loan Fund, Inc.—A pool of funds from archdiocesan parishes providing low interest loans for capital improvements and new construction by archdiocesan parishes. This nonprofit religious, charitable and educational corporation, whose president is the Archdiocese of Omaha, is duly constituted under the laws of the State of Nebraska. LEE KARRER, Business Mgr., *100 N. 62nd St., Omaha, 68132.* Tel: 402-558-3100; Fax: 402-558-3026.

Omaha. Archdiocesan Retreat and Conference Centers—Located in renovated Sheehan Center and Cathedral Center space, overnight, day and weekend accommodations for teens, young adults and adult groups, large and small meeting space, chapel and food service area. Deacon TOM FRANKENFIELD, *3330 N. 60th St., Omaha, 68104.* Tel: 402-558-1442; Fax: 402-551-1482.

Omaha Campus for Hope—Detoxification, inpatient treatment and extended care for low-income and indigent alcoholics. VICKI MACA, Contact Person, *1490 N. 16th St., Omaha, 68102.* Tel: 402-827-0570.

UCSS Counseling Services—JACK WRIGHT, *Sheehan Center, 3300 N. 60th St., Omaha, 68104.* Tel: 402-554-0520. RAY WILSON, Substance Abuse, *3300 N. 60th St., Omaha, 68104.* Tel: 402-554-0520.

Catholic Family Services—CARROLL BARNES, Contact Person, *1761 26th Ave., P.O. Box 573, Columbus, 68602-0573.* Tel: 402-563-3833.

Catholic Family Services—1255 4th St., Ste. 220, Norfolk, 68701. Tel: 402-371-3555.

Vocations—Rev. GREGORY P. BAXTER, S.T.L.

Youth-Young Adult Ministry—Ms. RITA RAMOS, *3216 N. 60th St., Omaha, 68104.* Tel: 402-551-5070.

CLERGY, PARISHES, MISSIONS AND PAROCHIAL SCHOOLS

CITY OF OMAHA
(Douglas County)

1—ST. CECILIA'S CATHEDRAL, Revs. Norman F. Hunke; Damien J. Cook; Ukachukwu Sebastian Onyeabor.
Res., 701 N. 40 St., 68131. Tel: 402-551-2313; Fax: 402-551-2306.
School—Tel: 402-556-6655.
Congregation of the Most Holy Rosary, (Sinsinawa, WI) 1; Lay Teachers 30; Students 527.
Catechesis/Religious Programs—Bonnie Pryor, D.R.E.
Students 70.

2—ST. ADALBERT, Rev. Frank A. Partusch. In res., Rev. Gregory Baxter.
Res., 2617 S. 31st St., 68105. Tel: 402-345-1621.
Catechesis/Religious Programs—2124 S. 32nd Ave., 68105. Tel: 402-341-5604.
Students 5.

3—ST. AGNES, Rev. Damian Zuerlein.
Res., 2215 Q St., 68107. Tel: 402-731-0100; Fax: 402-731-2196.

4—ST. ANN, Revs. John C. Rizzo; Gustavo Barrientos. In res., Rev. Nguyen Loi.
Res., 2247 Poppleton Ave., 68108. Tel: 402-341-6613; Fax: 402-341-1753.
School—All Saints Catholic School. See Elementary Schools, Interparochial Under Institutions Located in the Archdiocese.
Catechesis/Religious Programs—Students 14.

5—ST. ANTHONY, Rev. Carl F. Sodoro.
Res., 5401 S. 33rd St., 68107. Tel: 402-733-2423.

6—ASSUMPTION, B.V.M., Rev. J. Brian Beilman.
Res., 5434 S. 22nd St., 68107. Tel: 402-734-4500; Fax: 402-734-4501.
School—Tel: 402-734-4504.
Lay Teachers 12; Students 160.

7—ST. BENEDICT THE MOOR, Rev. Walter E. Boehme, S.J.
Res., 2423 Grant St., 68111. Tel: 402-348-0631.

8—ST. BERNADETTE, Revs. Robert F. Preisinger; Joseph Broudou; Deacons Ron Casart; Pete Digilio; Sebastian Enzolera. In res., Rev. Msgr. Albert L. Krejci.
Res., 7600 S. 42nd St., Omaha, 68147. Tel: 402-731-4694; Fax: 402-733-4890.
School—Tel: 402-731-3033; Fax: 402-731-8735. Mrs. Lisa Nelson, Prin.
Lay Teachers 22; Students 359.
Catechesis/Religious Programs—Tel: 402-731-9421; Fax: 402-733-4890.
Students 118.

9—ST. BERNARD, Revs. Jerome I. Spenner; Ryan Lewis; Deacons Donald Kemp; Skip Baughman; Carl Miller; Edward Osterhaus; Paul Dreismeier; Maurice Menke.
Res., 3601 N. 65 St., 68104. Tel: 402-551-0269; Fax: 402-551-2311.
School—Tel: 402-553-4993. James Palmer, Prin.
Lay Teachers 20; Students 306.
Catechesis/Religious Programs—Tel: 402-556-1679. JoAnne Raleigh, D.R.E.
Students 80.

10—BLESSED SACRAMENT, Rev. Edgar J. Wortmann.
Res., 3020 Curtis Ave., 68111. Tel: 402-455-5200; Fax: 402-455-6699.
School—Tel: 402-455-4030; Fax: 402-455-6699.
Lay Teachers 11; Students 109.

11—ST. BRIDGET, Rev. James L. Weeke. In res., Rev. Paul Begley.
Res., 4112 S. 26th St., 68107. Tel: 402-733-8811; Fax: 402-733-1272.
Catechesis/Religious Programs—Tel: 402-734-5227.
Students 22.

12—CHRIST THE KING, Revs. Thomas R. Ward; John L. Pietramale; Wayne W. Schlautman; Deacon Glenn Tylutki.
Res., 654 S. 86th St., 68114. Tel: 402-391-3606; Fax: 402-391-1498.
School—Tel: 402-391-0977; Fax: 402-391-2418. Mrs. Mary Anderson, Prin.
Lay Teachers 28; Students 332.
Catechesis/Religious Programs—Tel: 402-391-3624. Colleen Leise, D.R.E.
Students 90.

13—ST. ELIZABETH ANN, Revs. Joseph G. Hanefeldt; Joseph M. Wray; Deacons Jack Finney; Richard Nelson; Ernie Gencarelli; Martin Crowley; Dennis Connor; John Dagerman.
Res., 5425 North 114th St., 68164. Tel: 402-493-9103; Fax: 402-493-0630.
School—St. James-Seton School. See Elementary Schools, Interparochial Under Institutions Located in the Archdiocese.
Catechesis/Religious Programs—Tel: 402-572-0369; Fax: 402-572-0368. Mrs. Doris Grillo, D.R.E.
Students 742.

14—ST. FRANCES CABRINI, Rev. Roger Kalscheuer; Deacon Anthony Filipcic.
Res., 1334 S. Ninth St., 68108. Tel: 402-342-2464; Fax: 402-342-2470.
Catechesis/Religious Programs—Students 29.
School—All Saints Catholic School. See Elementary Schools, Interparochial Under Institutions Located in the Archdiocese.

15—ST. FRANCIS ASSISI, Revs. John C. Starostka; John R. Buckson, Hispanic Ministry; Deacon Timothy J. Koziel.
Res., 4513 S. 32nd St., 68107-1499. Tel: 402-731-2699; Fax: 402-731-2364.
School—Tel: 402-733-3345.
Sisters 1; Lay Teachers 2; Students 30.
Catechesis/Religious Programs—Students 102.

16—HOLY CROSS, Revs. Charles F. Swanson; Thomas S. Matt. In res., Rev. Ralph Librea; Deacon George Elster.
Res., 4803 William St., 68106. Tel: 402-553-7500; Fax: 402-553-7735.
School—Tel: 402-551-3773.
Lay Teachers 21; Students 364.
Catechesis/Religious Programs—Students 79.

17—HOLY FAMILY, Deacon Ralph L. Hueser, Admin.
Res., 1715 Izard St., 68102. Tel: 402-345-1062; Fax: 402-344-8136.

18—HOLY GHOST, Rev. Richard J. Reiser, Temporary Admin.; Deacons Tom Schulte; Paul Eubanks.
Res., 5219 S. 53rd St., 68117. Tel: 402-731-3176; Fax: 402-738-1409.

School—Tel: 402-731-5161; Fax: 402-738-1409. Jane Barreuther, Prin.
Lay Teachers 16; Students 250.
Catechesis/Religious Programs—Tel: 402-731-4574. Mary Gregg, D.R.E.
Students 268.

19—HOLY NAME, Revs. Richard Quinn, C.SS.R.; William Parker, C.SS.R.; John Morton, C.SS.R.; Bro. William Cloughley, C.SS.R.
Res., 3014 N. 45th St., 68104. Tel: 402-451-6622; Fax: 402-457-6901.
School—(Grades K-8). Tel: 402-451-5403; Fax: 402-453-7950. Sofia Kock, Prin.
Lay Teachers 13; Students 254.
Catechesis/Religious Programs—Tel: 402-453-0873. J. Diane Van Ornam, D.R.E.
Students 40.

20—IMMACULATE CONCEPTION, B.V.M., Rev. Wally G. Wancewicz; Deacon Paul Matukewicz.
Res., 2708 S. 24th St., 68108. Tel: 402-342-1074; Fax: 402-342-1074.
School—All Saints Catholic School. See Elementary Schools, Interparochial Under Institutions Located in the Archdiocese.
Catechesis/Religious Programs—Students 62.

21—ST. JAMES, Rev. Michael W. Grewe; Rt. Rev. Raphael Walsh, O.S.B.; Deacons Jerry Gau; Larry Heck; Stan Kurtz; Pat Lenz; Wayne Young. In res., Rev. James V. Brown, O.A.R.
Res., 9025 Larimore Ave., 68134. Tel: 402-572-0499; Fax: 402-573-9345.
School—St. James-Seton School. See Elementary Schools, Interparochial Under Institutions Located in the Archdiocese.
Catechesis/Religious Programs—Tel: 402-572-0369; Fax: 402-572-0368. Mrs. Doris Grillo, D.R.E.
Students 175.

22—ST. JOAN OF ARC, Rev. Emmett F. Meyer. In res., Rev. Patrick C. Harrison, J.C.L.
Res., 3122 S. 74th St., 68124. Tel: 402-393-2005; Fax: 402-398-9438.
School—Tel: 402-393-2314; Fax: 402-393-4405.
Sisters of Mercy 2; Lay Teachers 24; Students 338.
Catechesis/Religious Programs—Tel: 402-391-1906; 393-2315. Marilyn Opitz, D.R.E.
Students 147.

23—ST. JOHN, Revs. Bert Thelen, S.J.; Philip R. Amidon, S.J.; Thomas N. Schloemer, S.J.; Deacon Ken Kalkowski.
Office: 2500 California Pl., 68178. Tel: 402-280-3030; Fax: 402-280-2465.

24—ST. JOHN VIANNEY, Revs. R. Patrick McCaslin; Paul M. Albensius; Deacons Pete DesRosiers; Frank Telich. In res., Rev. James M. Sullivan (HEL).
Res., 5801 Oak Hills Dr., 68137. Tel: 402-895-0808; Fax: 402-895-0808.
Catechesis/Religious Programs—Tel: 402-895-0896. Anne Waldron, D.R.E.
Students 403.

25—ST. JOSEPH, Rev. Walter G. Wancewicz.
Res., 1723 S. 17th St., 68108. Tel: 402-342-1618; Fax: 402-342-2640.
School—All Saints Catholic School. See Elementary Schools, Interparochial Under Institutions Located in the Archdiocese.
Catechesis/Religious Programs—Students 64.

26—ST. LEO, Revs. Harold J. Buse; William D. Bond.
Res., 1920 N. 102nd St., 68114. Tel: 402-397-0407; Fax: 402-397-2887.
School—St. Pius X-St. Leo School. See Elementary Schools, Interparochial Under Institutions Located in the Archdiocese.
Catechesis/Religious Programs—Students 492.

27—ST. MARGARET MARY, Revs. Melvin Merwald; Rodney T. Adams; Michael Mukasa (Uganda).
Res., 6116 Dodge St., 68132. Tel: 402-558-2255; Fax: 402-551-5631.
School—Tel: 402-551-6663.
Lay Teachers 22; Students 542.
Catechesis/Religious Programs—Students 742.

28—ST. MARY, Rev. Carl F. Sodoro.
Res., 3529 Q St., 68107. Tel: 402-731-0204.
School—Tel: 402-738-9533; Fax: 402-738-1425.
Lay Teachers 13; Students 142.
Catechesis/Religious Programs—Students 167.

29—ST. MARY MAGDALENE, Revs. James E. Gilg; Fernando C. Benliro.
Res., 109 S. 19th St., 68102. Tel: 402-342-4807; Fax: 402-344-0941.
School—All Saints Catholic School. See Elementary Schools, Interparochial Under Institutions Located in the Archdiocese.

30—MARY OUR QUEEN, Revs. Carl A. Salanitro; Ralph B. O'Donnell; Deacons Paul Rooney; Ron Hesson; Robert Hamilton. In res., Rev. Michael F. Gutgsell.
Res., 3535 S. 119th St., 68144. Tel: 402-333-8662; Fax: 402-333-4504.
School—3405 S. 119th St., 68144. Tel: 402-333-8663; Fax: 402-334-3948.
Lay Teachers 27; Students 612.
Catechesis/Religious Programs—Tel: 402-333-8231. Barb Eastridge, D.R.E.
Students 450.

31—MOTHER OF PERPETUAL HELP. (Church of the Deaf).
Res., 5215 Seward St., 68104. Tel: 402-558-4214.

32—OUR LADY OF GUADALUPE, Revs. Damian Zuerlein; John R. Buckson; Anthony Espinosa; Gonzalo Ojeda (Mexico); Deacons Joe Ramirez; Duane Bronk.
Res., 2310 O St., 68107. Tel: 402-731-2196; Fax: 402-731-2196.
Catechesis/Religious Programs—Sr. Marcianne Trujillo, D.R.E.
Students 529.

33—OUR LADY OF LOURDES, Revs. Frank A. Partusch; Paul L. Vasquez; Deacon Frank Hilt.
Res., 2110 S. 32nd Ave., 68105. Tel: 402-346-0900; Fax: 402-344-3315.
School—2124 S. 32nd Ave., 68105. Tel: 402-341-5604. Mrs. Debra Turner, Prin.
Sisters 1; Lay Teachers 21; Students 411.

34—ST. PATRICK, Revs. Lucian S. Astuto; Eric Flood, F.S.S.P.
Res., 1404 Castelar St., 68108. Tel: 402-341-1305; Fax: 402-342-5510.
School—All Saints Catholic School. See Elementary Schools, Interparochial Under Institutions Located in the Archdiocese.
Catechesis/Religious Programs—Students 91.

35—ST. PETER, Revs. John C. Rizzo; Gustavo Barrientos; Deacon John Zak.
Res., 709 S. 28th St., 68105. Tel: 402-341-4560; Fax: 402-341-6483.

36—SS. PETER AND PAUL, Revs. Burnell B. Bisbee, S.J., Temporary Admin.; Norman B. Parr.
Res., 5912 S. 36th St., 68107. Tel: 402-731-4578; Fax: 402-738-8808.
School—Tel: 402-731-4713; Fax: 402-731-2633. Richard Leimbach, Prin.
Lay Teachers 17; Students 298.
Catechesis/Religious Programs—Tel: 402-733-3344. Mary Ellen Hartquist, D.R.E.
Students 129.

37—ST. PHILIP NERI, Revs. Daniel J. Kampschneider; Thomas A. Greisen; Deacon Fred Hendrick; Sr. Susan Ivis, Pastoral Min., Tel: 402-451-6921.
Res., 8200 N. 30th St., 68112. Tel: 402-455-1289; Fax: 402-455-8398.
School—Tel: 402-455-8666; Fax: 402-453-3620. Barbara Marchese, Prin.
Lay Teachers 13; Students 228.
Catechesis/Religious Programs—Tel: 402-455-2190. Marsha Moon, D.R.E.
Students 92.

38—ST. PIUS X, Revs. Lloyd A. Gnirk; William Safranek.
Res., 6905 Blondo St., 68104. Tel: 402-558-8446; Fax: 402-558-4986.
School—St. Pius X-St. Leo School. See Elementary Schools, Interparochial Under Institutions Located in the Archdiocese.
Catechesis/Religious Programs—Tel: 402-558-1898. Susan Naatz, D.R.E.
Students 816.

39—ST. RICHARD, Rev. Kenneth P. Vavrina.
Res., 4320 Fort St., 68111. Tel: 402-455-2865; Fax: 402-455-0679.
School—Tel: 402-451-0692. Ms. Sue McCaslin, Prin.
Sisters 2; Lay Teachers 11; Students 160.

40—ST. ROBERT BELLARMINE, Revs. Donald W. Shane; Mario D. Rapose; Deacons Fred Alexander, (Retired); William Fell. In res., Rev. Gerald P. Melchior.
Res., 11802 Pacific St., 68154. Tel: 402-333-8989; Fax: 402-333-5489.
School—(Grades PreK-8). Tel: 402-334-1929; Fax: 402-333-7188. Sandra Suiter, Prin.
Lay Teachers 30; Students 615.
Catechesis/Religious Programs—Tel: 402-333-1959. Wilma D. Smith, D.R.E.
Students 220.

41—ST. ROSE, Rev. Thomas J Adams.
Res., 4102 S. 13th St., 68107. Tel: 402-733-9327; Fax: 402-731-9937.

42—SACRED HEART, Rev. Thomas M. Fangman; Deacons Charles Weskirchen; James Chambers.
Res., 2218 Binney St., 68110. Tel: 402-451-5755; Fax: 402-451-1731.
School—Tel: 402-451-5858.
Lay Teachers 12; Students 135.
Catechesis/Religious Programs—Students 87.

43—ST. STANISLAUS, Rev. R. Michael Fitzpatrick, S.T.L.; Deacons Daniel Saniuk; James Staroski. Pastoral Ministers: Sr. Margaret Mary Ryan.
Res., 4002 J St., 68107. Tel: 402-731-4152; Fax: 402-731-4389.
School—Tel: 402-731-0484.
Lay Teachers 8; Students 128.
Catechesis/Religious Programs—Students 29.

44—ST. STEPHEN THE MARTYR, Revs. Gerald E. Gonderinger; Timothy M. Podraza.
Res., 17053 M St., 68135. Tel: 402-896-9682.
Church—16701 S St., 68135. Tel: 402-896-9675; Fax: 402-896-1990.
School—Tel: 402-896-0754. Mr. David Peters Prin.
Students 767.
Catechesis/Religious Programs—Tel: 402-896-9683.
Students 642.

45—ST. THERESE OF THE CHILD JESUS, Rev. Kenneth P. Vavrina.
Res., 5316 N. 14th Ave., 68110. Tel: 402-455-2865.

46—ST. THOMAS MORE, Revs. John E. Vernon; Alexander Wild. In res., Rev. Stanislaus Golik.
Res., 4804 Grover St., 68106. Tel: 402-556-1456; Fax: 402-556-1395.
School—Tel: 402-551-9504; Fax: 402-551-9507.
Lay Teachers 24; Students 379.
Catechesis/Religious Programs—Tel: 402-551-9816; Fax: 402-551-9507.
Students 135.

47—ST. VINCENT DE PAUL, Sarpy Co., Revs. Dennis A. Hanneman; Francis A. Nigli; Deacons Donald K. Clausen; William J. Barnes; Gary J. Hennessey. In res., Rev. Thomas F. O'Brien.
Res., 14330 Eagle Run Dr., 68164. Tel: 402-496-7988 (Pastoral Center); 498-8425 (Rectory); Fax: 402-496-9933.
School—Tel: 402-492-2111. Patricia Buttell, Prin.
Students 750.
Catechesis/Religious Programs—Tel: 402-493-1642; Fax: 402-496-9933.
Students 772.

48—ST. WENCESLAUS, Revs. Franklin A. Dvorak; Dermot J. Dunne; Richard J. Swolek; Deacons John Cerveny; Elvon Anderson; Donald Cowles; Joseph Friend.
Res., 15353 Pacific St., Omaha, 68154. Tel: 402-330-0304; Fax: 402-330-1476.
School—(Grades K-8). Tel: 402-330-4356. Mary McGuire, Prin.
Students 842.
Catechesis/Religious Programs—Tel: 402-330-1889. Judy Thorne, D.R.E.
Students 808.

OUTSIDE THE CITY OF OMAHA

Albion, Boone Co., St. Michael, Rev. Frank J. Baumert.
Res., 524 W. Church St., 68620. Tel: 402-395-2393; Fax: 402-330-1476.
School—Tel: 402-395-2926; Fax: 402-395-2926.
Priests 1; Lay Teachers 10; Students 90.
Catechesis/Religious Programs—Students 233.

Aloys, Cuming Co., St. Aloysius, Rev. Dennis DeGuzman.
Res., 700 Hwy. 32, West Point, 68788. Tel: 402-372-2789. [CEM]

Atkinson, Holt Co., St. Joseph, Rev. LuVerne W. Steffes; Deacons Gerald Gonderinger, (Retired); Art Villemure.
Res., 317 W. State St., P.O. Box 220, 68713. Tel: 402-925-2122; Fax: 402-925-5320. [CEM]
School—Tel: 402-925-2104.
Lay Teachers 10; Students 90.
Catechesis/Religious Programs—Tel: 402-925-5854. Patti Skrdla, D.R.E.
Students 123.

Bancroft, Cuming Co., Holy Cross, Rev. David W. LaPlante.
Res., P.O. Box 524, Lyons, 68038. Tel: 402-687-2102; Fax: 402-687-2102.
Catechesis/Religious Programs—Students 39.

Battle Creek, Madison Co., St. Patrick's, Rev. Michael P. Eckley.
Res., 107 N. Third St., P.O. Box 40, 68715. Tel: 402-675-2485.
Catechesis/Religious Programs—Marg Weber, D.R.E.
Students 105.
Mission—Schoolcraft, Madison Co., St. Francis de Sales.

Beemer, Cuming Co., Holy Cross, Revs. Mark K Merkel; Jeff Zyla, Temporary Admin.
Res., 517 Fraisier St. N., P.O. Box 212, 68716. Tel: 402-528-3475; Fax: 402-528-3374. [CEM]
Catechesis/Religious Programs—Students 62.

Bellevue, Sarpy Co., St. Mary, Revs. Francis W. Lordemann; Michael P. Keating; Deacons Ralph Hueser; Duane Iwanski; Chuck L'Archevesque; Andy Foray; John Huck; Eugene Hanson; John Wacha.
Res., 811 W. 23rd Ave., 68005. Tel: 402-291-1350; Fax: 402-291-1375.

School—(Grades PreK-8). Tel: 402-291-1666. Jean Seibel, Prin.
Lay Teachers 25; Students 281.
Catechesis/Religious Programs—Tel: 402-291-3964. Nina Tisinger, D.R.E.
Students 358.

Blair, Washington Co., St. Francis Borgia, Rev. Alfred J. Salanitro.
Res., P.O. Box 548, 68008. Tel: 402-426-3823; Fax: 402-426-5131. [CEM]
Catechesis/Religious Programs—Tel: 402-426-5145. David Kaslon, D.R.E.
Students 381.

Bellevue, Sarpy Co., St. Matthew The Evangelist Church of Bellevue, Rev. Dennis R. Stolinksi.
Res., 3605 Looking Glass Dr., 68123. Tel: 402-292-7418; Fax: 402-292-7418.
School—(Grades K-8) 12210 S. 36th St., 68123. Tel: 402-291-2030; Fax: 402-291-2047. Patrick J. Slattery, Prin.
Lay Teachers 16; Students 199.
Catechesis/Religious Programs—Students 174.

Bloomfield, Knox Co., St. Andrew, Rev. Stanley J. Schmit.
Res., 304 S. McNamara St., P.O. Box 416, 68718. Tel: 402-373-2233; Fax: 402-373-2233. [CEM]
Catechesis/Religious Programs—Tel: 402-373-2696. Barb Jackson, D.R.E.
Students 131.

Bow Valley, Cedar Co., SS. Peter and Paul. Merged with Sacred Heart, Wynot; Ss. Philip and James, St. James and Immaculate Conception, St. Helena to form Holy Family Church of Cedar County, Hartington.

Boys Town, Douglas Co., Immaculate Conception B.V.M., Rev. Valentine J. Peter. In res., Rev. Msgr. Peter F. Dunne; Rev. Eugene McReynolds, O.S.B.
Res., 68010. Tel: 402-498-1000; Fax: 402-498-1010.
Catechesis/Religious Programs—Tel: 402-498-1885.
Students 570.

Butte, Boyd Co, SS. Peter and Paul, Rev. Lydell T Lape.
Res., P.O. Box 8, 68722. Tel: 402-775-2452; Fax: 402-775-2452. [CEM]
Catechesis/Religious Programs—Students 64.
Mission—Naper, Boyd Co., Sacred Heart. [CEM]

Cedar Rapids, Boone Co., St. Anthony, Rev. Ralph J. Steffensmeier.
Res., P.O. Box 56, 68627. Tel: 308-358-0773; Fax: 402-358-0773. [CEM]
Catechesis/Religious Programs—Students 110.
Mission—Primrose, Boone Co., St. Mary, 68627. [CEM]

Central City, Merrick Co., St. Michael, Rev. Nelson A. Newman; Deacon Robert Flesch.
Res., 2402 20th Ave., 68826. Tel: 308-946-2855; Fax: 308-946-2214.
Catechesis/Religious Programs—D.R.E.: Janelle Benson; Dave Varley.
Students 104.

Clarks, Merrick Co., St. Peter, Rev. Donald M. Cleary.
Res., 315 N. Esther, Fullerton, 68638. Tel: 308-536-2574. [CEM]
Catechesis/Religious Programs—Tel: 308-548-2573. Linda Yrkoski, D.R.E.
Students 51.

Clarkson, Colfax Co., SS. Cyril and Methodius, Rev. Floyd A. Wessling.
Res., 120 Cherry St., P.O. Box 457, 68629. Tel: 402-892-3464; Fax: 402-892-9879.
School—St. John Neumann, Tel: 402-892-3474; Fax: 402-892-3090.
Lay Teachers 4; Students 62.
Catechesis/Religious Programs—Students 96.

Coleridge, Cedar Co., St. Michael, Rev. William E. Sanderson.
Res., 315 S. Madison, R.R. 1, 68727. Tel: 402-283-4614; Fax: 402-254-6553.
Mailing Address: P.O. Box 278, Harrington, 68739.
Catechesis/Religious Programs—Students 66.

Columbus, Platte Co., St. Anthony, Rev. Christopher J. Grimmond; Deacons Michael Placzek; Michael McGuire; Kelly McGowan.
Res., 562 17th Ave., 68601. Tel: 402-564-3313; Fax: 402-563-1005.
School—Tel: 402-564-4767; Fax: 402-563-1005. Norma Cremers, Prin.
Lay Teachers 7; Students 158.
Catechesis/Religious Programs—Lori Olson, D.R.E.
Students 144.

St. Bonaventure, Revs. Daniel E. Keller; Thomas Weisbecker; Deacons Arthur Spenner; Lawrence Mielak.
Res., 1565 18th Ave., 68601. Tel: 402-564-7151; Fax: 402-562-6025. [CEM]
School—Tel: 402-564-7153. Mr. Chris Vos, Prin.
Sisters 2; Lay Teachers 13; Students 226.
Catechesis/Religious Programs—D.R.E.: Rose V. Arp; Pat Williams.
Students 291.

St. Isidore, Revs. Joseph A. Miksch; Steven D. Emanuel.
Res., 3921 20th St., 68601. Tel: 402-564-8993; Fax: 402-564-8955.
School—Tel: 402-564-2604; Fax: 402-564-5349.
Missionary Benedictine Sisters 4; Lay Teachers 12; Students 228.
Catechesis/Religious Programs—Students 178.

Constance, Knox Co., St. Joseph. (Mission of Crofton). Rev. Robert K. English.
Mailing Address: Box 335, Crofton, 68730. Tel: 402-388-4814. [CEM]
School—West Catholic Elementary. See Elementary Schools, Interparochial Under Institutions Located in the Archdiocese.

Creighton, Knox Co., St. Ludger, Rev. Keith D. Rezac.
Res., 908 Lake St., 68729-2917. Tel: 402-358-3596.
School—410 Bryant Ave., 68729. Tel: 402-358-3501; Fax: 402-358-3501.
Sisters 1; Lay Teachers 4; Students 44.
Catechesis/Religious Programs—Tel: 402-358-3501. D.R.E.: Sharon Closter; LaDonna Ebel; Darla Frisch.
Students 112.
Mission—Brunswick, Antelope Co., St. Ignatius.

Crofton, Knox Co., St. Rose of Lima, Rev. Robert K. English.
Res., 1316 W. Fifth St., P.O. Box 335, 68730. Tel: 402-388-4814; Fax: 402-388-2680. [CEM]
School—Tel: 402-388-4393; Fax: 402-388-4393.
Lay Teachers 8; Students 154.
Catechesis/Religious Programs—D.R.E.: Cindy Stucky, (Grades 1-8); Arlene Dick.
Students 247.

Dodge, Dodge Co., St. Wenceslaus, Rev. Daniel Wittrock.
Res., 743 Second St., 68633. Tel: 402-693-2235; Fax: 402-693-2255. [CEM 2]
School—Tel: 402-693-2819; Fax: 402-693-2347. Elizabeth Gibney, Prin.
Lay Teachers 6; Students 79.
Catechesis/Religious Programs—Tel: 402-693-2347. Joan Ruskamp, D.R.E.
Students 104.

Duncan, Platte Co., St. Stanislaus, Rev. David M. Korth.
Res., P.O. Box 192, 68634. Tel: 402-897-2625; Fax: 402-897-2626. [CEM]
Catechesis/Religious Programs—Students 79.

Elgin, Antelope Co., St. Boniface, Rev. Thomas E. Bauwens; Deacons Dennis Wiehn; Bill Camp.
Res., P.O. Box B, 68636-0433. Tel: 402-843-2345; Fax: 402-843-2253. [CEM]
School—Tel: 402-843-5460; Fax: 402-843-5842.
Sisters 1; Lay Teachers 8; Students 122.
Catechesis/Religious Programs—Students 202.

Elkhorn, Douglas Co., St. Patrick, Rev. Ronald S. Wasikowski.
Res., 20500 W. Maple Rd., P.O. Box 10, 68022. Tel: 402-289-4289; Fax: 402-289-4288. [CEM]
School—(Grades PreK-3). Donald Ridder, Prin.
Students 82.
Catechesis/Religious Programs—Tel: 402-289-4947.
Students 367.

Emerson, Dakota Co., Sacred Heart, Rev. James V. Kramper.
Res., Sixth St. & Main St., P.O. Box 250, 68733. Tel: 402-695-2342; Fax: 402-695-2505. [CEM]
School—Tel: 402-695-2513.
Lay Teachers 4; Students 43.
Catechesis/Religious Programs—Students 107.

Ewing, Holt Co., St. Peter de Alcantara, Rev. Jay L. Kruse.
Res., P.O. Box 37, 68735. Tel: 402-626-7605; Fax: 402-626-7668.
Catechesis/Religious Programs—Tel: 402-626-7905. Elaine Thoendel, D.R.E.
Students 98.

Fordyce, Cedar Co., St. John the Baptist, Rev. Gregory Benkowski; Deacon Marcus Potts.
Res., P.O. Box 170, 68736. Tel: 402-357-3506; Fax: 402-357-3708. [CEM]
School—West Catholic Elementary. See Elementary Schools, Interparochial Under Institutions Located in the Archdiocese.
Catechesis/Religious Programs—Tel: 402-357-2548. Kathy Magorian, D.R.E.
Students 9.

Fort Calhoun, Washington Co., St. John the Baptist, Rev. Ronald J. Noecker.
Res., 215 N. 13th St., P.O. Box 148, 68023. Tel: 402-468-5348; Fax: 402-468-4619.
Catechesis/Religious Programs—Tel: 402-468-5659.
Students 169.

Fremont, Dodge Co., St. Patrick, Revs. Owen W. Korte; Carl Zoucha; Roland A. Peschel; Deacons Robert Chapman; Edward Gentrup; Justin Lauer; Hugh Robinson; LeRoy Spieker.
Res., 422 E. Fourth St., 68025. Tel: 402-721-6611; Fax: 402-727-8167. [CEM]
High School—Archbishop Bergan, (Grades 9-12). Tel: 402-721-9683; Fax: 402-721-5366. Don Cunningham, Prin.
Lay Teachers 26; Students 267.
School—Bergan Middle School, (Grades 6-8). Tel: 402-721-9766; Fax: 402-721-5366.
Catechesis/Religious Programs—Tel: 402-721-9710. Margaret Iossi, D.R.E.
Students 465.

Fullerton, Nance Co., St. Peter, Rev. Donald M. Cleary.
Res., 315 N. Esther, P.O. Box 368, 68638. Tel: 308-536-2574; Fax: 308-536-2574. [CEM]
Catechesis/Religious Programs—Tel: 308-536-2481.
Students 179.

Genoa, Nance Co., St. Rose of Lima, Rev. Robert H. Nienaber.
Res., 116 N. Elm St., P.O. Box 490, 68640-0490. Tel: 402-993-2323; Fax: 402-993-2323.
Catechesis/Religious Programs—Students 128.

Gretna, Sarpy Co., St. Patrick, Rev. Daniel F. Soltys; Deacon Joseph Krajicek.
Res., 416 Angus St., 68028. Tel: 402-332-4444; Fax: 402-332-5107. [CEM]
Catechesis/Religious Programs—Tel: 402-332-3242. Elaine Sedlacek, D.R.E.
Students 421.

Hartington, Cedar Co., Holy Family Church of Cedar County, Rev. Ross C. Burkhalter.
Parish Office: 106 W. 889th Rd., 68739-6079. Tel: 402-254-3311; Fax: 402-254-3311.
Catechesis/Religious Programs—Students 148.

Holy Trinity, Revs. William E. Sanderson; John S. Andrews.
Res., 404 S. Broadway Ave., P.O. Box 278, 68739. Tel: 402-254-6559; Fax: 402-254-6553. [CEM]
School—Tel: 402-254-6496.
Lay Teachers 10; Students 193.
Catechesis/Religious Programs—Students 145.

Heun, Colfax Co., Holy Trinity, Rev. Ray O. Bonham.
Res., 1733 Road 12, Clarkson, 68629. Tel: 402-986-1627; Fax: 402-986-1627. [CEM]
School—See Elementary Schools, Interparochial Under Institutions Located in the Archdiocese.
Catechesis/Religious Programs—Students 55.
Mission—Tabor, Colfax Co., St. Mary. [CEM]

Hooper, Dodge Co., St. Rose of Lima, Rev. William D. L'Heureux.
Res., 405 Elk St., P.O. Box 443, 68031. Tel: 402-654-3449. [CEM]
Catechesis/Religious Programs—Students 53.
Mission—Scribner, Dodge Co., St. Lawrence, 405 Elk St. Box 443, 68031. Tel: 402-654-3449. [CEM]
Catechesis/Religious Programs—Students 130.

Howells, Colfax Co., SS. Peter and Paul, Rev. Paul Ortmeier.
Res., 614 Center St., P.O. Box 40, 68641. Tel: 402-986-1653; Fax: 402-986-1653.
School—Howells Community Catholic School. See Elementary Schools, Interparochial Under Institutions Located in the Archdiocese.
Catechesis/Religious Programs—Students 123.

St. John Nepomucene, Rev. Paul Ortmeier.
Res., 614 Center St., P.O. Box 40, 68641. Tel: 402-986-1653; Fax: 402-986-1653. [CEM]
School—Howells Community Catholic School. See Elementary Schools, Interparochial Under Institutions Located in the Archdiocese.
Catechesis/Religious Programs—Students 89.

Humphrey, Platte Co., St. Francis, Rev. Stephen J. Gutgsell. In res., Rev. Wayne S. Pavela.
Res., P.O. Box 116, 68642. Tel: 402-923-0913; Fax: 402-923-1931. [CEM]
School—(Grades K-6). Tel: 402-923-0611; Fax: 402-923-1590.
Lay Teachers 8; Students 173.
High School—Tel: 402-923-0818.
Lay Teachers 16; Students 165.
Catechesis/Religious Programs—Students 43.

Jackson, Dakota Co., St. Patrick, Rev. Richard Whiteing, Temporary Admin.
Res., 203 E. Elk St., P.O. Box 87, 68743. Tel: 402-632-4292; Fax: 402-632-9254.
Catechesis/Religious Programs—Tel: 402-632-4258; Fax: 402-632-4312. Claudette Albenesius, D.R.E.
Students 125.
Mission—Hubbard, Dakota Co., St. Mary, P.O. Box 126, Hubbard, 68741. Tel: 402-632-4283. [CEM 2]

Krakow, Nance Co., SS. Peter and Paul, Rev. Robert H. Nienaber, Admin.
Res., P.O. Genoa, R.R. 2, P.O. Box 18, 68640. Tel: 402-993-6600.
Catechesis/Religious Programs—Students 23.

Laurel, Cedar Co., St. Mary, Rev. Mark A. Tomasiewicz; Deacon LeRoy Creamer.
Res., 406 Elm St., P.O. Box 828, 68745. Tel: 402-256-3303; Fax: 402-256-3019.
Catechesis/Religious Programs—Marietta Freeman, D.R.E.
Students 108.
Mission—Dixon, Dixon Co., St. Anne.

Leigh, Colfax Co., St. Mary, Rev. Melvern A. Weise.
Res., 220 W. Third St., P.O. Box 385, 68643. Tel: 402-487-2666; Fax: 402-487-2666. [CEM]
Catechesis/Religious Programs—Laurie Urban, D.R.E.
Students 75.

Lindsay, Platte Co., Holy Family, Rev. James F. Novotny.
Res., P.O. Box 68, 68644. Tel: 402-428-2455; Fax: 402-428-5205. [CEM]
School—(Grades 1-6). Tel: 402-428-3455; Fax: 402-428-3231.
Lay Teachers 7; Students 105.
High School—(Grades 7-12). Tel: 402-428-3215; Fax: 402-428-3231.
Lay Teachers 11; Students 113.
Catechesis/Religious Programs—Students 79.

Lynch, Boyd Co., Assumption B.V.M., Rev. Frank E. Jindra.
Res., P.O. Box 167, 68746. Tel: 402-569-2421; Fax: 402-569-2421. [CEM]

Lyons, Burt Co., St. Joseph, Rev. David W. LaPlante.
Res., 430 Lincoln St., P.O. Box 524, 68038. Tel: 402-687-2102; Fax: 402-687-2102.
Catechesis/Religious Programs—Students 80.

Madison, Madison Co., St. Leonard, Rev. Stanley L. Kasun; Deacon Frederick Ridder.
Res., 504 S. Nebr. St., P.O. Box 368, 68748. Tel: 402-454-3529; Fax: 402-454-3529. [CEM]
School—Tel: 402-454-3525; Fax: 402-454-6653.
Lay Teachers 5; Students 84.
Catechesis/Religious Programs—Students 156.

Menominee, Cedar Co., St. Boniface, Rev. Gregory Benkowski; Deacon Clarence Jansen.
Res., P.O. Box 170, Fordyce, 68736. Tel: 402-357-3506; Fax: 402-357-3507. [CEM]
School—West Catholic Elementary. See Elementary Schools, Interparochial Under Institutions Located in the Archdiocese.
Catechesis/Religious Programs—Tel: 402-357-2548. Kathy Magorian, D.R.E.
Students 70.

Monterey, Cuming Co., St. Boniface, Rev. Dennis DeGuzman.
Res., 450 12th Rd., West Point, 68788. Tel: 402-372-3681; Fax: 402-372-3681. [CEM]
Catechesis/Religious Programs—Students 4.

Neligh, Antelope Co., St. Francis, Rev. Craig Loecker; Deacon Bernard Burbach.
Res., 702 W. 11th St., P.O. Box 259, 68756. Tel: 402-887-4521; Fax: 402-843-2297.
Catechesis/Religious Programs—Students 240.
Mission—Neligh, Antelope Co., St. Theresa, 702 West 11th, P.O. Box 259, 68756.

Newcastle, Dixon Co., St. Peter, Rev. James J. Bartak.
Mailing Address: P.O. Box 898, Ponca, 68770-0898.
Res., P.O. Box 127, 405 Annie St., 68757. Tel: 402-355-2620 (Rectory); 755-2773 (Office); Fax: 402-755-2525.
Catechesis/Religious Programs—Tel: 402-355-2643. Angie Kneifl, D.R.E.
Students 69.

Norfolk, Madison Co., Sacred Heart, Revs. Rob A. Allgaier; Frank P. Parrinello; David D. Belt; Deacons Jim Doolittle; Richard Mueting; Irving St. Arnold; Donald Seamann.
Res., 202 S. Fifth St., 68701. Tel: 402-371-2621; Fax: 402-371-0403.
School—(Grades K-12). Tel: 402-371-4584 (K-6); 371-2784 (7-12); Fax: 402-379-8129 (K-6); 379-2929 (7-12). Principals: Ron Brewer, (Grades K-6); Jeff Bellar, (Grades 7-12).
Priests 4; Lay Teachers 56; Students 799.
Catechesis/Religious Programs—Tel: 402-371-8658. Mary Throener, D.R.E. (Grades K-12).
Students 657.

North Bend, Dodge Co., St. Charles Borromeo, Rev. Thomas J. Sellentin.
Res., P.O. Box 457, 68649. Tel: 402-652-8484; Fax: 402-652-3418.
Catechesis/Religious Programs—D.R.E.:, Tel: 402-652-8437. Betty Marxsen, (Grades K-6).
Students 215.

Olean, Colfax Co., Sacred Heart. (mission of St. Wenceslaus, Dodge). Rev. Daniel Wittrock.
Res., 743 Second St., Dodge, 68633. Tel: 402-693-2356. [CEM]
School—Howells Community Catholic School. See Elementary Schools, Interparochial Under Institutions Located in the Archdiocese.

O'Neill, Holt Co., St. Patrick, Revs. Mark D. Filips; Mark Bridgman; Lisa Lueninghoener, Liturgist.
Res., 301 E. Adams, 68763. Tel: 402-336-1602; Fax: 402-336-1613. [CEM]
School—Tel: 402-336-2664.
Sisters 1; Lay Teachers 11; Students 109.
High School—Tel: 402-336-4455.
Sisters 1; Lay Teachers 15; Students 120.
Catechesis/Religious Programs—Tel: 402-336-1602; Fax: 402-336-1513. Mary Novak, D.R.E.
Students 210.
Mission—Amelia, Holt Co., St. Joseph, Tel: 402-482-5283.

Osmond, Pierce Co., St. Mary of the Seven Dolors, Rev. James Buckley.
Res., 509 Hill St., P.O. Box 397, 68765. Tel: 402-748-3340; Fax: 402-748-3433. [CEM]
School—Tel: 402-748-3433.
Lay Teachers 4; Students 60.
Catechesis/Religious Programs—Students 127.

Papillion, Sarpy Co., St. Columbkille, Revs. Steven J. Stillmunks; Leo Rigatuso; Charles L. Jurgensmeier, S.J.; Deacons Frank Mascarello; Jerry Overkamp; Eldon Lauber; Roland Kaiser; Joseph Morley; Duane Thome; Steve Jordan; Paul Powers; Bob Steier; Yano DiGiacomo.
Res., 200 E. Sixth St., 68046. Tel: 402-339-3285; Fax: 402-592-4753.
School—Tel: 402-339-8706; Fax: 402-592-4147.
Lay Teachers 22; Students 521.
Catechesis/Religious Programs—Tel: 402-339-0990; Fax: 402-339-3977. Margie Altman, D.R.E.
Students 796.

Pender, Thurston Co., St. John, Rev. James V. Kramper.
Res., 108 N. Fifth St., P.O. Box 96, 68047. Tel: 402-385-3258.
Catechesis/Religious Programs—Students 80.

Petersburg, Boone Co., St. John the Baptist, Rev. Frank J. Baumert.
Res., 524 W.Church St., Albion, 68620. Tel: 402-395-2393; Fax: 402-395-2393. [CEM]
School—Tel: 402-386-5472.
Lay Teachers 3; Students 32.
Catechesis/Religious Programs—Students 71.

Pierce, Pierce Co., St. Joseph, Rev. Gerald A. Connealy.
Res., 118 W. Willow St., 68767. Tel: 402-329-4200; Fax: 402-329-4579. [CEM]
Catechesis/Religious Programs—Tel: 402-329-6655.
Students 184.

Plainview, Pierce Co., St. Paul, Rev. James M. Buckley.
Res., P.O. Box 387, 68769. Tel: 402-582-4413; Fax: 402-582-4413. [CEM]
Catechesis/Religious Programs—Tel: 402-748-3340.
Students 72.

Platte Center, Platte Co., St. Joseph, Rev. Rodney V. Kneifl.
Res., P.O. Box 155, 68653-0155. Tel: 402-246-2255; Fax: 402-246-2045. [CEM]
Catechesis/Religious Programs—Tel: 402-246-5700. Angela Dolezal, D.R.E.
Students 125.

Ponca, Dixon Co., St. Joseph, Rev. James J. Bartak; Deacon Paul Poulosky.
Res., P.O. Box 898, 68757. Tel: 402-355-2620; 755-2773 (Office); Fax: 402-755-2525. [CEM]
Catechesis/Religious Programs—Carol Conrad, D.R.E.
Students 98.

Raeville, Boone Co., St. Bonaventure, Rev. Thomas E. Bauwens.
Res., 301 So. 2nd St., Box B, Elgin, 68636. Tel: 402-386-5580; Fax: 402-843-2253. [CEM]

Ralston, Douglas Co., St. Gerald, Revs. Gary L. Ostrander; Michael D. Schmitz.
Res., 7859 Lakeview St., 68127. Tel: 402-331-1955; Fax: 402-331-8733.
School—Tel: 402-331-4223; Fax: 402-331-4523. David Garland, Prin.
Lay Teachers 17; Students 331.
Catechesis/Religious Programs—Students 494.

Randolph, Cedar Co., St. Frances de Chantal, Rev. Ronald A. Battiato; Deacon Vincent Schmit.
Res., 402 N. Bridge St., 68771. Tel: 402-337-0644; Fax: 402-337-1406. [CEM]
Catechesis/Religious Programs—Tel: 402-337-0341. Becky Nordhues, D.R.E.
Students 238.

St. Charles, Cuming Co., St. Anthony, Rev. Dennis DeGuzman.
Res., 445 15th Rd., West Point, 68788. Tel: 402-372-3681. [CEM]

St. Edward, Boone Co., St. Edward, Rev. James F. Novotny.
Res., 805 Washington St., P.O. Box A, 68660-0136. Tel: 402-678-2642; Fax: 402-678-2341. [CEM]
Catechesis/Religious Programs—Anita Cruise, D.R.E.
Students 75.

St. Helena, Cedar Co., Immaculate Conception. Merged with Ss. Philip and James, St. James; Ss. Peter and Paul, Bow Valley and Sacred Heart, Wynot to form Holy Family Church of Cedar County.

St. James, Cedar Co., SS. Philip and James. Merged with Immaculate Conception, St. Helena; Ss. Peter and Paul, Bow Valley and Sacred Heart, Wynot to form Holy Family Church of Cedar County.

St. John, Holt Co., St. John, Rev. Jay L. Kruse.
Res., P.O Box 37, Ewing, 68735. Tel: 402-626-7605; Fax: 402-626-7668.
Catechesis/Religious Programs—D.R.E.: Beth Schueth; Elaine Kimes.
Students 46.

Schuyler, Colfax Co., St. Augustine, Rev. William S. Whelan; Deacons Marvin Capoun; James DeBlauw.
Res., 619 Banner St., 68661. Tel: 402-352-3521; Fax: 402-352-3521. [CEM]
Catechesis/Religious Programs—320 W. 10 St., 68661. Tel: 402-352-2149.
Students 356.

St. Mary, Rev. Gerald A. Leise; Deacons Evan Drozda; Jim Conrad; Carl Perrin.
Res., 308 W. 10 St., 68661. Tel: 402-352-3540; Fax: 402-352-5971.
Catechesis/Religious Programs—Tel: 402-352-2149. Ann Lankford, D.R.E.
Students 192.

Silver Creek, Merrick Co., St. Lawrence, Rev. David M. Korth.
Res., P.O. Box 332, 68663. Tel: 308-773-2282; Fax: 308-733-2282. [CEM]
Catechesis/Religious Programs—Tel: 308-773-2430; Fax: 308-773-8281. Joan Sock, D.R.E.
Students 53.

Snyder, Dodge Co., St. Leo, Rev. Thomas J. Sellentin.
Res., P.O. Box 188, 68664. Tel: 402-568-2520. [CEM]
Catechesis/Religious Programs—Tel: 402-568-2586. Betty Marxsen, D.R.E.
Students 29.

South Sioux City, Dakota Co., St. Michael, Revs. David F. Liewer; Richard J. Whiteing.
Res., 1405 First Ave., 68776. Tel: 402-494-5423; Fax: 402-494-6342.
School—Tel: 402-494-1526; Fax: 402-494-4283.
Lay Teachers 14; Students 180.
Catechesis/Religious Programs—1414 Third Ave., 68776. Tel: 402-494-2827.
Students 300.
Mission—Homer, Dakota Co., St. Cornelius.

Spencer, Boyd Co., St. Mary, Rev. Frank E. Jindra.
Res., South St. & Harmon St., P.O. Box 149, 68777. Tel: 402-589-0067; Fax: 402-589-1013.
Catechesis/Religious Programs—D.R.E.: Mary Kirpatrick, (Grades 1-6), Tel: 402-589-1266; Bill Engelhaupt, (Grades 7-12), Tel: 402-589-9016.
Students 75.

Springfield, Sarpy Co., St. Joseph, Rev. James R. Cain.
Res., 102 S. Ninth St., P.O. Box 345, 68059. Tel: 402-253-2889.
Catechesis/Religious Programs—Tel: 402-253-2949. Linda Keller, D.R.E.
Students 160.

Stanton, Stanton Co., St. Peter, Rev. Timothy J. Lange.
Res., P.O. Box 557, 68779. Tel: 402-439-2147; Fax: 402-439-2149.
Catechesis/Religious Programs—D.R.E.: Valerie Morfeld Tel: 402-396-3207; Karen Petersen Tel: 402-439-2331.
Students 92.

Stuart, Holt Co., St. Boniface, Rev. Douglas P. Scheinost.
Res., 106 E. Fourth, P.O. Box 190, 68780. Tel: 402-924-3262; Fax: 402-924-3494. [CEM]
School—Tel: 402-924-3803.
Lay Teachers 5; Students 40.
Catechesis/Religious Programs—Students 96.

Tarnov, Platte Co., St. Michael, Rev. Leonard C. Ficenec, Admin.
Res., R.R. 1, P.O. Box 25c Humphrey, 68642. Tel: 402-246-4821; Fax: 402-246-4821. [CEM]
Catechesis/Religious Programs—Students 32.

Tekamah, Burt Co., St. Patrick, Rev. Martin P. Conley.
Res., 1323 R St., 68061-1542. Tel: 402-374-1692; Fax: 402-374-1692.
Catechesis/Religious Programs—Romaine Boerma, D.R.E.
Students 99.
Mission—Decatur, Burt Co., Holy Family.

Tilden, Madison Co., Our Lady of Mt. Carmel, Rev. Robert A. Schmitz.
Res., P.O. Box 458, 68781. Tel: 402-368-7710; Fax: 402-368-7710.
Catechesis/Religious Programs—Tel: 402-368-5919. Corine Frey, D.R.E.
Students 113.

Valley, Douglas Co., St. John, Rev. Robert Bester, Admin.
Res., 209 E. Sunset, 68064. Tel: 402-359-5783; Fax: 402-359-5217.
Catechesis/Religious Programs—Tel: 402-779-2814. Connie Schnoes, D.R.E.
Students 207.

Verdigre, Knox Co., St. Wenceslaus, Rev. Michael B. Malloy.
Res., 409 S. Third St., P.O. Box 9, 68783-0009. Tel: 402-668-2331; Fax: 402-668-2375. [CEM]
Catechesis/Religious Programs—Students 128.
Mission—Neobrara, Knox Co., St. William, P.O. Box 9, Verdigre 68783-0009.

Walthill, Thurston Co., St. Joseph, Rev. Thomas S. Gall.
Res., 501 Main St., 68067. Tel: 402-846-5550; Fax: 402-878-2760.
Mission—Macy, Thurston Co., Our Lady of Fatima.

Wayne, Wayne Co., St. Mary, Rev. James F. McCluskey.
Res., 412 E. 8th St., 68787. Tel: 402-375-2000; Fax: 402-375-5782. [CEM]
School—Tel: 402-375-2337.
Lay Teachers 8; Students 45.
Catechesis/Religious Programs—Students 209.

West Point, Cuming Co., Assumption B.V.M., Revs. James C. Ryberg; Mark J. McKercher; Deacons Vincent Maly; Kenneth Batenhorst.
Res., 343 N. Monitor St., 68788. Tel: 402-372-2188; Fax: 402-372-3563. [CEM]
School—Guardian Angel, Tel: 402-372-5328. Sr. Carol Seidl, Prin.
Priests 1; Sisters 2; Lay Teachers 18; Students 316.
Catechesis/Religious Programs—Sr. Thelma Wiese, D.R.E.
Students 116.

Winnebago, Thurston Co., St. Augustine's. (Indian Mission). Revs. Steven Boes, Dir.; Thomas S. Gall, Asst. Dir.
Res., P.O. Box GG, 68071. Tel: 402-878-2577; Fax: 402-878-2760.
School—Tel: 402-878-2291; Fax: 402-878-2760.
Missionary Benedictine Sisters 4; Lay Teachers 7; Students 75.
Catechesis/Religious Programs—Students 20.
Our Lady of Fatima of Macy, Thurston Co. (mission of St. Joseph, Walthill). Rev. Thomas S. Gall.
Res., P.O. Box GG, 68071. Tel: 402-878-2402; Fax: 402-846-5550.

Wisner, Cuming Co., St. Joseph, Rev. Jeffrey L. Zyla.
Res., 1318 G Ave. W., P.O. Box 623, 68791. Tel: 402-529-3242; Fax: 402-529-6239. [CEM]
Catechesis/Religious Programs—Tel: 402-529-3891. Anne McManigal, D.R.E.
Students 123.

Wynot, Cedar Co., Sacred Heart. Merged with Ss. Philip and James, St. James; Immaculate Conception, St. Helena and Ss. Peter and Paul, Bow Valley to form Holy Family Church of Cedar County.

Special Assignment:
Reverend Fathers—
Fitzpatrick, R. Michael, Dir. Catholic Cemeteries, 7710 W. Center Rd., Omaha, NE 68124. Tel: 402-391-3711

On Duty Outside the Archdiocese:
Reverend Fathers—
Fiala, John M., Society of Our Lady of Most Holy Trinity
McKamy, Eldon J., Providence St. Vincent Medical Center, Portland, OR

Graduate Studies:
Reverend Fathers—
Loseke, Jeffery S., Rome, Italy
Taphorn, Joseph C., Rome, Italy

Military Chaplains:
Reverend Fathers—
Dendinger, William J., Chap., U.S.A.F.
Dillon, Jerome V., Chap., U.S.N.R.
Hall, Douglas C., U.S.A.F.
Reeson, David G., U.S.A.F.

Absent on Leave:
Reverend Fathers—
Donner, Randall G.
Fiala, John M.
Herek, Daniel P.
Rush, Gerald V.
Whalen, John J.
Zaccone, Paul C., Congregation of the Sacred Hearts

Absent on Sick Leave:
Reverend Fathers—
Finch, Joseph E.
Lammers, Ralph A.
Stortz, Donald L.

Retired:
Reverend Monsignors—
Ariano, Joseph W.
Brodersen, Charles F., 9230 Burt St., #223, Omaha, NE 68114
Hupp, Robert P., 7232 Shirley, Omaha, NE 68124
Kelligar, William L., 7232 Shirley Ct., Omaha, NE 68124
Kerwin, Eugene H., 7232 Shirley Ct., Omaha, NE 68124
Krejci, Albert L., 7600 S. 42nd St., Omaha, NE 68147
Meister, Andrew H., P.O. Box 25D, Cedar Bluffs, NE 68015
Mickells, Anthony B., 2405 S. 48th Ave., Omaha, NE 68106
O'Donnell, Edward C., 1870 So. 75th St., Omaha, NE 68124
Werner, Cyril J., P.O. Box 562, Hartington, NE 68739
Wolbach, Richard A., 4001 S. 36th St., Omaha, NE 68107
Reverend Fathers—
Bartek, James F., 900 N. 90th St., Omaha, NE 68114
Bartek, William C., 7323 Shirley Ct., Omaha, NE 68124
Beacom, John F., 757 E. Decatur, West Point, NE 68788
Begley, Paul, 4112 S. 26th St., Omaha, NE 68107
Carroll, Patrick A., 4752 N. 14th Ave., Omaha, NE 68110
Ciurej, Richard S., 4107 S. 38th St., Omaha, NE 68107
Dickes, Jerome H., 500 E. 8th St., Yankton, SD 57078
Dunne, Peter F., Boys Town Center, Boys Town, NE 68010
Fangman, Paul J., Rte. 1, Box 139, Humphrey, NE 68642
Ficenec, Leonard C., R.R. 1, Box 202, Tarnov, NE 68642
Fitzgerald, William F., 7655 East Main, Scottsdale, AZ 85251
Flisiak, Stefan, R.R. 2, Box 18, Genoa, NE 68640
Furlong, Thomas D., 3605 Looking Glass Dr., Bellevue, NE 68123
Galas, Daniel D., 7924 Elm Plaza, #101, Omaha, NE 68124
Gass, Robert J., 14948 G St., Omaha, NE 68137
Golik, Stanislaus, 4804 Grover St., Omaha, NE 68106
Hebert, John M., 320 E. Decatur, West Point, NE 68788
Hunkeler, Edward J., 5605 105th Plaza-3, Omaha, NE 68134
Kelly, Michael J., 1870 S. 75th St., Omaha, NE 68124
Kenny, James E., 7232 Shirley St., Omaha, NE 68124
Koros, John J., 120 Citrus Rd., N.E., Lake Placid, FL 33852
Krajicek, Robert P., 5204 E. Mavi Ln., Glendale, AZ 85306
Kreikemeier, Leo A., Rte. 1, P.O. Box 25E, Cedar Bluffs, NE 68015
LaRocque, Benedict J., O.S.B., Saint Benedict Abbey, Atchison, KS 66002
McCaslin, John O., 7323 Shirley St., #305, Omaha, NE 68124
Meiergerd, Godfrey A., Rte. 1, Box 250, Cedar Bluffs, NE 68124
Micek, Joseph S., 1655 E. Sahara, Apt. 1056, Las Vegas, NV 89104
Moreci, Francis A., 2642 N. Newland Ave., Chicago, IL 60635
Musteikis, Leonard, 420 Preston Cir., Sunny Hills, FL 32428
Petrasic, Martin J., 2603 S. 50th St., Omaha, NE 68106
Petrusic, Anthony A., 322 Virginia St., Hollywood, FL 33019
Schwartz, Hugh F., 7323 Shirley St., #205, Omaha, NE 68124
Smith, Robert J., 2724 N. 98th St., Omaha, NE 68114
Stevens, Clifford J., 709 S. 28th St., Omaha, NE 68105
Tuma, Anthony F., 1870 S. 75th St., Omaha, NE 68124
Wilwerding, Anthony P., #8 Madonna Dr., Hardy, AR 72542

Permanent Deacons:
Abbott, Ernest, Jr.
Anderson, Andy
Archbold, Steve
Archibald, Joseph
Barbour, Frank
Barnes, William J.
Batenhorst, Kenneth F.
Baughman, Charles
Brich, James
Brisson, Ralph
Bronk, Duane
Burbach, Bernie
Camp, William J.
Capoun, Marvin
Casart, Ronald
Cerveny, John
Chambers, James
Chapman, Robert, (Retired)
Clausen, Donald
Connor, Dennis
Conrad, James J., Jr.
Cowles, Donald
Creamer, LeRoy
Crowley, Martin
Cuva, Fred
Dahlseid, John
Davis, Dennis, (Retired)
DeBlauw, James L.
DesRosiers, Peter
Dethlefs, Dennis
DiGiacomo, Yano
Digilio, Peter
Dineen, Lonnie
Doolittle, James
Dreifuerst, Lester, (Retired)
Dreismeier, Paul
Drozda, Evan
Dunn, Donald
Edgerton, Richard
Elster, George
Enzolera, Sebastian
Eubanks, Paul
Fell, William
Filipcic, Anthony
Finney, Jack
Fitzgerald, Thomas
Flesch, Robert
Foray, Andrew
Frankenfield, Thomas H.
French, Gary
Friend, Joseph
Gau, Jerome
Gencarelli, Ernest
Gentrup, Edward
Goldsmith, Edwin G.
Gonderinger, Gerald, (Retired)
Gurney, David
Guzman, Luis
Hamilton, Robert
Hanson, Eugene H.
Heck, Lawrence
Hendricks, Fred
Hennessey, Gary
Hesson, Ronald W.
Hills, Lyle
Hilt, Frank
Horner, Ron
Huck, John
Hueser, Ralph
Hughes, Thomas J.
Iwanski, Duane
Jansen, Clarence
Johnson, Donald
Jordan, Steve
Kaiser, Roland G.
Kalkowski, Kenneth
Kemp, Donald, (Retired)
Knockenhauer, George F.
Koziel, Timothy J.
Krajicek, Joseph
Kronschnabel, John
Kube, Norman
Kurtz, Stanley
L'Archevesque, Charles
Lauber, Eldon
Lauer, Justin, (Retired)
Lenz, Patrick
Livingston, Tom
Lukowski, Ray
Maly, Vince

Mascarello, Frank
Mascarello, John, (Retired)
Matukewicz, Paul
McGowan, Kelly
McGuire, Michael
Mendick, Daniel, (Retired)
Menke, Maurice
Mielak, Lawrence
Miles, Patrick
Miller, Carl
Miller, Ira
Morley, Joseph Edward
Mueting, Richard
Murphy, Thomas
Nelson, Richard
Newell, James M.
Osterhaus, Edwin
Overkamp, Jerry
Perchal, Daniel E.
Perrin, Carl A.
Placzek, Michael
Potts, Marcus
Poulosky, Paul
Powers, Paul
Preister, Tim
Purnell, Thomas, (Retired)
Ramirez, Joseph
Ridder, Frederick
Robinson, Hugh
Rooney, Paul
Sanders, Thomas, (Retired)
Saniuk, Daniel
Schimonitz, Eugene
Schmit, Vincent
Schulte, Thomas
Schumacher, Allan
Seamann, Donald M.
Sommer, Andrew
Sommer, Fred, (Retired)
Spenner, Arthur
Spicer, Ernest
Spieker, LeRoy
St. Arnold, Skip
Staroski, Jim
Steenson, Gerald
Steffen, Andrew
Steffen, Paul
Steier, Robert A.
Telich, Frank
Tharp, Bud
Thoene, Sylvan
Thome, Duane
Tylutki, Glenn
Villemure, Arthur
Wade, Thomas W.
Weskirchen, Charles
Wiehn, Dennis
Wocha, John
Zak, John J., Jr.

INSTITUTIONS LOCATED IN THE ARCHDIOCESE

[A] COLLEGES AND UNIVERSITIES

OMAHA. *College of St. Mary*, 1901 S. 72nd St., 68124. Tel: 402-399-2400; Fax: 402-399-2342.
E-mail: enroll@csm.edu
Web site: www.csm.edu
For a complete listing, refer to the Colleges and Universities section.

Creighton University, 2500 California Plaza, 68178. Tel: 402-280-2700; Fax: 402-280-2727.
E-mail: jpschlegel@creighton.edu
Web site: www.creighton.edu
For a complete listing, refer to the Colleges and Universities section.

[B] HIGH SCHOOLS, DIOCESAN

OMAHA. *Daniel J. Gross Catholic High School of Omaha*, 7700 S. 43rd St., 68147. Tel: 402-734-2000; Fax: 402-734-4270.
E-mail: cleve@gross.creighton.edu
Web site: www.gross.creighton.edu
Rebecca Cleveland, Pres. & Contact; Dorothy Ostrowski, Prin.; Joe Blazevich, Asst. Prin.; Tom Kerkman, Asst. Prin.; Cynthia Bvettner, Dir. of Development; Marie Angele, Campus Ministry; Rev. Joseph Brovdou. Lay Teachers 48; Students 604.

Roncalli Catholic High School of Omaha, 6401 Sorensen Pkwy., 68152. Tel: 402-571-7670; Fax: 402-571-3216.
E-mail: DGross@roncalli.creighton.edu
Web site: www.roncalli.creighton.edu
Dr. Duane Gross, Pres., & Contact; Larry Tuma, Prin.; Mrs. Paula Lenz, Dean; Rev. Ryan Lewis, Chap.; Mr. Clayton Freemen, Campus Min. Lay Teachers 26; Students 328.

V.J. & Angela Skutt Catholic High School of Omaha, 3131 S. 156th St., 68130. Tel: 402-333-0818; Fax: 402-333-1790.
E-mail: vjskutt@creighton.edu
Web site: www.skuttcatholic.com
Rev. James E. Gilg, Pres. & Contact; Sr. Clarice Faltus, O.S.F., Prin.; Rob Meyers, Activities Dir. Priests 1; Sisters 2; Lay Teachers 48; Students 620.

COLUMBUS. *Scotus Central Catholic High School*. (Grades 7-12), 1554 18th Ave., 68601. Tel: 402-564-7165; Fax: 402-564-6004.
E-mail: wgannon@gilligan.esu7.K12.ne.us
Web site: gillligan.esu.ne.us/~scoweb/scotus.html
Mr. William Gannon, Supt.; Mr. Wayne Morfield, Prin. & Contact; Revs. Steven D. Emanuel, Teacher-Campus Min.; David M. Korth, Asst. Campus Min. Priests 2; Lay Teachers 32; Students 475.

ELGIN. *Pope John XXIII Central Catholic High School at Elgin*, P.O. Box 179, 68636. Tel: 402-843-5325.
E-mail: dcannon@esu8.esu8.K12.ne.us.
Dennis Cannon, Prin. Priests 4; School Sisters of St. Francis 1; Lay Teachers 9; Students 115.

HARTINGTON. *Cedar Catholic High School*, 401 S. Broadway, P.O. Box 15, 68739. Tel: 402-254-3906; Fax: 402-254-3976.
E-mail: mike@cchs.esu1.K12.ne.us.
Web site: www.cchs.cedar.esu1.K12.ne.us
Mike McCabe, Admin. & Contact; Rev. Stanley J. Schmit, Spiritual Dir. Lay Teachers 22; Students 243.

NORFOLK. *Norfolk Catholic High School*, 2300 Madison Ave., 68701. Tel: 402-371-2784.
E-mail: jbellar@ncf.comm.com
Web site: www.ncknights.org
Mr. Jeff Beller, Prin. & Contact. Priests 3; Lay Teachers 35; Students 410.

WEST POINT. *Central Catholic High School*, 68788. Tel: 402-372-5326; Fax: 402-372-3563.
E-mail: central@cathschls.creighton.edu
Web site: www.pathfinder.esu2.K12.ne.us/ccatholic
Mrs. Peggy Thayer, Prin. & Contact. Franciscan Sisters of Christian Charity 22; Lay Teachers 13; Students 168.

[C] HIGH SCHOOLS, PRIVATE

OMAHA. *Creighton Preparatory School*, 7400 Western Ave., 68114. Tel: 402-393-1190; Fax: 402-393-0260.
E-mail: rtillman@creighton.edu
Web site: www.creightonprep.creighton.edu
Revs. Robert V. Hotz, S.J., Pres.; Robert J. Tillman, S.J., Supr. & Contact; Mr. John Naatz, Prin.; Revs. William J. Doran, S.J.; Willard J. Dressel, S.J.; Michael J. Marco, S.J.; Mark E. Niemann, S.J.; William F. O'Leary, S.J.; Kevin C. Schneider, S.J.; James A. Sinnerud, S.J.; James J. Strzok, S.J.; Bros. James E. Garvey, S.J.; Paul J. Kemper, S.J. Priests 10; Brothers 2; Scholastics 2; Lay Teachers 47; Students 979.

Duchesne Academy of the Sacred Heart, 36th & Burt Sts., 68131. Tel: 402-558-3800; Fax: 402-558-0051.
E-mail: duchesne@creighton.edu
Web site: www.duchesn.creighton.edu/dash.htm
Mrs. Sheila K. Haggas, Head of School & Contact. Society of the Sacred Heart 4; Lay Teachers 26; Girls 265.

Marian High School, 74th and Military Ave., 68134. Tel: 402-571-2618; Fax: 402-571-2978.
E-mail: ekmarian@marian.creighton.edu
Web site: http://marian.creighton.edu
Servants of Mary. Elizabeth Kish, Head of School, Prin. & Contact. Lay Teachers 46; Girls 723.

Mercy High School, 1501 S. 48th St., 68106. Tel: 402-553-9424; Fax: 402-553-0394.
E-mail: burnellj@mercy.creighton.edu
Web site: www.mercyhigh.org
Sr. Johanna Burnell, R.S.M., Pres. & Contact; Carolyn Jaworski, Prin. Sisters of Mercy of the Americas 4; Lay Teachers 25; Girls 325.

BOYS TOWN. *Father Flanagan's Boys' Home*, 68010. Rev. Valentine J. Peter, Contact.
See Protective Institutions.

ELKHORN. *Mount Michael High School*, 22520 Mt. Michael Rd., 68022-3400. Tel: 402-289-2544; Fax: 442-289-4539.
E-mail: bosborne@knightnet.creighton.edu
Web site: www.mountmichelhs.com
Rt. Rev. Theodore Wolff, O.S.B., Abbot; Brian Osborne, Prin. & Contact; Revs. Robert Halter, O.S.B.; Charles Zach, O.S.B., Pres.; Richard Thell, O.S.B.; John Hagemann, O.S.B.; Michael Liebl, O.S.B.; Daniel Lenz, O.S.B.; Louis L. Sojka, O.S.B.; Stephen J. Plank, O.S.B. Priests 4; Sisters 1; Professed Brothers 2; Lay Teachers 12; Students 150.

[D] ELEMENTARY SCHOOLS, INTER-PAROCHIAL

OMAHA. *All Saints Catholic School*, 1335 S. 10th St., 68108. Tel: 402-346-5757; Fax: 402-346-8794. John Palladino, Prin. & Contact. Serving parishes of St. Ann, St. Frances Cabrini, St. Joseph, St. Mary Magdalene Immaculate Conception, St. Patrick. Lay Teachers 15; Students 210.

Catholic Academy, 2326 S. 14th St., 68108. Tel: 402-345-3500; Fax: 402-342-8005. Craig Estee, Head Teacher.

St. James-Seton School, 9212 Tomahawk Blvd., 68134. Tel: 402-572-0339; Fax: 402-572-0347.
E-mail: tcrum@marian.creighton.edu
Terry Crum, Prin. & Contact. Servants of Mary 1; Lay Teachers 35; Students 777.

St. Pius X-St. Leo School, 6905 Blondo St., 68104. Tel: 402-551-6667; Fax: 402-551-8123.
E-mail: jgubbels@creighton.edu
Web site: www.SPSL.creighton.edu
Mrs. Joyce Gubbels, Prin. & Contact. Sisters 2; Lay Teachers 44; Students 836.

FORDYCE. *West Catholic Elementary*, 303 Omaha St., P.O. Box 167, 68736-0167. Tel: 402-357-3507; Fax: 402-357-3795. Serving parishes in Constance, Fordyce & Menominee. Mrs. Marilyn Wiebelhaus, Prin. & Contact. Lay Teachers 5; Students 66.

HARTINGTON. *East Catholic Elementary*, 108 W. 889th Rd., 68739-6079. Tel: 402-357-2146; Fax: 402-357-3758. Marilyn Wiebelhaus, Prin. Serving parishes in Bow Valley, St. Helena & Wynot. Lay Teachers 5; Students 55.

HOWELLS. *Howells Community Catholic School*, 114 N. 6th St., 68641. Tel: 402-986-1689; Fax: 402-986-1653. Serving parishes in Howells, Olean, Heun, Aloys & Tabor. Mrs. Mary Ann Spicka, Head Teacher (Grades 1-6). Lay Teachers 6; Students 109.

[E] ELEMENTARY SCHOOLS, PRIVATE

BOYS TOWN. *Father Flanagan's Boys' Home*. Rev. Valentine J. Peter, Contact. See Protective Institutions below.

[F] SPECIAL EDUCATION

OMAHA. *Christian Urban Education Service Foundation*, 2207 Wirt St., 68110. Tel: 402-451-5755; Fax: 402-451-1731. Rev. Thomas M. Fangman, Exec. Dir. of CUES. Sisters 1; Lay Teachers 10; Students 121.

The Jesuit Middle School of Omaha, 2311 N. 22nd St., 68110. Tel: 402-346-4464; Fax: 402-341-1817.
E-mail: skisj@yahoo.com
Rev. James L. Michalski, S.J., Pres. & Contact Person. Lay Teachers 6; Students 65.

Madonna School for Exceptional Children, 2537 N. 62nd, 68104. Tel: 402-556-1883.
E-mail: madonnaschool@home.com
Web site: www.discoveromaha.com/community/groups/madonnaschool/htm
Dr. Deirdre Milobar, Prin. Lay Teachers 10; Students 40.

Madonna Shop, 2014 N. 66th, 68104. Tel: 402-551-5441; Fax: 402-551-6910. Robin Moses, Mgr.

[G] GENERAL HOSPITALS

OMAHA. *Alegent Health - Bergen Mercy Health System*, 1010 N. 96th St., Ste. 200, 68114. Tel: 402-343-4430; Fax: 402-343-4337.
Web site: www.alegent.com
For a complete listing, refer to the Hospitals section.

Archbishop Bergan Mercy Medical Center, 7500 Mercy Rd., 68124. Tel: 402-398-6060; Fax: 402-398-6920
For a complete listing, refer to the Hospitals section.

Boys Town National Research Hospital, 555 N. 30 St., 68131. Tel: 402-498-6511; Fax: 402-498-6357
For a complete listing, refer to the Hospitals section.

NORFOLK. *Faith Regional Health Services*, 1500 Koenigstein Ave., 68701. Tel: 402-644-7205; Fax: 402-644-7468.
E-mail: proche@frhs.org
Web site: www.frhs.org
For a complete listing, refer to the Hospitals section.

O'NEILL. *St. Anthony's Hospital*, 2nd and Adams St., 68763. Tel: 402-336-2611; Fax: 402-336-2815
For a complete listing, refer to the Hospitals section.

WAYNE. *Providence Medical Center*, 1200 Providence Rd., 68787. Tel: 402-375-3800; Fax: 402-375-7989.
E-mail: MThomas@midlands.net
For a complete listing, refer to the Hospitals section.

WEST POINT. *Franciscan Care Services, Inc., dba St. Francis Memorial Hospital*, 430 N. Monitor St., 68788-1595. Tel: 402-372-2404; Fax: 402-372-2360.
E-mail: fc70656@navix.net
For a complete listing, refer to the Hospitals section.

[H] NURSING AND CONVALESCENT HOMES

OMAHA. *Bergan Mercy Care Center*, 1870 S. 75th St., 68124. Tel: 402-398-8500
For a complete listing, refer to the Special Care Facilities section.

Mercy Villa, 1845 S. 72nd St., 68124. Tel: 402-391-6224; Fax: 402-391-1872.
E-mail: johneenO@mercyoma.org
For a complete listing, refer to the Special Care Facilities section.

New Cassel Retirement Center, 900 N. 90th St., 68114. Tel: 402-393-2277; Fax: 402-393-3784.
Web site: www.newcassel.org
For a complete listing, refer to the Special Care Facilities section.

NORFOLK. *St. Joseph Nursing Home*, 401 N. 18th St., 68701. Tel: 402-371-9404.
E-mail: bdisch@frhs.org
For a complete listing, refer to the Special Care Facilities section.

WEST POINT. *Franciscan Care Services, Inc., (dba St. Joseph Retirement Community)*, 320 E. Decatur, 68788. Tel: 402-372-3477; Fax: 402-372-6600
For a complete listing, refer to the Special Care Facilities section.

[I] PROTECTIVE INSTITUTIONS

BOYS TOWN. *Father Flanagan's Boys' Home*, 68010. Tel: 402-498-1000; Fax: 402-498-1010.
E-mail: peterv@boustown.org
Web site: www.boustown.org
For a complete listing, refer to the Special Care Facilities section.

[J] FAMILY SERVICE CENTERS

OMAHA. *Catholic Charities*, Daniel E. Sheehan Center, 3300 N. 60th St., 68104. Tel: 402-554-0520; Fax: 402-551-8797.
E-mail: catholiccharities@ccomaha.org
Web site: www.ccomaha.org
Scot L. Adams, Contact.

COLUMBUS. *Catholic Charities*, 1761 26th Ave., P.O. Box 573, 68602-0573. Tel: 402-563-3833; Fax: 402-562-8714. Carroll Barnes, Dir. & Contact.

NORFOLK. *Catholic Charities Counselling Services*, 1109 S. 13th St., Ste. 302, 68701. Tel: 402-371-3555; Fax: 402-379-4662. Carroll Barnes, Dir. & Contact.

[K] MONASTERIES AND RESIDENCES OF PRIESTS AND BROTHERS

OMAHA. *Campion House*, 518 N. 19th St., 68102. Tel: 402-280-3900; Fax: 402-280-3911. Revs. Lawrence E. Gillick, S.J., Supr.; Thomas J. Hansen, S.J.; John P. Fitzgibbons, S.J.; Bro. Gerald E. Peltz, S.J.

Jesuit Community at Creighton University, 2500 California St., 68178. Tel: 402-280-2700; Fax: 402-280-5590.
E-mail: jesuits@creighton.edu
Web site: www.creighton.edu
Revs. Thomas J. Shanahan, S.J., Rector; David L. Smith, S.J., Min. & Contact; Albert A. Agresti, S.J. (New England); Philip R. Amidon, S.J.; Andrew Alexander, S.J.; Thomas E. Bannantine, S.J.; Burnell B. Bisbee, S.J.; Walter E. Boehme; Gail G. Bohr, S.J.; Robert E. Brodzeller, S.J.; Raymond A. Bucko, S.J. (NY); Robert O. Burns, S.J.; Neil Cahill, S.J.; Gregory I. Carlson, S.J.; James F. Clifton; Donald A. Doll, S.J.; Donald D. Driscoll, S.J.; Harry S. Eglsaer, S.J.; Lawrence W. Flanagan, S.J.; Michael J. Flecky, S.J.; Thomas A. Halley, S.J.; M. Dennis Hamm, S.J.; Robert P. Hart, S.J.; Jonathan Hasehka, S.J.; Richard J. Hauser, S.J.; Bro. James Heidrick, S.J.; Revs. Lawrence C. Helmueller, S.J.; Daniel S. Hendrickson, S.J.; Robert E. Hoene, S.J.; Thomas A. Hoffman, S.J.; John G. Holbrook, S.J.; John P. Horn, S.J.; Eugene J. Jakubek, S.J.; Charles L. Jurgensmeier, S.J. (California); Howard E. Kalb, S.J.; Charles T. Kestermeier, S.J.; William T. Kolarec, S.J.; James P. Kramper, S.J.; Edward A. Larkin, S.J.; Leland E. Lubbers, S.J.; John J. Lynch, S.J.; Paul A. Mahowald, S.J.; Thomas C. Manahan, S.J.; Robert F. McEniry, S.J.; Richard D. McGloin, S.J.; Dennis P. McNeilly, S.J.; Thomas S. McShane, S.J.; James L. Michalski, S.J.; Michael G. Morrison, S.J.; Charles F. Mullen, S.J.; Robert F. O'Connor, S.J.; Francis A. Prokes, S.J.; James J. Quinn, S.J.; Perry L. Robinson, S.J.; Luis Rodriguez, S.J.; Gregory A. Schissel, S.J.; John P. Schlegel, S.J.; Thomas N. Schloemer, S.J.; David G. Schultenover, S.J.; John M. Scott, S.J.; Edward A. Sharp, S.J.; Most Rev. John R. Sheets, S.J., D.D.; Bros. Robert E. Smith, S.J.; Edmund W. Stetzen, S.J.; Revs. Paul J. Strittmatter, S.J.; Albert R. Thelen, S.J.; Ernesto Travieso, S.J.; Martin O. Vaske, S.J.; Bros. Michael R. Wilmot, S.J.; James R. Zuercher, S.J.; Revs. M. John Wymelenberg, S.J.; John D. Zuercher, S.J. Priests 67; Brothers 5; Scholastics 1.
Legal Title: *Jesuit Community at Creighton University.*

ELKHORN. *Mount Michael Abbey*, 22520 Mount Michael Rd., 68022-3400. Tel: 402-289-2541; Fax: 402-289-4539.
E-mail: twolff@mountmike.creighton.edu
Web site: www.springwebdesign.com/MountMichael
Benedictine Fathers. Rt. Rev. Theodore J. Wolff, O.S.B., Abbot & Contact; Bro. Jerome Kmiecik, O.S.B., Prior; Rev. Michael Liebl, O.S.B., Sub-Prior; Rt. Rev. Raphael Walsh, O.S.B.; Revs. Benedict Dohle, O.S.B.; Albert Massmann, O.S.B.; Adrian Liable, O.S.B.; Nathanael Foshage, O.S.B.; Eugene McReynolds, O.S.B.; Bernard Sheehan, O.S.B.; Charles Zach, O.S.B.; Richard Thell, O.S.B.; John Hagemann, O.S.B.; Daniel Lenz, O.S.B.; Louis L. Sojka, O.S.B.; Stephen J. Plank, O.S.B. Priests 15; Professed Brothers 9.

ST. COLUMBANS. *St. Columban's Foreign Mission Society.* (Corporate Title: St. Columban's Foreign Mission Society), 68056. Tel: 402-291-1920; Fax: 402-291-8693.
E-mail: stcolneus@aol.com
Web site: www.stcolumban.org
Regional Headquarters and Administration Offices of the Columban Fathers in the United States. Revs. James J. Hastings, S.S.C., Vice Dir.; A. Aguilar, S.S.C., Hispanic Devel. & Vocation Dir.; Richard Steinhilber, S.S.C.; Denis Bartley, S.S.C.; John Burger, S.S.C., Editor Columban Mission; Paul E. Casey, S.S.C.; J. Donald Devine, S.S.C.; Edward Dolan, S.S.C.; Oliver Kennedy, S.S.C.; Donal O'Farrell, S.S.C.; Robert O'Rourke, S.S.C.; Colm Stanley, S.S.C.; Alban Sueper, S.S.C.; William Sweeney, S.S.C. Priests 14.
Other Assignments: Revs. W. Aedan McGrath, S.S.C., Legion of Mary; Thomas Normanly, S.S.C., Buffalo, NY; Clarence Beckley, S.S.C., Pending; Robert Clark, S.S.C., U.S. Navy; John Buckley, S.S.C. (Brazil); George Da Roza, S.S.C., Studies; Michael Donnelly, S.S.C. (Fabens, TX); Thomas Vaughan, S.S.C., Pending; Robert Burke, S.S.C., Joliet, IL; Vincent McCarthy, S.S.C., Pending; William Morton, S.S.C., El Paso, TX; Victor Gaboury, S.S.C., Pending; Cathal Gallagher (Sioux Falls, SD); Donald Kelley, S.S.C., Duouque; James Needham, S.S.C., St. Paul, MN; Paul O'Malley, S.S.C., Worcester; John Wanaurny (Fabens, TX).

SCHUYLER. *Benedictine Mission House*, Christ the King Priory, 68661. Tel: 402-352-2177; Fax: 402-352-2176.
E-mail: bmh.schuyler@alltel.net
Web site: www.megavision.com/benedict
Revs. Germar Neubert, Prior & Contact; Adam Patras, O.S.B., (Leave of Absence); Volker Futter, O.S.B., Sub-prior; Thomas Aquinas Leitner, O.S.B. Brothers 4.

[L] CONVENTS AND RESIDENCES FOR SISTERS

OMAHA. *Monastery of St. Clare*, 3626 N. 65th Ave., 68104. Tel: 402-558-4916; Fax: 402-558-5046.
Web site: www.poorclare.org/Omaha
Poor Clares (Second Order of St. Francis). Sr. Mary Clare Brown, Contact. Sisters 9. Attended by Jesuit Fathers.

Motherhouse of the Servants of Mary, Convent of Our Lady of Sorrows, 7400 Military Ave., 68134. Tel: 402-571-2547; Fax: 402-573-6055.
Web site: www.osms.org
Sr. Jean Morrow, O.S.M., Prov. & Contact; Sr. Doris Durant, O.S.M., Asst. Prov. Professed 111; Novice 1; Sisters in Motherhouse 36.

Provincial Motherhouse and Novitiate of the Notre Dame Sisters, 3501 State St., 68112. Tel: 402-455-2994; Fax: 402-455-3974.
E-mail: notredamesisters@juno.com
Web site: www.notredamesisters.org
Sr. Margaret Hickey, N.D., Prov. Pres. & Contact. Professed 64; Sisters living at Motherhouse 34.

Regional Office of the Sisters of Mercy of the Americas (Regional Community of Omaha), 7262 Mercy Rd., 68124-2312. Tel: 402-393-8225; Fax: 402-393-8145.
E-mail: patriciaf@mercyoma.org
Web site: www.mercyoma.org
Sr. Patricia Forret, R.S.M., Pres.; Brenda Gift, Contact. Perpetually Professed 238.

Sisters of the Annunciation of the Archdiocese of Omaha, 14849 "G" St., 68137. Tel: 402-891-0001; Fax: 402-891-0333. Revs. Robert J. Gass; Matthew J. Gutowski; Carl F. Sodoro; Sr. Maria Gabriel, Novice.

Sisters of the Good Shepherd (R.G.S.), 1106 N. 36th St., 68131. Tel: 402-551-2966; Fax: 402-551-2495.
Web site: www.goodshepherdsisters.org
Sr. Eileen Schiltz. Sisters 2.

NORFOLK. *Immaculata Convent*, 300 N. 18th St., 68701-3687. Tel: 402-371-3438; Fax: 402-379-2877.
E-mail: maryagnes@conpoint.com
Web site: www.norfolkosb.org
Sr. Agnes Salber, O.S.B., Prioress & Contact. Legal Title: *Immaculata Convent, Priory Motherhouse and Novitiate of the Missionary Benedictine Sisters.* Sisters 35; Postulants 1; Novices 3.

O'NEILL. *St. Anthony's Convent*, 210 E. Adams St., 68763. Tel: 402-336-3576; Fax: 402-336-2581. Sr. Margaret Schneider, Contact. Sisters of St. Francis of Penance and Christian Charity 3.

[M] SECULAR INSTITUTES

OMAHA. *Institute of the Apostolic Oblates*, 6762 Western Ave., 68132. Tel: 402-553-4418; Fax: 402-553-1388.
E-mail: ao-omaha@mitec.net
Teresa J. Monaghen, National Moderator. A secular institute for women with the aim of promoting the universal call to holiness, through working apostolate of the Pro Sanctity Movement.

Apostolic Sodales - Secular Institute for Priests, Boys Town Center, 68010. Tel: 402-498-1469. Rev. Peter Dunne; Palmira Tafani, Contact.

ELKHORN. *Pro Sanctity Movement*, 11002 N. 204th St., 68022. Tel: 402-289-2670; Fax: 402-289-1938.
E-mail: psm@mitec.net
Web site: www.prosanctitate.org
Teresa Monaghen, National Dir. Tel: 402-289-2670; Brian Lenz, Dir. Tel: 402-551-7398; Teresa Monaghen, Contact. Ecclesial organization: Promotes apostolates of holiness; teaches, supports and guides people seeking to deepen their spiritual life.

[N] EDUCATIONAL FOUNDATIONS AND TRUST FUNDS

OMAHA. *The Omaha Archdiocesan Educational Foundation, Inc.* The Office of Stewardship and Development, 3212 North 60th St., P.O. Box 4130, 68104-0130. Tel: 402-554-8493; Fax: 402-551-3426.
E-mail: jtamisie@creighton.edu

Archbishop Sheehan Adult Education Endowment Trust.

All Saints Catholic School Educational Endowment Trust. Tel: 402-346-5757.

Black Students Catholic Educational Endowment Trust.

Music in Catholic Schools Endowment Trust.

Roncalli Catholic High School Educational Endowment Trust. Tel: 402-571-7670.

Roncalli Catholic High School Scholarship Endowment Trust. Tel: 402-571-7670.

Religious Education Evangelization Commission Endowment Trust.

The Catholic Voice Educational Endowment Trust. Tel: 402-558-6611.

Marian High School Scholarship Endowment Trust. Tel: 402-571-2618.

Marian High School Endowment Trust. Tel: 402-571-2618.

West Point Central Catholic High School Activity Center Endowment Trust. Tel: 402-372-5326. The Omaha Archdiocesan Parish Foundation, Inc. The Office of Stewardship and Development, 3212 N. 60th St., P.O. Box 4130, 68104-0130. Tel: 402-554-8493; Fax: 402-551-3426.

St. Michael Church of Albion, NE, Educational Endowment Trust, Albion. Tel: 402-395-2393.

St. Michael Church of Albion, NE, Parish Endowment Trust, Albion. Tel: 402-395-2393.

St. Aloysius Parish Endowment Trust, Aloys. Tel: 402-372-3681.

St. Aloysius Parish Educational Endowment Trust. Tel: 402-372-3681.

St. Joseph Parish Endowment Trust, Amelia. Tel: 402-336-1602.

St. Joseph Parish Educational Endowment Trust, Amelia. Tel: 402-336-1602.

St. Joseph Church Educational Endowment Trust, Atkinson. Tel: 402-925-2122.

St. Joseph Parish Endowment Trust, Atkinson. Tel: 402-925-2122.

Holy Cross Parish Endowment Trust, Bancroft. Tel: 402-687-2102.

Holy Cross Parish Educational Endowment Trust, Bancroft. Tel: 402-687-2102.

St. Patrick Parish Endowment Trust, Battle Creek. Tel: 402-675-2495.

St. Patrick Parish Educational Endowment Trust, Battle Creek. Tel: 402-675-2485.

Holy Cross Parish Endowment Trust, Beemer; Fax: 402-528-3475.

Holy Cross Parish Educational Endowment Trust, Beemer. Tel: 402-528-3475.

St. Mary Church Educational Endowment Trust, Bellevue. Tel: 402-291-1350.

St. Mary Church Endowment Trust, Bellevue. Tel: 402-291-1350.

St. Matthew the Evangelist Parish Endowment Trust, Bellevue. Tel: 402-292-7418.

St. Francis Borgia Parish Endowment Trust, Blair. Tel: 402-426-3823.

St. Francis Borgia Parish Educational Endowment Trust, Blair. Tel: 402-426-3823.

St. Andrew Parish Endowment Trust, Bloomfield. Tel: 402-373-2233.

St. Andrew Parish Educational Endowment Trust, Bloomfield. Tel: 402-373-2233.

SS. Peter and Paul Parish Endowment Trust, Bow Valley. Tel: 402-254-3311.

SS. Peter and Paul Parish Educational Endowment Trust, Bow Valley. Tel: 402-254-3311.

East Catholic Elementary School Educational Endowment Trust, Bow Valley. Tel: 402-357-2146.

St. Ignatius Parish Endowment Trust, Brunswick. Tel: 402-582-4288.

St. Ignatius Parish Educational Endowment Trust, Brunswick. Tel: 402-582-4288.

SS. Peter and Paul Parish Endowment Trust, Butte. Tel: 402-775-2452.

SS. Peter and Paul Parish Educational Endowment Trust, Butte. Tel: 402-775-2452.
St. Anthony Parish Endowment Trust, Cedar Rapids. Tel: 308-358-0773.
St. Anthony Parish Educational Endowment Trust, Cedar Rapids. Tel: 308-358-0773.
St. Michael Catholic Church Parish Endowment Trust, Central City. Tel: 308-946-2855.
St. Michael Parish Educational Endowment Trust, Central City. Tel: 308-946-2855.
St. Peter Parish Endowment Trust, Clarks. Tel: 308-536-2574.
St. Peter Parish Educational Endowment Trust, Clarks. Tel: 308-536-2574.
SS. Cyril and Methodius Parish Endowment Trust, Clarkson. Tel: 402-892-3464.
SS. Cyril and Methodius Parish Educational Endowment Trust, Clarkson. Tel: 402-892-3464.
Church of St. Theresa of Avila Parish Educational Endowment Trust, Clearwater. Tel: 402-887-4521.
St. Theresa of Avila Parish Endowment Trust, Clearwater. Tel: 402-887-4521.
St. Michael Parish Endowment Trust, Coleridge. Tel: 402-283-4614.
St. Michael Parish Educational Endowment Trust, Coleridge. Tel: 402-283-4614.
St. Anthony Parish Endowment Trust, Columbus. Tel: 402-564-3313.
St. Anthony Parish Educational Endowment Trust, Columbus. Tel: 402-564-3313.
St. Anthony Elementary School Endowment Trust, Columbus. Tel: 402-564-3313.
St. Bonaventure Church Endowment Trust, Columbus. Tel: 402-564-7151.
St. Isidore Church Endowment Trust, Columbus. Tel: 402-564-8993.
St. Isidore Parish Educational Endowment Trust, Columbus. Tel: 402-564-8993.
St. Isidore Elementary School Endowment Trust, Columbus. Tel: 402-564-8993.
Scotus Central Catholic High School Endowment Trust, Columbus. Tel: 402-564-7165.
St. Joseph Parish Endowment Trust, Constance. Tel: 402-388-4814.
St. Joseph Parish Educational Endowment Trust, Constance. Tel: 402-388-4814.
St. Ludger Parish Endowment Trust, Creighton. Tel: 402-358-3596.
St. Ludger Parish Educational Endowment Trust, Creighton. Tel: 402-358-3596.
St. Ludger Elementary School Endowment Trust, Creighton. Tel: 402-358-3596.
St. Rose of Lima Parish Endowment, Crofton. Tel: 402-388-4814.
St. Rose of Lima Parish Educational Endowment Trust, Crofton. Tel: 402-388-4814.
Holy Family Parish Endowment Trust, Decatur. Tel: 402-374-1692.
Holy Family Parish Educational Endowment Trust, Decatur. Tel: 402-374-1692.
St. Anne Parish Endowment Trust, Dixon. Tel: 402-256-3303.
St. Anne Parish Educational Endowment Trust, Dixon. Tel: 402-256-3303.
St. Wenceslaus Parish Endowment Trust, Dodge. Tel: 402-693-2235.
St. Wenceslaus Church Educational Endowment Trust, Dodge. Tel: 402-693-2235.
St. Stanislaus Parish Endowment Trust, Duncan. Tel: 402-897-2625.
St. Stanislaus Parish Educational Endowment Trust, Duncan. Tel: 402-897-2625.
St. Boniface School Endowment Trust, Elgin. Tel: 402-843-2345.
St. Boniface Parish Endowment Trust, Elgin. Tel: 402-843-2345.
St. Boniface Parish Educational Endowment Trust, Elgin. Tel: 402-843-2345.
Pope John XXIII Central Catholic High School Endowment Trust, Elgin. Tel: 402-843-2345.
Mt. Michael Foundation, Inc., Elkhorn. Tel: 402-289-2541.
St. Patrick School Tuition Assistance Endowment Trust, Elkhorn. Tel: 402-289-4289.
St. Patrick School Endowment Trust, Elkhorn. Tel: 402-289-4289.
St. Patrick Parish Endowment Trust, Elkhorn. Tel: 402-289-4289.
Sacred Heart Parish Endowment Trust, Emerson. Tel: 402-695-2342.
Sacred Heart Parish Educational Endowment Trust, Emerson. Tel: 402-695-2342.
St. Peter de Alcantara Parish Endowment Trust, Ewing. Tel: 402-626-7605.
St. Peter de Alcantara Parish Educational Endowment Trust, Ewing. Tel: 402-626-7605.
St. John the Baptist Parish Endowment Trust, Fordyce. Tel: 402-357-3506.
St. John the Baptist Parish Educational Endowment Trust, Fordyce. Tel: 402-357-3506.
West Catholic Educational Endowment Trust, Fordyce. Tel: 402-357-3506.
St. John the Baptist Parish Endowment Trust, Fort Calhoun. Tel: 402-468-5348.
St. John the Baptist Church Educational Endowment Trust, Fort Calhoun. Tel: 402-468-5348.
St. Patrick Catholic Church Endowment Trust, Fremont. Tel: 402-721-6611.
St. Patrick Parish Educational Endowment Trust, Fremont. Tel: 402-721-6611.
St. Peter Catholic Church Endowment Trust, Fullerton. Tel: 308-536-2574.
St. Peter Parish Educational Endowment Trust, Fullerton. Tel: 308-536-2574.
St. Rose of Lima Parish Endowment Trust, Genoa. Tel: 402-993-2323.
St. Rose of Lima Parish Educational Endowment Trust, Genoa. Tel: 402-993-2323.
St. Patrick Parish Endowment Trust, Gretna. Tel: 402-332-4444.
St. Patrick Parish Educational Endowment Trust, Gretna. Tel: 402-332-4444.
Holy Trinity Parish Endowment Trust, Hartington. Tel: 402-254-6559.
Holy Trinity Parish Educational Endowment Trust, Hartington. Tel: 402-254-6559.
Holy Trinity Grade School Endowment Trust, Hartington. Tel: 402-254-6559.
Holy Trinity Parish Endowment Trust, Heun. Tel: 402-986-1627.
Holy Trinity Parish Educational Endowment Trust, Heun. Tel: 402-986-1627.
St. Cornelius Parish Endowment Trust, Homer. Tel: 402-494-5423.
St. Cornelius Parish Educational Endowment Trust, Homer. Tel: 402-494-5423.
St. Rose of Lima Parish Endowment Trust, Hooper. Tel: 402-654-3449.
St. Rose of Lima Parish Educational Endowment Trust, Hooper. Tel: 402-654-3449.
St. John Nepomucene Parish Endowment Trust, Howells. Tel: 402-986-1653.
St. John Nepomucene Parish Educational Endowment Trust, Howells. Tel: 402-986-1653.
SS. Peter and Paul Parish Endowment Trust, Howells. Tel: 402-986-1653.
SS. Peter and Paul Parish Educational Endowment Trust, Howells. Tel: 402-986-1653.
SS. Peter and Paul Catholic Church Endowment for Howells Community Catholic School, Howells. Tel: 402-986-1653.
St. Mary Parish Endowment Trust, Hubbard. Tel: 402-256-3303.
St. Mary Parish Educational Endowment Trust, Hubbard. Tel: 402-256-3303.
St. Francis Parish Endowment Trust, Humphrey. Tel: 402-923-0913.
St. Patrick Parish Endowment Trust, Jackson. Tel: 402-632-4292.
St. Patrick Parish Educational Endowment Trust, Jackson. Tel: 402-632-4292.
SS. Peter and Paul Parish Endowment Trust, Krakow. Tel: 402-993-6600.
SS. Peter and Paul Parish Educational Endowment Trust, Krakow. Tel: 402-993-6600.
St. Mary Parish Endowment Trust, Laurel. Tel: 402256-3303.
St. Mary Parish Educational Endowment Trust, Laurel. Tel: 402-256-3303.
St. Mary Parish Endowment Trust, Leigh. Tel: 402-487-2666.
Holy Family Parish Endowment Trust, Lindsay. Tel: 402-428-2455.
Holy Family Parish Educational Endowment Trust, Lindsay. Tel: 402-428-2455.
Assumption Parish Endowment Trust, Lynch. Tel: 402-569-2421.
Assumption Parish Educational Endowment Trust, Lynch. Tel: 402-569-2421.
St. Joseph Parish Endowment Trust, Lyons. Tel: 402-569-2421.
St. Joseph Parish Educational Endowment Trust, Lyons. Tel: 402-569-2421.
Our Lady of Fatima Parish Endowment Trust, Macy. Tel: 402-878-2402.
Our Lady of Fatima Parish Educational Endowment Trust, Macy. Tel: 402-878-2402.
St. Leonard Parish Endowment Trust, Madison. Tel: 402-454-3529.
St. Leonard Parish Educational Endowment Trust, Madison. Tel: 402-454-3529.
St. Boniface Parish Educational Endowment Trust, Menominee. Tel: 402-357-3506.
St. Boniface Parish Endowment, Menominee. Tel: 402-357-3506.
St. Boniface Parish Endowment Trust, Monterey. Tel: 402-372-3681.
St. Boniface Parish Educational Endowment Trust, Monterey. Tel: 402-372-3681.
Sacred Heart Parish Endowment Trust, Naper. Tel: 402-775-2452.
Sacred Heart Parish Educational Endowment Trust, Naper. Tel: 402-775-2452.
St. Francis of Assisi Parish Educational Endowment Trust, Neligh. Tel: 402-887-4521.
St. Francis of Assisi Parish Endowment Trust, Neligh. Tel: 402-887-4521.
St. Peter Parish Endowment Trust, Newcastle. Tel: 402-755-2773.
St. Peter Parish Educational Endowment Trust, Newcastle. Tel: 402-755-2773.
St. William Parish Endowment Trust, Niobrara. Tel: 402-668-2331.
St. William Parish Educational Endowment Trust, Niobrara. Tel: 402-668-2331.
Sacred Heart Parish Endowment Trust, Norfolk. Tel: 402-371-2621.
St. Charles Borromeo Parish Endowment Trust, North Bend. Tel: 402-652-8484.
St. Charles Borromeo Parish Educational Endowment Trust, North Bend. Tel: 402-652-8484.
Sacred Heart Parish Endowment Trust, Olean. Tel: 402-693-2235.
Sacred Parish Educational Endowment Trust, Olean. Tel: 402-693-2235.
Blessed Sacrament Parish Endowment Trust. Tel: 402-455-5200.
Blessed Sacrament Parish Educational Endowment Trust. Tel: 402-455-5200.
Blessed Sacrament School Educational Endowment Trust. Tel: 402-455-5200.
Christ the King Parish Endowment Trust. Tel: 402-391-3606.
Christ the King Educational Endowment Trust. Tel: 402-391-3606.
Church of the Assumption Educational Endowment Trust. Tel: 402-734-4500.
Church of the Assumption Endowment Trust. Tel: 402-734-4500.
Church of the Assumption Scholarship Educational Endowment Trust. Tel: 402-734-4500.
Holy Cross Parish Endowment Trust. Tel: 402-553-7500.
Holy Family Parish Endowment Trust. Tel: 402-345-1062.
Holy Family Parish Educational Trust. Tel: 402-345-1062.
Holy Ghost Parish Endowment Trust. Tel: 402-731-3176.
Holy Ghost Educational Endowment Trust. Tel: 402-731-3176.
Immaculate Conception Parish Endowment Trust. Tel: 402-342-1074.
Immaculate Conception Parish Educational Endowment Trust. Tel: 402-342-1074.
Mary Our Queen Educational Endowment Trust. Tel: 402-333-8662.
Mother of Perpetual Help Parish Endowment Trust. Tel: 402-333-8662.
Mother of Perpetual Help Parish Educational Endowment Trust. Tel: 402-558-4214.
Our Lady of Fatima Parish Endowment Trust. Tel: 402-341-5772.
Our Lady of Fatima Parish Educational Endowment Trust. Tel: 402-341-5772.
Our Lady of Guadalupe Parish Endowment Trust. Tel: 402-734-2196.
Our Lady of Guadalupe Educational Endowment Trust. Tel: 402-402-734-2196.
Our Lady of Lourdes Parish Endowment Trust, 402-346-0900.
Our Lady of Lourdes of Parish Educational Endowment Trust. Tel: 402-346-0900.
Our Lady of Lourdes School Educational Endowment Trust. Tel: 402-346-0900.
Sacred Heart Parish Endowment Trust. Tel: 402-451-5755.
Sacred Heart Parish Educational Endowment Trust. Tel: 402-451-5755.
St. Adalbert Parish Endowment Trust. Tel: 402-345-1621.
St. Adalbert Parish Educational Endowment Trust. Tel: 402-345-1621.
St. Agnes Parish Endowment Trust. Tel: 402-731-2196.
St. Agnes Parish Educational Endowment Trust. Tel: 402-731-2196.
St. Ann Parish Endowment Trust. Tel: 402-341-6613.
St. Ann Parish Educational Endowment Trust. Tel: 402-341-6613.
St. Anthony Parish Endowment Trust. Tel: 402-733-2433.
St. Anthony Parish Educational Endowment Trust. Tel: 402-733-2433.
St. Benedict Parish Endowment Trust. Tel: 402-348-0631.
St. Benedict Parish Educational Endowment Trust. Tel: 402-348-0631.
St. Bernadette Parish Endowment Trust. Tel: 402-731-4694.

St. Bernadette Parish Educaitonal Endowment Trust. Tel: 402-731-4694.
St. Bernard Parish Memorial Endowment Trust. Tel: 402-551-0269.
St. Bernard Parish Religious Educational Endowment Trust. Tel: 402-551-0269.
St. Bridget Parish Endowment Trust. Tel: 402-733-8811.
St. Bridget Parish Educational Endowment Trust. Tel: 402-733-8811.
St. Cecilia Cathedral Endowment Trust. Tel: 402-551-2313.
St. Elizabeth Ann Parish Endowment Trust. Tel: 402-493-2186.
St. Elizabeth Ann Parish Educational Endowment Trust. Tel: 402-493-2186.
St. Francis of Assisi Church of South Omaha Endowment Trust. Tel: 402-731-2699.
St. Francis of Assisi Church of South Omaha Educational Endowment Fund. Tel: 402-731-2699.
St. Frances Cabrini Parish Endowment Trust. Tel: 402-342-2464.
St. Frances Cabrini Parish Educational Endowment Trust. Tel: 402-342-2464.
St. James Parish Endowment Trust. Tel: 402-572-0499.
St. James Parish Educational Endowment Trust. Tel: 402-572-0499.
St. James/Seton School Educational Endowment Fund. Tel: 402-572-0499.
St. Joan of Arc Parish Educational Endowment Fund. Tel: 402-393-2005.
St. Joan of Arc Parish Endowment Trust. Tel: 402-393-2005.
St. Joan of Arc Grade School Educational Endowment Trust. Tel: 402-393-2005.
St. John Vianney Church of Millard Parish Endowment Trust. Tel: 402-895-0808.
St. John Vianney Parish Educational Endowment Trust. Tel: 402-895-0808.
St. Joseph Parish Endowment Trust. Tel: 402-342-2836.
St. Joseph Parish Educational Endowment Trust. Tel: 402-342-2836.
St. Leo Parish Endowment Trust. Tel: 402-397-0407.
St. Leo Parish Educational Endowment Trust. Tel: 402-397-0407.
St. Margaret Mary Parish Endowment Trust. Tel: 402-558-2255.
St. Margaret Mary Parish Educational Endowment Trust. Tel: 402-558-2255.
St. Margaret Mary School Educational Endowment Trust. Tel: 402-558-2255.
St. Mary Parish Endowment Trust. Tel: 402-731-0204.
St. Mary Parish Educational Endowment Trust. Tel: 402-731-0204.
St. Mary Elementary School Endowment Trust. Tel: 402-731-0204.
St. Patrick Church Educational Endowment Trust. Tel: 402-341-1305.
St. Peter Parish Endowment Trust. Tel: 402-341-4560.
St. Peter Parish Educational Endowment Trust. Tel: 402-341-4560.
SS. Peter and Paul Church Endowment Trust. Tel: 402-731-4578.
SS. Peter and Paul Parish Educational Endowment Trust. Tel: 402-731-4578.
SS. Peter and Paul Elementary School Educational Endowment Trust. Tel: 402-731-4578.
St. Philip Neri Church Endowment Trust. Tel: 402-455-1289.
St. Philip Neri Parish Educational Endowment Trust. Tel: 402-455-1289.
St. Pius X Parish Endowment Trust. Tel: 402-558-8446.
St. Pius X Parish Educational Endowment Trust. Tel: 402-558-8446.
St. Pius X/St. Leo School Educational Endowment Trust. Tel: 402-558-8446.
St. Richard Parish Endowment Trust. Tel: 402-455-2865.
St. Richard Parish Educational Endowment Trust. Tel: 402-455-285.
St. Richard Grade School Educational Endowment Trust. Tel: 402-455-2865.
St. Robert Bellarmine Parish Endowment Trust. Tel: 402-333-8989.
St. Rose Parish Endowment Trust. Tel: 402-733-9327.
St. Rose Parish Educational Endowment Trust. Tel: 402-733-9327.
St. Stanislaus Parish Endowment Trust. Tel: 402-731-4152.
St. Stanislaus Parish Educational Endowment Trust. Tel: 402-731-4152.
St. Stephen the Martyr Parish Endowment Trust. Tel: 402-896-9675.
St. Stephen the Martyr Parish Educational Endowment Trust. Tel: 402-896-9675.
St. Stephen the Martyr Elementary School Educational Endowment Trust. Tel: 402-896-9675.
St. Therese of the Child Jesus Parish Endowment Trust. Tel: 402-455-4966.
St. Therese of the Child Jesus Parish Educational Endowment Trust. Tel: 402-455-4966.
St. Thomas More Parish Endowment Trust. Tel: 402-556-1456.
St. Thomas More Parish Educational Endowment Trust. Tel: 402-556-1456.
St. Thomas More School Educational Endowment Trust. Tel: 402-556-1456.
St. Vincent de Paul Parish Endowment Trust. Tel: 402-496-7988.
St. Vincent de Paul Parish Educational Endowment Trust. Tel: 402-496-7988.
St. Wenceslaus Parish Endowment Trust. Tel: 402-330-0304.
St. Wenceslaus Parish Educational Endowment Trust. Tel: 402-330-0304.
St. Patrick Foundation, Inc., O'Neill. Tel: 402-336-1602.
St. Mary School Foundation, Inc., O'Neill. Tel: 402-336-1602.
St. Mary of the Seven Dolors Parish Endowment Trust, Osmond. Tel: 402-748-3340.
St. Columbkille Parish Endowment Trust, Papillon. Tel: 402-339-3285.
St. Columbkille Educational Endowment Trust, Papillion. Tel: 402-339-3285.
St. John the Baptist Parish Endowment Trust, Pender. Tel: 402-385-3285.
St. John the Baptist Parish Educational Endowment Trust, Pender. Tel: 402-385-3285.
St. John the Baptist Parish Endowment Trust, Petersburg. Tel: 402-386-5580.
St. John the Baptist Parish Educational Endowment Trust, Petersburg. Tel: 02-386-5580.
St. Joseph Parish Endowment Trust, Pierce. Tel: 402-329-4200.
St. Joseph Parish Educational Endowment Trust, Pierce. Tel: 402-329-4200.
St. Paul Parish Endowment Trust, Plainview. Tel: 402-582-4413.
St. Paul Parish Educational Endowment Trust, Plainview. Tel: 402-582-4413.
St. Joseph Parish Endowment Trust, Platte Center. Tel: 402-246-2255.
St. Joseph Parish Educational Endowment Trust, Platte Center. Tel: 402-246-2255.
St. Joseph Parish Endowment Trust, Ponca. Tel: 402-755-2773.
St. Joseph Parish Educational Endowment Trust, Ponca. Tel: 402-755-2773.
St. Mary Parish Endowment Trust, Primrose. Tel: 308-358-0773.
St. Mary Parish Educational Endowment Trust, Primrose. Tel: 308-358-0773.
St. Bonaventure Parish Endowment Trust, Raeville. Tel: 402-386-5254.
St. Bonvaventure Parish/Pope John XXIII High School Educational Endowment Trust, Raeville. Tel: 402-386-5254.
St. Gerald Parish Endowment Trust, Ralston. Tel: 402-331-1955.
St. Frances de Chantal Parish Endowment Trust, Randolph. Tel: 402-337-0644.
St. Frances de Chantal Parish Educational Endowment Trust, Randolph. Tel: 402-337-0644.
St. Anthony Parish Endowment Trust, St. Charles. Tel: 402-572-3681.
St. Anthony Parish Educational Endowment Trust, St. Charles. Tel: 402-572-3681.
St. Edward Parish Endowment Trust, St. Edward. Tel: 402-395-2926.
St. Edward Parish Educational Endowment Trust, St. Edward. Tel: 402-395-2926.
Immaculate Conception Parish Endowment Trust, St. Helena. Tel: 402-245-3311.
Immaculate Conception Parish Educational Endowment Trust, St. Helena. Tel: 402-245-3311.
SS. Philip and James Parish Endowment Trust, St. James. Tel: 402-357-2400.
SS. Philip and James Parish Educational Endowment, St. James. Tel: 402-357-2400.
St. Francis de Sales Parish Endowment Trust, Schoolcraft. Tel: 402-675-2485.
St. Augustine Parish Endowment Trust, Schuyler. Tel: 402-352-3521.
St. Augustine Parish Educational Endowment Trust, Schuyler. Tel: 402-352-3521.
St. Mary Parish Endowment Trust, Schuyler. Tel: 402-352-3540.
St. Mary Parish Educational Endowment Trust, Schuyler. Tel: 402-352-3540.
St. Lawrence Parish Endowment Trust, Scribner. Tel: 402-654-3449.
St. Lawrence Parish Educational Endowment Trust, Scribner. Tel: 402-654-3449.
St. Lawrence Parish Endowment Trust, Silver Creek. Tel: 402-897-2625.
St. Lawrence Parish Educational Endowment Trust, Silver Creek. Tel: 402-897-2625.
St. Leo Parish Endowment Trust, Snyder. Tel: 402-897-2625.
St. Leo Parish Educational Endowment Trust, Snyder. Tel: 402-568-2520.
St. Michael Educational Endowment, South Sioux City. Tel: 402-494-5423.
St. Mary Catholic Church Endowment Trust, Spencer. Tel: 402-589-0067.
St. Mary Parish Educational Endowment Trust, Spencer. Tel: 402-589-0067.
St. Joseph Parish Endowment Trust, Springfield. Tel: 402-253-2899.
St. Joseph Parish Educational Endowment Trust, Springfield. Tel: 402-253-2899.
St. Peter Parish Endowment Trust, Stanton. Tel: 402-439-2147.
St. Peter Parish Educational Endowment Trust, Stanton. Tel: 402-439-2147.
St. Boniface Parish Endowment Trust, Stuart. Tel: 402-924-3262.
St. Boniface Parish Educational Endowment Trust, Stuart. Tel: 402-924-3262.
St. Boniface Elementary School Endowment Trust, Stuart. Tel: 402-924-3263.
St. Mary Parish Endowment Trust, Tabor. Tel: 402-986-1627.
St. Mary Parish Educational Endowment Trust, Tabor. Tel: 402-986-1627.
St. Michael Parish Endowment Trust, Tarnov. Tel: 402-246-4821.
St. Michael Parish Educational Endowment Trust, Tarnov. Tel: 402-246-4821.
St. Patrick Parish Endowment Trust, Tekamah. Tel: 402-374-1692.
St. Patrick Parish Educational Endowment Trust, Tekamah. Tel: 402-374-1692.
Our Lady of Mt. Carmel Parish Endowment Trust, Tilden. Tel: 402-368-7710.
Our Lady of Mt. Carmel Parish Educational Endowment Trust, Tilden. Tel: 402-368-7710.
St. John the Evangelist Parish Endowment Trust, Valley. Tel: 402-359-5783.
St. John the Evangelist Parish Educational Endowment Trust, Valley. Tel: 402-359-5783.
St. Wenceslaus Church Parish Endowment Trust, Verdigre. Tel: 402-668-2331.
St. Wenceslaus Parish Educational Endowment Trust, Verdigre. Tel: 402-668-2331.
St. Joseph Parish Endowment Trust, Walthill. Tel: 402-878-2402.
St. Joseph Parish Educational Endowment Trust, Walthill. Tel: 402-878-2402.
St. Mary Parish Endowment Trust, Wayne. Tel: 402-375-2000.
St. Mary Educational Endowment Trust, Wayne. Tel: 402-375-2000.
Church of the Assumption of the B.V.M. Parish Endowment Trust, West Point. Tel: 402-372-2188.
Church of the Assumption of the B.V.M. Parish Endowment Trust, West Point. Tel: 402-372-2188.
Guardian Angels Grade School Educational Endowment Trust, West Point. Tel: 402-372-2188.
West Point Central Catholic High School Educational Endowment Trust, West Point. Tel: 402-372-5326.
St. Augustine Indian Mission Endowment Trust, Winnebago. Tel: 402-878-2402.
St. Augustine Indian Mission Educational Endowment Trust, Winnebago. Tel: 402-878-2402.
St. Augustine Indian Mission Tuition Relief Educational Endowment Trust, Winnebago. Tel: 402-878-2402.
St. Joseph Parish Endowment Trust, Wisner. Tel: 402-529-3242.
St. Joseph Parish Educational Endowment Trust, Wisner. Tel: 402-529-3242.
Sacred Heart Parish Endowment Trust, Wynot. Tel: 402-357-2400.
Sacred Heart Parish Educational Endowment Trust, Wynot. Tel: 402-357-2400.

ST. COLUMBANS. *Columban Fathers Regional Administration*, P.O. Box 10, 68056-0010. Tel: 402-291-1920; Fax: 402-291-8693.
E-mail: stcolneus@aol.com
Web site: www.st.columban.org.
St. Columban's Central Administration.
St. Columban's D-M-P Trust.
St. Columban's Gift Annuity Trust.
St. Columban's Education Trust.
St. Columban's Priests Health Program Trust.
St. Columban's Retirement Fund Trust.
St. Columban's Seminary Reserve Trust.
St. Columban's Masses in Trust.
St. Columban's Donors/Personal Trust.
St. Columban's Regional Trust.
St. Columban's Burse Estate Trust.
St. Columban's Gift Annuity Trust California.

[O] MISCELLANEOUS

OMAHA. Purpose: To provide affordable housing to the economically poor.

Archdiocesan Consultation Service, 3300 N. 60th St., 68104. Tel: 402-551-1135; Fax: 402-554-0365. E-mail: mmicheletto@omahaflo.creighton.edu
Sr. Marie Micheletto, R.S.M., Dir. & Contact.

Archdiocesan Hispanic Ministry Office, 3216 N. 60th St., 68104. Tel: 402-558-3134; Fax: 402-551-3050. E-mail: mcdp@omahahmo.creighton.edu
Sr. Angela Erevia, M.C.D.P., Dir.; Carolina Padilla, Sec.

Beginning Experience, 3214 N. 60th St., 68104. Tel: 402-551-9003; Fax: 402-551-3050. Sr. Barbara Markey, Contact.

Bergan Mercy Foundation, Inc. (Provides support to the mission of Bergen Mercy Health System dba Alegent Health), 7500 Mercy Rd., 68124. Tel: 402-343-4430; Fax: 402-343-4337.
E-mail: ncooney@alegent.org
Sr. Norita Cooney, R.S.M., Contact Person.

Black Student Catholic Scholarship Trust Fund, c/o Office of Stewardship and Development, P.O. Box 4130, 68104-0130. Tel: 402-554-8493. A trust for the purpose of providing eligible black Catholic students scholarships and assistance for Catholic high school education. The board of 10 trustees for a nonprofit religious and educational corporation, whose president is the Archbishop of Omaha oversees the affairs of this trust. Tessie Edwards, Contact.

Cathedral Arts Project, Inc., 100 N. 62nd St., 68132. Tel: 402-558-3100; Fax: 402-558-3026.
E-mail: WorshipOmaha@compuserve.com
Bro. William J. Woeger, F.S.C., Exec. Dir. & Contact.

Catholic Charities Foundation, 3300 N. 60th St., 68104. Tel: 402-554-0520; Fax: 402-551-8797.
E-mail: catholiccharities@ccomaha.org
Web site: www.ccomaha.org
Scot L. Adams, Ph.D., Pres. & Contact.

Catholic Jail and Prison Ministry, 701 S. 28th St., 68105-1511. Tel: 402-342-7142; Fax: 402-330-5842.
E-mail: cjpm@prodigy.net
Richard P. Vondenkamp, Dir.

Catholic Umbrella Pool, 4223 Center St., 68105. Tel: 402-551-8765; Fax: 402-551-2943. Mr. Dennis F. Atwood, Contact Person.

Christ Child Society of Omaha, 1248 S. 10th St., 68108. Tel: 402-342-4566; Fax: 402-342-4541. C. Timothy Connor, Exec. Dir. & Contact. Day Care Centers 2; Total Assisted 200. Special Care Centers 3; Total Assisted 5,000.

Christian Family Movement (CFM), 3514 N. 63rd St., 68104. Tel: 402-558-1710. Contacts: Edwin & Sheila Osterhaus.

Christian Urban Education Service, 2207 Wirt St., 68110. Tel: 402-451-5755; Fax: 402-451-1731. Rev. Thomas M. Fangman.

Christians Encounter Christ, 1938 S. 149th Cir., 68144. Tel: 402-334-2497. Jan Mitchell, Contact Person. Purpose: To promote the transferring of environments through Christian leaders who are willing to live and share their principles of being Christian. Through the ongoing development of their Christian Personality, strengthened by their 4th Day, these leaders strive to instill the spirit and sense of gospel to all environments in which they are actively involved.

Francis House. (Men's Sheltering.), 1702 Nicholas St., 68102. Tel: 402-341-1821; Fax: 402-341-5270.
E-mail: siena1702@aol.com
Paul A. Koch, Dir. & Contact.

Harrington Homes Program, 7262 Mercy Rd., Ste. 102, 68124-2348. Tel: 402-398-6614; Fax: 402-398-6370. Sr. Carolyn Coffey, R.S.M., Contact Person.

Health System of Mercy, 7262 Mercy Rd., 68124-2312. Tel: 402-393-8225; Fax: 402-393-8145.
E-mail: patriciaf@mercyoma.com
Web site: www.mercyoma.org
Sr. Patricia Forret, R.S.M., Contact Person.

Heart of Mary Publishing Company, Incorporated dba Heart of Mary Ministry, 2216 Poppleton Ave., 68108-3436. Tel: 402-342-9265; Fax: 402-342-9094.
E-mail: Srmarylucy@aol.com
Web site: www.heartofmaryministry.com
Sr. Mary Lucy Astuto, Contact.

Holy Family Shrine, P.O. Box 241212, 68124. A place of pilgrimage, prayer and resource for the public and private prayer. This nonprofit religious, charitable and educational corporation is duly constituted under the laws of the State of Nebraska and operated by a Board of Trustees. Sr. Renee Mirkes, O.S.F., Contact.

Holy Name Housing Corp., 3014 N. 45th St., 68104. Tel: 402-453-6100; Fax: 402-451-7187. Sr. Marilyn Ross, R.S.M., Exec. Dir. & Contact.

Holy Trinity Church of Colfax, County Parish and Cemetery Endowment Trust Fund, 100 North 62nd St., 68132. Tel: 402-986-1627.

The Institute for Priestly Formation, 320 North 20th St., #1208, 68178. Tel: 402-546-6384; Fax: 402-280-2423.
E-mail: rgabuzda@creighton.edu
Web site: www.creighton.edu/ipf
Rev. Richard J. Gabuzda, Contact Person. Purpose: To offer programs and support for the integration of theological study, spiritual growth and direction, and retreat experiences for diocesan seminarians and priests.

Intecessors of the Lamb, 4014 N. Post Rd., 68112. Tel: 402-455-5262; Fax: 402-455-1323.
E-mail: bellwether@novia.net
Web site: www.bellwetheromaha.org
Mother Nadine, Contact Person.

Marriage Encounter, 16404 Jefferson St., 68138. Tel: 402-896-3925.
E-mail: tmarble@radiks.net
Web site: www.geocities.com/capecanaveral/6748/mesect9/
Tom & Karen Marble, Exec. Team.

McAuley Bergan Center, 3552 Farnam St., 68131. Tel: 402-342-1688; Fax: 402-342-7043. Paul Maginn, Dir. & Contact. Adult Day Care Centers.

Mercy Housing Midwest, 7262 Mercy Rd., 68124. Tel: 402-398-6614; Fax: 402-398-6370.
E-mail: ccoffey@mercyhousing.org
Sr. Carolyn Coffey, R.S.M., Contact Person.

Mercy Housing, 2904 N. 45th St.

Omaha dba Mercy House, 7262 Mercy Rd., 68124. Tel: 402-398-6614; Fax: 402-398-6370. Sr. Carolyn Coffey, R.S.M., Contact Person.

Harrington Homes Program, 7262 Mercy Rd., 68124. Tel: 402-398-6614; Fax: 402-398-6370. Sr. Carolyn Coffey, R.S.M., Contact Person.

Mercy Northglen, 7262 Mercy Rd., 68124. Tel: 402-398-6614; Fax: 402-398-6370. Sr. Carolyn Coffey, R.S.M., Contact Person.

Mercy Western Manor, 7262 Mercy Rd., 68124. Tel: 402-398-6614; Fax: 402-398-6370. Sr. Carolyn Coffey, R.S.M., Contact Person.

Mercy Crestview Village, 7262 Mercy Rd., 68124. Tel: 402-398-6614; Fax: 402-398-6370. Sr. Carolyn Coffey, R.S.M., Contact Person.

Mercy Oakwood Gardens, 7262 Mercy Rd., 68124. Tel: 402-398-6614; Fax: 402-398-6370. To provide affordable housing to the economically poor. Sr. Carolyn Coffey, R.S.M., Contact Person.

New Cassel Foundation, 900 N. 90th St., 68114-2769. Tel: 402-393-2277; Fax: 402-393-3784. A nonprofit religious, charitable and educational corporation, duly constituted under the laws of the State of Nebraska, to provide support and benefit for the New Cassel Retirement Center and the Franciscan Adult Day Center. Rev. James R. Tiegs, Pres. & Contact.

New Covenant Center: Education for Justice and Peace, 703 S. 28th St., 68105-1528. Tel: 402-345-5111; Fax: 402-345-5111.
E-mail: mcosssf@juno.com
Sr. Maureen Connolly, S.S.S.F., Prog. Coord.

Notre Dame Housing, Inc., 3501 State St., 68112-1709. Tel: 402-455-2994; Fax: 402-455-3974.
E-mail: maz@creighton.edu
Web site: www.notredamesisters.org
Sr. Mary Ann Zimmer, N.D., Contact Person.
Purpose: To provide housing for elderly and persons of low-income or otherwise unable to afford market rate housing.

Notre Dame Living Center, Inc., 3501 State St., 68112-1709. Tel: 402-455-2994; Fax: 402-455-3974.
E-mail: maz@creighton.edu
Web site: www.notredamesisters.org
Sr. Mary Ann Zimmer, N.D., Contact Person & Pres. Purpose: Provides affordable housing to the elderly, particularly those of low-income status.

Pope Paul VI Institute for the Study of Human Reproduction, 6901 Mercy Rd., 68106. Tel: 402-390-6600; Fax: 402-390-9851.
E-mail: popepaul@mitec.net
Web site: www.popepaulvi.com
Thomas W. Hilgers, M.D., Dir.

St. Cecilia Schola Cantorum, Inc., 100 N. 62nd St., 68132. Tel: 402-558-3100; Fax: 402-551-4212. A nonprofit religious, charitable, educational center, duly constituted under the laws of the State of Nebraska, provides education and resources in church music and promoting the performance of church music in the Archdiocese of Omaha. Rev. Gerald P. Melchior, Contact.

St. James Manor, Inc., 3102 No. 60th St., 68104. Tel: 402-551-4243; Fax: 402-558-8023.
E-mail: JoeR@ccomaha.org
Joseph V. Rysavy, Pres. & Contact.

St. Mary's Church of Tabor Parish and Cemetery Endowment Trust Fund, 100 North 62nd St., 68132. Tel: 402-986-1627.

Siena - Francis House, Inc., P.O. Box 217, D.T.S., 68101. Tel: 402-341-1821; Fax: 402-341-5270.
E-mail: siena1702@aol.com
Paul A. Koch, Dir. & Contact.

Siena House. (Women's Sheltering), 1702 Nicholas St., 68102. Tel: 402-341-1821; Fax: 402-341-5270.
E-mail: siena1702@aol.com
Paul A. Koch, Dir. & Contact.

TEC, Box 4130, 68104. Tel: 402-554-8493; Fax: 402-554-8402.
E-mail: rramos@creighton.edu
Rita Ramos, Asst. Dir. Youth Ministry.

Widowed and Divorced Catholics of Omaha, 3214 N. 60th St., 68104. Tel: 402-551-9003; Fax: 402-551-3050.
Web site: jgould@omahaflo.creighton.edu
Jean Gould, Contact.

The Young Adult Beginning Experience, 3214 N. 60th St., 68104. Tel: 402-551-9003; Fax: 402-551-3050. Sr. Barbara Markey, Contact.

CROFTON. *Sacred Faith House of Prayer of the Brothers and Sisters of Charity*, 89574 545th Ave., 68730-3238. Tel: 402-388-2472; Fax: 402-388-2472.
E-mail: sfhop@bloomnet.com
A place of hermitage and retreat, public and private prayer and resources for spirituality through teaching, publishing and acts of charity. Contacts: Dr. Joseph Kelly; Neville Ann Kelly.

HUMPHREY. *St. Francis Church of Humphrey Cemetery Endowment Trust Fund*, P.O. Box 116, 68642. Tel: 402-923-0913; Fax: 402-923-1931.
E-mail: rectory@megavision.com
Rev. Stephen J. Gutgsell, Contact Person.

LYNCH. *Niobrara Valley House of Renewal*, P.O. Box 167, 68746. Tel: 402-569-2421.
E-mail: marypmin@threeriver.net
Web site: www.threeriver.net/retreat
Mary Hildman, Contact.

OAKDALE. *Tintern Retreat and Resource Center*, RR 1, Box 52, 68761. Tel: 402-776-2188.
E-mail: tintern@gpcom.net
Phyllis A. Camp, Contact.

PETERSBURG. *Rural Central Deanery Faith and Ministry Formation Center*, P.O. Box 9, 68652-0009. Tel: 402-386-5395.
E-mail: rcdeanery@yahoo.com
Sr. Patricia Throener, O.S.F., Contact.

St. John the Baptists' Church of Petersburg Cemetary Endowment Trust Fund. c/o St. John the Baptist Church, 524 West Church St., Albion, 60620. Tel: 402-395-2393. A trust for the purpose of providing for the support and benefit of the cemeteries maintained by St. John the Baptist Church of Petersburg. The nonprofit, charitable and educational corporation is duly constituted under the laws of the State of Nebraska and is operated by a 3 member Board of Trustees.

ST. EDWARD. *St. Edward's Church (of St. Edward) Cemetary Endowment Trust Fund*. 103 East 3rd St., Lindsay, 68644. Tel: 402-428-2455; Fax: 402-428-5205. A trust for the purpose of providing for the support and benefit of the cemetaries maintained by St. Edward Church, St Edward, NE. The nonprofit, charitable and educational corporation is duly constituted under the laws of the State of Nebraska and is operated by a 3 member Board of Trustees.

SCHUYLER. *St. Benedict Center Endowment Fund*, 1123 Rd. "I", P.O. Box 528, 68661-0528. An endowment for the purpose of providing for the support and benefit of development, maintenance and supplemental funding of programs and services of St. Benedict Center and the receipt and management of gifts and bequests to the same center. The nonprofit, charitable and educational corporation is duly constituted under the laws of the State of Nebraska. Very Rev. Germar Neubert, O.S.B., Contact at Benedictine Mission House/Christ the King Priory.

SILVER CREEK. *St. Lawrence Church of Silver Creek Cemetery Endowment Trust Fund*, P.O. Box 332, 68663. Tel: 308-773-2282.
E-mail: dkorth@megavision

WINNEBAGO. *Feathers*, c/o St. Augustine Indian Mission, P.O. Box GG, 68071. Tel: 402-878-2402; Fax: 402-878-2760. An endowment, duly constituted under the laws of the State of Nebraska as a nonprofit religious, charitable and educational corporation, to provide scholarships to Native American children of the Winnebago nation to attend high school. Rev. Steven Boes, Contact & Dir.

St. Augustine's Indian Mission, P.O. Box GG, 68071. Tel: 402-878-2402; Fax: 402-878-2760.
E-mail: sboes@mother.esul.org.
Web site: www.geocities.com/Athens/Parthenon/7144
Revs. Steven Boes, Contact & Dir.; Tom Gall, Asst. Dir.

[P] PUBLIC ASSOCIATIONS OF THE CHRISTIAN FAITHFUL

OMAHA. *Christian Life Community-North Central Region (CLC)*, 2500 California Plaza, 68178. Tel: 402-280-2692; Fax: 402-280-5590. A public association of the Christian faithful of Pontificial Right providing spiritual support and guidance in the Jesuit

tradition of the Spiritual Exercises. Rev. Jack Zurcher, S.J., Contact & Regional Ecclesial Asst.
Intercessors of the Lamb, 4014 North Post Rd., 68112. Tel: 402-455-1514; Fax: 402-455-1323.
Web site: www.bellwetheromaha.org
A community of the consecrated hermits and a center of formation with the charism of intercessory prayer; provides retreats, conferences and resources for charismatic, marian and spiritual warfare spirituality. Mother Nadine Brown, Contact.

CROFTON. *The Brothers and Sisters of Charity at Little Portion Heritage*, c/o Sacred Faith House of Prayer, 89574 545th Ave., 68730-3238. Tel: 402-388-2472; Fax: 402-388-2472.
E-mail: sfhop@bloomnet.com
Motherhouse: Little Portion Hermitage, 350 CR 248, Berryville, AR, 72616. Tel: 501-253-7710; Fax: 501-253-6640. An integrated monastic and domestic community established by the Bishop of the Diocese of Little Rock, Arkansas. Contacts in the Archdiocese of Omaha: Dr. Joseph Kelly; Neville Ann Kelly.

RELIGIOUS INSTITUTES OF MEN REPRESENTED IN THE ARCHDIOCESE

For further details refer to the corresponding bracketed number in the Religious Institutes of Men or Women section.

[0200]—*Benedictine Monks.*—O.S.B.
[0330]—*Brothers of the Christian Schools.* (St. Louis, MO).—F.S.C.
[0690]—*Jesuit Fathers and Brother.* (Wisconsin Prov.).—S.J.
[0150]—*Order of the Augustinian Recollects.* (St. Augustine Prov.).—O.A.R.
[1070]—*Redemptorist Fathers.* (St. Louis Prov.).—C.SS.R.
[0370]—*Society of St. Columban.*—S.S.C.

RELIGIOUS INSTITUTES OF WOMEN REPRESENTED IN THE ARCHDIOCESE

[0230]—*Benedictine Sisters of Pontifical Jurisdiction.*—O.S.B.
[1070-03]—*Dominican Sisters.*—O.P.
[1230]—*Franciscan Sisters of Christian Charity.*—O.S.F.
[1430]—*Franciscan Sisters of Our Lady of Perpetual Help.*—O.S.F.
[2575]—*Institute of the Sisters of Mercy of the Americas.*—R.S.M.
[0210]—*Missionary Benedictine Sisters.*—O.S.B.
[2960]—*Notre Dame Sisters.*—N.D.
[3760]—*Order of St. Clare.*—O.S.C.
[1680]—*School Sisters of St. Francis.* (Our Lady of Angels Prov.).—O.S.F.
[3580]—*Servants of Mary.*—O.S.M.
[1630]—*Sisters of St. Francis of Peace and Christian Charity.* (Denver Prov.).—O.S.F.
[1640]—*Sisters of St. Francis of Perpetual Adoration.* (Colorado Springs, CO).—O.S.F.
[1830]—*Sisters of the Good Shepherd.*—R.G.S.
[3270]—*Sisters of the Most Precious Blood.* (O'Fallon, MO).—C.PP.S.
[3320]—*Sisters of the Presentation of the B.V.M.*—P.B.V.M.
[4070]—*Society of the Sacred Heart.*—R.S.C.J.

ARCHDIOCESAN CEMETERIES

OMAHA. *Calvary.*
Holy Sepulchre.
Resurrection.
St. Mary.
St. Mary Magdalene.

NECROLOGY

✠ Sheehan, Most Rev. Daniel E., (Retired). —Died Oct. 24, 2000.
† Peter, Rev. Msgr. Paul F., (Retired). —Died Oct. 15, 2000.
† Price, Francis R., (Retired). —Died March 5, 2000.

Diocese of Orange in California

(Arausicanae in California)

Most Reverend

TOD DAVID BROWN, D.D.

Bishop of Orange; ordained May 1, 1963; appointed Bishop of Boise December 27, 1988; Episcopal Ordination April 3, 1989; appointed Bishop of Orange June 29, 1998; installed September 3, 1998. Marywood Center, 2811 E. Villa Real Dr., Orange, CA, 92867.

Most Reverend

NORMAN F. McFARLAND, D.D., J.C.D.

Retired Bishop of Orange; ordained June 15, 1946; appointed Titular Bishop of Bida and Auxiliary of San Francisco June 5, 1970; consecrated September 8, 1970; appointed Apostolic Administrator December 6, 1974; appointed Bishop of Reno-Las Vegas February 10, 1976; installed March 31, 1976; appointed Bishop of Orange December 29, 1986; installed February 24, 1987; retired June 30, 1998. *Res., 200 W. La Veta Ave., Orange, CA, 92866. Office: Marywood Center, 2811 E. Villa Real Dr., Orange, CA, 92867.*

Most Reverend

JAIME SOTO, M.DIV.

Auxiliary Bishop of Orange; ordained June 12, 1982; appointed March 23, 2000.

Chancellor's Office: 2811 E. Villa Real Dr., P.O. Box 14195, Orange, CA, 92863-1595. Tel.: 714-282-3000; Fax: 714-282-3029.

Web site address: www.rcbo.org

E-mail address: sr.kit@rcbo.org

ESTABLISHED JUNE 18, 1976.

Square Miles 782.

Comprises the County of Orange in the State of California.

DIOCESAN PATRON: Our Lady of Guadalupe.

Legal Titles: *(Prot. No. CD 528-76)*

The Roman Catholic Bishop of Orange, a Corporation Sole.

Diocese of Orange Education and Welfare Corporation.

Catholic Charities of Orange.

For legal titles of parishes and diocesan institutions, consult the Diocesan Pastoral Service Office.

STATISTICAL OVERVIEW

Personnel	
Bishop	1
Auxiliary Bishops	1
Retired Bishops	1
Abbots	1
Retired Abbots	1
Priests: Diocesan Active in Diocese	116
Priests: Active Outside Diocese	8
Priests: Retired, Sick or Absent	58
Number of Diocesan Priests	182
Religious Priests in Diocese	89
Extern Priests in Diocese	13
Ordinations:	
Diocesan Priests	5
Transitional Deacons	1
Permanent Deacons in Diocese	67
Total Brothers	12
Total Sisters	360
Parishes	
Parishes	55
With Resident Pastor:	
Resident Diocesan Priests	47
Resident Religious Priests	8
Missions	3
Pastoral Centers	4
Professional Ministry Personnel:	
Brothers	1
Sisters	35
Lay Ministers	191
Welfare	
Catholic Hospitals	3
Total Assisted	362,032
Homes for the Aged	1
Total Assisted	23
Day Care and Extended Day Care Centers	2
Total Assisted	171
Specialized Homes	5
Total Assisted	602
Special Centers for Social Services	3
Total Assisted	2,639,227
Residential Care of Disabled	1
Total Assisted	13
Other Institutions	1
Total Assisted	25
Educational	
Diocesan Students in Other Seminaries	38
Total Seminarians	38
High Schools, Diocesan and Parish	3
Total Students	4,658
High Schools, Private	3
Total Students	1,088
Elementary Schools, Diocesan and Parish	38
Total Students	14,673
Elementary Schools, Private	2
Total Students	725
Catechesis/Religious Education:	
High School Students	15,086
Elementary Students	37,515
Total Students Under Catholic Instruction	73,783
Teachers in the Diocese:	
Priests	10
Brothers	10
Sisters	40
Lay Teachers	984
Vital Statistics	
Receptions into the Church:	
Infant Baptism Totals	17,291
Adult Baptism Totals	710
Received into Full Communion	632
First Communions	13,082
Confirmations	11,281
Marriages:	
Catholic	2,626
Interfaith	677
Total Marriages	3,303
Deaths	2,948
Total Catholic Population	1,044,191
Total Population	2,760,948

Former Bishops—Most Rev. WILLIAM R. JOHNSON, appt. Titular Bishop of Biera and Auxiliary Bishop of Los Angeles, Feb. 9, 1971; cons. March 25, 1971; installed as first Bishop of Orange, June 18, 1976; died July 28, 1986.—Most Rev. NORMAN F. MCFARLAND, D.D., J.C.D., ord. June 15, 1946; appt. Titular Bishop of Bida and Auxiliary of San Francisco, June 5, 1970; cons. Sept. 8, 1970; appt. Apostolic Administrator, Dec. 6, 1974; appt. Bishop of Reno-Las Vegas, Feb. 10, 1976; installed March 31, 1976; appt. Bishop of Orange, Dec. 29, 1986; installed Feb. 24, 1987; retired June 30, 1998.

Vicar General—Rev. Msgr. JOHN URELL, Office: *Marywood Center.*

Chancellor—Sr. KATHERINE GRAY, C.S.J., Office: *Marywood Center.*

Moderator of the Curia—Rev. Msgr. JOHN URELL, Office: *Marywood Center.*

Director of Clergy Personnel—Rev. J. MICHAEL MCKIERNAN, Office: *Marywood Center.*

Secretary to the Bishop—Rev. J. MICHAEL MCKIERNAN, Office: *Marywood Center.*

Vicar for Religious Communities—Sr. EYMARD FLOOD, O.S.C., Office: *Marywood Center.*

Vicar for Hispanic Communities—Most Rev. JAIME SOTO, D.D., M.S.W., Office: *Marywood Center.*

Vicar for Priests—Rev. KERRY BEAULIEU, Office: *Marywood Center.*

Vicar for Religious Education—Rev. CHRISTOPHER SMITH, Office: *Marywood Center.*

Vicar for Pastoral and Community Affairs—Rev. Msgr. JOHN F. SAMMON, P.A., *Res., 200 W. La Veta Ave., Orange, 92866.*, Office: *Marywood Center.*

Diocesan Pastoral Service Office—2811 E. Villa Real Dr., P.O. Box 14195, Orange, 92863-1595. Tel: 714-282-3000; Fax: 714-282-3029. Office Hours: Mon.-Fri. 9-5.

Office of Canonical Services—2811 E. Villa Real Dr., P.O. Box 14195, Orange, 92863-1595. Tel: 714-282-3080; Fax: 714-282-3087.

Judicial Vicar—Rev. WILLIAM J. VOHSING, J.C.L.

Adjutant Judicial Vicars—Rev. Msgr. DANIEL J. MURRAY, J.C.L.; Rev. Msgr. DANIEL H. BRENNAN; Rev. DOUGLAS J. COOK, J.C.L.

Promoter of Justice—Rev. Msgr. HUGH O'CONNOR.

Judges—Rev. Msgr. DANIEL H. BRENNAN; Rev. Msgr. JOHN G. CAMPBELL, J.C.L.; Rev. Msgr. PAUL MARTIN; Rev. Msgr. JOHN URELL, M.S.W.; Rev. Msgr. DANIEL J. MURRAY, J.C.L.; Very Rev. ARTHUR A. HOLQUIN, S.T.L.; Revs. JAMES HARTNETT; THOMAS HA; DANIEL R. HOPCUS; JOHN R. KELLER; JOSEPH NETTEKOVEN; TED OLSON; KENNETH SCHMIT; WILLIAM J. VOHSING, J.C.L.; JOHN CARONAN, O.Praem.,

J.C.L.; MARGARET ANN RAMSDEN, S.F.C.C., J.C.L.; Ms. PEGGY JEAN PAOLI, J.C.L.; PAULA MODAFF, S.P., J.C.L.

Defenders of the Bond—Revs. TIMOTHY RAMAEKERS; JOHN A. BRADLEY; TUAN JOSEPH PHAM, J.C.L.; DOUGLAS COOK, J.C.L.

Ecclesiastical Notaries—SUE KIRRER; LINDA BRAUN; CAROL REDDICK; SANDRA DALTON; LILLIAN ESQUIVEL.

National Organization for Decent Literature—Rev. Msgr. JOHN F. SAMMON, Dir., Office: *Marywood Center.*

Newman Apostolate—Rev. PATRICK PHILBIN, S.M., Dir., *P.O. Box 6030, Irvine, 92616.* Tel: 714-856-0211.

Parish Councils and Parish Development—Sr. KATHERINE GRAY, C.S.J., Dir., Office: *Marywood Center.*

Diaconate—Mr. FRANK CHAVEZ, Office: *Marywood Center.*

Clergy Personnel Board—Rev. Msgr. JOHN URELL, V.G.; Revs. FRED BAILEY; CIRILO FLORES; MICHAEL HEHER; TIMOTHY MACCARTHY; TUYEN NGUYEN; EAMON O'GORMAN; J. MICHAEL MCKIERNAN, Auditor, Office: *Marywood Center.*

Communications Office—Rev. Msgr. LAWRENCE J. BAIRD, Dir., Office: *Marywood Center.*

Conciliation & Arbitration Office—Ms. DOLORES CHURCHILL, L.C.S.W., Office: *Marywood Center.*

Diocesan Council of Catholic Women—Sr. EYMARD FLOOD, O.S.C., Moderator; JACKIE REED, Pres., Office: *Marywood Center.*

Priests' Relief—Rev. KERRY BEAULIEU, Office: *Marywood Center.*

Council of Priests—Most Rev. TOD D. BROWN; Most Rev. JAIME SOTO, D.D., M.S.W.; Rev. Msgr. JOHN SAMMON; Rev. Msgr. PAUL MARTIN; Rev. WILLIAM VOHSING; Rev. Msgr. JOHN URELL; Rev. Msgr. PETER TIEN; Rev. Msgr. WILBUR DAVIS; Revs. ARTHUR HOLQUIN; JEROME KARCHER; AL BACA; RUDOLPH PRECIADO; JIM RIES; COLM CONLON; DICK KENNEDY; ENRIQUE SERA; ALEX KIM; DANIEL HOPCUS; JOHN MCANDREW; JEROME HENSON; MICHAEL HEHER; KERRY BEAULIEU; MARITO REBAMONTAN; JOHN LENIHAN; GERALD M. HORAN, O.S.M.; JOSEPH SCERBO, S.A.; JOHN CARONAN, O.Praem., Office: *Marywood Center.*

Consultors—Rev. WILLIAM VOHSING; Rev. Msgr. JOHN SAMMON; Most Rev. JAIME SOTO, D.D., M.S.W.; Rev. Msgr. PETER TIEN; Rev. Msgr. JOHN URELL; Rev. Msgr. WILBUR DAVIS; Revs. JOHN LENIHAN; KERRY BEAULIEU; MICHAEL HEHER; Very Rev. ARTHUR HOLQUIN; Revs. GERALD HORAN, O.S.M.; MARITO REBAMONTAN.

Propagation of the Faith—Rev. Msgr. JOHN F. SAMMON, Dir., Office: *Marywood Center.*

Council for Religious—Sr. EYMARD FLOOD, O.S.C., Dir.; Sr. RITA BURNHAM, R.S.M.; Sr. CLARE BRIODY, D.M.J.; Sr. YOLANDA MAGALLANES, S.D.S.H.; Sr. BLANCA RIVERA, M.C.; Bro. PASCAL BARRY, O.H.; Sr. BARBARA REDER, S.P.; Sr. JEAN SCHULTZ, S.P.; Sr. ROSALEEN STOIBER, O.P.

Society of St. Vincent de Paul of Orange County—Mr. DAN HARNEY, Pres.; Rev. PEREGRINE GRAFFIUS, O.S.M., Spiritual Dir., *180 S. Cypress, Orange, 92866.* Tel: 714-633-9194.

Schools Office—Bro. WILLIAM CARRIERE, F.S.C., Supt.; Mrs. SALLY TODD, Assoc. Supt., Office: *Marywood Center.*

Schools Advisory Board of Education—Office: *Marywood Center.*

Vocations Office—Rev. Msgr. WILBUR DAVIS, Dir., Office: *Marywood Center.*

Catholic Campaign for Human Development—Sr. KATHERINE GRAY, C.S.J., Dir.

Local Board—DOLORES CHURCHILL; Deacon FRANK CHAVEZ; WALTER DALY; DIETER MYERS GONZALES; EDWARD EGAN; WILLIAM ERICKSON; VIRGINIA FAULKNER; Sr. REBECCA RODRIGUEZ, C.S.J.; FRED VEGA, Office: *Marywood Center.*

Diocesan Offices and Directors

Apostleship of Prayer—Rev. Msgr. HUGH O'CONNOR, *2050 W. Ball Rd., Anaheim, 92804.* Tel: 714-774-2595.

Archivist—Rev. WILLIAM KREKELBERG, Office: *Mission Basilica San Juan Capistrano, 31522 Camino Capistrano, San Juan Capistrano, 92675-0691.*

Boy Scouts—Rev. Msgr. JOHN F. SAMMON, Office: *Marywood Center.*

Liturgical Commission—Very Rev. ARTHUR HOLQUIN, Chm.; Revs. ROD STEPHENS; KERRY BEAULIEU; MICHAEL HEHER; JOHN MCANDREW; J. MICHAEL MCKIERNAN; TUAN JOSEPH PHAM; Ms. JO ANN DAVIS; Mr. FRANK CHAVEZ; Ms. CHARLENE DUMITRU; Mr. FERMIN GOMEZ; Dr. PATRICIA LAMB; Ms. KATHY LEWIS; Ms. LESA TRUXAW; Mr. MICHAEL SHAFFER, Office: *Marywood Center.*

Building and Renovation Committee of the Liturgical Commission—Revs. ROD STEPHENS; KERRY BEAULIEU; J. MICHAEL MCKIERNAN; Very Rev. ARTHUR HOLQUIN; Dr. PATRICIA LAMB; Mr. MICHAEL SHAFFER, Office: *Marywood Center.*

Land Advisory Board—Most Rev. TOD D. BROWN; Rev. ED POETTGEN; Sr. KATHERINE GRAY, C.S.J., Auditor; Mr. ARTHUR BIRTCHER; Mr. TERENCE K. BARRY, Chm.; Ms. SHARON HENNESSEY; Mr. DANIEL HOLDEN; Mr. R. RAND SPERRY; Rev. Msgr. JOHN URELL; KENNETH TAIT. Staff: Mr. PHIL REIS; LILY FUNK; Rev. J. MICHAEL MCKIERNAN.

Diocesan Construction Board—Most Rev. TOD D. BROWN; Rev. THEODORE OLSON; Mr. TERRANCE BARRY; Mr. RON GAGNON; Mr. ARTHUR BIRTCHER, Chm.; Mr. MARKO E. BOTICH; Mr. EDWARD REYNOLD; Mr. HARRY G. KREIDER; Mr. RICHARD HUNSAKER. Staff: Mr. PHIL RIES; Mr. BRIAN ARII, Construction Mgr.; Rev. J. MICHAEL MCKIERNAN; Rev. Msgr. JOHN URELL; Sr. KATHERINE GRAY.

Diocesan Finance Council—Most Rev. TOD D. BROWN; Rev. JOSEPH JUSTICE; Sr. KATHERINE GRAY, C.S.J., Auditor; Mr. TOM KLEINBAUER; Mr. GORDON LEE; Rev. Msgr. JOHN URELL; Rev. JOSEPH JUSTICE; THERESA CAGNEY MORRISON; Mr. WILLIAM CRAWFORD; Mr. GUY WILSON; Mr. PAUL SCHLOEMER. Staff: Rev. J. MICHAEL MCKIERNAN; Mr. PHIL RIES, Dir.; Mr. CARLOS VASQUEZ.

Director of Finance—Mr. PHIL RIES, Dir.; Mr. CARLOS VASQUEZ, Controller, Office: *Marywood Center.*

Catholic Charities of Orange—KRISTAN SCHLICHTE, Exec. Dir., Office: *1506 Brookhollow, Ste. 112, Santa Ana, 92705.* Tel: 714-662-7500.

Cemeteries—Mr. MICHAEL SHAFFER, Dir., Office: *Marywood Center.*

Cemeteries Board—Rev. Msgr. JOHN F. SAMMON, Chm.

Ministry to Priests—Rev. KERRY BEAULIEU, Vicar, Priests; Rev. Msgr. DANIEL BRENNAN; Rev. Msgr. HUGH O'CONNOR; Revs. MICHAEL HOAN; RUDOLPH PRECIADO; LAURENCE DOLAN; ROY KIM; SIMON KIM; RICHARD DELAHUNTY; ROD KELLER; KEN SCHMIT; JOHN MCANDREW; JOHN MONEYPENNY; GORDON MORELAND, S.J.; TUAN NGUYEN; JOSEPH JUSTICE; MICHEL PECHARICH; STEVE SALLOT, Office: *Marywood Center.*

Cursillo Movement—Revs. RAYMOND SKONEZNY, Exec. Spiritual Dir. DAVID VUELVAS-ARIAS, Spiritual Dir., Hispanic Cursillo; PETER VU DINH TRAC, Spiritual Dir., Vietnamese Cursillo, Office: *Marywood Center.*

Office for Deaf Ministry—CONNIE WILD, Dir.; Deacon FRANK LUNA; Sr. JUDITH DUGAN, C.S.J., *2050 W. Chapman Ave., Ste. 217, Orange, 92868.* Tel: 714-940-0884; 940-0880 (TDD); Fax: 714-639-8670; 939-9905.

Office for Religious Education—Rev. CHRISTOPHER H. SMITH, Vicar; RUTH BRADLEY, Dir. OLIVIA CORNEJOS, Dir. Elementary/Junior High; MARY BROSSEAU, Consultant Spec. Rel. Educ. Assoc. Directors Youth & Young Adult Ministries: NANCY HORMUTH, Dir. JAVIER CASTILLO, Assoc. Dir.

Library/Media Center—DIANE MURRAY, Dir.

Institute of Pastoral Ministry—JOAN KULIK, Dir. NURIA CHEKOURAS, Assoc. Dir., Office: *Marywood Center.*

Ecumenical and Interreligious Affairs—Rev. RAFAEL LUEVANO, Chm.; Sr. MARYANNE HUEPPER, C.S.J.; Rev. JOHN MONESTERO; Dr. CHARLES FRAZEE; Mrs. SUE MONTANO FENWICK; Dr. GEORGE E. SAINT-LAURENT; Mrs. JOSEPHINE BALL, Office: *Marywood Center.*

Family Life—CARMELA TREANOR, Dir., Office: *Marywood Center.*

Marriage Preparation - Spanish—JULIA RAMIREZ, Coord.

Marriage Preparation - English—Coords.: Deacon JERRY PYNE; JOANN PYNE.

Natural Family Planning—MARY DAUSCH, Coord.

RAINBOWS—DOLORES CERVANTES, Coord.

Family Life Outreach—EILEEN PFAFF, Coord.

Engaged Encounter—VINNIE DEFALCO; MARY KAY DEFALCO.

Marriage Encounter - English—CATHY MAURER; STEVE MAURER.

Marriage Encounter - Spanish—SALVADOR GONZALES; DOLORES GONZALES.

Vietnamese Community Couples Retreat—Mr. PETER NHUE NGUYEN; Mrs. PETER NHUE NGUYEN, *Vietnamese Catholic Center, 1538 Century Blvd., Santa Ana, 92703-1301.* Tel: 714-554-4211.

Retrouvaille - English—BRIAN CHU; DINAH CHU; LARRY HERICH; ELLEN HERICH.

Retrouvaille - Spanish—ANGELES JUAREZ; ARNULFO JUAREZ; FRANCISCO LEYVA; ESPERANZA LEYVA.

Office of Hispanic Ministry—Mrs. JUANA MARIA AMEZQUITA, Admin., Office: *Marywood Center.*

Holy Childhood—Rev. Msgr. JOHN F. SAMMON, Dir., Office: *Marywood Center.*

Holy Name Society—Rev. Msgr. JOHN F. SAMMON, Dir., Office: *Marywood Center.*

Insurance—Mr. MICHAEL SHAFFER, Dir., Office: *Marywood Center.*

Legion of Mary—Rev. Msgr. PEDRO YRIGAN, Dir., *Res., 922 N. Newhope St., Santa Ana, 92703.* Tel: 714-554-3437. Rev. Msgr. HUGH O'CONNOR, *Res., 2050 W. Ball Rd., Anaheim, 92804.* Tel: 714-774-2595.

Worship & Evangelization—Rev. ROD STEPHENS, Dir., Office: *Marywood Center.*

Respect Life Program NCCB—Rev. Msgr. JOHN F. SAMMON, Dir., Office: *Marywood Center.*

Catecumenate—Rev. ROD STEPHENS, Dir., Office: *Marywood Center.*

Stewardship Office—BARBARA NELSON, Dir., Office: *Marywood Center.*

Development Office—Rev. Msgr. LAWRENCE BAIRD, Office: *Marywood Center.*

Perpetual Adoration Programs—Rev. Msgr. JOHN SAMMON, Dir., Office: *Marywood Center.*

CLERGY, PARISHES, MISSIONS AND PAROCHIAL SCHOOLS

CITY OF ORANGE

1—CATHEDRAL OF THE HOLY FAMILY (1921), Very Rev. Arthur Holquin, Rector; Rev. Robert Capone; Deacon Joseph Esparza. In res., Revs. Rod Stephens; Dominic DeLay, O.P.

Res., 566 S. Glassell St., 92866. Tel: 714-639-2900; Fax: 714-639-8022.

School—530 S. Glassell St., 92866. Tel: 714-538-6012; Fax: 714-633-5892.

Lay Teachers 27; Students 613.

Catechesis/Religious Programs—Tel: 714-538-2800.

Students 930.

2—LA PURISIMA (1964), Revs. Valentin Ramon, C.M.F.; Michael Philen; Leo Delgado, C.M.F.; Thomas De-Nguyen Dang; Deacon Dr. Anthony Bube; Deacons Clyde Davis; Juan Espinoza; Richard Lovett.

Res., 11712 N. Hewes, 92869. Tel: 714-633-5800; Fax: 714-633-8364.

School—Tel: 714-633-5411; Fax: 714-633-1588. Kathleen Manulkin, Prin.

Sisters of the Company of Mary 2; Lay Teachers 18; Students 309.

Catechesis/Religious Programs—Tel: 714-633-5344; Fax: 714-633-1588.

Students 1,189.

3—ST. NORBERT (1963), Revs. John M. Joyce; James R. Ries. In res., Most Rev. Peter Esterka; Deacon Timothy Carver.

Res., 300 E. Taft Ave., 92865. Tel: 714-637-4360; Fax: 714-637-0201.

School—Tel: 714-637-6822; Fax: 714-637-1604.

Lay Teachers 15; Students 303.

Catechesis/Religious Programs—Tel: 714-998-1070; Fax: 714-637-1604. D.R.E.: Carmen Estrada; Edith Marik.

Students 669.

ORANGE COUNTY OUTSIDE THE CITY

Anaheim, St. Anthony Claret (1955), Rev. Marito F. Rebamontan; Rev. Msgr. James F. Nash, Pastor Emeritus; Revs. Al S. Baca; Benjamin L. Benedicto; Deacon Jay L. Milam.

Res., 1450 E. La Palma Ave., 92805. Tel: 714-776-0270; Fax: 714-776-6022.

School—Tel: 714-535-3284; Fax: 714-535-8558.

Lay Teachers 13; Students 234.

Catechesis/Religious Programs—Tel: 714-778-0580. D.R.E.: Maria Holper; Leonard Beckman.

Students 851.

Aliso Viejo, Corpus Christi, Rev. Fred Bailey.

27101 Aliso Creek Rd., Suite 136, 92656. Tel: 949-389-9008; Fax: 949-831-6540.

Anaheim, St. Boniface (1860), Revs. Joseph Justice; Michael Hoan; John Procter.

Res., 120 N. Janss St., 92805. Tel: 714-956-3110; Fax: 714-956-3034. In res., Most Rev. Jaime Soto.

School—500 W. Chartres St., 92805. Tel: 714-772-3060; Fax: 714-956-5170.

Dominican Sisters (Mission San Jose) O.P. 1; Lay Teachers 14; Students 281.

Catechesis/Religious Programs—Tel: 714-956-3461; Fax: 714-956-3060.

Students 1,020.

St. Justin Martyr (1958), Rev. Joseph Nettekoven; Rev. Msgr. Hugh O'Connor, Pastor Emeritus; Revs. John Neneman; Antonio Zapata. In res., Rev. John Monestero.

Res., 2050 W. Ball Rd., 92804. Tel: 714-774-2595; Fax: 714-774-9849.

Church—Ball Rd. and Empire, 92804.

School—2030 W. Ball Rd., 92804. Tel: 714-772-4902; Fax: 714-772-2092.
Lay Teachers 12; Students 290.
Catechesis/Religious Programs—Tel: 714-535-6111.
Students 382.
Mission—Anaheim, Sacred Heart, 10852 Harcourt, 92804. Tel: 714-821-3133.

San Antonio (1977), Rev. Seamus A. Glynn. In res., Rev. William J. Vohsing; Deacon Doug Cook.
Res., 5800 E. Santa Ana Canyon Rd., 92807. Tel: 714-974-1416; Fax: 714-974-9630.
School—Please see St. Francis of Assisi School located under Multi-Parish Schools in the Institution Section.
Catechesis/Religious Programs—Tel: 714-974-2053. Carolyn Buehler, D.R.E.
Students 987.

Brea, St. Angela Merici (1962), Rev. Theodore Olson; Rev. Msgr. Emmett McCarthy, Pastor Emeritus; Revs. John McAndrew; Miguel Alvarez (Mexico); Deacons Fred von Voigt; Carlos Navarro.
Res., 585 Walnut St., 92821. Tel: 714-529-1821; Fax: 714-529-0569.
Church—Walnut and Fir, 92821.
School—575 S. Walnut Ave., 92821. Tel: 714-529-6372; Fax: 714-529-7755.
Lay Teachers 14; Religious 1; Students 301.
Catechesis/Religious Programs—Tel: 714-529-2311.
Students 896.

Buena Park, St. Pius V (1948), Revs. Thomas McManus, O.S.A.; Patrick Crilly, O.S.A.; Thomas Tevington, O.S.A.; Patrick A. Brennan, O.S.A.; Declan (Finbarr) Fogarty, O.S.A.
Res., 7691 Orangethorpe Ave., 90621. Tel: 714-522-2193; Fax: 714-522-1730.
School—Tel: 714-522-5313; Fax: 714-522-1767.
Lay Teachers 19; Students 627.
Catechesis/Religious Programs—Tel: 714-522-3971.
Students 639.

Capistrano Beach, San Felipe de Jesus (1950) (Hispanic), Rev. John A. Bradley; Rev. Msgr. John V. Coffield, Pastor Emeritus; Deacon Victor Samano.
Res., 27526 Paseo Verano, San Juan Capistrano, 92675-5314. Tel: 949-661-7500; Fax: 949-661-7500.
Church—Domingo St. & Sepulveda, 92624.
Catechesis/Religious Programs—Students 234.

Costa Mesa, St. Joachim (1947), Revs. Joseph R. Robillard; Douglas Dale; Ismael Silva, M.C.C.J.
Res., 1964 Orange Ave., 92627. Tel: 949-574-7400; Fax: 949-574-7408.
School—Tel: 949-574-7411; Fax: 949-646-8948.
Lay Teachers 13; Students 315.
Catechesis/Religious Programs—Tel: 949-574-7405 (English); 574-7416 (Spanish); Fax: 949-575-7407.
Students 625.

St. John the Baptist (1960), Revs. Jerome M. Henson, V.F.; John-Paul Hopping; Raphael Xuan Nguyen. In res., Rev. Msgr. Daniel H. Brennan; Rev. Tran Phuc Long.
Res., 1015 Baker St., 92626. Tel: 714-540-2214; Fax: 714-540-5902.
School—Tel: 714-557-5060; Fax: 714-557-9263. Sr. M. Vianney Ennis, S.M., Prin.
Sisters of Mercy 1; Lay Teachers 22; Students 615.
Catechesis/Religious Programs—Tel: 714-546-4102. D.R.E.: Sr. Sharon Richards, S.D.S.H.; Sr. Theresa Nguyen, L.H.C., (Vietnamese), Tel: 714-542-4455; Elira Diaz, (Spanish), Tel: 714-540-2292.
Students 560.

Cypress, St. Irenaeus (1961), Revs. Michael Heher; Simon Kim; Reynold E. Furrell.
Res., 5201 Evergreen Ave., 90630. Tel: 714-826-0760; Fax: 714-826-1608.
School—9201 Grindlay St., 90630. Tel: 714-827-4500; Fax: 714-827-2930.
Sisters 2; Lay Teachers 24; Students 570.
Catechesis/Religious Programs—9211 Grindlay St., 90630. Tel: 714-826-1140.
Students 1,006.

Dana Point, St. Edward (1969), Revs. John P. Lenihan; Steven Correz; Denis Lyons; Deacon Jesse Michel.
Res., 33926 Calle La Primavera, 92629. Tel: 949-496-1307; Fax: 949-496-1557.
School—33866 Calle La Primavera, 92629. Tel: 949-496-1241; Fax: 949-496-1819.
Lay Teachers 18; Students 475.
Catechesis/Religious Programs—Tel: 949-496-6011.
Students 1,000.

El Toro, Santiago de Compostela (1979), Revs. Kenneth A. Schmit; Gilberto Escobedo.
Res., 21682 Lake Forest Dr., Lake Forest, 92630. Tel: 949-951-8599; Fax: 949-951-2687.
School—Please see Serra Catholic School located under Multi-Parish schools, in the Institution Section.
Catechesis/Religious Programs—Tel: 949-951-0792.
Students 865.

Fountain Valley, Holy Spirit (1972), Revs. Joseph Knerr; Joseph Luan Nguyen. In res., Rev. Philip T. Smith, O.Praem., S.T.M.
Res., 17270 Ward St., 92708. Tel: 714-963-1811; Fax: 714-968-1775.
Catechesis/Religious Programs—Tel: 714-963-7871. Sr. Anna Tom, D.R.E.
Students 517.

Fullerton, St. Juliana Falconieri (1965), Revs. Jude M. Herlihy, O.S.M.; Donald M. Duplessis, O.S.M.; Patrick J. Donovan, O.S.M., Chap. (California State Univ. - Newman Club); Deacons William Schlater; Jay L. Milam. In res., Rev. David M. Kondik, O.S.M.
Office: 1319 N. Acacia Ave., 92831. Tel: 714-879-1965; Fax: 714-526-6673.
Res., 1316 N. Acacia Ave., 92831. Tel: 714-879-1965.
School—1320 N. Acacia Ave., 92831. Tel: 714-871-2829.
Lay Teachers 10; Students 324; Part-Time Teachers 3.
Catechesis/Religious Programs—Students 320.

St. Mary's (1912), Revs. Paul Goni, O.A.R.; Antonio Zauala, O.A.R.; Francis J. de la Vega, O.A.R.; Deacons Carlos Gonzalez; Manuel Chavira.
Res., 400 W. Commonwealth Ave., 92832. Tel: 714-525-2500; Fax: 714-525-3837.
School—Tel: 714-525-9689; Fax: 714-525-8944.
Sisters of St. Joseph of Orange 1; Lay Teachers 8; Students 182.
Catechesis/Religious Programs—Tel: 714-992-5070.
Students 710.

St. Philip Benizi (1958), Revs. Ignatius M. Kissel, O.S.M.; Manuel Maya, O.S.M.; Timothy Kremen, O.S.M.; Justin Pisciotta, O.S.M.; Deacons Jack Brennan; Richard Glaudini; Fidel Rodriguez.
Res., 235 S. Pine Dr., 92833-3294. Tel: 714-871-3610; Fax: 714-871-5827.
School—215 S. Pine Dr., 92833-3293. Tel: 714-871-6121; Fax: 714-992-4167. Sally Campos, Prin.
Lay Teachers 10; Students 208.
Catechesis/Religious Programs—Tel: 714-870-0561. Ms. Carmelita Yanez, D.R.E.
Students 488.

Garden Grove, St. Callistus (1961), Revs. Rudolph J. Preciado; Joseph Tuan Pham; Jude Lucier O. Praem; Viet-Peter Ho. In res., Rev. Msgr. John Urell.
Res., 12921 Lewis St., 92840. Tel: 714-971-2141; Fax: 714-971-9112.
Church—Garden Grove Blvd. and Lewis St., 92840.
St. Callistus Preschool—12132 Haster St., 92840. Tel: 714-750-6777.
School—12901 Lewis St., 92840. Tel: 714-971-2023; Fax: 714-971-2031.
Dominican Sisters 2; Lay Teachers 14; Students 343.
Catechesis/Religious Programs—Tel: 714-971-2091. Maureen Ross, D.R.E.
Students 1,414.

St. Columban (1953), Revs. Donald Romito; Michael P. Hanifin; Pascal B. Nguyen; Quang Chu; Deacons Robert Kelleher; William Cobbett.
Res., 10801 Stanford Ave., 92840. Tel: 714-534-1174; Fax: 714-534-1937.
School—10855 Stanford Ave., 92840. Tel: 714-534-3947; Fax: 714-590-9153.
Religious Sisters of Charity 1; Lay Teachers 15; Students 315.
Catechesis/Religious Programs—Tel: 714-537-2015.
Students 1,431.

Huntington Beach

1—St. Bonaventure (1965), Revs. Bruce Patterson; Martin R. Benzoni, O.Praem.; Tuan John Nguyen.
Res., 16400 Springdale St., 92649. Tel: 714-846-3350; 846-3359; Fax: 714-840-0480.
School—Tel: 714-846-2472; Fax: 714-840-0498.
Union of the Sisters of the Presentation of the Blessed Virgin Mary 6; Lay Teachers 24; Students 632.
Catechesis/Religious Programs—16377 Bradbury Ln., 92647. Tel: 714-846-2472. Virginia Curley, D.R.E.
Students 1,016.

2—St. Mary's by the Sea (1977), Revs. Daniel Johnson; Eamon Mackin, C.H.S.
Res., 321 10th St., 92648. Tel: 714-536-6913; Fax: 714-536-2464.
Catechesis/Religious Programs—Students 145.

3—SS. Simon and Jude (1912), Revs. Laurence P. Dolan, O.F.M.; Christian Mondor, O.F.M.; Lawrence R. Gosselin, O.F.M.; Michael L. Harvey, O.F.M. In res., Rev. Emery Tang, O.F.M.
Res., 20444 Magnolia St., 92646. Tel: 714-962-3333; Fax: 714-965-6456.
School—Tel: 714-962-4451; Fax: 714-968-1329.
Lay Teachers 27; Students 694.
Catechesis/Religious Programs—Tel: 714-963-0014. Rochelle Cafferty, D.R.E.
Students 496.

4—St. Vincent de Paul (1977), Revs. Jerome T. Karcher; James Overend; Deacon Scotty Bourne.
Res., 8345 Talbert Ave., 92646. Tel: 714-842-3000; Fax: 714-842-6780.
Catechesis/Religious Programs—Students 225.

Irvine, St. Elizabeth Ann Seton (1976), Revs. Thomas Pado; Alex H. Ha.
Res., 9 Hillgate, 92612-3265. Tel: 949-854-1000; Fax: 949-854-0079.
Catechesis/Religious Programs—Students 400.

St. John Neumann (1978), Revs. Colm Conlon; John E. Shetler; Ray Skonezny.
Res., 5101 Alton Pkwy., 92604-8605. Tel: 949-559-4006; Fax: 949-857-4788.
Catechesis/Religious Programs—Tel: 949-786-6105; Fax: 949-786-6102. Carolyn Lawmaster, D.R.E.
Students 730.

St. Thomas More (1996), Rev. John E. Janze. In res., Rev. William Krekelberg.
Res., 4112 Escudero Dr., 92620-3212. Tel: 949-551-8601; Fax: 949-551-5879.
Catechesis/Religious Programs—Tel: 949-551-8029.
Students 513.

Laguna Beach, St. Catherine of Siena (1923), Revs. Eamon T. O'Gorman; Timothy Freyer. In res., Rev. Thomas J. McIntyre, C.M.
Res., 990 Temple Ter., 92651. Tel: 949-494-9701; Fax: 949-497-2610.
School—3090 S. Coast Hwy., 92651. Tel: 949-494-7339; Fax: 949-376-5752.
Lay Teachers 17; Students 281.
Catechesis/Religious Programs—Tel: 949-499-5876.
Students 190.

Laguna Hills, St. Nicholas (1965), Revs. Juan Caboboy; Francis Moran; Tuan Joseph Pham; Deacons Ray Havert; Michael Fletcher. In res.,
Res., 24252 El Toro Rd., Laguna Woods, 92653. Tel: 949-837-1090; Fax: 949-837-9510.
Catechesis/Religious Programs—Tel: 949-837-7676.
Students 490.

Laguna Niguel, St. Timothy (1980), Revs. Bruce Lavery; Donald Kolda, S.J.; George Blais; Deacon Ed Salgado.
Res., 29102 Crown Valley Pkwy., 92677. Tel: 949-249-4091; Fax: 949-249-4094.
Catechesis/Religious Programs—Tel: 949-495-4126.
Students 860.

La Habra, Our Lady of Guadalupe (1947), Revs. Justin H. MacCarthy; John W. Moneypenny.
Res., 900 W. La Habra Blvd., 90631. Tel: 562-691-0533; Fax: 562-694-8328.
School—Tel: 562-697-9726; Fax: 562-905-0095.
Sisters of St. Joseph of Orange 1; Lay Teachers 22; Students 500.
Catechesis/Religious Programs—Tel: 562-691-2104; Fax: 562-697-6391.
Students 759.

Los Alamitos, St. Hedwig (1960), Revs. Daniel R. Hopcus; Thomas J. Keller, M.S.C.; Joseph Droessler.
Res., 11482 Los Alamitos Blvd., 90720. Tel: 562-430-0509; Fax: 562-431-9989.
School—Tel: 562-431-5001; Fax: 562-799-1791.
Lay Teachers 25; Students 601.
Catechesis/Religious Programs—Tel: 562-493-2521.
Students 575.

Mission Viejo, St. Kilian (1970), Rev. James P. Dunning. In res., Rev. Craig Butters.
Res., 26872 Estanciero Dr., 92691. Tel: 949-586-4440; Fax: 949-454-1043.
School—Please see Serra Catholic School located under Multi-Parish Schools, in the Institution Section.
Catechesis/Religious Programs—Tel: 949-586-4550. Marcia Burns, D.R.E.
Students 1,100.

Newport Beach, Our Lady of Mount Carmel (1923), Rev. Msgr. Daniel J. Murray; Rev. Patrick A. Doherty.
Res., 1441 W. Balboa Blvd., 92661-1010. Tel: 949-673-3775; Fax: 949-673-3137.
Catechesis/Religious Programs—Tel: 949-673-2719; Fax: 949-673-3801.
Students 180.

Our Lady Queen of Angels (1953), Rev. Msgr. William McLaughlin; Revs. Sean Condon; Vincent M. Gilmore, O.Praem.
Res., 2046 Mar Vista Dr., 92660. Tel: 949-644-0200; Fax: 949-644-1349.

School—750 Domingo Dr., 92660. Tel: 949-644-1166; Fax: 949-644-6213.
Lay Teachers 20; Students 350.
Catechesis/Religious Programs—Tel: 949-219-1497.
Students 582.
Convent—2108 Aralia St., 92660. Tel: 714-644-0660.
Chapel—St. John Vianney, Tel: 714-675-2221. Rev. Msgr. Lawrence J. Baird.

Placentia, St. Joseph (1953), Revs. Timothy Ramaekers; James Curran, C.M.F.; Deacon Ed Faulk.
Res., 717 N. Bradford Ave., 92870-4599. Tel: 714-528-1487; Fax: 714-528-1569.
School—801 N. Bradford Ave., 92870-4599. Tel: 714-528-1794; Fax: 714-528-0668.
Lay Teachers 18; Students 300.
Catechesis/Religious Programs—Tel: 714-993-0830; Fax: 714-993-0539. D.R.E.: Teri Kleckner; Eloisa Ramirez, (Spanish).
Students 350.
Mission—Atwood, Orange Co., St. Theresa Chapel, 636 Van Buren Ave., Atwood, 92811.

Rancho Santa Margarita, San Francisco Solano Church (1989), Revs. Michael Pecharich; Alex K. Kim; Sr. Barbara Reder, S.P., Pastoral Assoc.
Res., 22082 Antonio Pkwy., 92688-1993. Tel: 949-589-7767; Fax: 949-589-7768.
School—Serra Catholic School, 23652 Antonio Pkwy., 92688-1993. Tel: 949-888-1990; Fax: 949-888-1994. Audrey Tellers, Prin.
Lay Teachers 41; Students 775; Total Staff 85.
Catechesis/Religious Programs—Tel: 949-589-1709; Fax: 949-589-1709.
Students 1,826.

San Clemente, Our Lady of Fatima (1947), Revs. Jack Sewell; Christopher Heath; Rev. Msgr. Anthony McGowan, Pastor Emeritus.
Res., 105 La Esperanza, 92672. Tel: 949-492-4101; Fax: 949-492-4856.
School—Tel: 949-492-7320; Fax: 949-492-3793.
Lay Teachers 13; Students 313.
Catechesis/Religious Programs—Tel: 949-492-1663.
Students 454.

San Juan Capistrano, Mission Basilica (1776), Rev. Msgr. Paul M. Martin; Revs. Ramon Cisneros Alcaraz; Harold Fumo; Deacons Joseph Halka; David Sire; Viviano Mireles. In res., Rev. Joseph Scerbo, S.A.
Res., P.O. Box 697, 92693. Tel: 949-234-1360; Fax: 949-248-2008 (Parish Office). [CEM]
School—Tel: 949-234-1385; Fax: 949-248-2178.
Lay Teachers 16; Students 400.
Catechesis/Religious Programs—Tel: 949-234-1370; Fax: 949-248-2056. Linda Berkshire, D.R.E.
Students 575.

Santa Ana

1—Immaculate Heart of Mary (1960), Revs. Enrique Sera; Ignatius Lau; Gabriel Ramirez; Deacon Gerardo de Santos.
Res., 1100 S. Center St., 92704. Tel: 714-751-5335.
School—Tel: 714-545-8185.
Lay Teachers 10; Students 315.
Catechesis/Religious Programs—Tel: 714-546-5186.
Students 1,001.

2—Our Lady of Guadalupe (1927) (Hispanic), Rev. Alonso Caceres. In res., Rev. Msgr. Gerardo J. Tanilong.
Res., 541 E. Central Ave., 92707. Tel: 714-540-0902; Fax: 714-540-3053.
Catechesis/Religious Programs—Tel: 714-540-9231. Rosa Castro, D.R.E.
Students 1,128.

3—Our Lady of Guadalupe (1938) (Hispanic), Revs. Ramon Gaitan, O.A.R.; Alfonso Ramirez, O.A.R.
Res., 1322 E. Third St., 92701. Tel: 714-836-4142; Fax: 714-836-7417.
Catechesis/Religious Programs—Tel: 714-835-8933. Margarita Garza, D.R.E.
Students 1,100.

4—Our Lady of Lourdes (1985) (Hispanic), Rev. William Barman.
Res., 5021 W. 16th St., 92703. Tel: 714-636-3260; Fax: 714-539-0783.
Catechesis/Religious Programs—Students 374.

5—Our Lady of the Pillar (1965) (Hispanic), Revs. Alfredo de Dios, O.A.R.; Gabino Perez; Jose Luis Jimenez; Joachim Goni, O.A.R.; Deacon Ulises Feliciano, O.A.R.
Res., 1622 W. 6th St., 92703. Tel: 714-543-1700; Fax: 714-543-9640.
School—601 N. Western Ave., 92703. Tel: 714-542-5177; Fax: 714-541-5748.
Catechesis/Religious Programs—Tel: 714-542-4684.
Students 1,434.

6—St. Anne's (1923) (Hispanic), Revs. Cirilo B. Flores; Michael Galinada, S.M.; Lorenzo Hernandez; Deacon Carlos Euyoque.
Res., 109 Borchard Ave., P.O. Box 2425, 92707. Tel: 714-835-7434; Fax: 714-835-4506.
School—Tel: 714-542-9328; Fax: 714-542-3431.
Sisters 5; Lay Teachers 6; Students 304.
Catechesis/Religious Programs—Tel: 714-542-1213; Fax: 714-542-6608.
Students 807.

7—St. Barbara's (1962), Revs. Richard C. Kennedy; Salvador Landa; Kiem Van Tran; Joseph Truc Dinh, S.D.B.
Res., 730 S. Euclid St., 92704. Tel: 714-775-7733; Fax: 714-775-9467.
School—Tel: 714-775-9477; Fax: 714-775-9468.
Lay Teachers 21; Students 500.
Catechesis/Religious Programs—Tel: 714-775-9475.
Students 1,470.

8—St. Joseph's (1887), Revs. Christopher H. Smith; Cesar Salazar.
Res., 727 Minter St., 92701. Tel: 714-542-4411; Fax: 714-542-9770.
School—Tel: 714-542-2704; Fax: 714-542-2132.
Lay Teachers 11; Students 255.
Catechesis/Religious Programs—Tel: 714-550-8096.
Students 685.

Seal Beach, St. Anne's (1921), Rev. Robert S. Vidal; Rev. Msgr. Michael Collins, Pastor Emeritus.
Res., 340 Tenth St., 90740. Tel: 562-431-0721; Fax: 562-431-3050.
Catechesis/Religious Programs—Students 112.
Holy Family (1969), Rev. Msgr. Brian Coghlan; Rev. Msgr. James J. Pierse, Pastor Emeritus.
Res., 13900 Church Pl., 90740. Tel: 562-430-8170; Fax: 562-493-4643.

Stanton, St. Polycarp (1961), Revs. Edward Poettgen; Vincent Hung Pham; Deacon Javier Antunez. In res., Rev. Matthias Ho, (Retired).
Res., 8100 Chapman Ave., 90680. Tel: 714-893-2766; Fax: 714-898-6675.
School—8182 Chapman Ave., 90680. Tel: 714-893-8882; Fax: 714-897-3357.
Lay Teachers 9; Students 201.
Catechesis/Religious Programs—Tel: 714-892-3158.
Students 1,109.

Tustin, St. Cecilia (1957) (Spanish-Vietnamese), Revs. Timothy MacCarthy; Robert Puhlman; Tuyen Nguyen; Deacons Lee Meyer; Jerry Miller; Rafael Romero; Jon Schlemmer.
Res., 1301 Sycamore, 92780. Tel: 714-544-3250; Fax: 714-838-1996.
School—Tel: 714-544-1533; Fax: 714-544-0643.
Lay Teachers 15; Students 365.
Catechesis/Religious Programs—Tel: 714-838-4466.
Students 698.

Westminster, Blessed Sacrament (1947), Revs. James Hartnett; Sy Uy Nguyen; Anh Tran Tuan Nguyen; David Vuelvas-Arias.
Res., 14072 S. Olive St., 92683. Tel: 714-892-4489; Fax: 714-892-5560.
School—14146 S. Olive St., 92683. Tel: 714-893-7701; Fax: 714-891-7186. Roisin McAree, Prin.
Lay Teachers 14; Students 318.
Catechesis/Religious Programs—14144 S. Olive St., 92683. Tel: 714-897-2142. Dave Vellanoweth, D.R.E.
Students 1,272.

Yorba Linda, St. Martin (1970), Revs. Richard A. Delahunty; John T. Hiltz, (Retired); David Gruver.
Res., 19767 Yorba Linda Blvd., 92886. Tel: 714-970-2771; Fax: 714-970-5654.
School—St. Francis of Assisi, 5330 Eastside Cir., 92887. Tel: 714-695-3700; Fax: 714-695-3704. Debra Declues, Prin.
Lay Teachers 25; Students 518; Total Staff 49.
Catechesis/Religious Programs—Tel: 714-970-2521. D.R.E.: Pam Bender; Jackie Schultz, (Adult); David Glaudini, (Youth).
Students 2,801.

Chaplains Of Public Institutions

Orange. *Juvenile Hall* 331 The City Dr., 92868. Tel: 714-634-7611. Rev. Brendan Smith, S.T., 422 Almond, 92866. Tel: 714-633-6527.
Orange County Medical Center 101 The City Dr. S., 92868. Tel: 714-634-5678. Served by St. Callistus Parish. 12921 Lewis St., Garden Grove, 92840. Tel: 714-971-2141.
Theo Lacy Minimum Security Facility. (Branch Jail), 501 The City Dr., 92862. Tel: 714-834-3090. Rev. Brendan Smith, S.T., Chap., 422 Almond, 92866. Tel: 714-633-6527.

Costa Mesa. *Fairview Developmental Center* 2501 Harbor, 92626. Tel: 714-545-9331. Rev. Charles W. Willingham, O.Praem.

Special Assignment:
Reverend Monsignors—
Duc Tien, Peter, Dir., Vietnamese Center, 1538 N. Century Blvd., Santa Ana, CA 92703. Tel: 714-554-4211
Sammon, John F., P.A., Vicar for Pastoral and Community Affairs
Reverend Fathers—
Cheong, Antonius, St. Thomas Korean Catholic Center, Anaheim, CA 92801-6710
Cook, Douglas, Dir., Polish Center, Yorba Linda
Hogan, John, S.S.C., Dir., Korean Center, 7655 Trask Ave., Westminster, CA 92683
Moreland, J. Gordon, S.J., Dir., House of Prayer for Priests, 7734 Santiago Canyon Rd., Orange, CA 92869
Morrissey, Michael, S.S.C., Korean Martyrs, 7655 Trask Ave., Westminster, CA 92863

On Duty Outside the Diocese:
Reverend Fathers—
Buckman, Franklin J., Our Lady of Mt. Carmel, 503 W. Chocktoot, P.O. Box 396, Chiloquin, OR 79624
Hung, Joseph K., Gethsemane Abbey, KY

Military Chaplains:
Reverend Fathers—
Fry, James Q.
Shimotsu, John
Sweeney, Kevin

Absent on Sick Leave:
Reverend Fathers—
DiStefano, Joseph
Fee, Pat
Kinzer, Gary
Kolberg, Lawrence R.
Luongo, John
Monestero, John

Inactive Leave:
Reverend Monsignors—
Harris, Michael
Reverend Fathers—
Colleran, Desmond
Coughlin, Richard
Coulombe, Dale
Croal, James Joseph
Fama, Benjamin
Farris, James M.
Frost, Stephen
Geraughty, Michael
German, Timothy J.
Gibbons, Francis X.
Harvey, James
Jagosz, Mitchell
Levesque, Paul
Martinez, Carlos
Melito, Joseph
Nguyen, Dominic Hoa
Nguyen, Joseph Chuan
O'Callaghan, John
Perez, Henry
Pham, Huy Phi
Ramos, Eleuterio
Richards, Fabian
Ruhl, John
Ryder, Matthais
Schmidt, Nicholas
Thies, Jeffrey
Tressler, Robert
Widera, Siegfried

Retired:
Most Rev.—
McFarland, Norman F.
Reverend Monsignors—
Campbell, John
Coffield, John V.
Collins, Michael
Doyle, Timothy
Falvey, Sinon
Hughes, Michael
Keenan, John C.
McCarthy, Emmett
McGowan, Anthony
Nash, James F.
O'Connor, Hugh
Pierse, James J.
Scannell, Peter
Yrigan, Pedro
Reverend Fathers—
Chinh, Peter
Croal, Thomas
Ho, Matthias
Keller, J. Rod
Long, Tran Phuc
Sheahan, John A.

Trac, Peter Vu Dinh

Permanent Deacons:
Antunez, Jay, St. Polycarp, Stanton
Barth, John, On Duty Outside the Diocese
Bourne, Scotty, St. Vincent de Paul
Boyer, Charles, Our Lady Queen of Angels
Brenes-Rios, Anthony, Our Lady of Guadalupe, La Habra
Brennan, John, St. Philip Benizi, Fullerton
Bube, Anthony, La Purisima, Orange
Carver, Timothy, St. Norbert, Orange
Chavez, Frank, St. Martin de Porres, Yorba Linda
Chavira, Manuel, St. Mary, Fullerton
Cobbett, William, St. Columban
Cook, Douglas, San Antonio de Padua, Anaheim Hills
Coughlin, Charles, Blessed Sacrament, Westminster
Davis, Clyde, La Purisima
Dennis, Irving, On Duty Outside the Diocese
DeSantos, Gerardo, Immaculate Heart of Mary, Santa Ana
Duthoy, Raymond, St. Justin Martyr, Anaheim
Erwin, Glenn, Our Lady of Mt. Carmel, Newport Beach
Esparza, Joseph, Holy Family Cathedral
Espinoza, Juan, La Purisima
Esposito, Robert, (On duty outside the Diocese)
Euyoque, Carlos, St. Anne, Santa Ana
Faulk, Edward, St. Joseph, Placentia
Fletcher, Michael, St. Nicholas
Garza, Domingo, Our Lady of Guadalupe, Santa Ana
Glaudini, Richard, St. Philip Benizi, Fullerton
Gonzales, Carlos, St. Mary, Fullerton
Gonzalez, Miguel, St. Bonaventure and Our Lady of Guadalupe
Halka, Joseph, Tuscon
Havert, Raymond, St. Nicholas, Laguna Hills
Jones, Wesley, St. Boniface, Anaheim
Kelleher, Robert, St. Columban, Garden Grove
Lee, Moon Chul, Korean Martyrs
Leon, Ramon, St. Justin Martyr
Lovett, Richard, La Purisima
Luna, Frank, Catholic Deaf Center, Orange
Melton, Harold, On Duty Outside the Diocese
Merandi, Louis, Holy Cross Greek Melkite
Meyer, Leon, St. Cecilia, Tustin
Michel, Jesse, St. Edwards, Dana Point
Milam, Jay, St. Juliana Falconieri, Fullerton
Miller, Gerald, St. Cecilia, Tustin
Mireles, Viviano, Mission San Juan Capistrano, San Juan Capistrano
Myers, Paul, On Duty Outside the Diocese
Naumann, Richard, St. Kilian (SR)
Navarro, Carlos, St. Angela Merici, Brea
Porcella, Roger, On Duty Outside the Diocese
Pyne, Gerald, Our Lady of Guadalupe, La Habra
Reynoso, Jose Luis, St. Boniface, Anaheim
Richeson, James, (On duty outside the Diocese)
Rivera, Manuel
Rodriguez, Fidel, St. Philip Benizi
Romero, Rafael, St Cecilia, Tustin
Salgado, Fernando, St. Timothy, Laguna Niguel
Samano, Victor, San Felipe de Jesus, Capistrano Beach
Schlater, William, St. Juliana Falconieri, Fullerton
Schlemmer, Jon, St. Cecilia, Tustin
Sire, David, Mission San Juan Capistrano, San Juan Capistrano
Song, Thomas, St. Elizabeth Ann Seton
Stripling, Joseph, Blessed Sacrament, Westminster
Sullivan, Neill, Our Lady Queen of Angels, Newport Beach
Swift, Bernard, (Retired)
Tran, Vincent, St. Bonaventure
vonVoigt, Fred, St. Angela Merici, Brea
Zambrano, Jose, On Duty Outside the Diocese

INSTITUTIONS LOCATED IN THE DIOCESE

[A] SEMINARIES AND SCHOLASTICATES FOR RELIGIOUS

MIDWAY CITY. *St. Patrick's Novitiate and Scholasticate,* 7820 Bolsa Ave., 92655. Tel: 714-897-8181; Fax: 714-898-9020. Conducted by the Brothers of St. Patrick. Brothers 5.

SILVERADO. *St. Michael's Norbertine Postulancy, Novitiate and Juniorate,* 19292 El Toro Rd., 92676. Tel: 949-858-0222; Fax: 949-858-4583. Conducted by the Norbertine Fathers. Rt. Rev. Eugene J. Hayes, O.Praem., Abbot; Revs. Thomas W. Nelson, O.Praem., Dir. Formation; Augustine R. Puchner, O.Praem., Asst. Dir. Formation; Very Rev. Hugh C. Barbour, O.Praem, Ph.D., Prof. Philosophy; Revs. John E. Caronan, O.Praem., Prof. Latin; Gregory M. Dick, O.Praem, Prof. Scripture; Hubert S. Szanto, O.Praem., Prof. Latin. For listing of other Norbertine priests working in the Diocese, refer to St. Michael College Prep High School. Priests 6; Total Enrollment 18.

[B] COLLEGES AND UNIVERSITIES

ORANGE. *St. Joseph College, Orange,* 480 S. Batavia St., 92868. Tel: 714-633-8121; Fax: 714-744-3165
For a complete listing, refer to the Colleges and Universities section.

[C] HIGH SCHOOLS, DIOCESAN

FULLERTON. *Rosary High School.* (Girls), 1340 N. Acacia Ave., 92831. Tel: 714-879-6302; Fax: 714-879-0853.
E-mail: tmazzarella@rosaryhs.org
Web site: www.rc.net/orange/rosary
Mrs. Trudy Mazzarella, Prin. Sisters 1; Lay Teachers 41; Students 715; Total Staff 62.

RANCHO SANTA MARGARITA. *Santa Margarita Catholic High School,* 22062 Antonio Pkwy., 92688. Tel: 949-766-6000; Fax: 949-766-6005.
E-mail: information@smhs.org
Web site: www.smhs.org
Merritt V. Hemenway, Prin. Priests 1; Sisters 2; Lay Teachers 102; Students 1,850.

SANTA ANA. *Mater Dei High School.* (Coed), 1202 W. Edinger, 92707-2191. Tel: 714-754-7711; Fax: 714-754-1880.
E-mail: admissions@materdei.org
Web site: www.materdei.org
Norbertine Fathers; Franciscan Fathers; Brothers of St. Patrick; Sisters of St. Joseph of Orange; Religious Sisters of Charity; Sisters de l'Union Chretienne de St. Chaumond; Sisters of St. Louis; Sisters of the Company of Mary. Mr. Patrick Murphy, Prin.; Revs. Steven Sallot, Rector & Chap.; Eugene David Burnett, O.F.M.; Robert S. Hodges, O.Praem.; Luke S. Laslavich, O.Praem. Priests 4; Brothers 1; Sisters 5; Lay Teachers 126; Students 2,099; Total Staff 135.

[D] HIGH SCHOOLS, PRIVATE

ANAHEIM. *Cornelia Connelly School of the Holy Child.* (Girls), 2323 W. Broadway, 92804. Tel: 714-776-1717; Fax: 714-776-2534.
E-mail: cornelia@connellyhs.org
Sisters of the Holy Child Jesus. Sr. Francine Gunther, S.H.C.J., Head of School.
Cornelia Connelly School Development Fund.
Cornelia Connelly School Scholarship Fund. Lay Teachers 20; Students 213; Total Staff 43.
Servite High School; Servite High School Development Fund, 1952 W. La Palma, 92801. Tel: 714-774-7575; Fax: 714-774-1404.
E-mail: mail@servitehs.org
Web site: servitehs.org
Servite Friars. Rev. Gerald M. Horan, O.S.M., Pres.; Mr. Raymond Dunne, Prin.; Revs. Richard M. Boyle, O.S.M.; Edward M. Penonzek, O.S.M.; Michael M. Pontarelli, O.S.M.; Eugene M. Smith, O.S.M.; Bro. Joel A. Lechner, O.S.M. Priests 5; Brothers 1; Lay Teachers 52; Students 800; Total Staff 75.

SILVERADO. *St. Michael's College Preparatory High School.* (Grades 9-12). (Boarding school for boys), 19292 El Toro Rd., 92676-9710. Tel: 949-858-0222; Fax: 949-858-7365. Revs. Gabriel D. Stack, O.Praem., Prin.; Jordan S. Anderson, O.Praem.; Godfrey E. Bushmaker, O.Praem.; Adrian J. O'Connor, O.Praem.; Lawrence C. Johnson, O.Praem.; Justin R. Ramos, O.Praem; James G. Smith, O.Praem., Treas.; Hubert S. Szanto, O.Praem; Victor S. Szczurek, O.Praem.; Sebastian Walsh, O.Praem, Seminarian; Charles W. Willingham, O.Praem. Priests 10; Lay Teachers 10; Students 70; Total Staff 22.

[E] ELEMENTARY SCHOOLS AND DAY NURSERIES, PRIVATE

ANAHEIM. *St. Catherine's Military School,* 215 N. Harbor Blvd., 92805. Tel: 714-772-1363; Fax: 714-772-3004.
E-mail: scms215@earthlink.net
Legal Title: *St. Catherine's Military School, a Corp.* Sr. Carolyn Marie Monahan, Admin. & Prin. Dominican Sisters of Mission San Jose 12; Sisters 10; Lay Teachers 13; Students 175; Total Staff 55.

SANTA ANA. *Santa Clara Day Nursery and Kindergarten,* 1021 N. Newhope, 92703. Tel: 714-554-8850; Fax: 714-554-5886.
E-mail: clarisus@earthlink.net
Poor Clare Missionary Sisters (M.C.). Sisters 12; Children 100; Total Staff 14.

TUSTIN. *Saint Jeanne de Lestonnac School,* 16791 E. Main, 92870. Tel: 714-542-4271; Fax: 714-542-0644.
E-mail: jeanne@stjeanne.com
Web site: www.stjeanne.com
Sr. Cecilia Duran, O.D.N., Prin. Sisters of the Company of Mary 2; Lay Teachers 30; Students 500.

[F] MULTI-PARISH SCHOOLS

RANCHO SANTA MARGARITA. *Serra Catholic School,* 23652 Antonio Pkwy., 92688-1993. Tel: 949-888-1990; Fax: 949-888-1994.
E-mail: serra@serraschool.org
Web site: www.serraschool.org
Mrs. Audrey Tellers, Prin. Lay Teachers 41; Students 775; Total Staff 85.

YORBA LINDA. *St. Francis of Assisi School,* 5330 Eastside Circle, 92887. Tel: 714-695-3700; Fax: 714-695-3704. Ms. Debra Declues, Prin. Lay Teachers 25; Students 518; Total Staff 49.

[G] GENERAL HOSPITALS

ORANGE. *St. Joseph Hospital of Orange,* 1100 W. Stewart Dr., P.O. Box 5600, 92868-3995. Tel: 714-771-8000, Ext. 8020; Fax: 714-744-8600
For a complete listing, refer to the Hospitals section.

FULLERTON. *St. Jude Medical Center,* 101 E. Valencia Mesa Dr., 92835-3875. Tel: 714-871-3280; Fax: 714-446-5067.
Web site: www.stjudemc.com
For a complete listing, refer to the Hospitals section.

MISSION VIEJO. *Mission Hospital Regional Medical Center,* 27700 Medical Center Rd., 92691. Tel: 949-364-1400; Fax: 949-364-2056.
E-mail: srma@0103.stjoe.org
Web site: www.mhrmc.com
For a complete listing, refer to the Hospitals section.

[H] SPECIAL SERVICES

ORANGE. *Loyola Institute for Spirituality,* 480 S. Batavia St., 92868. Tel: 714-997-9587; Fax: 714-997-9588.
E-mail: loyinst@pacbell.net
Rev. Allan F. Deck, S.J., Exec. Dir.
St. Vincent de Paul Society, 180 S. Cypress, 92866. Tel: 714-547-5566; Fax: 714-771-2739. Mr. Edward C. Hartman, Pres.; Mr. Joseph D. Kay, Exec. Dir.; Rev. Tuyen Nguyen, Spiritual Advisor. Total Staff 106; Total Assisted 385,277.
Special Works of the St. Vincent de Paul Society:
Second Harvest Food Bank of Orange County, 426-A W. Almond, 92866. Tel: 714-771-1343; Fax: 714-771-2748. Mr. Thomas M. Seeberg.
St. Vincent de Paul Center for Community Reconciliation, 2525-N. North Grand Ave., Santa Ana, 92705. Tel: 714-288-5600; Fax: 714-288-5619. Joseph D. Kay, Dir. Programs include: Catholic Detention Ministry, Friends Outside and Institute for Conflict Management.
Stores and Workshops, 180 Cypress, 92866. Tel: 714-633-9194; Fax: 714-997-1703. Charles A. Reich, Dir.
Search of Orange County, Inc., P.O. Box 4191, 92867. Tel: 714-753-3533.
Web site: www.rc.net/orange/search

ANAHEIM. *St. Thomas Korean Catholic Center,* 412 N. Crescent Way, 92801. Tel: 714-772-3993; Fax: 714-772-3636. Revs. Antonius Cheong, Dir.; Roy Kim; John Lee, Admin.

SANTA ANA. *Holy Family Services, Adoption and Foster Care,* 1403 S. Main St., 92707. Tel: 714-835-5551; Fax: 714-973-4971.
E-mail: hfsadopt@aol.com
Web site: hfs.org
Debra Richardson, Exec. Dir.
St. Francis Home, 1718 W. 6th St., 92703. Tel: 714-542-0381; Fax: 714-542-4654. Franciscan Sisters of the Immaculate Conception, Inc. Sr. Elia Caro, O.S.F., Admin. Sisters 23.
Vietnamese Catholic Center, 1538 N. Century Blvd., 92703. Tel: 714-554-4211; 554-5565; Fax: 714-265-1161. Rev. Msgr. Peter Nguyen Duc Tien, Dir. Total in Residence 1; Total Staff 5.

SILVERADO. *St. Michael's Summer Camp,* St. Michael's Abbey, 19292 El Toro Rd., 92676-9701. Tel: 949-858-0222, Ext. 226; Fax: 949-858-4583. Boys aged 7-12 years. Capacity 120; Total in Residence 95; Total Staff 25.

WESTMINSTER. *Korean Catholic Ministry,* 7655 Trask Ave., 92683. Tel: 714-897-6510; Fax: 714-897-0832. Revs. John Hogan, S.S.C., Dir. Korean Martyrs Center; Michael Morrissey. Tel: 714-897-6961.

YORBA LINDA. *Polish Center,* 3999 Rose Dr., 92886. Tel: 714-996-8161; Fax: 714-996-8161. Rev. Douglas Cook, Dir.

[I] MONASTERIES AND RESIDENCES OF PRIESTS AND BROTHERS

ORANGE. *Claretian Missionaries*, La Purisima, 11712 N. Hewes, 92869. Tel: 714-633-5800.
E-mail: lps@ocweb.com
Web site: www.ocweb.com/.lps.
Total in Residence 3; Total Staff 12.

ANAHEIM. *Servite Fathers and Brothers*. Servite Friars, Servite Priory, 1922 W. La Palma Ave., 92801-3595. Tel: 714-774-8869; Fax: 714-774-6792. Revs. Eugene M. Smith, O.S.M.; Richard M. Boyle, O.S.M.; Gerald M. Horan, O.S.M.; Michael M. Pontarelli, O.S.M.; Bro. Joel A. Lechner, O.S.M.
De familia members of the community living outside the priory: Rev. Edward M. Penonzek, O.S.M., Servite High School, 1952 W. La Palma Ave., 92801-3595. Tel: 714-774-7575; Fax: 714-774-1404.

BUENA PARK. *Augustinian Fathers*, St. Pius V, 7691 Orangethorpe Ave., 90621. Tel: 714-522-2193; Fax: 714-522-1730.
E-mail: cherbers@pacbell.net
Total in Residence 5; Total Staff 12.

Order of Friar Servants of Mary (Servites), 5210 Somerset St., 90621-1498. Tel: 714-523-5810; Fax: 714-523-8129.
E-mail: osmwest@aol.com
Councillors: Bro. Brian M. Fitzpatrick, O.S.M.; Revs. Gerald M. Horan, O.S.M.; Christopher M. Krymski, O.S.M.; Bro. Joel Lechner, O.S.M.; Rev. Eugene M. Smith, O.S.M.; Bro. Edmund M. Baran, Prov. Co-Treas.; Rev. Ignatius M. Kissel, O.S.M., Prov. Co-Treas.; Bro. Michael M. Callary, O.S.M., Prov. & Corp. Sec.; Rev. Conrad M Borntrager, O.S.M., Prov. Archivist.

St. Juliana Falconieri Priory, 1316 N. Acacia Ave., Fullerton, 92831; Fax: 714-526-6673. Revs. Patrick M. Donovan, O.S.M. Tel: 714-879-1971; Donald M. Duplessis, O.S.M.; David M. Kondik, O.S.M.; Jude M. Herlihy, O.S.M.

St. Philip Benizi Priory, 235 S. Pine Dr., Fullerton, 92833-3294. Tel: 714-871-3613; Fax: 714-871-5827. Revs. Ignatius M. Kissel, O.S.M.; Justin M. Kremen, O.S.M.; Manuel Maya Chavez, O.S.M.

Seven Holy Founders Priory, 1922 W. LaPalma Ave., Anaheim, 92801-3595. Tel: 714-774-8869; Fax: 714-774-6792. Revs. Richard M. Boyle, O.S.M.; Paul M. Gins, O.S.M.; Gerald M. Horan, O.S.M.; Edward M. Penonzek, O.S.M.; Michael M. Pontarelli, O.S.M.; Eugene M. Smith, O.S.M.; Bro. Joel Lechner, O.S.M.

Sisters of St. Joseph - Chaplain, Regina Residence, 430 S. Batavia, Orange, 92868. Rev. Gerard M. Calkins, O.S.M.

The Grotto, 8840 N.E. Skidmore St., Portland, OR, 97220. Tel: 503-254-7371; Fax: 503-254-7948. Residents 7; Religious 7.

FULLERTON. *Augustinian Recollects*, St. Mary, 400 W. Commonwealth Ave., 92832-1713. Tel: 714-525-2500; Fax: 714-525-3837.

Servite Fathers and Brothers, St. Juliana Falconieri, 1316 N. Acacia, 92831. Tel: 714-879-1971; Fax: 714-526-6673. St. Philip Benizi, 235 S. Pine Dr., 92833-3294. Tel: 714-871-3613. Total in Residence 4; Total Staff 3.

HUNTINGTON BEACH. *Franciscan Fathers*, SS. Simon and Jude, 20444 Magnolia St., 92646. Tel: 714-962-3333; Fax: 714-965-6456.
E-mail: cmondor@scj.org

MIDWAY CITY. *Brothers of St. Patrick, St. Patrick's Novitiate and Scholasticate*, 7820 Bolsa Ave., 92655. Tel: 714-897-8181; Fax: 714-898-9020. Bros. Livinus Bellew, F.S.P.; Aquinas Cassin, F.S.P.; Edwin Guidera, F.S.P.; Ignatius Mulqueen, F.S.P.; Matthew Regan, F.S.P.

SANTA ANA. *Augustinian Recollects*, Our Lady of Guadalupe, 1322 E. 3rd St., 92701-5104. Tel: 714-836-4142; Fax: 714-836-7417. Our Lady of the Pillar, 1622 6th St., 92703. Tel: 714-543-1700; Fax: 714-543-9640.

Trinitarian Missionaries/Missionary Servants of the Most Holy Trinity, Trinitarian House, P.O. Box 1933, 92702. Tel: 714-543-7394; Fax: 714-973-2348. Revs. Brendan Smith, S.T.; John J. Seymour, S.T.; Clif Marquis, S.T.; Nicholas Barille, S.T.

SILVERADO. *Norbertine Fathers of Orange Inc.*, St. Michael's Abbey (O.Praem.), 19292 El Toro Rd., 92676-9710. Tel: 949-858-0222; Fax: 949-858-4583. Rt. Revs. Eugene J. Hayes, O.Praem., Abbot; Ladislas K. Parker, O.Praem., (Retired) Abbot Emeritus; Very Rev. Hugh C. Barbour, O.Praem., Prior; Rev. James G. Smith, O.Praem., Subprior. Parish Apostolates: Revs. Martin R. Benzoni, O.Praem., Parochial Vicar, St. Bonaventure; Vincent M. Gilmore, O.Praem., Parochial Vicar, Our Lady Queen of Angels; Raymond L. Perez, O.Praem., Parochial Vicar, Mary Star of the Sea, San Pedro; Philip T. Smith, O.Praem., Parochial Vicar, Holy Spirit; Jordan S. Anderson, O.Praem., Graduate Studies; Stephen M. Boyle, O.Praem., St. Michael's Prep; John E. Caronan, O.Praem., Abbey Treas.; Leo J. Celano, O.Praem., Prison Chap.; Adrian J. Connor, O.Praem., St. Michael's Prep; Raphael J. Davis, O.Praem., Graduate Studies; Gregory M. Dick, O.Praem., Plant Mgr.; Patrick D. Foutts, O.Praem., Mary Star of the Sea; Paul L. Gelencser, O.Praem., (Retired); Francis M. Gloudeman, O.Praem., Chap., St. Michael's Academy; Robert S. Hodges, O.Praem., Mater Dei; Joseph K. Horn, O.Praem., Computer Tech.; Gerlac A. Horvath, O.Praem., (Retired); Bernard M. Johnson, O.Praem., Mary Star of the Sea; Lawrence C. Johnson, O.Praem., St. Michael's Prep; Anthony Mary J. Kopp, O.Praem., Mary Star of the Sea; Luke S. Laslavich, O.Praem., Mater Dei; Jerome M. Molokie, O.Praem., Abbey Cantor; Peter D. Muller, O.Praem., Mary Star of the Sea; Thomas W. Nelson, O.Praem., Dir. Formation; Pascal B. Nguyen, O.Praem., Mary Star of the Sea; Michael U. Perea, O.Praem., Chap., Thomas Aquinas College; Augustine R. Puchner, O.Praem., Novice Master; Justin S. Ramos, O.Praem., St. Michael's Prep; Hermann-Joseph K. Rettig, O.Praem., Pastor, St. Stephen's, Los Angeles; Clement A. Rudnay, O.Praem., (Retired); Theodore R. Smith, O.Praem., Teaching in Hungary; Gabriel D. Stack, O.Praem., Prin., St. Michael's Prep; Hubert S. Szanto, O.Praem., (Retired); Nicholas M. Tacito, O.Praem., St. Michael's Prep; Werenfried P. van Straaten, O.Praem., Aid to the Church in Need; Charles W. Willingham, O.Praem., St. Michael's Prep; Norbert J. Wood, O.Praem., Rector, Mary Star of the Sea. Priests 41; Deacons 2; Clerics 9; Novices 9; Postulants 2.

WESTMINSTER. *Columban Fathers*, Korean Martyrs Catholic Center, 7655 Trask Ave., 92683. Tel: 714-897-6510; Fax: 714-897-0832. Revs. John Hogan, S.S.C. Tel: 714-897-2825; Michael Morrissey, S.S.C. Tel: 714-897-6961.

[J] CONVENTS AND RESIDENCES FOR SISTERS

ORANGE. *Servants of Mary*, Regina Residence, 430 S. Batavia St., 92668. Tel: 714-633-8121.

Sisters of Charity of Leavenworth, 2427 Northumberland Rd. N., 92865-2901. Tel: 714-974-8518; 974-3359 (voice mail).

Sisters of Providence, Marywood Center, 2811 E. Villa Real Dr., 92867. Tel: 714-282-3099; Fax: 714-282-3029.
E-mail: srconcetta@rcbo.org

Sisters of St. Joseph of Orange Motherhouse Community, 480 S. Batavia, 92868. Tel: 714-633-8121, Ext. 7735; Fax: 714-744-3165.
E-mail: mtochtro@corp.stjoe.org
Sr. Michelle Tochtrop, C.S.J., Gen. Sec. & Contact. Sisters 37. Regina Residence Community, 430 S. Batavia St., 92868. Tel: 714-744-3109; Fax: 714-744-3163.
E-mail: rreginares@earthlink.net
Sisters 62. Palmyra Community, 940 W. Palmyra, 92868. Tel: 714-771-4706.
E-mail: csjpalmyra@aol.com
Sisters 4. Casa Magnolia Community, 954 W. Palmyra, 92868. Tel: 714-639-1030.
E-mail: casamag@aol.com
Sisters 3. St. Joseph Hospital Community, P.O. Box 5600, 92868. Tel: 714-771-8040.
E-mail: cnvntsjo@corp.stjoe.org
Sisters 9. Greengrove Community, 2075 Greengrove St., 92665. Tel: 714-974-9079.
E-mail: csjgr@earthlink.net
Sisters 2. Valencia Community, 5742 E. Valencia Dr., 92869. Tel: 714-639-3665.
E-mail: csjval@yahoo.com
Sisters 4.

Sisters of the Company of Mary, La Purisima Convent, 11712 N. Hewes, 92869. Tel: 714-538-0811; Fax: 707-221-2096.
E-mail: lps@ocweb.com
Web site: ocweb.com/lps
Sisters 3.

Sisters of the Presentation of the Blessed Virgin Mary, St. Norbert Convent, 343 E. Chestnut, 92867. Tel: 714-637-7390; Fax: 714-637-7473.
E-mail: orangePBVM@aol.com
Sisters 4.

ANAHEIM. *Dominicans, Mission San Jose*, St. Catherine Military School, 215 N. Harbor Blvd., 92805-2596. Tel: 714-772-1363; Fax: 714-772-3004.
E-mail: stcatherine@artsci.com
Sisters 12.

Religious Sisters of Mercy of the Americas, St. Boniface Parish, 120 N. Janss St., 92805. Tel: 714-956-3110; Fax: 714-956-3034. St. Justin Martyr, 2050 W. Ball Rd., 92804. Tel: 714-774-2407; Fax: 714-774-9849.

BREA. *Sisters of St. Clare*, 446 South Poplar Ave., 92821-6649. Tel: 714-257-1113; Fax: 714-257-0681. Sisters 3.

BUENA PARK. *Sisters of Our Lady of Perpetual Help*, 6751 Western Ave., 90621. Tel: 714-521-1345; Fax: 714-521-7611. Sisters 9.

COSTA MESA. *Sisters of Mercy of Ireland*, St. John the Baptist Convent, 2960 Mendoza Dr., 92626. Tel: 714-545-2116; Fax: 714-557-9263. Sisters 4.

Sisters of the Company of Mary, St. Joachim Convent, 1943 Orange Ave., 92727. Tel: 949-574-7408; Fax: 949-574-7407.
E-mail: stjoachim@ioc.net
Sisters 4.

CYPRESS. *Sisters of the Blessed Virgin Mary*, St. Irenaeus Convent, 5151 Evergreen Ave., 90630. Tel: 714-527-4844; Fax: 714-527-5189.

DANA POINT. *Sisters of Social Service*, St. Edward, 33926 Calle La Primavera, 92629-2018. Tel: 949-496-1307; Fax: 949-496-1557.
E-mail: nrahn@stedward.com

Sisters of St. Joseph of Orange, Mission Hospital Community, 33392 Via Lenita, 92629. Tel: 949-488-0433.
E-mail: srma@mhr.stjoe.org
Sisters 3.

FOUNTAIN VALLEY. *Sisters of Social Service*, 9076 La Colonia, 92708-2719. Tel: 714-847-8981; Fax: 213-747-4499.

FULLERTON. *Sisters of St. Joseph of Orange*, Rosary Community, 1601 E. Alto Ln., 92831. Tel: 714-526-3141.
E-mail: csjoalto@earthlink.net
Sisters 4. Adrian Dominicans, 1925 Sunny Crest Dr., 92835. Tel: 714-680-9262. St. Jude Hospital Community, 3642 Coronado Dr., 92835. Tel: 714-879-7159. Sisters 5.

GARDEN GROVE. *Eucharistic Missionaries of the Most Holy Trinity*, 11892 E. Lampson Ave., 92840. Tel: 714-530-5727; Fax: 714-636-5192.
E-mail: orangemest@aol.com
Sisters 4.

Religious Sisters of Charity, St. Columban Convent, 12555 Westlake St., 92840. Tel: 714-534-1003. Sisters 5.

Sisters of the Presentation of the Blessed Virgin Mary, St. Columban Residence, 10871 Stanford Ave., #18, 92840-5139. Tel: 714-537-2015.

HUNTINGTON BEACH. *Sisters of Charity of the Blessed Virgin Mary*, SS. Simon & Jude Convent, 20512 Tobermory Cir., 92646-5837. Tel: 714-968-2237; Fax: 714-965-6456.

Sisters of the Presentation of the Blessed Virgin Mary, St. Bonaventure Convent, 16441 Bradbury Ln., 92647. Tel: 714-846-6212.
E-mail: presentation@linkline.com
Sisters 5.

LA HABRA. *Sisters of St. Joseph of Carondelet*, Villa Maria House of Prayer, 1252 N. Citrus Dr., 90631. Tel: 562-691-5838; Fax: 562-691-2572. Sisters 3.

Sisters of St. Joseph of Orange, Our Lady of Guadalupe Community, 920 W. La Habra Blvd., 90631. Tel: 562-691-8612; Fax: 562-905-0095.

LAGUNA HILLS. *Sisters of Little Company of Mary*, St. Nicholas Convent, 24652 La Cienega, 92653. Tel: 949-643-8688; Fax: 949-831-5022. Sisters 2.

LAKE FOREST. *School Sisters of St. Francis*, 24001 Muirlands Blvd. #146, 92630. Tel: 949-951-8681.
E-mail: sssf@earth.execpc.com
Web site: www.sssf.org

RANCHO PALOS VERDES. *Daughters of Mary and Joseph Provincialate*, 5300 Crest Rd., 90275-5004. Tel: 310-377-9968; Fax: 310-544-0387.
E-mail: dmjca@earthlink.net
Web site: www.home.earthlink.net/~dmjca

Daughters of Mary and Joseph, c/o Regina Residence 430 S. Batavia St., Orange, 92868. Tel: 714-744-3509, Ext. 2272.

RANCHO SANTA MARGARITA. *Sisters of Providence*, 252 Montana Del Lago, 92688. Tel: 949-589-3322; Fax: 949-589-7768.

SANTA ANA. *Dominicans, Mission San Jose*, St. Callistus Convent, 2541 N. Forest Ave., 92706. Tel: 714-953-4322. Sisters 4.

Franciscan Missionary Sisters of the Immaculate Conception, St. Francis Home for the Aged, 1718 W. 6th St., 92703. Tel: 714-542-0381; Fax: 714-542-4654. Sisters 23.

Lovers of the Holy Cross Sisters, 1401 S. Sycamore St., 92707. Tel: 714-542-4455; Fax: 714-542-4846. Sisters 12.

Poor Clare Missionary Sisters of the Blessed Sacrament, 1019 N. Newhope St., 92703-1534. Tel: 714-554-8850; Fax: 714-554-5886.
E-mail: clarisas@earthlink.net
Sisters 15.

Sisters of Mercy of the Americas, 16350 Harbor Blvd., #2602, 92704-3836. Tel: 714-839-7893.

Sisters of St. Joseph of Carondelet, Hogar de San Jose, 507 N. Linwood Ave., 92701. Tel: 714-541-6480. St. Joseph, 727 Minter St., 92701. Tel: 714-550-8096; Fax: 714-550-8095.

Sisters of St. Joseph of Orange, Casa Guadalupe Community, 414 S. Broadway, 92701. Tel: 714-834-9381.
E-mail: csj414@yahoo.com
Sisters 4. Olive Street Community, 2109 N. Olive St., 92706. Tel: 714-542-3380.
E-mail: csj2109@earthlink.net
Sisters 4.
Sisters of the Company of Mary, St. Anne's Convent, 1339 S. Broadway, 92707. Tel: 714-558-1340. Sisters 5.
Society Devoted to the Sacred Heart, Heart of Jesus Retreat Center, 2927 S. Greenville St., 92704. Tel: 714-557-4538; Fax: 714-668-9780. Sisters 7. Sacred Heart Convent, 2911 S. Greenville St., 92704. Tel: 714-751-6335. Sisters 6.

SEAL BEACH. *Franciscans, Syracuse*, St. Anne Convent, 328 1/2 10th St., 90740. Tel: 310-493-4630.

SILVERADO. *Rosarian Dominicans*, St. Michael's Convent, 19292 El Toro Rd., 92676. Tel: 949-858-0487. Sisters 7.

TUSTIN. *Adrian Dominicans*, St. Jeanne de Lestonnac Convent, 16791 E. Main St., 92780. Tel: 714-541-3125; Fax: 714-835-0648.
E-mail: odn@ocweb.com
Web site: www.ocweb.com/odnusa
Community of the Holy Spirit, 14692 Charloma Dr., 92780. Tel: 714-544-8339; Fax: 949-644-9218.
Sisters de L'Union-Chretienne de Saint Chaumond, 14391 Clarissa Ln., 92780. Tel: 714-730-1475; Fax: 714-731-7315. Sisters 4.
Sisters of Providence, 14692 Charloma Dr., 92780. Tel: 714-544-9021. Sisters 2.
Sisters of the Company of Mary, Provincial House, 16791 E. Main St., 92780. Tel: 714-541-3125; Fax: 714-835-0648.
E-mail: odn@ocweb.com
Web site: www.ocweb.com/odnusa
Sisters 16.

WESTMINSTER. *Korean Sisters of Our Lady of Perpetual Help*, 7655 Trask Ave., 92683. Tel: 714-373-2556; Fax: 714-897-0832. Sisters 2.

YORBA LINDA. *Sisters of Providence Residence*, Providence House, 4580 Casa Oro Dr., 92886. Tel: 714-996-5027; Fax: 714-996-1425.
E-mail: dpaula996@juno.com
Web site: spsmw.org
Sr. Jan Craven, S.P.; Sr. Paula Damiano, S.P. Sisters 2.

[K] CATHOLIC CHARITIES

SANTA ANA. *Catholic Charities of Orange County, Inc.*, 1506 Brookhollow Dr., Ste. 112, 92705. Tel: 714-662-7500; Fax: 714-662-1861.
E-mail: ccocinfo@ccoc.org
Web site: ccoc.org
Kristan Schlichte, M.S., Exec. Dir.; Most Rev. Jaime Soto, M.S.W., Vicar of Charities.
Counseling Services. Tel: 714-662-7500; Fax: 714-662-1861. Alice Thull, Program Dir.
Columbian House, Garden Grove. Tel: 714-530-8630; Fax: 714-530-8630. Fe Santos, Facility Mgr. Residential care for children with developmental disabilities.
Family Support Services. Tel: 714-662-7500; Fax: 714-957-4612. Berenice Olivas, Program Dir.
Employment Services, Anaheim. Tel: 714-635-5230; Fax: 714-635-9896. Xang Yang, Program Dir.
Family Service Center. Tel: 714-668-1130; Fax: 714-957-2523. Lupe Savastano, Program Dir.
Resettlement, Immigration & Citizenship Services. Tel: 714-662-7500; Fax: 714-662-1861. Thu Tran, Program Dir.
Community Social Action. Tel: 714-662-7500; Fax: 714-662-1861. Erik M. Giblin, Program Dir.
Parish Social Ministry. Tel: 714-662-7500; Fax: 714-662-1861. Josie Ngoc Tran, Program Dir. Total Staff 160; Total Assisted 34,277.

[L] RETREAT HOUSES

ORANGE. *Center for Spiritual Development*, 434 S. Batavia St., 92868-3907. Tel: 714-744-3175, Ext. 4404; Fax: 714-744-3176. Sr. Jane Delisle, C.S.J., Exec. Dir. Total Staff 12.
House of Prayer for Priests, 7734 Santiago Canyon Rd., 92869. Tel: 714-639-9740; Fax: 714-639-9313. Rev. J. Gordon Moreland, S.J., Dir. In res. Rev. Patrick B. Philbin, S.M. Total in Residence 2; Total Staff 1.
Marywood Retreat Center, 2811 E. Villa Real Dr., 92867. Tel: 714-282-3099 (Evenings & Weekends); Fax: 714-282-3029.
E-mail: sr.concetta@rcbo.org
Elizabeth Sandoval, Facilities Coord., Tel: 714-282-3098 (Days Mon.-Fri.); Fax: 714-282-3029. Sr. M. Concetta Banez, S.P., Res. Dir. Retreats for youth, men, women & married couple groups. Capacity 120.

LA HABRA. *Villa Maria House of Prayer*, 1252 N. Citrus Dr., 90631. Tel: 562-691-5838; Fax: 562-691-2572. Sisters of St. Joseph of Carondelet.

SANTA ANA. *Heart of Jesus Retreat Center*, 2927 S. Greenville St., 92704. Tel: 714-557-4538; Fax: 714-668-9780.
E-mail: sdshrc@juno.com
Society Devoted to the Sacred Heart. Sisters 7; Total Staff 7.

[M] NEWMAN CENTERS

FULLERTON. *California State University Fullerton, Newman Center*, St. Juliana Falconieri, 1316 N. Acacia Ave., 9283-1202. Tel: 714-526-7189; Fax: 714-526-6673.
E-mail: csufnewman@hotmail.com
Rev. Patrick J. Donovan, O.S.M.

IRVINE. *U.C.I. Interfaith Center*, P.O. Box 6030, 92616-6030. Tel: 949-856-0211; 753-3373, Ext. 3; Fax: 714-639-9313. Rev. Patrick B. Philbin, S.M., Diocesan Dir. Campus Ministry.

[N] SECULAR INSTITUTES

FULLERTON. *Pro Sanctity Spirituality Center, Retreat House*, 205 S. Pine Dr., 92833. Tel: 714-956-1020; Fax: 714-525-8948.
E-mail: ApostolicO@aol.com
Agnes Rus, Dir. Capacity: 27-40 for day use.
Pro Sanctity Movement. Tel: 714-956-1020; Fax: 714-525-8948. Barbara Wagner, Dir.

[O] MISCELLANEOUS LISTINGS

ORANGE. *Orange Catholic Foundation*, 2811 E. Villa Real Dr., 92867-1999. Tel: 714-282-3000; Fax: 714-282-3029.
E-mail: msgr.LBaird@rcbo.org
Rev. Msgr. Lawrence J. Baird, Dir. Devel.
Orange County Catholic Alumni Club, P.O. Box 6054, 92863-6054. Tel: 714-502-8086.
E-mail: orangecountyCAC@juno.com
Web site: www.netinsight.com/caci/occac/html
St. Joseph Health System, 500 S. Main St., Ste. 400, 92868. Tel: 714-347-7579; Fax: 714-347-7590.
Web site: www.stjhs.org
Sr. Marianna Gemmet, C.S.J., Chm. Bd.; Mr. Richard Statuto, Pres. & CEO.
St. Joseph Health System Foundation, 500 S. Main St., Ste. 400, 92868. Tel: 714-347-7579; Fax: 714-347-7590. Maya Dunn, Contact Person.
St. Jude Hospital Yorba Linda, St. Joseph Health System, 500 S. Main St., 92868-4515. Tel: 714-347-7579; Fax: 714-347-7590. Robert J. Frashetti.
Sisters of St. Joseph Healthcare Foundation, 480 S. Batavia St., 92868. Tel: 714-633-8121; Fax: 714-744-3165.
E-mail: dhejna@corp.stjoe.org
Sr. Diane Hejna, C.S.J., Exec. Dir.

FULLERTON. *Apostolic Oblates*, 2125 W. Walnut Ave., 92833. Tel: 714-871-5768; Fax: 714-525-8948.
E-mail: ApostolicO@aol.com
House of Formation for Professed Apostolic Oblates. Secular Institute of the Apostolic Oblates, Inc. Agnes Rus, Local Moderator.
St. Jude Memorial Foundation, P.O. Box 4138, 92834. Tel: 714-992-3033; Fax: 714-738-0691.

SILVERADO. *Norbertine Association of St. Joseph, Inc.*, St. Michael's Abbey, 19292 El Toro Rd., 92676-9710. Tel: 949-858-0222, Ext. 216; Fax: 949-858-4583. Officers: Rt. Rev. Eugene J. Hayes, O.Praem., Pres.; Rev. John E. Caronan, O.Praem., Sec.; Monique Petit, Moderator. A public association of the faithful for unmarried lay women wishing to live a more intense Norbertine spirituality in common.

RELIGIOUS INSTITUTES OF MEN REPRESENTED IN THE DIOCESE

For further details refer to the corresponding bracketed number in the Religious Institutes of Men or Women section.

[0530]—*Atonement Friars*.—S.A.
[0140]—*Augustinian Fathers*.—O.S.A.
[0150]—*Augustinian Recollects*.—O.A.R.
[1160]—*Brothers of St. Patrick*.—F.S.P.
[0330]—*Brothers of the Christian Schools*.—F.S.C.
[0360]—*Claretian Missionaries*.—C.M.F.
[0370]—*Columban Fathers*.—S.S.C.
[0380]—*Comboni Missionaries of the Heart of Jesus*. (Verona).—M.C.C.J.
[]—*Crusade of the Holy Spirit*.—C.H.S.
[]—*Divine Word*.—S.V.D.
[0520]—*Franciscan Fathers*.—O.F.M.
[0670]—*Hospitaller Brothers of St. John of God*.—O.H.
[0690]—*Jesuit Fathers and Brothers*.—S.J.
[0780]—*Marist Fathers*.—S.M.
[1110]—*Missionaries of the Sacred Heart*.—MSC.
[0900]—*Norbertine Fathers*.—O.Praem.
[0610]—*Priests of the Holy Cross*.—C.S.C.
[1190]—*Salesians of Don Bosco*.—S.D.B.
[1240]—*Servite Fathers and Brothers*.—O.S.M.
[0840]—*Trinity Missionaries*.—S.T.

RELIGIOUS INSTITUTES OF WOMEN REPRESENTED IN THE DIOCESE

[]—*Benedictine Sisters*. (Rapid City, SD).—O.S.B.
[2020]—*Community of the Holy Spirit*.—C.H.S.
[]—*Congregation of Divine Providence*.
[1920]—*Congregation of Sisters of the Holy Cross*.—C.S.C.
[0880]—*Daughters of Mary and Joseph*.—D.M.J.
[1070-13]—*Dominican Sisters*. (Adrian, MI).—O.P.
[]—*Dominican Sisters*. (Mission San Jose).—O.P.
[1070-03]—*Dominican Sisters*. (Sinsinawa).—O.P.
[]—*Dominican Sisters*. (Western Australia).—O.P.
[]—*Dominican Sisters*. (Caldwell, NJ).—O.P.
[]—*Eucharistic Missionaries of the Most Holy Trinity*.—M.E.S.S.T.
[1350]—*Franciscan Missionary Sisters of the Immaculate Conception*.—O.S.F.
[1540]—*Franciscan Sisters*. (Clinton, IA).—O.S.F.
[]—*Franciscan Sisters*. (Syracuse, NY).—O.S.F.
[1650]—*Franciscan Sisters, Philadelphia Foundation*.—O.S.F.
[2390]—*Lovers of the Holy Cross Sisters*.—L.H.C.
[2840]—*Poor Clare Missionaries of Blessed Sacrament*.—M.C.
[3280]—*Presentation Sisters of Blessed Virgin Mary*.—P.B.V.M.
[3400]—*Religious Sisters of Charity*.—R.S.C.
[]—*Religious Sisters of the Sacred Heart of Mary*.—R.S.H.M.
[]—*Rosarian Dominican Sisters*.—O.P.
[]—*St. Joseph Third Order of St. Francis*.—S.S.J.T.O.R.
[]—*School Sisters of Notre Dame*.—S.S.N.D.
[1680]—*School Sisters of St. Francis*.—S.S.S.F.
[3580]—*Servants of Mary*.—O.S.M.
[]—*Sisters de L'Union-Chretienne de Saint Chaumond*.—U.C.S.C.
[]—*Sisters for Christian Community*.—S.F.C.C.
[]—*Sisters of Charity of Leavenworth*. (KS).—S.C.L.
[0430]—*Sisters of Charity of the Blessed Virgin Mary*.—B.V.M.
[]—*Sisters of Mercy of Ireland*.—S.M.
[2575]—*Sisters of Mercy of the Americas*.—R.S.M.
[]—*Sisters of Our Lady of Perpetual Help*.—S.O.L.P.H.
[]—*Sisters of Providence*. (Montreal).—S.P.
[3340]—*Sisters of Providence*. IN.—S.P.
[]—*Sisters of Providence*. (Seattle).—S.P.
[4090]—*Sisters of Social Service*.—S.S.S.
[3770]—*Sisters of St. Clare*.—O.S.C.
[3830-03]—*Sisters of St. Joseph*. (Orange).—C.S.J.
[3840]—*Sisters of St. Joseph of Carondelet*.—C.S.J.
[3840]—*Sisters of St. Joseph of Carondelet*. (Albany Prov.).—C.S.J.
[3935]—*Sisters of St. Louis*.—S.S.L.
[0700]—*Sisters of the Company of Mary*.—O.D.N.
[1990]—*Sisters of the Holy Names of Jesus and Mary*.—S.N.J.M.
[2270]—*Sisters of the Little Company of Mary*.—L.C.M.
[4050]—*Sisters of the Society Devoted to the Sacred Heart*.—S.D.S.H.
[4060]—*Society of the Holy Child Jesus*.—S.H.C.J.

DIOCESAN CEMETERIES

ORANGE. *Holy Sepulcher*, 7845 Santiago Canyon Rd., 92869. Kevin Haynes, Supt.

ANAHEIM. *Holy Cross*.

HUNTINGTON BEACH. *Good Shepherd Cemetery and Mausoleum*, 8301 Talbert Ave., 92646. Guadalupe Ramirez, Supt.

LAKE FOREST. *Ascension*, 24754 Trabuco Rd., 92630. John D. Callaghan, Jr., Supt.

NECROLOGY

† Daley, Wallace J., (On Duty Outside the Diocese). —Died April 8, 2000.

† Gonzales, George, El Toro, CA Santiago de Compostela Church. —Died Jan. 21, 2000.

Diocese of Orlando

(Dioecesis Orlandensis)

Most Reverend

NORBERT M. DORSEY, C.P., D.D., S.T.D.

Bishop of Orlando; ordained April 28, 1956; appointed Auxiliary Bishop of Miami January 10, 1986; ordained Titular Bishop of Mactaris and Auxiliary Bishop of the Archdiocese of Miami March 19, 1986; appointed Bishop of Orlando March 20, 1990; installed as Third Bishop of Orlando May 25, 1990. *Office: 421 E. Robinson, P.O. Box 1800, Orlando, FL, 32802.*

Most Reverend

THOMAS J. GRADY, D.D.

Retired Bishop of Orlando; ordained April 23, 1938; appointed Auxiliary Bishop of Chicago June 21, 1967; ordained Titular Bishop of Vamalla August 24, 1967; appointed Bishop of Orlando November 9, 1974; installed as Second Bishop of Orlando December 16, 1974; retired May 25, 1990. *Mailing Address: 421 E. Robinson, P.O. Box 1800, Orlando, FL, 32802.*

ESTABLISHED JUNE 18, 1968.

Square Miles 11,255.66.

Comprises the Counties of Brevard, Lake, Marion, Orange, Osceola, Polk, Seminole, Sumter and Volusia in the State of Florida.

For legal titles of parishes and diocesan institutions, consult the Chancery.

Chancery: 421 E. Robinson, P.O. Box 1800, Orlando, FL, 32802-1800. Tel.: 407-246-4800; Fax: 407-246-4942.

Web site address: www.orlandodiocese.org

E-mail address: orldiofin@aol.com

STATISTICAL OVERVIEW

Personnel	
Bishop	1
Retired Bishops	1
Priests: Diocesan Active in Diocese	98
Priests: Active Outside Diocese	5
Priests: Retired, Sick or Absent	21
Number of Diocesan Priests	124
Religious Priests in Diocese	42
Extern Priests in Diocese	20
Ordinations:	
Diocesan Priests	2
Transitional Deacons	1
Permanent Deacons	7
Permanent Deacons in Diocese	116
Total Brothers	15
Total Sisters	124
Parishes	
Parishes	71
With Resident Pastor:	
Resident Diocesan Priests	61
Resident Religious Priests	10
Missions	10
New Parishes Created	1
Professional Ministry Personnel:	
Brothers	6
Sisters	31
Lay Ministers	171
Welfare	
Day Care and Extended Day Care Centers	10
Total Assisted	900
Specialized Homes	2
Total Assisted	325
Special Centers for Social Services	6
Total Assisted	45,658
Other Institutions	9
Total Assisted	900
Educational	
Diocesan Students in Other Seminaries	12
Total Seminarians	12
High Schools, Diocesan and Parish	5
Total Students	2,466
Elementary Schools, Diocesan and Parish	31
Total Students	12,753
Non-residential Schools for the Disabled	1
Total Students	60
Catechesis/Religious Education:	
High School Students	4,342
Elementary Students	21,342
Total Students Under Catholic Instruction	40,975
Teachers in the Diocese:	
Priests	1
Sisters	35
Lay Teachers	855
Vital Statistics	
Receptions into the Church:	
Infant Baptism Totals	5,878
Adult Baptism Totals	537
Received into Full Communion	737
First Communions	5,474
Confirmations	4,365
Marriages:	
Catholic	1,011
Interfaith	585
Total Marriages	1,596
Deaths	3,583
Total Catholic Population	340,448
Total Population	3,177,046

Former Bishops—Most Rev. WILLIAM D. BORDERS, D.D., ord. May 18, 1940; appt. Bishop of Orlando, May 2, 1968; cons. June 14, 1968; transferred to Baltimore, March 25, 1974 as Archbishop.—Most Rev. THOMAS J. GRADY, D.D., ord. April 23, 1938; appt. Second Bishop of Orlando, Nov. 9, 1974; installed Dec. 16, 1974; retired May 25, 1990.

Chancery—421 E. Robinson, P.O. Box 1800, Orlando, 32802-1800. Tel: 407-246-4800; Fax: 407-246-4942.

Vicar General—Rev. PATRICK J. CAVERLY, V.G., *P.O. Box 1800, Orlando, 32802.* Tel: 407-246-4800.

Archivist—JANE QUINN.

Chancellor—Sr. LUCY VAZQUEZ, O.P., J.C.D., *P.O. Box 1800, Orlando, 32802.* Tel: 407-246-4800.

Tribunal—421 E. Robinson, P.O. Box 1800, Orlando, 32802. Tel: 407-246-4850.

Judicial Vicar—Rev. MATTHEW J. CONNOLLY.

Adjutant Judicial Vicar—Rev. PAIGE BLAKELY, J.C.L.

Director of Tribunal—Sr. LUCY VAZQUEZ, O.P., J.C.D.

Promoter of Justice—Sr. LUCY VAZQUEZ, O.P., J.C.D.

Defenders of the Bond—Revs. FERNANDO GIL, J.D., J.C.D.; GREGORY PARKES, J.C.L.; Sr. LUCY VAZQUEZ, O.P., J.C.D.

Judges—Revs. PAIGE BLAKELY, J.C.L.; RONALD KRISMAN, J.C.L.; MATTHEW CONNOLLY; JOHN GIEL, J.C.L.; JOSE BAUTISTA, J.C.L.

Regional Advocate—Sr. ANN ENGLERT, O.P. Tel: 407-668-1426.

Chief Financial Officer—GERALD F. HILBRICH.

Comptroller—ROGER BARNES.

Deans—Rev. ROBERT FUCHECK, Northern Deanery; Rev. ROBERT MARKUNAS, Central Deanery South; Rev. RICHARD WALSH, Central Deanery North; Rev. RAYMOND O'LEARY, Eastern Deanery; Rev. ANTHONY BLUETT, Western Deanery; Rev. ROBERT J. HOEFFNER, Southern Deanery.

Priests' Council—Executive Committee: Most Rev. NORBERT M. DORSEY, C.P., Pres.; Revs. NICHOLAS KING, Chm. VAL SHEEDY, Vice Chm.; MIGUEL GONZALEZ, Sec.; PATRICK J. CAVERLY, V.G., Ex Officio; EMILE GENTILE, T.O.R., Ex Officio. Members: Revs. CARLOS BEDOYA; PHIL EGITTO; ANTHONY BLUETT; ROBERT FUCHECK; MIGUEL GONZALEZ; ROBERT HOEFFNER; NICHOLAS KING; ROBERT MARKUNAS; NICHOLAS O'BRIEN; PAUL HENRY; RAYMOND O'LEARY; VAL SHEEDY; PETER UNIOWSKI; RICHARD WALSH; RICHARD TROUT.

Consultors—Revs. PATRICK J. CAVERLY, V.G.; ROBERT HOEFFNER; ANTHONY BLUETT; ROBERT MARKUNAS; RAYMOND O'LEARY; RICHARD WALSH; ROBERT FUCHECK.

Bishop's Executive Staff—Most Rev. NORBERT M. DORSEY; Revs. PATRICK J. CAVERLY, V.G.; PAUL HENRY; EMILE GENTILE, T.O.R.; ROBERT WEBSTER; Sr. LUCY

VAZQUEZ, O.P., J.C.D.; THOMAS AGLIO; GERALD F. HILBRICH.

Vicar for Religious—Sr. LUCY VAZQUEZ, O.P., J.C.D., *P.O. Box 1800, Orlando, 32802.*

Vicar for Clergy—Rev. EMILE GENTILE, T.O.R.

Diocesan Offices and Organizations

Office of Stewardship & Development—MARILYN L. BLANCHETTE, Dir., *P.O. Box 1800, Orlando, 32802.* Tel: 407-246-4841.

Black Ministry—Rev. LEO HODGES, *1771 N. Semoran Blvd., Orlando, 32807.* Tel: 407-658-1818.

Haitian Community Ministry—Rev. PIERRE LOUIS JOSEPH, *1771 N. Semoran Blvd., Orlando, 32807.* Tel: 407-658-1818.

Building Commission—WILLIAM G. KRAMER, A.I.A., Coord., *P.O. Box 1800, Orlando, 32802.* Tel: 407-246-4870.

Campus Ministry—Rev. EMILE GENTILE, T.O.R., Dir., *P.O. Box 1800, Orlando, 32802.* Tel: 407-246-4875.

Catholic Charities—THOMAS AGLIO, Dir., *1771 N. Semoran Blvd., Orlando, 32807-3598.* Tel: 407-658-1818; Fax: 407-282-2891.

Cemeteries—Rev. THOMAS BARRETT, Dir., *P.O. Box 1800, Orlando, 32802.* Tel: 407-246-4870.

Censor of Books—Sr. LUCY VAZQUEZ, O.P., J.C.D., *Chancery Office, P.O. Box 1800, Orlando, 32802.*

Cursillos de Cristiandad—Rev. CARL VACEK, T.O.R., Dir., *San Pedro Center, 2400 Dike Rd., Winter Park, 32792.* Tel: 407-671-6322.

Prison & Jail Ministry—THOMAS GILLAN, *1771 N. Semoran Blvd., Orlando, 32807-3544.* Tel: 407-658-1818.

Diocesan Pastoral Council—Vacant, Bishop's Rep., *P.O. Box 1800, Orlando, 32802.* Tel: 407-246-4840.

Ecumenical Office—Rev. LARRY LOSSING, *P.O. Box 1800, Orlando, 32802.* Tel: 407-260-8422.

Education, Board of—Dr. CHUCK MOJOCK, Chm.

Education, Department of—MAUREEN HUNTINGTON, Ed.S., Supt., *P.O. Box 1800, Orlando, 32802.* Tel: 407-246-4900; Fax: 407-246-4940.

Family Life—ELAINE HENRIS, Dir., *P.O. Box 1800, Orlando, 32802.* Tel: 407-246-4865.

Catholic Gay & Lesbian Ministry—Rev. JOHN R. FLYNN, O.S.A., Dir., *P.O. Box 1800, Orlando, 32802-1800.* Tel: 407-695-3262; Fax: 407-246-4942.

Farmworker Ministry, Office for—Rev. ROBERT MARKUNAS, Dir., *P.O. Box 1800, Orlando, 32802.* Tel: 407-246-4930; Fax: 407-246-4932.

Finance Committee—GERALD F. HILBRICH, *P.O. Box 1800, Orlando, 32802.*

Fiscal Management—GERALD F. HILBRICH.

Hispanic Ministry Office—Rev. ROBERT MARKUNAS, Dir., *P.O. Box 1800, Orlando, 32802.* Tel: 407-246-4930; Fax: 407-246-4942.

Immigration Services—RICHARD LOGUE, Dir., *1771 N. Semoran Blvd., Orlando, 32807-3598.* Tel: 407-658-0110; Fax: 407-249-5699.

Insurance Committee—Vacant, Chm., *P.O. Box 1800, Orlando, 32802.* Tel: 407-246-4840.

Lay Ministry Development—Dr. LINDA PERRONE ROONEY, Dir., *P.O. Box 1800, Orlando, 32802.* Tel: 407-246-4880; Fax: 407-246-4884.

Liturgical Commission—Rev. ROBERT WEBSTER, Dir., *P.O. Box 1800, Orlando, 32802.* Tel: 407-246-4860.

Newspaper—"The Florida Catholic", STEVE E. PARADIS, Editor & Gen. Mgr., *P.O. Box 609512, Orlando, 32860-9512.* Tel: 407-660-9141; Fax: 407-660-2977.

Permanent Diaconate—Rev. EMILE GENTILE, T.O.R., Dir. Co-Directors: Deacons BOB KINSEY; GERRY KELLY, *P.O. Box 1800, Orlando, 32802.* Tel: 407-246-4875; Fax: 407-246-4942.

Priests' Continuing Education—Rev. RICHARD WALSH, *St. Margaret Mary, 526 Park Ave., Winter Park, 32789.* Tel: 407-647-3392.

Priests' Personnel—Rev. EMILE GENTILE, T.O.R., *P.O. Box 1800, Orlando, 32802.* Tel: 407-246-4875.

Propagation of the Faith—Rev. JOHN MCCORMICK, Dir., *Holy Redeemer, 1603 N. Thacker Ave., Kissimmee, 34741.* Tel: 407-846-3700.

Real Estate Committee—Rev. NICHOLAS KING, Chm., *St. Mary, 75 Barton Ave., Rockledge, 32955-2939.* Tel: 407-636-6834.

Refugee Resettlement—RICHARD LOGUE, Dir., *1771 N. Semoran Blvd., Orlando, 32807-3598.* Tel: 407-658-0110; Fax: 407-249-5699.

Religious Education—Sr. LINDA L. GAUPIN, C.D.P., Ph.D., Dir., *P.O. Box 1800, Orlando, 32802.* Tel: 407-246-4910; Fax: 407-246-4940.

Media Center—ROZAN JORDAN, Dir., *329 Broadway, Orlando, 32803.* Tel: 407-246-4895; Fax: 407-246-4942.

Respect Life Office—DEBORAH SHEARER, Dir., *1771 N. Semoran Blvd., Orlando, 32807-3544.* Tel: 407-277-7266; Fax: 407-658-5782.

Scouting—Office of Youth Ministry, P.O. Box 1800, Orlando, 32802. Tel: 407-246-4911.

Sister Diocese-Mission Office—Sr. BERNADETTE MACKAY, O.S.U., Dir., *P.O. Box 1800, Orlando, 32802.* Tel: 407-246-4890; Fax: 407-246-4942.

Sister's Council—Sr. PAT SIPAN, S.N.D., Pres., *Resurrection Catholic Church, P.O. Box 771257, Winter Garden, 34777-1257.* Tel: 407-656-3113.

Society of St. Vincent de Paul—DONALD LEAR, Pres., *P.O. Box 1800, Orlando, 32802.*

Spiritual Development—Rev. CARL VACEK, T.O.R., *2400 Dike Rd., Winter Park, 32792.* Tel: 407-671-6322.

Vietnamese Ministry—Rev. DUNG VAN "JOSEPH" BUI, *4001 Edgewater Dr., Orlando, 32804.* Tel: 407-293-9213.

Vocations—Revs. THOMAS BARRETT, Dir. CARLOS BEDOYA, Asst. Dir., *P.O. Box 1800, Orlando, 32802.* Tel: 407-246-4875; Fax: 407-246-4942.

Youth Ministry—Vacant, *P.O. Box 1800, Orlando, 32802.* Tel: 407-246-4911; Fax: 407-246-4940.

CLERGY, PARISHES, MISSIONS AND PAROCHIAL SCHOOLS

CITY OF ORLANDO
(Orange County)

1—ST. JAMES CATHEDRAL (1881), Revs. Sean Heslin; Frank J. Mutsko; Fernando Bonilla; Deacon Sam Ryan.
Church—215 N. Orange Ave., 32801. Tel: 407-422-2005; Fax: 407-422-2009.
School—Tel: 407-841-4432; Fax: 407-648-4603.
Lay Teachers 22; Students 462.
Catechesis/Religious Programs—Tel: 407-422-8624; Fax: 407-422-4009.
Students 365.
Mission—Orlando, Orange Co., St. Ignatius Kim Korean Mission, 1504 Muriel St., 32806. Tel: 407-897-6587; Fax: 407-897-6587. Rev. Zachariah Jeong Do-Sek.

2—BLESSED TRINITY (1965), Revs. Joe Aquino, M.S., Co-Pastor; Ron Gagne, M.S., Co-Pastor; Camillo Avitabile, M.S. In res., Rev. Matthew J. Connolly.
Res., 4545 E. Anderson Rd., 32812. Tel: 407-277-1702; Fax: 407-277-1973.
Catechesis/Religious Programs—Tel: 407-277-1702; Fax: 407-277-1973.
Students 450.

3—GOOD SHEPHERD (1956), Revs. Brian R. Sheridan, M.S.; Daniel P. Bradley, M.S.; Deacons Jose "Manny" Garcia; Wayne Phelps, Pastoral Assoc.
Mailing Address: 5900 Oleander Dr., 32807. Tel: 407-277-3939; Fax: 407-273-5148.
Res., 567 Hewett Dr., 32807. Tel: 407-275-5486.
School—Tel: 407-277-3973; Fax: 407-277-2605.
Sisters 2; Lay Teachers 33; Students 651.
Pre-School—Tel: 407-277-3939, Ext. 220.
Sisters 1; Lay Teachers 11; Students 96.
Catechesis/Religious Programs—Tel: 407-277-3939, Ext. 211. Maria Virgen Jimenez, D.R.E.
Students 670.

4—HOLY CROSS (1992), Rev. Robert Kurber.
Res., 12600 Marsfield Ave., 32837. Tel: 407-438-0990; Fax: 407-438-4090.
Catechesis/Religious Programs—Students 730.

5—HOLY FAMILY (1975), Revs. William Ennis; Gregory Parkes; Felicito Baybay; Deacons Charles Mallon; Robert Pleus.
Res., 5125 S. Apopka-Vineland Rd., 32819. Tel: 407-876-2211; Fax: 407-876-1167. [JC]
School—5129 S. Apopka-Vineland Rd., 32819. Tel: 407-876-9344; Fax: 407-876-8775. Sr. Dorothy Sayers, M.P.F., Prin.
Sisters 2; Lay Teachers 30; Students 645.
Catechesis/Religious Programs—Tel: 407-876-6331; Fax: 407-876-8775.
Students 1,040.

6—ST. ANDREW (1957), Revs. Ben Berinti, C.PP.S.; Sante Reale, C.PP.S.; Deacons James M. Flynn; Jose Cruz; Rafael Hernandez.
Res., 801 Hastings, 32808. Tel: 407-293-0730; Fax: 407-293-0739.
School—Tel: 407-295-4230; Fax: 407-290-0959.
Lay Teachers 25; Students 488.
Catechesis/Religious Programs—Students 223.

7—ST. CHARLES BORROMEO (1954) (English-Vietnamese), Revs. Thomas Barrett; J. P. Morgan; Joseph Dung Van Bui; Deacons Richard Rupp; James Smith.
Res., 4001 Edgewater Dr., 32804. Tel: 407-293-9556; Fax: 407-293-9213.
School—Tel: 407-293-7691; Fax: 407-295-9839.
Lay Teachers 30; Students 595.
Preschool—Tel: 407-295-7041.
Lay Teachers 2; Students 40.
Catechesis/Religious Programs—Tel: 407-297-0284.
Students 92.

8—ST. ISAAC JOGUES (1987), Revs. Robert Markunas; Phillip Nunez, III; Deacons Robert Kloznick; Orlando Lendoiro; Angel Pacheco.
Mailing Address: 4301 S. Chickasaw Tr., 32829. Tel: 407-249-0906; Fax: 407-273-3236.
Catechesis/Religious Programs—Students 690.

9—ST. JOHN VIANNEY (1959), Revs. Paul J. Henry; Bernard Byrne; Vidal Arboleda, (Retired); Miguel Gonzalez; Deacons Miguel Beltran; Kevin Mills; Tom Tagye, Dir. Ministry to the Sick & Plant Mgr.
Res., 6200 S. Orange Blossom Tr., 32809. Tel: 407-855-5391; Fax: 407-859-3631.
School—Tel: 407-855-4660; Fax: 407-857-7932. Sr. Elizabeth Murphy, Prin.
Sisters of St. Francis of Philadelphia 2; Lay Teachers 31; Students 703.
Catechesis/Religious Programs—Terri Tagye, D.R.E.
Students 474.

10—ST. JOSEPH (1962) (Polish-Filipino), Revs. Robert W. Brown; Larry Lossing; Joseph Piatek.
Res., 1501 N. Alafaya Tr., 32828. Tel: 407-275-0841.
Catechesis/Religious Programs—Tel: 407-282-7784.
Students 575.

OUTSIDE THE CITY OF ORLANDO

Altamonte Springs, Seminole Co., St. Mary Magdalen (1959), Revs. Charles I. Mitchell; Edward J. Thompson; Pedro J. Zapata; Thomas Smith; Deacons Henry Libersat; Norm Kazyk; Jerry Kelly.
Res., 861 Maitland Ave., 32701. Tel: 407-831-1212; Fax: 407-831-1560.
School—Tel: 407-339-7301; Fax: 407-339-9556.
Sisters 3; Lay Teachers 28; Students 534.
Catechesis/Religious Programs—Tel: 407-834-2211.
Students 533.

Annunciation (1982), Revs. Patrick J. Caverly; Stephen D. Parkes; Charles J. Deeney, O.M.I.
Mailing Address: P.O. Box 915887, Longwood, 32791-5887. Tel: 407-869-9472; Fax: 407-869-4661.
Res., 1020 Montgomery Rd., 32714.
School—Annunciation Catholic Academy, (Grades K-8). Tel: 407-774-2801; Fax: 407-774-2826.
Lay Teachers 29; Students 523.
Catechesis/Religious Programs—Tel: 407-869-0934.
Students 1,064.

Apopka, Orange Co., St. Francis of Assisi (1966), Revs. Clyde A. Bonar; Jose Bautista; Deacons Heriberto Santana; Laurence Herbert.
Res., 834 S. Orange Blossom Trail, 32703-6560. Tel: 407-886-4602; Fax: 407-886-9758.
Catechesis/Religious Programs—Students 378.

Barefoot Bay, Brevard Co., St. Luke (1986), Rev. Patrick J. O'Carroll; Deacon Roland Benoit.
Res., 5055 Micco Rd., 32976. Tel: 561-664-9310; Fax: 561-664-3374. [JC]
Catechesis/Religious Programs—Students 39.

Bartow, Polk Co., St. Thomas Aquinas (1956), Rev. Domingo Gonzalez.
Res., 1305 E. Mann Rd., 33830. Tel: 863-533-4514; Fax: 863-533-5090.
Catechesis/Religious Programs—Tel: 863-533-4514.
Students 149.
Missions—Fort Meade, Polk Co., St. Elizabeth Ann Seton, 101 Edgewood, Fort Meade, 33841. Tel: 863-285-7390; Wahneta, Polk Co., Our Lady of Guadalupe, 2150 State Rd. 559, Wahneta, 33880. Tel: 863-299-3854; Fax: 863-299-8247. Rev. Norman Farland.

Belleview, Marion Co., St. Theresa (1951), Rev. James MacLoughlin.
Res., 11526 S.E. U.S. Hwy. 301, 34420-4430. Tel: 352-245-2458; Fax: 352-245-1521.
Catechesis/Religious Programs—Tel: 352-245-5300; Fax: 352-245-1521.
Students 128.

Bushnell, Sumter Co., St. Lawrence (1959), Rev. Fabian Sheganoski, T.O.R.
320 E. Dade Ave., 33513. Tel: 352-793-7788; Fax: 352-793-4787.
Res., 223 E. Vermont Ave., 33513. Tel: 352-793-4636.
Catechesis/Religious Programs—Deborah Gibbons Moran, D.R.E.
Students 65.
Mission—Wildwood, Sumter Co., St. Vincent de Paul Mission.

Candler, Marion Co., Immaculate Heart of Mary (1983), Deacon Lou Bonneau.
Mailing Address: P.O. Box 310, 32111. Tel: 904-687-4031; Fax: 904-687-1811.
Catechesis/Religious Programs—Tel: 904-687-8818.
Students 31.
Mission—Citra, Marion Co., Christ the King.

Casselberry, Seminole Co., St. Augustine (1969), Revs. Michael J. Hughes, O.S.A.; John R. Flynn, O.S.A.; James R. Keating, O.S.A.
Res., 375 N. Sunset Dr., 32707. Tel: 407-695-3262; Fax: 407-699-8998.
Catechesis/Religious Programs—Students 322.

Clermont, Lake Co., Blessed Sacrament (1961), Rev. Andrew Wawrzycki; Deacons Paul Schneider; Rafael Gonzalez.
Res., 720 12th St., 34711. Tel: 352-394-3562; Fax: 352-394-3562.
Catechesis/Religious Programs—Tel: 352-394-1097.
Students 491.

Cocoa, Brevard Co., Blessed Sacrament (1967), Rev. Edmund S. Czarnecki; Deacon Richard J. Basso.
Mailing Address: P.O. Box 40, Sharpes, 32959.
Office: 5135 U.S. No. 1 N., 32927. Tel: 321-632-6333; Fax: 321-631-2560.
Catechesis/Religious Programs—Students 259.

Cocoa Beach, Brevard Co., Church of Our Saviour (1956), Rev. Eamon Tobin.
Res., 5301 N. Atlantic Ave., 32931. Tel: 321-783-4554; Fax: 321-868-6743.
School—Tel: 321-783-2330; Fax: 321-784-6330.
Lay Teachers 15; Students 268.
Catechesis/Religious Programs—Students 235.

Daytona Beach, Volusia Co., St. Paul's (1881), Revs. Robert E. Webster; Peter A. Sagorski; Jose Munoz; Deacon Robert Landers.
Res., 317 Mullally St., P.O. Box 646, 32115. Tel: 904-252-5422; Fax: 904-252-1936.
School—Tel: 904-252-7915; Fax: 904-238-7903.
Lay Teachers 17; Students 366.
Catechesis/Religious Programs—Students 80.

Our Lady of Lourdes (1953), Rev. Philip J. Egitto.
Res., 201 University Blvd., 32118. Tel: 904-255-0433; Fax: 904-238-1175.
School—Tel: 904-252-0391.
Lay Teachers 17; Students 282.
Catechesis/Religious Programs—Students 110.

DeBary, Volusia Co., St. Ann's (1959), Rev. Paige A. Blakely; Deacon William Cavins.
Office: 26 Dogwood Tr., P.O. Box 530218, 32753. Tel: 407-668-8270; Fax: 407-668-8471.
Res., 10 Larkspur Ln., 32713.
Catechesis/Religious Programs—Students 311.

De Land, Volusia Co., St. Peter's (1883), Revs. William Gohring; Ronald Oser; R. Alfredo Ortiz; Deacons Chester DeMarsh; Michael Alverez; Robert LaPlante; Gerard Smith; Robert Kinsey; Edward Rinderle; Wilfred Steinmetz; Ronald Keehner.
Mailing Address: P.O. Box 3700, 32721. Tel: 904-822-6000; Fax: 904-822-6034.
Res., 359 W. New York Ave., 32720.
School—Tel: 904-822-6010; Fax: 904-822-6013. Mrs. Joan Kinsey, Prin.
Lay Teachers 18; Students 297.
Catechesis/Religious Programs—Students 352.
Mission—Barberville, Volusia Co., San Jose Mission, 165 Emporia Rd., Barberville, 32005. Tel: 904-749-9372.

Deltona, Volusia Co., Our Lady of the Lakes (1970), Revs. Edward J. McCarthy; Ralph I. DuWell; Deacons Hervey Mondor; Ray Doyle; Bruno Wiencek; Dan Feinbaum; Gilberto Perez; Ricardo Gonzalez.
Res., 1310 Maximilian St., 32725. Tel: 407-574-2131; Fax: 407-860-0074.
Catechesis/Religious Programs—Tel: 407-574-4620.
Students 610.

St. Clare (1989), Rev. Christopher A. Hoffmann; Deacons Joseph Robert; Gilberto Torres.
Res., 2961 Day Rd., 32738. Tel: 904-789-9990; Fax: 904-789-2430.
Catechesis/Religious Programs—Students 200.

Dunnellon, Marion Co., St. John the Baptist (1976), Rev. Donald G. Mainardi; Deacon Fred Crawford, Jr.
Res., U.S. 41 N., P.O. Box 310, 34430. Tel: 352-489-3166; Fax: 352-489-3156.
Catechesis/Religious Programs—Students 108.

Eustis, Lake Co., St. Mary of the Lakes (1912), Revs. Manuel A. Fernandez; Anthony Farrell; Deacons Louis Klein; Francis McDonald.
Res., 218 Ocklawaha Ave., 32726-4802. Tel: 352-483-3500; Fax: 352-483-1370.
Catechesis/Religious Programs—Students 362.

Haines City, Polk Co., St. Ann (1969). (Formerly Transfiguration). Revs. Andrew O'Reilly, C.PP.S.; Frank Buck.
Res., 1311 E. Robinson Dr., P.O. Box 1285, 33845. Tel: 863-422-4370; Fax: 863-421-2522. [JC]
Catechesis/Religious Programs—Tel: 863-422-7743. Patricia Brabson, D.R.E.
Students 440.

Indialantic, Brevard Co., Holy Name of Jesus (1959), Revs. David Page; Thomas Connery; Raymond Hughes, C.R.; Deacons Charles Foy; Joseph Richiuso.
Res., 3050 Hwy. A1A, 32903. Tel: 321-773-2783; Fax: 321-777-0929.
School—(Grades K-8). Tel: 321-773-1630; Fax: 321-773-7148.
Lay Teachers 26; Students 445.
Catechesis/Religious Programs—Tel: 321-773-3905.
Students 782.

Kissimmee, Osceola Co., Holy Redeemer (1917) (Spanish), Revs. John McCormick; Pedro (Peter) Puntal; Rafael Villegas.
Res., 1603 N. Thacker Ave., 34741. Tel: 407-847-2500; 407-846-3700; Fax: 407-847-9687.
School—(1993) (Grades PreK-8) 1800 W. Columbia Ave., 34741. Tel: 407-870-9055; Fax: 407-870-2214. Maureen Kane, Prin.
Sisters of St. Joseph 1; Lay Teachers 22; Students 426.
Catechesis/Religious Programs—Tel: 407-870-8196; Fax: 407-870-2214. Bro. James Needham, D.R.E.
Students 760.

St. Catherine of Siena, Rev. Vidal Martinez, O.S.M.
Office: 2750 Osceola Pkwy., 34745.
Res., 430 Otter Creek Dr. P.O. Box 450698, 34745-0698. Tel: 407-344-9607; Fax: 407-344-9160.

Lady Lake, Lake Co., St. Timothy (1985), Revs. Robert Fucheck; Louis J. Gonter; James Mulvaney; Deacons John Sullivan; Frederick Giel; Nicholas Deutsch.
1351 Paige Pl., 32159. Tel: 352-753-0989; Fax: 352-753-9602.
Catechesis/Religious Programs—Students 36.

Lakeland, Polk Co.,

1—CHURCH OF THE RESURRECTION, (1963), Revs. Matthew Mello; Andrew Mallick; Deacon Joseph Wortman.
Res., 3855 S. Florida Ave., 33813-1109. Tel: 863-646-3556; Fax: 863-644-8697.
Catechesis/Religious Programs—Tel: 863-644-0585.
Students 290.

2—ST. ANTHONY'S, (1982), Revs. Vianney Cunningham, T.O.R.; Roderick Soha, T.O.R.; Joseph M. Hayden; Deacon Frank F. Oettinger. In res., Rev. Killian Perry, T.O.R.
Res., 820 Marcum Rd., P.O. Box 90164, 33804-0164. Tel: 863-858-8047; Fax: 863-859-1036. [JC]
School—(Grades PreK-7) 820 Marcum Rd., 33809. Tel: 863-858-0671. Sr. Michael Patrick Koegel, O.S.F., Prin.
Sisters 3; Lay Teachers 11; Students 191.
Catechesis/Religious Programs—Tel: 863-858-8611.
Students 212.

3—ST. JOHN NEUMANN, (1988), Rev. Peter Uniowski.
Res., P.O. Box 1064, Mulberry, 33860-1064. Tel: 863-644-7201; Fax: 863-647-0888.
Church—501 E. Carter Rd., 33813. Tel: 863-647-3400. [JC]
Catechesis/Religious Programs—Tel: 863-607-9458.
Students 159.

4—ST. JOSEPH'S, (1898), Revs. John Caulfield; Robert Moses; Reynord Araya-Morales; Deacon Antonio Martinez.
Res., 210 W. Lemon St., P.O. Box 30, 33802. Tel: 863-682-0555; Fax: 863-686-9546.
School—Tel: 863-686-6415; Fax: 863-687-8074.
Sisters of Notre Dame 1; Lay Teachers 19; Students 330.
Catechesis/Religious Programs—Tel: 863-687-8873.
Students 306.

Lake Wales, Polk Co., Holy Spirit (1927), Revs. Frank Cerio; Felix Banos, Pastor Emeritus; Leo Dobo, (Retired); Deacons Donald E. Raymond; Robert Demming; John Avery.
Res., 644 S. 9th St., P.O. Box 232, 33853. Tel: 863-676-1556; Fax: 863-676-2962.
Catechesis/Religious Programs—Tel: 863-678-1083.
Students 287.

Leesburg, Lake Co., St. Paul's (1954), Revs. John C. Giel; Nicholas J. O'Brien; Deacon Lawrence Holder.
Res., 1330 Sunshine Ave., 34748. Tel: 352-787-6354; Fax: 352-787-5971.
School—Tel: 352-787-4657; Fax: 352-787-0324.
Lay Teachers 16; Students 202.
Catechesis/Religious Programs—Tel: 352-787-6354; Fax: 352-787-5971.
Students 166.

Longwood, Seminole Co., Church of the Nativity (1960), Revs. Kenneth R. Schnipke, C.PP.S.; Henry L. Frantz, C.PP.S.; Deacon Constantino Ferriola. In res., Rev. Norbert Adelman.
Res., 3255 N. County Rd. 427, 32750. Tel: 407-322-3961; Fax: 407-322-3981.
Catechesis/Religious Programs—Students 830.

Melbourne, Brevard Co., Our Lady of Lourdes (1931) (Spanish), Revs. William Hanley; Carlos Bedoya. In res., Rev. Stephen Baumann; Deacon Michael Biennas.
Res., 1626 Oak St., 32901-4517. Tel: 321-723-3636; Fax: 321-951-8029.
School—420 E. Fee Ave., 32901. Tel: 321-723-3631; Fax: 321-723-7408.
Lay Teachers 16; Students 223.
Catechesis/Religious Programs—Students 146.

Ascension (1959), Revs. Francis X.J. Smith; Anthony Quinlivan, C.Ss.R.; Deacons Michael McElwee; Sergio Colon.
Mailing Address: 2950 N. Harbor City Blvd., 32935-6259. Tel: 321-254-1595; Fax: 321-255-3490.
School—Tel: 321-254-5495; Fax: 321-259-0993.
Sisters of Mercy (Ardee, Ireland) 2; Lay Teachers 27; Students 613.
Catechesis/Religious Programs—Tel: 321-259-6693.
Students 682.

Melbourne Beach, Brevard Co., Immaculate Conception (1978), Rev. Joseph A. Nolan; Deacon Howard Pettengill, Jr.
Res., 3780 S. Hwy. A1A, 32951. Tel: 321-725-0552; Fax: 321-727-8218.
Catechesis/Religious Programs—Students 135.

Merritt Island, Brevard Co., Divine Mercy (1964), Revs. Michael A. Farrell; Colin Kidd, O.F.M., (Retired).
Res., 1940 N. Courtenay Pkwy., 32953. Tel: 321-452-5955; Fax: 321-455-2268.
School—Tel: 321-452-0263; Fax: 321-453-7573.
Sisters of Mercy (Galway) 2; Lay Teachers 17; Students 271.
Catechesis/Religious Programs—Students 248.
Convent—1930 N. Courtenay Pkwy., 32953. Tel: 321-452-1279.
Sisters 4.

Mims, Brevard Co., Holy Spirit (1967), Rev. Bill Zamborsky.
Office & Res.: 2399 Holder Rd., 32754-2103. Tel: 321-269-2282; Fax: 321-269-2252.
Catechesis/Religious Programs—Tel: 321-269-7785.
Students 205.

Mount Dora, Orange Co., St. Patrick's (1973) (Hispanic), Revs. Emile A. Gentile, T.O.R.; Christopher Panagoplos, T.O.R.; Hugo Londono; Deacon William Fisher.
Res., 6801 Old Hwy. 441 S., P.O. Box 211, 32756. Tel: 352-383-8556; Fax: 352-383-8443. [CEM]
Catechesis/Religious Programs—Students 152.

New Smyrna Beach, Volusia Co., Sacred Heart (1926), Revs. Michael L. Dillon, C.Ss.R.; John G. Barry, C.Ss.R.; Alvaro Riquelme, C.Ss.R.; John Cavanaugh, C.Ss.R.; David J. Sharrock, C.Ss.R.; Eugene Daigle, C.Ss.R.; Deacon Thomas Murray.
Res., 998 Father Donlan Dr., Box 729, 32170. Tel: 904-428-6426; Fax: 904-423-4088.
School—Tel: 904-428-4732; Fax: 904-428-4087.
Sisters of Notre Dame(Toledo) 3; Lay Teachers 19; Students 243.
Catechesis/Religious Programs—Tel: 904-427-8372; Fax: 904-428-4087. Blake Buruazos, D.R.E.
Students 212.
Mission—Edgewater, Volusia Co., St. Gerard, 3171 S. Ridgewood Ave., Edgewater, 32141. Tel: 904-428-6930.

Our Lady Star of the Sea (1973), Rev. Thomas J. Bergin; Deacon Paul Rock.
Res., 3837 Sandstone Ct., 32169. Tel: 904-427-4530; Fax: 904-423-6245.
Catechesis/Religious Programs—Tel: 904-423-6245.
Students 80.

Ocala, Marion Co.,

1—BLESSED TRINITY, (1922), Revs. Patrick J. Sheedy; Luis A. Barerra; Deacons James Schwartz; James Boerstler; Heriberto Berrios; Primitiuo Perez.
Res., 5 S.E. 17th St., 34471. Tel: 352-629-8092; Fax: 352-351-8872.
School—Tel: 352-622-5808; Fax: 352-622-1660.
Lay Teachers 45; Students 752.
Catechesis/Religious Programs—Students 537.

2—OUR LADY OF THE SPRINGS, (1982), Revs. William J. Neumann; Mark R. Wegg.
Office—4047 N.E. 21st St., 34470. Tel: 352-236-2230; Fax: 352-236-1475.
Catechesis/Religious Programs—Fran Lopez, D.R.E. (Grades K-8).
Students 105.
Missions—Ocala National Forest, Marion Co., St. Joseph of the Forest, 17301 E. Hwy. 40, Silver Springs, 34488. Tel: 352-625-4222; Fax: 352-625-4922; Astor, Lake Co., St. Hubert of the Forest, P.O. Box 715, Astor, 32102. Tel: 352-759-3983.

3—QUEEN OF PEACE, (1987), Rev. Patrick J. O'Doherty.
Res., 6455 S.W. State Rd. 200, 34476. Tel: 352-854-2181; Fax: 352-854-7840. [JC]
Catechesis/Religious Programs—Students 110.

4—St. Jude's Catholic Community, (1983), Rev. Anthony Palmese; Deacon Santos Santiago.
Church & Res.: 443 Marion Oaks Dr., 34473-3203. Tel: 352-347-0154; Fax: 352-347-5211.
Catechesis/Religious Programs—Students 89.

Ormond Beach, Volusia Co., St. Brendan (1960), Rev. John J. Ryan; Deacon John J. Mann.
Res., 1000 Ocean Shore Blvd., 32176. Tel: 904-441-1505; Fax: 904-441-0774.
School—Tel: 904-441-1331.
Lay Teachers 25; Students 198.
Catechesis/Religious Programs—Students 125.

Prince of Peace (1966), Revs. Thomas P. McMackin; Timothy P. Daly; Deacon John J. Mann.
Res., 600 S. Nova Rd., 32174. Tel: 904-672-5272; Fax: 904-677-3224.
Catechesis/Religious Programs—Students 460.

Palm Bay, Brevard Co., Our Lady of Grace (1989), Rev. Leo Hodges; Deacons Richard C. Shaw; Francis Falotico; William T. Wanca, Sr.
Church & Mailing Address: 300 Malabar Rd. S.E., 32907-3005. Tel: 321-725-3066; Fax: 321-725-9534.
Res., 949 Haas St., 32907. Tel: 321-786-8742.
Catechesis/Religious Programs—Students 400.

St. Joseph (1914), Revs. Robert J. Hoeffner; Chau Nguyen; Deacon Alfred P. Somma.
Res., 5330 Babcock St. N.E., P.O. Box 060507, 32906. Tel: 321-727-1565; Fax: 321-676-2579. [CEM]
School—Tel: 321-723-8866; Fax: 321-727-1181.
Lay Teachers 25; Students 428.
Catechesis/Religious Programs—Students 250.

Poinciana, Kissimmee Co., St. Rose of Lima (1994), Rev. Fernando Gil.
Res., 140 Pompei Dr., 34758. Tel: 407-932-5004; Fax: 407-932-0407.
Catechesis/Religious Programs—Students 130.

Port Orange, Volusia Co., Epiphany (1962), Rev. Paul T. Kamide. In res., Rev. Peter Mitchell.
Res., 201 Lafayette St., 32127. Tel: 904-767-6111; Fax: 904-767-0017.
Catechesis/Religious Programs—Students 235.

Our Lady of Hope (1981), Rev. Raymond J. O'Leary.
Res., P.O. Box 290216, 32129. Tel: 904-788-6144; Fax: 904-761-8840.
Catechesis/Religious Programs—Tel: 904-788-6747.
Students 423.

Rockledge, Brevard Co., St. Mary's (1917), Rev. Nicholas King; Rev. Msgr. Terence J. Farrelly, Pastor Emeritus; Rev. Robert Mitchell.
Mailing Address: 75 Barton Ave., 32955. Tel: 321-636-6834; Fax: 321-632-4301. [JC]
School—Tel: 321-636-4208; Fax: 321-636-0591.
Sisters of Mercy (Limerick) 4; Lay Teachers 21; Students 540.
Catechesis/Religious Programs—Tel: 321-633-9985.
Students 423.

St. Cloud, Osceola Co., St. Thomas Aquinas (1968), Revs. Fabian G. Gimeno; Kent Walker.
Res., 701 Brown Chapel Rd., P.O. Box 700368, 34770-0368. Tel: 407-957-4495; Fax: 407-957-1771.
Church—700 Brown Chapel Rd., 34769.
School—800 Brown Chapel Rd., 34769. Tel: 407-957-1772; Fax: 407-957-0131.
Lay Teachers 25; Students 370.
Catechesis/Religious Programs—Tel: 407-957-4057.
Students 350.

Sanford, Seminole Co., All Souls (1911), Revs. Richard W. Trout; Albert J. Fornace; Hugo Londono; Stephen McNicholas.
Res., 301 W. 8th St., Ste. A, 32771. Tel: 407-322-3795; Fax: 407-322-1131. [CEM]
School—Tel: 407-322-7090; Fax: 407-321-7255.
Lay Teachers 17; Students 315.
Catechesis/Religious Programs—Students 234.

Titusville, Brevard Co., St. Teresa (1958), Revs. John S. Murray; Charles Viviano; Deacons Donald Boland; Charles I. Robichaud.
Res., 203 Ojibway Ave., P.O. Box 1598, 32781-1598. Tel: 321-268-3441; Fax: 321-268-3270.
School—Tel: 321-267-1643; Fax: 321-268-5124.
Sisters of Mercy (Gort, Ireland) 3; Lay Teachers 11; Students 344.
Catechesis/Religious Programs—Tel: 321-268-0440.
Students 270.
Convent—3380 Muirfield Dr., 32780. Tel: 321-267-1610; Fax: 321-267-1610.
Sisters 2.

Winter Garden, Orange Co., Resurrection (1967), Rev. John J. Franck, C.PP.S.
Church & Mailing Address: P.O. Box 771257, 34777. Tel: 407-656-3113; Fax: 407-654-4935.
Res., 358 Floral Dr., 34787.
Catechesis/Religious Programs—Students 370.

Winter Haven, Polk Co., St. Joseph's (1923), Revs. Anthony Bluett; Joseph Pinchock; Deacon Nuoc Van Dang.
Res., 532 Ave. M N.W., 33881. Tel: 863-294-3144; Fax: 863-299-9709.
School—Tel: 863-293-3311; Fax: 863-299-7894.
Sisters of Notre Dame, Chardon, Ohio Province 1; Lay Teachers 26; Students 492.
Catechesis/Religious Programs—Tel: 863-299-9709.
Students 226.

St. Matthew (1973), Rev. Fred R. Ruse.
Church & Mailing Address: 1991 Overlook Dr., 33884. Tel: 863-324-3040.
Res., 365 Pasco Ct., 33884. Tel: 863-324-0357; Fax: 863-324-9181.
Catechesis/Religious Programs—Tel: 863-324-3559.
Students 225.

Winter Park, Orange Co., St. Margaret Mary (1947), Revs. Richard Walsh; Michael E. Giglio; David Vivero, Jr.; Deacons Jack Timmes; Nemsy Gubatan; Ralph Eckoff.
Res., 526 N. Park Ave., 32789. Tel: 407-647-3392; Fax: 407-647-4492.
School—Tel: 407-644-7537; Fax: 407-644-7357.
Lay Teachers 30; Students 545.
Catechesis/Religious Programs—Tel: 407-647-5171; Fax: 407-647-4492.
Students 670.

Saints Peter and Paul, Seminole Co., (1967), Revs. Sean K. Cooney; David Scotchie; Deacons Al Castellana; James Campbell; Donald Warner; Jerry Vaughan.
Res., 5300 Old Howell Branch Rd., 32792. Tel: 407-657-6114; Fax: 407-657-9375.
Catechesis/Religious Programs—Tel: 407-657-9530; Fax: 407-657-9530.
Students 898.

Winter Springs, Seminole Co., St. Stephen (1985), Rev. John J. Bluett.
Res., 575 Tuskawilla Rd., 32708. Tel: 407-699-5683; Fax: 407-699-8408.
Catechesis/Religious Programs—Students 1900.

Shrines

1—Mary Queen of the Universe Shrine (1986), Revs. F. Joseph Harte; Barry Dowd; Fortune Frenoy, S.M.; William M. Boyle; Sr. Ita Hickey, O.S.C.
Res., 8300 Vineland Ave., 32821. Tel: 407-239-6600; Fax: 407-239-1362.

Special Assignment:
Reverend Fathers—
Barrett, Thomas, Office of Cemeteries & Office of Vocations
Connolly, Matthew J., Judicial Vicar
Gentile, Emile A., T.O.R., Vicar for Clergy
Lossing, Larry, Office of Ecumenism
Markunas, Robert, Hispanic & Farmworker Ministry
Walsh, Richard, Priests' Continuing Education
Webster, Robert E., Office of Liturgy

On Duty Outside the Diocese:
Reverend Fathers—
Bastos, Luiz C., Palm Beach
Henry, Peter, Switzerland
Kandel, Timothy, Miami
Mueller, Michael, U.S. Military
Olds, Steven, St. Vincent de Paul Seminary, Boynton Beach, FL
Stahl, Allen, U.S. Military
Traupman, Robert, Maryland

Sabbatical:
Reverend Fathers—
Bendixen, Arthur, Inactive
Cleare, Rudi, On Leave
Collins, Michael, Inactive
Coyle, James, Inactive
Danen, Lyle, Inactive
Ewen, Kurt, Inactive
Finley, William, Inactive
Granahan, Gerard, Inactive
LaBo, Timothy P., Inactive
Uhran, Vernon, Inactive

Retired:
Reverend Monsignors—
Bartok, Charles, 3753 Grove Circle, Zellwood, FL 32798
Campagnone, Francis, 215 Cherry Wood Ln., Edgewater, FL 32132
Cannon, Thomas, St. Peter, P.O. Box 3700, DeLand, FL 32723-3700. Tel: 904-822-6000
Denehy, John, 460 Grant Ave., Satellite Beach, FL 32937. Tel: 321-773-5069
Farrelly, Terence J., 56 Barton Ave., Rockledge, FL 32955. Tel: 407-636-9099
Farris, Semaan, 604 Tupelo Dr., Melbourne, FL 32935. Tel: 407-255-2505
Reverend Fathers—
Angles, Sebastian, 2601 Muscatello St., Orlando, FL 32837. Tel: 407-851-1934
Arboleda, Vidal, St. John Vianney, 6200 S. Orange Blossom Tr., Orlando, FL 32809. Tel: 407-855-5391
Banos, Felix, P.O. Box 232, Lake Wales, FL 33859. Tel: 863-676-1556
Benitez, Eduardo, P.O. Box 1524, Davenport, FL 33837
Cosgrove, J. Kelly, 4182 Mount Vernon Ave., Titusville, FL 32780. Tel: 407-267-8601
Dobo, Leo, 1070 Tequesta Tr., Lake Wales, FL 33853. Tel: 863-769-1919
Donnelly, Brendan, P.O. Box 686, Southbury, CT 06488-0686. Tel: 203-264-5071
Donohue, Peter, C.S.C., Christopher Lodge, 323 Arthur Ave., Cocoa Beach, FL 32931. Tel: 407-799-8383
Edwards, James F., P.O. Box 2188, Ormond Beach, FL 32175. Tel: 904-258-5293
Fanning, Leo M., 14 Polar Bear Pk., Ormond Beach, FL 32174. Tel: 904-672-1725
Foley, William A., S.M., 31 Fillmore Ct., Satellite Beach, FL 32937. Tel: 407-773-7631
Freitas, Daniel, 4905 Buttonwood Dr., Melbourne, FL 32940. Tel: 407-242-7365
Garvy, John, Blue Ridge Apartments, 108 N. Blue Ridge Rd., Black Mountain, NC 28711
Gonter, Louis J., 9980 S.E. 161st. Pl., Summerfield, FL 32691. Tel: 352-347-7289
Goodman, Frank, 900 Mosley Rd., Lake Alfred, FL 33850
Grasso, Richard E., 415 N. Halifax Dr., Ormond Beach, FL 32176. Tel: 904-677-0188
Hamilton, Edward A., 1600 Hagy's Ford Rd. Apt. 4N, Penn Valley, FL 19072. Tel: 610-949-0443
Hannon, Michael, 5216 Karlsburg Pl., Palm Harbor, FL 34685. Tel: 813-934-2469
Hayden, Joseph Mark, 4747 Road 33 N., #354, Lakeland, FL 33805. Tel: 941-686-8046
Holland, Cajetan, C.S.C., 325 Arthur Ave., Cocoa Beach, FL 32931-4065
Jennings, Francis, C.SS.R., St. Alphonsus Villa, P.O. Box 548, New Smyrna Beach, FL 32170
Karwacki, Marion T., 236 Lake Ira Dr. W., Winter Haven, FL 33884. Tel: 941-324-1385
Kidd, Colin, O.F.M., Divine Mercy, 1940 N. Courtenay Pkwy., Merritt Island, FL 32953. Tel: 407-452-5955
Knoll, Mark, C.SS.R., P.O. Box 1529, New Smyrna Beach, FL 32170-1529. Tel: 904-427-3094
Lambour, Stephen, C.S.C., 325 Arthur Ave., Cocoa Beach, FL 32931-4065
Lochner, Robert J., C.S.C., Christopher Lodge, 323 Arthur Ave., Cocoa Beach, FL 32931. Tel: 407-799-8383
McNicholas, Stephen, 5 Brighton Ter., Cobh, County Cork Ireland. Tel: 011-353-21-814-783
Mena, Jose, 501 N. Ocean St., Apt. 1703, Jacksonville, FL 32202
Moreau, George, (Jan.-May), P.O. Box 07267, Fort Myers, FL 33919
Moser, Charles J., S.M.A., 165 Bonita St., Titusville, FL 32780. Tel: 407-267-6863
Mulvaney, James, St. Timothy, 1351 Paige Pl., Lady Lake, FL 32159. Tel: 352-753-0989
Nebus, Vincent, P.O. Box 060507, Palm Bay, FL 32906-0507
Nolin, Joseph A., 219 Essex Dr., Ormond Beach, FL 32176. Tel: 904-441-2055
O'Reilly, P. J., 2891 Nokomis Ave., Palm Bay, FL 32905. Tel: 407-724-6702
Pawlak, Edwin F., 2465 S. Washington Ave., Unit A106, Titusville, FL 32780. Tel: 407-269-6089
Power, Virgil, Sandy Oaks Park, 6760 N. Lecanto Hwy., Beverly Hills, FL 32665
Quinn, Peter, P.O. Box 7022, Daytona Beach, FL 32116
Redmond, Lawrence, P.O. Box 4159, St. Augustine, FL 32085
Rimshaw, Joseph J., S.S.J., 411 E. Lincoln Ave., Melbourne, FL 32901-4536. Tel: 407-723-1708
Ross, Kenneth, 62 Archer St., Yonkers, NY 10701-1540. Tel: 914-969-4360
Serraino, Frederick, C.S.C., Christopher Lodge, 325 Arthur Ave., Cocoa Beach, FL 32931. Tel: 407-783-6312
Sheedy, Val, Oceans 3, 3043 S. Atlantic Ave., Apt. 202, Daytona Beach, FL 32118
Shine, Sean, P.O. Box 495, Candler, FL 32111. Tel: 352-687-4282
Slafkosky, Andrew L., 610 Pine Rd., Silver Springs Shores, FL 34472. Tel: 352-687-8677
Smith, Thomas, 621 Swallow Dr., Casselberry, FL 32707. Tel: 407-695-1720
VanNufflen, Albert, C.I.C.M., Aliki Condominium, 2828 N. Atlantic Ave., #202, Daytona Beach, FL 32118. Tel: 904-672-9098

Wallace, Harry, 4031 Saxson Dr., New Smyrna Beach, FL 32169. Tel: 904-426-7808
Whipple, Donald W., C.S.C., Christopher Lodge, 323 Arthur Ave., Cocoa Beach, FL 32931. Tel: 407-799-8383
Zammit, Francis X., P.O. Box 291242, Port Orange, FL 32129. Tel: 904-761-1388

Permanent Deacons:
Agers, Allen, (Retired), Holy Spirit, Mims
Almodovar, Ismael, Resurrection, Winter Garden
Alvarez, Jose M., St. Peter, DeLand
Barbieri, Robert, Inactive
Basso, Richard, Blessed Sacrament, Sharpes
Beltran, Miguel, St. John Vianney, Orlando
Berrios, Heriberto, Blessed Trinity, Ocala
Biennas, Michael, Our Lady of Lourdes, Melbourne
Boerstler, James, Blessed Trinity, Ocala
Boland, Donald, St. Teresa, Titusville
Bonneau, Louis, Immaculate Heart of Mary, Candler
Campbell, James, Sts. Peter & Paul, Winter Park
Casares, Gabriel, St. Catherine of Siena, Kissimmee
Castellana, Al, Sts. Peter & Paul, Winter Park
Cavins, William, St. Ann, DeBary
Collier, John, Unassigned
Colon, Hector, St. Ann, Haines City
Colon, Sergio, Ascension, Melbourne
Cooley, Benjamin, St. Matthew, Winter Haven
Crawford, Fred J., Jr., St. John the Baptist, Dunnellon
Crotty, John, St. Joseph, Orlando
Cruz, Jose F., St. Andrew, Orlando
Dang, Nuoc Van, St. Joseph, Winter Haven
Decatrel, Leon, St. Joseph, Orlando
DeMarsh, Chester, Prince of Peace, Ormond Beach
Demming, Robert, Holy Spirit, Lake Wales
Desjardins, Roland, On Duty Outside the Diocese
Deutsch, Nicholas, (Retired)
Diaz, Celso, Holy Cross, Orlando
Diaz, Frank, Resurrection, Winter Garden
Doyle, Raymond, (Retired), Our Lady of the Lakes, Deltona
Dwyer, Bruce, Holy Spirit, Mims
Falatico, Francis E., Our Lady of Grace, Palm Bay
Feinbaum, Daniel, Our Lady of the Lakes, Deltona
Ferriola, Constantino, Jr., Nativity, Longwood
Fisher, William, Jr., St. Patrick, Mount Dora
Flynn, James, St. Andrew, Orlando
Foy, Les, Holy Name of Jesus, Indialantic
Garcia, Jose M., Good Shepherd, Orlando
Gonzalez, Julio, Resurrection, Winter Garden
Gonzalez, Rafael, Blessed Sacrament, Clermont
Gonzalez, Ricardo, Our Lady of the Lakes, Deltona
Gubatan, Nemsy, St. Margaret Mary, Winter Park
Hamilton, James, Our Lady of the Springs, Ocala
Henry, Vernon, Our Saviour, Cocoa Beach
Herbert, Larry, St. Francis of Assisi, Apopka
Hernandez, Rafael, St. Andrew, Orlando
Hindes, John T., St. Joseph of the Forest Mission, Silver Springs
Holder, Lawrence, St. Paul, Leesburg
Kazyk, Norm, St. Mary Magdalen, Altamonte Springs
Keehner, Ron, St. Peter, DeLand
Kelly, Gerard, St. Mary Magdalen, Altamonte Springs
Kinsey, Robert, St. Peter, DeLand
Klein, Louis, St. Mary of the Lakes, Eustis
Kloznick, Robert, St. Isaac Jogues, Orlando
Lammers, Jack, St. Joseph of the Forest Mission, Silver Springs
Landers, Robert, St. Paul, Daytona Beach
LaPlante, Robert, St. Peter, DeLand
Lendoiro, Orlando, St. Issac Jogues, Orlando
Libersat, Henry, St. Mary Magdalen, Altamonte Springs
Maldonado, Eliezer, St. Catherine of Siena, Kissimmee
Mallon, Charles A., Holy Family, Orlando
Mann, John J., Prince of Peace, Ormond Beach
Martin, Jack, Holy Cross, Orlando
Martinez, Antonio, St. Joseph, Lakeland
McDonald, Francis L., St. Mary of the Lakes, Eustis
McElwee, Michael, Ascension, Melbourne
McMahon, George, On Duty Outside the Diocese
Messinger, George, Epiphany, Port Orange
Mills, Kevin, St. John Vianney, Orlando
Monat, Noe, St. Ann, Haines City
Mondor, Hervey, Our Lady of the Lakes, Deltona
Morales, Julio, On Duty Outside the Diocese
Morales, Ramon, Holy Cross, Orlando
Morales, Rene, St. Catherine of Siena Church, Kissimmee
Murello, Andy, St. Mary, Rockledge
Murray, Thomas, Sacred Heart, New Smyrna Beach
Neris, Susano, Blessed Trinity, Orlando
Ocasio, Roberto, St. Catherine of Siena, Kissimmee
Oettinger, Frank, St. Anthony, Lakeland
Otradovec, Byron, St. Lawrence, Bushnell
Pacheco, Angel, St. Isaac Jogues, Orlando
Pellosie, John, (Retired)
Perez, Gilberto, Our Lady of the Lakes, Deltona
Pettengill, Howard, Jr., Immaculate Conception, Melbourne Beach
Phelps, Wayne, Good Shepherd, Orlando
Pleus, Robert, Holy Family, Orlando
Ramos, Jose Vidal, St. Rose of Lima, Poinciana
Ramos, Pedro, St. Rose of Lima, Poinciana
Raymond, Donald, Holy Spirit, Lake Wales
Reilly, Eugene, Our Savior, Cocoa
Richiuso, Joseph, Holy Name of Jesus, Indialantic
Rinderle, Edward, St. Peter, DeLand
Robert, Joseph, St. Clare, Deltona
Robichaud, Charles, St. Teresa, Titusville
Rock, Paul J., Our Lady Star of the Sea, New Smyrna Beach
Rupp, Richard T., St. Charles Borromeo, Orlando
Ryan, Sam, St. James, Orlando
Sanborn, Philip, St. Theresa, Belleview
Santana, Heriberto, St. Francis of Assisi, Apopka
Santiago, Santos, St. Jude, Ocala
Schneider, Paul A., Blessed Sacrament, Clermont
Schwartz, James, Blessed Trinity, Ocala
Seidel, James B., Holy Name of Jesus, Indialantic
Shaw, Richard, Our Lady of Grace, Palm Bay
Simpson, Bruce, St. James, Orlando
Smith, Gerard F., St. Peter, DeLand
Smith, James, St. Charles Borromeo, Orlando
Somma, Alfred P., St. Joseph, Palm Bay
Steinmetz, Wilfred, St. Peter, DeLand
Sullivan, John, St. Timothy, Lady Lake
Swart, Homer, Epiphany, Port Orange
Tagye, Thomas, St. John Vianney, Orlando
Timmes, John, St. Margaret Mary, Winter Park
Timmis, Harold
Torres, Gilberto, St. Clare, Deltona
Vaughn, Jerry, Sts. Peter & Paul, Winter Park
Wanca, William T., Our Lady of Grace, Palm Bay
Warner, Donald, Sts. Peter & Paul, Winter Park
Wendel, David, St. John Neumann, Lakeland
Wiencek, Bruno, Our Lady of the Lakes, Deltona
Wortman, Joseph, Resurrection, Lakeland

INSTITUTIONS LOCATED IN THE DIOCESE

[A] HIGH SCHOOLS, DIOCESAN AND PAROCHIAL

ORLANDO. *Bishop Moore High School*, 3901 Edgewater Dr., 32804. Tel: 407-293-7561; Fax: 407-296-8135.
E-mail: halscottc@bishopmoore.org
Web site: www.bishopmoore.org
Rev. Thomas Barrett. Priests 1; Sisters 1; Lay Teachers 58; Students 1,190.

DAYTONA BEACH. *Father Lopez High School*, 960 Madison Ave., 32114. Tel: 904-253-5213; Fax: 904-252-6101.
E-mail: dgonsalves@fatherlopez.org
Web site: www.fatherlopez.org
Mr. David Gonsalves, Prin. Lay Teachers 35; Students 399.

LAKELAND. *Santa Fe Catholic High School*. (Grades 9-12), 3110 Highway 92 E., 33801. Tel: 863-665-4188; Fax: 863-665-4151.
E-mail: scarolann-sfhs@doschool.org
Sr. Carol Ann Ziecina, Prin. Sisters 2; Lay Teachers 21; Students 183.

MELBOURNE. *Central Catholic High School*, 100 E. Florida Ave., 32901. Tel: 407-727-0793; Fax: 407-727-1134.
E-mail: ManciniJ@melbournecc.org
Web site: melbournecc.org
Mr. Joe Mancini, Prin.; Rev. Stephen Bauman, School Pastor. Lay Teachers 41; Students 645.

OCALA. *Trinity Catholic High School*, 5 S.E. 17th St., 34471. Tel: 352-622-9025; Fax: 352-622-1660. Bro. Thomas Andrew Prendergrast, C.F.C., Prin.; Rev. Patrick J. Sheedy, School Pastor.

[B] SPECIAL SCHOOLS

ORLANDO. *Morning Star School*, 954 Leigh Ave., 32804-2299. Tel: 407-295-3077; Fax: 407-522-1700.
E-mail: mss954@aol.com
Sr. Elizabeth Marie Stoup, S.S.J., Prin. School for Exceptional Children. Sisters of St. Joseph of St. Augustine 2; Lay Teachers 7; Students 60.

[C] HOUSING ACCOMMODATIONS FOR THE ELDERLY

ORLANDO. *Bishop Grady Villas*, 954 Leigh Ave., 32804-2299
For a complete listing, refer to the Special Care Facilities section.

Monsignor Bishop Manor Apts., Inc., 824 Borders Cir., 32808. Tel: 407-293-3339; Fax: 407-293-0085.
E-mail: BishopMano@aol.com
Web site: www.orlandodawn.com/monsignorBishopManor
For a complete listing, refer to the Special Care Facilities section.

DAYTONA BEACH. *Casa San Pablo*, 401 N. Ridgewood Ave., 32114. Tel: 904-253-2828; Fax: 904-253-0842.
E-mail: bobbie0110@aol.com
For a complete listing, refer to the Special Care Facilities section.

MELBOURNE. *Ascension Manor*, 2960 Pineapple Ave., 32935. Tel: 321-757-9828; Fax: 321-752-9437.
E-mail: manorgang@aol.com
For a complete listing, refer to the Special Care Facilities section.

OCALA. *Trinity Villas I, Inc.*, 3728 N.E. 8th Pl., 34470-1093. Tel: 352-694-5507; Fax: 352-694-1434
For a complete listing, refer to the Special Care Facilities section.

Trinity Villas II, Inc., 3728 N.E. 8th Pl., 34470-1093. Tel: 352-694-5507; Fax: 352-694-7434
For a complete listing, refer to the Special Care Facilities section.

ORMOND BEACH. *Prince of Peace Housing, Inc. dba Prince of Peace Villas*, 664 S. Nova Rd., 32174. Tel: 904-673-5080; Fax: 904-673-2008.
E-mail: popvillas@aol.com
For a complete listing, refer to the Special Care Facilities section.

PORT ORANGE. *Epiphany Manor*, 4792 S. Ridgewood Ave., 32127. Tel: 904-767-2556; Fax: 904-761-0490
For a complete listing, refer to the Special Care Facilities section.

WINTER HAVEN. *Episcopal Catholic Apartments*, 500 Ave. L, N.W., 33881. Tel: 863-299-4481; Fax: 863-299-5719.
E-mail: BethW0345@aol.com
For a complete listing, refer to the Special Care Facilities section.

[D] RETREAT CENTERS

WINTER PARK. *San Pedro Spiritual Development Center*, 2400 Dike Rd., 32792. Tel: 407-671-6322; Fax: 407-671-3992.
E-mail: spcdove@aol.com
Web site: www.orlandodiocese.org
Revs. Carl Vacek, T.O.R., Dir.; Giles Schinelli, T.O.R.; Bro. David Liedl, T.O.R. In res. Rev. Robert J. D'Aversa, T.O.R. Total Staff 3; Total in Residence 4.

[E] NEWMAN CENTERS OF CENTRAL FLORIDA

ORLANDO. *Embry-Riddle Aeronautical University*. Office of the Chaplain, 600 S. Clyde Morris Blvd., Daytona Beach, 32114-3900. Tel: 904-226-6581.
E-mail: dalyt@cts.db.erau.edu
Rev. Timothy P. Daly, University Chap. & Dir. Catholic Campus Ministry.

University of Central Florida Catholic Campus Ministry, SRC Room 154, UCF Box 163235, 32816-3235. Tel: 407-657-6114, Ext. 226.
E-mail: davsco@catholicweb.com
Web site: pegasus.cc.ucf.edu/~ccm
Rev. David Scotchie.

University of Central Florida Newman Center, UCF P.O. Box 163235, 32816-3235. Tel: 407-823-5337; Fax: 407-897-2146.
E-mail: djscotchie@aol.com
Web site: pegasus.cc.ucf.edu/~newman
Rev. David Scotchie.

DE LAND. *Stetson University Catholic Campus Ministry*, Newman House, 523 N. Amelia Ave., 32724. Tel: 904-822-8156.
E-mail: choffman@stetson.edu
Rev. Christopher A. Hoffmann; Deacon Edward Rinderle, Co-Dir. Total Staff 1.

LAKELAND. *Florida Southern College Newman Center*, c/o St. Anthony, P.O. Box 90164, 33804-0164. Tel: 941-858-8047; Fax: 941-859-1036. Revs. Vianney Cunningham, T.O.R.; Roderick Soha, T.O.R. Total Staff 2; Total in Residence 2.

MELBOURNE. *Florida Institute of Technology Campus Ministry*, 150 W. University Blvd., 32901-6988. Tel: 321-674-8045; Fax: 321-984-8461.
E-mail: dbailey@fit.edu
Web site: www.fit.edu
Rev. Douglas Bailey, S.D.S. Total Staff 2.

WINTER PARK. *Rollins College Campus Ministry*, c/o St. Margaret Mary, 526 Park Ave. N., 32789. Tel: 407-647-3392; Fax: 407-647-4492.
E-mail: frmichael@stmargaretmary.org
Web site: stmargaretmary.org
Rev. Michael E. Giglio.

[F] MONASTERIES AND RESIDENCES OF PRIESTS AND BROTHERS

ORLANDO. *Bethany House of Beutel*, 1600 Lakeside Dr., 32803-1508. Tel: 407-894-8175; Fax: 407-897-1133. Revs. Jordan K. Grimes, C.P., Supr.; Warren Womack, C.P.; Bro. Philip Frank, C.P. Prayer Center for Passionist Priests and Brothers.

COCOA BEACH. *Holy Cross Fathers, Eastern Priests Province*, 325 Arthur Ave., 32931-4065. Tel: 407-799-8383; Fax: 407-783-6312. Revs. Robert J. Brennan, C.S.C., Supr.; Stephen Lambour, C.S.C.; Robert J. Lochner, C.S.C.; Peter Donohue, C.S.C.; Cajetan Holland, C.S.C.; Donald W. Whipple, C.S.C.; Bros. Jerome Healey, C.S.C.; Herman Zaccarelli, C.S.C.; Gerard Suddick, C.S.C. Total Staff 2; Total in Residence 7.

KISSIMMEE. *Presentation Brothers*, 1602 Pettis Blvd., 34701. Tel: 407-846-2033; Fax: 407-846-7473. Bros. Francis Schafer, F.P.M., Region Leader; Jude Collins, F.P.M.

NEW SMYRNA BEACH. *Redemptorist Fathers of the Vice Province of Richmond*, 313 Hillman St., P.O. Box 1529, 32170. Tel: 904-427-3094; Fax: 904-423-1270.
E-mail: vprichmond@aol.com
Very Rev. Edward J. Gray, C.SS.R.; Bro. Thomas Kuhn, C.SS.R., Vice Prov. Procurator; Revs. George Kelly, C.SS.R.; Robert M. Pagliari, C.SS.R. Total Staff 4; Total in Residence 45.

St. Alphonsus Villa-Redemptorist Fathers and Brothers, 318 N. Riverside Dr., P.O. Box 548, 32170-0548. Tel: 904-428-6481. Revs. George Dorn, C.SS.R., Supr.; Donald Bolton, C.SS.R.; Walter Bueche, C.SS.R.; Joseph Gribbon, C.SS.R.; Francis Jennings, C.SS.R.; Leo Lanigan, C.SS.R.; James McGonagle, C.SS.R.; Jerome Murphy, C.SS.R.; Henry O'Toole, C.SS.R.; Francis Sands, C.SS.R.; Alfred Sieradski, C.SS.R.; Bro. Thomas Kuhn, C.SS.R. Total Staff 8; Total in Residence 12.

Villa Madonna, 4385 Saxon Ave., 32169. Tel: 904-427-4660. Rev. Patrick Seelman, T.O.R., Contact Person; Bro. Regis Leonard, T.O.R.

OCALA. *Congregation of Christian Brothers.* (Eastern U.S. American Province), 1384 S.E. 54th Pl., 34480. Tel: 352-622-1374. Bro. Thomas A. Prendergast, C.F.C., Contact Person.

WINTER PARK. *Franciscan Friars, T.O.R., Provincial Residence, San Pedro Friary*, 2400 Dike Rd., 32792-8118. Tel: 407-671-6322; Fax: 407-671-3992.
Friars in Residence: Revs. Robert J. D'Aversa, T.O.R.; Giles Schinelli, T.O.R.; Carl Vacek, T.O.R.; Bro. David Liedl, T.O.R. Total Staff 3; Total in Residence 4.

San Pedro Center, Third Order Regular of St. Francis, 2400 Dike Rd., 32792. Tel: 407-671-6322; Fax: 407-671-3992.
E-mail: spcdove@aol.com
Revs. Carl Vacek, T.O.R., Dir.; Robert J. D'Aversa, T.O.R.; Giles Schinelli, T.O.R.; Bros. Terence Thielen, T.O.R., Admin.; David Liedl, T.O.R. Total Staff 3; Total in Residence 4.

[G] MISCELLANEOUS

ORLANDO. *Good Shepherd Corporation of Orlando, Inc.*, 599 Bablonica Dr., 32807. Tel: 407-658-2909; Fax: 407-658-0005.
E-mail: gssodeanne70@yahoo.com
Sr. Mary Brigid Lawlor, Pres. Total Assisted 72; Total Staff 4.

GOLDENROD.
Catholic Volunteers in Florida, Inc., P.O. Box 702, 32733-0702. Tel: 407-331-6444; Fax: 407-331-6446.
E-mail: volunteer@cvif.org
Web site: www.cvif.org
National recruitment for statewide (FL) placement of full-time volunteers in one-year service assignments. Co-sponsored by Florida's bishops, Sisters of the Living Word, Sisters of St. Joseph of St. Augustine, FL, and New Hope Charities. The Episcopal Advisor is Most Reverend John J. Snyder of the Diocese of St. Augustine. Ella Kalenberg, Volunteer Coord.; Mr. Richard Galentino, Exec. Dir. Staff 2; Lay Volunteers 6.

WINTER GARDEN. *Sisters of St. Joseph's Architectural Stained Glass*, 930 Carter Rd., Ste. 212, 34787. Tel: 407-877-3220; Fax: 407-877-3220.
E-mail: liteart@aol.com
Owned and operated by the Sisters of St. Joseph of St. Augustine, FL.

RELIGIOUS INSTITUTES OF MEN REPRESENTED IN THE DIOCESE

For further details refer to the corresponding bracketed number in the Religious Institutes of Men or Women section.

[0140]—*Augustinians.*—O.S.A.
[]—*Congregation of Christian Brothers.* (Eastern U.S. American Province).—C.F.C.
[0610]—*Congregation of the Holy Cross (Southern Province).*—C.S.C.
[1000]—*Congregation of the Passion.*—C.P.
[]—*Congregation of the Resurrection.*—C.R.
[0520]—*Franciscan Fathers.*—O.F.M.
[]—*Legionaries of Christ.*—L.C.
[0760]—*Marist Fathers Society of Mary.*—S.M.
[0720]—*Missionaries of Our Lady of LaSalette.*—M.S.
[]—*Missionhurst Congregation of the Immaculate Heart of Mary.*—C.I.C.M.
[0910]—*Oblates of Mary Immaculate.*—O.M.I.
[]—*Presentation Brothers.*—F.P.M.
[1070]—*Redemptorist Fathers (Baltimore Province).*—C.SS.R.
[]—*St. Joseph Society of the Sacred Heart.*—S.S.J.
[1240]—*Servants of Mary (Servites).*—O.S.M.
[0110]—*Society of African Missions.*—S.M.A.
[1200]—*Society of the Divine Savior.*—S.D.S.
[1060]—*Society of the Precious Blood (Cincinnati Province).*—C.PP.S.
[0560]—*Third Order Regular of Saint Francis (Province of the Immaculate Conception).*—T.O.R.

RELIGIOUS INSTITUTES OF WOMEN REPRESENTED IN THE DIOCESE

[]—*Alianza in Jesus through Mary (Secular Institution).*—A.J.M.
[0230]—*Benedictine Sisters of Pontifical Jurisdiction.* (St. Petersburg).—O.S.B.
[]—*Congregation of the Sisters of the Holy Family.*—S.S.F.
[1070]—*Dominican Sisters.*—O.P.
[1180]—*Franciscan Sisters of Allegany, New York.*—O.S.F.
[2720]—*Mission Helpers of the Sacred Heart.*—M.H.S.H.
[2750]—*Missionary Sisters of the Immaculate Heart of Mary.*—I.C.M.
[3770]—*Order of St. Clare.*—O.S.C.
[3130]—*Our Lady of Victory Missionary Sisters.*—O.L.V.M.
[3320]—*Presentation Sisters of the Blessed Virgin Mary.*—P.B.V.M.
[2070]—*Religious of the Holy Union of the Sacred Hearts.*—S.U.S.C.
[3430]—*Religious Teachers Filippini.*—M.P.F.
[3590]—*Servants of Mary (Servite Sisters).*—O.S.M.
[]—*Sisters for Christian Community.*—S.F.C.C.
[0440]—*Sisters of Charity of Cincinnati, Ohio.*—S.C.
[0430]—*Sisters of Charity of the Blessed Virgin Mary.*—B.V.M.
[0990]—*Sisters of Divine Providence.*—C.D.P.
[2360]—*Sisters of Loretto at the Foot of the Cross.*—S.L.
[2640]—*Sisters of Mercy from Ireland.* (Meath Community).—R.S.M.
[2535]—*Sisters of Mercy from Ireland.* (Galway).—R.S.M.
[2523]—*Sisters of Mercy from Ireland.* (Longford).—R.S.M.
[2530]—*Sisters of Mercy from Ireland.* (Ardee-Dundalk).—R.S.M.
[2560]—*Sisters of Mercy from Ireland.* (Ennis).—R.S.M.
[2550]—*Sisters of Mercy from Ireland.* (Limerick).—R.S.M.
[2575]—*Sisters of Mercy of the Americas.*—R.S.M.
[2990]—*Sisters of Notre Dame.* (Chardon, OH).—S.N.D.
[3000]—*Sisters of Notre Dame de Namur.*—S.N.D.deN.
[1630]—*Sisters of St. Francis of Penance & Christian Charity.*—O.S.F.
[1650]—*Sisters of St. Francis of Philadelphia.*—O.S.F.
[]—*Sisters of St. Francis of Syracuse.*—O.S.F.
[1570]—*Sisters of St. Francis of the Holy Family.*—O.S.F.
[3840]—*Sisters of St. Joseph of Carondelet.* (St. Louis, MO).—C.S.J.
[3850]—*Sisters of St. Joseph of Chambery.*—C.S.J.
[3900]—*Sisters of St. Joseph of St. Augustine, Florida.*—S.S.J.
[1830]—*Sisters of the Good Shepherd.*—R.G.S.
[1990]—*Sisters of the Holy Names of Jesus and Mary.*—S.N.J.M.
[4110]—*Ursuline Nuns.*—O.S.U.

NECROLOGY

(No Deaths)

Diocese of Owensboro

(Dioecesis Owensburgensis)

Most Reverend

JOHN J. McRAITH, D.D.

Bishop of Owensboro; ordained February 21, 1960; appointed October 23, 1982; consecrated December 15, 1982. *Res., 501 W. Fifth St., Owensboro, KY, 42301. Address correspondence to: 600 Locust St., Owensboro, KY, 42301; Fax: 270-683-6883.*

CREATED DECEMBER 9, 1937.

ERECTED FEBRUARY 23, 1938.

Square Miles 12,502.

Comprises the following thirty-two Counties in the western part of the State of Kentucky: Allen, Ballard, Breckinridge, Butler, Caldwell, Calloway, Carlisle, Christian, Crittenden, Daviess, Edmonson, Fulton, Graves, Grayson, Hancock, Henderson, Hickman, Hopkins, Livingston, Logan, Lyon, McCracken, McLean, Marshall, Muhlenberg, Ohio, Simpson, Todd, Trigg, Union, Warren and Webster.

For legal titles of parishes and diocesan institutions, consult the Catholic Pastoral Center.

Catholic Pastoral Center: 600 Locust St., Owensboro, KY, 42301. Tel.: 270-683-1545; Fax: 270-683-6883.

Web site address: www.owensborodio.org

E-mail address: ja@cpc.brescia.edu

STATISTICAL OVERVIEW

Personnel	
Bishop	1
Priests: Diocesan Active in Diocese	63
Priests: Active Outside Diocese	4
Priests: Retired, Sick or Absent	16
Number of Diocesan Priests	83
Religious Priests in Diocese	20
Extern Priests in Diocese	2
Ordinations:	
Diocesan Priests	1
Religious Priests	5
Total Brothers	4
Total Sisters	226
Parishes	
Parishes	79
With Resident Pastor:	
Resident Diocesan Priests	47
Resident Religious Priests	5
Without Resident Pastor:	
Administered by Priests	27
Pastoral Centers	2
Professional Ministry Personnel:	
Brothers	3
Sisters	39
Lay Ministers	49
Welfare	
Catholic Hospitals	1
Total Assisted	300,000
Health Care Centers	2
Total Assisted	8,000
Homes for the Aged	2
Total Assisted	170
Day Care and Extended Day Care Centers	3
Total Assisted	209
Special Centers for Social Services	2
Total Assisted	16,000
Educational	
Diocesan Students in Other Seminaries	19
Total Seminarians	19
Colleges and Universities	1
Total Students	750
High Schools, Diocesan and Parish	3
Total Students	1,091
Elementary Schools, Diocesan and Parish	19
Total Students	4,122
Catechesis/Religious Education:	
High School Students	1,299
Elementary Students	2,941
Total Students Under Catholic Instruction	10,222
Teachers in the Diocese:	
Priests	6
Sisters	13
Lay Teachers	401
Vital Statistics	
Receptions into the Church:	
Infant Baptism Totals	1,008
Adult Baptism Totals	176
Received into Full Communion	263
First Communions	1,016
Confirmations	1,058
Marriages:	
Catholic	197
Interfaith	230
Total Marriages	427
Deaths	559
Total Catholic Population	51,152
Total Population	778,235

Former Bishops—Most Rev. FRANCIS R. COTTON, D.D., First Bishop of Owensboro; ord. June 17, 1920; appt. Dec. 16, 1937; cons. Feb. 24, 1938; died Sept. 25, 1960.—Most Rev. HENRY J. SOENNEKER, D.D., Second Bishop of Owensboro; ord. May 26, 1934; appt. March 10, 1961; cons. April 26, 1961; installed May 9, 1961; retired June 17, 1982; died Sept. 24, 1987.

Catholic Pastoral Center—600 Locust St., Owensboro, 42301. Tel: 270-683-1545; Fax: 270-683-6883. Refer all official business to this address.

Vicar General—Rev. JOSEPH M. MILLS, J.C.L., *Res., Mount St. Joseph, 8001 Cummings Rd., Maple Mount, 42356.* Tel: 270-229-0125.

Chancellor—Sr. JOSEPH ANGELA BOONE, O.S.U.

Archivist—Sr. EMMA CECILIA BUSAM, O.S.U.

Diocesan Tribunal—

Judicial Vicar—Rev. J. PATRICK REYNOLDS, J.C.L.

Adjutant Judicial Vicar—Vacant.

Defenders of the Bond—Revs. JOSEPH M. MILLS, J.C.L.; GREGORY G. TRAWICK, J.C.L.

Judges—Revs. LEONARD ALVEY, Ed.S.; J. PATRICK REYNOLDS, J.C.L.; JOHN VAUGHAN, J.C.D.; RICHARD MEREDITH, Ph.D.

Advocates—Priests and pastoral ministers of the diocese.

Case Promoters—Sr. VIVIAN MARIE BOWLES, O.S.U.; Mrs. DONNA MURPHY.

Notaries—Mrs. MARY ANN KURZ; Ms. LOUANNE GELARDEN.

Clinical Psychologist—PATRICIA G. CAMPBELL; SHANNON SULLIVAN WRIGHT.

Diocesan Boards and Councils

Diocesan Pastoral Council—Sr. AUDREY RECKTENWALD, M.S.B.T; Bro. KEN GRONDIN, C.F.C.; Rev. JOHN VAUGHAN; Mr. CHARLES RUCKS; Mr. JIM SHANAHAN; Mr. DAN RALPH; Ms. DEBBIE RALPH; Mr. TOM HAYDEN; Mr. PERRY ELDER; Ms. SHARON EBELHAR; Ms. SUE GRAY; Ms. HELEN WILLETT; Ms. BARBARA PENNER; Ms. BETTY ELDER; Mr. JIM SCOTT; Mr. PAUL BACHI; Ms. CHARLOTTE HEDGES; Ms. MARILYN CHANDLER; Mr. JOE HANCOCK; Mr. STEVE SHOULTA; Mr. BILL CLARK.

Consultors—Revs. BRIAN ROBY; DARRELL VENTERS; JERRY RINEY; TIMOTHY SWEENEY, O.S.B.; Rev. Msgr. BERNARD POWERS; Rev. JOSEPH V. RHODES.

Deans—Rev. DENNIS HOLLY, G.H.M., Bowling Green; Rev. J. EDWARD BRADLEY, Central; Rev. TERRY DEVINE, Eastern; Rev. DELMA CLEMONS, Fancy Farm; Rev. JERRY BAKER, Hopkinsville; Rev. MAURICE TIELL, The Lakes; Rev. JOHN VAUGHAN, Owensboro; Rev. HENRY WIEDER, Paducah.

Priests' Council—Revs. JOSEPH M. MILLS; MAURICE TIELL; DENNIS HOLLY, G.H.M.; TERRY DEVINE; HENRY WIEDER; DELMA CLEMONS; JERRY BAKER; JOHN VAUGHAN; J. EDWARD BRADLEY; BRIAN ROBY; DARRELL VENTERS; JERRY RINEY; TIMOTHY SWEENEY, O.S.B.; Rev. Msgr. BERNARD POWERS; Rev. JOSEPH V. RHODES.

Council of Religious—Sr. MARY LOUISE ALVEY, O.S.U.; Sr. MARTHA SCHULER, G.H.M.S.; Sr. MARY MATTHIAS WARD, O.S.U.; Sr. DIANA NEWTON, R.S.M.; Sr. RITA LECHNER, S.P.; Sr. MARCAN FREKING, O.S.F.; Sr. AUDREY RECKTENWALD, M.S.B.T.; Bro. KEN GRONDIN, C.F.C.

Pastoral Office for Administration—Sr. JOSEPH ANGELA BOONE, O.S.U., Dir. AL THOMPSON, Assoc. Dir.

Pastoral Office for Stewardship—Mr. TOM LILLY, Dir.

Committee for Administration—Mr. HOMER BARTON; Ms. JANET BERRY; Ms. DONNA SAUER; Sr. BARBARA JEAN HEAD, A.S.C.; Mr. CHARLES KAMUF; Mr. JOSEPH HANCOCK; Mr. BOB OGLE; Revs. BRAD WHISTLE; JOE MILLS; MARTY HAYES; Mr. MIKE THOMPSON.

Pastoral Office for Education—

Superintendent of Schools—Mr. JOSEPH O'BRYAN.

Director of Office for Religious Education—Ms. PATTY BLAIR.

Committee for Education—Revs. LEONARD ALVEY; BRIAN JOHNSON; Bro. KEN GRONDIN; Sr. CABRINI FOUSHEE, O.S.U.; Mr. STEVE SHOULTA; ANNE O'BRYAN; ED CALHOUN; Ms. BONNIE MARKS; Ms. LORRAINE LUKEN; Ms. CAROL HIGDON; Mr. DAN POWELL; Ms. KAY VILLINES; Ms. BARBARA HERTEL; Ms. KELLEY HUFFORD.

Director of Ecumenism—Rev. JOSEPH O'DONNELL, Glmy., *9515 Ky. 144, Knottsville, 42366.* Tel: 270-281-4802; Fax: 270-281-9556.

Youth Ministry—Rev. HENRY WIEDER, Dir.; Ms. MELINDA PRUNTY, Assoc. Dir.

Director of Communications and Editor of the Diocesan Newspaper "Western Kentucky Catholic"—Mr. MEL HOWARD.

Director of Television and Radio Broadcast Communications—Mr. CLIFF RUSSELL.

Pastoral Office for Worship—Rev. LARRY MCBRIDE, Dir. MARTHA HAGAN, Assoc. Dir.; Mr. MIKE BOGDAN, Dir. Office for Music.

Diocesan Liturgical Committee—Revs. CARL MCCARTHY; LARRY MCBRIDE, Chm. TONY BICKETT; Sr. LARRAINE LAUTER, O.S.U.; Ms. MARTHA HAGAN; Ms. PATTY BROWN; Mr. MICHAEL BOGDAN; Ms. SUE ECKMANS; Sr. ANNALITA LANCASTER, O.S.U.; Rev. JOHN THOMAS; Ms. CLEO HIGDON; Sr. ALICIA COOMES, O.S.U.

Pastoral Office for Spiritual Life—Sr. AMELIA STENGER, O.S.U., Dir., *Mount St. Joseph, Maple Mount, 42356.* Tel: 270-229-0200; Fax: 270-229-0279.

Cursillo—Sr. ELAINE BURKE, O.S.U., *Mount St. Joseph, 8001 Cummings Rd., Maple Mount, 42356.* Tel: 270-229-0200.

Pastoral Office for Outreach—Sr. PATRICIA FRONING, O.S.F., Dir.

Catholic Charities—Vacant, Dir., *600 Locust St., Owensboro, 42301.* Tel: 270-683-1545. Board Members: MARK PFIEFER; Revs. ED BRADLEY; PHIL RINEY; Sr. LUCY BONIFAS; Sr. MAE KOENIG, G.H.M.S.; GRETCHEN BINEGAR; KAYE CASTLEN; CHARLIE REID; DICK MURPHY; STEVE TEASLEY; BOB HOWARD; MIKE BOONE; STEVE THOMPSON; PATRICIA ROOF; RITA HEINZ; Bro. KEN WOODS.

Catholic Campaign for Human Development—Vacant, Dir.

Catholic Relief Service—Vacant, Dir.

Pastoral Office for Social Concerns—RITA BROTHERS, Dir.

Social Concerns Committee—LIZ FRANCIS; Sr. ROSE JEAN POWERS; Sr. MARTHA SCHULER, G.H.M.S.; GLORIA ADAMS; MARILYN CHANDLER; MIKE MORROW; MARTHA CRABTREE; SARAH BAKER; Sr. CHRISTINE BECKETT; SHARRIE CINNAMOND; BERNADETTE HOWARD; BILL WATHEN.

Respect Life Office—RITA BROTHERS.

African-American Office—GLORIA ADAMS.

Hispanic Office—Rev. STAN PURYEAR, Dir., *St. Peter Parish, 81 Church St., Owensboro, 42301.* Tel: 270-764-1983.

Pastoral Office of Family Life—EDWINA HYLAND, Coord. BETTY MEDLEY, Assoc. Dir.

Family Life Committee—Mr. TOM HAYDEN; Ms. JOYCE HAYDEN; Revs. JOHN VAUGHAN; JOSEPH M. MILLS; BRIAN ROBY; Ms. GAIL CRITCHELOW; Ms. CAROL YANIK; Mr. DON WEAVER; Ms. MARY WEAVER; Ms. MARY YANIK; Mr. JERRY CRITCHELOW; Mr. DENNY MANN; BETTY MEDLEY; EDWINA HYLAND.

Natural Family Planning—GWEN JENNINGS; ANGIE SIMS; ANGIE WAHL.

Mission Office—Rev. JOSEPH M. MILLS.

Pastoral Office for Personnel—Rev. DARRELL VENTERS.

Priest Personnel Committee—Revs. GERALD CALHOUN; MIKE CLARK; FREDDIE BYRD; JERRY RINEY; BRAD WHISTLE; JOE MILLS; DARRELL VENTERS.

Vocations Office—Rev. BRAD WHISTLE, *Precious Blood Parish, 3306 Fenmore St., Owensboro, 42301.* Tel: 270-684-6888; Fax: 270-684-1304.

Continuing Education for Priests—Rev. RICHARD MEREDITH, *St. Pius Tenth Parish, 3512 E. 6th St., Owensboro, 42303.* Tel: 270-684-4745; Fax: 270-684-2709.

[*]Roman Catholic Diocese of Owensboro Charitable Trust Fund, Inc.—Most Rev. JOHN J. MCRAITH; Revs. JOE MILLS; JOE RHODES.

Organizations

St. Vincent de Paul Society—Rev. DARRELL VENTERS, Chap., *P.O. Box 10170, Bowling Green, 42102-4770.*

Scouting Activities—Rev. KENNETH MIKULCIK, Chap., *600 Locust St., Owensboro, 42301.* Tel: 270-683-1545.

Holy Childhood Association—Rev. JOSEPH M. MILLS.

Teens Encounter Christ—Rev. FREDDIE BYRD, *600 Locust St., Owensboro, 42301.* Tel: 270-683-1545.

Legion of Mary—Vacant.

CLERGY, PARISHES, MISSIONS AND PAROCHIAL SCHOOLS

CITY OF OWENSBORO
(Daviess County)

1—ST. STEPHEN CATHEDRAL, Revs. John R. Vaughan; Thomas Joseph Buckman, Jr. Pastoral Assocs.: Sr. Ann McGrew; Mr. Michael Conley; Mr. Ron Greenwell; Mr. Larry Lyon.
Res., 614 Locust St., 42301. Tel: 270-683-6525; Fax: 270-683-3621.
Chapel—Blessed Sacrament, 602 Sycamore St., 42301. Tel: 270-926-4741. [CEM] Rev. Brian Roby; Gloria Adams, Admin.

2—BLESSED MOTHER, Revs. Freddie Byrd; Eric Riley; Jan Storm, Admin. Asst.; Dr. Margaret Ayers, Pastoral Assoc.
Office: 515 E. 22nd St., 42303.
Res., 601 E. 23rd St., 42303. Tel: 270-683-8444; Fax: 270-688-0446.

3—THE IMMACULATE, Rev. Timothy Sweeney, O.S.B.; Sr. Julia Head, O.S.U., Pastoral Assoc.
Parish Office: 2516 Christie Pl., 42301. Tel: 270-683-0689; Fax: 270-926-9016.
Res., 2601 Christie Pl., 42301.

4—OUR LADY OF LOURDES, Rev. John R. Meredith.
Res., 4029 Frederica St., 42301. Tel: 270-684-5369; Fax: 270-683-8008.

5—PRECIOUS BLOOD, Revs. Brad Whistle; Pete Hughes. Pastoral Assocs.: Sr. Larraine Lauter, O.S.U.; Sr. Rosanne Spalding, O.S.U.
Res., 3306 Fenmore St., 42301. Tel: 270-684-6888; Fax: 270-684-1304.

6—ST. PIUS TENTH, Revs. Richard Meredith; Maury Riney.
Res., 3512 E. Sixth St., 42303. Tel: 270-684-5517; 684-4745 (Office); Fax: 270-684-2709.

7—SS. JOSEPH AND PAUL, Rev. Anthony Bickett; Martha McCarty, Pastoral Assoc.
Res., 609 E. 4th St., 42303. Tel: 270-683-5641; Fax: 270-685-4766.

OUTSIDE THE CITY OF OWENSBORO

Aurora, Marshall Co., St. Henry, Rev. Richard L. Cash.
Res., 16097 U.S. Hwy. 68 E., Hardin, 42048. Tel: 270-474-8058; Fax: 270-474-9876. [CEM]

Axtel, Breckinridge Co., St. Anthony, Rev. Bruce Fogle.
Res., R.R. 3, Hardinsburg, 40143. Tel: 270-257-2132. [CEM]

Bardwell, Carlisle Co., St. Charles, Rev. Anthony Stevenson.
Res., R.R. 2, Box 317, 42023. Tel: 270-642-2586; Fax: 270-642-2586. [CEM]

Beaver Dam, Ohio Co., Holy Redeemer, Rev. Fideles Levri, Glmy.; Sr. Luisa Bickett, O.S.U., Pastoral Assoc.
Office: P.O. Box 106, 42320. Tel: 270-274-3414; Fax: 270-274-4245.; 768 Horse Branch Loop, Horse Branch, 42349. Tel: 270-274-4285.

Big Clifty, Grayson Co., St. Mary. Closed. Records kept at St. Paul's Church, 1821 St. Paul Rd., Leitchfield, KY 42754. Tel: 270-242-7436.

Bowling Green, Warren Co., St. Joseph's, Revs. Anthony Shonis; Manuel D. Rivas (El Salvador) (Hispanic Min.).
Res., 434 Church Ave., 42101. Tel: 270-842-2525; Fax: 270-843-9624.
Holy Spirit, Revs. W. Jerry Riney; Brian Johnson; Ms. Anita Willoughby, Pastoral Assoc.
Res., 2232 Smallhouse Rd., 42104-4141. Tel: 270-842-7777; Fax: 270-842-6174.

Brown's Valley, Daviess Co., St. Anthony, Rev. Tony Jones; Sr. Martha Keller, O.S.U., Pastoral Assoc.
Church—261 St. Anthony Rd., Utica, 42376. Tel: 270-733-4341. [CEM]

Cadiz, Trigg Co., St. Stephen, Rev. Richard Cash.
Res., 1698 Canton Rd., 42211. Tel: 270-522-3801; Fax: 270-522-3801.

Calhoun, McLean Co., St. Sebastian, Rev. Anthony Jones; Sr. Martha Keller, O.S.U., Pastoral Assoc.
Res., 180 State Rte. 136 W., 42327-9521. Tel: 270-273-3185. [CEM]

Calvert City, Marshall Co., St. Pius Tenth, Rev. Robert Drury. Pastoral Assocs.: Sr. Lisa Marie Cecil, O.S.U.; Sr. Mary Angela Matthews, O.S.U.
Res., P.O. Box 495, 42029. Tel: 270-395-4727; Fax: 270-395-5747.
Stations—Kentucky State Penitentiary, Tel: 270-388-2211; Western Kentucky Correctional Complex, Tel: 270-388-9781.

Central City, Mulenberg Co., St. Joseph, Rev. Francis Mastrovito, T.O.R.; Sr. Rose Karen Johnson, O.S.U., Pastoral Assoc.; Sr. Rose Theresa Johnson, O.S.U., Pastoral Assoc.
Res., 113 S. Third St., 42330. Tel: 270-754-1164.

Clarkson, Grayson Co., St. Elizabeth of Hungary, Rev. Charles G. Fischer.
Res., 1821 St. Paul Rd., Leitchfield, 42754. Tel: 270-242-7436. [CEM]
Catechesis/Religious Programs—306 Clifty Ave., 42726. Tel: 270-242-4414.

Clinton, Hickman Co., St. Jude, Rev. J. Michael Clark; Sr. Cecelia J. Olinger, O.S.U., Pastoral Assoc.
Res., 42031. Tel: 270-653-6869.

Cloverport, Breckinridge Co., St. Rose, Rev. Bruce McCarty.
Res., 118 Chestnut St., 40111. Tel: 270-788-6422. [CEM]

Curdsville, Daviess Co., St. Elizabeth, Rev. Aloysius Powers, Admin.
Mailing Address: 6143 First St., P.O. Box 9-A, 42334. Tel: 270-229-4134.

Dawson Springs, Hopkins Co., Resurrection, Rev. Martin Mattingly.
Church—530 Industrial Park Rd., 42408. Tel: 270-383-4743; 797-8665.

Earlington, Hopkins Co., Immaculate Conception, Rev. Martin Mattingly.
Res., 125 S. Day St., 42410. Tel: 270-383-4743.

Eddyville, Lyon Co., St. Mark Church, Rev. Maurice J. Tiell.
Res., 302 Peachtree Ln., 42038. Tel: 270-388-2133.

Elkton, Todd Co., St. Susan, Rev. Frank Ruff, Glmy.; Bro. Ken Woods, Glemy., Pastoral Assoc.
Res., P.O. Box 788, 42220. Tel: 270-265-5263; Fax: 270-265-5288.

Fancy Farm, Hickman Co., St. Denis, Rev. Anthony Stevenson.
Res., St. Charles Church, R.R. 2, Box 317, Bardwell, 42023. Tel: 270-642-2586; Fax: 270-642-2586. [CEM]
St. Jerome, Graves Co., Rev. Delma Clemons.
Res., P.O. Box 38, 42039. Tel: 270-623-8181; Fax: 270-623-6341. [CEM]
Catechesis/Religious Programs—Lisa Morgan, D.R.E.
Students 279.

Fordsville, Ohio Co., St. John the Baptist, Revs. Richard M. Powers; Michael Williams; Sr. Clarita Browning, O.S.U., Pastoral Assoc.
Mailing Address: P.O. Box 127, 42343. Tel: 270-276-3619.

Franklin, Simpson Co., St. Mary of the Woods, Rev. Dennis Holly, Glmy.; Sr. Davida Loosbrock, O.S.F., Pastoral Assoc.
Res., Box 388, 42135. Tel: 270-586-4515. [CEM]

Fulton, Fulton Co., St. Edward, Rev. J. Michael Clark.
Res., 504 Eddings St., 42041. Tel: 270-472-2742; Fax: 270-472-2742.

Grand Rivers, Livingston Co., St. Anthony of Padua. (Grand Rivers Catholic Church). Rev. Msgr. George H. Hancock; Sr. Rosemary Esterkamp, G.H.M.S.
Res., 1518 J.H. O'Bryan Ave., P.O. Box 447, 42045. Tel: 270-362-0408; Fax: 270-362-0408.

Grayson Springs, Grayson Co., St. Augustine, Rev. Gary Hayes.
Res. & Mailing Address: c/o St. Anthony Church, 1256 St. Anthony Church Rd., Clarkson, 42726. Tel: 270-242-4791; Fax: 270-242-2601. [CEM]

Guthrie, Todd Co., Sts. Mary & James, Rev. Frank Ruff, Glmy. Pastoral Ministers: Sr. Bernadette Hengstebeck, G.H.M.S.; Sr. Catherine Schoenborn, G.H.M.S.
Res., P.O. Box 325, 42234. Tel: 270-483-2571.

Hardinsburg, Breckinridge Co., St. Romuald, Rev. Terry Devine.
Res., 40143. Tel: 270-756-2356; Fax: 270-756-2099. [CEM]

Hawesville, Hancock Co., Immaculate Conception, Rev. Carl McCarthy; Sr. Rita Lechner, S.P., Pastoral Assoc.
Res., 42348. Tel: 270-927-8419; Fax: 270-927-6783. [CEM]

Henderson, Henderson Co., Holy Name of Jesus, Revs. J. Edward Bradley; Andrew Ausenbaugh. Pastoral Assocs. Sr. Pauletta Kane, S.C.N.; Sr. Margaret Ann Aull, O.S.U.
Res., 511 Second St., 42420. Tel: 270-826-2096; Fax: 270-827-1494. [CEM]
School—618 Second St., 42420. Tel: 270-827-3425; Fax: 270-827-3432.
Ursuline Sisters 1; Lay Teachers 35; Students 612.

Henshaw, Union Co., St. Ambrose, Rev. Dan Kreutzer; Sr. Markan Freking, O.S.U., Pastoral Assoc.
Res., c/o St. Francis Borgia, 1308 N. Adams St., Sturgis, 42459. Tel: 270-333-4645; Fax: 270-333-4342. [CEM]

Hickman, Fulton Co., Sacred Heart, Rev. J. Michael Clark; Sr. Mary Agnes VonderHaar, O.S.U., Pastoral Assoc.
Res., 411 Moulton St., 42050-1327. Tel: 270-236-2071.

Hopkinsville, Christian Co., SS. Peter and Paul, Rev. Gerald H. Baker. In res., Rev. Sean Kopczynski, C.P.M.
Res., 902 E. Ninth St., 42240. Tel: 270-885-8522; Fax: 270-885-5296.
School—Tel: 270-886-0172; Fax: 270-887-9924.
Lay Teachers 10; Students 212.

Irvington, Breckinridge Co., Holy Guardian Angels, Rev. Bruce McCarty.
Mailing Address: 118 Chestnut St., Cloverport, 40111. Tel: 270-547-2132; Fax: 270-788-6422.
301 W. High St., 40146.

Knottsville, Daviess Co., St. William, Rev. Martin E. Hayes. In res., Rev. Joseph A. O'Donnell, Glmy.
Res., 9515 Kentucky 144, Philpot, 42366. Tel:

270-281-4802; Fax: 270-281-9556. [CEM]
School—Mary Carrico Memorial School, Tel: 270-281-5546.
Lay Teachers 9; Students 135.

LaCenter, Ballard Co., St. Mary, Revs. Henry Wieder; Ken Mikulcik; Sr. Sandy Compas, O.S.U., Pastoral Assoc.
Church—P.O. Box 570, 42056. Tel: 270-665-5551 (Office); 665-5654 (Res.); Fax: 270-665-9033. [CEM]

Leitchfield, Grayson Co., St. Joseph's, Rev. Dave Johnson; Sr. Ruth Mattingly, O.S.U., Pastoral Min.
Res., 109 W. Walnut St., 42754. Tel: 270-259-3028; Fax: 270-259-9860. [CEM]

Lewisport, Hancock Co., St. Columba, Rev. Carl McCarthy; Sr. Rita Lechner, S.P., Pastoral Assoc.
Res., 815 Pell St., P.O. Box 358, 42351. Tel: 270-927-8419; Fax: 270-295-3682. [CEM]

Livermore, McLean Co., St. Charles, Rev. Tony Jones.
Res., 261 St. Anthony Rd., Utica, 42376. Tel: 270-273-3185.
Church—506 Hill Ave., 42352.

McQuady, Breckinridge Co., St. Mary-of-the-Woods, Rev. Bruce Fogle.
Res., R.R. 3, Hardinsburg, 40143. Tel: 270-756-2093. [CEM 2]

Madisonville, Hopkins Co., Christ the King, Rev. Gerald Calhoun.
Res., 1600 Kingsway Dr., 42431. Tel: 270-821-5494; Fax: 270-825-8612.
School—Tel: 270-821-8271; Fax: 270-825-9394.
Lay Teachers 14; Students 138.
Preschool—Tel: 270-821-3954.
Students 75.

Marion, Crittenden Co., St. William, Rev. I. Daniel Kreutzer.
Res., 860 S. Main St., 42064. Tel: 270-965-2477; Fax: 270-965-0918. [CEM]

Mayfield, Graves Co., St. Joseph, Rev. Ray Clark.
Res., 702 W. Broadway St., 42066. Tel: 270-247-2843; Fax: 270-247-6835. [CEM]
School—Tel: 270-247-4420; Fax: 270-247-6835.
Lay Teachers 11; Students 163.

Morganfield, Union Co., St. Ann's, Rev. Patrick M. Bittel; Melissa Alvey, Pastoral Min.
Res., 304 Church St., 42437. Tel: 270-389-2287; Fax: 270-389-0219. [CEM]

Morgantown, Butler Co., Holy Trinity, Rev. Fideles Levri, Glmy.; Sr. Marie Colette Gerry, O.S.F., Pastoral Assoc.
Res., 766 Logansport Rd., P.O. Box 222, 42261. Tel: 270-526-3723; Fax: 270-274-4245.

Murray, Calloway Co., St. Leo, Rev. Ray Goetz; Sr. Mary Matthias Ward, O.S.U., Pastoral Assoc.
Res., 401 N. 12th St., 42071. Tel: 270-753-3876; Fax: 270-759-2074.

Oak Grove, Christian Co., St. Michael the Archangel, Rev. David William Kennedy, Admin.
Res., 448 State Line Rd., P.O. Box 505, 42262. Tel: 270-640-9580; 522-3801 (Rectory).

Paducah, McCracken Co.,

1—St. Francis de Sales, Revs. Larry McBride; Gregory Arflack.
Res., 116 S. Sixth St., 42001. Tel: 270-442-1923; Fax: 270-443-4616.

2—Rosary Chapel, Revs. Larry McBride; Gregory Arflack.
Mailing Address: P.O. Box 1481, 42002-1481.
Res., 711 Ohio St., 42001. Tel: 270-444-6383; Fax: 270-444-0553.

3—St. John the Evangelist, Rev. Benjamin F. Luther.
Res., 6705 Old U.S. Hwy. 45, 42003. Tel: 270-554-3810; Fax: 270-554-3810.
School—7450 St. John Church Dr., 42003. Tel: 270-554-8826; Fax: 270-554-8826.
Lay Teachers 9; Students 95.

4—St. Thomas More, Revs. Henry Wieder; Ken Mikulcik.
Church—5645 Blandville Rd., 42001. Tel: 270-534-9000; Fax: 270-534-4339.

Peonia, Grayson Co., St. Anthony's, Rev. Gary Hayes.
Res., 1256 St. Anthony Church Rd., Clarkson, 42726. Tel: 270-242-4791. [CEM]

Philpot, Daviess Co., St. Lawrence, Rev. Martin E. Hayes.
Res., 9515 Kentucky 144, Knottsville, 42366. Tel: 270-281-4802; Fax: 270-281-9556. [CEM]

Princeton, Caldwell Co., St. Paul, Rev. Richard T. Danhauer.
Res., 813 S. Jefferson, 42445. Tel: 270-365-6786.

Providence, Webster Co., Holy Cross, Rev. Paul P. Powell. Pastoral Assocs.: Bros. Ken Grondin, C.F.C.; Tim Smyth, C.F.C.
Church—730 North Highway 41A, 42450. Tel: 270-667-7308; Fax: 270-835-9919.

Reed, Henderson Co., St. Augustine, Rev. Msgr. Bernard Powers.
Res., 16777 Hwy. 60 E., 42451. Tel: 270-764-5599. [CEM]

Rome, Daviess Co., St. Martin, Rev. Leonard Arcilesi; Rose Ann Payne, Pastoral Assoc.
Res., 5856 Kentucky 81, Owensboro, 42301. Tel: 270-685-0339; Fax: 270-684-5444.

Russellville, Logan Co., Sacred Heart, Rev. Glenn Jarman, C.P.M.
Res., 296 W. 6th St., 42276. Tel: 270-726-6963; Fax: 270-726-2232.

Scottsville, Allen Co., Christ the King, Rev. Dennis Holly, Glmy.; Sr. Davida Loosbrock, O.S.F., Pastoral Assoc.
Res., P.O. Box 463, 42164. Tel: 270-237-4404.

Sebree, Webster Co., St. Michael, Rev. Paul P. Powell. Pastoral Assocs.: Bros. Ken Grondin, C.F.C.; Tim Smyth, C.F.C.
Res., P.O. Box 705, Church St., 42455. Tel: 270-835-2584; Fax: 270-835-9919.

St. Joseph, Daviess Co., St. Alphonsus, Rev. Gregory G. Trawick.
Res., 7950 Cummings Rd., Owensboro, 42301. Tel: 270-229-4566; Fax: 270-229-4164. [CEM]

St. Paul, Grayson Co., St. Paul, Rev. Charles G. Fischer.
Res., 1821 St. Paul Rd., Leitchfield, 42754. Tel: 270-242-7483. [CEM]
School—Tel: 270-242-7483.
Lay Teachers 4; Students 27.

Sorgho, Daviess Co., St. Mary Magdalene, Rev. J. Patrick Reynolds.
Res., 7232 Kentucky 56, Owensboro, 42301. Tel: 270-771-4436; Fax: 270-771-4438. [JC]

Stanley, Daviess Co., St. Peter of Alcantara, Rev. Stan Puryear.
Res., 81 Church St., Owensboro, 42301. Tel: 270-764-1983. [CEM 2]

Sturgis, Union Co., St. Francis Borgia, Rev. Dan Kreutzer; Sr. Marcan Freking, O.S.F., Pastoral Assoc.
Res., 1308 N. Adams St., 42459. Tel: 270-333-5915; Fax: 270-333-4342.

Sunfish, Edmonson Co., St. John the Evangelist, Rev. Dave Johnson; Sr. Mary Lou Ruck, S.P., Pastoral Assoc.
Church—430 St. John Church Rd., 42284. Tel: 270-286-4366. [CEM]

Uniontown, Union Co., St. Agnes, Rev. Robert Willett; Libby Downs, Pastoral Assoc.
Res., P.O. Box 607, 42461. Tel: 270-822-4416; Fax: 270-822-5316. [CEM]

Waverly, Union Co., Sacred Heart, Rev. Robert Willett.
Res., 201 E. Market St., 42462. Tel: 270-389-4224; Fax: 270-389-4224. [CEM]
St. Peter, Rev. Robert Willett.
Res., 201 E. Market St., 42462. Tel: 270-389-4224; Fax: 270-389-4224. [CEM]

Wax, Grayson Co., St. Benedict, Rev. Gary Hayes.
Res., St. Anthony Church, 1256 St. Anthony Church Rd., Clarkson, 42726. Tel: 270-242-4791. [CEM]

Whitesville, Daviess Co., St. Mary of the Woods, Revs. Richard M. Powers; Mike Williams.
Res., 10534 Main Cross, P.O. Box 1, 42378. Tel: 270-233-4196; Fax: 270-233-5557. [CEM]
School—St. Mary's Grade School, Tel: 270-233-5253; Fax: 270-233-9360.
Lay Teachers 12; Students 233.

Non-Parochial Assignments:
Reverend Fathers—
Alvey, Leonard J., Brescia College, 717 Frederica St., Owensboro, KY 42301
Hostetter, Larry, Brescia University, 717 Frederica St., Owensboro, KY 42301
Mills, Joseph M., Chap., Mount St. Joseph, Maple Mount, KY 42356
Piskula, Louis, Chap., St. Joseph Monastery, 8564 Crisp Rd., Whitesville, KY 42378
Reisz, Leonard, 617 E. 23rd St., Owensboro, KY 42301
Speaks, John, 2501 Old Hartford Rd., Owensboro, KY 42303

On Duty Outside the Diocese:
Reverend Fathers—
Roof, Frank, Chap., U.S. Penitentiary, 4200 Bureau Rd. N., Terre Haute, IN 47808
Thomas, John, St. Meinrad, IN, St. Meinrad Seminary

Absent on Leave:
Reverend Fathers—
Karl, Kevin
Little, John
Payne, Gary
Ulrich, Steve

Military Chaplains:
Reverend Fathers—
Wheatley, Carroll, COMNAVACTUK (A04), PSC 821 Box 1, FPO AE, England 09421-0001
Willett, William D., 5955 Wainwright Dr., Fort Hood, TX 76544

Retired:
Reverend Fathers—
Clements, Richard, Bishop Cotton Apartments, 2501 Old Hartford Rd., Owensboro, KY 42303
DeNardi, Charles A., Ambassador Shores, 1705 St. Paul Rd., Leitchfield, KY 42754
Glahn, Carl, Bishop Cotton Apts., 2501 Old Hartford Rd., Owensboro, KY 42303
Hagman, William J., Bishop Cotton Apts., 2501 Old Hartford Rd., Owensboro, KY 42303
Hancock, Walter, P.O. Box 241-A, Rte. 2, Irvington, KY 40146. Tel: 270-547-6724
Hayden, Lucian P., Carmel Home, 2501 Old Hartford Rd., Owensboro, KY 42303
Hite, James C., Bishop Cotton Apts., 2501 Old Hartford Rd., Owensboro, KY 42303
Miller, Joseph C., Box 319, Nevis, MN 56467
O'Bryan, Henry, P.O. Box 114, Owensboro, KY 42302-0114
Rhodes, Joseph, Bishop Cotton Apts., 2501 Old Hartford Rd., Owensboro, KY 42303
Riney, Philip C., P.O. Box 95, McDaniels, KY 40152-0095

INSTITUTIONS LOCATED IN THE DIOCESE

[A] COLLEGES AND UNIVERSITIES

Owensboro. *Brescia University*, 717 Frederica St., 42301. Tel: 270-685-3131; 800-264-1234; Fax: 270-686-4266.
E-mail: brescia.edu
Web site: www.brescia.edu
For a complete listing, refer to the Colleges and Universities section.

[B] HIGH SCHOOLS, INTER-PAROCHIAL

Owensboro. *Owensboro Catholic High School*, 1524 W. Parrish Ave., 42301. Tel: 270684-3215; Fax: 270-684-7050.
E-mail: staplh@cpc.brescia.edu
Web site: www.owensborodio.org/schools/ocs/index.htm
Mr. Harold Staples, Prin.; Rev. Brian Roby, Chm. Religion Dept. & Dean of Students; Mr. Charles A. Pride, Devel. Dir. Priests 1; Sisters 1; Lay Teachers 44; Students 701.

Paducah. *St. Mary High School*, 1243 Elmdale Rd., 42003. Tel: 270-442-1681; Fax: 270-442-7920.
E-mail: AWHIT@apex.net
Web site: www.smss.org
Mrs. Rosann Whiting, Prin. Sisters 1; Lay Teachers 16; Students 202.

Whitesville. *Trinity High School*, 42378. Tel: 270-233-5533; Fax: 270-233-9293. Mr. Mike Clark, Prin. Priests 1; Lay Teachers 14; Students 189.

[C] ELEMENTARY SCHOOLS, INTER-PAROCHIAL

Owensboro. *Catherine Spalding School.* (Grades K-6), 4017 Frederica St., 42301. Tel: 270-684-7583; Fax: 270-684-4938. Mr. P. J. Hayden, Prin. Lay Teachers 14; Students 243.
Francis R. Cotton School. (Grades K-6), 3418 E. 4th St., 42303. Tel: 270-683-2268; Fax: 270-684-8309. E-mail: thomsons@csp.brescia.edu
Mr. Ron Ryan, Prin. Lay Teachers 18; Students 234.
Henry J. Soenneker School. (Grades K-6), 3400 Fenmore St., 42301. Tel: 270-684-6487; Fax: 270-684-4957. Mrs. Sandy Fleming, Prin. Sisters 1; Lay Teachers 3; Students 44.
Holy Angels Elementary, 5712 Kentucky Hwy. 56, 42301. Tel: 270-771-4773; Fax: 270-771-4310. Bill Hagan, Prin. Lay Teachers 11; Students 167.
Holy Family (Middle) School. (Grades 7-8). (Owensboro Catholic Middle School), 2540 Christie Pl., 42301. Tel: 270-683-0480; Fax: 270-683-0495. Mr. James T. Duffy, Prin. Lay Teachers 19; Students 305.
St. Angela Merici School. (Grades K-6), 525 E. 23rd St., 42303. Tel: 270-683-6989; Fax: 270-684-5956. Ms. Tracy Conkright, Prin. Ursuline Sisters 1; Lay Teachers 17; Students 317.

Bowling Green. *St. Joseph School*, 416 Church Ave., 42101-1887. Tel: 270-842-1235; Fax: 270-842-9072.

Ms. Joanne Powell, Prin. Lay Teachers 15; Students 300.

HARDINSBURG. *St. Romuald School*, 295 N. Main St., 40143. Tel: 270-756-5504. Ms. Pam Fentress, Prin. Lay Teachers 10; Students 208.

MORGANFIELD. *St. Ann Interparochial School*, 320 S. Church St., 42437-1600. Tel: 270-389-1898; Fax: 270-389-1834.
E-mail: sais@kih.net
Mrs. Janet Gill, Prin. Lay Teachers 11; Students 221.

PADUCAH. *St. Mary Elementary*, 377 Highland Blvd., 42003. Tel: 270-442-1681, Ext. 252; Fax: 270-442-7920.
E-mail: burchett@apex.net
Web site: www.smss.org
Mrs. Marina Burchett, Prin. Lay Teachers 22; Students 370.

St. Mary Middle School. (Grades 6-8), 1243 Elmdale Rd., 42003. Tel: 270-442-1681, Ext. 231; Fax: 270-442-7920.
E-mail: awhit@apex.net
Ms. Rosann M. Whiting, Prin. Religious 1; Lay Teachers 7; Students 163.

[D] GENERAL HOSPITALS

PADUCAH. *Lourdes Hospital*, 1530 Lone Oak Rd., P.O. Box 7100, 42002-7100. Tel: 270-444-2444; Fax: 270-444-2980.
E-mail: mmoore@lourdes-pad.org
For a complete listing, refer to the Hospitals section.

[E] HOMES FOR AGED

OWENSBORO. *Carmel Home*, 2501 Old Hartford Rd., 42303. Tel: 270-683-0227; Fax: 270-688-0630
For a complete listing, refer to the Special Care Facilities section.

KNOTTSVILLE. *Bishop Soenneker Home*, 9545 Kentucky 144, 42366. Tel: 270-281-4881
For a complete listing, refer to the Special Care Facilities section.

[F] MONASTERIES AND RESIDENCES OF PRIESTS AND BROTHERS

HARTFORD. *Glenmary House*, 300 Peach Alley, 42347. Tel: 270-298-9886.
E-mail: idj44@juno.com
The Home Missioners of America. Bro. Larry Johnson, Dir. In res. Rev. Tom Kirkendoll, Glmy.

SOUTH UNION. *Fathers of Mercy*, 806 Shaker Museum Rd., 42283. Tel: 270-542-4146; Fax: 270-542-4147.
E-mail: fathers@fathersofmercy.com
Web site: www.fathersofmercy.com
Very Rev. William P. Casey, C.P.M., Supr. Gen. In res. Revs. David M. Wilton, C.P.M., Vicar Gen., Mission Dir.; Ben Cameron, C.P.M.; Louis Caporiccio, C.P.M.; John R. O'Brien, C.P.M.; Daniel Sheehan, C.P.M.; Francis Fusare, C.P.M.; Christopher Henderson, C.P.M.; Joseph Burgdorf, C.P.M.; Shannon Collins, C.P.M.; Denis Blais, C.P.M.; Wade Menezes, C.P.M.

[G] CONVENTS AND RESIDENCES FOR SISTERS

OWENSBORO. *The Glenmary Center*, P.O. Box 22264, 42304-2264. Tel: 270-686-8401; Fax: 270-686-8759.
E-mail: info@glenmarysisters.org
Web site: http://www.glenmarysisters.org
Home Mission Sisters of America, Inc. aka Glenmary Sisters. Sr. Christine Beckett, Pres.

Special Centers for Social Services & Assistance. Total Assisted 10,000; Total Staff 7. Professed Sisters in Community 11.

LIVERMORE. *The Glenmary Center for Mission Training*. Formation Program. 220 E. 7th St., P.O. Box 520, 42352-0520. Tel: 270-278-5239. Sr. Mae Koenig, Dir.; Sr. Patricia Leighton.

MAPLE MOUNT. *Mount St. Joseph*, 42356. Tel: 270-229-4103; Fax: 270-229-4127.
E-mail: rmarita@brescia.edu
Web site: www.owensborodio.org/msj
Motherhouse and Convent of the Ursuline Nuns of the Congregation of Paris. Sr. Rose Marita O'Bryan, O.S.U., Supr.; Rev. Joseph Mills, Chap.; Sr. Emma Cecilia Busam, O.S.U., Archivist. Professed Sisters in Community 202.

WHITESVILLE. *St. Joseph's Monastery*, 8564 Crisp Rd., 42378. Tel: 270-233-4571; Fax: 270-233-4356.
E-mail: nunstjo@mindspring.com
Web site: www.passionistnuns.org
Religious of the Passion of Jesus Christ, (Passionist Nuns, Cloistered Contemplative). Mother Mary Agnes Higgs, C.P., Supr.; Rev. Louis Piskula, Chap. Professed Sisters 18.

[H] RETREAT CENTERS

MAPLE MOUNT. *Mount St. Joseph Conference and Retreat Center, Inc.*, 42356. Tel: 270-229-0200; Fax: 270-229-0279.
E-mail: msjcenter@mindspring.com
Web site: www.owensborodio.org/msjcenter
Sr. Amelia Stenger, O.S.U., Dir. Assoc. Directors: Rev. Msgr. Bernard Powers; Sr. Elaine Burke, O.S.U.

[I] NEWMAN CENTERS

BOWLING GREEN. *Western Kentucky University Newman Center*, St. Thomas Aquinas Chapel, 1403 College St., P.O. Box 10170, 42102-4770. Tel: 270-843-3638; Fax: 270-843-3638.
E-mail: ventersd@home.com
Web site: www.premiernet.net/~wkucnc
Rev. Darrell Venters, Dir.; Sr. Elaine Byrne, O.S.U., Pastoral Min. Students 1,685.

MURRAY. *Murray State University Newman House*, 220 N. 13th St., 42071. Tel: 270-753-1391; Fax: 270-759-2074.
E-mail: smmward@apex.net
Web site: campus.murraystate.edu/org/nwman
Sr. Mary Matthias Ward, O.S.U.; Rev. J. Raymond Goetz. Students 800.

[J] MISCELLANEOUS LISTINGS

OWENSBORO. *Cathedral Preschool*, 600 Locust St., 42301. Tel: 270-926-1652.
E-mail: cathedralpreschool@cpc.brescia.edu
Students 206.

The Catholic Foundation of Western Kentucky, 600 Locust St., 42301. Tel: 270-683-1545; Fax: 270-683-6883.
E-mail: ja@cpc.brescia.edu
Web site: www.owensboro.org

Centro Latino, 524 Locust St., 42301. Tel: 270-683-2541. Total Staff 3; Total Assisted 1,500.

Daniel Pitino Shelter, Inc., 501 Walnut St., 42301. Tel: 270-688-9000; Fax: 270-688-0093. Provides soup kitchen seven days a week, shelter for 58 homeless, education facilities, legal aid and medical services for those unable to pay. Total Assisted 30,000; Employees 10; Volunteers 210.

Gideon Productions, Inc., 4029 Frederica St., 42301. Tel: 270-689-1622; Fax: 270-689-1622.
E-mail: rvjrm@mindspring.com
Web site: www.gideonproductions.com
Rev. John R. Meredith, Contact Person.

Glenmary Sisters Charitable Trust, P.O. Box 22264, 42301. Tel: 270-686-8401; Fax: 270-686-8759.
E-mail: srpatghms@juno.com
Mr. Frank Harris, Chm.; Sr. Patricia Leighton, Sec.; Mr. Charles Reid.

Interparish Deposit Loan Fund Corp., 600 Locust St., 42301-2130. Tel: 270-683-1545; Fax: 270-683-6883.
E-mail: ja@cpc.brescia.edu
Web site: www.owensborodio.org
Sr. Joseph Angela Boone, Contact Person.

Mercy Health Partners. Kentucky Indiana, Inc., The Corporate Center, Bldg. A, Ste. 202, 401 Frederica St., 42301. Tel: 270-683-7590; Fax: 270-683-5055.
E-mail: dborders@health-partners.org
Doug Borders, Pres. & CEO.

Elderly Cottage Housing Opportunity (ECHO), Sacred Heart Village, 2120 Payne St., Louisville, 40206. Tel: 502-895-9425. Leslie A. Wilson, Admin.

Owensboro Catholic Consolidated School System, 1524 W. Parrish Ave., 42301. Tel: 270-686-8896; Fax: 270-686-8997.
E-mail: mudds@bellsouth.net; mudd@cpc.brescia.edu
Web site: www.owensborodio.org/schools/ocs/index.htm
Sr. Susan Mary Mudd, O.S.U., Dir.

The Roman Catholic Diocese of Owensboro Kentucky Charitable Trust Fund, Inc., 600 Locust St., 42301. Tel: 270-683-1545; Fax: 270-683-6883. Sr. Joseph Angela Boone, O.S.U.

BOWLING GREEN. *Diocesan Shrine of Mary Mother of the Church and Model of all Christians*, St. Joseph, 434 Church St., 42101. Tel: 270-842-2525; Fax: 270-554-3810.
E-mail: bluther@apex.net

PADUCAH. *Our Lady of the Pines Prayer House, Inc.*, 717 S. 6th St., 42001. Tel: 270-443-3650.

St. Mary School System, 1243 Elmdale Rd., 42003. Tel: 270-442-1681, Ext. 225; Fax: 270-442-7920.
Web site: www.smss.org
Tom Fusco, Dir.

St. Mary School System Benefit Fund, 1243 Elmdale Rd., 42003. Tel: 270-442-1681; Fax: 270-442-7920.
E-mail: @smss.org

RELIGIOUS INSTITUTES OF MEN REPRESENTED IN THE DIOCESE

For further details refer to the corresponding bracketed number in the Religious Institutes of Men or Women section.

[0200]—*Benedictine Monks.*—O.S.B.
[0310]—*Congregation of Christian Brothers.*—C.F.C.
[0820]—*Congregation of the Fathers of Mercy.*—C.P.M.
[0570]—*Glenmary Home Missioners.* (Glendale OH).—Glmy.
[0560]—*Third Order Regular of Saint Francis.*—T.O.R.

RELIGIOUS INSTITUTES OF WOMEN REPRESENTED IN THE DIOCESE

[0360]—*Carmelite Sisters of the Divine Heart of Jesus.*—Carmel D.C.J.
[2080]—*Home Mission Sisters of America.*—G.H.M.S.
[2575]—*Institute of the Sisters of Mercy of the Americas.* (Cincinnati, OH; Detroit, MI).—R.S.M.
[2790]—*Missionary Servants of the Most Blessed Trinity.*—M.S.B.T.
[]—*Missioneras del Sagrado Corazon de Jesus Ad Gentes.*—M.A.G.
[3170]—*Religious of the Passion of Jesus Christ.*—C.P.
[]—*Sinsinawa Domincan Sisters.*—O.P.
[0500]—*Sisters of Charity of Nazareth.*—S.C.N.
[3360]—*Sisters of Providence of Saint Mary-of-the-Woods, Indiana.*—S.P.
[1650]—*Sisters of St. Francis of Philadelphia.* (PA).—O.S.F.
[2260]—*Sisters of the Lamb of God.*—A.D.
[1760]—*Sisters of the Third Order of St. Francis of Penance and Charity.* (Tiffin, OH).—O.S.F.
[1720]—*Sisters of the Third Order Regular of St. Francis of the Congregation of Our Lady of Lourdes.* (Rochester, MN).—O.S.F.
[4120]—*Ursuline Nuns, of the Congregation of Paris.*—O.S.U.
[1570]—*Sisters of St. Francis of the Holy Family.* (Dubuque, IA).—O.S.F.

INTERPAROCHIAL CEMETERIES

OWENSBORO. *Mater Dolorosa*, 1860 W. 9th St., 42301.

Resurrection, 5404 Leitchfield Rd., 42303. Mr. Art Hodde, Dir.

BOWLING GREEN. *St. Joseph Interparochial Cemetery*, St. Joseph Cemetary Foundation, P.O. Box 10334, 42102. Tel: 270-842-2525. Mr. Ray Grudzielaner, Pres.

NECROLOGY

† Hite, Clarence, (Retired). —Died Dec. 11, 2000.

Diocese of Palm Beach

Most Reverend

ANTHONY J. O'CONNELL, D.D.

Bishop of Palm Beach; ordained 1963; appointed Bishop of Knoxville May 27, 1988; ordained and installed September 8, 1988; appointed Bishop of Palm Beach November 6, 1998.

The Pastoral Center: Mailing Address: P.O. Box 109650, Palm Beach Gardens, FL, 33410-9650. Location: 9995 N. Military Tr., Palm Beach Gardens, FL, 33410. Tel.: 561-775-9500; Fax: 561-775-9556.

Web site address: diocese.maco.net

E-mail address: diocese@maco.net

ESTABLISHED OCTOBER 24, 1984.

Square Miles 5,115.

Comprises the Counties of Palm Beach, Martin, Indian River, Okeechobee and St. Lucie in the State of Florida.

Legal Corporate Title: *The Diocese of Palm Beach.*

For legal titles of parishes and diocesan institutions, consult the Chancery.

STATISTICAL OVERVIEW

Personnel	
Bishop	1
Retired Bishops	1
Priests: Diocesan Active in Diocese	69
Priests: Active Outside Diocese	8
Priests: Retired, Sick or Absent	18
Number of Diocesan Priests	95
Religious Priests in Diocese	38
Extern Priests in Diocese	18
Ordinations:	
Diocesan Priests	6
Transitional Deacons	2
Permanent Deacons	1
Permanent Deacons in Diocese	43
Total Brothers	5
Total Sisters	156
Parishes	
Parishes	48
With Resident Pastor:	
Resident Diocesan Priests	43
Resident Religious Priests	5
Missions	4
New Parishes Created	1
Professional Ministry Personnel:	
Brothers	2
Sisters	26
Lay Ministers	68
Welfare	
Catholic Hospitals	1
Total Assisted	230,000
Homes for the Aged	1
Total Assisted	240
Specialized Homes	1
Total Assisted	16
Special Centers for Social Services	23
Total Assisted	13,005
Residential Care of Disabled	3
Total Assisted	16
Other Institutions	3
Total Assisted	311
Educational	
Seminaries, Diocesan	1
Students from This Diocese	6
Students from Other Diocese	80
Diocesan Students in Other Seminaries	19
Total Seminarians	25
High Schools, Diocesan and Parish	3
Total Students	2,219
Elementary Schools, Diocesan and Parish	14
Total Students	5,568
Elementary Schools, Private	2
Total Students	581
Catechesis/Religious Education:	
High School Students	3,088
Elementary Students	13,761
Total Students Under Catholic Instruction	25,242
Teachers in the Diocese:	
Priests	6
Sisters	18
Lay Teachers	460
Vital Statistics	
Receptions into the Church:	
Infant Baptism Totals	4,624
Adult Baptism Totals	342
Received into Full Communion	384
First Communions	3,760
Confirmations	2,307
Marriages:	
Catholic	812
Interfaith	325
Total Marriages	1,137
Deaths	2,691
Total Catholic Population	244,771
Total Population	1,482,026

Former Bishop—Most Rev. THOMAS V. DAILY, D.D., ord. Jan. 10, 1952; appt. Titular Bishop of Bladia and Auxiliary Bishop of Boston, Dec. 31, 1974; cons. Feb. 11, 1975; appt. first Bishop of Palm Beach, July 17, 1984; installed Oct. 24, 1984; transferred to Bishop of Brooklyn, Feb. 20, 1990.—Most Rev. J. KEITH SYMONS, D.D., ord. May 18, 1958; appt. Auxiliary Bishop of St. Petersbury, Jan. 16, 1981; cons. March 19, 1981; appt. second Bishop of Pensacola-Tallahassee, Sept. 29, 1983; installed Nov. 8, 1983; appt. second Bishop of Palm Beach, June 2, 1990; installed July 31, 1990; resigned June 2, 1998.

The Pastoral Center—Mailing Address: P.O. Box 109650, Palm Beach Gardens, 33410-9650. Tel: 561-775-9500; Fax: 561-775-9556. *9995 N. Military Trail, Palm Beach Gardens, 33410.*

Vicar General—Rev. JAMES MURTAGH, V.G.

Episcopal Vicars—Rev. Msgr. JOHN R. MCMAHON; Revs. FRANCIS J. LECHIARA; TIMOTHY J. LYNCH; RICHARD MURPHY; ARTHUR J. VENEZIA.

Moderator of Curia—Rev. JAMES MURTAGH, V.G.

Executive Secretary to Bishop—Mrs. ANNETTE RUSSELL.

Matrimonial Tribunal—

Judicial Vicar—Rev. Msgr. THOMAS J. KLINZING, J.C.L.

Judges—Rev. Msgr. RAYMOND BLAIR, J.C.D.; Rev. Msgr. THOMAS KLINZING, J.C.L.; Revs. GLEN J. POTHIER, J.C.L.; DAMIAN TOWEY, C.P., J.C.D.

Defenders of the Bond—Rev. Msgr. JOSEPH MARBACH, J.C.D.; Revs. TIMOTHY J. LYNCH, J.C.L.; WILLIAM MARTIN, O.M.I., J.U.D.; CAESAR RUSSO, J.C.D.

Assessors—Rev. Msgr. JAMES BURKE; Rev. MICHAEL W. EDWARDS; Mrs. LORRAINE SABATELLA.

Promoter of Justice—Rev. DAMIAN TOWEY, C.P., J.C.D.

Director of the Tribunal—Mrs. LORRAINE SABATELLA, B.A.

Notaries—Rev. JAMES MURTAGH, V.G.; Ms. MARY LOU HUGHES; Mrs. LORRAINE SABATELLA.

Secretaries—Mrs. GEMA FERNANDEZ; Mrs. DEBORAH DUXBURY; Mrs. HELEN COUGHTER.

Advocates—Rev. Msgr. JAMES BURKE; Mr. BERNARD CONKO; Mrs. KATHLEEN CONTE; Ms. SYLVIA RAFTERY.

Chancellor—Rev. JAMES MURTAGH, V.G.

Vice Chancellor—Ms. MARY LOU HUGHES.

Archives—Ms. MARY LOU HUGHES.

Vicariate for Christ's Faithful

Episcopal Vicar—Rev. ARTHUR J. VENEZIA.

Diocesan Office of Evangelization—Rev. JOHN PALLARD, O.M.I., Dir.

Office for Vocations—Rev. IRVINE NUGENT, Deputy Dir.

Vicar for Permanent Deacons—Deacon JACK PIERCE, Vicar.

Vicar for Religious—Rev. MARK A. SZANYI, O.F.M.Conv.; Sr. MARIA CONSILIA MANTELLO, A.S.C.J., Assoc. Vicar for Religious.

Dir. for Religious Vocations—Sr. MARIA CONSILIA MANTELLO, A.S.C.J., Assoc. Vicar.

Diocesan Commission of Religious—Sr. JEANNE DREA, O.P., Chm.

Laity—

Office for Black Catholic Ministry—Mrs. LORRAINE LYLES, Dir.

Office for Haitian Ministry—Rev. ARTHUR VENEZIA, Dir.

Office for Hispanic Ministry—Sr. REGINA TUTZO, R.M.I.

Rural Life Migrant Ministry—P.O. Box 1203, Stuart, 34995. Mrs. MARIA CHRISTINA MARQUEZ, Coord.

Holy Childhood Association—Rev. JOHN A. BARROW, Dir., *P.O. Box 109650, Palm Beach Gardens, 33410-9650.*

Legion of Mary—Rev. KEVIN MACGABHANN, Spiritual Moderator.

Vicariate for Catholic Charities

Vicar—Rev. Msgr. JOHN R. MCMAHON.

Catholic Charities—Ms. MADELEINE SCHUTZ, L.C.S.W., Exec. Dir.; Mrs. NANCY MONICATTI, M.S.W., Assoc. Dir.

Belle Glade Office—Ms. EURANDA CLARKE.

Birthline Crisis Pregnancy Center—Mrs. ARLENE CONKLIN.

Counseling Services—Ms. DIANN JASINSKI, L.C.S.W.

Gladeskids (Belle Glade)—Sr. LAURA CAVANAUGH, S.B.S.

Indiantown Outreach Center—Ms. MARIA CHRISTINA MARQUEZ.

Indian River County Counseling—Mrs. ELIZABETH MAXWELL, M.S.W.

Office of Social Concerns/Campaign for Human Development & Catholic Relief Services—Sr. JEANNE DREA, O.P.

Elder Affairs Case Management & Guardianship—Sr. MARYROSE CROWLEY, S.S.N.D.

Emmaus Residence for Persons Living with AIDS—Ms. JUDY THOMPSON, Dir.

Lifeline Crisis Pregnancy Center—Mrs. ARLENE CONKLIN.

Martin County Offices (Hobe Sound, Indiantown, East Stuart, Stuart)—Ms. HELEN KELLY, L.C.S.W.

Maurawood Community Outreach for Pregnancy/Parenting—Ms. PEGGY O'NEILL, L.C.S.W., M.L.S.P., M.S.S.

Nazareth Homes-Adult Group Homes for People with Developmental Disabilties—Alhambra House: Sr. RITA BAUM, S.S.J. Bethlehem House: Sr. RITA BAUM, S.S.J. Columbia House: Sr. RITA BAUM, S.S.J.

Aim for the Best - Abstinence Program—Mrs. ELENA M. GARCIA.

Office of Housing Management & Development—Mrs. ROBIN LUNN.

Okeechobee Outreach Center/After School Program—Mr. EDWARD ISAMAN.

Refugee Resettlement & Immigration Services—Ms. ANNE MARIE ALEXANDRE.

Saint Lucie County Office—Ms. CARMEN SIBRUN, M.S.W.

Samaritan Center for Homeless Families—Mrs. JOYCE WILD.

Villa Assumpta Housing for the Elderly—Mrs. LINDA MATZ, Mgr.

Villa Franciscan Housing for the Elderly—Mr. WILLIAM KERR, Mgr.

Villa Madonna Housing for the Elderly—Mrs. ROSEMARY MCMAHON, Mgr.

Vicariate for Education

Vicar—Rev. FRANCIS J. LECHIARA.

Office of Catechesis and Leadership Development—Deacon JAMES CAMPBELL, Dir.

Missionary Cooperative Plan—Rev. JOHN A. BARROW, *P.O. Box 109650, Palm Beach Gardens, 33410-9650.*

Propagation of the Faith—Rev. JOHN A. BARROW, *P.O. Box 109650, Palm Beach Gardens, 33410-9650.*

Office of Communications—Deacon SAM BARBARO, Dir.

Office of "The Florida Catholic"—Mrs. IRENE HEY, Editor.

Office of the Catholic Schools—Sr. JOAN DAWSON, O.S.F., Supt.; Mrs. PATRICIA CANTIERI, Asst. Supt.

Office of Special Education - C.O.M.E.—Mrs. PATRICIA CANTIERI, Dir.

Vicariate for Marriage and the Family

Vicar—Rev. TIMOTHY J. LYNCH.

Family Life—

Engaged Encounter—Ms. JANICE PETERSEN, Coord.

Office of Youth Ministry and Young Adult Ministry—Rev. DONALD T. FINNEY, Spiritual Moderator; Sr. JUDE RUGGERI, A.S.C.J., Dir.; Mr. KEVIN DRISCOLL, Assoc. Dir.

Cursillo Movement—100 Crestwood Blvd., S., Royal Palm Beach, 33411. Rev. MICHAEL TSCHUDI, Spiritual Dir.

Cursillo Movement for Hispanics—Rev. MATTHEW DIDONE, C.S., Spiritual Dir., *9600 W. Atlantic Ave., Delray Beach, 33446.*

Office of Ministry with People with Disabilities—Sr. RITA BAUM, S.S.J., Dir.

Office of Prison Ministry—Sr. BETTY FRASCINO, O.S.F., Dir.

Office of Ecumenical and Inter-Faith Activities—Revs. BRIAN FLANAGAN, Dir. MICHAEL TSCHUDI, Assoc. Dir.

Office for Liturgy—Rev. MICHAEL DRISCOLL, O.Carm., Dir.

Office for Campus Ministry—

Florida Atlantic University—Rev. SEAN POLAND.

Chaplain for Catholic Scouting—Vacant.

Liaison to Charismatic Movement—Rev. WALTER DOCKERILL.

World Wide Marriage Encounter—Rev. FRANK B. GUINAN, Spiritual Moderator. Exec. Couple: LARRY BALIK; HERMIE BALIK, *220 Colony Way W., Jupiter, 33458.*

Office for Respect Life—Mr. DONALD KAZIMIR, Dir.

Vicariate for Pastoral Services

Vicar—Rev. RICHARD MURPHY.

Diocesan Financial Administrator—Mr. BASIL ZALOOM.

Financial Advisory Board—Rev. RICHARD MURPHY, Chm.

Office for Building and Renovations—Mr. PATRICK MOLAMPHY, Dir.

Commission for Building—Rev. RICHARD MURPHY, Chm.

Office of Cemeteries—Rev. THOMAS VENGAYIL, Dir.

Office of Data Processing—Rev. RICHARD MURPHY.

Office of Stewardship—Mr. EDWARD LOUGHLIN, Dir.

Legal Affairs—Mr. J. PATRICK FITZGERALD, ESQ., *110 Merrick Way, Ste. 3-B, Coral Gables, 33134.* Tel: 561-659-6438; Fax: 305-443-6613.

Consultative Bodies

College of Consultors—Rev. Msgr. THOMAS J. KLINZING, J.C.L.; Rev. Msgr. JOHN R. MCMAHON; Revs. JAMES MURTAGH, V.G.; CHRISTOPHER ALLEN; GERALD GRACE; FRANCIS LECHIARA; TIMOTHY LYNCH; RICHARD MURPHY; CHARLES NOTABARTOLO; ARTHUR VENEZIA.

Presbyteral Council—Rev. Msgr. THOMAS J. KLINZING, J.C.L.; Rev. Msgr. JOHN R. MCMAHON; Revs. JAMES MURTAGH, V.G.; FRANCIS LECHIARA; TIMOTHY LYNCH; RICHARD MURPHY; IRVINE NUGENT; WILLIAM O'SHEA; FRANCIS REARDON; NESTOR RODRIQUEZ; ARTHUR VENEZIA; VICTOR ULTO; MARTIN DEVERAUX; THOMAS VENGAYIL.

Miscellaneous

Society of St. Vincent de Paul, District Council of the Treasure Coast—Mrs. FRANCES ASKLAND, *1063 S.W. McCoy Ave., Port St. Lucie, 34953.* Tel: 561-336-9054.

CLERGY, PARISHES, MISSIONS AND PAROCHIAL SCHOOLS

CITY OF PALM BEACH GARDENS
(Palm Beach County)

1—CATHEDRAL OF ST. IGNATIUS LOYOLA (1984), Revs. John A. Kasparek, S.C.J., Rector; Timothy O'Toole; John Pallard, O.M.I.
Res., 9999 N. Military Tr., Palm Beach Gardens, 33410. Tel: 561-622-2565; Fax: 561-624-9489.
Catechesis/Religious Programs—Students 625.

OUTSIDE THE CITY OF PALM BEACH GARDENS

Belle Glade, Palm Beach Co., St. Philip Benizi, Revs. Luis Aineto, S.D.B.; James McKenna, S.D.B.; Jeremiah Reen, S.D.B.; Joseph Berruete, S.D.B; Bros. Michael Brinkman; Lino Seneci, S.D.B.
Res., 710 S. Main St., 33430. Tel: 561-996-3870; Fax: 561-996-3899.
Catechesis/Religious Programs—Students 324.

Boca Raton, Palm Beach Co.,

1—ASCENSION, Revs. Matthew A. Morgan; Charles Hawkins.
Res., 7250 N. Federal Hwy., 33487. Tel: 561-997-5486; Fax: 561-997-5862.

2—OUR LADY OF LOURDES, Revs. Francis Reardon; Brian M. Flanagan; Rev. Msgr. Joseph H. O'Shea, Pastor Emeritus.
Res., 20094 Lyons Rd., 33428. Tel: 561-483-2440; Fax: 561-482-0626.
Catechesis/Religious Programs—Students 1,200.

3—ST. JOAN OF ARC, Rev. Msgr. John McMahon; Revs. Roger McDonough (BGP); Giuseppe Savaia (Italy).
Res., 370 S.W. 3rd St., 33432. Tel: 561-392-0007; Fax: 561-392-0074.
School—Sisters of Mercy, Skibbereen. Sr. Ellen Murphy R.S.M., Prin.
Sisters 3; Lay Teachers 27; Students 639.
Catechesis/Religious Programs—Students 861.

4—ST. JOHN THE EVANGELIST, Rev. Michael O'Flaherty.
Res., 19785 Hampton Dr., Ste. #4, 33434. Tel: 561-488-1373.

5—ST. JUDE, Revs. Raymond Maher, O.Carm., Admin.; Michael Driscoll, O.Carm.; Timothy Johnson, O.Carm.; Christopher Stack, O.Carm.
Res., 21693 Club Villa Terrace, 33433.
Church—21689 Toledo Rd., 33433. Tel: 561-392-8172; Fax: 561-362-0845.
School—Tel: 561-392-9160. Miss Debbie Armstrong, Prin.
Sisters 1; Lay Teachers 16; Students 360.
Catechesis/Religious Programs—Students 604.

Boynton Beach, Palm Beach Co., St. Mark, Rev. Mark Szanyi, O.F.M.Conv. In res., Revs. Glen Pothier; Sean Poland (KNX).
Res., 643 N.E. 4th Ave., 33435. Tel: 561-734-9330; Fax: 561-735-3463.
School—Sisters of Charity of St. Elizabeth. Mrs. Marcia Seamans, Prin.
Sisters 2; Lay Teachers 18; Students 315.

St. Thomas More, Rev. Frank O'Loughlin. In res., Rev. Ronald Schulz.
Res., 10935 S. Military Tr., 33436. Tel: 561-737-3095; Fax: 561-737-8697.

Delray Beach, Palm Beach Co.,

1—EMMANUEL, Revs. James Fiore; Raymond Hubert, Pastor Emeritus.
Res., 15700 S. Military Tr., 33484. Tel: 561-496-2480.

2—OUR LADY OF PERPETUAL HELP MISSION, Rev. Roland Desormeaux, C.S.
Residence and Church—510 S.W. Eighth Ave., 33444. Tel: 561-276-4880; Fax: 561-276-7036.

3—OUR LADY QUEEN OF PEACE, Revs. Matthew DiDone, C.S., Admin.; Jose Marum, C.S.
Res., 9600 W. Atlantic Ave., 33446. Tel: 561-499-6234; Fax: 561-499-5513.
Claritian Missionaries 4.

4—ST. VINCENT FERRER, Revs. John A. Skehan; Donald R. Munro; D. Brian Horgan.
Res., 840 George Bush Blvd., 33483. Tel: 561-276-6892; Fax: 561-276-8068.
School—715 N.E. 8th Ave., 33483.
Sisters of Mercy (Kinsale, Ireland) 4; Lay Teachers 15; Students 322.

Fellsmere, Indian River Co., Our Lady of Guadalupe Mission, Rev. Jaime de Jesus Diaz (Colombia).
Mission—Fellsmere, Indian River Co., Rte. 512, P.O. Box 9, 32948. Tel: 561-571-9875; Fax: 561-571-8321.

Fort Pierce, St. Lucie Co., Notre Dame Mission, Rev. Danis Ridore.
Res., 217 N. U.S. Hwy. #1, 34950. Tel: 561-466-9617.

St. Anastasia, Revs. Michael Woodcock; Mark Christopher, Pastor Emeritus; John Gallagher (Ireland).
Res., 407 S. 33rd St., P.O. Box 430, 34954-0430. Tel: 561-461-2233; Fax: 561-461-2242.
School—Tel: 561-461-2232; Fax: 561-468-2037. Mrs. Vickie Guettler, Prin.
Sisters 1; Lay Teachers 24; Students 601.

St. Mark, Revs. Richard Murphy; Sean de Leis, C.S.Sp.
Res., 1924 Zephyr Ave., 34982. Tel: 561-461-8150.

Highland Beach, Palm Beach Co., St. Lucy, Revs. Gerald Grace; Anthony J. Chepanis, Pastor Emeritus.
Res., 3510 S. Ocean Blvd., 33487. Tel: 561-278-1280; Fax: 561-278-8509.

Hobe Sound, Martin Co., St. Christopher, Revs. Aidan Hynes; Richard Vilie (MIA). In res., Rev. Andrew Riley, P.I.M.E.
Res., 12001 S.E. Federal Hwy., 33455. Tel: 561-546-5150; Fax: 561-546-8820.

Indiantown, Martin Co., Holy Cross, Revs. Thomas Euteneuer; Juan de la Calle, Pastor Emeritus.
Mailing Address: P.O. Box 999, 34956.
Res., 15927 S.W. 150 St., 34956. Tel: 561-597-2798; Fax: 561-597-2741.

Jensen Beach, Martin Co., St. Martin de Porres, Revs. Robert L. Magee; Thomas J. Rynne, Pastor Emeritus.
Mailing Address: P.O. Box 1087, 34958.
Res., 2555 N.E. Savanna Rd., 34958. Tel: 561-334-4214; Fax: 561-334-8627.

Juno Beach, Palm Beach Co., St. Patrick, Rev. Frank Guinan.
Res., 2549 Hope Ln., W., Palm Beach Gardens, 33410. Tel: 561-626-8626; Fax: 561-622-6471.

Jupiter, Palm Beach Co., St. Peter, Rev. Charles Notabartolo.
Res., 1701 Indian Creek Pkwy., 33458. Tel: 561-575-0837; Fax: 561-575-6784.
Catechesis/Religious Programs—Students 950.

Lake Worth, Palm Beach Co.,

1—SACRED HEART, Revs. Peter Van Nguyen; Francis X. Fenech, Pastor Emeritus; Noel McGrath (Ireland); Ducasse Francois, I.V. Dei. (Haiti).
Res., 425 N. M St., 33460. Tel: 561-582-4736; Fax: 561-588-5238.
School—410 N. M St., 33460. Sr. Marilyn Reeves, S.F.C.C., Prin.
Sisters 4; Lay Teachers 13; Students 283.

2—ST. LUKE, Revs. David W. Carr; Daniel V. Cronin; Larkin Connolly, Pastor Emeritus; Robert Becerra (NEW); Juan Raul Cardenas.
Res., 2892 S. Congress Ave., 33461. Tel: 561-965-8980; Fax: 561-965-1384.
School—Tel: 561-965-8190; Fax: 561-965-2404. Sr. Janet Finely, O.S.F., Prin.
Lay Teachers 11; Students 284.

3—ST. MATTHEW, Rev. Clemens Hammerschmitt.
Res. & Mailing Address: 6090 Hypoluxo Rd., 33467-5654. Tel: 561-966-8878; Fax: 561-968-1238.

4—ST.THERESE DE LISIEUX,
Res., 9124 Winding Woods Dr., 33467. Tel: 561-649-6768; Fax: 561-649-6764. Rev. Louis Guerin.

Lantana, Palm Beach Co., Holy Spirit, Revs. Kevin MacGabhann; William O'Dea, Pastor Emeritus; Tomasz Makowski.
Res. and Mailing—1000 Lantana Rd., P.O. Box 2978, 33465. Tel: 561-585-5970; Fax: 561-575-8482.

North Palm Beach, Palm Beach Co., St. Clare, Revs. William D. O'Shea; John J. Pasquini.
Res., 821 Prosperity Farms Rd., 33408. Tel: 561-622-7477; Fax: 561-624-0022.
School—Tel: 561-622-7171; Fax: 561-627-4426. Mr. Andrew J. Houvouras, Prin.
Lay Teachers 25; Students 547.
St. Paul of the Cross, Revs. Arthur Venezia; Peter Troung; Thomas Otto.
Res., 10970 State Rd. 703, 33408. Tel: 561-626-1873; Fax: 561-622-7307.

Okeechobee, Okeechobee Co., Sacred Heart, Rev. Hugh Duffy.
Mailing Address: P.O. Box 716, 34973.
Res., 701 S.W. Sixth St., 34973. Tel: 863-763-3727; Fax: 863-763-9334.

Pahokee, Palm Beach Co., St. Mary, Rev. John J. Mericantante.
Res., 1200 E. Main St., 33476. Tel: 561-924-7305; Fax: 561-924-9394.

Palm Beach, Palm Beach Co., St. Edward, Rev. Francis J. Lechiara. In res., Rev. Yves Lapierre (Haiti).
Res., 144 N. County Rd., 33480. Tel: 561-832-0400; Fax: 561-833-3359.

Palm City, Martin Co., Holy Redeemer, Revs. Martin B. Mulqueen; Bernard F. Powell.
Mailing Address: P.O. Box 916, 34991.
Res., 1964 Capri St., 34990. Tel: 561-286-4590.

Port St. Lucie, St. Lucie Co., St. Lucie, Rev. Msgr. James M. Burke; Revs. Peter C. Dolan, Pastor Emeritus; Donald T. Finney, M.I.C.; Paul Chung Nguyen.
Res., 425 S.W. Irving St., 34983. Tel: 561-878-1215; Fax: 561-878-1299.
Catechesis/Religious Programs—Students 550.
St. Elizabeth Ann Seton, Rev. Edmund L. Szpieg.
Church—930 S.W. Tunis Ave., 34953. Tel: 561-336-0282; Fax: 561-336-1494.
Holy Family, Revs. Thomas F. Cauley; Rodney A. Titus.
Mailing Address: P.O. Box 8447, 34985. Tel: 561-335-2385; Fax: 561-335-2517.
Res., 2330 Mariposa Ave., 34953.

Riviera Beach, Palm Beach Co., St. Francis of Assisi, Revs. William P. McSweeney, O.M.I.; Rolland Bennett, O.M.I. In res., Rev. Robert Colfer, O.M.I.
Res., 200 W. 20th St., 33404. Tel: 561-842-2482; Fax: 561-863-2985.
School—Mrs. Judith Edelman, Prin. Lay Teachers 10; Students 160.

Royal Palm Beach, Palm Beach Co., Our Lady Queen of the Apostles, Revs. Thomas J. Skindeleski; Andrew Rudnicki, M.I.C.
Res., 172 Kings Way, 33411. Tel: 561-798-5661; Fax: 561-798-5663.
Mailing Address: 100 Crestwood Blvd. S., 33411.

Sebastian, Indian River Co., St. Sebastian, Revs. John Morrissey; Jaime de Jesus Diaz (Colombia).
Mailing Address: P.O. Box 78-1212, 32978-1212.
Res., 13075 U.S. Hwy. 1, 32958. Tel: 561-589-5790; Fax: 561-388-0084.

Stuart, Martin Co., St. Andrew (1999), Rev. John A. Barrow.
Mailing Address: P.O. Box 1204, Hobe Sound, 33455.
Church—6540 S.E. Federal Hwy., 34997. Tel: 561-781-4415; Fax: 561-781-2906.
St. Joseph, Revs. A. Christopher Allen; Victor A. Ulto (BRK); Kevin Nelson.
Res., 1200 E. 10th St., 34996. Tel: 561-287-2727; Fax: 561-278-4998.
School—Tel: 561-287-6975; Fax: 561-287-4733. Mrs. Marie Privuznak, Prin.
Lay Teachers 21; Students 423.

Tequesta, Palm Beach Co., St. Jude, Revs. Thomas Vengayil; John J. McAtavey, Pastor Emeritus; Julian P. Harris.
Mailing Address: P.O. Box 3726, 33469.
Res., 204 U.S. Hwy. 1, 33469. Tel: 561-746-7974; Fax: 561-743-6127.

Vero Beach, Indian River Co., St. Helen, Rev. Michael W. Edwards; Rev. Msgr. Irvine Nugent, Pastor Emeritus; Revs. Adrian Torres (Colombia); Brian Lehnert.
Res., 2085 Tallahassee Ave., P.O. Box 2927, 32961. Tel: 561-567-5129; Fax: 561-567-4823.
School—2050 Vero Beach Ave., 32960.
Lay Teachers 9; Students 265.
Holy Cross, Revs. Richard Murphy; John B. O'Hare, Pastor Emeritus; John Massaro, C.S.C.
Res., 500 Iris Ln., 32964. Tel: 561-231-0671; Fax: 561-234-5653.
St. John of the Cross, Rev. John A. Crowley.
Res., 950 82nd Ave., 32966. Tel: 561-563-0057; Fax: 561-563-0057.

Wellington, Palm Beach Co., St. Rita, Revs. Walter J. Dockerill; Luis Bastos (ORL).
Res., 13645 Paddock Dr., 33414. Tel: 561-793-8544; Fax: 561-793-4082.

West Palm Beach, Palm Beach Co.,

1—HOLY NAME OF JESUS, Revs. Aidan Lacy; Gavin Badway.
Res., 345 S. Military Tr., 33415. Tel: 407-683-3555; Fax: 407-683-1051.
School—Sr. Kathleen Cumins, R.S.H.M., Prin. Sisters 1; Lay Teachers 13; Students 300.

2—MARY IMMACULATE, Revs. Timothy J. Lynch; Jimmy Hababag (Philippines).
Res., 390 Sequoia Dr., 33409. Tel: 561-686-8128; Fax: 561-686-8406.

3—ST. ANN, Rev. James Murtagh.
Res., 310 N. Olive Ave., 33410. Tel: 561-832-3757; Fax: 561-659-1465.
School—Sisters 6; Lay Teachers 12; Students 200.

4—ST. JOHN FISHER, Revs. William Martin, O.M.I., Pastor; John Vereb, Pastor Emeritus; Harold Fisher, O.M.I.
Res., 4001 North Shore Dr., 33407. Tel: 561-842-1224.

5—ST. JULIANA, Revs. Alfredo Hernandez; Nestor Rodriguez; Brian King.
Res., 4500 S. Dixie Hwy., 33405. Tel: 561-833-9745.
School—Mrs. Mary Beth Quick, Prin. Sisters of St. Joseph 4; Lay Teachers 15; Students 261.

Special Assignment:
Reverend Monsignors—
Klinzing, Thomas, Judicial Vicar, Tribunal
Reverend Fathers—
Armbrust, Leo F., 11380 Prosperity Farms Rd., Palm Beach Gardens, FL 33410
Fitzgerald, Matthew
Kuczborski, Joseph
Poland, Sean, Campus Ministry
Schaefer, Richard, St. Mary's Medical Center
Schulz, Ronald, Permanent Deacon Formation Prog.
Tschudi, Michael

On Duty Outside the Diocese:
Reverend Fathers—
Barrett, Thomas
Block, John G.
McNally, Michael J., St. Charles Borromeo Seminary - Overbrook, 100 E. Wynnewood Rd., Wynnewood, PA 19096
O'Flanagan, Thomas
Ryan, Patrick
Sockol, Timothy, Angelicum (Rome)

Retired:
Reverend Monsignors—
Nugent, Irvine
O'Shea, Joseph H.
Reverend Fathers—
Aymanamkuzhy, Jacob
Calle, Juan de la
Chepanis, Anthony J.
Christopher, Mark
Connolly, Larkin
Dolan, Peter C.
Fenech, Francis X.
Flynn, Francis
Hubert, Raymond P.
Maloney, Francis E.
Malvey, James
McAtavey, John J.
O'Dea, William
O'Hare, John B.
Powell, Bernard
Profeta, Salvatore
Rynne, Thomas J.
Stack, Christopher
Vereb, John

Permanent Deacons:
Allgaier, John (NEW)
Ambroise, Emile
Barbaro, Sam
Beres, Ronald
Campbell, James
Collins, George (NY)
Crary, Lawrence
Daniels, Robert
Demes, Dennis
DiMauro, Joseph
Gallagher, Daniel (NY)
Gluhosky, Frank (HRT)
Hamilton, Jack (WDC)
Hayes, Stephen (RVC)
Kucera, John
Leone, Charles (MIA)
Lopez, Jesus
Lucente, Salvatore (PH)
Mancuso, Terry (PEO)
McMahon, Stephen
Melendez, Carlos
Mieses, Luis J. (Santo Domingo)
Mostler, John (RVC)
Ortiz, Jose
Pagliara, Daniel
Pfeiffer, Robert
Pierce, Jack
Raisch, Jack
Ramos, Geraldo (BGP)
Santana, Richard (NY)
Sawney, Ira (Grenada)
Seppanen, Henry (CAM)
Shellheimer, Bill (NEW)
Toussaint, Henk
Venezia, Richard
Wesley, Albert (FTW)
Whalen, Charles (ALB)

INSTITUTIONS LOCATED IN THE DIOCESE

[A] SEMINARIES, RELIGIOUS OR SCHOLASTICATES

BOYNTON BEACH. *St. Vincent de Paul Regional Seminary*, 10701 S. Military Tr., 33436. Tel: 561-732-4424; Fax: 561-737-2205.
E-mail: sudp.edu
Revs. Stephen C. Bosso, S.S.L. (PT), Rector & Pres.; Steven Olds (ORL), Dean, Pastoral Formation; Guillermo Arias, S.J., M.Ed., Dean, Spiritual Formation; Sr. Janet Sullivan, O.S.F., Continuing Education Dir.; Dr. Zoila Diaz, D.Min., Academic Dean; Dr. Sixto Garcia, Ph.D.; Dr. Antonio Lopez, Ph.D.; Mr. Art Quinn, L.S., Librarian; Rev. Msgr. William White, M.A. (NY); Most Rev. Raymond Lessard, J.C.L.; Revs. Steven O'Hala, S.T.D. (MIA), Vice Rector & Treas.; Nicholas Glisson, Ph.D. (STA); Caesar Russo, J.C.L., S.T.L. (STA); Jose Juan Quijano, S.T.L. (MIA); Juan Carlos Rios, S.T.L.; Sr. Margarita Gomez, R.M.I, S.T.L.; Dr. Emilio Chavez, Ph.D.; Dr. Miguel H. Diaz, Ph.D.

[B] HIGH SCHOOLS, DIOCESAN AND PAROCHIAL

BOCA RATON. *Pope John Paul II High School*, 4001 N. Military Tr., 33431. Tel: 561-994-8998; Fax: 561-989-8582. Revs. Guy Fiano, O.Carm., Pres.; Thomas Zalewski, O.Carm.; James Hess, O.Carm. Lay Teachers 57; Students 820.

FORT PIERCE. *John Carroll High School*, 3402 Delaware Ave., 34947-6116. Tel: 561-464-5200; Fax: 561-464-5233.
E-mail: jchs@gate.net
Web site: www.vero.com/com/vol/jchs
Rev. Michael Sajda, O.F.M.Conv., Pres.; Mr. Clyde L. Russell, Prin.; Bro. Joseph Colarossi, O.F.M.Conv. Sisters 2; Lay Teachers 29; Students 530.

WEST PALM BEACH. *Cardinal Newman High School*, 512 Spencer Dr., 33409. Tel: 561-683-6266; Fax: 561-683-7307.
E-mail: cnhs@flinet.com
Web site: http://www.flinet.com/~cnhs
Rev. David W. Carr, Pres.; John F. Clarke, Prin.; James E. Carver, Asst. Prin.; Rev. Richard George, Chap. Lay Teachers 62; Students 890.

[C] SCHOOLS, PRIVATE

INDIANTOWN. Oratory. *Hope Rural School*. (Grades K-6), 15929 S.W. 150th St., 34956. Tel: 561-597-2203; Fax: 561-597-2259.
E-mail: hopesch@gate.net
Web site: www.gate.net/~hopesch
Sr. Marie Celeste Gatti, O.P., Dir.; Sr. Marion Hangsterfer, O.P., Prin. Sisters 3; Lay Teachers 7; Students 190.

WEST PALM BEACH.
Rosarian Academy. (Grades PreK-8), 807 N. Flagler Dr., 33401. Tel: 561-832-5131. Sisters of St. Dominic (Adrian, MI). Rev. William Martin, O.M.I., Chap.; Mrs. Mary DeVault, Prin. Sisters 6; Lay Teachers 26; Students 317.

[D] GENERAL HOSPITALS

WEST PALM BEACH. *St. Mary's Foundation of Palm Beach County, Inc.*, 901 45th St., 33407-2495. Tel:

561-881-2894; Fax: 561-881-2864
For a complete listing, refer to the Hospitals section.

[E] HOMES FOR AGED

WEST PALM BEACH. *Noreen McKeen Residence for Geriatric Care*, 315 Flagler Dr. S., 33401. Tel: 561-655-8544; Fax: 561-650-8952
For a complete listing, refer to the Special Care Facilities section.

[F] ADULT GROUP HOMES

BOCA RATON. *Alhambra House*, 399 NE 25th Ter., 33431. Tel: 561-392-9497. Sr. Rita Baum, S.S.J., Contact.
Bethlehem House, 2280 NE 5th Ave., 33431. Tel: 561-392-9474. Sr. Rita Baum, S.S.J., Contact.
Columbia House, 424 N.E. 8th St., 33432. Tel: 561-417-2681; Fax: 561-392-9475.

[G] PERSONAL PRELATURES

DELRAY BEACH. *Opus Dei.* (Prelature of the Holy Cross and Opus Dei), 4409 Frances Dr., 33445. Tel: 561-498-1249; Fax: 561-498-0054. Legal Title: *The Work of God, Inc.* Revs. Salvador V. Serrano; Christopher Schmitt.

[H] MONASTERIES AND RESIDENCES OF PRIESTS AND BROTHERS

BOCA RATON. *St. Elias Priory-Order of Carmelites, NY*, 4944 Rabbit Hollow, 33487. Tel: 561-995-6762; Fax: 561-995-0769. Revs. Thomas Zalewski, O.Carm.; Guy Fiano, O.Carm., Prior; James Hess, O.Carm.

NORTH PALM BEACH. *Our Lady of Florida Spiritual Center*, 1300 U.S. Hwy. No. 1, 33408. Tel: 561-626-1300; Fax: 561-627-3956. Revs. Francis Finnigan, C.P., Dir. Retreats; Damian Towey, C.P.; Emmanuel Gordon, C.P.; Raphael Amrhein, C.P.; Bro. Matthew Krawchyk; Sr. Breda Eustace, C.P. Priests 4.

TEQUESTA. *P.I.M.E. Missionaries*, 1550 Beach Rd., 33469. Tel: 561-746-7767; Fax: 561-747-9549.
E-mail: nichom@aol.com
Web site: http://www.pime.org
Revs. Nicholas Maestrini, P.I.M.E., Rector; Pasquale Persico, P.I.M.E.

VERO BEACH. *Paulist Fathers Residence*, 1225 20th Ave., 32960. Tel: 561-562-0500; Fax: 561-794-9810. Revs. Thomas J. Marley, C.S.P.; William J. Cantwell, C.S.P.; George F. Helmich, C.S.P.; Thomas J. Connellan, C.S.P.

[I] CONVENTS AND RESIDENCES FOR SISTERS

DELRAY BEACH. *Christ the King Monastery of St. Clare.* (Solemn Vows, Papal Enclosure), 3900 Sherwood Blvd., 33445-5699. Tel: 561-498-3294; Fax: 561-498-2281. Sr. Mary Veronica Butler, O.S.C., Abbess. Cloistered Sisters 9; Extern Sisters 3.
Claretian Missionary, Sisters of Florida, Inc., 9600 W. Atlantic Ave., 33446. Tel: 561-498-9239; Fax: 561-637-5712.
E-mail: claretian.sr.delray@worldnet.att.net
Web site: www.claretiansisters.org

WEST PALM BEACH. *Adrian Dominican Sisters, Florida Mission Chapter*, 810 N. Olive Ave., 33401-3710. Tel: 561-832-6521; Fax: 561-832-0365.
E-mail: flmich@aol.com
Web site: http://www.op.org/adrian/
Sr. Mary Ann Caulfield, O.P., Chapter Prioress.

[J] RETREAT HOUSES

LANTANA. *The Cenacle Spiritual Life Center*, 1400 S. Dixie Hwy., 33462-5492. Tel: 561-582-2534; Fax: 561-582-8070.
E-mail: cebackefk@aol.com
Web site: www.gopbi.com/community/groups/cenacle/index.html
Spiritual Life Center for laity and religious. Sisters 7.

NORTH PALM BEACH. *Our Lady of Florida Spiritual Center*, 1300 U.S. Hwy. No. 1, 33408. Tel: 561-626-1300; Fax: 561-627-3956.
E-mail: finnigan@gate.net
Web site: http://www.webhighway.com/ourlady

[K] MISCELLANEOUS LISTINGS

PALM BEACH GARDENS. *Catholic Charities of the Diocese of Palm Beach, Inc.* Mailing Address: P.O. Box 109650, 34410-9650. 9995 N. Military Tr., 34410.
GladesKids Out of School Program, St. Philip Benizi, 710 S. Main St., Belle Glade, 33430. Tel: 561-996-3970. Sr. Laura Cavanaugh, S.B.S.
Con El, Inc. Mailing Address: P.O. Box 109650, 33410-9650.
Diocesan Council of Catholic Women. 17574 Lake Park Rd., Boca Raton, 33487. Rev. Clemens Hammerschmitt, Diocesan Moderator; Mrs. Mary Kanamine, Pres. Tel: 561-335-2085.
Diocesan Health Plan Trust. Mailing Address: P.O. Box 109650, 33410-9650. Rev. Francis J. Lechiara, Chm.
Diocesan Pension Plan Trust. Mailing Address: P.O. Box 109650, 33410. Rev. Francis J. Lechiara, Chm.
Diocesan Property & Liability Insurance Committee. Mailing Address: P.O. Box 109650, 33410-9650. Rev. Richard Murphy, Chm.
Diocese of Palm Beach Endowment Trust. Mailing Address: P.O. Box 109650, 33410-9650.
The Florida Catholic of Palm Beach, Inc. Mailing Address: P.O. Box 109650, 33410-9650.
Helping Hands Scholarship Fund, Diocese of Palm Beach. Tel: 561-775-9547. Mailing Address: P.O. Box 109650, 33410-9650.

BOCA RATON. *Christ Child Society of Boca Raton*, P.O. Box 811025, 33481-1025.
E-mail: cchildboca@aol.com

BOYNTON BEACH. *St. Vincent de Paul Regional Seminary Endowment Trust*, 10701 S. Military Tr., 33436.

DELRAY BEACH. *Mary's Room International, Inc.*, 840 George Bush Blvd., 33483.

JENSEN BEACH. *Villa Assumpta, Inc.*, 2539 N.E. Mission Dr., 9-8, 34957. Tel: 561-334-0009; Fax: 561-334-2168. Ms. Linda Matz, Res. Mgr.

LAKE WORTH. *Villa Madonna*, 4809 Lake Worth Rd., 33463-3455.

NORTH PALM BEACH. *Christ Child Society of Palm Beach*, P.O. Box 14441, 33408.

PALM CITY. *St. Raphael Family Life Center*, 9440 S.W. 48th Ave., 34991. Tel: 561-781-0350.

PORT ST. LUCIE. *District Council of the Treasure Coast, Society of St. Vincent de Paul*, 1063 S.E. McCoy Ave., 34953. Tel: 561-336-9054.

RIVIERA BEACH. *Society of St. Vincent de Paul, District Council*, 2567 Old Dixie Hwy., 33404. Tel: 561-845-0562; Fax: 561-845-0534.
Villa Franciscan, Inc., 2101 Avenue F, 33404. Tel: 561-840-0444; Fax: 561-840-9444.
E-mail: vfan@bellsouth.net
Web site: villafranciscan.catholicweb.com
Mr. William Kerr, Mgr.

VERO BEACH. *Society of St. Vincent de Paul, St. Sebastian Conference*, 5480 85th St., 32967. Tel: 561-589-3338.

WEST PALM BEACH. *Emmaus Residence*, P.O. Box 247, 33402-9998. Tel: 561-863-9227; Fax: 561-863-1680. Ms. Judy Thompson, Dir.

RELIGIOUS INSTITUTES OF MEN REPRESENTED IN THE DIOCESE

For further details refer to the corresponding bracketed number in the Religious Institutes of Men or Women section.

[0200]—*Benedictine Monks.*—O.S.B.
[1330]—*Congregation of Mission.*—C.M.
[1030]—*Congregation of St. Paul.*—C.S.P.
[1000]—*Congregation of the Passionists.*—C.P.
[0480]—*Conventual Franciscans.*—O.F.M.Conv.
[0520]—*Franciscan Friars.* (Holy Name Prov.).—O.F.M.
[0520]—*Franciscan Friars.* (Immaculate Conception Prov.).—O.F.M.
[0740]—*Marians of the Immaculate Conception.*—M.I.C.
[1210]—*Missionaries of St. Charles-Scalabrinians.*—C.S.
[0270]—*Order of Carmelites.*—O.Carm.
[0910]—*Order of Mary Immaculate.*—O.M.I.
[1050]—*Pontifical Institute for Foreign Missions.*—P.I.M.E.
[1190]—*Salesians of Don Bosco.*—S.D.B.
[0110]—*Society of African Missions.*—S.M.A.
[0690]—*Society of Jesus.*—S.J.

RELIGIOUS INSTITUTES OF WOMEN REPRESENTED IN THE DIOCESE

[0130]—*Apostles of the Sacred Heart of Jesus.*—A.S.C.J.
[0330]—*Carmelite Sisters for the Aged and Infirm.*—O.Carm.
[0685]—*Claretian Missionary Sisters.*—R.M.I.
[]—*Congregation of Sisters of the Passion.*—C.P.
[]—*Congregation of the Sisters of the Most Holy Soul of Christ the Lord.*—C.S.S.Ch.
[1070-03]—*Dominican Sisters.* (Sinsinawa, WI).—O.P.
[1070-13]—*Dominican Sisters.* (Adrian, MI.—O.P.
[1070-06]—*Dominican Sisters.* (Newburgh, NY).—O.P.
[1070-16]—*Dominican Sisters.* (Ossining, NY).—O.P.
[1070-22]—*Dominican Sisters.* (Fall River, MA).—O.P.
[]—*Dominican Sisters of St. Catherine de Ricci.*—O.P.
[1140]—*Eucharistic Missionaries of St. Dominic.*—O.P.
[]—*Franciscan Sisters.* (Milwaukee, WI).—O.S.F.
[1180]—*Franciscan Sisters of Allegany, NY.*—O.S.F.
[1310]—*Franciscan Sisters of Little Falls.*—O.S.F.
[1845]—*Guadalupana Missionaries of the Holy Spirit.*—M.G.Sp.S.
[]—*Hermitage of Diocese of Palm Beach.*
[2575]—*Institute of Sisters of Mercy of the Americas.*—R.S.M.
[3760]—*Order of St. Clare.*—O.S.C.
[3460]—*Religious of Mary Immaculate.*—R.M.I.
[3110]—*Religious of Our Lady of the Cenacle.*—R.C.
[3465]—*Religious of the Sacred Heart of Mary.*—R.S.H.M.
[2970]—*School Sisters of Notre Dame.*—S.S.N.D.
[1680]—*School Sisters of St. Francis.*—S.S.S.F.
[0500]—*Sisters of Charity of Nazareth.*—S.C.N.
[0430]—*Sisters of Charity of the Blessed Virgin Mary.*—B.V.M.
[2110]—*Sisters of Humility of Mary.*—H.M.
[2560]—*Sisters of Mary Reparatrix.*—S.M.R.
[3000]—*Sisters of Notre Dame de Namur.*—S.N.D.deN.
[3340]—*Sisters of Providence.*—S.P.
[0590]—*Sisters of St. Elizabeth, Convent Station.*—S.C.
[1800]—*Sisters of St. Francis of the Third Order Regular.* (Williamsville, NY).—O.S.F.
[3840]—*Sisters of St. Joseph of Carondelet.*—C.S.J.
[]—*Sisters of St. Joseph of St. Augustine.*—S.S.J.
[0260]—*Sisters of the Blessed Sacrament.*—S.B.S.
[1990]—*Sisters of the Holy Names of Jesus and Mary.*—S.N.J.M.
[]—*Sisters of the Most Holy Soul of Jesus.*
[2150]—*Sisters, Servants of the Immaculate Heart of Mary.*—I.H.M.
[2490]—*Society of Catholic Medical Missionaries.*—S.C.M.M.

DIOCESAN CEMETERIES

WEST PALM BEACH. *Our Lady Queen of Peace Catholic Cemetery, Inc.*, 10941 Southern Blvd., 33406. Tel: 561-793-0711. Deacon Jack Pierce, Admin.

NECROLOGY

† O'Donnell, Richard Joseph, (Retired). —Died Oct. 20, 2000.
† Sutton, John Joseph, Boca Raton, St. Joan of Arc. —Died Aug. 30, 2000.

Diocese of Paterson

(Dioecesis Patersonensis)

Most Reverend

FRANK J. RODIMER, D.D., J.C.D.

Bishop of Paterson; ordained May 19, 1951; appointed Bishop of Paterson December 13, 1977; ordained and installed February 28, 1978. *Res., 178 Derrom Ave., Paterson, NJ, 07504.*

ESTABLISHED DECEMBER 9, 1937.

Square Miles 1,214.

Comprises the Counties of Passaic, Morris and Sussex in the State of New Jersey.

For legal titles of parishes and diocesan institutions, consult the Chancery Office.

Diocesan Center: 777 Valley Rd., Clifton, NJ, 07013. Tel.: 201-777-8818; Fax: 201-777-8976.

Web site address: www.patersondiocese.org

STATISTICAL OVERVIEW

Personnel	
Bishop	1
Abbots	2
Retired Abbots	6
Priests: Diocesan Active in Diocese	163
Priests: Active Outside Diocese	19
Priests: Retired, Sick or Absent	76
Number of Diocesan Priests	258
Religious Priests in Diocese	199
Extern Priests in Diocese	13
Ordinations:	
Transitional Deacons	1
Permanent Deacons in Diocese	158
Total Brothers	48
Total Sisters	853
Parishes	
Parishes	111
With Resident Pastor:	
Resident Diocesan Priests	96
Resident Religious Priests	12
Without Resident Pastor:	
Administered by Priests	3
Pastoral Centers	5
Professional Ministry Personnel:	
Brothers	1
Sisters	59
Lay Ministers	141
Welfare	
Catholic Hospitals	3
Total Assisted	747,657
Homes for the Aged	8
Total Assisted	425
Residential Care of Children	3
Total Assisted	244
Day Care and Extended Day Care Centers	6
Total Assisted	561
Specialized Homes	2
Total Assisted	14,000
Special Centers for Social Services	13
Total Assisted	90,000
Residential Care of Disabled	10
Total Assisted	111
Educational	
Diocesan Students in Other Seminaries	13
Seminaries, Religious	2
Students Religious	5
Total Seminarians	18
Colleges and Universities	2
Total Students	1,852
High Schools, Diocesan and Parish	5
Total Students	2,512
High Schools, Private	5
Total Students	1,568
Elementary Schools, Diocesan and Parish	57
Total Students	16,783
Elementary Schools, Private	3
Total Students	519
Catechesis/Religious Education:	
High School Students	8,473
Elementary Students	36,908
Total Students Under Catholic Instruction	68,633
Teachers in the Diocese:	
Priests	24
Brothers	14
Sisters	133
Lay Teachers	1,129
Vital Statistics	
Receptions into the Church:	
Infant Baptism Totals	8,959
Adult Baptism Totals	225
Received into Full Communion	364
First Communions	7,943
Confirmations	4,411
Marriages:	
Catholic	1,603
Interfaith	457
Total Marriages	2,060
Deaths	3,720
Total Catholic Population	407,932
Total Population	1,093,309

Former Bishops—Most Rev. THOMAS H. MCLAUGHLIN, S.T.D., LL.D., cons. July 25, 1935; transferred to Paterson, Dec. 16, 1937; died March 17, 1947.—Most Rev. THOMAS A. BOLAND, S.T.D., cons. July 25, 1940; transferred to Paterson, June 21, 1947; transferred to Newark as Archbishop, Nov. 15, 1952; died March 16, 1979.—Most Rev. JAMES A. MCNULTY, D.D., appt. Auxiliary Bishop of Newark, Aug. 2, 1947; cons. Oct. 7, 1947; appt. Bishop of Paterson, April 9, 1953; transferred to Diocese of Buffalo, Feb. 12, 1963; died Sept. 4, 1972.—Most Rev. JAMES J. NAVAGH, D.D., cons. Sept. 24, 1952; appt. Bishop of Ogdensburg, May 8, 1957; transferred to Bishop of Paterson, Feb. 12, 1963; died Oct. 2, 1965.—Most Rev. LAWRENCE B. CASEY, D.D., appt. Auxiliary Bishop of Rochester, Feb. 10, 1953; cons. May 5, 1953; appt. Bishop of Paterson, March 9, 1966; died June 15, 1977.

Vicar General, Moderator of the Curia—Rev. Msgr. HERBERT K. TILLYER.

Vicar for Planning and Priorities—Rev. Msgr. JAMES T. MAHONEY.

Vicar for Retired Priests—Rev. Msgr. RAYMOND LOPATESKY.

Coordinator for Religious—Sr. EILEEN KELLY, P.B.V.M.

Vicar for Deacons—Rev. Msgr. ROBERT DIACHEK.

Deans—Rev. Msgr. THOMAS J. COLETTA, Paterson; Rev. VICTOR J. MAZZA, Clifton; Rev. HERNAN ARIAS, Passaic; Rev. Msgr. EUGENE BOLAND, Mid Passaic County; Rev. BERNARD SPLAWSKI, O.F.M., Northern Passaic County; Rev. DAVID MCDONNELL, Southwestern Morris County; Rev. Msgr. PATRICK E. BROWN, Southeastern Morris County; Rev. PATRICK RICE, Eastern Morris County; Rev. DENNIS J. HOGAN, Northeastern Morris County; Rev. JOSEPH T. ANGINOLI, Northern Morris County; Rev. P. CHRISTOPHER MULDOON, Western Morris County; Rev. STANLEY BARRON, Sussex County.

Diocesan Center—777 Valley Rd., Clifton, 07013. Tel: 973-777-8818; Fax: 973-777-8976. Office Hours: Mon.-Fri. 9-4:30. All mail should be addressed to this office.

Chancellor—Rev. JOHN E. HART.

Vice Chancellor—Rev. T. MARK CONDON.

Archivist—Rev. Msgr. RAYMOND J. KUPKE.

Secretary to the Bishop—Rev. T. MARK CONDON.

Admin. Asst. to the Bishop—Mrs. KIT SPRINGER.

Admin. Asst. to the Chancellor—Mrs. GRACE MAZZA.

Secretary to the Vice Chancellor—Ms. KERRY DOLAN.

Diocesan Counsel—Dwyre, Connell & Lisbona.

Diocesan Tribunal—

Judicial Vicar—Rev. Msgr. EDWARD J. KURTYKA, J.C.D.

Adjutant Judicial Vicar—Rev. JOSEPH T. ANGINOLI, J.C.L.

Advocates—Revs. JOHN T. CONNOLLY, M.Div.; MICHAEL BURKE, S.T.M., J.D.

Auditors—Revs. PAUL IOVINO; JOHN P. HANLEY; Deacon ANTHONY SALIERNO.

Defenders of the Bond—Rev. Msgr. KENNETH E. LASCH, J.C.D.; Revs. T. MARK CONDON, J.C.L.; EDWARD J. HINDS, J.C.L.; GEORGE F. HUNDT, J.C.L.

Pro-Synodal Judges—Rev. Msgr. JOHN J. CARROLL, Ed.D.; Revs. JOHN T. CATOIR, J.C.D.; MARK A. MANCINI, M.Div.; JOHN E. HART, J.C.L.; Rev. Msgr. JOHN J. DEMKOVICH; Rev. Msgr. JOHN H. DERICKS; Rev. Msgr. HERBERT K. TILLYER, M.Ch.A.; Rev. Msgr. THOMAS J. TRAPASSO, S.T.L.; Rev. REGIS P. WALLACE, O.S.B.

Administrative Assistants and Notaries—Mrs. SHAWN VACCA; Mrs. ROSE LUCIGNANI.

Consulting Psychologist—EDMUND J. RUBIN, Ph.D.; JAMES A. SAVAGE, Psy.D.

Presbyteral Council—Rev. Msgr. JOHN J. CARROLL; Rev. Msgr. PAUL KNAUER; Rev. Msgr. HERBERT K. TILLYER; Revs. Msgr. ELIAS TAMAYO; Rev. Msgr. PETER J. DOODY; Rev. Msgr. PAUL A. LONGUA; Revs. ROBERT J. GORDON; JOHN E. HART; WAYNE M. VARGA; PATRICK RICE; MARC MANCINI; RICHARD RENTO; SANTO FRAPAUL, O.F.M.Cap; ROBERT WISNIEFSKI.

College of Consultors—Rev. Msgr. PAUL A. LONGUA; Rev. Msgr. PAUL F. KNAUER; Rev. Msgr. HERBERT K TILLYER; Rev. Msgr. ELIAS TAMAYO; Rev. Msgr. PETER J. DOODY; Revs. JOHN E. HART; WAYNE M. VARGA; ROBERT J. GORDON; PATRICK RICE; MARC MANCINI; RICHARD RENTO; ROBERT WISNIEFSKI.

Diocesan Secretariats

Communications Secretariat—Mr. RICHARD A. SOKERKA, *597 Valley Rd., P.O. Box 1887, Clifton, 07015.* Tel: 973-278-3202; Fax: 973-279-2265.

"The Beacon"—Diocesan Newspaper, Mr. RICHARD A. SOKERKA, Editor & Gen. Mgr.; Ms. TERRI MAURO, Mng. Editor, *597 Valley Rd., P.O. Box 1887, Clifton, 07015.* Tel: 973-279-8845.

Communications Office—MARIANNA THOMPSON, Dir., *597 Valley Rd., P.O. Box 1887, Clifton, 07015.* Tel: 973-278-3202; Fax: 973-279-2265.

Secretariat For Parish Life—Mr. PHILIP A. RUSSO, Exec. Sec., *777 Valley Rd., Clifton, 07013.* Tel: 973-777-8818.

Office of Family Life—Rev. CHARLES J. PARR, Consultant.

Engaged Encounter—Rev. ROBERT J. MITCHELL, Spiritual Dir. Tel: 973-691-1561. Coordinators: TODD SCHMIDT; DEBBIE SCHMIDT. Tel: 973-726-7016. Registration Couple: DAVID DE MARTINO; LINDA DE MARTINO. Tel: 973-764-5711.

Respect Life—Mrs. MARIE RYAN, Consultant.

Office of Parish Catechetics—Mr. THOMAS BROWN, Consultant.

Catechetical Leaders Association—Ms. JOAN BUTKA. Tel: 973-427-0327.

Office of Ministry Among Hispanics—Rev. TERENCE MORAN, C.SS.R., Consultant; Ms. IVANNIA VEGA, Consultant for Hispanic Youth & Family Ministry.

Commission for Hispanic Catholic Ministry—Deacon JOSE GIRON, Chm. Tel: 973-742-0822.

Office of Worship and Spirituality—Dr. PATRICIA BARTLE, Consultant.

Liturgical Commission—Rev. EDWARD J. HINDS, Chm. Tel: 973-538-3231.

Environment & Architecture Commission—Rev. ROBERT GORDON. Tel: 973-779-6201.

RCIA Commission—Rev. EDWARD A. COLLINS. Tel: 973-696-1234.

Office of Youth Ministry—Consultants: Mr. PHILIP RUSSO; Ms. IVANNIA VEGA.

Young Prophets Catholic Youth Program in Paterson—Rev. GENO SYLVA, Dir. Tel: 973-694-3702, Ext. 13.

Catholic Scouting—Rev. WAYNE VARGA. Tel: 973-334-2090.

Office for Campus Ministry—Rev. LOUIS J. SCURTI, Coord., Catholic Campus Ministers. Tel: 973-595-6184.

Ecumenical Officer—Rev. CHARLES J. PARR, *737 Valley Rd., Clifton, 07013.* Tel: 973-777-5651.

Media Resourcing—Mrs. GINGER MOLL.

Related Organizations—

Catholic Deaf Society—Rev. Msgr. JOSEPH J. GOODE, Moderator, *651 Millbrook Ave., Randolph, 07869.* Tel: 973-895-1962. Rev. Msgr. THOMAS J. TRAPASSO, Asst. Moderator.

Charismatic Renewal—Rev. NICHOLAS BOZZA, Liaison. Tel: 973-347-0032.

English Cursillos—Mr. JACK LEONARD, Lay Dir. Tel: 908-637-6174. Spiritual Advisors: Rev. JOHN A. CONNELL; Deacon JOSEPH PARLAPIANO; Sr. MARIANNE JOYCE, S.C.

Spanish Cursillos—Vacant, Lay Dir. Tel: 973-361-9073. Rev. BRANDO IBARRA. Tel: 973-742-2142.

World Wide Marriage Encounter—Exec. Couple: BOB BROZON; LYNNE BROZON. Tel: 973-586-4016. Registration Couple: EILEEN PEREZ; RALPH PEREZ. Tel: 800-499-6552.

Pastoral Administration

Division of Clergy and Personnel—

Clergy Personnel Office—Rev. Msgr. THOMAS ZAZZELLA, Dir.; Mrs. ROSEMARY J. DONNELLY, Admin. Asst., *737 Valley Rd., Clifton, 07013.* Tel: 973-777-2955.

Deacon Internship Program—Rev. Msgr. FRANCIS J. DUFFY, Dir., *6 Sussex Ave., Morristown, 07960.* Tel: 973-538-4851.

Ministry for Priestly Formation and Education—Rev. CHARLES J. PARR, Dir., *737 Valley Rd., Clifton, 07013.* Tel: 973-777-5651.

Mission Office—Rev. Msgr. JOHN J. DEMKOVICH, Dir.; Mrs. ELEANOR MATAS, Office Mgr., *24 DeGrasse St., Paterson, 07505.* Tel: 973-278-3491.

Office of Health Care Ministry—Rev. Msgr. ROBERT M. DIACHEK, Dir., *205 Madison Ave., Madison, 07940-1003.* Tel: 973-443-9300.

Office of the Permanent Diaconate—Rev. Msgr. ROBERT M. DIACHEK, Vicar, *205 Madison Ave., Madison, 07940-1003.* Tel: 973-443-9300; Fax: 973-443-4140.

Vicar for Religious Communities—Sr. EILEEN KELLY, P.B.V.M., Coord. Tel: 973-777-8818.

Vocations Office—Rev. PAUL S. MANNING, Dir., *737 Valley Rd., Clifton, 07013.* Tel: 973-472-2812.

Division of Finance and Budget—

Business Office—Mr. WAYNE G. LONG, Finance Officer;Mr. JOSEPH LIPARI, Controller; Mrs. DEBORAH LOUGHEED, Bookkeeper; Mrs. BETTY ANN GREENE, Sec.; Mr. TIMOTHY POTTER, Dir. Devel., *777 Valley Rd., Clifton, 07013.*

Diocesan Facilities Manager—Mr. JAMES FIERRO.

Insurance Office—Mrs. EILEEN FOGARTY, Employee Benefits; Ms. DENISE SCHMIDT, Risk Mgr., *777 Valley Rd., Clifton, 07013.* Tel: 973-777-8818.

Diocesan Cemetery Office—Rev. Msgr. HERBERT K. TILLYER, Dir.; Mr. JOHN M. CAVANAUGH, Asst. Dir., *58 McLean Blvd., Paterson, 07513.* Tel: 973-279-2900.

School Division—Mr. FRANK PETRUCELLI, Supt.; Sr. DOROTHY BANASHAK, S.S.C., Asst. Supt. Secondary Educ. and Governmental Programs; Sr. JOSEPH SPRING, S.C.C., Asst. Supt. Elementary Educ.; Sr. NANCY GRASSIA, O.S.F., Asst. Supt.; Mr. JOHN FANELLI, Dir. Technology; Mr. PATRICK PEACE, Dir. Finances and Admin. Svcs.; Mr. PAUL OESTERLE, Educ. Council Pres.; Sr. MARGARET MURPHY, P.B.V.M., Elementary Principals' Assoc. Pres., *777 Valley Rd., Clifton, 07013.* Tel: 201-777-8818.

Secretariat for Catholic Charities—Mr. JOSEPH F. DUFFY, Exec. Sec.; Rev. EDWARD LAMBRO, Dir. Devel. & Public Rels., *24 De Grasse St., Paterson, 07505.* Tel: 973-279-7100; Fax: 973-523-1150.

Hispanic Information Center—Mr. LORENZO HERNANDEZ, Dir., *270 Passaic St., Passaic, 07055.* Tel: 973-779-7022.

Catholic Family and Community Services—Mr. JOSEPH F. DUFFY, Exec. Dir.; Mr. ROBERT JACOB, Assoc. Dir. & CFO; Ms. CATHERINE SPINA, Admin. Asst. Staff Attorneys: Rev. MICHAEL BURKE; Ms. VIRGINIA GROSSI, *24 De Grasse St., Paterson, 07501.* Tel: 973-279-7100.

Aging Services—Ms. PATRICIA REIDY, Dir. Tel: 973-279-4300.

Family Services—Rev. THOMAS MCGRATH, Dir., *476 17th Ave., Paterson, 07504.* Tel: 973-523-9595.

Friendship Corner—Ms. JANET TERRY, Dir., *279 Carroll St., Paterson, 07509.* Tel: 973-569-0001.

Parish Social Ministries—Mr. THOMAS MCCANN, Dir., *476 17th Ave., Paterson, 07504.* Tel: 973-523-7361.

Immigration and Refugee Services—Ms. MAI LIEU, Dir., *24 DeGrasse St., Paterson, 07501.* Tel: 973-279-7100.

Italian Catholic Center—Miss PHILOMENA DESOPO, Dir., *24 DeGrasse St., Paterson, 07501.* Tel: 973-278-4955.

Mt. St. Joseph's Children Center—Sr. DOROTHY SHEAHAN, S.C., *124 Shepherd Ln., Totowa, 07512.* Tel: 973-595-5720.

Multi-Lingual Center—Ms. ROSE KARDASHIAN, Dir., *24 DeGrasse St., Paterson, 07501.* Tel: 973-279-7100.

The Palloti Center—Ms. ANITA MORAWSKI, Dir., *476 17th Ave., Paterson, 07054.* Tel: 973-523-1544.

Partnership for Social Services—Sr. THOMASINA GEBHARD, S.S.M., Dir., *48 Wyker Rd., Franklin, 07416.* Tel: 973-827-4702.

Sancta Maria House of Mercy—Sr. MARIA WHILIFER, Dir., *360 E. 37th St., Paterson, 07504.* Tel: 973-523-1338.

Father English Multi-Purpose Community Center—Deacon ROBERT VESOTA, Exec. Dir., *435 Main St., Paterson, 07501.* Tel: 973-881-0280.

Preschool Day Care Center Programs—A Child's World-El Mundo del Nino; EUNICE RAMIREZ, Dir. A Child's Time-El Tiempo del Nino; LILA BANKS, Dir., *433 Main St., Paterson, 07501.* Tel: 973-278-3110. El Mundo de Colores; LAURA ZARIFE, Dir., *44 Ward St., Paterson, 07505.* Tel: 973-523-0919.

Passaic Teen Center—228 Hope Ave., Passaic, 07055. Tel: 973-473-5755.

Youth Haven—Shelter-Crisis Intervention, Ms. DENISE MEZA, Dir., *212 Slater St., Paterson, 07501.* Tel: 973-881-1611.

Catholic Social Services of Morris County, Inc. (Hope House)—Mrs. PHILOMENA D'SA, Exec. Dir.; Vacant, Dir. Devel. & Publicity; Mrs. BARBARA LONGO, Coord. Fix-It Prog.; Mr. STEPHEN T. DEATS, Coord. Alcoholism Programs; Miss KIM PRAITANO, Dir. AIDS Center; Mrs. RITA O'SHEA, Coord. Home Sharing Prog.; Ms. VERONICA CUNNINGHAM, Dir. Substance Abuse Prog.; Ms. NISHA ASWANI, Dir. Finance & Admin.; Ms. SUSAN DERAN, Coord. Chore Prog.; Ms. MELINDA STRANGEWAY, Dir. Gen. Counseling; Vacant, Clinical Supvr., *19-21 Belmont Ave., Dover, 07801.* Tel: 973-361-5555.

Department for Persons with Disabilities—Mr. THOMAS A. BARRETT, Exec. Dir.; Ms. JULIE TATTI, Assoc. Dir.; Sr. JOAN KATHLEEN GERCKE, S.S.J., Dir., Human Resources; Mr. ROCCO ZAPPILE, Comptroller, *1049 Weldon Rd., Oak Ridge, 07438.* Tel: 973-697-4394.

Group Homes—

Murray House—Ms. WANDA PEREZ, Dir., *86 Allwood Pl., Clifton, 07015.* Tel: 973-470-5694.

Wayne Marathon House—Mrs. MARIA ARCE, Dir., *648 Black Oak Ridge Rd., Wayne, 07470.* Tel: 973-628-9074.

Finnegan House—Ms. LYNNE OLIVARI, Dir., *1049 Weldon Rd., Oak Ridge, 07438.* Tel: 973-697-1246.

Alexander House—Ms. ARLENE GROSENBECK, Dir., *1049 Weldon Rd., Oak Ridge, 07438.* Tel: 973-697-1812.

Columbus House—Ms. CHERYL SLATE, Dir., *1049 Weldon Rd., Oak Ridge, 07438.* Tel: 973-697-1644.

Fitzpatrick House—Ms. PAMELA VAN ECK, Dir., *215 Mountain Ave., Pompton Lakes, 07442.* Tel: 973-248-1569.

Wehrlen House—Ms. MARGARET DOYLE, Dir., *18 Bisset Dr., West Milford, 07480.* Tel: 973-208-1883.

Gruenert Employment Center—Mrs. KATHY DE YOUNG, Dir., *725 Rte. 15 S., Lake Hopatcong, 07849.* Tel: 973-663-9102.

Basile Apartment—Mrs. JANET WASHINGTON, Dir., *Brittany Chase, Wayne, 07470.* Tel: 973-694-9591.

Calabrese House—Mr. THOMAS A. BARRETT, Exec. Dir., *829 Littleton Rd., Parsippany, 07054.* Tel: 973-299-8360.

Wallace House—Mr. THOMAS BARRETT, Exec. Dir., *447 Glen Rd., Sparta, 07871.* Tel: 973-726-3470.

Keleher Apartments—Ms. ISABEL ALMONTE, Dir., *67B Pike Dr., Wayne, 07470.* Tel: 973-697-4394.

Straight and Narrow, Inc.—Rev. NORMAN O'CONNOR, C.S.P., Exec. Dir. LORNA TONGARA, Exec. Asst.; Dr. RICHARD GUILD, Dir. Adult Residential Treatment; Mrs. KAREN HUTHER, Dir. Alpha-II Prog.; Ms. PHYLLIS ANDERSON, R.N., Dir. Mt. Carmel Hospital; Dr. RICHARD GUILD, Dir. Cedar Out-Patient Clinic; Bro. KENNETH HARDING, O.F.M., Dir. Juvenile Treatment Unit; Rev. GREG DROGON, Dir. Pastoral Care Unit; Dr. PAUL TEODORO, Medical Dir., *296 Straight St., Paterson, 07501.* Tel: 973-345-6000.

McNulty Half-Way House—Mr. PATRICK KELLY, Dir., *101 Cedar St., Paterson, 07501.* Tel: 973-279-7003.

Medical Day Care Center—HENRIETTA LEMON, R.N., Dir., *180 E. 19th St., Paterson, 07524-1537.*

Methadone Maintenance Centers—JACOB REED, Dir., *Bergen Pines Hospital, E. Ridgewood Ave., Paramus, 07652., Bergen Pines Hospital, 75 E. Broadway, Hackensack, 07601.*

Affiliated Organizations—

Apostleship of Prayer—Rev. Msgr. CHRISTOPHER DILELLA, Dir., *26 Green Village Rd., Madison, 07040.* Tel: 973-377-4000.

Diocesan Council of Catholic Women—Rev. Msgr. JOSEPH A. CIAMPAGLIO, Dir., *152 Mt. Pleasant Ave., Dover, 07801.* Tel: 973-366-7095. Mrs. MAUREEN JOYCE, *8 Glenwood Mountain Rd., Sussex, 07461.*

Justice and Peace Commission—Rev. PATRICK RICE.

Diocesan Holy Name Federation—Mr. FRANK STEINER, Pres.

Legion of Mary—Rev. Msgr. JOHN J. DEMKOVICH, Spiritual Dir.; Mrs. LUCY LEONE, Pres., *63 Monroe St., Passaic, 07055.* Tel: 973-779-0427.

Priests Eucharistic League—Rev. Msgr. CHRISTOPHER DILELLA, Dir., *26 Green Village Rd., Madison, 07040.* Tel: 973-377-4000.

Commission for Black Catholic Ministries—Mr. BRUCE B. LAWSON, Pres. Tel: 973-898-9260.

Commission for Hispanic Catholic Ministries—Deacon JOSE GIRON, Chm.

CLERGY, PARISHES, MISSIONS AND PAROCHIAL SCHOOLS

CITY OF PATERSON
(Passaic County)

1—CATHEDRAL OF ST. JOHN THE BAPTIST (1820), Rev. Msgr. Mark J. Giordani; Revs. Ruben Dario Cortez, S.X.; Luis A. Rendon (Colombia). In res., Deacons Manuel Santiago; Jose Pomales; Guido Pedraza.

Res., 381 Grand St., 07505. Tel: 973-345-4070; Fax: 973-345-7831. [CEM]

School—Pope John Paul II School. See Elementary Schools, Diocesan under Institutions Located in the Diocese for details.

Catechesis/Religious Programs—Students 350.

2—ST. AGNES (1883), Rev. Luciano Cruz; Deacon Gilberto Vazquez.

Res., 681 Main St., 07503. Tel: 973-279-0250; Fax: 973-357-1218.

Catechesis/Religious Programs—Students 184.

3—ST. ANTHONY'S (1909) (Italian), Revs. James Curran, S.D.B.; Vincent Duffy, S.D.B.; Jacinto Vaca, S.D.B.

Res., 138 Beech St., 07501. Tel: 973-742-9695; Fax: 973-881-0522.

School—(1921), 144 Beech St., 07501. Tel: 973-279-3510; Fax: 973-523-1757.

Salesian Sisters, Daughters of Mary Help of Christians 3; Lay Teachers 9; Students 280.

4—BLESSED SACRAMENT (1911) (Italian), Rev. Msgr. Richard A. Rusconi. In res., Rev. John F. Heusser.

Res., 224 E. 18th St., 07524. Tel: 973-523-5002; Fax: 973-523-3766.

School—(1953), 289-Sixth Ave., 07524. Tel: 973-278-8787; Fax: 973-278-6436.
Maestre Pie Filippini (Religious Teachers Filippini) 3; Lay Teachers 11; Students 250.
Catechesis/Religious Programs—Students 69.

5—St. Bonaventure (1877), Rev. John T. Piccione, O.F.M.; Deacon Joseph Balough. In res., Rev. Angelus Gambatese, O.F.M.
Res., 174 Ramsey St., 07501. Tel: 973-279-1016; Fax: 973-279-2507.
Catechesis/Religious Programs—Students 100.

6—St. Casimir's (1911) (Lithuanian), Rev. Paul O'Donnell Duggan.
Res., 147 Montgomery St., 07501. Tel: 973-279-1922.

7—St. George (1897), Revs. John J. Klein; Nelson Betancur; Deacon William Hussey.
Res., 408 Getty Ave., 07503. Tel: 973-742-0350; Fax: 973-754-0657.
School—(1897), 30 Michigan Ave., 07503. Tel: 973-684-6754; Fax: 973-684-1988.
Lay Teachers 12; Students 380.
Catechesis/Religious Programs—Students 90.

8—St. Gerard Majella (1962), Revs. George F. Hundt; John P. Hanley; Deacons Joseph Sisco; George Forshay.
Res., 501 W. Broadway, 07522. Tel: 973-595-8446; Fax: 973-790-0778.
School—(1965), Tel: 973-595-5640; Fax: 973-595-5475.
Sisters 2; Lay Teachers 8; Students 266.
Catechesis/Religious Programs—Students 95.

9—St. Joseph's (1867), Rev. Robert W. Wisniefski.
Res., 399 Market St., 07501. Tel: 973-278-0030.
School—Pope John Paul II School. See Elementary Schools, Diocesan under Institutions Located in the Diocese for details.

10—St. Mary's (1873). (Auxilium Christianorum). Revs. Joseph G. Buffardi; Jorge Rodriguez.
Res., 410 Union Ave., 07502. Tel: 973-790-8651; Fax: 973-790-8534.
School—(1874), 95 Sherman Ave., 07502. Tel: 973-956-1542; Fax: 973-956-1759.
Salesian Sisters of St. John Bosco 4; Lay Teachers 10; Students 307.
Catechesis/Religious Programs—Students 159.

11—St. Michael the Archangel (1903) (Italian), Rev. Joseph J. Orlandi. In res., Rev. Gregory Drogon.
Res., 70 Cianci St., 07501. Tel: 973-523-8413; Fax: 973-253-4279.

12—Our Lady of Lourdes (1882), Rev. Thomas Crangle, O.F.M.Cap.
Res., 440 River St., 07524. Tel: 973-742-2142; Fax: 973-345-9136.
School—(1883), Tel: 973-278-0164; Fax: 973-278-3030.
Lay Teachers 10; Students 270.
Catechesis/Religious Programs—Students 56.

13—Our Lady of Pompei (1916) (Italian), Rev. Sal J. Panagia; Deacon Henry Gallo.
Res., 70 Murray Ave., 07501. Tel: 973-742-1969; Fax: 973-742-1335.
Catechesis/Religious Programs—Students 160.

14—Our Lady of Victories (1882), Rev. Msgr. Thomas J. Coletta; Deacons Leo Gardner; Mario Munoz; Calvin Norris.
Res., 100 Fair St., 07501. Tel: 973-279-0487; Fax: 973-977-8506.

15—St. Stephen's (1903) (Polish), Rev. John T. Connolly. In res., Rev. Francis Maliszewski; Deacon Candelario Espinal.
Res., 86 Martin St., 07501. Tel: 973-742-2822; Fax: 973-742-1679.
Catechesis/Religious Programs—Students 62.

16—St. Therese (1926), Revs. Charles J. Waller; Donald J. Sella.
Res., 80-13th Ave., 07504. Tel: 973-881-0400.
School—(1953), 765 14th Ave., 07504. Tel: 973-278-4135; Fax: 973-278-3228. Deacon Nicholas Varsalona, Prin.
Lay Teachers 11; Students 320.
Catechesis/Religious Programs—Students 50.

OUTSIDE THE CITY OF PATERSON

Andover, Sussex Co., Good Shepherd (1979), Rev. Msgr. Richard A. Steiger; Deacon Thomas Sullivan.
Office: Rte. 517 (48 Tranquility Rd.), P.O. Box 464, 07821. Tel: 973-786-6631; 786-5520 (Res.).
Catechesis/Religious Programs—Tel: 973-786-6632.
Students 450.

Boonton, Morris Co., Our Lady of Mount Carmel (1847), Rev. Edward J. Hinds; Deacon Barry Costello.
Res., 910 Birch St., 07005. Tel: 973-334-1017; Fax: 973-335-1833. [CEM]
School—(1868), 205 Oak St., 07005. Tel: 973-334-2777; Fax: 973-334-0975.
Lay Teachers 12; Students 179.
Catechesis/Religious Programs—Tel: 973-334-0429.
Students 280.

SS. Cyril and Methodius (1907) (Slovak), Revs. James J. Termyna; Zdzislaw Nawrocki, S.CHR.; Sr. Ursula Carr, S.C., Pastoral Assoc.
Res., 215 Hill St., 07005. Tel: 973-334-0139; Fax: 973-402-9512. [CEM]
Catechesis/Religious Programs—Students 68.

Branchville, Sussex Co., Our Lady Queen of Peace (1951), Rev. Msgr. William P. Stober.
Res., 209 Rte. 206, 07826. Tel: 973-948-3185; Fax: 973-948-4799.
Catechesis/Religious Programs—Tel: 973-948-2741.
Students 340.

Budd Lake, Morris Co., St. Jude (1946), Rev. Robert J. Mitchell; Deacon Anthony C. Siino; Donna M. Cole, Pastoral Assoc. In res., Rev. Robert G. Hoffman.
Res., Mt. Olive Rd., 07828. Tel: 973-691-1561; Fax: 973-691-9060.
Catechesis/Religious Programs—Students 730.

Butler, Morris Co., St. Anthony (1878), Revs. Thomas R. Hartle, O.F.M.; John J. Doyle, O.F.M.; Sr. Joanne Beirne, O.P., Pastoral Assoc.
Res., 65 Bartholdi Ave., 07405. Tel: 973-838-0031; Fax: 973-838-0649. [CEM]
School—(1882), Tel: 973-838-0854; Fax: 973-838-1460.
Sisters 1; Lay Teachers 11; Students 220.
Catechesis/Religious Programs—Students 380.
Parish House—71 Bartholdi Ave., 07405. Tel: 973-838-8585.

Cedar Knolls, Morris Co., Notre Dame of Mt. Carmel (1917), Revs. Jude S. Salus, O.S.B.; Justin Capato, O.S.B.; Bro. James Konchalski, O.S.B.
Res., 75 Ridgedale Ave., 07927. Tel: 973-538-1358; Fax: 973-538-7403.
Catechesis/Religious Programs—Students 450.

Chatham, Morris Co., St. Patrick's (1874), Rev. Msgr. Ronald A. Amandolare; Rev. Owen Moran; Deacons Joseph A. Wisneski; Francis P. McQuade; Mark Nixon.
Res., 85 Washington Ave., 07928. Tel: 973-635-0625; Fax: 973-635-0119.
School—(1872), 45 Chatham St., 07928. Tel: 973-635-4623; Fax: 973-635-2311.
Lay Teachers 33; Students 373.
Catechesis/Religious Programs—Students 528.

Chatham Township, Morris Co., Corpus Christi (1966), Rev. Msgr. James Mahoney.
Res., 234 Southern Blvd., Chatham, 07928. Tel: 973-635-0070; Fax: 973-675-5518.
Catechesis/Religious Programs—Students 1,000.

Chester, Morris Co., St. Lawrence the Martyr (1950), Rev. Msgr. P. Kevin Flanagan; Rev. Lancelot Reis; Deacon Frank Owens.
Res., Main St., P.O. Box 730, 07930. Tel: 908-879-5371.
Catechesis/Religious Programs—Main St., P.O. Box 31, Tel: 908-879-6714; Fax: 908-879-7701.
Students 586.

Clifton, Passaic Co.,

1—Sacred Heart, (1897) (Italian), Rev. Msgr. Julian B. Varettoni; Revs. Andrew T. Perretta; Michael D. Joly.
Res., 145 Randolph Ave., 07011. Tel: 973-546-6012; Fax: 973-546-1814.
School—(1953), 43 Clifton Ave., 07011. Tel: 973-546-4695; Fax: 973-546-8774.
Lay Teachers 13; Students 276.
Catechesis/Religious Programs—Students 35.

2—St. Andrew the Apostle, (Allwood) (1938), Rev. Msgr. Peter J. McHugh; Rev. Boguslaw Kobus; Deacon Robert J. Ayers.
Res., 400 Mt. Prospect Ave., 07012. Tel: 973-779-6873; Fax: 973-779-0573.
School—(1953), 418 Mt. Prospect Ave., 07012. Tel: 973-473-3711; Fax: 973-473-6611.
Sisters of the Presentation 2; Lay Teachers 10; Students 252.
Catechesis/Religious Programs—Tel: 973-473-2863.
Students 169.

3—St. Brendan, (1945), Rev. Frank W. Weber. In res., Rev. Msgr. Francis Matarazzo; Rev. Alan F. Savitt.
Res., 154 E. First St., 07011. Tel: 973-772-1115; Fax: 973-772-0497.
School—(1946), 154 E. First St., 07011. Tel: 973-772-1149; Fax: 973-773-1163.
Sisters 1; Lay Teachers 13; Students 321.
Catechesis/Religious Programs—Tel: 973-772-6775; Fax: 973-772-5456.
Students 195.

4—St. Clare's, (1913), Rev. Msgr. Brendan P. Madden; Rev. Thomas J. Fitzgerald.
Res., 69 Allwood Rd., 07014. Tel: 973-777-7588.
School—(1959), Tel: 973-777-7582; Fax: 973-473-0127.
Lay Teachers 17; Students 220.
Catechesis/Religious Programs—Students 260.

5—SS. Cyril and Methodius, (1913) (Slovak), Rev. Msgr. John J. Demkovich, Admin.; Deacons John Teresinski; Edward Ramirez; Sr. Eleanor Goekler, Pastoral Assoc. In res., Rev. Jose Javier Nieves.
Res., 218 Ackerman Ave., 07011. Tel: 973-546-4390; Fax: 973-546-3269.

6—St. John Kanty, (1930) (Polish), Revs. Alex B. Cymerman, O.F.M.Conv.; Waclaw Sokolowski, O.F.M.Conv.; Roger Haas, O.F.M.Conv.; Deacon Robert Altilio.
Res., 49 Speer Ave., 07013. Tel: 973-779-4102; Fax: 973-779-2104.
School—(1958), 37 Speer Ave., 07013. Tel: 973-471-9407; Fax: 973-773-0857.
Felician Sisters 1; Lay Teachers 17; Students 234.
Catechesis/Religious Programs—Tel: 973-779-6214.
Students 250.

7—St. Paul, (1914), Revs. Victor J. Mazza; Brian Flanagan; Deacon Joseph Puskas. In res., Revs. Robert K. Hooper; Clement Cardillo, S.D.B.
Res., 124 Union Ave., 07011. Tel: 973-546-2746; Fax: 973-340-2083.
School—(1916), Tel: 973-546-2161; Fax: 973-546-0057.
Sisters of Charity 3; Lay Teachers 10; Students 200.
Catechesis/Religious Programs—Students 300.

8—St. Philip the Apostle, (1943), Rev. Msgr. Peter J. Doody; Revs. Robert J. Gordon; Thomas G. Rainforth; Deacon Gregory DeLorenzo.
Res., 797 Valley Rd., 07013. Tel: 973-779-6200; Fax: 973-779-2959.
School—(1954), Tel: 973-779-4700.
Lay Teachers 32; Students 565.
Catechesis/Religious Programs—Tel: 973-779-1439.
Students 528.

Convent Station, Morris Co., St. Thomas More (1966), Rev. Msgr. J. Francis Feenan. In res., Rev. Zbigniew Kluba.
Res., Madison Ave., Box 286-C, 07961. Tel: 973-267-5330.
Catechesis/Religious Programs—Students 220.

Denville, Morris Co., St. Mary's (1926), Rev. Msgr. James H. Murray; Rev. Richard V. Tartaglia; Deacons Al Klose; Charles Burrows.
Res., 15 Myers Ave., 07834. Tel: 973-627-0269; Fax: 973-627-6355.
School—(1954), Tel: 973-627-2606; Fax: 973-627-9316.
Lay Teachers 12; Students 210.
Catechesis/Religious Programs—Tel: 973-627-8276.
Students 660.

Dover, Morris Co., St. Mary's (1845), Revs. Richard H. Oliveri; John H. O'Connor.
Res., 425 W. Blackwell St., 07801. Tel: 973-366-0184; Fax: 973-366-5377. [CEM]
School—(1878), S. Main St., 07801. Tel: 973-366-0309; Fax: 973-366-6252.
Sisters of Christian Charity 1; Lay Teachers 17; Students 229.
Catechesis/Religious Programs—Tel: 973-366-0236.
Students 370.

Our Lady Queen of the Most Holy Rosary (1959) (Hispanic), Rev. Msgr. Elias Tamayo; Rev. Guillermo Velez; Deacon Percy Silva.
Res., 77 Richards Ave., 07801. Tel: 973-361-2725; Fax: 973-361-4058.
Catechesis/Religious Programs—Students 229.

Sacred Heart (1904), Rev. Msgr. Ronald J. Tully; Rev. Andrew Velez; Deacons Eugene P. Dolan; Brian Drury; Henry Hyle. In res., Rev. Msgr. Charles F. Powers, (Retired).
Res., 4 Richards Ave., 07801. Tel: 973-366-0060; Fax: 973-366-8636.
School—(1923), 30 N. Essex St., 07801. Tel: 973-366-2068; Fax: 973-366-9428.
Sisters of Sorrowful Mother 1; Lay Teachers 15; Students 230.
Catechesis/Religious Programs—Students 275.

East Hanover, Morris Co., St. Rose of Lima (1957), Rev. Msgr. William McCarthy; Deacons Robert A. Lang; Frank Puglia. Pastoral Assocs.: Sr. Dolores Alfone, F.S.R.; Sr. Concepta D'Amato, F.S.R.
Res., 312 Ridgedale Ave., 07936. Tel: 973-887-5572; Fax: 973-884-0476.
School—(1961), Tel: 973-887-6990.
Lay Teachers 28; Students 464.
Catechesis/Religious Programs—Tel: 973-887-0357.
Students 649.

Flanders, Morris Co., St. Elizabeth Ann Seton (1985), Rev. Msgr. John B. Wehrlen; Rt. Rev. Gerard P. Lair, O.S.B.; Deacons James McGrory; Stephen P. Natafalusy.

Res., 61 Main St., 07836. Tel: 973-927-1629; Fax: 973-927-1629.
Catechesis/Religious Programs—Tel: 973-927-7077; Fax: 973-927-0327.
Students 990.

Florham Park, Morris Co., Holy Family (1951), Rev. Msgr. Raymond J. Kupke; Rev. William J. Mooney. Pastoral Assocs.: Mrs. Barbara Froetscher; Mrs. Patricia Danishek; Mrs. Virginia Akhoury; Deacons William F. Ward; Mark McCabe.
Res., 1 Lloyd Ave., 07932. Tel: 973-377-1817; Fax: 973-377-6350.
School—(1954), Tel: 973-377-4181; Fax: 973-377-0273.
Sisters of Christian Charity 2; Lay Teachers 19; Students 293.
Catechesis/Religious Programs—Tel: 973-377-2498.
Students 577.

Franklin, Sussex Co., Immaculate Conception (1867), Rev. Martin G. Glynn.
Res., 75 Church St., 07416. Tel: 973-827-9575; Fax: 973-827-7375. [CEM]
Catechesis/Religious Programs—Tel: 973-827-9501.
Students 293.

Green Pond, Morris Co., St. Simon the Apostle (Rockaway Twp.) (1942), Rev. Joseph T. Anginoli.
Res., 1010 Green Pond Rd., 07435. Tel: 973-697-4699.
Catechesis/Religious Programs—Students 131.

Hainesville, Sussex Co., St. Thomas the Apostle (1941), Rev. Gerald F. Lewis.
Mailing Address: P.O. Box 187, Layton, 07851. Tel: 973-948-2296; Fax: 973-293-8933.
Catechesis/Religious Programs—Tel: 973-293-3536.
Students 71.

Hamburg, Sussex Co., St. Jude the Apostle (1966), Rev. William B. Collins.
Res., Beaver Run Rd., P.O. Box 1, 07419. Tel: 973-827-8030; Fax: 973-827-8382.
Catechesis/Religious Programs—Tel: 973-827-2280.
Students 325.

Haskell, Passaic Co., St. Francis of Assisi (1905), Rev. Msgr. Remigio G. Rocco; Deacon Jose Rivera.
Res., 868 Ringwood Ave., 07420. Tel: 973-835-0480; Fax: 973-835-3277.
School—(1912), Tel: 973-835-3268; Fax: 973-616-7644.
Lay Teachers 11; Students 216.
Catechesis/Religious Programs—Tel: 973-835-1946.
Students 323.

Hawthorne, Passaic Co., St. Anthony's (1908), Rev. Msgr. Elso C. Introini; Revs. T. Kevin Corcoran; Arthur J. Colaiacovo; Deacons Richard J. Brudzynski; Anthony E. Bernardin; Anthony Fadlalla.
Res., 276 Diamond Bridge Ave., 07506. Tel: 973-427-1478; Fax: 973-427-4826.
School—(1912), 268 Diamond Bridge Ave., 07506. Tel: 973-423-1818; Fax: 973-423-6065.
Sisters 1; Lay Teachers 12; Students 228.
Catechesis/Religious Programs—Tel: 973-427-7873.
Students 795.

Hewitt, Passaic Co., Our Lady Queen of Peace (1921), Rev. William Scully, O.F.M.; Deacons Charles Roche; Joseph Verboys.
Res., Friary, 1911 Union Valley Rd., 07421. Tel: 973-728-8162; Fax: 973-728-4650.
School—(1960), Tel: 973-728-9339; Fax: 973-728-6850.
Franciscan Sisters 1; Lay Teachers 9; Students 217.
Catechesis/Religious Programs—Tel: 973-728-8264.
Students 800.

Highland Lakes, Sussex Co., Our Lady of Fatima (1954), Rev. Msgr. Robert B. Carroll.
Mailing Address: P.O. Box 242, 07422. Tel: 973-764-4457; Fax: 973-764-4504.
Catechesis/Religious Programs—Tel: 973-764-7277.
Students 576.

Hopatcong, Sussex Co., St. Jude's (1931), Revs. George J. Gothie; John J. McGuigan.
Res., 40 Maxim Dr., 07843. Tel: 973-398-6377; Fax: 973-398-0121.
Catechesis/Religious Programs—Students 480.

Kinnelon, Morris Co., Our Lady of the Magnificat (1961), Rev. Msgr. John J. Carroll; Rev. Timothy Dowling; Deacon Joseph Richardson.
Res., 2 Miller Rd., 07405. Tel: 973-838-6838; Fax: 973-838-0710. [CEM]
School—(1964), Tel: 973-838-6222; Fax: 973-838-0409. Ms. Karen Fasanella, Prin.
Lay Teachers 11; Students 267.
Catechesis/Religious Programs—Tel: 973-838-0567. Sr. Ellen Denise O'Connor, F.S.P.
Students 610.

Lake Hopatcong, Morris Co., Our Lady Star of the Sea (Jefferson Twp.) (1910), Rev. P. Christopher Muldoon; Deacon Vincent Pisano.
Res., Espanong Rd., P.O. Box 337, 07849. Tel: 973-663-0211; Fax: 973-663-4302.
Catechesis/Religious Programs—Tel: 973-663-0124.
Students 510.

Lincoln Park, Morris Co., St. Joseph's (1922), Rev. Dennis J. Hogan; Sr. Eileen Halloran, F.S.P., Pastoral Assoc.; Deacons Stephen Marabeti; Joseph Parlapiano.
Res., 216 Comly Rd., 07035. Tel: 973-696-4411; Fax: 973-305-8466.
Catechesis/Religious Programs—Students 379.

Little Falls, Passaic Co., Our Lady of the Holy Angels (1883), Revs. Robert Sandoz, O.F.M.; Gregory Gebbia, O.F.M.; John Leonard, O.F.M.; Brian Cullinane, O.F.M.; Deacon Frank Muoio. Pastoral Assocs.: Sr. Margaret Lucille Peterson, O.P.; Sr. Mary Judith Lynch, O.P.
Res., 465 Main St., 07424. Tel: 973-256-5200; Fax: 973-256-0185.
School—(1903), 471 Main St., 07424. Tel: 973-256-1132; Fax: 973-890-0904. Sr. Mary Byrnes, P.B.V.M., Prin.
Sisters 1; Lay Teachers 8; Students 192.
Catechesis/Religious Programs—Students 926.

Long Valley, Morris Co., St. Luke (1982), Rev. Michael J. Drury.
Res., 3 Carl Ln., P.O. Box 416, 07853. Tel: 908-876-3515; Fax: 908-876-5277.
Church—265 W. Mill Rd., 07853.
Catechesis/Religious Programs—Students 612.

St. Mark the Evangelist (1986), Rev. Allen F. Stepien.
Res., 59 Spring Ln., 07853. Tel: 908-850-0652; Fax: 908-850-0648.
Catechesis/Religious Programs—Students 350.

Madison, Morris Co., St. Vincent Martyr (1805), Rev. Msgr. Christopher C. DiLella; Rev. Peter VB. Wells. In res., Rev. Anthony J. Clorra, O.P.M.CAP.
Res., 26 Green Village Rd., 07940. Tel: 973-377-4000; Fax: 973-377-8242. [CEM]
School—(1848), Tel: 973-377-1104; Fax: 973-377-2632.
Lay Teachers 25; Students 375.
Catechesis/Religious Programs—Tel: 973-966-1771.
Students 740.

McAfee, Sussex Co., St. Francis de Sales (1963), Rev. Msgr. John V. Boland; Rev. Frederick Walters.
Mailing Address: P.O. Box 785, 07428. Tel: 973-827-3248; Fax: 973-827-7534.
Catechesis/Religious Programs—Tel: 973-827-8300.
Students 1000.

Mendham, Morris Co., St. Joseph's (1853), Rev. Msgr. Kenneth E. Lasch; Deacons Robert F. Santos; William P. Long.
6 New St., 07945. Tel: 973-543-5950; Fax: 973-543-6025. [CEM]
School—(1963), Tel: 973-543-7474; Fax: 973-543-7817.
Lay Teachers 9; Students 260.
Catechesis/Religious Programs—Students 650.

Montague, Sussex Co., St. James the Greater (1943), Rev. Gerald F. Lewis.
Res., 75 River Rd., 07827. Tel: 973-293-3379; Fax: 973-293-8933.
Catechesis/Religious Programs—Tel: 973-293-3536.
Students 88.

Montville, Morris Co., St. Pius X (1959), Revs. Joseph J. Garbarino; John F. Tarantino; Deacons Andrew L. Cavaliere; Steven Madreperla.
Parish Ministry Office: Tel: 973-335-2894; Fax: 973-394-0069.
Res., 18 Changebridge Rd., 07045. Tel: 973-331-1706.
School—(1963), Tel: 973-335-1253; Fax: 973-335-2392. Sr. June Morrissey, S.C., Prin.
Lay Teachers 12; Students 250.
Catechesis/Religious Programs—24 Changebridge Rd.
Students 1000.

Morris Plains, Morris Co., St. Virgilius (1881), Rev. William L. Winston; Sr. Mary Larkin, Pastoral Assoc.; Deacons Sylvester Mazzoccoli; Daniel Scrone; Peter McNally; Merle Sisler. In res., Rev. Msgr. James L. Fallon, Pastor Emeritus.
Res., 250 Speedwell Ave., 07950. Tel: 973-538-1418; Fax: 973-538-2992.
School—(1910), Tel: 973-539-7267; Fax: 973-292-5157.
Sisters of St. Dominic 2; Lay Teachers 12; Students 246.
Catechesis/Religious Programs—Tel: 973-267-1366.
Students 554.

Morristown, Morris Co., Assumption of the Blessed Virgin Mary (1848), Rev. Msgr. Martin F. Rauscher; Rev. Dennis J. Crowley; Deacons P. Michael Hanly; Gabriel Lasch; William Harty; Tony DiLorenzo; Frank Para; Tom Spruiell. In res., Rev. Msgr. William P. Glennon; Rev. Joseph M. Casey.
Res., 91 Maple Ave., 07960. Tel: 973-539-2141; Fax: 973-984-0632. [CEM]
School—(1850), 63 MacCulloch Ave., 07960. Tel: 973-538-0590; Fax: 973-984-3632.
Sisters of Charity 3; Lay Teachers 34; Students 600.
Catechesis/Religious Programs—Tel: 973-267-5638.
Students 748.

St. Margaret's (1930), Rev. Msgr. Francis J. Duffy; Rev. J. Brando Ibarra. In res., Rev. Msgr. Thomas J. Trapasso.
Res., 6 Sussex Ave., 07960. Tel: 973-538-0874; Fax: 973-538-4581.
Catechesis/Religious Programs—Tel: 973-267-8354.
Students 240.

Mountain Lakes, Morris Co., St. Catherine of Siena (1956), Revs. Patrick Rice; Regis P. Wallace, O.S.B.
Res., 10 N. Pocono Rd., 07046. Tel: 973-334-7131; Fax: 973-334-3202.
Catechesis/Religious Programs—Tel: 973-334-5257.
Students 750.

Mount Arlington, Morris Co., Our Lady of the Lake (1888), Revs. Joseph Ryan; Desmond O'Connor, S.P.S.
Res., One Park Ave., 07856. Tel: 973-398-0240; Fax: 973-398-3667.
Catechesis/Religious Programs—Tel: 973-770-0291.
Students 361.

Mount Hope, Morris Co., St. Bernard's (1855), Rev. Joseph G. Farias, Admin.
Res., 446 Mt. Hope Rd., Wharton, 07885-2814. Tel: 973-627-0066; Fax: 973-627-3631.
Catechesis/Religious Programs—Students 84.

Netcong, Morris Co., St. Michael's (1873), Rev. Nicholas G. Bozza; Deacons Alex Buckholtz; Philip Pawlows; Joseph Keenan; Stuart Murphy.
Res., 4 Church St., 07857. Tel: 973-347-0032; Fax: 973-347-1560. [CEM]
School—(1922), Tel: 973-347-0039; Fax: 973-347-0054.
Sisters of Christian Charity 2; Lay Teachers 17; Students 460.
Catechesis/Religious Programs—Tel: 973-347-1465.
Students 560.

Newton, Sussex Co., St. Joseph's (1854), Rev. Peter Filipkowski; Deacons Gerald Hanifen; Alfred Kucinski; Raymond Biersbach. In res., Rev. Angelus Croce.
Res., 17 Elm St., 07860. Tel: 973-383-1985; Fax: 973-383-8164. [CEM]
Catechesis/Religious Programs—Tel: 973-383-8413.
Students 558.

New Vernon, Morris Co., Christ the King (1956), Rev. Patrick G. O'Donovan.
Res., Blue Mill Rd., P.O. Box 368, 07976. Tel: 973-539-4955; Fax: 973-267-7070.
Catechesis/Religious Programs—Tel: 973-539-5729.
Students 250.

Oak Ridge, Morris Co., St. Thomas, the Apostle (1949), Rev. Msgr. John E. Fitzpatrick.
Res., 5635 Berkshire Valley Rd., 07438. Tel: 973-208-0090; Fax: 973-208-0092. [CEM]
Catechesis/Religious Programs—Tel: 973-208-0096.
Students 332.

Ogdensburg, Sussex Co., St. Thomas of Aquin (1881), Rev. Stanley C. Barron; Deacon Edward Reading.
Res., 53 Kennedy Ave., 07439. Tel: 973-827-3190; Fax: 973-827-9738. [CEM]
Catechesis/Religious Programs—Students 151.

Parsippany, Morris Co., St. Christopher (1944), Rev. Msgr. Frank B. Ferraioli; Rev. Sean McDonnell (Ireland); Deacons John J. Kelly; Michael Pirylis; John Bernero; Edward Lally; Henry Rohrman. In res., Rev. George Kuzihappallil.
Res., 1050 Littleton Rd., 07054. Tel: 973-539-7050; Fax: 973-539-3601.
School—(1962), Tel: 973-539-7053; Fax: 973-539-0207.
Sisters of St. Dominic 4; Lay Teachers 15; Students 406.

Catechesis/Religious Programs—Tel: 973-539-6208.
Students 650.

St. Ann (1982), Rev. Msgr. Martin McDonnell; Sr. Frances Sanzo, S.S.C., Pastoral Assoc.; Deacons Donald O'Leary; Alfred Frank.
Res., 781 Smith Rd., 07054. Tel: 973-884-1986; Fax: 973-884-0940.
Catechesis/Religious Programs—Students 225.

St. Peter the Apostle (1938), Rev. Msgr. Herbert K. Tillyer; Revs. Wayne M. Varga; Ronald T. Sordillo; Sr. Sylvia Berzinski, S.S.C., Pastoral Assoc.; Sr. Regina McTiernan, C.S.J.B., Pastoral Assoc.; Deacons David Collins; Daniel Ferry; Timothy Manning.
Res., 179 Baldwin Rd., 07054. Tel: 973-334-2090; Fax: 973-334-5397.
School—(1958), Tel: 973-334-4704; Fax: 973-334-0622.
Sisters 1; Lay Teachers 20; Students 263.
Catechesis/Religious Programs—189 Baldwin Rd., 07054. Tel: 973-335-9713.
Students 617.

Passaic, Passaic Co.,

1—St. Nicholas, (1868), Rev. Msgr. Felipe N. Carvajal.
Res., 153 Washington Pl., 07055. Tel: 973-779-7867; Fax: 973-815-1893.
School—(1874), 123 Jefferson St., 07055. Tel: 973-779-1987; Fax: 973-779-1931.
Sisters of Charity 2; Lay Teachers 10; Students 260.
Catechesis/Religious Programs—Tel: 973-779-7867; Fax: 973-815-1893.
Students 250.

2—St. Anthony of Padua, (1917) (Italian), Revs. Hernan Arias; Ramilo Esplana.
Res., 95 Myrtle Ave., 07055. Tel: 973-777-4793; Fax: 973-779-6864.
School—(1960), 40 Tulip St., 07055. Tel: 973-773-0970.
Sisters 4; Lay Teachers 8; Students 220.
Catechesis/Religious Programs—Students 466.

3—Assumption of the Blessed Virgin Mary, (1891) (Slovak), Rev. Msgr. John J. Demkovich.
Res., 63 Monroe St., 07055. Tel: 973-779-0427; Fax: 973-472-5033.

4—Holy Rosary, (1918) (Polish), Revs. Stefan Las; Stanley Lesniowski.
Res., 6 Wall St., 07055. Tel: 973-473-1578; Fax: 973-779-5812.
Catechesis/Religious Programs—Students 350.

5—Holy Trinity, (1900) (German), Revs. Mark Olenowski; Antonio Rodriguez.
Res., 226 Harrison St., 07055. Tel: 973-778-9763; Fax: 973-778-7582.

6—St. Joseph's, (1892) (Polish), Rev. Msgr. Joseph Czerkies; Rev. Dariusz Kaminski.
Res., 7 Parker Ave., 07055. Tel: 973-473-0921; Fax: 973-473-4085.
Catechesis/Religious Programs—Students 245.

7—Our Lady Of Mt. Carmel, (1902) (Italian), Rev. Sam Frapaul, O.F.M.Cap.
Res., 10 St. Francis Way, 07055. Tel: 973-473-0246; Fax: 973-473-3404.
School—(1954), Tel: 973-473-8183; Fax: 973-473-0937.
Franciscan Sisters 4; Lay Teachers 12; Students 303.

8—Our Lady of Fatima, (1954) (Hispanic), Revs. Gilberto Gutierrez; Hector Melendez (Cuba).
Res., 32 Exchange Pl., 07055. Tel: 973-472-0815; Fax: 973-472-0250.
Catechesis/Religious Programs—Students 215.

9—St. Stephen's, (1902) (Magyar), Rev. Stephen N. Mustos, Sch.P.
Res., 223 Third St., 07055. Tel: 973-779-0332; Fax: 973-778-4263.
Catechesis/Religious Programs—Students 5.

Pequannock, Morris Co., Holy Spirit (1949), Revs. Alfred J. Lampron; Edward A. Collins; Deacons Gil Leifer; Michael Scruggs.
Res., 318 Tpke., 07440. Tel: 973-696-1234; Fax: 973-305-9390.
School—(1956), Tel: 973-835-5680; Fax: 973-835-1757.
Maestre Pie Filippini (Religious Teachers Filippini) 2; Lay Teachers 20; Students 350.
Catechesis/Religious Programs—330 Newark-Pompton Tpke., Tel: 973-835-5680.
Students 300.
Convent—Tel: 973-694-2111.

Our Lady of Fatima Chapel (Tridentine) (1994), Revs. Dennis Bouchard, F.S.S.P., Admin.; Nicholas Zolverowicz, F.S.S.P. In res., Rev. Kenneth Baker, S.J.
Res., 32 West Franklin Ave., 07440. Tel: 973-694-6727; Fax: 973-694-7629.
School—St. Maximilian Kolbe School, 18 First St., 07440. Tel: 973-694-1034; Fax: 973-694-1304. Mrs. Mary Lou Bednar, Prin.
Lay Teachers 4; Students 35.

Pompton Lakes, Passaic Co., Our Lady of the Assumption (1906), Revs. John Carnevale, O.F.M.; Jude Murphy, O.F.M.; Sean O'Brien, O.F.M.; Sr. Arlene Kollar, S.S.C., Pastoral Assoc.; Deacons Thomas Kimak; Hal Clark; Edward Higgins.
Parish Office: 64 Pompton Ave., 07442. Tel: 973-835-0374; Fax: 973-835-8173.
Res., St. Mary's Friary, 52 Lenox Ave., 07442. Tel: 973-839-1975.
School—(1951), Tel: 973-835-2010; Fax: 973-835-7529. Ms. Kathleen Berlino, Prin.
Lay Teachers 15; Students 235.
Catechesis/Religious Programs—Tel: 973-835-7750; Fax: 973-835-6307.
Students 1,735.

Pompton Plains, Morris Co., Our Lady of Good Counsel (1962), Rev. Msgr. Patrick J. Scott; Deacons Don X. Bancroft; Edward Jaroszewski; Charles Mallory. In res., Rev. Michael J. Lombardo.
Res., 155 W. Pkwy., P.O. Box 218, 07444. Tel: 973-839-2447; Fax: 973-839-9492.
Catechesis/Religious Programs—Tel: 973-839-3311.
Students 607.

Prospect Park, Passaic Co., St. Paul's (1924), Rev. Msgr. Edward J. Kurtyka; Rev. Marc Mancini. In res., Rev. Michael A. Burke.
Res., 286 Haledon Ave., Paterson, 07508. Tel: 973-790-8169.
Catechesis/Religious Programs—Tel: 973-790-8135.
Students 148.

Randolph, Morris Co., Resurrection (1978), Rev. Msgr. William M. Naughton; Revs. Brendan McLoughlin; Thomas A. Heffernan (BRK); Deacons Robert M. Flavin; Roger Lacouture; Kenneth Weaver.
Res., 651 Millbrook Ave., 07869. Tel: 973-895-4224; Fax: 973-895-3224.
Catechesis/Religious Programs—Tel: 973-895-4226; Fax: 973-895-9888.
Students 1,140.

St. Matthew the Apostle (1988), Rev. David McDonnell; Deacons Edward Keegan; William Peters; Patrick Sheehan.
Res., 267 Dover-Chester Rd., 07869. Tel: 973-584-1101; Fax: 973-584-0499.
Catechesis/Religious Programs—Students 638.

Ringwood, Passaic Co., St. Catherine of Bologna (1917), Rev. Msgr. Patrick G. Panos; Rev. Gerald B. Kanzic; Deacons James Elliott; Richard Michalski.
Res., 112 Erskine Rd., 07456. Tel: 973-962-7032; Fax: 973-962-1776.
School—(1948), Tel: 973-962-7131; Fax: 973-962-0585.
Franciscan Sisters of Ringwood 3; Lay Teachers 18; Students 345.
Catechesis/Religious Programs—Tel: 973-962-4966.
Students 510.

Rockaway, Morris Co., St. Cecilia's (1869), Revs. John E. Hart; Brendan J. Murray; J. Patrick Ryan. In res., Rev. Paul S. Manning.
Res., 70 Church St., 07866. Tel: 973-627-0313; 627-0316; Fax: 973-627-4811. [CEM]
School—(1958), Halsey Ave., 07866. Tel: 973-252-0760; Fax: 973-627-5217.
Sisters of Christian Charity 1; Lay Teachers 12; Students 316.
Catechesis/Religious Programs—Tel: 973-252-0760.
Students 770.

Sacred Heart (1923) (Slovak), Rev. John E. Hart, Admin.; Nannette Pierson, Pastoral Assoc. In res., Rev. Jeremiah C. O'Riordan; Bro. Luke Maher, F.S.C.
Res., 63 E. Main St., 07866. Tel: 973-627-0422; Fax: 973-627-6249.
School—(1965), Tel: 973-627-7689.
Sisters of the Sorrowful Mother 1; Lay Teachers 10; Students 335.

Rockaway Township, Morris Co., St. Clement, Pope and Martyr (1964), Rev. Msgr. Joseph A. Ciampaglio; Deacon Harry Dachisen.
Res., 154 Mt. Pleasant Ave., Dover, 07801. Tel: 973-366-7095; Fax: 973-366-6083.
Catechesis/Religious Programs—Tel: 973-366-7547; Fax: 973-366-7640.
Students 340.

Schooley's Mountain, Morris Co., Our Lady of the Mountain (1954), Rev. Ralph H. Sodano.
Res., Rte. 24, 07870. Tel: 908-876-4395. [CEM]
Catechesis/Religious Programs—Tel: 908-876-4003.
Students 950.

Sparta, Sussex Co., Our Lady of the Lake (1935), Rev. Msgr. Paul F. Knauer; Rev. Msgr. Paul Longua; Rev. A. Richard Carton. In res., Rev. Chukwudi Obiajunwa (Nigeria).
Res., 294 Sparta Ave., 07871. Tel: 973-729-6107; Fax: 973-729-7203.
School—(1954), Tel: 973-729-9174; Fax: 973-729-0318. Ms. Barbara Campione, Prin.
Lay Teachers 25; Students 492.
Catechesis/Religious Programs—Students 790.

Blessed Kateri Tekakwitha (1988), Revs. Daniel W. Murphy; John Andrew Connell, Admin.; Juan Carlos Ruiz; Sr. Barbara Moore, O.P., Pastoral Assoc.; Deacons Andrew Calandriello; Paul Puleo; Charles Mathias; William Pearson.
Res., 427 Stanhope Rd., 07871. Tel: 973-729-1682; Fax: 973-729-0702.
Catechesis/Religious Programs—Tel: 973-729-0489.
Students 1,267.

Stirling, Morris Co., St. Vincent de Paul (1886), Rev. Msgr. Patrick E. Brown; Rev. Albert Nix.
Res., Bebout Ave., 07980. Tel: 908-647-0118; Fax: 908-647-5992. [CEM]
School—(1955), Tel: 908-647-0421; Fax: 908-647-3878.
Lay Teachers 22; Students 281.
Catechesis/Religious Programs—Tel: 907-647-0772.
Students 703.

Stockholm, Sussex Co., St. John Vianney (1958), Rev. Matthew J. Twiggs; Deacons Edmund Galinski; Stanley Sisson.
Res., 07460. Tel: 973-697-6550; Fax: 973-697-6882.
Catechesis/Religious Programs—Tel: 973-764-7071.
Students 330.

Succasunna, Morris Co., St. Therese (1957), Revs. Joseph P. Davis; James A.D. Smith; Michael A. Walsh; Deacon Anthony Signorelli.
Res., 7 Hunter St., 07876. Tel: 973-584-8271; Fax: 973-584-0684.
School—(1963), Tel: 973-584-0812; Fax: 973-584-2029.
Sisters 2; Lay Teachers 8; Students 258.
Catechesis/Religious Programs—Tel: 973-584-8444; Fax: 973-584-9492.
Students 792.

Sussex, Sussex Co., St. Monica (1881), Rev. Charles A. Perricone; Deacon Jerome Schenker; Carol Bezak, Patoral Assoc.
Res., 33 Unionville Ave., 07461. Tel: 973-875-4521; Fax: 973-875-7538.
Catechesis/Religious Programs—Tel: 973-875-2252; Fax: 973-875-5531.
Students 950.

Swartswood, Sussex Co., Our Lady of Mt. Carmel (1951), Rev. John J. Quinlan; Deacons Ellis F. Schweitzer; Robert T. Davis; Edward J. Muller; Debra M. Tripi, Pastoral Assoc.
Mailing Address: P.O. Box 124, 07877. Tel: 973-383-3566; Fax: 973-383-3831.
Catechesis/Religious Programs—Tel: 973-579-2355.
Students 275.

Totowa Borough, Passaic Co., St. James of the Marches (1926), Rev. Msgr. Eugene M. Boland; Rev. Paul Iovino.
Res., 32 St. James Pl., Totowa, 07512. Tel: 973-790-0288; Fax: 973-790-7064.
School—(1956), Tel: 973-956-8824; Fax: 973-956-8824. Sr. Mary Ann Grimes, Prin.
Sisters 1; Lay Teachers 11; Students 180.
Catechesis/Religious Programs—31 St. James Pl., Tel: 973-790-4860; Fax: 973-790-4644.
Students 361.

Wayne, Passaic Co.,

1—Annunciation, (1963), Rev. Msgr. Stanislaus E. Schinski; Deacons Charles Tenga; Andrew Kostic; Paul Liotard.
Res., 45 Urban Club Rd., 07470. Tel: 973-694-5700; Fax: 973-694-5706.
Catechesis/Religious Programs—Tel: 973-694-0787.
Students 263.

2—Holy Cross, (1925), Rev. Charles J. Parr.
Res., 17 Van Duyne Ave., 07470. Tel: 973-696-1065.
Catechesis/Religious Programs—Tel: 973-696-3500.
Students 106.

3—Immaculate Heart of Mary, (1956), Rev. Msgr. Louis J. Bihr; Rev. Daniel A. Kelly; Deacons Joseph Sisco; Jaime Llanso. In res., Rev. Roger Hebert.
Res., 580 Ratzer Rd., 07470. Tel: 973-694-3400; Fax: 973-694-3459.
School—(1958), Tel: 973-694-1225; Fax: 973-872-9043.
Lay Teachers 15; Students 251.

Catechesis/Religious Programs—Tel: 973-694-4891.
Students 553.

4—OUR LADY OF CONSOLATION, (1963), Revs. James R. Hertel, J.C.D.; Philip Le Beau; Deacon Robert Pringle.
Res., 1799 Hamburg Tpke., 07470. Tel: 973-839-3444; Fax: 973-839-9695.
School—(1967), Tel: 973-839-2323; Fax: 973-839-2428.
Sisters 3; Lay Teachers 9; Students 217.
Catechesis/Religious Programs—Students 395.

5—OUR LADY OF THE VALLEY, (1960), Rev. Msgr. James H. O'Rorke; Deacons Michael Wallace; Vincent Cocilovo. In res., Rev. Eugene R. Sylva.
Res., 630 Valley Rd., 07470. Tel: 973-694-4585; Fax: 973-696-5451.
School—(1962), Tel: 973-696-2212; Fax: 973-696-0238.
Sisters of St. Joseph 1; Lay Teachers 22; Students 335.
Catechesis/Religious Programs—630 Valley Rd., Tel: 973-696-8307.
Students 770.

West Milford Township, Passaic Co., St. Joseph (1765), Rev. Bernard J. Splawski, O.F.M.; Deacons Milton Smilek; Anthony Curcio.
Res., 454 Germantown Rd., West Milford, 07480. Tel: 973-697-6100; Fax: 973-697-3716.
School—(1956), Tel: 973-697-6896.
Lay Teachers 11; Students 245.
Catechesis/Religious Programs—Tel: 973-208-0636.
Students 425.

Whippany, Morris Co., Our Lady of Mercy (1854), Revs. John DeMattia; John P. Pilipie; Sr. Ann McKeon, G.N.S.H., Youth Min.
Res., 9 Parsippany Rd., 07981. Tel: 973-887-0050; Fax: 973-887-0991. [CEM]
School—Tel: 973-887-2611; Fax: 973-887-6629. Sr. Catherine Duignan, C.S.J.P., Prin.
Lay Teachers 8; Students 175.
Catechesis/Religious Programs—94-96 Whippany Rd., Tel: 973-887-0767.
Students 390.

Chaplains of Public Institutions

Hospitals

PATERSON. *Preakness Hospital* P.O. Box V, 07509. Tel: 973-278-6800. Rev. John F. Heusser.
St. Joseph Hospital 703 Main St., 07503. Tel: 973-754-2000; 754-2060 (Office). Sr. Jane Frances Brady, Pres. & CEO; Rev. William N. Cramer, Dir. Pastoral Care; Sr. Marie Josetta Wethington, S.C.

DENVILLE. *St. Clare Hospital* Pocono Rd., 07834. Tel: 973-627-3000. Rev. Charles Lovato, Chap.

DOVER. *Dover General Hospital* Jardine St., 07801. Tel: 973-939-3000. Rev. Jeremiah C. O'Riordan.

MORRIS PLAINS. *Greystone Park Psychiatric Hospital* 07950. Tel: 973-538-1800. Rev. Joseph M. Casey.

MORRISTOWN. *Morristown Memorial Hospital* 100 Madison Ave., 07960. Tel: 973-540-5307. Rev. Zbigniew Kluba; Sr. Jo Mascera, S.S.C.

NEWTON. *Newton Memorial Hospital* 175 High St., 07860. Tel: 973-383-2121. Rev. John J. Quinlan.

PASSAIC. *Passiac General Hospital* 350 Blvd., 07055. Tel: 973-345-4300. Rev. Msgr. Francis Matarazzo; Rev. Robert K. Hooper.
St. Mary Hospital 211 Pennington Ave., 07055. Tel: 973-473-1000. Revs. Luke Guastella, O.F.M.Cap.; Vincent Liuzzo, O.F.M.Cap.

POMPTON PLAINS. *Chilton Memorial Hospital* 07444. Tel: 973-831-5000. Rev. Michael J. Lombardo.

TOTOWA. *North Jersey Developmental Center.* Rev. Louis J. Scurti.

WAYNE. *Wayne General Hospital* Hamburg Tpke., 07470. Tel: 973-942-6900. Rev. Michael J. Lombardo.

Correctional Facilities

PATERSON. *Passaic County Jail.* Rev. Msgr. Mark J. Giordani; Rev. Hernan Arias.

MORRIS PLAINS. *Morris County Youth Center.* Rev. Robert G. Hoffmann.

MORRISTOWN. *Morris County Jail.* Rev. Msgr. Patrick E. Brown.

NEWTON. *Sussex County Jail.* Rev. Robert G. Hoffmann.

Special Assignment:
Reverend Fathers—
Condon, T. Mark, 178 Derrom Ave., Paterson, NJ 07504
Diachek, Robert M., 205 Madison Ave., Madison, NJ 07940-1053. Tel: 973-236-1333
McGrath, Thomas M., 476 17th Ave., Paterson, NJ 07504. Tel: 201-523-9595

On Duty Outside the Diocese:
Reverend Fathers—
Brown, Patrick, Ellenville, NY
Coutinho, Absalom, Palmetto, FL
DiCristina, Frank A., Beaumont, CA
Erwin, Patrick O., Mayaguez, PR
Grasso, Richard, Daytona Beach, FL
Holterhoff, Edward G., Monterey, CA
Mastroeni, Anthony J., Christendom College, Front Royal, VA
McLeod, David, Manahawkin, NJ
Moss, James T., Saskatoon, Saskatchewan, Canada
Pavlick, Raymond A., Walden, NY
Reading, Edward, Ortley Beach, NJ
Stephenson, Alphonse J., Point Pleasant, NJ
Vitillo, Robert J., Washington, DC
Weis, John H., Bad Axe, MI

Military Chaplains:
Reverend Monsignors—
Cusack, John J., USAF
Reverend Fathers—
Briganti, Philip J., USA
O'Grady, Frank, USA
Parisi, Michael, USN

Sabbatical:
Reverend Fathers—
McLoughlin, Brendan

Absent on Leave:
Reverend Monsignors—
Alonso, Jose A.
Goode, Joseph J.
Reverend Fathers—
Coppola, David L.
Gorrell, Paul
Holliday, David D.
Pisarcik, John G.
White, Gregory A.

Unassigned:
Reverend Fathers—
Daly, M. Paul
Dillon, Edward J.
Mabango, Ashiono Anthony
Scolamiero, Dominic A.
Scott, James C.

Retired:
Reverend Monsignors—
Bertasius, Anthony
Biesiada, Louis W., 2001 N.E. 38th St., Lighthouse Point, FL 33064
Bischoff, Francis J., 140 Shepherd Ln., Totowa, NJ 07512
Busch, Aloysius J., Nazareth Village, Main St., Chester, NJ 07930
Carey, Leo P., Nazareth Village, Main St., Box 635, Chester, NJ 07930
Cassidy, Charles C., 516 Oak Hill Ct., Lanoka Harbor, NJ 08734
Conway, Michael, 3900 S. University Dr., Davie, FL 33328
Corr, John F., 83 Primose Tr., Morristown, NJ 07960
Dericks, John H., 288 Lackawanna Dr., Andover, NJ 07821
Doyle, James J., 140 Shepherd Ln., Totowa, NJ 07512
Dudak, George A., P.O. Box 257, Hibernia, NJ 07842
Fallon, James L., 10 W. Hanover Ave., Morris Plains, NJ 07950
Ferrito, Joseph L., 516 Oak Hill Ct., Lanoka Harbor, NJ 08734
Flek, Ladislaus J., 140 Shepherd Ln., Totowa, NJ 07512
Gallo, Louis J., Nazareth Village, Main St., Box 635, Chester, NJ 07930
Hayes, Denis A., 140 Shepherd Ln., Totowa, NJ 07512
Lee, Thaddeus, P.O. Box 2044, Beach Haven, NJ 08008
McBride, Peter A., Nazareth Village, Main St., Chester, NJ 07930
McQuaid, Eugene, P.O. Box 628, Dingmans Ferry, PA 18328
Meyer, Joseph J., 140 Shepherd Ln., Totowa, NJ 07512
Morris, John E., 140 Shepard Ln., Totowa, NJ 07512
Podgorny, John
Powers, Charles F., 4 Richards St., Dover, NJ 07801
Puma, Vincent E., 970 Black Oak Ridge Rd., Wayne, NJ 07470
Rugel, James J., 12 Grove Rd., Oak Ridge, NJ 07438
Russo, Charles J., 27 Livingston Rd., Morristown, NJ 07960
Ryan, John R., Nazareth Village, Main St. Box 635, Chester, NJ 07930
Ryan, Leo P., Nazareth Village, Main St. Box 635, Chester, NJ 07930
Trapasso, Thomas J., 6 Sussex Ave., Morristown, NJ 07960
Zazella, Thomas J.
Reverend Fathers—
Catoir, John T.
Colucci, Gregory
Costigan, George, St. Francis Convent, Windemere Ave., Mt. Arlington, NJ 07856
Davey, Edward M., Nazareth Village, Main St., Chester, NJ 07930
Fanning, Leo M., 14 Polar Bear Path, Ormond Beach, FL 32174
Feeney, Bernard, R.R. 6, Box 399, Branchville, NJ 07826
Hanley, James T.
Hebert, Roger, 580 Ratzer Rd., Wayne, NJ 07470
Heekin, John M.
Hewitt, Kenneth R., 490 Windemere Ave., Mount Arlington, NJ 07856
Jacobs, Richard A., 7 Middlesex Rd., East Greenbush, NY 12061
Jasaitis, Raymond J., Nazareth Village, Main St., Box 635, Chester, NJ 07930
Krajewski, Paul A., 10 Prime Rose Ln., Mount Arlington, NJ 07856
LoGatto, Joseph J., 424 Third St., Carlstadt, NJ 07072
Lugo, Joseph W., 78 Chestnut St., Bridgewater, NJ 08807
Maliszewski, Francis, 86 Martin St., Paterson, NJ 07501
McHugh, Dennis, Our Lady's Shrine, Knock, County Mayo, Ireland
Mullan, Patrick, Nazareth Village, Main St., Box 635, Chester, NJ 07930
Murphy, Joseph E., Narareth Village, Main St., Box 635, Chester, NJ 07930
Mushinsky, John E., 22 Boston Rd., Neptune, NJ 07753
O'Kielty, James P., Nazareth Village, Main St., Box 635, Chester, NJ 07930
O'Riordan, Jeremiah, 63 E. Main St., Rockaway, NJ 07866
Pruschowitz, Walter M., Beverwyck Nursing Home, 420 Beverwyck Rd., Parsippany, NJ 07054 Germany
Rento, Richard G., 33 Murray Ln., Lavalette, NJ 08735
Ruddy, Edward J., St. Attracta's Nursing Home, Knock Rd., Charlestown, County Mayo, Ireland
Shema, George T., Nazareth Village, Main St., Box 635, Chester, NJ 07930
Sullivan, John A., 730 Linnwood Ave., Brick, NJ 08723

Permanent Deacons:
Acevedo, Pedro, St. Agnes, Paterson
Altilio, Robert M., St. John Kanty, Clifton
Ayers, Robert, St. Andrew the Apostle, Clifton
Balough, Joseph, St. Bonaventure, Paterson
Bancroft, Don X., Our Lady of Good Counsel, Pompton Plains
Bernardine, Anthony E., St. Anthony, Hawthorne
Bernero, John, St. Christopher, Parsippany
Bianchi, Roland, Archdiocese of Newark, NJ
Biersbach, Raymond, St. Joseph, Newton
Brudzynski, Richard, St. Anthony, Hawthorne
Buckholtz, Alexander E., St. Michael Church, Netcong
Burrows, Charles, St. Mary, Denville
Calandriello, Andrew, Blessed Kateri Tekakwitha, Sparta
Cassidy, Joseph, Retired
Cavaliere, Andrew L., St. Pius X, Montville
Ciampa, Alfred, Unassigned
Clark, Hal G., St. Mary, Pompton Lakes
Cocilovo, Vincent, Our Lady of the Valley, Wayne
Collins, David, St. Peter the Apostle, Parsippany
Cortes, Jesus, Our Lady of Fatima, Passaic
Costello, Barry, Mt. Carmel Church, Boonton
Crowley, Joseph C., Jr., Our Lady of Consolation, Wayne
Curcio, Anthony, Jr., St. Joseph, West Milford
Dachisen, Harry, St. Clement Pope and Martyr, Rockaway Township
DaSilva, Joao, St. Matthew, Randolph
Davis, Robert T., Our Lady of Mount Carmel, Swartswood
de Mena, Henry, Unassigned
DeLorenzo, Gregory, St. Philip Church, Clifton
DiLorenzo, Anthony, Assumption, Morristown
Dolan, Eugene P., Sacred Heart, Dover
Drury, Brian, Sacred Heart, Dover
Elliott, James, St. Catherine of Bologna, Ringwood
Espinal, Candelario, St. Stephen, Paterson
Fadalla, Gerald J.

Fanelli, Alfredo, Notre Dame of Mt. Carmel, Cedar Knolls
Ferry, Daniel F., St. Peter the Apostle, Parsippany
Forshay, George W., St. Gerard Majella, Paterson
Frank, Alfred E., St. Ann, Parsippany
Galinski, Edmund V., St. John Vianney, Stockholm
Gallo, Henry, Our Lady of Pompei, Paterson
Gardner, Leo, Our Lady of Victories, Paterson
Gibbons, Thomas P., Our Lady of the Mountain, Schooley's Mountain
Giron, Jose D., St. Stephen, Paterson
Grish, Kevin, (Unassigned)
Hanifen, Gerald B., St. Joseph, Newton
Hanly, P. Michael, Assumption, Morristown
Harty, William, Assumption, Morristown
Head, Robert C., Our Lady of the Mountain, Schooley's Mountain
Healy, Philip, Immaculate Heart of Mary, Wayne
Healy, Thomas F., Jr., St. Luke, Long Valley
Higgins, Edward J., St. Mary, Pompton Lakes
Hilber, Joseph, Good Shepherd, Andover
Hussey, William E., St. George Church, Paterson
Hyle, Henry, Sacred Heart, Dover
Jaroszewski, Edward, Our Lady of Good Counsel Church, Pompton Plains
Jones, Frederick B., Jr., 6th ASG Chaplain Office, APO, AE 09107
Keegan, Edward, St. Matthew, Randolph
Keenan, Joseph, St. Michael, Netcong
Kelly, John, St. Christopher, Parsippany
Kimak, Thomas J., St. Mary, Pompton Lakes
Klose, Albert P., St. Mary, Denville
Kostic, Andrew, Annunciation, Wayne
Kronyak, Robert
Kronyak, Thomas, St. Jude, Hamburg
Lacouture, Roger, Resurrection, Randolph
Lally, Edward J., St. Christopher, Parsippany
Lang, Robert A., St. Rose of Lima, East Hanover
Larkin, John S., Diocese of Charleston, SC
Lasch, Gabriel L., Assumption BVM Church, Morristown
Lebron, Florencio G., (Unassigned)
Leifer, Gil, Holy Spirit, Pequannock
Liotard, Paul A., Annunciation, Wayne
Llanso, Jamie, Father English Center, Paterson
Llibre, John, Unassigned
Long, William P., St. Joseph, Mendham
Madreperla, Steven A., St. Pius X, Montville
Mallory, Charles, Our Lady of Good Counsel Church, Pompton Plains
Manning, Tim, St. Peter the Apostle, Parsippany
Marabeti, Stephen J., St. Joseph Church, Lincoln Park
Maron, Edward, Our Lady of the Lake, Sparta
Mathias, Charles T., Bl. Kateri Tekakwitha, Sparta
Mazzaccoli, Sylvester A., St. Virgil Church, Morris Plains
McCabe, Mark, Holy Family, Florham Park
McCaffrey, David
McGrory, James G., St. Elizabeth Ann Seton, Flanders
McMullin, Robert, St. Gerard Majella, Paterson
McNally, Peter J., St. Virgil, Morris Plains
McQuaid, Francis P., St. Patrick, Chatam
Meyer, John, Diocese of Charleston, SC
Michalski, Richard, St. Catherine of Bologna, Ringwood
Morris, James, Blessed Sacrament, Paterson
Muller, Edward J., Our Lady of Mount Carmel, Swartswood
Munoz, Mario, Our Lady of Victories, Paterson
Muoio, Frank, Holy Angels Church, Little Falls
Murphy, Stuart, St. Michael, Netcong
Natafalusy, Stephen P., St. Elizabeth Ann Seton, Flanders
Nixon, Mark G., St. Patrick, Chatham
Norris, Calvin P., Our Lady of Victories, Paterson
O'Leary, Donald, St. Ann, Parsippany
Ochner, Ronald, Diocese of Venice, FL
Owens, Frank, St. Lawrence the Martyr, Chester
Padden, Frank J.
Para, Frank, Assumption, Morristown
Parlapiano, Joseph J., St. Joseph, Lincoln Park
Pawlows, Philip T., St. Michael, Netcong
Pearson, William J., Blessed Kateri Tekakwitha, Sparta
Pedraza, Guido, St. John the Baptist, Paterson
Peters, William L., St. Matthew, Randolph
Pilek, John F., St. Luke, Long Valley
Pirylis, Michael, St. Christopher, Parsippany
Pisano, Vincent F., Our Lady Star of the Sea, Hopatcong
Pomales, Jose, St. John Cathedral, Paterson
Pringle, Robert H., Our Lady of Good Counsel, Pompton Plains
Puglia, Frank, St. Rose of Lima, East Hanover
Puleo, Paul A., Blessed Kateri Tekakwitha, Sparta
Puskas, Joseph, St. Paul, Clifton
Quinn, Joseph, Notre Dame of Mt. Carmel, Cedar Knolls
Ramirez, Edward, St. Nicholas, Passaic
Reading, Edward J., St. Thomas of Aquin, Ogdensburg
Reed, Daniel, Unassigned
Richardson, Joseph, Our Lady of Magnificat, Kinnelon
Rivera, Jose M., St. Francis of Assisi, Haskell
Roche, Charles, St. Francis of Assisi, Haskell
Rohrman, Harry, St. Christopher, Parsippany
Salierno, Anthony, St. Mary, Paterson
Sanchez, Armando, Blessed Sacrament, Paterson
Santiago, Manuel, St. John the Baptist Cathedral, Paterson
Santos, Robert F., St. Joseph, Mendham
Schenker, Jerome, St. Monica, Sussex
Schwietzer, Ellis F., Our Lady of Mount Carmel, Swartswood
Scrone, Daniel, St. Virgil, Morris Plains
Scruggs, Michael K., Holy Spirit, Pequannock
Sheehan, Patrick, St. Matthew, Randolph
Signorelli, Anthony, St. Therese, Succasunna
Siino, Anthony C., St. Jude, Budd Lake
Silva, Percy, Our Lady Queen of the Holy Rosary, Dover
Simeone, Enio, Passaic General Hospital
Sisco, Joseph, St. Gerard Majella, Paterson
Sisler, Merle F., St. Virgil, Morris Plains
Sisson, Stanley, St. John Vianney, Stockholm
Smilek, Milton, St. Joseph, West Milford
Spruiell, Thomas, Assumption, Morristown
Sullivan, Thomas, Good Shepherd, Andover
Tenga, Charles, Annunciation, Wayne
Teresinski, John S., SS. Cyril & Methodius Church, Clifton
Turner, John, Leave of Absence
Van Orman, Patrick, Our Lady of the Mountain, Schooleys Mountain
Van Vleet, Arthur H., St. Joseph, Newton
Varsalona, Nicholas, St. Therese Church, Paterson
Vazquez, Gilberto, St. Agnes, Paterson
Verboys, Joseph R., Our Lady Queen of Peace, Hewitt
Vesota, Robert, Father English Center, Paterson
Walker, John, (Unassigned)
Wallace, Michael J., Our Lady of the Valley, Wayne
Ward, William, Holy Family, Florham Park
Weaver, Kenneth, Resurrection, Randolph
Whelan, Edward, Sacred Heart, Dover
Wisneski, Joseph A., St. Patrick, Chatham

INSTITUTIONS LOCATED IN THE DIOCESE

[A] SEMINARIES, RELIGIOUS OR SCHOLASTICATES

OAK RIDGE. *Paulist Novitiate*, 243 Mount Paul Rd., 07438-9512. Tel: 973-697-6341.
E-mail: Jfoleycsp@cs.com
Missionary Society of St. Paul the Apostle (Paulist Fathers). Rev. John J. Foley, C.S.P., J.C.D., Dir. Ministries.

[B] COLLEGES AND UNIVERSITIES

HALEDON. *Salesian College*, 655 Belmont Ave., 07508. Tel: 973-790-7963; Fax: 973-790-6484.
E-mail: secretarysua@aol.com
For a complete listing, refer to the Colleges and Universities section.

MENDHAM. *Assumption College for Sisters*, 07945. Tel: 973-543-6528; Fax: 973-543-9459.
E-mail: socc@nac.net
Web site: www.acscollegeforsisters.org
For a complete listing, refer to the Colleges and Universities section.

MORRISTOWN. *College of Saint Elizabeth*, 2 Convent Rd., 07960-6989. Tel: 973-290-4000; Fax: 973-290-4488.
E-mail: smgeorge@112a.st-elizabeth.edu
Web site: www.st-elizabeth.edu
For a complete listing, refer to the Colleges and Universities section.

[C] HIGH SCHOOLS, DIOCESAN

PATERSON. *Paterson Catholic Regional High School*, 764-11th Ave., 07514. Tel: 973-278-1024; Fax: 973-684-7244.
E-mail: gperez@nettrip.net
Sr. Gloria Perez, P.B.V.M., Prin.; Teresa Kerr, Asst. Prin.; Michele R. Fierro, Asst. Prin..Priests 1; Sisters 2; Brothers 3; Lay Teachers 33; Students 470.

DENVILLE. *Morris Catholic High School*, 07834. Tel: 973-627-6674; Fax: 973-627-4351.
E-mail: morcath@morriscatholic.org
Web site: www.morriscatholic.org
Bro. Luke Maher, F.S.C., Dir.; Sr. Marie Pauline Demek, S.C.C., Asst. Prin.; Rev. Paul S. Manning, Chap..Priests 1; Brothers 1; Sisters 7; Lay Teachers 28; Students 395.

MADISON. *Bayley-Ellard High School*, 07940. Tel: 973-377-2486; Fax: 973-377-6639.
E-mail: bayley@nac.net
Web site: www.nac.net/bayley
Mr. Frank D. Mattiace, Exec. Dir. & Prin.; Rev. Msgr. John F. Corr; Rev. Msgr. James L. Fallon. Priests 2; Sisters 3; Lay Teachers 34; Students 250.

SPARTA. *Pope John XXIII High School*, 07871. Tel: 973-729-6125; Fax: 973-729-4313.
E-mail: dipathspj@impresso.com
Rev. Kieran A. McHugh, Prin..Lay Teachers 58; Students 822.

WAYNE. *De Paul High School*, 1512 Alps Rd., 07470. Tel: 973-694-3702; Fax: 973-633-5381.
E-mail: tsmithline@depaulcatholic.org
Web site: depaulcatholic.org
Thomas Smithline, Prin.; Rev. Eugene R. Sylva..Sisters 1; Lay Teachers 46; Students 575.

[D] HIGH SCHOOLS, PRIVATE

PATERSON. *Don Bosco Technical High School*, 202 Union Ave., 07502. Tel: 973-595-8800; 790-5508 (Residence); Fax: 973-595-8987.
E-mail: dbtpat@juno.com
Revs. Steve Schenck, S.D.B., Dir.; James Horan, S.D.B.; Paul P. Avallone, S.D.B.; Michael Mendl, S.D.B.; Thomas McGahee, S.D.B.; Adelard La Bonte, S.D.B.; Bros. Bruno Busatta, S.D.B.; John Andres, S.D.B.; John Cauda, S.D.B.; Henry VanDerVelden, S.D.B.; Andrew Bertello, S.D.B. Priests 6; Brothers 8; Sisters 2; Lay Teachers 20; Students 350.
Don Bosco Volunteers, Inc. Rev. Paul P. Avallone, S.D.B., Contact Person.

CONVENT STATION. *Academy of St. Elizabeth*, 07961. Tel: 973-290-5200; Fax: 973-290-5232. Sisters of Charity. Sr. Patricia Mary McMullen, S.C., Prin. Sisters 6; Lay Teachers 24; Students 230.

MORRISTOWN. *Delbarton School*, 230 Mendham Rd., 07960. Tel: 973-538-3231; Fax: 973-538-8836.
E-mail: homepage@delbarton.org
Web site: www.delbarton.org
Day School for Boys. (Grades 7-12). Rev. Luke L. Travers, O.S.B., Headmaster. Asst. Headmasters: Mr. John Kowalik, Dean of School; Mr. Edward Kim, Dean of Faculty; Mr. David Donovan, Dir. of Admissions; Rev. Edward Seton J. Fittin, O.S.B., Dir. Campus Min. Monks 18; Laymen 70; Students 541.

Villa Walsh Academy, 07960. Tel: 973-538-3680; Fax: 973-538-6733.
E-mail: villawalsh@aol.com
Web site: www.villawalsh.org
College Preparatory for girls (Grades 7-12). Conducted by Religious Teachers Filippini. Sr. Patricia Pompa, M.P.F., Prin. Sisters 9; Lay Teachers 25; Students 235.

NORTH HALEDON. *Mary Help of Christians Academy*, 659-723 Belmont Ave., 07508. Tel: 973-790-6200; Fax: 973-790-6125.
E-mail: tma24@maryhelp.net
Web site: www.maryhelp.org
Daughters of Mary Help of Christians (Salesian Sisters). Sr. Carmen Pena, F.M.A., Supr.; Sr. Margaret Wilhelm, F.M.A., Prin. Sisters 22; Lay Teachers 19; Students 212.

[E] ELEMENTARY SCHOOLS, DIOCESAN

CLIFTON. *Pope John Paul II School*. Serving St. John the Baptist Cathedral and St. Joseph, Paterson, 775 Valley Rd., 07013. Tel: 973-458-9282.
E-mail: principal@pjpii.com
Sr. Theresa Kelly, F.M.A., Prin. Asst. Principals: Ms. Kathleen Fields; Sr. Theresa Samson, F.M.A. Sisters 6; Lay Teachers 32; Students 800.

[F] REGIONAL ELEMENTARY SCHOOLS

FRANKLIN. *Immaculate Conception Regional School*, 65 Church St., 07416. Tel: 973-827-3777; Fax: 973-827-8728.
E-mail: so'leary@tapnet.net
Mrs. Sheila O'Leary, Prin. Serves Immaculate Conception, Franklin; Our Lady of Fatima, Highland Lakes; St. John Vianney, Stockholm; St. Monica, Sussex; St. Thomas of Aquin, Ogdensburg; St. Francis De Sales, McAfee; St. Jude, Hamburg. Sisters 2; Lay Teachers 12; Students 286.

NEWTON. *St. Joseph Regional School*, Jefferson St., 07860. Tel: 973-383-2909; Fax: 973-383-6353.
E-mail: sba@nac.net
Sr. Betty Ann Martinez, F.M.A., Prin. Serves St. Joseph, Newton; Our Lady Queen of Peace, Branchville; Our Lady of Mount Carmel, Swartswood. Sisters 1; Lay Teachers 10; Students 237.

PASSAIC. *Passaic Catholic Regional School*, 212 Market St., 07055. Tel: 973-773-4644. Sr. Joselle Ratka, C.S.S.F., Prin. Serves Holy Rosary, St. Joseph, St.

Stephen, St. Mary, Our Lady of Fatima, in Passaic. Sisters 1; Lay Teachers 10; Students 210.

[G] PRIVATE PRESCHOOL

FLORHAM PARK. *Magic Kingdom Day Nursery*, 88 Brooklake Rd., 07932. Tel: 973-966-9762; Fax: 973-377-3994. Vocationist Sisters. Sr. Gelsey Mosca, S.D.V., Prin. Sisters 11; Lay Teachers 2; Students 78.

NEWTON. *Camp Auxilium Learning Center*, 14 Old Swartswood Rd., 07860. Tel: 973-383-2621; Fax: 973-383-3214.
E-mail: campauxilium@nac.net
Web site: www.campauxilium.org
Salesian Sisters. Sr. Lou Ann Fantauzza, F.M.A., Prin. Sisters 3; Lay Teachers 12; Students 245.

PARSIPPANY. *St. Elizabeth's Nursery and Montessori School, Inc.*, 499 Park Rd., 07054. Tel: 973-540-0721; Fax: 973-540-9186. Mother Gina Maria Amico, F.S.S.E., Contact Person. Students 170.

[H] CHILDREN'S CENTERS

DENVILLE. *St. Peter's Village*, 170 Diamond Spring Rd., 07834. Tel: 973-627-0212; Fax: 973-627-3338.
E-mail: srkatherine@nac.net
Staffed by School Sisters of Notre Dame. Sr. Katherine M. Kinnally, S.S.N.D., Dir. Sisters 1; Residents 16.

TOTOWA. *Mt. St. Joseph Children's Center*, 124 Shepherd Ln., 07512. Tel: 973-595-5720. Residential Treatment Center for Emotionally Disturbed Boys. Under the direction of Catholic Family and Community Services. Sr. Dorothy Sheahan, S.C., Dir. Residents 37; Day Students 20.

[I] RETREAT HOUSES & HOUSES OF PRAYER

BRANCHVILLE. *Sanctuary of Mary-Our Lady of the Holy Spirit*, 252 Wantage Ave., 07826. Tel: 973-875-7625. Rev. Silvester J. Livolsi (NEW).

CHESTER. *Hermits of Bethlehem in the Heart of Jesus*, 82 Pleasant Hill Rd., 07930. Tel: 908-879-7059; Fax: 908-879-7059. Rev. Eugene L. Romano, Desert Father. Priests 1; Brother Candidates 1; Sisters 4; Candidates 1.

CONVENT STATION. *Xavier Center*, 07961. Tel: 973-290-5100; Fax: 973-290-5121.
E-mail: cahxavier@aol.com
A retreat & conference center. Sr. Carol Heller, S.C., Admin.

FLORHAM PARK. *Vocationist Fathers Retreat Center*, 90 Brooklake Rd., 07932. Tel: 973-966-6262; Fax: 973-593-8381.
E-mail: vocationist@aol.com
Web site: www.vocationist.org
Rev. Edgar da Cunha, S.D.V., Dir.

MENDHAM. *Villa Pauline*, 07945. Retreat House for Men & Women. Sisters of Christian Charity 7.

MORRISTOWN. *Loyola House of Retreats*, 161 James St., 07960. Tel: 973-539-0740; Fax: 973-898-9839.
E-mail: retreathouse@loyola.org
Web site: www.loyola.org
Society of Jesus. Revs. Patrick J. Sullivan, Supr. & Dir.; Donald G. Devine, S.J.; Edmund W. Nagle, S.J.; Emmet J. Norton, S.J.; William R. O'Leary, S.J., Admin.; Louis P. Sogliuzzo, S.J.; Thomas F. Walsh, S.J.; Richard J. Anable, S.J.; William P. Poorten, S.J.; Kirk R. Reynolds, S.J.; Sr. Barbara Connell, S.C.; Sr. Irene M. Garvey, O.P. Priests 9; Sisters 2.

St. Mary's Abbey Retreat Center, 230 Mendham Rd., 07960. Tel: 973-538-5231, Ext. 2100; Fax: 973-538-7109.
E-mail: abbeyretreat@juno.com
Web site: delbarton.org
Rev. Patrick M. Hurley, O.S.B., Dir. & Guestmaster.

MOUNT ARLINGTON. *Felician Retreat House*, 35 Windemere Ave., 07856. Tel: 973-398-9806. Sr. Mary Gilbert Szaroleta, C.S.S.F., Dir.

NEWTON. *Queen of Peace Retreat House*, St. Paul's Abbey, P.O. Box 7, 07860. Tel: 973-383-2470; 393-0660. Deacon Edward J. Reading.

Sacred Heart Retreat Center, 20 Old Swartswood Rd., 07860. Tel: 973-383-2620; Fax: 973-383-3083.
E-mail: shcenter@juno.com
Daughters of Mary Help of Christians (Salesian Sisters of St. John Bosco). Sr. Catherine Hurley, F.M.A., Supr. Sisters 4.

OAK RIDGE. *Mount Paul Retreat Center*, 243 Mount Paul Rd., 07438-9512. Tel: 973-697-6341.
E-mail: Jfoleycsp@cs.com
Rev. John J. Foley, C.S.P., J.C.D., Dir. Ministries.

RINGWOOD. *Mt. St. Francis Retreat Center*, 474 Sloatsburg Rd., 07456. Tel: 973-962-9778; Fax: 973-962-0445.
E-mail: fsrretreat@aol.com
Sr. Rosemary Napolitano, F.S.R., Admin.

[J] GENERAL HOSPITALS

PATERSON. *St. Joseph's Hospital and Medical Center*, 703 Main St., 07503. Tel: 973-754-2000; Fax: 973-754-3273
For a complete listing, refer to the Hospitals section.

DENVILLE. *Saint Clare's Community Care, Inc. dba Saint Clare's Health Services*, c/o 25 Pocono Rd., 07834. Tel: 973-989-3124; Fax: 973-989-3195.
E-mail: jmccaffrey@stclares.org
Web site: www.stclares.org
For a complete listing, refer to the Hospitals section.

Saint Clare's Hospital, Inc., 25 Pocono Rd., 07834. Tel: 973-625-6000; Fax: 973-625-0416.
E-mail: jmccaffrey@saintclares.org
Web site: www.saintclares.org
For a complete listing, refer to the Hospitals section.

PASSAIC. *St. Mary's Hospital*, 211 Pennington Ave., 07055. Tel: 973-470-3000.
E-mail: petersonp@smh-passaic.org
Web site: www.smh-passaic.org
For a complete listing, refer to the Hospitals section.

[K] HOMES FOR AGED

PATERSON. *St. Joseph Rest Home for Aged Women*, 46 Preakness Ave., 07522. Tel: 973-956-1921; Fax: 973-956-1582
For a complete listing, refer to the Special Care Facilities section.

DENVILLE. *Franciscan Oaks Independent Living Units & Health Center*, 21 Pocono Rd., 07834. Tel: 973-586-5000; Fax: 973-586-5039
For a complete listing, refer to the Special Care Facilities section.

St. Francis Residential Community, 07834 Fax: 973-625-9245.
E-mail: billmili@aol.com
For a complete listing, refer to the Special Care Facilities section.

TOTOWA. *St. Joseph's Home for the Elderly*, 140 Shepherd Ln., 07512. Tel: 973-942-0300; Fax: 973-942-7201
For a complete listing, refer to the Special Care Facilities section.

[L] RESIDENCES FOR WOMEN

PATERSON. *St. Frances Residence*, 25 Jackson St., 07501. Tel: 973-278-7074; Fax: 973-523-5848. Sr. Jeanette Swan, S.C., Admin. Sisters of Charity of St. Elizabeth, NJ 5; Residents 30.

MORRISTOWN. *Dericks Residence*, 70 MacCulloch Ave., 07960. Tel: 973-292-9517; Fax: 973-292-7510.
E-mail: dericksresidence@aol.com
Ms. Sarah Benjamin, Dir. Residents 25.

WAYNE. *Bethany Residence*, 738 Rte. 23, 07470. Tel: 973-628-8109. Sr. Joseph Loretto, M.S.B.T., Admin. Residents 12.

Kilroy Residence, 584 Ratzer Rd., 07470. Tel: 973-694-3594. Sr. Maria Francis Shebellock, F.S.P., Dir. Residents 12.

[M] MONASTERIES AND RESIDENCES OF PRIESTS AND BROTHERS

PATERSON. *St. Benedict the Moor Friary*, 146 Danforth Ave., 07501. Tel: 973-523-0808; Fax: 973-523-5904. Rev. Claude Lenehan, O.F.M.; Bros. Vincent Casamento, O.F.M.; Paul Santoro, O.F.M., Guardian.

BUTLER. *St. Anthony Friary*, 63 Bartholdi Ave., 07405. Tel: 973-838-4080; Fax: 973-492-5483. Order of Friars Minor. Revs. Frederick McKeever, O.F.M., Guardian; John S. Ahearn, O.F.M.; Emmett A. Barrett, O.F.M.; Giles F. Bello, O.F.M.; Alvin A. Black, O.F.M.; Maurice J. Brick, O.F.M.; Patrick M. Brown, O.F.M.; Bernard R. Creighton, O.F.M., Vicar; Emmanuel Duffy, O.F.M.; Matthew L. Gaskin, O.F.M.; Charles V. Hayes, O.F.M.; Cordius P. Kazanchy, O.F.M.; John J. Kull, O.F.M.; Joel Munzing, O.F.M.; Gerard R. McDonald, O.F.M.; Anthony McGuire, O.F.M.; Theodore A. McNally, O.F.M.; Alexius J. Mulrenan, O.F.M.; LaSalle O'Friel, O.F.M.; Neil Padden, O.F.M.; John J. Pierce, O.F.M.; Edwin F.D. Robinson, O.F.M.; Jude Smith, O.F.M.; Edward J. Sullivan, O.F.M.; Bros. Peter R. Butler, O.F.M.; Fintan Duffy, O.F.M.; Paschal Gallagher, O.F.M.; Thomas Sullivan, O.F.M.; Rosario Vieira, O.F.M. Priests 23; Brothers 5.

CLIFTON. *Holy Face of Jesus Monastery*, 1697 State Hwy. 3, P.O. Box 691, 07012. Tel: 973-778-1177; Fax: 973-778-3809. Sylvestrine Benedictine Monks. Revs. Hilary Conti, O.S.B.; Paul Karieakatt, O.S.B.; Thomas Toomey, O.S.B.; Joseph Kulathinal, O.S.B. Priests 4.

FLORHAM PARK. *Father Justin Vocationary*, 90 Brooklake Rd., 07932. Tel: 973-966-6262; Fax: 973-593-8381.
Web site: www.vocationist.org
Revs. Armando Palmieri, S.D.V., Supr.; Mario Muccitelli, S.D.V.; Ugo Fraraccio, S.D.V.; Robert Vass, S.D.V.

LAFAYETTE. *St. Francis Center*, 07848. Tel: 973-383-6465. Capuchin Friars. Bro. Julius Tkaczyk, O.F.M.Cap., Vicar; Rev. Brian Tomlinson, O.F.M.Cap., Local Minister. Priests 1; Brothers 1.

MORRISTOWN. *St. Mary's Abbey*, Delbarton, 230 Mendham Rd., 07960. Tel: 973-538-3231; Fax: 973-538-7109.
E-mail: osbmonks@delbarton.org
Web site: www.osbmonks.org
Rt. Revs. Thomas J. Confroy, O.S.B., Abbot; Brian H. Clark, O.S.B., Abbot Emeritus; Leonard G. Cassell, O.S.B., Abbot Emeritus; Martin J. Burne, O.S.B., Abbot Emeritus; Gerard P. Lair, O.S.B., Abbot Emeritus; Very Rev. Elias R. Lorenzo, O.S.B., Prior; Revs. Jerome Borski, O.S.B.; Benet W. Caffrey, O.S.B.; Gabriel M. Coless, O.S.B.; Michael J. Collins, O.S.B.; Mark W. Confroy, O.S.B.; Richard J. Cronin, O.S.B.; Edward Seton Fittin, O.S.B.; Germain L. Fritz, O.S.B.; Simon P. Gallagher, O.S.B.; Giles P. Hayes, O.S.B.; John E. Hesketh, O.S.B.; Patrick M. Hurley, O.S.B.; Joel J. Leikhim, O.S.B.; Beatus T. Lucey, O.S.B.; Adrian T. McLaughlin, O.S.B.; Kenneth H. Mayer, O.S.B.; Peter J. Meaney, O.S.B.; James O'Donnell, O.S.B.; Hilary O'Leary, O.S.B.; Rembert F. Reilly, O.S.B.; Joachim B. Schweitzer, O.S.B.; Andrew T. Smith, O.S.B.; Luke L. Travers, O.S.B.; Bros. John Babicz, O.S.B.; Eamon H. Drew, O.S.B.; Tarcisius Hoang-Hoa, O.S.B.; Jonathan M. Hunt, O.S.B.; Christopher K. Rosa, O.S.B.; Anthony S. Sargent, O.S.B.; Kieran M. Shiek, O.S.B.; Brendan A. Tumalty, O.S.B.
Resident Outside the Abbey: Revs. Damian B. Breen, O.S.B.; Timothy J. Brennan, O.S.B.; Justin Capato, O.S.B.; Conall R. Coughlin, O.S.B.; Donal R. Fox, O.S.B.; Karl J. Roesch, O.S.B.; Jude S. Salus, O.S.B.; Wilfred G. Schulz, O.S.B.; Bruno A. Ugliano, O.S.B.; Benedict M. Worry, O.S.B.; Regis P. Wallace, O.S.B.; Bros. James Konchalski, O.S.B.; Paul J. Diveny, O.S.B. Total Priests 41; Serving Out of Diocese 11; Brothers 9.

NEWTON. *St. Paul's Abbey*, 07860. Tel: 973-383-2470; Fax: 973-383-5782.
E-mail: spabbey@hotmail.com
(Formerly the Little Flower Monastery). Order of St. Benedict, Congregation of St. Ottilien. Rt. Revs. Joel P. Macul, O.S.B., Abbot; Justin E. Dzikowicz, O.S.B., (Resigned); Augustine J. Hinches, O.S.B., (Resigned); Revs. Boniface D. Cronin, O.S.B.; Andrew C. O'Sullivan, O.S.B.; Jude C. Bradley, O.S.B.; Patrick J. Bonner, O.S.B.; Bede E. Classick, O.S.B.; Basil J. Wallace, O.S.B.
Priests Residing Outside the Monastery: Mailing Address: P.O. Box 213, Lushoto, Tanzania. Rev. Damian J. Milliken, O.S.B., Inkamana Abbey, P/Bag X9333, Vryheid 3100, South Africa. Rev. Peter W. Blue, O.S.B. Priests 11; Lay Monks 2.

OAK RIDGE-MILTON. *St. Stanislaus B. M. Friary*, Manor Dr., 07438. Tel: 973-697-7757. Capuchin Fathers. Revs. Henry T. Krajewski, O.F.M.Cap., Superior; Francis Mucharski, O.F.M.Cap.; Francis J. Salwowski, O.F.M.Cap.; Sigmund M. Klimowicz, O.F.M.Cap.; Peter Gacki, O.F.M.Cap.; Francis Majewski, O.F.M.Cap., Vicar; Joseph M. Kubiak, O.F.M.Cap.; Stephen Laliberte, O.F.M.Cap.; Ivot Miszkel, O.F.M.Cap.; Norbert Karava, O.F.M.Cap. Priests 9.

RINGWOOD. *Holy Name Friary, Inc.*, 2 Morris Rd., 07456. Tel: 973-962-7200; Fax: 973-962-9766. Rev. A. Francis Soucy, O.F.M., Supr. & Contact Person; Most Rev. Thomas Manning, O.F.M., Bishop Emeritus, Coroico; Revs. Declan Bailey, O.F.M.; Amadeus Burke, O.F.M.; Urban Cain, O.F.M.; Flavian Colligan, O.F.M.; Michael Feeny, O.F.M.; Louis Foley, O.F.M.; Roland Fregault, O.F.M.; Fabian Joyce, O.F.M.; Leonard Kelly, O.F.M.; Hugh King, O.F.M.; Gerard Lewis, O.F.M.; Alban Maguire, O.F.M.; Edward McGuire, O.F.M.; Kieran F. McMahon, O.F.M.; Conor Mullaly, O.F.M.; Zachary O'Friel, O.F.M.; Lawrence F. Pafchik, O.F.M.; Evan Roche, O.F.M.; Vincent Shea, O.F.M.; Jude Smith, O.F.M.; Bernard Weinholtz, O.F.M.; Bros. Louis Black, O.F.M.; John Kries, O.F.M.; Gilbert McEvoy, O.F.M.; Joseph P. Trunk, O.F.M.; Agapitus Rothmann, O.F.M.; Paul Slaby, O.F.M.

STIRLING. *Holy Spirit Missionary Cenacle*, 1050 Long Hill Rd., 07980. Tel: 908-647-0208; Fax: 908-647-5770.
E-mail: religious@stshrine.org
Web site: stshrine.org
Missionary Servants of the Most Holy Trinity. Revs. Peter Krebs, S.T., Dir.; Stephen Ernst, S.T.; Vincent Fitzpatrick, S.T.; Cajetan McDyre, S.T.; Campion Murphy, S.T.; Stephen Quinn, S.T.; Bro. Martin Pacholek, S.T. Priests 6; Brothers 1.

Serenity Retreat League, 1292 Long Hill Rd., Box 10, 07980. Tel: 908-647-1539. Sr. Mary T. Lynch, S.F.C.C., Dir.

Shrine of St. Joseph, 1050 Long Hill Rd., 07980. Tel: 908-647-0208; Fax: 908-647-5770.
E-mail: religious@stshrine.org
Web site: stshrine.org

Rev. Peter Krebs, S.T., Custodian..Priests 6; Brothers 1; Sisters 6.

WAYNE. *P.I.M.E. Missionaries Residence*, 34 Grandview Dr., 07470. Tel: 973-694-1790; Fax: 973-694-0444.
E-mail: pimenj@bellatlantic.net
Web site: www.beamissionary.org
Revs. Luigi Acerbi, P.I.M.E.; Giancarlo Ghezzi, P.I.M.E.

Xaverian Missionary Fathers, Provincial House, 12 Helene Court, 07470. Tel: 973-942-2975; Fax: 973-942-5012.
E-mail: xavmissionoff@sigmaweb.net
Web site: www.sigmaweb.net/xavmissions
Revs. Ivan Marchesin, S.X., Prov.; Frank B. Grappoli, S.X.; Dario Maso, S.X.
Mission Assignments: Makeni, Sierra Leone: Most Rev. George Biguzzi, S.X.; Revs. Victor Mosele, S.X.; Luciano Peterlini, S.X.; Graziano Rossato, S.X.; James Tully, S.X.
Belem, Brazil: Revs. Francis Gugliotta, S.X.; Danilo Lago, S.X.; Mario Pezzotti, S.X.
Cameroon: Revs. Rene Lovat, S.X.; Pierino Zoni, S.X.
Sao Paulo, Brazil: Rev. Gino Nasini, S.X.
Jakarta, Indonesia: Revs. Bruno Orru, S.X.; Franco Qualizza, S.X.
Buenaventura, Colombia: Revs. Mark Marangone, S.X.; Mauro Loda, S.X.
Torreon, Mexico: Rev. Adolph Menendez, S.X.
Taiwan: Revs. Martino Roia, S.X.; Joseph Matteucig, S.X.
Japan: Revs. Pio Devoti, S.X.; Paolo Gobbo, S.X.; Greg Holm, S.X.
Philippines: Revs. Carl Chudy, S.X.; Kenneth Cannon, S.X.

[N] CONVENTS AND RESIDENCES FOR SISTERS

PATERSON. *Daughters of Charity of the Most Precious Blood*, 46 Preakness Ave., 07522. Tel: 973-956-1921; Fax: 973-956-1582. Sr. Maria Goretti Chaloux, D.C.P.B., Supr. Sisters 11.

Missionary Sisters of the Immaculate Conception of the Mother of God, 779 Broadway, 07509. Tel: 973-279-3790; Fax: 973-742-8231. Mailing Address: P.O. Box 3026, 07509-3026. Sr. Eleanor Goerler, S.M.I.C., Prov. Coord.

Missionary Sisters of the Immaculate Conception of the Mother of God, 396 E. 38th St., 07504. Tel: 973-279-2885. Sisters 5.

Missionary Sisters of the Immaculate Conception of the Mother of God, 374-18th Ave., 07504-1333. Tel: 973-523-4988. Sisters 6.

CHESTER. *Carmel of the Immaculate Heart of Mary*. Hermits of Our Lady of Mt. Carmel (Diocesan Community), 80 Pleasant Hill Rd., 07930-2135. Tel: 908-879-4990. Sr. Mary of Jesus and St. Joseph, H.O.Carm., Desert Mother. Sisters 4.

CONVENT STATION. *Motherhouse of the Sisters of Charity*. Mailing Address: P.O. Box 476, 07961. Tel: 973-290-5424; Fax: 973-290-5335.
E-mail: escharity@aol.com
Sr. Barbara Conroy, S.C., General Supr. Professed Sisters 90.

St. Anne Villa. Mailing Address: P.O. Box 476, 07961. Tel: 973-292-6501.
E-mail: srcsc@aol.com
Sisters of Charity of St. Elizabeth. Home for retired and infirm Sisters. Sr. Rosanne Caiazzo, S.C., Admin.; Rev. Wilfred Schulz, O.S.B., Chap. Bed Capacity 100.

DENVILLE. *Our Lady of Sorrows Convent, Sisters of Sorrowful Mother*, 9 Pocono Rd., 07834. Tel: 973-627-9008; Fax: 973-625-9245.
E-mail: olsconventnj@aol.com
Residences: 4 Pocono Rd., 07834. Tel: 973-983-8456. 45 N. Shore Dr., 07834. Tel: 973-625-8433. 1 Gregory Dr., Boonton, 07005. Tel: 973-331-9859. 40 E. Main St., Rockaway, 07866. Tel: 973-627-4643. 32 Wits End Dr., Hamburg, 07419. Tel: 973-827-0191. Sisters 35.

FLORHAM PARK. *Sister Joanna House of Formation*, 88 Brooklake Rd., 07932. Tel: 973-966-9762. Sr. Anna Maria Mancino, S.D.V., Delegate & Superior; Sr. Romilda A. Borges, S.D.V., Prin. Sisters 9.

GLADSTONE. *Mt. St. John Convent*, 22 St. John's Dr., 07934. Tel: 908-234-1074; 234-0640; Fax: 908-781-7814. Sisters of St. John the Baptist. Sr. Angelita Vazzano, C.S.J.B., Admin. Sisters 9.

HALEDON. *Institute of the Daughters of Mary Help of Christians*, 655 Belmont Ave., 07508. Tel: 973-790-7964; Fax: 973-790-6485.
E-mail: secretarysva@aol.com
Provincialate of Daughters of Mary Help of Christians. Sr. Judith Suprys, F.M.A., Prov.; Sr. Cecilia Besi, F.M.A., Supr.; Rev. Paul P. Avallone, S.D.B., Chap. Daughters of Mary Help of Christians (Salesian Sisters) 41.

MENDHAM. *Mallinckrodt Convent-Motherhouse and Novitiate of the Sisters of Christian Charity*, 07945. Tel: 973-543-6528; Fax: 973-543-9459.
E-mail: socc@nac.net
Web site: scceast.org
Daughters of the Blessed Virgin Mary of the Immaculate Conception. Sr. Mary Edward Spohrer, S.C.C., Prov. Supr. Sisters 53; Novices 2.

MORRISTOWN. *Monastery Discalced Carmelite Nuns of the Most Blessed Virgin Mary of Mt. Carmel*, 189 Madison Ave., 07960. Tel: 973-539-0773; Fax: 973-984-0509. Mother Mary Michael, O.C.D., Prioress. Professed Nuns 7; Extern Sisters 1; Novices 1.

St. Lucy Provincialate of the Religious Teachers Filippini, Novitiate, Villa Walsh Academy, 455 Western Ave., 07960-4928. Tel: 973-538-2886; Fax: 973-538-6107.
E-mail: lauretti@bellatlantic.net
Web site: www.filippiniusa.org
Legal Title: *Pontifical Institute of the Religious Teachers Filippini*. Sr. Frances Lauretti, M.P.F., Prov.; Sr. Ascenza Tizzano, M.P.F., Supr.; Sr. Dolores Potkay, M.P.F., Dir. Formation. Sisters 83; Junior Professed 2.

MOUNT ARLINGTON. *Felician Sisters of St. Francis of Assisi Convent*, 37 Windemere Ave., 07856. Sr. Mary Josita, C.S.S.F., Local Supr. Professed Sisters 7.

OAK RIDGE. *Society of the Sisters of the Church*, 15 Heritage Ct., 07438. Tel: 973-208-1456; Fax: 973-334-5397.
E-mail: SRBW@ssoc.org
Web site: www.ssoc.org
Sr. Sylvia Berzinski, S.S.C., Coord..Sisters 11.

PARSIPPANY. *St. Francis of Assisi Novitiate-Franciscan Sisters of St. Elizabeth*, 499 Park Rd., 07054. Tel: 973-539-3797; Fax: 973-539-3347.
E-mail: ludovico@garden.net
Mother Gina Maria Amico, F.S.S.E., Delegate General; Rev. Philip W. Nielsen, O.F.M., Chap., Tel: 973-605-8729; Fax: 973-539-3347. Perpetually Professed Sisters 16; Temp. Professed Sisters 9.

PASSAIC. *Our Lady of Mt. Carmel Convent, Franciscan Sisters of Ringwood*, 47 Reid Ave., 07055. Tel: 973-471-6352. Sr. M. Berard, F.S.R., Supr. Sisters 5.

St. Joseph Convent, 9 Quincy St., 07055. Sr. Krystyna Kwasniak, D.P.H.M., Supr.

RINGWOOD. *Mt. St. Francis*, 07456. Tel: 973-962-7411. General Motherhouse and Novitiate of the Franciscan Sisters. Sr. Annette Lucchese, F.S.R., Gen. Coord.; Rev. Lawrence Burke, O.F.M. Professed Sisters 32.

STIRLING. *Blessed Trinity Missionary Cenacle*, 1190 Long Hill Rd., 07980. Tel: 908-647-1165. Missionary Servants of the Most Blessed Trinity 1.

Holy Trinity Convent, 1026 Long Hill Rd., 07980. Tel: 908-647-6584. Sr. Anna Karusat, Supr. Servants of Jesus 6.

WEST PATERSON. *Missionary Sisters of the Immaculate Conception of the Mother of God*, Generalate, 48 Garden Ave., 07424. Tel: 973-279-1484; Fax: 973-279-2991.
E-mail: smicgen@worldnet.att.net
Sr. Corona Chung, S.M.I.C., Coord. Gen. Sisters 5.

The Society of Sisters for the Church, 396 Rifle Camp Rd., 07424. Tel: 973-345-1816.
E-mail: eustac@aol.com
Sr. Eleanor Ustach, S.S.C., Pres..Sisters 20; Companions 1.

[O] NEWMAN CENTERS

HALEDON. *William Paterson University of New Jersey*. Jesus Christ, Prince of Peace Chapel & Bishop Frank J. Ropimer Catholic Campus Ministry Center, 219 Pompton Rd., 07508.
E-mail: scurti@wpunj.edu
Web site: www.geocities.com/princeofpeace_07508
Rev. Louis J. Scurti.

MADISON. *Drew University Catholic Campus Ministry*. Chaplain's Office, President's House Annex, 07940. Tel: 973-408-3027; Fax: 973-627-3631.
E-mail: jfarias@drew.edu
Rev. Joseph G. Farias. Tel: 973-627-0066.

Fairleigh Dickinson University.
Catholic Campus Ministry, Fairleigh Dickinson University, 285 Madison Ave., 07940. Tel: 973-443-8651; Fax: 973-627-3631.
E-mail: jgusf@aol.com
Rev. Joseph G. Farias, Res: 446 Mt. Hope Rd., Wharton, 07885-2814. Tel: 973-627-0066; Fax: 973-627-3631.

[P] MISCELLANEOUS LISTINGS

PATERSON. *The Association of the Marian Apostolate of Mercy, Inc.*, 360 E. 37th St., 07504. Tel: 973-523-1338. Sr. Maria Elizabeth Whilifer, Pres.; Rev. John Gordon, Sec.; Judith A. Bonnesen, Treas.; Rev. Msgr. Mark Giordani, Spiritual Dir.

Martin de Porres Village Corporation, Green St., 07501. Tel: 973-881-8022. Rev. Msgr. Herbert K. Tillyer, Pres. Sponsoring Martin De Porres, Vill.

Riese Corporation, Twentieth Ave., 07501. Tel: 973-279-2262. Rev. Msgr. Herbert K. Tillyer, V.G., Pres. Sponsoring Governor Paterson Towers, Maurice Brick Residence, Brestel Residence, William F. Hinchcliffe Pavilion, Ralph J. Diverio Residence, Murray M. Bisgaier Residence, William Levine Residence.

St. Anthony's Guild, 07509. Tel: 973-777-3737; Fax: 212-594-2769.
E-mail: anthonian@aol.com
Web site: anthonian.org
Membership organization supports the work of The Franciscan Friars of Holy Name Province. Revs. Joseph M. Hertel, O.F.M., Dir.; Cassian A. Miles, O.F.M.; Allan G. Von Kobs, O.F.M.; Felician A. Foy, O.F.M.; Rayner F. Williams, O.F.M.

CHESTER. *Nazareth Village*, 6 Meadow Ln., Box 635, 07930. Tel: 908-879-6991; Fax: 908-879-7461.
Web site: www.nazarethvillage.com
Retirement residence for diocesan priests. Rev. Msgr. Raymond M. Lopatesky, Dir. In res. Rev. Msgr. Peter A. McBride; Rev. Msgr. Aloysius J. Busch; Revs. Walter Pruschowitz; John T. Catoir; Patrick Mullan; Raymond J. Jasaitis; Rev. Msgr. John R. Ryan; Rev. Msgr. Leo P. Ryan; Rev. Msgr. Leo P. Carey; Revs. M. Edward Davey; James P. O'Kielty; Joseph E. Murphy; George T. Shema.

CONVENT STATION. *Seton Health Care, Inc.*, Convent of Saint Elizabeth, P.O. Box 476, 07961. Tel: 973-290-5450; Fax: 973-290-5335.
E-mail: escharity@aol.com
Web site: www.scnj.org
Sr. Barbara Conroy, S.C., Pres.

DOVER. *Saint Clare's Health Services, Inc.*, 400 W. Blackwell St., 07801. Tel: 973-989-3124; Fax: 973-989-3195.
E-mail: jmccaffrey@saintclares.org
Web site: www.saintclares.org
(Parent Corporation: Marian Health System, Inc.).

Saint Clare's Hospital, Inc., Denville. Tel: 973-625-6000; Fax: 973-625-0416.

Saint Clare's Foundation, Inc., Denville. Tel: 973-983-5300; Fax: 973-983-5307.

St. Francis Life Care Corporation, Denville. Tel: 973-586-6003; Fax: 973-586-6030.

Saint Francis Health Resort, Inc., aka St. Francis Residential Community, Denville. Tel: 973-627-5000; Fax: 973-627-6389.

Saint Clare's Community Care, Inc., Denville. Tel: 973-442-2300; Fax: 973-442-2330.

Saint Clare's Management Services, Inc., Sparta. Tel: 973-729-6465; Fax: 973-729-7057.

Saint Clare's Home Care, Inc., Sparta. Tel: 973-729-6465; Fax: 973-729-7057.

Visiting Nurse Association of Sussex Co., Inc., Sparta. Tel: 973-792-6465; Fax: 973-729-7057.

MADISON. *Priests Residence*, 205 Madison Ave., 07940-1003. Tel: 973-443-9300; Fax: 973-443-4140.
E-mail: user567964@aol.com
Rev. Msgr. Robert M. Diachek.

MORRISTOWN. *College of St. Elizabeth, Center for Theological and Spiritual Development*, 2 Convent Rd., 07960. Tel: 973-290-4300; Fax: 973-290-4312.
E-mail: aciorra@liza.st-elizabeth.edu
Web site: csespirit.org
Rev. Anthony J. Ciorra, O.F.M.Cap.

PASSAIC. *St. Jude Media Ministries*, 63 Monroe St., 07055. Tel: 973-777-0303; Fax: 973-472-5033.
E-mail: jtcatoir@juno.com
Rev. John T. Catoir, Dir.

STIRLING. *Father Judge Apostolic Center*, 1292 Long Hill Rd., 07980. Tel: 908-647-7112; 647-2422 (Res.); Fax: 908-647-6045.
E-mail: fjac3@aol.com
Web site: www.fjac.org
Rev. Dennis Berry, S.T., Dir.; Sr. Gail Lambert, M.S.B.T., Co-Dir.; Bro. Odel Medina, S.T., Migrant Ministry; Jean T. Peterson, Program Liasion.

Trinity Mission Center, 1292 Long Hill Rd., 07980. Tel: 908-647-7003; Fax: 908-647-6045.
E-mail: trinityctr@aol.com
Web site: www.tmc3.org
Sponsored by: Missionary Servants of the Most Holy Trinity. Rev. Raymond Riding, S.T. Service opportunities through the Missionary Cenacle Family.

WAYNE. *Siena Village*, 1000 Siena Village, 07470. Tel: 973-696-2811; Fax: 973-696-2721. Sr. Alice Matthew, O.P., Dir.

RELIGIOUS INSTITUTES OF MEN REPRESENTED IN THE DIOCESE

For further details refer to the corresponding bracketed number in the Religious Institutes of Men or Women section.

[0200]—*Benedictine Monks*. (St. Mary, St. Paul Abbeys; Holy Face of Jesus Residence).—O.S.B.

[0470]—*The Capuchin Friars*. (Italian, Polish).—O.F.M.Cap.

[0480]—*Conventual Franciscans*(Polish).—O.F.M.Conv.
[0520]—*Franciscan Friars.* (Holy Name Prov.).—O.F.M.
[0690]—*Jesuit Fathers and Brothers.* (New York Prov.).—S.J.
[0840]—*Missionary Servants of the Most Holy Trinity.* (Silver Spring, MD).—S.T.
[1030]—*Paulist Fathers.* (New York).—C.S.P.
[1190]—*Salesians of Don Bosco.* (Turin, Italy).—S.D.B.
[1340]—*Vocationist Fathers.*—S.D.V.
[1360]—*Xaverian Missionary Fathers.* (Wayne).—S.X.

RELIGIOUS INSTITUTES OF WOMEN REPRESENTED IN THE DIOCESE

[0230]—*Benedictine Sisters of Pontifical Jurisdiction.*—O.S.B.
[0740]—*Daughters of Charity of the Most Precious Blood.*—D.C.P.B.
[0850]—*Daughters of Mary Help of Christians.*—F.M.A.
[]—*Daughters of the Most Pure Heart of the Most Holy Virgin Mary.* (Passaic).
[0420]—*Discalced Carmelite Nuns.*—O.C.D.
[1070-06]—*Dominican Sisters.*—O.P.
[1070-18]—*Dominican Sisters.*—O.P.
[1170]—*Felician Sisters.*—C.S.S.F.
[1400]—*Franciscan Missionary Sisters of the Sacred Heart.* (Peekskill).—F.M.S.C.
[1420]—*Franciscan Sisters of Ringwood.*—F.S.R.
[1460]—*Franciscan Sisters of St. Elizabeth.*—F.S.S.E.
[]—*Hermits of Our Lady of Mt. Carmel.*—H.O.Carm.
[2340]—*Little Sisters of the Poor.*—L.S.P.
[2790]—*Missionary Servants of the Most Blessed Trinity.*—M.S.B.T.
[2760]—*Missionary Sisters of the Immaculate Conception of the Mother of God.*—S.M.I.C.
[3430]—*Religious Teachers Filippini.*—M.P.F.
[2970]—*School Sisters of Notre Dame.*—S.S.N.D.
[1700]—*School Sisters of the Third Order of St. Francis.*—O.S.F.
[3560]—*Servants of Jesus.* (Starling).—S.J.
[3580]—*Servants of Mary.*—O.S.M.
[0590]—*Sisters of Charity of Saint Elizabeth, Convent Station.*—S.C.
[0660]—*Sisters of Christian Charity.*—S.C.C.
[3820]—*Sisters of St. John the Baptist.*—C.S.J.B.
[3830]—*Sisters of St. Joseph.* (Chestnut Hill, PA).—C.S.J.
[3890]—*Sisters of St. Joseph of Peace.*—C.S.J.P.
[1830]—*Sisters of the Good Shepherd.*—R.G.S.
[3320]—*Sisters of the Presentation of the B.V.M.*.—P.B.V.M.
[4100]—*Sisters of the Sorrowful Mother (Third Order of St. Francis).*—S.S.M.
[]—*The Society of the Sisters of the Church.* (Passaic).
[4210]—*Vocationist Sisters.*—S.D.V.

NECROLOGY

† Grieco, Charles, (Retired). —Died March 17, 2000.
† Guzman, Rev. Msgr. Raul, Pastor Emeritus, Passaic, NJ Our Lady of Fatima. —Died Aug. 24, 2000.
† Morris, Robert J., (Retired). —Died May 30, 2000.

Diocese of Pensacola-Tallahassee

(Dioecesis Pensacolensis-Tallaseiensis)

Most Reverend

JOHN H. RICARD, S.S.J., D.D., PH.D.

Bishop of Pensacola-Tallahassee; ordained May 25, 1968; ordained Auxiliary Bishop of Baltimore July 2, 1984; appointed Bishop of Pensacola-Tallahassee January 21, 1997.

Pastoral Center: P.O. Drawer 17329, Pensacola, FL, 32522. Tel.: 904-432-1515; Fax: 904-436-6424.

Web site address: www.cfi.net/ptdiocese/pt.html

E-mail address: CHNOF12529@aol.com

ESTABLISHED NOVEMBER 6, 1975.

Square Miles 14,044.

Comprises the following Counties: Bay, Calhoun, Escambia, Franklin, Gadsden, Gulf, Holmes, Jackson, Jefferson, Leon, Liberty, Madison, Okaloosa, Santa Rosa, Taylor, Wakulla, Walton and Washington Counties.

For legal titles of parishes and diocesan institutions, consult the Pastoral Center.

STATISTICAL OVERVIEW

Personnel	
Bishop	1
Priests: Diocesan Active in Diocese	50
Priests: Active Outside Diocese	8
Priests: Retired, Sick or Absent	15
Number of Diocesan Priests	73
Religious Priests in Diocese	9
Extern Priests in Diocese	31
Ordinations:	
Diocesan Priests	2
Permanent Deacons	17
Permanent Deacons in Diocese	53
Total Brothers	5
Total Sisters	51
Parishes	
Parishes	50
With Resident Pastor:	
Resident Diocesan Priests	41
Resident Religious Priests	10
Missions	9
Welfare	
Catholic Hospitals	1
Homes for the Aged	3
Total Assisted	210
Special Centers for Social Services	4
Total Assisted	21,968
Other Institutions	1
Total Assisted	2,420
Educational	
Diocesan Students in Other Seminaries	16
Total Seminarians	16
High Schools, Diocesan and Parish	1
Total Students	612
Elementary Schools, Diocesan and Parish	8
Total Students	2,457
Non-residential Schools for the Disabled	1
Total Students	16
Catechesis/Religious Education:	
High School Students	1,266
Elementary Students	5,346
Total Students Under Catholic Instruction	9,713
Teachers in the Diocese:	
Sisters	9
Lay Teachers	202
Vital Statistics	
Receptions into the Church:	
Infant Baptism Totals	1,258
Received into Full Communion	1,730
First Communions	1,251
Confirmations	990
Marriages:	
Catholic	201
Interfaith	187
Total Marriages	388
Deaths	593
Total Catholic Population	67,425
Total Population	1,274,000

Former Bishops—Most Rev. RENE H. GRACIDA, D.D., ord. May 23, 1959; appt. Titular Bishop of Masuccaba and Auxiliary of Miami, Dec. 6, 1971; cons. Jan. 25, 1972; appt. first Bishop of Pensacola-Tallahassee, Oct. 1, 1975; installed Nov. 6, 1975; transferred to Bishop of Corpus Christi, May 19, 1983.—Most Rev. J. KEITH SYMONS, D.D., Bishop of Pensacola-Tallahassee; ord. May 18, 1958; Titular Bishop of Siguritanus and Auxiliary of St. Petersburg; appt. Jan. 16, 1981; cons. March 19, 1981; Bishop of Pensacola-Tallahassee; appt. Sept. 29, 1983; installed Nov. 8, 1983; transferred to Bishop of Palm Beach, June 2, 1990.—Most Rev. JOHN M. SMITH, J.C.D., D.D., Bishop of Pensacola-Tallahassee; ord. May 27, 1961; Titular Bishop of Tre Taverne and Auxiliary of Newark; appt. Dec. 1, 1987; cons. Jan. 25, 1988; Bishop of Pensacola-Tallahassee; appt. June 25, 1991; installed July 31, 1991; transferred to Coadjutor of Trenton, Nov. 21, 1995.

Pastoral Center—11 N. B St., Pensacola, 32501. Tel: 850-432-1515; Fax: 850-436-6424., *Mailing Address: P.O. Drawer 17329, Pensacola, 32522.*

Chancellor—Rev. Msgr. JAMES AMOS, J.C.L., V.G.

Vicar for Priests—Rev. JOHN CASSIDY.

Vicar for Permanent Deacons—Deacon JOHN MORGAN.

Vicar for Religious—Rev. Msgr. JAMES AMOS, J.C.L., V.G.

Vice Chancellor & Notary—Rev. Msgr. MICHAEL REED, J.C.L.

Vicars Forane—Rev. Msgr. RICHARD J. BOWLES, V.F., Cathedral Vicariate Forane; Rev. Msgr. MICHAEL MOONEY, V.F., Northwest Vicariate Forane; Very Rev. STEVEN O'CONNOR, V.F., Southwest Vicariate Forane; Rev. Msgr. FRANCIS SZCZYKUTOWICZ, V.F., North Central Vicariate Forane; Very Rev. ROBERT MORRIS, West Central Vicariate Forane; Rev. Msgr. WILLIAM A. CROWE, V.F., East Central Vicariate Forane; Rev. Msgr. JOHN V. O'SULLIVAN, V.F., Eastern Vicariate Forane.

Diocesan Tribunal—1000 W. Garden St., Pensacola, 32501., Mailing Address: P.O. Drawer 17329, Pensacola, 32522. Tel: 850-436-6454; Fax: 850-436-6457.

Judicial Vicar—Rev. Msgr. JAMES J. FLAHERTY, J.C.L., J.V.

Associate Judicial Vicar—Vacant.

Advocates—Rev. EUGENE D. CASSERLY; Deacon DANIEL MCAULIFFE.

Judges—Rev. Msgr. JAMES J. FLAHERTY, J.C.L., J.V.; Rev. WILLIAM P. BROWN, J.C.L.

Promoter of Justice—Rev. Msgr. MICHAEL REED, J.C.L.

Auditors—Revs. THOMAS BONANTI; JOSEPH CALLIPARE; EUGENE D. CASSERLY, M.Ch.A.; Deacon DANIEL MCAULIFFE; Rev. Msgr. MICHAEL REED, J.C.L.

Defender of the Bond—Rev. Msgr. JAMES AMOS, J.C.L., V.G.

Notaries—Rev. JOSEPH CALLIPARE; Rev. Msgr. MICHAEL REED, J.C.L.; Deacons DANIEL MCAULIFFE; GERARD WILLIAMSON; RAMON BONANNO; Mrs. BECKY HICE.

College of Consultors—Rev. Msgr. JAMES AMOS, J.C.L., V.G.; Rev. Msgr. WILLIAM CROWE; Rev. Msgr. MICHAEL CHERUP; Rev. Msgr. MICHAEL MOONEY; Rev. ROY MARIEN; Rev. Msgr. JOHN O'SULLIVAN.

Administrative Council—Rev. Msgr. JAMES AMOS, J.C.L., V.G.; Rev. Msgr. MICHAEL CHERUP; Rev. Msgr. JAMES J. FLAHERTY, J.C.L.; Rev. Msgr. MICHAEL MOONEY; Rev. Msgr. MICHAEL REED, Sec.; Sr. ELLEN KIERAN, M.S.B.T.; Sr. MARY CAPLICE, C.N.D.; Deacon JOHN MCLELLAN.

Council of Permanent Deacons—Most Rev. JOHN H. RICARD, S.S.J.; Deacons JOHN MORGAN, Chm., Vicar for Deacons; GERALD WILLIAMSON; JOHN MCLELLAN; JOAQUIN TREVINO; MACK SHOOK.

Council of Sisters—Sr. ELAINE JORDAN, D.C., Chm.; Sr. CAROL HARBECK, R.S.M., Vice Chm.; Sr. MARYANN CALABRESE, C.N.D., Sec.; Sr. MARY GILLESPIE, C.N.D., Treas.

Diocesan Commissions, Departments, And Offices

Apostleship of the Sea, Office of the—Rev. Msgr. RICHARD J. BOWLES, V.F., Chap., *P.O. Drawer 17329, Pensacola, 32522.* Tel: 850-432-1515.

Archivist—Rev. Msgr. MICHAEL REED, J.C.L., *P.O. Drawer 17329, Pensacola, 32522.* Tel: 850-432-1515.

Black Catholics, Office of—Deacon BRADLEY SEABROOK, Dir., *P.O. Drawer 17329, Pensacola, 32522.* Tel: 850-432-1515.

Building & Renovation, Diocesan Commission for—Rev. Msgr. JAMES AMOS, J.C.L., V.G., Chm.; Rev. Msgr. LUKE HUNT; Mr. JOHN KENNEDY; Mr. THEODORE J. RUCKSTUHL; Mr. J. PATRICK REMICH; FELECIA C. SONNIER, *P.O. Drawer 17329, Pensacola, 32522.* Tel: 850-432-1515.

Building & Renovation, Office of—Rev. Msgr. JAMES AMOS, J.C.L., V.G., Dir., *P.O. Drawer 17329, Pensacola, 32522.* Tel: 850-432-1515.

Campaign for Human Development, Office of—Rev. Msgr. MICHAEL REED, J.C.L., Dir., *P.O. Drawer 17329, Pensacola, 32522.* Tel: 850-432-1515.

Campus Ministry—P.O. Drawer 17329, Pensacola, 32522. Tel: 850-432-1515. Pensacola-University of West Florida: Rev. JOHN CAYER, Dir., *9945 Hillview Dr., Pensacola, 32514.* Tel: 850-477-3221. Tallahassee-Florida Agricultural & Mechanical University, St. Eugene Chapel: Rev. SEMANHYIA BOATENG-MENSAH, Dir., *701 Gamble St., Tallahassee, 32310.* Tel: 850-222-6482. Florida State University: Rev. TOM COLLINS, Dir., *P.O. Box 2395, Tallahassee, 32316.* Tel: 850-222-9630.

Catholic Daughters of the Americas—Rev. ROBERT F. MORRIS, Court Chap.; Mrs. JOYCE PFEIFFER, Regent, *304 N. Sunset Blvd., Gulf Breeze, 32507.*

Catholic Women, Diocesan Council of—Rev. Msgr. RICHARD J. BOWLES, V.F., Spiritual Dir. TRICIA ZERMENO, Pres., *P.O. Drawer 17329, Pensacola, 32522.* Tel: 850-432-1515.

Catholic Charities, Department of—Sr. ELLEN KIERAN, M.S.B.T., M.S.W., Dir. Offices—Pensacola: *222 E. Government St., Pensacola, 32501.* Tel: 850-436-6410; Fax: 850-436-6419. Fort Walton Beach: Mrs. MARTI DEADRICK, Supvr., *11 First St., S.E., Fort Walton Beach, 32548.* Tel: 850-244-2825; Fax: 850-244-2963. Panama City: Mrs. MILLIE DICKENS, Supvr., *3218 E. 11th St., Panama City, 32401.* Tel: 850-763-0475; Fax: 850-763-2969. Tallahassee: Ms. WENDY J. BLAIR, Supvr., *P.O. Box 20165, Tallahassee, 32316.* Tel: 850-222-2180; Fax: 850-681-6963. Quincy: *27 N. Shadow St., Quincy, 32351.* Tel: 850-875-1353.

Cemetery Office—Deacon JEAN WHITE, Dir., *P.O. Drawer 17329, Pensacola, 32522.* Tel: 850-432-1515. *Holy Cross Cemetery, 1300 E. Hayes St., Pensacola, 32503.* Tel: 850-432-0878. Deacon JEAN WHITE, Dir., *Calvary Cemetery, 834 Sunny Hills Blvd., Sunny Hills, 32428.* Tel: 850-773-2165. Mr. FRED MCEVOY, Dir.

Charismatic Renewal, Diocesan Commission for—Rev. EUGENE PATHE, Moderator; JOE BROWN, Chm., *P.O. Drawer 17329, Pensacola, 32522.* Tel: 850-432-1515.

Christian Formation, Office of—Sr. MARGARET KUNTZ, A.S.C.J., Dir. GARY TAYLOR, Assoc. Dir. Leaven Facilitators: JULIAN SOLLOHUB; MAXINE LEBOUEF; JENNIFER MIHALCIK, Project Junior High Coord.; Mrs. RITA TOLBERT, Resource Center Coord., *P.O. Drawer 17329, Pensacola, 32522.* Tel: 850-436-6455.

Communications, Office of—Rev. MICHAEL MOONEY, Dir., *P.O. Drawer 17329, Pensacola, 32522.* Tel: 850-432-1515; Fax: 850-435-7756.

"The Florida Catholic"—MARY INABNIT, Reporter for the Diocese of Pensacola-Tallahassee Edition of *"The Florida Catholic", P.O. Drawer 17329, Pensacola, 32522.* Tel: 850-432-5215; Fax: 850-435-7756.

Cursillo Movement—Rev. PAUL STEWART, Spiritual Dir.; Mr. BOB MACKO, Diocesan Lay Dir., *P.O. Drawer 17329, Pensacola, 32522.* Tel: 850-432-1515.

Ecumenical & Interreligious Affairs, Office of—Rev. JOHN GRAY, Dir., *5200 Saufley Field Rd., Pensacola, 32526.* Tel: 850-456-5966; Fax: 850-453-3138.

Education, Department of—P.O. Drawer 17329, Pensacola, 32522. Tel: 850-432-1515.

Schools, Diocesan Commission for—Mrs. CYNTHIA LACOUR; Sr. MARY CAPLICE, C.N.D., Admin. Officer; Mr. RICHARD LURTON; Dr. NANCY ROBERTS; STEPHANY ALFT; STERLING BYRANT; ALAN MANNING; Revs. JOSEPH CAFFREY; MARTIN BRATEK, C.R.; MICHAEL CHERUP; ELEANOR GASI, Chm., *P.O. Drawer 17329, Pensacola, 32522.* Tel: 850-432-1515.

Superintendent of Schools, Office of the—Sr. MARY CAPLICE, C.N.D., Supt., *P.O. Drawer 17329, Pensacola, 32522.* Tel: 850-432-1515.

Marriage & Family Life Ministries, Department of—Mrs. LOUISE RITZ, Dir., *P.O. Drawer 17329, Pensacola, 32522.* Tel: 850-432-1515. Ministries: Engaged Encounter, Leadership Development for Family, Marriage Encounter and Natural Family Planning (NFP), Ministry to Aging, Ministry of Marriage Enrichment, The Third Option, Refocus, Evenings for the Engaged, For Better and Forever, Pre Cana, To Trust Again Consolation, Parenting Programs, New Beginnings New Outlook.

Pro-Life Activities—Rev. EUGENE CASSERLY, *P.O. Box 6117, Pensacola, 32503-0117.* Tel: 850-478-2797.

Respect Life Committee—Rev. Msgr. MICHAEL MOONEY; Rev. KEVIN JOHNSON; Deacons MIKE MURPHY; JEFFREY TRUMPS; Mr. BOB BRADY; Mr. MARK FARMER; Mrs. MARK FARMER; Mr. JIM KANE; Mrs. JIM KANE; Dr. MICHAEL MANGAN; Mrs. MICHAEL MANGAN; Dr. ROBERT SAYER; Mrs. MARTHA SEEP; Mrs. VALERIE SCHUMM.

Finance, Diocesan Commission for—Mr. ROBERT EMMANUEL, Chm.; Rev. Msgr. LUKE HUNT, Sec.; Rev. Msgr. JAMES AMOS, J.C.L., V.G.; Rev. JOHN CASSIDY; Mr. ROBERT HAMEL; Mr. ERIC NICKELSEN; Mr. VINCE WHIBBS, JR.; Mr. ALBERT WILLIAMS, JR.; Dr. DONALD FURY; J. PATRICK REMICH; Deacon JOHN MCLELLAN, *P.O. Drawer 17329, Pensacola, 32522.* Tel: 850-432-1515.

Finance, Department of—Deacon JOHN C. MCLELLAN, Dir., *P.O. Drawer 17329, Pensacola, 32522.* Tel: 850-432-1515.

Hispanic Ministry, Office of—Sr. MARIA LAUREN DONOHUE, M.S.B.T., Dir., *P.O. Drawer 17329, Pensacola, 32522.* Tel: 850-432-1515.

Holy Childhood Association—Sr. MARY CAPLICE, C.N.D., Dir., *P.O. Drawer 17329, Pensacola, 32522.* Tel: 850-432-1515.

Holy Name Society—Rev. Msgr. MICHAEL REED, J.C.L., *P.O. Drawer 17329, Pensacola, 32522.* Tel: 850-432-1515.

Justice and Peace, Office of—Vacant, *P.O. Drawer 17329, Pensacola, 32522.* Tel: 850-432-1515.

Knights of Columbus—Rev. Msgr. LUKE HUNT, Diocesan Chap., *P.O. Box 1057, Gulf Breeze, 32562.* Tel: 850-934-0222; Fax: 850-934-2804.

Legion of Mary—Rev. HECTOR R.G. PEREZ, S.T.D., Diocesan Spiritual Dir., *P.O. Drawer 12001, Pensacola, 32589.* Tel: 850-432-9362.

Liturgy, Office of—Rev. J. CRAIG WILLIAMS, Dir., *P.O. Drawer 17329, Pensacola, 32522.* Tel: 850-436-6455.

Permanent Diaconate Formation Board—Rev. Msgr. JAMES AMOS, J.C.L., V.G.; Very Rev. JAMES J. FLAHERTY, J.C.L., J.V.; Deacons HENRY BURRELL; JOHN MORGAN; THOMAS FRAITES; DALE JOHNSON; RAMON BONANNO; Rev. Msgr. LUKE HUNT; Rev. MARTIN HOLLEY; PATRICK REMICH; MINNIE SEABROOK; Rev. CRAIG WILLIAMS; Sr. CHRISTINE KELLY, S.S.J., *P.O. Drawer 17329, Pensacola, 32522.* Tel: 850-432-1515.

Permanent Diaconate, Office of—Deacon JOHN MORGAN, Vicar for Deacons, *P.O. Drawer 17329, Pensacola, 32522.* Tel: 850-432-1515.

Priestly Life and Ministry, Office of—Very Rev. ROBERT MORRIS, Dir., *P.O. Drawer 17329, Pensacola, 32522.* Tel: 850-432-1515.

Priests' Pension Plan, Board for—Most Rev. JOHN H. RICARD, S.S.J.; Rev. Msgr. LUKE HUNT; Rev. Msgr. JAMES AMOS, J.C.L., V.G.; Very Rev. MICHAEL MOONEY; Rev. Msgr. MICHAEL TUGWELL; Revs. JACK GRAY; JOHN T. CASSIDY; Rev. Msgr. JOHN O'SULLIVAN; Deacon JOHN MCLELLAN, Consultant.

Clergy Concerns—Rev. Msgr. MICHAEL CHERUP, Chm.; Rev. JOHN CASSIDY; Very Revs. C. SLADE CRAWFORD; ROBERT MORRIS; Rev. DENNIS O'BRIEN, *P.O. Drawer 17329, Pensacola, 32522.* Tel: 850-432-1515.

Propagation of the Faith, Office of—Rev. FRANCIS SZCZYKUTOWICZ, Dir., *P.O. Drawer 17329, Pensacola, 32522.* Tel: 850-432-1515.

Real Estate, Diocesan Commission for—Rev. Msgr. LUKE HUNT, Chm.; Rev. Msgr. WILLIAM A. CROWE, V.F.; Rev. Msgr. RICHARD J. BOWLES, V.F.; Rev. Msgr. JOHN V. O'SULLIVAN, V.F.; Rev. Msgr. FRANCIS SZCZYKUTOWICZ, V.F.; Mr. ROBERT EMMANUEL; Mr. J. PATRICK REMICH; Mr. JOHN DONOVAN; Mr. JOHN MORGAN, Sec., *P.O. Drawer 17329, Pensacola, 32522.* Tel: 850-432-1515.

Real Estate, Office of—Deacon JOHN MORGAN, Dir., *P.O. Drawer 17329, Pensacola, 32522.* Tel: 850-432-1515.

St. Vincent de Paul Society—Pensacola Particular Council, Rev. OLIVER BARRETT, C.S.Sp., Spiritual Dir. GREG PETERSON, Pres., *2200 W. Desoto St., Pensacola, 32505.* Tel: 850-434-6615. Tallahassee Chapter, Mr. ALBERT A. RELATION, Pres., *P.O. Box 2395, Tallahassee, 32316.* Tel: 850-576-6099.

Seminarian Candidate Review Board—Rev. ROY MARIEN, Chm.; Rev. Msgr. JAMES AMOS, J.C.L., V.G.; Very Rev. C. SLADE CRAWFORD; Mr. WILLIAM NADICKSBERND; Sr. MARY CAPLICE, C.N.D.; Mrs. ROSEMARY MASON, *P.O. Drawer 17329, Pensacola, 32522.* Tel: 850-432-1515.

Seminarians, Office of—Rev. SLADE CRAWFORD, Dir.; Mrs. LINDA BARREH, Sec., *P.O. Drawer 17329, Pensacola, 32522.* Tel: 850-432-1515.

Vocations, Office of—Rev. SLADE CRAWFORD, Dir.; Mrs. LINDA BARREH, Sec., *Drawer 17329, Pensacola, 32522.* Tel: 850-432-1515.

Serra Club—Pensacola: Rev. OLIVER BARRETT, Spiritual Dir.; Dr. WILLIAM RYAN, Pres.; Tallahassee: Mr. LOUISE FETE, Pres.; Fort Walton Beach-Niceville: Rev. KEVIN JOHNSON, Spiritual Dir. MARGARET MAULSHAGEN, Pres., *P.O. Drawer 17329, Pensacola, 32522.* Tel: 850-432-1515.

Youth Ministry, Office of—Rev. MICHAEL A. CHERUP, Dir.; Miss CINDY BAROCO, Sec., *P.O. Drawer 17329, Pensacola, 32522.* Tel: 850-432-1515.

CLERGY, PARISHES, MISSIONS AND PAROCHIAL SCHOOLS

GREATER PENSACOLA
(Escambia County)

1—CATHEDRAL OF THE SACRED HEART (1905), Revs. Michael V. Reed, Rector; Raymond Mullins; George Sindik; Deacons Jean White; Henry Burrell.
Res., 1101 E. Mallory St., P.O. Box 2248, 32503. Tel: 850-438-3131; Fax: 850-436-6428.
School—Sacred Heart Cathedral School, 1603 N. 12th Ave., 32503. Tel: 850-436-6440; Fax: 850-436-6444. Apostles of the Sacred Heart. Tel: 850-438-0560. Sr. Elizabeth Knight, A.S.C.J., Prin.
Catechesis/Religious Programs—Students 135.
Convent—1700 Conway Dr., 32503. Tel: 904-438-0560.

2—LITTLE FLOWER (1945), Revs. Michael J. Flynn; Martin D. Holley; Deacon Reymond Castellano.
Res., 6495 Lillian Hwy., P.O. Box 3009, 32516. Tel: 850-455-5641; Fax: 850-455-4508.
School—Tel: 850-455-4851; Fax: 850-457-8982. Mary Lou Tansey, Prin.
Lay Teachers 14; Students 239.
Catechesis/Religious Programs—Tel: 850-455-8434.
Students 121.

3—HOLY SPIRIT (Warrington) (1968), Rev. Msgr. James Amos, V.G.; Deacons Eugene Geri; Stanley Barrows.
Res., 10650 Gulf Beach Hwy., 32507. Tel: 850-492-0837 (Office); Fax: 850-492-4875.
Catechesis/Religious Programs—Tel: 852-492-5136.
Students 142.

4—NATIVITY OF OUR LORD (1969), Revs. Michael P. Mooney; John Cayer; Deacons Randall Comeau; Dennis Dobransky.
Res., 9945 Hillview Rd., 32514-5702. Tel: 850-477-3221; Fax: 850-494-1503.
Catechesis/Religious Programs—Tel: 850-478-5584, Ext. 20.
Students 370.

5—OUR LADY QUEEN OF MARTYRS, MISSION (1977), Rev. Augustine Nguyen Thanh Hue (Vietnamese).
Res., 3295 S. Barrancas Ave., 32507. Tel: 850-455-2712; Fax: 850-455-0264.

6—ST. ANNE'S (Bellview) (1964), Rev. John F. Gray; Deacon John C. McLellan. In res., Rev. Thomas O'Flaherty.
Res., 5200 Saufley Field Rd., 32526-1626. Tel: 850-456-5966; Fax: 850-453-3138.
Catechesis/Religious Programs—Students 177.

7—ST. ANNE (Brownsville) (1953), Rev. D. Oliver Barrett, C.S.Sp.
Res., 2910 W. Gadsden St., 32505. Tel: 850-433-5467; Fax: 850-453-3138.

8—ST. ANTHONY OF PADUA (1941) (African American), Rev. Thomas A. Bonanti.
Res., 1804 N. Davis St., 32503. Tel: 850-436-6422.
Catechesis/Religious Programs—Students 9.

9—ST. JOHN THE EVANGELIST (1859), Rev. Richard L. Altenbaugh; Deacon Gerard Williamson.
Res., 303 S. Navy Blvd., 32507. Tel: 850-455-0356; Fax: 850-453-5109. [CEM]
School—Sisters of Mercy, Tel: 850-456-5218; Fax: 850-456-5956. Sr. Patricia Ann Pepitone, R.S.M., Prin.
Sisters 2; Lay Teachers 18; Students 239.
Catechesis/Religious Programs—Students 84.
Convent—325 S. Navy Blvd., 32507. Tel: 850-455-0355; Fax: 850-456-3046.

10—ST. JOSEPH (1891) (African American), Rev. Thomas A. Bonanti; Sr. Maureen Joseph Kirwan, S.C., Pastoral Assoc.
Mailing Address: P.O. Box 13566, 32591. Tel: 850-436-6461; Fax: 850-436-6462. [CEM]
Res., 141 W. Intendencia St., 32501.
Catechesis/Religious Programs—Students 71.

11—ST. MARY (1941), Revs. Eugene D. Casserly; Dominic Dat Tran.
Mailing Address: P.O. Box 6117, 32503. Tel: 850-478-2797; Fax: 850-478-2739.
Res., 401 Van Pelt Ln., 32505. Tel: 850-478-2797; Fax: 850-478-2739.
Catechesis/Religious Programs—Tel: 850-478-1635.
Students 125.

12—ST. MICHAEL (1559), Very Rev. Richard J. Bowles, V.F.
Res., 19 N. Palafox St., P.O. Box 12423, 32582. Tel: 850-438-4985; Fax: 850-433-9758.

13—ST. PAUL (1963), Rev. Msgr. Michael W. Tugwell; Revs. Paul White; Douglas White; Douglas Halsema; Deacons John P. Morgan; Robert Leblanc.
Res., 3131 Hyde Park Rd., 32503. Tel: 850-434-2551; Fax: 850-436-6449.
School—Apostles of the Sacred Heart (Hamden, CT), Tel: 850-436-6435; Fax: 850-436-6437. Sr. M. Lizabeth Doty, A.S.C.J., Prin.
Sisters 1; Lay Teachers 15; Students 301.

Catechesis/Religious Programs—Tel: 850-436-6446.
Students 370.
Convent—1700 Conway Dr., 32503. Tel: 850-438-0560.
Mission—Pensacola, Escambia Co., Church of Our Savior, 6700 Old Spanish Tr., 32504.

14—ST. STEPHEN (1922), Rev. Hector R.G. Perez, S.T.D.
Res., 900 W. Garden St., 32501. Tel: 850-432-9362.
Catechesis/Religious Programs—Students 38.

15—ST. THOMAS MORE (1954), Rev. John T. Cassidy. In res., Rev. James R. Olnhausen.
Mailing Address: 510 Bayshore Dr., 32507. Tel: 850-456-2543; Fax: 850-455-5203.
Catechesis/Religious Programs—Students 39.

CITY OF TALLAHASSEE
(Leon County)

1—CO-CATHEDRAL OF ST. THOMAS MORE (1968), Revs. C. Slade Crawford, Rector; Thomas S. Collins.
Res., 900 W. Tennessee St., P.O. Box 2395, 32316. Tel: 850-222-7371; 222-9630 (Office); Fax: 850-222-6430.
Catechesis/Religious Programs—Students 147.
Chapel—St. Eugene, Florida A&M University, 701 W. Gamble St., 32310. Tel: 850-222-6482; Fax: 850-222-6482. [JC]
Rev. Semanhyia Boateng-Mensah, Chap.

2—BLESSED SACRAMENT, Very Rev. John V. O'Sullivan, V.F.; Revs. Michael Shaw; James F. Cregan.
Res., 624 Miccosukee Rd., 32308. Tel: 850-222-1321; Fax: 850-222-9772.
School—Trinity Catholic, Tel: 850-222-0444; Fax: 850-224-5067. Sr. Aileen McClain, O.P., Prin.
Sisters 2; Lay Teachers 34; Students 542.
Catechesis/Religious Programs—Students 235.

3—GOOD SHEPHERD (1973), Revs. Michael Foley; Thomas Guido; Philip Fortin; Deacon Andrew Radigan.
Office: 4665 Thomasville Rd., 32308. Tel: 850-893-1837; 893-2381.
Catechesis/Religious Programs—Bette Scaringe, D.R.E.
Students 703.

4—ST. LOUIS (1979), Rev. Paul E. Stewart; Deacons Nelson Madera, Ph.D.; Mack Shook.
Res., 4151 Miraflores Ln., 32303. Tel: 850-562-5140; Fax: 850-562-7356.
Catechesis/Religious Programs—Students 84.

OUTSIDE THE CITIES OF PENSACOLA AND TALLAHASSEE

Apalachicola, Franklin Co., St. Patrick (1851), Rev. Roger Latosynski.
Res., 27 Sixth St., P.O. Box 550, 32320. Tel: 904-653-9453; Fax: 850-653-4528. [JC]

Bayou George, Bay Co., Our Lady of the Rosary, Rev. W. P. Brown.
Res., 5622 Julie Dr., Panama City, 32404. Tel: 850-769-5067.
Catechesis/Religious Programs—Students 35.
Mission—Fountain, Bay Co., Our Lady Queen of Peace.

Blountstown, Calhoun Co., St. Francis of Assisi, Rev. John P. Selleck, (Retired).
Res., 334 Gaskin St., 32424. Tel: 850-674-4482.
Mission—Wewahitchka, Gulf Co., St. Lawrence, Box 651, Wewahitchka, 32465. Tel: 850-639-5787.

Bonifay, Holmes Co., Blessed Trinity (1979), Rev. Joseph Caffrey, Admin.
Res., 2331 Hwy. 177A, 32425. Tel: 850-547-3735; Fax: 850-547-7477.

Cantonment, Escambia Co., St. Jude Thaddeus (1966), Rev. Richard E. Dawson; Deacons John Bartoszewicz; Bradley Seabrook; Tom Simard.
Res., 303 Rocky Ave., 32533. Tel: 850-968-6189; Fax: 850-968-1578. [CEM]
Mission—Barrineau Park, Escambia Co., St. Elizabeth of Hungary, 303 Rocky Ave., 32533. Tel: 850-587-2550.
Catechesis/Religious Programs—Students 71.

Chattahoochee, Gadsden Co., Holy Cross Parish (1972), Rev. Jacob M. Pallivathukkall (India) Admin.
Res., R.R. 1, Box 1562, 32324. Tel: 850-663-4610.

Chipley, Washington Co., St. Joseph the Worker (1968), Rev. Patrick H. Foley.
Res., P.O. Box 266, 32428. Tel: 850-638-7654; Fax: 850-547-7477.
Catechesis/Religious Programs—Students 25.

Crestview, Okaloosa Co., Our Lady of Victory (1954), Rev. John F. Kelly.
550 Adams Dr., 32536.
Res., 143 Jeff Dr., 32536. Tel: 850-682-4622; Fax: 850-689-0335.
Catechesis/Religious Programs—Students 380.

De Funiak Springs, Walton Co., St. Margaret, Rev. Joseph P. Caffrey.
Mailing Address: Box 590, 32433. Tel: 850-892-9247.
Res., 267 U.S. Highway 331 N., 32433. Tel: 850-892-3028.
Catechesis/Religious Programs—Students 31.
Mission—Freeport, Walton Co., Christ the King, #15542 Hwy. 331 S., Freeport, 32439.

Destin, Okaloosa Co., Corpus Christi (1977), Rev. Robert F. Morris; Deacon Joseph Rose.
Res., 307 Beach Dr., 32541. Tel: 850-654-5422; Fax: 850-837-3807.
Catechesis/Religious Programs—Tel: 850-654-5423. Linda S. Shapiro, D.R.E.
Students 118.

Church of the Resurrection, Walton Co., (1981), Rev. Roy C. Marien; Deacon Matthew Rezmer.
Res., 259 Miramar Beach Dr., 32550. Tel: 850-837-0357; Fax: 850-837-2062.
Catechesis/Religious Programs—Students 76.

Fort Walton Beach, Okaloosa Co., St. Mary (1914), Very Rev. Michael Cherup; Rev. Kevin Johnson; Deacons Robert J. Saxer; Charles Wolf; John Howell; William Bodisch; Ramon Bonnano; Walter Richardson; Michael Murphy; Daniel McAuliffe; Anthony Restivo.
Res., 110 St. Mary Ave., S.W., 32548-6645. Tel: 850-243-3742; Fax: 850-243-1271.
School—Tel: 850-243-8913; Fax: 850-243-7895. Mrs. Regina Nadicksbernd, Prin.
Lay Teachers 22; Students 337.
Catechesis/Religious Programs—Tel: 850-244-1833. Sr. Evelyn Rogers, S.U.S.C., D.R.E.
Students 297.

Fountain, Bay Co., Our Lady Queen of Peace Mission, Rev. William P. Brown.
Mailing Address: P.O. Box 213, 32438. Tel: 850-769-5067.
Church—18005 Lazy Ln., 32438.

Freeport, Walton Co., Christ the King Mission (1984), Rev. Joseph P. Caffrey.
Hwy. 331 N., P.O. Box 590, De Funiak Springs, 32435-0590. Tel: 850-892-9247; Fax: 850-892-0412. See St. Margaret Parish, De Funiak Springs.

Gulf Breeze, Santa Rosa Co., St. Ann (1948), Rev. Msgr. Luke Hunt; Revs. Viet Huynh; William Condren; Deacon Robert Kostic, (Retired).
Res., 100 Daniel Dr., P.O. Drawer 1057, 32562. Tel: 850-932-2859; Fax: 850-934-2804.
St. Ann Discovery School—(Learning Center & Afterschool) (Ages 1-11). Tel: 850-932-9330. Mrs. Penny Geiger, Dir.
Teachers 34; Students 166.
Catechesis/Religious Programs—Students 227.
Mission—Gulf Breeze, Santa Rosa Co., Our Lady of the Assumption, 920 Via de Luna, P.O. Box 1057, Pensacola Beach, 32561. Tel: 850-934-0222; Fax: 850-934-6020.

Lanark Village, Franklin Co., Sacred Heart of Jesus (1960), Rev. James F. Cregan.
Res., 109 Newman Dr., P.O. Box 729, 32323. Tel: 850-697-3445.

Madison, Madison Co., St. Vincent de Paul (1907), Rev. Ernest Sylvestre, O.M.I. In res., Rev. Joseph C. Schwab, O.M.I.
Res., 402 N.W. Sumter St., P.O. Box 730, 32341. Tel: 850-973-2428; Fax: 850-973-9311.
Catechesis/Religious Programs—Students 30.

Marianna, Jackson Co., St. Anne (1947), Rev. Patrick H. Foley.
Res., 3009 Fifth St., P.O. Box 1547, 32447. Tel: 850-482-3734. [JC]
Catechesis/Religious Programs—Tel: 850-526-3291.
Students 66.

Mary Esther, Okaloosa Co., St. Peter (1975), Rev. Joseph P. Callipare; Deacon David P. Robinson.
Res., 100 Francis St., 32569. Tel: 850-581-2556; Fax: 850-581-2640.
Catechesis/Religious Programs—Tel: 850-581-7263.
Students 157.

Medart, Wakulla Co., St. Elizabeth Ann Seton (1975), Rev. James B. MacGee, O.M.I.
Mailing Address: 3609 Coastal Hwy., Crawfordville, 32327. Tel: 850-926-1797; Fax: 850-926-1737. [CEM]
Catechesis/Religious Programs—Students 55.
Mission—Woodville, Leon Co., St. Stephen the Protomartyr, Natural Bridge Rd., P.O. Box 1142, Woodville, 32362. Tel: 850-421-9094.

Mexico Beach, Bay Co., Our Lady of Guadalupe Mission. See St. Dominic, Panama City.

Milton, Santa Rosa Co., St. Rose of Lima (1957), Rev. Thom A. Crandall; Deacons David Davey; Thomas Kennell.
Res., 515 Park Ave., S.W., 32570. Tel: 850-623-3600; Fax: 850-983-3043. [JC]
Catechesis/Religious Programs—Students 300.

Monticello, Jefferson Co., St. Margaret (1917), Rev. Ernest Sylvestre, O.M.I.
Res., P.O. Box 730, Madison, 32341. Tel: 850-973-2428; Fax: 850-973-9311.
Church—U.S. Hwy. 90 E., 32334. Tel: 850-997-3622.

Niceville, Okaloosa Co., Christ Our Redeemer (1989), Rev. J. Craig Williams; Deacons Michael Carucci; Joaquin Trevino; James Murray; William Schaal.
Res., 1028 White Point Rd., 32578. Tel: 850-897-7797; Fax: 850-897-2422.
Catechesis/Religious Programs—Tel: 850-897-2974.
Students 272.

Holy Name of Jesus (1964), Revs. Daniel J. Butler; Eugene W. Pathe; Deacons Thomas Fraites; Louis Marini; Willie O'Neal; James Cox; Gary McBride.
Res., 1200 Valparaiso Blvd., P.O. Box 576, 32588. Tel: 850-678-7813; Fax: 850-678-5775.
Catechesis/Religious Programs—Students 330.

Panama City, Bay Co., St. Dominic (1917), Rev. Msgr. William A. Crowe, V.F.; Revs. James J. Lambert; Peter L. Zaleswki.
Res., 3308 E. 15th St., 32405-7414. Tel: 850-785-4574; Fax: 850-872-0800.
Catechesis/Religious Programs—Tel: 850-763-7393.
Students 325.
Mission—Mexico Beach, Bay Co., Our Lady of Guadalupe, 1500 N. 15th St., Mexico Beach, 32410. Tel: 850-648-3006. [CEM]

St. John the Evangelist (1945), Revs. Jerzy Zieba, C.R., Vicar; Martin Bratek, C.R.; Deacons Dale Johnson; Earl C. Mirus; John Kreppein.
Res., 1008 Fortune Ave., P.O. Box 978, 32401. Tel: 850-763-1821; Fax: 850-784-1739.
School—Tel: 850-763-1775; Fax: 850-784-4461. Miss Sally Lorei, Prin.
Lay Teachers 21; Students 289.
Catechesis/Religious Programs—Students 529.

SS. Peter & Paul Mission (1981) (Vietnam), Rev. Dominic P. Sa, Admin.
Mailing Address: P.O. Box 3627, FL. 32401. Tel: 850-914-0390.
Res., 1003 E. Ave., 32401. Tel: 850-785-4574. [JC]
Catechesis/Religious Programs—Students 50.

Panama City Beach, Bay Co., St. Bernadette (1956), Rev. David T. O'Shea.
Res., 1214 Moylan Rd., 32407. Tel: 850-234-3490; Fax: 850-234-3266.
Catechesis/Religious Programs—Tel: 850-234-3266.
Students 132.

Pensacola Beach, Escambia Co., Our Lady of the Assumption Mission (1979),
Mailing Address: P.O. Box 1057, Gulf Breeze, 32561.
920 Via de Luna, 32561. Tel: 850-934-0222; Fax: 850-934-6020. See St. Ann, Gulf Breeze.
Catechesis/Religious Programs—Students 37.

Perry, Taylor Co., Immaculate Conception (1914), Rev. Edward Hauf, O.M.I. In res., Rev. Francis Bagan, O.M.I.
Res., 2750 S. Byron Butler Pkwy., 32347. Tel: 850-584-3169; Fax: 850-584-5736.
Catechesis/Religious Programs—Tel: 850-584-8853.
Students 94.
Center—Tel: 850-584-8853.

Port St. Joe, Gulf Co., St. Joseph (1925), Rev. Thomas J. Guido.
Res., 2006 Monument Ave., P.O. Box 820, 32457-0820. Tel: 850-227-1417.
Church—20th & Monument Sts., 32457-0820. Tel: 850-229-8637.
Missions—Port St. Joe, Gulf Co., San Blas Catholic Mission, C30E, 32456.; Wewahitchka, Gulf Co., St. Lawrence Mission.

Quincy, Gadsden Co., St. Thomas the Apostle (1957), Rev. Dennis O'Brien.
Res. & Mailing Address: 27 N. Shadow St., P.O. Box 549, 32353. Tel: 850-627-2350; Fax: 850-627-6755.
Catechesis/Religious Programs—Tel: 850-627-8807.
Students 180.
Hispanic Ministry Office of St. Thomas—Religious Education Office, Tel: 850-627-8807.
Missions—Greensboro, Gadsen Co., Juan Diego, Outreach Center for the Hispanic Migrants/Farmworkers, Tel: 850-442-9023. Mrs. Mary Matthews, Contact.; Greensboro, Gadsen Co., Casa Guadalupe Catholic Center for Evangelization, P.O. Box 59, Greensboro, 32330. Tel: 850-442-4337.

Santa Rosa Beach, Walton Co., St. Rita (1982), Rev. Msgr. James J. Flaherty; Deacons Jeffrey Trumps; David Casey.
Mailing Address: 20 St. Rita Ln., P.O. Box 1223, 32459. Tel: 850-267-2558; 267-4592 (Rectory); Fax: 850-267-3711.
Catechesis/Religious Programs—Students 42.

Sunny Hills, Washington Co., St. Theresa (1972), Rev. Francis S. Szczykutowicz.
Res., 2056 Sunny Hills Blvd., 32428. Tel: 850-773-3406; Fax: 850-773-7008.

Tiger Point, Santa Rosa Co., St. Sylvester (1979), Very Rev. Steven J. O'Connor.
Res., 3551 Gulf Breeze Pkwy., Gulf Breeze, 32561. Tel: 850-932-6807; Fax: 850-932-6338.
Catechesis/Religious Programs—Students 237.

Wewahitchka, Gulf Co., St. Lawrence Mission, c/o 334 Gaskin St., Blountstown, 32424. See St. Francis of Assisi, Blountstown.

Woodville, Leon Co., St. Stephen the Protomartyr (1979),
Mailing Address: P.O. Box 1142, 32362. Tel: 850-421-9094. See St. Elizabeth Ann Seton, Medart.

Chaplains of Public Institutions

PENSACOLA. *Escambia County Jail.* Deacon Dennis Dobransky.

TALLAHASSEE. *Federal Correctional Institution.* Rev. Edward Fisher.

CHATTAHOOCHEE. *Florida State Hospital.* Vacant.
River Junction Correctional Institution. Vacant.

EGLIN. *Eglin Federal Prison Camp Eglin Air Force Base.* Deacon Thomas Fraites.

MARIANNA. *Dozier School for Boys Sunland Training Center, Jackson Vocation Center.* Vacant.
Florida Correctional Institutions. Sr. Ann Marie Raftery, O.S.F.

SNEADS. *Apalachee Correctional Institution.* Deacon Robert Moore.

On Duty Outside the Diocese:
Reverend Monsignors—
Kerr, William A., La Roche College, 9000 Babcock Blvd., Pittsburgh, PA 15237
Reverend Fathers—
Bosso, Stephen C., St. Vincent de Paul Regional Seminary, 10701 E. Military Tr., Boynton Beach, FL 33436
Roland, Charles, St. Joseph Church, 2011 Darling Ave., Waycross, GA 31501
Sarmiento, Oscar, St. Isidro Parish, 2310 Martin Luther King Blvd., Pompano Beach, FL 33609-1591

Military Chaplains:
Reverend Fathers—
Bluett, James K.
Krzywicki, Lance P., Chap., PSC 810, Box 14, FPO, AE 09169
McClanahan, Robert P., Jr., NAS, Patuxent River, MD 20670
Voyt, Stephen A., Major, Wright Patterson AFB, OH 45424

On Leave of Absence:
Reverend Fathers—
Castillo, Richard
Hevia, Todd O.
Wood, Peter N.

Retired:
Reverend Monsignors—
Cunningham, Patrick
Reverend Fathers—
Dzienkiewicz, Edwin
Halstead, Philip
Hogarty, Paul
Jorden, James A.
Joseph, William
Kiem, Anthony
Kirby, Edward A.
White, Philip

Permanent Deacons:
Barrows, Stanley, Holy Spirit, Pensacola
Bartoszewicz, John M., St. Jude Thaddeus, Cantonment
Bodish, William, St. Mary, Fort Walton Beach
Bonanno, Frederick R., St. Mary, Fort Walton Beach
Boughton, Grant, Christ our Redeemer, Niceville
Burrell, Henry N., Cathedral of the Sacred Heart, Pensacola
Carucci, Michael J., Christ Our Redeemer, Niceville
Casey, David R., Holy Name of Jesus, Niceville
Cloud, Millard F., Inactive
Comeau, Randall O., Nativity of Our Lord, Pensacola
Davey, David, St. Rose of Lima, Milton
Dealy, Michael J., (Retired)
Dobransky, Dennis, Nativity, Pensacola
Fraites, Thomas J., Holy Name of Jesus, Niceville
Gaines, William G., Leave of Absence
Gardner, James L., (Retired)
Geri, Eugene A., Holy Spirit, Pensacola
Greskovich, Frank J., Leave of Absence
Howell, John, St. Mary, Fort Walton Beach
Hromadka, Joseph J., St. Rita, Mexico Beach
Johnson, Dale R., St. John the Evangelist, Panama City
Kennell, Thomas H., St. Rose of Lima, Milton
Kreppein, John, St. John the Evangelist, Panama City
Madera, Nelson I., St. Louis, Tallahassee
Marini, Louis, Holy Name of Jesus, Niceville
McLellan, John, St. Anne, Bellview
Mirus, Earl C., St. John the Evangelist, Panama City
Morgan, John P., St. Paul, Pensacola
O'Neal, Willie, Holy Name of Jesus, Niceville
Packard, Russell C., St. Paul, Pensacola
Radigan, Terence A., Good Shepherd, Tallahassee
Restivo, Anthony, Corpus Christi, Destin
Richardson, Walter H., St. Mary, Fort Walton
Robinson, David P., St. Peter, Mary Esther
Rose, Joseph, Corpus Christi, Destin
Saxer, Robert J., St. Mary, Fort Walton Beach
Seabrook, Bradley M., St. Jude, Cantonment
Shettle, Charles G., (Retired)
Shook, Mack D., St. Louis, Tallahassee
Simard, Thomas, St. Jude, Cantonment
Trevino, Joaquin D., Christ Our Redeemer, Niceville
Vota, Joseph L., (Retired)
White, Jean F., Cathedral of the Sacred Heart, Pensacola
Williamson, Gerard, St. John the Evangelist, Warrington
Wines, Frank, St. Sylvester (Diocese of Lansing, MI)
Wolf, Charles R., St. Mary, Fort Walton Beach

INSTITUTIONS LOCATED IN THE DIOCESE

[A] HIGH SCHOOLS, DIOCESAN

PENSACOLA. *Pensacola Catholic High School*, 3043 W. Scott St., 32505. Tel: 850-436-6400; Fax: 850-436-6405.
E-mail: martinK5@juno.com
Web site: pensacolachs.org
Sr. Kierstin Martin, A.S.C.J., Prin. Sisters 2; Lay Teachers 37; Students 610.

[B] ELEMENTARY SCHOOLS, DIOCESAN

PENSACOLA. *St. Michael*, 601 N. Palafox St., 32501. Tel: 850-436-6464; Fax: 850-436-6458.
E-mail: StMichael@pen.net
Web site: wwwpensacolastmichael.org
Sisters of St. Joseph (Buffalo). S. Robert Anne, S.S.J., Prin. Sisters 2; Lay Teachers 14; Students 258.

[C] GENERAL HOSPITALS

PENSACOLA. *The Mother Seton Guild of Sacred Heart Hospital, Inc.*, 32504
For a complete listing, refer to the Hospitals section.
Sacred Heart Foundation, Inc., 4475 Bayou Blvd., 32503
For a complete listing, refer to the Hospitals section.
Sacred Heart Hospital of Pensacola, 5151 N. Ninth Ave., 32504. Tel: 850-416-7000; Fax: 850-416-6119.
E-mail: pmadden@shhpens.org
Web site: sacred-heart.org
For a complete listing, refer to the Hospitals section.

[D] HOMES FOR AGED

PENSACOLA. *Haven of Our Lady of Peace*, 5203 N. Ninth Ave., 32504. Tel: 850-477-0531; Fax: 850-477-6782.
E-mail: mfox@shhpens.org
For a complete listing, refer to the Special Care Facilities section.

[E] APARTMENTS FOR THE ELDERLY AND HANDICAPPED

TALLAHASSEE. *Casa Calderon, Inc.*, 800 W. Virginia St., 32304. Tel: 850-222-4026; Fax: 850-561-6868.
E-mail: karkoel@aol.com.
For a complete listing, refer to the Special Care Facilities section.

[F] CONVENT AND RESIDENCES FOR SISTERS

PENSACOLA. *Blessed Trinity Missionary Cenacle*, 412 Bayshore Dr., 32507. Tel: 850-456-4141. Sisters 5.
Notre Dame Convent, Sisters of the Congregation of Notre Dame, 1001 Deason St., 32505. Tel: 850-438-5906. Sisters 3.
Sacred Heart Hospital Convent, 1657 Trinity Dr., 32504. Tel: 850-416-7920; Fax: 850-416-6119.
E-mail: srjeanrh@sacred-heart.org
Web site: www.shhint.net
St. Michael Convent, 18 W. Jackson St., 32501-3956. Tel: 850-436-6460.
E-mail: stmichaelepen.net
Web site: pensacolastmichael.org
Sisters of Mercy of the Americas; Sisters of St. Joseph (Buffalo); Sisters of Charity of St. Elizabeth of New Jersey. Sisters 3.

APALACHICOLA. *Martin House*, 149 10th St., 32320. Tel: 850-653-8774.
E-mail: apalachop@digitalexp.com
Sinsinawa Dominicans Congregation of the Most Holy Rosary 2; Total Assisted 1,016.

MARIANNA. *Mission Helpers of the Sacred Heart Convent*, 3007 Fifth St., 32446. Tel: 850-526-3291. Sisters 2.

SUNNY HILLS. *Vestiarki Sisters of Jesus (Poland)*, 3919 Vistula Dr., 32428. Tel: 850-773-3302. Sisters 4; Total Assisted 3.

[G] HOMELESS SHELTERS

PANAMA CITY. *Naomi House*, 2941 11th St., 32401. Tel: 850-769-5756.
St. Barnabas House, 3128 E. 11th St., 32401. Tel: 850-763-0475; Fax: 850-763-2969.
E-mail: cathcharpc@aol.com
Sheila Harmon, Coord. Total in Residence 20; Total Staff 4.

[H] RETREAT HOUSES

TALLAHASSEE. *The Saint John Neumann Spiritual Renewal Center*, 685 Miccosukee Rd., 32308. Tel: 850-224-2971. Sr. Christine Kelly, S.S.J., Dir. Sisters 3.

NAVARRE. *Casa Stella Maris*, 7650 Clark St., 32566. Tel: 850-932-6807. Very Rev. Steven J. O'Connor, Dir. Total Staff 1.

[I] MISCELLANEOUS

PENSACOLA. *Diocese of Pensacola-Tallahassee Education Foundation, Inc.*, P.O. Drawer 17329, 32522. Tel: 850-432-1515; Fax: 850-436-6424.
E-mail: DIOPCTAL75@aol.com
Web site: www.cfi.net/ptdioccese/pt.html
St. Michael Cemetery Foundation, Inc., P.O. Drawer 17329, 32522. Tel: 850-432-1515.

RELIGIOUS INSTITUTES OF MEN REPRESENTED IN THE DIOCESE

For further details refer to the corresponding bracketed number in the Religious Institutes of Men or Women section.

[0340]—*Cistercian Fathers.*—O.Cist.
[1080]—*Congregation of the Resurrection.* (Chicago Prov.).—C.R.
[0650]—*Holy Ghost Fathers.*—C.S.Sp.
[0590]—*Missionaries of the Holy Apostles.*—M.Ss.A.
[0910]—*Oblates of Mary Immaculate.* (Eastern American Prov.).—O.M.I.
[0430]—*Order of Preachers-Dominicans.* (Southern Prov.).—O.P.

RELIGIOUS INSTITUTES OF WOMEN REPRESENTED IN THE DIOCESE

[0130]—*Apostles of the Sacred Heart of Jesus.*—A.S.C.J.
[0760]—*Daughters of Charity of St. Vincent de Paul.* (Eastern Prov.).—D.C.
[1070-03]—*Dominican Sisters.*—O.P.
[1070-13]—*Dominican Sisters.*—O.P.
[1070-14]—*Dominican Sisters.*—O.P.
[2720]—*Mission Helpers of the Sacred Heart.*—M.H.S.H.
[2790]—*Missionary Servants of the Most Blessed Trinity.*—M.S.B.T.
[0430]—*Sisters of Charity of Blessed Virgin Mary.*—B.V.M.
[0590]—*Sisters of Charity of Saint Elizabeth, Convent Station.*—S.C.
[0990]—*Sisters of Divine Providence.*—C.D.P.
[2575]—*Sisters of Mercy of the Americas.* (Baltimore, MD).—R.S.M.
[1660]—*Sisters of Saint Francis of the Providence of God.*—O.S.F.
[3900]—*Sisters of St. Joseph of St. Augustine, Florida.*—S.S.J.
[2980]—*Sisters of the Congregation de Notre Dame.* (Blessed Sacrament Prov.).—C.N.D.
[2070]—*Sisters of the Holy Union.*—S.U.S.C.
[3480]—*Sisters of the Resurrection.*—C.R.
[2150]—*Sisters, Servants of the Immaculate Heart of Mary.*—I.H.M.
[]—*Vestiarski Sisters of Jesus.* (Poland).—V.S.

NECROLOGY

† Gallagher, Rev. Msgr. James, Pensacola, FL Holy Spirit. —Died Feb. 8, 2000.
† McKeon, Alexander P. —Died Feb. 3, 2000.

Diocese of Peoria

(Dioecesis Peoriensis)

Most Reverend

JOHN J. MYERS, D.D., J.C.D.

Bishop of Peoria; ordained December 17, 1966; appointed July 14, 1987; consecrated September 3, 1987; acceded to See of Peoria January 23, 1990. *Res., 607 N.E. Madison Ave., Peoria, IL, 61603.* Tel.: 309-671-1550; Fax: 309-671-5079.

Chancery: 607 N.E. Madison Ave., P.O. Box 1406, Peoria, IL, 61655. Tel.: 309-671-1550; Fax: 309-671-5079.

ESTABLISHED 1877.

Square Miles 16,933.

A cross-section of Illinois, bounded on the north by the Counties of Whiteside, Lee, De Kalb, Grundy and Iroquois, and on the east by Kendall, Grundy, Kankakee and Ford, and on the south by Adams, Brown, Cass, Menard, Sangamon, Macon, Moultrie, Douglas and Edgar; comprising the Counties of Bureau, Champaign, Dewitt, Fulton, Hancock, Henderson, Henry, Knox, La Salle, Livingston, Logan, Marshall, Mason, McDonough, McLean, Mercer, Peoria, Piatt, Putnam, Rock Island, Schuyler, Stark, Tazewell, Vermilion, Warren and Woodford.

For legal titles of parishes and diocesan institutions, consult the Chancery.

STATISTICAL OVERVIEW

Personnel	
Bishop	1
Abbots	1
Retired Abbots	1
Priests: Diocesan Active in Diocese	168
Priests: Active Outside Diocese	13
Priests: Retired, Sick or Absent	66
Number of Diocesan Priests	247
Religious Priests in Diocese	49
Extern Priests in Diocese	1
Ordinations:	
Diocesan Priests	3
Transitional Deacons	3
Permanent Deacons in Diocese	81
Total Brothers	21
Total Sisters	321
Parishes	
Parishes	165
With Resident Pastor:	
Resident Diocesan Priests	133
Resident Religious Priests	21
Without Resident Pastor:	
Administered by Priests	11
Missions	39
Pastoral Centers	5
Professional Ministry Personnel:	
Brothers	2
Sisters	22
Lay Ministers	38
Welfare	
Catholic Hospitals	8
Total Assisted	1,409,004
Homes for the Aged	6
Total Assisted	500
Residential Care of Children	1
Total Assisted	55
Day Care and Extended Day Care Centers	2
Total Assisted	349
Special Centers for Social Services	1
Total Assisted	16,921
Residential Care of Disabled	1
Total Assisted	4
Other Institutions	3
Total Assisted	2,158
Educational	
Diocesan Students in Other Seminaries	34
Total Seminarians	34
Colleges and Universities	1
Total Students	150
High Schools, Diocesan and Parish	6
Total Students	2,588
High Schools, Private	1
Total Students	331
Elementary Schools, Diocesan and Parish	47
Total Students	12,440
Catechesis/Religious Education:	
High School Students	2,744
Elementary Students	10,616
Total Students Under Catholic Instruction	28,903
Teachers in the Diocese:	
Priests	16
Brothers	2
Sisters	40
Lay Teachers	1,033
Vital Statistics	
Receptions into the Church:	
Infant Baptism Totals	2,729
Adult Baptism Totals	455
Received into Full Communion	517
First Communions	2,515
Confirmations	3,041
Marriages:	
Catholic	475
Interfaith	448
Total Marriages	923
Deaths	2,011
Total Catholic Population	221,932
Total Population	1,440,518

Former Bishops—Most Rev. JOHN LANCASTER SPALDING, D.D., cons. May 1, 1877; resigned Sept. 11, 1908; Titular Archbishop of Scitopolis; appt. Oct. 14, 1908; died Aug. 25, 1916.—Most Rev. EDMUND M. DUNNE, D.D., ord. June 24, 1887; cons. Sept. 1, 1909; died Oct. 17, 1929.—Most Rev. JOSEPH H. SCHLARMAN, D.D., Ph.D., J.C.D., ord. June 29, 1904; cons. June 17, 1930; named Assistant at Papal Throne, Nov. 16, 1950; Archbishop *ad personam; appt. June 27, 1951; died Nov. 10, 1951.—Most Rev.* WILLIAM E. COUSINS, D.D., ord. April 23, 1927; Titular Bishop of Forma and Auxiliary Bishop of Chicago; appt. Dec. 17, 1948; cons. March 7, 1949; Bishop of Peoria; appt. May 19, 1952; Archbishop of Milwaukee; appt. Dec. 17, 1958; died Sept. 14, 1988.—Most Rev. JOHN B. FRANZ, D.D., ord. June 13, 1920; Bishop of Dodge City; appt. May 29, 1951; cons. Aug. 29, 1951; transferred Peoria, Aug. 8, 1959; retired June 1, 1971; died July 3, 1992.—Most Rev. EDWARD W. O'ROURKE, D.D., ord. May 28, 1944; Bishop of Peoria; appt. May 24, 1971; cons. July 15, 1971; retired Jan. 23, 1990; died Sept. 29, 1999.

Chancery—607 N.E. Madison Ave., P.O. Box 1406, Peoria, 61655. Tel: 309-671-1550. Please direct all calls for all departments to this number; Fax: 309-671-5079. Office Hours: Mon.-Fri. 8:30-4:30.

Vicar General—Rev. Msgr. JAMES F. CAMPBELL, Protonotary Apostolic, Vicar General. Tel: 309-671-1581; Fax: 309-671-1558. Rev. Msgr. STEVEN P. ROHLFS, S.T.D., Vicar General. Tel: 309-671-1550; Fax: 309-671-1558., Mailing Address:: *Sheen Pastoral Center, 412 N.E. Madison Ave., Peoria, 61603.*

Chancellor—Rev. Msgr. STEVEN P. ROHLFS, S.T.D., *Sheen Pastoral Center, 412 N.E. Madison Ave., Peoria, 61603.* Tel: 309-671-1550; Fax: 309-671-1558.

Moderator of the Curia—Rev. Msgr. STEVEN P. ROHLFS, S.T.D., *Sheen Pastoral Center, 412 N.E. Madison Ave., Peoria, 61603.* Tel: 309-671-1550; Fax: 309-671-1558.

Vice Chancellors—Rev. Msgr. JOSEPH A. ZUBE, J.C.L.; Revs. JOSEPH P. DONTON; MARK MERDIAN, *607 N.E. Madison Ave., Peoria, 61603.* Tel: 309-671-1550; Fax: 309-671-5079.

Director of Development—Mr. JOHN HOWARD, *Sheen Pastoral Center, 412 N.E. Madison Ave., Peoria, 61603.* Tel: 309-671-1550; Fax: 309-671-1595.

Director of Finance—Mr. TOBY GUALANDRI, *Sheen Pastoral Center, 412 N.E. Madison Ave., Peoria, 61603.* Tel: 309-671-1550; Fax: 309-671-1595.

Diocesan Tribunal—Sheen Pastoral Center, 412 N.E. Madison Ave., Peoria, 61603. Tel: 309-671-1550; Fax: 309-677-6798.

Judicial Vicar—Very Rev. RICHARD SOSEMAN, M.A., J.C.L.

Defender of the Bond—Rev. J. BRIAN REJSEK, J.C.L.

Adjutant Judicial Vicars—Rev. J. BRIAN REJSEK, J.C.L.; Rev. Msgr. JOSEPH A. ZUBE, J.C.L.; Rev. Msgr. RICK OBERCH, J.C.L.

Auditor—Sr. MARIANNE BURKHARD, O.S.B., J.C.L.

Judges—Rev. Msgr. RICHARD G. FITZSIMMONS; Rev. JEROME JUNG, J.C.D.; Rev. Msgr. CLARENCE J. HETTINGER, J.C.L.; Sr. MARIANNE BURKHARD, O.S.B., J.C.L.

Advocates—Mrs. CHERYL CRISS; Mr. DAVID REISING.

Notaries—Mrs. DEBRA WILLIAMS; Mrs. JANICE VICARY; Mrs. NANCY PAUL.

Diocesan College of Consultors—Most Rev. JOHN J. MYERS, D.D., J.C.D.; Rev. Msgr. STEVEN P. ROHLFS, V.G.; Rev. Msgr. STUART SWETLAND; Rev. Msgr. RICHARD SOSEMAN; Rev. Msgr. JEROME HAM; Rev. Msgr. DALE WELLMAN; Revs. THOMAS E. MACK; PHILIP HALFACRE; JEFFREY LAWRENCE; WILLIAM MILLER, L.C.; KENNETH MARCHULONES, *Sheen Pastoral Center, 412 N.E. Madison Ave., Peoria, 61603.* Tel: 309-671-1550; Fax: 309-671-1558.

Vicariates and Vicars—Rev. Msgr. THOMAS W. MALONEY, Bloomington; Rev. Msgr. ALBERT W. HALLIN, Champaign; Rev. THADDEUS PRACZ, Danville; Rev. WILLIAM M. GARDNER, Henry; Rev. DUANE C. JACK, Kewanee; Rev. J. BRIAN RESJEK, La Salle; Rev. Msgr. E. E. HIGGINS, Lincoln; Rev. RICHARD PRICCO, Macomb; Rev. ERNEST PIZZAMIGLIO, Monmouth; Rev. Msgr. RAYMOND BOYLE, Ottawa; Rev. Msgr. JAMES J. SWANER, Pekin; Rev. STEVE MCKINLEY, O.F.M.Conv., Peoria, N.W.; Rev. BENJAMIN B. REESE, Peoria, S.E.; Rev. THOMAS E. MACK, Pontiac; Rev. PAUL E. SHOWALTER, Rock Island.

Diocesan Offices and Directors

Finance Council (Canon 492)—Most Rev. JOHN J. MYERS, D.D., J.C.D., Pres.; Rev. Msgr. STEVEN P. ROHLFS, V.G.; Sr. DIANE MARIE MCGREW, O.S.F.; Rev. Msgr. THOMAS MILLER; Mr. MATTHEW LEVY; Mr. GERALD T. WOMBACHER; Ms. JEAN SOMERS; Mr. DANIEL REYNOLDS; Mr. TOBY GUALANDRI; Mr. ALLYN G. SCHMID; Mr. JOHN HOWARD, *Sheen Pastoral Center, 412 N.E. Madison Ave., Peoria, 61603.* Tel: 309-671-1550; Fax: 309-671-1595.

Art and Architecture Commission—Rev. Msgr. STEVEN ROHLFS, S.T.D., V.G., *412 N.E. Madison Ave., Peoria, 61603.* Tel: 309-671-1550; Fax: 309-671-1558.

Catholic Cemeteries—Rev. JOHN ANDERSON, *Sheen Pastoral Center, 412 N.E. Madison Ave., Peoria, 61603.* Tel: 309-671-1550; Fax: 309-671-1595.

Catholic Education Office—Dr. MELVIN KUHBANDER, Ph.D., Supt., Catholic Schools; Mrs. PATRICIA KAWCZYNSKI, Assoc. Supt.; Mr. WILLIAM A. JANICKI, Dir., Religious Education Dept.; Ms. BARBARA MCATEE, Assoc. Dir.; Mr. RONALD BOLSTER; Mr. DAVID MCCUTCHEN, *Sheen Pastoral Center, 412 N.E. Madison Ave., Peoria, 61603.* Tel: 309-671-1550; Fax: 309-671-1595.

Catholic Men, Council of—Rev. DONALD R. SCHLADEN, Moderator, *Box 26, Marseilles, 61341.* Tel: 815-795-2240.

Catholic Relief Services—Rev. JOHN C. ANDERSON, *412 N.E. Madison Ave., Peoria, 61603.* Tel: 309-671-1550; Fax: 309-671-1595.

Catholic Women, Council of—Rev. Msgr. DALE WELLMAN, Moderator, *312 W. 1st St., Milan, 61264.* Tel: 309-787-4593.

Censor Librorum—Rev. Msgr. STEVEN P. ROHLFS, S.T.D., V.G.

Clergymen's Aid Society—Most Rev. JOHN J. MYERS, D.D., J.C.D., Chm. & Ex Officio; Rev. Msgr. STEVEN P. ROHLFS, S.T.D., V.G., Exec. Sec., Treas. & Ex Officio; Revs. JEFF LAWRENCE; GERALD MEYER; MARK MERDIAN, Sec. ROBERT SPILMAN; THOMAS MALONEY; KENNETH MARCHELONES; Rev. Msgr. THOMAS MILLER; Rev. Msgr. ALBERT W. HALLIN, *412 N.E. Madison Ave., Peoria, 61603.* Tel: 309-671-1550; Fax: 309-671-1558.

Commission for Ecumenism—Rev. Msgr. ALBERT W. HALLIN, *405 W. Clark St., Champaign, 61820.* Tel: 217-352-8748.

Communications, Office of—Mrs. KATE KENNY, Dir., *Sheen Pastoral Center, 412 N.E. Madison Ave., Peoria, 61603.* Tel: 309-671-1550; Fax: 309-671-1595.

Council of Conciliation and Arbitration—Rev. Msgr. STEVEN P. ROHLFS, S.T.D., V.G., Chm., *Sheen Pastoral Center, 412 N.E. Madison Ave., Peoria, 61603-2720.* Tel: 309-671-1550; Fax: 309-671-1558.

Cursillo Program—Rev. BRIAN BROWNSEY, Spiritual Dir., *Spalding Renewal Center, 401 N.E. Madison Ave., Peoria, 61603.* Tel: 309-676-4001.

Diocesan Office of Development—Mr. JOHN HOWARD, Dir.; Mr. SHAWN RIEDELL, Assoc. Dir., *Sheen Pastoral Center, 412 N.E. Madison Ave., Peoria, 61603.* Tel: 309-671-1550; Fax: 309-671-1595.

Diocesan Education Commission—*Sheen Pastoral Center, 412 N.E. Madison Ave., Peoria, 61603.* Tel: 309-671-1550; Fax: 309-671-1595.

Diocesan Office of Finance—Mr. TOBY GUALDRI, Dir.; Vacant, Auditor, Finance Office: *Sheen Pastoral Center, 412 N.E. Madison Ave., Peoria, 61603.* Tel: 309-671-1550; Fax: 309-671-1595.

Diocesan Pastoral Council—Rev. Msgr. STEVEN P. ROHLFS, S.T.D., V.G., *Sheen Pastoral Center, 412 N.E Madison Ave., Peoria, 61603.* Tel: 309-671-1550; Fax: 309-671-1558.

Diocesan Personnel Board—Rev. Msgr. STEVEN P. ROHLFS, S.T.D., V.G., Dir., *Sheen Pastoral Center, 412 N.E. Madison Ave., Peoria, 61603.* Tel: 309-671-1550; Fax: 309-671-1558.

Diocesan Director of Music—RICK TOMIC.

Divine Worship, Office of—Vacant, Dir., *Sheen Pastoral Center, 412 N.E. Madison Ave., Peoria, 61603.* Tel: 309-671-1550; Fax: 309-671-1595.

Evangelization—Mr. DAVID MCCUTCHEN, Dir., *Sheen Pastoral Center, 412 N.E. Madison Ave., Peoria, 61603.* Tel: 309-671-1550; Fax: 309-671-1595.

Office of Marriage and Family—Mr. TIM RODER, Dir., *Sheen Pastoral Center, 412 N.E. Madison Ave., Peoria, 61603.* Tel: 309-671-1550; Fax: 309-671-1595.

Office of Pastoral Services—Ms. JEANNE WHALEN, Dir., *Sheen Pastoral Center, 412 N.E. Madison Ave., Peoria, 61603.* Tel: 309-671-1550; Fax: 309-671-1595.

Office of Chastity Formation and Family Planning—Mr. TODD AGLIALORO, Dir., *Sheen Pastoral Center, 412 N.E. Madison Ave., Peoria, 61603.* Tel: 309-671-1550; Fax: 309-671-1595.

Holy Childhood Association—Rev. JOHN C. ANDERSON, Dir., *412 N.E. Madison Ave., Peoria, 61603.* Tel: 309-671-1550; Fax: 309-671-1595.

Newspaper—"The Catholic Post"—Most Rev. JOHN J. MYERS, Publisher; Mr. THOMAS DERMODY, Editor-in-Chief, *409 N.E. Monroe Ave., Peoria, 61603.* Tel: 309-673-3603; Fax: 309-673-0334.

Nurses, Council of—Vacant.

Permanent Diaconate, Office of—Rev. Msgr. CHARLES J. BEEBE, Episcopal Vicar/Dir., *412 N.E. Madison Ave., Peoria, 61603.* Tel: 309-671-1582; Fax: 309-671-1595.

Priests' Eucharistic League—Rev. Msgr. JOSEPH A. ZUBE, J.C.L., *Sheen Pastoral Center, 412 N.E. Madison Ave., Peoria, 61603.* Tel: 309-671-1550; Fax: 309-671-1595.

Propagation of the Faith—Rev. JOHN C. ANDERSON, Dir., *412 N.E. Madison Ave., Peoria, 61603.* Tel: 309-671-1550; Fax: 309-671-1595.

Priests' Purgatorial Society—Rev. Msgr. STEVEN P. ROHLFS, S.T.D., V.G., Dir., *Sheen Pastoral Center, 412 N.E. Madison Ave., Peoria, 61603.* Tel: 309-671-1550; Fax: 309-671-1558.

Rural Life Conference—Rev. GREGORY K. KETCHAM, Dir., *Church of the Immaculate Conception, 218 W. Broadway, Monmouth, 61462.* Tel: 309-634-7533.

Presbyteral Council—Rev. Msgr. DALE WELLMAN, Pres.; Revs. PHILIP D. HALFACRE, Vice Pres. DWIGHT CAMPBELL, Sec./Treas., *Sheen Pastoral Center, 412 N.E. Madison, Peoria, 61603.* Tel: 309-671-1550; Fax: 309-671-1558.

Social Service—Miss PEGGY A. ARIZZI, Diocesan Dir. TRICIA FOX, Assoc. Dir., *2900 W. Heading Ave., P.O. Box 817, Peoria, 61652.* Tel: 309-671-5700., Rock Island Office: *816 20th St., Rock Island, 61201.* Tel: 309-788-9581., Bloomington Office: *106 W. Chestnut, Bloomington, 61701.* Tel: 309-788-9581., Champaign Office: *610 1-2 E. Park St., Champaign, 61820.* Tel: 217-352-5279., LaSalle Office: *535 3rd St., LaSalle, 61301.* Tel: 815-223-4007., Galesburg Office: *2401 N. Broad St., Galesburg, 61401.*, Macomb Office: *105 S. Johnson St., Macomb, 61455.* Tel: 309-833-1791.

TEC—Rev. BRIAN BROWNSEY, Dir., *Spalding Renewal Center, 401 N.E. Madison Ave., Peoria, 61603.* Tel: 309-676-4001.

Vocations—Rev. JOSEPH DONTON, Dir., *607 N.E. Madison Ave., P.O. Box 1406, Peoria, 61655.* Tel: 309-671-1568; Fax: 309-671-5079. Associate Directors: Rev. STANLEY DEPTULA, *604 E. Armory, Champaign, 61820.* Tel: 217-344-1184. Rev. BRIAN K. BROWNSEY, *303 Division St., P.O. Box 159, Utica, 61373.* Tel: 815-667-4677. Rev. CHRIS G. HAAKE, *5105 N. Sheridan, Peoria, 61603.* Tel: 309-691-8741.

CLERGY, PARISHES, MISSIONS AND PAROCHIAL SCHOOLS

CITY OF PEORIA
(Peoria County)

1—ST. MARY'S CATHEDRAL (1846), Most Rev. John J. Myers, S.T.L., J.C.D., Bishop of Peoria; Rev. Joseph P. Donton.
Res., 607 N.E. Madison Ave., 61603. Tel: 309-671-1568; Fax: 309-671-1577.

2—HOLY FAMILY (1956), Revs. Steve McKinley, O.F.M.Conv., V.F.; Patrick Stoffer, O.F.M.Conv.; Bro. Martin Schmitz, O.F.M.Conv.; Deacon James Maubach.
Res., 3720 N. Sterling, 61615. Tel: 309-688-3427; Fax: 309-688-2174.
School—2329 W. Reservoir, 61615. Tel: 309-688-2931; Fax: 309-681-5687. Gary Parmelee, Prin.
Lay Teachers 23; Students 415.

3—SACRED HEART (1879) (German), Revs. Sergius Scherpnenberg, O.F.M.; Marne Breckensiek, O.F.M.; Louis Bartko, O.F.M.; Deacon Michael Reid.
Res., 504 Fulton St., 61602. Tel: 309-673-6316; 6317.

4—ST. ANN (1994), Revs. Terry A Cassidy; Francis Gallogher; Deacon Joseph Koeppel.
Mailing Address: 1010 S. Louisa St., 61605. Tel: 309-674-5072; Fax: 309-655-1566.
St. Ann's Youth Center,: 1009 S. Louisa St., 61605. Tel: 309-674-0225.

5—ST. BERNARD'S, Rev. James G. Pallardy.
Res., 509 E. Kansas Ave., 61603. Tel: 309-682-1221; Fax: 309-682-3462.
School—Tel: 309-682-5823.
Lay Teachers 12; Students 150.

6—ST. BONIFACE'S (1881) (German). Closed. For inquiries for parish records contact St. Ann, Peoria.

7—ST. CECILIA'S. Closed. For Sacramental records write St. Philomena, 3300 N. Twelve Oaks Dr., Peoria, IL 61604.

8—ST. JOHN'S (1890) (Irish). Closed. For inquiries for parish records contact St. Ann, Peoria.

9—ST. JUDE'S (1975), Rev. Harry A Pierjok; Deacons Thomas Rapach; Roger Hunter.
Res., 1508 Wilhelm Rd., Dunlap, 61525. Tel: 309-243-7811; Fax: 309-243-7810. [CEM]
Catechesis/Religious Programs—Tel: 309-243-7324.
Students 301.

10—ST. MARK'S (1891), Rev. Benjamin B. Reese; Deacons Bernard Filzen; Charles Tuerk; John Skender.
Res., 1113 W. Bradley Ave., 61606. Tel: 309-673-1263; Fax: 309-673-2212.
School—Tel: 309-676-7131; Fax: 309-677-8060.
Lay Teachers 17; Students 310.
Catechesis/Religious Programs—Tel: 309-673-2212.
Students 60.

11—ST. MARTIN DE PORRES (1976), Rev. Glenn Fontana.
Res., 103 S. Sheridan, 61605. Tel: 309-676-0726; Fax: 309-676-4090.
Southside Catholic Child Care Center—1010 W. Johnson, 61605. Tel: 309-674-7340.

12—ST. PETER'S (1897), Rev. Mark J. Merdian; Deacon Richard Zimmerman.
Res., 2719 N.E. Madison Ave., 61603. Tel: 309-685-3861; Fax: 309-688-1502.

13—ST. PHILOMENA'S (1945), Rev. Msgr. Charles J. Beebe; Revs. Charles Klamut; Vien Van Do; Deacons Robert England; Richard Hammel; Harry Ohl; David Reising. In res., Rev. Timothy Nolan.
Res., 3300 N. Twelve Oaks Dr., 61604-1464. Tel: 309-682-8642; Fax: 309-682-8955. [JC]
School—Sisters of St. Francis, Tel: 309-685-1208; Fax: 309-681-5676. Sr. Mary Joseph Bickett, O.S.F., Prin.
Sisters 4; Lay Teachers 19; Students 485.
St. Philomena Endowment Trust—.

14—ST. THOMAS (1937), Revs. William A. Watson; Bowan Schmitt; Sr. Rachel Bergschneider, O.S.B., Pastoral Assoc. & D.R.E.; Deacons Donald Efinger; Robert Waldschmidt; Francis S. Eaton; Earl Hietter; William Kelley, Sr.
Res., 904 E. Lake Ave., Peoria Heights, 61614. Tel: 309-688-3446; Fax: 309-688-3467.
School—4229 N. Monroe, Peoria Heights, 61614. Tel: 309-685-2533.
Lay Teachers 26; Students 480.
Catechesis/Religious Programs—Students 169.

15—ST. VINCENT DE PAUL (1962), Rev. Msgr. Thomas R. Miller; Rev. Kenneth Hummel; Deacon Robert W. Myers, Sr. In res., Rev. Msgr. Clarence J. Hettinger.
Res., 6001 N. University St., 61614. Tel: 309-691-3602; Fax: 309-691-3687.
School—6003 N. University St., 61614. Tel: 309-691-5012.
Lay Teachers 26; Students 468.
Catechesis/Religious Programs—Tel: 309-691-6513.
Students 156.

OUTSIDE THE CITY OF PEORIA

Abingdon, Knox Co., Sacred Heart (1924), Rev. Frederick Bruce King, I.C.
Res., 506 N. Main St., 61410. Tel: 309-462-3421.
Mailing Address: P.O. Box 589, Galesburg, 61402-0589.

Aledo, Mercer Co., St. Catherine's Church (1914), Rev. Gregory J. Plunkett.
Res., 106 N.E. Fourth, 61231. Tel: 309-582-7500; Fax: 309-582-5155. [CEM]
Catechesis/Religious Programs—Students 150.
Missions—Keithsburg, Mercer Co., St. Mary's, 602 S. 10th St., Keithsburg, 61442. Tel: 309-374-2420; New Boston, Mercer Co., St. Theresa of the Little Flower, 109 Washington, New Boston, 61272.

Alexis, Warren Co., St. Theresa's (1877) (Swedish), Rev. Michael L. Menner.
Res., 131 Main St., P.O. Box 26, 61412. Tel: 309-482-3935. [CEM]
Mission—Wataga, Knoxville Co., St. Aloysius, N. Depot St., Wataga, 61488. Tel: 309-375-6835.

Andalusia, Rock Island Co., St. Patrick's (1974), Rev. Richard L. Barclift.
Mailing Address: Box 249, 61232.
Res., 9616 140th St. W., Taylor Ridge, 61284. Tel: 309-798-2098.
Catechesis/Religious Programs—Tel: 309-798-2630.
Students 150.

Annawan, Henry Co., Sacred Heart (1893), Rev. Timothy J. Sauppe.
Res., 305 W. South Ave., 61234. Tel: 309-935-6911. [CEM]

Arlington, Bureau Co., St. Patrick's (1864), Rev. Kevin D. Gorman, O.S.B.
Res., 106 Church St., P.O.Box 78, 61312. Tel: 815-638-2323. [CEM]

Atkinson, Henry Co., St. Anthony's (1870) (Belgian), Rev. Donnelly J. Fitzpatrick.
Res., 204 W. Main St., P.O. Box 210, 61235-0210. Tel: 309-936-7900; Fax: 309-936-7900. [CEM]

Bartonville, Peoria Co., St. Anthony (1969), Rev. Ronald L. Palmer; Deacons Richard Hammond; Louis Tomlianovich.
Res., 2525 Skyway Rd., 61607. Tel: 309-697-0645; Fax: 309-697-2188.
Catechesis/Religious Programs—Students 225.

Bement, Piatt Co., St. Michael, Rev. Joseph T. Hogan.
Res., 1301 N. Market St., Monticello, 61856. Tel: 217-762-2566.

Benson, Woodford Co., St. John (1873), Rev. Neri Greskoviak, O.F.M.
Res., c/o 506 W. Randolph, Roanoke, 61561. Tel: 309-394-2615; Fax: 309-923-3031. [CEM]

Blackstone, Livingston Co., St. Bernard. Closed. For inquiries for sacramental records contact Immaculate Conception, Streater.

Bloomington, McLean Co.,

1—Holy Trinity, (1853), Revs. David C. Heinz; Gregory E. Nelson; Deacons Brendan Carolan; Lewis Roesch.
Res., 704 N. Main St., 61701. Tel: 309-829-2197; Fax: 309-829-2243. [CEM]
School—705 N. Roosevelt, 61701. Tel: 309-828-7151; Fax: 309-827-8131.
1909 E. Lincoln St., 61701. Tel: 309-662-3712; Fax: 309-663-9115.
Sisters 2; Lay Teachers 26; Students 615.
Catechesis/Religious Programs—Tel: 309-828-8242. Mrs. Sharon Priester, D.R.E.
Students 290.

2—St. Mary's, (1867) (German), Rev. Ric Schneider, O.F.M.; Deacon Darrel Petri.
Res., 527 W. Jackson St., 61701. Tel: 309-827-8526; Fax: 309-829-3061. [CEM]
School—603 W. Jackson St., 61701. Tel: 309-828-5954.
Lay Teachers 10; Students 96.
Catechesis/Religious Programs—Students 158.

3—St. Patrick's, (1892), Revs. Jeffrey D. Stirniman; Vincent E. Dietzen, Pastor Emeritus. In res., Rev. Stephen A. Willard.
Res., 1209 W. Locust St., 61701. Tel: 309-829-1355; Fax: 309-828-0577. [JC]

4—St. Patrick Church of Merna, (1890), Rev. Gerald T. Ward.
Church—R.R. 1, Box 38, 61704. Tel: 309-662-7361; Fax: 309-664-6167. [CEM]
Catechesis/Religious Programs—Sr. Rita Ann Bregenhorn, O.S.U., Pastoral Assoc.
Students 480.

Bradford, Stark Co., St. John the Baptist (1876), Rev. John Thieryoung.
Res., 218 First St., Box 310, 61421. Tel: 309-897-4081; Fax: 309-897-8007. [CEM]

Brimfield, Peoria Co., St. Joseph's (1852) (Irish), Rev. Edward Roberts.
Res., 314 W. Clay St., 61517. Tel: 309-446-3275. [CEM]
Mission—Williamsfield, Knox Co., St. James, Williamsfield, 61489. Tel: 309-446-3275.

Budd, Livingston Co., St. Bernard's. Closed. For parish records contact Church of the Immaculate Conception, Streator.

Bushnell, McDonough Co., St. Bernard (1877), Rev. David L. Kurt.
Res., 376 W. Hail St., 61422. Tel: 309-772-2333.

Camp Grove, Marshall Co., St. Patrick (1866) (Irish), Rev. Michael J. Driscoll.
Res., 115 W. Camp St., 61424. Tel: 309-493-5261. [CEM]

Campus, Livingston Co., Sacred Heart (Irish), Rev. Donald Roszkowski.
Res., P.O. Box 68, 60920. Tel: 815-998-2197. [CEM]

Canton, Fulton Co., St. Mary's (1862), Rev. Arthur D. Meyer; Deacon Victor Kovachevich.
Mailing Address: 139 E. Chestnut St., 61520.
Res., 140 N. 2nd Ave., 61520. Tel: 309-647-1473; Fax: 309-647-1476. [CEM 2]
Catechesis/Religious Programs—Tel: 309-647-0261.
Students 185.

Carthage, Hancock Co., Immaculate Conception (1860), Rev. Jeffrey Small.
Res., 125 N. Fayette, 62321. Tel: 217-357-3087. [CEM]
Mission—West Point, Hancock Co., St. Mary.

Champaign, Champaign Co.,

1—Holy Cross, (1912), Rev. Msgr. Albert W. Hallin; Rev. David Henderson; Deacon Henry Hart.
Res., 405 W. Clark St., 61820. Tel: 217-352-8748; Fax: 217-366-2929.
School—410 W. White St., 61820. Tel: 217-356-9521; Fax: 217-356-1745.
Lay Teachers 25; Students 415.
Catechesis/Religious Programs—Sr. Joan Kaucher, C.S.J., D.R.E.
Students 173.

2—St. John's Catholic Chapel, (1918). (For Catholic Students at the University of Illinois). Rev. Msgr. Stuart W. Swetland, Chap.; Revs. Stanley L. Deptula; Ben Rodriguez; Antonio Dittmer; Fortunatus Bijura (Rulenge, Tanzania); Johndamascene Zilimu (Rulenge, Tanzania).
Res., Newman Hall, 604 E. Armory Ave., 61820. Tel: 217-344-1184; Fax: 217-344-4957.

3—St. Mary's, (1854), Rev. Thomas J. Royer.
Res., 612 E. Park Ave., 61820. Tel: 217-352-8364; Fax: 217-352-6859. [CEM]

4—St. Matthew, (1965), Revs. Anthony J. Trosley; Scott S. Engelbrecht.
Res., 1303 Lincolnshire Dr., 61821. Tel: 217-359-4224; Fax: 217-359-9846.
School—1307 Linconshire Dr., 61821. Tel: 217-359-4114; Fax: 217-359-7507.
Lay Teachers 17; Students 475.
Catechesis/Religious Programs—Tel: 217-359-8761.
Students 310.

Chatsworth, Livingston Co., SS. Peter and Paul (1877) (French), Rev. Richard W. Brunskill.
Res., 406 N. Fifth St., P.O. Box 546, 60921. Tel: 815-635-3127; Fax: 815-635-3756. [CEM]

Chenoa, McLean Co., St. Joseph's (1859), Rev. Carl LoPresti.
Res., 225 W. Owsley, 61726. Tel: 815-945-2561; Fax: 815-945-7634. [CEM]
Catechesis/Religious Programs—Students 96.
Mission—Lexington, McLean Co., St. Mary, Tel: 815-945-7987.

Cherry, Bureau Co., Holy Trinity (1904), Rev. Kevin D. Gorman, O.S.B.
Res., P.O. Box 159, 212 S. Main, 61317. Tel: 815-894-2006; Fax: 815-894-2090. [CEM]

Chillicothe, Peoria Co., St. Edward's (1900), Rev. Anthony M. Ego; Deacons Gregory Serangeli; Bob Pomazel.
Res., 1216 N. 6th St., 61523. Tel: 309-274-3809. [CEM]
School—Tel: 309-274-2994; Fax: 309-274-4150.
Lay Teachers 13; Students 212.

Clinton, De Witt Co., St. John the Baptist's (1879), Rev. Gordon Pillon.
Res., 502 N. Monroe St., 61727. Tel: 217-935-3727.
Catechesis/Religious Programs—Tel: 217-935-3727.
Students 105.

Coal Valley, Rock Island Co., St. Maria Goretti (1972), Rev. Richard F. Bresnahan; Sr. Sandra Brunenn, O.S.B., Pastoral Assoc.; Deacons Charles Breeden; Robert Zimmerman.
Res., P.O. Box 159, 210 E. 22nd Ave., 61240. Tel: 309-799-3414; Fax: 309-799-3436.
Catechesis/Religious Programs—Tel: 309-799-7283.
Students 102.

Colfax, McLean Co., St. Joseph's (1850), Rev. Robert D. Spilman.
Res., P.O. Box 169, 107 W. North, 61728. Tel: 309-723-6229; Fax: 309-723-6229.
Mission—Strawn, Livingston Co., St. Rose.

Colona, Henry Co., St. Patrick's (1941), Rev. Edward E. Bush.
Res., 201 First St., 61241. Tel: 309-792-3854. [JC]
Catechesis/Religious Programs—Tel: 309-949-2200. Jean Sottos, D.R.E.
Students 290.

Creve Coeur, Tazewell Co., Sacre Coeur (1954), Rev. James E. King.
Res., 301 Roosevelt St., 61610. Tel: 309-699-8223.
Church:—601 Rusche Ln., 61610. Tel: 309-699-8511.

Cullom, Livingston Co., St. John's (1881), Rev. Richard W. Brunskill.
Res., 113 Van Alstyne, P.O. Box 376, 60929. Tel: 815-689-2367.

Dalzell, Bureau Co., St. Thomas More (1934) (Italian), Rev. Placid W. Hatfield, O.S.B.; Deacon Robert Beltramini.
Res., 302 Chestnut, 61320. Tel: 815-663-6201.

Danville, Vermilion Co., Holy Family (1978), Rev. Ted Pracz; Deacons Herman Bott; Richard Smith.
Church—444 E. Main St., 61832. Tel: 217-431-5100; Fax: 217-431-5103. [CEM]
School—Tel: 217-431-5108.
Lay Teachers 14; Students 255.

St. Paul's (1915), Rev. Douglas J. Hennessy; Sr. Charles Allen, Pastoral Assoc.
Res., 1303 N. Walnut St., 61832. Tel: 217-442-5313; Fax: 217-442-5356.
School—1307 N. Walnut St., 61832. Tel: 217-442-3880; Fax: 217-442-5852.
Lay Teachers 26; Students 343.
Catechesis/Religious Programs—Students 128.

Delavan, Tazewell Co., St. Mary's (1859), Rev. Gerald J. Verdun.
Res., Box 769, 61734. Tel: 309-244-8516. [CEM]
Mission—Hopedale, Tazewell Co., St. Joseph's.

Depue, Bureau Co., St. Mary's (1908), Rev. Mubarak Anwar Amar.
Res., 312 Park St., Box 19, 61322. Tel: 815-447-2552. [CEM]

Downs, McLean Co., St. Mary's (1910), Rev. Stephen A. Willlard.
Church—101 N. Lincoln, P.O. Box 66, 61736. Tel: 309-378-4679; Fax: 309-378-4080.
Catechesis/Religious Programs—Students 168.

Dunlap, Peoria Co., St. Clement's. Closed. For inquiries for parish records contact St. Jude, 1508 W. Wilhelm Rd., 61525.

Dwight, Livingston Co., St. Patrick's (1862) (Irish), Rev. James E. Rickey.
Res., 126 W. Mazon Ave., P.O. Box 70, 60420. Tel: 815-584-3522; Fax: 815-584-3400. [CEM]
Catechesis/Religious Programs—Tel: 815-584-3110. Ginger Connor, D.R.E.
Students 266.

Eagle Township, La Salle Co., Annunciation of Blessed Virgin Mary (1869) (Irish), Rev. Charles A. McCarthy, C.S.Sp.
Church—Rte. 3, Eagle Township, Streator, 61364. Tel: 815-672-6500.
Res., Rte 1, 957 N. 17th Rd., Tonica, 61370. Tel: 815-856-2502. [CEM]

Earlville, La Salle Co., St. Theresa's (1904), Rev. Michael J. Driscoll.
Res., 221 Union St., Box 190, 60518. Tel: 815-246-4321; Fax: 815-246-9581. [CEM 2]

East Moline, Rock Island Co., St. Anne (1919), Rev. Robert D. O'Connor; Sr. Mary O'Connor, B.V.M, Pastoral Assoc.
Res., 555 18th Ave., 61244. Tel: 309-755-5071; Fax: 309-755-5343.
School—Tel: 309-755-9771; Fax: 309-755-7407.
Sisters of Charity of the B.V.M. 2; Lay Teachers 13; Students 242.

St. Mary's (1907) (Belgian-Spanish), Rev. Joseph Dondanville; Deacon Jerry Buyck.
Res., 1908 13th St., 61244. Tel: 309-755-4111; Fax: 309-755-2384. [JC]
School—Tel: 309-755-4352.
Lay Teachers 16; Students 140.
Catechesis/Religious Programs—1925 13th St., 61244.
Students 150.

East Peoria, Tazewell Co., St. Monica's (1898), Rev. Kenneth L. Marchulones; Sr. Marjorie Meismer, O.S.F., Pastoral Assoc.; Deacon Ronald Rager.
Res., 303 Campanile Dr., 61611. Tel: 309-694-2061.
Catechesis/Religious Programs—Tel: 309-699-8458. Sr. Marjorie Miesmer, O.S.F., D.R.E.
Students 144.

Elkhart, Logan Co., St. Patrick (1856), Rev. Patrick DeMeulemeester.
Res., 213 S. Bogardus, P.O. Box 19, 62634. Tel: 217-947-2714; Fax: 217-947-2714.
Missions—Mount Pulaski, Logan Co., St. Thomas Aquinas, St. Patrick's, 62634.; Middletown, Logan Co., St. John the Baptist, St. Patrick's, 62634.

Elmwood, Peoria Co., St. Patrick's (1870) (Irish), Rev. Paul Stiene, I.C.; Deacon Deane Keefer.
Res., P.O. Box 440, 61529. Tel: 309-742-4921; Fax: 309-742-8243. [CEM]

El Paso, Woodford Co., St. Mary's (1863), Rev. Lawrence P. Morrissey.
Res., 79 W. Third, P.O. Box 197, 61738. Tel: 309-527-4555; Fax: 309-527-7750. [CEM 2]
Catechesis/Religious Programs—Tel: 309-744-2490. Mrs. Judy Hinshaw, D.R.E.
Students 118.

Eureka, Woodford Co., St. Luke's (1982), Rev. Msgr. James Swaner, Admin.
Mailing Address: 705 E. Jefferson, Washington, 61571. Tel: 309-467-4855. [JC]
Church—904 E. Regan Dr., P.O. Box 226, 61530.

Fairbury, Livingston Co., St. John the Baptist (1857), Rev. Scott Archer.
Res., 110 E. Ash, 61739. Tel: 815-692-2555. [CEM]
Catechesis/Religious Programs—Students 125.
Mission—Forrest, Livingston Co., St. James, 322 S. William, Forrest, 61741.

Farmer City, De Witt Co., Sacred Heart (1899), Rev. Antonio Dittmer, Admin.
Res., 612 N. Plum St., 61842. Tel: 309-928-3855. [CEM]
Mission—Bellflower, McLean Co., St. John.

Farmington, Fulton Co., St. Matthew's (1904) (Italian), Rev. Paul Stiene, I.C.; Deacon John Burton.
Res., 156 E. Vernon St., 61531. Tel: 309-245-4351.

Galesburg, Knox Co., Corpus Christi (1885), Rev. Thomas E. Seibert, I.C.
Res., 273 S. Prairie St., 61401. Tel: 309-343-8256; Fax: 309-343-4793. [CEM]
School—Costa Catholic School. Operates with Immaculate Heart and St. Patrick. 2726 Costa Dr., 61401. Tel: 309-344-3151.
Sisters 1; Lay Teachers 22; Students 311.
Catechesis/Religious Programs—Students 150.
Immaculate Heart of Mary (1956), Rev. Ernest E. Pizzamiglio.
Mailing Address: P.O. Box 550, 61402. Tel: 309-344-3108; Fax: 309-344-1205.
Res., 2401 N. Broad St., 61401.
School—See Corpus Christi Parish.
Catechesis/Religious Programs—Students 123.
St. Patrick's (1863), Rev. Frederick Bruce King, I.C.; Deacon James D. Haneghan.
Mailing Address: P.O. Box 589, 61402-0589. Tel: 309-343-9874; Fax: 309-343-9944.
Res., 858 S. Academy St., 61401. [JC]
School—See Corpus Christi Parish.

Galva, Henry Co., St. John's (1882) (Swedish), Rev. Eugene Lopez.
Res., 212 N.E. 1st St., 61434. Tel: 309-932-2409; Fax: 309-932-8238. [CEM]

Geneseo, Henry Co., St. Malachy's (1866), Revs. Michael G. Pakula; John A. Mahoney, Pastor Emeritus; Deacons Harley Chaffee; Harley Harris; Thomas Wachtel; Larry Honzel.
Res., 595 E. Ogden Ave., 61254. Tel: 309-944-5393; Fax: 309-944-5319.
School—Tel: 309-944-3230.
Lay Teachers 7; Students 144.
Catechesis/Religious Programs—Tel: 309-944-3518. M. Elizabeth Fristensky, D.R.E.
Students 342.

Georgetown, Vermilion Co., St. Isaac Jogues (1942), Rev. John Paninski, M.S.
Res., 109 W. Seventh St., 61846. Tel: 217-662-6708.

Granville, Putnam Co., Sacred Heart Of Jesus (1908) (Italian), Rev. Howard C. Barch, Jr.
Res., P.O. Box 217, 61326. Tel: 815-339-2138; Fax: 815-339-2138. [CEM]
Catechesis/Religious Programs—Students 120.
Mission—Bureau, Bureau Co., St. Francis Xavier, P.O. Box 217, 61323.

Havana, Mason Co., St. Patrick's, Rev. Michael Monclova.
Res., P.O. Box 345, 437 S.Orange, 62644. Tel: 309-543-6373; Fax: 309-543-3241. [CEM]
Mission—Manito, Mason Co., Immaculate Conception, 505 S. Adams, P.O. Box 242, Manito, 61546. Tel: 309-968-6826. Deacon William Meyer.

Hennepin, Putnam Co., St. Patrick's (1865), Rev. Howard C. Barch, Jr.
Res., 10 St., P.O. Box 200, 61327. Tel: 815-925-7500; Fax: 815-339-6133. [CEM]
Mission—Mount Palatine, Putnam Co., Immaculate Conception, P.O. Lostant, Lostant, 61335. Tel: 815-882-2337. [CEM]

Henry, Marshall Co., St. Joseph's (1878) (Irish), Rev. John Verrier, Admin.
Res., 401 South St., Box 75, 61537. Tel: 309-246-5145. [CEM 2]
St. Mary's (1851) (German), Rev. John verrier, Admin.
Res., Box 75, 61537. Tel: 309-246-5145. [CEM 2]
Catechesis/Religious Programs—Tel: 309-364-2011. Sr. Anita D.R.E.
Students 228.

Hoopeston, Vermilion Co., St. Anthony's (1877), Rev. R. Anthony Lee; Deacon William C. Ringler.
Church—423 S. Third St., P.O. Box 414, 60942. Tel: 217-283-6211; Fax: 217-283-6252.

Hooppole, Henry Co., St. Mary's. Attended by Annawan.

Ivesdale, Champaign Co., St. Joseph's (1863) (Irish), Rev. Thomas J. Royer.
Res., 612 E. Park, Champaign, 61820. Tel: 217-352-8364; Fax: 217-352-6859. [CEM]

Kewanee, Henry Co., St. Francis of Assisi (1906) (Polish), Rev. John Burns.
Res., 1009 N. Burr, 61443. Tel: 309-852-2761; Fax: 309-852-0222.
Mission—Cambridge, Henry Co., St. John Vianney, 313 S. West St., Cambridge, 61238. Tel: 309-937-3304.
St. Mary's Catholic Church (1855), Rev. Duane C. Jack; Deacons Martin Van Meltebeck; John T. Mock; Raymond Van Wassenhove.
Res., 406 W. Central Blvd., 61443-2010. Tel: 309-852-4549; Fax: 309-853-4106. [CEM 2]
School—Visitation, 107 S. Lexington, 61443. Tel: 309-856-7451.
Lay Teachers 12; Students 220.
Catechesis/Religious Programs—Tel: 309-856-5451. Mrs. Phyllis Elliott, D.R.E.
Students 132.

Kickapoo, (Edwards) Peoria Co., St. Mary of Kickapoo (1837), Rev. Msgr. Eric S Powell. In res., Rev. Msgr. Robert C. Livingston.
Res., 9910 W. Knox St., Kickapoo (Edwards), 61528. Tel: 309-691-2030 (Church); Fax: 309-691-2898. [CEM]
School—Tel: 309-691-3015.
Lay Teachers 6; Students 78.

Lacon, Marshall Co., Immaculate Conception (1853), Rev. John M. Verrier; Deacon J. Robert Murphy.
Res., 418 N. Center St., 61540. Tel: 309-246-5145. [CEM 2]

Ladd, Bureau Co., St. Benedict's (1893), Rev. Harold L. Datzman, O.S.B.
Res., 314 Bureau St., 61329. Tel: 815-894-2319; Fax: 815-894-2265.
Mission—Seatonville, Bureau Co., St. Gertrude, 711 Railroad Ave., Seatonville, 61359.

La Salle, La Salle Co.,

1—QUEEN OF THE HOLY ROSARY, (1925) (Italian), Rev. Dale R. Maloy.
Res., 529 Fourth St., 61301. Tel: 815-223-7129. [JC]

2—ST. HYACINTH'S, (1875), Rev. Joseph W. Anderson; Deacon Charles Burgess.
Res., 927 10th St., 61301. Tel: 815-223-0934. [CEM]
School—LaSalle Catholic, Tel: 815-223-5088. Mr. John Ranger, Prin.
Sisters 1; Lay Teachers 16; Students 165.

3—RESURRECTION, (1979), Rev. John M. Onderko.
Res., 913 Fifth St., 61301. Tel: 815-223-1459.
School—LaSalle Catholic School, Tel: 815-223-5088.
Lay Teachers 15; Students 161.
Mission—Dimmick Township, Sacred Heart.

4—ST. PATRICK'S, (1838) (Irish), Rev. M. Duane Leclercq.
Res., 725-Fourth St., 61301. Tel: 815-223-0641; Fax: 815-223-0523. [CEM]
School—Daughters of Charity of St. Vincent de Paul, Tel: 815-223-1166.
Sisters 4; Lay Teachers 12; Students 207.

Leonore, La Salle Co., SS. Peter and Paul's (1860) (German), Rev. Charles A. McCarthy, C.S.Sp.
Res., Rte. 1, Tonica, 61370. Tel: 815-856-2502; Fax: 815-856-2502. [CEM]

Lewistown, Fulton Co., St. Mary's (1865), Rev. Robert W. O'Connor.
Res., 705 N. Broadway St., P.O. Box 106, 61542. Tel: 309-547-3226; Fax: 309-547-3226. [CEM]
Mission—St. David, Fulton Co., St. Michael.

Lincoln, Logan Co., Holy Family (1857), Revs. E. Edward Higgins; Thomas Taylor.
Res., 316 S. Logan St., 62656. Tel: 217-732-4019; Fax: 217-735-2650. [CEM 2]
School—Carroll Catholic School, Tel: 217-732-7518; Fax: 217-732-7518.
Lay Teachers 12; Students 219.
Catechesis/Religious Programs—Holy Family Religious Education Center, 103 Fourth St., 62656. Tel: 217-735-3520.
Students 90.
Missions—Atlanta, Logan Co., St. Mary, Atlanta, 61723.; Mason City, Mason Co., St. Columba, Mason City, 62664.

Loretto, Livingston Co., St. Mary's (1873) (German). Closed. For inquiries contact St. Patrick, Dwight.

Lostant, La Salle Co., St. John the Baptist's (1862), Rev. William M. Gardner.
Res., P.O. Box 486, Wenona, 61377. Tel: 815-853-4558.
Church—301 S. Sheridan, 61334. Tel: 815-368-3339. [CEM]

Macomb, McDonough Co., St. Paul's (1854), Rev. Richard A. Pricco.
Res., 309 W. Jackson, 61455. Tel: 309-833-2496; Fax: 309-833-1560. [CEM]
School—Tel: 309-833-2470.
Lay Teachers 8; Students 142.
Catechesis/Religious Programs—Tel: 309-837-1024.
Students 140.
Mission—Tennessee, McDonough Co., Sacred Heart.

Mahomet, Champaign Co., Our Lady of the Lake (1981), Rev. John C. Horton; Deacon Robert Baxley.
Res., 501 W. State St., P.O. Box 109, 61853. Tel: 217-586-5153; Fax: 217-586-5924.
Catechesis/Religious Programs—Tel: 217-586-6283. Mr. Roger L. Phelps, D.R.E.
Students 580.

Marseilles, La Salle Co., St. Joseph's (1902), Rev. Glenn H. Harris.
Res., 200 Broadway St., P.O. Box 26, 61341. Tel: 815-795-2240.
Catechesis/Religious Programs—Tel: 815-795-2251.
Students 73.

Matherville, Mercer Co., St. Anthony's Church (1916), Rev. Richard Slavish.
Office: P.O. Box 208, 61263. Tel: 309-754-8711. [CEM 2]
Mission—Viola, Mercer Co., St. John, Viola, 61486. Tel: 309-596-2950.

Mendota, La Salle Co., Holy Cross (1863), Revs. J. Brian Rejsek; Peter Pilon; Deacon Vincent Slomian.
Res., 1010 Jefferson St., 61342. Tel: 815-538-6151; Fax: 815-539-5014. [CEM]
School—1000 Jefferson St., 61342. Tel: 815-538-6016.
Sisters of the Third Order of St. Dominic (Springfield) 1; Lay Teachers 12; Students 275.
Catechesis/Religious Programs—Tel: 815-539-6050. Karen Zolper, D.R.E.
Students 110.

Metamora, Woodford Co., St. Mary's (1864) (German), Revs. Dacian Batt, O.F.M.; Matthew Holahan, O.F.M.; Deacon Marvin Smith.
Res., 415 W. Chatham St., P.O.Box 319, 61548. Tel: 309-367-4407; Fax: 309-367-4437. [CEM]
School—Tel: 309-367-2528; Fax: 309-367-4437.
Sisters of St. Francis of the Immaculate Conception 1; Lay Teachers 11; Students 150.
Catechesis/Religious Programs—Mr. Rodney Thompson, D.R.E.
Students 105.
St. Mary of Lourdes (1831), Rev. Robert Weakley, O.F.M.; Deacon Jack Gaetz; Bro. Xavier Gedeon, O.F.M.
Res., Rte. 2, 61548. Tel: 309-383-4460; Fax: 309-383-4467.

Milan, Rock Island Co., St. Ambrose (1924), Rev. Msgr. Dale L. Wellman; Sr. Charlotte Sonneville, O.S.B., Pastoral Assoc.; Deacon Frank Randazzo.
Res., 312 W. First St., 61264. Tel: 309-787-4593; Fax: 309-787-6403.
School—Operates as part of Jordan Catholic School of Rock Island, Tel: 309-793-7363.
Students 60.
Catechesis/Religious Programs—Tel: 309-787-6240. Diane Hansen, D.R.E.
Students 117.

Minonk, Woodford Co., St. Patrick's (1878), Rev. Robert F. Gilles.
Res., 420 E. Sixth St., Box 107, 61760-0107. Tel: 309-432-2700; Fax: 309-432-2700. [CEM]
Mission—Flanagan, Livingston Co., St. Joseph.
Catechesis/Religious Programs—Students 117.

Moline, Rock Island Co., Christ the King (1967), Rev. Donald L. Levitt.
Parish Center: 3205 60th St., 61265. Tel: 309-762-4634; Fax: 309-762-7848.
Catechesis/Religious Programs—Tel: 309-797-5202. D.R.E.: Janet Myers, (PreK-6 & Jr. High); David Cruse, (High School Youth Ministry); Sharon Cruise, (High School Youth Ministry).
Students 200.
Sacred Heart (1906) (Belgian), Revs. Robert E. Lee; Michael J. Andrejek; Robert Rayson; Sr. Kathleen Mullin, Pastoral Assoc.; Deacons John Landry; Dennis De Vooght.
Lee Parish Center—1608 13th St., 61265. Tel: 309-762-2362; Fax: 309-757-5502.
School—Seton Catholic School, (Grades PreK-8). Tel: 309-757-5500.
Sisters 1; Lay Teachers 30; Students 605.
Catechesis/Religious Programs—Rita Luebbers, D.R.E.
Students 231.
St. Mary's (18756) (Hispanic), Rev. Jerome R. Pilon; Deacon Russell W. Swim.
Res., 412 10th St., 61265. Tel: 309-764-1562; Fax: 309-764-0317. [CEM]
Catechesis/Religious Programs—Tel: 309-762-6575. Mrs. Claire Sally Van Oteghem, D.R.E.
Students 79.

Monmouth, Warren Co., Immaculate Conception, Revs. R. E. Enderlin; Bailey Clemens; Deacon William Clark.
Church—218 W. Broadway, 61462. Tel: 309-734-7533; Fax: 309-734-6082. [CEM]
School—Tel: 309-734-6037.
Lay Teachers 10; Students 140.
Mission—Oquawka, Henderson Co., St. Andrew.

Monticello, Piatt Co., St. Philomena, Rev. Joseph T. Hogan.
Res., 1301 N. Market St., 61856. Tel: 217-762-2566. [CEM]

Morton, Tazewell Co., Blessed Sacrament (1957), Rev. Mark A. DeSutter; Deacon Thomas Moran.
Res., 217 E. Greenwood St., 61550. Tel: 309-266-9721; Fax: 309-266-9201.
School—Tel: 309-263-8442; Fax: 309-263-8443.
Lay Teachers 13; Students 213.
Catechesis/Religious Programs—Tel: 309-266-6791. Judy Krumholz, D.R.E.
Students 334.

Nauvoo, Hancock Co., SS. Peter and Paul's (1848) (German), Rev. Gregory K. Ketcham.
Res., 150 N. Wells St., 62354. Tel: 217-453-2428; Fax: 217-453-2015. [CEM 2]
School—Tel: 217-453-2511.
Lay Teachers 7; Students 93.
Catechesis/Religious Programs—Students 75.
Mission—Dallas City, Hancock Co., Sacred Heart, Dallas City, 62330.

Normal, McLean Co., Epiphany (1966), Rev. Msgr. Tom Maloney; Deacon Richard Grimler.
Res., 1006 E. College Ave., 61761. Tel: 309-452-2585; 452-3223; Fax: 309-452-4851.
School—Tel: 309-452-3268.
Lay Teachers 14; Students 403.
Catechesis/Religious Programs—Mary Jean Kraft, D.R.E.
Students 350.

Odell, Livingston Co., St. Paul's (1901) (Irish), Rev. Donald Roszkowski.
Res., 313 W. Hamilton, 60460. Tel: 815-998-2197. [CEM 2]
School—Tel: 815-998-2194.
Lay Teachers 8; Students 110.

Oglesby, La Salle Co., Holy Family (1953), Rev. Gregory Jozefiak.
Res., 311 N. Woodland Ave., 61348. Tel: 815-883-8233.
School—Tel: 815-883-8916; Fax: 815-883-8943.
Lay Teachers 12; Students 226.

Ohio, Bureau Co., Immaculate Conception Church (1875) (Irish), Rev. Binh K. Tran.
Res., c/o St. John's, 204 N. Main St., Walnut, 61376-0370. Tel: 815-379-2602. [CEM]

Orion, Henry Co., Mary, Our Lady of Peace (1962), Rev. R. Michael Schaab.
Res., 1402 10th St., P.O.Box 175, 61273-0175. Tel: 309-526-8106.
Catechesis/Religious Programs—Students 177.

Ottawa, La Salle Co.,

1—St. Columba, (1844) (Irish), Revs. David Kipfer; Jason Gray; Deacon Estal C. Daron.
Res., 122 W. Washington St., 61350. Tel: 815-433-0700; Fax: 815-433-0305. [CEM]
School—1110 LaSalle St., 61350. Tel: 815-433-1199.
Lay Teachers 13; Students 230.
Catechesis/Religious Programs—Students 125.

2—St. Francis of Assisi, (1858), Rev. Gerald J. Meyer.
Res., 820 Sanger St., 61350. Tel: 815-434-0969; Fax: 815-434-1073. [CEM]

3—St. Mary's, (1927), Rev. Patrick K. O'Neal.
Res., 2005 Center St., Ottawa (Naplate), 61350. Tel: 815-433-2404; Fax: 815-433-9458.

4—St. Patrick's, (1893) (Irish), Revs. Philip Halfacre; Daniel Wilder; Robert J. Creager, Pastor Emeritus.
Res., 726 W. Jefferson St., 61350. Tel: 815-434-0768; Fax: 815-434-0793.
School—801 W. Jefferson St., 61350. Tel: 815-433-2889.
Dominican Sisters (Sinsinawa, WI) 2; Lay Teachers 10; Students 175.
Catechesis/Religious Programs—Mrs. Mary Jean Weihman, D.R.E.
Students 151.
Convent—727 W. Jefferson, 61350. Tel: 815-433-2637.

Pekin, Tazewell Co., St. Joseph's (1863), Revs. Timothy Nolan; James Kruse; Deacons Charles Murray; Martin Pogioli; Ernie Whited. In res., Rev. Brian Brownsey.
Res., 303 S. Seventh St., 61554. Tel: 309-347-6108; Fax: 309-347-6959. [CEM 2]
School—Tel: 309-347-7194. Joan Moore, Prin.
Lay Teachers 16; Students 342 (including Pre-school).
Catechesis/Religious Programs—Martha Novak, D.R.E.
Students 282.

Penfield, Champaign Co., St. Lawrence's (1898), Rev. William C. Keebler, Jr.
Res., P.O. Box 49, 61862. Tel: 217-595-5560; Fax: 217-595-5439. [CEM]

Peru, La Salle Co., St. Joseph's (1854), Revs. Henry H. Fritz, O.S.B.; Joseph J. Heyd, O.S.B.; Sr. Karen Marie Lanigan, O.S.F., Pastoral Assoc., Tel: 815-223-1317.
Res., 1925 5th St., P.O.Box 608, 61354. Tel: 815-223-0718; Fax: 815-223-5690. [CEM]
School—Peru Catholic School System, (Grades PreK-8). Operated jointly by the Peru parishes. 2003 Fifth St., 61354. Tel: 815-224-1914.
Sisters 1; Lay Teachers 18; Students 273.
Catechesis/Religious Programs—Sandra Weger, D.R.E.
Students 129.

St. Mary's (1867) (Irish), Rev. Richard Kolczaski; Deacon Fred Sims.
Res., 1319 Sixth St., 61354. Tel: 815-223-2672.
School—Peru Catholic School System. See St. Joseph's for details. Tel: 815-224-1914.

St. Valentine's (1891) (Polish), Rev. Thomas Badovsky.
Res., 1109 Pulaski St., 61354. Tel: 815-223-0315. [CEM]
School—Peru Catholic School System. See St. Joseph's for details. Tel: 815-224-1914.
Catechesis/Religious Programs—Tel: 815-223-8471. Lynda Martin, D.R.E.
Students 175.

Pesotum, Champaign Co., St. Mary (1875) (German), Rev. Joseph M. Mai Chi Thanh.
Res., P.O. Box 169, 61863. Tel: 217-867-2434. [CEM]

St. Joseph (1904) (German), Rev. Joseph M. Mai Chi Thanh.
Res., P.O. Box 619, 61863. Tel: 217-867-2434. [CEM]

Peterstown, La Salle Co., SS. Peter and Paul (1872), Rev. Richard Fitzsimmons.
Res., 1010 Jefferson St., Mendota, 61342. Tel: 815-538-6151; Fax: 815-539-5014. [CEM]

Philo, Champaign Co., St. Thomas (1869), Rev. Dwight P. Campbell.
Res., 310 E. Madison, P.O. Box 266, 61864. Tel: 217-684-2571; Fax: 217-684-2571. [CEM]
School—Tel: 217-684-2309; Fax: 217-684-2309.
Sisters of the Third Order of St. Dominic (Springfield) 1; Lay Teachers 9; Students 160.
Mission—Bongard, Champaign Co., Immaculate Conception, 61864. [CEM]

Pontiac, Livingston Co., St. Mary's (1877), Revs. Thomas E. Mack; Thomas Holloway.
Res., 119 E. Howard St., P.O. Box 374, 61764. Tel: 815-844-7683; Fax: 815-842-4345. [CEM]
School—414 N. Main St., 61764. Tel: 815-844-6585; Fax: 815-844-6987.
Lay Teachers 14; Students 244.
Catechesis/Religious Programs—Students 123.

Princeton, Bureau Co., St. Louis (1865), Rev. Edward O. Harkrader.
Res., 616 S. Gosse Blvd., 61356. Tel: 815-879-0181; Fax: 815-879-8010.
School—Tel: 815-872-8521.
Sisters 2; Lay Teachers 11; Students 142.
Catechesis/Religious Programs—Tel: 815-872-1033.
Students 217.

Princeville, Peoria Co., St. Mary of the Woods (1867), Rev. Richard Soseman.
Res., 407 S. Walnut, 61559. Tel: 309-385-4370. [CEM]

Ransom, La Salle Co., St. Patrick's (1883), Rev. William Arthur Ryan.
Res., 110 Wallace, P.O. Box 127, 60470. Tel: 815-586-4266. [CEM]
Mission—Grand Ridge, LaSalle Co., St. Mary, R.R. 1, Grand Ridge, 61325. Tel: 815-249-6871.

Rantoul, Champaign Co., St. Malachy's (1888), Revs. Jeffrey G. Laible; Stanley J. Malinowski, Pastor Emeritus; Deacon William Shipp Tel: 217-893-0741.
Office: Tel: 217-892-2023; Fax: 217-892-2378.
Res., 311 E. Grove Ave., 61866. Tel: 217-892-2044. [CEM]
School—340 E. Belle Ave., 61866. Tel: 217-892-2011.
Sisters 3; Lay Teachers 12; Students 191.
Convent—304 E. Belle Ave., 61866. Tel: 217-892-2870. Sisters of the Third Order of St. Dominic (Springfield)

Rapids City, Rock Island Co., St. John the Baptist (1857), Rev. James P. DeBisschop.
Res., 1416 Third Ave., P.O. Box 258, 61278. Tel: 309-496-2414; Fax: 309-755-1650. [CEM]
Catechesis/Religious Programs—Students 164.
Mission—Hampton, Rock Island Co., St. Mary, 708 State Ave., Rte. 84, Hampton, 61256. Tel: 309-755-5033. Deacon James Quinn.

Raritan, Henderson Co., Church of St. Patrick (1876) (Irish), Revs. E. E. Enderlin; Bailey Clemens; Deacon William Clark.
Res., P.O. Box 24, 61471. Tel: 309-734-7533.

Roanoke, Woodford Co., St. Joseph (1874), Rev. Neri Greskoviak, O.F.M.
Res., 506 W. Randolph, 61561. Tel: 309-923-3031; Fax: 309-926-3031.

Rock Island, Rock Island Co.,

1—St. Mary, (1851) (German). (Formerly Immaculate Conception). Revs. James K. Ramer; George J. Schroeder, Pastor Emeritus (Retired).
2208 Fourth Ave., 61201. Tel: 309-793-1897.
Rectory—2208 Fourth Ave., 61201-8904. Tel: 309-788-3322.

2—Sacred Heart, (1900), Rev. Ambrose Cunningham; Sr. Mary Veronica Grennan, Pastoral Assoc.
Res., 2810 Fifth Ave., 61201. Tel: 309-794-0660.
School—Jordan Catholic School of Rock Island, Tel: 309-793-7350.
Sisters 1; Lay Teachers 29; Students 594.

3—St. Joseph's, (1876), Rev. Lawrence A. Morlan; Sr. Germaine Cupp, O.S.B., Pastoral Assoc.
Res., 1316 Second Ave., 61201. Tel: 309-794-9793.
School—Operates as part of Jordan Catholic School of Rock Island.

4—St. Pius X, (1955), Rev. Msgr. Paul E. Showalter; Revs. Thomas Mizeur; David Whiteside; Deacons Timothy Granet; Paul Martin; Philip Sailer.
Res., 2502 29th Ave., 61201. Tel: 309-793-7373; Fax: 309-793-7376.
School—Operates as part of Jordan Catholic School of Rock Island. Tel: 309-793-7350.
Sisters 2; Lay Teachers 35; Students 248.
Catechesis/Religious Programs—Students 120.

Rushville, Schuyler Co., St. Rose (1870), Rev. Robert E. Reynolds.
Res., 319 N. Franklin St., P.O. Box 194, 62681-0292. Tel: 217-322-3424. [JC]

Rutland, La Salle Co., Sacred Heart (1895) (Irish), Rev. James C. Kretz.
Res., c/o 311 W. Santa Fe Ave., P.O. Box 165, Toluca, 61369. Tel: 815-452-2043. [CEM]

St. Augustine, Knox Co., St. Augustine (1863), Rev. David L. Kurt.
Mailing Address: 376 W. Hail, Bushnell, 61422. Tel: 301-462-3421. [CEM]

Seneca, La Salle Co., St. Patrick's (1853), Rev. Msgr. Raymond J. Boyle.
Parish Center: 183 W. Union, 61360. Tel: 815-357-8509; Fax: 815-357-6239. [CEM]
Res., 176 W. Union St., 61360. Tel: 815-357-6239; Fax: 815-357-6476.
Catechesis/Religious Programs—Tel: 815-357-8509; Fax: 815-357-8509.
Students 198.

Seymour, Champaign Co., St. Boniface (1878), Rev. George E. Wuellner, Pastor Emeritus.
Res., 416 County Rd., 1100 N., 61875. Tel: 217-863-2190. [CEM]

Sheffield, Bureau Co., St. Patrick's (1854), Rev. Jeff Windy.
Res., 231 W. Atkinson St., 61361. Tel: 815-454-2251; Fax: 815-454-2541. [CEM]
Mission—Wyanet, Bureau Co., St. Margaret Mary.

Silvis, Rock Island Co., Our Lady of Guadalupe (1927) (Hispanic), Rev. J. M. Logan; Deacon Henry Sandoval.
Res., 800 17th St., 61282. Tel: 309-792-3867.
Catechesis/Religious Programs—Students 56.

Spring Valley, Bureau Co.,

1—Immaculate Conception, (1884), Rev. Paul J. Meismer.
Res., 202 N. Greenwood St., 61362. Tel: 815-663-5351. [CEM]

2—St. Anne's. Closed. For sacramental records contact SS. Peter and Paul's, Spring Valley.

3—St. Anthony's, (1904) (Italian), Rev. Bruce Lopez.
Res., P.O. Box 150, 510 Richard A. Mautino Dr., 61362-0150. Tel: 815-663-3731; Fax: 815-663-0012.
Catechesis/Religious Programs—Charles Palia, D.R.E.
Students 129.

4—SS. Peter and Paul's, (1891) (Polish), Rev. Edward S. Kopec.
Res., 220 N. Terry St., P.O. Box 209, 61362. Tel: 815-663-3041. [CEM]

Streator, La Salle Co.,

1—Immaculate Conception, (1868) (Irish), Rev. Deo Gratias R. Mutefunya.
Res., 404 N. Park St., 61364. Tel: 815-672-2034; Fax: 815-673-3796. [CEM]
School—St. Mary's, Tel: 815-672-3811. Mrs. Anne Hale, Prin.
Lay Teachers 9; Students 85.

2—St. Anthony of Padua, (1881), Rev. Msgr. Jerome Ham; Revs. Vandennis Nguyen; Patrick Riordan.
Res., 407 S. Park St., 61364. Tel: 815-672-4523; Fax: 815-672-0378. [CEM]
School—410 S. Park St., 61364. Tel: 815-672-3847.
Sisters 1; Lay Teachers 14; Students 212.
Catechesis/Religious Programs—Students 140.

3—St. Casimir, (1916) (Polish), Rev. Jerome Ham.
Res., 405 Illinois St., 61364. Tel: 815-672-2206. [CEM]
Catechesis/Religious Programs—Students 7.

4—St. Stephen's, (1884) (Slovak), Rev. Msgr. Peter E. Bolerasky; Rev. Jeffrey C. Lawrence.
Res., 711 Lundy St., 61364. Tel: 815-672-2474. [CEM 2]
School—807 E. Lundy St., 61364. Tel: 815-672-3265.
Sisters 3; Lay Teachers 7; Students 232.

Thomasboro, Champaign Co., St. Elizabeth's (1893), Rev. William Keebler, Admin.
Res., 100 Church St., Box 367, 61878. Tel: 217-643-3395. [CEM]

Mission—Ludlow, Champaign Co., Sacred Heart, Ludlow, 60949.

Tiskilwa, Bureau Co., St. Mary's (1881), Rev. John Theiryoung.
Res., P.O. Box 179, 61368. Tel: 815-646-4451; Fax: 815-646-4376. [CEM]

Tolono, Champaign Co., St. Patrick's (1859), Rev. Dennis H. O'Riley.
Res., 212 E. Washington St., P.O. Box K, 61880. Tel: 217-485-5194. [CEM]
Mission—Homer, Champaign Co., St. Charles Borromeo, 110 S. East, Homer, 61849.

Toluca, Marshall Co., St. Ann's (1895) (Italian), Rev. James C. Kretz.
Res., 311 W. Santa Fe Ave., Box 165, 61369. Tel: 815-452-2043. [CEM]

Urbana, Champaign Co., St. Patrick's (1901), Revs. George F. Remm; Eugene Kane, (Retired); Sr. Charlene Cesario, S.S.C.M., Pastoral Assoc.; Deacon Dan Murphy.
Res., 708 W. Main St., 61801. Tel: 217-367-2665; Fax: 217-383-1002.
Catechesis/Religious Programs—Carolyn McElrath, D.R.E.
Students 450.

Utica, La Salle Co., St. Mary (1858), Rev. Patrick Hendian.
Res., 303 Division St., 61373. Tel: 815-667-4677; Fax: 815-667-4097. [CEM]

Walnut, Bureau Co., St. John's (1912), Rev. Binh K. Tran.
Res., P.O. Box 370, 204 N. Main St., 61376-0370. Tel: 815-379-2602.

Wapella, De Witt Co., St. Patrick's (1858), Rev. Gordon Pillon.
Res., 308 S. Locust St., 61777. Tel: 217-935-9242. [CEM]

Warsaw, Hancock Co., Sacred Heart (1874) (German), Rev. Raymond M. Lukoskie.
Res., 245 S. 9th St., 62379. Tel: 217-256-3657. [CEM]
Catechesis/Religious Programs—Students 150.
Mission—Hamilton, Hancock Co., St. Mary. Deacons William Gray; Eugene Heintz.

Washburn, Woodford Co., St. Elizabeth, Revs. Dacian Batt, O.F.M.; Matthew Holaham, O.F.M.
Mailing Address: P.O. Box 219, Metamora, 61548. Tel: 309-367-4407 (St. Mary's Metamora). [CEM]

Washington, Tazewell Co., St. Patrick's (1941), Rev. James J. Swaner; Deacon Paul Neakrase.
Res., 705 E. Jefferson, 61571. Tel: 309-444-3524; Fax: 309-444-7070.
School—Tel: 309-444-4345; Fax: 309-444-7100. Sisters of St. Mary of the Presentation 1; Lay Teachers 16; Students 227.
Catechesis/Religious Programs—Tel: 309-444-4139. Margaret Anguish, D.R.E.
Students 194.

Wedron, La Salle Co., St. Joseph's (1947), Rev. John G. Waugh.
Res., Box 60, 60557. Tel: 815-433-2962.

Wenona, Marshall Co., St. Mary's (1867), Rev. William M. Gardner. In res., Rev. Jerome V. Morrissey, (Retired).
Res., P.O. Box 486, 61377. Tel: 815-853-4558. [CEM]

Westville, Vermilion Co., St. Mary's (1903), Rev. David Erickson.
Res., 231 N. State St., 61883. Tel: 217-267-3334; Fax: 217-267-3335. [CEM]
School—225 N. State St., 61883. Tel: 217-267-7730; Fax: 217-267-3327.
Lay Teachers 14; Students 156.
SS. Peter and Paul. Closed. For inquiries for parish records contact St. Mary's, Westville.

Woodhull, Henry Co., St. John's (1889) (Swedish), Rev. Bruce D. Lopez.
Res., 390 E. Highway Ave., P.O. Box 249, 61490. Tel: 309-334-2180; Fax: 309-334-3317. [CEM 2]

Wyoming, Stark Co., St. Dominic's (1881), Rev. Charles Karl, Admin.
Res., 303 Galena Ave., 61491. Tel: 309-695-4031. [CEM]
Mission—Toulon, Stark Co., St. John, Toulon, 61483.

Chaplains of Public Institutions

DANVILLE. *Veterans' Administration Hospital* Tel: 217-442-8000. Rev. John Schultz, Military Chap.

DWIGHT. *Dwight Correctional Center.* Attended from St. Patrick's, Dwight. Tel: 815-584-3522. Rev. James E. Rickey.

LINCOLN. *Lincoln State School* Tel: 217-735-2361. Rev. Eugene Prendeville, O.M.I., Chap.
Logan Correctional Center. Vacant. Tel: 217-947-2714; 309-244-8516.

PONTIAC. *Illinois State Penitentiary.* Rev. Jonas Callanan, I.C., Chap., Res., 811 Hill St., 61704. Tel: 815-842-1150.

SHERIDAN. *Illinois Industrial School for Boys.* Rev. John G. Waugh, Chap.

Special Residence:
Reverend Fathers—
Carney, Edward
Zube, Joseph

Special Assignment:
Reverend Monsignors—
Hettinger, Clarence J., Diocesan Tribunal
Reverend Fathers—
Anderson, John C., Propagation of the Faith, Holy Childhood Assn., Catholic Relief Society

On Duty Outside the Diocese:
Reverend Monsignors—
Prendergast, John J., Chap., U.S. Air Force
Reverend Fathers—
Baer, M. Stuart, Providence Health Systems, 501 S. Buena Vista St., Burbank, CA 91505
Bird, Steven, North American College, Vatican City State
Collins, Patrick W., Archdiocese of Chicago
Guthrie, Raymond, Diocese of Rockford
Henseler, J. Thomas, Diocese of Springfield, IL
Hochstatter, Theodore
Myers, James E., 32 Middlefield Rd., Menlo Park, CA 94025
Ohm, Edward, Military
Pham, John-Peter, Studying for Diplomatic Corp.
Smith, Jerome, Diocese of Joliet
Virtue, William D., Mt. St. Mary Seminary, Emmitsburg, MA
Vitaliano, Dominic, Military
Williams, John Mark, North American College, Rome

Absent on Leave:
Reverend Fathers—
Engels, Francis C., P.O. Box 272, Kewanee, IL 61443-0272
Harbert, William S., 550 E. Carl Sandberg, Apt. 142, Galesburg, IL 61401
O'Brien, Terrance
Shea, Thomas, Rte. 1, Secor, IL 61771

Retired:
Reverend Monsignors—
Campbell, James F.
Duncan, Edward J.
Goodman, Norman D.
Hettinger, Clarence J., 6001 N. University, Peoria, IA 61614
Livingston, Robert C., St. Mary's Rectory, 8819 W. Knox St., Kickapoo, IL 61525
Morrissey, James L.
Motsett, C. Bourke, 1806 Washington, Danville, IL 61832
O'Dea, Joseph J., 2223 W. Heading Ave., W. Peoria, IL 61604
Render, Bernard A., 1301 N.E. Glendale Ave., Peoria, IL 61603
Reverend Fathers—
Aldrich, Ralph, 1817 Dale St., San Diego, CA 92102
Bawiec, Edward J., 424 W. First St., Oglesby, IL 61348
Blough, E. C., St. Augustine Manor, 1301 N.E. Glendale, Peoria, IL 61603
Brajkovich, Thomas R.
Breuning, Walter A.
Brom, D. Giles, St. Clare Nursing Home, 5533 N. Galena Rd., Peoria Hts., IL 61614
Ciesielski, Heinc, 1553 Sobieski, LaSalle, IL 61301
Colgan, Marvin, St. Joseph's, 401 9th St., Lacon, IL 61540
Condon, Louis M., P.O. Box 10319, 3538 70th St., Moline, IL 61265
Crawford, Richard E., 1414 S. Monroe, Streator, IL 61364
Creager, Robert J., 823 Canal St., Ottawa, IL 61350
Culleton, James P., 320 George St., Apt. W2, Morris, IL 60450
Dietzen, John J.
Dietzen, Vincent E., 436 South St., Danville, IL 61832
Divan, Anthony L.
Gaughran, John, 312 N. State St., Westville, IL 61883
Gildner, Leo H.
Graves, Joseph A., 5335 Red Sky Dr., Colorado Springs, CO 80915
Hettinger, Paul W., R.R. 2, 3888 E. 1st Rd., Mendota, IL 61342
Hiland, George, 374 Benchopst, Sebastian, FL 32958
Hoffman, Robert, 343 Hickory Ct., Oakwood, IL 61858
Hughes, Robert T., 1103 Peppertree Ln., Eureka, IL 61530
Jesiolowski, Sylvester E., 315 E. Second Ave., Box 21, Oglesby, IL 61348
Kane, Eugene, 1831 County Rd. 2500 N., Thomasboro, IL 61878
Karl, Charles E., 3633 Richwoods Blvd., Peoria, IL 61604
Kelly, Thomas F.
King, John, P.O. Box 79, Starrucla, PA 18462
Krewer, Edward M., 1177 N. Gooding St., La Salle, IL 61301-1581
Mahoney, John A., 620 E. Ogden, Geneseo, IL 61254-1145
Malinowski, Stanley J., 17 Golf Dr., Loda, IL 60948
Morrissey, Jerome V., St. Augustine Manor, 1301 N.E. Glendale Ave., Peoria, IL 61603
Mullen, Richard, 2414 Heritage Dr., Champaign, IL 61821
Niemeyer, John, 132 Mobile-Land Ct., Bloomington, IL 61701
O'Connor, John F., 407 N. Franklin, River Forest, IL 60305
O'Toole, John J., R.R. 2, P.O. Box 85-A, Lexington, IL 61753
Prendergast, Robert E., P.O. Box 548, Kewanee, IL 61443
Purcell, James, 19 Pinewood Park, Chillcothe, IL 61523
Raney, Richard E., 685 Mantanzas Ct., Fort Myers Beach, FL 33931
Reynolds, Robert E., 319 N. Franklin, Rushville, IL 62681-0292
Russo, Nicodemus A., 613 Fenwick, San Antonio, TX 78239
Ryan, Francis, 2223 W. Heading Ave., W. Peoria, IL 61604
Ryan, William A., 610 E. First St., Spring Valley, IL 61362
Schroeder, George J., 16 Waverly Dr., Rock Island, IL 61201
Sors, Vladimir, 308 S. Monroe St., Streator, IL 61364
Sprague, George Raymond, St. Augustine Manor, 1301 N.E. Glendale, Peoria, IL 61603
Thompson, George M., 3026 55th St., Moline, IL 61265
Verhoye, Gerard A., 202 N. State, Box 603, Atkinson, IL 61235
Weishar, John A., St. Francis Continuing Care, 210 S. Fifth St., Burlington, IA 52601
Wuellner, George E., St. Boniface Church, 416 County Rd. 1110 N., Seymour, IL 61875
Very Rev. Canon—
Flattery, John J., Canon in Perpetuum, 20967 Walnut Hill, Danville, IL 61834. Tel: 217-442-2603

Permanent Deacons:
Barr, Earl, Diocese of Phoenix
Baxley, Robert, Our Lady of the Lake, Mahomet
Beltramini, Robert, Leave of Absence
Bott, Herman J., Holy Family, Danville
Breeden, Charles, St. Maria Goretti, Coal Valley
Brinker, Kenneth, Diocese of Portland
Burgess, Charles E., St. Hyacinth's, LaSalle
Burton, John, St. Matthew, Farmington
Carolan, Brendan, Holy Trinity, Bloomington
Chaffee, Harley, St. Malachy, Genesco
Clark, William H., Immaculate Conception, Monmouth
Daron, Estal, St. Columba, Ottawa
DeVooght, Dennis, Sacred Heart, Moline
Eaton, Francis, St. Thomas, Peoria Heights
Efinger, Donald, St. Thomas, Peoria
England, Robert, (Retired)
Filzen, Bernard R., St. Mark's Church, Peoria
Gaetz, Dale, Co. Admin. of Permanent Deacons, St. Mary, Lourdes
Granet, Timothy, St. Pius X, Rock Island
Gratkowski, Daniel, Leave of Absence
Gray, William, St. Mary Mission, Hamilton
Grimler, Richard, Epiphany, Normal
Hammel, Richard F., Proctor Community Hospital, Peoria; St. Philomena, Peoria
Hammond, Richard G., St. Anthony's Church, Bartonville
Haneghan, James, St. Patrick, Galesburg
Harris, Harley, St. Malachy, Geneseo
Hart, Henry, Holy Cross, Champaign
Heintz, Eugene, St. Mary Mission, Hamilton
Hietter, Earl E., St. Thomas, Peoria Heights
Honzel, Larry, St. Malachy, Genesco
Hunter, Roger, St. Jude, Dunlop
Kauth, Richard, Leave of Absence
Keefer, Wesley, St. Patrick, Elmwood
Kelly, William, St. Thomas, Peoria Heights
Kettering, Jack M., Our Lady of Guadalupe, Silvis
Koeppel, Joseph, St. Ann's, Peoria

Kovachevich, Victor, St. Mary, Canton
La Hood, Joseph, St. Martin de Porres, Peoria & Prison Ministry
Lalande, John, Holy Cross, Champaign
Landry, John, Sacred Heart, Moline
Mancuso, Terry, Leave of Absence
Martin, Paul, St. Pius X, Rock Island
Maubach, James, Holy Family, Peoria
McClellan, William, Leave of Absence
Meyer, William, Immaculate Conception, Manito
Moch, John, St. Mary, Kewanee
Moran, Thomas, Blessed Sacrament, Morton
Murphy, John P., St. Louis, Princeton
Murphy, John R., Immaculate Conception, Lacon
Murphy, R. Daniel, St. Patrick, Urbana
Murray, Charles, St. Joseph, Pekin
Myers, Robert, St. Vincent de Paul, Peoria
Neakrase, Paul, St. Patrick, Washington
Nevinger, Ronald, Diocese of Lafayette, IN
Nichols, Ed, St. Philomena, Monticello
Oenning, Frank W., Leave of Absence
Ohl, Harry, St. Philomena, Peoria
Petri, Darrel, St. Mary, Bloomington
Pogioli, Martin, St. Joseph, Pekin
Pomazal, Robert, St. Edward, Chillicothe
Rager, Ronald L., St. Monica's Church, East Peoria
Ramirez, Jesse, St. Patrick's, Galesburg
Randazzo, Frank G., St. Ambrose, Milan
Rapach, Thomas, St. Jude's, Dunlap
Reid, Michael, Sacred Heart, Peoria; Prison Ministry
Reising, David, St. Philomena, Peoria
Ringler, William, St. Anthony's, Hoopeston
Roesch, Lewis, Holy Trinity, Bloomington
Sailer, Philip, St. Pius X, Rock Island
Sandoval, Henry, Our Lady of Guadalupe, Silvis
Scanlan, Richard, St. Matthew, Champaign
Serangeli, Gregory, St. Edward's, Chillicothe, Co-Admin. of Permanent Deacons
Shipp, William, St. Malachy's, Rantoul
Simon, Nicholas, St. Anthony, Atkinson
Sims, Fred, St. Mary, Peru
Skender, John, St. Mark, Peoria
Sloman, William, St. Francis Medical Center, Peoria
Slomian, Vincent, Holy Cross, Mendota
Smith, Frank, (Retired)
Smith, Marvin, St. Mary, Metamora
Smith, Richard, Holy Family, Danville
Swim, Russ, St. Mary, Moline
Tomlianovich, Louis A., St. Anthony's, Bartonville
Van Meltebeck, Martin, St. Mary, Kewanee
Van Wassenhove, Raymond, St. Mary, Kewanee
Verbeck, Walter, St. Malachy, Geneseo
Wachtel, Thomas, St. Malachy, Geneseo
Waldschmidt, Robert, St. Thomas, Peoria
Whited, Ernie, St. Joseph, Pekin
Zimmerman, Richard, St. Peter, Peoria
Zimmerman, Robert, St. Maria Goretti, Coal Valley

INSTITUTIONS LOCATED IN THE DIOCESE

[A] SEMINARIES, RELIGIOUS OR SCHOLASTICATES

PEORIA. *Rosminian Novitiate*, 2327 W. Heading Ave., 61604. Tel: 309-676-6341; Fax: 309-676-1087.
E-mail: wtmic@juno.com
Revs. James Nugent, I.C., Asst.; William T. Miller, I.C., Novice Master. In res. Priests 2; Laymen 3; Total Staff 5.

PERU. *St. Bede Abbey and Academy*, 61354. Tel: 815-223-3140; Fax: 815-223-8580.
E-mail: stbede@ivnet.com
Web site: www.theramp.net/stbede/index.html
Permanent Staff: Priests 11; Brothers 3; Sisters 2; Lay Staff 60. The Benedictine Society of St. Bede. Rt. Revs. Roger F. Corpus, O.S.B., Abbot; Marion E. Balsavich, O.S.B., (Resigned); Very Rev. Claude J. Peifer, O.S.B., Subprior; Bro. Nathaniel Grossman, O.S.B., Prior, Novice Master, Junior Master; Revs. Stephen J. Souse, O.S.B.; Eugene A. Lauer, O.S.B.; William J. Kirk, O.S.B.; Sebastian C. Lewis, O.S.B.; Kevin D. Gorman, O.S.B.; Alfred J. Scheidler, O.S.B.; Henry H. Fritz, O.S.B.; Bernard A. Horzen, O.S.B.; Dunstan R. Morrissey, O.S.B.; Joseph J. Heyd, O.S.B.; Arthur G. Schmit, O.S.B.; Allen J. Mattingly, O.S.B.; Ambrose B. Hessling, O.S.B.; Placid W. Hatfield, O.S.B.; Matthew C. Mazzuchelli, O.S.B.; Benedict B. McKean, O.S.B.; Gabriel G. Bullock, O.S.B.; Harold L. Datzman, O.S.B.; Philip D. Davey, O.S.B.; Ronald L. Margherio, O.S.B.; Samuel D. Pusateri, O.S.B.; Patrick A. Fennell, O.S.B.; Dominic M. Garramone, O.S.B.; James M. Murray, O.S.B.; Bros. George J. Matsouka, O.S.B.; Bede D. Schuda, O.S.B.; Mark F. Strassburger, O.S.B.; Luke E. McLachlan, O.S.B.; Michael M. Calhoun, O.S.B. Priests 28; Brothers 6.

[B] HIGH SCHOOLS, DIOCESAN AND INTER-PAROCHIAL

PEORIA. *Notre Dame High School*, 5105 N. Sheridan, 61614. Tel: 309-691-8741; Fax: 309-691-0875.
Web site: peorianotredame.com
Thomas Flanagan, Dir. Devel.; Rev. Chris Haake, Chap.
Peoria Notre Dame Scholarship Trust, 5105 N. Sheridan Rd., 61614. Rev. James J. Swaner, Pres.; Mary Putnam, Vice Pres.; Carl Anderson, Sec.; John Wagner, Treas. Priests 1; Sisters 3; Lay Teachers 59; Students 980.

BLOOMINGTON. *Central Catholic High School*, 712 N. Center St., 61701. Tel: 309-827-5373; Fax: 309-827-0173.
E-mail: CCHS@ice.net
Web site: www/ice.net/~cchs
Mrs. Joy Allen, Prin.; Rev. Stephen A. Willard. Priests 1; Lay Teachers 28; Students 314.

CHAMPAIGN. *High School of St. Thomas More*, 3901 N. Mattis, 61822. Tel: 217-352-7210. Dr. Ted Mittler, Prin.; Rev. Antoinio Dittmer, Chap. Priests 1; Lay Teachers 9; Students 73.

DANVILLE. *Schlarman High School*, 61832. Tel: 217-442-2725; Fax: 217-442-0293.
E-mail: stittp@SHS.com
Web site: www.schlarman.com
Lisa A. Green, Admin.; Rev. Anthony Lee. Lay Teachers 19; Students 200.

OTTAWA. *Marquette High School*, 1000 Paul St., 61350. Tel: 815-433-0125; Fax: 815-433-2632.
E-mail: xavmhs@roe35.lth2.k12.il.us
Web site: URL: marquettehs.com
Ronald Spander, Prin.; Rev. Patrick Henehan, Chap. Priests 4; Lay Teachers 22; Students 246.

ROCK ISLAND. *Alleman High School*, 1103 40th St., 61201. Tel: 309-786-7793; Fax: 309-786-7834. Colin Letendre, Prin.; Revs. Daniel J. Mirabelli, C.S.V., Dir. of Devel.; Michael J. Andrejek, Chap. Priests 2; Sisters 5; Deacons 2; Lay Teachers 30; Students 559.

[C] HIGH SCHOOLS, PRIVATE

NAUVOO. *St. Mary's Academy*, 62354. Tel: 217-453-6619; Fax: 217-453-2316. Sr. Roberta Bussan, O.S.B., Dir.

PERU. *St. Bede Academy*, 61354. Tel: 815-223-3140. Full-time Teachers: Priests 3; Sisters 2; Lay Teachers 17. Benedictine Fathers and Brothers. Rev. Philip Davey, O.S.B., Supt.; Mrs. Michelle Mershon, Prin.; Revs. Stephen J. Souse, O.S.B., Registrar; Patrick A. Fennell, O.S.B.; Bro. Bede Schuda, O.S.B., CFO; Mr. Bernie Moore, Asst. Prin.; Mr. Robert Leclercq, Dir. Guidance; Mr. Thomas McGunnigal, Business Mgr. Benedictine Priests 5; Brothers 2; Lay Teachers 18; Students 337.

[D] ELEMENTARY SCHOOLS, PRIVATE

PEORIA. *Father Sweeney School*, 403 N.E. Madison Ave., 61603. Tel: 309-637-6305; Fax: 309-637-6347.
E-mail: fsweeney@mtco.com
Web site: www.mtco.com/~fsweeney
(Grades 4-8). The Father John Sweeney Memorial Program for the Academically Gifted. Mrs. Mary Rogers, Prin. Lay Teachers 13; Students 117.

[E] ELEMENTARY SCHOOLS INTER-PAROCHIAL

LA SALLE. *La Salle Catholic School*, 1055 Sixth St., 61301. Tel: 815-223-5088.
E-mail: laser2@theramp.net
Web site: www.asd.com
John D. Ranger, Prin. Lay Teachers 14; Students 161.

MOLINE. *Seton Catholic School*, 1320-16th Ave., 61265. Tel: 309-757-5500; Fax: 309-762-0545.
E-mail: pvasquez@setonschool.com
Administrators: Sr. Paula Vasquez, O.S.F.; Mrs. Jane Barrett. Sisters 4; Lay Teachers 34; Students 625.

ROCK ISLAND. *Jordan Catholic School of Rock Island, Inc.* Facilities at St. Ambrose, St. Pius, and Sacred Heart. 2901-24th St., P.O. Box 3490, 61204-3490. Tel: 309-793-7350; Fax: 309-793-7361.
E-mail: JCSoffice@Revealed.net
Web site: http://home.revealed.netJCSoffice/index.html
Daniel Lievens, Admin.
Directs the Elementary School System for the Rock Island-Milan area, operating facilities at Sacred Heart, St. Pius X. Parishes in Rock Island and St. Ambrose in Milan.
Commission on Education for Jordan Catholic School, P.O. Box 3490, 61204-3490. Tel: 309-793-7350; Fax: 309-793-7361. Lay Teachers 31; Students 612.

WEST PEORIA. *Immaculate Conception Pre-Kindergarten*, 2408 W. Heading Ave., 61604-5096. Tel: 309-674-6168; Fax: 309-674-2006.
E-mail: smbicc@dave-world.net
Web site: osfsisterswpeoria.org
Sr. M. Elaine Haertjens, O.S.F., Dir. Sponsored by the Sisters of St. Francis of the Immaculate Conception. Students 10.

[F] RELIGIOUS EDUCATION CENTERS, PRIVATE

PERU. *Sisters of St. Benedict*, 26 W. U.S. Hwy. 6, 61354. Tel: 815-223-6741. Sr. Margaret Suerth, O.S.B., IVCC College; Sr. Mary Core, O.S.B., St. Bede Academy; Sr. Catherine Maloney, O.S.B., Hospice Care, Illinois Valley Community Hospital, Peru, IL.

[G] CATHOLIC SOCIAL SERVICE OF PEORIA

WEST PEORIA. *Catholic Social Service of Peoria*, 2900 W. Heading Ave., 61604. Tel: 309-671-5700; Fax: 309-674-1664.
E-mail: csspierson@aol.com
Ms. Peggy A. Arizzi, Exec Dir.; Ms. Tricia C. Fox, Assoc. Dir.
Catholic Social Service West, 2900 W. Heading Ave., 61604. Tel: 309-671-5700; Fax: 309-674-1664. Foster Home Programs. Tel: 309-671-5750; Fax: 309-671-1046.
Catholic Social Service Institutions, 2900 W. Heading Ave., 61604. Guardian Angel Home. Tel: 309-671-5700; Fax: 309-673-3405. Jesu Children's Enrichment Center. Tel: 309-686-7550.
Peoria Community Area Project/LaCasa Center, 1406 W. Antoinette St., Peoria, 61605. Tel: 309-637-2600; Fax: 309-637-6327. Family Counseling, Adoption Services, Senior Citizens In-Home Counseling, Women's Counseling & Support Services, Cabrini Maternity Services.
Catholic Social Service Counseling, 413 N.E. Monroe, Peoria, 61603. Tel: 309-671-5720; Fax: 309-671-0257.
Catholic Social Service Branch Offices: 603 N. Center St., Bloomington, 61701. Tel: 309-829-6307; Fax: 309-829-3254. 2714 McGraw Dr., Bloomington, 61704. Tel: 309-662-3840; Fax: 309-663-2883. 416 W. Locust St., Canton, 61520. Tel: 309-647-5014; Fax: 309-647-8287. 1315A Curt Dr., Champaign, 61820. Tel: 217-352-5179; Fax: 217-352-0318. 102 N. Robinson, Danville, 61832. Tel: 217-443-1772; Fax: 217-443-1701. 292 N. Chambers, Galesburg, 61401. Tel: 309-342-1136; Fax: 309-342-1891. 542 Crosat, LaSalle, 61301. Tel: 815-223-4007; Fax: 815-224-4550. 310 S. Logan, Lincoln, 62656. Tel: 217-732-3771; Fax: 217-735-1738. 527 Grant St., P.O. Box 355, Macomb, 61455-0355. Tel: 309-833-1791; Fax: 309-836-1462. 15 S. Capitol, Ste. 215, Pekin, 61554. Tel: 309-353-9500; Fax: 309-353-3528. 816 20th St., Rock Island, 61201. Tel: 309-794-2200; Fax: 309-786-9492. 823 20th St., Rock Island, 61201. Tel: 309-786-0770; Fax: 309-786-3856. Fort Armstrong, 1900 3rd Ave., Rock Island, 61201. Tel: 309-788-9581; Fax: 309-788-9608.
Catholic Social Service Outreach Offices: Dwight Outreach Office, 126 Mazon Ave., Dwight, 60420. Tel: 815-584-3110. Geneseo Outreach Office, 217 N. Russell, Geneseo, 61254. Tel: 309-944-3518. Kewanee Outreach Office, 223 W. Central Blvd., Kewanee, 61443. Tel: 309-852-2564. Pontiac Outreach Office, 501 N. Chicago, Pontiac, 61764. Tel: 815-844-3629. Streator Outreach Office, 111 E. Spring St., Streator, 61364. Tel: 815-673-2311. Total Institutional Staff 33; Other Staff 571.

[H] CHILDREN'S HOMES

WEST PEORIA. *Catholic Social Service Foster Care Program*, 2900 W. Heading Ave., 61604. Tel: 309-671-5700; Fax: 309-671-1046
For a complete listing, refer to the Special Care Facilities section.
Guardian Angel Home, 2900 W. Heading Ave., 309-671-5760 Fax: 309-673-3405
For a complete listing, refer to the Special Care Facilities section.

[I] DAY CARE CENTERS

PEORIA. *South Side Catholic Child Care Center*, 1010 W. Johnson St., 61605. Tel: 309-674-7340; Fax: 309-682-2065. Ollie Bracket, Dir. Children 103; Total Staff 15.

WEST PEORIA. *Jesu Children's Enrichment Centers*, 2900 W. Heading Ave., 61604. Tel: 309-671-5660. Staff 42; Capacity 158; Served 212.

[J] GENERAL HOSPITALS

PEORIA. *OSF Healthcare System*, 800 N.E. Glen Oak Ave., 61603-3200. Tel: 309-699-2852; Fax: 309-655-6869.
Web site: www.osfhealthcare.org
For a complete listing, refer to the Hospitals section.

St. Francis' Medical Center, 530 N.E. Glen Oak Ave., 61637. Tel: 309-655-2000; Fax: 309-655-2347.
E-mail: keith.e.steffen@osfhealthcare.org
For a complete listing, refer to the Hospitals section.

BLOOMINGTON. *OSF St. Joseph Medical Center*, 2200 E. Washington, 61701. Tel: 309-662-3311; Fax: 309-662-7143.
Web site: www.osfstjoseph.org
For a complete listing, refer to the Hospitals section.

DANVILLE. *Provena United Samaritans Medical Center*, 812 N. Logan, 61832. Tel: 217-443-5000; Fax: 217-443-1965
For a complete listing, refer to the Hospitals section.

GALESBURG. *St. Mary Medical Center*, 3333 N. Seminary St., 61401-1299. Tel: 309-344-3161; Fax: 309-344-9494
For a complete listing, refer to the Hospitals section.

PONTIAC. *Saint James Hospital*, 610 E. Water, 61764. Tel: 815-842-2828; Fax: 815-842-4912.
Web site: www.osfstjames.org
For a complete listing, refer to the Hospitals section.

SPRING VALLEY. *St. Margaret's Hospital*, 600 E. First St., 61362. Tel: 815-664-5311; Fax: 815-664-1335.
E-mail: admin@st.margarets.com
Web site: http://www.St.Margarets.com
For a complete listing, refer to the Hospitals section.

STREATOR. *St. Mary's Hospital*, 111 E. Spring St., 61364. Tel: 815-673-2311; Fax: 815-673-4541
For a complete listing, refer to the Hospitals section.

URBANA. *Provena Covenant Medical Center*, 1400 W. Park St., 61801. Tel: 217-337-2000; Fax: 217-337-4541.
E-mail: dianehfriedman@provenahealth.com
Web site: www.provenahealth.com
For a complete listing, refer to the Hospitals section.

[K] SPECIAL HOSPITALS AND SANATORIA

LACON. *St. Joseph's Nursing Home*, 401 Ninth St., 61540. Tel: 309-246-2175; Fax: 309-246-3609
For a complete listing, refer to the Special Care Facilities section.

PEORIA HEIGHTS. *Saint Clare Home*, 5533 N. Galena Rd., 61614. Tel: 309-682-5428
For a complete listing, refer to the Special Care Facilities section.

ROCK ISLAND. *St. Anthony's Continuing Care Center*, 767 30th St., 61201. Tel: 309-788-7631
For a complete listing, refer to the Special Care Facilities section.

[L] HOMES FOR AGED

PEORIA. *St. Augustine Manor*, 1301 N.E. Glendale Ave., 61603. Tel: 309-674-7069; Fax: 309-494-6547
For a complete listing, refer to the Special Care Facilities section.
St. Joseph's Home of Peoria, 2223 W. Heading Ave., 61604. Tel: 309-673-7425; Fax: 309-673-7430
For a complete listing, refer to the Special Care Facilities section.

[M] RETREAT HOUSES

GEORGETOWN. *LaSalette Missionaries*, 5065 Olivet Rd. (Olivet), 61846. Tel: 217-662-6671. Revs. John Paninski, c/o St. Issac Joques Parish, Georgetown; Thaddeus Plawny, M.S. Priests 2; Total Staff 2.

HENRY. *Christ the King Retreat Center - Diocese of Peoria*, Box 165, 61537. Tel: 309-364-3084. Rev. John C. Anderson, Admin.; Deacon Frederick J. Kruse, Dir. Priests 1; Total in Residence 2; Total Staff 3.

[N] MONASTERIES AND RESIDENCES FOR PRIESTS AND BROTHERS

PEORIA, IL. *Congregation of St. John*, 1116 W. College, 61606-1728. Tel: 309-674-0208; Fax: 309-497-3759.
E-mail: stjohn@bobcat.bradley.edu
Web site: www.stjean.com
Revs. Antoine Thomas, Prior; Joseph Mary Brown; Bros. Dominic Mary; Peter.

PRINCEVILLE, IL. *St. Joseph Priory and Novitiate*, 11223 W. Legion Hall Rd., 61559. Tel: 309-385-1193; Fax: 309-385-1830. Revs. Cominic Francis, Prior; Didier-Marie, Novice Master. Priests 2; Professed Brothers 5; Novices 7.

[O] CONVENTS AND RESIDENCES FOR SISTERS

PEORIA. *Immaculate Conception Convent*. Tel: 309-674-6168; Fax: 309-674-2006.
E-mail: smbicc@dave-world.net
Web site: osfsisterswpeoria.org
2408 W. Heading Ave., West Peoria, 61604-5096. Tel: 309-674-6168; Fax: 309-674-2006. Motherhouse of the Sisters of St. Francis of the Immaculate Conception. Sr. M. Barbara Buckley, O.S.F., Pres.; Rev. James F. Campbell, Chap. Sisters 15; Professed Sisters 54.
Missionaries of Charity Convent, 506 Hancock St., 61603. Tel: 309-674-7160. Sr. M. Danielle, M.C., Supr. Sisters 4; Total Assisted 17,058; Total Volunteer Staff 30.
The Poor Clares. Tel: 309-682-3182; Fax: 309-682-3182. Our Lady of the Angels Convent, 3432 W. Baskin Ridge, 61604. Tel: 309-682-3182; Fax: 309-682-3182. Sisters 4.
St. Francis Medical Center Hospital - Convent, 740 N. Glen Oak Ave., 61603. Tel: 309-655-4014; Fax: 309-655-2347. Sr. M. Ildefonsa Richter, O.S.F., Supr., Tel: 309-655-2083; 655-2044. The Sisters of the Third Order of St. Francis 9.

EAST PEORIA. *Motherhouse, The Sisters of the Third Order of St. Francis*, 1175 Saint Francis Ln., 61611-1299. Tel: 309-699-7215. Sr. Mary Ellen Flannery, O.S.F., Major Supr. Sisters in Residence 28; Total Sisters in Community 64.
Mt. Alverno Novitiate, 1175 Saint Francis Ln., 61611-1299. Tel: 309-699-9313.
E-mail: vocation.info@osfhealthcare.org
Web site: www.osfhealthcare.org
Rev. Msgr. Rick J. Oberch, Chap. Novitiate of The Sisters of the Third Order of St. Francis. Sisters 2; Novices 3.

LACON. *St. Joseph Motherhouse and Novitiate*, 61540. Tel: 309-246-2175; Fax: 309-246-2708. Congregation of the Daughters of St. Francis of Assisi - American Province. Sr. M. Vaclava Ballon, Prov. Supr. Sisters 15; Sisters in Community (Professed) 34.

NAUVOO. *St. Mary Monastery, Motherhouse and Novitiate*, 62354. Tel: 217-453-2227; Fax: 271-453-6552.
E-mail: smaryadm@nauvoo.net
Web site: www.stmarymonastery.org
Sr. Ruth Ksycki, O.S.B., Prioress. Benedictine Sisters of Pontifical Jurisdiction. Sisters in Community 69.

OTTAWA. *Sisters of Mercy of the Americas*, 906 Canal St., Apt. 516, 61350. Tel: 815-433-1357. Sisters 1; Total Asssisted 1,000; Total Staff 6.

PONTIAC. *Handmaids of Nazareth*, St. Mary Convent, 111 E. Howard St., 61764-1917. Tel: 815-842-1890; Fax: 815-842-1582.
E-mail: srdonnamarie@hotmail.com
Mailing Address: P.O. Box 507, Pittsford, NY, 14534. Sisters in Residence 4.

PRINCEVILLE. *St. Therese Convent*, 11227 W. Legion Hall Rd., 61559. Tel: 309-385-2550; Fax: 309-385-2550. Sr. Marie Agnes, Supr. Sisters 15.
Sisters of St. John, 11227 W. Legion Hall Rd., 61559; Fax: 309-385-2550. Sisters 12.

ROCK ISLAND. *St. Mary of the Angels Convent*, 1000-30th St., 61201. Tel: 309-786-3733. Sr. Mary Stephanie, O.S.F., Supr.; Rev. Raphael Fabish, Chap. Sisters in Residence 7.

STREATOR. *Franciscan Sisters*, 905 S. Park St., 61364. Tel: 815-673-1259. Mailing Address: St. Francis Convent, LaVerna Rd., P.O. Box 19431, Springfield, 62794-9431. Sr. Eleanora Marie Maurer, O.S.F.

WEST PEORIA. *Mother of Peace Home*, 2223 W. Heading Ave., 61604. Tel: 309-673-4657. Total Residents 13; Total Staff 14.

[P] NEWMAN CENTERS

PEORIA. *Newman Foundation at Bradley University & Illinois Central College*, 1116 W. College Ave., 61606-1728. Tel: 309-674-0208 (Office); Fax: 309-497-3759.
E-mail: bradleynewmancenter@hotmail.com
Web site: www.geocities.com/bradleynewmancenter/
Gina McKenna, Office Mgr. Congregation of St. John. Revs. Antoine Thomas; Joseph Mary Brown; Bro. Dominic Mary. Total Residence 4.

CHAMPAIGN. *St. John's Catholic Student Chapel and Newman Foundation, University of Illinois*, 604 E. Armory Ave., 61820. Tel: 217-344-1184; Fax: 217-344-4957.
E-mail: newmanfoundation.org
Rev. Msgr. Edward J. Duncan, Emeritus; Rev. Msgr. Stuart W. Swetland, Dir.; Revs. Ben Rodriguez; Stanley Deptula; Antonio Dittmer; Fortunatus Bijura; Johndamascene Zilimu. Total in Residence 6; Total Staff 6; Newman Center Residence 339; Newman Center Staff 95.

MACOMB. *St. Francis of Assisi Newman Center*, 1401 University Dr., 61455. Tel: 309-837-3988.
E-mail: frdon@priest.com
Web site: www.macomb.com/~newman
Rev. Daniel J. Wilder, Chap.

NORMAL. *St. Robert Bellarmine Newman Center, Illinois State University*, 501 S. Main St., 61761-2996. Tel: 309-452-5046; Fax: 309-452-3845.
E-mail: gccaste@ilstu.edu
Rev. Gary C. Caster, Chap. Total Staff 4.

ROCK ISLAND. *Augustana College Catholic Campus Ministry*, 61201. Tel: 309-794-7272.
E-mail: AMNMR@Augustana.edu
Sr. Marilyn Ring, O.S.B. Staff 1.

[Q] PERSONAL PRELATURES

URBANA. *Opus Dei*. Prelature of the Holy Cross and Opus Dei, Lincoln Green Center, 715 W. Michigan Ave., 61801. Tel: 217-367-6650; Fax: 217-344-2987.
E-mail: lincolngreen@net66.com
Web site: www.opusdei.org
In res. Rev. Jerome Jung.

[R] MISCELLANEOUS

PEORIA. *Northside Office of Christian Response*, 1825 N.E. Adams St., 61603. Tel: 309-637-0322; 800-637-5508; Fax: 309-637-0307. Mr. John Truitt, Dir. Total Assisted 151; Total Staff 1.
St. Augustine Community, 1301 N.E. Glendale, 61603. Tel: 309-674-7069; Fax: 309-494-6547.
Highwood Learning Center, 1301 N.E. Glendale Ave., 61603. Tel: 309-674-7069; Fax: 309-494-6547. Dick Langjahr, Admin. Total Assisted 80; Total Staff 30.
St. Vincent De Paul Society, 3612 N.E. Monroe St., 61603. Tel: 800-637-5508; Fax: 309-637-0307. Diocesan Council and Particular Council of Peoria. John and Mary Truitt, Co-Presidents. Total Assisted; over 800 Families in 12 parishes.
SHARE Food Program of Central Illinois, Inc., 1825 N.E. Adams St., 61603. Tel: 309-637-0282; 800-637-5508; Fax: 309-637-0307. Total Staff 5; Assisted: 156,000 Family Units of Food.

ALEDO. *Family of Mary Coredemptrix*, 1331 230th St., 61231. Tel: 309-372-4654.

BLOOMINGTON. *Homes of Hope, Inc.* Homes of Hope, 1570 Hunt Dr., Normal, 61761.

MOLINE. *The Order of the Legion of Little Souls of the Merciful Heart of Jesus*, 428 39th St., 61265-1641. Tel: 309-797-8491; Fax: 309-736-5570.
E-mail: littlesoul@home.org
Web site: www.littlesouls.org
Teresa I. Huyten, Dir.; Rev. Michael L. Menner, Diocesan Chap.

RELIGIOUS INSTITUTES OF MEN REPRESENTED IN THE DIOCESE

For further details refer to the corresponding bracketed number in the Religious Institutes of Men or Women section.

[0200]—*Benedictine Monks.* (St. Bede Abbey).—O.S.B.
[]—*Congregation of St. John.*—F.J.
[1320]—*Clerics of St. Viator.*—C.S.V.
[0480]—*Conventual Franciscans.*—O.F.M.Conv.
[0520]—*Franciscan Friars.* (Prov. of St. John the Baptist).—O.F.M.
[0300]—*Institute of Charity.* (Rome, Italy).—I.C.
[0720]—*The Missionaries of Our Lady of La Salette.*—M.S.
[0910]—*Oblates of Mary Immaculate.* (Central Prov.).—O.M.I.
[0430]—*Order of Preachers (Dominicans).* (Prov. of St. Albert the Great).—O.P.

RELIGIOUS INSTITUTES OF WOMEN REPRESENTED IN THE DIOCESE

[0230]—*Benedictine Sisters of Pontifical Jurisdiction.*—O.S.B.
[0920]—*Congregation of the Daughters of St. Francis of Assisi, (American Prov.).*—D.S.F.
[2100]—*Congregation of the Humility of Mary.*—C.H.M.
[1920]—*Congregation of the Sisters of the Holy Cross.*—C.S.C.
[1730]—*Congregation of the Sisters of the Third Order of St. Francis, Oldenburg, IN.*—O.S.F.
[1710]—*Congregation of the Third Order of St. Francis of Mary Immaculate, Joliet, IL.*—O.S.F.
[0760]—*Daughters of Charity of St. Vincent de Paul.*—D.C.
[1070-03]—*Dominican Sisters.*—O.P.
[1070-10]—*Dominican Sisters.*—O.P.
[1450]—*Franciscan Sisters of the Sacred Heart.*—O.S.F.
[1770]—*Hospital Sisters of the Third Order of St. Francis.*—O.S.F.
[2575]—*Institute of the Sisters of Mercy of the Americas.*—R.S.M.
[2710]—*Missionaries of Charity.*—M.C.
[3230]—*Poor Handmaids of Jesus Christ.*—P.H.J.C.
[2970]—*School Sisters of Notre Dame.*—S.S.N.D.
[1680]—*School Sisters of St. Francis.*—O.S.F.
[3520]—*Servants of the Holy Heart of Mary.*—S.S.C.M.
[0430]—*Sisters of Charity of the Blessed Virgin Mary.*—B.V.M.
[0660]—*Sisters of Christian Charity.*—S.C.C.
[2450]—*Sisters of Mary of the Presentation.*—S.M.P.
[3360]—*Sisters of Providence of Saint Mary-of-the-Woods, Indiana.*—S.P.
[1540]—*Sisters of Saint Francis, Clinton, Iowa.*—O.S.F.
[1705]—*The Sisters of St. Francis of Assisi.*—O.S.F.

[1580]—*Sisters of St. Francis of the Immaculate Conception.*—O.S.F.

[3840]—*Sisters of St. Joseph of Corondelet.*—C.S.J.

[]—*Sisters of the Community of St. John.*

[1820]—*Sisters of the Third Order of St. Francis (East Peoria, Illinois).*—O.S.F.

DIOCESAN CEMETERIES

PEORIA. *Catholic Cemetery Association of Peoria, IL.* Tel: 309-674-2760. Operates St. Mary's Cemetery, St. Joseph's Cemetery and Resurrection Cemetery in Peoria.

BLOOMINGTON. *Holy Cross Cemetery Association of Bloomington, IL.* Tel: 309-829-2197.

DANVILLE. *Resurrection Catholic Cemetery Association of Danville, IL.* Tel: 217-431-5100.

FARMER CITY. *St. Joseph Cemetery Association of Farmer City, IL.* Tel: 309-928-3855.

GALESBURG. *St. Joseph's Cemetery Association of Galesburg, IL.* Tel: 309-342-1913.

PEKIN. *Catholic Cemetery Association of Pekin, IL.* Tel: 309-347-6109.

ROCK ISLAND. *Calvary Cemetery Association of Rock Island, IL.* Tel: 309-788-6197; 764-1928.

NECROLOGY

† Carton, Rev. Msgr. George A., (Retired). —Died March 18, 2000.

† Huguet, Dean M., Westville, IL Church of St. Mary. —Died April 20, 2000.

† Lassuy, Raymond J., (Retired). —Died Aug. 17, 2000.

† McDermott, Paul B., (Absent on Leave). —Died May 19, 2000.

† Robards, Charles P., Thomasboro, IL Church of St. Elizabeth. —Died Dec. 31, 1999.

† Ryan, John J., (Absent on Leave). —Died Feb. 19, 2000.

Archdiocese of Philadelphia

(Archidioecesis Philadelphiensis)

His Eminence

ANTHONY CARDINAL BEVILACQUA, D.D., M.A., J.C.D., J.D.

Archbishop of Philadelphia; ordained June 11, 1949; appointed Titular Bishop of Aquaealba and Auxiliary Bishop of Brooklyn October 7, 1980; consecrated November 24, 1980; appointed Bishop of Pittsburgh October 7, 1983; installed December 12, 1983; installed Archbishop of Philadelphia February 11, 1988; Created Cardinal Priest June 28, 1991. *Office: 222 N. 17th St., Philadelphia, PA, 19103-1299; All official correspondence should be sent to this office.*

Most Reverend

ROBERT P. MAGINNIS, D.D., V.G.

Auxiliary Bishop of Philadelphia and Titular Bishop of Siminina; ordained May 13, 1961; consecrated March 11, 1996. *Res., St. Colman Rectory, 11 Simpson Rd., Ardmore, PA, 19003-2812.* Tel.: 610-642-0545.

Most Reverend

JOSEPH F. MARTINO, D.D., V.G.

Auxiliary Bishop of Philadelphia and Titular Bishop of Cellae in Mauritania; ordained December 18, 1970; consecrated March 11, 1996. *Res., St. Charles Borromeo Seminary, Overbrook, 100 E. Wynnewood Rd., Wynnewood, PA, 19096.* Tel.: 610-667-3394.

Most Reverend

MARTIN N. LOHMULLER, D.D.

Retired Auxiliary Bishop of Philadelphia and Titular Bishop of Ramsbury; ordained June 3, 1944; appointed Auxiliary Bishop of Philadelphia and Titular Bishop of Ramsbury February 11, 1970; consecrated April 2, 1970; retired October 11, 1994. *Res., Villa Maria House of Studies, King Rd., P.O. Box 701, Immaculata, PA, 19345.*

Most Reverend

LOUIS A. DE SIMONE, D.D.

Retired Auxiliary Bishop of Philadelphia and Titular Bishop of Cillio; ordained May 10, 1952; appointed Auxiliary Bishop of Philadelphia and Titular Bishop of Cillio June 27, 1981; consecrated August 12, 1981; retired April 2, 1997. *Res., St. Monica Church, 2422 S. 17th St., Philadelphia, PA, 19145.*

The Chancery: 222 N. 17th St., Philadelphia, PA, 19103-1299. Tel.: 215-587-4538; Fax: 215-587-3907.

Web site address: www.archdiocese-phl.org

E-mail address: chancery@adphila.org

DIOCESE ESTABLISHED APRIL 8, 1808.

ERECTED AN ARCHDIOCESE FEBRUARY 12, 1875.

Square Miles 2183.28.

Comprises all the City and County of Philadelphia, and the Counties of Bucks, Chester, Delaware and Montgomery in the State of Pennsylvania.

PATRONS OF THE DIOCESE: I. Immaculate Conception B.V.M., December 8; II. Saints Peter and Paul, Apostles, June 29. This Archdiocese was solemnly consecrated to the Sacred Heart of Jesus on the Feast of Saint Teresa of Avila, October 15, 1873. On May 23, 1952, the Archdiocese of Philadelphia was solemnly consecrated to the Immaculate Heart of Mary at the Shrine of Our Lady of Fatima, Portugal.

For legal titles of parishes and archdiocesan institutions, consult The Chancery.

STATISTICAL OVERVIEW

Personnel	
Cardinal	1
Auxiliary Bishops	2
Retired Bishops	2
Abbots	1
Retired Abbots	1
Priests: Diocesan Active in Diocese	567
Priests: Active Outside Diocese	24
Priests: Diocesan in Foreign Missions	5
Priests: Retired, Sick or Absent	177
Number of Diocesan Priests	773
Religious Priests in Diocese	407
Extern Priests in Diocese	40
Ordinations:	
Diocesan Priests	10
Religious Priests	1
Transitional Deacons	3
Permanent Deacons	14
Permanent Deacons in Diocese	188
Total Brothers	125
Total Sisters	3,711
Parishes	
Parishes	283
With Resident Pastor:	
Resident Diocesan Priests	260
Resident Religious Priests	23
Missions	7
Pastoral Centers	20
New Parishes Created	3
Closed Parishes	6
Professional Ministry Personnel:	
Brothers	4
Sisters	182

Lay Ministers	246
Welfare	
Catholic Hospitals	8
Total Assisted	830,526
Health Care Centers	9
Total Assisted	235
Homes for the Aged	20
Total Assisted	7,058
Residential Care of Children	5
Total Assisted	926
Day Care and Extended Day Care Centers	2
Total Assisted	165
Specialized Homes	5
Total Assisted	1,504
Special Centers for Social Services	15
Total Assisted	93,530
Residential Care of Disabled	5
Total Assisted	372
Other Institutions	7
Total Assisted	12,309
Educational	
Seminaries, Diocesan	1
Students from This Diocese	59
Students from Other Diocese	86
Seminaries, Religious	1
Students Religious	20
Total Seminarians	79
Colleges and Universities	11
Total Students	33,161
High Schools, Diocesan and Parish	22
Total Students	23,148

High Schools, Private	15
Total Students	7,259
Elementary Schools, Diocesan and Parish	214
Total Students	81,672
Elementary Schools, Private	20
Total Students	5,205
Non-residential Schools for the Disabled	5
Total Students	356
Catechesis/Religious Education:	
High School Students	7,596
Elementary Students	51,007
Total Students Under Catholic Instruction	209,483
Teachers in the Diocese:	
Priests	148
Brothers	55
Sisters	746
Lay Teachers	9,091
Vital Statistics	
Receptions into the Church:	
Infant Baptism Totals	18,074
Adult Baptism Totals	1,296
Received into Full Communion	684
First Communions	15,308
Confirmations	13,610
Marriages:	
Catholic	4,569
Interfaith	1,940
Total Marriages	6,509
Deaths	12,896
Total Catholic Population	1,430,161
Total Population	3,707,238

Former Bishops—Most Rev. MICHAEL FRANCIS EGAN, O.F.M., D.D., cons. Oct. 28, 1810; died July 22, 1814.—Most Rev. HENRY CONWELL, D.D., cons. Sept. 24, 1820; died April 22, 1842.—Most Rev. FRANCIS PATRICK KENRICK, D.D., cons. June 6, 1830; transferred to Baltimore in 1851; died July 8, 1863.—Saint JOHN NEPOMUCENE NEUMANN, C.SS.R., D.D., cons. March 28, 1852; died Jan. 5, 1860 Canonized June 19, 1977.—Most Rev. JAMES FREDERIC WOOD, D.D., cons. coadjutor, cum iure successionis, April 26, 1857; Bishop of Philadelphia, Jan. 5, 1860; appt. Archbishop Feb. 12, 1875; Sacred Pallium, June 17, 1875; died June 20, 1883.—Most Rev. PATRICK JOHN RYAN, D.D., cons. April 14, 1872 Bishop of Tricomia and Coadjutor with right of succession to the Archbishop of St. Louis; appt. Titular Archbishop of Salamis, Jan. 6, 1884 Archbishop of Philadelphia, June 8, 1884; died Feb. 11, 1911.—Most Rev. EDMOND FRANCIS PRENDERGAST, D.D., cons. Feb. 24, 1897, Titular Bishop of Scillio; Auxiliary Bishop of Philadelphia; Archbishop of Philadelphia, May 27, 1911; died Feb. 26, 1918.—His Eminence DENNIS CARDINAL DOUGHERTY, appt. Bishop of Nueva Segovia, P.I., April 7, 1903; cons. June 14, 1903; transferred to Jaro, P.I., April 19, 1908; transferred to Buffalo Nov. 30, 1915; transferred to Philadelphia April 30, 1918; installed as

Archbishop of Philadelphia July 10, 1918 Pallium conferred May 6, 1919; created Cardinal Priest, March 7, 1921; died May 31, 1951.—His Eminence JOHN CARDINAL O'HARA, C.S.C., appt. Military Delegate of Armed Forces and Titular Bishop of Mylasa Dec. 11, 1939; cons. Jan. 15, 1940; transferred to Buffalo Mar. 10, 1945; transferred to Philadelphia Nov. 28, 1951; installed as Archbishop of Philadelphia Jan. 9, 1952 Pallium conferred Jan. 12, 1953; created Cardinal Priest Dec. 15, 1958; died Aug. 28, 1960.—His Eminence JOHN CARDINAL KROL, D.D., J.C.D., ord. Feb. 20, 1937; appt. Titular Bishop of Cadi and Auxiliary Bishop of Cleveland July 11, 1953; cons. Sept. 2, 1953; appt. Archbishop of Philadelphia Feb. 11, 1961; created Cardinal Priest June 26, 1967; retired Feb. 11, 1988; died March 3, 1996.

Vicars General—Most Rev. ROBERT P. MAGINNIS, D.D., V.G. Tel: 610-642-0545. Most Rev. JOSEPH F. MARTINO, D.D., V.G. Tel: 610-667-3394. Rev. Msgr. JOSEPH R. CISTONE, V.G. Tel: 215-587-4507.

Office of the Cardinal Archbishop—His Eminence ANTHONY CARDINAL BEVILACQUA, D.D., M.A., J.C.D., J.D., Archbishop of Philadelphia; Rev. JOHN J. MCINTYRE, Admin. Sec. to the Cardinal Archbishop, *222 N. 17th St., Philadelphia, 19103-1299.* Tel: 215-587-3800.

Office of the Vicar for Administration—Rev. Msgr. JOSEPH R. CISTONE, V.G., Vicar General. Tel: 215-587-4507; Fax: 215-587-4545. Rev. Msgr. MICHAEL T. MCCULKEN, Asst. Vicar Admin. Tel: 215-587-4511. Assocs. to the Vicar Admin.: Rev. JOSEPH P. DUNCAN; Bro. JOSEPH WILLARD, F.S.C.; Mr. JAMES J. BOCK, JR.; Sr. LINDA M. SARIEGO, O.S.F., *222 N. 17th St., Philadelphia, 19103-1299.*

Regional Vicars—Rev. JAMES D. BEISEL, Vicar for Bucks County, *685 York Rd., Warminster, 18974.* Tel: 215-957-1525. Rev. Msgr. JAMES T. MCDONOUGH, A.C.S.W., Vicar for Chester County, *2 Forrest Lane, Strafford, 19087-2504.* Tel: 610-995-9450. Rev. THOMAS J. SMITH, Vicar for Delaware County, *1797 S. Sproul Rd., Springfield, 19064-1195.* Tel: 610-543-6759. Rev. Msgr. JOHN C. MARINE, Vicar for Montgomery County, *354 Conshohocken State Rd., Gladwyne, 19035.* Tel: 610-896-0567. Rev. Msgr. FRANCIS W. BEACH, Vicar for Philadelphia-North, *240 Hermitage St., Philadelphia, 19127.* Tel: 215-508-4250. Rev. Msgr. JOHN T. CONWAY, Vicar for Philadelphia-South, *525 Cobbs Pkwy., Philadelphia, 19143.* Tel: 215-476-7484. The Vicar for Philadelphia-South Supervises The St. Peter Claver Evangelization Center. *502 S. 12th St., Philadelphia, 19147.* Tel: 215-735-3164. The Vicar for Philadelphia-North Supervises The Catholic Institute for Evangelization. *4404 N. 5th St., Philadelphia, 19104.* Tel: 215-324-8291.

Office of the Vicar for Religious—

Vicar for Religious—Rev. Msgr. ALEXANDER J. PALMIERI, J.C.L.

Coordinator for Vocations to Religious Life—Sr. KATHLEEN LEARY, S.S.J., Office: *222 N. 17th St., Philadelphia, 19103-1299.* Tel: 215-587-3795; Fax: 215-587-3790.

The Chancery—Rev. Msgr. ALEXANDER J. PALMIERI, J.C.L., Chancellor; Rev. JAMES M. OLIVER, J.C.D., Vice Chancellor, *222 North 17th St., Philadelphia, 19103-1299.* Tel: 215-587-4538; Fax: 215-587-3907.

Catholic Heritage Center—Rev. Msgr. ALEXANDER J. PALMIERI, J.C.L., Chm. Exec. Committee; KATHLEEN S. KAHLAU, Project Coord., *320 Walnut St., Philadelphia, 19106.* Tel: 215-587-4538; Fax: 215-587-3907., *Mailing Address: 222 N. 17th St., Philadelphia, 19103-1299.* For complete entry, refer to "Miscellaneous" listings.

Archivist—JOSEPH J. CASINO, M.A., M.S.L.S., Office: *St. Charles Borromeo Seminary, 100 E. Wynnewood Rd., Wynnewood, 19096-3001.* Tel: 610-667-2125.

Metropolitan Tribunal—*222 N. 17th St., Philadelphia, 19103-1299.* Tel: 215-587-3750; Fax: 215-587-0508. Communications should be sent to the above address.

Judicial Vicar—Rev. Msgr. JAMES J. GRAHAM, J.C.D.

Assistant Judicial Vicars—Revs. JOSEPH C. DIECKHAUS, J.C.L.; PAUL A. DIGIROLAMO, J.C.D.; EDUARDO G. MONTERO, J.C.L.

Archdiocesan Judges—Revs. MICHAEL J. FITZGERALD, J.D., J.C.D.; STEVEN J. HARRIS, J.C.D.; ALEXANDER J. PALMIERI, J.C.L.; Rev. Msgr. SAMUEL E. SHOEMAKER, J.C.D.; Rev. Msgr. VINCENT M. WALSH, J.C.D.; Sr. CARLOTTA BARTONE, S.H.C.J., J.C.L.

Promoter of Justice—Rev. THOMAS A. KANE, J.C.D.; Rev. Msgr. VINCENT M. WALSH, J.C.D.

Defenders of the Bond—Revs. JOHN P. BOLAND, M.A.; THOMAS A. KANE, J.C.D.; GERARD C. MESURE, J.C.D.; JAMES M. OLIVER, J.C.D.; ROBERT J. POWELL, D.M.A.; JOHN D. REARDON, M.Div.; Ms. MELISSA L. TRUMAN, J.C.L.; Rev. VINCENT F. WELSH, J.C.L.

Approved Advocates—Revs. EDWARD H. BELL, M.Div.; JOSEPH W. BONGARD, M.A.; JOSEPH E. HOWARTH, M.A.L.S.; MARK J. HUNT, S.T.L.; W. FRED KINDON, M.A.; KENNETH P. MCATEER, M.Div.; JOSEPH J. NICOLO, M.Div.; DANIEL J. SULLIVAN, M.A.; THOMAS J. WISNIEWSKI, M.Div.; KARL A. ZEUNER, S.T.L.; Sr. CAROL MOCKUS, C.S.F.N.; Deacons EDWARD A. KONARSKI; JOHN C. HYNES.

Secretary—Rev. JOHN D. REARDON, M.Div.

Notaries—JOAN MCDOWELL; WINIFRED CANNON; MARY KAY DEVLIN.

Office of the Vicar for Renewal and Evangelization—Rev. Msgr. CHARLES V. DEVLIN, Vicar, *222 N. 17th St., Philadelphia, 19103-1299.* Tel: 215-587-0500; Fax: 215-587-0502.

Associate to the Vicar—Mr. JOHN J. TAGUE, M.A. Tel: 215-587-0547; Fax: 215-587-0502.

Assistant to the Vicar—Sr. ELLEN CAVANAUGH, R.S.M. Tel: 215-587-0551; Fax: 215-587-0502.

Program Coordinator—Sr. MERCEDES ROJO, O.S.F. Tel: 215-965-1707; Fax: 215-587-0502.

Coordinator and Financial Manager—Mrs. ANITA GUZZARDI. Tel: 215-587-0504; Fax: 215-587-0502.

Office for Ecumenical and Interreligious Affairs—Most Rev. JOSEPH F. MARTINO, D.D., H.E.D., Dir., *222 N. 17th St., Philadelphia, 19103-1299.* Tel: 215-587-3624; Fax: 215-587-3628.

Management Information Services—Mr. MARK S. HOJNOWSKI, Dir. Tel: 215-587-3567; Fax: 215-587-3808.

Office for Audit Services—Mr. PHILIP H. GALLAGHER, JR., C.P.A., Dir. Tel: 215-587-2474; Fax: 215-587-0512.

Office for General Services—Tel: 215-587-3633.

Special Projects—Rev. Msgr. LOUIS A. D'ADDEZIO, Dir. Tel: 215-587-3992; Fax: 215-587-2481. Mr. VINCENT E. PIERSANTE, Coord. Building Svcs. Tel: 215-587-3519. Mr. GEORGE G. SHARRETTS, Coord. Special Projects. Tel: 215-587-3962.

Ecclesiastical Exchange Program—Tel: 215-587-3996.

Office for Research and Planning—ROBERT J. MILLER, Ed.D., Dir. Tel: 215-587-3545; Fax: 215-587-3817.

Secretariat for Catholic Education

All addresses are: 222 N. 17th St., Philadelphia, PA 19103-1299 unless otherwise indicated

Secretary for Catholic Education—Rev. Msgr. PHILIP J. CRIBBEN, M.A. Tel: 215-587-3700; Fax: 215-587-5644; 587-5638.

Office of Catholic Education—Rev. Msgr. PHILIP J. CRIBBEN, M.A., Sec. for Catholic Educ.; Dr. RICHARD V. MCCARRON, JR., Supt. of Schools. Asst. Supts.: Dr. KATHLEEN CARDAMONE, Secondary Schools; Deacon THOMAS F. O'BRIEN, Ph.D., Ed.D., Elementary & Secondary Curriculum and Instruction; Dr. MARY RITA CLEARY, Elementary; Dr. ELIZABETH O'DONNELL, Spec. Educ.

Office for Youth and Young Adults—Rev. THOMAS M. HIGGINS, Dir.; Mr. LEONARD J. DIPAUL, Asst. Dir., *105 Argyle Rd., Ardmore, 19003.* Tel: 610-649-9476.

Parish Youth Ministry—Mr. LEONARD J. DIPAUL, Dir. Tel: 610-649-9410.

Archdiocesan Boy Scout—Rev. JOHN B. WENDRYCHOWICZ, Chap. Tel: 610-649-9476.

Camp Neumann Conference Center—STEPHEN TAYLOR, Dir. Tel: 215-343-6552.

Community Service Corps—KATHLEEN O'DONNELL, Dir. Tel: 215-567-4280.

Young Adult Ministry—MATTHEW MANION, Coord., *Office for Youth and Young Adults, 105 Argyle Rd., Ardmore, 19003.* Tel: 610-649-9476; Fax: 610-649-9520.

Secretariat For Catholic Human Services

All addresses are: 222 N. 17th St., Philadelphia, PA 19103-1299. Tel: 215-587-3900, unless otherwise indicated

Secretary for Catholic Human Services—Rev. Msgr. TIMOTHY C. SENIOR, L.S.W., M.B.A. Tel: 215-587-3903. Rev. JOSEPH A. TRACY, S.T.L., M.A., Deputy Sec. Tel: 215-587-3908.

Chief Financial Officer—Mr. EDWARD T. CAHILL. Tel: 215-587-3889.

Information Technology Services—*227 N. 18th St., Philadelphia, 19103.* Tel: 215-854-7067. LOUISE MAIA, M.S., Information Systems; LEE MYERS, Information Technologies.

Catholic Social Services (300)—

Catholic Charities of the Archdiocese of Philadelphia—Rev. Msgr. TIMOTHY C. SENIOR, L.S.W., M.B.A., Exec. Dir. Tel: 215-587-3903. JAMES AMATO, L.S.W., Deputy Sec. for Catholic Social Svcs. Tel: 215-587-3754. Mr. EDWARD T. CAHILL, Chief Financial Officer.Tel: 215-587-3889. TERESA THOMPSON, L.S.W., Dir. Children Svcs. Tel: 215-587-0529. KAREN K. BECKER, L.S.W., Dir. Family Svcs. Tel: 215-587-3590. Ms. LORRAINE KNIGHT, M.Ed., Dir. Administrative & Support Svcs. Tel: 215-587-3906. JOHN M. WAGNER, Dir. Housing & Homeless Svcs. Tel: 215-587-3589. Bro. DENNIS MALLOY, F.S.C., Dir. Juvenile Justice Svcs., *St. Gabriel's System, 117 S. 17th St., Philadelphia, 19103.* Tel: 215-665-8777. MARK E. FITZGERALD, N.H.A., Dir. Mental Retardation Svcs., Administrative Office: *1797 S. Sproul Rd., Springfield, 19064.* Tel: 610-543-5410.

Family Service Centers—

Philadelphia Family Services Center City—MARTIN R. FRICK, L.S.W., M.P.A., Admin., *227 N. 18th St., Philadelphia, 19103.* Tel: 215-854-7090.

North Philadelphia Service Center—*Casa del Carmen, 4400 N. Reese St., Philadelphia, 19140.* Tel: 215-329-5660. W. GIOVANNI MORANTE, M.A., Admin.

Northeast Philadelphia Service Center—*7340 Jackson St., Philadelphia, 19136.* Tel: 215-624-5920. AMY STONER, L.S.W., Admin.

Bucks County Service Center—*100 Levittown Pkwy., Levittown, 19054.* Tel: 215-945-2550., *607 W. Street Rd., Warminster, 18974.* Tel: 215-957-6699.

Sellersville—*427 N. Main St., Sellersville, 18960.* Tel: 215-453-7098. MARGUERITE POWERS, L.S.W., Asst. Dir.

Chester County Service Center—*141 E. Lancaster Ave., Downingtown, 19335.* Tel: 610-269-4060., *105 Prospect Ave., West Grove, 19390.* Tel: 610-869-6500. WILLIAM KEFER, L.S.W., Admin.

Delaware County Service Center—*130 E. 7th St., Chester City, 19013.* Tel: 610-876-9183., *240 N. Bishop Ave., Springfield, 19064.* Tel: 610-626-6550. JAMES MCMASTER, M.B.A., Admin.

Montgomery County Service Center—*353 E. Johnson Hwy., Norristown, 19401.* Tel: 610-279-7372. Sr. PATRICIA KELLY, M.S.B.T., M.S.W., Admin.

Specialized Services—

Senior Adult Services—GEORGE SALLOOM, L.S.W., Admin. Tel: 215-854-7070.

Immigration Services—*227 N. 18th St., Philadelphia, 19103.* PHYLLIS FORMAN, Esq. Tel: 215-854-7019.

Adoption Services—*227 N. 18th St., Philadelphia, 19103.* Tel: 215-854-7050. MARY LARK MERMAN, L.S.W., Admin.

Child Care—Tel: 215-587-3575. SUZANNE O'GRADY, M.S.S., Admin.

Housing/Homeless Services—*227 N. 18th St., Philadelphia, 19103.* Tel: 215-854-7060. DEBORAH WAGNER, L.S.W., Admin.

Office for Human Relations—VELMA J. CLARK, M.A., Dir. Tel: 215-587-5655.

Volunteer & Community Relations—*227 N. 18th St., Philadelphia, 19103.* Tel: 215-854-7058. WILLIAM TANGRADI, M.S.W., Mgr.

Nutritional Development Services—PATRICK F.E. TEMPLE-WEST, Dir., *111 S. 38th St., Philadelphia, 19104.* Tel: 215-895-3470.

Catholic Health Care Services—Rev. Msgr. TIMOTHY C. SENIOR, L.S.W., M.B.A., Exec. Dir. Tel: 215-587-3903. JUDITH A. PASSERINI, C.N.H.A., Deputy Sec. Catholic Health Care Svcs. Tel: 215-587-2436. JOSEPH J. SWEENEY, JR., Chief Financial Officer. Tel: 215-368-0900, Ext. 3104. LOUISE M. SULLIVAN, Dir. Facility Based Svcs., N.H.A. Tel: 215-587-2496. KENNETH P. LEWIS, Dir. Planning & Prog. Devel., M.S.W., B.C.D., N.H.A. Tel: 215-587-2487. BEVERLEE JOHANNSEN, R.N., Asst. Dir. Quality Assurance. Tel: 215-587-3663.

Secretariat For Catholic Life and Formation

All addresses are: 222 N. 17th St., Philadelphia, PA 19103-1299. Fax: 215-587-3561, unless otherwise indicated

Secretary for Catholic Life and Formation—BERNADETTE A. O'CONNELL, M.S., L.S.W. Tel: 215-587-5629.

Deputy Secretary for Catholic Life and Formation—THOMAS WAVRO, A.M. Tel: 215-587-5667.

Office for Black Catholics—Sr. BORETA A. SINGLETON, I.H.M., Dir. Tel: 215-587-3634.

Family Life Office—ELEANOR LEGATES, Dir., *100 E. Wynnewood Rd., Wynnewood, 19096-3069.* Tel: 610-660-9002.

Office for Hispanic Catholics—ANNA C. VEGA, Dir. Tel: 215-587-3786.

Office for Formation of the Laity—DOMINIC LOMBARDI, S.T.L., Dir. Tel: 215-587-5630.

Parish Pastoral Councils—MARY GINDHART, Program Coord. Tel: 215-587-3694.

Prison Ministry Program—LAURA FORD RUCINSKI, Coord. Tel: 215-331-3640.

Church Ministry Institute—MARYANNE HARRINGTON, Coord., *100 E. Wynnewood Rd., Wynnewood, 19096-3099.* Tel: 610-617-7275.

Office for Pastoral Care of Migrants and Refugees—Rev. THOMAS BETZ, O.F.M.Cap., Dir. Tel: 215-587-3540.

Apostleship of the Sea—Vacant, Coord., *Seamen's Church Institute, 249 Arch St., Philadelphia, 19106.* Tel: 215-922-2562.

Cambodian Apostolate—Sr. MARY THERESA NGUYEN, A.C.J., Contact, *St. Thomas Aquinas Rectory, 1719 Morris St., Philadelphia, 19145.* Tel: 215-334-2312.

Chinese Apostolates—During regular school hours call 215-922-0999; other times call St. John the Evangelist Rectory. Tel: 215-563-4145.

Filipino Apostolate—Sr. LORETTO MAPA, R.A., Coord., *St. Thomas Aquinas Rectory, 1719 Morris St., Philadelphia, 19145.* Tel: 215-334-2312.

Haitian Apostolate—Rev. JEAN-CLAUDE MOMPOINT, Coord., Office: *Incarnation of Our Lord, 5105 N. 5th St., Philadelphia, 19120.* Tel: 215-329-2320.

Indian Apostolate, Syro Malabar Rite—Rev. JOHN THARAYIL, C.M.I., *St. Thomas Aquinas, 601 Bristol Pike, Croydon, 19021-5496.*

Indian Apostolate, Syro Malankara Rite—Rev. CHACKO VARGHESE, Coord., *Incarnation of Our Lord, 5th St. & Lindley Ave., Philadelphia, 19120.* Tel: 215-329-2320.

Indian Apostolate-Knanayan Comm.—Rev. THOMAS VATTOTHUPARAMBIL, Coord., Office: *St. Anthony of Padua, 259 Forest Ave., Ambler, 19002.* Tel: 215-646-4742.

Indian Apostolate, Latin Rite—Rev. RAJU B. SELVARAJ, *St. Mary Medical Center, Langhorne-Newtown Rd., Langhorne, 19047.* Tel: 215-750-2000.

Irish Apostolate—Rev. GERARD BURNS, Coord., Office: *St. Cyril of Alexandria, 153 Penn Blvd., East Lansdowne, 19050.* Tel: 610-623-1929.

Korean Apostolate—Rev. MARTIN KIM, Coord., *Holy Angels, 7000 Old York Rd., Philadelphia, 19125.* Tel: 215-548-5535.

Laotian Apostolate—Contact: Office for Pastoral Care for Migrants & Refugees. Tel: 215-587-3540.

Portuguese Apostolate—Rev. JONAS V. DEMORAES, Coord., *Office: Incarnation of Our Lord Rectory, 5105 N. 5th St., Philadelphia, 19120.* Tel: 215-329-2320.

Vietnamese Apostolate—Rev. JOSEPH DINH, Coord., Office: *St. Thomas Aquinas, 1719 Morris St., Philadelphia, 19145.* Tel: 215-334-2312.

Respect Life Office—HELEN P. KELLEHER, Dir. Tel: 215-587-5661.

Department for AIDS Ministry—Vacant, Admin. Tel: 215-587-3839.

Department for Pastoral Care for Persons with Disabilities—HELEN P. KELLEHER, Admin. Tel: 215-587-3530 (Voice); 0510 (TDD).

Apostolate to Deaf Persons—Rev. ANTHONY RUSSO, C.SS.R., Coord., *St. Boniface Church, 174 Diamond St., Philadelphia, 19122.* Tel: 215-423-9547 (Voice/TDD).

Department for Pro-Life Activities—KAREN CAHILL, Admin. Tel: 215-587-3703. Rev. PAUL S. QUINTER, S.T.D., M.S., Delegate of the Cardinal to Pro-Life Organizations. Tel: 215-587-3703.

Pontifical Society for the Propagation of the Faith—Rev. Msgr. JAMES J. FITZPATRICK, Dir. Tel: 215-587-3944.

Pontifical Society of St. Peter Apostle—Rev. Msgr. JAMES FITZPATRICK, Dir. Tel: 215-587-3944.

Pontifical Missionary Society of the Holy Childhood (Holy Childhood Assn.)—Rev. Msgr. JAMES FITZPATRICK, Dir. Tel: 215-587-3944.

Pontifical Missionary Union—Rev. Msgr. JAMES FITZPATRICK, Dir. Tel: 215-587-3944.

Office for Worship—Rev. DANIEL E. MACKLE, Dir. Tel: 215-587-3537.

Secretariat For Clergy

All addresses are: 222 N. 17th St., Philadelphia, PA 19103-1299 unless otherwise indicated.

Secretary for Clergy—Rev. Msgr. WILLIAM J. LYNN. Tel: 215-587-4532.

Office for Clergy—

Department Priest Personnel—Rev. Msgr. WILLIAM J. LYNN, Dir.; Rev. VINCENT F. WELSH, Asst. Dir. Tel: 215-587-4532.

Priests' Personnel Board—Most Rev. ROBERT P. MAGINNIS; Most Rev. JOSEPH F. MARTINO; Rev. Msgr. FRANCIS W. BEACH; Revs. JAMES D. BEISEL; LOUIS P. BELLOPEDE; Rev. Msgr. JOHN J. CAULFIELD; Rev. Msgr. JOSEPH R. CISTONE; Rev. Msgr. JOHN T. CONWAY; Rev. Msgr. JAMES J. GRAHAM; Rev. Msgr. WILLIAM J. LYNN; Rev. Msgr. JOHN C. MARINE; Rev. Msgr. JAMES T. MCDONOUGH; Revs. THOMAS J. DUNLEAVY; JOSEPH P. MCGEOWN; THOMAS J. SMITH; CHARLES P. VANCE.

Department of Chaplaincies—Vacant.

Department of Continuing Formation for Diocesan Priests—Revs. JOSEPH P. GENTILI, Dir. MATTHEW J. KORNACKI, Asst. Dir.

Department Retired Clergy—Rev. Msgr. FRANCIS A. MENNA, Admin.

Department Permanent Deacons—Rev. DENNIS J. CARBONARO, Admin.; Sr. VERONICA GROSS, R.S.M., Asst. Admin., *St. Charles Borromeo Seminary, 100 E. Wynnewood Rd., Wynnewood, 19096.* Tel: 610-664-2213.

St. Charles Borromeo Seminary—Rev. Msgr. MICHAEL F. BURBIDGE, M.A., Ed.D., Rector, *100 E. Wynnewood Rd., Wynnewood, 19096.* Tel: 610-667-3394.

Vocation Office for Diocesan Priesthood—Rev. JOSEPH P. DEVLIN, Dir., *St. Charles Borromeo Seminary, 100 E. Wynnewood Rd., Wynnewood, 19096.* Tel: 610-667-5778.

Secretariat For Temporal Services

All addresses are: 222 N. 17th St., Philadelphia, PA 19103 unless otherwise indicated.

Temporal Services—Mr. GLENN J. MASAKOWSKI, M.MGT., Sec. & CFO. Tel: 215-587-3959; Fax: 215-587-0599. Ms. MAUREEN VAN THUYNE, Deputy Sec. Tel: 215-587-3958; Fax: 215-587-0599. Assistant Secretaries: Mr. EDWARD M. MERENDA, M.B.A., C.P.A., C.I.A. Tel: 215-587-2435; Fax: 215-587-3939. Mr. FRANCIS P. COUGHLIN, M.A., M.S. Tel: 215-587-5654; Fax: 215-587-0599.

Investment Services—Mr. ROBERT J. GUNN. Tel: 215-587-3969; Fax: 215-587-3939.

Capital Projects Office—Mr. ARTHUR FRIEDMAN, M.S., Dir. Tel: 215-587-3560; Fax: 215-587-0599.

Catholic Cemeteries Office—Mr. ROBERT WHOMSLEY, Dir., *111 S. 38th St., Philadelphia, 19104.* Tel: 215-895-3450; Fax: 215-895-3458.

Human Resources Office—Mrs. MARLENE M. LOGLISCI, S.P.H.R., Dir. Tel: 215-587-3910; Fax: 215-587-3572.

Office for Insurance Services—CHARLES J. DEBEVEC, C.P.C.U., Dir. Tel: 215-587-3644; Fax: 215-587-2498.

Office for Legal Services—Rev. MICHAEL J. FITZGERALD, J.D., J.C.D., Dir. Tel: 215-587-0511; Fax: 215-587-0512.

Real Estate Office—EUGENE F. BRAZIL, ESQ., Dir. Tel: 215-587-2453; Fax: 215-587-0512.

Office for Accounting Services—Mrs. LAURA J. MONTGOMERY, Dir. Tel: 215-587-3943; Fax: 215-587-3939.

Parish Financial Services—Mr. EDWARD M. MERENDA, M.B.A., C.P.A., C.I.A. Tel: 215-587-2435; Fax: 215-587-3939.

Educational Financial Services—DAVID J. MAGEE, M.B.A., Ed.D., Dir. Tel: 215-587-3755; Fax: 215-587-3525.

Secretariat for External Affairs

All addresses are: 222 N. 17th St., Philadelphia, PA 19103-1299 unless otherwise indicated.

Secretary for External Affairs—STAN H. RETIF. Tel: 215-587-3507; Fax: 215-587-3649.

Office for Public Affairs—GUY L. CIARROCCHI, Dir. Tel: 215-587-3509; Fax: 215-587-0515.

Office for Communications—CATHERINE L. ROSSI, Dir. Tel: 215-587-3747; Fax: 215-587-3871.

Newspaper - "Catholic Standard and Times"—Rev. PAUL S. QUINTER, S.T.D., M.S., Editor. Tel: 215-587-3660; Fax: 215-587-3979.

Office for Development—STAN H. RETIF, Dir. Tel: 215-587-5650; Fax: 215-587-3647.

Catholic Charities Appeal/Planned Giving—ANTONIA BUTTO. Tel: 215-587-5650; Fax: 215-587-3647.

Business Leadership Organized for Catholic Schools—MEGHAN CAMPBELL. Tel: 215-587-0590; Fax: 215-587-2442.

Parish and Diocesan Stewardship—JERRY BOTTO. Tel: 215-587-3651; Fax: 215-587-3647.

Archdiocesan Offices, Boards, Commissions and Committees

All addresses are: 222 N. 17th St., Philadelphia, PA 19103-1299 unless otherwise indicated.

Blind, Guild for all the—Rev. EDMUND J. MAHER. Tel: 215-854-7042.

Board of Trustees of Lay Employees Retirement Plan—His Eminence ANTHONY CARDINAL BEVILACQUA, D.D., M.A., J.C.D., J.D., Chm.; Mr. GLENN J. MASAKOWSKI, Vice Chm.

Diocesan Priests' Compensation and Benefits Committee—Rev. Msgr. WILLIAM J. LYNN, Chm.; Rev. Msgr. JOHN E. BRESLIN; Rev. Msgr. FRANCIS A. MENNA; Rev. Msgr. LEON J. PECK; Revs. GREGORY J. FAIRBANKS; CHARLES E. GORMLEY; FRANCIS P. GROARKE; KENNETH W. SHARP; Mr. GLENN MASAKOWSKI; Mr. ROBERT SIMS; Revs. DANIEL J. SULLIVAN; SAMUEL A. VERRUNI; ROBERT C. VOGAN.

Building Committee—Rev. Msgr. RICHARD J. SKELLY, Chm. (Drawings of building plans are reviewed by this committee).

Cardinal's Committee for Christian Home and Family—ELEANOR LEGATES, M.A., Dir., *Family Life Office, 100 E. Wynnewood Rd., Wynnewood, 19096.* Tel: 610-660-9002.

Catholic Health Association of the United States, The—Rev. Msgr. TIMOTHY C. SENIOR, M.S.W., M.B.A., Moderator.

Catholic Relief Services—Rev. Msgr. WILLIAM J. PAUL, Dir., *St. John the Evangelist Church, 752 Big Oak Rd., Morrisville, 19067.* Tel: 215-295-4102.

Censores Librorum—Rev. Msgr. JOSEPH J. ANDERLONIS, S.T.D.; Rev. Msgr. FRANCIS A. BARSZCZEWSKI, S.T.L., M.S.L.S.; Rev. JOSEPH G. PRIOR, S.T.D., S.S.L., M.A.

Charismatic Prayer Groups—Contact Office for Formation of the Laity: Tel: 215-587-5642.

Charismatic Publication Office - Key of David Publications—Rev. Msgr. VINCENT M. WALSH, J.C.D., *Presentation B.V.M. Church, 204 Haverford Rd., Wynnewood, 19096.* Tel: 610-642-8341.

Church Ministry Institute—MARYANNE HARRINGTON, Coord., *St. Charles Borromeo Seminary, 100 E. Wynnewood Rd., Wynnewood, 19096.* Tel: 610-617-7275.

College of Consultors—His Eminence ANTHONY CARDINAL BEVILACQUA, D.D., J.C.D., M.A., J.D., Presider; Most Rev. ROBERT P. MAGINNIS, D.D., V.G.; Most Rev. JOSEPH F. MARTINO, D.D., V.G.; Rev. Msgr. JOSEPH R. CISTONE, V.G.; Rev. Msgr. WALTER J. CONWAY; Rev. Msgr. WILLIAM J. LYNN; Rev. Msgr. ROBERT T. MCMANUS; Rev. Msgr. ALBERT V. NORRELL; Rev. Msgr. ALEXANDER J. PALMIERI, J.C.L.; Rev. Msgr. BERNARD J. TRINITY; Revs. EDWARD H. BELL; MATTHEW J. KORNACKI.

Council of Managers for Development—Rev. Msgr. JOSEPH R. CISTONE, V.G., Chm.; Most Rev. ROBERT P. MAGINNIS, D.D., V.G., Vice Chm. Tel: 215-587-4507.

Council of Priests—His Eminence ANTHONY CARDINAL BEVILACQUA, D.D., J.C.D., M.A., J.D., Presider; Most Rev. ROBERT P. MAGINNIS, D.D., V.G.; Most Rev. JOSEPH F. MARTINO, D.D., V.G.; Rev. Msgr. JOSEPH R. CISTONE, V.G.; Rev. Msgr. JOHN E. BRESLIN; Rev. Msgr. MICHAEL F. BURBIDGE; Rev. Msgr. WILLIAM A. DOMBROW; Rev. Msgr. THOMAS J. HILFERTY; Rev. Msgr. JOHN J. JAGODZINSKI; Rev. Msgr. ALEXANDER J. PALMIERI, J.C.L.; Rev. Msgr. WILLIAM J. LYNN; Rev. Msgr. CHARLES V. DEVLIN; Rev. Msgr. ROBERT T. MCMANUS; Rev. Msgr. ALBERT V. NORRELL; Revs. ROBERT J. CARROLL; JAMES D. BEISEL; JAMES R. BAJOREK; THOMAS R. BETZ, O.F.M.Cap.; HENRY B. DEGNAN; MICHAEL F. DIGREGORIA, O.S.A.; MICHAEL F. HENNELLY; JOSEPH C. MCLOONE; MICHAEL S. OLIVERE; CHARLES J. SULLIVAN; Rev. FRANCIS X. MEEHAN.

Educational Fund—Office for Financial Services. Tel: 215-587-3959.

Holy Name Society—Rev. MICHAEL J. FITZPATRICK, Spiritual Dir., *St. Timothy Rectory, 3001 Levick St., Philadelphia, 19149.* Tel: 215-624-6188.

Information Line, Archdiocesan—Tel: 215-587-3600.

Interparochial Cooperation, Commission for—Rev. DANIEL J. SULLIVAN, *Holy Innocents Rectory, 1337 E. Hunting Park Ave., Philadelphia, 19124-4938.* Tel: 215-743-2600.

Legion of Mary—Rev. FRANCIS G. LENDACKY, *St. Agnes-St. John Nepomucane Rectory, 319 Brown St., Philadelphia, 19123-2228.* Tel: 215-627-0340.

Moderator of Priests Conferences—Rev. Msgr. WILLIAM J. LYNN, Sec. for Clergy. Tel: 215-587-4532.

Parish Sites and Boundaries, Commission for—Rev. Msgr. JAMES P. MCCOY, Chm.

Pastors Review Board—Rev. Msgr. JOHN E. BRESLIN; Rev. ROBERT J. CARROLL; Rev. Msgr. WILLIAM A. DOMBROW; Rev. Msgr. JOHN J. JAGODZINSKI; Revs. FRANCIS X. MEEHAN; CHARLES J. SULLIVAN.

Pennsylvania Catholic Conference—(Harrisburg). Board of Governors: His Eminence ANTHONY CARDINAL BEVILACQUA, D.D., M.A., J.C.D., J.D. Administrative Board: Rev. Msgr. JOSEPH R. CISTONE, V.G.; GUY L. CIARROCCHI, Esq. Education Department: Rev. Msgr. PHILIP J. CRIBBEN, M.A.; Dr. RICHARD V. MCCARRON, JR. Social Concerns: Rev. Msgr. TIMOTHY C. SENIOR, M.A., M.S.W., M.B.A.; HELEN KELLEHER.

Priests Eucharistic League—Rev. Msgr. JOHN E. GILLESPIE, Dir., *Motherhouse, Grey Nuns of the Sacred Heart, 1750 Quarry Rd., Yardley, 19067-2016.* Tel: 215-968-4236.

The Papal Foundation—Rev. Msgr. THOMAS J. BENESTAD, Exec. Dir. Tel: 215-587-4501., *222 N. 17th St., Philadelphia, 19103-1299.*

CLERGY, PARISHES, MISSIONS AND PAROCHIAL SCHOOLS

CITY OF PHILADELPHIA
(Philadelphia County)

1—CATHEDRAL BASILICA OF SS. PETER AND PAUL (1846), Rev. Msgr. John A. Close; Revs. Joseph C. McLoone; Michael A. Chapman. In res., Rev. Msgr. John J. Caulfield; Rev. Daniel E. Mackle; Deacon Epifano DeJesus.

Res., 1723 Race St., 19103. Tel: 215-561-1313; 1314; Fax: 215-561-1580.

Catechesis/Religious Programs—Students 75.

Chapel—Our Lady of the Miraculous Medal, Tel: 215-972-8116.

2—ST. ADALBERT (1904) (Polish), Rev. Msgr. Francis S. Feret; Rev. Msgr. Anthony E. Jaworowski, Pastor

Emeritus; Revs. Jerome H. Pohl; Robert Marczewski. In res., Rev. Thaddeus Gorka.
Res., 2645 E. Allegheny Ave., 19134. Tel: 215-739-3500; Fax: 215-739-5706.
School—3236 Edgemont St., 19134. Tel: 215-739-1920; Fax: 215-739-0519.
Sisters of the Holy Family of Nazareth 3; Lay Teachers 14; Students 284.

3—ST. AGATHA-ST. JAMES (1976). Consolidated. Rev. Karl A. Zeuner; Deacon Andre Guillet; Ms. Eileen Harding, Parish Svcs. Dir. Pastoral Assocs.: Revs. Charles J. Brinkman; George Strausser; Charles J. Pfeffer.
Res., 3728 Chestnut St., 19104. Tel: 215-386-9732; Fax: 215-386-5899.

4—ST. AGNES-ST. JOHN NEPOMUCENE (1907) (Slovak). Consolidated January 1, 1980. Rev. Francis G. Lendacky.
Res., 319 Brown St., 19123. Tel: 215-627-0340.

5—ALL SAINTS (Bridesburg) (1860), Rev. Edward P. Burke.
Res., 2651 Buckius St., 19137. Tel: 215-535-4411; Fax: 215-744-6533. [CEM]
School—4623 E. Thompson St., 19137. Tel: 215-743-0715; 535-3699.
Sisters of St. Francis of Philadelphia 2; Lay Teachers 9; Students 216.
Catechesis/Religious Programs—Students 70.

6—ALL SAINTS CHAPEL. Closed. (1877-1977) Formerly located at Philadelphia General Hospital, 700 Civic Center Blvd. Spiritual records are kept at St. Agatha-St. James Church. Tel.: 215-386-9732; 386-9733.

7—ST. ALOYSIUS (1894) (German), Rev. Thomas J. Rossi, O.Praem.
Res., c/o 2530 Wharton St., 19146. Tel: 215-468-1088; Fax: 215-468-2882.
School—Our Lady of Angels. See Consolidated Parish Schools under Institutions Located in the Archdiocese. Tel: 215-468-7230; Fax: 215-468-2554.
Catechesis/Religious Programs—Our Lady of Angels School, 30th & Dickinson Sts., Tel: 215-334-0374.
Students 53.

8—ST. ALPHONSUS. Closed. (1852-1972) Formerly located at 1400 S. Fourth St. Spiritual records are kept at Sacred Heart of Jesus Church. Tel.: 215-465-4050; 465-4051.

9—ST. AMBROSE (1923), Revs. James N. Catagnus; John M. Harkins; Deacons Jose M. Mendez; Luis Ruiz.
Res., 363 E. Roosevelt Blvd., 19120. Tel: 215-329-7900; 7901; Fax: 215-329-9206.
Church—C St. & Roosevelt Blvd., 19120.
School—405 E. Roosevelt Blvd., 19120. Tel: 215-457-3083.
Sisters of St. Joseph 2; Lay Teachers 13; Students 378.
Catechesis/Religious Programs—Tel: 215-455-8160.
Students 80.

10—ST. ANDREW (1924) (Lithuanian), Rev. Peter M. Burkauskas.
Res., 1913 Wallace St., 19130. Tel: 215-765-2322; Fax: 215-765-0124.

11—ST. ANNE (1845), Rev. Patrick E. Sweeney. In res., Rev. Joseph Tracy.
Res., 2328 E. Lehigh Ave., 19125. Tel: 215-739-4590; Fax: 215-739-0983. [CEM]
School—2343 E. Tucker St., 19125. Tel: 215-634-4231.
Sisters of St. Joseph 1; Lay Teachers 19; Students 437.
Catechesis/Religious Programs—Cedar & Tucker Sts.
Students 603.

12—ANNUNCIATION B.V.M. (1860) (Italian), Rev. Anthony J. D'Angelico. In res., Revs. Michael J. Fitzgerald; Eduardo G. Montero.
Res., 1511 S. 10th St., 19147. Tel: 215-334-0159; Fax: 215-462-5065.
School—12th & Wharton Sts., 19147. Tel: 215-465-1416; Fax: 215-465-0308.
Sisters, Servants of the Immaculate Heart of Mary 3; Lay Teachers 13; Students 317.
Catechesis/Religious Programs—Students 367.

13—ST. ANSELM (1962), Rev. Msgr. James J. Shields; Revs. Peter J. DiMaria; James A. Lyons. In res., Rev. Msgr. William A. Doolin; Deacon Gerald J. Whartenby.
Res., 12669 Dunks Ferry Rd., 19154. Tel: 215-637-3525; Fax: 215-637-4915.
School—12670 Dunks Ferry Rd., 19154. Tel: 215-632-1133; Fax: 215-632-3264. Sr. Honora Marie Johnston, Prin.
Sisters of the Immaculate Heart of Mary 8; Lay Teachers 29; Students 840.
Catechesis/Religious Programs—Students 168.

14—ST. ANTHONY OF PADUA (1886). Closed. Formerly Located at 2321 Fitzwater St. Spiritual records are kept at St. Charles Borromeo Church. Tel. 215-735-0600.

15—ASCENSION OF OUR LORD (1899), Revs. Michael J. McCleane; Paul A. Castellani; Deacon Leo Gladnick; Sr. Joan Ruthmiller, S.S.J., Dir. Parish Svcs.
Res., 725 E. Westmoreland St., 19134. Tel: 215-739-1670; Fax: 215-739-1455.
School—735 E. Westmoreland St., 19134. Tel: 215-739-6226. Teresa Richardson, M.A., Prin.
Sisters 2; Lay Teachers 10; Students 242.
Catechesis/Religious Programs—Sr. Catherine Langle, S.S.J., D.R.E.
Students 50.

16—ASSUMPTION B.V.M. (1848). Closed. (1848-1995) Formerly located at 1131 Spring Garden St. Spiritual records are kept at St. John the Evangelist Church. Tel.: 215-563-4145.

17—ST. ATHANASIUS (1928), Rev. Herbert A. Bevard.
Res., 2050 Walnut Ln., 19138. Tel: 215-548-2700; Fax: 215-548-7453.
School—St. Athanasius-Immaculate Conception School. See Consolidated Parish Schools under Institutions Located in the Archdiocese. Tel: 215-424-5045; Fax: 215-927-6615.
Sisters 4; Lay Teachers 11; Students 278.
Catechesis/Religious Programs—Students 295.

18—ST. AUGUSTINE (1796). First foundation of Augustinian Order in U.S.A. Revs. John F. O'Rourke, O.S.A.; Pascal A. DeCicco, O.S.A., Pastoral Assoc.; William J. Krupa, O.S.A. In res., Rev. W. Howard McGraw, O.S.A.
Res., 243 N. Lawrence S., 19106-1195. Tel: 215-627-1838; Fax: 215-627-3911.
School—St. Mary Interparochial School. See Consolidated Parish Schools under Institutions Located in the Archdiocese.

19—ST. BARBARA (1921), Rev. Msgr. Wilfred J. Pashley; Rev. Thomas F. Loughrey, Pastor Emeritus.
Res., 5359 Lebanon Ave., 19131. Tel: 215-473-1044; Fax: 215-473-5252.
Catechesis/Religious Programs—Students 6.
Convent—5336 Diamond St., 19131. Tel: 215-477-3839.

20—ST. BARNABAS (1919), Revs. Bernard J. Herron; John F. Babowitch; Peter N. Quinn; Deacons Leonard J. Wolkowicz; John J. Ellis.
Res., 6300 Buist Ave., 19142-3098. Tel: 215-726-1119; 1120; Fax: 215-726-1180.
School—64th St. & Buist Ave., 19142-3097. Tel: 215-729-3603.
Sisters of Immaculate Heart of Mary 5; Lay Teachers 17; Students 450.
Worship Sites:—St. Mary of Czestochowa Church, 59th & Elmwood Ave., and Our Lady of Loreto Church, 6214 Grays Ave.
Catechesis/Religious Programs—Tel: 215-724-8728.
Students 120.
Convent—6328 Buist Ave., 19142-3097. Tel: 215-729-1572.

21—ST. BARTHOLOMEW (1919), Revs. Joseph P. Denny; James J. McGinnis; James J. Anziano. In res., Rev. Ildebrando E. Schifalacqua; Deacon John J. Bean.
Res., 5600 Jackson St., 19124. Tel: 215-831-1224; 1225; Fax: 215-831-0467.
School—Jackson & Sanger St., 19124. Tel: 215-744-6393.
Lay Teachers 21; Students 522.
Catechesis/Religious Programs—Students 185.

22—ST. BENEDICT (1922), Rev. George B. Moore; Deacons Stephen Hopkins; James T. Walker; Calvin C. Smith.
Res., 1940 E. Chelten Ave., 19138. Tel: 215-924-4401; Fax: 215-924-4390.
School—1935 Medary Ave., 19138. Tel: 215-424-8073.
Lay Teachers 9; Students 185.
Catechesis/Religious Programs—Students 13.
Convent—1942 E. Chelten Ave., 19138. Tel: 215-924-2876.

23—ST. BERNARD (1927), Revs. Charles J. Sullivan; Thomas J. Dunleavy; Alexander Masluk; David Machain, (Retired); Rev. Msgr. John B. Fee, Pastor Emeritus; Rev. John G. Fala, (Retired).
Res., 7341 Cottage St., 19136. Tel: 215-333-0446; Fax: 215-333-3215.
School—7340 Jackson St., 19136. Tel: 215-624-5204; Fax: 215-624-8806.
Lay Teachers 29; Students 635.
Catechesis/Religious Programs—Students 150.

24—ST. BONAVENTURE (1889-1993). Closed. Formerly located at 9th & Cambria Sts. Spiritual records are kept at St. Veronica Church. Tel: 215-228-4878.

25—ST. BONIFACE (1865), Revs. Sean J. McGillicuddy, C.SS.R.; Wenceslaus J. Smutny, C.SS.R.; Charles McDonald, C.SS.R.; Bro. Manuel Martinez, C.SS.R. In res., Revs. Anthony T. Russo, C.SS.R., Deaf Apostolate; Gerard J. Brinkmann, C.SS.R.; Alexander F. Ortiz, C.SS.R.; Kevin R. Murray, C.SS.R.
Res., 174 W. Diamond St., 19122. Tel: 215-739-6376; Fax: 215-739-5102.
School—142 W. Diamond St., 19122. Tel: 215-634-6588.
Lay Teachers 10.
Catechesis/Religious Programs—Students 180.

26—ST. BRENDAN (1925-1934). Closed. Formerly located at 507 Manheim St. Spiritual records are kept at St. Francis of Assisi Church. Tel.: 215-842-1287.

27—ST. BRIDGET (1853), Rev. Richard R. York, M.A., M.Div.
Res., 3667 Midvale Ave., 19129. Tel: 215-844-4126; Fax: 215-842-2536.
School—3636 Stanton St., 19129. Tel: 215-843-2828.
Sisters of St. Joseph 2; Lay Teachers 14; Students 203.
Catechesis/Religious Programs—Students 247.
Convent—3665 Midvale Ave., 19129. Tel: 215-844-5663.
St. Francis Friary—3685 Midvale Ave., Tel: 215-844-1125.

28—ST. CALLISTUS (1921), Rev. Eugene M. Tully; Deacon Francis J. Connors. In res., Revs. John C. Dougherty; Andrew Cosmos.
Res., 700 N. 67th St., 19151-3614. Tel: 215-473-4417; Fax: 215-473-6728.

29—ST. CARTHAGE (1915-2000). Closed. Formerly located at 525 Cobbs Creek Pkwy. Spiritual records are kept at St. Cyprian Church. Tel.: 215-747-3250.

30—ST. CASIMIR (1893) (Lithuanian), Revs. Peter M. Burkauskas; Eugene A. Wassel, Pastor Emeritus.
Res., 324 Wharton St., 19147. Tel: 215-468-2052; Fax: 215-468-0354.
School—Tel: 215-334-8407; Fax: 215-334-0521. Mrs. Ann O'Connor, Prin.
Lay Teachers 8; Students 115.
Catechesis/Religious Programs—Students 161.

31—ST. CATHERINE OF SIENA (1910-1972). Closed. Formerly located at 436 W. Penn St. Spiritual records are kept at St. Vincent de Paul Church. Tel.: 215-438-2925.

32—ST. CECILIA (1911), Rev. Msgr. Francis X. Dreger; Revs. Thomas C. Hagan; Thomas M. Sodano; Matthew W. Guckin; Deacon Louis Malfara.
Res., 535 Rhawn St., 19111. Tel: 215-725-1240; Fax: 215-725-2130.
School—525 Rhawn St., 19111. Tel: 215-725-8588; Fax: 215-725-2130.
Sisters of the Immaculate Heart of Mary 8; Lay Teachers 34; Students 958.
Catechesis/Religious Programs—Tel: 215-725-2580.
Students 197.

33—ST. CHARLES BORROMEO (1868), Rev. George A. Majoros.
Res., 902 S. 20th St., 19146. Tel: 215-735-0600; Fax: 215-735-6630.
Church—20th & Christian Sts., 19146.
School—2019 Montrose St., 19146. Tel: 215-735-6879; 735-1475; Fax: 215-735-5523. Sr. Denise Ware, S.F.C.C., Prin.
Lay Teachers 10; Students 170.
St. Charles Early Childhood Programs—1941 Christian St., 19146.
Lay Teachers 1; Students 4.
Catechesis/Religious Programs—Tel: 215-735-6898.
Students 35.

34—CHRIST THE KING (1963), Revs. Henry G. Birkhead, Pastor Emeritus; James A. Callahan; Stephen C. White; Deacon Walter C. Fulmer.
Res., 3252 Chesterfield Rd., 19114. Tel: 215-632-1144; Fax: 215-632-4933.
School—3205 Chesterfield Rd., 19114. Tel: 215-632-1375; 637-3838.
Sisters of St. Joseph 3; Lay Teachers 22; Students 465.
Catechesis/Religious Programs—Tel: 215-632-2144.
Students 90.

35—ST. CHRISTOPHER (1950), Rev. Msgr. Joseph P. Garvin; Revs. Kenneth G. Putz; John P. Gutekunst; Joseph F. Smith, Pastor Emeritus.
Res., 13301 Proctor Rd., 19116. Tel: 215-673-5177; Fax: 215-698-0585.
School—13307 Proctor Rd., 19116. Tel: 215-673-5787; Fax: 215-673-8511.
Sisters of Mercy 1; Lay Teachers 39; Students 933.
Catechesis/Religious Programs—Sr. Michele Fisher, C.S.F.N., D.R.E.
Students 198.

36—ST. CLEMENT (1865), Revs. John J. Cox; Steven J. Marinucci.
Res., 2210 S. 71st St., 19142-1108. Tel: 215-729-0500; Fax: 215-729-3003.
School—SS. Clement-Irenaeus Consolidated School.

See Consolidated Parish Schools under Institutions Located in the Archdiocese. Tel: 215-729-8368; Fax: 215-729-1274.
Sisters, Servants of the Immaculate Heart of Mary 5; Lay Teachers 10; Students 295.
Catechesis/Religious Programs—Students 56.

37—ST. COLUMBA (1895-1993). Closed. Formerly located at 2340 W. Lehigh Ave. Spiritual records are kept at St. Martin de Porres Church. Tel.: 215-228-8330; 228-8331.

38—CORPUS CHRISTI (1921-1987). Closed. (1912-1987) Formerly located at 29th & Allegheny Ave. Spiritual records are kept at St. Martin de Porres Church. Tel.: 215-228-8330; 228-8331.

39—SAINT CYPRIAN (2000), Rev. Msgr. Federico A. Britto. In res., Rev. John T. Conway.
Res., 525 Cobbs Creek Pkwy., 19143. Tel: 215-747-3250; Fax: 215-476-9974.
School—6225 Cedar Ave., 19143. Tel: 215-748-4450; Fax: 215-747-7794. Camille Brown, Prin.
Lay Teachers 27; Students 671.
Convent—5501 Cedar Ave., 19143. Tel: 215-472-2936.

40—ST. DOMINIC (1849), Revs. James J. Mulligan; Bernard J. Benischeck; Michael J. Heim; Timothy F. O'Sullivan.
Res., 8504 Frankford Ave., 19136. Tel: 215-624-5502; 5503; Fax: 215-333-1750. [CEM]
School—8512 Frankford Ave., 19136. Tel: 215-333-6703; Fax: 215-333-9930.
Sisters, Servants of the Immaculate Heart of Mary 9; Lay Teachers 24; Students 594.
Catechesis/Religious Programs—Students 86.
Convent—8510 Frankford Ave., 19136. Tel: 215-333-0144.

41—ST. DONATO (1910) (Italian), Rev. Ferdinand Buccafurni.
Res., 403 N. 65th St., 19151. Tel: 215-747-4131.
School—405 N. 65th St., 19151. Tel: 215-748-2994; Fax: 215-748-0288.
Sisters 2; Lay Teachers 9; Students 254.
Catechesis/Religious Programs—Students 254.

42—ST. EDMOND (1912), Rev. Francis P. Groarke. In res., Rev. Michael S. Olivere.
Res., 2130 S. 21st St., 19145. Tel: 215-334-3755; Fax: 215-334-2081.
Catechesis/Religious Programs—Students 20.

43—ST. EDWARD THE CONFESSOR (1865-1993). Closed. Formerly located at 8th & York Sts. Spiritual records are kept at Visitation B.V.M. Church. Tel.: 215-228-8330; 228-8331.

44—ST. ELIZABETH (1872-1993). Closed. Spiritual records are kept at St. Martin De Porres Church.

45—EPIPHANY OF OUR LORD (1889) (Italian), Revs. Dominic M. Chiaravalle; John E. Calabro.
Res., 1121 Jackson St., 19148. Tel: 215-334-1035; Fax: 215-334-7885.
School—13th & Jackson Sts., 19148. Tel: 215-467-5385; Fax: 215-336-5103.
Lay Teachers 19; Students 409.
Catechesis/Religious Programs—Students 110.

46—ST. FRANCIS OF ASSISI (1899), Rev. Richard J. Rock, C.M. In res., Revs. Joseph Foley, C.M.; Francis Sacks, C.M.; Bro. Joseph Tauraso, C.M.
Res., 4821 Greene St., 19144. Tel: 215-842-1287; Fax: 215-842-3338.
School—St. Martin De Porres School (Germantown). See Consolidated Parish Schools under Institutions Located in the Archdiocese. Tel: 215-842-1266; Fax: 215-842-1400. Sr. Nancy Cassidy, Prin.
Lay Teachers 9; Students 205.

47—ST. FRANCIS DE SALES (1890), Rev. Roland D. Slobogin; Sr. Alice Daly, I.H.M., Pastoral Assoc. In res., Revs. Albert Selvadasan; John Pidgeon; Damien Schill.
Res., 4625 Springfield Ave., 19143. Tel: 215-222-5819; Fax: 215-222-5821.
School—917 S. 47th St., 19143. Tel: 215-387-1749; 727-3929; Fax: 215-387-6605.
Sisters, Servants of the Immaculate Heart of Mary 7; Lay Teachers 17; Students 543.
Catechesis/Religious Programs—Students 8.

48—ST. FRANCIS XAVIER (1839), Rev. Paul C. Convery, C.O.; Deacon Vincent J. Thompson. In res., Revs. George G. Thiers, C.O.; Alberto Roya-Mojia, C.O., J.C.D.; Aaron Pfaff; Bros. Brian Gaffney, C.O.; Mario Crestani.
Res., 2319 Green St., 19130. Tel: 215-765-4568; Fax: 215-765-4049.
Oratory—2321 Green St., 19130.
School—24th & Wallace Sts., 19130. Tel: 215-763-6564; Fax: 215-236-2818.
Sisters, Servants of the Immaculate Heart of Mary 3; Lay Teachers 11; Students 238.
Worship Site:—Saint Hedwig, 802 N. 24th St.
Convent—2324 Green St., 19130. Tel: 215-665-1340.

49—ST. GABRIEL (1895), Rev. Michael J. Lee, O.Praem.; Sr. Rene Wentzel, I.H.M., Pastoral Min.; Sr. Linda Uhrin, I.H.M., Pastoral Min.; Rev. James C. Rodia, O.Praem.
Res., 2917 Dickinson St., 19146. Tel: 215-463-4060; Fax: 215-755-2680.
School—Our Lady of Angels. See Consolidated Parish Schools under Institutions Located in the Archdiocese. Tel: 215-468-7230.
Lay Teachers 22; Students 404.
Catechesis/Religious Programs—Students 40.
Convent—2916 Dickinson St., Tel: 215-334-2620.

50—ST. GEORGE (1902) (Lithuanian), Rev. Msgr. Joseph J. Anderlonis, S.T.D.
Res., 3580 Salmon St., 19134. Tel: 215-739-3102; Fax: 215-739-7217.
School—2700 E. Venango St., 19134. Tel: 215-634-8803.
Lay Teachers 10; Students 203.
Convent—3570 Salmon St., 19134. Tel: 215-739-0472.
Sisters 4.

51—GESU (1868-1993). Closed. Formerly located at 18th & Thompson Sts. Spiritual records are kept at St. Malachy Church. Tel.: 215-763-1305.

52—GOOD SHEPHERD (1925), Rev. J. Thomas Heron. In res., Rev. James C. Otto, S.J.
Res., 6667 Chester Ave., 19142. Tel: 215-727-8300; Fax: 215-727-5932.
School—66th St. & Chester Ave., 19142. Tel: 215-729-8766.
Lay Teachers 11; Students 245.
Catechesis/Religious Programs—Students 276.

53—ST. GREGORY. Closed. (1895-1981) Formerly located at 52nd and Warren Sts. Spiritual records are kept at St. Rose of Lima Church. Tel: 215-877-2991, 2992.

54—ST. HEDWIG (1907-2000) (Polish). Formerly located at 802 N. 24th St. Spiritual records are kept at St. Francis Xavier Church. Tel.: 215-765-4568.

55—ST. HELENA (1924), Revs. Craig F. Brugger; Albert C. DiGiacobbe; Joseph T. Trinh; Deacons Victor Seda; Francis Urmison. In res., Rev. Rayford E. Emmons.
Res., 6161 N. Fifth St., 19120-1497. Tel: 215-424-1300; Fax: 215-424-9152.
School—6101 N. Fifth St., 19120. Tel: 215-549-2947; Fax: 215-549-5947.
Sisters of St. Joseph 5; Lay Teachers 15; Students 485.
Catechesis/Religious Programs—Tel: 215-924-9530.
Students 84.

56—ST. HENRY (1916-1993) (German). Closed. Formerly located at 4400 N. 5th St. Spiritual records are kept at Incarnation Church. Tel.: 215-329-2320; 329-2321.

57—HOLY ANGELS (1906), Rev. Martin S. Kim. In res., Rev. Inchang Yu.
Res., 7000 Old York Rd., 19126. Tel: 215-548-5535; Fax: 215-224-6615.
Catechesis/Religious Programs—Students 200.

58—HOLY CHILD (1909-1993). Closed. Formerly located at 5200 N. Broad St. Spiritual records are kept at Our Lady of Hope Church. Tel.: 215-329-8100; 329-8164.

59—HOLY CROSS (1890), Rev. Leo P. Oswald; Deacon Richard Coyne. In res., Rev. Ronald M. Jakows.
Res., 154 E. Mt. Airy Ave., 19119. Tel: 215-247-0661; Fax: 215-247-1849.
School—144 E. Mt. Airy Ave., 19119. Tel: 215-242-0414; Fax: 215-242-0414.
Sisters of St. Joseph 4; Lay Teachers 10; Students 237.
Convent—148 E. Mt. Airy Ave., 19119. Tel: 215-247-0262.
Catechesis/Religious Programs—Tel: 215-247-3405; Fax: 215-247-3405. Mr. James Nelson, D.R.E. Students 42.

60—HOLY FAMILY (1885), Revs. Francis X. McKee; James J. Martin; John W. Gsell, Pastor Emeritus. In res., Rev. Thomas F. Gibbons, M.M.; Deacon Eugene R. Leahy.
Res., 234 Hermitage St., 19127. Tel: 215-482-0450; 482-8608; Fax: 215-482-7531.
School—242 Hermitage St., 19127. Tel: 215-487-2796; 483-0903; Fax: 215-487-9134.
Lay Teachers 13; Students 263.
Catechesis/Religious Programs—Interparochial C.C.D. Program - St. Josaphat's, Tel: 215-483-4470; Fax: 215-483-4471.
Students 30.

61—HOLY INNOCENTS (1927), Revs. Daniel J. Sullivan; Wilfred F. Maloney; James M. Cox.
Res., 1337 E. Hunting Park Ave., 19124. Tel: 215-743-2600; Fax: 215-743-8041.
School—1312 E. Bristol St., 19124. Tel: 215-743-5909.
Sisters, Servants of the Immaculate Heart of Mary 10; Lay Teachers 18; Students 516.
Catechesis/Religious Programs—Students 20.

62—HOLY NAME OF JESUS (Fishtown) (1904), Rev. Gregory J. Pariante.
Res., 701 E. Gaul St., 19125-2896. Tel: 215-739-3960; Fax: 215-739-7597.
School—E. Berks & Gaul Sts., 19125. Tel: 215-423-3334; Fax: 215-425-9353.
Sisters, Servants of the Immaculate Heart of Mary 6; Lay Teachers 8; Students 271.
Preschool:—Kensington, Tel: 215-423-3041. Sr. Janet Walters, I.H.M., Prin.

63—HOLY REDEEMER (1941) (Chinese). Unassigned. (Mission Chapel of the Church of St. John the Evangelist).
School—915 Vine St., 19107. Tel: 215-922-0999; Fax: 215-922-6674.
Lay Teachers 9; Students 249.
Parish House:—916 Wood St., 19107. Tel: 215-627-5293; Fax: 215-563-9980.

64—HOLY SPIRIT (1964), Revs. David C. Sicoli; Vijayakumar Tom Chithalan, C.M.I.
Res., 1900 Geary St., 19145. Tel: 215-334-4242; Fax: 215-334-8787.
School—1845 Hartranft St., 19145. Tel: 215-389-0715; Fax: 215-336-7719.
Lay Teachers 10; Students 221.
Catechesis/Religious Programs—Students 46.

65—HOLY TRINITY (1789) (German). Attended by Old St. Mary's Church, Sixth and Spruce Sts.
252 South Fourth St., 19106. Tel: 215-923-7930. [CEM]
School—St. Mary Interparochial School. See Consolidated Parish Schools under Institutions Located in the Archdiocese. Tel: 215-923-7522.

66—ST. HUBERT (1924). Closed. Formally located at Torresdale and Cottman Aves. from 1924-1940. Spiritual records transferred to St. Bernard Church. Tel: 215-333-0446.

67—ST. HUGH OF CLUNY (1922), Rev. Dennis M. Mooney; Deacon Jose L. Lozada-Figueroa. In res., Rev. Jonas V. DeMoraes.
Res., 145 W. Tioga St., 19140. Tel: 215-634-1800; Fax: 215-427-0303.
School—3533 N. Mascher St., 19140. Tel: 215-634-3060; 634-3183; Fax: 215-634-2690.
Sisters of St. Joseph 5; Lay Teachers 6; Students 288.
Catechesis/Religious Programs—Students 280.

68—ST. IGNATIUS OF LOYOLA (1893) (African American), Rev. James R. Bajorek.
Res., 636 N. 43rd St., 19104. Tel: 215-386-5065; 386-1058; Fax: 215-386-2832.
School—617 N. 43rd St., 19104. Tel: 215-222-3626. Sr. Lynn Marie Ralph, S.B.S., Prin.
Sisters of the Blessed Sacrament 5; Lay Teachers 9; Students 220.
Convent—644 N. 43rd St., 19104. Tel: 215-386-0302.
Chaplaincy—St. Ignatius Nursing Home, Tel: 215-349-8800; Fax: 215-222-3078.

69—IMMACULATE CONCEPTION (1869), Rev. Herbert J. Sperger. In res., Revs. Stanley M. Gana; Edmund C. Wesolowski; Bernard C. Farley; Michael F. Hennelly, M.Div.
Res., 1020 N. Front St., 19123. Tel: 215-627-2702; Fax: 215-627-7344.

70—IMMACULATE CONCEPTION (1902) (African-American), Rev. Timothy V. Lyons, C.M. In res., Revs. William J. O'Brien, C.M.; Charles T. Plock, C.M.; John W. Gouldrick, C.M.; Gregory P. Cozzubbo, C.M.
Res., 1020 E. Price St., 19138. Tel: 215-843-9468; Fax: 215-843-6570.
School—St. Athanasius-Immaculate Conception School. See Consolidated Parish Schools under Institutions located in the Archdiocese. Tel: 215-424-5045; Fax: 215-927-6615.
Catechesis/Religious Programs—Students 51.

71—IMMACULATE HEART OF MARY (1952), Rev. Msgr. Bartholomew J. O'Brien; Revs. John M. Donohie; Mark S. Kunigonis.
Res., 819 Cathedral Rd., 19128. Tel: 215-483-1000; Fax: 215-483-1732.
School—815 Cathedral Rd., 19128. Tel: 215-482-2029; Fax: 215-482-1075.
Lay Teachers 35; Students 560.
Catechesis/Religious Programs—Students 87.

72—INCARNATION OF OUR LORD (1900), Revs. John M. Halloran; Chacko Thadathil Varghese (India); William G. Ayres; Jean-Claude Mompoint, (Haitian Apostolate); Deacons Felipe Cruz; Jose A. Fontanez; Jose Hernandez. In res., Rev. Jonas De Morais, (Portuguese Apostolate).
Res., 5105 N. Fifth St., 19120. Tel: 215-329-2320; Fax: 215-329-6149.
School—Tel: 215-457-2779. Sr. Janet Regina, I.H.M., Prin.

Sisters, Servants of the Immaculate Heart of Mary 6; Lay Teachers 19; Students 550.
Catechesis/Religious Programs—Students 135.
Convent—401 W. Lindley Ave., 19120. Tel: 215-329-0672.

73—SAINT IRENAEUS (1966), Rev. Gavin W. Muir; Deacon Michael R. Arno.
Res., 2728 South 73rd St., 19153. Tel: 215-727-2888; Fax: 215-365-4751.
School—SS. Clement-Irenaeus Consolidated School. See Consolidated Parish Schools under Institutions Located in the Archdiocese. Tel: 215-729-8368; Fax: 215-729-1274.

74—ST. JAMES (1850-1976). Consolidated with St. Agatha to form St. Agatha-St. James. See separate listing for details.

75—ST. JEROME (1955), Revs. Joseph B. Graham; Lawrence F. Crehan, M.Div.; Martin F. O'Hara, Pastor Emeritus; Eugene J. McBride, O.S.F.S.; Deacons Charles Pavonarius; Raymond Gwynn. In res., Rev. Edward V. Avery.
Res., 8100 Colfax St., 19136. Tel: 215-333-4461; Fax: 215-333-6791.
School—3031 Stamford St., 19136. Tel: 215-624-0637; Fax: 215-624-5711. Sharon Nendza, Prin.
Sisters of St. Joseph 3; Lay Teachers 31; Students 774.
Catechesis/Religious Programs—Students 44.

76—ST. JOACHIM (1845), Revs. Robert Bazzoli, O.S.F.S.; Harold McGovern, O.S.F.S.; Deacon Steven P. Wetzel. In res., Rev. Mark Plaushin, O.S.F.S.
Res., 1527 Church St., 19124. Tel: 215-535-0580; Fax: 215-831-1788. [CEM]
School—Penn & Church Sts., 19124. Tel: 215-288-9501.
Sisters 4; Lay Teachers 11; Students 185.
Catechesis/Religious Programs—Tel: 215-288-5911.
Students 90.
Convent—1509 Church St., Tel: 215-535-6177.
Servants of the Immaculate Heart of Mary 9.

77—ST. JOAN OF ARC (1919), Rev. Edward H. Bell. In res., Rev. Msgr. Philip J. Cribben.
Res., 2025 E. Atlantic St., 19134. Tel: 215-535-4641; 535-5138; Fax: 215-535-7477.
School—3556 Frankford Ave., 19134. Tel: 215-533-3210; Fax: 215-533-3864.
Sisters, Servants of the Immaculate Heart of Mary 7; Lay Teachers 9; Students 246.
Catechesis/Religious Programs—Students 99.
Convent—3550 Frankford Ave., 19134. Tel: 215-533-0959.

78—ST. JOHN THE BAPTIST (1831), Revs. Frederick Kindon; James R. Casey; Sr. Kathy Claflin, S.S.J., Dir. Parish Svcs. In res., Rev. Thomas J. Grumm.
Res., 146 Rector St., 19127. Tel: 215-482-4600; Fax: 215-482-2976. [CEM]
School—119 Rector St., 19127. Tel: 215-482-0449; Fax: 215-482-2451.
Sisters, Servants of the Immaculate Heart of Mary 7; Lay Teachers 15; Students 510.

79—ST. JOHN CANTIUS (1892) (Polish), Rev. Joseph J. Zingaro; Rev. Msgr. Adam J. Bydlon, Pastor Emeritus; Revs. Dennis J. Witalec; Jan Palkowski.
Res., 4415 Almond St., 19137. Tel: 215-535-6667; Fax: 215-535-7107.
School—4435 Almond St., 19137. Tel: 215-535-3446.
Sisters of the Holy Family of Nazareth 2; Lay Teachers 9; Students 270; Kindergarten 24.
Catechesis/Religious Programs—Students 430.

80—ST. JOHN THE EVANGELIST (1830), Revs. James Menkhus, O.F.M.Cap.; Paul Dressler, O.F.M.Cap.; Benjamin Regotti, O.F.M.Cap.; Bro. James Gavin, O.F.M.Cap. In res., Revs. Thomas Betz, O.F.M.Cap.; Anselm Martin, O.F.M.Cap.
Res., 21 S. 13th St., 19107. Tel: 215-563-4145; Fax: 215-563-1770. [CEM]
School—St. Mary Interparochial School. See Consolidated Parish Schools under Institutions Located in the Archdiocese. Tel: 215-923-7522.
Mission—Philadelphia, Philadelphia Co., Holy Redeemer Chinese Church, 915 Vine St., 19107. Tel: 215-922-0999; Fax: 215-922-6674.

81—ST. JOHN NEPOMUCENE (Slovak). Consolidated with St. John Nepomucene and St. Agnes January 1, 1980. Spiritual records transferred to St. Agnes Church, 319 Brown St., Philadelphia, PA 19123. Tel.: 215-627-0340.

82—ST. JOSAPHAT (1898) (Polish), Rev. John B. Wendrychowicz. In res., Rev. Edward A. Pelczar.
Res., 124 Cotton St., 19127. Tel: 215-483-4470; Fax: 215-483-4037.
School—137 Grape St., 19127. Tel: 215-482-0285; Fax: 215-483-4053.
Bernardine Sisters of St. Francis 1; Lay Teachers 9; Students 260.
Catechesis/Religious Programs—Students 16.

83—OLD ST. JOSEPH'S (1733), Revs. Leo A. Murray, S.J., Admin.; William C. Carroll, S.J.; William F. Gavin, S.J. In res., Revs. Joseph P. Logan, S.J.; William C. Rickle, S.J.; Joseph C. Sands, S.J.
Res., 321 Willings Alley, 19106. Tel: 215-923-1733; 1734; Fax: 215-574-8529.
School—St. Mary Interparochial School. See Consolidated Parish Schools under Institutions Located in the Archdiocese.

84—ST. KATHERINE OF SIENA (1922), Rev. Msgr. James P. McBride; Revs. Paul J. Stenson; John P. O'Connor; Joseph L. Coffey; Jose Ainikkal, C.M.I. (India); Anne Rhodes, Business Mgr.; Deacon James J. Duffy.
Res., 9700 Frankford Ave., 19114. Tel: 215-637-7548; Fax: 215-637-0146.
School—9720 Frankford Ave., 19114. Tel: 215-637-2181; Fax: 215-637-4867. Sr. M. John, C.S.F.N., Prin.
Sisters of the Holy Family of Nazareth 4; Lay Teachers 29; Students 716.
Catechesis/Religious Programs—Tel: 215-637-1464. Donna Heeney, D.R.E.
Students 60.

85—KING OF PEACE (1926) (Italian), Revs. Ralph J. Chieffo; Thomas J. Rossi, O.Praem.
Res., 2530 Wharton St., 19146. Tel: 215-468-4107; Fax: 215-468-2882.
School—Our Lady of Angels. Please see Consolidated Parish Schools under Institutions Located in the Archdiocese. Tel: 215-468-7230; Fax: 215-468-2554.
Catechesis/Religious Programs—Our Lady of Angels School, 30th & Dickinson Sts., Tel: 215-334-0374.
Students 79.
Convent—1309 S. 26th St., 19146. Tel: 215-389-5414.

86—ST. LADISLAUS (1906) (Polish), Rev. John B. Wendrychowicz.
1650 W. Hunting Park Ave., 19140.
Res., 124 Cotton St., 19127. Tel: 215-225-8148.

87—ST. LAURENTIUS (1882) (Polish), Rev. Francis A. Gwiazda. In res., Rev. Joseph C. Stec, M.A.
Res., 1608 E. Berks St., 19125. Tel: 215-739-1776; 739-9387.
School—1612 E. Berks St., 19125. Tel: 215-423-8834; Fax: 215-426-4675.
Felician Sisters of St. Francis 6; Lay Teachers 9; Students 259.
Catechesis/Religious Programs—Students 322.
Convent—1648 E. Berks St., 19125. Tel: 215-739-4447.

88—ST. LEO (1884), Revs. John J. Farry; Joseph E. O'Brien; Matthew Chadwick, O.F.M.Conv.
Res., 6658 Keystone St., 19135. Tel: 215-333-0340; Fax: 215-333-7590.
School—6649 Tulip St., 19135. Tel: 215-624-8669.
Sisters of St. Joseph 4; Lay Teachers 11; Students 303.
Catechesis/Religious Programs—Students 56.
Convent—4900 Unruh St., 19135. Tel: 215-624-1253.

89—ST. LUCY (1905) (Italian), Rev. Francis J. Sabatini. In res., Rev. Paul G. Obrimski.
Res., 4503 Smick St., 19127. Tel: 215-483-0554; Fax: 215-483-2450.
School—146 Green Ln., 19127. Tel: 215-482-6578.
Lay Teachers 10; Students 232.
Catechesis/Religious Programs—Students 10.

90—ST. LUDWIG (1891-1975) (German). Closed. Formerly located at 28th & Master Sts. Spiritual records are kept at St. Francis Xavier Church. Tel.: 215-765-4568.

91—ST. MADELEINE SOPHIE (1925), Rev. Leo P. Oswald.
Res., 6440 Greene St., 19119. Tel: 215-438-9464; Fax: 215-848-7953.
School—St. Martin De Porres School (Germantown). See Consolidated Parish Schools under Institutions Located in the Archdiocese. Tel: 215-842-1266.

92—ST. MALACHY (1850) (African American), Rev. John P. McNamee.
Res., 1429 N. 11th St., 19122. Tel: 215-763-1305; Fax: 215-763-2023.
School—1419 N. 11th St., 19122. Tel: 215-232-0696; Fax: 215-236-1434.
Lay Teachers 11; Students 214.
Catechesis/Religious Programs—Students 55.
Convent—1415 N. 11th St., 19122. Tel: 215-763-5366.

93—SAINT MARTHA (1966), Revs. John Pwodziunas, O.F.M.; Richard J. Twlko, O.F.M. In res., Rev. Marcel Kolakowski, O.F.M., (Retired).
Res., 11301 Academy Rd., 19154-3304. Tel: 215-632-3720; Fax: 215-632-7737.
School—11321 Academy Rd., 19154-3304. Tel: 215-632-0320; Fax: 215-632-5546.
Lay Teachers 29; Students 639.
Catechesis/Religious Programs—Students 90.

94—ST. MARTIN DE PORRES (1993), Rev. Edward J. Hallinan; Deacons Edward J. Andrews; Thomas A. Shields. In res., Rev. Kevin C. Lawrence.
Res., 2340 W. Lehigh Ave., 19132. Tel: 215-228-8330; Fax: 215-221-6516.
School—23rd St. & Lehigh Ave., 19132. Tel: 215-223-6872.
Sisters of St. Joseph 4; Lay Teachers 18; Students 465.
Catechesis/Religious Programs—Students 55.

95—ST. MARTIN OF TOURS (1923), Revs. Anthony W. Janton; Marshall J. Kloda; John D. Hand; Vyjay Kumar Francis; Charles D. Smith; Rev. Msgr. Michael F. Marley, Pastor Emeritus. In res., Rev. Msgr. Nelson J. Perez.
Res., 5450 Roosevelt Blvd., 19124. Tel: 215-535-2962; Fax: 215-535-3091.
School—Loretto Ave. & Sanger St., 19124. Tel: 215-533-3050.
Sisters of the Immaculate Heart of Mary 18; Lay Teachers 47; Students 1,200.
Catechesis/Religious Programs—Tel: 215-535-3090. Sr. Phyllis Direnzo, I.H.M., D.R.E.
Students 210.

96—OLD ST. MARY'S (1763), Rev. Msgr. John A. Sharkey. In res., Rev. Gerard C. Mesure.
Res., 252 S. Fourth St., 19106. Tel: 215-923-7930. [CEM]
School—St. Mary Interparochial School. See Consolidated Parish Schools under Institutions Located in the Archdiocese. Tel: 215-923-7522.
Lay Teachers 9; Students 242.

97—ST. MARY OF THE ASSUMPTION (1849) (German), Revs. John J. Sibel; Emil C. Oestreich, Pastor Emeritus; Deacon Joseph Sexton.
Res., 176 Conarroe St., 19127. Tel: 215-482-4264; Fax: 215-508-1731. [CEM]
School—167 Conarroe St., 19127. Tel: 215-482-1611; Fax: 215-508-1536.
Sisters 3; Lay Teachers 10; Students 264.
Catechesis/Religious Programs—Students 284.

98—ST. MARY OF CZESTOCHOWA (Polish). Closed. (1927-2000) Formerly located at 59th St. and Elmwood Ave. Spiritual records are kept at St. Barnabas Church. Tel.: 215-726-1119; 1120.

99—ST. MARY OF THE ETERNAL (Italian). Closed. (1911-1976) Formerly located at 2222 W. Clearfield St. Spiritual records are kept at St. Martin de Porres. Tel.: 215-228-8330; 228-8331.

100—ST. MARY MAGDALEN DE PAZZI (Italian). Closed. (1852-2000). Formerly located at 712 Montrose St. Spiritual records are kept at Saint Paul Church. Tel.: 215-923-0355.

101—MATER DOLOROSA (1911) (Italian), Rev. Charles F. Engelhardt, O.S.F.S.
Res., 1676 Ruan St., 19124. Tel: 215-535-4036; 743-4718; Fax: 215-535-1267.
School—Paul & Ruan Sts., 19124. Tel: 215-743-4753; Fax: 215-535-1267. Miss Grace McGuirl, Prin.
Lay Teachers 12; Students 196.
Catechesis/Religious Programs—Students 236.

102—MATERNITY B.V.M. (1870), Rev. Msgr. Anthony W. McGuire; Revs. Edward E. Brady; Francis E. Fox; Edward C. Kelly; Deacons Victor Bonilla; Phillip Heaney; John C. Hynes. In res., Rev. Msgr. Bernard E. Witkowski.
Res., 9220 Bustleton Ave., 19115. Tel: 215-673-8127; 676-5144; Fax: 215-673-6597.
School—9322 Bustleton Ave., 19115. Tel: 215-673-0235; Fax: 215-671-1347. Miss Kathleen Veasy, Prin.
Sisters of Mercy 1; Lay Teachers 28; Students 867.
Catechesis/Religious Programs—Students 110.
Convent—Tel: 215-673-8118.

103—ST. MATTHEW (1927), Rev. Msgr. Charles E. McGroarty; Revs. James E. Goerner; James J. McLaughlin; Richard E. Rudy. In res., Rev. Thomas J. Kelley.
Res., 3000 Cottman Ave., 19149. Tel: 215-333-0585; Fax: 215-333-0757.
School—3040 Cottman Ave., 19149. Tel: 215-333-3142.
Sisters, Servants of the Immaculate Heart of Mary 10; Lay Teachers 43; Students 1,268.
Catechesis/Religious Programs—Students 78.

104—ST. MICHAEL (1831), Rev. Herbert J. Sperger; Sr. Angela Cordero A.C.J., Coord. Parish Svcs.; Deacon Zoilo Martes. In res., Rev. Francis Piro.
Res., 1445 N. Second St., 19122. Tel: 215-739-2358; Fax: 215-739-5766. [CEM]
Convent—1434 N. Second St., 19122. Tel: 215-739-3677.

105—ST. MICHAEL MISSION. (1923-1958) Formerly located at Red Lion & Knights Rd. in Torresdale. Spiritual records are kept at Our Lady of Calvary Church. Tel.: 215-637-7515.

106—ST. MICHAEL OF THE SAINTS. Closed. (1924-1982) Formerly located at 4811 Germantown Ave. Spiritual records kept at St. Francis of Assisi Church. Tel.: 215-842-1287.

107—ST. MONICA (1895), Most Rev. Louis A. De Simone; Revs. Anthony J. Cossavella; Albin J. Grous; Clement Kurowski, O.F.M.; Deacons John C. Orlando; Leonard D. DeMasi.
Res., 2422 S. 17th St., 19145. Tel: 215-334-4170.
School—1714 Ritner St., 19145. Tel: 215-467-5338; 334-3777; Fax: 215-467-4599.
Sisters, Servants of the Immaculate Heart of Mary 6; Lay Teachers 24; Students 784.
Catechesis/Religious Programs—Students 139.

108—MOST BLESSED SACRAMENT (1901) (African American), Rev. Roland D. Slobogin.
Res., 5628 Chester Ave., 19143. Tel: 215-729-0694; Fax: 215-729-0712.
School—5601 Kingsessing Ave., 19143. Tel: 215-727-1863.
Sisters, Servants of Immaculate Heart of Mary 2; Lay Teachers 8; Students 215.
Catechesis/Religious Programs—Students 12.

109—MOST PRECIOUS BLOOD OF OUR LORD (1907-1993). Closed. (1907-1993) Formerly located at 28th & Diamond Sts. Spiritual records are kept at St. Martin De Porres Church. Tel.: 215-228-8330.

110—MOTHER OF DIVINE GRACE (1926) (Italian), Rev. Angelo R. Citino; Deacon Joseph A. Micucci.
Res., 2918 E. Thompson St., 19134. Tel: 215-739-0353; Fax: 215-739-9910.
School—2612 E. Monmouth St., 19134. Tel: 215-426-7325; Fax: 215-426-0753.
Lay Teachers 10; Students 201.
Catechesis/Religious Programs—Students 8.

111—NATIVITY OF THE BLESSED VIRGIN MARY (1882), Revs. Richard J. McAndrews; Joseph F. Okonski. In res., Revs. Mardean E. Miller; Daniel J. Moriarity.
Res., 2535 E. Allegheny Ave., 19134. Tel: 215-739-2735; Fax: 215-739-2748.
School—2541 E. Madison St., 19134. Tel: 215-739-8761; Fax: 215-739-8781.
School Sisters of Notre Dame 2; Lay Teachers 17; Students 390.
Catechesis/Religious Programs—Tel: 215-739-4667. Mrs. Susan Campbell, D.R.E.
Students 85.
Convent—3224 Belgrade St., 19134. Tel: 215-427-3261; Fax: 215-427-3263. Novitiate-Sisters of Our Lady of Mercy

112—ST. NICHOLAS OF TOLENTINE (1912) (Italian), Revs. Nicholas Martorano, O.S.A.; John Brynes, O.S.A. In res., Rev. Anthony Gasparro, O.S.A., (Retired); Bro. John Holt, O.S.A.; Deacon Raymond Jacobucci.
Res., 910 Watkins St., 19148. Tel: 215-463-1326; Fax: 215-463-0888.
Church—Ninth St. below Morris St., 19148.
School—913 Pierce St., 19148. Tel: 215-468-0353; Fax: 215-334-9661.
Religious Sisters Filippini 3; Religious 1; Lay Teachers 22; Students 511.
Catechesis/Religious Programs—Students 61.

113—OUR LADY OF ANGELS (1907) (Italian), Rev. Ferdinand Buccafurni, Admin.
Res., St. Donato Church, 403 N. 65th St., 19151. Tel: 215-747-4131.
Church—4970 Master St., 19131.

114—OUR LADY OF THE BLESSED SACRAMENT (1910-1972). Closed. Formerly located at 712 N. Broad St. Spiritual records are kept at the Cathedral Basilica of SS. Peter and Paul. Tel.: 215-561-1313; 561-1314.

115—OUR LADY OF CALVARY (1958), Revs. John P. Paul; John S. Hutter; George J. Monahan.
Res., 11024 Knights Rd., 19154. Tel: 215-637-7515; Fax: 215-637-7517.
School—11027 Kipling Ln., 19154. Tel: 215-637-1648; Fax: 215-632-3810.
Sisters of the Holy Family of Nazareth 3; Lay Teachers 34; Students 924.
Catechesis/Religious Programs—Students 108.

116—OUR LADY OF CONSOLATION (1917) (Italian), Rev. Michael C. DiIorio.
Res., 7056 Tulip St., 19135. Tel: 215-333-0442; 333-5774; Fax: 215-333-2884.
School—Princeton & Edmund Sts., 19135. Tel: 215-624-0505. Ms. Margaret A. Clinton, Prin.
Sisters of St. Francis of Philadelphia 1; Lay Teachers 10; Students 265.
Catechesis/Religious Programs—Students 265.
Convent—7052 Tulip St., 19135. Tel: 215-332-4426.

117—OUR LADY OF GOOD COUNSEL (1898-1932). Closed. Formerly located at 816 Christian St. Spiritual records are kept at St. Paul Church. Tel.: 215-923-0355.

118—OUR LADY HELP OF CHRISTIANS (1885) (German), Rev. Leo J. McGee. In res., Rev. Robert W. Povish.
Res., 3160 Gaul St., 19134. Tel: 215-739-2211.
School—2424 E. Allegheny Ave., 19134. Tel: 215-427-3499.
Sisters of Christian Charity 4; Lay Teachers 9; Students 260.
Catechesis/Religious Programs—Students 342.
Convent—Tel: 215-739-7890.

119—OUR LADY OF THE HOLY SOULS (1909-1993). Closed. Formerly located at 19th & Tioga Sts. Spiritual records are kept at Our Lady of Hope Church. Tel.: 215-329-8100.

120—OUR LADY OF HOPE (1993), Rev. Msgr. Kenneth P. McAteer; Revs. James P. Gorman; Michael J. Kelly; Deacon William Champagne. In res., Rev. Alphonsus B. Dakora (Ghana).
Res., 5200 N. Broad St., 19141-1628. Tel: 215-329-8100; 329-8164; Fax: 215-324-4660.
School—5218 N. Broad St., 19141-1626. Tel: 215-324-4211.
Lay Teachers 12; Students 280.
Catechesis/Religious Programs—Students 102.

121—OUR LADY OF LORETO (1932-2000) (Italian). Closed. Formerly located at 6214 Grays Ave. Spiritual records are kept at St. Barnabas Church. Tel.: 215-726-1119; 1120.

122—OUR LADY OF LOURDES (1894), Revs. James C. Sherlock; George W. Crowe.
Res., 6315 Lancaster Ave., 19151. Tel: 215-473-1669; 1670; Fax: 215-473-1670.
School—1940 N. 63rd St., 19151. Tel: 215-877-2727; Fax: 215-877-6042.
Sisters of Mercy 2; Lay Teachers 12; Students 224.
Catechesis/Religious Programs—Students 30.

123—OUR LADY OF MERCY (1889-1984). Closed. Formerly located at Broad St. & Susquehanna Ave. Spiritual records are kept at St. Malachy Church. Tel.: 215-763-1305.

124—CHAPEL OF OUR LADY OF THE MIRACULOUS MEDAL (LA MILAGROSA) (1912) (Spanish). Attended by Cathedral Basilica of SS. Peter and Paul, 1723 Race St., Philadelphia, PA 19103. Tel: 215-561-1313; 1314. Rev. Michael A. Chapman.
Church—1903 Spring Garden St., 19130. Tel: 215-972-8116.
Catechesis/Religious Programs—Students 16.

125—OUR LADY OF MT. CARMEL (1896), Revs. Kenneth W. Sharp; Robert T. Feeney; Thomas Achandy, C.M.I. (India). In res., Rev. Quan H. Tran.
Res., 2319 S. Third St., 19148. Tel: 215-334-7766; Fax: 215-334-3269.
School—2329 S. Third St., 19148. Tel: 215-334-0584; Fax: 215-336-4519.
Sisters of Mercy 3; Lay Teachers 16; Students 451.
Convent—251 Ritner St., 19148. Tel: 215-334-6800.

126—OUR LADY OF POMPEII (1914-1993) (Italian). Closed. Formerly located at 6th St. & Erie Ave. Spiritual records are kept at St. Veronica Church. Tel.: 215-228-4878.

127—OUR LADY OF RANSOM (1955), Revs. William F. McGeown; Christopher M. Walsh.
Res., 6701 Calvert St., 19149. Tel: 215-332-6166; Fax: 215-332-6811.
School—6740 Roosevelt Blvd., 19149. Tel: 215-332-4352.
Sisters, Servants of the Immaculate Heart of Mary 4; Lay Teachers 14; Students 432.
Catechesis/Religious Programs—Tel: 215-708-2495.
Students 107.
Convent—Tel: 215-624-1954.

128—OUR LADY OF THE ROSARY (1886), Rev. Thomas P. Kletzel; Sr. Katherine Mary Chazotte, S.B.S., Dir. Parish Svcs. In res., Rev. Thomas M. Higgins.
Res., 345 N. 63rd St., 19139. Tel: 215-476-6511; 476-2050.
School—344 N. Felton St., 19139. Tel: 215-474-4011; Fax: 215-474-7807. Mrs. Margeuritte Henry, Prin.
Lay Teachers 10; Students 245.
Catechesis/Religious Programs—Students 27.

129—OUR LADY OF THE ROSARY (Germantown) (1928-1977) (Italian). Closed. Formerly located at 528 E. Haines St. Spiritual records are kept at Immaculate Conception Church. Tel.: 215-843-9468.

130—OUR LADY OF VICTORY (1899), Rev. Thomas P. Kletzel; Deacon Richard G. Nightingale.
Res., 5412 Vine St., 19139. Tel: 215-747-7567; 747-6731; Fax: 215-748-6269.
School—54th & Summer Sts., 19139. Tel: 215-747-8004. Sr. Barbara Farrell, S.S.J., Prin.
Sisters of St. Joseph 6; Lay Teachers 9; Students 245.
Catechesis/Religious Programs—Students 43.
Convent—5330 Vine St., 19139. Tel: 215-747-7040.

131—OUR MOTHER OF CONSOLATION (1855), Revs. James T. Dever, O.S.F.S.; John W. Brennan, O.S.F.S.; Michael J. McCue, O.S.F.S.; Deacons Clifford W. Brown; James M. Tormey.
Res., 9 E. Chestnut Hill Ave., 19118. Tel: 215-247-0430; Fax: 215-247-2506.
School—17 E. Chestnut Hill Ave., 19118. Tel: 215-247-1060; Fax: 215-247-0590. Mary P. Boyle, Prin.
Sisters of St. Joseph 5; Lay Teachers 7; Students 248.
Catechesis/Religious Programs—Tel: 215-248-4517.
Students 48.
Convent—23 E. Chestnut Hill Ave., 19118. Tel: 215-247-0552.

132—OUR MOTHER OF MERCY PRISON CHAPLAINCY. Unassigned.
Res., 1350 Vernon Rd., 19150. Tel: 215-549-3760; Fax: 215-549-1271. Ministry to Philadelphia County Prisons; House of Correction; Detention Center; Curran-Fromhold Correctional Facility; Philadelphia Industrial Correctional Center, Special Detention Facilities, Tel: 215-685-8385. Fax: 215-685-8938.

133—OUR MOTHER OF SORROWS (1852), Revs. James Bajorek; Alexander Masluk; Rev. Msgr. James P. Daly, Pastor Emeritus.
Res., 1030 N. 48th St., 19131. Tel: 215-878-0875; Fax: 215-878-7420.
School—1020 N. 48th St., 19131. Tel: 215-473-5828; Fax: 215-477-3096.
Sisters of St. Joseph 2; Lay Teachers 10; Students 260.
Catechesis/Religious Programs—Felicia Muldrow, D.R.E.
Students 30.

134—ST. PATRICK (1839), Rev. Msgr. Philip J. Dowling; Rev. Peter A. Fitzpatrick, Pastor Emeritus. In res., Rev. Milton Jordan.
Res., 242 S. 20th St., 19103. Tel: 215-735-9900; Fax: 215-732-0998.
School—St. Mary Interparochial School, Tel: 215-923-7522.

135—ST. PAUL (1843), Rev. Charles L. Sangermano. In res., Rev. Vincent F. Welsh, J.C.L., M.A.
Res., 808 S. Hutchinson St., 19147. Tel: 215-923-0355; Fax: 215-923-1803.
Worship Site:—Saint Mary Magdalen dePazzi Church, 712 Montrose St.
Catechesis/Religious Programs—Students 120.

136—ST. PETER THE APOSTLE (1842), Revs. Joseph C. Tizio, C.Ss.R.; Herman Brinkmann, C.Ss.R.; Seamus M. Quinn, C.Ss.R.; Michael Hopkins, C.Ss.R; John O'Toole; Mr. Eugene McGarvey, Business Mgr.; Deacons Miguel Betancourt; Juan Ramos. In res., Rev. Msgr. George Tomichek, D.C.; Revs. William C. Maggs, C.Ss.R.; Donald Miniscalco, C.Ss.R.
Church and Mailing Address: 5th St. & Girard Ave., 19123.; Rectory: 1019 N. Fifth St., 19123. Tel: 215-627-2386; 2387; 627-1176; Fax: 215-627-2366.
School—1009 N. Fifth St., 19123. Tel: 215-922-5958. Sr. Rosalia Federici, S.S.N.D.
School Sisters of Notre Dame 8; Lay Teachers 9; Students 294.
Catechesis/Religious Programs—Dianne Skripek, D.R.E.
Students 353.
Convent—1005 N. 5th St., 19123. Tel: 215-627-3954.
Shrine—St. John Neuman. Mary Arghenbright, Office Mgr.; Bridgette Day, Coord.

137—ST. PETER CLAVER (1889-1985). Closed. Formerly located at 12th & Lombard Sts. Spiritual records are kept at St. John the Evangelist Church. Tel.: 215-563-4145.

138—ST. PHILIP NERI (1840), Rev. Msgr. James J. Fitzpatrick. In res., Rev. Msgr. Louis A. D'Addezio.
Res., 218 Queen St., 19147. Tel: 215-468-1922; Fax: 215-465-3147.
Catechesis/Religious Programs—Twinned with Sacred Heart, Philadelphia.

139—ST. RAPHAEL (1904-1989). Closed. Formerly located at 86th St. & Tinicum Ave. Spiritual records are kept at St. Irenaeus Church. Tel.: 215-727-2888.

140—ST. RAYMOND OF PENAFORT (1941), Rev. Msgr. John F. O'Brien. In res., Rev. Paul S. Quinter.
Res., 1350 Vernon Rd., 19150. Tel: 215-549-3760; Fax: 215-549-1271.
School—7940 Williams Ave., 19150. Tel: 215-548-1919.
Sisters of Mercy 1; Lay Teachers 10; Students 295.
Catechesis/Religious Programs—Students 59.

141—RESURRECTION OF OUR LORD (1928), Revs. William C. Kaufman; Robert L. Brennan; Patrick S. McManus; John E. Fitzgerald.
Res., 2000 Shelmire Ave., 19152. Tel: 215-745-3211; Fax: 215-745-0587.
School—2020 Shelmire Ave., 19152. Tel: 215-742-1127; Fax: 215-742-0947. Stephen J. Hewitt, Prin.; Lucille Hillerman, Vice Prin.
Lay Teachers 34; Students 891.
Catechesis/Religious Programs—Students 224.

142—ST. RICHARD (1924), Revs. Joseph J. Gallagher; John J. Morley, Pastor Emeritus. In res., Rev. James P. Olson.
Res., 3010 S. 18th St., 19145. Tel: 215-468-4777; Fax: 215-468-3161.
School—19th & Pollock Sts., 19145. Tel: 215-467-5430.
Lay Teachers 10; Students 250.
Convent—1827 Pollock St., 19145. Tel: 215-465-5209.
Sisters of Mercy 5.

143—ST. RITA OF CASCIA (1907), Revs. Michael F. Di Gregorio, O.S.A., Pastor & Shrine Dir.; James L. Galligan, O.S.A.; Edward E. Doran, O.S.A.; Deacon Leroy F. O'Kedas. In res., Revs. Edward V. Griffin, O.S.A.; Joseph A. Genito, O.S.A.
Res., 1166 S. Broad St., 19146. Tel: 215-546-8333; Fax: 215-732-3510.

144—ST. ROSE OF LIMA (1921), Rev. Msgr. Wilfred J. Pashley.
Res., 1535 N. 59th St., 19151. Tel: 215-877-2991; Fax: 215-877-8255.
School—1522 N. Wanamaker St., 19131. Tel: 215-473-6030; Fax: 215-473-2338.
Sisters, Servants of the Immaculate Heart of Mary 2; Lay Teachers 8; Students 285.
Catechesis/Religious Programs—Students 10.

145—SACRED HEART OF JESUS (1871), Revs. Michael J. Sheehan; William E. Dean. In res., Rev. John J. Bradley.
Res., 1404 S. Third St., 19147-6099. Tel: 215-465-4050; 4051; Fax: 215-465-0400.
School—1329 Moyamensing Ave., 19147. Tel: 215-462-4129; Fax: 215-462-9429. Sr. Elizabeth Monica Acri, I.H.M., Prin.
Sisters of the Immaculate Heart of Mary 3; Lay Teachers 9; Students 236.
Catechesis/Religious Programs—Students 9.
Convent—1420 S. Third St., 19147. Tel: 215-463-8719.

146—SACRED HEART (1913-1977) (Hungarian). Closed. Formerly located at Mascher & Master Sts. Spiritual records are kept at St. Michael Church. Tel.: 215-739-2358.

147—ST. STANISLAUS (1891) (Polish), Rev. Joseph B. Jarosz.
Res., 242 Fitzwater St., 19147. Tel: 215-925-2631.
School—St. Mary Interparochial School. See Consolidated Parish Schools under Institutions Located in the Archdiocese.
Catechesis/Religious Programs—Students 10.

148—STELLA MARIS (1954), Rev. Msgr. James F. Connelly, S.T.L., H.E.D.; Revs. George B. Cadwallader, M.A.; John P. Collins, M.A., M.Div.; Deacon James Thompson.
Res., 2901 S. 10th St., 19148. Tel: 215-465-2336; 2337.
School—814 Bigler St., 19148. Tel: 215-467-6262; Fax: 215-389-6040.
Sisters of St. Joseph 3; Lay Teachers 12; Students 307.
Catechesis/Religious Programs—Students 105.
Convent—2929 S. 10th St., 19148. Tel: 215-462-1111.

149—ST. STEPHEN (1843-1993). Closed. Formerly located at Broad & Butler Sts. Spiritual records are kept at Our Lady of Hope Church. Tel: 215-329-8100.

150—ST. TERESA OF AVILA (1853-1972). Closed. Formerly located at Broad & Catherine Sts. Spiritual records are kept at St. Rita Church. Tel: 215-546-8333.

151—ST. THERESE OF THE CHILD JESUS (1925), Rev. Steven J. Harris, J.C.D.; Deacon Edward M. Purnell.
Res., 6611 Ardleigh St., 19119. Tel: 215-438-5279; Fax: 215-438-8031.
School—Anderson & Upsal Sts., 19119. Tel: 215-844-5654; Fax: 215-844-8461. Mrs. Donna-Maria Meyers, Prin.
Lay Teachers 12; Students 200.
Catechesis/Religious Programs—Tel: 215-438-5746.
Students 10.

152—ST. THOMAS AQUINAS (1885), Revs. Arthur I. Taraborelli; Joseph Dinh C. Huynh (Vietnam). In res., Rev. Joseph W. McCloskey.
Res., 1719 Morris St., 19145. Tel: 215-334-2312; Fax: 215-755-9369.
School—18th & Morris Sts., 19145. Tel: 215-334-0878; Fax: 215-334-2357.
Lay Teachers 19; Students 619.
Day Care—1700 Fernon St.; 1800 Morris St., Tel: 215-334-6480.
Staff 10; Children 52.
Catechesis/Religious Programs—Students 6.

153—ST. TIMOTHY (1928), Revs. Anthony W. Dieckhaus; Michael J. Fitzpatrick; John J. LaRosa; Joseph W. Callahan.
Res., 3001 Levick St., 19149. Tel: 215-624-6188; Fax: 215-624-1316.
School—Hawthorne & Levick Sts., 19149. Tel: 215-338-9797; Fax: 215-331-6457. Stephen DiCicco, Prin.; Margaret Presutti, Vice-Prin.
Sisters of St. Joseph 2; Lay Teachers 36; Students 1,030.
Catechesis/Religious Programs—Students 148.
Convent—3033 Levick St., 19149. Tel: 215-624-8333.

154—TRANSFIGURATION OF OUR LORD (1905-2000). Formerly located at 5533 Cedar Ave. Spiritual records are kept at St. Cyprian Church. Tel.: 215-747-3250.

155—ST. VERONICA (1872), Revs. Eduardo Coll, I.V.E.; Raul Montfort; Mrs. Maureen Maher, Business Mgr.; Deacons Javier Correa; Rafael Maldonado; Alfonso Fernandez.
Res., 533 W. Tioga St., 19140. Tel: 215-228-4878; 225-5677; Fax: 215-228-0381.
School—Sixth & Tioga St., 19140. Tel: 215-225-1575; Fax: 215-225-2595. Sr. Virginia Paschall, I.H.M., Prin.
Sisters, Servants of the Immaculate Heart of Mary 3; Lay Teachers 7; Students 231.
Catechesis/Religious Programs—Tel: 215-228-4878. Sr. Alba M. Bonilla, O.P., D.R.E.
Students 179.
Convents—3521 N. Sixth St., 19140. Tel: 215-223-9107. Sisters, Servants of the Immaculate Heart of Mary Sr. Helen Maureen Campbell, I.H.M., Superior.; 632 W. Erie Ave., 19140. Tel: 215-226-3507. Dominican Sisters of Our Lady of the Rosary of Fatima Sr. Cruz Maria Vega, O.P., Superior.
Casila Outreach Program—606 W. Eric Ave., 19140. Tel: 215-226-3507. Sr. M. Ester Ortiz, O.P.

156—ST. VINCENT DE PAUL (1851), Revs. Aidan R. Rooney, C.M.; Joseph V. Cummins, C.M.; Stephen M. Grozio, C.M.; Bro. Alfred J. Smith, C.M.
Res., 109 E. Price St., 19144. Tel: 215-438-2925; Fax: 215-438-4856.
School—St. Martin De Porres School (Germantown). See Consolidated Parish Schools under Institutions Located in the Archdiocese. Tel: 215-842-1266.

157—VISITATION B.V.M. (1874), Rev. Msgr. Edward M. Deliman; Revs. Augusto Concha; Stephan B. Perzan; Deacons Edwin Manzano; Apolonio Collazo.
Res., 2625 B St., 19125. Tel: 215-634-1133; Fax: 215-634-6622.
School—300 E. Lehigh Ave., 19125. Tel: 215-634-7280; Fax: 215-634-4062.
Sisters of St. Joseph 5; Lay Teachers 18; Students 464.
Catechesis/Religious Programs—Sr. Margaret Doherty, S.H.C.J., D.R.E.
Students 171.

158—ST. WILLIAM (1920), Rev. Msgr. James E. Mortimer; Revs. Winson Parekkat, C.M.I.; Clemens J. Gerdelmann; Angelo Hernandez. In res., Rev. Edmund J. Maher.
Res., 6200 Rising Sun Ave., 19111. Tel: 215-745-1389; Fax: 215-745-2650.
Primary School—6200 Palmetto St., 19111. Tel: 215-342-3369.
Intermediate School—Rising Sun and Robbins Aves., 19111. Tel: 215-342-4488.
Middle School—Rising Sun and Devereaux Aves., 19111. Tel: 215-725-2574.
Sisters, Servants of the Immaculate Heart of Mary 11; Lay Teachers 35; Students 843.
Catechesis/Religious Programs—Students 82.
Day Care Center—514 McKinley St., 19111. Tel: 215-745-7708.
Convent—6226 Rising Sun Ave., 19111. Tel: 215-745-3513.
Pastoral Care Ministry: Tel: 215-742-9992.

OUTSIDE THE CITY OF PHILADELPHIA

Abington, Montgomery Co., Our Lady Help of Christians (1953), Rev. Joseph D. Bowen; Rev. Msgr. J. Clement Bennington, Pastor Emeritus; Deacon Joseph T. Rooney. In res., Rev. Albert J. Santorsola.
Res., 1500 Marian Rd., 19001. Tel: 215-886-3456; Fax: 215-886-7312.
Preschool—Tel: 215-887-8503.
Lay Teachers 4; Students 60.
School—Elkins & Crater Rds., 19001. Tel: 215-887-3067.
Lay Teachers 10; Students 249.
Catechesis/Religious Programs—Students 200.

Ambler, Montgomery Co., St. Anthony of Padua (1886), Revs. Stephen P. McHenry; Thomas Vattothuparambil (India); Deacon David E. Jones.
Res., 259 Forest Ave., 19002-5999. Tel: 215-646-4742; Fax: 215-646-4864. [CEM]
School—Ambler Catholic Elementary School. See Consolidated Parish Schools under Institutions Located in the Archdiocese. Tel: 215-646-6150; Fax: 215-654-5254.
Sisters of St. Joseph 3; Lay Teachers 14; Students 297.
Catechesis/Religious Programs—Tel: 215-646-0586.
Students 249.
Convent—251 Forrest Ave., 19002. Tel: 215-646-0426.

St. Joseph (1920), Rev. Daniel J. Cavanaugh; Deacon Francis Clark. In res., Rev. James R. Jugenheimer.
Res., 16 S. Spring Garden St., 19002-4797. Tel: 215-646-0494; Fax: 215-643-6389.
School—Ambler Catholic Elementary School. See Consolidated Parish Schools under Institutions Located in the Archdiocese. Tel: 215-646-2007.
Catechesis/Religious Programs—Students 328.

Ardmore, Montgomery Co., St. Colman (1907), Most Rev. Robert P. Maginnis; Rev. Joseph M. Arnholt; Rev. Msgr. Francis J. Statkus, Pastor Emeritus; Deacon James T. Owens. In res., Rev. Richard J. Wright.
Res., 11 Simpson Rd., 19003. Tel: 610-642-0545; Fax: 610-642-6853.
School—SS. Colman-John Neumann School. See Consolidated Parish Schools under Institutions Located in the Archdiocese. Tel: 610-642-0545.

Ardsley, Montgomery Co., Queen of Peace (1954), Revs. James P. Matteo; Michael H. Spitzer, M.A., M.Div.; Rev. Msgr. Joseph E. Lynaugh, Pastor Emeritus; Rev. Msgr. Thomas J. Hilferty, Pastor Emeritus. In res., Rev. Msgr. William J. Lynn.
Res., 820 North Hills Ave., 19038. Tel: 215-887-1838; Fax: 215-887-8328.
School—835 North Hills Ave., Tel: 215-886-4782.
Sisters of the Holy Family of Nazareth 2; Sisters, Servants of the Immaculate Heart of Mary 2; Lay Teachers 13; Students 211.
Catechesis/Religious Programs—Tel: 215-886-3014. Sr. Jean Marie, C.S.F.N., D.R.E.
Students 276.
Convent—825 North Hills Ave., Tel: 215-887-4785.

Aston, Delaware Co., St. Joseph (1947), Revs. Robert C. Vogan; Geraldo J. Pinero.
Res., 256 Concord Rd., 19014. Tel: 610-497-3340; Fax: 610-497-3383. [CEM]
School—Tel: 610-494-0147. Ms. Anne Cook, Prin.
Lay Teachers 22; Students 459.
Catechesis/Religious Programs—Tel: 610-494-4358. Ms. Patricia McGeever, D.R.E.
Students 379.

Bala Cynwyd, Montgomery Co., St. Matthias (1906), Rev. Arthur E. Rodgers; Rev. Msgr. Thomas A. Kane, Pastor Emeritus, (Retired); Mr. John Yura, Dir. Parish Svcs.; Deacon Gerald Kelly. In res., Revs. Charles E. Gormley, (Retired); Philip J. Lowe, Ed.D.
Res., 128 Bryn Mawr Ave., 19004-3099. Tel: 610-664-0207; Fax: 610-664-3559.
Catechesis/Religious Programs—120 Bryn Mawr Ave., 19004-3098. Tel: 610-664-1942. Marie Faiss, D.R.E.
Convent—108 Highland Ave., 19004. Tel: 610-667-1399.

Bensalem, Bucks Co.,

1—ST. CHARLES BORROMEO, (1903), Rev. Msgr. Francis A. Carbine; Rev. Patrick G. McCormick. In res., Rev. John F. Meyers.
Res., 1731 Hulmeville Rd., 19020. Tel: 215-638-3625; Fax: 215-245-8578.
School—(Grades PreK-8) 1704 Bristol Pike, Tel: 215-639-3456; Fax: 215-639-0496.
Sisters, Servants of the Immaculate Heart of Mary 5; Lay Teachers 17; Students 474.
Catechesis/Religious Programs—Tel: 215-638-3650.
Students 184.
Convent—1080 Kings Ave., Tel: 215-639-0113.

2—ST. ELIZABETH ANN SETON, (1902), Rev. John J. Duffy, Pastor Emeritus; Deacons Francis C. Klauder; Joseph W. Niland; Lawrence J. Gibson. In res., Rev. Michael J. Lonergan.
1200 Park Ave. E., 19020-4652. Tel: 215-245-6122; Fax: 215-245-4211.
Catechesis/Religious Programs—Tel: 215-638-1498.
Students 182.

3—SAINT EPHREM, (1966), Rev. James E. McGuire; Rev. Msgr. Edward S. Musial, Pastor Emeritus; Revs. Joseph E. Howarth; Anthony F. Orth; Deacons Edward J. Dymek; James Debow.
Res., 5400 Hulmeville Rd., 19020. Tel: 215-245-1698; Fax: 215-245-4787. [CEM]

School—5340 Hulmeville Rd., 19020. Tel: 215-639-9488; Fax: 215-639-0206.
Sisters, Servants of the Immaculate Heart of Mary 4; Lay Teachers 25; Students 650.
Catechesis/Religious Programs—Tel: 215-639-4895.
Students 360.
Convent—5300 Hulmeville Rd., 19020. Tel: 215-638-1024.

4—OUR LADY OF FATIMA, (1954), Revs. Thomas D. Homa; Victor Warkulwiz, M.S.S.
Res., Fatima Acres, 2933 Street Rd., 19020. Tel: 215-639-4254; Fax: 215-639-4589.
School—Tel: 215-638-3256; Fax: 215-639-6424.
Sisters, Servants of the Immaculate Heart of Mary 5; Lay Teachers 8; Students 235.
Catechesis/Religious Programs—2915 Street Rd., Tel: 215-639-8814.
Students 117.
Convent—2915 Street Rd., 19020. Tel: 215-639-1916. Fatima Acres

Berwyn, Chester Co., St. Monica (1897), Rev. George G. Hagenbach.
Res., 635 First Ave., 19312. Tel: 610-644-0110; Fax: 610-695-0850. [CEM]
School—First and Woodside Aves., Tel: 610-644-8848; Fax: 610-695-8515. Mrs. Diana Thompson, Prin.
Lay Teachers 16; Students 245.
Catechesis/Religious Programs—Tel: 610-647-4757. Sr. Constance Davis, O.S.F., D.R.E.
Students 260.

Boothwyn, Delaware Co., St. John Fisher (1971), Rev. John T. Lyons.
Res., 4225 Chichester Ave., 19061. Tel: 610-485-0441; Fax: 610-859-2109.
School—Holy Saviour-St. John Fisher School. See Consolidated Parish Schools under Institutions Located in the Archdiocese. Tel: 610-485-0363; Fax: 610-485-7809.
Catechesis/Religious Programs—Tel: 610-485-0581.
Students 286.

Bridgeport, Montgomery Co., St. Augustine (1892), Rev. Msgr. Francis X. Schmidt; Rev. Francis H. Gallen, Pastor Emeritus. In res., Rev. Charles J. Kennedy.
Res., 464 Ford St., 19405. Tel: 610-272-4088; Fax: 610-272-6396. [CEM]
School—Holy Trinity Catholic School. See Consolidated Parish Schools under Institutions Located in the Archdiocese. Tel: 610-279-4630 (Upper); 277-4133 (Lower); Fax: 610-279-5579 (Upper); 277-4725 (Lower).
Sisters, Servants of the Immaculate Heart of Mary 4; Lay Teachers 11; Students 275.
Catechesis/Religious Programs—Students 85.

Our Lady of Mt. Carmel (1924) (Italian), Rev. Salvatore J. Pronesti.
Res., 502 Ford St., 19405. Tel: 610-272-3479; Fax: 610-272-5449.
School—Holy Trinity Catholic School. See Consolidated Parish Schools under Institutions Located in the Archdiocese. Tel: 610-279-4630; Fax: 610-279-5579.
Catechesis/Religious Programs—Students 65.

Our Mother of Sorrows (1926) (Slovak), Rev. Paul A. DiGirolamo, Admin.
Res., 504 Holstein St., 19405. Tel: 610-275-3170.
School—St. Augustine-Our Lady of Mount Carmel School. See Consolidated Parish Schools under Institutions Located in the Archdiocese. Tel: 610-279-4630; Fax: 610-279-5579.

Bristol, Bucks Co., St. Ann (1906) (Italian), Revs. James R. Day, O.SS.T.; John DiMatteo, O.SS.T., Pastor Emeritus; Claude J. Gravel, O.S.S.T.
Res., 357 Dorrance St., P.O. Box 1175, 19007. Tel: 215-788-2128; Fax: 215-781-9782.
School—418 Jefferson Ave., 19007. Tel: 215-788-2030; Fax: 215-788-2979.
Sisters of the Most Holy Trinity 3; Lay Teachers 7; Students 215.
Catechesis/Religious Programs—Students 90.
Convent—430 Jefferson Ave., 19907. Tel: 215-788-2531.
Mission—Tullytown, Bucks Co., Sacred Heart of Jesus, Main St., 19007.

St. Mark (1845), Rev. Francis C. Lewis. In res., Rev. Vincent Tung The Pham.
Res., 1025 Radcliffe St., 19007. Tel: 215-788-2319;788-2493; Fax: 215-785-4121. [CEM]
School—1024 Radcliffe St., 19007. Tel: 215-785-0973; Fax: 215-781-0268.
Lay Teachers 11; Students 193.
Catechesis/Religious Programs—Students 150.
Convent—921 Radcliffe St., 19007.

Brookhaven, Delaware Co., Our Lady of Charity (1952), Rev. Msgr. Andrew J. Hanlon; Revs. James J. Kelly, Pastor Emeritus; John D. Schiele.
Res., 231 Upland Rd., 19015. Tel: 610-872-6192; Fax: 610-872-1120.
School—249 Upland Rd., 19015. Tel: 610-874-0410; Fax: 610-874-5879.
Sisters, Servants of the Immaculate Heart of Mary 7; Lay Teachers 18; Students 390.
Catechesis/Religious Programs—Students 210.
Convent—245 Upland Rd., 19015. Tel: 610-874-8101.

Brookline, Delaware Co., Annunciation B.V.M. (1927), Rev. Msgr. Ignatius L. Murray; Rev. George J. Boyle. In res., Rev. Msgr. Michael T. McCulken; Rev. Joseph P. Devlin.
Res., 410 Sagamore Rd., Havertown, 19083. Tel: 610-449-1613; Fax: 610-449-7041.
School—411 Brookline Blvd., Havertown, 19083. Tel: 610-446-8430.
Sisters of Mercy 1; Lay Teachers 18; Students 312.
Catechesis/Religious Programs—Tel: 610-449-9858.
Students 301.
Convent—421 Brookline Blvd., Havertown, 19083. Tel: 610-449-4065.

Broomall, Delaware Co., St. Pius X (1955), Revs. James Hutchins; Joseph M. Derrig; William T. Small; Deacon Joseph E. Iannucci.
Res., 220 Lawrence Rd., 19008. Tel: 610-353-4880; Fax: 610-356-1084.
School—204 Lawrence Rd., 19008. Tel: 610-356-7222; Fax: 610-356-5380.
Sisters, Servants of the Immaculate Heart of Mary 4; Lay Teachers 27; Students 609.
Catechesis/Religious Programs—Tel: 610-353-6950.
Students 466.

Bryn Mawr, Delaware Co., St. John Neumann (1964), Rev. Msgr. James H. Meehan; Sr. Carol Kelly, S.S.J., Coord. In res., Rev. Msgr. David E. Walls; Rev. Michael J. Matz.
Res., 380 Highland Ln., 19010. Tel: 610-525-3100; Fax: 610-525-6363.
School—SS. Colman-St. John Neumann School. See Consolidated Parish Schools under Institutions Located in the Archdiocese. Tel: 610-525-3266; Fax: 610-525-6103. Mrs. Mary Ann DeAngelo, Prin.
Sisters 1; Lay Teachers 17; Students 252.
Catechesis/Religious Programs—Students 123.
Convent—340 Highland Ln., 19010. Tel: 610-527-1220; 527-3115.

Our Mother of Good Counsel, Montgomery Co., (1885), Revs. James E. Martinez, O.S.A.; Adrian Gilligan, O.S.A. In res., Revs. Anthony P. Burrascano, O.S.A.; Harry A. Cassel, O.S.A., (Retired); Joseph A. Duffey, (Retired).
Res., 31 Pennswood Rd., 19010. Tel: 610-525-0147; Fax: 610-525-0157.
School—St. Thomas-Good Counsel School. See Consolidated Parish Schools under Institutions Located in the Archdiocese. Tel: 610-525-1407; Fax: 610-525-4701.
Lay Teachers 14; Students 204.
Catechesis/Religious Programs—Fax: 610-525-0157.
Students 173.

Buckingham, Bucks Co., Our Lady of Guadalupe (2000), Revs. Joseph J. Quindlen; Robert B. McDermott; Deacon Joseph N. Gousie.
Mailing Address: P.O. Box 406, 18912-0406.
Parish Office: 5667 York Rd., Lahaska, 18931. Tel: 215-794-2004; Fax: 215-794-5004.
Res., 3686 W. Long Ln., Doylestown, 18901-1292.

Center Square, Montgomery Co., St. Helena (1919), Revs. Joseph J. Nicolo; John T. Coates, Pastor Emeritus; Deacon A. Kenneth Belanger. In res., Rev. Gregory J. Hickey.
Res., P.O. Box 5085, 19422-0809. Tel: 610-275-7711; Fax: 610-275-7610.
School—Tel: 610-279-3345.
Sisters of Mercy 1; Lay Teachers 18; Students 378.
Catechesis/Religious Programs—Tel: 215-277-3573.
Students 291.
Convent—Tel: 610-272-1383.

Chadds Ford, Delaware Co., St. Cornelius (1963), Rev. James E. Locke.
Res., 110 Ridge Rd., 19317. Tel: 610-459-2502; Fax: 610-459-3942.
School—St. Cornelius Academy, Tel: 610-459-8663.
Catechesis/Religious Programs—Students 90.

Chalfont, Bucks Co., St. Jude (1962), Rev. Msgr. James P. McCoy; Rev. Mark S. Gaspar; Mr. Robert T. O'Sullivan, Business Mgr.; Deacons Vincent G. Ceneviva; John T. Riordan; Claude B. Granese. In res., Rev. Robert P. Lepleiter, (Retired).
Res., 321 W. Butler Ave., 18914-2329. Tel: 215-822-0179; Fax: 215-822-0638.
School—323 W. Butler Ave., 18914. Tel: 215-822-9225; Fax: 215-822-0722. Sr. Marie Melanie, R.S.M., Prin.
Sisters 3; Lay Teachers 25; Students 526.
Catechesis/Religious Programs—Tel: 215-822-7553. Mrs. Helen Rosenbaum, Prin.
Students 637.

Cheltenham, Montgomery Co., St. Joseph (1953), Rev. William S. Harrison.
Res., 120 Hilldale Rd., 19012. Tel: 215-635-5533; Fax: 215-635-4578.
School—Boncouer & Water Rds., Tel: 215-635-0102; Fax: 215-635-4881.
Daughters of Our Lady of the Sacred Heart 2; Lay Teachers 8; Students 143.
Catechesis/Religious Programs—Students 37.
Convent—7633 Waters Rd., Tel: 215-224-2159.

Presentation of Blessed Virgin Mary (1890), Revs. William S. Harrison; John R. McFadden; Sr. Joan Anne Melley, S.S.J., Parish Service Dir.
Res., 100 Old Soldiers Rd., 19012. Tel: 215-379-1364; 379-1599; Fax: 215-379-1456.
School—Hasbrook Ave. & Old Soldiers Rd., 19012. Tel: 215-379-3798; Fax: 215-379-4430.
Lay Teachers 20; Students 460.
Catechesis/Religious Programs—Tel: 215-379-2054.
Students 149.
Convent—107 Old Soldiers Rd., 19012. Tel: 215-379-8343.

Chester, Delaware Co.,

1—ST. ANTHONY OF PADUA, (1908-1993) (Italian). Closed. Formerly located at 308 W. 3rd St. Spiritual records are kept at Saint Katharine Drexel Church, Chester. Tel: 610-872-3731.

2—SAINT KATHARINE DREXEL, (1993), Revs. Kevin P. Murray; Stephen D. Thorne; Peter J. Welsh; Deacon Michael J. Finn.
1920 Providence Ave., 19013. Tel: 610-872-3731; Fax: 610-872-0545.
School—Tel: 610-872-7358; Fax: 610-872-7833.
Catechesis/Religious Programs—Students 387.
Convent—1902 Providence Ave., 19013. Tel: 610-876-4916.
Mission—Chester, Delaware Co., Saint Katharine Drexel Center for Evangelization, 2nd & Norris St., 19013. Tel: 610-872-3731; Fax: 610-872-0545.

3—ST. HEDWIG, (1902-1993) (Polish). Closed. Formerly located at 4th & Hayes Sts. Spiritual records are kept at Sacred Heart Church, Clifton Heights. Tel: 610-623-0409.

4—IMMACULATE HEART OF MARY, (1873-1993). Closed. Formerly located at 2nd & Norris Sts. Spiritual records are kept at Saint Katharine Drexel Church, Chester. Tel: 610-872-3731.

5—ST. MICHAEL, (1842-1993). Closed. Formerly located at 7th St. & Avenue of the States. Spiritual records are kept at Saint Katharine Drexel Church, Chester. Tel: 610-872-3731.

6—OUR LADY OF VILNA, (1924-1972) (Lithuanian). Closed. Formerly located at 4th & Madison Sts. Sacramental records are kept at Saint Katharine Drexel Church, Chester. Tel: 215-872-3731.

7—RESURRECTION OF OUR LORD, (1911-1993). Closed. Formerly located at 9th St. & Highland Ave. Spiritual records are kept at Saint Katharine Drexel Church, Chester. Tel: 610-872-3731.

8—ST. ROBERT, (1922-1993). Closed. Formerly located at 20th St. & Providence Ave. Spiritual records are kept at Saint Katharine Drexel Church, Chester. Tel: 610-872-3731.

Chester Heights, Delaware Co., St. Thomas the Apostle (1729), Revs. Richard C. Williams; Francis J. Cauterucci; Deacons Anthony DiIenno; Charles Devine.
Res., 430 Valley Brook Rd., Glen Mills, 19342. Tel: 610-459-2224; Fax: 610-459-2677. [CEM]
School—Tel: 610-459-8134; Fax: 610-459-8120.
Lay Teachers 14; Students 304.
Catechesis/Religious Programs—Tel: 610-459-3477. Joseph Doyle, D.R.E.
Students 550.
Chaplaincies—Glen Mills Schools; Delaware County Prison; Brinton Manor; Rosehill.

Clifton Heights, Delaware Co., Sacred Heart (1910) (Polish), Rev. Msgr. Francis A. Barszczewski, S.T.L.; Rev. Jan Palkowski; Deacon Boleslaw S. Wojewodka.
Res., 316 E. Broadway, 19018. Tel: 610-623-0409; Fax: 610-623-2926.
Kindergarten & Preschool—301 E. Berkley Ave., 19018. Tel: 610-623-4861.
Convent—300 E. Berkley Ave., 19018. Tel: 610-623-8804.
Mission—Chester, Delaware Co., St. Hedwig Chapel, 4th & Hayes Sts., Chester, 19013.

Coatesville, Chester Co.,

1—ST. CECILIA, (1870), Revs. Francis J. Schlett; Nicholas J. Dininni.
Res., 99 N. 6th Ave., 19320. Tel: 610-384-0422; Fax: 610-384-4415. [CEM]
School—Coatesville Area Catholic Elementary

School. See Consolidated Parish Schools under Institutions Located in the Archdiocese. Tel: 610-384-5961.
Sisters, Servants of the Immaculate Heart of Mary 4; Lay Teachers 16; Students 560.
Catechesis/Religious Programs—Students 240.
Convent—603 E. Lincoln Hwy., Tel: 610-384-0733; Fax: 610-384-5730.

2—OUR LADY OF THE ROSARY, (1917) (Italian), Rev. Harry A. Romano; Deacon Richard Stoughton.
Res., 80 S. 17th Ave., 19320. Tel: 610-384-1415; Fax: 610-383-6592.
School—Coatesville Area Catholic Elementary School. See Consolidated Parish Schools under Institutions Located in the Archdiocese. Tel: 610-384-5961.
Catechesis/Religious Programs—Tel: 610-384-1415.
Students 270.

3—ST. JOSEPH, (1924) (Slovak), Rev. John V. Oulds.
Res., 404 Charles St., 19320. Tel: 610-384-0360.
School—Coatesville Area Catholic Elementary School. See Consolidated Parish Schools under Institutions Located in the Archdiocese. Tel: 610-384-5961.
Catechesis/Religious Programs—Students 55.

4—ST. STANISLAUS KOSTKA, (1907) (Polish), Rev. John V. Oulds.
Res., 209 W. Lincoln Hwy., 19320. Tel: 610-384-1172; Fax: 610-384-1172 (Call First). [CEM]
School—Coatesville Area Catholic Elementary School. See Consolidated Parish Schools under the Institutions Located in the Archdiocese. Tel: 610-384-5961.
Catechesis/Religious Programs—Students 7.

Collegeville, Montgomery Co., St. Eleanor (1911), Revs. John A. Franey; James P. McKelvey; Deacons Gerald McGrath; James Burns; Michael Woodal; Gerard P. McGrath; Joseph R. DeRosa. In res., Revs. Joseph Bongard; Francis P. Lennon, Pastor Emeritus.
Res., 647 Locust St., 19426. Tel: 610-489-1647; Fax: 610-489-7469.
School—Tel: 610-489-9434.
Lay Teachers 23; Students 550.
Catechesis/Religious Programs—Tel: 610-489-4677.
Students 815.
Convent—111 Sixth Ave., 19426. Tel: 610-489-1573.

Collingdale, Delaware Co., St. Joseph (1916), Revs. James E. McVeigh; David A. Fernandes; Michael J. Davis.
Res., 500 Woodlawn Ave., 19023. Tel: 610-583-4530; Fax: 610-583-7730.
School—Bartram & Woodlawn Aves., Tel: 610-586-0356. Sr. Susan Immaculate, I.H.M., Prin.
Sisters, Servants of the Immaculate Heart of Mary 13; Lay Teachers 26; Students 755.
Catechesis/Religious Programs—Students 270.

Conshohocken, Montgomery Co., SS. Cosmas and Damian (1912) (Italian), Rev. Gasper A. Genuardi. In res., Rev. Msgr. Alexander J. Palmieri, M.A., J.C.L.; Deacon Armand J. Maresca.
Res., 209 W. Fifth Ave., 19428. Tel: 610-828-0101; Fax: 610-828-5294.
School—See Consolidated Parish Schools under Institutions Located in the Archdiocese. Conshohocken Catholic School, Tel: 610-828-2007; Fax: 610-825-8796.
Catechesis/Religious Programs—Students 126.

St. Mary (1905) (Polish), Rev. Msgr. Robert J. Grudowski. In res., Rev. Msgr. Edward S. Musial.
Res., 140 W. Hector St., 19428. Tel: 610-828-0260; Fax: 610-828-9665. [CEM]
Catechesis/Religious Programs—Students 45.

St. Matthew (1851), Rev. James W. Donlon. In res., Revs. John J. Ames; Gerard C. Chapman.
Res., 219 Fayette St., 19428. Tel: 610-828-0424; Fax: 610-825-5168. [CEM]
School—Conshohocken Catholic School. See Consolidated Parish Schools under Institutions Located in the Archdiocese. Tel: 610-828-2007; Fax: 610-825-8796.
Catechesis/Religious Programs—Students 148.
Convent—Third Ave. & Harry St., Tel: 610-828-0174.

Croydon, Bucks Co., St. Thomas Aquinas (1922), Revs. Francis M. Gallagher, M.A.; John Tharayil, C.M.I.; Peter Talocci.
Res., 601 Bristol Pike, 19021-5496. Tel: 215-788-2989; 788-5813; Fax: 215-788-7626.
School—Walnut Ave. & Bristol Pike, Tel: 215-785-1130; Fax: 215-785-2564. Barbara A. Rutecki, Prin.
Lay Teachers 12; Students 250.

Darby, Delaware Co., Blessed Virgin Mary (1913), Rev. Joseph Corley. In res., Rev. Edward Kennedy.
Res., 1101 Main St., 19023. Tel: 610-583-2128; Fax: 610-583-9829.
School—47 MacDade Blvd., 19023. Tel: 610-586-0638.
Sisters, Servants of the Immaculate Heart of Mary 3; Lay Teachers 15; Students 289.
Catechesis/Religious Programs—Tel: 610-461-2490.
Students 83.

Delphi, Montgomery Co., St. Mary (1926), Revs. Charles J. McElroy; Thomas J. Furey.
Res., 40 Spring Mount Rd., Schwenksville, 19473. Tel: 610-287-8156; Fax: 610-287-4226.
School—Tel: 610-287-7757.
Lay Teachers 15; Students 298.
Catechesis/Religious Programs—Tel: 610-287-4517.
Students 456.

Downingtown, Chester Co., St. Joseph (1851), Rev. Msgr. Robert T. McManus; Revs. William J. Smith, Pastor Emeritus; Walter J. Benn; Vito J. Carbone; James D. Tortorici; Deacon Edward R. Schiappa. In res., Rev. James J. McGuinn.
Res., 338 Manor Ave., 19335. Tel: 610-269-8294; Fax: 610-269-2487. [CEM]
School—340 Manor Ave., 19335. Tel: 610-269-8999; Fax: 610-269-2252.
Sisters, Servants of the Immaculate Heart of Mary 4; Lay Teachers 27; Students 800.
Catechesis/Religious Programs—Tel: 610-873-8798.
Students 1,412.
Convent—336 Manor Ave., 19335. Tel: 610-363-6559.

Doylestown, Bucks Co., Our Lady of Mount Carmel (1850), Rev. Msgr. John E. Breslin; Revs. John J. Davids; Philip G. Bochanski; Daniel J. Gallagher; Bro. Richard C. Ekmann, O.S.A.; Deacons George Corwell; Joseph Gousie, Sr.; Walter Kelly.
Res., 235 E. State St., 18901. Tel: 215-348-4190; Fax: 215-348-3104. [CEM]
School—E. Ashland St., 18901. Tel: 215-348-5907; Fax: 215-348-5671.
Sisters of St. Francis of Philadelphia 4; Lay Teachers 23; Students 560.
Catechesis/Religious Programs—Tel: 215-345-7089; Fax: 215-345-4216. Sr. Christa DeBacher, D.R.E.
Students 1,085.
Convent—209 E. State St., 18901. Tel: 215-348-4663.

Drexel Hill, Delaware Co.,

1—ST. ANDREW, (1916), Rev. Msgr. D. James McGettigan; Revs. Joseph M. Glatts, Admin.; Girard J. Cusatis; Deacon Daniel N. DeLucca.
Res., 3500 School Ln., 19026. Tel: 610-259-1169; Fax: 610-259-0556.
School—529 Mason Ave., 19026. Tel: 610-259-5145. Mrs. Eileen Wilson, Prin.
Sisters of St. Joseph 3; Lay Teachers 22; Students 545.
Catechesis/Religious Programs—Students 405.
Convent—535 Mason Ave., 19026. Tel: 610-259-6130.

2—ST. BERNADETTE, (1947), Revs. William A. Wright; John H. Roebuck; Deacon Frank B. Burke, Business Mgr.
Res., 1035 Turner Ave., 19026. Tel: 610-789-7676; Fax: 610-789-9539.
School—1015 Turner Ave., 19026. Tel: 610-449-6126; Fax: 610-789-0890.
Oblate Sisters of St. Francis de Sales 4; Lay Teachers 23; Students 456.
Catechesis/Religious Programs—Tel: 610-853-1740. John Blisard, D.R.E.
Students 306.
Convent—Tel: 610-789-2325.

3—ST. CHARLES BORROMEO, (1849), Rev. Msgr. Daniel A. Murray, S.T.L., S.S.L.; Rev. Stephen A. Moerman; Deacons Francis Fabrizio; Peter Calabrese.
Res., 3422 Dennison Ave., 19026. Tel: 610-623-3800; Fax: 610-284-9583. [CEM]
School—3400 Dennison Ave., 19026. Tel: 610-626-4687; Fax: 610-626-1935.
Sisters, Servants of the Immaculate Heart of Mary 5; Lay Teachers 21; Students 415.
Catechesis/Religious Programs—Tel: 610-259-4389.
Students 254.
Convent—3407 Dennison Ave., 19026. Tel: 610-623-0965.

4—ST. DOROTHY, (1947), Rev. Msgr. Frederick J. Helduser; Rev. Michael D. Murphy; Deacon John J. Davaro. In res., Rev. Daniel J. Dougherty.
Res., 4910 Township Line, 19026. Tel: 610-789-7788; 789-7338; Fax: 610-789-6936.
School—Tel: 610-789-4100.
Lay Teachers 22; Students 442.
Catechesis/Religious Programs—Tel: 610-853-1499.
Students 350.
Convent—1201 Burmont Rd., 19026. Tel: 610-789-4112.

East Goshen, Chester Co., SS. Peter and Paul (1967), Revs. James J. Foley; Louis D. Kovacs, Pastor Emeritus; Joseph W. Dragon; Deacons Arthur G. Harrison; Thomas J. Horan; Robert J. Kefer; Robert F. Pierce.
Res., 1325 Boot Rd., West Chester, 19380. Tel: 610-692-2216; Fax: 610-692-7103.
Catechesis/Religious Programs—Tel: 610-692-5886.
Students 507.

East Lansdowne, Delaware Co., St. Cyril of Alexandria (1928), Revs. Peter D. Burke; Donald J. Farrell, Pastor Emeritus; Dennis Z. Fedak; Gerard Burns (Ireland); Deacon James E. Dalton.
Res., 153 Penn Blvd., 19050-2698. Tel: 610-623-5160; Fax: 610-622-2479.
School—716 Emerson Ave., 19050. Tel: 610-623-1113; Fax: 610-623-2427.
Sisters, Servants of the Immaculate Heart of Mary 2; Lay Teachers 14; Students 310.
Catechesis/Religious Programs—19050. Tel: 610-623-1406.
Students 225.
Convent—171 Penn Blvd., 19050. Tel: 610-623-6590.

Eddystone, Delaware Co., St. Rose of Lima (1890), Rev. Gerald D. Canavan.
Res., 1901 Chester Pike, 19013. Tel: 610-876-6170; Fax: 610-876-6128.
School—St. Madeline-St. Rose School. See Consolidated Parish Schools under Institutions Located in the Archdiocese.
Catechesis/Religious Programs—Students 216.

Elkins Park, Montgomery Co., St. James (1923), Rev. Raymond J. Himsworth.
Res., 8320 Brookside Rd., 19027. Tel: 215-635-6210; Fax: 215-635-3346.
School—8304 Brookside Rd., 19027. Tel: 215-635-4673; Fax: 215-635-3521.
Lay Teachers 11; Students 225.

Essington, Delaware Co., St. Margaret Mary Alacoque (1921), Revs. John J. Nevins; Francis J. Cornely, Pastor Emeritus.
Res., 500 Wanamaker Ave., 19029. Tel: 610-521-9177; Fax: 610-595-0230.

Exton, Chester Co., SS. Philip and James (1959), Rev. Msgr. Michael J. Burke; Rev. Msgr. John J. Caulfield, Pastor Emeritus; Revs. Christopher B. Rogers; Jeffrey M. Stecz; Deacons Frank M. Bizal; Charles W. Polley, Jr.; William C. Fahy. In res., Rev. Samuel A. Verruni, Chap.
Res., 107 N. Ship Rd., 19341. Tel: 610-363-6536; Fax: 610-524-7359.
School—721 N. Ship Rd., 19341. Tel: 610-363-6530; Fax: 610-363-6495. Sr. Mary Anne Winterberg, I.H.M., Prin.
Sisters, Servants of the Immaculate Heart of Mary 5; Lay Teachers 24; Students 732.
Catechesis/Religious Programs—Tel: 610-363-1307. Sr. Eunice Marie, I.H.M., D.R.E.
Students 577.
Convent—105 N. Ship Rd., 19341. Tel: 610-363-7068.

Fairless Hills, Bucks Co., St. Frances Cabrini (1952), Rev. Msgr. John J. Miller; Rev. Leo P. Oswald.
Res., 325 S. Oxford Valley Rd., 19030. Tel: 215-946-4040; 943-1116.
School—10 Goble Ct., 19030. Tel: 215-946-6334.
Lay Teachers 21; Students 395.
Catechesis/Religious Programs—Tel: 215-946-1115.
Students 285.

Fallsington, Bucks Co., St. Joseph the Worker (1956), Rev. Donald G. Birch. In res., Rev. Thomas J. Rooney.
Res., 9172 New Falls Rd., 19054. Tel: 215-945-4486; Fax: 215-945-3292.
School—9160 New Falls Rd., 19054. Tel: 215-945-4312; Fax: 215-945-8733.
Lay Teachers 20; Students 252.
Catechesis/Religious Programs—Tel: 215-945-4680.
Students 200.

Feasterville, Bucks Co., Assumption B.V.M. (1950), Revs. Daniel P. Devine; Albert T. Kostelnick; James J. Brennan. Pastoral Assocs.: Sr. Diane Wolf, S.S.J.; Sr. Madeline Dolores, I.H.M. In res., Rev. Robert H. Roedel.
Res., 1900 Meadowbrook Rd., 19053. Tel: 215-357-1221; Fax: 215-357-2283.
School—Tel: 215-357-5499.
Sisters, Servants of the Immaculate Heart of Mary 5; Lay Teachers 18; Students 434.
Catechesis/Religious Programs—Tel: 215-357-3445. Sr. Kathryn Benham, I.H.M., D.R.E.
Students 313.
Convent—55 Bristol Rd., 19053. Tel: 215-355-3898.

Flourtown, Montgomery Co., St. Genevieve (1953), Rev. Robert J. Carroll. In res., Revs. John D. Reardon; Carl F. Janicki; Deacon Joseph Manson.

Res., 1225 Bethlehem Pike, 19031. Tel: 215-836-2828; Fax: 215-836-7218.
School—1237 Bethlehem Pike, 19031. Tel: 215-836-5644; Fax: 215-836-0159.
Sisters of St. Joseph 4; Lay Teachers 16; Students 207.
Catechesis/Religious Programs—Tel: 215-836-1994.
Students 198.
Convent—1301 Bethlehem Pke., 19031. Tel: 215-233-4392; Fax: 215-233-4392.

Gladwyne, Montgomery Co., St. John Baptist Vianney (1927), Rev. Donald E. Leighton; Deacon Paul Kern. In res., Rev. Msgr. Joseph A. Shields.
Res., 1110 Vaughans Ln., 19035. Tel: 610-642-0938; Fax: 610-642-1432.
Catechesis/Religious Programs—1222 Hagysford Rd., Penn Valley, 19072. Tel: 610-664-0165; Fax: 610-664-5612. Sr. Mary Sarah, R.S.M., D.R.E.

Glenolden, Delaware Co., St. George (1923), Rev. Michael P. McCormac.
Res., 22 E. Cooke Ave., 19036-1497. Tel: 610-237-1633; Fax: 610-237-9626.
School—15 Lamont Ave., 19036-1497. Tel: 610-583-0419.
Lay Teachers 10; Students 243.
Catechesis/Religious Programs—Students 211.
Convent—11 E. Lamont Ave., 19036-1497. Tel: 610-583-5160.

Glenside, Montgomery Co., St. Luke the Evangelist (1905), Revs. J. Michael Flood; Joseph T. Murphy; Joseph D. Brandt. In res., Rev. Daniel J. Kearns.
Res., 2316 Fairhill Ave., 19038. Tel: 215-572-0128; Fax: 215-572-0482.
School—2330 Fairhill Ave., 19038. Tel: 215-884-0843; Fax: 215-884-4607. Sr. Helen Frederick, S.S.J., Prin.
Sisters of St. Joseph 4; Lay Teachers 22; Students 439.
Catechesis/Religious Programs—2324 Fairhill Ave., 19038. Tel: 215-884-2080. Mary Jane Dean, D.R.E.
Students 350.
Convent—2324 Fairhill Ave., 19038. Tel: 215-884-0225.

Hatboro, Montgomery Co., St. John Bosco (1953), Revs. Charles H. Hagan; Louis J. Kolenkiewicz; Deacons Daniel J. Rouse; William F. Kruckenberger.
Res., 235 E. County Line Rd., 19040. Tel: 215-672-7280; Fax: 215-675-7084.
School—215 E. County Line Rd., 19040-1298. Tel: 215-675-1484.
Sisters, Servants of the Immaculate Heart of Mary 3; Lay Teachers 8; Students 249.
Catechesis/Religious Programs—Students 350.
Convent—189 E. County Line Rd., 19040. Tel: 215-675-2301.

Hatfield, Montgomery Co., St. Maria Goretti (1953), Revs. Leonard N. Peterson; Brian P. Hennessy.
Res., 1601 Derstine Rd., 19440. Tel: 215-721-0199; Fax: 215-721-4320.
School—2980 Cowpath Rd., 19440. Tel: 215-721-9098; Fax: 215-721-3394.
Sisters, Servants of the Immaculate Heart of Mary 5; Lay Teachers 10; Students 265.
Catechesis/Religious Programs—Tel: 215-721-6559.
Students 693.
Convent—2990 Cowpath Rd., 19440. Tel: 215-723-8873.

Havertown, Delaware Co., St. Denis (1825), Rev. Msgr. Joseph T. Marino; Rev. Joseph C. McCaffrey; Deacons John F. Schlegel; David B. Schaffer.
Res., 2401 St. Denis Ln., 19083. Tel: 610-446-0200; Fax: 610-446-4638. [CEM]
School—300 E. Eagle Rd., 19083. Tel: 610-446-4608; Fax: 610-446-5705.
Sisters of Mercy 2; Lay Teachers 30; Students 560.
Catechesis/Religious Programs—Tel: 610-449-7892.
Students 269.
Convent—Tel: 610-446-1263.

Highland Park, Delaware Co., St. Laurence (1917), Rev. Msgr. Thomas J. Herron; Revs. Francis J. Mulranen; John D. Silcox, Jr.
Res., 30 St. Laurence Rd., Upper Darby, 19082. Tel: 610-449-0600; 0601; Fax: 610-449-4299.
School—8245 W. Chester Pike, 19082. Tel: 610-789-2670; Fax: 610-789-1128.
Sisters, Servants of the Immaculate Heart of Mary 9; Lay Teachers 18; Students 520.
Catechesis/Religious Programs—Tel: 610-789-4854.
Students 238.
Convent—Tel: 610-449-7042.
H.O.P.E. Program—.

Hilltown, Bucks Co., Our Lady of the Sacred Heart (1919), Rev. John F. McBride.
Res., Rte. 152 & Broad St., 18927. Tel: 215-822-9224; Fax: 215-712-0278. [CEM]
School—St. Agnes-Sacred Heart School. See Consolidated Parish Schools under Institutions Located in the Archdiocese. Tel: 215-822-9174; Fax: 215-822-7942.
Catechesis/Religious Programs—Tel: 215-822-9020.
Students 385.

Holland, Bucks Co., St. Bede the Venerable (1966), Revs. Eugene G. Cusick; Gary Pacitti; Andrew McCormick.
Res., 1054 Holland Rd., 18966. Tel: 215-357-5720; Fax: 215-396-0704.
School—1053 Holland Rd., 18966. Tel: 215-357-4720.
Sisters of St. Casimir 1; Lay Teachers 22; Students 516.
Catechesis/Religious Programs—Tel: 215-357-2130.
Students 830.
Convent—35 Vanderveer Dr., 18966. Tel: 215-355-2132.

Honey Brook, Chester Co., St. Peter (1963), Rev. William J. Cox; Virginia L. Giles, Business Mgr.; Deacon Richard L. Fremont.
Res., 1080 N. Manor Rd., 19344-9610. Tel: 610-942-2112.
Catechesis/Religious Programs—Tel: 610-942-4518. Patrice A. Peterson, D.R.E.
Students 502.

Horsham, Montgomery Co., St. Catherine of Siena (1963), Revs. John C. Wilz; Laurence Gleason; Deacons Timothy Urbanski; Richard Haddon. In res., Rev. Joseph Kelley.
Res., 321 Witmer Rd., 19044. Tel: 215-672-2881; Fax: 215-674-1025.
School—317 Witmer Rd., 19044. Tel: 215-674-1904; Fax: 215-674-1466.
Sisters of Mercy 1; Lay Teachers 22; Students 424.
Catechesis/Religious Programs—Tel: 215-674-8549.
Students 660.
Convent—319 Witmer Rd., 19044. Tel: 215-672-7221.

Huntingdon Valley, Montgomery Co., St. Albert the Great (1962), Rev. Msgr. Paul F. Curran; Revs. John J. Kelly; John P. Gallagher; Sr. Marie Rachfalski, O.S.F., Parish Svcs. Dir.
Res., 212 Welsh Rd., 19006. Tel: 215-947-3500; Fax: 215-938-9071.
School—216 Welsh Rd., 19006. Tel: 215-947-2332; Fax: 215-938-9360. Mary Randles, Prin.
Lay Teachers 23; Students 515.
Catechesis/Religious Programs—Tel: 215-947-3641.
Students 262.

Jamison, Bucks Co., St. Cyril of Jerusalem (1965), Rev. Robert J. Powell, D.M.A., M.A., M.Div.; Deacon Joseph F. Windish. In res., Rev. Charles Zlock, M.A., M.I.B.S.
Res., 1410 Almshouse Rd., 18929. Tel: 215-343-1288; Fax: 215-343-3924.
Catechesis/Religious Programs—Tel: 215-343-3139.
Students 813.

Jenkintown, Montgomery Co., Immaculate Conception (1866), Rev. Msgr. John J. Conahan; Deacon Paul Hagerty. In res., Revs. William J. Chiriaco; Nicholas Martino.
Res., 604 West Ave., 19046. Tel: 215-884-4022; 887-0181; Fax: 215-887-4163.
School—606 West Ave., 19046. Tel: 215-887-1312.
Lay Teachers 15; Students 235.
Catechesis/Religious Programs—Tel: 215-885-5586.
Students 285.

Kennett Square, Chester Co., St. Patrick (1869), Revs. Victor F. Sharrett; David H. Benz; Deacon James K. Madonna.
Res., 218 S. Meredith St., 19348. Tel: 610-444-2128; Fax: 610-444-4941. [CEM]
Parish Office: 212 Meredith St., 19348. Tel: 610-444-4364; Fax: 610-444-2129.
School—210 Meredith St., 19348. Tel: 610-444-3104; Fax: 610-444-3166.
Lay Teachers 10; Students 265.
Catechesis/Religious Programs—Tel: 610-444-2214. Mrs. Patricia Lohr, D.R.E.
Students 305.

Kimberton, Chester Co., St. Basil the Great (1965), Rev. Robert A. McLaughlin; Deacon Barry R. Midwood. In res., Rev. William E. Grogan.
Res., 2300 Kimberton Rd., Box 637, 19442-0637. Tel: 610-933-2110; 933-4730; Fax: 610-933-0627.
School—Tel: 610-933-2453; Fax: 610-933-7590.
Lay Teachers 12; Students 300.
Catechesis/Religious Programs—Tel: 610-935-1261.
Students 273.
Convent—Tel: 610-933-2345. Sisters of St. Francis Residence

King of Prussia, Montgomery Co., Mother of Divine Providence (1954), Revs. Thomas P. Gaynard; James F. Sullivan.
Res., 333 Allendale Rd., 19406. Tel: 610-265-4178; Fax: 610-265-1653.
School—405 Allendale Rd., 19406. Tel: 610-265-2323; Fax: 610-265-1816.
Grey Nuns of the Sacred Heart 2; Lay Teachers 14; Students 361.
Catechesis/Religious Programs—Tel: 610-337-2173.
Students 244.
Convent—Tel: 610-278-9439.

Lafayette Hill, Montgomery Co., St. Philip Neri (1945), Revs. Charle P. Vance; Edward J. Kelly. In res., Rev. Paul C. Brandt.
Res., 437 Ridge Pike, 19444. Tel: 610-828-5717; 834-1975; Fax: 610-834-0392.
School—3015 Chestnut St., 19444. Tel: 610-828-3082; Fax: 610-828-2943.
Sisters of St. Joseph 6; Lay Teachers 20; Students 495.
Catechesis/Religious Programs—Tel: 610-834-9868.
Students 156.
Convent—Tel: 610-828-2866.

Lansdale, Montgomery Co., St. Stanislaus (1876), Rev. Msgr. Joseph W. Murray; Revs. David A. Doyne; John C. Nguyen; Joseph T. Shenosky; Deacons Mathieu Tielemans; C. Stephens Vondercrone.
Res., 51 Lansdale Ave., 19446. Tel: 215-855-3133; Fax: 215-855-5478. [CEM]
School—493 E. Main St., 19446. Tel: 215-368-0995; Fax: 215-393-4869. Diane McCaughan, Prin.; Mrs. Barbara Kelly, Asst. Prin.
Lay Teachers 34; Students 787.
Catechesis/Religious Programs—Tel: 215-855-9893.
Students 388.

Lansdowne, Delaware Co., St. Philomena (1898), Rev. Robert J. Chapman. In res., Rev. A. Jason Kulczynski.
Res., 41 E. Baltimore Ave., 19050. Tel: 610-622-2420; Fax: 610-622-1215.
School—21 N. Highland Ave., 19050. Tel: 610-259-6817; Fax: 610-259-5656. Mrs. Mary Rose Worrilow, Prin.
Lay Teachers 11; Students 244.
Catechesis/Religious Programs—Students 54.

Lenni, Delaware Co., St. Francis de Sales (1894), Revs. William J. Teverzczuk; Joseph E. Walsh, Pastor Emeritus.
Res., 35 New Rd., P.O. Box 97, 19052. Tel: 610-459-2203; Fax: 610-459-5029. [CEM]
School—Tel: 610-459-0799; Fax: 610-558-3058.
Sisters of St. Francis of Philadelphia 2; Lay Teachers 11; Students 190.
Catechesis/Religious Programs—Tel: 610-459-0554.
Students 250.
Convent—28 New Rd., Aston, 19014. Tel: 610-459-2501.
Stations—Delco Juvenile Detention Center.; Fair Acres Geriatric Center, Tel: 610-891-5600; Sleighton Farms, Tel: 610-558-6500; Granite Farms Est., Tel: 610-358-3440; Riddle Village, Tel: 610-891-3777; Senior Quarters, Tel: 610-358-9933; Riddle Hospital, Tel: 610-566-9400; Penn State Lima Campus, Tel: 610-892-1350; Williamson School, Tel: 610-566-1776.

Levittown, Bucks Co., Immaculate Conception B.V.M. (1954), Revs. Joseph L. Logrip; John Mulholland.
Res., 5201 Emilie Rd., 19057-2505. Tel: 215-946-1638; 1639; Fax: 215-946-2149.
School—3810 Oxford Valley Rd., 19057. Tel: 215-949-2848.
Sisters, Servants of the Immaculate Heart of Mary 2; Lay Teachers 15; Students 302.
Catechesis/Religious Programs—Tel: 215-945-0826.
Students 175.
Convent—Tel: 215-945-4664.

St. Michael the Archangel (1953), Rev. Msgr. Richard T. Powers; Revs. Luke L. Chow; Francis X. Trauger; Michael J. Saban; Deacon Harry J. Simpson.
Res., 66 Levittown Pkwy., 19054. Tel: 215-945-1166; Fax: 215-945-6988.
School—130 Levittown Pkwy., 19054. Tel: 215-943-0222; Fax: 215-943-9068.
Lay Teachers 32; Students 720.
Catechesis/Religious Programs—Tel: 215-547-2518.
Students 458.
Convent—88 Levittown Pkwy., 19054. Tel: 215-943-8232.

Queen of the Universe (1955), Revs. Paul A. Wiedmann; John C. Moloney; Deacon Joseph Upcavage. In res., Rev. Henry E. Dougherty.
Res., 2443 Trenton Rd., 19056. Tel: 215-945-8750; Fax: 215-945-0413.
School—Tel: 215-945-1866.

Sisters of St. Joseph 1; Lay Teachers 12; Students 209.
Catechesis/Religious Programs—Tel: 215-945-2704.
Students 521.
Convent—Tel: 215-945-6116.

Linfield, Montgomery Co., St. Clare (1963), Rev. Thomas J. Duffy.
Res., 1228 Main St., 19468-1020. Tel: 610-495-7263; Fax: 610-495-9928.
Catechesis/Religious Programs—Students 158.

Linwood, Delaware Co., Holy Saviour (1915), Rev. Thomas P. McKelvey.
Res., 108 E. Ridge Rd., 19061. Tel: 610-485-2520; 2521.
School—Holy Saviour-St. John Fisher School. See Consolidated Parish Schools under Institutions Located in the Achdiocese. Tel: 610-485-0363; Fax: 610-485-7809. Joann Hummel, B.A., Prin.
Catechesis/Religious Programs—Students 440.
Convent—122 E. Ridge Rd., 19061. Tel: 610-485-7320.

Lower Makefield, Bucks Co., St. John the Evangelist (1964), Rev. Msgr. William J. Paul; Rev. Michael Gerlach; Deacons James E. Hartman; Robert P. Gellentien. In res., Rev. Robert J. Conner.
Res., 752 Big Oak Rd., Morrisville, 19067. Tel: 215-295-4102; Fax: 215-295-3128.
School—728 Big Oak Rd., Morrisville, 19067. Tel: 215-295-0629; Fax: 215-295-6258.
Bernardine Sisters of St. Francis 1; Lay Teachers 17; Students 295.
Catechesis/Religious Programs—Tel: 215-295-9239.
Students 637.
Convent—Tel: 215-295-8201.

Malvern, Chester Co., St. Patrick (1915), Revs. James J. Ambrogi; James T. McCabe; Francis N. McDevitt, Pastor Emeritus; Deacons Lawrence P. Froio; Paul Cox.
Res., 126 Woodland Ave., 19355. Tel: 610-647-2345; Fax: 610-647-4997.
School—115 Channing Ave., 19355. Tel: 610-644-5797; Fax: 610-647-0535.
Catechesis/Religious Programs—Tel: 610-296-8899; Fax: 610-296-8384.
Students 525.

Manoa, Delaware Co., Sacred Heart (1927), Revs. Henry J. McKee; George J. Boyle, Pastor Emeritus; Rev. Msgr. James McGrath, Pastor Emeritus; Rev. Msgr. Thomas B. Falls, Pastor Emeritus; Rev. James J. Whelan; Deacons John J. Suplee; Thomas J. Woods; Louis F. Verna. In res., Rev. Joseph Duncan.
Res., 105 Wilson Ave., Havertown, 19083. Tel: 610-449-3000; Fax: 610-449-2364.
School—Tel: 610-446-9198; Fax: 610-446-4861.
Sisters, Servants of the Immaculate Heart of Mary 1; Lay Teachers 14; Students 269.
Catechesis/Religious Programs—Tel: 610-446-7597; Fax: 610-446-3176. Eileen V. Lynch, D.R.E.
Students 310.
Convent—108 Shelbourne Rd., 19083. Tel: 610-446-3694.

Maple Glen, Montgomery Co., St. Alphonsus (1963), Revs. Peter J. Foley; J. Jerome Wild; Thomas J. Kelly, Pastor Emeritus; Wilfred F. Maloney, Pastor Emeritus.
Res., 33 Conwell Dr., 19002. Tel: 215-646-4600; Fax: 215-646-0180.
School—29 Conwell Dr., 19002. Tel: 215-646-0150.
Lay Teachers 24; Students 417.
Catechesis/Religious Programs—Tel: 215-643-7938.
Students 282.
Convent—1349 Somneytown Pike, Gwymedd Valley, 19437. Tel: 215-646-5259.

Marcus Hook, Delaware Co., Immaculate Conception (1917) (Italian), Rev. Joseph A. Amalfitano.
Res., 21 W. Eighth St., P.O. Box 355, 19061. Tel: 610-485-1026.

Media, Delaware Co., St. Mary Magdalen (1963), Revs. Ralph J. Chieffo; James F. Hughes, Pastor Emeritus; John E. Mulgrew, M.A.; Deacon E. Peter Zurbach.
Res., 2400 N. Providence Rd., 19063. Tel: 610-566-8821; Fax: 610-566-1005.
School—2430 N. Providence Rd., 19063. Tel: 610-565-1822; Fax: 610-627-9670.
Lay Teachers 26; Students 440.
Catechesis/Religious Programs—Tel: 610-565-5782.
Students 160.

Nativity of the Blessed Virgin Mary (1868), Rev. Msgr. Francis A. Giliberti; Revs. Patrick J. Welsh; James F. Bradley, Pastor Emeritus. In res., Rev. Joseph J. Kennedy, Pastor Emeritus.
Res., 30 E. Franklin St., 19063. Tel: 610-566-0185; Fax: 610-566-2873. [CEM]
School—Gayley St., 19063. Tel: 610-566-6881; Fax: 610-566-2010.
Servants of the Most Sacred Heart of Jesus 5; Lay Teachers 8; Students 185.
Catechesis/Religious Programs—Tel: 610-566-3910.
Students 331.
Convent—Tel: 610-565-8399.

Milmont Park, Delaware Co., Our Lady of Peace (1922), Revs. Charles M. O'Rourke; David W. Givey.
Res., 501 Belmont Ave., 19033-3308. Tel: 610-532-8081; 8082.
School—Milmont and Reese Aves., 19033-3395. Tel: 610-534-0689; Fax: 610-534-4856. Sr. Denise Clifford, S.S.J., Prin.
Sisters of St. Joseph 3; Lay Teachers 12; Students 250.
Catechesis/Religious Programs—Students 190.
Convent—Tel: 610-532-4699.

Morrisville, Bucks Co., Holy Trinity (1900), Rev. John C. Eckert; Deacon Warren C. Leonard.
Res., 201 N. Pennsylvania Ave., 19067. Tel: 215-295-3045; Fax: 215-295-8317. [CEM]
School—Osborne Ave. & Stockham Ave., 19067. Tel: 215-295-6900; Fax: 215-337-9079. Mrs. Barbara Nuzzolo, Prin.
Lay Teachers 12; Students 281.
Catechesis/Religious Programs—Students 120.

Morton, Delaware Co., Our Lady of Perpetual Help (1907), Rev. Msgr. Richard J. Skelly; Rev. John R. DiOrio; Deacon Joseph M. Oliver. In res., Rev. Msgr. Joseph P. McFadden.
Res., O.L.P.H. Ct., 2130 Franklin Ave., 19070. Tel: 610-543-1046; Fax: 610-543-6150.
School—#5 O.L.P.H. Ct., 2130 Franklin Ave., 19070. Tel: 610-543-8350; Fax: 610-544-3203.
Sisters of St. Francis of Philadelphia 2; Lay Teachers 19; Students 440.
Catechesis/Religious Programs—Tel: 610-543-5448.
Students 390.
Convent—#3 O.L.P.H. Ct., 2130 Franklin Ave., 19070. Tel: 610-543-0186.

Narberth, Montgomery Co., St. Margaret (1900), Rev. Msgr. James J. Flood; Sr. Elizabeth Pflieger, R.S.M., Dir. Parish Svcs. In res., Revs. Stephen J. Dougherty; Thomas J. McManus.
Res., 208 N. Narberth Ave., 19072. Tel: 610-664-3770.
School—227 N. Narberth Ave., 19072. Tel: 610-664-2640; Fax: 610-664-4677.
Sisters of Mercy 1; Lay Teachers 14; Students 229.
Catechesis/Religious Programs—Tel: 610-664-5715. Ms. Mary Katherine Roach, D.R.E.
Students 155.
Convent—506 Haverford Ave., 19072. Tel: 610-664-2748.

New Garden Township, Chester Co., St. Gabriel of the Sorrowful Mother (1988), Rev. Richard J. Maisano. Mailing Address: P.O. Box 709, Avondale, 19311. Tel: 610-268-0296; Fax: 610-268-5022.
Catechesis/Religious Programs—Students 209.

New Hope, Bucks Co., St. Martin of Tours (1885), Revs. John P. Schmeer; Paul J. Carey, Pastor Emeritus. W. Bridge St. & Riverstone Cir., 18938. [CEM]
Res., 111 New St., 18938. Tel: 215-862-5472; Fax: 215-862-1829.
Catechesis/Religious Programs—Students 212.

Newtown, Bucks Co., St. Andrew (1880), Revs. Michael C. Picard; Joseph V. Accardi; Edward T. Kearns. In res., Rev. Christopher Redcay.
Res., 81 Swamp Rd., 18940. Tel: 215-968-2262; Fax: 215-579-9344. [CEM]
School—51 Wrights Rd., 18940. Tel: 215-968-2685; Fax: 215-968-4795.
Preschool—138 S. Sycamore St., 18940. Tel: 215-968-3464; Fax: 215-968-8606.
Sisters, Servants of the Immaculate Heart of Mary 4; Lay Teachers 48; Students 1,050.
Catechesis/Religious Programs—Tel: 215-968-6929.
Students 1,175.
Convent—Tel: 215-968-6568.

Newtown Square, Delaware Co., St. Anastasia (1912), Revs. John J. Shellem; Michael A. Colagreco; Rev. Msgr. Richard J. Simons, Pastor Emeritus; Rev. Joseph F. Fitzpatrick, S.J. In res., Rev. Joseph F. Rymdeika.
Res., 3301 W. Chester Pike, 19073. Tel: 610-356-1613; Fax: 610-356-8332.
School—Tel: 610-356-6225; Fax: 610-356-5748.
Sisters of St. Joseph 3; Lay Teachers 32; Students 680.
Catechesis/Religious Programs—Tel: 610-356-5069.
Students 425.
Convent—3305 W. Chester Pike, 19073. Tel: 610-356-0273.

Norristown, Montgomery Co.,

1—St. Francis of Assisi, (1923), Revs. George P. Ettorre; Kevin C. Trautner. In res., Rev. Dominick F. Finn, O.S.F.S.
Res., 600 Hamilton St., 19401. Tel: 610-272-0402; Fax: 610-272-1794.
School—Oak & Buttonwood Sts., 19401. Tel: 610-272-0501; Fax: 610-272-8011.
Sisters of St. Joseph 1; Lay Teachers 15; Students 278.
Catechesis/Religious Programs—Students 146.
Convent—Tel: 610-272-3686.

2—Holy Saviour, (1903) (Italian), Rev. Msgr. Arthur J. Centrella; Rev. Louis P. Bellopede; Rev. Msgr. J. John Busco; Deacons John Parker; Donald Kretsch.
Res., 407 E. Main St., 19401. Tel: 610-275-0958; Fax: 610-275-8464.
School—Airy & Walnut Sts., 19401. Tel: 610-272-8864; Fax: 610-272-0311.
Lay Teachers 12; Students 180.
Catechesis/Religious Programs—Students 550.
Mission—Black Horse, Montgomery Co., Our Lady of Mount Carmel, 460 Fairfield Rd., 19401. Tel: 610-277-7739.

3—St. Patrick, (1835), Revs. Louis C. Bier; Ignatius Marneni; Bernard Kranicka, Business Mgr.
Res., 714 DeKalb St., 19401. Tel: 610-272-1408; Fax: 610-275-0238. [CEM]
Catechesis/Religious Programs—Religious Educ. Bldg., Chestnut & Green Sts., 19401. Tel: 610-272-4500. Dennis Mueller, D.R.E.
Students 71.
Convent—630 DeKalb St., 19401. Tel: 610-277-5962. Missionaries of Charity

4—St. Paul, (1963), Rev. Harry E. McCreedy; Sr. Rosellen Bracken, R.S.M., Parish Svcs. Dir.; Mary Rose Edmonds, Business Mgr.; Deacon Michael Dayoc. In res., Revs. Henry B. Degnan; Frank A. Giuffre.
Res., 2007 New Hope St., 19401. Tel: 610-279-6725; Fax: 610-275-6771.
School—351 E. Johnson Hwy., 19401. Tel: 610-275-2990; Fax: 610-275-0470.
Lay Teachers 12; Students 200.
Catechesis/Religious Programs—Students 101.

5—St. Titus, (1962), Rev. Msgr. Thomas J. Scanlon; Rev. Edward A. Windhaus.
Res., 3006 Keenwood Rd., East Norritown, 19403. Tel: 610-279-4990; Fax: 610-279-8640.
School—Keenwood Rd. & Norriton Dr., East Norritown, 19403. Tel: 610-279-6043; Fax: 610-279-8090.
Lay Teachers 18; Students 375.
Catechesis/Religious Programs—3000 Keenwood Rd., 19401. Tel: 610-279-5662.
Students 65.

North Wales, Montgomery Co., Mary, Mother of the Redeemer (1987), Revs. Philip C. Ricci; Francis J. Gallagher.
Res., 1325 Upper State Rd., 19454. Tel: 215-362-7400; 362-8966; Fax: 215-362-4127.
Catechesis/Religious Programs—Tel: 215-362-4895.
Students 890.

St. Rose of Lima (1919), Rev. Msgr. John P. Boland. In res., Rev. Msgr. James J. Graham; Rev. Gerald S. Smith; Deacons Edward A. Konarski; John J. Campbell.
Res., 428 S. Main St., 19454-3224. Tel: 215-699-4617; Fax: 215-699-4452.
School—425 W. Pennsylvania Ave., 19454-3498. Tel: 215-699-8831; Fax: 215-661-1691.
Lay Teachers 14; Students 249.
Catechesis/Religious Programs—Tel: 215-699-4434.
Students 325.

Norwood, Delaware Co., St. Gabriel (1891), Revs. Daniel M. Dooley; John J. Large; Christopher J. Papa, M.A.
Res., 233 Mohawk Ave., 19074. Tel: 610-586-1225; Fax: 610-586-6068.
School—Cleveland Ave., Tel: 610-532-3234; Fax: 610-532-5523.
Lay Teachers 18; Students 440.
Catechesis/Religious Programs—Tel: 610-532-5057.
Students 580.

Oreland, Montgomery Co., Holy Martyrs (1949), Rev. Michael J. Ryan. In res., Revs. Raymond F. Tribuiani; Ignatius J. Szal, Pastor Emeritus.
Res., 120 Allison Rd., 19075. Tel: 215-884-8575; Fax: 215-884-5924.
School—121 Allison Rd., 19075. Tel: 215-887-2044; Fax: 215-887-0024. Sr. Sharon McCarthy, S.S.J., Prin.
Lay Teachers 12; Students 149.
Preschool—207 Ulmer Ave., 19075. Tel: 215-572-8605.
Catechesis/Religious Programs—Students 200.

Ottsville, Bucks Co., St. John the Baptist (1743), Rev. Joseph Tobias, M.S.C.; Deacon Ernest D'Angelo.
Res., 4050 Durham Rd., 18942. Tel: 610-847-5521; Fax: 610-847-5521. [CEM]
School—Tel: 610-847-5523; Fax: 610-847-5523.
Lay Teachers 13; Students 229.
Catechesis/Religious Programs—Tel: 610-847-5522; Fax: 610-847-5522.
Students 265.

Oxford, Chester Co., Sacred Heart (1914), Rev. John F. Hummell, Ed.D.; Deacon Francis Murphy.
Res., 203 Church Rd., 19363. Tel: 610-932-5040; Fax: 610-932-5041.
Catechesis/Religious Programs—Tel: 610-932-5863.
Students 405.

Paoli, Chester Co., St. Norbert (1956), Revs. Domenic A. Rossi, O.Praem.; Walter J. Burke, O.Praem, Pastor Emeritus; Maurice C. Avicolli, O.Praem.
Res., 50 Leopard Rd., 19301. Tel: 610-644-1655; Fax: 610-644-1928.
School—Greenlawn & Leopard Rds., 19301. Tel: 610-644-1670; Fax: 610-644-0201.
Lay Teachers 16; Students 265.
Catechesis/Religious Programs—Tel: 610-664-1342.
Students 476.

Parkesburg, Chester Co., Our Lady of Consolation (1853), Revs. Victor J. Eschbach; George P. Schneider, Pastor Emeritus. In res., Rev. John Van De Paer, C.I.C.M.
Res., 603 Second Ave., 19365. Tel: 610-857-3510; Fax: 610-857-2353. [CEM]
School—Coatesville Area Catholic Elementary School. See Consolidated Parish Schools under Institutions Located in the Archdiocese. Tel: 610-384-5961; Fax: 610-384-5730.
Catechesis/Religious Programs—10 Cemetery Rd., 19365. Tel: 610-857-1003.
Students 302.
Mission—Doe Run, Chester Co., St. Malachy, 76 St. Malachi Rd., 19330. [CEM]

Penndel, Bucks Co., Our Lady of Grace (1908), Revs. William B. Dooner; Robert A. Roncase; Anthony M. Bozeman; Robert J. Conner, Pastor Emeritus.
Res., 225 Bellevue Ave., 19047. Tel: 215-757-7700; 757-7786; Fax: 215-757-5377. [CEM]
School—300 Hulmeville Ave., 19047. Tel: 215-757-5287; Fax: 215-757-6199. Mrs. Margaret M. Secoda, Prin.
Lay Teachers 26; Students 579.
Catechesis/Religious Programs—Tel: 215-757-5530.
Students 573.
Parish Service Center—338 Hulmeville Ave., 19047. Tel: 215-757-5052.

Pennsburg, Montgomery Co., St. Philip Neri (1919), Rev. John J. Scarcia.
Res., 1325 Klinerd Rd., 18073. Tel: 215-679-9275; 679-9330; Fax: 215-679-0386. [CEM]
School—Sixth & Washington Sts., East Greenville, 18041. Tel: 215-679-7481; Fax: 215-679-8370.
Students 146.
Catechesis/Religious Programs—Tel: 215-541-3120.
Students 236.

Penn Valley, Montgomery Co., St. Justin Martyr (1964), Rev. Donald E. Leighton, M.A.; Sr. Mary Sarah, R.S.M., Parish Svcs. Dir.; Bernice Mintzer, Business Mgr. In res., Rev. Thomas J. Wisniewski, M.Div.
Res., 1222 Hagysford Rd., Narberth, 19072. Tel: 610-664-0165; Fax: 610-664-5612.

Phoenixville, Chester Co.,

1—St. Ann, (1905), Revs. John J. Newns; Michael G. Murtha.
Res., 502 Main St., 19460. Tel: 610-933-3732; Fax: 610-935-7958. [CEM]
School—Holy Family School. See Consolidated Parish Schools under Institutions Located in the Archdiocese. Tel: 610-933-7562; Fax: 610-933-8823.
Lay Teachers 17; Students 426.
Catechesis/Religious Programs—Tel: 610-933-2543; Fax: 610-935-7958.
Students 260.
Parish Center—602 S. Main St., 19460. Tel: 610-983-3751.

2—Holy Trinity, (1903) (Polish), Rev. Msgr. John M. Galyo.
Res., 219 Dayton St., 19460. Tel: 610-933-3023; Fax: 610-935-9261. [CEM]
School—Holy Family School. See Consolidated Parish Schools under Institutions Located in the Archdiocese. Tel: 610-933-7562; Fax: 610-933-8823.
Catechesis/Religious Programs—Students 12.
Convent—221 Dayton St., 19460. Tel: 610-983-9446. Bernardine Sisters of the Third Order of St. Francis

3—St. Mary of the Assumption, (1840), Rev. Thomas J. Brennan.
Res., 212 Dayton St., 19460. Tel: 610-933-2526; Fax: 610-935-1706. [CEM 2]
School—Holy Family School. See Consolidated Parish Schools under Institutions Located in the Archdiocese. Tel: 610-933-7562.
Catechesis/Religious Programs—Students 115.

4—Sacred Heart, (1900) (Slovak), Rev. Msgr. John M. Galyo. In res., Rev. James V. Leary.
Res., 148 Church St., 19460. Tel: 610-933-3830; Fax: 610-935-9261. [CEM]
School—Holy Family School. See Consolidated Parish Schools under Institutions Located in the Archdiocese. Tel: 610-933-7562; Fax: 610-933-8823.
Catechesis/Religious Programs—Students 70.

Plymouth Meeting, Montgomery Co., Epiphany of Our Lord (1957), Rev. Msgr. James F. Baldrick; Rev. Dominic L. Rossi; Deacons William R. Radetzky; Kenneth P. Clancy; Joel M. Ziff; Emil J. Wernert. In res., Rev. James J. Kelly.
Res., 3050 Walton Rd., 19462-2361. Tel: 610-828-8634; Fax: 610-828-1802.
School—3040 Walton Rd., 19462-2361. Tel: 610-825-0160.
Lay Teachers 12; Students 225.
Catechesis/Religious Programs—Tel: 610-825-6790. Mr. James Orgera, D.R.E.
Students 331.

Pottstown, Montgomery Co., St. Aloysius (1856), Revs. John F. McCole; Dominic Tran Minh Duc; Francis E. Kelly; Deacon Ismael Fuentes.
Res., 214 N. Hanover St., 19464. Tel: 610-326-5877; Fax: 610-326-0901. [CEM 2]
School—Third & Hanover Sts., 19464. Tel: 610-326-6167.
Sisters of St. Francis of Philadelphia 1; Lay Teachers 22; Students 506.
Catechesis/Religious Programs—Tel: 610-473-9049.
Students 326.
Convent—223 Beech St., 19464. Tel: 610-326-1498; Fax: 610-326-0901.

Holy Trinity (1899) (Slovak), Revs. John F. McCole; Andrew L. Slafkosky, Pastor Emeritus.
Res., 370 South St., 19464. Tel: 610-326-2432; Fax: 610-326-4106. [CEM]
Catechesis/Religious Programs—St. Aloysius School, Tel: 610-326-6167.
Students 4.

St. Peter (1924) (Polish), Rev. Edward P. Kuczynski; Deacon David M. Kubczak.
Res., 1128 South St., 19464. Tel: 610-326-5023; Fax: 610-323-4297.
School—1126 South St., 19464. Tel: 215-323-6730.
Bernardine Sisters of St. Francis 1; Lay Teachers 9; Students 200.
Catechesis/Religious Programs—Students 95.
Convent—1124 South St., 19464. Tel: 610-323-9378.

Primos, Delaware Co., St. Eugene (1955), Rev. Joseph J. Meehan. In res., Rev. Joseph C. Bordonaro.
Res., 200 S. Oak Ave., 19018. Tel: 610-626-2866; Fax: 610-626-1904.
School—110 S. Oak Ave., 19018. Tel: 610-622-2909; Fax: 610-622-6358.
Lay Teachers 9; Students 231.
Catechesis/Religious Programs—Students 200.

Quakertown, Bucks Co., St. Isidore (1886), Revs. Frederick J. Riegler; John F. Wackerman.
Res., 531 W. Broad St., 18951. Tel: 215-536-4389; Fax: 215-536-4137. [CEM]
School—603 W. Broad St., Tel: 215-536-6052; Fax: 215-536-8647.
Lay Teachers 13; Students 270.
Catechesis/Religious Programs—Tel: 215-536-6498.
Students 350.

Richboro, Bucks Co., St. Vincent de Paul (1968), Revs. Joseph J. McLaughlin; John D. Gabin.
Res., 654 Hatboro Rd., 18954-1039. Tel: 215-357-5905; Fax: 215-953-8190.
Catechesis/Religious Programs—Tel: 215-322-1932.
Students 609.

Ridley Park, Delaware Co., St. Madeline (1908), Revs. George J. Mazzotta; Joseph P. Gallagher; Gary J. Kramer; Deacons William J. Guinane; Gregory R. O'Brien. In res., Rev. Sidney C. Burgoyne.
Res., 110 Park St., 19078. Tel: 610-532-6880; Fax: 610-532-6653.
Church—Penn St. & Morton Ave., 19078.
School—St. Madeline-St. Rose School. See Consolidated Parish Schools under Institutions Located in the Archdiocese. Tel: 610-583-3662; Fax: 610-583-3683.
Lay Teachers 18; Students 426.
Catechesis/Religious Programs—Tel: 610-583-6120.
Students 350.

Riegelsville, Bucks Co., St. Lawrence (1974), Rev. Robert H. Breen.
Res., 345 Elmwood Ln., P.O. Box 126, 18077. Tel: 610-749-2684. [JC]
Catechesis/Religious Programs—Twinned with St. John the Baptist, Ottsville.

Roslyn, Montgomery Co., St. John of the Cross (1953), Rev. Msgr. Thomas J. Duane; Rev. John J. Kilgallon. In res., Rev. Ronald M. Vierling, M.F.C.
Res., 2741 Woodland Rd., 19001. Tel: 215-659-4460; Fax: 215-659-2551.
School—2805 Woodland Rd., Tel: 215-659-1365; Fax: 215-659-7996. Mrs. Christine Weiseman, Prin.
Lay Teachers 15; Students 307.
Catechesis/Religious Programs—Tel: 215-659-1451.
Students 212.
Convent—2803 Woodland Rd., Tel: 215-659-4483. Grey Nuns of the Sacred Heart

Royersford, Montgomery Co., Sacred Heart (1973), Rev. Thomas F. Doyle; Deacon Michael J. Conroy. In res., Rev. Robert H. Mulligan.
Res., 838 Walnut St., P.O. Box 64, 19468. Tel: 610-948-5915; 948-4087; Fax: 610-948-9177.
School—Area Catholic Elementary School of the Sacred Heart, Lewis Rd. & Washington St., 19468. Tel: 610-948-7206; Fax: 610-948-6508.
Lay Teachers 14; Students 240.
Catechesis/Religious Programs—Tel: 610-792-2997. Douglass Dunn, D.R.E.
Students 426.

Rydal, Montgomery Co., St. Hilary of Poitiers (1962), Rev. Msgr. Michael J. Carroll. In res., Rev. Paul M. Kennedy, M.A.
Res., 820 Susquehanna Rd., 19046. Tel: 215-884-3252.
School—920 Susquehanna Rd., 19046. Tel: 215-887-4520; Fax: 215-887-6337.
Students 249.

Secane, Delaware Co., Our Lady of Fatima (1952), Revs. Engelbert G. Michel; William S. Kirk. In res., Rev. Thomas R. Urian.
Res., 1 Fatima Dr., 19018. Tel: 610-532-5800.
School—10 Fatima Dr., 19018. Tel: 610-586-7539; Fax: 610-586-0117.
Sisters, Servants of the Immaculate Heart of Mary 4; Lay Teachers 15; Students 460.
Catechesis/Religious Programs—Tel: 610-532-7430.
Students 248.
Convent—5 Fatima Dr., 19018. Tel: 610-532-1190.

Sellersville, Bucks Co., St. Agnes (1919), Rev. Msgr. James E. Molloy; Rev. John F. Bowe; Deacon Harry Tucker.
Res., 445 N. Main St., 18960. Tel: 215-257-2128; Fax: 215-257-4561. [CEM]
School—St. Agnes-Sacred Heart School. See Consolidated Parish Schools under Institutions Located in the Archdiocese. Tel: 215-257-3571; Fax: 215-257-8036.
Lay Teachers 25; Students 532.
Catechesis/Religious Programs—Tel: 215-257-1811.
Students 527.

Sharon Hill, Delaware Co., Holy Spirit (1892), Revs. Martin E. Woodeshick; Daniel J. Kehoe, Pastor Emeritus; Deacons Albert Rayner; Thomas Butcavage.
Res., 1028 School St., 19079. Tel: 610-583-2220; Fax: 610-583-5130.
School—1036 School St., 19079. Tel: 610-532-7557; Fax: 610-532-3614.
Lay Teachers 14; Students 217.
Catechesis/Religious Programs—Tel: 610-532-1154.
Students 80.

Southampton, Bucks Co., Our Lady of Good Counsel (1923), Rev. Msgr. Bernard J. Trinity; Revs. James T. Henry; Francis X. Herron; Brian A. Izzo. In res., Rev. Mark J. Hunt.
Res., 611 Knowles Ave., 18966-4198. Tel: 215-357-1300, Ext. 100; Fax: 215-357-4452.
School—Second St. Pike, 18966. Tel: 215-357-1300, Ext. 101. Mr. Frank Mokriski, Prin.
Lay Teachers 25; Students 578.
Catechesis/Religious Programs—Tel: 215-357-1300, Ext. 126.
Students 527.

South Coventry, Chester Co., St. Thomas More (1968), Rev. Hugh J. Dougherty; Deacon George W. Leonhardt, Jr.
Res., 2101 Pottstown Pike, Pottstown, 19465. Tel: 610-469-9304; Fax: 610-469-9315.
Catechesis/Religious Programs—Tel: 610-469-9302.
Students 290.

Spring City, Chester Co., St. Joseph (1919), Rev. John J. Dinda. In res., Revs. Michael W. Rzonca; Robert I. Riedy, Pastor Emeritus; Donato P. Silveri.

Res., 3640 Schuylkill Rd., 19475. Tel: 610-948-7760; Fax: 610-948-8509.

Springfield, Delaware Co., St. Francis of Assisi (1923), Revs. Salvatore M. Riccio; Michael A. Filippello; Deacons James D. Kane, Sr.; Arthur M. McGuire. In res., Rev. Thomas J. Smith.
Res., 136 Saxer Ave., 19064. Tel: 610-543-0848; Fax: 610-604-0283.
School—112 Saxer Ave., Tel: 610-543-0546; Fax: 610-544-9431.
Lay Teachers 18; Students 393.
Catechesis/Religious Programs—Students 340.

Holy Cross (1948), Revs. Edward B. Cahill; Mark G. Swope; Sr. Antoinette Marie, R.S.M., Pastoral Min. In res., Deacon Robert Frankenberger.
Res., 651 E. Springfield Rd., 19064. Tel: 610-626-3321; Fax: 610-622-2920.
School—Bishop & Springfield Rds., 19064. Tel: 610-626-1709.
Sisters of Mercy 1; Lay Teachers 18; Students 411.
Catechesis/Religious Programs—Tel: 610-626-1057; Fax: 610-626-8057.
Students 250.
Convent—Tel: 610-626-2492.

St. Kevin (1955), Rev. Anthony G. Flynn; Sr. Eleanor McFadden, S.S.J., Pastoral Assoc.; Deacons Thomas Eichman; Leonard Diana; Joseph Coyle. In res., Revs. Thomas P. Gillin; John A. Fitzgibbons.
Res., St. Kevin Rectory, 200 W. Sprowl Rd., 19064-2016. Tel: 610-544-8777; 8778; Fax: 610-544-7832.
School—Tel: 610-544-4455; Fax: 610-544-7092.
Sisters of St. Joseph 9; Lay Teachers 17; Students 369.
Convent—Tel: 610-544-4535.

Stowe, Montgomery Co., St. Gabriel of the Sorrowful Mother (1929), Revs. James W. Gormley; Patrick A. Duddy, Pastor Emeritus. In res., Rev. James A. Murphy, (Retired); Deacon Charles H. Rebuck.
Parish Center: 127 E. Howard St., 19464. Tel: 610-326-5127; Fax: 610-326-5749.
Res., 421 Jefferson St., 19464. Tel: 610-327-2248.
Catechesis/Religious Programs—Students 93.

Strafford, Chester Co., Our Lady of the Assumption (1908) (Italian), Rev. Joseph A. Vadino. In res., Rev. Msgr. James T. McDonough; Rev. Daniel J. Hoy, (Retired).
Res., 35 Old Eagle School Rd., 19087. Tel: 610-688-1178; 688-6147; Fax: 610-293-9680. [CEM]
Preschool—135 Fairfield Ln., 19087. Tel: 610-688-5277.
Catechesis/Religious Programs—Tel: 610-688-6590.
Students 170.

Swarthmore, Delaware Co., Notre Dame de Lourdes (1959), Rev. William J. Benonis; Deacons Michael McAndrews; James Basilio. In res., Rev. John Flanagan.
Res., 950 Michigan Ave., 19081. Tel: 610-544-1270; Fax: 610-544-4310.
School—990 Fairview Rd., 19081. Tel: 610-328-9330.
Lay Teachers 13; Students 296.
Catechesis/Religious Programs—Tel: 610-544-9739.
Students 301.

Swedesburg, Montgomery Co., Sacred Heart (1907) (Polish), Rev. Leonard A. Lewandowski; Rev. Msgr. Anthony E. Jaworowski, (Retired); Deacon T. Eric Makoid.
Res., 120 Jefferson St., 19405. Tel: 610-275-1750; Fax: 610-275-0480.
School—Holy Trinity Catholic School. See Consolidated Parish Schools under the Institutions Located in the Archdiocese. Tel: 610-277-4133; Fax: 610-277-4725.
Lay Teachers 11; Students 208.
Catechesis/Religious Programs—Students 55.
Convent—635 E. Fourth St., 19405. Tel: 610-275-3348; Fax: 610-272-6166.

Trooper, Montgomery Co., Visitation B.V.M. (1954), Rev. Msgr. Francis J. Clemins, Pastor Emeritus; Rev. Msgr. Thomas A. Murray; Revs. Zachary W. Navit; Eugene C. Wilson. In res., Rev. Henry C. Schuyler.
Res., 196 N. Trooper Rd., Norristown, 19403. Tel: 610-539-5572; Fax: 610-539-3240.
School—N. Trooper Rd., R.D. 1, Norristown, 19403. Tel: 610-539-6080; Fax: 610-630-7946.
Sisters of the Holy Family of Nazareth 2; Lay Teachers 34; Students 760.
Catechesis/Religious Programs—Tel: 610-539-6211. Roseanne Terranova, D.R.E.
Students 560.
Convent—Tel: 610-539-5558.

Upper Darby, Delaware Co., St. Alice (1922), Revs. William P. Donnelly; Joseph Tran Kim Thien, Pastoral Assoc.; Rev. Msgr. William A. Doolin, Pastor Emeritus. In res., Deacon Joseph F. Coyle.
Res., 150 Hampden Rd., 19082. Tel: 610-352-1431.
School—135 Copley Rd., 19082. Tel: 610-352-0725; Fax: 610-352-7288.
Sisters, Servants of the Immaculate Heart of Mary 4; Lay Teachers 8; Students 237.
Catechesis/Religious Programs—Students 178.

Upper Gwynedd, Montgomery Co., Corpus Christi (1964), Rev. Msgr. Thomas P. Flanigan, Ed.D.; Revs. Joseph L. Farrell; Francis J. Loughran, Pastor Emeritus; Gerald P. Carey; Sr. Mary Corbett, S.S.J., Dir. Human Svcs. In res., Rev. Martin T. Cioppi, Ed.D.
Res., 900 Sumneytown Pike, Lansdale, 19446. Tel: 215-855-1311; Fax: 215-855-3631.
School—920 Sumneytown Pike, Lansdale, 19466. Tel: 215-368-0582; Fax: 215-361-5927.
Sisters of St. Joseph 3; Lay Teachers 17; Students 519.
Catechesis/Religious Programs—Tel: 215-362-2292. Trish Keen, D.R.E.
Students 797.
Convent—1622 Supplee Rd., Lansdale, 19446. Tel: 215-368-0737.

Upper Uwchlan, Chester Co., Saint Elizabeth (2000), Rev. Msgr. Thomas M. Mullin.
Res., 2 Fox Ridge Rd., Glenmoore, 19343-9546. Tel: 610-321-9616; Fax: 610-321-1275.
Parish Office: 941 Pottstown Pike, P.O. Box 695, Uwchlan, 19480-0695. Tel: 610-321-0283; Fax: 610-321-0257.

Valley Forge, Montgomery Co., St. Teresa of Avila (1918), Rev. Msgr. Andrew J. Golias, S.T.D., S.T.L.; Revs. Francis E. Kelly, Pastor Emeritus; Thomas F. Walsh, Pastor Emeritus. In res., Rev. Michael P. O'Malley, M.A.
Mailing Address: Box 248, 19481. Tel: 610-666-5820; Fax: 610-666-7511.
Res., 1260 S. Trooper Rd., Norristown, 19403.
School—2550 S. Parkview Dr., Norristown, 19403. Tel: 610-666-6069. Maria Brown, Prin.
Lay Teachers 8; Students 232.
Catechesis/Religious Programs—Tel: 610-666-0644. Nance Morrisroe, D.R.E.
Students 284.

Villanova, Delaware Co., St. Thomas of Villanova Parish (1848), Revs. Dennis J. Harten, O.S.A.; Michael Bielecki, O.S.A. In res., Rev. Anthony M. Genovese, O.S.A.
Res., 1229 W. Lancaster Ave., Rosemont, 19010. Tel: 610-525-4801; Fax: 610-525-6041.
School—St. Thomas-Good Counsel School. See Consolidated Parish Schools under Institutions Located in the Archdiocese.
St. Thomas of Villanova Preschool—1236 Montrose Ave., Rosemont, 19010. Tel: 610-525-7554.

Wallingford, Delaware Co., St. John Chrysostom (1952), Revs. Joseph P. McGeown; Efren V. Esmilla; Deacons Raymond Vadino; Walter Lance.
Res., 617 S. Providence Rd., 19086. Tel: 610-874-3418; Fax: 610-872-1741.
School—607 Providence Rd., 19086. Tel: 610-876-7110.
Sisters of St. Joseph 4; Lay Teachers 21; Students 352.
Catechesis/Religious Programs—605 S. Providence Rd., 19086. Tel: 610-872-4673.
Students 559.
Convent—Tel: 610-872-7194.

Warminster, Bucks Co., Nativity of Our Lord (1956), Revs. William J. O'Donnell; John J. Shelley, Pastor Emeritus; Stephen F. Katziner. In res., Rev. James F. Endres.
Res., 625 W. Street Rd., 18974. Tel: 215-675-1925; Fax: 215-674-3787.
School—585 W. Street Rd., 18974. Tel: 215-675-2820; Fax: 215-675-9413.
Sisters of St. Joseph 1; Lay Teachers 32; Students 663.
Catechesis/Religious Programs—Tel: 212-672-5316.
Students 386.
Convent—605 W. Street Rd., 18974. Tel: 215-672-0147.

Warrington, Bucks Co., St. Joseph (1922), Revs. James A. Grant; Robert G. Suskey; Rev. Msgr. Leon J. Peck, Pastor Emeritus; Deacon Karl Hartmann. In res., Rev. Raymond J. Overstreet.
Res., 1795 Columbia Ave., 18976. Tel: 215-672-3020; Fax: 215-672-3114.
School—St. Joseph/St. Robert Bellarmine School. See Consolidated Parish Schools under Institutions Located in the Archdiocese. Tel: 215-672-0724.
Lay Teachers 21; Students 500.
Catechesis/Religious Programs—Tel: 215-672-9990. Sr. Anna Marie McDermott, I.H.M., D.R.E.
Students 230.
Station—Willow Grove Naval Air Station, Tel: 215-443-6002.

St. Robert Bellarmine (1968), Rev. Msgr. Joseph T. Kane; Rev. Joseph M. McDermott; Deacon George E. Morris.
Res., 856 Euclid Ave., 18976. Tel: 215-343-0315; Fax: 215-343-8592.
School—St. Joseph & St. Robert Bellarmine School. See Consolidated Parish Schools under Institutions Located in the Archdiocese. Tel: 215-672-0724.
Catechesis/Religious Programs—Euclid Ave. & Carriage Way, 18976. Tel: 215-343-9433.
Students 558.

Wayne, Chester Co., St. Isaac Jogues (1970), Rev. Msgr. Joseph C. Cunningham; William McLaughlin, Business Mgr.; Deacon George F. McAndrews. Parish Svc. Directors: Mary D. Schachinger; Joan M. Carey. In res., Rev. Paschal U. Onunwa.
Res., 50 W. Walker Rd., 19087. Tel: 610-687-3366; Fax: 610-293-9529.
Preschool—Tel: 610-687-2481.
Catechesis/Religious Programs—Tel: 610-687-2481. Louis M. Valenti, D.R.E.
Students 246.

St. Katharine of Siena, Delaware Co., (1893), Rev. Msgr. John J. Jagodzinski; Rev. Appiah Asante; Sr. Elizabeth O'Hara, S.S.J., Parish Svcs. Dir. In res., Rev. Pascal A. Monteleone.
Res., 104 S. Aberdeen Ave., 19087. Tel: 610-688-4584; Fax: 610-688-7951.
School—229 Windermere Ave., 19087. Tel: 610-688-5451; Fax: 610-688-6796. Sr. William Therese, I.H.M., Prin.
Sisters, Servants of the Immaculate Heart of Mary 6; Lay Teachers 21; Students 367.
Catechesis/Religious Programs—Tel: 610-688-7890. Sr. Rose Marie Adams, I.H.M., D.R.E.
Students 323.
Convent—235 Windermere Ave., 19087. Tel: 610-688-0655.

West Chester, Chester Co., St. Agnes (1793), Rev. Msgr. Thomas P. Craven; Rev. Msgr. Thomas J. Hilferty; Revs. William B. Lange; Christopher J. Papa; Deacon Victor Gonzalez.
Res., 233 W. Gay St., 19380. Tel: 610-692-2990; Fax: 610-692-9623. [CEM]
School—211 W. Gay St., 19380. Tel: 610-696-1260.
Sisters, Servants of the Immaculate Heart of Mary 4; Lay Teachers 25; Students 589.
Catechesis/Religious Programs—207 W. Gay St., 19380. Tel: 610-436-4640; Fax: 610-719-1961.
Students 616.
Convent—205 W. Gay St., 19380. Tel: 610-692-9430.

SS. Simon and Jude (1961), Revs. Francis X. Meehan; Joseph Watson; Mr. Ronald B. Avellino, Business Mgr.; Deacons James Lyon; Ben Stam. In res., Rev. Msgr. Richard LaHart; Rev. Dennis O'Donnell.
Res., 8 Cavanaugh Ct., 19382. Tel: 610-696-3624; Fax: 610-696-3971.
School—6 Cavanaugh Ct., Tel: 610-696-5249; Fax: 610-696-4682.
Sisters, Servants of the Immaculate Heart of Mary 6; Lay Teachers 21; Students 621.
Catechesis/Religious Programs—Tel: 610-692-3118. Sr. Rose Caritas, I.H.M., D.R.E.
Students 525.
Convent—Tel: 610-692-4394.

West Conshohocken, Montgomery Co., St. Gertrude (1888), Rev. James J. McKeaney.
Res., 209 Merion Ave., 19428. Tel: 610-828-0268; Fax: 610-828-7024.
PreK-Kindergarten—150 Cedar Ave., 19428. Tel: 610-828-2161.

West Grove, Chester Co., Assumption B.V.M. (1873), Rev. Msgr. John W. Graf; Rev. James J. Melle; Joyce Malchione, Business Mgr. In res., Rev. Francis J. Depman.
Res., 107 Evergreen St., 19390. Tel: 610-869-2722; Fax: 610-869-3252. [CEM]
School—290 State Rd., 19390. Tel: 610-869-9576; Fax: 610-869-4049. Sr. Francis Eileen Tiernan, I.H.M., Prin.
Sisters, Servants of the Immaculate Heart 3; Lay Teachers 17; Students 315.
Catechesis/Religious Programs—Tel: 610-869-8575. Sharon Hannan, D.R.E.
Students 595.
Convent—105 Evergreen St., 19390. Tel: 610-869-9832.
Mission—Avondale, Chester Co., Santa Maria, Madra de Dios, P.O. Box 1019, Avondale, 19311. Tel: 610-268-3365; Fax: 610-869-9395.

Westtown, St. Maximilian Kolbe (1986), Rev. Msgr. Hugh P. Campbell; Rev. William A. Trader; Deacons Lawrence Brandon; Alfred Mauriello; William Hickey.
Res., 15 E. Pleasant Grove Rd., West Chester, 19382. Tel: 610-399-6936; Fax: 610-399-4828.
School—(Grades PreK-8). Tel: 610-399-8400; Fax: 610-399-4684.
Students 415.
Catechesis/Religious Programs—Tel: 610-399-9642.
Students 608.

Willow Grove, Montgomery Co., St. David (1919), Revs. Richard T. Bolger; Francis V. Bielski; Deacon William F. Eliason. In res., Rev. Richard P. Connors.
Res., 316 N. Easton Rd., 19090. Tel: 215-657-0252; Fax: 215-659-6516.
School—401 N. Easton Rd., 19090. Tel: 215-659-6393.
Sisters, Servants of the Immaculate Heart of Mary 5; Lay Teachers 19; Students 349.
Catechesis/Religious Programs—Tel: 215-659-4059.
Students 402.
Convent—400 N. Easton Rd., 19090. Tel: 215-659-0445.

Wyndmoor, Montgomery Co., Seven Dolors (1916), Rev. Robert J. Carroll. In res., Revs. John D. Reardon; Carl F. Janicki.
1200 E. Willow Grove Ave., 19038-7614. Tel: 215-233-2552; Fax: 215-233-2553.
Catechesis/Religious Programs—Students 30.

Wynnewood, Montgomery Co., Presentation B.V.M. (1954), Rev. Msgr. Vincent M. Walsh, J.C.D.; Rev. Msgr. John C. Kavanagh, Pastor Emeritus; Sr. Alice Price, R.S.M., Dir.
Res., 204 Haverford Rd., 19096. Tel: 610-642-8341; Fax: 610-896-1970.
School—230 Haverford Rd., 19096. Tel: 610-642-8040. Kay Kelly, Prin.
Lay Teachers 13; Students 184.
Catechesis/Religious Programs—Students 130.
Convent—240 Haverford Rd., 19096. Tel: 610-642-3803.
Sisters 3.

Yardley, Bucks Co., St. Ignatius of Antioch (1920), Rev. Msgr. Samuel E. Shoemaker, J.C.D.; Revs. Joseph R. Hess, M.Div.; Alan J. Okon, Jr., M.Div.; Deacons Robert J. Skawinski; Robert J. Stewart.
Res., 999 Reading Ave., 19067. Tel: 215-493-3377; Fax: 215-493-0450. [CEM][JC]
School—Tel: 215-493-3867.
Lay Staff 21; Students 305.
Catechesis/Religious Programs—Tel: 215-493-5204; Fax: 215-493-0956.
Students 671.

Yeadon, Delaware Co., St. Louis (1928), Rev. Charles E. Bonner. In res., Rev. John J. Delli Carpini.
Res., 821 W. Cobbs Creek Pkwy., 19050. Tel: 610-623-0553; Fax: 610-623-8191.
Catechesis/Religious Programs—Students 21.

Chaplains of Public Institutions

PHILADELPHIA. *Philadelphia Prison System* 8001 State Rd., 19136. Tel: 215-276-2288. Rev. Mardean E. Miller.
Veterans Administration Medical Center University & Woodland Aves., 19104. Tel: 215-823-5800, Ext. 2776. Rev. Damien Schill.

COATESVILLE. *Veterans Administration Medical Center* 19320. Tel: 215-384-7711, Ext. 190. Rev. Joseph S. Hasiebar.

GRATERFORD. *Graterford State Correctional Institution* 19426. Tel: 215-489-4151. Rev. Michael W. Rzonca, Chap.

NORRISTOWN. *Norristown State Hospital* 19401. Tel: 215-270-1104. Rev. Dominick F. Finn, O.S.F.S., Chap.

SPRING CITY. *Southeastern Pennsylvania Veterans Center* 19475. Tel: 215-948-2400. Rev. Donato P. Silveri.

On Special or Other Archdiocesan Assignment:
Reverend Monsignors—
Beach, Francis W., Regl. Vicar, Philadelphia-North, 240 Hermitage St., Philadelphia, PA 19127
Cistone, Joseph R., Vicar for Admin. Ridley Park, Spiritual Life Center, 405 Tome St., Ridley Park, PA 19078
Devlin, Charles V., Vicar for Renewal & Evangelization, Archdiocesan Office Center, 222 N. 17th St., Philadelphia, PA 19103-1299
Marine, John C., Vicar for Montgomery Co., 354 Conshohocken State Rd., Gladwyn, PA 19035
Reverend Fathers—
McIntyre, John J., Admin. Sec., Office of the Archbishop, 222 N. 17th St., Philadelphia, PA 19103

On Duty Outside the Archdiocese:
Reverend Monsignors—
Bransfield, Michael J., National Shrine of the Immaculate Conception, Fourth St. & Michigan Ave., N.E., Washington, DC 20017
Green, James P., Apostolic Nunciature, Immortellevej, 11, 2950 Vedbaek, Denmark Spain
Pepe, Joseph A., Tribunal, Archodiocese of Santa Fe, 4000 Saint Joseph Pl., N.W., Albuquerque, NM 87120
Thomas, Daniel E., Official, Congregation for Bishops, Pontifical North American College, Vatican City State, 00120 Europe. Tel: 011-39-6849-3846
Reverend Fathers—
Brennan, James J., Mepkin Abbey, 1098 Mepkin Abbey Rd., Moncks Corner, SC 29461
Brockson, Scott D., Our Lady of Mount Carmel, Box 2062, Barceloneta, PR 00617
Donofrio, Michael J., Parroquia San Pedro, Apartado 13, Andanuaylas, Apurimac, Peru
Funk, Peter C., 9920 N. Major Dr., Beaumont, TX 77713-7618
Garzarelli, Santo R., Bishop's House, P.O. Box 205, Vanimo, Papua New Guinea
Hamill, Gregory J., c/o Secretary for Clergy, 222 North 17th St., Philadelphia, PA 19103
Kutys, Daniel J., N.C.C.B. Office for the Catechism, 3211 4th St., N.E., Washington, DC 20017
Magee, Michael K., Congregation for Divine Worship, Via Tor de' Conti, 17/1, Focolare Sacerdotale, Rome 00184 Italia
McGann, Thomas A., Our Lady of Guadalupe, 3200 E. 91st St., Chicago, IL 60617
McNamara, Donald P., Misioneros De Maryknoll, Apartado Postal 20.273, San Martin, Caracas 1020-A Venezuela, S.A.
Mendez, Rafael, Diocese of Arecibo, PR 00613
Menei, Francis T., Trinity Spiritual Center, 3609 Simpson Ferry Rd., Shiremanstown, PA 17011
Murphy, William S., Our Lady of Mount Carmel, P.O. Box 2062, Barleloneta, PR 00617
Shields, Hugh Joseph, Society of St. James the Apostle, 24 Clark St., Boston, MA 02109

Military Chaplains:
Reverend Fathers—
Boyle, Dennis P.
Burns, Vincent P.
Concha, Alfonso J.
DiGregorio, Joseph L.
Foley, Francis P.
McManus, Gerald D.

Graduate Studies:
Reverend Fathers—
Brady, Patrick J., Casa Santa Maria, Via dell'Umilta 30, Rome 00187
Bransfield, Brian J., Casa Santa Maria, Via dell'Umilta 30, Rome, 00187
Donovan, William G., Casa Santa Maria, Via dell'Umilta 30, Rome 00187 Italy
Emmons, Rayford E., St. Helena Rectory, 6161 N. 5th St., Philadelphia, PA 19120-1422
Fairbanks, Gregory J., Casa Santa Maria, Via dell'Umilta 30, Rome, 00187
Gill, G. Dennis, Casa Santa Maria, Via dell'Umilta 30, Rome 00187 Italy
Mesure, Gerard C., Villanova University, Villanova, PA 19085

Absent on Sick Leave:
Reverend Monsignors—
Nace, Arthur J.
Reverend Fathers—
Bloh, Stephen R.
DeMayo, John B.
Kohler, Thomas M.
McCarthy, Michael J.
Mills, Donald J.
Moriarity, Daniel J.
Noone, Charles J.
Roedel, Robert H.
Satchell, Martin J.
Smart, Raymond W.
Sweeney, Joseph J.
Van Thuyne, Dennis G.

Absent on Leave:
Reverend Monsignors—
Walls, David E.
Reverend Fathers—
Blaine, Michael J.
Bonavitacola, John M.
DePaoli, Edward M.
Donnelly, Russell J.
Dougherty, William J.
Fisher, Craig B.
Freeman, John A.
Haynes, Mark J.
Iannarella, James M.
Jablonski, Edward J.
Martino, Nicholas J.
McLoughlin, Richard J.
O'Brien, Mark J.
Swierzy, Michael W.
Taraborelli, Carmen F.
Wiejata, Sylwester

Retired:
Reverend Monsignors—
Bennington, J. Clement, Villa St. Joseph, 1436 Lansdowne Ave., Darby, PA 19023-1298
Busco, John J., Holy Savior Rectory, 407 E. Main St., Norristown, PA 19041-5119
Bydlon, Adam J., Villa Saint Joseph, 1436 Lansdowne Ave., Darby, PA 19023-1298
Carbo, Eugene J., 8 Joseph Dr., Norristown, PA 19401
Caufield, John J., Cathedral Basilica SS. Peter and Paul, 1723 Race St., Philadelphia, PA 19103
Clemins, Francis J., Villa Saint Joseph, 1436 Lansdowne Ave., Darby, PA 19023-1298
Conway, Walter J., Saint Francis Country House, 1412 Lansdowne Ave., Darby, PA 19023-1218
Daly, James P., Villa Saint Joseph, 1436 Lansdowne Ave., Darby, PA 19023-1298
Doolin, William A., Saint Anselm Rectory, 12669 Dunks Ferry Rd., Philadelphia, PA 19154
Falls, Thomas B., Villa Saint Joseph, 1436 Lansdowne Ave., Darby, PA 19023-1298
Fee, John B., Villa Saint Joseph, 1436 Lansdowne Ave., Darby, PA 19023-1298
Fitzmaurice, Francis J., Villa Saint Joseph, 1436 Lansdowne Ave., Darby, PA 19023
Howard, James J., 9224 Grace Ln., Philadelphia, PA 19115
Jaworowski, Anthony E., Sacred Heart Rectory, 120 Jefferson St., Swedesburg, PA 19405
Kane, Thomas A., Villa Saint Joseph, 1436 Lansdowne Ave., Darby, PA 19023-1298
Kavanaugh, John C., Presentation B.V.M. Rectory, 204 Haverford Rd., Wynnewood, PA 19096
Keul, Francis X., Regina Coeli Residence for Priests, 685 York Rd., Warminster, PA 18974
LaHart, Richard T., SS. Simon and Jude Rectory, 8 Cavanaugh Ct., West Chester, PA 19382
Lynaugh, Joseph E., Villa Saint Joseph, 1436 Lansdowne Ave., Darby, PA 19023-1298
Marley, Michael F., Villa Saint Joseph, 1436 Lansdowne Ave., Darby, PA 19023-1298
McGrath, James, 6101 34th St. W., 10 E, Bradenton, FL 34210-3701
Monaghan, Charles J., Villa Saint Joseph, 1436 Lansdowne Ave., Darby, PA 19023-1298
Musial, Edward S., Saint Mary Rectory, 140 W. Hector St., Conshohocken, PA 19428
Mynaugh, Charles B., Villa Saint Joseph, 1436 Lansdowne Ave., Darby, PA 19023-1298
Norrell, Albert V., Villa Saint Joseph, 1436 Lansdowne Ave., Darby, PA 19023-1298
Nugent, Arthur W., 1341 Osbourne Ave., Roslyn, PA 19001
Peck, Leon J., Regina Coeli Residence for Priests, 685 York Rd., Warminster, PA 18974
Pryor, Thomas P., Villa Saint Joseph, 1436 Lansdowne Ave., Darby, PA 19023
Schaeflein, Charles J., Mount Nazareth, 2775 Holme Ave., Philadelphia, PA 19152
Shields, Joseph A., Saint John the Baptist, Vianney Rectory, 1110 Vaughan Ln., Gladwyne, PA 19035
Simons, Richard J., Villa Saint Joseph, 1436 Lansdowne Ave., Darby, PA 19023-1298
Statkus, Francis J., 208 E. Trenton Ave., Wildwood Crest, NJ 08260
Vizzard, James J., Saint Francis Country House, 1412 Lansdowne Ave., Darby, PA 19023-1218
Reverend Fathers—
Barnes, Gerard J., Villa Saint Joseph, 1436 Lansdowne Ave., Darby, PA 19023-1298
Barr, Philip R., 1511 Grant Rd., West Chester, PA 19382
Bartos, Francis J., Villa Saint Joseph, 1436 Lansdowne Ave., Darby, PA 19023-1298
Benonis, Richard R., 7207 Southern Ridge Dr., Converse, TX 78109
Birkhead, Henry G., Regina Coeli Residence for Priests, 685 York Rd., Warminster, PA 18974
Boyle, George J., Annunciation B.V.M. Rectory, 410 Sagamore Rd., Havertown, PA 19083-3998
Brackenridge, David F., Villa Saint Joseph, 1436 Lansdowne Ave., Darby, PA 19023-1298
Bradley, James F., Saint Francis Country House, 1412 Lansdowne Ave., Darby, PA 19023-1218
Burgoyne, Sidney C., Saint Madeline Rectory, 110 Park St., Ridley Park, PA 19078
Carey, Paul J., Regina Coeli Residence for Priests, 685 York Rd., Warminster, PA 18974
Catullo, Pasquale R., Villa Saint Joseph, 1436 Lansdowne Ave., Darby, PA 19023-1298
Cellucci, Carl D., 902 Surf Ave., North Wildwood, NJ 08260
Chwieroth, Edward J., 4323 Vista St., Philadelphia, PA 19136
Coates, John T., Saint Mary's Manor, 701 Lansdale Ave., Lansdale, PA 19446-2900
Conner, Robert J., Saint John the Evangelist Rectory, 752 Big Oak Rd., Morrisville, PA 19067
Cornely, Francis J., Regina Coeli Residence for Priests, 685 York Rd., Warminster, PA 18974
Cudemo, Nicholas V., 1310 Grovania Ave., Abington, PA 19001
Cullen, John F., Regina Coeli Residence for Priests, 685 York Rd., Warminster, PA 18974

Daly, John J., Villa Saint Joseph, 1436 Lansdowne Ave., Darby, PA 19023-1298
Degnan, Henry B., St. Paul Rectory, 2007 New Hope St., Norristown, PA 19401
Devlin, Joseph F., Villa St. Joseph, 1436 Lansdowne Ave., Darby, PA 19023-1298
Dougherty, Henry E., Queen of the Universe Rectory, 2443 Trenton Rd., Levittown, PA 19056
Dougherty, John C., Saint Callistus Rectory, 700 North 67th St., Philadelphia, PA 19151-3614
Dougherty, Joseph D., Regina Coeli Residence for Priests, 685 York Rd., Warminster, PA 18974
Duddy, Patrick A., Villa Saint Joseph, 1436 Lansdowne Ave., Darby, PA 19023-1298
Duffy, John J., Five Whalerman Cove, Brigantine, NJ 08203
Dunne, Peter J., 815 Haycock Run Rd., Kintnersville, PA 18930
Durney, Charles W., P.O. Box 138, Tuscarora, PA 17982
Dux, James M., Villa Saint Joseph, 1436 Lansdowne Ave., Darby, PA 19023-1298
Dziadosz, Edward T., 438 W. Mahanoy Ave., Mahanoy City, PA 17948-0095
Fala, John G., Saint Bernard Rectory, 7341 Cottage St., Philadelphia, PA 19136
Farrell, Donald J., Saint Cyril of Alexandria Rectory, 153 Penn Blvd., East Lansdowne, PA 19050
Feeney, Thomas M., 1341 Osbourne Ave., Roslyn, PA 19001
Fitzpatrick, Peter A., St. Patrick Rectory, 242 S. 20th St., Philadelphia, PA 19103
Foster, John J., Regina Coeli Residence for Priests, 685 York Rd., Warminster, PA 18974
Gallen, Francis H., Hershey Mill, 118 Chandler Dr., West Chester, PA 19380
Glynn, John P., 137 105th St., Stone Harbor, NJ 08247
Gormley, Charles E., Saint Matthias Rectory, 128 Bryn Mawr Ave., Bala Cynwyd, PA 19004
Graf, Henry C., Regina Coeli Residence for Priests, 685 York Rd., Warminster, PA 18974
Graham, Thomas D., Villa Saint Joseph, 1436 Lansdowne Ave., Darby, PA 19023-1298
Griffin, Richard J., Villa Saint Joseph, 1436 Lansdowne Ave., Darby, PA 19023-1298
Gsell, John W., Villa Saint Joseph, 1436 Landsdowne Ave., Darby, PA 19023-1298
Hartnett, Walter J., Villa Saint Joseph, 1436 Lansdowne Ave., Darby, PA 19023-1298
Heim, John S., 4527 Salmon St., Philadelphia, PA 19137
Hoy, Daniel J., Our Lady of the Assumption Rectory, 35 Old Eagle School Rd., Strafford, PA 19087
Hughes, James F., 1060 Lenape Dr., East Stroudsburg, PA 18301
Jaworowski, Leon E., Villa Saint Joseph, 1436 Lansdowne Ave., Darby, PA 19023-1298
Joseph, William T., Villa Saint Joseph, 1436 Lansdowne Ave., Darby, PA 19023-1298
Jung, Joseph B., Villa Saint Joseph, 1436 Lansdowne Ave., Darby, PA 19023-1298
Kane, Aloysius T., Villa Saint Joseph, 1436 Lansdowne Ave., Darby, PA 19023-1298
Kehoe, Daniel J., Holy Spirit Rectory, 1028 School St., Sharon Hill, PA 19079
Kelley, Thomas J., Saint Matthew Rectory, 3000 Cottman Ave., Philadelphia, PA 19149
Kelly, James J., Villa Saint Joseph, 1436 Lansdowne Ave., Darby, PA 19023-1298
Kelly, James Joseph, Epiphany of Our Lord Rectory, 3050 Walton Rd., Norristown, PA 19462
Kelly, Thomas J., Saint Francis Country House, 1412 Lansdowne Ave., Darby, PA 19023-1298
Kennedy, Joseph J., Villa St. Joseph, 1436 Lansdowne Ave., Darby, PA 19023-1298
Klapp, John S., Saint Francis Country House, 1412 Lansdowne Ave., Darby, PA 19023-1218
Koob, Edward H., 6612 Pleasure Ave., Sea Isle City, NJ 08243-1450
Kovacs, Louis D., Saint Francis Country, 1412 Lansdowne Ave., Darby, PA 19023-1218
Krick, Howard K., 123 Brackenridge Apt. 116, San Antonio, TX 78209
Leary, James V., Sacred Heart Rectory, 148 Church St., Phoenixville, PA 19460
Lennon, Francis P., St. Eleanor Rectory, 647 Locust St., Collegeville, PA 19426-2541
Lepleiter, Robert P., St. Jude Rectory, 321 W. Butler Ave., Chalfont, PA 18914-2329
Loughran, Francis J., Saint Francis Country House, 1412 Lansdowne Ave., Darby, PA 19023-1218
Loughrey, Thomas F., 651 W. Pine Ave., West Wildwood, NJ 08260
Machain, David B., Saint Bernard Rectory, 7341 Cottage St., Philadelphia, PA 19136
Maguire, Connell J., 2800 N. Ocean Dr., Apt. B15a, Riviera Beach, FL 33404
Maher, Edmund J., St. William Rectory, 6200 Rising Sun Ave., Philadelphia, PA 19111
McDevitt, Francis N., Villa Saint Joseph, 1436 Lansdowne Ave., Darby, PA 19023-1298
Morley, John J., Saint Francis Country House, 1412 Lansdowne Ave., Darby, PA 19023-1218
Morrison, Francis X., Villa Saint Joseph, 1436 Lansdowne Ave., Darby, PA 19023-1298
Morrison, Robert A., Villa Saint Joseph, 1436 Lansdowne Ave., Darby, PA 19023-1298
Murphy, James A., St. Gabriel Rectory, 421 Jefferson St., Stowe, PA 19464
Murphy, James J., 227 Brazilian Ave., Palm Beach, FL 33480
Murphy, Joseph T., 812 Rowland Ave., Cheltenham, PA 19012
Murray, John J., Villa Saint Joseph, 1436 Lansdowne Ave., Darby, PA 19023-1298
O'Connor, John P., Saint Katherine of Siena Rectory, 9700 Frankford Ave., Philadelphia, PA 19114-2896
O'Halloran, Martin J., Regina Coeli Residence for Priests, 685 York Rd., Warminster, PA 18974
O'Hara, Martin F., St. Jerome Rectory, 8100 Colfax St., Philadelphia, PA 19136-1801
Oestreich, Emil C., Villa St. Joseph, 1436 Lansdowne Ave., Darby, PA 19023-1298
Ostaszewski, George, 4255 Richmond St., Philadelphia, PA 19137
Reino, Joseph C., 910 Wynnewood Rd., Philadelphia, PA 19151-4501
Riedy, Robert I., Saint Francis Country House, 1412 Lansdowne Ave., Darby, PA 19023-1218
Rilley, John F., Villa St. Joseph, 1436 Lansdowne Ave., Darby, PA 19023
Rodo, Anthony C., c/o Mary & Sylvia, 23 Psalja St. - BKR 02, Birkirkara, Malta Europe
Rogers, Francis P., Villa Saint Joseph, 1436 Lansdowne Ave., Darby, PA 19023-1298
Rossi, Anthony M., Villa Saint Joseph, 1436 Lansdowne Ave., Darby, PA 19023-1298
Ryan, Robert F., St. Gabriel's Hall, P.O. Box 7280, Audubon, PA 19407
Schifalacqua, Ildebrando E., St. Bartholomew Rectory, 5600 Jackson St., Philadelphia, PA 19124
Schneider, George P., 109 Chestnut St., Parkesburg, PA 19365
Schuyler, Henry C., Visitation B.V.M. Rectory, 196 N. Trooper Rd., Norristown, PA 19403-2665
Scully, Philip A., Villa Saint Joseph, 1436 Lansdowne Ave., Darby, PA 19023-1298
Senske, Joseph A., Gillet Convent, Immaculata College, P.O. Box 731, Immaculata, PA 19345
Shea, Thomas F., Villa Saint Joseph, 1436 Lansdowne Ave., Darby, PA 19023-1298
Sheridan, James B., Villa Saint Joseph, 1436 Lansdowne Ave., Darby, PA 19023-1298
Slafkosky, Andrew L., 610 Pine Rd., Silver Spring Shores, Ocala, FL 34472-6167
Smith, Joseph F., Viilla Saint Joseph, 1436 Lansdowne Ave., Darby, PA 19023-1298
Smith, William J., 9 Church Rd., Marmora, NJ 08223
Smyth, Henry J., Regina Coeli Residence for Priests, 685 York Rd., Warminster, PA 18974
Speitel, Edmond J., 805 3rd St., Ocean City, NJ 08226
Stanton, William J., Regina Coeli Residence for Priests, 685 York Rd., Warminster, PA 18974
Stec, Joseph C., Saint Laurentius Rectory, 1608 East Berks St., Philadelphia, PA 19125-2499
Szal, Ignatius J., 460 Sunbury St., Minersville, PA 17954
Van Stone, John J., Villa Saint Joseph, 1436 Lansdowne Ave., Darby, PA 19023-1298
Walsh, George J., Villa Saint Joseph, 1436 Lansdowne Ave., Darby, PA 19023
Walsh, John M., Villa Saint Joseph, 1436 Lansdowne Ave., Darby, PA 19023-1298
Walsh, Joseph E., Saint Francis de Sales Rectory, 35 New Rd., P.O. Box 97, Lenni, PA 19052
Walsh, Michael L., Camilla Hall, Immaculata, PA 19345
Walsh, Thomas F., 730 Salem Ct., Yardley, PA 19067
Wassel, Eugene A., Saint Francis Country House, 1412 Lansdowne Ave., Darby, PA 19023-1298
Wesolowski, Edmund C., Immaculate Conception Rectory, 1020 North Front St., Philadelphia, PA 19123-1717
Wright, Richard J., Saint Colman Rectory, 11 Simpson Rd., Ardmore, PA 19003

Permanent Deacons:
All locations are Philadelphia unless otherwise indicated.

Andrews, Edward J., St. Martin De Porres Church
Arno, Michael R., St. Irenaeus Church
Basilio, James A., Notre Dame De Lourdes Church, Swarthmore
Bean, John J., St. Bartholomew Church
Belanger, A. Kenneth, St. Helena Church, Center Square
Bentancourt, Miguel, St. Peter the Apostle Church
Bianco, Salvatore R., Immaculate Heart of Mary Church
Bizal, Francis M., SS. Philip and James Church, Exton
Bolter, George A., St. Monica Church, Berwyn
Bonilla, Victor M., Maternity B.V.M. Church
Brandon, Lawrence G., St. Maximilian Kolbe Church, West Chester
Brown, Clifford W., Our Mother of Consolidation Church
Burke, Francis B., St. Bernadette, Drexel Hill
Burns, James H., St. Eleanor Church, Collegeville
Butcavage, Thomas E., Holy Spirit Church, Sharon Hill
Calabrese, Peter J., St. Charles Borromeo Church, Drexel Hill
Campbell, John J., St. Rose of Lima, North Wales
Cavaliere, Francis M., St. Joseph Church, Warrington
Cella, Joseph M., Our Lady of Ransom Church
Ceneviva, Vincent G., St. Jude Church, Chalfont
Champagne, William E., Our Lady of Hope Church
Clancy, Kenneth P., Epiphany of Our Lord Church, Norristown
Clark, Francis T., St. Joseph Church, Ambler
Collazo, Apolonio, Visitation B.V.M. Church
Connors, Francis J., St. Callistus
Conroy, Michael F., Sacred Heart Church, Royersford
Corwell, George V., Our Lady of Mt. Carmel Church, Doylestown
Cox, Paul R., St. Patrick, Malvern
Coyle, Joseph P., St. Alice Church, Upper Darby
Coyne, Richard C., Holy Cross Church
Cruz, Felipe, Incarnation of Our Lord Church
D'Angelo, Ernest, St. John the Baptist Church, Ottsville
Dalton, James E., St. Cyril of Alexandria Church, East Lansdowne
Davaro, John J., St. Dorothy Church, Drexel Hill
Dayoc, Michael J., St. Paul Church, Norristown
DeBow, James P., St. Ephrem Church, Bensalem
DeJesus, Epifanio, Cathedral Basilica of SS. Peter & Paul
DeLucca, Daniel N., St. Andrew Church, Drexel Hill
DeMasi, Leonard, St. Monica Church
Derivan, Albert T., St. Andrew Church, Newtown
DeRosa, Joseph R., St. Eleanor, Collegeville
Devine, Charles F., St. Thomas the Apostle Church, Chester Heights
Diana, Leonard J., St. Kevin Church, Springfield
DiIenno, Anthony J., St. Thomas the Apostle, Glen Mills
Duffy, James J., St. Katherine of Siena
Dymek, Edward J., St. Ephrem Church, Bensalem
Eichman, Thomas E., St. Kevin Church, Springfield
Eliason, William F., St. David Church, Willow Grove
Ellis, John J., St. Barnabas Church
Fabrizio, Francis S., St. Charles Borromeo Church, Drexel Hill
Fahy, William C., SS. Philip and James Church, Exton
Favinger, M. Eugene, Our Lady of Consolation Church, Parkesburg
Fernandez, Alfonzo, St. Veronica Church
Finn, Michael J., Blessed Katharine Drexel Church, Chester
Fontanez, Jose, Incarnation of Our Lord Church
Frankenberger, Robert J., Holy Cross Church, Springfield
Franks, Michael J., Sr., St. Philip Neri Church, Pennsburg
Fremont, Richard L., St. Peter Church, Honey Brook
Froio, Lawrence P., St. Patrick Church, Malvern
Fuentes, Ismael, St. Aloysius Church, Pottstown
Fulmer, Walter C., Christ the King Church
Garritano, Dominic A., Our Lady of Ransom Church
Gellentien, Robert P., St. John the Evangelist Church, Morrisville
George, Albert J., Holy Spirit Church
Gibson, Lawrence J., St. Elizabeth Ann Seton Church, Bensalem
Gladnick, Leo T., Ascension of Our Lord Church
Gonzalez, Victor M., St. Agnes Church, West Chester
Gousie, Joseph N., Our Lady of Guadalupe Church, Buckingham
Granese, Claude B., St. Jude Church, Chalfont
Gravlin, John J., Unassigned
Guillet, Andre J.P., St. Agatha/St. James
Guinane, William J., St. Madeline Church, Ridley Park
Gwynn, Raymond F., St. Jerome Church
Haddon, Richard S., St. Catherine of Siena Church, Horsham

Hagerty, Paul B., Immaculate Conception Church, Jenkintown
Hannan, Thomas J., Assumption B.V.M. Church, West Grove
Harper, Sidney M., St. Athanasius Church
Harrison, A. Gerald, SS. Peter and Paul Church, West Chester
Hartmann, James E., St. John the Evangelist Church, Morrisville
Hartmann, Karl J., St. Joseph Church, Warrington
Heaney, Philip E., Maternity B.V.M. Church
Hernandez, Jose, Incarnation of Our Lord Church
Hickey, William L., St. Maximilian Kolbe, West Chester
Hoelzle, Louis F., St. Frances Cabrini Church, Fairless Hills
Hopkins, Stephen, St. Benedict Church
Horan, Thomas J., SS. Peter & Paul Church, West Chester
Huynh, Trac Mai, St. Francis De Sales Church
Hynes, John, Maternity B.V.M. Church
Iannucci, Joseph E., St. Pius X Church, Broomall
Jacobucci, Raymond, St. Nicholas of Tolentine Church
Jones, David E., St. Anthony of Padua Church, Ambler
Kane, James D., Sr., St. Francis of Assisi Church, Springfield
Kefer, Robert J., SS. Peter & Paul Church, West Chester
Kelly, Gerald F., St. Matthias Church, Bala Cynwyd
Kelly, Walter E., Our Lady of Mount Carmel Church, Doylestown
Kern, Paul R., St. John Baptist Vianney Church, Gladwyne
Kerr, Frederick H., St. Cecilia Church, Coatesville
Klauder, Francis, St. Elizabeth Ann Seton Church, Bensalem
Konarski, Edward A., St. Rose of Lima Church, North Wales
Kretsch, Donald J., Holy Savior Church, Norristown
Kruckenberger, William F., St. John Bosco Church, Hatboro
Kubczak, David M., St. Peter Church, Pottstown
Lance, Walter C., St. John Chrysostom Church, Wallingford
Leahy, Eugene R., Holy Family Church
Leonard, Warren C., Holy Trinity, Morrisville
Leonhardt, George W., St. Thomas More Church, South Coventry
Lozada, Jose Luis, St. Hugh of Cluny Church
Lyon, James E., SS. Simon & Jude Church, West Chester
Madonna, James K., St. Patrick Church, Kennett Square
Makoid, T. Eric, Sacred Heart Church, Swedesburg
Maldonado, Rafael, St. Veronica Church
Malfara, Louis S., St. Cecilia Church
Manson, Joseph J., St. Genevieve Church, Flourtown
Manzano, Edwin R., Visitation B.V.M. Church
Maresca, Armand J., SS. Cosmas & Damian Church, Conshohocken
Martes, Zoilo, St. Michael Church
Mauriello, Alfred J., St. Maximilian Kolbe, West Chester
McAndrews, Michael J., Notre Dame DeLourdes Church, Swarthmore
McGovern, Clement J., St. Cornelius Church, Chadds Ford
McGrath, Gerard P., St. Eleanor Church, Collegeville
McGuire, Arthur M., St. Francis of Assisi Church, Springfield
Mendez, Jose M., St. Ambrose Church
Micucci, Joseph A., Mother of Divine Grace Church
Morris, George E., St. Robert Bellarmine Church, Warrington
Murphy, Francis X., Sacred Heart Church, Oxford
Nightingale, Richard G., Our Lady of Victory Church
Niland, Joseph W., St. Elizabeth Ann Seton Church, Bensalem
O'Brien, Gregory R., St. Madeline Church, Ridley Park
O'Kedas, Leroy F., St. Rita of Cascia Church
Oliver, Joseph M., Our Lady of Perpetual Help, Morton
Orlando, John C., St. Monica Church
Orlando, Joseph P., St. Bede the Venerable Church, Holland
Owens, James T., St. Colman, Ardmore
Parker, John, Holy Saviour Church, Norristown
Pavonarius, Charles A., St. Jerome Church
Pierce, Robert F., SS. Peter & Paul Church, West Chester
Polley, Charles W., Jr., Ss. Philip and James Church, Exton
Purnell, Edward M., St. Theresa of the Child Jesus Church
Radetsky, William R., Epiphany of Our Lord Church, Norristown
Ramos, Juan F., St. Peter the Apostle
Rayner, Albert E., Holy Spirit Church, Sharon Hill
Rebuck, Charles H., St. Gabriel Church, Stowe
Riordan, John T., St. Jude Church, Chalfont
Rooney, Joseph T., Our Lady Help of Christians Church, Abington
Rouse, Daniel J., St. John Bosco Church, Hatboro
Ruiz, Luis, St. Ambrose Church
Schaffer, David B., St. Denis Rectory, Havertown
Schiappa, Edward R., St. Joseph Church, Downingtown
Schlegel, John F., St. Denis Rectory, Havertown
Seda, Victor, St. Helena Church
Sexton, Joseph F., St. Mary of the Assumption Church
Shields, Thomas A., St. Martin De Porres Church
Simpson, Harry J., St. Michael the Archangel, Levittown
Skawinski, Robert J., St. Ignatius Church, Yardley
Smith, Calvin C., St. Benedict Church
Stam, Bernardus C., SS. Simon & Jude Church, West Chester
Stewart, James J., St. Edmond Church
Stewart, Robert J., St. Ignatius Church, Yardley
Stoughton, Richard L., Our Lady of the Rosary Church, Coatesville
Suplee, John J., Sacred Heart Church, Havertown
Thompson, James A., Stella Maris
Thompson, Vincent J., St. Francis Xavier Church
Tielemans, Mathieu M., St. Stanislaus Church, Lansdale
Tobin, Charles A., St. Philomena Church, Lansdowne
Tormey, James M., Our Mother of Consolation Church
Tucker, Henry E., St. Agnes Church, Sellersville
Upcavage, Joseph R., Queen of the Universe Church, Levittown
Urbanski, Timothy E., St. Catherine of Siena Church, Horsham
Urmson, Francis B., St. Helena
Vadino, Raymond M., St. John Chrysostom Church, Wallingford
Verna, Louis, Sacred Heart Church, Havertown
Vondercrone, C. Stephens, St. Stanislaus Church, Lansdale
Walker, James T., St. Benedict Church
Wernert, Emil J., Epiphany of Our Lord, Norristown
Whartenby, Gerald J., St. Anselm Church
Windish, Joseph F., St. Cyril of Jerusalem Church, Jamison
Wirth, Richard D., St. Cornelius Church, Chadds Ford
Wojewodka, Boleslaw S., Sacred Heart Church, Clifton Heights
Wolkowicz, Leonard J., St. Barnabas Church
Woodall, Michael V., St. Eleanor Church, Collegeville
Woods, Thomas J., Sacred Heart Church, Havertown
Ziff, Joel M., Epiphany of Our Lord Church, Norristown
Zurbach, E. Peter, St. Mary Magdalen Church, Media

INSTITUTIONS LOCATED IN THE ARCHDIOCESE

[A] SEMINARIES, ARCHDIOCESAN

WYNNEWOOD. *Theological Seminary of St. Charles Borromeo, Overbrook*, Administration: 100 E. Wynnewood Rd., 19096. Tel: 610-667-3394; Fax: 610-667-7635.
E-mail: frmburbi@adphila.org
Web site: www.scs.edu
Rev. Msgr. Michael F. Burbidge, M.A., Ed.D., Rector; Rev. Christopher J. Schreck (SAV), S.T.B., S.S.L., Ph.D., S.T.D., Vice Rector, Educational Admin.; Elaine K. Rice, M.B.A., Vice Pres., Finance; Ruth Suder, B.S., Vice Pres., Operations; Revs. Joseph Prior, M.Div., M.A., S.S.L., S.T.D., Academic Dean, Theology Division; David E. Diamond, M.Div., M.A., Ph.D., Academic Dean, College Division; Frederick L. Miller, M.A., S.T.L., S.T.D. (NEW), Academic Dean, Religious Studies Division; Thomas J. Owens, M.Div., M.A., Dean of Formation, Theology Division; Joseph L. Maloney, M.Div., Dean of Formation, College Division; John C. O'Driscoll, M.Div., S.L.L., Dir. Liturgy; Joseph F. Gleason, M.Div., M.S., Dir. Spiritual Formation, Theology Division; Paul V. Dougherty, M.Div., M.A., Dir. Spiritual Formation, College Division; Joseph P. Gentili, M.Div., S.T.L., S.T.D., Dir. Pastoral and Apostolic Formation; Cait Kokolus, M.S.L.S., M.A., Dir. Library Svcs.; Lawrence A. Heyman, Ed.M., Registrar; Revs. John M. Savinski, M.Div., M.A., Dir., Spirituality Year Prog.; Anthony J. Costa, M.Div., M.A., S.T.L., Spiritual Dir., Spirituality Year Prog. Full Time Instructional Faculty: Rev. Andrew R. Baker (ALN), M.Div., M.A., S.T.L., S.T.D.; Mark E. Bradford, M.Mus.; Revs. Stephen F. Brett, S.S.J., Ph.D, J.D.; Augustine M. Esposito, O.S.A., M.Div., M.A., Ph.D.; Mary Ellen Fattori, M.A.; Janet Haggerty, M.A., Ph.D.; Atherton C. Lowry, M.A., Ph.D.; Revs. Matthew J. Kornacki, M.Div.; Shaun L. Mahoney, M.Div., S.T.L.; Rev. Msgr. Richard Malone, M.A., J.C.L., S.T.D.; Rev. Kevin T. McMahon, S.T.B., S.T.L., S.T.D. (WIL), John Cardinal Krol Chair Prof. of Moral Theology; Gerald H. Malsbary, M.A., Ph.D.; Rev. Michael J. McNally, M.Div., M.Th., M.A., Ph.D (PMB); Elizabeth M. Nagel, M.A., S.S.L., S.S.D.; Revs. James M. Oliver, M.Div., M.A., J.C.L., J.C; Robert A. Pesarchick, M.Div., M.A., S.T.L., S.T.D.; John H. Sceski, M.A., Ph.D.; Christine A. Shwartz, M.A., M.Div., M.L.S. Adjunct Faculty: J. Brian Benestad, M.A., Ph.D.; Rev. Dennis J. Carbonaro, M.Div., M.A.; Rev. Msgr. Michael J. Chaback (ALN), Ph.B., S.T.B., S.T.L., S.T.D.; Rev. Stephen J. Dougherty, M.Div., M.A.; Bro. Michael T. Duffy, O.F.M.Conv., M.S.; Sr. Mary Elizabeth Kratzinger, S.S.J., M.A.; Rev. Daniel E. Mackle, M.Div., M.A.; Rev. Msgr. Stephen P. McHenry, M.A., Ph.D.; Rev. Thomas J. McManus, M.Div., M.A., S.T.L.; Rev. Msgr. Alexander J. Palmieri, M.Div., M.A., J.C.L.; Rev. Joseph F. Rymdeika, M.Div., M.A.; Sr. Suzanne Shaffer, I.H.M., B.A.; Sr. Rita Small, R.S.M., M.A.; Rabbi David A. Wortman, M.A., M.Phil.; Shawn Weldon, M.A. In res. Most Rev. Joseph F. Martino, D.D., S.T.L., H.E.D.; Rev. Msgr. Charles V. Devlin; Rev. Msgr. Thomas J. Benestad, M.Div. (ALN). Priests 31; Brothers 1; Sisters 3; Lay Staff 15; College and Theology Division Students 157; Religious Studies Division Students 326; Seminarians from Archdiocese 59; Seminarians from other Dioceses 86; Religious Communities 12.

[B] SEMINARIES, RELIGIOUS OR SCHOLASTICATES

PHILADELPHIA. *Brothers of the Christian Schools Scholasticate*, Jeremy House, 6633 Ardleigh St., 19119-3898. Tel: 215-843-1884; Fax: 215-843-1617.
E-mail: jeremyhouse@juno.com
Bro. Dennis Malloy, F.S.C., Dir. Professed Brothers 4.

DePaul Novitiate, 5710 Magnolia St., 19144. Tel: 215-843-1581; Fax: 215-844-9634.
E-mail: semnov@erols.com
Revs. John P. Timlin, C.M., Dir.; Charles M. Shanley, C.M., Asst. Dir. In res. Revs. Charles P. Strollo, C.M.; Thomas F. McKenna, C.M.; Bro. Peter A. Campbell, C.M. National Novitiate for the Congregation of the Mission (Vincentians). Priests 2; Novices 2.

St. Vincent's Seminary, 500 E. Chelten Ave., 19144-1296. Tel: 215-848-1985; Fax: 215-844-2085.
E-mail: cmphila88@aol.com
Very Rev. Thomas F. McKenna, C.M., Prov.; Revs. Charles P. Strollo, C.M., Asst. Prov.; William W. Sheldon, C.M., Supr.; Francis W. Sacks, C.M., Dir. Missions; Senior Confreres Liaison; John W. Gouldrick, C.M., Treasurer; William J. O'Brien, C.M., Dir. Miraculous Medal Association; John W. Carven, C.M., Provincial Archivist. Central House of the Eastern Province of the Congregation of the Mission, (Vincentians).

PAOLI. *Daylesford Abbey*, 220 S. Valley Rd., 19301-1900. Tel: 610-647-2530; Fax: 610-651-0219.
E-mail: nobertines@daylesford.org
Web site: www.daylesford.org
Legal Title: *Norbertine Fathers, Inc.* Ronald J. Rossi, O.Praem., Abbot; Very Rev. John J. Novielli, O.Praem., Prior; Rt. Rev. John E. Neitzel, O.Praem., Abbot Emeritus; Revs. Steven J. Albero, O.Praem., Vocation Dir.; Joseph A. Serano, O.Praem., Treas. Priests 21; Brothers 3.

SPRINGFIELD. *Don Guanella House of Formation*, 1795 S. Sproul Rd., 19064. Tel: 610-328-3406; Fax: 610-328-1019. Congregation of the Servants of Charity. Rev. Silvio De Nard, S.C. Priests 1.

VILLANOVA. *St. Augustine Friary*, 214 Ashwood Rd., 19085. Tel: 610-527-0325; Fax: 610-527-0640. Rev. James D. McBurney, O.S.A., Prior; Bro. John Konwerski, O.S.A.; Revs. Daniel E. Doyle, O.S.A.; Edward J. Enright, O.S.A.; Thomas F. Martin, O.S.A.; Stanley C. Smith, O.S.A.; Peter J. Toscani, O.S.A. Priests 6; Brothers 1.

[C] COLLEGES AND UNIVERSITIES

PHILADELPHIA. *Chestnut Hill College*, 9601 Germantown Ave., 19118-2693. Tel: 215-248-7000; Fax: 215-248-7155.
E-mail: apply@chc.edu
Web site: www.chc.edu
For a complete listing, refer to the Colleges and Universities section.

Holy Family College, (1954) Grant and Frankford Aves., 19114. Tel: 215-637-7700; Fax: 215-637-3787.
E-mail: fonley@hfc.org
Web site: www.hfc.edu
For a complete listing, refer to the Colleges and Universities section.

LaSalle University, 1900 W. Olney Ave., 19141. Tel: 215-951-1000; Fax: 215-951-1783
For a complete listing, refer to the Colleges and Universities section.

St. Joseph's University, 5600 City Ave., 19131. Tel: 610-660-1000; Fax: 610-660-1201.
Web site: www.sju.edu
For a complete listing, refer to the Colleges and Universities section.

ASTON. *Neumann College*, One Neumann Dr., 19014-1298. Tel: 610-459-0905; Fax: 610-459-1370.
E-mail: neumann@neumann.edu
Web site: www.neumann.edu
For a complete listing, refer to the Colleges and Universities section.

GWYNEDD VALLEY. *Gwynedd-Mercy College*, 19437. Tel: 215-646-7300; Fax: 215-641-5573.
E-mail: hoffman.r@gmc.edu
Web site: www.gmc.edu
For a complete listing, refer to the Colleges and Universities section.

IMMACULATA. *Immaculata College*, (1920), 19345. Tel: 610-647-4400; Fax: 610-251-1668.
Web site: www.immaculata.edu
For a complete listing, refer to the Colleges and Universities section.

RADNOR. *Cabrini College*, (1957) 610 King of Prussia Rd., 19087-3698. Tel: 610-902-8100; Fax: 610-902-8309.
E-mail: nancy.gardner@cabrini.edu
Web site: www.cabrini.edu
For a complete listing, refer to the Colleges and Universities section.

ROSEMONT. *Rosemont College of the Holy Child Jesus*, 19010-1699. Tel: 610-526-2984; Fax: 610-527-0341.
E-mail: jtrogers@rosemont.edu
Web site: www.rosemont.edu
For a complete listing, refer to the Colleges and Universities section.

VILLANOVA. *Villanova University*, 19085. Tel: 610-519-7499; Fax: 610-519-5333.
E-mail: Stephen.Merritt@Villanova.edu
For a complete listing, refer to the Colleges and Universities section.

[D] HIGH SCHOOLS, ARCHDIOCESAN

PHILADELPHIA. *Archbishop Ryan High School*, 11201 Academy Rd., 19154-3397. Tel: 215-637-1800; Fax: 215-637-8833.
E-mail: archryanlib@zdnetmail.com
Web site: www.ryanhs.org
Opened September 7, 1966. Franciscan Friars, Order of Friars Minor. Revs. Charles Newman, O.F.M., Prin.; Rene Barczak, O.F.M.; Carl Graczyk, O.F.M.; Francis Kelly, O.F.M.; Gabriel A. Rosetti, O.F.M.; Louis Stislow, O.F.M., Chap. Priests 3; Brothers 1; Sisters 4; Lay Teachers 110; Total Staff 119; Students 2,592.

Cardinal Dougherty High School, 6301 N. 2nd St., 19120-1599. Tel: 215-276-2300; Fax: 215-276-2306.
E-mail: cdhs@libertynet.org
Web site: www.libertynet.org/~cdhs
(Coed) Opened September 1956. Rev. Paul M. Kennedy, M.A., M.Div., Pres.; Mrs. Mary Harkins, M.A., Prin.; Rev. Carl F. Janicki, School Min. Priests 5; Sisters 15; Lay Teachers 47; Students 1,152.

Father Judge High School for Boys, 3301 Solly Ave., 19136-2396. Tel: 215-338-9494; Fax: 215-338-0250.
E-mail: principal@fjquest.com
Web site: fjquest.com
Opened September 1954. Oblates of St. Francis de Sales. Revs. Joseph D. Bowler, O.S.F.S.; Thomas P. Gallagher, O.S.F.S.; Eugene L. Kelly, O.S.F.S.; Dennis W. Killion, O.S.F.S.; Gerard J. Mahoney, O.S.F.S.; David M. Merchant, O.S.F.S.; Edward L. Rauch, O.S.F.S., Pres.; William O. Seelaus, O.S.F.S.; John J. Dennis, O.S.F.S.; Gerald M. Dunne, O.S.F.S. (SUP); Bro. Thomas Brophy, O.S.F.S.; Revs. Robert G. Mulligan, O.S.F.S., Prin.; Joseph G. Campellone, O.S.F.S., Chap. Priests 12; Brothers 1; Lay Teachers 59; Students 1,360.

John W. Hallahan Catholic Girls High School, 311 N. 19th St., 19103-1198. Tel: 215-563-8930; Fax: 215-563-3809. Opened September 18, 1901. Dr. Lorraine S. Rice, Pres.; Sr. Marita Carmel, I.H.M., Prin.; Rev. Michael F. Hennelly, School Min. Priests 1; Sisters 7; Lay Teachers 26; Students 640.

Little Flower Catholic High School for Girls, 1000 W. Lycoming St., 19140. Tel: 215-455-6900; Fax: 215-329-0478.
Web site: littleflowerhighschool.org
Opened September 1, 1939. Sr. Kathleen Klarich, R.S.M., Prin.; Sr. Donna Shallo, I.H.M., Pres.; Rev. Robert W. Povish, School Min. Sisters 22; Lay Teachers 31; Students 786.

Northeast Catholic High School for Boys, 1842 E. Torresdale Ave., 19124-4418. Tel: 215-831-1234; Fax: 215-743-0926.
E-mail: preznechs@aol.com
Web site: www.northcatholic.com
Opened September 7, 1926. Oblates of St. Francis de Sales. Res., 1840 E. Torresdale Ave., 19124-4418. Revs. Mark J. Wrightson, O.S.F.S, Pres.; Nicholas R. Waseline, O.S.F.S., Prin.; Very Rev. William E. Davis, O.S.F.S., Supr.; Rev. William T. McCandless, O.S.F.S., School Min. Priests 11; Brothers 2; Sisters 2; Lay Faculty 42; Students 850.

Roman Catholic High School for Boys, 301 N. Broad St., 19107. Tel: 215-627-1270; 627-1570; Fax: 215-627-4979.
E-mail: mail@cahillite.com
Web site: www.cahillite.com
Opened September 8, 1890. Revs. Paul C. Brandt, M.A., Pres. & Rector; Gerard J. Hoffman, M.Div.; Robert Mulligan, M.A., School Minister; Ronald M. Jakows, Teacher. Priests 4; Sisters 2; Lay Teachers 40; Students 872.

St. Hubert's Catholic High School for Girls, 7320 Torresdale Ave., 19136. Tel: 215-624-6840; Fax: 215-624-5940.
E-mail: sthubert@nni.com
Web site: www.asd.com
Opened September 1941. Sr. Alma Rose Schlosser, S.S.J., Pres.; Rev. Christopher D. Lucas, O.F.M.Conv., Dir. School Ministry; Sr. Marie Esther Hart, I.H.M., Prin. Priests 1; Sisters 10; Lay Teachers 56; Students 1,171.

St. John Neumann High School. (Formerly Southeast Catholic High School), 2600 Moore St., 19145-1798. Tel: 215-389-4900; Fax: 215-462-3577.
E-mail: neumann@netaxs.com
Web site: www.netaxs.com~neumann
(Boys) Opened September 1, 1934. Canons Regular of Premontre Diocesan Priests forming Faculty. Revs. Michael S. Olivere, Pres.; Quan H. Tran, School Ministry; James C. Otto. Priests 3; Sisters 1; Lay Teachers 33; Students 678.

St. Maria Goretti High School, 1736 S. 10th St., 19148. Tel: 215-465-8437; Fax: 215-462-2410.
E-mail: mgpres@adphila.org
Web site: www.goretti.com
(Girls) Opened September 1955. Sr. M. Sheila Foy, I.H.M., Pres.; Jane M. Pellegrino, Prin.; Rev. James Olson, School Min. Sisters 20; Lay Teachers 32; Students 670.

West Philadelphia Catholic High School, 4501 Chestnut St., 19139. Tel: 215-386-2244; Fax: 215-222-1651.
Web site: www.westcatholic.org
Opened September 6, 1989. Bro. Richard Kestler, F.S.C.; Rev. John Pidgeon, Dir. School Ministry. Priests 1; Religious 21; Lay Teachers 34; Students 863.

DOWNINGTOWN. *Bishop Shanahan High School*, 220 Woodbine Rd., 19335. Tel: 610-518-1300.
E-mail: hrapine@shanahan.org
Web site: www.shanahan.org
(Coed) Formerly St. Agnes High School opened in 1909; became diocesan high school September 1957, moved from West Chester to Downingtown in 1998. Sr. Helen Rapine, I.H.M., Pres.; Sr. Nancy McFadden, I.H.M., Prin.; Revs. Joseph F. Rymdeika; James J. Melle; Joseph D. Brandt. Sisters, Servants of the Immaculate Heart of Mary 13; Priests 3; Lay Teachers 48; Students 1106.

DREXEL HILL. *Archbishop Prendergast High School*, 401 N. Lansdowne Ave., 19026. Tel: 610-259-0265; Fax: 610-259-3676.
E-mail: prendie@nni.com
Web site: www.prendie.com
Open September 1956. Sr. Catherine Robinson, S.S.J., Pres.; Mrs. Mary Berner, Prin.; Rev. Jason Kulczynski, Dir. School Ministry. Priests 1; Sisters 14; Lay Teachers 44; Girls 930.

Monsignor Bonner High School, 403 N. Lansdowne Ave., 19026-1196. Tel: 610-259-0280; Fax: 610-259-1630.
Web site: www.bonnerhigh.com
(Boys) Opened September 1953 as Archbishop Prendergast High School for Boys. New name adopted September 1956. Revs. John T. Denny, O.S.A., Pres.; William E. Atkinson, O.S.A., Prior; Francis X. Devlin, O.S.A.; John J. Ferrence, O.S.A.; Daniel McLaughlin, O.S.A. Priests 5; Sisters 3; Lay Teachers 45; Students 1,050.

FAIRLESS HILLS. *Conwell-Egan Catholic High School*, 611 Wistar Rd., 19030. Tel: 215-945-6200; Fax: 215-945-6206. Formerly Bishop Egan High School, Fairless Hills, and Bishop Conwell High School, Levittown. Mr. William L. Galante, Pres.; Sr. John Ann Proach, O.S.F., Prin.; Rev. Fidelis F. Weber, T.O.R., Guidance Dir. Sisters 8; Brothers 1; Deacons 1; Lay Teachers 57; Students 1,190.

NORRISTOWN. *Kennedy-Kenrick Catholic High School*, 250 E. Johnson Hwy., 19401. Tel: 610-275-2846; Fax: 610-277-6699.
E-mail: ghickey810@aol.com
Web site: webaddress.com/kkchs
Formerly Bishop Kenrick High School, Norristown, and Archbishop Kennedy High School, Conshohocken. Rev. Gregory J. Hickey, Pres.; Helen T. Chaykowsky, Prin.; Revs. Gerard C. Chapman, Campus Min.; Frank A. Giuffre. Priests 2; Sisters 3; Lay Teachers 26; Students 556; Administrators 5.

POTTSTOWN. *St. Pius X High School*, 844 N. Keim St., 19464. Tel: 610-326-8990. Opened 1954. Rev. Philip J. Lowe, Ed.D., Prin.; Mr. Salvatore DiNenna, Pres. Priests 3; Sisters 1; Lay Teachers 32; Students 578.

RADNOR. *Archbishop John Carroll High School*, 211 Matson Ford Rd., 19087. Tel: 610-688-7610; Fax: 610-688-8326 (Prin.); 971-0827 (Pres.).
Web site: www.jcarroll.org
Opened September 1967. Rev. Thomas P. Gillin, Dir. of School Ministry. Priests 3; Sisters 6; Lay Teachers 50; Students 1,113.

SPRINGFIELD. *Cardinal O'Hara High School*, 1701 S. Sproul Rd., 19064. Tel: 610-544-3800; Fax: 610-544-1189.
E-mail: cohs.com
(Coed) Opened September, 1963. Rev. Msgr. Joseph P. McFadden, Pres.; Revs. Joseph C. Bordonaro; John B. Flanagan; Thomas R. Urian. Priests 4; Sisters 5; Lay Teachers 91; Students 2,030.

WARMINSTER. *Archbishop Wood Catholic High School*, 655 York Rd., 18974. Tel: 215-672-5050.
E-mail: jbeisel@archwood.org
Web site: www.archwood.org
Opened September 1964. Revs. James D. Beisel, Pres.; John P. Paul, Campus Min.; James F. Endres; J. Brian Bransfield; Charles Zlock. Priests 5; Sisters 10; Brothers 1; Lay Teachers 57; Students 1,240.

WYNCOTE. *Bishop McDevitt High School*, 125 Royal Ave., 19095-1198. Tel: 215-887-5575; Fax: 215-887-1371.
E-mail: APMcDev30@nni.com
Web site: www.mcdevitths.org
Opened September 1958. Frederick J. Ciao, Ph.D., Pres.; Revs. William J. Chiriaco; James R. Jugenheimer; Albert J. Santorsola. Priests 3; Sisters 4; Lay Teachers 45; Students 827.

[E] VOCATIONAL HIGH SCHOOLS

PHILADELPHIA. *Mercy Vocational High School*, 2900 W. Hunting Park Ave., 19129-1803. Tel: 215-226-1225; Fax: 215-228-6337.
E-mail: apmervoc@nni.com
Web site: www.mercyvocational.com
Sr. Rosemary Herron, R.S.M., Prin.; Miss Joan Pilkington, Vice Prin. Sisters of Mercy 12; Lay Teachers 30; Students 381.

[F] HIGH SCHOOLS, PAROCHIAL

LANSDALE. *Lansdale Catholic High School*, 700 Lansdale Ave., 19446-2995. Tel: 215-362-6160; 242-6160 (Philadelphia); Fax: 215-362-5746. Opened 1949 as a school of St. Stanislaus Parish. Mr. Frank Giovonizzi, Prin.; Rev. Martin T. Cioppi, Pres. Priests 3; Lay Teachers 45; Students 985.

[G] HIGH SCHOOLS, PRIVATE

PHILADELPHIA. *Nazareth Academy High School*, 4001 Grant Ave., 19114-2999. Tel: 215-637-7676; Fax: 215-637-8523.
E-mail: sjlawlor@juno.com
Web site: www.nazarethacademyhs.org
Sr. M. Jeanette Lawlor, C.S.F.N., Prin. Sisters 11; Lay Teachers 55; Girls 480.

St. Joseph's Preparatory School, Office of the President, 1733 W. Girard Ave., 19130. Tel: 215-978-1950; Fax: 215-765-1710.
Web site: www.sjprep.org
Rev. David A. Sauter, S.J., Pres.; Dr. Michael J. Coury, Prin.; Mr. Daniel A. Brennan, Vice Pres. for Devel.; Mr. Charles J. Johnson, Treas.; Mrs. Rose Marie Kettinger, Registrar; Mr. John P. Petruzzelli, Dean of Students; Revs. Stephen A. Garber, S.J.; Bernard J. Boyle, S.J.; Thomas F. Clifford, S.J.; Robert W. Mattingly, S.J.; Francis E. Skechus, S.J.; Justin Whittington, S.J. Priests 7; Sisters 1; Lay Teachers 58; Students 967.

BENSALEM. *Holy Ghost Preparatory School*, 2429 Bristol Pike, 19020. Tel: 215-639-2102; Fax: 215-639-4225.
Web site: www.holyghostprep.bensalem.pa.us
Rev. James P. McCloskey, C.S.Sp., Headmaster. Tel: 215-639-2102. Holy Ghost Fathers 4; Lay Teachers 38; Boys 474.

BRYN MAWR. *Country Day School of the Sacred Heart*, 480 Bryn Mawr Ave., 19010. Tel: 610-527-3915; Fax: 610-527-0942.
E-mail: smacdonald@cdssh.com
Web site: www.cdssh.org
Sr. Matthew Anita MacDonald, S.S.J., Head of School; Rev. Thomas P. Gillin. Sisters 2; Lay Teachers 32; Total Staff 58; Students 320.

DEVON. *Devon Preparatory School*, 19333. Tel: 610-688-7337; Fax: 610-688-2409.
E-mail: sjcalasanctius@juno.com
Piarist Fathers. Revs. James P. Shea, Sch.P., Headmaster; Richard S. Wyzykiewicz, Sch.P., Chap. & Rector; Ferdinand Negrillos, Sch.P.; Louis G. Mesko, Sch.P.; Geza Pazmany, Sch.P. Priests 3; Lay Teachers 30; Students 266.

FLOURTOWN. *Mt. St. Joseph Academy*, 120 W. Wissahickon Ave., 19031. Tel: 215-233-3177; Fax: 215-233-4734.
E-mail: mdacey@msjacad.org
Web site: www.msja.org
Sr. Mary Dacey, S.S.J., Pres.; Sr. Karen Dietrich, S.S.J., Prin. Sisters of St. Joseph 15; Lay Teachers 42; Students 549.

GWYNEDD VALLEY. *Gwynedd-Mercy Academy*, 1345 Sumneytown Pike, 19437-0902. Tel: 215-646-8815; Fax: 215-646-4361.
Web site: www.gmahs.com
Sr. Kathleen Boyce, R.S.M., Prin. Sisters 14; Lay Teachers 36; Girls 392.

HOLLAND. *Villa Joseph Marie High School for Girls*, 18966. Tel: 215-357-8810; Fax: 215-357-2477.
E-mail: vjmhs@nni.com
Web site: vjmhs.org
Sr. M. Elaine, S.S.C., Prin.; Rev. John A. Cannon, Chap. Priests 1; Sisters of St. Casimir 3; Lay Teachers 21; Students 300.

MALVERN. *Malvern Preparatory School for Boys*, 418 S. Warren Ave., 19355-2707. Tel: 610-644-5454.
Web site: www.malvernprep.com
Revs. David J. Duffy, O.S.A., Pres.; Stephen M. Curry, O.S.A.; James R. Flynn, O.S.A., Asst. Head; James D. McBurney, O.S.A., Campus Min.; John R. Liggio, O.S.A., Prior, Chair of Theology. Priests 5; Lay Teachers 68; Students 590.

Villa Maria Academy High School, 370 Old Lincoln Hwy., 19355. Tel: 610-644-2551; Fax: 610-644-2866.
E-mail: info@vmahs.org
Web site: www.vmahs.org
Sr. Mary Kelly, I.H.M., Prin. Sisters, Servants of the Immaculate Heart of Mary 15; Lay Teachers 35; Total Staff 50; Girls 420.

MERION. *Merion Mercy Academy*, 19066. Tel: 610-664-6655; Fax: 610-664-6322.
E-mail: mma@merion-mercy.com
Web site: www.merion-mercy.com
Day School for Girls. Sr. Regina Ward, Prin. Sisters of Mercy 10; Lay Teachers 40; Students 431.

VILLANOVA. *Academy of Notre Dame de Namur*, 560 Sproul Rd., 19085. Tel: 610-687-0650; Fax: 610-687-1912.
E-mail: hprusak@usa.net
Web site: ndspa.org
Sr. Regina Finnegan, Pres.; Miss Jean Phalan, Prin. Sisters 10; Lay Teachers 65; Girls 490.

WYNDMOOR. *LaSalle College High School*, 8605 Cheltenham Ave., 19038. Tel: 215-233-2911; Fax: 215-233-1418.
E-mail: labs@lschs.org
Web site: www.lschs.org
Bro. Rene Sterner, F.S.C., Pres.; Mr. Fred Assaf, Prin.; Bro. Brendan Garwood, F.S.C., Religious Supr. Priests 1; Brothers of the Christian Schools 10; Lay Teachers 76; Students 990.

[H] CONSOLIDATED PARISH SCHOOLS

PHILADELPHIA. *Our Lady of Angels School*, 30th and Dickinson Streets, 19146. Tel: 215-468-7230; Fax: 215-755-2680. Sr. Bernadette Anne Keane, I.H.M., Prin. Consolidated school for St. Gabriel Parish, St. Aloysius Parish, King of Peace Parish, Philadelphia, PA.

St. Athanasius-Immaculate Conception School, 7105 Limekiln Pike, 19138. Tel: 215-424-5045; Fax: 215-927-6615.
E-mail: appthanic05@nni.com
Consolidated school for St. Anthanasius Parish and Immaculate Conception Parish. Sisters 4; Lay Teachers 11; Students 279.

St. Martin de Porres School (Germantown), 44 W. Logan St., 19144. Tel: 215-842-1266. Consolidated school for St. Francis of Assisi Parish, St. Madeleine Sophie Parish and Saint Vincent de Paul Parish. Sisters 1; Lay Teachers 9; Priests 1; Students 200.

St. Mary Interparochial School, 5th & Locusts Sts., 19106. Tel: 215-923-7522; Fax: 215-923-8502.
E-mail: smips@earthlink.net
Consolidated school for St. Stanislaus Parish, Old St. Joseph Parish, Old St. Mary Parish, St. John the Evangelist Parish, St. Augustine Parish, Holy Trinity Parish, St. Mary Magdalen dePazzi and St. Patrick. Lay Teachers 10; Students 238.

St. Matthew Elementary Campus. Tel: 610-828-2007; Fax: 610-825-8796.

St. Cosmas & Damian Primary Campus. (Grades PreK-K). Tel: 610-828-0755. Mrs. Jacqueline Kerrigan, Prin.

SS. Clement-Irenaeus School, 72nd St. & Paschall Ave., 19142-1108. Tel: 215-729-8368. Consolidated school for St. Clement Parish and St. Irenaeus Parish. Servants of the Immaculate Heart of Mary 5; Lay Teachers 13; Students 300.

AMBLER. *Ambler Catholic Elementary School*, 260 Forest Ave., 19002. Tel: 215-646-6150; Fax: 215-646-7435.
E-mail: kaleslie@amblercatholic.org
Web site: www.amblercatholic.org
Consolidated school for St. Anthony of Padua Parish and St. Joseph Parish. Sisters of St. Joseph 3; Lay Teachers 13; Students 277.

BRIDGEPORT. *Holy Trinity Catholic School*. Tel: 610-277-4133; Fax: 610-277-4725.
Web site: holytrinitycatholic.com

Holy Trinity Lower School. (Grades PreK-3), 631 E. Fourth St., Swedesburg, 19405. Tel: 610-277-4133; Fax: 610-277-4725.

Holy Trinity Upper School. (Grades 4-8), 504 Ford St., 19405. Tel: 610-279-4630; Fax: 610-279-5579. Sr. Patricia Mengel, I.H.M., Prin. Servants of the Immaculate Heart of Mary 4; Lay Teachers 12; Students (PreK-4) 125; Students (5-8) 83. Consolidated schools for St. Augustine, Bridgeport; Our Lady of Mount Carmel, Bridgeport; Sacred Heart, Swedesburg.

Holy Trinity School, 504 Ford St., 19405. Tel: 610-279-4630; Fax: 610-279-5579.
E-mail: pmnostop@juno.com
Web site: holytrinitycatholic.com
Sr. Patricia Mengel, I.H.M., Prin. Consolidated school for St. Augustine, Bridgeport; Our Lady of Mount Carmel, Bridgeport; Sacred Heart, Swedesburg. Sisters 4; Lay Teachers 14; Students 208.

BRYN MAWR. *St. Thomas-Good Counsel School*, 575 Lancaster Ave., 19010. Tel: 610-525-1407; Fax: 610-525-4701.
E-mail: stgc@stgcschool.org
Consolidated school for St. Thomas of Villanova Parish and Our Mother of Good Counsel Parish. Lay Teachers 10; Students 203.

SS. Colman-John Neumann School, 372 Highland Ln., 19010. Tel: 610-525-3266; Fax: 610-525-6103.
E-mail: maangelo@exario.net
Mrs. Mary Ann DeAngelo, Prin. Consolidated school for St. Colman Parish and St. John Neumann Parish. Sisters 1; Lay Teachers 20; Students 270.

COATESVILLE. *Coatesville Area Catholic Elementary School*, 605 E. Lincoln Hwy., 19320. Tel: 610-384-5961; Fax: 610-384-5730.
E-mail: apcaces09@aol.com
Web site: www.coatesvillecatholicsch.org
Consolidated for St. Cecilia Parish, St. Joseph Parish, Our Lady of Consolation, Parksburg, St. Stanislaus and Our Lady of Rosary, Coatesville. Servants of the Immaculate Heart of Mary 4; Lay Teachers 16; Students 561.

CONSHOHOCKEN. *Conshohocken Catholic School*.
E-mail: apconsho13@nni.com
Mrs. Jacqueline Kerrigan, Prin., St. Matthew Elementary Campus. (Grades 1-8), 205 Fayette St., 19428. Tel: 610-828-2007; Fax: 610-825-8796. SS. Cosmas & Damian Primary Campus. (Grades PreK-K), 5th Ave. & Maple St., 19428. Tel: 610-828-0755; Fax: 610-828-5191. Mrs. Michele Slattery, Coord. Consolidated school for SS. Cosmas & Damian Parish and St. Matthew Parish. Sisters 3; Lay Teachers 16; Students 258.

LINWOOD. *Holy Saviour-St. John Fisher School*, 122 E. Ridge Rd., 19061. Tel: 610-485-0363; Fax: 610-485-7809. Ms. Jo-Ann Hummel, Prin. Consolidated school for Holy Saviour Parish and St. John Fisher Parish. Lay Teachers 20; Students 360.

PHOENIXVILLE. *Holy Family School*, 221 Third Ave., 19460. Tel: 610-933-7562. Consolidated school for St. Ann Parish, Holy Trinity Parish, St. Mary of the Assumption Parish and Sacred Heart Parish. Lay Teachers 14; Students 350.

RIDLEY PARK. *St. Madeline-St. Rose School*, Tome & Rogers Sts., 19078. Tel: 610-583-3662; Fax: 610-583-3683.
E-mail: smsrcs@yahoo.com
Consolidated School for St. Madeline Parish and St. Rose of Lima Parish. Lay Teachers 20; Students 426.

SELLERSVILE. *St. Agnes-Our Lady of the Sacred Heart*, 393 N. Main St., 18960. Tel: 215-257-3571; Fax: 215-822-7942. Consolidated school for St. Agnes Parish and Our Lady of the Sacred Heart, Hilltown. Lay Teachers 23; Students 532.

WARRINGTON. *SS. Joseph-St. Robert School*, 850 Euclid Ave., 18976. Tel: 215-343-5100; Fax: 215-343-7434. Consolidated school for St. Joseph Parish and St. Robert Bellarmine Parish. Lay Teachers 18; Students 500.

[I] ELEMENTARY SCHOOLS, PRIVATE

PHILADELPHIA. *Cecilian Academy*, 100-144 W. Carpenter Ln., 19119. Tel: 215-849-3252; Fax: 215-849-7043. (K-8 and Learning Disabilities Program). Sr. Colleen Dauerbach, Prin. Convent, 6818 Chesheim Rd., 19119. Sisters of St. Joseph 11; Lay Teachers 13; Students 150.

The Gesu School, 18th & Thompson Sts., 19121. Tel: 215-763-3660; 763-9077(Development); Fax: 215-763-9844.
E-mail: 110344.1406@compuserve.com
Rev. George W. Bur, S.J., Pres.; Sr. Ellen Convey, I.H.M., Prin.; Rev. Neil Ver-Schneider, S.J.; Sr. Patricia McGrenra, I.H.M. Priests, Society of Jesus 2; Sisters, Servants of the Immaculate Heart of Mary 2; Lay Teachers 29; Students 435.

Nazareth Academy Grade School, 4701 Grant Ave., 19114. Tel: 215-637-7777; Fax: 215-637-5696.
Web site: www.nazarethacademy.net
Sr. M. Martin, C.S.F.N., Prin. Sisters of the Holy Family of Nazareth 4; Lay Teachers 12; Students 235.

Norwood-Fontbonne Academy for Boys and Girls, 8891 Germantown Ave., 19118. Tel: 215-247-3811; 242-1611; Fax: 215-247-8405; 248-9721.
E-mail: nfaprin@erols.com
Sr. Kathy McShane, S.S.J., Prin. Sisters of St. Joseph 13; Lay Teachers 34; Students 551.

BRYN MAWR. *St. Aloysius Academy*. (Grades PreK-8), 401 S. Bryn Mawr Ave., 19010. Tel: 610-527-0506; 525-1670; Fax: 610-525-5140.
E-mail: soar@staloysiusacademy.org
Sr. Carolyn M. Dimick, I.H.M., Prin. Sisters, Servants of the Immaculate Heart of Mary 11; Lay Teachers 26; Students 325.

DREXEL HILL. *School of the Holy Child Jesus*. (Grades PreK-8), 450 Penn Ave., 19026. Tel: 610-259-2712; Fax: 610-259-1862.
E-mail: shcadm@hotmail.com
Web site: www.holychildonline.com
Mrs. Anita P. Coll, Head. Lay Teachers 31; Students 251.

IMMACULATA. *Villa Maria Academy*, 19345. Tel: 610-644-4864; Fax: 610-647-6403.
E-mail: mburke@villamaria.org
Web site: www.villamaria.org
Sr. Mary A. Burke, I.H.M., Prin. Sisters, Servants of the Immaculate Heart of Mary 6; Lay Teachers 24; Girls 368.

MERION. *Waldron Mercy Academy*, 513 Montgomery Ave., 19066. Tel: 610-664-9847; Fax: 610-664-6364.
E-mail: waldronmercy.org
Web site: www.waldronmercy.org
Sr. Patricia Smith, R.S.M., Prin.; Mr. Stephen Stritch, Vice Prin. Sisters of Mercy 2; Lay Teachers 42; Students 550.

RADNOR. *Armenian Sisters Academy*, 440 Upper Gulph Rd., 19087. Tel: 610-687-4100; Fax: 610-687-2430.
E-mail: asaphila@aol.com
Web site: www.armeniansrsacademy.org
Montessori for ages 3-6. Ungraded Elementary for ages 7-14. Sr. Louisa Kassarjian, Prin. Sisters 4; Lay Teachers 22; Students 187.

ROSEMONT. *Rosemont School of the Holy Child*, 1344 Montgomery Ave., 19010. Tel: 610-525-1876; Fax: 610-525-7128.
E-mail: mbroderi@rosemont-sch.org
Web site: www.rosemont-sch.org
Sr. Mary Broderick, S.H.C.J., Prin. Sisters of the Holy Child Jesus 2; Lay Teachers 34; Students 301.

SPRING HOUSE. *Gwynedd-Mercy Academy*. (Grades K-8), Elementary Division, 816 Norristown Rd., P.O. Box 241, 19477. Tel: 215-646-4916; 646-2406 (Business Office); Fax: 215-628-8441.
E-mail: mkenney@gmaelem.org
Web site: www.gmaelem.org
Sr. Anne Crampsie, R.S.M., Prin. Sisters of Mercy 2; Lay Teachers 39; Total Staff 50; Students 450.

WYNCOTE. *Ancillae-Assumpta Academy*. (Grades PreK-8). (Coed), 2025 Church Rd., 19095. Tel: 215-885-1636; Fax: 215-885-2740.
E-mail: emccoy@erols.com
Web site: www.ancillae.org
Sr. Elizabeth McCoy, A.C.J., Dir.; Sr. Maureen Gillespie, A.C.J., Prin. Handmaids of the Sacred Heart of Jesus 5; Lay Teachers 56; Students 564.

YARDLEY. *Grey Nun Academy*, 1750 Quarry Rd., 19067. Tel: 215-968-4151; Fax: 215-860-7418.
E-mail: sdb@gnaedu.org
Web site: www.gnaedu.org
(Coed Day School). Sr. Dolores Beatty, G.N.S.H., Prin. Grey Nuns of the Sacred Heart 3; Lay Teachers 25; Students 246.

[J] SPECIAL EDUCATION

PHILADELPHIA. *Our Lady of Confidence Day School*, 19140.
E-mail: apconf01@nni.com
Mentally Handicapped and/or Developmentally Delayed. Main School and Office, 314 N. Easton Rd., Willow Grove, 19090-2506. Tel: 215-657-9311; Fax: 215-657-9312.
E-mail: apconf01@nni.com
High School Site, 6301 N. Second St., 19020-1599. Tel: 215-276-2300, Ext. 262; 285. Sr. Francis Christi, S.S.J., Prin. Sisters of St. Joseph 1; Lay Teachers 10; Students 130.

LEVITTOWN. *Queen of the Universe Day Center*, 2477 Trenton Rd., 19056. Tel: 215-945-6090; Fax: 215-945-7320. Mrs. Sharon Quay, Prin. Mentally Retarded and Developmental Delay Students. Lay Teachers 4; Students 45.

NORWOOD. *Archbishop Ryan School for Children with Hearing Impairment*, 233 Mohawk Ave., 19074. Tel: 610-586-7044; Fax: 610-586-7053.
E-mail: APRyanGab01@nni.com
Web site: www.ces/msaorg
Sr. Margaret Langer, I.H.M., Prin. Convent. Tel: 610-583-5160. Sisters of St. Joseph 4; Sisters of St. Francis 1; Lay Teachers 8; Students 46.

UPPER DARBY. *St. Lucy Day School for Children with Visual Impairments*, 130 Hampden Rd., 19082. Tel: 610-352-4550; 352-4555; Fax: 610-352-4582.
E-mail: APLucy1@nni.com
Web site: www.netslink.com/stlucy
Day school for children who are blind or visually impaired. Sr. M. Margaret Fleming, I.H.M., Prin. Sisters, Servants of the Immaculate Heart of Mary 6; Lay Teachers 4; Students 34.

WYNNEWOOD. *St. Katherine Day School*, 930 Bowman Ave., 19096. Tel: 610-667-3958; Fax: 610-667-3625.
E-mail: APKath01@nni.com
Children with Developmental Delay/Mental Retardation. James S. Kane, Prin. Lay Teachers 12; Students 122.

[K] THE CATHOLIC SOCIAL SERVICES OF THE ARCHDIOCESE OF PHILADELPHIA

PHILADELPHIA. *The Catholic Social Services of the Archdiocese of Philadelphia*, 222 N. 17th St., 19103. Tel: 215-587-3900; Fax: 215-587-2479.
E-mail: Chumsrv@adphila.org
Web site: www.archdiocese-phl.org
All addresses unless otherwise indicated. Rev. Msgr. Timothy C. Senior, M.B.A., M.S.W., M.A., Exec. Dir.; Edward T. Cahill, Chief Fin. Officer; James Amato, L.S.W., Deputy Sec.; Teresa Thompson, L.S.W., Dir. Children Svcs.; Karen K. Becker, L.S.W., Dir. Family Svcs.; Lorraine Knight, Dir. Administrative & Support Svcs.; John M. Wagner, Dir. Housing & Homeless Svcs.; Bro. Dennis Malloy, F.S.C., Dir. Juvenile Justice Svcs., St. Gabriel's System, 117 S. 17th St., 19103. Tel: 215-665-8777; Fax: 215-665-8821. Mark E. Fitzgerald, Dir. Mental Retardation Svcs., Administrative Office, 1797 S. Sproul Rd., Springfield, 19064. Tel: 610-543-5410; Fax: 610-543-5397. Suzanne O'Grady, M.S.S., Admin. Child Care Dept.; Velma J. Clark, M.A., Dir., Office for Human Relations.
Office for Human Relations. Tel: 215-587-5655; Fax: 215-587-5626.
Northeast Philadelphia, 7340 Jackson St., 19136. Tel: 215-624-5920; Fax: 215-624-9197. Amy Stoner, L.S.W., Admin.
North Philadelphia, Casa del Carmen, 4400 N. Reese St., 19140. Tel: 215-329-5660; Fax: 215-329-6722. W. Giovanni Morante, M.A., Admin.
Bucks County:
Levittown, 100 Levittown Pkwy., Levittown, 19054. Tel: 215-945-2550; Fax: 215-945-3595. Marguerite Powers, L.S.W., Asst. Dir.
Middle Bucks County:
Sellersville, 427 N. Main St., Sellersville, 18960. Tel: 215-453-7098; Fax: 215-453-6572. Marguerite Powers, L.S.W., Asst. Dir.
Warminster, 607 W. Street Rd., Warminster, 18974. Tel: 215-957-6699; Fax: 215-957-9189. Marguerite Powers, L.S.W., Admin.
Chester County:
West Grove, 105 Prospect Ave., West Grove, 19390. Tel: 610-869-6500; Fax: 610-869-6258. William Kefer, L.S.W., Admin.
Downingtown, 141 E. Lancaster Ave., Downingtown, 19335. Tel: 610-269-4060; Fax: 610-269-4065. William Kefer, L.S.W., Admin.
Delaware County:
Chester City, 130 E. 7th St., Chester, 19013. Tel: 610-876-9183; Fax: 610-876-9243. James McMaster, M.B.A., Admin.
Springfield, 240 N. Bishop Ave., Springfield, 19064. Tel: 610-626-6550; Fax: 610-626-2069. James McMaster, M.B.A., Admin.
Montgomery County:
Norristown, 353 E. Johnson Hwy., Norristown, 19401. Tel: 215-279-7372; Fax: 610-270-0626. Sr. Patricia Kelly, M.S.B.T., L.S.W., Admin.
Holy Family Center, 227 N. 18th St., 19103. Tel: 215-587-3900; Fax: 215-854-7100.
Volunteer & Community Relations Services. Tel: 215-854-7058; Fax: 215-854-7100. William Tangradi, M.S.W., Mgr. Tel: 215-854-7058.
Immigration Services, 19103. Tel: 215-854-7010; Fax: 215-854-7100. Phyllis Forman, Esq., Admin.
Family Services. Tel: 215-854-7090; Fax: 215-854-7100. Martin R. Frick, L.S.W., M.P.A., Admin. Tel: 215-854-7067; Fax: 215-854-7100.
Adoption Services. Tel: 215-854-7050; Fax: 215-854-7100. Mary Lark Merman, L.S.W., Admin.
Senior Adult Services. Tel: 215-854-7070; Fax: 215-854-7100. George Salloom, L.S.W., Admin.
Housing/Homeless Services. Tel: 215-854-7080; Fax: 215-854-7100. Deborah Wagner, Admin. Total Assisted 93,530; Total Staff 1,735.

[L] INSTITUTIONS FOR DEPENDENT CHILDREN

PHILADELPHIA. *St. Joseph Catholic Home for Children*, 5238 N. Broad St., 19141. Tel: 215-324-2610; Fax: 215-457-8240.
E-mail: srlouise@adphila.org
For a complete listing, refer to the Special Care Facilities section.
St. Vincent's Orphanage Tacony, 7201 Milnor St., 19135. Tel: 215-624-5600
For a complete listing, refer to the Special Care Facilities section.

AMBLER. *St. Mary's Villa for Children*, 701 Bethlehem Pike, P.O. Box 388, 19002-0388. Tel: 215-643-7676; Fax: 215-542-9219
For a complete listing, refer to the Special Care Facilities section.

BENSALEM. *St. Francis Homes for Boys*, 857 Langstroth Ln., 19020-5735. Tel: 215-638-9310
For a complete listing, refer to the Special Care Facilities section.
St. Joseph's House for Boys, 857 Langstroth Ln., 19020-5735. Tel: 215-244-8690; Fax: 215-244-8694
For a complete listing, refer to the Special Care Facilities section.

[M] RESIDENTIAL SCHOOLS FOR MENTALLY HANDICAPPED CHILDREN AND ADULTS

SPRINGFIELD. *Cardinal Krol Center*, 1799 S. Sproul Rd., 19064. Tel: 610-543-3380; Fax: 610-544-1207.
Web site: www.cssmrserv.org
Rev. Dennis M. Weber, S.C., Admin. A residential facility for 131 mentally retarded male adults which provides an environment, both day and residential, that contributes to the individuals own growth and development by fulfilling their potential in the physical, mental, emotional, social, psychological, and spiritual areas of their lives. Priests 3; Residential Capacity 131; Day Program 41; Total Assisted 171; Total Staff 150.
Divine Providence Village, 686 Old Marple Rd., 19064. Tel: 610-328-7730; Fax: 610-544-1710. Sr. Gertrude LaBarbera, D.S.M.P., Admin.; Rev. Msgr. Timothy C. Senior, M.B.A., M.S.W., M.A., Chap. Care & specialized training for developmentally disabled females. Sisters 7; Capacity 108.
Don Guanella School for Retarded Boys, 1797 S. Sproul Rd., 19064-1195. Tel: 610-543-1418. Rev. Romano DiRuscio, S.C., M.A., Admin. Provides specialized care and treatment program for mentally retarded boys ages 6-21. Capacity: Residents 40; Day Students 35.

[N] RESIDENTIAL HOMES FOR PHYSICALLY HANDICAPPED CHILDREN

ROSEMONT. *St. Edmond's Home for Children*, 320 S. Roberts Rd., 19010. Tel: 610-525-8800; Fax: 610-525-2693
For a complete listing, refer to the Special Care Facilities section.

[O] PROTECTIVE INSTITUTIONS

PHILADELPHIA. *St. Gabriel's System*, Administrative Offices, 117 S. 17th St., Ste. 1701, 19103. Tel: 215-665-8777; Fax: 215-665-8821
For a complete listing, refer to the Special Care Facilities section.

AUDUBON. *St. Gabriel's Hall*, Box 7280, 19407-7280. Tel: 215-247-2776 (Philadelphia); 610-666-7970 (Audubon)
For a complete listing, refer to the Special Care Facilities section.

[P] DAY TREATMENT CENTERS

PHILADELPHIA. *De La Salle-In-Towne Day Treatment Center*, 25 S. Van Pelt St., 19103. Tel: 215-567-5500; Fax: 215-567-6922.
E-mail: delvoc@nni.com
Bro. Robert J. Kinzler, F.S.C., M.S.W., Exec. Dir.; Charles E. Gaus, Dir. A community based day treatment program for court-committed delinquent boys, ages 14-17. Capacity 110; Total Staff 35; Total Assisted 260.

BENSALEM. *De La Salle Vocational Day Treatment Center*, Box 344, 19020. Tel: 215-464-0344. Bros. Robert Kinzler, F.S.C., M.S.W., Exec. Dir.; Dennis Malloy, F.S.C., A.C.S.W., M.A., Dir. A community based day treatment program for court-committed delinquent boys, ages 15-18. Capacity 125; Total Staff 40.

[Q] RESIDENCES FOR UNMARRIED MOTHERS

HAVERTOWN. *St. Vincent's Maternity Residence*, 104 E. Township Line Rd., 19083. Tel: 610-446-0105; Fax: 610-446-0105. Sr. Louise Kane, S.S.J., L.S.W., Admin. Capacity 11. Information and Referrals. Tel: 215-324-2610; Fax: 215-457-8240. Total Assisted 100; Total Staff 12.

[R] SENIOR CITIZEN CENTERS

PHILADELPHIA. *Norris Square Senior Citizens Center*, 2121 N. Howard St., 19133. Tel: 215-423-7241; Fax: 215-634-7751.
Web site: cconstable/po/web/aoc
Carmen Constable, Coord. Total Assisted 100; Total Staff 9.
St. Anne's Center, 2607 E. Cumberland St., 19125. Tel: 215-423-2772; Fax: 215-423-2423. Barbara Jo Hartzell, Center Coord. Total Staff 6; Total Assisted 11,288.
St. Bernard's Senior Adult Program, 7340 Jackson St., 19136. Tel: 215-624-5920; Fax: 215-624-9197. Susan A. Lawson-Jock, Prog. Dir.
St. Rita's Senior Citizen Center, 1150-1154 S. Broad St., 19146. Tel: 215-735-4300; Fax: 215-735-0935. Daryl Kezell, L.S.W., Coord. Total Staff 11; Total Assisted 400.
Star Harbor Senior Center, 4700 Springfield Ave., 19143. Tel: 215-726-7468; Fax: 215-726-7496. Elizabeth Miller, Coord.

[S] OUTREACH CENTERS

PHILADELPHIA. *Casa del Carmen*, 4400 N. Reese St., 19140. Tel: 215-329-5660. W. Giovanni Morante, M.A. Offers emergency crisis social services to the Spanish speaking community in Philadelphia and surrounding areas.
Catholic Center for the Deaf and Hard of Hearing, St. Boniface Rectory, 174 W. Diamond St., 19122. Tel: 215-423-9547. Rev. Anthony T. Russo, C.SS.R., Dir. Mass and Homily in Sign Language: Resurrection Church, Castor Ave. & Vista St., 19152. St. Mary's Manor, 701 Lansdale Ave., Lansdale, 19446. Tel: 215-368-0900. St. Stanislaus Church, Main St. and Lansdale Ave., Lansdale, 19446. Tel: 215-855-3133. St. Charles Borromeo Church, Burmont Rd and Dennison Ave., Drexel Hill, 19026. Tel: 215-623-3800. Rev. Paul V. Dougherty, M.A.
Mass with Sign Language Interpreter: St. Francis of Assisi Church, Marshall and Buttonwood Sts., Norristown, 19401. Tel: 215-272-0402. S.S. Peter and Paul, Boot Rd. & Rte. 202, West Chester, 19380. Tel: 610-692-2216. St. Francis of Assisi, Marshall St. & Buttonwood St., Norristown, 19401. Tel: 610-272-0402. St. Joseph's Church, Bartram and Woodlawn Ave., Collingdale, 19023. Tel: 610-583-4530. St. Thomas Aquinas Church, Bristol Pike and Walnut Ave., Croydon, 19021.
Drueding Center/Project Rainbow, 413 W. Master St., 19122. Tel: 215-769-1830; 769-1931; Fax: 215-787-0999.
Web site: www.holyredeemer.com
Sr. Ellen M. Marvel, C.S.R., Vice Pres.
Subsidiary of Holy Redeemer Health System. Sponsor: Sisters of the Holy Redeemer, C.S.R. Marketing/Public Affairs Department, c/o 1602 Huntingdon Pike, Meadowbrook, 19046. Tel: 215-938-3226; Fax: 215-938-3232. Provides transitional housing and support services for homeless women with children; daycare is provided for the children.
Mercy Hospice, 334 S. 13th St., 19107. Tel: 215-545-5153. Suzanne O'Grady, Dir. Provides temporary and extended shelter care, hot meals, clothing, casework and referral services to homeless and transient women and women with children. Total Staff 33; Total Assisted 2,700.
St. John's Hospice for Men, 1221 Race St., 19107. Tel: 215-563-7763; Fax: 215-563-0108. Staffed by Catholic Social Services Archdiocese of Philadelphia. Rev. Kevin C. Lawrence, Program Dir. Total Assisted 50,000; Total Staff 32.

Women of Hope, 1210 Lombard St., 19147. Tel: 215-732-1341; Fax: 215-592-0650. Una Edwards, Dir. Residential Facility for chronically mentally ill homeless women. Capacity 24.

Women of Hope, 251 N. Lawrence St., 19106. Tel: 215-592-9116. Sr. Maureen Crissy, R.S.M., Prog. Dir. Residential facility for chronically mentally ill homeless women. Capacity 22; Total Staff 21; Total Assisted 22.

CHESTER. *Bernardine Center*, 2625 Ninth St., 19013. Tel: 215-497-3225; Fax: 610-497-3659.
E-mail: officemanager@bee.net
Eleanor C. Missimer, Dir. Svcs. Hospitality Room, Emergency Food Cupboard, Supercupboard Program, After-School Tutoring, Computer Use Skill Building, Advocacy, Social Justice and Spirituality Education. Sisters 3.

[T] DAY CARE CENTERS

PHILADELPHIA. *Bambino Gesu Child Development Center*, 5210 N. Broad St., 19141. Tel: 215-457-4330; Fax: 215-457-4216. Sr. Mary Julia Apolonio, O.S.P., Admin. Total Staff 15.

St. Monica Day Care Center, 1441 Porter St., 19145. Tel: 215-334-6001; Fax: 215-467-4599. Sister, Servants of the Immaculate Heart of Mary. Sr. Colleen Dougherty, I.H.M., Admin. Total Staff 12; Total Assisted 120.

St. Vincent's Day Care Center, 7201 Milnor St., 19135. Tel: 215-624-5600; Fax: 215-624-8355. Rev. Msgr. William A. Koenig, Pres., Bd. of Mgrs.; Agnes Healey, Dir. Day Care.

[U] GENERAL HOSPITALS

PHILADELPHIA. *Mercy Hospital of Philadelphia*, 501 S. 54th St., 19143. Tel: 215-748-9000
For a complete listing, refer to the Hospitals section.

Nazareth Hospital, 2601 Holme Ave., 19152. Tel: 215-335-6000; Fax: 215-335-6598
For a complete listing, refer to the Hospitals section.

St. Agnes Medical Center, 1900 S. Broad St., 19145. Tel: 215-339-4100
For a complete listing, refer to the Hospitals section.

DARBY. *Mercy Catholic Medical Center*, 19023
For a complete listing, refer to the Hospitals section.

HAVERTOWN. *Mercy Community Hospital*, 2000 Old W. Chester Pike, 19083. Tel: 610-853-7000; Fax: 610-449-0415
For a complete listing, refer to the Hospitals section.

HUNTINGDON VALLEY. *Holy Redeemer Health Care Corporation and Foundation*, 521 Moredon Rd., 19006. Tel: 215-914-4000; Fax: 215-914-4020.
Web site: www.holyredeemer.com
For a complete listing, refer to the Hospitals section.

HRH Management Corporation, 667 Welsh Rd., 19006. Tel: 215-938-4650; Fax: 215-938-4671.
Web site: www.holyredeemer.com
For a complete listing, refer to the Hospitals section.

LANGHORNE. *St. Mary Medical Center* Langhorne-Newton Rd., 19047. Tel: 215-750-2000.
For a complete listing, refer to the Hospitals section.

MEADOWBROOK. *Holy Redeemer Hospital and Medical Center*, 1648 Huntingdon Pike, 19046. Tel: 215-947-3000.
Web site: www.holyredeemer.com
For a complete listing, refer to the Hospitals section.

[V] SPECIAL HOSPITALS AND SANATORIA

PHILADELPHIA. *Mount Nazareth*, 2755 Holme Ave., 19152. Tel: 215-338-8992; Fax: 215-338-8752
For a complete listing, refer to the Special Care Facilities section.

ASTON. *Assisi House*, 600 Red Hill Rd., 19014. Tel: 215-459-8990; Fax: 610-558-5344.
E-mail: jmmcdevi@osfphila.org
For a complete listing, refer to the Special Care Facilities section.

DARBY. *Villa Saint Joseph*, 1436 Lansdowne Ave., 19023-1298. Tel: 610-586-8535; Fax: 610-586-2810
For a complete listing, refer to the Special Care Facilities section.

DOWNINGTOWN. *St. John Vianney Center*, 151 Woodbine Rd., 19335. Tel: 610-269-2600; Fax: 610-873-8028.
Web site: sjvcenter.org
For a complete listing, refer to the Special Care Facilities section.

FLOURTOWN. *St. Joseph Villa*, 110 W. Wissahickon Ave., 19031-1898. Tel: 215-836-4179; Fax: 215-248-7802.
E-mail: rudegeairm@stjosephvilla.org
For a complete listing, refer to the Special Care Facilities section.

IMMACULATA. *Camilla Hall Nursing Home*, P.O. Box 100, 19345-0100. Tel: 610-644-1152; Fax: 610-695-0691
For a complete listing, refer to the Special Care Facilities section.

MERION STATION. *McAuley Convent*, 517 Montgomery Ave., 19066. Tel: 610-667-2775
For a complete listing, refer to the Special Care Facilities section.

VENTNOR. *Villa St. Joseph by the Sea*, 114 S. Princeton Ave., 08406. Tel: 609-822-7184
For a complete listing, refer to the Special Care Facilities section.

WARMINSTER. *Regina Coeli Residence for Priests*, 685 York Rd., 18974. Tel: 215-441-4642
For a complete listing, refer to the Special Care Facilities section.

[W] AFFILIATED SERVICES

PHILADELPHIA.

Holy Redeemer Home Health & Hospice Services. Holy Redeemer Support Services, 12265 Townsend Rd., Ste. 400, 19154. Tel: 215-671-9200; Fax: 215-671-1950.
Web site: www.holyredeemer.com
Subsidiary of Holy Redeemer Health System, Inc. Sponsor: Sisters of the Holy Redeemer. Denise Collins, COO, Marketing/Public Affairs Department, c/o 1602 Huntingdon Pike, Meadowbrook, 19046. Tel: 215-938-3226; Fax: 215-938-3232. Medicare certified home health agency serving patients in their own homes; Medicare certified hospice program serving terminally ill patients and their families.

Order of Friars Minor - Holy Name Province. Tel: 215-423-2859; Fax: 215-423-3875.

St. Francis Inn, 2441 Kensington Ave., 19125. Tel: 215-423-5845; Fax: 215-423-2289. Rev. Michael A. Duffy, O.F.M., Contact Person. Priests 3; Brothers 3. A hot meal and shelter service for the poor.

Thea Bowman's Women's Center, 2858 Kensington Ave., 19134. Sr. Xavier Kozubal, C.S.F.N., Contact Person. Women's day activity center.

St. Benedict's Thrift Store, 437 W. Girard Ave., 19122. Tel: 215-235-1848.

St. Benedict Thrift Shop, 437 W. Girard Ave., 19122. Tel: 215-235-1848. Karen Pushaw, Contact Person. A clothing and furniture thrift store operated by Franciscans.

LANGHORNE. *St. Mary's Child Development Center*, c/o St. Mary's Hospital, Langhorne-Newton Rd., 19047. Tel: 215-750-5720; Fax: 215-891-6955. Elaine Karmilowicz.

PHOENIXVILLE. *St. Mary's Franciscan Shelter*, 209 Emmett St., 19460. Tel: 610-933-3097; Fax: 610-917-9845. Sr. Emma Mary Steckel, O.S.F., Staff; Sr. Mary Teresa Coll, O.S.F., Housekeeping; Sr. Christine Kranichfeld, Dir.; Rose Dougherty, Case Mgr. Total Staff 4; Families Assisted 26.

[X] NURSING AND CONVALESCENT HOMES

PHILADELPHIA. *Sacred Heart Free Home for Incurable Cancer*, 1315 W. Hunting Park Ave., 19140. Tel: 215-329-3222; Fax: 215-329-4197
For a complete listing, refer to the Special Care Facilities section.

St. Ignatius Nursing Home, 4401 Haverford Ave., 19104. Tel: 215-349-8800; Fax: 215-222-3078
For a complete listing, refer to the Special Care Facilities section.

St. John Neumann Nursing Home, 10400 Roosevelt Blvd., 19116. Tel: 215-698-5600; Fax: 215-698-5755.
E-mail: adminsec.sjnh@erols.com
For a complete listing, refer to the Special Care Facilities section.

DARBY. *St. Francis Country House*, 1412 Lansdowne Ave., 19023-1218. Tel: 610-461-6510; Fax: 610-461-3558
For a complete listing, refer to the Special Care Facilities section.

DOWNINGTOWN. *St. Martha Manor*, 470 Manor Ave., 19335. Tel: 610-873-8490; Fax: 610-873-5927
For a complete listing, refer to the Special Care Facilities section.

FLOURTOWN. *Sisters of St. Joseph of Philadelphia, St. Joseph Villa Staff Visitation Community*, 110 W. Wissahickon Ave., 19031-1898. Tel: 215-836-4179; Fax: 215-248-7802
For a complete listing, refer to the Special Care Facilities section.

[Y] BOARDING HOMES FOR THE AGED

PHILADELPHIA. *Holy Family Home*, 5300 Chester Ave., 19143-4993. Tel: 215-729-5153
For a complete listing, refer to the Special Care Facilities section.

Immaculate Mary Home, 2990 Holme Ave., 19136-1829. Tel: 215-335-2100; Fax: 215-331-1016
For a complete listing, refer to the Special Care Facilities section.

Sacred Heart Manor, 6445 Germantown Ave., 19119. Tel: 215-438-5268; Fax: 215-951-0798.
E-mail: michaelshm@aol.com
For a complete listing, refer to the Special Care Facilities section.

St. Joseph Housing Corporation. Tel: 215-248-7200; Fax: 215-248-7277.
E-mail: msvc19118@aol.com
Web site: www.ssjphila.org
For a complete listing, refer to the Special Care Facilities section.

DARBY. *Little Flower Manor*, 1201 Springfield Rd., 19023. Tel: 610-534-6000; Fax: 610-534-6039
For a complete listing, refer to the Special Care Facilities section.

Villa St. Teresa, 1215 Springfield Rd., 19023. Tel: 610-583-0700; Fax: 610-583-5011
For a complete listing, refer to the Special Care Facilities section.

ELVERSON. *St. Mary of Providence Center*, 227 Isabella Rd., 19520. Tel: 610-942-4166; Fax: 610-942-4268
For a complete listing, refer to the Special Care Facilities section.

FLOURTOWN. *Bethlehem Retirement Village*, 100 W. Wissahickon Ave., 19031. Tel: 215-233-0998; Fax: 215-233-9052.
E-mail: JoanGrelis@aol.com
For a complete listing, refer to the Special Care Facilities section.

HOLLAND. *St. Joseph Home for the Aged*, 1182 Holland Rd., 18966. Tel: 215-357-5511; Fax: 215-357-1701
For a complete listing, refer to the Special Care Facilities section.

HUNTINGDON VALLEY. *Redeemer Village - Redeemer Village II*, 1551 Huntingdon Pike, 19006. Tel: 215-947-8168.
Web site: www.holyredeemer.com
For a complete listing, refer to the Special Care Facilities section.

LANSDALE. *St. Mary Manor*, 701 Lansdale Ave., 19446. Tel: 215-368-0900; Fax: 215-362-2891
For a complete listing, refer to the Special Care Facilities section.

YARDLEY. *D'Youville Manor*, 1750 Quarry Rd., 19067. Tel: 215-579-1750; Fax: 215-579-3054
For a complete listing, refer to the Special Care Facilities section.

[Z] RESIDENCES FOR WOMEN

PHILADELPHIA. *Lucy Eaton Smith, The*, 1929 Sansom St., 19103. Tel: 215-564-0561; Fax: 215-567-4529. Dominican Sisters of the Congregation of St. Catherine de Ricci. Total Staff 7; Residents 150.

Saint Katharine Drexel Residence, 7919 Forrest Ave., 19150. Tel: 215-549-5765; Fax: 215-549-2375. Carolyn Harrington, Dir.

St. Mary's Convent: Residence for Women, 5th and Locust Sts., 19106. Tel: 215-922-4228; Fax: 215-922-5131. Religious Sisters of Mercy. Sr. Catherine Rawley, R.S.M., Admin. Residents 33; Total Staff 6.

[AA] MONASTERIES AND RESIDENCES OF PRIESTS AND BROTHERS

PHILADELPHIA. *Augustinian Community (O.S.A.)*, 910 Watkins St., 19148. Tel: 215-463-1326; Fax: 215-463-0888. Rev. Nicholas Martorano, O.S.A., Prior.

Brothers of Charity (F.C.), 6522 Belmar St., 19142. Tel: 215-729-4417. Bro. William Riley, F.C.

Brothers of the Christian Schools, St. Mary's Hall, 7018 Boyer St., 19119-1801. Tel: 215-248-2434; Fax: 215-248-4327. Bro. Edward Davis, F.S.C., Dir. Total in Residence 5.

Congregation of the Mission, St. Vincent's Seminary, 500 E. Chelten Ave., 19144-1203. Tel: 215-848-1985; Fax: 215-844-2085.
E-mail: cmphila88@aol.com
Central House of the Congregation of the Mission (Vincentian Community), Eastern Province. Novitiate, Central Shrine of the Miraculous Medal in the United States, The Central Association of the Miraculous Medal and St. Catherine's Infirmary, The Brother Bertrand Ducournau Archives of the Eastern Province of the Congregation of the Mission.
Provincial Administration: Very Rev. Thomas F. McKenna, C.M., Prov.; Revs. Charles P. Strollo, C.M., Asst. Prov.; John W. Gouldrick, C.M., Prov. Treas.
House Administration: Revs. William W. Sheldon, C.M., Supr.; William J. Bamber, C.M., Asst. Supr.; Gerald E. Deitzer, C.M., Treas. In res. Revs. William J. Bamber, C.M.; Robert J. Brandenberger, C.M.; Joseph L. Boegel, C.M.; George E. Browne, C.M.; Stephen F. Cantwell, C.M.; John W. Carven, C.M., Prov. Archivist; John J. Cusack, C.M.; Gerald E. Deitzer, C.M.; Walter F. Dirig, C.M.; Donald L. Doyle, C.M.; John A. Doyle, C.M.; Daniel E. Donovan, C.M.; Thomas M. Finley, C.M.; William P. Finn; Frederick J. Gaulin, C.M.; Aloysius P. Grass, C.M.; John J. Hodnett, C.M.; John V. Kennedy, C.M.; Thomas R. Kennedy, C.M.; John F. King, C.M.; Daniel J. Kramer, C.M.; Edward C. Mannion, C.M.; William E. McKeon, C.M.; Paul M. Murphy, C.M.; Charles J. O'Connor, C.M.; Bartholomew J. O'Malley, C.M.; John S. Pearce, C.M.; William W.

Sheldon, C.M.; Joseph J. Symes, C.M.; Joseph R. Wright, C.M.

St. Catherine Infirmary. Tel: 215-848-1985, Ext. 142; Fax: 215-848-6078. Revs. Patrick J. Fleming, C.M.; Joseph P. McCaffrey, C.M.; Terence J. Mooney, C.M.; Vincent J. Nugent, C.M.; Daniel J. Renaldo, C.M.; Vincent E. Trunk, C.M.
Vincentian Fathers of the Eastern Province of the Congregation of the Mission serving on special assignments other than the Motherhouse:
Ethiopia: Rev. Francis X. Maguire, C.M.
Rome, Italy: Very Rev. Robert P. Maloney, C.M.; Rev. Elmer Bauer, III, C.M.
District of Columbia: Rev. David M. O'Connell, C.M.
Florida: Revs. Lester T. DeMott, C.M.; Robert P. Galchus, C.M.; Edward F. McQuillan, C.M.; Jose Sanchez, C.M.
Illinois: Rev. Patrick S. Flanagan, C.M.
Michigan: Revs. Richard J. Kehoe, C.M.; Michael M. Shea, C.M.
New York: Rev. William J. Gormley, C.M.
South Carolina: Rev. John J. Lawlor, C.M.
Texas: Rev. Carl L. Pieber, C.M. Total in Residence 36.

Father Judge Faculty House, 3301 Solly Ave., 19136. Tel: 215-624-1604; Fax: 215-332-3478. Revs. Joseph D. Bowler, O.S.F.S.; Joseph G. Campellone, O.S.F.S.; John J. Dennis, O.S.F.S.; Gerald M. Dunne, O.S.F.S.; Thomas P. Gallagher, O.S.F.S.; Eugene L. Kelly, O.S.F.S.; Dennis W. Killion, O.S.F.S.; Gerard J. Mahoney, O.S.F.S.; Eugene J. McBride, O.S.F.S.; David M. Merchant, O.S.F.S.; Robert G. Mulligan, O.S.F.S.; Edward L. Rauch, O.S.F.S.; William O. Seelaus, O.S.F.S.; Bro. Thomas Brophy, O.S.F.S. Total Staff 7; Total in Residence 13.

Gesu School Jesuit Community and Outreach Center(S.J.), 1700 W. Thompson St., 19121. Tel: 215-763-3660; Fax: 215-763-9844.
E-mail: 110344.1406@compuserve.com
Rev. George W. Bur, S.J., Contact Person. Total Assisted 500; Total Staff 2.

Holy Ghost Fathers, 8101 Cresco Ave., 19136. Tel: 215-331-1039. Rev. Francis R. Duffy, C.S.Sp., Ph.D. Total in Residence 1.

Holy Spirit Missonary Cenacle, 1301 Oak Ln., 19126. Tel: 215-924-2257; Fax: 215-224-6808. Missionary Servants of the Most Holy Trinity. Bro. Paul Michalenko, S.T.

Inner City House, 1904 N. 22nd St., 19121. Tel: 215-765-1904. Rev. David I. Hagan, O.S.F.S., Dir. Total in Residence 1; Total Assisted 700.

Jesuit Community at St. Joseph's University, 5600 City Ave., 19131. Tel: 610-660-1400; Fax: 610-664-6640.
E-mail: jesuits@sju.edu
Web site: www.sju.edu/JESUIT_COMMUNITY
Loyola Center: Revs. Joseph J. Godfrey, S.J., Rector; Harry F. Geib, S.J., Dir. Infirmary; Nicholas J. Rashford, S.J., Pres.; H. Cornell Bradley, S.J., Asst. to the Rector; Richard J. Comboy, S.J., Father Min.; Joseph A. Arroyo, S.J. (Spain); Michael L. Barber, S.J.; John E. Bennett, S.J.; Bruce M. Bidinger, S.J.; Edward C. Bradley, S.J.; Francis F. Burch, S.J.; Peter A. Clark, S.J.; Donald G. Clifford, S.J.; Richard J. Colgan, S.J.; Jerome B. Coll, S.J.; John M. Comey, S.J.; William M. Davish, S.J.; Thomas J. Doyle, S.J.; Gerald F. Finnegan, S.J.; Stephen A. Garber, S.J.; Vincent J. Genovesi, S.J.; Paul J. Gilvary, S.J.; James J. Gormley, S.J.; Howard J. Heim, S.J.; Frederick A. Homann, S.J.; Albert H. Jenemann, S.J.; Francis X. Knott, S.J.; Frederick C. Koehler, S.J.; Joseph L. Lombardi, S.J.; John J. Mawhinney, S.J.; Bernard J. McConnell; John W. McDaniel, S.J.; John P. McGinty, S.J.; Dennis E. McNally, S.J.; James W. Moore, S.J.; Patrick F. Murray, S.J.; Anthony P. Roberts, S.J.; William A. Ryan, S.J.; Patrick R. Shaules, S.J.; Francis E. Skechus, S.J.; Herbert F. Smith, S.J.; Robert A. Thoman; Edward J. Tinney, S.J.; Martin R. Tripole, S.J.; Thomas FX Wheeler, S.J.; Bros. Robert J. Fitzgerald, S.J.; Bartholomew Sheehan, S.J. Priests 45; Brothers 2.

St. Alphonsus House, 5800 Overbrook Ave., 19131. Tel: 215-477-9220; Fax: 215-477-1519. Revs. David E. Barry, S.J.; Anthony J. Berret, S.J.; Joseph J. Feeney, S.J.; James J. Neville, S.J.; Bro. John J. McLane, S.J. Priests 4; Brothers 1.

Residing Elsewhere. Rev. Edward C. Bradley, S.J., Counselor for Students and Faculty, Thomas Jefferson Univ., Orlowitz Hall, 1000 Walnut St., Apt. 1513, 19107. Tel: 215-928-1614. Rev. Patrick R. Shaules, S.J., Dir. Operation HELP, Inc., P.O. Box 134, Harly, DE, 19953. Tel: 302-492-8985; Fax: 302-492-8360. Rev. Thomas Wheeler, S.J., Infirmary Chap., McAuley Convent, 517 Montgomery Ave., Merion Station, 19066-1296. Tel: 610-660-7841; Fax: 610-667-9680.

Jesuit Community, Arrupe House, 1226 N. 18th St., 19121. Tel: 215-765-1875; Fax: 215-763-9844.
E-mail: gburl@juno.com
Residence of Jesuit Fathers and Brother. Revs. George W. Bur, S.J., Supr.; Thomas F. Clifford, S.J.; Bernard J. Boyle, S.J.; Robert W. Mattingly, S.J.; Renato T. Oliveros, S.J.; Bro. Walter F. Quistgaard, S.J.; Revs. David A. Sauter, S.J.; Neil L. Ver'Schneider, S.J.; Justin Whittington, S.J.

Maryknoll House, 6367 Overbrook Ave., 19151. Tel: 215-477-5892.
E-mail: mklphil@igc.apc.org
Web site: http://www.maryknoll.org
Maryknoll Fathers and Brothers (Catholic Foreign Mission Society of America, Inc.). Rev. Francis Higdon, M.M.

Monastery of Our Lady of Mercy, 6398 Drexel Rd., 19151-2596. Tel: 215-879-0594; Fax: 215-877-7625.
Web site: www.orderofmercy.org
Order of the B.V.M. of Mercy (Mercedarian Friars). Post Novitiate formation house for the Order. Revs. Wayne C. Genereux, O.de.M., Local Supr.; James W. Mayer, O.de.M., Master of Students, Philosophy & Theology. Total in Residence 9; Total Staff 2.

Oblates of St. Francis De Sales, Northeast Catholic High School Faculty House, 1840 E. Torresdale Ave., 19124-4418. Tel: 215-535-9080; Fax: 215-535-9042. Oblates of St. Francis De Sales. Very Rev. W. E. Davis, O.S.F.S., Supr.; Revs. Robert D. Ashenbrenner, O.S.F.S.; Leon V. Bonikowski, O.S.F.S.; John V. DiFilippo, O.S.F.S.; Joseph J. Griffin, O.S.F.S.; William T. McCandless, O.S.F.S.; Francis J. Pileggi, O.S.F.S.; William G. Scholl, O.S.F.S.; Vincent E. Smith, O.S.F.S.; John J. Sullivan, O.S.F.S.; Cornelius F. Kilty, O.S.F.S.; Nicholas R. Waseline, O.S.F.S.; Bros. Harry G. Schneider, O.S.F.S.; James F. Williams, O.S.F.S.; Rev. Mark J. Wrightson, O.S.F.S. Total in Residence 15.

Order of Friars Minor of the Province of the Most Holy Name aka Holy Name Province, The Franciscans, 1802 E. Hagert St., 19125. Tel: 215-423-2859. Revs. Michael A. Duffy, O.F.M.; Francis Pompei, O.F.M.; Paul Lostritto; Bros. Xavier de la Huerta, O.F.M.; Thomas Ennis, O.F.M.; John Gill.

The Philadelphia Congregation of The Oratory of St. Philip Neri, 2321 Green St., 19130-3196. Tel: 215-765-4568; Fax: 215-765-4049. Very Rev. George G. Thiers, C.O., Provost; Revs. Paul C. Convery, C.O., Vicar; Alberto Royo-Mejia, C.O., J.C.D.; Aaron J. Pfaff; Bros. Brian Gaffney, C.O.; Mario Crestani.

St. Michael's Passionist Residence, 6300 N. Seventh St., 19126. Tel: 215-549-1761; Fax: 215-549-2141.
E-mail: crcp@erols.com
Web site: passionists.org
Revs. Christopher Cleary, C.P., Dir.; Columkille Regan, C.P.; Lucian Clark, C.P. Total Staff 2; Total in Residence 3.

St. Norbert Priory, 1815 S. 27th St., 19145. Tel: 215-389-5575.
E-mail: snpriory@netaxs.com
Canons Regular of Premontre Faculty residence for Norbertine Fathers who teach at St. John Neumann High School. Revs. Hubert N. Beaudoin, O.Praem.; Richard J. Antonucci, O.Praem., Supr.; Michael J. Lee, O.Praem.; John M. Cagney, O.Praem.; James C. Rodia, O.Praem.; John C. Zagarella, O.Praem.; Bros. William Kelly, O.Praem.; John B. Ginder, O.Praem.

St. Pius X Friary, 11051 Academy Rd., 19154. Tel: 215-632-1300; Fax: 215-632-2550.
E-mail: Frank19114@worldnet.att.net
Order of Friars Minor, Assumption B.V.M. Province. Faculty Residence for Archbishop Ryan High School. Revs. Rene Barczak, O.F.M.; Roderick Drag, O.F.M.; Carl Graczyk, O.F.M.; Francis X. Kelly, O.F.M., Guardian; Linus E. Kopczewski, O.F.M.; Charles Newman, O.F.M.; Warren Rector, O.F.M.; Gabriel A. Rosetti, O.F.M.; Joel F. Szydlowski, O.F.M.; Rudolph Wieszczek, O.F.M.; Frank Berna, O.F.M.

Society of the Brother Servants of the Holy Spirit (B.H.S.), Providence House, 3531 N. 19th St., 19140. Tel: 215-225-7231. Bro. Darryl-Joseph Branch, B.H.S., Contact Person. Total in Residence 4.

AUDUBON. *Christian Brothers (F.S.C.)*, St. Gabriel Hall Community, Pawlings Rd., P.O. Box 7280, 19407-7280. Tel: 215-247-2776: 610-666-7970.

BENSALEM. *Congregation of the Holy Ghost*, Spiritan Hall, 2401 Bristol Pike, 19020. Tel: 215-638-0232; 0233; Fax: 215-638-0241.
E-mail: rnroach@aol.com
Faculty Residence for Priests & Brothers Teaching at Holy Ghost Preparatory School; Also Residence for Retired Priests and Brothers.
School Community: Revs. James P. McCloskey, C.S.Sp., Supr.; Christopher H. McDermott, C.S.Sp., Bursar.
Retirement Community: Revs. Robert N. Roach, C.S.Sp., Supr.; John R. Muka, C.S.Sp.; Albert M. Seichepine, C.S.Sp.; Stephen A. Zamborsky, C.S.Sp.; Francis R. Duffy.

BRYN MAWR. *Augustinians Friars (O.S.A.)*, Our Mother of Good Counsel Community, 31 Pennswood Rd., 19010-3475. Tel: 610-525-0327; Fax: 610-525-0157.
E-mail: augustiniansomgc@prodigy.net
Rev. James E. Martinez, O.S.A., Contact Person.

DEVON. *Piarist Fathers (Order of the Pious Schools)*, 363 Valley Forge Rd., 19333. Tel: 610-688-6807; Fax: 610-688-2409.
E-mail: sjcalasanctius@juno.com
Web site: azeg@juno.com
Priests who teach at Devon Preparatory School: Revs. James J. Shea, Sch.P., Headmaster; Richard S. Wyzykiewicz, Sch.P., Rector & Prov. Asst.; Louis G. Mesko, Sch.P.; Ferdinand Negrillos, Sch.P.; Geza Pazmany, Sch.P.; Stephen Mustos, Sch.P.

Piarist Fathers Latin Mission. Tel: 305-279-2333; Fax: 305-279-0925. Revs. David Powers, Sch.P.; Mario B. Vizcaino, Sch.P. Total Staff 6; Total in Residence 5.

DOYLESTOWN. *Pauline Fathers Monastery, Shrine of Our Lady of Czestochowa*, 654 Ferry Rd., P.O. Box 2049, 18901. Tel: 215-345-0607; Fax: 214-348-2148.
E-mail: cshrine@aol.com
Web site: www.polishshrine.com
Office. Tel: 215-345-0600; 0601; Fax: 215-348-2148. Revs. Lucius Tyrasinski, O.S.P.P.E., Prov.; Jan Kolmaga, O.S.P.P.E., Prior; Stephen Z. Wozniczka, O.S.P.P.E., Shrine Dir.; Christopher Drybka, O.S.P.P.E.; Bartlomiej Marciniak, O.S.P.P.E.; Tadeusz Olzacki, O.S.P.P.E.; Albert P. Ostatek, O.S.P.P.E.; Simon Shaner, O.S.P.P.E.; Mikolaj Socha, O.S.P.P.E.; Marian Zalecki, O.S.P.P.E.; Michael Zembrzuski, O.S.P.P.E.; Bros. Casimir Pasnik; Didak Turi; Luke Mitura; Peter Lisiecki; Tomasz Fabiszewski, O.S.P.P.E.

FAIRLESS HILLS. *St. Anthony Friary*, 607 Wistar Rd., 19030. Tel: 215-943-4810. Franciscan Friars T.O.R. Revs. Fidelis F. Weber, T.O.R., Guidance Dir. & Local Min.; Neil Saller, T.O.R.; M. Gerald Gordon, T.O.R.; John Grinnen, T.O.R.; Donald F. Vuketich, T.O.R.; Gabriel Zeis, T.O.R.; Bros. John Paul McMahon, T.O.R.; John T. Carosella, T.O.R.; Lawrence Hilferty, T.O.R. Faculty residence for priests and brothers who teach at Conwell-Egan Catholic High School. Total in Residence 9.

LANGHORNE. *Society of Mary, Marist Fathers*, St. Mary's Hospital, 19047. Tel: 215-750-2558. Rev. George Wallace, S.M., Contact.

LAVEROCK. *Brothers of Charity (F.C.)*, Triest Hall, 7720 Doe Ln., 19038. Tel: 215-887-6361; 887-6372; Fax: 215-877-6372.
E-mail: mlonswayfc@aol.com
Web site: www.fracarita.com
Total Staff 4; Total in Residence 3.

MALVERN. *Augustinian Friars (O.S.A.)*, Malvern Prep School Community, St. Augustine Friary, 418 S. Warren Ave., 19355-2707. Tel: 610-644-5454; 647-8281; Fax: 610-647-8281.
E-mail: jlig@erols.com
Revs. David J. Duffy, O.S.A., Pres.; Stephen M. Curry, O.S.A.; James R. Flynn, O.S.A., Asst. Head; John R. Liggio, O.S.A., Prior. In res. Rev. Francis A. Sirolli, O.S.A. Total in Residence 5; Students 590.

PAOLI. *Daylesford Abbey*, 220 S. Valley Rd., 19301-1900. Tel: 610-647-2530; Fax: 610-651-0219.
E-mail: norbertines@daylesford.org
Web site: www.daylesford.org
Legal Title: *Norbertine Fathers, Inc.* Rt. Rev. Ronald J. Rossi, O.Praem., Abbot; Very Rev. John J. Novielli, O.Praem., Prior; Revs. Steven J. Albero, O.Praem., Vocation Dir.; Joseph A. Serano, O.Praem., Treas.; Andrew D. Ciferni, O.Praem.; Joseph P. McLaughlin, O.Praem.; Richard J. Antonucci, O.Praem.; Maurice C. Avicolli, O.Praem.; Hubert N. Beaudoin, O.Praem.; John M. Cagney, O.Praem.; Francis X. Cortese, O.Praem.; William J. Fischer, O.Praem.; Edward J. Kimpel, O.Praem.; Joseph C. Laenen, O.Praem.; David T. Lawlor, O.Praem.; Michael J. Lee, O.Praem.; Rt. Rev. John E. Neitzel, O.Praem., Abbot Emeritus; Revs. James C. Rodia, O.Praem.; Domenic A. Rossi, O.Praem.; Thomas J. Rossi, O.Praem.; Nicholas R. Terico, O.Praem.; Charles T. Urban, O.Praem.; John C. Zagarella, O.Praem.; Bros. Blase G. Corso, O.Praem.; John B. Ginder, O.Praem.; William J. Kelly, O.Praem. Priests 24; Brothers 3.

SPRINGFIELD. *Servants of Charity (S.C.)*, Don Guanella Village, 1795 S. Sproul Rd., 19064. Tel: 610-328-3406. Rev. Romano DiRuscio, S.C., Contact Person. Total in Residence 6.

VILLANOVA. *Fray de Leon Community*, Villanova University, 19085. Tel: 610-519-5020; Fax: 215-587-3907. Augustinians. Revs. Richard T. O'Leary, O.S.A., Prior; Arthur B. Chappell, O.S.A.; Peter M. Donohue, O.S.A.; Patrick B. McStravog, O.S.A.; Joseph S. Mostardi, O.S.A. In res. Rev. Edward T. Hastings, O.S.A. Total in Residence 6.

Provincial Offices of the Order of St. Augustine, Province of St. Thomas of Villanova, P.O. Box 340, 19085-0340. Tel: 610-527-3330; Fax: 610-520-0618.
E-mail: secretary@augustinian.org
Web site: www.augustinian.org
Very Rev. John E. Deegan, O.S.A., Prior Prov.; Revs. Anthony P. Burrascano, O.S.A., Treas. & Mission Procurator; John J. Sheridan, O.S.A., Prov. Archivist; John E. Rotelle, O.S.A., Contact Person, Prov. Sec., Dir. Augustinian Press; Richard D. Appicci, O.S.A., Mission Office; Patrick B. McStravog, O.S.A., Dir. Vocations. Tel: 610-527-3330 Ext. 284, St. Augustine Friary, 214 Ashwood Rd., P.O. Box 40, 19085. Tel: 610-527-0325; Fax: 610-527-0640. James D. McBurney. Total in Residence 8.

St. John Stone Friary, 37 Aldwyn Ln., 19085. Tel: 610-527-7925; Fax: 610-527-2307. Revs. John E. Deegan, O.S.A., Prior Prov.; Kail C. Ellis, O.S.A.; John E. Rotelle, O.S.A.; Michael J. Scanlan, O.S.A.; T. Shawn Tracy, O.S.A., Prior.

St. Thomas Monastery, 19085. Tel: 610-519-7500; Fax: 610-519-5040. Revs. Richard D. Appicci, O.S.A.; John P. Betoni, O.S.A.; Salvatore S. Bonaccorsi; John E. Bresnahan, O.S.A.; George F. Burnell, O.S.A.; Donald X. Burt, O.S.A.; Jan H. Busch, O.S.A.; George J. Callaghan, O.S.A.; Angus N. Carney, O.S.A.; James T. Deery, O.S.A.; Russell J. DeSimone, O.S.A.; Edmund J. Dobbin, O.S.A., Pres., Villanova University; John M. Driscoll, O.S.A.; Gerard M. Duff, O.S.A.; Francis A. Eigo, O.S.A.; Augustine M. Esposito, O.S.A.; John J. Farrell, O.S.A.; Francis A. Farsaci, O.S.A.; John J. Fitzgerald, O.S.A.; Dennis J. Gallagher, O.S.A.; John J. Gallagher, O.S.A.; Karl A. Gersbach, O.S.A.; Dante L. Girolami, O.S.A.; Edwin T. Grimes, O.S.A.; John J. Hagen, O.S.A.; Joseph A. Jordan, O.S.A., Treas.; Patrick J. Kenny, O.S.A.; Charles P. Laferty, O.S.A.; Martin S. Laird, O.S.A.; Joseph F. Laverty, O.S.A.; Bernard A. Lazor, O.S.A.; John F. Lipp, O.S.A.; John F. McAtee, Prior; Neil J. McGettigan, O.S.A.; Francis X. McGuire, O.S.A.; John J. McKenzie, O.S.A.; Thomas M. Mahoney, O.S.A.; Thomas J. Mahony, O.S.A.; Lee J. Makowski, O.S.A.; Francis L. Melcher, O.S.A.; John J. Melton, O.S.A.; Thomas M. Murnane, O.S.A.; Alfred E. Murphy, O.S.A.; Robert J. Murray, O.S.A.; William J. Murray, O.S.A.; James L. Nolan, O.S.A.; Bernard J. O'Dowd, O.S.A.; John M. Quinn, O.S.A.; Walter J. Quinn, O.S.A.; Patrick J. Rice, O.S.A.; George F. Riley, O.S.A.; Joseph C. Schnaubelt, O.S.A.; Albert C. Shannon, O.S.A.; Joseph L. Shannon, O.S.A.; Thomas J. Shea, O.S.A.; John J. Sheridan; Ralph V. Shuhler, O.S.A.; Ralph C. Shurer, O.S.A.; Arthur F. Smith, O.S.A.; John P. Stack, O.S.A.; Robert E. Steinman, O.S.A.; Michael P. Sullivan, O.S.A.; William C. Van Breda, O.S.A.; Dennis G. Wilde, O.S.A.; Eugene M. Zega, O.S.A.; Bros. Nicholas Osuna, O.S.A.; Richard C. Ekmann, O.S.A. Total Staff 17; Total in Residence 67.

St. Thomas of Villanova Friary, 109 Willowburn Rd., 19085-1313. Tel: 610-527-0856; Fax: 610-527-8812. Revs. Donald F. Reilly, O.S.A.; Richard G. Cannuli, O.S.A.; Joseph D. Calderone, O.S.A.

WYNDMOOR. *Christian Brothers (F.S.C.)*, LaSalle High School Community, 8605 Cheltenham Ave., 19038. Tel: 215-233-3030; Fax: 215-233-0297.
E-mail: brotherbrendan@juno.com
Web site: lschs.org
Bro. Brendan Garwood, F.S.C., Contact Person. Total in Residence 15.

Oblates of St. Francis de Sales (O.S.F.S.). Villa de Sales Oblate Residence, 8501 Flourtown Ave., 19038. Tel: 215-836-1472; Fax: 215-836-7213. Very Rev. Joseph F. Chorpenning, O.S.F.S., S.T.L., Ph.D., Religious Supr. & Contact Person. Total in Residence 7.

Villa de Sales Oblate Residence, 8501 Flourtown Ave., 19038. Tel: 215-836-1472; Fax: 215-836-7213. Very Rev. Joseph F. Chorpenning, O.S.F.S., S.T.L., Ph.D.; Rev. Raymond J. Christ, O.S.F.S.; Bro. Robert J. Drelich, O.S.F.S.; Revs. William A. Guerin, O.S.F.S.; Richard T. Reece, O.S.F.S.; William F. Walsh, O.S.F.S.; Albert J. Smith, O.S.F.S. Total in Residence 7.

[BB] CONVENTS AND RESIDENCES OF SISTERS

PHILADELPHIA. *Assumption Hall*, Sisters of St. Joseph, 8900 Norwood Ave., 19118-2711. Tel: 215-247-3665; 248-2564. Sr. Ann Sweeney, S.S.J., Contact. Residence for Norwood-Fontbonne Academy Faculty. Total Staff 15; Total in Residence 19.

Blessed Trinity Missionary Cenacle, 804 N. 24th St., 19130. Tel: 215-765-2237. Missionary Servants of the Most Blessed Trinity, Ministry in Catholic Social Services and various parish ministries.

Blessed Trinity Mother Missionary Cenacle, 3501 Solly Ave., 19136. Tel: 215-335-7550; Fax: 215-335-7559.
E-mail: msbtphl@aol.com
Generalate, Novitiate and Candidacy of the Missionary Servants of the Most Blessed Trinity. Mother Boniface Center. Sr. Barbara DeMoranville, M.S.B.T., Gen. Custodian; Sr. Mary E. Butler, M.S.B.T., Gen. Sec. Total Staff 25; Total in Residence 113.

Carmelite Monastery, 66th Ave. and Old York Rd., 19126. Tel: 215-424-6143; Fax: 215-424-6143; 424-6145, Ext. 5. Mother Barbara of the Holy Ghost, Prioress.

Carmelite Sisters for the Aged and Infirm (O.Carm.), Sacred Heart Manor, 6445 Germantown Ave., 19119. Tel: 215-236-5268; Fax: 215-438-7743.
E-mail: michaelshm@aol.com

Congregation of the Sisters of St. Felix, St. Ignatius Convent, 4401 Haverford Ave., 19104. Tel: 215-222-2296; Fax: 215-222-3078. Sr. Mary Agatha Cebula, Local Min.

Convent of the Daughters of Charity, 449 E. Locust Ave., 19144-1323. Tel: 215-438-3536.
E-mail: dc449@gateway.net
Web site: dc-northeast.org
Sr. Patricia Bouza, D.C., Supr. Total in Residence 8.

Convent of the Little Sisters of the Assumption, 6300 Drexel Rd., 19151. Tel: 215-877-8655. Total in Residence 6.

Daughters of St. Paul, 9171 A Roosevelt Blvd., 19114. Tel: 215-676-9494; Fax: 215-676-9928.
E-mail: philadelphia@pauline.org
Web site: www.pauline.com
Sr. Marjorina Zanatta, F.S.P., Supr.

Daughters of St. Paul Convent, 9610 Evans St., 19115. Tel: 215-969-5068.
E-mail: philadelphia@pauline.org
Web site: www.pauline.org
Sr. Marjorina Zanatta, F.S.P., Supr. Sisters 4.

Dominican Sisters of Our Lady of the Rosary of Fatima, Convent of Mother M. Dominga, 606 W. Erie Ave., 19140-4431. Tel: 215-226-3507; Fax: 215-226-3507.
E-mail: fatimapa@juno.com
Web site: www.madredominga.org/
Dominican Sisters of Our Lady of the Rosary of Fatima. Sr. M. Angelica Perez, O.P., Local Supr. Total in Residence 4.

Emmaus Convent, 5358 Cedar Ave., 19143. Tel: 215-471-7260. Sisters of Mercy (R.S.M.). Total in Residence 3.

Franciscan Sisters of Allegany (O.S.F.), 2622 Potter St., 19125. Tel: 215-739-6441; Fax: 215-739-5607.

Grey Nuns of the Sacred Heart. Tel: 215-269-9783; Fax: 215-269-9789.
E-mail: mel@greynun.org
Web site: www.greynun.org
St. Joseph the Worker Convent, 9168 New Falls Rd., Fallsington, 19054. Tel: 215-269-9783; Fax: 215-269-9789. Total in Residence 8.

Handmaids of the Sacred Heart of Jesus, Provincial Residence, 1242 S. Broad St., 19146-3119. Tel: 215-468-6368; Fax: 215-271-1488.
E-mail: acjphilly@juno.com
Web site: acjusa.org
Sr. Gloria Petrone, A.C.J., Prov. Supr. Total in Residence 7.

Hannah House, Sisters of St. Joseph, 2458 N. 16th St., 19132. Tel: 215-221-0211. Sr. Virginia Jenkins, S.S.J., Contact Person. Sisters 2.

Immaculate Heart Convent, 7310 Torresdale Ave., 19136. Tel: 215-332-8299.
E-mail: smarie@integra-net.com
Sr. Marie de Lourdes, I.H.M., Contact Person. Faculty Residence for Sisters, Servants of the Immaculate Heart of Mary, teaching at St. Hubert High School. Total in Residence 14.

Immaculate Heart Convent, 4904 Chestnut St., 19139. Tel: 215-474-8971. Sr. Regina Havens, I.H.M., Supr. Faculty Residence for Sisters, Servants of the Immaculate Heart of Mary, who teach at West Philadelphia Catholic High School and Archbishop Prendergast High School. Total Staff 8; Total in Residence 8.

Little Servants of the Holy Family of Seoul, 70th & Old York Rd., 19126. Tel: 215-548-5535. Sr. Andrew Kim, L.S.H.F., Local Supr.

Little Sisters of the Assumption, 1211 S. 15th St., 19146-3116. Tel: 215-218-9157; Fax: 215-218-9159.
E-mail: lsaritner@aol.com
Web site: www.littlesisters.org
Sr. Marie Gervasi, L.S.A., Contact. Total in Residence 4.

Little Sisters of the Poor, Holy Family Home, 5300 Chester Ave., 19143. Tel: 215-729-5753; Fax: 215-729-5158.

Little Workers of the Sacred Hearts, Sacred Hearts Convent, 160 Carpenter Ln., 19119. Tel: 215-843-2266.

Mary Immaculate Convent, 1731 S. 11th St., 19148. Tel: 215-468-9133. Sr. M. Ann Bernadette, I.H.M., Supr. Faculty Residence for Sisters, Servants of the Immaculate Heart of Mary, who teach at St. Maria Goretti High School and John W. Hallahan High School. Total Staff 24; Total in Residence 24.

Medical Mission Sisters (M.M.S.), 217 E. Price St., 19144. Tel: 215-844-3672.
E-mail: barb@medicalmissionsisters.org
Sr. Barbara Ann Brigham, M.M.S., Contact Person. Total in Residence 5.

Medical Mission Sisters, North American Sector, 8400 Pine Rd., 19111. Tel: 215-742-6100; Fax: 215-342-3948.
E-mail: mmsorg@medicalmissionsisters.org
Web site: www.medicalmissionsisters.org
Sr. Maria Hornung, M.M.S., Sector Coord.; Sr. Denise Elliott, M.M.S., District Coord. Sisters in Sector 142; Total in Residence 58.

Missionary Sisters of the Most Sacred Heart, Trinity House, 518 Devereaux Ave., 19111. Tel: 215-342-3498. Total in Residence 4.

Missionary Sisters of the Sacred Heart (Cabrini Sisters), 67th and Callowhill Sts., 19151. Tel: 215-472-7911; Fax: 215-472-4289. Sr. Christine Perazzoli, M.S.C., Supr.

Monastery of the Visitation Nuns, 5820 City Ave., 19131-1295. Tel: 215-473-5888; Fax: 215-473-7512. Mother Antoinette Marie Walker, V.H.M., Supr.; Rev. Howard J. Heim, S.J., Chap. Total Staff 11; Total in Residence 9.

Mother of Peace House, 2622 Potter St., 19125. Tel: 215-739-6441; Fax: 215-739-5607. Franciscan Sisters of Allegany.

Mt. St. Joseph Convent, 9701 Germantown Ave., 19118-2694. Tel: 215-248-7200; Fax: 215-248-7277.
E-mail: MSJC19118@aol.com
Web site: home.earthlink.net/~roredassj/homepage/
Motherhouse of the Sisters of St. Joseph of Chestnut Hill, Philadelphia. Sr. Patricia Kelly, S.S.J., Supr.

Nazareth Convent, Religious Sisters of Mercy, 6369 Woodbine Ave., 19151. Tel: 215-477-3022. Sr. Patricia Smith, R.S.M., Contact Person.

Peace Hermitage, Society of Catholic Medical Missionaries, 8400 Pine Rd., 19111. Tel: 215-742-6100; 342-0961; 342-2039; Fax: 215-342-3948.
E-mail: ednav@juno.com
Sr. Edna C. Villafuerte, S.C.M.M., Contact Person. Total in Residence 5.

Poor Servants of the Mother of God, 832 N. Judson St., 19130. Tel: 215-763-4526.

Provincial House of the Sisters of the Holy Family of Nazareth. Immaculate Conception Province, 4001 Grant Ave., 19114. Tel: 215-637-6464; Fax: 215-637-8475.
Web site: http://www.integra-net.com/csfn.phila
Sr. M. Michaelann Delaney, Prov. Supr.; Rev. Ronald J. Ferrier, Chap. Total in Residence 160.

Religious Sisters of the Assumption, Assumption Convent, 914 S. 49th St., 19143. Tel: 215-727-9430.
E-mail: revait27@aol.com
Sr. Ann Palmer, Supr.

St. Francis Convent, 1727 S. 11th St., 19148. Tel: 215-463-7343.
E-mail: gpfrancis@alt.net
Residence of Sisters of St. Francis of Philadelphia employed at St. Maria Goretti and Hallahan High Schools, St. Agnes Hospital, Sacred Heart School, (Child/Family Treatment), and Archdiocesan Office, Grant Writing in Aston and Southern Homes.

St. Isaac House, Society of the Daughters of the Heart of Mary. Tel: 610-664-9546; Fax: 610-617-0504. 226 N. Essex Ave., #106, Narberth, 19072. Tel: 610-664-9546. Sr. Kathleen F. Devine, D.H.M., Supr.

St. Joseph Convent, 7300 Torresdale Ave., 19136. Tel: 215-338-4884.
E-mail: ssjtorr@netcarrier.com
Faculty Residence for Sisters of St. Joseph, who teach at St. Hubert and Father Judge High School, St. Vincent's Orphanage and Nazareth Academy.

St. Joseph the Worker Convent, 2846 W. Allegheny Ave., 19132. Tel: 215-228-4030. Sisters of Mercy (R.S.M.). Sr. Raymond Mary, Coord.

St. Michael Hall, 9001 Germantown Ave., 19118. Tel: 215-247-3698.
E-mail: SSJsmhall@aol.com
Sr. James Agnes Campbell, S.S.J., Contact Person. Faculty Residence for Sisters of St. Joseph who staff Chestnut Hill College. Total in Residence 9.

School Sisters of Notre Dame, Nativity Community, 6346 Hegerman St., 19135. Tel: 215-333-5742; Fax: 215-739-8781.
E-mail: atgroves@netscape.net
Sr. Kathleen Groves, S.S.N.D., Prin.

School Sisters of Notre Dame, St. Vincent Community, 7201 Milnor St., 19135. Tel: 215-624-5635. Total in Residence 5.

School Sisters of Notre Dame, 2141 N. Howard St., 19122. Tel: 215-634-2227; Fax: 215-426-8031.
E-mail: ckeck@hotmail.com

School Sisters of Notre Dame, 158 E. Huntingdon St., 19125. Tel: 215-425-1350.

School Sisters of Notre Dame, Visitation Community, 3978 Constance Rd., 19114. Tel: 215-824-0754.
E-mail: sisterbernie@yahoo.com
Web site: www.ssnd.org
Sr. Bernadette Marie Ravenstahl, S.S.N.D., Contact.

Shalom Convent, 5342-44 Cedar Ave., 19143-1918. Tel: 215-474-5538. Residence of Religious Sisters of Mercy. Sisters 6.

Sister Servants of the Holy Spirit of Perpetual Adoration (S.Sp.S.A.P.), Convent of Divine Love, 2212 Green St., 19130. Tel: 215-567-0123; Fax: 215-569-8314.
E-mail: cdl2212@earthlink.net
Web site: www.holyspiritadorationsisters
Sr. Mary Catherine, S.Sp.S.A.P., Supr.; Rev. Joseph C. Dieckhaus, Chap.

Sisters of Charity of Nazareth, 1905 Brown St., 19130. Tel: 215-236-0993.

Sisters of Our Lady of Mercy, S.O.L.M., 3224 Belgrade St., 19134-5299. Tel: 215-427-3261; Fax: 215-427-3263. Total in Residence 4.

Sisters of St. Francis of Philadelphia. Franciscan Formation House. 338 Warton St., 19147. Tel: 215-336-8915. Total in Residence 6.

Sisters of St. Francis of Philadelphia, Santa Chiara, 2238 S. 12th St., 19148. Tel: 215-465-2227. Sisters Residence for those who work at St. Agnes Medical Center and Epiphany Church.

Sisters of St. Francis of Philadelphia, St. Agnes Convent, 1900 S. Broad St., 19145. Tel: 215-465-1597. Total in Residence 13.

Sisters of St. Francis of Philadelphia (O.S.F.), 1342 Castle Ave., 19148. Tel: 215-755-2352.
E-mail: srmargesullivan@chi-east.org

Sisters of St. Francis of Philadelphia, Canticle House.
E-mail: mlucey@osfphila.org
Web site: www.osfphila.org
Congregational Minister's Office, 609 S. Convent Rd., Aston, 19014. Tel: 610-558-7701; Fax: 640-459-0195.
Convent, 1626 Mifflin St., 19145. Tel: 215-551-2586.

Sisters of St. Joseph, Neumann Hall, 58 E. Northwestern Ave., 19118. Tel: 215-248-7282. Total in Residence 4.

Sisters of St. Joseph of Philadelphia. Divine Shepherd Convent, 927 Bethlehem Pike, Erdenheim, 19038. Tel: 215-836-2082. Total in Residence 6.

Sisters of St. Joseph of Philadelphia, Immaculate Heart of Mary Convent, 823 Cathedral Rd., 19128. Tel: 215-482-8540. Sisters in Residence 7.

Sisters of St. Joseph of Philadelphia, Cecilian Academy, 6818 Cresheim Rd., 19119. Tel: 215-438-7515. Total in Residence 10.

Sisters of St. Joseph of Philadelphia, Fournier Community, Administration, 9701 Germantown Ave., 19118-2694. Tel: 215-248-7200; Fax: 215-248-7277.
E-mail: MSJC19118@aol.com
Web site: home.earthlink.net/~roredassj/homepage/
Sr. Margaret Fleming, S.S.J., Supr. Gen. Sisters 4.

Sisters of St. Joseph of Philadelphia, Nazareth House. Tel: 215-836-2613.
E-mail: nazareth@peoplepc.com
931 Bethlehem Pike, Erdenheim, 19038. Tel: 215-836-2613. Total in Residence 5.

Sisters of the Blessed Sacrament, Acacia Community, 3533 N. 19th St., 19140. Tel: 215-223-9132. Total in Residence 3.

Sisters of the Good Shepherd, 733 Susquehanna Rd., 19111-1399. Tel: 215-742-4774. Total in Residence 2.

Sisters of the Good Shepherd, 5356 Chew Ave., 19138. Tel: 215-843-9411; Fax: 215-843-3141.
E-mail: marynorad@juno.com
Neighborhood ministry, mediation program. Total in Residence 4.

Sisters of the Good Shepherd (Contemplative), 715 Susquehanna Rd., 19111. Tel: 215-722-3970. Sr. Jude Ellen Golumbieski, C.G.S., Supr. Total in Residence 16.

Sisters of the Good Shepherd (R.G.S.), P.O. Box 44258, 19144. Tel: 215-849-2070; Fax: 215-849-4385. Sr. M. Loretta Clancy, R.G.S., Contact Person. Total in Residence 2.

Sisters of the Holy Child, 2362 E. York St., 19125. Tel: 215-423-9514.
E-mail: shcjyorkst@juno.com

Response-Ability Residence, 4724 Cedar Ave., 19143. Tel: 215-726-3947.
E-mail: ra96@erols.com
Residence for volunteers for Teacher Service Project sponsored by the Society of Holy Child.

Sisters of the Holy Family of Nazareth, St. Joseph Convent, Grant and Frankford Aves., 19114. Tel: 215-637-6262; Fax: 215-637-5689.

Sisters of the Holy Family of Nazareth, Jesus of Nazareth Convent (aka Mount Nazareth), 2755 Holme Ave., 19152. Tel: 215-338-8992; Fax: 215-338-8752. Total in Residence 51.

Sisters of the Holy Family of Nazareth, Infant Jesus Convent, 2723 Holme Ave., 19152-2015. Tel: 215-335-6380; Fax: 215-335-3764.
E-mail: nazcon@aol.com
Web site: www.csfn.org
Total in Residence 25.

Sisters of the Holy Redeemer, Emmaus Convent, 1117 Wakeling St., 19124. Tel: 215-288-5564; Fax: 215-787-0999.
Web site: www.sistersholyredeemer.org

Sisters of the Holy Redeemer, Angelus-Formation Community, 705 Medary Ave., 19126. Tel: 215-276-0262; Fax: 215-914-4111.
E-mail: amariecsr@aol.com
Web site: www.sistersholyredeemer.org
1; Total in Residence 3.

AMBLER. *Sisters of the Holy Family of Nazareth (C.S.F.N.)*, St. Mary's Villa for Children, 701 Bethlehem Pike, Box 388, 19002. Tel: 215-643-7676; Fax: 215-542-9219. Residential Treatment Center for Children.

ARDMORE. *Missionary Sisters of the Holy Rosary (M.S.H.R.)*, 205 Cricket Ave., 19003. Tel: 610-896-1786; Fax: 610-896-9063. Total in Residence 6.

ASTON. *Convent of Our Lady of Angels.* (Formerly Glen Riddle), 609 S. Convent Rd., 19014. Tel: 215-459-4125.
E-mail: ekulacz@osfphila.org
Web site: www.osfphila.org
Motherhouse of the Sisters of St. Francis of Philadelphia. Sr. Marie Lucey, O.S.F., Congregational Min.

Mt. Alvernia Convent, 602A S. Convent Rd., 19014. Tel: 215-459-5989.
E-mail: hherberi@home.com
Sisters of St. Francis of Philadelphia. Sr. Helen St. Paul, O.S.F., Contact Person. Total in Residence 3.

Sisters of St. Francis of Philadelphia, Our Lady of the Valley Convent, 10 Red Hill Rd., 19014-1119. Sr. Margarita Guggy, O.S.F., Contact. Total in Residence 4; Total Staff 4.

Sisters of St. Francis of Philadelphia, Portiuncula Convent, 610 Red Hill Rd., 19014. Tel: 610-558-5350. Sisters 9.

Sisters of St. Francis of Philadelphia, Assisi House, 600 Red Hill Rd., 19014. Tel: 610-459-8990; Fax: 610-558-5344.
E-mail: jmmcdevi@osfphila.org
Total Staff 117; Total in Residence 126.

Sisters of St. Francis of Philadelphia, TAU Convent, 886 Concord Rd., 19014. Tel: 610-494-7322. Sr. Helen Budzik, O.S.F., Contact. Total in Residence 5.

BENSALEM. *St. Elizabeth Convent*, 1663 Bristol Pike, 19020-8502. Tel: 215-244-9900; Fax: 215-244-8174.
E-mail: kathdrexel@aol.com
Web site: www.katharinedrexel.org
Motherhouse of the Sisters of the Blessed Sacrament for Indians and Colored People. Sr. Monica Loughlin, S.B.S., Pres.; Sr. Barbara Specker, S.B.S., Local Dir. Total in Residence 43; Total Staff 13.

St. Michael Hall, 1663 Bristol Pike, 19020-8502. Tel: 215-244-9900; 638-0865; Fax: 215-244-8174.
E-mail: SBS@libertynet.org
Web site: www.liberty.org/SBS
The Infirmary of the Sisters of the Blessed Sacrament.

Sisters of the Blessed Sacrament Novitiate, 1663 Bristol Pike, 19020. Mailing Address: P.O. Box 8502, 19020. Sr. Amedee Maxwell, S.B.S. Professed Sisters 4; Novices 1; Total in Residence 5.

BRANDAMORE. *Medical Mission Sisters*, P.O. Box 216, 19316. Tel: 215-742-6100. Sr. Kathryn Gates, M.M.S., Personnel Asst.

BROOKHAVEN. *Sisters of St. Francis of Philadelphia*, Claddagh House, 160 Meadowbrook Ln., 19015. Tel: 610-490-5367.
E-mail: mirmurray@home.com
Web site: www.osfphila.org
Total in Residence 3.

BRYN MAWR. *Missionary Sisters of the Holy Rosary*, 741 Polo Rd., 19010. Tel: 610-520-1974; Fax: 610-520-2002.
E-mail: berniemurd@aol.com
Web site: www.icdc.com/~mshr
Total in Residence 8.

Sisters of the Holy Child Jesus, Bryn Mawr Center, 105 County Line Rd., 19010. Tel: 610-525-9955. Sr. Alice Penrose, S.H.C.J., Contact Person. Retirement Residence for Sisters of the Holy Child Jesus.

Society of the Holy Child Jesus, 700 Old Lancaster Rd., 19010. Tel: 610-527-5076; Fax: 610-527-4671.
E-mail: countyline@juno.com
Retirement Residence for Sisters of the Holy Child Jesus. Total in Residence 6.

CHELTENHAM. *Daughters of Our Lady of the Sacred Heart*, St. Joseph Convent, 7633 Waters Rd., 19012. Tel: 215-224-2159.
E-mail: fdnsc@aol.com
Total in Residence 2.

CHESTER. *Bernardine Sisters of St. Francis*, Sacred Heart Convent, 2601 W. Tenth St., 19013. Tel: 610-497-2368; Fax: 610-497-3434.
E-mail: conlab1@juno.com
Total in Residence 18.

Bernardine Sisters of St. Francis, Bernardine Center, 2625 W. Ninth St., 19013. Tel: 610-497-3225.

Bernardine Sisters of St. Francis, Blessed Katharine Drexel Convent, 2061 W. 10th St., 19013. Tel: 610-497-2368.

Missionaries of Charity, Gift of Mary, 2714 W. 9th St., 19013. Tel: 610-494-7424. Sr. M. Aloka, M.C., Contact. Total Assisted 247; Total Staff 5.

COATESVILLE. *Comboni Missionary Sisters*, 58 S. 6th Ave., 19320. Tel: 610-380-9229. Sr. Joan Ramus, C.M.S., Supr.

DARBY. *Religious Sisters of Mercy*, Bethlehem Convent, 3 Golf Rd., 19023. Tel: 610-461-7634; Fax: 610-567-6333. Sr. Mary Elizabeth Burke, R.S.M., Coord. Residence of Sisters, majority of whom minister at Mercy Health Corporation. Sisters 2.

Sisters of the Divine Redeemer, Divine Redeemer Convent, 1209 Springfield Rd., 19023. Tel: 610-534-1688.

DEVON. *Congregation of the Benedictines of Jesus Crucified, O.S.B.*, Regina Mundi Priory, Inc., 550 S. Waterloo Rd., 19333-1798. Tel: 610-688-5130; Fax: 610-995-0477. Sr. M. Rita Syn, O.S.B., Prioress. Total in Residence 14.

DREXEL HILL. *Holy Child Convent*, 453 Shadeland Ave., 19026. Tel: 610-259-1732.
E-mail: SHCJ.453@juno.com
Residence of Sisters of the Holy Child Jesus (S.H.C.J.).

St. Joseph Convent, 435 N. Lansdowne Ave., 19026-1190. Tel: 610-622-0440. Sr. Gertrude Friel, S.S.J., Local Coord. Faculty Residence for Sisters of St. Joseph who teach at Archbishop Prendergast High School, Msgr. Bonner High School, and Bishop Neuman.

Sisters of Notre Dame de Namur, 435 N. Lansdowne Ave., 19026-1190. Tel: 610-237-4760.

Society of the Holy Child Jesus, Provincial Office, 460 Shadeland Ave., 19026. Tel: 610-626-1400; Fax: 610-626-1454.
E-mail: Shci460@cs.com
Web site: www.shcj.org
Sr. Marcia Sichol, S.H.C.J., Prov. Leader. Legal Title: *Society of the Holy Child Jesus American Province, Inc.*

Xavier House Provincial Offices, 460 Shadeland Ave., 19026. Tel: 610-626-1400; Fax: 610-626-0451.
E-mail: mwsichol@cs.com
Web site: www.shcj.org
Society of the Holy Child Jesus.

ELKINS PARK. *Dominican Retreat House, Convent of Our Lady of Prouille*, 750 Ashborne Rd., 19027-2596. Tel: 215-782-8520; 224-0945. Total Staff 38; Total in Residence 20.

Dominican Sisters Administrative Offices, Dominican Congregation of St. Catherine de Ricci, 750 Ashbourne Rd., 19027-2596. Tel: 215-635-6027; Fax: 215-635-2071.
E-mail: mebennettop@cswebmail.com
Sr. Mary Ellen Bennett, O.P., Pres.

St. Catherine Hall, 750 Ashbourne Rd., 19027-2596. Tel: 215-635-4540; Fax: 215-635-2372.
E-mail: stcathall@aol.com
Retirement Residence for Dominican Sisters of St. Catherine de Ricci. Total Staff 5; Total in Residence 26.

ELVERSON. *Daughters of St. Mary of Providence (D.S.M.P.)*, St. Mary of Providence Center, 227 Isabella Rd., 19520. Tel: 610-942-4166; Fax: 610-942-4268. Sr. Bernadine Ugolini, D.S.M.P., Contact Person. Total in Residence 5; Total Staff 15.

ESSINGTON. *Bernardine Sisters of St. Francis*, St. Margaret Mary Convent, 546 Wanamaker Ave., 19029. Tel: 610-521-3286; Fax: 610-497-3659.
E-mail: jperose@aol.com

FEASTERVILLE. *Grey Nuns of the Sacred Heart*, 1825 Bridgetown Pike, 19053.

FLOURTOWN. *St. Rita Convent*, 1410 Bethlehem Pike, 19031. Tel: 215-836-1615; Fax: 215-641-5579.
E-mail: mccannm@gmc.edu
Sisters of Mercy of the Americas. Sr. Maureen B. McCann, R.S.M. Total in Residence 2.

Sisters of St. Joseph of Philadelphia, Mt. St. Joseph Academy, 120 W. Wissahickon Ave., 19031-1922. Tel: 215-233-4368; Fax: 215-233-4734. Total in residence 15.

FOX CHASE MANOR. *Sisters of St. Basil (O.S.B.M.).* Motherhouse of the Sisters of St. Basil. 710 Fox Chase Rd., 19046-4198. Tel: 215-663-9153; Fax: 215-728-6129.
E-mail: basilians@aol.com
Sr. Dorothy Ann Busowski, O.S.B.M., Prov.

Basilian Spirituality Center, 710 Fox Chase Rd., 19046. Tel: 215-342-8381.

GLENSIDE. *Medical Mission Sisters.* (Society of Catholic Medical Missionaries, Inc.), 15 E. Glenside Ave., 19038. Tel: 215-886-4036.
E-mail: eunice@medicalmissionsisters.org
Web site: medicalmissionsisters.org
Total in Residence 3.
Sisters of St. Francis of Assisi (Milwaukee), 229 Edge Hill Rd., 19038. Tel: 215-866-7388.

GWYNEDD VALLEY. *Sisters of Mercy of the Americas - Annunciation Convent*, Gwynedd Mercy College, Evans Rd., 19437. Tel: 215-646-8894.
Religious Sisters of Mercy - St. Joseph Convent, Evans Rd. & Sumneytown Pike, 19437. Tel: 215-646-5259.
Religious Sisters of Mercy - Treweryn Convent, Gwynedd Mercy College, Sumneytown Pike, 19437. Tel: 215-641-5529; 641-5544; 641-5507.
Religious Sisters of Mercy-Tabor Convent, Gwynedd Mercy College, Sumneytown Pike, 19437. Tel: 215-641-5516.
Religious Sisters of Mercy - Transfiguration Convent, Gwynedd Mercy College, Sumneytown Pike, 19437. Tel: 215-641-5512.
Religious Sisters of Mercy - Visitation Convent, Gwynedd Mercy College, 19437. Tel: 215-641-5537.

HOLLAND. *Villa Joseph Marie*, 1180 Holland Rd., 18966. Tel: 215-357-8810; Fax: 215-357-1707. Sr. Ann Therese, S.S.C., Supr.; Rev. John A. Cannon, Chap.

HUNTINGDON VALLEY. *Sisters of the Holy Redeemer Provincialate*, 521 Moredon Rd., 19006. Tel: 215-914-4100; Fax: 215-914-4111.
E-mail: rheilman@holyredeemer.com
Web site: www.sistersholyredeemer.org
Sr. M. Regina Heilman, C.S.R., Prov. Supr. Chaplains: Revs. Michael C. Bolesta; Timothy M. Judge; James J. Coonan. Total in Residence 15.

IMMACULATA. *Sisters, Servants of the Immaculate Heart of Mary (I.H.M.)*, Pacis Hall, 19345. Tel: 610-889-1668; Fax: 610-695-0691 (Camilla Hall). Sr. Eliz Seton, I.H.M., Contact. Total in Residence 48.
Sisters, Servants of the Immaculate Heart of Mary, (I.H.M.), Camilla Hall, Box 100, 19345. Tel: 610-644-1152; Fax: 610-695-0691.
Sisters, Servants of the Immaculate Heart of Mary (I.H.M.), Gillet Hall, Box 400, 19345-0400. Tel: 610-647-4400. Total in Residence 57.
Villa Maria House of Studies, 1140 King Rd., 19345-0200. Tel: 610-647-2160; Fax: 610-889-4874.
E-mail: betmc97@aol.com
Legal Title: *Villa Maria House of Studies, Motherhouse of the Sisters, Servants of the Immaculate Heart of Mary.* Ministry in the field of Academic Education at all levels, Early Childhood Center, Congregation Retirement and Health Care Center, Pastoral Ministry, Diocesan and Parish Administration, Literacy Center, Spirituality Center, Directors of Religious Education, Drug and Alcohol Counseling, Ministry to Hispanics. Total in Residence 1,216.

JENKINTOWN. *Grey Nuns of the Sacred Heart*, Immaculate Conception Convent, 600 West Ave., 19046. Tel: 215-884-9145. Sr. Maureen Quigley, G.N.S.H., Coord.
Sisters of the Holy Redeemer, St. Elizabeth Convent, 615 Fox Chase Rd., 19046. Tel: 215-379-0112; Fax: 215-914-4111.
E-mail: bdeitrich@holyredeemer.com
Web site: www.sistersholyredeemer.org
Total in Residence 3.

KING OF PRUSSIA. *The Bernardine Sisters of the Third Order of St. Francis.* (also known as Bernardine Franciscan Sisters), 403 Allendale Rd., 19406. Tel: 610-337-3864; Fax: 610-337-4359.
E-mail: bfgeneralate@aol.com
Web site: www.bfranciscan.org
Sr. Madonna Marie Harvath, O.S.F., Gen. Min. General Councilors: Sr. Amalia Vivian, O.S.F.; Sr. Charlene Dalrymple, O.S.F.; Sr. Marilisa Helena da Silva, O.S.F. Legal Title: *The Bernardine Sisters of the Third Order of St. Francis, Generalate.*

LANGHORNE. *Monastery of St. Clare, Poor Clares.* Prayer and Altar Bread Ministry. 1271 Langhorne-Newton Rd., 19047-1297. Tel: 215-968-5775; Fax: 215-968-6254.
E-mail: stclare@voicenet.com
Web site: www.voicenet.com/~stclare
Cloistered Contemplative Nuns.
San Damiano Convent, 104 Alberts Way, 19047. Tel: 215-860-7185. Total in Residence 3.
Sisters of St. Francis of Philadelphia, St. Mary Convent, 19047. Tel: 215-757-9494. Total in Residence 10.
Sisters of St. Francis of Philadelphia, Franciscan Residence, 113 Alberts Way, 19047. Tel: 215-860-1059. Sisters serving at St. Mary Medical Center.

LANSDALE. *Religious of the Assumption*, Assumption Convent, 500 E. Main St., 19446. Tel: 215-368-4427.
E-mail: ralansdale@juno.com

MALVERN. *Villa Maria Convent*, 370 Old Lincoln Hwy., 19355. Tel: 610-647-4878; Fax: 610-644-2866.
E-mail: info@VMHS.org
Web site: www.vmahs.org
Sisters, Servants of the Immaculate Heart of Mary (I.H.M.). Total in Residence 14.

MEADOWBROOK. *Sisters of the Holy Redeemer*, Emmanuel Convent, 1600 Huntingdon Pike, 19046. Tel: 215-938-5650; Fax: 215-914-4111.
Web site: www.sistersholyredeemer.org
Total in Residence 9.

MERION. *Sisters of Mercy of the Americas, Merion Regional Community, Convent*, 19066. Tel: 610-664-6650; Fax: 610-664-3429. Sr. Christine McCann, R.S.M., Regl. Pres.; Sr. Juliet Ferrari, R.S.M., Local Coord.; Rev. John J. McIntyre, Chap. Motherhouse of the Sisters of Mercy of Merion, PA. Sisters 89.
Sisters of Mercy of the Americas, Merion Regional Community, Agape, 515 Montgomery Ave., 19066. Tel: 610-664-2861.
E-mail: ryann38318@aol.com
Sisters 2.

MERION STATION. *Religious of the Assumption.* Assumption Convent and Spiritual Center. 227 N. Bowman Ave., 19066. Tel: 610-664-3074; 664-1736; Fax: 610-664-7328.
E-mail: rabowman227@juno.com
Sr. Anne Francoise, R.A., Supr.; Sr. Francis Joseph, R.A., Center Dir. Total in Residence 7; Total Staff 3.
Religious Sisters of Mercy, St. Anne Convent, 276 Meeting House Ln., 19066. Tel: 610-667-4531.
Religious Sisters of Mercy, Bethany House of Prayer, 272 Meeting House Ln., 19066. Tel: 610-667-3066.
Religious Sisters of Mercy, McAuley Convent (Infirmary), 517 Montgomery Ave., 19066. Tel: 610-667-2775; Fax: 610-667-9680. Rev. Thomas F.X. Wheeler, S.J., Chap.
Agape Convent, 515 Montgomery Ave., Merion, 19066. Tel: 610-664-2861.

MORTON. *Sisters of St. Francis of Philadelphia (O.S.F.)*, 2130 Franklin Ave., Ct. No. 3, 19070-1217. Tel: 610-543-0186. Total In Residence 7; Total Staff 7.

NEWTOWN. *Grey Nuns of the Sacred Heart*, 135 S. Sycamore St., 18940. Tel: 215-968-0735. Sr. Patricia Geary, G.N.S.H.; Sr. Jean Liston, G.N.S.H.; Sr. Dolores Beatty, G.N.S.H. Total in Residence 3.

NORRISTOWN. *Immaculate Heart Convent*, 1834 Arch St., 19401. Tel: 610-279-2616. Sr. Francis Bernard, I.H.M., Supr. Faculty Residence for Sisters, Servants of the Immaculate Heart of Mary, who teach at Kennedy-Kenrick Catholic High School.
Missionaries of Charity, 630 DeKalb St., 19401-3944. Tel: 610-277-5962. Sr. M. Carmelina, M.C., Supr. Services include Food Distribution and Emergency Night Shelter. Sisters 4.

OVERBROOK. *Little Sisters of the Assumption (L.S.A.)*, 6300 Drexel Rd., 19151. Tel: 215-877-8655; 0958. Total in Residence 5.

RADNOR. *Armenian Sisters of the Immaculate Conception*, 440 Upper Gulph Rd., 19087. Tel: 610-688-9360; Fax: 610-687-2430.
E-mail: asasisters@aol.com
Sr. Louisa Kassarjian, Supr. Total in Residence 4.
Missionary Sisters of the Sacred Heart of Jesus (Cabrini Sisters), Cabrini College Convent, 610 King of Prussia Rd., 19807-3698. Tel: 610-995-1210 (convent); 971-0281 (vocation office); Fax: 610-995-1210.
E-mail: vandusen49@aol.com
Total in Residence 2.

ROSEMONT. *American Province Archives, Sisters of the Holy Child Jesus.* Residence for Sisters of the Holy Child Jesus in varied apostolates, 1316 Wendover Rd., 19010. Tel: 610-525-5601.
Daughters of St. Mary of Providence (D.S.M.P.), 320 Roberts Rd., 19010. Tel: 610-525-8800. Sr. Martha Scheessele, D.S.M.P., Contact Person. Sisters who work at St. Edmond's Home for Children.
Holy Child Infirmary, 1341 Montgomery Ave., 19010. Tel: 610-525-1329.
E-mail: cmmshcj@cs
Total Staff 20; Total in Residence 33.
Sisters of the Holy Child Jesus (S.H.C.J.), New Sharon Community, 1341 Montgomery Ave., 19010. Tel: 610-525-9900.
E-mail: cmmshcj@cs
Sr. Catherine M. Murray, S.H.C.J., Coord. Total in Residence 15.
Infirmary - Community. Tel: 610-525-1329. Total in Residence 33.
Sisters of the Holy Child Jesus (S.H.C.J.), Carroll House Convent, 1301 Wendover Ave., 19010. Tel: 610-527-1025.
E-mail: shcj@cs.com
Total in Residence 5.
Sisters of the Holy Child Jesus (S.H.C.J.), Gracemere Convent, 1316 Wendover Rd., 19010. Tel: 610-525-5601.
E-mail: gracemere@juno.com
Total in Residence 6.
Sisters of the Holy Child Jesus (S.H.C.J.), Midhill Convent, 1355 Montgomery Ave., 19010. Tel: 610-527-3486; Fax: 610-527-2428.
E-mail: cmmshc@cs
Total in Residence 10.

SELLERSVILLE. *Bernardine Sisters of St. Francis.* House of Contemplation/Prayer. St. Agnes Convent, 427 N. Main St., 18960. Tel: 215-257-0845; Fax: 215-257-8880.
E-mail: stagnessel@aol.com
Open to lay and religious for days of prayer, hermitage retreats, private retreats, and prayer weekends. Call to inquire. Total in Residence 2.

SHARON HILL. *Poor Servants of the Mother of God S.M.G. Novitiate*, 209 Felton Ave., 19079. Tel: 610-532-6769; Fax: 610-532-6765. Sr. Teresa Conner, S.M.G., Contact.

SPRINGFIELD. *Daughters of St. Mary of Providence*, Divine Providence Village, 686 Old Marple Rd., 19064. Tel: 610-328-7730.
Immaculate Heart of Mary Convent, 1725 S. Sproul Rd., 19064. Tel: 610-544-0275. Sr. Marie Jerome, I.H.M., Supr. Faculty Residence for Sisters, Servants of the Immaculate Heart of Mary, who teach in Cardinal O'Hara High School and Archbishop Prendergast High School.
Our Lady of Mercy Convent, 1735 S. Sproul Rd., 19064. Tel: 610-544-0238. Faculty Residence for Sisters of Mercy who teach in Cardinal O'Hara and Mercy Vocational High Schools.
St. Anthony Convent, 1715 S. Sproul Rd., 19064. Tel: 610-544-4066.
E-mail: sasisters@rcn.com
Residence for Sisters of St. Francis of Philadelphia who teach in Cardinal O'Hara High School and other Ministries. Total Staff 7; Total in Residence 7.
St. Joseph Convent, 1705 S. Sproul Rd., 19064. Tel: 610-544-4230.
E-mail: ssjoh@nni.com
Sr. Joyce Ballerino, S.S.J. Sisters of St. Joseph Faculty House, Cardinal O'Hara High School. Total in Residence 10.

STRAFFORD. *Our Lady of the Assumption Convent*, 139 Fairfield Ln., 19087. Tel: 610-688-7889. Sisters, Servants of the Immaculate Heart of Mary. Sr. Patricia Hughes, I.H.M., Supr. Total in Residence 6.

VILLANOVA. *Sisters of Notre Dame de Namur*, Notre Dame Convent, 560 Sproul Rd., 19085. Tel: 610-688-8810; Fax: 610-687-1912.
Web site: ndapa.org
Residence for Sisters of Notre Dame de Namur who teach at Academy of Notre Dame.

WARMINSTER. *Immaculate Heart of Mary Convent*, 657 York Rd., 18974-2001. Tel: 215-674-0717; 674-0665. Sr. Mary Joannes Toner, I.H.M., Supr. Faculty Residence for Sisters, Servants of the Immaculate Heart of Mary, who teach at Archbishop Wood High School. Total in Residence 7.
Sisters of St. Joseph of Philadelphia, Nativity of Our Lord Convent, 605 W. Street Rd., 18974. Tel: 215-672-0147. Residence of Sisters St. Joseph.

WYNCOTE. *Handmaids of the Sacred Heart of Jesus*, 2025 Church Rd., 19095. Tel: 215-576-6250; Fax: 215-576-8052.
E-mail: acjwyncote@erols.com
Web site: www.ancillae.org
Sr. Elizabeth McCoy, A.C.J., Supr. Total in Residence 9.

WYNNEWOOD. *Sisters of the Holy Child Jesus (S.H.C.J.)*, Connell House, 105 Old Forest Rd., 19096. Tel: 610-649-8462.
Web site: www.shcj.org
Total in Residence 4.

YARDLEY. *Grey Nuns of the Sacred Heart (GNSH)*, St. Joseph Community, 1750 Quarry Rd., 19067-3998. Tel: 215-968-4237; Fax: 215-968-6656.
E-mail: annmckee@greynun.org
Web site: www.greynun.org
Sr. Marie Cecil Egan, GNSH, Coord. Total in Residence 22.
Motherhouse of the Grey Nuns of the Sacred Heart, 1750 Quarry Rd., 19067-3998. Tel: 215-968-4236; Fax: 215-968-6656.
E-mail: annmckee@greynun.org
Web site: www.greynun.org
Sr. Marlene G. Butler, GNSH, Pres.; Sr. Dolores Fitzpatrick, GNSH, Coord., St. Mary's Community. Total in Residence 33.

YEADON. *St. Michael Convent*, 14 Baily Rd., 19050. Tel: 610-623-3631. Sr. Barbara McGeever, R.S.M., Supr. Residence of Religious Sisters of Mercy who staff Mercy Health Corporation of Southeastern PA.

[CC] RETREAT HOUSES

PHILADELPHIA. *Center for Marianist Spirituality & Communities (CMSC)*, 1341 N. Delaware Ave., Ste. 308, 19125-4300. Tel: 610-634-4116; Fax: 610-634-4955.
E-mail: CMARSCOM@aol.com
Web site: www.marianist-cmsc.org

CMSC is committed to the misssion and spirit of Mary. This spirit fosters spiritual growth and formation, the building of lay faith/action communities and social justice according to the unique gifts of the Marianist tradition. Programs offered in Spirituality, Mary & Community Building for groups, staff, faculty, and parishes. Bro. Jack Ventura, S.M. Total Staff 3; Total Assisted 600.

Mother Boniface Center, 3501 Solly Ave., 19136. Tel: 215-335-7541; Fax: 215-335-7511. Sr. Rebecca Betz, M.S.B.T. Sponsored by Missionary Servants of the Most Blessed Trinity. Mid-week and weekend programs; retreats, days of recollection, scripture study, meetings, workshops and hosting programs. Capacity 80; Total Staff 5; Total in Residence 2.

Urban House of Prayer, 1919 Cambridge St., 19130. Tel: 215-236-8328. Sisters of Notre Dame de Namur. Sr. Marie Bodell, S.N.D.deN., Dir.; Rev. George W. Bur, S.J. Total in Residence 1.

ASTON. *Clare House*, 608 B. Legion Rd., 19014. Tel: 610-459-4077; Fax: 610-558-6122.
E-mail: ccrine@osphila.org
Web site: www.osphila.org
Sr. Celeste Crine, O.S.F., Dir. Directed and Private Retreats. Staffed by Sisters of St. Francis of Philadelphia. Capacity 4; Total Staff 3; Total Guests 320.

ELKINS PARK. *Dominican Retreat House*. Convent of Our Lady of Prouille, 750 Ashbourne Rd., 19027-2596. Tel: 215-782-8520; Fax: 215-782-1744.
E-mail: retreathouse@msn.com
Retreat house for laity and religious. Total Staff 31; Total in Residence 11.

HAVERFORD. *Saint Raphaela Center*, 616 Coopertown Rd., 19041. Tel: 610-642-5715; Fax: 610-642-6788.
E-mail: acihaverford@juno.com
Handmaids of the Sacred Heart of Jesus. Sr. Dorothy Beck, A.C.J., Dir.

MALVERN. *St. Joseph's-in-the-Hills*. (The Malvern Retreat House), 313 Warren Ave., 19355-0315. Tel: 610-644-0400; Fax: 610-644-4363.
E-mail: malvernlrl@aol.com
Web site: www.st-joseph-in-the-hills.org
Owned and Operated by the Laymen's Retreat League. Rev. Dennis J.W. O'Donnell, Ph.D., Rector. Tel: 610-647-8581; Stephen Tulli, Chm.; Chuck Burgy, Ex. Dir. Offers weekend and weekday, overnight, twilight programs for men, women, students, seniors and clergy. Daily Capacity 300; Annual Retreatants over 20,000.

YARDLEY. *Providence Center*, 1750 Quarry Rd., 19067-3998. Tel: 215-968-4236; Fax: 215-968-6656.
E-mail: tmckittrick@greynun.org
Tom McKittrick, Dir. Providence Center shares space at the Grey Nuns Motherhouse. Limited overnight accomodations available. Individually directed retreats available on a limited basis. Able to provide space for Days of Prayer for groups up to 25 persons.

[DD] CAMPS

JAMISON. *Camp Neumann Conference Center*. Tel: 215-343-6552; Fax: 215-343-8849.
E-mail: campneumann@yahoo.com
Mailing Address: P.O. Box 297, 18929. Tel: 215-343-6552. Summer resident camp for boys and girls.

[EE] NEWMAN APOSTOLATE

PHILADELPHIA. *Newman Center at Drexel University*, 30 S. 33rd St., 19104-2509. Tel: 215-590-8760; Fax: 215-590-8634.
E-mail: newmanap@adphila.org
Web site: www.archdiocese-phl.org/offices/na.htm
Rev. Charles J. Brinkman, Archdiocesan Dir.
Full Time Chaplaincies:

University of Pennsylvania, Newman Hall, 3720 Chestnut St., 19104-6189. Tel: 215-898-7575; Fax: 215-386-5899.
E-mail: cpfeffer@newman.upenn.edu
Web site: www.newman.upenn.edu
Rev. Charles J. Pfeffer, Newman Chap.; Ms. Susan Harte, Asst. to the Chap.

Drexel University, Newman Center, 30 S. 33rd St., 19104-2509. Tel: 215-590-8760; Fax: 215-590-8634.
E-mail: FB@CyberPriest.com
Web site: www.drexel.edu/newmancenter
Rev. Charles J. Brinkman, Chap.

Temple University, Newman Center, 2129 N. Broad St., 19122-1193. Tel: 215-232-3779; Fax: 215-235-7302.
E-mail: gfairb01@astro.temple.edu
Web site: www.templenewmancenter.org
Rev. Gregory J. Fairbanks, Chap.; Sr. Helen Victor, S.S.J., Asst. to Chap.

West Chester University, Newman Center, 409 Trinity Dr., West Chester, 19382-5362. Tel: 610-436-0891; Fax: 610-436-6247.
E-mail: 103624.2035@compuserve.com
Web site: iws.wcupa.edu/stu/newman
Rev. Samuel A. Verruni, Chap.; Ms. Christine M. Silsby, M.A., Assoc. to Chap.

Tri-College Newman Cluster-Bryn Mawr, Haverford and Swarthmore Colleges, 219 Fayette St., Conshohocken, 19042. Tel: 610-828-0424; Fax: 610-825-5168.
E-mail: james1@swarthmore.edu
Rev. John J. James, Chap.
Part-time Chaplaincies:

Allegheny University of the Health Sciences, Hahnemann.

MCP-Hahnemann Univeristy (Center City Campus). Chaplaincy Vacant.

MCP-Hahnemann University, (East Falls Campus), St. Bridget Church, 3667 Midvale Ave., 19129-1712. Tel: 215-844-4126. Rev. Richard R. York, Chap.

Allegheny University Hospitals, Bucks County, St. John Bosco Church, 235 East County Line Rd., Hatboro, 19040-1298. Tel: 215-672-7280. Rev. Joseph D. Dougherty, Chap.

Allegheny University Hopitals, Elkins Park, St. James Church, 8320 Brookside Dr., Elkins Park, 19027. Tel: 215-635-6210. Rev. Raymond J. Himsworth, Chap.

Beaver College, St. Luke the Evangelist Church, 2316 Fairhill Ave., Glenside, 19038-4107. Tel: 215-572-0128. Rev. J. Michael Flood, Chap.

Bucks County Community College, St. Andrew Church, 81 Swamp Rd., Newtown, 18940. Tel: 215-968-2262.

Cheney University. Tel: 610-399-2353. Dr. O'dell Edward Jack, Dean, School of Education. Tel: 610-399-2353.

Community College of Philadelphia. Chaplaincy Vacant.

Delaware County Community College, St. Anastasia Church, 3301 W. Chester Pk., Newtown Square, 19073. Tel: 610-356-3303; 359-5206. Frank Mulvaney, D.C.C.C., Contact, Math/Science Dept., Delaware County Community College, Math Science Dept., Media, 19063. Tel: 610-359-5206. Rev. Leonard N. Peterson, Chap.

St. Anastasia Church, 3301 West Chester Pike, Newtown Square, 19073. Tel: 610-356-1613; 356-3303; Fax: 610-356-8332.

Delaware Valley College of Science and Agriculture, St. Jude Church, 321 W. Butler Ave., Chalfont, 18914-2329. Tel: 215-822-0179; Fax: 215-822-0638. Rev. James B. McCoy.

Harcum Junior College, Our Mother of Good Counsel, 31 Pennswood Rd., Bryn Mawr, 19010. Tel: 610-525-0147.

Harcum College. Chaplaincy Vacant.

Haverford College. Chaplaincy Vacant.

Thomas Jefferson University. Chaplaincy Vacant.

Lincoln University, Sacred Heart Church, 101 Church Rd., Oxford, 19363. Tel: 610-932-5040. Rev. John F. Hummell, Chap.

Montgomery County Community College. Chaplaincy Vacant. St. Helena Church, P.O. Box 5085, Center Square, 19422. Tel: 610-275-7711. Pennsylvania State University-Abington. Chaplaincy Vacant.

Pennsylvania State University - Ogontz Campus, Our Lady Help of Christians, 1500 Marian Rd., Abington, 19001. Tel: 215-886-3456.

Pennsylvania State University - Delaware County Campus, St. Francis de Sales Church, New Rd., Box 97, Lenni, 19062. Tel: 610-459-2203.

Pennsylvania State University-Great Valley Campus. Chaplaincy Vacant.

Philadelphia College of Pharmacy and Science, St. Francis de Sales Church, 4625 Springfield Ave., 19143. Tel: 215-222-5819.

Philadelphia College of Textiles and Science, St. Bridget Church, 3667 Midvale Ave., 19129-1712. Tel: 215-844-4126. Rev. Richard R. York.

Philadelphia University, St. Bridget Church, 3667 Midvale Ave., 19129-1712. Tel: 215-844-4126. Rev. Richard R. York.

Roxborough Memorial School of Nursing, St. John the Baptist, 146 Rector St., 19107. Tel: 215-482-4600.

Swarthmore College. Chaplaincy Vacant.

Temple University, Ambler Campus, St. Alphonsus Church, 33 Conwell Dr., Maple Glen, 19002. Tel: 215-646-4600; Fax: 215-646-0180.
Web site: www.libertynet.org/~tunewman

University of the Arts, Assoc. Dean's Office, Broad and Pine Sts., 19102. Tel: 215-875-2236.

St. John the Evangelist Church, 21 S. 13th St., 19107. Tel: 215-563-4145. Dr. Annelte DiMedio, Ph.D., Contact.

University of the Sciences in Philadelphia, Newman Center, 30 S. 33rd St., 19104-2509. Tel: 215-590-8760. Rev. Charles J. Brinkman.

Ursinus College, St. Eleanor Church, 647 Locust St., Collegeville, 19426-2541. Tel: 610-489-1647; Fax: 610-489-7469. Rev. John A. Franey, Chap.

Widener University, Blessed Katherine Drexel Church, 20th and Providence Ave., Chester, 19013-5695. Tel: 610-872-0545. Rev. Stephen D. Thorne, Chap.

[FF] MISCELLANEOUS LISTINGS

PHILADELPHIA. *Alpha House Kindergarten*, Grant and Frankford Aves., 19114. Tel: 215-632-3366. Mrs. Sara LaSalle-Tarantin, Prin. Total in Residence 123; Total Staff 7.

Apostleship of Prayer, St. Joseph's University, 5600 City Ave., 19131. Tel: 610-660-1436; 660-1400; Fax: 610-664-6640. Rev. Herbert F. Smith, S.J., Dir.

Catholic Health Care Services, 222 N. 17th St., 19103. Tel: 215-587-3663; Fax: 215-587-3773.

Catholic Heritage Center, 320 Walnut St., 19106. Tel: 215-587-4538; Fax: 215-587-3907. Mailing Address: 222 N. 17th St., 19103-1299. Rev. Msgr. Alexander J. Palmieri, J.C.L., Chm., Exec. Committee; Kathleen S. Kahlau, Project Coord. Catholic Heritage Center is a state-of-the-art, multi-purposed facility, owned and operated by the Archdiocese of Philadelphia, for the preservation and exhibition of Catholic art, history, and culture. It includes an interactive museum, a special exhibits gallery, an archival and research center, and a rooftop reception area with a commanding view of Independence Hall and its surroundings. This facility, which is located in Philadelphia's historic district, will provide visitors with an experience that is both educational and entertaining.

Catholic Kolping Society, 1285 Southampton Rd., 19115. Tel: 215-676-8977. Rev. Engelbert G. Michel, Praeses; Mrs. Catherine Pinkerton, Pres.; Mr. Alphonse Ellerkamp, Vice-Praeses; Mr. Earl Asimos, Treas.; Mr. Alex Eli, Vice Pres.

Catholic League For Persons With Disabilities, 4110 Glenview St., 19135. Tel: 215-331-2617. Board of Directors 15; Total Membership 85.

Catholics United for the Faith. (St. John Neumann Philadelphia Area Chapter), 183 Hillcrest Ave., 19118. Tel: 215-247-2585; Fax: 215-247-6335.
E-mail: annemwilson@yahoo.com
Mrs. Anne M. Wilson, Chm.

Center for Human Integration, 8400 Pine Rd., 19111. Tel: 215-742-3505; Fax: 215-742-3507.
E-mail: Connectchi@cs.com
Web site: www.centerforhumanintegration.org
Sr. Mary Em McGlone, MMS Dir. School of integrative body mind therapies, classes and client services.

The Central Association of the Miraculous Medal, 475 E. Chelten Ave., 19144-5785. Tel: 215-848-1010; Fax: 215-848-1014; 1-800-523-3674.
E-mail: wobrien@enter.net
Web site: www.tcam.org
Rev. William J. O'Brien, C.M., Dir.; Mr. Charles P. Kelly, Gen. Mgr. & Contact Person Miraculous Medal Magazine.

CORA Services, 733 Susquehanna Rd., 19111. Tel: 215-342-7660; 535-2957 (Neumann Center); Fax: 215-745-9857.
E-mail: mck71@erols.com
Anthony F. Chunn, Ph.D., CEO; Sr. Mary Charity Kohl, Founding Admin. Legal Title: *CORA Services, Inc., Philadelphia, Pennsylvania*. Services provided for children, families and teen pregnancy. Programs available: counseling, speech and language, remediation and GED. Total Assisted 30,000; Total Staff 264.

Euphrasia House, Inc., P.O. Box 44258, 19144-3016. Tel: 215-849-3371; Fax: 215-849-7708. Sr. Mary Loretta Clancy, Dir. & Contact Person. Women-in-Transition. Sponsored by the Sisters of the Good Shepherd. Residential and Outreach Services. Total Staff 8; Total in Residence 12.

Fournier Retirement Fund Corporation, Mount St. Joseph Convent, 9701 Germantown Ave., 19118-2694. Tel: 215-248-7205; Fax: 215-248-7277.
E-mail: msjc19118@aol.com
Web site: www.ssjphila.org
Sr. Eugenie Madeleine Gaddi, S.S.J., Gen. Sec. & Contact Person.

Franciscan Volunteer Ministry, Inc., P.O. Box 29276, 19125. Tel: 215-427-3070; Fax: 215-427-3059.
E-mail: fvmpd@aol.com
Web site: www.fvm89.org
Katie Sullivan, Prog. Dir. Purpose: To create and run a Franciscan lay volunteer program in the United States.

Good Shepherd Mediation Program, 5356 Chew Ave., 19138. Tel: 215-843-5413; Fax: 215-843-2080.
E-mail: shepherd@libertynet.org
Web site: www.libertynet/~shepherd/
Cheryl Cutrona, Exec. Dir. Legal Title: *Good Shepherd Corporation, Philadelphia, Pennsylvania*.

IHM Center for Literacy and GED Programs, 425 W. Lindley Ave., 19120. Tel: 215-457-2232; Fax: 215-457-5209.
E-mail: ihmcenter@dca.net
Sr. M. Anne Smith, I.H.M., M.A., Dir., 929 S.

Farragut St., 19143. Tel: 215-382-0292; Fax: 215-726-4811. Full-time program with courses in Adult Basic Education (ABE); English for Speakers of Other Languages (ESOL) and General Educational Development (GED).

Katherine Kiernan Chateau, Inc., c/o Catholic Social Services, 222 N. 17th St., Ste. 300, 19103. Tel: 215-587-3903; Fax: 215-587-2479.
E-mail: chumsrv@adphila.org
Web site: www.archdiocese-phl.org

Ladies of Charity, 227 N. 18th St., 19103. Tel: 215-854-7025. His Eminence Anthony J. Bevilacqua, D.D., M.A., J.C.D., J.D.; Rev. Msgr. Timothy C. Senior, M.B.A., M.S.W., M.A.; Rev. Msgr. James T. McDonough, A.C.S.W., Moderator; Mrs. Dominick Lazanski, Pres. Emeritus; Miss Marie E. Bergmaier, Pres. Purpose is to provide volunteer services for hopitals, nursing homes and home-bound individuals.

Missionary Cenacle Apostolate, 3501 Solly Ave, 19136. Tel: 215-708-8225; Fax: 215-708-8226.
E-mail: josiemorales@juno.com
Web site: www.mcenacle.org/mca/mca.htm
Mrs. Josie Morales, Gen. Custodian, 1602 E. Helmick St., Carson, CA, 90746. Tel: 310-632-0641; Fax: 310-258-4096. The MCA is a branch of the Missionary Cenacle Family. Lay people called to be missionaries in the Church in the providence of everyday life. MCA members live and work in the United States, Mexico, Puerto Rico and Colombia.

National Communicators Network for Women Religious, 360 Longshore Ave., 19111. Tel: 215-725-4239.
E-mail: AMckenzie115@aol.com
Web site: www.ncnwr.org
Audrey K. McKenzie, Contact Person. Sponsor: Communication personnel of congregations of Women Religious who are members. NCNWR is organized to promote and assist in the understanding of women religious and specifically to enhance their image and advance their mission. The organization is also provides a network of professional support and education for its members.

St. Agnes Foundation, 1900 S. Broad St., 19145. Tel: 215-339-4225. James M. Wilson, Pres.

St. Vincent's Orphan Asylum-St. Vincent's Comprehensive Emergency Shelter Program, 7201 Milnor St., 19135. Tel: 215-MA4-5600; Fax: 215-624-8355. Rev. Eduardo G. Montero, J.C.L. Beds 48; Total Assisted 475; Total Staff 105.

Society of Catholic Medical Missionaries Generalate, Inc. (Effective 1991), 8400 Pine Rd., 19111. Tel: 215-742-6100; Fax: 215-342-3948.
E-mail: medmisisters@gn.apc.org
Web site: www.medicalmissionsisters.org
Sr. Clarita Hackman, M.M.S., Contact Person; Sr. Elizabeth Koothanam, M.M.S., Pres. Corporation collects funds for charitable and missionary work, for Medical Mission Sisters; Assists in operation of hospitals, clinics and primary health care programs; Assists in care of poor, sick and infirm, in U.S. and overseas; Assists in training and educating men and women in medicine and nursing, and other health professions; Trains candidates for the Community; Provides assisted living care to sick and elder Medical Mission Sisters.

Society of St. Vincent de Paul of Philadelphia, 901 E. Luzerne St., 19124. Tel: 215-288-9540; Fax: 215-288-9540.
E-mail: SVDpphila@cs.com
Most Rev. Robert P. Maginnis, D.D., Spiritual Advisor; Albert P. Federico, Jr., Pres.; Carey G. Roberts, Exec. Dir.; Robert Lanzilotta, Gen Mgr. Catholic Lay Organization serving those in need with spiritual, moral, material and financial support regardless of race, creed, etc.

The Warner Perpetual Trust for the Benefit of Catholic Charities, Provident National Bank, P.O. Box 7648, 19101. Tel: 610-585-5698; Fax: 610-358-4275. Legal Title: *The Warner Perpetual Trust for the Benefit of Catholic Charities of the Archdiocese of Philadelphia.*
(The "Perpetual" Trust).

ASTON. *Franciscan Ministries Foundation, Inc.*, 609 S. Convent Rd., 19014. Tel: 610-558-7713; Fax: 610-558-5357.
E-mail: mmayer@osfphila.org
Web site: www.osfphila.org
Sr. Eileen Valerie, Contact. Tel: 610-558-7701; Sr. Madonna Marie Cunningham, O.S.F., Acting Dir. Purpose: Raises funds to fulfill the needs of the Ministries and Retired Sisters of the Sisters of St. Francis of Philadelphia.

Sisters of St. Francis of Philadelphia, Charitable Trust I and Charitable Trust II, Our Lady of Angels Convent, 19014. Tel: 610-558-6794; Fax: 610-459-0195.
E-mail: mlucey@osfphila.org
Web site: www.osfphila.org
Sr. Marie Lucey, O.S.F., Congregational Minister.

CONSHOHOCKEN. *Mercy Health System of Southeastern PA*, One West Elm St., 19428. Tel: 610-567-6106; Fax: 610-567-6150.
Web site: www.mercyhealth.org
Sr. Mary Christine McCann, R.S.M., Chm. Bd.; Mark T. O'Neil, Jr., Pres. & CEO. Holding Company for diversified health care subsidiaries including Mercy Fitzgerald Hospital, Mercy Hospital of Philadelphia, Mercy Community Hospital, Mercy Suburban Hospital, Mercy Eastwick, Mercy Home Health Services. Mercy Health System operates Mercy Court, a 100-unit apartment building for independent, low-income elderly adults.

FLOURTOWN. *Saint Joseph Guild*, Stenton and Wissahickon Aves., P.O. Box 36, 19031-0036. Tel: 215-248-7838; Fax: 215-248-7802.
E-mail: sjguild19@aol.com
Sr. Ann Marguerite, S.S.J., Dir.

FORT WASHINGTON. *John Paul II Foundation for Peace, Justice & Human Rights*, The Copernicus House, P.O. Box 267, 19034. Tel: 215-646-4101.

HUNTINGDON VALLEY.

Holy Redeemer Health System, 667 Welsh Rd., 19006. Tel: 215-938-4650; Fax: 215-938-4671.
Web site: www.holyredeemer.com
Mailing Address: Marketing/Public Affairs Department, c/o 1602 Huntingdon Pike, Meadowbrook, 19046. Sponsor: Sisters of the Holy Redeemer, C.S.R. Michael B. Laign, Pres. & CEO. Parent organization which maintains, manages, and operates the health care system composed of the various corporations sponsored and established by the Sisters of the Holy Redeemer, C.S.R. as follows: Drueding Center; Holy Redeemer Home Health and Hospice Services; Holy Redeemer Health Care Corporation and Foundation; HRH Management Corp.; Holy Redeemer Visiting Nurse Agency (NJ); Holy Redeemer Managed Care Org.; HR Physician Services; Holy Redeemer Hosp. & Med. Ctr.; Redeemer Med. Supply Co.

Holy Redeemer Hospital and Medical Center. Tel: 215-947-3000.

Redeemer Center.

St. Joseph's Manor. Tel: 215-938-4000.

The Lafayette - Redeemer. Tel: 215-214-2877. Benjamin Pieczynski, Div. Oper. Officer.

Holy Redeemer Foundation. Tel: 215-914-4000.

Holy Redeemer Home Health and Hospice Services. Tel: 215-671-9200.

Holy Redeemer Transitional Care Unit.

Holy Redeemer Multicare.

Holy Redeemer Visiting Nurse Agency. Tel: 609-465-2082.

Holy Redeemer Hospice. Tel: 215-671-9200.

Redeemer Village - Redeemer Village II. Tel: 215-947-8168.

Drueding Center/Project Rainbow. Tel: 215-769-1830.

HRH Management Corporation.

HR Physician Services (aka Holy Redeemer Physician and Ambulatory Services). Tel: 215-938-4600.

Holy Redeemer Managed Care Organization. Tel: 215-938-4600.

IMMACULATA. *Enserv Inc.*, King Rd., 19345. Tel: 610-647-4400, Ext. 3147; Fax: 610-251-1668.

KING OF PRUSSIA. *Bernardine Franciscan Sisters Mission and Ministries Charitable Trust*, 403 Allendale Rd., 19406. Tel: 610-337-3864; Fax: 610-337-4359.
E-mail: bfgeneralate@aol.com
Web site: www.bfranciscan.org
Sr. Madonna Marie Harvath, Contact Person.

Bernardine Franciscans, Delaware County, 403 Allendale Rd., 19406. Tel: 610-337-3864; Fax: 610-337-4359.
E-mail: bfgeneralate@aol.com
Web site: www.bfranciscan.org
Bernadine Center, 2625 W. Ninth St., Chester, 19013. Sr. Madonna Marie Harvath, Contact Person. Total Staff 12; Total Assisted 7,914.

MEADOWBROOK.

Holy Redeemer Physician and Ambulatory Services, 1602 Huntington Pike, 2nd Floor, 19046. Tel: 215-938-4600; Fax: 215-938-4610.
Web site: www.holyredeemer.com
Subsidiary of Holy Redeemer Health System. Sponsor: Sisters of the Holy Redeemer C.S.R. Michele Urofsky, Sr. Vice Pres. Nonprofit corporation formed to establish, operate and maintain family health clinics and practices, laboratories, dispensaries, buildings, and facilities relating to these purposes, and provide the services of physicians and other health care professionals in connection with the provision of health care services at Holy Redeemer Hospital and Medical Center, and other hospitals, clinics and health care facilities.

MERION. *Greaton Properties, Inc.*, 701 City Line Ave., 19066. Tel: 610-660-1321. Mr. Timothy W. Joyce, Pres.

NEWTOWN SQUARE. *Catholic Health East*, 14 Campus Blvd., Ste. 300, 19073-3277. Tel: 610-355-2004; Fax: 610-355-2050.
E-mail: sfoti@che.org
Web site: che.org
Mr. Daniel F. Russell, Pres. & CEO.

Eastern Mercy Health System, 14 Campus Blvd., Ste. 300, 19087. Tel: 610-355-2000; Fax: 610-355-2050. Deacon Joel Ziff, Pres. & CEO. Eastern Mercy Health System is a multi-institutional Catholic health system sponsored by nine Regional Communities of the Sisters of Mercy of the Americas and the Franciscan Sisters of St. Joseph (Hamburg, NY). Founded in 1986 for the purpose of preserving and strengthening the Catholic health ministry. Eastern Mercy provides programs, services, and expertise, which enhance the sponsorship, stewardship and strategic positioning of participating health care organizations.

YEADON. *Mercy Court*, 550 S. Lansdowne Ave., 19050. Tel: 610-623-3083; Fax: 640-259-1414.
E-mail: mercycourt@rcm.com
Sisters of Mercy. Sr. Mary Carmela, R.S.M., Prog. Mgr. Low income apartments for independent living for older adults. Total Apartments 100; Total Staff 5.

RELIGIOUS INSTITUTES OF MEN REPRESENTED IN THE ARCHDIOCESE

For further details refer to the corresponding bracketed number in the Religious Institutes of Men or Women section.

[0140]—*The Augustinians*(Provs. of St. Thomas Villanova & Our Mother of Good Counsel).—O.S.A.
[0290]—*Brothers of Charity*.—F.C.
[0330]—*Brothers of the Christian Schools*. (Baltimore Prov.).—F.S.C.
[]—*Brothers of the Holy Spirit*.—B.H.S.
[0900]—*Canons Regular of Premontre*.—O.Praem.
[0470]—*Capuchin Friars*.—O.F.M.Cap.
[0275]—*Carmelites of Mary Immaculate*.—C.M.I.
[0860]—*Congregation of the Immaculate Heart of Mary (Missionhurst)*.—C.I.C.M.
[1330]—*Congregation of the Mission*. (Eastern Prov.).—C.M.
[1000]—*Congregation of the Passion*.—C.P.
[0650]—*Holy Ghost Fathers*. (Eastern Prov.).—C.S.Sp.
[]—*Institute of the Incarnate Word*.—V.E.
[0800]—*Maryknoll Fathers and Brothers*.—M.M.
[0850]—*Missionaries of Africa*.—M.Afr.
[0825]—*Missionaries of the Blessed Sacrament*.—M.S.S.
[1110]—*Missionaries of the Sacred Heart*. (American Prov.).—M.S.C.
[0840]—*Missionary Servants of the Most Holy Trinity*.—S.T.
[0920]—*Oblates of St. Francis de Sales*.—O.S.F.S.
[0520]—*Order of Friars Minor*. (Assumption B.V.M. & Most Holy Name Provs.).—O.F.M.
[0480]—*Order of Friars Minor, Conventual*.—O.F.M.Conv.
[0970]—*Order of Our Lady of Mercy*.—O.deM.
[1310]—*Order of the Holy Trinity*.—O.SS.T.
[1010]—*Pauline Fathers*.—O.S.P.P.E.
[0950]—*The Philadelphia Congregation of the Oratory of Saint Philip Neri*.—C.O.
[1040]—*Piarist Fathers*.—Sch.P.
[1070]—*Redemptorist Fathers*. (Baltimore Prov.).—C.SS.R.
[1220]—*Servants of Charity*.—S.C.
[0690]—*Society of Jesus (Jesuits)*. (Maryland Prov.).—S.J.
[0760]—*Society of Mary (Marianists)*.—S.M.
[0780]—*Society of Mary (Marists)*.—S.M.
[0700]—*Society of St. Joseph of the Sacred Heart*.—S.S.J.
[0560]—*Third Order Regular of Saint Francis*. (Prov. of the Most Sacred Heart).—T.O.R.

RELIGIOUS INSTITUTES OF WOMEN REPRESENTED IN THE ARCHDIOCESE

[1070-13]—*Adrian Dominican Sisters*.
[]—*Armenian Sisters of the Immaculate Conception*.—C.I.C.
[1810]—*Bernardine Sisters of the Third Order of St. Francis*.—O.S.F.
[0330]—*Carmelite Sisters for the Aged and Infirm*.—O.Carm.
[0690]—*Comboni Missionary Sisters*.—C.M.S.
[0270]—*Congregation of Bon Secours*.—C.B.S.
[2250]—*Congregation of the Benedictines of Jesus Crucified*.—O.S.B.
[]—*Contemplative Sister of the Good Shepherd*.—C.G.S.
[0760]—*Daughters of Charity of St. Vincent de Paul*.—D.C.

[0900]—*Daughters of Our Lady of the Sacred Heart.*—F.D.N.S.C.
[0940]—*Daughters of St. Mary of Providence.*—D.S.M.P.
[0810]—*Daughters of the Heart of Mary.*—D.H.M.
[0420]—*Discalced Carmelite Nuns.*—O.C.D.
[1070-17]—*Dominican Sisters.*—O.P.
[1070-23]—*Dominican Sisters.*—O.P.
[1105]—*Dominican Sisters of Hope.*—O.P.
[]—*Dominican Sisters of Our Lady of the Rosary.*—O.P.
[]—*Dominican Sisters of St. Catherine de Ricci.* (Elkins Park, PA).—O.P.
[1170]—*Felician Sisters.*—C.S.S.F.
[1180]—*Franciscan Sisters of Alleghany, New York.*—O.S.F.
[1840]—*Grey Nuns of the Sacred Heart.*—G.N.S.H.
[1870]—*Handmaids of the Sacred Heart of Jesus.*—A.C.J.
[]—*Little Servants of the Holy Family of Seoul.*—L.S.H.F.
[2300]—*Little Servants Sisters of the Immaculate Conception.*—L.S.I.C.
[2310]—*Little Sisters of the Assumption.*—L.S.A.
[2340]—*Little Sisters of the Poor.*—L.S.P.
[2345]—*Little Workers of the Sacred Hearts.*—P.O.S.C.
[2490]—*Medical Mission Sisters.*—M.M.S.
[2710]—*Missionaries of Charity.*—M.C.
[1360]—*Missionary Franciscan Sisters of the Immaculate Conception.*—M.F.I.C.
[2790]—*Missionary Servants of the Most Blessed Trinity.*—M.S.B.T.
[2730]—*Missionary Sisters of the Holy Rosary.*—M.S.H.R.
[2800]—*Missionary Sisters of the Most Sacred Heart of Jesus of Hiltrup.*—M.S.C.
[2860]—*Missionary Sisters of the Sacred Heart.* (Eastern Prov.).—M.S.C.
[3060]—*Oblates Sisters of St. Francis de Sales.*—O.S.F.S.
[3730]—*Order of St. Basil the Great.*—O.S.B.M.
[3760]—*Order of St. Clare.*—O.S.C.
[1705]—*Order of St. Francis of Assisi.*—O.S.F.
[0950]—*Pious Society Daughters of St. Paul.*—F.S.P.
[3640]—*Poor Servants of the Mother of God.*—S.M.G.
[3390]—*Religious of the Assumption.*—R.A.
[3430]—*Religious Teachers Filippini.*—M.P.F.
[2970]—*School Sisters of Notre Dame.*—S.S.N.D.
[1700]—*School Sisters of St. Francis.*—O.S.F.
[]—*Servants of the Lord and of the Virgin of Matara.*—S.S.V.M.
[3540]—*Sister Servants of the Holy Spirit of Perpetual Adoration.*—S.Sp.S.deA.P.
[2160]—*Sister Servants of the Immaculate Heart of Mary.* (Scanton).—I.H.M.
[3630]—*Sister Servants of the Most Sacred Heart of Jesus.*—S.S.C.J.
[0500]—*Sisters of Charity of Nazareth.*—S.C.N.
[0660]—*Sisters of Christian Charity.*—S.C.C.
[2575]—*Sisters of Mercy of the Americas, Merion, PA.*—R.S.M. [0820]—*Daughters of the Holy Spirit.*—D.H.S.
[3000]—*Sisters of Notre Dame de Namur.*—S.N.D.deN.
[2670]—*Sisters of Our Lady of Mercy.*—S.O.L.M.
[3893]—*Sisters of Saint Joseph of Chestnut Hill, Philadelphia.*—S.S.J.
[3740]—*Sisters of St. Casimir.*—S.S.C.
[1650]—*Sisters of St. Francis of Philadelphia.*—O.S.F.
[0260]—*Sisters of the Blessed Sacrament for Indians and Colored People.*—S.B.S.
[0970]—*Sisters of the Divine Compassion.*—R.D.C.
[1020]—*Sisters of the Divine Redeemer.*—S.D.R.
[1830]—*Sisters of the Good Shepherd.*—R.G.S.
[1970]—*Sisters of the Holy Family of Nazareth.*—C.S.F.N.
[2000]—*Sisters of the Holy Redeemer.*—C.S.R.
[2060]—*Sisters of the Most Holy Trinity.*—O.SS.T.
[2170]—*Sisters, Servants of the Immaculate Heart of Mary (Immaculta).*—I.H.M.
[4060]—*Society of the Holy Child Jesus.*—S.H.C.J.
[4120]—*Ursuline Sisters of the Immaculate Conception.*—O.S.U.
[4190]—*Visitation Nuns.*—V.H.M.

ARCHDIOCESAN CEMETERIES

PHILADELPHIA. *Cathedral*, 48th St. and Lancaster Ave., 19131. Tel: 215-477-8918.
Holy Sepulchre, Cheltenham Ave. & Ivy Hill Rd., 19150. Tel: 215-247-0691.
New Cathedral, 2nd & Butler Sts., 19140. Tel: 215-634-3212.
BENSALEM. *Resurrection*, 5201 Hulmeville Rd., 19020. Tel: 215-639-0965.
CHALFONT. *St. John Neumann*, 3797 County Line Rd., 18914. Tel: 215-822-0680.
NEWTOWN. *All Saints*, R.R. 413, Twining Bridge Rd., 18940.
SPRINGFIELD. *SS. Peter and Paul*, 1600 S. Sproul Rd., 19064. Tel: 610-544-4933.
WEST BRANDYWINE TWP. *All Souls*, R.R. 322, 19343.
WEST CONSHOHOCKEN. *Calvary*, Gulph & Matsonford Rd., 19428. Tel: 610-525-2214.
WEST GROVE. *Holy Saviour* Penn Township.
YEADON. *Holy Cross*, 626 Bailey Rd., 19050. Tel: 610-626-2206; 215-476-3656.

NECROLOGY

✠ Graham, Most Rev. John J., Retired Auxiliary Bishop. —Died Aug. 4, 2000.
† Bartos, Rev. Msgr. John V, Sellersville, PA St. Agnes. —Died Sept. 9, 2000.
† Bones, James J, Levittown, PA Immaculate Conception. —Died March 18, 2000.
† Brennan, Robert E, Norristown, PA St. Titus. —Died July 11, 2000.
† Calpin, Thomas J., Pastor Emeritus, Morrisville, PA Holy Trinity. —Died Jan. 6, 2000.
† Chapman, A. James, Pastor Emeritus, Philadelphia, PA St. Irenaeus. —Died Feb. 23, 2000.
† Gough, James F., (Retired). —Died Jan. 10, 2000.
† Henry, Joseph A., Pastor Emeritus, Riegelsville, PA St. Lawrence. —Died Dec. 7, 1999.
† Lazzaro, NIcholas A., Pastor Emeritus, Conshohocken, PA SS. Cosmas/Damian. —Died Nov. 15, 1999.
† Marszalek, Francis G, King of Prussia, PA Mother of Divine Providence. —Died Jan. 3, 2000.
† Matsko, John M., Pastor Emeritus, Bridgeport, PA Our Mother of Sorrows. —Died Dec. 31, 1999.
† McCaffrey, Gerard D., (Retired). —Died March 9, 2000.
† McDermott, Francis A., Pastor Emeritus, Philadelphia, PA Assumption B.V.M. —Died Sept. 9, 2000.
† Mullen, L. James, Chap, Philadelphia, PA St. John Neumann Nursing Home. —Died June 2, 2000.
† Murphy, James F., (Retired). —Died Oct. 19, 2000.
† Reynolds, Ignatius C., Pastor Emeritus, Gladwyne, PA St. John Baptist Vianney. —Died Aug. 6, 2000.
† Smith, Martin G., (Retired). —Died Dec. 22, 1999.
† Spaits, George S., (Retired). —Died March 29, 2000.
† St. Clair, Joseph A., Pastor Emeritus, Ardmore, PA St. Colman. —Died March 9, 2000.
† Stevenson, Rev. Msgr. Frederick J., Pastor Emeritus, Wallingford, PA St. John Chrysostom. —Died Feb. 13, 2000.

Diocese of Phoenix

(Dioecesis Phoenicensis)

Most Reverend

THOMAS J. O'BRIEN, D.D.

Bishop of Phoenix; ordained May 7, 1961; consecrated January 6, 1982; installed January 18, 1982. *Res., 48 E. Wagon Wheel Dr., Phoenix, AZ, 85020. All correspondence to be sent to: 400 E. Monroe, Phoenix, AZ, 85004-2376.*

Diocesan Office: 400 E. Monroe, Phoenix, AZ, 85004-2376. Tel.: 602-257-0030; Fax: 602-256-1340.

Web site address: www.catholicsun.org

E-mail address: tbow@cathdioc.org

ESTABLISHED DECEMBER 2, 1969.

Square Miles 43,967.

Comprises the Counties of Maricopa; Mohave; Yavapai & Coconino not to include the territorial boundaries of the Navajo Indian Reservation; Pinal—that portion of land known as the Gila River Indian Reservation in the State of Arizona.

Patroness of Diocese: Our Lady of Guadalupe.

For legal titles of parishes and diocesan institutions, consult the Chancery Office.

STATISTICAL OVERVIEW

Personnel	
Retired Archbishops	1
Bishop	1
Retired Bishops	1
Priests: Diocesan Active in Diocese	102
Priests: Active Outside Diocese	2
Priests: Retired, Sick or Absent	28
Number of Diocesan Priests	132
Religious Priests in Diocese	98
Extern Priests in Diocese	67
Ordinations:	
Diocesan Priests	5
Transitional Deacons	3
Permanent Deacons	20
Permanent Deacons in Diocese	207
Total Brothers	9
Total Sisters	233
Parishes	
Parishes	87
With Resident Pastor:	
Resident Diocesan Priests	61
Resident Religious Priests	19
Without Resident Pastor:	
Administered by Deacons	5
Completely Vacant	1
Missions	27
New Parishes Created	1
Professional Ministry Personnel:	
Brothers	8
Sisters	194
Lay Ministers	416
Welfare	
Catholic Hospitals	1
Total Assisted	415,019
Health Care Centers	1
Total Assisted	97,000
Homes for the Aged	11
Total Assisted	723
Day Care and Extended Day Care Centers	27
Total Assisted	1,012
Specialized Homes	8
Total Assisted	615
Special Centers for Social Services	10
Total Assisted	2,128,679
Residential Care of Disabled	1
Total Assisted	27
Educational	
Diocesan Students in Other Seminaries	27
Total Seminarians	27
High Schools, Diocesan and Parish	4
Total Students	2,868
High Schools, Private	1
Total Students	1,196
Elementary Schools, Diocesan and Parish	25
Total Students	8,087
Catechesis/Religious Education:	
High School Students	6,727
Elementary Students	34,185
Total Students Under Catholic Instruction	53,090
Teachers in the Diocese:	
Priests	13
Scholastics	3
Brothers	1
Sisters	43
Lay Teachers	619
Vital Statistics	
Receptions into the Church:	
Infant Baptism Totals	10,838
Adult Baptism Totals	563
Received into Full Communion	1,033
First Communions	8,143
Confirmations	4,118
Marriages:	
Catholic	1,353
Interfaith	526
Total Marriages	1,879
Deaths	3,609
Total Catholic Population	462,780
Total Population	3,335,125

Former Bishops—Most Rev. EDWARD A. MCCARTHY, D.D., installed Bishop of the Diocese of Phoenix, Dec. 2, 1969; transferred Coadjutor Archbishop of Miami, July 7, 1976; installed Sept. 17, 1976.—Most Rev. JAMES S. RAUSCH, D.D., Ph.D., installed March 22, 1977; died May 18, 1981.

Vicar General—Rev. Msgr. RICHARD MOYER, V.G., *Diocesan Center.* Tel: 602-257-0030., *Our Lady of Joy, P.O. Box 1359, Carefree, 85377.* Tel: 602-488-2229. Rev. DALE FUSHEK, V.G., *St. Timothy, 1730 W. Guadalupe Rd., Mesa, 85202-7424.* Tel: 480-775-5200.

Diocesan Office—400 E. Monroe, Phoenix, 85004. Tel: 602-257-0030; Fax: 602-257-5645.

Chancellor—Sr. MARY ANN WINTERS, S.C., *400 E. Monroe, Phoenix, 85004.* Tel: 602-257-0030; Fax: 602-257-5645.

Assistant Chancellor—Rev. MICHAEL L. DISKIN, *400 E. Monroe, Phoenix, 85004.* Tel: 602-257-0030; Fax: 602-257-5645.

College of Consultors—Rev. Msgr. RICHARD W. MOYER, V.G.; Revs. ALAN MALONE, J.V.; DALE FUSHEK, V.G.; ROBERT SKAGEN; CHARLES KIEFFER; NATHAN CASTLE, O.P.; DOUGLAS LORIG; MICHAEL STRALEY.

Finance and Administration—Rev. Msgr. RICHARD MOYER, Vicar; Deacon RONALD D. HENDERSON, Dir., *400 E. Monroe, Phoenix, 85004.* Tel: 602-257-5594; Fax: 602-258-3425.

Vicars Forane—Revs. FRANK FERNANDEZ, V.F.; MICHAEL O'GRADY; ROBERT SKAGEN; CHARLES GORAIEB, V.F.; MICHAEL STRALEY; MICHAEL DEPTULA; CHRIS COX, C.S.C.; DOUGLAS LORIG; BLASE MEYER; FRANK BARTEL; ROBERT CLEMENTS; JOHN SHETLER.

Diocesan Tribunal—Office: *400 E. Monroe, Phoenix, 85004.* Tel: 602-257-5585; Fax: 602-257-5646.

Judicial Vicar—Rev. ALAN MALONE.

Adjutant Judicial Vicars—Revs. PHILIP ACQUARO, C.S.B., J.C.L.; TIMOTHY R. DAVERN, J.C.L.; PAUL OREL, J.C.L.

Diocesan Judges—Revs. PHILIP ACQUARO, C.S.B., J.C.L.; TIMOTHY R. DAVERN, J.C.L.; ALAN MALONE; PAUL OREL, J.C.L.; Deacon DOUGLAS LECLAIR, J.C.L.

Defenders of the Bond—Revs. PETER DOBROWSKI; CHARLES G. KIEFFER; FRANK P. SIMLIK; Sr. FRANCES WETZEL, O.P.

Advocates—Rev. MICHAEL L. DISKIN; Deacon PAUL HURSH; Sr. MARY DELBERT WEISENSEL, S.S.N.D.; Sr. RUTH KARNITZ, S.S.N.D.; Mrs. SANDRA CONSIGLIO.

Auditors—Sr. RUTH KARNITZ, S.S.N.D.; Sr. MARY DELBERT WEISENSEL, S.S.N.D.; Deacon PAUL HURSH.

Notaries—Sr. M. ANTHONY POERIO, I.B.V.M.; Ms. DOROTHY DALTON; Mrs. JUSTINA SANCHEZ; Ms. BECKY CRUZ; Mrs. WALDA SWEENEY.

Appellate Court Administrator-Diocese of Phoenix—Mrs. MAUREEN HAMILTON.

Presbyteral Council—Most Rev. THOMAS J. O'BRIEN, D.D.; Rev. Msgr. RICHARD W. MOYER, V.G.; Revs. MICHAEL O'GRADY; ROBERT SKAGEN; MICHAEL DEPTULA; NATHAN CASTLE, O.P.; ROBERT CLEMENTS; DAVID COONEY, S.D.S.; DALE FUSHEK, V.G.; GREG MENEGAY; BLASE MEYER; MICHAEL J. STRALEY; THOMAS ZURCHER; TIMOTHY CONLON, O.S.C.; CHRIS COX, C.S.C.; DOUGLAS LORIG; JOHN SHETLER; JOHN HALL; MICHAEL DISKIN, Asst. Chancellor; FRANK FERNANDEZ, V.F.; CHARLES GORAIEB, V.F.; CHARLES KIEFFER; ALAN MALONE, J.V.; Sr. MARY ANN WINTERS, Chancellor.

Diocesan Pastoral Council—Most Rev. THOMAS J. O'BRIEN, D.D.; Rev. Msgr. RICHARD W. MOYER, V.G.; Revs. MICHAEL L. DISKIN; PAUL OREL; PATRICK ROBINSON; Bro. RICHARD ARMSTRONG, C.S.C.; Sr. MARY ANN WINTERS, S.C., Chancellor; WILLIAM DOOLEY, M.D.; JULIA GARCIA; SYLVIA LOPEZ, Chm. HARVEY LESAN; MEGAN O'CONNOR; ARMIDA MEDINA; GLORIA COLLINS; KEVIN MCCARTHY; Sr. NANCY PERLICK, R.S.M.; MICHAEL SILLS-TRAUSCH; ART STINE;

MARVIN VENS; MANUEL MONTOYA; Sr. PATRICIA C. SMITH, O.P.; Rev. DALE FUSHEK, V.G.; THOMAS NASH; MARY V. THOMAS, Exec. Sec.

Arizona Catholic Conference—Rev. Msgr. EDWARD RYLE, M.S.W., Exec. Dir., *400 E. Monroe, Phoenix, 85004.* Tel: 602-257-0030; Fax: 602-257-5540.

Buildings & Property—JOHN MINIERI, Dir. JOSEPH GALANO, Assoc. Dir., *Diocesan Center, 400 E. Monroe, Phoenix, 85004.* Tel: 602-257-0030; Fax: 602-462-5207. Rev. LARRY WEIDNER, Vicar, *4633 N. 54th St., Phoenix, 85018.* Tel: 602-840-5066.

Catholic Community Foundation—Most Rev. THOMAS J. O'BRIEN, D.D., Pres. JOHN SCOLA, C.F.R.E., Exec. Dir., *400 E. Monroe, Phoenix, 85004.* Tel: 602-257-5640; Fax: 602-256-1356.

Catholic Cemeteries—Rev. MICHAEL L. DISKIN, Spiritual Advisor; GARY L. BROWN, Exec. Dir. St. Francis, Holy Cross, Holy Redeemer and Queen of Heaven. Office: *2033 N. 48th St., Phoenix, 85008.* Tel: 602-267-1329; Fax: 602-267-7942., Calvary Cemetery: *201 W. University, Flagstaff, 86001.* Tel: 520-774-9125.

"The Catholic Sun"—(Diocesan Newspaper); Mr. CHRISTOPHER GUNTY, Assoc. Publisher, *400 E. Monroe, Phoenix, 85004.* Tel: 602-257-0030; 257-5565; Fax: 602-258-6404.

Communications—MARGE INJASOULIAN, Dir., *400 E. Monroe, Phoenix, 85004.* Tel: 602-257-0030; Fax: 602-257-5645.

Information Systems—KIM BRISWALTER, Dir., *400 E. Monroe, Phoenix, 85004.* Tel: 602-257-5598; Fax: 602-257-5561.

Stewardship Office—(Charity & Development Appeal); BILL SCHWANEKAMP, Dir., *400 E. Monroe St., Phoenix, 85004.* Tel: 602-257-5573; Fax: 602-256-1356. (Endowments/Planned Giving); JOHN SCOLA, Exec Dir., *400 E. Monroe St., Phoenix, 85004.* Tel: 602-257-5640. JIM CRUTHOFF, Assoc. Dir. Tel: 602-257-5641.

Ecumenical and Interreligious Affairs—Rev. MICHAEL L. DISKIN, Dir., *400 E. Monroe, Phoenix, 85004.* Tel: 602-257-0030; Fax: 602-257-5645.

Vicariate of Christian Formation and Education—Sr. DOLORETTE FARIAS, S.S.N.D., Exec. Dir., *400 E. Monroe, Phoenix, 85004.* Tel: 602-257-0030; Fax: 602-462-5207.

Diaconate Ministry—Deacon DANIEL PETERSON, Dir., *400 E. Monroe, Phoenix, 85004.* Tel: 602-257-0030; Fax: 602-257-5540. JAMES E. FOGLE, Asst. to Dir. Tel: 623-465-0602. CHARLES VAN DYKE, Asst. in Formation. Tel: 480-951-8711. Deacon BUDDY CLAPHAM, Assoc. Dir. of Formation.

Vocations—Rev. DONALD KLINE, Dir., *400 E. Monroe, Phoenix, 85004.* Tel: 602-257-0030; Fax: 602-257-5540.

Office of Worship—Rev. SCOTT BRUBAKER, Vicar; Sr. MARY ANTHONY POERIO, I.B.V.M., Dir., *400 E. Monroe, Phoenix, 85004.* Tel: 602-257-0030; Fax: 602-462-5207.

Schools—MARYBETH MUELLER, Supt. Schools; MARY CATHERINE KEATING, Asst. Supt. JOANNE JOHNSON, Coord. Instructional Svcs., *400 E. Monroe, Phoenix, 85004.* Tel: 602-257-0030; Fax: 602-462-5207.

Catechetical Ministry—Deacon JOHN MEYER, Dir. CAROL GASTELUM, Assoc. Dir. STACY FILEWICZ-ROSS, Assoc. Dir., *400 E. Monroe, Phoenix, 85004.* Tel: 602-257-0030; Fax: 602-462-5207.

Youth-Young Adult Campus Ministry—LARRY FRAHER, Dir. BARBARA STANLEY, Asst. Dir., *400 E. Monroe, Phoenix, 85004.* Tel: 602-257-5559; Fax: 602-462-5207.

The Catholic Scouting Program—Rev. DENNIS O'ROURKE, Liaison, *St. Benedict, 6400 W. Del Rio St., Chandler, 85226.* Tel: 602-961-1610; Fax: 602-961-1794.

Family Life Office—RICHARD BERGKESSEL, Dir., *400 E. Monroe, Phoenix, 85004.* Tel: 602-257-0030; Fax: 602-462-5207.

Life Issues—JUDY GIFFORD, Coord., *400 E. Monroe, Phoenix, 85004.* Tel: 602-257-0030; Fax: 602-462-5207.

Mount Claret Center—Directors: Rev. Msgr. JOHN J. McMAHON; Rev. EUGENE MAGUIRE; Ms. JO SWIGER, Asst. Dir.; Sr. REGINA MARIE BOSLET, S.C., Asst. Dir. Cursillo Movement: Revs. Msgr. JOHN J. McMAHON, Spiritual Dir.; Sr. JANICE BOHN, S.N.D-.deN., Assoc. Spiritual Dir., *4633 N. 54th St., Phoenix, 85018.* Tel: 602-840-5066; Fax: 602-840-5732.

Office of Disability Ministry—ISABELLA RICE, Dir., *400 E. Monroe, Phoenix, 85004.* Tel: 602-257-5558; 602-744-6314 (TTY); Fax: 602-462-5207.

Native American Ministry Office—Rev. JOHN J. HALL, Vicar; Sr. ANNE FISCHER, S.S.N.D., Dir.; Sr. ROSE MARIE DEIBEL, S.N.D., Assoc. Dir. Tel: 602-810-0471., *400 E. Monroe, Phoenix, 85004.* Tel: 602-257-0030; Fax: 602-462-5207.

Native American Ministry - Field Office—Sr. ANNE FISCHER, S.S.N.D., Dir., *120 Church St., P.O. Box 545, Sacaton, 85247.* Tel: 520-562-3716.

Diocesan Office of Social Ministry—Mr. GUY MIKKELSEN, *77 E. Thomas Rd., Ste. 100, Phoenix, 85012.* Tel: 602-285-1800; Fax: 602-285-1838.

Diocesan Attorney—GREGORY J. LEISSE, *400 E. Monroe, Phoenix, 85004.* Tel: 602-257-0030; Fax: 602-257-5645.

Priests' Assurance Association—Rev. MICHAEL L. DISKIN, Sec., *400 E. Monroe, Phoenix, 85004.* Tel: 602-257-0030.

Polish Pastoral Mission—Rev. EUGENIUSZ BOLDA, S.Ch., Admin., *Our Lady of Czestochowa, 6530 N. 7th St., Phoenix, 85014.* Tel: 602-212-1172; Fax: 602-212-1173.

Priest Personnel—Rev. THOMAS ZURCHER, C.S.C., Vicar, *400 E. Monroe, Phoenix, 85004.* Tel: 602-257-0030; Fax: 602-257-5645.

Advisory Board for the Continuing Formation of Priests—Rev. THOMAS ZURCHER, C.S.C., *400 E. Monroe, Phoenix, 85004.* Tel: 602-257-0030.

Priestly Life and Ministry Board—Rev. THOMAS ZURCHER, C.S.C., *400 E. Monroe, Phoenix, 85004.* Tel: 602-257-0030.

Priests' Placement Board—Rev. THOMAS ZURCHER, C.S.C., *400 E. Monroe, Phoenix, 85004.* Tel: 602-257-0030.

Prisons, Catholic Ministries To—Deacon PETER MURPHY, Dir. Tel: 602-256-2321.

Youth at Risk—KEVIN STARRS, Coord., *320 N. 20th Dr., Phoenix, 85009-3881.* Tel: 602-267-1531.

State Adult Facilities—Phoenix Prison Complex, Perryville Prison (female), Lewis Prison, ACW Prison.

State Juvenile Facilities—Adobe Mountain, Black Canyon, Encanto, Eagle Point, Sunrise.

County Jails (Adult & Juvenile)—Madison Jail, Durango Jail, Estrella Jail (female), Towers Jail.

Federal Prison (Adult)—Federal Correction Institute (male & female).

Private Prison (Adult)—Phoenix West.

Diocesan Prison Ministry Staff—Black Canyon Hwy., 2800 W. Pinnacle Peak Rd., Phoenix, 85027. Tel: 602-869-9050, Ext. 270.

County Juvenile Detention Center—3125 W. Durango, Phoenix, 85009. Diocesan Prison Ministry Staff.

Propagation of the Faith—Sr. JEAN STEFFES, C.S.A., *400 E. Monroe, Phoenix, 85004.* Tel: 602-257-0030; Fax: 602-257-5540.

Holy Childhood Association—Sr. JEAN STEFFES, C.S.A, *400 E. Monroe, Phoenix, 85004.* Tel: 602-257-0300; Fax: 602-257-5540.

Hispanic Ministry—

Office of Hispanic Ministry—Rev. TIMOTHY CONLON, O.S.C., Vicar, *400 E. Monroe, Phoenix, 85004.* Tel: 602-257-0030; Fax: 602-462-5207.

Office of Human Resources (Personnel)—JOHN UNGVARY, Dir., *400 E. Monroe, Phoenix, 85004.* Tel: 602-257-0030; Fax: 602-257-5561.

Religious, Office of—Sr. JEAN STEFFES, C.S.A., Dir., *400 E. Monroe, Phoenix, 85004.* Tel: 602-257-0030; Fax: 602-257-5540.

Catholic Tuition Organization of the Diocese of Phoenix (CTODP)—Mrs. JENNIFER KRAUS, Coord., *Diocesan Center, 400 E. Monroe St., Phoenix, 85004.* Tel: 602-744-6342.

Office of Black Catholic Ministry—Mrs. MARIE AUSBERRY, Coord.; Mr. JIM BOOZER, Chm., *Diocesan Center, 400 E. Monroe St., Phoenix, 85004.* Tel: 602-257-5554.

CLERGY, PARISHES, MISSIONS AND PAROCHIAL SCHOOLS

CITY OF PHOENIX
(Maricopa County)

1—SS. SIMON AND JUDE CATHEDRAL (1953), Revs. Michael O'Grady, Rector; Patrick Mowrer; Deacons Earl Barr; Rick Curran. In res., Revs. Francis A. Peacock; Donald Kline.
Res., 6351 N. 27th Ave., 85017. Tel: 602-242-1300; Fax: 602-249-3768.
School—Tel: 602-242-1299. Sr. Raphael Quinn, I.B.V.M., Prin.
Sisters 2; Lay Teachers 23; Students 565.
Convent—Tel: 602-242-2544.
Mission—Phoenix, Maricopa Co., Santa Rosa Chapel, 1901 W. Ocotillo, 85017.

2—CORPUS CHRISTI (1985), Revs. Albert F.H. Hoorman; Thaddeus McGuire; Sr. Frances Ellsperman, O.P., Pastoral Assoc.; Deacons Alexander Gaudio; Patrick Flynn; Philip Simeone.
Res., 3550 E. Knox, 85044. Tel: 480-893-8770; Fax: 480-893-3291.

3—HOLY FAMILY (1968), Rev. Jorge Canez.
Res., 6802 S. 24th St., 85040. Tel: 602-268-2632; Fax: 602-268-8909.

4—IMMACULATE HEART OF MARY (1924), Rev. George Highberger.
Res., 909 E. Washington St., 85034. Tel: 602-253-6129; Fax: 602-253-4210.

5—MOST HOLY TRINITY (1951), Revs. Roberto Corral, O.P.; Vincent Foerstler, O.P.; Joseph Thuan Nguyen, O.P.; Bros. Pasquale Manalio, O.P.; Francis Le, O.P.
Res., 8620 N. Seventh St., 85020. Tel: 602-944-3375; Fax: 602-943-2323.
School—535 E. Alice Ave., 85020. Tel: 602-943-9058. Ms. Jane Segovia, Prin.
Lay Teachers 23; Students 366.
McHugh Hall / Small Hall—8820 N. Seventh St., 85020. Tel: 602-997-6726.

6—ST. AGNES (1940), Revs. Tiernan O'Callaghan, O.Carm.; Patrick Gavin, O.Carm. In res., Revs. Ernest Larkin, O.Carm.; Michael Kwiecien, O.Carm.
Res., 1954 N. 24th St., 85008. Tel: 602-244-0349; Fax: 602-244-0054.
School—2311 E. Palm Ln., 85006. Tel: 602-244-1451. Catherine Downey, Prin.
Lay Teachers 11; Students 263.
Convent—1818 N. 23rd St., 85006. Tel: 602-244-1174.

7—SS. ANTHONY AND PIUS X (1943), Rev. George Highberger.
Church & Res.—909 S. First Ave., 85003. Tel: 602-252-1771; Fax: 602-252-1669.
Missions—Phoenix, Maricopa Co., St. Pius X, 809 S. Seventh Ave., 85007.; Phoenix, Maricopa Co., Our Lady of Fatima, 1418 S. 17th Ave., 85007. Tel: 602-254-4944. Rev. Francis A. Peacock, Admin.

8—ST. AUGUSTINE (1970), Revs. David Sanfilippo; Nick Floridi; Mrs. Dorothy Allen, Parish Admin.; Deacons Al Gonzales; Juan Guzman.
Res., 3630 N. 71st Ave., 85033. Tel: 623-849-3131; Fax: 623-849-5689.

9—ST. CATHERINE OF SIENA (1947), Revs. Charles Goraieb; Kevin Ikpah; Deacons George Lazok; Manuel Vasquez.
Res., 6401 S. Central Ave., 85040. Tel: 602-276-5581; Fax: 602-276-2119.
School—6413 S. Central Ave., 85040. Tel: 602-276-2241, Ext. 251; Fax: 602-268-7886. Roberta Walker, Prin.
Lay Teachers 10; Students 225.

10—ST. EDWARD CONFESSOR (1976), Rev. Jorge Canez; Deacon Peter Fejes.
Res., 4410 E. Southern Ave., 85040. Tel: 602-438-0043; Fax: 602-438-9305.

11—ST. FRANCIS XAVIER (1928), Revs. Edward E. Callanan, S.J.; Patrick J. Reuse, S.J.; Philip Blake, S.J.; Joseph Dube, S.J.
Res., 4715 N. Central Ave., 85012-1796. Tel: 602-279-9547; Fax: 602-248-8968.
School—Tel: 602-266-5364. Mrs. Kristen Spucces, Prin.
Lay Teachers 28; Students 540.

12—ST. GREGORY (1947), Revs. John J. Dougherty, C.S.C.; Stephen Wilbricht, C.S.C.; Deacons Edward Bolton; Lee Kloft. In res., Rev. Thomas K. Zurcher, C.S.C.
Res., 3424 N. 18th Ave., 85015. Tel: 602-264-4488; Fax: 602-264-4489 (Call first).
School—3440 N. 18th Ave., 85015. Tel: 602-266-9527. Mrs. Judy Setzkorn, Prin.
Sisters 2; Lay Teachers 15; Students 286.
Convent—3437 N. 18th Ave., 85015. Tel: 602-265-2396. Sisters of the Institute of B.V.M.

13—ST. JEROME (1962), Revs. L. Pierre Hissey; Greg Menegay; Deacons Michael Phelan; Theodore Micek; Richard Rein; Bill Bidleman.
Church—10815 N. 35th Ave., 85029. Tel: 602-942-5555; Fax: 602-504-9115.
School—Tel: 602-942-5644. Carl Hodus, Prin.
Sisters 1; Lay Teachers 12; Students 315.

14—ST. JOAN OF ARC (1979), Revs. Larry W. Weidner; John Cullinan; John McDonough; Gena McGowan, Pastoral Assoc.; Deacons Phil Locascio; Guy Goubeaux.
Parish Center: 3801 E. Greenway Rd., 85032-4698. Tel: 602-867-9171; Fax: 602-482-7930.

15—ST. JOSEPH (1969), Rev. Frank Fernandez; Deacons Harry Schwan; Charles Kelly.
Res., 11001 N. 40th St., 85028. Tel: 602-996-5120; Fax: 602-996-4011 (Call first).

16—ST. LUKE (1985), Rev. Richard A. Milligan.
Res., 19644 N. Seventh Ave., 85027. Tel: 623-582-0561.
Mission—New River, Maricopa Co., Good Shepherd Mission, 45033 N. 12th St., 85087. Tel: 623-465-9740; Fax: 623-742-7031. Rev. Valentine L. Boyle, O.Carm., Admin.

17—St. Mark (1946), Rev. David Cooney, S.D.S.; Deacon Jose Hernandez. In res., Rev. Fred Peters, S.D.S.; Bro. Roger Pelky, S.D.S.
Res., 400 N. 30th St., 85008. Tel: 602-267-0503.
Mission—Phoenix, Maricopa Co., St. Philip the Deacon Catholic Center, 615 N. 20th St., 85006. Tel: 602-253-1076. Deacon Louis Pardini, Admin.

18—St. Martin de Porres (1973), Deacon Jose Olivarez, Admin.
Res., 3851 W. Wier Ave., 85041. Tel: 602-276-2466 (Church); Fax: 602-232-2147.

19—St. Mary's Basilica (1881), Rev. Evan Howard, O.F.M. In res., Revs. Lester Mitchell, O.F.M.; Lucius Grosso, O.F.M.; Luis Baldonado, O.F.M.; Javier Reyes-Ruiz, O.F.M.; Alonso De Blas, O.F.M.; Garrett Edmunds, O.F.M.; Bro. Kevin Dunne O.F.M.
Res., 231 N. Third St., 85004. Tel: 602-252-7651; Fax: 602-256-2773.

20—St. Matthew (1939), Rev. Raymond Ritari; Sr. Ginger Downey, O.L.V.M., Pastoral Assoc.; Deacon Tony Beltran.
Res., 320 N. 20th Dr., 85009. Tel: 602-258-1789; Fax: 602-258-6507.
School—2038 W. Van Buren, 85009. Tel: 602-254-0611. Dr. Robert Sherman, Prin.
Sisters 2; Lay Teachers 7; Students 211.
Convent—2106 W. Van Buren, 85009. Tel: 602-253-9124.

21—St. Paul (1976), Revs. Eugene O'Carroll; Joseph McGaffin; Deacons Robert England; Bill Vivio.
Res., 330 W. Coral Gables Dr., 85023. Tel: 602-942-2608; Fax: 602-548-0708.

22—Our Lady of the Valley (1973), Rev. Scott Brubaker.
Church—3220 W. Greenway Rd., 85053. Tel: 602-993-1213; Fax: 602-993-1223.

23—Sacred Heart (1954), Revs. Luis Baldonado, O.F.M.; Javier Reyes-Ruiz, O.F.M.
Church—1421 S. 12th St., 85034. Tel: 602-258-2089.

24—St. Theresa (1955), Revs. Charles G. Kieffer; James Wall; Deacons Colin Campbell; Sione Hola. In res., Rev. Michael L. Diskin.
Res., 5045 E. Thomas Rd., 85018. Tel: 602-840-0850; Fax: 602-840-0871.
School—5001 E. Thomas Rd., 85018. Tel: 602-840-0010. Gerald Streit, Prin.
Lay Teachers 26; Students 580.

25—St. Thomas the Apostle (1950), Revs. John Spaulding; John T. Ehrich; Joseph Fichtner, O.S.C.; Deacons Americo Gouveia; Anthony Dudzic; Kenneth Miller; Leonard Zbiegien. In res., Rev. Oliver Mohan, O.M.I.
Res., 2312 E. Campbell Ave., 85016-5597. Tel: 602-954-9089; Fax: 602-956-3454.
School—4510 N. 24th St., 85016. Tel: 602-954-9088. Sr. Patricia Gehling, S.S.N.D., Prin.
Sisters 3; Lay Teachers 30; Students 580.

26—St. Vincent de Paul (1957), Revs. John V. Shine, C.M.; John O'M. Sharpe, C.M.; Ruben Dario Restrepo, C.M. In res., Rev. Michael J. Boyle, C.M.; Deacons Bill Jenkins; Ray Roger; Lorenzo Salazar.
Res., 3140 N. 51st Ave., 85031. Tel: 623-247-6871; Fax: 623-247-4457.
School—3130 N. 51st Ave., 85031. Tel: 623-247-8595. Sr. Louise Camous, D.C., Prin.
Sisters 2; Lay Teachers 13; Students 263.
Convent—3130 N. 51st Ave., 85031. Tel: 623-247-8916. Daughters of Charity

OUTSIDE THE CITY OF PHOENIX

Bagdad, Yavapai Co., St. Francis of Assisi (1949), Deacon Thomas Phelan, Parish Life Coord.
Mailing Address: P.O. Box 768, 86321.
Church & Rectory: 220 Cook St., 86321. Tel: 520-633-2389.

Bapchule, Pinal Co., St. Peter's (1949), Deacon Edward Burgin, Admin.
Mailing Address: P.O. Box 545, Sacaton, 85247. Tel: 520-562-3716; 602-319-0742 (Mobile); Fax: 520-315-3963.
School—P.O. Box 10840, 85221. Tel: 520-315-3835; Fax: 520-315-3963. Sr. Martha Mary Carpenter, O.S.F., Prin.
Franciscan Sisters of Christian Charity (Manitowoc, WI) 4; Lay Teachers 7; Students 189.
Missions of Gila River Catholic Community Team—.
Missions—Blackwater, Holy Family; Sacaton Flats, Our Lady of Victory; Santan, St. Anne; Sacaton, St. Anthony.

Buckeye, Maricopa Co., Saint Henry (1956), Rev. Richard Driscoll, S.D.S., Admin.
Res., 128 S. Third St., 85326. Tel: 623-386-6407; Fax: 623-386-4328.
Mission—Harquahala Valley, San Isidoro Labrador.

Bullhead City, Mohave Co., St. Margaret Mary (1947), Rev. Peter P. Dobrowski; Deacons Richard Eckert; Philip Wisely.
Res., 1691 N. Oatman Rd., 86442. Tel: 520-758-7117; Fax: 520-758-2345.

Camp Verde, Yavapai Co., St. Frances Cabrini (1962), Rev. James Kelly.
Res., P.O. Box 1677, 86322. Tel: 520-567-3543.
Church—608 W. General Crook Trail, 86322. Tel: 520-567-3543; Fax: 520-567-7058.
Mission—Black Canyon City, Yavapai Co., St. Philip Benizi, P.O. Box 138, Black Canyon City, 85324. Tel: 623-374-5392; Fax: 623-374-9768. Rev. Kevin Hunt Diaz.

Carefree, Maricopa Co., Our Lady of Joy (1972), Rev. Msgr. Richard W. Moyer, V.G.
Res., P.O. Box 1359, 85377. Tel: 480-488-2229 (Church); 488-0469(Rectory); Fax: 480-488-1085.

Cashion, Maricopa Co., St. William (1973), Rev. Thomas G. Bielawa, S.D.S., Admin.
Mailing Address: P.O. Box 329, 85329.
Res., 11003 W. Third St., 85329. Tel: 623-936-6115; Fax: 623-936-8308.
Mission—Santa Maria, Our Lady of Guadalupe, 6807 Lower Buckeye Rd., Phoenix, 85043.

Chandler, Maricopa Co., St. Andrew the Apostle (1985), Revs. Joseph I. Hennessy; Camille Prat, S.J.; Deacon Gary Jacobs.
Res., 3450 W. Ray Rd., 85226. Tel: 480-899-1990; Fax: 480-917-8475.

St. Mary's (1937), Revs. Robert Clements; Alonso Saenz; Deacons Craig Hintze; J. Patrick Garber.
Res., 230 W. Galveston, 85224. Tel: 480-963-3207; Fax: 480-814-9417.
School—St. Mary-Basha Catholic Elementary, 200 W. Galveston, 85224. Tel: 480-963-4951. Sr. Mary Norbert Long, S.C., Prin.
Sisters of Charity, Seton Hill 3; Lay Teachers 19; Students 532.

St. Benedict (1985), Rev. Dennis J. O'Rourke; Deacon Dwight Morton.
Church—6400 W. Del Rio St., 85226. Tel: 480-961-1610; Fax: 480-961-1794.

Cottonwood, Yavapai Co., Immaculate Conception (1966), Rev. Emile "Bud" Pelletier; Deacons James Anderson; Onofre Duran; Ron Pelton.
Mailing Address: P.O. Box 995, 86326.
Res., 421 N. Willard St., 86326. Tel: 520-634-2933; Fax: 520-634-3326.
Mission—Clarkdale, Yavapai Co., St. Cecilia, P.O. Box 366, Clarkdale, 86324-0366. Tel: 520-634-2142. Rev. Michael F. Hurley, Admin.

El Mirage, Maricopa Co., Santa Teresita (1968), Rev. David Kelash; Deacon Jose Garza.
Church—14016 N. Verbena St., 85335.
Res., P.O. Box 67, 85335. Tel: 623-583-8183; Fax: 623-583-2963.

Flagstaff, San Francisco de Asis (1997), Revs. Michael Straley; Stephen Schack; Gary Regula.
Mailing Address: P.O. Box 1946, 86002-1946. Tel: 520-779-1341; Fax: 520-779-2903.
Rectory: 520 W. Riordan Rd., 86002.
School—St. Mary's Catholic School, 320 N. Humphrey, 86001. Tel: 520-779-1337. Ms. Marilyn Johnson, Prin.
Sisters 1; Lay Teachers 13; Students 239.
Convent—202 S. Kendrick, 86001. Tel: 520-744-3680. Institute of the Blessed Virgin Mary Loretto Sisters
Chapels—Nativity of B.V.M., 16 W. Cherry Ave., 86001.; Our Lady of Guadalupe, 225 S. Kendrick, 86001.; St. Pius X, 2257 E. Cedar Ave., 86004.

Fountain Hills, Maricopa Co., Ascension (1976), Rev. Thomas O'Dea; Leann Gratz, Parish Mgr. Pastoral Assocs: Sr. Kathleen Storan; Patricia Mullen. In res., Rev. William Healy.
Church—12615 Fountain Hills Blvd., 85268. Tel: 480-837-1066; Fax: 480-837-9093.
Mission—Rio Verde, St. Dominic, 25603 N. Danny Ln., Ste. 2, Rio Verde, 85263. Tel: 602-471-1516.

Gila Bend, Maricopa Co., St. Michael (1963). Unassigned.
Res., 515 W. Norma St., P.O. Drawer F, 85337. Tel: 520-683-6463.
Church—314 Dodson St., 85337.
Mission—Tohono O'Odham, St. Lucy, Paloma Ranch. (Native American Village). Deacon Tom Swisher, Admin., Tel: 602-319-1876.

Gilbert, Maricopa Co., St. Anne (1943), Revs. Douglas E. Lorig; Julio Higuera; Christopher Shappard, O.S.B.; Stephen Adrian; Matthew Plathottam; Deacons Ken Kulinowski; Gerald O'Toole; James Salamone; Tom Phelan; Bob Carey; John Berger; Bobbi Friedrich, Pastoral Assoc.
Mailing Address: P.O. Box 228, 85299-0228. Tel: 480-892-4970; Fax: 480-892-6736.
Church—440 E. Elliot Rd., 85299-0228.

Mission—Queen Creek, Maricopa Co., Our Lady of Guadalupe, P.O. Box 856, Queen Creek, 85242. Tel: 480-963-3207. Deacon Roman Jimenez.

Glendale, Maricopa Co.,

1—Our Lady of Perpetual Help, (1948), Revs. Fausto Penafiel; John Ebbesmier; Deacons Tony Lopez; Robert Myers; Eddie Molina; Charles Heeter; Vincent Torres.
Res., 5614 W. Orangewood Ave., 85301. Tel: 623-939-9785; Fax: 623-934-8854.
School—7521 N. 57th Ave., 85301. Tel: 623-931-7288. Cecilia Frakes, Prin.
Sisters 1; Lay Teachers 16; Students 358.
Chapel—Our Lady of Guadalupe, 55th Ave. & Lamar.

2—St. Helen, (1974), Revs. Robert Skagen; Louis Mraz, O.S.C.; Sr. Patricia Oliver, R.S.M., Pastoral Assoc.; Deacons Joseph Shinske; Robert Rudolph Campas; Paul Csuy; Tim Seibold.
Res., 5510 W. Cholla, 85304. Tel: 623-979-4202; Fax: 623-412-1226.

3—St. James, (1982), Rev. Kenneth A. Van De Ven; Deacons John O'Connor; Alan Bowslaugh; Frank Devine.
Church—19640 N. 35th Ave., 85308. Tel: 623-581-0707; Fax: 623-581-0110.
Res., 18225 N. 35th Dr., 85308. Tel: 623-843-0421.

4—St. Louis The King, (1962), Revs. John Slobig; Robert J. Bliven, O.S.C.; Deacon Gene Messer.
Mailing Address: 4331 W. Maryland Ave., 85301. Tel: 623-930-1127; Fax: 623-930-1129.
School—Tel: 623-939-4260. Sr. Jean Perry, C.S.A., Prin.
Sisters 1; Lay Teachers 10; Students 252.

5—St. Raphael, (1974), Rev. Cyprian Hibner, O.Carm.; Deacons Forrest Briesch; Richard Meidle.
Res., 5504 W. Acoma, 85306.
Church—5525 W. Acoma, 85306. Tel: 602-938-4227; Fax: 602-978-0305.

6—St. Thomas More, (1997), Rev. James Turner; Deacon Roy Drapeau; Judith Casar, Pastoral Assoc.
P.O. Box 11887, 85318-1887. Tel: 623-566-8222.

Goodyear, Maricopa Co., Saint John Vianney (1956), Revs. Joseph V. Corpora, C.S.C.; Christopher Cox; Deacon James Cascio.
Office: 539 La Pasada Blvd., 85338. Tel: 602-932-3313; Fax: 602-932-1896.
Res., 11 Loma Linda Blvd., Avondale, 85323. Tel: 602-925-0418.
School—Tel: 623-932-2434. Patricia Waldmann, Prin.
Brothers 1; Sisters 3; Lay Teachers 11; Students 321.
Convent—15 W. Loma Linda Blvd., Avondale, 85323. Tel: 623-932-2652; Fax: 623-932-1243.

Grand Canyon, Coconino Co., El Cristo Rey (1960), Rev. Don Felix Perera, Admin.
Mailing Address: P.O. Box 505, 86023. Tel: 520-638-2390.

Guadalupe, Maricopa Co., Our Lady of Guadalupe (1970), Rev. Joseph A. Baur, O.F.M., Admin.; Deacon Santo Bernasconi.
Office: 5445 San Angelo, St. Guadelupe, 85283. Tel: 480-839-2860.
Res., 9004 Calle Maravilla, 85283. Tel: 480-839-2376.

Jerome, Yavapai Co., Holy Family (1908). Unassigned.
St. Cecilia Mission: (Sacramental Records) P.O. Box 366, Clarkdale, 86324. Tel: 520-634-2142.

Kingman, Mohave Co., St. Mary's (1906), Rev. James Alling; Deacons Bill Del Monaco; Jose Rodriguez; Brian Lewiz.
Res., 302 E. Spring St., 86401. Tel: 520-753-3359; Fax: 520-753-2581.
Mission—Dolan Springs, Mohave Co., Our Lady of the Desert, P.O. Box 491, Dolan Springs, 86441. Tel: 520-767-3154.

Lake Havasu City, Mohave Co., Our Lady of the Lake (1969), Revs. Michael Deptula; Lawrence Baumann; Eugene A. Burke, C.S.C.; Deacons Thomas C. Coe; Thomas DeFilippis.
Res., 1975 Daytona Dr., 86403. Tel: 520-855-2685; Fax: 520-855-7172.

Laveen, Maricopa Co., St. John The Baptist (1910), Deacon Joseph "Tom" Swisher, Admin.
Res., P.O. Box 693, 85339-0693. Tel: 520-550-2034.
Missions—Santa Cruz, St. Catherine; Ak-Chin, St.Francis; Gila Bend, San Lucy; Gila River, Indian Care Center.
Station—Lone Butte, St. Francis Xavier.

Litchfield Park, Maricopa Co., St. Thomas Aquinas, Rev. Kieran Kleczewski; Deacons Chuck Shaw; Bill Phares.
Res., 447 S. Litchfield Rd., 85340. Tel: 623-935-2151; 935-3625; Fax: 623-935-5044.

Mesa, Maricopa Co.,

1—ALL SAINTS, (1972), Rev. Robert Caruso; Deacons Donnan Lukaszewski; T. Vincent Neeley; Ray Semmler; Reed Santa.
Church—1534 N. Recker Rd., 85205. Tel: 480-985-7655; Fax: 480-396-0837.

2—CHRIST THE KING, (1959), Revs. Christopher Carpenter; William Kosco; Deacons Joseph August; Philip Van Der Heyden; Stanley Humpal.
Res., 1505 E. Dana Ave., 85204.
Church—1551 E. Dana Ave., 85204. Tel: 480-964-1719; Fax: 480-844-4498.
School—Tel: 480-844-4480. Casimir (Casey) Kozlik, Prin.
Lay Teachers 12; Students 286.

3—HOLY CROSS, (1978), Rev. Dennis Riccitelli; Deacon James Battista.
Res., 1244 S. Power Rd., 85206. Tel: 480-981-2021; Fax: 480-981-6844.

4—QUEEN OF PEACE, (1934), Revs. Karl LeClaire, S.D.S.; Lloyd P. Kramlich, S.D.S.; Paul Portland, S.D.S.; Deacons John Reidel; Buddy Clapham. In res., Bro. Ervan Digman, S.D.S.
Res., 141 N. Macdonald St., 85201. Tel: 480-969-9166; Fax: 480-969-8102.
School—109 N. Macdonald St., 85201. Tel: 602-969-0226. Mr. Michaels Evans, Prin.
Lay Teachers 9; Students 173.

5—ST. BRIDGET, (1985), Rev. John F. Cunningham; Deacons Joe Scaccia; William Shea; Len Liszewski.
Res., 2850 E. Lockwood St., 85213. Tel: 480-924-9138.
Church—2213 N. Lindsay Rd., 85213. Tel: 480-924-9111; Fax: 480-924-3103.

6—ST. TIMOTHY, (1978), Revs. Dale J. Fushek; Neil McGarrity; Deacons Ollie Babbitts; Thomas Bolduc; Barry Smith; Dutch Hurrish; Richard Petersen; Chris Bassett. In res., Revs. Paul Orel; Fred Gaglia.
Res., 1730 W. Guadalupe, 85202. Tel: 480-775-5200; Fax: 480-820-7984.
Convent—2754 S. Pennington, 85202.
Sisters 4.
Catholic Life Productions, Inc. dba LIFE TEEN Program—Tel: 480-820-7001. Phil Baniewicz, Exec. Dir.

Peoria, Maricopa Co., St. Charles Borromeo (1968), Rev. Hugo Gonzalez.
Mailing Address: P.O. Box 819, 85380-0819.
Res., 8617 W. Peoria Ave., 85345. Tel: 623-979-3418.
Church—8615 W. Peoria Ave., 85345. Fax: 623-412-2397.

Prescott, Yavapai Co., Sacred Heart (1877), Revs. Fred LeClaire, C.M.F.; James Griffin, C.M.F.; Richard Farrell, C.M.F.; Joseph Gamm, C.M.F.; Darrin Merlino, C.M.F.; Deacons William Davis; Thomas Kayser; John Lamon; Tony Humphrey; Tom Gregory; Bill Starrs.
Res., 150 Fleury Ave., 86301. Tel: 520-445-3141; Fax: 520-717-1074.
School—131 N. Summit Ave., 86301. Tel: 520-445-2621. Ms. Donna Walsh, Prin.
Institute of the Blessed Virgin Mary Sisters 1; Lay Teachers 9; Students 164.
Convent—229 N. Summit St., 86301. Tel: 520-445-7861.
Missions—Congress Junction, Yavapai Co., Good Shepherd of the Desert. Rev. John Vogt.; Yarnell, Yavapai Co., St. Mary's, P.O. Box 706, Yarnell, 85362. Tel: 520-427-0276. Rev. Peter Taylor.; Chino Valley, Yavapai Co., St. Catherine Laboure, P.O. Box 152, Chino Valley, 86323. Tel: 520-636-4071. Rev. John Salvador, C.M.F.

Prescott Valley, Yavapai Co., St. Germaine (1984), Revs. John Shetler; Kevin Hunt Diaz.
Res., 7997 E. Dana Dr., 86314. Tel: 520-772-6350; Fax: 520-772-4413.
Mission—Mayer, St. Joseph, S. Hwy. 69, P.O. Box 446, Mayer, 86333. Tel: 520-632-4018. Rev. Kevin Hunt Diaz.

Scottsdale, Maricopa Co.,

1—BLESSED SACRAMENT, (1974), Rev. Patrick Robinson; Deacons Pat Hughes; Harry Hude; Tom Walsh; Jack Ehrlich.
Res., 11300 N. 64th St., 85254. Tel: 480-948-8370; Fax: 480-951-3844.

2—OUR LADY OF PERPETUAL HELP, (1949), Revs. Thomas Hever; John Bernbrock, S.J.; Patrick Colleary; Deacons Irving Fleming; James Hoyt.
Res., 7655 E. Main St., 85251. Tel: 480-947-4331; Fax: 480-874-3798.
School—3801 N. Miller Rd., 85251. Tel: 480-874-3720. Sr. Marian Grace Brandt, S.C., Prin.
Sisters of Charity 1; Lay Teachers 24; Students 589.
Convent—7634 E. Second St., 85251. Tel: 480-945-3867.

3—ST. BERNADETTE, (1995), Rev. Richard Felt; Deacons John Meyer; Roy Rooker. In res., Rev. Thomas A. Walsh, (Retired).
Office: 16245 N. 60th St., 85254. Tel: 480-905-0221; Fax: 480-905-0249.

4—ST. BERNARD OF CLAIRVAUX, (1994), Rev. Robert Voss; Deacon Fred Giesner.
Res., 10755 N. 124th St., 85259. Tel: 480-661-9843; Fax: 480-614-8092.

5—ST. DANIEL THE PROPHET, (1961), Revs. Francis R. Zappitelli; Eugene Young; Deacons Roy Anderson; Ranald Guldan; Charles Raymond; Richard Regan; Martin Dippre; Jesse Sanchez. In res., Rev. Patrick Smith.
Res., 7923 E. Latham St., 85257. Tel: 480-945-8437; Fax: 480-945-4335.
School—Tel: 480-949-8034. Sr. Mary Lucilla Wertz, S.C., Prin.
Lay Teachers 10; Students 242.
Convent—7830 E. Roosevelt, 85257. Tel: 480-423-5240.
Korean Catholic Community: Rev. Lawrence Kang.

6—ST. MARIA GORETTI, (1967), Revs. Blase Myer; John M. Picardi; Deacons Herve Lemire; Tom Bills; Clem Czapinski.
Res., 8344 E. Edward Ave., 85250.
Church—6261 N. Granite Reef Rd., 85250. Tel: 480-948-8380; Fax: 480-948-8815.

7—ST. PATRICK, (1980), Rev. Eric Tellez; Deacon Jim Buchanan.
Office: 10815 N. 84th St., 85260. Tel: 480-998-3843; Fax: 480-998-5218.

Sedona, Yavapai Co., St. John Vianney (1965), Rev. J.C. Ortiz.
Res., 180 Soldiers Pass Rd., P.O. Box 3909, W. Sedona, 86340. Tel: 520-282-7545; Fax: 520-282-1798.
Chapel—Holy Cross, 780 Chapel Rd., P.O. Box 1043, 86339. Tel: 520-282-4069; Fax: 520-282-3701.

Seligman, Yavapai Co., St. Francis (1940), Rev. Andres Hejdak, Admin.
Res., P.O. Box 308, 86337. Tel: 520-422-3354.
Church—104 Schoney, 86337.
Mission—Ashfork, St. Anne, 47047 7th St., Ashfork, 86320.

Sun City, Maricopa Co., St. Clement of Rome (1970), Revs. Earl D'Eon; Mathew Mampara; Matthias Feit, (Ret.); Deacons Irving Dennis; Stanley Giza.
Res., 15800 Del Webb Blvd., 85351. Tel: 623-974-5867; Fax: 623-974-0562.
St. Elizabeth Seton (1976), Revs. Franklin Bartel; Ed Coleman, O.M.I.; William Harnischfeger; Deacon William Tone.
Res., 9728 Palmeras Ln., 85373. Tel: 623-972-2129; Fax: 623-974-0654.
Church of St. Joachim & St. Anne (1961), Revs. Frank P. Simlik; Richard Ryan.
Mailing Address: P.O. Box 748, 85372.
Res., 11625 111th Ave., 85351-3746. Tel: 623-972-1179; Fax: 623-972-1170.

Sun City West, Maricopa Co., Our Lady of Lourdes (1979), Revs. Michael Minogue; Harold Graf; Deacons Maurice Arnold; Jack Cummings; George Koch; Peter Murphy; Stephen Martin.
Res., 19002 N. 128th Ave., 85375. Tel: 623-546-2767; Fax: 623-214-1246.

Sun Lakes, Maricopa Co., St. Steven (1988), Rev. Emmett J. FitzPatrick.
Mailing Address: 24827 S. Dobson Rd., 85248. Tel: 480-895-9266.
Res., 10324 E. Michigan Ave., 85248. Tel: 480-895-9304.

Surprise, Maricopa Co., St. Clare of Assisi, Rev. John Coleman.
P.O. Box 1427, 85378-1427. Tel: 623-546-3444.

Tempe, Maricopa Co.,

1—HOLY SPIRIT, (1973), Rev. John Hanley; Deacon Frank Danna.
Office: 1815 E. Gemini Dr., 85283. Tel: 480-838-7474; Fax: 480-838-6720.; Rectory: 1871 E. Libra Dr., 85283.
Church—1800 E. Libra Dr., 85283.

2—OUR LADY OF MT. CARMEL, (1932), Rev. Mark Dippre.
Res., 2121 S. Rural Rd., 85282. Tel: 480-967-8791; Fax: 480-967-4919.
School—2117 S. Rural Rd., 85282. Tel: 480-967-5567. Dr. Vincent Sheridan, Prin.
Lay Teachers 25; Students 539.
Tongan Catholic Community: Rev. Timothy R. Davern, J.C.L., Liaison.

3—RESURRECTION, (1970), Revs. Leo Brogan; Timothy R. Davern, J.C.L. In res., Rev. Joseph G. Krijnen.
Res., 3201 S. Evergreen Rd., 85282. Tel: 480-838-0207; Fax: 480-756-1501.

4—ST. MARGARET, (1972), Deacons Frank G. Galarza, Admin.; Pedro Mesa; Manuel Olivas.
Res., 2435 E. McArthur Dr., 85281. Tel: 480-967-0379; Fax: 480-967-3825.
Missions—Salt River Indian, St. Francis, P. O. Box 3334, Scottsdale, 85271. Tel: 520-562-3716; Lehi, St. Paschal Baylon, P.O. Box 545, Sacaton, 85247.

Tolleson, Maricopa Co., Blessed Sacrament (1953), Rev. Daniel McBride; Deacon Antonio M. Chavez, Sr.
Res., 512 N. 93rd Ave., 85353. Tel: 623-936-7107; Fax: 623-936-9536.

Wickenburg, Maricopa Co., St. Anthony of Padua (1941), Rev. John Vogt.
Res., 232 N. Tegner St., 85390. Tel: 520-684-2096; Fax: 520-684-3539.
Mission—Aguila, Our Lady of Guadalupe, 50627 Eagle Eye Rd., P.O. Box 294, Aguila, 85320.

Williams, Coconino Co., St. Joseph's (1928), Rev. J.F. Michael Bain.
Res., 900 W. Grant, 86046. Tel: 520-635-2430; Fax: 520-635-0177, Ext. 51.

Chaplains of Public Institutions

PHOENIX. *Arizona State Hospital* 2500 E. Van Buren St., 85008. Tel: 602-220-6190. Chaplains: Sr. Patricia Pieper, S.N.D.deN.; Charles R. Johnson.
Good Samaritan Medical Center. Vacant. 1111 E. McDowell Rd., 85006. Tel: 602-239-4324.
Maricopa Medical Center 2601 E. Roosevelt St., 85008. Tel: 602-267-5011. Rev. Fred Peters, S.D.S., Chap.
Phoenix Indian Medical Center. (For Sacramental Records Contact St. Francis Xavier at 602-279-9547) 4212 N. 16th St., 850. Tel: 602-263-1017. Jim White, Chap., Tel: 602-263-1576.
St. Joseph's Hospital P.O. Box 2071, 85001. Tel: 602-406-3690. Rev. Cornelius Draves-Arpaia, Chap., Directors Chaplaincy Svcs.: Sr. Margaret McBride; Sr. Michaelle Hennessey.
St. Luke's Medical Center 1800 E. Van Buren St., 85006. Tel: 602-251-8480. Don Mitchum, Chap. Coord.
United States Veterans Affairs Medical Center 650 E. Indian School Rd., 85012. Tel: 602-222-6422. Revs. Peter Morello, Chief of Chap. Svcs.; Kenneth Klieber, Chap.

CHANDLER. *Chandler Regional Hospital* 475 S. Dobson Rd., 85224. Tel: 480-821-7639. Sr. Joan Pfeiffer, S.N.D.deN., Chap.

LUKE AIR FORCE BASE. *Luke Catholic Community* 58 FW/HC, 13968 Shooting Star St., 85309-1932. Tel: 623-856-6211; Fax: 623-856-6968. Revs. Brian Bell, Chap.; John Regan, Auxiliary Chap.; Deacons Thomas Henn; James Pfleger.

PRESCOTT. *United States Veterans Hospital (Prescott)* Veterans Administration Medical Center, 86313. Tel: 520-776-6029. Rev. Gerald Caffrey, C.M.F., Chap.

SCOTTSDALE. *Scottsdale Memorial Hospital* 7400 E. Osborn Rd., 85251. Tel: 480-481-4000; 602-945-8437. Rev. Patrick Smith, Chap.

Special Assignment:
Reverend Monsignors—
McMahon, John J., Dir. Mount Claret Center, 4633 N. 54th St., Phoenix, AZ 85018. Tel: 602-840-5066
Moyer, Richard W., V.G., Vicar Amin. Svcs., 400 E. Monroe, Phoenix, AZ 85004. Tel: 602-257-0030
Reverend Fathers—
Acquaro, Philip A., C.S.B., Diocesan Ctr., Tribunal Office, 400 E. Monroe, Phoenix, AZ 85004. Tel: 602-257-0030
Conlon, Timothy, O.S.C., Vicar, Hispanic Ministry, Diocesan Center, 400 E. Monroe, Phoenix, AZ 85004. Tel: 602-257-0030
Diskin, Michael L., Asst. Chancellor & Ecumenical Officer, Diocesan Center, 400 E. Monroe, Phoenix, AZ. Tel: 602-257-0030
Fushek, Dale, V.G., St. Timothy, 1730 W. Guadalupe Rd., Mesa, AZ 85202. Tel: 480-775-5200
Goulet, Wayne F., 8540 N. Central Ave., #13, Phoenix, AZ 85020
Hall, John, Vicar, Native American Ministry, 400 E. Monroe, Phoenix, AZ 85004. Tel: 602-257-0030
Kline, Donald, Vocation Dir., 400 E. Monroe St., Phoenix, AZ 85004. Tel: 602-257-0030
Makacinas, Stanley, O.Carm., Exec. Dir. Kino Institute, 1224 E. Northern Ave., Phoenix, AZ 85020. Tel: 602-997-7397
Malone, Alan, Judicial Vicar, 400 E. Monroe, Phoenix, AZ 85004. Tel: 602-257-0030
Orel, Paul, Diocesan Center Tribunal Office, 400 E. Monroe, Phoenix, AZ
Parker, Charles, Tribunal Office, 400 E. Monroe St., Phoenix, AZ 85004. Tel: 602-257-0030
Ryle, Edward J., Exec. Dir., Arizona Catholic Conference, 400 E. Monroe St., Phoenix, AZ 85004. Tel: 602-257-0030
Sharp, David L., C.S.B., Campus Min., Glendale Community College, 6000 W. Olive Ave., Glendale, AZ 85302. Tel: 623-435-3525

On Duty Outside the Diocese:
Reverend Fathers—
Lessard, Joseph M.

On Leave:
Reverend Fathers—
Gauthier, John
Meyer, Vernon

Unassigned:
Reverend Fathers—
Boulanger, Andre
Bredemann, George
Briceno, Joseph
Lehman, Mark A.
Sherwood, Lan S.

Retired:
Reverend Fathers—
Bormann, Charles P., 5029 E. Smokehouse Tr., Cave Creek, AZ 85331
Boyle, Thomas, 325 W. Holly St., Phoenix, AZ 85003
Colton, Bernard, 122A Clanabogan Rd., Omagh, Co. Tyrone, BT 7815 N Northern Ireland
Cullinan, John F., St. Joan of Arc, 3801 E. Greenway Rd., Phoenix, AZ 85032-4698
Faustina, John M., P.O. Box 135, Island Pond, VT 05846-0135
Feit, Matthias, 12036 103rd Ave., Sun City, AZ 85351
Florez, Laurence A., P.O. Box 74, Youngtown, AZ 85363
Gillespie, Joseph, 13605 N. Del Webb Blvd., Sun City, AZ 85351
Glass, Gerald J., 8141 N. 16th St., #7, Phoenix, AZ 85020
Groves, Edmund, St. Paul's Convent, Bushmount, Clonakilty, Co. Cork, Ireland
Kelly, Martin C., O'Callaghans Mills, Count Clare, Ireland
Kotnis, Gregory M., P.O. Box 3081, Lake Havasu City, AZ 86405-3081
Krijnen, Joseph G., Resurrection Parish, 3201 S. Evergreen Rd., Tempe, AZ 85282
Long, Francis C., 2345 W. Orangewood Ave., Phoenix, AZ 85021-7659
Maguire, Eugene, 4701 N. 68th St., #147, Scottsdale, AZ 85251
McCready, Daniel A., 918 E. Broadmor, Tempe, AZ 85282
McKay, William E., 6457 E. Dodge St., Mesa, AZ 85205
Mitchell, William J., 1675 Leisure World, Mesa, AZ 85206
Morales, Raul, P.O. Box 6412, Mesa, AZ 85216-6412
O'Reilly, Francis J., 3633 N. 6th Ave., #B23, Phoenix, AZ 85013-3743
Pirrung, George, P.O. Box 1144, Cottonwood, AZ 86326
Portmann, Frederick, 1825 W. Emelita Ave., Mesa, AZ 85202
Sigman, Louis A., 1272 E. La Costa Pl., Chandler, AZ 85226
Wajda, Edward J., 214 S. Laveen Ave., Chandler, AZ 85226
Walsh, Thomas A., St. Bernadette Parish, 16245 N. 60th St., Scottsdale, AZ 85254. Tel: 602-905-0221
Wasielewski, Henry R., P.O. Box 939, Tempe, AZ 85280-0939

Permanent Deacons:
Aird, Gordon, St. Bridget, Mesa
Anderson, James, Immaculate Conception, Cottonwood
Anderson, Roy, (Retired), St. Daniel the Prophet, Scottsdale
Anselmo, Clement, St. John the Baptist, Laueen
Arnold, James, San Francisco de Asis, Flagstaff
Arnold, Maurice, (Retired), Our Lady of Lourdes, Sun City West
August, Joe, (Retired), Christ the King, Mesa
Babbits, Oliver, (Retired), St. Timothy, Mesa
Barelli, John, St. Philip Benizi Mission, Black Canyon City
Barr, Earl, SS. Simon & Jude Cathedral, Phoenix
Barraza, David, St. Anne, Gilbert
Bassett, Chris, St. Timothy, Mesa
Battista, James, Holy Cross, Mesa
Beard, Stephen, St. Benedict, Chandler
Beltran, Anthony N., St. Matthew's, Phoenix
Bennett, Bruce, St. Mary, Chandler
Berger, Don, St. Anne, Gilbert
Bernasconi, Santo R., Our Lady of Guadalupe, Guadalupe
Bidleman, William, St. Jerome, Phoenix
Bilinski, John, On leave
Bills, Tom, St. Maria Goretti, Scottsdale
Bolduc, Thomas, St. Timothy, Mesa
Bolton, Edward L., St. Gregory, Phoenix
Boswell, Keith, St. Anne, Gilbert
Bowslaugh, Alan P., St. James, Glendale
Brett, James, Resurrection, Tempe
Briesch, Forrest, St. Raphael, Glendale
Buchanan, James, St. Patrick, Scottsdale
Burgin, Edward, St. Francis Indian Mission, Scottsdale
Burke, Edward, St. Joseph Hospital, Phoenix
Cameron, George, St. Henry, Buckeye
Campas, Rudolph, St. Helen, Glendale
Campbell, Colin, St. Theresa, Phoenix
Carey, Robert, St. Ann, Gilbert
Carr, Michael, St. Timothy, Mesa
Cascio, James, St. John Vianney, Avondale
Chavez, Antonio, Blessed Sacrament, Tolleson
Clapham, Buddy, Queen of Peace, Mesa
Coe, Tom, Our Lady of the Lake, Lake Havasu City
Crawford, Don, St. Timothy, Mesa
Csuy, Paul E., St. Helen, Glendale
Cummings, Jack, Our Lady of Lourdes, Sun City West
Cuprak, Richard, St. Benedict, Chandler
Curran, Richard, Ss. Simon & Jude Cathedral, Phoenix
Czapinski, Clemens, St. Maria Goretti, Scottsdale
Dana, Frank, Holy Spirit, Tempe
Davey, Bob, (Retired), Our Lady of the Lake, Lake Havasu City
Davis, Keith, St. Thomas More, Glendale
Davis, William, Sacred Heart, Prescott
DeFelippis, Thomas, Our Lady of the Lake, Lake Havasu City
Del Monaco, William, St. Mary, Kingman
Dennis, Irving, St. Clement of Rome, Sun City
Devine, Frank, St. James, Glendale
Dippre, Martin, St. Daniel the Prophet, Scottsdale
Drapeau, Roy, St. Thomas More, Glendale
Dudzic, Anthony, St. Thomas the Apostle, Phoenix
Duran, Onofre, Immaculate Conception, Cottonwood
Eckert, Dick, St. Margaret Mary, Bullhead City
England, Robert E., St. Paul, Phoenix
Fejes, Peter, St. Edward, Phoenix
Ferski, Andy, (Retired), Most Holy Trinity, Phoenix
Fischer, Donald, St. Joan of Arc, Phoenix
Fleming, Irving, Our Lady of Perpetual Help Church, Scottsdale
Flynn, Patrick F., Corpus Christi, Phoenix
Franks, William, Queen of Peace, Mesa
Galarza, Frank, St. Margaret, Tempe
Garber, J. Pat, (Retired), St. Mary, Chandler
Garcia, Ernie, St. Andrew the Apostle, Chandler
Garza, Jose, Santa Teresita, El Mirage
Gaudio, Alexander L., Corpus Christi, Phoenix
Giesner, Fred, St. Bernard of Clairvaux, Scottsdale
Giza, Stanley, St. Clement of Rome, Sun City
Gonzales, Albert, St. Augustine, Phoenix
Goubeaux, Guy, St. Joan of Arc, Phoenix
Gouveia, Americo, St. Thomas the Apostle, Phoenix
Gregory, Tom, (Retired), Sacred Heart, Prescott
Guldan, Ranald, (Retired), St. Daniel the Prophet, Scottsdale
Guzman, Juan, St. Augustine, Phoenix
Hamilton, Jim, Office of the Diaconate
Heeter, Charles, Our Lady of Perpetual Help, Glendale
Henderson, Ron, Diocesan Center, Phoenix; St. Benedict, Chandler
Henn, Thomas, Luke Air Force Base, Litchfield
Hernandez, Jose, St. Mark, Phoenix
Hickcox, Edward M., San Francisco de Asis, Flagstaff
Hintze, Craig, St. Mary, Chandler
Hola, Sione, St. Theresa, Phoenix
Holgin, Alex, Our Lady of Mount Carmel, Tempe
Hoyt, James, Our Lady of Perpetual Help, Scottsdale
Hude, Harry, Blessed Sacrament, Scottsdale
Hughes, Patrick, Blessed Sacrament, Scottsdale
Humpal, Stanley, Christ the King, Mesa
Humphrey, Charles A., Sacred Heart, Prescott
Hurley, Dan A., (Retired), St. Joachim & St. Anne, Sun City
Hurrish, Dutch, St. Timothy, Mesa
Hursh, Paul, St. Timothy, Mesa
Jacobs, Gary, St. Andrew the Apostle, Chandler
Jenkins, William, St. Vincent de Paul, Phoenix
Jimenez, Ramon H., St. Ann, Gilbert
Johnson, Gary, Holy Spirit, Tempe
Kaminsky, David, St. Francis Cabrini, Camp Verde
Kayser, Thomas E., Assoc. Dir. of the Permanent Diaconate, Sacred Heart, Prescott
Kelly, Charles, St. Joseph, Phoenix
Kloft, Lee, St. Gregory Parish, Phoenix
Koch, George, Our Lady of Lourdes, Sun City West
Kuban, Donald, St. Thomas the Apostle, Phoenix
Kulinowski, Kenneth, St. Anne, Gilbert
Lamon, John, Sacred Heart Parish, Prescott
Lazok, George, St. Catherine of Siena, Phoenix
LeClair, Douglas, St. Thomas Byzantine, Gilbert
Lemire, Herve, St. Maria Goretti, Scottsdale
Leone, Robert, All Saints Newman Center, Tempe
Lessard, Joseph M., Mount Claret Retreat Center, Phoenix
Lewis, Brian, St. Mary, Kingman
Liszewski, Leonard, St. Bridget, Mesa
LoCascio, Phil, St. Joan of Arc, Phoenix
Lopez, Ed, St. Agnes, Phoenix
Lopez, Tony, Our Lady of Perpetual Help, Glendale
Lukaszewski, Don, All Saints, Mesa
Marion, Kenneth, (Retired), St. Paul, Phoenix
Marth, Jim, Santa Teresita, El Mirage
Martin, Sidney, St. Anthony, Sacaton
Martin, Stephen J., Our Lady of Lourdes, Sun City West
Meidl, Richard, St. Raphael, Glendale
Meli, John, (Retired), Our Lady of the Valley, Glendale, Mesa, Pedro, St. Margaret
Messer, Gene, St. Louis the King, Glendale
Meyer, John A., Diocesan Dir. of Catechetical Ministry, St. Bernadette, Scottsdale
Micek, Theodore, St. Jerome, Phoenix
Miller, John, (Retired), St. Thomas the Apostle, Byzanzine, Gilbert
Miller, Kenneth, St. Thomas the Apostle, Phoenix
Molina, Eddie, Our Lady of Perpetual Help, Glendale
Morton, Dwight, St. Benedict, Chandler
Mosley, William, Office of the Diaconate
Murphy, Peter, Director, Prison Ministry; Our Lady of the Lourdes, Sun City West
Myers, Robert P., Our Lady of Perpetual Help, Glendale
Neely, Vincent, All Saints, Mesa
O'Connor, John, St. James, Glendale
O'Toole, Gerald, St. Anne Parish, Gilbert
Olivarez, Jose D., St. Martin de Porres, Phoenix
Olivas, Manuel, St. Margaret Tempe
Ortega, Elisandro G., (Retired), St. Mark, Phoenix
Pardini, Louis, Ph.D., St. Philip the Deacon, Phoenix
Pelton, Ron, Immaculate Conception, Cottonwood
Petersen, Richard, St. Timothy, Mesa
Peterson, Daniel, Dir. Diaconate
Pfleger, James, Luke Air Force Base, Litchfield
Phares, William, Santa Teresita, El Mirage
Phelan, Mike, St. Jerome, Phoenix
Phelan, Thomas J., St. Francis of Assisi, Bagdad; St. Mary Mission, Yarnell
Rade, Douglas, San Francisco de Asis, Flagstaff
Raymond, Charles J., (Retired), St. Daniel the Prophet, Scottsdale
Raymond, Robert, (Retired), Office of the Diaconate
Regan, W. Richard, (Retired), St. Daniel the Prophet, Scottsdale
Rein, Richard, St. Jerome, Phoenix
Reinert, George, (Retired), St. Bernard of Clairvaux, Scottsdale
Riedel, John, Queen of Peace, Mesa
Rocha, Felix, Office of the Diaconate
Rodriguez, Jose, St. Mary, Kingman
Roger, Ray, St. Vincent de Paul, Phoenix
Rooker, Roy, St. Bernadette, Scottsdale
Roy, Alex, Scottsdale
Ruiz, Ron, Christ the King, Mesa
Salamone, James, St. Anne Parish, Gilbert
Salazar, Lorenzo, St. Vincent de Paul, Phoenix
Sanchez, Harry E., St. Agnes, Phoenix
Sanchez, Jesse, St. Daniel the Prophet, Scottsdale
Santa, Reed, All Saints, Mesa
Scaccia, Joe, St. Bridget, Mesa
Schwan, Harry, St. Joseph, Phoenix
Seibold, Tim, St. Helen, Glendale
Sejba, Jim, Our Lady of Joy, Carefree
Semmler, Raymond, (Retired), All Saints, Mesa
Shaw, Chuck, St. Thomas Aquinas, Litchfield Park
Shea, William, St. Bridget, Mesa
Shinske, Joseph, St. Helen's, Glendale
Simeone, Philip, Corpus Christi, Phoenix
Smith, Barry, St. Timothy, Mesa
Snyder, George, Holy Spirit, Tempe
Springer, James, St. Joan of Arc, Phoenix
Starrs, William, Sacred Heart, Prescott
Swisher, Thomas, Prison Ministry, St. John the Baptist
Terrazas, Carlos, Immaculate Heart, Phoenix
Tone, William, (Retired), St. Elizabeth Seton, Sun City
Torres, Vincent, Our Lady of Perpetual Help, Glendale
Treichel, Robert, (Retired), Our Lady of the Lake, Lake Havasu City
Valle, Matias, Ss. Simon & Jude, Phoenix
Valverde, W. George, St. Martin de Porres, Phoenix
Van Der Hayden, Philip, Christ the King, Mesa
Vasquez, Manuel, St. Catherine of Siena, Phoenix
Vera, Emidio B., (Retired), St. Catherine of Sienna, Phoenix

Vivio, William, St. Paul, Phoenix
Walsh, Thomas, Blessed Sacrament, Scottsdale
West, Tony, SS. Simon & Jude Cathedral, Phoenix
Whelan, Laurence, San Francisco de Asis, Flagstaff
White, Jim, All Saints, Mesa
Wisely, Phil, St. Margaret Mary, Bullhead City
Wood, Stewart, St. Elizabeth Seton, Sun City
Zbiegien, Leonard J., St. Thomas the Apostle, Phoenix

INSTITUTIONS LOCATED IN THE DIOCESE

[A] HIGH SCHOOLS, DIOCESAN

PHOENIX. *Bourgade Catholic High School*, 4602 N. 31st Ave., 85017. Tel: 602-973-4000; Fax: 602-973-5854.
E-mail: srmary@bourgade.org
Sr. Mary McGreevy, S.S.N.D., Prin.; Sr. Kathleen Janiak, R.S.M., Dir. Studies; Mr. Charles Hetzer, Dir. Studies; Mr. Robert Guyton, Dir. Students; Rev. John Ebbesmier, Chap. Sisters 4; Lay Teachers 28; Students 349.

St. Mary's High School, 2525 N. Third St., 85004. Tel: 602-254-6371; Fax: 602-253-0337.
E-mail: st_mary_hs_p@diocesephoenix.org
Web site: www.smks.org
Mr. Bill Lehman, Prin.; Mrs. Suzanne Fessler, Asst. Prin.; Mr. William Mueller, Dir. Guidance & Counseling; Rev. Marv Knighton, Campus Min. Academic Advisors: Sr. Linda Campbell, O.S.B.; Justin DiBianco; Daniel Johansen; Thomas Reilly. Priests 2; Sisters 1; Lay Teachers 50; Students 825.

Xavier College Preparatory, 4710 N. Fifth St., 85012. Tel: 602-277-3772; Fax: 602-279-1346.
E-mail: sjfphx@xcp.org
Web site: www.xcp.org
Sr. M. Joan Fitzgerald, B.V.M., Prin.; Sr. Lynn Winsor, B.V.M., Vice Prin. Sisters 10; Lay Teachers 63; Students 1,157.

CHANDLER. *Seton Catholic High School*, 1150 N. Dobson Rd., 85224. Tel: 480-963-1900; Fax: 480-963-1974.
E-mail: setoncatholic@diocesephoenix.org
Web site: www.setoncatholic.org
Dr. Richard Riley, Prin.; Mrs. Regina Wainwright, Asst. Prin.; Mrs. Shelley Connor, Fin. Admin. Priests 1; Sisters of Charity of Seton Hill 3; Lay Teachers 41; Students 537.

[B] HIGH SCHOOLS, PRIVATE

PHOENIX. *Brophy College Preparatory*, 4701 N. Central Ave., 85012. Tel: 602-264-5291; Fax: 602-266-3642.
Web site: www.brophyprep.org
Jesuit Fathers. Boys day school. Rev. Edward Reese, S.J., Pres.; Mr. Edwin J. Hearn, Prin.; Mr. William Kopas, Asst. Prin.; Mrs. Dorothy Dunnion, Asst. Prin.; Mr. A. Joseph Helm, Jr., Treas.; James Gmelich, Dean of Students; Revs. E. Louis Bishop, S.J.; Christopher Cartwright, S.J.; Kevin Dilworth, S.J.; J. Cameron Ayers, S.J.; James E. Flynn, S.J.; John J. Perlite, S.J., Sub-Min.; Lan Ngo, S.J., Scholastic; Anton J. Renna, S.J.; John R. Becker, S.J.; Harry T. Oliver, S.J.; Jesus Palomino, S.J., Scholastic; Minh Dang, S.J., Scholastic. Priests 10; Scholastics 3; Lay Teachers 75; Students 1,196.

[C] ELEMENTARY SCHOOLS, PAROCHIAL

PHOENIX. *St. John Bosco Catholic School Community*, P.O. Box 50537, 85076-0537. Tel: 602-257-5578. MaryBeth Mueller, Supt. of Schools. Intraparish school for Corpus Christi, Phoenix; Holy Spirit, Tempe; St. Andrew, Chandler and St. Benedict, Chandler.

SCOTTSDALE. *Pope John XXIII Catholic School Community*, 16235 N. 60th St., 85254. Tel: 480-905-0939; Fax: 480-905-0955.
E-mail: popejohnXXIII@diocesephoenix.org
Web site: www.popejohnXIII.org
Rev. Richard Felt, Liaison Pastor; Mr. William C. Langley, Prin. Intraparish School for St. Bernadette, Scottsdale; Blessed Sacrament, Scottsdale; St. Joan of Arc, Phoenix and Our Lady of Joy, Carefree. Sisters 1; Lay Teachers 20; Students 480.

[D] GENERAL HOSPITALS

PHOENIX. *St. Joseph's Hospital and Medical Center*, 350 W. Thomas Rd., P.O. Box 2071, 85001. Tel: 602-285-3000
For a complete listing, refer to the Hospitals section.

[E] HOMES FOR THE AGED & HANDICAPPED

PHOENIX. *Desert Crest Apartments*, 2101 E. Maryland Ave., 85016. Tel: 602-264-6427
For a complete listing, refer to the Special Care Facilities section.

Guadalupe Senior Village, 222 W. Thomas Rd., Ste. 214, 85103. Tel: 602-406-6218; Fax: 602-406-4119.
Web site: www.mercyhousing.org
For a complete listing, refer to the Special Care Facilities section.

Mesa Senior Meadows, 222 W. Thomas Rd., Ste. 214, 85013. Tel: 602-406-6218; Fax: 602-406-4119.
Web site: www.mercyhousing.org
For a complete listing, refer to the Special Care Facilities section.

Senior Village, 3541 W. Vogel, 85051. Tel: 602-843-3008
For a complete listing, refer to the Special Care Facilities section.

Sweetwater Gardens Apartments, 2035 E. Sweetwater, 85022. Tel: 602-867-4549
For a complete listing, refer to the Special Care Facilities section.

AVONDALE. *Vianney Villas Apartments*, 750 S. Fourth St., 85323. Tel: 623-932-2036
For a complete listing, refer to the Special Care Facilities section.

KINGMAN. *Kingman Heights Apartments*, 1020 Detroit Ave., 86401. Tel: 520-753-2425
For a complete listing, refer to the Special Care Facilities section.

LAKE HAVASU CITY. *Becket House Apartments*, 865 Cashmere Dr., 86403. Tel: 520-855-7178
For a complete listing, refer to the Special Care Facilities section.

WICKENBURG. *Padua Hills Apartments*, 460 S. West Rd., 85390. Tel: 520-684-7034
For a complete listing, refer to the Special Care Facilities section.

WILLIAMS. *St. Agnes Apartments*, 200 S. Ninth, 86046. Tel: 520-635-2913
For a complete listing, refer to the Special Care Facilities section.

[F] CONVENTS AND RESIDENCES OF SISTERS

PHOENIX. *Institute of Blessed Virgin Mary (I.B.V.M.)*. (Regional House), 2521 W. Maryland Ave., 85017. Tel: 602-433-0658; Fax: 602-864-8620. Sisters 4.

Missionaries of Charity, 1414 S. 17th Ave., 85007. Tel: 602-258-5504. Sisters 3.

Our Lady of Guadalupe Monastery. Sisters of St. Benedict, 8502 W. Pinchot, 85037. Tel: 623-848-9608.
E-mail: bensrs@aol.com
Sr. Linda Campbell, O.S.B., Prioress.
Day Care Center. Capacity 12; Children 12. Sisters 2.

Sisters of Charity of the Blessed Virgin Mary. (Xavier Convent), 4712 N. Third St., 85012. Tel: 602-264-0445. Sisters 7.

Sisters of Divine Savior, 323 E. Elm St., 85012-1703. Tel: 602-274-0228.
E-mail: sdselmst@fastq.com
Sr. Georgene Faust, S.D.S., Cluster Coord. for Region. Sisters 5.

Union of Sisters of the Presentation of the Blessed Virgin Mary. (Provincial House), 729 W. Wilshire Dr., 85007. Tel: 602-271-9687; 258-9476; Fax: 602-253-9166. Sr. Joan O'Sullivan, P.B.V.M., Prov. Sisters 2.

MESA. *Sisters of Notre Dame de Namur*. (Casa Guadalupe), 548 W. Third St., 85201. Tel: 480-964-3685; Fax: 480-655-9975.
E-mail: mesasnd@aol.com
Students 2.

TEMPE. *Sisters of Charity*. (Seton House), 1014 S. George Dr., 85281. Tel: 480-967-5538. Sisters 3.

[G] MONASTERIES AND RESIDENCES OF PRIEST AND BROTHERS

PHOENIX. *Carmelite Community*, 1717 W. Flower, 85015. Revs. Valentine L. Boyle, O.Carm., (Retired); John R. Larkin, O.Carm., (Retired). Priests 2.

Crosier Community of Phoenix (Canons Regular of the Order of the Holy Cross), 2617 E. Campbell Ave., 85016. Tel: 602-224-0434; Fax: 602-224-0722.
E-mail: frkunkel@amug.org
Revs. Joseph P. Cain, O.S.C.; Joseph J. Bruemmer, O.S.C.; Richard N. Ohlemacher, O.S.C.; Louis R. Mraz, O.S.C.; Robert J. Bliven, O.S.C.; Leo W. Kapphahn, O.S.C.; Joseph A. Fichtner, O.S.C.; Neil Emon, O.S.C., Prior; Robert V. Zylla, O.S.C.; John Vincent, O.S.C.; Timothy Conlon, O.S.C.; Bros. James Scher, O.S.C.; Fernando Rivera, O.S.C.; Gabriel Guerrero, O.S.C. Priests 11; Brothers 3.

Holy Cross Congregation/Casa Santa Cruz, 7126 N. Seventh Ave., 85021. Tel: 602-944-6000; Fax: 602-944-1221. Revs. Eugene A. Burke, C.S.C.; Milton N. Adamson, C.S.C.; Joseph F. O'Donnell, C.S.C., Dir.; David Schlaver, C.S.C., Supr.; John P. Schuneman, C.S.C.; Ambrose J. Wheeler, C.S.C.; Robert L. Kramer, C.S.C.; Louis W. Rink, C.S.C., (Retired); Bros. Robert Woodward; Timothy O'Connell, C.S.C. Priests 8; Brothers 2.

TEMPE. *Dominicans (Dominican Community-Jordan House)*, 1042 E. Campus, 85282. Tel: 480-829-1804. Revs. Nathan G. Castle, O.P., Supr.; Jordan Vajda, O.P. Priests 2.

[H] RETREAT HOUSES

PHOENIX. *Mt. Claret Center*, 4633 N. 54th St., 85018. Tel: 602-840-5066; Fax: 602-840-5732. Rev. Msgr. John J. McMahon, Dir.; Rev. Eugene Maguire, Dir.; Sr. Regina Marie Boslet, S.C., Assoc. Dir.; Jo Swiger, Assoc. Dir.
Cursillo Movement: Rev. Msgr. John J. McMahon, Spiritual Dir.; Sr. Janice Bohn, S.N.D.deN., Assoc. Spiritual Dir. Priests 2.

BLACK CANYON CITY. *Contemplative House of Prayer*. (Our Lady of Solitude), P.O. Box 1140, 85324. Tel: 623-374-9204. Sr. Mary Therese Sedlock, O.S.F., Dir.

SCOTTSDALE. *Franciscan Renewal Center, Inc. (Casa de Paz Y Bien)*, 5802 E. Lincoln Dr., 85253. Tel: 480-948-7460; Fax: 480-948-2325.
E-mail: pazybien@aol.com
Web site: www.thecasa.org
Bro. Joseph Schwab, O.F.M., Dir.; Revs. Micah Muhlen, O.F.M.; Peter Kirwin, O.F.M.; William Shaughnessy, O.F.M.; Bro. Mario Vasquez, O.F.M. Priests 3; Brothers 2.

[I] NEWMAN CENTERS

PHOENIX. *Office of Youth and Young Adult Ministries*, 400 E. Monroe, 85004. Tel: 602-257-5559; Fax: 602-462-5207.
E-mail: lfraher@diocesephoenix.org
Directors: Larry Fraher; Barbara Stanley. Mesa Community College, Chandler; Gilbert Community College; Glendale Community College; Scottsdale Community College; Paradise Valley Community College; ASU West.

American Graduate School of International Management. (Glendale), Thunderbird Campus, 15249 N. 59th Ave., Glendale, 85306. Tel: 602-978-7011. Joaquin Duarte. Tel: 602-978-7184.

Glendale Community College, 35949 S. Ricon Rd., Wickenburg, 85390. Tel: 520-684-7779. Rev. David L. Sharp, C.S.B.

Yavapai College, Emery Riddle Aeronautical University. (Prescott), Sacred Heart Parish, 150 Fleury Ave., Prescott, 86301. Tel: 520-445-3141. Mr. Ed Johanson.

Arizona State University. (Tempe), All Saints Catholic Newman Center, 230 E. University Dr., P.O. Box 1987, Tempe, 85281. Tel: 480-967-7823. Revs. Nathan Castle, O.P., Dir.; Jordan Vajda, O.P.

Catholic Committee on Scouting. Tel: 602-961-1610. Rev. Dennis J. O'Rourke, Chap.

[J] ACADEMIES OF RELIGIOUS TEACHING

PHOENIX. *Kino Institute*, 1224 E. Northern Ave., 85020-4295. Tel: 602-997-7397; Fax: 602-870-8871.
E-mail: kino@cathdioc.org
Rev. Stanley Makacinas, O.Carm., Exec. Dir. Tel: 602-212-1745; Teofilo Argueta-Ramirez, Dir. La Programa de Formacion Pastoral; Kathy Brown, Dean School of Theological Studies; Pat Julian, Dir. Spirituality Program Art of Spiritual Direction: An Ecumenical Program; Rev. Michael Kwiecien, O.Carm., Faculty; Margaret Newman, Business Mgr.; Sr. Bibiane Roy, O.P., Librarian. Tel: 602-906-9798; Terry Temple, Dir. Survival School of Church Mgmt. Tel: 602-874-3719; Marilyn Crawford, Dir. Bookstore. Tel: 602-906-9798; Diana Stickney, Dir. University San Francisco Graduate Program. Tel: 602-870-4123; Fax: 602-678-5675; Joe Velazquez, Emeritus Faculty. Total Staff 18.

[K] MISCELLANEOUS LISTINGS

PHOENIX. *Andre House of Arizona*, 213 S. 11th Ave., 85007-3132. Hospitality House, Indiana Province of the Congregation of Holy Cross. Mailing Address: P.O. Box 2014, 85001-2014. Tel: 602-255-0580; Fax: 602-254-3834. Rev. Brent Allan Kruger, C.S.C., Dir.; Bro. Richard Armstrong, C.S.C.

Avondale Senior Village, 222 W. Thomas Rd., Suite 214, 85013. Tel: 602-406-6218. Cherie Kirschbaum, Pres.; Stephen L. Hastings, Vice Pres.

Camelot Casitas, 222 W. Thomas Rd., Suite 214, 85013. Tel: 602-406-6218. Cherie Kirschbaum, Pres.; Stephen L. Hastings, Vice Pres.

Casa De Merced, 222 W. Thomas Rd., #214, 85013. Tel: 602-406-6218; Fax: 602-406-4119.
Web site: www.mercyhousing.org
Cherie Kirschbaum, Pres.

Catholic Social Services of Central and Northern Arizona, Inc., 1610 W. Camelback Rd., 85015. Tel: 602-285-1999; Fax: 602-285-0311. Kathryn Byrne, Pres.; Paul Martodam, M.P.A., CEO; Kristen Schmidt, M.S.W., Ph.D., COO.
Regional Agencies:
Catholic Social Service of Phoenix, 1825 W. Northern Ave., 85021. Tel: 602-997-6105; Fax: 602-870-3891.

West Valley Office, 14010 N. El Mirage Rd., El Mirage, 85323. Tel: 623-972-1576.

Head Start Office, 8438 N. 39th Ave., 85051. Tel: 602-937-5230. Maureen Webster, A.C.S.W., C.I.S.W., Regl. Dir.

East Valley Catholic Social Service, 430 N. Dobson Rd., Ste. 110, Mesa, 85201. Tel: 480-964-8771; Fax: 480-964-8865. 24 hour Domestic Violence Hotline Tel: 480-821-1024. Ellie Gersten, A.C.S.W., Regl. Dir.

Catholic Social Service Flagstaff, 43 S. San Francisco, Flagstaff, 86001. Tel: 520-774-9125; Fax: 520-774-0697. Tara Fairfield, Ed.D., Regl. Dir.

Catholic Social Service of Yavapai, 116 N. Summit, Prescott, 86301. Tel: 520-778-2531; Fax: 520-771-9531.

Verde Valley Office, 736 North Main St., Cottonwood, 86326. Tel: 520-634-4254; Fax: 520-639-4368. John Allen, M.C., Regl. Dir.

Catholic Social Service of Mohave, 1370 Ramar Rd., Ste. D, Bullhead City, 86442. Tel: 520-758-4176; Fax: 520-758-5141.

2438 Kingman Ave., Kingman, 86401. Tel: 520-718-1117; Fax: 520-718-1124.

Westside Head Start, 7400 W. Olive Ave., Ste. 10, Peoria, 85345. Tel: 623-486-9868; Fax: 623-486-9988. 27 Head Start Centers. Linda Brown, Dir.

Pregnancy Parenting & Adoption Services, 1825 W. Northern Ave., 85021. Tel: 602-997-6105; Fax: 602-331-4071. Adrienne Kraft, A.S.C.W., C.I.S.W., Dir.

Office of Peace & Justice, 1610 W. Camelback Rd., 85015. Tel: 602-285-1999; Fax: 602-285-0311. Sr. Carmen Ferrante, M.S.C., Dir.

Residential Facilities:

Casa Linda Lodge. Tel: 602-943-6461; Fax: 602-943-4173. Pregnant and parenting teens. Diane Ellis, C.I.S.W., Res. Prog. Supvr.

Sundance Lodge. Tel: 602-870-0376; Fax: 602-870-3891. Group Transitional living for homeless mothers and their children. Diane Ellis, C.I.S.W., Res. Prog. Supvr.

My Sister's Place. Tel: 480-821-1024; Fax: 480-963-9532. Domestic Violence Shelter.

Spring Haven Group Home. Tel: 602-997-6105; Fax: 602-870-3891. Abused and neglected adolescent girls. Diane Ellis, C.I.S.W., Res. Prog. Supvr.

Aspen House, 304 S. O'Leary, Flagstaff, 86001. Tel: 520-226-8600. Tara Fairfield, Ed.D., Regl. Dir.

The Catholic Tuition Organization of the Diocese of Phoenix, 400 E. Monroe, 85004. Tel: 602-744-6342; Fax: 602-258-3425.
E-mail: ctodp@diocesephoenix.org
Web site: www.ctodp.org
Jennifer Kraus, Dir.; Rev. Msgr. Richard Moyer, Pres.

Christ Child Society, 4633 N. 54th St., 85018-1904. Tel: 602-667-3355. Ann Schwanekamp, Pres.

El Mirage Senior Village, 222 W. Thomas Rd, #214, 85013. Tel: 602-406-6218; Fax: 602-406-4119.
Web site: www.mercyhousing.org
Cherie Kirschbaum, Pres.

Foundation for Senior Living, 77 E. Thomas Rd., Ste. 100, 85012. Tel: 602-285-1800; Fax: 602-285-1838.
E-mail: gmikkelsen@diocesephoenix.org
Murray Gibson, Chm.; Guy Mikkelsen, Pres.

Foundation for Senior Adult Living, Inc. Sweetwater Gardens (Apartments for the Handicapped), Phoenix; Kingman Heights Apartments, Kingman. Tel: 602-285-1800; Fax: 602-285-1838.
E-mail: chollinger@diocesephoenix.org
Charles Hollinger, Contact Person.

FSAL Desert Crest. Tel: 602-285-1800; Fax: 602-285-1838. Charles Hollinger, Contact Person.

FSAL Development Corp. (Sun Terrace Apartments, Mesa). Tel: 602-285-1800; Fax: 602-285-1838.

FSAL Management. Tel: 602-285-1800; Fax: 602-285-1838.
E-mail: switt@diocesephoenix.org
Selina Witt, Contact Person.

FSAL Programs. Adult Day Health Care Centers; In-Home Care Services; Home Safety & Repair Program; Community Action Programs/Senior Centers; Adult Foster Care; Oasis (Older Adult Service & Information System); Pathways Program (Resources and Referral-Care Management). Tel: 602-285-1800; Fax: 602-285-1838.
E-mail: lmartin@diocesephoenix.org
Linda Martin, Dir.

FSAL Rural Development. Becket House Apartments, Lake Havasu City; Vianney Villas Apartments, Avondale; Padua Hills Apartments, Wickenburg; St. Agnes Apartments, Williams, Amy Neal Retirement Center, Kingman. Tel: 602-285-1850; Fax: 602-285-1838.

Payson Senior Living, Inc. (Pineview Manor Apartments, Payson). Tel: 602-285-1800; Fax: 602-285-1838. Charles Hollinger, Contact Person.

FSL Pathways. Assisted Group Living Program (11 Houses), Phoenix. Tel: 602-285-1800; Fax: 602-285-1838. Charles Hollinger, Contact Person.

Guadalupe Senior Village, 222 W. Thomas Rd., Ste. 214, 85013. Tel: 602-406-6218.
Web site: www.mercyhousing.org
Cherie Kirschbaum, Pres.

Mercy Housing Southwest, 222 W. Thomas, #214, 85013. Tel: 602-406-6218; Fax: 602-406-4119.
Web site: www.mercyhousing.org
Cherie Kirschbaum, Pres.

Mercy Properties Arizona, 222 W. Thomas Rd., #214, 85013. Tel: 602-406-6218; Fax: 602-406-4119.
Web site: www.mercyhousing.org
Cherie Kirschbaum, Pres.

Mesa Senior Meadows, 222 W. Thomas Rd., Ste. 214, 85013. Tel: 602-406-6218.
Web site: www.mercyhousing.org
Cherie Kirschbaum, Pres.

National Catholic Council for Hispanic Ministry, Inc., 2929 N. Central Ave., Suite 1500, 85012. Tel: 602-266-8623; Fax: 602-266-8670.
E-mail: ncchmi@aol.com
Web site: www.ncchm.org
Mr. Armando Contreras, Exec. Dir.

Natural Family Planning, 400 N. 30th St., 85008. Tel: 602-225-0636; Fax: 602-225-0175.
E-mail: phxnfp@aol.com
Web site: www.phxnfp.org
Peggy Frei, Dir. & Diocesan Coord. for N.F.P. Svcs. Center provides Natural Family Planning Services, Instructional Series, Introductions to Natural Family Planning for Marriage Preparation. Program is endorsed by the Diocesan Development Plan for N.F.P., National Council of Catholic Bishops.

Peoria Place, 222 W. Thomas Rd., Suite 214, 85013. Tel: 602-406-6218. Cherie Kirschbaum, Pres.; Stephen L. Hastings, Vice Pres.

Plazas de Merced, 222 W. Thomas Rd., #214, 85013. Tel: 602-402-6218; Fax: 602-406-4119.
Web site: www.mercyhousing.org
Cherie Kirschbaum, Pres.

St. Joseph the Worker. (Job Service), 213 S. 11th Ave., 85007-3503. Tel: 602-257-4390; Fax: 602-254-3834.
E-mail: the_worker_jobs@bigfoot.com
Mailing Address: P.O. Box 13503, 85002-3503. Michael Barlow, Chm. Bd. of Dir.; Janet M. Gray, Exec. Dir.; Tom Ryan, Vice Pres.; Bro. Richard Armstrong, C.S.C., Treas. To assist homeless people and those on the verge of homelessness, in their efforts to secure and keep full-time, meaningful employment.

St. Mary's Scholarship & Benefit Fund, 2525 N. Third St., 85004. Tel: 602-254-6371; Fax: 602-253-0337. David Cantelme, Pres.

St. Vincent De Paul Society, P.O. Box 13600, 85002. Tel: 602-254-3338; Fax: 602-261-6829.
Web site: www.stvincentdepaul.net
Stephen J. Zabilski, Exec. Dir.; Nancy B. Spencer, Pres.; Rev. Msgr. John J. McMahon, Spiritual Advisor.

Southwest Catholic Health Network Corp., 2800 N. Central Ave., Ste. 400, 85004. Tel: 602-263-3066; Fax: 602-263-2098. Katherine J. Byrne, Pres.

Vista Alegre, 222 W. Thomas Rd., Ste. 214, 85013. Tel: 602-406-6218. Cherie Kirschbaum, Pres.

GOODYEAR. *St. John Vianney School Development Fund*, 539 La Pasada Blvd., 85338. Tel: 623-932-3313; Fax: 623-932-1896.
E-mail: frcorpora@cathdioc.org
Rev. Joseph V. Corpora, C.S.C., Pres.

MESA.

Life Teen, Inc., 1730 W. Guadalupe Rd., 85202. Tel: 480-820-7001.
E-mail: pbaniewicz@diocesephoenix.org
Mr. Phil Baniewicz, Exec. Dir.

PEORIA. *The Catholic Retreat for Young Singles, Inc.*, 8219 W. Salter Dr., 85382. Tel: 623-825-3889.
E-mail: Davidjgannon@uswest.net
David Gannon, Liaison.

TEMPE.

City of the Lord, 711 W. University Dr., 85281-3411. Tel: 480-968-5895; 968-5990; Fax: 480-921-9175.
E-mail: cotled@aol.com
Edward Wilmowski, Pres. Vice Presidents: James R. Jones; Robert Carmody.

Friends of the Orphans. Mailing Address: P.O. Box 25507, 85285-5507. 424 E. Southern Ave, Ste. 102, 85282. Tel: 480-967-9449; Fax: 480-967-9288.
E-mail: fotoaz@fotoaz.org
Web site: www.fotoaz.org
Dee Campbell, Exec. Dir.

RELIGIOUS INSTITUTES OF MEN REPRESENTED IN THE DIOCESE

For further details refer to the corresponding bracketed number in the Religious Institutes of Men or Women section.

[0170]—*Basilian Fathers*. (Western Prov.).—C.S.B.
[0200]—*Benedictine Monks*. (St. Meinrad Archabbey).—O.S.B.
[0600]—*Brothers of the Congregation of Holy Cross*.—C.S.C.
[0400]—*Canons Regular of the Order of the Holy Cross*.—O.S.C.
[0270]—*Carmelite Fathers and Brothers*. (Prov. of St. Elias).—O.Carm.
[0350]—*Cistercian Order of the Strict Observance (Trappists)*.—O.C.S.O.
[0360]—*Claretian Missionaries*. (Western Prov.).—C.M.F.
[1330]—*Congregation of the Mission*. (Prov. of the West).—C.M.
[0520]—*Franciscan Friars*. (Prov. of Santa Barbara).—O.F.M.
[0650]—*Holy Ghost Fathers*. (Western Prov.).—C.S.Sp.
[0690]—*Jesuit Fathers and Brothers*. (California, Oregon & Chicago Provs.).—S.J.
[0910]—*Oblates of Mary Immaculate*. (Our Lady of Hope).—O.M.I.
[0430]—*Order of Preachers (Dominicans)*. (Western Prov.).—O.P.
[0610]—*Priests of the Congregation of Holy Cross*.—C.S.C.
[1240]—*Servites*. (Western Prov.).—O.S.M.
[1200]—*Society of the Divine Savior*. (North American Prov.).—S.D.S.
[1060]—*Society of the Precious Blood*. (Cincinnati Prov.).—C.PP.S.

RELIGIOUS INSTITUTES OF WOMEN REPRESENTED IN THE DIOCESE

[0230]—*Benedictine Sisters of Pontifical Jurisdiction*. (Duluth, St. Paul, MN).—O.S.B.
[0990]—*Congregation of Divine Providence*. (Pittsburgh, PA).—C.D.P.
[2715]—*The Congregation of Missionary Sisters of Christ the King for Polish Immigrants*. (Poznan, Poland; Chicago, IL).—M.Chr.
[1780]—*Congregation of Sisters of the Third Order of St. Francis of Perpetual Adoration*. (La Crosse, WI).—F.S.P.A.
[3710]—*Congregation of the Sisters of St. Agnes*. (Fond du Lac, WI).—C.S.A.
[1920]—*Congregation of the Sisters of the Holy Cross*. (Notre Dame, IN).—C.S.C.
[1710]—*Congregation of the Third Order of St. Francis of Mary Immaculate*. (Joliet, IL).—O.S.F.
[0760]—*Daughters of Charity*. (Los Altos Hills, CA).—D.C.
[0850]—*Daughters of Mary Help of Christians*. (San Antonio, TX).—F.M.A.
[0810]—*Daughters of the Heart of Mary*. (Holyoke, MA).—D.H.M.
[1070-03]—*Dominican Sisters*. (Sinsinawa, WI).—O.P.
[1070-11]—*Dominican Sisters*. (Sparkill, NY).—O.P.
[1070-13]—*Dominican Sisters*. (Adrian, MI).—O.P.
[1070-24]—*Dominican Sisters*. (Great Bend, KS).—O.P.
[1070-28]—*Dominican Sisters*. (Akron, OH).—O.P.
[1070-30]—*Dominican Sisters*. (Mountain View, CA).—O.P.
[1120]—*Dominican Sisters of Roman Congregation*. (Iowa City, IA).—O.P.
[1230]—*Franciscan Sisters of Christian Charity*. (Manitowoc, WI).—O.S.F.
[1310]—*Franciscan Sisters of Little Falls, Minnesota*. (Little Falls, MN).—O.S.F.
[1430]—*Franciscan Sisters of Our Lady of Perpetual Help*. (St. Louis, MO).—O.S.F.
[1440]—*Franciscan Sisters of the Poor*. (Brooklyn, NY).—F.S.P.
[2370]—*Institute of the Blessed Virgin Mary (Loretto Sisters)*. (Toronto, Ont., Canada).—I.B.V.M.
[2380]—*Institute of the Blessed Virgin Mary (Loretto Sisters)*. (Rathfarnham, Dublin, Ireland).—I.B.V.M.
[2740]—*Maryknoll Sisters of St. Dominic*. (Maryknoll, NY).—M.M.
[]—*Missionarias Carmelitas de Santa Teresa del Nino Jesus*. (Pueblo, Mexico).—M.C.S.T.N.J.
[]—*Missionarias del Espiritu Santo y la Familia Sagrada*. (Coahuila, Mexico).—M.E.S.F.S.
[2710]—*Missionaries of Charity*. (Calcutta, India).—M.C.
[]—*Missionaries of the Kingship of Christ, a Secular Institute*. (Bethesda, MD).—S.I.M.
[2860]—*Missionary Sisters of the Sacred Heart of Jesus*. (New York, NY).—M.S.C.
[3130]—*Our Lady of Victory Missionary Sisters*. (Huntington, IN).—O.L.V.M.
[2970]—*School Sisters of Notre Dame*. (Milwaukee, WI; Irving, TX; Mankato, MN; Wilton, CT).—S.S.N.D.
[1680]—*School Sisters of St. Francis*. (Milwaukee, WI).—S.S.S.F.
[1690]—*School Sisters of the Third Order of St Francis*. (Pittsburgh, PA).—O.S.F.
[0440]—*Sisters of Charity of Cincinnati, Ohio*.—S.C.
[0570]—*Sisters of Charity of Seton Hill, Greensburg, Pennsylvania*.—S.C.
[0430]—*Sisters of Charity of the B.V.M.* (Dubuque, IA).—B.V.M.

[2575]—*Sisters of Mercy of the Americas.* (Pittsburgh, PA; Burlingame, CA; Chicago, IL; Omaha, NE).—R.S.M.

[3000]—*Sisters of Notre Dame de Namur.* (Cincinnati, OH).—S.N.D.deN.

[1540]—*Sisters of St. Francis.* (Clinton, IA).—O.S.F.

[1705]—*The Sisters of St. Francis of Assisi.* (Milwaukee, WI).—O.S.F.

[1630]—*Sisters of St. Francis of Penance and Charity.* (Redwood City, CA).—O.S.F.

[1570]—*Sisters of St. Francis of the Holy Family.* (Dubuque, IA).—O.S.F.

[3830-05]—*Sisters of St. Joseph.* (Brentwood, NY).—C.S.J.

[3830-11]—*Sisters of St. Joseph.* (Nazareth, MI).—S.S.J.

[3830-15]—*Sisters of St. Joseph.* (Concordia, KS).—C.S.J.

[3840]—*Sisters of St. Joseph of Carondelet.*—C.S.J.

[3930]—*Sisters of St. Joseph of the Third Order of St. Francis.* (South Bend, IN).—S.S.J.-T.O.S.F.

[1030]—*Sisters of the Divine Savior.* (Milwaukee, WI).—S.D.S.

[1990]—*Sisters of the Holy Names of Jesus and Mary.* (Los Gatos,CA).—S.N.J.M.

[3730]—*Sisters of the Order of St. Basil the Great.* (Uniontown, PA).—O.S.B.M.

[3260]—*Sisters of the Precious Blood.* (Dayton, OH).—C.PP.S.

[3320]—*Sisters of the Presentation of the B.V.M.* (San Francisco, CA).—P.B.V.M.

[2150]—*Sisters, Servants of the Immaculate Heart of Mary.*—I.H.M.

[3330]—*Union of the Sisters of the Presentation of the B.V.M.* (Phoenix, AZ).—P.B.V.M.

NECROLOGY

† Bourbon, Arthur, (Retired). —Died Jan. 18, 2000.

† Smith, Paul, (Retired). —Died July 8, 2000.

Diocese of Pittsburgh

(Dioecesis Pittsburgensis)

Most Reverend

DONALD W. WUERL, S.T.D.

Bishop of Pittsburgh; ordained December 17, 1966; appointed Titular Bishop of Rosemarkie and Auxiliary Bishop of Seattle December 3, 1985; consecrated January 6, 1986; appointed and canonically installed Bishop of Pittsburgh February 12, 1988; liturgically installed March 25, 1988. *Office: 111 Blvd. of the Allies, Pittsburgh, PA, 15222-1618. All official correspondence should be sent to this office.*

Most Reverend

JOHN B. MCDOWELL, PH.D.

Retired Auxiliary Bishop of Pittsburgh; Titular Bishop of Tamazuca; ordained November 4, 1945; appointed July 18, 1966; consecrated September 8, 1966; resigned September 30, 1996. *Mailing Address: c/o Diocese of Pittsburgh, 111 Blvd. of the Allies, Pittsburgh, PA, 15222-1618.*

Most Reverend

WILLIAM J. WINTER, V.G., S.T.D.

Auxiliary Bishop of Pittsburgh and Titular Bishop of Uthina; ordained December 17, 1955; appointed December 27, 1988; consecrated February 13, 1989. *Res., Sacred Heart Church, 310 Shady Ave., Pittsburgh, PA, 15206-4389.*

Most Reverend

DAVID A. ZUBIK, V.G., D.D.

Auxiliary Bishop of Pittsburgh; ordained May 3, 1975; appointed February 18, 1997; installed April 6, 1997. *Mailing Address: c/o 111 Blvd. of the Allies, Pittsburgh, PA, 15222-1618.*

ESTABLISHED AUGUST 8, 1843.

Square Miles 4,092.

Comprises the Counties of Allegheny, Beaver, Lawrence, Washington, Greene, and Butler in the State of Pennsylvania.

For legal titles of parishes and diocesan institutions, consult the Legal Office.

Pastoral Center: 111 Blvd. of the Allies, Pittsburgh, PA, 15222-1618. Tel.: 412-456-3000.

Web site address: www.diopitt.org

E-mail address: communications@diopitt.org

STATISTICAL OVERVIEW

Personnel	
Bishop	1
Auxiliary Bishops	2
Retired Bishops	1
Priests: Diocesan Active in Diocese	338
Priests: Active Outside Diocese	27
Priests: Diocesan in Foreign Missions	2
Priests: Retired, Sick or Absent	112
Number of Diocesan Priests	479
Religious Priests in Diocese	123
Extern Priests in Diocese	51
Ordinations:	
Diocesan Priests	6
Permanent Deacons in Diocese	52
Total Brothers	37
Total Sisters	1,606
Parishes	
Parishes	216
With Resident Pastor:	
Resident Diocesan Priests	198
Resident Religious Priests	11
Without Resident Pastor:	
Administered by Priests	7
New Parishes Created	2
Closed Parishes	2
Professional Ministry Personnel:	
Brothers	3
Sisters	67
Lay Ministers	242
Welfare	
Catholic Hospitals	7
Total Assisted	1,039,870
Homes for the Aged	11
Total Assisted	1,444
Day Care and Extended Day Care Centers	22
Total Assisted	2,139
Specialized Homes	7
Total Assisted	7,199
Special Centers for Social Services	11
Total Assisted	92,638
Residential Care of Disabled	1
Total Assisted	307
Educational	
Seminaries, Diocesan	1
Students from This Diocese	9
Diocesan Students in Other Seminaries	18
Total Seminarians	27
Colleges and Universities	3
Total Students	13,829
High Schools, Diocesan and Parish	8
Total Students	3,574
High Schools, Private	3
Total Students	630
Elementary Schools, Diocesan and Parish	106
Total Students	26,078
Elementary Schools, Private	4
Total Students	950
Non-residential Schools for the Disabled	2
Total Students	154
Catechesis/Religious Education:	
High School Students	6,862
Elementary Students	50,154
Total Students Under Catholic Instruction	102,258
Teachers in the Diocese:	
Priests	5
Brothers	9
Sisters	95
Lay Teachers	1,946
Vital Statistics	
Receptions into the Church:	
Infant Baptism Totals	8,598
Adult Baptism Totals	378
Received into Full Communion	776
First Communions	8,797
Confirmations	9,083
Marriages:	
Catholic	2,223
Interfaith	1,035
Total Marriages	3,258
Deaths	9,699
Total Catholic Population	753,147
Total Population	1,939,656

Former Bishops—Rt. Rev. MICHAEL J. O'CONNOR, D.D., ord. June 1, 1833; cons. Aug. 15, 1843; transferred to Erie and then to Pittsburgh Dec. 20, 1853; resigned May 23, 1860; entered the Society of Jesus Dec. 22, 1860; died at Woodstock College, MD, Oct. 18, 1872.—Rt. Rev. MICHAEL DOMENEC, C.M., D.D., ord. June 30, 1839; cons. Dec. 9, 1860; transferred to Allegheny, Jan. 11, 1876; resigned July 29, 1877; died at Tarragona, Spain, Jan. 5, 1878.—Rt. Rev. JOHN TUIGG, D.D., ord. May 14, 1850; cons. March 19, 1876; transferred as Apostolic Administrator of Allegheny 1877; died at Altoona Dec. 7, 1889.—Rt. Rev. RICHARD PHELAN, D.D., ord. May 4, 1854; cons. Aug. 2, 1885; Titular Bishop of Cibyra and Coadjutor to the Rt. Rev. John Tuigg; succeeded to Bishop Tuigg, Dec. 7, 1889; died Dec. 20, 1904.—Most Rev. J. F. REGIS CANEVIN, D.D., ord. June 4, 1879; cons. Titular Bishop of Sabrata and Coadjutor, Feb. 24, 1903; succeeded to the See of Pittsburgh, Dec. 20, 1904; resigned Nov. 26, 1920; Titular Archbishop of Pelusium; appt. Jan. 9, 1921; died March 22, 1927.—Most Rev. HUGH C. BOYLE, D.D., ord. July 2, 1898; succeeded to the See of Pittsburgh, June 16, 1921; cons. June 29, 1921; died Dec. 22, 1950.—His Eminence JOHN CARDINAL DEARDEN, S.T.D., ord. Dec. 8, 1932; Titular Bishop of Sarepta and Coadjutor Bishop of Pittsburgh; appt. March 13, 1948; cons. May 18, 1948; succeeded to the See, Dec. 22, 1950; assistant at the Pontifical Throne, Oct. 15, 1957; installed at the Archdiocese of Detroit, Dec. 18, 1958; created Cardinal, April 28, 1969; died Aug. 2, 1988.—His Eminence JOHN CARDINAL WRIGHT, S.T.D., ord. Dec. 8, 1935; Titular Bishop of Aegeae and Auxiliary of Boston; appt. May 10, 1947; cons. June 30, 1947; transferred to Bishop of Worcester, Jan. 28, 1950; transferred to Pittsburgh, Jan. 23, 1959; to the Roman Curia as Prefect of the Sacred Congregation for the Clergy; appt. April 23, 1969; created Cardinal, April 28, 1969; died at Cambridge, MA, Aug. 10, 1979.—Most Rev. VINCENT M. LEONARD, D.D., ord. June 16, 1935; appt. Titular Bishop of Arsacal and Auxiliary, Feb. 28, 1964; cons. April 21, 1964; succeeded to the See, June 1, 1969; resigned June 30, 1983; died Aug. 28, 1994.—His Eminence ANTHONY CARDINAL BEVILACQUA, D.D.,

J.C.D., J.D., ord. June 11, 1949; Titular Bishop of Aquae Albae and Auxiliary Bishop of Brooklyn; appt. Oct. 4, 1980; cons. Nov. 24, 1980; Bishop of Pittsburgh; appt. Oct. 10, 1983; installed Dec. 12, 1983; appt. Archbishop of Philadelphia, Feb. 11, 1988; created Cardinal, June 29, 1991.

Pastoral Center—111 Blvd. of the Allies, Pittsburgh, 15222-1618. Tel: 412-456-3000. All official correspondence should be directed to this office.

Chancellor—Sr. MARGARET HANNAN, R.S.M. Tel: 412-456-3129.

Vicars General—Most Rev. WILLIAM J. WINTER, V.G., S.T.D.; Most Rev. DAVID A. ZUBIK, V.G., D.D.

Bishop's Office—Most Rev. DONALD W. WUERL, S.T.D.; Revs. ROBERT J. GRECCO, M.Div., Admin. Sec. EDWARD L. YUKAS, Master of Ceremonies, Direct all official correspondence to the Bishop at this address: *111 Blvd. of the Allies, Pittsburgh, 15222-1618.* Tel: 412-456-3010.

General Secretary—Most Rev. DAVID A. ZUBIK, V.G., D.D. Tel: 412-456-3131; Fax: 412-456-3197.

Associate General Secretary—Sr. MARGARET HANNAN, R.S.M. Tel: 412-456-3129.

Vicar for Canonical Services—Very Rev. LAWRENCE A. DINARDO, V.E., J.C.L.,Address all correspondence to: *111 Blvd. of the Allies, Pittsburgh, 15222-1698.* Tel: 412-456-3135; Fax: 412-456-3173.

Matrimonial Concerns, Office for—Canonical Consultants: Revs. RICHARD M. LELONIS, J.C.L.; JAMES P. MCDONOUGH, S.T.L., J.C.L.

Tribunal Office—Address all correspondence to: *111 Blvd. of the Allies, Pittsburgh, 15222-1698.* Tel: 412-456-3033; Fax: 412-456-3173.

Judicial Vicar—Very Rev. ROBERT J. AHLIN, J.C.L.

Director of Cases—Mrs. RITA FERKO JOYCE, J.D., J.C.L.

Judges—Very Rev. PAUL J. BRADLEY, V.F., M.S.W.; Very Rev. LAWRENCE A. DINARDO, V.E., J.C.L.; Very Rev. WILLIAM P. FEENEY, V.F., M.Div.; Very Rev. ROBERT F. GUAY, V.F., M.Div.; Revs. JAMES L. AARON, M.S.Ed.; JAMES R. BEDILLION, J.C.L.; TIMOTHY G. EVANS, S.T.L.; JAMES E. KUNKEL, S.T.M.; RICHARD M. LELONIS, J.C.L.; JOSEPH R. LEMP, S.T.L.; THOMAS M. O'DONNELL, M.Div.; THEODORE A. RUTKOWSKI, S.T.L.; JOSEPH C. SCHEIB; CHARLES W. SPEICHER, Ph.D., S.T.M.; LEO V. VANYO, J.C.D.; BENEDETTO P. VAGHETTO, J.C.L.; ROBERT R. WERTHMAN, M.Div.; Mrs. RITA FERKO JOYCE, J.D., J.C.L.

Promoter of Justice—Rev. JAMES P. MCDONOUGH, S.T.L., J.C.L.

Defenders of the Bond—Revs. MARTIN F. BARKIN, M.Div.; J. LAWRENCE BRUNEY, M.Div.; DENNIS J. COLAMARINO, M.Div.; LOUIS L. DENINNO, M.Div.; ROBERT M. FRANCO, M.Ch.A.; JAMES P. MCDONOUGH, S.T.L., J.C.L.; JOHN R. RUSHOFSKY, M.S.Ed.

Auditors-Assessors—Revs. FRANK D. ALMADE, Ph.D.; CHARLES S. BOBER, S.T.D.; ROBERT J. CEDOLIA, M.A.; DAVID D. DEWITT, M.Div.; KEVIN J. DOMINIK, M.Div.; MARK A. ECKMAN, M.Div.; EDWARD L. KRYSTON, M.Div.

Advocates—Revs. CARMEN A. D'AMICO, M.Div.; MICHAEL W. DECEWICZ, M.Div.; ANDREW C. FISCHER, M.Div.; JOSEPH F. KEENAN, M.Div.; PAUL J. ZYWAN, M.Div.; Deacon DAVID E. LAMM, J.D.

Notaries—Ms. MARTHA J. BRAUN; Ms. ANNETTE W. SEMAN; Mrs. THERESE M. BINKNEY; Mrs. DARLENE WILCE.

Secretary for Clergy and Religious—Very Rev. JAMES S. RUGGIERO, V.E., M.Div., *111 Blvd. of the Allies, Pittsburgh, 15222-1618.* Tel: 412-456-3060; Fax: 412-456-3188.

Secretary for Education—Rev. KRIS D. STUBNA, S.T.D., *111 Blvd. of the Allies, Pittsburgh, 15222-1618.* Tel: 412-456-3100; Fax: 412-456-3101.

Secretary for Pastoral Life—Rev. RONALD P. LENGWIN, M.Div., *111 Blvd. of the Allies, Pittsburgh, 15222-1618.* Tel: 412-456-3021; Fax: 412-456-3168.

Secretary for Social Concerns—Rev. FRANK D. ALMADE, Ph.D., *111 Blvd. of the Allies, Pittsburgh, 15222-1618.* Tel: 412-456-3156; Fax: 412-456-3180.

Deans and Deaneries—Most Rev. WILLIAM J. WINTER, V.G., S.T.D., Chm., College of Deans; Very Rev. EDWARD M. BRYCE, V.F., S.T.L., Central (Allegheny County); Very Rev. THOMAS B. FERRIS, V.F., Northside (Allegheny County); Very Rev. ROBERT G. DUCH, V.F., Ph.D., Allegheny Valley (Allegheny County); Very Rev. PAUL J. BRADLEY, V.F., M.S.W., Northwest (Allegheny County); Very Rev. JAMES W. GARVEY, V.F., M.Div., East Suburban (Allegheny County); Very Rev. ROBERT J. MEYER, V.F., South Pittsburgh (Allegheny County); Very Rev. HUGH J. LANG, V.F., M.Ed., Steel Valley (Allegheny County); Very Rev. WALTER A. SOBON, V.F., M.S.Ed., Southwest (Allegheny County); Very Rev. DONALD P. BREIER, V.F., M.Div., South Hills (Allegheny County); Very Rev. STEPHEN M. CHERVENAK, V.F., S.T.L., Mon Yough (Allegheny County); Very Rev. ROBERT F. GUAY, V.F., M.Div., Beaver County; Very Rev. JAMES F. MURPHY, V.F., M.Div., Butler County; Very Rev. MAURO J. CAUTELA, V.F., M.Div., Lawrence County; Very Rev. ALBIN C. MCGINNIS, V.F., Greene County; Very Rev. WILLIAM P. FEENEY, V.F., M.Div., Washington County East; Very Rev. PHILIP J. DONATELLI, V.F., M.Div., Washington County West.

Office for the Delegate for Religious—2900 Noblestown Rd., Pittsburgh, 15205-4227. Tel: 412-928-5844.

Priest Council—Most Rev. DONALD W. WUERL, S.T.D., Pres.; Most Rev. WILLIAM J. WINTER, V.G., S.T.D.; Most Rev. DAVID A. ZUBIK, V.G., D.D.; Revs. NORMAN E. BEVAN, C.S.Sp.; CHARLES S. BOBER, S.T.D.; Very Rev. PAUL J. BRADLEY, V.F., M.S.W.; Very Rev. EDWARD M. BRYCE, V.F., S.T.L.; Rev. CARMEN A. D'AMICO, M.Div.; Very Rev. LAWRENCE A. DINARDO, V.E., J.C.L.; Revs. JOHN R. HANEY, M.Div.; DAVID J. KRISS, M.Div.; JOHN P. MALONEY; JOSEPH R. MCCAFFREY, M.A., M.Div.; THOMAS R. MILLER, M.Div.; Rev. Msgr. WILLIAM M. OGRODOWSKI, S.T.L.; Rev. KENNETH E. OLDENSKI, M.A.; Very Rev. JAMES S. RUGGIERO, V.E., M.Div.; Revs. GEORGE E. SALADNA, S.T.L., S.S.L.; JOHN W. SKIRTICH; DANIEL SULLIVAN, C.P.; DAVID H. TAYLOR, M.Div.; JAMES G. YOUNG, M.Div.

College of Consultors—Most Rev. DONALD W. WUERL, S.T.D.; Most Rev. WILLIAM J. WINTER, V.G., S.T.D.; Most Rev. DAVID A. ZUBIK, V.G., D.D.; Rev. CHARLES S. BOBER, S.T.D.; Very Revs. PAUL J. BRADLEY, V.F., M.S.W.; EDWARD M. BRYCE, V.F., S.T.L.; Revs. JOHN R. HANEY, M.Div.; JOHN P. MALONEY; JOSEPH R. MCCAFFREY, M.A., M.Div.; Rev. Msgr. WILLIAM M. OGRODOWSKI, S.T.L.; Revs. DAVID H. TAYLOR, M.Div.; JAMES G. YOUNG, M.Div.

Diocesan Development Board—Revs. RONALD P. LENGWIN, M.Div., Chm. FRANK D. ALMADE, Ph.D.; Mrs. NANCY F. BECK; Sr. PATRICIA CAIRNS, C.S.J.; Sr. MARGARET HANNAN, R.S.M.; Mr. CHARLES A. KOEMPEL, C.P.A.; Mr. JOSEPH G. LUTTRINGER; Mr. AMBROSE MURRAY; Revs. JOHN M. O'TOOLE; KRIS D. STUBNA, S.T.D.; GEORGE A. WILT, M.A.

Diocesan Finance Council—Most Rev. DONALD W. WUERL, S.T.D., Pres.; Most Rev. DAVID A. ZUBIK, V.G., D.D., Chm.; Ms. KATHLEEN GEIS; Sr. MARGARET HANNAN, R.S.M.; Mr. MICHAEL J. HANNON; Mr. JAMES MCLAUGHLIN; Mr. HARRY F. MURRAY; Mr. FRED O'BRIEN; Rev. ROBERT J. REARDON, M.S.Ed.; Mr. FRANK J. SCHNEIDER; Mr. LEO W. YOCHUM.

Diocesan Pastoral Council—Most Rev. DONALD W. WUERL, S.T.D., Chm.; Most Rev. WILLIAM J. WINTER, V.G., S.T.D.; Most Rev. DAVID A. ZUBIK, V.G., D.D.; Ms. MARYANN C. BOBER; Sr. ROBERTA BRADLEY, C.D.P.; Mr. BRAD R. CATON; Mr. JAMES CAVANAUGH; Rev. STEPHEN M. CHERVENAK, S.T.L.; Deacon DALE J. DISANTO; Mrs. NICOLA ESTES; Rev. PHILIP N. FARRELL; Bro. RICHARD GRZESKIEWICZ, F.S.C.; Mr. RICHARD P. JACOB; Mr. KENNETH M. KORAB; Dr. ROBERT A. KORCHECK; Mr. LEON W. KOSAKOWSKI; Mrs. MARY RUTH LACKNER; Mr. KENNETH G. OGILVIE; Rev. STEVEN M. PALSA; Sr. MARY CABRINI PROCOPIO, C.S.S.F.; Ms. LINDA L. RENDULIC; Mrs. LINDA L. RITZER; Mr. JOHN SEARLES; Mrs. IRENE Z. SLEZICK; Sr. JOHN MARTIN SULLIVAN, A.S.C.J.; Mr. THOMAS J. URAM; Mr. JAMES WEILAND.

Clergy Personnel Board—Most Rev. DONALD W. WUERL, S.T.D.; Most Rev. WILLIAM J. WINTER, V.G., S.T.D.; Most Rev. DAVID A. ZUBIK, V.G., D.D.; Very Rev. JAMES S. RUGGIERO, V.E., M.Div., Chm.; Revs. CHARLES S. BOBER, S.T.D.; CHARLES J. BAPTISTE; RICHARD A. INFANTE, M.Div., M.A.; RONALD P. LENGWIN, M.Div.; G. MALCOLM MCDONALD, M.Div., Exec. Sec.; Very Rev. ROBERT J. MEYER, V.F.; Rev. ROBERT J. MILLER, M.A., M.Div.; Rev. Msgr. WILLIAM M. OGRODOWSKI, S.T.L.; Revs. KENNETH E. OLDENSKI, M.A.; JOHN R. RUSHOFSKY, V.F., M.S.Ed., Exec. Sec.

Diocesan Administration

Administrative Procedures, Office for—Very Rev. LAWRENCE A. DINARDO, V.E., J.C.L., Admin.; Mrs. RITA F. JOYCE, J.D., J.C.L., Consultant. Tel: 412-456-3135.

Adult and Family Catechesis, Office for—Rev. RONALD D. LAWLER, O.F.M.Cap., Ph.D., Dir.; Deacon PAUL M. HOOVER, M.D., Asst. Tel: 412-456-3117.

Archives and Records Center—Mr. KENNETH A. WHITE, Dir.; Mr. BURRIS E. ESPLEN, Archivist, *125 N. Craig St., Pittsburgh, 15213-1555.* Tel: 412-621-6217.

Bishop, Office of the Diocesan—Revs. ROBERT J. GRECO, M.Div., Admin. Sec. EDWARD L. YUHAS, Master of Ceremonies. Tel: 412-456-3010.

Bishop Boyle Career Center—Mr. JOSEPH A. CARR, Dir., *120 E. 9th Ave., Homestead, 15120-1600.* Tel: 412-462-8516.

Black Catholic Ministries, Office for—Mrs. MARGRETTA STOKES TUCKER, M.Ed., Dir. Tel: 412-456-3170.

Budget and Planning - Secretariat for Education, Office for—Mr. ROY CARTIER, M.B.A., M.R.P., Dir. Tel: 412-456-3108.

Building Commission—Most Rev. DAVID A. ZUBIK, V.G., D.D., Chm.; Mr. JAMES J. ZIELINSKI, Exec. Sec., *4721 5th Ave., Pittsburgh, 15213.* Tel: 412-621-6206.

Building Services, Office for—Mrs. DARLENE M. HOLZER, Mgr. Tel: 412-456-3016.

Campus Ministry, Office for—Rev. W. PETER HORTON, M.A., Dir., *Newman Center, 342 Normal Ave., Slippery Rock, 16057.* Tel: 724-794-6620; 412-536-1050.

Canonical Services, Department for—Very Rev. LAWRENCE A. DINARDO, V.E., J.C.L. Tel: 412-456-3135.

Catechesis, Office for—Mr. KENNETH M. OGOREK, M.A., Dir. Tel: 412-456-3115.

Catechetical Ministries, Office for—Ms. SHARON T. TYBOROWSKI, Dir. Tel: 412-456-3110.

Catholic Charities—Sr. PATRICIA CAIRNS, C.S.J., Exec. Dir., *212 9th St., Pittsburgh, 15222.* Tel: 412-456-6999., Allegheny County: *212 9th St., Pittsburgh, 15222.* Tel: 412-456-6999., Beaver County: *1260 N. Brodhead Rd., Monaca, 15601.* Tel: 724-775-0758., Butler County: *407 A W. Jefferson St., Butler, 16001.* Tel: 724-287-4011., Greene County: *32 Church St., Ste. 3, Waynesburg, 15370.* Tel: 724-627-6410., Lawrence County: *413 Highland Ave., New Castle, 16101.* Tel: 724-658-5526., Washington County: *331 S. Main St., Washington, 15301.* Tel: 724-228-7722., Roselia Center: *624 Clyde St., Pittsburgh, 15213.* Tel: 412-682-4410; 4411. Services for single pregnant women. Maryhouse Residence for Women: *1113 Creedmoor Ave., Pittsburgh, 15226.* Tel: 412-563-3312., St. Joseph's House of Hospitality, Inc.: *1635 Bedford Ave., Pittsburgh, 15219.* Tel: 412-471-0666., Ozanam Cultural Center: *1833 Wylie Ave., Pittsburgh, 15219.* Tel: 412-281-4046.

Challenges: Options in Aging—15 W. Washington St., Ste. 201, New Castle, 16101. Tel: 724-658-3729.

Catholic Cemeteries Assoc., The—Ms. ANNABELLE MCGANNON, Exec. Dir., *718 Hazelwood Ave., Pittsburgh, 15217-2807.* Tel: 412-521-9133.

Catholic Schools, Department for—Mr. ROBERT L. PASERBA, Ed.D., Supt. Schools; Sr. MARY JO MUTSCHLER, S.C., Asst. Supt. Elementary Schools; Mrs. ANNA MARIE CATANZARO, M.Ed., Asst. Supt. Secondary Schools; Mr. RONALD T. BOWES, D.A., Asst. Supt. Public Policy & Devel. Tel: 412-456-3090.

Educational Consultants—Sr. BENITA DEMATTEIS, O.S.B., M.Ed.; Sr. URSULA KELLY, S.S.N.D., M.A.; Sr. CATHERINE ANN KOLLER, C.D.P., M.A.; Sr. LORETTA KRALL, C.S.J., M.A.; Mr. WILLIAM C. LLOYD, M.Ed.; Sr. M. DENISE MAHER, C.S.J., M.A.; Mr. KENNETH M. OGOREK, M.A.; Sr. IRENE MARY WILBURN, S.C., M.A., *135 1st Ave., Pittsburgh, 15222.* Tel: 412-456-3070.

Chaplaincies, Office for—Vacant, *4721 5th Ave., Pittsburgh, 15213.* Tel: 412-621-6209.

Charismatic Prayer Groups—Rev. JOHN P. SWEENEY, Moderator, *St. Titus Parish, 952 Franklin St., Aliquippa, 15001-3359.* Tel: 724-378-8561.

Chief Financial Officer—Mr. CHARLES A. KOEMPEL, C.P.A. Tel: 412-456-3137.

Clergy and Ministerial Formation, Department for—Rev. KEVIN J. DOMINIK, M.Div., Dir., *St. Paul Seminary, 2900 Noblestown Rd., Pittsburgh, 15205-4227.* Tel: 412-928-5840.

Clergy Personnel, Dept. for—Rev. JOHN R. RUSHOFSKY, M.S.Ed. Tel: 412-456-3060.

Communications Commission, Office for—Rev. KRIS D. STUBNA, S.T.D., Chm. Communications Commission. Tel: 412-456-3100. Mr. WILLIAM W. HILL, Sr. Staff Communicator; Mr. CRAIG T. MAIER, Staff Communicator. Tel: 412-456-3020.

Cultural Diversity, Commission on—Rev. RONALD P. LENGWIN, M.Div., Chm. Tel: 412-456-3021.

Deaf Persons, Office for—Mrs. KAREN M. MCGANN, Dir.; Rev. WALTER G. RYDZON, M.Div., Chap., *135 1st Ave., Pittsburgh, 15222.* Tel: 412-456-3119 (Voice); 456-3122 (TTY).

Development, Office for—Mr. GREGORY R. DUFOUR, Dir. Tel: 412-456-3085.

Diaconate, Office for the—Rev. DAVID J. BONNAR, S.T.B., Dir., *St. Paul Seminary, 2900 Noblestown Rd., Pittsburgh, 15205-4227.* Tel: 412-928-5840.

Diocesan National Black Catholic Congress Leadership Team—Ms. BARBARA A. ANTROM, Team Leader, *324 Baker Ave., Clairton, 15025.* Tel: 412-233-3492.

Diocesan Purchasing Commission—Mr. JAMES W. PEARCE, Exec. Dir., *2900 Noblestown Rd., Pittsburgh, 15205.* Tel: 412-922-6400.

Disabilities, Department for Persons with—Ms. GRACE T. HARDING, M.A., Dir., *135 1st Ave., Pittsburgh, 15222.* Tel: 412-456-3119 (Voice); 456-3122 (TTY).

Ecumenical and Interfaith Commission—Rev. RONALD P. LENGWIN, M.Div., Chm. Tel: 412-456-3021.

Educational Media, Department for—Mr. JEFFREY A. HIRST, Dir., *St. Paul Seminary, 2900 Noblestown Rd., Pittsburgh, 15205-4227.* Tel: 412-928-5817.

Educational Special Events, Office for—Sr. M. IGNATIUS ROONEY, R.S.M., M.Ed., Dir. Tel: 412-456-3075.

Electronic Media, Office for—Mrs. NANCY K. LIPPERT, Dir., *St. Paul Seminary, 2900 Noblestown Rd., Pittsburgh, 15205-4227.* Tel: 412-928-5923.

Employment Development and Community Concerns, Office for—Mr. JOSEPH A. CARR, Dir. Tel: 412-456-3164.

Evangelization and Christian Initiation, Office for—Rev. M. ERIC DISKIN, M.Div., Dir. Tel: 412-456-3083.

Family Life and Family Concerns, Office for—Mrs. MAUREEN H. WOOD, M.R.E., Dir. Tel: 412-456-3160.

Financial Services, Office for—Mr. JOSEPH G. LUTTRINGER, Dir. Tel: 412-456-3025., *Central Accounting Dept.* Tel: 412-456-3032., *Parish Accounting Dept.* Tel: 412-456-3025., *Auditing Dept.* Tel: 412-456-3028.

Foundation, Catholic Diocese of Pittsburgh—Mr. GREGORY R. DUFOUR, Exec. Dir. Tel: 412-456-3085.

Gilmary Diocesan Center—Mr. RONALD W. RAGAN, M.P.A., Dir., *601 Flaugherty Run Rd., Coraopolis, 15108-3899.* Tel: 412-264-8400.

Health Care Ministries—Rev. FRANK D. ALMADE, Ph.D., Coord. Tel: 412-456-3156.

Information Technology, Office for—Mr. JOHN F. ZDILLA, M.S., Dir. Tel: 412-456-3152.

Insurance/Employee Benefits, Office for—Mr. DAVID S. STEWART, Mgr. Tel: 412-456-3045.

Justice and Peace Commission—Mrs. VERONICA MORGAN-LEE, Ph.D., Chm. Tel: 412-456-3162.

Learning Media Center—Mr. JEFFREY A. HIRST, Dir., *St. Paul Seminary, 2900 Noblestown Rd., Pittsburgh, 15205-4227.* Tel: 412-928-5817.

Legal Office—Mr. WILLIAM A. STEIDLE, JR., ESQ., Gen. Counsel. Tel: 412-456-3126.

Matrimonial Concerns, Office for—Canonical Consultants: Revs. RICHARD M. LELONIS, J.C.L.; JAMES P. MCDONOUGH, S.T.L., J.C.L.

Mental Retardation and Special Religious Education, Office for Persons with—Mrs. JOSEPHINE K. CRAME, Dir., *135 1st Ave., Pittsburgh, 15222.* Tel: 412-456-3119.

Ministries, Institute for—Sr. PATRICIA ROGAN, O.S.F., Dir., *St. Paul Seminary, 2900 Noblestown Rd., Pittsburgh, 15205-4227.* Tel: 412-928-5827.

Missions, Office for—Rev. JOHN E. KOZAR, M.Div., Dir. Tel: 412-456-3065.

Music Ministry, Office for—Rev. JAMES J. CHEPPONIS, M.Div., M.A., Dir. Tel: 412-456-3042.

Natural Family Planning Advisory Committee—Deacon PAUL M. HOOVER, M.D., Chm. Tel: 412-456-3160.

Parish Services, Office for—Sr. MARILYN HOEING, O.S.F., Dir. Tel: 412-456-3057.

Payroll, Office for—Mr. JOHN G. CVETIC, Mgr. Tel: 412-456-3006.

Personnel, Office for—Mrs. DARLENE M. HOLZER, Mgr. Tel: 412-456-3016.

Physical Disabilities, Office for Persons with—Rev. PATRICK F. RAGER, Chap. Tel: 412-461-6393.

Pilgrimage Office—Rev. JOHN E. KOZAR, M.Div., Dir. Tel: 412-456-3065.

Pornography, Commission to Counter—Mrs. NORMA NORRIS, Chm. Tel: 412-456-3160.

Pre-Ordination Formation, Department for—Rev. DAVID J. BONNAR, S.T.B., Dir., *St. Paul Seminary, 2900 Noblestown Rd., Pittsburgh, 15205-4227.* Tel: 412-928-5840.

Property Planning and Development, Office for—Mr. JAMES J. ZIELINSKI, Dir., *4721 5th Ave., Pittsburgh, 15213.* Tel: 412-621-6206.

Public Affairs, Department for—Rev. RONALD P. LENGWIN, M.Div., Dir. Tel: 412-456-3021.

Religious Education/CCD, Department for—Mrs. JUDITH A. KIRK, Dir.; Deacon STEPHEN J. BYERS, Asst. Tel: 412-456-3112.

Research and Planning, Office for—Mr. JOHN P. FLAHERTY, M.A., Dir. Tel: 412-456-3146.

Retired Clergy, Office for—Very Rev. THOMAS J. KRAM, V.E., M.Div., Vicar; Deacon JAMES R. GRAB, Asst. Tel: 412-881-3675.

Retired Priests, Residences for—Mr. PAUL MERLO, Admin., *St. John Vianney Manor, 2600 Morange Rd., Pittsburgh, 15205.* Tel: 412-928-0825. Rev. H. MICHAEL KERNAN, Dir., *Cardinal Dearden Center, 4721 5th Ave., Pittsburgh, 15213.* Tel: 412-687-8022.

St. Paul Seminary—Revs. DAVID J. BONNAR, S.T.B., Rector; KEVIN J. DOMINIK, M.Div., Vice Rector; Sr. JUDITH WORDEN, R.S.M., Coord. of Apostolic Works; Mrs. MARY ALICE BUCK, Admin. Asst. to Rector, *2900 Noblestown Rd., Pittsburgh, 15205-4227.* Tel: 412-921-5800.

Social Awareness, Department for—Ms. SUSAN L. RAUSCHER, Dir. Tel: 412-456-3161.

Social Programs and Community Development, Department for—Mr. W. JOHN HANNIGAN, M.S.W., Dir. Tel: 412-456-3162.

Society for the Propagation of the Faith—Rev. JOHN E. KOZAR, M.Div., Dir. Tel: 412-456-3065.

Television and Radio Production—Refer to Electronic Media, Office for.

Theological Commission—Rev. JOSEPH J. KLEPPNER, S.T.L., Ph.D., Chm. Tel: 724-775-6363.

Vision Impairments, Office for Persons with—Rev. Msgr. PAUL M. LACKNER, Chap., *135 1st Ave., Pittsburgh, 15222.* Tel: 412-456-3119.

Vocations, Office for—Rev. DAVID J. BONNAR, S.T.B., Dir., *St. Paul Seminary, 2900 Noblestown Rd., Pittsburgh, 15205-4227.* Tel: 412-928-5840.

Worship, Office for—Rev. M. ERIC DISKIN, Dir. Tel: 412-546-3041.

Worship Commission—Rev. M. ERIC DISKIN, Chm. Tel: 412-456-3041.

Youth and Young Adult Ministry, Office for—Mrs. JOYCE A. GILLOOLY, M.S.Ed., Dir.; Rev. EDWARD M. CZEMERDA, M.Div., Assoc. Dir.; Mr. GARY M. SLIFKEY, Assoc. Dir., *Gilmary Diocesan Center, 601 Flaugherty Run Rd., Coraopolis, 15108-3899.* Tel: 412-264-9530.

CLERGY, PARISHES, MISSIONS AND PAROCHIAL SCHOOLS

CITY OF PITTSBURGH, PROPER
(Allegheny County)

1—ST. PAUL CATHEDRAL (1834), Revs. Leo V. Vanyo, Rector; Daniel J. Maurer. In res., Revs. Robert J. Grecco; James J. Chepponis.
Res., 108 N. Dithridge St., 15213. Tel: 412-621-4951; Fax: 412-621-4951.

2—ST. AGNES. Closed. For sacramental records contact St. Paul Cathedral.

3—ST. ANN (Hungarian). Closed. See St. Stephen.

4—ST. AUGUSTINE (German). Closed. See Our Lady of the Angels.

5—ST. BEDE (1922), Rev. Edward M. Bryce. In res., Revs. Joseph C. Beck; Felix Owino, A.J.
Res., 509 S. Dallas Ave., 15208. Tel: 412-661-7222; Fax: 412-661-9337.
School—6920 Edgerton Ave., 15208. Tel: 412-661-9425; Fax: 412-661-0447.
Lay Teachers 19; Students 308.

6—ST. BENEDICT THE MOOR (1889) (African American), Rev. Carmen A. D'Amico; Deacon Reynold Wilmer.
Res., 91 Crawford St., 15219. Tel: 412-281-3141; Fax: 412-391-7151.
School—2900 Webster Ave., 15219. Tel: 412-682-3755; Fax: 412-682-4058.
Sisters of St. Joseph 6; Lay Teachers 7; Students 211.
Convent—Tel: 412-621-0519.

7—ST. CATHERINE OF SIENA (Beechview) (1902), Rev. Robert M. Franco. In res., Rev. Louis DeNinno.
Res., 1901 Broadway Ave., 15216. Tel: 412-531-2135; Fax: 412-531-8543.

8—ST. CHARLES LWANGA PARISH (1992). Consolidated from the following churches: Corpus Christi, Holy Rosary, Mother of Good Counsel, Our Lady Help of Christians, Our Lady of the Most Blessed Sacrament and SS. Peter & Paul. Revs. David H. Taylor; Michael John Lynam. In res., Revs. Gregory Ugah (Nigeria); Cornelius Okochi (Nigeria).
Res., 7114 Kelly St., 15208. Tel: 412-731-3020; Fax: 412-731-1615.
School—Holy Rosary, 7120 Kelly St., 15208. Tel: 412-731-2567; Fax: 412-731-3476.
Lay Teachers 12; Students 259.

9—CORPUS CHRISTI. Closed. See St. Charles Lwanga.

10—ST. ELIZABETH OF HUNGARY (Slovak). Closed. See St. Patrick-St. Stanislaus Kostka.

11—EPIPHANY (1903) (Irish), Rev. Daniel L. Sweeney, Admin. In res., Revs. John F. Walsh, Hospital Chap.; James McDonough.
Res., 1018 Centre Ave., 15219. Tel: 412-471-0257; Fax: 412-471-1345.

12—OUR LADY HELP OF CHRISTIANS (Italian). Closed. See St. Charles Lwanga.

13—HOLY FAMILY (Polish). Closed. See Our Lady of the Angels.

14—HOLY ROSARY. Closed. See St. Charles Lwanga.

15—ST. HYACINTH (Polish). Closed. See St. Regis.

16—IMMACULATE CONCEPTION (1905) (Italian), Revs. Dale E. DeNinno, Admin.; Edward J. Kunco.
Res., 4712 Liberty Ave., 15224. Tel: 412-682-5353; Fax: 412-682-6766.
School—Tel: 412-621-5199; Fax: 412-621-5601.
Sisters of the Holy Spirit, Pittsburgh 4; Lay Teachers 16; Students 372.

17—IMMACULATE HEART OF MARY (1897) (Polish), Rev. Joseph E. Swierczynski.
Res., 3058 Brereton Ave., 15219. Tel: 412-621-5170; Fax: 412-621-7445.

18—ST. JOACHIM. Closed. See St. Rosalia.

19—ST. JOHN THE BAPTIST. Closed. See Our Lady of the Angels.

20—ST. JOSEPH (1872) (German), Revs. Dale E. DeNinno, Admin.; Edward J. Kunco.
Res., 4712 Liberty Ave., 15224. Tel: 412-682-2354; Fax: 412-682-6766.

21—ST. KIERAN. Closed. See St. Matthew.

22—ST. LAWRENCE O'TOOLE (East End) (1897), Rev. James G. Graham.
Res., 5323 Penn Ave., 15224. Tel: 412-363-1771; Fax: 412-363-7552.

23—ST. LOUISE DE MARILLAC (Upper St. Clair) (1961), Revs. Thomas E. Kredel; George R. Dalton; J. Lawrence Bruney; Sr. Mary Andrew Budinski, C.S.S.F., Pastoral Assoc.
Res., 312 McMurray Rd., 15241. Tel: 412-833-1010; Fax: 412-833-6624.
School—310 McMurray Rd., 15241. Tel: 412-835-0600.
Felician Sisters 3; Lay Teachers 25; Students 582.

24—ST. MARTIN (West End). Closed. See Guardian Angels.

25—ST. MARY'S (Lawrenceville). Closed. See Our Lady of the Angels.

26—ST. MARY ASSUMPTION (Lawrenceville). Closed. See St. Matthew.

27—ST. MARY OF MERCY (1870), Revs. John M. O'Toole; Francis A. Siler. In res., Revs. Ronald P. Lengwin; Andre Quenum (West Africa) (Cotonou).
Res., 202 Stanwix St., 15222. Tel: 412-261-0110; Fax: 412-261-0113.

28—ST. MATTHEW (1993). Consolidated from St. Kieran and St. Mary Assumption. Rev. Joseph J. Janiszeski, T.O.R.
Res., 5322 Carnegie St., 15201. Tel: 412-781-6701; Fax: 412-781-1331.

29—MOTHER OF GOOD COUNSEL (Italian). Closed. See St. Charles Lwanga.

30—OUR LADY OF THE ANGELS (1993). Consolidated from St. Augustine, Holy Family, St. John the Baptist and St. Mary. Revs. John Getsy, O.F.M.Cap.; Gervase Degenhardt, O.F.M.Cap.; Michael P. Masich, O.F.M.Cap.; Deacon Francis J. Dadowski. In res., Revs. Ralph Zehe, O.F.M.Cap.; Kenan Crowley, O.F.M.Cap.; Reginald Russo, O.F.M.Cap.
Res., 225 37th St., 15201. Tel: 412-682-0929; Fax: 412-682-6889. [CEM]
School—St. John Neumann Regional Catholic Elementary School. See Consolidated Schools under Institutions Located in the Diocese. Tel: 412-682-5096; Fax: 412-682-0811.

31—OUR LADY OF THE MOST BLESSED SACRAMENT. Closed. See St. Charles Lwanga.

32—ST. PATRICK (Strip District). Closed. See St. Patrick-St. Stanislaus Kostka.

33—SS. PETER AND PAUL (East Liberty). Closed. See St. Charles Lwanga.

34—ST. PHILOMENA Squirrel Hill. Closed. See St. Bede.

35—ST. RAPHAEL (1911), Revs. Joseph V. Kurutz; Daniel Vallecorsa. In res., Rev. John J. Charnoki.
Res., 1118 Chislett St., E., 15206. Tel: 412-661-3100; Fax: 412-661-4105.
School—1154 Chislett St., 15206. Tel: 412-661-0288; Fax: 412-661-0428.
Sisters of St. Joseph 2; Lay Teachers 10; Students 165.

36—ST. REGIS (1993). Merged with St. Hyacinth. Rev. Donald C. Fisher, M.A.
Res., 3235 Parkview Ave., 15213. Tel: 412-681-9365; Fax: 412-681-1175.

37—ST. ROSALIA (1993). Merged with St. Joachim. Rev. Joseph W. Reschick.
Res., 411 Greenfield Ave., 15207. Tel: 412-421-5766; Fax: 412-421-4529.
School—Tel: 412-521-3005; Fax: 412-521-2763.
Sisters of the Immaculate Heart of Mary 2; Lay Teachers 11; Students 163.

38—SACRED HEART (1872), Most Rev. William J. Winter, V.G.; Rev. John J. Baver, M.Div. In res., Revs. John A. Reifsnyder; Miles Eric Diskin.
Res., 310 Shady Ave., 15206. Tel: 412-661-0187; Fax: 412-661-7932.
School—325 Emerson St., 15206. Tel: 412-441-1582.
Sisters of Charity 2; Lay Teachers 21; Students 475.

39—ST. STANISLAUS (Strip District) (Polish). Closed. See St. Patrick-St. Stanislaus Kostka.

40—ST. PATRICK-ST. STANISLAUS KOSTKA (1993). Consolidated of St. Stanislaus, St. Patrick and St. Elizabeth of Hungary. Rev. Thomas J. McKenna, Admin.
Res. & Parish Office: 57 21st St., 15222. Tel: 412-471-4767; Fax: 412-471-1209.

41—ST. STEPHEN (1993). Merged with St. Ann. Rev. Cornelius W. McCaulley, S.T.L.
Mailing Address: 5115 Second Ave., 15207.

Res., 131 E. Elizabeth St., 15207. Tel: 412-421-9210.
School—134 E. Elizabeth St., 15207. Tel: 412-421-9447; Fax: 412-421-4748.
Sisters of Charity 1; Lay Teachers 10; Students 99.

SOUTH SIDE

42—ST. ADALBERT (Polish). Closed. See Prince of Peace.

43—ST. BASIL (1907) (German), Revs. Robert J. Meyer; Thomas J. Lewandowski. In res., Rev. Joseph C. Scheib.
Res., 1735 Brownsville Rd., 15210. Tel: 412-882-9763; Fax: 412-882-2476.
School—1803 Concordia St., 15210. Tel: 412-884-4434; Fax: 412-884-4799.
Lay Teachers 11; Students 182.
Convent—30 W. Willock Rd., 15227. Tel: 412-881-0638.

44—ST. CANICE (Knoxville). Closed. See St. John Vianney.

45—ST. CASIMIR (Lithuanian). Closed. See Prince of Peace.

46—ST. GEORGE (Allentown). Closed. See St. John Vianney.

47—GUARDIAN ANGELS (West End) (1994). Merged with St. James and St. Martin. Rev. John E. Hissrich. In res., Rev. Joseph Marie Obama (Cameroon).
Res., 1030 Logue St., 15220. Tel: 412-921-4077; Fax: 412-922-4945. [CEM]
School—Elizabeth Seton Elementary. See Consolidated Schools under Institutions Located in the Diocese.

48—ST. HENRY. Closed. See St. John Vianney.

49—HOLY ANGELS (1903), Rev. J. David Crowley, M.A. In res., Rev. Richard J. Czapinski.
Res., 408 Baldwin Rd., 15207. Tel: 412-461-6906; Fax: 412-461-0961.

50—HOLY INNOCENTS (1900), Revs. Donald N. Buchleitner; John B. Corbett.
Res., 3011 Landis St., 15204. Tel: 412-331-0268; Fax: 412-331-1219.
School—Elizabeth Seton Elementary. See Consolidated Schools under Institutions Located in the Diocese.

51—ST. JAMES (West End). Closed. See Guardian Angels.

52—ST. JOHN THE EVANGELIST. Closed. See Prince of Peace.

53—ST. JOSAPHAT (Polish). Closed. See Prince of Peace.

54—ST. JOHN VIANNEY (Hilltop) (1994). Consolidation of the the following churches: St. Canice, St. George, St. Henry, and St. Joseph. Revs. Charles S. Bober; Douglas A. Boyd; John L. McKenna; Deacon Ralph W. Bachner. In res., Revs. William R. Terza; Jerome A. Dixon.
823 Climax St., 15210. Tel: 412-381-8300; Fax: 412-431-3790. [JC]
School—Bishop Leonard Catholic School, 434 Ormsby Ave., 15210. Tel: 412-381-3541; Fax: 412-381-8611.
Students 315.

55—ST. JUSTIN (Mt. Washington) (1917), Rev. Walter C. Rydzon.
Res., 539 Boggs Ave., 15211. Tel: 412-381-9878; 412-381-9825 (TTY); Fax: 412-431-8017.

56—ST. MARY OF THE MOUNT (Mt. Washington) (1873), Rev. Louis F. Vallone; Deacon Robert Barth. In res., Revs. Clement Okoye (Nigeria); Bernadine Eikhuenelo (Nigeria).
Res., 403 Grandview Ave., 15211. Tel: 412-381-0212; Fax: 412-381-9921.
School—Bigham St. & Grandview Ave., 15211. Tel: 412-431-4645; Fax: 412-381-0770.
Sisters of the Immaculate Heart of Mary 2; Lay Teachers 10; Students 187.

57—ST. MATTHEW (Slovak). Closed. See Prince of Peace.

58—ST. MICHAEL (German). Closed. See Prince of Peace.

59—OUR LADY OF LORETO (1959), Rev. George F. Chortos.
Res., 1905 Pioneer Ave., 15226. Tel: 412-341-6161; Fax: 412-341-3399.

60—ST. PAMPHILUS (1960), Rev. Alexis Anania, O.F.M. In res., Revs. R. Stephen Almagno, O.F.M.; Tae Woo Jung (Korea); Friar John-Michael Pinto, O.F.M.
Res., 1000 Tropical Ave., 15216. Tel: 412-341-1000; Fax: 412-341-6956.
Church—1000 Tropical Ave., 15216. Tel: 412-531-8449.

61—ST. PETER. Closed. See Prince of Peace.

62—ST. PIUS X (1954), Rev. Thomas M. Marpes. In res., Rev. Evaristus Mushi (Tanzania).
Res., 3040 Pioneer Ave., 15226. Tel: 412-563-5423; Fax: 412-561-3868.
School—Brookline Regional Catholic School, (Grades PreK-8). See Consolidated Schools under Institutions Located in the Diocese.

63—PRINCE OF PEACE (1992). Consolidated from the following churches: St. Adalbert, St. Casimir, St. John the Evangelist, St. Josaphat, St. Matthew, St. Michael and St. Peter. Revs. Bernard M. Harcarik; John B. Lendvai. In res., Rev. Reginald U. Nwauzor (Nigeria).
Res., 81 S. 13th St., 15203-1897. Tel: 412-481-8380; Fax: 412-431-0209. [CEM 6]
School—85 S. 14th St., 15203. Tel: 412-481-1269.
Sisters 4; Lay Teachers 9; Students 131.

64—RESURRECTION (Brookline) (1909), Revs. Joseph P. Grosko; Joseph G. Luisi; Deacon Richard Very.
Res., 1100 Creedmoor Ave., 15226. Tel: 412-563-4400; Fax: 412-563-4403.

65—ST. VINCENT (Esplen). Closed. See St. John of God, McKees Rocks.

66—ST. WENDELIN (Carrick) (1873), Rev. Gary W. Oehmler. In res., Revs. Severo Kuupuo (Ghana); Deo Gratias Kiwanuke (Uganda).
Res., 2728 Custer Ave., 15227. Tel: 412-882-1480; Fax: 412-884-2334. [CEM]
School—Bishop John B. McDowell Regional School. See Consolidated Schools under Institutions Located in the Diocese.

NORTH SIDE

67—ST. AMBROSE. Merged with St. Boniface to form Holy Wisdom.

68—ANNUNCIATION. Closed. See Incarnation of the Lord.

69—ST. BONIFACE. Merged with St. Ambrose to form Holy Wisdom.

70—ST. CYRIL OF ALEXANDRIA (1924), Very Rev. Thomas B. Ferris, V.F.
Res., 3854 Brighton Rd., 15212. Tel: 412-761-1552; Fax: 412-761-3318.
School—Tel: 412-761-5043; Fax: 412-761-0840.
Sisters of Mercy of the Diocese of Pittsburgh 1; Lay Teachers 15; Students 245.
Convent—3830 Parviss St., 15212. Tel: 412-766-8338.

71—ST. FRANCIS XAVIER. Closed. See Risen Lord.

72—ST. GABRIEL ARCHANGEL (Slovak). Closed. See Risen Lord.

73—HOLY WISDOM (1994), Very Rev. Lawrence A. DiNardo, M.Ch.A., J.C.L., V.E.; Rev. Msgr. Donald W. Kraus, S.T.D., Ph.D. In res., Rev. Eugene J. Dougherty.
Res., 1025 Haslage Ave., 15212-3429. Tel: 412-231-1116; Fax: 412-231-1072. [CEM]

74—INCARNATION OF THE LORD (1993). Consolidated from Annunciation and Nativity of Our Lord. Rev. John M. Bachkay.
Res., 4071 Franklin Rd., 15214. Tel: 412-931-2911; Fax: 412-931-2832.
School—4072 Franklin Rd., 15214. Tel: 412-931-2330; Fax: 412-931-2832. Sr. Roberta Kardell, S.F.C.C.
Sisters 1; Lay Teachers 12; Students 156.

75—ST. JOSEPH. Closed. See St. Peter.

76—ST. LEO. Closed. See Risen Lord.

77—OUR LADY QUEEN OF PEACE. Closed. See St. Peter.

78—MOST HOLY NAME OF JESUS (Troy Hill) (1868) (German), Rev. W. David Schorr; Deacon G. Gregory Jelinek. In res., Revs. James L. Aaron, (Retired); Benedict Ndeyekiyo, A.L.C.P.
Res., 1700 Harpster St., 15212-4393. Tel: 412-231-2994; Fax: 412-231-7180. [CEM]
School—Cardinal Wright Regional School. See Consolidated Schools under Institutions Located in the Diocese.
Chapel—St. Anthony's, (1880), Tel: 412-323-9504. Sr. Margaret Liam Glenane, S.A., Asst. Dir.

79—NATIVITY OF OUR LORD. Closed. See Incarnation of the Lord.

80—ST. NICHOLAS (Croatian). Closed. See St. Nicholas.

81—ST. PETER (1993). Consolidated from St. Cyprian, St. Mary's, Mary Immaculate & Our Lady, Queen of Peace, St. Joseph, St. Peter and St. Wenceslaus. Revs. Benjamin R. Walker, O.S.B.; Richard Ulam, O.S.B.; Job Foote, O.S.B.
Res., 720 Arch St., 15212. Tel: 412-321-0711; Fax: 412-321-7807. [CEM]
School—Cardinal Wright Regional School. See Consolidated Schools under Institutions Located in the Diocese.

82—REGINA COELI (Italian). Closed. For sacramental records contact St. Cyril of Alexandria.

83—RISEN LORD (1993). Consolidated from the following churches: St. Francis Xavier, St. Gabriel Archangel, St. Leo and Our Lady of Perpetual Help. Rev. Thomas J. Galvin; Deacon David Gruseck. In res., Rev. Frank A. Mitolo.
Res., 3250 California Ave., 15212. Tel: 412-761-1507; Fax: 412-761-6454.

84—ST. WENCESLAUS. Closed. See St. Peter.

OUTSIDE THE CITY OF PITTSBURGH

Aleppo Township, Allegheny Co., St. Mary (1852), Rev. John E. Kozar.
Res., 444 Glenfield Rd., Sewickley, 15143. Tel: 412-741-6460. [CEM]

Aliquippa, Beaver Co., St. Titus (1994). Merged with St. Joseph, West Aliquippa. Revs. John P. Sweeney; James M. Bachner.
Res., 952 Franklin Ave., 15001. Tel: 724-378-8561; Fax: 724-378-4851. [JC 2]
School—107 Sycamore St., 15001. Tel: 724-378-7940; Fax: 724-375-8893.
Lay Teachers 13; Students 170.

Allison Park, Allegheny Co., St. Ursula (1908), Revs. Garrett D. Dorsey; Ernest Strelinski, P.A. In res., Rev. Msgr. John C. McCarren.
Res., 3937 Kirk Ave., 15101. Tel: 412-486-6700; Fax: 412-486-2562.
School—Tel: 412-486-5511; Fax: 412-492-1295.
Sisters 1; Lay Teachers 22; Students 244.

Ambridge, Beaver Co.,

1—ST. VERONICA. Closed. See Good Samaritan.

2—DIVINE REDEEMER. Closed. See Good Samaritan.

3—ST. STANISLAUS. Closed. See Good Samaritan.

4—CHURCH OF CHRIST THE KING. Closed. See Good Samaritan.

5—HOLY TRINITY, (Croatian). Closed. See Good Samaritan.

6—GOOD SAMARITAN, (1994). Consolidated from the following churches: St. Veronica, Divine Redeemer, St. Stanislaus, Christ the King and Holy Trinity. Revs. James Kunkel; John Skirtich; Kenneth R. Keene.
Res., 725 Glenwood Ave., 15003. Tel: 724-266-6565; Fax: 724-266-5570. [CEM][JC]
School—Glenwood Ave. & 8th St., 15003. Tel: 724-266-1670; Fax: 724-266-5570. Susan Ebel, Prin.
Sisters 2; Lay Teachers 11; Students 132.

Aspinwall, Allegheny Co., St. Scholastica (1903), Rev. Robert G. Duch, Ph.D.
Res., 309 Brilliant Ave., 15215. Tel: 412-781-0186; Fax: 412-781-4316.
School—Christ the Divine Teacher Academy. See Consolidated Schools under Institutions Located in the Diocese.

Avella, Washington Co., St. Michael (1917), Rev. Pierre G. Sodini, S.T.L.
Res., 95 Highland Ave., 15312. Tel: 724-587-3570. [CEM]

Baden, Beaver Co., St. John the Baptist (1866), Rev. Joseph J. Dascenzo.
Res., 375 Linmore Ave., P.O. Box 171, 15005. Tel: 724-869-2280; Fax: 724-869-0305. [CEM]

Bairdford, Allegheny Co., St. Victor (1919), Rev. Bartley A. Sorensen; Deacon Silverio Rubio.
Res., Box 149, 15006. Tel: 724-265-2070; Fax: 724-265-6316.

Baldwin Boro, Allegheny Co., St. Albert the Great (1956), Rev. Edward Kryston; Deacon Robert J. Becker.
Res., 3171 Churchview Ave., 15227. Tel: 412-884-7744; Fax: 412-884-2300.
School—Bishop John B. McDowell Regional School. See Consolidated Schools under Institutions Located in the Diocese.

Beaver, Beaver Co., SS. Peter and Paul (1830), Rev. Msgr. William M. Ogrodowski (STL). In res., Revs. Regis R. Alberth; Kenneth E. Myers, M.S.Ed.
Res., 200 Third St., 15009. Tel: 724-775-4111; Fax: 724-775-1117. [CEM]
School—370 E. End Ave., 15009. Tel: 724-774-4450; Fax: 724-774-5192.
Sisters of St. Francis of Providence of God 1; Lay Teachers 11; Students 189.

Beaver Falls, Beaver Co., Divine Mercy (1994). Consolidated from St. Mary and Holy Trinity. Rev. Donald R. Bischof. In res., Rev. Paul J. Savage, S.T.L.
Res., 605 Tenth St., 15010. Tel: 724-846-4585; Fax: 724-846-6868. [CEM]
School—609 Tenth St., 15010. Tel: 724-846-5955; Fax: 724-846-1896.
Lay Teachers 9; Students 115.
Holy Trinity (Polish). Closed. See Divine Mercy.
St. Philomena (1948), Rev. David E.F. Scharf.
Res., 3908 Sixth Ave., 15010. Tel: 724-843-7375; Fax: 724-843-7575.
School—Tel: 724-846-2272.
Lay Teachers 8; Students 90.

Bellevue, Allegheny Co., Assumption of the Blessed Virgin Mary on the Beautiful River (1903), Revs. Dennis M. Buranosky; John P. Hickey; Michael L. Yaksick.

Res., 45 N. Sprague Ave., 15202. Tel: 412-766-6660; Fax: 412-766-4836.
School—35 N. Jackson Ave., 15202. Tel: 412-761-7887; Fax: 412-761-7620.
Lay Teachers 25; Students 250.

Bentleyville, Washington Co., St. Luke. Closed. See Ave Maria, Ellsworth.

Bessemer, Lawrence Co., St. Anthony (1909). Merged with St. Lawrence, Hillsville to form Christ the King, Hillsville.

Bethel Park, Allegheny Co., St. Germaine (1957), Rev. Nicholas A. Pesanka; Sr. Mary Faith Balawejder, C.S.S.F., Pastoral Assoc.
Res., 7003 Baptist Rd., 15102. Tel: 412-833-0661; Fax: 412-833-4036.
School—7001 Baptist Rd., 15102. Tel: 412-833-0223.
Lay Teachers 16; Students 186.

St. Thomas More (1953), Revs. Kenneth R. White; Steven M. Palsa; Joseph B. Cordori.
Res., 126 Fort Couch Rd., Pittsburgh, 15241. Tel: 412-833-0031; Fax: 412-833-5995.
School—134 Fort Couch Rd., Pittsburgh, 15241. Tel: 412-833-1412; Fax: 412-833-5597.
Lay Teachers 19; Students 309.

St. Valentine (1931), Revs. J. Francis Frazer; Robert M. Miller.
Res., 2710 Ohio St., 15102. Tel: 412-835-4415; Fax: 412-835-4417.
School—(Grades PreK-8) 2709 Mesta St., 15102. Tel: 412-835-3780.
Lay Teachers 17; Students 280.

Blawnox, Allegheny Co., St. Edward (1938), Rev. Russell J. Maurer. In res., Rev. Thomas M. Kirby.
Res., 450 Walnut St., Pittsburgh, 15238. Tel: 412-828-4066; Fax: 412-828-3084.

Bobtown, Greene Co., St. Ignatius of Antioch (1924), Rev. Lawrence V. Holpp.
Res., Box 63, 15315. Tel: 724-839-7122; Fax: 724-839-7315.
Mission—Bobtown, Greene Co., Holy Family.

Boyers, Butler Co., St. Alphonsus (1841). Merged with Epiphany, St. Paschal and St. Louis, W. Sunbury. Rev. Albert C. Koser.
Mailing Address: P.O. Box 46, 16020.
Res., 2709 W. Sunbury Rd., 16020. Tel: 724-791-2393. [CEM][JC 3]

Braddock, Allegheny Co., Good Shepherd (1985), Revs. Thomas A. Wagner; Robert J. Zajdel. In res., Revs. Joseph D. Karabin; Anthony N. Mghanga.
Res., 416 Verona St., 15104. Tel: 412-271-1515; Fax: 412-271-1222.
School—1025 Braddock Ave., 15104. Tel: 412-271-2492; Fax: 412-271-3248. Sr. Marie Diane Novachek, V.S.C., Prin.
Sisters 3; Lay Teachers 8; Students 132.
Convent—Tel: 412-271-1736.

Braddock Hills, Allegheny Co., Sacred Heart (1897) (Polish), Rev. Thomas A. Wagner, Admin.
Res., 1600 Brinton Rd., 15221-4902. Tel: 412-271-4222; Fax: 412-271-1222.

Brentwood, Allegheny Co., St. Sylvester (1924), Revs. Mark A. Eckman; Leroy A. DiPietro. In res., Very Rev. Robert J. Ahlin; Deacon Joseph R. Mueller.
Res., 3754 Brownsville Rd., 15227. Tel: 412-882-8593; Fax: 412-882-0153.
School—30 W. Willock Rd., 15227. Tel: 412-882-9900.
Sisters of Divine Providence 1; Lay Teachers 12; Students 225.

Bridgeville, Allegheny Co.,

1—St. Agatha, (1894). Closed. See Holy Child.

2—Holy Child, (1994). Consolidated from St. Agatha and St. Anthony. Revs. Frederick L. Cain; Nicholas A. Spirko.
Res., 212 Station St., 15017. Tel: 412-221-5213; Fax: 412-257-2461. [CEM]
School—Tel: 412-221-4720; Fax: 412-257-9742.
Sisters 2; Lay Teachers 14; Students 236.
Convent—509 Coulter St., 15017. Tel: 412-221-8930.

3—St. Anthony, (1915) (Lithuanian). Closed. See Holy Child.

4—St. Barbara, (1894), Rev. William F. Kohler.
Res., 45 Prestley Rd., 15017-1971. Tel: 412-221-5152; Fax: 412-221-7935. [CEM]

Bulger, Washington Co., St. Ann (1917), Rev. Rudolph M. Silvers.
Res., 967 Grant St., Box 488, 15019-0488. Tel: 724-796-3791; 9151 (Hall).

Burgettstown, Washington Co., Our Lady of Lourdes (1916), Rev. Richard J. Tusky.
Res., 621 S. Main St., 15021. Tel: 724-947-3363; Fax: 724-947-9348. [CEM]
School—620 Main St., 15021. Tel: 724-947-5076; Fax: 724-947-5065.
Lay Teachers 10; Students 162.

Butler, Butler Co.,

1—St. Fidelis of Sigmaringen, (1995), Revs. James F. Murphy; George Palick.
Res., 125 Buttercup Rd., 16001. Tel: 724-482-2690; Fax: 724-482-2315.

2—St. Michael the Archangel, (1909) (Italian-French), Rev. James W. Dolan.
Res., 432 Center Ave., 16001. Tel: 724-282-4107; Fax: 724-282-3156. [CEM]
School—Butler Catholic School. See Consolidated Schools under Institutions Located in the Diocese.

3—St. Paul, (1867) (Territorial), Revs. Hugh M. Gloninger; Norbert J. Campbell; Robert M. Staszewski; Deacon Gerald C. Stein, (Retired). In res., Rev. Henry S. Preneta (GBG) Hospital Chap.
Res., 128 N. McKean St., 16001. Tel: 724-287-1759.
School—Butler Catholic School. See Consolidated Schools under Institutions Located in the Diocese.

4—St. Peter, (1821) (German), Rev. Jack Nanz.
Res., 127 Franklin St., 16001. Tel: 724-287-2743; Fax: 724-287-8447. [CEM]
School—Butler Catholic School. See Consolidated Schools under Institutions Located in the Diocese.

5—St. Wendelin, (1863), Rev. Harry R. Bielewicz.
Res., 210 St. Wendelin Rd., 16002. Tel: 724-287-0820; Fax: 724-287-6253. [CEM]
Preschool—Tel: 724-285-4986.
Students 56.
School—(Grades K-7) 211 St. Wendelin Rd., 16002. Tel: 724-285-4986.
Lay Teachers 8; Students 91.

Cabot, Butler Co., St. Joseph (1904), Rev. Michael Greb, O.F.M.Cap.
Res., 315 Stoney Hollow Rd., 16023. Tel: 724-352-2149; Fax: 724-352-7174.

California, Washington Co., St. Thomas Aquinas (1888), Rev. Mark J. Skertich.
Res., 213 Fourth St., 15419. Tel: 724-938-3204; Fax: 724-938-0434. [CEM]

Canonsburg, Washington Co., St. Patrick (1993). Merged with St. Genevieve. Revs. Philip J. Przybyla; Kenneth A. Sparks; Alfred C. Cicola; Deacon Joseph C. Meyer, Jr.
Res., 317 W. Pike St., 15317. Tel: 724-745-6560; Fax: 724-746-1112. [CEM]
School—Hutchinson & Murdock Sts., 15317. Tel: 724-745-7977; Fax: 724-746-1112.
Priests 3; Lay Teachers 11; Students 217.

St. Genevieve (Polish). Closed. See St. Patrick.

Carmichaels, Greene Co., St. Hugh (1951), Revs. John M. Bauer; Paul F. Merkovsky.
Res., 408 Rte. 88, 15320. Tel: 724-966-7270; Fax: 724-966-9118.

Carnegie, Allegheny Co.,

1—St. Elizabeth Ann Seton, (1992) (Italian-German). Consolidated from the following churches: Holy Souls, St. Ignatius de Loyola, Immaculate Conception, St. Joseph, St. Luke and St. Vincent de Paul, Walkers Mill. Revs. Rudolph F. Smoley; Raymond M. Utz. In res., Rev. James S. Ruggiero, V.E.
Res., 206 Mary St., 15106-2489. Tel: 412-276-1011; Fax: 412-276-0816. [CEM][JC 4]

2—Holy Souls. Closed. See St. Elizabeth Ann Seton.

3—St. Ignatius de Loyola, (Polish). Closed. See St. Elizabeth Ann Seton.

4—Immaculate Conception, (Polish). Closed. See St. Elizabeth Ann Seton.

5—St. Joseph, (German). Closed. See St. Elizabeth Ann Seton.

6—St. Luke. Closed. See St. Elizabeth Ann Seton.

Castle Shannon, Allegheny Co., St. Anne (1889), Very Rev. Donald P. Breier, V.F.; Revs. James R. Gretz; James P. Holland. In res., Rev. Msgr. Charles O. Rice, Pastor Emeritus.
Res., 400 Hoodridge Dr., Pittsburgh, 15234. Tel: 412-531-5964; Fax: 412-531-6136. [CEM]
School—4040 Willow Ave., Pittsburgh, 15234. Tel: 412-561-7720; Fax: 412-561-7927.
Lay Teachers 15; Students 285.

Cecil, Washington Co., St. Mary (1909), Rev. Robert P. Connolly.
Res., 10 St. Mary's Ln., 15321. Tel: 412-221-1560; Fax: 412-221-9544. [CEM]

Center Township, Beaver Co., St. Frances Cabrini (1961), Revs. Joseph J. Kleppner, S.T.L., Ph.D.; Chuck Baptiste.
Res., 115 Trinity Dr., Aliquippa, 15001. Tel: 724-775-6363; Fax: 724-775-3848.

St. Andrew, Butler Co., (1964), Rev. James G. Salberg.
Res., 1660 N. Main St., Ext., Butler, 16001. Tel: 724-287-7781; Fax: 724-287-7346.

Charleroi, Washington Co.,

1—St. Jerome. Closed. See Mary Mother of the Church.

2—SS. Cyril and Methodius, (Slovak). Closed. See Mary Mother of the Church.

3—Mary Mother of the Church, (1992). Consolidated from SS. Cyril & Methodius, St. Jerome and Mother of Sorrows. Revs. David F. Dzermejko; Michael A. Caridi.
Res., 624 Washington Ave., 15022-1989. Tel: 724-483-4572; 724-483-5533; Fax: 724-483-0122. [CEM]

4—Mother of Sorrows, (Italian). Closed. See Mary Mother of the Church.

Chicora, Butler Co., Mater Dolorosa (1910), Rev. David D. DeWitt.
Res., P.O. Box 243, 16025. Tel: 724-445-2275; Fax: 724-445-7507.

Chippewa Township, Beaver Co., Christ the Divine Teacher (1969), Rev. Harry R. Sangl.
Res., 116 Thorndale Dr., Beaver Falls, 15010. Tel: 724-846-7540.

Churchill Borough, Allegheny Co., St. John Fisher (1960), Rev. Carl J. Gentile.
Res., 33 Lewin Ln., Pittsburgh, 15235. Tel: 412-241-4722; Fax: 412-241-4653.

Clairton, Allegheny Co., St. Clare of Assisi (1994). Consolidated from the following churches: St. Joseph, St. Paulinus and St. Clare. Revs. Emil W. Fischer, O.F.M.Cap.; James Kurtz, O.F.M.Cap.
Office: 314 Wilson Ave., 15025. Tel: 412-233-7870; Fax: 412-233-0742. [CEM]
School—336 Wilson Ave., 15025. Tel: 412-233-7598.

St. Joseph. Closed. See St. Clare of Assisi.

St. Paulinus. Closed. See St. Clare of Assisi.

Clarksville, Washington Co., St. Thomas (1992) (Polish-Italian), Rev. Thomas R. Miller.
Res., R.D. No. 1, 15322. Tel: 724-377-2588; Fax: 724-377-0707.

Conway, Beaver Co., Our Lady of Peace (1941), Revs. Robert Guay; Patrick Barkey. In res., Rev. David C. Menegay.
Res., 1000 Third Ave., 15027. Tel: 724-869-3024; Fax: 724-869-3025.

Coraopolis, Allegheny Co., St. Joseph (1891), Rev. G. Malcolm McDonald.
Res., 1304 Fourth Ave., 15108. Tel: 412-264-6162; Fax: 412-264-5370. [CEM]
School—Tel: 412-264-6141; Fax: 412-264-1518.
Felician Sisters 2; Lay Teachers 9; Students 168.

Coylesville, Butler Co., St. John (1853), Rev. Louis F. Pascazi, Admin.
Res., 455 Clearfield Rd., Fenelton, 16034-9735. Tel: 724-287-7590. [CEM]

Crafton, Allegheny Co., St. Philip (1839) (Irish), Revs. Walter W. Dworak; Daniel W. Whalen.
Res., 50 W. Crafton Ave., Pittsburgh, 15205. Tel: 412-922-6300; Fax: 412-920-7310. [CEM]
School—52 W. Crafton Ave., Pittsburgh, 15205. Tel: 412-928-2742.
Sisters of Charity 4; Lay Teachers 25; Students 407.

Cranberry Township, Butler Co., St. Ferdinand (1961), Revs. John P. Gallagher; Kevin F. McKnight; Joseph P. Newell; Deacon John J. Walsh; Barbara McCarthy, Pastoral Assoc.
Res., 2535 Rochester Rd., 16066-6496. Tel: 724-776-2888; Fax: 724-776-2378.

Creighton, Allegheny Co., Holy Family (East Deer Twp.) (1949) (Territorial), Rev. Miroslaw Stelmaszczyk.
Res., 787 Freeport Rd., 15030. Tel: 724-224-1626; Fax: 724-224-0609.

Darlington, Beaver Co., St. Rose of Lima (1871), Rev. James B. Krah.
Res., 3357 Constitution Blvd., 16115. Tel: 412-843-0152.
St. Ann (Worship Site):New Galilee, 16141.

Donora, Washington Co.,

1—St. Charles. Closed. See Our Lady of the Valley.

2—St. Dominic, (Slovak). Closed. See Our Lady of the Valley.

3—Holy Name of the Blessed Virgin Mary. Closed. See Our Lady of the Valley.

4—Our Lady of the Valley, (1992). Consolidated from the following churches: St. Charles Borromeo, St. Dominic, Holy Name of the Blessed Virgin Mary and St. Philip Neri. Rev. David J. Kriss. In res., Rev. Kenneth Agede (Nigeria).
Res., 571 Thompson Ave., 15033. Tel: 724-379-4777; 379-7777; Fax: 724-379-6242. [CEM]

5—St. Philip Neri, (Italian). Closed. See Our Lady of the Valley.

Duquesne, Allegheny Co., Holy Name. Closed. See Christ the Light of the World.

St. Joseph (1897) (German), Rev. Dennis Colamarino. In res., Rev. Emmanuel C. Agbakwuru (Nigeria).
Res., 817 W. Grant Ave., 15110. Tel: 412-466-1304. [CEM]
School—Duquesne Catholic School. See Consolidated Schools under Institutions Located in the Diocese. Tel: 412-466-3895.

Christ the Light of the World (1994). Consolidated from St. Hedwig and Holy Name. Rev. Dennis Colamarino.
Res., 32 S. First St., 15110. Tel: 412-469-0196. [CEM 2]

East McKeesport, Allegheny Co., St. Robert Bellarmine (1951), Rev. John G. Oesterle.
Res., 1313 Fifth Ave., 15035. Tel: 412-824-2644; 824-2635; Fax: 412-824-4786.

East Pittsburgh, Allegheny Co., St. William. Closed. See Holy Cross.
St. Helen (Slovak). Closed. See Holy Cross.
Holy Cross (1994). Consolidated from St. William and St. Helen. Rev. Miroslaus A. Wojcicki.
Res., 905 Main St., 15112. Tel: 412-829-1146; Fax: 412-816-2059.
Convent—(Allison Park) 515 Howard St., 15112. Tel: 412-829-0815. Sisters of Divine Providence Sisters 3.

Elizabeth, Allegheny Co., St. Michael (1849), Revs. Timothy G. Evans; R. Donald Jones.
Res., 101 McLay Dr., 15037. Tel: 412-751-0663; Fax: 412-751-2161. [CEM]
School—Sixth & Bayard St., 15037. Tel: 412-384-9400; Fax: 412-384-3727.
Lay Teachers 8; Students 110.

Ellsworth, Washington Co., Ave Maria (1994). Consolidated from St. Luke, St. Clement, and St. Joseph. Rev. Pierre M. Falkenhan.
Mailing Address: P.O. Box 650, 15331-0650.
Res., 126 Church St., Bentleyville, 15314. Tel: 724-239-3591. [CEM 2]
School—Box 590, 15331. Tel: 724-239-2226; Fax: 724-239-2272.
Lay Teachers 5; Students 62; Preschool Students 30.

Ellwood City, Lawrence Co., Holy Redeemer Parish, Very Rev. Mauro J. Cautela, V.F.; Rev. Mark L. Thomas.
300 Crescent Ave., Ste. 1, 16117. Tel: 724-758-4411; Fax: 724-752-1466.
St. Agatha (1895) (Territorial). Merged with Purification of the Blessed Virgin Mary, Ellwood City to form Holy Redeemer, Ellwood City.
Purification of the Blessed Virgin Mary (1914). Merged with St. Agatha, Ellwood City to form Holy Redeemer, Ellwood City.

Elrama, Allegheny Co., St. Isaac Jogues (1950), Rev. Robert Andrew Kohuch.
Res., Box 600, 15038. Tel: 412-384-4406; Fax: 412-384-5740.

Emsworth, Allegheny Co., Sacred Heart (1891), Revs. John P. Skaj, C.S.Sp.; Francis P. Meenan, C.S.Sp. In res., Rev. Iordepuun J. Akpagher, C.S.Sp.
Res., 154 Orchard Ave., Pittsburgh, 15202. Tel: 412-761-6651; Fax: 412-766-8298.

Etna, Allegheny Co., All Saints (1902), Rev. John Vojtek.
Res., 19 Wilson St., Pittsburgh, 15223-1798. Tel: 412-781-0530; Fax: 412-784-8769.
Preschool—20 Wilson St., Pittsburgh, 15223. Tel: 412-781-4692.
School—19 Dewey St., Pittsburgh, 15223. Tel: 412-782-0939.
Lay Teachers 9; Students 127.
Social Service—Tel: 412-781-0530.

Evans City, Butler Co., St. Matthias (1939), Rev. William J. Ritzert.
Res., 417 E. Main St., 16033. Tel: 724-538-5331.

Finleyville, Washington Co., St. Francis of Assisi (1893), Rev. Robert J. Boyle; Deacon Victor P. Satter.
Res., 3609 Washington Ave., 15332. Tel: 724-348-7145; Fax: 724-348-7522. [CEM]

Forest Hills, Allegheny Co., St. Maurice (1949), Rev. Charles T. Geiselhart, M. Div. In res., Rev. Pachomius Okogie, O.S.B.
Res., 2001 Ardmore Blvd., Pittsburgh, 15221. Tel: 412-271-0809; Fax: 412-271-2415.
School—Tel: 412-351-5403.
Sisters 5; Lay Teachers 19; Students 334.

Franklin Park Borough, Allegheny Co., Saints John and Paul (1994), Rev. Albert J. Semler.
Res., 2586 Wexford-Bayne Rd., Sewickley, 15143. Tel: 724-935-2104; Fax: 724-935-8320.
St. John Neumann (1979), Revs. William R. Bovard; Robert R. Coyne.
Res., 1543 Old Orchard Rd., Pittsburgh, 15237. Tel: 412-366-2020; Fax: 412-366-2866.

Fredericktown, Washington Co., St. Michael the Archangel. Closed. See St. Oliver Plunkett, Marianna.

Freedom, Beaver Co., St. Felix (1906) (Italian), Rev. Leon Leitem, O.F.M.Cap.
Res., 450 13th St., 15042. Tel: 724-775-1476; Fax: 724-775-5684. [CEM]

Glade Mills, Butler Co., Holy Sepulcher (1944), Rev. John P. Maloney. In res., Rev. Thomas Akpen (Nigeria).
Res., 1304 E. Cruikshank Rd., Butler, 16002. Tel: 724-586-7610; Fax: 724-586-7247.
School—Tel: 724-586-5022.
Lay Teachers 13; Students 161.

Glassport, Allegheny Co., St. Cecilia. Closed. See Queen of the Rosary.
Queen of the Rosary (1994). Consolidated from Holy Cross and St. Cecilia. Rev. Casimir Kedzierski.
Res., 530 Michigan Ave., 15045. Tel: 412-672-7209; Fax: 412-672-6390.
School—St. Joseph Regional School. See Consolidated Schools under Institutions Located in the Diocese. 15133. Tel: 412-678-0659.

Glenshaw, Allegheny Co., St. Bonaventure (1957), Revs. George C. Newmeyer; Mark A. Thomas.
Res., 2001 Mount Royal Blvd., 15116. Tel: 412-486-2606; Fax: 412-492-9329.
School—Tel: 412-486-2608; Fax: 412-487-8657.
Sisters of Divine Providence 1; Lay Teachers 27; Students 555.
St. Mary of the Assumption (1834), Revs. John A. Marcucci; Paul Grunebach; Philip N. Farrell.
Res., 2510 Middle Rd., 15116. Tel: 412-486-4100; Fax: 412-486-4150. [CEM]
School—Tel: 412-486-7611; Fax: 412-487-9509.
Sisters of Divine Providence 1; Lay Teachers 26; Students 422.

Green Tree, Allegheny Co., St. Margaret (1938), Rev. Harry E. Nichols.
Res., 310 Mansfield Ave., Pittsburgh, 15220. Tel: 412-921-0745; Fax: 412-921-0707.
School—915 Alice St., Pittsburgh, 15220. Tel: 412-922-4765; Fax: 412-922-4647.
Lay Teachers 21; Students 284.

Harmarville, Allegheny Co., St. Francis of Assisi (1940), Rev. Hugh J. McCormley.
Res., 2599 Freeport Rd., Pittsburgh, 15238. Tel: 412-828-3123; Fax: 412-828-0527.

Harwick, Allegheny Co., Our Lady of Victory (1944), Rev. Albert L. Zapf.
Res., 1319 Low Grade Rd., Box 198, 15049. Tel: 724-274-8575; Fax: 724-274-0529.

Herman, Butler Co., St. Mary of the Assumption (1842), Rev. Lester Knoll, O.F.M.Cap.
Res., 821 Herman Rd., P.O. Box 26, 16039. Tel: 724-285-3285; Fax: 724-285-4715. [CEM]
School—Tel: 724-283-2129.
Lay Teachers 9; Students 130; PreK 34.

Hillsville, Lawrence Co., Christ the King, Rev. James A. Downs.
P.O. Box 23, 16132. Tel: 724-667-7721; Fax: 724-667-0827.
St. Lawrence (1904) (Italian). Merged with St. Anthony, Bessemer to form Christ the King, Hillsville.

Holiday Park, Allegheny Co., Our Lady of Joy (1968), Rev. Robert J. Cedolia.
Res., 2000 O'Block Rd., Pittsburgh, 15239. Tel: 412-795-3388; Fax: 412-793-5308.

Homestead, Allegheny Co.,

1—St. Anne. Closed. See St. Maximilian Kolbe, Homestead.

2—St. Anthony. Closed. See St. Maximilian Kolbe, Homestead.

3—St. Mary Magdalene. Closed. See St. Maximilian Kolbe, Homestead.

4—SS. Peter and Paul, (Lithuanian). Closed. See St. Maximilian Kolbe, Homestead.

Hopewell Township, Beaver Co., Our Lady of Fatima (1954), Revs. David A. Driesch; James B. Farnan.
Res., 2270 Brodhead Rd., Aliquippa, 15001. Tel: 724-375-7626; Fax: 724-375-0219.
School—Tel: 724-375-7565.
Lay Teachers 15; Students 189.

Imperial, Allegheny Co., St. Columbkille (1908), Revs. Domenic Mancini; Richard J. Wesoloski.
Res., 103 Church Rd., 15126. Tel: 724-695-7325; Fax: 724-695-9202. [CEM]

Industry, Beaver Co., St. Christine. Closed. See St. Blaise, Midland.

Ingram, Allegheny Co., Ascension (1967), Rev. Walter A. Sobon.
Res., 114 Berry St., Pittsburgh, 15205. Tel: 412-921-1230; Fax: 412-922-1279.

Jefferson Boro, Allegheny Co., St. Thomas A'Becket (1957), Rev. Robert L. Seeman.
Res., 509 Gill Hall Rd., Jefferson Hills, 15025. Tel: 412-655-2885; Fax: 412-655-0615.

Kennedy Township, Allegheny Co., St. Malachy (1953), Revs. Richard S. Jones; Michael S. Suslowicz; Deacon David Lamm.
Res., 343 Forest Grove Rd., Coraopolis, 15108. Tel: 412-771-5483; Fax: 412-331-7312.
School—Tel: 412-771-4545.
Lay Teachers 12; Students 288.

Koppel, Beaver Co., Queen of Heaven (1992). Consolidated from St. Monica, Wampum and St. Teresa, Koppel. Rev. Joseph R. Lemp, S.T.L.
Res., 6421 Sixth Ave., P.O. Box A, 16136-0601. Tel: 724-846-5702; Fax: 724-846-2219. [CEM]
St. Teresa. Closed. See Queen of Heaven.

Lawrence, Washington Co., St. Elizabeth. Closed. See St. Mary, Cecil.

Liberty Boro, Allegheny Co., St. Eugene. Closed. See St. Mark, Port Vue.

Lyndora, Butler Co., St. John (1904) (Slovak). Closed. See St. Fidelis of Sigmaringen, Butler.
St. Stanislaus Kostka (1919) (Polish). Merged with St. Conrad, Meridian, and St. John, Lyndora, to form St. Fidelis, Butler.

McDonald, Washington Co., St. Alphonsus (1892), Rev. John A. Harvey.
Res., 219 W. Lincoln Ave., 15057. Tel: 724-926-2984; Fax: 724-926-5120.

McKeesport, Allegheny Co.,

1—St. Martin de Porres, (1993). Consolidated from St. Mary, Holy Trinity, Sacred Heart and St. Peter. Revs. John L. Gudewicz; F. Raymond Trance; Deacons Ken Gleason; Steve Pikula; Dale DiSanto. In res., Revs. John A. Palko; Anthony Naaeke (Ghana).
Res., 704 Market St., 15132. Tel: 412-672-9763; Fax: 412-672-2817. [CEM 3]
School—St. Joseph Regional School. See Consolidated Schools under Institutions Located in the Diocese.

2—St. Peter. Closed. See St. Martin de Porres.

3—St. Mary, (German). Closed. See St. Martin de Porres.

4—St. Mary Czestochowa, (1893) (Polish), Rev. Francis B. Lachowicz.
Res., 2515 Versailles Ave., 15132. Tel: 412-672-0765; Fax: 412-672-2220. [CEM]
School—McKeesport Central Catholic School. See Consolidated Schools under Institutions Located in the Diocese.

5—Holy Trinity. Closed. See St. Martin de Porres.

6—St. Patrick, (1993). Merged with St. Denis, Versailles and St. Perpetua, McKeesport. Rev. Vincent P. Velas.
Res., 310 32nd St., 15132. Tel: 412-673-4110; Fax: 412-678-7259. [CEM]

7—St. Pius V, (1903). Merged with St. Stephen. Rev. John J. Keane, Admin.
Res., 2911 Versailles Ave., 15132. Tel: 412-673-8878; Fax: 412-673-8704. [CEM]
School—McKeesport Central Catholic School. See Consolidated Schools under Institutions Located in the Diocese.

8—St. Stephen, (1899) (Hungarian). Closed. See St. Pius V.

9—Sacred Heart, (Croatian). Closed. See St. Martin de Porres.

10—St. Perpetua. Closed. See St. Patrick, Versailles.

McKees Rocks, Allegheny Co.,

1—St. Mary Help of Christians, (German). Closed. See St. John of God.

2—St. Francis de Sales. Closed. See St. John of God.

3—St. John of God, (1993). Consolidated from the following churches: St. Francis de Sales, SS. Cyril & Methodius, St. Maria Goretti Chapel, St. Mark, St. Mary Help of Christians, Mother of Sorrows and St. Vincent, Pittsburgh. Revs. Paul C. Householder; Lawrence R. Smith. In res., Revs. Harold Baily; Regis J. Ryan; Christopher Mbogu (Nigeria).
Parish Office: 1 Desiderio Way, 15136. Tel: 412-771-5646; Fax: 412-331-0678. [CEM 2]
School—3 Desiderio Way, 15136. Tel: 412-331-8501; Fax: 412-331-0678.
Lay Teachers 6; Students 102.

4—St. Maria Goretti Chapel. Closed. See St. John of God.

5—Mother of Sorrows, (Italian). Closed. See St. John of God.

6—St. Mark, (Slovak). Closed. See St. John of God.

7—SS. Cyril and Methodius, (Polish). Closed. See St. John of God.

Fredericktown, Washington Co., St. Oliver Plunkett (1994). Consolidated from Saints Mary & Ann, Marianna, and St. Michael Archangel, Fredericktown. Rev. Edward S. Litavec. In res., Rev. Francis A. Nazimek.
Res., Box 638, 15333. Tel: 724-377-0128; Fax: 724-377-0129. [CEM]

Mars, Butler Co., St. Kilian (1920), Rev. John W. Rebel.
Res., Clarke & Cherry Sts., P.O. Box 394, 16046. Tel: 724-625-1665; Fax: 724-625-1922.

Meadowlands, Washington Co., Our Lady of the Miraculous Medal (1949), Rev. John L. O'Shea.
Res., Box 366, 15347. Tel: 724-222-1911; Fax: 724-222-5688. [JC]

Meridian, Butler Co., St. Conrad. Merged with St. John and St. Stanislaus Kostka, Lyndora to form St. Fidelis, Butler.

Midland, Beaver Co., St. Blaise (1994), Rev. Dennis J. Bradley.
Res., 772 Ohio Ave., 15059. Tel: 724-643-4050; Fax: 724-643-6533.

Millvale, Allegheny Co.,

1—St. Ann. Closed. See Holy Spirit.

2—St. Anthony, (German). Closed. See Holy Spirit.

3—Holy Spirit, (1994). Consolidated from St. Anthony and St. Ann. Revs. John R. Weber, C.S.Sp.; John Nader, C.S.Sp. In res., Rev. Dominic A. Lih (Nigeria).
Res., 608 Farragut St., Pittsburgh, 15209. Tel: 412-821-4424; Fax: 412-821-8258.
School—100 Howard St., Pittsburgh, 15209. Tel: 412-821-4805; Fax: 412-821-4714.
Lay Teachers 13; Students 201.

4—St. Nicholas, (Croatian). Closed. See the new St. Nicholas.

5—St. Nicholas, (1894) (Croatian), Very Rev. Gabriel Badurina, T.O.R.
Administrative Center: 24 Maryland Ave., Pittsburgh, 15209. Tel: 412-821-3438; Fax: 412-821-8726. [JC 2]

Monaca, Beaver Co., St. John the Baptist (1888), Revs. Frank M. Kurimsky; Robin S. Evanish.
Res., 1409 Pennsylvania Ave., 15061. Tel: 724-775-3940; Fax: 724-775-6886. [CEM]
School—Virginia Ave. & 15th St., 15061. Tel: 724-775-5774; Fax: 724-775-2997.
Lay Teachers 13; Students 269.

Monongahela, Washington Co., Transfiguration (1865), Rev. William P. Feeney.
Res., 722 W. Main St., 15063. Tel: 724-258-7742; Fax: 724-258-8733. [CEM 2]
School—Madonna Regional Catholic School. See Consolidated Schools under Institutions Located in the Diocese.

St. Anthony (1905) (Italian-Slavic), Rev. Joseph E. Feltz, Admin.
Res., 225 Park Ave., 15063. Tel: 724-258-9710; Fax: 724-258-3362.

Monroeville, Allegheny Co., St. Bernadette (1955), Revs. Michael W. Decewicz; Kenneth E. Kezmarsky; Joseph F. Keenan.
Res., 245 Azalea Dr., 15146. Tel: 412-373-0050; Fax: 412-374-8113.
School—(Grades PreK-8). Tel: 412-372-7255.
Sisters 2; Lay Teachers 20; Students 380.

North American Martyrs (1960), Rev. Francis J. Murhammer. In res., Rev. Thomas V. Manning.
Res., 2526 Haymaker Rd., 15146. Tel: 412-373-0330; Fax: 412-380-1306.
School—(Grades K-6). Tel: 412-373-0889.
Lay Teachers 9; Students 141.

Moon Township, Allegheny Co., St. Margaret Mary (1956), Rev. John Ayoob.
Res., One Parish Pl., 15108-2697. Tel: 412-264-2573; Fax: 412-264-4327.

Mt. Lebanon, Allegheny Co., St. Bernard (1919), Revs. George A. Wilt; John W. Markell; John E. Suhoza.
Res., 311 Washington Rd., Pittsburgh, 15216. Tel: 412-561-3301; Fax: 412-563-0211.
School—(Grades PreK-8) 315 Washington Rd., Pittsburgh, 15216. Tel: 412-341-5444; Fax: 412-341-2044.
Lay Teachers 31; Students 564.

St. Winifred (Pittsburgh) (1960), Rev. Jeremiah T. O'Shea; Deacon Joseph Kosko.
Res., 550 Sleepy Hollow Rd., Pittsburgh, 15228. Tel: 412-344-5010; Fax: 412-563-7279.

Munhall, Allegheny Co.,

1—St. Margaret. Closed. See St. Maximilian Kolbe, Homestead.

2—St. Maximilian Kolbe, (1992). Consolidated from the following churches: St. Anne, Homestead; St. Anthony, Homestead; St. Margaret, Homestead;St. Mary Magdalene, Homestead; St. Michael, Homestead; SS. Peter & Paul, Homestead. Rev. Henry R. Krawczyk. In res., Revs. Mark W. Glasgow Tel: 412-462-1807; Thomas O'Donnell Tel: 412-462-9258.
Church—129 E. 10th Ave., Homestead, 15120-1996. Tel: 412-461-1054; Fax: 412-462-1744. [CEM 3]

3—St. Michael, (Slovak). Closed. See St. Maximilian Kolbe, Homestead.

4—St. Rita, (1936) (Slovak), Rev. Alvin J. Adams.
Res., 219 W. Schwab Ave., 15120. Tel: 412-461-4204; Fax: 412-462-5484.

5—St. Therese of Lisieux, (1925), Very Rev. Hugh J. Lang; Rev. Nicholas Mastrangelo. In res., Rev. Joseph C. Girdis, (Retired).
Res., One St. Therese Ct., 15120. Tel: 412-462-8161; Fax: 412-462-4817.
School—Three St. Therese Ct., 15120. Tel: 412-462-8163.
Sisters of Charity 3; Lay Teachers 19; Students 342.

Muse, Washington Co., Holy Rosary (1963), Rev. George T. DeVille.
Res., Orchard St., P.O. Box 447, 15350-0447. Tel: 724-745-3531.

Natrona, Allegheny Co., St. Joseph (1992). Merged with St. Ladislaus and St. Mathias. Rev. Donald J. Sotak.
Res., 96 Pond St., 15065-2630. Tel: 724-224-1336; Fax: 724-224-6926. [CEM]
High School—800 Montana Ave., Natrona Heights, 15065. Tel: 724-224-5552; Fax: 724-224-0235.

St. Ladislaus (Polish). Closed. See St. Joseph.

St. Mathias. Closed. See St. Joseph.

Natrona Heights, Allegheny Co., Blessed Sacrament. Closed. See Our Lady of the Most Blessed Sacrament.

Our Lady of the Most Blessed Sacrament (1992) (Polish-Slovak). Consolidated from Most Blessed Sacrament and Our Lady of Perpetual Help. Revs. Stan M. Gregorek; Aaron J. Kriss; Bernard B. Costello; Deacon Patrick Wood.
Res., 1526 Union Ave., 15065-2008. Tel: 724-226-4900; Fax: 724-224-3559.

Our Lady of Perpetual Help. Closed. See Our Lady of the Most Blessed Sacrament.

Nemacolin, Greene Co., Our Lady of Consolation (1923), Revs. John M. Bauer; Paul Merkovsky.
Mailing Address: c/o St. Hugh, 408 Rte. 88, Carmichael, 15320.
Res., 837 Wood Ext., 15351. Tel: 724-966-7909. [CEM]

Neshannock, Lawrence Co., St. Camillus (1959), Rev. Robert J. Miller. In res., Rev. Francis C. Graff.
Res., 314 W. Englewood Ave., New Castle, 16105. Tel: 724-652-9471; Fax: 724-654-1430.

New Bedford, Lawrence Co., St. James (1844), Rev. Joseph R. McCaffrey.
Res., P.O. Box 207, 16140. Tel: 724-964-8276; Fax: 724-964-1108. [CEM]

New Brighton, Beaver Co., Holy Family (1994). Consolidated from St. Joseph and SS. Cyril and Methodius. Rev. James R. Orr.
Rectory & Office: 1851 3rd Ave., 15066. Tel: 724-847-3538; 847-3548; Fax: 724-847-3585.
Church—521 7th Ave., 15066. [CEM]

SS. Cyril and Methodius (Slovak). Closed. See Holy Family.

New Castle, Lawrence Co.,

1—Mary, Mother of Hope, (1993). Consolidated from St. Mary and Madonna of Czestochowa. Rev. Victor J. Molka, Jr.
Res., 124 N. Beaver St., 16101. Tel: 724-658-2564; Fax: 724-658-9024. [CEM][JC]

2—St. Mary. Closed. See Mary, Mother of Hope.

3—St. Joseph the Worker, (1888), Rev. Robert J. Schweitzer.
Res., 1111 S. Cascade St., 16101. Tel: 724-658-1683; Fax: 724-658-1684. [JC]

4—St. Vitus, (1901) (Italian), Rev. John D. Petrarulo.
Res., 910 S. Mercer St., 16101. Tel: 724-652-3422; Fax: 724-652-2322. [JC]
School—915 S. Jefferson St., 16101. Tel: 724-654-9297; Fax: 724-654-9364.
Apostles of the Sacred Heart of Jesus 4; Lay Teachers 9; Students 151.

5—Madonna of Czestochowa. Closed. See Mary, Mother of Hope.

6—St. Michael, (Slovak). Closed. See St. Vincent de Paul.

7—SS. Philip and James, (Polish). Closed. See St. Vincent de Paul.

8—St. Lucy, (Italian). Closed. See St. Vincent de Paul.

9—St. Margaret. Closed. See St. Vincent de Paul.

10—St. Vincent de Paul, (1993). Consolidated from the following churches in New Castle: St. Lucy, St. Michael, SS. Philip & James, St. Margaret; and Holy Cross, West Pittsburg. Revs. Benedetto P. Vaghetto, J.C.L.; Michael J. Maranowski, M.Div.; Frank G. Erdeljac, M.Div.; Deacon S. Daniel Kielar.
Res., One Lucymont Dr., 16102. Tel: 724-652-5829; Fax: 724-656-0413. [CEM 2]

North Oakland, Butler Co., St. Joseph (1872), Rev. David D. DeWitt, Admin.
Res., Main St., P.O. Box 243, Chicora, 16025. Tel: 724-445-2275. [CEM]

North Rochester, Beaver Co., St. Pudentiana. Closed. See St. Cecilia, Rochester.

Oakdale, Allegheny Co., St. Patrick (1866), Rev. William J. Schwartz.
Res., 7322 Noblestown Rd., 15071. Tel: 724-693-9260; Fax: 724-693-9247. [CEM]

Oakmont, Allegheny Co., St. Irenaeus (1908), Rev. Paul D. Cwynar; Deacon Mario W. Giconi.
Res., 387 Maryland Ave., 15139. Tel: 412-828-3065; Fax: 412-828-1587.
School—Tel: 412-828-8444; Fax: 412-828-9461. Ms. Mary Frances Panian, Prin.
Lay Teachers 13; Students 110.

O'Hara Township, Allegheny County, St. Joseph (1845), Rev. James R. Bedillion, J.C.L.
Res., 330 Dorseyville Rd., Pittsburgh, 15215. Tel: 412-963-8885; Fax: 412-963-1945. [CEM]

Overbrook, Allegheny Co., St. Norbert (1914) (German), Revs. Michael C. MacVeigh; Joseph P. Pudichery.
Res., 2413 Off Saw Mill Run Blvd., Pittsburgh, 15234. Tel: 412-881-1316; 881-2474; Fax: 412-881-6728.

Penn Hills, Allegheny Co., St. Bartholomew (1950), Revs. James W. Garvey; Vincent F. Kolo. In res., Rev. Diego Cadri (Uganda).
Res., 111 Erhardt Dr., Pittsburgh, 15235. Tel: 412-242-3374; Fax: 412-242-1488.
School—Tel: 412-242-2511; Fax: 412-242-8317.
Sisters 4; Lay Teachers 20; Students 339.

St. Gerard Majella (1964), Rev. John D. Brennan.
Res., 121 Dawn Dr., Verona, 15147. Tel: 412-793-3333; Fax: 412-793-4726.

St. Susanna (1960), Rev. Martin F. Barkin.
Res., 200 Stotler Rd., 15235-3554. Tel: 412-731-7465; Fax: 412-798-0479.

Perrysville, Allegheny Co., St. Teresa of Avila (1867), Revs. Thaddeus S. Maida; David J. Jastrab; William P. Siple.
Res., 1000 Avila Ct., Pittsburgh, 15237. Tel: 412-367-9001; Fax: 412-366-8415. [CEM]
School—800 Avila Ct., Pittsburgh, 15237. Tel: 412-367-9001, Ext. 530; Fax: 412-364-1172.
Religious 2; Lay Teachers 24; Students 462.

Peters Township, Washington Co., St. Benedict the Abbot (1962), Revs. Philip J. Donatelli; John J. Arnott; Deacon John Layton; Dennis Gehlrlein, Pastoral Assoc.
Res., 120 Abington Dr., McMurray, 15317. Tel: 724-941-9406; Fax: 724-941-9517.

Pitcairn, Allegheny Co., St. Michael (1895), Rev. James E. Somma.
Church—750 Wall Ave., 15140. Tel: 412-373-3400.
Res., 740 Wall Ave., 15140. Tel: 412-373-2610; Fax: 472-373-3400.

Pleasant Hills, Allegheny Co., St. Elizabeth (1942), Revs. Roy H. Conley; David Cillo; John Batykefer.
Res., Grove Pl., Pittsburgh, 15236. Tel: 412-881-7728; Fax: 412-882-8320.
School—Tel: 412-881-2958; Fax: 412-882-0111.
Lay Teachers 32; Students 581.
Chapel of Convenience—St. David, Baldwin Boro., Pittsburgh, Tel: 412-882-8744.

Plum, Allegheny Co., St. Januarius (1950), Rev. Peter R. Pilarski.
Res., 1450 Renton Rd., 15239. Tel: 412-793-4439; Fax: 412-793-7135.

Port Vue, Allegheny Co., St. Joseph. Closed. See St. Mark.

St. Mark (1993), Revs. Gerald S. Mikonis; Innocent Anyanwu, C.S.Sp. (Nigeria).
Administration Center: 1101 Romine Ave., 15133. Tel: 412-678-6275; Fax: 412-673-1393.; St. Joseph Worship Site: 1125 Romine Ave., 15133.
Res. & St. Eugene Worship Site—3210 Liberty Way, Liberty Borough, 15133. Tel: 412-678-6275.
School—St. Joseph Regional School. See Consolidated Schools under Institutions Located in the Diocese. Tel: 412-678-0659.

Prospect, Butler Co., St. Christopher at the Lake (1974), Rev. Matthew Tosello.
Res., 229-232 N. Franklin St., 16052. Tel: 724-865-2430; Fax: 724-865-1120.

Rankin, Allegheny Co., Visitation of the Blessed Virgin Mary (Croatian). Closed. See Word of God, Swissvale.

Reserve Township, Allegheny Co., St. Aloysius (1892), Rev. William G. Rutledge.
Res., 3616 Mt. Troy Rd., Pittsburgh, 15212. Tel: 412-821-2351; Fax: 412-821-6480.

Richeyville, Washington Co., St. Agnes (1994), Rev. Francis Z. Jurewicz.
Res., Box 406, 15358. Tel: 724-632-5858; Fax: 724-632-5858. [CEM]

Richland Township, Allegheny Co., Saint Richard (1992), Rev. Kenneth E. Oldenski.
Res., 3841 Dickey Rd., Gibsonia, 15044. Tel: 724-444-1971; Fax: 724-444-6001.

Robinson Township, Allegheny Co., Holy Trinity (Moon Run) (1944), Revs. Robert W. Herrmann; William J. Scholz. In res., Rev. John Fitzgerald.

Res., 5718 Steubenville Pike, P.O. Box 15567, Pittsburgh, 15244. Tel: 412-787-2140; 787-2143; Fax: 412-787-3799.
School—(Grades PreK-8). Tel: 412-787-2656; Fax: 412-787-9487.
Sisters of Charity 1; Lay Teachers 22; Students 436.

Rochester, Beaver Co., St. Cecilia (1856) (German-Italian). Merged with St. Pudentiana. Revs. Ward Stakem, O.F.M.Cap.; William Gillum, O.F.M.Cap.; Philip Fink, O.F.M.Cap.; Scott Seethaler, O.F.M.Cap.
Res., 303 Jackson St., 15074. Tel: 724-775-0801; Fax: 724-774-3056. [CEM]

Roscoe, Washington Co., St. Joseph (1904), In res., Rev. George J. Moneck, Admin.
Res., Box 486, 15477. Tel: 724-938-2324; Fax: 724-938-2983.

Ross Township, Allegheny Co., St. Sebastian (North Hills) (1952), Very Rev. Paul J. Bradley, V.F.; Revs. Thomas A. Sparacino; James M. Stover.
Res., 311 Siebert Rd., Pittsburgh, 15237. Tel: 412-364-8999; Fax: 412-364-6330.
School—307 Siebert Rd., Pittsburgh, 15237. Tel: 412-364-7171; Fax: 412-364-5891.
Sisters 6; Lay Teachers 26; Students 439.

Russellton, Allegheny Co., Transfiguration (1916), Rev. Robert W. Habe.
Res., 15 Poma St., 15076. Tel: 724-265-1030; Fax: 724-265-1030. [CEM]
School—(Grades K-8) McKrell Rd., 15076. Tel: 724-265-3350.
Lay Teachers 10; Students 119.

Scott Township, Allegheny Co., SS. Simon and Jude (1955), Rev. Richard E. Ward. In res., Rev. Kris D. Stubna.
Res., 1607 Greentree Rd., Pittsburgh, 15220. Tel: 412-563-3189; Fax: 412-563-8524.
School—1625 Greentree Rd., Pittsburgh, 15220. Tel: 412-563-1353; Fax: 412-563-8617.
Lay Teachers 18; Students 252.

Our Lady of Grace (1947), Revs. Theodore A. Rutkowski; Howard W. Campbell.
Res., 310 Kane Blvd., Pittsburgh, 15243. Tel: 412-279-7070; Fax: 412-276-0278.
School—1734 Bower Hill Rd., Pittsburgh, 15243. Tel: 412-279-6611; Fax: 412-279-6755.
Lay Teachers 22; Students 364.

Sewickley, Allegheny Co., St. James (1863), Revs. Raymond Rhoden; William Hausen; Deacon Robert Sabatelle.
Res., 200 Walnut St., 15143. Tel: 412-741-6650; Fax: 412-741-4782. [CEM]
School—201 Broad St., 15143. Tel: 412-741-5540.
Sisters of St. Joseph 3; Lay Teachers 12; Students 299.

Sharpsburg, Allegheny Co., St. John Cantius (1906) (Polish), Rev. Andrew C. Fischer, Admin.
Res., 201 9th St., 15215. Tel: 412-784-8700; Fax: 412-781-1101.

St. Mary (1994), Rev. Andrew C. Fischer, Admin.
Res., 201 Ninth St., 15215. Tel: 412-784-8700; Fax: 412-781-1101. [CEM][JC]

Madonna of Jerusalem (1904) (Italian), Rev. Andrew C. Fischer, Admin.
Res., 201 Ninth St., 15215. Tel: 412-784-8700; Fax: 412-781-1101.

Slippery Rock, Butler Co., St. Peter (1938), Rev. James L. Armstrong, D.Min.
Res., 670 S. Main St., 16057. Tel: 724-794-2880; Fax: 724-794-1255. [CEM]

South Park, Allegheny Co., Nativity (1905), Rev. Richard A. Infante.
Res., 5802 Curry Rd., Pittsburgh, 15236. Tel: 412-655-3000; Fax: 412-650-4658.
School—(Grades PreK-8) 5811 Curry Rd., Pittsburgh, 15236. Tel: 412-653-1500; Fax: 412-653-2619.
Lay Teachers 13; Students 166.

St. Joan of Arc (1923), Rev. Phillip Pribonic.
Res., 6414 Montour St., 15129. Tel: 412-833-2400; Fax: 412-835-1764.
School—6470 Library Rd., 15129. Tel: 412-833-2433.
Lay Teachers 16; Students 147.

Springdale, Allegheny Co., St. Alphonsus (1901), Rev. George E. Saladna, S.T.L., S.S.L.
Res., 750 Pittsburgh St., 15144-1699. Tel: 724-274-5084; Fax: 724-274-7035.

Swissvale, Allegheny Co.,

1—St. Anselm. Closed. See Word of God.

2—Word of God, (1994) (Irish-Croatian). Consolidated from the following churches: St. Anselm, St. Barnabus and Visitation of the Blessed Virgin Mary, Rankin. Revs. Frank J. Drabiska; Dam Nguyen; Paul Henne. In res., Rev. Peter Debo (Uganda).
Res., 7446 McClure Ave., Pittsburgh, 15218. Tel: 412-241-1372; Fax: 412-241-0168.
School—7438 McClure Ave., Pittsburgh, 15218. Tel: 412-371-8587.
Sisters of Charity 2; Lay Teachers 19; Students 400.

3—Saint Barnabas, (Slovak). Closed. See Word of God.

4—Madonna del Castello, (1920) (Italian), Rev. John J. Cassella, M.Div.
Res., 2021 S. Braddock Ave., Pittsburgh, 15218. Tel: 412-271-5666; Fax: 412-271-5667.

Tarentum, Allegheny Co., Holy Martyrs (1992) (Slovak). Consolidated from St. Clement and Sacred Heart, St. Peter. Rev. Donald Chortos.
Res., 353 W. Ninth Ave., 15084. Tel: 724-224-0770; Fax: 724-224-7070. [CEM][JC 2]

Sacred Heart - St. Peter. Closed. See Holy Martyrs.
St. Clement. Closed. See Holy Martyrs.

Turtle Creek, Allegheny Co., St. Colman (1882), Rev. Patrick J. Hynes.
Res., 100 Tri-Boro Ave., 15145. Tel: 412-823-2564; Fax: 412-823-6436.
School—(Grades PreK-8) 547 Hunter St., 15145. Tel: 412-823-4871; Fax: 412-823-6326.
Sisters of Mercy of the Americas 1; Lay Teachers 18; Students 320.

Unity, Allegheny Co., St. John the Baptist (1915), Revs. Charles W. Speicher; David Poecking. In res., Rev. Peter Nwachukwu (Nigeria).
Res., 444 St. John St., Pittsburgh, 15239. Tel: 412-793-4511; 793-4580; Fax: 412-793-4311. [CEM]
School—418 Unity Center Rd., Pittsburgh, 15239. Tel: 412-793-0555; Fax: 412-793-4001.
Lay Teachers 22; Students 357.

Upper St. Clair, Allegheny Co., St. John Capistran (1968), Rev. Robert J. Reardon.
Res., 1610 McMillan Rd., Pittsburgh, 15241. Tel: 412-221-6275; Fax: 412-257-3789.

Verona, Allegheny Co., St. Joseph (1866), Revs. Edwin J. Wichman; Trieu Ngoc Le.
Res., 825 Second Ave., 15147-1498. Tel: 412-795-5114. [CEM]
School—Tel: 412-828-7213.
Lay Teachers 13; Students 193.

Versailles, Allegheny Co., St. Denis. Closed. See St. Patrick, McKeesport.

Wampum, Lawrence Co., St. Monica. Closed. See Queen of Heaven, Koppel.

Washington, Washington Co., Immaculate Conception (1854), Revs. James G. Young; John E. Dinello; John E. Forbidussi; Deacons Leon Abraham, (Retired); Joseph Cerenzia; John Manion. In res., Rev. Evaristus Obi (Nigeria).
Res., 119 W. Chestnut St., 15301. Tel: 724-225-1425; Fax: 724-229-7946. [CEM 3]
School—111 W. Spruce St., 15301. Tel: 724-225-1680.
Lay Teachers 30; Students 500.

St. Hilary (1919), Rev. Thomas D. O'Neil.
Res., 320 Henderson Ave., 15301. Tel: 724-222-4087; Fax: 724-222-2130.

Waynesburg, Greene Co., St. Ann (1839), Rev. Albin C. McGinnis.
Res., 232 E. High St., 15370. Tel: 724-627-7568. [CEM]

West Aliquippa, Beaver Co., St. Joseph. Closed. See St. Titus, Aliquippa.

West Mifflin, Allegheny Co.,

1—St. Agnes, (1867), Rev. Michael J. Polak.
Res., 622 St. Agnes Ln., 15122. Tel: 412-466-2655. [CEM]
School—653 St. Agnes Ln., 15122. Tel: 412-466-6238; Fax: 412-466-2013.
Sisters of the Holy Spirit 5; Lay Teachers 8; Students 167.
Convent—635 St. Agnes Ln., 15122. Tel: 412-466-3554.

2—Holy Spirit, (1963), Rev. Daniel A. Valentine.
Res., 2603 Old Elizabeth Rd., 15122-2598. Tel: 412-466-5048; Fax: 412-466-4983.

3—Holy Trinity, (1901) (Slovak), Rev. Edward P. Bunchek.
Res., 529 Grant Ave. Ext., 15122. Tel: 412-466-6545; Fax: 412-466-6968. [CEM]

4—Resurrection, (1936), Rev. Robert G. Turner.
Res., 3909 Donna Ave., 15122. Tel: 412-461-8087; Fax: 412-461-0142.
School—James LaVelle, One Majka Dr., 15122. Tel: 412-462-4344; Fax: 412-461-1230.
Lay Teachers 11; Students 195.

West Pittsburg, Lawrence Co., Holy Cross. Closed. See St. Vincent de Paul, New Castle.

West Sunbury, Butler Co., St. Louis. Closed. See St. Alphonsus, Boyers.

West View, Allegheny Co., St. Athanasius (1905), Revs. Robert A. Norton; Martin R. Conley.
Res., 7 Chalfonte Ave., Pittsburgh, 15229. Tel: 412-931-4624; Fax: 412-939-3516.
School—2 Wentworth Ave., Pittsburgh, 15229. Tel: 412-931-6633. Ms. Gabrielle Yingling, Prin.
Lay Teachers 12; Students 203.

Wexford, Allegheny Co., St. Alexis (1961), Rev. Paul J. Zywan. In res., Rev. Harry F. Petrie.
Res., 10090 Old Perry Hwy., 15090. Tel: 724-935-4343; Fax: 724-935-1270. [CEM]
School—(Grades PreK-7). Tel: 724-935-3940; Fax: 724-935-6070.
Lay Teachers 19; Students 313.

St. Alphonsus (1840), Revs. Peter P. Murphy; Richard J. Thompson.
Res., 201 Church Rd., 15090. Tel: 724-935-1151; Fax: 724-934-3877. [CEM][JC]
School—Tel: 724-935-1152; Fax: 724-935-1110.
Sisters 2; Lay Teachers 23; Students 530.

Whitehall, Allegheny Co., St. Gabriel of the Sorrowful Virgin (1944), Revs. John R. Haney; Alan E. Morris; Deacon James F. Leonard.
Res., 5200 Greenridge Dr., Pittsburgh, 15236. Tel: 412-881-8115; 881-8117; Fax: 412-881-8115 (call first).
School—Tel: 412-882-3353; Fax: 412-882-2125.
Lay Teachers 23; Students 487.

White Oak Boro, Allegheny Co., St. Angela (1958), Rev. Stephen M. Chervenak.
Res., 1732 Fawcett Ave., White Oak, 15131. Tel: 412-672-2365; Fax: 412-672-1576.
School—1640R Fawcett Ave., White Oak, 15131. Tel: 412-672-2360; Fax: 412-672-0880.
Lay Teachers 12; Students 297.

Wildwood, Allegheny Co., St. Catherine of Sweden (1953), Revs. Regis M. Farmer; Gregory C. Swiderski.
Res., 2308 W. Hardies Rd., 15091. Tel: 412-961-0399; 724-443-2087; 443-5876; Fax: 724-443-3633.

Wilkinsburg, Allegheny Co., St. James (1869), Rev. Warren W. Metzler.
Res., 718 Franklin Ave., Pittsburgh, 15221. Tel: 412-241-1392; Fax: 412-241-6625.
School—721 Rebecca Ave., Pittsburgh, 15221. Tel: 412-242-3515; Fax: 412-241-3199.
Lay Teachers 21; Students 240.

Wilmerding, Allegheny Co., St. Jude the Apostle (1994). Consolidated from St. Aloysius and St. Leocadia. Rev. John J. O'Malley.
Res., 405 Westinghouse Ave., 15148. Tel: 412-823-8390; 823-1117; Fax: 412-823-2485. [CEM]

St. Leocadia (Polish). Closed. See St. Jude the Apostle.

Wireton, Allegheny Co., St. Catherine of Siena (1911), Rev. Thomas R. Wilson.
Res., 199 McGovern Blvd., Crescent, 15046. Tel: 724-457-7026; 724-457-0106 (Church Hall); Fax: 724-457-3292.

Zelienople, Butler Co., St. Gregory (1906), Rev. Charles B. Bergman.
Res., 2 W. Beaver St., 16063. Tel: 724-452-7245; Fax: 724-452-4064. [CEM]
School—115 Pine St., 16063. Tel: 724-452-9731; Fax: 724-452-4064.
Lay Teachers 10; Students 199.

Chaplains of Public Institutions

Allegheny County. *Depaul Institution* Tel: 412-561-4848. Rev. Richard L. Conboy Tel: 412-299-7846.
St. Joseph House of Hospitality Tel: 412-471-0666. Rev. Daniel B. Dixon.
Seneca Hills Village. Attended by St. Bartholomew Parish. Tel: 412-242-3343. Tel: 412-793-1700.

Beaver County. *McGuire Memorial Home* Tel: 724-843-3400. Rev. Regis R. Alberth Tel: 724-775-4111.

Hospitals

Allegheny County. *Allegheny General* Tel: 412-359-3131. Revs. Frank A. Mitolo Tel: 412-359-4269; Thomas J. McKenna Tel: 412-359-4269.
Jefferson Hospital Tel: 412-469-5000. Rev. Robert Andrew Kohuch Tel: 412-384-4406; Sr. Nancy Kline, Pastoral Care, Tel: 412-469-5855.
McKeesport Hospital Tel: 412-664-2000. Rev. John M. Elanjileth (ROM) Tel: 412-673-5552.
Mercy Health System of Pittsburgh-Mercy Providence Hospital. Attended by St. Peter. Tel: 412-321-0711 Tel: 412-323-5600.
Mercy Health System of Pittsburgh-Pittsburgh Mercy Hospital Tel: 412-232-8111. Revs. Joseph Monahan, T.O.R.; John L. McKenna.
Ohio Valley General Hospital. Attended by St. Malachy. Tel: 412-771-5483 Tel: 412-777-6161.
St. Clair Memorial Hospital. Attended by Our Lady of Grace, Pittsburgh. Tel:412-279-7070 Tel: 412-561-4900. Rita Torres, Social Services, Tel: 412-344-6600.
St. Francis Medical Center Tel: 412-622-4343. Revs. Robert Craig, O.F.M.Cap. Tel: 412-682-6430; Bonaventure Stefun, O.F.M.Cap. Tel: 412-471-4390; Greg Chervenak, O.F.M.Cap.; Sr. Mary Joseph Trimbur, O.S.F. Tel: 412-622-4741.
Sewickley Valley Hospital. Attended by St. James. Tel: 412-741-6656 Tel: 412-741-6600.

UPMC Braddock Tel: 412-636-5000. Rev. Joseph D. Karabin Tel: 412-271-1515.

UPMC Children's Hospital Tel: 412-647-5326. Sr. Nora Egan, C.S.J. Tel: 412-372-6758.

UPMC Magee-Women's Hospital Tel: 412-647-1000. Sr. Nora Egan, C.S.J. Tel: 412-372-6758.

UPMC Passavant Hospital. Sacramental coordination by St. Sebastian, Ross Township. Tel: 412-367-6700. Sr. Caritas Marshall, C.S.J. Tel: 412-364-5938.

UPMC Shadyside Hospital Tel: 412-623-2121. Revs. Gilbert Puznakoski Tel: 412-621-5679; Michael McDermott.

UPMC Southside Hospital Tel: 412-488-5550. Rev. John F. Walsh Tel: 412-471-0654.

UPMC St. Margaret Hospital Tel: 412-784-4000. Deacon Louis Kriston, Jr.

UPMC University of Pittsburgh Medical Center Tel: 412-647-2020. Revs. Samuel J. Esposito Tel: 412-621-5679; Michael McDermott Tel: 412-621-5679; Richard Terdine Tel: 412-621-5679; Sr. Mary Kay Hamond, C.S.J. Tel: 412-882-7593.

West Penn Allegheny Health System-Allegheny Valley Hospital. Attended by Our Lady of the Most Blessed Sacrament, Natrona Heights. Tel: 724-224-5100.

West Penn Allegheny Health System-Forbes Metro. Attended by St. James, Wilkinsburg. Tel:412-241-1392 Tel: 412-247-2424.

West Penn Allegheny Health System-Forbes Regional. Sacramental coordination by St. Bartholomew. Tel: 412-858-2000. Sr. Monique Dietz, L.B. Tel: 412-781-4022; Rev. James E. Somma Tel: 412-373-2610.

West Penn Allegheny Health System-Suburban General Hospital. Attended by Assumption of the Blessed Virgin Mary on the Beautiful River, Bellevue. Tel:412-766-6660.

West Penn Allegheny Health System-West Penn Hospital Tel: 412-578-5000. Revs. John M. Jordan Tel: 412-621-5679; Edward L. Hoffman Tel: 412-621-5679.

BEAVER COUNTY. *The Medical Center Beaver* Tel: 724-728-7000. Rev. Kenneth Myers Tel: 724-775-4111.

UPMC Beaver. Attended by St. Titus, Aliquippa. Tel:724-378-8561 Tel: 724-875-1212.

BUTLER COUNTY. *Butler Memorial Hospital*. Attended by St. Fidelis Parish. Tel. 724-482-2690 Tel: 724-283-6666. Ethel Galli, Pastoral Care.

GREENE COUNTY. *Greene County Memorial*. Attended by St. Ann, Waynesburg. Tel:724-627-7568 Tel: 724-627-3101. Very Rev. Albin C. McGinnis; Rev. Paul Merkovsky.

LAWRENCE COUNTY. *Ellwood City Hospital*. Attended by St. Agatha, Ellwood City. Tel:724-758-7587. Tel: 724-752-0081.

Jameson Memorial Hospital Tel: 724-658-9001. Rev. Frank G. Erdeljac Tel: 724-535-4786.

St. Francis Hospital Tel: 724-658-3511. Rev. Frank G. Erdeljac Tel: 724-535-4786.

WASHINGTON COUNTY. *Mon Valley Hospital*. Attended by Transfiguration, Monongahela. Tel:724-258-7742 Tel: 724-258-2000.

Washington County East Deanery Tel: 724-377-0128. Deacon Thomas W. Raymond.

Washington Hospital. Attended by Immaculate Conception, Washington. Tel:724-225-1425 Tel: 724-225-7000.

West Penn Allegheny Health System-Canonsburg Hospital Tel: 724-745-6100. Rev. Thomas Kirby Tel: 724-745-0950.

Veterans Administration Hospitals

ALLEGHENY COUNTY. *Department of Veterans Affairs Medical Center Aspinwall* Tel: 412-688-6000, Ext. 6729. Revs. Ralph Zehe, O.F.M.Cap. Tel: 412-682-0929; Emitt Schuler, O.F.M.Cap. Tel: 412-531-4545.

Department of Veterans Affairs Medical Center Oakland Tel: 412-683-3000. Revs. Ralph Zehe, O.F.M.Cap. Tel: 412-682-6430; Mark W. Glasgow Tel: 412-461-1054; Emitt Schuler, O.F.M.Cap. Tel: 412-531-4545.

BUTLER COUNTY. *Department of Veterans Affairs- Deshon Hospital* Tel: 724-287-4781. Rev. William J. Ritzert Tel: 724-538-5331.

Rehabilitation, Nursing and Geriatric Care Facilities

ALLEGHENY COUNTY. *Asbury Heights*. Attended by St. Bernard, Mt. Lebanon. Tel: 412-561-3300. Tel: 412-341-1030.

Atrium I Nursing Research and Rehabilitation Center Tel: 412-787-2483.

Baldwin Health Care. Attended by St. Elizabeth of Hungary, Pittsburgh. Tel: 412-882-8744. Tel: 412-885-8400.

Beverly Manor of Monroeville Tel: 412-856-7570. Rev. Thomas V. Manning.

Collins Nursing Center Tel: 412-661-1740. Rev. Edward L. Hoffman Tel: 412-621-5679.

DT Watson Rehab Hospital. Attended by St. James, Sewickley. Tel: 412-741-6650. Tel: 412-741-9000.

Forbes Nursing Center Tel: 412-665-3232. Rev. Joseph C. Beck Tel: 412-661-7222.

Greater Pittsburgh Rehab Hospital Tel: 412-856-2400. Rev. Joseph C. Beck Tel: 412-661-7222.

Hamilton Hills Personal Care. Rev. Thomas V. Manning Tel: 412-373-0330.

Healthsound Harmarville Rehabilitation Hospital. Attended by St. Mary of the Assumption. Tel: 412-486-4100 Tel: 412-781-5700.

Heartland Health Care Center Tel: 412-665-2400. Rev. Edward L. Hoffman Tel: 412-621-5679.

Heritage Shadyside. Attended by Sacred Heart, Pittsburgh. Tel: 412-661-0187. Also attended by St. Rosalia, Pittsburgh. Tel: 412-421-5766. Tel: 412-422-5100.

Independence Court of Mt. Lebanon. Attended by St. Ann, Castle Shannon. Tel: 412-531-5964; St. Thomas More, Bethel Park. Tel: 724-883-0031 Tel: 412-341-4400.

Independent Court of Monroeville Tel: 412-373-3030. Rev. Joseph C. Beck Tel: 412-661-7222.

James P. Wall Home for the Aged Tel: 412-761-5373. Rev. Alvin P. Gutierrez.

Kane Regional Center - Glen Hazel Tel: 412-422-6800. Rev. Joseph C. Beck Tel: 412-661-7222; Sr. Donna Marie Mulligan, S.C. Tel: 412-461-0968.

Kane Regional Center - McKeesport Tel: 412-675-8600. Sr. Thomas Joseph Gaines, S.C. Tel: 412-675-8600.

Kane Regional Center - Ross. Attended by St. Sabastian. Tel: 412-369-2000.

Kane Regional Center - Scott Tel: 412-429-3000. Rev. Richard L. Conboy, S.T.L. Tel: 412-429-3040.

Ladies of the Grand Army Republic (LGAR). Rev. Thomas V. Manning Tel: 412-373-0330.

Manorcare Health Services. Attended by SS. Simon & Jude. Greentree Rd., Tel: 412-344-7744. Rev. Richard E. Ward Tel: 412-563-3189.

Manorcare Health Services. Vacant. McMurray Rd., Tel: 412-941-3080.

Manorcare Health Services. Attended by St. Thomas More. Tel: 412-833-0031. Highland Dr., Tel: 412-831-6050. Rev. Kenneth R. White.

Manorcare Health Services Perry Hwy., Tel: 412-369-9955. Rev. Joseph C. Beck Tel: 412-661-7222.

Manorcare Health Services. Attended by North American Martyrs, Monroeville. Tel: 412-373-0330. Tel: 412-856-7071.

Marian Manor, Inc Tel: 412-563-6866. Rev. Robert R. Werthman Tel: 412-388-1292.

Mercy Senior Care Tel: 412-665-5100. Rev. Edward L. Hoffman Tel: 412-621-5679.

Mt. Lebanon Manor Convalescent Center. Attended by St. Thomas More. Tel: 412-833-0031. Tel: 412-257-4444. Rev. Kenneth R. White.

Oakmont Nursing Center. Attended by St. Irenaeus, Oakmont. Tel: 412-828-3085. Tel: 412-828-7300.

Presbyterian Seniorcare Westminister Place. Attended by St. Irenaeus, Oakmont. Tel: 412-826-6088. Rev. Thomas V. Manning Tel: 412-373-0334.

Ridgepoint. Attended by Nativity, South Park Twp. Tel: 412-655-3000. Tel: 412-653-6870.

Riverview Center for Jewish Seniors. Attended by St. Rosalia, Pittsburgh. Tel: 412-421-5766. Tel: 412-521-5900.

St. Margaret Senca Place. Attended by St. Bartholomew, Penn Hills. Tel: 412-242-3374. Tel: 412-798-8000. Rev. Thomas V. Manning.

Shadyside Nursing and Rehabilitation Center Tel: 412-362-3500. Rev. Edward L. Hoffman Tel: 412-621-5679.

Southwestern Nursing and Rehabilitation Center. Attended by Holy Spirit, West Mifflin. Tel: 412-466-0600, Ext. 5989. Rev. Daniel A. Valentine.

UPMC Canterbury Place. Attended by Our Lady of the Angels, Pittsburgh. Tel: 412-682-0929. Tel: 412-622-9000.

UPMC Rehabilitation Hospital (The Childrens Institute). Attended by St. Bede, Pittsburgh. Tel: 412-661-7222. Tel: 412-420-2400.

Vincentian Home for the Chronically Ill Tel: 412-366-5600. Revs. Paul G. Spisak Tel: 724-935-4343; David C. Dixon, Asst., Tel: 412-928-0825.

Vincentian Regency Home Tel: 412-366-8540. Revs. Paul G. Spisak Tel: 724-935-4343; David Dixon, Asst., Tel: 412-928-0825.

Woodhaven Convalescent Center Tel: 412-856-4770. Rev. Joseph C. Beck Tel: 412-661-7222.

BEAVER COUNTY. *Beaver Valley Geriatric Center* Tel: 724-775-7100. Revs. Paul J. Savage Tel: 724-846-4585; Kenneth E. Myers Tel: 724-775-4111.

BUTLER COUNTY. *Sunnyview Home*. Attended by St. Fidelis. Tel: 724-482-2690. Tel: 724-282-1800. Ethel Galli, Pastoral Care.

GREENE COUNTY. *Curry Memorial Home*. Attended by St. Ann, Waynesburg. Tel: 724-627-7568. Tel: 724-627-3153.

Franklin Care Center. Attended by St. Ann, Waynesburg. Tel: 724-627-7568. Tel: 724-852-2020.

LAWRENCE COUNTY. *Almira Home* Tel: 724-652-4131. Rev. Francis C. Graff Tel: 724-652-9471.

Belvedere Residence, Inc Tel: 724-924-2191. Rev. Francis C. Graff Tel: 724-652-9471.

Castle Manor Tel: 724-654-4377. Rev. Francis C. Graff Tel: 724-652-9471.

Cedar Manor Tel: 724-654-8050. Rev. Francis C. Graff Tel: 724-652-9471.

Golden Hill Nursing, Inc Tel: 724-654-7791. Rev. Francis C. Graff Tel: 724-652-9471.

Haven Convalescent Home Tel: 724-654-8833. Rev. Francis C. Graff Tel: 724-652-9471.

Highland Hall Care Center Tel: 724-658-4781. Rev. Francis C. Graff Tel: 724-652-9471.

Hill View Manor Tel: 724-658-1521. Rev. Francis C. Graff Tel: 724-652-9471.

Indian Creek Nursing Center Tel: 724-653-6340. Rev. Francis C. Graff Tel: 724-652-9471.

Jack Rees Nursing and Rehabilitation Services Tel: 724-652-3863. Rev. Francis C. Graff Tel: 724-652-9472.

Majors Manor Tel: 724-924-9568. Rev. Francis C. Graff Tel: 724-652-9471.

Overlook Nursing Home Tel: 724-946-3511. Rev. Francis C. Graff Tel: 724-652-9471.

Shenango United Presbyterian Home Tel: 724-946-3516. Rev. Francis C. Graff Tel: 724-652-9471.

Silver Oak Nursing Tel: 724-652-3863. Rev. Francis C. Graff Tel: 724-652-9471.

WASHINGTON COUNTY. *Beverly South Hills* Tel: 724-746-1300. Rev. Thomas M. Kirby Tel: 724-745-0950.

Canon House Tel: 724-745-7771. Rev. Thomas M. Kirby Tel: 724-745-0950.

Charles House Home for the Aged Tel: 724-745-6355. Rev. Thomas M. Kirby Tel: 724-745-0950.

Greenery Nursing Home Tel: 724-745-8000. Rev. Thomas M. Kirby Tel: 724-745-0950.

Horizon Senior Care Tel: 724-746-5040. Rev. Thomas M. Kirby Tel: 724-745-0950.

Pine Lawn Home Tel: 724-746-1460. Rev. Thomas M. Kirby Tel: 724-745-0950.

Rest Haven Personal Care Home I Tel: 724-745-3333. Rev. Thomas M. Kirby Tel: 724-745-0950.

Rest Haven Personal Care Home II Tel: 724-746-3233. Rev. Thomas M. Kirby Tel: 724-745-0950.

Rest Haven Personal Care Home V Tel: 724-746-4666. Rev. Thomas M. Kirby Tel: 724-745-0950.

Various Nursing Homes. Rev. Richard Ragni Tel: 724-343-9588.

Mental Health Facilities

ALLEGHENY COUNTY. *Mayview State Hospital* Tel: 412-257-6500. Revs. George T. DeVille Tel: 724-745-3531; Harold Bailey Tel: 412-771-5646.

Western Psychiatric Hospital. Attended by UPMC Chaplains. Tel: 412-647-9071. Tel: 412-624-2100.

WASHINGTON COUNTY. *The Bradley Center* Tel: 724-746-1212; 746-2400. Rev. Thomas M. Kirby Tel: 724-745-0950.

Correctional Institutions

ALLEGHENY COUNTY. *Allegheny County Jail* Tel: 412-350-2000. Rev. George F. Chortos Tel: 412-350-2051; Deacons James A. Kenny; Thomas J. O'Neill.

Shuman Center. Social Services. Tel: 412-665-4135. Tel: 412-661-6806. Deacon Patrick Wood Tel: 724-226-4900.

State Correctional Institute at Pittsburgh Tel: 412-381-8300. Rev. William R. Terza Tel: 412-761-1955.

BEAVER COUNTY. *Beaver County Jail*. Vacant.

BUTLER COUNTY. *Butler County Jail*. Rev. Hugh M. Gloninger Tel: 724-287-1759.

GREEN COUNTY. *State Correctional Institute at Green* Tel: 724-852-2902. Rev. George J. Moneck Tel: 724-938-2324.

State Correctional Institution at Waynesburg (Women's Facility) Tel: 724-627-6185. Revs. Albin C. McGinnis Tel: 724-627-7568; Paul Merkovsky; Sr. Yvonne Dursh, O.S.F. Tel: 724-882-3470.

Waynesburg County Jail Tel: 724-627-7780. Revs. Albin C. McGinnis Tel: 724-627-7568; Paul Merkovsky.

LAWRENCE COUNTY. *Lawrence County Jail* Tel: 724-654-5384. Rev. James A. Downs Tel: 724-667-7737.

Youth Development Center Tel: 412-656-7300. Rev. Joseph R. McCaffrey Tel: 412-964-8276; Sr. Noreen Sterns, H.M.

WASHINGTON COUNTY. *Washington County Jail*. Attended by Immaculate Conception, Washington. Tel: 412-225-1425. Tel: 412-561-7557.

On Duty Outside the Diocese:

Reverend Fathers—

Bleichner, Howard P., Theological College of Catholic University, 401 Michigan Ave., N.E., Washington, DC 20017

Burns, Edward J., N.C.C.B., 3211 4th St. N.E., Washington, DC 20017-1194

Cellini, Ronald R., St. Peter Parish, 70 Lady's Island Dr., Beauford, SC 29901

Cizik, Ladis, Exec. Dir., Blue Army of Our Lady of Fatima, Lanteri House, 668 Mountain View Rd., E., Asbury, NJ 08802-1400

Connolly, Brian W., 2444 Madison Rd., Apt. 911, Cincinnati, OH 45208
Fay, William J., St. Vincent Seminary, Frasier Purchase Rd., Latrobe, PA 15650
Friday, Robert M., Catholic University, 620 Michigan Ave., N.E., Washington, DC 20064-0001
Hebda, Bernard A., Palazzo Delle Congregazioni, Piazza pio XII, 00120 Citta' del Vaticano, Italy
Lauer, Eugene F., Catholic Theological Union, 5401 S. Cornell Ave., Chicago, IL 60615
Mazurek, James K., SS. Cyril & Methodius Seminary, 3535 Indian Tr., Orchard Lake, MI 48324
Mueller, Richard J., St. Peter the Apostle, 5130 Rattlesnake Hammond Rd., Naples, FL 34113
Paone, Ernest C., 1556 Glacier Rd., Oceanside, CA 92054
Roos, H. Jules, Centro de Obras Sociales, Apartado 473, Chimbote, Peru
Seeger, James E., Bishop's House, P.O. Box 69, Mendi S. Highlands 251, Papua, New Guinea
Taylor, Augustus R., Jr., 1812 W. 48th St., Los Angeles, CA 90062
Whalen, Timothy F., Chancellor, Orchard Lake School, 3535 Indian Tr., Orchard Lake, MI 48324

Graduate Studies:
Reverend Fathers—
Wehner, James A., Casa Santa Maria, Via dell'Umilta 30, Rome, Italy 00187
Welding, Brian J., Casa Santa Maria, Via dell'Umilta 30, Rome, Italy 00187

Military Chaplains:
Reverend Fathers—
Brzek, Jon J., Office of the Chaplain, PSC 817, Box 43, FPO AE, 09622-0043
Dansak, Thomas E., PSG 1008, Box 3031, FPO AA, 34051
Fix, Donald P., National Naval Medical Center, 8901 Wisconsin Ave., Bethesda, MD 20889-5000
Geinzer, John A., Chap., USN, La Maddalena, PSC 816 Box 209, FPO, AE 09612
Glasgow, Mark W., Chap. VA Medical Center, c/o St. Maximilian Kolbe, 303 E. 1oth Ave., Homestead, PA 15120
Laboon, Joseph D., VA Medical Center, 1601 Perdido St., New Orleans, LA 70146
Lamonde, Joseph R., 4413 49th St., N.W., Washington, DC 20016
Malinsky, Gregory J., 1818 Belle Chez, Mt. Pleasant, SC 29464
Sagala, James F., 136 Celia Ter., Apt. B, Belleville, NJ 07109
Valko, Robert A., CHC USNR, 107 Caravel Ct., Havelock, NC 28532
Yagesh, Richard C., Rel Min Dept.-NAS Brunswick Chapel, 901 Fitch Ave., Brunswick, ME 04011

On Sabbatical:
Reverend Fathers—
Brennan, John D., c/o 304 Baker Dr., Aliquippa, PA 15001
Gudewicz, John A., c/o 346 Finley Ave., Carnegie, PA 15106

Absent on Sick Leave:
Reverend Fathers—
Patriquin, Garry D.
Rager, Patrick F.

Retired:
Reverend Monsignors—
Darkowski, Leon S., 235 The Boulevard, Pittsburgh, PA 15210
Dravecky, Michael A., 1471 Guffey Rd., North Huntingdon, PA 15642
Findlan, Joseph G., St. John Vianney Manor, 2600 Morange Rd., Pittsburgh, PA 15205
Garland, Robert P., 96 S.W. 15th Ct., Boynton Beach, FL 33426
Lackner, Paul M., Cardinal Dearden Center, 4721 Fifth Ave., Pittsburgh, PA 15213-2915
McCarren, John C., St. Ursula, 3937 Kirk Ave., Allison Park, PA 15101-3691
Rice, Charles O., St. Anne Church, 400 Hoodridge Dr., Pittsburgh, PA 15234-1794
Seli, John J., Cape Hacienda #202, 6655 Ridgewood Ave., Cocoa Beach, FL 32931
Reverend Fathers—
Aaron, James L., Most Holy Name of Jesus, 1700 Harpster St., Pittsburgh, PA 15212
Blough, William G., 421 Washington Ave., Oakmont, PA 15139
Boccard, Raymond C., 616 Fourth St., Apt. A, Ellwood City, PA 16117-2051
Bolvary, Paul L., 1013 Budapest, Krisztina KRT, 161A Hungary
Burchianti, Leo R., St. John Vianney Manor, 2600 Morange Rd., Pittsburgh, PA 15205
Charnoki, John J., St. Raphael, 1118 Chislett St., Pittsburgh, PA 15206-1304
Cheetham, William J., Cardinal Dearden Center, 4721 Fifth Ave., Pittsburgh, PA 15213
Conner, Glenn T., St. John Vianney Manor, 2600 Morange Rd., Pittsburgh, PA 15205
Deblasio, Dominck A., 605 Market St., Freeport, PA 16229
DeCarlo, Philip J., 801 Somerville Dr., Pittsburgh, PA 15243
DeLuca, Anthony, 409 Shady Ridge Dr., Monroeville, PA 15146
Dougherty, Eugene J., Holy Wisdom, 1025 Haslage Ave., Pittsburgh, PA 15212-3429
Fording, John D., St. John Vianney Manor, 2600 Morange Rd., Pittsburgh, PA 15205
Garbin, Arthur L., Felician Sisters, 1500 Woodcrest Ave., Coraopolis, PA 15108
Gelati, Dario, Parrocchia de Birbesi, 46030 Sustinente, Italy
Getty, Roy G., Cardinal Dearden Center, 4721 Fifth Ave., Pittsburgh, PA 15213-2915
Gibson, John W., St. John Vianney Manor, 2600 Morange Rd., Pittsburgh, PA 15205
Girdis, Joseph C., St. Therese, 1 St. Therese Ct., Munhall, PA 15120
Gualtieri, Raymond A., 4940 Brightwood Rd., Apt. A102, Bethel Park, PA 15102
Gubanich, Michael T., 106 S. Pine St., Ellsworth, PA 15331
Henry, Leo G., St. John Vianney Manor, 2600 Morange Rd., Pittsburg, PA 15205
Hutnik, William J., Vincentian Home, Perrymont Rd., Pittsburgh, PA 15237
Jackovic, George V., 124 Bennington Dr., Canonsburg, PA 15317
Jones, Patrick J., Cardinal Dearden Center, 4721 Fifth Ave., Pittsburgh, PA 15213
Jozwiak, Stanislaus J., 2103 Fawcett Ave., White Oak, PA 15131-1819
Kato, Stephen M., St. Stephen Rectory, 2125 Beacon St., McKeesport, PA 15132
Kelly, Gerard D., St. John Vianney Manor, 2600 Morenge Rd., Pittsburgh, PA 15205
Kernan, Michael H., Cardinal Dearden Center, 4721 Fifth Ave., Pittsburg, PA 15213-2915
Kilarecki, George W., Vincentian Home, Perrymont Rd., Pittsburgh, PA 15237
Kopecky, Joseph A., 1503 Sylvan Ave., Natrona Heights, PA 15065-1642
Kuczynski, Francis I., Vincentian Home, Perrymont Rd., Pittsburgh, PA 15237
Kuenzig, Aloysius A., 2715 Custer Ave., Pittsburgh, PA 15227
Kuenzig, Peter A., 2715 Custer Ave., Pittsburgh, PA 15227
Lackner, Francis J. X., St. John Vianney Manor, 2600 Morange Rd., Pittsburgh, PA 15205
Lech, Ferdinand F., St. John Vianney Manor, 2600 Morange Rd., Pittsburgh, PA 15205
Lech, George T., 28 Emerson Ave., Pittsburgh, PA 15205
Luteri, Evaristo, St. John Vianney Manor, 2600 Morange Rd., Pittsburgh, PA 15205
Lutz, Gerald J., 1422 Lakeside Dr., Allison Park, PA 15101
Majda, Francis A., 1809 Hanna St., New Castle, PA 16101
Maliszewski, Edward C., Fox Hills Towers, Apt. 216, 1120 Fox Hill Dr., Monroeville, PA 15146-1075
Manion, Thomas F., Cardinal Dearden Center, 4721 Fifth Ave., Pittsburgh, PA 15213-2915
Marchuronis, Francis V., 239 Rainprint Sq., Murrysville, PA 15668
Marconyak, Albert J., Little Sisters of the Poor, 1028 Benton Ave., Pittsburgh, PA 15212
Massung, Francis G., St. John Vianney Manor, 2600 Morange Rd., Pittsburgh, PA 15205
Mastrangelo, Joseph A., 1111 S. Mercer St., New Castle, PA 16101
McColligan, Raymond A., 98 S.W. 15th Ct., Boynton Beach, FL 33426
McIlvane, Donald W., 5700 Bunkerhill St., Apt. 1005, Pittsburgh, PA 15206-1166
McSweeney, Edward F., St. Athanasius, 7 Chalfonte Ave., Pittsburgh, PA 15229-1824
Michaels, John L., St. John Vianney Manor, 2600 Morange Rd., Pittsburgh, PA 15205
Miller, Joseph W., Vincentian Home, Perrymont Rd., Pittsburgh, PA 15237
Miller, William J., St. John Vianney Manor, 2600 Morange Rd., Pittsburgh, PA 15205
Murphy, Thomas R., 6346 Walnut St., Pittsburgh, PA 15206
Nazimek, Francis A., St. Oliver Plunkett, P.O. Box 638, Fredericktown, PA 15333-0638
Nee, Thomas M., St. John Vianney Manor, 2600 Morange Rd., Pittsburgh, PA 15205
O'Brien, John, Cardinal Dearden Center, 4721 Fifth Ave., Pittsburgh, PA 15213-2915
O'Connell, Thomas C., Vincentian Home, Perrymont Rd., Pittsburgh, PA 15237
Palko, John A., St. Martin de Porres, c/o 705 Shaw Ave., McKeesport, PA 15132-2334
Paluse, Richard V., 37 Forsythe Rd., Pittsburgh, PA 15220
Parme, George J., Villa St. Joseph, 1030 State St., Baden, PA 15005
Parsons, Harry E., St. John Vianney Manor, 2600 Morange Rd., Pittsburgh, PA 15205
Petrie, Harry F., St. Alexis, 10090 Old Perry Hwy., Wexford, PA 15090-9320
Plantes, Francis P., St. John Vianney Manor, 2600 Morange Rd., Pittsburgh, PA 15205
Pucci, Francis L., Sisters of Divine Redeemer, 999 Rock Run Rd., Elizabeth, PA 15037
Rishel, Robert F., St. John Vianney Manor, 2600 Morange Rd., Pittsburgh, PA 15205
Rocha, Victor J., Resurrection, 1100 Creedmoor Ave., Pittsburgh, PA 15213-2299
Rodgers, Francis M., St. John Vianney Manor, 2600 Morange Rd., Pittsburgh, PA 15205
Rodgers, Thomas M., Cardinal Dearden Center, 4721 Fifth Ave., Pittsburgh, PA 15213-2915
Schirra, Peter M., Vicentian Home, 111 Perrymount Rd., Pittsburgh, PA 15237
Sedlak, Valentine G., Cardinal Dearden Center, 4721 Fifth Ave., Pittsburgh, PA 15213-2915
Smith, Thomas E., 221 Lake Faith Dr., Maitland, FL 32751
Soisson, Clifford F., St. John Vianney Manor, 2600 Morange Rd., Pittsburgh, PA 15205
Szarnicki, Henry A., St. John Vianney Manor, 2600 Morange Rd., Pittsburgh, PA 15205
Szarnicki, Zygmunt V., St. John Vianney Manor, 2600 Morange Rd., Pittsburgh, PA 15205
Trzeciakowski, Edward J., St. John Vianney Manor, 2600 Morange Rd., Pittsburgh, PA 15205
Turlik, Andrew J., Vincentian Regency Nursing Home, 9399 Babcock Blvd., Allison Park, PA 15101
Unger, John M., St. John Vianney Manor, 2600 Morange Rd., Pittsburgh, PA 15205
Vecchio, Michael J., 502 Sewickley Heights Dr., Sewickley, PA 15143
Vollmer, Raymond A., 148 Monastery Ave., Pittsburgh, PA 15203-1432
Weirauch, William P., 181 44th St., Pittsburgh, PA 15201
Wichmanowski, Walter F., St. John Vianney Manor, 2600 Morange Rd., Pittsburgh, PA 15205

Permanent Deacons:
Abraham, Leon B., Immaculate Conception, Washington
Bachner, Ralph W., St. John Vianney
Bane, John J., St. Bernard, Mount Lebanon
Barth, Robert V., Catholic Cemeteries
Becker, Robert J., St. Albert the Great, Baldwin Boro
Brabender, Herbert C., Allegheny General Hospital
Brueckner, Joseph P.
Byers, Stephen J., Dept. for Religious Education/CCD
Cerenzia, Joseph A., Immaculate Conception, Washington
Cessar, Richard R., Northwest Deanery
Compomizzi, Joseph, St. John of God, McKees Rocks
Cunningham, Regis C., North American Martyrs, Monroeville
Dadowski, Francis J., Our Lady of the Angels, Lawrenceville
Deskevich, Stephen M., Holy Family Institute
DiSanto, Dale J., Mon Yough Deanery
Giconi, Mario W.
Gleason, Kenneth V., The Intersection, McKeesport
Grab, James R., Vicar for Retired Clergy
Gruseck, David J., Risen Lord, North Side
Hoover, Paul M., Office for Adult & Family Catechesis
Jelineck, G. Gregory, Most Holy Name of Jesus, Troy Hill
Kelly, Michael W., East Suburban Deanery
Kenny, James A., Allegheny County Jail
Kielar, S. Daniel, St. Vincent de Paul, New Castle
Killmeyer, Tim M., St. John of God, St. Malachy, Holy Trinity
Kosko, Joseph J., St. Winifred, Mt. Lebanon
Kriston, Louis H., Allegheny Valley Deanery
Kuhns, Elbert A., Greene County Deanery
Lamm, David E., Office for the Tribunal
Layton, John, St. Benedict the Abbot, Peters Twp.
Leonard, James F., St. Gabriel of the Sorrowful Virgin, Whitehall
Manion, John F., Washington & Jefferson College
McKelvey, Albert T.
Meyer, Joseph C., St. Patrick, Canonsburg
Miles, Leon F., St. Pamphilus, Beechview
Mueller, Joseph R., St. Sylvester, Brentwood
O'Keefe, Charles L., Little Sisters of the Poor

O'Neill, Thomas J., Allegheny County Jail
Pikula, Stephen C., Catholic Charities of the Diocese of Pittsburgh
Rice, Raymond C., St. Paul, Butler
Rubio-Roman, Silverio, St. Victor, Bairdford
Sabatelle, Robert C., Northwest Deanery
Satter, Victor P., St. Francis of Assisi, Finleyville
Sheil, James M., Greene County Deanery
Stein, Gerald C., St. Paul, Butler
Strathmann, William F., St. John Capistran, Upper Saint Clair
Sutton, Lawrence R., Our Lady of Grace, Scott Township
Very, Richard, Resurrection, Brookline
Walsh, John, St. Ferdinand, Cranberry Twp.
Wilmer, Reynold, St. Benedict the Moor, Hill District
Witter, David R., St. Alexis, Wexford
Wood, Patrick G., Shuman Juvenile Detention Center

INSTITUTIONS LOCATED IN THE DIOCESE

[A] SEMINARIES, RELIGIOUS OR SCHOLASTICATES

PITTSBURGH. *Saint Paul Seminary*, College & Pre-Theology, 2900 Noblestown Rd., 15205. Tel: 412-921-5800; Fax: 412-928-5842.
E-mail: seminaryprog@diopitt.org
Web site: www.diopitt.org
Revs. David J. Bonnar, Rector; Kevin J. Dominik, Vice Rector & Dir. Spiritual Formation; Sr. Judith Worden, R.S.M., Coord. Apostolic Works. Priests 2; Sisters 1; Students (attending Duquesne University) 8.

[B] COLLEGES AND UNIVERSITIES

PITTSBURGH. *Carlow College*, 3333 5th Ave., 15213. Tel: 412-578-6005; Fax: 412-578-6048.
Web site: www.carlow.edu
For a complete listing, refer to the Colleges and Universities section.

Duquesne University of the Holy Ghost, 600 Forbes Ave., 15282. Tel: 412-396-6000; Fax: 412-396-4334.
Web site: www.duq.edu
For a complete listing, refer to the Colleges and Universities section.

La Roche College, 9000 Babcock Blvd., 15237. Tel: 412-367-9300; Fax: 412-536-1038.
E-mail: admsas@laroche.edu
Web site: www.laroche.edu
For a complete listing, refer to the Colleges and Universities section.

[C] HIGH SCHOOLS, DIOCESAN

PITTSBURGH. *Canevin Catholic High School*, 2700 Morange Rd., 15205. Tel: 412-922-7400; Fax: 412-922-7403.
E-mail: diopghcanhs@impresso.com
Web site: www.cavein.com
Mr. John Maurer, Headmaster; Rev. Alvin J. Adams, Chap..Priests 1; Sisters 1; Lay Teachers 32; Students 469.

Central District Catholic High School. (Boys), 4720 Fifth Ave., 15213. Tel: 412-621-8189; Fax: 412-208-0555.
E-mail: principal@pittcentralcatholic.org
Web site: www.pittcentralcatholic.org
The school is a Diocesan institution under the care of the Christian Brothers. Bro. Richard Grzeskiewicz, F.S.C., Prin. Brothers 8; Lay Teachers 53; Students 860.

North Catholic High School. (Coed), 1400 Troy Hill Rd., 15212. Tel: 412-321-4823; Fax: 412-321-0599.
E-mail: diopghnochs@impresso.com
Web site: www.north-catholic.org
Sisters 2; Lay Teachers 29; Students 475.

Oakland Catholic High School, 144 N. Craig St., 15213. Tel: 412-682-6633; Fax: 412-682-2496.
E-mail: diopghoakchs@impresso.com
Web site: www.oaklandcath.org
Madeline M. Vincunas, Prin.; Katherine D. Freyvogel, Pres..Priests 1; Lay Teachers 35; Students 475.

BADEN. *Quigley Catholic High School*, 200 Quigley Dr., 15005. Tel: 724-869-2188; Fax: 724-869-3091.
E-mail: diopghquighs@impresso.com
Web site: www.qchs.org
Rev. David C. Menegay, Prin..Sisters 1; Lay Teachers 18; Students 216.

MCKEESPORT. *Serra Catholic High School*, 200 Hershey Dr., 15132. Tel: 412-751-2020; Fax: 412-751-3488.
E-mail: diopghserra@impresso.com
Web site: www.serrahs.com
Under the direction of the Franciscan Friars (Province of the Most Sacred Heart). Bro. James Boyle, T.O.R., Headmaster. Priests 2; Brothers 2; Sisters 2; Lay Teachers 19; Students 375.

MT. LEBANON. *Seton-LaSalle Catholic High School*, 1000 McNeilly Rd., 15226. Tel: 412-561-3583; Fax: 412-561-9097.
Under care of Sisters of Charity. Rev. John Batykefer, Chap. Priests 1; Sisters 3; Lay Teachers 32; Students 558.

[D] HIGH SCHOOLS, PRIVATE

PITTSBURGH. *Mt. Alvernia High School*, 146 Hawthorne Rd., 15209. Tel: 412-821-3858; Fax: 412-821-2910.
E-mail: MtAlvernHS@aol.com
Web site: mtalvernia.com
Sisters of St. Francis. Kimberly Minick, Prin. Sisters 2; Lay Teachers 15; Students 87.

Vincentian Academy - Duquesne University, Peebles & McKnight Rds., 15237. Tel: 412-364-1616; Fax: 412-367-5722. Vincentian Sisters of Charity 4; Lay Teachers 24; Students 245.

CORAOPOLIS. *Our Lady of the Sacred Heart High School*, 1504 Woodcrest Ave., 15108. Tel: 412-264-5140; Fax: 412-264-4143.
E-mail: olsh@nauticom.net
Felician Sisters, C.S.S.F. State approved day high school. Sr. Mary Francine Horos, C.S.S.F., Prin. Priests 1; Sisters 3; Lay Teachers 23; Students 300.

[E] ELEMENTARY SCHOOLS, DIOCESAN

PITTSBURGH. *St. Agnes Diocesan School*, 120 Robinson St., 15213. Tel: 412-682-1129; Fax: 412-687-8091.
E-mail: diopghstage@impresso.com
Sr. Elizabeth Ann Herbert, R.S.M., Prin..Sisters 1; Lay Teachers 11; Students 225.

[F] CONSOLIDATED SCHOOLS

PITTSBURGH. *Bishop McDowell Regional School* Baldwin. (Grades (PreK-8)), 3198 Schieck St., 15227. Tel: 412-884-5676; Fax: 412-884-8610.
E-mail: diopghbsmcd@impresso.com
Berenice Maroney-Turkaly, Prin. Serving the parishes of St. Albert the Great and St. Wendelin. Lay Teachers 13; Students 215.

Brookline Regional Catholic School Brookline. (Grades (PreK-8)), 3021 Landis St., 15226. Tel: 412-563-0858; Fax: 412-341-6063.
Web site: www.nauticom.net/www/pius/BRChome.htm
Janet Salley, Prin. Serving the parishes of Our Lady of Loreto, St. Pius X, and Resurrection. Religious 1; Lay Teachers 25; Students 449.

Cardinal Wright Regional School North Side. (Grades (PreK-8)), 711 West Commons, 15212. Tel: 412-231-8248; Fax: 412-231-0835. Mr. Kenneth E. Macek, Prin. Serving the parishes of St. Aloysius, Most Holy Name of Jesus and St. Peter. Religious 1; Lay Teachers 14; Students 244.

Christ the Divine Teacher Catholic Academy Aspinwall. (Grades K-8), 205 Brilliant Ave., 15215. Tel: 412-781-7927; Fax: 412-781-0891. William F. Miller, Prin. Serving the parishes of St. Edward, St. John Cantius, St. Joseph, Madonna of Jerusalem, St. Mary, and St. Scholastica. Religious 1; Lay Teachers 10; Students 171.

Elizabeth Seton Regional Elementary School. (Grades (PreK-8)), 3021 Landis St., 15204. Tel: 412-331-4529; Fax: 412-331-8734. Dr. Madonna Helbling, Prin. Serving the parishes of Guardian Angels and Holy Innocents. Lay Teachers 13; Students 264.

St. John Neumann Regional, Catholic Elementary. (Grades PreK-8). Serving the parishes of Our Lady of Angels, St. Matthew and St. Lawrence O'Toole. 250 44th St., 15201. Tel: 412-682-5096; Fax: 412-682-0811. Sr. Coletta Adelsberg, C.S.J., Prin. Sisters 1; Lay Teachers 10; Students 219.

BUTLER. *Butler Catholic School*. Tel: 724-285-4276; Fax: 724-285-4896.
E-mail: bcs@butlercatholic.org
Web site: www.butlercatholic.org
St. Michael. (Grades K-2), 130 Glenn Ave., 16001. Tel: 724-287-6614; Fax: 724-287-6334. St. Paul. (Grades 3-8), 515 E. Locust St., 16001. Tel: 724-285-4276; Fax: 724-285-4896. Butler Montessori School, St. Paul Bldg., 515 E. Locust St., 16001. Tel: 724-283-1846. Serving the parishes of St. Paul, St. Michael, St. Fidelis, St. Andrew, and St. Peter's, Butler. Sisters 2; Lay Teachers 26; Students 396.

DONORA. *Madonna Catholic Regional School*. (Grades K-8), 1 Park Manor Rd., 15033. Tel: 724-379-5977; Fax: 724-379-7633. M. A. Knoll, Prin. Serving the parishes of St. Anthony, Mary, Mother of the Church, Our lady of the Valley, and Transfiguration. Lay Teachers 22; Students 287.

DUQUESNE. *Duquesne Catholic School*. (Grades PreK-8), 12 Norman St., 15110. Tel: 412-466-3895; Fax: 412-466-3839.
E-mail: diopghduqc@impresso.com
Ms. Jo-Anne Dellaidotti, Prin. Serving the Parishes of Christ the Light of the World and St. Joseph, Duquesne. Lay Teachers 8; Students 135.

MCKEESPORT. *McKeesport Central Catholic*, 2412 Versailles Ave., 15132. Tel: 412-672-4612; Fax: 412-672-6158. Serving the parishes of St. Stephen, St. Pius V, St. Mary Czestochowa. Lay Teachers 7; Students 140.

PORT VUE. *St. Joseph Regional School*. (Grades PreK-8), 1125 Romine Ave., 15133. Tel: 412-678-0659; Fax: 412-678-1301.
E-mail: kinolem@stjoesregional.org
Mrs. Elizabeth M. Kinol, Prin. Serving the parishes of Queen of Rosary, St. Martin de Porres, St. Mark, St. Patrick. Lay Teachers 16; Students 372.

[G] ELEMENTARY SCHOOLS, PRIVATE

PITTSBURGH. *Carlow College Campus School*. (Grades PreK-8), 3333 5th Ave., 15213. Tel: 412-578-6157; Fax: 412-578-8850.
E-mail: bgirard@carlow.edu
Web site: www.carlow.edu/~ccs
Sisters of Mercy. Sisters 2; Lay Teachers 29; Students 258.

ALLISON PARK. *Providence Heights Alpha School*, 9000 Babcock Blvd., 15101. Tel: 412-366-4455; Fax: 412-635-6317. Sisters of Divine Providence. Sr. Rita Adams, C.D.P., Prin.; Sisters 4; Lay Teachers 12; Students 206.

BADEN. *Mount Gallitzin Academy*. (Grades PreK-8), 1016 State St., 15005-1399. Tel: 724-869-2505; 869-2151; Fax: 724-869-0924.
E-mail: mtgallitzin@stargate.net
Sisters of St. Joseph. Sr. Norma Zanieski, C.S.J., Prin. Sisters 7; Lay Teachers 15; Students 315; Preschool Students 25.

Mount Gallitzin Academy Corp., 1016 State St., 15005-1399. Tel: 724-869-2505; Fax: 724-869-0924.
E-mail: mtgallitzin@stargate.net
Sr. Norma Zanieski, C.S.J. Purpose: to engage in educational activities and the operation of educational program of the Sisters of St. Joseph. Funds, distributions, gifts, bequests, endowments, grants, and contributions from other charitable organizations and student tuitions will be used to support applicant organization's programs and ministry outreach.

[H] DEPARTMENT OF SPECIAL EDUCATION

PITTSBURGH. *The De Paul Institute*, 2904 Castlegate Ave., 15226. Tel: 412-561-4848; Fax: 412-561-4662. Oral day school for children with hearing, speech and language impairments. Philip S. Boggio, Ph.D., Supt.; Sr. Virginia Pascaretta, S.C., Educational Dir. Sisters 3; Lay Teachers 10; Students 76.

St. Anthony School Programs, 2718 Custer Ave., 15227. Tel: 412-882-1333; Fax: 412-882-1668.
E-mail: stanthbus@impresso.com
Resource rooms for students with special needs in 6 elementary schools and 2 high schools. Kim Scanlon Lieb, Exec. Dir. Lay Teachers 8; Students 79.

NEW BRIGHTON. *McGuire Memorial*, 2119 Mercer Rd., 15066-3437. Tel: 724-843-3400; Fax: 724-847-2004.
E-mail: mcgm@hotmail.com
Web site: www.trfn.clpgh.org/mmhf
Residential Facility- Intermediate Care for Developmentally Challenged. Sisters 7; Lay Staff 300; Residents 89.

[I] CHILD CARE INSTITUTIONS

PITTSBURGH. *Franciscan Child Day Care Center*, 1401 Hamilton Rd., 15234-2399. Tel: 412-882-5085; Fax: 412-885-7210.
E-mail: srsosfprov@aol.com
Web site: www.srsosfprov.org
For a complete listing, refer to the Special Care Facilities section.

Mt. Alvernia Day Care & Learning Center, 146 Hawthorne Rd., 15209. Tel: 412-821-4302; Fax: 412-821-3318.
Web site: www.millvaleFranciscans.org
For a complete listing, refer to the Special Care Facilities section.

Providence Connections, Inc., Corporate Office, 3113 Brighton Rd., 15212-2456. Tel: 412-766-3860; Fax: 412-766-6775
For a complete listing, refer to the Special Care Facilities section.

Vincentian Child Care, Inc., 8200 McKnight Rd., 15237. Tel: 412-366-8588; Fax: 412-366-8588.
Web site: vincentiansrspgh.org/childcare/index.html
For a complete listing, refer to the Special Care Facilities section.

EMSWORTH. *Holy Family Institute*, 8235 Ohio River Blvd., 15202. Tel: 412-766-4030; Fax: 412-766-5434.
E-mail: schott.sandra@hfi-pgh.org
Web site: www.hfi-pgh.org
For a complete listing, refer to the Special Care Facilities section.

[J] GENERAL HOSPITALS

PITTSBURGH. *Mercy Hospital of Pittsburgh*, 1400 Locust St., 15219. Tel: 412-232-8111; Fax: 412-232-7380. Web site: www.mercylink.org
For a complete listing, refer to the Hospitals section.
Mercy Providence Hospital, 1004 Arch St., 15212. Tel: 412-323-5600; Fax: 412-323-5685.
E-mail: ksweeney@mercy.pmhs.org
For a complete listing, refer to the Hospitals section.
Pittsburgh Mercy Foundation, 1709 Blvd. of the Allies, Ste. 100, 15219-5947. Tel: 412-232-7504; Fax: 412-232-7810.
E-mail: dbalcom@mercy.pmhs.org
Web site: www.mercylink.org
For a complete listing, refer to the Hospitals section.
Pittsburgh Mercy Health System, Inc., 1400 Locust St., 15219. Tel: 412-232-8111; Fax: 412-232-7380. Web site: www.mercylink.org
For a complete listing, refer to the Hospitals section.
St. Francis Medical Center, 400 45th St., 15201. Tel: 412-622-4343
For a complete listing, refer to the Hospitals section.
St. Francis Nursing Center-East, 745 N. Highland Ave., 15206. Tel: 412-362-6622
For a complete listing, refer to the Hospitals section.
St. Francis Health System, 4401 Penn Ave., 15224-1380. Tel: 412-622-4343; Fax: 412-622-4858.
Web site: www.sfhs.edu
For a complete listing, refer to the Hospitals section.

CRANBERRY TOWNSHIP. *St. Francis Hospital Cranberry*, One St. Francis Way, 16066. Tel: 412-772-5300
For a complete listing, refer to the Hospitals section.
St. Francis Nursing Center Cranberry, 5 St. Francis Way, 16066. Tel: 724-772-5350
For a complete listing, refer to the Hospitals section.

NEW CASTLE. *St. Francis Hospital of New Castle*, 1000 S. Mercer St., 16101. Tel: 724-658-3511
For a complete listing, refer to the Hospitals section.

[K] SPECIAL HOSPITALS AND SANATORIA FOR INVALIDS

PITTSBURGH. *Vincentian de Marillac*, 5300 Stanton Ave., 15206. Tel: 412-361-2833; Fax: 412-361-2833.
E-mail: villa@sgi.net
For a complete listing, refer to the Special Care Facilities section.
Vincentian Home Inc., 111 Perrymont Rd., 15237. Tel: 412-366-5600; Fax: 412-366-1408
For a complete listing, refer to the Special Care Facilities section.

[L] HOMES FOR THE AGED

PITTSBURGH. *Little Sisters of the Poor Home for the Aged*, 1028 Benton Ave., 15212. Tel: 412-761-5373; Fax: 412-734-1030.
E-mail: littlesisters1@mindspring.com
For a complete listing, refer to the Special Care Facilities section.
Marian Manor Corp., 2695 Winchester Dr., 15220-4099. Tel: 412-563-6866 (Admin.); 563-1244 (Nursing Service); Fax: 412-563-1250.
E-mail: marianmanr@aol.com
Web site: www.marianmanor.com
For a complete listing, refer to the Special Care Facilities section.
Mercy Senior Care: St. Joseph's, 5324 Penn Ave., 15224-1798. Tel: 412-665-5100; Fax: 412-665-4627
For a complete listing, refer to the Special Care Facilities section.
St. Pius X Residence, Inc., 2681 Waddington Ave., 15226. Tel: 412-563-5040; Fax: 412-563-3776
For a complete listing, refer to the Special Care Facilities section.

ALLISON PARK. *Vincentian Regency*, 9399 Babcock Blvd., 15101. Tel: 412-366-8540; Fax: 412-369-9789.
Web site: www.vcs.org
For a complete listing, refer to the Special Care Facilities section.

BADEN. *Villa St. Joseph of Baden, Inc.*, 1030 State St., 15005. Tel: 724-869-6300; Fax: 724-869-6399
For a complete listing, refer to the Special Care Facilities section.

[M] REHABILITATION, NURSING AND GENERIC CARE FACILITIES

PITTSBURGH. *Marian Hall Home, Inc.*, 934 Forest Ave., 15202-1118. Tel: 412-761-1999; Fax: 412-761-2556
For a complete listing, refer to the Special Care Facilities section.

[N] PERSONAL PRELATURES

PITTSBURGH. *Opus Dei.* Prelature of the Holy Cross and Opus Dei. Warwick House, 5090 Warwick Terr., 15213. Tel: 412-683-8448; Fax: 412-687-3806.
Web site: www.opusdei.org
Revs. Joseph Landauer; Martin J. Miller.

[O] MONASTERIES AND RESIDENCES OF PRIESTS AND BROTHERS

PITTSBURGH. *Congregation of the Oratory of St. Philip Neri*, The Pittsburgh Oratory, 4450 Bayard St., 15213. Tel: 412-681-3181; Fax: 412-681-2922.
E-mail: bsummers@andrew.edu
Web site: www.andrew.cmu.edu/USER/oratory
Very Rev. Bryan F. Summers, C.O., Provost; Revs. Drew P. Morgan, C.O.; David S. Abernethy, C.O.; Joseph E. Sioli, C.O.; Bro. Michael J. Darcy, C.O-..Total Staff 4.
Croatian Commissariate, T.O.R., 24 Maryland Ave., 152090. Tel: 412-821-3438; Fax: 412-821-8276. Very Rev. Gabriel Badurina, T.O.R., Commissary Prov.
Franciscan Friars, T.O.R., Queen of Peace Friary, 5324 Carnegie St., 15201. Tel: 412-782-4755; Fax: 412-782-2377. Bro. Albert Gentile, T.O.R., Local Min. Retreat Ministry: Revs. Bernard Tickerhoof, T.O.R.; Joseph A. Markalonis, T.O.R. In res. Rev. William Weider, T.O.R.; Bro. Michael Tripka, T.O.R.
St. Augustine Friary, 221 36th St., 15201. Tel: 412-682-6430; Fax: 412-682-6148. Revs. Robert Craig, O.F.M.Cap., Chap., VA Hospital & St. Francis Medical Center; Paul Farkas, O.F.M.Cap., Jubilarian; Francis Fugini, O.F.M.Cap., Sec. Missions & Dir. Seraphic Mass Assoc.; Paul Kuppe, O.F.M.Cap., Min. Prov.; Brendan Malloy, O.F.M.Cap., Fraternity Guardian & Prov. Spiritual Asst. S.F.O.; John Pavlik, O.F.M.Cap., Vicar Prov.; John J. Petrikovic, O.F.M.Cap., Prov. Sec.; Louis Petruha, O.F.M.Cap., Cont. Educ.; Benedict Pope, O.F.M.Cap.; Bertin Roll, O.F.M.Cap., Dir. Archconfraternity of Christian Mothers; Pascal Schaller, O.F.M.Cap.; Roy R. Schuster, O.F.M.Cap., Pastor St. Patrick Parish, Coalton, WV; Bonaventure Stefun, O.F.M.Cap., Chap. St. Francis Medical Center; DeSales Young, O.F.M.Cap., Chap. Sisters of St. Francis, Mt. Alvernia, Millvale, PA; Armand Yeaglin, O.F.M.Cap, Jubiliarian; Bros. James Allman, O.F.M.Cap., Fraternity Svcs.; David Cira, O.F.M.Cap., Chap. Mercy Health System; Joseph Day, O.F.M.Cap., Fraternity Svs.; Richard Lubomski, O.F.M.Cap., Prov. Dir. Finances; Thomas Tomasunas, O.F.M.Cap., Fraternity Svs.
St. Conrad Friary. 9448 Babcock Blvd., Allison Park, 15101. Tel: 412-364-8240; Fax: 412-366-8331.
Web site: www.capuchin.com
Revs. W. David Nestler, O.F.M.Cap., Guardian & Dir. Novices; Remo DiSalvatore, O.F.M.Cap., Asst. Dir. Novices; Gregory Chervenak, O.F.M.Cap., Chap. St. Francis Hospital, Millvale; Emil Fischer, O.F.M.Cap..Novices 5; Total in Residence 12; Total Staff 1. Jubilarians: Revs. Blaise J. Fusco, O.F.M.Cap.; Gabriel Giles, O.F.M.Cap; Roland Raible, O.F.M.Cap.
St. Francis Friary, 2905 Castlegate Ave., 15226. Tel: 412-531-4545; Fax: 412-531-0998. Revs. Thomas A. Dutkiewicz, O.F.M.Cap., Confessor, St. Mary of Mercy Church, Pittsburgh; Ronald Lawler, O.F.M.Cap., Dir. Diocesan Office for Adult & Family Catechesis; Guardian; Emitt Schuler, O.F.M.Cap., VA Chap.; Maurice Sheehan, O.F.M.Cap., Dean, Holy Apostles Seminary, Cromwell, CT; Edward Laurent, O.F.M.Cap., Dir. St. Fidelis Devel. Office & Vicar. Residents 5.
St. John Vianney Manor, 2600 Morange Rd., 15205. Tel: 412-928-0825; 928-0908; Fax: 412-928-1947. Retired priests' residence. In res. Revs. Leo R. Burchianti; Glenn T. Conner; David C. Dixon; Rev. Msgr. Joseph G. Findlan; Revs. John D. Fording; John W. Gibson; Leo G. Henry; Gerard D. Kelly; Francis J. X. Lackner; Evaristo Luteri; Michael C. MacVeigh; Francis G. Massung; John L. Michaels; William M. Miller; Thomas M. Nee; William P. O'Malley; Harry E. Parsons; Francis P. Plantes; Francis M. Rodgers; Bernard P. Shulik; Clifford F. Soisson; Henry A. Szarnicki; Zygmunt V. Szarnicki; Edward J. Trzeciakowski; John M. Unger; William P. Weirauch; Walter F. Wichmanowski. Total in Residence 27; Total Staff 8.
St. Paul of the Cross Monastery. Retreat Center, Passionist Overseas Missions. 148 Monastery Ave., S.S., 15203. Tel: 412-381-1188; Fax: 412-481-5049. Very Rev. Richard Burke, C.P., Local Supr.; Revs. William Davin, C.P.; Timothy Fitzgerald, C.P.; John F. McMillan, C.P., Dir. Confraternity of the Passion; Edwin Moran, C.P.; Anthony Neary, C.P.; Dan Sullivan, C.P.; Bros. Leo Di Fiore, C.P., Passionist Overseas Missions Dir.; Joseph Holzer, C.P.; Angelo Sena, C.P.
Mission Band: Revs. Timothy Fitzgerald, C.P.; Edwin Moran, C.P.; Dan Sullivan, C.P.
Retreat Center: Revs. Michael Salvagna, C.P., Dir. Tel: 412-381-7676; Paul Vaeth, C.P., Assoc. Dir.
Passionist Overseas Missions: Bro. Leo Di Fiore, C.P., Rel. Admin. Coord. Tel: 412-381-1189 Ext. 21. Total Assisted 5,000; Residents 12; Total Staff 15.
Society of The Divine Word, 207 Lytton, 15213. Tel: 412-683-4030. Rev. Walter Ostrowski, S.V.D., Mission Dir. Tel: 412-683-0640. Total in Residence 4.
Third Order Regular of Saint Francis - Province of the Most Sacred Heart of Jesus, 128 Woodshire Dr., 15215-1714. Tel: 412-781-8333; Fax: 412-781-1219.
E-mail: MinProvSHP@aol.com
Very Rev. Edmund F. Carroll, T.O.R., Prov. Min.; Revs. Joseph A. Markalonis, T.O.R., Retreat Min.; Joseph Monahan, T.O.R., Chap. Mercy Hospital; Bernard Tickerhoof, T.O.R., Retreat Min.; Bro. Albert Gentile, T.O.R., Local Min. In res. Bro. Michael Tripka, T.O.R.; Rev. William Wieder, T.O.R., Queen of Peace Friary, 5324 Carnegie St., 15201. Tel: 412-782-4755; Fax: 412-782-2377. Residents 7; Total Staff 2.

AVALON. *Holy Family Friary.* (Friars Minor), The Franciscans. 232 S. Home Ave., Pittsburgh, 15202-2899. Tel: 412-761-2550; 761-8470; Fax: 412-761-2959.
E-mail: sjbsec@franciscan.org
Friars Allan Schmitz, O.F.M.; Francis Duchala, O.F.M.; David Kohut, O.F.M.; Lawrence Pollak, O.F.M.; Jerome Pavlik, O.F.M.; Matthew Brozovic, O.F.M.; Roland Maruscak, O.F.M. Friars 7.
Franciscan House of Evangelization, 2428 Arlington Ave., Pittsburgh, 15210. Tel: 412-431-4476; Fax: 412-431-4478.
E-mail: ofmpgh@prodigy.net
Friars Daniel Barrett, O.F.M.; Thomas Gerchak, O.F.M.; Paschal Dierks, O.F.M.; David Moczulski, O.F.M. Friars 4.

BEN AVON. *St. Anthony Friary and Mission House.* 226 Rostrevor Pl., Pittsburgh, 15202-1920. Tel: 412-761-4831; Fax: 412-761-9130. Franciscan Friars of the Assumption of the Blessed Virgin Mary Province (Order of Friars Minor). Revs. Michael Derbish, O.F.M.; Joachim C. Studwell, O.F.M., Local Min.; Felix J. Reczek, O.F.M., (Living in Bellows Falls, VT). In res. Bro. Stephen Dupuis, O.F.M. Fathers 3; Brothers 1.

BETHEL PARK. *Holy Ghost Fathers and Brothers Provincialate*, 6230 Brush Run Rd., 15102. Tel: 412-831-0302; Fax: 412-831-0970.
E-mail: cppromis@aol.com
Very Rev. Donald J. McEachin, C.S.Sp., Prov. Supr.; Revs. Girard J. Kohler, C.S.Sp., Mission Procurator; Henry J. Koren, C.S.Sp., Archivist..Residents 3; Total Staff 6.

HERMAN. *St. Mary's Friary*, P.O. Box 26, 16039. Tel: 724-282-1485; Fax: 724-285-4715.
E-mail: stmarys11@aol.com
Capuchin Friars. Revs. Lester Knoll, O.F.M.Cap., Vicar; Michael Greb, O.F.M.Cap.; Wendel Moliski, O.F.M.Cap., Guardian; DePaul Ripko, O.F.M.Cap.; Gary Stakem, O.F.M.Cap.

MCKEESPORT. *Franciscan Friars*, Serra Friary, 200 Hershey Dr., 15132-7400. Tel: 412-751-1250; Fax: 412-751-3488.
E-mail: diopghserra@impresso.com
Web site: www.serrahs.org
Friars Patrick George, T.O.R., Local Minister; Terrance Adams, T.O.R.; Bros. Sean Fitzwater, T.O.R.; James Boyle, Headmaster.

ROCHESTER. *St. Cecilia Friary*, 303 Jackson St., 15074. Tel: 724-775-0801; 774-6046; Fax: 724-774-3056.
E-mail: stcecilia@access995.com
Capuchin Friars. Revs. Ward Stakem, O.F.M.Cap.; William Gillum, O.F.M.Cap.; Leon Leitem, O.F.M.Cap., Vicar, St. Felix Friary, Freedom, 15042. Tel: 724-775-1476; Fax: 724-775-1476. In res. Revs. Philip Fink, O.F.M.Cap.; Scott Seethaler, O.F.M.Cap.

[P] CONVENTS AND RESIDENCES FOR SISTERS

PITTSBURGH. *Convent of Mercy*, 3333 Fifth Ave., 15213. Tel: 412-578-6225; Fax: 412-578-6180.
E-mail: gscarpino@carlow.edu
Motherhouse of Sisters of Mercy of the County of Allegheny. Established in 1843. Sr. Georgine Scarpino, R.S.M.; Rev. Robert J. George, Chap. Total Professed Sisters 190.
Holy Family Manor, 301 Bellevue Rd., 15229-2194. Tel: 412-931-6996; Fax: 412-931-2399. Residence for Retired Sisters. Sisters 48.
Ladies of Bethany, 1004 Oglethorpe Ave., 15201-2151. Tel: 412-781-4022; Fax: 412-858-2532.
Other Convents: 276 Bruin Rd., Petrolia, 16050. Tel: 724-753-2294. 1509 Trinity Ave., Pittsburgh, 15206-1362. Tel: 412-441-2287.
Motherhouse and Novitiate of the Vincentian Sisters of Charity, 8200 McKnight Rd., 15237. Tel: 412-364-3000; Fax: 412-364-9055.
E-mail: creebel@vincentiansrspgh.org
Web site: www.vincentiansrspgh.org
Sr. Charlene Reebel, V.S.C., Gen. Supr.; Rev. Reginald Russo, O.F.M.Cap., Chap.
Motherhouse, Sisters of the Holy Spirit (S.H.S.) Ross Township, 5246 Clarwin Ave., 15229-2208. Tel: 412-931-1917; Fax: 412-931-3711.
E-mail: SRSHS@aol.com
Sr. Marita Juras, S.H.S., Gen. Supr.; Most Rev. David A. Zubik, Chap. Professed Sisters 58; Total in Community 59.

Our Lady of Sorrows Convent of the Passionist Nuns, 2715 Churchview Ave., 15227. Tel: 412-881-1155. Motherhouse and Novitiate of the Religious of the Passion. (Passionist Nuns). Mother Joyce Foga, C.P., Supr. Professed Sisters 9.

St. Benedict Monastery, Benedictine Sisters of Pontifical Jurisdiction, 4530 Perrysville Ave., 15229-2296. Tel: 412-931-2844; Fax: 412-931-8970.
E-mail: osbpgh@osbpgh.org
Web site: www.osbpgh.org
Motherhouse and Novitiate of the Benedictine Sisters in the Diocese. Sr. Roberta Campbell, O.S.B., Prioress. Sisters 78.

Benedictine Center, Inc. Tel: 412-931-6051; Fax: 412-931-6003. Sr. Roberta Campbell, O.S.B., Pres.

Sisters of Our Lady of Charity, N.A.U., 4100 Vinceton St., 15214. Tel: 412-931-2299; Fax: 412-931-6044. North American Union of the Sisters of Our Lady of Charity, Inc. Sr. Lynn Reid, Supr. Sisters 10.

Sisters of St. Francis of the Providence of God, St. Francis Convent Motherhouse, 3603 McRoberts Rd., 15234-2398. Tel: 412-882-9911; Fax: 412-885-7210.
E-mail: srsosfprov@aol.com
Web site: www.srsosfprov.org
Sr. Joanne Brazinski, O.S.F., Gen. Min.; Rev. Thomas Kram, Chap..Sisters 109.

Sisters of the Holy Family of Nazareth of Western Pennsylvania, 285 Bellevue Rd., 15229-2195. Tel: 412-931-4775; Fax: 412-931-9746.
E-mail: srmichelec@aol.com
Web site: www.pgh-csfn.org
Sr. Michele Collins, C.S.F.N., Prov. Supr. Tel: 412-931-4778; Fax: 412-931-0690. Legal Title: *Sisters of the Holy Family of Nazareth of Western Pennsylvania*. Professed Sisters in Provincialate 29; Total Professed Sisters 130.

ALLISON PARK. *The Sisters of Divine Providence*, Providence Heights Motherhouse, 9000 Babcock Blvd., 15101-2793. Tel: 412-931-5241; Fax: 412-635-5416.
E-mail: divine_providence@email.msn.com
Web site: www.sistersofdivineprovidence.org
Motherhouse and Novitiate of the Sisters of Divine Providence in the Diocese (Pittsburgh Province). Sr. Mary Ellen Rufft, C.D.P., Prov. Dir. & Pres.; Rev. Frank D. Almade, Chap. In Motherhouse 103; In Province (including Puerto Rico) 244.

BADEN. *St. Joseph Convent*, 1020 State St., 15005. Tel: 724-869-2151; 412-761-3700; Fax: 724-869-3336.
E-mail: secofcsj@usaor.net
Web site: www.stjoseph-baden.orgl
Sr. Anna Marie Gaglia, Congregational Moderator. Motherhouse of Sisters of St. Joseph. Rev. Philp Fink, O.F.M.Cap., Chap. Residents 99. In Community 286 (Final Professed); Temporary 1; Novices 1; Candidates 1.

BELLEVUE. *Mount Assisi Convent.* Motherhouse of the School Sisters of the Third Order of St. Francis, 934 Forest Ave., Pittsburgh, 15202. Tel: 412-761-6004; Fax: 412-761-0290.
E-mail: mtassisi@sgi.net
Web site: www.franciscansisters-pa.org
In res. Rev. Richard Lelonis, Chap. Sisters 82; Residents 47; Total Staff 8.

CORAOPOLIS. *Our Lady of the Sacred Heart Convent.* 1500 Woodcrest Ave., Pittsburgh, 15108. Tel: 412-264-2890; 269-2881; Fax: 412-264-7047.
E-mail: cssfpa@nauticom.net
Provincial House and Novitiate of the Felician Sisters of Pennsylvania C.S.S.F. Sr. Mary Cabrini Procopio, C.S.S.F., Prov. Min.; Rev. Arthur L. Garbin, Chap. Professed 130; Total in Residence 83; Total Staff 36.

Infirmary of St. Joseph Hall, 1500 Woodcrest Ave., 15108. Tel: 412-264-2890; 269-2881; Fax: 412-264-6108. Rev. Richard L. Conboy, S.T.L., Chap.

ELIZABETH. *Divine Redeemer Motherhouse*, 999 Rock Run Rd., 15037. Tel: 412-751-8600; Fax: 412-751-0355. Motherhouse and Novitiate of the Sisters of the Divine Redeemer. Sr. M. Monica Kosztolnyik, S.D.R., Prov. In res. Rev. Francis L. Pucci, Chap. In the Community 52.

EMSWORTH. *Mother Frances Convent.* 140 Allegheny Ave., Pittsburgh, 15202-1402. Tel: 412-766-6702; Fax: 412-766-6702.

MILLVALE. *St. Francis Convent.* Mt. Alvernia, 146 Hawthorne Rd., Pittsburgh, 15209. Tel: 412-821-2200; Fax: 412-821-3318.
E-mail: magill@dewey.cc.duq.edu
Web site: www.millvalefranciscans.com
Sisters of St. Francis of Millvale, PA. Motherhouse and Novitiate of the Order in the Diocese. In the Community: Professed Sisters 207; Juniors 1; Associates 37; In the Motherhouse: Professed Sisters 94. Attended by Capuchin Fathers from St. Augustine, Pittsburgh. Chaplains: Revs. DeSales Young, O.F.M.Cap.; Gregory Chervenak, O.F.M.Cap.

VILLA MARIA. *Sisters of the Humility of Mary*, Villa Maria Community Center, P.O. Box 914, 16155. Tel: 724-964-8861; Fax: 724-964-8082.
E-mail: info@humilityofmary.org
Web site: www.humilityofmary.org
Sr. Ruthmary Powers, H.M., Major Supr.; Rev. Frank G. Erdeljac. Tel: 724-535-4786. Professed Sisters 235; Novices 1; Residents 42; Total Staff 151.

[Q] RETREAT HOUSES

PITTSBURGH. *Franciscan Spirit and Life Center*, 3605 McRoberts Rd., 15234-2340. Tel: 412-881-9207; Fax: 412-885-7210.
E-mail: FSLCCOM@aol.com
Sisters of St. Francis of the Providence of God. Rev. Bernard Tickerhoof, T.O.R., Dir.
Purpose: To provide a facility to individuals for retreats and spiritual programs. Overnight accomodations for 23. Conference room and dining facility. Three hermitages available on daily, overnight or weekly basis. Total Staff 4.

Martina Spiritual Renewal Center, Inc., 5244 Clarwin Ave., 15229-2208. Tel: 412-931-9766; Fax: 412-931-1823.
Conducted by Sisters of the Holy Spirit.
Purpose: To provide a facility to individuals and groups for retreats and spiritual programs. Sr. Marita Juras, S.H.S., Pres.; Sr. Mary Richard Mehelich, S.H.S., Dir. Staff: Sr. Madalyn Chlebowski, S.H.S.

St. Paul of the Cross Retreat Center, 148 Monastery Ave., 15203. Tel: 412-381-7676; 381-7677; Fax: 412-431-3044.
E-mail: stpaulrc@sgi.net
Web site: trfn.clpgh.org/stpaulrc/
Revs. Michael Salvagna, C.P., Dir.; Paul Vaeth, C.P. Assocs.: Dr. Susan Stangl; Dr. Salvatore Mascari. Total in Residence 2; Total Staff 32.

The Burning Bush: Franciscan House of Prayer, 32-40 Pius St., 15203-1617. Tel: 412-381-3819; Fax: 412-381-1585.
E-mail: burnbush@nb.net
Purposes: A Franciscan-oriented House of Prayer and retreat facility for contemplation, rest, prayer and spiritual nourishment; motherhouse for formation and prayer of Lay Franciscans of Adoration. Contact Persons: Fred Koerner, L.F.A., Mod.; Sr. Damian Tosi, O.L.C., L.F.A., Asst. Mod. Total in Residence 3.

ALLISON PARK. *Kearns Spirituality Center*, 9000 Babcock Blvd., 15101-2713. Tel: 412-366-1124; Fax: 412-635-6318.
E-mail: kearnsscl@juno.com
Web site: www.sistersofdivprovidence.org
Sisters of Divine Providence. Directors: Sr. Agnes Raible, C.D.P.; Sr. Rose Michele Seiber, C.D.P. Conference room for 250; overnight accommodations for 60; dining facilities for 200. Call for more information on programs offered. Total Staff 6.

BETHEL PARK. *Holy Ghost Animation Center*, 6230 Bush Run Rd., 15102. Tel: 412-835-3510; Fax: 412-835-3541.
E-mail: bethel41@juno.com
Revs. Norman E. Bevan, C.S.Sp., Dir.; Constantine J. Conan, C.S.Sp.; Jeremiah A. Falvey, C.S.Sp.; Charles S. Giambrone, C.S.Sp.; John M. Jendzura; John R. Kanda, C.S.Sp.; Girard J. Kohler, C.S.Sp.; Henry J. Koren, C.S.Sp.; John P. McAndrew, C.S.Sp.; James F. Pergl, C.S.Sp.; John S. Rondeau, C.S.Sp.; J. Gerald Walsh, C.S.Sp. Total in Residence 12; Total Staff 23.

CORAOPOLIS. *Gilmary Diocesan Center*, 601 Flaugherty Run Rd., 15108-3899. Tel: 412-264-8400; Fax: 412-264-8415.
E-mail: gilmary@diopitt.org
Web site: www.diopitt.org
Ronald W. Ragan, Dir.
Overnight facilities for 219; meeting rooms for one-day programs; separate adult and youth facilities; 150 seat dining room, 150 seat chapel, indoor heated swimming pool, gymnasium, outdoor volleyball and basketball courts and ballfield.

Office for Adolescent Formation & Youth Ministry. Tel: 412-264-9530; Fax: 412-264-9539. Joyce Gillooly, Dir. Tel: 412-264-9530: Fax: 412-264-9539. Total Staff 10.

[R] OFFICES FOR CAMPUS MINISTRY

PITTSBURGH. *Office for Campus Ministry.* LaRoche College, 9000 Babcock Blvd., 15237. Tel: 412-536-1050, Ext. 141; Fax: 412-536-1048.
E-mail: hortonp1@laroche.edu
Rev. W. Peter Horton, Dir., Art Institute of Pittsburgh, St. Peter Church, 720 Arch St., 15212-5296. Tel: 412-321-0711. Rev. Benjamin R. Walker, O.S.B., Carlow College, 3333 5th Ave., 15213. Tel: 412-578-6069. Sr. Eleanore Loftos, R.S.M., Carnegie-Mellon University, Ryan Catholic Newman Center, 4450 Bayard St., 15213. Tel: 412-681-3181; Fax: 412-681-2922. Very Rev. Bryan F. Summers, C.O.; Sr. Bernadette Young, C.D.P.; Revs. David S. Abernethy, C.O.; Drew P. Morgan, C.O.; Joseph E. Sioli, C.O., Chatham College, Ryan Catholic Newman Center, 4450 Bayard St., 15213. Tel: 412-681-3181; Fax: 412-681-2922. Very Rev. Bryan F. Summers, C.O.; Sr. Bernadette Young, C.D.P.; Revs. David S. Abernethy, C.O.; Drew P. Morgan, C.O.; Joseph E. Sioli, C.O., Community College of Allegheny County - Boyce Campus, St. Bernadette Church, 5245 Azalea Dr., Monroeville, 15146. Tel: 412-373-0050; Fax: 412-374-8113. Rev. Michael W. Decewicz, Community College of Allegheny County - Northside Campus, St. Peter Church, 720 Arch St., 15212-5296. Tel: 412-321-0711; Fax: 412-321-7807. Rev. Job V. Foote, O.S.B., Community College of Allegheny County- South Campus, Holy Spirit Church, 2603 Old Elizabeth Rd., West Mifflin, 15122. Tel: 412-466-5048; Fax: 412-466-4983. Rev. Daniel A. Valentine, Community College of Allegheny County - North Hills Campus, St. Teresa of Avila, 1000 Avila Ct., 15237-2176. Tel: 412-367-9001; Fax: 412-366-8415. Ms. Joan Pilat, Duquesne University, Campus Ministry, 15282. Tel: 412-396-6020. Revs. Raymond D. French, C.S.Sp., Dir.; Timothy Hickey, C.S.Sp.; Matthias Idyu, C.S.Sp.; Sr. Bernadette Campbell, O.P., Geneva College, Campus Ministry, 289 Ridge Rd, New Brighton, 15066. Tel: 724-846-5978. Patrick Corcoran, Dir.; Rev. David E. Scharf, Pennsylvania State University, Beaver Campus, Campus Ministry, 289 Ridge Rd., New Brighton, 15066. Tel: 724-846-5978. Mr. Patrick W. Corcoran, Dir., Point Park College, St. Mary of Mercy Church, 202 Stanwix St., 15222. Tel: 412-261-0110; Fax: 412-261-0113. Rev. John M. O'Toole, C.O., Robert Morris College, Moon Township Campus, St. James Church, 200 Walnut St., Sewickley, 15143. Tel: 412-741-0836; 262-8313. Rev. Harold E. Baily, Robert Morris College, Downtown Pittsburgh Campus, St. Benedict the Moor Church, 1500 Centre Ave., 15219. Tel: 412-281-3141; Fax: 412-391-7151. Rev. Carmen A. D'Amico, University of Pittsburgh, Ryan Catholic Newman Center, 4450 Bayard St., 15213. Tel: 412-681-3181; Fax: 412-681-2922. Very Rev. Bryan F. Summers, C.O., Dir.; Sr. Bernadette Young, C.D.P.; Revs. David S. Abernethy, C.O.; Drew P. Morgan, C.O.; Joseph E. Sioli, C.O., California University (California), St. Thomas Aquinas Church, 4th & Union Streets, California, 15419. Tel: 724-938-3204; Fax: 724-938-0434. Rev. Mark J. Skertich, Dir., Westminster College, St. Camillus Church, 313 W. Englewood Ave., New Castle, 16105. Tel: 724-652-9471; Fax: 724-654-1430. Rev. Robert J. Miller, Slippery Rock University, Newman Center (Slippery Rock), 342 Normal Ave., Slippery Rock, 16057. Tel: 724-794-8459; Fax: 724-794-1150. Rev. James L. Armstrong, Dir.; Ms. Diane Magliocca, Campus Min., Washington and Jefferson College (Washington), Newman Center, 1 S. College St., Washington, 15301. Tel: 724-228-5004. Rev. John E. Forbidussi; Deacon John Manion, Waynesburg College (Waynesburg), St. Ann Church, 232 E. High St., Waynesburg, 15370. Tel: 724-627-7568. Revs. Albin C. McGinnis; Paul W. Merkovsky.

Office of Chaplaincies, 4721 Fifth Ave., 15213. Tel: 412-621-6209; Fax: 412-621-9541.
E-mail: kwinwood@diopitt.org

[S] MISCELLANEOUS LISTINGS

PITTSBURGH. *The Capuchin Franciscan Volunteer Corps, Inc.*, 220 37th St., 15201. Tel: 412-682-6011; Fax: 412-682-0506.
E-mail: volunteers@capuchin.com
Web site: www.capuchin.com
Province of St. Augustine of the Capuchin Order. Bro. Robert Toomey, O.F.M.Cap., Dir.
Purpose: To promote, train, supervise and support Catholic lay missions and missionaries throughout the world, especially in conjunction with the ministries and fraternities of the Capuchin Order.

Cardinal Tardini Charitable Trust, St. Mary of Mercy Church, 202 Stanwix St., 15222-1381.

Catholic Diocese of Pittsburgh Foundation, 111 Blvd. of the Allies, 15222. Tel: 412-456-3085; Fax: 412-456-3169.
E-mail: development@diopitt.org
Web site: www.diopitt.org

The Catholic Historical Society of Western Pennsylvania, Synod Hall, 125 N. Craig St., 15213. Tel: 412-242-3374. Rev. James W. Garvey, Sec.
Purpose: To promote the teaching of the Catholic Church in the United States, especially the Church in Western Pennsylvania; to recognize the growth, development and contribution of the Catholic Church by the preservation of artifacts, records and documents related to that history; to make available the results of research and study.

Catholic Long Term Care Network of Western Pennsylvania, Inc. A collaborative effort of nine religious communities and the Diocese of Pittsburgh. The sponsors operate thirteen skilled nursing facilities and seven assisted living-personal care homes. Sponsors: Diocese of Pittsburgh, Felician Sisters, Little Sisters of the Poor, School Sisters of St. Francis, Sisters of St. Joseph, Sisters of the Holy Spirit, Sisters of Mercy, Sisters of St. Basil the Great, Sisters of St. Francis of Millvale, Vincentian Sisters of Charity. 8200 McKnight Rd., 15237. Tel: 412-366-8540; Fax: 412-369-9789.

Chimbote Foundation, 111 Blvd. of the Allies, 15222-1618. Tel: 412-456-3065; Fax: 412-456-3069.
E-mail: jkozar@diopitt.org
Web site: www.diopitt.org

Christ Child Society of Pittsburgh, P.O. Box 11324, 15238-1324. Tel: 412-682-4102; Fax: 412-682-4102. Mrs. Ellen O'Brien, Contact; Rev. Frank D. Almade, Chap.
Purpose: To foster a personal love of Christ expressed in service for needy children and youths. Total Assisted 800; Volunteers 60.

The City of God Foundation, 285 Bellevue Rd., 15229. Tel: 412-828-8380; Fax: 412-828-8381. Veronica M. Rocks, Contact Person.

Elizabeth Seton Center Inc., 1900 Pioneer Ave., 15226. Tel: 412-561-8400; Fax: 412-561-8488.
E-mail: SrBarb@setoncenter.com
Sr. Barbara Ann Boss, S.C., Exec. Dir. Day Care Programs for Children and Adults; Senior Citizens Center; Suzuki School of Music. Sisters of Charity 15; Total Assisted 1,030; Total Staff 54.

The Epiphany Association, 947 Tropical Ave., 15216-3031. Tel: 412-341-7494; Fax: 412-341-7495.
E-mail: smuto@epiphanyassociation.org
Web site: www.epiphanyassociation.org
Total Staff 4; Total in Residence 1.

Holy Family Foundation, 8325 Ohio River Blvd., Ste. 200, 15202-1594. The Holy Family Foundation was formed in 1992 to promote & support the public charitable works & educational purposes of Holy Family Institute.

Mercy Hospital School of Nursing Alumni Association, 1401 Blvd. of Allies, 15219. Tel: 412-232-7948; Fax: 412-232-7951.
E-mail: cshallenberger@mercy.pmhs.org
Sr. Carolyn Schallenberger, R.S.M., Vice Pres., Nursing Svcs.

Mount Assisi Academy Preschool, 934 Forest Ave., 15202. Tel: 412-761-0381; Fax: 412-761-0290. Sr. Elaine Hromulak, O.S.F. Sisters 3; Lay Teachers 3; Students 102.

Mount Nazareth Center, Inc., 285 Bellevue Rd., 15229-2195. Tel: 412-931-9761; Fax: 412-931-7255.
E-mail: fjust@mtnazarethcenter.org
Web site: www.mtnazarethcenter.org
Mr. Fred D. Just, Exec. Dir. Tel: 412-931-1039. Total Staff 75.

Mt. Nazareth Learning Center. Child Care: Infants; Toddlers; Pre-School; Kindergarten. Tel: 412-931-9761; 931-9241; Fax: 412-931-7255. Total Assisted 517; Total Staff 28.

Nazareth Housing Services. Housing Counseling; Low Income Home Ownership. Tel: 412-931-3510; Fax: 412-931-7255. Total Assisted 2,139; Total Staff 4.

Nazareth Family Services. Family Counseling; Family Life Education. Tel: 412-931-1026; Fax: 412-931-7255. Total Assisted 2,569; Total Staff 4.

Nazareth Family Foundation, 285 Bellevue Rd., 15229. Tel: 412-931-4778; Fax: 412-931-9746. Sr. Maria Kruszewski, Pres. Purpose: To promote family life through financial support of facilities, programs, and services which enhance individual and family well-being. Total Assisted 8,802 Families; Total Staff 3.

North Catholic Endowment Fund, 111 Blvd. of the Allies, 15222. Tel: 412-456-3100; Fax: 412-456-3101.
E-mail: education@diopitt.org
Web site: www.diopitt.org

Pension Plan for the Diocese of Pittsburgh. (Lay Pension Plan), 111 Blvd. of the Allies, 15222. Tel: 412-456-3137; Fax: 412-456-3130.
E-mail: benefits@diopitt.org
Mr. Charles A. Koempel, Dir.

Pittsburgh Catholic Publishing Associates. Purpose: To promote for Catholics and other readers an understanding of the mission and teachings of the Church and its role in the community. 135 First Ave., Ste. 200, 15222-1506. Tel: 412-471-1252; Fax: 412-471-4228.
E-mail: pghcatholic@pittsburgh.net
Web site: www.pghcatholic.com
Mr. Greg Brown, Editor; Ms. Carmella A. Weismantle, Comptroller.
Purpose: To promote for Catholics and other readers an understanding of the mission and teachings of the Church and its role in the community.

Pittsburgh Diocese Knights of Columbus Bishop Wright Project, (Incorporated), 2718 Custer Ave., 15227. Tel: 412-882-1333; Fax: 412-882-1668.
E-mail: diopghstanth@impresso.com
Project for benefit of St. Anthony School for Programs and McGuire Memorial.

Priests' Benefit Plan of the Diocese of Pittsburgh, 111 Blvd. of the Allies, 15222. Tel: 412-456-3060; Fax: 412-456-3139.
E-mail: centralaccounting@diopitt.org
Rev. James S. Ruggiero, Chm.
Purpose: To provide certain retirement and health-related benefits to eligible priests.

St. Francis Academy Corporation, 1401 Hamilton Rd., 15234. Tel: 412-882-9911; Fax: 412-885-7210.
E-mail: srsosfprov@aol.com
Web site: www.srsosfprov.org
Sr. Mary Ann Lostoski, O.S.F., Pres.

St. Joseph's House of Hospitality, Inc., 1635 Bedford Ave., 15219. Tel: 412-471-0666; Fax: 412-471-8556.
E-mail: sjhh@stargate.net
Web site: trfn.clpgh.org/sjhh
A subsidiary of Catholic Charities. Ms. Phyllis A. Malchano, Exec. Dir. Seton Hill Sisters of Charity 3; Residents 60; Total Assisted 97; Total Staff 17.

Maryhouse Residence for Women, 1113 Creedmoor Ave., 15226. Tel: 412-563-3312; Fax: 412-563-8527. Residents 30; Total Assisted 33; Sisters of St. Francis 1.

St. Regis Residence. (Non-Sectarian), 50 Congress St., 15219. Tel: 412-281-9888. Accommodations for 53 renters, and is under the direction of a Board of Lay Managers. Luella Buck, Dir. Permanent Residents 25; Staff 3.

Saint Thomas More Society, Three Gateway Center, 401 Liberty Ave., Ste. 1460, 15222-1004. Tel: 412-391-7445; Fax: 412-391-7461.
E-mail: jwgesqpc@usaor.net
Mr. John W. Giltinan, Pres.

Sisters of Mercy Continuing Support Trust Fund, 3333 Fifth Ave., 15213. Tel: 412-578-6224; Fax: 412-578-6180.
E-mail: gscarpino@carlow.edu
Sr. Georgine Scarpino, Pres.

Sisters of St. Francis of the Providence of God Ministries Corporation, 3603 McRoberts Rd., 15234-2398. Tel: 412-882-9911; Fax: 412-885-7210.
E-mail: srsosfprov@aol.com
Web site: www.srsosfprov.org
Sr. Marian Blodis, O.S.F., Pres. Program: Franciscan Spirit and Life Center.

Society of Saint Vincent de Paul, Council of Pittsburgh, 1243 N. Franklin St., 15233. Tel: 412-321-1071; Fax: 412-321-9131. Jack Bosley, Pres.; Deacon Thomas O'Neill, Spiritual Advisor. Total Assisted 20,800; Total Staff 40.

St. Francis Plaza, Inc., 451 44th St., 15201-1122. Tel: 412-683-6252; Fax: 412-683-4269. Sr. M. Sylvia Schuler, Chm. Sisters 2; Residents 103.

Vincentian Collaborative Services, 8200 McKnight Rd., 15237. Tel: 412-630-9980. Sr. Theresa Novak, Pres.
Purpose: To provide coordination and supervision of facilities and services operating under the auspices of the Vincentian Sisters of Charity.

ALLISON PARK. *Congregations of Religious Women Charitable Trust*, 9000 Babcock Blvd., 15101. Tel: 412-931-5241; Fax: 412-635-5406. Dorothy M. Antonucci, Chm.

Divine Providence Foundation, 9000 Babcock Blvd., 15101. Tel: 412-931-5241; Fax: 412-635-5416. Sr. Mary Ellen Rufft, C.D.P., Pres.
Purpose: To perform public charitable works in the area of health care and education.

Sisters of Divine Providence Charitable Trust, 9000 Babcock Blvd., 15101-2793. Tel: 412-931-5241; Fax: 412-635-5416.
E-mail: bbastin@juno.com
Sr. Mary Ellen Rufft, C.D.P., Pres.

BADEN.

Girls Hope of Pittsburgh, Inc., 1020 Baden St., 15005. Tel: 412-869-2868; Fax: 724-869-6576.
E-mail: girlshope@bhgh.org
Sr. Donna Marie Tahaney, Contact Person.
Purpose: To provide a supportive home environment and a quality education through college for girls who have potential for leadership but who because of poverty, abuse, neglect or abandonment cannot remain in their own homes. Total Assisted 15; Total Staff 6.

Sisters of St. Joseph Charitable Trust, c/o St. Joseph Convent, 1020 State St., 15005. Tel: 724-869-6594. Sr. Anna Marie Gaglia, C.S.J.

BETHEL PARK. *Spiritan Support Trust*, 6320 Brush Run Rd., 15102. Tel: 412-831-0302; Fax: 412-831-0970.
E-mail: csspeast@sgi.net
Web site: www.spiritans.org
Very Rev. Donald J. McEachin, C.S.Sp., Prov. Supr.

CLAIRTON. *Sisters Place, Inc.*, 460 Reed St., 15025. Tel: 412-233-3903; Fax: 412-233-3904.
E-mail: kboyle9519@aol.com
Purpose: To provide hospitality, housing and advocacy to women and children who are homeless or of low income. Alice M. Kulikowski, Pres.; Kathi Boyle, Exec. Dir. Total Staff 8; Total Assisted 65.

ELIZABETH. *Divine Redeemer Health Care Ministeries Corp.*, 999 Rock Run Rd., 15037. Tel: 412-751-8600; Fax: 412-751-0355.

Sisters of Divine Redeemer Charitable Trust, 999 Rock Run Rd., 15037. Tel: 412-751-8600; Fax: 412-751-0355.

MCKEESPORT. *Auberle*, 1101 Hartman St., 15132-1500. Tel: 412-673-5800; Fax: 412-673-5805.
E-mail: aubadmin@sgi.net
Web site: trfn.clpgh.org/auberle
Mr. Lynn M. Knezevich, Exec. Dir.
Purpose: To provide services to at risk children and their families. Total in Residence 118; Total Staff 215.

Pauline Auberle Foundation, 2513 Fifth Ave., 15132. Tel: 412-673-1992; Fax: 412-673-1996.
E-mail: raymondn@auberle.org
Web site: trfn.clpgh.org/auberle
Raymond M. Niedenberger, Exec. Dir. Continues mission of Pauline Auberle Foundation while providing support to Auberle through fundraising, rental agreements, and overall management and leadership services. Total Staff 15.

VILLA MARIA. *The Center for Learning*, Evergreen Rd., Box 910, 16155. Tel: 800-767-9090; 724-964-8083; Fax: 888-767-8080.
E-mail: cfl@stratos.net
Web site: www.centerforlearning.org
Educational Publisher of values-based curriculum: Religion for Catholic schools and parishes; English/Language Arts, Social Studies and Novel/Drama Curriculum Units for all schools. Sr. Rose Schaffer, H.M., M.A., Pres. & CEO; Sr. Bernadette Vetter, H.M., M.A., Vice Pres. Owned and operated by the Sisters of the Humility of Mary. Directed by an Ecumenical Lay Board. Shipping-business office in Villa Maria. Administrative-Editorial Office, 21590 Center Ridge Rd., Rocky River, OH, 44116. Tel: 440-331-1404; Fax: 440-331-5414.

Sisters of the Humility of Mary Charitable Trust, Villa Maria Community Center, P.O. Box 313, 16155. Tel: 724-964-8861; Fax: 724-964-8082.
Web site: www.humilityofmary.org
Sr. Mildred Ely, H.M., Contact.

Villa Maria Education Center, 16155. Tel: 724-964-8886; Fax: 724-964-8815.
E-mail: RKramer@humilityofmary.com
Sr. Rose Marie Kramer, H.M., Dir. A center for adolescents and pre-adolescents which provides programs to foster the development of strong spiritual and personal values, self-worth, respect for others, and social awareness. Total Assisted 2,500; Total Staff 10.

Villa Maria Residential Services. (Villa Maria Apartments), P.O. Box 230, 16155. Tel: 724-964-8099; Fax: 724-964-8082.
E-mail: MSchaffer@humilityofmary.com
Web site: www.humilityofmary.org
Housing for low & moderate income for senior citizens 58 & over. Sr. Mary Ida Schaffer, H.M., Pres. & CEO. Apartments 37.

RELIGIOUS INSTITUTES OF MEN REPRESENTED IN THE DIOCESE

For further details refer to the corresponding bracketed number in the Religious Institutes of Men or Women section.

[0200]—*Benedictine Monks*. (St. Vincent Archabbey).—O.S.B.

[0330]—*Brothers of the Christian Schools*. (Prov. of Baltimore).—F.S.C.

[0470]—*The Capuchin Friars*. (Prov. of St. Augustine).—O.F.M.Cap.

[1000]—*Congregation of the Passion*. (Eastern Prov.).—C.P.

[]—*Croatian Franciscans*. Croatian Commissariate.—T.O.R.

[0520]—*Franciscan Friars*. (Provs. of Assumption B.V.M. & Immaculate Conception; St. John the Baptist).—O.F.M.

[0650]—*Holy Ghost Fathers*. (Eastern Prov.).—C.S.Sp.

[0950]—*Oratorians*.—C.O.

[]—*Society of the Brother Servants of the Holy Spirit*.—B.H.S.

[0420]—*Society of the Divine Word*.—S.V.D.

[0560]—*Third Order Regular of Saint Francis*. (Prov. of Sacred Heart of Jesus).—T.O.R.

RELIGIOUS INSTITUTES OF WOMEN REPRESENTED IN THE DIOCESE

[0130]—*Apostles of the Sacred Heart of Jesus*.—A.S.C.J.

[0230]—*Benedictine Sisters of Pontifical Jursidiction*.—O.S.B.

[]—*Dominican Sisters, Congregation of the Most Holy Rosary*.

[]—*Dominican Sisters, St. Mary of the Springs*. (Columbus, OH).—O.P.

[1170]—*Felician Sisters*.—C.S.S.F.

[1190]—*Franciscan Sisters of Atonement*.—S.A.

[2575]—*Institute of the Sisters of Mercy of the Americas*. (Pittsburgh, PA; Erie, PA; Scranton, PA).—R.S.M.

[]—*Ladies of Bethany*.—L.B.

[2340]—*Little Sisters of the Poor*.—L.S.P.

[2720]—*Mission Helpers of the Sacred Heart.*—M.H.S.H.

[3071]—*North American Union Sisters of Our Lady of Charity.*—O.L.C.

[3170]—*Religious of the Passion of Jesus Christ.*—C.P.

[3430]—*Religious Teachers Filippini.* (St. Lucy Filippini Prov.).—M.P.F.

[2970]—*School Sisters of Notre Dame.*—S.S.N.D.

[1690]—*School Sisters of St. Francis.*—O.S.F.

[0570]—*Sisters of Charity of Seton Hill, Greensburg, Pennsylvania.*—S.C.

[0990]—*Sisters of Divine Providence.*—C.D.P.

[1660]—*Sisters of Saint Francis of the Providence of God.*—O.S.F.

[3830-13]—*Sisters of Saint Joseph.*—C.S.J.

[1620]—*Sisters of St. Francis of Millvale, Pennsylvania.*—O.S.F.

[]—*Sisters of St. Francis of the Third Order of Buffalo.*—O.S.F.

[3840]—*Sisters of St. Joseph of Carondelet.* (St. Paul, MN & Albany, NY Prov.).—C.S.J.

[1020]—*Sisters of the Divine Redeemer.*—S.D.R.

[1970]—*Sisters of the Holy Family of Nazareth.*—C.S.F.N.

[2040]—*Sisters of the Holy Spirit.*—S.H.S.

[2110]—*Sisters of the Humility of Mary.*—H.M.

[2160]—*Sisters, Servants of the Immaculate Heart of Mary.*—I.H.M.

[4120-03]—*Ursuline Nuns of the Congregation of Paris.*—O.S.U.

[]—*Ursuline Sisters of the Immaculate Conception.* (Cleveland).—O.S.V.

[4160]—*Vincentian Sisters of Charity.*—V.S.C.

DIOCESAN CEMETERIES

PITTSBURGH. *The Catholic Cemeteries Association,* Central Office, 718 Hazelwood Ave., 15217-2807. Tel: 412-521-9133; Fax: 412-521-7019.

All Saints Catholic Cemetery & Mausoleum (Braddock), 1560 Brinton Rd., 15221-4899. Tel: 412-271-5950; Fax: 412-271-8219.

Calvary Catholic Cemetery & Mausoleum, 718 Hazelwood Ave., 15217-2807. Tel: 412-421-9959; Fax: 412-421-3670.

Christ Our Redeemer Catholic Cemetery & Mausoleum (North Side), 204 Cemetery Ln., 15237-2722. Tel: 412-931-2206; Fax: 412-931-2229.

St. Mary Catholic Cemetery, c/o Calvery Cemetery, 718 Hazelwood Ave., 15217-2807. Tel: 412-421-9959; Fax: 412-621-6439.

St. Stanislaus Catholic Cemetery & St. Anthony Catholic Cemetery, 700 Soose Rd., 15209-1544. Tel: 412-821-4324; Fax: 412-821-4718.

Queen of Heaven Catholic Cemetery & Mausoleum, 2900 Washington Rd., McMurray, 15317-3278. Tel: 412-831-3360; 724-941-7601; Fax: 724-942-2550.

Resurrection Catholic Cemetery & Mausoleum, 100 Resurrection Rd., Moon Township, 15108. Tel: 724-695-2999; Fax: 724-695-3032.

Sacred Heart Catholic Cemetery and Mausoleum, 97 Sacred Heart Rd., Monongahela, 15063-9605. Tel: 724-258-2885; Fax: 724-258-2275.

Good Shepherd Catholic Cemetery & Mausoleum, 733 Patton St., Monroeville, 15146-4530. Tel: 412-824-0355; Fax: 412-823-9083.

Saint Joseph Catholic Cemetery & Mausoleum, 1443 Lincoln Hwy., North Versailles, 15137-2448. Tel: 412-823-9111; Fax: 412-823-6655.

Holy Souls Catholic Cemetery, c/o Resurrection Catholic Cemetery & Mausoleum, 100 Resurrection Rd., Moon Township, 15108. Tel: 724-695-3063; Fax: 724-695-3032.

Our Lady of Hope Catholic Cemetery & Mausoleum, 1898 Bakerstown Rd., Tarentum, 15084. Tel: 724-224-2785; Fax: 724-224-0211.

Holy Savior Catholic Cemetery, 4629 Bakerstown Rd., Gibsonia, 15044. Tel: 724-625-3822; Fax: 724-625-3880.

Mount Carmel Catholic Cemetery & Mausoleum, 7601 Mt. Carmel Rd., Verona, 15147. Tel: 412-241-1260; Fax: 412-241-5041.

NECROLOGY

† Berk, Aloysius B., Beechview, PA St. Catherine of Siena. —Died Aug. 27, 1999.

† Carey, Thomas F., Scott Township, PA SS. Simon and Jude. —Died Sept. 9, 1999.

† Dismachek, Francis M., (Retired). —Died Feb. 4, 2000.

† Romero, Michael C., Carrick, PA St. Basil. —Died June 17, 2000.

† Scanlon, John J., East McKeesport, PA St. Robert Bellarmine. —Died Nov. 22, 1999.

† Schultz, Rev. Msgr. Raymond T., Beaver, PA SS. Peter and Paul. —Died Oct. 27, 1999.

Diocese of Portland (In Maine)

(Dioecesis Portlandensis)

Most Reverend

JOSEPH JOHN GERRY, O.S.B.

Bishop of Portland; ordained June 12, 1954; ordained Titular Bishop of Praecausa and Auxiliary Bishop of Manchester April 21, 1986; appointed Bishop of Portland December 21, 1988; installed February 21, 1989. *Res., 199 Western Promenade, Portland, ME, 04102. Mailing Address: P.O. Box 11559, Portland, ME, 04104-7559.*

Most Reverend

EDWARD CORNELIUS O'LEARY, D.D.

Bishop Emeritus; ordained June 15, 1946; appointed Titular Bishop of Moglaena and Auxiliary November 17, 1970; consecrated January 25, 1971; succeeded to See December 4, 1974; installed December 18, 1974; resigned September 27, 1988. *Res., Cathedral Residence, 307 Congress St., Portland, ME, 04101.*

Chancery: 510 Ocean Ave., P.O. Box 11559, Portland, ME, 04104-7559. Tel.: 207-773-6471; Fax: 207-773-0182.

Most Reverend

MICHAEL RICHARD COTE, D.D.

Auxiliary Bishop of Portland; ordained June 29, 1975; ordained Titular Bishop of Cebarades and Auxiliary Bishop of Portland July 27, 1995. *Mailing Address: P.O. Box 11559, Portland, ME, 04104-7559. Res., Holy Family Rectory, 262 S. Main St., Old Town, ME, 04468.*

ESTABLISHED JULY 29, 1853.

Square Miles 33,040.

Comprises the State of Maine.

Corporate Title: *Roman Catholic Bishop of Portland, a Corporation Sole.*

For the legal titles of other diocesan-related institutions, please consult Chancery.

STATISTICAL OVERVIEW

Personnel	
Bishop	1
Auxiliary Bishops	1
Retired Bishops	1
Priests: Diocesan Active in Diocese	104
Priests: Active Outside Diocese	4
Priests: Retired, Sick or Absent	66
Number of Diocesan Priests	174
Religious Priests in Diocese	45
Extern Priests in Diocese	8
Ordinations:	
Diocesan Priests	1
Transitional Deacons	1
Permanent Deacons in Diocese	19
Total Brothers	30
Total Sisters	416
Parishes	
Parishes	136
With Resident Pastor:	
Resident Diocesan Priests	93
Resident Religious Priests	13
Without Resident Pastor:	
Administered by Priests	28
Administered by Women Religious	1
Administered by Lay People	1
Missions	51
Closed Parishes	2
Professional Ministry Personnel:	
Brothers	1
Sisters	14
Lay Ministers	63
Welfare	
Catholic Hospitals	3
Total Assisted	156,432
Health Care Centers	1
Total Assisted	830
Homes for the Aged	8
Total Assisted	1,025
Day Care and Extended Day Care Centers	4
Total Assisted	353
Special Centers for Social Services	7
Total Assisted	4,116
Other Institutions	1
Total Assisted	12
Educational	
Diocesan Students in Other Seminaries	14
Total Seminarians	14
Colleges and Universities	1
Total Students	3,941
High Schools, Diocesan and Parish	1
Total Students	279
High Schools, Private	2
Total Students	745
Elementary Schools, Diocesan and Parish	17
Total Students	4,032
Elementary Schools, Private	1
Total Students	171
Catechesis/Religious Education:	
High School Students	2,241
Elementary Students	13,812
Total Students Under Catholic Instruction	25,235
Teachers in the Diocese:	
Scholastics	1
Sisters	15
Lay Teachers	252
Vital Statistics	
Receptions into the Church:	
Infant Baptism Totals	2,737
Adult Baptism Totals	354
Received into Full Communion	464
First Communions	3,132
Confirmations	5,589
Marriages:	
Catholic	824
Interfaith	451
Total Marriages	1,275
Deaths	2,782
Total Catholic Population	212,253
Total Population	1,227,927

Former Bishops—The first Bishop-Elect, Very Rev. J. COSKERY V.G.,of Baltimore, declined the nomination.—Rt. Rev. DAVID W. BACON, D.D., cons. April 22, 1855; died Nov. 5, 1874.—Rt. Rev. JAMES AUGUSTINE HEALY, D.D., cons. June 2, 1875; died Aug. 5, 1900.—His Eminence WILLIAM CARDINAL O'CONNELL, cons. Bishop of Portland, May 19, 1901; named Coadjutor Archbishop of Boston, Feb. 8, 1906; succeeded to the See of Boston, Aug. 30, 1907; created Cardinal, Nov. 27, 1911; died April 22, 1944.—Rt. Rev. LOUIS S. WALSH, D.D., cons. Oct. 18, 1906; died May 12, 1924.—Rt. Rev. JOHN GREGORY MURRAY, D.D., ord. April 14, 1900; cons. April 28, 1920; transferred to the Archdiocese of St. Paul, Oct. 29, 1931; died Oct. 11, 1956.—Most Rev. JOSEPH EDWARD MCCARTHY, D.D., ord. July 4, 1903; cons. Aug. 24, 1932; died Sept. 8, 1955.—Most Rev. DANIEL JOSEPH FEENEY, D.D., LL.D., Bishop of Portland; ord. May 21, 1921; appt. Titular Bishop of Sita and Auxiliary of Portland, June 22, 1946; cons. Sept. 12, 1946; Apostolic Administrator of the Diocese; appt. July 27, 1948; Coadjutor "cum jure successionis"; appt. March 4, 1952; succeeded to See, Sept. 8, 1955; died Sept. 15, 1969.—Most Rev. PETER LEO GERETY, D.D., ord. June 29, 1939; appt. March 4, 1966; cons. June 1, 1966; appt. Apostolic Administrator, Feb. 18, 1967; succeeded to See, Sept. 15, 1969; transferred Archdiocese of Newark, April 2, 1974.—Most Rev. EDWARD C. O'LEARY, D.D., ord. June 15, 1946; Titular Bishop of Moglaena and Auxiliary Bishop of Portland; appt. Nov. 17, 1970; cons. Jan. 25, 1971; Apostolic Administrator; appt. June 29, 1974 ninth Bishop of Portland, Dec. 4, 1974; installed Dec. 18, 1974; resigned Sept. 27, 1988.

Vicar General—Most Rev. MICHAEL R. COTE.

Chancery—510 Ocean Ave., P.O. Box 11559, Portland, 04104-7559. Tel: 207-773-6471; Fax: 207-773-0182.

Office Hours: Mon.-Fri. 9-4:30. Closed Holidays.

Co-Chancellors—Rev. MARC B. CARON, S.T.L.; Sr. RITA-MAE BISSONNETTE, R.S.R., J.C.L.

Vice Chancellor—Rev. MARK P. NOLETTE, J.C.L.

Bishop's Delegate for Clergy—Rev. PAUL F. STEFANKO, J.C.L.

Public Affairs—Mr. MARC R. MUTTY.

Diocesan Tribunal—510 Ocean Ave., P.O. Box 11559, Portland, 04104-7559. Tel: 207-773-6471.

Officialis—Rev. PAUL F. STEFANKO, J.C.L.

Promoter of Justice—Rev. MARK P. NOLETTE, J.C.L.

Defenders of the Bond—Sr. RITA-MAE BISSONNETTE, R.S.R., J.C.L.; Sr. CLAUDIA BARBRE, R.S.M., J.C.L.; Rev. PAUL F. STEFANKO, J.C.L.; Sr. ANN KEEVAN, C.S.J., J.C.D.; Rev. MARK P. NOLETTE, J.C.L.; Most Rev. MICHAEL R. COTE, J.C.L., D.D.; Mr. GEORGE G. PAVLOFF, J.C.D.

Advocates—Sr. Claudia Barbre, R.S.M., J.C.L.; Sr. Ann Keevan, C.S.J., J.C.D.; Revs. Mark P. Nolette, J.C.L.; Paul F. Stefanko, J.C.L.; Mr. George G. Pavloff, J.C.D.; Sr. Rita-Mae Bissonnette, R.S.R., J.C.L.

Office Coordinator—Rev. Paul F. Stefanko, J.C.L.

Notaries—Mrs. Najlia Kerrigan; Mrs. Mary Delaney.

Associate Judges—Rev. Msgr. Raymond F. Begin, S.T.L., J.C.D.; Rev. Joseph J. Koury, J.C.D.; Sr. Rita-Mae Bissonnette, R.S.R., J.C.L.; Rev. Mark P. Nolette, J.C.L.; Most Rev. Michael R. Cote, J.C.L., D.D.; Mr. George G. Pavloff, J.C.D.; Rev. Michael J. Henchal, J.C.L.

Guardian—Rev. Marc B. Caron, S.T.L.

Deans—Rev. Msgr. Charles M. Murphy, V.F.; Very Revs. Richard C. Malo, V.F.; Rene T. Mathieu, V.F.; Michael J. Seavey, V.F.; Richard P. Rice, V.F.; Normand Carpentier, V.F.; James S. Plourde, V.F.; Brian D. Blanchette, V.F.; Alfred Jacques, V.F.; Frank J. Murray, V.F.

Diocesan Consultors—Rev. Msgr. Vincent A. Tatarczuk; Rev. Msgr. Charles M. Murphy, V.F.; Revs. Georges J. Plante; Clement D. Thibodeau; Rene T. Mathieu; Most Rev. Michael R. Cote, J.C.L., D.D.; Revs. Marc B. Caron; James J. Morrison; Paul F. Stefanko; John R. Skehan.

Diocesan Offices and Directors

Campaign for Human Development—Ms. Gloria A. Dugan, L.C.S.W., *P.O. Box 10660, Portland, 04104.* Tel: 207-781-8550; Fax: 207-781-8560.

Catholic Stewardship Appeal—Mr. William S. Richard, C.P.A., Dir.; Mrs. Annette DiMillo, Coord., *510 Ocean Ave., P.O. Box 11559, Portland, 04104-7559.* Tel: 207-773-6471.

Catholic Relief Services—Mrs. Carleen E. Cook, *510 Ocean Ave., P.O. Box 11559, Portland, 04104-7559.* Tel: 207-773-6471.

Catholic Schools Office—Sr. Rosemary T. Donohue, S.N.D., Supt., Schools, *510 Ocean Ave., P.O. Box 11559, Portland, 04104-7559.* Tel: 207-773-6471.

Catholic Scouting—Melvin Montpelier, Co-Chm., *36 Smokehouse Cir., South Portland, 04106.* Susan Vogel, Co-Chm., *39 Pillsbury St., South Portland, 04106.*

Catholic Charismatic Renewal Diocesan Liaison—Rev. Richard P. Rice, *144 Lincoln St., Bath, 04530-2198.*

Catholic Charities Maine—Central Services: Gloria A. Dugan, L.C.S.W., A.C.S.W., Exec. Dir.; Mr. Paul L. Morgan, Contracting Dir.; Ms. Bonnie J. Bagley, Svcs. Dir.; Ms. Sandra L. Boyd, Oper. Dir.; Mrs. Kathy Miller, Pub. Rels. Dir., *P.O. Box 10660, Portland, 04104.* Tel: 207-781-8550; Fax: 207-781-8560. Connie Jones, Human Resources Dir., *P.O. Box 10660, Portland, 04104.* Tel: 207-781-8550; Fax: 207-781-8560.

Clergy Benefit Plan-Clergy Pension Plan—Prudential Committee: Most Rev. Joseph J. Gerry, O.S.B., Pres.; Most Rev. Michael R. Cote; Revs. J. Joseph Ford, Chm. Bd. Claude J. Albert, Treas. Normand E. Carpentier, Sec. Members: Rev. Msgr. Paul D. Gleason; Rev.Msgr. Vincent A. Tatarczuk; Revs. Richard R. Ouellette; Lionel G. Chouinard; Georges J. Plante, V.F.; Marcel G. Chouinard; Daniel Greenleaf; Timothy Nadeau; Mark Reinhardt; Marc B. Caron; James E. Knox; George Pelletier; Mr. Timothy R. Cotnoir, Plan Accountant; Ms. Lisa C. Boucher, Plan Admin.

Diocesan Archivist—Sr. Therese Pelletier, S.C.I.M.

Diocesan Board of Education—Mr. Charles Kennedy, Chm.; Sr. Rosemary T. Donohue, S.N.D., Exec. Sec. Kellie M. Pizzo, Recording Sec. Members: Rev. Stephen Concannon; Priscilla Denton; Patricia Adams; Patricia Berthiaume; Joseph Donahue, Esq.; Susan Hudson; Daniel Bastarache; Lisa Braley; Mark Rioux; Rev. Theodore Corley, O.F.M.Cap.; Deborah Sanford; Rev. Richard McLaughlin; Susan Gajewski; Robert Smith.

Diocesan Bureau of Housing—Most Rev. Joseph J. Gerry, O.S.B., Bishop of Portland Pres.; Mr. David P. Twomey, Treas. Robert C. Robinson, Esq., Clerk, *P.O. Box 11559, Portland, 04104-7559.*

Diocesan Council of Priests—Rev. Msgr. Vincent A. Tatarczuk; Rev. Msgr. Robert Lavoie; Revs. Philip A. Tracy; Scott Mower; Georges J. Plante; Alfred Irving; Rene T. Mathieu, Chm. Clement D. Thibodeau; Joseph J. Koury; Francis P. Morin; Walter Gaudreau, S.M.; Raymond Picard; Robert D. Lariviere; Timothy Nadeau; James J. Morrison. Ex Officio: Most Rev. Michael R. Cote, J.C.L., D.D.; Rev. Msgr. Charles M. Murphy, V.F.; Revs. Marc B. Caron; John R. Skehan; Paul F. Stefanko.

Diocesan Director of Pastoral and Educational Services—Rev. John Skehan, *Chancery Office, 510 Ocean Ave., P.O. Box 11559, Portland, 04104-7559.*

Diocesan Finance Council—Most Rev. Joseph J. Gerry, O.S.B.; Most Rev. Michael R. Cote; Rev. Claude Albert; Mr. William Stoloski; Mr. Arthur Bordeuas; Mary Arnold; David Warren; John Deckro, Chm.; Rev. James J. Morrison; Charles Prinn; Gregg H. Ginn; John Schiavi; Richard Roderick; Gregory St. Angelo, Vice Chm.; Sr. Jude Murray, R.S.M.; Mr. Timothy Healy; Mr. Dan Roux; Mr. Edward Snook. Ex Officio Members: Rev. Marc B. Caron; Sr. Rita-Mae Bissonnette, R.S.R. Staff: David P. Twomey, C.P.A., Finance Officer; Mrs. Laurie J. Downey, C.P.A.; Mr. Timothy R. Cotnoir; William S. Richards.

Diocesan Office of Catechetics and Initiation—Barbara A. Smith, Diocesan Dir.; Mrs. Kathy Dyer, Region I Resource Person, *25 Coolidge Ave., Caribou, 04736.* Tel: 207-496-0520. Sr. Catherine Green, R.S.M., Region II Resource Person, *44 Bennoch Rd., P.O. Box 333, Stillwater, 04489-0333.* Tel: 207-827-5257. Region III Resource Persons: Agnes Dinn; James Dinn, *24 Hayford St., Farmingdale, 04344.* Tel: 207-622-2874. Barbara A. Smith, Region IV Resource Person, *Chancery Office, 510 Ocean Ave., P.O. Box 11559, Portland, 04104-7559.* Tel: 207-773-6471.

Diocesan Office of Public Affairs—Mr. Marc R. Mutty, Dir., *510 Ocean Ave., P.O. Box 11559, Portland, 04104-7559.*

Diocesan Office of Ministry to Persons with Disabilities—Ms. Claire P. Blais, *P.O. Box 11559, Portland, 04104-7559.*

Bishop's Delegate for Priests—Rev. Paul F. Stefanko, J.C.L., Dir., *510 Ocean Ave., P.O. Box 11559, Portland, 04104-7559.* Tel: 207-773-6471.

Diocesan Office of Small Christian Communities—Ms. Barbara A. Smith, Coord., *P.O. Box 11559, Portland, 04104-7559.* Tel: 207-773-6471.

Diocesan Office for Worship—Rev. Marc B. Caron, S.T.L., Dir., *510 Ocean Ave., P.O. Box 11559, Portland, 04104-7559.* Tel: 207-773-6471.

Diocesan Office of Youth Ministry—Mrs. Jeanne S. Bigelow, Dir. Youth Ministry Regional Coordinators: Region I, Karen Ouellette. Tel: 207-834-8355; Fax: 207-834-6835. Region II, William Romano, *P.O. Box 623, Waterville, 04901.* Tel: 207-862-6149; Fax: 207-862-4041. Region III, Veronica Carbonneau, *357 Fairway Dr., Auburn, 04210.* Tel: 207-782-2696; Fax: 207-782-2696.

Financial Management—Mr. David P. Twomey, Finance Officer; Mrs. Laurie J. Downey, C.P.A., Controller; Mr. Timothy R. Cotnoir, Asst. Controller, *510 Ocean Ave., P.O. Box 11559, Portland, 04104-7559.* Tel: 207-773-6471.

General Counsel—Mr. Robert C. Robinson, *12 Portland Pier, P.O. Box 568, Portland, 04112-0568.*

Maine Diocesan Council of Catholic Women—Most Rev. Joseph J. Gerry, Episcopal Chm.; Rev. Lawrence Conley, V.F., Diocesan Moderator, *St. Catherine Parish, 29 Paris St., Norway, 04268-1132.* Mrs. Jeanne P. Stephens, Diocesan Pres.

Newman Apostolate—Rev. Joseph J. Koury, J.C.D., Coord. Pastoral Assocs.: Revs. Philip A. Tracy; Lawrence Conley; Roger P. Chabot; James Murphy, C.S.C.; Michael Sheridan; Stephen Concannon; John F. O'Hara; John J. Topaz, O.F.M.Cap.; Sr. Mary Sweeney; Sr. Sylvia Comer; Ms. Rachel Nelson.

Vicar for Religious—Most Rev. Michael R. Cote.

Personnel Board—Revs. John R. Skehan; Michael J. Henchal, J.C.L.; Andrew Dubois; Paul Coughlin; Frank Murray; Paul F. Stefanko, J.C.L.; Marc B. Caron; Very Revs. Rene T. Mathieu, V.F.; Michael J. Seavey, V.F.; Revs. Lawrence J. Conley; Claude Gendreau; Normand Carpentier. Officio Members: Most Rev. Joseph J. Gerry, Pres.; Most Rev. Michael R. Cote, Vice Pres.; Rev. Msgr. Charles M. Murphy, V.F., Dir., Seminarians.

Pontifical Association of Holy Childhood—Mrs. Carleen E. Cook, Dir., *510 Ocean Ave., P.O. Box 11559, Portland, 04104-7559.* Tel: 207-773-6471.

Pontifical Society for the Propagation of the Faith—Mrs. Carleen E. Cook.

Seminarians, Director of—Rev. Msgr. Charles M. Murphy, V.F., *510 Ocean Ave., P.O. Box 11559, Portland, 04104-7559.* Tel: 207-773-6471.

Vocations—Revs. Daniel P. Greenleaf, Diocesan Dir., *St. Dominic Regional High School, 179 Blake St., Lewiston, 04240.* Tel: 207-782-6911; Fax: 207-795-6439., *Res., St. Patrick Rectory, 1 Walnut St., Lewiston, 04240.*

CLERGY, PARISHES, MISSIONS AND PAROCHIAL SCHOOLS

CITY OF PORTLAND
(Cumberland County)

1—Cathedral of the Immaculate Conception, Rev. James L. Nadeau, Rector. In res., Most Revs. Edward C. O'Leary, (Retired); Michael R. Cote; Revs. Robert E. Lee; Albin A. Andrus; Patrick J. Barrett; Harold D. Moreshead; Joseph E. Whitlock; Vincent McCann, M.H.H.; Marc B. Caron.
Res., 307 Congress St., 04101-3695. Tel: 207-773-7746 (Rectory); 774-5101 (Res.); Fax: 207-879-5547.
School—14 Locust St., 04101. Tel: 207-775-1491. Sr. Theresa Rand, R.S.M., Prin.
Sisters of Mercy 1; Sisters of the Holy Rosary 1; Lay Teachers 10; Students 211.
Catechesis/Religious Programs—Tel: 207-772-6597. Donna Lebel, D.R.E.
Students 125.

2—St. Dominic's. Merged to form Sacred Heart/St. Dominic's, Portland.

3—St. Joseph's, Revs. Patrick Glavin, O.F.M.Cap.; Don Bosco Duquette, O.F.M.Cap.; Theodosius Corley, O.F.M.Cap.; John Tokaz, O.F.M.Cap.; Anthony Egan, O.F.M.Cap.
Res., 673 Stevens Ave., 04103. Tel: 207-797-7026; Fax: 207-797-2679.
School—697 Stevens Ave., 04103. Tel: 207-797-7073; Fax: 207-797-7078. Ms. Lori Ann Lee, Prin.
Sisters of Mercy 1; Lay Teachers 14; Students 246.
Catechesis/Religious Programs—Tel: 207-797-9509. D.R.E.: Marha Turner; Sylvia Harlow.
Students 250.

4—St. Louis (Polish), Rev. Ireneusz Chodakowski, M.I.C.
Res., 279 Danforth St., 04102. Tel: 207-773-4176.

5—St. Patrick's, Revs. Coleman P. O'Toole; John D. Civiello.
Res., 1342 Congress St., 04102. Tel: 207-772-6325.
School—1251 Congress St., 04102. Tel: 207-772-2521; Fax: 207-828-8917. Mrs. Barbara Ann Arnoldo, Prin.
Sisters of Mercy 1; Lay Teachers 11; Students 208.
Catechesis/Religious Programs—Tel: 207-772-3521. Cynthia McGarry, D.R.E.
Students 208.

6—St. Peter's (Italian), Rev. Roland V. Petinge, O.F.M.; Bro. Mark Brown, O.F.M.
Res., 72 Federal St., 04101. Tel: 207-773-0748; Fax: 207-879-0557.
Catechesis/Religious Programs—Bro. Mark Brown, D.R.E.
Students 160.

7—Sacred Heart/St. Dominic. Merged with St. Dominic, Portland. Rev. Frederick H. Morse.
Res., 80 Sherman St., 04101-2216. Tel: 207-772-6182; Fax: 207-772-9615.
Catechesis/Religious Programs—Students 38.

8—St. Christopher's (Peaks Island), Rev. Frederick H. Morse.
15 Central St., P.O. Box 37, Peaks Island, 04108-0037. Tel: 207-766-2585; 772-9615.
Mailing Address: 80 Sherman St., 04101.
Catechesis/Religious Programs—Students 15.
Mission—Long Island, Great Diamond Island.

9—St. Pius X, Revs. Arthur H. Pare, S.J., Pastor; Robert F. Regan, S.J. In res., Rev. John W. Keegan, S.J.
Res., 492 Ocean Ave., 04103. Tel: 207-775-3032; Fax: 207-874-7514.
Catechesis/Religious Programs—Tel: 207-775-2185. Donna Beattie, D.R.E.
Students 220.

OUTSIDE THE CITY OF PORTLAND

Ashland, Aroostook Co., St. Mark's, Rev. Scott Mower.
Res., 68 School St., P.O. Box 190, 04732-0190. Tel: 207-435-3591. [CEM]
Catechesis/Religious Programs—Tel: 207-435-6440.
Students 35.
Missions—Portage, Our Lady of the Lakes; Washburn, St. Catherine.

Auburn, Androscoggin Co., St. Louis, Revs. Gerald A. Levesque; Louis J. Phillips.
Mailing Address: Auburn Catholic Community, P.O. Box 828, 04212-0828.
Res., 267 Minot Ave., 04210. Tel: 207-782-8096; Fax: 207-777-6307.
Catechesis/Religious Programs—Tel: 207-784-0012.
Students 22.
Parish Center—101 Second St., 04210.

St. Philip's, Revs. Gerald A. Levesque; Louis J. Phillips.
Mailing Address: Auburn Catholic Community, P.O. Box 828, 04212-0828.
Res., 365 Turner Rd., 04210-8410. Tel: 207-784-6486; Fax: 207-784-6487.
Catechesis/Religious Programs—Students 79.

Sacred Heart, Revs. Gerald A. Levesque; Louis J. Phillips; Sr. Elizabeth Platt, C.O.C., Pastoral Assoc. & RCIA Coord.

Mailing Address: Auburn Catholic Community, P.O. Box 828, 04212-0828.
Res., 267 Minot Ave., 04210. Tel: 207-782-8096; Fax: 207-782-8096.
Catechesis/Religious Programs—Sandra Tardiff, D.R.E., Tel: 207-786-9045.
Students 106.

Augusta, Kennebec Co., St. Mary's, Rev. Michael P. Gendreau. In res., Deacon Dean Lachance.
Res., 41 Western Ave., P.O. Box 555, 04332-0555. Tel: 207-623-8823; Fax: 207-623-7574. [CEM 2]
School—56 Sewall St., 04332. Tel: 207-623-3491; Fax: 207-626-5818. Sr. Barbara Brennan, R.S.M., Prin.
Sisters of Mercy 2; Lay Teachers 11; Students 264.
Catechesis/Religious Programs—D.R.E.: Mary-Ellen Mahon Tel: 207-626-5940; Monique Lemieuv, (Grades K-5); Melanie Baillargeon, (Grades 6-12).
Students 120.

St. Andrew's, Rev. Michael J. Seavey.
Res., St. Andrew St., R.F.D. 12, Box 1350, 04330-9752. Tel: 207-623-8543; Fax: 207-626-0287.
Catechesis/Religious Programs—Tel: 207-623-3159. Majorie H. Gallagher, D.R.E.
Students 70.

St. Augustine's, Rev. Richard E. St. Cyr.
Res., One Kendall St., 04330. Tel: 207-622-2184; Fax: 207-621-4064. [CEM 2]
School—24 Washington St., 04330. Tel: 207-622-1771. Sr. Rachel Boucher, Prin.
Sisters of the Presentation of Mary 2; Lay Teachers 9; Students 190.
Catechesis/Religious Programs—Tel: 207-621-4075. Lisa Couture, D.R.E.
Students 116.

Baileyville, Washington Co., St. James the Greater, Rev. Francis P. Morin, Sacramental Min.; Ms. Patricia Phillips, Parish Coord.
Res., 56 Summit St., P.O. Box 369, 04694-0369. Tel: 207-427-6908; Fax: 207-427-6908.
Catechesis/Religious Programs—Tel: 207-427-3481. Ms. Mary White, D.R.E.
Students 79.

Bangor, Penobscot Co., St. John's, Revs. Gerard G. Gosselin; Richard M. O'Brien. Pastoral Assocs.: Sr. Celestine Theriault, R.S.M.; Mr. Andre Vigneault. In res., Rev. John J. Austin.
Res., 207 York St., 04401. Tel: 207-942-6941; Fax: 207-947-5984.
School—All Saints Catholic School, P.O. Box 1749, 04401. Tel: 207-947-7063; Fax: 207-942-2398. Mr. John O'Connor, Prin.
Lay Teachers 13; Students 282.
Catechesis/Religious Programs—Tel: 207-945-0023. Joan Winstead, D.R.E.
Students 350.

St. Mary's, Rev. Frank J. Murray.
Res., 768 Ohio St., 04401-3106. Tel: 207-945-5018; Fax: 207-942-9781.
School—All Saints Catholic School of St. John's.
Catechesis/Religious Programs—Tel: 207-942-1643.
Students 400.

Bar Harbor, Hancock Co., Holy Redeemer, Rev. Joseph E. Daniels.
Res., 21 Ledgelawn Ave., 04609-1303. Tel: 207-288-3535; Fax: 207-288-3324. [CEM]
Catechesis/Religious Programs—Tel: 207-288-3421.
Students 47.

Bath, Sagadahoc Co., St. Mary, Rev. Richard P. Rice.
Res., 144 Lincoln St., 04530-2198. Tel: 207-443-3423.
Catechesis/Religious Programs—Tel: 207-443-4987. Nancy Lewis, D.R.E.
Students 139.

Belfast, Waldo Co., St. Francis of Assisi, Rev. Costanzo J. Piselli.
Res. & Mailing Address—81 Court St., 04915-6134. Tel: 207-338-4433; Fax: 207-338-9846.
Catechesis/Religious Programs—Tel: 207-338-9846.
Students 145.
Mission—Isleboro, St. Mary of the Isles.

Benedicta, Aroostook Co., St. Benedict's, Rev. Alfred Irving.
Res., P.O. Box 27, 04733-0024. Tel: 207-365-4128. [CEM]
Catechesis/Religious Programs—Tel: 207-365-4269. Anna Robinson, D.R.E.
Students 75.
Mission—Sherman Station, Penobscot Co., St. Joseph's Church, P.O. Box 27, Sherman Station, 04733.

Berwick, York Co., Our Lady of Peace, Rev. Hilary J. Cameron.
Res., 25 Berwick St., 03901-2109. Tel: 207-698-1072.
Catechesis/Religious Programs—Students 105.

Biddeford, York Co., St. Andre's, Rev. Reginald R. Brissette.
Mailing Address: 41 Sullivan St., 04005.
Res., 73 Bacon St., 04005. Tel: 207-282-3333; Fax: 207-286-8679. [JC]
School—St. James School. See St. Joseph's for details.
Catechesis/Religious Programs—Twinned with St. Joseph, Biddeford.

St. Joseph's, Rev. Renald D. Labarre; Sr. June Rita Fortier, S.C.I.M. In res., Revs. Raymond D. Auger; Patrick Martin.
Office—41 Sullivan St., P.O. Box 408, 04005. Tel: 207-282-9352; Fax: 207-286-8679.
Res., 43 Center St., 04005. Tel: 207-282-4817.
School—New Consolidated School - St. James, (Grades K-8) 25 Graham St., 04007. Tel: 207-282-4084. Ms. Marie Klement, Prin.
Sisters 1; Lay Teachers 28; Students 450.
Catechesis/Religious Programs—Tel: 207-282-4812. D.R.E.: Nancy P. Labbe, Pastoral Assoc.; Jeanne O'Keefe; Mary Milton.
Students 198.

St. Mary's, Rev. Brendan G. Harnett, Admin.
Office: 41 Sullivan St., 04005.
Res., P.O.Box 515, 04005. Tel: 207-284-5363; Fax: 207-286-8679. [CEM]
School—St. James School. See St. Joseph's for details. Tel: 207-282-4084.
Catechesis/Religious Programs—Twinned with St. Joseph, Biddeford.
Mission—Biddeford Pool, York Co., St. Brendan.

Bingham, Somerset Co., St. Peter's, Rev. Maurice N. Morin.
Res., Owens St., Box No. 667, 04920. Tel: 207-672-3912.
Catechesis/Religious Programs—Students 20.
Mission—West Forks, SS. Philip & James.

Boothbay Harbor, Lincoln Co., Our Lady, Queen of Peace, Rev. Raymond Picard.
Res., 82 Atlantic Ave., 04538-0165. Tel: 207-633-2680; Fax: 207-633-1164.
Catechesis/Religious Programs—Students 50.

Bradley, Penobscot Co., St. Ann, Rev. Paul R. Kearns.
Mailing Address: P.O. Box 137, 04411.
Res., 68 Main St., 04411. Tel: 207-827-2087. [JC]
Catechesis/Religious Programs—Tel: 207-827-7643. Mary Shorette, D.R.E.
Students 41.

Brewer, Penobscot Co., St. Joseph's, Rev. Joel R. Cyr.
Res., 531 N. Main St., 04412. Tel: 207-989-5388; Fax: 207-989-5343. [JC]
Catechesis/Religious Programs—Tel: 207-989-5343.
Students 130.

St. Teresa's, Rev. Joel R. Cyr. In res., Revs. Paul R. Marquis; Richard M. O'Brien.
Res., 440 S. Main St., 04412. Tel: 207-989-7049; Fax: 207-989-4992.
Catechesis/Religious Programs—Tel: 207-989-6129.
Students 103.

Bridgton, Cumberland Co., St. Joseph, Rev. Robert C. Vaillencourt.
Mailing Address: P.O. Box 310, 04009-0310. Tel: 207-647-2334.
Catechesis/Religious Programs—Tel: 207-925-3138.
Students 95.
Mission—Fryeburg, Oxford Co., St. Elizabeth Ann Seton, P.O. Box 332, Fryeburg, 04037. Tel: 207-935-4245.

Brownville Junction, Piscataquis Co., St. Francis Xavier, Rev. James P. Robichaud, O.M.I.; Deacon John Guerin, Pastoral Assoc.
Res., Front St., Box 385, 04415. Tel: 207-965-2341; Fax: 207-965-2341.
Catechesis/Religious Programs—Tel: 207-943-5160. Deborah Moulton, D.R.E.
Students 14.
Mission—Milo, St. Paul.

Brunswick, Cumberland Co., St. John the Baptist, Revs. Walter Gaudreau, S.M.; Edward Sheehan, S.M.; Kenneth Ridgeway, S.M.
Res., 39 Pleasant St., 04011. Tel: 207-725-8756; Fax: 207-798-4792. [CEM]
School—St. John's School, 39 Pleasant St., 04011. Tel: 207-725-5507. Mr. Edward P. Buckley, Prin.
Lay Teachers 22; Students 238.
Catechesis/Religious Programs—Tel: 207-729-5966. Carolyn Ruggles, D.R.E.
Students 160.
Mission—Pejepscot, Topsham Co., St. Andrew, Rte. 196, Pejepscot, 04086.

St. Charles, Rev. Stephen F. Concannon.
Office: 132 McKeen St., 04011. Tel: 207-725-2624; Fax: 207-725-4436.
Catechesis/Religious Programs—Tel: 207-725-4436.
Students 354.

Mission—Harpswell, Cumberland Co., St. Katharine Drexel.

Bucksport, Hancock Co., St. Vincent de Paul, Rev. John F. O'Hara, V.F.
Res., 158 Franklin St., P.O. Box S, 04416. Tel: 207-469-3322. [CEM]
Catechesis/Religious Programs—MaryAnn Ullo, D.R.E.
Students 93.

Calais, Washington Co., Immaculate Conception, Rev. Brian D. Blanchette.
Res., 17 Calais Ave., 04619. Tel: 207-454-3413.
Catechesis/Religious Programs—Leah McLean, D.R.E.
Students 109.

Camden, Knox Co., Our Lady of Good Hope, Rev. Eugene F. Gaffey.
Res., 7 Union St., 04843. Tel: 207-236-4785; Fax: 207-236-9422.
Catechesis/Religious Programs—Tel: 207-236-4889.
Students 114.
Mission—North Haven, Our Lady of Peace.
Station—Vinalhaven, Our Lady of Peace.

Cape Elizabeth, Cumberland Co., St. Bartholomew, Rev. Michael J. Henchal; Deacon John S. Brennan.
Res., 8 Two Lights Rd., 04107. Tel: 207-799-5528; Fax: 207-799-1532.
Catechesis/Religious Programs—Students 255.

Caribou, Aroostook Co., Holy Rosary, Rev. Leopold G. Nicknair. In res., Rev. Msgr. Gilman J. Chaloult.
Res., 31 Thomas Ave., P.O. Box 625, 04736. Tel: 207-498-2536; Fax: 207-498-2537.
Catechesis/Religious Programs—Tel: 207-498-8655. D.R.E.: Michael McCormack; Gail Langley.
Students 165.

Sacred Heart, Rev. Joachim Thanh Nguyen.
Res., 1143 Van Buren Rd., 04736. Tel: 207-498-2763.
Catechesis/Religious Programs—Betty Thompson, D.R.E., Tel: 207-498-8741.
Students 68.

Daigle, Aroostook Co., Holy Family. Closed. For inquiries for parish records please contact St. Louis, Fort Kent.

Dexter, Penobscot Co., St. Anne's, Rev. Raymond P. Morency.
Res., 59 Free St., 04930. Tel: 207-924-7104.
Catechesis/Religious Programs—Tel: 207-924-7993.
Students 49.

Dover-Foxcroft, Piscataquis Co., St. Thomas, Rev. James P. Robichaud, O.M.I.
Res., 45 High St., 04426. Tel: 207-564-2842.
Catechesis/Religious Programs—Tel: 207-564-0867. Louise DuLac, D.R.E.
Students 60.
Mission—Sangerville, Holy Family.

Eagle Lake, Aroostook Co., St. Mary's, Rev. James R. Albert.
Res., Church St., 04739. Tel: 207-444-5119. [CEM]
Catechesis/Religious Programs—Tel: 207-444-6083. Mildred Pelletier, D.R.E.
Students 68.

East Millinocket, Penobscot Co., St. Peter's, Rev. Richard C. Malo; Deacon Daniel Watson.
Res., 56 Cedar St., P.O. Box 400, 04430. Tel: 207-746-3333; Fax: 207-746-8188.
Catechesis/Religious Programs—Julie Fiske, D.R.E.
Students 80.

Eastport, Washington Co., St. Joseph, Rev. Paul M. Sullivan, S.J.
Res., 51 Washington St., 04631. Tel: 207-853-2825. [JC]
Catechesis/Religious Programs—Students 24.
Mission—Pembroke, St. John the Evangelist.

Ellsworth, Hancock Co., St. Joseph's, Rev. Leo James Michaud.
Res., 231 Main St., 04605. Tel: 207-667-2342; Fax: 207-667-2043. [CEM]
Catechesis/Religious Programs—Students 102.
Missions—Green Lake, Our Lady of the Lake; Winter Harbor, St. Margaret.

Fairfield, Somerset Co., Immaculate Heart of Mary, Rev. Marcel L. Dumoulin; Kimberly Suttie, Pastoral Assoc.
Res., 21 High St., 04937. Tel: 207-453-6131; Fax: 207-453-8334.
Catechesis/Religious Programs—Tel: 207-453-7940.
Students 153.

Falmouth, Cumberland Co., Holy Martyrs, Rev. Msgr. Charles M. Murphy, S.T.D.; Deacon Dennis J. Popadak.
Catechesis/Religious Programs—266 Foreside Rd., 04105. Tel: 207-781-4573; Fax: 207-781-3961.
Students 483.

Farmington, Franklin Co., St. Joseph's, Rev. Roger P. Chabot.
Mailing Address: c/o The Pastoral Center, 133 Middle St., 04938-1598. Tel: 207-778-2778; Fax: 207-778-0268.
Catechesis/Religious Programs—David Levensalor, D.R.E.
Students 128.

Fort Fairfield, Aroostook Co., St. Denis, Rev. William J. Carrigg, Admin.
Res., 43 Main St., 04742-1223. Tel: 207-473-7329. [CEM 2]
Catechesis/Religious Programs—Students 95.

Fort Kent, Aroostook Co., St. Louis, Rev. James S. Plourde.
Res., 11 E. Main St., 04743. Tel: 207-834-5656; Fax: 207-834-7461. [CEM]
Catechesis/Religious Programs—Tel: 207-834-3970. D.R.E.: Ziona Straub, (Grades K-6/SPRED); Irene Harvey, (Grades 7-12); Nancy Thibodeau.
Students 610.

Frenchville, Aroostook Co., St. Luce's (Upper), Rev. Claude R. Gendreau.
Mailing Address: P.O. Box 98, 04745-0098. Tel: 207-543-7313; Fax: 207-543-9332. [CEM]
Catechesis/Religious Programs—Tel: 207-543-7313. Marie Textor, D.R.E.
Students 199.

Gardiner, Kennebec Co., St. Joseph's, Rev. Clement D. Thibodeau. In res., Rev. Robert P. Bouchard.
Res., One Lincoln Ave., 04345-2188. Tel: 207-582-2385; Fax: 207-588-0650. [CEM]
Catechesis/Religious Programs—Tel: 207-582-1149.
Students 320.

Gorham, Cumberland Co., St. Anne, Rev. Lawrence J. Conley.
Res., 299 Main St., 04038. Tel: 207-839-4857; 839-3082; Fax: 207-839-3082.
Catechesis/Religious Programs—Tel: 207-839-3082; Fax: 207-839-4857. Claire Sirois, D.R.E.
Students 370.
Mission—East Sebago, Our Lady of Sebago.

Grand Isle, Aroostook Co., St. Gerard-Mt. Carmel, Rev. Richard R. Ouellette.
Res., 04746. Tel: 207-895-3436. [CEM]
Catechesis/Religious Programs—Verna Beaulieu, D.R.E.
Students 74.

Gray, Cumberland Co., St. Gregory, Rev. Msgr. Robert G. Lavoie.
Res., 24 N. Raymond Rd., P.O. Box 345, 04039-0345. Tel: 207-657-4241.
Catechesis/Religious Programs—Tel: 207-657-5659.
Students 130.

Greenville, Piscataquis Co., Holy Family, Rev. Eddy J. Morin.
Res., Pritham Rd., P.O. Box 457, 04441-0457. Tel: 207-695-2262.
Catechesis/Religious Programs—Tel: 207-695-2009. Lucy Fay, D.R.E.
Students 30.
Mission—Rockwood, Somerset Co., St. Joseph's. [CEM]

Hallowell, Kennebec Co., Sacred Heart, Rev. George W. Hickey.
Res., 12 Summer St., 04347. Tel: 207-623-3424.
Catechesis/Religious Programs—Tel: 207-623-3807. Michael Gilbert, D.R.E.
Students 80.

Hamlin, Aroostook Co., St. Joseph, Revs. Joseph S. Chasse, S.M.; David Lajoie, S.M.; Robert McDonald, S.M.; Souvenir Jean-Paul, S.M.
Res., 336 Main St., Van Buren, 04785. Tel: 207-868-2718. [CEM]
Catechesis/Religious Programs—Tel: 207-868-2835.
Students 10.

Hampden, Penobscot Co., St. Matthew, Rev. Jean Paul Labrie.
Res., 70 Western Ave., P.O. Box 280, 04444. Tel: 207-862-3517; Fax: 207-862-4576.
Catechesis/Religious Programs—Tel: 207-862-5404. Mrs. Pam Smith, D.R.E.
Students 175.

Houlton, Aroostook Co., St. Mary's, Rev. L. Philip Cyr; Sr. Carol Martin, P.F.M., Pastoral Assoc.
Res., 112 Military St., 04730. Tel: 207-532-2871; Fax: 207-532-4401.
Catechesis/Religious Programs—Students 291.

Howland, Penobscot Co., St. Leo, Rev. Andre L. Houle, O.M.I.
P.O. Box 329, 04448. Tel: 207-732-3495; Fax: 207-732-5112. [CEM]
Catechesis/Religious Programs—Tel: 207-732-4636.
Students 60.

Indian Township, Washington Co., St. Ann (1929), Rev. Francis P. Morin; Deacon George Stevens, Jr.
Church—P.O. Box 358, 04668-0358. Tel: 207-796-5013.
Mission—Indian Township, St. Theresa's Chapel.

Island Falls, Aroostook Co., St. Agnes, Rev. Alfred Irving.
Mailing Address: P.O. Box 27, Benedicta, 04733-0027. Tel: 207-365-4128. [CEM]
Catechesis/Religious Programs—Students 15.
Mission—Patten, St. Paul.

Jackman, Somerset Co., St. Anthony, Rev. William F. Modlin.
Mailing Address: P.O. Box 338, 04945-0338.
Res., 04945. Tel: 207-668-2881. [CEM]
Catechesis/Religious Programs—Students 63.

Jay, Franklin Co., St. Rose of Lima, Rev. Richard E. Senghas.
Res., One Church St., 04239. Tel: 207-897-2173; Fax: 207-897-2478.
Catechesis/Religious Programs—Tel: 207-897-3940.
Students 110.

Kennebunk, York Co., St. Martha's, Rev. Laurent R. Laplante.
Res., 34 Portland Rd., P.O. Box 510, 04043. Tel: 207-985-6252; Fax: 207-985-7740.
Catechesis/Religious Programs—Mrs. Rosanne Smith, D.R.E.
Students 280.

Kittery, York Co., St. Raphael's, Rev. Real J. Nadeau.
Res., 6 Whipple Rd., 03904-1739. Tel: 207-439-0442; Fax: 207-439-0442.
Catechesis/Religious Programs—Faith Formation Center, 6 Whipple Rd., 03904-1739.
Students 128.

Lewiston, Androscoggin Co.,

1—St. Joseph's, Rev. Richard McLaughlin.
Res., 253 Main St., 04240. Tel: 207-784-5328; Fax: 207-795-5078. [JC]
School—393 Main St., 04240. Tel: 207-784-8811; Fax: 207-783-9522. Mrs. Andree Tostevin, Prin.
Lay Teachers 15; Students 213.
Catechesis/Religious Programs—Tel: 207-782-2286. Connie Ayotte, D.R.E.
Students 101.

2—Holy Cross, Revs. Rene T. Mathieu; Wilfred P. Labbe.
Res., 16 Ste. Croix St., P.O. Box 1540, 04241-1540. Tel: 207-782-9463; Fax: 207-782-5968. [JC]
School—17 Baird St., 04241. Tel: 207-783-9323. Ms. Patricia Berthiaume, Prin.
Sisters 2; Lay Teachers 29; Students 468.
Catechesis/Religious Programs—Tel: 207-783-7241. Ms. Ruth Oakley, D.R.E.
Students 280.

3—Holy Family, Rev. Andrew DuBois; Doreen Gagne, Pastoral Assoc.
Res., 607 Sabattus St., 04240. Tel: 207-782-8928; Fax: 207-782-3179.
Catechesis/Religious Programs—Tel: 207-783-7330. Marie Beaulieu, D.R.E.
Students 275.

4—St. Mary's. Closed.

5—St. Patrick's, Revs. Robert D. Lariviere; Roland P. Nadeau. In res., Revs. Bertrand R. Poussard; Daniel P. Greenleaf.
Pastoral Center: 135 Ash St., 04240. Tel: 207-777-1200.
Res., 220 Bates St., 04240. Tel: 207-782-1997. [CEM]
Catechesis/Religious Programs—Fax: 207-786-9223. Rita Desjarding, D.R.E.
Students 25.

6—SS. Peter and Paul, Revs. Robert D. Lariviere; Roland P. Nadeau.
Mailing Address: 135 Ash St., 04240. Tel: 207-777-1200; Fax: 207-786-9223.
Res., 220 Bates St., 04240.
School—135 Western Ave., Auburn, 04210. Tel: 207-782-0721; Fax: 207-782-0110. Sr. Margaret Walsh, R.S.M., Prin.
Lay Teachers 10; Students 143.
Catechesis/Religious Programs—Rita Desjarding, D.R.E.
Students 50.

Limerick, York Co., St. Matthew, Rev. Richard A. Nadeau.
Res., 19 Dora Ln., 04048. Tel: 207-793-2244; Fax: 207-793-2191.
Catechesis/Religious Programs—Tel: 207-642-3231; Fax: 207-286-2349. Marc Hildreth, D.R.E.
Students 245.

Limestone, Aroostook Co., St. Louis, Rev. William J. Carrigg, Admin.; Janet Beckwith, Pastoral Assoc. In res., Rev. L. Chanel Cyr.
Res., 302 Main St., 04750-1116. Tel: 207-325-4843.
Catechesis/Religious Programs—Tel: 207-325-4656.
Students 94.

Lincoln, Penobscot Co., St. Mary, Revs. Myles Cyr, O.M.I.; Roger Cyr; Deacon Thomas Krapf.
Res., 168 Main St., 04457. Tel: 207-794-6333; Fax: 207-794-8044.
Catechesis/Religious Programs—Carl Cooper, D.R.E.
Students 90.
Missions—Kingman, St. James; Winn, Sacred Heart; Danforth, St. Ann; Vanceboro, Guardian Angel.

Lisbon, Androscoggin Co., St. Anne's. Merged with Holy Family and SS. Cyril and Methodius to form Holy Trinity, Lisbon Falls.

Lisbon Falls, Androscoggin Co., Holy Trinity (1995), Rev. Lionel G. Chouinard.
Res., 51 Main St., 04252-1597. Tel: 207-353-2792 (Office); Fax: 207-353-6192. [CEM 3]
Catechesis/Religious Programs—Tel: 207-353-6306.
Students 80.

SS. Cyril and Methodius (Slovak). Merged with St. Anne's and Holy Family to form Holy Trinity, Lisbon Falls.

Lubec, Washington Co., Sacred Heart, Rev. Richard A. Lembo.
Res., 19 Church St., 04652. Tel: 207-733-2214.
Catechesis/Religious Programs—Tel: 207-853-2494.
Students 6.
Mission—Campobello, St. Timothy's, New Brunswick, Canada E09 3H0.

Lyman, York Co., St. Philip, Rev. Thomas M. Lee.
Res., 404 Goodwins Mills Rd., 04002. Tel: 207-499-2940. [JC]
Catechesis/Religious Programs—Lucille Prescott, D.R.E.
Students 92.

Machias, Washington Co., Holy Name of Jesus, Rev. Michael J. Sheridan, Admin.
Res., 11 Free St., P.O. Box 248, 04654. Tel: 207-255-3731; Fax: 207-255-3337.
Catechesis/Religious Programs—Dan Hogan, D.R.E.
Students 46.
Mission—Cherryfield, St. Michael's.

Madawaska, Aroostook Co., St. David's, Rev. Richard R. Ouellette.
Res., 774 Main St., 04756. Tel: 207-728-3366. [CEM]
Catechesis/Religious Programs—Tel: 207-728-4012. Sharon M. Oullettte, D.R.E.
Students 108.

St. Thomas Aquinas, Rev. John L. Audibert.
Mailing Address: P.O. Box 128, 04756. Tel: 207-728-7531; Fax: 207-728-4217. [CEM]
Catechesis/Religious Programs—Tel: 207-728-7135. Ann Marie Clavette, D.R.E.
Students 314.

Madison, Somerset Co., St. Sebastian, Rev. Georges J. Plante; Elisabeth Crowley, Pastoral Assoc.
Res., 149 Main St., 04950-1599. Tel: 207-696-3203. [CEM]
Catechesis/Religious Programs—Tel: 207-696-3206; Fax: 207-696-5560.
Students 82.

Mars Hill, Aroostook Co., St. Joseph, Rev. Thomas Lequin.
Mailing Address: St. Mary's Rectory, P.O. Box 813, Presque Isle, 04769. Tel: 207-768-3671; 429-9805 (Church).
Catechesis/Religious Programs—Tel: 207-764-0161; Fax: 207-764-8092.
Students 13.

Mechanic Falls, Androscoggin Co., Our Lady of Ransom, Rev. Antonio Amato.
Res., 117 Elm St., P.O. Box 206, 04256. Tel: 207-345-2691.
Catechesis/Religious Programs—D.R.E.: Sandy Ferland; Judy Emch; Ellen Theriault.
Students 80.
Mission—Mechanic Falls, Oxford Co., St. Mary, P.O. Box 206, 04256.

Mexico, Oxford Co., St. Theresa, Rev. L. Joseph Lange.
Res., 3 Brown St., 04257. Tel: 207-364-2593. [JC]
Catechesis/Religious Programs—Kathleen Bisson, D.R.E.
Students 28.
Mission—Dixfield, St. Joseph.

Millinocket, Penobscot Co., St. Martin of Tours, Rev. Richard C. Malo; Deacon Daniel Watson.
Mailing Address: 112 Maine Ave., 04462.
Res., 18 Colby St., 04462. Tel: 207-723-5902 (Office); 723-9533 (Rectory); Fax: 207-723-5902.
Catechesis/Religious Programs—Tel: 207-723-9904. Paula Miller, D.R.E.
Students 170.

Newcastle, Lincoln Co., St. Patrick, Rev. Raymond Picard.
Mailing Address: P.O. Box 598, 04553. Tel: 207-563-3240. [CEM]
Catechesis/Religious Programs—St. Patrick's Parish Ctr., Academy Hill Rd., 04553. Tel: 207-563-6038.
Students 74.

Northeast Harbor, Hancock Co., St. Ignatius, Rev. Joseph E. Daniels; Deacon Joseph LaPlante.
Res., 21 Ledgelawn Ave., Bar Harbor, 04609-1303. Tel: 207-288-3535; Fax: 207-288-3324.
Catechesis/Religious Programs—436 Seawall Rd, 04679. Tel: 207-244-0445.
Students 29.
Missions—Islesford, Our Lady Star of the Sea; Manset, St. Peter's.

North Vassalboro, Kennebec Co., St. Bridget's, Rev. Joseph W. Cahill.
Mailing Address: P.O. Box 159, 04962. Tel: 207-873-3204; Fax: 207-861-8182.
Catechesis/Religious Programs—Tel: 207-465-9751. Mrs. Anna M. Anderson, D.R.E.
Students 98.
Mission—China Lake, St. Peter.

Norway, Oxford Co., St. Catherine of Sienna, Rev. Maurice T. Lebel.
Res., 32 Paris St., 04268-1132. Tel: 207-743-2606; Fax: 207-743-6601.
Catechesis/Religious Programs—Students 107.
Mission—Bethel, Oxford Co., Our Lady of the Snows, Rte. 26, Bethel, 04217. Tel: 207-824-2933.

Oakland, Kennebec Co., St. Theresa, Rev. Joseph W. Cahill.
Res., 25 Church St., 04963. Tel: 207-465-3856.
Catechesis/Religious Programs—Tel: 207-465-7951. Anna H. Anderson, D.R.E., Tel: 207-397-2041.
Students 115.
Mission—Belgrade Lakes, St. Helena.

Old Orchard Beach, York Co., St. Margaret's, Rev. Normand E. Carpentier; Deacon Daniel J. Delargy.
Res., 6 Saco Ave., P.O. Box 289, 04064-0289. Tel: 207-934-2322; Fax: 207-934-8322.
Catechesis/Religious Programs—Tel: 207-934-4232.
Students 151.
Chapel—Old Orchard, St. Luke's.

Old Town, Penobscot Co.,

1—HOLY FAMILY, Rev. Normand P. Richard. In res., Most Rev. Michael R. Cote.
Res., 262 S. Main St., 04468. Tel: 207-827-4000. [JC]
Catechesis/Religious Programs—Tel: 207-827-2377; Fax: 207-827-2113.
Students 210.

2—ST. JOSEPH'S. Closed. See Holy Family.

3—ST. MARY'S. Closed. See Holy Family.

4—ST. ANN CHURCH, INDIAN ISLAND, Rev. Paul R. Kerns.
Mailing Address: P.O. Box 560, 04468-0560. Tel: 207-827-2172.
Catechesis/Religious Programs—Mrs. Terry Paul, D.R.E.
Students 31.

Oquossoc, Franklin Co., Our Lady of the Lakes, Rev. John E. Harris.
Res., Box 333, 04964. Tel: 207-864-3795.
Catechesis/Religious Programs—Students 10.
Missions—Rangeley, St. Luke, Tel: 207-864-2622; Stratton, St. John, Tel: 207-246-4892; Sugarloaf U.S.A., Richard H. Bell Memorial Chapel.

Orono, Penobscot Co., St. Mary's, Rev. Joseph J. Koury, Pastor.
Res., 83 College Ave., 04473. Tel: 207-866-3372; Fax: 207-866-4543.
Church—89 Main St., 04473. [JC]
Catechesis/Religious Programs—Students 22.

Our Lady of Wisdom Personal Campus Parish, Rev. Joseph J. Koury; Sr. Mary Sweeney, S.C.
Res., University of Maine, Newman Center, 83 College Ave., 04473. Tel: 207-866-2155; Fax: 207-866-4543.
Catechesis/Religious Programs—Margaret Hallee, D.R.E.
Students 90.
Newman Campus Ministry Center—Tel: 207-866-2155; Fax: 207-866-4543.

Perry, Washington Co., St. Ann (Pleasant Point), Rev. Francis P. Morin; Deacon Francis Nicholas; Sr. Janice Murphy, R.S.M., Parish Coor.
Res., 04667. Tel: 207-853-4718.
Catechesis/Religious Programs—Students 50.

Pittsfield, Somerset Co., St. Agnes, Rev. C. James Martel.
Res., 5 High St., P.O. Box 369, 04967. Tel: 207-487-2777.
School—6 Pine St., 04967. Tel: 207-487-3899. Sr. Elizabeth Cobb, R.S.M., Prin.
Diocesan Sisters of Mercy 2; Lay Teachers 4; Students 44.
Catechesis/Religious Programs—Students 100.

Presque Isle, Aroostook Co., Nativity of B.V.M., Rev. Thomas Lequin.
Res., 6 Roberts St., P.O. Box 813, 04769-0813. Tel: 207-768-3671; Fax: 207-764-8092. [CEM 2]
Catechesis/Religious Programs—Tel: 207-764-0161. Ann Albert, D.R.E.
Students 280.

Richmond, Sagadahoc Co., St. Ambrose, Rev. George C. Pelletier.
Res., 27 Kimball St., P.O. Box 38, 04357. Tel: 207-737-4713.
Catechesis/Religious Programs—Tel: 207-737-8364.
Students 80.
Mission—Litchfield, Kennebec Co., St. Leo, Litchfield, 04350. Tel: 207-268-4727.

Rockland, Knox Co., St. Bernard's, Rev. Mark S. Reinhardt.
Res., 150 Broadway, 04841. Tel: 207-594-4322; Fax: 207-594-0234. [CEM]
Catechesis/Religious Programs—Suzanne Edwards, D.R.E.
Students 190.
Mission—Thomaston, Knox Co., St. James.

Rumford, Oxford Co., St. Athanasius-St. John, Rev. Alfred Jacques.
Res., 126 Maine Ave., 04276. Tel: 207-364-4555; Fax: 207-364-4555. [JC]
School—115 Maine Ave., 04276. Tel: 207-364-2528. Walter Buotte, Prin.
Lay Teachers 12; Students 137.
Catechesis/Religious Programs—Michelle Walton, D.R.E.
Students 259.
Mission—Roxbury Pond, St. Mary's Chapel.

Sabattus, Androscoggin Co., Our Lady of the Rosary, Rev. Angelo B. LeVasseur.
Res., 131 High St., 04280. Tel: 207-375-6951; Fax: 207-373-6951.
Catechesis/Religious Programs—Tel: 207-375-6581.
Students 82.
Mission—Greene, St. Francis, Tel: 207-946-5758.

Saco, York Co., Most Holy Trinity, Revs. James J. Doherty, C.S.C.; Patrick Walsh, C.S.C.; Sr. Rita Bujold, C.S.J., Pastoral Assoc. In res., Rev. James F. Murphy, C.S.C.
Res., 271 Main St., Box 310, 04072. Tel: 207-282-3321; Fax: 207-284-2274.
Catechesis/Religious Programs—Tel: 207-282-6392.
Students 315.

Notre Dame de Lourdes, Rev. Paul E. Cote.
Res., 16 Cutts Ave., 04072. Tel: 207-282-1392; Fax: 207-282-0353. [JC]
School—50 Beach St., 04072. Tel: 207-283-3111; Fax: 207-286-2750. Sr. Linda Mae Plourde, P.M., Prin.
Sisters of the Presentation of Mary 1; Lay Teachers 12; Students 178.
Catechesis/Religious Programs—Tel: 207-282-0911. Marcel Bertrand, D.R.E.
Students 40.

St. Agatha, Aroostook Co., St. Agatha's, Rev. Claude R. Gendreau.
Res., 04772. Tel: 207-543-7447; Fax: 207-543-9392.
Catechesis/Religious Programs—Tel: 207-543-6119. Judy Michaud, D.R.E.
Students 93.
Mission—Madawaska, Aroostook Co., St. Michael's Chapel, Birch Point Rd., Madawaska, 04756. Tel: 207-728-7845. [CEM 2]

St. Francis, Aroostook Co., St. Charles, Rev. Michael L. Doucette.
Res., P.O. Box 100, 04774. Tel: 207-398-3530. [CEM 2]
Catechesis/Religious Programs—Students 50.
Mission—Allagash Plantation, St. Paul.

St. John, Aroostook Co., St. John, Rev. Michael L. Doucette.
Mailing Address: P.O. Box 100, St. Francis, 04774. Tel: 207-398-3530. [CEM]

Sanford, York Co., Holy Family, Revs. Claude J. Albert; Timothy J. Nadeau.
Res., 66 North Ave., 04073. Tel: 207-324-2420; Fax: 207-324-5318. [JC]
School—St. Thomas Consolidated School. For Holy Family, St. Ignatius and Notre Dame, Springvale. Tel: 207-324-2549; Fax: 207-324-2549. Norman Provost, Prin.
Sisters 1; Lay Teachers 16; Students 263.
Catechesis/Religious Programs—Tel: 207-324-5832. Joyce M. St. Pierre, D.R.E.
Students 100.

St. Ignatius Martyr, Revs. Claude J. Albert; Timothy J. Nadeau; Gerald Coutu, Pastoral Assoc. & D.R.E.
Res., 10 St. Ignatius St., 04073. Tel: 207-324-6040; Fax: 207-324-6041. [CEM]
Catechesis/Religious Programs—Tel: 207-324-6231. Gerald Coutu, D.R.E.
Students 69.

Scarborough, Cumberland Co., St. Maximilian Kolbe, Rev. James J. Morrison.
Mailing Address: P.O. Box 57, 04070-0057. Tel: 207-883-2597 (Res.); 207-883-0334 (Parish Office); Fax: 207-883-4246.
Catechesis/Religious Programs—Tel: 207-883-1742. Kathy Sparda, D.R.E.
Students 806.
Mission—Pine Point, Scarborough Co., St. Jude, Rte. 9, 04074.

Sinclair, Aroostook Co., St. Joseph, Rev. Claude R. Gendreau.
Res., St. Agatha, 04772. Tel: 207-543-7447; Fax: 207-543-6119. [CEM]
In res., P.O. Box 61, 04779. Tel: 207-243-7563
Catechesis/Religious Programs—Students 23.

Skowhegan, Somerset Co., Notre Dame De Lourdes, Rev. Marcel G. Chouinard; Sr. Claudette Darisse, A.S.V., Pastoral Assoc.
Res., 222 Water St., P.O. Box 369, 04976. Tel: 207-474-2039; Fax: 207-474-2039. [CEM]
Catechesis/Religious Programs—Tel: 207-474-9844. Beth Crowe, D.R.E.
Students 133.

South Berwick, York Co., St. Michael, Rev. Philip Michael Tracy.
Res., 29 Young St., 03908. Tel: 207-384-4241; Fax: 207-384-4289. [CEM]
Catechesis/Religious Programs—Students 143.

South Portland, Cumberland Co., Church of the Holy Cross, Rev. Paul E. Coughlin, Pastor.
Mailing Address: 124 Cottage Rd., P.O. Box 2708, 04116-2708. Tel: 207-772-7489; Fax: 207-772-7480.
Parish Office: 29 Aspen Ave., S. Portland, 04106.
Res., 11 Aspen Ave., 04106. Tel: 207-871-8923; Fax: 207-871-0235.
School—436 Broadway, 04106. Tel: 207-799-6661; Fax: 207-799-8345. Deacon Steven G. Harnois, Prin.
Lay Teachers 17; Students 287.
Catechesis/Religious Programs—Tel: 207-773-8710; Fax: 207-772-7480. Joseph Draper, D.R.E.
Students 215.

St. John the Evangelist, Rev. Paul E. Coughlin.
Res., 11 Aspen Ave., 04106. Tel: 207-772-7489; Fax: 207-871-0235.
Catechesis/Religious Programs—Twinned with Holy Cross, South Portland. Tel: 207-773-8710; Fax: 207-772-7480. Joseph Draper, D.R.E.

Springvale, York Co., Notre Dame, Revs. Claude A. Albert; Timothy J. Albert.
Res., 10 Payne St., Box 278, 04083. Tel: 207-324-6630. [CEM]
Catechesis/Religious Programs—Rebecca Carlson, D.R.E.
Students 298.

Stockholm, Aroostook Co., St. Therese, Rev. Joachim Thanh Nguyen.
Mailing Address: 1143 Van Buren Rd., Caribou, 04736.
Church—04783. Tel: 207-498-2763.
Catechesis/Religious Programs—Diane Dickinson, D.R.E.
Students 23.

Stonington, Hancock Co., St. Mary Star of the Sea, Rev. John F. O'Hara.
Res., Thurlow Hill, Box 25, 04681. Tel: 207-367-2343.
Mission—Castine, Hancock Co, Our Lady of Holy Hope, Pleasant St., Box 413, Castine, 04421. Tel: 207-326-8228.

Van Buren, Aroostook Co., St. Bruno - St. Remi, Revs. Joseph S. Chasse, S.M.; David Lajoie, S.M.; Robert McDonald, S.M.; Souvenir Jean-Paul, S.M.
Res., 336 Main St., 04785. Tel: 207-868-2718; Fax: 207-868-9713. [CEM]
Catechesis/Religious Programs—Tel: 207-868-2835. Rebecca Devost, D.R.E.
Students 142.
Mission—Van Buren, Aroostook Co., St. Rose Chapel.

St. Remi. Merged with St. Bruno. For further details see separate listing under St. Bruno.

Wallagrass, Aroostook Co., St. Joseph's, Rev. James R. Albert.
Church—R.R. 1, Box 1205, Soldier Pond, 04781. Tel: 207-444-5135. [CEM 3]
Res., Church St., P.O. Box 249, Eagle Lake, 04739. Tel: 207-444-5119. [CEM]
Catechesis/Religious Programs—Students 30.

Waterville, Kennebec Co., Parish of the Holy Spirit. Merging St. Francis de Sales, Sacred Heart and Notre Dame Parishes. Revs. Philip A. Tracy; Ralph Boisvert; Paul Clogan; Sr. Line Rioux, C.S.J., Pastoral Assoc.
Res., 70 Pleasant St., 04901-5405. Tel: 207-872-2281; Fax: 207-877-0675. [JC]
Catechesis/Religious Programs—Tel: 207-872-2264; Fax: 207-872-2264. D.R.E.: Rachel Matthews; Monica Bolduc.
Students 198.
Sacred Heart. Merged with Notre Dame and St. Francis de Sales to form Parish of the Holy Spirit, Waterville.
Notre Dame. Merged with Sacred Heart and St. Francis de Sales to form Parish of the Holy Spirit, Waterville.

Wells, York Co., St. Mary, Rev. J. Joseph Ford.
Res., Eldredge Rd., P.O. Box 368, 04090. Tel: 207-646-5605; Fax: 207-646-9437.
Catechesis/Religious Programs—Students 177.
Mission—Ogunquit, All Saints.

Westbrook, Cumberland Co., St. Edmund (Prides Corner), Rev. Richard D. Bertrand, S.J.
Res., 355 Bridgton Rd., 04092. Tel: 207-797-8233; Fax: 207-797-8356.
Catechesis/Religious Programs—Tel: 207-797-4539. Mrs. Sandra Bois, D.R.E.
Students 140.
St. Hyacinth, Rev. James P. Brewer; Sr. Christine Plouffe, O.P., Pastoral Assoc.
Res., 295 Brown St., 04092. Tel: 207-854-2003; Fax: 207-854-4899. [CEM]
Catechesis/Religious Programs—Tel: 207-854-4925. D.R.E.: Cynthia Crockett; Ann Marie Leach.
Students 150.
St. Mary's, Rev. Joseph Manship.
Res., 625 Main St., 04092. Tel: 207-854-2753; Fax: 207-856-7318. [JC]
Catechesis/Religious Programs—Tel: 207-854-8669. Larry Guertin, D.R.E.
Students 128.

Whitefield, Lincoln Co., St. Denis, Rev. Donald R. Daigle; Deacon Joseph Reid.
Res., 298 Grand Army Rd, 04353-3419. Tel: 207-549-7425. [CEM]
Catechesis/Religious Programs—Students 55.

Wilton, Franklin Co., St. Mary. Closed. For further details see separate listing for St. Joseph, Farmington.

Windham, Cumberland Co., Our Lady of Perpetual Help, Rev. Edward A. Thomson.
Res., Rte. 302, 919 Roosevelt Tr., P.O. Box 1030, 04062-1030. Tel: 207-892-8288; Fax: 207-893-1072.
Catechesis/Religious Programs—Tel: 207-892-8922.
Students 390.
Mission—East Raymond, St. Raymond Chapel, Rte. 85 at Crescent Lake, East Raymond, 04071.

Winslow, Kennebec Co., St. John the Baptist, Rev. Paul A. Plante; Mrs. Elaine Gordon, Pastoral Assoc.
Res., 47 Monument St., 04901. Tel: 207-872-2373; 877-0953; Fax: 207-873-7301. [JC]
School—36 1/2 Garand St., 04901. Tel: 207-872-7115; Fax: 207-872-2500. Mr. Kevin Scully, Prin.
Lay Teachers 10; Students 118.
Catechesis/Religious Programs—Students 275.

Winterport, Waldo Co., St. Gabriel, Rev. Jean Paul Labrie.
Res., St. Matthew's, 70 Western Ave., P.O. Box 280, Hampden, 04444. Tel: 207-862-3517; Fax: 207-862-4576.
Catechesis/Religious Programs—Tel: 207-223-4087. Beth Thieme, D.R.E.
Students 35.

Winthrop, Kennebec Co., St. Francis Xavier, Rev. Sylvio J. Levesque.
Res., 10 Lake St., 04364. Tel: 207-377-2922; Fax: 207-377-7087. [JC]
Catechesis/Religious Programs—Tel: 207-377-6844. Nancy Lynn Yocono, D.R.E.
Students 164.
Mission—Monmouth, Kennebec Co., St. Stanislaus.

Yarmouth, Cumberland Co., Sacred Heart, Rev. Paul F. Stefanko. Pastoral Assocs.: Ann Peacock; Cherie Piper.
Res., 326 Main St., 04096. Tel: 207-846-5584; Fax: 207-846-6003. [CEM]
Catechesis/Religious Programs—Tel: 207-846-6003. D.R.E.: Ann Peacock; Debra Gagnon.
Students 298.
Mission—Freeport, St. Jude's.

York Harbor, York Co., St. Christopher-by-the-Sea, Rev. Albert B. Colpitts.
Res., One Lilac Ln., York, 03909-1020. Tel: 207-363-2111; Fax: 207-363-1586.
Catechesis/Religious Programs—Tel: 207-363-4177; Fax: 207-363-8934. Rose Cronin, D.R.E.
Students 282.
Mission—York Beach, St. Mary, Star of the Sea.

Chaplains of Public Institutions

PORTLAND. *Maine Medical Center* Tel: 207-871-0111. Chaplains: Revs. Patrick Glavin, O.F.M.Cap.; Thomas M. Murphy; Albin A. Andrus.
Mercy Hospital Tel: 207-879-3358. Rev. Donald McAllister; Mrs. Agnes LaStoria; Sr. M. Michael Connelly, R.S.M.
St. Joseph's Manor Tel: 207-797-0600. Rev. Robert E. Lee.

AUGUSTA. *Augusta Mental Health Institute*. Vacant. Tel: 207-289-7334.
Kennebec Valley Medical Center Tel: 207-626-1000. Mr. Stephen Vinette, Pastoral Assoc.

BANGOR. *Eastern Maine Medical Center*. Taylor Hospital, Bangor Convalescent Center, Tel: 207-942-6941. Rev. John J. Austin.
St. Joseph's Hospital Tel: 207-262-1798. Rev. Richard V. Rokos; Sr. Mary Edmund, C.S.S.F., Pastoral Assoc.

BIDDEFORD. *Southern Maine Medical Center* Tel: 207-283-3663. Lewella Daigle.

LEWISTON. *Central Maine Medical Center* Tel: 207-795-0111. Mrs. Kathleen O'Wril.
St. Mary's Regional Medical Center. Rev. Donald Gagnon, S.M., Campus Ave., P.O. Box 291, 04243-0291. Tel: 207-777-8520. Sr. Madeline Normand, P.M.; Sr. Huguette Allard, S.G.M.; Mr. Kenneth Rancort.

SOUTH PORTLAND. *Maine Youth Center*. Deacon John McAuliffe, Jr.
Men's Correctional Center Tel: 207-828-4921. Rev. Robert P. Bouchard.

THOMASTON. *Maine State Prison* Tel: 207-828-4921. Rev. Robert P. Bouchard.

TOGUS. *Dept. of Veteran Affairs* Tel: 207-622-1134, Ext. 5176. Rev. Raymond R. Lagace, O.F.M.

WARREN. *Super Maximum Facility & Minimum Facility* Tel: 207-828-4921. Rev. Robert P. Bouchard.

WATERVILLE. *Mid-Maine Medical Center* Tel: 207-872-1000. Mrs. Angeline Hubert.

Special or Other Diocesan Assignment:
Reverend Fathers—
Beaudet, George W., P.O. Box 11559, Portland, ME 04104-7559
Caron, Marc B., P.O. Box 11559, Portland, ME 04104-7559. Tel: 207-773-6471; 772-5104
Nolette, Mark P., P.O. Box 11559, Portland, ME 04104-7559
Roux, G. Albert, P.O. Box 127, St. Francis, ME 04774-0127
Skehan, John R., P.O. Box 11559, Portland, ME 04104-7559
Therriault, Ronald P., 27 Riverside St., Lewiston, ME 04240

On Duty Outside the Diocese:
Reverend Fathers—
Carrigan, Fredrick, 342 Willis Ave., P.O. Box 172, Bronx, NY 10454. Tel: 212-927-3875

Military Chaplains:
Reverend Fathers—
Cote, David P., USAF Academy, 412 33rd Ave. NE, Great Falls, MT 59404-4203
Goudreau, Joseph L., 3704 2nd St. South, Arlington, VA 22204-1604. Tel: 703-696-3532; Fax: 703-696-5996
Welch, Bernard J., USCG Tracen, 1 Munro Ave., Cape May, NJ 08204-5001

Sabbatical:
Reverend Fathers—
Beaudet, George W.
Girouard, Robert J.
Robitaille, Marcell L.

On Leave:
Reverend Fathers—
Carter, Joseph F.
Laroche, Christopher J.

Retired:
Reverend Monsignors—
Begin, Raymond F., 4951 Summertree Rd., Venice, FL 34293-4254
Chaloult, Gilman J., 31 Thomas Ave., Caribou, ME 04736. Tel: 207-498-2536
Gleason, Paul D., P.O. Box 1938, Hampton, NH 03842-0019. Tel: 613-926-5442
Tatarczuk, Vincent A., P.O. Box 218, Raymond, ME 04071. Tel: 207-655-3672
Tracy, George E., 11 Bangor Mall Blvd., Suite 400, Bangor, ME 04401-2596. Tel: 207-866-3100; Fax: 207-866-3105
Reverend Fathers—
Auger, Gaston E., Box 476, West Kennebunk, ME 04094. Tel: 207-985-7059
Auger, Raymond D., St. Joseph, 43 Center St., Biddeford, ME 04005
Barrett, Patrick J., Cathedral Residence, 307 Congress St., Portland, ME 04101. Tel: 207-874-2830
Berube, Louis F., 11 Windsor Pl., Lewiston, ME 04240. Tel: 207-777-1692
Bill, J. Armand, 402A Sandpiper Dr., Fort Pierce, FL 34948. Tel: 561-467-1011
Bureau, Germain H., Mount St. Joseph Home, 7 Highwood St., Waterville, ME 04901. Tel: 207-872-0742
Burns, T. Lee, 22357 Peachland Blvd., Port Charlotte, FL 33952. Tel: 941-236-2521
Caron, Antonin R., 79 Fairlawn Ave., P.O. Box 2267, Lewiston, ME 04241-2267
Carrier, Herve G., P.O. Box 3061, Lewiston, ME 04243-3061. Tel: 207-795-0657
Cormier, Norman R., Pleasant Hill Rd., R.R. 1, Box 441, Limerick, ME 04048-9735. Tel: 207-793-2377
Cyr, L. Chanel, 302 Main St., Limestone, ME 04750-1116. Tel: 207-325-4843
Davis, John P., 68 Webster Ave., Lewiston, ME 04240. Tel: 207-784-6235
Feeney, John J., 175 A Pine St., Portland, ME 04102. Tel: 207-780-1494
Frechette, Leonard A., St. Andre Healthcare Facility, 409 Pool Rd., Biddeford, ME 04005
Gilbert, Valmont R., Tahitian Garden Circle, #4359B, Holiday, FL 34691. Tel: 727-938-5213
Gorham, Peter P., P.O. Box 515, Ellsworth, ME 04605-0515. Tel: 207-667-2050
Goudreau, George W., P.O. Box 28, Rumford, ME 04276
Gower, James M., 23 High Brook Rd., Bar Harbor, ME 04609. Tel: 207-288-9780
Harvey, Richard R., 12 Bayberry Rd., Brewer, ME 04412-1202. Tel: 207-989-8007
Huot, Leopold J., St. Andre Healthcare Facility, 409 Pool Rd., Biddeford, ME 04005
Jacques, Donald W., 17 Lorisa Ln., Milford, NH 03055. Tel: 603-672-1981
Kane, Francis J., 677 Cherry Valley Rd., #47, Guilford, NH 03246. Tel: 603-293-8614
Knox, James, 31 Clearview Dr., Scarborough, ME 04074-8319. Tel: 207-883-9652
L'Heureux, Ernest L., 64 Lebonan St., Sanford, ME 04073. Tel: 207-459-7090
Lauzon, Raymond J., Pranceskona Vienuolynus, Vilniaus 2, Kretinga, 5700 Lithuania
Lavoie, Rene G., 4808 NW 48th Ave., Tamarac, FL 33319-3635. Tel: 954-735-4580
Lee, Robert E., Cathedral Residence, 307 Congress St., Portland, ME 04101. Tel: 207-773-6980
Leveille, Rudolph J., 69 Juniper St., Bangor, ME 04401. Tel: 207-942-9715
Marquis, J. Alphee, Forest Hill Manor, 20 Bolduc Ave., Fort Kent, ME 04743
Martel, Robert T., Mount St. Joseph Home, Highwood St., Waterville, ME 04901. Tel: 207-873-0006
McCarthy, Richard C., 58 Pitt St., Portland, ME 04103. Tel: 207-772-1211
McGarrigle, Michael, 76 Ward Cir., Brunswick, ME 04011-9343. Tel: 207-725-5764
McInnis, Richard W., 16 Lochness Rd., Rumford, ME 04276. Tel: 207-364-8717
McKenna, Joseph R., 100 State St. # 321, Portland, ME 04101. Tel: 207-775-1084
Moreshead, Harold D., 757 Main St. # 22, S. Portland, ME 04106. Tel: 207-828-8638
Mulkern, Stephen M., P.O. Box 474, New Harbor, ME 04554. Tel: 207-677-2881
Neautl, Armand R., 54 Blacksmith Rd. # 11, Wells, ME 04090 207-646-6417
Nicknair, Bernard L., 135 Willard Rd., Auburn, ME 04210. Tel: 207-795-6394
Nicknair, Harold, 5725 80th St. N., Unit # 411, St. Petersburg, FL 33709. Tel: 727-545-7876
O'Donnell, Richard A., 61 Cleveland Cir., S. Portland, ME 04106
Ouellette, Roger J., Mount St. Joseph Home, Highwood St., Waterville, ME 04901-5797. Tel: 207-873-0432
Paquet, Hubert J., 46 Wentworth St., Biddeford, ME 04405. Tel: 207-286-9674
Pare, Paul U., 5731 So. SR 7., Ft. Lauderdale, FL 33314
Pare, Paul M., St. Paul Center, 136 State St., Augusta, ME 04330

Parent, Royal J., Golden Gate Mobile Home Community, 82010 A. St., Pinella Pk, Fl 33781-1718. Tel: 727-568-9163
Patenaude, Gilbert A., 47 River St., Augusta, ME 04330. Tel: 207-622-3832
Romani, Joseph, St. Joseph Manor, 1133 Washington Ave., Portland, ME 04103
Rotunno, Anthony R., P.O. Box 297, Rockwood, ME 04478-0297. Tel: 207-534-8831
Soucy, D. Wilfrid, 5027 Reseda Dr., New Port Richey, FL 34652-6251. Tel: 727-842-1497
St. Pierre, Romeo A., 15 Garden Circle N, Caribou, ME 04736
Whitlock, Joseph E., Cathedral Residence, 307 Congress St., Portland, ME 04101-3695

INSTITUTIONS LOCATED IN THE DIOCESE

[A] COLLEGES AND UNIVERSITIES

STANDISH. *Association of Mercy Colleges and Universities*, 278 Whites Bridge Rd., 04084-5263. Tel: 207-893-7711; Fax: 207-893-7867
For a complete listing, refer to the Colleges and Universities section.

Saint Joseph's College, 278 Whites Bridge Rd., 04084-5263. Tel: 207-893-7711; Fax: 207-893-7867.
Web site: www.sjcme.edu
For a complete listing, refer to the Colleges and Universities section.

[B] HIGH SCHOOLS, REGIONAL

LEWISTON. *St. Dominic Regional High School*, 179 Blake St., 04240. Tel: 207-782-6911; Fax: 207-795-6439.
E-mail: gmwelch@explorehaine.com
Web site: www.st-dominic.net
Rev. Daniel P. Greenleaf, Chap.; Mr. G. Michael Welch, Prin. Priests 1; Sisters 1; Lay Teachers 23; Students 270.

[C] HIGH SCHOOLS, PRIVATE

PORTLAND. *Catherine McAuley High School*, 631 Stevens Ave., 04103. Tel: 207-797-3802; Fax: 207-797-3804. Sr. Edward Mary Kelleher, R.S.M., Prin. Sisters of Mercy 3; Lay Teachers 24; Girls 317.

Cheverus High School, 267 Ocean Ave., 04103. Tel: 207-774-6238; Fax: 207-828-0207.
E-mail: info@cheverus.org
Web site: www.cheverus.org
Faculty resides at St. Ignatius Residence. See separate listing for details. Rev. John W. Keegan, S.J., Pres.; Mr. John H.R. Mullen, Prin.; Revs. Richard H. Roos, S.J., Supr.; William Eagan, S.J.; John W. Keegan, S.J. Priests 1; Lay Teachers 30; Students 398.

[D] ELEMENTARY SCHOOLS, PRIVATE

WATERVILLE. *Mount Merici Elementary School*, 142 Western Ave., 04901. Tel: 207-873-3773; Fax: 207-873-6377.
E-mail: mmpvt-mm@mount-merici.pvt.k12.me.us
Web site: www.mount-merici.pvt.k12.me.us
Susan H. Cote, Prin. Lay Teachers 14; Students 172.

[E] CATHOLIC CHARITIES MAINE, INC.

FALMOUTH. *Catholic Charities Maine*. Mailing Address: P.O. Box 10660, Portland, 04104-6060. 356 U.S. Rte. 1, 04105. Tel: 207-781-8550. Most Revs. Joseph J. Gerry, O.S.B., Pres.; Michael R. Cote, Vice Pres.; Mr. Michael Poulin, Esq., Chm.; Mr. Gregory M. Smith, C.P.A., Treas.; Ms. Gloria A. Dugan, Exec. Dir.; Ms. Connie Jones, Human Resources Dir. Tel: 207-781-8550.

St. Elizabeth's Child Development Center, 87 High St., Portland, 04101. Tel: 207-871-7444. Daniel Murphy, Dir.

St. Michael's Center Emergency Foster Care, 1066 Kenduskeag Ave., Bangor, 04401. Tel: 207-941-2855.
E-mail: pvestal@ccmaine.org
Web site: www.ccmaine.org
Mr. Paul K. Vestal, Jr., Dir. Legal Title: *St. Michael's Center Emergency Foster Care, Juvenile Jail Diversion Program and Home Based Family Services and Tracker Services.*

[F] SPECIAL RESIDENTIAL SERVICES

PORTLAND. *McAuley Residence, Inc.*, 91 State St., 04101. Tel: 207-773-5289; Fax: 207-773-2672.
E-mail: mcauleyr@maine.rr.com
Transitional Housing and support services for women with or without children. Sr. Miriam T. Callnan, R.S.M., Dir.

AUBURN. *St. Joseph Child Care Center*, 270 Minot Ave., 04210. Tel: 207-782-2711. Ms. Constance R. Ouellette, Dir.

BIDDEFORD. *St. Andre Home, Inc.*, Admin. Office, 283 Elm St., 04005-3093. Tel: 207-282-3351.
E-mail: SaintAndre@yahoo.com
Dr. Gregory C. Foltz, Exec. Dir. Pregnant and Parenting Young Women, Adoption Services, Service to Troubled Teens, Infant Foster Care Homes, Emergency Placement; Public Information-Education; Community Outreach Services; Residences in Biddeford, Lewiston, Bangor.

[G] HOMES FOR THE AGED

PORTLAND. *Deering Pavilion Apartment House for Senior Citizens*, 880 Forest Ave., 04103. Tel: 207-797-8777; Fax: 207-797-8963.
E-mail: oren@maine.rr.com
For a complete listing, refer to the Special Care Facilities section.

St. Joseph's Manor, 1133 Washington Ave., 04103. Tel: 207-797-0600; Fax: 207-797-4168
For a complete listing, refer to the Special Care Facilities section.

BANGOR. *St. Xavier's Home*, 119 Somerset St., 04401. Tel: 207-942-4815
For a complete listing, refer to the Special Care Facilities section.

BIDDEFORD. *St. Andre Health Care & Rehab Center*, 407 Pool St., 04005-9716. Tel: 207-282-5171; Fax: 207-282-5372
For a complete listing, refer to the Special Care Facilities section.

LEWISTON. *Maison Marcotte*, 100 Campus Ave., 04240. Tel: 207-786-0062
For a complete listing, refer to the Special Care Facilities section.

St. Marguerite d'Youville Pavilion, 102 Campus Ave., 04240. Tel: 207-777-4200
For a complete listing, refer to the Special Care Facilities section.

WATERVILLE. *Mt. St. Joseph Holistic Care Community*, Highwood St., 04901. Tel: 207-873-0705; Fax: 207-873-6626.
E-mail: msj@mtsj.org
Web site: www.mtsj.org
For a complete listing, refer to the Special Care Facilities section.

Seton Village Inc., 1 Carver St., 04901. Tel: 207-873-0178; Fax: 207-873-1233
For a complete listing, refer to the Special Care Facilities section.

[H] GENERAL HOSPITALS

PORTLAND. *Mercy Hospital*, 144 State St., 04101. Tel: 207-879-3000
For a complete listing, refer to the Hospitals section.

BANGOR. *St. Joseph Hospital*, 360 Broadway, 04401. Tel: 207-262-1000
For a complete listing, refer to the Hospitals section.

BUCKSPORT. *Bridgewell, Inc.*, Box 836, 04416. Tel: 207-469-7616; Fax: 207-469-7616
For a complete listing, refer to the Hospitals section.

LEWISTON. *Community Clinical Services, Inc.*, 100 Campus Ave, Ste. #1, 04240. Tel: 207-777-8841
For a complete listing, refer to the Hospitals section.

Sisters of Charity Health System, Inc., 97 Campus Ave., 04240. Tel: 207-777-8802; Fax: 207-777-8595
For a complete listing, refer to the Hospitals section.

St. Mary's Regional Medical Center, Campus Ave., P.O. Box 291, 04243-0291. Tel: 207-777-8100; Fax: 207-777-8595
For a complete listing, refer to the Hospitals section.

[I] MONASTERIES AND RESIDENCES OF PRIESTS AND BROTHERS

PORTLAND. *St. Ignatius Residence*, 77 Read St., 04103-3433. Tel: 207-777-0473; Fax: 207-775-1229. Jesuit Fathers (New England Prov.). Revs. Richard H. Roos, S.J., Supr.; William J. Eagan. Priests 2; Seminarians 1.

ALFRED. *Notre Dame Institute*, Shaker Hill Rd., P.O. Box 159, 04002. Tel: 207-324-6612; Fax: 207-490-2370. Provincial House of Brothers of Christian Instruction. Bros. Daniel Caron, F.I.C., Prov. Tel: 207-324-0067; James Lacasse, F.I.C., Supr. Tel: 207-324-6612; Rev. Theodore Letendre, F.I.C., Dir., Notre Dame Spiritual Center. Tel: 207-324-6160; Fax: 207-324-5044. Revs. Henry Vanasse, F.I.C., Chap. Tel: 207-324-1017; Theodore Letendre, F.I.C. Brothers 21.

KENNEBUNKPORT. *St. Anthony's Friary*.
E-mail: jbacev@ispchannel.com
Franciscan Vice-Province of St. Casimir in Lithuania, Canada and United States, Office of the Magazine "The Bell of St. Francis" (in Lithuanian language). St. Anthony's Friary, Guest House and St. Anthony's Shrine. 28 Beach Ave., P.O. Box 980, 04046. Tel: 207-967-2011. Revs. Placid Barius, O.F.M., Vice Prov. Lithuanian Vice-Province; Leonard Andriekus, O.F.M., Dir. Art Gallery; George S. Gailiusis, O.F.M., Dir. Gift Shop; Gabriel Baltrusaitis, O.F.M., Vicar of the Friary, Procurator & Dir. Guest House; Raphael J. Sakalys, O.F.M., Sec. of Vice Province in USA; John J. Bacevicius, O.F.M., Guardian; Dennis Arambasick, O.F.M.; Andrew R. Bisson, Parish Ministry. Priests 8.

LEWISTON. *SS. Peter and Paul House*, 10 Richmond Ave, 04240-5346. Tel: 207-784-7309; Fax: 207-777-0056. Residence for Dominican Fathers or Friar Preachers. Revs. James Donovan, O.P. (Canada); Raymond Corriveau, O.P., Supr.; Rosaire Pelletier, O.P.; Bro. Irenee Richard, O.P., Treas. Priests 3; Brothers 1.

American Dominican Friars Serving in Canada. Revs. Thomas Demers, O.P.; Thomas R. Potvin, O.P.; Bernard M. Remillard, O.P.; Claude Richard, O.P.; Bro. Robert Beaulieu, O.P.

PEAKS ISLAND. *Mother of the Good Shepherd Monastery by the Sea*, 235 Pleasant Ave., 04108. Tel: 207-766-2717; Fax: 207-766-2707.
E-mail: monks@gwi.net
Web site: www.augustinianmonks.org
The Servants of God of St. Augustine. Rev. A.M. Seamus Kuebler, O.S.A., Prior; Bro. Nicholas Druin, O.S.A., Subprior. Purpose is to especially pray and minister to priests and brothers.

WATERVILLE. *Mt. St. Joseph Priest Retirement Home*, 7 Highwood St., 04901-5797. Tel: 207-873-0705. Revs. Germain H. Bureau; Robert T. Martel; Roger J. Ouellette; Marcel Robitaille.

[J] CONVENTS AND RESIDENCES OF SISTERS

PORTLAND. *House of Formation*, 605 Stevens Ave., 04103. Tel: 207-797-6957; Fax: 207-797-0146. Sr. Mary M. Morey, R.S.M., Contact Person. Sisters of Mercy of the Americas 3.

Mercy Convent, 144 State St., 04101. Tel: 207-879-3566. Sr. Mary Michael Connelly, R.S.M., Coord. Sisters of Mercy of the Americas 4.

Monastery of the Precious Blood, 166 State St., 04101-3794. Tel: 207-774-0861; Fax: 207-774-3253. Sr. Mary Jo Divney, A.P.B., Supr. Adorers of the Precious Blood 3; Novices 2.

Motherhouse of the Sisters of Mercy of the Americas, 605 Stevens Ave., 04103-0146. Tel: 207-797-7861; Fax: 207-797-0416.
E-mail: jlittle@maine.77.com
Sr. Jean Little, R.S.M., Regional Pres.; Sr. Mary Gemma Connelly, R.S.M., Local Coord. Motherhouse; Rev. Theodosius Corley, O.F.M.Cap., St. Joseph Rectory, Stevens Ave. Sisters in Residence at Motherhouse 72.

St. Patrick, 17 Frances St., 04102. Tel: 207-772-0723. Sr. Phyllis Doyle, R.S.M., Coord. Sisters of Mercy of the Americas 3.

Sisters of Charity, 1137 Washington Ave., 04103. Tel: 207-797-8607; Fax: 207-797-6086.
E-mail: jacquied@juno.com
Sr. Jacqueline Peloquin, Contact Person. Sisters 4.

Sisters of Mercy of the Americas, 186 Lane Ave., 04103. Tel: 207-878-6630. Sr. Theresa Rand, R.S.M., Contact Person. Sisters of Mercy of the Americas 4.

Sisters of Our Lady of the Holy Rosary, 20 Thomas St., 04102. Tel: 207-774-3756. Sr. Carole Jean Lappa, R.S.R., Regl. Supr. Tel: 207-772-3130. Sisters of Our Lady of the Holy Rosary 4.

AUBURN. *Companions of Christ*, 133 Western Ave., 04210. Tel: 207-784-5960. Sr. Elizabeth Platt, C.O.C., Contact Person. Sisters 2.

AUGUSTA. *St. Augustine*, 5 Kendall St., 04330. Tel: 207-622-2494. Sisters of the Presentation of Mary. Sr. Rachel Boucher, P.M., Supr. Sisters 2.

St. Mary, 8 Lincoln St., 04330. Tel: 207-623-4033. Sr. Barbara Brennan, R.S.M., Contact Person. Sisters of Mercy of the Americas 2.

BANGOR. *St. Joseph Convent*, 360 Broadway, 04401-3900. Tel: 207-262-1124; Fax: 207-262-1925.
E-mail: sebarb@mint.net
Sr. Barbara Theresa Martis, C.S.S.F., Contact Person. Felician Sisters 10.

BIDDEFORD. *Marie Fitzbach Convent*, 290 Elm St., 04005. Tel: 207-282-2714. Sr. Simmone Janelle, S.C.I.M., Supr. Servants of the Immaculate Heart of Mary (Good Shepherd) 8.

Marie Joseph Spiritual Center, R.F.D. 2, Evans Rd., 04005. Tel: 207-284-5671; Fax: 207-286-1371.
E-mail: mjsc@cybertours.com
Sr. Cecile Plasse, P.M., Supr.; Rev. James Murphy, C.S.C., Chap. Sisters of the Presentation of Mary 12.

St. Joseph's Convent, 409 Pool St., 04005. Tel: 207-284-8381; Fax: 207-286-9418. Sr. Claire Ouellette, S.C.I.M., Supr. Sections A, B & C. Sisters of the Immaculate Heart of Mary (Good Shepherd) 44.

BRUNSWICK. *St. John the Baptist Convent,* 37 Pleasant St., 04011. Tel: 207-725-5484.
E-mail: lauri@gwi.net
Sr. Laurianne Michaud, O.S.U., Supr. Ursuline Sisters 8.

CASCO. *Community of the Resurrection,* P.O. Box 284, 04015-0284. Tel: 207-627-7184; Fax: 207-627-4840. Sr. Renata Camenzind, Supr. Total in Residence 7.

HOULTON. *Marie Claire Residence,* 7 Cleveland St., 04730. Tel: 207-532-2324; Fax: 207-532-4401. Sr. Carol Martin, P.F.M., Contact Person. Little Franciscans of Mary 3.

INDIAN ISLAND. *St. Ann's Convent.*
E-mail: edesjardins@iisbia.edu
Penobscot Reservation, P.O. Box 3039, Old Town, 04468. Tel: 207-827-4862. Sisters of Mercy of the Americas.

LEWISTON. *Dominican Sisters of the Roman Congregation,* Provinvial Residence, 123 Dumont Ave., 04240. Tel: 207-782-3535; Fax: 207-782-0435.
E-mail: moniqueb@mogalink.net
Sr. Monique Belanger, O.P., Regional Supr. Sisters 5.

Holy Cross, 15 Baird Ave., 04240. Tel: 207-782-0263. Sr. Nora Dumais, Supr. Sisters of the Presentation of Mary 5.

Sisters of Charity, Sisters' Residence, 98 Campus Ave., P.O. Box 701, 04243-0701. Tel: 207-782-0798. Sr. Estelle Lamothe, Supr. Sisters 2.

OLD ORCHARD BEACH. *Sisters of Our Lady of the Holy Rosary.* Regional House, 25 Portland Ave., 04064-2211. Tel: 207-934-0592. Sr. Olla Laplante, Supr. Sisters 3.

PITTSFIELD. *St. Agnes,* 9 High St., 04967-1213. Tel: 207-487-4790. Sr. Elizabeth Cobb, Contact Person. Diocesan Sisters of Mercy 2.

PLEASANT POINT. *St. Ann's Convent.* P.O. Box 126, Perry, 04667. Tel: 207-853-2944.
E-mail: sisterjanice@ola.
Sr. Janice Murphy, R.S.M., Coord.

SABATTUS. *Dominican Sisters,* 61 Lisbon Rd., 04280-9761. Tel: 207-375-6583; Fax: 207-375-2694.
E-mail: Lucille@cybertours.com
Sr. Marguerite Gregoire, O.P., Prioress. Dominican Sisters of the Roman Congregation 10.

SACO. *Bay View Community,* 187 Bay View Rd., 04072. Tel: 207-283-3636; Fax: 207-282-7376.
E-mail: scimbv@gwi.net
Sr. Lucille Gamache, S.C.I.M., Supr.; Rev. James E. Connor, Chap., Tel: 207-284-8863. Servants of the Immaculate Heart of Mary (Good Shepherd Sisters) 34.

Notre Dame de Lourdes, 27 Thornton Ave., 04072. Tel: 207-284-8943. Sr. Marie-May Lausier, Dir. Sisters of the Presentation of Mary 4.

Provincial Residence, 313 Seaside Ave., 04072-3410. Tel: 207-284-6429; Fax: 207-282-7376.
E-mail: scimpro@gwi.net
Servants of the Immaculate Heart of Mary. Sr. Theresa Rounds, S.C.I.M., Prov. Supr. Sisters 3.

ST. AGATHA. *Our Lady of Wisdom Convent,* 380 Main St., P.O. Box 108, 04772-0108. Tel: 207-543-7523. Sr. Candide Corriveau, D.W., Coord. Daughters of Wisdom 6.

SOUTH PORTLAND. *Our Lady of Mercy Convent,* 265 Cottage Rd., 04106. Tel: 207-767-5804. Sr. M. Eunice Boyd, R.S.M., Supr. Gen. Diocesan Sisters of Mercy of Portland 9.

VAN BUREN. *St. Bruno Convent,* 300 Main St., 04785. Tel: 207-868-5266.
E-mail: scimvb@gwi.net
Sr. Dorina Chasse, S.C.I.M., Supr. Servants of the Immaculate Heart of Mary 7.

WATERVILLE. *Blessed Sacrament Convent,* 101 Silver St., 04901. Tel: 207-872-7072; Fax: 207-873-2317.
E-mail: blesac@mint.net
Web site: www.members.mint.net/blesac
Servants of the Blessed Sacrament. Rev. Richard G. Lonsdale, Chap. Tel: 207-872-5742; Sr. Patricia Ann Keane, S.S.S., Supr. Sisters 9.

Mt. Merici Convent, 142 Western Ave., 04901-4617. Tel: 207-873-3515; Fax: 207-873-4926. Sr. Mary Anne Poulin, O.S.U., Prioress. Ursuline Sisters 12.

Mt. St. Joseph Fontbonne Community, Highwood St., 04901. Tel: 207-873-5377. Sr. Marcelle Roy, C.S.J., Coord. Sisters of St. Joseph 9.

Mt. St. Joseph Sisters' Residence, 7 Highwood St., 04901. Tel: 207-873-4804. Sr. Yvette Poulin, C.S.J., Coord. Sisters of St. Joseph 3.

Ursuline Sisters Care Center, 142 Western Ave., 04901. Tel: 207-873-1931; Fax: 207-873-4926. Sr. Patricia Couture, O.S.U., Supr. Ursuline Sisters 9.

Ursuline Sisters' Residence, 140 1/2 Western Ave., 04901. Tel: 207-872-9375. Sr. Mary Ann Poulin, O.S.U., Contact Person. Sisters 3.

WINSLOW. *Provincialate of the Sisters of St. Joseph,* 93 Halifax St., 04901. Tel: 207-872-4512; Fax: 207-873-1976.
E-mail: csjwinme@mint.net
Sr. Laurette Levasseur, C.S.J., Prov. Supr.; Sr. Gilla Dube, Coord. Sisters 4.

[K] HERMITAGES

ELLSWORTH. *John of the Cross Monastery,* 19 Trinity Way, 04605-9523. Tel: 207-664-0026.
E-mail: gaudeamus@altavista.com
Sr. Margaret Dorgan, D.C.M. Carmelite Sisters 2.

ST. ALBANS. *Divine Mercy Hermitage,* 57 Bryant Rd., 04971. Tel: 207-938-3730; Fax: 207-938-3730.
E-mail: srmm@somtel.com
Sr. Margaret Mary Cuddeback.

Sky-Arch Hermitage, 47 Byrant Rd., 04971. Tel: 207-938-3458.
E-mail: srhermit@somtel.com
Web site: www.somtel.com/~srhermit
Sr. B. Emmanuel Bryant.

THORNDIKE. *Transfiguration Hermitage,* 548 Files Hill Rd., 04986-9709. Tel: 207-568-3731.
E-mail: srewagner@uninets.net
Sr. Elizabeth Wagner, Contact Person.

[L] RETREAT HOUSES

ALFRED. *Notre Dame Retreat & Spiritual Center,* P.O. Box 159, 04002-0159. Tel: 207-324-6160; Fax: 207-324-5044. Bro. Theodore Letendre, F.I.C., Dir.

AUGUSTA. *St. Paul Center.* (Men and Women), 136 State St., 04330-7496. Tel: 207-622-6235; Fax: 207-622-6735. Deacon Dean Lachance, Dir.

BIDDEFORD. *Marie Joseph Spiritual Center,* R.F.D. #2, Lester Orcutt Blvd., 04005. Tel: 207-284-5671; Fax: 207-286-1296. Sr. Claire Vanasse, P.M., Dir.; Rev. James F. Murphy, C.S.C., Chap. Sisters of the Presentation of Mary.

FRENCHVILLE. *Christian Life Center.* P.O. Box 530, 04745-0530. Tel: 207-543-6193; Fax: 207-543-6193.
E-mail: clc@ainop.com
Web site: www.ainop.com/users/clc
Rev. James S. Plourde, Dir.

SACO. *Bay View Villa, Guest and Retreat House,* 187 Bay View Rd., 04072. Tel: 207-286-8762.
E-mail: brv@gwi.net
Servants of the Immaculate Heart of Mary. Sr. Claire Lambert, S.C.I.M., Dir.

[M] NEWMAN CENTERS

PORTLAND. *University of New England-Westbrook College.* Res. St. Joseph Church, 673 Stevens Ave., 04103. Tel: 207-797-7026; Fax: 207-797-2679. Revs. Theodosius Corley, O.F.M.Cap.; Don Bosco Duquette, O.F.M.Cap.

University of Southern Maine. Portland Campus, c/o Sacred Heart/St. Dominic Rectory, 80 Sherman St., 04101-2216. Tel: 207-772-6182; Fax: 207-772-9615.
E-mail: shsdp@ime.net
Rev. Frederick H. Morse.
Gorham Campus. Vacant.

BIDDEFORD. *University of New England.* Res. St. Joseph Rectory, P.O. Box 408, 04005. Rev. James Murphy, C.S.C., Chap.

BRUNSWICK. *Bowdoin College,* St. Charles Parish, 132 McKeen St., 04011.
E-mail: frchris@aol.com
Newman Center, 04011. Tel: 207-576-3135. Rev. Stephen F. Concannon. Tel: 207-725-2624.

CASTINE. *Maine Maritime Academy,* 158 Franklin St., P.O. Box S, 04416. Tel: 207-469-3322. Rev. John F. O'Hara, V.F., Chap.

FARMINGTON. *University of Maine at Farmington.* c/o The Pastoral Center, 133 Middle St., 04938. Tel: 207-778-2778; Fax: 207-778-0268.
E-mail: gal@somtel.com
Rev. Roger P. Chabot, Chap.; Susan Anzivino, Moderator.

FORT KENT. *University of Maine at Fort Kent.* RR #2 Box 80, 04743. Karen Ouellette, Chap.

LEWISTON. *Bates College,* 163 Wood St., 04240. Tel: 207-786-8272; Fax: 207-786-8282.
E-mail: mdescha@bates.edu
Web site: www.bates.edu/admin/offices/chaplain
Rev. Wilfred Labbe.

MACHIAS. *University of Maine at Machias,* c/o Holy Name, P.O. Box 248, 04654. Tel: 207-255-3731. Rev. Michael Sheridan.

ORONO. *University of Maine.* Our Lady of Wisdom Parish/Newman Center, 83 College Ave., 04473-1596. Tel: 207-866-2155; Fax: 207-866-4543.
E-mail: koury@saturn.caps.maine.edu
Web site: www.ume.maine.edu/newman
Rev. Joseph J. Koury; Sr. Mary Sweeney, S.C., Campus Min.

PRESQUE ISLE. *University of Maine at Presque Isle.* St. Mary's Rectory, 6 Roberts St., P.O. Box 813, 04769. Tel: 207-768-3671.

SOUTH PORTLAND. *Southern Maine Technical College.* Holy Cross Rectory, 11 Aspen St., 04106. Tel: 207-799-4611; Fax: 207-799-2818. Rev. Paul E. Coughlin.

STANDISH. *Saint Joseph's College.* Campus Ministry Office., 04084-5263. Tel: 207-893-7791. Rev. John Tokaz, O.F.M.Cap.; Sr. Sylvia Comer, R.S.M., Dir. of Campus Ministry; Deacon John McAuliffe.

WATERVILLE. *Colby College,* Mid Maine Campus Ministry, 04901. Tel: 207-872-3559.
E-mail: patracy@colby.edu
Dean of Students Office, Colby College. Rachel Nelson, Assoc. Campus Min.; Rev. Philip A. Tracy, Chap.

Thomas College, Mid Maine Campus Ministry, 04901. Tel: 207-872-3559. Dean of Students Office, Colby College. Rev. Philip A. Tracy, Chap.

[N] MISCELLANEOUS LISTINGS

PORTLAND. *St. Elizabeth's Child Development Center,* 87 High St., 04101. Tel: 207-871-7444. Daniel Murphy.

BANGOR. *St. Michael's Center,* 1066 Kenduskeag Ave., 04401. Tel: 207-941-2855; Fax: 207-941-2835.
E-mail: pvestal@main.org
Web site: www.ccmaine.org
Paul Vestal, Jr., Dir. Emergency Foster Care, Juvenile Intensive Supervision Services, Home Based Family Services and Case Management Services.

BIDDEFORD. *St. Andre Housing, Inc.,* 39 Sullivan St., 04005. Tel: 207-773-6471. David Twomey, Contact Person, P.O. Box 1159, Portland, 04104-7559. Sponsored by: Roman Catholic Diocese of Portland. Purpose: to provide low income housing for the elderly in a deprived area of the state.

LEWISTON. *Wisdom's Center,* 91 Sabattus St., 04240. Tel: 207-784-0155.
E-mail: wisdomscenter@prodigy.net
Sr. Irene Arsenault, D.W., Dir.

RELIGIOUS INSTITUTES OF MEN REPRESENTED IN THE DIOCESE

For further details refer to the corresponding bracketed number in the Religious Institutes of Men or Women section.

[0320]—*Brothers of Christian Instruction.*—F.I.C.
[0470]—*The Capuchin Friars.* (Prov. of St. Mary).—O.F.M.Cap.
[0740]—*Congregation of Marians of the Immaculate Conception* (St. Stanislaus Kostka Prov.).—M.I.C.
[0480]—*Conventual Franciscans.*—O.F.M.Conv.
[0520]—*Franciscan Friars.* (Custody of St. Casimer).—O.F.M.
[0690]—*Jesuit Fathers and Brothers.* (New England Prov.).—S.J.
[0780]—*Marist Fathers.* (Boston Prov.).—S.M.
[0910]—*Oblates of Mary Immaculate.* (Prov. of St. John the Baptist).—O.M.I.
[0430]—*Order of Preachers (Dominicans).* (Canadian Prov.).—O.P.
[]—*Order of St. Augustine.*—O.S.F.
[0610]—*Priests of the Congregation of the Holy Cross.* (Eastern Prov.).—C.S.C.

RELIGIOUS INSTITUTES OF WOMEN REPRESENTED IN THE DIOCESE

[]—*Community of the Resurrection.*
[]—*Companions of Christ.*—C.O.C.
[3100]—*Congregation of Our Lady of the Holy Rosary.*—R.S.R.
[2230]—*Congregation of the Infant Jesus.*—C.I.J.
[0750]—*Daughters of the Charity of the Sacred Heart of Jesus.*—F.C.S.C.J.
[0960]—*Daughters of Wisdom.*—D.W.
[]—*Diocesan Carmelites of Maine.*—D.C.M.
[]—*Diocesan Sisters of Mercy.*—R.S.M.
[1120]—*Dominican Sisters of the Roman Congregation.*—O.P.
[1170]—*Felician Sisters.*—C.S.S.F.
[2575]—*Institute of the Sisters of Mercy of the Americas.*—R.S.M.
[2280]—*Little Franciscan of Mary.*—P.F.M.
[2760]—*Missionary Sisters of the Immaculate Conception of the Mother of God.*—S.M.I.C.
[3500]—*Servants of the Blessed Sacrament.*—S.S.S.
[3550]—*Servants of the Immaculate Heart of Mary.*—S.C.I.M.
[0490]—*Sisters of Charity of Montreal (Grey Nuns).*—S.G.M.
[0610]—*Sisters of Charity of St. Hyacinthe (Grey Nuns).*—S.C.S.H.
[3000]—*Sisters of Notre Dame de Namur.*—S.N.D.deN.
[3750]—*Sisters of St. Chretienne.*—S.S.Ch.
[3870]—*Sisters of St. Joseph (Lyons, France).*—C.S.J.

[0150]—*Sisters of the Assumptions.*—S.A.S.V.

[0110]—*The Sisters of the Precious Blood.*—A.P.B.

[3310]—*Sisters of the Presentation of Mary.*—P.M.

[4110]—*Ursuline Nuns (Roman Union).* (Northeastern Prov.).—O.S.U.

[0640]—*Sisters of Charity of St. Vincent de Paul.* (Halifax).—S.C.

DIOCESAN CEMETERIES

BANGOR. *Mount Pleasant,* 449 Ohio St., 04401. Tel: 207-947-4322. Mr. William Foley.

BIDDEFORD. *St. Joseph,* West St., P.O. Box 391, 04005. Tel: 207-282-0747.

LEWISTON. *St. Peter,* Switzerland Rd., 04240. Tel: 207-782-8721. Gerry Raymond.

SOUTH PORTLAND. *Calvary,* 1461 Broadway, 04106. Tel: 207-773-5796. Mr. Richard Nee.

WATERVILLE. *St. Francis,* 78 Grove St., 04901. Tel: 207-872-2770. Mr. Clarence Hebert, Mailing Address: P.O. Box 575, 04903-0575.

NECROLOGY

† Conroy, Peter C., Lewiston, ME Holy Family Church. —Died Nov. 18, 1999.

† O'Brien, Edward J., (Retired). —Died Dec. 28, 1999.

† Pollard, Daniel E., (Retired). —Died May 22, 2000.

† Scahill, John J., Portland, ME Cathedral of the Immaculate Conception. —Died Feb. 26, 2000.

Archdiocese of Portland in Oregon

(Archidioecesis Portlandensis in Oregon)

Most Reverend

JOHN G. VLAZNY, D.D.

Archbishop of Portland in Oregon; ordained December 20, 1961; appointed Auxiliary Bishop of Chicago and Titular Bishop of Stagno October 31, 1983; consecrated December 13, 1983; appointed Bishop of Winona May 19, 1987; installed July 29, 1987; appointed Archbishop of Portland in Oregon October 28, 1997; installed December 19, 1997.

Most Reverend

KENNETH D. STEINER, D.D.

Archdiocesan Administrator; ordained May 19, 1962; appointed Titular Bishop of Avensa and Auxiliary December 6, 1977; ordained March 2, 1978. *Office: 2838 E. Burnside St., Portland, OR, 97214.*

ERECTED AS A VICARIATE-APOSTOLIC DECEMBER 1, 1843.

CREATED ARCHDIOCESE OF OREGON CITY, JULY 24, 1846; NAME CHANGED BY PAPAL DECREE TO "ARCHDIOCESE OF PORTLAND IN OREGON," SEPTEMBER 26, 1928.

Square Miles 29,717.

Comprises that part of the State of Oregon lying between the summit of the Cascades and the Pacific Ocean.

For legal titles of parishes and archdiocesan institutions, consult the Archdiocesan Pastoral Center.

Archdiocesan Pastoral Center: 2838 E. Burnside St., Portland, OR, 97214-1895. Tel.: 503-234-5334; Fax: 503-234-2545.

Web site address: www.archdpdx.org/

E-mail address: @archdpdx.org

STATISTICAL OVERVIEW

Personnel	
Archbishop	1
Auxiliary Bishops	1
Abbots	2
Retired Abbots	1
Priests: Diocesan Active in Diocese	100
Priests: Active Outside Diocese	5
Priests: Diocesan in Foreign Missions	1
Priests: Retired, Sick or Absent	46
Number of Diocesan Priests	152
Religious Priests in Diocese	181
Extern Priests in Diocese	26
Ordinations:	
Diocesan Priests	3
Religious Priests	1
Transitional Deacons	4
Permanent Deacons in Diocese	26
Total Brothers	79
Total Sisters	531
Parishes	
Parishes	125
With Resident Pastor:	
Resident Diocesan Priests	77
Resident Religious Priests	34
Without Resident Pastor:	
Administered by Priests	9
Administered by Lay People	4
Completely Vacant	1
Missions	26
Pastoral Centers	1
New Parishes Created	1
Professional Ministry Personnel:	
Brothers	1
Sisters	25
Lay Ministers	171
Welfare	
Catholic Hospitals	9
Total Assisted	2,063,583
Health Care Centers	5
Total Assisted	2,867
Homes for the Aged	7
Total Assisted	1,803
Day Care and Extended Day Care Centers	4
Total Assisted	3,163
Specialized Homes	6
Total Assisted	3,154
Special Centers for Social Services	14
Total Assisted	1,028,589
Residential Care of Disabled	3
Total Assisted	47
Educational	
Seminaries, Diocesan	1
Students from This Diocese	17
Students from Other Diocese	131
Diocesan Students in Other Seminaries	1
Students Religious	36
Total Seminarians	54
Colleges and Universities	2
Total Students	4,549
High Schools, Diocesan and Parish	3
Total Students	1,535
High Schools, Private	6
Total Students	3,365
Elementary Schools, Diocesan and Parish	41
Total Students	8,938
Elementary Schools, Private	1
Total Students	382
Catechesis/Religious Education:	
High School Students	3,090
Elementary Students	13,092
Total Students Under Catholic Instruction	35,005
Teachers in the Diocese:	
Priests	49
Brothers	9
Sisters	62
Lay Teachers	1,388
Vital Statistics	
Receptions into the Church:	
Infant Baptism Totals	5,591
Adult Baptism Totals	760
Received into Full Communion	763
First Communions	4,206
Confirmations	2,433
Marriages:	
Catholic	845
Interfaith	512
Total Marriages	1,357
Deaths	1,982
Total Catholic Population	297,841
Total Population	2,869,750

Former Bishops—Most Rev. FRANCIS NORBERT BLANCHET, D.D., First Vicar Apostolic of Oregon Territory; cons. July 25, 1845, Titular Bishop of Drasa; appt. Archbishop of Oregon City, July 24, 1846 when the Vicariate was erected into an ecclesiastical province; resigned 1880; died June 18, 1883.—Most Rev. CHARLES JOHN SEGHERS, D.D., cons. June 29, 1873; Bishop of Vancouver Island, British Columbia; coadjutor to the Archbishop of Oregon City, Dec. 10, 1878; Archbishop, Dec. 20, 1880; resigned 1884 and transferred to Vancouver Island, British Columbia; died Nov. 28, 1886.—Most Rev. WILLIAM H. GROSS, C.SS.R., D.D., Archbishop of Oregon City; cons. Bishop of Savannah, GA April 27, 1873 promoted by His Holiness Leo XIII Feb. 1, 1885 from Savannah to the Archiepiscopal See of Oregon City; died Nov. 14, 1898.—Most Rev. ALEXANDER CHRISTIE, D.D., Archbishop of Oregon City; cons. June 29, 1898, Bishop of Vancouver Island, B. C. promoted by His Holiness Leo XIII February 12, 1899 from Vancouver Island to the Archiepiscopal See of Oregon City; died April 6, 1925.—Most Rev. EDWARD D. HOWARD, D.D., LL.D., Titular Archbishop of Albule; ord. June 12, 1906; cons. Titular Bishop of Isauria and Auxiliary Bishop of Davenport, April 6, 1924; appt. to the See of Oregon City, April 30, 1926 asst. at the Pontifical Throne, May 2, 1939; transferred to the Titular See of Albule and as Archbishop of Portland in Oregon, Dec. 9, 1966; died Jan. 2, 1983.—Most Rev. ROBERT

JOSEPH DWYER, D.D., Ph.D., ord. June 11, 1932; cons. Bishop of Reno, August 5, 1952; appt. Archbishop of Portland in Oregon, Dec. 9, 1966; resigned Jan. 22, 1974; died March 24, 1976.—Most Rev. CORNELIUS MICHAEL POWER, D.D., J.C.D., ord. June 3, 1939; appt. Bishop of Yakima, Feb. 5, 1969; cons. May 1, 1969; appt. Archbishop of Portland in Oregon, Jan. 22, 1974; retired July 3, 1986; died May 22, 1997.—Most Rev. WILLIAM J. LEVADA, S.T.D., ord. Dec. 20, 1961; appt. Titular Bishop of Capri and Auxiliary Bishop of Los Angeles, March 29, 1983; appt. Archbishop of Portland in Oregon, July 1, 1986; installed Sept. 21, 1986; appt. Coadjutor Archbishop of San Francisco, Aug. 17, 1995; transferred Oct. 24, 1995.—Most Rev. FRANCIS E. GEORGE, O.M.I., Ph.D., S.T.D., ord. Dec. 21, 1963; appt. Bishop of Yakima July 10, 1990; installed Sept. 21, 1990; appt. Archbishop of Portland in Oregon, April 29, 1996; installed May 27, 1996; appt. Archbishop of Chicago April 8, 1997; installed May 7, 1997.

Office of the Archbishop

Archdiocesan Pastoral Center—2838 E. Burnside St., Portland, 97214-1895. Tel: 503-234-5334; Fax: 503-234-2545.

Vicars and Directors

Vicar General—Rev. DENNIS O'DONOVAN.
Vicar for Clergy—Rev. CHARLES LIENERT.
Finance Officer—LEONARD VUYLSTEKE.
Department Directors—
Business Affairs—PAULETTE FURNESS.
Clergy—Rev. CHARLES LIENERT.
Education—ROBERT MIZIA.
Chancellor/Public Services—MARY JO TULLY.
Pastoral Services—Rev. MICHAEL MASLOWSKY.
Evangelization—Deacon THOMAS GORNICK.
Vicariate For Southeast Asians—Rev. VINCENT MINH, C.SS.R., Episcopal Vicar, *5404 N.E. Alameda Dr., Portland, 97213.* Tel: 503-249-5892.
Chancellor—MARY JO TULLY.
College of Consultors—Most Rev. JOHN G. VLAZNY; Most Rev. KENNETH D. STEINER; Rev. Msgr. FRANK CAMPBELL; Revs. JOSEPH BROWNE, C.S.; DONALD BUXMAN; JOSEPH JACOBBERGER; CHARLES LIENERT; GREGORY MOYS; DENNIS O'DONOVAN; PAUL PERI; GEORGE WOLF.
Area Vicars—Rev. JOSEPH JACOBBERGER, Downtown Portland; Vacant, North Portland; Rev. ROBERT KRUEGER, Northeast Portland; Rev. STEPHEN BOSSI, C.S.P., Southeast Portland; Rev. RICHARD SIRIANNI, East Portland Suburban; Most Rev. KENNETH STEINER, South Portland Suburban; Rev. RICHARD ROSSMAN, West Portland Suburban; Rev. WAYNE FORBES, Beaverton Suburban; Rev. THOMAS FARLEY, Yamhill County; Rev. J. PATRICK MOORE, Tualatin Valley; Rev. HEIKO JUNGE, Columbia County; Rev. RICHARD THOMPSON, O.F.M.Conv., North Coast; Rev. VINCENT TRUJILLO, O.S.B., Marion County; Rev. GEORGE WOLF, Metropolitan Salem; Rev. PANNEER SELVAM, Santiam; Rev. JOHN HENDERSON, O.F.M.Conv., Albany-Corvallis; Rev. STEPHEN CLOVIS, Metropolitan Eugene; Rev. JACK WELLS, Middle Coast; Rev. JOHN MCGUIRE, South Coast; Rev. WILLIAM RYAN, O.S.A., Douglas County; Rev. RAYMOND FINERTY, O.P., Southern Oregon.
Personnel Board—Revs. ROBERT KRUEGER; JACK MOSBRUCKER; PAUL PERI; MARK BACHMEIER; MICHAEL JOHNSTON; CHARLES LIENERT, Ex Officio.

Tribunal

Judicial Vicar—Rev. PATRICK BRENNAN, J.C.L.; LINDA WEIGEL, J.C.L., Dir. Tel: 503-233-8380.
Adjutant Judicial Vicar—Revs. CARL FLACH; KELLY VANDEHEY, J.C.L.
Judges—Revs. PATRICK BRENNAN, J.C.L.; CARL J. FLACH; CARL GIMPL; GARY JACOBSON; THOMAS BROCKHAUS, O.S.B., J.C.D.; JOSEPH JACOBBERGER; HENRY LACERTE, J.C.D.; Rev. Msgr. EDMUND VAN DER ZANDEN; MICHAEL PATRICK, J.C.L.; KELLY VANDEHEY, J.C.L.
Defenders of the Bond—Revs. JAMES MAYO; GREGORY MOYS; Sr. MAUREEN ABBOTT, S.P.; LINDA WEIGEL, J.C.L.
Auditors—ALEXANDRIA GUERRA-SUNDBERG; PEG WILLS.
Case Instructor—Sr. MAUREEN ABBOTT, S.P.
Notaries—MARGARET PALMER; SUSAN OUFFOUE; MARY ANN LARGUIER.
Advocates—All priests with Archdiocesan assignments and pastoral ministers by appointment.

Archdiocesan Offices and Agencies

Archives—MARY A. GRANT, Archivist. Tel: 503-233-8334., *2838 E. Burnside St., Portland, 97214-1895.*
Building Commission—Most Rev. JOHN G. VLAZNY; Revs. THEODORE WEBER, Chm. DENNIS O'DONOVAN; JOSEPH HEUBERGER; ALEXANDER PLASKER, O.S.B.; A. P. DIBENEDETTO, F.A.I.A.; JOHN BROCKAMP; FRED SHIPMAN; TAI FUNATAKE; ROBERT BOILEAU; JOSEPH GEHLEN; DAVID HODGIN; DONALD BENZ; PAULETTE FURNESS, Ex Officio; KEN SCOTT, Sec. Tel: 503-234-5334.
Business Affairs—PAULETTE FURNESS, Dir., *2838 E. Burnside St., Portland, 97214-1895.* Tel: 503-234-5334.
Campus Ministry—Rev. MICHAEL MASLOWSKY, Dir., *2838 E. Burnside St., Portland, 97214-1895.* Tel: 503-233-8385.
Catholic Charities, Inc.—DENNIS KEENAN, Exec. Dir., *231 S.E. 12th Ave., Portland, 97214-9813.* Tel: 503-231-4866.
Catholic Deaf Ministry—Sr. LINDA ROBY, B.V.M., Dir., *2408 S.E. 16th Ave., Portland, 97214.* Tel: 503-236-7527 (V-TDD).
"Catholic Sentinel"—(Official Newspaper of the Archdiocese), Most Rev. JOHN G. VLAZNY, Publisher-in-Chief; JOHN J. LIMB, Publisher; ROBERT PFOHMAN, Editor, *5536 N.E. Hassalo, Portland, 97213-3638.* Tel: 503-281-1191.
Catholic Youth Organization—KRISTA VON BORSTELL, Exec. Dir., *Oregon Plaza, 825 N.E. 20th St., Ste. 320, Portland, 97232.* Tel: 503-231-9484.
Cemeteries—TIM CORBETT, Supt., *Mt. Calvary Cemetery, 333 S.W. Skyline Blvd., Portland, 97221.* Tel: 503-292-6621.
Clergy Personnel—Rev. CHARLES LIENERT, Vicar for Clergy, *2838 E. Burnside St., Portland, 97214-1895.* Tel: 503-233-8366.
Communications—BUD BUNCE, Dir., *2838 E. Burnside St., Portland, 97214-1895.* Tel: 503-233-8373.
Continuing Education for Clergy—Rev. SLIDER STEURNOL, Dir. Board Members: Revs. ED SCHWAB; MICHAEL SPRAVER; TODD MOLINARI; JOSEPH JACOBBERGER; PAT DONOGHUE, *2838 E. Burnside St., Portland, 97214-1895.* Tel: 503-234-5334.
Diaconate Office—Rev. RICHARD HUNEGER, Dir.; Deacon JOHN RIES, Assoc. Dir., *2838 E. Burnside St., Portland, 97214-1895.* Tel: 503-233-8344.
Ecumenical and Interreligious Affairs—Rev. RICHARD SIRIANNI, Dir. MARY JO TULLY, Assoc. Dir., *2838 E. Burnside St., Portland, 97214.* Tel: 503-233-8323.
Evangelization—Deacon THOMAS GORNICK, Dir., *2838 E. Burnside St., Portland, 97214-1895.* Tel: 503-233-8335.
Finance Council—Most Rev. JOHN G. VLAZNY, Chair; Revs. PAUL PERI; PATRICK WALSH; DENNIS O'DONOVAN; DOUG WHITE; DONNA RAGAN; PAULETTE FURNESS; DOUG TOLLEFSON; ARTHUR SCHULTE, JR., Ph.D.; LEO C. SHERRY, JR.; MYRON FLECK; LEONARD VUYLSTEKE; DENNIS FERGUSON; EDWARD HERINCKX, *2838 E. Burnside St., Portland, 97214-1895.* Tel: 503-233-8350.
Financial Services—LEONARD VUYLSTEKE, Dir., *2838 E. Burnside St., Portland, 97214-1895.* Tel: 503-233-8359.
Hispanic Ministries—RAUL VELAZQUEZ, Dir., *2838 E. Burnside St., Portland, 97214.* Tel: 503-233-8324.
Historical Commission—MARY-CATHERINE CUTHILL, Pres., *2838 E. Burnside St., Portland, 97214-1895.*
Holy Childhood, Pontifical Association of—MARY JO TULLY, Dir., *2838 E. Burnside St., Portland, 97214-1895.* Tel: 503-233-8323.
Housing—Rev. MICHAEL MASLOWSKY, Dir., *2838 E. Burnside St., Portland, 97214-1895.* Tel: 503-233-8385.
Human Resources—BARBARA BALTZ, Dir., *2838 E. Burnside St., Portland, 97214-1895.* Tel: 503-234-5334.
Immigration Counseling Services—SUSAN ROSSITER, Dir., *321 S.W. 4th Ave., No.701, Portland, 97204.* Tel: 503-221-1689.
Justice and Peace—FRANK FROMHERZ, Dir., *2838 E. Burnside St., Portland, 97214-1895.* Tel: 503-233-8361.
Liturgical Commission—Revs. PAUL PERI, Chm. JOHN DOMIN; Sr. JEREMY GALLET, S.P., Ex Officio; Revs. JAMES MAYO; JOSEPH S. MCMAHON; RICHARD RUTHERFORD, C.S.C.; Sr. LORETTA SCHAFF, O.S.F.; MARY JO TULLY; JAMES WILDE, *2838 E. Burnside St., Portland, 97214-1895.*
Marriage and Family Life Office—JAY WONACOTT, Dir., *2838 E. Burnside St., Portland, 97214-1895.* Tel: 503-233-8393.
Ministry Formation—Revs. PAUL PERI, Dir. MICHAEL JOHNSTON, Asst. Dir., *2838 E. Burnside St., Portland, 97214-1895.* Tel: 503-233-8341.
Ministry to the Aging—RUTH HAYES-BARBA, Dir., *2838 E. Burnside St., Portland, 97214-1895.* Tel: 503-233-8394.
Mission Office—MARY JO TULLY, Dir., *2838 E. Burnside St., Portland, 97214-1895.* Tel: 503-233-8323.
Oregon Catholic Conference—Most Rev. JOHN G. VLAZNY, Pres.; Most Rev. ROBERT F. VASA (BAK), Vice Pres. ROBERT CASTAGNA, Gen. Counsel & Exec. Dir., *2838 E. Burnside St., Portland, 97214-1895.* Tel: 503-233-8387.
Oregon Catholic Press—Most Rev. JOHN G. VLAZNY, Publisher-in-Chief; JOHN J. LIMB, Publisher, *5536 N.E. Hassalo, Portland, 97213.* Tel: 503-281-1191.
Pastoral Services, Pastoral Councils, Charismatic Renewal—Rev. MICHAEL MASLOWSKY, Dir., *2838 E. Burnside St., Portland, 97214-1895.* Tel: 503-233-8385.
People with Disabilities—DOROTHY DESMARTEAU-COUGHLIN, Dir. LYNDA BROWN, Asst. Dir.; Rev. PATRICK DONOGHUE, Rel. Outreach Coord., *2838 E. Burnside St., Portland, 97214-1895.* Tel: 503-233-8396 (V/TTY).
Pro-Life Activities—Rev. MICHAEL MASLOWSKY, Dir., *2838 E. Burnside St., Portland, 97214-1895.* Tel: 503-233-8385.
Project Rachel—*447 N.E. 47th Ave., Ste. 100, Portland, 97213.* Tel: 1-800-249-8074.
Propagation of the Faith, Pontifical Society for the—MARY JO TULLY, Dir., *2838 E. Burnside St., Portland, 97214-1895.* Tel: 503-233-8323.
Religious Education—CATHY SHANNON, Dir., *2838 E. Burnside St., Portland, 97214-1895.* Tel: 503-234-5334.
Refugee Resettlement—CECILIA BARICEVIC, *231 S.E. 12th Ave., Portland, 97214-1342.* Tel: 503-231-4866.
Resource Development—DOUG TOLLEFSON, Dir., *2838 E. Burnside St., Portland, 97214-1895.* Tel: 503-233-8336.
St. Mary's Home for Boys—EMMA DENNIS, Exec. Dir., *16535 S.W. Tualatin Valley Hwy., Beaverton, 97006.* Tel: 503-649-5651.
School Office—ROBERT MIZIA, Supt. Tel: 503-233-8300. Bro. WILLIAM CAMPBELL, S.M., Asst. Supt., School Personnel & Technology; Sr. RITA RAE SCHNEIDER, R.S.M., Asst. Supt., Faith Formation & Curriculum, *2838 E. Burnside St., Portland, 97214-1895.*
Special Projects—TODD COOPER, Dir., *2838 E. Burnside St., Portland, 97214-1895.* Tel: 503-233-8386.
Stewardship Office—Deacon TOM GORNICK, Dir., *2838 E. Burnside St., Portland, 97214-1895.* Tel: 503-233-8335.
Vocations—Rev. TIMOTHY MOCKAITIS, Dir., *2838 E. Burnside St., Portland, 97214-1895.* Tel: 503-233-8368.
Worship—Sr. JEREMY GALLET, S.P., Dir., *2838 E. Burnside St., Portland, 97214-1895.* Tel: 503-233-8342.
Youth Ministry—Vacant, Dir., *2838 E. Burnside St., Portland, 97214-1895.* Tel: 503-233-8395.

CLERGY, PARISHES, MISSIONS AND PAROCHIAL SCHOOLS

CITY OF PORTLAND
(Multnomah County)

1—CATHEDRAL OF THE IMMACULATE CONCEPTION (1851), Revs. Joseph Jacobberger; Binh Hoang; Deacons John Ries; Robert Lucas.
Res., 1716 N.W. Davis St., 97209. Tel: 503-228-4397; Fax: 503-242-2568.
School—110 N.W. 17th Ave., 97209. Tel: 503-227-4297; Fax: 503-243-3819.
Order of Servants of Mary 2; Lay Teachers 10; Students 225.

2—ST. AGATHA (1911), Rev. Joseph A. Baccellieri. In res., Revs. Timothy Murphy; Richard Paperini.
Office: 1430 S.E. Nehalem St., 97202. Tel: 503-236-4747; Fax: 503-235-3218.
School—(Grades K-8). Tel: 503-234-5500.
Lay Teachers 12; Students 201.
Catechesis/Religious Programs—Students 12.

3—ALL SAINTS (1917), Rev. John Kerns.
Res., 3847 N.E. Glisan, 97232. Tel: 503-232-4305; Fax: 503-238-8847.
School—601 N.E. 39th Ave., 97232. Tel: 503-236-6205; Fax: 503-236-0781.
Lay Teachers 22; Students 388.
Catechesis/Religious Programs—Students 73.

4—ST. ANDREW (1907), Rev. Robert W. Krueger.
Res., 806 N.E. Alberta St., 97211. Tel: 503-281-4429; Fax: 503-281-4411.
Catechesis/Religious Programs—Students 60.

5—ST. ANTHONY (1917), Rev. Michael Maslowsky.
Res., 3600 S.E. 79th Ave., 97206. Tel: 503-771-6039; Fax: 503-772-0107.
Catechesis/Religious Programs—Students 30.

6—ASCENSION (1892), Revs. Gus Krumm, O.F.M.; Charles Talley, O.F.M.; Bro. Jeff Macnab, O.F.M. In res., Revs. Loren Kerkof, O.F.M.; Robert Beltrami, O.F.M.; Bros. Mark Schroeder, O.F.M.; Didicus Clavel, O.F.M.; Robert Rodrigues, O.F.M.; Tom Nichols, O.F.M.; Maria Solis, Hispanic Min.; Thom Gaueler, Business Mgr.
Church: 7507 S.E. Yamhill, 97215. Tel: 503-256-3897; Fax: 503-257-4681.

Res., 404 S.E. 68th, 97215. Tel: 503-253-8305.
Catechesis/Religious Programs—Tel: 503-256-3897; Fax: 503-257-4681.
Students 173.

7—ASSUMPTION (1909). (North Portland Catholic Community). Rev. David Gutmann.
Mailing Address: 5227 N. Bowdain St., 97203. Tel: 503-289-2834; Fax: 503-283-7056.

8—ST. BIRGITTA (1954), Rev. Joseph P. Browne, C.S.C.
Res., 11820 N.W. St. Helens Rd., 97231-2319. Tel: 503-286-3929.
Chapel—Portland, Chapel of Our Lady of Sinj.
Catechesis/Religious Programs—Students 53.

9—BLESSED SACRAMENT (1913). Closed. For inquiries for parish records please contact Holy Cross, Portland (North Portland Catholic Community).

10—ST. CHARLES (1914), Rev. Kelly Vandehey; Martha Stephenson, Pastoral Assoc.
Parish Center: 5310 N.E. 42nd, 97218. Tel: 503-281-6461; Fax: 503-281-6828.
Catechesis/Religious Programs—Students 70.

11—CHURCH OF KOREAN MARTYRS (1990) (Korean), Rev. Andrew Sung Han Kim.
Res., 10840 S.E. Powell Blvd., 97266. Tel: 503-762-6880; Fax: 503-760-6601. [JC]
Catechesis/Religious Programs—Students 65.

12—ST. CLARE (1913), Rev. Donald A. Durand.
Res., 8535 S.W. 19th Ave., 97219. Tel: 503-244-1037; Fax: 503-246-2665.
School—Tel: 503-244-7600; Fax: 503-246-2665.
Sisters of Charity 1; Lay Teachers 15; Students 223.
Catechesis/Religious Programs—Students 305.

13—ST. ELIZABETH OF HUNGARY (1953), Rev. Louis J. Urbanski.
Res., 4112 S.W. Sixth Ave. Dr., 97201. Tel: 503-222-2168; Fax: 503-274-2438.

14—ST. FRANCIS OF ASSISI (1876), Rev. Charles J. Lienert, Mod.; Valerie Chapman, Pastoral Admin.; Sr. Phyllis Jaszkowiak, Pastoral Assoc.
Res., 330 S.E. 11th Ave., 97214. Tel: 503-232-5880; Fax: 503-232-6449.
Catechesis/Religious Programs—Students 35.

15—HOLY CROSS (1901). (North Portland Catholic Community.). Rev. David Gutmann.
Office: 5227 N. Bowdoin St., 97203. Tel: 503-289-2834; Fax: 503-283-7056.
School—Tel: 503-289-3010; Fax: 503-286-5006.
Sisters 4; Lay Teachers 11; Students 205.
Chapel—Christ The Teacher, University of Portland, 5000 N. Willamette Blvd., 97203. Tel: 503-283-7311; Fax: 503-283-7399.
Catechesis/Religious Programs—Students 80.

16—HOLY FAMILY (1931), Rev. Robert Barricks.
3732 S.E. Knapp, 97202. Tel: 503-774-1428; Fax: 503-774-1854.
Res., 3732 Knapp St., 97202. Tel: 503-788-2051; Fax: 503-774-1854.
School—Tel: 503-774-8871; Fax: 503-774-8872. Kathleen Lockie, Prin.
Lay Teachers 16; Students 240.
Catechesis/Religious Programs—Fax: 503-774-7804 (Youth).
Students 130.

17—HOLY REDEEMER (1906), Revs. John Amsberry; Charles Wood.
Res., 25 N. Portland Blvd., 97217. Tel: 503-285-4539; Fax: 503-285-0666.
School—Tel: 503-283-5197; Fax: 503-283-9479.
Sisters of the Holy Names of Jesus and Mary 7; Franciscan Sisters 1; Lay Teachers 14; Students 399.
Catechesis/Religious Programs—Students 35.

18—HOLY ROSARY PARISH & DOMINICAN PRIORY (1894), Very Revs. Emmerich W. Vogt, O.P., Pastor & Prior; Paul Raftery, O.P.; Rev. Aquinas Costello, O.P. In res., Revs. Paul A. Duffner, O.P.; Lawrence E. Banfield, O.P.; Christopher H. Moschini, O.P.; Christopher Terry, O.P.
1333 N.E. MLK Jr. Blvd., 97232.
Res., 375 N.E. Clackamas St., 97232. Tel: 503-235-3163; Fax: 503-235-3164.
Confraternity of the Most Holy Rosary—P.O. Box 3617, 97208. Tel: 503-236-8393; Fax: 503-236-8394.
Catechesis/Religious Programs—Tel: 503-635-7993; Fax: 503-635-7993.
Students 161.

19—ST. IGNATIUS (1907), Revs. Roy Antunez, S.J.; Jerry Graham, S.J.
Res., 3400 S.E. 43rd Ave., 97206. Tel: 503-777-1491; Fax: 503-777-3142. [JC]
School—3330 1/2 S.E. 43rd St., 97206. Tel: 503-774-5533; Fax: 503-788-1134.
Sisters of the Holy Names of Jesus and Mary 2; Lay Teachers 16; Students 241.
Convent—4130 S.E. Brooklyn, 97206. Tel: 503-231-6538. Sisters of the Holy Names of Jesus and Mary Sisters 4.
Catechesis/Religious Programs—Students 55.

20—IMMACULATE HEART OF MARY (1888), Rev. Nicolaus Marandu.
Res., 2926 N. Williams Ave., 97227-1628. Tel: 503-287-3724; Fax: 503-287-5011.

21—ST. JOHN FISHER (1959), Rev. Wayne A. Forbes; Deacon Richard Heames, Pastoral Assoc., Tel: 503-244-5784.
Res., 7007 S.W. 46th Ave., 97219. Tel: 503-246-4686; Fax: 503-452-8570.
School—Tel: 503-246-3234; Fax: 503-246-4117.
Lay Teachers 14; Aides 7; Students 267.
Catechesis/Religious Programs—Tel: 503-244-5784; Fax: 503-452-8570.
Students 90.

22—CHURCH OF ST. JOSEPH THE WORKER (1885), Rev. Jack Krall.
Res., 2310 S.E. 148th, 97233. Tel: 503-761-8710; Fax: 503-761-8545.
Catechesis/Religious Programs—Tel: 503-762-2704.
Students 173.

23—ST. MARY MAGDALENE (1911). (The Madeleine). Rev. E. B. Painter, S.J.
Res., 3123 N.E. 24th Ave., 97212. Tel: 503-281-5777; Fax: 503-281-0673.
School—3240 N.E. 23rd Ave., 97212. Tel: 503-288-9197; Fax: 503-280-1196. Bernadette Kunnen, Prin.; Marietta Debruhl, Vice Prin.
Sisters of the Holy Name 2; Lay Teachers 16; Students 243.
Catechesis/Religious Programs—Students 63.

24—CHURCH OF ST. MICHAEL, THE ARCHANGEL (1894) (Italian), Rev. Dennis O'Donovan, Mod.; Celeste Granato, Admin.
Res., 424 S.W. Mill St., 97201. Tel: 501-228-8629; Fax: 501-827-7689.

25—OUR LADY OF LAVANG (1999) (Vietnamese), Revs. Vincent Minh, C.SS.R.; James Pham-Van-Ninh, S.E.; Joseph Nguyen Duc Hau, S.E.
5404 N.E. Alameda Dr., 97213. Tel: 503-249-5892; Fax: 503-249-1776.
Catechesis/Religious Programs—Students 850.

26—OUR LADY OF SORROWS (1917), Rev. Amancio Rodrigues.
Res., 5221 S.E. Knight St., 97206. Tel: 503-775-6731; Fax: 503-775-6732.
School—Tel: 503-771-3592; Fax: 503-774-5390.
Sisters 1; Lay Teachers 10; Students 172.
Catechesis/Religious Programs—Students 53.

27—ST. PATRICK (1885), Rev. Michael T. Patrick (Canada).
Res., 1623 N.W. 19th Ave., 97209. Tel: 503-222-4086.
Catechesis/Religious Programs—Students 37.

28—ST. PETER (1911), Rev. Dale T. Waddill; Brendan Mallon, Pastoral Assoc.; Roberto Minero, O.S.F., Hispanic Min.
Mailing Address: 8648 S.E. Foster Rd., 97266. Tel: 503-777-3321; Fax: 503-777-3321.
Res., 5736 S.E. 86th St., 97266. Tel: 503-777-1026.
Catechesis/Religious Programs—Tel: 503-777-3322.
Students 180.

29—ST. PHILIP NERI (1912), Revs. Stephen E. Bossi, C.S.P.; Vincent J. Sampietro, C.S.P. Pastoral Assocs.: Revs. Richard W. Chilson, C.S.P.; Ricky Manalo, C.S.P.
Res., 2408 S.E. 16th Ave., 97214. Tel: 503-231-4955; Fax: 503-736-1383.

30—ST. PIUS X (Cedar Mill) (1953), Revs. Ronald C. Millican; Angelo Gomes; Deacon Robert Little.
Office: 1280 N.W. Saltzman Rd., 97229. Tel: 503-644-5264; Fax: 503-626-6540.
School—1260 N.W. Saltzman Rd., 97229. Tel: 503-644-3244; Fax: 503-646-6568.
Lay Teachers 13; Students 268.
Catechesis/Religious Programs—Tel: 503-626-3154.
Students 740.

31—QUEEN OF PEACE. (North Portland Catholic Community.). Rev. David Gutmann.
Mailing Address: 5227 N. Bowdain St., 97203. Tel: 503-289-2834; Fax: 503-283-7056.

32—ST. RITA (1924), Rev. Damian M. Kobus, O.S.M.
Mailing Address: 10029 N.E. Prescott St., 97220. Tel: 503-252-3403; Fax: 503-256-9682.
Catechesis/Religious Programs—Students 40.

33—ST. ROSE OF LIMA (1911), Rev. Richard J. Huneger.
Res., 2727 N.E. 54th Ave., 97213. Tel: 503-281-5318; Fax: 503-284-8350.
School—Archbishop Howard School, Tel: 503-281-1912; Fax: 503-281-0554.
Lay Teachers 12; Students 278.
Catechesis/Religious Programs—Students 69.

34—SACRED HEART (1893), Rev. Joseph A. Baccellieri.
Res., 3910 S.E. 11th Ave., 97202. Tel: 503-231-9636; Fax: 503-231-1766.
Catechesis/Religious Programs—Students 17.

35—ST. STANISLAUS (1907) (Polish), Rev. Henry Kociolek, S.Ch.
Res., 3916 N. Interstate Ave., 97227-1063. Tel: 503-281-7532; Fax: 503-281-7532.
Catechesis/Religious Programs—Christ Our Life.
Students 94.

36—ST. STEPHEN (1907), Rev. Morton Park.
Res., 1112 S.E. 41st Ave., 97214. Tel: 503-234-5019; Fax: 503-239-5985.
School—4235 S.E. Salmon, 97214. Tel: 503-235-7040; Fax: 503-239-5985.
Lay Teachers 5; Students 114.
Catechesis/Religious Programs—Fax: 503-236-0843.
Students 26.

37—ST. THERESE OF THE CHILD JESUS (1955), Rev. Jacob A. Mosbrucker; Deacon Vernard Korchinski, Pastoral Assoc.
Res., 1260 N.E. 132nd Ave., 97230. Tel: 503-256-5850; Fax: 503-253-3560.
School—Tel: 503-253-9400; Fax: 503-253-9571.
Dominican Sisters of Mission San Jose 2; Lay Teachers 12; Students 245.
Catechesis/Religious Programs—Students 70.

38—ST. THOMAS MORE (1936), Rev. Michael P. Johnston.
Church—3525 S.W. Patton Rd., 97221. Tel: 503-222-2055; Fax: 503-242-1831.
School—Tel: 503-222-6105; Fax: 503-227-5661.
Lay Teachers 15; Students 225.
Catechesis/Religious Programs—Students 80.

39—ST. VINCENT DE PAUL (1919). (Downtown Chapel). Revs. Richard F. Berg C.S.C.; Jeffrey Schneibel, C.S.C. In res., Bro. Ronald Whelan, C.S.C., Pastoral Assoc.; Rev. Gary N. Smith, S.J.
Res., 601 W. Burnside St., 97209. Tel: 503-228-0746; Fax: 503-402-1607.
Catechesis/Religious Programs—Students 2.

OUTSIDE THE CITY OF PORTLAND

Albany, Linn Co., Our Lady of Perpetual Help (1885), Rev. John C. Betts; Kathleen Reilly, Pastoral Assoc.
Res., 728 Ellsworth St., 97321. Tel: 541-926-1449; Fax: 541-926-2191.
School—815 S. Broadalbin, Tel: 541-928-7474. Sharon Tebb, Prin.
Sisters 2; Lay Teachers 4; Students 144.
Catechesis/Religious Programs—Tel: 541-926-9327. Ellen Ketsdever, D.R.E.
Students 280.

Aloha, Washington Co., St. Elizabeth Ann Seton (1982), Rev. J. Pat Moore.
Res., 3145 S.W. 192nd Ave., 97006. Tel: 503-649-9044; 649-6211; Fax: 503-848-2915.
Catechesis/Religious Programs—Tel: 503-848-3766.
Students 253.

Ashland, Jackson Co., Our Lady of the Mountain (1887), Revs. Gerald A. Buckley, O.P.; Raymond Finerty, O.P., Newman Center; Brendan McAnerney, O.P. In res., Rev. Paschal Donald Salisbury, O.P.
Res., 987 Hillview Dr., 97520. Tel: 541-482-1146; Fax: 541-488-5174.
Catechesis/Religious Programs—Students 175.

Astoria, Clatsop Co., St. Mary, Star of the Sea (1874), Rev. Richard B. Thompson.
Res., 1465 Grand Ave., 97103. Tel: 503-325-3671; Fax: 503-325-7983. [JC]
School—Tel: 503-325-3771.
Lay Teachers 8; Students 119.
Mission—Hammond, Clatsop Co., St. Francis de Sales, 867 5th Ave., 97121.
Catechesis/Religious Programs—Students 90.

Bandon, Coos Co., Holy Trinity (1883), Rev. William E. Karath.
Res., 355 Oregon Ave., Box 1037, 97411. Tel: 541-347-2309; Fax: 541-347-9256. [CEM]
Mission—Port Orford, Curry Co., St. John the Baptist, P.O. Box 884, Port Orford, 97465.
Catechesis/Religious Programs—Students 49.

Beaverton, Washington Co., St. Cecilia (1876), Revs. Scott Vandehey; Joseph Betschart.
Res., 5105 S.W. Franklin Ave., 97005. Tel: 503-644-2619; Fax: 503-626-7204.
School—Tel: 503-644-7647; Fax: 503-646-4217.
Sisters 1; Lay Teachers 15; Students 260.
Catechesis/Religious Programs—Tel: 503-644-0203.
Students 420.

Holy Trinity (1962), Rev. John Waldron.
Res., 13715 S.W. Walker Rd., 97005. Tel: 503-643-9528; Fax: 503-644-8486. [CEM]
School—Tel: 503-644-5748; Fax: 503-643-4475.
Lay Teachers 16; Students 255.
Catechesis/Religious Programs—Tel: 503-646-0331; Fax: 503-626-2030.
Students 215.

Brookings, Curry Co., Star of the Sea (1923), Rev. Edmund K. Ryan, O.P.
Mailing Address: Box 1066, 97415.
Mission—Gold Beach, Curry Co., St. Charles Borromeo, 94323 Gauntlet, P.O. Box 33, Gold Beach, 97444. Tel: 541-247-2453. Rev. Thomas F. Mannion.
Catechesis/Religious Programs—Students 25.

Canby, Clackamas Co., St. Patrick (1882), Rev. Thomas D. Yurchak.
Res., 498 N.W. Ninth, P.O. Box 730, 97013. Tel: 503-266-9411; Fax: 503-263-2293. [CEM]
Catechesis/Religious Programs—488 N.W. 9th, 97013. Tel: 503-266-2401.
Students 286.

Central Point, Jackson Co., Shepherd of the Valley (1978), Rev. James Clifford, O.S.A.
Office: 600 Beebe Rd., 97502. Tel: 541-664-1050; Fax: 541-664-9312.
Catechesis/Religious Programs—Students 72.

Coos Bay, Coos Co., St. Monica (1888), Rev. Terry J. O'Connell.
Mailing Address: 357 S. 6th St., 97420.
Church—97420. Tel: 541-267-7421; Fax: 541-267-8491.
Catechesis/Religious Programs—Students 81.

Coquille, Coos Co., Holy Name (1915), Rev. John F. McGuire.
Res., 12 N. Dean St., 97423. Tel: 541-396-3849; Fax: 541-396-4620.
Catechesis/Religious Programs—Students 47.
Missions—Myrtle Point, Coos Co., Sts. Ann and Michael, 209 Second St., Myrtle Point, 97458. Tel: 541-396-3849; Powers, Coos Co., St. Bridget, 580 Third & Spruce, Powers, 97466.

Cornelius, Washington Co., St. Alexander (1881) (Hispanic), Revs. Mark J. Cach; Meliton (Enrique) Ceballos (Mexico).
Mailing Address: P.O. Box 644, 97113. Fax: 503-992-8634.
Res., 183 N. 11th, 97113. Tel: 503-359-0304; Fax: 503-359-0304.
Catechesis/Religious Programs—Students 312.

Corvallis, Benton Co., St. Mary (1861), Revs. John Henderson, O.F.M. Conv.; Michael Walker; Deacons Francis Potts; Chris Anderson; Gloria J. Holt, Contact Person.
Res., 501 N.W. 25th St., 97330. Tel: 541-757-1988; Fax: 541-757-2788. [CEM]
Catechesis/Religious Programs—Tel: 541-757-1675.
Students 682.

Cottage Grove, Lane Co., Our Lady of Perpetual Help (1897), Rev. James Dowd; Sr. Elizabeth Hecker, S.N.J.M., Pastoral Assoc.
Res., 1025 N. 19th St., 97424. Tel: 541-942-3420; Fax: 541-942-4712.
Mission—Creswell, Lane Co., St. Philip Benizi, Cresswell.
Catechesis/Religious Programs—Students 112.

Dallas, Polk Co., St. Philip (1920), Rev. Gerald Quintal.
Office: 825 S.W. Mill St., 97338. Tel: 503-623-2440. [JC]
Catechesis/Religious Programs—Students 100.

Estacada, Clackamas Co., St. Aloysius (1924), Rev. Robert J. Palladino.
Res., P.O. Box 1199, 97023. Tel: 503-630-2416. [JC]
Catechesis/Religious Programs—Students 85.

Eugene, Lane Co.,

1—St. Jude, (1969), Rev. John E. McGrann.
Office: 4330 Willamette, 97405. Tel: 541-344-1191; Fax: 541-345-6001.
Catechesis/Religious Programs—Students 115.

2—St. Mark, (1962), Rev. Daniel Reynolds.
Res., 1760 Echo Hollow Rd., 97402. Tel: 541-689-0725; Fax: 541-689-0569.
Catechesis/Religious Programs—Tel: 541-689-2345.
Students 74.

3—St. Mary, (1887), Revs. Mark V. Bachmeier; Victor Perez.
Res., 1062 Charnelton St., 97401. Tel: 541-342-1139; Fax: 541-334-6996. [CEM]
Catechesis/Religious Programs—Students 139.

4—St. Paul, (1955), Rev. Stephen Clovis.
Res., 1201 Satre St., 97401. Tel: 541-686-2345; Fax: 541-686-0037.
School—Tel: 541-344-1401; Fax: 541-344-2572.
Sisters 1; Lay Teachers 18; Students 263.
Catechesis/Religious Programs—Students 183.

5—St. Peter, (1955), Rev. David Ronald Cullings.
Res., 1150 Maxwell Rd., 97404. Tel: 541-688-1051; Fax: 541-689-0782 (call first). [JC]
Catechesis/Religious Programs—Tel: 541-689-0782.
Students 117.

6—St. Thomas More, (1915). (University Parish). Rev. Michael Fones, O.P.; Stefani Catone, Pastoral Assoc. In res., Revs. Bede Wilks, O.P.; Thomas More McGreevy, O.P.
Res., 1850 Emerald St., 97403. Tel: 541-343-7021; 346-4468; Fax: 541-686-8028.
Catechesis/Religious Programs—Students 32.

Florence, Lane Co., St. Mary, Our Lady of the Dunes (1951), Rev. Donald K. Gutmann.
Res., 85060 U.S. Hwy. 101 S., Box 2640, 97439. Tel: 541-997-2312; Fax: 541-902—0417.
Catechesis/Religious Programs—Students 75.

Forest Grove, Washington Co., St. Anthony (1908), Rev. Elwin Schwab; Sandra S. Zajdel, Pastoral Assoc., Tel: 503-357-8147; Jim Cammond, Business Mgr.
Res., 1660 Elm St., 97116. Tel: 503-357-2989; Fax: 503-357-2217. [JC]
Catechesis/Religious Programs—Students 196.

Gervais, Marion Co., Sacred Heart-St. Louis (1847), Rev. Kenneth Jacques, O.S.B.
Res., 680 Elm Ave., P.O. Box 236, 97026. Tel: 503-792-4231; Fax: 503-792-3749. [CEM]
School—Tel: 503-792-4541; Fax: 503-792-3826. Nicki Medeiros, Prin.
Lay Teachers 4; Students 112.
Catechesis/Religious Programs—Tel: 503-463-8525.
Students 115.

Grand Ronde, Yamhill Co., St. Michael (1860), Rev. Raymond Elam, O.S.A.
Res., 48520 S.W. Hebo Rd., 97347. Tel: 503-843-2206.

Grants Pass, Josephine Co., St. Anne (1896), Revs. Gregory Moys; John Cihak.
Res., 1131 N.E. 10th St., 97526. Tel: 541-476-2240; Fax: 541-476-2194.
Parish Center—1133 N.E. 10th St., 97526. Tel: 541-479-4848.
School—(Grades PreK-8). Tel: 541-479-1582; Fax: 541-479-1582. Ms. Frankie Bytheway, Prin.
Lay Teachers 11; Students 175.
Kelly Youth Center—1129 N.E. 10th St., 97526. Tel: 541-476-5802.
Catechesis/Religious Programs—Tel: 541-479-4848.
Students 154.
Missions—Cave Junction, Josephine Co., St. Patrick, 407 W. River St., Cave Junction, 97523. Tel: 541-592-3658; Fax: 541-592-3580. Rev. Harry Holwell.; Rogue River, Jackson Co., Rogue River Catholic Community, P.O. Box 1596, Rogue River, 97537. Tel: 541-582-1373. Deacon Robert Chapin.

Gresham, Multnomah Co., St. Anne (1957), Revs. J. Michael Morrissey; Cirilo Bailon (Mexico).
Res., 1015 S.E. 182nd Ave., 97233-5099. Tel: 503-665-4935; Fax: 503-661-2116.
Catechesis/Religious Programs—Students 220.

St. Henry (1913), Revs. Richard D. Sirianni; E. Slider Steuernol. In res., Rev. Charles J. Lienert; Deacon Donald Philip.
Office: 346 N.W. First St., 97030. Tel: 503-665-9129; Fax: 503-665-8238.
Catechesis/Religious Programs—Students 263.

Hillsboro, Washington Co., St. Matthew (1902), Revs. Jose Ortega, M.Sp.S.; Gerardo Alberto, M.Sp.S.
Res., 447 S.E. 3rd Ave., 97123-4499. Tel: 503-648-1998; Fax: 503-648-4489. [CEM]
School—Tel: 503-648-2512; Fax: 503-648-4518.
Lay Teachers 10; Students 258.
Catechesis/Religious Programs—Tel: 503-648-6213.
Students 285.

Independence, Polk Co., St. Patrick (1908), Rev. Galdino Monteiro, S.F.X.
Office: 1275 E St., 97351. Tel: 503-838-1242; Fax: 503-838-6873.
Res., 1258 E St., 97351. Tel: 503-838-5137.
Catechesis/Religious Programs—Students 140.

Jordan, Linn Co., Our Lady of Lourdes (1885), Rev. Kevin O'Conor, O.M.I., Mod.; Deacon Ron Bentz, Admin., Tel: 503-394-2488.
Res., 39043 Jordan Rd., 97374. Tel: 503-394-2437; Fax: 541-327-2343. [CEM][JC 2]
Catechesis/Religious Programs—Tel: 503-394-3853. Linda Duman, D.R.E.
Students 34.
Mission—Lyons, Linn Co., St. Patrick, 7th St., Lyons, 97358.

Junction City, Lane Co., St. Helen (1916), Rev. Joseph Black.
Res., 1350 W. Sixth Ave., 97448. Tel: 541-998-8053; Fax: 541-998-9474. [CEM]
Catechesis/Religious Programs—Students 90.

Keizer, Marion Co., St. Edward (1967), Rev. Philip M. Hemming.
Office: 5303 River Rd. N., 97303. Tel: 503-393-5323; Fax: 503-393-5323.
Catechesis/Religious Programs—Fax: 503-463-5439.
Students 120.

Lake Oswego, Clackamas Co., Our Lady of the Lake (1890), Revs. Joseph S. McMahon; Peter Makala.
Mailing Address: 650 A Ave., 97034-2943. Tel: 503-636-7687; Fax: 503-636-9415. [CEM]
School—715 A Ave., 97034-2943. Tel: 503-636-2121; Fax: 503-635-7760. Joan M. Codd, Prin.
Lay Teachers 19; Students 249.
Catechesis/Religious Programs—Students 550.

Lebanon, Linn Co., St. Edward (1903), Rev. Paul P. Maher, O.M.I.; Deacon Richard E. Triska.
Mailing Address: Office, 100 Main St., 97355. Tel: 541-258-5333; Fax: 541-258-2511.
Res., 251 Second St., 97355.
Catechesis/Religious Programs—Tel: 541-258-2224.
Students 125.

Lincoln City, Lincoln Co., St. Augustine (1925), Rev. Mell Stead.
Res., 1139 N.W. Hwy. 101, 97367. Tel: 541-994-2216. [CEM]
Catechesis/Religious Programs—Students 43.

McMinnville, Yamhill Co., St. James (1876), Rev. Thomas B. Farley.
Res., 1145 E. First St., 97128. Tel: 503-472-5232; Fax: 503-472-4414. [CEM]
School—Tel: 503-472-2661.
Lay Teachers 10; Students 134.
Catechesis/Religious Programs—Students 75.
Mission—Dayton, Yamhill Co., St. Martin de Porres, 407 Ferry St., Dayton, 97114. Tel: 503-864-2378; Fax: 503-864-3211.

Medford, Jackson Co., Sacred Heart of Jesus (1928), Revs. Liam Cary; William Dillard.
Res., 449 S. Ivy St., 97501. Tel: 541-779-4661; Fax: 541-774-9474. [JC]
School—Tel: 541-772-4105; Fax: 541-732-0633. Perry Martin, Prin.
Lay Teachers 15; Students 262.
Mission—Jacksonville, Jackson Co., St. Joseph, 280 N. 4th, Jacksonville, 97530.
Catechesis/Religious Programs—Students 360.

Milwaukie, Clackamas Co., Christ the King (1960), Rev. Donald R. Buxman; Deacon William Moisant.
Res., 7414 S.E. Michael Dr., 97222. Tel: 503-659-1475; Fax: 503-659-6138.
School—Tel: 503-659-1475, Ext. 501. Ruth Gill, Prin.
Lay Teachers 14; Students 251.
Catechesis/Religious Programs—Tel: 503-786-0102.
Students 160.

St. John the Baptist (1912), Kenneth Steiner; Rev. Francis Chun; Sr. Rae Skinner, S.N.J.M., R.C.I.A. Dir.
Res., 10955 S.E. 25th, 97222. Tel: 503-654-5449; Fax: 503-653-9567.
School—10956 S.E. 25th, 97222. Tel: 503-654-0200; Fax: 503-654-8419.
Lay Teachers 18; Students 190.
Catechesis/Religious Programs—Tel: 503-659-2760; Fax: 503-653-9567.
Students 243.

Molalla, Clackamas Co., St. James (1962), Rev. R. Ed Coleman.
Res., 301 Frances St., 97038. Tel: 503-829-2080; Fax: 503-829-2806.
Catechesis/Religious Programs—Tel: 503-829-2880.
Students 128.

Monroe, Benton Co., St. Rose (1883), Rev. Joseph Black; William J. Richardson, Jr., Admin.
Mailing Address: P.O. Box 516, 97456. Tel: 541-847-5454.
Res., 00470 S. Fifth, 97456. Tel: 541-847-5454. [CEM]

Mt. Angel, Marion Co., St. Mary (1880) (German), Revs. Edmund Smith, O.S.B.; Vincent Trujillo, O.S.B.
Res., 575 East College St., 97362. Tel: 503-845-2296; Fax: 503-845-2297. [CEM 2]
Catechesis/Religious Programs—Tel: 503-845-9248.
Students 253.
Mission—Scotts Mills, Marion Co., Holy Rosary. [CEM]

Myrtle Creek, Douglas Co., All Souls (1952), Rev. William A. Ryan, O.S.A.
Res., 1242 N.E. Spruce St., P.O. Box 810, 97457. Tel: 541-863-3271; Fax: 541-863-6759. [JC]
Catechesis/Religious Programs—Students 31.
Mission—Glendale, Douglas Co., Holy Family, 243 Marshall Ave., Glendale, 97442.

Newberg, Yamhill Co., St. Peter (1909), Rev. Gregory A. Gage; Matthew Floyd, Pastoral Assoc.
Res., 2315 N. Main, 97132-6081. Tel: 503-538-4312; Fax: 503-538-5693.

Catechesis/Religious Programs—Tel: 503-538-2988.
Students 155.

Newport, Lincoln Co., Sacred Heart Parish (1889), Rev. Jack M. Wells.
Res., 927 N. Coast Hwy., P.O. Box 843, 97365. Tel: 541-265-5101; Fax: 541-265-7582. [JC]
Mission—Siletz, Lincoln Co., St. Mary, 231 E. Logsden Rd, Siletz, 97380. Tel: 541-444-1164.
Catechesis/Religious Programs—Students 115.

North Bend, Coos Co., Holy Redeemer (1906), Rev. Karl Schray.
Res., 2250 16th St., 97459. Tel: 541-756-6901; Fax: 541-756-3234. [JC]
Catechesis/Religious Programs—Tel: 541-756-0161; 756-8904 (Youth Min.).
Students 177.

North Plains, Washington Co., St. Edward (1913), Rev. Msgr. Frank Campbell.
Res., P.O. Box 507, 97133. Tel: 503-644-1932; 647-2131 (Parish). [CEM]
Catechesis/Religious Programs—Tel: 503-647-2131.
Students 65.

Oakridge, Lane Co., St. Michael (1941). Unassigned.
Res., 76387 Crestview St., P.O. Box 422, 97463. Tel: 541-782-3262.
Mission—Dexter, Lane Co., St. Henry, 38925 Dexter Rd., P.O. Box 65, Dexter, 97431. Tel: 541-937-3033. [JC] Rev. Francis J. Falsetto, S.J.
Catechesis/Religious Programs—Students 84.

Oregon City, Clackamas Co., St. John the Apostle (1842), Rev. Richard J. Wallace.
Res., 417 Washington St., 97045. Tel: 503-656-3474; Fax: 503-656-0486. [CEM]
School—Tel: 503-656-5123. Alan Loboy, Prin.
Lay Teachers 10; Students 203.
Catechesis/Religious Programs—Tel: 503-656-7755.
Students 247.

Rainier, Columbia Co., Nativity B.V.M. (1909), Rev. Luan Q. Tran.
Res., 204 E. C St., P.O. Box 340, 97048. Tel: 503-556-5641.
Mission—Clatskanie, Columbia Co., St. John the Baptist, High St., Clatskanie, 97016.

Redland, Clackamas Co., St. Philip Benizi (1969), Rev. Carl J. Flach.
Res., 18211 S. Henrici Rd., Oregon City, 97045. Tel: 503-631-2882; Fax: 503-631-7443.
Catechesis/Religious Programs—Tel: 503-631-7124.
Students 193.

Reedsport, Douglas Co., St. John the Apostle (1924), Rev. Don Gutmann; Charlotte Fogarty, Pastoral Assoc.
Res., 12 St. Johns Way, 97467. Tel: 541-271-5621.
Catechesis/Religious Programs—Students 15.

Rockaway, Tillamook Co., St. Mary by the Sea (1927), Revs. William A. Maat, O.S.B.; George W. Carr, O.F.M.
Mailing Address: P.O. Box 390, 97136. Tel: 503-355-2345. [JC]
Church—275 S. Pacific St., Tel: 503-355-2661 (Office); Fax: 503-355-9611.
Catechesis/Religious Programs—Students 10.

Roseburg, Douglas Co., St. Joseph (1867), Revs. Juniper Schneider, O.F.M.Conv.; William Holtzinger.
Res., 800 W. Stanton St., 97470. Tel: 541-673-5157; Fax: 541-672-5022. [CEM]
School—Tel: 541-672-1751; Fax: 541-673-5229.
Lay Teachers 10; Students 152.
Catechesis/Religious Programs—Tel: 541-672-7239.
Students 343.

Roy, Washington Co., St. Francis of Assisi (1908), Rev. Todd Molinari.
Res., 39135 N.W. Harrington Rd., Banks, 97106. Tel: 503-324-2231. [CEM]
School—39085 N.W. Harrington Rd., Banks, 97106. Tel: 503-324-2182; Fax: 503-324-7032.
Lay Teachers 5; Students 107.
Catechesis/Religious Programs—Students 71.

St. Helens, Columbia Co., St. Frederic (1910), Rev. Heiko Junge.
Res., 175 S. 13th St., 97051. Tel: 503-397-0148; Fax: 503-366-3870.
Catechesis/Religious Programs—Tel: 503-397-0366.
Students 80.

St. Louis, Marion Co., St. Louis. Closed. For sacramental records contact Sacred Heart-St. Louis, Gervias.

St. Paul, Marion Co., St. Paul (1839), Rev. Charles D. Borho.
Res., 20217 Christie St., N.E., P.O. Box 454, 97137. Tel: 503-633-4611. [CEM]
School—20327 Christie St., N.E., P.O. Box 188, 97137. Tel: 503-633-4622; Fax: 503-633-4624. Ms. Christina Meadows, B.S., M.A., Prin.
Lay Teachers 7; Students 101.
Catechesis/Religious Programs—Students 17.

Salem, Marion Co., St. Joseph (1864), Revs. Carl Gimpl; Joseph Hoang.
Res., 721 Chemeketa St. N.E., 97301. Tel: 503-581-1623; Fax: 503-581-7271. [JC]
School—Tel: 503-581-2147.
Sisters of the Holy Names of Jesus and Mary 2; Lay Teachers 28; Students 278.
Catechesis/Religious Programs—Tel: 503-585-5095.
Students 375.
Mission—Salem, Marion Co., San Jose, Tel: 503-399-6288.

Queen of Peace (1963), Rev. George Wolf. Pastoral Assocs.: Sr. Theresa Calouri, B.V.M.; Darlene Joynt. Office: P.O. Box 3016, 97302. Tel: 503-364-7202; Fax: 503-364-5882.
School—4227 Lone Oak Rd., S.E., Tel: 503-362-3443; Fax: 503-589-9411. Debilyn Janota, Prin.
Lay Teachers 10; Students 145.
Catechesis/Religious Programs—Tel: 503-364-7202; Fax: 503-364-5882. D.R.E.: Tricia Boyle, Preschool-Elem.; Martin Gay, Youth Min., Young Adult (Grades 7-12); Cheri Posedel, Youth Min., Young Adult (Grades 7-12).
Students 560.

St. Vincent de Paul (1925), Rev. Patrick McNamee; Sr. Joyce Barsotti, S.S.M.O., Pastoral Assoc.
Res., 1025 Columbia St., 97303-5198. Tel: 503-363-4589; Fax: 503-363-9493. [JC]
School—Tel: 503-363-8457; Fax: 503-363-1516.
Lay Teachers 7; Students 91.
Catechesis/Religious Programs—1015 Columbia St. N.E., 97303. Tel: 503-363-2166; Fax: 503-363-2339.
Students 192.

Sandy, Clackamas Co., St. Michael the Archangel (1898), Rev. J. Aidan Mayo.
Res., 18090 S.E. Langensand Rd., 97055-9427. Tel: 503-668-4446; Fax: 503-668-5018.
Mission—Welches, Clackamas Co., St. John the Evangelist, Box 1278, 97067. Tel: 503-622-6338.
Catechesis/Religious Programs—Students 59.

Scappoose, Columbia Co., St. Wenceslaus (1911), Rev. James R. Stange.
Parish Office: Tel: 503-543-2110; Fax: 503-543-5159.
Res., 51555 Old Portland Rd., 97056. [CEM]
Catechesis/Religious Programs—Tel: 503-534-7425.
Students 123.

Scio, Linn Co., St. Bernard (1912), Rev. Kevin O'Conner, O.M.I.
Res., P.O. Box 45, 97374. Tel: 503-394-2625.
Catechesis/Religious Programs—Students 20.
Mission—Jefferson, Marion Co., St. Thomas, 647 Third St., Jefferson, 97352. Tel: 541-327-2343.

Seaside, Clatsop Co., Our Lady of Victory (1913), Rev. Nicholas Nilema, A.L.C.P.; Deacon Alton Stromberg.
Res., 120 Ocean Way, 97138. Tel: 503-738-6161; Fax: 503-738-6182.
Parish Office—Tel: 503-738-6161.
Mission—Seaside, Clatsop Co., St. Peter the Fisherman, P.O. Box 117, Archcape, 97102. Tel: 503-436-2876.
Mailing Address: 120 Ocean Way, 97138.
Catechesis/Religious Programs—Students 109.

Shady Cove, Jackson Co., Our Lady of Fatima (1955), Rev. William McHugh, O.M.I.
Res., 37 Church Ln., P.O. Box 116, 97539. Tel: 541-878-2479.
Catechesis/Religious Programs—Students 53.

Shaw, Marion Co., St. Mary (1906), Rev. G. James Brady, C.S.C.
Mailing Address: P.O. Box 338, Aumsville, 97325-0338. Tel: 503-362-6159.
Res., 9168 Silver Falls Hwy., S.E., Aumsville, 97325. Tel: 503-371-6435. [CEM]
Catechesis/Religious Programs—Students 45.

Sheridan, Yamhill Co., Good Shepherd (1908), Rev. Raymond Elam, O.S.A.
Res., 127 N.E. Hill St., 97378. Tel: 503-843-2206.

Sherwood, Washington Co., St. Francis (1921), Rev. Thomas McCarthy, S.J.
Mailing Address: P.O. Box 279, 97140. Tel: 503-625-6185; Fax: 503-625-6187.
Res., 400 S. Pine St., 97140. Tel: 503-625-6186.
Church—400 N.E. Oregon St., 97140. Tel: 503-625-5914.
Catechesis/Religious Programs—Tel: 503-625-6187; Fax: 503-625-6187.
Students 293.

Silverton, Marion Co., St. Paul (1914), Rev. Cosmas White, O.S.B.; Deacon Loris A. Buccola.
Res., 1410 Pine St., 97381. Tel: 503-873-2044; Fax: 503-873-0304. [CEM]
Catechesis/Religious Programs—Students 203.

Springfield, Lane Co., St. Alice (1947), Rev. Patrick Walsh.
Res., 1520 F St., 97477. Tel: 541-747-7041; Fax: 541-746-5213.
Catechesis/Religious Programs—Students 170.

Stayton, Marion Co., Immaculate Conception (1903), Rev. Panneer Selvam.
Res., 1077 N. Sixth Ave., 97383. Tel: 503-769-2656; Fax: 503-769-5621. [CEM]
School—Tel: 503-769-2718; Fax: 503-769-0560.
Sisters of St. Mary of Oregon 1; Lay Teachers 17; Students 286.
Catechesis/Religious Programs—Students 120.

Sublimity, Marion Co., St. Boniface (1879), Rev. Arthur P. Dernbach; Deacon Donald T. Triggs.
Res., 375 E. Church St., 97385. Tel: 503-769-5664. [CEM]
Catechesis/Religious Programs—Students 92.
Missions—Mill City, Marion Co., St. Catherine of Siena, First & Ivy, Mill City, 97360.; Detroit, Marion Co., St. Christopher, Santiam Ave., Detroit, 97342.

Sutherlin, Douglas Co., St. Francis Xavier (1957), Revs. Juniper Schneider, O.F.M.Conv.; Bill Holtzinger.
Mailing Address: 800 Stanton St., Roseburg, 97470. Tel: 541-673-5157 (Office).
Mission—Drain, Douglas Co., St. John the Apostle. [JC]

Sweet Home, Linn Co., St. Helen (1953), Rev. Andrew Harris, O.M.I.
Res., 815 Fifth Ave., 97386. Tel: 541-367-2530.
Catechesis/Religious Programs—Students 66.
Mission—Brownsville, Linn Co., Holy Trinity, 104 Blakely Ave., P.O. Box 145, Brownsville, 97327.

Tigard, Washington Co., St. Anthony (1910), Rev. Leslie M. Sieg.
Res., 9905 S.W. McKenzie St., 97223. Tel: 503-639-4179; Fax: 503-624-2364. [CEM]
School—Fax: 503-620-5117. Jeananne Bloudek, Prin.
Lay Teachers 26; Students 392.
Catechesis/Religious Programs—Students 432.

Tillamook, Tillamook Co., Sacred Heart (1890), Rev. Gary Zerr.
2411 Fifth St., 97141. Tel: 503-842-6647; Fax: 503-842-3897. [CEM]
Catechesis/Religious Programs—Tel: 503-842-8984.
Students 175.
Mission—Cloverdale, Tillamook Co., St. Joseph, P.O. Box 9, Cloverdale, 97112. Tel: 503-392-3685. Rev. Menino George A. Nazareth.

Tualatin, Clackamas Co., Church of the Resurrection (1981), Rev. Richard Rossman.
Mailing Address: 21060 S.W. Stafford Rd., 97062. Tel: 503-638-1579; Fax: 503-638-8754.
Catechesis/Religious Programs—Students 301.

Veneta, Lane Co., St. Catherine of Siena (1954), Rev. Dan Reynolds, Mod.; Gene Modrich, Parish Admin.
Res., 25181 E. Broadway, P.O. Box 277, 97487. Tel: 503-935-3933.
Catechesis/Religious Programs—Students 36.

Verboort, Washington Co., Visitation B.V.M. (1875) (Dutch), Rev. Joseph Heuberger.
Res., 4285 N.W. Visitation Rd., Forest Grove, 97116. Tel: 503-357-3860; Fax: 503-359-0819. [CEM]
School—Tel: 503-357-6990; Fax: 503-359-0819.
Sisters of St. Mary of Oregon (S.S.M.O.) 1; Lay Teachers 9; Students 125.
Catechesis/Religious Programs—Students 12.

Vernonia, Columbia Co., St. Mary (1923), Rev. Heiko Junge, Mod.; Juanita Dennis, Pastoral Assoc.
Church—960 Missouri Ave., P.O. Box 312, 97064. Tel: 503-429-8841; Fax: 503-429-8841 (Call First).
Catechesis/Religious Programs—Students 36.
Mission—Our Lady of the Woods. [JC]

Waldport, Lincoln Co., St. Anthony (1949), Rev. Gerard Steckler, S.J., Admin.
Mailing Address: P.O. Box 770, 97394. Tel: 541-563-3246; Fax: 541-563-3246.
685 N. Broadway, 97394.
Catechesis/Religious Programs—Students 30.

Wilsonville, Clackamas Co., St. Cyril (1926), Rev. Paul Peri.
Res., 9210 S.W. Fifth St., 97070. Tel: 503-682-2332; Fax: 503-682-0898 (Call First).
Catechesis/Religious Programs—Students 133.

Woodburn, Marion Co., St. Luke (1899), Revs. David Zegar; Jaime Rojas (Mexico); Deacon Jerry McKenzie.
Office: 417 Harrison St., 97071. Tel: 503-981-5011; Fax: 503-981-5012.
Res., 417 Harrison St., 97071. Tel: 503-981-1531. [CEM]
School—529 Harrison St., 97071. Tel: 503-981-7441; Fax: 503-982-4697.

Sisters 4; Lay Teachers 10; Students 174.
Catechesis/Religious Programs—Students 156.
Mission—Hubbard, Marion Co., St. Agnes, 3052 D St., Hubbard, 97032.

Yamhill, Yamhill Co., St. John (1910), Rev. David Janes, Admin.
Mailing Address: P.O. Box 580, 97148. Tel: 503-662-4291.
Catechesis/Religious Programs—Students 63.

SOUTHEAST ASIAN VICARIATE

1—SOUTHEAST ASIAN VICARIATE, Multnomah Co., (1982). Please refer to Our Lady of Lavang Church, Portland, OR.

Chaplains of Public Institutions

PORTLAND. *Department of Veterans' Affairs Medical Center* 3710 S.W. U.S. Veterans' Hospital Rd., Box 1034, 97207. Tel: 503-220-8262, Ext: 57027, 57021; Fax: 503-721-1049. Rev. William E. Wickham, C.S.C.
Oregon Health Sciences University St. Elizabeth, 4112 Sixth Ave. Drive, 97201. Tel: 503-222-2168. Rev. Louis Urbanski.

ROSEBURG. *U.S. Veterans' Administration Hospital* 913 N.W. Garden Valley Blvd., 97470-6513. Tel: 541-440-1000, Ext. 4720. Deacon John Stenbeck.

SALEM. *Mill Creek Correctional Facility* 5465 Turner Rd., 97310-9400. Tel: 503-378-2333. Rev. James Jacobson, S.J.
Oregon State Correctional Institution 3405 Deer Park Dr. S.E., 97310. Tel: 503-373-0105.
Oregon State Penitentiary 2605 State St., 97310. Tel: 503-378-2333; Fax: 503-378-3897. Rev. James Jacobson, S.J.
Oregon Women's Correction Center 2809 State St., 97310. Tel: 503-378-6482, Ext. 7139. Rev. Kenneth Jacques, O.S.B.
Santiam Correctional Institution 4005 Aumsville Hwy. S.E., 97310-9112. Tel: 503-378-2333. Rev. James Jacobson, S.J.
Youth Correctional Facility 2450 Strong Rd., 97310. Tel: 503-986-0421; Fax: 503-986-0406. Rev. Ted Frison.

SHERIDAN. *Federal Correctional Institution* 27072 Ballston Rd., 97378-9601. Tel: 503-843-4442, Ext. 254. Rev. Perry McCoy, O.S.M.

WHITE CITY. *U.S. Veternan's Affairs Domiciliary* 97503. Tel: 541-826-2111, Ext. 3321. Revs. Joseph E. Shirey, S.J.; Paschal Donald Salisbury, O.P.

WOODBURN. *MacLaren Youth Correctional Facility* 2630 N. Pacific Hwy., 97071. Tel: 503-981-9531, Ext. 316. Rev. Ted Frison.

Special Assignment:
Reverend Fathers—
Carey, Raymond, P.O. Box 3019, Salem, OR 97302
Donoghue, Patrick, 2838 E. Burnside, Portland, OR 97214-1895

On Duty Outside the Archdiocese:
Reverend Fathers—
Adams, Daniel, St. Benedict, 1801 Octavia St., San Francisco, CA 94109
Brennan, Patrick, North American College, 00120 Vatican City, Europe
Clark, David, St. Vincent de Paul Church, 36 Altenburg Gardens, Clapham Common, London, SWII IJJ England
Coleman, James, Padres de Santiago Apostol, Castilla 919, Santa Cruz, Bolivia
Dare, Glenn O., Diocese of Sacramento
King, Martin, 6 ARW/HC, 2204 Administration Ave., MacDill AFB, FL 33621
Kueber, Michael, St. John the Evangelist, Little Canada, MN

Absent on Leave:
Reverend Fathers—
Galluzzo, James, c/o 4545 S.E. Tibbetts, Portland, OR 97206
Knusel, Frank, 34799 N. Honeyman Rd., Scappoose, OR 97056
Stobie, Steve, 103-215 Bolton St., Ottawa, ON KIN5B5

Retired:
Reverend Fathers—
Alvares, Augustine, 12075 Mount Hamilton Rd., San Jose, CA 95140
Beno, Joseph, 484 S. 17th St., P.O. Box 1012, St. Helens, OR 97051
Bliven, Edmond, 3311 S.W. First Ave., Portland, OR 97201
Brennan, Cathal, 14544 S.E. Brightwood Ave., Milwaukie, OR 97267
Brouillard, John, 17704 N.W. Shadyfir Loop, Space 39, Beaverton, OR 97006
Cieslinski, Robert, St. John Vianney Residence, 4630-D S.W. St. John Vianney Way, Beavertown, OR 97007
Crunican, James, Mount St. Joseph Residence, 3060 S.E. Stark St., Portland, OR 97214
Cunniff, Vincent, 4655-D S.W. St. John Vianney Way, Beaverton, OR 97007
Denman, Donald, St. John Vianney Residence, 4630-B S.W. St. John Vianney Way, Beaverton, OR 97007
DePra, Italo, 1148 Third Ave. #62, Chula Vista, CA 91911
Dieringer, James J., P.O. Box 683, Pacific City, OR 97135
Domin, John M., 14645 S.W. Farmington, Beaverton, OR 97007
Engel, John, 17704 N.W. Shadyfir Loop, Space 39, Beaverton, OR 97006
Fleming, Brendan, St. John Vianney Residence, 4525-D. S.W. St. John Vianney Way, Beaverton, OR 97007 Ireland
Fritz, Norbert, McCauley Terrace, 3120 S.E. Stark #3007, Portland, OR 97214
Gothe, Marcus, St. John Vianney Residence, 4655-B S.W. St. John Vianney Way, Beaverton, OR 97007
Grammond, Maurice, Encore Senior Village, 1808 S.E. 182nd, Portland, OR 97233
Hume, Kenneth, 19453 Stillmeadow Dr., Oregon City, OR 97045
Hwang, Bernard, O.S.B., 19526 Lazy Creek Ln., Oregon City, OR 97045
Jacobson, Gary, St. John Vianney Residence, 4595 S.W. St. John Vianney Way, Beaverton, OR 97007
Kennedy, Alan, Maryville Nursing Home, 14645 S.W. Farmington Rd., Beaverton, OR 97007
Kies, Emil, Evergreen Court, No. 101, 451 O'Connell St., North Bend, OR 97459
Kolasinski, Daniel, P.O. Box 526, Reedsport, OR 97467
Lau, Michael, 19885 S.W. Oak Ct., Aloha, OR 97007
Linehan, Cornelius, 8736 N.E. Russell Pl., Portland, OR 97220
Linehan, Jeremiah, 6908 N.E. Tillamook St., Portland, OR 97210
McHugh, Donald, 1623 S.E. Miller St., Portland, OR 97202
McKean, Louis, P.O. Box 1121, Chula Vista, CA 91912
McMahon, Joseph M., 4525-B St. John Vianney Way, Beaverton, OR 97007
Moore, Neil, 1619 N.W. Bridgeway Ln., Beaverton, OR 97006
Neuville, Joseph, P.O. Box 586, Aurora, OR 97002
Reedy, John J., Maryville Nursing Home, 14645 S.W. Farmington Rd., Beaverton, OR 97007
Ridi, Pio, 6806 N. Sedro, Portland, OR 97203
Rodakowski, Louis, P.O. Box 177, Vida, OR 97488
Saalfeld, Lawrence, 14506 S.E. Carol Ave., Milwaukie, OR 97267
Sassano, Rock, 71403 Fishhawk Rd., Birkenfeld, OR 97016
Senko, Martin, 20964 S. W. Rock Rd., Aloha, OR 97606
Taaffe, Charles Q, 1085 Columbia St. N.E., Salem, OR 97303
Thielen, Martin, 4655-C S.W. St. John Vianney Way, Beaverton, OR 97007
Van Der Zanden, Edmund, St, John Vianney Residence, 4525-C S.W. St. John Vianney Way, Beaverton, OR 97007
Vandehey, Ervin S., Maryville Nursing Home, 14645 S.W. Farmington Rd., Beaverton, OR 97007
Weber, Theodore, 14460 S.E. Sieben Creek Dr., Clackamas, OR 97015
Williams, Alfred, 900 S.W. Liberty Bell Dr., Beaverton, OR 97006
Wraszczak, Chester, Summerplace #204, 15727 N.E. Russell, Portland, OR 97230

Permanent Deacons:
Anderson, Chris, St. Mary, Corvallis
Bentz, Ron, Our Lady of Lourdes, Scio
Buccola, Loris, St. Paul, Silverton
Chapin, Robert L., Jr., St. Anne, Grants Pass
Ciffone, Donald, St. Rose, Portland
Cummings, Owen, St. Paul, Silverton
Filardi, Ronald, Sacred Heart, Medford
Gornick, Thomas, Unassigned
Jacob, Ramon, St. Andrew, Portland
Korchinski, Vernon, St. Therese, Portland
Little, Robert, St. Pius X, Portland
Lucas, Robert, The Cathedral, Portland
Luz, John, St. Paul, Eugene
McKenzie, Gerald, St. Luke, Woodburn
Mendez, Jose R., St. Joseph, Salem
Morin, Edward, (Retired)
Myers, James, Church of Resurrection, Tualatin
Philip, Donald, St. Henry, Gresham
Potts, Francis, St. Mary, Corvallis
Ries, John D., The Cathedral, Portland
Rodriguez, Raul, St. Martinde Porres, Dayton
Soper, Leonard, St. Benedict Lodge, McKensie Bridge
Stenbeck, John H., St. Joseph, Roseburg
Stromberg, Alton, Our Lady of Victory, Seaside
Triggs, Donald J., St. Boniface, Sublimity
Triska, Richard, St. Edward, Lebanon

INSTITUTIONS LOCATED IN THE ARCHDIOCESE

[A] SEMINARIES, RELIGIOUS, ARCHDIOCESAN OR SCHOLASTICATES

PORTLAND. *Franciscan Formation Community*, 827 N.E. Alberta, 97211. Tel: 503-287-9223; Fax: 503-284-7278.
E-mail: Postulancy@sbfranciscans.org
Web site: www.sbfranciscans.org
Rev. Javier Reyes, O.F.M., Dir. & Contact Person. Priests 2; Brothers 1; Postulants 4.
Jesuit Novitiate of St. Francis Xavier, 3301 S.E. 45th Ave., 97206. Tel: 503-774-5699; Fax: 503-788-2596.
E-mail: orenev@teleport.com
Revs. Patrick J. Lee, S.J., Dir. Novices; Steven C. Dillard, S.J., Socius/Minister. In res. Rev. John J. Kindall, S.J. Priests 3; Novices 14.

MOUNT ANGEL. *Felix Rougier House of Studies*, 585 E. College St., 97362. Mailing Address: P.O. Box 499, St. Benedict, 97373. Revs. Gustavo Garcia, M.Sp.S., Supr. of the Vicariate; Antonio Armendariz, M.Sp.S., Rector & Supr. House of Studies; Juan Jose Gonzalez, Assoc. Rector. Brothers 10.

ST. BENEDICT. *Mount Angel Seminary*, 97373. Tel: 503-845-3951; Fax: 503-845-3126.
E-mail: registrar@mtangel.edu
Rt. Rev. Joseph Wood, O.S.B., Abbot & Chancellor; Rev. Nathan Zodrow, O.S.B., Admin.; Marina Keys, Admin. Asst. & Contact Person; Dr. Elaine Park, S.S.L., S.T.D., Academic Dean; Revs. Richard Paperini, Dir. Spiritual Life; Philip Waibel, O.S.B., Dir. Pastoral Education; Odo Recker, O.S.B., Admissions Dir.; Mrs. Dorene Preis, Registrar; Sr. Teresa Gould, F.M., Coordinator Liturgy; Bro. Robert Rodriguez, O.F.M., Asst. Dir. Pastoral Educ.; Mr. Thomas Bolton, Alumni Dir. Formation Directors: Revs. Dave Rogerson (SEA), Dir. Personal Formation; William Hammelman, O.S.B.; Liem Nguyen, O.S.B.; Richard Paperini; William Miller, S.J.; Vitaliano Ola'aiga; Karl Nielson, O.S.B. Priests 24; Sisters 4; Brothers 7; Lay Teachers 18.

[B] COLLEGES AND UNIVERSITIES

PORTLAND. *University of Portland*, 5000 N. Willamette Blvd., 97203. Tel: 503-943-7911; Fax: 503-943-7401.
E-mail: webmaster@up.edu
Web site: www.up.edu
For a complete listing, refer to the Colleges and Universities section.

MARYLHURST. *Marylhurst University*, 97036. Tel: 503-636-8141; Fax: 503-636-9526.
E-mail: president@marylhurst.edu
Web site: www.marylhurst.edu
For a complete listing, refer to the Colleges and Universities section.

[C] HIGH SCHOOLS, DIOCESAN

PORTLAND. *Central Catholic High School*. (Coed), 2401 S.E. Stark St., 97214. Tel: 503-235-3138; Fax: 503-233-0073.
E-mail: centralcatholichigh.org
Web site: www.centralcatholichigh.org
Rev. Timothy Murphy, Pres.; Ron Edwards, Prin. & Contact Person. Priests 1; Sisters 3; Lay Teachers 58; Students 800.

MEDFORD. *St. Mary's School*. (Coed), 816 Black Oak Dr., 97504. Tel: 503-773-7877; Fax: 503-772-8973.
Web site: www.stmarys.medford.or.us
Barbara W. Callaway, Prin. Sisters 1; Lay Teachers 40; Lay Staff 12; Students 346.

STAYTON. *Regis High School*. (Coed), P.O. Box 65, 97383. Tel: 503-769-2159; Fax: 503-769-1706.
E-mail: regis@wvi.com
Mr. Douglas J. Wasko, Prin. Lay Teachers 15; Students 181.
Regis High School Foundation, P.O. Box 65, 97383. Tel: 503-769-2159; Fax: 503-769-1706.

[D] HIGH SCHOOLS, PRIVATE

PORTLAND. *Jesuit High School*. (Coed), 9000 S.W. Beaverton-Hillsdale Hwy., 97225-2491. Tel: 503-292-2663; Fax: 503-292-0134.
E-mail: dgedrose@jesuitportland.com
The Society of Jesus. Mr. Richard Gedrose, Pres. &

Contact Person; Rev. Richard H. Ganz, S.J., Rector; Mrs. Sandra Satterberg, Prin.; Mr. Paul Hogan, Academic Vice Prin.; Mr. Steve Beaird, Vice Pres. Development; Mr. James Naggi, Vice Prin. Student Life; Mrs. Shirley Poppe, Admissions Dir.; Mr. Donald Clarke, Campus Min. Faculty: Revs. Richard H. Ganz, S.J.; William E. Hayes, S.J., Chancellor; David S. Olivier, S.J.; Lawrence F. Robinson, S.J. In res. Revs. Joseph R. DeJardin, S.J.; Edward P. McTighe, S.J.
School: Priests 4; Lay Staff 106; Students 1,079.
Community: Priests 6.

St. Mary's Academy. (Girls), 1615 S.W. Fifth Ave., 97201. Tel: 503-228-8306; Fax: 503-223-0995.
Web site: www.stmaryspdx.org
Sr. Mollie Reavis, S.N.J.M., Prin. Sisters 5; Lay Teachers 42; Students 540.

BEAVERTON. *Valley Catholic Middle & High Schools.* (Coed), 4275 S.W. 148th Ave., 97007. Tel: 503-644-3745; Fax: 503-646-4054.
Web site: www.ssmo.org
Sisters of St. Mary of Oregon. Mrs. Marty Karlin, Prin. Sisters 3; Lay Teachers 41; Students 480.

EUGENE. *Marist High School.* (Coed), 1900 Kingsley Rd., 97401. Tel: 541-686-2234; Fax: 541-342-6451.
E-mail: marisths@rio.com
Web site: www.rio.com/~marist
Rev. Vincent Benoit, O.P.; Cheryl Brelsford, Prin. Priests 1; Lay Teachers 37; Students 554.

MILWAUKIE. *LaSalle High School.* (Coed), 11999 S.E. Fuller Rd., 97222. Tel: 503-352-1432; Fax: 503-659-2535.
E-mail: lasalle@lasalle.pvt.k12.or.us
Web site: lasalle.pvt.k12.or.us
William S. George, Prin.; Gregory R. VanderZanden, Pres. Sisters 1; Lay Teachers 36; Students 642.

SALEM. *Salem Catholic Schools Foundation,* P.O. Box 13207, 97309. Tel: 503-371-9068.

[E] ELEMENTARY SCHOOLS, AREA

EUGENE. *O'Hara Area Elementary Catholic School,* 715 W. 18th, 97402. Tel: 541-485-5291; Fax: 541-484-9138. Dr. Anselmo Villanueva, Prin. Comprised of students from the following parishes in Eugene: St. Jude, St. Mark, St. Mary, St. Paul, St. Peter, St. Alice and the Newman Center. Lay Teachers 21; Students 340.

[F] ELEMENTARY SCHOOLS, PRIVATE

PORTLAND.
St. Andrew Nativity School, 806 NE Alberta St., 97211. Tel: 503-335-9600; Fax: 503-335-9494.
E-mail: kconnellsj@yahoo.com
Rev. Kevin Connell, S.J., Pres.

Franciscan Montessori Earth School, 14750 S.E. Clinton St., 97236. Tel: 503-760-8220; Fax: 503-760-8333. Staffed by Franciscan Sisters of the Eucharist. Mother Francine Cardew, F.S.E., Dir. Franciscan Sisters of the Eucharist 5; Seminarians 2; Lay Teachers 19; Students 335.

BEAVERTON. *St. Mary of the Valley Grade School.* (Grades K-6), 4440 S.W. 148th Ave., 97007. Tel: 503-626-7781; Fax: 503-626-5731.
E-mail: smvgsprincipal@ssmo.org
Sisters of St. Mary of Oregon. Jean Bomber, Prin. & Contact Person; Susan A. Castagna, Supt. SSMO Campus Schools. Sisters 2; Lay Teachers 20; Students 384.

Valley Catholic School. (Grades 7-12), 4275 S.W. 148th Ave., 97007. Tel: 503-644-3745; Fax: 503-646-4054. Sue Harris, Prin. & Contact Person; Susan A. Castagna, Supt. SSMO Campus Schools. Sisters 2; Lay Teachers 41; Students 494.

[G] SOCIAL AND MINISTERIAL SERVICES

PORTLAND. *Catholic Charities of the Archdiocese of Portland in Oregon,* 231 S.E. 12th Ave., 97214. Tel: 503-231-4866; Fax: 503-231-4327. Dennis B. Keenan, M.S.W., Exec. Dir.; Richard Deml, C.P.A., Controller; Chance Schmidt, Pub. Rels. Mgr. CSS Group Homes 344; Resettlement Services 461; CCS Foundation Homes 39; Total persons annually served by CSS 132,467.

Catholic Charities Social Service Division of Portland, 231 S.E. 12th Ave., 97214. Tel: 503-231-4866; Fax: 503-231-4327. Douglas Alles, Social Svc. Dir.; Rev. Bruce Cwiekowski, AIDS Ministry Coordinator. Programs include: maternity and aftercare home, adoption, mental health, case management, domestic violence intervention, refugee resettlement, Hispanic health outreach, AIDS ministry, ministry to the elderly, Asian social services, Project Rachel, Immigration Legal Services, Rose Haven day shelter for homeless women, and low income housing.

Catholic Youth Organization/Camp Howard, 825 N.E. 20th, Ste. 320, 97232-2295. Tel: 503-231-9484; Fax: 503-231-9531. Krista Von Borstel, Exec. Dir. Programs include: Youth recreation & camping.

Immigration Counseling Services, 321 S.W. 4th Ave., Ste. 701, 97204. Tel: 503-221-1689; Fax: 503-221-3063. Susan Rossiter, Exec. Dir. Programs include: Immigration legalization advocacy, court hearing representation.

Catholic Community Services of Lane County, 945 W. Seventh Ave., Eugene, 97402. Tel: 541-345-3642; Fax: 541-345-2891. Jeanne Benson, Exec. Dir. Programs include: Emergency shelter, utilities, and food, single mothers shelter, drug dependent mothers shelter, family shelter, young parents program, family self-sufficiency program.

Catholic Community Services of Mid-Willamette Valley and the Central Coast, 142 Glenbrook N., Keizer, 97307. Tel: 503-390-2600; Fax: 503-304-1343. Jim Seymour, Exec. Dir. Programs include: Center for delinquent youth, developmentally & physically disabled group homes, shelter for displaced youth, counseling center, Hispanic mental health outreach, child abuse prevention program.

Catholic Community Services of Southern Oregon, 440 S. Ivy St., Medford, 97501. Tel: 541-779-0803; Fax: 541-779-0803. Maria Aranda, Dir. Programs include: Emergency services, health clinics, community education, immigration legal services.

[H] CHILD DEVELOPMENT CENTERS

PORTLAND.
Providence Child Center, 830 N.E. 47th Ave., 97213. Tel: 503-215-2400; Fax: 503-215-0660. Legal Title: *Sisters of Providence in Oregon.* Patricia Budo, Operations Admin. Sisters 1; Total Staff 168. Children's Nursing Center providing skilled nursing care and habilitation/rehabilitation services for children who have physical and mental disabilities and multiple care needs. Long-term chronic care, short-term care for respite, transition, or pediatric hospice provided.

Providence Montessori School. Tel: 503-215-2409; Fax: 503-215-0660. Preschool and elementary education for children ages 2 1/2 to 8 with a broad array of developmental needs and abilities.

Wee Care. Tel: 503-215-6832; Fax: 503-215-0660. Day-care center for children of employees of Providence Medical Center, ages 6 weeks to 6 years.

[I] RESIDENTIAL SCHOOLS FOR YOUTHS WITH EMOTIONAL-SOCIAL PROBLEMS

BEAVERTON. *St. Mary's Home for Boys, Inc.,* 16535 S.W. Tualatin Valley Hwy., 97006. Tel: 503-649-5651. Residential & day treatment center for behaviorally & emotionally disturbed children. Emma Dennis, Exec. Dir. & Contact Person. Students 500.

[J] GENERAL HOSPITALS

PORTLAND. *Providence Portland Medical Center,* 4805 N.E. Glisan St., 97213. Tel: 503-215-1111; 215-6833; Fax: 503-215-5619
For a complete listing, refer to the Hospitals section.

Providence St. Vincent Medical Center, 9205 S.W. Barnes Rd., 97225. Tel: 503-297-4411; Fax: 503-291-2468
For a complete listing, refer to the Hospitals section.

EUGENE. *Sacred Heart Medical Center,* 1255 Hilyard St., P.O. Box 10905, 97440. Tel: 541-686-7300; Fax: 541-686-7391
For a complete listing, refer to the Hospitals section.

FLORENCE. *Peace Harbor Hospital,* 400 Ninth St., 97439. Tel: 541-997-8412; Fax: 541-997-9155
For a complete listing, refer to the Hospitals section.

MEDFORD. *Providence Medford Medical Center,* 1111 Crater Lake Ave., 97504-6225. Tel: 541-732-5000; Fax: 541-732-5872
For a complete listing, refer to the Hospitals section.

MILWAUKIE. *Providence Milwaukie Hospital,* 10150 S.E. 32nd Ave., 97222. Tel: 503-513-8300; Fax: 503-513-8463
For a complete listing, refer to the Hospitals section.

NEWBERG. *Providence Newberg Hospital,* 501 Villa Rd., 97132. Tel: 503-537-1701; Fax: 503-537-1811
For a complete listing, refer to the Hospitals section.

ROSEBURG. *Mercy Medical Center, Inc.,* 2700 Stewart Pkwy., 97470. Tel: 541-673-0611; Fax: 541-677-4830
For a complete listing, refer to the Hospitals section.

SEASIDE. *Providence Seaside Hospital,* 725 S. Wahanna Rd., 97138-7735. Tel: 503-717-7000; Fax: 503-717-7505.
E-mail: jrenner@providence.org
Web site: www.providence.org/northcoast
For a complete listing, refer to the Hospitals section.

[K] HOMES FOR AGED

PORTLAND. *Mt. St. Joseph, Inc.,* 3060 S.E. Stark St., 97214-3099. Tel: 503-535-4700; Fax: 503-797-6702
For a complete listing, refer to the Special Care Facilities section.

BEAVERTON. *Maryville Nursing Home,* 14645 S.W. Farmington Rd., 97007. Tel: 503-643-8626; Fax: 503-520-1435
For a complete listing, refer to the Special Care Facilities section.

MOUNT ANGEL. *Providence Benedictine Nursing Center,* 540 S. Main St., 97362-9523. Tel: 503-845-6841; Fax: 503-845-9229
For a complete listing, refer to the Special Care Facilities section.

NORTH BEND. *Evergreen Court for Retirement Living, Inc.,* 451 O'Connell St., 97459. Tel: 541-756-4466; Fax: 541-756-5669
For a complete listing, refer to the Special Care Facilities section.

St. Catherine's Residence and Nursing Center, 3959 Sheridan Ave., 97459. Tel: 541-756-4151; Fax: 541-756-5669
For a complete listing, refer to the Special Care Facilities section.

[L] MONASTERIES AND RESIDENCES OF PRIESTS

PORTLAND. *Colombiere Community,* 2222 N.W. Hoyt St., 97210. Tel: 503-221-2323; Fax: 503-228-6741.
E-mail: jrlaudwein@cs.com
Web site: www.nwjesuits.org
Revs. James R. Laudwein, S.J., Supr.; J. Patrick Stewart, S.J., Min.; Arnold R. Beezer, S.J.; Peter D. Byrne, S.J.; Kevin G. Connell, S.J.; James R. Conyard, S.J.; Thomas R. Garvin, S.J.; Robert B. Grimm, S.J.; James E. Jacobsen, S.J.; David G. King, S.J.; John McBride, S.J.; William T. Miller, S.J.; John V. Murphy, S.J.; Ignatius F. Ohno, S.J.; Brad R. Reynolds, S.J.; Wilfred P. Schoenberg, S.J.

The Grotto, The National Sanctuary of Our Sorrowful Mother, 85th and N.E. Sandy Blvd., P.O. Box 20008, 97294-0008. Tel: 503-254-7371; 7372 (Monastery); Fax: 503-254-7948. Revs. John M. Topper, O.S.M., Prior & Exec. Dir.; Patrick M. McNamara, O.S.M. In res. Revs. Louis Breton, O.S.M.; Damian M. Kobus, O.S.M.; Perry McCoy, O.S.M. Brothers 2; Sisters 4.

Holy Cross Fathers & Brothers, C.S.C. - University of Portland, 5000 N. Willamette Blvd., 97203. Tel: 503-943-8024; Fax: 503-943-7313.
E-mail: csc@up.edu
Revs. Michael M. DeLaney, C.S.C., Supr.; Robert Antonelli, C.S.C.; George C. Bernard, C.S.C.; Frederick Barr, C.S.C.; Thomas Bill, C.S.C.; Joseph P. Browne, C.S.C.; James Connelly, C.S.C.; John Donato, C.S.C; Barry J. Hagan, C.S.C.; Thomas Hosinski, C.S.C.; William Hund, C.S.C.; John Kurtzke, C.S.C.; James Lackenmier, C.S.C.; Edwin Obermiller, C.S.C.; Dennis P. O'Hare, C.S.C.; Claude Pomerleau, C.S.C.; Chester Prusynski, C.S.C.; Richard Rutherford, C.S.C.; Charles D. Sherrer, C.S.C.; Arthur Schoenfeldt, C.S.C.; Adrien Ste. Marie, C.S.C.; David T. Tyson, C.S.C.; Ronald Wasowski, C.S.C.; Arthur F. Wheeler, C.S.C.; Bros. Ken Allen, C.S.C.; Flugence Dougherty, C.S.C.; Frederick Williams, C.S.C.; Donald Stabrowski, C.S.C.; Shawn Priggel, C.S.C.

Holy Rosary Priory, 375 N.E. Clackamas St., 97232. Tel: 503-235-3163; Fax: 503-235-3164.

Jesuit Provincial Office (Society of Jesus, Oregon Prov.), 2222 N.W. Hoyt, 97210. Tel: 503-226-6977; Fax: 503-228-6741.
E-mail: breynolds@nwjesuits.org
Web site: http://www.nwjesuits.org
Very Rev. Robert B. Grimm, S.J., Prov.; Revs. Brad R. Reynolds, S.J., Asst. for Formation, Socius; Ignatius F. Ohno, S.J., Exec. Asst.; Stephen C. Lantry, S.J., Dir. of Vocations; Michael A. Tyrrell, S.J., Prov. Treasurer; Joel K. Adams, S.J., Asst. for Secondary Schools; Mr. Matthew Senecal, Dir. of Devel.; Mr. William Lockyear, Chief Fin. Officer; Mrs. Joyceann Hagen, Asst. for Ministries.
Oregon Province priests not listed elsewhere: Rev. David A. Myers, S.J., 5441 San Angelo St., Guadalupe, AZ, 85283. Tel: 602-838-3143. Rev. Anthony Anh, S.J., c/o Rocky Mountain Mission, N.W., 323 Edmonds St., Omak, WA, 98841-9661. Tel: 509-826-6401.
Oregon Province priests serving outside the US: Revs. Francis E. Case, S.J.; Joseph B. Danel, S.J.; William L. Loyens, S.J.; John J. Morris, S.J.; Bartholomew J. Murphy, S.J.; John J. Navone, S.J.; Michael J. Schultheis, S.J.; Joseph H. Small, S.J.; Gary N. Smith, S.J.; Anthony P. Via, S.J.; Thomas E. Zeyen, S.J.; Bros. Frederick O. Mercy, S.J.; James P. Selinsky, S.J.

AMITY. *Brigittine Priory of Our Lady of Consolation - The Order of the Most Holy Savior,* 23300 Walker Ln., 97101. Tel: 503-835-8080; Fax: 503-835-9662.
E-mail: monks@brigittine.org
Web site: www.brigittine.org
Bro. Steven Vargo, O.Ss.S., Prior. Professed 9; Novices 1.

LAFAYETTE. *The Cistercian (Trappist) Abbey of Our Lady of Guadalupe*, 97127. Tel: 503-852-7174; Fax: 503-852-7748. Order of Cistercians of the Strict Observance. Rev. John-Baptist Hasbrouck, O.C.S.O., Prior; Rt. Rev. Peter McCarthy, O.C.S.O.; Revs. Casey Bailey, O.C.S.O.; Martin Cawley, O.C.S.O.; Timothy Clark, O.C.S.O.; Howard Curtis, O.C.S.O.; Joseph-Benedict Donnelly, O.C.S.O.; Jerome Ebacher, O.C.S.O.; Dismas Gannon, O.C.S.O.; Francis King, O.C.S.O.; Richard Layton, O.C.S.O.; Timothy Michell, O.C.S.O.; Romain Payant, O.C.S.O.; Peter Plakut, O.C.S.O.; Mark Weidner, O.C.S.O.; Arnold Weller, O.C.S.O. Solemnly Professed 34; Priests 16; Simply Professed 1; Novices 2; Total in Community 37.

MOUNT ANGEL. *Missionaries of the Holy Spirit, M.Sp.S.*, 585 E. College St., 97362. Mailing Address: P.O. Box 499, St. Benedict, 97373. Tel: 503-845-1181; 503-845-1182; Fax: 503-845-1189.
E-mail: msps@teleport.com
Web site: www.teleport.com/~msps/
Serving the Felix Rougier House of Studies and St. Matthew Parish, Hillsboro. Rev. Gustavo Garcia, M.Sp.S., Supr. of the Vicariate.

ST. BENEDICT. *Mt. Angel Abbey*, 97373. Tel: 503-845-3030; Fax: 503-845-3594.
Web site: www.mtangel.edu
Rt. Revs. Joseph Wood, O.S.B., Abbot; Peter Eberle, O.S.B., (Retired); Very Revs. Paul Thomas, O.S.B., Prior; Paschal Cheline, O.S.B., Subprior; Revs. Bruno Becker, O.S.B.; Thomas Aq. Brockhaus, O.S.B.; Isaac Jogues Brown, O.S.B.; Dominic Broxmeyer, O.S.B.; Athanasius Buchholz, O.S.B.; Matthias Burger, O.S.B.; Matthew Butsch, O.S.B.; Thien Dang, O.S.B.; Marian Del Monaco, O.S.B.; Augustine De Noble, O.S.B.; Jeremy Driscoll, O.S.B.; Gregory Duerr, O.S.B.; Richard Galvin, O.S.B.; William Hammelman, O.S.B.; Pius X Harding, O.S.B.; Daniel Hasenoehrl, O.S.B.; Stephen Hofmann, O.S.B.; Kenneth Jacques, O.S.B.; Ezekiel Lotz, O.S.B.; Joachim McCann, O.S.B.; Michael Mee, O.S.B.; Lawrence Minder, O.S.B.; Liem Nguyen, O.S.B.; David Nicholson, O.S.B.; Karl Nielson, O.S.B.; Bede Partridge, O.S.B.; Alexander Plasker, O.S.B.; Odo Recker, O.S.B.; Leo Rimmele, O.S.B.; Bernard Sander, O.S.B.; Timothy Sander, O.S.B.; Edmund Smith, O.S.B.; Benedict Suing, O.S.B.; Vincent Trujillo, O.S.B.; Philip Waibel, O.S.B.; Marius Walter, O.S.B.; Cosmas White, O.S.B.; Jerome Young, O.S.B.; Placidus Zach, O.S.B.; Nathan Zodrow, O.S.B. Monks in perpetual vows 61 (divided as follows:); Priests 44; Brothers 17.

SHERIDAN. *Augustinian Community*, c/o Good Shepherd, 127 N.E. Hill St., 97378-1333. Tel: 503-843-2206. Revs. Raymond Elam, O.S.A., Reg. Supr.; James Clifford, O.S.A.; William Ryan, O.S.A.

[M] CONVENTS AND RESIDENCES FOR SISTERS

PORTLAND. *"Rose Hall" Reparation and Prayer Center*, 2120 S.E. 24th Ave., 97214-5504. Tel: 503-236-4207; Fax: 503-236-3400. Mother Mary of the Angels, S.R., Dir.
Convent of Sisters of Reparation of the Sacred Wounds of Jesus.
E-mail: repsrs@juno.com
Novitiate, 2120 S.E. 24th Ave., 97214-5504. Tel: 503-236-4207; Fax: 503-236-3400. Mother Mary of the Angels, S.R., Supr. Gen. Sisters 3; Donne Members 90.
Convent of the Good Shepherd, 562 N. Portland Blvd., 97217. Tel: 503-283-4931; Fax: 503-283-4894. Sisters 4.
Convent of the Society of the Holy Child Jesus, 5431 N. Strong St., 97203. Tel: 503-289-9975.
Holy Cross Convent (1670), 7408 S.E. Alder, 97215. Tel: 503-254-3284; Fax: 503-255-3097.
E-mail: mtgth@aol.com
Legal Title: *Sisters Adorers of the Holy Cross.* Sr. M. Agathe, Supr. Sisters 25; Novices 1; Candidates 6. First foundation in the United States in 1976, founded by Bishop Pierre Lambert de la Motte. Represented in the Archdiocese of Portland in Oregon and the Diocese of Arlington, VA.
Sisters of Mercy Convent, 3080 S.E. Stark St., 97214. Tel: 503-236-1972; Fax: 503-797-6702.
Sisters of Social Service, 14405 S.W. Sexton Mt. Dr., Apt. A, 97005-7493. Tel: 503-641-6509.
Other Address: 1776 Madras St. S.E., Salem, 97306. Tel: 503-391-7498. Sisters 3.

BEAVERTON. *Convent, Franciscan Missionary Sisters of Our Lady of Sorrows*, 3600 S.W. 170th Ave., 97006-5099. Tel: 503-649-1634; Fax: 503-649-8382. Sr. Anne Marie, O.S.F., Supr. Gen.; Sr. Maristella Saya, O.S.F., Local Supr. Sisters 14; Novitiate 3.
St. Mary of the Valley Convent, 4440 S.W. 148th Ave., 97007. Tel: 503-644-9181; Fax: 503-464-1102. Motherhouse of the Sisters of St. Mary of Oregon. Sr. Barbara Jean Laughlin, S.S.M.O., Supr. Gen.; Sr. Adele Marie Altenhofen, Local Supr.; Most Rev. Basil Meeking, Chap. Professed Sisters 90.

BRIDAL VEIL. *Convent, Franciscan Sisters of the Eucharist.* Administrative Center, 48100 E. Crown Point Hwy., 97010. Tel: 503-695-2375; Fax: 503-695-2368.
E-mail: fsebvo@transport.com
Sr. Mary Michael Costello, F.S.E., Supr.; Sr. Janet Siepker, Contact Person. Sisters 7.

EUGENE. *Carmel of Maria Regina.* (Contemplative Order), 87609 Green Hill Rd., 97402. Tel: 541-345-8649; Fax: 541-345-4857. Mother Maria Teresa, O.C.D., Prioress. Professed Sisters 9.

MARYLHURST. *Convent of the Holy Names*, 97036. Tel: 503-636-8105; Fax: 503-675-2453. Provincial House of the Sisters of the Holy Names of Jesus & Mary, S.N.J.M. Leadership Council: Sr. Mary Breiling; Sr. Jane Hibbard; Sr. Lynda Thompson. Professed Sisters 212; Temporarily professed 3.

MT. ANGEL. *Queen of Angels Monastery*, 840 S. Main St., 97362-9527. Tel: 503-845-6141; Fax: 503-845-6585.
E-mail: qam@open.org
Web site: www.benedictine-srs.org
Monastery of the Benedictine Sisters of Mt. Angel. Sr. Dorothy Jean Beyer, O.S.B., Prioress & Contact Person. See separate listing for Shalom Prayer Center (retreat center) and St. Joseph Shelter (special center for social services and assistance). Sisters 55; Postulants 1; Novices 2.

[N] RETREAT HOUSES

PORTLAND. *The Jesuit Spirituality Center*, 424 S.W. Mill St., 97201. Tel: 503-242-1973; Fax: 503-242-1996. Legal Title: *Loyola Retreat Association, S.J., Inc. dba The Jesuit Spirituality Center.* Rev. Peter D. Byrne, S.J., Co-Dir.; Marilyn Kirvin-Quamme, Co-Dir. & Contact Person.

BEAVERTON. *Our Lady of Peace Retreat*, 3600 S.W. 170th Ave., 97006-5099. Tel: 503-649-7127; Fax: 503-649-8382. Sr. Maristella Sayo, O.S.F., Supr.; Sr. Cordea Wang, O.S.F., Asst. Supr. Franciscan Missionary Sisters of Our Lady of Sorrows 14.

GOLD HILL. *St. Rita's Retreat Center*, P.O. Box 310, 97525. Tel: 541-855-1333. Rev. Edward D. Altstock, Dir. & Contact Person.

MCKENZIE BRIDGE. *St. Benedict Lodge-Dominican Retreat & Conference Center*, 56630 North Bank Rd., 97413-9614. Tel: 541-822-3572 (Office & Dominican Res.); Fax: 541-822-3631.
Web site: http://www.op.org/stbenedicts
Dominican Retreat & Conference Center. Lodge-retreat guests: 541-822-6151. Bro. Daniel Thomas, O.P., Dir. & Contact Person; Rev. Vincent Benoit, O.P., Assoc. Dir.; Deacon Leonard Soper, 46052 McKenzie Hwy., Vida, 97488. Tel: 541-896-0284.
E-mail: dcnlgjms@earthlink.net
Sr. John Maureen Backenstos, S.N.J.M., Spiritual & Temporal Ministry, 91683 Alma Dr., 97413. Tel: 541-822-3937.

MT. ANGEL. *Benedictine Sisters Shalom Prayer Center*, 840 S. Main St., 97362-9527. Tel: 503-845-6773; Fax: 503-845-6585.
E-mail: shalom@open.org
Web site: www.open.org/shalom
Sr. Joan Pokorny, O.S.B., Dir. & Contact Person. Sisters 5.

PACIFIC CITY. *Nestucca Sanctuary*, P.O. Box 670, 97135-0670. Rev. Andrew J. Dufner, S.J., Retreat Dir. & Contact Person.

ST. BENEDICT. *Mount Angel Abbey Retreat House*, 97373. Tel: 503-845-3025. Rev. Alexander Plasker, O.S.B., Dir.

[O] SOCIETY OF ST. VINCENT DE PAUL

PORTLAND. *Macdonald Center*, 605 N.W. Couch St., 97209. Tel: 503-222-5720; Fax: 503-241-7375. Rev. Richard F. Berg, C.S.C., Exec. Dir.; Mary Sue Richen, Prog. Dir.
Society of St. Vincent de Paul. Portland Council, 3601 S.E. 27th Ave., 97202. Tel: 503-235-7837; Fax: 503-233-5581.
E-mail: svdp@northwest.com
Web site: rogue.northwest.com/~svdp
Total people served annually 458,600.

EUGENE. *Society of St. Vincent de Paul.* Archdiocesan Council. 705 S. Seneca St., 97402. Tel: 541-687-5820; Fax: 541-683-9423.
E-mail: svdp@svdplanecounty.org
Web site: www.svdp@svdplancounty.org
Donald Lamb, Pres.
Society of St. Vincent de Paul. Eugene Council. 705 S. Seneca St., 97402. Tel: 541-687-5820; Fax: 541-683-9423.
E-mail: svdp@svdplancounty.org
Web site: www.svdp@svdplanecounty.org
Donald Lamb, Pres.; Terrence R. McDonald, Exec. Dir.; Rebecca Larson, Contact Person.

MEDFORD. *Society of St. Vincent de Paul.* Rogue Valley Council, P.O. Box 1663, 97501. Tel: 541-772-3828; Fax: 541-772-6886.
E-mail: vincent@mind.net
Web site: www.sovicariate.org/svop/saintvincent.
William J. Howe, Treas. Total people served annually 50,000.

SALEM.
Society of St. Vincent de Paul. Council of Mid-Willamette Valley, 730 Front St. N.E., 97301. Tel: 503-364-1062; Fax: 503-364-2708.
E-mail: SVD@open.org
Joseph Glandorf, Pres.; Nancy Cooney, Exec. Dir. & Contact Person. Total people served annually 92,000.

[P] NEWMAN CENTERS

PORTLAND. *University of Portland*, Campus Ministry, 5000 N. Willamette Blvd., 97203. Tel: 503-943-7131; Fax: 503-943-7399.
E-mail: ministry@up.edu
Web site: www.up.edu
Revs. Edwin Obermiller, C.S.C., Dir.; John Donato, C.S.C., Assoc.; Bro. Shawn Priggel, C.S.C., Assoc.; Maureen Briare, Choir Dir.; Deacon William Dailey, C.S.C. Prog. Assistants: Andrew Sebesta; Kent Heli; Diane Zbasnik.
Southern Oregon University (Ashland), Walsh Memorial Newman Center, 1150 Ashland St., Ashland, 97520. Tel: 541-482-0825; Fax: 541-488-5256.
E-mail: rfinerty@mind.net
Web site: www.sou.edu/su/newman/newman.htm
Rev. Raymond Finerty, O.P., Dir. & Chap.
Oregon State University (Corvallis), Newman Center, 2111 N.W. Monroe St., Corvallis, 97330. Tel: 541-752-6818.
E-mail: giffords@peak.org
Sue Gifford, Pastoral Dir.
University of Oregon (Eugene), Newman Center, 1850 Emerald St., Eugene, 97403. Tel: 541-343-7021; Fax: 541-686-8028.
E-mail: newman@efn.org
Web site: www.efn.org/~newman
Revs. Michael Fones, O.P.; Juan Carlos Diaz Flores, O.P., Assoc.; Stephani Catone, Pastoral Assoc.
Lane Community College, 4000 E. 30th Ave., Eugene, 97405. Tel: 541-747-4501, Ext. 2850.
E-mail: wormant@worldnet.att.net
Web site: members.tripod.com/~campus_ministry/catholic.html
Tara Worman, Coord.
Pacific University (Forest Grove).
E-mail: kathyyee@juno.com
Rev. Elwin Schwab, Chap.; Kathy Yee, Campus Min., Res. St. Anthony Church, 1660 Elm St., Forest Grove, 97116. Tel: 503-357-8075; Fax: 503-357-2217.
Lewis & Clark (Lake Oswego). Rev. Joseph S. McMahon, Chap., Our Lady of the Lake Church, 650 A Avenue, Lake Oswego, 97034. Tel: 503-636-7687; Fax: 503-636-9415.
Linfield College (McMinnville).
E-mail: mdouglass@onlinemac.com
Michael Douglas, Campus Min., St. James Church, 1145 N.E. First St., McMinnville, 97128. Tel: 503-472-5232.
Marylhurst University (Marylhurst), Durocher Center for Campus Ministry. Rev. Denis Lawrence, Chap., Marylhurst, 97036. Tel: 800-634-9982.
E-mail: dlawrence@marylhurst.com
Western Oregon State College (Monmouth). Rev. Galdino Monteiro, S.F.X., Chap., 1258 E St., Independence, 97351. 245 W. Main, Monmouth, 97361. Tel: 503-838-1242; Fax: 503-838-3856.
Willamette University (Salem). Rev. Carl Gimpl, Chap.; Chrissy Weston, Campus Min., St. Joseph Church, 721 Chemeketa St., N.E., Salem, 97301. Tel: 501-581-1623.

[Q] MISCELLANEOUS

PORTLAND.
St. Joseph the Worker Job Service, c/o Archdiocesan Pastoral Center, 2838 E. Burnside St., 97214-1895. Tel: 503-234-5334; Fax: 503-234-2545.
Blanchet House of Hospitality, 340 N.W. Glisan St., 97209. Tel: 503-226-3911. Bill Muir, Dir. Tel: 503-807-4330.
Catholic Broadcasting Northwest, Inc., 88.3 KBVM-FM, P.O. Box 5888, 97228-5888. Tel: 503-285-5200; Fax: 503-285-3322.
E-mail: info@kbvm.com
Web site: www.kbvm.com
Caron M. Fox, Exec. Dir.
Cordero Corporation (dba De LaSalle North Portland High School), 900 S.W. Fifth Ave., Ste. 2600, 97204-1268. Tel: 503-224-3380. Charles F. Hinkle, Contact Person.
Franciscan Enterprise of Oregon, Inc., P.O. Box 11268, 97211. Tel: 503-284-8642; Fax: 503-284-4092.
E-mail: feo@teleport.com
Julia Wexler, Contact Person.
Franciscan Ministry Network, 4725 N.E. 9th Ave., 97211. Tel: 503-287-5062.
E-mail: tumultym@aol.com
Rev. Matt Tumulty, O.F.M., Exec. Dir. & Contact Person.

Jesuit Development & Communications Office, P.O. Box 4408, 97208. Tel: 503-227-1174; Fax: 503-228-6741.
E-mail: msenecal@nwjesuits.org
Web site: www.nwjesuits.org
Mr. P. Matthew Senecal, Dir. Devel.; Ms. Donna Wiench, Com. Dir.; Revs. J. Patrick Stewart, S.J., Assoc. Dir. Devel.; Daniel C. Weber, S.J., Assoc. Dir. Devel.; Ignatius F. Ohno, S.J., Liaison for Jesuit Intl. Min.

Jesuit Volunteer Corps: Northwest, P.O. Box 3928, 97208-3928. Tel: 503-335-8202; Fax: 503-249-1118. John Matcovich, Exec. Dir.

Northeast Catholic Counseling Center, 8383 N.E. Sandy Blvd., Suite 205, 97220. Tel: 503-253-0964; Fax: 503-253-7659. Sr. Barbara Kennedy, O.S.M., Dir. & Contact Person. Sisters 2; Lay Counselors 4.

Oregon Catholic Conference, 2838 E. Burnside St., 97214. Tel: 503-233-8387; Fax: 503-235-2630. Most Revs. John G. Vlazny, Pres.; Robert Vasa, Vice Pres.; Kenneth D. Steiner, Dir.; Rev. Dennis O'Donovan, Sec. & Treas.; Mr. Robert Castagna, Gen. Counsel & Exec. Dir.

Paulist Fathers Catholic Center for Evangelization, 2408 S.E. 16th Ave., 97214. Tel: 503-231-4955; Fax: 503-736-1383.
E-mail: phlneri@aol.com
Web site: www.paulist.org/portland/paulists.html
Revs. Stephen E. Bossi, C.S.P.; Richard W. Chilson, C.S.P.; Ricky Manalo, C.S.P.

St. Andrew Legal Clinic, 807 N.E. Alberta, 97211. Tel: 503-281-1500; Fax: 503-282-5642. Joel K. Overlund, Dir. & Contact Person.

The Gamelin-Oregon Association-Emilie House, 5520 N.E. Glisan, 97213-3169. Tel: 503-236-9779; Fax: 503-239-1867. Sisters of Providence. Sr. Alexis Melancon, S.P., Dir. & Contact Person. 41 apartments for the elderly and subsidized by the Department of Housing and Urban Development.

Women's Intercommunity AIDS Resource, 1608 S.E. Ankeny, 97214. Tel: 503-238-4420; 888-303-4420; Fax: 503-238-4610. Catharine Keane, Contact Person.

BEAVERTON. *Our Lady of Peace Institute in Catholic Teaching*, 3600 S.W. 170th Ave., 97006. Tel: 503-649-7127; Fax: 503-649-8382. Rev. Leo Slatterie, Dir.; Sr. Anne Marie, O.S.F., Coord. & Contact Person. Staff 7; Students 60.

CORVALIS.
Teen Life/Teen Faith Youth Ministries, 501 NW 25th St., Ste. 7, 97330. Tel: 541-766-5271; Fax: 541-766-5271.
E-mail: tltf@proaxis.com
Web site: www.tltf.org
Deacon Francis Potts, Exec. Mgr. & Contact Person.

LAKE OSWEGO. *Catholic Engaged Encounter of Oregon, Inc.*, 18 Walking Woods Dr., 97035. Tel: 503-697-3545; Fax: 503-699-7500.
E-mail: jbsax1aol.com
Web site: www.visionww.com/ceeore
Marriage Preparation Program providing weekend retreats to engaged couples. John Saxman; Mary Saxman. Couples served 428; Volunteers 85.

Cornelia Connelly Counseling Center, 3975 S.W. Mercantile Dr., Ste. #154, 97035. Tel: 503-636-1157; Fax: 503-675-9691.
E-mail: spearing@teleport.com
Web site: www.teleport.com/~spearing/
Sr. Joan Spearing, S.H.C.J., Dir. & Contact Person. Total people assisted annually 812.

MARYLHURST.
Mary's Woods at Marylhurst, Inc., P.O. Box 25, 97036. Tel: 503-635-3621; Fax: 503-635-2279.
E-mail: snjmorepa@impresso.com
Web site: www.maryswoods.com
Sr. Mary Breiling, S.N.J.M., Pres.

MILWAUKIE. *La Salle High School Educational Foundation*, 11999 SE Fuller Rd., 97222. Tel: 503-353-1417; Fax: 503-659-2535.
E-mail: lasalle@lasalle.pvt.k12.or.us
Web site: lasalle.pvt.k12.or.us
Mr. Bruce Michieli, Contact Person & Dir. Finance.

MT. ANGEL. *Benedictine Foundation of Oregon*, Box 912, 97362. Tel: 503-845-2556; Fax: 503-845-2815.
E-mail: bfo@teleport.com
Web site: www.benedictine-srs.org
Steven Ritchie, Exec. Dir. & Contact Person.

St. Joseph's Shelter, 925 S. Main, P.O. Box 1005, 97362-9527. Tel: 503-845-6147; Fax: 503-845-2815.
E-mail: sjsch@open.org
Sr. Adele Mansfield, O.S.B., Admin. & Contact Person. Special center for social services and assistance. Total Staff 12; Total People Served 1,239; Total Shelter Nights 28,752; Total Meals Served 20,718.

MYRTLE CREEK. *Council of Douglas County of the Society of St. Vincent dePaul*, 116 N. Main, P.O. Box 1258, 97457. Tel: 541-863-5489; Fax: 541-863-5489.
E-mail: STTESS@INTERNETCDS.com
Mr. David Santos, Contact Person & Council Pres. Total people served annually 11,760.

RELIGIOUS INSTITUTES OF MEN REPRESENTED IN THE ARCHDIOCESE

For further details refer to the corresponding bracketed number in the Religious Institutes of Men or Women section.

[]—*Apostolic Life Community Of Priests (Holy Spirit Fathers)*.—A.L.C.P.
[0140]—*The Augustinians*.—O.S.A.
[0200]—*Benedictine Monks*. (Mt. Angel, OR).—O.S.B.
[0895]—*Brigittine Monastery of Our Lady of Consolidation*.—O.Ss.S.
[0350]—*Cistercians Order of the Strict Observance (Trappists)*.—O.C.S.O.
[]—*Conventual Franciscans*.—O.F.M.Conv.
[]—*Discalced Carmelite Friars*.—O.C.D.
[0520]—*Franciscan Friars*. (Prov. of Santa Barbara).—O.F.M.
[0690]—*Jesuit Fathers and Brothers*. (Oregon Prov.).—S.J.
[0660]—*Missionaries Of The Holy Spirit*.—M.Sp.S.
[0910]—*Oblates of Mary Immaculate*.—O.M.I.
[0430]—*Order of Preachers (Dominicans)*. (Western Prov.).—O.P.
[1030]—*Paulist Fathers*.—C.S.P.
[0610]—*Priests of the Congregation of Holy Cross*.—C.S.C.
[1070]—*Redemptorist Fathers*. (Oakland Prov.).—C.SS.R.
[1240]—*Servites*. (Western Prov.).—O.S.M.
[1260]—*Society of Christ*.—S.Ch.
[]—*Society Of Mary*.—S.M.

RELIGIOUS INSTITUTES OF WOMEN REPRESENTED IN THE ARCHDIOCESE

[0230]—*Benedictine Sisters of Pontifical Jurisdiction*. (Mount Angel, OR).—O.S.B.
[1920]—*Congregation of the Sisters of Holy Cross*.—C.S.C.
[1780]—*Congregation of the Sisters of the Third Order of St. Francis of Perpetual Adoration*.—F.S.P.A.
[0420]—*Discalced Carmelite Nuns*.—O.C.D.
[1070-12]—*Dominican Sisters*.—O.P.
[]—*Dominican Sisters Congregation of the Holy Cross*.—O.P.
[]—*Dominican Sisters Of Caldwell, NJ*.—O.P.
[1390]—*Franciscan Missionary Sisters of Our Lady of Sorrows*.—O.S.F.
[]—*Holy Spirit Sisters*.
[1250]—*The Institute of the Franciscan Sisters of the Eucharist*.—F.S.E.
[2575]—*Institute of the Sisters of Mercy of the Americas*. (Omaha, NE).—R.S.M.
[]—*Oblates of Saint Martha*.—O.S.M.
[2519]—*Religious Sisters of Mercy of Alma, MI*.—R.S.M.
[3590]—*Servants of Mary (Servite Sisters)*.—O.S.M.
[]—*Sisters For Christian Community*.—S.F.C.C.
[0430]—*Sisters of Charity of the Blessed Virgin Mary*.—B.V.M.
[3350]—*Sisters of Providence*. (Prov. of the Sacred Heart).—S.P.
[3360]—*Sisters of Providence of St.-Mary-of-the-Woods, IN*.—S.P.
[3475]—*Sisters of Reparation of the Sacred Wounds of Jesus*.—S.R.
[4080]—*Sisters of Social Service of Los Angeles, Inc*.—S.S.S.
[]—*Sisters of St. Dominic*. (Akron, Ohio).—O.P.
[]—*Sisters of St. Dominic*. (Blauvelt, NY).—O.P.
[1630]—*Sisters of St. Francis of Penance and Christian Charity*.—O.S.F.
[1650]—*The Sisters of St. Francis of Philadelphia*.—O.S.F.
[1530]—*Sisters of St. Francis of the Congregation of Our Lady of Lourdes, Sylvania, Ohio*.—O.S.F.
[1570]—*Sisters of St. Francis of the Holy Family*. (Dubuque, IA).—O.S.F.
[3890]—*Sisters of St. Joseph of Peace*. (Western Prov.).—C.S.J.P.
[3960]—*Sisters of St. Mary of Oregon*.—S.S.M.O.
[1830]—*The Sisters of the Good Shepherd*.—R.G.S.
[1990]—*Sisters of the Holy Names of Jesus and Mary*.—S.N.J.M.
[3320]—*Sisters of the Presentation of the B.V.M*.—P.V.B.M.
[4060]—*Society of the Holy Child Jesus*. (American Prov.).—S.H.C.J.
[4155]—*Vietnamese Adorers of the Holy Cross*.—M.T.G.
[]—*Vietnamese Holy Cross Sisters*.

ARCHDIOCESAN CEMETERIES

PORTLAND. *Gethsemani*.
Mount Calvary.
EUGENE. *Mount Calvary*.
SALEM. *St. Barbara*.

NECROLOGY

† Griffin, Bertram F., Portland, OR St. Michael the Archangel. —Died July 28, 2000.

Diocese of Providence

(Dioecesis Providentiensis)

Most Reverend

ROBERT E. MULVEE, D.D., J.C.D.

Bishop of Providence; ordained June 30, 1957; appointed Auxiliary Bishop of Manchester and Titular Bishop of Summa February 15, 1977; consecrated April 14, 1977; appointed Bishop of Wilmington February 19, 1985; installed April 11, 1985; appointed Coadjutor Bishop of Providence February 9, 1995; succeeded to See June 11, 1997. *Res., 30 Fenner St., Providence, RI, 02903-3603. Mailing Address: One Cathedral Sq., Providence, RI, 02903-3695.* Tel.: 401-278-4545; Fax: 401-278-4548.

Most Reverend

ROBERT J. McMANUS, D.D., S.T.D.

Auxiliary Bishop of Providence; Titular Bishop of Allegheny; ordained May 27, 1978; appointed December 1, 1998; consecrated February 22, 1999. *Res., Seminary of Our Lady of Providence, 485 Mt. Pleasant Ave., Providence, RI, 02908. Mailing Address: One Cathedral Sq., Providence, RI, 02903-3695.* Tel.: 401-278-4587; Fax: 401-278-4582.

Most Reverend

LOUIS E. GELINEAU, D.D., S.T.L., J.C.L.

Former Bishop of Providence; ordained June 5, 1954; appointed December 6, 1971; consecrated January 26, 1972; retired June 11, 1997. *Res., 30 Fenner St., Providence, RI, 02903-3603. Mailing Address: One Cathedral Sq., Providence, RI, 02903-3695.* Tel.: 401-278-4545; Fax: 401-278-4548.

Most Reverend

GEORGE H. PEARCE, S.M., D.D.

Former Archbishop of Suva; ordained February 3, 1947; appointed Titular Bishop of Attalea in Pamphilia February 29, 1956; promoted to Suva June 22, 1967; resigned April 10, 1976. *Res. & Mailing Address: 30 Fenner St., Providence, RI, 02903-3603.* Tel.: 401-331-2434; Fax: 401-278-4530.

Corporate Title: *Roman Catholic Bishop of Providence, a corporation sole.*

ESTABLISHED APRIL 16, 1872.

Square Miles 1,085.

Comprises the State of Rhode Island .

Bishop's Office & Chancery Office: One Cathedral Square, Providence, RI, 02903-3695. Tel.: 401-278-4500; Fax: 401-278-4548.

Web site address: www.dioceseofprovidence.org

E-mail address: jlplante@dioceseofprovidence.org

STATISTICAL OVERVIEW

Personnel	
Retired Archbishops	1
Bishop	1
Auxiliary Bishops	1
Retired Bishops	2
Abbots	1
Retired Abbots	1
Priests: Diocesan Active in Diocese	195
Priests: Active Outside Diocese	17
Priests: Diocesan in Foreign Missions	1
Priests: Retired, Sick or Absent	92
Number of Diocesan Priests	305
Religious Priests in Diocese	116
Extern Priests in Diocese	18
Ordinations:	
Diocesan Priests	3
Transitional Deacons	4
Permanent Deacons in Diocese	96
Total Brothers	122
Total Sisters	682
Parishes	
Parishes	157
With Resident Pastor:	
Resident Diocesan Priests	138
Resident Religious Priests	7
Without Resident Pastor:	
Administered by Priests	12
Missions	8
Pastoral Centers	20
Professional Ministry Personnel:	
Brothers	1
Sisters	46
Lay Ministers	140
Welfare	
Catholic Hospitals	1
Total Assisted	253,767
Health Care Centers	1
Total Assisted	25
Homes for the Aged	13
Total Assisted	870
Day Care and Extended Day Care Centers	9
Total Assisted	672
Specialized Homes	2
Total Assisted	170
Special Centers for Social Services	11
Total Assisted	56,722
Residential Care of Disabled	1
Total Assisted	3
Other Institutions	12
Total Assisted	152,470
Educational	
Seminaries, Diocesan	1
Students from This Diocese	7
Students from Other Diocese	1
Diocesan Students in Other Seminaries	20
Total Seminarians	27
Colleges and Universities	2
Total Students	7,693
High Schools, Diocesan and Parish	4
Total Students	2,158
High Schools, Private	8
Total Students	3,803
Elementary Schools, Diocesan and Parish	42
Total Students	11,980
Elementary Schools, Private	4
Total Students	1,365
Catechesis/Religious Education:	
High School Students	9,216
Elementary Students	32,283
Total Students Under Catholic Instruction	68,525
Teachers in the Diocese:	
Priests	38
Brothers	38
Sisters	103
Lay Teachers	1,617
Vital Statistics	
Receptions into the Church:	
Infant Baptism Totals	6,129
Adult Baptism Totals	195
Received into Full Communion	356
First Communions	6,448
Confirmations	4,825
Marriages:	
Catholic	1,652
Interfaith	373
Total Marriages	2,025
Deaths	5,695
Total Catholic Population	623,752
Total Population	987,429

Former Bishops—Rt. Rev. THOMAS F. HENDRICKEN, D.D., cons. first Bishop of Providence, April 28, 1872; died June 11, 1886.—Rt. Rev. MATTHEW HARKINS, D.D., cons. second Bishop of Providence, April 14, 1887; died May 25, 1921.—Most Rev. WILLIAM A. HICKEY, D.D., ord. Dec. 22, 1893; appt. Coadjutor Bishop of Providence, *Cum jure successionis,* March 10, 1919; cons. Titular Bishop of Claudiopolis, April 10, 1919; succeeded to the See of Providence, May 25, 1921; died Oct. 4, 1933.—Most Rev. FRANCIS P. KEOUGH, D.D., cons. fourth Bishop of Providence, May 22, 1934; appt. Archbishop of Baltimore, Nov. 29, 1947; died Dec. 8, 1961.—Most Rev. RUSSELL J. MCVINNEY, D.D., appt. May 29, 1948; cons. July 14, 1948 fifth Bishop of Providence; died Aug. 10, 1971.—Most Rev. LOUIS E. GELINEAU, D.D., appt. Dec. 6, 1971; cons. sixth Bishop of Providence, Jan. 26, 1972; retired June 11, 1997.

Vicars General—Most Rev. ROBERT J. MCMANUS, D.D., S.T.D.; Rev. Msgr. WILLIAM I. VARSANYI, J.C.D.

Episcopal Vicars and Secretary—

Vicar for Canonical Affairs—Rev. Msgr. WILLIAM I. VARSANYI, J.C.D.

Vicar for Education—Most Rev. ROBERT J. MCMANUS, D.D., S.T.D.

Vicar for Judicial Matters—Very Rev. JOEL A. LECUIVRE, J.C.L.

Vicar for Planning & Finance—Rev. Msgr. WILLIAM J. MCCAFFREY, S.T.B., M.A.

Vicar for Spirituality and Evangelization—Rev. Msgr. JOHN C. ALLARD.
Secretary for Social Ministry—Mr. JOHN J. BARRY, III.
Vicars for Deaneries—Very Rev. JOHN A. KILEY, Deanery No. I; Very Rev. JOHN E. UNSWORTH, Deanery No. II; Very Rev. EUGENE J. MCKENNA, Deanery No. III; Very Rev. RAYMOND C. THEROUX, Deanery No. IV; Very Rev. CHARLES E. DOWNING, Deanery No. V; Very Rev. RAYMOND B. BASTIA, Deanery No. VI; Very Rev. RANDOLPH G. CHEW, Deanery No. VII; Very Rev. JOHN C. HALLORAN, Deanery No. VIII; Very Rev. JOHN W. LOLIO, Deanery No. IX; Very Rev. GERALD E. BEIRNE, Deanery No. X; Very Rev. DANIEL M. TRAINOR, Deanery No. XI; Very Rev. PAUL R. GRENON, Deanery No. XII.
Bishop's Office & Chancery Office—One Cathedral Sq., Providence, 02903-3695. Office Hours: Mon.-Fri. 8:30-4:30. Tel: 401-278-4500; Fax: 401-278-4548.
Vicars General—Most Rev. ROBERT J. MCMANUS, D.D., S.T.D. Tel: 401-278-4587. Rev. Msgr. WILLIAM I. VARSANYI, J.C.D. Tel: 401-278-4520.
Vicar for Canonical Affairs—Rev. Msgr. WILLIAM I. VARSANYI, J.C.D. Tel: 401-278-4520.
Moderator of the Curia—Rev. Msgr. PAUL D. THEROUX, S.T.B., J.C.L. Tel: 401-278-4535.
Chancellors—Rev. Msgr. JACQUES L. PLANTE, M.A. Tel: 401-278-4515. Rev. Msgr. ROBERT C. EVANS, J.C.L. Tel: 401-278-4517.
Diocesan Tribunal—One Cathedral Sq., Providence, 02903-3695. Tel: 401-278-4666.
Judicial Vicar—Very Rev. JOEL A. LECUIVRE, J.C.L.
Judges—Rev. Msgr. PAUL D. THEROUX, S.T.B., J.C.L.; Revs. JOHN J. DARCY, M.A., J.C.L.; JOSEPH A. HOWARTH, J.C.L., S.T.B.; FRANCIS P. KAYATTA, M.A., M.C.L., J.C.L.; RONALD P. SIMEONE, M.Div., J.C.L.
Assessors and Auditors—Rev. EDWARD J. MCGOVERN, S.T.L, M.S.W.
Promoter of Justice—Rev. Msgr. WILLIAM I. VARSANYI, J.C.D.
Defenders of the Bond—Most Rev. LOUIS E. GELINEAU, D.D., J.C.L., S.T.L.; Rev. Msgr. MARTIN A. CANAVAN, S.T.L., J.C.L.; Rev. JOHN J. LAVIN, J.C.D.
Assessors and Counselors—Sr. MADONNA CRAWFORD, R.S.M., M.A.; Mrs. DIANE DIFIORE, B.S.
Notary—Mrs. LINDA L. NASTARI.
Secretary—Very Rev. JOEL A. LECUIVRE, J.C.L.
Council of Priests—One Cathedral Sq., Providence, 02903-3695. Tel: 401-278-4517.
Officers—Most Rev. ROBERT E. MULVEE, Pres.; Very Rev. RANDOLPH G. CHEW, Moderator; Rev. Msgr. ROBERT C. EVANS, J.C.L., Sec. & Treas.
Council Members—Most Rev. ROBERT J. MCMANUS, D.D., S.T.D.; Rev. Msgr. ROBERT C. EVANS, J.C.L.; Rev. Msgr. WILLIAM J. MCCAFFREY, S.T.B., M.A.; Rev. Msgr. ROBERT C. NEWBOLD, Ph.D., J.D.; Rev. Msgr. PAUL D. THEROUX, S.T.B., J.C.L.; Rev. Msgr. WILLIAM I. VARSANYI, J.C.D.; Very Revs. RANDOLPH G. CHEW; JOHN C. HALLORAN; JOEL A. LECUIVRE, J.C.L.; DANIEL M. TRAINOR; Revs. STEPHEN P. AMARAL; JOSEPH A. ESCOBAR; ROBERT F. HAWKINS; EDWARD J. MCGOVERN; BERNARD A. HEALEY; ANTHONY D. IWUC; JAMES T. RUGGIERI; JOHN P. SOARES.
College of Consultors—Most Rev. ROBERT J. MCMANUS, D.D., S.T.D.; Rev. Msgr. ROBERT C. EVANS, J.C.L.; Rev. Msgr. WILLIAM J. MCCAFFREY, S.T.B., M.A.; Rev. Msgr. ROBERT C. NEWBOLD, Ph.D., J.D.; Rev. Msgr. PAUL D. THEROUX; Rev. Msgr. WILLIAM I. VARSANYI, J.C.D.; Very Revs. RANDOLPH G. CHEW; JOHN C. HALLORAN; Revs. ROBERT F. HAWKINS; ANTHONY D. IWUC; JAMES T. RUGGIERI.
Diocesan Finance Council—Most Rev. ROBERT E. MULVEE, Pres.; Most Rev. ROBERT J. MCMANUS, D.D., S.T.D.; Rev. Msgr. WILLIAM I. VARSANYI, J.C.D.; Rev. Msgr. ROBERT C. EVANS, J.C.L.; Rev. Msgr. WILLIAM J. MCCAFFREY, S.T.B., M.A., Sec.; Rev. Msgr. JACQUES L. PLANTE, M.A.; Rev. Msgr. PAUL D. THEROUX, J.C.L.; Revs. EDWARD S. CARDENTE; BERTRAND L. THEROUX; Sr. M. THERESE ANTONE, R.S.M.; Mr. JOSE ALEX ARIZA; Mr. JOHN W. FLYNN; Hon. ANTHONY A. GIANNINI; Mr. ANTHONY T. GWIAZDOWSKI; Ms. MARIE J. LANGLOIS; Mr. THOMAS J. SKALA; Hon. PAUL J. TAVARES.
Deputy Finance Officer—Mr. MICHAEL F. SABATINO, C.P.A.

Diocesan Offices and Directors

AIDS Ministry—(cf. Community Services and Advocacy).
Alzheimer's Respite Care—(cf. Community Services and Advocacy).
Apostolate for Deaf and Hearing Impaired—Rev. GERARD O. SABOURIN, Dir., *One Cathedral Sq., Providence, 02903-3695.* Tel: 401-278-4630; 331-3283 (Voice & TTD).
Apostolate for Persons with Handicaps—(Legal Title: The Mercy Home and School). Rev. GERARD O. SABOURIN, Dir., *One Cathedral Sq., Providence, 02903-3695.* Tel: 401-278-4630.
SPRED (Special Religious Education)—Ms. COLLEEN TOUCHETTE, *One Cathedral Sq., Providence, 02903-3695.* Tel: 401-658-1174.
Archives—Rev. Msgr. JACQUES L. PLANTE, M.A., Archivist; Ms. VERONICA LIMA, Archive Clerk, *One Cathedral Sq., Providence, 02903-3695.* Tel: 401-278-4522.
Black Catholic Ministry—Mrs. LOIS TABELA, Coord., *One Cathedral Sq., Providence, 02903-3695.* Tel: 401-278-4552.
Building Commission, Office of—Mr. GEORGE W. STAPLES, Dir., Facilities; Mr. MICHAEL D. FALCONE, Facilities Engineer; Ms. CAROL ANN NELSON, Facilities Mgr.; Mr. MAXIME E. GIROUARD, JR., Environmental Engineer, *One Cathedral Sq., Providence, 02903-3695.* Tel: 401-278-4636.
Catholic Campaign for Human Development Grants—(cf. Community Services and Advocacy).
Catholic Campus Ministry—Rev. JOHN P. SOARES, Dir., *Catholic Student Center, 90 Chapel Way, University of Rhode Island, Kingston, 02881-1228.* Tel: 401-874-2324.
Catholic Chaplaincy Team (Correctional Facilities)—(cf. Community Services and Advocacy).
Catholic Charity Fund—Mr. ANTHONY T. GWIAZDOWSKI, Exec. Dir.; Rev. Msgr. WILLIAM J. MCCAFFREY, S.T.B., M.A., Moderator, *Stewardship and Development Office, 80 St. Mary Dr., Cranston, 02920.* Tel: 401-943-6550.
Catholic Foundation of Rhode Island—Mr. ANTHONY T. GWIAZDOWSKI, Dir.; Ms. KAREN R. COOPER, Asst. Dir., *Stewardship and Development Office, 80 St. Mary's Dr., Cranston, 02920.* Tel: 401-943-6550.
Catholic-Jewish Relations—Rev. THOMAS J. TREPANIER, Dir., *191 School St., P.O. Box 67, Albion, 02802-0062.* Tel: 401-333-1568.
Catholic Mutual Group—Mr. GREG CARLSON, Claims & Risk Mgr., *80 St. Mary's Dr., Cranston, 02920-5200.* Tel: 401-944-5375; 944-5379; Fax: 401-944-5380.
Catholic Relief Services—Rev. Msgr. WILLIAM I. VARSANYI, J.C.D., Dir., *One Cathedral Sq., Providence, 02903-3695.* Tel: 401-278-4519.
Catholic School Office—Bro. WILLIAM DYGERT, C.S.C., Supt., *One Cathedral Sq., Providence, 02903-3695.* Tel: 401-278-4550.
Catholic Scouting-Boy Scouts, Girl Scouts, Camp Fire—One Cathedral Sq., Providence, 02903-3695. Tel: 401-278-4626.
Catholic Youth Organization—(Legal title: *Catholic Youth Organization of the Diocese of Providence);* Miss LOUISE M. DUSSAULT, Dir., Youth Ministry, *One Cathedral Sq., Providence, 02903-3695.* Tel: 401-278-4626.
Cemeteries—(Legal title: *Catholic Cemeteries);* Rev. ANTHONY W. VERDELOTTI, Dir., *One Cathedral Sq., Providence, 02903-3695.* Tel: 401-278-4575.
Censors of Books—Rev. Msgr. JOHN F. COX, Ph.D.; Rev. Msgr. ROBERT C. NEWBOLD, Ph.D., J.D.
Charismatic Renewal—Rev. RAYMOND M. KELLY, *152 Holden St., Providence, 02908.* Tel: 401-421-7070.
Charisnewal RI—Co-Dirs.: Mr. BOB LAFAZIA; Mr. TED CARLSON, *244 Smith St., Providence, 02908.* Tel: 401-253-9457.
Child Care, Office of—Mrs. ALEXANDRA F. MOSER, Exec. Dir., *485 Mt. Pleasant Ave., Providence, 02908.* Tel: 401-274-3094.
Clearinghouse Program—(cf. Community Services and Advocacy).
Clergy Benefit Fund: Medical and Pension—(Legal Title: *Our Lady, Queen of the Clergy); 128 Greene St., Woonsocket, 02895-4565.* Tel: 401-769-7487; Fax: 401-765-3646.
Medical Advisory Board—Rev. Msgr. WILLIAM I. VARSANYI, Chm.; Rev. Msgr. GEORGE L. FRAPPIER, Sec.
Pension Advisory Board—Rev. Msgr. WILLIAM I. VARSANYI, Chm.; Rev. Msgr. GEORGE L. FRAPPIER, Sec.
Clergy Resource Advisor—Rev. Msgr. GEORGE L. FRAPPIER, *128 Greene St., Woonsocket, 02895.* Tel: 401-769-7487; Fax: 401-765-3646.
Communications—(Legal title: *Diocesan Catholic Telecommunications Network of Rhode Island);* (News Media, Radio, TV, Public Relations); Mr. WILLIAM G. HALPIN, Dir., *One Cathedral Sq., Providence, 02903-3695.* Tel: 401-278-4600; Fax: 401-278-4649.
Media Services Department—(Media Production, Audio-Visual, Photography, Creative Media Programming and Consultation); Mrs. ANN FORTE, *One Cathedral Sq., Providence, 02903-3695.* Tel: 401-278-4678.
Telecommunications Department—(Produces "Called to Serve" and other Catholic programming, Liaison with State Interconnect and CATV Companies, EWTN Liaison); Miss SUSAN MCCARTHY, Program Coord.; Mr. ANTHONY RIZZINI, Asst. to Dir., Radio & TV Prod., *One Cathedral Sq., Providence, 02903-3695.* Tel: 401-278-4608.
Community Services and Advocacy—(Legal Title: *Diocesan Bureau of Social Services);* Mrs. MARY BRAY, Program Monitor/Supvr., *83 Stewart St., Providence, 02903-4006.* Tel: 401-421-7833; Fax: 401-453-6135.
AIDS Ministry—Bro. RICHARD GAGNON, A.A. Tel: 401-421-7833.
Alzheimer's Respite Care—Ms. CHERYL ALBRIGHT. Tel: 401-421-7866.
Catholic Campaign for Human Devleopment Grants—Mr. JOHN J. BARRY, III. Tel: 401-421-4808.
Catholic Chaplaincy Team (Correctional Facilities)—Rev. GERALD G. HARBOUR; Mr. ROLAND COMEAU, R.I. Training School.
Clearinghouse Program—Mrs. MARY BRAY.
Community Advocacy—Mr. JOHN HANLEY.
Information Specialist—Sr. PATRICIA ONYEJE, D.M.M.M.
Immigration and Refugee Services—Mr. MARK MORRISON, . Fax: 401-277-9027.
Interfaith Community Dire Emergency Fund / Emergency Assistance Network—Mr. DOUGLAS LAPIERRE.
Justice and Peace Education—Ms. PAT JAEHNIG.
Neighborhood Friendly Visitor Program—Ms. CHERYL ALBRIGHT. Tel: 401-421-7886.
Respite Care Services—Ms. CHERYL ALBRIGHT. Tel: 401-421-7886.
Cursillo Movement—Rev. FRANK S. SALMANI, Spiritual Dir., *538 Broadway, Providence, 02909.* Tel: 401-274-3434. Mrs. KATHRYN ROBBIO, Lay Coord., *100 Empress Dr., E. Greenwich, 02818.* Tel: 401-884-2424.
Ecumenical Commission—Rev. LIONEL A. BLAIN, Chm., *1200 Mendon Rd., Woonsocket, 02895.* Tel: 401-766-0626.
Education and Compliance—Lt. ROBERT N. MCCARTHY, Dir., *433 Elmwood Ave., Providence, 02907.* Tel: 401-941-0760.
Education, Department of—Most Rev. ROBERT J. MCMANUS, D.D., S.T.D., Vicar for Education, *One Cathedral Sq., Providence, 02903.* Tel: 401-278-4587. Bro. WILLIAM DYGERT, C.S.C., Supt., Schools. Tel: 401-278-4550. Sr. SHEILA DURANTE, R.S.M., Asst. Supt.; Rev. JOHN P. SOARES, Dir., Campus Min., *URI Catholic Student Center.* Tel: 401-874-2324. Rev. Msgr. JACQUES L. PLANTE, Office of Ministerial Formation. Tel: 401-278-4613. Mr. JOSEPH P. SINWELL, Dir., Office of Religious Education, C.C.D. Tel: 401-278-4646. Rev. GERARD O. SABOURIN, Dir., Diocesan Apostolate Persons with Handicapped. Tel: 401-278-4630. Ms. COLLEEN TOUCHETTE, SPRED (Special Religious Education). Tel: 401-658-1174.
Evangelization—Sr. MARTA INES TORO, O.P., Dir., *One Cathedral Sq., Providence, 02903-3695.* Tel: 401-278-4624.
Finance Office—(cf. Planning and Finance Office).
Fiscal Office—Mr. J. TIMOTHY KOCAB, Diocesan Controller, *One Cathedral Sq., Providence, 02903-3695.* Tel: 401-278-4616.
Government Liaison—Rev. Msgr. ROBERT C. NEWBOLD, Ph.D., J.D., Diocesan Dir.
Grievance Committee—Very Rev. GERALD E. BEIRNE, Chm., *622 Putnam Pike, Greenville, 02828-1401.* Tel: 401-949-1500.
Health Care Ministries, Office of—Rev. JOHN E. WATTERSON, Dir., *103 Pine Street, P.O. Box 518, Pawtucket, 02862.* Tel: 401-725-0160; Fax: 401-729-0341.
Hispanic Ministry—Mrs. AIDA HIDALGO, Dir., *One Cathedral Sq., Providence, 02903-3695.* Tel: 401-278-4526.
Holy Childhood Association—Rev. Msgr. WILLIAM I. VARSANYI, J.C.D., Dir., *One Cathedral Sq., Providence, 02903-3695.* Tel: 401-278-4519.
Holy Name Society—Rev. ANTHONY D. IWUC, Dir., *391 High St., Central Falls, 02863.* Tel: 401-723-5427.
Human Resources Office—Mr. WILLIAM G. MEYER, Dir., *One Cathedral Square, Providence, 02903-3695.* Tel: 401-278-4584; Fax: 401-751-0049.
Immigration and Refugee Services—(Legal Title: *Diocesan Bureau of Social Services);* (cf. Community Services and Advocacy).
Insurance Commission—Rev. Msgr. WILLIAM J. MCCAFFREY, S.T.B., M.A., Chm., *One Cathedral Sq., Providence, 02903-3695.* Tel: 401-278-4616.
Justice and Peace Education—(cf. Community Services and Advocacy).
Life and Family Ministry—(Legal Title: *Retreat House of the Immaculate Heart of Mary);* Mr. STEPHEN A. BURKE, M.S.W., Dir., *433 Elmwood Ave. & 1 Carter, Providence, 02907.* Tel: 401-467-7203; Fax: 401-467-7205.
Natural Family Planning—SHEILA BURKE, *433 Elmwood Ave., Providence, 02907.* Tel: 401-467-7203.
Neighborhood Friendly Visitor Program—(cf. Community Services and Advocacy).
Parish Outreach—SILVIO CUELLAR; ELIZABETH LEBRON, *433 Elmwood Ave., Providence, 02907.* Tel: 401-467-7203.

Peace and Justice—CATHERINE FOLCHER MCELROY, *433 Elmwood Ave., Providence, 02907.* Tel: 401-467-7203.

Project Rachel—JOAN PENDERGAST, *433 Elmwood Ave., Providence, 02907.* Tel: 401-467-7203.

Respect Life—Vacant, *433 Elmwood Ave., Providence, 02907.* Tel: 401-467-7203.

Marriage Preparation—Deacon STEPHEN COTE, *1 Carter St., Providence, 02907.* Tel: 401-467-7203; Fax: 401-467-7205.

Divorce and All Other Losses—Ms. DOROTHY J. LEVESQUE, *1 Carter St., Providence, 02907.* Tel: 401-467-7204.

Management Information Services—Ms. PEG RYAN, Dir., *One Cathedral Sq., Providence, 02903-3695.* Tel: 401-278-4611.

Media Services Department—(cf. Communications).

Ministerial Formation—(Continuing Education of Priests, Permanent Deacons, Lay Ministers). Rev. Msgr. JACQUES L. PLANTE, Dir., *One Cathedral Sq., Providence, 02903-3695.* Tel: 401-278-4613.

Occult Awareness Ministry—Rev. PAUL E. DESMARAIS, *c/o One Cathedral Sq., Providence, 02903-3695.* Tel: 401-273-1702.

Pastoral Planning—Ms. CONNIE THORNTON, Dir., *One Cathedral Sq., Providence, 02903-3695.* Tel: 401-278-4610.

Planning and Finance—Rev. Msgr. WILLIAM J. MCCAFFREY, S.T.B., M.A., Vicar; Mr. MICHAEL F. SABATINO, C.P.A., Finance Officer, *One Cathedral Sq., Providence, 02903.* Tel: 401-278-4540; Fax: 401-831-1947.

Priests, Minister for—Rev. NORMAND J. GODIN, *1045 Douglas Pike, Mohegan, Harrisville, 02830.* Tel: 401-568-7101.

Priests' Eucharistic League—Rev. JOSEPH P. HYNES, Dir., *358 Newport Ave., Pawtucket, 02861.* Tel: 401-722-4470.

Priests' Personnel Board—Rev. Msgr. ROBERT C. EVANS, J.C.L., Dir., *One Cathedral Sq., Providence, 02903-3695.* Tel: 401-278-4527. Constituency 1: Rev. FRANCIS W. O'HARA,Constituency 2: Rev. STANLEY T. NAKOWICZ,Constituency 3: Rev. HENRY J. BODAH-,Constituency 4: Rev. BERNARD A. HEALEY,Appointed Member: Very Rev. JOHN E. UNSWORTH.

Project Hope/Projecto Esperanza—(Legal Title: *Project Hope/Projecto Esperanza);* Mrs. MARY BRAY, Dir., *400 Dexter St., Center Falls, 02863.* Tel: 401-728-0515; Fax: 401-722-2330.

Propagation of the Faith—(Legal title: *Society for the Propagation of the Faith, Diocese of Providence);* Rev. Msgr. WILLIAM I. VARSANYI, J.C.D., Dir., *One Cathedral Sq., Providence, 02903-3695.* Tel: 401-278-4519.

Radio & T.V. Producer—(cf. Communications).

Respite Care Services—(cf. Community Services and Advocacy).

Religious, Office of—Sr. JACQUELINE DICKEY, S.S.C.H., Dir., *One Cathedral Sq., Providence, 02903-3695.* Tel: 401-278-4633.

Religious Education—Mr. JOSEPH P. SINWELL, *34 Fenner St., Providence, 02903.* Tel: 401-278-4646.

Renewal in the Spirit—Rev. JOHN F. RANDALL, *Res., 178 Dexter St., Providence, 02907.* Tel: 401-421-6441.

Respect Life—(cf. Life and Family Ministry).

Retreat House Program—Sr. JEAN MARIE MCGEE, R.S.M., Admin., *Our Lady of Peace Spiritual Life Center, Narragansett, 02882.* Tel: 401-884-7676; 783-2871.

Senior Care, Office of—Miss MARY ANN ALTRUI, Exec. Dir., *400 Mendon Rd., North Smithfield, 02896-6999.* Tel: 401-767-3500.

St. Vincent de Paul Society—(Emergency Assistance Network), *20 River Ave., Providence, 02908.* Tel: 401-521-1301; Fax: 401-521-1300.

Social Ministry—Mr. JOHN J. BARRY, III, Sec., *83 Stewart St., Providence, 02903.* Tel: 401-421-4808; Fax: 401-274-5450.

Spirituality and Evangelization—Rev. Msgr. JOHN C. ALLARD, Vicar; Sr. MARTA INES TORO, O.P., Dir., Evangelization, *One Cathedral Sq., Providence, 02903-3695.* Tel: 401-278-4625.

SPRED (Special Religious Education)—(cf. Apostolate for Persons with Handicaps).

Stewardship and Development—(Annual Appeal, Planned Giving, Bishop's Partnership in Charity); Mr. ANTHONY T. GWIAZDOWSKI, Dir.; Rev. Msgr. WILLIAM J. MCCAFFREY, Moderator, *80 St. Mary's Dr., Cranston, 02920.* Tel: 401-943-6550.

Telecommunications—(cf. Communications).

Vocations—Revs. ALBERT A. KENNEY, Dir. MARCEL L. TAILLON, Vocations Recruiter, *485 Mt. Pleasant Ave., Providence, 02908.* Tel: 401-831-8011. Sr. JACQUELINE DICKEY, S.S.C.H., Assoc. Dir., Religious, *One Cathedral Sq., Providence, 02903-3695.* Tel: 401-278-4633.

Worship, Office for—Rev. PETER J. ANDREWS, Dir., *One Cathedral Sq., Providence, 02903-3695.* Tel: 401-278-4640.

Young Adult Ministry—Ms. LORA MORGAN, Coord., *One Cathedral Sq., Providence, 02903-3695.* Tel: 401-278-4525.

Youth Ministry—Miss LOUISE DUSSAULT, Dir., *One Cathedral Sq., Providence, 02903-3695.* Tel: 401-278-4636.

CLERGY, PARISHES, MISSIONS AND PAROCHIAL SCHOOLS

CITY OF PROVIDENCE
(Providence County)

1—CATHEDRAL OF SS. PETER AND PAUL (1837). (Legal title: SS. Peter and Paul's Church, Providence, Rhode Island). Rev. Francis J. Giudice, Rector. In res., Revs. Normand W. Valois; John J. Darcy.
Res., 30 Fenner St., 02903. Tel: 401-331-2434 (Office); 278-4510 (Cathedral Residence); Fax: 401-331-2435.
Convent—Tel: 401-272-4502.
Sisters of St. Joseph 6.
Catechesis/Religious Programs—Students 7.

2—ST. ADALBERT (1902) (Polish). (Legal Title: Saint Adalbert's Church). Rev. Frederick V. Slota.
Res., 866 Atwells Ave., 02909-2596. Tel: 401-351-9306; Fax: 401-351-9306.
Convent—Tel: 401-831-3336. Sr. Mary Alexander, Supr.
Felician Sisters of St. Francis 2.
Catechesis/Religious Programs—864 Atwells Ave., 02909-2596.
Students 97.

3—ST. AGNES (1904). (Legal title: St. Agnes Church). Rev. Normand J. Godin, Admin.
Res., 351 Branch Ave., 02904. Tel: 401-861-7265; Fax: 401-454-6839.
Catechesis/Religious Programs—Tel: 401-331-2547.
Students 93.

4—ST. ANN (1895) (Italian). (Legal title: Saint Ann's Catholic Church of Providence, Rhode Island). Revs. Raymond B. Bastia; Angelo N. Carusi.
Res., 2 Russo St., 02904. Tel: 401-861-5111; Fax: 401-751-5453.
School—525 Branch Ave., 02904. Tel: 401-331-0891; Fax: 401-854-0870.
Lay Teachers 15; Students 215.
Catechesis/Religious Programs—Tel: 401-521-5220.
Students 77.

5—ST. ANTHONY (Olneyville) (1900). (Legal title: Saint Anthony's Church Corporation, Rhode Island). Rev. Joseph Protano, Jr.
Res., 549 Plainfield St., 02909. Tel: 401-943-2300; Fax: 401-943-2301.
Catechesis/Religious Programs—Students 131.

6—ASSUMPTION OF THE BLESSED VIRGIN MARY (1871). (Legal title: The Church of the Assumption, Providence, Rhode Island). Revs. Daniel M. Trainor; Guillermo L. Corrales Bedoya (Colombia).
Res., 791 Potters Ave., 02907. Tel: 401-941-1248; Fax: 401-781-4887.
Catechesis/Religious Programs—Tel: 401-941-3768.
Students 272.

7—ST. AUGUSTINE (1929). (Legal title: Saint Augustine's Church, Providence, Rhode Island). Revs. Barry R.L. Connerton; Bernard A. Healey. In res., Rev. Msgr. Salvatore R. Matano; Rev. Joseph A. Howarth.
Res., 20 Old Rd., 02908. Tel: 401-831-3503; Fax: 401-421-9060.
School—635 Mt. Pleasant Ave., 02908. Tel: 401-831-1213; Fax: 401-831-4256. Mrs. Paul F. Morry, Prin.
Sisters 2; Lay Teachers 26; Students 323.
Catechesis/Religious Programs—Students 382.

8—ST. BARTHOLOMEW (1907) (Italian). Silver Lake District (Legal title: Saint Bartholomew's Church Corporation). Revs. Joseph F. Pranzo, C.S.; Francis Minchiatti, C.S.; Deacon Robert L. Gallo.
Res., 297 Laurel Hill Ave., 02909-3897. Tel: 401-944-4466; Fax: 401-946-5866.
School—315 Laurel Hill Ave., 02909-3898. Tel: 401-944-5662; Fax: 401-946-6422. Mr. Frank D. Spaziano, Prin.
Sisters 1; Lay Teachers 13; Students 193.
Catechesis/Religious Programs—Tel: 401-943-6211. Maryann Califano, D.R.E.
Students 150.

9—BLESSED SACRAMENT (1888). (Legal title: The Church of the Blessed Sacrament in Providence, Rhode Island). Rev. Charles E. Maher; Deacons Thomas F. Boutier; Vincente Caban.
Res., 239 Regent Ave., 02908. Tel: 401-751-7575; Fax: 401-621-9605.
School—240 Regent Ave., 02908. Tel: 401-831-3993. Jacqueline Colicci, Prin.
Sisters Faithful Companions of Jesus 1; Lay Teachers 21; Students 337.
Catechesis/Religious Programs—Tel: 401-751-7567.
Students 89.
Convent—350 Mount Pleasant Ave., 02908. Tel: 401-274-6578.
Sisters Faithful Companions of Jesus 4.

10—ST. CASIMIR (1919) (Lithuanian). (Legal title: Saint Casimir's Church, Providence, Rhode Island). Rev. Adolph Klimanskis (NOR) Admin.
Res., 350 Smith St., 02908. Tel: 401-331-1051.

11—ST. CHARLES BORROMEO (1874) (French). (Legal title: Saint Charles Borromeo Roman Catholic Church, Providence, Rhode Island). Revs. John F. Randall; John W. Gray; Deacons Jose Rico, Pastoral Assoc.; Rony Lopez; Joseph Braga.
Res., 178 Dexter St., 02907. Tel: 401-421-6441; Fax: 401-454-4986.
Catechesis/Religious Programs—Students 285.

12—ST. EDWARD (1874). (Legal title: The Church of St. Joseph Geneva Rhode Island). Revs. Edward S. Cardente; C. Brian Lagasse; Hugo Carmona.
Res., 10 Caxton St., 02904. Tel: 401-331-4035.
Church—997 Branch Ave., 02904.
Catechesis/Religious Programs—Tel: 401-353-5215.
Students 100.

13—GENESIS COMMUNITY. Closed. For inquiries for parish records contact Cathedral of SS. Peter & Paul, Providence.

14—ST. HEDWIG. Closed. For inquiries for sacramental records contact St. Adalbert Parish, Providence.

15—HOLY CROSS (1949) (Italian). (Legal Title: Corporation of the Church of the Holy Cross). Rev. Anthony Mancini, Admin.; Deacon John J. Natalizia.
Res., 18 King Philip St., 02909. Tel: 401-274-5225; Fax: 401-274-6635.
Catechesis/Religious Programs—Tel: 401-751-1144. Mrs. June Carnevale, D.R.E.
Students 174.

16—HOLY GHOST (1889) (Italian). (Legal title: Corporation of the Church of the Holy Ghost, Rhode Island). Rev. Ignatius Battaglia, C.S.
Res., 472 Atwells Ave., 02909. Tel: 401-421-3551; Fax: 401-421-3557.
School—35 Swiss St., 02909. Tel: 401-421-4455; Fax: 401-421-5444. Mrs. Carol Wood-Soltys, Prin.
Sisters of Mercy of the Americas 1; Lay Teachers 9; Students 186.
Day Care Center—Tel: 401-521-9510.
Lay Teachers 3; Children 40.
Catechesis/Religious Programs—Mr. Alfred Casinelli, D.R.E.
Students 45.

17—HOLY NAME OF JESUS (1882). (Legal title: Church of the Holy Name of Jesus at Providence, Rhode Island). Rev. Kevin R. Fisette; Deacon Frederick A. Young.
Res., 99 Camp St., 02906-1799. Tel: 401-272-4515; Fax: 401-272-4616.
School—Tel: 401-351-0533; Fax: 401-351-0371.
Lay Teachers 12; Students 156.
Catechesis/Religious Programs—Students 55.

18—IMMACULATE CONCEPTION. Closed. For inquiries for sacramental records contact St. Patrick Parish, Providence.

19—ST. JOHN. Closed. (Legal title: St. John Church of Providence Rhode Island). Sacramental records are located at St. Mary Church, Providence.

20—ST. JOSEPH (Foxpoint) (1851). (Legal title: St. Joseph's Church Providence Rhode Island). Rev. Msgr. William J. McCaffrey; Sr. Mary Ann Hosey, R.S.M., Pastoral Min. In res., Revs. Henry J. Bodah; John J. Rainone.
Res., 92 Hope St., 02906. Tel: 401-421-9137; Fax: 401-621-5349.
Catechesis/Religious Programs—Students 42.

21—ST. MARON. (Legal title: Church of St. Maron in Providence). Rev. Msgr. Jacques L. Plante.
Res., One Cathedral Square, 02903-3695.

22—ST. MARY (Broadway) (1853). (Legal title: St. Mary's Church Providence Rhode Island). Rev. Frank S. Salmani; Deacon Robert Nicholson.
Res., 538 Broadway, 02909-3329. Tel: 401-274-3434.
School—30 Barton St., 02909. Tel: 401-274-5250. Mr. Robert Waldraff, Prin.
Sisters of the Congregation de Notre Dame 1; Lay Teachers 11; Students 166.
Catechesis/Religious Programs—Students 36.

23—ST. MICHAEL THE ARCHANGEL (South Providence) (1859). (Legal title: St. Michael's Providence, Rhode Island). Revs. Raymond B. Malm; Jacques E. Chavannes; Deacon Juan Andres Perez.
Res., 239 Oxford St., 02905. Tel: 401-781-7210; Fax: 401-461-6164.
Catechesis/Religious Programs—Students 350.

24—OUR LADY OF CHARITY. (Legal title: Church of Our Lady of Charity of Providence). Rev. Msgr. William I. Varsanyi.
Res., One Cathedral Sq., 02903-3695.

25—OUR LADY OF LOURDES (1904) (French). (Legal title: Church of Our Lady of Lourdes). Rev. Msgr. Paul D. Theroux; Deacon Anthony Wendolowski.
Res., 901 Atwells Ave., 02909. Tel: 401-272-8127; Fax: 401-861-0226.

26—OUR LADY OF MT. CARMEL (1921) (Italian). (Legal title: Church of Our Lady of Mount Carmel, Providence). Revs. Raymond P. Luft; Hugo Carmona (Colombia); Fredy Jimenez (Columbia); Deacon Jose Turcios.
Res., 12 Spruce St., 02903. Tel: 401-274-2113.
Catechesis/Religious Programs—Students 70.

27—OUR LADY OF THE ROSARY (Portuguese). (Legal title: Church of Our Lady of the Rosary). Rev. Antonio M. Paiva.
Res., 463 Benefit St., 02903. Tel: 401-421-5621.
Convent—17 Traverse St., 02903. Tel: 401-751-9342, 401-751-6432.
Sisters of St. Dorothy 2.
Catechesis/Religious Programs—Sr. Fatima Simas, S.S.D., D.R.E.
Students 216.

28—ST. PATRICK (1841). (Legal title: St. Patrick's Church, Providence, Rhode Island). Rev. Raymond M. Kelly.
Res., 152 Holden St., 02908. Tel: 401-421-7070.
Church—244 Smith St., 02908.
School—Tel: 401-421-9300. Mr. Stephen M. Raymond, Prin.
Lay Teachers 14; Students 185.
Catechesis/Religious Programs—Students 85.

29—ST. PIUS V (1918). (Legal title: Saint Pius Church, Providence, Rhode Island). Revs. Vincent G. DeLucia, O.P.; Gabriel Pivarnik, O.P.; John Baptist Ku, O.P. In res., Bro. Denis Swann, O.P.; Rev. John L. Sullivan, O.P.; Very Rev. John P. Burchill, O.P., Prior.
Res., 55 Elmhurst Ave., 02908. Tel: 401-751-4871; Fax: 401-273-1089.
School—49 Elmhurst Ave., 02908. Tel: 401-421-9750; Fax: 401-455-3928. Mrs. Helina Cobery, Prin.
Lay Teachers 20; Students 270.
Catechesis/Religious Programs—Students 250.
Convent—30 Elmhurst Ave., 02908. Tel: 401-751-0362.

30—ST. RAYMOND (1911). (Legal title: Saint Raymond's Church Corporation). Rev. Edward L. Pieroni.
Res., 2 Matilda St., 02904-1812. Tel: 401-351-4224; Fax: 401-274-3350.
Church—1240 N. Main St., 02906. Tel: 401-351-4224; Fax: 401-274-3350.
Catechesis/Religious Programs—Students 48.

31—ST. SEBASTIAN (1915). (Legal title: Church of Saint Sebastian). Rev. Robert W. Hayman, M.A., Ph.D.; Rev. Msgr. Martin A. Canavan, S.T.L., J.C.L (P.H.U.).
Res., 67 Cole Ave., 02906. Tel: 401-751-0196; Fax: 401-273-7406.
Catechesis/Religious Programs—Tel: 401-272-6062.
Students 117.

32—ST. TERESA OF AVILA (Olneyville) (1883). (Legal title: Saint Teresa's Church Providence Rhode Island). Rev. Raymond L. Tetrault.
Res., 18 Pope St., 02909. Tel: 401-831-7714; Fax: 401-831-7727.
Catechesis/Religious Programs—Students 89.

33—ST. THOMAS (Fruit Hill) (1886). (Legal title: St. Thomas' Church of Manton Rhode Island). Rev. Francis P. Kayatta; Deacon Albert DePetrillo.
Res., 65 Fruit Hill Ave., 02909. Tel: 401-272-7118; Fax: 401-272-8431.
School—See St. Thomas Regional School. Tel: 401-351-0403.
Catechesis/Religious Programs—Tel: 401-272-1443.
Students 327.
Convent—41 Edendale Ave., 02911. Tel: 401-272-1722.

OUTSIDE THE CITY OF PROVIDENCE

Barrington, Bristol Co., Holy Angels (1913) (Italian). (Legal title: Holy Angel's Church Corporation). Rev. Raymond J. Ferrick.
Res., 341 Maple Ave., 02806. Tel: 401-245-7743; Fax: 401-245-9698.
Catechesis/Religious Programs—341 Maple Ave., 02806. Tel: 401-247-1764.
Students 71.

St. Luke (West Barrington) (1942). (Legal title: Saint Luke's Church Corporation, Barrington). Revs. William R. Jenkinson; David F. Gaffney.
Res., 108 Washington Rd., 02806-1133. Tel: 401-246-1212.
School—Waldron Ave., 02806. Tel: 401-246-0990; Fax: 401-246-2120. Mrs. Margaret C. Halpin, Prin.
Lay Teachers 17; Students 299.
Catechesis/Religious Programs—Tel: 401-246-1363. D.R.E.: Patricia Grattan, (Grades 1-5); Diane Comerford, (Grades 6-10).
Students 666.

Bristol, Bristol Co., St. Elizabeth (1913) (Portuguese). (Legal title: Saint Elizabeth's Church of Bristol). Revs. Thomas J. Ferland; Robert L. Bailey; Deacon John Sardinha.
Res., 577 Wood St., 02809-2395. Tel: 401-253-8366; Fax: 401-253-7695.
School—10 Monroe Ave., 02809. Tel: 401-253-7622; Fax: 401-253-5910. Mrs. Magdalen Chianese, Prin.
Lay Teachers 12; Students 198.
Catechesis/Religious Programs—Tel: 401-253-3501; Fax: 401-253-7630. D.R.E.: Mrs. Genevieve Souza; Mrs. Lisa Correira.
Students 546.

St. Mary (1869). (Legal title: Saint Mary's Church, Bristol, Rhode Island). Rev. Barry J. Gamache; Deacon Bernard G. Theroux.
Res., 330 Wood St., 02809. Tel: 401-253-3300; Fax: 401-253-3300. [CEM]
Catechesis/Religious Programs—Tel: 401-253-2270.
Students 249.
Mission—Prudence Island, Our Lady of Prudence, 02872.

Our Lady of Mount Carmel (1917) (Italian). (Legal title: Church of Our Lady of Mount Carmel, Bristol). Revs. James J. Verdelotti; James D. Capoverdi, Jr.; Deacon Paul Bisbano.
Res., 141 State St., 02809. Tel: 401-253-9449; Fax: 401-253-5687. [JC]
School—Maestre Pie Filippini. (Religious Teachers Filippini) 117 State St., 02809. Tel: 401-253-8455; Fax: 401-254-8234. Sr. Concetta Millemaggi, M.P.F., Prin.
Sisters 2; Lay Teachers 12; Students 212.
Catechesis/Religious Programs—131 State St., 02809. Tel: 401-624-3664.
Students 177.

Burrillville, Providence Co.,

1—ST. JOSEPH, (Pascoag) (1884). (Legal title: Saint Joseph's Roman Catholic Church of Pascoag). Rev. Clifford J. Cabral.
Res., 183 Sayles Ave., P.O. Box 188, Pascoag, 02859. Tel: 401-568-2411; Fax: 401-568-2586.
Catechesis/Religious Programs—Students 266.

2—OUR LADY OF GOOD HELP, (Mapleville) (1905). (Legal title: Eglise de Notre Dame de Bonsecours). Rev. Timothy J. Lemlin; Deacon Richard J. Lapierre.
Res., 1063 Victory Hwy., Box 158, Mapleville, 02839. Tel: 401-568-5272; Fax: 401-568-5351.
Catechesis/Religious Programs—Mrs. Patricia Ducharme, D.R.E.
Students 246.

3—ST. PATRICK, (Harrisville) (1854). (Legal title: St. Patrick's Church, Burrillville, Rhode Island). Rev. Bernard M. O'Reilly, M.A., Ph.D., D.Min.
Res., 45 Main St., Harrisville, 02830. Tel: 401-568-5600; Fax: 401-568-7132. [CEM][JC 2]
Catechesis/Religious Programs—Tel: 401-568-5580.
Students 220.
Mission—Glendale, St. Louis Chapel, Old Victory Hwy., Glendale, 02826.

4—ST. THERESA OF THE CHILD JESUS, (Nasonville) (1923). (Legal title: Church of Saint Teresa of the Child Jesus, Nasonville). Rev. Roland L. Simoneau.
Res., 35 Dion Dr., Harrisville, 02830. Tel: 401-568-8280; Fax: 401-567-9238. [CEM]
Catechesis/Religious Programs—Tel: 401-568-3057.
Students 162.

Central Falls, Providence Co.,

1—THE HOLY SPIRIT CATHOLIC COMMUNITY, (1997). Consolidation of the following three parishes: Holy Trinity, (Legal Title: Church of the Holy Trinity, Central Falls); Notre Dame, (Legal Title: Notre Dame Church); and St. Matthew, (Legal Title: Saint Matthew's Church of Central Falls). Revs. Robert P. Perron, Admin.; Ontoniel J. Gomez-Serna; Eugene R. Lessard; Deacon Luis A. Hernandez. In res., Rev. Robert A. Rochon.
Res., 1030 Dexter St., 02863-1717. Tel: 401-726-2600; 725-1748; 723-5326; Fax: 401-722-0224. [CEM]
Catechesis/Religious Programs—Tel: 401-722-3717.
Students 365.

2—HOLY TRINITY, (1989). Merged with Notre Dame, Central Falls and St. Matthew, Central Falls to form The Holy Spirit Catholic Communtity, Central Falls. (Legal title: Church of the Holy Trinity, Central Falls).

3—ST. JOSEPH, (1906) (Polish). (Legal title: St. Joseph's Church of Central Falls). Rev. Anthony D. Iwuc. In res., Rev. Krzysztof Krauzowicz, S.D.B.
Res., 391 High St., 02863-3109. Tel: 401-723-5427.

4—ST. MATTHEW'S, (1906) (French). Merged with Holy Trinity, Central Falls and Notre Dame, Central Falls to form The Holy Spirit Catholic Community, Central Falls. (Legal title: Saint Matthew's Church of Central Falls).

5—NOTRE DAME, (1873) (French). Merged with Holy Trinity, Central Falls and St. Matthew, Central Falls to form The Holy Spirit Catholic Community, Central Falls. (Legal title: Notre Dame Church).

Charlestown, Washington Co., St. Mary (Carolina) (1946). (Legal title: Saint Mary's Church Corporation, Carolina). Rev. John F. Heaney.
Res., P.O. Box 475, Carolina, 02812. Tel: 401-364-7214; Fax: 401-364-0182.
Catechesis/Religious Programs—Tel: 401-783-1849.
Students 415.
Mission—Charlestown, Washington Co., St. James, 2079 Mat. School House Rd., Charlestown, 02813. Tel: 401-364-7214.

Coventry, Kent Co., SS. John and Paul (1955). (Legal title: SS. John and Paul Parish Corporation, Coventry). Revs. Joseph P. Henry; Michael J. Menna; David C. Procaccini; Deacon Robert A. Turbitt, II.
Res., 341 S. Main St., 02816. Tel: 401-821-5764; Fax: 401-828-5351.
School—Father John V. Doyle School, Tel: 401-821-3756. Mr. J. Robert McDermott, Prin.; Mrs. Vivian Ryan, Vice Prin.
Lay Teachers 25; Students 480.
Catechesis/Religious Programs—Tel: 401-821-4780.
Students 1,402.

Our Lady of Czenstochowa (Quidnick) (1905) (Polish). (Legal title: Church of Our Lady of Czenstochowa). Rev. Stephen P. Amaral.
Res., 445 Washington St., 02816. Tel: 401-821-7991; Fax: 401-821-8714.
Catechesis/Religious Programs—Students 70.

St. Vincent de Paul (Anthony) (1937) (French). (Legal title: Church of Saint Vincent de Paul, Anthony, Rhode Island). Rev. Paul J. Laporte; Deacon Edward Sadowski, Jr.
Res., 6 St. Vincent de Paul St., 02816. Tel: 401-821-8719; Fax: 401-827-5071.
Convent—8 St. Vincent de Paul St., 02816. Tel: 401-828-6506. Sr. Lorette Soucy, P.M., Supr.
Sisters of the Presentation of Mary 2.
Catechesis/Religious Programs—2 St. Vincent de Paul St., 02816. Tel: 401-828-3090.
Students 190.

Cranston, Providence Co.,

1—ST. ANN, (1858). (Legal title: St. Anne's Church, Cranston, Rhode Island). Rev. John G. Greaves.
Res., 1493 Cranston St., 02920. Tel: 401-942-2767; Fax: 401-942-2773.
Catechesis/Religious Programs—Tel: 401-942-0655.
Students 308.

2—HOLY APOSTLES, (1991). (Legal title: Holy Apostles Church, Cranston, Rhode Island). Rev. Richard D. Sheahan.
Res., 800 Pippin Orchard Rd., 02921. Tel: 401-946-5586; Fax: 401-946-5066.
Catechesis/Religious Programs—Students 1,326.

3—IMMACULATE CONCEPTION, (Oaklawn) (1958). (Legal title: Immaculate Conception Church Corporation, Cranston). Rev. Ronald E. Brassard; Deacons Carmine Forlingieri; Thomas R. Raspallo.
Res., 237 Garden Hills Dr., 02920. Tel: 401-942-1854; Fax: 401-942-2897.
Catechesis/Religious Programs—Tel: 401-942-1958. D.R.E.: Barbara Prata; Jonathan Jenkins.
Students 452.

4—ST. MARK, (Garden City) (1950). (Legal title: Saint Mark's Church Corporation of Cranston). Revs. Richard A. Donnelly; Michael J. Woolley; Deacon Robert C. Persson.
Res., 9 Garden Ct., 02920. Tel: 401-942-1616.
Catechesis/Religious Programs—Tel: 401-942-3231.
Students 414.

5—ST. MARY, (Knightsville) (1925) (Italian). (Santa Maria della Civita) (Legal title: Saint Mary's Church, Cranston). Revs. Alfred C. Lonardo; Daniel M. Azzarone; Deacon Peter A. Ceprano.
Res., 1525 Cranston St., 02920-5297. Tel: 401-942-1492; Fax: 401-946-2531.

School—Tel: 401-944-4107; Fax: 401-944-2395. Mrs. Elizabeth Mizzoni, Prin.
Lay Teachers 19; Students 303.
Catechesis/Religious Programs—Tel: 401-944-1323. Phyllis Ann Persson, D.R.E.
Students 510.

6—St. Matthew, (Auburn) (1909). (Legal title: St. Matthew's Church Corporation). Revs. James R. Collins; William J. Ledoux.
Res., 15 Frances Ave., 02910. Tel: 401-461-7172; Fax: 401-461-7339.
Church—Elmwood & Park Ave., 02910.
School—1301 Elmwood Ave., 02910. Tel: 401-941-8954; Fax: 401-781-7722. Ms. Elaine P. Dykstra, Prin.
Lay Teachers 19; Students 254.
Catechesis/Religious Programs—Tel: 401-781-4568; Fax: 401-461-7173. Sr. Rita E. McCoy, R.S.M., D.R.E.
Students 400.

7—St. Paul, (Edgewood) (1907). (Legal title: Saint Paul's Church of Edgewood). Revs. Randolph G. Chew; Mark A. Sauriol; Sr. Mary Ann Rossi, C.N.D., Pastoral Assoc. In res., Rev. Robert J. Maynard.
Res., One St. Paul Pl., 02905. Tel: 401-461-5734; Fax: 401-785-3613.
School—1789 Broad St., 02905. Tel: 401-941-2030. Mrs. Jean Patterson, Prin.
Lay Teachers 15; Students 193.
Catechesis/Religious Programs—Tel: 401-941-5576. Ann Holland, D.R.E.
Students 349.

Cumberland, Providence Co.,

1—St. Aidan, (1962). (Legal title: St. Aidan Church Corporation, Cumberland). Rev. Donald L. Depatie.
Res., 1460 Diamond Hill Rd., 02864. Tel: 401-333-5897; Fax: 401-333-5078.
Catechesis/Religious Programs—Tel: 401-333-9030.
Students 286.

2—St. Joan of Arc, (Cumberland Hill) (1929). (Legal title: Saint Joan's Church, Cumberland, Rhode Island). Rev. Norman W. Bourdon.
Res., 3357 Mendon Rd., 02864-2195. Tel: 401-658-2084; Fax: 401-658-2086.
Catechesis/Religious Programs—Tel: 401-658-0734.
Students 557.

3—St. John Baptist Mary Vianney, (Diamond Hill) (1953). (Legal title: Saint John Baptist Mary Vianney Church Corporation, Diamond Hill). Rev. J. Raymond Theroux; Deacon Paul H. Lambert.
Res., 3609 Diamond Hill Rd., 02864. Tel: 401-333-6060; Fax: 401-333-0766.
Catechesis/Religious Programs—3587 Diamond Hill Rd., 02864. Tel: 401-333-2347.
Students 675.

4—St. Joseph, (Ashton) (1872). (Legal title: St. Joseph's Church, Ashton, Rhode Island). Rev. John W. Hunt.
Res., Mendon Rd., P.O Box 7005, 02864. Tel: 401-333-4013; Fax: 401-333-4013. [CEM]
Catechesis/Religious Programs—Tel: 401-333-4014.
Students 293.

5—Our Lady of Fatima, (Valley Falls) (1953) (Portuguese). (Legal title: Church of Our Lady of Fatima, Valley Falls). Revs. Dennis J. Kieton; Domingos M. da Cunha.
Res., Fatima Dr., 02864. Tel: 401-723-6719; Fax: 401-723-1698. [JC]
Catechesis/Religious Programs—Tel: 401-724-3454; Fax: 401-724-3454.
Students 420.

6—St. Patrick, (Valley Falls) (1861). (Legal title: St. Patrick's Church Corporation, Valley Falls, Rhode Island). Revs. Lawrence E. Toole; Joseph E. Davis.
Res., 301 Broad St., 02864. Tel: 401-725-0344; 725-7802. [CEM 2]
Catechesis/Religious Programs—Tel: 401-725-0344.
Students 280.

East Greenwich, Kent Co., Our Lady of Mercy (1853). (Legal title: Our Lady of Mercy, Greenwich, Rhode Island). Revs. John W. Lolio; Anthony W. Verdelotti. In res., Rev. Msgr. Robert C. Evans.
Res., 65 Third St., 02818. Tel: 401-884-4968; Fax: 401-884-1415. [CEM]
Catechesis/Religious Programs—Tel: 401-884-1061.
Students 744.
Convents—36 Fourth Ave., 02818. Tel: 401-884-9292.; 66 Fifth Ave., 02818. Tel: 401-886-4753.

East Providence, Providence Co.,

1—St. Brendan, (Riverside) (1909). (Legal title: St. Brendan's Church). Revs. John E. Unsworth; Michael A. Kelley. In res., Rev. W. Douglas Grant.
Res., 60 Turner Ave., Riverside, 02915. Tel: 401-433-2600; Fax: 401-433-3336.
School—55 Turner Ave., Riverside, 02915. Tel: 401-433-1290; Fax: 401-433-4600.
Lay Teachers 12; Students 231.
Catechesis/Religious Programs—Tel: 401-433-2680. John D. Sousa, D.R.E.
Students 715.

2—St. Francis Xavier, (1915) (Portuguese). (Legal title: Saint Francis Xavier's Church). Revs. Victor M. Vieira; Jay A. Finelli. In res., Revs. Michael A. Sisco; Louis M. Diogo.
Res., 81 N. Carpenter St., 02914. Tel: 401-434-1878; Fax: 401-438-1950.
Catechesis/Religious Programs—Tel: 401-434-3153; 434-9421.
Students 825.

3—St. Margaret, (Rumford) (1888). (Legal title: Saint Margaret's Church Corporation, East Providence Rhode Island). Rev. Thomas L. Keenan; Deacon John F. Needham.
Res., 1098 Pawtucket Ave., Rumford, 02916. Tel: 401-438-3230; Fax: 401-438-4221.
School—42 Bishop Ave., Rumford, 02916. Tel: 401-434-2338; Fax: 401-431-0266. Mr. John Rezendes, Prin.
Lay Teachers 25; Students 272.
Catechesis/Religious Programs—Tel: 401-435-4755.
Students 234.

4—St. Martha, (1956). (Legal title: St. Martha's Church Corporation, East Providence). Revs. Jude P. McGeough; Normand J. Demers.
Res., 2595 Pawtucket Ave., 02914. Tel: 401-434-4060; Fax: 401-434-4849.
Catechesis/Religious Programs—Tel: 401-434-7030.
Students 247.

5—Our Lady of Loreto, (1920) (Italian). (Legal title: Church of Our Lady of Loreto, East Providence). Rev. Stanley T. Nakowicz.
Res., 346 Waterman Ave., 02914. Tel: 401-434-3535; Fax: 401-434-8204.
Catechesis/Religious Programs—Students 117.

6—Sacred Heart, (1876). (Legal title: Church of the Sacred Heart). Rev. Peter S. DiTullio, S.C.
Res., 118 Taunton Ave., 02914. Tel: 401-434-0326; Fax: 401-434-5240.
School—56 Purchase St., 02914. Tel: 401-434-1080; Fax: 401-434-4638.
Lay Teachers 14; Students 190.
Nursery-Day Care—101 Taunton Ave., 02914. Tel: 401-434-2462.
Staff 8; Children 90.
Catechesis/Religious Programs—Students 77.

Exeter, Washington Co., Blessed Kateri Tekakwitha Mission. (An operation of Saint Hedwig's Church Corporation). Rev. Gerard O. Sabourin, Admin.
84 Exeter Rd., 02822. Tel: 401-295-0234.

Foster, Providence Co., St. Paul the Apostle (1972). (Legal title: St. Paul's Church Corporation, Foster). Rev. Paul A. Charland.
Res., 116A Danielson Pike, 02825-1421. Tel: 401-647-3664; Fax: 401-647-3680.
Catechesis/Religious Programs—Students 270.

Glocester, Providence Co., St. Eugene (Chepachet) (1956). (Legal title: St. Eugene's Church Corporation, Chepachet). Rev. Charles P. Quinn; Deacon Norman Bacon.
Res., 1251 Putnam Pike, P.O. Box A, Chepachet, 02814. Tel: 401-568-5102; Fax: 401-567-7847.
Catechesis/Religious Programs—Students 280.

Hopkinton, Washington Co., St. Joseph (Hope Valley) (1939). (Legal title: Saint Joseph's Church, Hope Valley). Rev. Michael J. Leckie.
Res., P.O. Box 388, 1105 Main St., Hope Valley, 02832. Tel: 401-539-8311.
Catechesis/Religious Programs—Tel: 401-539-8312.
Students 301.

Our Lady of Victory (Ashaway) (1946). (Legal title: Church of Our Lady of Victory, Ashaway). Rev. James V. Farley.
Res., 169B Main St., P.O. Box 276, Ashaway, 02804. Tel: 401-377-8830; Fax: 401-377-8830.
Catechesis/Religious Programs—Tel: 401-377-8435; Fax: 401-377-8830.
Students 121.

Jamestown, Newport Co., St. Mark (Jamestown) (1909). (Legal title: Saint Mark Church of Jamestown). Rev. William J. O'Neill.
Res., 60 Narragansett Ave., 02835. Tel: 401-423-1421; Fax: 401-423-2067. [CEM]
Catechesis/Religious Programs—Tel: 401-423-1518.
Students 316.

Johnston, Providence Co.,

1—St. Brigid, (Thornton) (1915). (Legal title: Saint Brigid's Church of Johnston). Rev. James L. Kelleher.
Res., 1231 Plainfield, 02919. Tel: 401-944-2232.
Catechesis/Religious Programs—Students 108.

2—Our Lady of Grace, (1913) (Italian). (Legal title: Church of Our Lady of Grace). Rev. Douglas J. Spina; Deacon Robert P. Troia.
Res., 4 Lafayette St., 02919. Tel: 401-231-2220; Fax: 401-231-3905.
Catechesis/Religious Programs—Tel: 401-231-8959.
Students 203.

3—St. Robert Bellarmine, (1963). (Legal title: St. Robert Bellarmine Church Corporation, Johnston). Rev. John G. LaPointe.
Res., 1804 Atwood Ave., 02919-3215. Tel: 401-232-5600; Fax: 401-231-5793.
Catechesis/Religious Programs—Students 476.

4—St. Rocco, (1903) (Italian). (Legal title: Saint Rocco Church of Johnston). Revs. Alfred P. Almonte, C.S.; Hector Sartori, C.S.; Sr. Patricia Cigrand, A.S.C.J., Pastoral Assoc.; Deacon Robert P. Troia.
Res., 927 Atwood Ave., 02919. Tel: 401-942-5203; Fax: 401-464-6422.
School—931 Atwood Ave., 02919. Tel: 401-944-2993; Fax: 401-944-3019. Sr. Mary Carol Gentile, A.S.C.J., Prin.
Apostles of the Sacred Heart of Jesus 3; Lay Teachers 25; Students 510.
Catechesis/Religious Programs—Tel: 401-944-6040. Sr. Rose Alfieri, C.P., D.R.E.
Students 325.

Lincoln, Providence Co., St. Ambrose (Albion) (1905). (Legal title: St. Ambrose Church, Albion, Rhode Island). Rev. Thomas J. Trepanier.
Res., 191 School St., Albion, 02802. Tel: 401-333-1568; Fax: 401-333-8941. [CEM]
Catechesis/Religious Programs—Tel: 401-334-3735.
Students 250.

St. James (Manville) (1874). (Legal title: Saint James Church of Manville, Rhode Island). Rev. Richard P. Desaulniers; Deacon Gregory Horton.
Res., 33 Division St., Box 60, Manville, 02838. Tel: 401-766-1558; Fax: 401-766-1561. [CEM]
Catechesis/Religious Programs—57 Division St., Manville, 02838. Tel: 401-769-2676.
Students 200.

St. Jude (Lincoln) (1946). (Legal title: St. Jude's Church, Lincoln). Rev. Bernard C. Lavin; Deacon James T. Walsh.
Res., 301 Front St., 02865. Tel: 401-725-8140; Fax: 401-726-4946.
Catechesis/Religious Programs—Tel: 401-725-8120. Sr. Mary Higgins, R.S.M., D.R.E.
Students 764.

Little Compton, Newport Co., St. Catherine of Siena (1930). (Legal title: St. Catherine's Church Corporation, Little Compton). Rev. Gerald W. Hussey; Deacon Joseph A. Goulart.
Res., 74 Simmons Rd., P.O. Box 208, 02837-0208. Tel: 401-635-4420; Fax: 401-635-2214. [CEM]
Catechesis/Religious Programs—Students 145.

Middletown, Newport Co., St. Lucy (Middletown) (1952). (Legal title: Saint Lucy's Church Corp.). Rev. Eugene J. McKenna.
Res., 909 W. Main Rd., 02842-6351. Tel: 401-847-6153; Fax: 401-846-1545.
Catechesis/Religious Programs—Tel: 401-847-6154. D.R.E.: Sr. Mary T. Burns, C.P.; Sr. Rosemary Burnham, R.S.M.; Sr. Assunta Riley, R.S.M.
Students 409.

Narragansett, Washington Co., St. Mary, Star of the Sea (Point Judith) (1960). (Legal title: St. Mary, Star of the Sea Church Corporation, Point Judith). Rev. Donald J. Bouressa.
Res., P.O. Box 3329, 02882. Tel: 401-783-4449; Fax: 401-783-0986.
Catechesis/Religious Programs—Tel: 401-789-7308; Fax: 401-783-0986.
Students 301.

St. Thomas More (1917). (Legal title: St. Thomas More Church, Narragansett Pier, Rhode Island). Rev. John C. Halloran; Deacon Paul J. Sullivan.
Res., 53 Rockland St., 02882. Tel: 401-789-7682; Fax: 401-783-8646.
Catechesis/Religious Programs—Tel: 401-783-2113.
Students 272.
Chapel—Bonnet Shores, St. Veronica Summer Chapel.

New Shoreham, Washington Co., St. Andrew (Block Island) (1917). (Legal title: Saint Andrew's Church Corporation, Block Island). Rev. Donal R. Kehew, Admin.
Res., Spring St., Block Island, 02807. Tel: 401-466-5519. [JC]
Catechesis/Religious Programs—Students 21.

Newport, Newport Co.,

1—St. Augustin, (1911). (Legal title: Saint Augustin's Church of Newport). Rev. John McNulty; Sr. Josephine St. Leger, S.J.C., Pastoral Assoc.

Res., 2 Eastnor Rd., 02840. Tel: 401-847-0518; Fax: 401-848-2411.
Catechesis/Religious Programs—Students 107.

2—Jesus Saviour, (1926) (Portuguese). (Legal title: Church of Jesus-Saviour, Newport). Rev. Francis A. O'Loughlin; Deacon James N. Dunbar.
Res., One Vernon Ave., 02840. Tel: 401-847-1267; Fax: 401-846-3375.
Catechesis/Religious Programs—Tel: 401-846-4095.
Students 110.

3—St. Joseph, (1885). (Legal title: Saint Joseph's Church of Newport, Rhode Island). Rev. John J. Lavin.
Res., 5 Mann Ave., 02840. Tel: 401-847-0065; Fax: 401-849-2195.
Catechesis/Religious Programs—Tel: 401-847-9248; Fax: 401-849-2195.
Students 320.

4—St. Mary, (1826). (Legal title: St. Mary's, Newport, Rhode Island). Rev. George B. McCarthy.
Res., 12 William St., P.O. Box 547, 02840. Tel: 401-847-0475; Fax: 401-845-9497. [CEM]
Catechesis/Religious Programs—Tel: 401-846-6057.
Students 187.

North Kingstown, Washington Co., St. Bernard (Wickford) (1874). (Legal title: St. Bernard's Roman Catholic Church of Wickford, Rhode Island). Rev. Dennis A. Reardon; Deacons Ronald DePietro; Joseph Turcotte.
Office: 415 Tower Hill Rd., Wickford, 02852. Tel: 401-295-0387; Fax: 401-295-1713.
Catechesis/Religious Programs—Tel: 401-295-5235. Michelle Sandham, D.R.E.
Students 445.

St. Francis De Sales (Davisville) (1960). (Legal title: St. Francis de Sales Church Corporation, North Kingstown). Revs. Bertrand Theroux; John C. Codega; Deacon Raymond LaFrance.
Res., 381 School St., 02852. Tel: 401-884-2105; Fax: 401-885-4315.
Catechesis/Religious Programs—Tel: 401-885-3639. D.R.E.: Cathleen Dowd; Sara Kirtlink.
Students 920.

North Providence, Providence Co.,

1—St. Anthony, (1944) (Italian). (Legal title: Saint Anthony's Church Corporation, North Providence). Revs. Edward S. Cardente; C. Brian Lagasse.
Res., 5 Gibbs St., 02904. Tel: 401-353-3120; Fax: 401-353-5126.
Catechesis/Religious Programs—D.R.E., Tel: 401-353-5125. Maryann Pallotta, D.R.E.
Students 550.

2—St. Lawrence, (Centredale) (1907). (Legal title: Saint Lawrence Church of Centredale). Rev. David Piacentini. In res., Rev. Peter G. Young.
Res., 624 Woonasquatucket Ave., 02911-1652. Tel: 401-231-9126; Fax: 401-231-7425.
Catechesis/Religious Programs—Tel: 401-231-5255.
Students 281.

3—Mary, Mother of Mankind, (1967). (Legal title: Mary, Mother of Mankind Church Corporation, North Providence). Rev. Stephan A. Silipigni.
Res., 25 Fourth St., 02911. Tel: 401-231-3542; Fax: 401-232-0965.
Catechesis/Religious Programs—Tel: 401-231-3544.
Students 266.

4—Presentation of the Blessed Virgin Mary, (Marieville) (1912) (French). (Legal title: Church of the Presentation of the Blessed Virgin Mary). Rev. Louis T. Natalizia; Deacon Louis A. Vani.
Res., 1081 Mineral Spring Ave., 02904. Tel: 401-722-7140; Fax: 401-722-6617.
Catechesis/Religious Programs—Tel: 401-722-8824; 722-7007 (Rel. Ed. Center).
Students 239.

North Smithfield, Providence Co., St. John the Evangelist (Slatersville) (1872). (Legal title: St. John's Church Society, Rhode Island). Rev. Raymond A. Tetreault; Deacon Normand R. LaFleur.
Res., 63 Church St., Slatersville, 02876. Tel: 401-762-0946; Fax: 401-762-0944. [CEM]
Catechesis/Religious Programs—Tel: 401-762-0966. Mrs. Sara D. Hickey, D.R.E.
Students 525.

Pawtucket, Providence Co.,

1—St. Anthony, (1926) (Portuguese). (Legal title: Saint Anthony's Church Corporation, Pawtucket). Rev. Joseph A. Escobar, O.P., Admin.; Deacon Manuel Martins.
Res., 32 Lawn Ave., 02860. Tel: 401-723-9138; Fax: 401-725-5616.
Catechesis/Religious Programs—Students 226.

2—St. Cecilia, (1910) (French). (Legal title: Saint Cecilia's Church Corporation). Rev. Francis C. Santilli; Deacon Louis P. Serra.
Res., 1253 Newport Ave., 02861. Tel: 401-722-1101; Fax: 401-727-3844.
School—755 Central Ave., 02861. Tel: 401-723-9463; Fax: 401-722-1444.
Sisters 3; Lay Teachers 26; Students 419.
Catechesis/Religious Programs—Students 411.

3—St. Edward, (1904). (Legal title: St. Edward's Church of Pawtucket). Rev. M. Kevin Lynch; Deacon Raymond E. Batalon.
Office: 58 Hancock St., 02860. Tel: 401-725-7036.
Catechesis/Religious Programs—58 Hancock St., 02860.
Students 104.

4—Immaculate Heart of Mary, (1979) (Cape Verdean). (An operation of Church of St. Maron in Providence). Rev. Arlindo A. Amaro, C.S.Sp., Admin.
Res., 35 Clay St., Central Falls, 02863. Tel: 401-725-1126; Fax: 401-726-4119.
Church—291 High St., 02860. Tel: 401-725-5456.
Catechesis/Religious Programs—Students 115.

5—St. John the Baptist, (1884) (French). (Legal title: The Church of St. John the Baptist of Pawtucket Rhode Island). Very Rev. Joel A. Lecuivre, J.C.L.; Rev. Jose Omar Zuluaga (Colombia); Deacon Raymond M. Lagesse.
Res., 69 Quincy Ave., 02860. Tel: 401-722-9054; Fax: 401-724-3514.
Catechesis/Religious Programs—Students 242.

6—St. Joseph, (1873). (Legal title: St. Joseph's Church). Revs. Charles B. McDermott; Philip Bonvouloir, A.A., Hispanic Apostolate. In res., Revs. Timothy L. Gillen; Richard C. Maynard; John J. McElroy, Pastor Emeritus.
Res., 193 Walcott St., 02860. Tel: 401-724-9190.
Catechesis/Religious Programs—Students 225.

7—St. Leo the Great, (1916). (Legal title: Church of Saint Leo the Great in Pawtucket). Very Rev. John A. Kiley; Rev. Christopher M. Davenport.
Res., 697 Central Ave., 02861. Tel: 401-722-1220; Fax: 401-726-3392.
School—723 Central Ave., 02861. Tel: 401-725-3620; Fax: 401-725-1696. Sr. Marie Lorraine Halpin, R.S.M., Prin.
Sisters 4; Lay Teachers 15; Students 297.
Catechesis/Religious Programs—Tel: 401-722-0744. Mrs. Janet Ricca, D.R.E.
Students 275.

8—St. Maria Goretti, (1953). (Legal title: St. Maria Goretti Church Corporation, Pawtucket). Rev. Kenneth J. Suibielski.
Res., 165 Power Rd., 02860. Tel: 401-725-4355; Fax: 401-729-5711.
Catechesis/Religious Programs—Tel: 401-729-5713.
Students 256.

9—St. Mary of the Immaculate Conception, (1829). (Legal title: The Church of the Immaculate Conception of Pawtucket, Rhode Island). Rev. John E. Watterson. In res., Rev. Msgr. Jacques L. Plante; Deacon C. Patrick Sheehy.
Res., 103 Pine St., P.O. Box 518, 02862. Tel: 401-722-5425; Fax: 401-729-0341. [CEM]
School—(Grades PreK-8) 167 George St., 02862. Tel: 401-723-6695. Mrs. Patricia Baumgartel, Prin.
Sisters 1; Lay Teachers 14students240.
Catechesis/Religious Programs—Tel: 401-722-5426. Mrs. Lisa Woodhead.
Students 158.

10—Our Lady of Consolation, (1895) (French). (Legal title: Church of Our Lady of Consolation Rhode Island). Rev. Normand L. Courtemanche.
Res., 10 Webster St., 02860. Tel: 401-722-2804; Fax: 401-722-2804.
Catechesis/Religious Programs—Tel: 401-725-2409.
Students 96.

11—Sacred Heart of Jesus, (1872). (Legal title: The Church of the Sacred Heart of Jesus of Pawtucket, Rhode Island). Rev. Paul E. Desmarais. In res., Revs. William H. Tanguay, Dir., Hmong Apostolate, Tel: 401-723-5480; Dreher.
Res., 38 Park St., 02860. Tel: 401-722-3226.
Catechesis/Religious Programs—Tel: 401-722-9861.
Students 218.

12—St. Teresa of the Child Jesus, (1929). (Legal title: Church of Saint Teresa of the Child Jesus, Pawtucket, Rhode Island). Revs. Joseph Paquette; Charles H. Galligan.
Res., 358 Newport Ave., 02861. Tel: 401-722-4470; Fax: 401-722-2958.
School—150 Wood Haven Rd., 02861. Tel: 401-726-1414; Fax: 401-722-6998. Sr. Kathleen Farley, R.S.M., Prin.
Sisters of Mercy of the Americas 2; Lay Teachers 15; Students 190.
Catechesis/Religious Programs—Tel: 401-723-2266. Ms. Mary Kretzer, D.R.E.
Students 309.

Portsmouth, Newport Co., St. Anthony (1901). (Legal title: Saint Anthony's Church of Portsmouth). Rev. Daniel J. Gray.
Res., P.O. Box 570, 2836 E. Main Rd., 02871. Tel: 401-683-0089; Fax: 401-683-9680.
Catechesis/Religious Programs—Tel: 401-683-3636.
Students 245.

St. Barnabas (1963). (Legal title: St. Barnabas Church Corporation, Portsmouth). Rev. Kevin J. Brassil.
Res., 1697 E. Main Rd., 02871. Tel: 401-683-1343; Fax: 401-683-5065.
Catechesis/Religious Programs—Tel: 401-683-3147.
Students 517.

Scituate, Providence Co., St. Joseph (North Scituate) (1940). (Legal title: Saint Joseph's Church Corporation, North Scituate). Rev. Francis J. Keefe.
Res., Danielson Pk., P.O. Box 236, North Scituate, 02857. Tel: 401-647-2255; Fax: 401-647-2968.
Catechesis/Religious Programs—Tel: 401-647-2650.
Students 478.

Smithfield, Providence Co., St. Michael (Georgiaville) (1875). (Legal title: St. Michael's Church, Georgiaville, Rhode Island). Rev. Richard A. Valentine; Deacon William Small, Ph.D.
Res., 80 Farnum Pike, Georgiaville, 02917. Tel: 401-231-5119; Fax: 401-231-0523.
Catechesis/Religious Programs—Tel: 401-231-1340.
Students 550.

St. Philip (Greenville) (1852). (Legal title: St. Philip's Church Greenville Rhode Island). Revs. Gerald E. Beirne; Robert E. Lacombe; Deacons Harris J. Gederman; Carlo J. Sabetti.
Res., 622 Putnam Ave., Greenville, 02828-1403. Tel: 401-949-1500; Fax: 401-949-3504.
School—618 Putnam Ave., Greenville, 02828. Tel: 401-949-1130; Fax: 401-949-1141.
Sisters of Mercy of the Americas 1; Lay Teachers 17; Students 254.
Catechesis/Religious Programs—Tel: 401-949-0330. Jean Cedor, D.R.E.
Students 1,039.

South Kingstown, Washington Co., Christ the King (Kingston) (1950). (Legal title: Christ the King Church Corporation, Kingston). Rev. Joseph D. Creedon.
Res., 180 Old North Rd., Kingston, 02881. Tel: 401-783-7459; Fax: 401-789-3671.
Catechesis/Religious Programs—Tel: 401-789-0417.
Students 856.

St. Francis of Assisi (Wakefield) (1879). (Legal title: Saint Francis's Church). Revs. Nicholas P. Smith; Jared J. Costanza; Deacon Paul O. Iacono.
Mailing Address: 114 High St., Wakefield, 02879-3141. Tel: 401-783-4411; Fax: 401-783-9667. [CEM]
Catechesis/Religious Programs—Tel: 401-792-8684.
Students 551.
Mission—Matunuck, Washington, St. Romuald, 61 Atlantic Ave., Wakefield, 02879.

Tiverton, Newport Co.,

1—St. Christopher, (1925). (Legal title: Saint Christopher's Church of Tiverton). Rev. Francis P. Kanda, C.S.Sp.
Res., 1660 Main Rd., 02878. Tel: 401-624-6644.
Catechesis/Religious Programs—Students 160.

2—Holy Ghost, (North Tiverton) (1913). (Legal title: Church of the Holy Ghost, North Tiverton). Rev. Henry P. Zinno, Jr.; Deacon Raymond E. Levesque.
Res., 311 Hooper St., 02878. Tel: 401-624-8131; Fax: 401-625-5156.
Catechesis/Religious Programs—Tel: 401-624-3664.
Students 330.

3—St. Madeleine Sophie, (1948). (Legal title: Saint Madeleine's Church Corporation of Tiverton). Rev. Gerald W. Hussey.
Res., 35 Lake Rd., 02878. Tel: 401-624-4226.
Catechesis/Religious Programs—Students 82.

4—St. Theresa, (1960). (Legal title: St. Theresa's Parish Corporation, Tiverton). Rev. Peter J. Andrews; Deacon Jesse L. Martins.
Res., 265 Stafford Rd., 02878. Tel: 401-624-8746; Fax: 401-625-5384.
Catechesis/Religious Programs—Tel: 401-625-5576.
Students 177.

Warren, Bristol Co.,

1—ST. ALEXANDER, (1915) (Italian). (Legal title: Saint Alexander's Church Corporation, Warren). Rev. David W. Masello, Admin.
Res., 221 Main St., 02885. Tel: 401-245-6369; Fax: 401-247-5455. [CEM]
Catechesis/Religious Programs—Tel: 401-247-1764.
Students 37.

2—ST. CASIMIR, (1908) (Polish). (Legal title: Saint Casimir's Church of Warren). Rev. Matthew J. Strumski.
Res., 228 Child St., 02885-9998. Tel: 401-245-4422. [JC]
Catechesis/Religious Programs—21 Liberty St., 02885. Tel: 401-245-3925.
Students 13.

3—ST. JEAN BAPTISTE, (1877) (French). (Legal title: The Church of Saint Jean Baptiste of Warren Rhode Island). Revs. Peter J. Gower; Dariusz G. Jonczyk.
Res., 328 Main St., 02885. Tel: 401-245-8392; Fax: 401-245-6582. [CEM]
Catechesis/Religious Programs—Students 136.

4—ST. MARY OF THE BAY, (1851). (Legal title: Church of Saint Mary of the Bay). Revs. Peter J. Gawer; Dariusz G. Jonczyk.
Res., 645 Main St., 02885. Tel: 401-245-7000; Fax: 401-245-7093. [CEM]
Catechesis/Religious Programs—Tel: 401-245-7000, Ext. 17.
Students 411.
Convent—430R Water St., 02885. Tel: 401-245-8629. Sisters of Mercy of the Americas

5—ST. THOMAS THE APOSTLE, (1952) (Portuguese). (Legal title: Saint Thomas the Apostle Church Corporation). Rev. John E. Abreu; Deacon Benjamin Barboza.
Res., 500 Metacom Ave., 02885. Tel: 401-245-4469; Fax: 401-245-4527.
Catechesis/Religious Programs—Tel: 401-245-4488. Anne Furtado, D.R.E.
Students 95.

Warwick, Kent Co.,

1—ST. BENEDICT, (Conimicut) (1914). (Legal title: St. Benedict's Church, Conimicut). Rev. Pierre J. Plante.
Res., 135 Beach Ave., P.O. Box 9485, 02889. Tel: 401-737-9492; Fax: 401-739-0974.
Catechesis/Religious Programs—70 Transit St., 02889. Tel: 401-738-2545.
Students 280.

2—ST. CATHERINE, (Apponaug) (1916). (Legal title: Saint Catherine's Roman Catholic Church of Warwick, Rhode Island). Rev. Roger G. Champigny; Deacon John F. Baker.
Res., 3252 Post Rd., 02886. Tel: 401-737-4455; Fax: 401-732-7739.
Catechesis/Religious Programs—Tel: 401-737-6234. D.R.E.: Brenda Newbury; Martha Capaldi.
Students 283.

3—ST. CLEMENT'S, (1961). Merged with St. Rose of Lima to form St. Rose of Lima/St. Clement, Warwick. (Legal title: St. Clement Church Corporation, Warwick).

4—ST. FRANCIS OF ASSISI, (Hillsgrove) (1943). (Legal title: Saint Francis Church Corporation, Hillsgrove). Rev. Timothy J. Gorton; Sr. Arlene Kalin, S.S.J., Pastoral Assoc.; Deacon Kevin P. Masse.
Res., 596 Jefferson Blvd., 02886. Tel: 401-737-5191; Fax: 401-737-1159.
School—610 Jefferson Blvd., 02886. Tel: 401-737-2721; Fax: 401-737-2721. Mr. Thomas Meagher, Prin.
Sisters of St. Joseph 2; Lay Teachers 19; Students 165.
Catechesis/Religious Programs—Students 117.
Convent—249 Chestnut St., 02888. Tel: 401-781-2464.

5—ST. GREGORY THE GREAT, (Cowesett) (1961). (Legal title: St. Gregory the Great Church Corporation, Warwick). Revs. Alfred V. Ricci; Roger M. Fortin; Deacon Robert V. Stone.
Res., 360 Cowesett Rd., 02886. Tel: 401-884-1666; Fax: 401-884-2448.
Catechesis/Religious Programs—Tel: 401-884-0797.
Students 640.

6—ST. KEVIN, (1956). (Legal title: St. Kevin's Church Corporation, Warwick). Revs. Robert F. Hawkins; Francis W. O'Hara.
Res., 333 Sandy Ln., 02889. Tel: 401-737-2638; Fax: 401-732-2832.
School—39 Cathedral Rd., 02889. Tel: 401-737-7172; Fax: 401-738-2832.
Lay Teachers 24; Students 411.
Catechesis/Religious Programs—Tel: 401-739-6309. Harriet Duffy, D.R.E.
Students 492.

7—ST. PETER, (Pawtuxet) (1933). (Legal title: St. Peter's Church, Warwick, Rhode Island). Rev. Roger C. Gagne. In res., Rev. Msgr. John F. Cox, Pastor Emeritus; Rev. Nicholas J. Iacovacci.
Res., 350 Fair St., 02888. Tel: 401-467-4895; Fax: 401-785-9282.
School—Tel: 401-781-9242; Fax: 401-467-5673. Mrs. Maureen Jannetta, Prin.
Lay Teachers 18; Students 286.
Catechesis/Religious Programs—120 Mayfair Rd., 02888. Tel: 401-461-5691.
Students 395.

8—ST. RITA, (Oakland Beach) (1935). (Legal title: Saint Rita's Church Corporation, Oakland Beach). Rev. Bertil J. Anderson.
Res., 722 Oakland Beach Ave., 02886. Tel: 401-738-1800; Fax: 401-738-1806.
Catechesis/Religious Programs—Students 349.

9—ST. ROSE OF LIMA, (Greenwood) (1950). Merged with St. Clement to form St. Rose of Lima/St. Clement, Warwick. (Legal title: Saint Rose's Church Corporation, Warwick).

10—SS. ROSE & CLEMENT, (1998). Consolidation of St. Rose of Lima and St. Clement. (Legal title: St. Clement's Church Corporation, Warwick) (Legal title: St. Rose's Church Corporation, Warwick). Rev. Robert L. Marciano.
Res., 171 Inman Ave., 02886-1700. Tel: 401-739-0213; Fax: 401-732-4144.
School—St. Rose of Lima, 200 Brentwood Ave., 02886. Tel: 401-739-6937; Fax: 401-737-4632. Mrs. Linda E. LeBeau, Prin.
Lay Teachers 15; Students 280.
Catechesis/Religious Programs—111 Long St., 02886. Tel: 401-737-1330. Mrs. Sue Jarbean, D.R.E.
Students 442.

11—ST. TIMOTHY, (Hoxie) (1950). (Legal title: Saint Timothy's Church Corporation, Warwick). Revs. James J. Hamilton; David E. Green.
Res., 1799 Warwick Ave., 02889. Tel: 401-739-9552; Fax: 401-738-2466.
Catechesis/Religious Programs—101 Lake Shore Dr., 02889. Tel: 401-738-9079.
Students 274.

12—ST. WILLIAM, (Norwood) (1933). (Legal title: Saint William Church Corporation, Norwood). Rev. George P. Behan; Deacon Thomas P. O'Hara.
Res., 200 Pettaconsett Ave., 02888. Tel: 401-781-7226; Fax: 401-781-4177.
Catechesis/Religious Programs—Tel: 401-781-0343.
Students 165.

Westerly, Washington Co.,

1—ST. CLARE, (Misquamicut) (1946). (Legal title: Saint Clare's Church Corporation, Misquamicut). Revs. Peter M. Cavanaugh; Bernard M. Dore (India).
Res., 4 Saint Clare Way, Misquamicut, 02891. Tel: 401-348-8765.
Catechesis/Religious Programs—Tel: 401-596-1838.
Students 212.

2—IMMACULATE CONCEPTION, (1885) (Italian). (Legal title: Church of the Immaculate Conception of Westerly, Rhode Island). Revs. Wilfrid G. Gregoire; Ronald J. Bengford; Deacons Robert G. Alessio; John D. McGregor.
Mailing Address: P.O. Box 556, 02891-0556.
Res., 111 High St., 02891. Tel: 401-596-2130; Fax: 401-348-2351. [CEM]
Catechesis/Religious Programs—Tel: 401-596-0900. D.R.E.: Mrs. Rosemary Buonocore, (Grades 1-6); Mrs. Catherine Kimmel, (Grades 7-10).
Students 565.

3—ST. PIUS X, (1955). (Legal title: St. Pius X Parish Corporation, Westerly). Rev. Raymond N. Suriani.
Res., 44 Elm St., 02891. Tel: 401-596-2535; Fax: 401-596-9930.
School—32 Elm St., 02891. Tel: 401-596-5735; Fax: 401-596-5791.
Lay Teachers 12; Students 193.
Catechesis/Religious Programs—Tel: 401-596-8530.
Students 193.

4—ST. VINCENT DE PAUL, (Bradford) (1946). (Legal title: Saint Vincent's Church Corporation, Bradford). Rev. James V. Farley.
Res., P.O. Box 277, 7 Church St., Bradford, 02808. Tel: 401-377-2289; Fax: 401-377-8830.
Catechesis/Religious Programs—Tel: 401-377-8435.
Students 155.

West Warwick, Kent Co.,

1—ST. ANTHONY, (Riverpoint) (1925) (Portuguese). (Legal title: Saint Anthony's Church Corporation, River Point). Rev. Reinaldo M. Cardoso.
Res., 10 Sunset Ave., 02893. Tel: 401-821-8342.
Catechesis/Religious Programs—Students 146.

2—CHRIST THE KING, (Centreville) (1931) (French). (Legal title: Church of Christ the King, West Warwick). Rev. George L. Allard. In res., Rev. David F. Ricard, Chap., Kent County Memorial Hospital, Warwick.
Res., 120 Legris Ave., 02893. Tel: 401-821-9228; Fax: 401-821-0866. [JC]
Catechesis/Religious Programs—130 Legris Ave., 02893. Tel: 401-823-3443. D.R.E.: Mrs. Janice Rousselle; Mrs. Jeanne Carrier.
Students 226.

3—ST. JAMES, (Arctic) (1908). (Legal title: Saint James Church Corporation of Arctic). Revs. Barry M. Meehan; Alphonse O. LaThiez; Ferrell E. McLaughlin.
Res., 20 Washington St., 02893-4919. Tel: 401-821-7323; Fax: 401-826-7274.
Catechesis/Religious Programs—Tel: 401-828-5059.
Students 129.

4—ST. JOHN THE BAPTIST, (Arctic) (1874) (French). (Legal title: St. John the Baptist Church of Centreville, Rhode Island). Revs. Barry M. Meehan; Alphonse O. Lethiez (Haiti); Ferrell McLaughlin.
Res., 20 Washington St., 02893. Tel: 401-821-7661; Fax: 401-826-7274. [CEM]
School—St. John the Baptist School, 17 St. John St., 02893. Tel: 401-821-5285. Mr. John Mitchell, Prin.
Sisters of Mercy 1; Lay Teachers 15; Students 140.
Catechesis/Religious Programs—Tel: 401-822-1619.
Students 125.

5—ST. JOSEPH, (Natick) (1873). (Legal title: St. Joseph's Church, Natick RI). Revs. Charles H. Downing; Fredy Jimenez-Londono, Hispanic Ministry; Deacon Laurence O. Gagnon.
Res., 854 Providence St., 02893-1140. Tel: 401-821-4072; Fax: 401-821-2408.
School—(Grades PreK-8) Wakefield St., 02893. Tel: 401-821-3450.
Deacons 1; Lay Teachers 20; Students 285.
Catechesis/Religious Programs—Students 250.

6—ST. MARY, (Crompton) (1844). (Legal title: St. Mary's Church, Crompton Rhode Island). Rev. Paul F. Reynolds.
Res., 70 Church St., 02893. Tel: 401-821-5555; 822-1006. [CEM][JC]
Catechesis/Religious Programs—Tel: 401-828-8756.
Students 212.

7—OUR LADY OF GOOD COUNSEL, (Phenix) (1897) (French). (Legal title: Church of Our Lady of Good Counsel, Warwick RI). Rev. Paul R. Lemoi.
Res., 60 Pleasant St., 02893. Tel: 401-821-6428. [CEM]
Catechesis/Religious Programs—Tel: 401-822-1869.
Students 115.

8—SS. PETER AND PAUL, (Phenix) (1853). (Legal title: SS. Peter and Paul's Church, Phoenixville, Rhode Island). Rev. Richard A. Bucci, Admin.
Res., 48 Highland St., 02893-5699. Tel: 401-821-2198. [CEM]
Catechesis/Religious Programs—Students 105.

9—SACRED HEART CHURCH, (Natick) (1929) (Italian). (Legal title: Church of the Sacred Heart, Natick RI). Rev. Robert J. Giardina; Deacon Armand Ragosta.
Res., 820 Providence St., 02893. Tel: 401-821-4184; Fax: 401-828-8883.
Catechesis/Religious Programs—Tel: 401-828-5202.
Students 144.

Woonsocket, Providence Co.,

1—ST. AGATHA, (1953). (Legal title: Saint Agatha's Church Corporation, Woonsocket). Rev. Msgr. John C. Allard; Rev. Gerard J. Caron; Deacon Eugene Garceau. In res., Rev. Joseph P. Heaney.
Res., 34 Joffre Ave., 02895. Tel: 401-767-2950; Fax: 401-767-2951.
Catechesis/Religious Programs—Students 162.

2—ALL SAINTS CATHOLIC COMMUNITY, (1998). An alliance of the following three parishes: Our Lady of Victories, (French), est. 1909, (Legal title: Church of Notre Dame des Victoires); St. Aloysius, (French) est. 1902, (Legal title: Saint Aloysius Church of Woonsocket); and St. Ann, (French) est. 1890 (Legal title: St. Ann's Church Corporation of Woonsocket RI). Revs. Roger A. Houle; James T. Ruggieri; Deacon N. David Bouley. In res., Rev. J.A. Roger Lacasse.
Res., 82 Cumberland St., 02895. Tel: 401-762-1100; 766-0370; Fax: 401-765-6321. [JC]
Catechesis/Religious Programs—Tel: 401-766-5771.
Students 292.
Convent—120 Gaulin Ave., 02895. Tel: 401-766-2485. St. Ann Convent Sr. Celia Laliberte, P.M., Supr.
Sisters of the Presentation of Mary 5.

3—ST. ALOYSIUS. Merged with Our Lady of Victories, Woonsocket and St. Ann, Woonsocket, to form All Saints Catholic Community, Woonsocket.

4—ST. ANN. Merged with Our Lady of Victory, Woonsocket and St. Aloysius, Woonsocket to form All Saints Catholic Community, Woonsocket.

5—ST. ANTHONY, (1924) (Italian). (Legal title: Saint Anthony's Church, Woonsocket RI). Rev. Ronald P. Simeone; Deacon Bernard Archambault. In res.,
Res., 128 Greene St., 02895. Tel: 401-766-2640. [JC]
Catechesis/Religious Programs—Fax: 401-765-3646.
Students 53.

6—ST. CHARLES, (1846). (Legal title: St. Charles Borromeo's Church, Woonsocket RI). Rev. D. Bryan Finerty.
Res., 190 N. Main St., 02895-3140. Tel: 401-766-0176; Fax: 401-766-0185. [CEM]
Catechesis/Religious Programs—Tel: 401-766-3088.
Students 54.

7—HOLY FAMILY, (1902) (French). (Legal title: Church of the Holy Family). Rev. Edward G. St-Godard.
Res., 414 S. Main St., 02895. Tel: 401-762-0830; Fax: 401-762-3441. [JC]
Catechesis/Religious Programs—Students 100.

8—ST. JOSEPH, (East Woonsocket) (1929) (French-Canadian). (Legal title: Saint Joseph's Church, Woonsocket). Revs. Lionel A. Blain; Maurice L. Brindamou.
Res., 1200 Mendon Rd., 02895-3999. Tel: 401-766-0626; Fax: 401-766-1632.
Catechesis/Religious Programs—1210 Mendon Rd., 02895. Tel: 401-766-8233. Michelle T. Barrette, D.R.E.
Students 400.
Station—Woonsocket Health Center, Tel: 401-765-2100; Fax: 401-232-7275.

9—OUR LADY OF VICTORIES. Merged with St. Alyosius, Woonsocket and St. Ann, Woonsocket to form All Saints Catholic Community, Woonsocket.

10—OUR LADY, QUEEN OF MARTYRS, (1953). (Legal title: Our Lady, Queen of Martyrs Church Corporation, Woonsocket). Rev. Paul R. Grenon. In res., Rev. Joseph A. Pescatello.
Res., 1409 Park Ave., 02895-6597. Tel: 401-762-5117; Fax: 401-765-8875.
Catechesis/Religious Programs—Tel: 401-767-2576; Fax: 401-765-8875.
Students 272.

11—PRECIOUS BLOOD, (1843) (French). (Legal title: The Church of the Precious Blood of Woonsocket, Rhode Island). Rev. Msgr. John C. Allard, Admin.; Rev. Gerard J. Caron. In res., Revs. Henri D. Morin; Albert H. Brindamour.
Res., 94 Carrington Ave., 02895. Tel: 401-762-0326; 883-6600; Fax: 401-767-2951. [CEM]
Catechesis/Religious Programs—34 Joffre Ave., 02895. Tel: 401-767-2950.
Students 42.

12—SACRED HEART, (1895). (Legal title: Church of the Sacred Heart Woonsocket RI). Rev. Roger L. Bacon.
Res., 415 Olo St., 02895. Tel: 401-766-3150; Fax: 401-766-6864.
Catechesis/Religious Programs—Tel: 401-766-3151.
Students 155.

13—ST. STANISLAUS, (1905) (Polish). (Legal title: Saint Stanislaus Kostka Church of Woonsocket). Rev. Boguslaw T. Gibowski, Admin.
Res., 174 Harris Ave., 02895. Tel: 401-762-0021. [JC]
Catechesis/Religious Programs—Students 53.

Chaplains of Public Institutions

PROVIDENCE. *Miriam Hospital* 164 Summit Ave., 02906. Tel: 401-274-3700. Rev. Edward L. Pieroni, Res., 2 Matilda St., 02904-1812.
Rhode Island Hospital 593 Eddy St., 02902. Tel: 401-277-4000. Rev. Gerald G. Harbour, Res., 60 Turner Ave., Riverside, 02915. Rev. W. Douglas Grant, Res., 2615 Warwick Ave., Warwick, 02889. Rev. Jose Q. Dos Reis, Res., 2615 Warwick Ave., Warwick, 02889. Sr. Perpetua Lester, R.S.M., Res., 81 N. Carpenter St., East Providence, 02914-4598. Rev. Michael A. Sisco, Res., 367 Kenyon Ave., Pawtucket, 02861. Ms. Janice Hart, Chap.
Roger Williams Hospital. Pastoral care provided by local parishes. 825 Chalkstone Ave., 02908. Tel: 401-456-2000.
Veterans Administration Hospital Davis Park, 02908. Tel: 401-273-7100. Revs. Francis J. Crowley (BO); Dennis Murphy (RIC).

BURRILLVILLE. *Rhode Island-Zambarano State Hospital.* Vacant. Pastoral care provided by Office of Health Ministries. Wallum Lake, 02859.

CRANSTON. *Department of Corrections.* c/o 83 Steward St., Providence, 02903. Rev. Philip E. Bonvouloir, A.A., 9 Alma Ave., East Providence, 02916. Archdeacon George Yany, 111 Cross St., Central Falls, 02863. Sr. Agnes Bonville, R.S.M., 716 Brayton Ave., Somerset, MA 02726. Sr. Claire Dugan, S.S.J.
Rhode Island State Institutions Eleanor Slater Hospital, 02893. Rev. John J. Rainone, Res., 92 Hope St., Providence, 02906-2099. Tel: 401-421-9137.

JOHNSTON. *Port of Providence Catholic Chaplain* 927 Atwood Ave., 02919-6291. Tel: 401-942-5203. Rev. Hector Sartori, C.S.

NEWPORT. *Newport Hospital.* Rev. Francis A. O'Loughlin, Res., 5 Mann Ave., 02840. Tel: 401-847-0065.

NORTH SMITHFIELD. *Landmark Medical Center, Fogarty Unit.* Pastoral care provided by local parishes.

PAWTUCKET. *Memorial Hospital of Rhode Island.* Pastoral care provided by local parishes.

SOUTH KINGSTOWN. *South County Hospital.* Rev. Nicholas P. Smith, Res., 114 High St., Wakefield, 02879-3141. Tel: 401-782-8000.

WARWICK. *Kent County Memorial Hospital.* Rev. David F. Ricard, Res., 120 Legris Ave., West Warwick, 02893.

WESTERLY. *The Westerly Hospital.* Pastoral care provided by local parishes. 25 Wells St., 02891. Tel: 401-596-6000.

WOONSOCKET. *Landmark Medical Center, Woonsocket Unit.* Pastoral care provided by local parishes.

On Duty Outside the Diocese:
Reverend Monsignors—
Matano, Salvatore R., Apostolic Nunciature, Washington, DC
Reverend Fathers—
Baker, John C., St. Anthony's Church, 901 N.E. Second St., Ft. Lauderdale, FL 53301
Beirne, Robert M., Young Christian Movement, Baltimore, MD
Berthelette, Ernest H., Chap., U.S. Air Force
Blais, Robert L., c/o Priests' Personnel Office, One Cathedral Sq., Providence, RI 02903
Bolton, Paul J., Chap., U.S. Army
Brodeur, Dennis A., 477 N. Lindbergh Blvd., St. Louis, MO 63141
Collins, Raymond F., Catholic University of America, Washington, DC
Haberek, Jerome A., Chap., U.S. Army
Kelley, Edward J., Chap., U.S. Army
LaMontagne, Bernard L., St. Mary of Woods, IN 47876
Montecalvo, Carlo F., Chap., U.S. Air Force
O'Neill, Thomas D., Diocese of Victoria
Pincince, Gerald P., 191 Hadley Rd., Sugar Hill, NH 03585
Prendiville, Edmond P., St. Helen Church, 3033 NW 33rd Ave., Fort Lauderdale, FL 33310-1123
Rochon, Robert A., St. Ann's Hospital, Fall River, MA
Sistare, John A., Pontifical North American College, Rome
Tanguay, William H., Dir. Hmong Ministry, c/o Sacred Heart Rectory, 38 Park St., Pawtucket, RI 02860

Absent on Leave:
Reverend Fathers—
Abruzzese, Joseph A.
Allaire, Robert A.
Carpentier, Robert A.
LaMountain, Michael V.
Lepire, Roland M.
Scagnelli, Peter J.
Sweet, Douglas S.

Retired:
Reverend Monsignors—
Carey, William J., P.O. Box 16, Jamestown, RI 02835
Cavallaro, Galliano J., 7 Lees Farm Commons Dr., Providence, RI 02904
Cerrito, Albert J., 402 Elm Ave., Port Charlotte, FL 33952
Cox, John F., 350 Fair St., Warwick, RI 02888
Dunn, Louis W., c/o One Cathedral Sq., Providence, RI 02903-3695
Dziob, Michael W., St. John Vianney Residence, 493 Mt. Pleasant Ave., Providence, RI 02908
Egan, Edward F., St. John Vianney Residence, 493 Mt. Pleasant Ave., Providence, RI 02908
Frappier, George L., St. Anthony Rectory, 128 Greene St., Woonsocket, RI 02895
Geoghegan, Arthur T., 1900 S. Ocean Ave., Ft. Lauderdale, FL 33316
Guilbault, Oscar A., 860 N. Quidnessett Rd., North Kingstown, RI 02852
Lloyd, Paul A., Jeanne Jugen Residence, 964 Main St., Pawtucket, RI 02860
Metsy, Norman G., 6467 Oak Shore Dr., Panama City, FL 32404
Murray, William F., P.O. Box 1366, Mashpee, MA 02649
Newbold, Robert C., St. John Vianney Residence, 493 Mt. Pleasant Ave., Providence, RI 02908-3329
Tavares, John E., P.O. Box 1193, Eastham, MA 02642
Reverend Fathers—
Beaulieu, Raymond, P.O. Box 433, Jamestown, RI 02835
Belhumeur, Roger E., 1650 Douglas Ave., North Providence, RI 02904
Besse, Joseph A., 70 Landmark Ave., Warwick, RI 02886
Boland, Edward F., St. John Vianney Residence, 493 Mt. Pleasant Ave., Providence, RI 02908
Borkowski, John A., 19 Helen Ave., Freehold, NJ 07728
Brindamour, Albert H., P.O. Box 14, Manville, RI 02838-0014
Bushee, Richard J., 650 E. Greenwich Ave., Bldg. 7, Unit 310, West Warwick, RI 02893
Carmone, Anthony F., P.O. Box 9177, Port Charlotte, FL 33949-9177
Carnevale, Thomas J., 1 Vernon Ave., Newport, RI 02840
Carty, John T., 43 Phillips Rd., East Greenwich, RI 02818-0472
de Serpa, Roberto, Rua Recreio dos Artistas 46-10.D, 9700 Angra do Heroismo, Terceira, Azores
Dean, Frederic D., St. John Vianney Residence, 493 Mt. Pleasant Ave., Providence, RI 02908-3329
DeLellis, Francis V., 190 S. Weeden Rd., Wakefield, RI 02880
Deneault, Normand J., St. John Vianney Residence, 493 Mt. Pleasant Ave., Providence, RI 02908
Desrosiers, Alfred R., c/o One Cathedral Sq., Providence, RI 02903-3695
Diogo, Louis M., 81 N. Carpenter St., East Providence, RI 02914
Doucet, Ovila T., Jeanne Jugan Residence, 964 Main St., Pawtucket, RI 02860
Doyle, John V., Mt. St. Rita Health Center, 15 Sumner Brown Rd., Cumberland, RI 02864
Dreher, John D., Sacred Heart Rectory, 38 Park St., Pawtucket, RI 02860
Duhaime, James H., 173B Harrisville Main St., Harrisville, RI 02830
Dyer, Raymond E., Mt. St. Rita Health Center, 15 Sumner Brown Rd., Cumberland, RI 02864
Ethier, Robert D., 49 Farm St., Blackstone, MA 01504
Farrell, John F., Box 689, West Kingstown, RI 02892
Fioretti, Jerome, Scalabrini Villa, 860 No. Quidnessett Rd., North Kingstown, RI 02852
Fitzgerald, Edmund H., 171 School House Rd., Warren, RI 02885
Freitas, Fernando P., 29 Bullocks Pt. Ave., Apt. 3A, Riverside, RI 02915-5341
Gagne, Rene E., St. John Vianney Residence, 493 Mt. Pleasant Ave., Providence, RI 02908
Gallagher, Joseph T., P.O. Box 80066, South Dartmoutth, MA 02748
Gallagher, William M., P.O. Box 80066, South Dartmouth, MA 02748
Gillen, Timothy L., St. Joseph Rectory, 193 Walcott St., Pawtucket, RI 02860-3266
Gorman, George F., St. John Vianney Residence, 493 Mt. Pleasant Ave., Providence, RI 02908
Hart, Thomas B., P.O. Box 921, Portsmouth, RI 02871
Hazebrouck, Maurice L., 41 Hazebrouck St., Cumberland, RI 02864
Heaney, Joseph P., St. Agatha Rectory, 34 Joffre Ave., Woonsucket, RI 02895
Hogan, Ralph R., 30 Kingstown Rd., Narragansett, RI 02882
Horgan, Joseph E., 25 Leading St., Johnston, RI 02919
Hunt, Patrick J., 23 Willis Dr., Cumberland, RI 02964
Hynes, James P., 12 Lane F Ramblewood Estates, Coventry, RI 02816
Hynes, Joseph P., 12 Lane F Ramblewood Estates, Coventry, RI 02816
Iacovacci, Nicholas J., 350 Fair St., Warwick, RI 02888
Johnson, Edward A., 719 Deer Run Villa, St. Simons Is., GA 31522
King, Donald J., St. John Vianney Residence, 493 Mt. Pleasant Ave., Providence, RI 02908
Lacasse, Roger, St. Ann Rectory, 82 Cumberland St., Woonsocket, RI 02895
Lynch, Cornelius B., 125 Bucklin St., Apt. 15, Pawtucket, RI 02861
Marot, Roger L., Father Marot CYO Center, 53-77 Federal St., Woonsocket, RI 02895
Maynard, Leon C., St. John Vianney Residence, 493 Mt. Pleasant Ave., Providence, RI 02908

Maynard, Richard C., St. Joseph Rectory, 193 Walcott St., Pawtucket, RI 02860-3266
Maynard, Robert J., 1 St. Paul Pl., Cranston, RI 02905
McElroy, John J., 193 Walcott St., Pawtucket, RI 02860
McGovern, Edward J., St. John Vianney Residence, 493 Mt. Pleasant Ave., Providence, RI 02908
Mendonsa, August F., 67 Howland Ave., East Providence, RI 02914
Micarelli, Edmond C., c/o One Cathedral Sq., Providence, RI 02903-3695
Moniz, Hyacinth, 825 Wakefield St., Box 84, West Warwick, RI 02893
Morin, Henri D., 94 Carrington Ave., Woonsocket, RI 02895
Murphy, Joseph F., St. John Vianney Residence, 495 Mt. Pleasant Ave., Providence, RI 02908
Murphy, William F., St. John Vianney Residence, 493 Mount Pleasant Ave., Providence, RI 02908
Narewski, Peter J., St. John Vianney Residence, 493 Mt. Pleasant Ave., Providence, RI 02908
Rafferty, Raymond J., St. James Well, Greenore, County Louth, Ireland
Randall, Robert J., 2322 Oliver Hazzard Perry Hwy., Wakefield, RI 02880
Raspallo, Domenic, 38 Oaklawn Ave., Cranston, RI 02920
Robert, Emile A., 259 Park Ave., Woonsocket, RI 02895
Schenick, Joseph D., St. John Vianney Residence, 495 Mt. Pleasant Ave., Providence, RI 02908
Sears, William F., 92 Hope St., Providence, RI 02906
Shanley, Joseph D., 167 Blackstone St., Woonsocket, RI 02895
Silva, James M., c/o One Cathedral Sq., Providence, RI 02903
Thadeu, Joseph S., 62 Griffith Dr., East Providence, RI 02915
Turillo, B. Samuel, 215 Old Succotash Rd., South Kingstown, RI 02880
Valois, Normand W., 30 Fenner St., Providence, RI 02903
Walsh, Clyde J., St. John Vianney Residence, 493 Mt. Pleasant Ave., Providence, RI 02908
Young, Peter G., 624 Woonasquatucket Ave., North Providence, RI 02911

Permanent Deacons:
Alessio, Robert G., Immaculate Conception, Westerly
Andrade, Charles, St. Patrick, Providence
Archambault, Bernard L., St. Joseph's, Woonsocket
Bacon, Normand J., St. Eugene, Chepachet
Baker, John F., St. Catherine, Warwick
Barboza, Benjamin, St. Thomas, Warren
Batalon, Raymond E., St. Edward, Pawtucket
Bisbano, Paul, Our Lady of Mount Carmel, Bristol
Blais, Robert, Our Lady, Queen of Martyrs, Woonsocket
Bouchard, Thomas, St. Joseph, Woonsocket
Bouley, David N., All Saints Catholic Community, Woonsocket
Boutier, Thomas F., Blessed Sacrament, Providence
Braga, Joseph F., St. Charles, Providence
Caban, Vincente, Holy Spirit Catholic Community, Central Falls
Ceprano, Peter A., St. Mary, Cranston
Conley, James E., St. Mary of the Bay, Warren
Corey, John A., St. Kevin, Warwick
Cote, Stephen R., Immaculate Conception, Westerly
Dadlez, Mark A., St. Alexander, Warren
Daidone, Salvatore A., St. Joseph, Jacksonville, FL
DePetrillo, Albert, St. Thomas, Providence
DePietro, Ronald H., St. Francis de Sales, North Kingstown
DiOrio, Dominic P., Our Lady of Loreto, East Providence
Dufour, John, St. Joan, Cumberland
Dunbar, James N., St. Theresa, Tiverton
Edsall, Noel, St. Francis de Sales, North Kingstown
Forlingieri, Carmine, Immaculate Conception, Cranston
Gagnon, Laurence O., Sr., St. Joseph, West Warwick
Gallo, Robert L., St. Bartholomew, Providence
Garceau, Eugene, St. Agatha, Woonsocket
Garcia, Luis, Assumption, Providence
Gauthier, Clovis, Our Lady of Consolation, Pawtucket
Gederman, Harris J., St. Philip, Greenville
Gomez, Oscar, St. Teresa, Providence
Goulart, Joseph, Sr., St. Catherine's, Little Compton
Hernandez, Luis A., Holy Spirit Catholic Community, Central Falls
Holder, Lawrence C., Diocese of Orlando, FL
Horton, Gregory, St. James, Manville
Iacono, Paul, St. Francis of Assisi, South Kingstown
Johnson, Loring F., Assumption, Providence
Keogh, Richard B., Christ the King, Kingston
LaFleur, Norman R., St. John the Evangelist, Slatersville
LaFrance, Raymond J., St. Francis de Sales, North Kingstown
Lagesse, Raymond M., St. John's, Pawtucket
Lambert, Paul H., St. John Vianney, Cumberland
Lapierre, Richard J., Our Lady of Good Help, Mapleville
Lennon, Thomas J., St. Benedict, Warwick
Levesque, Raymond E., Holy Ghost, Tiverton
Lopez, Pedro, Our Lady of Mt. Carmel, Providence
Lopez, Rony, St. Charles, Providence
Lucian, Robert C., Diocese of St. Augustine, FL
MacLure, Robert, St. Patrick, Providence
Martins, Jesse L., St. Theresa, Tiverton
Martins, Manuel, St. Anthony, Pawtucket
Masse, Kevin P., St. Francis, Warwick
Masse, Paul, St. John the Evangelist, Slatersville
Maynard, Jacques, St. Mary's, West Warwick (Crompton)
McAdam, Robert, St. Augustine's, Providence
McGregor, John D., Immaculate Conception, Westerly
Millard, Charles E., M.D., St. Mary of the Bay, Warren
Morisseau, Robert M., St. Peter, Warwick
Mulcahy, Robert, St. Joseph's, Woonsocket
Napolitano, Michael D., Our Lady of Good Counsel, West Warwick
Natalizia, John J., Holy Cross, Providence
Needham, John F., St. Margaret, East Providence
Nicholson, Robert E., St. Teresa, Pawtucket
Nova, Leocadio, Diocese of St. Petersburg, FL
O'Hara, Thomas P., St. William, Warwick
Ouellette, Lucien, St. Maria Goretti, Pawtucket
Perez, Juan Andres, St. Michael, Providence
Persson, Robert C., St. Mark, Cranston
Ragosta, Armand, St. Mary, Cranston
Raspallo, Thomas R., Immaculate Conception, Cranston
Riccio, Raymond L., St. Rocco, Johnston
Rico, Jose, St. Charles Borromeo, Providence
Sabetti, Carlo J., St. Philip, Greenville
Sadowski, Edward J., Jr., St. Vincent de Paul, Coventry
Sardinha, John, St. Elizabeth's, Bristol
Serra, Louis P., St. Margaret, Rumford
Sheehy, C. Patrick, St. Mary, Pawtucket
Sinesi, Rugiero A., Christ the King, West Warwick
Small, William A., St. Michael, Esmond
Stone, Francis J., St. Peter, Warwick
Stone, Robert V., St. Peter, Warwick
Sullivan, Paul J., St. Thomas More, Narragansett
Tanguay, Paul A., Our Lady of Consolation, Pawtucket
Theroux, Bernard G., St. Mary, Bristol
Theroux, Paul A., St. Francis of Assisi, Wakefield
Tribelli, Anthony A., St. Ann's, Cranston
Troia, Robert, St. Rocco's, Thornton
Tumminelli, Joseph P., St. Robert Bellamine, Johnston
Turbitt, Robert A., II, SS. John and Paul, Coventry
Turcios, Jose, St. Charles, Providence
Turcotte, Joseph G., St. Bernard, North Kingstown
Urrico, Francis X., Diocese of Venice, FL
Vani, Louis A., Presentation of the Blessed Virgin Mary, North Providence
Walsh, James T., St. Jude, Lincoln
Wendoloski, Anthony, Jr., Our Lady of Lourdes, Providence
West, Harry A., Jr., St. Teresa, Providence
Young, Frederick A., Holy Name, Providence

INSTITUTIONS LOCATED IN THE DIOCESE

[A] SEMINARIES, DIOCESAN

PROVIDENCE. *Seminary of Our Lady of Providence*, 485 Mt. Pleasant Ave., 02908. Tel: 401-331-1316; Fax: 401-521-4192.
Web site: www.catholicpriest.com
Most Rev. Robert J. McManus, D.D., S.T.D., Rector; Revs. Albert A. Kenney, Vocation Dir. & Dir. Spiritual Formation; Marcel L. Taillon, Vocations Recruiter. Legal Title: *Seminary of Our Lady of Providence*. House of Formation for College Students and Pre-Theologians. Staff 3; Students 8.

[B] COLLEGES AND UNIVERSITIES

PROVIDENCE. *Providence College*, River Ave. & Eaton St., 02918. Tel: 401-865-1000; Fax: 401-865-2057.
E-mail: pcadmiss@providence.edu
Web site: www.providence.edu
For a complete listing, refer to the Colleges and Universities section.

NEWPORT. *Salve Regina University*, 02840-4192. Tel: 401-847-6650; Fax: 401-847-0372.
E-mail: sruadmis@salve.edu
Web site: www.salve.edu
For a complete listing, refer to the Colleges and Universities section.

[C] HIGH SCHOOLS, DIOCESAN

PAWTUCKET. *St. Raphael Academy*, 123 Walcott St., 02860. Tel: 401-723-8100; Fax: 401-723-8740.
Web site: www.saintraphaelacademy.org
Rev. Charles Galligan; Bro. Daniel Aubin, F.S.C., Prin. Conducted by the Brothers of the Christian Schools with Sisters of Mercy of the Americas. Legal Title: *Saint Raphael Academy*. Priests 1; Brothers 4; Sisters 1; Lay Teachers 42; Students-Boys 322; Girls 237.

SOUTH KINGSTOWN. *The Prout School*. 4640 Tower Hill Rd., Wakefield, 02879. Tel: 401-789-9262; Fax: 401-782-2262.
E-mail: ddemers@theproutschool.org
Web site: www.theproutschool.org
Bro. Edmond Precourt, F.S.C., Prin. Brothers 3; Sisters 1; Lay Teachers 42; Students-Boys 205; Girls 305. Legal Title: *The Prout School*.

WARWICK. *Bishop Hendricken High School*, 2615 Warwick Ave., 02889. Tel: 401-739-3450; Fax: 401-732-8261.
E-mail: hawks@hendricksen.com
Web site: www.hendricken
Revs. Marcel L. Taillon, Chap.; Jose Q. dos Reis, Chap. of the Brothers; Bro. Thomas R. Leto, Pres. Congregation of Christian Brothers. Legal Title: *Bishop Hendricken High School*. Priests 1; Brothers 5; Sisters 2; Lay Teachers 63; Boys 1,014.

[D] HIGH SCHOOLS, REGIONAL

PAWTUCKET. *Bishop Francis P. Keough Regional High School*, 145 Power Rd., 02860. Tel: 401-726-0335; Fax: 401-726-0336.
E-mail: biskeo@netscape.net
Jeanne H. Leclerc, Prin. Sisters 1; Lay Teachers 5; Girls 75.

[E] HIGH SCHOOLS, PRIVATE

PROVIDENCE. *La Salle Academy*. (Grades 7-12), 612 Academy Ave., 02908. Tel: 401-351-7750; Fax: 401-444-1782.
E-mail: diaroche@loa.com
Web site: http://www.loa.com/lasalle
Bro. Michael McKenery, F.S.C., Pres.; Mr. Donald Kavanagh, Prin.; Rev. Albert A. Kenney, Chap. Conducted by the Brothers of the Christian Schools. Legal Title: *St. John Baptist de LaSalle Institute*. Priests 1; Brothers 8; Lay Teachers 87; Students 1,275; Total Staff 126.

COVENTRY. *St. Xavier Academy*, 2 Saint Vincent de Paul St., 02816. Tel: 401-826-2130; Fax: 401-826-2131.
E-mail: ksiok@sxa.org
Web site: www.sxa.org
Friends of St. Xavier. Mrs. Kathleen Siok, Prin. Lay Teachers 10; Girls 50.

EAST PROVIDENCE. *St. Mary Academy*. (Grades 6-12). Tel: 401-434-0113; Fax: 401-438-5936.
Web site: www.stmaryacademy.bayview.org
Bayview, 3070 Pawtucket Ave., Riverside, 02915. Tel: 401-434-0113; Fax: 401-483-5936. Sisters of Mercy of the Americas and Sisters of St. Joseph. Sr. Elizabeth McAuliffe, R.S.M., Pres.; Ms. Colleen Gribbon, Prin. Sisters 9; Lay Teachers 55; Girls 818.

PORTSMOUTH. *Portsmouth Abbey School*, Cory's Ln., 02871. Tel: 401-683-2000; Fax: 401-683-5888.
E-mail: abbotmark@portsmouthabbey.org
Web site: www.portsmouthabbey.org
Rt. Rev. F. Mark Serna, O.S.B., Abbot. Legal Title: *Order of St. Benedict in Portsmouth, Rhode Island*. Priests 8; Brothers 2; Lay Teachers 50; Students 313.

SOUTH KINGSTOWN. *Immaculate Conception Academy*. Tel: 401-782-6200; Fax: 401-782-6208.
E-mail: mbrackett@interedu.com
4780 Tower Hill Rd., Wakefield, 02879. Tel: 401-782-6200; Fax: 401-782-6205. Ms. Maria Bracket, Prin.; Rev. Javier Fayos, L.C., Chap. Boarding School Students 68.

WARREN. *Our Lady of Fatima High School*. (Grades 7-12), 360 Market St., Rte. 136, 02885. Tel: 401-245-4449; Fax: 401-245-1380. Sr. Mary Margaret Souza, S.S.D., Prin. Sisters of St. Dorothy. Sisters 5; Lay Teachers 12; Students 165.

WOONSOCKET. *Mt. St. Charles Academy*. (Grades 7-12), 02895-5599. Tel: 401-769-0310; Fax: 401-762-2327.
E-mail: mtstcharlesadmin@edgenet
Web site: mountsaintcharles.org

Bros. Robert R. Croteau, S.C., Pres.; Mark E. Hilton, S.C., Prin. Brothers of the Sacred Heart. Legal Title: *Mount Saint Charles Academy, Inc.* Brothers 16; Sisters 1; Lay Teachers 45; Students 940.

[F] ELEMENTARY SCHOOLS, PRIVATE

PROVIDENCE. *San Miguel School*, 12 Carter St., 02907. Tel: 401-467-9777; Fax: 401-785-4976.
E-mail: lgoyette@rinet36.org
Web site: www.sanmiguelprov.org
Bro. Lawrence Goyette, F.S.C. Students 62; Brothers 2; Sisters 1; Lay Teachers 7; Students 62.

CUMBERLAND. *Mercymount Country Day School*, Wrentham Rd., 02864. Tel: 401-333-5919; Fax: 401-333-5150.
E-mail: ride5179@ride.ri.net
Web site: www.ri.net/RInet/Mercymount/mcd1.html
Sr. Martha Mulligan, R.S.M., Prin. Sisters of Mercy of the Americas. Sisters 5; Brothers 1; Lay Teachers 23; Students 393.

EAST PROVIDENCE. *St. Mary Academy.* (Grades PreK-12). Day Pupils. Bayview, 3070 Pawtucket Ave., Riverside, 02915. Tel: 401-434-0113. Sisters of Mercy of the Americas. Sr. Norma Fleming, R.S.M., Prin., Elementary School; Miss Colleen Gribbon, Prin., High School; Sr. Elizabeth McAuliffe, R.S.M., Ed.D., Pres. Sisters 24; Lay Teachers 71; Students 1,066.

NEWPORT. *St. Joseph of Cluny Sisters' School, Inc.* (Grades PreK-8). (Day School), Brenton Rd., 02840. Tel: 401-847-6043; Fax: 401-848-5678.
E-mail: clunyone@n2mail.com
Web site: www.ri-net/Rinet/Cluny
Sr. Marie Cooper, S.J.C., Pres.; Sr. Regina Brunelle, Vice Pres.; Mr. Michael Segerson, Prin.; Sr. Josephine St. Leger, Sec. & Treas. Trustees: Sr. Luke Parker; Sr. Anne Lobsinger. Sisters 2; Lay Teachers 18; Students 235.

PORTSMOUTH. *St. Philomena School*, 324 Cory's Lane, 02871. Tel: 401-683-0268; Fax: 401-683-6554. Sisters Faithful Companions of Jesus. Sr. Ann Marie Walsh, F.C.J., Prin. Teaching Sisters 1; Lay Teachers 30; Students 449.

[G] REGIONAL ELEMENTARY SCHOOLS

PROVIDENCE. *Bishop McVinney Regional School.* (Grades PreK-8), 155 Gordon Ave., 02905. Tel: 401-781-2370; Fax: 401-785-2618.
E-mail: bmv155@aol.com
Sr. Theresina Scully, C.P., Prin. Sisters 2; Lay Teachers 15; Students 359. Legal Title: *Catholic Association for Regional Education.*

St. Thomas Regional School, 15 Edendale Ave., 02911. Tel: 401-351-0403; Fax: 401-351-0403 (call first).
E-mail: strspw@rinet36.org
Patricia A. Wolfert, Prin. Sisters 1; Lay Teachers 9; Students 265.

CENTRAL FALLS. *St. Elizabeth Ann Seton Academy*, 909 Lonsdale Ave., 02863. Tel: 401-728-6230; Fax: 401-723-9532. Sr. Ann McKenna, R.S.M., Prin. Sisters 4; Lay Teachers 10; Students 270.

CRANSTON. *Cranston-Johnston Catholic Regional School*, 43 Poplar Dr., 02920. Tel: 401-942-7245; Fax: 401-943-5738.
E-mail: cjcrraspallo@aol.com
Deacon Thomas R. Raspallo, Prin. Sisters 1; Lay Teachers 24; Students 455.

EAST GREENWICH. *Our Lady of Mercy Regional School.* (Grades PreK-6), Fourth Ave., 02818. Tel: 401-884-1618. Miss Barbara C. Dwyer, Prin. Sisters 4; Lay Teachers 22; Students 341.

MIDDLETOWN. *All Saints Academy.* (Grades K-8), 915 W. Main Rd., 02842. Tel: 401-848-4300; Fax: 401-848-5587.
E-mail: rid40001@ride.ri.net
Web site: allsaintsacademy.org
Sr. Mildred Morrissey, F.M.M., Prin. Sisters 3; Lay Teachers 7; Students 160.

PAWTUCKET. *Woodlawn Catholic Regional School.* (Grades K-8), 61 Hope St., 02860. Tel: 401-723-3759; Fax: 401-722-4090.
E-mail: pawcaool@llushe.wsbe.org
Web site: members.home.net/regionals
Sr. Martha M. Serbst, R.S.M., Prin. Sisters 3; Lay Teachers 7; Students 248.

SOUTH KINGSTOWN. *Monsignor Matthew F. Clarke Regional School.* (Grades PreK-6), Tower Hill Rd., 02879. Tel: 401-789-0860; Fax: 401-789-3164. Henry Fiore, Jr., Prin. Lay Teachers 18; Students 392.

WARWICK. *Overbrook Academy at Our Lady of Providence Center.* (Boarding School), 836 Warwick Neck Ave., 02889. Tel: 401-737-2850.
E-mail: overbrook@ids.net
Miss Ann Donaldson, Prin. & Dir.; Rev. Javier Fayos, L.C., Chap. Lay Teachers 16; Students 146.

WEST WARWICK. *Notre Dame Regional School.* (Grades K-8), 59 Pleasant St., 02893. Tel: 401-821-6334; Fax: 401-821-1248. Sr. Patricia Langton, O.P., Prin. Sisters 1; Lay Teachers 9; Students 168.

[H] THE GREATER WOONSOCKET CATHOLIC REGIONAL SCHOOL SYSTEM

Member Schools

BURRILLVILLE. *Father Holland Catholic Regional Elementary School.* (Grades PreK-7). Tel: 401-568-4589; Fax: 401-567-9069.
E-mail: fr.holland@tp.net
Web site: www.users.tp.net/fr.holland
180 Sayles Ave., Pascoag, 02859. Tel: 401-568-4589; Fax: 401-567-9069.
Web site: www.users.tp.net/fr.holland
Lay Teachers 9; Students 227. Mailing Address: Regional Administration, P.O. Box 487, Woonsocket, 02895. Tel: 401-762-1095. Shawn A. Capron, Prin.

WOONSOCKET. *Good Shepherd Catholic Regional Middle School.* (Grades 6-8), 1210 Mendon Rd., 02895. Tel: 401-767-5906. Mrs. Marianne Alger, Admin.; Mrs. Louise P. Kane, Prin. Lay Teachers 9; Students 199.

Monsignor Gadoury Regional Primary School. (Grades PreK-3), 1371 Park Ave., 02895. Tel: 401-767-5902; Fax: 401-767-5902. Mary Chabot, Prin. Lay Teachers 6; Students 167.

Our Lady of Victories Regional Primary School. (Grades K-3), 148 Spring St., 02895. Tel: 401-767-5904. Mr. Armand B. Houle, Prin. Lay Teachers 9; Students 202.

St. Joseph Intermediate Regional School. (Grades 4-5), 1210 Mendon Rd., 02895. Tel: 401-767-5907. Mrs. Louise Kane, Prin. Lay Teachers 6; Students 121.

[I] CHILD CARING FACILITIES

PROVIDENCE. *Group Home for Adolescent Boys.* (Whitmarsh House), 1055 N. Main St., 02904. Tel: 401-351-7230; Fax: 401-421-0198. Bro. John McHale, O.L.P., Dir. Boys 68.

NARRAGANSETT. *Ocean Tides*, 635 Ocean Rd., 02882-1314. Tel: 401-789-1016; Fax: 401-788-0924.
E-mail: brob@oceantides.org
Bros. Brendan Gerrity, F.S.C., Pres.; John McGann, F.S.C., Social Svcs.; John Norton, F.S.C., Court Liaison. Legal Title: *Ocean Tides, Inc.* Brothers 3; Lay Teachers 23; Lay Staff 39; Students 102.

[J] DAY NURSERIES

PROVIDENCE. *Carter Day Nursery*, 239 Public St., 02905. Tel: 401-751-9752; Fax: 401-351-6110.
E-mail: ncurran@dioceseofprovidence.org
Nicole F. Curran, B.S., Dir.; Mrs. Alexandra Moser, B.A., Exec. Dir. Day care provided for 126 children. Legal Title: *The Nazareth Home.* Total Asisted 100; Total Staff 17.

St. Vincent Day Care Center, 485 Mt. Pleasant Ave., 02908. Tel: 401-274-3094; Fax: 401-274-3092.
E-mail: alexandraf@msn.com
Mrs. Alexandra F. Moser, B.A., Exec. Dir. Day care provided for 71 children. Legal Title: *Saint Vincent de Paul Infant Asylum.* Total Assisted 71; Total Staff 21.

LINCOLN. *Mount St. Francis Day Care Center*,. Tel: 401-767-2829; Fax: 401-767-3748.
E-mail: marie@intap.net
57 Division St., Manville, 02838. Tel: 401-767-2829; Fax: 401-767-3748. Mrs. Alexandra Moser, B.A., Exec. Dir. & Program Dir. Day care provided for 121 children 6 weeks old through Kindergarten full day. Legal Title: *Mount St. Francois of Woonsocket, RI.* Total Assisted 121; Total Staff 15.

NEWPORT. *Garrettson Memorial Day Care Nursery*, 299 Spring St., 02840. Tel: 401-846-6470. Mary Ann Altrui, M.S.W., Dir. Day care & licensed kindergarten provided for 90 children between the ages of 2-6 years old. Legal Title: *The Saint Clare Home.* Lay Teachers 12.

[K] GENERAL HOSPITALS

PROVIDENCE. *St. Joseph Health Services of Rhode Island - St. Joseph Hospital for Specialty Care*, 21 Peace St., 02907. Tel: 401-456-4080; Fax: 401-456-4089.
Web site: www.stjosephri.com
For a complete listing, refer to the Hospitals section.

NORTH PROVIDENCE. *St. Joseph Health Services of Rhode Island - Our Lady of Fatima Hospital*, 200 High Service Ave., 02904. Tel: 401-456-3000.
Web site: www.fatimahospital.com
For a complete listing, refer to the Hospitals section.

[L] VISITING AND NURSING OF THE SICK

PROVIDENCE. *Holy Spirit Convent*, 43 Westerly Ave., 02909. Tel: 401-946-5639. Daughters of the Holy Spirit. Sr. Louis Ernest Brodeur, D.H.S., Contact Person; Sr. Louis Ernest Brodeur, D.H.S.; Sr. Caroline Devinez, D.H.S. Sisters 2; Visits 302; Number of patients 25.

[M] HOMES FOR AGED

PROVIDENCE. *St. Joseph Living Center*, 153 Dean St., 02903. Tel: 401-272-3335
For a complete listing, refer to the Special Care Facilities section.

CUMBERLAND. *Mount St. Rita Health Centre*, 15 Sumner Brown Rd., 02864. Tel: 401-333-6352.
E-mail: mail@mountstrita.org
Web site: www.mountstrita.org
For a complete listing, refer to the Special Care Facilities section.

NEWPORT. *St. Clare Home*, 309 Spring St., 02840. Tel: 401-849-3204; Fax: 401-849-5780.
E-mail: clarehome@rcn.com
For a complete listing, refer to the Special Care Facilities section.

NORTH KINGSTOWN. *Scalabrini Villa*, 860 N. Quidnessett Rd., 02852. Tel: 401-884-1802; Fax: 401-884-4727.
E-mail: villa@efortress.com
Web site: www.freeyellow.com/members3/scalabrini/
For a complete listing, refer to the Special Care Facilities section.

NORTH SMITHFIELD. *St. Antoine Residence*, 400 Mendon Rd., 02896. Tel: 401-767-3500; Fax: 401-769-5249.
E-mail: Antoine@tiac.net
For a complete listing, refer to the Special Care Facilities section.

The Villa at Saint Antoine, 400 Mendon Rd., 02896-6999. Tel: 401-767-2574; Fax: 401-767-2581
For a complete listing, refer to the Special Care Facilities section.

PAWTUCKET. *Jeanne Jugan Apartments*, 310 Sayles Ave., 02860
For a complete listing, refer to the Special Care Facilities section.

Jeanne Jugan Residence, 964 Main St., 02860. Tel: 401-723-4314; Fax: 401-727-2885
For a complete listing, refer to the Special Care Facilities section.

WOONSOCKET. *Saint Francis House*, 167 Blackstone St., 02895. Tel: 401-762-5255; Fax: 401-767-2911.
E-mail: st.francis@fortress.com
For a complete listing, refer to the Special Care Facilities section.

[N] CAMPS AND COMMUNITY CENTERS

PROVIDENCE. *McAuley House*, 163 Niagara St., 02907. Tel: 401-941-9013; Fax: 401-941-6862. Legal Title: *The McAuley Corporation.* Sr. Ann L. Welch, R.S.M., Admin. Total under care annually 25,000.

McAuley Village, 325 Niagara St., 02907-2000. Tel: 401-467-3630; Fax: 401-467-2760.
E-mail: mcauley@ids.net
Web site: users.ids.net/~mcauley
Legal Title: *The McAuley Corporation.* Sr. Dolores Crowley, R.S.M., Exec. Dir. Families assisted 22; Children in day care center 46; Total Staff in village and day care center 20.

St. Francis Chapel & City Ministry Center, 58 Weybosset St., 02903. Tel: 401-331-6510; Fax: 401-453-0034.
E-mail: dcprovri@aol.com
Web site: stfrancischapel.com
Rev. David I. Covertino, O.F.M., Guardian & Dir.

St. Martin de Porres Multi-Purpose Center, 160 Cranston St., 02907. Tel: 401-274-6783; Fax: 401-274-5930.
E-mail: stmartinwh@aol.com
Legal Title: *St. Martin de Porres Center.* Wayne B. Houle, Dir. Total under care 2,100; Total Assisted 2,300; Total Staff 12.

BURRILLVILLE. *Mater Spei Day Camp.* Tel: 401-568-3580. Box W, Chepachet, 02814. Maria Piccirilli, Dir.

CRANSTON. *Rejoice in Hope Youth Center*, 804 Dyer Ave., 02920. Tel: 401-942-6571; 1-800-230-6590; Fax: 943-8686.
E-mail: rejoiceinhope@juno.com
Patricia Kane, Dir.

EAST PROVIDENCE. *Emmaus Youth Center - Region 4.* Tel: 401-433-4327; Fax: 401-433-1320.
E-mail: emmauscyo@juno.com
Web site: www.oso.com./community/groups/emmaus
25 Metropolitan Park Dr., Riverside, 02915. Tel: 401-433-4327; Fax: 401-433-1320.
E-mail: emmauscyo@juno.com
Maria Piccirilli, Dir.

PAWTUCKET. *Father Barry CYO Center*, 38 Denver St., 02860. Tel: 401-723-5111; 723-5119; Fax: 401-723-1757.
E-mail: frbarrycyo@juno.com
Legal Title: *Father Barry CYO Center.* Ms. Colette M. Savaria, Dir.

SOUTH KINGSTOWN. *St. Dominic Savio Youth Center.* Tel: 401-783-4055; Fax: 401-789-4630.
E-mail: stdomsavio@juno.com
60 St. Dominic Rd., Peace Dale, 02883. Tel: 401-783-4055; 783-9123; Fax: 401-789-4630. Legal Title: *St.*

Dominic Savio Boys' Center. Ms. Marie L. Lachapelle, Dir.

Tower Hill Camp. Tel: 401-783-9123; Fax: 401-789-4630.
E-mail: stdomsavio@juno.com
60 St. Dominic Rd., Peace Dale, 02883. Tel: 401-783-9123; Fax: 401-789-4630. Legal Title: *Rhode Island Home for Working Boys*. Ms. Marie L. Lachapelle, Dir.

WARWICK. *OLP Center, Inc.*, 836 Warwick Neck Ave., 02889. Tel: 401-739-6850; Fax: 401-738-8058.
E-mail: Aldrichman@ids.net
Web site: Aldrichmansion.com
Legal Title: *OLP Center, Inc.* Mrs. Paulette M. Turcotte, Dir.

WOONSOCKET. *Fr. Marot CYO Center*, 53 Federal St., 02895. Tel: 401-762-3252; Fax: 401-762-3255.
E-mail: fmcyocenter@juno.com
Legal Title: *CYO of Northern Rhode Island, Inc.* Co-Directors: Miss Fern Dery; Mr. Roland Berard; Rev. Roger L. Marot, Spiritual Dir.

[O] PERSONAL PRELATURES

PROVIDENCE. *Prelature of the Holy Cross and Opus Dei*, Mathewson House, 224 Bowen St., 02906. Tel: 401-272-7834; Fax: 401-272-7854.
E-mail: info@opusdei.org
Web site: www.opusdei.org
Rev. Thomas J. Lamb.

[P] MONASTERIES AND RESIDENCES OF PRIESTS AND BROTHERS

PROVIDENCE. *Brothers of Our Lady of Providence*, 164 Massachusetts Ave., 02907. Tel: 401-461-6638. Office, 20 Eighth St., 02906. Tel: 401-351-7230. Bro. John McHale, O.L.P., Supr. Brothers 2.

St. Francis Friary, 58 Weybosset St., 02903. Tel: 401-331-6510; Fax: 401-453-0034.
E-mail: stfrancis@ids.net
Web site: stfrancischapel.com
Legal Title: *St. Francis Weybosset Street Chapel, Inc.* Franciscan Friars. Revs. David I. Convertino, O.F.M., Guardian; William Beaudin, O.F.M., Vicar; Severin Brady, O.F.M.; Hugh Eller, O.F.M.; Stephen Lynch, O.F.M.; Ambrose Donehue, O.F.M.; Michael Putich, O.F.M.; Charles V. (Thomas) Finnegan, O.F.M.; Eric T. Carpine, O.F.M.; Bros. John Capozzi, O.F.M.; Thomas Cole, O.F.M.; Scott Brookbank, O.F.M. Priests 12.

St. John Vianney Residence, 493 Mt. Pleasant Ave., 02908. Tel: 401-331-9870. Residence for Senior Priests. Rev. Edward J. McGovern, Coord. Residents: Rev. Msgr. Michael W. Dziob; Rev. Msgr. Edward F. Egan; Rev. Msgr. Robert Newbold; Revs. Edward F. Boland; Frederic D. Dean; Normand J. Deneault; Rene E. Gagne; George F. Gorman; Donald J. King; Leon C. Maynard; Joseph F. Murphy; William F. Murphy; Peter J. Narewski; Joseph D. Schenick; Clyde J. Walsh. Priests 16.

St. Pius Priory, 55 Elmhurst Ave., 02908. Tel: 401-751-4871; Fax: 401-273-1089. Legal Title: *Dominican Fathers*. Revs. John P. Burchill, O.P., Prior; Gabriel Pivarnik, O.P., Subprior; John L. Sullivan, O.P.; John Baptist Ku, O.P.; Vincent G. DeLucia, O.P.; Bro. Denis Swann, O.P. Priests 5; Brothers 1.

St. Thomas Aquinas Priory at Providence College, 333 Eaton St., 02918-0001. Tel: 401-865-2101 (office); Fax: 401-865-2959. Legal Title: *Priory of St. Thomas Aquinas*. Dominican Friars.
Assigned & Residing in the Priory: Very Rev. Edward T. Myers, O.P., Prior; Most Rev. Ernest B. Boland, O.P., Retired Bishop of Multan; Revs. Jon Alexander, O.P. (Chicago Prov.); J. Iriarte Andujar, O.P.; Albino F. Barrera, O.P.; Timothy F. Bellamah, O.P.; Robert E. Bond, O.P.; Daniel J. Cassidy, O.P.; Edward L. Cleary, O.P. (Chicago Prov.); George L. Cochran, O.P.; Paul M. Conner, O.P. (Oakland Prov.); Thomas M. Coskren, O.P.; John F. Cunningham, O.P.; G. Adrian Dabash, O.P.; James J. Davis, O.P.; James A. Driscoll, O.P.; Francis C. Duffy, O.P.; Thomas J. Ertle, O.P.; William David Folsey, O.P.; Joseph J. Guido, O.P.; Kenneth R. Gumbert, O.P. (Oakland Prov.); Ralph T. Hall, O.P.; Curtis E. Henritzy, O.P.; G. Nicholas Ingham, O.P.; P. Augustine Judd, O.P.; Terence Keegan, O.P.; John A. Langlois, O.P.; Bernard F. Langton, O.P.; Joseph L. Lennon, O.P.; Richard A. McAlister, O.P.; James R. McAvey, O.P.; Thomas D. McGonigle, O.P. (Chicago Prov.); J. Stuart McPhail, O.P.; William P. Marquis, O.P.; Robert A. Morris, O.P.; Matthew F. Morry, O.P.; Robert D. Myett, O.P.; Mark D. Nowel, O.P.; John S. Peterson, O.P.; Matthew D. Powell, O.P. (Chicago Prov.); James Ferrer Quigley, O.P.; George P. Schommer, O.P.; Paul E. Seaver, O.P.; Kenneth Sicard, O.P.; A. Philip Smith, O.P.; James T. Sullivan, O.P.; Walter Urban Voll, O.P.; Bros. M. Francis Liebold, O.P.; F. Kevin O'Connell, O.P.
Assigned but Living Outside the Priory: Revs. Brian Chrzastek, O.P., (St. Vincent Ferrer Priory, River Forest, IL); P. Augustine Judd, O.P., (Albertinum, Fribourg, Switzerland). Bishops in Residence 1; Priests in Residence 48; Brothers in Residence 2; Priests residing outside Priory 3.

BRISTOL. *St. Columban's Retirement House*, Box 65, Ferry Rd., 02809. Tel: 401-253-6909; Fax: 401-253-7099. Legal Title: *St. Columban's Foreign Mission Society*. Revs. William F. Sullivan, S.S.C., Supr.; Thomas L. Convery, S.S.C.; Joseph Crehan, S.S.C.; Norbert F. Feld, S.S.C.; Brian Gallagher, S.S.C.; Michael Harrison, S.S.C.; Rudolph Hoza, S.S.C.; Otto J. Imholte, S.S.C., Vicar/Bursar; Stephen Kealy, S.S.C.; Francis Keaney, S.S.C.; Fintan Keegan, S.S.C.; Joseph McSweeney, S.S.C.; Joseph Murrin, S.S.C.; John O'Doherty, S.S.C.; Hugh O'Rourke, S.S.C.; Paul J. O'Rourke, S.S.C.; Matthew Quinn, S.S.C.; David E. Richers, S.S.C.; James Roddy, S.S.C. Priests 19.

BURRILLVILLE. *Brothers of the Sacred Heart Provincial House*. Tel: 401-568-8686; Fax: 401-568-9810.
E-mail: loulaperle@aol.com
Legal Title: *The Order of the Brothers of the Sacred Heart of New England, Inc.* Mailing Address: 685 Steere Farm Rd., Pascoag, 02859-4601. Tel: 401-568-8686; 568-3361; Fax: 401-568-9810. Revs. Ronald S. Dupuis, S.C., Chap.; Nelson Dionne, S.C., Asst. Chap.; Bros. Robert F. Breault, S.C., Prov. Supr. of New England Prov.; Louis J. Laperle, S.C., Exec. Asst. for Finances; Fred U. Bouchard, S.C., Local Supr.; Edward Breault, S.C., Prov. Sec.; Paul F. Hebert, S.C., Exec. Asst. for Missions; John Louis Collignon, S.C., Devel. Dir.; Roland Ouellette, S.C., Vocation Dir. Brothers 32.

NARRAGANSETT. *Christian Brothers' Center*, 635 Ocean Rd., 02882. Tel: 401-789-0244; Fax: 401-783-5303.
E-mail: cbcjdl@aol.com
Legal Title: *Brothers of the Christian Schools, Long Island-New England Province*. Brothers of the Christian Schools. Rev. Owen F. Goodwin, SS.CC., Chap.; Bros. Daniel Casey, F.S.C., Acting Prov.; Peter Iorlano, F.S.C., Vocation & Formation Counselor; Mr. Lee Grossi, Dir. Finance; Mrs. Mary Yakey, Health Care Coord. Brothers 44; Brothers in the Province 94.

PORTSMOUTH. *Abbey of St. Gregory the Great*, 285 Cory's Lane, 02871. Tel: 401-683-2000; Fax: 401-683-5888.
E-mail: abbotmark@portsmouthabbey.org
Web site: www.portsmouthabbey.org
Legal Title: *Order of St. Benedict in Portsmouth, Rhode Island*. Benedictines of the English Congregation. Rt. Rev. F. Mark Serna, O.S.B., Abbot; Very Rev. R. Ambrose Wolverton, O.S.B., Prior; Rt. Rev. Matthew Stark, O.S.B., Retired Abbot; Revs. H. David Hurst, O.S.B.; Julian Stead, O.S.B.; B. Benedict Lang, O.S.B.; F. Philip Wilson, O.S.B.; A. Damian Kearney, O.S.B.; Michael Stafford, O.S.B.; P. Geoffrey Chase, O.S.B.; Christopher Davis, O.S.B.; T. Edmund Adams, O.S.B.; Caedmon Holmes; P. Paschal Scotti, O.S.B. Abbots 2; Priests 12; Brothers 2.

WARWICK. *Augustinians of the Assumption*, 639 Jefferson Blvd., 02886. Tel: 401-737-6014; Fax: 401-737-1680. Revs. Philip Bonvouloir, A.A.; Peter Precourt, A.A.; Bro. Richard Gagnon, A.A.

WOONSOCKET. *Brothers of the Sacred Heart*, 800 Logee St., 02895. Tel: 401-769-0313; Fax: 401-769-0065.
E-mail: ride7859@ride.ri.net
Bro. Willie A. Morin, S.C., Local Supr. Brothers 13.

St. John's Residence, 159 Earle St., 02895. Tel: 401-766-9677. Bro. Alan Aubin, S.C., Supr. Brothers 7.

[Q] CONVENTS AND RESIDENCES FOR SISTERS

BARRINGTON. *Monastery of Discalced Carmelites*, Nayatt Ave., 02806. Tel: 401-245-3421; Fax: 401-245-6872. Legal Title: *Monastery of Discalced Carmelites at Nayatt, Barrington, RI.* Sr. Vilma Seelaus, O.C.D., Prioress. Professed Sisters 15.

BRISTOL. *Mt. St. Joseph Provincialate*, 13 Monkeywrench Ln., 02809. Tel: 401-253-7835; Fax: 401-253-7835.
E-mail: sr.dot@att.net
Sisters of St. Dorothy. Sr. Dorothy Schwarz, S.S.D., Prov. Coord.; Sr. Isabel Borg Cardona, S.S.D., Local Coord. Sisters 5.

CUMBERLAND. *Sisters of Mercy of the Americas, Regional Community of Providence*, 15 Highland View Rd., 02864-1124. Tel: 401-333-6333; Fax: 401-333-6450.
E-mail: administration@mercyri.org
Legal Title: *Sisters of Mercy of Providence, Inc.* Sr. Patricia Combies, R.S.M., Pres. Councilors: Sr. Maureen McElroy, R.S.M.; Sr. Joan Bailey, R.S.M.; Sr. Marlene Laliberte, R.S.M.; Sr. Christina Costigan, R.S.M. Sisters 382; Temporary Vows 1; Candidates 1. Sisters of Mercy, 15 Highland View Rd., 02864-1124. Tel: 401-333-2439. Sisters of Mercy 1. Mercycrest Convent, 255 Wrentham Rd., 02864. Tel: 401-333-5283. Sisters of Mercy 2. Mercyknoll Convent, Highland View Rd., 02864. Tel: 401-333-6804. Sisters of Mercy 2. Mercymount Convent, Wrentham Rd., 02864. Tel: 401-333-0158. Sisters of Mercy 6.

EAST PROVIDENCE. *St. Mary Convent*. Tel: 401-434-0486; Fax: 401-434-2658. Bay View, 3070 Pawtucket Ave., Riverside, 02915. Tel: 401-434-0486; Fax: 401-434-2658. Sr. Rose Marie Rocha, R.S.M., Admin. Sisters of Mercy of the Americas 39.

NARRAGANSETT. *Sisters of the Cross & Passion Convent*, 24 Castle Rd., 02882. Tel: 401-783-6668. Sisters 3.

Sisters of the Cross and Passion, 21 Starr Dr., 02882. Tel: 401-783-5457. Sr. Margaret Mary Hanley, C.P., Coord. Sisters 2.

NEWPORT. *Benedictines of Jesus Crucified*, St. Paul's Priory, 61 Narragansett Ave., 02840-4099. Tel: 401-847-2423; Fax: 401-847-3897. Legal Title: *Benedictines of Jesus Crucified Inc.* Benedictine Sisters of Pontifical Jurisdiction. Convent of the Congregation of the Benedictines of Jesus Crucified, O.S.B. Sr. Marie Agathe Karunaratne, O.S.B., Prioress. Sisters 12.

Cluny Provincial House, 90 Brenton Rd., 02840-4256. Tel: 401-846-4757; 401-846-4826 (Prov.); Fax: 401-846-2276; 401-845-4826 (Office).
E-mail: clunyusa@hotmail.com
Sisters of St. Joseph of Cluny.
Provincial House. Sr. Marie Cooper, S.J.C., Prov. Supr.; Sr. Josephine St. Leger, S.J.C., Prov. Councilor, St. Joseph of Cluny Convent. Tel: 401-847-3637; Fax: 401-847-4072. Sr. Gisele Menos, S.J.C., Local Supr. Sisters 8; Sisters in Diocese 14; Sisters in Cluny Prov. of U.S.A. & Canada 40.

Corpus Christi Carmel, 516 Broadway, 02840. Tel: 401-847-6165. Corpus Christi Carmelite Sisters. Sr. Teresa Winefride, O.Carm., Supr.; Sr. Delphine, O.Carm., Regl. Supr., U.S.A. Sisters 3.

St. Clare Convent, Cutting Memorial, 301 Spring St., 02840. Tel: 401-846-1025. Legal Title: *The Saint Clare Home*. Daughters of the Holy Spirit 4.

NORTH KINGSTOWN. *Holy Family Convent*, 1 Wright Ln., 02852. Tel: 401-294-3554; Fax: 401-295-2077.
E-mail: ellend5@juno.com
Legal Title: *Sisters of the Holy Cross and Passion*. Provincial Office of the Sisters of the Cross and Passion. Sr. Ellen Downes, C.P., Prov. Sisters 2.

NORTH PROVIDENCE. *Daughters of Mary Mother of Mercy*, 2 Pope St., 02904. Tel: 401-353-8654; Fax: 401-353-5126. Sisters 3.

Franciscan Missionaries of Mary, 399 Fruit Hill Ave., 02911. Tel: 401-353-5800; Fax: 401-353-2674.
E-mail: fmmalc@aol.com
Web site: www. fmmusa.org
Legal Title: *Franciscan Missionaries of Mary*.

Holy Family Community, 399 Fruit Hill Ave., 02911. Tel: 401-353-5800. Sr. Virginia Daly, F.M.M., Supr. Sisters 10.

Our Lady, Queen of Peace, Assisted Living Community, 399 Fruit Hill Ave., 02911. Tel: 401-353-5800; Fax: 401-354-8296. Sr. Mary Bayer, F.M.M., Supr.; Sr. Lois Ann Pereira, F.M.M., Admin. Sisters 19.

Trinity Community, Assisted Living Community, 399 Fruit Hill Ave., 02911. Tel: 401-353-5800. Sr. Josephine Iozzo, F.M.M., Supr. Sisters 14.

Our Lady of the Lourdes Convent, 385 Fruit Hill Ave., 02911. Tel: 401-353-6381. Sr. Rosemarie Higgins, F.M.M., Supr. Sisters 2.

Bethany, (House of On-Going Formation), 397 Fruit Hill Ave., 02911. Tel: 401-353-5860.
E-mail: fmmbethany@aol.com
Sr. Joyce Gardella, F.M.M., Dir.

De Chappotin Community, 399 Fruit Hill Ave., 02911. Tel: 401-353-9412. Sr. Rosalie McNaughton, F.M.M., Supr. Sisters 7.

NORTH SMITHFIELD. *Franciscan Missionaries of Mary*, Ein Karim Community, 318 Mendon Rd., 02895. Tel: 401-766-8242; Fax: 401-766-6492.
E-mail: fmmkarim@juno.com
Sr. Agnes Begley, F.M.M., Coord. Sisters 4.

PAWTUCKET. *St. John the Baptist Convent*, 85 Slater St., 02860-2863. Tel: 401-722-1850.
E-mail: fmmpawt@aol.com
Sr. Mary E. Ward, F.M.M., Coord.; Sr. Helen Kalogaras, F.M.M.; Sr. Mary Nancy Cabral, F.M.M.; Sr. Bernice Moreau, F.M.M.; Sr. Philomena Agudo, F.M.M.; Sr. Aline Giroux, F.M.M.; Sr. Ann Tarnauskas, F.M.M.; Sr. Carol Flaherty, F.M.M. Franciscan Missionaries of Mary 8.

SOUTH KINGSTOWN. *Congregation of the Sisters of Divine Providence Generalate*. Tel: 401-782-1785; Fax: 401-782-6967.
E-mail: cdpgen@hotmail.com
Web site: www.divineprovidence-cdp.org
Mother of Providence Convent, 12 Christopher St., Wakefield, 02879. Tel: 401-782-1785; Fax: 401-782-6967. Sr. Myra Rodgers, C.D.P., Gen. Supr.

WOONSOCKET. *Emmanuel House*, 67 Highland St., 02895. Tel: 401-766-0525.

Franciscan Apostolic Sisters, 89 Morris St., 02895. Tel: 401-769-9395; Fax: 401-884-3573.
E-mail: fasv1@cs.com
Sr. Nemesia Licayu, F.A.S., Regl. Animator. Sisters 7.

[R] RETREAT HOUSES

CUMBERLAND. *Mercy Lodge*, Summer Brown Rd., P.O. Box 7651, 02864. Tel: 401-333-2801.

NARRAGANSETT. *Our Lady of Peace Spiritual Life Center*, Ocean Rd., Box 507, 02882. Tel: 401-884-7676; Fax: 401-792-8682. Legal Title: *Our Lady of Peace Retreat House*. Sr. Jean Marie McGee, R.S.M., Dir. Team Members: Revs. Robert F. Caul; Richard M. Friedrichs; Ms. Veneta Lorraine.

NEWPORT. *St. Paul Priory Guest House*, 61 Narragansett Ave., 02840-4099. Tel: 401-847-2423; Fax: 401-847-3897. Benedictines of Jesus Crucified, O.S.B. Sr. Marie Agathe Karunaratne, O.S.B., Prioress.

NORTH PROVIDENCE. *Bethany Renewal Center*, 397 Fruit Hill Ave., 02911. Tel: 401-353-5860.
E-mail: bethanyfmm@aol.com
Web site: www.fmmusa.org
Conducted by the Franciscan Missionaries of Mary. Sr. Joyce C. Gardella, F.M.M., Dir.; Sr. Yvette Hubert, F.M.M., Co. Dir.

[S] NEWMAN CENTERS

PROVIDENCE. *Brown University*, Office of Chaplains & Rel. Life, Box 1931, 02912. Tel: 401-863-2344; Fax: 401-863-9359.
E-mail: catholic@brown.edu
Web site: www.brown.edu/students/Brown_Catholic
Rev. Henry J. Bodah, Chap.; Mary Beth Reynolds, Catholic Campus Min.

Johnson & Wales University. Tel: 401-598-1830; Fax: 401-598-1171. Catholic Campus Ministry-CBCSI Bldg., 8 Abbott Park Pl., 02903. Tel: 401-598-1830; Fax: 401-598-1171.
E-mail: sgaumont@jwu.edu
Sandra Gaumont, Campus Min.

Rhode Island College, Catholic Campus Ministry, Student Union 300, 600 Mt. Pleasant Ave., 02908. Tel: 401-456-8168; Fax: 401-456-8168 (Call first).
Web site: www.ric.edu/student/chaplain
Deacon Michael Napolitano.

BRISTOL. *Roger Williams University*, Catholic Chaplain's Office, 1 Old Ferry Rd., 02809. Tel: 401-254-3433.
E-mail: frbj6@aol.com
Rev. Barry J. Gamache.

SMITHFIELD. *Bryant College*, Chaplain's Office, 1150 Douglas Pike, Box 33, 02917-1284. Tel: 401-232-6045; Fax: 401-232-6362.
E-mail: revjp@bryant.edu
Rev. Joseph A. Pescatello, Chap.

SOUTH KINGSTOWN. *University of Rhode Island Catholic Center*. Tel: 401-874-2324; Fax: 401-874-9099.
E-mail: jso9365u@postoffice.uri.edu
Web site: www.uricatholiccenter.org
Kingston, 02881. Tel: 401-874-2324; Fax: 401-874-9099.
E-mail: jso9365u@postoffice.uri.edu
Chaplains: Revs. John P. Soares; Joseph D. Creedon; Mrs. Carol Maddock, Campus Min.

[T] SECULAR INSTITUTES

LINCOLN. *Oblate Missionaries of Mary Immaculate*. P.O. Box 303, Manville, 02838. Miss Ruth A. Valois.

PAWTUCKET. *Opus Spiritus Sancti-East Coast USA Region*, 103 Pine St., P.O. Box 518, 02860. Tel: 401-278-4515; Fax: 401-278-4548.
E-mail: Iacobvs@aol.com
Rev. Msgr. Jacques L. Plante, Regl. Coord.

SMITHFIELD. *Regnum Christi*. 60 Austin Dr., Greenville, 02828. Tel: 401-949-2820; Fax: 401-949-2310. Ms. Maria Lourdes Fernandez, Dir.

[U] MISCELLANEOUS LISTINGS

PROVIDENCE. *Miscellaneous Listings for the Diocese of Providence*. Mailing address for all Providence listings, Chancery Office: 1 Cathedral Sq., 02903. Tel: 401-278-4500; Fax: 401-278-4548.
E-mail: jlplante@dioceseofprovidence.org
For further information contact. Rev. Msgr. Jacques L. Plante, Chancellor.
Catholic Charity Fund.
Catholic Information Center of Newport.
Catholic Inner City Apostolate, Inc.
Catholic Investment Trust, Inc.
Catholic Teachers' College of Providence.
The Church of the Immaculate Conception, North Providence.
De LaSalle Academy Corporation.
Diocesan Administration Corporation. Tel: 401-278-4616; Fax: 401-751-6808. J. Timothy Kocab, Diocesan Controller.
Diocesan Service Corporation.
House of the Good Shepherd of Providence.
Homes for Hope Foundation.
Inter-Parish Loan Fund, Inc.
LaSalle Academy.
Little Sisters of the Assumption of Woonsocket.
Marian Association of Northern Rhode Island.
Mary, Mother of Youth Center.
The Mercy Home and School.
Mother of Hope Novitiate.
New England Conference of Diocesan Directors of Religious Education.
Our Lady of Providence Preparatory Seminary.
Our Lady, Queen of the Clergy.
Pius X Salvage Bureau.
Providence Catholic Schools Collaborative.
The Rhode Island Catholic Orphan Asylum (St. Aloysius Home).
Roman Catholic Bishop of Providence. A Corporation Sole.
St. Benedict's Hearth Corporation, East Providence.
Saint Hedwig's Church Corporation, Providence.
St. John's Church of Providence.
Saint Margaret's Home.
Saint Maria Society.
St. Mary Academy of the Visitation.
Saint Raphael's Industrial Home and School.
St. Vincent de Paul Home, Woonsocket.
Stella Maris Home for Convalescents.
Vision of Hope, Inc.

BURRILLVILLE. *Father Andre Coindre Charitable Trust*. Tel: 401-568-2379; Fax: 401-568-9810.
E-mail: loulaperle@aol.com
685 Steere Farm Rd., Pascoag, 02859-4601. Bro. Louis J. Laperle, S.C., Corp. Sec.

CUMBERLAND. *Conference of Regional Treasurers*, 15 Highland View Rd., 02864-1124. Tel: 401-333-9145; Fax: 401-333-6450.
E-mail: mpmurphy@mercyri.org
Sr. Marypatricia Murphy, R.S.M.

NARRAGANSETT. *Saint Benilde Community Support Charitable Trust*, 635 Ocean Rd., 02882-1314. Tel: 401-789-0244; Fax: 401-783-5303.
E-mail: cbclee@aol.com

NORTH PROVIDENCE. *Franciscan Missionaries of Mary*, 399 Fruit Hill Ave., 02911. Tel: 401-353-5800; Fax: 401-354-8296.
E-mail: mmotte@aol.com
Mission Resource Center. Tel: 401-353-4470; Fax: 401-353-8779. Sr. Alma Dufault, F.M.M., Dir.

PASCOAG. *The Charles Lwanga Charitable Trust*, 658 Steere Farm Rd., 02859-4601. Tel: 401-568-2379; Fax: 401-568-9810. Bro. Louis J. Laperle, S.C., Exec. Asst. Finances.

SMITHFIELD. *Domus Mariae Formation Center ("Mater Ecclesiae")*. 60 Austin Dr., Greenville, 02828. Tel: 401-949-2820; Fax: 401-949-2310. Members 65. (Regnum Christi Movement). Ms. Maria Lourdes Fernandez, Dir.; Revs. Jose A. Alonso, L.C., Chap.; Andrew McNair, L.C.

LC Pastoral Services, Inc. 60 Austin Ave., Greenville, 02828. Tel: 401-949-2820; Fax: 401-949-2310. Bro. Juan Sabadell, L.C., Contact Person.

Mater Ecclesiae, Inc. 60 Austin Dr., Greenville, 02828. Tel: 401-949-2820; Fax: 401-949-2310. Bro. Juan Sabadell, L.C., Contact Person.

Pro Values, Inc. 60 Austin Ave., Greenville, 02828. Tel: 914-773-1368; Fax: 914-773-1438. Bro. Juan Sabadell, L.C., Sec., Treas. & Contact Person.

SOUTH KINGSTOWN. *Compass USA, Inc.*, 47 Crest Ave., 02879. Tel: 203-281-4798. Bro. Juan Sabadell, L.C., Contact Person.

Hombre Nueva (RI), Inc., 47 Crest Ave., 02879. Tel: 203-281-4798. Bro. Juan Sabadell, L.C., Contact Person.

The Legion of Christ (RI) Incorporated. 4780 Tower Hill Rd., Wakefield, 02879. Tel: 203-281-4798. Bro. Juan Sabadell, L.C., Contact Person.

Overbrook, Incorporated. 60 Austin Ave., Greenville, 02828. Tel: 203-281-4798. Bro. Juan Sabadell, L.C., Contact Person.

WEST WARWICK. *Tides Family Services*, Family Counseling, 215 Washington St., 02893. Tel: 401-822-1360; Fax: 401-823-4694.
E-mail: tidesfs@netzero.net
Bro. Michael Reis, F.S.C., Pres. & Treas.
Branch Offices: Youth New Futures, 790 Broad St., Providence, 02907. Tel: 401-467-8888; Fax: 401-467-8899. Youth New Futures, 242 Dexter St., Pawtucket, 02860. Tel: 401-724-8100; Fax: 401-724-8899. Tides' Hispanic Outreach Project, 242 Dexter Ave., Pawtucket, 02860. Tel: 401-724-8100; Fax: 401-724-8899. Learning Center, 242 Dexter St., Pawtucket, 02860. Tel: 401-724-8060; Fax: 401-724-8899. Woonsocket Outreach Project, 1 Social St., Woonsocket, 02895. Tel: 401-766-9320; Fax: 401-766-9324. Staff 50; Assisted 1,500.

RELIGIOUS INSTITUTES OF MEN REPRESENTED IN THE DIOCESE

For further details refer to the corresponding bracketed number in the Religious Institutes of Men or Women section.

[]—*Apostolic Life Community of Priests in the Opus Spiritus Sancti.*—O.S.S.
[0130]—*Assumptionists* (Augustinians of the Assumption).—A.A.
[0200]—*Benedictine Monks.*—O.S.B.
[]—*Brothers of Our Lady of Providence.*—O.L.P.
[0330]—*Brothers of the Christian Schools.* (New England-Long Island Prov.).—F.S.C.
[1100]—*Brothers of the Sacred Heart.*—S.C.
[0310]—*Congregation of Christian Brothers.*—C.F.C.
[0520]—*Franciscan Friars.* (Prov. of the Most Holy Name).—O.F.M.
[0600]—*Holy Cross Brothers.*—C.S.C.
[0650]—*Holy Ghost Fathers.* (Eastern Prov.).—C.S.Sp.
[0730]—*Legionaires of Christ.*—L.C.
[0720]—*Missionaries of Our Lady of LaSalette.*—M.S.
[1210]—*Missionaries of St. Charles (Scalabrinians).*—C.S.
[1110]—*Missionaries of the Sacred Heart.*—M.S.C.
[0430]—*Order of Preachers (Dominicans).* (Prov. of St. Joseph).—O.P.
[1220]—*Servants of Charity.*—S.C.
[0370]—*Society of St. Columban.*—S.S.C.

RELIGIOUS INSTITUTES OF WOMEN REPRESENTED IN THE DIOCESE

[0130]—*Apostles of the Sacred Heart of Jesus.*—A.S.C.J.
[]—*Apostolic Life Community of Sisters in the Opus Spiritus Sancti.*—O.S.S.
[2250]—*Benedictines of Jesus Crucified.*—O.S.B.
[0350]—*Carmelite Sisters (Corpus Christi).*—O.Carm.
[0990]—*Congregation of Divine Providence.*—C.D.P.
[]—*Daughters of Mary Mother of Mercy.*—D.M.M.M.
[0940]—*Daughters of St. Mary of Providence.*—D.S.M.P.
[0820]—*Daughters of the Holy Spirit.*—D.H.S.
[0420]—*Discalced Carmelite Nuns.*—O.C.D.
[1070-15]—*Dominican Sisters.*—O.P.
[1170]—*Felician Sisters.*—C.S.S.F.
[]—*Franciscan Apostolic Sisters.*—F.A.S.
[1370]—*The Franciscan Missionaries of Mary.*—F.M.M.
[]—*Franciscan Sisters.*—O.S.F.
[3790]—*Institute of the Sisters of St. Dorothy.*—S.S.D.
[2340]—*Little Sisters of the Poor.*—L.S.P.
[3450]—*Religious of Jesus and Mary.*—R.J.M.
[3110]—*Religious of the Cenacle.*—R.C.
[2070]—*Religious of the Holy Union of the Sacred Hearts.*—S.U.S.C.
[4070]—*Religious of the Sacred Heart.*—R.S.C.J.
[3430]—*Religious Teachers Filippini.*—M.P.F.
[2970]—*School Sisters of Notre Dame.*—S.S.N.D.
[3650]—*Servants of Our Lady, Queen of the Clergy.*—S.R.C.
[2575]—*Sisters of Mercy of the Americas.*—R.S.M.
[3000]—*Sisters of Notre Dame de Namur.*—S.N.D.deN.
[3720]—*Sisters of Saint Anne.*—S.S.A.
[3750]—*Sisters of St. Chretienne.*—S.S.CH.
[3815]—*Sisters of St. Jeanne d'Arc.*—S.J.A.
[3860]—*Sisters of St. Joseph of Cluny.*—S.J.C.
[3830]—*Sisters of St. Joseph of Springfield.*—S.S.J.
[2980]—*Sisters of the Congregation of Notre Dame.*—C.N.D.
[3180]—*Sisters of the Cross and Passion.*—C.P.
[1010]—*Sisters of the Divine Providence of Kentucky.*—C.D.P.
[3310]—*Sisters of the Presentation of Mary.*—P.M.
[3320]—*Sisters of the Presentation of the B.V.M.*—P.B.V.M.
[4040]—*Society of St. Ursula.*—S.U.
[4048]—*Society of the Sisters, Faithful Companions of Jesus.*—F.C.J.

DIOCESAN CEMETERIES

PROVIDENCE. *St. Patrick's.*
BARRINGTON. *Maria Del Campo.*
CRANSTON. *St. Ann's.*
CUMBERLAND. *Resurrection.*
EAST PROVIDENCE. *Gate of Heaven.*
MIDDLETOWN. *St. Columba.*
PAWTUCKET. *Mount St. Mary's.*
St. Francis.
WEST GREENWICH. *St. Joseph.*

NECROLOGY

† Hurley, Paul T., Burrillville, RI St. Theresa of the Child Jesus Church. —Died Jan. 29, 2000.
† Marcantonio, Robert A. —Died Oct. 20, 1999.
† Richman, Bertrand N., Tiverton, RI St. Theresa Church. —Died July 3, 2000.
† Sullivan, Rev. Msgr. Arthur A., (Retired). —Died Jan. 30, 2000.
† Thomson, Paul van K., (Retired). —Died Dec. 22, 1999.
† Ventre, Armand V., North Providence, RI Our Lady of Fatima Hospital. —Died Dec. 27, 1999.

Diocese of Pueblo

(Dioecesis Pueblensis)

Most Reverend

ARTHUR N. TAFOYA, D.D.

Bishop of Pueblo; ordained May 12, 1962; appointed July 1, 1980; consecrated and installed September 10, 1980. *Mailing Address: 1001 Grand Ave., Pueblo, CO, 81003.* Tel.: 719-544-9861; Fax: 719-544-1220.

Catholic Pastoral Center: 1001 N. Grand Ave., Pueblo, CO, 81003. Tel.: 719-544-9861; Fax: 719-544-5202.

Web site address: www.pueblo-diocese.com

E-mail address: diocesepueblo@usa.net

Most Reverend

CHARLES A. BUSWELL, D.D.

Retired Bishop of Pueblo; ordained July 9, 1939; appointed August 8, 1959; consecrated September 30, 1959; installed October 6, 1959; retired September 18, 1979. *Res., Villa Pueblo Towers, 1111 Bonforte Blvd., #210, Pueblo, CO, 81001-1837.*

DIOCESAN PATRON: St. Therese of the Child Jesus. Secondary Patroness: Our Lady of Guadalupe.

ERECTED A DIOCESE NOVEMBER 15, 1941.

Square Miles 48,155.

Comprises the 29 Counties of Alamosa, Archuleta, Baca, Bent, Conejos, Costilla, Crowley, Custer, Delta, Dolores, Fremont, Gunnison, Hinsdale, Huerfano, Kiowa, La Plata, Las Animas, Mesa, Mineral, Montezuma, Montrose, Otero, Ouray, Prowers, Pueblo, Rio Grande, Saguache, San Juan and San Miguel in the southern part of the State of Colorado.

For legal titles of parishes and diocesan institutions, consult the Business Office.

STATISTICAL OVERVIEW

Personnel	
Bishop	1
Retired Bishops	1
Abbots	1
Retired Abbots	1
Priests: Diocesan Active in Diocese	34
Priests: Active Outside Diocese	2
Priests: Diocesan in Foreign Missions	1
Priests: Retired, Sick or Absent	34
Number of Diocesan Priests	71
Religious Priests in Diocese	32
Extern Priests in Diocese	4
Ordinations:	
Diocesan Priests	1
Transitional Deacons	1
Permanent Deacons in Diocese	15
Total Brothers	7
Total Sisters	100
Parishes	
Parishes	52
With Resident Pastor:	
Resident Diocesan Priests	33
Resident Religious Priests	14
Without Resident Pastor:	
Administered by Priests	3
Administered by Deacons	1
Administered by Women Religious	1
Missions	56
Closed Parishes	1
Professional Ministry Personnel:	
Sisters	9
Lay Ministers	49
Welfare	
Catholic Hospitals	5
Total Assisted	935,217
Homes for the Aged	2
Total Assisted	1,353
Specialized Homes	1
Total Assisted	215
Special Centers for Social Services	3
Total Assisted	4,200
Educational	
Diocesan Students in Other Seminaries	6
Total Seminarians	6
High Schools, Diocesan and Parish	1
Total Students	53
High Schools, Private	1
Total Students	99
Elementary Schools, Diocesan and Parish	3
Total Students	713
Elementary Schools, Private	1
Total Students	392
Catechesis/Religious Education:	
High School Students	2,148
Elementary Students	5,376
Total Students Under Catholic Instruction	8,787
Teachers in the Diocese:	
Brothers	1
Sisters	14
Lay Teachers	102
Vital Statistics	
Receptions into the Church:	
Infant Baptism Totals	1,832
Adult Baptism Totals	162
Received into Full Communion	464
First Communions	1,356
Confirmations	768
Marriages:	
Catholic	276
Interfaith	139
Total Marriages	415
Deaths	1,286
Total Catholic Population	108,153
Total Population	601,000

Former Bishops—Most Rev. JOSEPH CLEMENT WILLGING, D.D., First Bishop of Pueblo; ord. June 20, 1908; appt. Dec. 6, 1941; cons. Feb. 24, 1942; Assistant at Pontifical Throne, Feb. 20, 1958; died March 3, 1959.

Catholic Pastoral Center—1001 N. Grand Ave., Pueblo, 81003. Tel: 719-544-9861; 1-800-354-2729; Fax: 719-544-5202. Office Hours: Mon.-Fri. 8-12 & 1-5.

Vicar General—Rev. Msgr. EDWARD H. NUNEZ, V.G.

Chancellor—Rev. Msgr. MARK A. PLEWKA, J.C.L., Ext. 162.

Vice Chancellor—Mrs. LORRAINE GUERIN, Ext. 151.

Diocesan Tribunal—

Judicial Vicar—Rev. Msgr. MARK A. PLEWKA, J.C.L.

Promotor Justitiae—Rev. Msgr. JOSEPH P. McGUINNESS.

Defensores Vinculi—Rev. GEORGE V. FAGAN, J.C.L.; Ms. DONI R. NEEDHAM, Ext. 161.

Judicial Experts—Rev. Msgr. MARVIN J. KAPUSHION, M.S.W., J.C.L., L.C.S.W.; Dr. MICHAEL MILLARD, Ph.D.

Secretarial to the Tribunal—Ms. DONI NEEDHAM, Ext. 161.

Judges—Revs. RICHARD F. BECKER; ROGER P. DORCY; Rev. Msgr. EDWARD H. NUNEZ, V.G.

Ecclesiastical Notaries—Mrs. LORRAINE GUERIN; Ms. DONI NEEDHAM; Rev. MARK T. BETTINGER.

Presbyteral Council-College of Consultors—Ex Officio: Most Rev. ARTHUR N. TAFOYA, D.D.; Rev. Msgr. MARK A. PLEWKA, J.C.L., Ext. 162. Rev. Msgr. EDWARD H. NUNEZ, V.G., Vacant, Vice Chm. & Treas.; Revs. THOMAS M. ADRIANS, Vice Chm. & Treas. JOHN J. COSTANZO; ROGER DORCY; JOHN FARLEY; NATHANAEL FOSHAGE, O.S.B.

Deans—Rev. THOMAS R. HINNI, C.M., V.F., Pueblo Deanery; Rev. WILLIAM T. GLEESON, V.F., Alamosa Deanery; Rev. MICHAEL McCLEARY, V.F., Durango Deanery; Rev. MICHAEL N. SMITH, S.J., V.F., Grand Junction Deanery; Rev. CHARLES A. SENA, V.F., La Junta Deanery; Rev. RICHARD L. WEHRMEYER, C.M., V.F., Trinidad Deanery.

Archivist—Mrs. LORRAINE GUERIN, Ext. 151.

Diocesan Offices

Department of Pastoral Life—Rev. RAY VAN DORPE, C.M., Ext. 116.

Stewardship—Vacant.

Social Justice—Mr. LARRY HOWE-KERR, Coord., Ext. 112.

Office of Worship—Mr. DAVID K. WOOD, Coord., Ext. 117.

Evangelization—Vacant.

Catechetical Ministry—Sr. LAETITIA SLUSSER S.C., Co-ord. Formation, Ext. 115.

Administrative Services—

Business and Finance—Mrs. BARBARA J. DUFF, Ext. 141.

Human Resources—Mrs. THERESA FARLEY, Ext. 171.

Clergy Services—Rev. J. WILLIAM HUBER, Ext. 181.

Tribunal—Rev. Msgr. MARK A. PLEWKA, J.C.L., Ext. 162.

The Bishop of Pueblo, a Corporation Sole—1001 N. Grand Ave., Pueblo, 81003. Tel: 719-544-9861.

Diocesan Office for Development—Mr. BRUCE F. BRANDT, Dir., Ext. 131.

Finance Advisory Council—Mr. DAN CARLEO, Chm., *514 Thatcher Bldg., Pueblo, 81003*. Tel: 719-543-4842. Ms. PRISCILLA R. LUCERO, Vice Chm., *Wells Fargo Bank, 201 W. 8th St., Pueblo, 81003*. Tel: 719-549-3908.

Diocesan Newspaper—"The Chronicle of Catholic Life"; Most Rev. ARTHUR N. TAFOYA, D.D., Publisher, *1001 Grand Ave., Pueblo, 81003*. Tel: 719-544-9861. Mng. Editor: *109 Pawnee Ave., Manitou Springs, 80829*. Tel: 719-685-5202.

Coordinator for Schools—Sr. ANDREA VASQUEZ, O.S.B., Ext. 123.

Liaison for Organizations—Mrs. LORRAINE GUERIN, Contact Person.

Missions—Sr. ANDREA VASQUEZ, O.S.B., Dir., *1001 N. Grand Ave., Pueblo, 81003*. Tel: 719-544-9861, Ext. 123.

Holy Childhood, Association—Sr. ANDREA VASQUEZ, O.S.B., Contact, *1001 N. Grand Ave., Pueblo, 81003*. Tel: 719-544-9861, Ext. 123.

Propagation of the Faith—Sr. ANDREA VASQUEZ, O.S.B., Contact, *1001 N. Grand Ave., Pueblo, 81003*. Tel: 719-544-9861, Ext. 123.

Family Life Ministry—Vacant, *1001 Grand Ave., Pueblo, 81003*. Tel: 719-544-9861, Ext. 113.

Migrant Ministry—Mr. LARRY HOWE-KERR, Coord., Ext. 112.

Religious Education / Youth and Young Adult Ministry—Vacant, Contact, Resource Library; Mr. JOHN CHAVEZ. Tel: 719-544-9861, Ext. 121.

R.C.I.A.—Mr. DAVID K. WOOD, Coord., Ext. 117.

Diocesan Liturgical Council—Most Rev. ARTHUR N. TAFOYA, D.D., Contact Person.

Campus Ministry—Sr. ANDREA VASQUEZ, O.S.B., Ext. 122.

Vocations—Rev. RAYMOND VANDORPE, C.M., Dir., Ext. 116.

Catholic Charities of the Diocese of Pueblo, Inc.—JANE MAZUR, Dir., *429 W. 10th St., Ste. 101, Pueblo, 81003*.

Division—Family Counseling Center, 429 W. 10th St., Ste. 101, Pueblo, 81003. Tel: 719-544-4233.

The Bishop Charles A. Buswell Trust—Villa Pueblo Towers, 1111 Bonforte Blvd., #210, Pueblo, 81001-1837. Tel: 719-543-2804.

Boy Scouts of America—Deacon MIKE ROVELLA, Chap., *P.O. Box 638, Montrose, 81402*.

Catholic Charismatic Renewal Center—Rev. ROBERT A. HAGAN, S.J., Dir., *235 N. Convent, Trinidad, 81082*. Tel: 719-846-3369.

Clergy Benefit Society of the Diocese of Pueblo, Inc.—Rev. EDWARD G. PETTIT, *919 E. Evans Ave., Pueblo, 81004*. Tel: 719-542-4702.

Clergy Formation Council—Rev. RAYMOND VANDORPE, C.M., *1001 N. Grand Ave., Pueblo, 81003*. Tel: 719-544-9861, Ext. 116.

Diocesan Catechetical Council—Most Rev. ARTHUR N. TAFOYA, D.D., Contact Person, *1001 N. Grand Ave., Pueblo, 81003*. Tel: 719-544-9861, Ext. 151.

Diocesan Council of Catholic Women—Rev. RICHARD F. BECKER, Moderator, *1145 S. Aspen Rd., Pueblo, 81006*. Tel: 719-544-1886.

Diocesan Pastoral Council—Mr. DAVID HURR, Chm., *P.O. Box 773, Paonia, 81428*. Tel: 970-527-4468. PEG HAUTMAN, Vice Chm., *238 1/2 E. 5th, Walsenburg, 81089*. Tel: 719-738-2702.

Father John Powers Memorial Basketball League, Inc.—Mr. ROBERT J. DOUGLASS, Contact Person, *144 Harvard Ave., Pueblo, 81004*. Tel: 719-544-7192.

Girl Scouts of America—Mrs. SANDY RICHMOND, *106 Carrillon Ln., Pueblo, 81005-3352*. Tel: 719-564-8553.

John Neumann Catholic School Foundation—330 Lake Ave., Pueblo, 81004. Tel: 719-543-8407; Fax: 719-543-8864.

Human Development Commission of the Diocese of Pueblo—Ms. AURORA MARTINEZ, Chm., *2341 E. Drive, Monte Vista, 81144*. Tel: 719-852-5323.

Catholic Campaign for Human Development—Mr. LARRY HOWE-KERR, Chm.

Nocturnal Adoration Society—Sr. JOSEPHINE RONEY, S.S.S., *311 E. Mesa Ave., Pueblo, 81006*. Tel: 719-545-PRAY.

Presbyteral Council—Most Rev. ARTHUR N. TAFOYA, D.D., Pres.; Revs. JOHN J. COSTANZO, Chm. THOMAS M. ADRIANS, Vice Chm. & Treas. ROGER P. DORCY; JOHN B. FARLEY; Rev. Msgr. EDWARD H. NUNEZ, V.G., Ex Officio; Rev. Msgr. MARK A. PLEWKA, J.C.L., Ex Officio.

Standing Committees—

Clergy Assemblies—Revs. JOHN COSTANZO, Chm. WILLIAM DOLL, Sec. LEONARD RACKI, Treas.

Continuing Education and Formation—Revs. KEVIN NOVAK, Chm. BARBARA J. DUFF, Ex Officio; Revs. CHARLIE SENA; RAY VANDORPE; TONY WOJCINSKI.

Personnel—Revs. TOM ADRIANS, Chm. JOHN COSTANZO; WILLIAM NELSON; JAMES KOENIGSFELD; EDWARD G. PETTIT; Rev. Msgr. EDWARD NUNEZ, V.G.

[*]Posada Shelter—Ms. ANNE STATTELMAN, Dir., *1008 N. Grand Ave., Pueblo, 81003*. Tel: 719-545-8776.

Clergy Conference of the Diocese of Pueblo—Rev. KEVIN NOVAK, *40 E. Montezuma, Cortez, 81321*. Tel: 970-565-7308; Fax: 970-565-0822.

Las Hermanas de Pueblo—Mrs. ROSEANNA PADILLA, Pres., *P.O. Box 4116, Pueblo, 81001*. Tel: 719-544-2014.

SEARCH—Ms. SANDY HANSEN, *917 E. Evans, Pueblo, 81004*. Tel: 719-546-1015; 544-8246.

Sisters' Council—Sr. ANDREA VASQUEZ, O.S.B., *1001 N. Grand Ave., Pueblo, 81003-2948*. Tel: 719-544-9861, Ext. 123.

Legion of Mary—Ms. MARINA ZAMORA, Pres., *2944 Aster St., Pueblo, 81005*. Tel: 719-564-7248.

CLERGY, PARISHES, MISSIONS AND PAROCHIAL SCHOOLS

CITY OF PUEBLO
(Pueblo County)

1—SACRED HEART CATHEDRAL (1872), Rev. Anthony A. Wojcinski.
Parish Office: 414 W. 11th St., 81003. Tel: 719-544-5175; Fax: 719-586-9922.

2—CHRIST THE KING (1957), Rev. Thomas M. Adrians.
1708 Horseshoe Dr., 81001. Tel: 719-542-9248; Fax: 719-545-9826.
Convent—11 MacNaughton Rd., 81001. Tel: 719-543-2466; Fax: 719-545-9826.

3—HOLY FAMILY (1954), Rev. Jesse L. Perez.
2827 Lakeview Ave., 81005. Tel: 719-564-2696; Fax: 719-564-4396.
Catechesis / Religious Programs—Pam Evanoff, D.R.E.
Students 350.
Mission—Rye, Pueblo Co., St. Aloysius, (1936). Rev. Msgr. Marvin J. Kapushion.
Res., P.O. Box 186, Rye, 81069.

4—HOLY ROSARY (1954), Rev. Msgr. Mark A. Plewka, J.C.L.
Office: 2400 W. 22nd St., 81003. Tel: 719-545-7219.
Res., 3123 Cascade, 81008. Tel: 719-546-2330.

5—OUR LADY OF THE ASSUMPTION (1949), Rev. Edward G. Pettit; Deacon Phil Reynolds, Pastoral Assoc.
Mailing Address: & Parish Office: 919 E. Evans, 81004. Tel: 719-543-2168; Fax: 719-562-1195.
Res., 324 E. Mesa Ave., 81006. Tel: 719-595-0217.

6—OUR LADY OF GUADALUPE CHAPEL (1968). Unassigned.
Mailing Address: 1402 E. 7th St., 81001.
914 E. Second St., 81001. Tel: 719-544-8411.

7—OUR LADY OF THE MEADOWS (1979), Rev. Roger P. Dorcy; Sr. Jeanne M. Wiest, O.P., Pastoral Assoc.; Deacon Rick Oreskey.
23 Starling Dr., 81005. Tel: 719-561-3580; Fax: 719-561-1271.

8—OUR LADY OF MT. CARMEL (1902), Rev. John Waters, S.J.
421 Clark St., 81003. Tel: 719-542-5952; Fax: 719-542-2310.

9—ST. ANNE (1956), Rev. James E. Friel.
Res., 2701 E. 12th St., 81001. Tel: 719-545-2644; Fax: 719-542-8089.

10—ST. ANTHONY OF PADUA. Closed. For inquiries for parish records contact the Chancery.

11—ST. FRANCIS XAVIER (1903), Rev. Thomas R. Hinni, C.M., V.F.; Jack Blanc, Business Mgr. In res., Rev. Joseph Williams, C.M.
611 Logan Ave., 81004. Tel: 719-564-1125; Fax: 719-564-1141.
Mission—Beulah, Pueblo Co., Our Lady of Lourdes.

12—ST. JOSEPH (1960), Revs. Richard F. Becker; Robert J. Carden.
Office: 1145 S. Aspen Rd., 81006. Tel: 719-544-1886; Fax: 719-544-5137.
Res., 1165 S. Aspen Rd., 81006. Tel: 719-543-0835.

13—ST. LEANDER (1921), Rev. Ben Bacino; Deacons Robert Myscofski; Edward Riccillo.
Office: 1402 E. Seventh St., 81001. Tel: 719-544-8411; Fax: 719-544-8202.

14—ST. MARY (1895), Rev. Edward G. Pettit.
Office & Mailing Address: 919 E. Evans, 81004. Fax: 719-562-1195.; 217 E. Mesa Ave., 81006. Tel: 719-543-3601.

15—ST. PATRICK (1882), Rev. Edward G. Pettit.
Office & Mailing Address: 919 E. Evans, 81004. Fax: 719-562-1195.
Res., 304 E. Routt Ave., 81004. Tel: 719-542-4702.

16—ST. PIUS X (1955), Rev. J. William Huber, Ph.D.
Parish Center: 3130 Morris Ave., 81008. Tel: 719-542-4264; Fax: 719-583-8103.
Mission—Pueblo West, Pueblo Co., St. Paul the Apostle, 3130 Morris Ave., Pueblo West, 81008. Tel: 719-547-3725.

17—SHRINE OF ST. THERESE (1948), Rev. Vicente Paz en La Casa; Linda Davis, Pastoral Assoc.
300 Goodnight Ave., 81004. Tel: 719-542-1788; Fax: 719-542-2130.

OUTSIDE THE CITY OF PUEBLO

Aguilar, Las Animas Co., St. Anthony (1875) (Spanish-Italian), Rev. Philip Coury, C.M.
P.O. Box 577, 81020. Tel: 719-941-4124; Fax: 719-941-4124. [CEM]
Missions—Trujillo Creek, Mount Carmel; Gulnare, Las Animas Co., San José.

Alamosa, Alamosa Co., Sacred Heart (1887), Rev. Gary L. Kennedy; Mrs. Marianne Dunne, Pastoral Assoc.
P.O. Box 547, 81101. Tel: 719-589-3211; 589-5829 (Parish Center); Fax: 719-589-5820.
Station—Mosca, Adams State College, (Alamosa), Tel: 719-587-7011.

Avondale, Pueblo Co., Sacred Heart (1960) (Spanish), Rev. Maurice O. Gallagher, Supvr.; Mr. John L. Sullivan, Parish Dir.
P.O. Box 279, 81022. Tel: 719-947-3092; Fax: 719-947-3082.
Mission—Boone, Pueblo Co., St. William, Mailing Address: 52950 Basgal Rd., Boone, 81025. Tel: 719-947-3548.

Canon City, Fremont Co., St. Michael (1880), Rev. James E. King; Deacon Merle E. Runck.
611 N. 11th St., 81212. Tel: 719-275-7549; Fax: 719-275-7540.; 138 Gere Ct., 81212. Tel: 719-276-2527.

Capulin, Conejos Co., St. Joseph (1912), Rev. William T. Gleeson, V.F.; Sr. Rene Weeks, O.P., Pastoral Assoc.
Mailing Address: P.O. Box 40, 81124. Tel: 719-274-5304; Fax: 719-274-4454. [CEM]
Missions—La Jara, Conejos Co., Our Lady of the Valley, 19617 S. Hwy. 285, La Jara, 81140. Tel: 719-274-5647; Manassa, Conejos Co., St. Therese of the Child Jesus, 115 Main St., Manassa, 81141.; Los Sauces, St. Anthony, 18900 County Rd. 28, Los Sauces, 81151.; Romeo, Conejos Co., Our Lady of the Immaculate Conception, 211 Blanca St., Romeo, 81148.

Center, Saguache Co., St. Francis Jerome (1951), Revs. John J. Costanzo; William R. Nelson.
781 Warden St., 81125. Tel: 719-754-3969; Fax: 719-754-3152.
Mission—Saguache, Saguache Co., St. Agnes, P.O. Box 22, 81149.
Station—Crestone, Tel: 719-256-4778; Fax: 719-256-4719.

Conejos, Conejos Co., Our Lady of Guadalupe (1857), Rev. Bud A. Jaramillo, C.R., Admin.
Mailing Address: P.O. Box 305, Antonito, 81120. Tel: 719-376-5985; Fax: 719-376-2530. [CEM]
6633 Co. Rd. 13, 81129.
Missions—Antonito, Conejos Co., St. Augustine, 305 W. 8th, Antonito 81120.; Lobatos, Sagrada Familia; Ortiz, San Juan Nepomuceno y San Cayetano; San Antonio, San Antonio de Padua; San Rafael, San Pedro y San Rafael; San Miguel, San Miguel.

Cortez, Montezuma Co., St. Margaret Mary (1945), Revs. Kevin Novak; Thomas N. Munson. In res., Rev. Msgr. Joseph P. McGuinness Tel: 970-564-1284.
Mailing Address: 40 E. Montezuma, 81321.
28 E. Montezuma Ave., 81321. Tel: 970-565-7308 (Office); Fax: 970-565-0822.
Mission—Dove Creek, Dolores Co., St. Jude, 313 N. Pine, Dove Creek, 81324.

Crested Butte, Gunnison Co., Queen of All Saints (1883). Attended by St. Peter Parish, Gunnison. Rev. James F. Koenigsfeld, V.F.
Church—P.O. Box 271, 81224. Tel: 970-641-0808; Fax: 970-641-4592.

Del Norte, Rio Grande Co., Holy Name of Mary (1879), Revs. John J. Costanzo; William R. Nelson.
645 Pine Ave., P.O. Box 97, 81132. Tel: 719-657-3147; Fax: 719-657-2855. [CEM]
Missions—Los Valdeses, Rio Grande Co., St. Francis of Assisi; South Fork, Rio Grande Co., Holy Family; Creede, Mineral Co., Immaculate Conception.

Delta, Delta Co., St. Michael (1911), Rev. Mark T. Bettinger.
Parish Office: 628 Meeker St., 81416. Tel: 970-874-3300; Fax: 970-874-7848.

Res., 560 Meeker St., 81416. Tel: 970-874-5116.
Mission—Cedaredge, Delta Co., St. Philip Benizi, P.O. Box 713, Cedaredge, 81413. Tel: 970-856-6495.

Durango, La Plata Co., St. Columba (1881), Rev. Michael L. McCleary, V.F.
1830 E. Second Ave., 81301. Tel: 970-247-0044; Fax: 970-385-5737.
School—Tel: 970-247-5527; Fax: 970-382-9355.
Sisters of St. Dominic 2; Lay Teachers 20; Students 254.

Sacred Heart (1906), Rev. Joseph Gallegos, C.R.
254 Fifth Ave., 81301. Tel: 970-247-3997; Fax: 970-375-2385.

Florence, Fremont Co., St. Benedict (1895), Rev. Michael Murray, O.S.B.; Deacon Vernon Dobelmann, Pastoral Assoc.
622 W. Second St., P.O. Box 189, 81226. Tel: 719-784-4879; Fax: 719-784-2070.
Mission—Rockvale, Fremont Co., St. Patrick.

Fruita, Mesa Co., Sacred Heart (1890), Rev. Msgr. Edward H. Nunez, Supvr.
Mailing Address: 513 E. Aspen Ave., 81521. Tel: 970-858-9605; Fax: 970-858-9605.

Gardner, Huerfano Co., Sacred Heart (1912), Rev. Richard Wehrmeyer, C.M., V.F.
Mailing Address: P.O. Box 86, Walsenburg, 81089. Tel: 719-738-1204; Fax: 719-738-1206.

Grand Junction, Mesa Co., Immaculate Heart of Mary (1955), Revs. James H. Plough; Steven J. Murray.
790 26 1/2 Rd., 81501. Tel: 970-242-6121.
Mission—Palisade, Mesa Co., St. Ann, 535 W. 1st St., Palisade, 81526. Tel: 970-464-5157. Sr. Celine Regan, O.P., Pastoral Assoc.
Stations—Debeque.; Collbran.

St. Joseph (1884), Rev. Msgr. Edward H. Nunez; Rev. William (Liam) Hugh Courtney; Deacons William Pewters, Pastoral Assoc.; Stanley G. Neumann.
Mailing Address: 230 N. Third, 81501.
253 White Ave., 81501. Tel: 970-243-0209; Fax: 970-243-7493.
School—Holy Family School.
North: 800 Bookcliff, 81501. Tel: 970-242-6168; Fax: 970-242-4244. Margie Shean, Prin.; South: 303 Grand Ave., 81501. Tel: 970-241-1489.
Sisters 1; Lay Teachers 21; Students 298.

Gunnison, Gunnison Co., St. Peter (1881), Rev. James F. Koenigsfeld, V.F.
303 N. Wisconsin St., 81230. Tel: 970-641-0808; Fax: 970-641-4592.
Mission—Lake City, Hinsdale Co., St. Rose of Lima, Tel: 970-944-2555.

Holly, Prowers Co., St. Frances of Rome (1910), Rev. Msgr. William P. Doll.
130 S. Fifth St., 81047. Tel: 719-537-6688.
Mailing Address: P.O. Box 130.
Mission—Bristol, Prowers Co., St. Mary.

Ignacio, La Plata Co., St. Ignatius Parish (1898), Rev. Edward J. Andary.
P.O. Box 1350, 81137. Tel: 970-563-4241; Fax: 970-563-1032.
Missions—Bayfield, La Plata Co., St. Bartholemew, P.O. Box 214, Bayfield, 81122.; Arboles, Archuleta Co., SS. Peter & Rose, R.R. 2, 81137.
Station—Tiffany.

La Junta, Otero Co., Our Lady of Guadalupe/ St. Patrick (1889), Rev. Charles A. Sena, V.F.
222 Lincoln St., Box 1181, 81050. Tel: 719-384-4342; 384-4372; Fax: 719-384-7894.

Lamar, Prowers Co., St. Francis De Sales-Our Lady of Guadalupe (1930), Rev. George V. Uralikunnel.
600 E. Parmenter St., 81052. Tel: 719-336-7759; Fax: 719-336-0291.

Las Animas, Bent Co., St. Mary (1910), Rev. George S. Reynolds, O.P.
714 Elm St., 81054. Tel: 719-456-0357.

Mancos, Montezuma Co., St. Rita (1914), Rev. Kevin Novack. In res., Rev. Msgr. Joseph P. McGuinness Tel: 970-564-1284; Rev. Tom Munson.
P.O. Box 150, 81328. Tel: 970-533-7388 (Rectory); Fax: 970-565-0822.
Missions—Dolores, Montezuma Co., Our Lady of Victory Church, 101 N. 7th, Dolores, 81323. Tel: 970-565-7308; Rico, Dolores Co., Immaculate Heart of Mary Chapel.
Station—Mesa Verde, National Park.

Monte Vista, Rio Grande Co., St. Joseph (1920), Revs. John J. Costanzo Tel: 719-852-2673; William R. Nelson; Thomas J. Quinn; Deacon Don Lamb.
425 Batterson, P.O. Box 587, 81144. Tel: 719-852-2523 (Rectory); 719-852-2673 (Parish); Fax: 719-852-0623.
Stations—Lariate.; Morada.; Mountain Meadows, Tel: 719-852-5138; Homelake, Tel: 719-852-5118; High Valley, Tel: 719-852-5711.

Montrose, Montrose Co., St. Mary (1906), Rev. Msgr. Daniel R. Huber; Deacons Dennis Putnam, Parish Assoc.; Michael Rovella.
Mailing Address: P.O. Box 638, 81402-0638.
547 S. Fifth St., 81401. Tel: 970-249-3319; Fax: 970-249-9088.; Parish Center: 1855 St. Mary's Dr., 81402.
Mission—Olathe, Montrose Co., Our Lady of Fatima, c/o St. Mary Church, P.O. Box 638, Olathe, 81402.

Ouray, Ouray Co., St. Daniel the Prophet (1883), Rev. Nathanael Foshage, O.S.B.
P.O. Box 565, 81427. Tel: 970-325-4373.
Mission—Silverton, San Juan Co., St. Patrick, 1005 Reece, Silverton, 81433.

Pagosa Springs, Archuleta Co., Immaculate Heart of Mary (1923), Rev. John C. Bowe, C.R.; Deacon Tom Bomkamp Tel: 970-731-3115.
P.O. Box 451, 81147. Tel: 970-264-5702; Fax: 970-264-4876. [CEM]
Catechesis/Religious Programs—Students 147.
Missions—Frances, Archuleta Co., St. Francis. Fax: 970-264-3166; Pagosa Junction, Archuleta Co., St. John Baptist; Trujillo, Archuleta Co., St. James.
Station—Chromo.

Paonia, Delta Co., Sacred Heart (1923), Rev. Michael N. Smith, S.J., V.F., Admin.
235 N. Fork Ave., P.O. Box 988, 81428. Tel: 970-527-3214; Fax: 970-527-5468.
Mission—Hotchkiss, Delta Co., St. Margaret Mary, 331 Bridge St., Hotchkiss, 81419.

Rocky Ford, Otero Co., St. Peter (1910), Rev. John B. Farley.
1209 Swink Ave., 81067. Tel: 719-254-3565; Fax: 719-254-3921.
Missions—Manzanola, Otero Co., St. Joseph the Worker, P.O. Box 265, Manzanola, 81058.; Ordway, Crowley Co., St. Peter Chapel, P.O. Box 218, Ordway, 81063. Tel: 719-267-4645; Fowler, Otero Co., Mary Queen of Heaven, P.O. Box 214, Fowler, 81039. Tel: 719-263-4455.

San Luis, Costilla Co., Sangre de Cristo (1881) (Hispanic), Revs. Patrick M. Valdez, C.R.; Sergio Robles, C.R.
Res., P.O. Box 326, 81152. Tel: 719-672-3685; Fax: 719-672-0300. [CEM]
Catechesis/Religious Programs—Students 59.
Missions—Blanca, Costilla Co., St. James; Fort Garland, Costilla Co., Holy Family; Chama, Costilla Co., Immaculate Conception; San Acacio, Costilla Co., San Acacio; San Pedro, Costilla Co., SS. Peter and Paul; San Isidro, Costilla Co., St. Isidro; San Francisco, Costilla Co., St. Francis of Assisi; Garcia, Costilla Co., Sacred Heart of Jesus.

Silverton, San Juan Co., St. Patrick (1883), Rev. Nathanael Foshage, O.S.B.
Mailing Address: P.O. Box 565, Ouray, 81427. Tel: 970-325-4373.

Springfield, Baca Co., Annunciation (1932), Rev. J. Patrick Walsh, S.J.
140 Kansas St., 81073. Tel: 719-523-6645.
Station—Walsh.

Telluride, San Miguel Co., St. Patrick (1896), Rev. Nathanael Foshage, O.S.B., Supvr.; Deacon Michael Doehrman, Parish Dir.
P.O. Box 398, 81435. Tel: 970-728-3387; Fax: 970-728-8029.
Mission—Nucla, Montrose Co., Our Lady of Sorrows, P.O. Box 451, Nucla, 81424.

Trinidad, Las Animas Co., Most Holy Trinity, Trinidad Area Catholic Community (Trinidad Cluster) (1885), Revs. James Costello, S.J., Supr.; Eugene C. Renard, S.J.; Robert A. Hagan, S.J.
235 N. Convent St., 81082. Tel: 719-846-3369; Fax: 719-846-4856. [CEM]
School—237 Church St., 81082. Tel: 719-846-7541.
Sisters 3; Lay Teachers 18; Students 216.
Missions—Vigil, Las Animas Co., St. Isidore; Segundo, Las Animas Co., St. Ignatius.

Our Lady of Mt. Carmel, Trinidad Area Catholic Community (Trinidad Cluster). Closed. For inquiries for parish records contact Most Holy Trinity, 719-846-3369.

St. Joseph, Trinidad Area Catholic Community (Trinidad Cluster). Closed. For inquiries for parish records contact Most Holy Trinity, 719-846-3369.

Vineland, Pueblo Co., St. Therese (1928), Revs. Richard F. Becker; Robert F. Carden.
1133 Lane 36, Pueblo, 81006. Tel: 719-948-2410; 544-1886; Fax: 719-544-5137.

Walsenburg, Huerfano Co., St. Mary (1896), Rev. Richard Wehrmeyer, C.M., V.F.; Sr. Carol Tlach, S.N.D., Senior Outreach Dir.
P.O. Box 86, 81089. Tel: 719-738-1204; Fax: 719-738-1206. [CEM]
Missions—La Veta, Huerfano Co., Christ the King, P.O. Box 752, La Veta, 81055.; Gardner, Huerfano Co., Sacred Heart, P.O. Box 228, Gardner, 81040.; Chama, Huerfano Co., Our Lady of Guadalupe.

Westcliffe, Custer Co., Our Lady of the Assumption (1870), Rev. Louis M. Kirby, O.S.B.
P.O. Box 359, 81252. Tel: 719-783-2340.

Chaplains of Public Institutions

PUEBLO. *Colorado State Hospital*. Vacant. Tel: 719-546-4434.
Parkview Hospital. Michael C. DeSciose, Res., 1024 Oxford St., #6, 81005.

CANON CITY. *Fremont Correctional Facility*. Vacant. St. Dismas Chapel.

CROWLEY. *Arkansas Valley Correctional Facility*. Vacant.

FLORENCE. *Federal Correctional Institute at Florence*. Rev. John O'Flynn.

FORT LYON. *Veterans Administration Hospital*. Vacant. Mailing Address:Mailing Address: P.O. Box 147, 81038. Tel: 719-456-1260, Ext. 3939.

TRINIDAD. *State Home for the Aged*. Administered by priests from Trinity area Catholic community.

On Duty Outside the Diocese:
Reverend Fathers—
Haberman, C. Robert, San Rafael, CA
Norman, Clifford A., Mexico

Absent on Leave:
Reverend Fathers—
Bonfadini, Leo
Bouchard, Norman
Groves, William
Thill, Richard
Trujillo, Carlos B.
Vandenberg, James

Military Chaplains:
Reverend Fathers—
Cerwonka, Clarence G., U.S. Army

Retired:
Reverend Monsignors—
Delaney, Howard L., 7-C Bonnymede, Pueblo, CO 81001
Holland, George T., 2204 Wyoming Ave., Pueblo, CO 81004
McGuinness, Joseph P., 28 E. Montezuma Ave., Cortez, CO 81321-3299. Tel: 970-564-1284
Reverend Fathers—
Blanpied, Robert D., Harrison Regent, 4481 Harrison Blvd., #124, Ogden, UT 84403. Tel: 801-475-9963
Cavanagh, Michael J., 56 Wentworth, Westwood, MA 02090
Corbett, Michael E., 2110 "B" Chatalet Lane, Pueblo, CO 81005. Tel: 719-566-9836
Danowski, Alexander J., 653 Country Court, Grand Junction, CO 81504-5907
Grimes, Raymond P., 805 S. Aguilar Dr., Pueblo West, CO 81007-1701
Kiernan, John G., 2185 Linda Ln., Grand Junction, CO 81501
Kukucka, Joseph G., Maple Manor Villa, 212 Maple Ave., Apt. 17, La Junta, CO 81050
Marcantonio, Clement, LRMC 799 CMR 402, APO AE, 09180
McDevitt, James J., St. Vincent's Church, 840 George Bush Blvd., Delray Beach, FL 33483
Mendrick, Paul P., 1312 Lakeview Ave., Apt. 204, Pueblo, CO 81004
Montoya, Jose J., Forrest Park Care Center, 7045 Stuart St., Westminister, CO 80030
Munson, Thomas N., Res., 16098 County Rd. 28.3, Dolores, CO 81323
O'Sullivan, John C., Livingston Baker Apts. #608, 1925 First Ave., Seattle, WA 98101
Powers, William V., 1414 E. 8th St., Pueblo, CO 81001
Racki, Leonard E., 31 Terrace Dr., Pueblo, CO 81001
Roche, Ron, 1912 Vinewood Lane, Pueblo, CO 81005. Tel: 719-565-0813
Rykowski, Jerome A., 587 Eastwood St., Grand Junction, CO 81504-4814. Tel: 970-243-6234
Schmitt, Ervin J., 1024 Oxford St., #9, Pueblo, CO 81005. Tel: 719-564-0885
Schoening, Sylvester H., Hermitage, 1250 Mountain View Ln., P.O. Box 553, Norwood, CO 81423
Smigiel, Walter J., 3517 Atlantic Dr., Colorado Springs, CO 80910
Sutton, John H., 310 3rd Ave., Cando, ND 58324
Sweeney, Eugene J., 120 Ashley Dr., Fairhope, AL 36532
Tomalonis, John, Tremont Nursing Home, 44 Donaldson Rd., Tremont, PA 17981
Wichmann, Edward W., 1225 Central Blvd., Apt. 903, Brownsville, TX 78520

Permanent Deacons:
Boies, James A., Sr., V.A. Hospital Chap.
Bomkamp, Thomas, Immaculate Heart of Mary, Pagosa Springs
Dobelmann, Vernon, St. Benedict, Florence
Doehrman, Michael J., Parish Dir., Telluride/Nucla
Dunn, Joseph, Sacred Heart, Durango

Hawes, Lloyd, St. Peter, Gunnison
LaConte, Michael, Christ the King, Pueblo
Lamb, Donald, St. Joseph, Monte Vista
Luginbill, John, St. Mary, Walsenburg
Lumbert, Steven, Holy Family, Pueblo
Myscofski, Robert, Our Lady of the Meadows, Pueblo
Neumann, Stan, St. Joseph, Grand Junction
Newport, Gary, St. Columba, Durango
Oreskey, Richard, Our Lady of the Meadows, Pueblo
Pewters, William, St. Joseph, Grand Junction
Putnam, Dennis, St. Mary, Montrose
Reynolds, Philip, Christ the King, Pueblo
Riccillo, Edward, St. Leander, Pueblo
Romero, Toby, Sacred Heart, Durango
Rovella, Mike, St. Mary, Montrose
Runck, Merle, Unassigned
Shafer, Jacob, Sacred Heart Cathedral, Pueblo
Stroop, John, Queen of All Saints, Crested Butte
Swindells, George A., St. Pius X/St. Paul, Pueblo
VanHouten, Douglas, Immaculate Heart of Mary, Grand Junction
Wertin, Henry, St. Francis de Sales, Lamar

INSTITUTIONS LOCATED IN THE DIOCESE

[A] HIGH SCHOOLS, DIOCESAN

TRINIDAD. *Trinidad Catholic Schools*, 201 Church St, 81082. Tel: 719-846-7541; Fax: 719-846-4856. Ms. Joanne Romero, Prin. Sisters 2; Lay Teachers 9; Students 53.

[B] HIGH SCHOOLS, PRIVATE

CANON CITY. *St. Scholastica Academy*, 615 Pike Ave., 81212. Tel: 719-275-7461; Fax: 719-269-9531.
E-mail: ssacad@iex.net
Web site: www.stscholastica.net
Girls boarding and day school. (Grades 6-12). Ms. Virginia T. Wilkinson. Benedictine Sisters of Chicago 8; Lay Teachers 13; Students 92.

[C] ELEMENTARY SCHOOLS, DIOCESAN

PUEBLO. *The Shrine of St. Therese Catholic School*, 320 Goodnight Ave., 81004. Tel: 719-561-1121; Fax: 719-561-2252. Mr. Peter Iten, Prin.

DURANGO. *St. Columba.* (Grades PreK-8), 1801 E. 3rd Ave., 81301-5072. Tel: 970-247-5527; Fax: 970-382-9355.
E-mail: saintc@frontier.net
Sr. Edith Marie Hauser, O.P., Prin. Sisters 2; Lay Teachers 18; Students 254.

GRAND JUNCTION. *Holy Family*. North Campus. (Grades K-2 & 6-8), 800 Bookcliff Ave., 81501. Tel: 970-242-6168; Fax: 970-242-4244. Ms. Margie Shean, Prin. Sisters 1; Lay Teachers 15; Students 198. South Campus. (Grades 3-5), 3rd & Grand, 81501. Tel: 970-241-1489; Fax: 970-241-1480. Ms. Margie Shean, Prin. Sisters 1; Lay Teachers 6; Students 100.

TRINIDAD. *Trinidad Catholic Elementary*. (Grades K-6), 201 Church St., 81082-2606. Tel: 719-846-7218; Fax: 719-846-7541. Ms. Joanne Romero, Prin. Sisters 1; Lay Teachers 12; Students 161.

[D] ELEMENTARY SCHOOLS, PRIVATE

PUEBLO. *John Neumann Catholic Schools*, 330 Lake Ave., 81004. Tel: 719-543-8407; Fax: 719-543-8864.
E-mail: admissions@johnneumann.org
Mr. Arthur Sanchez, Interim Admin.
Elementary School, 2415 E. Orman Ave., 81004. Tel: 719-561-9419; 566-9636; Fax: 719-561-4718. Dr. Geraldine Aragon, Dir. Lay Teachers 18; Students 213.
Middle School, 330 Lake Ave., 81004. Tel: 719-543-8864; 543-8407; Fax: 719-543-8864. Mr. Jack Pecoraro, Dir. Lay Teachers 7; Students 98.
Preschool, 2415 E. Orman Ave., 81004. Tel: 719-561-9419; Fax: 719-561-4718. Connie Lauer, Dir. Lay Teachers 3; Students 81.

[E] GENERAL HOSPITALS

PUEBLO. *Centura Health-St. Mary-Corwin Medical Center*, 1008 Minnequa Ave., 81004. Tel: 719-560-4000; Fax: 719-560-4646.
E-mail: chaplainsmc@centura.org
Web site: www.stmarycorwin.org
For a complete listing, refer to the Hospitals section.

CANON CITY. *Centura Health-St. Thomas More Hospital*, 1338 Phay Ave., 81212. Tel: 719-269-2000; Fax: 719-269-2016
For a complete listing, refer to the Hospitals section.

DURANGO. *Centura Health-Mercy Medical Center*, 375 E. Park Ave., 81301. Tel: 970-247-4311; Fax: 970-382-1082.
E-mail: kirkdignum@mercydurango.org
Web site: www.mercydurango.org
For a complete listing, refer to the Hospitals section.

GRAND JUNCTION. *Marillac Clinic, Inc.*, 2333 N. 6th St., 81501. Tel: 970-243-7803; Fax: 970-255-1711.
E-mail: jcameron@stmarygj.com
For a complete listing, refer to the Hospitals section.
St. Mary Hospital and Medical Center, P.O. Box 1628, 81502. Tel: 970-244-2273; Fax: 970-244-7510
For a complete listing, refer to the Hospitals section.

[F] SPECIAL CARE FACILITIES

PUEBLO. *Villa Pueblo*, 1111 Bonforte Blvd., 81001. Tel: 719-545-5911; Fax: 719-544-1354
For a complete listing, refer to the Special Care Facilities section.

CANON CITY. *Centura Health-Progressive Care Center*, 1338 Phay Ave., 81212. Tel: 719-269-2000; Fax: 719-269-2016.
E-mail: barbaracarochi@centura.org
For a complete listing, refer to the Special Care Facilities section.

FLORENCE. *Centura Health-St. Joseph Manor*, 600 W. 3rd St., 81226-1117. Tel: 719-784-4893; Fax: 719-784-4308
For a complete listing, refer to the Special Care Facilities section.

[G] MONASTERIES AND RESIDENCES OF PRIESTS AND BROTHERS

CANON CITY. *Holy Cross Abbey*, P.O. Box 1510, 81215-1510. Tel: 719-275-8631; Fax: 719-275-7125.
E-mail: hcabbey@juno.com
Web site: www.holycrossabbey.org
Kenneth C. Hein, O.S.B., Abbot; Rt. Rev. Edward J. Vollmer, O.S.B., Retired Abbot; Revs. Ignatius J. Smith, O.S.B., Prior; William L. Thompson, O.S.B.; Bernard P. Gervais, O.S.B.; Louis M. Kirby, O.S.B.; Henry W. Lacerte, O.S.B., Subprior; Gregory Legge, O.S.B.; Paul J. Montez, O.S.B.; Michael D. Murray, O.S.B.; Martin de Porres J. Muheim, O.S.B.; Bros. Bernard A.F. Best, O.S.B.; Matthew Bach, O.S.B.; Kevin J. Bachmann, O.S.B.; David J. Downey, O.S.B.; Francis Shaw, O.S.B. Priests of Monastery 12; Professed Brothers 4.

TRINIDAD. *Trinidad Area Catholic Community*, Rectory, 615 E. Goddard Ave., 81082. Tel: 719-846-3360. Business Address: 235 N. Convent St., 81082. Tel: 719-846-3369; Fax: 719-846-4856. Revs. James Costello, S.J., Supr.; Robert A. Hagan, S.J.; Eugene C. Renard, S.J.

[H] CONVENTS AND RESIDENCES FOR SISTERS

PUEBLO. *Servants of the Blessed Sacrament*, 311 E. Mesa Ave., 81006. Tel: 719-545-7729; Fax: 719-542-3094. Sr. Josephine Roney, S.S.S., Supr. Sisters 3; Postulants 3; Novices 1.

GRAND JUNCTION. *Adrian Dominican Sisters, Southwest Mission Chapter*, 1983 S. Broadway, 81503-9592. Tel: 970-241-6152; Fax: 970-257-0812.
E-mail: gmesaop@aol.com
Web site: www.op.org/adrian
Sr. Barbara Stanek, O.P., Chapter Prioress.

[I] NEWMAN CENTERS

GUNNISON. *Campus Ministry - Diocese of Pueblo*, 600 E. Georgia, 81230. Tel: 970-641-0325.
E-mail: newman@frontier.net
Ms. Janet Johnson.
Adams State College (Alamosa), United Campus Ministry College Center, Rm. 329, Alamosa, 81102. Tel: 719-589-7516; 274-5304. Shirley Atencio.
Fort Lewis College (Durango). Fort Lewis College Center for Campus Ministry, North Complex #7, 1000 Rim Dr., Box 7211, Durango, 81301. Tel: 970-247-7460. Ms. Lisa Sauer, Campus Min.
Mesa State College (Grand Junction), Newman Center, 1135 College Pl., Grand Junction, 81501. Tel: 970-241-3670. Ms. Janet Johnson, Campus Min.
Western State College (Gunnison), Campus Ministry Center, 600 E. Georgia, 81230. Tel: 970-641-0325. Ms. Sheilagh McGlynn, Campus Min.
Otero Junior College (La Junta), P.O. Box 1181, La Junta, 81050. Tel: 719-384-4342. Mr. F. Anthony Gallegos, Contact Person.
Lamar Junior College (Lamar). (Contact Parish, St. Francis de Sales), 600 E. Parmenter, Lamar, 81052. Tel: 719-336-7759.
University of Southern Colorado (Pueblo). Christ the King, 1708 Horseshoe Dr., Pueblo, 81001. Tel: 719-542-9248. Joyce Archuleta, Contact Person.
Trinidad State Junior College Campus Ministry (Trinidad), 600 Prospect, Trinidad, 81082. Tel: 719-846-5624.

[J] RETREAT WORK

CANON CITY. *Trinity Ranch Conference & Renewal Center, Inc.*, P.O. Box 1510, 81215. Tel: 719-275-8631; Fax: 719-275-7125.
E-mail: hcabbey@juno.com
Rt. Rev. Kenneth C. Hein, O.S.B., Chm. & CEO.

CRESTONE. *Spiritual Life Institute of America, Inc.*, P.O. Box 219, 81131. Tel: 719-256-4778; Fax: 719-256-4719.
E-mail: nada@fone.net
Web site: www.spirituallifeinstitute.org
Revs. David Denny, Prior; John Meoska. Priests 2; Brothers 1; Sisters 8.

MONTROSE. *Spes in Deo Franciscan Family Retreat Center, Inc.*, 21661 Hwy. 550, 81401. Tel: 970-249-3526.
E-mail: joyce@spesindeoretreat.com
Web site: www.spesindeoretreat.com
M. Joyce Martin, Pres., Bd. of Directors.

WHITEWATER. *Whitewater Community, Inc.*, 8250 Kannah Creek Rd., 81527. Tel: 970-241-3847. Sisters 2.

[K] MISCELLANEOUS

PUEBLO.
Catholic Diocese of Pueblo Foundation, 1001 N. Grand Ave., 81003. Tel: 719-544-9861, Ext. 53; Fax: 719-544-5202.
E-mail: diopueblo-foundation@usa.net
Web site: pueblo-diocese.com
Mr. Bruce F. Brandt, Dir.
Deacon Candidate Formation Council, 1001 N. Grand Ave., 81003. Tel: 719-544-9861, Ext. 116. Rev. Ray VanDorpe, C.M., Deacon Dir.
Historic Southside Catholic Community, 919 East Evans Ave., 81004. Tel: 719-296-8778; Fax: 719-562-1195. The Historic Southside Catholic Community is an organization which clusters the pastoral and administrative functions for 3 parishes: Our Lady of the Assumption, St. Mary Help of Christians, and St. Patrick Catholic Churches/ Parishes. Robert J. Salle, Pastoral Admin. & Contact; Rev. Edward G. Pettit, Pastor; Deacon Philip Reynolds.
John Neumann Catholic School (Administration & Middle School), 330 Lake Ave., 81004. Tel: 719-543-8407; Fax: 719-543-8864.
E-mail: admissions@johnneumann.org
Web site: www.johnneumann.org
Mr. J. Arthur Sanchez, Admin. (John Neumann Catholic Schools housed at Seton Education Center).
Pueblo Community Soup Kitchen, Inc., 422 W. Seventh, 81003. Tel: 719-545-6540. Wanda Mercer, Coord.
S.E.T. of Pueblo, Inc. A division of Catholic Health Initiatives Mountain Region. 1902 E. Orman Ave., 81004. Tel: 719-560-5886; Fax: 719-564-4709.
E-mail: noreenellisonsc@centura.org
Sr. Jacqueline Riggio, S.C., Exec. Dir. Purpose: A ministry to low-income, disadvantaged, and underserved persons, providing educational and health maintenance for empowerment and transformation.
St. Anthony Community, 18 Dartmouth, 81005. Tel: 719-566-1620. Mr. Ed Sajbel, Contact Person.
SEARCH of Pueblo, 917 E. Evans, 81004. Tel: 719-544-8246.
E-mail: searchofpueblo@aol.com
Ms. Sandy Hansen, Coord.
Serra Club of Pueblo, 5426 Stonemoor Dr., 81005. Tel: 719-566-0511. Mrs. Sally Stricca, Pres.
Sisters for Christian Community, 1081 S. Lynx Dr., 81007. Tel: 719-547-2416; Fax: 719-547-4401.
E-mail: salliewatkins@juno.com
Sr. Sallie Watkins, S.F.C.C., Ph.D., Sec.

CENTER. *Artes Del Valle (Hispanic Craft Cooperative)*, P.O. Box 627, 81125. Tel: 719-589-4769; 754-3191. Miss Shirley Ortega, Mgr. Artes del Valle is under the auspices of St. Francis Jerome Church, Center.

DURANGO. *Mercy Health Foundation*, 375 E. Park Ave., 81301. Tel: 970-382-2091; Fax: 970-385-5392.
E-mail: karenmidkiff@mercydurango.org
Affiliate of Catholic Health Initiatives. Ms. Karen Midkiff, Exec. Dir.

GRAND JUNCTION. *Grand Valley Catholic Outreach*, 240 White Ave., 81501. Tel: 970-241-3658; Fax: 970-242-3908.
E-mail: gvco@juno.com
Sr. Karen Bland, Exec. Dir., P.O. Box 246, 81502. Tel: 970-241-3658; Fax: 970-242-3908.
Grand Valley Peace and Justice, 253 White Ave., P.O. Box 246, 81501. Tel: 970-243-4378; Fax: 970-243-7493.
E-mail: bevg3@prodigy.net
Mrs. Bev Goodrich, Dir.

St. Mary's Hospital Foundation, 2635 N. 7th St., P.O. Box 1628, 81502-1628. Tel: 970-244-2015; Fax: 970-244-6108.
E-mail: mmccarthy@stmarygj.com
Mary Frances McCarthy, Exec. Dir.
St. Mary's Rehabilitation Center, Inc., P.O. Box 1628, 81502.

PAGOSA SPRINGS. *Archuleta Housing Corporation*, 713 San Juan Ave. P.O. Box 355, 81147-0355. Tel: 970-264-2195.

RELIGIOUS INSTITUTES OF MEN REPRESENTED IN THE DIOCESE

For further details refer to the corresponding bracketed number in the Religious Institutes of Men or Women section.

[0200]—*Benedictine Monks.*—O.S.B.
[1330]—*Congregation of the Mission.* (Missouri Prov.).—C.M.
[0260]—*Discalced Carmelite Monks.*—O.C.D.
[0690]—*Jesuit Fathers and Brothers.* (Missouri Prov.).—S.J.
[1300]—*Theatine Fathers.* (Rome, Italy).—C.R.

RELIGIOUS INSTITUTES OF WOMEN REPRESENTED IN THE DIOCESE

[0230]—*Benedictine Sisters of Pontifical Jurisdiction.* (Chicago, IL; Covington, KY; Colorado Springs, CO; Yankton, SD).—O.S.B.
[1710]—*Congregation of the Third Order of St. Francis of Mary Immaculate, Joliet, IL.*—O.S.F.
[0420]—*Discalced Carmelite Nuns.*—O.C.D.
[1070-13]—*Dominican Sisters.*—O.P.
[1070-24]—*Dominican Sisters.*—O.P.
[1845]—*Guadalupanas Missionaries of the Holy Spirit.*—M.G.Sp.S.
[2575]—*Institute of the Sisters of Mercy of the Americas.*—R.S.M.
[2960]—*Notre Dame Sisters.*—N.D.
[3130]—*Our Lady of Victory.*—O.L.V.M.
[3580]—*Servants of Mary.*—O.S.M.
[3500]—*Servants of the Blessed Sacrament.*—S.S.S.
[]—*Sisters for Christian Community.*—S.F.C.C.
[0440]—*Sisters of Charity of Cincinnati, Ohio.*—S.C.
[0480]—*Sisters of Charity of Leavenworth, Kansas.*—S.C.L.
[2360]—*Sisters of Loretto At the Foot of the Cross.*—S.L.
[1570]—*Sisters of St. Francis of the Holy Family.*—O.S.F.
[3830-15]—*Sisters of St. Joseph.*—C.S.J.
[3830-18]—*Sisters of St. Joseph.*—C.S.J.
[1720]—*Sisters of the Third Order Regular of St. Francis of the Congregation of Our Lady of Lourdes.*—O.S.F.
[]—*Sisters of Whitewater Community.*
[4060]—*Society of the Holy Child Jesus.*—S.H.C.J.

CEMETERIES, DIOCESAN AND PAROCHIAL

PUEBLO. *Gate of Heaven.* Legal Title: *Gate of Heaven Section, Roselawn Cemetery Assoc.*
AGUILAR. *St. Anthony.* (St. Anthony Parish).
CAPULIN. *St. Anthony; St. Francis; St. Joseph; and Capulin.* (St. Joseph Parish).
CONEJOS. *Conejos; Las Mesitas; San Antonio; Ortiz; and Labatos.* (Our Lady of Guadalupe Parish).
DEL NORTE. *St. Francis of Assisi.* (Holy Name of Mary Parish).
FRUITA. *Fruita Catholic.* (Sacred Heart Parish).
PAGOSA SPRINGS. *St. John the Baptist; St. Andrew Avelino; St. Francis; and St. James.* (Immaculate Heart of Mary Parish).
RYE. *Mount Olivet.* (St. Daniel Mission Parish). Legal Title: *The Rye Mount Olivet Cemetery.*
SAN LUIS. *San Luis; San Pedro; San Acacio; San Francisco; and Chama.* (Sangre de Cristo Parish).
TRINIDAD. *Trinidad Catholic.* Legal Title: Trinidad Catholic Cemetery Assoc. (Holy Trinity Parish).
WALSENBURG. *St. Mary.* Legal Title: St. Mary Cemetery Association, Inc. (St. Mary Parish).
WESTCLIFFE. *Silver Cliff Assumption Catholic.* (Our Lady of the Assumption Parish).

NECROLOGY

† Beno, John R., (Retired). —Died Dec. 5, 2000.

Diocese of Raleigh

(Dioecesis Raleighiensis)

Most Reverend

F. JOSEPH GOSSMAN, D.D., J.C.D.

Bishop of Raleigh; ordained December 17, 1955; appointed Titular Bishop of Aguntum and Auxiliary Bishop of Baltimore July 15, 1968; ordained Bishop, September 11, 1968; appointed Fourth Bishop of Raleigh April 8, 1975; installed May 19, 1975. *Res., 1601 Westbridge Ct., Raleigh, NC, 27606. Office: 715 Nazareth St., Raleigh, NC, 27606.* Tel.: 919-821-9702.

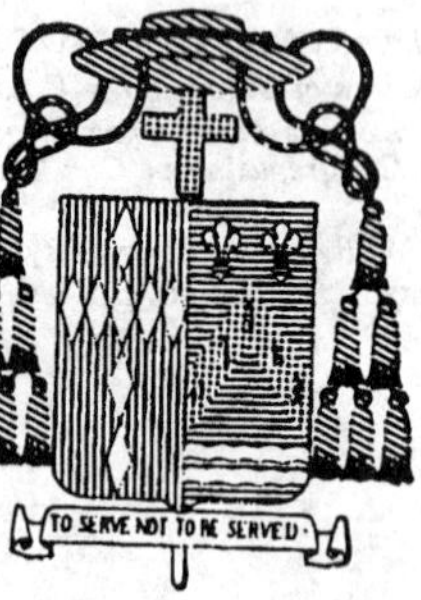

Most Reverend

GEORGE E. LYNCH, D.D.

Retired Auxiliary Bishop of Raleigh; Titular Bishop of Satafi; ordained May 29, 1943; appointed October 20, 1969; consecrated January 6, 1970; retired July 10, 1985. *Res., P.O. Box 3, Woodlawn Station, Bronx, NY, 10470.*

ESTABLISHED AS VICARIATE-APOSTOLIC OF NORTH CAROLINA BY POPE PIUS IX, MARCH 3, 1868.

ESTABLISHED AS DIOCESE OF RALEIGH BY POPE PIUS XI, DECEMBER 12, 1924.

Square Miles 31,875.

Comprises the following Counties in the State of North Carolina: Alamance, Beaufort, Bertie, Bladen, Brunswick, Camden, Carteret, Caswell, Chatham, Chowan, Columbus, Craven, Cumberland, Currituck, Dare, Duplin, Durham, Edgecombe, Franklin, Gates, Granville, Greene, Halifax, Harnett, Hertford, Hoke, Hyde, Johnston, Jones, Lee, Lenoir, Martin, Moore, Nash, New Hanover, Northampton, Onslow, Orange, Pamlico, Pasquotank, Pender, Perquimans, Person, Pitt, Robeson, Sampson, Scotland, Tyrrell, Vance, Wake, Warren. Washington, Wayne and Wilson.

For legal titles of parishes and diocesan institutions, consult the Chancery.

Catholic Center: 715 Nazareth St., Raleigh, NC, 27606. Tel.: 919-821-9700; Fax: 919-821-9705.

Web site address: www.raldioc.org

E-mail address: chancery@raldioc.org

STATISTICAL OVERVIEW

Personnel	
Bishop	1
Retired Bishops	1
Priests: Diocesan Active in Diocese	63
Priests: Active Outside Diocese	4
Priests: Retired, Sick or Absent	20
Number of Diocesan Priests	87
Religious Priests in Diocese	53
Extern Priests in Diocese	2
Ordinations:	
Diocesan Priests	2
Permanent Deacons in Diocese	23
Total Brothers	9
Total Sisters	77
Parishes	
Parishes	75
With Resident Pastor:	
Resident Diocesan Priests	45
Resident Religious Priests	20
Without Resident Pastor:	
Administered by Women Religious	10
Missions	12
Pastoral Centers	5
New Parishes Created	1
Professional Ministry Personnel:	
Brothers	1
Sisters	11
Lay Ministers	116
Welfare	
Special Centers for Social Services	12
Total Assisted	46,508
Educational	
Seminaries, Diocesan	1
Students from This Diocese	3
Diocesan Students in Other Seminaries	19
Total Seminarians	22
High Schools, Diocesan and Parish	1
Total Students	862
Elementary Schools, Diocesan and Parish	29
Total Students	6,943
Catechesis/Religious Education:	
High School Students	2,730
Elementary Students	14,061
Total Students Under Catholic Instruction	24,618
Teachers in the Diocese:	
Priests	6
Brothers	4
Sisters	14
Lay Teachers	386
Vital Statistics	
Receptions into the Church:	
Infant Baptism Totals	3,998
Adult Baptism Totals	263
Received into Full Communion	418
First Communions	2,898
Confirmations	1,470
Marriages:	
Catholic	451
Interfaith	436
Total Marriages	887
Deaths	1,006
Total Catholic Population	167,537
Total Population	3,697,588

Former Bishops of Diocese—Most Rev. WILLIAM J. HAFEY, D.D., cons. June 24, 1925; transferred to the See of Scranton, PA, Oct. 2, 1937; installed Nov. 15, 1937; died May 12, 1954.—Most Rev. EUGENE J. MCGUINNESS, D.D., cons. Dec. 21, 1937; transferred to the See of Oklahoma City and Tulsa, OK, Dec. 8, 1944; installed Jan. 10, 1945; died Dec. 27, 1957.—Most Rev. VINCENT S. WATERS, D.D., cons. May 15, 1945; installed June 6, 1945; died Dec. 3, 1974.

Former Bishops of Vicariate-Apostolic—His Eminence JAMES CARDINAL GIBBONS, cons. Aug. 16, 1868, Titular Bishop of Adramyttum, first Vicar-Apostolic; transferred to Richmond, VA, July 30, 1872; promoted to the See of Baltimore, Oct. 3, 1877; created Cardinal-Priest of S. Maria in Trastevere, June 7, 1886; died March 24, 1921.—Most Rev. JOHN J. KEANE, cons. Bishop of Richmond and Vicar-Apostolic of North Carolina, Aug. 25, 1878; transferred to the Titular See of Jasso, Aug. 12, 1888; elevated to the Archepiscopal Dignity with the title of Archbishop of Damascus, Jan. 9, 1897; transferred to the See of Dubuque, July 24, 1900; resigned April 3, 1911; appt. Titular Archbishop of Cios, April 28, 1911; died June 23, 1918.—Rt. Rev. H. P. NORTHROP, cons. Titular Bishop of Rosalia and Vicar-Apostolic of North Carolina, Jan. 8, 1882; transferred to Charleston, Jan. 27, 1883; died June 7, 1916.—Rt. Rev. LEO HAID, O.S.B., Vicar Apostolic of North Carolina and Abbot-Ordinary of Belmont Abbey; cons. Titular Bishop of Messene, July 1, 1888; died July 24, 1924.

Office of the Bishop—715 Nazareth St., Raleigh, 27606. Tel: 919-821-9702; Fax: 919-821-9705.

Vicar General & Moderator of the Curia—Rev. Msgr. GERALD L. LEWIS, *715 Nazareth St., Raleigh, 27606.* Tel: 919-821-9708.

Chancellor—RUSSELL C. ELMAYAN, *715 Nazareth St., Raleigh, 27606.* Tel: 919-821-9704.

Vice Chancellor for Canonical Affairs—Very Rev. GIRARD M. SHERBA, J.C.D., *715 Nazareth St., Raleigh, 27606.* Tel: 919-821-9756.

Chancery—715 Nazareth St., Raleigh, 27606. Tel: 919-821-9703; Fax: 919-821-9779.

Deans—Very Rev. MICHAEL A. BUTLER, Albermarle; Very Rev. JAMES M. LABOSKY, Cape Fear; Very Rev. THOMAS J. GAUL, Fayetteville; Very Rev. ERNEST J. RUEDE, New Bern; Very Rev. JOHN MCGEE, O.S.F.S, Piedmont; Rev. Msgr. JOHN F. O'CONNOR, Raleigh; Very Rev. JOSEPH G. MULRONEY, J.C.L., Tar River.

Diocesan Attorney—CHARLES F. POWERS, III, *P.O. Box 1471, Raleigh, 27602.* Tel: 919-828-0684.

Diocesan Consultors—Rev. PHILLIP M. LEACH; Rev. Msgr. GERALD L. LEWIS, V.G.; Rev. Msgr. JOHN F. O'CONNOR; Rev. Msgr. MICHAEL P. SHUGRUE; Revs. DONALD F. STAIB; JOSEPH G. VETTER.

Diocesan Tribunal—715 Nazareth St., Raleigh, 27606. Tel: 919-821-9700. All rogatorial commissions should be directed to the Tribunal.

Defenders of the Bond—Very Rev. JOSEPH G. MULRONEY, J.C.L.; Rev. ALBAN HARMON, C.P., J.C.L.; Sr. PATRICIA WILSON, S.C.

Diocesan Judges—Rev. Msgr. GERALD L. LEWIS, S.T.L., V.G.; Rev. Msgr. THOMAS P. HADDEN; Rev. MICHAEL CONNOLLY, O.S.F.S.

Director of the Tribunal—Sr. PATRICIA M. WILSON, S.C.

Notaries—VIKKI NEWELL; ANNE SPEICHER.

Officialis—Very Rev. GIRARD M. SHERBA, J.C.D.

Promoter of Justice—Vacant.

Priests' Council—Rev. DAVID BROCKMAN; Very Rev. MICHAEL A. BUTLER, V.F.; Revs. MICHAEL CLAY; MICHAEL C. CONNOLLY, O.S.F.S.; Very Rev. THOMAS J. GAUL, V.F.; Rev. JEFFREY A. INGHAM; Very Rev. JAMES M. LABOSKY, V.F.; Rev. PHILLIP M. LEACH; Very Revs. JOHN MCGEE, O.S.F.S.; JOSEPH G. MULRONEY, V.F.; Rev. Msgr. JOHN O'CONNOR, V.F.; Very Rev. ERNEST RUEDE, V.F.; Revs. WILLIAM J. RUHL, O.S.F.S.; BERNARD E. SHLESINGER; Rev. Msgr. MICHAEL SHUGRUE; Revs. DONALD STAIB; JOSEPH G. VETTER. Ex Officio: Rev. Msgr. GERALD LEWIS, V.G.; Very Rev. D. ROBERTO KEENAN; Rev. Msgr. THOMAS P. HADDEN.

Sisters' Council—Sr. MARY MARGARET WEBER, C.S.C.; Sr. MARY JEAN KOREJWO, S.N.D.

Vicar for Priests—Rev. Msgr. MICHAEL SHUGRUE, *1610 Castalia Dr., Cary, 27513.*

Vicars for Religious—Sr. DAMIAN MARIE JACKSON, O.S.F., *711 Mason Rd., Durham, 27712.* Sr. MARGARET GALLAGHER, I.H.M., *124 Marshall St., Warrenton, 27589.*

Diocesan Divisions and Departments

Business Services Division—THOMAS POTOSKY, Dir., *Catholic Center, 715 Nazareth St., Raleigh, 27606.* Tel: 919-821-9722.

Computer Services—JOHN ALLAN TALLANT. Tel: 919-821-9719.

Fiscal Services—Tel: 919-821-9727.

Development Office—DEBORAH ROSSI. Tel: 919-821-9721.

Property/Construction—ARTHUR WESCHE. Tel: 919-821-9726.

Communications Division—FRANK MOROCK, Dir., *Catholic Center, 715 Nazareth St., Raleigh, 27606.* Tel: 919-821-9732.

Ecumenical Commission—Rev. DAVID MCBRIAR, O.F.M. Tel: 919-682-3449.

Evangelization Office—TERRENCE JACKSON, Dir. Tel: 919-821-9746.

Freeman Media Resource Center—TERRI RING. Tel: 919-821-9743.

Graphic Services—TAMMY S. STANLEY. Tel: 919-821-9735.

Human Resources—LEO TAPLER, Dir. Tel: 919-821-9711.

NC Catholic Newspaper—JOHN STRANGE, Editor. Tel: 919-821-9736.

Campus Ministry—Rev. PHILLIP LEACH, Dir., *Newman Catholic Student Center, 218 Pittsboro St., Chapel Hill, 27516-2738.* Tel: 919-929-3730.

Catholic Schools—MICHAEL J. FEDEWA, Supt. Tel: 919-821-9748.

Faith Development—MARY DOWLING. Tel: 919-821-9771.

Catechesis & Catechist Formation—JAN VALLERO. Tel: 919-821-8145.

Marriage Preparation—Mrs. LINDA BEDO. Tel: 919-821-9753.

Youth Ministry—MICHAEL HAGARTY. Tel: 919-821-9770.

Young Adult Ministry—MICHELE A. CASTLE. Tel: 919-821-9772.

Adult Faith Development—ROBERT JONES. Tel: 919-821-9740.

African-American Ministry—Sr. MAXINE TOWNS, S.A., *St. Alphonsus Center, 810 N. Reid St., Wilson, 27893.* Tel: 919-821-9762.

Hispanic Ministry—TERESA ALDAHONDO, *Catholic Center, 715 Nazareth St., Raleigh, 27606.* Tel: 919-821-9764.

Vicar for Hispanics—Very Rev. D. ROBERTO KEENAN, *c/o Diocese of Raleigh, Hispanic Ministry, 715 Nazareth St., Raleigh, 27606.* Tel: 919-821-9738.

Office of Liturgy—Rev. Msgr. JOHN F. O'CONNOR, *Our Lady of Lourdes, 2718 Overbrook Dr., Raleigh, 27608.* Tel: 919-782-1973.

Vicar for African Americans—Rev. Msgr. THOMAS P. HADDEN, *St. Mary Church, 412 Ann St., Wilmington, 28401-4596.* Tel: 910-762-5491.

Vocations—Rev. MICHAEL G. CLAY, Dir. of Formation, *740 Gimghoul Rd., Chapel Hill, 27514-3811.* Tel: 919-967-2203. Rev. BERNARD E. SHLESINGER, III, Dir. of Recruitment, *P.O. Box 100, Newton Grove, 28366.* Tel: 910-594-0152.

Catholic Social Ministries—KATHLEEN WALSH, A.C.S.W., Dir., *Catholic Center, 715 Nazareth St., Raleigh, 27606.* Tel: 919-821-9752.

Peace and Justice—Sr. JOAN JURSKI, O.S.F., *Catholic Center, 715 Nazareth St., Raleigh, 27606.* Tel: 919-821-9751.

Senior Housing—KATHLEEN WALSH, *Catholic Center, 715 Nazareth St., Raleigh, 27606.* Tel: 919-821-9752.

Miscellaneous Offices—

Apostleship of the Sea—Rev. FRANCIS R. MOESLEIN, *2106 Joslyn Dr., Morehead City, 28557-9200.* Tel: 919-726-3579.

Boy Scouts—HALL MOORE, JR., Scout Chap., *329 Meredith St., Raleigh, 27606.*

Censor Librorum—Vacant.

Engaged Encounter—Marriage Preparation and Enrichment Office, *Catholic Center, 715 Nazareth St., Raleigh, 27606.* Tel: 919-821-9753.

Holy Childhood Pontifical Association—Rev. WILLIAM L. PITTS, *Sacred Heart, P.O. Box 1768, Pinehurst, 28374-1768.* Tel: 910-295-6550.

Marriage Encounter—MICHAEL WALLACE; REGINA WALLACE. Tel: 252-454-0430.

Human Resources—LEO TAPLER, *Catholic Center, 715 Nazareth St., Raleigh, 27606.* Tel: 919-821-9711.

Propagation of the Faith—Rev. WILLIAM L. PITTS, *Sacred Heart, P.O. Box 1768, Pinehurst, 28374-1768.* Tel: 910-295-6550.

CLERGY, PARISHES, MISSIONS AND PAROCHIAL SCHOOLS

CITY OF RALEIGH
(Wake County)

1—CATHEDRAL OF THE SACRED HEART (1924), Very Rev. Girard M. Sherba, Rector; Rev. Jonathan A. Woodhall.
Office: 219 W. Edenton St., 27603-1724. Tel: 919-832-6030; Fax: 919-833-4667.
Res., 219 W. Edenton St., 27603. Tel: 919-836-1790; Fax: 919-833-4667.
School—Tel: 919-832-4711; Fax: 919-832-8329. Mrs. Donna Moss, Prin.
Lay Teachers 18; Students 265.
Catechesis/Religious Programs—D.R.E.: Barbara Shamburger; Sue O'Neill.
Students 234.

2—CATHOLIC STUDENT CENTER, NORTH CAROLINA STATE UNIVERSITY (1974), Rev. Alan J. Dash.
Mailing Address: 600 Bilyeu St., 27606. Tel: 919-833-9668; Fax: 919-833-1194.
Res., 136 N. King Charles Rd., 27610. Tel: 919-833-3248.
Doggett Center at Aquinas House: 600 Bilyeu St., 27606. Tel: 919-833-9668; Fax: 919-833-1194.

3—OUR LADY OF LOURDES (1954), Rev. Msgr. John F. O'Connor; Rev. Frank M. Raffo; Deacon Myles J. Charlesworth.
Office: 2718 Overbrook Dr., 27608. Tel: 919-782-1973; Fax: 919-571-9957.
Res., 2912 Anderson Dr., 27608. Tel: 919-781-9784.
School—2710 Overbrook Dr., 27608. Tel: 919-782-1670. Mrs. Susan Goethals, Prin.
Sisters of Notre Dame 2; Lay Teachers 20; Students 537.
Catechesis/Religious Programs—D.R.E.: Gail Halada, (PreK-8); Al Benthal, (Adult).
Students 521.

4—ST. FRANCIS OF ASSISI (1982), Revs. Daniel Kenna, O.F.M.; Mark Reamer, O.F.M.
Res., 11401 Leesville Rd., 27613. Tel: 919-847-8205; Fax: 919-870-1790. [CEM]
Catechesis/Religious Programs—Tel: 919-847-8205. D.R.E.: Maureen Leahy, (Grades PreK-6); Ann Danyluk, (Grades 7-9); Cathy Felder, (Grades 10-12); Colleen McCarthy, (High School); Peggy Dunbeck Monti, (Dir. of Evangelization); Ann Murray, (Family).
Students 1,116.

5—ST. JOSEPH (1968), Rev. Thanh N. Nguyen.
Res., 630 Peartree Ln., 27610. Tel: 919-231-6364; Fax: 919-231-9884.
Catechesis/Religious Programs—Ken Killinger, D.R.E.
Students 80.

6—ST. LUKE THE EVANGELIST (1985), Rev. David D. Brockman.
Res., 12317 Bayleaf Church Rd., 27614-9165. Tel: 919-870-1490.
Church—12333 Bayleaf Church Rd., 27614-9165. Tel: 919-848-1533; Fax: 919-848-0662.
Catechesis/Religious Programs—Tel: 919-848-3197.
Students 250.

7—ST. RAPHAEL (1966), Revs. Robert S. Curry, S.J.; Shay W. Auerbach, S.J.; William R. Ryan, S.J. Pastoral Assocs.: Deacons Robert T. Madey; Frank Barnes; William A. Abel; Marion Danforth; Marge Wood. In res., Rev. Robert Hussey, S.J.
Res., 5801 Falls of Neuse Rd., 27609. Tel: 919-876-1581; Fax: 919-872-3723. [CEM]
School—St. Raphael, Tel: 919-876-1581, Ext. 713. John Pendergrass, Prin.
Students 257.
St. Raphael Catholic Early Childhood Center—Tel: 919-876-1581, Ext. 728; Fax: 919-872-3723. Carrie Griffith, Dir.
Students 156.
Catechesis/Religious Programs—Tel: 919-876-1668; Fax: 919-872-3723. Mary Lynn Whittaker, D.R.E. (PreK-5).
Students 768.

OUTSIDE THE CITY OF RALEIGH

Ahoskie, Hertford Co., St. Charles Borromeo (1944), Rev. Stephen C. Worsley.
Res., P.O. Box 605, 27910. Tel: 252-332-2939.
Catechesis/Religious Programs—Students 54.
Mission—Scotland Neck, Halifax Co., St. Anne.

Apex, Wake Co., St. Andrew the Apostle (1983), Revs. David E. Fitzgerald, S.A.; Alban Carroll, S.A.; Francis Eldridge, S.A.
Res., 3008 Old Ralegh Rd., 27502. Tel: 919-362-0414; Fax: 919-362-5778.
Catechesis/Religious Programs—Tel: 919-362-1673.
Students 1308.

St. Mary Magdalene (1997), Rev. Donald F. Staib.
625 Magdala Pl., 27502. Tel: 919-657-4800; Fax: 919-657-4805.
School—
Catechesis/Religious Programs—Students 217.

Burgaw, Pender Co., St. Joseph (1908), Rev. Drew Perry.
Church & Res.: 1303 Hwy. 117 S., 28425. Tel: 910-259-2601; Fax: 910-259-7695. [CEM]
Catechesis/Religious Programs—D.R.E.: Brian Wright, (St. Joseph); Marcia Hatcher, (Transfiguration).
Students 45.
Mission—Wallace, Duplin Co., Transfiguration, (1953) 506 E. Main St., Wallace, 28466. Tel: 910-285-1876.

Burlington, Alamance Co., Blessed Sacrament (1928), Revs. Briant Cullinane, O.F.M. Conv.; Carlos Arce, O.F.M.Conv.; Robert Benko, O.F.M.Conv. In res., Revs. Terence Pescatore, O.F.M. Conv.; John Ruffo, O.F.M.Conv.
Mailing Address: P.O. Box 619, 27216. Tel: 336-226-8796; Fax: 336-227-2896.
Res., 1236 Westbrook Ave., Elon College, 27244. Tel: 336-446-6753.
School—Tel: 336-570-0019; Fax: 336-570-9623. Mr. George Boschini, Prin.
Lay Teachers 27; Students 346.
Catechesis/Religious Programs—Tel: 336-570-0013. Mrs. Mary Key, D.R.E.
Students 364.

Buxton, Dare Co., Our Lady of the Seas, Rev. Andre C. Izac.
Mailing Address: P.O. Box 399, 27920. Tel: 252-995-6370.

Cary, Wake Co., St. Michael the Archangel (1962), Rev. Msgr. John A. Wall; Revs. Philip M. Tighe; William J. Upah.
Res., 804 High House Rd., 27513. Tel: 919-468-6100; Fax: 919-468-6130.
Catechesis/Religious Programs—Tel: 919-468-6120. Mollie Berry, D.R.E.
Students 1,680.

Castle Hayne, New Hanover Co., St. Stanislaus Kostka (1914) (Polish), Rev. Ryszard Kolodziej.
Church & Res.: 4849 Castle Hayne Rd., 28429-4849. Tel: 910-675-2336 (Office); Fax: 910-675-3116. [CEM]
Catechesis/Religious Programs—Students 60.

Chapel Hill, Orange Co., St. Thomas More (1940), Revs. John G. Durbin; Christopher J. Flanagan. Pastoral Assocs.: Ms. Theresa Keller; Sr. Marie St. Paul Alspaugh, S.S.J.
Parish Offices: 940 Carmichael St., 27514-4203. Tel: 919-942-1040; Fax: 919-942-6193.
Res., 301 Rossburn Way, 27516. Tel: 919-967-8485.
School—(Grades K-8) 920 Carmichael St., 27514. Tel: 919-929-1546; Fax: 919-929-1783. Sr. Catherine Michael Fee, S.S.J., Prin.
Sisters 1; Lay Teachers 28; Students 452.
Catechesis/Religious Programs—Tel: 919-933-1041. D.R.E.: Jim Hynes; Leo Moreda.
Students 507.

Newman Catholic Student Center, University of North Carolina (1968), Revs. Phillip M. Leach; Edward P. Mahoney.
Res., 218 Pittsboro St., 27516-2738. Tel: 919-929-3730; Fax: 919-929-3778.
Catechesis/Religious Programs—Tel: 919-933-1041.
Students 140.

Clinton, Sampson Co., Immaculate Conception (1910), Revs. John Williams; Jose Antonio Galvez, O.F.M. Conv.
Mailing Address: P.O. Box 859, 28329. Tel: 910-592-1384; Fax: 910-592-8725.
Mission—Mount Olive, Duplin Co., Posada Guadalupana, (1993).
Station—San Juan, Old Hwy. 701, Ingold, Tel: 910-592-1384.

Dunn, Harnett Co., Sacred Heart (1916), Rev. Paul M. Parkerson.
Mailing Address: P.O. Box 535, 28335. Tel: 910-891-1972; Fax: 910-891-5767.
Res., 209 S. Ellis Ave., 28334. Tel: 910-892-3414.
Catechesis/Religious Programs—Mrs. Jan Rebman, D.R.E.
Students 115.

Durham, Durham Co.,

1—Holy Cross, (1938) (African American), Rev. Brendan R. Horan, S.J.
Res., 1400 S. Alston Ave., 27707. Tel: 919-682-4852; Fax: 919-688-6160.
Catechesis/Religious Programs—Tel: 919-688-6160. Helen Hudson, D.R.E.
Students 90.

2—Holy Infant, (1970), Revs. John E. McGee, O.S.F.S.; Richard E. Cleary, O.S.F.S.
Res., 5000 South Park Dr., 27713-9470. Tel: 919-544-7135; Fax: 919-544-1799. [CEM]
Catechesis/Religious Programs—Students 205.

3—Immaculate Conception, (1906), Revs. David J. McBriar, O.F.M.; John J. Heffernan, O.F.M.; Patrick E. Tuttle, O.F.M.; Deacon Laurence DeCarolis.
Res., 725 Burch Ave., 27701. Tel: 919-682-3449; Fax: 919-682-7999.
School—Immaculata, 721 Burch Ave., 27701. Tel: 919-682-5847; Fax: 919-956-7073. Mr. John Castranio, Prin.
Lay Teachers 32; Students 433.
Catechesis/Religious Programs—Barbara Pegg, D.R.E.
Students 377.

4—St. Matthew, (1990), Rev. John G. Parish (LA).
Res., 1001 Mason Rd., 27712. Tel: 919-479-1001; Fax: 919-479-4848. [CEM]
Catechesis/Religious Programs—Lynn Sale, D.R.E.
Students 180.

Edenton, Chowan Co., St. Anne (1858), Rev. Roch T. Drozdzik.
Mailing Address: P.O. Box 422, 27932. [CEM]
Church—207 N. Broad St., 27932. Tel: 919-482-2617; Fax: 252-482-8702.
Catechesis/Religious Programs—Students 62.
Mission—Columbia, Tyrrell, All Souls, Helen Randlett, 462 Old Cherry Rd., Creswell, 27928. Tel: 252-797-4068.

Elizabeth City, Pasquotank Co., Holy Family (1915), Rev. John L. Gillespie.
Mailing Address: 1453 N. Road St., 27906-1525. Tel: 252-338-2521; Fax: 252-338-4183.
Res., 1453 N. Road St., 27909. Tel: 919-335-4419.
Catechesis/Religious Programs—Nicole Lavinder, D.R.E.
Students 215.
Station—Currituck, Currituck Senior Citizens Center, Tel: 919-232-3505.

Farmville, Pitt Co., St. Elizabeth (1931) (Lebanese), Sr. Grace Campbell, I.H.M., Pastoral Admin.
Mailing Address: P.O. Box 189, 27828. Tel: 252-753-4367; Fax: 252-753-4367.
Catechesis/Religious Programs—Students 17.

Fayetteville, Cumberland Co., St. Ann (1940) (African American), Revs. Thomas R. Davis; Joseph J. Yaeger.
Office:—365 N. Cool Spring St., 28301. Tel: 910-483-3216; Fax: 910-483-4185.
Res., 365 N. Cool Spring St., 28301. Tel: 910-483-5871.
School—Tel: 910-483-3902; Fax: 910-483-3195. Sr. Ann Claire D.C., Prin.
Daughters of Charity 3; Lay Teachers 12; Students 180.
Catechesis/Religious Programs—Tel: 910-488-7137; Fax: 910-483-4185. Michael Patterson, D.R.E.
Students 130.
Convent—1933 Martindale Dr., 28304. Tel: 910-484-1675.

St. Elizabeth Ann Seton (1981), Rev. Willard Rucinski, O.S.F.S.
Res., 700 Carnegie St., 28311. Tel: 910-488-8274; Fax: 910-488-7116.
Catechesis/Religious Programs—Dianne VanPelt, D.R.E.
Students 239.

St. Patrick (1824), Revs. John R. Kelly; Frank M. Raffo, Jr.
Mailing Address: 2840 Village Dr., 28304-3813. Tel: 910-323-2410; Fax: 910-323-3006.
Res., 433 Holly Ln., 28305. Tel: 910-484-8253.
School—1620 Marlborough Rd., 28304. Tel: 910-323-1865. Mr. Tom Manion, Prin.
Lay Teachers 12; Students 262.
Catechesis/Religious Programs—Tel: 910-323-2410, Ext. 107; Fax: 910-323-3006. Margaret Blanc, D.R.E.
Students 392.

Fuquay-Varina, Wake Co., St. Bernadette (1987), Sr. Claudia Bronsing, Pastoral Admin.; Deacon Anthony Meier.
Mailing Address: 1005 Wilbon Rd., 27526-9702. Tel: 919-552-8758; Fax: 919-552-1846.
Catechesis/Religious Programs—Tel: 919-552-8758. Mrs. Michele Dexter, D.R.E.
Students 285.
Hispanic Office—Tel: 919-552-2922.

Garner, Wake Co., St. Mary, Mother of the Church (1966), Rev. Robert T. Schriber; Deacon Leo Tapler.
Res., 1008 Vandora Springs Rd., 27529. Tel: 919-772-5777; 919-772-5524 (Office); Fax: 919-772-5534.
Catechesis/Religious Programs—Tel: 919-772-5199. Kathy Hardy, D.R.E.
Students 343.

Goldsboro, Wayne Co., St. Mary (1889), Revs. William J. Ruhl, O.S.F.S.; Thomas P. Norris, O.S.F.S.
Res., 1000 N. Jefferson Ave., 27530-3141. Tel: 919-734-5033; Fax: 919-580-0730.
School—Tel: 919-735-1931; Fax: 919-735-1917. Lynn P. Magoon, Prin.
Sisters, Servants of the Immaculate Heart of Mary 3; Lay Teachers 14; Students 263.
Catechesis/Religious Programs—Mrs. Carole M. Sears, D.R.E.
Students 182.

Greenville, Pitt Co., St. Gabriel (1936), Rev. Thomas McCann, C.P.; Lucille Gorham, Pastoral Assoc.
Res., 1120 Martin Luther King Jr. Dr., 27834. Tel: 252-758-1504; Fax: 252-758-1479.
Catechesis/Religious Programs—Students 45.

St. Peter's (1884), Revs. Justin Kerber, C.P.; Patrick Geinzer, C.P.
Res., 2700 E. Fourth St., 27858. Tel: 252-757-3259; Fax: 252-752-1499.
School—Tel: 252-752-3529; Fax: 252-752-7604. Ramon Espinosa, Prin.
Lay Teachers 33; Students 540.
Catechesis/Religious Programs—Tel: 252-752-1718. Sarah McPherson, D.R.E.
Students 292.

Hampstead, Pender Co., St. Jude the Apostle (1992), Rev. Terrence Collins.
Mailing Address: 18737 Hwy. 17 N., 28443. Tel: 910-270-1477; Fax: 910-270-1424.
Res., 557 Osprey Dr., Hempstead, 28443. Tel: 910-273-1689.
Catechesis/Religious Programs—Students 70.
Mission—Surf City, Pender Co., St. Mary, Gate of Heaven.

Havelock, Craven Co., Annunciation (1953), Rev. Peter McKeown, M.S.; Bro. Robert Belliveau, M.S.
Mailing Address: P.O. Box 720, 28532-0177. Tel: 252-447-2112; Fax: 252-447-2595.
School—Tel: 252-447-3137; Fax: 252-447-3137. Mrs. June Pietras, Prin.
Lay Teachers 15; Students 247.
Catechesis/Religious Programs—246 E. Main St., 28532. Tel: 252-447-2436; Fax: 252-447-2436. Mrs. Maureen McInerney, D.R.E.
Students 160.

Henderson, Vance Co., St. James the Greater (1925). Consolidated St. Paul and St. Catherine of Siena, Oxford merged to form St. James the Greater. Rev. J. William Long.
Res., 3275 Hwy. 158 Bypass, 27536. Tel: 252-438-3124; Fax: 252-438-3214. [CEM][JC]
Catechesis/Religious Programs—Students 160.
Mission—Warrenton, Warren Co., St. Joseph, Norlina Rd., Warrenton, 27589. Tel: 252-438-3124.

Hillsborough, Orange Co., Holy Family (1989), Sr. Marie Therese Bugge, O.S.U., Pastoral Admin.
Mailing Address: 216 Governer Burke Rd., 27278. Tel: 919-732-1030; Fax: 919-732-7852.
Catechesis/Religious Programs—Students 120.

Hope Mills, Cumberland Co., Good Shepherd (1981), Very Rev. Thomas J. Gaul, V.F.
Res., 5050 Oak St., 28348. Tel: 910-425-1590; Fax: 910-423-9973.
Catechesis/Religious Programs—Tel: 910-425-5617. Janice Carnahan, D.R.E.
Students 416.

Jacksonville, Onslow Co., Shrine of the Infant of Prague, Church of the Holy Spirit (1941), Revs. Thomas R. Davis; Douglas J. Smiley.
Mailing Address: P.O. Drawer 556, 28541. Tel: 910-347-4196; Fax: 910-347-9338.
Res., 205 Chaney Ave., 28540. Tel: 910-347-8881.
School—St. Francis of Assisi, Tel: 910-353-1300; 455-0838; Fax: 910-353-1305. Michele Estep, Prin.
Lay Teachers 20; Students 180.
Catechesis/Religious Programs—Tel: 910-455-1296. Sr. Cecilia McClain, S.C., D.R.E.
Students 416.

Kinston, Lenoir Co., Holy Spirit Catholic Church (1921) (African American-Hispanic). (Formerly Holy Trinity-Our Lady of the Atonement). Rev. Douglas Reed; Sr. Augustine Serrano, O.S.F.
Mailing Address: 400 Academy Heights Rd., 28504. Tel: 252-523-8898; Fax: 252-527-9495.
Res., 137 Rae Rd., 28504.
Church—400 Academy Heights Rd., 28504.
Catechesis/Religious Programs—Pat Kaspryzk, D.R.E.
Students 115.

Kitty Hawk, Dare Co., Holy Redeemer (1935), Very Rev. Michael A. Butler, V.F.; Thomas Herrity, Bus. Mgr.
Mailing Address: P.O. Box 510, 27949. Tel: 252-261-4700; Fax: 252-261-1405.
Office: 301 W. Kitty Hawk Rd., 27949.
Res., 109 Sunrise View, 27949. Tel: 252-261-8935.
Catechesis/Religious Programs—Sr. Mary Kay Bush S.C., D.R.E.
Students 384.
Missions—Nags Head, Dare Co., Holy Trinity, 73315 Virginia Dare Tr., Nags Head, 27959.; Buxton, Dare Co., Our Lady of the Seas, P.O. Box 399, Buxton, 27920-0399. Tel: 919-995-6370.
Stations—Ocracoke, Annunciation, Tel: 919-995-6370; Corolla, Corolla Chapel, Tel: 919-441-7220.

Laurinburg, Scotland Co., St. Mary (1946), Rev. Kevin Fahey.
Mailing Address: P.O. Box 1148, 28353-1148. Tel: 910-276-1478; 276-4468 (Office); Fax: 910-276-9519. [JC]
Catechesis/Religious Programs—Students 105.

Louisburg, Franklin Co., Our Lady of the Rosary (1999), Sr. Elizabeth Bullen, I.H.M., Admin.
Church—408 W. Noble St., 27549. Tel: 919-497-3124; Fax: 919-497-3124.
Catechesis/Religious Programs—Students 30.

Lumberton, Robeson Co., St. Francis De Sales (1938), Revs. Robert J. Yankevitch, S.J.; Marcus Ayala, O.F.M. Conv.
Mailing Address: P.O. Box 2249, 28359-2249. Tel: 910-739-4723; Fax: 910-739-5443.
Res., 2000 Elizabethtown Rd., 28358.
Catechesis/Religious Programs—Tel: 910-739-4713.
Students 99.
Mission—Red Springs, Robeson Co., St. Andrew, 506 E. 4th Ave., Red Springs, 28377. Tel: 910-843-3440.

Morehead City, Carteret Co., St. Egbert (1929), Very Revs. Gregory D. Spencer, Admin.; Francis R. Moeslein, Pastor Emeritus; Deacon Albert Feneis.
Parish Hall—1706 Evans St., 28557. Tel: 252-726-3559; Fax: 252-726-2232.
Res., 1612 Evans St., 28557. Tel: 252-726-2535.
School—Tel: 252-726-3418. Mrs. Lesley Ferguson, Prin.
Lay Teachers 7; Students 136.
Catechesis/Religious Programs—Tel: 919-726-9696. Jeanette Fugate, D.R.E.
Students 155.

New Bern, Craven Co., St. Paul (1821), Very Rev. Ernest J. Ruede, V.F.; Rev. Msgr. James R. Jones, Pastor Emeritus; Sr. Monique Dissen, H.M., Pastoral Assoc.; Deacon William Hunt, Pastoral Assoc.
Rectory: 3108 Farrior Cir., 28562. Tel: 252-638-4436.
Church—3005 Country Club Rd., 28562. Tel: 252-638-1984; Fax: 252-638-2144. [CEM]
School—3007 Country Club Rd., 28562. Tel: 252-633-0100; Fax: 252-633-4457. Sr. Susan Therese Armbruster, I.H.M., Prin.
Sisters, Servants of the Immaculate Heart of Mary 3; Lay Teachers 12; Students 310.
Catechesis/Religious Programs—Tel: 252-633-3030. Joy Harsen, D.R.E.
Students 215.

Newton Grove, Sampson Co., Our Lady of Guadalupe (1871), Rev. Bernard (Ned) Shlesinger, III.
Office: P.O. Box 100, 28366. Tel: 910-594-0287; Fax: 910-594-1749.
Res., 211 Irwin Dr., 28366. Tel: 910-594-0152. [CEM]
Catechesis/Religious Programs—Students 143.

Oriental, Saint Peter the Fisherman, Sr. Maria Goretti Timperio, I.H.M., Pastoral Assoc.
Res., 504 Broad St., 28571. Tel: 252-249-3687.

Pinehurst, Moore Co., Sacred Heart (1919), Revs. William L. Pitts; Robert W. Diegelman.
Mailing Address: P.O. Box 1768, 28370. Tel: 910-295-6550; Fax: 910-255-0299.
Catechesis/Religious Programs—Tel: 910-295-3072. Mrs. Barbara Kemple, D.R.E.
Students 254.
Mission—Robbins, Moore Co., Blessed Juan Diego, 100 S. Ross, Robbins, 27325.

Plymouth, Washington Co., St. Joan of Arc (1959), Sr. Dolores Glick, M.H.S.H., Pastoral Admin.
Mailing Address: P.O. Box 822, 27962. Tel: 919-793-4052; Fax: 919-793-4052.
Catechesis/Religious Programs—Students 7.

Raeford, Hoke Co., St. Elizabeth of Hungary (1959), Sr. Jeanne Morgan, S.S.J., Pastoral Admin.
Res., 124 Palmer St., 28376-9322. Tel: 910-875-8803; Fax: 910-875-8803.
Catechesis/Religious Programs—Students 50.

Riegelwood, Columbus Co., Christ the King (1964), Rev. J. Douglas Lawson, Admin.
Mailing Address: P.O. Box 155, 28456. Tel: 910-655-3313.

Roanoke Rapids, Halifax Co., St. John the Baptist (1931), Rev. Mark J. Betti.
Res., 115 E. Ninth St., 27870. Tel: 252-537-4667; Fax: 252-535-2076.
Catechesis/Religious Programs—Teri Bales, D.R.E. Students 55.

Rocky Mount, Nash & Edgecombe Cos., Our Lady of Perpetual Help (1892), Revs. JaVan J. Saxon; Richard W. Turner.
Mailing Address: 331 Hammond St., 27804. Tel: 252-972-0452; Fax: 252-972-4780.
Res., 501 Hammond St., 27804. Tel: 252-972-1949; Fax: 252-972-4780.
School—Tel: 252-972-1971. Mr. Steve Coryell, Prin. Lay Teachers 8; Students 120.
Catechesis/Religious Programs—Tel: 252-972-0498. Dianne Young, D.R.E.
Students 250.
Mission—Rocky Mount, Nash & Edgecombe Cos., Immaculate Conception, 723 Virginia Ave., 27804.

Roxboro, Person Co., SS. Mary and Edward (1935), Rev. Robert P. Staley.
Res., 611 N. Main St., 27573-5040. Tel: 336-599-4122; Fax: 336-598-0412.
Mission—Butner, St. Bernadette.

Sanford, Lee Co., St. Stephen (1932), Rev. John J. Forbes.
Res., 2402 Wicker St. Ext., 27330-9352. Tel: 919-776-1532; Fax: 919-775-1399.
Catechesis/Religious Programs—Tel: 919-776-3843.
Students 378.

Shallotte, Brunswick Co., St. Brendan the Navigator (1983), Rev. Michael C. Connolly, O.S.F.S.
Mailing Address: Box 2984, 28459-9999. Tel: 910-754-8544; Fax: 910-755-6046.
Church & Office: 5101 Ocean Hwy. W., 28459. [JC]
Catechesis/Religious Programs—Tel: 910-754-8544.
Students 70.

Siler City, Chatham Co., St. Julia (1961) (Hispanic), Revs. Daniel M. Quackenbush, O.F.M.Conv.; Conall C. McHugh, O.F.M. Conv.
Mailing Address: 1002 W. Third St., 27344. Tel: 919-742-5584; Fax: 919-742-4917.
Catechesis/Religious Programs—Students 108.

Smithfield, Johnston Co., St. Ann (1935), Rev. Joseph G. Mulroney, J.C.L.
Res., 113 N. Seventh St., 27577. Tel: 919-934-2084; Fax: 919-934-4639.
Catechesis/Religious Programs—Students 237.

Southern Pines, Moore Co., St. Anthony of Padua (1895), Rev. James F. Butler; Sr. Mary Anne Pierson, M.S.B.T., Admin.
Mailing Address: P.O. Box 29, 28388-0029. Tel: 910-692-6613; Fax: 910-692-4964.
Res., 23 Village in the Woods, 28387. Tel: 910-693-7789; Fax: 910-692-4361.
Catechesis/Religious Programs—Tel: 910-692-6241. Mary Sue Riddle, D.R.E.
Students 127.

Southport, Brunswick Co., Sacred Heart (1941), Rev. J. Douglas Lawson; Deacon Eugene Gillis (CHL); Patricia Ciemnicki, Dir. Pastoral Svcs.
Mailing Address: 5269 Dosher Cutoff, S.E., 28461. Tel: 910-457-6173; Fax: 910-457-6421.
Res., 213 Yaupon Dr., 28461. Tel: 910-457-0223.
Catechesis/Religious Programs—Tel: 910-457-6173. D.R.E.: Patricia Novotny; Ruthann Horan.
Students 141.

Swansboro, Onslow Co., St. Mildred (1947), Rev. Donald G. Baribeau, M.S.
Res., 616 Sabiston Dr., 28584-9674. Tel: 910-326-4370; Fax: 910-326-7825. [CEM]
Catechesis/Religious Programs—Tel: 910-326-5589. Laura Leblanc, D.R.E.
Students 140.

Tarboro, Edgecombe Co., St. Catherine (1934), Rev. Edward Deviny, C.P.
Res., 1004 St. David St., 27886. Tel: 919-823-3866; Fax: 919-824-0412.
Catechesis/Religious Programs—Students 32.

Wake Forest, Wake Co., St. Catherine of Siena (1940), Rev. Robert J. Kus.
Church—520 W. Holding Ave., 27587. Tel: 919-570-0070; Fax: 919-570-0071.
Catechesis/Religious Programs—Susan Gammon, D.R.E.
Students 546.

Washington, Beaufort Co., Mother of Mercy (1963), Rev. Gerald R. Biron, M.S.
Res., 112 W. Ninth St., 27889. Tel: 252-946-2941; Fax: 252-946-1399.
Church—111 W. Ninth St., 27889.
Catechesis/Religious Programs—Tel: 919-946-8808. Dana Lawson, D.R.E.
Students 46.

Wendell, Wake Co., St. Eugene (1948), Rev. Thomas F. Watkins; Deacon Willie Foggie.
Mailing Address: P.O. Box 188, 27591. Tel: 919-365-7114; Fax: 919-365-9431.
Catechesis/Religious Programs—Tel: 919-365-9431. Gail Hernandez, D.R.E.
Students 173.

Whiteville, Columbus Co., Sacred Heart (1938), Rev. James P. Byrne, O.S.F.S.
Res., 402 N. Lee St., 28472. Tel: 910-642-3895; Fax: 910-640-1948.
Catechesis/Religious Programs—Students 61.
Mission—Elizabethtown, Bladen Co., Our Lady of the Snows, 701 Broad St., Elizabethtown, 28337. Tel: 910-862-4998; Fax: 910-862-7298.

Williamston, Martin Co., Holy Trinity (1951), Sr. Kieran Williams, I.H.M., Pastoral Admin.
Mailing Address: P.O. Box 894, 27892-0894. Tel: 252-792-4091; Fax: 252-792-4091.
Church—Hwy. 17-13 Bypass, 27892. Tel: 252-792-4306.
Catechesis/Religious Programs—Students 101.

Wilmington, New Hanover Co., Immaculate Conception (1925), Revs. Jim Behan, O.S.F.S.; Barry R. Strong, O.S.F.S.
Church—6650 Carolina Beach Rd., 28412. Tel: 910-791-1003; Fax: 910-791-0081.
Catechesis/Religious Programs—6336 Myrtle Grove Rd., Wilm, 28409. Carol Cholette, D.R.E.
Students 201.

St. Mark (1978) (Hispanic), Revs. Matthew D. Hendrick; M. Arturo Cabra.
Church—1011 Eastwood Rd., 28403. Tel: 910-392-0720; Fax: 910-392-6777.
Catechesis/Religious Programs—Tel: 910-793-5974. Ms. Anne Doyle, D.R.E.
Students 561.
Mission—Riegelwood, Columbus Co., Christ the King, P.O. Box 155, Riegelwood, 28456-0155.

St. Mary (1821), Very Rev. James M. Labosky, V.F.; Rev. Msgr. Thomas P. Hadden, Pastor Emeritus; Daniel M. Bifalco, Parish Admin.
Res., 405 Ann St., 28401-4592. Tel: 910-762-5491; Fax: 910-762-9664.
School—Tel: 910-762-6517; Fax: 910-762-9646. Gina DeLong, Prin.
Lay Teachers 24; Students 380.
St. Thomas Preschool—Tel: 910-762-7764; Fax: 910-762-9646. Helen Pennington, Dir.
Lay Teachers 4; Students 48.
Catechesis/Religious Programs—Tel: 910-251-9992. Sr. Barbara Marie Cady, S.U., D.R.E.
Students 191.

Wilson, Wilson Co., St. Alphonsus De Liguori. Closed. For sacramental records contact St. Therese, Wilson.

Church of St. Therese (1923), Revs. Trent L. Watts; Eduardo Marrugo Ripoll (Columbia).
Church and Office: 700 Nash St., N.E., 27893-3047. Tel: 252-237-3019; Fax: 252-237-2042.
Res., 200 Gray St., N.E., 27893-3710. Tel: 252-237-0143.
School—(Grades PreK-5). Tel: 252-237-3019, Ext. 18; Fax: 252-237-2042.
Lay Teachers 11; Students 131.
Catechesis/Religious Programs—Tel: 252-237-3019.
Students 166.

Wrightsville Beach, New Hanover Co., St. Therese (1939), Rev. Eugene Grabowski.
Res., 209 S. Lumina Ave., 28480. Tel: 910-256-2471; Fax: 910-256-2459.

Catechesis/Religious Programs—Students 110.

Special Assignment:
Reverend Fathers—
Clay, Michael G., 744 Gimghoul St., Chapel Hill, NC
Lewis, Gerald, Vicar Gen., 715 Nazareth St., Raleigh, NC 27606
Mahoney, Edward P., Duke University, Durham, NC 27706

On Duty Outside the Diocese:
Reverend Fathers—
Carlson, Steven V., HHC 122nd Signal BN, Unit 15089, Apo, AP 96258-0350
Fitzgerald, R. Martin, 87 Fox Rd. #716, Waltham, MA 02451
Garneau, F. James, Pontifical College Josephinum, 7625 North High St., Columbus, OH 43235
Ingham, Jeffrey A., The Presbytery, 45 Lee Rd., Lynton, Devon EX356BX England

Absent on Leave:
Reverend Fathers—
Dorsel, John F.
Klaus, Joseph J.

Retired:
Reverend Monsignors—
Hadden, Thomas P., 1506 Village Dr., #4, Wilmington, NC 28401-7556
Jones, James, 2228 Fox Horn Rd., New Bern, NC 28562. Tel: 252-635-5318
Reverend Fathers—
Bryon, Paul J., 211 McCauley St., Chapel Hill, NC 27516. Tel: 919-968-1657
Carcich, G. John, 592 Central Dr., Villa F1, Southern Pines, NC 28387. Tel: 910-692-6434
Creel, Jesse, St. Albans, 120-32 193rd St., Jamaica, NY 11412-3637. Tel: 708-525-0880
Ghisalberti, Giacomo G., 10820 N.Kings Rd., #2, P.M.B. 143, Myrtle Beach, SC 29572
Giacomini, Antonio, O.F.M.Cap., Stratford Arms, Apt. 9-B, Greenville, NC 27858
Harper, John, St. Joseph of the Pines, 103 Gossman St., Room 860, Southern Pines, NC 28387. Tel: 910-692-5814
Keaney, James P., 1316 E. Ninth St., Roanoke Rapids, NC 27870. Tel: 252-535-4093
Ketchersid, Corbin W., 146-C Wayan Creek Dr., Fayetteville, NC 28314. Tel: 910-488-1797
Lawson, Robert T., 590 Central Ave., Villa E-3, Southern Pines, NC 28389. Tel: 910-695-4340
Maloney, Francis G., 592 Central Ave., Villa F.3, Southern Pines, NC 28387
Moeslein, Francis R., 2106 Joslyn Dr., Morehead City, NC 26557-9200. Tel: 252-726-3579
Mulholland, Charles H., Sunrise Assisted Living of Raleigh, 4801 Edwards Mill Rd., Raleigh, NC 27612. Tel: 919-834-7545
Parker, Kenneth, 704 McIntosh Rd., Carthage, NC 28327. Tel: 910-245-4640
Richardson, John L., 1889 Norwood St., S.W., Schooner's Pointe, Ocean Isle Beach, NC 28469
Shea, Robert F., 592 Central Ave., Villa F.4, Southern Pines, NC 28387

Permanent Deacons:
Barnes, Frank, St. Rafael, Raleigh
Broering, Harry, Mother of Mercy, Washington
Charlesworth, Myles, Our Lady of Lourdes, Raleigh
Davis, William, St. Stanislaus, Castle Hayne
DeCarolis, Lawrence, Immaculate Conception, Durham
Evans, Forest, Holy Family, Hillsborough
Feneis, Al, St. Egbert, Morehead City
Foggie, Willie, St. Eugene, Wendell
Gillis, Eugene, Sacred Heart, Southport
Goodrow, Joseph, Infant of Prague, Jacksonville
Hanemann, Louis, St. Michael, Cary
Hubisz, John, N.C.S.U. Aquinas House, Raleigh
Hunt, William, St. Paul, New Bern
Junginger, George, St. Michael, Cary
Lewandowski, Stephen, St. Joseph, Raleigh
Madey, Robert, St. Raphael, Raleigh
McGahran, Robert, St. Brendan, Shallotte
Meier, Anthony, St. Bernadette, Fuquay-Varina
Rodriguez, Jorge, Unassigned
Schoebel, James, Ft. Bragg, Fayetteville
Tapler, Leopold, St. Mary, Garner
Wobser, Don, Holy Redeemer, Kitty Hawk

INSTITUTIONS LOCATED IN THE DIOCESE

[A] HIGH SCHOOLS

RALEIGH. *Cardinal Gibbons Memorial High School*, 1401 Edwards Mill Rd., 27607. Tel: 919-834-1625; Fax: 919-834-9771.
E-mail: aj1401@hotmail.com
Bro. Michel Bettigole, O.S.F., Prin. Priests 1; Brothers 4; Sisters 3; Deacons 1; Lay Teachers 62; Students 861.

[B] CHILD CARE CENTERS

RALEIGH. *St. Joseph Pre-School*, 624 Peartree Ln., 27610. Tel: 919-231-4545; Fax: 919-231-9884.
E-mail: margie@ibm.net

Mrs. Marjorie Shaughnessy, Dir. Students 12.

St. Raphael Catholic School and Early Childhood Center, 5801 Falls of the Neuse Rd., 27609. Tel: 919-876-3526; Fax: 919-872-3723. Mr. John Pendergrass, Prin.; Mrs. Carrie Griffith, Dir. Lay Teachers 38; Students 490.

APEX. *Saint Andrew Early Childhood Center*, 3008 Old Raleigh Rd., 27502. Tel: 919-387-8656. Eileen Vaughan, Co-Dir.; Ann Graf, Co-Dir. Total Staff 23; Students 132.

CARY. *St. Michael's Early Childhood Center*, 804 High House Rd., 27513. Tel: 919-468-6110; Fax: 919-468-6130. Ms. Elana O'Connell, Dir. Total Staff 23; Students 216.

GARNER. *St. Mary Child Development Center*, 1008 Vandora Springs Rd., 27529. Tel: 919-772-0009; Fax: 919-772-5534. Ms. Karen Williams, Dir. Lay Teachers 7; Total Staff 16; Students 132.

WILMINGTON. *St. Thomas Child Development Center*, 109 S. Second St., 28401. Tel: 910-799-9843; Fax: 910-762-9664. Helen F. Pennington, Dir. Total Staff 10; Lay Teachers 6; Students 55.

[C] GENERAL HOSPITALS

SOUTHERN PINES. *St. Joseph of the Pines*, 590 Central Dr., 28387-2899. Tel: 910-295-3920; Fax: 910-695-2371.
Web site: www.sjp.org
For a complete listing, refer to the Hospitals section.

[D] CATHOLIC SOCIAL SERVICES

RALEIGH. *Catholic Social Ministries of the Diocese of Raleigh, Inc.*, 715 Nazareth St., 27606-2187. Tel: 919-821-9750; Fax: 919-821-9712. Kathleen Walsh, A.C.S.W, Diocesan Dir. Total Staff 50; Total Assisted 46,508.

Regional Office, 226 Hillsborough St., 27605. Tel: 919-832-0225; Fax: 919-832-0736. Rick Miller-Haraway, L.C.S.W.

Regional Office, 4000 Princess Pl. Dr., Wilmington, 28405. Tel: 910-251-8130; Fax: 910-251-8491. Diane Pisczek, M.Ed., Dir.

Regional Office, 1424 Broad St., P.O. Box 647, Durham, 27702. Tel: 919-286-1964; Fax: 919-286-4001. Susan Gilbertson, L.C.S.W.

Regional Office, 3830 Boone Trail, Fayetteville, 28306-2791. Tel: 910-424-2020; Fax: 910-424-8435. Stephen Dow, L.C.S.W.

Angel Place, 226 Hillsborough St., 27603. Tel: 919-832-0225; Fax: 919-832-0736.

Regional Office, 3405 Trent Rd., P.O. Box 14930, New Bern, 28561. Tel: 252-638-2188; Fax: 252-638-2417. Linda Fornaciari, L.C.S.W.

Regional Office, 2717 S. Memorial Dr., Greenville, 27835-8241. Tel: 252-355-5111; Fax: 252-355-1088. Elaine Franzetti, L.C.S.W.

Regional Office, 123 Market St., Hertford, 27944. Tel: 252-426-7717; Fax: 252-426-9940. Julian Miller, L.C.S.W.

Peace and Justice Office, 715 Nazareth St., 27606-2198. Tel: 919-821-9751; Fax: 919-821-9712. Sr. Joan Jurski, O.S.F.

Senior Housing Office, 715 Nazareth St., 27606-2187. Tel: 919-821-9752; Fax: 919-821-9712.

[E] MONASTERIES AND RESIDENCE OF PRIESTS AND BROTHERS

RALEIGH. *Dominican Community*, De Porres House, 304 E. Park Dr., 27605-2927. Tel: 919-571-8123. Revs. Michael M. Burke, O.P.; James D. Campbell, O.P.; Martin J. Iott, O.P.; Arthur R. Kirwin, O.P.; Jude Siciliano, O.P.; Steve Smith, O.P.

Jesuit Community, 5801 Falls of the Neuse Rd., 27609. Tel: 919-876-1581; Fax: 919-872-3723.
E-mail: tierneya@raldioc.org
Jesuits in Eastern North Carolina: Revs. Robert Curry, S.J., Supr.; Paul W. Brant, S.J.; Shay W. Auerbach, S.J.; William R. Ryan, S.J.; John J. McLain, S.J.; James A. Devereux, S.J.; Robert J. Yankevitch, S.J.; Henry B. Haske, S.J.; Brendan R. Horan, S.J.; Robert M. Hussey, S.J.

BURLINGTON. *Conventual Franciscans*, Blessed Sacrament Church, 408 W. Davis St., P.O. Box 619, 27216. Tel: 336-226-8796; Fax: 336-227-2896. Revs. Briant Cullinane, O.F.M.Conv.; Terence Pescatore, O.F.M.Conv.; Robert Benko, O.F.M.Conv.; Carlos Arce, O.F.M.Conv.; John Ruffo, O.F.M. Conv. Total in Residence 5.

CARY. *Franciscan Brothers of Brooklyn*, 108 Springbrook Pl., 27511-9482. Tel: 919-859-4750. Bros. Michel Bettigole, O.S.F.; Gary Cregan, O.S.F.; Richard Contino, O.S.F.; Hugh McGraft, O.S.F.

SURF CITY. *Marianist Community*, 130 N. Oak Dr., 28445. Tel: 910-328-6030.
E-mail: topsailmarianists@juno.com
Rev. Richard Kuhn, S.M.; Bros. Ray McQuade, S.M., Dir.; Frank Smith, S.M.

[F] CONVENTS AND RESIDENCES FOR SISTERS

RALEIGH. *Sisters of Charity of Seton Hill*, 2433 Milburnie Rd., 27610. Tel: 919-829-8005.
E-mail: wilson@raldioc.org

Sisters of Divine Providence, 109 Autumn Chase Dr., 27613. Tel: 919-571-0325.
E-mail: ljschorr@bellsouth.net

Sisters of Notre Dame, 3905 Yew Circle, 27612. Tel: 919-781-3739. Sisters 2.

Sisters of the Holy Cross, 6200 Valley Estates Dr., 27612. Tel: 919-518-1829. Sisters 2.

AHOSKIE. *Sisters of St. Louis—California Region*, 409 W. Church St., 27910. Tel: 919-332-2220.
E-mail: tmssl@yahoo.com

CARY. *Sisters of St. Francis of Sylvania, Ohio*, 1204-C Village Greenway, 27511. Tel: 919-460-6218; Fax: 919-821-9705.
E-mail: jurski@raldioc.org

CHAPEL HILL. *St. Thomas More Sisters' Residence*, 301 Colony Woods Dr., 27514. Tel: 919-929-1547. Sisters 2.

Sisters, Servants of the Immaculate Heart of Mary, 6 St. James Pl., 27514-3426. Tel: 919-933-8240; Fax: cgellings@aol.com.

DURHAM. *Dominican Congregation of St. Catherine De-Ricci*, 711 Mason Rd., 27712-9229. Tel: 919-477-1285; Fax: 919-477-9485.
E-mail: camay711@aol.com

Sisters of St. Francis of Philadelphia, 711 Mason Rd., 27712-9229. Tel: 919-477-1285; Fax: 919-477-9485.
E-mail: djack127@aol.com

FARMVILLE. *Sisters, Servants of the Immaculate Heart of Mary*, P.O. Box 189, 27828-0189. Tel: 252-753-4367; Fax: 252-753-4367.
E-mail: elizabet@greenvillenc.com

FAYETTEVILLE. *Daughters of Charity*, Marguerite Naseau House, 1933 Martindale Dr., 28304. Tel: 910-484-1675.
E-mail: susanpugh@usa.net
Daughters of Charity of St. Vincent de Paul. Sisters 5.

FUQUAY-VARINA. *Sisters of Saint Francis*, 4704 Tee Box Ct., 27526. Tel: 919-557-5372.

GARNER. *Adrian Dominican Sisters*, House of Preachers, 1411 Kenbrook Dr., 27529. Tel: 919-661-9324; Fax: 919-661-0817.
E-mail: adncpreach@aol.com
Congregation of the Most Holy Rosary.

GOLDSBORO. *St. Mary's Convent*, 1603 Edgerton St., 27530. Tel: 919-735-0838. Sisters, Servants of the Immaculate Heart of Mary. Sisters 2.

GREENVILLE. *Daughters of Wisdom*, 303 Oak St., 27858. Tel: 252-758-8097. Sisters 2.

JACKSONVILLE. *Holy Spirit Convent*, 3 East Dr., 28546. Tel: 910-353-1200; Fax: 910-347-9338.
E-mail: ceilsc@phoenixcon.net
Total in Residence 2.

KITTY HAWK. *Sisters of Charity*, 5110 Lindbergh Ave., 27949. Tel: 919-261-3335. Sr. Mary Kay Bush, S.C.; Sr. Francis Agnes Anthony, S.C.

NEW BERN. *St. Paul Convent*, 3003 Country Club Rd., 28562. Tel: 252-637-3726. Total in Residence 5.

RAEFORD. *St. Elizabeth of Hungary Parish House*, 124 Palmer St., 28376. Tel: 910-875-8803; Fax: 910-875-8803.
E-mail: srjmorgan@juno.com
Web site: www.members.tripod.com/jubilee/st.eliz/index.html

ROLESVILLE. *Sisters For Christian Community*, P.O. Box 517, 27571.

SANFORD. *St. Mark's Convent*, 893 Valley Rd., 27330. Tel: 919-776-5350. Sisters of St. Joseph of St. Mark 2.

SOUTHERN PINES. *Missionary Servants of the Most Blessed Trinity*, 565 N. May St., 28387-5611. Tel: 910-692-4032. P.O. Box 816, 28388.

St. Joseph of the Pines, 590 Central Dr., 28387. Tel: 910-692-6848.
E-mail: smzeno@hwy5.net
Sisters of Providence 2.

TARBORO. *Congregation of St. Agnes*, 701 Cedar Ln., 27886. Tel: 919-823-8801; Fax: 282-823-0989.
E-mail: tcoutreach@earthlink.net

WARRENTON. *Sisters, Servants of the Immaculate Heart of Mary*, 124 Marshall St., 27589; Fax: 252-257-5605.
E-mail: stjoseph@3rd.com

WILLIAMSTON. *Sisters, Servants of the Immaculate Heart of Mary*, P.O. Box 894, 27892. Tel: 919-792-4091; Fax: 919-792-4091.
E-mail: kieran@williamstonnc.com

WILMINGTON. *Sisters of St. Ursula*, 216 S. Fifth Ave., 28401. Tel: 910-251-9992; Fax: 910-762-9664.
E-mail: bmcady@aol.com
Web site: sisterofstursula.com
Sisters 4.

WILSON. *Franciscan Sisters of the Atonement*, 810 Reid St. E., 27893. Tel: 252-243-1962; Fax: 252-243-0378.

Sisters of Notre Dame, 911 Branch St. N.W., 27893-2925. Tel: 252-206-1771.
E-mail: sndwilson@simflex.com
Total in Residence 3.

[G] RETREAT HOUSES

RALEIGH. *Madonna House*, 424 Rose Ln., 27610. Tel: 919-231-4049.
E-mail: madonnah@mv.igs.net
Web site: www.mv.igs.net/~madonnah
Carolyn Desch; Carol Gordon; Miss Theresa Davis, Dir.

DURHAM. *Avila Retreat Center*, 711 Mason Rd., 27712-9229. Tel: 919-477-1285; Fax: 919-477-9485.
E-mail: jacksond@raldioc.org
Web site: www.raldioc.org/avila.html
Sr. Damian Marie Jackson, O.S.F., Dir. Total Staff 8; Total in Residence 2.

[H] COLLEGE CAMPUS MINISTRY CENTERS

RALEIGH. *Doggett Center for Catholic Campus Ministry at Aquinas House*, North Carolina State University, 600 Bilyeu St., 27606-2152. Tel: 919-833-9668; Fax: 919-833-1194.
E-mail: ajdash@unity.ncsu.edu
Web site: www2.ncsu.edu/ncsu/stud_orgs/aquinas_house/
Rev. Alan J. Dash.

CHAPEL HILL. *Newman Catholic Student Center*, University of North Carolina, 218 Pittsboro St., 27516. Tel: 919-929-3730; Fax: 919-929-3778.
Web site: www.newman-chapelhill.org
Revs. Phillip M. Leach; Edward P. Mahoney.

DURHAM. *Newman Catholic Student Center Duke University*, Box 90974, 27708-9074. Tel: 919-684-8959; Fax: 919-681-8661.
E-mail: joev@duke.edu
Web site: www.duke.edu/web/catholic/
Rev. Joseph G. Vetter, Dir.; Sr. Joanna Walsh, F.C.J., Associate.

North Carolina Central University, 1400 S. Alston Ave., 27707. Tel: 919-682-4852; Fax: 919-688-6160.
E-mail: sjdurham@juno.com
Rev. Brendan R. Horan, S.J.

ELON COLLEGE. *Elon College*. Tel: 336-278-7355; Fax: 336-278-7299.
E-mail: jruffo@elon.edu
Web site: www.elon.edu/ccm
Mailing Address: Catholic Campus Ministry, Campus Box 2960, 27244-2010. Tel: 336-278-7355. Rev. John Ruffo, O.F.M.Conv., Campus Min.

GREENVILLE. *Catholic Student Center for Students at East Carolina University*, P.O. Box 2605, 27836-2605. Tel: 252-757-1991; Fax: 252-757-3135.
E-mail: ecunewman@hotmail.com
Web site: www.newman-ecu.org
Center, 953 E. 10th St., 27858. Tel: 252-757-3760; Fax: 252-757-3125. Office, 955 E. 10th St., 27858. Tel: 252-757-1991; Fax: 252-757-3735. Rev. Thomas P. Bonacci, C.P. Priests 1.

WILMINGTON. *Newman Catholic Student Center*, University of North Carolina at Wilmington, 4802 College Acres Dr., 28403. Tel: 910-792-0507; Fax: 910-792-0507.
E-mail: fourqureanm@uncwil.edu
Web site: www.newman-uncw.org
Mary Pat Fourqurean, M.S., M.P.S.

[I] MISCELLANEOUS

RALEIGH. *Catholic Housing Corporation*, 715 Nazareth St., 27606. Tel: 919-821-9704; Fax: 919-821-9705.
E-mail: lmaan@raldio.org

Catholic Parish Outreach, 408 Capital Blvd., 27603. Tel: 919-834-9680; Fax: 919-834-9680. Total Staff 90; Total Assisted 20,797.

The Clergy Retirement Plan of Diocese of Raleigh, 715 Nazareth St., 27606. Tel: 919-821-9711; Fax: 919-821-9712.
E-mail: tapler@raldioc.org

CHAPEL HILL. *Vocations Office*, 740 Gimbhoul Rd., 27514-3811. Tel: 919-967-2205; Fax: 919-967-3048.
E-mail: clay@raldioc.org
Rev. Michael G. Clay, Dir.

DURHAM. *The Burch Avenue Center, Inc.*, c/o Immaculate Conception Church, 725 Burch Ave., 27701-2811. Tel: 919-682-3449; Fax: 919-682-7999.

NORTH TOPSAIL BEACH. *Marianist Family Ministry, Inc.* Christian Family Living Center, 2006 Wicker St., 28460. Tel: 910-328-1584; Fax: 910-328-3481.
E-mail: cf12@juno.com
Joseph Dicostanzo. Total Staff 291; Total in Residence 1,968.

PINEHURST. *Duke and St. Joseph Home Care, Inc.*, 95 Aviemore Dr., 28374. Mr. George Kecatos, Pres. Home Health Agencies 14.

St. Joseph of the Pines Home Health Agency, 95 Aviemore Dr., 28374. Tel: 910-295-3920. Retirement Villas, Low-income Housing for elderly. Legal

Title: *St. Joseph of the Pines, Inc.* Lorena Moree, Exec. Dir. & Chief Oper. Officer.
Serving Moore, Lee, Hoke, Anson, Harnett, Davidson, Randolph, Montgomery, Robeson, Scotland, Chatham, Richmond, Mecklenburg and Cumberland Counties. Long Term Care Facilities 1.

SMITHFIELD. *Short Journey Center*, 2323 Cleveland Rd., 27577. Tel: 919-934-7463; Fax: 919-934-7464.

SOUTHERN PINES. *St. Joseph of the Pines Retirement Villa*, 592 Central Dr., 28387. Tel: 910-692-6455; Fax: 910-695-2371. Pat Newton, Dir. Total Staff 8; Total in Residence 71.

RELIGIOUS INSTITUTES OF MEN REPRESENTED IN THE DIOCESE

For further details refer to the corresponding bracketed number in the Religious Institutes of Men or Women section.

[1000]—*Congregation of the Passion.*—C.P.
[0480]—*Conventual Franciscans.*—O.F.M.Conv.
[0520]—*Franciscan Friars.*—O.F.M.
[0530]—*Franciscan Friars of the Atonement.*—S.A.
[0690]—*Jesuit Fathers and Brothers.* (Maryland & New York Provs.).—S.J.
[0720]—*The Missionaries of Our Lady of La Salette.*—M.S.
[0920]—*Oblates of St. Francis De Sales.* (American Prov.).—O.S.F.S.
[0430]—*Order of Preachers (Dominicans).*—O.P.

RELIGIOUS INSTITUTES OF WOMEN REPRESENTED IN THE DIOCESE

[3710]—*Congregation of the Sisters of Saint Agnes.*—C.S.A.
[]—*Adrian Dominican Sisters of the Most Holy Rosary.* (Adrian, MI).—O.P.
[3935]—*Congregation of the Sisters of St. Louis.*—S.S.L.
[1920]—*Congregation of the Sisters of the Holy Cross.*—C.S.C.
[0760]—*Daughters of Charity of St. Vincent de Paul.*—D.C.
[0960]—*Daughters of Wisdom.*—D.W.
[1070-13]—*Dominican Sisters.*—O.P.
[1070-17]—*Dominican Sisters.*—O.P.
[1190]—*Franciscan Sisters of the Atonement.*—S.A.
[]—*Mission Helpers of the Sacred Heart.*—M.H.S.H.
[2790]—*Missionary Servants of the Most Blessed Trinity.*—M.S.B.T.
[]—*Sisters for Christian Community.*—S.F.C.C.
[0570]—*Sisters of Charity of Seton Hill, Greensburg, Pennsylvania.*—S.C.
[0990]—*Sisters of Divine Providence.*—C.D.P.
[2990]—*Sisters of Notre Dame.* (Chardon, OH).—S.N.D.
[3340]—*Sisters of Providence.*—S.P.
[1650]—*Sisters of St. Francis of Philadelphia.*—O.S.F.
[3830]—*Sisters of St. Joseph.*—S.S.J.
[3910]—*Sisters of St. Joseph of St. Mark.*—S.J.S.M.
[1830]—*Sisters of the Good Shepherd.* (Silver Spring, MD).—R.G.S.
[1990]—*Sisters of the Holy Names of Jesus and Mary.*—S.N.J.M.
[2150]—*Sisters, Servants of the Immaculate Heart of Mary.*—I.H.M.
[2160]—*Sisters, Servants of the Immaculate Heart of Mary.*—I.H.M.
[2170]—*Sisters, Servants of the Immaculate Heart of Mary.*—I.H.M.
[4048]—*Society of Sisters Faithful Companions of Jesus.*—F.C.J.
[4040]—*Society of St. Ursula.*—S.U.
[]—*Ursuline Sisters.*—O.S.U.

NECROLOGY

(No Deaths)

Diocese of Rapid City

(Dioecesis Rapidopolitana)

Most Reverend

BLASE J. CUPICH

Bishop of Rapid City; ordained August 16, 1975; appointed July 7, 1998; ordained and installed September 21, 1998.

FORMERLY THE DIOCESE OF LEAD.

ERECTED AUGUST 4, 1902; SEE TRANSFERRED TO RAPID CITY, AUGUST 1, 1930.

Square Miles 43,000.

Comprises the Counties of Bennett, Butte, Corson, Custer, Dewey, Fall River, Gregory, Haakon, Harding, Jackson, Jones, Lawrence, Lyman, Meade, Mellette, Pennington, Perkins, Stanley, Shannon, Todd, Tripp and Ziebach in the State of South Dakota.

For legal titles of parishes and diocesan institutions, consult the Chancery Office.

Chancery Office: 606 Cathedral Dr., Rapid City, SD, 57701. Tel.: 605-343-3541; Fax: 605-348-7985.

E-mail address: diocese@enetis.net

STATISTICAL OVERVIEW

Personnel	
Bishop	1
Priests: Diocesan Active in Diocese	31
Priests: Active Outside Diocese	1
Priests: Retired, Sick or Absent	13
Number of Diocesan Priests	45
Religious Priests in Diocese	27
Ordinations:	
Diocesan Priests	2
Transitional Deacons	1
Permanent Deacons in Diocese	27
Total Brothers	6
Total Sisters	59
Parishes	
Parishes	97
With Resident Pastor:	
Resident Diocesan Priests	24
Resident Religious Priests	7
Without Resident Pastor:	
Administered by Priests	65
Administered by Women Religious	1
Missions	32
Pastoral Centers	4
Professional Ministry Personnel:	
Brothers	3
Sisters	10
Lay Ministers	27
Welfare	
Residential Care of Children	1
Total Assisted	6
Day Care and Extended Day Care Centers	1
Total Assisted	20
Specialized Homes	2
Total Assisted	992
Special Centers for Social Services	10
Total Assisted	6,673
Other Institutions	2
Educational	
Diocesan Students in Other Seminaries	13
Total Seminarians	13
High Schools, Diocesan and Parish	1
Total Students	207
High Schools, Private	1
Total Students	190
Elementary Schools, Diocesan and Parish	1
Total Students	508
Elementary Schools, Private	1
Total Students	217
Catechesis/Religious Education:	
High School Students	1,556
Elementary Students	3,430
Total Students Under Catholic Instruction	6,121
Teachers in the Diocese:	
Priests	1
Scholastics	1
Sisters	4
Lay Teachers	108
Vital Statistics	
Receptions into the Church:	
Infant Baptism Totals	626
Adult Baptism Totals	86
Received into Full Communion	124
First Communions	674
Confirmations	499
Marriages:	
Catholic	190
Interfaith	121
Total Marriages	311
Deaths	458
Total Catholic Population	31,607
Total Population	222,683

Former Bishops—Most Rev. JOHN STARIHA, D.D., cons. Oct. 28, 1902; retired March 29, 1909 and named Titular Bishop of Antipatride; died in Laibach, Austria, Nov. 28, 1915.—Most Rev. JOSEPH F. BUSCH, D.D., cons. May 19, 1910; transferred to Saint Cloud, MN, Feb. 21, 1915; died May 31, 1953.—Most Rev. JOHN J. LAWLER, S.T.D., cons. Titular Bishop of Greater Hermopolis and Auxiliary Bishop of St. Paul, Minnesota, May 19, 1910; transferred to the See of Lead, Jan. 29, 1916; died March 11, 1948.—Most Rev. LEO F. DWORSCHAK, D.D., cons. Titular Bishop of Tium and Coadjutor Bishop of Rapid City "cum jure successionis," Aug. 22, 1946; transferred to Fargo, ND, April 10, 1947.—Most Rev. WILLIAM T. MCCARTY, C.SS.R., D.D., appt. Titular Bishop of Anaea and Delegate to the Military Vicar, Jan. 2, 1943; appt. Coadjutor Bishop of Rapid City "cum jure successionis," April 10, 1947; succeeded to March 11, 1948; retired Sept. 17, 1969; appt. Titular Bishop of Rotdon; died Sept. 14, 1972.—Most Rev. HAROLD J. DIMMERLING, D.D., appt. Bishop of Rapid City, Sept. 17, 1969; ord. May 2, 1940; cons. Oct. 30, 1969; died Dec. 13, 1987.—Most Rev. CHARLES J. CHAPUT, D.D., appt. Bishop of Rapid City, April 11, 1988; appt. Archbishop of Denver, Feb. 18, 1997.

Vicar General—Rev. DANIEL JUELFS, J.C.L.

Chancery Office—606 Cathedral Dr., P.O. Box 678, Rapid City, 57709. Tel: 605-343-3541; Fax: 605-348-7985. Office Hours: Mon.-Fri. 8-5 Address all official business to this office.

Chancellor—MARGARET SIMONSON.

Diocesan Tribunal—606 Cathedral Dr., P.O. Box 678, Rapid City, 57709-0678. Tel: 605-343-3541; Fax: 605-348-7985.

Officialis—Rev. DANIEL JUELFS.

Diocesan Consultors—Revs. WILLIAM PAULY, S.J.; MICHEL MULLOY; DANIEL JUELFS; LEO HAUSMANN; KERRY PRENDIVILLE; STEVE BIEGLER.

Deaneries—Rev. RONALD GARRY, Piedmont; Rev. GARY ORESHOSKI, Sturgis; Rev. MARK MCCORMICK, Hot Springs; Rev. ROBERT BADEN, Wall; Rev. DENNIS RISS, Lemmon; Rev. RAYMOND DEISCH, Gregory.

Presbyteral Council—Rev. RAYMOND DEISCH, Pres.

Vicar for Retired Priests—Rev. D. CRAIG COWER.

Permanent Diaconate Program, Sioux Spiritual Center—Rev. STEVE MITTEN, S.J., *HCR 77, Box 271, 20100 Center Rd., Howes, 57748.* Tel: 605-985-5906.

Development and Stewardship Program—GRANT TROTTER, Dir.

Continuing Education of Clergy—Rev. Msgr. MICHAEL B. WOSTER.

Vocation Program—Rev. TIMOTHY HOAG, Dir., *P.O. Box 399, Presho, 57568-0399.* Tel: 605-895-2534.

Diocesan Finance Manager—SUZANNE LAMBERT.

Diocesan Finance Council—Ms. IONA LANGER; CHRIS SCHMID; SHIRLEY STEC; JEFFREY VIKEN; ARTHUR KROETCH; RAY HILLENBRAND; PETE LIEN, JR.; STEVE HAYES; Rev. BRIAN LANE; FRANK SHORT; Mrs. CAROL VARLAND; Mrs. AGNES MOUSEL.

Holy Childhood Pontifical Association—Rev. PAUL DAHMS.

Propagation of the Faith—Rev. PAUL DAHMS.

Beginning Experience—606 Cathedral Dr., P.O. Box 678, Rapid City, 57709-0678. Tel: 605-343-3541.

Birthright—606 Cathedral Dr., P.O. Box 678, Rapid City, 57709-0678. Tel: 605-343-3541.

Bereavement—606 Cathedral Dr., P.O. Box 678, Rapid City, 57709-0678. Tel: 605-343-3541.

Couple to Couple—606 Cathedral Dr., P.O. Box 678, Rapid City, 57709-0678. Tel: 605-343-3541.

Cursillo—606 Cathedral Dr., P.O. Box 678, Rapid City, 57709-0678. Tel: 605-343-3541.

Engaged Encounter—606 Cathedral Dr., P.O. Box 678, Rapid City, 57709-0678. Tel: 605-343-3541.

Marriage Encounter—606 Cathedral Dr., P.O. Box 678, Rapid City, 57709-0678. Tel: 605-343-3541.

Catholic Relief Service—Rev. PAUL DAHMS, Dir., *606 Cathedral Dr., Rapid City, 57701-5498.*

Native Concerns Office—PHYLLIS DECORY, Dir., *606 Cathedral Dr., Rapid City, 57701.* Tel: 605-343-3541.

Pro-Life Commission—SUE JIMMERSON, Chm., *606 Cathedral Dr., Rapid City, 57701.*

Retreat Ministry—606 Cathedral Dr., P.O. Box 678, Rapid City, 57709-0678. Tel: 605-343-3541.

Retrouvaille—606 Cathedral Dr., P.O. Box 678, Rapid City, 57709-0678. Tel: 605-343-3541.

Right to Life—606 Cathedral Dr., P.O. Box 678, Rapid City, 57709-0678. Tel: 605-343-3541.

Director of Ongoing Formation—Rev. Msgr. WILLIAM J. O'CONNELL, *P.O. Box 539, McLaughlin, 57642-0539.* Tel: 605-823-4401.

Vicar of Education—THOMAS LANE.

Supt. of Schools—DICK THOMPSON, *300 Fairmont Blvd., Rapid City, 57701.* Tel: 605-343-8484.

Director of Rural Life—Rev. DENNIS RISS, *P.O. Box 210, Lemmon, 57638-0210.* Tel: 605-374-3767.

Office of Family Life—HARRIET YOUNG, Dir., *606 Cathedral Dr., P.O. Box 678, Rapid City, 57709-0678.* Tel: 605-343-3541; Fax: 605-348-7985.

Diocesan Office of Religious Education—JEAN BERRY, Dir., *300 Fairmont Blvd., Rapid City, 57701.* Tel: 605-341-2508.

Campaign for Human Development—Rev. PAUL DAHMS, Dir., *606 Cathedral Dr., Rapid City, 57701-5498.* Tel: 605-343-3541.

West River Catholic Newspaper—EILEEN SULLIVAN ROTERT, Editor, *606 Cathedral Dr., Rapid City, 57701.*

West River Catholic Youth Commission—*606 Cathedral Dr., Rapid City, 57701.*

Archives—SR. CELINE ERK, O.S.B.

CLERGY, PARISHES, MISSIONS AND PAROCHIAL SCHOOLS

CITY OF RAPID CITY
(Pennington County)

1—CATHEDRAL OF OUR LADY OF PERPETUAL HELP (1890), Rev. Msgr. Michael Woster, J.C.L., Rector; Revs. Michael Hight; Valentine Young, O.F.M.; Brian Patrick Christensen; Deacons Tom Lane; George Gladfelter; Mike Curtin.
Church—520 Cathedral Dr., 57701-5499. Tel: 605-342-0507; Fax: 605-343-9677.
School—St. Elizabeth Seton Central School. See separate listing under Institutions Located in the Diocese.
Catechesis/Religious Programs—Pat Roe, D.R.E. Students 295.
Chapel—Immaculate Conception.
Mission—Hermosa, St. Michael's.

2—BLESSED SACRAMENT (1947), Rev. Michel Mulloy. In res., Revs. David Orians; Andrzej Stanislaw Wyrostek.
Res., 4500 Jackson Blvd., 57702-4999. Tel: 605-342-3336; Fax: 605-341-5668.
Catechesis/Religious Programs—Students 608.
Mission—Keystone, Pennington Co., Our Lady of Mt. Carmel.

3—ST. THERESE THE LITTLE FLOWER (1941). Formerly known as The Church of St. John the Evangelist. Rev. Brian Lane; Deacon Claude Sauer.
Res., 532 Adams St., 57701. Tel: 605-342-1556; Fax: 605-348-6272. [JC]
Catechesis/Religious Programs—Tel: 605-348-6272.
Students 258.

4—ST. ISAAC JOGUES (1949) (Native American), Rev. Patrick M. McCorkell, S.J.; Deacons James Garnett; Leroy Decory; Luis Usera. In res., Rev. John Hatcher, S.J.
Res., 221 Knollwood Dr., P.O. Box 1304, 57709-1304. Tel: 605-343-2165; Fax: 605-343-3257.
Catechesis/Religious Programs—Students 117.
Mother Butler Center—Catechetical and Social Center for Indians. Tel: 605-343-2165; Fax: 605-313-3257.
Mission—Rapid City, Pennington Co., Indian Health Service, Sioux San Hospital and Pennington County Jail.

OUTSIDE THE CITY OF RAPID CITY

Belle Fourche, Butte Co., St. Paul (1905), Rev. Arnold A. Kari.
Res., 855 Fifth St., 57717-1701. Tel: 605-723-3226. [JC]
Also attends St. Mary, Newell and St. Joseph's, Mud Butte.
Catechesis/Religious Programs—Tel: 605-892-3226.
Students 96.
Missions—Newell, St. Mary, Star of the Sea; Mud Butte, St. Joseph.

Bison, Perkins Co., Blessed Sacrament (1918), Rev. Ed Vanorny.
Res., P.O. Box 297, 57620. Tel: 605-244-5546. [JC]
Catechesis/Religious Programs—Students 21.
Mission—Drew, Perkins Co., St. James, Tel: 605-244-5546.

Bonesteel, Gregory Co., Immaculate Conception (1906), Rev. James D. Becht.
Res., P.O. Box 376, 57317-0376. Tel: 605-654-2204. [CEM]
Also attends Church of St. Anthony, Fairfax and St. Francis Xavier, Ponca Creek.
Catechesis/Religious Programs—Students 65.

Buffalo, Harding Co., St. Anthony (1917). Attended by Blessed Sacrament, Bison. Revs. Ed Varnorny; Andrew Morvay, (Retired).
Res., P.O. Box 297, Bison, 57620-0297. Tel: 605-244-5546. [CEM][JC]
Catechesis/Religious Programs—Students 34.
Missions—Cox, Harding Co., St. Agnes; Ralph, Harding Co., St. Isidore; Reva, Harding Co., Our Lady of the Prairie.

Burke, Gregory Co., Sacred Heart (1905). Attended by St. Joseph, Gregory.
Res., P.O. Box 354, 57523-0354. Tel: 605-775-2532. [CEM 2]
Catechesis/Religious Programs—Students 55.

Clearfield, Tripp Co., St. Boniface. Closed. For sacramental records contact Immaculate Conception, Winner.

Colome, Tripp Co., St. Isidore (1909). Attended by Immaculate Conception, Winner. Revs. Leo Hausmann; Janusz Korban.
Res., P.O. Box 405, 57528-0405. Tel: 605-842-1437. [JC]
Catechesis/Religious Programs—Tel: 605-842-2452.
Students 58.

Custer, Custer Co., St. John the Baptist (1911). Attended by St. Anthony's, Hot Springs. Revs. Mark McCormick; John Joseph Heying.
Res., P.O. Box 632, 57730-0632. Tel: 605-673-4426. [JC]
Also attends St. Rose of Lima, Hill City.
Catechesis/Religious Programs—Tel: 605-673-4426.
Students 88.

Deadwood, Lawrence Co., St. Ambrose (1877), Rev. Paul G. Dahms.
Res., 760 W. Main St., 57732-1003. Tel: 605-578-1519. [CEM]
Catechesis/Religious Programs—732 Main St., 57732-0320. Tel: 605-578-1921.
Students 50.

Eagle Butte, Dewey Co., All Saints (1911) (Native American), Revs. Thomas Westhoven, S.C.J.; Anthony Kluckman, S.C.J.; Bro. Frank Presto, S.C.J.
Res., P.O. Box 110, 57625-0110. Tel: 605-964-3391; Fax: 605-964-3300. [JC]
Catechesis/Religious Programs—Students 64.
Missions—Bridger, Ziebach Co., Immaculate Conception; Cherry Creek, Ziebach Co., St. Joseph; Dupree, Ziebach Co., Sacred Heart; Promise, Dewey Co., St. Catherine; Red Scaffold, Ziebach Co., Sacred Heart; Ridgeview, Dewey Co., St. Joseph; Thunder Butte, Ziebach Co., St. Luke; White Horse, Dewey Co., St. Therese.

Fairfax, Gregory Co., St. Anthony's (1904). Attended by Immaculate Conception, Bonesteel. Rev. James D. Becht.
Mailing Address: c/o P.O. Box 376, Bonesteel, 57317-0376. Tel: 605-654-2204. [CEM]
Catechesis/Religious Programs—Students and adults attend religious education at Immaculate Conception, Bonesteel.

Faith, Meade Co., St. Joseph (1917), Rev. Brian Fawcett.
Res., P.O. Box 307, 57626-0307. Tel: 605-967-2201; Fax: 605-967-2208. [CEM]
Catechesis/Religious Programs—Students 37.
Missions—Red Owl, Meade Co., St. Anthony; Plainview, Meade Co., Our Lady of Victory.

Fort Pierre, Stanley Co., St. John (1905), Rev. Dale Kutil.
Res., 206 W. Main, P.O. Box 670, 57532-0670. Tel: 605-223-2176. [JC]
Catechesis/Religious Programs—Students 149.

Gregory, Gregory Co., St. Joseph (1905), Rev. Raymond J. Deisch.
Res., 414 Church St., 57533. Tel: 605-835-9290. [CEM 3]
Catechesis/Religious Programs—Mary Vale Hall, 411 Church St., Tel: 605-835-9396.
Students 93.

Hermosa, Custer Co., St. Michael's. Attended by Our Lady of Perpetual Help Cathedral, Rapid City.

Hill City, Pennington Co., St. Rose of Lima (1898). Attended by St. Anthony's, Hot Springs. Revs. Mark McCormick; John Joseph Heying.
Res., P.O. Box 632, Custer, 57730. Tel: 605-673-4426. [JC]
Catechesis/Religious Programs—Tel: 605-574-2479.
Students 54.

Hot Springs, Fall River Co., St. Anthony's (1890), Revs. Mark McCormick; John Joseph Heying.
Res., P.O. Box 969, 57747-0969. Tel: 605-745-3393; Fax: 605-745-3393. [JC]
Catechesis/Religious Programs—Deacon Earl F. Witte.
Total Enrollment (Elem./H.S.) 184.
Mission—Edgemont, Fall River Co., St. James, 310 3rd St., Edgemont, 57735.

Kadoka, Jackson Co., Our Lady of Victory (1908). Attended by St. Patrick's, Wall. Rev. Robert D. Baden; Deacon Eugene A. Heckathorne.
Res., P.O. Box 159, 57543-0159. Tel: 605-837-2219. [JC]
Catechesis/Religious Programs—Students 30.

Kennebec, Lyman Co., St. Michael's (1906). Attended by St. Mary, Lower Brule.
Mailing Address: P.O. Box 185, Lower Brule, 57548-0185. Tel: 605-473-5335; Fax: 605-473-5453. [CEM]
Catechesis/Religious Programs—Students 26.

Kenel, Corson Co., Assumption of the Blessed Virgin Mary (1879) (Native American). Attended by St. Bernard, McLaughlin.
Res., P.O. Box 539, McLaughlin, 57642-0539. Tel: 605-823-4401; Fax: 605-823-2325.
Catechesis/Religious Programs—Students 30.

Kyle, Shannon Co., Our Lady of Sorrows (1910) (Native American), Rev. Joseph Damhorst, S.J.; Deacon Lawrence Whiting, (Retired). In res., Revs. James Ryan, S.J.; Paul Manhart, S.J.
Res., P.O. Box 398, 57752-0398. Tel: 605-455-2888. [CEM 2]
Catechesis/Religious Programs—Students 25.
Missions—Allen, Bennett Co., St. John of the Cross; Medicine Root, Shannon, St. Stephens.

Lead, Lawrence Co., St. Patrick's (1878), Rev. William A. Zandri.
Res., 141 S. Siever St., 57754. Tel: 605-584-2002. [CEM][JC]
Catechesis/Religious Programs—Students 89.

Lemmon, Perkins Co., St. Mary's (1909), Rev. Dennis Riss; Deacons Carl Orthman; Bill Dustman.
Res., P.O. Box 210, 57638. Tel: 605-374-3767; Fax: 605-374-3768. [JC]
Catechesis/Religious Programs—Peggy Falvey, D.R.E.
Students 121.
Missions—Morristown, Corson Co., Sacred Heart; Watauga, Corson Co., St. Michael.

Lower Brule, Lyman Co., St. Mary's (1923) (Native American), Revs. Yvon Sheehy, S.C.J.; James L. Walters, S.C.J.
Office: P.O. Box 185, 57568. Tel: 605-473-5335; Fax: 605-473-5453. [CEM]
Catechesis/Religious Programs—Students 21.

Manderson, Shannon Co., St. Agnes (1901) (Native American). Attended by Our Lady of Sorrows, Kyle. Rev. James Ryan, S.J.
Res., P.O. Box 398, Kyle, 57752. Tel: 605-455-2888. [CEM]
Catechesis/Religious Programs—Students 35.
Missions—Wounded Knee, Shannon Co., Sacred Heart, P.O. Box 88, 57756. Tel: 605-867-2267; Rockyford, Shannon Co., St. Peter's.

Martin, Bennett Co., Our Lady of the Sacred Heart (1918), Rev. John J. Hennessy, S.J.; Deacons Calvin Clifford; Lawrence Kocer.
Mailing Address: P.O. Box 567, 57551. Tel: 605-685-6232. [CEM][JC]
Catechesis/Religious Programs—Tel: 605-685-6274.
Students 148.

McIntosh, Corson Co., St. Bonaventure's (1913), Rev. Msgr. William O'Connell; Rev. Steven Biegler.
Res., P.O. Box 320, 57641. Tel: 605-273-4334; Fax: 605-823-2325. [CEM]
Catechesis/Religious Programs—Students 40.

McLaughlin, Corson Co., St. Bernard (1918), Rev. Msgr. William O'Connell; Rev. Steven Biegler; Deacons Vern Rath; Paul Keller.
Res., P.O. Box 539, 57642. Tel: 605-823-4401; Fax: 605-823-2325. [CEM]
Catechesis/Religious Programs—Tel: 605-823-4210; Fax: 605-823-4757.
Sisters of St. Francis of the Immaculate Conception 2; Lay Teachers 16; Students 124.
Missions—Bullhead, Corson Co., St. Aloysius; Wakpala, Corson Co., St. Bede; Kenel, Corson Co., Our Lady of the Assumption Parish; McIntosh, Corson Co., St. Bonaventure, P.O. Box 320, McIntosh, 57641. Tel: 605-273-4334.

Midland, Haakon Co., St. William (1911). Attended by Sacred Heart, Philip.
Mailing Address: P.O. Box 309, Philip, 57567. Tel: 605-859-2664; Fax: 605-859-2812.

Mission, Todd Co., St. Thomas the Apostle (1933) (Native American). Attended by St. Francis, Mission. Rev. David H. Gau, S.J.; Deacon Marlon J. Leneaugh.
Church—P.O. Box 151, 57555. Tel: 605-856-4618. [CEM]
Catechesis/Religious Programs—Tel: 605-856-2273. Gladys Bordeaux, D.R.E.
Students 56.

Mission—Okreek, Todd Co., St. Peter's, P.O. Box 499, St. Francis, 57572. Tel: 605-747-2362.

Morristown, Corson Co., Sacred Heart (1912). Attended by St. Mary's, Lemmon.
Mailing Address: P.O. Box 210, Lemmon, 57638. Tel: 605-374-3767. [JC]
Catechesis/Religious Programs—Students 25.

Murdo, Jones Co., St. Martin (1906). Attended by Christ the King, Presho.
Mailing Address: P.O. Box 399, Presho, 57568. Tel: 605-669-2436. [CEM]
Catechesis/Religious Programs—Tel: 605-895-2534.
Students 25.

Newell, Butte Co., St. Mary Star of the Sea (1910). Attended by St. Paul, Belle Fourche.
Mailing Address: P.O. Box 72, 57760. Tel: 605-456-2221.
Catechesis/Religious Programs—Students 58.
Mission—Mud Butte, Meade Co., St. Joseph's Catholic Church, (1921) Mud Butte, 57758.

New Underwood, Pennington Co., St. John the Evangelist (1921), Rev. Daniel Juelfs.
Res., P.O. Box 305, 57761. Tel: 605-754-6446. [JC]
Catechesis/Religious Programs—Students 44.
Mission—Lakeside, Meade Co., St. Margaret.

Norris, Melette Co., Sacred Heart (1955). Attended by St. Francis Mission, St. Francis, S.D. Rev. Ronald S. Seminara, S.J.
Res., HCR 76, Box 11A, Belvidere, 57521-9701. Tel: 605-747-2118. [JC]

Oglala, Shannon Co., Our Lady of the Sioux (1916) (Native American). Attended by Holy Rosary Mission, Pine Ridge. Sr. Julianne Brockamp, P.B.V.M., Pastoral Coord.
Res., P.O. Box 140, 57764. Tel: 605-867-5673. [CEM]
Catechesis/Religious Programs—Students 5.

Parmelee, Todd Co., St. Agnes, Rev. Neal J. Wilkinson, S.J.
Res., P.O. Box 115, 57566. Tel: 605-747-2118; Fax: 605-747-5057.
Catechesis/Religious Programs—Students 90.
Missions—Upper Cutmeat, Sacred Heart; He Dog, St. Patrick Hall; Black Pipe-Corn Creek, St. Joseph Hall.

Philip, Haakon Co., Sacred Heart (1907), Rev. John Anthony Grossenburg.
Res., 307 W. Elm, P.O. Box 309, 57567. Tel: 605-859-2664; Fax: 605-859-2812. [JC]
Catechesis/Religious Programs—Students 144.
Missions—Milesville, Haakon Co., St. Mary; Midland, Haakon Co., St. William.

Piedmont-Black Hawk, Meade Co., Our Lady of the Black Hills (1916), Rev. Ronald Garry; Deacon Walt Wilson.
Res., HCR 80, Box 481, 57769. Tel: 605-787-5168. [JC]
Catechesis/Religious Programs—Students 195.

Pine Ridge, Shannon Co., Sacred Heart (1890) (Lakota). Attended from Holy Rosary Mission. Rev. Stephen J. Sanford, S.J.
Res., P.O. Box 359, 57770. Tel: 605-867-5551; Fax: 605-867-1969. [JC]
Catechesis/Religious Programs—Students 70.

Porcupine, Shannon Co., Church of Christ the King (1901) (Native American), Rev. James Ryan, S.J.
Res., P.O. Box 398, Kyle, 57752-0398. Tel: 605-867-1614; 455-2888; Fax: 605-867-5874. [CEM]
School—Our Lady of Lourdes Mission School, Tel: 605-867-5568. Cynthia Hillman, Prin.
Sisters 2; Lay Teachers 8; Students 174.
Catechesis/Religious Programs—Students 30.
Mission—Porcupine, Shannon Co., St. Paul, P.O. Box 7, 57772. Tel: 605-867-1614. [CEM]

Presho, Lyman Co., Christ the King (1906), Rev. Timothy Hoag.
Res., P.O. Box 399, 57568-0399. Tel: 605-895-2534. [CEM]
Catechesis/Religious Programs—Students 30.
Missions—Murdo, Jones Co., St. Martin of Tours; Draper, Jones Co., St. Anthony of Padua.

Reliance, Lyman Co., St. Mary's (1911). Attended by St. Mary's, Lower Brule.
Mailing Address: P.O. Box 185, Lower Brule, 57548-0185. Tel: 605-473-5335; Fax: 605-473-5453. [CEM]
Catechesis/Religious Programs—Students 22.

Rosebud, Todd Co., St. Bridget, Rev. David H. Gau, S.J.
Res., P.O. Box 340, 57570-0340. Tel: 605-747-2496.
Catechesis/Religious Programs—Students 115.
Mission—Soldier Creek, St. Rose.

St. Francis, Todd Co., St. Charles (1886) (Native American), Rev. Joseph C. Gill, S.J.; Deacon Ben Black Bear, Jr.
Res., Box 499, 57572. Tel: 605-747-2533; Fax: 605-747-5057. [CEM]
Missions—See listing under Indian Missions for Rosebud Reservation, St. Francis regarding details on personnel and missions.; Soldier Creek, Todd Co., St. Rose; Spring Creek, Todd Co., St. Patrick.

Spearfish, Lawrence Co., St. Joseph (1907), Rev. Kerry Prendiville.
Res., 844 5th St., 57783-2005. Tel: 605-642-2306; Fax: 605-642-1024. [JC]
Catechesis/Religious Programs—Students 400.

Sturgis, Meade Co., St. Francis of Assisi (1840), Rev. Gary Oreshoski; Deacon Roger Heidt.
Res., 1049 Howard St., 57785-1999. Tel: 605-720-3579. [CEM]
Catechesis/Religious Programs—Tel: 605-720-3996. Debi Dauer, D.R.E.
Students 247.

Timber Lake, Dewey Co., Holy Cross (1910), Rev. Peter Kovarik.
Res., P.O. Box 70, 57656-0070. Tel: 605-865-3653.
Catechesis/Religious Programs—Students 115.
Missions—Isabel, Dewey Co., St. Mary; Trail City, Corson Co., Holy Rosary.

Wall, Pennington Co., St. Patrick's (1917), Rev. Robert D. Baden.
Res., P.O. Box 405, 57790-0405. Tel: 605-279-2542. [JC]
Catechesis/Religious Programs—Students 77.
Mission—Interior, Jackson Co., Holy Rosary.

Wanblee, Jackson Co., Ignatius Loyola (1920) (Native American), Rev. Joseph Damhorst, S.J.
Res., P.O. Box 229, 57577. Tel: 605-462-6170. [CEM 3][JC 5]
Catechesis/Religious Programs—Tel: 605-455-2831.
Students 20.
Mission—Potato Creek, Jackson Co., St. Henry.

Watauga, Corson Co., St. Michael (1912). Attended by St. Mary's, Lemmon.
Mailing Address: P.O. Box 210, Lemmon, 57638-0210. Tel: 605-374-3767; Fax: 605-374-3768. [CEM]
Catechesis/Religious Programs—Students 27.

White River, Mellette Co., St. Ignatius (1899) (Native American), Rev. Ronald S. Seminara, S.J.
Res., P.O. Box 245, 57579-0245. Tel: 605-259-3381. [CEM][JC]
Catechesis/Religious Programs—Tel: 605-259-3313.
Students 22.
Mission—Wood, Melette Co., Our Lady of Good Counsel, Wood, 57585.

Sacred Heart, Melette Co., (1919), Rev. Ronald S. Seminara, S.J.
P.O. Box 245, 57579-0245. Tel: 605-259-3213. [CEM][JC]
Catechesis/Religious Programs—Students 12.

Winner, Tripp Co., Immaculate Conception (1910), Revs. Leo Hausmann; Janusz Korban.
Res., 302 W. Fourth, P.O. Box 765, 57580. Tel: 605-842-3520.
Catechesis/Religious Programs—Students 214.
Mission—Keyapaha, Tripp Co., St. Ann. [JC]

INDIAN MISSIONS

Eagle Butte, Dewey Co., Cheyenne River Reservation (1911) (Native American), Revs. Thomas Westhoven, S.C.J.; Anthony Kluckman, S.C.J.; Bro. Frank Presto; Deacon Ted Knife, Sr.
Mailing Address: All Saints, P.O. Box 110, 57625. Tel: 605-964-3391; Fax: 605-964-3300. [CEM 8][JC 2]
Catechesis/Religious Programs—Students 149.
Missions—Bridger, Ziebach Co., Immaculate Conception; Dupree, Ziebach Co., Sacred Heart; Promise, Dewey Co., St. Catherine; Ridgeview, Dewey Co., St. Joseph; Cherry Creek, Ziebach Co., St. Joseph; Thunder Butte, Ziebach Co., St. Luke; Red Scaffold, Ziebach Co., Sacred Heart; White Horse, Ziebach Co., St. Therese.

Lower Brule, Lyman Co., Lower Brule Reservation (1895) (Native American), Revs. Yvon Sheehy, S.C.J.; James L. Walters, S.C.J.
Mailing Address: P.O. Box 185, 57548. Tel: 605-473-5335; 473-5215; Fax: 605-473-5453. [CEM]
Sisters 3.
Catechesis/Religious Programs—Students 21.

Pine Ridge, Shannon Co., Holy Rosary (Pine Ridge Reservation) (1888) (Native American), Revs. Peter J. Klink, S.J.; Patrick Burns, S.J.; Tom Simonds, S.J.; Steve Sanford, S.J.; Earl J. Kurth, S.J.; Joseph Damhorst, S.J., (Kyle, Wamblee); William Pauly, S.J., Supr.; Paul Manhart, S.J., (Kyle, Wamblee); James Ryan, S.J., (Manderson, Wounded Knee, Porcupine).; Thomas Merkel, S.J., Supt. of Red Cloud School.
Mailing Address: 100 Mission Dr., 57770-2100. Tel: 605-867-5491; Fax: 605-967-1291.
Priests 10; Lay Teachers 42; Brothers 3; Scholastics 1.
School—Red Cloud Indian School, Tel: 605-867-5491; Fax: 605-867-1291. Sr. Monica O.S.F., Coord. Sisters of St. Francis of Penance and Christian Charity 1; Sisters of Charity of Cincinnati 1; School Sisters of Notre Dame of St. Louis 1; Congregation of Notre Dame 5; Lay Teachers 43; Students: Elementary 217; High School 190.
Catechesis/Religious Programs—Students 65.
Missions—Cuny Table, Shannon Co., St. Joseph; Oglala, Shannon Co., Our Lady of Sioux, P.O. Box 140, Oglala, 57764. Tel: 605-867-5673; No Water, Shannon Co., Our Lady of Good Counsel; Slim Butte, Shannon Co., Our Lady of Lourdes; Red Shirt Table, Shannon Co., St. Bernard.

St. Francis, Todd Co., Rosebud Reservation (1886) (Native American). St. Francis Mission and Rosebud Educational Society. Revs. Ronald S. Seminara, S.J., Supr., Mission.; Joseph C. Gill, S.J.; John A. Hennessy, S.J., Our Lady of the Sacred Heart, Martin.; Richard T. Jones, S.J.; Robert G. Gilroy, S.J.; Glendon R. Welshons, S.J.; David H. Gau, S.J.; Neal Wilkinson; Bro. Edward C. Gill, S.J.; Deacons Ben Black Bear, Jr.; Marlon Leneaugh.
Mailing Address: P.O. Box 499, 57572-0499. Tel: 605-747-2361; Fax: 605-747-5057. [CEM]
Priests 8; Permanent Deacons 2; Brothers 2; Sisters 2.
Catechesis/Religious Programs—Tel: 605-747-2142.
Students 669.
Missions—St. Francis, Todd Co., St. Charles, Tel: 605-747-2533; Okreek, Todd Co., St. Peter, Tel: 605-747-2362; Soldier Creek, Todd Co., St. Rose, Tel: 605-747-2362; Spring Creek, Todd Co., St. Patrick, Tel: 605-747-2845; Parmelee, Todd Co., St. Agnes, Box 115, Parmelee, 57566. Tel: 605-747-2118; Upper Cutmeat, Todd Co., Sacred Heart, Box 115, Parmelee, 57566. Tel: 605-747-2118; Rosebud, Todd Co., St. Bridget, P.O. Box 340, Rosebud, 57570. Tel: 605-747-2439; White River, Mellette Co., St. Ignatius; White River, Mellette Co., Sacred Heart; Wood, Mellette Co., Our Lady of Good Counsel, Tel: 605-747-2362; Norris, Mellette Co., Sacred Heart, HCR 76, Box 11A, Belvidere, 57560-0141. Tel: 605-462-6353; Mission, Todd Co., St. Thomas, Box 151, Mission, 57555. Tel: 605-856-4618.

Standing Rock, Corson Co., Standing Rock Reservation (1918), Rev. Msgr. William J. O'Connell; Rev. Steven Biegler.
St. Bernard's Church: P.O. Box 539, McLaughlin, 57642. Tel: 605-823-4401; Fax: 605-823-2325.
Missions—Wakpala, Corson Co., St. Bede; Bullhead, Corson Co., St. Aloysius; Kenel, Corson Co., Assumption of the Blessed Virgin Mary Church.

Chaplains of Public Institutions

ELLSWORTH. *Ellsworth AFB*. Rev. David A. Voelker, 28th BW/HC, Ellsworth AFB, 57706.

On Duty Outside the Diocese:
Reverend Fathers—
Novotny, Richard

Retired:
Reverend Fathers—
Birdsall, John M., 2110-C St. Martin Dr., Rapid City, SD 57702
Corry, John J., 2110-C St. Martin Dr., Apt. 107, Rapid City, SD 57702
Cower, D. Craig, 824 Columbus, #204, Rapid City, SD 57701-3578
Jordan, Collins P., c/o Lionel Bordeaux, Mission, SD 57555
Lambert, William, 163 Vondera St., Robertsville, MO 63072
Morvay, Andrew, P.O. Box 85, Buffalo, SD 57720-0085
Philbin, William, 428 W. Kenilworth Ave., Palatine, IL 60067
Plante, Richard A., C/O John J. Feehan P.O. Box 8475, Rapid City, SD 57709-8475
Scadron, Christopher, 8220 W. Staterd 48, Bloomington, IN 47404-9735
Scherer, Gerald N., P.O. Box 268, Hermoso, SD 57744-0268
Staricek, Andrew, P.O. Box 7, Bison, SD 57620-0007
Valades, Reuben, 304 Denver St. Apt. 101, Rapid City, SD 57701

Permanent Deacons:
Black Bear, Ben, Jr., St. Francis Mission, St. Francis
Clifford, Calvin, Martin
Condon, Harold, Parmelee
Coy, Patrick, Hill City
Curtin, Michael, Rapid City
DeCory, Leroy, Rapid City
Dustman, Bill, Lemmon

Garnet, James W., Rapid City
Gladfelter, George, Rapid City
Grant, Albert, Hot Springs
Heckathorne, Eugene A., Kadoka
Heidt, Roger, Sturgis
Hill, Ken, Albuquerque, New Mexico
Keller, Paul, McLaughlin
Knife, Theodore, Faith
Kocer, Lawrence, Martin
Lane, Thomas, Silver City
Leneaugh, Marlon, Mission
Murray, Chet, (Retired), Rapid City
Orthman, Carl, Lemmon
Rath, Vern, McLaughlin
Sauer, Claude, (Retired), St. Therese, Rapid City
Tully, Frederick G., Hill City
Usera, Luis, Rapid City
Whiting, Lawrence, Kyle
Wilson, Walt, Piedmont
Witte, Earl Joseph, St. James, Edgemont

INSTITUTIONS LOCATED IN THE DIOCESE

[A] DIOCESAN CATHOLIC SCHOOL SYSTEM

RAPID CITY. *St. Thomas More High School*, 300 Fairmont Blvd., 57701. Tel: 605-343-8484; Fax: 605-348-1318.
E-mail: stm@stm.k12.sd.us
Web site: stm.k12.sd.us
Richard Thompson, Supt. Lay Teachers 22; Students 207; Total Staff 43.

St. Elizabeth Elementary and Middle School, 431 Oakland, 57701. Tel: 605-348-1477; Fax: 605-342-4367. Lay Teachers 31; Students 508; Staff 59.

[B] MONASTERIES AND RESIDENCES OF PRIESTS & BROTHERS

EAGLE BUTTE. *Sacred Heart Community House*, P.O. Box 110, 57625-0110. Tel: 605-964-3391; Fax: 605-964-3300. Revs. Thomas Westhoven, S.C.J.; Anthony Kluckman, S.C.J.; Bro. Frank Presto, S.C.J. Priests 2; Brothers 1.

HOWES. *Kino Jesuit Community*, HCR 77 Box 271, 57748-9505. Tel: 605-985-5906; Fax: 605-985-5908.
E-mail: smitten@basec.net
In res. Revs. Thomas Lawler, S.J.; Thomas J. Tierney, S.J.; Stephen F. Mitten, S.J.; Patrick M. McCorkell, S.J.; John Hatcher, S.J., Dir. of Inculturation. Priests 5.

LOWER BRULE. *SCJ Community House*, P.O. Box 185, 57548-0185. Tel: 605-473-5335; 473-5487; Fax: 605-473-5453.
E-mail: pastteam@gwtc.net
Revs. Yvon Sheehy, S.C.J.; James L. Walters, S.C.J.; Bro. Duane Lemke, S.C.J. Priests 2; Total in Residence 3; Total Staff 3.

PIEDMONT. *Holy Nativity Monastery*, Bethlehem Rd., P.O. Box 170, 57769-0170. Tel: 605-787-4606. Revs. Louis Marie, Supr.; Giles Goyette; Elias Havel; Bros. Ephraim Martin; Augustine Martin; Robert Nortz; Joseph Brady. Priests 3; Brothers 4.

PINE RIDGE. *Jesuit Community of Holy Rosary Mission*, 100 Mission Dr., 57770-0001. Tel: 605-867-5491; Fax: 605-867-1291.
E-mail: holyrosary@basec.net
Web site: www.redcloudindianschool
Revs. William Pauly, S.J., Supr.; Peter J. Klink, S.J., Pastor, Pres.; Earl J. Kurth, S.J.; Stephen Sandford, S.J.; Joseph Damhorst, S.J.; Paul Manhart, S.J.; Patrick Burns, S.J.; Tom Simonds, S.J.; Tom Merkel, S.J., Supt., Red Cloud School; James Ryan, S.J.; Bros. Bill Fostes, S.J.; Clair Simon, S.J.; Michael Zimmerman, S.J. Priests 10; Brothers 3; Total in Residence 17; Scholastics 1.

[C] CONVENTS AND RESIDENCES FOR SISTERS

RAPID CITY.
Benedictine Convent of St. Martin, 2110 C St. Martin Dr., 57702-9660. Tel: 605-343-8011; Fax: 605-399-2723.
E-mail: fmartin620@aol.com
Web site: www.catholic-church.org/stmartins
Motherhouse and Novitiate of the Sisters of St. Benedict. Sr. Lorane Cofin, O.S.B., Prioress. Sisters 36.

Benedictine Convent of St. Martin Retirement Trust, 2110-C St. Martin Dr., 57702-9660. Tel: 605-343-8011; Fax: 605-399-2723. Sr. Mary Wegher, Trustee & Contact Person.

St. Martin's Community Center, 2110-C St. Martin Dr., 57702-9660. Tel: 605-343-8011; Fax: 605-399-2723. Total Assisted 20; Total Staff 2.

Kateri Convent, 624 Adams, 57701-0809. Tel: 605-343-6261. Home Visitations, particularly Native Americans, Communion to Homebound. Oblate Sisters of the Blessed Sacrament 2.

PORCUPINE. *Our Lady of Lourdes School Convent*, P.O. Box 7, 57772-0007. Tel: 605-867-1056; Fax: 605-867-5874. Notre Dame Sisters.

[D] MISCELLANEOUS

RAPID CITY. *The Catholic Education Fund, Inc.*, P.O. Box 678, 57709-0678. Tel: 605-343-8484; Fax: 605-343-1315.

Catholic Parish Association Contingency Fund, Inc., P.O. Box 678, 57709-0678. Tel: 605-343-3541; Fax: 605-348-7985.

Catholic Social Service of the Diocese of Rapid City, 918 5th St., 57701. Tel: 605-348-6086; Fax: 605-348-1050.
E-mail: css@rapidnet.com
James Kinyon, Dir.

Priest Retirement and Aid Association, Westhills Village, F211, 255 Texas St., 57701. Tel: 605-721-3456. Most Rev. Blase Cupich; Revs. Dale Kutil, Pres.; D. Craig Cower, Exec. Sec.; Rev. Msgr. Michael Woster; Revs. Brian Lane; Leo Hausmann, Vice Pres. & Recorder.

St. Martin's Community Center, 2110 C St. Martin Dr., 57702-9392. Tel: 605-343-8011; Fax: 605-399-9660. Sr. Edna Marie Stephenson, O.S.B., Dir.

St. Martin's Learning Center, 2110-C St. Martin Dr., 57702-9392. Tel: 605-343-2243.
E-mail: ckovarik@gwtc.net
Sr. Carol Kovarik, O.S.B., Dir. Sisters 2; Students 20.

Western South Dakota Catholic Foundation, Inc., P.O. Box 678, 57709-0678. Tel: 605-343-3541; Fax: 605-348-7985.
E-mail: gtrotter@enetis.net

EAGLE BUTTE. *Sacred Heart Center*, 121 Landmark St., P.O. Box 2000, 57625-2000. Tel: 605-964-6062; Fax: 605-964-6060.
E-mail: shc@rapidnet.com
Bro. Francis J. Presto, S.C.J., Dir. Total Assisted 992; Total Staff 33.

HOWES. *The Diocese of Rapid City Mahpiya na Maka Okoigna*. Sioux Spiritual Center, HC 77, Box 271, 57748-9505. Tel: 605-985-5906; Fax: 605-985-5908.
E-mail: smitten@basec.net
Revs. Thomas A. Lawler, S.J.; Stephen F. Mitten, S.J.; John Hatcher, S.J. Total in Residence 2; Total Staff 6.

MANDERSON. *St. Francis Home*, P.O. Box 122, 57756-0122. Tel: 605-455-2077. Sr. Geraldine Clifford, O.S.F., Minister; Sr. Colleen Mahoney, O.S.F. Sisters of St. Francis Marycrest. Home for abandoned and abused children (Licensed) 2-18 years of age.

RELIGIOUS INSTITUTES OF MEN REPRESENTED IN THE DIOCESE

For further details refer to the corresponding bracketed number in the Religious Institutes of Men or Women section.

[1350]—*Brothers of St. Francis Xavier*.—C.F.X.
[1130]—*Congregation of the Priests and Brothers of the Sacred Heart*.—S.C.J.
[0690]—*Jesuit Fathers and Brothers*.—S.J.

RELIGIOUS INSTITUTES OF WOMEN REPRESENTED IN THE DIOCESE

[0230]—*Benedictine Sisters of Pontifical Jurisdiction*. (Rapid City, SD).—O.S.B.
[1070-13]—*Dominican Sisters*. (Adrian, MI).—O.P.
[2960]—*Notre Dame Sisters*. (Omaha, NE).—N.D.
[3010]—*Oblate Sisters of the Blessed Sacrament*. (Marty, SD).—O.S.B.S.
[2970]—*School Sisters of Notre Dame*. (St. Louis, MO).—S.S.N.D.
[1680]—*School Sisters of St. Francis*. (Milwaukee, WI).—S.S.S.F.
[]—*Sisters of Charity of Cincinnati (Ohio)*.—S.C.
[0660]—*Sisters of Christian Charity*. (Wilmette, IL).—S.C.C.
[1630]—*Sisters of St. Francis of Penance and Christian Charity*. (Denver, CO).—O.S.F.
[1580]—*Sisters of St. Francis of the Immaculate Conception*. (Peoria, IL).—O.S.F.
[2980]—*Sisters of the Congregation of Notre Dame*. (Ridgefield, CT).—C.N.D.
[1030]—*Sisters of the Divine Savior*. (Milwaukee, WI).—S.D.S.
[3320]—*Sisters of the Presentation of the B.V.M.*. (Aberdeen, SD; Dubuque, IA; Fargo, ND).—P.B.V.M.
[]—*Sisters of St. Francis of the Holy Family*. (Dubuque).

DIOCESAN CEMETERIES

RAPID CITY. Catholic Cemeteries (all Diocesan) are located in the following parishes: Bear Butte, Belle Fourche, Bonesteel, Buffalo, Burke, Cherry Creek, Cheyenne Agency, Clearfield, Colome, Custer, Dallas, Deadwood, Dupree, Eagle Butte, Fairfax, Faith, Gregory, Glencross, Kadoka, Kenel, Kennebec, Lemmon, McIntosh, Martin Mission, Murdo, Pine Ridge, Porcupine, Presho, Reliance, St. Francis, Sturgis, Timber Lake, Trail City, Wakpala, Watauga, Winner, and Witten.

NECROLOGY

(No Deaths)

Diocese of Reno

(Dioecesis Renensis)

Most Reverend

PHILLIP F. STRALING, D.D.

Bishop of Reno; ordained March 19, 1959; appointed Bishop of San Bernardino July 18, 1978; installed November 6, 1978; appointed Bishop of Reno March 21, 1995; installed June 29, 1995. *290 S. Arlington Ave., Ste. 200, Reno, NV, 89501.*

Pastoral Center: 290 S. Arlington Ave., Ste. 200, Reno, NV, 89501. Tel.: 775-329-9274; Fax: 775-348-8619.

Web site address: catholicreno.com

E-mail address: dioceseofreno@pyramid.net

ERECTED AS THE DIOCESE OF RENO BY HIS HOLINESS POPE PIUS XI MARCH 27, 1931. CANONICAL ERECTION OF THE DIOCESE AUGUST 19, 1931; REDESIGNATED DIOCESE OF RENO-LAS VEGAS BY POPE PAUL VI, OCTOBER 13, 1976; REFORMED DIOCESE OF RENO BY HIS HOLINESS POPE JOHN PAUL II MARCH 21, 1995.

Square Miles 70,852.

Legal Title: "The Roman Catholic Bishop of Reno and His Successors, a Corporation Sole".

Comprises the Counties of: Carson City, Churchill, Douglas, Elko, Eureka, Humboldt, Lander, Lyon, Mineral, Pershing, Storey, and Washoe.

PATRONS OF THE DIOCESE: *Our Lady of the Snows (August 5); The Holy Family (Sunday in the Octave of Christmas); Established through an Apostolic brief dated August 24, 1933.*

For legal titles of parishes and diocesan institutions, consult the Pastoral Center.

STATISTICAL OVERVIEW

Personnel	
Bishop	1
Priests: Diocesan Active in Diocese	15
Priests: Active Outside Diocese	1
Priests: Retired, Sick or Absent	8
Number of Diocesan Priests	24
Religious Priests in Diocese	12
Extern Priests in Diocese	13
Ordinations:	
Transitional Deacons	1
Permanent Deacons in Diocese	7
Total Brothers	3
Total Sisters	38
Parishes	
Parishes	28
With Resident Pastor:	
Resident Diocesan Priests	18
Resident Religious Priests	7
Without Resident Pastor:	
Administered by Priests	1
Administered by Deacons	2
Missions	8
Professional Ministry Personnel:	
Brothers	1
Sisters	4
Lay Ministers	4
Welfare	
Catholic Hospitals	1
Total Assisted	199,234
Health Care Centers	3
Total Assisted	199,234
Day Care and Extended Day Care Centers	2
Total Assisted	233
Special Centers for Social Services	7
Total Assisted	32,250
Educational	
Diocesan Students in Other Seminaries	7
Total Seminarians	7
High Schools, Diocesan and Parish	1
Total Students	655
Elementary Schools, Diocesan and Parish	4
Total Students	1,123
Catechesis/Religious Education:	
High School Students	1,162
Elementary Students	4,357
Total Students Under Catholic Instruction	7,304
Teachers in the Diocese:	
Brothers	1
Sisters	4
Lay Teachers	115
Vital Statistics	
Receptions into the Church:	
Infant Baptism Totals	1,839
Adult Baptism Totals	143
Received into Full Communion	120
First Communions	1,359
Confirmations	681
Marriages:	
Catholic	226
Interfaith	92
Total Marriages	318
Deaths	340
Total Catholic Population	71,997
Total Population	573,630

Former Bishops—Most Rev. THOMAS K. GORMAN, D.D., D.Sc.Hist., ord. June 23, 1917; appt. Bishop, April 24, 1931; cons. July 22, 1931; appt. Coadjutor Bishop of Dallas "cum jure successionis," Feb. 8, 1952; succeeded to the See, Aug. 19, 1954; resigned Aug. 27, 1969; died Aug. 16, 1980.—Most Rev. ROBERT J. DWYER, D.D., Ph.D., ord. June 11, 1932; appt. May 20, 1952; cons. Aug. 5, 1952; elevated to Archiepiscopal Dignity and promoted to Portland in Oregon, Dec. 14, 1966; resigned Jan. 22, 1974; died March 24, 1976.—Most Rev. JOSEPH GREEN, D.D., ord. July 14, 1946; appt. Titular Bishop of Trisipa and Auxiliary of Lansing, June 22, 1962; cons. Aug. 28, 1962; appt. Bishop of Reno, March 10, 1967; installed May 5, 1967; resigned Dec. 6, 1974; died Aug. 31, 1982.—Most Rev. NORMAN F. McFARLAND, D.D., J.C.D., ord. June 15, 1946; appt. Titular Bishop of Bida and Auxiliary of San Francisco, June 5, 1970; ord. Bishop, Sept. 8, 1970; appt. Apostolic Admin. of Reno, Dec. 6, 1974; appt. Bishop of Reno, Feb. 10, 1976; transferred to Orange, Dec. 29, 1986; appt. Bishop of Orange, Feb. 24, 1987; retired June 30, 1998.—Most Rev. DANIEL F. WALSH, D.D., ord. March 30, 1963; appt. Titular Bishop of Tigia and Auxiliary of San Francisco; ord. Bishop, Sept. 24, 1981; appt. Bishop of Reno-Las Vegas, June 9, 1987; installed Aug. 6, 1987; appt. first Bishop of the newly established Diocese of Las Vegas, March 21, 1995; installed June 28, 1995.

Bishop's Office—

Bishop—Most Rev. PHILLIP F. STRALING.

Secretary—HELEN SCHMITT, Ext. 428.

Vicar-General—Rev. GEORGE WOLF, V.G.

Chancellor—Bro. MATTHEW CUNNINGHAM, F.S.R., Ext. 429.

Secretary—JOAN TOPOIAN, Ext. 410.

Tribunal—

Judicial Vicar/Officialis—Rev. THOMAS FRANSISCUS, C.SS.R., J.C.L.

Secretary/Notary—JENY HILL, Ext. 419.

Promoter of Justice—Rev. GEORGE WOLF, V.G.

Defenders of the Bond—Rev. Msgr. ROBERT A. BOWLING; Revs. GEORGE WOLF, V.G.; GARY M. LUIZ, C.PP.S., J.C.L.

Judges—Revs. ALBERT M. FOSSELMAN, J.C.L.; STEPHEN FROST, J.C.L.

Advocates—Bro. MATTHEW CUNNINGHAM, F.S.R.; Revs. DAVID SCHUYLER, S.M., S.T.L., J.C.D.; JAMES SETELIK; CHARLES DURANTE.

Education, Department of—

Superintendent of Schools—Bro. MATTHEW CUNNINGHAM, F.S.R., Ext. 429.

Diocesan Planning Office/Pastoral Service—Rev. FRANK J. MURPHY, Dir., Ext. 418. MAUREEN KECK, Assoc. Dir., Ext. 418.

Office of Adult Formation and Catechesis—MARY MARGARET SWOGGER, Ph.D., Dir., Ext. 431.

Diocesan Youth Ministry—JOSE OJEDA, Dir., Ext. 426.

Office of Hispanic Ministry—JOSE OJEDA, Dir., Ext. 426. MARIA DODSON, Sec., Ext. 415.

Diocesan Coordinator Hispanic Youth—MARIPAZ RAMOS, Ext. 423.

Department of Religious Education-Secretary—LETTY ANGUIANO, Ext. 413.

Department of Religious Education-Audio/Visual—PAT COLEMAN, Ext. 434.

Archives—Br. MATTHEW CUNNINGHAM, F.S.R., Chancellor, Ext. 429.

Curia—Most Rev. PHILLIP F. STRALING; Revs. GEORGE WOLF, V.G., Moderator; FRANCIS MURPHY; TOM FRANSISCUS, C.SS.R.; Bro. MATTHEW CUNNINGHAM, F.S.R.; Ms. MARY MARGARET SWOGGER, Ph.D.; Mr. KEVIN DAY; Mr. JOSE OJEDA; Mr. TIM WANNER.

Department of Stewardship and Development—Vacant, Ext. 432.

Diaconate—Rev. GERALD HANLEY.

Diocesan Communications—Bro. MATTHEW CUNNINGHAM, F.S.R., Ext. 429.

Diocesan Board of Consultors—Rev. Msgr. ROBERT BOWLING; Revs. GEORGE WOLF, V.G.; ARIEL ARIAS; RICHARD DEMOLEN; VIKTOR PEREZ, O.F.M.Conv.; JOHN BAIN; JOHN CORONA; CHARLES DURANTE; TOM FRANSISCUS, C.SS.R.

Diocesan Development Committee—Most Rev. PHILLIP F. STRALING; Mr. LEROY ARRASCADA; Rev. Msgr. ROBERT BOWLING; Mr. BOB CAPURRO; Bro. MATTHEW CUNNINGHAM, F.S.R.; Mr. KEVIN DAY; Rev. Msgr. LEO MCFADDEN; Mr. MARTIN BARRETT; Mr. TIM WANNER; MARY CONKLIN; HELAINE JESSE.

Finance Office—

Finance Committee—Most Rev. PHILLIP F. STRALING; Rev. GEORGE WOLF, V.G.; Ms. VIRGINIA ZORIO; Mr. ED HOUSTON; Mr. BOB ARMSTRONG; Bro. MATTHEW CUNNINGHAM, F.S.R.; Mr. TIM WANNER; Mr. RICHARD KWAPIL.

Business Manager—TIM WANNER, Ext. 420.

Personnel Administrator—CINDI MITCHELL, Ext. 424.
Administrative Assistant—JUDY LUBICH, Ext. 414.
Bookkeeper—JACKIE BURRIS, Ext. 422.

Frontier of the Faith—310 W. 2nd St., Reno, NV, 89503. Tel: 775-348-6628., *Mailing Address: P.O. Box 10930, Reno, NV, 89510.*
Director—BETTIE ENGEBRETSON.

Missionary Co-Op—Bro. MATTHEW CUNNINGHAM, F.S.R., Ext. 429.

"Northern Nevada Catholic" Newspaper—Vacant, Editor-in-Chief, *232 E. Plumb Ln., Reno, NV, 89502-3406.* Tel: 775-826-1010; Fax: 775-825-6100.

Our Mother of Sorrows Cemetery—2700 N. Virginia St., Reno, NV, 89503. Tel: 775-323-0133., *P.O. Box 8505, Reno, NV, 89507;* Fax: 775-323-1229. SOPHIE MITCHELL, Oper. Mgr.; Sr. OFELIA ROIBAS, Counselor.

Presbyteral Council—Rev. Msgr. ROBERT A. BOWLING; Revs. MIKE MAHONE; JOHN CORONA; CHARLES DURANTE; RICHARD DEMOLEN; GEORGE WOLF, V.G.; ARIEL ARIAS; VIKTOR PEREZ, O.F.M.Conv.; TOM FRANSISCUS, C.SS.R.

Priests' Personnel Board—Most Rev. PHILLIP F. STRALING; Rev. Msgr. ROBERT A. BOWLING; Revs. CHARLES DURANTE; MIKE MAHONE; GEORGE WOLF, V.G.; Bro. MATTHEW CUNNINGHAM, F.S.R.

Prison Ministry—Carson City Area: Rev. JIM SETELIK, *Corpus Christi Church.* Tel: 775-882-1967. MARGARET SANBORN; RUSS SANBORN. Tel: 775-885-0480.
Lovelock Prison—Rev. LORENZO TORRENTE. Tel: 775-273-2189.
State Prison Chaplain—Rev. JAMES KELLY. Tel: 775-882-9203, Ext. 287.

Property Management—TIM WANNER.

Respect Life Core Committee—Most Rev. PHILLIP F. STRALING; Revs. RICHARD DEMOLEN; CHARLES DURANTE; Sr. PATRICIA KELLY, O.C.D.; Mr. ROSS BARKER; Mrs. MARGARET GRAHAM; Ms. JULIANNA JERVIS; Mrs. MARILEE RAILTON; Ms. MARY CLARK; Ms. PAT GLENN.

Seminary Board—Most Rev. PHILLIP F. STRALING; Revs. CHARLES DURANTE; ROBERT SIMPSON; PAUL MCCOLLUM; ARTHUR HERKOWSKI; Mr. JOSE OJEDA; Ms. MARGARET GRAHAM.

Vocations Awareness Board—Revs. CHARLES DURANTE, Dir. PAUL MCCOLLUM; RICHARD DEMOLEN; Sr. MARIE MCGLOIN; Sr. MARIE LOUISE BISHOP; MIKE NEESER; ROSS BARKER; RICHARD PENDORF.

CLERGY, PARISHES, MISSIONS AND PAROCHIAL SCHOOLS

CITY OF RENO
(Washoe County)

1—ST. THOMAS AQUINAS CATHEDRAL (1907), Revs. Viktor Perez, O.F.M.Conv., Rector; Danut Benedic, O.F.M.Conv.; Charles Shelton, O.F.M.Conv. In res., Revs. John Farao, O.F.M. Conv.; Alphonse VanGuilder, O.F.M.Conv.
Res., 310 W. Second St., 89503-5398. Tel: 775-329-2571; Fax: 775-329-2456.
Catechesis/Religious Programs—D.R.E. Irma Alvarado, (Spanish); Maria Dodson, (English). Students 91.

2—OUR LADY OF THE SNOWS (1939), Revs. Robert E. Buchanan; John Farao, O.F.M.Conv.; Deacon Edmundo Valera. In res., Rev. Francis J. Murphy.
Office: 1138 Wright St., 89509. Tel: 775-323-6894; Fax: 775-323-6749.
School—1125 Lander St., 89509. Tel: 775-322-2773; Fax: 775-322-0827. Mary E. Clark, Prin.
Religious 1; Lay Teachers 14; Students 294.
Catechesis/Religious Programs—Tel: 775-329-6147; Fax: 775-323-6749. Lauri-Ann Reinhart, D.R.E.
Students 383.

3—OUR LADY OF WISDOM (1965), Rev. Frank Murphy; Linda Wanner, Pastoral Assoc.
Mailing Address: P.O. Box 8879, 89507.
Office: 1101 N. Virginia St., 89503. Tel: 775-322-4336; Fax: 775-322-3616.

4—ST. ALBERT THE GREAT (1948), Rev. Robert A. Simpson.
Mailing Address: 1259 St. Albert Dr., 89503.
Res., 1250 Wyoming Ave., 89503. Tel: 775-747-0722; Fax: 775-746-3976.
School—1255 St. Albert Dr., 89503. Tel: 775-747-3392; Fax: 775-747-6209. Colleen Welsh, Prin.; Cheryl Garlock, Vice Prin.
Lay Teachers 12; Students 310.
St. Albert's Child Development Center—1259 St. Albert Dr., 89503. Tel: 775-747-1617; Fax: 775-746-3976. Kristen Mareno, Dir.
Catechesis/Religious Programs—D.R.E.: Marcy Welch, (Grades K-6); Margaret Tharaldson, (Grades 7-12).
Students 342.

5—ST. ROSE OF LIMA (1996), Rev. Thomas Donnelly.
Mailing Address: P.O. Box 18790, 89511-0790. Tel: 775-851-1874; Fax: 775-851-1727.
Catechesis/Religious Programs—Tel: 775-849-1653. Rita Sloan, D.R.E.
Students 120.
Mission—Washoe Valley, Washoe Co., Holy Spirit, 1025 N. U.S. Hwy. 395, Washoe Valley, 89704.

6—ST. THERESE CHURCH OF THE LITTLE FLOWER (1947). (St. Jude Shrine). Rev. Msgr. Robert A. Bowling, V.F.; Revs. Richard DeMolen; Cyril Apassa; Deacon Robert Ruggiero.
Office: 875 E. Plumb Ln., 89502. Tel: 775-322-2255; Fax: 775-322-0196.
Res., 339 Urban Rd., 89509. Tel: 775-826-1432.
School—1300 Casazza Dr., 89502. Tel: 775-323-2931; Fax: 775-323-2997. Sr. Margaret Oates, R.S.M., Prin.
Sisters of Mercy 3; Lay Teachers 8; Students 315.
Catechesis/Religious Programs—Tel: 775-322-3415. Sr. Carol Bettencourt, S.H.F., D.R.E.
Students 510.

OUTSIDE THE CITY OF RENO

Battle Mountain, Lander Co., St. John Bosco (1940), Rev. John Keefe, C.S.C., Admin.
Mailing Address: P.O. Box 428, 89820.
Office: 392 S. Reese St., 89820.
Res., 384 S. Resse St., 89820. Tel: 775-635-2576; Fax: 775-635-5729.
Catechesis/Religious Programs—Tel: 775-635-0109. Izabel Murillo, D.R.E.
Students 144.
Mission—Austin, St. Augustine, 113 Virginia St., Austin, 89310. Tel: 775-635-2576.

Carlin, Elko Co., Sacred Heart (1910), Rev. John O'Keefe, C.S.C., Presbyteral Mod.; Deacon Craig LaGier, Parish Life Coord.
Mailing Address: P.O. Box 235, 89822.
Office: 651-3rd St., 89822. Tel: 775-754-6425; Fax: 775-754-2942.
Res., 315 Peters, 89822.

Carson City, Corpus Christi (1949), Rev. James Setelik.
Res., 5335 Snyder Ave., 89701. Tel: 775-882-1967; Fax: 775-882-2435.
Catechesis/Religious Programs—Barbara Reitzig, D.R.E.
Students 242.

St. Teresa's of Avila (1858), Rev. Gerald T. Hanley; Sr. Marie McGloin, S.A., Pastoral Assoc.; Deacon Bob Evans.
Res., 108 N. Minnesota St., 89703. Tel: 775-882-1968; Fax: 775-883-7063.
School—567 S. Richmond Ave., 89703. Tel: 775-882-2079; Fax: 775-882-6135. Ms. Madeleine Brennan, Prin.
Lay Teachers 11; Students 227.
Catechesis/Religious Programs—400 W. King St., Ste. 104, 89703. Tel: 775-882-2130; Fax: 775-882-3258. Mary Ann Randall D.R.E.
Students 590.

Dayton, Lyon Co., St. Ann, Rev. Michael Dallmeier, O.F.M.; Deacon Roger Porcella.
Mailing Address: P.O. Box 309, 89403. Tel: 775-246-7578.

Elko, Elko Co., St. Joseph's (1917), Deacon Don Tzinski, Pastoral Assoc.
Office: 1035 C St., 89801. Tel: 775-738-6432; Fax: 775-738-3356.
Res., 986 Highland Dr., 89801. Tel: 775-738-9545.
Catechesis/Religious Programs—Deacon Don Tzinski, D.R.E.
Students 754.
Missions—Wells, St. Thomas Aquinas, 619 Sixth St., P.O. Box 369, Wells, 89835. Tel: 775-752-3400. Rev. Brian Kennedy, C.S.S.R, Admin.; Jackpot, Elko Co., Our Lady of Guadalupe, P.O. Box 462, Jackpot, 89825. Sr. Rosemary Boessen, R.S.M., Admin. & Pastoral Assoc.

Eureka, Eureka Co., St. Brendan's (1872), Rev. John O'Keefe, C.S.C., Presbyteral Mod.; Deacon Craig LaGier, Parish Life Coord.
Mailing Address: P.O. Box 305, 89316.
Res., 70 N. O'Neill Ave., 89316. Tel: 775-237-5278.

Fallon, Churchill Co., St. Patrick (1920), Rev. Ariel Arias.
Church & Mailing Address—850 W. Fourth St., 89406. Tel: 775-423-2846; Fax: 775-423-5210.
Res., 375 Tedford Ln., 89406.
Catechesis/Religious Programs—D.R.E. Candy Cramer; Patty Fleming.
Students 206.

Fallon Naval Air Station Base Chapel (1977). Unassigned.
Office: Naval Air Station, 4755 Pasture Rd., Bldg. 351, 89496-5000. Tel: 775-426-2813; Fax: 775-426-2742.

Fernley, Lyon Co., St. Robert Bellarmine (1957), Rev. Thomas Cronin, Pastoral Admin.
Mailing Address: P.O. Box 473, 89408.
Office: 190 S. West St., 89408. Tel: 775-575-4011; Fax: 775-575-7601.
Catechesis/Religious Programs—Sherry Hall, D.R.E.
Students 71.
Mission—Empire, St. Joseph the Worker.

Gardnerville, Douglas Co., St. Gall (1917), Rev. William Nadeau, O.M.I., Pastoral Admin.
Office & Mailing Address: 1343 Centerville Rd., 89410. Tel: 775-782-2852; Fax: 775-782-2622.
Catechesis/Religious Programs—Tel: 775-782-3784. Julie Davis, D.R.E.
Students 314.

Hawthorne, Mineral Co., Our Lady of Perpetual Help (1938), Rev. Joseph C. Abraham (India) Pastoral Admin.
Mailing Address: P.O. Box 850, 89415.
Office: 804 A St., 89415. Tel: 775-945-2020; Fax: 775-945-3559.
Res., 794 A St., 89415.
Mission—Gabbs, St. Michael, P.O. Box 612, Gabbs, 89409.

Incline Village, Washoe Co., St. Francis of Assisi (1965), Rev. Michael Q. Mahone.
Mailing Address: P.O. Box 4226, 89450. Tel: 775-831-0490; Fax: 775-831-2045.
Church—Mt. Rose Hwy. at Kelly Dr., 89450.
Catechesis/Religious Programs—Students 137.

Lovelock, Pershing Co., St. John the Baptist (1875), Rev. Lorenzo Torrente.
Mailing Address: P.O. Box 177, 89418-0177.
Res., 1045 Franklin Ave, 89419-0177. Tel: 775-273-2189; Fax: 775-273-1154.
Church—1085 Franklin Ave., 89419-0177.
Catechesis/Religious Programs—Students 90.

Sparks, Washoe Co., Holy Cross Catholic Community (1967), Rev. George C. Wolf; Deacon Ron Schmitt.
Res., 3175 Goldy Way, 89434. Tel: 775-358-2544; Fax: 775-358-8239.
Catechesis/Religious Programs—Tel: 775-358-2883. D.R.E.: Laura Balmut, (Liturgy of the Word & Grades 1-7); Jill McAboy, (Grades 8-10 & Confirmation).
Students 405.

Immaculate Conception (1932), Rev. Norm King.
Res., 590 Pyramid Way, 89431. Tel: 775-358-5977; Fax: 775-359-3951.
Catechesis/Religious Programs—D.R.E.: Marilyn Heywood, (Elementary), Tel: 775-324-0555; Pat Giannotti, (High School), Tel: 775-358-3107.
Students 263.

Stead, Washoe Co., St. Michael's (1967), Rev. Thomas J. Fransiscus, C.Ss.R.
Res., 14075 Mt. Vida St., Reno, 89506. Tel: 775-972-7462; Fax: 775-972-9373.
Catechesis/Religious Programs—Constance West, D.R.E.
Students 87.

Sun Valley, Washoe Co., St. Peter Canisius (1976), Rev. Larry Morrison.
Res., 225 E. Fifth Ave., 89433. Tel: 775-673-6800; Fax: 775-673-2028.
Catechesis/Religious Programs—Tel: 775-673-2280. Christine Luna, D.R.E.
Students 178.

Virginia City, Storey Co., St. Mary in the Mountains (1862), Rev. Michael Dallmeier, O.F.M.
Mailing Address: P.O. Box 510, 89440.
Res., Taylor St. & E St., 89440. Tel: 775-847-9099; Fax: 775-847-7441.

Winnemucca, Humboldt Co., St. Paul (1883), Rev. Jose Issac (India) Pastoral Admin.
Mailing Address: 350 Melarkey St., 89445.
Res., Fourth St. & Melarkey St., 89445. Tel: 775-623-2928; Fax: 775-623-6816. Louise Good, Office Mgr.
Catechesis/Religious Programs—Virginia Perez, D.R.E.
Students 212.
Missions—Paradise Valley, Humboldt Co., St. Alphonsus, 89426.; McDermitt, Humboldt Co., Sacred Heart, 89421.

Yerington, Lyon Co., Holy Family (1901), Rev. Paul McCollum.
Res., 37 N. West St., 89447. Tel: 775-463-2882; Fax: 775-463-2162.
Catechesis/Religious Programs—Cindy Hitchcock, D.R.E.
Students 163.
Mission—Smith Valley, Lyon Co., St. John the Baptist, Hwy. 208, P.O. Box 36, Wellington, 89444. Tel: 775-465-2222; Fax: 775-465-9989.

Zephyr Cove, Douglas Co., Our Lady of Tahoe (1966), Rev. John K. Bain.
Mailing Address: P.O. Box 115, 89448.
Res., 630 Don Dr., 89448. Tel: 775-588-2080; Fax: 775-588-0211.

Catechesis / Religious Programs—Mary Beth Crosby, D.R.E., Tel: 530-542-2620.
Students 75.

On Duty Outside the Diocese:
Reverend Fathers—
Hoffman, Frank, 917 Torrence St. #20, San Diego, CA 92103

Leave of Absence:
Reverend Fathers—
Perrier, Martin
Vieages, Harold

Absent on Sick Leave:
Reverend Monsignors—
Meger, Thomas

Retired:
Reverend Monsignors—
McFadden, Leo E., 3363 Spring Creek Cir., Reno, NV 89509
Reverend Fathers—
Avella, William, 64 Jasper Ln., Dayton, NV 89403
Corona, John, 1740 Lavender Ct., Minden, NV 89423
Fosselman, Albert, Double Diamond/The Meadows, 1162 Tule Dr., Reno, NV 89511
Herkowski, Arthur M., 1299 Flora Glen Dr., Sparks, NV 89434
Wright, Thomas, P.O. Box 481, Yerington, NV 89447

Permanent Deacons:
Evans, Robert, 877 Thompson St, Carson City, NV 89703. Tel: 775-883-2341
Lagier, Craig, P.O. Box 235, Carlin, NV 89822. Tel: 775-754-6425
Porcella, Roger, 986 Ridgeview Dr., Carson City, NV 89705. Tel: 775-267-5110
Ruggiero, Robert L., 1095 Thoma St., Reno, NV 89502. Tel: 775-348-7119
Schmitt, Ron, 1095 E. York Way, Sparks, NV 89434. Tel: 775-358-1625
Schreiner, Dennis, 1780 Grandview, Reno, NV 89503. Tel: 775-624-6864
Schumacher, Wendell, (Retired)
Tzinski, Don, 974 Highland Dr., Elko, NV 89801. Tel: 775-777-1799

INSTITUTIONS LOCATED IN THE DIOCESE

[A] HIGH SCHOOLS, DIOCESAN

RENO. *Bishop Manogue High School*, 400 Bartlett St., 89512. Tel: 775-329-0011; Fax: 775-329-5961.
E-mail: manogue@powernet.net
Mr. Jim Williams, Pres.; Richard L. Squires, Prin.; Martin Barrett, Devel. Dir.; Susan Smith, Business Mgr. Brothers 1; Clergy 1; Sisters 1; Lay Teachers 45; Students 653.

[B] GENERAL HOSPITALS

RENO. *St. Mary's Central Nevada Health Care Corp.*, 235 W. Sixth St., 89520-0108. Tel: 775-770-3554; Fax: 775-770-3621
For a complete listing, refer to the Hospitals section.
St. Mary's Foundation, 235 W. Sixth St., 89520-0108. Tel: 775-789-3020; Fax: 775-770-3545.
E-mail: stephanie.hauk@saintmarysreno.com
For a complete listing, refer to the Hospitals section.
St. Mary's Health Care Corp., dba St. Mary's Health Network, 235 W. Sixth St., 89520-0108. Tel: 775-770-3004.
Web site: www.saintmarysreno.com
For a complete listing, refer to the Hospitals section.
St. Mary's Regional Medical Center, 235 W. Sixth St., 89520-0108. Tel: 775-323-2041; Fax: 775-770-3963
For a complete listing, refer to the Hospitals section.

[C] DAY NURSERIES

RENO. *Holy Child Day Home*, 440 Reno Ave., 89509. Tel: 775-329-2979; Fax: 775-329-8537. Mrs. Karen L. Barreras, Dir. Lay Teachers 33; Boys 93; Girls 82.

[D] MONASTERIES AND RESIDENCES FOR PRIESTS AND BROTHERS

RENO. *Brothers of Our Lady of the Holy Rosary Monastery*, 232 Sunnyside Dr., 89503-3510. Tel: 775-747-4441.
E-mail: bros-reno@moondog.net
Bros. Philip Napolitano, F.S.R., Supr.; Matthew Cunningham, F.S.R.; Edward Zuber, F.S.R. Brothers 3.

[E] CONVENTS AND RESIDENCES FOR SISTERS

RENO. *Carmelite Monastery (O.C.D.)*, 1950 La Fond Dr., 89509-3099. Tel: 775-323-3236; Fax: 775-322-1532.
E-mail: jarc@pyramid.net
Sr. Ann Weber, Prioress. Discalced Carmelite Nuns 15.
Little Flower Convent (S.M.), 660 Casazza Dr., 89502. Tel: 775-322-5966; Fax: 775-322-5265. Sisters of Mercy. Sr. Elizabeth O'Neill, S.M., Contact Person. Sisters 3.
St. Mary's Convent (O.P.), 411 W. Sixth St., 89503. Tel: 775-323-5196. Sr. Patricia Simpson, O.P., Supr. Dominican Sisters of San Rafael. Sisters 9.
Sisters of the Holy Family, S.H.F., 6730 S. McCarran Blvd., 89509. Tel: 775-827-5370.
E-mail: renoshf@juno.com
Sr. M. Carmen Baca, S.H.F.; Sr. Carol Bettencourt, S.H.F.; Sr. M. Christopher Schmidt, S.H.F. Holy Family Sisters. Sisters 3.

SPARKS. *Sisters of St. Philip Neri*, 135 Pascus Pl., 89431. Tel: 775-331-0708; Fax: 775-331-7073.
E-mail: sisterr@nsn.k12.nv.us
Sisters 2.

[F] CAMPUS MINISTRY

RENO. *University of Nevada, Newman Community.* Served by Our Lady of Wisdom, 1101 N. Virginia St., 89503. Tel: 775-322-4336; Fax: 775-322-3616. Mailing Address: P.O. Box 8879, 89507.
E-mail: ladyofwisdom@worldnet.att.net
Rev. Frank Murphy, Chap.

[G] CATHOLIC COMMUNITY SERVICES OF NORTHERN NEVADA

RENO. *Catholic Community Services of Northern Nevada.* Mailing Address: P.O. Box 5099, 89513-5099. 500 E. Fourth St., 89512. Tel: 775-322-7073; Fax: 775-322-8197.
E-mail: ccsnn@gbis.com
Adoption. Linda Maisel, Dir. Tel: 775-322-7073.
Emergency Assistance. Ida Yoas, Dir. Tel: 775-322-0553.
St. Vincent's Food Pantry. Grace Turner, Dir. Tel: 775-786-5266.
St. Vincent's Thrift Shop. James Baker, Dir. Tel: 775-322-9824.
Holy Child Day Home, 440 Reno Ave., 89509. Tel: 775-329-2979; Fax: 775-329-8537. Karen Barreras, Dir.
St. Vincent's Dining Room. Mailing Address: P.O. Box 5099, 89513-5099. 505 W. Third St., 89503. Tel: 775-329-5363. Ray Trevino, Dir.
St. Vincent's Haven. Mailing Address: P.O. Box 5099, 89513-5099. 1865 Montello Ave., 89506. Tel: 775-329-1189. Mark Klebofski, Dir.
St. Vincent's Residence, 395 Gould St., 89502. Ron Griffin, Dir. Tel: 775-322-2143.

[H] MISCELLANEOUS

RENO.
Fertility Care Center of Reno, Inc., 3680 Grant Dr., Ste. O, 89509. Tel: 775-827-5111; Fax: 775-827-5111.
E-mail: fertilityR@aol.com
Juliana Jervis, Contact Person.
Nevada Catholic Conference, 290 S. Arlington Ave., Ste. 200, 89501-1713. Tel: 775-326-9416; Fax: 775-348-8619.
E-mail: bpayant@pyramid.net
Bob Payant, Exec. Dir.

RELIGIOUS INSTITUTES OF MEN REPRESENTED IN THE DIOCESE

For further details refer to the corresponding bracketed number in the Religious Institutes of Men or Women section.
[0960]—*Brothers of the Congregation of Our Lady of the Holy Rosary.*—F.S.R.
[0480]—*Conventual Franciscans.*—O.F.M.Conv.
[0520]—*Franciscan Friars.*—O.F.M.
[0910]—*Oblates of Mary Immaculate.*—O.M.I.
[0610]—*Priests of the Congregation of the Holy Cross.*—C.S.C.
[1070]—*Redemptorist Fathers.*—C.Ss.R.
[0990]—*Society of the Catholic Apostolate.* (Irish Prov.).—S.A.C.

RELIGIOUS INSTITUTES OF WOMEN REPRESENTED IN THE DIOCESE

[0420]—*Discalced Carmelite Nuns.*—O.C.D.
[1070-04]—*Dominican Sisters of San Rafael.*—O.P.
[1190]—*Franciscan Sisters of the Atonement.*—S.A.
[2523]—*Sisters of Mercy of Ardagh and Clonmacnois.*—R.S.M.
[1705]—*Sisters of St. Francis of Assisi.*—O.S.F.
[1650]—*Sisters of St. Francis of Philadelphia.*—O.S.F.
[]—*Sisters of St. Philip Neri.* (Madrid, Spain).—R.F.
[1960]—*Sisters of the Holy Family.*—S.H.F.

DIOCESAN CEMETERIES

RENO. *Our Mother of Sorrows Cemetery & Mausoleum*, 2700 N. Virginia St., 89503. Mailing Address: P.O. Box 8505, 89507. Tel: 775-323-0133; Fax: 775-323-1229. Sophia Mitchell, Operations Mgr.; Sr. Ofelia Roibas, Counselor.

NECROLOGY

† Fanning, Gerard F., (Retired). —Died Oct. 15, 2000.

Diocese of Richmond

(Dioecesis Richmondiensis)

Most Reverend

WALTER F. SULLIVAN, D.D.

Bishop of Richmond; ordained May 9, 1953; appointed Titular Bishop of Selsey and Auxiliary Bishop of Richmond October 20, 1970; consecrated December 1, 1970; appointed Apostolic Administrator of Richmond April 30, 1973; succeeded to the See, June 6, 1974. *Res., 800 Cathedral Pl., Richmond, VA, 23220. Office: 811 Cathedral Pl., Suite B, Richmond, VA, 23220-4801.*

ESTABLISHED IN 1820.

Square Miles 36,711.

Comprises the State of Virginia, with the exception of the Counties of Arlington, Clarke, Culpeper, Fairfax, Fauquier, Frederick, King George, Lancaster, Loudoun, Madison, Northumberland, Orange, Page, Prince William, Rappahannock, Richmond, Shenandoah, Spottsylvania, Stafford, Warren and Westmoreland.

For legal titles of parishes and diocesan institutions, consult the Chancery Office.

The Chancery: 811 Cathedral Pl., Richmond, VA, 23220-4801. Tel.: 804-359-5661; Fax: 804-358-9159.

Web site address: www.diocric.org

E-mail address: aedwards@diocric.org

STATISTICAL OVERVIEW

Personnel	
Bishop	1
Abbots	1
Priests: Diocesan Active in Diocese	122
Priests: Active Outside Diocese	12
Priests: Retired, Sick or Absent	31
Number of Diocesan Priests	165
Religious Priests in Diocese	39
Extern Priests in Diocese	13
Ordinations:	
Diocesan Priests	2
Permanent Deacons	2
Permanent Deacons in Diocese	29
Total Brothers	12
Total Sisters	198
Parishes	
Parishes	143
With Resident Pastor:	
Resident Diocesan Priests	106
Resident Religious Priests	8
Without Resident Pastor:	
Administered by Priests	16
Administered by Deacons	1
Administered by Women Religious	7
Administered by Lay People	5
Completely Vacant	1
Missions	7
Pastoral Centers	2
Professional Ministry Personnel:	
Brothers	1
Sisters	16
Lay Ministers	140
Welfare	
Catholic Hospitals	10
Total Assisted	619,549
Homes for the Aged	15
Total Assisted	2,733
Residential Care of Children	2
Total Assisted	460
Day Care and Extended Day Care Centers	9
Total Assisted	867
Special Centers for Social Services	8
Total Assisted	10,000
Residential Care of Disabled	5
Total Assisted	240
Educational	
Diocesan Students in Other Seminaries	8
Total Seminarians	8
High Schools, Diocesan and Parish	6
Total Students	1,382
High Schools, Private	3
Total Students	869
Elementary Schools, Diocesan and Parish	22
Total Students	8,519
Elementary Schools, Private	1
Total Students	431
Non-residential Schools for the Disabled	1
Total Students	140
Catechesis/Religious Education:	
High School Students	5,922
Elementary Students	18,779
Total Students Under Catholic Instruction	36,050
Teachers in the Diocese:	
Priests	4
Sisters	7
Lay Teachers	740
Vital Statistics	
Receptions into the Church:	
Infant Baptism Totals	3,538
Adult Baptism Totals	701
Received into Full Communion	1,134
First Communions	3,619
Confirmations	1,917
Marriages:	
Catholic	578
Interfaith	699
Total Marriages	1,277
Deaths	1,545
Total Catholic Population	200,342
Total Population	4,555,139

Former Bishops—Rt. Rev. PATRICK KELLY, D.D., first Bishop; cons. Aug. 24, 1820; transferred Waterford and Lismore in 1822; died Oct. 8, 1829.—Rt. Rev. RICHARD V. WHELAN, D.D., second Bishop; cons. March 21, 1841; transferred Wheeling, July 23, 1850; died July 7, 1874.—Rt. Rev. JOHN MCGILL, D.D., cons. Nov. 10, 1850; died Jan. 14, 1872.—His Eminence JAMES CARDINAL GIBBONS, D.D., cons. August 16, 1868 Bishop of Adramyttum, and Vicar-Apostolic of North Carolina; transferred the See of Richmond, July 30, 1872; transferred the See of Baltimore, Oct. 3, 1877; created Cardinal Priest of S. Maria in Trastevere, June 7, 1886; died March 24, 1921.—Rt. Rev. JOHN J. KEANE, D.D., cons. Aug. 25, 1878; resigned August, 1888 rector of the Catholic University, Washington, DC; transferred to Archbishopric of Dubuque, July 24, 1900; died June 27, 1918.—Rt. Rev. AUGUSTINE VAN DE VYVER, D.D., cons. Oct. 20, 1889; died Oct. 16, 1911.—Rt. Rev. DENIS JOSEPH O'CONNELL, D.D., cons. May 3, 1908 Titular Bishop of Sebaste and Auxiliary Bishop of San Francisco; appt. Bishop of Richmond, Jan. 19, 1912; resigned Jan. 15, 1926 and appointed Titular Archbishop of Marianne; died Jan. 1, 1927.—Most Rev. ANDREW J. BRENNAN, D.D., ord. December 17, 1904; cons. Titular Bishop of Thapsus and Auxiliary Bishop of Scranton, April 25, 1923; appt. Bishop of Richmond, May 28, 1926; resigned April 14, 1945; appt. Titular Bishop of Telmissus; died May 23, 1956.—Most Rev. PETER L. IRETON, D.D., ord. June 20, 1906; appt. Titular Bishop of Cime Coadjutor Bishop and Apostolic Administrator of Richmond, August 3, 1935; cons. October 23, 1935; named Bishop of Richmond, April 14, 1945; named Assistant at the Pontifical Throne, May 21, 1956; died April 27, 1958.—Most Rev. JOHN J. RUSSELL, D.D., ord. July 8, 1923; appt. Bishop of Charleston, Jan. 28, 1950; cons. March 14, 1950; appt. Bishop of Richmond, July 3, 1958; retired April 3, 1973; died March 17, 1993.

Central Administrative Offices

All Diocesan Offices are located at: 811 Cathedral Place, Richmond, VA 23220-4801. Tel: 804-359-5661; Fax: 804-358-9159, unless otherwise indicated

Vicars General—Rev. Msgr. THOMAS F. SHREVE, V.G., J.C.L.; Rev. Msgr. CHARLES A. KELLY, V.G.

Episcopal Vicars—Rev. Msgr. THOMAS J. CAROLUZZA, Eastern Vicariate; Rev. Msgr. CHARLES A. KELLY, Central Vicariate; Rev. Msgr. ROBERT M. PERKINS, Southside Vicariate; Rev. Msgr. J. KENNETH RUSH, Western Vicariate.

Diocesan Tribunal Central Offices—3805 Cutshaw Ave., Ste. 307, Richmond, 23230-3938. Tel: 804-355-9155; Fax: 804-359-2810.

Judicial Vicar—Rev. Msgr. WILLIAM V. SULLIVAN, J.C.L., M.Ch.A.

Adjutant Judicial Vicars—Revs. J. SCOTT DUARTE, J.C.D; R. FRANCIS MUENCH, J.C.L.

Judges—Revs. MARTIN E. LAVIN, J.C.D.; J. SCOTT DUARTE, J.C.D.; J. KENNETH RUSH, D.Min.; R. FRANCIS MUENCH, J.C.L.; RUSSELL E. SMITH, S.T.D.; MICHAEL M. DUFFY, J.C.L.; KEVIN J. O'BRIEN, S.T.B., Ph.D.

Defenders of the Bond—Deacon JOHN H. THOMAS; H. ROBERTA SMALL, J.C.L.

Field Offices—

Roanoke—P.O. Box 21784, Roanoke, 24018-0180.

Tidewater—145 Dupre Ave., Norfolk, 23503-3423. Tel: 804-588-2941.

Ecclesiastical Notaries—Mrs. BARBARA A. LEE; Mrs. DENISE RYAN; ANTHONY K. SPRATLEY; Ms. BARBARA WATTS.

Auditors—Ms. VALERIE MCAVOY.

Vicar for the Hispanic Apostolate—Rev. Msgr. MICHAEL S. SCHMIED; ELISA MONTALVO, Dir. Tel: 804-359-5661, Ext. 204.

Ethnic and Special Liturgies—Filipino, Hispanic, Korean, Vietnamese; Tridentine Latin Mass, Deaf/ Hearing Impaired—Please contact the Chancery office for locations and schedules.

Vicar for Ecumenism—Rev. Msgr. RAYMOND A. BARTON.

Chancellor—Mrs. ANNE C. EDWARDS.

Secretary to the Bishop—Rev. PASQUALE J. APUZZO.

Special Assistant to the Bishop—Dr. STEPHEN M. COLECCHI.

Vicar for Vocations—Rev. MICHAEL A. RENNINGER.

Vocation Director for Promotion and Recruitment—Rev. Msgr. MICHAEL MCCARRON.

Department of Communication & Administrative—Rev. PASQUALE J. APUZZO, Moderator.

Office of Communication—Rev. PASQUALE J. APUZZO, Dir.

Office of Human Resources—Mr. MICHAEL BECHELLI, Dir.; Mrs. ETTA SHEPPERD, Benefits Admin.

Office of Development—Ms. CAROLE KAHWAJY, Dir.

Office of Information Technology—Ms. JOAN PARDUE, Dir.; Mrs. KAREN BISHOP, Programmer/Analyst; Mr. NICK KURIGER, Network Admin.

Office of Printing—Mr. NORMAN HOWARD, Dir.

Department of Financial & Fiscal Services—Mr. JOHN F. BARRETT, Moderator.

Office of Finance—Mr. JOHN F. BARRETT, Dir.

Office of Plant Management—Mrs. SUSAN R. TEAL, Dir.

Office of Risk Management—Mr. KURT HICKMAN, Dir.

Department of Pastoral Services—Ms. DIANE BIALKOWSKI, Moderator.

Office of Christian Formation—Mr. DENNIS BEEMAN, Dir. Assoc. Dirs.: Mrs. EMILY FILIPPI; Ms. PATRICIA NOVAK.

Office of Catholic Schools—Ms. DIANE BIALKOWSKI, Supt. Assistant Superintendents: Ms. MAUREEN MCCABE; Mrs. PATRICIA AVERY.

Office of Campus and Young Adult Ministry—Bro. COSMAS RUBENCAMP, C.F.X., Dir.; Sr. DIANE GUY, S.N.D., Assoc. Dir.

Department of Social Action—Dr. STEPHEN M. COLECCHI, Moderator.

Office of Justice and Peace—Dr. STEPHEN M. COLECCHI, Dir. Assoc. Dirs.: Mr. MICHAEL E. STONE; Dr. KATHLEEN KENNEY.

Appalachian Office of Justice & Peace—MUZAFFAR FAZALUDDIN, Dir., *P.O. Box 660, St. Paul, 24283.* Tel: 540-762-5050.

Migrant Ministry Office—Mr. JAMES ALBRIGHT, Dir., *P.O. Box 584, Accomac, 23301.* Tel: 757-787-7862.

Office of Refugee Resettlement & Immigration Services—Mrs. MARILYN BRESLOW, Exec. Dir.

Richmond Regional Dir.—KATHLEEN JACKSON.

Norfolk Regional Dir.—JANE COOK, *1801 Ashland Ave., Norfolk, 23509.* Tel: 757-623-9131.

Roanoke Regional Dir.—BARBARA SMITH, *1106 9th St., S.E., Roanoke, 24013.* Tel: 540-342-7561.

Ministry with Older Adults—MARY ELLEN COX, Coord. Tel: 804-227-3116.

Office of Black Catholics—Sr. CORA MARIE BILLINGS, R.S.M., Dir.

Diocesan Councils and Organizations

Apostleship of the Sea—STELLA MARRIS; Rev. SANTIAGO C. FRIAS, *155 W. Government Ave., Norfolk, 23503.* Tel: 757-623-4222.

Campaign for Human Development—Mr. MICHAEL STONE, Diocesan Dir.

Catholic Relief Services—Dr. KATHLEEN KENNEY.

Catholic Historical Society of the Roanoke Valley—Mrs. MARGARET M. COCHENER, Pres., *400 W. Campbell Ave., Roanoke, 24016.*

Catholic Daughters of America—Ms. MARIAN E. NOWLAND, State Regent, *4617 Seminary Rd., Apt. 207, Alexandria, 22304.*

Catholic Golden Age—Ms. JEAN CAHEN, *2821 Hilliard Rd., Richmond, 23228.*

"Catholic Virginian" (Diocesan Newspaper)—Mr. CHARLES MAHON, Editor, *P.O. Box 26843, Richmond, 23261.* Tel: 804-359-5654; Fax: 804-359-5689. Mr. STEPHEN S. NEILL, Assoc. Editor; Mrs. JUDITH LINDFORS, Business Mgr. & Circulation Dir.

Council of Catholic Women—Mrs. CHARLENE FOUGHNER, *408 Loura Ct., Hampton, 23666.*

Catholic Women's Club—Mrs. WILLIAM A. LOTH, Pres., *8503 Academy Rd., Richmond, 23229.*

Cemeteries—Rev. GEORGE E. ZAHN, Dir. Tel: 804-329-0473.

Councilium Board for Education—MAUREEN MCCABE, *811 Cathedral Pl., Richmond, 23220.* Tel: 804-359-5661.

Council of Priests—See Presbyteral Council.

Cursillio—Lay Co-Dirs.: JAMES MCGROGAN; ALBERTA MCGROGAN, *Rte. 1, Box 65-A, Fairfield, 24435.* Tel: 540-348-5939.

Commonwealth Catholic Charities—1512 Willow Lawn Dr., Richmond, 23230-0565. Tel: 804-285-5900. Rev. DAVID J. BERGNER, S.D.S., Exec. Dir.; Dr. STEPHEN M. COLECCHI, Diocesan Dir.

Catholic Charities of Hampton Roads, Inc.—4855 Princess Anne Rd., Virginia Beach, 23462. Tel: 757-467-7707. Mrs. MARGARET ROBERTSON, Exec. Dir.

Ecumenical Officer—Rev. RAYMOND A. BARTON, *712 Little Neck Rd., Virginia Beach, 23452.*

Finance Council—JAMES F. BETTS, *1417 Floyd Ave., Richmond, 23220.*

Haitian Ministry Commission—Bro. COSMOS RUBENCAMP, Exec. Sec., *811 Cathedral Pl., Richmond, 23220.* Tel: 804-359-5661.

Holy Childhood Association—Rev. Msgr. THOMAS F. SHREVE, J.C.L., V.G.

Knights of Columbus—JAMES P. MCCUSKER, State Deputy, *9237 Bayberry Ave., Manasas, 22110.*

Nocturnal Adoration Society—Rev. JAMES KAUFFMANN, *300 N. Sheppard St., Richmond, 23220.*

Diocesan Pastoral Council—Mrs. PATTY HUFFMAN, *825 Elmwood Dr., Harrisonburg, 22801.*

Diocesan School Board—Mr. ERNIE DREW, Chm., *1602 Marblehead Ct., Richmond, 23235.*

Pax Christi Richmond—Mr. JOHN GALLINI, *2425 Triton Dr., Richmond, 23235.*

Pax Christi Virginia—ADELE DELLA-VALLE RAUTH; BOB DELLA-VALLE RAUTH, *110 Lee Dr., Huddleston, 24104.*

Presbyteral Council—Rev. JOHN A. GRACE, Chm., *1052 S. Main St., Harrisonburg, 22801.*

Propagation of the Faith—Rev. Msgr. THOMAS F. SHREVE, J.C.L., V.G.

Respect Life—MICHAEL E. STONE, Coord.

Diocesan AIDS Task Force—Dr. STEPHEN LENTON, Chm., *P.O. Box 7087, Richmond, 23221-0087.*

Richmond Catholic Heritage Foundation—Contact Mrs. Anne Edwards at the Chancery.

Secular Carmelite Communities—

Community of the Holy Spirit—SUNNI COWLING, O.C.D.S., Pres., *1211 Mt. Erin Dr., Richmond, 23231.*

Community of Our Lady of the Annunication—TIRA KNIPSEL, O.C.D.S., Pres., *1288 Alanton Dr., Virginia Beach, 23454.*

Serra Club of Richmond—GERARD J. MULLEN, *12749 Walton Ridge Lane, Midlothian, 23113.*

Scouting—Rev. DAVID MCGUIRE; Mr. JOHN CONRON, Diocesan Lay Chm. Tel: 804-272-5075.

Youth Ministry Council—Ms. PATRICIA NOVAK, *811 Cathedral Pl., Richmond, 23220.*

CLERGY, PARISHES, MISSIONS AND PAROCHIAL SCHOOLS

CITY OF RICHMOND

1—CATHEDRAL OF THE SACRED HEART (1906), Most Rev. Walter F. Sullivan, D.D.; Rev. Msgr. Charles A. Kelly, Rector; Revs. Michael A. Renninger, Vice-Rector; Alexander Pereira.
Bishop's Office: 811 Cathedral Pl., 23220-4801. Tel: 804-359-5661; Fax: 804-358-9159.; Cathedral Office: 823 Park Ave., 23220. Tel: 804-359-5651; Fax: 804-359-8043. [JC]
Church—18 N. Laurel, 23220.
Catechesis/Religious Programs—Students 129.

2—CHURCH OF THE EPIPHANY (Chesterfield Co) (1979), Rev. Msgr. Thomas F. Shreve.
Mailing Address: 11000 Smoketree Dr., 23236-3144. Tel: 804-794-0222; Fax: 804-378-2013.
School—See St. Edward, Richmond.
Catechesis/Religious Programs—Students 1,050.

3—HOLY ROSARY (1953) (African American), Rev. Louis Ruoff.
Mailing Address: P.O. Box 23116, 23223.
Parish Office: 1209 N. 33rd St., 23223-0416. Tel: 804-222-1105; Fax: 804-226-2204.
Res., 917 Old Denny St., 23231. Tel: 804-222-6568.
Church—N. 33rd & S St., 23223.
Child Care Center—1218 N. 34th St., 23223. Tel: 804-222-2590. Ms. Cynthia Rascoe, Dir.
Students 120.

4—OUR LADY OF LOURDES (Henrico Co.) (1944), Rev. Thomas McDonnell, S.J.
Church—8200 Woodman Rd., 23228-3237. Tel: 804-262-7315; Fax: 804-262-7337. [JC]
School—Tel: 804-262-1770; Fax: 804-262-1437. Lucy R. Reilley, Prin.
Lay Teachers 19; Students 302.
Catechesis/Religious Programs—Students 304.

5—SACRED HEART (1901), Rev. David Stokes, S.J. In res., Rev. G. Harry Hock, S.J.
Mailing Address: 1415 Perry St., 23224-2057.
Res., 1409 Perry St., 23224. Tel: 804-230-6430; 232-8964 (Office); Fax: 804-231-9931. [JC]
Church—1401 Perry St., 23224.

6—ST. AUGUSTINE (Chesterfield Co.) (1973), Rev. Msgr. Michael S. Schmied.
Mailing Address: 4400 Beulah Rd., 23237-1850.
Res., 9608 Verlinda Ct., 23237. Tel: 804-778-4842.
Church—Corner of Hopkins & Beulah Rd., 23237. Tel: 804-275-7962; Fax: 804-271-4604.
Catechesis/Religious Programs—Students 391.

7—ST. BENEDICT (1911), Rev. James Kauffmann.
Mailing Address: 206 N. Belmont Ave., 23221.
Res., 1129 West Ave., 23220. [JC]
Church—300 N. Sheppard St., 23221-2407. Tel: 804-254-8810; Fax: 804-355-5112.
Church Mailing Address: 206 N. Belmont Ave., 23221.
School—3100 Grove Ave., 23221. Tel: 804-254-8850. Mrs. Mary Claire Robinson, Prin.
Lay Teachers 15; Students 254.
Catechesis/Religious Programs—Students 78.

8—ST. BRIDGET (Henrico Co.) (1949), Rev. Msgr. Thomas G. Miller.
Church—6006 Three Chopt Rd., 23226-2797. Tel: 804-282-9511; Fax: 804-285-7227.
School—6011 York Rd., 23226. Fax: 804-288-5730. Ms. Anne T. Carroll, Prin.
Sisters 1; Lay Teachers 30; Students 472.
Catechesis/Religious Programs—Students 448.

9—ST. EDWARD THE CONFESSOR (1959), Revs. Donald H. Lemay; Charles L. Breindel; Deacon Robert Ewan.
Mailing Address: 2700 Dolfield Rd., 23235-2618. Tel: 804-272-2948; Fax: 804-560-3565.
Res., 10908 Ashburn Rd., 23235-2618. Tel: 804-330-0772.
Church—Hugeunot Rd. & Dolfield Dr., 23235.
School—Regional School St. Edward-Epiphany, 10701 Huguenot Rd., 23235. Tel: 804-272-2881; Fax: 804-272-2904. Ms. Georgette Richards, Prin.
Catechesis/Religious Programs—Students 740.

10—ST. ELIZABETH (1923) (African American), Rev. Pasquale Apuzzo; Sr. Cora Marie Billings, R.S.M., Pastoral Coord.
Mailing Address: 1301 Victor St., 23222-3935. Tel: 804-329-4599; Fax: 804-321-0741. [JC]
Church—2712 Second Ave., 23222.
School—All Saints, 3418 Noble Ave., 23222. Tel: 804-329-7524; Fax: 804-321-1538. Mr. Kenneth Soistman, Prin.

11—ST. GABRIEL (Chesterfield Co.) (1997), Rev. John M. DeGiorgio.
Mailing Address: P.O. Box 129, Moseley, 23120. Tel: 804-639-6712; Fax: 804-639-6591.
Catechesis/Religious Programs—Students 788.

12—ST. JOSEPH TRIDENTINE CHAPEL, Rev. Adrian W. Harmening, O.S.B., Chap.
12829 River Rd., 23233. Tel: 804-342-1319; 784-7172; Fax: 804-355-5112; 784-7173.
Catechesis/Religious Programs—Students 88.

13—ST. KIM TAEGON (1986) (Korean), Rev. Paul Pyung Ki Cho.
Mailing Address: 3103 Maury St., 23224-3542. Tel: 804-232-0993; Fax: 804-232-0995.
Church—3100 Logandale Ave., 23224.
Catechesis/Religious Programs—Students 49.

14—ST. MARY (1962), Rev. Walter G. Lewis.
Mailing Address: 9505 Gayton Rd., 23229-5319. Tel: 804-740-4044; Fax: 804-740-2197.
School—9501 Gayton Rd., 23229. Tel: 804-740-1048. Mrs. Hazel Lewane, Prin.
Lay Teachers 21; Students 274.
Catechesis/Religious Programs—Students 550.

15—ST. MICHAEL (Glen Allen) (1992), Rev. John E. Leonard.
Mailing Address: 4491 Springfield Rd., Glen Allen, 23060. Tel: 804-527-1037; Fax: 804-527-1039.
Catechesis/Religious Programs—Students 1,035.

16—ST. PATRICK (1859), Rev. Robert Gloisten.
Mailing Address: 213 N. 25th St., 23223-7115. Tel: 804-648-0504; Fax: 804-648-5216.
School—2600 E. Grace St., 23223. Tel: 804-648-3621; Fax: 804-648-3622. Mrs. Bettijo Loving, Prin.

17—ST. PAUL (1921), Rev. George E. Zahn. In res., Rev. Frederick J. Feusahrens.
Mailing Address: 909 Rennie Ave., 23227. Tel: 804-329-0473; 329-5512; Fax: 804-321-6454.
School—All Saints, 3418 Noble Ave., 23227. Tel: 804-329-7524; Fax: 804-321-1538. Mr. Kenneth Soistman, Prin.
Catechesis/Religious Programs—Students 65.

18—ST. PETER (1834), Rev. Robert A. Brownell.
Mailing Address: P.O. Box 933, 23218-0933. Tel: 804-643-4315; Fax: 804-783-6120.
Res., 4030 Forest Hill Ave., Apt. 27, 23225. Tel: 804-231-3941. [JC]
Church—800 E. Grace St., 23219.
Catechesis/Religious Programs—Students 10.

19—CHURCH OF THE VIETNAMESE MARTYRS (1983) (Vietnamese), Rev. Joseph Than Xuan Pham. In res., Rev. Anthony Ngo.
Mailing Address: 12500 Patterson Ave., 23233. Tel: 804-784-5450; Fax: 804-784-9822.
Catechesis/Religious Programs—Students 101.

OUTSIDE THE CITY OF RICHMOND

Abingdon, Christ the King (1983), Rev. Robert L. Krenik.
Mailing Address: P.O. Box 1201, 24212-1201.
Res., 124 Park Blvd., Marion, 24354. Tel: 540-783-7282; 628-2941; Fax: 540-783-7282.
Church—820 E. Main St., 24212.
Catechesis/Religious Programs—Students 53.

Amelia, Good Samaritan (1980), Deacon Peter Menting, Admin.
Mailing Address: P.O. Box 759, 23002. Tel: 804-298-0684; Fax: 804-292-5078.
Catechesis/Religious Programs—Students 9.

Amherst, Amherst Co., St. Francis of Assisi (1995), Rev. Daniel Kelly. In res., Rev. Saul Anleu.
P.O. Box 663, 24521. Tel: 804-263-8509.
Catechesis/Religious Programs—Students 10.

Appomattox, Our Lady of Peace (1982), Rev. Robert Dillon; Deacon William K. Hayes.
Mailing Address: P.O. Box 668, 24522-0668. Tel: 804-352-0104.
Res., Rte. 3, Box 7250, Dillwyn, 23936. Tel: 804-969-2168; Fax: 804-969-2168.
Church—Intersection of Rte. 631 & Rte. 627, 24522.
Catechesis/Religious Programs—Students 3.

Ashland, Hanover Co., St. Ann (1892), Rev. Msgr. William V. Sullivan.
Church & Mailing Address—105 S. Snead St., 23005-1811. Tel: 804-798-5039; Fax: 804-798-5072.
Res., 202 Thompson St., 23005-1514. Tel: 804-752-5902.
Catechesis/Religious Programs—Students 175.

Bedford, Holy Name of Mary (1874), Rev. James Cowles.
Mailing Address: 1307 Oakwood St., 24523-1613. Tel: 540-586-8988; Fax: 540-587-9080.
Res., 1531 Newton Cir., 24523. Tel: 540-586-9271.
Church—1301 Oakwood St., 24523.
Catechesis/Religious Programs—Students 63.

Big Stone Gap, Wise Co., Sacred Heart (1902), Rev. Anthony Rodrigues. In res., Rev. Leslie Schmidt, Glmy.
Mailing Address: 1821 Holton Ave., 24219-2611. Tel: 540-523-6546; Fax: 540-523-1602.
Catechesis/Religious Programs—Students 30.

Blacksburg, Montgomery Co., St. Mary & Newman Community (1938), Rev. James M. Arsenault; Deacon Mike Ellerbrock. Campus Ministers: Rev. James Griffin; Mr. Peter Court.
Mailing Address: 706 Harding Ave., N.E., 24060-3618. Tel: 540-552-1091; Fax: 540-953-2962.
Res., 213 Price St., 24060. Tel: 540-951-2136.
Newman Community: 203 Otey St., 24060. Tel: 540-951-0032.
Catechesis/Religious Programs—Students 274.

Blackstone, Nottoway Co., Immaculate Heart of Mary (1947), Rev. Anthony Dinges; Mrs. Therese Mansfield, Pastoral Coord.
Mailing Address: P.O. Box 266, 23824-0266. Tel: 804-292-5535; Fax: 804-292-5535.
Church—903 S. Main St., 23824.
Catechesis/Religious Programs—Students 20.

Bristol, St. Anne (1903), Rev. Thomas A. Ianucci; Deacon Harry Hall.
Mailing Address: 350 Euclid Ave., 24201-4014. Tel: 540-669-8200; Fax: 540-669-7825. [CEM]
Res., 922 Chester St., 24201. Tel: 540-466-4776.
School—300 Euclid Ave., 24201. Tel: 540-669-0048; Fax: 540-669-3523. Mrs. Jean Green, Prin.
Lay Teachers 21; Students 199.
Catechesis/Religious Programs—Students 128.

Brookneal, Campbell Co., St. Elizabeth of Hungary (1989), Rev. Matthias Newell; Sr. Edna M. Maier, Pastoral Coord.
Mailing Address: 800 John Randolph Blvd., South Boston, 24592-2943. Tel: 804-572-2285; Fax: 804-572-1725.
Res., 3302 W. Main St., South Boston, 24592. Tel: 804-517-0349.
Church—374 Juniper Cliff Rd., 24528.
Catechesis/Religious Programs—Students 6.

Buckingham, Church of the Nativity (1981), Rev. Robert Dillon.
Mailing Address: P.O. Box 241, 23921-0241. Tel: 804-969-3306; 969-2168 (Rectory); Fax: 804-968-2168.
Church—Rte. 60 E., 23921.

Buckner, Immaculate Conception (1876), Rev. Rodney Rodis.
Mailing Address: P.O. Box 40, Mineral, 23117-0040. Tel: 540-894-4266; Fax: 540-894-4993.
Res., 106 Loving St., Louisa, 23093. Tel: 540-894-4266.
Church—1107 Frederick Hall Rd., 23024.

Cape Charles, Northampton Co., St. Charles (1886), Rev. J. Michael Breslin.
Mailing Address: 545 Randolph Ave., 23310-3305. Tel: 757-331-1724.
Catechesis/Religious Programs—Students 18.

Caroline County, St. Mary of the Annunciation (1914), Rev. J. Scott Duarte.
Mailing Address: P.O. Box 396, Ladysmith, 22501.
Office & Church—10306 Ladysmith Rd., Ladysmith, 22501. Tel: 804-448-9064; Fax: 804-364-3553.
Catechesis/Religious Programs—Students 66.

Charlottesville, Albemarle Co., Church of the Holy Comforter (1880), Rev. Julian B. Goodman, Jr.
Mailing Address: 208 E. Jefferson St., 22902-5105. Tel: 804-295-7185; Fax: 804-295-7001.
Res., 660 Evergreen Ave., 22902. Tel: 804-977-5859.
Catechesis/Religious Programs—Students 147.

Church of the Incarnation (1976), Rev. William E. La Fratta.
Office: 1465 Incarnation Dr., 22901-1716. Tel: 804-973-4381; Fax: 804-973-1757.
Res., 2414 Commonwealth Dr., 22901. Tel: 804-978-7544.
Catechesis/Religious Programs—Students 776.

St. Thomas Aquinas (1963), Revs. Gregory Salomone, O.P.; Michael McCormack, O.P.; Thomas J. Blau. In res., Rev. Augustine Thompson.
Mailing Address: 331 Kent Rd., 22903. Tel: 804-293-8081.
Office: Tel: 804-293-6472; 293-8081; Fax: 804-296-1941.
Res., 308 Alderman Rd., 22903. Tel: 804-977-5658.
Church—401 Alderman Rd., 22903.
Catechesis/Religious Programs—Students 486.

Chesapeake, Chesapeake Co.,

1—PRINCE OF PEACE, (1975), Rev. Christian Haydinger.
Mailing Address: 621 Cedar Rd., 23322. Tel: 757-547-0356; 547-3903; Fax: 757-436-6477.
Res., 303 Elberon Ct., 23322. Tel: 757-547-2951.
Catechesis/Religious Programs—Students 860.

2—ST. MARY, (1915), Rev. James Geiger; Sr. Bernice McCourt, S.N.D., Pastoral Coord.
Mailing Address: P.O. Box 174-B, 23321-0174. Tel: 757-488-2663; 548-8426 (Rectory); Fax: 757-488-9237.
Church—536 Homestead Rd., 23321.
Catechesis/Religious Programs—Students 38.

3—ST. STEPHEN, MARTYR, (1997), Rev. James E. Gordon.
Mailing Address: 1544 S. Battlefield Blvd., 23322. Tel: 757-421-7416; Fax: 757-421-7488.
Res., 1117 Vineyard Dr., 23322. Tel: 757-546-9400.
Catechesis/Religious Programs—Students 410.

4—ST. THERESE OF LISIEUX, Rev. Robert L. Cummins.
Mailing Address: 4137 Portsmouth Blvd., 23321-2127. Tel: 757-488-2553; Fax: 757-465-4086.
Res., 3908 Parkway Rd., 23321. Tel: 757-488-5413.
Catechesis/Religious Programs—Students 410.

Chincoteague, Accomack Co., St. Andrew (1977), Rev. Louis Benoit.
Mailing Address: P.O. Box 229, 23336-0229. Tel: 757-336-5432; Fax: 757-336-3515.
Res., 6319 Mumford St., 23336.
Church—6288 Church St., 23336.
Catechesis/Religious Programs—Students 28.

Christiansburg, Holy Spirit Catholic Church (1995), Rev. John Prinelli.
Mailing Address: P.O. Box 98, 24068.
Church—Our Savior Lutheran Church, 1845 Cambria Rd., 24073. Tel: 540-381-0299; 921-3547; Fax: 540-921-3547.
Catechesis/Religious Programs—Students 48.

Clarksville, Mecklenburg Co., St. Catherine of Siena (1947), Rev. James Fosnot.
Mailing Address: P.O. Box 1537, 23927.
Res., 810 Market St., 23927. Tel: 804-374-5040.
Church—805 Virginia Ave., 23927. Tel: 804-374-8408; Fax: 804-374-9442.
Catechesis/Religious Programs—Students 16.

Clifton Forge, Alleghany Co., St. Joseph (1889), Rev. Robert Warren; Sr. Eveline Murray, Pastoral Coord.
Mailing Address: 620 Jefferson Ave., 24422-1715. Tel: 540-863-5371; Fax: 540-863-8963. [CEM]
Catechesis/Religious Programs—Students 30.

Clintwood, Dickenson Co., St. Joseph (1979), Rev. Robert B. Rademacher, Glmy.; Christine Ramirez, Pastoral Coord.
Mailing Address: Box 1250, 24228-1250. Tel: 540-926-5451; Fax: 540-926-6518.
Church—Main St., 24228.
Catechesis/Religious Programs—Students 10.

Colonial Heights, St. Ann (1925), Rev. Msgr. Robert M. Perkins. In res., Rev. William Nolte.
Mailing Address: 17111 Jefferson Davis Hwy., 23834-5396. Tel: 804-526-2548; Fax: 804-526-1922.
Res., 12861 Percival St., Chester, 23831. Tel: 804-796-9342.
Catechesis/Religious Programs—Students 460.

Columbia, Fluvanna Co., St. Joseph (1967), Rev. Gerald A. Przywara.
Mailing Address: P.O. Box 808, 23038-0808. Tel: 804-842-3970.
Res., 15 Dogleg Rd., Palmyra, 22963. Tel: 804-589-5200.

Covington, Alleghany Co., Sacred Heart (1924), Rev. David L. Nott.
Office: 214 W. Locust St., 24426-1537. Tel: 540-965-5821; Fax: 540-962-2147.
Res., 222 W. Locust St., 24426-1537.
Catechesis/Religious Programs—Students 36.

Crewe, Nottoway Co., St. John the Baptist (1939), Rev. Anthony Dinges; Ms. Therese Mansfield, Pastoral Coord.
Mailing Address: 102 Oliver Ave., 23930-1410. Tel: 804-645-7509; Fax: 804-292-5535.
Catechesis/Religious Programs—Students 4.
Mission—Meherrin, Sacred Heart, (1913) P.O. Box 62, Meherrin, 23954. Tel: 804-736-9390.

Danville, Pittsylvania Co., Sacred Heart (1878), Rev. David V. McGuire.
Mailing Address: 288 W. Main St., 24541-2848. Tel: 804-792-9456; Fax: 804-792-9463.
Res., 154 College Ave., 24541. Tel: 804-792-0081.
School—540 Central Blvd., 24541. Tel: 804-793-2656; Fax: 804-793-2658. Marguerite S. Dees, Prin.
Lay Teachers 23; Students 281.
Catechesis/Religious Programs—Students 84.

Dinwiddie Co., St. John (1907), Rev. John J. Martinez, S.J.
Mailing Address: 7215 Squirrel Level Rd., Petersburg, 23805-7035. Tel: 804-861-0123; Fax: 804-861-0123.
Church—Squirrel Level Rd. & Flank Rd., Dinwiddie, 23805.
Catechesis/Religious Programs—Students 32.

Elkton, Rockingham Co., Holy Infant (1953), Rev. Daniel Bain.
Mailing Address: 101 W. Marshall Ave., 22827-1221. Tel: 540-298-1341.
Church—Rte. 33 & Rte. 340, 22827.
Catechesis/Religious Programs—Students 13.

Emporia, Greensville Co., St. Richard (1940), Rev. Leo T. Cervantes.
Mailing Address: 117 Laurel St., 23847-2506. Tel: 804-634-3524; Fax: 804-634-0114.
Catechesis/Religious Programs—Students 8.
Mission—Lawrenceville, Greensville Co., St. Bernard, (1945) 117 Laurel St., 23847.

Farmville, Prince Edward Co., St. Theresa (1939), Rev. Richard T. Mooney.
Church and Mailing Address: 709 Buffalo St., 23901-1109. Tel: 804-392-3934; Fax: 804-392-1611.
Res., 400 Putney St., 23901. Tel: 804-315-5161.
Catechesis/Religious Programs—Students 100.

Fincastle, Botetourt Co., Church of the Transfiguration (1989), Rev. Robert J. Warren; Sr. Eveline Murray, Pastoral Coord.
Mailing Address: P.O. Box 416, 24090-0416. Tel: 540-473-2656; 473-3691 (Res.); Fax: 540-473-2193.
Church—7624 Roanoke Rd., 24090.
Catechesis/Religious Programs—Students 160.

Fort Monroe, St. Mary Star of the Sea (1860), Rev. Joseph L. Clark.
Mailing Address: 7 Frank Ln., 23651-1010. Tel: 757-722-9855; 722-3138; Fax: 757-726-0083.
School—St. Mary Star of the Sea, 14 N. Willard Ave., Hampton, 23663. Tel: 757-723-6358; Fax: 757-723-7580. Sr. Marie Blanchette Cummings, Prin.
Sisters 2; Lay Teachers 15; Students 265.
Catechesis/Religious Programs—Students 42.

Franklin, Southampton Co., St. Jude (1948), Rev. Carl De Souza.
Mailing Address: 1014 Clay St., 23851-1309. Tel: 757-569-9600; Fax: 757-562-6974.
Catechesis/Religious Programs—Students 90.
Mission—Wakefield, Infant of Prague.

Gate City, Scott Co., St. Bernard (1956), Rev. Roland Hautz, Glmy.
Mailing Address: 105 Linda St., 24251. Tel: 540-386-9665; Fax: 540-386-3902.
Catechesis/Religious Programs—Students 8.
Mission—Dungannon, St. Patrick, (1946) Rte. 1, Box 135, Dungannon, 24245. Tel: 540-995-2305.

Gloucester, St. Therese, the Little Flower (1939), Rev. Lee Guarnieri.
Church & Mailing Address: 6262 Main St., 23061.; Office: Tel: 804-693-5939; 693-9043 (Hall); Fax: 804-693-4766.

Res., 8051 Belroi Rd., 23061. Tel: 804-695-3380.
Catechesis/Religious Programs—Students 237.

Greene County, Shepherd of the Hills (1980), Rev. Daniel Bain.
Mailing Address: P.O. Box 83, Quinque, 22965-0083. Tel: 804-985-3929.
Res., 101 W. Marshall Ave., Elkton, 22827. Tel: 540-298-1341.
Church—Rte. 633, Quinque.
Catechesis/Religious Programs—Students 30.

Hampton

1—Catholic Community of the Korean Martyrs (1989), Rev. Steven Kang-Jin Suh.
Mailing Address: 2018 Bay Ave., 23661. Tel: 757-245-4485; 303-3423; Fax: 757-247-7928.

2—Immaculate Conception (1968), Rev. Robert E. French.
Mailing & Res.: P.O. Box 7382, 23666-0382. Tel: 757-826-0050.
Church—2150 Cunningham Dr., 23666. Tel: 757-826-0393; 826-0455; Fax: 757-825-0855.
Catechesis/Religious Programs—Students 152.

3—St. Joseph (1968), Revs. Joseph J. Majewski, C.SS.R.; Donald Winter, C.SS.R.; Anthony Morris, C.SS.R.
Mailing Address: P.O. Box 4126, 23664-0126.
Res., 410 Buckroe Ave., 23664-0126. Tel: 757-851-1711.
Church—414 Buckroe Ave., 23664-0126. Tel: 757-851-8800; Fax: 757-851-1875.
Catechesis/Religious Programs—Students 245.

4—St. Rose of Lima (1948), Rev. Donald J. Cavey.
Mailing Address: 2114 Bay Ave., 23661. Tel: 757-245-5513; Fax: 757-245-1277.
Res., 2108 Bay Ave., 23661. Tel: 757-245-2810.
Catechesis/Religious Programs—Students 55.

5—Our Lady of Vietnam Chapel (1994), Rev. Joseph Hai Nguyen.
Mailing Address: P.O. Box 1937, 23699. Tel: 757-622-5345; 722-2657; Fax: 757-247-9612.
Chapel—1307 LaSalle Ave., 23669.

Harrisonburg, Rockingham Co., Blessed Sacrament (1906), Revs. Kenneth E. Wood; John A. Grace.
Mailing Address: & Church: 154 N. Main St., 22802. Tel: 540-434-4341; 434-8601; Fax: 540-434-0849.
Res., 843 Meadowlark Dr., 22802. Tel: 540-433-5666.
Catechesis/Religious Programs—Students 450.

Highland Springs, Henrico Co., St. John (1929), Rev. James R. Guttendorf.
Mailing Address: P.O. Box 190, 23075-0190. Tel: 804-737-8028; 5732; Fax: 804-328-4683.
Res., 24 N. Oak, 23075. Tel: 804-737-4077.
Church—813 W. Nine Mile Rd., 23075.
Catechesis/Religious Programs—Students 127.

Hopewell, St. James Church (1918), Rev. Daniel Bond.
Mailing Address: 510 W. Poythress St., 23860-2508.
Res., 102 N. Fifth Ave., 23860. Tel: 804-458-9286.
Church—500 W. Poythress St., 23860. Tel: 804-458-9223; 458-9286 (evening); Fax: 804-458-1216.
Catechesis/Religious Programs—Students 119.
Mission—Claremont, St. Anne, (1950).

Hot Springs, Bath Co., The Shrine of the Sacred Heart (1922), Rev. David L. Nott.
Mailing Address: Drawer B, 24445-0047. Tel: 540-839-2603; Fax: 540-962-2147.

Hurt, Pittsylvania Co., St. Victoria (1964), Rev. Robert E. Dillon.
Mailing Address: P.O. Box 640, 24563-0640. Tel: 804-969-2168; Fax: 804-324-4759.
Res., 305 Victoria Dr., 24563.
Catechesis/Religious Programs—Students 38.

Lake Gaston, Mecklenberg Co., St. Peter The Apostle (1995), Rev. Leo T. Cervantes.
Church—Rte. 903, Ebony, Tel: 804-634-3524; Fax: 804-634-0114.

Lebanon, Russell Co., Good Shepherd (1959), Rev. Paul Maier.
Mailing Address: P.O. Box 730, 24266-0730. Tel: 540-889-1690; 889-0127.
Church—479 N.W. Main St., 24266.
Catechesis/Religious Programs—Students 7.

Lexington, Rockbridge Co., St. Patrick (1873), Rev. N. Alan Lipscomb.
Mailing Address: P.O. Box 725, 24450-0725. Tel: 540-463-3533; Fax: 540-463-6384.
Office: 219 W. Nelson St., 24450.
Res., 225 Denny Lane, 24450. Tel: 540-463-6819.
Church—219 W. Nelson St., 24450.
Catechesis/Religious Programs—Students 141.

Lovingston, Nelson Co., St. Mary (1979), Rev. Daniel Kelly. In res., Rev. Saul Anleu.
P.O. Box 375, 22949-0735. Tel: 804-263-4008.
Catechesis/Religious Programs—Students 19.

Lynchburg, Campbell Co., Holy Cross (1859), Rev. Msgr. J. Kenneth Rush.
Office: 710 Clay St., 24504-2530. Tel: 804-846-5245; Fax: 804-846-7022. [CEM]
Res., 3766 Fort Ave., 24501. Tel: 804-846-5966.
Church—710 Clay St., 24504.
School—Regional School, (Grades PreK-12) 2125 Langhorne Rd., 24501. Tel: 804-847-5436. Mr. John P. Jones, Prin.
Lay Teachers 45; Students 317.
Catechesis/Religious Programs—Students 288.
St. Thomas More (1978), Rev. Kevin J. O'Brien.
3015 Roundelay Rd., 24502-2036. Tel: 804-237-5911; Fax: 804-237-8854.
Catechesis/Religious Programs—Students 333.

Marion, Smyth Co., St. John the Evangelist Church (1974), Rev. Robert L. Krenik.
124 Park Blvd., 24354. Tel: 540-783-7282.
Church—120 Park Blvd., 24354.
Catechesis/Religious Programs—Students 18.

Martinsville, Henry Co., St. Joseph (1949), Rev. Martin Lavin.
Mailing Address: 704 E. Church St., 24112-3107. Tel: 540-638-4779; 638-1192; Fax: 540-638-2218.
Res., 9 Booker Rd., 24112. Tel: 540-632-3710.
Catechesis/Religious Programs—Students 95.

Mathews, Mathews Co., Church of Francis de Sales (1983), Rev. John D. Boddie.
Mailing Address: P.O. Box 158, 23109-0158. Tel: 804-725-2776; Fax: 804-725-5463.
Church—Rte. 647 & Lover's Ln., 23109.
Catechesis/Religious Programs—Students 29.

Mechanicsville, Hanover Co., Church of the Redeemer (1976), Rev. James J. Begley.
Church & Mailing Address: 8275 Meadowbridge Rd., 23116. Tel: 804-746-4911; Fax: 804-746-8657.
Res., 8222 N. Mayfield Ln., 23111. Tel: 804-730-1844.
Catechesis/Religious Programs—Students 605.

Middlesex County, Church of the Visitation (1983), Rev. John D. Boddie.
Mailing Address: P.O. Box 38, Topping, 23169-0038. Tel: 804-758-5160; Fax: 804-758-0676.
Res., Box 34, Cobbs Creek, 23035. Tel: 804-725-5463; Fax: 804-725-5463. [CEM]
Church—Rte. 33, Harmony Grove, 23035.
Catechesis/Religious Programs—Students 33.

Mineral, St. Jude (1974), Rev. Rodney Rodis.
Mailing Address: P.O. Box 40, 23117-0040. Tel: 540-894-4266; Fax: 540-894-4993.
Res., 106 Loving St., Louisa, 23093. Tel: 540-967-2465.
Church—1937 Davis Hwy., 23117.
Catechesis/Religious Programs—Students 72.

Moneta, Bedford Co., Resurrection (1984), Sr. Elizabeth Bagen, G.N.S.H., Pastoral Coord.
Mailing Address: 15353 Moneta Rd., 24121-9804. Tel: 540-297-5530; Fax: 540-297-6316.
Catechesis/Religious Programs—Students 52.

Newport News, Newport Co., Our Lady of Mount Carmel (1953), Rev. Msgr. Michael D. McCarron; Revs. Peter Tran; Timothy Keeney; Deacon Paul Larkin.
100 Harpersville Rd., 23601-2324. Tel: 757-595-0385; 0387; Fax: 757-599-9285.
School—Tel: 757-596-2754; Fax: 757-596-1727. Sr. Mary Aquinas, O.P., Prin.
Sisters of St. Dominic 4; Lay Teachers 16; Students 392.
Catechesis/Religious Programs—Students 453.
St. Jerome (1966), Rev. Joseph B. Majewski; Deacon Peter Kwon.
Mailing Address: 116 Denbigh Blvd., 23608-3333. Tel: 757-877-5021; Fax: 757-898-1437.
Catechesis/Religious Programs—Students 557.
St. Vincent de Paul (1881), Rev. Lloyd F. Stephenson.
Mailing Address: P.O. Box 258, 23607-0258. Tel: 757-245-4234; Fax: 757-245-0039.
Church—230 33rd St., 23607.
Catechesis/Religious Programs—Students 96.

Norfolk, Norfolk City Co.,

1—Blessed Sacrament, (1921), Rev. Joseph H. Metzger, III.
Mailing Address: 170 Painter St., 23505-4557. Tel: 757-423-8305; Fax: 757-451-3335. [JC]
Res., 110 W. Severn Rd., 23505. Tel: 757-489-9636.
Church—Newport Ave. & Painter St., 23505.
Catechesis/Religious Programs—Students 48.

2—Christ the King, (1949), Rev. Brian Rafferty.
Office & Mailing Address—1803 Columbia Ave., 23509-1298. Tel: 757-622-1120; 622-9196; Fax: 757-627-8808.
Res., 1804 Ashland Ave., 23509. Tel: 757-627-1723.
School—3401 Tidewater Dr., 23509. Tel: 757-625-4951; Fax: 757-623-5212. Mrs. Patricia Suraci, Prin.
Lay Teachers 19; Students 301.
Catechesis/Religious Programs—Students 160.

3—Holy Trinity, (1921), Rev. Wayne Ball. In res., Rev. Msgr. Santiago C. Frias Tel: 757-480-3434.
Mailing Address: 155 W. Government Ave., 23503-2905. Tel: 757-480-3433; Fax: 757-480-8749. [JC]
Res., 175 W. Government Ave., 23503. Tel: 804-480-3433.
School—154 W. Government Ave., 23503. Tel: 757-583-1873; Fax: 757-587-3677. Ms. Deneane Nofplot, Prin.
Lay Teachers 17; Students 230.
Catechesis/Religious Programs—Students 150.

4—Sacred Heart, (1894), Rev. John J. Wagner, III, Admin.
Office: 520 Graydon Ave., 23507-1711. Tel: 757-625-6763; Fax: 757-627-1965.
Catechesis/Religious Programs—Students 285.

5—Basilica of St. Mary, (1791) (African American), Rev. John J. Dorgan, Rector.
Office: 1000 Holt St., 23504-4241. Tel: 757-622-4487; Fax: 757-625-7679. [JC]
Church—232 Chapel St., 23504.
School—St. Mary's Academy, 921 Holt St., 23504. Fax: 757-587-3677. Sr. Inez Dicks, Prin.
Sisters 1; Lay Teachers 18; Students 211.
Catechesis/Religious Programs—Students 118.
Convent—1000 Holt St., 23504. Tel: 757-627-5213.

6—Our Lady of Lavang, (1991), Rev. Joseph Hai-Nguyen.
1806 Ashland Ave., 23509-1236.
Church—409 Compostella Rd., 23518. Tel: 757-622-5345; 545-5606; Fax: 757-622-4248.

7—St. Pius X, (1955), Rev. R. Francis Muench.
Mailing Address: 7800 Halprin Dr., 23518-4408. Tel: 757-583-0291; Fax: 757-583-0293.
Res., 1615 Longdale Dr., 23518. Tel: 757-855-3297.
School—7800 Halprin Dr., 23518. Tel: 757-588-6171; Fax: 757-587-6580. Sr. Marie Renee Murphy, I.H.M., Prin.
Sisters Servants of the Immaculate Heart of Mary 2; Lay Teachers 26; Students 525.
Catechesis/Religious Programs—Students 135.

Norge, James City Co., St. Olaf, Patron of Norway (1992), Rev. John E. Ridgell.
Mailing Address: 104 Norge Ln., 23188-7229. Tel: 757-564-3819; Fax: 757-565-1099.
Catechesis/Religious Programs—Students 125.

Norton, Wise Co., St. Anthony (1938), Rev. Joseph C. Facura.
Mailing Address: & Church: 1009 Virginia Ave., 24273-1897. Tel: 540-679-2336; Fax: 540-679-4501.
Mission—Coeburn, Wise Co., St. Mary. E. Front St. at Beech Ave.
Station—Wise, Clinch Valley College of the University of Virginia.

Onley, Accomac Co., St. Peter's the Apostle (1942), Revs. Frank Wiggins; Francisco Valle.
Mailing Address: P.O. Box 860, 23418-0860. Tel: 757-787-4592; Fax: 757-787-2899.
Church—U.S. Business Rte. 13, 23418.
Catechesis/Religious Programs—Students 64.

Palmyra, Fluvanna Co., Ss. Peter & Paul (1986), Rev. Gerald A. Przywara.
Mailing Address: Rte. 7, Box 7142, 22963-9506. Tel: 804-589-5201; Fax: 804-589-4463.
Catechesis/Religious Programs—Students 108.

Pearisburg, Giles Co., Holy Family (1965), Rev. John Prinelli.
Mailing Address: 516 Mason Court Dr., 24134-1832. Tel: 540-921-3547.
Catechesis/Religious Programs—Students 17.

Pennington Gap, Lee Co., Church of the Holy Spirit (1956), Rev. Anthony Rodrigues. In res., Rev. Leslie Schmidt.
Mailing Address: P.O. Box 923, Jonesville, 24263.
Res., 1821 Holton Ave., Big Stone Gap, 24219. Tel: 540-523-6546; Fax: 540-523-1602.
Church—1010 Morgan Ave., 24277.
Catechesis/Religious Programs—Students 12.

Petersburg, Prince George Co., St. Joseph (1842), Rev. Robert M. Spencer.
Mailing Address: P.O. Box 2006, 23804-1306.
Church & Office: 11 N. Market St., PA 23803. Tel: 804-733-3115; Fax: 804-862-9931.
Res., 19 Centre Hill Ct., 23803. Tel: 804-732-5127. [CEM]
School—Tel: 804-732-3931; Fax: 804-863-2635. Ms. Ruth Bonner, Prin.
Lay Teachers 10; Students 192.
Catechesis/Religious Programs—Students 45.

Pocahontas, Tazewell Co., St. Elizabeth (1896), Rev. Daniel O. Brady.
Mailing Address: P.O. Box 608, 24635-0608. Tel: 540-988-4626; 988-1844 (evenings); Fax: 540-988-4626.
Catechesis/Religious Programs—Students 7.

Portsmouth, Holy Angels (1917), Rev. Ven Ilano.
Office: 34 Afton Pkwy., 23702-2739. Tel: 757-485-2142; 2143; Fax: 757-485-3699.
Catechesis/Religious Programs—Students 90.

Church of the Resurrection (1971), Rev. James V. Carr.
Mailing Address: 3501 Cedar Ln., 23703. Tel: 757-484-7335; Fax: 757-484-5857.
Res., 5130 Castleway, 23703. Tel: 757-484-7336.
School—Portsmouth Catholic Elementary School, 2301 Oregon Ave., 23701. Tel: 757-488-6744; Fax: 757-465-8833. Ms. Thea Haubrich, Prin.
Catechesis/Religious Programs—Students 144.
St. Paul (1824), Rev. Joseph S. Slowik.
Res., 518 High St., 23704-3516. Tel: 757-397-7066; Fax: 757-393-4334. [CEM]
Church—522 High St., 23704.
Catechesis/Religious Programs—Students 148.

Powhatan, St. John Neumann (1948), Rev. J. Morton Biber; Deacon John H. Thomas Tel: 804-379-9811.
Church—2480 Batterson Rd., 23139-7513. Tel: 804-598-3754; 794-9098; Fax: 804-598-1467.
Catechesis/Religious Programs—Students 129.

Prince George County, Church of the Sacred Heart (1906), Rev. James E. Gallagher.
Mailing Address: 4415 County Dr., Petersburg, 23805-7567. Tel: 804-732-6385; Fax: 804-732-6385. [CEM]
Catechesis/Religious Programs—Students 161.

Quinton, New Kent Co., St. Elizabeth Ann Seton (1986), Rev. Russell E. Smith.
Mailing Address: & Church: 2631 Pocahontas Trail, 23141-0245. Tel: 804-932-4125; Fax: 804-932-8126.
Catechesis/Religious Programs—Students 23.

Radford, St. Jude (1967), Rev. Robert Judge, S.J.
Mailing Address: 1740 Tyler Rd., Christiansburg, 24073-6154. Tel: 540-639-5341; Fax: 540-639-4738.
Res., 900 Berkley St., 24141. Tel: 540-731-9541.
Catechesis/Religious Programs—Students 80.

Richlands, Tazewell Co., St. Mary (1962), Rev. Thomas R. Collins.
Mailing Address: 1118 Farmer St., 24641. Tel: 540-935-2815; 963-8545 (Rectory).
Catechesis/Religious Programs—Students 9.
Mission—Richlands, Buchanan Co., St. Joseph, (1966).

Roanoke, Roanoke Co., Our Lady of Nazareth (1914), Rev. Joseph P. Lehman.
Mailing Address: 2505 Electric Rd., S.W., 24018-3599. Tel: 540-774-0066 (Office); 774-0857 (Res.); Fax: 540-774-2148.
Catechesis/Religious Programs—Students 576.
St. Andrew (1890), Rev. Steven R. Rule.
Mailing Address: 631 N. Jefferson St., 24016-1401. Tel: 540-344-9814; 345-9714; Fax: 540-344-7879. [JC]
Res., 3025 Bancroft Dr., 24014. Tel: 540-344-9814.
Catechesis/Religious Programs—Students 369.
St. Gerard (1946), Rev. Thomas Mattingly.
809 Orange Ave., N.W., 24016-1117. Tel: 540-343-7744; Fax: 540-343-3599.
School—Roanoke Catholic Regional Elementary and High School, 621 N. Jefferson St., 24016. Tel: 540-982-3756. Ms. Karen Mabry, Prin.
Catechesis/Religious Programs—Students 71.

Rocky Mount, Franklin Co., Francis of Assisi (1984), Rev. Rolo B. Castillo.
Mailing Address: 15 Glennwood Dr., 24151-2111. Tel: 540-483-9591; 483-8981; Fax: 540-483-5232.
Catechesis/Religious Programs—Students 45.

St. Paul, Wise Co., St. Therese (1954), Rev. Paul Maier.
Mailing Address: P.O. Box 56, 24283-0056. Tel: 540-762-5932; Fax: 540-762-5932.
Res., 3107 Sixth Ave., 24283.
Catechesis/Religious Programs—Students 12.

Salem, Our Lady of Perpetual Help (1947), Rev. Jeremiusz H. Sojka.
Mailing Address: 314 Turner Rd., 24153-2399. Tel: 540-387-0491; Fax: 540-389-8237.
Res., 1408 Kathryn Ln., 24153. Tel: 540-387-1020.
Catechesis/Religious Programs—Students 243.

Scottsville, Albemarle Co., St. George (1975), Rev. Joseph Torretto.
Mailing Address: P.O. Box 9, 24590-0009. Tel: 804-286-3724; Fax: 804-263-6928.
Catechesis/Religious Programs—Students 7.
Missions—Lovingston, Nelson Co., St. Mary, (1979) P.O. Box 375, Lovingston, 22949-0735. Tel: 804-263-4008. Rev. Daniel Kelly.; Amherst, St. Francis of Assisi, (1995) P.O. Box 663, 24521. Tel: 804-263-8059.

Smithfield, Good Shepherd (1984). Unassigned. Ms. Joanne R. Gordon, Pastoral Coord.
Mailing Address: P.O. Box 840, 23431-0840. Tel: 757-365-0579; Fax: 757-365-4749.
Church—300 Smithfield Blvd., 23430.
Catechesis/Religious Programs—Students 122.

South Boston, Halifax Co., St. Paschal Baylon (1981). Unassigned. Sr. Edna N. Maier, Pastoral Coord.
Mailing Address: 800 John Randolph Blvd., 24592-2943.
Res., 3302 N. Main St., 24592. Tel: 804-572-3313; 572-2285 (Office); Fax: 804-572-1725.
Catechesis/Religious Programs—Students 14.

South Hill, Mecklenburg Co., Good Shepherd (1922), Rev. James Fosnot.
Mailing Address: P.O. Box 621, 23970-0621. Tel: 804-447-3622; Fax: 804-447-4729.
Church—1664 N. Mecklenburg Ave., 23970.
Catechesis/Religious Programs—Students 26.

Staunton, Augusta Co., St. Francis of Assisi (1844), Rev. John Adam Abe.
Church & Mailing Address—121 N. Augusta St., 24401-3636. Tel: 540-886-2262; Fax: 540-885-5743.
Res., 126 N. New St., 24401. Tel: 540-886-9121.
Catechesis/Religious Programs—Students 225.

Suffolk, St. Mary of the Presentation (1927), Rev. Patrick Golden.
Office: 202 S. Broad St., 23434-5715. Tel: 757-539-5732; Fax: 757-538-0103.
Church—200 S. Broad St., 23434.
Catechesis/Religious Programs—Students 149.

Tabb, York Co., Blessed Kateri Tekawitha (1986), Rev. Lawrence J. Mullany.
Church & Office: 3800 Big Bethel Rd., 23693-3814. Tel: 757-766-3800; 766-1384; Fax: 757-766-1125.
Catechesis/Religious Programs—Students 208.

Tappahannock, Essex Co., St. Timothy (1972), Rev. Michael M. Duffy.
Mailing Address: P.O. Box 129, 22560-0129.
Church—Rte. 17 & Airport Rd., 22560. Tel: 804-443-2760; Fax: 804-443-2022.
Catechesis/Religious Programs—Students 45.

Tazewell, St. Theresa (1980), Rev. Daniel O. Brady.
Mailing Address: P.O. Box 345, 24651-0345. Tel: 540-988-4626; Fax: 540-988-4626.
Church—304 Tazewell Ave., 24651.
Catechesis/Religious Programs—Students 31.

Virginia Beach

1—CHURCH OF THE ASCENSION (1972), Revs. James E. Parke; Charles Faul; Constantine Silayo.
Office: 4853 Princess Anne Rd., 23462-4446. Tel: 757-495-1887; 1886; Fax: 757-495-1516.
Catechesis/Religious Programs—Students 462.

2—CHURCH OF THE HOLY APOSTLES, Virginia Co., (1977). (Anglican-Roman Catholic Congregation of Hampton Roads). Rev. Charles Faul.
Church—1598 Lynnhaven Pkwy., 23456-2008. Tel: 757-427-0963; Fax: 757-427-9434.
Catechesis/Religious Programs—Students 23.

3—HOLY FAMILY, Virginia Co., (1977), Rev. Thomas J. Quinlan.
Parish Center: 1279 N. Great Neck Rd., 23454-2117. Tel: 757-481-5702; 481-0799; Fax: 757-481-3989.

4—HOLY SPIRIT, Virginia Co., (1975), Rev. Msgr. Thomas J. Caroluzza; Rev. Romeo Jazmin.
Office: 1396 Lynnhaven Pkwy., 23456-2710. Tel: 757-468-3600; 3601; Fax: 757-468-3342.
Res., 3345 Clubhouse Rd., 23452. Tel: 757-340-3933.
Catechesis/Religious Programs—Students 427.

5—ST. GREGORY THE GREAT, Virginia Co., (1957), Revs. Mario Fulgenzi; Paschal Kneip, O.S.B.; Damian Abbaticchio, O.S.B.; John Mary Tompkins; Philip Ghys, O.S.B.; Deacon Raymond Check.
Office: 5345 Virginia Beach Blvd., 23462. Tel: 757-497-8330; Fax: 757-490-1492.
School—5349 Virginia Beach Blvd., 23462-1896. Tel: 757-497-1811; Fax: 757-497-7517. Sr. Patricia O'Donnell, I.H.M., Prin.
Sisters 3; Lay Teachers 28; Students 694.
Catechesis/Religious Programs—Students 970.
Chapel—Chesapeake, St. Benedict Tridentine Chapel, (1992), 521 McCosh St., Chesapeake, Tel: 757-543-0561.
Catechesis/Religious Programs—Students 43.

6—ST. JOHN THE APOSTLE CHURCH, Virginia Co., (1989), Rev. Dwight E. Shrader. In res., Rev. Paul Gaughan, (Retired), Tel: 757-426-2550.
Church—800 Los Conaes Way, 23456-6421. Tel: 757-426-2180; Fax: 757-426-6857.
Catechesis/Religious Programs—Students 907.

7—ST. LUKE, Virginia Co., (1986), Rev. Eugene J. Teslovic.
Mailing Address: 2304 Salem Rd., 23456-1215. Tel: 757-427-5776; Fax: 757-427-2260.
Catechesis/Religious Programs—Students 223.

8—ST. MARK, Virginia Co., (1978), Rev. Daniel N. Klem.
Mailing Address: 1505 Kempsville Rd., 23464-7210. Tel: 757-479-1010; 479-0414; Fax: 757-479-9453.
Res., 4901 Whitewood Ln., 23464. Tel: 757-467-4932.
Catechesis/Religious Programs—Students 481.

9—ST. MATTHEW, Virginia Co., (1924), Rev. Timothy A. Drake; Deacon Daniel F. McCormick.
Office: 3314 Sandra Ln., 23464-1736. Tel: 757-420-6310; 6311; Fax: 757-420-7734.
Res., 806 Bridgeport Place, 23464. Tel: 757-523-1723.
School—3316 Sandra Ln., 23464. Tel: 757-420-6310; Fax: 757-420-4880. Ms. Barbara White, Prin.
Lay Teachers 28; Students 526.
Catechesis/Religious Programs—Students 300.

10—ST. NICHOLAS, Virginia Co., (1963), Rev. Msgr. Raymond A. Barton.
Office & Church—712 Little Neck Rd., 23452. Tel: 757-340-7231; Fax: 757-340-2727.
Res., 3340 Old Kirkwood Dr., 23452-5807. Tel: 757-498-7834.
Catechesis/Religious Programs—Students 473.

11—STAR OF THE SEA, Virginia Co., (1915), Rev. James E. Dorson.
Office: 1404 Pacific Ave., 23451-3439. Tel: 757-428-8547; Fax: 757-428-0788.
School—309 15th St., 23451. Tel: 757-428-8400. Mrs. Susan Fentress, Prin.
Sisters 2; Lay Teachers 15; Students 265.
Catechesis/Religious Programs—Students 248.

Waynesboro, Augusta Co., St. John the Evangelist (1946), Rev. William S. O'Brien.
Mailing Address: 344 Maple Ave., 22980-4706.
Office: Tel: 540-949-6145; 6146; Fax: 540-932-8512.
Res., 320 Maple Ave., 22980. Tel: 540-943-4051.
Church—300 Maple Ave., 22980.
Catechesis/Religious Programs—Students 215.
Station—Fishersville, Woodrow Wilson Rehabilitation Center.

West Point, King William Co., Our Lady of the Blessed Sacrament (1918), Rev. Gregory Kandt, Admin. In res., Rev. John Brieffies.
Mailing Address: 207 W. Euclid Blvd., 23181.
Church—3570 King William Ave., 23181. Tel: 804-843-3125; Fax: 804-843-9158. [CEM]
Catechesis/Religious Programs—Students 66.

Williamsburg, York Co., St. Bede's (1932), Revs. William H. Carr; Antonio R. Malabad; Ernest Bulinda; James P. Curran.
Mailing Address: 10 Harrison Ave., 23185-3530. Tel: 757-229-3631; Fax: 757-229-5361.
Res., 601 College Ter., 23185. Tel: 757-220-4233.
Church—500 Richmond Rd., 23185.
Catechesis/Religious Programs—Students 461.

Woodlawn, Carroll Co., St. Joseph's (1981), Rev. Charles W. Brickner.
Mailing Address: 99 Joy Ranch Rd., 24381-1213. Tel: 540-236-7814; Fax: 540-238-8711.
Catechesis/Religious Programs—Students 15.
Mission—Patrick Springs, Church of the Risen Lord, U.S. 58 and County 625, Patrick Springs.
Catechesis/Religious Programs—Students 13.
Mission—Floyd, Floyd Co., Church of All Saints. Rt. 615 & Rt. 693.
Catechesis/Religious Programs—Students 9.

Wytheville, St. Mary's (1845), Rev. Rene Castillo.
Mailing Address: P.O. Box 7, 24382-0007. Tel: 540-228-3104; Fax: 540-228-3322. [CEM]
Church—370 E. Main St., 24382.
Catechesis/Religious Programs—Students 55.
Mission—Pulaski, Davis Co., St. Edward, P.O. Box 1670, Pulaski, 24301. Tel: 540-980-6511.
Catechesis/Religious Programs—Students 40.

Yorktown, York Co., St. Joan of Arc (1954), Rev. Don Michael Hanna.
Office: 315 Harris Grove Ln., 23692-4014. Tel: 757-898-5570; Fax: 757-898-0737.
Catechesis/Religious Programs—Students 240.

Chaplains of Public Institutions

HAMPTON. *VA Medical Center* Chaplain Service, Bldg. 69, 23667. Tel: 804-722-9961, Ext. 3600. Revs. Lloyd F. Stephenson; Donald J. Cavey.

PETERSBURG. *Federal Correctional Institution*. Rev. John P. Blankenship.

SALEM. *Salem VA Medical Center* Tel: 540-982-2463. Rev. Thomas Mattingly, Chap.

On Special or Other Diocesan Assignment:
Reverend Fathers—
Apuzzo, Pasquale, Chancery Office
Lane, Mark

On Duty Outside the Diocese:
Reverend Fathers—
Funk, Virgil C., Washington, DC
McNally, Stephen, Bonn, Germany
Murphy, Dennis, Providence, RI
Natale, Samuel, New York
Slattery, Joseph A., Pretoria, South Africa
Thuy, Pham Quang
Williams, McKinley

Graduate Studies:
Reverend Fathers—
Trinh, Thai Q., Cailifornia Institute of Integral Studies, San Francisco

Military Chaplains:
Reverend Fathers—
Caiazzo, Nickolas (NOR)
Dang, Chin Van
Hickman, J. Stephen
Huan, Joseph Van Tran
Kanicki, Philip A.
Moran, Edward C.

Unassigned:
Reverend Fathers—
Bostwick, John

Retired:
Reverend Monsignors—
Michael, Chester P., Rte. 2, Box 225, Afton, VA 22920
Reverend Fathers—
Beardsley, Frederick, 5910 Kensington Ave., Richmond, VA 23226
Bowers, Vernon J., Mailing Address: U.S. Post Office, Ware Neck, VA 23178
Cassidy, Patrick, 628 Toll Gate Ln., Petersburg, VA 23865
Chmura, Stanislaus, 717 Cooper Ave., Inverness, FL 34450
Condon, William F., P.O. Box 1742, Clarksville, VA 23927
Connelly, William P., 4605 Truman Ln., Virginia Beach, VA 23445
Dinga, William, 1324 Debree Ave., Norfolk, VA 23517
Dinges, Anthony, 102 Oliver Ave., Crewe, VA 23920
Ditty, James, 1316 Mill Lake Quarter, Chesapeake, VA 23320
Gallagher, Paul V., 34 Oakland Dr., Pulaski, VA 24301
Gaughan, Paul, St. John's Rectory, 800 Los Conaes Way, Virginia Beach, VA 23456
Hamlet, Ralph, 141 Green Turtle Ln., #10, Charlottesville, VA 22901
Henry, Thomas, Our Lady of Peace, Charlottesville, VA 22901
Higgins, Phillip, P.O. Box 5141, Richmond, VA 23220
Kloepfer, John S., P.O. Box 1742, Clarksville, VA 23927
Kruc, James, 326 Wolf St., Philadelphia, PA 19148-3315
McEleney, Robert J., Rt. 5, Box 432, Appomattox, VA 24522
McIntyre, Raymond T., 62 Manhattan Dr., Ashley, PA 18706
Naro, Carl J., 153 Mayo Creek Ln., Wingina, VA 24599
Naylor, Ronald J., 100 E. Ocean View Ave., #904, Norfolk, VA 23503
Nee, Thomas B., 1133 Lassiter Ln., Suffolk, VA 23434
Newell, Matthias, 833 N. Main St., South Boston, VA 24592
Pereira, Albert F., 4713 Clintwood Dr., Portsmouth, VA 23703
Rodriguez, D. Andres G., San Martin de Tabara, Zamora, Spain
Ruth, Robert F., 201 Lazewell St., #115, Norfolk, VA 23510
Stickle, William, 128 Clipper Ct., Kill Devil Hills, NC 27948
Warren, Robert, P.O. Box 6194, Charlottesville, VA 22906
Welch, Thomas David, 351 Buntontown, Butler, TN 37640

Permanent Deacons:
Birx, Charles R., Radford
Carini, Albert J., St. Joseph, Columbia
Cartwright, Gordon, Lynchburg
Check, Raymond P., St. Gregory the Great, Virginia Beach
Donovan, Donald, St. Charles, Cape Charles
Dwyer, Bruce K., St. Joseph, Woodlawn
Ellerbrock, Michael, St. Mary, Blacksburg
Ewan, Robert, St. Edward, Richmond
Flanary, Barron, Sacred Heart, Big Stone Gap
Glynn, John, Church of the Resurrection, Portsmouth
Hall, Harry, St. Anne, Bristol
Hanzlik, Edward, Sacred Heart, New Bohemia
Hayes, William, Our Lady of Peace, Appomattox
Heise, George, Church of the Transfiguration, Fincastle
King, Walker, St. Pius X, Norfolk
Krajeski, Vernon, St. John the Apostle, Virginia Beach
Kwon, Peter H., Dr., St. Jerome, Newport News Korean Community
La Spina, Fred, Blessed Sacrament, Harrisonburg
Larkin, Paul V., Langley AFB
McCormick, Daniel F., St. Mark, Virginia Beach
Menting, Peter J., Good Samaritan, Amelia
Nemetz, David, St. Michael, Glen Allen
Ports, Francis J., Bedford
Roderique, Raymond, Forest
Shearer, David, St. Peter the Apostle, Onley
Thomas, John H., Diocesan Tribunal; St. John Neumann, Powhatan
Torres, Patricio-Lisboa, Bishop's Office
Vercart, Frank, St. Thomas Aquinas, Charlottesville
Weir, Robert, Virginia Beach

INSTITUTIONS LOCATED IN THE DIOCESE

[A] HIGH SCHOOLS, DIOCESAN

LYNCHBURG. *Holy Cross Regional School.* (Grades PreK-12), 2125 Langhorne Rd., 24501. Tel: 804-847-5436; 845-8862; Fax: 804-847-4156.
E-mail: hc@inmind.com
John P. Jones, Prin. Lay Teachers 31; Students 400.

NEWPORT NEWS. *Peninsula Catholic High School.* (Grades 8-12), 600 Harpersville Rd., 23601. Tel: 757-622-7246; Fax: 757-591-9718.
Web site: www.widomaker.com~pchs
Mrs. Francine Conway, Prin. Lay Teachers 32; Staff 8; Students 375.

PETERSBURG. *St. Vincent de Paul High School.* (Grades 7-12), 240 Wagner Rd., 23803-9232. Tel: 804-733-4305; Fax: 804-862-3634. Ms. Jeanette Coleman, Prin. Sisters 3; Lay Teachers 10; Lay Administrators 2; Students 101.

ROANOKE. *Roanoke Catholic School.* (Grades PreK-12), 621 N. Jefferson St., 24016. Tel: 540-982-3532; Fax: 540-345-0785.
E-mail: rcs1@rbnet.com
Ms. Karen Mabry, Prin. Lay Teachers 46; Students 576.

VIRGINIA BEACH. *Catholic High School.* (Grades 9-12), 4552 Princess Anne Rd., 23462. Tel: 757-467-2881; Fax: 757-467-0284.
E-mail: mailbox@chsvb.org
Rev. Msgr. William L. Pitt, Prin. Priests 1; Lay Teachers 41; Students 505.

[B] HIGH SCHOOLS, PRIVATE

RICHMOND. *Benedictine High School.* (Grades 9-12), 304 N. Sheppard St., 23221. Tel: 804-342-1300; Fax: 804-355-2407.
E-mail: info@benedictinehighschool.org
Web site: www.benedictinehighschool.org
A Military High School in the Charge of the Benedictine Monks. Rt. Rev. Benedict R. McDermott, O.S.B., Pres.; Dr. Rickey A. Kolb, Headmaster. Priests 1; Lay Teachers 31; Students 273.

Saint Gertrude High School. (Grades 9-12), 3215 Stuart Ave., 23221. Tel: 804-358-9114; Fax: 804-355-5682.
E-mail: stgert@mindspring.com
Web site: www.saintgertrude.org
Sr. Charlotte Lange, O.S.B., Prin. Benedictine Sisters 3; Lay Teachers 27; Students 291.

WILLIAMSBURG. *Walsingham Academy Upper School.* (Grades 8-12), 1100 Jamestown Rd., P.O. Box 8702, 23187-8702. Tel: 757-229-6026; Fax: 757-259-1401.
E-mail: umk@walsingham.org
Web site: walsingham.org
(Grades 8-12). Private Day School for Boys and Girls. Sr. Virginia Marie Kauffmann, R.S.M., Prin. Sisters of Mercy 4; Lay Teachers 28; Students 300.

[C] ELEMENTARY SCHOOLS, DIOCESAN

BLACKSBURG. *St. Mary Catholic School,* 706 Harding Ave., N.E., 24060-3618. Tel: 540-951-5345; Fax: 540-953-2962.
E-mail: smcs@bburg.net
Dr. H. E. Bauer, Prin. Lay Teachers 12; Students 110.

CHARLOTTESVILLE. *Charlottesville Catholic Elementary School.* (Grades K-4), 200 Four Seasons Dr., 22901. Tel: 804-964-0400; Fax: 804-964-1373.
E-mail: boschert@cfw.com
Web site: www.cvillecatholic.com
Kermit V. Boschert, Prin. Lay Teachers 16; Aides 4; Students 214.

POWHATAN. *Blessed Sacrament/Huguenot School.* (Grades PreK-12), 2501 Academy Rd., 23139. Tel: 804-598-4211; Fax: 804-598-1053. Dr. Lou Ross Hopewell, Pres.; Mr. Samuel Keller, Jr., Headmaster; Mr. James Fortune, Prin. Lay Teachers 40; Students 400.

[D] ELEMENTARY SCHOOLS, PRIVATE

WILLIAMSBURG. *Walsingham Academy Lower School,* P.O. Box 8702, 23187-8702. Tel: 757-229-2642; Fax: 757-259-1404.
E-mail: walsingham@aol.com
(Grades PreK-7). Day School for Boys and Girls. Sr. Mary Jeanne Oesterle, R.S.M., Prin. Sisters 2; Lay Teachers 34; Students 433.

[E] GENERAL HOSPITALS

RICHMOND. *St. Mary's Hospital,* 5801 Bremo Rd., 23226. Tel: 804-285-2011; Fax: 804-283-8327
For a complete listing, refer to the Hospitals section.

NEWPORT NEWS. *Mary Immaculate Hospital,* 2 Bernardine Dr., 23602-4499. Tel: 757-886-6600; Fax: 757-886-6751.
Web site: www.bonsecourshamptonroads.com
For a complete listing, refer to the Hospitals section.

NORFOLK. *Bon Secours De Paul Medical Center, Inc.,* 150 Kingsley Ln., 23505. Tel: 757-889-5000; Fax: 757-889-5837
For a complete listing, refer to the Hospitals section.

NORTON. *St. Mary's Hospital, Inc.,* P.O. Box 620, 24273. Tel: 540-679-9100; Fax: 540-679-7549.
E-mail: alester@st_maryshospital.com
Web site: www.st_maryshospital.com
For a complete listing, refer to the Hospitals section.

PORTSMOUTH. *Maryview Medical Center,* 3636 High St., 23707. Tel: 757-398-2200; Fax: 757-398-2359
For a complete listing, refer to the Hospitals section.

Maryview Psychiatric Hospital, 3636 High St., 23707
For a complete listing, refer to the Hospitals section.

[F] ORPHANAGES AND INFANT HOMES

RICHMOND. *St. Joseph's Villa,* 8000 Brook Rd., 23227-1338. Tel: 804-553-3200; Fax: 804-553-3259
For a complete listing, refer to the Special Care Facilities section.

NORFOLK. *St. Mary's Home for Disabled Children,* 317 Chapel St., 23504. Tel: 757-622-2208
For a complete listing, refer to the Special Care Facilities section.

ROANOKE. *De Paul Family Services, Inc.,* 5650 Hollins Rd., 24019. Tel: 540-265-8923; Fax: 540-265-7663
For a complete listing, refer to the Special Care Facilities section.

[G] CHILD LEARNING CENTERS

RICHMOND. *Holy Angels,* 1307 Lakeside Ave., 23228. Tel: 804-266-7200. Sr. Juliana Paladini, Dir. Comboni Missionary Sisters 4; Lay Teachers 2; Children 44.

Holy Rosary Child Care Center, 1218 N. 34th St., Box 8046, 23223. Tel: 804-222-2590; Fax: 804-222-1836. Ms. Shirley Daniels, Dir. Children 120.

Sacred Heart Center, Inc., 1400 Perry St., 23224. Tel: 804-230-4399; Fax: 804-231-7247.
E-mail: shcexecutive@mindspring.com
Naomi Chambers-Taylor, Exec. Dir. Neighboring Communities Day Care, After School Care, Adult Education, Social Services and K-2.

NORFOLK. *Christ the King Extended Care,* 3401 Tidewater Dr., 23509. Tel: 757-627-0119. Mrs. Uli Williford, Admin. Children 80.

POWHATAN. *St. John Neumann Family Life Center,* 2480 Batterson Rd., 23139. Tel: 804-598-3754; Fax: 804-598-1467.
E-mail: sjn_powua@juno.com
Rev. J. Morton Biber, Board Pres.

ROANOKE. *The Achievement Center-St. Vincent's Home, Inc.* Tel: 540-982-0128; Fax: 540-982-3629.
E-mail: tacenter@rev.net
Web site: www.achievementcenter.org
Mailing Address: P.O. Box 12368, 24025. Tel: 540-982-0128. 615 N. Jefferson St., 24016. Barbara Ann Whitwell, Dir. Private day school for children with learning disabilities. Total Assisted 140.

[H] HOMES FOR THE AGED

RICHMOND. *Marywood Apartments,* 1261 Marywood Ln., 23229. Tel: 804-740-5567; Fax: 804-740-9016.
E-mail: marywood@MSN.com
For a complete listing, refer to the Special Care Facilities section.

Our Lady of Hope Health Center, Inc., 13700 N. Gayton Rd., 23233. Tel: 804-360-1960
For a complete listing, refer to the Special Care Facilities section.

St. Francis Home, Inc., 2511 Wise St., 23225-3952. Tel: 804-231-1043; Fax: 804-231-1065
For a complete listing, refer to the Special Care Facilities section.

St. Joseph's Home for the Aged, 1503 Michael Rd., 23229. Tel: 804-288-6245; Fax: 804-288-8906
For a complete listing, refer to the Special Care Facilities section.

St. Mary Wood's, 1257 Marywood Ln., 23229. Tel: 804-741-8624; Fax: 804-740-7912.
E-mail: stmw@mindspring.com
For a complete listing, refer to the Special Care Facilities section.

CHARLOTTESVILLE. *Our Lady of Peace*, 751 Hillsdale Dr., 22901. Tel: 804-973-1155; Fax: 804-973-3397.
Web site: our-lady-of-peace
For a complete listing, refer to the Special Care Facilities section.

HAMPTON. *Seton Manor*, 215 Marcella Rd., 23666. Tel: 757-827-6512
For a complete listing, refer to the Special Care Facilities section.

LYNCHBURG. *McGurk House Apartments*, 2425 Tate Springs Rd., 24501. Tel: 804-846-2425; Fax: 804-847-5046.
E-mail: mcgurkhouse@worldnet.att.net
For a complete listing, refer to the Special Care Facilities section.

NEWPORT NEWS. *St. Francis Nursing Center*, 4 Ridgewood Pkwy., 23602
For a complete listing, refer to the Special Care Facilities section.

NORFOLK. *Madonna Home*, 814 W. 37th St., 23508. Tel: 757-623-6662; Fax: 757-623-4966
For a complete listing, refer to the Special Care Facilities section.

ROANOKE. *Our Lady of the Valley Retirement Community*, 650 N. Jefferson St., 24016. Tel: 540-345-5111; Fax: 540-985-6561.
Web site: ourladyofthevalley.com
For a complete listing, refer to the Special Care Facilities section.

SUFFOLK. *Bon Secours-Maryview Nursing Care*, 4775 Bridge Rd., 23435. Tel: 757-686-0488
For a complete listing, refer to the Special Care Facilities section.

VIRGINIA BEACH. *Marian Manor*, 5345 Marian Ln., 23462. Tel: 757-456-5018; Fax: 757-497-7561
For a complete listing, refer to the Special Care Facilities section.

Our Lady of Perpetual Help Health Center, Inc., 4560 Princess Anne Rd., 23462-7905
For a complete listing, refer to the Special Care Facilities section.

Russell House, 900 First Colonial Rd., 23454. Tel: 757-481-0770; Fax: 757-496-0859.
E-mail: russellhouse@erols.com
For a complete listing, refer to the Special Care Facilities section.

[I] HOME FOR HANDICAPPED ADULTS

RICHMOND. *St. Joseph's Villa Housing Corp.*, 8000 Brook Rd., 23227-1399. Tel: 804-553-3283; Fax: 804-553-3259
For a complete listing, refer to the Special Care Facilities section.

[J] SERVICES FOR THE DISABLED

RICHMOND. *Hollybrook I & II.* Tel: 804-553-3200; Fax: 804-553-3259.
E-mail: thevilla@i2020.net
St. Joseph Villa, 7700 Brook Rd., 23229. Tel: 804-553-3200; Fax: 804-553-3259. Mr. Ramon E. Pardue, Program Dir. Residents 80.

Outreach in Love. c/o Epiphany Church, 11000 Smoketree Dr., 23236. Tel: 804-794-0222. Lynda D. Heithaus, Coord. Religious education for people with disabilities.

Sean's Place, 713 N. First St., 23219. Tel: 804-344-8164. Mr. Pete Jones, Prog. Coord.

LYNCHBURG. *Nott Homes, Inc.*, 3009-3011 Roundelay Rd., 24502. Tel: 804-239-0722. Mrs. Helen Smith, Residential Mgr. Residents 8.

[K] SPECIALIZED SERVICES

RICHMOND. *Commonwealth Catholic Charities*, 1512 Willow Lawn Dr., 23230-0565. Tel: 804-285-5900; Fax: 804-285-9130.
E-mail: comcathric@aol.com
Web site: members.aol.com/COMCATHRIC/index.html
Rev. David J. Bergner, S.D.S., Exec. Dir.
Satellite Offices: 820 Campbell Ave., S.W., Roanoke, 24016. Tel: 540-344-5107; Fax: 540-344-2748. Woodbrook Shopping Center, 1859-C3 Seminole Tr., Charlottesville, 22901. Tel: 804-974-6880. Connections, 302 McClanahan St., S.W., Roanoke, 24014. Tel: 540-342-0411; Fax: 540-342-3307. 1024 Park Ave., N.W., Norton, 24273. Tel: 540-679-0967; Fax: 540-679-2719. Total Assisted 8,763.

VIRGINIA BEACH. *Catholic Charities of Hampton Roads, Inc.*, 4855 Princess Anne Rd., 23462. Tel: 757-467-7707; Fax: 757-495-3206. Margaret M. Robertson, Exec. Dir.
Branch Offices: 12829 Jefferson Ave., Ste. 101, Newport News, 23608. Tel: 757-875-0060. 1301 Colonial Ave., Norfolk, 23517. Tel: 757-625-2568. 3804 Poplar Hill Rd., Ste. A, Chesapeake, 23321. Tel: 757-484-0703. 1315 Jamestown Rd., Suite 202, Williamsburg, 23185. Tel: 757-253-2847. Total Assisted 24,000.

[L] MONASTERIES AND RESIDENCES OF PRIESTS AND BROTHERS

RICHMOND. *Mary Mother of the Church Abbey*, 12829 River Rd., 23233. Tel: 804-784-3508; Fax: 804-784-2214.
E-mail: bmcd@erols.com
Web site: www.richmondmonks.org
Benedictine Monks. Rt. Rev. Benedict R. McDermott, O.S.B., Abbot, Novice Master; Revs. Donald F. Scales, O.S.B., Prior; Thomas W. Stumpf, O.S.B.; Adrian W. Harmening, O.S.B., Procurator; Theophile W. Brown, O.S.B.; Augustine W. Cunningham, O.S.B.; Augustine W. Ludwig, O.S.B.; Elliot Needham, O.S.B.; Bros. Matthew Miller, O.S.B.; David Owen, O.S.B.; Mark Purcell, O.S.B.; Barry Butler, O.S.B.; Jeffery Williams, O.S.B.; James Glass. Priests 8; Brothers 6; Novices 5.

WEST POINT. *Missionaries of the Holy Family, General Mission Office—M.S.F., Inc.*, P.O. Box 918, 23181. Tel: 804-843-2622. Rev. John Brieffies, M.S.F., Pres. & Dir.

[M] CONVENTS AND RESIDENCES FOR SISTERS

RICHMOND. *Benedictine Sisters of Virginia, St. Gertrude Convent*, 3215 Stuart Ave., 23221. Tel: 804-355-7227. Sr. M. Gertrude Mueller. Sisters 3.

Comboni Missionary Sisters, Provincial House, 1307 Lakeside Ave., 23228. Tel: 804-266-2975; 262-8827; Fax: 804-264-2906. Sr. Maria Teresa Goffi, C.M.S., Provincial. Sisters 26.

Daughters of Charity. St. Patrick School Community, 207 N. 26th St., 23223. Tel: 804-649-7437. Sr. Clara Pedo, Supr.

CROZET. *Our Lady of the Angels Monastery*, Cistercian Nuns of the Strict Observance (Virginia), 3365 Monastery Dr., 22932. Tel: 804-823-1452; Fax: 804-823-6379.
E-mail: angels@esinet.net
Web site: www.esinet.net/angels.html
Mother Marion Rissetto, Prioress. Professed 8.

NEWPORT NEWS. *Bernardine Sisters of the Third Order of St. Francis*, 6E Ridgewood Pkwy., 23602. Tel: 757-886-6895; Fax: 757-886-6751.
Web site: www.bfranciscan.org
Sisters 15.

Bethlehem Monastery of the Poor Clare Nuns, 28 Harpersville Rd., 23601. Tel: 757-596-5942. Observing the Primitive Rule of St. Clare, Constitutions of the Poor Clare Federation of Mary Immaculate (strictly cloistered, solemn vows). Rev. Mother Mary Colette, Abbess. Solemnly Professed 12; Novices 3. Attended by Our Lady of Mt. Carmel Church, Newport News.

NORFOLK. *Sisters Servants of the Immaculate Heart of Mary.* St. Pius X Convent, 7813 Halprin Dr., 23518. Tel: 757-587-8657. Sr. Marie Kenee Murphy, Supr. Sisters 6.

NORTON. *Poor Servants of the Mother of God*, P.O. Box 620, 24273. Tel: 540-679-0477; Fax: 540-679-3581. Sr. Gabriella Hogan, S.M.G., Sister in Charge. Sisters 6.

PETERSBURG. *Daughters of Charity of St. Vincent de Paul*, St. Joseph Convent, 127 Franklin St., 23803-3307. Tel: 804-732-8501.
E-mail: stjpburg@ren.com
Sr. Mary Beard, Local Supr. Students 4.

PORTSMOUTH. *Sisters of Bon Secours*, 412 West Rd., 23707. Tel: 804-397-3869.
E-mail: rita_thomas@bshsi.com
Sr. Rita Thomas, Pres. Sisters 2.

ROCKVILLE. *Monastery of the Visitation Monte Maria*, 12221 Bienvenue Rd., 23146. Tel: 804-749-4885; Fax: 804-749-8606. Mother Mary Paula Zemienieuski, Supr. Visitation Sisters 17; Novices 1.

VIRGINIA BEACH. *Sisters Servants of I.H.M.*, St. Gregory the Great, 5349 Virginia Beach Blvd., 23462. Tel: 757-497-7517; Fax: 757-490-1492.
E-mail: sbrendaihm@aol.com
Sr. Brenda Anne Query, Supr.

WILLIAMSBURG. *Sisters of Mercy*, Walsingham Academy, P.O. Box 8702, 1100 Jamestown Rd., 23187-8702. Tel: 757-229-2642; Fax: 757-259-1401. Sr. Josephine Hynes, R.S.M. Sisters 7.

[N] RETREAT HOUSES

RICHMOND. *Benedictine Retreat and Conference Center*, Mary Mother of the Church Abbey, 12829 River Rd., 23233. Tel: 804-784-3508. Bro. Jeffery Williams.

The Dwelling Place, 601 Holly Grove Ln., 23235. Tel: 804-323-3360.
Conducted by: Patricia Carreras; Audrey Stech.

Richmond Hill. Ecumenical Center, 2209 E. Grace St., 23235. Tel: 804-783-7903. Rev. Benjamin Campbell, Pastoral Dir.

HAMPTON. *Holy Family Retreat*, 1414 N. Mallory St., P.O. 3151, 23663. Tel: 757-722-3997; Fax: 757-723-2478.
E-mail: gerry134@juno.com
Rev. Gerard H. Schreiber, C.Ss.R., Supr. & Dir. Asst. Retreat Directors: Revs. Charles J. Brinkman, C.Ss.R.; James H. Geiger, C.Ss.R.; Vang C. Trang, C.Ss.R.

LYNCHBURG. *Tabor Retreat Center*, 2125 Langhorne Rd., 24501. Tel: 804-846-6475. Deacon Gordon Cartwright.

MONTPELIER. *Shalom House.* Retreat Center, P.O. Box 196, 23192. Tel: 804-883-6149. Ms. Catherine Cawley, Dir.

ROANOKE. *Madonna House*, 828 Campbell Ave., S.W., 24016. Tel: 540-343-8464. Elizabeth Holmes, Dir.

SMITHFIELD. *The Well*, 18047 Quiet Way, 23430. Tel: 757-255-2366; Fax: 757-255-2366.
E-mail: staff@thewellretreatcenter.org
Web site: www.thewellretreatcenter.org
Co-Directors: Sr. Nancy Healy, S.F.C.C.; Diane Weymouth.

[O] MISCELLANEOUS

RICHMOND. *The Catholic Foundation of the Diocese of Richmond*, 811 Cathedral Pl., 23220. Tel: 804-359-5661; Fax: 804-358-9159. Ms. Carole Kahwajy, Contact Person.

St. Francis Home of Richmond Foundation, Ltd., 2511 Wise St., 23224. Tel: 804-231-1043; Fax: 804-231-1065. David Cran, Dir. Provides grants to subsidize cost of care for aged, infirm and disabled residents of limited means.

Shroud of Turin Center, Mary Mother of the Church Abbey, 12829 River Rd., 23233. Tel: 804-784-3366; Fax: 804-784-3431. Bryan Walsh, Dir. Provides educational services and conducts historical reseach into the Shroud of Turin.

Transitional Housing. Flagler Home-St. Joseph's Villa, 8000 Brook Rd., 23227-1399. Tel: 804-553-3258; Fax: 804-553-3259.
E-mail: thevilla@izozo.net
Linda Saltonstall, Dir. Women & Children in residence 70.

NORFOLK. *Catholic Worker Hospitality House*, 1321 W. 38th St., 23508. Tel: 804-423-5420. Coordinators: Steve Baggerly; Kim Williams.

PORTSMOUTH. *Catholic Elementary Education Foundation of Hampton Roads*, 2301 Oregon Ave., 23701. Sr. Carol Durkin, Chm.

ROANOKE. *Catholic Historical Society of the Roanoke Valley.* (Museum & Religious Goods), 400 W. Campbell Ave., 24016. Tel: 504-982-0152; Fax: 504-982-0152. Margaret M. Cochener, Pres.

St. Francis House, Inc., P.O. Box 2215, 24009. Tel: 540-345-9090. Eileen Stone, Dir. Food Distribution & Social Svcs.

VIRGINIA BEACH. *Catholic Diocese of Richmond Boy Scouts, Inc.*, 6300 Bucknell Cir., 23464. Paul Janka, Contact.

WILLIAMSBURG.
Little Sisters of St. Francis, United States and Canada Regional Center, P.O. Box 1356, 23185.

RELIGIOUS INSTITUTES OF MEN REPRESENTED IN THE DIOCESE

For further details refer to the corresponding bracketed number in the Religious Institutes of Men or Women section.

[0200]—*Benedictine Monks.* (Latrobe, PA).—O.S.B.
[1350]—*Brothers of St. Francis Xavier.*—C.F.X.
[0630]—*Congregation of the Missionaries of the Holy Family.*—M.S.F.
[0570]—*The Glenmary Home Missioners.*—Glmy.
[0690]—*Jesuits Fathers and Brothers.*—S.J.
[0430]—*Order of Preachers (Dominicans).* (Province of St. Joseph).—O.P.
[1070]—*Redemptorist Fathers.* (Baltimore Prov.).—C.SS.R.

RELIGIOUS INSTITUTES OF WOMEN REPRESENTED IN THE DIOCESE

[0230]—*Benedictine Sisters of Pontifical Jurisdiction.*—O.S.B.
[1810]—*Bernardine Sisters of the Third Order of St. Francis.*—O.S.F.
[0670]—*Cistercian Nuns of the Strict Observance.*—O.C.S.O.
[0690]—*Comboni Missionary Sisters.*—C.M.S.
[0270]—*Congregation of Bon Secours.*—C.B.S.
[1070-09]—*Congregation of St. Catherine of Siena, Racine.*—O.P.
[1070-07]—*Congregation of St. Cecelia, Nashville.*—O.P.
[1070-13]—*Congregation of the Most Holy Rosary, Adrian.*—O.P.
[1920]—*Congregation of the Sisters of the Holy Cross.*—C.S.C.
[0760]—*Daughters of Charity of St. Vincent de Paul.*—D.C.
[0820]—*Daughters of the Holy Spirit.*—D.H.S.

[0960]—*Daughters of Wisdom.*—D.W.
[1180]—*The Franciscan Sisters.*—O.S.F.
[1840]—*Grey Nuns of the Sacred Heart.*—G.N.S.H.
[2575]—*Institute of the Sisters of Mercy of the Americas.*—R.S.M.
[2340]—*Little Sisters of the Poor.*—L.S.P.
[2490]—*Medical Mission Sisters.*—S.C.M.M.
[2490]—*Medical Mission Sisters.*—M.M.S.
[2480]—*Medical Missionaries of Mary.*—M.M.M.
[2790]—*Missionary Servants of the Most Blessed Trinity.*—M.S.B.T.
[3760]—*Order of St. Clare.*—P.C.C.
[3640]—*Poor Servants of the Mother of God.*—S.M.G.
[3465]—*Religious of the Sacred Heart of Mary.* (Eastern American Prov.).—R.S.H.M.
[2970]—*School Sisters of Notre Dame.*—S.S.N.D.
[1070-03]—*Sinsinawa Dominican Congregation of the Most Holy Rosary.*—O.P.
[]—*Sisters for Christian Community.*—S.F.C.C.
[0500]—*Sisters of Charity of Nazareth.*—S.C.N.
[0590]—*Sisters of Charity of St. Elizabeth, Convent Station.*—S.C.
[0990]—*Sisters of Divine Providence.* (Our Lady of Divine Providence Prov.).—C.D.P.
[2990]—*Sisters of Notre Dame.*—S.N.D.
[3000]—*Sisters of Notre Dame de Namur.*—S.N.D.deN.
[1530]—*Sisters of St. Francis of the Congregation of Our Lady of Lourdes, Sylvania, Ohio.*—O.S.F.
[3840]—*Sisters of St. Joseph of Carondelet.*—C.S.J.
[2980]—*Sisters of the Congregation of Notre Dame.*—C.N.D.
[1990]—*Sisters of the Holy Names of Jesus and Mary.*—S.N.J.M.
[2110]—*Sisters of the Humility of Mary.*—H.M.
[2170]—*Sisters, Servants of the Immaculate Heart of Mary.* (Immaculata, PA).—I.H.M.
[4130]—*Ursuline Sisters of the Congregation of Tildonk, Belgium.*—O.S.U.
[4190]—*Visitation Nuns.*—V.H.M.

DIOCESAN CEMETERIES

RICHMOND. *Holy Cross*, First Ave. & Daniels St., 23222. Tel: 804-321-5936.
Mount Calvary, 1400 S. Randolph St., 23220. Tel: 804-355-5271.

LYNCHBURG. *Holy Cross.* Mailing Address: 710 Clay St., 24504. Tel: 804-846-5245.

NORFOLK. *St. Mary's*, 722 E. 30th St., 23504. Tel: 757-627-2874.

PORTSMOUTH. *Portsmouth Catholic.* Mailing Address: P.O. Box 155, 23705. Tel: 757-488-1723.

ROANOKE. *St. Andrew*, 3601 Salem Tpke., N.W., 24017. Tel: 540-342-9180.

NECROLOGY

† Conrad, Arthur D., Richmond, VA Holy Rosary. —Died Jan. 5, 2000.
† Noto, James, (Retired). —Died March 6, 2000.
† Ruth, Ronald A., Richmond, VA St. Edward. —Died March 9, 2000.

Diocese of Rochester

(Dioecesis Roffensis)

Most Reverend

MATTHEW H. CLARK, D.D.

Bishop of Rochester; ordained December 19, 1962; appointed Bishop of Rochester April 23, 1979; consecrated May 27, 1979; installed June 26, 1979. *Res., 1150 Buffalo Rd., Rochester, NY, 14624.*

ESTABLISHED MARCH 3, 1868.

Square Miles 7,107.

Comprises the Counties of Monroe, Livingston, Wayne, Ontario, Seneca, Cayuga, Yates, Steuben, Chemung, Tioga, Schuyler and Tompkins in the State of New York.

For legal titles of parishes and diocesan institutions, consult the Pastoral Center.

Legal Title of Diocese: The Diocese of Rochester.

Pastoral Center: 1150 Buffalo Rd., Rochester, NY, 14624-1890. Tel.: 716-328-3210; 800-388-7177; Fax: 716-328-3149.

Web site address: www.dor.org

STATISTICAL OVERVIEW

Personnel

Bishop	1
Abbots	2
Priests: Diocesan Active in Diocese	152
Priests: Active Outside Diocese	9
Priests: Retired, Sick or Absent	90
Number of Diocesan Priests	251
Religious Priests in Diocese	31
Extern Priests in Diocese	21
Ordinations:	
Diocesan Priests	2
Transitional Deacons	2
Permanent Deacons	3
Permanent Deacons in Diocese	126
Total Brothers	37
Total Sisters	666

Parishes

Parishes	157
With Resident Pastor:	
Resident Diocesan Priests	100
Resident Religious Priests	5
Without Resident Pastor:	
Administered by Priests	38
Administered by Deacons	1
Administered by Women Religious	9
Administered by Lay People	3
Missions	11
New Parishes Created	1
Closed Parishes	6
Professional Ministry Personnel:	
Sisters	68
Lay Ministers	322

Welfare

Catholic Hospitals	2
Total Assisted	280,000
Health Care Centers	2
Total Assisted	900
Homes for the Aged	4
Total Assisted	1,500
Residential Care of Children	2
Total Assisted	40
Day Care and Extended Day Care Centers	1
Total Assisted	120
Specialized Homes	7
Total Assisted	500
Special Centers for Social Services	42
Total Assisted	85,000
Residential Care of Disabled	10
Total Assisted	100

Educational

Seminaries, Diocesan	1
Students from This Diocese	5
Diocesan Students in Other Seminaries	5
Total Seminarians	10
Colleges and Universities	1
Total Students	149
High Schools, Diocesan and Parish	1
Total Students	132
High Schools, Private	6
Total Students	3,454
Elementary Schools, Diocesan and Parish	49
Total Students	11,951
Elementary Schools, Private	5
Total Students	927
Catechesis/Religious Education:	
High School Students	4,420
Elementary Students	30,936
Total Students Under Catholic Instruction	51,979
Teachers in the Diocese:	
Priests	3
Brothers	16
Sisters	61
Lay Teachers	1,096

Vital Statistics

Receptions into the Church:	
Infant Baptism Totals	5,250
Adult Baptism Totals	398
Received into Full Communion	714
First Communions	5,012
Confirmations	4,860
Marriages:	
Catholic	1,426
Interfaith	585
Total Marriages	2,011
Deaths	4,239
Total Catholic Population	338,501
Total Population	1,470,304

Former Bishops—Rt. Rev. BERNARD J. MCQUAID, D.D., cons. July 12, 1868; died Jan. 18, 1909.—Most Rev. THOMAS F. HICKEY, D.D., ord. March 25, 1884; cons. May 24, 1905; succeeded to the See, Jan. 18, 1909; appt. assistant at the Pontifical Throne, May 4, 1925 made Archbishop of the Titular See of Viminacium, Oct. 30, 1928; died Dec. 10, 1940.—Most Rev. JOHN FRANCIS O'HERN, D.D., ord. Feb. 17, 1901; appt. Bishop of Rochester, Jan. 8, 1929; cons. March 19, 1929; died May 22, 1933.—His Eminence EDWARD CARDINAL MOONEY, appt. Aug. 28, 1922; transferred to Detroit, May 26, 1937; installed Archbishop of Detroit, Aug. 3, 1937; created Cardinal, Feb. 18, 1946; died Oct. 25, 1958.—Most Rev. JAMES E. KEARNEY, D.D., ord. Sept. 19, 1908; appt. Bishop of Salt Lake, Utah, July 1, 1932; cons. Oct. 28, 1932; transferred to Rochester, July 31, 1937; installed Nov. 11, 1937; retired Oct. 26, 1966; died Jan. 12, 1977.—Most Rev. FULTON J. SHEEN, D.D., ord. Sept. 30, 1919; appt. Titular Bishop of Cesariana and Auxiliary of New York, May 28, 1951; cons. June 11, 1951; appt. to Rochester, Oct. 26, 1966; installed Dec. 15, 1966; resigned Oct. 15, 1969; appt. Titular Archbishop of Newport; died Dec. 9, 1979.—Most Rev. JOSEPH L. HOGAN, S.T.D., D.D., ord. June 6, 1942; appt. to Rochester, Oct. 6, 1969; cons. and installed Nov. 28, 1969; retired Nov. 28, 1978; died Aug. 27, 2000.

Pastoral Office Administration

Pastoral Center—1150 Buffalo Rd., Rochester, 14624-1890. Tel: 716-328-3210; 800-388-7177 (Toll Free within Diocese); Fax: 716-328-3149.

Vicar General and Pastoral Office Moderator—Rev. JOSEPH A. HART.

Vicar General—Rev. JOHN M. MULLIGAN.

Chancellor—Rev. KEVIN E. MCKENNA, J.C.D.

Judicial Vicar—Rev. LOUIS A. SIRIANNI, J.C.L.

Priest Secretary to the Bishop and Vice Chancellor—Rev. TIMOTHY T. BROWN.

Secretary to the Bishop—Mrs. MARY MOORHOUSE.

Diocesan Archives—Sr. CONNIE DERBY, R.S.M., Dir.; Rev. WILLIAM GRAF, Archivist, *63 Mason Rd., Fairport, 14450-9567.* Tel: 716-223-5500. Rev. ROBERT F. MCNAMARA, Archivist, *4536 St. Paul Blvd., Rochester, 14617.* Tel: 716-338-1602.

Bishop's Stewardship Council—Most Rev. MATTHEW H. CLARK, Pres.; Mr. ANTHONY J. ADAMS, JR.; Mr. MATTHEW AUGUSTINE; Mr. MARTIN K. BIRMINGHAM; Dr. PAUL BURGETT; Mr. WILLIAM CARPENTER; Mr. JOSEPH CLAYTON; Mr. JOSE CORONAS; Mr. CUTBERTO GARZA; Mr. JOHN GOUGH; Dr. JEROME E. HAAS; Rev. JOSEPH A. HART, V.G.; Ms. BARBARA KELLEY; Dr. KATHERINE E. KEOUGH; Mr. LAURENCE KIRWAN; Mr. LOUIS LANGIE, JR.; Ms. PATRICIA MALIGIERI; Mr. THOMAS MCDERMOTT; Ms. CONSTANCE MITCHELL; Sr. JANICE MORGAN, S.S.J.; Rev. JOHN M. MULLIGAN, V.G.; Ms. JANE F. NAPIER; Sr. PATRICIA A. SCHOELLES, S.S.J.; Mr. RANDAL SIMONETTI; Ms. JOYCE SINICROPI; Sr. SHEILA STEVENSON, R.S.M.; Rev. ROBERT T. WERTH.

Catholic Charities of the Diocese of Rochester—1150 Buffalo Rd., Rochester, 14624. Tel: 716-328-3210. JACK BALINSKY, Diocesan Dir. MARTIN BIRMINGHAM, Chm. Bd. of Directors.

Campaign for Human Development—JACK BALINSKY.

Catholic Relief Services—JUDY TAYLOR.

Communications Manager—JUDY TAYLOR.

Consistent Life Ethic Coordinator—Ms. JANN K. ARMANTROUT.

Catholic Charities Regional Offices

Catholic Charities Community and Residential Services—1945 E. Ridge Rd., Ste. 24, Rochester, 14622. Tel: 716-339-9800. PAUL T. PICKERING, Exec. Dir.

Administrative Services—BARBARA POLING.

Finances—JAMES CROWLEY, Dir.

Developmental Disabilities Services—KATHLEEN TERMINE, Dir.

AIDS Services—JANE HALLINEN, Dir.
Community Awareness Program—LYN ZYLA; ANNE SAWYKO, Devel. Coord.
Traumatic Brain Injury—TRACY COLOMBO, Dir.
Catholic Family Center—All offices at: *25 Franklin St., Rochester, 14604.* Tel: 716-546-7220. unless otherwise indicated. Ms. CAROLYN A. PORTANOVA, Pres. & CEO; Ms. JUDITH AZOFF, Vice Pres. Admin. Svcs. RITA AUGUSTINE, Vice Pres. Prog. Svcs. BEVERLY LUDKE, Vice Pres. Human Resources; BARBARA MURPHY, Vice Pres. Finance; CHRISTINE LICATA, Chm. Bd. Directors.

Departments of Catholic Family Center—
Catholic Youth Organization (CYO)—DEBORAH CUMMING-BROWN, Dir. Tel: 716-262-7008.
Children and Family Services—KAREN EMERTON, Dir. Tel: 716-262-7100.
Elder Services—IRENE COVENY, Dir. Tel: 716-262-7058.
Employee Assistance & Counseling—WENDY STRAUSS, Dir. Tel: 716-262-7034.
Homeless & Housing Services—SUSAN BENNETT, Dir. Tel: 716-423-9590.
Office of Social Policy & Research—MARV MICH, Dir. Tel: 716-262-7021.
Refugee and Immigration Services—EDWARD A. PATANE, Dir. Tel: 716-262-7082.
Restart Substance Abuse Services—CARL A. HATCH, Dir. Tel: 716-546-3046.
Fund Development & Community Relations—WILLIAM P. KEENAN. Tel: 716-262-7056.
Wayne County Office—M. JOSH MCCROSSEN, Dir. Tel: 315-331-4867.
Catholic Charities of the Finger Lakes—Serving Yates, Ontario, Wayne, Seneca and Cayuga Counties. Main Office: *One Franklin Sq., Geneva, 14456.* Tel: 315-789-2686., Satellite offices at: *33 William St., Auburn, 13021.* Tel: 315-262-0018., *4440 E. Ridge Rd., Williamson, 14589.* Tel: 315-589-2600. GIOVINA CAROSCIO, Exec. Dir. SCARLET EMERSON, Parish & Community Devel. Coord. THERESA MANGAPORA, Prog. Devel. Dir. ALMA KUNES, Prog. Coord. JACK SHARKEY, C.S.W., Prog. Mgr. THOMAS CASS, Chm. Regl. Bd. Directors.
Catholic Charities of the Southern Tier—Serving Chemung, Schuyler, Steuben, Tompkins and Tioga Counties. *215 E. Church St., Ste. 101, Elmira, 14901.* Tel: 607-734-9784. Mr. JOSEPH CAPARULO, Chm. Bd. Directors; ANTHONY T. BARBARO, Exec. Dir., , Ext. 129. CHRISTOPHER WILKINS, Devel. Office Dir., , Ext. 123. LEE RANDALL, Fin. Svc. Dir., , Ext. 140. DONNA RIEKER, Human Resources Dir., , Ext. 130. MARY M. NYBECK, Office Coord., , Ext. 126. KATHLEEN DUBEL, Justice & Peace Dir., , Ext. 135. MARILYN TERKOSKI, First Time Homebuyers, Housing Coun., , Ext. 133. JEFFREY EATON, Gateways Community Living Dir., , Ext. 110. SARAH CONLEY, First Step Victim Svcs. of Schuyler Cty. Coord. Tel: 607-535-2050.
Food Bank of the Southern Tier—PAUL HESLER, Dir. Tel: 607-796-6061. AMY V. DENENBERG, Transitions, Counseling for Healthy Living Dir. Tel: 607-936-4695. JOSEPH FEDEROWICZ, Catholic Charities/Tioga Office Dir. Tel: 607-689-0272. LAURA OPELT, Catholic Charities/Steuben Office Dir. Tel: 607-776-8085. GEORGE FERRARI, Catholic Charities/Tompkins Office Dir. Tel: 607-272-5062.

Catholic Charities of Livingston County—*10 Chapel St., Mt. Morris, 14510.* Tel: 716-658-4466. TIMOTHY MCMAHON, M.S.W., Exec. Dir.

Departments of Catholic Charities of Livingston County—
Livingston County Rural Outreach—Sr. NANCY O'BRIEN, R.S.M., Dir.
Community of Caring—CHERYL KELLER.
Partnership Success—DAWN KAVANAUGH.
Youth Mentoring Program—KIM RULIFFSON.
Hispanic Latino Outreach—ROBERT ANDINO.
Partnership for Success—DONNA SEVENSMA.
Host Home Program—JACKIE KLUBE.

Bishop Sheen Ecumenical Housing Foundation—*935 East Ave., Rochester, 14607.* Tel: 716-461-4263; Fax: 716-461-5177. ALLYNN SMITH, Exec. Dir. DOMINIC CAROSELLI, Pres. Bd. Directors Subsidiaries: Brentland Woods, Inc., Bloomfield Meadows, Inc.

Camp Stella Maris—*4395 E. Lake Rd., Livonia, 14487.* Tel: 716-346-2243; 346-2251; 346-9643. MATTHEW FLANIGAN, Exec. Dir. SUE VANDUSEN, Pres. Bd. Directors.

Kinship Family and Youth Services, Inc.—*2 Bethesda Dr., Ste. 10, Hornell, 14843.* Tel: 607-324-0909; Fax: 607-324-0983. JOSEPH WEIDER, Exec. Dir; RALPH P. KERR, Pres. Bd. Directors.

Mercy Center With The Aging—*327 Warrington Dr., Rochester, 14618-1536.* Tel: 716-244-5190. Sr. ANNE MALOY, R.S.M., M.S.W., Dir.; Sr. GRATIA L'ESPERANCE, R.S.M., M.Div., Asst. Dir.

Providence Housing Development Corporation—*1150 Buffalo Rd., Rochester, 14624.* Tel: 716-328-3210. MAGGIE BRINGEWATT, Exec. Dir. JACK BALINSKY, Pres. Bd. Directors; DONNA HALL, Dir. Operations & Legal Devel. JANE LANGE, Devel. & Mktg. Dir.

Shelter & Care Program—MARY JO CARBONARO, Monroe County Coord.

Homeownership—LISA ALCOTT, Monroe County Program Coord.

St. Ann's Home and The Heritage—*1500 Portland Ave., Rochester, 14621.* Tel: 716-342-1700. Ms. BETTY MULLIN, Pres. BARBARA PURVIS, Pres. Bd. Directors.

"Catholic Courier"—Tel: 716-328-4340. KAREN FRANZ, Gen. Mgr. & Editor Board of Directors: Most Rev. MATTHEW H. CLARK, Pres.; Rev. JOSEPH HART, Vicar General & Vice Pres.; Rev. KEVIN E. MCKENNA, J.C.D., Sec.; Ms. MUSETTE CASTLE; Rev. PATRICK CONNOR; Miss ELLEN DEBUONO; Rev. JOHN V. FORNI; Mr. RICHARD HARE; Mr. MARK HARE; Mr. WILLIAM KEDLEY; Mr. DAVID MACK; Mr. MARTIN Q. MOLL, SR.; Mr. GEORGE A. PARK, JR.; Mr. LEON SAWYKO; Ms. JULIE THANEY; Sr. ROBERTA TIERNEY, S.S.N.D.

Catholic Schools Office—Mr. TIMOTHY W. DWYER, Supt. Schools.
Assistant Superintendents—Sr. PATRICIA CARROLL, S.S.J., Asst. Supt. Government Svcs. & Admin.; Sr. VIRGINIA STEINWACHS, S.S.J., Asst. Supt. Human Resources; Sr. MARGARET MANCUSO, S.S.J., Asst. Supt. Curriculum & Instruction; Ms. PATRICIA JONES, Asst. Supt. Professional Devel.; Sr. ANNE GUERIN, S.S.J., Asst. Supt. School Advancement; Sr. ELAINE ENGLERT, S.S.J., Asst. Supt. WIN Program.
Assistant Superintendent for Business—Mr. GARY B. SMITH.

Clergy Relief Society—Most Rev. MATTHEW H. CLARK, D.D., Pres.; Revs. ROBERT KRECKEL, Vice Pres. THOMAS H. WHEELAND, Treas. JOHN FIRPO, Sec. RICHARD R. BRICKLER; JOHN H. HAYES; CHARLES MANNING; WILLIAM B. LEONE; RAYMOND BOOTH.

Office of Communications—
Director of Communications—Mr. MICHAEL TEDESCO.
Communications Assistant—MARY DAWES.

Conciliation Board—Rev. LANCE GONYO, *105 W. Main St., Sodus, 14551.* Tel: 315-483-6111.

Diocesan Consultors—Revs. JOSEPH A. HART, V.G.; WILLIAM DONNELLY; KEVIN MCKENNA, J.C.D.; JOHN MULLIGAN, V.G.; JOHN J. PHILLIPS; ROBERT SCHRADER; DANIEL TORMEY.

Office of Development—
Diocesan Director of Development—Mr. DANIEL HEALY.
Director of Major and Planned Giving—Vacant.
Director of Annual Giving—Vacant.
Administrative Assistant—Mrs. NANCY A. NASH.
Donor Relations Coordinator—Mrs. MICHELE GAMET.

Diocesan Building Commission—ERIC PATCHKE, Sec. DAVID ANDREWS; JOSEPH KIZINSKI; WILLARD STEANE; Sr. ESTELLE MARTIN, R.S.M.; WILLIAM MATTHEWS; Rev. WILLIAM J. AMANN.

Office Of Ecumenical And Interreligious Affairs—Vacant.

Commission for Ecumenical and Interreligious Affairs—DAVID VALVO, Chm.; Mrs. MICKIE CHRISTIANSEN; Ms. MARY COWDEN; Ms. JAYNE DEMAKOS; Sr. MARIE SUSANNE HOFFMAN, S.S.J.; Mr. MICHAEL NEARY; Dr. SUSAN NOWAK, S.S.J.; Mr. J. PATRICK O'CONNOR; Mrs. SUZANNE SHADY; Ms. ELAINE YAW.

Department of Evangelization and Catechesis—Ms. MARIBETH MANCINI, Dir.
Coordinator for Sacramental Catechesis—Sr. KAREN DIETZ, S.S.J.
Coordinator of Catechetical Programs and Resources—SCOTT RUTAN.
AV Resource Librarian—Sr. CONNIE DERBY, R.S.M.
Coordinator of Youth Ministry—MICHAEL THEISEN.

Faith Development Ministry—TIMOTHY DWYER, Diocesan Dir. of Faith Devel. Ministry, Supt. Catholic Schools; MARIBETH MANCINI, Diocesan Dir. of Faith Devel. Ministry, Evangelization & Catechesis.

Department of Financial Services—
Chief Financial Officer—Mr. JAMES M. RINEFIERD.
Controller—Ms. MARY ZIARNIAK.
Buildings and Properties—Mr. ERIC PATCHKE, Mgr.

Holy Sepulchre Cemetery—Most Rev. MATTHEW H. CLARK, D.D., Pres.; Rev. PETER T. BAYER, Vice Pres., Treas. & Sec.; Mr. JAMES WEISBECK, Dir. & Asst. Treas.; Mr. MARTIN BIRMINGHAM; Mr. DONALD BOLGER; Mr. ALFRED M. HALLENBECK; Mr. WILLIAM MCGINN; Mr. JAMES M. RINEFIERD; Mr. LARRY O. STID; Mrs. MICHAEL TOMAINO; Rev. THOMAS H. WHEELAND.

Information Systems And Research—
Diocesan Director—Ms. JOAN A. ZAIA.
Network Administrator—Mr. THOMAS VEEDER.
AS/400 Coordinator—Mrs. LYNNE SUORSA.
Parish Computer Coordinators—Mr. MARK DARLING; Ms. MAUREEN EASTERLY; Mr. FRED STRINGER.

Commission on Christian/Jewish Relations—Rev. JOSEPH P. BRENNAN; Ms. SUZANNE SCHNITTMAN.

Human Resources—Mr. WILLIAM OLSEN, Dir.
Department of Recruitment and Staff Services—Mrs. BARBARA PEDEVILLE, Dir.
Department of Priest Personnel—Rev. MICHAEL CONBOY.
Benefits Administration—Ms. PATRICIA HOSKING, Admin.
Coordinator of Clergy Services—Mrs. SANDRA GROCKI.
Priests' Personnel Board—Revs. MICHAEL F. CONBOY, Chm. ALEXANDER BRADSHAW; RICHARD BRICKLER; F. JAMES LAWLOR; THOMAS MULL; EDWARD PALUMBOS; JAMES SCHWARTZ.
Intern Process—Rev. EDWARD L. PALUMBOS, Dir., *3003 Dewey Ave., Rochester, 14616.* Tel: 716-663-3230.
Ministry to Priests—Rev. R. RICHARD BRICKLER, *330 Gregory St., Rochester, 14620.* Tel: 716-473-4271.
Priests' Pension Committee—Revs. ROBERT P. RING; JAMES MARVIN; ROBERT O'NEILL; MICHAEL BAUSCH; Mrs. SANDRA GROCKI; JAMES RINEFIERD; JAMES CROWLEY; WILLIAM NOONAN.
Priests' Sabbatical Committee—Mrs. JUDITH ANN KOLLAR, Chm.; Revs. R. RICHARD BRICKLER; JAMES E. BOYLE; WILLIAM DONNELLY; ROBERT P. RING; GEORGE WIANT.
Office of Vocations—Rev. JOHN A. DESOCIO, Dir., *Becket Hall, 314 Gregory St., Rochester, 14620.* Tel: 716-461-2890.
Office of Vocations Awareness—Mrs. PATRICIA FINNERTY, Dir. Tel: 716-328-3210.
Office of Seminarians—Rev. JOHN A. DESOCIO, Dir., *Becket Hall, 314 Gregory St., Rochester, 14620.* Tel: 716-461-2890.
Vicar for Religious—Human Resources.
Deacon Personnel—Deacon DAVID A. PALMA, Dir.
Deacon Personnel Board—Deacon THOMAS BECK; NANCY BECK; Deacon ANTHONY CARUSO; MARY ANN CARUSO; Deacon DAVID CADREGARI; REBECCA CADREGARI; Deacons CHARLES DISPENZA; CHRIS FISHER; LYNN FISHER; Deacon JAMES FITCH; DONNA FITCH; Deacon GREGORY KILEY; ELENA KILEY; Deacon DICK SCHULER; KATHY SCHULER. Ex Officio: Deacons THOMAS CASS; JIM CHATTERTON; MARY CHATTERTON; Deacon MICHAEL MANGIONE; SHARON MANGIONE.

Department of Legal Services—
Director—Rev. KEVIN E. MCKENNA, J.C.D., Chancellor.
Administrative Assistant—Miss CATHERINE L. SOLAN.
Tribunal—
Judges—Rev. LOUIS A. SIRIANNI, J.C.L., Judicial Vicar; Mr. RENATO AOANAN, J.C.L., Promoter of Justice; Revs. R. RICHARD BRICKLER, Adjutant Judicial Vicar; DONALD J. CURTISS, J.C.L.; Rev. Msgr. GERARD C. KRIEG, J.C.L.; Rev. WILLIAM F. LAIRD, J.C.L.; Ms. RENEE LISS-SIRACO, J.C.L.; Revs. JOHN A. LYNCH; JOHN M. MULLIGAN, V.G.; ROBERT F. O'NEILL, M.CH.A.; T. PIUS PATHMARAJAH, J.C.L.; Mr. JOHN G. SKVORAK, J.C.L.
Defenders of the Bond—Mr. RENATO AOANAN, J.C.L.; Revs. WILLIAM J. GORDINIER; M. GERARD HAFNER; WILLIAM LUM.
Staff—Rev. THOMAS CORBETT, Notary, Judicial Asst.; Ms. BARBARA FULLE, Administrative Asst.; Ms. MARY ELLEN GOVERTS, Case Instructor, Notary; Rev. WILLIAM E. GRAF, D.Min., Advocate; Miss CATHERINE L. SOLAN, Notary; Ms. LINDA ZILLIOUX, Administrative Asst.

Director Office of Liturgy—Ms. JOAN WORKMASTER; Ms. VIRGINIA MILLER, Assoc. Dir.

Liturgical Commission—Revs. EDWARD PALUMBOS, Chm. ROBERT BOURCY, Environment & Art; CHARLOTTE BRUNEY; CATHY CAIN; Sr. KAREN DIETZ, S.S.J.; HELEN HALLIGAN, Music; DEIRDRE HETZLER, Liturgical Preaching; JUDY HOFFEND; RITA MANNERS; Sr. ESTELLE MARTIN, R.S.M., Liturgy Newsletter; VIRGINIA MILLER; PAUL MURA; MICHAEL NICOSIA; SUSAN REED, Eucharist; Rev. ROBERT RING; Sr. MARY KAY RYAN, S.S.J.; Rev. NORMAN TANCK; JUDITH TOYER; YOLANDA VARGAS; TERYLE WATSON; JOAN A. WORKMASTER; SHERYL ZABEL, Inclusive Language.

Diocesan Missions Office (Propagation Of The Faith)—Rev. ROBERT C. BRADLER. Tel: 716-436-9200. World and Diocesan Missions. Sr. JANET KORN, R.S.M., Mission Awareness Coord. JOSEPHINE C. CONLON, Sec. & Bookkeeper.

Parish Support Ministries—
Director—Ms. KATHLEEN CANNON. Tel: 716-328-3228, Ext. 787 TDD (English); 716-328-3210 (Spanish).
Office Of Black Ministries—Vacant.
Office of Spanish Apostolate—Ms. GABRIELA JARAMILO, Dir.; Ms. LOURDES DECHATEAUVIEUX, Translator and Assoc. Dir., Field Office: *873 N. Clinton Ave., Rochester, 14605.* Tel: 716-232-4844.
Urban Subsidy Program—Ms. HA NGUYEN, Dir.
Office of Asian Pacific Ministry—Ms. HA NGUYEN, Dir.
Office of Pastoral Council Formation—J. EDWARD BELL, Consultant.
Office of Interdiocesan Hispanic Migrant Ministry—Mrs. MACRINA CARDENAS DE ALARCON, Dir., Field Office: *152 Main St., Brockport, 14420.* Tel: 716-637-3714. Sr. MARLENA ROGER, S.S.J., Assoc.

Dir., Field Office: *14 Ann St., Lockport, 14094.* Tel: 716-433-3136.

Pastoral Planning—Dr. WILLIAM PICKETT, Dir. Tel: 716-328-3228, Ext. 214. Mrs. MARY MOORHOUSE, Administrative Asst. Pastoral Planning Liaisons: Mr. CASEY LOPATA; Ms. KAREN RINEFIERD.

Priests' Council—Rev. WILLIAM DONNELLY, Chm.

Regional Coordinator—Rev. TIMOTHY BROWN, Liaison.

Commission of Women—Ms. KATHLEEN M. CANNON, Liaison.

Diocesan Women's Commission—Sr. MARY LOUISE HEFFERNAN, S.S.J., Chm.; Ms. CHRISTINE BOCHEN, Vice Chm. DIANE BURKE; CHARLOTTE BRUNEY; GINNY CORNYN, Sec./Treas. MACRINA CARDENAS DE ALARCON; GIOVINA CAROSIO; PAT REDMOND CLARK; EDITH FINDEIS; Rev. GEORGE HEYMAN; MONETTE MAHONEY; ELIZABETH MUNOZ; KATHERINE FRANCES OTIS; XOCHITL PALACIOS; GUY KEVIN REED; Sr. KAY SCHWENZER, S.S.J.; NORA SHANNON; Sr. EDNA SLYCK, S.S.J.

CLERGY, PARISHES, MISSIONS AND PAROCHIAL SCHOOLS

METROPOLITAN ROCHESTER
(Monroe County)

1—SACRED HEART CATHEDRAL (1910), Revs. John M. Mulligan; Gerald T. Connor; Thomas P. Mull; Sr. Joan Hilbert, R.S.M., Pastoral Assoc. In res., Most Rev. Matthew H. Clark, D.D.; Rev. Timothy T. Brown.
Res., 296 Flower City Pk., 14615. Tel: 716-254-3221; Fax: 716-254-8970.
School—Tel: 716-458-8088; Fax: 716-458-7155. Sr. M. Stephanie Riley, S.S.J., Prin.
Lay Teachers 21; Students 350; Preschool 44.
Catechesis/Religious Programs—D.R.E. Mrs. Mary Anne Taylor; Ms. Marianne Himmelsbach.
Students 110.
Convent—287 Flower City Pk., 14615. Tel: 716-254-5048.

2—ST. AMBROSE (1921), Revs. Michael J. Schramel; John L. Dugan, C.S.B.; Sr. Gertrude Erb, R.S.M., Pastoral Assoc.; Laurie Maier, Business Mgr.
Res., 25 Empire Blvd., 14609. Tel: 716-288-5000; Fax: 716-654-7658.
School—Tel: 716-288-0580; Fax: 716-288-2612. Rebecca Maloney, Prin.
Lay Teachers 22; Students 255; Preschool 58.
Catechesis/Religious Programs—Tel: 716-288-1620. D.R.E.: Mary Kay Oberst; Vicki Iannettone.
Students 210.
Convent—61 Waldo Ave., 14609. Tel: 716-288-9149.

3—ST. ANDREW (1914), Rev. Timothy E. Horan; Deacon William Schmitz; Sr. Anne Marie Lennon, R.S.M., Pastoral Assoc.
923 Portland Ave., 14621.
School—Tel: 716-467-9201; Fax: 716-467-4191. Thomas G. Bahr, Prin.
Lay Teachers 18; Students 224.
Catechesis/Religious Programs—Tel: 718-342-6665. Sr. Lucille Nalbone, M.P.F., D.R.E.
Students 34.

4—ST. ANNE (1930), Revs. Frank E. Lioi; John Colacino, C.PP.S.; Dominic Jung, C.PP.S., Korean Min.; Sr. Roberta Rodenhouse, R.S.M., Pastoral Assoc.; Deacon Gregory R. Sampson. In res., Revs. Joseph M. Sasso; Thomas Hoctor; Louis A. Sirianni.
Res., 1600 Mt. Hope Ave., 14620-4598. Tel: 716-271-3260; Fax: 716-271-7160. [CEM]
Catechesis/Religious Programs—Alice L. Leistman, D.R.E.
Students 75.

5—CHURCH OF THE ANNUNCIATION (1917) (Italian), Revs. Dennis R. Sewar; Emmaneul Nyong (Nigeria); Ernest P. Udoh (Nigeria). Pastoral Assocs.: Mary Linder; Norman Dunn.
Res., 1754 Norton St., 14609. Tel: 716-544-1050; Fax: 716-544-5923.
Catechesis/Religious Programs—Gerri Grandi, D.R.E.
Students 19.

6—ST. ANTHONY OF PADUA (1906) (Italian-Vietnamese), Revs. Paul J. Tomasso; Donald J. Curtise; Louis Nhien, Vietnamese Min.; Andrew An, Vietnamese Min.; Barbara Smullen, Pastoral Assoc.; Deacons John Antenucci; Joseph Hac Thai Nguyen; Kate Knowlton, Business Mgr.
Res., 60 Lorimer St., 14608. Tel: 716-458-1180; Fax: 716-458-7836.

7—ST. AUGUSTINE (1898). Clustered with Our Lady of Good Counsel and St. Monica to form Roman Catholic Community of the 19th Ward on July 1, 1992.
Office: 410 Chili Ave., 14611. Tel: 716-328-2442.

8—BLESSED SACRAMENT (1902), Revs. Robert J. Kennedy; Bruce F. Ammering. Pastoral Assocs.: Sr. Margaret Rose; Christopher Hoo; Beverly LaBelle. In res., Rev. George Norton; Rev. Msgr. John F. Duffy.
Parish: 534 Oxford St., 14607.
Res., 259 Rutgers St., 14607. Tel: 716-271-7240; Fax: 716-442-7517 (call first).
Catechesis/Religious Programs—Tel: 716-442-7517. Deacon David Paluskiewicz, D.R.E.
Students 71.

9—ST. BONIFACE (1860) (German), Rev. R. Richard Brickler.
Res., 330 Gregory St., 14620. Tel: 716-473-4271. [CEM]
School—(Grades PreK-6). Tel: 716-271-6370; Fax: 716-271-8099. Sr. Mary Smith, S.S.N.D., Prin.
School Sisters of Notre Dame 1; Sisters of St. Joseph 1; Lay Teachers 9; Students 182; Preschool 31.
Catechesis/Religious Programs—Students 40.

10—ST. BRIDGET (1854), Rev. Anthony P. Mugavero; Deacon Charles R. Dispenza.
Res., 8 Mark St., 14605.
Church—14 Mark St., 14605. Tel: 716-454-4236; Fax: 716-454-0835.
Catechesis/Religious Programs—Students 41.

11—ST. CECILIA (1949), Revs. Kevin E. McKenna; Michael Murimi; Sr. Marie Therese S.S.N.D., Pastoral Assoc.; Sr. Roberta Tierney, S.S.N.D., Parish Life Coord.; Suzanne Mackey, Business Mgr.; Donald Metzger, Parish Finance Dir. In res., Rev. Walter F. Cushing.
Res., 2732 Culver Rd., 14622. Tel: 716-467-4286; Fax: 716-544-8889. [CEM]
Catechesis/Religious Programs—Tel: 716-338-1051. D.R.E.: Ann G. Kubiak; Mary Ann Noto.
Students 178.

12—ST. CHARLES BORROMEO (1925), Revs. Edward L. Palumbos; Douglas Della Pietra; Francis E. Blighton; William F. McGrath, Jr.; Deacon Tom Schrage. Pastoral Assocs.: Sr. Barbara Baker, M.H.S.H.; Sr. Miriam Nugent, R.S.M. In res., Revs. Elmer W. Heindl; Thomas R. Statt.
Res., 3003 Dewey Ave., 14616. Tel: 716-663-3230; Fax: 716-663-8055.
School—64 Maiden Ln., 14616. Tel: 716-663-1220. Mary Barrese-Frame, Prin.
Students 205; Preschool 36.
Catechesis/Religious Programs—Tel: 716-663-8000. Margaret A. Gray, D.R.E.
Students 225.

13—CHRIST THE KING (1955), Revs. Norman C. Tanch, C.S.B.; Joseph A. Trovato, C.S.B.
Res., 445 Kings Hwy., 14617. Tel: 716-266-1288; Fax: 716-266-1074.
School—Tel: 716-467-8730; Fax: 716-467-5392. Colleen D'Hondt, Prin.
Sisters of St. Joseph 2; Lay Teachers 16; Students 210; Preschool 61.
Catechesis/Religious Programs—Tel: 716-338-1146. Mrs. Mary Ann Obark, D.R.E.
Lay Teachers 62; Students 475.

14—CORPUS CHRISTI (1888), Rev. Daniel McMullin. Pastoral Assocs.: Marie Suzanne Hoffman, S.S.J.; Sr. Martha Teresa Gomez, O.L.C., Hispanic Min.; Rosalee C. Magee, Business Mgr.
Res., 80 Prince St., 14605. Tel: 716-325-2424; Fax: 716-262-3576.
Church—864 Main St. E., 14605.
Catechesis/Religious Programs—Tel: 716-232-3032; Fax: 716-262-3576. Pam Cooper-Vince, D.R.E.
Students 61.

15—ST. FRANCIS ASSISI (1929), Rev. Paul J. Tomasso.
Res., 60 Lorimer St., 14608. Tel: 716-436-6693.
Catechesis/Religious Programs—Students 70.

16—ST. FRANCIS XAVIER. (Canonically merged in 1985 and now known as Holy Redeemer-St. Francis Xavier). All inquiries should be directed to the listed address: 34 Teresa St., 14605-1696.

17—ST. GEORGE (1907) (Lithuanian), Revs. Charles L. Mockevicius; Dominic F. Mockevicius.
Res., 545 Hudson Ave., 14605. Tel: 716-232-4111.

18—GUARDIAN ANGELS (1960), Mr. Dean Condon, Pastoral Admin.; Rev. Louis A. Sirianni; Mary Bills, Pastoral Assoc.; Deacon Tony Mercadel.
Res., 2061 E. Henrietta Rd., 14623. Tel: 716-334-1412; Fax: 716-334-7145.

19—ST. HELEN (1940), Rev. John A. Firpo; Deacon Richard Schuler, Pastoral Assoc.; Tracey Sheehan, Busines Mgr. In res., Revs. Kevin E. McKenna, Chancellor; Damian Ilokada (Africa).
Res., 310 Hinchey Rd., 14624. Tel: 716-235-1210.
School—Quadrant School, 150 Lettington Dr., 14624. Tel: 716-235-2391; Fax: 716-235-2417. Mary Beth Sullivan, Prin.
Lay Teachers 17; Students 210; Preschool 38.
Catechesis/Religious Programs—Fax: 716-235-8018. D.R.E.: Patricia Rodman; Gina Jennison.
Students 157.

20—HOLY APOSTLES (1884), Revs. Paul J. Tomasso; Donald J. Curtise; Sr. Dorothy Mary Leising, S.S.N.D., Pastoral Assoc.; Deacons John Antenucci; Salvador Otero; Carlos Vargas; Brunilda Martinez, Spanish Min.; Kate Knowlton, Business Mgr.
Parish: 530 Lyell Ave., 14606.
Res., 7 Austin St., 14606. Tel: 716-254-7170; Fax: 716-254-5813.

21—HOLY CROSS (1873), Revs. Thomas H. Wheeland; Frederick F. Eisemann; John Reif; Sr. Kathleen Mary O'Connell, Pastoral Assoc.; Sr. Rita Biel, Pastoral Visitor; Deacon Ed Giblin.
Res., 4492 Lake Ave., 14612. Tel: 716-663-2244; Fax: 716-865-5379.
School—4488 Lake Ave., 14612. Tel: 716-663-6533; Fax: 716-663-7948. Mrs. Mary Dayton, Prin.
Sisters 1; Lay Teachers 31; Students 426; Preschool 72.
Catechesis/Religious Programs—Tel: 716-621-8133. Karen Henrichs, D.R.E.
Students 335.
Convent—4490 Lake Ave., 14612. Tel: 716-663-5351.

22—HOLY FAMILY (1864) (German), Rev. Paul J. Tomasso; Deacons Robert Schrader; Angelo Coccia.
Res., 415 Ames St., 14611. Tel: 716-328-3110; Fax: 716-328-3112.
School—899 Jay St., 14611. Tel: 716-328-4800; Fax: 716-328-4728. Sr. Lorraine Burns, S.S.N.D., Prin.
Lay Teachers 18; Students 185; Preschool 52.
Catechesis/Religious Programs—D.R.E.: Bernard Grizard; Debbie Difilippo.
Students 64.

23—HOLY GHOST (1875), Revs. Albert Delmonte; Alexander H. Bradshaw; Irene Goodwin, Pastoral Assoc.; Deacon David Cadregari.
Res., 220 Coldwater Rd., 14624. Tel: 716-247-3535; Fax: 716-247-4223. [CEM]
Catechesis/Religious Programs—Tel: 716-426-1289. D.R.E.: Rosanne Young; Laurie Orman.
Students 41.

24—HOLY NAME OF JESUS (1964), Rev. Charles T. Manning; Michele Berlot, Pastoral Assoc.
Res., 15 St. Martin's Way, 14616. Tel: 716-621-4040; Fax: 716-621-6343; 621-1339.
Catechesis/Religious Programs—Tel: 716-621-6343. Joann White, D.R.E.
Students 322.

25—HOLY REDEEMER-ST. FRANCIS XAVIER (1867-1888). Merged in 1985. Revs. Dennis J. Shaw; Laurence Tracy; Sr. Zito Toto, O.L.C., Pastoral Assoc.; Deacon Agenol Rodriguez; Carmen Sanchez, Business Mgr.
Res., 34 Teresa St., 14605. Tel: 716-482-3211; Fax: 716-325-5771.
Church—300 Bay St., 14605.

26—HOLY ROSARY (1889), Rev. Lawrence V. Murphy; Deacon James Fitch; Rose Culligan Davis, Pastoral Assoc.
Res., 414 Lexington Ave., 14613. Tel: 716-458-4422; Fax: 716-458-8209.
School—420 Lexington Ave., 14613. Tel: 716-254-8180; Fax: 716-254-4604. Miss Mary Beth Fuehrer, Prin.
Lay Teachers 8; Students 162.
Catechesis/Religious Programs—Students 73.

27—IMMACULATE CONCEPTION (1849), Rev. Michael G. Upson.
Office: 445 Frederick Douglass St., 14608. Tel: 716-325-3893; Fax: 716-325-2082.

28—ST. JAMES (1949), Rev. John A. Lynch.
Res., 109 Brockley Rd., 14609. Tel: 716-482-9796.
School—Northeastern Quadrant Catholic School.
Catechesis/Religious Programs—Students 70.

29—ST. JOHN THE EVANGELIST (1914), Rev. William V. Spilly. Pastoral Assocs.: Sr. Chris Treichel, O.S.F.; Patricia Curtis; Anne-Marie Brogan; Sr. Elaine Kolesnick, R.S.M. In res., Rev. Edward A. Zimmer.
Mailing Address: 150 Floverton St., 14610.
Res., 549 Humboldt St., 14610. Tel: 716-482-6211; Fax: 716-482-8213.
School—Tel: 716-654-9437; Fax: 716-654-8787.
Lay Teachers 15; Students 165; Pre-School 26.
Catechesis/Religious Programs—Students 87.

30—ST. JOHN EVANGELIST (1865), John V. Forni; Revs. Joseph F. D'Aurizio; Dennis Bonsignore.
Res., 2400 Ridge Rd., W., 14626. Tel: 716-225-8980; Fax: 716-723-9825.
School—2376 W.Ridge Rd., 14626. Tel: 716-225-3450; Fax: 716-225-6301. Mrs. Eileen Preston, Prin.
Lay Teachers 19; Students 318.
Catechesis/Religious Programs—Tel: 716-225-4200. Rose Battisto, D.R.E.
Students 541.

31—ST. JOSEPH (1836). Closed. For inquiries for parish records contact Our Lady of Victory.

32—ST. JUDE THE APOSTLE (1968), Rev. John J. Steger. Res., 4100 Lyell Rd., 14606. Tel: 716-247-4322; Fax: 716-429-5111.
Catechesis/Religious Programs—Tel: 716-247-5275.
Students 247.

33—OUR LADY OF GOOD COUNSEL (1928). Clustered with St. Augustine and St. Monica to form Roman Catholic Community of the 19th Ward on July 1, 1992.
Office: 75 Ernestine St., 14619. Tel: 716-235-1130.

34—OUR LADY OF LOURDES (1928), Rev. John L. O'Connor; Deacon Robert Schrader. In res., Revs. Otto J. Vogt; William Amann.
Res., 150 Varinna Dr., 14618. Tel: 716-473-9656; Fax: 716-271-6472.
School—Seton Catholic School, (Grades PreK-6). See St. Thomas More for Grades 7 & 8. 165 Rhinecliff Dr., 14618. Tel: 716-473-6604; Fax: 716-473-3347; 473-2361. Sr. Kathleen Lurz, S.S.J., Prin.
Sisters 2; Lay Teachers 35; Students 340; Preschool 100.
Catechesis/Religious Programs—Tel: 716-244-2361. Mrs. Suzanne Regan, D.R.E.
Students 207.

35—OUR LADY OF MERCY (1957), Rev. Stanley G. Kacprzak. Pastoral Assocs.: Roni Antenucci; Carole Sampson.
Res., 36 Armstrong Rd., 14616. Tel: 716-865-0775; Fax: 716-865-0403.
Catechesis/Religious Programs—Tel: 716-865-2917; Fax: 716-865-9403. Sr. Kathryn Wahl, R.S.M., D.R.E.
Students 150.

36—OUR LADY OF MOUNT CARMEL (1909), Revs. Dennis Shaw; Laurence Tracy; Sr. Julia Norton, R.S.M.; Sr. Regis Straughn, R.S.M.; Deacons Nemesio Martinez; Felix Medero.
Res., 53 Ontario St., 14605. Tel: 716-232-1133; Fax: 716-232-1554.
Catechesis/Religious Programs—Tel: 716-224-0177. Yolanda Ortiz-Vargas, D.R.E.
Students 77.
Convent—59 Ontario St., 14605. Tel: 716-454-6766.
St. Martin's Soup Kitchen—Tel: 716-325-6500.

37—OUR LADY OF PERPETUAL HELP (1905), Rev. Neil Miller; Sr. Livia Ann Ruocco, R.S.M., Pastoral Assoc.
Res., 1089 Joseph Ave., 14621. Tel: 716-467-2725; Fax: 716-467-6841.
Catechesis/Religious Programs—Students 60.

38—OUR LADY QUEEN OF PEACE (1960), Sr. Jacqulyn Reichart, R.S.M., Pastoral Admin.; Very Rev. Joseph A. Hart, S.T.D., V.G.; Margaret Ostromecki, Pastoral Assoc. In res., Rev. John T. Walsh, M.Div.
Parish: 601 Edgewood Ave., 14618-4329.
Res., 95 Warren Ave., 14618-4311. Tel: 716-244-3010; Fax: 716-242-7733.
Catechesis/Religious Programs—Students 199.

39—OUR LADY OF VICTORY-ST. JOSEPH (1848), Rev. Winfried M. Kellner, Admin.; Carl J. Conde, Pastoral Assoc.
Res., 210 Pleasant St., 14604. Tel: 716-454-2244; Fax: 716-454-2246.

40—OUR MOTHER OF SORROWS (1829) (Irish), Revs. Alexander H. Bradshaw; Thomas R. Statt; John F. Gagnier; Peter M. DeBillis; Sr. Mary Doran, S.S.J., Pastoral Assoc. In res., Rev. Edwin S. Obiorah (Nigeria).
Res., 5000 Mt. Read Blvd., 14612. Tel: 716-663-5432; Fax: 716-663-7683. [CEM]
School—1701 Latta Rd., 14612. Tel: 716-621-3495. Samuel Zalacca, Prin.
Lay Teachers 27; Students 360.
Catechesis/Religious Programs—Tel: 716-621-3495. Mrs. Claudia Adams, D.R.E.
Students 433.

41—ST. LAWRENCE (1959), Revs. Frank J. Falletta; Michael J. Volino; Donald J. Haycock, C.S.C.
Res., 1000 N. Greece Rd., 14626. Tel: 716-723-1350; Fax: 716-723-1361.
School—Tel: 716-225-3870; Fax: 716-225-1336. Mr. Joseph P. Holleran, Prin.
Religious 2; Lay Teachers 23; Students 437; Preschool 120.
Catechesis/Religious Programs—Tel: 716-225-7320. Mrs. Jamie O'Mara, D.R.E.
Students 638.

42—ST. LUCY (1912). Closed. For inquiries for parish records contact Immaculate Conception Church.

43—ST. MARGARET MARY (1929), Nancy J. DeRycke, Temp. Admin. In res., Revs. Peter Bayer; John Rosse.
Res., 401 Rogers Pkwy., 14617. Tel: 716-342-2100; Fax: 716-467-7694.
School—School at Monroe County Catholic Schools: St. Margaret Mary's, (Grades PreK-6) 400 Rogers Pkwy., 14617. Tel: 716-266-0413; Fax: 716-266-9322. Sr. Mary Alice O'Brien, R.S.M., Prin.
Religious 1; Lay Teachers 9; Students 187; Preschool 55.
Catechesis/Religious Programs—Tel: 716-342-7114.
Students 410.

44—ST. MARK (1964), Rev. Thomas M. Erdle; Mary Chatterton, Pastoral Assoc.; Deacons James L. Chatterton; Thomas Kluchko.
Res., 54 Kuhn Rd., 14612. Tel: 716-225-3710; Fax: 716-227-6824.
Catechesis/Religious Programs—Tel: 716-227-6824; Fax: 716-225-8910; 227-6824. Charles Territo, D.R.E.
Students 602.

45—ST. MARY (1834), Rev. William Donnelly. Pastoral Assocs.: Mary Lu Coffey; Sr. Catherine Heverin, S.S.J.; Deacon William Coffey.
Res., 15 St. Mary's Pl., 14607. Tel: 716-232-7142; Fax: 716-232-6289.

46—EMMANUEL CHURCH OF THE DEAF OF THE DIOCESE OF ROCHESTER (1981), Rev. Raymond H. Fleming; Deacon Patrick A. Graybill.
Parish: 75 Ernestine St., 14619.
Res., 34 St. Monica St., 14619. Tel: 716-235-3244; 235-1812.
Catechesis/Religious Programs—Students 18.

47—ST. MICHAEL (1872) (German-Hispanic), Revs. Dennis J. Shaw; Laurence Tracy; Sr. Kay E. Schwenzer, R.S.M., Pastoral Assoc.; Deacon Jorge Malave.
Office and Res.: 124 Evergreen St., 14605-1196. Tel: 716-325-4040; Fax: 716-325-5771.
Church—869 N. Clinton Ave., 14605-1196.
Catechesis/Religious Programs—Students 109.

48—ST. MONICA (1898) (Irish). Clustered with Our Lady of Good Counsel and St. Augustine to form Roman Catholic Community of the 19th Ward on July 1, 1992. In res., Revs. Robert T. Werth; Raymond H. Fleming; Richard C. O'Connell.
Res., 34 Monica St., 14619. Tel: 716-235-3322.
School—841 Genesee St., 14611. Tel: 716-235-4140. Sr. Mary Marvin, R.S.M., Prin.
Lay Teachers 16; Students 225.

49—ROMAN CATHOLIC COMMUNITY OF THE 19TH WARD (1992). Consolidation of Our Lady of Good Counsel, St. Augustine, and St. Monica. Revs. Robert T. Werth; Raymond Fleming; Mary Ellen Fischer, Pastoral Assoc.; Deacon Joseph Fiz H. Glasgow; Eileen Dillio, Business Mgr. In res., Rev. Richard O'Connell.
Office: 34 Monica St., 14619. Tel: 716-235-3322; Fax: 716-235-3322.

50—ST. PATRICK (1832). Closed. (Old Cathedral). Records can be obtained from St. Anthony of Padua Church, 60 Lorimer St., Rochester, NY 14608. Tel: 716-458-1180.
1150 Buffalo Rd., 14624.

51—SS. PETER AND PAUL (1843), Craig Bullock, Admin.; Kate Knowlton, Business Mgr.
Res., 720 Main St., W., 14611. Tel: 716-436-3110; Fax: 716-436-0373.
Catechesis/Religious Programs—Craig Bullock, D.R.E.
Students 29.

52—ST. PIUS TENTH (1954), Revs. Foster P. Rogers; Michael Mayer; Mary Anne Bookman, C.S.J., Pastoral Assoc.; Deacons Victor Yanaitis; John E. Zierle.
Res., 3032 Chili Ave., 14624. Tel: 716-247-2511; 247-2566 (Office); Fax: 716-247-8848. [CEM]
Catechesis/Religious Programs—3000 Chili Ave., 14624. Tel: 716-247-5269; Fax: 716-247-7409. Mary Cumbo, D.R.E.
Students 409.
School—(Grades PreK-6). Tel: 716-247-5650; Fax: 716-247-7409. Mr. Stephen Oberst, Prin.
Sisters of St. Joseph 1; Lay Teachers 21; Students 435.
Catechesis/Religious Programs—3000 Chili Ave., 14624. Tel: 716-247-5269; Fax: 716-247-7409.
Students 409. D.R.E. Ms. Ann Hastee; Sr. Mary Cumbo.

53—ST. PHILIP NERI (1929) (Italian), Rev. Timothy E. Horan.
Res., 1782 Clifford Ave., 14609. Tel: 716-328-4142.
Catechesis/Religious Programs—Students 22.

54—MOST PRECIOUS BLOOD (1930) (Italian), Revs. Lawrence V. Murphy; John Milligan.
Parish: 219 Stenson St., 14606.
Res., Holy Rosary Rectory, 414 Lexington Ave., 14606. Tel: 716-458-6079; Fax: 716-458-5339.
Catechesis/Religious Programs—Students 34.

55—ST. SALOME (1925), Rev. William G. Darling; Deacon Laurence Feasel.
Res., 4282 Culver Rd., 14622. Tel: 716-323-1160.
Catechesis/Religious Programs—Annette Truby, D.R.E.
Students 79.

56—ST. STANISLAUS (1890) (Polish), Rev. Adam Ogorzaly; Deacon Raymond Mielcarek.
Res., 34 St. Stanislaus St., 14621. Tel: 716-467-3068; Fax: 716-467-3072.
Catechesis/Religious Programs—919 Norton St., 14621. Tel: 716-544-2614.
Students 57.

57—ST. THEODORE (1924), Revs. Daniel F. Holland; Frederick Helfrich; Jack Quinn; Deacon Tony Caruso. Pastoral Assocs.: Sr. Catherine Pfleger, R.S.M.; Sr. Barbara Bartkowiak, O.S.F.; Sr. Mary Jean Smith, S.S.J. In res., Revs. Gerald T. Connor; Celestine Obi (Nigeria).
Res., 168 Spencerport Rd., 14606. Tel: 716-429-6811; Fax: 716-429-7726.
Catechesis/Religious Programs—Tel: 716-429-5650.
Students 428.

58—ST. THERESA (1927) (Polish). Closed. For inquiries for parish records contact St. Stanislaus, Rochester.

59—ST. THOMAS THE APOSTLE (1922), Revs. Robert C. Bradler; Ralph J. Fraats; Deacon Thomas H. Beck; Barbara Kelly, Business Mgr. In res., Rev. Robert F. McNamara.
Res., 4536 St. Paul Blvd., 14617. Tel: 716-342-2323; Fax: 716-342-0356.
Catechesis/Religious Programs—Tel: 716-342-1704. Mr. David Higbee, D.R.E.
Students 101.

60—ST. THOMAS MORE (1953), Rev. Lee P. Chase; Sr. Ellen Galvin, S.S.J., Pastoral Assoc. In res., Revs. Richard J. Orlando; George Okoth (Kenya); Mark Miller.
Res., 2617 East Ave., 14610. Tel: 716-381-4200; Fax: 716-381-6327.
School—Siena Catholic Academy, (Grades 7-8). See Our Lady of Lourdes for Grades PreK-6. Tel: 716-381-1220; Fax: 716-381-1223.
Lay Teachers 25; Students 388; Preschool 5.
Catechesis/Religious Programs—Tel: 716-381-0470. Deacon Stephen Carroll, D.R.E.
Students 86.

OUTSIDE METROPOLITAN ROCHESTER

Addison, Steuben Co., St. Catherine of Siena (1854), Rev. Gerald T. O'Connor.
Res., 49 Maple St., 14801. Tel: 607-359-2115. [CEM]
Catechesis/Religious Programs—Tel: 607-359-2550.
Students 72.

Apalachin, Tioga Co., St. Margaret Mary (1955), Rev. Robert P. Ring. In res., Deacon Joseph F. Federowicz.
Res., 1110 Pennsylvania Ave., 13732. Tel: 607-625-3191; Fax: 607-625-5717.
Catechesis/Religious Programs—Tel: 607-625-3192.
Students 151.

Auburn, Cayuga Co.,

1—HOLY FAMILY, (1834), Rev. James C. Burke, Admin.
Parish: 85 N. St., 13021. Tel: 315-259-9576; Fax: 315-255-1506.
School—Cayuga County Catholic School, Tel: 315-253-8327; Fax: 315-253-2401.
Catechesis/Religious Programs—Tel: 315-252-9578; Fax: 315-255-1506.
Students 76.

2—SACRED HEART, (1955), Revs. William Laird; Paul Brennan; James Enright; Sr. Chris J. Treichel, O.S.F., Pastoral Assoc.; Deacon Nicholas Valvo; Maureen Collins, Business Mgr.
Res., 90 Melrose Rd., 13021. Tel: 315-252-7271; Fax: 315-255-0716. [JC]
School—St. Joseph Primary School. A consolidation of the following parishes: Holy Family; Sacred Heart; and St. Alphonsus. 17 Clymer St., Auburn, NY 13021, Tel: 315-253-8327; Fax: 315-253-2401.
Catechesis/Religious Programs—Tel: 315-253-2712. Sr. Nancy Emerick, O.S.F., D.R.E.
Students 425.
Mission—Owasco, Cayuga Co., St. Ann, (1912) 90 Melrose Rd., 13021. Tel: 315-252-7271.

3—ST. MARY, (1868) (Irish), Rev. Robert J. Schrader. In res., Rev. James C. Enright (BUF).
Res., 15 Clark St., 13021. Tel: 315-252-9545; Fax: 315-252-9546.
School—St. Joseph's. Also serving the parishes of Auburn. Tel: 315-253-8357.
Catechesis/Religious Programs—17 Clymer St., 13021. Tel: 315-252-3439.
Students 367.

4—ST. ALPHONSUS, (1853) (German), Rev. Louis A. Vasile; Deacon Gregg Lawson; Jill A. Dello Stritto, Business Mgr. In res., Revs. Clarence W. Gardner, Pastor Emeritus; Joseph T. Gaynor; Paul J. Freemesser Tel: 315-255-3159; Edward J. Foy; Robert M. Egan.

Parish: 85 E. Genesee St., 13021.; Mailing And Res.: 10 S. Lewis St., 13021. Tel: 315-252-7261; Fax: 315-252-7262. [JC]
School—St. Joseph's Elementary School. A consolidation of the parishes of Cayuga County. 89 Genesee St., 13021. Tel: 315-253-8327; Fax: 315-253-2401.
Lay Teachers 24; Students 325; Preschool 110.
Catechesis/Religious Programs—Tel: 315-253-6147. Marie Venaglia, D.R.E.
Students 105.

5—St. Aloysius. Closed. For inquiries for parish records contact the Chancery.

6—St. Hyacinth, (1905) (Polish), Rev. Xavier Nawrocki, O.F.M.Conv.
Res., 61 Pulaski St., 13021. Tel: 315-252-7297; Fax: 315-255-3781. [JC]
School—St. Joseph School. A consolidation of the following parishes: Holy Family; Sacred Heart; St. Alphonsus; and St. Hyacinth. Tel: 315-253-8327.
Catechesis/Religious Programs—Tel: 315-252-5132.
Students 155.

7—St. Francis of Assisi, (1907) (Italian), Rev. Robert L. Beligotti.
Res., 299 Clark St., 13021. Tel: 315-252-7593; Fax: 315-252-7593. [JC]
Catechesis/Religious Programs—Tel: 315-252-7594.
Students 72.

Aurora, Cayuga Co., Good Shepherd Catholic Community, Rev. Brian E. Jeffers; Deacon John Prave.
Main St., Box 296, 13026-0296. Tel: 315-364-7197; Fax: 315-364-7179. [CEM]
St. Patrick (1858). Closed. For inquiries for parish record contact Good Shepherd Catholic Community, Aurora.

Avon, Livingston Co., St. Agnes (1866), Rev. Ronald P. Harley; Mary Lou Marks, Pastoral Assoc.; Deacon Edward Mathis; Barbara Swiecki, Temp. Admin.; Lynne Siragusa, Business Mgr.
Res., 108 Prospect St., 14414. Tel: 716-226-2100; Fax: 716-226-6436. [CEM]
School—Tel: 716-226-8500. Gerald E. Benjamin, Ph.D., Prin.
Lay Teachers 8; Students 100; Preschool 47.
Catechesis/Religious Programs—Tel: 716-226-3232. Michael Drexler, D.R.E.
Students 117.

Bath, Steuben Co., St. Mary (1860), Rev. Richard J. Shatzel.
Res., 32 E. Morris St., 14810. Tel: 607-776-3327; Fax: 607-776-3409. [CEM]
School—Tel: 607-776-4767.
Catechesis/Religious Programs—36 E. Morris St., 14810. Tel: 607-776-4767; Fax: 607-776-3409.
Students 172.

Bradford, Steuben Co., St. Stanislaus (1922) (Polish), Revs. Gerald T. O'Connor; Andrew J. Kalafsky.
Res., Main St., P.O. Box 153, 14815-0153. Tel: 607-359-2115.
Mission—Campbell, Steuben Co., St. Joseph, (1870) P.O. Box 153, 14815-0153.
Catechesis/Religious Programs—Students 101.

Brockport, Monroe Co., Nativity of the Blessed Virgin Mary (1848), Rev. Peter Enyan-Boadu; Cathy Cerame, Business Mgr.
Res., 152 Main St., 14420-1972. Tel: 716-637-4500; Fax: 716-637-4232. [CEM]
School—Holley & Utica St., 14420. Tel: 716-637-2100; Fax: 716-637-7420.
Lay Teachers 8; Students 140.
Catechesis/Religious Programs—Tel: 716-637-8490. Joan Tannous, D.R.E.
Students 348.

Caledonia, Livingston Co., St. Columba (1885), Rev. Walter J. Plominski, Admin.
Res., 198 North St., 14423. Tel: 716-538-2126. [CEM]
Catechesis/Religious Programs—Students 135.
Mission—Mumford, Monroe Co., St. Patrick, (1854) Church St., Mumford, 14511.

Canandaigua, Ontario Co., St. Mary (1844), Revs. Thomas P. Mull; Walter L. Wainwright; Douglas DellaPietra; Deacon Claude Lester, Pastoral Assoc. In res., Rev. Emmett J. Halloran.
Res., 95 N. Main St., Canadaigua, 14424. Tel: 716-394-1220; Fax: 716-396-3230. [CEM]
School—16 Gibson St., 14424. Tel: 716-394-4300. Ann Marie Deutsch, Prin.
Lay Teachers 15; Students 205.
Catechesis/Religious Programs—16 Gibson St., 14424. Tel: 716-394-4590.
Students 579.

Canisteo, Steuben Co., St. Joachim (1880), Revs. James Yeager; Elias Menuba; Audrey B. Tilden, Pastoral Assoc.
Res., 32 W. Main St., 14823. Tel: 607-698-4034; Fax: 607-698-4768.
Catechesis/Religious Programs—Students 42.

Cato, Cayuga Co., St. Patrick (1875), Rev. William B. Leone; Deacon John Tomandl.
Parish: Mechanic St.; Mailing and Res.: 2667 Hamilton St., Weedsport, 13166. Tel: 315-834-6266; Fax: 315-689-7090.
Catechesis/Religious Programs—Tel: 315-834-9203. Walter Sheehan, D.R.E.
Students 117.

Cayuga, Cayuga Co., St. Joseph (1870). Closed. For inquiries for parish records contact Good Shepherd Catholic Community, Aurora.

Churchville, Monroe Co., St. Vincent De Paul (1869), Revs. William F. Laird; Theodore J. Auble; M. Gerard Hafner; Charlotte M. Bruney, Pastoral Admin.
Res., 11 N. Main St., P.O. Box 609, 14428. Tel: 716-293-1400; Fax: 716-293-0531. [CEM]
Catechesis/Religious Programs—Tel: 716-293-1180. D.R.E.: Kathleen Kuntz; Patricia VerWeire.
Students 164.

Clifton Springs, Ontario Co., St. Felix (1856). Merged with St. Francis to form St. Felix / St. Francis Parish Cluster, Clifton Springs.
St. Felix / St. Francis Parish Cluster (1992), Rev. Edward J. Dillon; Deacon Robert Cyrana.
Catechesis/Religious Programs—Students 181.

Clyde, Wayne Co., St. John the Evangelist (1852) (Italian), Revs. James E. Hewes; Leo J. Reinhardt.
Res., 114 Sodus St., 14433. Tel: 315-923-3941; Fax: 315-923-3941. [CEM]
Catechesis/Religious Programs—Sr. Catherine Gibbons, D.R.E.
Students 65.
Mission—Savannah, Wayne Co., St. Patrick, (1875) Grand Ave., Savannah, 13146. Tel: 315-365-3244.

Cohocton, Steuben Co., Holy Family Catholic Community, Revs. Stephen Kraus; Gennaro J. Ventura, (Retired); C. A. Quintus; Deacon Dan Slattery.
Churches—St. Pius V, 35 Maple Ave., P.O. Box 387, 14826.; St. Joseph, 206 Fremont St., Wayland, 14572.; Sacred Heart of Jesus, Chapel St., P.O. Box 189, Perkinsville, 14529.
Office: 206 Fremont St., Wayland, 14572. Tel: 716-728-2228; Fax: 716-728-2232.; St. Mary's Rectory: 40 Elizabeth St., Dansville, 14437. Tel: 716-335-2700.
Catechesis/Religious Programs—Ann Carey, D.R.E.
Students 69.
St. Pius V (1861) (German). Consolidated with St. Joseph, and Sacred Heart of Jesus to form Holy Family Catholic Community.

Corning, Steuben Co., St. Mary (1848), Revs. Michael F. Conboy; Michael R. Brown; Donald J. Curtiss; Mark Miller; Sr. Joan Cawley, S.S.J., Pastoral Assoc.; Deacons Raymond Defendorf; James Hankey. In res., Rev. Francis R. Davis.
Mailing Address: c/o 222 Dodge Ave., 14830. Tel: 607-936-4689; Fax: 607-936-0222. [CEM]
School—All Saints Academy, State St., 14830. Tel: 607-936-9234; Fax: 607-936-1797.
Catechesis/Religious Programs—Clustered with St. Patrick's. Tel: 602-936-4689; Fax: 602-936-0222. Mary Ann Hinkley, D.R.E.
Students 166.
St. Patrick (1903), Revs. Michael F. Conboy; Michael R. Brown; Donald Curtiss; Mark Miller; Sr. Joan Cawley, Pastoral Assoc.; Deacons Raymond Defendorf; James Hankey.
Office & Mailing Address: c/o 222 Dodge Ave., 14830. Tel: 607-936-4689; Fax: 607-936-0222.
School—All Saints Academy, Denison Pkwy., 14830. Tel: 607-962-6377; Fax: 607-962-0174.
Lay Teachers 6; Students 72; Preschool 32.
Catechesis/Religious Programs—Clustered with St. Mary's. Tel: 607-936-4683. Mary Ann Hinkley, D.R.E.
Students 125.
St. Vincent de Paul (1913), Revs. Michael F. Conboy; Michael R. Brown; Donald J. Curtiss; Mark A. Miller; Deacons Ray Defendorf; James Hankey. Pastoral Assocs.: Barbara Hesenius; Sr. Joan Cawley, S.S.J.; Patricia LaFortune.
Res., c/o 222 Dodge Ave., 14830. Tel: 607-936-4688; Fax: 607-936-0222. [JC]
Catechesis/Religious Programs—Tel: 607-936-4689. Alene Goodman, D.R.E.
Students 39.

Dansville, Livingston Co., St. Mary (1845), Revs. Stephen Kraus; Lance Gonyo; C.A. Quintus Fernando; Deacon Dan Slattery.
Res., 40 Elizabeth St., 14437. Tel: 716-728-2228; Fax: 716-728-2232. [CEM]
School—St. Mary's School, Tel: 716-335-6800; Fax: 716-335-9381.
Lay Teachers 9; Students 105; Preschool 26.
Catechesis/Religious Programs—Tel: 716-335-8700; Fax: 716-335-3092.
Students 123.
Mission—Holy Family Catholic Community.

Dryden, Tompkins Co., Holy Cross (1962), Rev. Bernard L. Carges; Barbara J. Stinard, R.S.M., Admin.
Parish: 375 S.George Rd., Freeville, 13068.; c/o Fr. Carges: 212 Locke Rd., Groton, 13073. Tel: 607-844-8314; Fax: 607-844-8358.
Catechesis/Religious Programs—Barbara Ivers, D.R.E.
Students 148.

East Bay, Wayne Co., St. John Fisher (1935). Closed. All inquiries for mission records can be made at St. Mary Magdalen, Wolcott.

East Bloomfield, Ontario Co., St. Bridget (1850), Revs. Richard J. Beligotti, Admin.; Douglas DellaPietra; Sr. Diane Dennie, Admin.; Deacon Claude Lester.
Res., 15 Church St., 14443. Tel: 716-657-7626; Fax: 716-657-5349. [CEM]
Catechesis/Religious Programs—Students 111.

East Rochester, Monroe Co., St. Jerome (1905), Revs. Albert L. Delmonte; Michael F. Conboy; Sr. Mary Ann Brunett, S.S.J., Pastoral Assoc.; Deacon Tom Ecker. In res., Rev. Edward Steinkirchner.
Res., 207 S. Garfield St., 14445. Tel: 716-586-3231; Fax: 716-586-0537.
Catechesis/Religious Programs—206 West Ave., 14445. Tel: 716-586-1625.
Students 281.

Elmira, Chemung Co.,

1—Sts. Peter and Paul of Eastside Catholic Parish, (1848), Rev. Patrick L. Connor; Sr. Kathleen Bayer, R.S.M., Pastoral Assoc.; Deacons Michael Campanelli, (Retired); George Welch.
Office: 161 High St., Elimira, 14901. Tel: 607-732-1994; Fax: 607-732-2629.
Res., 950 Lake St., 14901. Tel: 607-732-2455.
School—Holy Family Catholic Schools. Serving the parishes in Elmira. See St. Mary, St. Casimir, and Our Lady of Lourdes for details.
Catechesis/Religious Programs—Clustered with St. Cecilia & St. John the Baptist. Cecilia Ryan, D.R.E.
Students 74.

2—St. Patrick, (1871) (Irish), Revs. Joseph P. McCaffrey; Walter Wainwright; Sr. Maureen Mylott, S.C., Pastoral Assoc.; Deacon I. Michael Mangione; Faith-Louise Eaton, Business Mgr.
Res., 604 Park Pl., 14901. Tel: 607-733-0300; Fax: 607-733-3606.
School—Holy Family Catholic Schools. Serving the parishes in Elmira. See St. Mary, St. Casimir, and Our Lady of Lourdes for details. Tel: 607-734-4414.
Catechesis/Religious Programs—Tel: 607-737-0536; Fax: 607-733-3606. Rose Bennett, D.R.E.
Students 134.

3—St. Mary, (1873) (Irish), Rev. Richard T. Farrell; Deacon Robert Stowell; Jeannette Meck, Business Mgr. In res., Rev. Joseph F. Brodnick.
Res., 224 Franklin St., 14904. Tel: 607-734-6254.
School—Holy Family Primary, (Grades PreK-3). See St. Casimir and Our Lady of Lourdes for Intermediate and Jr. High. 421 Fulton St., 14904. Tel: 607-732-3588; Fax: 607-732-1850. Constance Dunn, Prin.
Lay Teachers 18; Students 240; Preschool 68.
Catechesis/Religious Programs—Tel: 607-734-5220; Fax: 607-733-8890. D.R.E.: Donna Bennett; Bonnie Collins.
Students 215.

4—St. John the Baptist of Eastside Catholic Parish, (1866) (German), Rev. Patrick L. Connor; Sr. Kathleen Bayer, R.S.M., Pastoral Assoc.; Deacons Michael Campanelli, (Retired); George Welch; Judy Butler, Business Mgr.
Church & Mailing Address: 161 High St., 14901. Tel: 607-732-1994 (Office); Fax: 607-732-2629 (Office).
Res., 950 Lake St., 14901. Tel: 607-732-2455.
School—Holy Family Catholic Schools. Serving the parishes in Elmira. See St. Mary, St. Casimir, and Our Lady of Lourdes for details.
Catechesis/Religious Programs—Clustered with Sts. Peter & Paul.

5—St. Casimir, (1890) (Polish), Rev. Christopher E. Linsler; Sr. Mary O'Brien, S.S.J., Pastoral Assoc.; Deacon William P. Dougherty; Anne Bremer, Business Mgr. In res., Revs. Severine S. Msemwa; Thadeus F. Mkamwa.
Res., 1012 Davis St., 14901. Tel: 607-734-1622; Fax: 607-733-5870.
School—Holy Family Jr. High. See St. Mary and Our Lady of Lourdes for Primary and Intermediate. 1008 Davis St., 14901. Tel: 607-734-0336; Fax: 607-734-4977. Mrs. Elizabeth Berliner, Prin.
Lay Teachers 14; Students 170.

Catechesis/Religious Programs—Jean Keenan, D.R.E.
Students 84.

6—ST. CECILIA OF EASTSIDE CATHOLIC PARISH, (1904), Rev. Patrick L. Connor; Sr. Kathleen Bayer, R.S.M., Pastoral Assoc.; Deacons Michael Campanelli, (Retired); George Welch; Judy Butler, Business Mgr.
Office: 161 High St., 14901. Tel: 607-732-1994; Fax: 607-732-2629.
Res., 950 Lake St., 14901. Tel: 607-732-2455.
School—Holy Family Catholic Schools. Serving the parishes in Elmira. See St. Mary, St. Casimir, and Our Lady of Lourdes for details.
Catechesis/Religious Programs—Clustered with Sts. Peter & Paul.

7—ST. ANTHONY, (1908) (Italian). Clustered with St. Patrick's Church. Revs. Walter L. Wainwright; Joseph J. McCaffrey; Sr. Maureen Mylott, S.C., Pastoral Assoc.; Deacon I. Michael Mangione; Faith-Louise Eaton, Business Mgr.
Res., 604 Park Pl., 14901. Tel: 607-733-0300; Fax: 607-733-3606.
School—Holy Family Catholic Schools. Serving the parishes in Elmira. See St. Mary, St. Casimir, and Our Lady of Lourdes for details. Tel: 607-734-4414.
Catechesis/Religious Programs—Clustered with St. Patrick. Rose Bennett, D.R.E.
Students 124.

8—OUR LADY OF LOURDES, (1940), Rev. Jerimiah P. Moynihan; Lisa Rustici, Admin.
Parish: 304 Demarest Pkwy., 14905.
Res., 120 Fairmont Rd., 14905. Tel: 607-732-6261; Fax: 607-732-7256.
School—Holy Family Intermediate. See St. Mary and St. Casimir for Primary and Junior High. 301 Demarest Pkwy., 14905. Tel: 607-734-0841; Fax: 607-732-5432. Miss Brenda Lisi, Prin.
Lay Teachers 10; Sisters 1; Students 171.
Catechesis/Religious Programs—Tel: 607-734-0727. Margaret Johnson, D.R.E.
Students 200.

Elmira Heights, Chemung Co., St. Charles Borromeo (1904), Rev. Christopher E. Linsler; Sr. Mary O'Brien, C.S.J., Pastoral Assoc.; Deacon William P. Dougherty.
Res., 130 Oakwood Ave., 14903. Tel: 607-734-7619.
Catechesis/Religious Programs—Tel: 607-734-1622; Fax: 607-733-5870.
Students 100.

Fairport, Monroe Co., Assumption of the Blessed Virgin Mary (1866), Revs. Edward Golden; Gary Tyman, Vicar; Deacon Ronald J. Tocci. Pastoral Assocs.: Sheryl Zabel; Sheila Cody. In res., Rev. Msgr. George A. Cocuzzi.
Res., 20 East Ave., 14450. Tel: 716-388-0040; Fax: 716-388-0248. [CEM]
Catechesis/Religious Programs—Assumption School of Religion, 10 Baumer Place, 14450. Tel: 716-223-0525; Fax: 716-223-5253. Cathy Tocci, D.R.E.
Students 870.

Church of the Resurrection (1973), Rev. William E. Graf.
Res., 52 Mason Rd., 14450. Tel: 716-223-6686; Fax: 716-223-6958.
Church—63 Mason Rd., 14450. Tel: 716-223-5500; Fax: 716-223-6958.
Catechesis/Religious Programs—Students 227.

St. John of Rochester (1962), Rev. James E. Boyle; Sr. Barbara Hesenius, Pastoral Assoc.; Deacons Thomas J. Cleary; Daniel M. Kinsky. In res., Revs. John J. Phillips; Michael C. Hogan.
Res., Ministry Bldg., 8 Wickford Way, 14450. Tel: 716-248-5993; Fax: 716-387-0517.
Rectory: 18 Wickford Way, 14450.
School—10 Wickford Way, 14450. Tel: 716-248-8836; Fax: 716-248-8839. Mrs. Eileen O'Neill, Prin.
Lay Teachers 13; Students 200; Preschool 20.
Catechesis/Religious Programs—Tel: 716-248-8850. Judith Swagler, D.R.E.
Students 814.

Fleming, Cayuga Co., St. Isaac Jogues (1946), Rev. Albert J. Shamon, Admin.
Parish: Rt. 34.
Mailing Address: 5043 State Rt. 34, Auburn, 13021.
Res., 5 S. Marvine Ave., Auburn, 13021. Tel: 315-255-2912; Fax: 315-255-2912.

Geneseo, Livingston Co., St. Mary (1854), Rev. William Gordinier. In res., Rev. Eugene H. McFarland Tel: 716-243-2551.
Office: 13 North St., 14454. Tel: 716-243-1100; Fax: 716-243-0240.
Res., 4 Avon Rd., 14454. [CEM]
Catechesis/Religious Programs—Students 210.

Geneva, Ontario Co., St. Francis de Sales (1835), Rev. Roy Kiggins. Pastoral Assocs.: Sr. Lucy Jean, C.S.C.; Sr. Ruth A. Page. In res., Rev. Paul Bonnacci, Vicar.
Parish: 130 Exchange St., 14456.
Res., 48 Pultney St., 14456. Tel: 315-789-5787; Fax: 315-781-1985. [CEM][JC 2]
School—Consolidated School. See St. Stephen and St. Francis de Sales. Tel: 315-789-2818.
Catechesis/Religious Programs—Tel: 315-789-0903.
Students 232.

St. Stephen (1904). Consolidated with the following parishes: St. Francis de Sales and St. Stephen. Rev. Roy Kiggins; Rev. Msgr. Gerard C. Krieg; Rev. Paul Bonacci. Pastoral Assocs.: Ruth A. Page; Sr. Lucy Jean, C.S.C.
Office: 130 Exchange St., 14456.; Res. & Church: 48 Pulteney St., 14456. Tel: 315-789-1124; Fax: 315-781-1985. [JC]
School—(Grades PreK-8) 17 Elmwood Ave., 14456. Tel: 315-789-1828; Fax: 315-789-2186. Mrs. Elaine Morrow, Prin.
Sisters of St. Joseph 1; Lay Teachers 17; Students 200; Preschool 15.
Catechesis/Religious Programs—110 Exchange St., 14456. Tel: 315-781-2624. Walter Savaria, D.R.E.
Students 263.

Groton, Tompkins Co., St. Anthony (1873), Rev. Bernard L. Carges.
Res., 312 Locke Rd., R.D. 2, 13073. Tel: 607-898-5135; Fax: 607-898-7608. [CEM]
Catechesis/Religious Programs—Students 120.

Hamlin, Monroe Co., St. Elizabeth Ann Seton (1982), Revs. Paul J. Ryan; M. Gerard Hafner; Deacons Christopher Fisher; Klaus Schulz.
Res., 3747 Brick Schoolhouse Rd., 14464. Tel: 716-964-8627; Fax: 716-964-3352.
Catechesis/Religious Programs—Tel: 716-964-8200. Cynthia Lazzaro, D.R.E.
Students 233.

Hammondsport, Steuben Co., St. Gabriel (1845), Sr. Anne Michelle McGill, Pastoral Admin.; Rev. Richard Shatzel; Sr. Margaret Kunder, S.S.J., Pastoral Assoc.
Res., 78 Shethar St., 14840. Tel: 607-569-3501; Fax: 607-569-3226. [JC]
Catechesis/Religious Programs—Fax: 607-569-3501.
Students 59.

Henrietta, Monroe Co., Church of the Good Shepherd (1911), Revs. Michael J. Bausch; Steve W. Lape; Walter Stacker, Business Mgr. Pastoral Assocs.: Sr. Barbara Stinard, R.S.M.; Susan Reed; Mary Ann Klee.
Res., 3318 E. Henrietta Rd., 14467. Tel: 716-334-3518; Fax: 716-334-6015. [CEM]
School—3288 E. Henrietta Rd., 14467. Tel: 716-334-5100. Marie Arcuri, Prin.
Lay Teachers 12; Students 235; Preschool 40.
Catechesis/Religious Programs—Tel: 716-334-3023. D.R.E.: Carolyn Hahn; Margaret Churnetski.
Students 550.

Hilton, Monroe Co., St. Leo (1884), Revs. John J. Glogowski; M. Gerald Hafner; Deacon James P. Steiger. In res., Rev. Joseph D'Aurizio.
Res., 167 Lake Ave., 14468. Tel: 716-392-2710; Fax: 716-392-9254.
Catechesis/Religious Programs—Tel: 716-392-9694.
Students 240.

Honeoye, Ontario Co., St. Mary, Our Lady of the Hills (1868), Rev. Edward B. Zenkel; Deacon Roger Loomis.
Parish: 8961 Main St., 14471.
Res., Rte. 20A, Box 725, 14471. Tel: 716-229-5007. [CEM]
Catechesis/Religious Programs—Students 88.

Honeoye Falls, Monroe Co., St. Paul of the Cross (1870), Rev. Lawrence A. Gross; Sr. Yvonne Nadeau, S.S.N.D., Pastoral Assoc.; Deacon Albro C. Wilson, Jr.
Res., 29 Monroe St., 14472. Tel: 716-624-1443; Fax: 716-624-5169. [CEM]
Catechesis/Religious Programs—Students 231.

Hornell, Steuben Co., St. Ann (1849), Revs. James P. Jaeger; Paul Schnacky, (Retired); Kip Corriveau, Vicar; Elias Menuba; Sr. Mary Jude Rodenbrock, R.S.M., Pastoral Assoc.; Deacon Robert W. McCormick; John Buchko, Business Mgr. In res., Rev. Robert Kanka, (Retired).
Res., 31 Erie Ave., P.O. Box 605, 14843. Tel: 607-324-0410; Fax: 607-324-6784. [CEM][JC 2]
School—27 Erie Ave., 14843. Tel: 607-324-0733; Fax: 607-324-0985. Sr. Dolores Ann Stein, Prin.
Lay Teachers 13; Students 133; Preschool 33.
Catechesis/Religious Programs—Tel: 607-324-7121. Marianne Logan, D.R.E.
Students 203.

St. Ignatius Loyola (1931), Rev. James P. Jaeger; John Buchko, Business Mgr.
Parish: 343 Canisteo St., 14843.
Res., 31 Erie Ave., 14843. Tel: 607-324-5811.
Catechesis/Religious Programs—Tel: 607-324-7121.
Students 94.

Horseheads, Chemung Co., St. Mary Our Mother (1866), Rev. Thomas W. Burr; Rosemary Bloise, Pastoral Assoc.; Deacon Daniel R. Hurley. In res., Rev. Robert C. MacNamara, (Retired).
Res., 816 W. Broad St., 14845. Tel: 607-739-3817; Fax: 607-739-5628. [CEM]
School—811 Westlake St., 14845. Tel: 607-739-9157. Mary Canali, Prin.
Lay Teachers 13; Students 192; Preschool 30.

Interlaken, Seneca Co., St. Francis Solanus (1875), Rev. Bernard Maloney, O.F.M.Cap.
Parish: Orchard St., 14847.
Mailing Address: c/o Holy Cross Church, P.O. Box 337, Ovid, 14521.
Office: P.O. Box 357, Ovid, 14521-0337. Tel: 607-869-2261; Fax: 607-869-9825.
Res., St. Fidelis Friary, 7790 County Rd. 153, 14847. Tel: 607-532-4423; Fax: 607-532-9271.
Church—Orchard St., 14847.

Ithaca, Tompkins Co., St. Catherine of Siena (1960), Rev. Ronald E. Gaesser; Patricia Cote, Business Mgr. Pastoral Assocs.: Mary Boris; Candace Galik; Diane Schafer.
Res., 302 St. Catherine Cir., 14850. Tel: 607-257-2493; Fax: 607-257-5901.
Catechesis/Religious Programs—Students 165.

Immaculate Conception (1848), Revs. Leo J. Reinhardt; George P. Heyman; Ghana R. Pentareddy (India); Deacon George Kozak. Pastoral Assocs.: Sr. Edna Slyck, R.S.M.; Ann Kozak; Gregory Wesley.
Res., 113 N. Geneva St., 14850. Tel: 607-273-6121; Fax: 607-273-0185. [CEM 2]
School—320 W. Buffalo St., 14850. Tel: 607-273-2707; Fax: 607-272-8456. John Farrelly, Prin.
Lay Teachers 17; Students 184; Preschool 35.
Catechesis/Religious Programs—Tel: 607-273-0303.
Students 160.

King Ferry, Cayuga Co., Our Lady of the Lake, King Ferry (1868). Closed. For inquiries for parish records contact Good Shepherd Catholic Community, Aurora.

Lansing, All Saints (1913), Mary E. Wintish, R.S.M., Pastoral Admin.; Rev. Scott Kubinski.
Res., 347 Ridge Rd., 14882. Tel: 607-533-7344.
Catechesis/Religious Programs—Students 70.

Leicester, Livingston Co., St. Thomas Aquinas (1897), Revs. George N. Okoth; Desmond O'Neill; Mabel Treadwell, Pastoral Assoc.
Res., 175 Main St. Box 195, 14481. Tel: 716-382-3400; Fax: 716-382-3349.
Mission—Retsof, Livingston Co., St. Lucy, (1912) 2770 Retsof Ave., Retsof, 14539. Tel: 716-243-4068.

Lima, Livingston Co., St. Rose (1848), Rev. Lawrence F. Gross; Deacon Eugene Edwards.
1985 Lake Ave., P.O. Box 8A, 14485.
Res., 29 Monroe St., Honeoye Falls, 14472. Tel: 716-624-1443; Fax: 716-582-2663. [CEM]
Catechesis/Religious Programs—Tel: 716-624-1005.
Students 75.

Livonia, Livingston Co., St. Joseph (1911), Revs. John H. Hayes; Jerome F. Schifferli, Pastor Emeritus; Alice Miller Nation, Pastoral Assoc.
Res., 14 Washington St., P.O. Box 77, 14487. Tel: 716-346-3815; Fax: 716-346-9445. [CEM]
Catechesis/Religious Programs—41 Spring St., 14487. Tel: 716-346-2500; Fax: 716-346-3723.
Students 225.
Mission—Conesus, Livingston Co., St. William, P.O. Box 77, 14487. Tel: 716-346-3757.

Livonia Center, Livingston Co., St. Michael (1848). Closed. For inquiries for parish records contact St. Mary's, Honeoye.

Lyons, Wayne, St. Michael (1852) (Italian), Rev. William M. Barrett. In res., Rev. James E. Hewes Tel: 315-946-4299.
Res., 3 Holley St., 14489-1505. Tel: 315-946-4182; Fax: 315-946-4736.
Catechesis/Religious Programs—Students 62.

Macedon, Wayne Co., St. Patrick (1883), Rev. Robert Scott Bourcy; Donna Fitch, Pastoral Assoc.; Deacon Dominick N. Abballe.
Res., 52 Main St., 14502. Tel: 315-986-5671; Fax: 315-986-4398. [CEM]
Catechesis/Religious Programs—Tel: 315-986-2021.
Students 235.

Marion, Wayne Co., St. Gregory (1914), Rev. Robert Gaudio; Dr. Denise Mack, Pastoral Assoc.
Mailing Address: 136 Church St., Palmyra, 14522. Tel: 315-597-4571.
Office: 3806 Union St., 14505. Tel: 315-926-4323.
Catechesis/Religious Programs—Students 115.

Mendon, Monroe Co., St. Catherine of Siena (1902), Rev. F. James Lawlor; Sr. Ruth Maier, S.S.J., Pastoral Assoc. In res., Rev. John P. Norris.
Res., 26 Mendon-Ionia Rd., 14506. Tel: 716-624-4990; Fax: 716-624-4996.

Catechesis/Religious Programs—Mrs. Gail Brooks, D.R.E.
Students 350.
Convent—15 Mendon-Ionia Rd., 14506. Tel: 716-624-1538.

Montezuma, Cayuga Co., St. Michael (1865). Closed. For inquiries for parish records contact St. Joseph, Weedsport.

Moravia, Cayuga Co., St. Patrick (1872). Closed. For inquiries for parish records contact Good Shepherd Catholic Community, Aurora.

Mount Morris, Livingston Co., St. Patrick (1869), Rev. Michael J. Brown.
Res., 46 Stanley St., 14510. Tel: 716-658-2110. [CEM]
Parish Center, 33 Murray St., Mt. Morris, 14510.
Catechesis/Religious Programs—Students 96.

Naples, Ontario, Our Lady of the Lakes Catholic Community, Revs. Philip J. Billotte; Sean Garrity, C.S.B.; Deacons Michael McGuire; Claude Curtin. In res., Rev. Peter Deckman.
Res., 180 N. Main St., P.O. Box 459, 14512. Tel: 716-374-2414; Fax: 716-374-2415.
Catechesis/Religious Programs—Students 91.

Newark, Wayne Co., St. Michael (1863), Revs. Peter C. Clifford; Peter M. DeBellis; Jesus Flores, Rgnl. Hispanic Min.; Sr. Lucilla Romero Ponce, Rgnl. Hispanic Min.; Deacon Thomas Cass; Deborah Housel, Pastoral Assoc.
Res., 401 Main St., 14513. Tel: 315-331-6753; Fax: 315-331-2925.
School—320 S. Main St., 14513. Tel: 315-331-2297. Mrs. Kathleen Peters, Prin.
Lay Teachers 20; Students 352.
Catechesis/Religious Programs—Tel: 315-331-3408. D.R.E.: Rose Leisenring Tel: 315-331-6753; Jeanette Housecamp.
Students 355.

Newark Valley, Tioga County, St. John the Evangelist (1880), Revs. William A. Moorby; Timothy L. Niven; Betty D'Arcy, Pastoral Assoc.; Deacon Warren M. Rutan.
Parish: 24 Rock St.
Res., 300 Main St., Owego, 13827. Tel: 607-687-1068; Fax: 607-687-8122.
Catechesis/Religious Programs—Tel: 607-642-3258; Fax: 607-642-3258.
Students 113.
Mission—Catatonk, Tioga Co., St. Francis of Assisi, (1930).

North Chili, Monroe Co., St. Christopher (1968), Rev. Robert F. O'Neill, Admin.; Sr. Carol Fox, R.S.M., Pastoral Assoc.
Res., 3350 Union St., P.O. Box 399, 14514. Tel: 716-594-1400.
Catechesis/Religious Programs—Tel: 716-594-1441.
Students 571.

Nunda, Livingston Co., Holy Angels (1854). Clustered with St. Patrick's. Rev. Michael R. Brown.
Mailing Address: c/o St. Patrick's Church, 46 Stanley St., Mount Morris, 14510. Tel: 716-658-2110.
Catechesis/Religious Programs—21 Massachusetts St., 14517. Tel: 716-468-3450.
Students 61.

Odessa, Schuyler Co., St. Benedict (1965), Rev. David L. Bonin; Catherine Paul Theiss, C.S.J., Pastoral Assoc.
Mailing Address: 905 N. Decatur St., P.O. Box 288, Watkins Glen, 14891.
Res., 1101 1/2 Tenth St., Watkins Glen, 14891. Tel: 607-535-2786; Fax: 607-535-2990.
Church—Speedway, 14869. Tel: 607-594-2226.
Catechesis/Religious Programs—Tel: 607-387-5957.
Students 5.

Ontario, Wayne Co., St. Mary of the Lake (1869), Rev. Robert G. Kreckel; Lee Skerritt, Pastoral Assoc.; Deacon Gerald J. Skerrett.
Res., 5823 Walworth Rd., P.O. Box 499, 14519. Tel: 315-524-2611; Fax: 607-524-8353. [CEM]
Catechesis/Religious Programs—5823 Walworth Rd., 14519. Tel: 315-524-7421.
Students 340.

Ovid, Seneca Co., Holy Cross (1849), Rev. Bernard Maloney, O.F.M. Cap.
7239 Main St., P.O. Box 337, 14521-0337.
Res., St. Fidelis Friary, 7790 County Rd. 153, Interlaken, 14847. Tel: 607-869-2261; Fax: 607-869-9825. [CEM]
Catechesis/Religious Programs—Students 38.

Owego, Tioga Co., St. Patrick (1842), Revs. William A. Moorby; Timothy L. Niven; Betty D'Arcy, Pastoral Assoc.; Deacon Warren M. Rutan.
Res., 300 Main St., 13827. Tel: 607-687-1068; Fax: 607-687-8122. [CEM]
School—Tel: 607-687-1770; Fax: 607-687-4305. Gary Foote, Prin.
Lay Teachers 7; Students 99; Preschool 45.
Catechesis/Religious Programs—Students 174.

Painted Post, Steuben Co., Immaculate Heart of Mary (1952), Revs. Michael F. Conboy; Michael R. Brown; Donald J. Curtiss; Mark A. Miller; Sr. Mary Kay Ryan, S.S.J., Pastoral Assoc.; Sr. Joan Cawley, S.S.J., Admin.; Deacons Raymond Defendorf; James Hankey.
Mailing Address: c/o 222 Dodge Ave., Corning, 14830. Tel: 607-962-4689; Fax: 607-936-0222. [CEM][JC]
Catechesis/Religious Programs—Alene Goodman, D.R.E.
Students 203.

Palmyra, Wayne Co., St. Anne (1850), Revs. Robert Gaudio; Francis H. Vogt, Pastor Emeritus; Dr. Denise Mack, Pastoral Assoc.
Res., 136 Church St., 14522. Tel: 315-597-4571; Fax: 315-597-4571. [CEM]
Catechesis/Religious Programs—Mrs. Pam McKechney, D.R.E.
Students 155.

Penfield, Monroe Co., Holy Spirit (1965), Revs. Frederick W. Bush; Ronald A. Antinarelli. In res., Rev. Gerard J. McMahon.
Res., 1355 Hatch Rd., Webster, 14580. Tel: 716-671-5520; Fax: 716-671-7262.
Catechesis/Religious Programs—Tel: 716-671-5680.
Students 217.

St. Joseph (1860), Rev. Kevin P. Murphy; Deacon Ken Arnold. Pastoral Assocs.: Sr. Patricia M. Switzer, R.S.M.; Nancy Giordano. In res., Revs. L. John Hedges; Edward E. Steinkirchner; Eric C. Phillips; Pius Pathmarajah (India).
Parish: 43 Gebhardt Rd., 14526.
Res., 35 Gebhardt Rd., 14526. Tel: 716-586-8089; Fax: 716-586-0674. [CEM]
School—39 Gebhardt Rd., 14526. Tel: 716-586-6968; Fax: 716-586-4619. Marilyn Dewey, Prin.
Sisters 1; Lay Teachers 24; Students 438.
Catechesis/Religious Programs—Patrick B. Fox, D.R.E.
Students 975.

Penn Yan, Yates Co., St. Michael (1850), Revs. Philip J. Billotte, Pastor; Sean M. Garrity, Pastor; Peter Deckman; Deacon Claude Curtin.
Mailing Address: 210 Keuka St., 14527.
Res., 312 Liberty St., 14527. Tel: 315-536-7459; Fax: 315-536-6964. [CEM 2]
School—214 Keuka St., 14527. Tel: 315-536-6112; Fax: 315-536-6112. JoAnn Struck, Prin.
Lay Teachers 7; Students 107.
Catechesis/Religious Programs—210 Keuka St., 14527. Tel: 315-536-3794. Mary Tyrrell, D.R.E.
Students 100.
Mission—Dundee, Yates Co., St. Andrew, (1877) Union St., Penn Yan, 14837.

Phelps, Ontario Co., St. Francis (1869). Merged with St. Felix to form St. Felix / St. Francis Parish Cluster, Clifton Springs.

Pittsford, Monroe Co., St. Louis (1911), Rev. James A. Schwartz; Deacon John Payne. Pastoral Assocs.: Deacon Thomas J. Driscoll; Sr. Judith Ann Kenrick, R.S.M. In res., Rev. Raymond Booth; Rev. Msgr. Gerard C. Krieg.
Res., 60 S. Main St., 14534. Tel: 716-586-5675; Fax: 716-387-9888.
School—11 Rand Pl., 14534. Tel: 716-586-5200. Kathleen Carroll, Prin.
Lay Teachers 24; Students 369; Preschool 70.
Catechesis/Religious Programs—64 S. Main St., 14534. Tel: 716-381-4455; Fax: 716-387-9888.
Students 365.

Church of the Transfiguration (1983), Rev. Gerald J. Appelby; Deacons Michael Piehler; Anthony Scicolino; Barbara Swiecki, Pastoral Assoc.
Res., 50 W. Bloomfield Rd., 14534. Tel: 716-248-2427; Fax: 716-385-9870.
Catechesis/Religious Programs—Tel: 716-248-2465. Mary Presutti-Lancto, D.R.E.
Students 940.

Red Creek, Wayne Co., St. Thomas the Apostle (1882), Revs. John V. Forni; George P. Heyman.
Mailing Address: 11956 Washington St., Wolcott, 14590-1133. Tel: 315-594-9430. [CEM]
Catechesis/Religious Programs—Students 40.
Mission—Fair Haven, Cayuga Co., St. Jude Chapel, (1962). All inquiries for sacramental records for St. Thomas and St. Jude prior to July 1, 1985 can be made at Cayuga Cluster 2667 Hamilton St., Weedsport, NY 13166. Telephone: 716-594-9430. 11956 Washington St., Wolcott, 14590.

Rexville, Steuben Co., St. Mary (1845) (Irish), Revs. James Yeager; Elias Menuba; Audrey Tilden, Pastoral Assoc.; John Buchko, Business Mgr.
Res., 32 W. Main St., Canisteo, 14823. Tel: 607-698-4034. [CEM 4]
Catechesis/Religious Programs—Students 29.

Rush, Monroe Co., St. Joseph (1863), Revs. Robert Kennedy, Sacramental Min.; Richard Kinsky, C.S.B.; Sr. Alice Cooney, S.S.J., Pastoral Admin.; James Aroune, Pastoral Assoc.
Res., 1209 Rush West Rush Rd., 14543-0320. Tel: 716-533-1719.
Catechesis/Religious Programs—Fax: 716-533-1790.
Students 267.

Scipio Center, Cayuga Co., St. Bernard (1867). Closed. For inquiries for parish records contact Good Shepherd Catholic Community, Aurora.

Scottsville, Monroe Co., St. Mary of the Assumption (1853), Revs. Kevin E. McKenna; Damian Ilokoba; Deacon Michael Mahoney, Admin.
Res., 99 Main St., P.O. Box 23, 14546. Tel: 716-889-3100; Fax: 716-889-7806. [CEM]
Catechesis/Religious Programs—Tel: 716-889-8440; Fax: 716-889-7806.
Students 154.

Seneca Falls, Seneca Co., St. Patrick (1831), Revs. David Gramkee; Richard Murphy.
Res., 97 W. Bayard St., 13148. Tel: 315-568-5203; Fax: 315-568-4893. [CEM]
School—Tel: 315-568-6295; Fax: 315-568-6295.
Lay Teachers 16; Students 140; Preschool 25.
Catechesis/Religious Programs—81 W. Bayard St., 13148. Tel: 315-568-2573.
Students 184.

Shortsville, Ontario Co., St. Dominic (1885), Revs. William J. Cosgrove; John F. Gagnier; Maura Sweeney, Pastoral Assoc.; Deacon Edward A. Smith.
Res., 6 Canandaigua St., 14548. Tel: 716-289-4164. [CEM]
Catechesis/Religious Programs—Andrea Record, D.R.E.
Students 155.

Sodus, Wayne Co., Epiphany (1922), Revs. Lance M. Gonyo; David J. Faraone; Deacon Edward R. Sergeant.
Parish: 105 W. Main St., 14551.
Res., 26 Orchard Park, 14551. Tel: 315-483-6111; Fax: 315-483-6111.
Catechesis/Religious Programs—Ann Wilkins, D.R.E.
Students 154.
Mission—Sodus Point, Wayne Co., St. Rose, (1886).

Spencerport, Monroe Co., St. John the Evangelist (1867), Rev. William C. Michatek; Marnie Suss, Pastoral Assoc.; Deacon Larry Van Etten. In res., Revs. Paul G. Wohlrab; M. Gerard Hafner.
Parish: 55 Martha St., 14559.
Res., 60 Martha St., 14559. Tel: 716-352-5481; Fax: 716-352-3759. [CEM]
School—65 Martha St., 14559. Tel: 716-352-4550; Fax: 716-349-2275. Linda Boone, Prin.
Lay Teachers 15; Students (K-8) 150; Students (PreK) 15.
Catechesis/Religious Programs—Tel: 716-352-0225; 352-7468 (Youth Min.); Fax: 716-352-3759. D.R.E.: Shirley Curatolo; Susan Versluys.
Students 610.

Stanley, Ontario Co., St. Theresa (1875), Revs. Sean M. Garrity; Philip J. Billotte; Peter Deckman; Deacon Claude Curtin.
Res., 2050 Main St., P.O. Box 416, 14561. Tel: 716-526-5566; Fax: 716-526-5566. [CEM]
Catechesis/Religious Programs—Students 65.
Mission—Rushville, Ontario Co., St. Mary, (1869) Gilbert St., 14561.

Trumansburg, Tompkins Co., St. James the Apostle (1857), Rev. Eugene O'Hara, O.F.M. Cap.
Res., 17 Whig St., P.O. Box 1, 14886. Tel: 607-387-6781; Fax: 607-387-3763. [CEM]
Catechesis/Religious Programs—Students 79.

Union Springs, Cayuga Co., St. Michael's (1851). Closed. For inquiries for parish records contact Good Shepherd Catholic Community, Aurora.

Van Etten, Chemung Co., St. Pius the Tenth (1954), Rev. Thomas H. Watts.
Mailing Address: c/o 132 Main St., 14889. Tel: 607-589-4494; Fax: 607-565-8660.
Res., 503 Clark St., Waverly, 14892. Tel: 607-565-2014; Fax: 607-565-2014.
Catechesis/Religious Programs—Students 12.

Victor, Ontario Co., St. Patrick (1856) (Irish), Rev. George Wiant; Ruth Anne Dupre-Trippe, Pastoral Assoc.
Res., 115 Maple Ave., 14564. Tel: 716-924-7111; Fax: 716-742-3296. [CEM]
School—Preschool 68.
Catechesis/Religious Programs—115 Maple Ave., 14564. Tel: 716-924-2800.
Students 320.

Waterloo, Seneca Co., St. Mary (1868), Rev. Eugene R. Weis; Patricia Albrecht, Pastoral Assoc.; Deacon Gary DiLallo.
Res., 23 Center St., 13165. Tel: 315-539-2944; Fax:

315-539-8841. [CEM]
School—Tel: 315-539-3772; Fax: 315-539-8403. Fred J. Smith, Prin.
Lay Teachers 13; Students 129; Preschool 34.
Catechesis/Religious Programs—Tel: 315-539-8146. Lena Shipley, D.R.E.
Students 163.

Watkins Glen, Schuyler Co., St. Mary of the Lake (1846) (Irish-Italian), Rev. David L. Bonin; Sr. Catherine Paul Theiss, C.S.J., Pastoral Assoc.; Deacons Dan Hurley; Fran Haber.
Parish: 905 N. Decatur St., P.O. Box 289, 14891.
Res., 110 1/2 Tenth St., 14891. Tel: 607-535-2786; Fax: 607-535-2990. [CEM 2]
Parish Center—10th St., 14891.
Catechesis/Religious Programs—Tel: 607-535-4367.
Students 151.

Waverly, Tioga Co., St. James (1881), Rev. Thomas H. Watts; Sr. Agnes Catherine Battersby, Pastoral Assoc. In res., Rev. William A. Burns.
Res., 503 Clark St., 14892. Tel: 607-565-2014; Fax: 607-565-8660. [CEM]
Catechesis/Religious Programs—Tel: 604-565-2521.
Students 98.

Wayland, Steuben Co., St. Joseph's (1881) (German). Consolidated with St. Pius V and Sacred Heart of Jesus to form Holy Family Catholic Community.

Webster, Monroe Co., Holy Trinity (1861), Rev. Thomas F. Nellis; Judith Kiehl, Pastoral Assoc.; Deacon Leo Kester. In res., Rev. Thomas Hoctor.
Res., 1460 Ridge Rd., 14580. Tel: 716-265-0391; Fax: 716-265-1627. [CEM]
School—1456 Ridge Rd., 14580. Tel: 716-265-2002; Fax: 716-265-3405. Mr. Chris Meagher, Prin.
Lay Teachers 14; Students 262.
Catechesis/Religious Programs—Tel: 716-265-4750.
Students 297.

St. Paul (1967), Rev. David Simon; Sr. Diane Branch, S.S.J., Pastoral Assoc.
Res., 783 Hard Rd., 14580. Tel: 716-671-2112; Fax: 716-787-8907.
Catechesis/Religious Programs—Scott Rutan, D.R.E.
Students 648.

Weedsport, Cayuga Co., St. John (1865), Rev. William B. Leone; Deacon John Tomandl.
Parish: Rochester St., Port Byron, 13140.; Mailing and Res.: 2667 Hamilton St., P.O. Box 266, 13166. Tel: 315-834-6266; Fax: 315-834-6278.
Catechesis/Religious Programs—Tel: 315-834-9203; Fax: 315-689-7090. Walter B. Sheehan, D.R.E.
Students 105.

St. Joseph (1854), Rev. William B. Leone; Deacon John Tomandl.
Res., 2667 Hamilton St., P.O. Box 266, 13166. Tel: 315-834-6266; Fax: 315-834-6278. [CEM]
Catechesis/Religious Programs—Tel: 315-834-9203; Fax: 315-689-7090. Walter Sheehan, D.R.E.
Students 183.

Webster, Monroe Co., St. Rita (1950), Revs. Charles J. Latus; Donald E. McCarthy, C.S.B.; Deacons Richard Mahany; Stan Douglas, Sr. Pastoral Assocs.: Sr. Judith Whalen, S.S.J.; Rose Leisenring. In res., Donald E. McCarthy, C.S.B.
Res., 1008 Maple Dr., 14580. Tel: 716-671-1100; Fax: 716-671-5446.
School—Tel: 716-671-3132; Fax: 716-671-3134. Sr. Katherine Ann Rappl, R.S.M., Prin.
Sisters of Mercy 1; Lay Teachers 22; Students 357; Preschool 80.
Catechesis/Religious Programs—Tel: 716-671-2079. Andrew Desmarais, D.R.E.
Students 595.

Wolcott, Wayne Co., St. Mary Magdalene (1940), Revs. George P. Heyman; John V. Forni.
Parish: Washington St. and Northup Ave., 14590-1133.; Mailing and Res.: 11956 Washington St., 14590-1133. Tel: 315-594-9430.
Catechesis/Religious Programs—Students 50.

Chaplains of Public Institutions

Health Care Facilities

ROCHESTER. *Genesee Hospital Via Health*. Rev. George Norton, Dir. Spiritual Care, 224 Alexander St., 14607. Tel: 716-922-7660.
Highland Hospital. Vacant. 1000 South Ave., 14620. Tel: 716-461-6890.
Monroe Community Hospital. Rev. Damian I. Lokoba; Mrs. Suzanne Shady, 435 E. Henrietta Rd., 14620. Tel: 716-760-6500.
Park Ridge Hospital/Unity Health System 1555 Long Pond Rd., 14626. Betsy MacKinnon, D.C., Dir. Spiritual Care; Rev. Celestine Obi; Jeanne Marie Jongen, Chap., Tel: 716-723-7969; Rev. Harriet McConnochie, Coord., Tel: 716-723-7967.
Rochester General Hospital/Via Health. Rev. William Endres, 1425 Portland Ave., 14621. Tel: 716-338-4080.
St. Ann's Home/Heritage. Rev. Peter Bayer, Dir. Spiritual Care, 1500 Portland Ave., 14621. Tel: 716-342-1700. RoseMarie Zlotnick, Patoral Care Assoc.
Strong Memorial Hospital. Rev. Kip Corriveau, 601 Elmwood Ave., 14642. Tel: 716-275-2187.
Unity Health System St. Mary's Genesee St. Campus. Rev. Celestine Obi; Sr. Barbara Gulino, S.S.J., Chap., 89 Genesee St., 14611. Tel: 716-328-3268.

AUBURN, CAYUGA CO. *Mercy Health and Rehabilitation Center*. Cayuga Co. Rev. Richard Beligotti; Sr. Mary Norbert, O.S.F., 3 St. Anthony St., 13021. Tel: 315-253-0351.

BATH, STEUBEN CO. *Soliders' Home and Veterans' Hospital* Tel: 607-776-2111, Ext. 1382. Revs. Ronald Marecki; David Carson.

CANANDAIGUA, ONTARIO CO. *Veteran's Hospital* Tel: 716-394-2000, Ext. 3052. Revs. Miecislaus I. Curzydio; Francis H. Vogt.

ELMIRA, CHEMUNG CO. *St. Joseph Hospital*. Chemung Co. Rev. Joseph F. Brodnick; Sr. Margot Mann, S.S.J., 555 E. Market St., 14902. Tel: 607-733-6541.

HORNELL, STEUBEN CO. *St. James Mercy Hospital*. Steuben Co. Rev. Brian Diffenbacher; Sr. Elaine Hollis, S.S.J., Chap., 411 Canisteo St., 14843. Tel: 607-324-8153.

State Facilities

ROCHESTER. *Finger Lakes DDSO - Rochester Site*. Vacant. 620 Westfall Rd., 14620. Tel: 716-461-8676.
Rochester Psychiatric Center 1111 Elmwood Ave., 14620. Tel: 716-473-3230. Deacon Brian McNulty, Chap.

AUBURN. *Auburn Correctional Facility* 135 State St., 13021. Tel: 315-253-8401. Revs. Joseph McCaffrey; James C. Enright.

ELMIRA. *Elmira Correctional Facility, Center and Camp Monterey* P.O. Box 500, 14902. Tel: 607-734-3901. Rev. Joseph Brodnick; Mr. Peter G. Ladley; Mr. Michael Stanley.
Elmira Psychiatric Center 100 Washington St., 14901. Tel: 607-737-4991. Deacon Joseph Federowicz, Chap.

GENESEO, LIVINGSTON CO. *Finger Lakes DDSO - Geneseo Site* 3 Park St., 14454-1217. Tel: 716-243-6405. Deacon Edward Sergent.

INDUSTRY. *State Agricultural & Industrial School, Div. of Youth*. Vacant. 14474. Tel: 716-533-1700.

MORAVIA, CAYUGA CO. *Cayuga Correctional* P.O. Box 1150, 13118. Tel: 315-497-1110. Rev. John Dillon.

NEWARK, WAYNE CO. *Finger Lakes DDSO - Newark Site* 703 E. Maple Ave., 14513. Tel: 315-331-1700. Deacon Edward Sergeant.

PINE CITY. *Southport Correctional Facility* P.O. Box 2000, 14871-2000. Tel: 607-737-0850. Chaplains: Rev. Richard T. Farrell; Mrs. Theresa Stanley.

RED CREEK. *Butler Correctional Facility* P.O. Box 388, 13143. Tel: 315-754-6216, Ext. 288. Rev. Joseph McCaffrey.

ROMULUS. *Five Points Correctional Facility* State Rte. 96, 14541. Tel: 607-869-5111. Rev. Vincent Panepinto; Deacon Gregory Kiley, Chap.

SONYEA, LIVINGSTON CO. *Groveland Correctional Facility* Rt. 36, P.O. Box 50, 14556. Tel: 716-658-2871, Ext. 4003. Rev. William I. Onuh; Deacon Paul Clement.
Livingston Correctional Facility and Seneca Correctional Facility Rt. 36, P.O. Box 49, 14556. Tel: 716-658-2731. Rev. William I. Onuh; Deacon Nemesio Martinez.

WILLARD, SENECA CO. *Drug Treatment Center* 7116 County Rd. 132, P.O. Box 303, 14588-0303. Tel: 607-869-5500, Ext. 4800. Rev. Vincent Panepinto.

County Jail Chaplains

ROCHESTER. *Livingston County Jail*. Vacant. 4 Church St., Geneseo, 14454. Tel: 716-243-1100.
Monroe County Jail. Deacons William Baker; Brian Mahoney.
Tompkins County Jail. Vacant.
Yates County Jail. Vacant.

On Duty Outside the Diocese:
Reverend Fathers—
Bartollotta, Victor W., Jr., Bishop Lynch High School, 9750 Ferguson Rd., Dallas, TX 75228-3891
Brown, Lewis, Office of the Chaplain, Naval District Washington, 2270 Enterprise Way SE, Ste. 134, Washinton, DC 20373-5804
Celso, Thomas B., 163 Patterson St., Newark, NY 14513-9119
Curran, Charles E., Southern Methodist University, 4125 Woodcreek Dr., Dallas, TX 75220
Fleming, Terence K., Bayfront-St. Anthony's Health Center, 1200 Seventh Ave. N., St. Petersburg, FL 33705
Valenti, Thomas J., Church of Notre Dame, 405 W. 114th St., New York, NY 10025

Graduate Studies:
Reverend Fathers—
Condon, Daniel, Catholic Univ., Washington DC
Lum, William, St. Paul Univ., Ottawa Canada
VanDurme, Patrick, The American College - Catholic University of Louvain, Naamsestraat 100, 300 Leuven, Belgium

---

Military Chaplains:
Reverend Fathers—
Brown, Lewis E., CHC, USNR, Regional Support Group, 9170 2nd St., Ste. 120, Norfolk, VA 23511-2393
Zygadlo, Mitchell, United States Air Force, PSC3, Box 7264, APO, AP, 96266

Absent on Leave:
Reverend Fathers—
Emo, Eugene
Mulligan, Charles
Walczak, Melvin

Retired:
Reverend Monsignors—
Cirrincione, Joseph A., Mailing Address: 81 Whitney St., Rochester, NY 14611
Cocuzzi, George A., Church of the Assumption Rectory, 20 East Ave., Fairport, NY 14450
Duffy, John F., McAuley Center, 1437 Blossom Rd., Rochester, NY 14610
Gefell, Gerard J., 2332 Humphrey Rd., Cape Vincent, NY 13618
Gefell, Joseph G., 2332 Humphrey Rd., Cape Vincent, NY 13618
Murphy, J. Emmett, S.S.J. Convent Infirmary, 4199 East Ave., Rochester, NY 14618-3733
Quinn, Richard M., Sisters of Mercy Infirmary, 1437 Blossom Rd., Rochester, NY 14610
Roche, William M., Our Lady of Mt. Carmel Rectory, 300 Fulton St., Redwood City, CA 94062
Shannon, William H., Sisters of St. Joseph Motherhouse, 4095 East Ave., Rochester, NY 14618
Reverend Fathers—
Alletto, Nicholas P., Lakeshore Nursing Home, 425 Beach Ave., Rochester, NY 14612
Amann, William, 150 Varianna Dr., Rochester, NY 14618
Ammering, Bruce, 1600 East Ave., #1008, Rochester, NY 14618
Booth, Raymond, 64 N. Main St., Pittsford, NY 14534
Brennan, Joseph P., 251 Bay Village Dr., Rochester, NY 14609
Brennan, Paul, 345 Waters Edge, Auburn, NY 13021
Burns, William A., St. James Rectory, 503 Clark St., Waverly, NY 14892
Calimeri, Anthony F., P.O. Box 24, Phelps, NY 14532
Callan, L. James, 500 Cook Rd., Hamlin, NY 14464
Cloonan, Joseph F., 16608 Juarez Dr., San Diego, CA 92128
Connor, Gerald T., 168 Spencerport Rd., Rochester, NY 14606
Cosgrove, James, 295 Chestnut Ridge Rd., Rochester, NY 14624
Cushing, Walter, St. Cecilia's Rectory, 2732 Culver Rd., Rochester, NY 14622
D'Aurizio, Joseph F., St. Leo's Rectory, 167 Lake Avenue, Hilton, NY 14468
Davis, Francis R., St. Mary's Rectory, 155 State St., Corning, NY 14830
Dollen, Bernard, 4477 Buffalo Rd., North Chili, NY 14514
Donovan, Joseph D., S.S.J. Convent Infirmary, 4199 East Ave., Rochester, NY 14618-3733
Donovan, Robert, McAuley Residence, 1437 Blossom Rd., Rochester, NY 14610
Downs, Robert, Southfield Apartments, Quill Ave. & Clymer St., Apt. D-13, Auburn, NY 13021
Doyle, James, Chapel Oaks #1110, 1550 Portland Ave., Rochester, NY 14621
Egan, Joseph M., St. Alphonsus Rectory, 85 E. Genesee St., Auburn, NY 13021
Egan, Robert, Holy Family, 85 North St., Auburn, NY 14580
Ehmann, Benedict A., S.S.J. Convent Infirmary, 4199 East Ave., Rochester, NY 14618-3733
Elsemann, Frederick F., 151 Sheppler St., Rochester, NY 14612

Erb, Francis J., P.O. Box 665, Savona, NY 14879
Falcone, Sabastian, 214 Alaimo Dr., Rochester, NY 14625
Foy, Edward J., St. Alphonsus Rectory, 10 Lewis St., Auburn, NY 13021
Freemesser, Paul J., 10 S. Lewis St., Auburn, NY 13021
Gardner, Clarence W., St. Alphonsus Rectory, 10 Lewis St., Auburn, NY 13021
Gaynor, Joseph T., St. Alphonsus Rectory, 10 Lewis St., Auburn, NY 13021
Grace, Patrick J., 3742 Wildwood Rd., San Diego, CA 92107
Halloran, Emmett J., St. Mary's Rectory, 95 North Main St., Canandaigua, NY 14424
Hanna, Austin B., McAuley Residence, 1437 Blossom Rd., Rochester, NY 14610
Hedges, L. John, McAuley Residence, 1437 Blossom Rd., Rochester, NY 14610
Heindl, Elmer W., St. Charles Borromeo Rectory, 3003 Dewey Ave., Rochester, NY 14616
Hempel, John L., 109 Edgewood Ct., Forest Lakes, Oldsmar, FL 34677
Hoctor, Thomas D., c/o 1150 Buffalo Rd., Rochester, NY 14624
Hogan, Michael C., St. John of Rochester Rectory, 8 Wickford Way, Fairport, NY 14450
Holberton, William B., 555 Spring St., Apt. 806, Bethlehem, PA 18018
Kalafsky, Andrew J., 414 Lakeview Ave., Watkins Glen, NY 14891
Kanka, Robert, St. Ann's Rectory, 31 Erie Ave., P.O. Box 605, Hornell, NY 14843
Kelly, Gerald G., 434 Pine Glen Ln., Apt. B1, Lake Worth, FL 33463
Krieg, Gerald, St. Louis Rectory, 64 S. Main St., Pittsford, NY 14534
MacNamara, Robert C., St. Mary Our Mother Rectory, 816 W. Broad St., Horseheads, NY 14845
Mans, Leo, P.O. Box 2307, Winter Park, FL 32709-2307
Marvin, James J., 294 E. Lake Rd., P.O. Box 463, Honcoye, NY 14471
McDonald, Elmer J., 6145 Sun Blvd., #505B, St. Petersburg, FL 33715
McDonnell, Joseph M., McAuley Residence, 1437 Blossom Rd., Rochester, NY 14610
McFarland, Eugene H., St. Mary Rectory, 13 North St., Geneseo, NY 14454
McMahon, Gerald J., 1355 Hatch Rd., Webster, NY 14580
McNamara, Elmer A., McAuley Residence, 1437 Blossom Rd., Rochester, NY 14610
McNamara, Joseph M., St. Pius X Home, 714 E. Brighton St., Syracuse, NY 13205
McNamara, Robert F., St. Thomas the Apostle Rectory, 4536 St. Paul Blvd., Rochester, NY 14617
Meng, Robert A., 7 Harwood Ln., East Rochester, NY 14445
Metzger, Edwin, St. Mary's Church, P.O. Box 152, Fredericksburg, TX 78624
Mockevicius, Charles L., 1156 Plank Rd., Webster, NY 14580
Mockevicius, Dominic F., 1156 Plank Rd., Webster, NY 14580
Morgan, John A., St. Mary Magdalen Rectory, 2532 Ventura Blvd., Camarillo, CA 93010
Murphy, David M., 45 Smith Ave., Newton, MA 02165
Nacca, John J., Cathedral of the Sacred Heart, P.O. Box 2248, Pensacola, FL 32513
Nolan, Norbert L., 120 Holyoke St., Bldg. 4, Apt. 2, Rochester, NY 14615
Norris, John P., St. Catherine of Siena Rectory, 26 Mendon-Ionia Rd., Mendon, NY 14506
O'Brien, Bartholomew J., c/o 1150 Buffalo Rd., Rochester, NY 14624
O'Connell, Richard C., St. Monica Rectory, 34 Monica St., Rochester, NY 14619
Orlando, Richard J., St. Thomas More Rectory, 2617 East Ave., Rochester, NY 14610
Phillips, John, 8 Wickford Way, Fairport, NY 14450
Rosse, John, 401 Rogers Pkwy., Rochester, NY 14616
Sansom, Lawrence W., 58 Green Knolls Dr., Rochester, NY 14620
Sasso, Joseph M., 8112 Oatka Tr., LeRoy, NY 14482
Schifferli, Jerome F., 7 Washington St., Box 311, Livonia, NY 14487
Schmidt, Elmer J., McAuley Residence, 1437 Blossom Rd., Rochester, NY 14610
Schnacky, Paul, 31 Erie Ave., Hornell, NY 14843
Shamon, Albert J., 5 S. Marvine Ave., Auburn, NY 13021
Slattery, James F., St. Joseph Infirmary, 4199 East Ave., Rochester, NY 14618
Smith, Robert, RR1, Box 180D, Red Creek, NY 13143
Steinkirchner, Edward E., St. Jerome Rectory, 207 S. Garfield St., East Rochester, NY 14445
Sundholm, Conrad, 3465 Treetop Cir., Spring Hill, Fl 14445
Tormey, Daniel, 48 Holiday Harbour, Canandaigua, NY 14424
Ventura, Gennaro J., 8247 Dutch Hollow Rd., Wayland, NY 14572
Vogt, Francis H., 115 Throop St., Palmyra, NY 14522
Vogt, Otto J., St. Thomas More Rectory, 2617 East Ave., Rochester, NY 14610-3199
Wahl, Raymond J., S.S.J. Convent Infirmary, 4199 East Ave., Rochester, NY 14618-3733
Walsh, John T., 95 Warren Ave., Rochester, NY 14618
Wohlrab, Paul G., St. John the Evangelist Rectory, 60 Martha St., Spencerport, NY 14559
Wolfe, James, 19 Bly St., Rochester, NY 14620
Zimmer, Edward A., St. John the Evangelist Rectory, 549 Humboldt St., Rochester, NY 14610

Permanent Deacons:
Abballe, Dominic, (Retired)
Almeter, Robert C., Diocese of Syracuse
Aman, Leo, Nazareth College, Pittsford
Antenucci, John, Holy Apostles/St. Anthony Cluster, Rochester
Arnold, Kenneth, St. Joseph's Church, Penfield
Baker, William, Monroe County Jail Min.
Beck, Thomas, St. Thomas the Apostle, Rochester
Bergeron, Albert, (Retired)
Birx, Charles, Diocese of Richmond
Bowers, Owen F., St. Joseph, Rusk; St. James, Irondequoit
Burke, Robert, St. Rita's Church, Webster
Burnett, George, Leave of Absence
Cadregari, David, Holy Ghost, Gates
Campanelli, Michael, (Retired)
Carrol, Stephen, St. Thomas More, Rochester
Caruso, Anthony, St. Theodore, Rochester
Casey, Lawrence B., Diocese of Atlanta
Cass, K. Thomas, Leave of Absence
Chatterton, James, St. Mark's, Rochester
Cleary, Thomas J., St. John of Rochester, Fairport; St. Rita's, Webster
Clement, Paul F., Groveland Correctional Facility, Sonyea
Coccia, Angelo, Holy Family, Rochester; St. Francis House
Coffey, William, St. Mary's, Rochester
Cunningham, John, St. Christopher, North Chili
Curtin, Claude, St. Michael's, Penn Yan
Cyrana, Robert, St. Felix and St. Francis, Clifton Springs
Datz, Ramon, On Leave of Absence
Defendorf, Raymond, St. Mary & St. Patrick, Corning
DiLallo, Gary R., St. Mary's, Waterloo
Dispenza, Charles, St. Bridget's, Rochester
Dizer, Robert, Inactive
Dougherty, William P., St. Charles Borromeo and St. Casimir, Elmira Heights
Douglas, Stanley, St. Rita's, Webster
Doyle, Gregory J., Matt Talbot Ministry, Rochester
Driscoll, Joseph, St. Louis Church, Pittsford
Dwyer, Joseph, Immaculate Conception, Rochester
Ecker, Thomas R., Bethany House, Penfield; St. Jerome's, East Rochester
Edwards, Eugene L., Jr., St. Rose, Lima
Elhilow, Edward, St. Nicholas the Wonderworker, Gates
Erb, John, Unassigned
Feasel, Laurence, St. Salome's Church; Rochester Gen. Hospital
Federowicz, Joseph F., Elmira Psychiatric Center, Elmira
Fisher, Christopher, St. Elizabeth Ann Seton, Hamlin
Fitch, James E., Holy Rosary, Rochester
Fuerst, Eugene C., (Retired)
Giblin, Edward, Holy Cross Church, Rochester
Giugno, John M, Most Precious Blood, Rochester
Glasgow, Joseph H., Fitz, RCC of the 19th Ward, Rochester
Graff, Stephen J., Diocese of Syracuse
Graybill, Patrick A., Emmanuel Church of the Deaf
Green, Stanley J., Diocese of Augustine
Haber, Francis, St. Mary's of the Lake, Watkins Glen
Hankey, James D., Painted Post Roman Catholic Community, Corning
Hoerner, Gerard A., Diocese of Buffalo
Holmes, John, Jr., Diocese of St. Augustine
Homick, Willis, SS. Peter and Paul, Auburn
Hunt, William R., Diocese of Raleigh
Hurley, Daniel R., St. Mary Our Mother, Horseheads; St. Mary's of the Lake, Watkins Glen
Jewell, Thomas, Leave of Absence
Kester, Leo A., (Retired)
Kiley, Gregory, Five Points Correctional Facility, Romulus
Kinsky, Daniel M., St. John of Rochester, Fairport
Kluchko, Thomas J., St. Mark, Rochester
Kohlmeier, Charles P., Mercy Prayer Center
Kozak, George, Immaculate Conception, Ithaca
Krupiarz, Michael J., Unassigned
Lawson, Gregg K., St. Alphonsus, Auburn
Lebron, Juan, On Duty Outside the Diocese
Lester, Claude E., St. Bridget/St. Joseph, Bloomfield
Lombard, Richard J., Newman Catholic Community, Rochester Institute of Technology
Loomis, Roger, St. Mary's, Honeoye
Mahany, Richard E., (Retired)
Mahoney, Brian, Monroe County Jail
Mahoney, I. Michael, St. Mary of the Assumption, Scottsville
Malave, Jorge, St. Michael's, Rochester
Mangione, Michael, St. Anthony / St. Patrick, Elmira
Marini, Anthony, Diocese of Charlotte
Martinez, Nemesio, Livingston Correctional Facility
Mathis, Edward, Groveland Correctional Institution and St. Agnes, Avon
Maune, William D., Diocese of Chicago
McCormick, Robert W., St. Ann's, Hornell
McGuire, Michael R., St. Januarius, Naples; St. Patrick's, Prattsburg
McNulty, Brian J., Newman Catholic Community, Rochester Institute of Technology
Medero, Felix, Community of Hope, Rochester
Melendez, Eliseo, Diocese of Ogdensburg
Mercadel, Anthony J., Guardian Angels, Rochester
Mercado, Conrado, On Duty Outside the Diocese
Mielcarek, Raymond, St. Stanislaus, Rochester
Morin, Kenneth, On Leave of Absence
Nguyen, Hoc Thai, St. Anthony of Padua, Rochester
Ona, Fernando V., On Leave of Absence
Otera, Salvador, To be assigned
Palma, David, Pastoral Center
Paluskiewicz, David L., Blessed Sacrament, Rochester
Payne, David L., F.X., St. Louis, Pittsford
Piehler, Michael J., Transfiguration, Pittsford
Prave, John J., Cayuga Team Ministry, Auburn
Rodriguez, Agenol, Holy Redeemer, Rochester
Rutan, Warren, St. John the Evangelist, Newark Valley
Sampson, Gregory R., St. Anne, Rochester
Scarciotta, Kenneth A., (Retired)
Schmitz, William F., St. Andrew's, Rochester
Schrader, Robert, Holy Family Church, Rochester
Schrage, Thomas, St. Charles Borromeo, Rochester
Schuler, Richard, St. Helen, Rochester
Schultz, Klaus D., St. Elizabeth Ann Seton, Hamlin
Sciolino, Anthony, Transfiguration, Pittsford
Sergeant, Edward R., Newark Development Center, Newark; Church of the Epiphany, Sodus
Shanley, Patrick M., St. Boniface, Rochester
Skerrett, Jerry, St. Mary's of the Lake, Ontario
Slattery, Daniel P., St. Joseph's, Wayland
Smith, Edward A., St. Dominic's, Shortsville
Steiger, James P., St. Leo, Hilton
Stowell, Robert, St. Mary's, Elmira
Strode, Walter E., Diocese of Cincinnati
Swift, John G., (Retired)
Tocci, Ronald, Church of the Assumption, Fairport
Tomandl, John D., Northern Cayuga Cluster, Auburn
Valvo, Nicholas, Sacred Heart Church, Auburn
Van Etten, Laurence A., St. John the Evangelist, Spencerport
Vargas, Carlos H., St. Francis of Assisi, Rochester
Verkon, Ronald, Diocese of Scranton
Welch, George J., Eastside Catholic Parish, Elmira
Wight, Edward, St. Mary's, Bath
Wilson, Albro C., Jr., St. Paul of the Cross, Honeoye Falls
Yanaitis, Victor M., St. Pius X, Chili
Zierle, John E., St. Pius Tenth, Rochester

INSTITUTIONS LOCATED IN THE DIOCESE

[A] GRADUATE SCHOOL OF THEOLOGY

ROCHESTER. *St. Bernard's Institute*, 1100 S. Goodman St., 14620. Tel: 716-271-3657; Fax: 716-271-2045.
Web site: www.sbi.edu
For a complete listing, refer to the Colleges and Universities section.

[B] COLLEGES AND UNIVERSITIES

ROCHESTER. *St. John Fischer College*, 3690 E. Ave., 14618. Tel: 716-385-8010; Fax: 716-385-8289.
Web site: www.sjfc.edu
Katherine E. Keough, Pres.; J. David Arnold, Provost & Dean.

[C] HIGH SCHOOLS

ROCHESTER. *The Aquinas Institute*, 1127 Dewey Ave., 14613-9989. Tel: 716-254-2020; Fax: 716-254-7401.
E-mail: ellend@frontiernet.net
Patrick A. Hanley, Pres.; Vilma Goetting, Prin..Lay Teachers 62; Students 899.

Bishop Kearney High School. (Coed), 125 Kings Hwy., 14617-5596. Tel: 716-342-4000; Fax: 716-342-4694.
E-mail: kearney@frontiernet.net
Web site: www.bkhs.org
Sponsored by the Congregation of Christian Brothers in association with the School Sisters of Notre Dame, Wilton Province. Mark S. Peterson, Pres.; Louis D'Angelo, Prin.; Mrs. Donna Gmelin, Asst. Prin. Brothers 2; Sisters 1; Lay Teachers 35; Students 450.

McQuaid Jesuit High School, 1800 S. Clinton Ave., 14618. Tel: 716-473-1130; Fax: 716-256-6171.
E-mail: jesuitres@mcquaid.org
Web site: www.mcquaid.org
Jesuit Fathers. Revs. William J. McCurdy, S.J., Supr.; James J. Fischer, S.J., Pres.; Philip G. Judge, S.J., Prin.; Frederick G. Betti, S.J.; John P. Carriero, S.J.; John M. Costello, S.J.; James R. Dolan, S.J.; Joseph DeMaio, O.Carm.; Jack Healy, O.Carm.; Leon J. Hogenkamp, S.J.; William C. McCusker, S.J.; Francis J. McNamara, S.J., Alumni Dir.; Brian Murphy, O.Carm.; William Spong; Lawrence J. Wroblewski, S.J. Priests 2; Lay Teachers 50; Students 853.

Nazareth Schools: The Hall; The Academy, 1001 Lake Ave., 14613. Tel: 716-647-8733; Fax: 716-647-8737.
E-mail: nazsac@rochester.rr.com
Web site: nazarethschools.org
Sisters of St. Joseph 7; Lay Teachers 65; Students 750.

Our Lady of Mercy High School. (Grades 7-12), 1437 Blossom Rd., 14610. Tel: 716-288-7120; Fax: 716-288-7966.
E-mail: mercycom@netacc.net
Web site: www.mercyhs.com
Mrs. Evelyn J. Kirst, Prin..Sisters of Mercy 12; Lay Teachers 57; Students 605.

ELMIRA. *Notre Dame High School*, 1400 Maple Ave., 14904. Tel: 607-734-2267; Fax: 607-737-8903.
E-mail: ndhs@hotmail.com
Sr. Mary Walter Hickey, R.S.M., Prin.; Rev. Vincent McDonough, S.J., Chap..Priests 1; Sisters of Mercy 2; Lay Teachers 25; Students 400.

GENEVA. *De Sales High School*. (Incorporated under the laws of the State of New York), 14456. Tel: 315-789-5111; Fax: 315-789-8230.
E-mail: desales@epix.net
Web site: dhsoffice@lynnet.com
Daniel E. Skinner, Prin..Lay Teachers 18; Students 142.

[D] JUNIOR HIGH SCHOOLS

ROCHESTER. *All Saints Catholic Jr. High*, 170 Spencerport Rd., 14606. Tel: 716-429-6010; Fax: 716-429-6761.
E-mail: allsaintsjh@hotmail.com
Web site: www.mypage.goplay.com/allsaintsjrhigh
Sisters 1; Lay Teachers 11; Total Staff 12; Students 145.

Catholic Schools of Monroe County, 1150 Buffalo Rd., 14624. Tel: 716-328-3210; Fax: 716-328-3149.
E-mail: guerin@dor.org
Web site: www.dor.org
Priests 1; Sisters 42; Lay Teachers 802; Students 13,265.

Northeastern Catholic Jr. High, 125 Kings Hwy. S., 14617. Tel: 716-544-0560; Fax: 716-544-0411.
E-mail: gotto125@aol.com
Total Staff 23; Students 205.

[E] ELEMENTARY SCHOOLS, PRIVATE

ROCHESTER. *Corpus Christi School*, 546 Oxford St., 14607. Tel: 716-473-3937; Fax: 716-442-0538.
E-mail: ccdcs@dor.org
Sr. Eileen Daly, S.S.J., Prin..Sisters 2; Lay Teachers 7; Students 180.

School of the Holy Childhood, 100 Groton Pkwy., 14623. Tel: 716-359-3710; Fax: 716-359-3722.
E-mail: admin@holychildhood.org
Web site: www.holychildhood.org
Day Programs and School for Mentally Retarded Children and Adults. Sr. M. Seraphine, S.S.J., Dir. Sisters of St. Joseph 5; School Sisters of Notre Dame 1; Lay Teachers 24; Children 116; Adults 80.

EAST ROCHESTER. *Trinity Montessori School*, 501 S. Garfield St., 14445. Tel: 716-586-1004; Fax: 716-586-1821.
E-mail: tms@frontiernet.net
Web site: www.trinitymontessori.org
Sr. Clare Francis Mogenhan, S.S.J., Admin..Sisters 4; Lay Teachers 19; Students 163.

ELMIRA. *Holy Family Catholic School System-Diocese of Rochester*, 301 Demarest Pkwy. (Business Office), 14905. Tel: 607-734-4414; Fax: 607-732-5432. 421 Fulton St., 14904. Sisters 1; Lay Teachers 34; Students 590.

[F] HOMES FOR AGED

ROCHESTER. *St. Ann's Home for the Aged*, 1500 Portland Ave., 14621. Tel: 716-342-1700; Fax: 716-342-9585.
Web site: www.stannsrochester.org
For a complete listing, refer to the Special Care Facilities section.

St. Ann's Nursing Home Co., Inc., 1450 Portland Ave., 14621. Tel: 716-342-1700; Fax: 716-342-9585.
Web site: www.stannsrochester.org
For a complete listing, refer to the Special Care Facilities section.

[G] CAMPS

LIVONIA. *Camp Stella Maris*, Conesus Lake, 4395 E.Lake Rd., 14487. Tel: 716-346-2243; Fax: 716-346-6921.
E-mail: starotsea@aol.com
Web site: campstellamaris.org
Conesus Lake, 4395 E. Lake Rd., 14487. Tel: 716-346-2243; Fax: 716-346-6921. Matthew J. Flanigan, Exec. Dir.; John Caselli, Board Pres.; Heather Jones, Summer Camp Dir.
Purpose: Residential camping under Catholic auspices, for boys and girls (ages 7-14) of all faiths. Encampment period: Eight weeks during summer (July/August). Rental of facility available September-June for family/youth development retreats. ACA accredited. Day Camp Center for boys and girls (ages 5-10). Encampment period: Eight weeks during July/August in conjunction with resident camp. Adventure-Based Learning Experience (ABLE) high and low challenge ropes courses ideal for building trust, confidence, cooperation, teamwork, self-esteem, communication, and leadership skills. Total Staff 8; Total Assisted 272.

[H] GENERAL HOSPITALS

AUBURN. *Mercy Health & Rehabilitation Center Nursing Home Co., Inc.*, (1972) St. Anthony St., 13021. Tel: 315-253-0351; Fax: 315-258-3904.
E-mail: mercy@tds.net
For a complete listing, refer to the Hospitals section.

ELMIRA. *St. Joseph's Hospital*, 55 E. Market St., 14902. Tel: 607-733-6541; Fax: 607-737-7837.
E-mail: srmarie@stjosephs.org
Web site: www.stjosephs.org
For a complete listing, refer to the Hospitals section.

St. Joseph's Hospital Foundation, Inc., 200 Madison Ave., Ste. 1c, 14901. Tel: 607-737-7004; Fax: 607-324-8115.
E-mail: dsullivan@stjosephs.org
For a complete listing, refer to the Hospitals section.

HORNELL. *St. James Mercy Health System*, 411 Canisteo St., 14843. Tel: 607-324-8000; Fax: 607-324-8115
For a complete listing, refer to the Hospitals section.

[I] MONASTERIES AND RESIDENCES OF PRIESTS AND BROTHERS

ROCHESTER. *Basilian Residence*, 3497 East Ave., 14618. Tel: 716-586-4600; Fax: 716-385-6383. Revs. Angelo D. Bovenzi, C.S.B.; T. Paul Broadhurst, C.S.B.; Albert W. Cylwicki, C.S.B., Supr.; John L. Dugan, C.S.B.; Leo A. Hetzler, C.S.B., Councilor; Richard C. Kinsky, C.S.B; Richard C. Lanzalaco, C.S.B., Councilor; John R. Lee, C.S.B.; Thomas M. Miller, C.S.B.; John C. Murray, C.S.B.; John A. Poluikis, C.S.B. In res. Rev. James K. Kiarie.
Priests of the Region Serving Elsewhere: Rev. William J. Sheehan, C.S.B., Collegio San Clemente, Via Labicana, 95, 00184, Rome, Italy. Rev. George Kosicki, C.S.B., c/o Companions of Christ the Lamb, P.O. Box 12, Paradise, MI, 49768. Tel: 906-492-3647. Rev. J. Gareth Poupore, C.S.B., 16 Village Trail, Honeoye Falls, 14472. Rev. Donald E. McCarthy, C.S.B., St. Rita's Church, 1008 Maple Dr., Webster, 14580. Basilian Fathers of Fisher House, 224 Fairport Rd., East Rochester, 14445. Tel: 716-381-9283. Revs. Paul F. English, Rector. Tel: 716-264-9185; John R. Cavanaugh. Tel: 716-385-1353.

Becket Hall, 314 Gregory St., 14620. Tel: 716-461-2890; Fax: 716-328-3149.
E-mail: beckethall@juno.com
Web site: www.dor.org
Residence for Pre-Theologate candidates. Rev. John A. DeSocio, Dir. Students 8.

Missionaries of the Precious Blood, 1261 Highland Ave., 14620. Tel: 716-461-2750; Fax: 716-461-0318.
E-mail: Jac56@rochester.rr.com
Revs. John A. Colacino, C.PP.S. Tel: 716-461-2750; Joseph Grasso, C.PP.S. Tel: 716-461-9250.

St. George's Rectory, 545 Hudson Ave., 14605. Tel: 716-232-4111. Revs. Dominic F. Mockevicius, Admin.; Charles L. Mockevicius, Co-Admin.

Whitefriars Priory, 625 Colebrook Dr., 14617. Tel: 716-266-2560. Revs. Brian Murphy, O.Carm.; Joseph DeMaio, O.Carm.; Jack Healy, O.Carm., Prior; Matthew Temple, O.Carm. Total in Residence 4.

INTERLAKEN. *St. Fidelis Friary*, 7790 County Rd. 153, 14847. Tel: 607-532-4423; Fax: 607-532-9271. Capuchin Friars-Province of St. Mary (Order of Friars Minor Capuchin). Revs. Eugene O'Hara, O.F.M.Cap., Supr.; Regis J. Armstrong, O.F.M.Cap., Vicar; Oliver J. O'Connor, O.F.M.Cap., Preaching Ministry; Julian Phelan, O.F.M.Cap., Preaching Ministry; Bernard Maloney, O.F.M.Cap. Priests 5.

PIFFARD. *Abbey of the Genesee*, 14533. Tel: 716-243-0660; 243-2220 (Retreat House); Fax: 716-243-4816.
E-mail: abbeygen@frontiernet.net
Web site: www.lemoyne.edu/~bucko/genesee.htm
The Order of Cistercians of the Strict Observance (Trappists). Rt. Rev. John Eudes Bamberger, O.C.S.O., Abbot; Revs. Francis R. Steger, O.C.S.O.; Thomas Aquinas Bond, O.C.S.O.; John J. Denburger, O.C.S.O.; Marcellus R. Earl, O.C.S.O.; Raymond J. Fournier, O.C.S.O.; Jerome J. Machar, O.C.S.O.; Robert J. Moore, O.C.S.O.; Regis C. Tompkins, O.C.S.O.; Justin R. Sheehan, O.C.S.O.; Joseph F. Stanton, O.C.S.O.; Aelred W. Wentz, O.C.S.O. Absent on Leave: Rev. Michael M. Hayden, O.C.S.O. Total Staff 2; Professed Monks 37; Priests 13; Oblates 1; Total in Community (Piffard) 41.

PINE CITY. *Mount Saviour Monastery*, 231 Monastery Rd., 14871-9770. Tel: 607-734-1688; Fax: 607-734-1689.
E-mail: msaviour@servtech.com
Web site: www.servtech.com/~/msaviour
Very Rev. Martin Boler, O.S.B., Prior; Revs. James Cronin, O.S.B.; James Kelly, O.S.B..Professed Monks 12; Professed Priests 3; Total in Community 15.

WATKINS GLEN. *St. Anthony of Padua Residence*, 225 Lakeview Ave. Ext., P.O. Box 41, 14891. Tel: 607-535-2073; Fax: 607-535-2073.
E-mail: fraustin@juno.com
Franciscan Friars. Rev. Austin J. Budnick, O.F.M. Affiliated with the Assumption of the B.V.M. Province, with headquarters in Pulaski, Wisconsin. Priests 1.

[J] CONVENTS AND RESIDENCES FOR SISTERS

ROCHESTER. *Nazareth Convent*, 16 Lake View Park, 14613-1798. Tel: 716-458-3443; Fax: 716-254-6446.
E-mail: nazarethconvent@hotmail.com
Sr. Susan Schantz, S.S.J., Local Coord..Sisters 38.

North American Union-Sisters of Our Lady of Charity, OLC Holy Angels Convent, 1280 N. Winton Rd., 14609-5897. Tel: 716-654-8600. Sr. Zita Toto, Supr. Professed Sisters 4.

St. Joseph Convent Infirmary, 4199 East Ave., 14618-3733. Tel: 716-381-4064; Fax: 716-381-3273. Rev. Bruce Ammerling, Chap. Infirmary and home for retired Sisters of Saint Joseph of Rochester, Inc. Sr. Joseph Gilmary Russell, S.S.J., Local Coord.; Rev. Donald J. Curtiss, Chap. Sisters 71; Priests 7.

Sisters of Mercy of the Americas Regional Community of Rochester, 1437 Blossom Rd., 14610. Tel: 716-288-2710; Fax: 716-288-2756. Sr. Sheila Stevenson, Pres. In res. Rev. Kip F. Corriveau, Chap. Tel: 716-482-0553. Professed Sisters 207; Perpetual Vows 207.

Sisters St. Joseph Motherhouse, 4095 East Ave., 14618-3798. Tel: 716-586-1000; Fax: 716-586-1193.
E-mail: ssjcong@ssjrochester.org
Web site: www.ssjvolunteers.org
Motherhouse of the Sisters of St. Joseph of the Diocese of Rochester. Sr. Janice Morgan, Congregational Pres.; Rev. Msgr. William H. Shannon, Chap. Professed Sisters in Community 394.

Spirit House, Inc., 72 Dorvid Rd., 14617. Tel: 716-544-5698; Fax: 716-266-2611.
E-mail: spirithouse1@juno.com
Web site: www.wounded-in-spirit.com
Sr. Mary Ann Ayers, R.S.M., Dir.

ELMIRA. *Monastery of Mary the Queen, Dominican Nuns,* 1310 W. Church St., 14905. Tel: 607-734-9506; Fax: 607-734-1452.
E-mail: elmiraop@juno.com
Web site: www.op.org/maryqueen/default.htm
Sr. Mary of the Sacred Heart, O.P., Prioress..Solemn Vows 12; Perpetual Vows 1; In Formation 3.

PITTSFORD. *Monastery of Our Lady and St. Joseph Carmelite Monastery,* 1931 W. Jefferson Rd., 14534. Tel: 716-427-7094. Discalced Carmelite Nuns. Mother Miriam of the Angels, O.C.D., Prioress. Professed Nuns with Solemn Vows 7; Externs with Simple Vows 1; Simple Professed Novice 1; Novices 1.

[K] RETREAT HOUSES

ROCHESTER. *Borromeo Prayer Center,* 3011 Dewey Ave., 14616. Tel: 716-663-5856; Fax: 716-663-8055.
E-mail: bpc98@juno.com
Web site: www.frontiernet.net/~stcharls
Patricia W. Scouten, Admin.

Mercy Prayer Center, 65 Highland Ave., 14620. Tel: 716-473-6893; Fax: 716-473-6414. Conducted and subsidized by Sisters of Mercy. Total in residence 3; Total Staff 6.

S.S.J. Spirituality Center, 402 Rogers Pkwy., 14617. Tel: 716-336-4370.
E-mail: MLHSSJ@juno.com
Mary Louise Heffernan, S.S.J., Dir..; Total in residence 1; Total Staff 6.

CANANDAIGUA. *Notre Dame Retreat House,* Box 342, 5151 Foster Rd., 14424. Tel: 716-394-5700; Fax: 716-394-9215.
E-mail: redemptorists@aol.com
Web site: nortredameretreathouse.org
Revs. Frederick C. Brinkmann, C.Ss.R., Dir.; Paul A. Miller, C.Ss.R.; Leo F. Dunn, C.Ss.R.; Jack J. Fiske, C.Ss.R.

CORNING. *Anawim Community Center,* 122 E. First St., 14830. Tel: 607-936-4965; Fax: 607-936-0207.
E-mail: anawimcorning@exotrope.net
Web site: www.anawim.com
Rev. Richard M. Rusk (MET), Admin..Total In Residence 5; Total Staff 11.

[L] MISCELLANEOUS LISTINGS

ROCHESTER. *Apostleship of Prayer,* Diocesan Pastoral Center, 1150 Buffalo Rd., 14624. Tel: 716-328-3210. Rev. Thomas P. Mull.

Archivist (Diocese of Rochester Archives), 1150 Buffalo Rd., 14624. Tel: 716-328-3210, Ext. 204; Fax: 716-328-3149.
E-mail: graf@sjfc.edu
Sr. Connie Derby, R.S.M., Dir. of Archives and Records; Rev. William E. Graf, Archivist, 52 Mason Rd., Fairport, 14450. Tel: 716-223-6686. Rev. Robert F. McNamara, Archivist, 4536 St. Paul Blvd., 14617. Tel: 716-338-1602.

Catherine McAuley Housing dba Mercy Residential Services. Melita Residential Services/Melita House, 198 Oriole St., 14613-1923. Tel: 716-254-2175; Fax: 716-254-2229.
E-mail: meresvc@juno.com
Sisters of Mercy of Rochester. Florence R. Koenig, Exec. Dir., Pres. & Contact Person. Total Staff 13; Total assisted in residence 40; Total assisted in aftercare 25.

Catherine McAuley Housing dba Mercy Residential Services, 198 Oriole St., 14613-1923. Tel: 716-254-2175; Fax: 716-254-2229.
E-mail: meresvc@juno.com
Florence R. Koenig, Exec. Dir. & Pres. Transitional Housing for Single Mothers and their Children. Total Staff 13; Families assisted 40.

Catholic Charismatic Renewal, 115 Woodbine Ave., 14619. Tel: 716-235-0235.
E-mail: kindleinuse@aol.com
Diocesan Liaison Team: Betty Bunce; Ann Bartholomew. Tel: 716-377-9504; Mary Haywood. Tel: 716-247-2941; Rev. Stan Kacarzak, Spiritual Advisor.

Catholic Committee on Scouting, 1150 Buffalo Rd., 14624. Tel: 716-328-3210; Fax: 716-328-3149.
E-mail: theisen@dor.org
Web site: www.dor.org
Rev. John A. DeSocio.

Catholic Gay & Lesbian Family Ministry, 1150 Buffalo Rd., 14624. Tel: 716-271-7363; Fax: 716-271-7363.
E-mail: cglfm@aol.com
Karen Rinefierd, Diocesan Liaison.

Censores Librorum, 1150 Buffalo Rd., 14624. Revs. Joseph A. Hart; William F. Laird; Rev. Msgr. William H. Shannon; Rev. William E. Graf.

Corpus Christi Center, Inc., 142 Webster Ave., 14609. Tel: 716-288-2634; Fax: 716-288-0252.
E-mail: cccwebster@juno.com
Sr. Kathleen Ann Kolb, R.S.M., Exec. Dir. and Pres. Health and dental services for the uninsured and advocacy.

Dunn Tower Apartments, Inc., 100 Dunn Tower Dr., 14606. Tel: 716-429-5520; Fax: 716-429-9720 (Call first).
E-mail: dt1@mindex.com
Ann R. Huber, Mgr. Housing for Seniors. Total Staff 6; Total in Residence 199.

Family Rosary For Peace, Inc., P.O. Box 11007, 14611. Tel: 716-436-6693; Fax: 716-254-7170. Rev. Paul J. Tomasso, Dir.; Dolores Mary Brien, Sec.

Holy Childhood Association, 1150 Buffalo Rd., 14624. Tel: 716-436-9200; Fax: 716-529-9501. Rev. Robert C. Bradler, Dir.

Marriage Encounter Apostolate. (Worldwide).
E-mail: johnstacey@eznet.net
Web site: www.wwme.org
154 West Ave., Hilton, 14468. Tel: 716-392-8146.
E-mail: johnstacey@eznet.net
John and Stacey Ayers, Contact; Rev. John Murray, C.S.B.

Providence Housing Development Corporation, 1150 Buffalo Rd., 14624. Tel: 716-328-3210; Fax: 716-328-4142.
E-mail: bringewatt@dor.org
Programs offered: Property Management, Shelter & Care for the Homeless, First-time Homebuyers and Housing Information, Credit Repair and Housing Development. Units of Housing 175.

Rochester Catholic Worker Bethany House, 169 St. Bridget's Dr., 14605. Tel: 716-454-4197; Fax: 716-454-4197, Ext. [*]51.
E-mail: rbethan1@rochester.rr.com
Donna Ecker, Contact Person..Total staff 4.

St. Joseph's House of Hospitality (1941), 402 South Ave., 14620. Tel: 716-232-3262.
E-mail: jtmalt@hotmail.com
Web site: www.catholicworker.com
Mailing Address: P.O. Box 31062, 14603. Tel: 716-232-3262. Services provide soup kitchen, personal assistance to the needy, temporary housing and social justice advocacy. Total Staff 9; Total Assisted 120.

St. Theodore's Apartment Housing Development Fund Co., Inc. (Dunn Tower II Apts.), 200 Dunn Tower Dr., 14606. Tel: 716-429-6840.
E-mail: dt2@mindex.com

Union Meadows Housing Development Fund Corp., 1150 Buffalo Rd., 14624. Tel: 716-328-3210; Fax: 716-328-4142.
E-mail: bringewatt@dor.org
Maggie Bringewatt, Exec. Dir.; Jack Balinsky, Pres. & Board of Directors..Total Staff 2; Total in Residence 48.

GENEVA. *DeSales Institution Foundation,* 90 Pulteney St., 14456. Tel: 315-789-5111; Fax: 315-789-8230.
E-mail: hockpg@aol.com
Peter Koch, Pres.; Robert Anania, Vice Pres.; Edward Smaldone, Jr., Sec. & Treas.

OWEGO. *Tioga County Rural Ministry, Inc.,* 60 North Ave., 13827. Tel: 607-687-3021; Fax: 607-687-3033. Sr. Lisette O'Brien, R.S.M., Pres. This ministry serves as a food pantry and an emergency outreach to the poor and elderly of the county. Total Staff 3; Total Assisted 7,005.

SENECA FALLS. *Patrician Fund Trust,* St. Patrick's Church, 97 W. Bayard St., 13148. Tel: 315-568-5203; Fax: 315-568-4893.
E-mail: sstpatri@dor.org
Web site: www.senecafallsonline.com/stpats/
Rev. David Gramkee.

SPENCERPORT. *Legion of Mary,* 60 Martha St., 14559. Tel: 716-352-9052. Rev. Paul G. Wohlrab, Spiritual Dir. - Rochester Comitium, Rochester Comitium, 6 Martha St., 14559-1329. Tel: 716-266-8087. Mrs. Joan Stanton, Pres., 1381 Beach Ave., Rochester, 14612. Tel: 716-663-0371.

[M] CAMPUS MINISTRY

ROCHESTER. *Diocesan Department of Campus Ministry,* Pastoral Center, 1150 Buffalo Rd., 14624. Tel: 716-328-3210; Fax: 716-328-3149.
E-mail: olsen@dor.org
William Olsen, Dir. Assoc. Directors: Rev. Michael Mahler; Mary Humenay.

Catholic Newman Community at the University of Rochester, Interfaith Chapel, 320 Wilson Blvd., 14627. Tel: 716-275-4321; Fax: 716-442-4279. Rev. Brian Cool; Sr. Kathleen Wayne, R.S.M., Contact Person.

Eastman School of Music Catholic Students Organization, c/o Rev. William Donnelly, St. Mary's Pl., 14607. Tel: 716-232-7140; Fax: 716-232-6289. Rev. William Donnelly, Contact Person; Helen Halligan, Contact Person.

Nazareth College of Rochester, 4245 East Ave., 14618. Tel: 716-389-2305; Fax: 716-389-2300. Rev. Lee P. Chase, Sacramental Min.; Deacon Leo Aman, Chap. Tel: 716-389-2306; Lynne Boucher. Tel: 716-389-2308.

Newman (Catholic Campus) Parish, RIT/NTID, Interfaith Center, 40 Lomb Memorial Dr., 14623. Tel: 716-475-2135; Fax: 716-475-5485.
E-mail: newman@rit.edu
Web site: www.rit.edu/~newman/
Rev. Joseph Catanise. Tel: 716-475-5172 (V/TTY); Deacon Richard Lombard. Tel: 716-475-7606.

Monroe Community College - Office of the Chaplain, 1000 E. Henrietta Rd., 14623. Tel: 716-292-2558, Ext. 292; Fax: 716-292-2509.

St. John Fisher College, 3690 East Ave., 14618. Tel: 716-385-8368; Fax: 716-385-5209. Rev. Paul F. English, C.S.B., Dir., Campus Ministry. Tel: 716-385-8367; Deirdre McKiernan Hetzler. Tel: 716-385-8249; Sally Vaughan, Coord. of Community Svc. Tel: 716-385-8196.

State University College at Brockport, the Newman Oratory of Brockport, NY, Inc., 101 Kenyon St., 14420. Tel: 716-637-5036; Fax: 716-637-7866.
E-mail: neuman@rpa.net
Margot Van Etten, Full-time Chap.; Rev. Celestine Obi; Shelley J. Meiers, Office Mgr.

State University College at Geneseo (Geneseo), Newman Catholic Community at the Interfaith Center, 11 Franklin St., Box 265, Geneseo, 14454. Tel: 716-243-1460.
E-mail: neuman@geneseo.edu
Rev. George Okoth, Sacramental Min.; Shannon Loughlin, Dir.; Jamie Fazio, Full-time Min.

The Cornell Catholic Community, Inc. (Ithaca), Cornell University, G-22 Anabel Taylor Hall, Ithaca, 14853. Tel: 607-255-4228; Fax: 607-255-7793. Revs. Michael Mahler, Chap. Dir. Tel: 607-255-6013; Edward J. Ondrako, O.F.M.Conv., Ph.D., Chap., Theologian-in-Residence. Tel: 607-255-9380; Sr. Donna M. Fannon, M.H.S.H., Chap., Assoc. Dir. for Programming. Tel: 607-255-4256; Theresa Miller, Chap., Liturgy & Outreach. Tel: 607-255-9240; Dawn Redlin, Assoc. Dir. Admin. & Devel. Tel: 607-255-6012; Kristen Werkowich, Dir. of Devel. Tel: 607-255-6012; Barbara Reed, Chap., Social Justice Ministries. Tel: 607-255-9240; Danielle Waight, Admin. Asst. Tel: 607-255-6012.

The Catholic Community of Ithaca College, 100 Muller Chapel, Ithaca College, 453 Danby Rd., Ithaca, 14850. Tel: 607-274-3103; Fax: 607-274-1901. Rev. Scott M. Kubinski. Tel: 607-274-3184; Ms. Mary Humenay, Dir. Tel: 607-274-1117.

Elmira College, 1 Park Place, Elmira, 14901. Tel: 607-735-1824, Ext. 1824. Rev. Severine Msemwa, St. Casimir Church, 1004 Davis St., Elmira, 14901-1096.

Finger Lakes Community College c/o St. Mary's Church, 95 N. Main St., Canandaigua, 14424.

Corning Community College, One Academic Dr., Corning, 14830.

Hobart and William Smith College, c/o St. Stephen's Church, 48 Pulteney St., Geneva, 14456. Rev. Roy Kiggins. Tel: 315-789-1124.

Keuka College c/o St. Michael's Church, 312 Liberty St., Penn Yan, 14527. Tel: 315-536-7459; Fax: 315-536-6964. Revs. Phil Bilotte; Peter Deckman. Tel: 315-536-7459.

Roberts Wesleyan College, 2301 Westside Dr., North Chili, 14514.
Campus Ministry Personnel, 2301 Westside Dr., North Chili, 14514. Rev. Bernard Dollen; Sr. Carol Fox. Tel: 716-594-9125.

Wells College, c/o St. Patrick Church, Main St., P.O. Box 296, Aurora, 13026-0296. Rev. Brian E. Jeffers. Tel: 315-364-7197.

Cayuga Community College, P.O. Box 1000, Auburn, 13021. Sr. Chris Lloyd, S.S.J., Chap. Tel: 315-255-1743.

New York Chiropractic College, c/o St. Patrick's Church, 97 W. Bayard St., Seneca Falls, 13148. Tel: 315-568-5203 (Rectory); 568-3124 (College); Fax: 315-568-4893. Rev. Richard Murphy.

RELIGIOUS INSTITUTES OF MEN REPRESENTED IN THE DIOCESE

For further details refer to the corresponding bracketed number in the Religious Institutes of Men or Women section.

[0170]—*Basilian Fathers.*—C.S.B.
[0200]—*Benedictine Monks.*—O.S.B.
[0470]—*The Capuchin Friars.* (Province of St. Mary).—O.F.M.Cap.
[0270]—*Carmelite Fathers and Brothers.*—O.Carm.
[0350]—*Cistercians Order of the Strict Observance (Trappists).*—O.C.S.O.
[0310]—*Congregation of Christian Brothers.* (Eastern Prov.).—C.F.C.
[1140]—*Congregation of the Sacred Hearts of Jesus and Mary.*—SS.CC.
[0480]—*Conventual Franciscans.* (Buffalo & Immaculate Conception Provinces).—O.F.M.Conv.
[0520]—*Franciscan Friars.* (Assumption B.V.M. Prov.).—O.F.M.

[0690]—*Jesuit Fathers and Brothers.* (New York Province).—S.J.
[0610]—*Priests of the Congregation of Holy Cross.*—C.S.C.
[1070]—*Redemptorist Fathers.* (Baltimore Province).—C.SS.R.
[0760]—*Society of Mary (Marianists).*—S.M.
[1060]—*Society of the Precious Blood.*—C.PP.S.
[0560]—*Third Order Regular of Saint Francis.*—T.O.R.

RELIGIOUS INSTITUTES OF WOMEN REPRESENTED IN THE DIOCESE

[3110]—*Congregation of Our Lady of the Retreat in the Cenacle.*—R.C.
[0760]—*Daughters of Charity of St. Vincent de Paul.*—D.C.
[0420]—*Discalced Carmelite Nuns.*—O.C.D.
[1050]—*Dominican Contemplative Nuns.*—O.P.
[1070-13]—*Dominican Sisters (Adrian, MI).*—O.P.
[1070-05]—*Dominican Sisters (Amityville, NY).*—O.P.
[2575]—*Institute of the Sisters of Mercy of the Americas.* (Rochester, NY).—R.S.M.
[2470]—*Maryknoll Sisters of St. Dominic.*—M.M.
[]—*Misioneras Guadalupanas del Espiritu Santo.*
[3070]—*North American Union Sisters of Our Lady of Charity.*—N.A.U.-O.L.C.
[3430]—*Religious Teachers Filippini.*—M.P.F.
[2970]—*School Sisters of Notre Dame.*—S.S.N.D.
[3950]—*Sisters of Saint Mary of Namur.*—S.S.M.N.
[1800]—*Sisters of St. Francis of the Third Order Regular (Williamsville, New York).*—O.S.F.
[3830-14]—*Sisters of St. Joseph (Rochester).*—S.S.J.
[3840]—*Sisters of St. Joseph of Carondolet.*—C.S.J.
[3730]—*Sisters of the Order of St. Basil the Great.*—O.S.B.M.
[1490]—*Sisters of the Third Franciscan Order.*—O.S.F.
[3620]—*Sisters, Servants of Mary Immaculate.*—S.S.M.I.
[2160]—*Sisters, Servants of the Immaculate Heart of Mary.*—I.H.M.

DIOCESAN CEMETERIES

ROCHESTER. *Holy Sepulchre.*

REGIONAL CEMETERIES

AUBURN. *St. Joseph's.*
CORNING. *St. Mary.*
ELMIRA. *SS. Peter and Paul's.*
GENEVA. *St. Mary's and St. Patrick's.*

NECROLOGY

† Blighton, Francis E, Rochester, NY St. Charles Borromeo Prayer Center. —Died Jan. 11, 2000.
† Cosgrove, James R., Chap, Rochester, NY St. Mary's Hospital/Unity Health System. —Died Nov. 2, 1999.
† Egan, Joseph M., (Retired). —Died Dec. 20, 1999.
† Faraone, David J, Sodus, NY Church of the Epiphany. —Died Dec. 19, 1999.
† Harley, Ronald P, Avon, NY St. Agnes Church. —Died Sept. 26, 2000.
† Hickey, Most Rev. Dennis W., (Retired Auxiliary Bishop). —Died Oct. 6, 1999.
† Hogan, Most Rev. Joseph L., (Retired). —Died Aug. 27, 2000.
† Holberton, William B., (Retired). —Died March 6, 2000.
† O'Neill, Desmond R, Leicester, NY St. Thomas Aquinas/St Lucy. —Died March 31, 2000.
† Wahl, Raymond J., (Retired). —Died Dec. 24, 1999.

Diocese of Rockford

(Dioecesis Rockfordiensis)

Most Reverend

THOMAS G. DORAN, D.D., J.C.D.

Bishop of Rockford; ordained December 20, 1961; appointed Bishop of Rockford April 19, 1994; consecrated and installed June 24, 1994. *Res., 1243 N. Court St., Rockford, IL, 61103.*

Most Reverend

ARTHUR J. O'NEILL, D.D., V.G.

Retired Bishop of Rockford; ordained March 27, 1943; appointed Bishop of Rockford August 19, 1968; consecrated and installed October 11, 1968; retired April 19, 1994. *Res., 14 Country Club Beach, Rockford, IL, 61103.* Tel.: 815-877-5078.

Diocesan Chancery: 1245 N. Court St., P.O. Box 7044, Rockford, IL, 61126-7044. Tel.: 815-962-3709; Fax: 815-968-2824.

Web site address: www.rockforddiocese.org

E-mail address: chancery99@aol.com

ESTABLISHED SEPTEMBER 23, 1908.

Square Miles 6,457.

Comprises Jo Daviess, Stephenson, Winnebago, Boone, McHenry, Carroll, Ogle, DeKalb, Kane, Whiteside and Lee Counties in the State of Illinois.

For legal titles of parishes and diocesan institutions, consult the Chancery Office.

STATISTICAL OVERVIEW

Personnel	
Bishop	1
Retired Bishops	2
Abbots	1
Retired Abbots	2
Priests: Diocesan Active in Diocese	115
Priests: Active Outside Diocese	3
Priests: Retired, Sick or Absent	39
Number of Diocesan Priests	157
Religious Priests in Diocese	58
Extern Priests in Diocese	11
Ordinations:	
Diocesan Priests	8
Transitional Deacons	4
Permanent Deacons in Diocese	112
Total Brothers	16
Total Sisters	260
Parishes	
Parishes	105
With Resident Pastor:	
Resident Diocesan Priests	86
Resident Religious Priests	9
Without Resident Pastor:	
Administered by Priests	10
Pastoral Centers	1
Welfare	
Catholic Hospitals	3
Total Assisted	499,606
Health Care Centers	21
Total Assisted	43,752
Homes for the Aged	8
Total Assisted	789
Day Care and Extended Day Care Centers	1
Total Assisted	56
Specialized Homes	1
Total Assisted	252
Special Centers for Social Services	10
Total Assisted	303,832
Educational	
Diocesan Students in Other Seminaries	40
Total Seminarians	40
High Schools, Diocesan and Parish	6
Total Students	3,335
High Schools, Private	2
Total Students	895
Elementary Schools, Diocesan and Parish	41
Total Students	12,181
Catechesis/Religious Education:	
High School Students	5,329
Elementary Students	26,958
Total Students Under Catholic Instruction	48,738
Teachers in the Diocese:	
Priests	12
Brothers	2
Sisters	22
Lay Teachers	838
Vital Statistics	
Receptions into the Church:	
Infant Baptism Totals	6,105
Adult Baptism Totals	254
Received into Full Communion	428
First Communions	6,347
Confirmations	4,352
Marriages:	
Catholic	989
Interfaith	446
Total Marriages	1,435
Deaths	2,153
Total Catholic Population	363,430
Total Population	1,298,208

Former Bishops—Most Rev. PETER J. MULDOON, D.D., ord. Dec. 18, 1886; cons. Titular Bishop of Tamassus and Auxiliary Bishop of Chicago, July 25, 1901; appt. Bishop of Rockford, Sept. 28, 1908; made Assistant to the Pontifical Throne, June 8, 1921; died Oct. 8, 1927.—Most Rev. EDWARD F. HOBAN, S.T.D., ord. July 11, 1903; cons. Titular Bishop of Colonia and Auxiliary Bishop of Chicago, Dec. 21, 1921; appt. Bishop of Rockford, Feb. 10, 1928; appt. Assistant at the Pontifical Throne, Nov. 25, 1937; appt. Titular Bishop of Listra and Coadjutor Bishop of Cleveland, Nov. 16, 1942; succeeded to the See of Cleveland, Nov. 2, 1945; died Sept. 22, 1966.—Most Rev. JOHN J. BOYLAN, D.D., Ph.D., ord. July 28, 1915; appt. Nov. 21, 1942; cons. Feb. 17, 1943; died July 19, 1953.—Most Rev. RAYMOND P. HILLINGER, D.D., ord. April 2, 1932; appt. Nov. 3, 1953; cons. Dec. 29, 1953; appt. Titular Bishop of Derbe and Auxiliary Bishop of Chicago, June 27, 1956; died Nov. 13, 1971.—Rt. Rev. DONALD M. CARROLL, D.D., appt. June 27, 1956; resigned Sept. 25, 1956.—Most Rev. LORAS T. LANE, D.D., ord. March 19, 1937; appt. Titular Bishop of Bencenna and Auxiliary of Dubuque, May 29, 1951; cons. Aug. 20, 1951; appt. to Rockford, Oct. 11, 1956; died July 22, 1968.

Diocesan Chancery—1245 N. Court St., P.O. Box 7044, Rockford, 61126-7044. Tel: 815-962-3709; Fax: 815-968-2824. Address all official business to this office. Office Hours: Mon.-Fri. 9-12, 1-3.

Vicars General—Most Rev. ARTHUR J. O'NEILL, D.D., V.G.; Rev. Msgr. THOMAS C. BRADY, P.A., V.G., Ph.D.; Rev. Msgr. DAVID D. KAGAN, V.G., J.C.L., *1245 N. Court St., P.O. Box 7044, Rockford, 61126-7044.* Tel: 815-962-3709.

Moderator of the Curia—Rev. Msgr. DAVID D. KAGAN, V.G., J.C.L.

Vicar for Clergy and Religious—Rev. Msgr. ERIC R. BARR.

Parish Services and Directors—Mr. THOMAS MCKENNA, Dir. Social Svcs., *921 W. State St., Rockford, 61102.* Mr. JASON CHRISTENSEN, Asst. Dir. Social Svcs., *921 W. State St., Rockford, 61102.* Rev. JOHN SLAMPAK, Dir. Pastoral Svcs., *921 W. State St., Rockford, 61102.* Mrs. LORRIE GRAMER, Asst. Dir. Pastoral Svcs., *Bishop Lane Retreat Center, 7708 E. McGregor Rd., Rockford, 61102.* Sr. PATRICIA DOWNEY, O.P., Dir. Educational Svcs., *Catholic Education Office, 1260 N. Church St., Rockford, 61103.* Mr. JOHN MCGRATH, Asst. Dir. Educational Svcs., *Catholic Education Office, 1260 N. Church St., Rockford, 61103.* Dr. WAYNE LENELL, Dir. Financial & Admin. Svcs., *921 W. State St., Rockford, 61102.* Mrs. JODI RIPPON, Asst. Dir. Financial & Admin. Svcs., *921 W. State St., Rockford, 61102.*

Chancellor—Very Rev. GLENN L. NELSON, J.C.L.

Bishop's Secretary for Retired Priests—Rev. Msgr. CHARLES W. MCNAMEE, P.A., J.C.L.

Secretary to the Bishop—Rev. JOSEPH P. NAILL.

Diocesan Tribunal—850 N. Church St., Rockford, 61103. Tel: 815-963-8960; Fax: 815-963-9962. Address all official business to this office.

Judicial Vicar—Rev. Msgr. DAVID D. KAGAN, J.C.L.

Adjutant Judicial Vicar—Rev. MICHAEL KURZ, J.C.L.

Secretary and Director of the Tribunal—Sr. AUDREY STRAUB, S.S.N.D., J.C.L.

Secretary for Administrative Processes—Rev. ROBERT J. SWEENEY.

Promoter of Justice—Rev. Msgr. JOHN J. MITCHELL, V.F.

Defenders of the Bond—Sr. AUDREY STRAUB, S.S.N.D., J.C.L.; Sr. ELAINE KERSCHER, O.S.F., J.C.L.; Sr. BEVERLY JEANNE HOWE, O.P., J.C.L.

Pro Synodal Judges—Rev. Msgr. RAYMOND J. WAHL, P.A., J.C.D.; Revs. GERALD P. KOBBEMAN; WILLIAM A. KRIEGSMANN; FRANCIS E. MCDONNELL; ARQUIMEDES VALLEJO.

Advocates—Sr. MARGARET ANNE FLOTO, O.S.F.; Sr. JEANNINE WEIDNER, O.S.F.

Experts—Rev. THOMAS J. MONAHAN, Ph.D.; Mr. MICHAEL M. KAGAN, M.A.; Mr. DANIEL J. APPINO, M.S.Ed.

Notaries—Mrs. DENISE GEORGE; Mrs. DONNA HAYES; Mrs. CINDY FELDMILLER.

Diocesan Consultors—Rev. Msgr. THOMAS E. BALES; Rev. Msgr. THOMAS C. BRADY; Rev. Msgr. DAVID D. KAGAN; Rev. Msgr. DANIEL J. HERMES; Rev. Msgr. JOHN J. MITCHELL; Rev. Msgr. WILLIAM H. SCHWARTZ; Rev. Msgr. RAYMOND J. WAHL; Revs. LEO J. BARTEL; JOHN W. CAHILL; DANIEL J. DEUTSCH; STEPHEN J. KNOX; GEOFFREY D. WIRTH.

Deans—Rev. Msgr. EDWARD S. WRIGHT, Aurora Deanery; Rev. Msgr. WILLIAM J. CLAUSEN, DeKalb Deanery; Rev. Msgr. ROBERT B. HOFFMAN, Elgin Deanery; Rev. Msgr. P. WILLIAM MCDONNELL, Freeport Deanery; Rev. Msgr. PHILIP E. O'NEIL, McHenry County Deanery; Rev. Msgr. JOHN J. MITCHELL, Rockford Deanery; Rev. Msgr. THOMAS E. BALES, Sterling Deanery.

Episcopal Delegate for Women Religious—Sr. JAMES MARIE O'CONNOR, S.S.N.D., *1245 N. Court St., P.O. Box 7044, Rockford, 61126-7044.* Tel: 815-962-3709; Fax: 815-968-2824.

Diocesan Offices and Directors

Black Catholic Ministry—SANDRA WRIGHT, Dir., *2505 School St., Rockford, 61101.* Tel: 815-965-9539; Fax: 815-964-9705.

Campaign for Human Development—Rev. HARLAN CLAPSADDLE, Dir., *921 W. State St., Rockford, 61102.* Tel: 815-965-0895; Fax: 815-965-6141.

Catholic Charismatic Renewal Services—Mr. RON BERGMAN, Diocesan Liaison, *1910 Bracknel Blvd., Rockford, 61103.* Tel: 815-654-4111.

Catholic Office of the Deaf—Very Rev. GLENN L. NELSON, J.C.L., Dir., *1245 N. Court St., P.O. Box 7044, Rockford, 61126-7044.* Tel: 815-962-3709; 962-2994 (TTY).

Catholic Relief Services—Mr. THOMAS MCKENNA, *921 W. State St., Rockford, 61102.* Tel: 815-965-0895; Fax: 815-965-6141.

Cemeteries—Rev. Msgr. THOMAS C. BRADY, P.A., Dir.; Mr. WAYNE LENELL, C.P.A., Ph.D., Admin., *8616 W. State St., Winnebago, 61088.* Tel: 815-965-1637; Fax: 815-965-9632.

Censores Librorum—Rev. Msgr. CHARLES W. MCNAMEE, P.A., J.C.L.; Rev. FRANCIS E. MCDONNELL.

Charities—Mr. BRISTON FERNANDES, Dir. Offices: *921 W. State St., Rockford, 61102.* Tel: 815-965-0895; Fax: 815-965-6141., *1700 N. Farnsworth Ave., Ste. 18, Aurora, 60505., 1315 Pleasant St., DeKalb, 60115., 566 Dundee Ave., Elgin, 60120., 1231 S. Walnut Ave., Freeport, 61032., 202 Summit St., Galena, 61036., 5215 W. Bull Valley Rd., McHenry, 60050., 801 W. 11th St., Sterling, 61081.*

Satellite Offices—*860 Biester Dr., #206 C, Belvidere, 61008., 315 S. Peoria Ave., Dixon, 61021.*

Clergy Relief Society, Priests' Retirement Committee—Rev. Msgr. CHARLES W. MCNAMEE, P.A., J.C.L., Exec. Sec., *1245 N. Court St., P.O. Box 7044, Rockford, 61126-7044.* Tel: 815-962-3709; Fax: 815-968-2824.

Communications—Dr. OWEN PHELPS, Dir., *921 W. State St., Rockford, 61102.* Tel: 815-963-3471; Fax: 815-968-2808.

Conciliation and Arbitration Council—Sr. ELAINE KERSCHER, O.S.F., J.C.L., Exec. Sec., *850 N. Church St., 2nd Fl., Rockford, 61103.* Tel: 815-963-8960; Fax: 815-963-9962.

Council of Catholic Women, Diocesan—Rev. Msgr. THOMAS L. DZIELAK, Moderator, *708 10th Ave., Rock Falls, 61071.* Tel: 815-625-4508. RITA PESAVENTO, *8421 Eddington Dr., Machesney Park, 61115.*

Cursillo Movement—Rev. ROBERT N. SHERRY, Dir., *5211 W. Bull Valley Rd., McHenry, 60050.* Tel: 815-385-LORD.

Development Office—Mr. DAVID HOUGAN, Dir., *921 W. State St., Rockford, 61102.* Tel: 815-964-6711; Fax: 815-968-2808.

Divine Worship, Office for—(and RCIA Resources)—Rev. JOHN A. SLAMPAK, S.T.L., Dir., *921 W. State St., Rockford, 61102.* Tel: 815-963-0344; Fax: 815-963-9747.

Ecumenism, Office of—Rev. Msgr. THOMAS DZIELAK, Dir., *St. Andrew, 708 Tenth Ave., Rock Falls, 61071.* Tel: 815-625-4508; Fax: 815-625-1569.

Education—Sr. PATRICIA DOWNEY, O.P., Supt. Schools; Sr. EILEEN SULLIVAN, O.P., Asst. Supt. Schools; Mr. JOHN MCGRATH, Dir., Rel. Educ. & Formation, *1260 N. Church St., Rockford, 61103.* Tel: 815-962-7791; Fax: 815-962-1767.

Ethicist for Health Care Issues, Diocesan—Rev. TIMOTHY L. DOHERTY, Ph.D., *921 W. State St., Rockford, 61102.* Tel: 815-963-4007; Fax: 815-962-2966.

Family Life—Mrs. LORRIE GRAMER, Dir., *7708 E. McGregor Rd., Rockford, 61102.* Tel: 815-965-5011; Fax: 815-965-5811.

Finance and Administration—Mr. WAYNE LENELL, C.P.A., Ph.D., Dir. Fin. & Admin. Svcs., *921 W. State St., Rockford, 61102.* Tel: 815-964-5231; Fax: 815-964-5501.

Hispanic Ministry Offices—Rev. WILLIAM R. SCHUESSLER, *921 W. State St., Rockford, 61102.* Tel: 815-962-8142. Offices in Diocese: Aurora Deanery: *Centro Cristo Rey, 315 N. Root St., Aurora, 60505.* DeKalb Deanery: *Centro Cuerpo de Cristo, 308 Fisk Ave., DeKalb, 60115.* Elgin Deanery: *Centro Jesus Resucitado, 90 N. Kennedy Dr., Carpentersville, 60110.* McHenry Deanery: *Centro San Jose, 207 E. Brainard St., Harvard, 60033.* Rockford Deanery: *Centro Sembrador, 921 W. State St., Rockford, 61102.* Sterling Deanery: *Tu C.A.S.A., 202 W. 6th St., Sterling, 61081.*

Holy Childhood Association—Sr. PATRICIA DOWNEY, O.P., Dir., *1260 N. Church St., Rockford, 61103.* Tel: 815-962-7791; Fax: 815-962-1767.

Investment and Loan—Mr. WAYNE LENELL, C.P.A., Ph.D., *921 W. State St., Rockford, 61102.* Tel: 815-964-5231; Fax: 815-964-5501.

Legion of Mary—Rev. WILLIAM P. COLLINS, Dir., *2505 School St., Rockford, 61101.* Tel: 815-965-9539.

Liturgical Commission, Diocesan—Rev. JOHN A. SLAMPAK, S.T.L., Dir., *921 W. State St., Rockford, 61102.* Tel: 815-963-0344; Fax: 815-963-9747.

Ministry Formation, Office of—Mr. JOHN MCGRATH, Dir., *921 W. State St., Rockford, 61102.* Tel: 815-962-8873; Fax: 815-962-2966.

Ministry to Priests Program—Rev. Msgr. ERIC R. BARR, Vicar, Clergy Sabbaticals and Diocesan Priests' Retreats, *1226 N. Church St., Rockford, 61103.* Tel: 815-965-5767; Fax: 815-965-5768.

Newman-Campus Ministry—Rev. STEPHEN J. KNOX, Dir., *512 Normal Rd., DeKalb, 60115.* Tel: 815-758-6667.

Newspaper—*"The Observer"*; Dr. OWEN PHELPS, Mng. Editor, *921 W. State St., Rockford, 61102.* Tel: 815-963-3471; Fax: 815-968-2808.

Permanent Diaconate Program Diocesan—*1204 N. Church St., Rockford, 61103.* Tel: 815-965-5837; Fax: 815-965-0085.

Priests' Eucharistic League—Rev. THOMAS J. MONAHAN, *2696 Aldersgate Dr., Rockford, 61103.* Tel: 815-282-9972.

Priest Personnel—Rev. Msgr. ERIC R. BARR, Vicar, Clergy and Religious, *1226 N. Church St., Rockford, 61103.* Tel: 815-965-5767; Fax: 815-965-5768.

Pro-Life Activities, Office of—Rev. DAVID A. PECK, Dir., *1245 N. Court St., P.O. Box 7044, Rockford, 61126.* Tel: 815-877-LIFE; Fax: 815-968-2824.

Propagation of the Faith—Rev. ROBERT J. SWEENEY, Dir., *921 W. State St., Rockford, 61102.* Tel: 815-962-2934; Fax: 815-962-2966.

Research and Planning—Mr. MICHAEL CIESLAK, Ph.D., Dir., *921 W. State St., Rockford, 61102.* Tel: 815-963-7799; Fax: 815-962-2966.

Rural Life Conference—Mr. THOMAS MCKENNA, Dir., *921 W. State St., Rockford, 61102.* Tel: 815-965-0895.

Scouts—Rev. Msgr. WILLIAM H. SCHWARTZ, P.A., Dir., *1243 N. Church St., Rockford, 61103.* Tel: 815-965-2765; Fax: 815-965-0743.

Seton Center—Mr. RONALD DI TOMASSI, Building Mgr., *921 W. State St., Rockford, 61102.* Tel: 815-965-2778.

Vocations—Revs. MARTIN G. HEINZ, Dir. AARON R. BRODESKI, Asst. Dir., *850 N. Church St., Rockford, 61103.* Tel: 815-963-1009; Fax: 815-963-9962.

CLERGY, PARISHES, MISSIONS AND PAROCHIAL SCHOOLS

CITY OF ROCKFORD
(Winnebago County)

1—ST. PETER CATHEDRAL (1922), Rev. Msgr. William H. Schwartz, P.A., Rector; Rev. Brian Geary; Deacons Charles Cooper; Martin Czerniewski.
Res., 1243 N. Church St., 61103. Tel: 815-965-2765; Fax: 815-965-0743.
School—1231 N. Court St., Tel: 815-963-3620; Fax: 815-963-0551. Mr. Michael Kagan, Prin.
Lay Teachers 15; Students 301.
Catechesis/Religious Programs—Mr. William Easton, D.R.E.
Students 90.

2—ST. ANTHONY OF PADUA (1909) (Italian), Revs. Luke Poczworowski, O.F.M.Conv.; James Jankowski, O.F.M.Conv. In res., Rev. Dominic Wisz, O.F.M.Conv.; Deacons Sam Cassaro; Frank Barone.
Res., 1010 Ferguson St., 61102. Tel: 815-965-2761; Fax: 815-968-2798.
Catechesis/Religious Programs—Tel: 815-965-8032.
Students 173.

3—ST. BERNADETTE (1957), Revs. John L. Stringini; Robert J. McClellan; Deacon Richard Gerdeman.
Res., 2400 Bell Ave., 61103. Tel: 815-968-0904; Fax: 815-987-9476.
Church—Rockton Ave. & Bell Ave., 61103.
School—2300 Bell Ave., Tel: 815-968-2288; Fax: 815-987-9453. Mrs. Elizabeth Adams-Young, Prin.
Lay Teachers 20; Students 344.
Catechesis/Religious Programs—2300 Bell Ave., 61103. Tel: 815-968-2289. Mrs. Alice Kaczmarek, D.R.E.
Students 97.

4—ST. EDWARD (1929), Rev. Msgr. Raymond J. Wahl, P.A.; Revs. James J. Murphy, Pastor Emeritus; James R. Keenan; Deacons Lambert Verstynen; Fred Skrade.
Parish Office: 3004 11th St., 61109. Tel: 815-229-0282; Fax: 815-229-8912.
Res., 3026 11th St., 61109. Tel: 815-398-1249.
School—3020 S. 11th St., Tel: 815-396-2631; Fax: 815-398-3134. Mr. John Fitzsimmons, Prin.
Lay Teachers 15; Students 280.
Catechesis/Religious Programs—Tel: 815-229-8914. Lynette M. Conner, D.R.E.
Students 215.

5—HOLY FAMILY (1963), Rev. Msgr. Daniel J. Hermes; Rev. Stephen Olutade Folorunso; Deacon Bob Bracken.
Office: 4401 Highcrest Rd., 61107. Tel: 815-398-4280; Fax: 815-398-4287.
School—4407 Highcrest Rd., Tel: 815-398-5331; Fax: 815-398-5902. Mr. Anthony Smerko, Prin.
Lay Teachers 28; Students 573.
Catechesis/Religious Programs—Tel: 815-397-9395. Joellen Lansing, D.R.E.
Students 302.

6—ST. JAMES (1853), Rev. David E. Beauvais; Deacon Ronald Magee. In res., Rev. William M. McKinstra.
Res., 428 N. Second St., 61107. Tel: 815-962-1214; Fax: 815-962-1236. [JC]
School—409 N. First St., Tel: 815-962-8515. Ms. Margo Shifo, Prin.
Lay Teachers 17; Students 280.
Catechesis/Religious Programs—Tel: 815-962-5588. Julie Fisher, D.R.E.
Students 149.

7—ST. MARY SHRINE, INSTITUTE OF CHRIST THE KING SOVEREIGN PRIEST (1997). For parish records, contact St. Anthony, Rockford. Rev. Brian Bovee.
Res., 517 Elm St., 61102. Tel: 815-965-5971; Fax: 815-965-6029.

8—ST. PATRICK (1919), Rev. William P. Collins; Deacon Ron Graw.
Res., 2505 School St., 61101. Tel: 815-965-9539; Fax: 815-964-9705. [JC]
Catechesis/Religious Programs—Tel: 815-964-6591.
Students 115.

9—SS. PETER AND PAUL (1911) (Hispanic Hogar), Rev. Timothy Piasecki.
Res., 617 Lincoln Ave., 61102. Tel: 815-962-7171; Fax: 815-962-7171.
Catechesis/Religious Programs—Students 120.

10—ST. RITA (1914), Revs. Gerald P. Kobbeman; Dean M. Smith; Deacons Alex Hainchek; Robert Martin. In res., Rev. Michael Kurz.
Res., 6254 Valley Knoll Dr., 61109-1898. Tel: 815-398-0853; Fax: 815-397-7499.
School—6284 Valley Knoll Dr., 61109-1898. Tel: 815-398-3466; Fax: 815-398-6104. Ms. Joan Leonard, Prin.
Lay Teachers 15; Students 360.
Catechesis/Religious Programs—Tel: 815-398-6483; Fax: 815-397-7499. Sr. Dorothy Bertsch, S.M.P., D.R.E.
Students 220.

11—ST. STANISLAUS KOSTKA (1912) (Polish), Rev. John J. Mikula, O.F.M.Conv.; Deacon James Hudzinski. In res., Rev. Hippolite Kuras, O.F.M.Conv.
Res., 201 Buckbee, 61104. Tel: 815-965-3913; Fax: 815-965-3915 (Call first).

OUTSIDE THE CITY OF ROCKFORD

Algonquin, McHenry Co., St. Margaret Mary (1954), Revs. Michael J. Tierney; Moises Apostol; Rodel Peji; Deacons Howard Fischer; Simon Grossmayer; Patrick Maher.
Parish Office: 111 S. Hubbard St., 60102. Tel: 847-658-7625; Fax: 847-658-7882.
School—(Grades (PreK-8)) 113 Hubbard St., Tel: 847-658-5313; Fax: 847-854-0501. Mrs. Kathleen McMahon, Prin.
Lay Teachers 13; Students 291.
Catechesis/Religious Programs—Tel: 847-658-9339. D.R.E.: Mrs. Sharon Prykop; Mrs. Teresa Chiappone (Junior & High School).
Students 1,262.

Amboy, Lee Co., St. Patrick (1857), Rev. Francis Daleiden, O.S.B.
Res., 32 N. Jones Ave., 61310. Tel: 815-857-2315; Fax: 815-857-2315. [CEM]
Catechesis/Religious Programs—Students 195.

Apple River, Jo Daviess Co., St. Joseph (1868), Rev. Miroslaw A. Reikowski.
Res., 107 Webster St., P.O. Box 3867, 61001. Tel: 815-594-2312. [CEM]
Catechesis/Religious Programs—Students 41.

Aurora, Kane Co.,

1—ANNUNCIATION OF THE BLESSED VIRGIN MARY, (1875), Rev. Mario Pedi, O.S.B.; Deacons Raymond Johnson; Harold Poss; Larry Motyka.
Res., 1820 Church Rd., 60504. Tel: 630-851-1436; Fax: 630-851-2435. [CEM]
School—1840 Church Rd., Tel: 630-851-4300; Fax: 630-851-4316. Mr. Paul Barton, Prin.
Lay Teachers 10; Students 300.
Catechesis/Religious Programs—Students 125.

2—HOLY ANGELS, (1892), Revs. Martin G. Heinz; Joseph P. Nicolosi; Dean Elno Russell; Deacons Tim White; Tom Hawksworth; Luke Cordes, (Retired). In res., Rev. Dennis Brown.
Res., 720 Hardin Ave., 60506-4997. Tel: 630-897-1194; Fax: 630-897-1370.
School—720 Kensington Pl., 60506. Tel: 630-897-3613; Fax: 630-897-8233. Mrs. Rosemary Hauser, Prin.
Lay Teachers 33; Students 762.
Catechesis/Religious Programs—Students 290.

3—ST. JOSEPH, (1899), Revs. Jerome I. Leake; Pierre G. Polycarpe; Deacon Norbert Szudarski, Pastoral Assoc., Tel: 630-897-0484.
Mailing Address: P.O. Box 4395, 60507.
Res., 405 St. Joseph Ave., 60505. Tel: 630-844-3780; Fax: 630-844-1338. [CEM]
School—706 High St., 60507. Tel: 630-844-3781. Miss Marie Bockhaus, Prin.
Lay Teachers 16; Students 370.
Catechesis/Religious Programs—Tel: 630-844-3782.
Students 48.

4—ST. MARY, (1872) (Irish), Deacons Richard Groom; William Rees. In res., Rev. Joseph M. Lessard.
Res., 430 E. Downer Pl., 60505-3475. Tel: 630-892-0480; Fax: 630-892-8664.
Catechesis/Religious Programs—430 E. Downer Pl., Tel: 630-859-3922.
Students 65.

5—ST. NICHOLAS, (1862) (Hispanic), Rev. Bernardo Fuentes Patino.
Res. & Mailing Address: 308 High St., 60505. Tel: 630-898-8707; Fax: 630-585-6423. [CEM]
School—Archbishop Romero School, 312 N. High St., Tel: 630-898-8690; Fax: 630-898-8866. Mr. Gary Widing, Prin.
Lay Teachers 10; Students 207.
Catechesis/Religious Programs—Sr. Rita Mary Phalen, O.S.F., D.R.E.
Students 603.

6—OUR LADY OF GOOD COUNSEL, (1909), Rev. Edward F. Gillespie; Deacon James J. Valesano.
Res., 620 S. Fifth St., 60505. Tel: 630-851-1100; Fax: 630-851-4069.
School—601 Talma St., Tel: 630-851-4400; Fax: 630-851-8220. Lucille Plachetka, Prin.
Students 399.
Catechesis/Religious Programs—Tel: 630-851-7567.
Students 75.

7—ST. PETER, (1929), Rev. Ronald A. Jones; Deacon Carlos Navarro.
Res., 925 Sard Ave., 60506. Tel: 630-896-6816; Fax: 630-896-2534.
School—915 Sard Ave., Tel: 630-892-1283. Sr. Margaret Fabrizius, O.P., Prin.
Sisters 3; Lay Teachers 5; Students 112.

8—ST. RITA OF CASCIA, (1927), Rev. Robert J. Willhite.
Res., 750 W. Old Indian Trail Rd., 60506. Tel: 630-892-5918.
School—770 W. Old Indian Trail Rd., Tel: 630-892-0020; Fax: 630-892-4236. Ms. Elizabeth Baney, Prin.
Lay Teachers 18; Students 358.
Catechesis/Religious Programs—Tel: 630-892-9507. Judith Feiden, D.R.E.
Students 383.

9—SACRED HEART, (1861) (French), Revs. David R. Engbarth; Robert Camacho; Deacon Richard Groom.
Res., 771 Fulton St., 60505. Tel: 630-898-4165; Fax: 630-898-4165. [CEM]
School—Archbishop Romero School, Tel: 630-898-8690; Fax: 630-898-8866.
Catechesis/Religious Programs—Tel: 630-898-4165; Fax: 630-898-3940. Conchita Hurtado, D.R.E.
Students 173.

10—ST. THERESE OF JESUS, (1925), Revs. Joseph T. Muller, M.S.C.; Brian D. Grady; Deacon Bruce M. Watermann.
Res., 271 N. Farnsworth Ave., 60505. Tel: 630-898-5422; Fax: 630-898-5327.
School—255 N. Farnsworth Ave., Tel: 630-898-0620; Fax: 630-898-3087. Mrs. Cheryl Zuiker, Prin.
Lay Teachers 5; Students 73.
Catechesis/Religious Programs—Students 320.

Batavia, Kane Co., Holy Cross (1854), Revs. Stephen St. Jules; Brian Donlin Grady; Deacons Raymond Martin; Edward Lober; William L. Jacobson, Business Mgr.
Res., 2300 Main St., 60510-7625. Tel: 630-879-4750; Fax: 630-879-9502. [JC]
Catechesis/Religious Programs—Tel: 630-879-4751. D.R.E.: Mrs. Diane E. Downey; Mrs. Theresa A. Palicka.
Students 1,394.

Belvidere, Boone Co., St. James (1886), Revs. Bernard J. Mullane; Ricardo F. Hernandez.
Office: 535 Caswell St., 61008. Tel: 815-547-6397; Fax: 815-547-0607.
Res., 514 Caswell St., 61008. Tel: 815-547-6397. [CEM]
School—320 Logan Ave., 61008. Tel: 815-547-7633; Fax: 815-544-2294. Mrs. Sandra Krekeler, Prin.
Lay Teachers 12; Students 212.
Catechesis/Religious Programs—Tel: 815-544-3698. Frank Zimmerman, D.R.E.
Students 532.

Byron, Ogle Co., St. Mary (1895), Rev. Timothy L. Doherty; Deacon Bob Smits, Jr.
Res., P.O. Box 1070, 232 E. Second St., 61010. Tel: 815-234-7431; Fax: 815-234-2133. [CEM]
Catechesis/Religious Programs—Tel: 815-234-5349. D.R.E.: Marilyn Herrmann; Beth Murbach.
Students 352.

Carpentersville, Kane Co., St. Monica (1957), Revs. William R. Schuessler; Fabio H. Garzon, S.D.B.; Deacons John Bach; J. Michael Frazier; Dennis Garber.
Res., 90 N. Kennedy Dr., 60110-1695. Tel: 847-428-2646; Fax: 847-428-0039. [JC]
Catechesis/Religious Programs—Tel: 847-428-7562. Gene Traversa, D.R.E.
Students 681.

Cary, McHenry Co., SS. Peter & Paul (1904), Revs. Donald M. Ahles; Jerome P. Koutnik; Deacon Howard Ganschow, II.
Res., 410 N. First St., 60013. Tel: 847-516-2636; Fax: 847-639-3474.
School—416 N. First St., 60013. Tel: 847-639-3041; Fax: 847-639-5329. Sr. Katrina Lamkin, O.P., Prin.
Dominican Sisters 1; Lay Teachers 11; Students 280.
Catechesis/Religious Programs—Tel: 847-639-0414; Fax: 847-639-3474. Terri Zbylut, D.R.E.
Students 1,435.

Crystal Lake, McHenry Co., St. Elizabeth Ann Seton (1978), Rev. Msgr. Michael A. Binsfeld; Rev. Perfecto Vasquez; Deacon Charles Gagnon; George Ross, Business Mgr.
Office: 800 McHenry Ave., 60014. Tel: 815-459-3033; Fax: 815-459-3040.
Res., 445 Dartmoor Dr., 60014. Tel: 815-459-6223.
Catechesis/Religious Programs—Tel: 815-459-3096; Fax: 815-459-3040. Monica Ebelhack, D.R.E.
Students 1,465.

St. Thomas the Apostle, Revs. Geoffrey Wirth; Mark A. Campobello; Keith Roscoe.
Res., 200 Washington St., 60014. Tel: 815-455-5407; Fax: 815-455-2733.
Pastoral Center: 272 King St., 60014. Tel: 815-455-5400; Fax: 815-455-2733.
School—265 King St., Tel: 815-459-0496; Fax: 815-459-0591. Mr. Warren Smith, Prin.
Lay Teachers 26; Students 487.
Catechesis/Religious Programs—Tel: 815-455-9787. Janet Kayser, D.R.E.
Students 900.

DeKalb, DeKalb Co., Christ the Teacher, University Parish of Northern Illinois University (1963), Revs. Stephen J. Knox; Addison H. Hart; Deacons James Dombek; Terrence Beer.
Office: 512 Normal Rd., 60115. Tel: 815-787-7770; Fax: 815-758-2053.
Catechesis/Religious Programs—Dr. Laura Bird, D.R.E.
Students 180.

St. Mary (1861), Rev. Karl P. Ganss. In res., Rev. Anthony Vu Khac Long.
Office: 302 Fisk Ave., 60115. Tel: 815-758-5432; Fax: 815-758-2487.
Res., 321 Pine St., 60115. Tel: 815-748-5654. [CEM]
School—210 Gurler Rd., Tel: 815-756-7905; Fax: 815-758-1459. Ms. Catherine Mutter, Prin.
Lay Teachers 21; Students 319.
Catechesis/Religious Programs—Tel: 815-758-8504.
Students 323.

Dixon, Lee Co., St. Anne (1928), Rev. Kenneth J. Anderson.
Res., 1104 N. Brinton Ave., 61021. Tel: 815-288-3131; Fax: 815-288-3139.
School—1112 N. Brinton Ave., Tel: 815-288-5619; Fax: 815-288-5820. Sr. Marcianne Bzdon, S.S.N.D., Prin.
Lay Teachers 13; Students 154.
Catechesis/Religious Programs—Students 96.

St. Patrick (1856), Rev. Daniel J. Deutsch; Deacons Sam Berard; Bob Brandenburg.
Office: 612 S. Highland, 61021. Tel: 815-284-7719; Fax: 815-284-4758. [JC]
School—St. Mary Elementary & Junior High, (Grades PreK-8) 704 Peoria Ave., Tel: 815-284-6986; Fax: 815-288-2940. Mrs. Jean Spohn, Prin.
Lay Teachers 17; Students 205.
Catechesis/Religious Programs—Tel: 815-284-2867. Mrs. Jacqueline Schauff, D.R.E.
Students 133.

Dundee, Kane Co., St. Catherine of Siena (1914), Revs. Richard A. Rosinski; William Antillon. In res., Rev. Max Striedl, Jr.
Office: 845 W. Main St., 60118. Tel: 847-426-2217; Fax: 847-426-1130.
Res., 833 Royal Ln., 60118.
School—Tel: 847-426-4808; Fax: 847-426-0437. Mrs. Magaret Sanders, Prin.
Lay Teachers 14; Students 285.
Catechesis/Religious Programs—Tel: 847-426-4712.
Students 752.
Mission—Gilbert, Kane Co., St. Mary, c/o 845 W. Main St., West Dundee, 60118. Tel: 847-836-8315. [CEM]

Durand, Winnebago Co., St. Mary (1862) (Irish), Rev. Msgr. Eric R. Barr.
Mailing Address: St. Mary's & St. Patrick's Cemeteries are jointly administered by St. Mary's Church, Durand. 606 W. Main St., 61024. Tel: 815-248-2490; Fax: 815-248-9100.
Catechesis/Religious Programs—Students 169.
Mission—Irish Grove Rd., Stephenson Co., St. Patrick. [CEM]

East Dubuque, Jo Daviess Co., St. Mary (1868), Rev. Raymond O. Holmgren.
Res., 170 Montgomery Ave., 61025. Tel: 815-747-3221; Fax: 815-747-6188. [JC]
School—701 Rte. 35 N., 61025. Tel: 815-747-3221. Sr. Maryann Tranel, O.P., Prin.
Lay Teachers 8; Students 110.
Catechesis/Religious Programs—Tel: 815-747-3010.
Students 75.

Elburn, Kane Co., St. Gall (1870) (Irish), Rev. Richard W. Paddock.
Res., 120 W. Shannon, P.O. Box 8020, 60119. Tel: 630-365-6030; Fax: 630-365-5483. [CEM]
Catechesis/Religious Programs—Tel: 630-365-9166.
Students 418.

Elgin, Kane Co.,

1—ST. JOSEPH, (1887) (German-Spanish), Revs. David W. Huber; Hector Moreno; Deacons John Sauceda; Armando Martinez.
Res., 272 Division St., 60120. Tel: 847-931-2800; Fax: 847-931-2810.
School—274 Division St., Tel: 847-931-2804; Fax: 847-931-2811. Janine M. Bolchazy, Prin.
Lay Teachers 12; Students 228.
Catechesis/Religious Programs—Tel: 847-931-2808; Fax: 847-931-2801.
Students 700.

2—ST. LAURENCE, (1929), Rev. Joseph F. Kulak.
Office: 226 Orchard St., 60123. Tel: 847-468-6900; Fax: 847-468-6904.
Res., 1213 Oakdale Dr., 60123. Tel: 847-468-6105.

School—572 Standish St., 60123. Tel: 847-468-6100; Fax: 847-468-6104. Mrs. Phyllis Jensen, Prin.
Lay Teachers 14; Students 247.
Catechesis/Religious Programs—Tel: 847-468-6900.
Students 178.

3—ST. MARY, (1851), Revs. Thomas J. Dempsey; Stanislaus Kos.
Parish Office—397 Fulton St., 60120. Tel: 847-888-2828; Fax: 847-888-2883.
Res., 390 Fulton St., 60120. Tel: 847-888-0502.
School—103 S. Gifford St., Tel: 847-695-6609; Fax: 847-695-6623. Mrs. Mary Beth Mitchell, Prin.
Lay Teachers 10; Students 236.
Catechesis/Religious Programs—Tel: 847-888-2718. Lesli Wiseman, D.R.E.
Students 257.

4—ST. THOMAS MORE, (1959), Rev. Richard M. Russo; Deacons William Joynt; Robert Plazewski.
Office: 215 Thomas More Dr., 60123. Tel: 847-888-1682; Fax: 847-888-3198. [JC]
School—1625 W. Highland Ave., Tel: 847-742-3959. Ms. Penelope Reid, Prin.
Lay Teachers 14; Students 287.
Catechesis/Religious Programs—Tel: 847-888-4887. Mr. Ron Becker, D.R.E.
Students 540.

Elizabeth, Jo Daviess Co., St. Mary (1886), Rev. Christopher J. Kuhn.
Res., 112 E. Washington St., Box 246, 61028. Tel: 815-858-3422; Fax: 815-858-2622. [CEM]
Catechesis/Religious Programs—Students 82.

Freeport, Stephenson Co.,

1—ST. CATHERINE. Closed. For inquiries for parish records contact the Chancery.

2—ST. JOSEPH, (1862) (German), Rev. John W. Cahill.
Res., 229 W. Washington Pl., 61032. Tel: 815-232-7622; Fax: 815-235-4690. [CEM]
School—Freeport Catholic Elementary School, 202 W. Pleasant St., Tel: 815-232-6416. Mrs. Kathy Runte, Prin.; Mr. Randall Musser, Admin. Prin.
Lay Teachers 12; Students 246.
Catechesis/Religious Programs—Tel: 815-235-4324.
Students 63.

3—ST. MARY, (1846), Rev. Joseph L. Lutz.
Office: 813 S. State Ave., 61032. Tel: 815-235-7544; Fax: 815-233-0005.
Res., 704 S. State Ave., 61032. [CEM]
Catechesis/Religious Programs—(Freeport Catholic School System).
Students 32.

4—ST. THOMAS AQUINAS, (1921), Rev. Msgr. P. William McDonnell; Deacons H. Donald Brunette; Richard Dinneen; Vincent Drees.
Res., 1400 Kiwanis Dr., 61032. Tel: 815-232-3225; Fax: 815-232-3231.
Catechesis/Religious Programs—Vincent Drees, D.R.E.
Students 173.

Fulton, Whiteside Co., Immaculate Conception (1863), Rev. Louis F. Tosto.
Res., 703 12th Ave., 61252. Tel: 815-589-3542; Fax: 815-589-4915.
Mission—Albany, Whiteside Co., St. Patrick, 1445 Waller Rd., 61230. Tel: 309-887-4072.
Catechesis/Religious Programs—Students 90.

Galena, Jo Daviess Co., St. Mary (1851) (German), Rev. Daniel D. Tranel.
Res., 406 Franklin St., 61036. Tel: 815-777-0134. [CEM]
Catechesis/Religious Programs—Tel: 815-777-2219. Patricia Schuler, D.R.E.
Students 158.

St. Michael (1832) (Irish), Rev. Daniel D. Tranel.
Res., 227 S. Bench St., 61036. Tel: 815-777-2053. [CEM]
Catechesis/Religious Programs—Tricia Tranel, D.R.E.
Students 90.

Geneva, Kane Co., St. Peter (1912), Rev. Msgr. Joseph F. Jarmoluk; Rev. John Christopher Fritz.
Office: 1891 Kaneville Rd., 60134. Tel: 630-232-0124; Fax: 630-232-9262.
Res., 1771 Kaneville Rd., 60134. Tel: 630-208-1625. [JC]
School—1881 Kaneville Rd., Tel: 630-232-0476; Fax: 630-208-5681. Mrs. Deborah Bray, Prin.
Lay Teachers 20; Students 460.
Catechesis/Religious Programs—Tel: 630-232-0124. Mr. John N. Lamperis, D.R.E.
Students 1,431.

Genoa, DeKalb Co., St. Catherine of Genoa (1912), Revs. Aloysius J. Neumann; Harold L. Nilges, Pastor Emeritus; Deacons John Kohler; Larry Zitkus.
Res., 340 S. Stott St., 60135. Tel: 815-784-2355; Fax: 815-784-2045. [CEM]
Catechesis/Religious Programs—Tel: 815-784-2045. D.R.E.: Joseph Phelan; Kris Phelan.
Students 253.

Hampshire, Kane Co., St. Charles Borromeo (1878), Rev. Thomas E. Brantman.
Res., 297 E. Jefferson Ave., 60140-7646. Tel: 847-683-2391; Fax: 847-683-2396. [CEM]
School—(Grades K-8) 288 E. Jefferson Ave., 60140. Tel: 847-683-3450; Fax: 847-683-3209. Mrs. Karen Behrns, Prin.
Lay Teachers 11; Students 110.
Catechesis/Religious Programs—295 E. Jefferson Ave., 60140. Tel: 847-683-1536. Joyce Donahue, D.R.E.
Students 285.

Hanover, Jo Daviess Co., St. John the Evangelist (1925), Rev. Christopher J. Kuhn.
Res., 103 Savanna Rd., 61041. Tel: 815-591-2258; Fax: 815-858-2622.
Catechesis/Religious Programs—Students 26.

Harmon, Lee Co., St. Flannen (1898), Rev. Thomas P. Dolan.
Res., P.O. Box 130, 61042. Tel: 815-359-7819. [CEM]

Hartland, McHenry Co., St. Patrick (1837), Rev. Paul M. Lipinski, Admin.; Deacons Arthur Holt; Joseph Kayser.
Res., 15012 St. Patrick Rd., Woodstock, 60098. Tel: 815-338-7883; Fax: 815-338-5570. [CEM]
Catechesis/Religious Programs—Tel: 815-338-5570.
Students 50.

Harvard, McHenry Co., St. Joseph (1866), Rev. Richard R. Kramer; Deacons Anthony Koss; Jack O'Leary.
Res., 206 E. Front St., 60033. Tel: 815-943-6406; Fax: 815-943-1604. [CEM]
School—201 N. Division St., Tel: 815-943-6933. Mrs. Marilyn Knapp, Prin.
Lay Teachers 7; Students 124.
Catechesis/Religious Programs—Tel: 815-943-1644. Beverly O'Leary, D.R.E.
Students 153.

Huntley, McHenry Co., St. Mary (1873), Rev. Robert M. Garrity; Deacons Thomas W. O'Brien; John A. McPhee.
Res., 10911 N. Woodstock St., 60142. Tel: 847-669-3137; Fax: 847-669-3138. [CEM]
Catechesis/Religious Programs—Students 380.

Johnsburg, McHenry Co., St. John the Baptist (1841), Rev. Robert A. Balog.
Res., 2302 W. Church St., McHenry, 60050. Tel: 815-385-1477; Fax: 815-363-3333. [CEM]
School—Tel: 815-385-3959; Fax: 815-363-3337. Pamela Dvonch, Prin.
Sisters 1; Lay Teachers 12; Students 251.
Catechesis/Religious Programs—Tel: 815-385-4870. D.R.E.: Sr. Clara Bauman, O.P.; Marge Dickinson.
Students 463.

Lee, Lee Co., St. James (1878), Rev. Norbert B. Weber, M.S.C.
Res., P.O. Box 108, 60530. Tel: 815-824-2053; Fax: 815-824-8488. [CEM 2]
Catechesis/Religious Programs—Tel: 815-824-8389.
Students 98.

Lena, Stephenson Co., St. Joseph (1870), Rev. Michael A. Librandi.
Res., 410 W. Lena St., 61048. Tel: 815-369-2810; Fax: 815-369-9137. [CEM]
Catechesis/Religious Programs—Tel: 815-443-2892. Louise Kloepping, D.R.E.
Students 122.

Loves Park, Winnebago Co., St. Bridget (1946), Rev. Msgr. John J. Mitchell; Rev. Akan S. Simon. In res., Rev. John J. Calkins.
Res., 600 Clifford Ave., 61111. Tel: 815-633-6311; Fax: 815-633-6314.
School—604 Clifford Ave., 61111. Tel: 815-633-8255; Fax: 815-633-5847. Sr. Mary Ann Hettel, S.S.C.M., Prin.
Religious 1; Lay Teachers 22; Students 485.
Catechesis/Religious Programs—Tel: 815-633-4006.
Students 370.

McHenry, McHenry Co., Church of Holy Apostles (1989), Rev. Robert N. Sherry; Deacons Joseph Phelan; Kenneth McNealy.
Church—5211 W. Bull Valley Rd., 60050. Tel: 815-385-5673; Fax: 815-385-6045.
Catechesis/Religious Programs—Tel: 815-385-4273. Jeanne Fraser, D.R.E.
Students 727.

St. Mary (1894) (German), Rev. Thomas E. Burr.
Res., 1401 N. Richmond Rd., 60050. Tel: 815-385-0024; Fax: 815-385-7809. [CEM]
School—Montini-Middle Grades, 1405 N. Richmond Rd., 60050. Tel: 815-385-1022.
Lay Teachers 9; Students 214. School Sisters of St. Francis, Tel: 815-385-0407. Mrs. Sheila Murphy, Prin.
Catechesis/Religious Programs—Tel: 815-385-2959. Anne Chrzan, D.R.E.
Students 177.

St. Patrick (1840) (Irish), Rev. Stephen K. Potter.
Res., 3500 W. Washington St., 60050. Tel: 815-385-0025; Fax: 815-385-0861. [CEM 2]
School—Montini Primary Center, Tel: 815-385-5380; Fax: 815-385-5017. Mrs. Sheila Murphy, Prin.; Mrs. Luann Gavula, Asst. Prin.
Sisters 1; Lay Teachers 27; Students 557.
Catechesis/Religious Programs—Tel: 815-385-2959. Anne Chrzan, D.R.E.
Students 389.

Maple Park, DeKalb Co., St. Mary (1850), Rev. Msgr. William J. Clausen.
Mailing Address: 123 S. County Line Rd., 60151-8024.
Res., 205 S. County Line Rd., 60151-8024. Tel: 815-827-3218; Fax: 815-827-3218.
Novak Center: 211 S. County Line Rd., 60151-8024. Tel: 815-827-3205. [CEM 2]
Catechesis/Religious Programs—Students 113.

Marengo, McHenry Co., Sacred Heart (1902), Rev. Msgr. Philip E. O'Neil; Deacon Robert Anchor.
Res., 323 N. Taylor St., 60152. Tel: 815-568-7878; Fax: 815-568-7929. [CEM]
Catechesis/Religious Programs—Tel: 815-568-6230. D.R.E.: Robert Olsen; Christine Murphy.
Students 463.

Maytown, Lee Co., St. Patrick (1840), Rev. Thomas P. Dolan.
Res., P.O. Box 130, Harmon, 61042. Tel: 815-359-7819. [CEM][JC 2]
Catechesis/Religious Programs—Students 20.

Menominee, Jo Daviess Co., Nativity of the Blessed Virgin Mary (1864), Rev. Theodore V. Lewandowski, Admin.
Res., 15406 W. Creek Valley Rd., East Dubuque, 61025. Tel: 815-747-3676; Fax: 815-747-3670. [CEM]
School—15390 W. Creek Valley Rd., Tel: 815-747-3670. Louise McCormick, Prin.
Lay Teachers 4; Students 100.

Morrison, Whiteside Co., St. Mary (1904), Rev. Leo J. Bartel.
Office: 126 E. Lincolnway, P.O. Box 248, 61270. Tel: 815-772-3095; Fax: 815-772-4890.
Res., 611 Greenwood Dr., 61270. Tel: 815-772-3095.
Catechesis/Religious Programs—Tel: 815-772-4890.
Students 110.

Mount Carroll, Carroll Co., SS. John and Catherine (1923). Attended by Savanna. Rev. Timothy J. Seigel.
Res., 314 S. Main St., P.O. Box 193, 61053. Tel: 815-244-1835 (Church); Fax: 815-273-3503.
Catechesis/Religious Programs—Students 73.

North Aurora, Kane Co., Blessed Sacrament (1970), Rev. Msgr. Edward S. Wright, V.F.
Res., 801 Oak St., 60542-1063. Tel: 630-897-1029; Fax: 630-897-1062.
Catechesis/Religious Programs—Sr. Rose Marie Weber, O.S.F., D.R.E.
Students 323.

Oregon, Ogle Co., St. Mary (1862), Rev. William A. Budden.
Mailing Address: P.O. Box 419, 61061. Tel: 815-732-7383; Fax: 815-732-4742.
Res., 303 N. Fourth St., 61061. Tel: 815-732-2234; Fax: 815-732-6332. [CEM]
Catechesis/Religious Programs—Tel: 815-732-7909.
Students 120.

Pecatonica, Winnebago Co., St. Mary (1872) (Irish-German), Rev. Robert J. Sweeney; Deacon Warren LaMont.
Res., 126 W. Fifth St., P.O. Box 656, 61063. Tel: 815-239-1271. [CEM]
Catechesis/Religious Programs—Students 144.

Polo, Ogle Co., St. Mary's (1854), Rev. John A. Hanrahan; Deacon John Gilmour.
Res., 211 N. Franklin Ave., 61064. Tel: 815-946-2535. [CEM]
Catechesis/Religious Programs—Students 75.

Prophetstown, Whiteside Co., St. Catherine (1917), Rev. Daniel E. Peters.
Res., 308 E. Third St., 61277. Tel: 815-537-2077.
Catechesis/Religious Programs—Tel: 815-537-2077. Jan Halpin, D.R.E.
Students 38.
Mission—Erie, Whiteside Co., St. Ambrose, 5th & Main St., Erie, 61250. Tel: 309-659-2781. [JC]

Richmond, McHenry Co., St. Joseph (1930), Rev. Joseph W. Kaiser; Deacon Lawrence Geinosky.
Res., 10519 Main St., 60071. Tel: 815-678-7421; Fax: 815-678-7421. [CEM]

Catechesis/Religious Programs—Tel: 815-678-6961. Roberta Schroeder, D.R.E.
Students 170.

Rochelle, Ogle Co., St. Patrick (1868), Rev. David A. Peck; Deacon Higinio Perez.
Res., 250 Kelley Dr., 61068. Tel: 815-562-2370; Fax: 815-562-5250. [CEM]
Catechesis/Religious Programs—Tel: 815-562-7677. Kalah Williams, D.R.E.
Students 374.

Rock Falls, Whiteside Co., St. Andrew (1950), Rev. Msgr. Thomas L. Dzielak.
Res., 708 10th Ave., 61071. Tel: 815-625-4508; Fax: 815-625-1569. [JC]
School—701 11th Ave., 61071. Tel: 815-625-1456; Fax: 815-625-1569. Mr. Philip D. Bellini, Prin.
Lay Teachers 7; Students 106.
Catechesis/Religious Programs—Tel: 815-625-4508.
Students 62.

St. Charles, Kane Co., St. John Neumann (1977), Rev. Msgr. Robert B. Hoffman; Rev. Edward J. Seisser; Deacons Martin Hetzel; Paul Iwanski; Ronald Williams.
Res., 2900 E. Main St., 60174. Tel: 630-377-2797; Fax: 630-377-2834.
Catechesis/Religious Programs—Tel: 630-377-2803. Jan Donovan, D.R.E.
Students 1,480.

St. Patrick (1851), Revs. Joseph B. Linster; Raymond P. Guthrie; Carl Edward Beekman.
Res. & Church Address: 408 Cedar St., 60174. Tel: 630-584-0092; Fax: 630-513-2246.
School—State St. & Fifth St., Tel: 630-584-6367; Fax: 630-584-9759. Mr. Joseph Battisto, Prin.
Sisters 1; Lay Teachers 24; Students 540.
Catechesis/Religious Programs—Tel: 630-513-2247. D.R.E. Sr. Joelyn Hayes; Patricia Mulheran.
Students 1,700.

Sandwich, DeKalb Co., St. Paul (1925), Rev. John T. Heraty.
Res., 110 N. Eddy St., 60548. Tel: 815-786-9266; Fax: 815-786-2977. [CEM]
Catechesis/Religious Programs—Tel: 815-786-8964.
Students 227.

Savanna, Carroll Co., St. John the Baptist (1884), Rev. Timothy J. Seigel.
Res., 318 Chicago Ave., 61074. Tel: 815-273-3961; Fax: 815-273-3503. [CEM]
Catechesis/Religious Programs—Tel: 815-273-3582.
Students 49.

Scales Mound, Jo Daviess Co., Holy Trinity (1863), Rev. Michael A. Librandi.
Mailing Address: St. Joseph Church, 410 W. Lena St., Lena, 61048. Tel: 815-369-2810; Fax: 815-369-9137. [CEM 2]
Catechesis/Religious Programs—Tel: 815-845-2347. Carol Bilgri, D.R.E.
Students 90.

Shannon, Carroll Co., St. Wendelin (1870), Rev. Michael J. Bolger.
18 S. Linn St., P.O. Box 23, 61078. Tel: 815-864-2548 (Church). [CEM]
Catechesis/Religious Programs—Students 41.

Somonauk, DeKalb Co., St. John the Baptist (1865), Rev. Donald D. DeSalvo.
Res., 320 S. Depot St., Box 276, 60552. Tel: 815-498-2010; Fax: 815-498-2770. [CEM]
Catechesis/Religious Programs—Tel: 815-498-2627.
Students 306.

South Beloit, Winnebago Co., St. Peter (1909), Rev. Msgr. Thomas C. Brady, P.A.; Revs. Carlos Hoffner; Luis Vasquez; Deacon Peter Calgaro.
Res., 620 Blackhawk Blvd., 61080. Tel: 815-389-2024; Fax: 815-389-2024.
School—320 Elmwood Ave., Tel: 815-389-3193. Sr. David Ennis, C.S.A., Prin.
Lay Teachers 10; Students 112.
Catechesis/Religious Programs—Tel: 815-389-9091. Jeanne Pulkrabek, D.R.E.
Students 338.
Mission—Roscoe, Winnebago Co., Church of the Holy Spirit, P.O. Box 478, Roscoe, 61073. Tel: 815-623-6930; Fax: 815-623-6930.

Spring Grove, McHenry Co., St. Peter (1900) (German), Rev. Andrew J. Plesa.
Church—2206 Main St., P.O. Box 129, 60081. Tel: 815-675-2288; Fax: 815-675-6774. [CEM]
Catechesis/Religious Programs—Tel: 815-675-2576.
Students 338.

Sterling, Whiteside Co., Sacred Heart (1870) (German), Rev. Paul C. White.
Res., 2224 Avenue J, 61081. Tel: 815-625-0631; 625-1134; Fax: 815-625-1138. [CEM]
Catechesis/Religious Programs—Tel: 815-625-4385.
Students 75.

St. Mary (1898), Rev. Msgr. Thomas E. Bales, V.F.; Rev. Uriel Lopez; Deacons John Kellen; James Lopez; Jane Olson, Pastoral Assoc.
Res., 507 Ave. B, 61081. Tel: 815-625-0640; Fax: 815-625-1684. [CEM]
School—6 W. Sixth St., Tel: 815-625-2253; Fax: 815-625-8942. Mrs. Rebecca Scmitt Tel: 815-626-6373.
Lay Teachers 24; Students 352.
Catechesis/Religious Programs—600 Ave. B, 61081. Tel: 815-625-6688.
Students 269.

Stockton, Jo Daviess Co., Holy Cross (1893) (German), Rev. Robert W. Jones.
Res., 216 E. Benton Ave., 61085. Tel: 815-947-2545; Fax: 815-947-3705. [CEM]
Catechesis/Religious Programs—Students 106.

Sublette, Lee Co., Our Lady of Perpetual Help, Rev. Edward R. Hughes.
Mailing Address: Box 80, West Brooklyn, 61378. Tel: 815-628-3901. [CEM]
Catechesis/Religious Programs—Students 93.

Sycamore, De Kalb Co., St. Mary (1885), Rev. Frank John Timar, M.S.C.
Res., 244 Waterman St., 60178. Tel: 815-895-3275; Fax: 815-895-4561. [CEM]
School—222 Waterman St., Tel: 815-895-5215. Mrs. Roseann Feldman, Prin.
Lay Teachers 12; Students 191.
Catechesis/Religious Programs—Tel: 815-895-3726.
Students 268.

Tampico, Whiteside Co., St. Mary (1875), Rev. Anthony Pantyra, Admin.; Deacon William Lemmer.
Res., 105 Benton St., P.O. Box 159, 61283. Tel: 815-438-5425. [CEM]
Catechesis/Religious Programs—Students 33.

Virgil, Kane Co., SS. Peter and Paul (1909), Rev. Les Suberi Echevia, Admin.; Deacons Clark Reynolds; Jim Newhouse.
Res., 5 N. 939 Meredith Rd., P.O. Box 26, 60182. Tel: 630-365-6618; Fax: 630-365-6659. [CEM]
Catechesis/Religious Programs—Students 148.

Walton, Lee Co., St. Mary (1913), Rev. Thomas P. Dolan.
Res., P.O. Box 130, Harmon, 61042. Tel: 815-359-7819.
Catechesis/Religious Programs—Students 26.

Warren, Jo Daviess Co., St. Ann (1914), Rev. Miroslaw A. Reikowski.
Res., 608 Railroad St., P.O. Box 665, 61087. Tel: 815-745-2312. [CEM]
Catechesis/Religious Programs—Students 72.

West Brooklyn, Lee Co., St. Mary, Rev. Edward R. Hughes.
Mailing Address: P.O. Box 80, 61378. Tel: 815-628-3901. [CEM]
Catechesis/Religious Programs—Students 34.

Wonder Lake, McHenry Co., Christ the King (1949), Rev. Dorrance E. Tranel.
Res., 5006 E. Wonder Lake Rd., 60097. Tel: 815-653-2561; Fax: 815-653-9401. [CEM]
Catechesis/Religious Programs—Tel: 815-653-2581. Ms. Maureen Mclain, D.R.E.
Students 160.

Woodstock, McHenry Co., Resurrection (1978), Rev. Jerzy Zieba, C.R.
Mailing Address: 2918 S. Country Club Rd., 60098. Tel: 815-338-7330; Fax: 815-338-7365.
Catechesis/Religious Programs—Nancy Neumeister, D.R.E.
Students 153.

St. Mary (1853), Revs. James W. McLoughlin; Michael Gerard Black; Deacons Eugene Wedoff; Hans Rokus.
Res., 312 Lincoln Ave., 60098. Tel: 815-338-3377; Fax: 815-338-3497. [CEM]
School—313 Tryon St., 60098. Tel: 815-338-3598; Fax: 815-338-3408. Mrs. Susan Rancak, Prin.
Lay Teachers 21; Students 349.
Catechesis/Religious Programs—Tel: 815-338-3413. Mrs. Diane O'Donnell, D.R.E.
Students 385.

Chaplains of Public Institutions

ELGIN. *Elgin State Hospital*. Vacant. 750 S. State St., 60123.

MOOSEHEART. *School of the Loyal Order of Moose*. Vacant. 301 Fifth Ave., 60539.

ST. CHARLES. *Illinois State Youth Center*. Records kept at St. Patrick, St. Charles. Chapel of the Immaculate Conception.

Special Assignment:
Reverend Monsignors—
Barr, Eric R., Vicar for Clergy & Religious, 1226 N. Church St., Rockford, IL 61103. Tel: 815-965-5767
Kagan, David D., Vicar Gen., Moderator of the Curia, 1245 N. Court St., P.O. Box 7044, Rockford, IL 61126-7044. Tel: 815-962-3709
Reverend Fathers—
Fuller, Michael J.K., Graduate Dept., Pontifical North American College, Casa Santa Maria, Via dell' Umilta, 30, Rome 00187 Italy
Maldonado, Leonardo, Hispanic Ministry for McHenry County, 235 Washington St., Woodstock, IL 60098. Tel: 815-338-8312
Naill, Joseph P., Sec. to the Bishop, 1245 N. Court St., P.O. Box 7044, Rockford, IL 61126-7044. Tel: 815-962-3709
Slampak, John A., Office of Divine Worship, 921 W. State St., Rockford, IL 61102. Tel: 815-963-0344
Very Rev. Msgr.—
Nelson, Glenn L., Chancellor, 1245 N. Court St., P.O.Box 7044, Rockford, IL 61126-7044. Tel: 815-962-3709

Active Outside the Diocese:
Reverend Fathers—
Donahugh, Donald E., 100 Gifford Pond Ln., Port Arthur, TX 77642
Myers, William F., 17445 S.W. 254 St., Homestead, FL 33031
Simonini, Michael F., St. Bernard, 1617 W. Pine St., Appleton, WI 54914. Tel: 414-739-0331

On Disability Leave:
Reverend Fathers—
Joffe, William I.

Absent on Leave:
Reverend Fathers—
Holdren, John C.
Tripodi, Frank J.
Wakitsch, Randall
Waser, Frank A.

Retired:
Reverend Monsignors—
McNamee, Charles W., Pastoral Assoc., Unit 15, 4718 Covey Ridge Ct., Loves Park, IL 61111. Tel: 815-639-9690
Reverend Fathers—
Becker, Anthony J., Vianney Oaks, 7712 E. McGregor Rd., Rockford, IL 61102
Calkins, John J., 600 Clifford Ave., Loves Park, IL 61111. Tel: 815-633-6311
Falcone, Emilio, PSC2 Box 7192, APO, AE 09012
Fitzgibbons, Al. L., 7527 N. Menominee Rd., East Dubuque, IL 61025. Tel: 815-747-3387
Gorinas, Vytautas, 700 S. Pauline, Apt. 1004, Chicago, IL 60612. Tel: 312-738-0788
Guagliardo, Salvatore J., Vianney Oaks, 7712 E. McGregor Rd., Rockford, IL 61102. Tel: 815-963-5618
Hiller, Everett J., 2520 W. Council Hill Rd., Scales Mound, IL 61075
Knott, William P., 15528 W. Sky Hawk Dr., Sun City West, AZ 85375. Tel: 602-214-2520
Kraemer, John A., 6167 N. Broadway, Unit 417, Chicago, IL 60660. Tel: 773-561-9857
Kriegsmann, William A., 1439 Rohde, Berkeley, IL 60163. Tel: 708-544-3039
Larson, James F., 1226 N. Church St., Rockford, IL 61103. Tel: 815-963-4346
London, Lawrence, Vianney Oaks, 7712 E. McGregor Rd., Rockford, IL 61102. Tel: 815-963-4820
McCarren, Charles K., Cor Mariae Center, 3330 Maria Linden Dr., Rockford, IL 61114
McGowan, John J., Health Center, 5100 John Ryan Blvd., #108, San Antonio, TX 78245. Tel: 512-677-8855
McKinstra, William M., 428 N. Second St., Rockford, IL 61107. Tel: 815-962-1214
McKitrick, James V., N.1555 Shadow Ln., Fontana, WI 53125. Tel: 262-275-6711
Millen, Edwin F., 615 Gates Ave., Aurora, IL 60505. Tel: 630-906-6558
Monahan, Thomas J., 2696 Aldersgate Dr., Rockford, IL 61103. Tel: 815-282-9972
Murphy, James L., 4449 Charles St., Rockford, IL 61108. Tel: 815-397-8126
Neville, Thomas W., Vianney Oaks, 7712 E. McGregor Rd., Rockford, IL 61102. Tel: 815-965-1108
Nilges, Harold L., 350 S. Stott St., Genoa, IL 60135. Tel: 815-784-4837
Peterson, William F., 147 Shadowood Dr., Martinez, GA 30907. Tel: 706-860-4738
Petit, Edmund P., 111 W. Park Ave., Aurora, IL 60506. Tel: 630-897-8052
Ratazak, Bernard A., Vianney Oaks, 7712 E. McGregor Rd., Rockford, IL 61102. Tel: 815-965-0910
Regnier, William H., Cor Mariae Center, 3330 Maria Linden Dr., Rockford, IL 61114. Tel: 815-633-4573

Rennell, Albert F., 1060 N. Farnsworth Ave., Apt. 1104, Aurora, IL 60505. Tel: 708-898-0664
Richter, Norbert M., 1230 Hillcrest Dr., Freeport, IL 61032. Tel: 815-232-6765
Rudden, Matthew T., P.O. Box 4111, Rockford, IL 61110. Tel: 815-964-5422
Schlade, Joseph F., 1109 N. Ashland Ave., Chicago, IL 60622. Tel: 312-384-7967
Shindelar, Vincent J., Vianney Oaks, 7712 E. McGregor Rd., Rockford, IL 61102. Tel: 815-962-9132
Thennes, Clarence J., 659 E. Jefferson St., Freeport, IL 61032. Tel: 815-232-6181
Urbaniak, Lawrence M., 4210 W. Marshall Ave., Phoenix, AZ 85019
Verstynen, Robert J., 4444 Brendenwood Rd., Rockford, IL 61107. Tel: 815-394-0447
Vlasz, Melvyn J., 4060 Hidden Hollow Dr., Unit C, Gainsville, GA 30506. Tel: 770-297-0752

Permanent Deacons:
Anchor, Robert, Sacred Heart, Marengo
Bach, John, St. Monica, Carpentersville
Barone, Frank, St. Anthony of Padua, Rockford
Beer, Terry, Christ the Teacher, DeKalb
Berard, Samuel, St. Parick, Dixon
Boyes, Eugene, (Retired)
Bracken, Robert, Holy Family, Rockford
Brandenburg, Robert, St. Patrick, Dixon
Brunette, Donald J., St. Thomas, Freeport
Buga, John, Port Richey, FL
Calgaro, Peter, St. Peter, South Beloit; Church of the Holy Spirit, Roscoe
Callahan, Donald J., St. James, Belvidere
Cassaro, Sam, St. Anthony of Padua, Rockford
Ciochon, Thaddeus, (Retired)
Cooper, Charles, St. Peter Cathedral, Rockford
Cordes, Luke, (Retired)
Cristoforo, Michael, St. Peter Cathedral, Rockford
Czerniewski, Martin, St. Peter Cathedral, Rockford
Dean, William, St. James, Rockford
Demming, Robert, Lake Wales, FL
Devine, John E., Houston, TX
Dinneen, Richard, St. Thomas Aquinas, Freeport
Dolan, Robert J., (Retired)
Dombek, James, Christ the Teacher, DeKalb
Drees, Vincent, St. Thomas Aquinas, Freeport
Ekstrom, Richard, St. Mary, McHenry
Felix, Ignacio, St. Rita of Cascia, Aurora
Fischer, Howard, St. Margaret Mary, Algonquin
Frazier, J. Michael, St. Monica, Carpentersville
Freund, Walter, St. Peter, Spring Grove
Gagnon, Charles, St. Elizabeth Ann Seton, Crystal Lake
Ganshow, Howard, SS. Peter & Paul, Cary
Garber, Dennis, St. Monica, Carpentersville
Gartland, William, St. Patrick, St. Charles
Geinosky, Lawrence, St. Joseph, Richmond
Gerdeman, Richard, St. Bernadette, Rockford
Giambalvo, Michael, St. Mary, Elgin
Gilmour, John, St. Mary, Polo
Graw, Ronald, St. Patrick, Rockford
Groom, Richard, Sacred Heart and St. Mary, Aurora
Grossmayer, Simon, St. Margaret Mary, Algonquin
Hainchek, Alex J., (Retired)
Hawksworth, Thomas, Holy Angels, Aurora
Hetzel, Martin, St. John Neumann, St. Charles
Hoefler, Ben, Springfield
Holt, Arthur, St. Patrick, Hartland
Hudzinski, James, St. Stanislaus, Rockford
Hurley, Dan A., Surprise, AZ
Iwanski, Paul, St. John Neumann, St. Charles
Johnson, Raymond R., Annunciation, Aurora
Johnson, William, St. Patrick, St. Charles
Kayser, Joseph, St. Patrick, Hartland
Kellen, John, St. Mary, Sterling
Kohler, John, (Retired)
Koss, Anthony, St. Joseph, Harvard
Krupka, James, London, England
Kulpin, John, St. Patrick, St. Charles
LaMont, Warren R., St. Mary, Pecatonica
LaPlante, Joseph A., Brimley, MI
Lemmer, William, St. Mary, Tampico
Linstad, Richard E., Sr., Moutain Home, AK
Lober, Edward, Holy Cross, Batavia
Lopez, James, St. Mary, Sterling
Magee, Ronald, St. James, Rockford
Maher, Patrick, St. Margaret Mary, Algonquin
Martin, Richard, St. Rita of Cascia, Aurora
Martin, Robert H., (Retired)
Martinez, Armando, St. Joseph, Elgin
McElroy, Robert D., Aurora, IL
McNealy, Kenneth, Holy Apostles, McHenry
McPhee, John, St. Mary, Huntley
Milano, Robert, St. Patrick, Amboy
Mosley, William, (On Duty Outside the Diocese)
Motyka, Larry, Annunciation, Aurora
Muehler, Gerald, (Retired)
Mulcahey, Richard, St. Mary, Durand
Murphy, Melvin J., (Retired)
Navarro, Carlos, St. Peter, Aurora
Newhouse, James, SS Peter & Paul, Virgil
O'Brien, Thomas, St. Mary, Huntley
O'Leary, Jack, St. Joseph, Harvard
Olson, James D., St. James, Belvidere
Perez, Higinio, St. Patrick, Rochelle
Phelan, Joseph, Church of Holy Apostles, McHenry
Plazewski, Robert, St. Thomas More, Elgin
Porter, John, (Retired)
Poss, Harold, Annunciation of the B.V.M., Aurora
Prendergast, John, Schoolcraft, MI
Real, Robert, St. Laurence, Elgin
Rees, William, St. Mary, Aurora
Reilly, Eugene, (Unassigned)
Rokus, Hans, St. Mary, Woodstock
Sauceda, John, St. Joseph, Elgin
Schaffer, Stephen, Montreal, Quebec, CANADA
Skrade, Fred, St. Edward, Rockford
Smith, Daniel, St. James, Belvidere
Smits, Robert, St. Mary, Byron
Statter, Ralph, St. Thomas, Crystal Lake
Szudarski, Norbert, St. Joseph, Aurora
Trost, Ray, Hampshire
Valesano, James J., Our Lady of Good Counsel, Aurora
Verstynen, Lambert, St. Edward, Rockford
Vondra, Edward
Waterman, John, St. Patrick, McHenry
Watermann, Bruce, St. Therese, Aurora
Weaver, Raymond, St. Nicholas, Aurora
Wedoff, Eugene, (Retired)
Welch, Thomas, Holy Family, Rockford
White, Thomas, Holy Angels, Aurora
Whitehead, William, Jr., St. Catherine of Siena, Dundee
Wilbricht, David, St. John the Evangelist, Hanover
Williams, Ronald, St. John Neumann, St. Charles
Zitkus, Lawrence, St. Catherine of Genoa, Genoa

INSTITUTIONS LOCATED IN THE DIOCESE

[A] SEMINARIES, RELIGIOUS OR SCHOLASTICATES

AURORA. *Marmion Abbey*, 850 Butterfield Rd., 60504. Tel: 630-897-7215; Fax: 630-897-0393.
E-mail: vincent58@aol.com
Web site: www.marmion.org
Rt. Rev. Vincent Bataille, O.S.B., Abbot; Very Rev. Kenneth Theisen, O.S.B., Prior. Priests 31; Brothers 16.

WOODSTOCK. *Resurrection Center Retreat House*, 2710 S. Country Club Rd., 60098. Tel: 815-338-1032; Fax: 815-338-1017.
E-mail: rescenter@stans.com
Web site: www2.stans.com/rescenter
Mr. James F. Ivers, Exec. Dir.; Revs. Richard Grek, C.R., Coord., Adult Programs in Spirituality; Gene Majewski, C.R., Spiritual Dir. Priests 2; Sisters 1; Lay Staff 7.

[B] HIGH SCHOOLS, DIOCESAN

ROCKFORD. *Boylan Central Catholic High School*, 4000 St. Francis Dr., 61103. Tel: 815-877-0531; Fax: 815-877-2544.
E-mail: boylan@hughestech.net
Web site: www.boylan.org
Sr. M. Anthony Marelli, O.P., Prin.; Mr. Vincent E. McGuire, Asst. Prin., Student Affairs; Revs. William H. Schwartz, Asst. Prin.; Christopher Kuhn, Spiritual Dir.; Mr. William C. Thumm, Dean of Students; Mr. Dan Appino, Guidance Dir.; Mr. Dennis Hiemenz, Asst. Prin., Academic Affairs; Mrs. Mary Gavan, Admin. Asst. Priests 1; Sisters 1; Lay Teachers 85; Students 1,382.

AURORA. *Aurora Central Catholic High School*, 1255 N. Edgelawn Dr., 60506. Tel: 630-907-0095; Fax: 630-907-1076.
E-mail: AuroraCentralCatholicHS@worldnet.att.net
Rev. F. William Etheredge, Prin.; Mr. Mark Krebs, Asst. Prin. Priests 1; School Sisters of St. Francis 1; Lay Teachers 28; Students 386.

ELGIN. *St. Edward Central Catholic High School*, 335 Locust St., 60123. Tel: 847-741-7535; Fax: 847-741-8658.
E-mail: GeoLaird@aol.com
Dr. George D. Laird, Supt.& Prin.; Donald Huber, Dean of Students; Rev. Max J. Striedl, Asst. Prin. & Spiritual Dir. Priests 5; Lay Teachers 33; Students 460.

FREEPORT. *Aquin Central Catholic Junior-Senior High School*, 1419 S. Galena Ave., 61032. Tel: 815-235-3154; Fax: 815-235-3185.
E-mail: aquinhs@aeroinc.net
Kathleen Runte, Supt. Prin.; Rev. Michael J. Bolger, Asst. Prin. & Chm. Religious Studies Dept. Priests 1; Sisters 1; Lay Teachers 17; Students 167.

STERLING. *Newman Central Catholic High School*, 1101 W. 23rs St., 61081-9002. Tel: 815-625-0500; Fax: 815-625-8444.
E-mail: dloftus@newmancches.org
Mr. Donald E. Loftus, Prin.; Rev. Paul C. White, Asst. Prin. & Spiritual Dir. Priests 2; Lay Teachers 16; Students 238.

WOODSTOCK. *Marian Central Catholic High School*, 1001 McHenry Ave., 60098. Tel: 815-338-4220; Fax: 815-338-4253.
E-mail: tlanders@marian.com
Web site: www.marian.com
Mr. Thomas E. Landers, Supt.; Mr. Charles Rakers, Prin.; Rev. Paul M. Lipinski, Asst. Prin. & Spiritual Dir.; Mr. Charles Maveus, Dean of Students; Mrs. Alana Flatley, Devel. Dir. Priests 1; Sisters 1; Lay Teachers 38; Students 769.

[C] HIGH SCHOOLS, PRIVATE

AURORA. *Marmion Academy*, 1000 Butterfield Rd., 60504. Tel: 630-897-6936; Fax: 630-897-7086.
E-mail: maalumni@marmion.org
Web site: www.marmion.org
Boarding and Day School. Rt. Rev. Vincent Bataille, O.S.B., Abbot & Pres.; Rev. Basil Yender, O.S.B., Headmaster. Benedictines 17; Lay Teachers 31; Students 448.

Rosary High School, 901 N. Edgelawn Ave., 60506. Tel: 630-896-0831; Fax: 630-896-8372.
E-mail: smfarrelly@juno.com
Web site: www.aurora.il.us/rosary/index/html
Sr. M. Megan Farrelly, O.P., Prin.; Sr. Mary Joseph Weigand, O.P., Asst. Prin.; Sandra Iwanski, Chm. Religious Studies. Sisters of St. Dominic 2; Lay Teachers 25; Girls 448.

[D] GENERAL HOSPITALS

ROCKFORD. *Saint Anthony College of Nursing*, 5658 E. State St., 61108. Tel: 815-395-5090; Fax: 815-395-2275.
E-mail: Terriburch@sacn
Web site: www.sacn.edu
For a complete listing, refer to the Hospitals section.

Saint Anthony Medical Center, 5666 E. State St., 61108. Tel: 815-226-2000; Fax: 815-395-5449.
E-mail: info@osfhealth.com
Web site: osfhealth.com
For a complete listing, refer to the Hospitals section.

AURORA. *Provena Mercy Center*, 1325 N. Highland Ave., 60506. Tel: 630-859-2222; Fax: 630-859-9014
For a complete listing, refer to the Hospitals section.

ELGIN. *Provena St. Joseph Hospital*, 77 N. Airlite St., 60123. Tel: 847-695-3200; Fax: 847-888-5475.
E-mail: edhunter@provena.org
Web site: www.provenasaintjoseph.org
For a complete listing, refer to the Hospitals section.

[E] SCHOOLS FOR EXCEPTIONAL ADOLESCENTS AND ADULTS

FREEPORT. *St. Vincent's Community Living Facility and Supported Living Arrangement*, 659 E. Jefferson St., 61032. Tel: 815-232-6181; Fax: 815-232-6143. Ms. Diane Cushman, Prog. Dir.; Rev. Clarence J. Thennes, Chap. Sisters 2; Patients assisted annually 35.

[F] HOMES FOR AGED AND ADULT DAY CARE CENTERS

ROCKFORD. *Provena Cor Mariae Center*, 3330 Maria Linden Dr., 61114. Tel: 815-877-7416; Fax: 815-877-4299.
E-mail: cormariaectr@aol.com
For a complete listing, refer to the Special Care Facilities section.

Provena St. Anne Center, 4405 Highcrest Rd., 61107. Tel: 815-229-1999; Fax: 815-229-1560
For a complete listing, refer to the Special Care Facilities section.

St. Anne Place, 4444 Brendenwood Rd., 61107. Tel: 815-399-6167; Fax: 815-399-6169.
E-mail: eric@stanneplace.org
Web site: www.stanneplace.org
For a complete listing, refer to the Special Care Facilities section.

Vianney Oaks, 7712 E. McGregor Rd., 61102. Tel: 815-965-0910
For a complete listing, refer to the Special Care Facilities section.

AURORA. *Provena Fox Knoll*, 421 N. Lake St., 60506. Tel: 630-844-0380; Fax: 630-844-0702
For a complete listing, refer to the Special Care Facilities section.

FREEPORT. *Provena St. Joseph Adult Day Care Services*, 659 E. Jefferson St., 61032. Tel: 815-266-8067; Fax: 815-232-6143
For a complete listing, refer to the Special Care Facilities section.

Provena St. Joseph Center, 659 E. Jefferson St., 61032. Tel: 815-232-6181; Fax: 815-232-6143
For a complete listing, refer to the Special Care Facilities section.

GENEVA. *Provena Geneva Care Center*, 1101 E. State St., 60134. Tel: 630-232-7544; Fax: 630-232-4409
For a complete listing, refer to the Special Care Facilities section.

ST. CHARLES. *Provena Pine View Care Center*, 611 Allen Ln., 60174. Tel: 630-377-2211; Fax: 630-377-4352.
Web site: Provenahealth.com
For a complete listing, refer to the Special Care Facilities section.

WHEATON. *Assisi Homes-Batavia Apartments, Inc.*, 26 W. 171 Roosevelt Rd., 60189. Tel: 708-462-9271
For a complete listing, refer to the Special Care Facilities section.

[G] MONASTERIES AND RESIDENCES OF PRIESTS AND BROTHERS

AURORA. *Marmion Abbey-St. Augustine's Abbey*, 850 Butterfield Rd., 60504. Tel: 630-897-7215; Fax: 630-897-0393.
E-mail: vincent58@aol.com
Web site: www.marmion.org
Legal Title: *Marmion*. Rt. Revs. Vincent Bataille, O.S.B., Abbot; Gerald Benkert, O.S.B., Abbot Emeritus; David J. Cyr, O.S.B., Abbot Emeritus; Very Rev. Kenneth Theisen, O.S.B., Prior; Revs. Barnabas Lundergan, O.S.B.; Andrew Wahmhoff, O.S.B.; Bede Stocker, O.S.B.; Alcuin Deck, O.S.B.; Luke Bohr, O.S.B.; Augustine Jones, O.S.B.; Martin Witting, O.S.B.; Hugh Schuck, O.S.B.; Terence Stanton, O.S.B.; Matthias Zinkan, O.S.B.; Bernard Schaefer, O.S.B.; Gregory Obee, O.S.B.; Philip Kremer, O.S.B.; Mario Pedi, O.S.B.; Francis Daleiden, O.S.B.; David Palmatier, O.S.B.; Charles Reichenbacher, O.S.B.; Basil Yender, O.S.B.; Joel Rippinger, O.S.B.; Christian Pusateri, O.S.B.; Michael Burrows, O.S.B.; John Brahill, O.S.B.; Thomas McLaughlin, O.S.B.; Rene Otzoy Colaj, O.S.B.; Cristobal Coche Quic; George Glover, O.S.B.; Frederick Peterson, O.S.B. Priests 31; Brothers 16.

Missionaries of the Sacred Heart Community, 305 S. Lake St., 60507. Tel: 630-892-2371; Fax: 630-892-1678.
E-mail: PROMSC@aol.com
Web site: www.misacor-usa.org
Provincial Administrative Office of the Missionaries of the Sacred Heart. Very Rev. David Foxen, M.S.C., Prov. Supr.; Revs. Edward Ball, M.S.C.; Peter E. Campbell, M.S.C.; David DeLuca, M.S.C.; Raymond Diesbourg, M.S.C.; Anthony Gendusa, M.S.C.; Joseph Jablonski, M.S.C.; Ronald Leinen, M.S.C.; Joseph Muller, M.S.C.; Gerald Paul, M.S.C.; Leo Petit, M.S.C.; Frank John Timar, M.S.C.; Norbert B. Weber, M.S.C.; Mark Zacker, M.S.C.; Bros. George Farkas, M.S.C.; James Hall, M.S.C.; Nicholas Lanese, M.S.C. Priests 14; Brothers 3.
Priests of the Province Serving Elsewhere - In Bogota, Colombia: Very Rev. German Barona, M.S.C., Sectional Supr.; Revs. Howard Fath, M.S.C.; Luis Alfonso Segura, M.S.C.; Tito Medina, M.S.C.; Michael Miller, M.S.C.; Wilson Tascon, M.S.C. In Papua, New Guinea. Revs. Hilary Fischer, M.S.C.; Joseph Gleixner, M.S.C.; Richard Kennedy, M.S.C.; Bernard Miller, M.S.C.; Leon Weisenberger, M.S.C.; Bros. Anton Frietas, M.S.C.; James Miller, M.S.C.; Patrick O'Hara, M.S.C.; Daniel Rakow, M.S.C.; Joseph Tesar, M.S.C. In Issoudun, France: Rev. Mark McDonald, M.S.C. In the Marshall Islands: Rev. James Campbell, M.S.C. In Rome, Italy. Bro. Michael Tomcics, M.S.C.

MCHENRY. *Villa Desiderata Retreat House*, 3015 N. Bayview Ln., 60050. Tel: 815-385-2264. Rev. Daniel F. Reardon, C.S.V., Resident Priest; Bro. Patrick Drohan, C.S.V., Facilities Mgr.

[H] CONVENTS AND RESIDENCES FOR SISTERS

ROCKFORD. *The Poor Clares of Rockford*, Corpus Christi Monastery, 2111 S. Main St., 61102-3591. Tel: 815-963-7343; Fax: 815-963-7369. Franciscan Colettine Poor Clares. Mother Mary Regina Dice, P.C.C., Abbess; Rev. Msgr. Al F. Harte, Chap., Res., 2223 S. Main St., 61102. Tel: 815-964-5003. Cloistered Sisters 20; Extern Sisters 1.

AURORA. *Provena McAuley Manor*, 400 W. Sullivan Rd., 60506. Tel: 630-859-3700; Fax: 630-264-1862. Legal Title: *Provena Senior Services dba Provena McAuley Manor*. Rev. James A. Boyle, Admin.; Sr. Judy Niemet, Asst. Admin. Nursing Care for the Aged, Chronically Ill or Invalid. Bed Capacity 87.

BATAVIA. *Holy Heart of Mary Novitiate*, 717 N. Batavia Ave., 60510. Tel: 630-879-1296; Fax: 630-879-7831.
E-mail: hatton@inil.com
Web site: www.inil.com/users/hatton
Servants of the Holy Heart of Mary. Sr. Linda K. Hatton, S.S.C.M., Supr. & Formation Dir. Professed Sisters 6; Candidate 1; Novices 2.

FREEPORT. *Congregation of the Sisters of the Immaculate Heart of Mary, Mother of Christ-Nigeria*, 1209 South Walnut St., 61032. Tel: 815-297-8287. Sr. M. Providentia Marinze, Regional Supr.

ST. CHARLES. *Our Lady of Creek Bend*, 37 W. 584 Dean St., 60175. Tel: 630-584-5699. Felician Sisters Residence. Sisters 4.

[I] COMMUNITY SERVICES

ROCKFORD. *St. Elizabeth's Catholic Community Center*, 1536 S. Main St., 61102. Tel: 815-969-6526; Fax: 815-969-6522. Mr. Thomas McKenna, Consultant. Total Staff 18; Total assisted 25,028.

AURORA. *Hesed House, Inc.*, 659 S. River St., 60506. Tel: 630-897-2156; Fax: 630-801-9759.
E-mail: hesedhouse@ntsource.com
Sr. Rose Marie Lorentzen, B.V.M., Exec. Dir. Ecumenical Center for ministry to the poor. Total assisted 244,095.

Public Action to Deliver Shelter, Inc. (PADS), 659 S. River St., 60506. Tel: 630-897-2165; Fax: 630-801-9759.
E-mail: hesedhouse@ntsource.com
Sr. Rose Marie Lorentzen, B.V.M., Exec. Dir. Ecumenical advocacy, overnight and transitional shelters and daytime drop-in center for homeless persons. Total Assisted 37,331.

[J] RETREAT HOUSES

ROCKFORD. *Bishop Lane Retreat Center*, 7708 E. McGregor Rd., 61102. Tel: 815-965-5011; Fax: 815-965-5811. Lorrie Gramer, Dir.

[K] FOUNDATIONS

ROCKFORD. *Boylan Educational Foundation, Inc.*, 4000 St. Francis Dr., 61103. Tel: 815-877-8008; Fax: 815-877-2544.

The Catholic Foundation for the People of the Diocese of Rockford, 921 W. State St., 61102. Tel: 815-964-6711; Fax: 815-968-2308.
E-mail: plannedgiving@mindspring.com
Web site: stewardshiprockford.com
Mr. John Sentovich, Exec. Dir.

AURORA. *Aurora Catholic Education Foundation*, P.O. Box 234, 60507. Tel: 630-898-2998.

Provena Mercy Foundation of Aurora, 1325 N. Highland Ave., 60506. Tel: 630-801-2662; Fax: 630-801-5621.
E-mail: ChristinesBork@ProvenaHealth.com
Web site: provenamercy.com
Ms. Christine Bork, Exec. Dir.

CRYSTAL LAKE. *St. Thomas the Apostle School Foundation, Inc.*, 272 King St., 60014. Tel: 815-455-5400; Fax: 815-455-2733.

DEKALB. *Newman Center of Northern Illinois University Educational Program*, 512 Normal Rd., 60115. Tel: 815-787-7770; Fax: 815-753-2053.
E-mail: sknox1@niu.edu
Web site: www.niu.student_orgs/newman/newman.html
Legal Title: *Newman Center of Northern Illinois University Educational Program and Development Fund, Inc.* Total Staff 11.

ELGIN. *St. Edward Central Catholic High School Education Foundation*, 100 Perry St., 60123. Tel: 847-695-4653; Fax: 847-695-4682.
E-mail: StEdMarket@aol.com
Margaret Floyd, Foundation Chairperson.

FREEPORT. *Education Through the 90's Foundation*, 1419 S. Galena Ave., 61032. Tel: 815-235-3154; Fax: 815-235-3185.
E-mail: aquinhs@aeroinc.net
The foundation provides financial support for the Freeport Catholic School System.

Freeport Catholic Education Foundation, 1419 S. Galena Ave., 61032. Tel: 815-235-3154; Fax: 815-235-3185.
E-mail: aquinhs@aeroinc.net
The foundation provides financial support for the Freeport Catholic School System.

STERLING. *Sauk Valley Catholic Education Foundation*, 1101 St. Mary's Rd., 61081. Tel: 815-626-5570; Fax: 815-626-5570.
E-mail: mhenson@roe55.K12.IL.US

Sauk Valley Area Religious Education Center, 1101 St. Mary Rd., 61081. Tel: 816-626-5570; Fax: 816-626-5570.

SYCAMORE. *St. Mary's Educational Foundation, Ltd.*, 244 Waterman St., 60178. Tel: 815-895-3275; Fax: 815-895-4561.

WOODSTOCK. *McHenry County Catholic Education Foundation*, 1005 McHenry Ave., 60098. Tel: 815-338-4220; Fax: 815-338-4253.
E-mail: tlanders@marian.com
Mr. Thomas Landers, Exec. Officer.

[L] NEWMAN CENTERS

DEKALB. *Newman Foundation for Catholic Students of Northern Illinois University*, 512 Normal Rd., 60115. Tel: 815-787-7770; Fax: 815-758-2053.
E-mail: sknox1@niu.edu
Web site: www.niu.edu/student_orgs/newman/newman/html.
Revs. Stephen J. Knox, Dir. Campus Ministries; Addison H. Hart, Assoc. Dir. Campus Ministries. Pastoral Assocs.: Mr. Terry Beer; Ms. Mary Sue Seibert; Ms. Jenna Regis.

[M] MISCELLANEOUS

ROCKFORD. *Catholic Diocese of Rockford, Mary's Messengers*, P.O. Box 8834, 61126. Tel: 815-874-7678. 3224 Ironwood Ave., 61109. Connie Austin, Contact & Chairwoman.

Catholic Office of the Deaf, 1245 N. Court St., P.O. Box 7044, 61126. Tel: 815-962-3709 (Voice); 962-2994 (TTY); Fax: 815-968-2824.
E-mail: RockfordHI@aol.com
Web site: members.aol.com/RockfordHI

National Association of Diaconate Directors, 1204 N. Church St., 61103. Tel: 815-965-0075; Fax: 815-965-0085.
E-mail: NADD@Execpc.com
Web site: NADD.fp.execpc.com

Vineyard Books, Gifts & Church Supplies, Highcrest Centre, 1638 N. Alpine Rd., 61107. Tel: 815-398-4030; Fax: 815-398-8477; 1-800-587-9777.
E-mail: books4cath@aol.com
Joann Toti, Mgr. Total Staff 11.

AURORA. *Association of the Communications Congregation*, P.O. Box 1775, 60507. Tel: 630-859-3657; Fax: 630-859-3657.
E-mail: evangelization@aol.com
Rev. Dennis Brown, Primary Supvr.

Joseph Corporation of Illinois, Inc., P.O. Box 525, 60507. Tel: 630-906-9400; Fax: 630-906-9406.
E-mail: joco@xnet.com
(Ecumenical not-for-profit housing developer). Gregory Schiefelbin, Exec. Dir.; Jerria Donelson, Admin. Asst.; Leticia Lara-Reyes, Dir. of Home Ownership Educ.; Jesus Fernandez, Dir. of Neighborhood Lending.

MOUNT CARROLL. *Samaritan Homecare / Hospice*. Sponsor: Mercy Health Services, Sisters of Mercy, Regional Community of Detroit, 102 E. Washington St., 60153. Tel: 815-244-2749; Fax: 815-244-2839.
E-mail: noej@mercyhealth.com
Vicki Johnson, R.N., B.S.N., Dir.; Joan Noe, Admin.; Tom Hesselmann, Pres.

ST. CHARLES. *Cultivation Ministries*, P.O. Box 662, 60174. Tel: 630-513-8222; Fax: 630-513-8233.
E-mail: info@cultivationministries.com
Web site: www.cultivationministries.com
Frank Mercadante, Exec. Dir. To cultivate team-based, comprehensive, and disciple-making Catholic youth ministries by training, resourcing and supporting adult and student leaders.

Queen of Americas Guild, 345 Kautz Rd., P.O. Box 851, 60174. Tel: 630-584-1822; Fax: 630-584-0648. Most Rev. Joseph J. Madera, M.Sp.S., Bishop for the Archdiocese for the Military Services, USA, Episcopal Moderator; Mr. Frank Smoczynski, Pres.; Mr. Stephen Banaszak, Vice Pres.; Mr. Alan Napleton, Sec.; Beverly Smoczynski, Treas. & Dir.
Board of Directors: Revs. Christopher Rengers, O.F.M.Cap.; Jacob Joerger, O.P.; George M. Hastrich; Sr. M. Theresa Alonso, M.C.M.; Mrs. Ruth Sloan.

STERLING. *St. Vincent DePaul Society*. Tel: 815-625-0311. St. Mary's Conference, 600 Ave. B, 61081. Tel: 815-625-0640; Fax: 815-625-1684. Total Staff 15; Total assisted 2,719.

STOCKTON. *Christ in the Wilderness*, 7500 S. Randecker Rd., 61085-8922. Tel: 815-947-2476. Frank Schwirtz, Dir., Center of Solitude and Prayer.

RELIGIOUS INSTITUTES OF MEN REPRESENTED IN THE DIOCESE

For further details refer to the corresponding bracketed number in the Religious Institutes of Men or Women section.

[0200]—*Benedictine Monks.* (Marmion Abbey, Aurora).—O.S.B.

[1320]—*Clerics of St. Viator.*—C.S.V.

[1080]—*Congregation of the Resurrection.* (Chicago Prov.).—C.R.

[0480]—*Conventual Franciscans.* (St. Bonaventure Province).—O.F.M.Conv.

[0520]—*Franciscan Friars.* (Assumption of the B.V.M. Prov.).—O.F.M.

[]—*Institute of Christ the King Sovereign Priest (Provincial House-Italy).*

[0720]—*The Missionaries of Our Lady of La Salette.*—M.S.

RELIGIOUS INSTITUTES OF WOMEN REPRESENTED IN THE DIOCESE

[]—*Auxiliaries of the Blessed Sacrament.*—A.S.B.
[0230]—*Benedictine Sisters.*—O.S.B.
[0350]—*Carmelite Sisters (Corpus Christi).*—O.Carm.
[2100]—*Congregation of the Humility of Mary.*—C.H.M.
[1920]—*Congregation of the Sisters of the Holy Cross.*—C.S.C.
[1710]—*Congregation of the Third Order of St. Francis of Mary Immaculate.*—O.S.F.
[1070-02]—*Dominican Sisters.*—O.P.
[1070-03]—*Dominican Sisters.*—O.P.
[1070-10]—*Dominican Sisters.*—O.P.
[1070-13]—*Dominican Sisters.*—O.P.
[1070-01]—*Dominican Sisters of St. Catharine.*—O.P.
[1170]—*Felician Sisters.*—C.S.S.F.
[2575]—*Institute of the Sisters of Mercy of the Americas.* (Chicago, IL).—R.S.M.
[]—*Mexican Passionist Sisters.*—C.F.P.
[2865]—*Missionaries of the Sacred Heart & Our Lady of Guadalupe.*—M.S.C.Gpe.
[2790]—*Missionary Servants of the Most Blessed Trinity.*—M.S.B.T.
[3760]—*Poor Clare Colettines.*—P.C.C.
[2970]—*School Sisters of Notre Dame.*—S.S.N.D.
[1680]—*School Sisters of St. Francis.*—O.S.F.
[3520]—*Servants of the Holy Heart of Mary.*—S.S.C.M.
[0430]—*Sisters of Charity of the Blessed Virgin Mary.*—B.V.M.
[2360]—*Sisters of Loretto at the Foot of the Cross.*—S.L.
[2450]—*Sisters of Mary of the Presentation.*—S.M.P.
[3360]—*Sisters of Providence of Saint Mary-of-the-Woods, Indiana.*—S.P.
[3710]—*Sisters of St. Agnes.*—C.S.A.
[1760]—*Sisters of St. Francis.*—O.S.F.
[1705]—*The Sisters of St. Francis of Assisi.*—O.S.F.
[1640]—*Sisters of St. Francis of Perpetual Adoration.*—O.S.F.
[1570]—*Sisters of St. Francis of the Holy Family.*—O.S.F.
[1660]—*Sisters of St. Francis of the Providence of God.*—O.S.F.
[3830-02]—*Sisters of St. Joseph.*—C.S.J.
[3830-15]—*Sisters of St. Joseph.*—C.S.J.
[3930]—*Sisters of St. Joseph of the Third Order of St. Francis.*—S.S.J.-T.O.S.F.
[1970]—*Sisters of the Holy Family of Nazareth.*—C.S.F.N.
[2350]—*Sisters of the Living Word.*—S.L.W.
[1770]—*Sisters of the Third Order of St. Francis.* (Peoria, Illinois).—O.S.F.
[3530]—*Spirit Missionary Sisters.*—S.Sp.S.

DIOCESAN CEMETERIES

ROCKFORD. *Calvary-St. Mary's/St. James.*
AURORA. *Mount Olivet.*
BATAVIA. *Geneva-St. Charles Resurrection.*
ELGIN. *Mount Hope.*
WINNEBAGO. *Calvary.*

NECROLOGY

† Conro, Ronald J., (Retired). —Died Nov. 13, 2000.
† Morrissey, William F., Aurora, IL St. Mary. —Died Nov. 4, 2000.
† Risley, L. Thomas, Carpentersville, IL St. Monica. —Died Jan. 22, 2000.
† Smithes, Donald F., Polo, IL St. Mary. —Died Aug. 9, 2000.

Diocese of Rockville Centre

(Dioecesis Petropolitana In Insula Longa)

Most Reverend

JAMES J. DALY, D.D.

Retired Auxiliary Bishop of Rockville Centre and Vicar General; ordained May 22, 1948; appointed Titular Bishop of Castra Nova and Auxiliary to the Bishop of Rockville Centre February 28, 1977; ordained Bishop May 9, 1977; retired July 1, 1996. *Res., 25 Lanes Rd., Blue Point, NY, 11715.* Tel.: 631-363-5150.

Most Reverend

EMIL A. WCELA, D.D.

Auxiliary Bishop of Rockville Centre and Episcopal Vicar of Eastern Vicariate; appointed Titular Bishop of Filaca and Auxiliary to the Bishop of Rockville Centre October 21, 1988; ordained Bishop December 13, 1988. *Res., Eastern Vicariate - Diocese of Rockville Centre, P.O. Box 780, Riverhead, NY, 11901.* Tel.: 516-369-0071.

(Vacant See)

Chancery Office: 50 N. Park Ave., Rockville Centre, NY, 11570. Tel.: 516-678-5800; Fax: 516-678-1786.

Web site address: drvc.org

E-mail address: chancellor@drvc.org

Most Reverend

JOHN R. McGANN, D.D.

Retired Bishop of Rockville Centre; ordained June 3, 1950; appointed Titular Bishop of Morosbisdus and Auxiliary to the Bishop of Rockville Centre November 12, 1970; ordained Bishop January 7, 1971; appointed Bishop of Rockville Centre May 3, 1976; installed June 24, 1976; retired January 4, 2000. *Res., St. Agnes Cathedral, 29 Quealy Pl., Rockville Centre, NY, 11570.* Tel.: 516-766-0205.

Most Reverend

JOHN C. DUNNE, D.D.

Auxiliary Bishop of Rockville Centre and Episcopal Vicar of Central Vicariate; appointed Titular Bishop of Abercorn and Auxiliary to the Bishop of Rockville Centre October 21, 1988; ordained Bishop December 13, 1988. *Res., Central Vicariate - Diocese of Rockville Centre, P.O. Box 39, Farmingdale, NY, 11735-0039.* Tel.: 516-249-1700.

ESTABLISHED APRIL 6, 1957.

Square Miles 1,222.

THE ROMAN CATHOLIC DIOCESE OF ROCKVILLE CENTRE, NEW YORK.

Comprises the Counties of Nassau and Suffolk (excepting Fishers Island) in the State of New York.

For legal titles of parishes and diocesan institutions, consult the Chancery Office.

STATISTICAL OVERVIEW

Personnel	
Auxiliary Bishops	2
Retired Bishops	2
Priests: Diocesan Active in Diocese	281
Priests: Active Outside Diocese	12
Priests: Diocesan in Foreign Missions	2
Priests: Retired, Sick or Absent	107
Number of Diocesan Priests	402
Religious Priests in Diocese	74
Extern Priests in Diocese	56
Ordinations:	
Diocesan Priests	2
Transitional Deacons	5
Permanent Deacons	11
Permanent Deacons in Diocese	219
Total Brothers	94
Total Sisters	1,433
Parishes	
Parishes	134
With Resident Pastor:	
Resident Diocesan Priests	130
Resident Religious Priests	4
Missions	1
Professional Ministry Personnel:	
Brothers	3
Sisters	265
Lay Ministers	427
Welfare	
Catholic Hospitals	4
Total Assisted	1,219,082
Health Care Centers	34
Total Assisted	175,725
Homes for the Aged	4
Total Assisted	9,462
Residential Care of Children	4
Total Assisted	10,562
Day Care and Extended Day Care Centers	102
Total Assisted	4,322
Specialized Homes	6
Total Assisted	1,326
Special Centers for Social Services	21
Total Assisted	48,706
Residential Care of Disabled	17
Total Assisted	198
Other Institutions	103
Total Assisted	194,000
Educational	
Seminaries, Diocesan	1
Students from This Diocese	19
Students from Other Diocese	19
Students Religious	5
Total Seminarians	24
Colleges and Universities	2
Total Students	5,358
High Schools, Diocesan and Parish	4
Total Students	3,851
High Schools, Private	8
Total Students	7,365
Elementary Schools, Diocesan and Parish	59
Total Students	28,057
Elementary Schools, Private	4
Total Students	1,072
Non-residential Schools for the Disabled	3
Total Students	103
Catechesis/Religious Education:	
High School Students	3,319
Elementary Students	116,331
Total Students Under Catholic Instruction	165,480
Teachers in the Diocese:	
Priests	12
Brothers	53
Sisters	174
Lay Teachers	1,952
Vital Statistics	
Receptions into the Church:	
Infant Baptism Totals	22,522
Adult Baptism Totals	627
Received into Full Communion	517
First Communions	22,181
Confirmations	16,595
Marriages:	
Catholic	5,034
Interfaith	1,331
Total Marriages	6,365
Deaths	13,098
Total Catholic Population	1,404,361
Total Population	3,008,203

Former Bishops—Most Rev. WALTER P. KELLENBERG, D.D., first Bishop of Rockville Centre; ord. June 2, 1928; appt. Titular Bishop of Joannina and Auxiliary Bishop of New York, Aug. 25, 1953; cons. Oct. 5, 1953; appt. Bishop of Ogdensburg, Jan. 19, 1954; appt. first Bishop of Rockville Centre, April 16, 1957; installed May 27, 1957; retired May 3, 1976; died Jan. 11, 1986.—Most Rev. JOHN R. McGANN, D.D., second Bishop of Rockville Centre; ord. June 3, 1950; appt. Titular Bishop of Morosbisdus and Auxiliary to the Bishop of Rockville Centre, Nov. 12, 1970; cons. Jan. 7, 1971; appt. second Bishop of Rockville Centre, May 3, 1976; installed June 24, 1976; retired Jan. 4, 2000.—Most Rev. JAMES T. McHUGH, S.T.D., third Bishop of Rockville Centre; ord. May 25, 1957; appt. Titular Bishop of Morosbisdo and Auxiliary Bishop of Newark, Nov. 20, 1987; cons. Jan. 25, 1988; appt. Bishop of Camden, May 13, 1989; installed June 20, 1989; appt. Coadjutor Bishop of Rockville Centre, Dec. 7, 1998; installed Feb. 22, 1999; succeeded to the See, Jan. 4, 2000; died Dec. 10, 2000.

Diocesan Administrator—Rev. Msgr. JOHN A. ALESANDRO, S.T.L., J.C.D., J.D., *120 Fifth St., Garden City, 11530.* Tel: 516-873-0972; Fax: 516-873-0975.

Diocesan Bishop Emeritus—Most Rev. JOHN R. McGANN, D.D.

Auxiliary Bishops—Most Rev. EMIL A. WCELA, D.D.; Most Rev. JOHN C. DUNNE, D.D.; Most Rev. JAMES J. DALY, D.D., Emeritus.

Secretary to the Bishop—Rev. Msgr. ROBERT J. BRENNAN. Tel: 516-678-5800, Ext. 402; Fax: 516-678-3138.

Episcopal Vicars—Vicar General/Western Vicariate: Rev. Msgr. JOHN A. ALESANDRO, S.T.L., J.C.D., J.D., Central Vicariate: Most Rev. JOHN C. DUNNE, D.D., *P.O. Box 39, Farmingdale, 11735-0039.* Tel: 516-249-1700; Fax: 516-249-1701. Eastern Vicariate: Most Rev. EMIL A. WCELA, D.D., *P.O. Box 780, Riverhead, 11901.* Tel: 631-369-0071; Fax: 631-727-8483.

Chancellor's Office—

Chancellor—Rev. Msgr. FRANCIS J. SCHNEIDER, J.C.D. Tel: 516-678-5800, Ext. 583; Fax: 516-764-3316.

Vice Chancellors—Rev. ROBERT O. MORRISSEY, J.C.D. Tel: 516-678-5800, Ext. 580. Rev. Msgr. ALAN J. PLACA, J.D., Rev. Msgr. ROBERT J. BRENNAN, M.Div., Sr. LUCY BLYSKAL, C.S.J., J.C.D.

Censors of Books—Rev. Msgr. JOHN A. ALESANDRO, S.T.L., J.C.D.; Rev. Msgr. FRANCIS X. GLIMM, S.T.L.; Rev. Msgr. GEORGE P. GRAHAM, J.C.D., Ph.D.; Rev. ROBERT O. MORRISSEY, J.C.D.; Rev Msgr. FRANCIS J. SCHNEIDER, J.C.D.; Rev. ROBERT J. SMITH, S.T.D.

Diocesan Tribunal—50 N. Park Ave., Rockville Centre, 11570. Tel: 516-678-5800; Fax: 516-594-1548.

Judicial Vicar—Rev. Msgr. EDWARD A. SWEENY, M.Div., J.C.D., Ph.D., Ext. 566.

Judicial Vicar Emeritus & Diocesan Judge—Rev. Msgr. MICHAEL MANZELLI, M.A., S.T.L., J.C.D., Ext. 559.

Adjutant Judicial Vicars—Revs. THOMAS V. ARNAO, M.Div., J.C.D., Ext. 558. JAMES F. PEREDA, M.Div., J.C.D., Ext. 565.

Diocesan Judge—Sr. LUCY BLYSKAL, C.S.J., J.C.D.

Judges for Interdiocesan Tribunal—Rev. Msgr. RICHARD C. BAUHOFF, J.C.D., Ph.D.; Rev. Msgr. THOMAS D. CANDREVA, S.T.L., J.C.D.; Rev. Msgr. CHARLES A. GUARINO, M.Div., M.A., J.C.D.; Rev. RICHARD P. KOPINSKI, M.S., M.A.; Rev. Msgr. FRANCIS S. MIDURA, M.Div., M.Ch.A.; Rev. Msgr. THOMAS E. MOLLOY, S.T.B., J.C.D.; Rev. Msgr. JOHN C. NOSSER, M.S.; Rev. JOHN J. TUTONE, M.Div., J.C.D.

Promoter of Justice—Rev. DONALD F. DIEDERICH, J.C.D.

Defenders of the Bond—Sr. LOIS KELLER, R.S.M., J.C.L., Ph.D., Ext. 563. Rev. ANTONIO S. PASCUAL, J.C.L.

Notaries—Sr. RUTH BORGERSEN, R.S.M., M.A.; Mrs. NANNO HAYES; Mrs. HELEN HOWE; Mrs. GRACE ROHE; Mrs. TONI TUZZOLINO.

In-Take Secretary—Mrs. NANNO HAYES, Ext. 571.

Medical Experts—CHRISTOPHER DEEG, Ph.D.; SIMEON RYAN, Ph.D.; JOHN MCDONAGH, Ph.D.; MAUREEN KALEY, Ph.D.; WILLIAM VAN ORNUM, Ph.D.

Coordinator of Post-Annulment Counseling Program—Mrs. BARBARA BUTLER. Tel: 631-754-9765.

Procurator & Advocates—Deacons JOSEPH T. BARTOLOTTO; EDWARD BILLIA; Mrs. MARIAN BOPP; Rev. WILLIAM G. BRESLAWSKI; Sr. MARY JANE BRUSTMAN, C.I.J.; Sr. IMELDA BUETOW, R.G.S.; Mrs. BARBARA BUTLER; Deacon JAMES BUTLER; Sr. HELEN BYRNE, C.S.J.; Deacon FRANCISCO CALES; Mrs. GAIL CARTON; Deacon TONY CEDRONE; Mrs. VIRGINIA CONLIN; Mrs. DOLORES CONNORS; Sr. MIRIAM HONORA CORR, C.S.J.; Rev. THOMAS C. COSTA; Deacons FRANK COVE; ANTHONY CUSEO; Sr. LUCILLE D'AMELIO, O.P.; Deacon GREGORY D'ANGELO; Mr. RICHARD DEMARCO; Rev. JOHN DERASMO; Ms. ANITA DOS SANTOS; Rev. Msgr. JOHN R. DREASEN; Rev. LAWRENCE T. DUNCKLEE; Sr. JUDY ENTERLIN, C.S.J.; Rev. JOHN J. FITZGERALD; Deacon ANDREW GARGIULO; Sr. MARGARET GERARD VON ACHEN, O.P.; Deacon RONALD J. GILLETTE; Rev. THOMAS HAGGERTY; Sr. ANN HORN, O.P.; Sr. BONNIE KELLY, C.S.J.; Sr. JANE LYONS, C.I.J.; Rev. JAMES P. MANNION, JR.; Deacon SALVATORE MARINO; Mr. JOHN J. MARTIN; Mr. JAMES J. MAUNE; Rev. Msgr. JAMES MCDONALD; Mr. STEVE MCGIFF; Deacon JAMES MCQUADE; Rev. Msgr. JOHN J. MIRECKI; Revs. JOSEPH A. MIRRO; JOHN R. MOORE; Deacon CHARLES MUSCARNERA; Mrs. NANCY NEWBERT; Mrs. MARY ANN O'CONNOR; Mr. THOMAS O'CONNOR; Mrs. MARY O'GRADY; Rev. VITALIS PEDZIK; Deacon THOMAS RICH; Ms. VILMA RIVERA; Rev. ROBERT ROMEO; Sr. MARY RONALD, C.S.F.N.; Rev. THOMAS J. ST. PIERRE; Deacon NEIL SQUITIERI; Sr. MARIA STAPLETON, C.S.J.; Rev. JOSEPH W. STAUDT; Mrs. ANN MARY STRIEDER; Sr. KATHLEEN T. SULLIVAN, C.S.J.; EILEEN TRACY; Sr. EUGENIA M. TRAVERS, O.P.; Rev. Msgr. EDMOND J. TRENCH; Sr. PATRICIA TURLEY, C.S.J.; Rev. MICHAEL VETRANO; Sr. ELLEN ZAK, C.S.F.N.; Rev. ANDRZEJ ZGLEJSZEWSKI.

Senate of Priests (Presbyteral Council/College of Consultors)—Most Rev. JOHN C. DUNNE, D.D.; Most Rev. EMIL A. WCELA, D.D.; Rev. Msgr. JOHN A. ALESANDRO, S.T.L., J.C.D., J.D.; Rev. Msgr. JOHN C. NOSSER; Rev. Msgr. ROBERT E. FAGAN; Rev. Msgr. PABLO M. RODRIQUEZ; Rev. Msgr. EDWARD J. DONNELLY; Rev. Msgr. THOMAS L. SPADARO; Rev. Msgr. JAMES MCDONALD; Revs. LAWRENCE CHADWICK; PAUL F. RAHILLY; GERARD LUTTENBERGER, C.M.; THOMAS GROENEWOLD; WILLIAM E. KOENIG; Rev. Msgr. FRANCIS J. SCHNEIDER, Exec. Sec.

Deans—Rockville Centre Deanery: Rev. Msgr. JAMES P. KELLY, North Hempstead Deanery: Rev. KENNETH WINKLER, Oyster Bay Deanery: Rev. Msgr. RICHARD C. BAUHOFF, Belmont Deanery: Rev. Msgr. JOHN R. DREASEN, Hicksville Deanery: Rev. Msgr. JAMES E. BOESEL, Five Towns Deanery: Rev. Msgr. CHARLES R. FINK, Seaford Deanery: Rev. Msgr. ROBERT E. GUGLIEMONE, Huntington Deanery: Rev. Msgr. T. PETER RYAN, Smithaven Deanery: Rev. Msgr. ELLSWORTH R. WALDEN, Babylon Deanery: Rev. Msgr. JAMES M. MCNAMARA, Islip Deanery: Rev. Msgr. JOHN C. NOSSER, North Brookhaven Deanery: Rev. WILLIAM HANSON, South Brookhaven Deanery: Rev. Msgr. THOMAS L. SPADARO, Peconic Deanery: Rev. DONALD J. DESMOND.

Diocesan Offices

Pastoral Center—50 N. Park Ave., Rockville Centre, 11570. Tel: 516-678-5800; Fax: 516-678-1786.

Director of Administration—Mr. KEVIN T. MURPHY. Tel: 516-678-5800, Ext. 404; Fax: 516-678-9647. Mr. MATTHEW BUONOCORE, Internal Auditor, Ext. 291.

Archives—Ms. JEAN WASSONG, *Seminary of the Immaculate Conception, 440 W. Neck Rd., Huntington, 11743.* Tel: 631-423-0483, Ext. 109; 516-678-5800, Ext. 594 (Satellite Office); Fax: 631-423-7922.

Bishop's Annual Appeal—Mrs. KATHY MULVEY, Dir. Tel: 516-678-5800, Ext. 514; Fax: 516-763-5689.

Building Office—CHESTER J. STRZEPEK, Dir. Tel: 516-678-5800, Ext. 603; Fax: 516-594-1128.

Campus Ministry—Rev. JOSEPH J. D'ANGELO, Campus Ministry Dir. Tel: 516-678-5800, Ext. 614.

Catechesis—Mr. GEORGE RAND, Dir. Tel: 516-678-5800, Ext. 506; Fax: 516-255-3786. Sr. ANNE MARIE DEAN, C.S.J., Catechetical Coord.-Eastern Vicariate, Personnel Svcs., Textbook Consultant, Ext. 502. Sr. JOAN MARY FINN, O.P., Coord. Pastoral Ministry for the Deaf, Ext. 205. Sr. SALLY RYAN, R.S.M., Pastoral Ministry for Persons with Disabilities, Catechetical Coord.- Central Vicariate, Ext. 540. Mr. TIMOTHY CARROLL, Adult Catechesis, Catechetical Svc. Awards, Catechetical Coord. Western Vicariate, Ext. 542. Sr. JUDITH O'BRIEN, I.H.M., Coord. Human Sexuality Education, Ext. 229. Vacant, Media Center Asst., Ext. 213.

Catholic Charities—Ms. LAURA A. CASSELL, Exec. Dir., *90 Cherry Ln., Hicksville, 11801.* Tel: 516-733-7013. See separate listing below.

Catholics of African Ancestry—Mrs. VANESSA BAIRD-STREETER, Dir. Tel: 516-678-5800, Ext. 239; Fax: 516-255-3780.

Cemeteries—Mr. NEAL S. BARLIN, Acting Dir., *Catholic Cemeteries, Diocese of Rockville Centre, P.O. Box 182, Westbury, 11590.* Tel: 516-334-7990; Fax: 516-334-4383., *Holy Rood Cemetery, 111 Old Country Rd., Box 182, Westbury, 11590-0182.* Tel: 516-334-7990., *Holy Sepulchre Cemetery, 3442 Rte. 112, Coram, 11727.* Tel: 631-732-3460; Fax: 631-732-3476., *Queen of All Saints Cemetery, 115 Wheeler Rd., Central Islip, 11722.* Tel: 631-234-8297; Fax: 631-234-8632.

Charismatic Renewal—Mr. STEVE BENTHAL, Dir.; Deacon FILIPE J. SIN, Hispanic Charismatic Renewal, *P.O. Box 1301, Brentwood, 11717.* Tel: 631-952-7400; Fax: 631-952-7403.

Consultation Service for Religious Personnel—Sr. THOMAS MORE, R.G.S., Exec. Dir., *P.O. Box 467, Rockville Centre, 11571.* Tel: 516-678-2135.

Deacons—Deacon JAMES W. FLANNERY, Dir. Tel: 516-678-5800, Ext. 607; Fax: 516-678-4347. Deacon GEORGE RIEGGER, Coord., Diaconate Formation, Ext. 282.

Diocesan Attorney—Mr. GEORGE RICE, *Bennette, Rice and Schure, 255 Merrick Rd., P.O. Box 710, Rockville Centre, 11570.* Tel: 516-766-0081; Fax: 516-766-2484.

Diocesan Services, Inc.—Mr. KEVIN T. MURPHY, Dir. Tel: 516-678-5800, Ext. 543.

Due Process (Conciliation-Arbitration)—Sr. LUCY BLYSKAL, C.S.J., J.C.D., Admin., *St. Joseph Renewal Center, 1725 Brentwood Rd., Brentwood, 11717-5587.* Tel: 631-273-1187, Ext. 32; Fax: 631-273-1451.

Ecumenical & Interreligious Affairs—Rev. Msgr. DONALD M. BECKMANN, D.Min., Dir. Tel: 516-678-5800, Ext. 613; Fax: 516-763-1078.

Education—Sr. JOANNE CALLAHAN, O.S.U., M.S., P.D., Supt. Tel: 516-678-5800, Ext. 548; Fax: 516-678-7362. Dr. JOANNE O'BRIEN, M.A., M.Ed., Ed.D., Assoc. Supt., Ext. 546. Sr. KATHLEEN EGAN, C.S.J., Asst. Supt. Public Policy & Govt. Programs, Ext. 555. Mr. BIAGIO ARPINO, M.S., P.D., Dir. Teacher Personnel, Ext. 553. Sr. TERESA RORKE, C.S.J., M.S., P.D., Dir. Regl. School Planning, Ext. 545. Ms. ROSEMARY DAMM, M.A., Dir. Curriculum & Instruction, Ext. 551. Sr. CATHERINE STARE, S.C., M.S., M.A., Dir. Curriculum & Testing, Ext. 550. Sr. ANTOINETTE DE AVEIRO, O.P., M.S., Dir. Early Childhood Programs, Ext. 277. Mrs. PENNY CURRY, M.S., Dir. Technology, Ext. 404.

Family Ministry—Mr. PATRICK DELZOPPO, Ph.D., C.A.S., Dir., Ext. 509. Coords.: Mrs. CATHY DANOWSKI, Parenting Education, Ext. 224. Dr. NANCY M. DEFLON, Retrouvaille and Separated/Divorced Catholics, Ext. 202. Mrs. ELLEN FRANK, Respect Life Ministry, Ext. 221. Mrs. ALYCIA GORMAN, Marriage Preparation, Ext. 223. Ms. MAUREEN RUSSELL, Youth Respect Life Ministry, Ext. 234. Mrs. ELAINE STILLWELL, Bereavement, Ext. 224.

Financial Affairs—Mr. KEVIN T. MURPHY, CFO, Ext. 543; Fax: 516-536-6554.

Finance Department—Vacant, Dir., Ext. 534; Fax: 516-536-6554.

Treasury Operations—Mrs. MAUREEN T. SCADUTO, Dir., Ext. 526; Fax: 516-536-6554.

Risk Management—Mr. WILLIAM G. CHAPIN, Dir., Ext. 261; Fax: 516-763-2606.

Human Resources—Mr. PETER FITZPATRICK, Dir., Ext. 529; Fax: 516-678-9566. Mrs. DOROTHY O'LEARY, Dir. Personnel, Ext. 500.

Diocesan Service, Inc.—Mr. KEVIN T. MURPHY, Sec. & Treas., Ext. 543.

Haitian-American Apostolate Ministry—Rev. MOISE AIME, Dir.; Ms. MARYSE EMMANUEL-GARCY, Coord.; Ms. MARYSE SAJOUS, Sec., *333 N. Main St., Freeport, 11520.* Tel: 516-868-8076; Fax: 516-868-0075.

Health Care Apostolate—Catholic Health Services, One Huntington Quadrangle, Ste. 4CO4, Melville, 11714. Tel: 631-396-2600; Fax: 631-396-5040. Mr. RONALD ALDRICH, Pres. & CEO, Catholic Health Svcs.; Rev. Msgr. ALAN J. PLACA, Bishop's Sec. for Health Affairs, Corp. Sec., Sr. EILEEN DONOVAN, O.P., Dir. Chaplaincy Svcs. Tel: 516-678-5800, Ext. 521. For individual hospitals and other healthcare institutions see separate listings below.

Information Bureau—Mrs. JOANNE C. NOVARRO, Dir., Office Public Information, Ext. 632; Fax: 516-594-0984.

Information Technology—PAUL J. LYNCH, Dir. Tel: 516-678-5800, Ext. 244; Fax: 516-536-6554. BRIAN WASSON, Asst. Dir., EDWARD TOMCZYK, Network Asst.

Marian Renewal—Sr. MARCELLA PURPURA, C.S.J., Coord., *P.O. Box 1301, Brentwood, 11717.* Tel: 631-952-7400.

Migration Office—Mr. JOHN K. BINGHAM, Dir. Immigrant Svcs. Catholic Charities, *143 Schleigel Blvd., Amityville, 11701.* Tel: 631-789-5210; Fax: 631-789-5245.

Mission Office—Society for the Propagation of the Faith, Holy Childhood Association, Catholic Relief Services Diocesan Mission in the Dominican Republic. Sr. CATHERINE G. KELLY, S.S.J., Dir. Tel: 516-678-5800, Ext. 513; Fax: 516-594-0064.

Newspaper - "The Long Island Catholic", (published by the Catholic Press Association of the Diocese of Rockville Centre, Inc.)—ELIZABETH O'CONNOR, Assoc. Publisher & Editor, *200 W. Centennial Ave., Ste. 201, P.O. Box 9000, Roosevelt, 11575.* Tel: 516-594-1000; Fax: 516-594-1092.

Parish Stewardship—200 W. Centennial Ave., Roosevelt, 11575. Tel: 516-763-6795; Fax: 516-763-6799. Mr. ROBERT P. CAMMARATA, Dir.; Ms. LAURIE WHITFIELD, Assoc. Dir.; Mr. ANTHONY J. DINO, Training & Support Specialist; Mrs. GEORGENA MCCANDLESS, Program Svcs. Coord.; Mrs. CAROLYN STRAUCH-REISER, Data Mgmt. Sec.

Pastoral Formation—Sr. LAUREN HANLEY, C.S.J., Dir. Tel: 516-678-5800, Ext. 539; Fax: 516-594-8385. Sr. MAUREEN JESSNIK, R.S.M., Coord., Ministry Tracks and Leadership Skill Training, Ext. 210. Sr. ANN HORN, O.P., Coord. Curriculum and Spiritual Formation, Ext. 538. Ms. PAULINE KOLLER, Coord. Instruction and Alumni Affairs, Ext. 592. Mrs. CLAIRE STIGLIC, Coord. Collaborative Formation, Ext. 596. Ms. SUZANNE RICHARDS, Coord. Formation Weekends and Multi-Cultural Ministry, Ext. 200. Mrs. ELENA SANCHEZ, Nassau Regl. Dir.; Mrs. DOT HORSTMANN, S. Suffolk Regl. Dir.; Mrs. MARCIA JOHNSON, Central Regl. Dir.; Ms. CAROL CALLAN, Eastern Suffolk Regl. Dir. Consultants: Bro. EDWARD BACON, O.S.F.; Rev. Msgr. VINCENT RUSH; Mrs. PATRICIA MEGALE.

Priest Personnel—Rev. Msgr. FRANCIS J. CALDWELL, C.S.W., Dir. Tel: 516-678-5800, Ext. 585; Fax: 516-764-3467.

Priestly Life and Ministry—Rev. THOMAS F. MULVANERTY, Dir., *St. Elizabeth Church, 175 Wolf Hill Rd., Melville, 11747.*

Priests' Personnel Assignment Board—Most Rev. JOHN C. DUNNE, D.D.; Most Rev. EMIL A. WCELA, D.D.; Rev. Msgr. JOHN A. ALESANDRO, J.C.D., J.D.; Rev. Msgr. FRANCIS J. CALDWELL, C.S.W., Chm.; Rev. Msgr. DANIEL J. HURLEY; Rev. BRIAN J. MCNAMARA; Rev. Msgr. JOHN C. NOSSER; Revs. GERARD A. RINGENBACK; JOSEPH M. SCHLAFER; KENNETH H. WINKLER; Mrs. PATRICIA FERGUS, Sec.

Priests' Personnel Policy Board—Rev. Msgr. FRANCIS J. CALDWELL, C.S.W.; Revs. THOMAS M. FUSCO; MICHAEL R. HANDS; ROBERT L. HAYDEN; THOMAS G. MCCORMICK; THOMAS F. MULVANERTY; CHARLES E. PAPA.

Priests' Retirement Board—Most Rev. JOHN C. DUNNE, D.D.; Rev. Msgr. JOHN A. ALESANDRO, Sec.; Rev. ROBERT Y. BLYMAN, M.D.; Rev. Msgr. FRANCIS J. CALDWELL, C.S.W.; Revs. ROBERT J. CLERKIN; THOMAS W. GROENEWOLD; Rev. Msgr. CHARLES A. GUARINO, J.C.D.; Rev. Msgr. ROBERT E. GUGLIELMONE; Rev. Msgr. JOHN P. MARTIN; Rev. Msgr. THADDEUS ROONEY; Rev. Msgr. JAMES P. SWIADER.

Prison Ministry and Criminal Justice Affairs—26 S. Saxon Ave., Bay Shore, 11706-8920. Tel: 631-969-0837; Fax: 631-666-5073. Bro. JACK MOYLAN, O.S.F., D.Min., Dir. SUZANNE D. JONES, Ministerial Svcs. Coord.

Nassau County Correctional Center—100 Carman Ave., East Meadow, 11554-1146. Tel: 516-572-4145; 572-3622. Chaplains: Rev. RALPH FERRO; Deacon JOHN SULLIVAN; Sr. VIRGINIA WATERS, F.S.P.; Bro. BILL CAWLEY, S.C.

Nassau County Juvenile Detention Center—61 Carman Ave., Westbury, 11590. Tel: 516-571-9153. Bro. JACK MOYLAN, O.S.F., Chap.

Suffolk County Correctional Facility—100 Center Dr., Riverhead, 11901. Tel: 631-852-2294; 852-2728. Chaplains: Sr. MICHELLE BREMER, C.S.F.N.; Deacon CHRIS VIGLIOTTA.

Suffolk County Minimum Security Facility—P.O. Box 69, Yaphank, 11980. Tel: 631-852-4713. Chaplains: Sr. MICHELLE BREMER, C.S.F.N.; Deacon JOHN SULLIVAN.

Religious—Vicars for Religious: Sr. MARYANNE FITZGERALD, S.C. Tel: 516-678-5800, Ext. 589. Bro. WILLIAM BOSLET, O.S.F. Tel: 516-678-5800, Ext. 588.

RENEW 2000—Rev. RALPH R. SOMMER, Coord., *P.O. Box 1312, Brentwood, 11717-1312.* Tel: 631-273-6396; Fax: 631-952-7403.

Research & Planning—Mr. CHESTER J. STRZEPEK, M.S., P.D., Dir., Ext. 603; Fax: 516-594-1128.

Spanish Apostolate—Sr. MARGARET MAYCE, O.P., Dir. Tel: 516-678-5800, Ext. 618. Rev. Msgr. PABLO M. RODRIQUEZ, Vicar for Hispanics. Tel: 516-489-3675.

Television (Telecare)—1200 Glenn Curtis Blvd., Uniondale, 11553. Tel: 516-538-8700; Fax: 516-489-9701. Rev. Msgr. THOMAS J. HARTMAN, Dir. VERONICA ALLOCCA, Vice Pres. Devel. KATHY DULANTO, Vice Pres. Sponsorship; LANCE HODGES, Vice Pres. & Dir. Operations; RICHARD HAEMMERLE, Vice Pres. & Bus. Mgr.

Vocations—Rev. THOMAS J. HAROLD, Dir. Tel: 516-678-5800, Ext. 586; Fax: 516-764-3467. Associate Vocation Directors: Revs. BRIAN P. BARR; ROBERT J. BATULE; THOMAS M. COOGAN; THOMAS M. FUSCO; ROBERT KUZNIK; Rev. Msgr. JAMES M. MCDONALD; Revs. BRIAN J. MCNAMARA; JOSEPH J. NIXON; MICHAEL J. RIEDER; THOMAS G. SALOY; Rev. Msgr. EDMOND J. TRENCH; Revs. JAMES C. VLAUN; EDWARD J. WALSH; Mrs. THERESE FUSCO ZAID, Vocation Program Coord., Ext. 242.

Worship—Rev. Msgr. RONALD HAYDE, Dir. Tel: 516-678-5800, Ext. 503. Sr. SHEILA BROWNE, R.S.M., Coord., Catechumenate, Ext. 231.

Youth and Young Adult Ministry—Mr. MICHAEL G. MCCARTHY, Dir. Tel: 516-678-5800, Ext. 522. Mrs. MARIANNE COLLINS, CYO, Ext. 238. Mr. AUSTIN CANNON, Scouting, Ext. 245. Mr. LAWRENCE CURRAN, Young Adult Ministry, Ext. 616.

Diocesan Organizations

Apostleship of Prayer—Rev. Msgr. JAMES M. MCDONALD, Dir., *35 N. Service Rd., Dix Hills, 11746.* Tel: 631-499-8520; Fax: 631-499-1530.

Catholic Accountants' Guild—Miss MARY R. GOELLER, Contact Person, *155 Garfield Ave., Mineola, 11501.* Tel: 516-746-1223.

Catholic Lawyer's Guild—Rev. Msgr. GEORGE P. GRAHAM, Chap., *3100 Hempstead Turnpike, Levittown, 11756.* Tel: 516-731-4220.

Nocturnal Adoration Society—Rev. Msgr. JAMES M. MCDONALD, Dir., *35 N. Service Rd., Dix Hills, 11746.* Tel: 631-499-8520; Fax: 631-499-1530.

Legion of Mary—Rev. JAMES MANNING, S.M.M., Dir., *26 S. Saxon Ave., Bayshore, 11706.* Tel: 631-666-7500; Fax: 631-665-4349.

Society of St. Vincent de Paul—249 Broadway, Bethpage, 11714. Tel: 516-822-3132; Fax: 516-822-2728.

SOFIA Institute—Rev. ROBERT S. SMITH, Dir., *440 W. Neck Rd., Huntington, 11743.*

CLERGY, PARISHES, MISSIONS AND PAROCHIAL SCHOOLS

VILLAGE OF ROCKVILLE CENTRE (Nassau County)

1—ST. AGNES CATHEDRAL (1894), Rev. Msgr. James P. Kelly, Rector; Most Rev. John R. McGann, D.D.; Revs. German Villabon, O.S.A.; Gerald Cestare; Bruce Reed; Deacons Thomas McDaid; Vincent Smyth. In res., Rev. Msgr. Frank J. Caldwell; Rev. Msgr. Ronald E. Hayde; Rev. Msgr. Robert J. Brennan.
Res., 29 Quealy Pl., 11570. Tel: 516-766-0205; Fax: 516-763-0745.
School—Tel: 516-678-5550; Fax: 516-678-0437.
Sisters of St. Dominic 3; Lay Teachers 44; Students 884. Co-Principals: Sr. Kathleen Carlin; Helen Newman.
Catechesis/Religious Programs—Tel: 516-678-2306. Mrs. Donna Eschenauer, D.R.E.
Students 1,300.

2—CAMPUS PARISH OF LONG ISLAND (1972), Rev. Joseph J. D'Angelo, M.Div.,M.S.,CASAC,M.A.C.
Office Address—(For details, please refer to Campus Ministries and Newman Centers under the Institution section.) 50 N. Park Ave., 11570. Tel: 516-678-5800, Ext. 614; Fax: 516-763-1078.

OUTSIDE VILLAGE OF ROCKVILLE CENTRE

Amityville, Suffolk Co., St. Martin's (1897), Rev. Msgr. Robert J. Saccacio; Rev. Richard T. Stelter.
Res., 37 Union Ave., 11701. Tel: 631-264-0124; Fax: 631-264-0139.
School—Tel: 631-264-7166.
Sisters of St. Dominic (Union Ave.) 4; Lay Teachers 21; Students 524.
Catechesis/Religious Programs—Tel: 631-691-1617.
Students 388.

Babylon, Suffolk Co., St. Joseph's (1877), Revs. John J. Barrett; Martin L. Klein; Gerald F. DeGiralamo, S.A.; Thomas P. Maloney; Deacons Michael J. Leyden; John F. Sullivan. In res., Rev. John J. Gorman. Pastoral Assocs.: Joseph Milazzo; Sr. Anna O'Connell.
Res., 39 N. Carll Ave., 11702-2701. Tel: 631-669-0068; Fax: 631-669-9175. [CEM]
Catechesis/Religious Programs—Tel: 631-587-4717. Marianne Mione, D.R.E.
Students 1,427.
Missions—Oak Beach, Suffolk Co. (Summer) 11702.; West Gilgo Beach, Suffolk Co. (Summer) 11702.

Baldwin, Nassau Co., St. Christopher (1915), Rev. Msgr. John F. Bennett; Rev. Msgr. Joseph F. Lawlor, Pastor Emeritus; Revs. Brian McQuade; Robert Kuznik; Deacons Charles Muscarnera; Joseph Pellegrino; Anthony Banno.
Res., 11 Gale Ave., 11510. Tel: 516-223-0723; Fax: 516-867-5678.
School—21 Pershing Blvd., 11510. Tel: 516-223-4404. Sr. Dolores McLaughlin, Prin.; Miss Joan Hanlon, Asst. Principal.
Sisters of St. Joseph 4; Lay Teachers 23; Students 422.
Catechesis/Religious Programs—Tel: 516-223-5813. D.R.E.: Mrs. Julianne Markey; Mrs. Gail Milne.
Students 1,177.

Bay Shore, Suffolk Co., St. Patrick's (1883), Rev. Msgr. John C. Nosser; Revs. Thomas M. Coogan; Rozario Chinnappan (India); Deacons Joseph Peralta; Michael Mahoney; Frank Keach. In res., Rev. Msgr. James F. Coffey, Pastor Emeritus; Rev. Msgr. Richard P. Hendel, (Retired).
Res., 9 N. Clinton Ave., 11706. Tel: 631-665-4911; Fax: 631-665-8388. [CEM]
School—6 N. Clinton Ave., 11706. Tel: 631-665-0569; Fax: 631-665-1456. Ms. Cathleen Quinn, Prin.
Lay Teachers 27; Students 502.
Catechesis/Religious Programs—Tel: 631-665-4914; Fax: 631-665-9009.
Students 1,109.

Bayville, Nassau, St. Gertrude's (1959), Rev. Peter Kaczmarek; Deacon Theodore Kolakowski. In res., Rev. Msgr. James Brassil, (Retired).
Res., 28 School St., 11709. Tel: 516-628-1113; Fax: 516-628-9032.
Catechesis/Religious Programs—Tel: 516-628-2432; Fax: 516-628-0224.
Students 500.

Bellmore, Nassau Co., St. Barnabas the Apostle (1912), Revs. Peter C. Dooley; Edward J. Muhs, Pastor Emeritus; Brian Ingram; Anthony Iaconis; Deacons Bernard Sherlock; Thomas Coleman.
Res., 2320 Bedford Ave., 11710. Tel: 516-785-0054; Fax: 516-221-7789.
Schools—St. Elizabeth Ann Seton Regional School, Bellmore Campus, (1992), 2341 Washington Ave., Tel: 516-785-5709; Fax: 516-785-4468.; St. Elizabeth Ann Seton Regional School, East Meadow Campus, 600 Newbridge Road, East Meadow, Tel: 516-785-7006; Fax: 516-785-7008. See Regional Schools under Institutions Located in the Diocese.
Catechesis/Religious Programs—Tel: 516-785-0130.
Students 1,530.

Bellport, Suffolk Co., Mary Immaculate (1905), Rev. Msgr. Bernard J. Ryan; Rev. Constantino Nieva.
Res., 16 Brown's Ln., 11713. Tel: 631-286-0154; Fax: 631-286-2937.
School—Holy Angels Regional School, Patchogue, Tel: 631-475-0422; Fax: 631-475-2641. See Regional Schools under Institutions Located in the Diocese.
Catechesis/Religious Programs—Tel: 631-286-3504.
Students 475.

Bethpage, Nassau Co., St. Martin of Tours (1923), Revs. Thomas J. Siconolfi, C.SS.R.; Thomas Schmidt, C.SS.R.; John Patton, C.SS.R.; Vincent Crotty, C.SS.R.; Deacons James A. Biggin; Eugene Capobianco; Frank Carrello.
Res., 40 Seaman Ave., 11714. Tel: 516-931-0818; Fax: 516-931-0559.
School—St. John Baptist de LaSalle Regional School, Bethpage/Farmingdale. See Regional Schools under Institutions Located in the Diocese. Tel: 516-931-0983.
Catechesis/Religious Programs—208 Broadway, 11714. Tel: 516-822-9768; Fax: 516-932-8454. D.R.E.: Dr. Elizabeth Lukaschek; Rosanne Sciaretta.
Students 1,200.

Blue Point, Suffolk Co., Our Lady of the Snow (1917), Revs. Diarmuid F. McGann; Richard M. Scanlon, Pastor Emeritus; Deacons Robert Gronenthal; Steve Kramer; Frank Hartmann.
Res., 175 Blue Point Ave., 11715. Tel: 631-363-6385; Fax: 516-363-7394.
School—Prince of Peace Regional School, Sayville, Tel: 516-589-3426. See Regional Schools under Institutions Located in the Diocese.
Catechesis/Religious Programs—Tel: 516-363-6394; Fax: 516-589-3426.
Students 900.

Bohemia, Suffolk Co., St. John Nepomucene (1919), Revs. James L. Wood; Louis L. Reuss, Pastor Emeritus; Charles N. Mangano; Sr. Phyllis Esposito, C.S.J., Pastoral Assoc.; Deacons James Bohuslaw; Anthony Cusumano.
Res., 1140 Locust Ave., 11716. Tel: 631-589-0540; Fax: 631-244-8086. [CEM]
School—Prince of Peace Regional School, Sayville. See Regional Schools under Institutions Located in the Diocese. Tel: 631-589-0422.
Catechesis/Religious Programs—1150 Locust Ave., 11716. Tel: 631-567-1765. Doris Petrocelli, D.R.E.
Students 1,692.

Brentwood, Suffolk Co., St. Anne's (1895), Revs. Thomas J. St. Pierre; Gerald S. Twomey; James J. Hannon; Deacons Jesus Alvarado; Juan Diaz, Spanish Apostolate; Terence A. Rasanen; Thomas R. Samson; John Walters.
Res., 88 Second Ave., 11717. Tel: 631-273-8113; Fax: 631-436-7914.
School—Our Lady of Providence Regional School, Central Islip, Tel: 631-234-6324; Fax: 631-234-6360. See Regional Schools under Institutions Located in the Diocese.
Catechesis/Religious Programs—Tel: 631-231-7344. Ms. Virginia Conzo, D.R.E.
Students 1,005.

St. Luke (1965), Revs. Lawrence Duncklee; Saul Londono, Associate, Colombian Missionary Soc.; Deacons John Trodden; Richard A. Luken; Wenceslao Rivera.
Res., 266 Wicks Rd., 11717. Tel: 631-273-1110; Fax: 631-951-2779. [JC]
School—Our Lady of Providence Regional School, Central Islip, Tel: 631-234-6535. See Regional Schools under Institutions Located in the Diocese.
Catechesis/Religious Programs—Tel: 631-273-4333.
Students 686.

Bridgehampton, Suffolk Co., Queen of the Most Holy Rosary (1922), Rev. Msgr. Ronald Richardson; Dr. Regina Wieman-Voegele, Pastoral Assoc.
Mailing Address: P.O. Box 3035, 11932. Tel: 631-537-0156; Fax: 631-537-7116.
School—Stella Maris Regional School, Sag Harbor, Tel: 631-725-2525; Fax: 631-725-4587. See Regional Schools under Institutions Located in the Diocese.

Brookville, Nassau Co., St. Paul the Apostle (1962), Revs. Mario Costa; Arthur C. Anderson.
Res., Cedar Swamp Rd., Brookville, Glen Head, 11545. Tel: 516-935-1880; Fax: 516-938-3683.
Catechesis/Religious Programs—Tel: 516-938-4531. D.R.E.: Sr. Regina Kraft; Mr. Len Tufaro.
Students 500.

Carle Place, Nassau Co., Church of Our Lady of Hope (1987), Rev. Donald M. Hanson; Deacons John T. Hickey; Thomas B. Rich; Raymond J. Tirelli; Patrick J. Dunphy.
Church—Cherry Ln. & Broadway, P.O. Box 352, 11514-0352. Tel: 516-334-6288; Fax: 516-997-4622.
School—St. Brigid/ Our Lady of Hope Regional School, 101 Maple Ave., Westbury, 11590. Tel: 516-333-0580; Fax: 516-333-0590.
Catechesis/Religious Programs—Tel: 516-334-4781. Donna Manley, D.R.E.
Students 720.

Cedarhurst, Nassau Co., St. Joachim (1894), Rev. Paul Rahilly; Deacon Frank J. Bono.
Res., 614 Central Ave., 11516. Tel: 516-569-1845; Fax: 516-569-0117.
School—620 Central Ave., 11516. Tel: 516-569-2290; Fax: 516-374-5158.
Sisters of St. Joseph 2; Lay Teachers 14; Students 204.
Catechesis/Religious Programs—Tel: 516-295-0878.
Students 204.

Centereach, Suffolk Co., Assumption of the Blessed Virgin Mary (1955), Rev. Msgr. Joseph K. Curley; Revs. William F. Shean; Paul J. Mijas.

Res., 20 Chestnut St., 11720. Tel: 631-585-8760; Fax: 631-585-3601.
Catechesis/Religious Programs—Tel: 631-588-6408. Mrs. Miriam Selig, D.R.E.
Students 1,365.

Center Moriches, Suffolk Co., St. John the Evangelist (1898), Revs. Joseph C. Coschignano; John J. Corcoran, Pastor Emeritus; John J. McCartney; Deacons Galvin Murphy; Chris Vigliotta.
Res., 25 Ocean Ave., 11934. Tel: 631-878-0009; Fax: 631-874-2466.
School—Our Lady, Queen of Apostles Regional School, Center Moriches. See Regional Schools under Institutions Located in the Diocese. Tel: 631-878-1033; Fax: 631-878-1059.
Catechesis/Religious Programs—Tel: 631-878-4141.
Students 1,500.

Centerport, Suffolk Co., Our Lady Queen of Martyrs (1966), Rev. Msgr. T. Peter Ryan; Rev. Harold J. Heindel, Assoc. Pastor; Sr. Eileen Corcoran, O.P., Pastoral Assoc.; Deacons Joseph Montesano; James Butler. In res., Rev. Msgr. Joseph F. Colligan, Pastor Emeritus.
Res., Prospect and Mill Dam Rds., P.O. Box 609, 11721. Tel: 631-757-8184; Fax: 631-262-0155.
School—Trinity Regional School, East Northport, Tel: 631-261-5130; Fax: 631-266-5345. See Regional Schools under Institutions Located in the Diocese.
Catechesis/Religious Programs—Tel: 631-757-0720; Fax: 631-757-3512. Margaret Dritto, D.R.E.
Students 1,100.

Central Islip, Suffolk Co., St. John of God (1904), Revs. Joseph P. Granata; Michael J. Rieder. Pastoral Assocs.: Sr. Catherine Peluso, O.P.; Sr. Agnes Claudia Allen, C.S.J., (Spanish Apostolate); Deacons Ronald J. Gillette; Frank Gariboldi. In res., Revs. John P. Halpin, Chap., Pilgrim Psychiatric Center; Marc-Arthur Jerome.
Res., 84 Carleton Ave., 11722. Tel: 631-234-6535; Fax: 631-234-7474. [CEM]
School—Our Lady of Providence Regional School, Central Islip. See Regional Schools under Institutions Located in the Diocese. Tel: 631-234-6324; Fax: 631-234-6360.
Catechesis/Religious Programs—Tel: 631-234-4040. Sr. Diane Morgan, O.P., D.R.E.
Students 680.
Parish Outreach Office—Tel: 631-234-1884. Sr. Julianne Spiess, S.S.N.D.
Convent—330 St. John St., 11722. Tel: 631-234-6533. Sisters of St. Joseph

Commack, Suffolk Co., Christ the King (1959), Rev. Msgr. Dennis M. Regan; Revs. Joseph W. Staudt; Simon Fernando; Sean Gann.
Res., 2 Indian Head Rd., 11725. Tel: 631-864-1623; Fax: 631-864-8891.
School—Holy Family Regional School, Commack, Tel: 631-543-0202; Fax: 631-543-0203. See Regional Schools under Institutions Located in the Diocese.
Catechesis/Religious Programs—Tel: 631-864-3696. Mrs. Margaret Marconi, D.R.E.
Students 1,213.

Copiague, Suffolk Co., Our Lady of the Assumption (1928), Revs. Michael Flynn; Andrew Waszczenko, S.D.S.; Camillo Lugo.
Res., Molloy St., 11726. Tel: 631-842-5211; 842-5476; Fax: 631-789-5326.
Catechesis/Religious Programs—Tel: 631-842-3545. Ruth Durago, D.R.E.
Students 990.

Coram, Suffolk Co., St. Frances Cabrini (1953), Rev. Nicholas J. Figliola; Deacons Fred Molina; Carmen L. Pagrotta; Monte Naylor, Jr.
Res., 134 Middle County Rd., 11727. Tel: 631-732-8445; Fax: 631-732-8978.
School—Holy Angels Regional School, Patchogue, Tel: 631-475-0422. See Regional Schools under Institutions Located in the Diocese.
Catechesis/Religious Programs—Tel: 631-698-3149. Vincent J. Whitfield, D.R.E.
Students 738.

Cutchogue, Suffolk Co., Sacred Heart (1901), Revs. Peter A. Allen; John P. Henry, Pastor Emeritus; Sr. Anne Lynch, R.S.M., Pastoral Assoc.; Deacon John Bopp.
Res., 27905 Main Rd., P.O. Box 926, 11935-0926. Tel: 631-734-6722; Fax: 631-734-7906. [CEM]
School—Our Lady of Mercy Regional School, Tel: 631-734-5166. See Regional Schools under Institutions Located in the Diocese.
Catechesis/Religious Programs—Tel: 631-734-2568. Sr. Ann Lynch, D.R.E.
Students 450.
Mission—Mattituck, Suffolk Co., Our Lady of Good Counsel, Main Rd., 11952.

Our Lady of Ostrabrama (1909) (Polish), Rev. Wladyslaw Rudnicki, Admin.
Res., 3000 Depot Ln., Box 997, 11935. Tel: 631-734-6446; Fax: 631-734-4117. [JC]
School—North Fork Regional Catholic School, Cutchogue, Tel: 631-734-5166. See Regional Schools under Institutions Located in the Diocese.
Catechesis/Religious Programs—Students 102.

Davis Park, Fire Island Suffolk Co., Most Precious Blood (1962). (Summer Mission). Rev. Francis Pizzarelli, S.M.M.
Mailing Address: P.O. Box 358, Port Jefferson, 11777. Tel: 631-928-2377; Fax: 631-473-5210.
Res., Spindrift Walk, Fire Island, 11728. Tel: 631-597-6525.

Deer Park, Suffolk Co., SS. Cyril and Methodius (1956), Rev. Msgr. Domenick T. Graziadio; Revs. Joseph K. Baidoo; Dominic U. Amadi (Nigeria); Caetano F. Costa (India); Francis D. Sang (Vietnam). In res., Rev. Msgr. Thaddeus Rooney.
Res., 125 Half Hollow Rd., 11729-4288. Tel: 631-667-4044; Fax: 631-667-6237.
School—Tel: 631-667-6229; Fax: 631-667-0093.
Sisters of St. Joseph 1; Lay Teachers 30; Students 504; Nursery 15; PreK 43.
Catechesis/Religious Programs—Tel: 631-667-6264; Fax: 631-667-7767.
Students 1,846.

Dix Hills, Suffolk Co., St. Matthew (1965), Rev. Msgr. James M. McDonald; Revs. Lawrence A. Chadwick; William G. Dailey; Bonaventure Thekkeveetil; Francis B. Nuss; Robert Kayser; Deacons James M. McQuade; Arnold Quaranta; James Hanly.
Res., 35 N. Service Rd., 11746. Tel: 631-499-8520; Fax: 631-499-1530.
School—Holy Family Regional School. See Regional Schools under Institutions Located in the Diocese. Tel: 631-453-0202.
Catechesis/Religious Programs—Tel: 631-499-8521. Mr. Anthony C. D'Amico, D.R.E.
Students 1,426.

East Hampton, Suffolk Co., Most Holy Trinity (1894), Rev. Donald J. Desmond, Pastor.
Res., 57 Buell Ln., 11937. Tel: 631-324-0134; Fax: 631-329-3552. [CEM]
Business: 79 Buell Ln., 11937. Tel: 631-324-1444.
School—Stella Maris Regional School, Sag Harbor. See Regional Schools under Institutions Located in the Diocese. Tel: 631-725-2525; Fax: 631-725-4587.
Catechesis/Religious Programs—Tel: 631-324-7994; Fax: 631-329-3552. Sharon Burns, D.R.E.
Students 380.
Mission—Amagansett, Suffolk Co., St. Peter the Apostle, Main St., Amagansett, 11930. Tel: 631-324-0134; Fax: 631-329-3552.

East Islip, Suffolk Co., St. Mary's (1898), Rev. Steven J. Peterson; Rev. Msgr. Peter A. Chiara, Pastor Emeritus; Revs. Lucian Fernandes; Raymond H. Nugent; John R. Moore; Dorothy Horstmann, Pastoral Assoc.
Res., 20 Harrison Ave., 11730. Tel: 631-581-4266; Fax: 631-581-0112.
School—Tel: 631-581-3423; Fax: 631-581-7509. Biagio Arpino, Prin.
Lay Teachers 43; Students 915.
Catechesis/Religious Programs—Tel: 631-581-3304.
Students 1,435.

East Meadow, Nassau Co., St. Raphael (1941), Revs. Thomas J. Haggerty; Charles Srion; Michael Hands; Sr. Judith Enterlin, C.S.J., Pastoral Assoc.; Mary-Ann O'Brien, Business Mgr.
Res., 600 Newbridge Rd., 11554. Tel: 516-785-0236; Fax: 516-783-9578.
School—St. Elizabeth Ann Seton Regional School, East Meadow Campus. See Regional Schools under Institutions Located in the Diocese. Tel: 516-785-7006; Fax: 516-785-7008.
Catechesis/Religious Programs—Tel: 516-221-9096. D.R.E.: Sr. Elizabeth McNeill, R.S.M.; Mrs. Arlene Vosilla.
Students 968.

East Northport, Suffolk Co., St. Anthony of Padua (1951), Revs. Richard P. Hoerning; James Atkins; James M. Kissane; Deacon Robert Braun; Hans Lindstrom, Business Mgr.
Res., 20 Cheshire Pl., 11731-2591. Tel: 631-261-1077; Fax: 631-757-0572.
School—Trinity Regional School, East Northport. See Regional Schools under Institutions Located in the Diocese. Tel: 631-261-5130.
Catechesis/Religious Programs—Tel: 631-261-1306. D.R.E.: Mrs. Judith Corbellini; Mrs. Eileen Schlee; Mrs. Patricia Seibert.
Students 1,544.

East Patchogue, Suffolk Co., St. Joseph the Worker (1955), Revs. Michael Connolly, O.F.M.Cap.; William Winters, O.F.M.Cap.; Robert Phelps, O.F.M.Cap.
Res., 510 Narragansett Ave., 11772. Tel: 631-286-9133; Fax: 631-286-9145.
School—Holy Angels Regional School, Patchogue. See Regional Schools under Institutions Located in the Diocese. Tel: 631-475-0422; Fax: 631-475-2036.
Catechesis/Religious Programs—Mrs. Mary Mensch, D.R.E.
Students 703.

East Rockaway, Nassau Co., St. Raymond's (1909), Rev. Msgr. William W. Jablonski; Rev. William V. Singleton, Pastor Emeritus. Pastoral Assocs.: Rev. Msgr. Thomas D. Candreva; Rev. Antonio S. Pascual; Deacons Robert C. Campbell; Richard W. LaRossa; Guy Donza.
Res., 263 Atlantic Ave., 11518. Tel: 516-593-5000; Fax: 516-887-0554.
School—Tel: 516-593-9010; Fax: 516-593-0986.
Sisters, Servants of the Immaculate Heart of Mary 4; Lay Teachers 15; Students 475.
Catechesis/Religious Programs—Tel: 516-593-9075. Mrs. Evelyn Contaldi, D.R.E.
Students 1,115.

Elmont, Nassau Co., St. Boniface (1898), Rev. Msgr. John R. Dreasen, V.F.; Revs. Lawrence B. Rafferty; Douglas Dower; Georgereau Thevenin (Haiti); Sr. Evelyn Lamoureux, D.W., Human Svcs. In res., Revs. George Punti; Francis Odufuye (Nigeria).
Res., 631 Elmont Rd., 11003. Tel: 516-354-0715; Fax: 516-354-0446. [CEM]
School—Tel: 516-354-6084; Fax: 516-437-5554. Mrs. Christine Faber, Prin.
Sisters of St. Dominic 2; Lay Teachers 18; Students 277.
Catechesis/Religious Programs—Tel: 516-437-7112. Sr. Margaret Fanning, C.S.J., D.R.E.
Students 800.

St. Vincent de Paul (1951), Revs. Donald E. Babinski, M.Div.; Daniel P. Sheridan, M.A., M.Div. In res., Rev. Msgr. Francis J. Schneider, J.C.D., M.Div.
Res., 1500 DePaul St., 11003. Tel: 516-352-2127; Fax: 516-352-2358.
Catechesis/Religious Programs—Tel: 516-352-2265. Ms. Mary Alice Burchell, M.A., D.R.E.
Students 637.

Farmingdale, Nassau Co., St. Kilian (1896), Rev. Msgr. Charles W. Swiger; Revs. Augustine Fernando (India); Angel V. Resultay (Philippines); Gerard J. Gentleman, Jr.; Deacons Frank D. Barone; Lucio Cotone; William Griffin; Herman Rodenburg; Donald Zirkel; George Owen; Frank Shanley, Business Mgr. In res., Most Rev. John C. Dunne.
Res., 485 Conklin St., 11735. Tel: 516-249-0127; Fax: 516-249-7131.
School—St. John Baptist de LaSalle Regional School, Bethpage/Farmingdale. See Regional Schools under Institutions Located in the Diocese. Tel: 516-931-0983 (Bethpage); 516-694-3610 (Farmingdale); Fax: 516-931-1502 (Bpg); 516-694-3614 (Fmdl).
Catechesis/Religious Programs—Tel: 516-694-0633; Fax: 516-454-8612. Mrs. Joanne Kolasa, D.R.E.
Students 1,541.
Parish Social Ministy/Outreach—Tel: 516-756-9656. Lisa Molluso, Dir.

Farmingville, Suffolk Co., Church of the Resurrection (1988), Rev. John M. Derasmo; Deacons Daniel Macellaro; Walter Williams.
Church—50 Granny Rd., 11738. Tel: 631-696-0232; Fax: 631-696-0271.
Catechesis/Religious Programs—Tel: 631-696-0270. Maryanne Trezza, D.R.E.
Students 922.

Floral Park, Nassau Co., St. Hedwig's (1902) (Polish), Revs. Francis E. Filmanski; Chester Diadia.
Res., One Depan Ave., 11001. Tel: 516-354-0042; Fax: 516-327-2458.
Catechesis/Religious Programs—Students 240.

Our Lady of Victory (1921), Rev. Msgr. Charles J. Nosser; Revs. Thomas Moriarty; John Hein (Vietnam); Deacon Lawrence P. Mulligan.
Res., 2 Floral Pkwy., 11001-3198. Tel: 516-354-0482; 354-0479; Fax: 516-354-7450.
School—2 Bellmore St., 11001. Tel: 516-352-4466; 354-2150; Fax: 516-352-2998. Margaret M. Augello, Prin.
Religious 1; Lay Teachers 27; Students 491.
Catechesis/Religious Programs—Tel: 516-352-0510. Sr. Barbara Kaiser, C.S.J., D.R.E.
Students 1,050.

Franklin Square, Nassau Co., St. Catherine of Sienna (1908), Rev. Thomas W. Groenewold; Rev. Msgr. William F. Costello, Pastor Emeritus; Rev. Edward J. Walsh; Rev. Msgr. Thomas S. Kane; Rev. Dennis Whelan; Deacons John Fodale; James DiGiovanna; Joseph Benincasa; Douglas Ferreiro.
Res., 33 New Hyde Park Rd., 11010. Tel: 516-352-0146; Fax: 516-326-7427.
School—990 Holzhimer, Tel: 516-437-2733. Mrs. Diane Staudinger, Prin.
Sisters of St. Dominic 1; Lay Teachers 25; Students 410.
Catechesis/Religious Programs—Tel: 516-354-4554. Helen Giordano, D.R.E.
Students 1,425.

Freeport, Nassau Co., Our Holy Redeemer (1903) (Hispanic), Revs. Richard Figliozzi; Celestine C. Anyanwu (Nigeria); Freddy Lozano (Columbia). In res., Rev. Msgr. Michael Manzelli; Deacons James Dunne; Francisco Cales; Bruce A. Burnham; Cristobal Sanchez.
Res., 37 S. Ocean Ave., 11520. Tel: 516-378-0665; Fax: 516-546-1416. [CEM]
Catechesis/Religious Programs—Tel: 516-546-1057; Fax: 516-546-1416.
Students 712.

Garden City, Nassau Co., St. Joseph's (1901), Revs. Joseph M. Schlafer; Brian J. McNamara. In res., Rev. Msgr. John A. Alesandro.
Res., 130 Fifth St., 11530. Tel: 516-747-3535; Fax: 516-746-0719.
School—450 Franklin Ave., 11530. Tel: 516-747-2730; Fax: 516-747-2854. Sr. Mary O'Donnell, O.P., Prin.; Ms. Florence Puff, Asst. Prin.
Lay Teachers 23; Students 415.
Catechesis/Religious Programs—Tel: 516-741-7787. Susan Mirabella, D.R.E.
Students 962.

St. Anne (1929), Revs. John D. Gilmartin; Richard R. Donovan; Deacons Edward Cunningham; Jack McGowan; George Browne; James O'Brien. In res., Rev. Msgr. William F. Costello; Rev. James C. Miller.
Res., 35 Dartmouth St., 11530. Tel: 516-352-5904; Fax: 516-352-1360.
School—25 Dartmouth St., 11530. Tel: 516-352-1205; Fax: 516-352-5969. Miss Jacqueline Lucarelli, Prin.
Religious of the Sacred Heart of Mary 3; Lay Teachers 22; Students 523.
Catechesis/Religious Programs—Tel: 516-488-1032. Sr. Kathleen Corr, O.P., D.R.E.
Students 915.

Glen Cove, Nassau Co., St. Patrick's (1856), Revs. Thomas C. Costa; Marian Bicz; Sr. Rena Perrone, O.P., Business Mgr.; Mr. Cantalicio Gamarra, Spanish Min. In res., Revs. Edison Santiago Londono (Columbia); Henry I. Benack, (Retired).
Res., 235 Glen St., 11542. Tel: 516-676-0276; Fax: 516-674-9137. [CEM]
For Hispanic Ministry—Tel: 516-759-6039.
School—All Saints Regional Catholic School, Glen Cove. See Regional Schools under Institutions Located in the Diocese. Tel: 516-676-0762; Fax: 516-676-0660.
Catechesis/Religious Programs—Tel: 516-671-7223. Sr. Teresa Raftery, I.H.M., D.R.E.
Students 600.
Convent—Amityville, Tel: 516-671-0501. Sisters of St. Dominic
Sisters 4.

St. Rocco (1937) (Italian), Rev. Aaron T. Vellarampampil. In res., Rev. Juniper J. Thomas.
Res., 18 Third St., 11542. Tel: 516-676-2482; Fax: 516-676-2117.
School—All Saints Regional Catholic School, Glen Cove. See Regional Schools under Institutions Located in the Diocese. Tel: 516-676-0762; Fax: 516-676-0660. Sr. Maureen Zellon, R.S.H.M., Prin.
Catechesis/Religious Programs—Students 290.

Glen Head, Nassau Co., St. Hyacinth (1909) (Polish), Revs. Richard Kopinski; Francis Podgorski; Joseph P. Kozlowski, Pastor Emeritus; Deacon Robert J. Heintz, (Retired).
Res., 319 Cedar Swamp Rd., 11545. Tel: 516-676-0361; Fax: 516-674-4728.
School—All Saints Regional Catholic School, Glen Cove. See Regional Schools under Institutions Located in the Diocese. Tel: 516-671-3033.
Catechesis/Religious Programs—Tel: 516-676-0361, Ext. 37. Miss Eileen Meserole, D.R.E.
Students 200.

Great Neck, Nassau Co., St. Aloysius (1876) (Hispanic-Korean), Rev. Msgr. Brendan P. Riordan; Rev. Simon Kim Han Ki (Korea). In res., Rev. Msgr. Alan J. Placa.
Res., 592 Middle Neck Rd., 11023. Tel: 516-482-2770; Fax: 516-829-3504.
Catechesis/Religious Programs—Tel: 516-482-5660; Fax: 516-829-4054.
Students 250.

Greenlawn, Suffolk Co., St. Francis of Assisi (1966) (Haitian), Rev. Msgr. Patrick J. Armshaw; Rev. Gregory Yacyshyn; Deacon Allan Longo.
Res., 29 Northgate Dr., 11740. Tel: 631-757-7435; Fax: 631-757-0469.
School—Trinity Regional School, East Northport. See Regional Schools under Institutions Located in the Diocese. Tel: 631-261-5130; Fax: 631-266-5345.
Catechesis/Religious Programs—Tel: 631-754-6436. Mrs. Theresa DeMayo, D.R.E.
Students 670.

Greenport, Suffolk Co., St. Agnes (1886), Rev. Msgr. Charles A. Guarino, J.C.D.
Res., Front St., 11944. Tel: 631-477-0048; Fax: 631-477-8519. [CEM]
School—Our Lady of Mercy, Cutchogue. See Regional Schools under Institutions Located in the Diocese. Tel: 631-734-5166.
Catechesis/Religious Programs—Tel: 631-477-1422.
Students 217.

Hampton Bays, Suffolk Co., St. Rosalie's (1901), Revs. William J. Gill; Sabbas Rodrigues.
Res., 31 Montauk Hwy., 11946. Tel: 631-728-9461; Fax: 631-728-2559.
School—Our Lady of the Hamptons Regional School. See Regional Schools under Institutions Located in the Diocese. Tel: 631-283-9140; Fax: 631-287-3958.
Catechesis/Religious Programs—Tel: 631-728-9461. Sarah Cunliffe, D.R.E.
Students 578.
Mission—East Quogue, Suffolk Co., 31 Montauk Hwy., 11946. Tel: 631-653-4471.

Hauppauge, Suffolk Co., St. Thomas More (1967), Rev. Msgr. Ellsworth R. Walden; Rev. Michael Boyle; Joan Dorr, Pastoral Assoc.; Deacon Robert Weisz. In res., Rev. Ralph Sommer.
Res., 115 Kings Hwy., 11788. Tel: 631-234-5551; Fax: 631-234-6412.
School—Holy Family Regional School, Commack. See Regional Schools under Institutions Located in the Diocese. Tel: 631-678-5800; Fax: 631-678-7362.
Catechesis/Religious Programs—119 Kings Hwy., 11788. Tel: 631-234-0397; Fax: 631-234-1199. D.R.E.: Mrs. Mary Ellen Carroll; Mrs. Patricia Chapin.
Students 1,256.

Hempstead, Nassau Co., Our Lady of Loretto (1870), Rev. Msgr. Pablo M. Rodriguez; Rev. Fruto Rosales; Sr. Teresa Logue, S.C., Pastoral Assoc.; Sr. Mary Therese Von Holdt, B.V.M.; Deacon Jose Roa; Mrs. Rosemary Viola; Miss Cathie Blackman.
Res., 104 Greenwich St., 11550. Tel: 516-489-3675; Fax: 516-485-8371.
School—St. Martin de Porres Regional School, Uniondale. See Regional Schools under Institutions Located in the Diocese. Tel: 516-481-3303.
Catechesis/Religious Programs—Tel: 516-483-3643.
Students 324.

St. John Chrysostom Malankara Mission (1999), 115 Greenwich St., 11550. Tel: 516-539-0414; Fax: 516-568-1906. Rev. Saji M. George, Admin.

St. Ladislaus (1915) (Polish), Rev. Msgr. Edward Wawerski. In res., Rev. John Siebor.
Res., 18 Richardson Pl., 11550. Tel: 516-489-0368; Fax: 516-292-9193.
School—St. Martin de Porres Regional School, Uniondale. See Regional Schools under Institutions Located in the Diocese.

Hewlett, Nassau Co., St. Joseph's (1872), Rev. Msgr. Charles R. Fink; Deacon Thomas Costello.
Res., 1346 Broadway, 11557. Tel: 516-374-0290; Fax: 516-374-2598.
Catechesis/Religious Programs—1355 Noel Ave., 11557. Tel: 516-569-6080; Fax: 516-374-3664. Frances Acquafredda, D.R.E.
Students 440.

Hicksville, Nassau Co., St. Ignatius Loyola (1859), Rev. Msgr. Donald T. Bennett; Revs. James Carmody; Gerard A. Gordon; Frederic J. Harrer, Pastor Emeritus; Rev. Msgr. Edward L. Tarrant, Pastor Emeritus.
Res., 129 Broadway, 11801. Tel: 516-931-0056; Fax: 516-939-0852.
School—30 Cherry St., 11801. Tel: 516-931-0831; Fax: 516-933-6528. Ms. Jacqueline Burdi, Prin.
Lay Teachers 24; Students 329.
Catechesis/Religious Programs—Tel: 516-935-6873. Mary Jane Mastrodomenico, D.R.E.
Students 750.

Holy Family (1951) (Irish-Italian), Rev. Msgr. Edward J. Donnelly; Revs. Vincent Schifano; Varghese Kocherry. In res., Rev. James A. Kirrane (BRK).
Res., 5 Fordham Ave., 11801. Tel: 516-938-3846; Fax: 516-938-6241.
School—Tel: 516-938-3881; Fax: 516-938-5041. Sr. Eileen McMahon, O.P., Prin.
Sisters of Saint Dominic 3; Lay Teachers 23; Students 582.
Catechesis/Religious Programs—Tel: 516-938-3854. Mrs. Carol Nealon, D.R.E.
Students 1,003.

Our Lady of Mercy (1953), Rev. Msgr. James E. Boesel; Revs. Charles A. Gartner, (Retired); Basil C. Colasito; Thomas P. Tuite, Jr.
Res., 500 S. Oyster Bay Rd., 11801. Tel: 516-931-4351; Fax: 516-433-8702.
School—Tel: 516-433-7040; Fax: 516-433-8286. Sr. Mary Joanne Deegan, R.S.M., Prin.
Sisters of Mercy 9; Lay Teachers 25; Students 644.
Catechesis/Religious Programs—Tel: 516-681-1228. Sr. Suzanne LePre, D.R.E.
Students 792.
Youth Ministry—Tel: 516-935-2444.
Lay Teachers 5; Students 98.

Holbrook, Suffolk Co., Good Shepherd (1970), Revs. Thomas L. Spadaro; Brian J. Brinker; Robert C. Scheckenback; Deacon Robert Hernandez.
Res., 1370 Grundy Ave., 11741. Tel: 631-588-7689; Fax: 631-588-7603.
School—Prince of Peace Regional School, Sayville. See Regional Schools under Institutions Located in the Diocese. Tel: 631-589-3426; Fax: 631-589-4523.
Catechesis/Religious Programs—Tel: 631-981-3889. D.R.E.: Sr. Lillian Delorme, O.P.; Sr. Dorothy Marie Schnell, C.S.J.
Students 2,300.

Huntington, Suffolk Co., St. Patrick's (1849), Rev. John Denniston; Rev. Msgr. Martin J. Flynn, Pastor Emeritus; Rev. Msgr. James B. Richter; Revs. Steven A. Berbig; Brian Barr; Deacon Jules Gagnon; Alan Jones, Business Mgr. In res., Rev. Thomas Edamattan (India).
Res., 400 Main St., 11743-3298. Tel: 631-673-5320; Fax: 631-673-4102. [CEM]
School—360 Main St., 11743-3298. Tel: 631-673-5325; Fax: 631-673-4609. Sr. Maureen McDade, Prin.
Sisters 2; Lay Teachers 30; Students 636.
Catechesis/Religious Programs—Tel: 631-673-5323. D.R.E.: Sr. Frances Viola; Sr. Peggy Ford; Robert Mahoney.
Students 1,300.

Huntington Station, Suffolk Co., St. Hugh of Lincoln (1913), Rev. Msgr. Vincent Rush; Revs. Joseph Arevalo; Joseph V. Davanzo; Deacons Edward W. Billia; Vito B. Taranto; Thomas Reilly; Luis Giraldo.
Res., 21 E. Ninth St., 11746. Tel: 631-427-0638; Fax: 631-427-1319.
Parish Center—1450 New York Ave., 11746.
School—Trinity Regional School, East Northport. See Regional Schools under Institutions Located in the Diocese. Tel: 631-261-5130; Fax: 631-266-5345.
Catechesis/Religious Programs—Tel: 631-271-6081. Miss Eileen McNamara, D.R.E.
Students 1,043.

Inwood, Nassau Co., Our Lady of Good Counsel (1910), Rev. Richard Nilsson; Deacon George Bruck.
Res., 68 Wanser Ave., 11096. Tel: 516-239-0953; Fax: 516-239-0386.
Catechesis/Religious Programs—Sr. Kathryn Slevin, C.S.J., D.R.E.
Students 378.

Island Park, Nassau Co., Sacred Heart (1938), Rev. John J. Tutone.
Res., 282 Long Beach Rd., 11558. Tel: 516-432-0655; Fax: 516-897-7567.
Catechesis/Religious Programs—Tel: 516-431-7877. Mrs. Carmel Caracciolo, D.R.E.
Students 359.

Islip Terrace, Suffolk Co., St. Peter the Apostle (1962), Rev. Gerard A. Ringenback; Deacon Joseph Marfoglio.
Res., 94 Valley Stream St., 11752. Tel: 631-277-9448; Fax: 631-224-1594.
School—Our Lady of Providence Regional School, Central Islip. See Regional Schools under Institutions Located in the Diocese. Tel: 631-234-6324; Fax: 631-234-6360.
Catechesis/Religious Programs—Tel: 631-581-5715. Sr. Ellen Zak, C.S.F.N., D.R.E.
Students 30.

Kings Park, Suffolk Co., St. Joseph's (1888), Rev. Msgr. Alex F. Manly; Revs. Francis P. Vattakudiyil; Paul A. Dolan; Deacons W. Donald Bennettson; Roy Smith.
Parish Center—59 Church St., 11754. Tel: 631-269-6635; Fax: 631-269-7508.
School—Holy Family Regional School, Commack. See Regional Schools under Institutions Located in the Diocese. Tel: 631-543-0202; Fax: 631-543-0203.
Catechesis/Religious Programs—Tel: 631-269-4383.
Students 1,828.

Lake Ronkonkoma, Suffolk Co., St. Elizabeth Ann Seton (1988), Rev. Patrick J. Whitney; Deacon Joseph Maffeo.
Res., 800 Portion Rd., 11779. Tel: 631-737-4388; Fax: 631-737-4389.
Catechesis/Religious Programs—Tel: 631-737-8915. Mrs. Michelle Hahn, D.R.E.
Students 1,000.

Levittown, Nassau Co., St. Bernard (1948), Rev. Msgr. George P. Graham, J.C.D., Ph.D.; Revs. Paul G. Driscoll, M.A.; Thomas G. McCormick, M.A. In res., Rev. Martin J. Hall, M.A.
Res., 3100 Hempstead Tpke., 11756. Tel: 516-731-4220; Fax: 516-731-4355.
School—Tel: 516-731-4322.
Lay Teachers 17; Students 246.
Catechesis/Religious Programs—Tel: 516-731-8511.
Students 1,400.

Lindenhurst, Suffolk Co., Our Lady of Perpetual Help (1871), Rev. Msgr. Daniel S. Hamilton; Revs. Vitalis B. Pedzik; Edward M. Seagriff; Richard F. Kammerer; Damian L. Cooper.
Res., 210 S. Wellwood Ave., 11757-4989. Tel: 631-226-7725; Fax: 631-225-9597.
School—Tel: 631-226-0208.
Sisters of St. Dominic 2; Lay Teachers 28; Students 680.
Catechesis/Religious Programs—Tel: 631-226-2384. Diana Castellano, Coord. Program Admin.; Biagio Arpino, Coord. Teaching Training & Curriculum Planning.
Students 2,013.

Long Beach, Nassau Co., St. Ignatius Martyr (1926), Rev. William R. Logan; Deacon Thomas J. Evrard. In res., Rev. Thomas P. O'Donnell; Rev. Msgr. Edward A. Sweeny.
Res., 721 W. Broadway, 11561. Tel: 516-432-0045; Fax: 516-432-0358.
School—Long Beach Regional Catholic School, Long Beach. See Regional Schools under Institutions Located in the Diocese. Tel: 516-432-8900; Fax: 516-432-8926.
Catechesis/Religious Programs—Tel: 516-432-6788. Pam Shannon, D.R.E.
Students 495.

St. Mary of the Isle (1915) (Spanish), Rev. Thomas E. Donohoe; Deacons John P. Dunlop; Nelson Daza; Sr. Frances Monuszko, O.P., Dir. St. Mary of the Isle Community Center, Pastoral Assoc.
Res., 315 E. Walnut St., 11561. Tel: 516-432-0157; Fax: 516-897-0566.
School—Long Beach Regional Catholic School, Long Beach. See Regional Schools under Institutions Located in the Diocese. Tel: 516-432-8900.
Catechesis/Religious Programs—Tel: 516-432-1320. Maryann Specht, D.R.E.
Students 437.

Lynbrook, Nassau Co., Our Lady of Peace (1941), Revs. Lawrence M. Penzes; Mark P. Rowan; Deacons Aniello Squitieri; Thomas Bast. In res., Rev. Antony Asir.
Res., 25 Fowler Ave., 11563. Tel: 516-599-6414; Fax: 516-596-1847.
School—Tel: 516-593-4884; Fax: 516-593-9861.
Sisters of Mercy 1; Lay Teachers 16; Students 338.
Catechesis/Religious Programs—Tel: 516-593-5150.
Students 600.

Malverne, Nassau Co., Our Lady of Lourdes (1926), Revs. Donald M. Baier; Edwin J. Collins, Pastor Emeritus; John F. Whelan; John F. Wymes, M.M.; John F. Meade (NY); Deacons Frank Cove; Theodore J. Van De Ven.
Res., 65 Wright Ave., 11565. Tel: 516-599-1269; Fax: 516-887-9517.
School—76 Park Blvd., 11565. Tel: 516-599-7328; Fax: 516-599-3813. Mr. John A. McQuillan, Prin.
Lay Teachers 19; Students 344.
Catechesis/Religious Programs—Tel: 516-599-7222; Fax: 516-599-2256. Mrs. Margaret DeStefano, D.R.E.
Students 517.

Manhasset, Nassau Co., St. Mary's (1853), Rev. Msgr. John J. McCann; Rev. Msgr. John J. Skelly, Pastor Emeritus; Rev. Msgr. John J. Wiest, Pastor Emeritus; Revs. Kevin M. Smith; Peter Dugandzic. In res., Rev. Cajetan Uchendu (Nigeria).
Res., 1300 Northern Blvd., 11030. Tel: 516-627-0385; Fax: 516-627-6070.
School—1340 Northern Blvd., 11030. Tel: 516-627-0184; Fax: 516-627-3795.
Sisters of the Immaculate Heart of Mary 2; Lay Teachers 30; Students 455.
High Schools—(Coed) 25 Second St., 11030. Tel: 516-627-2092; Fax: 516-627-4383.; 51 Clapham Ave., 11030. Tel: 516-627-2711; Fax: 516-627-3209.
Sisters of the Immaculate Heart of Mary 3; Dominican Sisters 2; Marist Brothers 3; Franciscan Brothers 1; Lay Teachers 56; Students 840.
Catechesis/Religious Programs—Tel: 516-627-4028; Fax: 516-627-5543.
Students 975.

Manorhaven, Nassau Co., Our Lady of Fatima (1948), Rev. Kenneth T. Nee.
Res., 6 Cottonwood Rd., Port Washington, 11050. Tel: 516-767-0781; Fax: 516-767-2981.
Catechesis/Religious Programs—Tel: 516-944-8322.
Students 212.

Manorville, Suffolk Co., St. Peter & Paul (1912), Rev. John J. McGratty; Deacons James McLaughlin; Robert Dejewski; Eda Lorello, Pastoral Assoc.
Res., 781 Wading River Rd., P.O. Box 207, 11949. Tel: 631-369-1273; Fax: 631-369-7141.
Catechesis/Religious Programs—Students 600.

Massapequa, Nassau Co., St. Rose of Lima (1952), Rev. Msgr. Daniel J. Hurley; Revs. Glenn Kennedy; Lawrence A. Sheehan, S.J.; Thomas P. Tuite; Kenneth M. Zach; Deacons Thomas J. Forbes; Thomas J. Quinn; Frank J. Flood; Francis B. McGuiness; Dennis R. O'Connor.
Res., 2 Bayview Ave., 11758-7299. Tel: 516-798-4992; Fax: 516-795-7836.
School—Tel: 516-541-1546; Fax: 516-797-0351. Sr. Kathleen Gallina, Prin.
Sisters of St. Dominic 3; Lay Teachers 29; Students 460.
Catechesis/Religious Programs—Tel: 516-541-1712.
Students 2,100.

Massapequa Park, Nassau Co., Our Lady of Lourdes (1955), Revs. Robert E. Mason; Thomas J. Reynolds, (Retired); Anthony J. Heinlein; Deacon Domenick Valdano.
Res., 855 Carmans Rd., 11762. Tel: 516-541-3270; Fax: 516-797-9851.
School—Tel: 516-798-7926; Fax: 516-798-8159.
Lay Teachers 20; Students 328.
Catechesis/Religious Programs—379 Linden St., 11762. Tel: 516-799-5179.
Students 670.

Mastic Beach, Suffolk Co., St. Jude (1949), Rev. Joseph A. Mirro; Rev. Msgr. Robert E. Fagan; Revs. Joseph Baidoo; Franklin Salazar; Deacons Thomas Gross; Thomas Gillen; Kenneth Geoghan.
Res., 89 Overlook Dr., 11951. Tel: 631-281-5743; Fax: 631-395-5786.
School—Our Lady, Queen of Apostles Regional School, Center Moriches. See Regional Schools under Institutions Located in the Diocese.
Catechesis/Religious Programs—Tel: 631-281-2835. Debra Crean, D.R.E.
Students 1,910.
Parish Human Services Center—89 Overlook Dr., 11951. Tel: 516-281-5634. Helen Mahon, Coord.

Medford, Suffolk Co., St. Sylvester (1948), Revs. Michael F. Holzmann; Edward J. Kealey; Deacons George J. Riegger; Francis P. Roettinger.
Res., 68 Ohio Ave., P.O. Box 336, 11763. Tel: 631-475-4506; Fax: 631-475-1057.
School—Holy Angels Regional School, Patchogue. See Regional Schools under Institutions Located in the Diocese. Tel: 631-475-0422; Fax: 631-475-2038.
Catechesis/Religious Programs—Tel: 631-475-8191. Mrs. Patricia A. Desmond, D.R.E.
Students 1,638.

Melville, Suffolk Co., St. Elizabeth (1962), Revs. Bruce J. Powers; Delfin Perras (Philippines); Deacons Richard Johnston; Joseph Mercolino.
Res., 181 Wolf Hill Rd., 11747. Tel: 631-271-4455; Fax: 631-271-1415.
School—Trinity Regional School, East Northport. See Regional Schools under Institutions Located in the Diocese. Tel: 631-261-5130; Fax: 631-266-5345.
Catechesis/Religious Programs—Students 800.

Merrick, Nassau Co., Cure of Ars (1926), Rev. Msgr. James P. Swiader; Rev. Robert A. Romeo. Pastoral Assocs.: Sr. Miriam Michael Joos, O.P.; Sr. Peggy Tully, O.P.
Res., 2323 Merrick Ave., 11566. Tel: 516-623-1400; Fax: 516-623-1107.
School—St. Elizabeth Ann Seton Regional School, Bellmore/East Meadow. See Regional Schools under Institutions Located in the Diocese. Tel: 516-679-1990; Fax: 516-679-2082.

Mineola, Nassau Co., Corpus Christi (1901) (Spanish-Portugese), Revs. Kenneth H. Winkler; Tomaz Gomide; Robert J. Batule; Rev. Msgr. Eugene F. Murphy; Rev. Thomas F. Murphy; Deacon John C. Reinhart. In res., Rev. Msgr. Edward L. Tarrant.
Res., 155 Garfield Ave., 11501. Tel: 516-746-1223; Fax: 516-294-5311.
School—120 Searing Ave., 11501. Tel: 516-746-2966; Fax: 515-739-3363. Sr. Laura Helbig, O.P., Prin.
Sisters of St. Dominic 1; Lay Teachers 30; Students (Nursery to 8th) 431.
Catechesis/Religious Programs—Tel: 516-294-0631; Fax: 516-294-0631. D.R.E.: Mrs. Ursula Bordonaro; Mrs. Joan O'Brien.
Students 769.

Montauk, Suffolk Co., St. Therese of Lisieux (1929), Rev. Peter Libasci.
Res., 55 S. Etna Ave., P.O. Box 5027, 11954. Tel: 631-668-2200; Fax: 631-668-2384.
School—Stella Maris Regional School, Sag Harbor. See Regional Schools under Institutions Located in the Diocese. Tel: 516-725-2525.
Day Care/Nursery School—Tel: 631-668-5353.
Children (3 & 4 years old) 42.
Catechesis/Religious Programs—Tel: 631-668-6141.
Students 214.

Nesconset, Suffolk Co., Church of the Holy Cross (1988), Pastoral Team: Rev. William G. Breslawski; Sr. Marion Snow, C.S.J., Pastoral Assoc.
Res., 95 Old Nichols Rd., 11767. Tel: 631-265-2200; Fax: 631-265-2229.
Catechesis/Religious Programs—Tel: 631-265-2200, Ext. 12. Mrs. Judith Pickel, D.R.E.
Students 1,217.

New Hyde Park, Nassau Co., Holy Spirit (1893), Rev. Msgr. John P. Martin, Co-Pastor; Rev. Msgr. Anthony M. Stangnelli, Co-Pastor. In res., Rev. Robert O. Morrissey.
Res., 500 Jericho Tpke., 11040. Tel: 516-354-0359; Fax: 516-354-2611 (Rectory).
School—13 S. Sixth St., 11040. Tel: 516-354-5566; Fax: 516-354-0325. Sr. Judy Flanagan, O.P., Prin.
Sisters of St. Dominic (Amityville) 6; Lay Teachers 23; Students 357.
Catechesis/Religious Programs—13 S. 6th St., 11040. Tel: 516-354-2363.
Students 660.

Notre Dame (1941), Rev. Msgr. Peter Pflomm; Revs. John Murray, Pastor Emeritus; William T. Slater; Stephen H. Donnelly; Anthony Kim (Korea); Sr. Judith A. Golden, O.P., Pastoral Assoc.; Deacon Gilbert McGaffney.
Res., 45 Mayfair Rd., 11040. Tel: 516-352-7203; Fax: 516-326-7988.
School—Tel: 516-354-5618; Fax: 516-354-5952. Sr. Lorraine McDonald, O.P., Prin.
Sisters of St. Dominic (Amityville) 5; Lay Teachers 28; Students 612.
Catechesis/Religious Programs—25 Mayfair Rd., 11040. Tel: 516-437-5604. Sr. Mary Jane Coleman, R.S.M., D.R.E.
Students 900.

North Merrick, Nassau Co., Sacred Heart (1952), Revs. Thomas G. Gallagher; Kevin W. Gruber; Deacon Daniel J. Delargy.
Res., 720 Merrick Ave., 11566. Tel: 516-379-1356; Fax: 516-379-1610.
School—Tel: 516-378-5797; Fax: 516-378-5797. Sr. Mary Morrin, C.S.J., Prin.
Sisters of St. Joseph 8; Lay Teachers 16; Students 341.
Catechesis/Religious Programs—Tel: 516-868-9406. Mrs. Cecelia Lerro, D.R.E.
Students 1,150.

Northport, Suffolk Co., St. Philip Neri (1894), Rev. Peter J. Garry; Deacons John F. Burkart; Andrew Schneider; Sr. Grace Vagnini, C.S.J., Pastoral Assoc. In res., Rev. Thomas J. Colgan.
Res., 344 Main St., 11768. Tel: 631-261-7753; Fax: 631-261-7420. [CEM]
School—Trinity Regional School, East Northport. See Regional Schools under Institutions Located in the Diocese. Tel: 631-261-5130 (main); 8520; Fax: 631-261-8560.
Catechesis/Religious Programs—Tel: 631-261-7800; Fax: 631-261-7836. D.R.E.: Kathleen Reid; Marianne Devine.
Students 780.

Ocean Beach, (Fire Island) Suffolk Co., Our Lady of the Magnificat (1921), Rev. Msgr. Ronald E. Hayde; Rev. Robert O. Morrissey, J.C.D.
Mailing Address: P.O. Box 445, 11770. Tel: 631-583-5868.

Oceanside, Nassau Co., St. Anthony (1927), Revs. Carsten Martensen, S.J.; Vincent J. Ritchie, S.J.; Rev. Msgr. Conrad R. Dietz; Revs. Martin F. Kirby; Pierce A. Brennan, S.J.; Matthew F. Roche, S.J.; Deacon James W. Flannery; Anna Maria Sirianni, C.S.W., Parish Outreach Coord., Tel: 516-764-9257.
Res., 110 Anchor Ave., 11572. Tel: 516-764-0048; 764-0665; Fax: 516-764-7726.
Catechesis/Religious Programs—Tel: 516-678-3388. Kathy Logan, D.R.E.
Students 1,128.

Oyster Bay, Nassau Co., St. Dominic's (1895), Rev. Msgr. Charles A. Ribaudo; Rev. Msgr. James E. Collins, Pastor Emeritus; Rev. Malcolm J. Burns.
Res., 96 Anstice St., 11771. Tel: 516-922-4488; Fax: 516-922-9491.
School—35 School St., 11771. Tel: 516-922-4233; Fax: 516-624-7613.
Sisters of the Immaculate Heart of Mary 2; Lay Teachers 19; Students 366.
High School—110 Antice St., 11771. Tel: 516-922-4888; Fax: 516-922-4898.
Sisters 2; Lay Teachers 40; Students 490.
Catechesis/Religious Programs—Tel: 516-922-7788.
Students 735.

Patchogue, Suffolk Co., St. Francis de Sales (1888), Rev. Robert J. Clerkin; Deacons Martin McIndoe; Fernando J. Quinones; Francisco Diaz-Granados; Sr. Joanna Ohlandt, C.S.J.; Sr. Marie Lourdes Vanston, I.H.M., Pastoral Assoc.
Res., 7 Amity St., P.O. Box 71, 11772. Tel: 631-475-0161; Fax: 631-475-1481. [CEM]
School—Holy Angels Regional School, Patchogue. See Regional Schools under Institutions Located in the Diocese. Tel: 631-475-0422; Fax: 631-475-2036.

Catechesis/Religious Programs—Tel: 631-289-4339. D.R.E.: Anne Boyce; Elaine Heschl. Students 700.

Our Lady of Mt. Carmel (1925) (Italian), Revs. Robert J. O'Connell; Alexander L. Sledzaus, Pastor Emeritus; Deacons Joseph Mystkowski; Bela Kalman; Barbara Cotsifas, Business Mgr.
Res., 495 New North Ocean Ave., 11772. Tel: 631-475-4739; Fax: 631-447-1030.
School—Holy Angels Regional School, Patchogue. See Regional Schools under Institutions Located in the Diocese. Tel: 631-475-0422; Fax: 631-475-2036.
Catechesis/Religious Programs—Tel: 631-289-7327. Frances McMahon, D.R.E.
Students 790.

Plainview, Nassau Co., St. Pius X (1955), Rev. Hugh D. Cannon. In res., Revs. David L. Mani (India) Chap. VA Hospital at Northport; Jose Simon Palliparambil, Chap., North Shore University Hospital at Plainview; Moise Aime (Haiti) Haitian Apostolate; Elaine D. Hallisey, Pastoral Assoc.
Res., One St. Pius Ct., 11803. Tel: 516-938-3959; Fax: 516-433-6138.
School—St. John Baptist de LaSalle Regional School, Bethpage/Farmingdale. See Regional Schools under Institutions Located in the Diocese. Tel: 516-931-0983 (Bethpage); 516-694-3610 (Farmingdale); Fax: 516-931-1502 (Bthpg.); 694-3614 (Fmgdl.).
Catechesis/Religious Programs—Tel: 516-822-8348.
Students 312.
Spirit Life Center: 300 Washington Ave., Tel: 516-938-7119. Rev. Robert A. McGuire, S.J.

Point Lookout, Nassau Co., Our Lady of the Miraculous Medal (1937) (Irish), Revs. William Gomes; Andrew J. Gallagher, Pastor Emeritus.
Res., 75 Parkside Dr., 11569. Tel: 516-431-2772; Fax: 516-432-8669.
School—Long Beach Regional Catholic School, Long Beach. See Regional Schools under Institutions Located in the Diocese. Tel: 516-432-8900; Fax: 516-432-8926.
Catechesis/Religious Programs—Students 60.

Port Jefferson, Suffolk Co., Infant Jesus (1903), Revs. Charles Romano; Andrew Nierengarten; John Worthley; Eric Dadson; Deacons William J. Powers; Richard E. Waldmann.
Res., 110 Myrtle Ave., 11777. Tel: 631-473-0165; Fax: 631-331-8094.
School—Our Lady of Wisdom Regional School, Port Jefferson. See Regional Schools under Institutions Located in the Diocese. Tel: 631-473-1211; Fax: 631-473-1064.
Catechesis/Religious Programs—Tel: 631-928-0447. Mrs. Barbara Saulino, D.R.E.
Students 1,400.

St. Gerard Majella (1968), Co-Pastors: Revs. William A. Hanson; Christopher J. Heller; Deacon Thomas O'Connor.
Res., 300 Terryville Rd., Port Jefferson Station, 11776. Tel: 631-473-2900; Fax: 631-473-0015.
School—Our Lady of Wisdom Regional School, Port Jefferson. See Regional Schools under Institutions Located in the Diocese. Tel: 631-473-1211; Fax: 631-473-1064.
Catechesis/Religious Programs—Tel: 631-928-2550. Alice Meyer, D.R.E.
Students 1,157.

Port Washington, Nassau Co., St. Peter of Alcantara (1901), Rev. Msgr. Daniel A. Picciano; Rev. Msgr. Walter E. Simmons, Pastor Emeritus; Rev. James F. Drew; Deacons Frank G. D'Angelo; Francis B. McGuinness, Business Mgr.
Res., 1327 Port Washington Blvd., 11050. Tel: 516-883-6675; Fax: 516-944-7461.
School—Tel: 516-944-3772; Fax: 516-767-8075. Sr. Agnes Shaw, I.H.M., Prin.
Sisters 8; Lay Teachers 19; Students 660.
Catechesis/Religious Programs—Tel: 516-883-5584. Dr. Timothy B. Kunz, D.R.E.
Students 480.
Convent—1317 Port Washington Blvd., 11050. Tel: 516-762-1282. Sisters, Servants of the Immaculate Heart of Mary (Scranton, PA)

Riverhead, Suffolk Co., St. John the Evangelist (1861), Revs. Thomas W. Coby; Jeffrey Madley. In res., Most Rev. Emil A. Wcela; Deacon John Lovett.
Res., 546 St. John's Pl., 11901. Tel: 631-727-2030; Fax: 631-369-5228. [CEM]
School—Tel: 631-727-4144; Fax: 631-727-3851.
Sisters of St. Dominic (Amityville) 1; Lay Teachers 9; Students 251.
Catechesis/Religious Programs—Tel: 631-727-6774.
Students 435.

St. Isidore's (1903) (Polish), Rev. Msgr. John Mirecki; Rev. Joseph Walas (Poland) Pastoral Assoc.
Res., 622 Pulaski St., 11901. Tel: 631-727-2114; Fax: 631-369-3566. [CEM]
School—515 Marcy Ave., 11901. Tel: 631-727-1650; Fax: 631-727-3945. Sr. Linda Joseph Chichi, C.S.F.N., Prin.
Sisters of the Holy Family of Nazareth 3; Lay Teachers 8; Students 260.
Catechesis/Religious Programs—Students 70.

Rocky Point, Suffolk Co., St. Anthony of Padua (1948), Revs. Patrick J. Callahan, Admin.; Michael Maffeo.
Res., 614 Rte. 25A, 11778. Tel: 631-744-2609; Fax: 631-744-5782.
Catechesis/Religious Programs—Tel: 631-821-0872.
Students 1,520.

Ronkonkoma, Suffolk Co., St. Joseph's (1910), Rev. Msgr. Francis S. Midura; Revs. Paul F. Butler; Peter Devaras; Peter T. Liu; Deacons James Altonji; Michael J. DeBellis; Joseph Dougherty; John Erdman. In res., Rev. Thomas F. Mulvanerty.
Res., 45 Church St., 11779-3300. Tel: 631-588-8456; Fax: 631-471-2569.
School—25 Church St., 11779. Tel: 631-588-4760; Fax: 631-588-0543. Mrs. Marie Salvietti, Prin.
Lay Teachers 27; Students 528.
Catechesis/Religious Programs—Tel: 631-981-1805. Linda Cussen, D.R.E.
Students 1,310.

Roosevelt, Nassau Co., Queen of the Most Holy Rosary (1919), Rev. Msgr. Thomas E. Molloy, J.C.D.; Sr. Kathleen O'Donnell, S.C., Pastoral Assoc.; Deacons Louis Sandberg; Clinton Lewis; Thomas Jackson. In res., Rev. Ralph Ferro.
Res., 196 W. Centennial Ave., 11575. Tel: 516-378-1315; Fax: 516-378-5754.
Catechesis/Religious Programs—200 W. Centennial Ave., 11575. Tel: 516-623-1391.
Students 335.

Roslyn, Nassau Co., St. Mary's (1871), Rev. Msgr. Richard C. Bauhoff; Deacons Edward M. Case; Jorge Coyoy.
Res., 110 Bryant Ave., P.O. Box 387, 11576-0387. Tel: 516-621-2222; Fax: 516-621-7892.
School—All Saints Regional Catholic School, Glen Cove. See Regional Schools under Institutions Located in the Diocese. Tel: 516-676-0762; Fax: 516-676-0660.
Catechesis/Religious Programs—Tel: 516-621-6798. Nora Toal, D.R.E.
Students 306.

Sag Harbor, Suffolk Co., St. Andrew's (1859), Rev. Msgr. Ronald A. Richardson; Sr. Lucille D'Amelio, O.P., Pastoral Assoc. In res., Rev. Andrew P. Blake, Pastor Emeritus.
Res., 122 Division St, 11963-3154. Tel: 631-725-0123; Fax: 631-725-3310. [CEM]
School—Stella Maris Regional School, Sag Harbor. See Regional Schools under Institutions Located in the Diocese. Tel: 631-725-2525; Fax: 631-725-4587.
Catechesis/Religious Programs—Tel: 631-725-0123, Ext. 22.
Students 250.

St. James, Suffolk Co., SS. Philip and James (1907), Revs. Robert J. Giuntini; Michael A. Carroll; James C. Bowman; Deacons Charles Brown; Kenneth Maher; Frank Crivello; Robert Heschl; John Keenan; Anthony Chamberlain. In res., Rev. Ladislaus Cser, S.J.
Res., One Carow Pl., 11780. Tel: 631-584-5454; Fax: 631-862-9675.
School—(Grades PreK-8). Tel: 631-584-7896; Fax: 631-584-3258. Mr. Anthony Giordano, Prin.
Lay Teachers 17; Students 418.
Catechesis/Religious Programs—Tel: 631-584-5486.
Students 1,500.

Saltaire, Suffolk Co., Our Lady Star of the Sea, Mission Chapel. (Summer Mission). Rev. Richard R. Viladesau, S.T.D., Admin.
Res., St. Anastasia Church, 45-14 245th St., Douglaston, 11362. Tel: 718-631-4454.

Sayville, Suffolk Co., St. Lawrence the Martyr (1895), Rev. Msgr. John Rowan; Rev. Msgr. John T. Heinlein; Rev. Donald C. Hayden; Deacon William F. Fullam, Jr.
Res., 27 Handsome Ave., 11782. Tel: 631-589-0042; 589-8135; 589-3887; Fax: 631-589-5318. [CEM]
School—Prince of Peace Regional School, Sayville. See Regional Schools under Institutions Located in the Diocese. Tel: 631-589-3926.
Catechesis/Religious Programs—Tel: 631-589-3160. Mrs. Lorraine Gallagher, D.R.E.
Students 1,460.

Sea Cliff, Nassau Co., St. Boniface Martyr (1898), Rev. Michael J. Torpey.
Res., 145 Glen Ave., 11579. Tel: 516-676-0676; Fax: 516-674-6742.
School—All Saints Regional Catholic School, Glen Cove. See Regional Schools under Institutions Located in the Diocese.
Catechesis/Religious Programs—Tel: 516-671-0418. Julia Byrne, D.R.E.
Students 320.

Seaford, Nassau Co., St. William, the Abbot (1928), Rev. William E. Koenig; Rev. Msgr. Thomas G. Leavey, Pastor Emeritus; Revs. Steven Camp; Jeffrey W. Johnston; Deacons William Brennan; Thomas Buchenberger.
Res., 2000 Jackson Ave., 11783. Tel: 516-785-1266; Fax: 516-785-4824.
School—2001 Jackson Ave., 11783. Tel: 516-785-6784; Fax: 516-785-2752. Mrs. Anna Guardino, Prin.
Ursuline Sisters 1; Lay Teachers 25; Students 600.
Catechesis/Religious Programs—Tel: 516-679-9558; Fax: 516-679-1649. Mrs. Georgette Levesque, D.R.E.
Students 1,400.

Maria Regina (1954), Revs. Gennaro J. DiSpigno; Joseph E. Nohs; Deacons Gerald F. Whitfield; John A. Weigel; John R. Nuzzi. In res., Rev. Francis M. Casey.
Res., 3945 Jerusalem Ave., 11783. Tel: 516-798-2415; Fax: 516-798-7493.
School—4045 Jerusalem Ave., 11783. Tel: 516-541-1229; Fax: 516-541-1235. Diane DeCandia, Prin.; Diane F. Ragonnet, Asst. Prin.
Sisters of Mercy 1; Lay Teachers 27; Students 576.
Catechesis/Religious Programs—3945 Jerusalem Ave., 11783. Tel: 516-541-0921; Fax: 516-795-2510.
Students 1,800.

St. James (1951), Rev. Robert S. Hewes; Rev. Dr. Francis Samuel; Rev. Gene Vollmer; Deacons James G. Beirne; John G. Leahy; Allen J. Helmbrecht, Business Mgr.
Res., 80 Hicksville Rd., 11783. Tel: 516-731-3710; Fax: 516-731-4828.
School—St. John Baptist de LaSalle Regional School, Bethpage/Farmingdale. See Regional Schools under Institutions Located in the Diocese. Tel: 516-931-0983; Fax: 516-931-1502.
Catechesis/Religious Programs—Tel: 516-796-2979; Fax: 516-731-4828. Sr. Rosemary Traynor, C.P., D.R.E.
Students 1,810.

Selden, Suffolk Co., St. Margaret of Scotland (1948), Revs. Christopher Aridas; Joseph Alenchery (India); Deacons William E. Kogler; Biagio Muratore; Phil Paolicelli; Joseph Scollan; Dennis Laderwager, Pastoral Assoc.
Res., 81 College Rd., 11784. Tel: 631-732-3131; Fax: 631-732-8827.
School—Holy Angels Regional School, Patchogue. See Regional Schools under Institutions Located in the Diocese. Tel: 631-475-0422; Fax: 631-475-2036.
Catechesis/Religious Programs—Tel: 631-698-0798; Fax: 631-732-8827. D.R.E.: Cathy DePasquale; Barbara Mahon; Marilynne Schaefer; Peggy Scheiner.
Students 1,500.

Setauket, Suffolk Co., St. James (1949), Revs. Donald Diederich, J.C.D.; Matthew Kotiaram; John Fitzgerald; Thomas F. McGlade, Pastor Emeritus; Philip J. Reehil, Pastor Emeritus; Deacons Gerry Coates; Thomas Owens; Joseph Ingulli.
Res., 429 Rte. 25-A, 11733. Tel: 631-941-4141; Fax: 631-751-6607. [CEM]
School—Our Lady of Wisdom Regional School, Port Jefferson. See Regional Schools under Institutions Located in the Diocese. Tel: 631-473-1211.
Catechesis/Religious Programs—Tel: 631-751-7287. D.R.E.: Louise DiCarlo; Joan Harley.
Students 1,291.

Shelter Island, Suffolk Co., Our Lady of the Isle (1907), Rev. Charles Dougherty, C.P.
Shelter Island Heights, Box 3027, Shelter Island Heights, 11965. Tel: 631-749-0001; Fax: 631-749-4218. [CEM]
School—Stella Maris Regional School, Sag Harbor. See Regional Schools under Institutions Located in the Diocese.

Shoreham, Suffolk Co., St. Mark (1973), Revs. Theodore J. Howard; William E. McCarthy; Deacon Patrick Gerace.
Res., 105 Randall Rd., 11786. Tel: 631-744-2800; Fax: 631-821-1628.
Catechesis/Religious Programs—Tel: 631-821-0550. Mrs. Lynn Fein, D.R.E.
Students 1,110.

Smithtown, Suffolk Co., St. Patrick (1952) (Irish/Italian), Rev. Msgr. Paul Walsh; Revs. Douglas Arcoleo; Frank J. Parisi; Deacons Richard Sanders; Fred Jackman; John Chott; Owen Farley; Vincent Abrahams. In res., Revs. Vincent Liu; Frederick Hill.
Res., 280 E. Main St., 11787. Tel: 631-265-2271; Fax: 631-863-1586. [CEM]
School—Tel: 631-724-0285; Fax: 631-265-4841. Mrs. Eileen Sadicario, Prin.
Sisters of St. Joseph 3; Lay Teachers 24; Students 708.
Catechesis/Religious Programs—Tel: 631-724-7454; Fax: 631-265-1250. Paula Billyard, D.R.E.
Students 1,708.

Sound Beach, Suffolk Co., St. Louis de Montfort (1971), Rev. Charles E. Papa; Rev. Msgr. John A. McGuire, Pastor Emeritus; Rev. Thomas P. Murray; Deacons Joseph T. Bartolotto; Peter F. Schultz; Gary F. Swane.
Mailing Address: 75 New York Ave., 11789. Tel: 631-744-8566; Fax: 631-744-8611.
School—Our Lady of Wisdom Regional School, Port Jefferson. See Regional Schools under Institutions Located in the Diocese. Tel: 631-473-1211; Fax: 631-473-1064.
Catechesis/Religious Programs—Tel: 631-744-9515; Fax: 631-821-6089. Mr. John McNamara, D.R.E.
Students 2,022.

Southampton, Suffolk Co., Sacred Hearts of Jesus and Mary (1896), Rev. Jeffrey J. Madley; Rev. Msgr. Edmond J. Trench, Pastor Emeritus; Deacons John W. McGauvran; John P. Moran.
Res., 168 Hill St., 11968. Tel: 631-283-0097; Fax: 631-283-3836. [CEM]
School—Our Lady of the Hamptons Regional School. See Regional Schools under Institutions Located in the Diocese. Tel: 631-283-9140.
Catechesis/Religious Programs—Tel: 631-283-3836.
Students 430.

Our Lady of Poland (1918) (Polish), Rev. Stanley Kondeja; Deacon James Ashe.
Res., 35 Maple St., 11968. Tel: 631-283-0667; Fax: 631-287-4146.
School—Our Lady of the Hamptons Regional School. See Regional Schools under Institutions Located in the Diocese. Tel: 631-283-9140; Fax: 631-287-3958.
Catechesis/Religious Programs—Tel: 631-283-5230; Fax: 631-283-5230.
Students 382.

Southold, Suffolk Co., St. Patrick's (1865), Revs. George J. Michell; Martin J. Osborne, Pastor Emeritus.
Res., Main Rd., P.O. Box 1117, 11971-1401. Tel: 631-765-3442; Fax: 631-765-9631. [CEM]
School—Our Lady of Mercy, Cutchogue. See Regional Schools under Institutions Located in the Diocese. Tel: 631-734-5166.
Catechesis/Religious Programs—Tel: 631-765-2338.
Students 262.

Syosset, Nassau Co., St. Edward Confessor (1952), Revs. Joseph C. McComiskey; Felix Weerasinghe; Deacons James Murphy; Lionel Roberts.
Res., 205 Jackson Ave., 11791-4218. Tel: 516-921-4420 (Information Line), 921-0756 (Rectory Office); Fax: 516-921-4549.
School—2 Teibrook Ave., 11791. Tel: 516-921-7767; Fax: 516-496-0001. Mrs. Anne Schaefer, M.S., Prin.
Sisters of Mercy (Brooklyn) 1; Lay Teachers 17; Students 257.
Parish Social Ministry Office:—Tel: 516-921-5628; Fax: 516-364-7326. Ms. Dawn Ravella, Dir.
Youth Ministry Office—Tel: 516-921-7631. Gerald Giglio, Dir.
Catechesis/Religious Programs—Tel: 516-364-1790 (Grades 1-5); 364-6803 (Grades 6-8). D.R.E.: Mrs. Dorothy Kuchler, (Grades 1-5); Ms. Maureen Moore, (Grades 6-8).
Students 825.

Uniondale, Nassau Co., St. Martha (1949), Revs. Edward C. Fitzpatrick; Edward G. Sullivan; Deacons Miguel Angel Romero; Trevor St. Evef Mathurin.
Res., 546 Greengrove Ave., 11553. Tel: 516-481-2550; Fax: 516-564-4552.
School—St. Martin de Porres Regional School, Uniondale. See Regional Schools under Institutions Located in the Diocese. Tel: 516-481-3303; Fax: 516-483-4138.
Catechesis/Religious Programs—Tel: 516-481-6608. Sr. Eileen Curley, R.S.M., D.R.E.
Students 251.

Valley Stream, Nassau Co., Holy Name of Mary (1902), Revs. Thomas J. Harold; Theodore J. LeTure, Pastor Emeritus; James L. Maltese; Stephen J. Brigandi, Jr.; Saji George; Deacons Anthony W. Cuseo; James O'Hara; Clyde Ruggieri; Richard F. Raad; Robert Walsh.
Res., 55 E. Jamaica Ave., 11580. Tel: 516-825-1450; Fax: 516-568-1906.
School—90 S. Grove St., 11580. Tel: 516-825-4009. Sr. Elizabeth Marie Lynch, C.S.J., Prin.
Lay Teachers 18; Students 275.
Catechesis/Religious Programs—90 S. Grove St., 11580. Tel: 516-825-1810. Sr. Barbara Shea, O.P., D.R.E.
Students 1,250.
Parish Outreach—90 S. Grove St., 11580. Tel: 516-825-0177; Fax: 516-825-5092. Sr. Margie Kelly, C.S.J., Dir.

Blessed Sacrament (1950), Revs. Gregory J. Cappuccino; Frank M. Nelson; Aloysius P. Pakianather (Sri Lanka); Deacons Anthony M. Cedrone; Salvatore A. Marino.
Res., 201 N. Central Ave., 11580. Tel: 516-568-1027; Fax: 516-872-1499.
School—50 Rose Ave., 11580. Tel: 516-825-7334. Melanie Maione, Prin.
Sisters of St. Joseph 1; Lay Teachers 18; Students 353.
Catechesis/Religious Programs—Tel: 516-561-1407. Lucille Vavosa, D.R.E.
Students 1,000.

Wading River, Suffolk Co., St. John Baptist (1922), Rev. Msgr. John P. Sullivan; Sr. Sheila Molloy, O.S.U., Pastoral Assoc.; Deacons Frederick Finter; Gregory Senholzi.
Res., 1488 North Country Rd., 11792. Tel: 631-929-4339; Fax: 631-369-6961.
Catechesis/Religious Programs—Students 694.

Wantagh, Nassau Co., St. Frances de Chantal (1952), Rev. Msgr. Robert E. Guglielmone; Revs. Joseph DeGrocco; James Mannion; Deacon Robert O'Donovan; Sr. Jocelyn Panzetta, C.I.J. In res., Rev. Thomas V. Arnao.
Res., 1309 Wantagh Ave., 11793. Tel: 516-785-2333; Fax: 516-826-7645.
School—St. Elizabeth Ann Seton Regional School, Bellmore/East Meadow. See Wantagh Regional Schools under Institutions Located in the Diocese. Tel: 516-785-5709; Fax: 516-785-4468.
Catechesis/Religious Programs—Judith Brady, D.R.E.
Students 2,018.

West Babylon, Suffolk Co., Our Lady of Grace (1963), Rev. Msgr. James McNamara; Revs. Thomas Saloy; William O'Rourke; Robert Lubrano; Deacons Peter DiGiuseppe, Pastoral Assoc.; John Morrow; Charles Graff; William Austin.
Res., 702 Albin Ave., 11704. Tel: 631-587-5185; Fax: 631-587-1427.
Catechesis/Religious Programs—Tel: 631-661-9353. D.R.E.: Barbara McGrellis; Patricia Callahan; Lee Abseck.
Students 2,305.

Westbury, Nassau Co., St. Brigid (1850), Revs. Francis X. Gaeta; James Stachacz; Augustine Savarimuthu, S.J. (India); Deacons Eugene Capobianco; Michael Metzdorff; Felix Matheis; James Morris; Frank Pesce.
Res., 75 Post Ave., 11590. Tel: 516-334-0021; Fax: 516-334-0082.
School—St. Brigid/ Our Lady of Hope Regional School, 101 Maple Ave., 11590. Tel: 516-333-0580; Fax: 516-333-0590. Paul P. Clagnaz, Prin.
School Sisters of Notre Dame 1; Lay Teachers 30; Students 534.
Catechesis/Religious Programs—Tel: 516-333-9434. D.R.E.: Stephanie Clagnaz; Jennifer Gallagher.
Students 1,700.

Westhampton Beach, Suffolk Co., Immaculate Conception (1891), Rev. Msgr. Joseph Murray.
Res., 580 Main Rd., 11978. Tel: 631-288-1423; Fax: 631-288-5498.
School—Our Lady, Queen of Apostles Regional School, Center Moriches. See Regional Schools under Institutions Located in the Diocese.
Catechesis/Religious Programs—Tel: 631-288-4188; Fax: 631-288-8215. Sr. Virginia Baeder, D.R.E.
Students 518.

West Hempstead, Nassau Co., St. Thomas, the Apostle (1931), Rev. Msgr. James P. Lisante; Revs. Andrzej Zglejszewski; Paul R. Bie. In res., Revs. Martin W. Curley; William I. Delaney.
Res., 24 Westminster Rd., 11552. Tel: 516-489-8585; Fax: 516-292-2651.
School—12 Westminster Rd., 11552. Tel: 516-481-9310; Fax: 516-481-8769. Mrs. Christina Teisch, Prin.
Sisters 3; Lay Teachers 22; Students 494.
Catechesis/Religious Programs—Tel: 516-538-7460. Mrs. Mary Ann Pellegrino, D.R.E.
Students 950.
Mission—Lakeview, Nassau Co., Chapel, Nassau Blvd. & Hempstead Ave., 11552. Tel: 516-483-4091.

West Islip, Suffolk Co., Our Lady of Lourdes (1956), Revs. Michael A. Vetrano; Francis X. Eisele; Richard P. Whitney; Deacons Stephen M. Behar; John Teufel; John DeGuardi. In res., Rev. James C. Vlaun.
Res., 455 Hunter Ave., 11795. Tel: 631-661-3224; Fax: 631-661-7143.
School—44 Toomey Rd., 11795. Tel: 631-587-7200; Fax: 631-587-4531. Regina A. Cioffi, Prin.
Lay Teachers 15; Students 363.
Catechesis/Religious Programs—Tel: 631-661-5440; Fax: 631-661-3606. D.R.E.: Sr. Diane Liona; Sr. Nancy Campkin.
Students 2,431.

Williston Park, Nassau Co., St. Aidan's Church (1929), Revs. Robert L. Hayden; Stephen Pietrowski; Bruno Dekrem; Rev. Msgr. Charles E. Bermingham, Pastor Emeritus; Rev. Msgr. Robert J. Kirwin, Pastor Emeritus; Deacons Herman J. Determann; Richard T. Blake; Salvatore Villani. In res., Rev. James Nunes.
Res., 505 Willis Ave., 11596. Tel: 516-746-6585; Fax: 516-746-6055.
Schools—(Grades Nursery-3) 525 Willis Ave., 11596. Tel: 516-746-6270.; (Grades 4-8) 510 Willis Ave., 11596. Tel: 518-747-6150. Eileen Oliver, Prin.
Sisters 2; Lay Teachers 28; Students 609.
Catechesis/Religious Programs—Tel: 516-747-3272. D.R.E.: Mrs. Elaina Kedjierski; Ms. Claire Schirtzer.
Students 1,035.
Convent—16 Pembroke St., 11596. Tel: 518-741-6869. Sisters of Charity

Woodbury, Nassau Co., Holy Name of Jesus (1962), Rev. Msgr. Donald M. Beckmann, D.Min.; Diane M. Vella, Pastoral Assoc.
Res., 690 Woodbury Rd., 11797-2504. Tel: 516-921-2334; Fax: 516-921-2408.
Catechesis/Religious Programs—Students 160.

Wyandanch, Suffolk Co., Our Lady of the Miraculous Medal (1932), Rev. William F. Brisotti; Deacon Richard Lamb.
Res., 1434 Straight Path, 11798. Tel: 631-643-7568; Fax: 631-643-5935.
Gerald Ryan Outreach Center, Inc.—Tel: 631-643-7591. Mrs. Ann Druckenmiller, Dir.; Sr. Elizabeth Myles, C.S.J., Religious Education & Youth Ministry, Tel: 631-643-3364.
Catechesis/Religious Programs—Tel: 631-643-3364.
Students 220.

Chaplains of Public Institutions

ROCKVILLE CENTRE. *Mercy Medical Center* 50 North Park Ave., Tel: 516-678-5800, Ext. 521. Sr. Eileen Donovan, O.P., Dir., Chaplaincy, Chaplains: Revs. Antony Asir; Michael Aggrey; Sr. Mary Alice Aschenbach, C.I.J., Dir.; Sr. Mary Morrow, D.W.; Sr. Norma Jean Lokcinski, C.I.J.; Sr. Elizabeth Scanlan, R.S.M.; Mary Ellen Eichman,
Mercy Hospice, Tel: 516-485-3060. Mrs. Edith Mi-ozzi, Dir.; Sr. Eleanor Boegel, Chap.

AMITYVILLE. *Brunswick Hospital*. (Vacant) 366 Broadway, 11701. Tel: 631-789-7000; 264-0124; 842-8488.
South Oaks Psychiatric Hospital Sunrise Hwy., 11701. Tel: 631-264-4000. Rev. Robert A. Hyatt, Res., Our Lady of Consolation Home, Tel: 631-598-0497.

BAY SHORE. *Southside Hospital* Montauk Hwy., 11706. Tel: 631-435-3484. Revs. Harold E. McBride, S.M.M.; Peter J. McCrann, S.M.M.

BETHPAGE. *New Island Hospital*. Rev. John Patton.

EAST MEADOW. *Nassau County Medical Center* 2201 Hempstead Tpke., 11554. Tel: 516-572-3195; 572-6069. Revs. Angelo J. Ditta; Brian A. McKeon; Sr. Maureen Chase.
Nassau County Police Department. Rev. Msgr. John A. Alesandro; Rev. Joseph J. D'Angelo.
Nassau County, Fire Chiefs, Council of. Rev. Kevin M. Smith.

GLEN COVE. *North Shore Community Hospital at Glen Cove* Tel: 516-676-5000. Rev. Juniper J. Thomas.

HUNTINGTON. *Huntington Hospital* 11743. Tel: 631-351-2000. Rev. Thomas Edamattan; Deacon Edward Billia.

MANHASSET. *North Shore Univ. Hospital* 1554 Community Dr., 11030. Tel: 516-562-0100. Revs. Antony Xavier; Isaac Mensah, Res., North Shore Hospital, Tel: 516-562-4713.

MELVILLE. *Long Island Developmental Center*. (Vacant) Box 788, 11747. Tel: 516-385-2700.

MINEOLA. *Winthrop Hospital* First St., 11501. Tel: 516-663-0333. Rev. Msgr. Eugene F. Murphy; Rev. Thomas Murphy, Res., Corpus Christi, 155 Garfield Ave., 11501-2583. Tel: 516-746-1223.

NESCONSET. *Nesconset Nursing Home*. Vacant. 11767. Tel: 516-361-8800.

NORTHPORT. *Veteran's Administration Hospital* 11768. Tel: 516-261-4400. Revs. John S. Malone, C.S.C.; Fozar David Moni; Augustine J. Sheehan.

OCEANSIDE. *South Nassau Communities Hospital* Tel: 516-763-2030. Deacon Charles Muscarnera.

PATCHOGUE. *Brookhaven Memorial Hospital* 100 Hospital Rd., 11772. Tel: 631-654-7100. Bro. Richard J. Crawley, O.F.M.Cap.

PLAINVIEW. *North Shore Hospital at Plainview* 888 Old Country Rd., 11083. Tel: 516-681-8900. Rev. Jose Simon Palliparambil, Res., St. Pius X, 1 St. Pius Ct., 11803-4023. Tel: 516-938-3959.

PORT JEFFERSON. *Maryhaven Center of Hope* 11777. Tel: 631-474-3400. Sr. Maryaline Zierle, O.P.
Mather Memorial Hospital 11777. Tel: 631-473-1320, Ext. 4007. Mrs. Theresa Helldorfer.
St. Charles Hospital, Port Jefferson, New York 11777. Tel: 631-474-6411. Revs. Eric Dadson; Jose Mappilamattel; Sr. Martha Winum, D.W.; Sr. Mary Jo O'Connor, D.W.; Sr. Josefita Rodriguez.

ROSLYN. *St. Francis Hospital* 11576. Sr. Lois Ann Van Delft, F.M.M., Dir.; Revs. Gabriel Miah; Augustine Kuriapilly; Sr. Rita Sculti, O.P.; Sr. Nancy Exconde, F.M.M.; Sr. Elizabeth Burke, P.B.V.M.; Sr. Mari Garesche, F.M.M.; Sr. Veronica Hanlon, R.S.M.

SAYVILLE. *Good Samaritan Nursing Home* 11782. Tel: 631-567-6600. Sr. Elizabeth Toohig, S.C.; Rev. Francis B. Nuss.

SMITHTOWN. *St. Catherine of Siena Hospital* 11787. Tel: 631-360-2000. Rev. Frederick Hill, Res., St. Patrick, 280 E. Main St., 11787. Tel: 631-862-3000; 979-1292. Sr. Patricia McDonnell, O.P.

STONY BROOK. *L.I. State Veterans' Home* Tel: 631-444-8500. Rev. Charles F. Kohli.

Stony Brook University Hospital SUNY at Stony Brook, 11790. Tel: 631-444-2765. Revs. Steve Unger; Anthony Ewherido; Thoms Aidoo; Sr. Marjorie Devlin; Cathy Granjean.

UNIONDALE. *Holly Patterson Geriatric Center* 875 Jerusalem Ave., 11553. Tel: 631-572-1500. Revs. R. Michael Reid; Ernest Robinson, Res., Holy Trinity High School, Hicksville. Tel: 516-433-2900.

VALLEY STREAM. *Franklin Medical Center Hospital* 11580. Tel: 516-256-6000. Rev. Francis Odufuye; Kathryn Martino, Res., St. Boniface Rectory, 631 Elmont Rd., Elmont, 11003-4028. Tel: 516-825-8800.

WEST BRENTWOOD. *Pilgrim Psychiatric Center* P.O. Box A, 11717. Tel: 631-434-5134. Rev. Lawrence J. O'Leary; Sr. Mary Summerville, C.S.J.; Rev. John P. Halpin.

WEST ISLIP. *Consolation Nursing Home* 11795. Tel: 613-587-1600. Rev. Robert A. Hyatt; Sr. Cecilia Gutman, O.P.

Good Samaritan Hospital Medical Center 11795. Tel: 631-376-3000. Revs. Lawrence Bellew, C.P.; Bernard M. Blood, S.M.M.; Vincent P. Cunningham, S.M.M.; Paul Dahn; Sr. Gertrude O'Brien, D.W.; Sr. Ellen Moore, O.P.; Sr. Felicia Moore, R.G.S.; Sr. Betty Keegan, F.M.M.; Sr. Ann Marie Pierce; Sr. Rosemary Jermusryk; Sr. Mary Anna Euring, O.P.; Monica Belber,

Good Samaritan Hospice Program, 175 Beach Dr., 11795. Tel: 631-376-3850. Sr. Joyce Osgood,

Good Samaritan Home Health Agency, Tel: 631-376-4300. Sr. Margaret Bickar, Chap.

Prison Ministry

BAY SHORE. *Office of Prison Ministry and Criminal Justice Affairs* 26 S. Saxon Ave., 11706-8920. Tel: 631-666-5073; Fax: 631-666-5073. Bro. John Moylan, O.S.F., D. Min., Dir.; Suzanne D. Jones, Coord. of Ministerial Svcs.

EAST MEADOW. *Nassau County Correctional Center* 100 Carman Ave., 11554-1146. Tel: 516-572-4145. Chaplains: Rev. Ralph Ferro; Sr. Virginia Waters, F.S.P.; Bro. Bill Cawley, S.C.; Deacon John Sullivan.

RIVERHEAD. *Suffolk County Correctional Facility* 100 Center Dr., 11901. Tel: 631-852-2294; 2728. Chaplains: Sr. Michelle Bremer, C.S.F.N.; Deacon Chris Vigliotta.

WESTBURY. *Nassua County Juvenile Detention Center* 61 Carman Ave., 11590. Tel: 516-571-9153. Bro. Jack Moylan, O.S.F., Chap.

YAPHANK. *Suffolk County Minimum Security Facility* P.O. Box 69, 11980. Tel: 631-852-4713. Chaplains: Sr. Michelle Bremer, C.S.F.N.; Deacon John Sullivan.

Absent on Leave:
Reverend Fathers—
Ball, Matthew J.
Gabriele, John J.
Houghton, Timothy
Huneke, Robert D.
Lennon, Charles
Mann, Peter
McDonnell, Stephen
MIller, James
Parkinson, Todd
Passamonte, Philip B.
Rebaldo, Ronald
Rogers, John
Rogers, Paul
White, John

Priests Released from Diocesan Assignment:
Reverend Monsignors—
Boccafola, Kenneth
Cervini, John
Maniscalco, Francis
Reverend Fathers—
Alarcon, Felix
Bogert, James
Cassar, Julian
Connolly, Andrew
Coyle, Robert
Ehrhart, Charles, Chap. Major
McMullen, Francis R.
Miraglia, Salvatore J.
Newman, Louis I.
Trapani, Anthony, Lt., CHC, USNR
Viladesau, Richard R.

Military Chaplains:
Reverend Fathers—
Coyle, Robert
Erhart, Charles M., U.S.M.C.A.-N.B.G.
Trapani, Anthony

Graduate Studies:
Reverend Fathers—
Henning, Richard, Rome, Italy

Retired:
Most Rev.—
Daly, James, Diocese of Rockville Centre, 50 N. Park Ave., Rockville Centre, NY 11570
McGann, John R., Cathedral of St. Agnes, 29 Quealy Place, Rockville Centre, NY 11570-4021
Reverend Monsignors—
Ballweg, Lawrence F., St. Pius X Residence, 1220 Front St., Uniondale, NY 11553-2097
Bermingham, Charles E., 101 Executive Center Dr., #4-511, W. Palm Beach, FL 33401
Brassil, James A., St. Gertrude, 28 School St., Bayville, NY 11709-1931
Chiara, Peter A., St. Mary, 20 Harrison Ave., East Islip, NY 11730-2314
Coffey, James F., St. Patrick, Nine North Clinton Ave., Bay Shore, NY 11706-7899
Colligan, Joseph F., Our Lady Queen of Martyrs, P.O. Box 0609, Centerport, NY 11721-1130
Collins, James E., St. Dominic, 93 Anstice St., Oyster Bay, NY 11771-3099
Costello, William F., St. Anne, 35 Dartmouth St., Garden City, NY 11530-5109
Flynn, Martin J., Carillon Nursing Home, 830 Park Ave., Huntington, NY 11743
Glimm, Francis X., St. Joseph Guest House, 350 Cuba Hill Rd., Huntington, NY 11743-4896
Hendel, Richard P., St. Patrick, Nine N. Clinton Ave., Bay Shore, NY 11706-7899
Kirwin, Robert J., St. Aidan, 505 Willis Ave., Williston Park, NY 11596-1786
Lawlor, Joseph F., St. Joseph Guest House, 350 Cuba Hill Rd., Huntington, NY 11743-4896
Leavey, Thomas G., St. William the Abbot, 2000 Jackson Ave., Seaford, NY 11783-2688
McCarren, Edgar P., Our Lady of Peace, 2800 Mission College Rd., Santa Clara, CA 95054
McGuire, John A., St. Louis de Montfort, 75 New York Ave., Sound Beach, NY 11789-0810
Richter, James B., St. Patrick, 400 Main St., Huntington, NY 11743-3298
Rooney, Thaddeus, Ss. Cyril & Methodius, 125 Half Hollow Rd., Deer Park, NY 11795-4288
Savastano, Anthony J., 80 Park Ave., Manhasset, NY 11030
Simmons, Walter E., St. Peter of Alcantara, 1327 Port Washington Blvd., Port Washington, NY 11050-3096
Skelly, John J., P.O. Box 5217, Rocky Point, NY 11778
Tarrant, Edward L., Corpus Christi, Mineola
Trench, Edmond J., P.O. Box 1503, East Quogue, NY 11942
Villar, Demetrio, 8528 Riverside Rd., Alexandria, VA 22308
Wiest, John J., St. Mary, 1300 Northern Blvd., Manhasset, NY 11030-3020
Reverend Fathers—
Barry, Ronald A., P.O Box 1708, Chandler, AZ 85244-1708
Benack, Henry I., St. Patrick, 235 Glen St., Glen Cove, NY 11542-3091
Blake, Andrew P., St. Andrew, 122 Division St., Sag Harbor, NY 11963-3154
Buckley, Harold P., St. Rose of Lima, Two Bayview Ave., Massapequa, NY 11758-7299
Callahan, Zachary, St. Pius X Residence, 1220 Front St., Uniondale, NY 11553-2097
Casey, Francis M., Maria Regina, 3945 Jerusalem Ave., Seaford, NY 11783-1627
Colgan, Thomas J., St. Philip Neri, 344 Main St., Northport, NY 11768-1779
Collins, Edwin J., 14295 Aster Ave., Wellington, FL 33414
Corali, Serafino A., St. Pius X Residence, 1220 Front St., Uniondale, NY 11553-2097
Cser, Ladislaus, S.J., Sts. Philip & James, One Carow Pl., St. James, NY 11780-1707
Curley, Martin W., St. Thomas the Apostle, 24 Westminister Rd., West Hempstead, NY 11552-1694
Curley, Robert
Curry, Thomas P., St. Pius X Residence, 1220 Front St., Uniondale, NY 11553-2097
Daley, John T.
De Vita, James C., C.V.E., Grantham B., 331, Deerfield Beach, FL 33442
Delaney, Richard, St. Brigid, 75 Post Ave., Westbury, NY 11590-4353
Delaney, William I., St. Thomas the Apostle, 24 Westminister Rd., West Hempstead, NY 11552-1694
Dineros, Santiago A., 107 Midland Blvd., Ronkonkoma, NY 11779
Dolan, James J., St. Pius X Residence, 1220 Front St., Uniondale, NY 11553-2097
Drab, John P., 24 Pheasant Rd., Noyac, NY 11963-2908
Duvelsdorf, Peter L., St. Pius X Residence, 1220 Front St., Uniondale, NY 11553-2097
Flaherty, Malachy C., O.F.M.Cap., St. Francis of Assisi, Greenlawn
Flynn, Edward J., St. Pius X Residence, 1220 Front St., Uniondale, NY 11553-2097
Gallagher, Andrew J., Our Lady of Miraculous Medal, 75 Parkside Dr., Point Lookout, NY 11569-9999
Gallagher, William G., 9949 Shore Rd., Brooklyn, NY 11209
Gartner, Charles A., Our Lady of Mercy, 500 South Oyster Bay Rd., Hicksville, NY 11801-3570
Gfroerer, Gerard J., St. Pius X Residence, 1220 Front St., Uniondale, NY 11553-2097
Gorman, John J., St. Joseph, 39 N. Carll Ave., Babylon, NY 11702-2701
Govern, William H., Maria Regina Convent, Brentwood Rd., Brentwood, NY 11717-5589
Hall, Martin J., St. Bernard, 3100 Hempstead Tpke., Levittown, NY 11756-1339
Harrer, Frederic J., 377D Woodbridge Dr., Ridge, NY 11961
Heenan, Michael F., 2021 Bonisle Cir., Palm Beach Gardens, FL 33418
Henesy, William P., Sunrest Health Facility, 70 N. Country Rd., Port Jefferson, NY 11777
Henry, John P., St. Ignatius, 715 E. Orange St., Tarpon Springs, FL 34689
Hourihane, Francis, 8170 Summerlin Village, Unit 602, Fort Myers, FL 33919
Kayser, Robert, Manor Park, 215 Carll's Path, Apt. 4C, Deer Park, NY 11729
Korycki, Walter R., 7 Susan Dr., Northport, NY 11768
Kozlowski, Joseph P., St. Hyacinth, 319 Cedar Swamp Rd., Glen Head, NY 11545-2296
LeTure, Theodore J., 2443 S.W. Sansome Ln., Port St. Lucie, FL 34953
Liu, Vincent, St. Patrick, 280 E. Main St., Smithtown, NY 11787-2920
McCabe, John H., Holy Trinity High School, 98 Cherry Lane, Hicksville, NY 11801-6297
McCarthy, Thomas, 215 W. Santa Barbara Rd., Lindenhurst, NY 11757
McGlade, Thomas F., P.O. Box 2414, Amagansett, NY 11930
McManus, Eugene J., St. Pius X Residence, 1220 Front St., Uniondale, NY 11553-2097
Meade, James C., Queen of Peace Residence, 110-30 221 St., Queens Village, NY 11429-1655
Millar, Andrew, Diocese of Rockville Centre, 50 N. Park Ave., Rockville Centre, NY 11570
Minturn, Joseph, 107 Colonial Pkwy., Manhasset, NY 11030
Mockevicius, Charles L., 1156 Plank Rd., Webster, NY 14580
Muhs, Edward J., St. Barnabas the Apostle, 2320 Bedford Ave., Bellmore, NY 11710-3617
Murphy, William T., 288 Court House Rd., Franklin Square, NY 11010
Murray, John E., Notre Dame, 45 Mayfair Rd., New Hyde Park, NY 11040-2094
Murray, John P., 19 Redfield Rd., Island Park, NY 11558
Navarroli, Frederick, 3900 Forest Grove Dr., Annandale, VA 22003
Niewczas, Taddeus, 84 Berry St., Brooklyn, NY 11211
O'Brien, Denis J., St. Anthony's Friary, 275 Wolf Hill Rd., South Huntington, NY 11743-1363
O'Donnell, Thomas, St. Ignatius Martyr, 721 W. Broadway, Long Beach, NY 11561-2897
Osborne, Martin J., St. Patrick, P.O. Box 117, Southold, NY 11971
Pai, Simon, Nathan Hale Senior Village, 30 Doxsey Pl., Apt. 231, Lynbrook, NY 11563
Parrini, Warren, 142 Shore Way, Oakdale, NY 11769
Pazo, John T., P.O. Box 525, Clairton, PA 15025-0525
Power, Virgil, Sandy Oaks Mobile Park, #16, 6760 N. Lecanto Hwy., Beverly Hills, FL 34465
Punti, George, St. Boniface, 631 Elmont Road, Elmont, NY 11003-4028
Reehil, Philip J., St. James, 429 Rte. 25A, Setauket, NY 11733-2850
Reuss, Louis L., St. John Nepomucene, 1140 Locust Ave., Bohemia, NY 11716-2139

Reynolds, Thomas, Our Lady of Lourdes, 855 Carmans Rd., Massapequa Park, NY 11762-1498
Scanlon, Richard M., Consolation Nursing Home, 111 Beach Dr., West Islip, NY 11795-4860
Serrano, John J., St. Pius X Residence, 1220 Front St., Uniondale, NY 11553-2097
Shane, Donald R., St. Pius X Residence, 1220 Front St., Uniondale, NY 11553-2097
Sheehan, Augustine J., Department of Veterans Affairs, Medica, 79 Middleville Rd., Northport, NY 11768
Sheehan, Lawrence A., S.J., St. Rose Lima, Two Bayview Ave., Massapequa, NY 11758-7299
Sheridan, Denis J., St. Pius X Residence, 1220 Front St., Uniondale, NY 11553-2097
Singleton, William V., St. Raymond, 263 Atlantic Ave., East Rockaway, NY 11518-1117
Sledzaus, Alexander L., Our Lady of Mount Carmel, 495 New N. Ocean Ave., Patchogue, NY 11772-1793
Swiatocha, Bruno, 34 Country Club Dr., Shallotte, NC 28470
Tortora, Raymond, 230 Cardinal Lane, Delray Beach, FL 33445
Traynor, John J., 25 Pitch Pine Pl., Medford, NY 11763
Wickman, Robert T., 14 Abergele Dr., Toms River, NJ 08757
Wilutis, John P., St. Pius X Residence, 1220 Front St., Uniondale, NY 11553-2097
Wodziak, Michael, c/o Mrs. R. Sircovics, 1148 5th Ave., Berwick, PA 18603
Yang, Paul, 35 E. Broadway, Apt. 21, Long Beach, NY 11561-4105

Permanent Deacons:
Abrahams, Vincent, St. Patrick, Smithtown
Altonji, James F., St. Joseph, Ronkonkoma
Alvarado, Jesus, St. Anne, Brentwood
Ashe, James C., Our Lady of Poland, Southampton
Austin, William, Our Lady of Grace, West Babylon
Banno, Anthony, St. Christopher, Baldwin
Barone, Frank D., St. Kilian, Farmingdale
Bartolotto, Joseph T., St. Louis De Montfort, Sound Beach
Bast, Thomas J., St. Frances de Chantal, Wantagh
Bedell, Paul, Campus Parish
Behar, Stephen, Our Lady of Lourdes, West Islip
Beirne, James G., St. James, Seaford
Benincasa, Joseph, St. Catherine of Sienna, Franklin Square
Bennettson, Donald W., St. Joseph's, Kings Park
Biggin, James A., St. Martin of Tours, Bethpage
Billia, Edward W., St. Hugh of Lincoln, Huntington Station
Blake, Richard T., St. Aidan, Williston Park
Bohuslaw, James, St. John Nepomucene, Bohemia
Bono, Frank J., St. Joachim, Cedarhurst
Bopp, John T., Sacred Heart, Cutchogue
Bowe, Martin J.
Braun, Robert G., St. Anthony of Padua, East Northport
Brennan, William V., St. William the Abbot, Seaford
Brown, Charles, SS. Philip & James, St. James
Browne, George J., St. Ann, Garden City
Bruck, George P., Our Lady of Good Counsel, Inwood
Buchenberger, Thomas E., St. William the Abbot, Seaford
Burkart, John F., St. Philip Neri, Northport
Burnham, Bruce A., Our Holy Redeemer, Freeport
Butler, James, Our Lady Queen of Martyrs, Centerport
Cales, Francisco, Our Holy Redeemer, Freeport
Campbell, Robert, St. Raymond, East Rockaway
Capobianco, Eugene, St. Martin of Tours, Bethpage
Carrello, Frank, St. Martin of Tours, Bethpage
Case, Edward M., St. Mary, Roslyn
Cedrone, Anthony M., Blessed Sacrament, Valley Stream
Cepeda, Jose A., Our Lady of Assumption, Copiague
Chamberlain, Anthony J., SS. Philip & James, St. James
Chott, John, St. Patrick, Smithtown
Coates, Gerard, St. James, Setauket
Coleman, Thomas, St. Barnabas the Apostle, Bellmore
Connolly, George P., Our Lady of Perpetual Help, Lindenhurst
Costello, Thomas P., St. Joseph, Hewlett
Cotone, Louis, St. Kilian, Farmingdale
Cove, Francis K., Our Lady of Lourdes, Malverne
Coyoy, Jorge, St. Mary, Roslyn
Crivello, Frank, Sts. Philip & James, St. James
Cunningham, Edward F., St. Anne, Garden City
Cuseo, Anthony W., Holy Name of Mary, Valley Stream
Cusumano, Anthony P., St. John, Nepomucene
D'Angelo, Frank G., St. Peter of Alcantara, Port Washington
D'Angelo, Gregory R., St. Raymond, East Rockaway
Daza, H. Nelson, St. Mary of the Isle, Long Beach
DeBellis, Michael J., St. Joseph, Ronkonkoma
DeGuardi, John P., Our Lady of Lourdes, Islip
Deignan, Thomas F., SS. Cyril and Methodius, Deer Park
Dejewski, Robert, Ss. Peter & Paul, Manokville
Determann, Herman J., St. Aidan, Williston Park
Diaz, Juan, St. Anne, Brentwood
Diaz-Granados, Francisco, St. Francis de Sales, Patchogue
DiGiovanna, James R., St. Catherine of Siena, Franklin Square
DiGiuseppe, Peter A., Our Lady Grace, West Babylon
Donza, Gaetano, St. Raymond, East Rockaway
Dougherty, Joseph M., St. Joseph, Ronkonkoma
Dunlop, John P., St. Mary of the Isle, Long Beach
Dunne, James A., Our Holy Redeemer, Freeport
Dunphy, Patrick J., Our Lady of Hope, Carle Place
Earley, George G.
Erdman, John P., St. Joseph, Ronkonkoma
Evard, Thomas J., St. Ignatius Martyr, Long Beach
Evers, Jeffrey, SS. Cyril & Methodius, Deer Park
Farley, Owen, St. Patrick, Smithtown
Ferreiro, Douglas, St. Catherine of Sienna, Franklin Square
Ferri, Richard, St. Martin of Tours, Amityville
Finter, Frederick E., St. John the Baptist, Wading River
Fitzpatrick, John, Ss. Cyril & Methodius, Deer Park
Flannery, James W., St. Anthony, Oceanside
Flood, Frank J., St. Rose of Lima, Massapequa
Fodale, John E., St. Catherine of Siena, Franklin Square
Forbes, Thomas J., St. Rose of Lima, Massapequa
Fullam, William F., Jr., St. Lawrence the Martyr, Sayville
Gagnon, Jules O. A., St. Patrick, Huntington
Garcia, Ricardo L., Holy Spirit, New Hyde Park
Gargiulo, Andrew T., Our Lady of Perpetual Help, Lindenhurst
Gariboldi, Frank, St. John of God, Central Islip
Gaudioso, Robert, St. Elizabeth Ann Seton, Lake Ronkonkoma
Geoghan, Kenneth, St. Jude, Mastic Beach
Gerace, Patrick C., St. Mark, Shoreham
Giambalvo, Anthony M., Christ the King, Commack
Gillen, Thomas J., St. Jude's, Mastic Beach
Gillette, Ronald J., St. John of God, Central Islip
Giraldo, Luis D., St. Hugh of Lincoln, Huntington Station
Graff, Charles J., Our Lady of Grace, West Babylon
Griffin, William, St. Kilian, Farmingdale
Gronenthal, Robert W., Our Lady of Snow, Blue Point
Gross, Thomas A., Jr., St. Jude, Mastic Beach
Guntert, Joseph F.
Hammel, Lawrence V., Our Lady of Hope, Carle Place
Hanly, James, St. Matthew, Dix Hills
Hartmann, Frank C., Our Lady of the Snow, Bluepoint
Hennessy, Thomas R., St. Martin of Tours, Amityville
Hernandez, Robert, Good Shepherd, Holbrook
Herrmann, Mark, St. John the Evangelist, Center Moriches
Heschl, Robert J., Sts. Philip & James, St. James
Hickey, John, Our Lady of Hope, Carle Place
Huber, Charles F., SS. Cyril & Methodius, Deer Park
Ingulli, Joseph, St. James, Setauket
Jackman, Frederick, St. Patrick, Smithtown
Jackson, Thomas H., Queen of the Most Holy Rosary, Roosevelt
Johnston, Richard J., St. Elizabeth, Melville
Kalman, Bela, Our Lady of Mount Carmel, Patchogue
Keach, Frank, St. Patrick, Bay Shore
Keenan, John, Sts. Philip & James, St. James
Kogler, William E., St. Margaret of Scotland, Selden
Kolakowski, Theodore, St. Gertrude, Bayville
Kramer, Steven L., Our Lady of the Snow, Blue Point
Lamb, Richard W., Our Lady of the Miraculous Medal, Wyandanch
LaRossa, Richard W., St. Raymond, East Rockaway
Leahy, John G., St. James, Seaford
Lewis, Clinton, Queen of the Most Holy Rosary, Roosevelt
Leyden, Michael J., St. Joseph, Babylon
Logsdon, Patrick B.
Longo, Allan D., St. Francis of Assisi, Greenlawn
Lovett, John J., St. John the Evangelist, Riverhead
Luken, Richard A., St. Luke, Brentwood
Macellaro, Daniel A., Resurrection, Farmingdale
Maffeo, Joseph R., St. Elizabeth Ann Seton, Ronkonkoma
Maher, Kenneth, SS. Philip & James, St. James
Mahoney, Michael A., St. Patrick, Bay Shore
Mannix, Briand, Corpus Christi, Mineola
Marfoglio, Joseph, St. Peter the Apostle, Islip Terrace
Marino, Salvatore A., Blessed Sacrament, Valley Stream
Maro, Robert R., St. Patrick, Huntington
Matheis, Felix J., St. Brigid, Westbury
Mathurin, Trevor S., St. Martha, Uniondale
McDaid, Thomas P., St. Agnes, Rockville Centre
McGaffney, Gilbert, Notre Dame, New Hyde Park
McGauvran, John W., Sacred Hearts of Jesus and Mary, Southampton
McGowan, John, St. Anne, Garden City
McGuinness, Francis B., St. Rose of Lima, Massapequa
McIndoe, Martin B., St. Francis de Sales, Patchogue
McKenna, Michael A., St. Boniface, Elmont
McLaughlin, James, Sts. Peter & Paul, Manorville
McNicholas, Joseph G., Holy Family, Hicksville
McQuade, James J., St. Matthew, Dix Hills
Mercolino, Joseph T., St. Elizabeth, Melville
Metzdorff, Michael C., St. Brigid, Westbury
Micucci, Raymond R., St. Boniface, Elmont
Mildeberger, William H., Jr., St. Boniface, Elmont
Molina, Fernando, St. Frances Cabrini, Coram
Montesano, Joseph A., Our Lady Queen of Martyrs, Centerport
Moran, John, Sacred Hearts of Jesus and Mary, Southampton
Morris, James P., St. Brigid, Westbury
Morrow, John W., Our Lady of Grace, West Babylon
Mulligan, Lawrence P., Our Lady of Victory, Floral Park
Muratore, Biagio V., St. Margaret of Scotland, Selden
Murphy, Galvin C., St. John the Evangelist, Center Moriches
Murphy, James, St. Edward the Confessor, Syosset
Muscarnera, Charles, St. Christopher, Baldwin
Mystkowski, Joseph J., Our Lady of Mt. Carmel, Patchogue
Naylor, Montford D., St. Francis Cabrini, Coram
Nuzzi, John, Maria Regina, Seaford
O'Brien, James J., St. Anne, Garden City
O'Connor, Dennis R., St. Rose of Lima, Massapequa
O'Connor, Thomas F., St. Gerard Majella, Port Jefferson Station
O'Donovan, Robert S., St. Frances de Chantal, Wantagh
O'Hara, James, Holy Name of Mary, Valley Stream
Odin, Frank A., Our Lady of Perpetual Help, Lindenhurst
Owen, George, St. Kilian, Farmingdale
Owens, Thomas F., St. James, Setauket
Pagano, Joseph, St. Joseph, Ronkonkoma
Pagnotta, Carmen, St. Frances Cabrini, Coram
Paolicelli, Philip, St. Margaret of Scotland, Selden
Pellegrino, Joseph C., St. Christopher, Baldwin
Peralta, Joseph F., St. Patrick, Bay Shore
Pesce, Frank V., St. Brigid, Westbury
Pettorino, John C., SS. Peter and Paul, Manorville
Pickel, James D.
Powers, William J., Infant Jesus, Port Jefferson
Quaranta, Arnold T., St. Matthew, Dix Hills
Quinn, Thomas J., St. Rose of Lima, Massapequa
Quinones, Fernando J., St. Francis de Sales, Patchogue
Raad, Richard, Holy Name of Mary, Valley Stream
Rasanen, Terence A., St. Anne, Brentwood
Reich, George F., St. John Nepomucene, Bohemia
Reilly, Thomas J., St. Hugh of Lincoln, Huntington Station
Reinhart, John C., Corpus Christi, Mineola
Rich, Thomas B., Our Lady of Hope, Carle Place
Riegger, George J., St. Sylvester, Medford
Rivera, Wenceslao, St. Luke, Brentwood
Roa, Jose, Our Lady of Loretto, Hempstead
Roberts, Lionel V., St. Edward the Confessor, Syosset
Rodenburg, Herman I., St. Kilian, Farmingdale
Roettinger, Francis P., St. Sylvester, Medford
Romero, Miguel A., St. Martha, Uniondale
Ruggieri, Clyde, Holy Name of Mary, Valley Stream
Samson, Thomas R., St. Anne, Brentwood
Sanchez, Cristobal, Our Holy Redeemer, Freeport
Sandberg, Louis C., Queen of the Most Holy Rosary, Roosevelt
Sanders, Richard W., St. Patrick's, Smithtown
Schneider, Andrew M., St. Philip Neri, Northport
Schultz, Peter F., St. Louis de Montfort, Sound Beach
Scollan, Joseph M., St. Margaret of Scotland, Selden
Senholzi, Gregory B., St. John the Baptist, Wading River
Severe, Max

Sherlock, Bernard F., St. Barnabas Apostle, Bellmore
Shortell, Michael V.
Smith, Edward W., St. Lawrence the Martyr, Sayville
Smith, Robert, St. Rosalie, Hampton Bays
Smith, Roy, St. Joseph, Kings Park
Smyth, Vincent P., St. Agnes, Rockville Centre
Squiteri, Aniello, Our Lady of Peace, Lynbrook
Sullivan, John F., St. Joseph, Babylon
Sullivan, Kenneth R., St. Martha, Uniondale
Swane, Gary, St. Louis de Montfort, Sound Beach
Taranto, Vito, St. Hugh, Huntington Station
Taylor, Bernard H., Our Lady Miraculous Medal, Wyandanch
Teufel, John G., Our Lady of Lourdes, West Islip
Tirelli, Raymond J., Our Lady of Hope, Carle Place
Trodden, John E., St. Luke, Brentwood
Valdaro, Dominick, Our Lady Lourdes, Massapequa Park
Van De Ven, Theodore, Our Lady of Lourdes, Malverne
Vargas, Daniel E., Our Lady of Assumption, Copiague
Vigliotta, Albert C., St. Mark, Shoreham
Vigliotta, Crescenzo T., St. John the Evangelist, Center Moriches
Villani, Salvatore B., St. Aidan, Williston Park
Voegele, Richard, St. Rosalie, Hampton Bays
Waldmann, Richard E., Infant Jesus, Port Jefferson
Walsh, Robert P., Holy Name of Mary, Valley Stream
Walters, John, St. Anne, Brentwood
Weigel, John A., Maria Regina, Seaford
Weisz, Robert D., St. Thomas More, Hauppauge
Wetzel, Edward V., St. Martin of Tours, Amityville
Whitfield, Gerald F., Maria Regina, Seaford
Williams, Walter B., Jr., Resurrection, Farmingville
Wilson, Gerard R.
Zirkel, Donald E., St. Kilians, Farmingdale

INSTITUTIONS LOCATED IN THE DIOCESE

[A] SEMINARIES, DIOCESAN

HUNTINGTON. *Diocesan Seminary of the Immaculate Conception*, 440 West Neck Rd., 11743. Tel: 631-423-0483; Fax: 631-423-2346. Most Rev. John R. McGann, D.D., Chm., Board of Governors; Rev. Msgr. Vincent F. Fullam, J.D. (BRK), Rector; Revs. Robert J. Smith, S.T.L.; S.T.D., Vice Rector & Academic Dean; Edward R. D'Andrea, M.Div., Dir. Spiritual Formation; Thomas M. Fusco, M.Div., Dir. Pastoral Formation & Dean of Seminarians; Sr. Nivard Stabile, O.P., Assoc. Dean; Jiri Lipa, Ph.D., Library Dir.; Mrs. Bernadette M. Grodman, Business Officer; Mrs. Joan Innvar, Registrar; Revs. William T. Donavan, S.T.B.; Patrick J. Griffin, C.M., Ph.D.; Joseph R. Gibino, Ph.D. (BRK); Katherine M. Hayes, Ph.D.; Rev. Gerard H. Luttenberger, C.M., S.T.D.; Sr. Mary Alice Piil, C.S.J., Ph.D.; Revs. Peter I. Vaccari, S.T.L. (BRK); Richard G. Henning, M.A., M.Div. Priests 10; Sisters 2; Lay Professor 1; Support Lay Staff 35; Seminarians 44; M.A. Students 102; D.Min. Students 8.

[B] COLLEGES AND UNIVERSITIES

ROCKVILLE CENTRE. *Molloy College*, 1000 Hempstead Ave., 11571-5002. Tel: 516-678-5000; 888-4-MOLLOY.
Web site: www.molloy.edu
For a complete listing, refer to the Colleges and Universities section.

PATCHOGUE. *St. Joseph's College*, 155 W. Roe Blvd., 11772-2399. Tel: 631-447-3200; Fax: 631-654-1782.
E-mail: lmcgrann@sjcny.edu
Web site: www.sjcny.edu
For a complete listing, refer to the Colleges and Universities section.

[C] HIGH SCHOOLS, DIOCESAN

NASSAU COUNTY

HICKSVILLE. *Holy Trinity*, 98 Cherry Ln., 11801. Tel: 516-433-2900; Fax: 516-433-2827.
E-mail: hths98@holytrinityhs.org
Web site: www.holytrinityhs.org
Mr. James J. Boglioli, Prin.; Rev. Joseph J. Nixon, Chap. In res. Rev. Msgr. Thomas J. Hartman; Revs. John H. McCabe; Michael Reid. Sisters 7; Lay Teachers 93; Students 1,500.

SUFFOLK COUNTY

WEST ISLIP. *St. John the Baptist*, 1170 Montauk Hwy., 11795. Tel: 631-587-8000; Fax: 631-587-8996.
E-mail: stjohns@earthlink.net
Web site: home.earthlink.net/~stjohns/
Walter D. Lace, Prin.; Rev. James C. Vlaun, Chap. Sisters 5; Priests 1; Lay Teachers 58; Students 1,097.

[D] HIGH SCHOOLS, PRIVATE

BRENTWOOD. *Academy of St. Joseph*. Independent; (Coed school grades PreK-6; Girl's school grades 7-12), 1725 Brentwood Rd., 11717. Tel: 631-273-2406; Fax: 631-231-4155.
E-mail: stjoseph@ix.netcom.com
Web site: home.earthlink.net/~stjoseph
Directed by the Sisters of St. Joseph. Sr. Valerie Scholl, C.S.J., Dir.; Sr. Joanne Forker, C.S.J., Prin. Sisters of St. Joseph 9; Lay Teachers 33; Students 398.

HEMPSTEAD. *Sacred Heart Academy*. College preparatory-girls, 47 Cathedral Ave., 11550. Tel: 516-483-7383; Fax: 516-483-1016.
E-mail: sha@li.net
Web site: www.li.net/~sha
Sr. Jeanne Marie Ross, C.S.J., Prin. Sisters 10; Lay Teachers 57; Students 768.

MINEOLA. *Chaminade High School (Boys)*. Directed by the Society of Mary (Marianists), 340 Jackson Ave., 11501. Tel: 516-742-5555; Fax: 516-742-1989.
E-mail: flyers@chaminade-hs.org
Web site: http://www.chaminade-hs.org
Rev. James C. Williams, S.M., Pres.; Bro. Joseph D. Bellizzi, S.M., Prin.; Mr. Salvatore Trentacoste, Asst. Prin.; Bros. Michael J. Gillen, S.M., Dir. Guidance; Thomas J. Cleary, S.M., Dean of Students; James W. Conway, S.M., Dir. Student Svcs.; Rev. Garrett J. Long, S.M., Chap.; Bro. Peter H. Heiskell, S.M., Dir. of Apostolic Action. Brothers 22; Priests 3; Lay Teachers 47; Students 1,600.

OAKDALE. *LaSalle, A Global Learning Community*. (Grades K-12), 500 Montauk Hwy., 11769. Tel: 631-218-7700; Fax: 631-218-7705.
E-mail: Lasaladm@li.net
Web site: www.LaSalle-Oakdale.org
Directed by the De La Salle Christian Brothers. Bros. A. Jerome, F.S.C., Pres.; Dennis Cronin, F.S.C., Headmaster; Mr. Donald Puleio, Dir. of Finance; Mr. James Abbatiello, Dir. of Admissions. Lay Teachers 34; Students: Upper School 145; Middle School 51; Primary School 73.

RIVERHEAD. *Mercy High School*. (Coed), 1225 Ostrander Ave., 11901. Tel: 631-727-5900; Fax: 631-727-8483.
E-mail: mercy@northeast.net
Web site: mercy.ws
Directed by the Sisters of Mercy. Sr. Mary Elaine, R.S.M., Prin.; Sr. Marie E. Parrino, R.S.M., Dean of Students; Sr. Marie E. Perrino, R.S.M., Asst. Prin. Sisters of Mercy (Brooklyn) 11; Other Sisters 2; Lay Teachers 28; Students 380.

SOUTH HUNTINGTON. *St. Anthony's High School*. College Prep. 275 Wolf Hill Rd., 11747-1394. Tel: 631-271-2020; Fax: 631-351-1507.
E-mail: 75017.3061@compuserve.com
Directed by the Franciscan Brothers of Brooklyn. Bro. Shane Burke, O.S.F., Ed.D., Prin. Priests 1; Brothers 18; Intercommunity Sisters 7; Lay Teachers 106; Students 2,162.

SYOSSET. *Our Lady of Mercy Academy*. Girls-day students. 815 Convent Rd., 11791. Tel: 516-921-1047; Fax: 516-921-3634.
Web site: www.OLMA.org
Directed by the Sisters of Mercy. Principals: Sr. Kieran Hartigan, R.S.M.; Sr. Margaret Ann Hartigan, R.S.M. Sisters of Mercy 11; Sisters of Charity 1; Sisters of St. Joseph 1; Lay Teachers 34; Students 480.

UNIONDALE. *Kellenberg Memorial High School*, 1400 Glenn Curtiss Blvd., 11553. Tel: 516-292-0200; Fax: 516-292-0877.
E-mail: kmhs@li.net
Web site: www.kellenberg.org
Directed by the Society of Mary. Rev. Philip K. Eichner, S.M., Pres.; Bros. Kenneth M. Hoagland, S.M., Prin.; Richard Hughes, Asst. Prin. Academics; Mr. Kenneth Conrade, Asst. Prin. Admissions; Rev. Albert Bertoni, S.M., Asst. Prin. Guidance; Ms. Maria Korzekwinski, Asst. Prin. Latin School; Bro. Roger Poletti, S.M., Asst. Prin. Activities; Rev. Thomas A. Cardone, S.M., Chap.; Mrs. Marina Trentacoste, Dean of Students; Mr. Edward Solosky, Dean of Men; Mr. Kevin A. Hearn, Athletic Dir.; Mr. Richard Kotlarz, Supvr. of Building Maintenance and Landscaping; Bro. Donald Nussbaum, S.M., Suprv. New Construction, Vehicles; Mr. Jim Payne, Supvr. Cleaning Maintenance; Mrs. Catherine Zabrouski, Financial Supvr. Priests 4; Brothers 9; Lay Teachers 90; Students 2,100.

[E] REGIONAL SCHOOLS

BELLMORE. *St. Elizabeth Ann Seton Regional School*. Tel: 516-785-5709; Fax: 516-785-4468.
E-mail: ctk@seas.edruc.org
Supported by the following parishes: St. Barnabas, Bellmore; St. Raphael, East Meadow; Cure of Ars, Merrick; St. Frances de Chantal, Wantagh.
Bellmore Campus, 2341 Washington Ave., 11710. Tel: 516-785-5709; Fax: 516-785-4468. Dr. Eileen Kilbride, Prin. Sisters 2; Lay Teachers 31; Students 664.
East Meadow Campus, 600 Newbridge Ave., East Meadow, 11554. Tel: 516-785-7006; Fax: 516-785-7008. Sr. William Noreen, S.C.H., Prin. Sisters 4; Lay Teachers 24; Students 480.

BETHPAGE. *St. John Baptist de LaSalle Regional School*. Tel: 516-931-0983; Fax: 516-931-1502.
E-mail: Lasallet@aol.com
Supported by the following parishes: St. Martin of Tours, Bethpage; St. Kilian, Farmingdale; St. Pius X, Plainview; St. James, Seaford.
Bethpage Campus, Central Ave., 11714. Tel: 516-931-0983; Fax: 516-931-1502. Dr. Victor Lana, Headmaster. Lay Teachers 23; Students 300.
Farmingdale Campus, 50 Cherry St., Farmingdale, 11735. Tel: 516-694-3610; Fax: 516-694-3614. Mrs. Susan Anaischik, Prin. Sisters 1; Lay Teachers 31; Students 325.

CENTER MORICHES. *Our Lady, Queen of Apostles Regional School*, 2 St. Johns Pl., 11934. Tel: 631-878-1033; Fax: 631-878-1059.
E-mail: sreileen@olqa.edruc.org
Sr. Eileen Martin, S.C., Prin. Sisters 1; Lay Teachers 16; Students 309. Supported by the following parishes: St. John Evangelist, Center Moriches; St. Jude, Mastic Beach; Immaculate Conception, Westhampton Beach; Ss. Peter & Paul, Manorville.

CENTRAL ISLIP. *Our Lady of Providence Regional School*, 82 Carleton Ave., 11722. Tel: 631-234-1113; 234-6324; Fax: 631-234-6360.
E-mail: provcsj@aol.com
Sr. Kerry Handal, C.S.J., Prin.-Upper School; Sr. Stephen Mary Puglisi, C.S.J., Prin.-Lower School. Sisters 1; Lay Teachers 28; Students 582. Supported by the following parishes: St. Anne, Brentwood; St. Luke, Brentwood; St. John of God, Central Islip; St. Peter the Apostle, Islip Terrace.

COMMACK. *Holy Family Regional School*, Indian Head Rd., P.O. Box 729, 11725. Tel: 631-543-0202; Fax: 631-543-0203.
E-mail: hfrs@aol.com
Ms. Agatha Cavoli, Prin. Sisters 4; Lay Teachers 19; Students 515. Supported by the following parishes: Christ the King, Commack; St. Matthew, Dix Hills; St. Thomas More, Hauppauge; St. Joseph, Kings Park.

CUTCHOGUE. *Our Lady of Mercy Regional School*, P.O. Box 970 - Main St., 11935. Tel: 631-734-5166. Sr. Mary Christi, Prin. Lay Teachers 8; Students 204. Supported by the following parishes: Sacred Heart, Cutchogue; Our Lady of Ostrabrama, Cutchogue; St. Agnes, Greenport; and St. Patrick, Southold.

EAST NORTHPORT. *Trinity Regional School*, 1025 Fifth Ave., 11731. Tel: 631-261-5130; Fax: 631-266-5345.
E-mail: tregion@optonline.net
Ms. Jeanne Morcone, Prin. Sisters 5; Lay Teachers 40; Students 850. Supported by the following parishes: Our Lady Queen of Martyrs, Centerport; St. Anthony of Padua, East Northport; St. Francis of Assisi, Greenlawn; St. Hugh of Lincoln, Huntington Station; St. Elizabeth, Melville; St. Philip Neri, Northport.
Satellite campuses exist at: 1450 New York Ave., Huntington Station, 11746. Tel: 631-549-7450. 364 Main St., Northport, 11768. Tel: 631-261-8520.

GLEN COVE. *All Saints Regional Catholic School*, 12 Pearsall Ave., 11542-3052. Tel: 516-676-0762; Fax: 516-676-0660. Sisters 1; Lay Teachers 27; Students 462. Supported by the following parishes: St. Boniface, Sea Cliff; St. Hyacinth, Glen Head; St. Mary, Roslyn; St. Patrick, Glen Cove; St. Rocco, Glen Cove.
Primary Campus. (Grades Nursery-Pr), 319 Cedar Swamp Rd., Glen Head, 11545-2298. Tel: 516-671-4247; Fax: 516-671-4247.
Upper Campus. (Grades K-8), 12 Pearsall Ave., 11542-3052. Tel: 516-676-0762; Fax: 516-676-0660. Sr. Maureen Vellon, R.S.H.M., Prin.

LONG BEACH. *Long Beach Catholic Regional School*. (Grades PreK-8), 735 W. Broadway, 11561. Tel: 516-432-8900; Fax: 516-432-3841. Mrs. Veronica Danca, Prin. Sisters 2; Lay Teachers 20; Students 455. Supported by the following parishes: St. Ignatius, Long Beach; St. Mary of the Isle, Long Beach, and Our Lady of the Miraculous Medal, Point Lookout.

PATCHOGUE. *Holy Angels Regional School*. (Grades K-8), Division St., 11772. Tel: 631-475-0422; Fax: 631-475-2036.
E-mail: smelise@holyangels.edrvc.org
Sr. Elise Bier, R.S.M., Prin. Sisters 2; Lay Teachers

16; Students 350. Supported by the following parishes: Mary Immaculate, Bellport; St. Frances Cabrini, Coram; St. Joseph the Worker, E. Patchogue; St. Sylvester, Medford; Our Lady of Mount Carmel, Patchogue; St. Frances de Sales, Patchogue, and St. Margaret of Scotland, Selden.

PORT JEFFERSON. *Our Lady of Wisdom Regional School*, 114-116 Myrtle Ave., 11777. Tel: 631-473-1211; Fax: 631-473-1064. Mrs. Nina Edwards, Prin. Lay Teachers 17; Students 250. Supported by the following parishes: Infant Jesus, Port Jefferson; St. Louis de Montfort, Sound Beach; St. James, Setauket; St. Gerard Majella, Port Jefferson Station.

SAG HARBOR. *Stella Maris Regional School*, Division St., 11963. Tel: 631-725-2525; Fax: 631-725-0568.
E-mail: stella@peconic.net
Judith Curtin, Prin. Sisters 1; Lay Teachers 12; Students 250. Supported by the following parishes: St. Therese of Lisieux, Montauk; Most Holy Trinity, East Hampton; St. Andrew, Sag Harbor; Queen of the Most Holy Rosary, Bridgehampton; Our Lady of the Isle, Shelter Island.

SAYVILLE. *Prince of Peace Regional School*, 200 Main St., 11782. Tel: 631-589-3426. Sr. Mary Kelly, S.S.N.D., Prin. Sisters 2; Lay Teachers 14; Students 320. Supported by the following parishes: Our Lady of Snow, Blue Point; St. John Nepomucene, Bohemia; Good Shepherd, Holbrook; St. Lawrence, Sayville.

SOUTHAMPTON. *Our Lady of the Hamptons Regional School*. (Grades K-8), 160 N. Main St., 11968. Tel: 631-283-9140; Fax: 631-283-3958.
E-mail: sks@hamptons.com
Web site: www.olh.com
31 Montauk Hwy., Hampton Bays, 11946. Tel: 631-723-3740; Fax: 631-728-2559. Nursery and PreK. Sr. Kathryn Schlueter, C.S.J., Prin. Sisters 3; Lay Teachers 16; Students 406. Supported by the following parishes: St. Rosalie, Hampton Bays; Our Lady of Poland, Southampton, and Sacred Hearts Jesus Mary, Southampton.

UNIONDALE. *St. Martin de Porres Regional School*, 530 Hempstead Blvd., 11553. Tel: 516-481-3303; Fax: 516-483-4138.
E-mail: wkemmerer@stmartdep.edrvc.org
Lay Teachers 19; Students 314. Supported by the following parishes: Our Lady of Loretto, Hempstead; St. Ladislaus, Hempstead; St. Martha, Uniondale.

[F] ELEMENTARY SCHOOLS, PRIVATE

MANHASSET. *Our Lady of Grace Montessori School and Center*. (Grades PreK-3), 29 Shelter Rock Rd., 11030. Tel: 516-365-9832; Fax: 516-365-9329. Sisters, Servants of the Immaculate Heart of Mary 4; Lay Teachers 17; Students 230.

OLD WESTBURY. *Old Westbury School of the Holy Child*. (Grades Nursery-8), 25 Store Hill Rd., 11568. Tel: 516-626-9300; Fax: 516-626-7814.
E-mail: oldwestburyschoolhc.com
Mr. Michael O'Donoghue, Head of School; Palma Gartland, Dir. Lower Grades; Gail Walker, Dir. Upper Grades. Lay Teachers 25; Students 135.

[G] SPECIALIZED CHILD CARE AGENCIES

NESCONSET. *Cleary Deaf Child Center, Inc.*, 301 Smithtown Blvd., 11767. Tel: 631-588-0530 (Voice and TTY); Fax: 631-588-0016.
E-mail: catherinef@clearyschool.org
Web site: www.clearyschool.org
For a complete listing, refer to the Special Care Facilities section.

PORT JEFFERSON STATION. *Maryhaven Center of Hope*, Administrative Offices, 1010 Rte. 112, 11776. Tel: 631-474-4120; Fax: 631-474-4110.
Web site: www.maryhaven@org.
For a complete listing, refer to the Special Care Facilities section.

SYOSSET. *St. Mary's Children and Family Services*, 525 Convent Rd., 11791-3864. Tel: 516-921-0808; Fax: 516-921-4542.
E-mail: stmlg@cs.com
Web site: stmaryscfs.com
For a complete listing, refer to the Special Care Facilities section.

WADING RIVER. *Little Flower Children's Services of New York*, 11792. Tel: 631-929-6200; Fax: 631-929-6121.
Web site: www.LittleFlowerNY.org
For a complete listing, refer to the Special Care Facilities section.

[H] CATHOLIC CHARITIES

HICKSVILLE. *Catholic Charities*, 90 Cherry Ln., 11801-6299. Tel: 516-733-7000; Fax: 516-733-7099. Laura A. Cassell, Exec. Dir. Tel: 516-733-7013; David P. Nelson, Chief Ministries Officer. Tel: 516-733-7012; Paul Englehart, Chief Program Officer. Tel: 516-733-7084; 733-7098 (fax).

Administrative Services, 90 Cherry Ln., 11801-6299. Michael Young, Dir. Administrative Services. Tel: 516-733-7003; 733-7099 (Fax); Robert J. Manfredi, MIS Admin. Tel: 516-733-7003; 733-7098 (Fax); John Gonta, Purchasing/Facilities Admin. Tel: 516-733-7090; 733-7099 (Fax).

Human Resources NY, 90 Cherry Lane, 11801-6299. Edward Moore, Human Resource Admin. Tel: 516-733-7005; 733-7038 (Fax); Carol Ann Radziewicz, Human Resource Coord. Tel: 516-733-7006; 733-7099 (Fax).

Finance, 90 Cherry Ln., 11801-6299. Tel: 516-733-7015; Fax: 516-733-7099. Edwin M. Kennedy, Dir. Finance; Jo Ann Parda, Financial Admin. Tel: 516-733-7017; Maureen Angelillo, Payroll Coord. Tel: 516-733-7030.

Office of Mental Health Residences. Tel: 631-665-5902; Fax: 631-665-3890. Howard G. Duff, Program Coord.
Residence for people who are psychiatrically impaired:

Siena Residence, 12 Mechanicsville Rd., Bay Shore, 11706. Tel: 631-968-8007; Fax: 631-968-8009. Anita DiMatteo, Contact.
Residences for children who are seriously emotionally disturbed:

Teaching Family Home Program. 269 W. Main St., Bay Shore, 11706. Tel: 631-665-5902; Fax: 631-665-3890. Howard G. Duff, Program Coordinator.

Maternity Services, 29 Kirkwood Ave., Merrick, 11566. Tel: 516-223-7888; Fax: 516-223-2752. Kathleen Ryan, Prog. Admin.; Carole Hendler, Mentoring of Moms Contact.
Residence for Pregnant Women:

Regina Residence, 29 Kirkwood Ave., Merrick, 11566. Tel: 516-223-7888; Fax: 516-223-2752. Kathleen Ryan, Prog. Admin.
Residence for Mothers and Babies:

Malta House. Tel: 516-223-7888; Fax: 516-223-2752. Kathleen Ryan, Prog. Admin.

Alcohol & Substance Abuse Services, 155 Indian Head Rd., Commack, 11725. Tel: 631-543-6200; Fax: 631-543-6203. Kathleen Ayers-Lanzilotta, Program Admin.; Barbara Raphael Gilson, Outpatient Clinic Contact.
Outpatient Clinics: 31 E. Main St., P.O. Box 758, Hampton Bays, 11956-0701. St. Therese of Lisieux Parish House, South Etna Ave., Montauk, 11954. St. Ann's Episcopal Church Parish House, 2463 Main St., Bridgehampton, 11932. Tel: 631-723-3362; Fax: 631-723-3365. Wayne Cavaliere, Contact, Talbot House Alcohol Crisis Center, 30-C Carlough Rd., Bohemia, 11716. Tel: 631-589-4144; Fax: 631-589-3281. Kathleen Brown, Contact.

Mental Health Services, 1729 N. Ocean Ave., Medford, 11763. Tel: 631-654-2944; Fax: 631-654-2966. Denis Demers, Mental Health Services Admin.
Supportive Case Management (For deinstitutionalized people with chronic mental illness): 269 W. Main St., Bay Shore, 11706. Tel: 631-665-5320; Fax: 631-665-5370. Kate Bishop, Contact, 1729 N. Ocean Ave., Medford, 11763. Tel: 631-654-2944; Fax: 631-654-2966.
Mental Health Clinics (Suffolk): 9 Fourth Ave., Bay Shore, 11706. Tel: 631-665-6707; Fax: 631-665-3564. Adelaide Corvelle, Contact, 1727 N. Ocean Ave., Medford, 11763. Tel: 631-654-1919; Fax: 631-475-8407. Jodi Kennedy, Contact.
Mental Health Clinics (Nassau):
259 Mineola Blvd., Mineola, 11501. Tel: 516-248-7100; Fax: 516-877-0717. 333 N. Main St., Freeport, 11520. Tel: 516-623-3322, Ext. 151; Fax: 516-623-3526. Patricia Quinn, Contact.

HIV/AIDS Services, 333 N. Main St., Freeport, 11520. Tel: 516-623-4820; Fax: 516-623-9607. Michael S.H. Young, Dir.

Special Dental Services Program, 333 N. Main St., Freeport, 11520. Tel: 516-623-4820; Fax: 516-623-9607. Dr. Samantha Ifill, Dental Dir.

AIDS Adult Day Health Care Program, 333 N. Main St., Freeport, 11520. Tel: 516-623-7400; Fax: 516-623-9607. Michael Ingrassea, Prog. Coord.

Housing Services, 90 Cherry Ln., 11801-6299. Tel: 516-733-7076; Fax: 516-733-7098. Paul A. Chedda, Dir. Tel: 516-733-7075; Robert Lulley, Pastoral Care Coord. (Suffolk Co.). Tel: 516-789-7059; Lynn Reddy, Housing Coord. Tel: 516-733-7081.

Senior Housing: St. Agnes Village, 100 St. Agnes Rd., Uniondale, 11553. Tel: 516-485-4721. Virginia Schultz, Contact, St. Joseph's Village, 2000 Boyle Rd., Selden, 11784. Tel: 631-736-0524. Angela Cammarata, Contact, Bishop Kellenberg Gardens, 2477 Long Beach Rd., Oceanside, 11572. Tel: 516-766-0777. Eileen Frost, Contact, Peternana Terrace, 45 Wallace St., Freeport, 11520. Tel: 516-378-4072. Bishop Ryan Village, 10 Squiretown Rd., Hampton Bays, 11946. Tel: 631-728-2413. Joan Lucas, Contact, St. Paul's Gardens, 702 St. Paul's Ct., Brentwood, 11717. Tel: 631-436-9074. Eileen Grabow, Contact, George Link Jr. Apts., George Link Jr. Cir., Coram, 11727. Tel: 631-732-6878. Deborah Chilcott, Contact, Mary's Manor, 60 Doughty Blvd., Inwood, 11696. Tel: 516-239-4291. Juanita Warren, Contact, Msgr. Henry J. Reel, 590 Christopher Ct., Medford, 11763. Tel: 631-475-6504. Deborah Chilcott, Contact, St. Hedwig's Gardens, 8 Linden Ave., Floral Park, 11001. Tel: 516-616-9023. Richard DeGennaro, Contact, Bishop McGann Village, Carleton Ave., Central Islip, 11722. Tel: 631-232-9356. Eileen Donaldson, Contact, Thea Bowman Residence, Schleigel Blvd., Amityville, 11701. Tel: 516-733-7075. Celeste Martin, Contact.

Food and Nutrition (FAN) Program, 143 Schleigel Blvd., Amityville, 11701. Tel: 516-789-9533; Fax: 516-789-9542. Robert H. Horn, Opers. Coord. Tel: 516-789-9533/9535; Linda Westervelt, Prog. Admin. Tel: 631-789-0520; 789-3844(Fax).
Food Center Locations: 66 N. 19th St., Wyandanch, 11798. Tel: 631-491-4166; Fax: 631-491-4950. 61-C Brightside Ave., Central Islip, 11722. Tel: 631-232-2797. 127 Bedell St., Hempstead, 11550. Tel: 516-489-9660. Blanco Dr., Mastic Beach, 11951. Tel: 631-399-5141. 38 St. John's Pl., Freeport, 11520. Tel: 516-623-4568; Fax: 516-623-2125.
Health Services:

Office for Persons with Disabilities, 143 Schleigel Blvd., Amityville, 11701. Tel: 631-789-5219; Fax: 631-789-3844. Bro. Alan J. Thomas, O.F.M., Contact, Services for Persons Blind/Visually Impaired. Tel: 516-789-5213; Fax: 516-789-3844. Services for Persons Deaf and Hard of Hearing. Tel: 516-789-5219; Fax: 516-789-3844. Bro. Alan J. Thomas, O.F.M., Contact.

Residential Services, 269 W. Main St., Bay Shore, 11706. Tel: 631-665-3434; Fax: 631-665-3586. Diane Ammirati, Program Admin.
Community residences for people who are developmentally disabled: Alhambra House, 3 Forest Pl., Huntington Station, 11746. Tel: 631-673-5240; Fax: 631-425-9628. Judith D'Agrosa, Contact, Caritas Residence, P.O. Box 2383, 4 Hilton Ct., Aqueboque, 11931. Tel: 631-722-5366. Jerry Bilinsky, Contact, Christopher Residence, 70 McKeon Ave., Valley Stream, 11580. Tel: 516-825-8282; Fax: 516-825-5383. Fernella St. Aimee, Contact, Msgr. R. Emmet Fagan Residence, 1504 DePaul St., Elmont, 11003. Tel: 516-358-2559; Fax: 516-616-0304. Adriene Wall, Contact, Rev. Thomas Helfrick Residence, 1 E. Moriches Blvd., East Moriches, 11940. Tel: 631-874-0292; Fax: 631-874-0292. Kelly McLaren, Contact, Mako Residence, 380 Ed's Rd., Southold, 11971. Tel: 631-765-1783; Fax: 631-765-1783. Kelly McLaren, Contact, Neumann Residence. (For Deaf Adults), 30 Brinkerhoff Ln., Manhassett, 11030. Tel: 516-627-5038; Fax: 516-869-0709. Marlowe Morrison, Contact, Bishop Ryan Residence, 258 Deauville Blvd., Copiague, 11726. Tel: 631-691-2126; Fax: 631-691-0860. Kathleen O'Mahony, Contact, Seton Residence, 3 Lombardi Pl., Amityville, 11701. Tel: 631-598-8216; Fax: 631-264-7967. Sr. Margaret Stadelman, Contact, Ted Hansler Residence, 24 Gardiners Ln., Hampton Bays, 11946. Tel: 631-728-8125; Fax: 631-728-0861. Linda Leone, Contact, Joseph Virdone Residence, 27 North Carll Ave., Babylon, 11702. Tel: 631-661-2826; Fax: 631-661-2952. James Kelly, Contact.

Senior Services, 147 Schleigel Blvd., Amityville, 11701. Tel: 631-789-0520; Fax: 631-789-3844. Livia Westervelt, Program Admin. Tel: 631-733-7057.

Bi-County Alliance of Senior Clubs. Tel: 631-789-0520; Fax: 631-789-3844. Liivia Westervelt, Contact.

Link-Age Case Management, 90 Cherry Ln., 11801-6299. Tel: 516-733-7064; Fax: 615-733-7098. John Sheridan, Contact, Meals-On-Wheels (Nassau). (For Seniors and People with AIDS), 124 Greenwich St., Hempstead, 11550. Tel: 516-485-7555; Fax: 516-485-7598. Jackie Blount, Contact, Meals-On-Wheels (Suffolk), 147 Schleigel Blvd., Amityville, 11701. Tel: 631-842-4123. MaryAnn McGrenra, Contact.
Senior Community Service Centers: 145 Schleigel Blvd., Amityville, 11701. Tel: 516-842-7331; 7332. Dennis Sullivan, Contact, 379 Linden St., Massapequa Park, 11762. Tel: 516-797-5357; Fax: 516-797-5529. Marline Evangelista, Contact, 619 Fenworth Blvd., P.O. Box 183, Franklin Square, 11010. Tel: 516-481-3322; Fax: 516-481-3236. Sue Bouffier, Contact, P.O. Box 243, 25 Nassau Ln., Island Park, 11558. Tel: 516-432-3388; Fax: 516-432-3958. Marie Frangella, Contact, 80 Anchor Ave., Oceanside, 11572. Tel: 516-764-9792; Fax: 516-764-9853. Margaret Keffel, Contact, P.O. Box 524, 2197 Jackson Ave., Seaford, 11783. Tel: 516-679-8373; Fax: 516-679-8374. Patricia Nadeau, Contact.

Immigrant Services, 143 Schleigel Blvd., Amityville, 11701. Tel: 631-789-5210; Fax: 631-789-5245. John K. Bingham, Dir. Tel: 631-789-5224; Carmen Maquilon, Coor. Tel: 631-789-5225.

Parish Social Ministry, 90 Cherry Ln., 11801. Tel: 516-733-7045; Fax: 516-733-7098. Anthony Mullen, Dir. Tel: 516-738-7051; Richard Koubek, Public Policy Education Network Coord. Tel: 516-733-7077; Judy Mazzarella, Special Projects, Parish Outreach. Tel: 516-733-7037; Brian Paradine, Volunteer Lawyers Initiative & Special Projects. Tel: 516-733-7046; George Reich, Developer, Parish Outreach. Tel: 516-733-7048; Patricia Oliviero, Developer, Parish Outreach. Tel: 516-733-7048; Kathy McIntyre, Developer; Connie Loos, Parish Outreach, Catholic Campaign for Human Development. Tel: 516-733-7054; Marisol Martinez, Developer, Parish Outreach. Tel: 516-733-7054; Marisa Zumbo, Developer, Parish Outreach. Tel: 516-733-7037; Margaret Melkonian, Justice & Peace Developer. Tel: 516-733-7049; Sharon Mullon, PPEN Developer. Tel: 516-733-7049; Ann Rose Bacani, Central Intake Coord. Tel: 516-733-7049.

Public Affairs and Development, 90 Cherry Ln., 11801. Tel: 516-733-7042; Fax: 516-733-7098. Scott A. Stepp, Coord. Tel: 516-733-7042; Helene A., Canberg, Communications/PR Specialist. Tel: 516-733-7043.

[I] CATHOLIC HEALTHCARE APOSTOLATE

NASSAU COUNTY

MELVILLE. *Catholic Health Services of Long Island*, One Huntington Quadrangle, Ste. 4C04, 11714. Tel: 631-396-5600; Fax: 631-396-5040
For a complete listing, refer to the Hospitals section.

SMITHTOWN. *Siena Village, Inc.*, 52 Rte. 25 A, 11787-1346. Tel: 516-396-5600
For a complete listing, refer to the Hospitals section.

[J] RESIDENCES FOR AGED

AMITYVILLE. *Dominican Village, Inc.*, 565 Albany Ave., 11701. Tel: 631-842-6091; Fax: 631-842-6131.
E-mail: dv@dominicanvillage.org
For a complete listing, refer to the Special Care Facilities section.

HUNTINGTON. *St. Joseph's Guest Home for the Aged, Inc.*, 350 Cuba Hill Rd., 11743. Tel: 631-368-9528; Fax: 931-266-1015
For a complete listing, refer to the Special Care Facilities section.

WEST ISLIP. *Our Lady of Consolation Geriatric Care Center*, 111 Beach Dr., 11795. Tel: 631-587-1600; Fax: 631-587-5960.
E-mail: olcl@villagenet.com
Web site: ourladyofconsolation.org
For a complete listing, refer to the Special Care Facilities section.

[K] SOCIETY OF ST. VINCENT DE PAUL

BETHPAGE. *Central Council*, Diocese of Rockville Centre, 249 Broadway, 11714. Tel: 516-822-3132; Fax: 516-822-2728.
E-mail: Bellis@svdprvc.org
Web site: svdprvc.org
Rev. Msgr. Patrick J. Armshaw, Spiritual Dir.; Thomas J. Lilly, Pres.; Robert S. Ellis, Exec. Dir. Total Assisted 107,744; Total Staff 112; Volunteers 1,033.

[L] HOME HEALTH SERVICES

HAMPTON BAYS. *Dominican Sisters Family Health Service*, 103-6 W. Montauk Hwy., P.O. Box 209, 11946. Tel: 631-728-0181; Fax: 631-723-0866. Montauk Hwy. & Cross Hwy., P.O. Box 866, Amagansett, 11930. Tel: 631-267-1090; Fax: 631-267-2004. Mrs. Joanna O'Connell, R.N., B.S.N., Admin., Suffolk Offices.

WESTBURY. *Nursing Sisters Home Care*. Tel: 516-683-1300; Fax: 516-683-1366.
Web site: TBD
Administrative Office, 1600 Stewart Ave., 11590. Tel: 516-683-1300; Fax: 516-683-1366. Keith Kertland, Pres. & CEO.
Nursing Service Offices: Kings County, 500 19th St., Brooklyn, 11215. Tel: 718-768-7271; Fax: 718-965-2035. Nassau County, 1600 Stewart Ave., 11590. Tel: 516-683-1300; Fax: 516-683-1367. Suffolk County. Medford Office, 3241 Rte. 112, Medford, 11763. Tel: 516-696-1002; Fax: 516-696-1007. Commack Office, 2171 Jericho Tpke., Ste. 100, Commack, 11725. Tel: 631-462-9000; Fax: 631-462-6947. Riverhead Office, 1394C Roanoke Ave., Riverhead, 11901. Tel: 631-591-4440; Fax: 631-591-4446.

[M] MONASTERIES AND RESIDENCES OF PRIESTS AND BROTHERS

BAY SHORE. *Montfort Missionaries*, 26 S. Saxon Ave., 11706. Tel: 631-666-7500; Fax: 631-665-4349.
E-mail: PRETRE@worldnet.att.net
Montfort Spiritual Center and Headquarters of magazine "Queen of All Hearts" and "Montfort Publications". Tel: 516-665-0726; Fax: 516-665-4349. Revs. Roger M. Charest, S.M.M., Mng. Editor; J. Patrick Gaffney, S.M.M., Assoc. Edit. & Preaching Team; George J. Werner, S.M.M., Supr., Preaching Team; Bernard M. Blood, S.M.M., Preaching Team; William M. Dilgen, S.M.M., Marriage Encounter; Maurice A. Landry, S.M.M.; James Manning, S.M.M., Preaching Team; Francis J. Allen, S.M.M., Preaching Team; Francis Pizzarelli, S.M.M., Hope House Ministry. Hospital Chaplains: Revs. Vincent P. Cunningham, S.M.M.; Harold E. McBride, S.M.M.; Peter J. McCrann, S.M.M.; Theodore Murphy, S.M.M. Priests 13.

Montfort Missionaries - Retreat Center, 26 S. Saxon Ave., 11706. Tel: 516-666-7500; Fax: 516-666-4349.

EASTPORT. *Shrine of Our Lady of the Island*, Montfort Missionaries; Eastport-Manor Rd., 11941. Tel: 631-325-0661; Fax: 631-325-5592. Revs. William J. Vigliotta, S.M.M., Dir.; Raymond Graham, S.M.M.

GLEN COVE. *St. Josaphat's Monastery, Novitiate and Retreat House*, East Beach Dr., 11542. Tel: 516-671-0545; Fax: 516-676-7465. Basilian Fathers. Revs. Cyril Tseszczuk, O.S.B.M. (Brazil), Supr. & Master of Novices; Hilarion Bebedik, O.S.B.M.; Januario Lucavei, O.S.B.M., Asst. Master of Novices; Athanasius B. Pekar, O.S.B.M.

MINEOLA. *Provincial Residence and Novitiate*, 240 Emory Rd., 11501. Tel: 516-742-5555; Fax: 516-742-1989.
E-mail: frthomas@kellenberg.org
Society of Mary (Marianists). Very Rev. Thomas A. Cardone, S.M., Prov.; Bro. Kenneth M. Hoagland, S.M., Asst. Prov. & Asst. Education; Rev. James C. Williams, S.M., Asst. Religious Life; Bro. Richard J. Hughes, S.M., Asst. Temporalities; Rev. Philip K. Eichner, S.M., Councilor; Bros. Michael J. Gillen, S.M., Councilor; Thomas J. Clearly, S.M., Councilor. In res. Revs. Ernest P. Lorfanfant, S.M.; Garrett J. Long, S.M.

OYSTER BAY. *St. Francis Monastery, Novitiate and Apostolic Center*, Planting Fields Rd., R.F.D. 1, Box 1365, 11771-1302. Tel: 516-922-3545; Fax: 516-922-9649. Franciscan Brothers. Bro. Roman Morris, O.S.F., Dir., St. Francis Center. Tel: 516-922-3545. In res. Bros. Jeffrey M. Pedersen, O.S.F. Tel: 516-624-9807; Christopher Thurneau, O.S.F. Tel: 516-922-3342.

Vincentian Community, 104 Anstice St., 11771. Tel: 516-992-3494; Fax: 516-992-5715.
E-mail: vinchouse@aol.com
Revs. Gerard H. Luttenberger, C.M.; Patrick J. Griffin, C.M.

POINT LOOKOUT. *Franciscan Friars*, 128 Hewlett Ave., P.O. Box 211, 11569. Tel: 516-432-3719; Fax: 516-432-1377.

UNIONDALE. *St. Pius X Residence*, 1220 Front St., 11553. Tel: 516-485-4200; Fax: 516-485-0596. Rev. Robert Y. Blyman, Vicar for Senior Priests. In res. Rev. Msgr. Lawrence F. Ballweg; Revs. Serafino A. Corali; Edward J. Flynn; John J. Serrano; John P. Wilutis; James J. Dolan; Brian A. McKeon; Donald R. Shane; Gerard J. Gfroerer; Thomas P. Curry; Zachary Callahan; Angelo J. Ditta; Peter L. Duvelsdorf; Denis J. Sheridan; Eugene J. McManus.

WEST HEMPSTEAD. *Maryknoll Residence*, 813 Myrna Dr., 11552. Tel: 516-489-7799.
E-mail: aschiavonemm@aol.com
Rev. Alphonse A. Schiavone, M.M., Dir.

[N] CONVENTS AND RESIDENCES FOR SISTERS

ROCKVILLE CENTRE. *Villa St. Joseph*, 984 N. Village Ave., 11570. Tel: 516-823-3800; Fax: 516-594-0412.
E-mail: DBTCCIJ@aol.com
Congregation of the Infant Jesus (Nursing Sisters of the Sick Poor). Professed Sisters 64.

AMITYVILLE. *Queen of the Rosary, Motherhouse*, 555 Albany Ave., 11701-1197. Tel: 631-842-6000; Fax: 631-842-0240.
E-mail: prioress@aol.com
Web site: www.amityvilleop.org
Sisters of St. Dominic. Legal Titles: *Dominican Sisters Community Support Corporation.; Amityville Dominican Sisters, Inc.* Sr. Mary Hughes, O.P., Prioress; Sr. Mary Arline Hornidge, O.P., Admin.; Rev. Msgr. Dominick J. Adessa, Chap. Total in Residence 134.

BAY SHORE. *New Jerusalem*, 106 N. Penataquit Ave., 11706-6939. Tel: 631-968-8859. Sisters 6.

BLUE POINT. *Ursuline Sisters, St. Ursula Center*, Middle Rd., P.O. Box 86, 11715. Tel: 631-363-2422; Fax: 631-363-7403. Congregation of Tildonk. Sr. Eileen C. Gallagher, O.S.U., Dir., St. Ursula R. Center; Sr. Agnes Seebach, O.S.U., Coord., St. Ursula Convent.

BRENTWOOD. *Maria Regina Convent*, 1725 Brentwood Rd., Bldg. 1, 11717-5589. Tel: 631-273-4500; Fax: 631-952-2378.
E-mail: MariaRegCo@cs.com
Sisters of St. Joseph. Sr. Joan Hackett, C.S.J., Local Supr. Sisters 112.

Saint Joseph Convent, Motherhouse, Brentwood Rd., 11717. Tel: 631-273-4531; Fax: 631-273-1451.
E-mail: BrentCSJ@aol.com
Web site: www.csjbrentwoodny.org
Sisters of Saint Joseph Generalate. Sr. Jean Amore, Pres.; Sr. Miriam Lucille Montella, Gen. Sec.; Sr. Joanne Feulner, Gen. Treas.; Sr. Edna McKeever, C.S.J., Community Archivist. Sisters 883.

Saint Joseph Novitiate, 1725 Brentwood Rd., 11717. Tel: 631-273-1187, Ext. 42; Fax: 631-273-1451.
E-mail: brentcsj@aol.com
Sr. Maryann Rogers, C.S.J., Coord.

DIX HILLS. *Contemplative Sisters of the Good Shepherd*, 151 Burrs Ln., P.O. Box 8020, 11746-9020. Tel: 631-643-1071; Fax: 631-643-9563. Sr. Virginia Agnes Turinese, Supr. Sisters 21.

Sisters of the Good Shepherd, 151 Burrs Ln., P.O. Box 8020, 11746-9020. Tel: 631-491-6850; Fax: 631-643-9199. Coordinators: Sr. Yvette Arnold; Sr. Karen Keegan. Sisters 25. Legal Title: *Sisters of the Good Shepherd, Huntington, NY, Inc.*

FRANKLIN SQUARE. *Spiritual Life Center*, 1031 Mosefan St., 11010. Tel: 516-328-7438. Sisters of St. Dominic. Sr. Kathleen Murphy, O.P., Dir. Sisters 2.

HAMPTON BAYS. *St. Joseph's Villa Retreat and Renewal Center*, 81 Lynn Ave., 11946. Tel: 631-728-6447. Sisters of St. Joseph 2.

HUNTINGTON. *Missionary Sisters of St. Benedict*, 350 Cuba Hill Rd., 11743. Tel: 631-368-9528; Fax: 631-266-1015. Sr. M. Bernarda Krajewska, O.S.B., Supr. Sisters 25.

ISLIP. *Daughters of Wisdom (Administration)*, 385 Ocean Ave., 11751. Tel: 631277-2660; Fax: 631-277-3274.
E-mail: wisdomsisters@cs.com
Sr. Evelyn Eckhardt, D.W., Prov. Administration Offices. Sisters 3.

OCEANSIDE. *St. Anthony's Parish House*, 111 Anchor Ave., 11572. Tel: 631-536-3308. Dominican Sisters (Amityville).

RONKONKOMA. *Religious of Our Lady of the Retreat in the Cenacle*, 310 Cenacle Rd., 11779-2203. Tel: 631-588-8366; Fax: 631-588-1729.

Cenacle Retreat House. Tel: 631-588-8366; Fax: 631-588-1729. Sr. Marie T. Halligan, Supr. Professed Sisters in Residence 39.

Cenacle Formation House, 312 Cenacle Rd., 11779-2203. Tel: 631-737-8491; Fax: 631-737-3375. Professed Sisters 4.

ROOSEVELT. *Oblate Sisters of the Most Holy Redeemer*, Mother of Good Counsel Home, 290 Babylon Tpke., P.O. Box 329, 11575-0329. Tel: 516-223-1013; Fax: 516-223-4254.
E-mail: ossr290@earthlink.net
Sr. Celina Ardila, O.SS.R., Exec. Dir. Mother of Good Counsel Home is a small group home for pregnant and parenting teenage mothers and their infants.

SEAFORD. *Sisters of St. Joseph*, 2316 Hampton Ave., 11783. Tel: 516-826-1773.
E-mail: murphkath@aol.com
Sisters 5.

SELDEN. *Providence Newman Center*, 76 College Rd., 11784. Tel: 631-732-2386. Sr. Grace Maria Dolan, C.S.J.

SOUND BEACH. *Our Lady of Perpetual Help Convent*, 49 Hilltop Dr., Box 926, 11789. Tel: 631-744-2477.
E-mail: dwsndbch@netscape.net
Sr. Virginia Marie Dunn, D.W., Coord. Daughters of Wisdom 23.

[O] RETREAT HOUSES

BLUE POINT. *St. Ursula Retreat Center, Inc.*, Middle Rd. and Blue Point Ave., P.O. Box 86, 11715-0086. Tel: 631-363-6544(Convent); 363-2422 (Retreat Center); Fax: 631-363-7403. Directed by Ursuline Sisters of Tildonk. Sr. Eileen Gallagher, O.S.U., Retreat Dir. Weekend retreats; private retreats; directed retreats; days and evenings of prayer. Sr. Agnes Seebach, O.S.U., Coord. of Sisters Ursuline Convent. Total in Residence 15.

MANHASSET. *St. Ignatius Retreat House, Inisfada*, 251 Searingtown Rd., 11030. Tel: 516-621-8300; Fax: 516-521-7201.
E-mail: inisfada@inisfada.net
Web site: www.inisfada.net
The Society of Jesus. Revs. Joseph S. Constantino, S.J., Dir.; Edward J. Quinnan, S.J.; Damian O. Halligan, S.J.; William P. Walsh, S.J. Sisters 1; Total Staff 5.

MOUNT SINAI. *House of the Holy Innocents, Inc.*, 722 Mt. Sinai-Coram Rd., Box 174, 11766. Tel: 516-331-1745; Fax: 516-331-0964.
E-mail: monkpeace@yahoo.com

OYSTER BAY. *St. Francis Center, Inc.*, 1365 Planting Fields Rd., 11771-1302. Tel: 516-922-3708; Fax: 516-922-9649. Directed by Franciscan Bros. of Brooklyn. Bro. Roman Morris, O.S.F., Dir.

PATCHOGUE. *St. Joseph's Prayer Center*, 312 Maple Ave., 11772. Tel: 631-207-3751; Fax: 631-764-3316. Mrs. Suzanne Reilly, Dir.; Rev. James J. Wheeler, S.J., Apostolic Dir. Total Staff 15.

RONKONKOMA. *Cenacle Retreat Center*, 310 Cenacle Rd., 11779-2203. Tel: 631-588-8366; Fax: 631-585-8485.
E-mail: srjosephine@cenaclesisters.org

Web site: www.cenaclesisters.org
Religious of the Cenacle. Sr. Josephine Daspro, C.S.J., Dir. of Ministry. Ministry Staff 5.

SAG HARBOR. *Cormaria Retreat House*, 11963. Tel: 631-725-4206; Fax: 631-725-1837.
E-mail: cormaria@aol.com
Web site: www.RSHM.org
Directed by the Religious of the Sacred Heart of Mary. Sr. Ann Thaddeus Marino, R.S.H.M., Retreat Dir. Religious of the Sacred Heart of Mary 5; Total Staff 12.

SHELTER ISLAND HEIGHTS. *St. Gabriel's Youth House*, 64 Burns Rd., P.O. Box 3015, 11965. Tel: 631-749-0850; Fax: 631-749-3154. A Youth Retreat Ministry directed by the Passionists. Retreats available for youth and young adult; women, men and married couples. Private retreats available at 3 bedroom, waterfront, "Star of the Sea" House of Prayer. Sr. Maureen Kervick, S.S.J., Retreat Dir. & Admin. Retreat Team: Ms. Patricia Krupski; Ms. Carmela Isabella; Mr. Henry Jacobs; Rev. Blaine Brezinski, C.P.

WATER MILL. *Siena Spirituality Center*, 615 Montauk Hwy., 11976. Tel: 631-726-4740; Fax: 631-726-1930.
E-mail: sienawater@aol.com
Mailing Address: P.O. Box 660, 11976. Richard M. Lawless, Th.D., Exec. Dir.; Sr. Honora Nolty, O.P., Prog. Dir. Dominican Sisters O.P. 3. Center offers private/directed retreats, recollection days, special interest programs and hosts business conferences. Also, Sabbatical (100 days) in Dominican tradition.

[P] CAMPUS MINISTRIES AND NEWMAN CENTERS

ROCKVILLE CENTRE. *The Campus Parish of Long Island*, Office of Campus 50 N. Park Ave., 11570. Tel: 516-678-5800, Ext. 614; Fax: 516-763-1068.
E-mail: CHAJJD@hofstra.edu
Web site: www.drvc.org/campusparish
Rev. Joseph J. D'Angelo, M.Div., M.S., C.A.S.A.C., M.A.C., Pastor & Dir. Canonical Institute of Non-territorial Campus Parishes.
Adelphi University, Rm. 312, University Center, Chaplain's Center, Garden City, 11530. Tel: 516-877-3116; Fax: 516-877-3659. Deacon Paul Bedell; Sr. Eileen M. Connor, O.P.
Hofstra University. Tel: 516-463-6920;463-6814; Fax: 516-463-6291. Chaplains' Office, Student Center 213, 200 Hofstra University, Hempstead, 11549. Tel: 516-463-6841; Fax: 516-463-6291. Joseph J. D'Angelo, M.Div.,M.S., C.A.S.A.C., Pastor & Director; Sr. Kathleen Riordan, O.P.
Nassau Community College. Tel: 516-572-7234; Fax: 516-463-6030. Stewart Avenue-Nursing Department, Garden City, 11530-6793. Tel: 516-572-7234;572-6814. Deacon Thomas Rich.
NY Institute of Technology, P.O. Box 8000, Old Westbury, 11548. Tel: 516-686-7794. Bro. Padraic Campbell, III, O.S.F.
LIU/C.W. Post College and New York Institute of Technology - Old Westbury. Tel: 516-299-2229; Fax: 516-299-2228. Interfaith Center, Brookville, 11548. Tel: 516-299-2229; Fax: 516-299-2228. Rev. Edward J. Brown, M.S.
Southampton Campus of Long Island University. Tel: 516-287-8110. Office of the Cathlolic Chaplain, Southampton, 11968. Tel: 516-287-8110.
Student Activities, Wood Hall, 239 Montauk Hwy., Southampton, 11968. Ms. Sally McGuire.
Suffolk Community College. Tel: 516-732-2386. 533 College Rd., Selden, 11784. Tel: 516-732-2386. Sr. Grace Dolan, C.S.J.
SUNY at Farmingdale. Tel: 516-420-2638; Fax: 516-420-2157. Memorial Hall, Rm. 211, Melville Rd., Farmingdale, 11735. Tel: 516-420-2638; Fax: 516-420-2157.
SUNY at Old Westbury. Interfaith Chaplaincy, Marshall Hall-Store Front, #10, Old Westbury, 11568-0219. Tel: 516-876-3031; Fax: 631-929-3188. Deacon Fred Finter.
SUNY at Stony Brook - Catholic Campus Ministry. Tel: 631-632-6562; Fax: 631-632-6524. Interfaith Center, 158 Humanities, Stony Brook, 11794-8033. Tel: 631-632-6562. Sr. Margaret Ann Landry, R.S.H.M.; Rev. John Fitzgerald.
Dowling College. Curtin Center, Ste. 116, Oakdale, 11769-1999. Tel: 516-244-5034. Deacon James Pickel.

[Q] MISCELLANEOUS

AMITYVILLE. *Amityville Dominican Sisters, Inc.*, 555 Albany Ave., 11701. Tel: 631-842-6000; Fax: 631-842-0240.
E-mail: prioress@aol.com
Web site: www.amityvilleop.org
Sr. Mary Hughes, O.P., Pres.; Sr. Francis Ann Gorman, O.P., Vice Pres.; Sr. Barbara C. Suessmann, O.P., Sec. & Treas.
Benincasa Family Services, Inc., 555 Albany Ave., 11701. Tel: 631-842-6000, Ext. 351; Fax: 631-842-1596.
E-mail: mkbenin555@aol
Sr. Margaret A. Krajci, O.P., Contact.
Dominican Sisters Community Support Corp., 555 Albany Ave., 11701. Tel: 631-842-6000; Fax: 631-842-0240.
E-mail: prioress@aol.com
Web site: www.amityvilleop.org
Sr. Mary Hughes, O.P., Pres.; Sr. Francis Ann Gorman, O.P., Vice Pres.; Sr. Barbara C. Suessmann, O.P., Sec. & Treas.
Siena Spirituality Center, Inc., c/o Sisters of the Order of St. Dominic, 555 Albany Ave., 11701. Tel: 631-842-6043. Sr. Barbara Suessman, O.P., Treas.

BAY SHORE. *Pronto of Long Island, Inc.*, 128 Pine Aire Dr., 11706. Tel: 631-231-8290; Fax: 631-231-8390. Mrs. Nilda Alvarez, Contact Person.

BRENTWOOD. *Thomas I. Conerty Outreach Center of Brentwood, Inc.*, 88 Second Ave., 11717. Tel: 631-273-8113; Fax: 631-435-3575. Ligia Guerrero, Contact Person.

CENTERPORT. *Mt. Alvernia, Inc.*, Prospect Rd., P.O. Box 301, 11721. Tel: 631-261-5730; Fax: 631-754-4204.
E-mail: alvernia@juno.com
Web site: www.alvernia.org
Directed by the Franciscan Brothers.
Camp Alvernia. Tel: 631-261-5730; Fax: 631-754-4204.
Mt. Alvernia Center for Retreats. Tel: 631-261-5730; Fax: 631-754-4204.

FARMINGVILLE. *Religious Computer Systems*, P.O. Box 508, 11738-0508. Tel: 631-732-7270; Fax: 631-732-6591.
E-mail: rcsjane@compuserve.com
Sr. Jane Muller, O.P. Social Security and computer services for Religious institutions under sponsorship of the Amityville Dominicans.

ISLIP. *Wisdom Charitable Trust*, 385 Ocean Ave., 11751. Tel: 631-277-2660; Fax: 631-277-3274.
E-mail: wisdomsisters@cs.com

NEW HYDE PARK. *Apostleship of Prayer, National Office for the U.S.* (Directed by the Society of Jesus), 3 Stephen Ave., 11040-3130. Tel: 516-328-9777; Fax: 516-328-6039.
E-mail: aposprayer@aol.com
Web site: www.cin.org/ap/
Rev. John H. Rainaldo, S.J., Nat'l Dir. Total Staff 4.

OAKDALE. *Saint John Baptist De La Salle of New York, Inc.*, 500 Montauk Hwy., 11769. Tel: 401-789-0244; Fax: 401-783-5303.
E-mail: cbcdcasey@aol.com
Bro. Daniel Casey, F.S.C.

RONKONKOMA. *Catholic Press Association of the United States and Canada, Inc.*, 3555 Veterans Memorial Hwy., Unit O, 11779. Tel: 631-471-4730; Fax: 631-471-4802.
E-mail: CathJourn@aol.com
Web site: www.catholicpress.org
Karen Franz, Pres.; Mr. Owen P. McGovern, Exec. Dir.

ROOSEVELT. *Friends of Mother of Good Counsel Home, Inc.*, 290 Babylon Tpke., 11575. Tel: 516-223-1013. Sr. Celina Ardila, Exec. Dir.

UNIONDALE. *TELEcare of the Diocese of Rockville Centre*. Tel: 516-538-8700; Fax: 516-489-9701.
E-mail: info@telecaretv.org
Web site: telecaretv.org
1200 Glenn Curtiss Blvd., 11553. Richard Haemmerle, Vice Pres. & Business Mgr.

WEST BABYLON. *Christa House, Inc.*, 720 Albin Ave., 11704. Tel: 631-376-0114; Fax: 631-376-0115.
Web site: ChristaHouse.org
Sr. Patricia A. Ryan, C.S.J.

WESTBURY. *Sisters, Lovers of the Holy Cross*. Tel: 516-333-9464; Fax: 516-624-9042.
E-mail: theresamartin@worldnet.att.net
St. Theresa Convent, 43 Crown Ln., 11590. Tel: 516-333-9464; Fax: 516-624-9042. Sr. Theresa Nguyen, Pres.

WYANDANCH. *Gerald J. Ryan Outreach Center, Inc.*, 1434 Straight Path, 11798. Total Assisted 16,000; Total Staff 3.
The Opening Word Program, Inc., 1434 Straight Path, 11798. Tel: 631-643-0541; Fax: 631-643-0541.
E-mail: opword@aol.com
Directed by the Sisters of St. Dominic. Sr. Mary Ryan, O.P., Exec. Dir.; Sr. Leonore Toscano, O.P., Treas.; Sr. Mary Hughes, O.P., Chairperson.

RELIGIOUS INSTITUTES OF MEN REPRESENTED IN THE DIOCESE

For further details refer to the corresponding bracketed number in the Religious Institutes of Men or Women section.

[0330]—*Brothers of the Christian Schools*.—F.S.C.
[1100]—*Brothers of the Sacred Heart*. (Province of New York).—S.C.
[0470]—*The Capuchin Friars*. (St. Mary Prov.).—O.F.M.Cap.
[1330]—*Congregation of the Mission-Vincentians*. (Eastern Prov.).—C.M.
[1000]—*Congregation of the Passion*. (Prov. of St. Paul of the Cross).—C.P.
[0490]—*Franciscan Brothers of Brooklyn*.—O.S.F.
[0520]—*Franciscan Friars*. (Holy Name Province).—O.F.M.
[0690]—*Jesuit Fathers and Brothers*. (NY Prov.).—S.J.
[0770]—*The Marist Brothers*.—F.M.S.
[0800]—*Maryknoll*.—M.M.
[0720]—*Missionaries of Our Lady of La Salette*.—M.S.
[0870]—*Montfort Missionaries*.—S.M.M.
[0430]—*Order of Preachers-Dominicans*.—O.P.
[1070]—*Redemptorist Fathers*.—C.SS.R.
[0760]—*Society of Mary*. (Provs. of NY; Meribah).—S.M.

RELIGIOUS INSTITUTES OF WOMEN REPRESENTED IN THE DIOCESE

[3110]—*Congregation of Our Lady of the Retreat in the Cenacle*.—R.C.
[1920]—*Congregation of the Sisters of the Holy Cross*.—C.S.C.
[]—*Daughters of Mary*. (Haiti).—F.de M.
[0960]—*Daughters of Wisdom*.—D.W.
[1070-05]—*Dominican Sisters*. (Amityville).—O.P.
[1070-11]—*Dominican Sisters*. Sparkille.—O.P.
[1070-15]—*Dominican Sisters*. (Blauvelt).—O.P.
[1070-16]—*Dominican Sisters*. (Hope).—O.P.
[1370]—*Franciscan Missionaries of Mary*.—F.M.M.
[1180]—*Franciscan Sisters of Allegany, New York*.—O.S.F.
[1425]—*Franciscan Sisters of Peace*.—F.S.P.
[1840]—*Grey Nuns of the Sacred Heart*.—G.N.S.H.
[2070]—*Holy Union Sisters*.—S.U.S.C.
[2575]—*Institute of the Sisters of Mercy of the Americas*. (Brooklyn, NY).—R.S.M.
[0210]—*Missionary Benedictine Sisters*.—O.S.B.
[3030]—*Oblate Sisters of M.H. Redeemer*.—O.S.S.R.
[3465]—*Religious of the Sacred Heart of Mary*.—R.S.H.M.
[2970]—*School Sisters of Notre Dame*.—S.S.N.D.
[0640]—*Sisters of Charity of St. Vincent de Paul*. (Halifax).—S.C.
[0650]—*Sisters of Charity of St. Vincent de Paul, of New York*.—S.C.
[0430]—*Sisters of Charity of the Blessed Virgin Mary*.—B.V.M.
[2575]—*Sisters of Mercy of the Americas*. (Dallas Region).—R.S.M.
[2575]—*Sisters of Mercy of the Americas*. (NY Region).—R.S.M.
[2990]—*Sisters of Notre Dame de Namur*.—S.N.D.
[3000]—*Sisters of Notre Dame de Namur*. (Baltimore & Base Communities Provinces).—S.N.D.deN.
[3830-05]—*Sisters of St. Joseph*. (Brentwood, NY).—C.S.J.
[3830-16]—*Sisters of St. Joseph*. (Springfield, MA.—S.S.J.
[3840]—*Sisters of St. Joseph of Carondelet*. (Province of Albany).—C.S.J.
[3393]—*Sisters of St. Joseph of Chestnut Hill*. (Philadelphia, PA).—S.S.J.
[3830-11]—*Sisters of St. Joseph of Nazareth*.—S.S.J.
[3180]—*Sisters of the Cross and the Passion*.—C.P.
[1830]—*Sisters of the Good Shepherd*.—R.G.S.
[1970]—*Sisters of the Holy Family of Nazareth*.—C.S.F.N.
[2240]—*Sisters of the Infant Jesus*.—C.I.J.
[3320]—*Sisters of the Presentation of the BVM*. (New Windsor, N.Y.).—P.B.V.M.
[2390]—*Sisters, Lovers of the Holy Cross*. (Brookville, N.Y.).—L.H.C.
[2160]—*Sisters, Servants of the Immaculate Heart of Mary*.—I.H.M.
[2150]—*Sisters, Servants of the Immaculate Heart of Mary*. (Monroe, MI).—I.H.M.
[4130]—*Ursuline Sisters of the Congregation of Tildonk, Belgium*.—O.S.U.

DIOCESAN CEMETERIES

CENTRAL ISLIP. *Queen of All Saints*, 115 Wheeler Rd., 11722. Tel: 631-234-8297.

CORAM. *Holy Sepulchre*, 3443 Rte. 112, 11727. Tel: 631-732-3460.

WESTBURY. *Holy Rood*, Old Country Rd., Box 182, 11590. Tel: 516-334-7990.

NECROLOGY

✠ McHugh, Most Rev. James T., Bishop of Rockville Centre. —Died Dec. 10, 2000.

† Fagan, Rev. Msgr. Daniel E., Valley Stream, NY Holy Name of Mary. —Died April 25, 2000.

† Flynn, Rev. Msgr. Martin J., (Retired). —Died Nov. 8, 2000.

† Huntington, Rev. Msgr. Christopher, (Retired). —Died March 10, 2000.

† Joseph, Ramon A., (Retired). —Died Sept. 13, 2000.

† Lukaszewski, Joseph C., (Retired). —Died April 26, 2000.

† Mahoney, John F., (Retired). —Died June 4, 2000.

† Mattei, Rev. Msgr. Saverio C, Dix Hills, NY St. Matthew. —Died April 10, 2000.

† Monteleone, Raphael D., (Retired). —Died Nov. 23, 1999.

† O'Farrell, Michael J., Northport, NY St. Philip Neri. —Died Feb. 13, 2000.

† Staiger, Charles, (Retired). —Died April 24, 2000.

† Stegmann, Rev. Msgr. Raymond V., (Retired). —Died June 9, 2000.

† Werring, Edward J., Rockville Centre, NY Our Lady of Mt. Carmel. —Died June 13, 2000.

Diocese of Sacramento

(Dioecesis Sacramentensis)

Most Reverend

WILLIAM K. WEIGAND, D.D.

Bishop of Sacramento; ordained May 25, 1963; appointed Bishop of Salt Lake City September 3, 1980; ordained and installed November 17, 1980; appointed Bishop of Sacramento November 30, 1993; installed January 27, 1994. *Mailing Address: Diocesan Pastoral Center, Office of the Bishop, 2110 Broadway, Sacramento, 95818-2541.* Tel.: 916-733-0200; Fax: 916-733-0215.

Most Reverend

RICHARD J. GARCIA, D.D.

Auxiliary Bishop of Sacramento; ordained June 15, 1973; appointed Titular Bishop of Bapara and Auxiliary Bishop of Sacramento November 25, 1997; ordained Auxiliary Bishop of Sacramento January 28, 1998. *Office: 2110 Broadway, Sacramento, CA, 95818-2541.* Tel.: 916-733-0200.

Most Reverend

FRANCIS A. QUINN, D.D., ED.D.

Retired Bishop of Sacramento; ordained June 15, 1946; appointed Titular Bishop of Numana and Auxiliary Bishop of San Francisco April 28, 1978; Episcopal ordination June 29, 1978; appointed Bishop of Sacramento December 18, 1979. *Office: 2110 Broadway, Sacramento, CA, 95818-2541.* Tel.: 916-733-0200.

Diocesan Pastoral Center: 2110 Broadway, Sacramento, CA, 95818-2541. Tel.: 916-733-0100 (General); Fax: 916-733-0195.

Web site address: www.diocese-sacramento.org

E-mail address: bishopweigand@diocese-sacramento.org

ERECTED BY HIS HOLINESS, LEO XIII, MAY 28, 1886.

Square Miles 42,597.

Legal Title: "Roman Catholic Bishop of Sacramento, A Corporation Sole".

Comprises the Counties of Amador, Butte, Colusa, El Dorado, Glenn, Lassen, Modoc, Nevada, Placer, Plumas, Sacramento, Shasta, Sierra, Siskiyou, Solano, Sutter, Tehama, Trinity, Yolo and Yuba in the State of California.

CO-PATRONS OF DIOCESE: St. Patrick; Our Lady of Guadalupe.

For legal titles of parishes and diocesan institutions, consult the Diocesan Pastoral Center.

STATISTICAL OVERVIEW

Personnel	
Bishop	1
Auxiliary Bishops	1
Retired Bishops	1
Abbots	1
Retired Abbots	1
Priests: Diocesan Active in Diocese	107
Priests: Active Outside Diocese	6
Priests: Retired, Sick or Absent	50
Number of Diocesan Priests	163
Religious Priests in Diocese	72
Extern Priests in Diocese	35
Ordinations:	
Diocesan Priests	4
Religious Priests	1
Transitional Deacons	6
Permanent Deacons	18
Permanent Deacons in Diocese	115
Total Brothers	31
Total Sisters	184
Parishes	
Parishes	98
With Resident Pastor:	
Resident Diocesan Priests	86
Resident Religious Priests	10
Without Resident Pastor:	
Administered by Women Religious	2
Missions	42
Professional Ministry Personnel:	
Brothers	5
Sisters	40
Lay Ministers	79
Welfare	
Catholic Hospitals	6
Total Assisted	427,059
Homes for the Aged	1
Total Assisted	118
Residential Care of Children	1
Total Assisted	21
Day Care and Extended Day Care Centers	3
Total Assisted	1,289
Specialized Homes	1
Total Assisted	23
Special Centers for Social Services	8
Total Assisted	109,150
Educational	
Diocesan Students in Other Seminaries	51
Seminaries, Religious	1
Students Religious	12
Total Seminarians	63
High Schools, Diocesan and Parish	4
Total Students	1,831
High Schools, Private	3
Total Students	2,450
Elementary Schools, Diocesan and Parish	47
Total Students	12,752
Catechesis/Religious Education:	
High School Students	2,631
Elementary Students	16,267
Total Students Under Catholic Instruction	35,994
Teachers in the Diocese:	
Priests	13
Scholastics	2
Brothers	7
Sisters	23
Lay Teachers	860
Vital Statistics	
Receptions into the Church:	
Infant Baptism Totals	9,326
Adult Baptism Totals	691
Received into Full Communion	848
First Communions	7,049
Confirmations	5,218
Marriages:	
Catholic	1,177
Interfaith	527
Total Marriages	1,704
Deaths	2,724
Total Catholic Population	477,330
Total Population	3,020,340

Former Bishops—Rt. Rev. EUGENE O'CONNELL, D.D., cons. Titular Bishop of Flaviopolis and appt. Vicar Apostolic of Marysville, Feb. 3, 1861; appt. First Bishop of Grass Valley, March 22, 1868; resigned March 17, 1884 and appt. Titular Bishop of Joppa; died Dec. 4, 1891.—Rt. Rev. PATRICK MANOGUE, D.D., cons. Titular Bishop of Ceremos, Coadjutor to Bishop O'Connell of Grass Valley, Jan. 16, 1881; succeeded to the See of Grass Valley on Bishop O'Connell's resignation, March 17, 1884; became the first Bishop of Sacramento, May 1886; died Feb. 27, 1895.—Rt. Rev. THOMAS GRACE, D.D., cons. June 16, 1896; died Dec. 27, 1921.—Rt. Rev. PATRICK J. KEANE, D.D., ord. June 20, 1895; cons. Bishop of Samaria, Dec. 14, 1920; appt. to See of Sacramento, March 17, 1922; died Sept. 1, 1928.—Most Rev. ROBERT J. ARMSTRONG, D.D., Litt.D., ord. Dec. 10, 1910; cons. March 12, 1929; died Jan. 14, 1957.—Most Rev. JOSEPH T. MCGUCKEN, D.D., S.T.D., LL.D., ord. Jan. 16, 1928; cons. Titular Bishop of Sanavo and Auxiliary Bishop of Los Angeles, March 19, 1941; Coadjutor Bishop of Sacramento, Oct. 26, 1955; succeeded to Jan. 14, 1957, as Bishop of Sacramento; promoted to the See of San Francisco, Feb. 21, 1962; died Oct. 6, 1983.—Most Rev. ALDEN J. BELL, D.D., M.S.S.W., ord. May 14, 1932; appt. Titular Bishop of Rhodopolis and Auxiliary Bishop of Los Angeles, April 18, 1956; cons. June 4, 1956; appt. Bishop of Sacramento, March 30, 1962; retired March 15, 1979; died Aug. 28, 1982.—Most Rev. JOHN S. CUMMINS, D.D., ord. Jan. 24, 1953; appt. Titular Bishop of Lambesi and Auxiliary Bishop of Sacramento, Feb. 26, 1974; cons. May 26,

1974; appt. Bishop of Oakland, May 3, 1977.—Most Rev. FRANCIS A. QUINN, D.D., Ed.D., ord. June 15, 1946; appt. Titular Bishop of Numana and Auxiliary Bishop of San Francisco, April 28, 1978; Episcopal Ordination, June 29, 1978; appt. Bishop of Sacramento, Dec. 18, 1979; retired Nov. 30, 1993.—Most Rev. ALPHONSE GALLEGOS, O.A.R., D.D., ord. May 24, 1958; appt. Titular Bishop of Sassabe and Auxiliary Bishop of Sacramento, Sept. 1, 1981; cons. Nov. 4, 1981; died Oct. 6, 1991.

Diocesan Pastoral Center—Rev. BERNARD TAPE, *2110 Broadway, Sacramento, 95818-2541.* Office Hours: Mon.-Fri. 8:30-4:30. Tel: 916-733-0100; Fax: 916-733-0195.

Vicar General and Moderator of the Curia—Rev. Msgr. ROBERT P. WALTON. Tel: 916-733-0200; Fax: 916-733-0215.

Chancellor and Secretary to the Bishop—Sr. EILEEN ENRIGHT, R.S.M. Tel: 916-733-0200; Fax: 916-733-0215.

Vice Chancellor—Rev. MARK R. RICHARDS, J.C.L. Tel: 916-733-0261; Fax: 916-733-0224.

Vicar Episcopal for Theological and Canonical Affairs—Rev. CHARLES S. MCDERMOTT, S.T.D. Tel: 916-733-0200; Fax: 916-733-0215.

Personnel Director for Priests—Vacant.

Vicar for Priests—Most Rev. RICHARD J. GARCIA. Tel: 916-733-0200; Fax: 916-733-0215.

Vicar for Religious—Sr. EILEEN ENRIGHT, R.S.M. Tel: 916-733-0200; Fax: 916-733-0215.

Vicar for Retired Priests—Rev. NICHOLAS PHELAN. Tel: 530-271-0167.

Vicar for Deacons—Deacon GERALD PAULY, *2110 Broadway, Sacramento, 95818-2541.* Tel: 916-733-0244; Fax: 916-733-0224.

Vicars Forane—Revs. AIDAN O'REILLY, (Siskiyou); MICHAEL KIERNAN, (Shasta); ROY R. DONER, (North Valley); MANUEL SORIA, (South Valley); RODNEY HALL, (Ridge); PATRICK O'CONNOR, (Northern Mines); JOHN P. SULLIVAN, (Southern Mines); JOHN E. BOLL, (Yolo); EDWARD J. LEWIS, (Solano); Rev. Msgr. ALBERT O'CONNOR, (Southern Suburbs); Revs. T. BRENDAN O'SULLIVAN, (City); LEO MCALLISTER, (American River); IGNATIUS HARAN, (Northern Suburbs).

Vicar for Hispanics and Other Ethnic Ministries—Most Rev. RICHARD J. GARCIA. Tel: 916-733-0200; Fax: 916-733-0215.

Diocesan Tribunal—Please direct all requests to the Tribunal. *2110 Broadway, Sacramento, 95818-2541.* Tel: 916-733-0225; Fax: 916-733-0224.

Judicial Vicar—Rev. DAVID L. DEIBEL, J.D., J.C.L.

Adjutant Judicial Vicar—Rev. MARK R. RICHARDS, J.C.L.

Pro-Synodal Judges—Rev. Msgr. PATRICK M. NOLAN; Revs. RODOLFO DELGADO, J.C.L.; LIAM MACCARTHY; MARK RICHARDS, J.C.L.; KRYSTYNA AMBORSKI, J.C.L.

Promoter of Justice—Rev. CHARLES S. MCDERMOTT, S.T.D.

Defenders of the Bond—Rev. Msgr. JAMES C. KIDDER; Revs. JOHN BOLL; BRENDAN MCKEEFRY; JOHN FOLMER, J.C.D.; JOSEPH HUYEN NGUYEN; DEBORAH A. BARTON, J.C.L.

Approved Advocates—SUSAN BOONE; CAROL SCOTT; JOANNE FANKHAUSER.

Notaries—CAROL CHEEVER; EVA GREINER; MAUREEN KUBASAK.

Civil Law—EDWARD G. HEIDIG, ESQ., Diocesan Attorney.

College of Consultors—Rev. Msgr. JAMES CHURCH; Revs. MICHAEL J. CORMACK; HUMBERTO GOMEZ; POLYCARPO GUMAPO; MICHAEL KIERNAN; PATRICK O'CONNOR; Rev. Msgr. ROBERT P. WALTON.

Diocesan Offices and Directors

AIDS, Ministry to—Rev. JOHN HEALY, Coord., *Mercy General Hospital, 4001 J St., Sacramento, 95819.* Tel: 916-453-4753.

Alcoholism Advisory Board—Most Rev. RICHARD J. GARCIA. Tel: 916-733-0200. Rev. THOMAS MAGUIRE. Tel: 916-985-2561, Ext. 4206.

Archives—Rev. WILLIAM BREAULT, S.J., Archivist, *2110 Broadway, Sacramento, 95818-2541.* Tel: 916-733-0299; 480-2165.

Black Catholic Council—BRENDA ELAZIER, *Office, 2110 Broadway, Sacramento, 95818-2541.* Tel: 916-733-0160; 227-2288; Fax: 916-733-0195. Rev. INNOCENT EMECHETE, Chap. Tel: 707-448-6841, Ext. 2976.

Building Committee—Direct inquiries to: Mr. THOMAS MCNAMARA, Staff, *Diocesan Pastoral Center, 2110 Broadway, Sacramento, 95818-2541.* Tel: 916-733-0277; Fax: 916-733-0295.

California Catholic Conference—*1119 K St., Sacramento, 95814.* Tel: 916-443-4851; Fax: 916-443-5629. Most Rev. SYLVESTER D. RYAN, Pres.; Most Rev. WILLIAM K. WEIGAND, Vice Pres.; Most Rev. STEPHEN E. BLAIRE, Sec. & Treas.; Mr. EDWARD "NED" E. DOLEJSI, Exec. Dir.; Mr. DAVID A. POLLARD, Assoc. Dir. for Public Policy; Mr. ROBERT TEEGARDEN, Assoc Dir. for Educ. CAROL HOGAN, Dir., Pastoral Projects & Com.; Vacant, Assoc. Dir., Office of Hispanic Affairs; Mr. RICHARD MOCKLER, Exec. Dir. Catholic Charities of California, Inc.

Alliance of Catholic Health Care—WILLIAM J. COX, Pres. & CEO, *1215 K St., Sacramento, 95814.* Tel: 916-552-2630; Fax: 916-552-7652.

Campus Ministry—Rev. MICHAEL NEWMAN, S.D.S., Diocesan Dir., *Newman Catholic Ctr., 346 Cherry St., Chico, 95928.* Tel: 530-342-5180; Fax: 530-342-3016.

Catholic Faith Formation—Mr. ROBERT MEANEY, Dir., *2110 Broadway, Sacramento, 95818-2541.* Tel: 916-733-0123; Fax: 916-733-0195. Mrs. LINDA SHUMATE, Consultant for Catechesis. Hispanic Catechesis: Deacon ANTONIO RAMIREZ, Consultant for Hispanic Catechesis; Sr. MARTHA JUAREZ, H.C.J.C., Consultant for Hispanic Adult Catechesis; Sr. ANITA MINIHANE, R.S.M., Coord. for Lay Ministry; Vacant, Coord. for Adult Faith Formation; Mrs. MILAGROS CALVETTI, Coord. Hispanic Youth/Young Adult Ministry; Mrs. CHERYL THOLCKE, Coord. Youth Ministry; Mr. STEPHEN THOLCKE, Dir. Pendola Center. Coordinators of Deaf Ministry: DEBBIE VANDERFORD; Ms. JEAN NELSON; Mr. STANLEY SIMONET; Mr. FELICIANO TAPIA, Hispanic Lay Ministry; Mrs. MICHELLE HENDRICKS, Catechesis, People with Special Needs; Mr. JOHN DONAHOE, Coord. for Camp Recreation; DEBBIE GLAUZ, Coord. for Camp Recreation.

Office of Evangelization—Sr. SUSAN MCCARTHY, R.S.M., Dir.; Rev. RICARDO GIRALDO, Hispanic Programs Coord., *2110 Broadway, Sacramento, 95818.* Tel: 916-733-0154.

Catholic Charities of Sacramento, Inc.—JAMES SWEENEY, Pres. & Chm. Bd. of Directors; JAMES F. RODGERS, Exec. Dir., *5890 Newman Ct., Sacramento, 95819.* Tel: 916-452-4621; Fax: 916-736-0282.

Cemeteries—Mr. PHILIP NIEDERBERGER, Dir., *2110 Broadway, Sacramento, 95818.* Tel: 916-733-0247; Fax: 916-733-0224.

Censor Librorum—Rev. CHARLES S. MCDERMOTT, S.T.D., *2110 Broadway, Sacramento, 95818-2541.* Tel: 916-733-0200; Fax: 916-733-0215.

Communications and Media—Rev. JAMES T. MURPHY, Dir., *1017 11th St., Sacramento, 95814.* Tel: 916-444-3071; Fax: 916-443-2749.

Council of Priests—Rev. EDWARD LEWIS, Chm. Tel: 707-644-8396. Most Rev. WILLIAM K. WEIGAND, D.D., Pres.; Most Rev. RICHARD GARCIA; Revs. POLYCARPO GUMAPO; ERIC LOFGREN; DANIEL A. LOONEY; LIAM MACCARTHY; CHARLES S. MCDERMOTT; VINCENT O'REILLY; JOSEPH MITCHELL, C.P.; Rev. Msgr. PATRICK NOLAN; Revs. BRENDAN O'SULLIVAN; MICHAEL HEBDA; MANUEL SORIA; GERALD RYLE; JAMES P. SHEETS; MIGUEL SILVA; Rev. Msgr. ROBERT P. WALTON; Rev. Msgr. JAMES CHURCH; Deacon WILLIAM RIEHL, Deacon Observor Direct all correspondence to: *2110 Broadway, Sacramento, 95818-2541.*

Detention Service—Vacant, Coord., *2110 Broadway, Sacramento, 95818-2541.* Tel: 916-733-0256; Fax: 916-733-0224.

Development—MIMI SCHERBER, Diocesan Dir., *2110 Broadway, Sacramento, 95818-2541.* Tel: 916-733-0266; Fax: 916-733-0295.

Diocesan Pastoral Council—Please direct all inquiries to: Sr. EILEEN ENRIGHT, R.S.M., Staff, Office of the Bishop: Tel: 916-733-0200.

Diocesan Priests' Trust Fund—Most Rev. WILLIAM K. WEIGAND, D.D., Pres. Ex Officio Please direct all inquiries to: Rev. Msgr. MURROUGH WALLACE, Treas., *St. Theresa Church, 1041 Lyons Ave., South Lake Tahoe, 96150.* Tel: 530-544-3533; Fax: 916-544-4662.

Divorced and Separated, Ministry to—Direct inquiries to: *Family Life Office, 2110 Broadway, Sacramento, 95818-2541.* Tel: 916-733-0155; Fax: 916-733-0195.

Due Process Conciliation, Council of—Rev. Msgr. MURROUGH WALLACE, Chm.; Rev. MICHAEL KIERNAN; Dr. WILLIAM MARIANO; ELAINE MASSEY; Sr. KATHLEEN HORGAN R.S.M.,Direct all correspondence to: Rev. CHARLES S. MCDERMOTT, S.T.D., *2110 Broadway, Sacramento, 95818-2541.* Tel: 916-733-0200.

Office of Arbitration—Revs. CHARLES S. MCDERMOTT, Chm. DANIEL A. LOONEY; Rev. Msgr. JAMES C. KIDDER; Rev. FRED OLIVER; Mrs. SHEILA NOLAN, Office: *2110 Broadway, Sacramento, 95818-2541.* Tel: 916-733-0200.

Eastern Catholic Churches—Rev. CHARLES S. MCDERMOTT, Liaison Officer, *2110 Broadway, Sacramento, 95818-2541.* Tel: 916-733-0200.

"Ecclesia Dei" Community (Latin Mass)—Rev. JOSEPH TERRA, F.S.S.P., *P.O. Box 5382, Sacramento, 95817.* Tel: 916-457-7824; Fax: 916-737-8930.

Ecumenical & Interreligious Affairs—Rev. JOHN KEANE, S.A., Diocesan Dir., *2110 Broadway, Sacramento, 95818-2541.* Tel: 916-733-0200; Fax: 916-733-0215.

Family Life—JOHN RIESCHICK, Dir., *2110 Broadway, Sacramento, 95818-2541.* Tel: 916-733-0155.

Finance Council—Members: Rev. BRENDAN MCKEEFRY; ROBERT GRANUCCI, ESQ.; Rev. IGNATIUS HARAN; ANNE HECK LONG; Ms. BETH LEONARD; Mr. MICHAEL PROFUMO; ROBERT SLAKEY; Mr. CHARLES SYLVA; Mr. PETE PADILLA; Ms. JULIE NAUMAN. Ex Officio: Rev. Msgr. ROBERT P. WALTON; Mr. THOMAS J. MCNAMARA, *Chancery Office, 2110 Broadway, Sacramento, 95818-2541.* Tel: 916-733-0277.

Investment Review Committee—Direct inquiries to: Mr. THOMAS MCNAMARA, *2110 Broadway, Sacramento, 95818-2541.* Tel: 916-733-0277; Fax: 916-733-0295.

Finance Office—Mr. THOMAS MCNAMARA, Dir., *2110 Broadway, Sacramento, 95818-2541.* Tel: 916-733-0277; Fax: 916-733-0295.

Social Justice—BILL SOUSA, *2110 Broadway, Sacramento, 95818-2541.* Tel: 916-733-0255; Fax: 916-733-0224.

Hispanic Apostolate—Deacon GERMAN TORO, *2110 Broadway, Sacramento, 95818-2541.* Tel: 916-733-0177; Fax: 916-733-0195.

Holy Childhood Association—Mr. THOMAS BUTLER, *2110 Broadway, Sacramento, 95818-2541.* Tel: 916-733-0110; Fax: 916-733-0120.

Hospitals, Diocesan Liaison for Catholic—Rev. JOHN J. HEALY, *Mercy General Hospital, 4001 J St., Sacramento, 95819.* Tel: 916-453-4753.

Lay Personnel—Mr. JOHN HALE, Dir., *2110 Broadway, Sacramento, 95818-2541.* Tel: 916-733-0240; Fax: 916-733-0295.

Marriage Preparation—JOHN RIESCHICK, Dir., Family Life Office, *2110 Broadway, Sacramento, 95818-2541.* Tel: 916-733-0155.

Newspapers—"Catholic Herald" and "El Heraldo Catolico"; Ms. JULIE SLY, Editor; RICARDO OLVERA, Editor, El Heraldo, Office: *5890 Newman Ct., Sacramento, 95819-2608.* Tel: 916-452-3344; Fax: 916-452-2945.

Ongoing Education of Clergy—Rev. T. BRENDAN O'SULLIVAN, Dir., *St. Anthony Church, 660 Florin Rd., Sacramento, 95831.* Tel: 916-428-5678.

Opus Sanctorum Angelorum—Rev. J. DERMOT DWYER, Spiritual Dir., *P.O. Box 752, Colfax, 95713.* Tel: 916-346-2286.

Permanent Diaconate Program—Sr. PAULINA HURTADO, O.P., Dir. Asst. Directors: Deacon LOU DEL GAUDIO; Mrs. SUSAN DEL GAUDIO, Office: *2110 Broadway, Sacramento, 95818-2541.* Tel: 916-733-0244.

Priests' Diocesan Aid Society—Ex Officio Officer: Most Rev. WILLIAM K. WEIGAND, D.D.,Please direct inquiries to: Rev. Msgr. JAMES F. CHURCH, Sec. & Treas., *7584 Center Pkwy., Sacramento, 95823.* Tel: 916-421-5177; Fax: 916-392-4831.

Priests' Personnel Board, Diocesan—Please direct all inquiries to: Priest Personnel, *Office of the Bishop, 2110 Broadway, Sacramento, 95818.* Tel: 916-733-0200. Revs. JOHN BOLL; TROY POWERS; JOSE KARIKATTIL; MICHAEL KIERNAN; ERIC LOFGREN; MIGUEL SILVA; BRENDAN T. O'SULLIVAN, Chm.; Rev. Msgr. ROBERT P. WALTON.

Propagation of the Faith—Rev. Msgr. JAMES CHURCH, Dir., *2110 Broadway, Sacramento, 95818-2541.* Tel: 916-733-0200; Fax: 916-733-0215.

Properties Committee—Please direct all inquiries to: Mr. THOMAS MCNAMARA, Staff, *2110 Broadway, Sacramento, 95818-2541.* Tel: 916-733-0277.

Radio and Television—See Communications and Media.

Research and Planning—Sr. EILEEN ENRIGHT, R.S.M., Chancellor, *2110 Broadway, Sacramento, 95818-2541.* Tel: 916-733-0200; Fax: 916-733-0215.

Respect Life—CHRISTINE CIPPERLY, Diocesan Coord., *Family Life Office, 2110 Broadway, Sacramento, 95818-2541.* Tel: 916-733-0155.

Schools—Mr. THOMAS BUTLER, Supt.; Mr. DOMINIC PUGLISI, Assoc. Supt., *2110 Broadway, Sacramento, 95818-2541.* Tel: 916-733-0110; Fax: 916-733-0120.

Vocations—Sr. MAUREEN MCINERNEY, O.P., Co-Dir.; Rev. MARK RICHARDS, Co-Dir.; Rev. JOHN KOUBA, S.D.S., Dir., Hispanic Seminarians, *2110 Broadway, Sacramento, 95818-2541.* Tel: 916-733-0258.

Worship, Office of—Mr. JACKSON SCHOOS, Dir., *2110 Broadway, Sacramento, 95818-2541.* Tel: 916-733-0220; Fax: 916-733-0295.

Lay Organizations—

Beginning Experience—SHARON THOMAS, Pres. Tel: 916-723-6745. LINDA DICKINSON, Public Rels. Tel: 916-774-9513.

Catholic Alumni Club—HEIDI KLEIN, Pres., *P.O. Box 1777, Carmichael, 95609-1777.* Tel: 916-427-6396; 863-3040(Hotline).

Catholic Daughters of the Americas—SHIRLEY GODFREY, *6600 Greenhaven Dr., Sacramento, 95831.* Tel: 916-428-5044.

Charismatic Renewal—Rev. Msgr. ANDREW V. COFFEY, Diocesan Liaison; Deacon JERRY PAULY, Assoc. Diocesan Liaison. Tel: 916-451-3738. Mr. MICHAEL DONEEN, Treas.

Cursillo Movement—Office: *2110 Broadway, Sacramento, 95818-2541.* Tel: 916-733-0181.

Daughters of Isabella—CAROLYN HADDEN, Regent, *P.O. Box 276, Galt, 95632.* Tel: 209-744-1802.

Diocesan Council of Catholic Nurses—Mrs. ELEANOR HAVEY, *4935 61st St., Sacramento, 95820.* Tel: 916-457-8649.

Diocesan Council of Catholic Women—Rev. Msgr. EDWARD J. KAVANAGH, Moderator; SUE WESTERFELD, *97 Dean Rd., Sacramento, 95815.* Tel: 916-657-0366.

Handicapables (Dept. of Catholic Faith Formation)—BOB KNAPIK. Tel: 916-422-5011. THERESA LOZOYA. Tel: 916-725-1898.

Italian Catholic Federation—Vacant, Chap. RICKI ZARELLI-DUGGAN, Dist. Pres., *3337 Bristol Rd., Sacramento, 95864.* Tel: 916-489-6213.

Knights of Peter Claver and Ladies Aux.—Mr. FRED MCLAURIN, Sacramento, Area Deputy, *P.O. Box 13471, Sacramento, 95813.* Tel: 916-971-4954. Mrs. ALBERTINE TAYLOR, Area Deputy, Ladies Div., *2606 Escobar Way, Sacramento, 95827.* Tel: 916-362-8426.

Knights of Columbus—Mr. DANNY J. THOMPSON, Northern California Chapter Pres., *5843 Wildwood Way, Marysville, 95901-7337.* Tel: 530-743-8324.

Legion of Mary—Rev. Msgr. CORNELIUS P. HIGGINS, *3027 Olive Glen Ct., Sacramento, 95821.* Tel: 916-487-9493. BETTY FRIEZ, Pres., *6090 S. Southland Park Dr., #2, Sacramento, 95822.* Tel: 916-422-7437. Three Curiae attached: Marysville-Yuba City, North Sacramento, Solano.

Marriage Encounter Worldwide—Contact Family Life Office, *2110 Broadway, Sacramento, 95818-2541.* Tel: 916-733-0155.

Scouting, Catholic Committee on—Rev. MARK RICHARDS, *2110 Broadway, Sacramento, 95818.* Tel: 916-733-0258.

Secular Franciscan Order—
Grass Valley-St. Patrick Parish—San Damiano Fraternity; LIZ HENGESBACH, SFO. Tel: 530-273-0787.
Sacramento-St. Francis of Assisi Parish—Fraternidad De San Juan Bautista (Spanish); GENARO GONZALEZ, SFO. Tel: 916-392-9632. St. Francis of Assisi Fraternity (English); BILL TURNER, SFO. Tel: 916-447-4637.

Secular Order of Discalced Carmelites—HAROLD HUNT, Pres., *P.O. Box 25, Rancho Cordova, 95741.* Tel: 916-362-5631.

Serra Club of Sacramento—YOUNG D. STEWART, Pres., *5903 Via Casitas, Carmichael, 95608.* Tel: 916-332-8732.

Young Ladies Institute—Mrs. PATRICIA CARVO, District 21 Deputy, *2768 Lincoln Rd., Yuba City, 95993.* Tel: 530-673-7147.

St. Thomas More Society—HERB BOLZ, Pres. Tel: 530-753-6094. Rev. CHARLES S. MCDERMOTT. Tel: 916-733-0200.

CLERGY, PARISHES, MISSIONS AND PAROCHIAL SCHOOLS

CITY OF SACRAMENTO
(Sacramento County)

1—CATHEDRAL OF THE BLESSED SACRAMENT (1889), Most Rev. William K. Weigand; Revs. James Murphy, Rector; Paul Ricks; Deacon Don De Haven.
Res., 1017 Eleventh St., 95814. Tel: 916-444-3071; Fax: 916-443-2749. Catechetical Center Cathedral Parish Hall Conducted by parish CCD and Daughters of Charity of Canossa.
Res., 1949 North Ave., 95838. Tel: 916-925-4001.
Catechesis/Religious Programs—Tel: 916-444-5364.
Students 130.

2—ALL HALLOWS (1942), Rev. Polycarpo Gumapo; Deacons Michael Donovan; George Kriske.
Res., 5500 13th Ave., 95820. Tel: 916-456-7206; Fax: 916-456-7325.
School—5700 13th Ave., 95820. Tel: 916-457-5621. Stephanie C. Jones, Prin.
Lay Teachers 10; Students 245.
Catechesis/Religious Programs—Tel: 916-736-0204.
Students 61.
Station—California State Youth Authority Center, 3001 Ramona Ave., 95820. Tel: 916-733-2350; Fax: 916-227-2511. Rev. William P. McSweeney, Chap.

3—HOLY SPIRIT (1940), Rev. Charles Brady; Deacon Bernard J. Weeks. In res., Rev. Leo O'Sullivan, O.S.A.
Res., 3159 Land Park Dr., 95818. Tel: 916-443-5442; Fax: 916-446-9015.
School—3920 W. Land Park Dr., 95822. Tel: 916-448-5663; Fax: 916-444-9631. Stephanie Pappas, Prin.
Lay Teachers 12; Students 299.
Catechesis/Religious Programs—Tel: 916-448-8257.
Students 130.
Convent—Tel: 916-448-3578. Sisters of Mercy (Auburn, CA)

4—IMMACULATE CONCEPTION (1909), Revs. Enrique Perez; Ricardo Giraldo; Deacons Gerald Pauly; Ramon Vega.
Parish Office: 3263 First Ave., 95817. Tel: 916-452-6866; Fax: 916-452-3879.
School—3263 First Ave., 95817. Tel: 916-452-7308. Anthony Hinojosa, Prin.
Sisters 2; Lay Teachers 7; Students 151.
Catechesis/Religious Programs—Tel: 916-682-9860.
Students 135.

5—OUR LADY OF GUADALUPE SHRINE (1958) (Hispanic), Rev. John Joe Monaghan, L.C.; Sr. Leonor Quijada Fernandez, Parochial Assoc.
Res., 711 T St., 95814. Tel: 916-442-3211; Fax: 916-442-3679.
Catechesis/Religious Programs—730 S St., 95814. Tel: 916-446-3500.
Students 542.

6—OUR LADY OF LOURDES (1957), Rev. Anthony Traynor; Deacon James Lalonde.
Res., 1951 North Ave., 95838. Tel: 916-925-5313; Fax: 916-922-0625.
Catechesis/Religious Programs—Tel: 916-925-4001.
Students 165.
Convent—1949 North Ave., 95838. Tel: 916-925-4001; Fax: 916-925-8897. Daughters of Charity of Cannosa

7—PRESENTATION OF THE BLESSED VIRGIN MARY (1961), Rev. Michael Carroll. In res., Rev. Msgr. Cornelius P. Higgins, Pastor Emeritus; Rev. Bernardin Mugabowakigeri Rowanda.
Mailing Address: P.O. Box 214208, 95821-0208.
Res., 4123 Robertson Ave., 95821. Tel: 916-481-7441; Fax: 916-481-2841.
School—3100 Norris Ave., 95821. Tel: 916-482-0351; Fax: 916-482-0377. Theresa Altieri, Prin.
Lay Teachers 15; Students 316.
Parish Center—3110 Norris Ave., 95821. Tel: 916-428-8883.
Catechesis/Religious Programs—Tel: 916-482-8883. Sr. Juliana Clancy.
Students 150.

8—SACRED HEART OF JESUS (1926), Rev. Michael O'Hara; Sr. Mary Martin, R.S.M., Pastoral Assoc., Tel: 916-452-4830; Deacons Gilbert Parra; William Riehl.
Res., 1040 39th St., 95816. Tel: 916-452-4136.
School—Sacred Heart, 3933 I St., 95816. Tel: 916-456-1576; Fax: 916-456-4773. Maureen Douglass, Prin.
Sisters of Mercy (Auburn, CA) 1; Lay Teachers 9; Students 312.
Catechesis/Religious Programs—Tel: 916-454-3640. Sr. O'Meara, R.S.M., D.R.E.
Students 42.

9—ST. ANNE (1961), Rev. Januarius E. Rodrigues; Deacon Pedro Manriquez.
Res., 7724 24th St., 95832. Tel: 916-422-8380; Fax: 916-422-7538.
School—7720 24th St., 95832. Tel: 916-422-3142. Mrs. Donna Nelson, Prin.
Religious 2; Lay Teachers 7; Students 220.
Catechesis/Religious Programs—Tel: 916-422-2419.
Students 60.

10—ST. ANTHONY (1974), Rev. T. Brendan O'Sullivan; Deacons James Healy; Richard Koppes; Michael Crowley. In res., Rev. John J. Keane, S.A.
Res., 660 Florin Rd., 95831. Tel: 916-428-5678; Fax: 916-428-0312.
Catechesis/Religious Programs—Tel: 916-392-6362.
Students 366.

11—ST. CHARLES BORROMEO (1960), Rev. Msgr. James Church; Revs. Cesar Ageas; Fernando Meza; Deacons Manuel Ocon; Don DeHaven.
Res., 7584 Center Pkwy., 95823. Tel: 916-421-5177; Fax: 916-392-4831.
School—7580 Center Pkwy., 95823. Tel: 916-421-6189; Fax: 916-421-3954. Susan Halfman, Prin.
Lay Teachers 12; Students 309.
Catechesis/Religious Programs—Students 400.

12—ST. ELIZABETH (1909) (Portuguese), Rev. Eduino Silveira.
Res., 1817 12th St., 95814. Tel: 916-442-2333; Fax: 916-498-0676.
Catechesis/Religious Programs—Students 41.

13—ST. FRANCIS OF ASSISI (1894), Friars Kenneth J. Laverone, O.F.M.; Anthony Garibaldi, O.F.M.
1066 26th St., 95816. Tel: 916-443-8084; Fax: 916-443-7356.
School—2500 K St., 95816. Tel: 916-442-5494; Fax: 916-442-1390. Ms. Barbara O'Donnell, Prin.
Lay Teachers 17; Students 320.
Catechesis/Religious Programs—Tel: 916-443-8084, Ext. 105.
Students 17.

14—ST. IGNATIUS OF LOYOLA (1954), Revs. Gerald H. Robinson, S.J.; Paul F. Belcher, S.J.; David W. MacDonald, S.J.; Deacon Jackson Gualco.
Res., 3235 Arden Way, 95825-2014. Tel: 916-482-9666; Fax: 916-482-6573.
School—3245 Arden Way, 95825. Tel: 916-488-3907; Fax: 916-488-0569. Patricia Lane, Prin.
Lay Teachers 16; Students 353.
Catechesis/Religious Programs—Tel: 916-482-9666, Ext. 238; Fax: 916-482-4869. Fatima Avila-Ohlsen, D.R.E.
Students 240.
Ignatian Institute for Family Life—Tel: 916-482-9666, Ext. 205.

15—ST. JEONG-HAE ELIZABETH (1993) (Korean), Rev. Anselmus Hak-rok Kim.
Res., 9354 Kiefer Blvd., 95826. Tel: 916-368-9204; Fax: 916-368-8304.
Catechesis/Religious Programs—Students 65.

16—ST. JOSEPH'S (1924), Rev. Robert A. Copsey; Sr. Ellen Philbin, R.S.M., Parish Min.; Deacon Henry Garcia.
Res., 1717 El Monte Ave., 95815. Tel: 916-925-3584; Fax: 916-925-1045.
School—1718 El Monte Ave., 95815. Tel: 916-925-1465; Fax: 916-925-0963. Mrs. Marsha J.B. Cornelius, Prin.
Sisters of Mercy (Auburn, CA) 1; Lay Teachers 8; Students 288.
Catechesis/Religious Programs—Tel: 916-924-8541. Sr. Martha Lopez, D.R.E.
Students 198.

17—ST. MARY (1906), Rev. Arnold Ortiz, O.S.J.; Deacon Luigi Del Gaudio.
Res., 1333 58th St., 95819. Tel: 916-452-0296; Fax: 916-452-3908.
School—5815 N St., 95819. Tel: 916-452-1100; Fax: 916-453-2750. Laura Allen, Prin., Tel: ext. 11.
Sisters 1; Lay Teachers 15; Aides 6; Students 321.
Convent—5801 N St., 95819. Tel: 916-451-5881; Fax: 916-453-2750. Sisters of the Presentation of the Blessed Virgin Mary (Monastereven, Ireland)
Catechesis/Religious Programs—Tel: 916-452-4115.
Students 140.

18—ST. PAUL (1958), Rev. Nicholas Duggan; Deacons Charles Morrison; Thomas Ferreira.
Res., 7200 Gardner Ave., P.O. Box 292280, 95829. Tel: 916-381-5200; Fax: 916-381-0332.
Catechesis/Religious Programs—Students 250.

19—ST. PETER (1955), Revs. Sidney Peter Hall; Francisco Hernandez Tovar; Deacons Deogracia "Ray" Ramos; Alejandro Reynoso; Tou Moua.
Res., 6210 McMahon Dr., 95824. Tel: 916-455-3001; Fax: 916-455-4721.
School—6200 McMahon Dr., 95824. Tel: 916-455-2915; Fax: 916-455-2915.
Sisters 4; Lay Teachers 8; Students 226.
Catechesis/Religious Programs—Tel: 916-455-0175.
Students 322.
Convent—5929 61st St., 95824. Tel: 916-457-0182. Sisters Servants of the Blessed Sacrament (Guadalajara, Mexico)

20—ST. PHILOMENE (1948), Rev. John Hannan; Rev. Msgr. Patrick M. Nolan, Pastor Emeritus; Deacons Charles Cheever; Keith Burke.
Res., 2428 Bell St., 95825. Tel: 916-481-6757; Fax: 916-481-1603.
School—2320 El Camino Ave., 95825. Tel: 916-489-5466; Fax: 916-489-2642. Debra Mosbrucker, Prin.
Lay Teachers 15; Students 295.
Catechesis/Religious Programs—Students 300.

21—ST. ROBERT (1955), Rev. Kieran M. McMahon; Deacon Martin Rodriguez.
Res., 2243 Irvin Way, 95822. Tel: 916-451-1475, Ext. 10,11.
School—2251 Irvin Way, 95822. Tel: 916-452-2111; Fax: 916-452-5765. Brian James, Prin.
Lay Teachers 9; Students 291.

22—ST. ROSE (1942), Rev. Msgr. Edward J. Kavanagh; Rev. Francis Lawlor. In res., Rev. Charles S. McDermott.
Res., P.O. Box 5037, Oak Park Station, 95817. Tel: 916-421-1414; Fax: 916-421-0460.
School—St. Patrick, 5945 Franklin Blvd., 95824. Tel: 916-421-4963; Fax: 916-421-3849. Dave Hoffman, Prin.
Lay Teachers 19; Students 381.

Catechesis/Religious Programs—Tel: 916-392-5679.
Students 507.

23—VIETNAMESE CATHOLIC MARTYRS (Vietnamese), Rev. Jude Ban Nguyen, C.M.C.; Deacon Anthony Huy Nguyen.
Res., 10371 Jackson Rd., 95827. Tel: 916-366-3162.
Catechesis/Religious Programs—Students 450.

OUTSIDE THE CITY OF SACRAMENTO

Alturas, Modoc Co., Sacred Heart (1883), Rev. Patrick J. Henry.
Res., 507 E. Fourth St., 96101. Tel: 530-233-2119.
Catechesis/Religious Programs—Students 25.
Mission—Cedarville, Modoc Co., St. James, Bonner St. & Garfield St., Cedarville, 96104.

Anderson, Shasta Co., Sacred Heart (1949), Rev. Michael F. Kiernan; Deacons Michael Evans; Anthony Short; Ray Hemenway.
Res., 3141 St. Stephen's Dr., 96007. Tel: 530-365-8573; Fax: 530-365-9544.
Schools—(Grades PreK-5) 3167 St. Stephen's Dr., 96007. Tel: 530-365-1429; Fax: 530-365-3039. Mrs. Elizabeth White, Prin.
Lay Teachers 7; Students 95; St. Francis Middle School, 21945 Old 44 Dr., Palo Cedro, 96073. Tel: 530-547-2900; Fax: 530-547-5439.
Students 194.
Catechesis/Religious Programs—Students 105.
Missions—Cottonwood, Shasta Co., St. Anne, 2nd St. & Main St., Cottonwood, 96022.; Shingletown, Shasta Co., Mary Queen of Peace, Shingletown Ridge Rd., Shingletown, 96088. Tel: 916-474-1870.

Antelope, Sacramento Co., St. Clare (1992), Rev. Colin MacDonald.
Res., 4313 Shandwick Dr., 95843. Tel: 916-721-4771; Fax: 916-721-4288. [JC]
Catechesis/Religious Programs—Tel: 916-339-2457; 722-0559.
Students 80.

Auburn, Placer Co., St. Joseph (1861), Revs. Noel T. Lynch; Tuikolongahau Kaniseli (New Zealand); Juan Manuel Ponce; Deacon Ed Morgado.
Res., 1162 Lincoln Way, 95603. Tel: 530-885-2956; Fax: 530-823-6676. [CEM]
School—11610 Atwood Rd., 95603. Tel: 530-885-4490; Fax: 530-885-0182. Mrs. Joan Walthers, Prin.
Lay Teachers 14; Students 285.
Catechesis/Religious Programs—Tel: 530-885-0362.
Students 269.
Mission—Auburn, Placer Co., St. Teresa of Avila, (1994) 11600 Atwood Rd., 95603.
Station—Forest Hill.

Benicia, Solano Co., St. Dominic (1854), Revs. David J. Farrugia, O.P.; Victor Cavalli; Eugene W. Sousa, O.P.; Deacons Ed Lazarek; John Flanagan.
P.O. Box 756, 94510-0756.; Res. & Church: 475 E. I St., 94510. Tel: 707-747-7220; Fax: 707-745-5642. [CEM]
School—935 E. 5th St., 94510. Tel: 707-745-1266. Sr. Elizabeth Curtis, C.H.F., Prin.
Lay Teachers 13; Students 342.
Catechesis/Religious Programs—433 E. I St., 94510. Tel: 707-747-7240.
Students 376.

Burney, Shasta Co., St. Francis of Assisi (1949), Rev. Eric D. Lofgren.
c/o P.O. Drawer 160, 96013.; Res. & Church: 37464 Juniper Ave., 96013. Tel: 530-335-2372.
Catechesis/Religious Programs—Students 50.
Missions—Bieber, Lassen Co., St. Stephen, Hwy. 299, Bieber, 96009.; Fall River Mills, Shasta Co., Our Lady of the Valley, 43434 Main St., Fall River Mills, 96028. Tel: 530-336-6212.

Carmichael, Sacramento Co., Our Lady of the Assumption (1952), Rev. Leo McAllister; Deacons Michael Tateishi; James Meucci. In res., Revs. William Broderick, (Retired); Mathew Maramkulan.
Res., 5057 Cottage Way, 95608. Tel: 916-481-5115; Fax: 916-481-4026.
School—5055 Cottage Way, 95608. Tel: 916-489-8958. Theresa Sparks, Prin.
Lay Teachers 9; Students 305.
Catechesis/Religious Programs—Tel: 916-488-4626.
Students 300.
Convent—Tel: 916-488-8188. Ladies of Loretto (Toronto, Canada)

St. John the Evangelist (1960), Revs. John Lagomarsino, S.S.C., Parochial Admin.; Ambrose Ugwuegbu; Deacon James Weeks, (Retired).
Res., 5751 Locust Ave., 95608. Tel: 916-483-8454; Fax: 916-481-8326.
School—5701 Locust Ave., 95608. Tel: 916-481-8845; Fax: 916-481-1319. Mrs. Ellen Gemma.
Lay Teachers 12; Students 289.
Catechesis/Religious Programs—Tel: 916-483-4628. Sr. Hannah O'Donohuge, D.R.E.
Students 202.

Chico, Butte Co., Our Divine Savior (1967), Rev. Roy R. Doner.
Office: 566 E. Lassen Ave., 95973. Tel: 530-343-4248; Fax: 530-343-3538.
Catechesis/Religious Programs—Tel: 530-345-6201.
Students 189.

St. John the Baptist (1878), Rev. Terry Fulton; Deacons Jesus Campos Padilla; Stephen Schwartz.
Res., 435 Chestnut St., 95928. Tel: 530-343-8741; Fax: 530-345-8602.
School—(Grades K-8) 435 Hazel St., 95928. Tel: 530-342-2502; Fax: 530-342-6292. Colleen Waugh, Prin.
Lay Teachers 13; Students 300.
Catechesis/Religious Programs—Students 683.
Mission—Durham, Butte Co., St. James, P.O. Box 562, Durham, 95938. [JC]

Citrus Heights, Sacramento Co., Holy Family (1949), Rev. Troy Powers; Rev. Msgr. Vito F. Mistretta, Pastor Emeritus; Rev. Christian Paul Egegl.
Res., 7817 Old Auburn Rd., 95610. Tel: 916-723-2494; Fax: 916-723-0199.
School—Tel: 916-722-7788; Fax: 916-722-5297. Sr. Arlene Connelly, I.B.V.M., Prin.
Lay Teachers 25; Students 646.
Preschool—Tel: 916-722-4620; Fax: 916-722-4509. Patricia Peterson, Preschool Dir., Tel: 916-722-4620.
Lay Teachers 9; Students 120.
Catechesis/Religious Programs—Tel: 916-726-7217; Fax: 916-721-3292. Linda Pulido, D.R.E.
Students 290.

Clarksburg, Yolo Co., St. Joseph (1893), Rev. Daniel Madigan.
Res. & Church Address—32890 S. River Rd., 95612. Tel: 916-665-1132; Fax: 916-665-9264.

Colfax, Placer Co., St. Dominic (1951), Rev. Dermot Dwyer, Admin.
c/o P.O. Box 752, 95713.; Res. & Church: 58 E. Oak St., 95713. Tel: 530-346-2286; Fax: 530-346-2286. [CEM]
Catechesis/Religious Programs—Tel: 530-346-2915.
Students 147.

Colusa, Colusa Co., Our Lady of Lourdes (1870), Revs. Edward Pepka, Admin.; Juan Perez; Deacon Miguel Fernandez.
Res., 745 Ware Ave., 95932. Tel: 530-458-4170; Fax: 530-458-8728.
Church—345 Oak St., 95932. Tel: 530-458-7901.
School—(Grades PreK-8). Tel: 530-458-8208; Fax: 530-458-8657. Mrs. Barbara Genera, Prin.
Lay Teachers 6; Students 113.
Catechesis/Religious Programs—Students 45.
Mission—Princeton, Colusa Co., St. Joseph, 1st St. & Center St., Princeton, 95970.
Station—Sycamore, Our Lady of Sorrows. [CEM]

Corning, Tehama Co., Immaculate Conception (1946), Rev. Thomas L. Seabridge, Co-Pastor. In res., Rev. Miguel Silva, Co-Pastor.
Res., 814 Solano St., 96021. Tel: 530-824-5879. [JC]
Catechesis/Religious Programs—Students 129.
Mission—Tehama, Tehama Co., St. Stanislaus, 4th St. & D St., Tehama, 96090.

Davis, Yolo Co., St. James (1912), Rev. Daniel A. Looney; Rev. Msgr. Andrew V. Coffey, Pastor Emeritus; Revs. Richard J. Blinn, S.J.; Rey Bersabal; Deacons Paul Taloff; Sam Colenzo; Clark Goecker.
Res., 200 W. 14th St., 95616. Tel: 530-756-3636; Fax: 530-756-5342. [JC]
School—1215 B St., 95616. Tel: 530-756-3946; Fax: 530-753-9765. Mary Kay Bolz, Prin.
Lay Teachers 14; Students 290.
Catechesis/Religious Programs—Tel: 916-756-9000. Linda O'Hara, D.R.E.
Students 550.
Newman Center—514 C St., 95616. Tel: 916-753-7393; Fax: 916-753-2794.

Dixon, Solano Co., St. Peter (1877), Revs. Maurice O'Brien; John J. Kyne, Pastor Emeritus; Deacons Robert H. Ikelman; John King.
Res., 105 S. 2nd St., 95620. Tel: 707-678-9424; Fax: 707-678-9432.
Catechesis/Religious Programs—Students 270.

Downieville, Sierra Co., Immaculate Conception (1853), Rev. Godwin Xavier.
Mailing Address: P.O. Box 48, North San Juan, 95960.
Res., Flume St., North San Juan, 95960. Tel: 530-292-3227; Fax: 530-292-3560.
Church—Church St., 95936. Tel: 530-289-3102. [CEM][JC]
Missions—North San Juan, Nevada Co., St. John, 10047 Flume St., North San Juan, 95960.; Sierra City, Sierra Co., St. Thomas, 108 Butte Aly, Sierra City, 96125.; Challenge, Yuba Co., St. Anthony, La Porte Rd., Challenge, 95925. Tel: 530-675-2001. Deacon George Lucas.

Dunsmuir, Siskiyou Co., St. John the Evangelist (1899), Rev. Aidan O'Riley.
Res., 5605 Shasta Ave., 96025. Tel: 530-235-4705; Fax: 530-235-4759. [JC]

El Dorado Hills, El Dorado Co., Holy Trinity (1992), Rev. Msgr. James C. Kidder; Greg Jensen, M.Div, Pastoral Assoc.; Deacon Neil Zachary. In res., Rev. John P. Sullivan.
Church—3111 Tierra de Dios Dr., 95762-8008. Tel: 530-677-3234; Fax: 530-677-3570.
Catechesis/Religious Programs—Tel: 530-677-3234, Ext. 205.
Students 365.

Elk Grove, Sacramento Co., St. Joseph (1962), Rev. Msgr. Albert G. O'Connor; Rev. Timothy Nondorf. In res., Rev. Msgr. Robert Walton; Deacon Paul Imrisek.
Res., 9961 Elk Grove-Florin Rd., 95624. Tel: 916-685-3681; Fax: 916-685-7254.
Catechesis/Religious Programs—Tel: 916-685-5636.
Students 820.
Mission—Rancho Murieta, Sacramento Co., 14673 Cantova Way, Rancho Murieta, 95683. Tel: 916-354-2403.

Good Shepherd Catholic Church (1993), Rev. Philip Wells.
Res., 9539 Racquet Ct., 95758. Tel: 916-684-5722; Fax: 916-684-4472.
School—St. Elizabeth Ann Seton Elementary School, 9539 Raquet Ct., 95758. Tel: 916-684-7903; Fax: 916-684-4472. Gail Sherman, Prin.
Students 202.
Catechesis/Religious Programs—Tel: 916-684-5722, Ext. 30.
Students 500.

Fairfield, Solano Co., Holy Spirit (1950), Revs. Michael Downey; Felipe Paraguya (Philippines); Umberto Penunuri.
c/o P.O. Box X, 94533.; Res. & Church: 1050 N. Texas St., 94533. Tel: 707-425-3138; Fax: 707-425-2029. [CEM]
School—(Grades K-8). Tel: 707-422-5016; Fax: 707-422-0874. Sr. Mairead Langley, C.H.F., Prin.
Sisters 3; Lay Teachers 12; Students 360.
Catechesis/Religious Programs—Tel: 707-425-9042. Suselia Hernandez, D.R.E.
Students 1,000.
Convent—Tel: 707-425-3572. Sisters of the Holy Faith (Dublin, Ireland)

Our Lady of Mount Carmel, (1979). (Carmelite Fathers). Revs. Sebastian Meyer, O.Carm.; Joseph Joyce, O.Carm.
Parish Office—Tel: 707-422-7767; Fax: 707-422-7946.
Res., 2700 Dover Ave., 94533. Tel: 707-426-3639.
Church—2700 Dover Ave., 94533.
Catechesis/Religious Programs—Tel: 707-422-2814.
Students 445.

Fair Oaks, Sacramento Co., St. Mel (1948), Revs. Richard Doheny; Carroll Keating, S.J.; Deacons Patrick Henning; David Lehman.
c/o P.O. Box 1180, 95628.; Res. & Church: 4745 Pennsylvania Ave., 95628. Tel: 916-967-1229; Fax: 916-967-5659.
School—Tel: 916-967-2814; Fax: 916-967-0705. Janet Nagel, Prin.
Lay Teachers 16; Students 315.
Catechesis/Religious Programs—Tel: 916-966-4314.
Students 225.

Folsom, Sacramento Co., St. John the Baptist (1857), Revs. Ignatius Haran; Alfredo Tamayo; Deacons Leslie White; Dennis Merino.
Mailing Address: Office, 307 Montrose Dr., 95630. Tel: 916-985-2065; Fax: 916-985-7579.
Res., 107 Joseph Way, 95630. Tel: 916-351-1939. [CEM]
School—St. John's-Notre Dame, Tel: 916-985-4129; Fax: 916-985-7958. Chris Maricle, Prin.
Lay Teachers 14; Students 322.
Catechesis/Religious Programs—Tel: 916-985-7338.
Students 576.
Station—Folsom State Prison, P.O. Box W, Represa, 95671. Tel: 916-985-2561; Fax: 916-351-3070.
Mailing Address: Folsom State Prison, P.O. Box 29, Represa, 95671. Tel: 916-985-8610, Ext. 6425; Fax: 530-647-0763. Rev. Thomas Maguire, Chap., Tel: 916-989-6564; Deacon Dennis Merino, Chap.
Station—California State Prison, P.O. Box 29, Sacramento, 95671. Tel: 916-985-8610; Fax: 916-985-6425.

Fort Jones, Siskiyou Co., Sacred Heart (1921), Rev. John M. Lawrence.
Res., 101 Carlock St., P.O. Box 126, 96032-0126. Tel: 530-468-2605; Fax: 530-468-5577. [CEM]
Catechesis/Religious Programs—Students 59.
Missions—Etna, Siskiyou Co., St. Mary's, 386 Center St., Etna, 96027. Tel: 530-467-3561; Happy

Camp, Siskiyou Co., All Saints, 1321 Indian Creek Rd., Happy Camp, 96093. Tel: 530-493-2657; Sawyer's Bar, Siskiyou Co., St. Joseph, Sawyer's Bar Rd., Etna, 96027.

Galt, Sacramento Co., St. Christopher (1885), Rev. Gerald Ryle; Deacon Thomas McGill.
c/o P.O. Box 276, 95632.
Res., 211 Sterling Grove, P.O. Box 276, 95632. Tel: 209-745-1389; Fax: 209-744-2183.
Church—950 S. Lincoln Way, 95632.
Catechesis/Religious Programs—Students 392.

Grass Valley, Nevada Co., St. Patrick (1855), Revs. Nicholas Phelan, Pastor Emeritus; Alfred D. Kaster; Simon Twomey; Sr. Geneva Paluka, R.S.M., Pastoral Min.; Deacons Carlos Astesana; James Chatigny; Brian Moore.
Res., 235 Chapel St., 95945. Tel: 530-273-2347; Fax: 530-272-9681. [CEM]
School—Mt. St. Mary's, Tel: 530-273-4694; Fax: 530-273-1724. Jude Mikal, Prin.
Lay Teachers 11; Students 225.
Preschool/Day Care—Tel: 530-273-6244; Fax: 530-273-1724.
Lay Teachers 4; Students 24.
Catechesis/Religious Programs—Students 348.

Gridley, Butte Co., Sacred Heart (1926), Rev. Rodolfo Delgado.
c/o P.O. Box 205, 95948.; Res. & Church: 1560 Hazel St., 95948. Tel: 530-846-2140; Fax: 530-846-5615.
Catechesis/Religious Programs—Students 300.
Mission—Live Oak, Sutter Co., Our Lady of Guadalupe, 9660 Broadway, Live Oak, 95953.

Ione, Amador Co., Sacred Heart (1932), Rev. Thomas Relihan.
Res., Church and Washington Sts., P.O. Box 4, 95640. Tel: 209-274-2158. [CEM][JC]
Catechesis/Religious Programs—Students 50.
Missions—Ione, Amador Co., Preston School of Industry, California Youth Authority, 201 Waterman Rd., 95640. Tel: 209-274-4771, Ext. 250. Rev. Humberto Gomez.; Ione, Amador Co., Mule Creek State Prison, P.O. Box 409099, 95640. Tel: 209-274-4911. Rev. Diego Baptista.

Isleton, Sacramento Co., St. Therese's (1953), Rev. Mario Nunez, Ph.L.
Res., P.O. Box 697, 95641. Tel: 916-777-6871.
Church—4th St. & Jackson Blvd., 95641.
Catechesis/Religious Programs—Students 80.

Jackson, Amador Co., St. Patrick's (1864), Revs. Thomas A. Bland; Polycarp Ndugbu (Nigeria); Deacons William Thompson; Don Gercich.
Res., 115 Court St., 95642. Tel: 209-223-0168; Fax: 209-223-2548. [CEM 2]
Catechesis/Religious Programs—Students 170.
Missions—Buckhorn, Amador Co., Our Lady of the Pines, 26750 Tiger Creek Rd., Pioneer, 95666.; Volcano, Amador Co., St. Bernard, Plug-Emigrant St., Volcano, 95689.

Knights Landing, Yolo Co., St. Paul (1949), Rev. Joseph Huong Nguyen; Deacon Antonio Gonzalez.
Res., 222 Sycamore Way, P.O. Box 176, 95645. Tel: 530-735-6478.
Catechetical Center—6th St. & Locust St., 95645.
Catechesis/Religious Programs—Students 80.
Mission—Zamora, Yolo Co., St. Agnes, 95645.

Lincoln, Placer Co., St. Joseph (1892), Revs. Vincent Brady; James Rockenstein, O.F.M.; Deacons Jesus Rodriguez; Roberto Ruiz; Kenneth Boone.
Res., 585 D St., 95648. Tel: 916-645-2102; Fax: 916-645-1422. [JC]
Catechesis/Religious Programs—412 6th St., 95648. Tel: 916-645-7754.
Students 280.
Missions—Nicolaus, Sutter Co., St. Boniface, 1028 Marcum Rd., Nicolaus, 95659. Tel: 916-656-2368; Wheatland, Yuba Co., St. Daniel, 214 Main St., Wheatland, 95692. Tel: 916-633-0344.
Shrine—Our Lady of Guadalupe, 3rd St. & K St., 95648.

Marysville, Yuba Co., St. Joseph (1852), Revs. Leon Juchniewicz; Juan Perez; Deacons Jesus Munoz; David Perez.
Mailing Address: Office, 223 Eighth St., 95901.
Res., 319 Seventh St., 95901. Tel: 530-742-6461; Fax: 530-742-0346. [CEM]
School—(Grades K-8) 715 C St., 95901. Tel: 530-743-4484; Fax: 530-743-4485. Mr. Jaime Arostegui, Prin.
Lay Teachers 9; Students 203.
Catechesis/Religious Programs—Tel: 530-742-7100.
Students 221.
Mission—Dobbins, Yuba Co., Sacred Heart Church, P.O. Box 208, Dobbins, 95953.

Maxwell, Colusa Co., Sacred Heart (1881), Revs. John Myles; Heriberto Serrano.
c/o P.O. Box 607, 95955.; Res. & Church: 45 Elm St., 95955. Tel: 530-438-2432; Fax: 530-438-2432. [CEM]
Missions—Arbuckle, Colusa Co., Holy Cross, 408 Laurel St., Arbuckle, 95912.; Williams, Colusa Co., Annunciation, 617 8th St., Williams, 95987. Tel: 530-473-2925; Stonyford, Colusa Co., St. Mary of the Mountain, 2nd St. & Geary St., Stonyford, 95979.

McCloud, Siskiyou Co., St. Joseph (1933), Rev. Michael O'Reilly.
213 Colombero Dr., P.O. Box 518, 96057. Tel: 530-235-4705; Fax: 530-235-4759.
Res., 5605 Shasta Ave., Dunsmuir, 96025. [JC]
Catechesis/Religious Programs—Students 21.

Mount Shasta, Siskiyou Co., St. Anthony (1954), Rev. Aidan O'Reilly.
Res., P.O. Box 467, 96067. Tel: 530-926-4477; Fax: 530-926-4234.
Church—Pine St. & Alma St., 96067. Tel: 530-926-4477.
Catechesis/Religious Programs—Tel: 530-926-3061.
Students 85.

Nevada City, Nevada Co., St. Canice (1851), Rev. James McKnight.
c/o P.O. Box 1597, 95959.; Res. & Church: 317 Washington St., 95959. Tel: 530-265-2049; Fax: 530-265-3697. [CEM]
Church—Coyote St., 95959.
Catechesis/Religious Programs—Tel: 916-265-2712.
Students 130.

North Highlands, Sacramento Co., St. Lawrence (1955), Revs. Joseph P. Ternullo; Francisco Velazquez, V.D.M.F.; Deacon Gary Fracolli.
Res., 4325 Don Julio Blvd., 95660. Tel: 916-332-4777; Fax: 916-332-8325.
School—(Grades K-8) 4325 Don Julio Blvd., 95660. Tel: 916-332-4779. Mrs. Marilyn Fleming, Prin.
Lay Teachers 10; Students 239.
Catechesis/Religious Programs—Tel: 916-332-4777.
Students 500.

Orangevale, Sacramento Co., Divine Savior (1987), Revs. Thomas Tureman, S.D.S.; Jeffrey Wocken, S.D.S.
Office & Mailing: 9079 Greenback Ln., 95662. Tel: 916-989-7400; Fax: 916-989-7410.
Res., 8680 Hickory Leaf Pl., 95662. Tel: 916-989-5425.
Catechesis/Religious Programs—Students 501.
Counseling Center—Tel: 916-989-7414.

Orland, Glenn Co., St. Dominic (1919), Revs. Thomas L. Seabridge, Co-Pastor; Miguel Silva, Co-Pastor.
c/o Box 816, 95963.; Res. & Church: 822 A St., 95963. Tel: 530-865-4550; Fax: 530-865-8451.
Catechesis/Religious Programs—Tel: 530-865-7115.
Students 178.
Mission—Hamilton City, Glenn Co., St. Mary, 400 Los Robles, 95951.

Oroville, Butte Co., St. Thomas the Apostle (1857). Unassigned.
Res., 1330 Bird St., 95965. Tel: 530-533-0262; Fax: 530-533-1148. [CEM]
School—1380 Bird St., 95965. Tel: 530-534-6969; Fax: 530-534-9374. Joani Briggs, Prin.
Lay Teachers 9; Students 147.
Catechesis/Religious Programs—Students 75.

Paradise, Butte Co., St. Thomas More (1949), Rev. Brendan McKeefry.
Res., 767 Elliott Rd., 95969. Tel: 530-877-4501; Fax: 530-877-5633.
School—771 Elliott Rd., 95969. Tel: 530-877-5328; Fax: 530-877-1485. Mrs. Michelle John, Prin.
Lay Teachers 9; Students 148.
Catechesis/Religious Programs—Tel: 530-877-6023.
Students 100.

Placerville, El Dorado Co., St. Patrick's (1855), Rev. John Cantwell; Deacon Stan S. Rudger.
Res., 3109 Sacramento St., 95667. Tel: 530-622-0373; Fax: 530-621-7770. [CEM]
Catechesis/Religious Programs—Tel: 530-622-7692; Fax: 530-621-7771.
Students 607.
Mission—Georgetown, El Dorado Co., St. James, 2831 Harkness St., Georgetown, 95634. Tel: 530-333-9432.

Portola, Plumas Co., Holy Family (1929), Rev. Glenn O. Dare.
c/o P.O. Box 1077, 96122.; Res. & Church: 108 Taylor Ave., 96122. Tel: 530-832-5006; Fax: 530-832-5520.
Catechesis/Religious Programs—Students 77.
Mission—Loyalton, Sierra Co., Holy Rosary, 4th St., 96118.

Quincy, Plumas Co., St. John (1947), Rev. Andrzej A. Koziczuk.
c/o Box 510, 95971.; Res. & Church: 170 Lawrence St., 95971. Tel: 530-283-0890; Fax: 530-283-4204.
Catechesis/Religious Programs—Tel: 530-283-2341.
Students 70.
Mission—Greenville, Plumas Co., St. Anthony, 209 Jesse St., Greenville, 95947. Tel: 530-284-6882.
Station—Buck's Lake, Quincy.

Rancho Cordova, Sacramento Co., St. John Vianney (1958), Revs. Martin J. Moroney; David Klein, S.J.; Deacons Walter Little; Phil Moseley.
Res., 10497 Coloma Rd., 95670. Tel: 916-362-1385; Fax: 916-361-8102.
School—10499 Coloma Rd., 95670. Tel: 916-363-4610; Fax: 916-363-3243. Mrs. Vicky Andrews, Prin.
Lay Teachers 13; Students 307.
Catechesis/Religious Programs—Tel: 916-362-3827.
Students 193.

Red Bluff, Tehama Co., Sacred Heart (1867), Revs. Michael J. Hebda; Eugenio Lopez.
Res. & Parish Hall: 2355 Monroe St., 96080. Tel: 530-527-2209; 527-1351 (Parish Hall); Fax: 530-529-2586. [CEM]
School—2255 Monroe St., 96080. Tel: 530-527-6727; Fax: 530-527-5026. Mrs. Kate Grimes, Prin.
Lay Teachers 9; Students 169.
Catechesis/Religious Programs—Students 106.

Redding, Shasta Co., Our Lady of Mercy (1980), Rev. Michael Canny.
Office: 2600 Shasta View Dr., 96002. Tel: 530-222-3424; Fax: 530-221-5717.
School—St. Francis Middle School, 21945 Old 44 Dr., Palo Cedro, 96073. Tel: 530-547-2900; Fax: 530-547-5349.
Lay Teachers 11; Students 195.
Catechesis/Religious Programs—Tel: 530-222-2497.
Students 50.

St. Joseph (1907), Rev. Msgr. Russell G. Terra; Deacons David Gasman; Frank Lopez; Michael Mangas.
Res., 2040 Walnut Ave., 96001. Tel: 530-243-3463; Fax: 530-243-7999. [CEM]
Schools—2460 Gold St., 96001. Tel: 530-243-2302; Fax: 530-243-2747. Mr. Tom Schwerdt, Prin.
Lay Teachers 16; Students 306; St. Francis Middle School, 21945 Old 44 Dr., Palo Cedro, 96073. Tel: 530-547-2900; Fax: 530-547-5349.
Students 194.
Catechesis/Religious Programs—Students 95.
Mission—Shasta Lake City, Shasta Co., St. Michael, 3440 Shasta Dam Blvd., 96019.

Rio Vista, Solano Co., St. Joseph (1885), Revs. Julian Medina; William K. Walsh, Pastor Emeritus.
Res., 130 S. 4th St., 94571. Tel: 707-374-2155; Fax: 707-374-5071. [CEM 2]
Catechesis/Religious Programs—Students 128.

Rocklin, Placer Co., SS. Peter and Paul (1981), Rev. Michael J. Dillon.
c/o Box 824, 95677.; Res. & Church: 4450 Granite Dr., 95677. Tel: 916-624-5827; Fax: 916-624-5924.
Catechesis/Religious Programs—Tel: 916-624-3093.
Students 865.

Roseville, Placer Co., St. Rose of Lima (1907) (Mexican), Revs. Michael McKeon; Roberto Jaramillo; Blaise Berg; Deacons William H. Boudier; Peter M. Silott; Juan Tamayo. In res., Rev. Michael J. Cormack, Pastor Emeritus.
Res., 615 Vine Ave., 95678. Tel: 916-783-5211; Fax: 916-783-5212.
School—633 Vine Ave., 95678. Tel: 916-782-1161; Fax: 916-782-7862. Charles Suarez, Prin.
Sisters 1; Lay Teachers 15; Students 304.
Catechesis/Religious Programs—Tel: 916-786-0650.
Students 500.

South Lake Tahoe, El Dorado Co., St. Theresa (1951), Rev. Msgr. Murrough C. Wallace; Revs. Charles Kelly; John J. Grace, Pastor Emeritus.
Res., 1041 Lyons Ave., 96150. Tel: 530-544-3533; Fax: 530-544-4662.
School—1081 Lyons Ave., 96150. Tel: 530-544-8944; Fax: 530-544-8909. Dr. Jeannette Holmes, Prin.
Lay Teachers 13; Students 170.
Catechesis/Religious Programs—Tel: 530-544-4788; Fax: 530-544-8909.
Students 435.
Mission—Camp Sacramento, El Dorado Co., Our Lady of the Sierras.

Susanville, Lassen Co., Sacred Heart (1912), Rev. Robert E. Brooks.
c/o P.O. Box 501, 96130.; Res. and Church: 120 N. Union St., 96130. Tel: 530-257-3230; Fax: 530-257-9213.

Catechesis/Religious Programs—Msgr. Moran Hall, 140 N. Weatherlow St., 96130. Tel: 530-257-8008. Students 95.
Station—Herlong.

Sutter Creek, Amador Co., Immaculate Conception (1864), Revs. Liam MacCarthy; Ronan P. Brennan, Pastor Emeritus; Deacon Ed Pogue.
Res., P.O. Box 127, 95685. Tel: 209-267-5602; Fax: 209-267-1278. [CEM 4]
Catechesis/Religious Programs—Spanish St. & Amelia St., 95685. Students 81.
Mission—Plymouth, Amador Co., St. Mary of the Mountains, Church St., Plymouth, 95669.

Tahoe City, Placer Co., Corpus Christi (1961), Rev. Patrick J. O'Connor.
P.O. Box 1878, 96145.
Church & Res.—905 W. Lake Blvd., 96145. Tel: 530-583-4409; Fax: 530-583-1408.
Catechesis/Religious Programs—Tel: 530-581-4637. Students 90.
Mission—Olympic Valley, Placer Co., Queen of the Snows, 1550 Squaw Valley Rd., 96146.
Station—Tahoma.

Truckee, Nevada Co., Assumption of the Blessed Virgin Mary (1870), Revs. Stanley Poltorak; Guillermo Rodriguez; Deacon Ray Craig.
P.O. Box 34014, 96160.; Res. & Church: 10116 E. St., 96160. Tel: 530-587-3595; Fax: 530-582-8648.
Catechesis/Religious Programs—Students 265.
Mission—Kings Beach, Placer Co., Our Lady of the Lake, 8363 Steelhead, Kings Beach, 96143.

Tulelake, Siskiyou Co., Holy Cross (1949), Rev. Brent C. Nall.
P.O. Box 266, 96134.; Res. & Church: 765 First St., 96134. Tel: 530-667-2727.
Catechesis/Religious Programs—Students 50.
Mission—Dorris, Siskiyou Co., Our Lady of Good Counsel, W. 3rd St., Dorris, 96023.

Vacaville, Solano Co., St. Joseph (1992), Rev. Vincent O'Reilly.
Res., 1771 Marshall Rd., 95687. Tel: 707-447-2354; Fax: 707-447-9322. [JC]
School—Notre Dame, 1781 Marshall Rd., 95687. Tel: 707-447-1460; Fax: 707-447-1498. Maryalice Clare, Prin.
Lay Teachers 12; Students 338.
Catechesis/Religious Programs—Students 224.

St. Mary (1947), Revs. Benedict DeLeon; Oscar Gutierrez; Lawrence A. Ryan, Pastor Emeritus; William Feeser; Deacons Domingo Cabrera; Pelagio Verba.
Res., 350 Stinson Ave., 95688. Tel: 707-448-2390; Fax: 707-448-2818.
Catechesis/Religious Programs—Tel: 707-446-1881. Students 420.
Catechetical Center—300 Hemlock St., 95688. Tel: 707-446-1881. Students 420.

Vallejo, Solano Co., St. Basil (1941), Revs. William P. Storan; Stephen M. Borlang; Deacons Michael Carlomagno; Mike Urick.
Res., 1200 Tuolumne St., 94590. Tel: 707-644-5251; Fax: 707-644-1423.
School—1230 Nebraska St., 94590. Tel: 707-642-7629; Fax: 707-642-8635. Mrs. Susan M. Hill, Prin.
Lay Teachers 12; Students 353; Preschool 93.
Catechesis/Religious Programs—Tel: 707-644-8309. Students 238.

St. Catherine of Siena (1964), Revs. William P. Kinane; Jesus Soriano.
Mailing Address: & Res.: 3450 Tennessee St., 94591. Tel: 707-553-1355; Fax: 707-557-6896.
School—(Grades K-8) 3460 Tennessee St., 94591. Tel: 707-643-6691; Fax: 707-647-4441. Mrs. Lee Roark, Prin.
Lay Teachers 13; Students 339.
Catechesis/Religious Programs—Tel: 707-647-4445. Students 332.

St. Vincent Ferrer (1855), Revs. Edward J. Lewis; Erwin Mesiona; Oscar Figueroa.
Res., 925 Sacramento St., 94590. Tel: 707-644-8396; Fax: 707-644-1330.
School—420 Florida St., 94590. Tel: 707-642-4311; Fax: 707-642-1329. Mrs. Susan Fulton, Prin.
Lay Teachers 11; Students 357.
Catechesis/Religious Programs—Tel: 707-643-0188. Students 518.
Mission—South Vallejo, Solano Co., St. Louis Bertrand, 643 Sonoma Blvd., 94590.

Walnut Grove, Sacramento Co., St. Anthony (1931), Rev. Cornelius O'Donnell, Admin.
P.O. Box 436, 95690.; Res. & Church: 14012 Walnut Ave., 95690. Tel: 916-776-1330.
Catechesis/Religious Programs—Students 79.

Weaverville, Trinity Co., St. Patrick (1853), Rev. Keith Canterbury; Deacon Everett Layne.
Res., P.O. Box 1219, 96093-1219. Tel: 916-623-4383.
Church—102 Church St., 96093. Tel: 530-623-4383.
Catechesis/Religious Programs—Students 35.
Missions—Hayfork, Trinity Co., Holy Trinity; Lewiston, Trinity Co., St. Gilbert.
Station—Mad River.

Weed, Siskiyou Co., Holy Family (1933), Rev. Michael O'Reilly.
Res., 1051 N. Davis Ave., 96094. Tel: 530-938-2076; Fax: 530-938-3837.
Catechesis/Religious Programs—Tel: 530-938-4334. Students 90.

West Sacramento, Yolo Co., Holy Cross (1913), Rev. Chad C. Puthoff, S.D.S.; Bro. William Hoefgen, S.D.S.; Deacon Raul Leon.
Res., 1321 Anna St., 95605. Tel: 916-371-1211; Fax: 916-371-9277.
School—800 Todhunter Ave., 95605. Tel: 916-371-1313. Sr. Jane Golden, R.S.M., Prin.
Sisters 3; Lay Teachers 8; Students 180.
Catechesis/Religious Programs—Students 205.
Convent—Tel: 916-371-1931; 933-0971. Sisters of Mercy (Auburn, CA)

Our Lady of Grace (1949), Rev. J. B. Walsh.
Res., 911 Park Blvd., 95691. Tel: 916-371-4814; Fax: 916-371-4814.
School—1990 Linden Rd., 95691. Tel: 916-371-9416; Fax: 916-371-1319. Sr. Michael Henry Moulin, D.H.S., Prin.
Sisters 1; Lay Teachers 11; Students 218.
Catechesis/Religious Programs—Fax: 916-371-4816. Students 103.
Convent—Tel: 916-371-9715.

Westwood, Lassen Co., Our Lady of the Snows (1929), Rev. Rodney Hall.
Res., 307 Fifth St., P.O. Box 905, 96137. Tel: 530-256-3344; Fax: 530-256-3344.
Church—425 Cedar St., 96137.
Catechesis/Religious Programs—Students 38.
Mission—Chester, Plumas Co., Christ the King, Melissa St., Chester, 96020. Tel: 530-258-3231.

Willows, Glenn Co., St. Monica (1877), Revs. Matthias J. O'Callaghan; Heriberto Serrano.
Res., 1129 W. Wood St., 95988. Tel: 530-934-3314; Fax: 530-934-3205. [CEM]
Catechesis/Religious Programs—Tel: 530-934-2239; Fax: 530-934-2253. Students 210.
Catechetical School—1151 W. Wood St., 95988. Tel: 530-934-5916; Fax: 530-934-3205. Students 190.

Winters, Yolo Co., St. Anthony (1913), Rev. Luciano Valenzuela, Admin.; Sr. Anne Chester, R.S.M., Pastoral Assoc.; Deacon Alejandro Arroyo.
Res., 306 Abbey St., P.O. Box 986, 95694. Tel: 530-795-2230; Fax: 530-795-5470.
Church—301 Main St., 95694.
Parish Center—511 Main St., 95694.
Catechesis/Religious Programs—Marie Valenzuela, D.R.E. Students 320.
Mission—Esparto, Yolo Co., St. Martin, 25633 Grafton Rd., Esparto, 95627. Tel: 530-787-3750.

Woodland, Yolo Co., Holy Rosary (1870), Revs. John E. Boll; Colm O'Kelly; Rodolfo DCL Llamas, V.D.C. (Mexico); Deacons Edward Kull; Gonzalo Chavez; Antonio Fernandez.
Res. & Parish Center: 503 California St., 95695. Tel: 530-662-2805. [CEM]
Church—(Corner of Walnut & Court Sts.) 301 Walnut St., 95695. Fax: 530-662-0796.
School—505 California St., 95695. Tel: 530-662-3494; Fax: 530-668-2442. Jeannie Venturini, Prin.
Lay Teachers 15; Students 270.
Catechesis/Religious Programs—Tel: 530-662-5394. Nancy Johnson, Coord. (English); Patricia Arriaga, Coord. (Spanish), Tel: 530-662-2894. Students 1,028.
Mission—Yolo, Yolo Co., Our Lady of Guadalupe. Sacramento St.

Yreka, Siskiyou Co., St. Joseph (1855), Rev. Sean O'Leary.
Res., 314 Fourth St., 96097. Tel: 530-842-3842; Fax: 530-842-3842.
Catechetical Center—308 Fourth St., 96097. Tel: 530-842-4874.
Catechesis/Religious Programs—Tel: 530-842-4874. Students 72.
Mission—Hawkinsville, Siskiyou Co., Immaculate Conception.

Yuba City, Sutter Co., St. Isidore (1952), Revs. Manuel B. Soria; Loreto Businos Rojas, Jr. In res., Rev. Joseph E. Bishop, Pastor Emeritus.
Res., 222 Clark Ave., 95991. Tel: 530-673-1573; Fax: 530-673-2512.
School—200 Clark Ave., 95991. Tel: 530-673-2217; Fax: 530-673-2217. Mrs. Terry Anderson, Prin.
Lay Teachers 11; Students 251.
Catechesis/Religious Programs—Students 500.

Chaplains of Public Institutions

SACRAMENTO. *California Youth Authority* Northern Reception Center-Clinic, 3001 Ramona Ave., 95826. Tel: 916-739-2104. Rev. Liam P. McSweeney.
Mule Creek State Prison. P.O. Box 409099, Ione, 95640. Tel: 209-274-4911. Rev. Diego Baptista.
Sacramento Juvenile Hall 9601 Kiefer Blvd., 95827. Tel: 916-875-5083. Matt Sanders, Youth Chap. & Contact Person, Tel: 916-489-3394.
Sutter General Hospital 2801 L St., 95816. Tel: 916-454-2222. Rev. James P. Sheets.
Sutter Memorial Hospital 52nd & F Sts., 95819. Tel: 916-454-3333. Rev. James P. Sheets.
University of California, Davis Medical Center 2315 Stockton Blvd., 95817. Tel: 916-453-2011. Rev. William J. Dinelli.

ELK GROVE. *Rio Consumnes Correctional Center* 12500 Bruceville Rd, 95758. Tel: 916-684-2001. Rev. Philip Wells, Contact Person, Tel: 916-684-5722.

FOLSOM. *California State Prison* Tel: 916-985-8610, Ext. 6025. P.O. Box 29, Represa, 95671. Deacon Denis Merino.
Folsom State Prison Tel: 916-985-2561, Ext. 4206. P.O. Box 71, Represa, 95671. Tel: 916-985-2561. Rev. Thomas Maguire.

PRESTON. *School of Industry* California Youth Authority, Tel: 209-274-8250. Rev. Humberto Gomez.

SUSANVILLE. *California Correctional Center* P.O. Box 790, 96130. Tel: 530-257-2181, Ext. 1180. Rev. Anthony B. Warnakula, C.H.S.P.
High Desert State Prison P.O. Box 750, 96130. Tel: 916-251-5100, Ext. 6722. Deacon Colby Smith.
Sierra Army Depot. Attended by Army & Navy Chaplains and Sacred Heart Parish.

VACAVILLE. *California Medical Facility* P.O. Box 2000, 95688. Tel: 707-448-6841, Ext. 2976. Rev. Innocent Emechete, Chap.
California State Prison, Solano P.O. Box 4000, 95696. Tel: 707-457-0182, Ext. 6462.

Special Assignment:
Reverend Fathers—
Silveira, Eduino, Chap. to Sheriff Deputies, St. Elizabeth Church, 1817 12th St., Sacramento, CA 95814
Tape, Bernard, Diocesan Pastoral Center, 2110 Broadway, Sacramento, CA 95818
Traynor, Anthony, Chap. to Firefighters & Sacramento Metro Airport, Our Lady of Lourdes Church, 1951 North Ave., Sacramento, CA 95838

On Duty Outside the Diocese:
Reverend Fathers—
Dermody, Thomas, San Diego Diocese
Leslie, Patrick J., Santa Rosa Diocese
McGrath, Patrick, Limerick, Ireland
Stevenson, R. Francis, Monterey Diocese

Military Chaplains:
Reverend Fathers—
Higgins, Richard B., U.S. Air Force

Awaiting Assignment:
Reverend Fathers—
Schloeder, Paul

Absent on Leave:
Reverend Fathers—
Brusato, Martin
Conway, Malachy
Garcia, Javier
Lee, Patrick
McCarthy, D. Joseph
Molumby, John
Mosher, Mark
Nguyen, Charles
Steinauer, Carl J.

Retired and in Senior Ministry:
Reverend Monsignors—
Coffey, Andrew V., 520 C St., Davis, CA 95616
Higgins, Cornelius P., 3027 Olive Glen Ct., Sacramento, CA 95821
Mennis, James F., 1601 Ocean Dr. S. #203, Jacksonville, FL 32250
Mistretta, Vito F., 7760 Woodchuck Way, Citrus Heights, CA 95610
Nolan, Patrick M., P.O. Box 215231, Sacramento, CA 95821
O'Neill, Patrick J., 350 Locust Dr., Apt. #L-104, Vallejo, CA 94591
Peters, Roy V., 469 Ena Rd. #3010, Honolulu, HI 96815
Schons, Gerard, 627 3rd St., Galt, CA 95632

Reverend Fathers—
Albrecht, Walter H., 722 State St., Aberdeen, WA 98520
Batch, Thomas A., 223 Hooper Rd., Yuba City, CA 95993
Bishop, Joseph E., 222 S. Clark Ave., Yuba City, CA 95991
Brennan, Ronan P., 2007 Country Villa, Auburn, CA 95603
Broderick, William, 5057 Cottage Way, Carmichael, CA 95608
Burke, Walter Dev, Courhill Rd., Kincon Ballina, Mayo, Ireland
Burns, Bernard J., Swellan, Co. Cavan, Ireland Ireland
Carrigan, Thomas C., Clarabricken House, Clifden Co., Kilkenny Ireland
Casey, Daniel, P.O. Box 5006 Fair Oaks, CA
Connelly, Robert J., P.O. Box 5037, Oak Park Sta., Sacramento, CA 95817
Cormack, Michael J., 7413 Timberrose, Roseville, CA 95747
Delahunty, Thomas P., 3247 Sandhurst Ct., Cameron Park, CA 95682
Dermody, Michael, Rocklin
Grace, John J., 3035 Berkeley Ave., South Lake Tahoe, CA 96150
Gurnell, Anthony, P.O. Box 437, Cayucos, CA 93430
Hold, William, 873 Colombine Way, Central Pointe, OR 97502
Keaney, Denis P., 1521 Lake Vista Ln., Eldorado Hills, CA 95762
Kyne, John J., 1960 Butte St. #27, Corning, CA 96021
Lanigan, Patrick J., 1182 Hartford Pl., Fairfield, CA 94533
Lenehan, Vincent, 5500 13th Ave., Sacramento, CA 95820
Lyons, Vincent, 1147-A Porter St., Vallejo, CA 94590
Maio, Anthony V., 110 Village Ct., Vacaville, CA 95687
Moloney, Sean, 2440 Cottage Way, #160, Sacramento, CA 95825
O'Donnell, Cornelius, St. Anthony, P.O. Box 436, Walnut Grove, CA 95690
O'Dowd, Brendan, 246 Cypress St., Brookings, OR 97415
O'Hara, Edward, Kilsonna, Longford, Granard, Ireland
O'Rafferty, Patrick, 39100 Orchard Ave., Cherry Valley, CA 92223-3797
Phelan, Nicholas, Vicar for Retired Priests, 439 Mill St. Apt. A, Grass Valley, CA 95945
Ramos, Cipriano, P.O. Box 684, Roseville, CA 95678
Ryan, Lawrence A., P.O. Box 8050, Santa Cruz, CA 95061
Sullivan, John P., 3111 Tierra de Dios Dr., El Dorado Hills, CA 95762
Vereker, Tobias, 2728 Elvyra Way, #55, Sacramento, CA 95821
Walsh, William K., 50 River Rd., #30, Rio Vista, CA 94571
Wdowiak, Boleslaw, 2404 Ruby Ct., Rocklin, CA 95677

Permanent Deacons:
Adams, James V., Chaminade, Chatsworth
Arroyo, Alejandro, St. Anthony, Winters
Astesana, Carlos, St. Patrick's, Grass Valley
Boone, Kenneth, St. Joseph, Lincoln
Boudier, William, St. Rose of Lima, Roseville
Burke, Keith, St. Philomene, Sacramento
Burkett, James, Our Divine Savior Parish, Chico
Cabrera, Domingo, St. Mary, Vacaville
Carlomagno, Michael, St. Basil, Vallejo
Cavanagh, Paul, St. Vincent Ferrer, Vallejo
Chatigny, James, St. Patrick, Grass Valley
Chavarria, Modesto, St. Anne, Sacramento
Chavez, Gonzalo, Holy Rosary, Woodland
Cheever, Charles, St. Philomene, Sacramento
Colenzo, Sam, St. James, Davis
Craig, Ray, Assumption, Truckee
Crowley, Michael, St. Anthony, Sacramento
David, Rudy, St. Catherine of Siena, Vallejo
DeHaven, Donald, St. Charles Borromeo, Sacramento
Del Gaudio, Lou, St. Mary, Sacramento
Donovan, Michael, All Hallows, Sacramento
Driggs, Richard, St. Francis of Assisi, Sacramento
Dufault, Duane, St. Anthony, Mount Shasta
Evans, Michael, Sacred Heart, Anderson
Fernandez, Antonio, Holy Rosary, Woodland
Fernandez, Miguel, Our Lady of Lourdes, Colusa
Fracolli, Gary, St. Lawrence, North Highlands
Garcia, Henry, St. Joseph, Sacramento
Gasman, David H., St. Joseph, Redding
Gercich, Don, St. Patrick, Jackson
Goecker, Clark, St. James, Davis
Gonzalez, Antonio, St. Paul, Knights Landing
Gualco, Jack, St. Ignatius of Loyola, Sacramento
Healy, James, St. Anthony's, Sacramento
Helgeson, Raymond, Stuebenville, OH
Hemenway, Raymond, Sacred Heart, Anderson
Henning, Patrick, St. Mel, Fair Oaks
Hernandez, Jesus, Holy Spirit, Fairfield
Ikelman, Robert, St. Peter, Dixon
King, John, St. Peter, Dixon
Koppes, Richard, St. Anthony, Sacramento
Kriske, George, All Hallows, Sacramento
Kull, Edward, Holy Rosary, Woodland
Lalonde, James, Our Lady of Lourdes, Sacramento
Layne, Everett H., Holy Trinity Mission; St. Patrick, Weaverville
Lazarek, Edward, St. Dominic, Benicia
Lehman, David, St. Mel, Fair Oaks
Leon, Raul, Holy Cross, West Sacramento
Link, Robert, Chicago, IL
Little, Walter, St. John Vianney, Rancho Cordova
Lobo, Pete, St. Catherine of Siena, Vallejo
Lopez, Frank, St. Joseph, Redding
Lucas, George, Immaculate Conception, Downieville
Mangas, Michael, St. Joseph, Redding
Mangoba, Leo, St. Vincent Ferrer, Vallejo
Manriquez, Pedro, St. Anne, Sacramento
Masla, John, Woodbury, MN
McGill, Thomas, St. Christopher, Galt
Merino, Dennis, St. John the Baptist, Folsom
Meucci, James, Our Lady of the Assumption, Carmichael
Morgado, Edwin, St. Joseph, Auburn
Morris, Douglas, Austin, TX
Morrison, Charles, St. Paul, Sacramento
Moseley, Philip, St. John Vianney, Rancho Cordova
Moua, Tou, St. Peter, Sacramento
Munoz, Jesus, St. Joseph, Marysville
Nguyen, Anthony, Vietnamese Catholic Martyrs, Sacramento
Niekamp, Lawrence, Our Divine Savior, Orangevale
Padilla, Jesus, St. John the Baptist, Chico
Parra, Gilbert, Sacred Heart, Sacramento
Pauly, Gerald, Immaculate Conception, Sacramento
Peregrino, Bobby, St. Catherine of Siena, Vallejo
Perez, Ben, St. Catherine, Vallejo
Perez, David, St. Joseph's, Marysville
Ramirez, Antonio, St. Joseph, Elk Grove
Ramirez, Jose, Our Lady of Guadalupe, Sacramento
Ramos, Ray, St. Peter, Sacramento
Rasmussen, Charles, Eagle, ID
Redling, Ralph, Kelseyville, CA
Reyna, Pedro, Sacred Heart, Maxwell
Reynoso, Alejandro, St. Peter, Sacramento
Riehl, William, Sacred Heart, Sacramento
Rodriquez, Jesus, St. Joseph, Lincoln
Rodriquez, Martin, St. Robert, Sacramento
Rudger, Stanley, St. Patrick, Placerville
Ruiz, Roberto, St. Joseph, Lincoln
Sanchez, Miguel, Mexico
Schaeffer, William, Abbey of New Clairvaux, Vina
Schwartz, Steve, St. John the Baptist, Chico
Sheldon, Lawrence, San Diego, CA
Shields, Floyd, St. John the Evangelist, Carmichael
Short, Anthony, Our Lady of Mercy, Anderson
Silott, Peter, St. Rose of Lima, Roseville
Sims, Robert, St. Vincent Ferrer, Vallejo
Smith, Colby, High Desert State Prison
Sorensen, David, Oregon
Sousa, William, Good Shepherd, Elk Grove
Stackhouse, Milton, St. Patrick, Grass Valley
Symkowick, Joseph, Newman Catholic Community, CSUS, Sacramento
Taloff, Paul, St. James, Davis
Tamayo, Juan, Our Lady of Guadalupe, Sacramento
Tateishi, Michael, Our Lady of the Assumption, Carmichael
Thompson, William, St. Patrick, Jackson
Travins, David, St. Thomas More, Paradise
Trueworthy, Len, Couer'D Alene, ID
Urick, Michael, St. Basil, Vallejo
Van Hook, Mark, St. Rose of Lima, Roseville
Vega, Ramon, Immaculate Conception, Sacramento
Verba, Phil, Jr., St. Mary, Vacaville
Vignery, Eldon, St. Isidore, Yuba City
Weeks, Bernard J., Holy Spirit, Sacramento
Weeks, James, St. John the Evangelist, Carmichael
White, Leslie, St. John the Baptist, Folsom
Wortman, Richard, St. Philip the Apostle, Sacramento
Zachary, Neil, Holy Trinity, El Dorado Hills
Zellmer, Gary, Sequim, WA

INSTITUTIONS LOCATED IN THE DIOCESE

[A] SEMINARY, RELIGIOUS

LOOMIS. *Mount St. Joseph Novitiate and Seminary*, 6530 Wells Ave., P.O. Box 547, 95650. Tel: 916-652-6336; Fax: 916-652-0620.
E-mail: fbrian@osjoseph.org
Web site: osjoseph.org
Novitiate of Oblates of St. Joseph. Revs. Mariusz Beczak, O.S.J.; Brian Crawford, O.S.J.; Horacio Trejo, O.S.J.; Bro. Marcello DiNardo, O.S.J. Priests 2; Brothers 1; Seminarians 6; Novices 6.

VINA. *Abbey of New Clairvaux, Trappist Seminary*, P.O. Box 80, 96092. Tel: 530-839-2161; Fax: 530-839-2332.
E-mail: txd@maxinet.com
Web site: www.maxinet.com/trappist/
Rt. Rev. Thomas X. Davis, O.C.S.O., J.C.L., Abbot. In res. Rt. Rev. Bernard Johnson, O.S.C.O., J.C.L., Abbott Emeritus; Revs. Timothy VanderVennett, O.C.S.O., S.T.L.; Lawrence A. Glaser, O.C.S.O.; Paul Jerome Konkler, O.C.S.O.; Harold K. Meyer, O.C.S.O.; Anthony R. Bellesorte, O.C.S.O.; Paul Mark Schwan, O.C.S.O. Seminarians 1.

[B] HIGH SCHOOLS, DIOCESAN

SACRAMENTO. *St. Francis High School.* (Girls), 6051 M St., 95819. Tel: 916-452-3461; Fax: 916-452-1591.
E-mail: sfhssac@connect.com
Web site: www.saintfrancishs.org
Kathleen Gaines, Prin. Lay Teachers 63; Girls 788.

PALO CEDRO. *Bishop Quinn High School*, 21893 Old 44 Dr., 96073. Tel: 530-547-2900; Fax: 530-547-5349.
E-mail: BQSF@impresso.com
Dr. Raymond L. John, Prin. Lay Teachers 8.

RED BLUFF. *Mercy High School*, 233 Riverside Way, 96080. Tel: 530-527-8313; Fax: 530-527-3058.
Web site: www.mercy-high.org
Dr. Paul Broughton, Prin. Lay Teachers 13; Students 220.

VALLEJO. *St. Patrick-St. Vincent High School*, 1500 Benicia Rd., 94591. Tel: 707-644-4425; Fax: 707-644-3107.
E-mail: spsvhs@impresso.com
Web site: www.spsv.pvt.k12.ca.us
Sr. Sue Pixley, O.P., Prin. Sisters 1; Lay Teachers 46; Students 668.

[C] HIGH SCHOOLS, PRIVATE

SACRAMENTO. *Christian Brothers High School of Sacramento, Inc.*, 4315 Martin Luther King Jr. Blvd., 95820. Tel: 916-733-3630; Fax: 916-733-3609.
Web site: www.cbhs-sacramento.org
Mr. Mark L. Warren, Pres.; Tom J. Rutten, Prin. Brothers 5; Sisters 1; Lay Teachers 63; Students 980.

Jesuit High School. Tel: 916-482-6060; Fax: 916-482-2310.
E-mail: kuntzj@jhssac.org
Web site: www.jhssac.org
Mailing Address: P.O. Box 254647, 95865-4647. Tel: 916-482-6060. 1200 Jacob Ln., Carmichael, 95608. Tel: 916-482-6060; Fax: 916-482-2310. (Boys). Revs. James F. Kuntz, S.J., Pres.; Gregory R. Bonfiglio, S.J., Rector; James A. Doogan, S.J.; Reynold J. Gatto, S.J.; Francis G. Hernandez, S.J.; David F. Klein, S.J.; Richard L. McCurdy, S.J.; John P. McGarry, S.J., Prin.; Charles R. Olsen, S.J.; Lorenzo J. Palafox, S.J.; William K. Stolz, S.J.; George V. Wanser, S.J. Jesuit Priests 12; Brothers 3; Scholastics 2; Lay Teachers 67; Boys 1,000.

Loretto High School. (Girls), 2360 El Camino Ave., 95821. Tel: 916-482-7793; Fax: 916-482-3621.
E-mail: LorettoHS@aol.com
Web site: www.Loretto.Room.Net
Religious of the Institute of the Blessed Virgin Mary. Sr. Helen Timothy, I.B.V.M., Pres.; Sr. Barbara Nelson, I.B.V.M., Prin. Sisters 2; Lay Teachers 51; Girls 470.

[D] ELEMENTARY SCHOOLS

ELK GROVE. *St. Elizabeth Ann Seton Elementary*, 9539 Raquet Ct., 95758. Tel: 916-684-7903; Fax: 916-684-4472. Gail Sherman, Prin.

[E] DAY NURSERY AND CHILD CARE HOMES

SACRAMENTO. *Grace Day Home*, 1909 7th St., 95814. Tel: 916-442-6557; Fax: 916-442-0924.
E-mail: graceday@pacbell.net
Ms. Nancy DeArmond, Exec. Dir. Lay Staff 34; Children 1,067.

St. Patrick Children's Home, Inc., 5945 Franklin Blvd., 95824. Tel: 916-421-1620; Fax: 916-421-3849.
E-mail: cmaloney@saintpatricks.net
Rev. Msgr. Edward J. Kavanagh, Exec. Dir.; Colleen Maloney, Financial Officer.
Two Residential Group Homes for Girls: Veda Cannon, Dir., Lopresti, 5036 Lemon Hill Ave., 95828. Tel: 916-421-1620; Fax: 916-421-3729. McMahon, 8529 Florin Rd., 95828. Tel: 916-421-1620;

Fax: 916-421-3729. Total Residents 16; Total Assisted 21; Total Staff 42.

St. Patrick's Child Care Centers, 5945 Franklin Blvd., 95824. Tel: 916-422-0123; Fax: 916-421-3849. Erin Young, Dir. Children (ages 2-5) 68; Children in after school care program 32; Total Assisted 101.

St. Patrick's Infant Toddler Program, 5945 Franklin Blvd., 95824. Tel: 916-422-0123; Fax: 916-421-3849. Children (ages 6 weeks-2 years) 24; Total Assisted 27.

St. Patrick's Infant-Toddler Program, 8201 Florin Rd., 95828. Tel: 916-383-3254. Erin Young, Dir. Children (ages 6 weeks-2 years 9 months) 34; Total Assisted 94. State funded for low income families-12 children ages 2-5. Private care: non-state funded.

St. Patrick's Foster Care Program. Tel: 916-386-1603; Fax: 916-386-0654. Stephen Isbell, Dir. Tel: 916-386-1603. Families providing care 49; Children 115; Total Staff 12.

[F] HOMES FOR SENIOR CITIZENS

SACRAMENTO. *Mercy-McMahon Terrace*, 3865 J St., 95816. Tel: 916-733-6510; Fax: 916-733-6515.
E-mail: mfgexcalibur@aol.com
Web site: www.mercysacramento.org
For a complete listing, refer to the Special Care Facilities section.

[G] GENERAL HOSPITALS

SACRAMENTO. *Mercy General Hospital*, 4001 J St., 95819. Tel: 916-453-4545; Fax: 916-453-4587.
E-mail: mhs@mercysacramento.org
Web site: www.mercysacramento.org
For a complete listing, refer to the Hospitals section.

CARMICHAEL. *Mercy American River/Mercy San Juan Hospital/Mercy American River Campus*, 6501 Coyle Ave., 95608. Tel: 916-537-5000; Fax: 916-537-5111.
E-mail: mhs@mercysacramento.org
Web site: www.mercysacramento.org
For a complete listing, refer to the Hospitals section.

FOLSOM. *Mercy Hospital of Folsom*, 1650 Creekside Dr., 95630. Tel: 916-983-7400; Fax: 916-983-7406.
E-mail: mhs@mercysacramento.org
Web site: www.mercysacramento.org
For a complete listing, refer to the Hospitals section.

MT. SHASTA. *Mercy Hospital of Mount Shasta dba Mercy Medical Center Mt. Shasta*, 914 Pine St., P.O. Box 239, 96067. Tel: 530-926-6111; Fax: 530-926-0517.
Web site: ntmhn1.mercy.org
For a complete listing, refer to the Hospitals section.

RANCHO CORDOVA. *Mercy Healthcare Sacramento*, 10540 White Rock Rd., 95670. Tel: 916-851-2000; Fax: 916-851-2727.
E-mail: mhs@mercysacramento.org
Web site: www.mercysacramento.org
For a complete listing, refer to the Hospitals section.

RED BLUFF. *Catholic Healthcare West North State dba St. Elizabeth Community Hospital*, 2550 Sr. Mary Columba Dr., 96080-4397. Tel: 530-529-8000; Fax: 530-529-8009
For a complete listing, refer to the Hospitals section.

REDDING. *Catholic Healthcare West North State dba Mercy Medical Center Redding*. Tel: 530-225-6000; Fax: 530-225-6125.
Web site: www.mercy.org
Mailing Address: P.O. Box 496009, 96049-6009.
For a complete listing, refer to the Hospitals section.

[H] MONASTERIES AND RESIDENCES OF PRIESTS AND BROTHERS

CARMICHAEL. *Jesuit High School Community of Sacramento*. Tel: 916-482-6060; Fax: 916-972-8037. (California Prov., Los Gatos). Mailing Address: P.O. Box 254647, Sacramento, 95865. Tel: 916-482-6060. 1200 Jacob Ln., 95608. Tel: 916-482-6060; Fax: 916-972-8037. Revs. Gregory R. Bonfiglio, S.J., Rector; William F. Breault, S.J.; James A. Doogan, S.J.; Reynold J. Gatto, S.J.; Edwin B. Harris, S.J.; Francis G. Hernandez, S.J.; James F. Kuntz, S.J.; David F. Klein, S.J.; Richard L. McCurdy, S.J.; John P. McGarry, S.J.; Charles R. Olsen, S.J.; Lorenzo J. Palafox, S.J.; William K. Stolz, S.J.; George V. Wanser, S.J.; Bros. Justin DeChance, S.J.; Charles Onorato, S.J.; Jeffrey Allen, S.J.; Tan Pham, S.J.; Marc Reeves, S.J. Priests 14; Brothers 3; Scholastics 2.

CITRUS HEIGHTS. *Christ the King Retreat*, 6520 Van Maren Ln., 95621. Tel: 916-723-5162; Fax: 916-723-6368. The Passionists (Chicago, IL). A community residence for the Passionist priests and brothers who conduct missions and retreats. Very Rev. Blaise Czaja, C.P.; Revs. Neil J. Parsons, C.P.; Thomas More Newbold, C.P.; James G. Strommer, C.P.; Joseph O. Mitchell, C.P., Retreat Dir.; Emil Womack, C.P.; Cedric Pisegna, C.P.; Ronan Newbold, C.P.; San Juan Alfonso, C.P.; Ronald Cork, C.P. Priests 10.

VINA. *Abbey of New Clairvaux, Trappist*, P.O. Box 80, 96092. Tel: 530-839-2161; Fax: 530-839-2332.
E-mail: txdavis@maxinet.com
Web site: www.maxinet.com/trappist/
Cistercian Abbey, Cistercians of the Strict Observance. Rt. Revs. Thomas X. Davis, O.C.S.O., J.C.L., Abbot; Bernard Johnson, O.S.C.O., J.C.L., Abbott Emeritus; Revs. Harold K. Meyer, O.C.S.O., Prior; Timothy VanderVennett, O.C.S.O., S.T.L.; Lawrence A. Glaser, O.C.S.O.; Paul Jerome Konkler, O.C.S.O.; Anthony R. Bellesorte, O.C.S.O.; John Baptist Porter, O.C.S.O.; Paul Mark Schwan, O.C.S.O. Priests 8; Professed Brothers 13.

[I] CONVENTS AND RESIDENCES FOR SISTERS

SACRAMENTO. *Canossian Daughters of Charity*, Our Lady of Lourdes Convent, 1949 North Ave., 95838. Tel: 916-925-4001; Fax: 916-925-8897.
E-mail: fdcc_sac@charliefish.com
Sisters 4.

Presentation Sisters, St. Mary's Convent, 5801 N St., 95819. Tel: 916-451-5881. Sisters 4.

Religious of the Virgin Mary, 7580 Center Pkwy., 95823. Tel: 916-421-7174. Sisters 4.

St. Charles Borromeo Convent, 7580 Center Pkwy., 95823. Tel: 916-421-7174; Fax: 916-421-3954.

Sister Servants of the Blessed Sacrament, St. Peter's Convent, 5929 61st St., 95824. Tel: 916-457-0182; Fax: 916-453-8950.
E-mail: sisbs@pacbell.net
Sisters 4.

Sisters Catechists of Jesus Crucified, St. Francis Convent, 5945 M St., 95819. Tel: 916-456-6485. Sisters 4.

Sisters of Social Service. Tel: 916-489-3714; Fax: 916-485-0363. 5349 Sedona Ct., Carmichael, 95608. Tel: 916-489-3714; Fax: 916-485-0363.

Sisters of the Holy Rosary of Fatima, 1708 U St., 95818. Tel: 916-442-8646.
E-mail: vlemus@diocese-sacramento.org
Sisters 4.

Sisters of the Sacred Hearts of Jesus & Mary, St. Paul's Convent, P.O. Box 292280, 95829. Tel: 916-381-5200; Fax: 916-381-0332. Sisters 2.

AUBURN. *Institute of the Sisters of Mercy of the Americas*. Tel: 530-887-2000; Fax: 530-887-0789.
E-mail: mercy.aub@onemain.com
Auburn Regional Community. Motherhouse: 535 Sacramento St., 95603-5699. Tel: 530-887-2000; Fax: 530-887-0789. Sr. Sheila Browne, R.S.M., Pres. Sisters in Community 19; Sisters in Diocese 80.

Russell House, 2223 L St., Sacramento, 95816-4926. Tel: 916-446-9251. Sisters 5.

McAuley Convent, 3846 H St., Sacramento, 95816-4613. Tel: 916-455-2843. Sisters 4.

Sisters of Mercy, 5625 Frontier Way, Carmichael, 95608. Tel: 916-489-0844. Sisters 3.

Our Lady of Fatima Convent, 2240 Hawthorne St., Sacramento, 95815-2910. Tel: 916-924-8541. Sisters 2.

Holy Spirit Convent, 3920 W. Land Park Dr., Sacramento, 95822-1123. Tel: 916-448-3578. Sisters 7.

Mercy Convent, 750 41st St., Sacramento, 95819-2738. Tel: 916-457-8274. Sisters 8.

Mercy San Juan, 6620 Oakbrook Dr., Fair Oaks, 95628. Tel: 916-962-7144. Sisters 7.

Holy Cross Convent, 800 Todhunter Ave., West Sacramento, 95605-2299. Tel: 916-371-1931. Sisters 6.

Sisters of Mercy, 212 Bittercreek Dr., Folsom, 95630-2353. Tel: 916-983-9268. Sisters 3.

Coolock Community, 848 39th St., Sacramento, 95816. Tel: 916-454-1723. Sisters 2.

Trocaire Cottage, 319 Elk Dr., Redding, 96003-3431. Tel: 530-244-1058. Sisters 2.

Kinsale Convent, 5256 H St., Sacramento, 95819-3539. Tel: 916-455-2715. Sisters 4.

CARMICHAEL. *Religious of the Institute of the Blessed Virgin Mary*, Assumption Convent, 5055 Cottage Way, 95608. Tel: 916-488-8188; Fax: 916-488-6983. Sisters 5.
Other Locations: 3606 Chadsworth Way, Sacramento, 95821. Tel: 916-485-6384; Fax: 916-485-6385. Sisters 3. 9190 Sebastiani Way, Sacramento, 95829. Tel: 916-618-2016; Fax: 916-739-1708.

FAIR OAKS. *Sisters of Mercy of Cashel*, St. Mel's Convent, P.O. Box 1180, 95628. Tel: 916-967-9504; Fax: 916-967-9504. Sisters 2.

FAIRFIELD. *Sisters of the Holy Faith*, Holy Spirit Convent, 1050 N. Texas St., 94533. Tel: 707-425-3572.
E-mail: hssf@impresso.com
Web site: www.hsschool.org
Sisters 5.

GEORGETOWN. *Discalced Carmelite Nuns*, P.O. Box 1720, 95634. Tel: 530-333-1617; Fax: 530-333-1617. Carmel of the Holy Family and Saint Therese. Sisters 13.

WEST SACRAMENTO. *Daughters of the Holy Spirit*, Our Lady of Grace Convent, 1990 Linden Rd., 95691. Tel: 916-371-9416; Fax: 916-371-1319.
E-mail: olgws@connect.com

[J] RETREAT HOUSES

SACRAMENTO. *Pendola Center*, 2110 Broadway, 95818-2541. Tel: 916-733-0123; 916-PEN-DOLA; Fax: 916-733-0195.
E-mail: campendola@aol.com
Web site: www.pendola.org
Center located in Sierra-Nevada foothills near Camptonville. Summer camp for boys and girls 6-16. Available for teenage and young adult retreats, school midweek retreats, field trips. Contact: Stephen Tholcke, Dir. of Pendola Center, Dept. of Catholic Faith Formation.

APPLEGATE. *Our Lady of the Oaks Villa*, P.O. Box 128, 95703. Tel: 530-878-2776; Fax: 530-878-1615.
E-mail: appvillia@pacbell.net
Available for retreats and conferences from September 1 to May 15. Rev. Gerald H. Robinson, S.J., Dir. Tel: 916-482-9666; Bro. James Sanders, S.J., Asst. Dir. Tel: 916-482-6060; Ronald W. Weingart, Resident Manager. Tel: 530-878-2776.

AUBURN. *Mercy Center Auburn*, 535 Sacramento St., 95603-5699. Tel: 530-887-2019; Fax: 530-887-1154.
E-mail: mercycenter@onemain.com

CITRUS HEIGHTS. *Christ the King Retreat Center*, 6520 Van Maren Ln., 95621. Tel: 916-725-4720; Fax: 916-725-4812.
Web site: www.passionist.org
Rev. Joseph O. Mitchell, C.P., Dir.; Sr. Marcella Fabing, C.S.J., Assoc. Dir.; Rev. Ronan Newbold, C.P.; Mr. Thomas Borkowski, Admin.

Christ the King Institute for Counseling & Spiritual Direction, 6520 Van Maren Ln., 95621. Tel: 916-783-9005. Rev. Jim Strommer, C.P., Dir.; Elizabeth Evans, M.A., Assoc.

Spiritual Life Institute at Christ the King Retreat Center, 6520 Van Maren Ln., 95621. Tel: 916-725-4720. Programs and courses in contemporary spirituality. Sr. Marcella Fabing, C.S.J., Coord.

[K] CAMPUS MINISTRIES AND NEWMAN CENTERS

CHICO. *Newman Centers*, 346 Cherry St., 95928-5113. Tel: 530-342-5180; Fax: 530-342-3016.
E-mail: mikenewsds@aol.com
Rev. Michael J. Newman, S.D.S., Diocesan Dir. Campus Ministry.

California State University (Sacramento), Newman Catholic Community. Tel: 916-454-4188; Fax: 916-454-4180. 5900 Newman Ct., Sacramento, 95819. Tel: 916-454-4188; Fax: 916-454-4180. Deacon Joseph Symkowick; Ms. Mary Ann Williams, Business Mgr.

California State University (Chico), Newman Catholic Community. Tel: 530-342-5180; Fax: 530-342-3016. Ms. Marge Flynn, Sec., 346 Cherry St., 95928. Tel: 530-342-5180; Fax: 530-342-3016.
E-mail: newmancm@aol.com
Web site: now2000.com/newman

University of California (Davis), Newman Catholic Community, 514 C St., Davis, 95616. Tel: 530-753-7393; Fax: 530-753-2794. Rev. Rey Bersabal, Interim Dir.

[L] CATHOLIC SOCIAL WELFARE ACTIVITIES

SACRAMENTO. *Catholic Charities of Sacramento, Inc.*, 5890 Newman Ct., 95819. Tel: 916-452-4621; Fax: 916-736-0282.
E-mail: ccsacjr@pacbell.net
James F. Sweeney, Chm. Bd. of Directors; James F. Rodgers, Exec. Dir.
Member Agencies of Catholic Charities of Sacramento, Inc.:

Catholic Social Service of Sacramento, 5890 Newman Ct., 95819-2608. Tel: 916-452-7481; Fax: 916-452-4099. Patricia Keast, Chm. Bd. of Directors; James F. Rodgers, Exec. Dir. Total Staff 19; Total Assisted 27,746.

Northern Valley Catholic Social Service, 1020 Market St., Redding, 96001. Tel: 530-241-0552; Fax: 530-247-3354. David Gasman, Chm. Bd. of Directors; Jan Maurer Watkins, Exec. Dir. Total Staff 167; Total Served 7,058.

Catholic Social Service of Solano County, 745 Georgia St., Vallejo, 94590. Tel: 707-644-8909; Fax: 707-644-6314. Daniel Healy, Chm. Bd. of Directors; Caroline Kieffer-Rosal, Exec. Dir. Total Staff 21; Total Assisted 7,791.
Subsidiaries of Catholic Charities of Sacramento:

Sacramento Food Bank Services, 3333 Third Ave., 95817. Tel: 916-456-1980; Fax: 916-451-5920. Charles Sylva, Chm. Bd. of Directors; Peter Berghuis, Exec. Dir. Total Staff 25; Total Served 28,993.
Administrative Project of Catholic Charities of Sacramento:

Mother Teresa Maternity Home, 3109 Sacramento St., Placerville, 95667. Tel: 530-662-0373. Lucille

Mosbacher, Chm. Bd. of Directors. Total Staff 3; Total Served 23.

Mercy Education Resource Center, 6007 Folsom Blvd. #200, 95819. Tel: 916-737-6026; Fax: 916-737-6507. E-mail: anne@mercyeducation.com
Web site: mercyeducation.com
Sponsored by the Sisters of Mercy Auburn Regional Community. Provides marriage counseling and individual counseling, and psycho-educational assessment. Sr. Anne Sekul, R.S.M., Dir. Total Staff 17; Total Assisted 2,700.

Society of St. Vincent de Paul, Sacramento District Council. Main Office: 2620 Fulton Ave., 95821. Tel: 916-972-1212; Fax: 916-972-1255. Phil Niederberger, Pres.

St. Vincent de Paul Thrift Store, 2620 Fulton Ave., 95821. Tel: 916-972-1212.

MARYSVILLE. *Grand Council, Catholic Ladies Relief Society of the Diocese of Sacramento*, 2074 Virgilia Ln., 95901. Tel: 530-742-9377. Doris Bitterman, Grand Pres. Tel: 530-742-9377; Rev. Leon Juchniewicz, Chap., 223 8th S.W. St., 95901.

ROSEVILLE. *Society of St. Vincent DePaul*, 139 Riverside, 95678. Tel: 916-781-3303; 781-3368 (dining room & thrift store); 781-3335 (food locker). Mr. Richard Roccucci, Pres. Total Assisted 23,129.

VALLEJO. *Society of St. Vincent de Paul Solano District Council*, 1225 Tualumne St., 94590. Tel: 707-644-5251. Mr. Michael Hayes, Pres.; John Elizalde. Total Assisted 1,733.

[M] YOUTH AND YOUNG ADULT MINISTRIES

SACRAMENTO. *Catholic Committee on Scouting*, 2110 Broadway, 95818. Tel: 916-733-0258; Fax: 916-733-0244. Rev. Mark Richards, Diocesan Chap.

Department of Catholic Faith Formation, 2110 Broadway, 95818. Tel: 916-733-0123; Fax: 916-733-0195. Mr. Robert Meaney, Dir.; Mrs. Linda Shumate, Consultant for Catechetics; Deacon Antonio Ramirez, Consultant, Hispanic Catechesis; Ms. Milagros Calvetti, Coord. Hispanic Youth/Young Adult Ministry; Mrs. Cheryl Tholcke, Coord. Youth Ministry; Mr. Stephen Tholcke, Dir. Pendola Center; Stanley Simonet, Pastoral Worker; Debbie Vanderford, Coord. Deaf Ministry; Feliciano Tapia, Hispanic Lay Ministry; Mrs. Michelle Hendricks, Coord. for the Ministry to Persons with Special Needs; Mr. John Donahoe, Coord. Camp Recreation.

[N] CAMPS

SACRAMENTO. *Pendola Center*, Office, 2110 Broadway, 95818-2541. Tel: 916-733-0123; 736-3652; Fax: 916-733-0195.
E-mail: campendola@aol.com
Web site: www.pendola.org
Located at Camptonville, Yuba County. Mr. Stephen F. Tholcke, Dir. Diocesan youth & young adult retreat center (September-April). Summer camp for boys and girls 6-16 (June, July, August). Outdoor school (September, October, November), available for parish youth and young adult retreats, school field trips and retreats.

[O] MISCELLANEOUS

SACRAMENTO. *Catholic Charities of California, Inc.*, 1119 K St., 2nd Flr., 95814. Tel: 916-313-4005; Fax: 916-443-4731.
E-mail: rmockler@cacatholic.org
Web site: www.cccalifornia.org
Rev. Msgr. Gregory A. Cox, Pres.; Richard Mockler, Exec. Dir.; Martina O'Sullivan, Vice Pres.; Maureen Shaw, Treas. & Sec.

Stanford Settlement, 450 W. El Camino, 95833-2299. Tel: 916-927-1303; Fax: 916-922-1694. Sr. Jeanne Felion, S.S.S., Dir. Assisted annually 10,000.

RANCHO CORDOVA. *Mercy Foundation*, 10540 White Rock Rd., Ste. 100, 95670. Tel: 916-851-2700; Fax: 916-851-2724.
E-mail: mhs@mercysacramento.org
Web site: www.mercysacramento.org
Mr. H. John Shaw, III, Pres.

RELIGIOUS INSTITUTES OF MEN REPRESENTED IN THE DIOCESE

For further details refer to the corresponding bracketed number in the Religious Institutes of Men or Women section.

[]—*Assumptionist Fathers.*—A.A.
[0330]—*Brothers of the Christian Schools.* (Napa, CA).—F.S.C.
[0270]—*Carmelite Fathers & Brothers.* (Barrington, IL).—O.Carm.
[0350]—*Cistercians Order of the Strict Observance-Trappists.* (Rome, Italy).—O.C.S.O.
[0370]—*Columban Fathers.*—S.S.C.
[]—*Congregation of Mother Coredemptrix.*—C.M.C.
[1000]—*Congregation of the Passion.* (Chicago, IL).—C.P.
[0520]—*Franciscan Friars.* (Prov. of St. Barbara).—O.F.M.
[]—*Franciscan Order of the Atonement.*—S.A.
[0690]—*Jesuit Fathers and Brothers.* (California Prov., Los Gatos, CA).—S.J.
[0730]—*Legionaries of Christ.*—L.C.
[0930]—*Oblates of St. Joseph.* (Santa Cruz, CA).—O.S.J.
[]—*Oratorians.* (Colombia).
[0950]—*Oratorians.*—C.O.
[0430]—*Order of Preachers-Dominicans.*—O.P.
[1065]—*Priestly Fraternity of St. Peter.*—F.S.S.P.
[1200]—*Society of the Divine Savior.* (Milwaukee, WI).—S.D.S.
[]—*Society of the Divine Word.*—S.V.D.

RELIGIOUS INSTITUTES OF WOMEN REPRESENTED IN THE DIOCESE

[1940]—*Congregation of the Sisters of the Holy Faith.*—C.H.F.
[0730]—*Daughters of Charity of Canossa.*—Fd.CC. (Rome, Italy).
[0820]—*Daughters of the Holy Spirit.* (Putnam, CT).—D.H.S.
[0420]—*Discalced Carmelite Nuns.*—O.C.D.
[1070-03]—*Dominican Sisters.* (Sinsinawa, WI).—O.P.
[1070-04]—*Dominican Sisters.* (San Rafael, CA).—O.P.
[]—*Dominican Sisters of Charity of the Presentation of the Blessed Virgin Mary.*—O.P.
[1190]—*Franciscan Sisters of the Atonement.* (Garrison, NY).—S.A.
[]—*Handmaids of the Holy Child Jesus.*—H.H.C.J.
[2370]—*Institute of the Blessed Virgin Mary (Loretto Sisters).*—I.B.V.M.
[2575]—*Institute of the Sisters of Mercy of the Americas.*—R.S.M.
[]—*Religious of the Virgin Mary.* (Quezon City, Philippines).—R.V.M.
[3499]—*Sister Servants of the Blessed Sacrament.*—S.S.B.S.
[]—*Sisters Catechists of Jesus Crucified.* (Mexico).—S.J.C.
[]—*Sisters of Mercy.* (Omaha).—R.S.M.
[]—*Sisters of Mercy of Cashel.* (U.S. Province).—R.S.M.
[]—*Sisters of Social Service.*—S.S.S.
[4080]—*Sisters of Social Service of Los Angeles, Inc.*—S.S.S.
[1630]—*Sisters of St. Francis of Penance and Christian Charity.* (Redwood City, CA).—O.S.F.
[]—*Sisters of St. Joseph of Carondelet.*—C.S.J.
[1960]—*Sisters of the Holy Family.* (San Jose, CA).—S.H.F.
[]—*Sisters of the Holy Name of Jesus & Mary.*—S.N.J.M.
[]—*Sisters of the Holy Rosary of Fatima.* (Salvatierra, Mexico).—H.R.F.
[3680]—*Sisters of the Sacred Hearts of Jesus and Mary.* (Essex).—S.H.J.M.
[3330]—*Union of the Sisters of the Presentation of the Blessed Virgin Mary.*—P.B.V.M.
[4110]—*Ursuline Nuns of the Congregation of Paris.*—O.S.U.

DIOCESAN CEMETERIES

SACRAMENTO. *St. Joseph*, 2615 21st St., 95818. Tel: 916-455-8324.

St. Mary's Cemetery & Mausoleum, 6700 21st Ave., 95820. Tel: 916-452-4831.

CITRUS HEIGHTS. *Calvary Cemetery & Mausoleum*, 7101 Verner Ave., P.O. Box 41303, 95841. Tel: 916-969-6541.

VALLEJO. *All Souls Cemetery & Mausoleum*, Glen Cove Rd., 94590. Tel: 707-644-5209.

St. Vincent, 550 Glen Cove Rd., 94590. Tel: 707-644-5209.

NECROLOGY

† Dowling, John. —Died April 5, 2000.
† Terwilliger, Rev. Msgr. John G., (Retired). —Died Oct. 7, 2000.

Diocese of Saginaw

(Dioecesis Saginavensis)

Most Reverend

KENNETH E. UNTENER, S.T.D., D.D.

Bishop of Saginaw; ordained June 1, 1963; ordained and installed as Bishop of Saginaw November 24, 1980. *Res., 5800 Weiss St., Saginaw, MI, 48603-2799.*

ESTABLISHED FEBRUARY 26, 1938.

Square Miles 6,955.

Comprises the following Counties in the State of Michigan: Arenac, Bay, Clare, Gladwin, Gratiot, Huron, Isabella, Midland, Saginaw, Sanilac and Tuscola.

For legal titles of parishes and diocesan institutions, consult the Chancery Office.

Chancery: 5800 Weiss St., Saginaw, MI, 48603-2799. Tel.: 517-799-7910; Fax: 517-797-6670.

Web site address: www.dioceseofsaginaw.org

STATISTICAL OVERVIEW

Personnel	
Bishop	1
Priests: Diocesan Active in Diocese	75
Priests: Active Outside Diocese	1
Priests: Diocesan in Foreign Missions	2
Priests: Retired, Sick or Absent	34
Number of Diocesan Priests	112
Religious Priests in Diocese	15
Extern Priests in Diocese	4
Ordinations:	
Transitional Deacons	1
Permanent Deacons in Diocese	14
Total Sisters	125
Parishes	
Parishes	108
With Resident Pastor:	
Resident Diocesan Priests	72
Resident Religious Priests	8
Without Resident Pastor:	
Administered by Priests	13
Administered by Deacons	1
Administered by Women Religious	13
Administered by Lay People	1
Professional Ministry Personnel:	
Sisters	23
Lay Ministers	22
Welfare	
Catholic Hospitals	1
Total Assisted	263,120
Health Care Centers	1
Total Assisted	10,750
Homes for the Aged	1
Total Assisted	100
Residential Care of Children	4
Total Assisted	191
Day Care and Extended Day Care Centers	7
Total Assisted	274
Specialized Homes	1
Total Assisted	1,262
Educational	
Diocesan Students in Other Seminaries	2
Total Seminarians	2
High Schools, Diocesan and Parish	3
Total Students	1,138
Elementary Schools, Diocesan and Parish	30
Total Students	5,007
Catechesis/Religious Education:	
High School Students	2,362
Elementary Students	9,790
Total Students Under Catholic Instruction	18,299
Teachers in the Diocese:	
Priests	1
Sisters	19
Lay Teachers	303
Vital Statistics	
Receptions into the Church:	
Infant Baptism Totals	1,928
Adult Baptism Totals	251
Received into Full Communion	252
First Communions	2,125
Confirmations	3,401
Marriages:	
Catholic	471
Interfaith	267
Total Marriages	738
Deaths	1,680
Total Catholic Population	142,505
Total Population	685,532

Former Bishops—Most Rev. WILLIAM F. MURPHY, S.T.D., J.C.L., LL.D., ord. June 13, 1908; appt. first Bishop of Saginaw, March 17, 1938; cons. May 17, 1938; died Feb. 7, 1950.—Most Rev. STEPHEN S. WOZNICKI, D.D., second Bishop; ord. Dec. 22, 1917; appt. Titular Bishop of Pelte and Auxiliary Bishop of Detroit, Dec. 13, 1937; cons. Jan. 25, 1938; transferred to Saginaw, March 28, 1950 Assistant at the Pontifical Throne, Dec. 22, 1967; resigned and transferred to the Titular See of Tiava, Oct. 30, 1968; died Dec. 10, 1968.—Most Rev. FRANCIS F. REH, S.T.L., J.C.D., third Bishop; ord. Dec. 8, 1935; appt. Bishop of Charleston, June 4, 1962; cons. June 29, 1962; transferred to the Titular See of Macrinna in Maurentania; Rector Pontifical North American College in Rome, Sept. 5, 1964; transferred to Saginaw, Dec. 18, 1968; installed Feb. 26, 1969; retired April 29, 1980; died Nov. 14, 1994.

Delegate to Senior Priests—Rev. ROBERT S. GOHM, *5800 Weiss St., Saginaw, 48603.* Tel: 517-799-7910.

Vicars General—Rev. JAMES F. GAVIT, J.C.D., *2872 N. Euclid Ave., Bay City, 48706-1342.* Tel: 517-684-1523. Rev. THOMAS E. SUTTON, J.C.L., *84 W. Midland Rd., Auburn, 48611.* Tel: 517-662-6861.

Episcopal Vicars—

Vicar for Hispanics—MARIA CEPEDA, Pastoral Minister, Coord., *Our Lady of Guadalupe Chapel & Center, 1619 Broadway, Bay City, 48708-8538.* Tel: 517-894-0661.

Vicar for Religious—Sr. JANET FULGENZI, O.P., Ph.D., *5800 Weiss St., Saginaw, 48603-2799.* Tel: 517-799-7910.

Vicar of Administration—Rev. THOMAS E. SUTTON, *c/o 5800 Weiss St., Saginaw, 48603-2799.*

Vicar for Canonical Affairs—Rev. JAMES F. GAVIT, J.C.D., *c/o 5800 Weiss St., Saginaw, 48603-2799.*

Vicars for Vicariates—Revs. DENNIS KUCHARCZYK, Vicariate 1; T. J. FLEMING, Vicariate 2; RICHARD BOKINSKIE, Vicariate 3; PAUL BALA, Vicariate 4; FREDERICK J. KAWKA, Vicariate 5; DANIEL ANHOLZER, O.F.M.Cap., Vicariate 6; DAVID PARSCH, Vicariate 7; JAMES HELLER, Vicariate 8; JOSEPH GRIFFIN, Vicariate 9; JEFFREY DONNER, Vicariate 10; JOHN R. JOHNSON, Vicariate 11; THOMAS KOWALCZYK, Vicariate 12.

Chancery—*5800 Weiss St., Saginaw, 48603-2799.* Tel: 517-799-7910; Fax: 517-797-6670.

Chancellor—Rev. THOMAS E. SUTTON, J.C.L.

Administrative Assistant to the Chancellor—CONNIE HUISKENS WOJDA.

Administrative Assistant to the Bishop—LEONA JONES.

Director of Finance—Mr. BRIAN BUCKINGHAM.

Administrative Assistant—KAREN SCHULTZ.

General Accountant—MARY JANE TACEY.

Accounting Assistant—JOSEPHINE MENDOZA.

Finance Council—RICHARD DOLINSKI, Chm.

Catholic Services Appeal—ADRIENNE JESCHKE, Coord., *5800 Weiss St., Saginaw, 48603-2799.* Tel: 517-799-7910.

Diocesan Building Commission—JOHN PROFFER, Chm., *5800 Weiss St., Saginaw, 48603-2799.* Tel: 517-799-7910.

Tribunal—*5800 Weiss St., Saginaw, 48603-2799.* Tel: 517-799-7910.

Judicial Vicar—Rev. RICHARD M. FILARY, J.C.L.

Defenders of the Bond—Very Rev. JAMES F. GAVIT, J.C.D.; Rev. ROBERT J. DELAND, J.C.L.

Judges—Revs. THOMAS E. SUTTON, J.C.L.; EUGENE A. FORBES, J.C.D.; ROBERT J. MEISSNER; ROBERT W. DAVEY, M.A.; RICHARD M. FILARY, J.C.L.

Promoter of Justice—Rev. JAMES F. GAVIT, J.C.D.

Notary—PATRICIA D. PRESTON.

Advocate—Rev. ROBERT W. DAVEY, M.A.

Diocesan Council—THERESA NOWAK, Chm., *5800 Weiss, Saginaw, 48603-2799.* Tel: 517-799-7910.

Diocesan Presbyteral Council—Rev. LEONARD WILKUSKI, Chm., *1008 S. Wenonah St., Bay City, 48706-5094.*

Diocesan Consultors—Revs. ROBERT S. GOHM; ROBERT H. BYRNE; RANDY J. KELLY; LOREN KALINOWSKI; JERRY KUKLA.

Clergy Personnel Board—Rev. WILLIAM TAYLOR, Chm., *1525 S. Washington, Saginaw, 48601-2895.* Tel: 517-755-8020.

Diocesan Council of Catholic Women—Mrs. BETTY LAFAVE, Pres., *754 Frank St., Caro, 48723.* Rev. DONALD J. EPPENBROCK, Moderator, *5366 Main St., Box 399, Lexington, 48450-0399.* Tel: 313-359-8101.

Office of Communication—Mrs. CATHERINE HAVEN, Dir., *5800 Weiss St., Saginaw, 48603-2799.* Tel: 517-797-6666.

Mission Office—Ms. JEAN SEMAN, Dir. for Missions, *5800 Weiss St., Saginaw, 48603-2799.* Tel: 517-797-6633.

Office of Education-Formation—BARBARA GEARY, Supt. of Schools, *5800 Weiss St., Saginaw, 48603-2799.* Tel: 517-797-6651. BARBARA MINCZENSKI, Dir. Rel. Educ. Formation; ANDREA MOLINARI, Catechetical Ministry Dir.

Director of Family-Youth Ministry—PEGGY MCCOURTNEY.

Family Life Ministry—Refer to: Catholic Family Service, *5800 Weiss St., Saginaw, 48603-2799.* Tel: 517-797-6638.

Evangelization Ministry—Contact Office of Education.

Ecumenism Ministry—Rev. GEORGE SEROUR, *8370 Unionville Rd., Sebewaing, 48759-9553.* Tel: 517-883-2746.

Ministry to Charismatic Renewal—MARGE FOBEAR, Dir., *Charismatic Renewal Center, 1110 State St., Bay City, 48706.* Tel: 517-686-4640.

Ministry to Priests—Rev. ROBERT S. GOHM,Saginaw Diocesan Center, *5800 Weiss St., Saginaw, 48603-2799.* Tel: 517-799-7910.

Financial Council—RICHARD DOLINSKI.

Diocesan Building Commission—JOHN PROFFER.

Office of Church Ministries—Rev. ROBERT S. GOHM, Dir. of Church Ministries Office, Ministry to Priests Program, Continuing Education for Priests; Rev. THOMAS MOORE, O.S.F.S., Dir. Seminarians & Vocations; Sr. ROBERTA KOLASA, S.J., Dir., Diocesan Ministries Institute; Sr. JOSEPHINE GAUGIER, O.P., English Language Lay Ministry Program.

Office of Christian Service—THOMAS CONKLIN, Dir. DIANE BELKNAP, Sec. Outreach Workers: BETTY DEVOTA, Vic. 3, 4, 5, 9, 12; SANDY BUZA, Vic. 1, 2, 8, 10, 11; Sr. LEONA SULLIVAN, Vic. 6, 7, *5800 Weiss St., Saginaw, 48603-2799.* Tel: 517-797-6672.

Office of Liturgy—MARY SELLARS MALLOY, Dir. CONNIE KACZYNSKI, Sec., *5800 Weiss St., Saginaw, 48603-2799.* Tel: 517-797-6664.

Catholic Family Services—THOMAS CONKLIN, Exec. Dir., *5800 Weiss St., Saginaw, 48603-2799.* Tel: 517-797-6636.

Saginaw Counseling Center—THOMAS CONKLIN, Dir., *710 N. Michigan Ave., Saginaw, 48602-4372.* Tel: 517-753-8446.

Bad Axe Counseling Center—123 Scott St., Bad Axe, 48413-1329. Tel: 517-269-7931.

Bay City Counseling Center—512 N. Lincoln St., Bay City, 48708-6615. Tel: 517-892-2504.

Midland Counseling Center—220 W. Main St., Midland, 48640-5165. Tel: 517-631-4711.

Mt. Pleasant Counseling Center—120 S. University St., Mt. Pleasant, 48858-2305. Tel: 517-773-9328.

Sandusky Counseling Center—119 E. Sanilac, Sandusky, 48471-1147. Tel: 810-648-2304.

Hispanic Ministries Cultural Center—MARIA CEPEDA, Dir.; Mr. GILBERTO GUEVARA, Dir. of Social Awareness, Youth & Immigration, *405 Hayes St., Saginaw, 48602.* Tel: 517-755-4477. MIGUEL MORENO, Dir. Hispanic Lay Ministry.

St. Francis Home (for elderly)—Sr. JANE MARIE LEBIEDZINSKI, C.S.S.F., Admin., *915 N. River Rd., Saginaw, 48609-6865.* Tel: 517-781-3150.

St. Vincent Home-Boysville of Michigan (for children)—Mr. RICK L. BOONE, M.S.W., North Reg. Dir., *925 N. River Rd., Saginaw, 48609-6866.* Tel: 517-781-0490.

St. Vincent de Paul Store—Mr. THOMAS M. SCHREMS, Mgr., *122 S. Hamilton St., Saginaw, 48602-2013.* Tel: 517-793-9585.

Organizations and Services—

Association of Saginaw Priests—Rev. JOHN A. EDERER, Pres.

Catholic Cemeteries—KENNETH GROYA, Dir. BETSY VANDER WOUDE, Admin., *5800 Weiss St., Saginaw, 48603-2799.* Tel: 517-797-6627.

Catholic Newspaper—KATHLEEN A. SOCHA, Editor, *1520 Court St., P.O. Box 1405, Saginaw, 48605-1405.* Tel: 517-793-7661; Fax: 517-793-7663.

Censor—Rev. Msgr. FRANCIS J. MURRAY, *5965 W. Michigan Ave., Saginaw, 48603-7500.* Tel: 517-791-5002.

Clergy Benefit Society—Rev. ROBERT MEISSNER, *2956 E. North Union Rd., Bay City, 48706-9246.* Tel: 517-684-1170.

Conciliation-Arbitration—ANN M. SCHULTE, Conciliation Clerk, *5800 Weiss, Saginaw, 48603.*

Holy Childhood Association—Sr. CORINNE WEISS, S.J., *5800 Weiss St., Saginaw, 48603-2799.*

Marriage Encounter—Rev. JOSEPH A. SCHABEL, Spiritual Dir. Tel: 517-753-8446.

St. Vincent de Paul Society—Mr. THOMAS LEFEVRE, Pres., *523 Michigan Ave., Bay City, 48708.* Tel: 517-893-5772.

Office of Stewardship/Development—ANNETTE O'BRIEN, *5800 Weiss St., Saginaw, 48603-2799.* Tel: 517-797-6679.

CLERGY, PARISHES, MISSIONS AND PAROCHIAL SCHOOLS

CITY OF SAGINAW
(Saginaw County)

1—ST. MARY CATHEDRAL (1853), Rev. Ronald F. Wagner.
Res., 615 Hoyt Ave., 48607-1713. Tel: 517-752-8119; Fax: 517-752-2165.

2—HOLY FAMILY, Rev. William R. Taylor.
Res., 1525 S. Washington Ave., 48601-2895. Tel: 517-755-8020; Fax: 517-755-7193. [CEM]

3—HOLY ROSARY. Closed. For inquiries for parish records contact SS. Simon and Jude Parish, Saginaw.

4—SS. SIMON AND JUDE, Rev. Robert Schramm, O.S.F.S.; Sr. Teresita Weind, S.N.D.deN., Pastoral Assoc. In res., Revs. John S. Mancini, O.S.F.S.; Thomas M. Moore, O.S.F.S.
Res., 2395 S. Outer Dr., 48601-6643. Tel: 517-752-7424; Fax: 517-753-8601.

5—OUR LADY HELP OF CHRISTIANS. Closed. For inquiries for parish records contact SS. Simon and Jude Parish, Saginaw.

6—OUR LADY OF MOUNT CARMEL. Closed. For inquiries for parish records contact SS. Simon and Jude Parish, Saginaw.

7—SACRED HEART. Closed. For inquiries for parish records contact SS. Simon and Jude Parish, Saginaw.

8—ST. ANDREW, Rev. Donald L. Christensen.
Res., 612 N. Michigan Ave., 48602-4387. Tel: 517-754-0487; Fax: 517-754-0308.

9—ST. ANTHONY OF PADUA, Rev. Walter Balduck, O.F.M.Cap.
Res., 3680 S. Washington Rd., 48601-4997. Tel: 517-752-1971; Fax: 517-752-1441. [JC]

10—ST. CASIMIR, Rev. John S. Sarge.
Res., 2122 S. Jefferson Ave., 48601-3498. Tel: 517-752-6648; Fax: 517-752-6691. [JC]

11—ST. GEORGE, Rev. John S. Sarge; Nanette Navarre, Pastoral Assoc.
Res., 2120 Erie St., 48601-4497. Tel: 517-753-3865; Fax: 517-753-6903. [JC]

12—ST. HELEN, Rev. Emmet L. Marceau.
Res., 2445 N. Charles St., 48602-5096. Tel: 517-793-0618; Fax: 517-793-5487. [JC]
School—Sr. Corinne Weiss, S.J., Prin. Servants of Jesus 1; Lay Teachers 11; Students 201.

13—ST. JOHN VIANNEY, Rev. Loren M. Kalinowski.
Church—6400 McCarty Rd., 48603-9621. Tel: 517-790-5086; Fax: 517-790-1681.
Res., 4477 McCarty Rd., 48603. Tel: 517-792-6582.

14—ST. JOSEPH, Rev. Daniel Anholzer, O.F.M.Cap. In res., Rev. Arthur Cooney, O.F.M.Cap.
Res., 910 N. Sixth Ave., 48601-1103. Tel: 517-753-4418; Fax: 517-755-1090.
Convent—903 N. Seventh St., 48601. Tel: 517-752-5470.
Sisters 6.

15—SS. PETER AND PAUL, Rev. Robert J. DeLand; Sr. Betty Zeestraten, O.S.F., Pastoral Assoc.
Res., 4735 W. Michigan Ave., 48603-6370. Tel: 517-799-5448; Fax: 517-799-1495.
School—Lee Ann Berg, Prin. Sisters 1; Lay Teachers 11; Students 195.

16—ST. RITA. Closed. For inquiries for parish records contact SS Simon & Jude Parish, Saginaw.

17—ST. STEPHEN, Rev. Patrick C. O'Connor. Pastoral Assocs: Sr. Sharon Haskins, D.C.; Hank J. Messing.
Res., 2711 Mackinaw St., 48602-3146. Tel: 517-799-2334; Fax: 517-793-3611.
School—Tel: 517-793-2811; Fax: 517-793-8463. Susan Nash, Prin.
Lay Teachers 23; Students 515.

18—ST. THOMAS AQUINAS, Revs. Robert Konopa, O.F.M.; Leonard Stunek, O.F.M.
Res., 5376 State Rd., 48603-3771. Tel: 517-799-2460; Fax: 517-799-0207. [JC]
School—Bernardine Sisters of Third Order of St. Francis. (Farmington, MI). Sr. Ann De Guise, O.S.F., Prin.
Sisters 2; Lay Teachers 20; Students 453.

OUTSIDE THE CITY OF SAGINAW

Albee, Saginaw Co., St. Mary, Rev. Robert W. Shine.
Res., 5661 Fergus Rd., Rte. 2, St. Charles, 48655-9624. Tel: 517-770-4453; Fax: 517-770-5111.

Alma, Gratiot Co., St. Mary, Rev. Jack Hammer.
Res., 517 N. Prospect Ave., 48801-1694. Tel: 517-463-5370; Fax: 517-463-8297.
School—220 W. Downie St., 48801. Tel: 517-463-4579. Cynthia Araway, Prin.
Lay Teachers 9; Students 186.

Argyle, Sanilac Co., St. Joseph, Rev. Steven Fillion.
Res., 4960 N. Ubly Rd., 48410-0007. Tel: 517-658-8145; Fax: 517-658-8105. [CEM]
Mission—Freiburg, Sanilac Co., St. Ignatius.

Auburn, Bay Co., St. Joseph, Rev. Thomas E. Sutton.
Res., 84 W. Midland Rd., 48611. Tel: 517-662-6861; Fax: 517-662-0064.
School—Area School. Annette Carbary, Prin.
Students 164.

AuGres, Arenac Co., St. Mark, Rev. James E. Falsey.
Res., 415 S. Court St., 48703-9598. Tel: 517-876-7925; Fax: 517-876-7778.

Bad Axe, Huron Co., Sacred Heart, Rev. Jack J. Leipert.
Res., 311 Whitelam St., 48413-1205. Tel: 515-269-7729; Fax: 517-269-4010. [CEM]

Bannister, Gratiot Co., St. Cyril, Rev. Wolfgang Streichardt.
Res., 517 E. Main St., 48807-9762. Tel: 517-862-5270; Fax: 517-862-4534.

Bay City, Bay Co.,

1—HOLY TRINITY, Rev. Leonard F. Wilkuski. In res., Rev. Kevin Kerbawy.
Res., 1008 S. Wenona Ave., 48706-5094. Tel: 517-893-4073; Fax: 517-893-7087.
School—Tel: 517-892-3018. Sally Preston, Prin.
Lay Teachers 7; Students 164.

2—ST. BONIFACE, Rev. Dale A. Orlik.
Res., 510 N. Lincoln Ave., 48708-6694. Tel: 517-893-4851; Fax: 517-893-1781.

3—ST. HEDWIG, Rev. Richard M. Filary.
Res., 1504 S. Kiesel, 48706-5240. Tel: 517-893-1072; Fax: 517-893-4710.

4—ST. HYACINTH, Rev. Edward J. Konieczka.
Res., 1515 Cass Ave., 48708-8740. Tel: 517-895-5581; Fax: 517-895-5583. [CEM]
School—Sr. Maurita Grabowski, C.S.S.F., Prin. Felician Sisters (Livonia, MI) 1; Lay Teachers 4; Students 86.
Convent—912 S. Farragut St., 48708.

5—ST. JAMES, (1983), Rev. Peter J. Gaspeny.
Res., 710 Columbus Ave., 48708-6483. Tel: 517-893-4693; Fax: 517-893-1504. [CEM]
School—Sr. Maureen Donovan, S.C., Prin. Sisters of Charity of Cincinnati, OH 3; Lay Teachers 11; Students 205.
Convent—200 S. Farragut St., 48708.

6—ST. JOSEPH, Rev. Raymond S. Fron. In res., Rev. John Killop, O.F.M.
Res., 1005 Third St., 48708-6006. Tel: 517-895-5783; Fax: 517-895-8837.

7—ST. MARIA GORETTI, Rev. James F. Gavit.
Res., 2872 N. Euclid Rd., 48706-1342. Tel: 517-684-1523; Fax: 517-684-8286.

8—ST. MARY, Rev. James Heller.
Res., 501 N. Walnut St., P.O. Box 1092, 48706-1092. Tel: 517-892-6031; Fax: 517-892-4005.

9—ST. STANISLAUS, Revs. William J. Rutowski; Steven S. Killey.
Res., 1503 Kosciuszko Ave., Ste. 100, 48708-8027. Tel: 517-893-6421; Fax: 517-893-3985.
School—Sr. Annette Marie Myrand, C.S.S.F., Prin. Felician Sisters (Livonia, MI) 2; Lay Teachers 10; Students 145.

10—ST. VINCENT DE PAUL, Rev. Robert J. Meissner.
Res., 2956 E. North Union Rd., 48706-9246. Tel: 517-684-1170; Fax: 517-684-4925.

11—OUR LADY OF GUADALUPE CHAPEL AND CENTER, Mrs. Maria Cepeda, Vicar for Hispanics.
Res., 1619 Broadway, 48708-8538. Tel: 517-894-0661; Fax: 517-894-0771.

12—OUR LADY OF THE VISITATION, Rev. Gerald E. Balwinski.
Res., 1106 State St., 48706-3697. Tel: 517-684-5184; Fax: 517-684-5189.
School—Visitation Academy, 1110 State St., 48706. John Leaman, Prin.
Lay Teachers 12; Students 73.

Beal City, Isabella Co., St. Joseph the Worker, Rev. John F. Cotter.
Res., 2163 N. Winn Rd., Mount Pleasant, 48858-9730. Tel: 517-644-2041; Fax: 517-644-2026. [CEM]
School—Mrs. Mary Hauck, Prin. Lay Teachers 6; Students 130.

Beaver, Bay Co., St. Valentine, Rev. Richard C. Ratajczak.
Res., 999 S. 9 Mile Rd., Kawkawlin, 48631-9756. Tel: 517-662-6843; Fax: 517-662-0152. [CEM]
School—1010 S. 9 Mile Rd., Kawkawlin, 48631. Tel: 517-662-6966; Fax: 517-662-0152. Sr. Elise Milostan, C.S.S.F., Prin.
Felician Sisters (Livonia, MI) 2; Lay Teachers 3; Students 62.

Birch Run, Saginaw Co., Sacred Heart, Rev. James R. Carlson.
Res., 12157 Church St., 48415-8706. Tel: 517-624-9098; Fax: 517-624-9427.

Bridgeport, Saginaw Co., Assumption of the Blessed Virgin Mary, Rev. Ligouri Mierzwiak, O.F.M.
Res., 7945 Bell Rd., P.O. Box 602, 48722-0602. Tel: 517-777-1200; Fax: 517-777-6280.
St. Christopher, Rev. Mason L. Vaughn.
Res., 3926 Williamson Rd., Saginaw, 48601-5839. Tel: 517-777-2605; Fax: 517-777-9691.

Caro, Tuscola Co., Sacred Heart, Rev. Kenneth E. Yaroch.
Res., 140 Atwood, 48723-1742. Tel: 517-673-2346; Fax: 517-673-5669. [CEM]
Convent—919 W. Frank St., 48723. Tel: 517-673-7813.

Carrollton, Saginaw Co., St. John the Baptist, Rev. Richard T. Szafranski; Sr. Honora Remes, D.C., Pastoral Admin.
Res., 545 Maple Ridge, P.O. Box 248, 48724-0248. Tel: 517-752-9350; Fax: 517-753-4943.
St. Josaphat, Rev. Richard E. Jozwiak.
Res., 469 Shattuck Rd., Saginaw, 48604-2391. Tel: 517-753-2497; Fax: 517-753-2498.
School—Joanna Jaskiewicz, Prin. Lay Teachers 10; Students 200.

Caseville, Huron Co., St. Roch, Rev. Dennis Kucharczyk.
Res., 6253 Main St., 48725. Tel: 517-856-4933.

Cass City, Tuscola Co., St. Pancratius, Rev. Paul W. Bala.
Res., 4292 S. Seeger St., 48726-1423. Tel: 517-872-3336; Fax: 517-872-1852.

Chesaning, Saginaw Co., Our Lady of Perpetual Help, Rev. Joseph M. Griffin.
Res., 404 S. Wood, 48616-1399. Tel: 517-845-6894; Fax: 517-845-7787. [CEM]
School—802 Lockwood St., 48616. Keith Valentine, Prin.
Lay Teachers 9; Students 114.

Clare, Clare Co., St. Cecilia, Rev. Joseph Ryan.
Res., 902 N. McEwan St., 48617-1297. Tel: 517-386-7681. [CEM]
School—Walt Smith, Prin. Lay Teachers 6; Students 110.

Coleman, Midland Co., St. Philip Neri, Rev. Todd Arnberg.
Res., 5199 W. Shaffer Rd., P.O. Box M, 48618-0512. Tel: 517-465-1768; Fax: 517-465-6311.
Mission—Edenville, Gladwin Co., St. Anne.

Croswell, Sanilac Co., St. Patrick, Rev. Donald G. Dueweke.
Res., 105 W. Sanborn Ave., 48422-1399. Tel: 810-679-3849; Fax: 810-679-3903. [CEM]
Mission—Peck, Sanilac Co., St. John. [CEM]

Essexville, Bay Co., St. John the Evangelist, Rev. Thomas J. McNamara. In res., Rev. Michael H. Wolf.
Res., 1600 Hudson St., 48732-1377. Tel: 517-892-1893; Fax: 517-894-5558.
School—619 Main St., 48732. Sue Grzegorczyk, Prin.
Lay Teachers 8; Students 74.

Fisherville, Bay Co., St. Anthony, Rev. Msgr. Eugene A. Forbes, J.C.D., V.G., P.A.
Res., 4699 S. 11 Mile Rd., Auburn, 48611-9535. Tel: 517-662-6480; Fax: 517-662-4335. [CEM]
School—Auburn Area Catholic, West Campus, 1492 W. Midland Rd., Auburn, 48611-9560. Tel: 517-662-6581; Fax: 517-662-4335.

Frankenmuth, Saginaw Co., Blessed Trinity, Rev. Frederick J. Kawka.
Res., 958 E. Tuscola Rd., 48734-9770. Tel: 517-652-3259; Fax: 517-652-2206.

Freeland, Saginaw Co., St. Agnes, Rev. Lawrence M. Pashak.
Res., 335 Johnson, 48623-9006. Tel: 517-695-5652; Fax: 517-695-6275.

Gagetown, Tuscola Co., St. Agatha, Rev. Paul W. Bala, Sacramental Min.; Sr. Joan Maher, M.Ss.P., Pastoral Admin.
Res., 4618 South St., Box 139, 48735-0139. Tel: 517-665-9966.

Gladwin, Gladwin Co., Sacred Heart, Rev. Patrick Jankowiak.
Res., 300 N. Silverleaf St., 48624-1697. Tel: 517-426-7154; Fax: 517-426-0896.
School—Sr. Mary Elizabeth Klier, O.S.F., Prin. Bernardine Sisters of Third Order of St. Francis (Farmington, MI) 1; Lay Teachers 5; Students 106.

Harbor Beach, Huron Co., Our Lady of Lake Huron, Rev. Gerald F. Kukla; Sr. Eileen Houlihan, I.H.M., Pastoral Assoc.
Res., 413 S. First St., 48441-1325. Tel: 517-479-3393; Fax: 517-479-3335. [CEM]
School—Mr. Lawrence E. Kish, II, Prin. Lay Teachers 10; Students 235.
Convent—406 S. First St., 48441.

Harrison, Clare Co., St. Athanasius, Rev. Daniel Nowak, O.F.M.
Res., 310 S. Broad St., 48625-0528. Tel: 517-539-6232.

Helena, Huron Co., St. Anthony, Rev. Charles Hammond.
Res., 4190 Parisville Rd., Ruth, 48470-9759. Tel: 517-479-6781; Fax: 517-864-3164. [CEM]

Hemlock, Saginaw Co., St. Mary, Rev. Robert S. Gohm.
Res., 151 St. Mary's Dr., 48626-9614. Tel: 517-642-5606; Fax: 517-642-5240. [CEM]
St. Mary Center—245 St. Mary's Dr., 48626.

Ithaca, Gratiot Co., St. Paul the Apostle, Rev. Julius A. Spleet; Sr. Virginia Scally, S.N.D.deN., Pastoral Admin.
Res., 621 E. Center St., 48847-1596. Tel: 517-875-3654; Fax: 517-875-7027.
Mission—Perrinton, Gratiot Co., St. Martin De Porres.

Kawkawlin, Bay Co., Sacred Heart, Rev. Chester J. Pilarski.
Res., 2510 S. Fraser Rd., 48631-9115. Tel: 517-684-1402; Fax: 517-684-0038.

Kinde, Huron Co., St. Mary-St. Edward, Rev. Mieczyslaw Oniskiewicz; Sr. Judy O'Brien, I.H.M., Pastoral Assoc.
Res., 1709 Moeller Rd., P.O. Box 68, 48445-0068. Tel: 517-874-4744; Fax: 517-874-4010.

Lexington, Sanilac Co., St. Denis, Rev. Donald J. Eppenbrock.
Res., 5366 Main St., P.O. Box 399, 48450-0399. Tel: 810-359-5400; Fax: 810-359-5833. [CEM]

Linwood, Bay Co., St. Anne, Rev. Thomas M. Kowalczyk.
Res., 315 W. Center St., 48634-9813. Tel: 517-697-4443.
School—Tel: 517-697-3100. Sr. Rose Ellen Dzwieleski, O.S.F., Prin.
Bernardine Sisters of Third Order of St. Francis (Farmington, MI) 3; Lay Teachers 8; Students 161.

Maple Grove, Saginaw Co., St. Michael, Rev. Randy J. Kelly.
Res., 17994 Lincoln Rd., New Lothrop, 48460-9600. Tel: 517-845-7011; Fax: 517-845-4729. [CEM]

Marlette, Sanilac Co., St. Elizabeth, Rev. Richard Bokinskie.
Res., 6785 W. Marlette St., 48453-1296. Tel: 517-635-7581; Fax: 517-635-5808.

Mayville, Tuscola Co., St. Joseph, Rev. Richard Bokinskie; Sr. Ruth Adamites, O.P., P.A.
Mailing Address: 315 Ohmer Rd., P.O. Box 283, 48744-0283. Tel: 517-843-6565; Fax: 517-683-2556.

Merrill, Saginaw Co., Sacred Heart, Rev. Craig L. Albrecht.
Res., 419 S. Midland St., 48637-0099. Tel: 517-643-5366; Fax: 517-643-5171. [CEM]

Midland, Midland Co., Assumption Blessed Virgin Mary, Rev. Robert W. Davey.
Res., 3516 Monroe, Rd. 8, 48642. Tel: 517-631-4447; Fax: 517-631-4323.
Blessed Sacrament, Rev. John R. Johnson.
Res., 3109 Swede Ave., 48642-3888. Tel: 517-835-6777; Fax: 517-835-2451.
School—Michael J. Knoff, Prin. Lay Teachers 13; Students 250.
St. Brigid, Rev. James Bessert.
Res., 207 Ashman St., 48640-5185. Tel: 517-835-7121; Fax: 517-835-9141.
School—130 W. Larkin St., 48640-6579. Tel: 517-835-9481; Fax: 517-835-9141. Christine Szatkowski, Prin.
Lay Teachers 18; Students 150.

Mount Pleasant, Isabella Co., Sacred Heart, Revs. Robert H. Byrne; Donald E. Henkes (MEM).
Res., 302 S. Kinney, 48858-2773. Tel: 517-772-1385; Fax: 517-773-9118. [CEM]
School—(Grades PreK-6) 200 S. Franklin St., 48858-2529. Eileen Ball, Prin.
Sisters 1; Lay Teachers 15; Students 284.
High School—Sacred Heart Academy, (Grades 7-12) 316 E. Michigan, 48858-2640. Tel: 517-772-1457. Virginia Chamberlain, Prin.
Priests 1; Sisters 1; Lay Teachers 19; Students 226.
St. Mary University Parish, Rev. Jeffrey Donner.
Res., 1405 S. Washington, 48858-4280. Tel: 517-773-3931; Fax: 517-772-2745.

Munger, Bay Co., St. Norbert, Rev. William J. Gruden.
Res., 126 W. Munger Rd., 48747-9767. Tel: 517-659-2193; Fax: 517-659-3417.

Nine Mile, Bay Co., St. Mary, Rev. Joseph K. Miller.
Res., 739 W. Cody-Estey Rd., Pinconning, 48650-8925. Tel: 517-879-5596; Fax: 517-879-6151. [CEM]
Station—Pinconning, St. Agnes, 216 E. Fifth St., Piconning, 48650.

Oakley, Saginaw Co., St. Michael, Rev. Joseph Griffin; M. Katherine Paul, M.Div., Pastoral Admin.
Res., Box 75, 48649-0075. Tel: 517-845-3545; Fax: 517-845-5499. [CEM]

Palms, Sanilac Co., St. Patrick, Rev. Steven M. Gavit, Sacramental Min.; Sr. Theresa Carlow, S.N.D.deN., Pastoral Admin.
Res., 1801 Palms Rd., 48465. Tel: 810-376-4853; Fax: 517-864-3526.

Parisville, Huron Co., St. Mary, Rev. Charles Hammond.
Res., 4190 Parisville Rd., Ruth, 48470-9759. Tel: 517-864-3523; Fax: 517-864-3164.

Pigeon, Huron Co., St. Francis Borgia, Rev. George J. Serour, Sacramental Min.; Sr. Theresa Fox, O.P., P.A.
Res., 25 Moeller St., Box U, 48755. Tel: 517-453-2151; Fax: 517-453-2156. [CEM]

Pinconning, Bay Co., St. Michael, Rev. Ramon Matuszewski.
Res., 225 Jennings St., 48650-9408. Tel: 517-879-2141; Fax: 517-879-6633.
School—Joan Turmell, Prin. Lay Teachers 9; Students 165.

Pinnebog, Huron Co., St. Felix, Rev. Dennis Kucharczyk, Sacramental Min.; Sr. Mary Schwartz, S.S.J., Pastoral Min.
Res., 3515 Limerick, Kinde, 48445-9723. Tel: 517-874-5833. [CEM]

Port Austin, Huron Co., St. Michael, Rev. Michael J. Bell.
Res., 8637 Garfield, P.O. Box 298, 48467-0298. Tel: 517-738-7521; Fax: 517-738-5886. [CEM]
Parish Center—8661 Independence Ave., P.O. Box 350, 48467.

Port Sanilac, Sanilac Co., St. Mary, Rev. Ronald J. Dombrowski.
Res., 7066 W. Main St., P.O. Box 467, 48469-0467. Tel: 810-622-9904; Fax: 810-622-7953. [CEM]
Mission—Forestville, Sanilac Co., St. John Chrysostom.

Rapson, Huron Co., St. Joseph, Rev. John Weis.
Res., 3455 Rapson Rd., Rte. 3, Bad Axe, 48413-9149. Tel: 517-269-8084. [CEM]
Mission—Smiths Corners, Huron Co., Holy Trinity. [CEM]

Reese, Tuscola Co., St. Elizabeth, Rev. William J. Gruden; Sr. Tereska Wozniak, O.P., Pastoral Assoc.
Res., 12835 E. Washington, 48757-9712. Tel: 517-868-4081; Fax: 517-868-9785. [CEM]
School—Jerry Miller, Prin. Lay Teachers 6; Students 145.

Rosebush, Isabella Co., St. Henry, Sr. Mary Ellen McDonald, O.P., Pastoral Admin.; Rev. Jeffrey Donnar, Sacramental Min.
Res., 4079 E. Vernon Rd., 48878-0067. Tel: 517-433-2229; Fax: 517-433-2229. [CEM]
School—Sr. Mary Ellen McDonald, O.P., Prin. Lay Teachers 5; Students 69.
Mission—Leaton, Isabella Co., St. Charles.

Ruth, Huron Co., SS. Peter and Paul, Rev. Steven W. Gavit.
Res., 7115 Atwater Dr., P.O. Box 55, 48470-0055. Tel: 517-864-3650; Fax: 517-864-8600. [CEM]
School—Lay Teachers 8; Students 122.

Ryan, Midland Co., St. Patrick, Sr. Janet Brown, O.P., Pastoral Admin.; Rev. Craig L. Albrecht, Sacramental Min.
Res., 4708 N. Meridian Rd., Rte. 2, Merrill, 48637-9546. Tel: 517-643-5652; Fax: 517-643-5652, Ext. 111. [CEM]

St. Charles, Saginaw Co., Immaculate Conception, Rev. Joseph J. Kearns.
Res., 708 Sanderson St., 48655-1895. Tel: 517-865-9460. [CEM]
School—H. Ross Klemko, Prin. Lay Teachers 6; Students 53.
Convent—712 Sanderson St., 48655. Tel: 517-865-6166.

St. Louis, Gratiot Co., St. Joseph, Rev. John E. Hammer.
Office: 605 S. Franklin, 48880-1747. Tel: 517-681-5080; Fax: 517-681-2887.

Sandusky, Sanilac Co., St. Joseph, Rev. R. Keith LeFleur.
Res., 511 N. Sandusky Rd., P.O. Box 249, 48471-0249. Tel: 810-648-4293; Fax: 810-648-4293.

Sanford, Midland Co., St. Agnes, Rev. Francis Voris, O.F.M.Cap.
Res., 2500 W. River Rd., 48657-9497. Tel: 517-687-5657; Fax: 517-687-2450.

Sebewaing, Huron Co., Holy Family, Rev. George J. Serour.
Res., 8370 Unionville Rd., 48759-9553. Tel: 517-883-2746; Fax: 517-883-3117. [CEM]

Shepherd, Isabella Co., St. Vincent De Paul, Rev. Robert J. Howe.
Res., 168 Wright, 48883-9079. Tel: 517-828-5720; Fax: 517-828-4652. [CEM]
School—Michael C. Smith, Prin. Lay Teachers 7; Students 70.
Missions—Winn, Isabella Co., St. Leo. [CEM]
Irishtown, Gratiot Co., St. Patrick.

Shields, Saginaw Co., Holy Spirit, Revs. David L. Parsch; John Mancini, O.S.F.S.
Res., 1035 N. River Rd., Saginaw, 48609-6864. Tel: 517-781-2457; Fax: 517-781-5518.

Standish, Arenac Co., Resurrection of the Lord, Rev. James M. Fitzpatrick.
Res., 423 Cedar, Box 306, 48658-0306. Tel: 517-846-9565; Fax: 517-846-9566. [CEM]

Ubly, Huron Co., St. Columbkille, Rev. Thomas J. Fleming.
Res., 4470 Washington St., 48475. Tel: 517-658-8824; Fax: 517-658-2088. [CEM]
St. John the Evangelist, Rev. Thomas J. Fleming.
Res., 4470 Washington St., 48475. Tel: 517-658-8824; Fax: 517-658-2088. [CEM]

Vassar, Tuscola Co., St. Frances Xavier Cabrini, Rev. John Ederer.
Res., 165 W. Maple St., 48768-1203. Tel: 517-823-2911; Fax: 517-823-2999.
Mission—Millington, Tuscola Co., St. Bernard. Closed.

Wilmot, Tuscola Co., St. Michael, Rev. Paul W. Bala, Sacramental Min.; Sr. Ruth Adamites, O.P., Pastoral Admin.
Res., 1951 Kingston Rd., Deford, 48729. Tel: 517-683-2475; Fax: 517-683-2556. [CEM]

Zilwaukee, Saginaw Co., St. Matthew, Rev. Richard T. Szafranski.
Res., 511 W. Cornell, Saginaw, 48604-1311. Tel: 517-755-7336; Fax: 517-755-4228.

Chaplains of Public Institutions

BAY CITY. *Bay Medical Center and Bay Osteopathic Hospital* 1201 S. Erie, 48706. Sr. Beth Pero, S.S.J.

On Duty Outside the Diocese:
Reverend Fathers—
Friske, Joseph P., Damaschkestr. 20, 8000 Munchen 82, Germany
Loos, Frederick C., Ave. Naucalpan #84, Col. La Canada, Naucalpan, Mexico, C.P. 53570
Mullet, John, Palm Beach, FL 33480

Retired:
Reverend Monsignors—
Murdick, Olin J.
Murray, Francis
Reverend Fathers—
Boucher, Edward F.
Bur, Stanislaus
Eickholt, Henry C.
Favara, Joseph F.
Frego, Max
Friske, Joseph P.
Ganley, Charles
Greiner, Lawrence
Hoogterp, John P.
Janowicz, Barney J.
Klimas, George H.
Kryszak, Marian
LaMarre, Theodore E.
Maher, Michael L.
McEachin, Cornelius
Navarre, Robert G.
Rabideau, Richard L.
Roach, Joseph W., S.A.G.
Rudy, Noel T.
Schabel, Joseph A.
Sierminski, Vernon
Sikorski, Harold R.
Skornia, Bernard L.
Spleet, Julius A.
Surman, Stanley
Thome, John J.
Van Mullekom, Richard
Welna, Floyd
Welsmiller, Francis F.
Wolf, Michael H.
Woloszyk, Ignatius J.

Permanent Deacons:
Alex, Frank, St. Anne, Edenville; & St. Philip Neri, Coleman
Arnold, Michael, St. Valentine Church, Beaver
Belanger, Stanley, (Retired)
Cremin, John J., St. Mary, Alma
DeNeut, Gerard H., St. Matthew, Zilwaukee
Emmeot, Dale, Blessed Sacrament Church, Midland
Fussman, Lawrence, Sacred Heart Church, Mount Pleasant
Hudson, Francis W., St. Brigid, Midland
Jankowiak, Michael, Blessed Sacrament, Midland
Kasprzyk, David, On Duty Outside the Diocese
Kebblish, Edward
Keller, George, Bay County Jail Ministry
Kuhr, Lambert, Jr., (Retired), Out of the Diocese
Masserang, Lawrence, Blessed Trinity, Frankenmuth
Middleton, Allan, St. Cecilia, Clare
Moeggenberg, John, On Duty Outside the Diocese
Stilwell, Lee, St. Norbert, Munger
Wilberding, John, St. Vincent dePaul, Shepherd
Winkler, Frank, (Retired)

INSTITUTIONS LOCATED IN THE DIOCESE

[A] HIGH SCHOOLS, INTER-PAROCHIAL

SAGINAW. *Nouvel Catholic Central High School*, 2555 Wieneke Rd., 48603. Charles C. Sorentino, Prin.; John Cuthbertson, Asst. Prin.; Kathy Myles, Campus Min. Lay Teachers 29; Students 495.

BAY CITY. *All Saints Central High School*, 217 S. Monroe St., 48708. Tel: 517-892-2533; Fax: 517-892-7188.
E-mail: allsaints@concentric.net
Web site: www.concentric.net/~Aschs
Thomas Grange, Prin. Sisters 1; Lay Teachers 12; Students 162.

[B] MIDDLE SCHOOLS

BAY CITY. *Holy Family Middle School*, 1503 Kosciuszko Ave., Ste. 200, 48708. Tel: 517-892-8332. Barbara Rakowski, Prin.; Sr. Irene Chrusciel, O.P., Pastoral Counselor. Sisters 1; Lay Teachers 10; Students 181.

[C] ELEMENTARY SCHOOLS, PRIVATE

AUBURN. *Auburn Area Catholic Schools*, East Campus: 114 Midland Rd., 48611. Tel: 517-662-6431. West Campus: 1492 W. Midland Rd., 48611. Tel: 517-662-6581. Sr. Anne Marie La Hai, R.S.N., Prin. Sisters 1; Lay Teachers 12; Students 195.

[D] CHILDREN'S HOMES

SAGINAW. *St. Vincent Home-Boysville of Michigan, Inc.*, 925 N. River Rd., 48609. Tel: 517-781-2780; Fax: 517-781-5422
For a complete listing, refer to the Special Care Facilities section.

[E] GENERAL HOSPITALS

SAGINAW. *St. Mary's Medical Center of Saginaw, Inc.*, 800 S. Washington, 48601-2594
For a complete listing, refer to the Hospitals section.

[F] HOMES FOR AGED

SAGINAW. *St. Francis Nursing Home*, 915 N. River Rd., 48609 Fax: 517-781-3791
For a complete listing, refer to the Special Care Facilities section.

[G] MONASTERIES AND RESIDENCES OF PRIESTS AND BROTHERS

SAGINAW. *Queen of Angels Friary and Retreat House*, 3400 S. Washington Rd., P.O. Box 2026, 48605. Tel: 517-755-2149; Fax: 517-755-1640.
Web site: www.rc.net/saginaw/retreat
Capuchin Friars of the Province of St. Joseph (Detroit) of the Capuchin Order of Friars Minor Capuchin.
Retreat Team: Revs. Thomas Zelinski, O.F.M.Cap., Dir.; Francis Voris, O.F.M.Cap.; Malcolm Maloney, O.F.M.Cap. In res. Rev. Vernon Wagner, O.F.M.Cap. Priests 5.

[H] CONVENTS AND RESIDENCES FOR SISTERS

SAGINAW. *Franciscan Poor Clare Nuns, O.S.C.*, 4875 Shattuck Rd., 48603-2962. Tel: 517-797-0593; Fax: 517-797-0527.
E-mail: srsclare@saginaw.cnchost.com
Web site: www.rc.net/saginaw/srsclare
Sr. Dianne Doughty, O.S.C., Supr./Abbess. Sisters 4.
Motherhouse and Novitiate of the Mission Sisters of the Holy Spirit, 1030 N. River Rd., 48609. Tel: 517-781-0934. Sr. Margo Tafoya, M.S.Sp., Community Coord. Sisters 12.

ALMA. *Motherhouse and Novitiate of the Religious Sisters of Mercy of Alma, Michigan*, 1835 Michigan Ave., 48801. Tel: 517-463-6035; Fax: 517-463-5811. Mothers Mary Quentin Sheridan, R.S.M.; Mary McGreevy, R.S.M., Vicar. Sisters 14.

[I] CATHOLIC EDUCATION ENDOWMENT FUNDS

SAGINAW. *Nouvel Catholic Central Educational Foundation Catholic School Foundation Endowment Fund*, 2555 Wieneke Rd., 48603-2897. Tel: 517-791-4330.
Roman Catholic Diocese of Saginaw Catholic School Foundation, 5800 Weiss St., 48603-2799. Tel: 517-797-6679. Annette M. O'Brien, Contact Person.
St. Helen Catholic School Foundation Endowment Fund, 2415 N. Charles St., 48602-5009. Tel: 517-792-7781.
St. Josaphat Catholic School Foundation Endowment Fund, 479 Shattuck St., 48604-2390. Tel: 517-754-9931.
St. Stephen Catholic School Foundation Endowment Fund, 1300 Malzahn St., 48602. Tel: 517-793-2811.
St. Thomas Aquinas Catholic School Foundation Endowment Fund, 2136 Berberovich St., 48603-3699. Tel: 517-792-2361.
SS. Peter and Paul Catholic School Foundation Endowment Fund, 4735 W. Michigan Ave., 48603-6370. Tel: 517-799-9006.

AUBURN. *Auburn Area Catholic Schools Catholic School Foundation Endowment Fund*, 1492 W. Midland Rd., 48611-9560. Tel: 517-662-6581.

BAY CITY. *All Saints Central High Catholic School Foundation Endowment Fund*, 217 S. Monroe St., 48708-7298. Tel: 517-892-2533.
Bay Catholic Educational Foundation Catholic School Foundation Endownment Fund, 2306 S. Monroe St., 48708-8786. Tel: 517-894-8777.
Holy Family Middle School Catholic School Foundation Endowment Fund, 1503 Kosciuszko Ave., Ste. 200, 48708-8027. Tel: 517-892-8332.
Holy Trinity Catholic School Foundation Endowment Fund, 1004 S. Wenona, 48706-5096. Tel: 517-892-3018.
St. Hyacinth Catholic School Foundation Endowment Fund, 2307 S. Monroe St., 48708-8786. Tel: 517-893-9503.
St. James Catholic School Foundation Endowment Fund, 715 14th St., 48708-7288. Tel: 517-892-4371.
St. Stanislaus Catholic School Foundation Endowment Fund, 900 S. Grant St., 48708-7393. Tel: 517-893-5085.
Visitation Academy/Sister Bernita Catholic School Foundation Endowment Fund, 1110 State St., 48706-3699. Tel: 517-684-3543.

BEAL CITY. *St. Joseph the Worker Catholic School Foundation Endowment Fund*, 2091 N. Winn Rd., Mt. Pleasant, 48858-9730. Tel: 517-644-3970.

CLARE. *St. Cecilia Catholic School Foundation Endowment Fund*, 106 E. Wheaton St., 48617-1398. Tel: 517-386-9862.

ESSEXVILLE. *St. John the Evangelist Catholic School Foundation Endowment Fund*, 619 Main St., 48732-1398. Tel: 517-892-0363.

GLADWIN. *Sacred Heart Catholic School Foundation Endowment Fund*, 330 N. Silverleaf St., 48624-1626. Tel: 517-426-8574.

HARBOR BEACH. *Our Lady of Lake Huron Catholic School Foundation Endowment Fund*, 222 Court St., 48441-1361. Tel: 517-479-3427.

KAWKAWLIN. *St. Valentine Catholic School Foundation Endowment Fund*, 1010 S. 9 Mile Rd., 517-662-6966.

LINWOOD. *St. Anne Catholic School Foundation Endowment Fund*, P.O. Box 548, 48634-0548. Tel: 517-697-3100.

MIDLAND. *Blessed Sacrament Catholic School Foundation Endowment Fund*, 3109 Swede Ave., 48642-3888. Tel: 517-832-8283.
The James Cardinal Hickey Educational Endowment Fund for St. Brigid Catholic School, 130 W. Larkin St., 48640-6579. Tel: 517-835-9481. Rev. James W. Bessert, Pastor.

PINCONNING. *St. Michael Catholic School Foundation Endowment Fund*, 310 E. 2nd St., 48650-9409. Tel: 517-879-3063.

REESE. *St. Elizabeth Catholic School Foundation Endowment Fund*, P.O. Box 409, 48757-9547. Tel: 517-868-4108.

ROSEBUSH. *St. Henry Catholic School Foundation Endowment Fund*, 4039 E. Vernon Rd., 48878-9774. Tel: 517-433-5469.

RUTH. *SS. Peter & Paul Catholic School Foundation Endowment Fund*, 7135 E. Atwater Rd., 48470-9777. Tel: 517-864-3649.

ST. CHARLES. *Immaculate Conception Catholic School Endowment Fund*, 712 Sanderson St., 48655-1898. Tel: 517-865-6181. H. Ross Klemko, Prin.

SHEPHERD. *St. Vincent de Paul Catholic School Foundation Endowment Fund*, 205 E. Maple St., 48883-9007. Tel: 517-828-5970.

[J] MISCELLANEOUS LISTINGS

SAGINAW. *Emmaus House*, 733 S. 14th St., 48601. Tel: 517-755-7538; Fax: 517-755-7538. Sr. Marietta Fritz, S.N.D.deN., Dir.
Jail Ministry, 1325 Cherry St., 48601. Tel: 517-755-3305. Sr. Mary Ruth Rault, D.C., Chap.
Holy Spirit Sisters Charitable Trust, 1030 N. River Rd., 48609. Sr. Margo Tafoya, M.S.Sp., Pres.

St. Mary's Medical Center of Saginaw, Inc., 800 S. Washington Ave., 48601.
Seton Health Corporation of East Central Michigan, 800 S. Washington Ave., 48601. Tel: 517-776-8176; Fax: 517-776-1704.
E-mail: Hratzer@saintmarys-saginaw.org
Web site: www.saintmarys-saginaw.org
Fred Fraizer, Pres. & CEO.

ALMA. *Religious Sisters of Mercy of Alma Corporation*, 1835 Michigan Ave., 48801. Tel: 517-463-6035. Mothers Mary Quentin Sheridan, R.S.M., Pres.; Mary McGreevy, R.S.M., Vice Pres.
Sacred Heart Mercy Health Care Center, 7320 N. Alger Rd., 48801. Tel: 517-463-3451; 463-8464. Sr. Mary Judith O'Brien, R.S.M.

BAY CITY. *Society of St. Vincent de Paul*, 523 Michigan Ave., 48708. Mr. Thomas Lefevre, Pres.
Member Conferences: Bay City-Holy Trinity, St. Hyacinth, St. James, St. Joseph's, St. Mary, St. Stanislaus, Visitation, St. Vincent de Paul; Essexville-St. John.

RELIGIOUS INSTITUTES OF MEN REPRESENTED IN THE DIOCESE

For further details refer to the corresponding bracketed number in the Religious Institutes of Men or Women section.

[0470]—*The Capuchin Friars.* (St. Joseph Prov.).—O.F.M.Cap.
[0480]—*Conventual Franciscans.*—O.F.M.
[0520]—*Franciscan Friars.* (Assumption Prov.).—O.F.M.
[0920]—*Oblates of St. Francis De Sales.*—O.S.F.S.

RELIGIOUS INSTITUTES OF WOMEN REPRESENTED IN THE DIOCESE

[1810]—*Bernadine Sisters of Third Order of St. Francis.*—O.S.F.
[0760]—*Daughters of Charity of St. Vincent de Paul.* (Evansville).—D.C.
[1070-03]—*Dominican Sisters.* (Sinsinawa, WI).—O.P.
[1070-09]—*Dominican Sisters.* (Racine, WI).—O.P.
[1070-13]—*Dominican Sisters.* (Adrian, MI).—O.P.
[1070-14]—*Dominican Sisters.* (Grand Rapids).—O.P.
[1070-26]—*Dominican Sisters.* (Oxford, MI).—O.P.
[1170]—*Felician Sisters.*—C.S.S.F.
[]—*Franciscan Poor Clare Nuns.*—O.S.C.
[2740]—*Mission Sisters of the Holy Spirit.*—M.S.Sp.
[3130]—*Our Lady of Victory Missionary Sisters.* (Huntington, IN).—O.L.V.M.
[3560]—*Servants of Jesus.*—S.J.
[0440]—*Sisters of Charity of Cincinnati, Ohio.*—S.C.
[2519]—*Sisters of Mercy of Alma, Michigan.*—R.S.M.
[2575]—*Sisters of Mercy of the Americas.* (Detroit, MI).—R.S.M.
[3000]—*Sisters of Notre Dame de Namur.* (Boston, MA; Cincinnati, OH).—S.N.D.deN.
[1570]—*Sisters of St. Francis of the Holy Family.* (Dubuque, IA).—O.S.F.
[3830-11]—*Sisters of St. Joseph.* (Nazareth, MI).—S.S.J.
[1030]—*Sisters of the Divine Savior.* (Milwaukee, WI).—S.D.S.
[1990]—*Sisters of the Holy Name of Jesus and Mary.* (Spokane, WA).—S.N.J.M.
[3260]—*Sisters of the Precious Blood (Dayton, Ohio).*—C.PP.S.
[2150]—*Sisters, Servants of the Immaculate Heart of Mary.* (Monroe).—I.H.M.

DIOCESAN CEMETERIES

SAGINAW. *St. Andrew's, Mt. Olivet & Calvary.*
BAY CITY. *St. Patrick's, Calvary & St. Stanislaus.*
LINWOOD. *St. Anne.*
MIDLAND. *Calvary.*

NECROLOGY

† Bauer, Joseph O., (Retired). —Died April 23, 2000.
† Hart, Harry J., (Retired). —Died Sept. 16, 1999.
† Howard, Thomas C., (Retired). —Died Oct. 14, 1999.
† Trombley, Jerome E., (Retired). —Died June 26, 2000.

Diocese of St. Augustine

(Dioecesis Sancti Augustini)

(Vacant See)

Catholic Center: P.O. Box 24000, Jacksonville, FL, 32241-4000. Tel.: 904-262-3200; Fax: 904-262-0698.

Web site address: staugustine.ml.org/diocese

E-mail address: krb9953@aol.com

Square Miles 11,032.

Florida, east of the Apalachicola River, was erected by Pope Pius IX into a Vicariate-Apostolic in the year 1857, and in 1870 into the Diocese of St. Augustine.

Comprises all of the northeastern Counties of the State of Florida including Alachua, Baker, Bradford, Clay, Columbia, Dixie, Duval, Flagler, Gilchrist, Hamilton, Lafayette, Levy, Nassau, Putnam, St. Johns, Suwannee and Union Counties.

For legal titles of parishes and diocesan institutions, consult the Catholic Center.

STATISTICAL OVERVIEW

Personnel	
Retired Bishop	1
Priests: Diocesan Active in Diocese	70
Priests: Active Outside Diocese	9
Priests: Retired, Sick or Absent	12
Number of Diocesan Priests	91
Religious Priests in Diocese	28
Extern Priests in Diocese	18
Ordinations:	
Diocesan Priests	1
Permanent Deacons in Diocese	26
Total Brothers	2
Total Sisters	111
Parishes	
Parishes	51
With Resident Pastor:	
Resident Diocesan Priests	47
Resident Religious Priests	4
Missions	8
Welfare	
Catholic Hospitals	1
Total Assisted	229,596
Homes for the Aged	2
Total Assisted	43,548
Special Centers for Social Services	6
Total Assisted	60,000
Residential Care of Disabled	4
Total Assisted	21
Other Institutions	5
Total Assisted	275
Educational	
Diocesan Students in Other Seminaries	23
Total Seminarians	23
High Schools, Diocesan and Parish	2
Total Students	2,012
Elementary Schools, Diocesan and Parish	24
Total Students	7,978
Non-residential Schools for the Disabled	1
Total Students	115
Catechesis/Religious Education:	
High School Students	8,282
Elementary Students	1,501
Total Students Under Catholic Instruction	19,911
Teachers in the Diocese:	
Priests	2
Sisters	19
Lay Teachers	540
Vital Statistics	
Receptions into the Church:	
Infant Baptism Totals	2,242
Adult Baptism Totals	415
Received into Full Communion	660
First Communions	2,329
Confirmations	1,967
Marriages:	
Catholic	417
Interfaith	353
Total Marriages	770
Deaths	1,035
Total Catholic Population	142,886
Total Population	1,598,247

Former Bishops—Rt. Rev. AUGUSTIN VEROT, S.S., D.D., cons. April 25, 1858; Vicar-Apostolic of Florida; translated to the See of Savannah in July, 1861; appt. Bishop of St. Augustine March, 1870; died June 10, 1876.—Rt. Rev. JOHN MOORE, D.D., cons. May 13, 1877; died July 30, 1901.—Rt. Rev. WILLIAM JOHN KENNY, D.D., ord. Jan. 15, 1879; cons. May 18, 1902; died Oct. 23, 1913.—Rt. Rev. M. J. CURLEY, D.D., cons. June 30, 1914; promoted to See of Baltimore Aug. 10, 1921; died May 16, 1947.—Most Rev. PATRICK BARRY, D.D., ord. June 9, 1895; appt. Feb. 22, 1922; cons. May 3, 1922; died Aug. 13, 1940.—Most Rev. JOSEPH P. HURLEY, D.D., ord. May 25, 1919; appt. Aug. 16, 1940; cons. Oct. 6, 1940 Received Personal title of Archbishop Aug. 18, 1950; died Oct. 30, 1967.—Most Rev. PAUL F. TANNER, D.D., ord. May 30, 1931; appt. Titular Bishop of Lamasba, Oct. 18, 1965; appt. Bishop of Saint Augustine, Feb. 21, 1968; retired April 21, 1979 Remained as Administrator to Dec. 4, 1979; died July 29, 1994.

Catholic Center—11625 Old St. Augustine Rd., Jacksonville, 32258., Mailing Address: P.O. Box 24000, Jacksonville, 32241-4000. Office Hours: Mon.-Fri. 9-4:30. Tel: 904-262-3200; Fax: 904-262-0698.

Vicar General and Moderator of Curia—Rev. Msgr. VINCENT J. HAUT, V.G., M.S.W.

Chancellor—Rev. KEITH R. BRENNAN, J.C.D.

Secretary to the Bishop—NANCY MADDEN.

Secretary to the Chancellor—JUDY T. PINSON.

Fiscal Office—IRENE G. PULEO, Fiscal Mgr.

Diocesan Tribunal—P.O. Box 24000, Jacksonville, 32241-4000. Tel: 904-262-3200.

Judicial Vicar—Rev. RALPH L. BESENDORFER, J.C.D.

Associate Judges—Rev. Msgr. DANIEL B. LOGAN; Rev. PETER H. COLASURDO, J.C.L.

Defenders of the Bond—Revs. JAMES R. BODDIE, JR.; KEITH R. BRENNAN, J.C.D.

Advocates—Revs. GREGORY J. FAY; DONAL SULLIVAN.

Promoter of Justice—Rev. Msgr. PATRICK M. MADDEN, S.T.L.; VERONICA DOSKOCIL, Administrative Asst. MARY C. SLEEPER, Sec.

Diocesan Consultors—Rev. Msgr. JOHN J. LENIHAN, M.S.W.; Rev. Msgr. EUGENE C. KOHLS, P.A., J.C.D.; Rev. Msgr. VINCENT HAUT, V.G., M.S.W.; Revs. JAMES R. BODDIE, JR.; DANIEL CODY; ROLAND M. JULIEN, V.F.; MICHAEL J. LARKIN.

Diocesan Pastoral Council—EDWARD TRENT, Chm., *Diocese of St. Augustine Catholic Center, P.O. Box 24000, Jacksonville, 32241-4000.* Tel: 904-262-3200; Fax: 904-262-0698.

Presbyteral Council—Revs. TIMOTHY LINDENFELSER, Chm. MOISES PALAROAN, Vice Chm. KEITH R. BRENNAN, J.C.D., Chancellor & Treas. WILLIAM HOCHHEIM, Sec.; Rev. Msgr. VINCENT J. HAUT, V.G., M.S.W.; Revs. EDWARD MURPHY; JOSEPH MEEHAN; WILLIAM A. KELLY, V.F.; GLENN PARKER, C.SS.R.; ROLAND M. JULIEN, V.F.; MARK WATERS.

Deans—Rev. DONAL SULLIVAN, V.F., St. Augustine Deanery; Rev. ROLAND M. JULIEN, V.F., Gainesville Deanery; Rev. THOMAS SULLIVAN, V.F., North Jacksonville Deanery; Rev. WILLIAM A. KELLY, V.F., South Jacksonville Deanery.

Building Commission—Most Rev. JOHN J. SNYDER, Chm.; Rev. Msgr. VINCENT J. HAUT, V.G., M.S.W., Vice Chm.; Rev. KEITH R. BRENNAN, J.C.D., Chancellor; Rev. Msgr. DANIEL B. LOGAN; Rev. THOMAS CODY; Mr. ARTHUR TODD; Revs. MICHAEL J. LARKIN; GREGORY J. FAY.

Catholic Foundation of Diocese of St. Augustine—Most Rev. JOHN J. SNYDER; Rev. Msgr. VINCENT J. HAUT, V.G., M.S.W.; Rev. KEITH R. BRENNAN, J.C.D., Chancellor; Dr. GASTON ACOSTA-RUA; ROLF ENGMANN; PATRICK CUSICK; KAY ZAMBETTI; MARJORIE MORALES; JOHN ANDERSON; FRANCIS SCHOLTZ; ANNE CONNOLLY; S. P. BRAUD, III; JACK DEMETREE; CAROL SHIRCLIFF; ERNEST P. BONO; DIANNE T. RICE; DENIS PLUMB; IRENE G. PULEO, Fiscal Mgr., *P.O. Box 24000, Jacksonville, 32241-4000.* Tel: 904-262-3200.

Finance Committee—Rev. Msgr. VINCENT J. HAUT, V.G., M.S.W.; Revs. KEITH R. BRENNAN, J.C.D.; WILLIAM A. KELLY; ROBERT MCDERMOTT; Dr. GASTON ACOSTA-RUA; MARIA ALLEN; ROBERT A. DEVEREUX; NATHANIEL HERRING, JR.; NEIL CRONIN; CLYDE E. LOWER; MARY V. SIEREDZINSKI; IRENE G. PULEO, Fiscal Mgr. FRANCIS N. SCHOLTZ, *P.O. Box 24000, Jacksonville, 32241-4000.* Tel: 904-262-3200.

Insurance Committee, Diocesan—Rev. KEITH R. BRENNAN, J.C.D.; Rev. Msgr. VINCENT J. HAUT, V.G., M.S.W.; Rev. MICHAEL R. HOULE; PATRICIA A. TIERNEY; WILLIAM J. TIERNEY; IRENE G. PULEO; JANET P. MORTON; SANDRA WARD; Sr. MAUREEN KELLEY, O.P., *P.O. Box 24000, Jacksonville, 32241-4000.* Tel: 904-262-3200.

Stewardship Council, Diocesan—Most Rev. JOHN J. SNYDER; Revs. PAT ECCLESTON; JOSEPH FINLAY; ROBERT MCDERMOTT; JOSEPH MEEHAN; ROBERT ARMSTRONG; TRESSIE BRUMFIELD; Sr. ENDA EGAN, R.S.M.; NANCY J. KEARNEY; JOHN MILANI; DENIS M. PLUMB; FRANCIS SCHOLTZ; CHRIS STENFTENAGEL; MARGARET GAYLORD; PAT THOMAS; GERALD WEEDON, *P.O. Box 24000, Jacksonville, 32241-4000.* Tel: 904-262-3200.

Diocesan Offices and Directors

Alcohol and Other Drug Abuse Commission—Co-Chairmen: MARIE WEBER; JAMES MCDADE, *P.O. Box 24000, Jacksonville, 32241-4000.* Tel: 904-262-3200.

Apostleship of the Sea—Deacon DALE WAMSTAD, O.F.M., *Providence Center, 134 E. Church St., Jacksonville, 32202-3130.* Tel: 904-356-3104.

Archives of Diocese—Vacant, *P.O. Box 24000, Jacksonville, 32241-4000.* Tel: 904-262-3200.

Bioethics Commission—T. JAMES GALLAGHER, M.D., Chm., *P.O. Box 24000, Jacksonville, 32241-4000.* Tel: 904-262-3200.

African and Native American Ministries—Rev. JAMES R. BODDIE, JR., Vicar of the Black Apostolate; ELLA SIMMONS, Dir., *P.O. Box 24000, Jacksonville, 32241-4000.* Tel: 904-262-3200.

Campaign for Human Development—Rev. EDWARD K. ROONEY, Dir., *1606 Blanding Blvd., Middleburg, 32068.* Tel: 904-282-0439.

Campus Ministry—Mr. PETER BLAY, Dir. PETER W. MORGAN, Campus Min., *Jacksonville University, Jacksonville, 32211.* Tel: 904-744-3950, Ext. 2258; 646-2638.

Christian Formation—Sr. LUCILLE CLYNES, D.W, Dir., *P.O. Box 24000, Jacksonville, 32241-4000.* Tel: 904-262-3200.

Catholic Burse Endowment Fund, Inc.—(Education of Priests), *P.O. Box 24000, Jacksonville, 32241-4000.* Tel: 904-262-3200.

Catholic Charities Bureau, Inc.—WILLIAM J. TIERNEY, Exec. Dir., *P.O. Box 24000, Jacksonville, 32241-4000.* Tel: 904-262-3200. See Separate Listing for more details.

Catholic Relief Services—WILLIAM J. TIERNEY, Dir., *P.O. Box 24000, Jacksonville, 32241-4000.* Tel: 904-262-3200.

Catholic Women, Council of—Rev. LUKE MCLOUGHLIN, Spiritual Moderator, *St. Matthew Church, 1773 Blanding Blvd., Jacksonville, 32210.* Tel: 904-388-8698.

Charismatic Renewal—Rev. Msgr. HAROLD F. JORDAN, Diocesan Coord., *Mission of Nombre de Dios, 30 Ocean Ave., St. Augustine, 32084.* Tel: 904-824-3045.

Civil Institutions—Rev. JOSE MANIYANGAT, M.A., *St. Mary Parish, P.O. Box 1120, Macclenny, 32063.* Tel: 904-259-6414.

Communications Commission—ART MARSHALL, Chm., *P.O. Box 24000, Jacksonville, 32241-4000.* Tel: 904-262-3200.

Communications, Office of—KATHLEEN BAGG-MORGAN, Dir., *P.O. Box 24000, Jacksonville, 32241-4000.* Tel: 904-262-3200.

Continuing Education for Priests—Rev. Msgr. R. JOSEPH JAMES, Dir., *9401 Staples Mill Dr., Jacksonville, 32244.* Tel: 904-777-3168.

Cursillos de Cristiandad—Rev. Msgr. R. JOSEPH JAMES, Spiritual Dir., *Mary Queen of Heaven, 9401 Staples Mill Dr., Jacksonville, 32244.* Tel: 904-777-3168. Rev. TIMOTHY R. LOZIER, Asst. Spiritual Dir., *St. Augustine Parish, P.O. Box 13888, Gainesville, 32604.* Tel: 904-372-3533. Deacon HAROLD BRODEUR, Asst. Spiritual Dir., *P.O. Drawer 330005, Atlantic Beach, 32233.* Tel: 904-246-6014.

Disabilities, Ministry of Persons with—PATRICK KENNEDY, Dir., *Providence Center, 134 E. Church St., Jacksonville, 32202-3130.* Tel: 904-356-0810; Fax: 904-358-7302.

Ecumenism—Dr. GLENN KUHNEL, Chm., *134 E. Church St., Jacksonville, 32202-3130.* Tel: 904-359-0068.

Educational Services—PATRICIA A. TIERNEY, M.S.Ed., Supt. Schools, *P.O. Box 24000, Jacksonville, 32241-4000.* Tel: 904-262-3200.

The Guardian of Dreams—Mr. JIM SELZER, Exec. Dir., *Providence Center, 134 E. Church St., Jacksonville, 32202-3130.* Tel: 904-354-4788; Fax: 904-358-7302.

Family Life, Diocesan Center for—Mr. JOSEPH C. PAYNE, Dir.; Rev. DANIEL CODY, Consultant, *P.O. Box 24000, Jacksonville, 32241-4000.* Tel: 904-262-3200. Regional Office: St. Vincent's Health System. Tel: 904-308-7474.

Farmworker Services Program—Mrs. CHIQUI MALDONADO, Dir., *40 Sanford St., St. Augustine, 32084.* Tel: 904-829-6300.

Florida Catholic Conference—D. MICHAEL MCCARRON, Ph.D., Exec. Dir., *890 Tallahassee Bank Bldg., P.O. Box 1638, Tallahassee, 32302-1638.* Tel: 850-222-3803.

Health Care Task Force—WILLIAM J. TIERNEY, Chm., *P.O. Box 24000, Jacksonville, 32241-4000.* Tel: 904-262-3200.

Hispanic Ministry—Rev. LUIS FLOREZ, Dir.; Ms. ALBA OROZCO, Coord., *P.O. Box 53257, Jacksonville, 32201.* Tel: 904-262-3200; 353-3243.

Holy Childhood Association, The—Rev. BRIAN EBURN, Dir., *P.O. Box 908, Crescent City, 32112.* Tel: 904-698-2055.

Holy Name Societies—Rev. Msgr. PATRICK M. MADDEN, S.T.L., Spiritual Dir., *Sacred Heart Rectory, 5752 Blanding Blvd., Jacksonville, 32244.* Tel: 904-771-2152.

Investment Committee—Rev. Msgr. VINCENT J. HAUT, M.S.W., V.G.; Rev. KEITH R. BRENNAN, J.C.D., Chancellor; IRENE G. PULEO, Fiscal Mgr. THOMAS TIERNEY; LOUIS V. WALSH; ROBERT A. DEVEREAUX; CLYDE LOWER.

Justice and Peace Commission—ELIZABETH O'BRIEN, Chm., *Providence Center, 134 E. Church St., Jacksonville, 32202-3130.* Tel: 904-358-7410; 7409; Fax: 904-358-7302.

Justice and Reconciliation, Ministry for—Sr. DOROTHEA MURPHY, R.S.M., Dir. Advocacy Office, *1717 N.E. 9th, Suite 123, Gainesville, 32609-3719.* Tel: 352-372-6006; Fax: 352-379-9670.

Pastoral Office—Rev. GROVER B. TIPTON, Dir., *P.O. Box 5216, Gainesville, 32627-5216.* Tel: 352-372-1469.

Legalization—NANCY VALDIVIESO, Dir., *Providence Center, 134 E. Church St., Rm. D-21, Jacksonville, 32202.* Tel: 904-354-5904; Fax: 904-356-2092.

Legion of Mary—Rev. JOSE MANIYANGAT, Spiritual Dir., *P.O. Box 1120, Macclenny, 32063.* Tel: 904-259-6414.

Liturgy Commission—Rev. THOMAS WILLIS, Chm. LUCILLE BARRETT, Vice-Chm.; Dr. GLENN KUHNEL, Exec. Sec., *Providence Center, 134 E. Church St., Jacksonville, 32202-3130.* Tel: 904-359-0068; Fax: 904-358-7302.

Planned Giving Office—Mrs. DENIS PLUMB, Dir., *P.O. Box 24000, Jacksonville, 32241-4000.* Tel: 904-262-3200.

Marriage Encounter—Mr. JOSEPH C. PAYNE, Exec. Dir. Exec. Team: TOM HUGHS; SUSAN HUGHS, *1851 King St., Room 103, Jacksonville, 33204.* Tel: 904-308-7474.

Parish Social Ministry—Sr. MARLENE PAYETTE, S.S.J., Dir., *Providence Center, 134 E. Church St., Jacksonville, 32202-3130.* Tel: 904-354-3416.

Priests' Spirituality Committee—Rev. JOSEPH MEEHAN, *P.O. Drawer 330005, Atlantic Beach, 32233.* Tel: 904-246-6014.

Propagation of the Faith—Rev. BRIAN EBURN, Dir., *P.O. Box 908, Crescent City, 32112.* Tel: 904-698-2055.

Refugee Resettlement—WILLIAM C. BEITZ, Dir., *Providence Center, 134 E. Church St., Jacksonville, 32202-3130.* Tel: 904-354-3416.

Respect Life Activities—BONNIE SEAVER, Dir.; Rev. THOMAS S. WILLIS, Spiritual Moderator, *P.O. Box 24000, Jacksonville, 32241-4000.* Tel: 904-262-3200.

Rural Life Director—Rev. MICHAEL PENDERGRAFT, *P.O. Box 1179, Live Oak, 32064.* Tel: 904-364-1108.

St. Vincent de Paul Societies—Tel: 904-262-3200.

Scouts—Revs. JAMES R. BODDIE, JR., Chap. EDWARD MURPHY, Asst. Chap., *P.O. Box 24000, Jacksonville, 32241-4000.* Tel: 904-262-3200.

Seminarians—Rev. JOHN H. TETLOW, Dir., *P.O. Box 24000, Jacksonville, 32241-4000.* Tel: 904-262-3200.

Stewardship, Office of—FRANCIS N. SCHOLTZ, Dir., *P.O. Box 24000, Jacksonville, 32241-4000.* Tel: 904-262-3200.

Vicar for Clergy—Rev. RALPH L. BESENDORFER, J.C.D., *P.O. Box 24000, Jacksonville, 32241-4000.* Tel: 904-262-3200.

Vicar for Religious—Sr. MAUREEN KELLEY, O.P., *P.O. Box 24000, Jacksonville, 32241-4000.* Tel: 904-262-3200.

Vicar for Senior Priests—Rev. Msgr. EUGENE C. KOHLS, P.A., J.C.D., *P.O. Box 5040, Jacksonville, 32247-5040.* Tel: 904-398-1963.

Vocations—Rev. JOHN H. TETLOW, Dir., *P.O. Box 24000, Jacksonville, 32241-4000.* Tel: 904-262-3200.

Youth and Young Adult Ministry—Mr. PETER BLAY, Dir., *134 E. Church St., Jacksonville, 32202.* Tel: 904-355-1100; Fax: 904-358-7302.

CLERGY, PARISHES, MISSIONS AND PAROCHIAL SCHOOLS

CITY OF ST. AUGUSTINE

(St. John's County)

1—CATHEDRAL OF ST. AUGUSTINE (1565). (A Minor Basilica). Revs. D. Terrence Morgan; Timothy M. Lindenfelser; James Orumpakkatt, C.M.I.; Patrick Cooke, C.S.Sp.; Alan Bower; Deacons Thomas Richards; John Pelletier. In res., Rev. Msgr. Harold F. Jordan.
Res., 35 Treasury St., 32084. Tel: 904-824-2806; Fax: 904-824-0761. [CEM]
School—Cathedral Parish School, (Grades K-8) 259 St. George St., 32084. Tel: 904-824-2861; Fax: 904-824-2862. Sr. Mary Victor Azar, S.S.J., Prin.
Sisters 1; Lay Teachers 26; Students 412.
Cathedral Parish Early Education Center—(Preschool and After School Care) 10 San Sabastian Ave., 32084. Tel: 904-829-2933. Jill Valley, Dir.
Lay Teachers 15; Students 100.
Catechesis/Religious Programs—Tel: 904-829-3338. Sr. Marilyn Dingman, S.S.J., Dir.
Students 130.
Missions—St. Augustine, St. Johns Co., Prince of Peace, San Marco Ave., 32084.; St. Augustine, St. Johns Co., St. Benedict the Moor, Martin Luther King Ave., 32084.

2—MISSION OF NOMBRE DE DIOS AND SHRINE OF OUR LADY OF LA LECHE (1565), Rev. Msgr. Harold F. Jordan, Dir.
Office: 30 Ocean Ave., 32084. Fax: 904-829-0819.
Res., 35 Treasury St., 32084. Tel: 904-824-3045; Fax: 904-824-0761.

3—ST. ANASTASIA (1988), Rev. Seamus O'Flynn; Sr. Enda Egan, Pastoral Assoc.; Deacons Bob Lucian; Ron Gagne.
Mailing Address: 5205 A1A S., 32080-7107.
Res., 5319 Fifth St., 32084. Tel: 904-471-3747; 471-5364 (Office); Fax: 904-471-7448.
Catechesis/Religious Programs—Sr. Enda Egan, R.S.M., D.R.E.
Students 150.

4—SAN SEBASTIAN (1968), Rev. Thomas P. Walsh; Deacon James Swanson.
Res., 1112 State Rd. 16, 32084. Tel: 904-824-6625; Fax: 904-829-0459.
Catechesis/Religious Programs—Students 110.

OUTSIDE THE CITY OF ST. AUGUSTINE

Atlantic Beach, Duval Co., St. John the Baptist (1967), Rev. Joseph Meehan; Deacon Harold Brodeur.
Mailing Address: P.O. Drawer 330005, 32233. Tel: 904-246-6014; Fax: 904-246-1219.
Catechesis/Religious Programs—Carole Fuchs, D.R.E.
Students 266.

Branford, Suwannee Co., San Juan Mission (1980), Rev. Michael Morse.
Mailing Address: P.O. Box 949, 32008. Tel: 904-935-2632; 752-4470; Fax: 904-935-2632.
Catechesis/Religious Programs—Students 60.

Bunnell, Flagler Co., St. Stephen (1957), Rev. Frederick Parke.
Mailing Address: 4600 Belle Terre Pkwy., Palm Coast, 32164.
Res., Rte. 100, 32110. Tel: 904-445-2246; Fax: 904-445-7808.

Callahan, Nassau Co., Our Lady of Consolation (1974), Rev. Ralph L. Besendorfer, J.C.D.
Res., 11625 Old St. Augustine Rd., Jacksonville, 32258. Tel: 904-262-3200; Fax: 904-262-0698.
Catechesis/Religious Programs—Tel: 904-879-3662. Sr. Helen Marie Kling, D.C., D.R.E.
Students 70.

Chiefland, Levy Co., St. John the Evangelist (1981), Rev. Joseph Maniangat.
Res., P.O. Box 863, 32644-0863. Tel: 352-493-1561; 493-9723 (Office); Fax: 352-493-9258.
Catechesis/Religious Programs—Students 71.
Mission—Cross City, Dixie Co., Holy Cross, 2090 S.W. Hwy. 19, Cross City, 32628. Tel: 352-498-5671.

Crescent City, Putnam Co., St. John the Baptist (1910), Rev. Brian Eburn; Sr. Bridie Ryan, Pastoral Assoc.
Res., P.O. Box 908, 32112. Tel: 904-698-2055; Fax: 904-698-4146. [CEM]
Catechesis/Religious Programs—Tel: 904-698-4334.
Students 109.

Elkton, St. John Co., St. Ambrose (1875) (Minorcan), Rev. Patrick Carroll, C.S.Sp., Admin.
Res., 6070 Church Rd., 32033. Tel: 904-692-1366; Fax: 904-692-1136. [CEM]
Catechesis/Religious Programs—Students 36.
Mission—Millcreek, St. Johns Co., Our Lady of Good Counsel, 5950 SR16, St. Augustine, 32092. [CEM]

Fernandina Beach, Amelia Island, Nassau Co., St. Michael's (1872), Revs. Mark S. Waters; Robert L. Napier; Neil Cornelli.
Res., 505 Broome St., 32034. Tel: 904-261-3472; Fax: 904-321-1901. [JC]
School—St. Michael's Academy:, (Grades PreK-5). Tel: 904-321-2102; Fax: 904-321-2330. Sr. Elizabeth Dunn, O.P., Prin.
Catechesis/Religious Programs—Janice Balota, Pastoral Assoc.
Students 243.

Flagler Beach, Flagler Co., Santa Maria Del Mar (1970), Rev. John O'Flaherty.
Res., 1681 N. Central Ave., P.O. Box 130, 32136. Tel: 904-439-2791; Fax: 904-439-2791. [CEM]
Catechesis/Religious Programs—Students 55.

Gainesville, Alachua Co.,

1—ST. PATRICK'S, (1887), Revs. Roland M. Julien; Issac Puchamkulam.
Res., 500 N.E. 16th Ave., 32601. Tel: 352-372-4641; 376-0575; Fax: 352-376-0575.
School—Tel: 352-376-9878; Fax: 352-371-6177. Elaine Baumgartner, Prin.
Lay Teachers 28; Students 581.
Catechesis/Religious Programs—Tel: 352-376-9878, Ext. 60. Diane St. Onge, D.R.E.
Students 43.
Mission—Hawthorne, Alachua Co., St. Philip Neri, U.S. 301 S., Hawthorne, 32640.

2—HOLY FAITH, (1973), Revs. Michael S. Williams; Ignatius J. Plathanam, C.M.I.; Deacon Philippe D. Fleury.
Res., 700 N.W. 39 Rd., 32607. Tel: 352-376-5405; Fax: 352-375-7568.
Catechesis/Religious Programs—Tel: 352-376-5405; Fax: 352-375-7568. Carmen M. Delgado, D.R.E.
Students 332.

3—QUEEN OF PEACE, (1987), Rev. Jeffrey A. McGowan.
Church—10900 S.W. 24th Ave., 32607. Tel: 352-332-6279; Fax: 352-331-7347. [JC]
School—Tel: 352-332-8808. Sr. Nancy Elder, I.H.M., Prin.
Catechesis/Religious Programs—Tel: 352-332-6279, Ext. 17. Sr. Beatrice Caulson, I.H.M., D.R.E.
Students 550.

4—ST. AUGUSTINE, (1923), Revs. John D. Gillespie; John M. Phillips; Timothy R. Lozier.
Res., 1738 W. University Ave., P.O. Box 13888, 32604. Tel: 352-372-3533; Fax: 352-378-9010.
Catechesis/Religious Programs—Fax: 352-378-0435. Anne Viera, D.R.E.
Students 241.

Green Cove Springs, Clay Co., Sacred Heart (1874), Rev. Donal Sullivan.
Res., 314 Cypress St., P.O. Box 276, 32043. Tel: 904-284-3811; Fax: 904-529-8845.
Catechesis/Religious Programs—Tel: 904-529-7629. Mrs. Sherry Latta-Raines, D.R.E.
Students 223.

High Springs, Alachua Co., St. Madeleine Sophie Parish (1925), Rev. Noel Cox, C.S.Sp.
Mailing Address: P.O. Box 892, 32655-0892.
Res., 3330 E. Martin Luther King Blvd., 32643. Tel: 904-454-2358; Fax: 904-454-4985.
Catechesis/Religious Programs—Students 104.

Interlachen, Putnam Co., St. John's Mission (1968), Rev. James E. O'Neal. In res., Rev. Richard J. Powers, S.J (New York).
Res., P.O. Box 207, 32148. Tel: 904-684-2528; Fax: 904-684-2528. [JC]
Catechesis/Religious Programs—Students 45.

Jacksonville, Duval Co.,

1—ASSUMPTION, (South Jacksonville) (1913), Rev. Msgr. Eugene C. Kohls; Rev. Edward W. Murphy. In res., Rev. Luis Florez, Dir., Hispanic Apostolate.
Res., 2403 Atlantic Blvd., P.O. Box 5040, 32247-5040. Tel: 904-398-1963; Fax: 904-398-6115.
School—Tel: 904-398-1774; Fax: 904-398-6712. Dr. William E. Howes, Prin.
Lay Teachers 32; Students 610.
Catechesis/Religious Programs—Mrs. Kathleen K. Lyons, D.R.E.
Students 80.

2—BLESSED TRINITY, (1957), Rev. Denis O'Regan.
Res., 10472 Beach Blvd., P.O. Box 16466, 32245. Tel: 904-641-1414; Fax: 904-641-8171.
School—(Grades PreK-2). Tel: 904-641-6458; Fax: 904-645-3762. Marie Davis, Prin.
Students 100.
Catechesis/Religious Programs—Tel: 904-646-4320. Mrs. Joanne Davis, D.R.E.
Students 192.

3—CHRIST THE KING, (1954) (Hispanic-Vietnamese), Revs. Robert J. McDermott, Jr.; Brian Carey, C.S.Sp.; Thanh T. Nguyen; Sr. Therese M. Horan, R.S.M. In res., Rev. Msgr. Joseph R. Lamonde; Rev. John H. Tetlow.
Res., 742 Arlington Rd., 32211. Tel: 904-724-0080; Fax: 904-721-2326.
School—Tel: 904-724-2954; Fax: 904-721-8004. Mrs. Janet Morton, Prin.
Lay Teachers 31; Teachers Aids 6; Students 609.
Catechesis/Religious Programs—D.R.E.: Deacon Dave McNamara; Lucille Guzzone.
Students 300.

4—CHURCH OF THE CRUCIFIXION, (1974) (African American), Rev. Cletus M. Watson, T.O.R.
Mailing & Rectory address: 6079 Bagley Rd., 32209-1805. Tel: 904-765-5284; Fax: 904-765-1680.
Catechesis/Religious Programs—Students 20.

5—HOLY FAMILY, (1974), Rev. Gregory Fay.
Office: 9800 Baymeadows Rd., 32256. Tel: 904-641-5838; Fax: 904-641-9704.
Catechesis/Religious Programs—Teresa Olson, D.R.E.
Students 140.

6—HOLY ROSARY, (1921), Revs. Glenn D. Parker, C.SS.R.; George Phillips, C.SS.R.; Bro. Martin Smith, C.SS.R.
Res., 746 W. 41st St., 32206. Tel: 904-764-3241; Fax: 904-765-4995.
School—Sisters of Notre Dame. (Toledo Prov.) 4920 Brentwood Ave., 32206. Tel: 904-765-6522; 353-6933; Fax: 904-765-9486. Sr. Patricia Marie McClain, S.N.D., Prin.
Sisters 4; Lay Teachers 15; Students 190.
Catechesis/Religious Programs—Students 25.

7—HOLY SPIRIT, (1966), Rev. Msgr. James J. Heslin; Deacon Gjet Bajraktari.
Res., 11665 Fort Caroline Rd., 32225. Tel: 904-641-7244; Fax: 904-641-7266.
School—(Grades PreK-8). Tel: 904-642-9165. Therese Moore, Prin.
Lay Teachers 17; Students 285.
Catechesis/Religious Programs—Judy Altmiller, D.R.E.
Students 336.

8—IMMACULATE CONCEPTION, (1854), Revs. Antonio Leon; Warren Keene. In res., Revs. Philip R. Gagan; Jose Mena.
Res., 121 E. Duval St., P.O. Box 100, 32201. Tel: 904-359-0331; Fax: 904-356-8133. [CEM][JC]

9—MARY QUEEN OF HEAVEN, (1988), Rev. Msgr. R. Joseph James.
Res., 9401 Staples Mill Dr., 32244. Tel: 904-777-1272.
Catechesis/Religious Programs—Tel: 904-777-3168; Fax: 904-778-7691.
Students 109.

10—MOST HOLY REDEEMER, (1962), Rev. Thomas S. Willis.
Res., 8523 Normandy Blvd., 32221-6701. Tel: 904-786-1192; Fax: 904-786-4224.
Catechesis/Religious Programs—Sharon Tomore, D.R.E.
Students 101.

11—OUR LADY OF THE ANGELS, (1917), Rev. Joseph Notarpole.
Res., 430 Crystal St., 32254. Tel: 904-389-4878; Fax: 904-389-4878. [CEM]

12—PRINCE OF PEACE, (1970), Rev. Michael J. Larkin.
Res., 6320 Bennett Rd., 32216. Tel: 904-733-6860; Fax: 904-367-0215.
Catechesis/Religious Programs—Tel: 904-733-6011.
Students 109.

13—RESURRECTION, (1959), Revs. Thomas Cody; Anthony Sebra; Deacon Stan Grenn.
Res., 3383 University Blvd. N., 32277. Tel: 904-744-0833; Fax: 904-744-7235.
School—Tel: 904-744-1266; Fax: 904-744-5800. Rosemary Nowotny, Prin.
Lay Teachers 16; Students 300.
Catechesis/Religious Programs—Tel: 904-744-5800. Noreen Thurson, D.R.E.
Students 215.

14—SACRED HEART, (1959), Rev. Msgr. Patrick M. Madden; Revs. Victor Z. Narivelil, C.M.I.; Conrad Cowart.
Res., 5752 Blanding Blvd., 32244. Tel: 904-771-2152; Fax: 904-573-8816.
School—Sisters of Mercy (Clonakilty, Ireland), Tel: 904-771-5800; Fax: 904-771-5323. Sr. Josephine O'Leary, R.S.M., Prin.
Sisters 1; Lay Teachers 28; Students 628.
Catechesis/Religious Programs—Sr. Mary of Mercy, D.R.E.
Students 256.

15—ST. FRANCIS CHOE CHAPEL, (1997) (Korean), Rev. Cheon Bong Benedic Jeong (Korea).
Res., 8051 Rampart Rd., 32244. Tel: 904-573-1833; Fax: 904-573-1833.

16—ST. JOSEPH'S, (1883), Rev. Daniel Cody.
Res., 11730 Old St. Augustine Rd., 32258-2002. Tel: 904-268-5422; Fax: 904-292-0248. [CEM]
School—Tel: 904-268-6688; Fax: 904-268-8989. Mrs. Jeanine Dineen, Prin.
Lay Teachers 26; Students 600.
Catechesis/Religious Programs—Carole Ginzl, D.R.E.
Students 647.

17—ST. MATTHEW'S, (Lake Shore) (1949), Rev. Luke McLoughlin.
Res., 1773 Blanding Blvd., 32210. Tel: 904-388-8698; Fax: 904-384-1233.
School—Tel: 904-387-4401; Fax: 904-388-4404. David Yazdiya, Prin.
Lay Teachers 18; Students 320.
Catechesis/Religious Programs—Tel: 904-388-1207. Onie Rodriguez, D.R.E.
Students 128.

18—ST. PATRICK, (1959), Rev. Ronald A. Camarda.
Res., 1429 Broward Rd., 32218. Tel: 904-768-2593; Fax: 904-786-2144.
School—Sisters of Mercy, (Grades K-8). Tel: 904-768-6323; Fax: 904-768-2144. Sr. Carmel O'Callahan, C.S.M., Prin.
Lay Teachers 14; Students 223.
Catechesis/Religious Programs—Tel: 904-757-4720.
Students 75.

19—ST. PAUL'S, (1923), Revs. Thomas K. Sullivan; James J. Corry, C.S.Sp.
Res., 2609 Park St., P.O. Box 40705, 32203. Tel: 904-387-2554; Fax: 904-388-6871.
School—Tel: 904-387-2841; Fax: 904-387-1781. Mr. John C. Lippincott, Prin.
Lay Teachers 18; Students 235.
Catechesis/Religious Programs—Students 12.

20—ST. PIUS THE FIFTH, (1919) (African American), Rev. James R. Boddie, Jr.
Res., 2110 Blue Ave., 32209. Tel: 904-354-1501; Fax: 904-354-7240.
School—1470 W. 13th St., 32209. Tel: 904-354-2613; Fax: 904-356-4522. Sr. Elise Kennedy, S.S.J., Prin.
Sisters 2; Lay Teachers 13; Students 196.
Catechesis/Religious Programs—Tel: 904-354-1501; Fax: 904-354-7240.
Students 45.

21—SAN JOSE, (1959), Revs. James Moss; Anthony P. Palazzolo; Rodolfo Godinez Fuentes.
Res., 3619 Toledo Rd., 32217. Tel: 904-733-1630; Fax: 904-733-7973.
School—Sisters of Mercy, Tel: 904-733-2510. Sr. Eithne Lowther, R.S.M., Prin.
Sisters 3; Lay Teachers 24; Students 613.
Catechesis/Religious Programs—Tel: 904-733-1630, Ext. 18; Fax: 904-731-4335. Nancy Cronin, D.R.E.
Students 200.

22—SYRIAC ANTIOCHIAN-RITE MISSION ST. EPHREM, (1986). Closed. For inquiries for parish records contact the Chancery.

Jacksonville Beach, Duval Co., St. Paul's (1930), Revs. William A. Kelly; James M. May; Dai Mai, I.C.
Res., 224 N. Fifth St., 32250. Tel: 904-249-2600; Fax: 904-249-0422.
School—Tel: 904-249-5394; Fax: 904-241-2911. Mrs. Katherine Boice, Prin.
Lay Teachers 27; Students 552.
Catechesis/Religious Programs—Tel: 904-249-2660. Mary Coleman, D.R.E.
Students 560.

Keystone Heights, Clay Co., St. William (1948), Rev. Moises Palaroan.
Res., P.O. Box 721, 32656. Tel: 352-473-4136; Fax: 352-473-4119. [JC]
Catechesis/Religious Programs—Students 117.

Korona, Flagler Co., St. Mary's (1914) (Polish), Revs. John O'Flaherty; Walter C. Bayer (Poland).
Mailing Address: P.O. Box 1537, Bunnell, 32110-1537. Tel: 904-437-5098 (Tues. & Thurs., 9:00am - 12:00pm).
Res., 801 N. Central Ave., P.O. Box 130, Flagler Beach, 32136. Tel: 904-439-2791. [CEM]

Lake City, Columbia Co., Epiphany (1965), Revs. Michael Morse; George Kuruvilla, C.M.I.
Res., Malone Dr., Rte. 10, Box 161-B, 32025. Tel: 904-752-4470; Fax: 904-752-4652.
School—Tel: 904-752-2320; Fax: 904-752-2364. Mrs. Rita Klenk, Prin.
Lay Teachers 15; Students 138.
Catechesis/Religious Programs—Tel: 904-752-3893.
Students 86.

Live Oak, Suwannee Co., St. Francis Xavier (1979), Rev. W. Michael Pendergraft.
Res., P.O. Box 1179, 32064. Tel: 904-364-1108; Fax: 904-364-1836.
Catechesis/Religious Programs—Tel: 904-362-7287. Nancy Roberts, D.R.E.
Students 52.
Mission—Jasper, Hamilton Co., St. Therese of Jesus, P.O. Box 890, Jasper, 32052. Tel: 904-364-1108.

Macclenny, Baker Co., St. Mary's (1960) (Vietnamese-Philippine), Rev. Jose Maniyangat.
Res., 104 Jacqueline Cir., P.O. Box 1120, 32063. Tel: 904-259-6414; Fax: 904-259-9712. [JC]
Catechesis/Religious Programs—Tel: 904-259-3217. Janet DeBoe, D.R.E.
Students 75.
Chaplaincy—Northeast Florida State Hospital, Macclenny; Union Correctional Institute, Raiford; and Florida State Prison, Starke. Tel: 904-964-8125.

Middleburg, Clay Co., St. Luke's (1982), Rev. Edward Rooney.
Res., 1606 Blanding Blvd., 32068. Tel: 904-282-0439; Fax: 904-291-9711.
Catechesis/Religious Programs—Sr. Mary Murphy, R.S.M., D.R.E.
Students 352.

Orange Park, Clay Co., St. Catherine's (1877), Rev. Msgr. Vincent J. Haut, V.G.; Rev. Jose Kulathinal, C.M.I. (India).
Res., 1649 Kingsley Ave., 32073. Tel: 904-264-0577; Fax: 904-264-7999.
Catechesis/Religious Programs—Tel: 904-264-2470. Bro. Dominic M. O'Brien, F.M.S., D.R.E.
Students 892.
Mission—Orange Park, Clay Co., Moosehaven Chapel, 1700 Park Ave., 32073. Tel: 904-278-1210.

Palatka, Putnam Co., St. Monica's (1858), Rev. Joseph F. Finlay.
Office: 114 S. 4th St., 32177. Tel: 904-325-9777; Fax: 904-329-1960. [CEM]
Catechesis/Religious Programs—Tel: 904-325-7777; Fax: 904-325-7777. Rev. Joseph F. Finlay, D.R.E.
Students 85.

Palm Coast, Flager Co., St. Elizabeth Ann Seton (1978), Revs. Frederick Parke; Michael Thompson; Sebastian Kaithamatton, C.M.I. Pastoral Ministers: Deacons John Holmes; James Casapulla; Robert McDermott.
Res., 4600 Belle Terre Pkwy., 32164. Tel: 904-445-2246; Fax: 904-445-7808. [CEM]
Catechesis/Religious Programs—Tel: 904-446-5854. D.R.E.: Mrs. Rosaire Downey; Mrs. Dee Casapulla.
Students 585.

Ponte Vedra Beach, St. John Co., Our Lady Star of the Sea (1972), Rev. Msgr. Daniel B. Logan; Rev. Timothy J. Cusick; Deacon Frank Harla.
Mailing Address: 545 Hwy. A1A N., 32082. Tel: 904-285-2698; Fax: 904-285-2502.
Preschool—Tel: 904-273-0034; Fax: 904-273-9740. Mrs. Laurie Kelley, Dir.
School—Palmer Catholic Academy, Tel: 904-543-8515; Fax: 904-543-8750. Mrs. Linda Earp, Prin.
Catechesis/Religious Programs—Tel: 904-273-0590; Fax: 904-273-0590.
Students 460.

St. Augustine Shores, St. John Co., Corpus Christi (1975), Rev. William C. Mooney; Deacon Joseph Cross.
Res., P.O. Box 3064, St. Augustine, 32085. Tel: 904-797-4842; Fax: 904-797-2746. [CEM]
Catechesis/Religious Programs—Students 200.

Starke, Bradford Co., St. Edward's (1941), Rev. William A. Hochheim.
Res., 441 N. Temple Ave., 32091-3207. Tel: 904-964-6155; Fax: 904-964-1411.
Catechesis/Religious Programs—Students 5.

Switzerland, St. John Co., San Juan Del Rio (1977), Rev. Edward Booth.
Res., 1714-3 State Rd., No. 13, 32259. Tel: 904-287-1589; 287-0519 (Office); Fax: 904-287-1504.
School—1714-2 State Rd. 13, Jacksonville, 32259. Tel: 904-287-8081; Fax: 904-287-4574.
Lay Teachers 15; Students 247.
Catechesis/Religious Programs—Tel: 904-287-2801.
Students 484.

Williston, Levy Co., Holy Family (1970), Rev. Paul V. Donnelly.
Res., 17353 N.E. 27 A, 32696. Tel: 352-528-2893; Fax: 352-528-6002.
Catechesis/Religious Programs—Students 82.
Mission—Inglis, Levy Co., St. Anthony the Abbot, P.O. Box 1070, Inglis, 34449. Tel: 352-447-3630; Fax: 352-447-4573.

Special Assignment:
Reverend Fathers—
Brennan, Keith R., Chancellor, The Catholic Center, P.O. Box 24000, Jacksonville, FL 32241-4000. Tel: 904-262-3200
Revilla, Francisco
Tipton, Grover B., Chap. of Prison Ministry

On Duty Outside the Diocese:
Reverend Fathers—
Carlo, Raymond J., Diocese of Charleston
Dux, John H., 311 Ayers Cir., Summerville, S.C. 29485
Fernandez, Marcellus, Diocese of Boise
Foley, Patrick H., Diocese of Pensacola-Tallahassee
Glisson, Nicholas J., St. Francis of Assisi, 860 Oak Grove Rd., Concord, CA 94518
Moore, Frederick Thomas, Pensacola, FL
Russo, Caesar, St. Vincent de Paul Seminary, Boynton Beach, FL
Walsh, Flannan J.
Young, Dennis M., Chap., V.A. Medical Center, Augusta, GA

Absent on Sick Leave:
Reverend Fathers—
Pollard, John L.

Retired:
Reverend Monsignors—
Conesa, Diego
Danaher, Mortimer, 7843 Fawn Oaks Ct., Jacksonville, FL 32256
Danaher, T. Leo, P.O. Box 330929, Atlantic Beach, FL 32233
Dawson, Joseph, S.T.D., 301 Elizabeth, Folkston, GA 31537
Lenihan, John J., 102 Hammock Circle, St. Augustine, FL 32095
Reverend Fathers—
Couture, Fernand, Hwy. 17, Orange Park, FL 32073
Ducci, Alex, c/o Cesare Ducci, Via Piemonte #4, Chiari, Breseia 25032 Italy
Haryasz, Francis S., 397 Village Drive St., Augustine, FL 32095
Shashy, Daniel, 671 D'Orleans Court, Jacksonville, FL 32211

INSTITUTIONS LOCATED IN THE DIOCESE

[A] HIGH SCHOOLS, DIOCESAN

ST. AUGUSTINE. *St. Joseph Academy*, 155 State Rd. 207, 32084. Tel: 904-824-0431; Fax: 904-826-4477.
E-mail: sja1874@juno.com
Web site: geocities.com/sja_32095
Day School. Sisters 2; Lay Teachers 21; Students 295.

JACKSONVILLE. *Bishop Kenny High School*, 1055 Kingman Ave., P.O. Box 5544, 32247. Tel: 904-398-7545; Fax: 904-398-5728. Rev. Michael R. Houle, M.A., M.Ed., M.Div., Pres.; Miss Jane Marnett, M.S., Prin.; Robert West, M.Ed., Vice Prin. & Athletic Dir.; Ms. Deborah Coffey, M.Ed., Academic Dean; Dave Williams, M.Ed., Dean of Students. Priests 2; Sisters 1; Lay Teachers 93; Students 1,640.

[B] ELEMENTARY SCHOOLS, INTERPAROCHIAL

MIDDLEBURG. *Annunciation School*. (Grades PreK-8), 1610 Blanding Blvd., 32068. Tel: 904-282-0504; Fax: 904-282-6808.
E-mail: spowell3@juno.com
Web site: home.catholicweb.com/annunciationangels
Interparish school composed of students from Sacred Heart, Green Cove Springs; St. Catherine's, Orange Park; and St. Luke, Middleburg. Susan Altieri, Prin. Lay Teachers 15; Students 310.

[C] CATHOLIC CHARITIES

ST. AUGUSTINE. *Catholic Charities Regional Office*, 225 W. King St., P.O. Box 543, 32085. Tel: 904-829-6300; Fax: 904-829-0494.
E-mail: ccbstaug@aol.com
Rebecca Stringer, Exec. Dir.

GAINESVILLE. *Catholic Charities Regional Office*. Emergency services, counseling, respite care, and adoptions. 1717 N.E. 9th St., 32609. Tel: 352-372-0294; Fax: 352-371-3157.
E-mail: cathchar@juno.com
Web site: www.afn.org/cathchar
Geralyn Ryan, Dir.

JACKSONVILLE. *Catholic Charities Bureau, Inc.*, 11625 Old St. Augustine Rd., P.O. Box 24000, 32241-4000. Tel: 904-262-3200; Fax: 904-262-0372.
E-mail: charities@CXP.COM
Mr. William J. Tierney, Diocesan Dir. Tel: 904-262-3200. Total Assisted 50,000; Total Staff 200.

Catholic Charities Regional Office, 134 E. Church St., 32202. Tel: 904-354-4846, Ext. 233; Fax: 904-354-4718.
E-mail: bbeitz@ccbjax.org
Web site: www.@ccbjax.org
William C. Beitz, Exec. Dir. Provides counseling services for substance abuse, marriage, families, maternity & aging. Also, emergency financial assistance for housing/utilities, food pantry, & adoption programs.

New Hope Program, 134 East Church St., 32202. Tel: 904-354-3464. Deacon Stanley Grenn, Dir. Total Assisted 900; Total Staff 2.

Office of Aging Services, 134 E. Church St., 32202-3130. Tel: 904-354-4846; Fax: 904-354-4718.
E-mail: kstrayer@ccbjax.org
Ms. Kathryn Strayer, L.C.S.W., Dir.

Office of AIDS Ministry, 134 E. Church St., 32202-3130. Tel: 904-354-4846, Ext. 229; Fax: 904-354-4718.
E-mail: mpayette@ccbjax.org
Sr. Marlene Payette, S.S.J., Dir.

Office of Justice and Peace, 134 E. Church St., 32202-3130. Tel: 904-358-7409; 358-7410; Fax: 904-358-7302.
E-mail: peace@cxp.com
Delena Stephens, Dir.

[D] SPECIAL APOSTOLATES

ST. AUGUSTINE. *Religious Education for Catholic Deaf and Blind*, 207 N. San Marco Ave., 32084-2799. Tel: 904-827-2607 (Voice/TDD); Fax: 904-827-2607.
E-mail: cathdb@juno.com
Web site: catholicdeaf.org; catholicblind.org
Rev. Rene Robert, Chap. Tel: 904-825-0359 (Voice/TDD); Jontal Hillard, Pastoral Worker and Teacher. Tel: 904-827-2607. Florida School for the Deaf and Blind.

JACKSONVILLE. *L'Arche Harbor House I, II, III and IV*, 700 Arlington Rd., 32211. Tel: 904-744-4435; Fax: 904-744-4470.
E-mail: larchfl@aol.com
Dorothy B. Klein, Exec. Dir. Total Staff 17; Total in Residence 21. A community residence for mentally retarded adults.

Morning Star School, 725 Mickler Rd., 32211. Tel: 904-421-2144; Fax: 904-421-1040.
E-mail: t.achliman@juno.com
Web site: users.fdn.com/~mss
Dr. Teri Aschliman, Prin. A school for exceptional children. Lay Teachers 12; Students 110.

[E] GENERAL HOSPITALS

JACKSONVILLE. *St. Vincent's Medical Center, Inc.*, 1800 Barrs St., P.O. Box 2982, 32203. Tel: 904-308-7300; Fax: 904-308-7326.
E-mail: jlogue@stvincentshealth.com
For a complete listing, refer to the Hospitals section.

[F] HOMES FOR AGING

JACKSONVILLE. *All Saints Nursing Home & Rehabilitation Center, Inc.*, 5888 Blanding Blvd., 32244. Tel: 904-772-1220; Fax: 904-772-6334.
E-mail: fish6@bellsouth.net
For a complete listing, refer to the Special Care Facilities section.

Casa San Pedro, P.O. Box 24000, 32241-4000. Tel: 904-262-3200; Fax: 904-262-9270
For a complete listing, refer to the Special Care Facilities section.

St. Catherine Laboure Manor, 1750 Stockton St., 32204. Tel: 904-308-4700; Fax: 904-308-2987.
E-mail: stvincentshealth.com
For a complete listing, refer to the Special Care Facilities section.

[G] CATHOLIC CHARITIES OFFICE OF HOUSING

JACKSONVILLE. *Jacksonville, Family Housing Management Co.*, 134 E. Church St., 32202. Tel: 904-632-1255; Fax: 904-632-2135.
E-mail: fahomaco@aol.com
Sandra B. Bonna, Dir., Jacksonville, Office of Housing Development, 134 E. Church St., 32202. Tel: 904-632-1255; Fax: 904-632-2135. Sandra B. Bonna, Dir.

Hurley Manor I, 3333 University Blvd. N., 32277. Tel: 904-744-6022; Fax: 904-744-6037. Norma Sullivan, Res. Mgr.
Parent Co., Catholic Charities Housing Association of Jacksonville, Inc. William Damato, Pres.

Hurley Manor II, 3335 University Blvd. N., 32277. Tel: 904-744-6022; Fax: 904-744-6037. Norma Sullivan, Res. Mgr.
Parent Co., Diocesan Housing Bureau, Inc. Nadine Swan, Pres.

Barry Manor, 1000 Husson Ave., Palatka, 32277. Tel: 904-328-5137; Fax: 904-328-5138. Patty Osborne, Res. Mgr.
Parent Co., Palatka Retirement Villas, Inc. Lou Ginn, Pres.

St. Clare House, 2064 Dellwood Ave., 32204. Tel: 904-632-1255; Fax: 904-632-2135.

Providence Center, 134 E. Church St., 32202. Tel: 904-632-1255; Fax: 904-632-2135.

San Jose Manor I. (Parent company: Housing Association of the Diocese of St. Augustine.), 3630 Galicia Rd., 32217. Tel: 904-739-0555; Fax: 904-739-0559.

San Jose Manor II. (Parent company: San Jose Catholic Housing Assoc., Inc.), 3622 Galicia Rd., 32217. Tel: 904-739-0555; Fax: 904-739-0559.

[H] MONASTERIES AND RESIDENCES OF PRIESTS AND BROTHERS

JACKSONVILLE. *Maryknoll Fathers & Brothers*, 2243 Saragossa Ave., 32217-2685. Tel: 904-739-1112; Fax: 904-739-9083.
E-mail: mklflorida@aol.com
Web site: maryknoll.org
In res. Revs. Joseph McGahren, M.M.; Michael J. Sloboda, M.M.; Henry Murphy, M.M. Total in Residence 3.

[I] CONVENTS AND RESIDENCES FOR SISTERS

ST. AUGUSTINE. *Motherhouse of the Sisters of St. Joseph of St. Augustine, Florida*, 241 St. George St., P.O. Box 3506, 32085. Tel: 904-824-1752; Fax: 904-826-0949.
E-mail: ssjfl@aol.com
Web site: ballingerr.xray.ufl.edu/sisters.html
Sr. Florence Bryan, S.S.J., Gen. Supr. Professed Sisters 100.
The Sisters of St. Joseph Continuing Community Support Trust Fund. Tel: 904-824-1752; Fax: 904-826-0949.

[J] RETREAT HOUSES

BUNNELL. *Discalced Carmelite Fathers of Florida*, HC 1 Box 70 - Korona, 32110. Tel: 904-437-2910; Fax: 904-437-5125. Revs. Joseph F. Zawada, O.C.D., Prior; Benedict Jurkiewicz; Augustine Kwiatkowski; Bro. Anthony Gemmato. Total Staff 4.

JACKSONVILLE. *Marywood Center for Spirituality and Ministry*, 1714-5 State Rd. 13, 32259. Tel: 904-287-2525; Fax: 904-287-9738.
E-mail: marywoodctr@ilnk.com
Mr. David E. Nowak, Dir.; Sr. Kathleen Power, Prog. Coord. Total Staff 12.

[K] MISCELLANEOUS

GAINESVILLE. *The Center for the Study of the Passion of Christ and the Holy Shroud*, 1738 W. University, 32603. Tel: 352-372-3533; Fax: 352-378-0435. Mrs. Gerry DeGraff, Exec. Sec.
Spirit Radio of North Florida, Inc., 500 N.E. 16th Ave., 32601. Tel: 352-372-4641; Fax: 352-376-0575. Rev. Roland M. Julien.

JACKSONVILLE. *The Florida Catholic AIDS Network*, Catholic Charities, 134 E. Church St., 32202-3130. Tel: 904-358-7410, Ext. 229; Fax: 904-358-7302.
E-mail: peace@cxp.com
Delena Stephens, Dir.

[L] NEWMAN CENTERS

ST. AUGUSTINE. *Flagler College Newman Center*, c/o Cathedral of St. Augustine, 35 Treasury St., 32084. Tel: 904-461-5795.
E-mail: ccfis@juno.com
Rev. D. Terrence Morgan.

GAINESVILLE. *University of Florida-St. Augustine Parish and Student Center*, 1738 W. University Ave., P.O. Box 13888, 32604. Tel: 352-372-3533; Fax: 352-378-9010.
E-mail: stucent@aol.com
Web site: staugustine_uf.org
Revs. John D. Gillespie; Timothy R. Lozier; John M. Phillips.

JACKSONVILLE. *Jacksonville Univ. & Univ. of North Florida Catholic Campus Ministry*, 32211. Tel: 904-744-3950, Ext. 7258.
E-mail: pmorgan@mail.ju.edu
Web site: http://www.unf.edu/groups/ccm/
Mr. Pete Morgan, Dir. Catholic Campus Ministry.

RELIGIOUS INSTITUTES OF MEN REPRESENTED IN THE DIOCESE

For further details refer to the corresponding bracketed number in the Religious Institutes of Men or Women section.

[0275]—*Carmelites of Mary Immaculate.*—C.M.I.
[1330]—*Congregation of the Mission.*—C.M.
[0260]—*Discalced Carmelite Friars.*—O.C.D.
[0650]—*Holy Ghost Fathers.*—C.S.Sp.
[0690]—*Jesuit Fathers and Brothers.*—S.J.
[0780]—*Marist Fathers.*—S.M.
[0800]—*Maryknoll.*—M.M.
[1070]—*Redemptorist Fathers.*—C.SS.R.
[0560]—*Third Order Regular of St. Francis.*—T.O.R.

RELIGIOUS INSTITUTES OF WOMEN REPRESENTED IN THE DIOCESE

[0230]—*Benedictine Sisters of Pontifical Jurisdiction.*—O.S.B.
[2515]—*Cashel Mercy Sisters.*—C.M.S.
[0760]—*Daughters of Charity of St. Vincent de Paul.* (Eastern Prov.).—D.C.
[0960]—*Daughters of Wisdom.*—D.W.
[1070-13]—*Dominican Sisters.*—O.P.
[]—*Holy Handmaids of the Child Jesus.*—H.H.C.J.
[2490]—*Medical Mission Sisters.*—M.M.S.
[2170]—*Servants of the Immaculate Heart of Mary.*—I.H.M.
[]—*Sisters for Christian Community.*—S.F.C.C.
[2517]—*Sisters of Mercy.*—S.M.
[2600]—*Sisters of Mercy.* (Cork and Ross).—S.M.
[2990]—*Sisters of Notre Dame.* (Toledo Prov.).—S.N.D.
[3900]—*Sisters of St. Joseph of St. Augustine, FL.*—S.S.J.
[3890]—*Sisters of St. Joseph of Peace.*—C.S.J.P.

NECROLOGY

† Barry, Joseph A., (Retired). —Died Aug. 17, 2000.

Diocese of St. Cloud

(Dioecesis S. Clodoaldi)

Most Reverend

JOHN F. KINNEY, D.D., J.C.D.

Bishop of St. Cloud; ordained February 2, 1963; appointed Titular Bishop of Caorle and Auxiliary Bishop of St. Paul and Minneapolis November 16, 1976; consecrated January 25, 1977; appointed Bishop of Bismarck June 28, 1982; installed August 23, 1982; appointed Bishop of St. Cloud May 9, 1995; installed July 6, 1995. *Office: 214 Third Ave. S., P.O. Box 1248, St. Cloud, MN, 56302-1248.* Tel.: 320-251-2340.

Most Reverend

GEORGE H. SPELTZ

Former Bishop of St. Cloud; ordained June 2, 1940; appointed Auxiliary Bishop of Winona and Titular Bishop of Claneus February 13, 1963; consecrated March 25, 1963; appointed Coadjutor of St. Cloud April 4, 1966; succeeded January 31, 1968; resigned January 13, 1987. *Res., 224 Third Ave. S., St. Cloud, MN, 56302.* Tel.: 320-251-3871.

Chancery: 214 Third Ave. S., P.O. Box 1248, St. Cloud, MN, 56302. Tel.: 320-251-2340; Fax: 320-251-0470.

Web site address: www.stcdio.org

Corporate Title: *"The Diocese of St. Cloud."*

ERECTED AS THE VICARIATE OF NORTHERN MINNESOTA, FEBRUARY 12, 1875.

CREATED AS THE DIOCESE OF ST. CLOUD, SEPTEMBER 22, 1889.

Square Miles 12,251.

Comprises the Counties of Stearns, Sherburne, Benton, Morrison, Mille Lacs, Kanabec, Isanti, Pope, Stevens, Traverse, Grant, Douglas, Wilkin, Otter Tail, Todd and Wadena in the State of Minnesota.

For legal titles of parishes and diocesan institutions, consult the Chancery Office.

STATISTICAL OVERVIEW

Personnel	
Bishop	1
Retired Bishops	1
Abbots	1
Retired Abbots	2
Priests: Diocesan Active in Diocese	88
Priests: Active Outside Diocese	1
Priests: Retired, Sick or Absent	48
Number of Diocesan Priests	137
Religious Priests in Diocese	116
Extern Priests in Diocese	2
Ordinations:	
Transitional Deacons	1
Permanent Deacons	1
Permanent Deacons in Diocese	34
Total Brothers	76
Total Sisters	646
Parishes	
Parishes	139
With Resident Pastor:	
Resident Diocesan Priests	77
Resident Religious Priests	13
Without Resident Pastor:	
Administered by Priests	49
Professional Ministry Personnel:	
Sisters	11
Lay Ministers	99
Welfare	
Catholic Hospitals	4
Total Assisted	215,011
Homes for the Aged	14
Total Assisted	1,298
Residential Care of Children	2
Total Assisted	157
Special Centers for Social Services	7
Total Assisted	401,706
Residential Care of Disabled	7
Total Assisted	51
Other Institutions	8
Total Assisted	745
Educational	
Diocesan Students in Other Seminaries	12
Seminaries, Religious	1
Students Religious	1
Total Seminarians	13
Colleges and Universities	2
Total Students	4,044
High Schools, Diocesan and Parish	1
Total Students	589
High Schools, Private	1
Total Students	292
Elementary Schools, Diocesan and Parish	33
Total Students	5,493
Catechesis/Religious Education:	
High School Students	7,722
Elementary Students	15,717
Total Students Under Catholic Instruction	33,870
Teachers in the Diocese:	
Priests	30
Brothers	8
Sisters	35
Lay Teachers	803
Vital Statistics	
Receptions into the Church:	
Infant Baptism Totals	2,382
Adult Baptism Totals	84
Received into Full Communion	237
First Communions	2,684
Confirmations	2,774
Marriages:	
Catholic	712
Interfaith	328
Total Marriages	1,040
Deaths	1,483
Total Catholic Population	147,047
Total Population	488,181

Former Bishops—Rt. Rev. RUPERT SEIDENBUSCH, O.S.B., D.D., cons. Bishop of Halia, Vicar-Apostolic of Northern Minnesota, May 30, 1875; resigned Nov. 15, 1888; died June 2, 1895.—Rt. Rev. OTTO ZARDETTI, D.D., cons. Oct. 20, 1889; transferred to Bucharest, Roumania, and raised to the Archiepiscopal Dignity, Feb. 23, 1894; died May 9, 1902.—Rt. Rev. MARTIN MARTY, O.S.B., D.D., cons. Bishop of Tiberias, Feb. 1, 1880; Bishop of Sioux Falls, 1889; transferred to St. Cloud, Jan. 21, 1895; died Sept. 19, 1896.—Rt. Rev. JAMES TROBEC, D.D., ord. Sept. 8, 1865; cons. Bishop of St. Cloud, Sept. 21, 1897; resigned April 15, 1914; appt. Titular Bishop of Lycopolis; died Dec. 14, 1921.—Most Rev. JOSEPH F. BUSCH, D.D., ord. July 28, 1889; appt. Bishop of Lead, S. D., April 9, 1910; cons. May 19, 1910; transferred to See of St. Cloud, Jan. 19, 1915; died May 31, 1953.—Most Rev. PETER W. BARTHOLOME, D.D., ord. June 12, 1917; appt. Titular Bishop of Lete and Coadjutor Bishop of St. Cloud "cum jure successionis", Dec. 6, 1941; cons. March 3, 1942; succeeded to See May 31, 1953; appt. Assistant at the Pontificial Throne July 23, 1954; resigned Jan. 31, 1968; died June 17, 1982.—Most Rev. GEORGE H. SPELTZ, D.D., Ph.D., appt. Auxiliary Bishop of Winona and Titular Bishop of Claneus February 13, 1963; cons. March 25, 1963; appt. Coadjutor of St. Cloud April 4, 1966 succeeded Jan. 31, 1968; resigned Jan. 13, 1987.—Most Rev. JEROME HANUS, O.S.B., D.D., appt. Bishop of St. Cloud, July 6, 1987; ord. and installed Aug. 24, 1987; appt. Coadjutor Archbishop of Dubuque, IA, Aug. 23, 1994.

Chancery—P.O. Box 1248, 214 Third Ave. S., St. Cloud, 56302. Tel: 320-251-2340; 259-5227 (after hours); Fax: 320-251-0470. Office Hours: Mon.-Fri. 9-12 & 1-4:30.

Vicar General—Rev. Msgr. DANIEL J. TAUFEN, S.T.L.

Chancellor—Rev. ROBERT ROLFES, J.C.L.

Vice Chancellor—Rev. MARVIN ENNEKING, J.C.L.

Assistant Chancellor—Sr. MARY MANDERNACH, O.S.B.

Diocesan Tribunal—316 Seventh Ave. N., St. Cloud, 56303. All marriage cases are to be directed to: *The Tribunal, Box 576, St. Cloud, 56302.* Tel: 320-251-6557.

Judicial Vicar—Rev. VIRGIL HELMIN, J.C.L.

Adjutant Judicial Vicar—Rev. WILLIAM VOUK, III, J.C.L.

Promoter Justitiae—Rev. Msgr. DANIEL J. TAUFEN, S.T.L.

Defensor Vinculi—Revs. NICHOLAS LANDSBERGER; ALFRED HELTEMES; GREGORY LIESER; THOMAS OLSON.

Judges—Revs. PAUL SCHMELZER; ROBERT LANDSBERGER; WILLIAM VOUK, III, J.C.L.; JONATHAN LICARI, O.S.B.; MARVIN ENNEKING, J.C.L.; THERESA A. WYBURN.

Notaries—Revs. VIRGIL HELMIN, J.C.L.; WILLIAM VOUK, III, J.C.L.; JILL LENTNER; DIANA SKAJA.

Advocates—Revs. JOSEPH KORF; LEON SLOMINSKI; ROGER KLASSEN, O.S.B.

Marriage Counseling—Caritas Family Services, *Pastoral Center, Diocese of St. Cloud, 305 N. Seventh Ave., St. Cloud, 56303.* Tel: 320-252-4121.

Diocesan Consultors—Rev. Msgr. DANIEL J. TAUFEN, S.T.L.; Revs. THOMAS BECKER; JOHN CASKEY; MARVIN ENNEKING; BERNARD GRUENES; LAURN VIRNIG; FRANCIS BRITZ; LLOYD HAUPT; GREGORY MASTEY.

Deans—Rev. KEVIN ANDERSON, St. Cloud; Rev. BERNARD GRUENES, Melrose; Rev. THOMAS BECKER, Alexandria; Rev. CLETUS CONNORS, O.S.B., Cold Spring; Rev. ROBERT KIEFFER, Fergus Falls; Rev. FRANCIS BRITZ, Foley; Rev. LAURN VIRNIG, Little Falls; Rev. FRANK TOMASIEWICZ, St. Joseph; Rev. ARLIE SOWADA, Morris; Rev. MARVIN ENNEKING, Princeton; Rev. JOHN CASKEY, Sauk Centre; Rev. JEROME NORDICK, Wadena.

Diocesan Corporate Board—Most Rev. JOHN KINNEY, Pres.; Rev. Msgr. DANIEL J. TAUFEN, S.T.L., Vice Pres.; Revs. ROBERT ROLFES, J.C.L., Sec. TIMOTHY BALTES; GREGORY LIESER.

Diocesan Finance Council—Most. Rev. JOHN F. KINNEY, Vacant, Finance Officer; Rev. Msgr. DANIEL J. TAUFEN, S.T.L.; Rev. JOSEPH KORF; Sr. RITA KRAEMER, O.S.F.; Mr. ALEX DIDIER; Mr. HUB LEVANDOWSKI; Mr. RICHARD GRUBER; Mr. THOMAS REIF; Mrs. SHARON HESS; Mrs. LUANN POPP; Mr. LOREN LIESEMEYER.

Due Process Service—Rev. MARVIN ENNEKING, J.C.L., Chm.

Presbyteral Council—Revs. JOHN CASKEY, Chm. FRANCIS BRITZ, Vice Chm. GREGORY MASTEY, Sec. THOMAS BECKER; JEROME NORDICK; ROBERT KIEFFER; FRANK TOMASIEWICZ; BERNARD GRUENES; MARVIN ENNEKING; CLETUS CONNORS, O.S.B.; ARLIE SOWADA; LAURN VIRNIG; KEVIN ANDERSON; KENNETH THIELMAN; WILLIAM MCNIFF, O.S.C.; Rev. Msgr. DANIEL J. TAUFEN, S.T.L.,Address correspondence to: *Church of Christ the King, P.O. Box 83, Browerville, 56438.*

Pastoral Council—Mrs. LEMAY BECHTOLD, Exec. Sec.; Revs. GREGORY MASTEY; KENNETH RIEDEMANN; RICHARD JOHN, O.S.C.; Sr. MARY ZIRBES, O.S.F.; Deacon LEO KOSIBA; MICHAEL BARTEN; MICHAEL CRUZEN; PATRICK DOMBROVSKI; JANET A. FAULHABER; JEROME HENDRICKSON; PETER HERMES; CHELSEA KELLER; JUDITH KORKOWSKI; SARAH KRYCH; KATHERINE MOENKEDICK; JOAN ZETTEL; BETTY ZWILLING.

Diocesan Offices and Programs

Archives—LOUISE THEISEN, Archivist. Tel: 320-251-2340.

Boy Scouts—Rev. LEROY SCHEIERL, Dir., *St. Francis DeSales, P.O. Box 69, Belgrade, 56312-0069.*

Building Commission—DONALD KAINZ, Chm.; Rev. TIMOTHY BALTES; Sr. DELORES DUFNER, O.S.B.; SYLVESTER JANOCHOSKI; MARILYN SUTTON; BRADLEY FORBROOK,Address correspondence to: DONALD KAINZ, *10105 Hedge Rd., N.W., Rice, 56367.*

Catholic Campaign for Human Development—Rev. ROBERT ROLFES, J.C.L., Dir., *P.O. Box 1248, St. Cloud, 56302.*

Campus Ministry—Rev. KEVIN ANDERSON, *Newman Center, 396 First Ave. S., St. Cloud, 56301.*

Catholic Charities—Mr. STEVEN BRESNAHAN, Dir., *1730 Seventh Ave. S., St. Cloud, 56301.* Tel: 320-252-0412. Caritas Family Services: Adoption, Counseling (Individual, Family, Financial, Pregnancy), Food Shelf and Women's Guild Clothing, P.M.I.'s, Services to Widowed and Divorced. JOAN COLLINS-MAROTTE, Dir., *305 Seventh Ave. N., St. Cloud, 56303.* Tel: 320-650-1660; Fax: 320-252-4508.

Women's Guild—ROSANNE HEALEY, Coord., *157 Roosevelt Rd., Ste. 100, St. Cloud, 56303.* Tel: 320-229-4560; Fax: 320-229-4562.

Catholic Relief Services—Rev. RICHARD LEISEN, Dir., *P.O. Box 39, Paynesville, 56362.* Tel: 320-243-4413.

Catholic Women, Council of—Rev. THOMAS MEYER, Moderator, *30325 Pan Dr., Cushing, 56443.* BETTY ZWILLING, Pres., *6523 32nd Ave. N., Sauk Rapids, 56379.*

Cemeteries Assumption-Calvary—*2341 Roosevelt Rd., St. Cloud, 56301.* Tel: 320-251-5511.

Censores Librorum—Revs. PAUL ZYLLA, S.T.D.; ROBERT C. HARREN, J.C.L.; Rev. Msgr. DANIEL J. TAUFEN, S.T.L.

Charismatic Renewal, Bishop's Liaison To—Rev. ANTHONY OELRICH, *St. Mary's Parish, P.O. Box 308, Holdingford, 56340-0308.*

Clerical Aid Association—Most Rev. JOHN F. KINNEY, Pres.; Rev. Msgr. DANIEL J. TAUFEN, S.T.L., Sec.; Rev. ROBERT ROLFES, J.C.L., Treas. Directors: Revs. SYLVESTER KLEINSCHMIDT; RICHARD LEISEN; ALEXANDER LUDWIG; PETER KIRCHNER; ELMER TORBORG; SILVERIUS SCHMITT, Address mail to: *The Chancery, P.O. Box 1248, St. Cloud, 56302.*

Commission for the Catholic Mission Among the Black and Indian Mission—Rev. RAYMOND STEFFES, O.S.C., Dir., *Crosier Monastery, P.O. Box 500, Onamia, 56359.*

Communications Office—(Radio, Television, Public Information, CTNA Affiliate), STEVE GOTTWALT, Dir., *Pastoral Center, Diocese of St. Cloud, 305 N. Seventh Ave., St. Cloud, 56303.* Tel: 320-251-0558.

Continuing Formation of Priests—Rev. RALPH ZIMMERMAN, Dir., *Church of Our Lady of the Lake, Box 100, Big Lake, 55309-0100.*

Development Office—Vacant, Dir. Devel.

Diocesan Education Council—Sr. CATHERINE KALLHOFF, S.S.N.D.; Deacon GREGORY STEELE; JOAN HEIPER; AIMEE BATES; NOELLA FATH; GERALYN NATHE-EVANS; JOANNE KRAVA.

Diocesan Foundation—CATHERINE COGHLAN, Exec. Dir.

Office of Catholic Education Ministries—Sr. CATHERINE KALLHOFF, S.S.N.D., Supt. Educ. LINDA KAISER, School Consultant; LORI DAHLHOFF, Consultant for Ministries/Persons with Disabilities & Catechist Formation; TIMOTHY WELCH, Consultant Media/Computer & Ministry Formation Program; BARBARA SIMON-JOHNSON, Office Coord. PATRICK FLYNN, Consultant for the Formation of Youth; LUANN TRUTWIN, Media Coord., Address all correspondence to: *Catholic Education Ministries, Pastoral Center, Diocese of St. Cloud, 305 N. Seventh Ave., St. Cloud, 56303.* Tel: 320-251-0111.

Diocesan Ecumenical Commission—Rev. GERALD DALSETH, Chm. Address all correspondence to: *P.O. Box 428, Pierz, 56364-0428.*

Diocesan Planning Council—Mr. THOMAS KEAVENY, Dir.; Revs. JONATHAN LICARI, O.S.B., Chm. ROBERT KIEFFER; JAMES REMMERSWAAL, O.S.C.; Sr. GEN MAIERS, O.S.B.; Ms. RITA CLASEMANN; Sr. RITA BARTHEL, O.S.F.; Deacon STANLEY HENNEN; Mr. ROBERT BARRETT; Ms. MARY JO COBB; Mr. MEL EUTENEUER; Mr. VICTOR KLIMOSKI.

Diocesan Priests Pension Plan Trustees—Most Rev. JOHN KINNEY; Rev. Msgr. DANIEL J. TAUFEN, S.T.L.; Revs. JAMES HAHN; SYLVESTER KLEINSCHMIDT; THOMAS OLSON; KENNETH THIELMAN; ROBERT ROLFES; STANLEY WIESER; ELMER TORBORG.

Director of Retired Priests—Rev. LLOYD HAUPT.

Eucharistic League—Rev. RAYMOND SCHULZETENBERG, Dir., *S.S. Peter & Paul Church, Gilman, 56333.*

Family Life Bureau—CHRISTINE CODDEN, Dir., *Pastoral Center, Diocese of St. Cloud, 305 N. Seventh Ave., St. Cloud, 56303.* Tel: 320-252-4721.

Health Ministry—Sr. MICHAEA BYRON, O.S.F., Coord., *214 3rd Ave. S., St. Cloud, 56301.* Tel: 320-252-7644. Rev. THOMAS KNOBLACH, Consultant for Healthcare Ethics.

Holy Childhood Association—Rev. WILLIAM VOS, Dir., *11-Eighth Ave., S., St. Cloud, 56301.*

Koinonia Program of Central Minnesota—Rev. DAVID MACIEJ, *P.O. Box 188, Rice, 56367.*

Legion of Decency—Rev. ROBERT E. ROLFES, J.C.L., *P.O. Box 1248, St. Cloud, 56302.*

Legion of Mary—Rev. RAYMOND STEFFES, O.S.C., *Crosier Monastery, Onamia, 56359.*

Natural Family Planning—Mrs. KAY EK, Dir., *316 Seventh Ave. N., St. Cloud, 56303.* Tel: 320-252-2100.

Newspaper "St. Cloud Visitor"—JOE TOWALSKI, Editor & Business Mgr., *Pastoral Center, Diocese of St. Cloud, 305 N. Seventh Ave., Box 1068, St. Cloud, 56302.* Tel: 320-251-3022.

Office of Diaconate—Deacon MICHAEL KEABLE, Dir.; Rev. RALPH ZIMMERMAN, Vicar for Permanent Deacons, *Church of Our Lady of the Lake, P.O. Box 100, Big Lake, 55309-0100.* Deacon DAVID LINDMEIER, Pres. Diaconal Community, *305 Seventh Ave. N., St. Cloud, 56303.* Tel: 612-252-4721.

Personnel Committee—Revs. LEROY KREMER, Dir. JONATHAN LICARI, O.S.B.; PETER KIRCHNER; DAVID RIEDER; MARVIN ENNEKING, J.C.L.; Rev. Msgr. DANIEL J. TAUFEN, *Mailing Address: 208 W. Broadway, Little Falls, 56345.*

Respect Life Program—JANE MARRIN, *316 7th Ave N., St. Cloud, 56303.* Tel: 320-259-0976.

Propagation of the Faith—Rev. WILLIAM VOS, Dir., *11 Eighth Ave. S., St. Cloud, 56301.* Tel: 320-251-1100; Fax: 320-251-2061.

Rural Life Program—*214 3rd Ave. S., St. Cloud, 56301.* Tel: 320-251-2340.

Spanish Migrant Program—Sr. ADELE GROSS, O.S.F., Consultant, *116 8th Ave., S.E., Little Falls, 56345.* Tel: 320-632-2981; Fax: 320-632-1714.

TEC (Central Minnesota TEC) (Together Encountering Christ)—Rev. KENNETH OPAT, O.S.C., Coord., *516 School St., Anoka, 55303.* Tel: 763-323-8178; Fax: 763-421-4230.

Vocations—Rev. DONALD WAGNER, Dir., *305 Seventh Ave. N., Ste. 102B, St. Cloud, 56303-3633.* Tel: 320-251-5001; Fax: 320-251-0424.

Worship, Office of—Mr. GARY FELDHEGE, Dir., *Pastoral Center, Diocese of St. Cloud, 305 N. Seventh Ave., St. Cloud, 56303.* Tel: 320-255-9068.

CLERGY, PARISHES, MISSIONS AND PAROCHIAL SCHOOLS

CITY OF ST. CLOUD
(Benton, Stearns, Sherburne Counties)

1—ST. MARY'S CATHEDRAL OF ST. CLOUD, Rev. Steven Binsfeld; Deacon Leo Kosiba. In res., Rev. Le Roy Maus.
Res., 25 Eighth Ave. S., 56301-4279. Tel: 320-251-1840; Fax: 320-251-1840, Ext. 6.
School—Tel: 320-251-1840, Ext. 150; Fax: 320-251-1840, Ext. 151.
Lay Teachers 10; Students 110.

2—HOLY ANGELS. Closed. For inquiries for parish records contact St. Mary's Cathedral, St. Cloud.

3—HOLY SPIRIT, Rev. Virgil A. Helmin; Deacons Charles Bobertz; Vernon Schmitz.
Office: 2405 Walden Way, 56301. Tel: 320-251-3764; Fax: 320-252-5143.
School—St. Elizabeth Ann Seton. Inter-Parochial school. See separate listing.

4—ST. ANTHONY OF PADUA, Revs. Robert C. Harren; Mark Innocenti; Deacon Carl S. Nord.
Res., 114 25th Ave. No., 56303. Tel: 320-251-5966; Fax: 320-251-0664.
School—St. Elizabeth Ann Seton Inter-Parochial School. See separate listing.

5—ST. AUGUSTINE, Rev. Simon Bischof, O.S.B.; Deacon Jeff Hennes.
Office: 443 Second St., S.E., 56304. Tel: 320-251-8335; Fax: 320-529-3231.
Res., 210 Fifth Ave., S.E., 56304.
School—Tel: 320-251-2376; Fax: 320-529-3222.
Lay Teachers 13; Students 196.

6—ST. JOHN CANTIUS, Rev. Peter Snyers; Deacon Fred Reker.
Res., 1515 N. Third St., 56303. Tel: 320-251-4455; Fax: 320-240-1238.

7—ST. MICHAEL, Rev. Mark Ostendorf.
Res., 1036 Co. Rd. 4, 56303. Tel: 320-251-6923; Fax: 320-202-1104.
School—Sts. Peter & Paul & Michael Inter-Parochial School. See separate listing.

8—ST. PAUL, Rev. Timothy Baltes; Deacons Michael Keable; Todd Warren; David Lindmeier.
Res., 1125 11th Ave. N., 56303. Tel: 320-251-4831; Fax: 320-251-2648.
School—Sts. Peter & Paul & Michael Inter-Parochial School. See separate listing.

9—ST. PETER, Rev. Gregory Lieser; Deacon John Woods.
Res., 930 31st Ave. N., 56303. Tel: 320-252-2113; Fax: 320-529-0796.
School—Sts. Peter & Paul & Michael Inter-Parochial School. See separate listing.

10—CHRIST CHURCH, Rev. Kevin Anderson.
Res., 396 S. First Ave., 56301. Tel: 320-251-2712; Fax: 320-252-3930.

OUTSIDE THE CITY OF ST. CLOUD

Albany, Stearns Co., Seven Dolors, Rev. Corwin Collins, O.S.B.
Res., Box 277, 56307. Tel: 320-845-2705. [CEM]
School—Holy Family, Tel: 320-845-2011.
Lay Teachers 8; Students 128.

Alexandria, Douglas Co., St. Mary's, Rev. Alexander P. Ludwig.
Res., 411 Hawthorne St., P.O. Box 669, 56308. Tel: 320-763-5781; Fax: 320-763-4833. [CEM]
School—Tel: 320-763-5861; Fax: 320-763-7992.
Lay Teachers 13; Students 205.

Avon, Stearns Co., St. Benedict's, Rev. James Reichert, O.S.B.
Church—P.O. Box 98, 56310. Tel: 320-356-7121. [CEM]

Battle Lake, Otter Tail Co., Our Lady of the Lake, Rev. Paul Folsom.
Res., 409 Lake Ave. N., P.O. Box 671, 56515. Tel: 218-864-5619; Fax: 218-864-5747.

Becker, Sherbune Co., Immaculate Conception, Rev. Marvin Enneking; Deacon Gregory Steele.
Res., 12100 Sherburne Ave., Box 426, 55308. Tel: 763-261-4242; Fax: 763-261-4314. [CEM]

Belgrade, Stearns Co., St. Francis De Sales, Rev. LeRoy Scheierl.
Res., 541 Martin Ave., P.O. Box 69, 56312. Tel: 320-254-8218. [CEM]

Belle Prairie, Morrison Co., Holy Family, Rev. Leroy Kremer, Admin.
Res., 18777 Riverwood Dr., Little Falls P.O., 56345. Tel: 320-632-5720. [CEM]

Belle River, Douglas Co., St. Nicholas, Rev. Jeff Ethen.
Church—9473 County Rd. 3, N.E., Box 339, Carlos, 56319. Tel: 612-852-7041. [CEM]

Bertha, Todd Co., St. Joseph's, Rev. Thomas Knoblach. Res., P.O. Box 158, 56437-0158. Tel: 218-924-2605; Fax: 218-924-2144. [CEM]

Big Lake, Sherburne Co., Our Lady of the Lake, Rev. Ralph Zimmerman.
Res., 411 Minnesota Ave., Box 100, 55309. Tel: 763-263-2863; Fax: 763-263-3187. [CEM]

BlueGrass, Wadena Co., St. Hubert's, Rev. Peter K. Kirchner, Jr.
Res., 20 Brown St. N., P.O. Box C, Verndale, 56481. Tel: 218-445-5786. [CEM]

Bluffton, Otter Tail Co., St. John the Baptist, Rev. Kevin Schwartz.
Res., 56518. Tel: 218-385-2608. [CEM]

Bowlus, Morrison Co., St. Stanislaus Kostka, Revs. Gregory Mastey; Joseph Herzing.
Res., 8550 State Hwy. 238, 56314-9801. Tel: 320-573-2975; Fax: 320-584-8231. [CEM]

Braham, Isanti Co., St. Peter & Paul, Rev. Nicholas M. Zimmer.
Res., 55006. Tel: 320-396-3105. [CEM]

Brandon, Douglas Co., Church of St. Ann, Rev. Eugene Lemm. In res., Rev. Richard J. Heid.
Res., P.O. Box 256, 56315. Tel: 320-524-2462. [CEM]

Breckenridge, Wilkin Co., St. Mary of the Presentation, Rev. Leo Moenkedrick.
Res., 221 N. Fourth St., 56520-1496. Tel: 218-643-5173. [CEM 2]
School—Tel: 218-643-5443; Fax: 218-643-5443.
Lay Teachers 11; Students 160.

Brennyville, Benton Co., St. Elizabeth, Rev. Thomas F. Olson.
Res., 16426 125 Ave., N.E., Foley, 56329. Tel: 320-355-2454; Fax: 320-355-2819. [CEM]

Brooten, Stearns Co., St. Donatus, Rev. James Statz.
Res., 301 Eastern Ave. S., P.O. Box 159, 56316. Tel: 320-352-2521. [CEM]

Browerville, Todd Co., Christ the King, Rev. John Caskey.
Res., P.O. Box 83, 56438. Tel: 320-594-2291. [CEM]
School—Tel: 320-594-6114; Fax: 320-594-6114.
Lay Teachers 6; Students 69.

Brown's Valley, Traverse Co., St. Anthony's, Rev. Arlie Sowada.
Res., Box 359, 56219. Tel: 320-695-2621. [CEM]

Buckman, Morrison Co., St. Michael's, Rev. Ronald Dockendorf.
Res., P.O. Box 638, 56317-0638. Tel: 320-468-2316; Fax: 320-468-2316. [CEM]

Butler, Otter Tail Co., Holy Cross, Rev. Kevin Schwartz.
Res., P.O. Box 36, Bluffton, 56518. Tel: 218-385-2608. [CEM]

Cambridge, Isanti Co., Christ the King, Rev. James David Hahn.
Res., 230 N. Fern St., 55008-1094. Tel: 612-689-1221; Fax: 612-689-8950. [CEM]

Chokio, Stevens Co., St. Mary's, Rev. Nathan Packard.
Res., P.O. Box 187, 56221. Tel: 320-324-2680; Fax: 320-324-2732. [CEM]

Clarissa, Todd Co., St. Joseph, Rev. Eugene A. Meemken.
Res., 107 S. John St., P.O. Box 5, 56440. Tel: 218-756-2205. [CEM]

Clear Lake, Sherburne Co., St. Marcus, Rev. LeRoy Scholz.
Res., 55319. Tel: 320-743-2481. [CEM]

Cold Spring, Stearns Co., St. Boniface, Rev. Cletus Connors, O.S.B.; Deacon John Salchert.
Res., 418 Main St., 56320. Tel: 320-685-3280; Fax: 320-685-7792. [CEM]
School—Tel: 320-685-3541.
Lay Teachers 14; Students 242.

Collegeville, Stearns Co., St. John the Baptist, Rev. Jonathan Licari, O.S.B.
Res., 56321. Tel: 320-363-2765. [JC]

Dent, Otter Tail Co., Sacred Heart, Rev. Jerome Nordick.
Res., 36963 State Hwy. 108, 56528. Tel: 218-758-2700. [CEM]

Donnelly, Stevens Co., St. Theresia. Closed. For inquiries for parish records contact St. Charles, Herman.

Duelm, Benton Co., St. Lawrence's, Rev. Marvin Enneking, Admin.
Res., 10915 Duelm Rd., N.E., Foley, 56329. Tel: 320-968-7502. [CEM]

Dumont, Traverse Co., St. Peter's, Rev. Stanley Wieser.
Res., 201 Ninth St. S., Wheaton, 56296. Tel: 320-563-4421.

Eden Valley, Stearns Co., The Church of the Assumption, Rev. Virgil R. Braun.
Res., 55329. Tel: 320-453-2788. [CEM]

Elbow Lake, Grant Co., St. Olaf, Rev. Andrew Marthaler.
Res., 18 Sixth Ave. N., 56531. Tel: 218-685-4318. [CEM]

Elizabeth, Otter Tail Co., St. Elizabeth, Rev. Todd Schneider.
Res., Pelican Rapids, 56572. Tel: 218-736-5230. [CEM]

Elk River, Sherburne Co., The Church of St. Andrew, Rev. Joseph Korf; Deacon Frederick St. Jean.
Res., 566 Fourth St., 55330. Tel: 763-441-1483; Fax: 763-441-1485. [CEM]
School—Tel: 612-441-2216; Fax: 612-441-1146.
Sisters 1; Lay Teachers 15; Students 315.

Elmdale, Morrison Co., St. Edward's, Revs. Gregory Mastey; Joseph Herzing.
Res., 8550 Hwy. 238, Bowlus, 56314. Tel: 320-573-2975. [CEM]

Elrosa, Stearns Co., SS. Peter and Paul, Rev. LeRoy Scheierl. In res., Rev. Lawrence Botz.
Res., 56325. Tel: 320-697-5541. [CEM]

Farming, Stearns Co., St. Catherine's, Rev. Michael Kwatera, O.S.B.
Res., Rte. 1, Richmond P.O., 56368. Tel: 320-548-3467. [CEM]

Fergus Falls, Otter Tail Co., Our Lady of Victory, Rev. Robert Kieffer.
Res., 207 Vine St. N., 56537. Tel: 218-736-2429; Fax: 218-736-4407. [JC]
School—Tel: 218-736-6661; Fax: 218-736-4407.
Lay Teachers 8; Students 133.

Flensburg, Morrison Co., Sacred Heart, Rev. David Grundman.
Res., 9406 Church Circle, Little Falls, 56345-9803. Tel: 320-632-5086. [CEM 2]

Foley, Benton Co., St. John's, Rev. Alfred J. Heltemes.
Res., Box 337, 56329. Tel: 320-968-7913. [CEM]
School—St. John's Area School. Consolidation of the following parishes: St. John's, Foley; St. Lawrence, Dvelm; St. Elizabeth, Brennyville; St. Joseph, Morrill; SS. Peter & Paul, Gilman; St. Patrick of Minden Township. Tel: 320-968-7972.
Lay Teachers 8; Students 108.

Foreston, Mille Lacs Co., St. Louis Bertrand, Rev. James Cashman, O.S.C.
Res., 187 First St. S., P.O. Box 128, 56330. Tel: 320-294-5460; Fax: 320-294-5588. [CEM]

Foxhome, Wilkin Co., St. Joseph. Closed. For inquiries for parish records contact St. Mary of the Presentation, Breckenridge.

Freeport, Stearns Co., Sacred Heart, Rev. Roger Klassen, O.S.B.
Res., 56331-0155. Tel: 320-836-2143; Fax: 320-836-2142. [CEM]
School—Tel: 320-836-2591.
Lay Teachers 5; Students 55.

Gilman, Benton Co., SS. Peter and Paul, Rev. Raymond A. Schulzetenberg.
Res., P.O. Box 86, 56333. Tel: 320-387-2255. [CEM]
School—St. John's. (Foley) Area School. Tel: 320-968-7972.

Glenwood, Pope Co., Sacred Heart, Rev. Thomas G. Becker; Deacon Frank Schmainda.
Res., 105 N. Franklin, 56334. Tel: 320-634-3813; Fax: 320-634-0590. [CEM]

Greenwald, Stearns Co., St. Andrew's, Rev. Kenneth J. Popp.
Res., 56335. Tel: 320-987-3160; Fax: 320-987-3306. [CEM]
School—Tel: 320-987-3133.
Sisters 1; Lay Teachers 1; Students 29.

Grey Eagle, Todd Co., St. Joseph's, Rev. Bernard Gruenes; Deacon Vincent Leisen.
Res., P.O. Box 366, 56336. Tel: 320-285-2545; Fax: 320-285-5255. [CEM]

Harding, Morrison Co., Holy Cross, Rev. Roger Thoennes.
Res., Rte. 4, Pierz, 56364. Tel: 320-277-3701. [CEM]

Henning, Otter Tail Co., Church of St. Edward of Henning, Rev. Thomas Knoblach.
Res., 56551. Tel: 218-583-2490. [CEM]

Herman, Grant Co., St. Charles, Rev. Nathan Packard.
Res., P.O. Box 187, Chokio, 56221. Tel: 320-677-2433; Fax: 320-324-2732. [CEM]

Hillman, Morrison Co., St. Rita's, Rev. Raymond Steffes, O.S.C.
Mailing Address: 16691 371st Ave., 56338. Tel: 320-277-3807. [CEM]

Holdingford, Stearns Co., St. Hedwig's, Co-Pastors: Revs. Gerald Mischke; Anthony Oelrich; Deacons Jeffrey Fromm; Jerome Schwarzbauer.
Res., 56340. Tel: 320-746-2231; Fax: 320-746-2449. [CEM]

St. Mary's, Co-Pastors: Revs. Gerald Mischke; Anthony Oelrich; Deacons Jeffrey Fromm; Jerome Schwarzbauer.
Res., 56340. Tel: 320-746-2231; Fax: 320-746-2449. [CEM]

Isanti, Isanti Co., St. Elizabeth Ann Seton, Rev. Jose Edayadiyil, Admin.
Res., 109 Fifth Ave. S., 55040. Tel: 763-444-5226; Fax: 763-444-5226. [CEM]

Jacob's Prairie, Wakefield Township, Stearns Co., St. James, Rev. Florian Muggli, O.S.B.
Res., 25042 County Rd. 2, Cold Spring, 56320. Tel: 320-685-3479. [CEM]

Kensington, Grant Co., Our Lady of the Runestone, Rev. Kenneth Riedemann.
Res., 25890 110th St., Lowry, 56349-4580. Tel: 320-283-5273. [CEM]

Kent, Wilkin Co., St. Thomas, Rev. Anthony Kroll.
Res., 56553. Tel: 218-557-8312. [CEM]

Kimball, Stearns Co., Church of Saint Anne, Rev. Frank S. Tomasiewicz.
Res., 441 Hazel Ave. E., 55353. Tel: 320-398-3860. [CEM]

Lake Henry, Stearns Co., St. Margaret's, Rev. Leo Leisen. In res., Rev. Walter Bednark.
Res., 100 Lillie Ave., Roscoe, 56371. Tel: 320-243-4574. [CEM]

Lake Reno, Pope Co., St. John Nepomuk, Rev. Kenneth Riedemann.
Res., 25890 110th St., Lowry, 56349-4580. Tel: 320-283-5273. [CEM]

Lastrup, Morrison Co., St. John Nepomuk, Rev. Roger Thoennes.
Res., P.O. Box 38, 56344. Tel: 320-468-2111. [CEM]

Little Falls, Morrison Co., St. Mary, Rev. Nicholas Landsberger.
Res., 305 Fourth St., S.E., 56345. Tel: 320-632-5640; Fax: 320-632-6002. [CEM 3]
School—See Inter-Parochial Schools under Institutions Located in the Diocese.

Our Lady of Lourdes, Rev. Leroy M. Kremer; Deacon Bruce Geyer.
Res., 208 W. Broadway, 56345. Tel: 320-632-8243; Fax: 320-616-2129. [CEM]
School—See Inter-Parochial Schools under Institutions Located in the Diocese.

Long Prairie, Todd Co., St. Mary of Mt. Carmel, Rev. Mark Stang; Deacon Mark Zenner.
Res., 409 Central Ave., 56347. Tel: 320-732-2635; Fax: 320-732-2025. [CEM][JC]
School—Tel: 320-732-3478; Fax: 320-732-3894.
Lay Teachers 9; Students 112.

Luxemburg, Stearns Co., St. Wendelin's, Rev. Leon Slominski.
Res., 22714 State Hwy. 15, St. Cloud, 56301. Tel: 320-251-6944. [CEM]
School—Tel: 612-251-9175.
Sisters 1; Lay Teachers 5; Students 105.

Maine, Otter Tail Co., Church of Saint James at Maine, Rev. Paul Folsom.
Res., 409 Lake Ave. N., P.O. Box 671, Battle Lake, 56515. Tel: 218-864-5619. [CEM]

Mayhew Lake, Benton Co., Annunciation, Rev. Francis Britz.
Res., 9965 Mayhew Lake Rd., N.E., Sauk Rapids, 56379. Tel: 320-252-1729. [CEM]

Meire Grove, Stearns Co., St. John's, Rev. Kenneth J. Popp.
Res., Greenwald, 56335. Tel: 320-987-3160. [CEM]
School—Tel: 320-987-3491.
Lay Teachers 2; Students 40.

Melrose, Stearns Co., St. Mary's, Rev. Vincent Lieser.
Res., 211 S. Fifth Ave. E., 56352-1427. Tel: 320-256-4207; Fax: 320-256-4208. [CEM 2]
School—Tel: 320-256-4257.
Lay Teachers 12; Students 198.

Menahga, Wadena Co., The Church of the Assumption of Our Lady of Menahga, Rev. Kevin Schwartz.
Res., St. John the Baptist, Bluffton, 56518. Tel: 218-385-2608. [CEM]

Milaca, Mille Lacs Co., St. Mary's, Rev. Richard John, O.S.C.
Res., 625 3rd Ave., S.E., 56353. Tel: 320-983-3255. [CEM]

Millerville, Douglas Co., Seven Dolors, Rev. Eugene Lemm.
Res., 16921 County Rd. 7, N.W., Brandon, 56315. Tel: 320-876-2240. [CEM]

Mora, Kanabec Co., St. Mary's, Rev. William Vos.
Res., 201-E. Forest Ave., 55051. Tel: 320-679-1593. [CEM]
Mission—Ogilvie, Kanabec Co., St. Kathryn.

Moran, Todd Co., St. Isidore, Rev. Eugene A. Meemken; Deacon Robert Shaffer.
Res., St. Joseph's Church, P.O. Box 5, Clarissa, 56440. Tel: 218-756-2205. [CEM]

Morrill, Morrison Co., St. Joseph's, Rev. Thomas F. Olson.
Res., 16454 - 125th Ave., N.E., Foley, 56329. Tel: 320-355-2454; Fax: 320-355-2819. [CEM]

Morris, Stevens Co., Assumption of the Blessed Virgin Mary, Rev. Alan Wielinski; Deacon Stanley Hennen.
Res., 207 E. Third, Box 287, 56267. Tel: 320-589-3003; Fax: 320-589-1822. [CEM]
School—Tel: 320-589-1704.
Lay Teachers 9; Students 89.

Motley, Morrison Co., St. Michael's, Rev. Robert Landsberger.
Res., P.O. Box 218, 56466. Tel: 218-352-6143; Fax: 218-352-6520.

New Munich, Stearns Co., Immaculate Conception, Rev. Roger Klassen, O.S.B.
Res., Freeport, 56331-0155. Tel: 320-836-2143; Fax: 320-836-2142. [CEM]

North Prairie, Morrison Co., Holy Cross, Revs. Gregory Mastey; Joseph Herzing.
Res., 8550 State Hwy. 238, Bowlus, 56314-9801. Tel: 320-573-2975; Fax: 320-584-8231. [CEM]

Ogilvie, Kanabec Co., St. Kathryn's, Rev. William Vos.
Res., 201 Forest Ave. E., Mora, 55051. Tel: 320-679-1593. [CEM]

Onamia, Mille Lacs Co., The Church of the Holy Cross of Onamia, Rev. William T. McNiff, O.S.C.
Res., 56359. Tel: 320-532-3122. [CEM]

Opole, Stearns Co., Our Lady of Mt. Carmel, Co-Pastors: Revs. Gerald Mischke; Anthony Oelrich; Deacons Jeffrey Fromm; Jerome Schwarzbauer.
Res., St. Mary's Rectory, Holdingford, 56340. Tel: 320-746-2231; Fax: 320-746-2449. [CEM]

Osakis, Douglas Co., Immaculate Conception, Rev. Richard McGuire.
Res., 316 Third Ave. W., P.O. Box F, 56360. Tel: 320-859-2390. [CEM]
School—St. Agnes, Tel: 320-859-2130; Fax: 320-859-5850.
Sisters 1; Lay Teachers 6; Students 89.

Padua, Stearns Co., Church of St. Anthony of Padua, Rev. James Statz.
Res., 33932 County Rd. 18, Sauk Centre, 56378. Tel: 320-352-2521. [CEM]

Parkers Prairie, Otter Tail Co., Church of St. William, Rev. Jeff Ethen.
Res., 56361. Tel: 218-338-2761. [CEM]

Paynesville, Stearns Co., St. Louis, Rev. Richard Leisen.
Res., 505 Burr St., Box 39, 56362. Tel: 320-243-4413. [CEM]

Pearl Lake, Stearns Co., Holy Cross, Rev. Charles Padathuruthy, Admin.; Deacon Andrew Kunkel.
Res., 10651 County Rd. 8, Kimball, 55353. Tel: 320-398-7986; Fax: 320-398-7873. [CEM]
School—Tel: 320-398-7885; Fax: 320-398-7873.
Lay Teachers 4; Students 61.

Pelican Rapids, Otter Tail Co., St. Leonard's, Rev. Todd Schneider.
Res., 56572. Tel: 218-863-5161. [CEM]

Perham, Otter Tail Co., St. Henry's, Rev. David J. Rieder.
Res., Box 216, 56573. Tel: 218-346-4240; Fax: 218-346-4240. [CEM]
School—Area School, Tel: 218-346-6190; Fax: 218-346-6190.
Lay Teachers 8; Students 107.

St. Stanislaus, Rev. David J. Rieder.
Res., P.O. Box 216, 56573. Tel: 218-346-4240; Fax: 218-346-4240. [CEM]

Pierz, Morrison Co., St. Joseph's, Rev. Gerald Dalseth.
Res., 68 Main St., P.O. Box 428, 56364. Tel: 320-468-6033; Fax: 320-468-2296. [CEM]
School—See Inter-Parochial School under Institutions Located in the Diocese.

Princeton, Mille Lacs Co., St. Edward's, Rev. Mark Willenbring.
Res., 804-S. Seventh Ave., 55371. Tel: 763-389-2115; Fax: 763-389-5137. [CEM]

Randall, Morrison Co., St. James, Rev. Alvin Quade.
Res., Box 225, 56475. Tel: 320-749-2720. [CEM]

Rice, Benton Co., Immaculate Conception, Rev. David Maciej; Deacon Russell Hackett.
Res., 130 First Ave., N.E., P.O. Box 189, 56367. Tel: 320-393-2725. [CEM]

Richmond, Stearns Co., SS. Peter and Paul's, Rev. Dominic Ruiz, O.S.B.
Res., P.O. Box 69, 56368. Tel: 320-597-2575; Fax: 320-597-5231. [CEM]
School—Tel: 320-597-2565.
Lay Teachers 7; Students 128.

Rockville, Stearns Co., Mary of the Immaculate Conception, Rev. Msgr. Daniel J. Taufen, S.T.L., Admin.; Deacon Bruce Maltzen.
Res., 113 Broadway, P.O. Box 7, 56369. Tel: 320-251-7801. [CEM]

Roscoe, Stearns Co., St. Agnes, Rev. Leo Leisen.
Res., 100 Lillie Ave., 56371. Tel: 320-243-4574. [CEM]

Royalton, Morrison Co., Holy Trinity, Rev. Laurn Virnig.
Res., 56373. Tel: 320-584-5484. [CEM]

Rush Lake, Otter Tail Co., St. Lawrence, Rev. Jerome Nordick.
Res., 36963 Hwy. 108, Dent, 56528. Tel: 218-758-2700. [CEM]

St. Anna, Stearns Co., Immaculate Conception, Co-Pastors: Revs. Gerald Mischke; Anthony Oelrich; Deacons Jeffrey Fromm; Jerome Schwarzbauer.
Res., St. Mary's Rectory, Holdingford, 56340. Tel: 320-746-2231; Fax: 320-746-2449. [CEM]

St. Anthony, Stearns Co., St. Anthony's, Rev. William Vouk, III.
Res., 24328 Trobec St., Albany, 56307. Tel: 320-845-2416. [CEM]

St. Augusta, Stearns Co., St. Mary Help of Christians, Rev. Robert E. Rolfes.
Res., 24588 County Rd. 7, St. Cloud, 56301. Tel: 320-252-1799; Fax: 320-252-1992. [CEM]
School—Tel: 320-251-3937.
Sisters of St. Benedict 2; Lay Teachers 5; Students 127.

St. Francis, Stearns Co., St. Francis of Assisi, Rev. William Vouk, III.
Res., 44055 State Hwy. 238, Freeport P.O., 56331. Tel: 320-573-2203. [CEM]

St. Joseph, Stearns Co., St. Joseph's, Rev. Gregory Miller, O.S.B.; Deacon Thomas Murray.
Res., 12 W. Minnesota St., 56374. Tel: 320-363-7505; Fax: 320-363-0710. [CEM]
School—Tel: 320-363-7769.
Lay Teachers 12; Students 191.

St. Martin, Stearns Co., St. Martin's, Rev. Michael Kwatera, O.S.B.
Res., 119 Maine St., Box 290, 56376. Tel: 320-548-3550. [CEM]

St. Nicholas, Stearns Co., St. Nicholas, Rev. Charles Padathuruthy, Admin.
Res., 15862 County Rd. 165, Watkins, 55389. Tel: 320-398-7986; 764-7345. [CEM]

St. Rosa, Stearns Co., St. Rose of Lima, Rev. Roger Klassen, O.S.B.
Res., Freeport, 56331-0155. Tel: 320-836-2143; Fax: 320-836-2142. [CEM]

St. Stephen, Stearns Co., St. Stephen's, Rev. John Miller.
Res., 56375. Tel: 320-251-1520. [CEM]

St. Wendel, Stearns Co., St. Columbkille's, Co-Pastors: Revs. Gerald Mischke; Anthony Oelrich; Deacons Jeffrey Fromm; Jerome Schwarzbauer. In res., Rev. Donald Wagner.
Res., St. Mary's Rectory, Holdingford, 56340. Tel: 320-746-2231; Fax: 320-746-2449. [CEM]

Sartell, Stearns Co., St. Francis Xavier, Rev. Eberhard Schefers.
Res., P.O. Box 150, 56377. Tel: 320-252-1363; Fax: 320-259-7090. [CEM]
School—Tel: 320-252-9940.
Lay Teachers 14; Students 170.

Sauk Centre, Stearns Co., Our Lady of the Angels, Rev. Bernard Kahlhamer; Deacon Lawrence Kaas.
Res., 211 S. Seventh, 56378-1505. Tel: 320-352-3502. [CEM]

St. Paul's, Rev. Timothy Wenzel.
Res., 304 Sinclair Lewis Ave., 56378. Tel: 320-352-2196.
School—Holy Family School. Inter-Parochial School: St. Paul's Sauk Centre, Our Lady of Angels, Sauk Center. 231 Sinclair Lewis Ave., 56378. Tel: 320-352-6535; Fax: 320-352-6537.
Lay Teachers 17; Students 280.

Sauk Rapids, Benton Co., Sacred Heart, Rev. Eugene Doyle; Deacon Kurt Kedrowski.
Res., 216 Third Ave. S., 56379. Tel: 320-251-8115; Fax: 320-252-0710. [CEM]
School—324 Third Ave. S., 56379. Tel: 320-251-2854; Fax: 320-251-0705.
Lay Teachers 15; Students 228.

St. Patrick, Rev. Marvin Enneking, Admin.
Res., 7286 Duelm Rd., N.E., 56379. Tel: 320-252-2069. [CEM]

Sedan, Pope Co., Immaculate Conception. Closed. For inquiries for parish records contact Sacred Heart, Glenwood.

Sobieski, Morrison Co., St. Stanislaus, Rev. David Grundman.
Res., 9406 Church Cir., Little Falls, 56345-9803. Tel: 320-632-5086. [CEM]

Spring Hill, Stearns Co., St. Michael's, Rev. Leo Leisen. In res., Rev. Edward Ramacher.
Res., 100 Lillie Ave., Roscoe, 56371. Tel: 320-243-4574. [CEM]

Staples, Todd Co., Sacred Heart, Rev. Lauren A. Germann.
Res., 310 Fourth St. N.E., Box 177, 56479. Tel: 218-894-2296. [JC]
School—Tel: 218-894-2077.
Lay Teachers 7; Students 110.

Swanville, Morrison Co., St. John the Baptist, Rev. Bernard Gruenes.
Res., 22 1st St., P.O. Box 68, 56382. Tel: 320-547-2920; Fax: 320-547-2578. [CEM]

Tintah, Traverse Co., St. Gall's, Rev. Andrew Marthaler.
Res., 56583. Tel: 218-369-2188. [CEM]

Upsala, Morrison Co., St. Mary, Revs. Gregory Mastey; Joseph Herzing.
Res., 8550 Hwy. 238, Bowlus, 56314. Tel: 320-573-2975; Fax: 320-584-8231. [CEM]

Urbank, Otter Tail Co., Sacred Heart, Rev. Jeff Ethen.
Res., Rte. 2, Box 133, P.O. Parkers Prairie, 56361. Tel: 218-267-2661. [CEM]

Verndale, Wadena Co., St. Frederick's, Rev. Peter K. Kirchner, Jr.
Res., 20 Brown St. N., P.O. Box C, 56481. Tel: 218-445-5786. [CEM]

Villard, Pope Co., St. Bartholomew's, Rev. Joseph Vandeberg.
Res., St. Alexius Church, West Union, 56389. Tel: 320-352-2563. [CEM]

Vineland, Mille Lacs Co., St. Therese, Little Flower Indian Mission,
P.O. Box 500, Onamia, 56359. Tel: 320-532-3614; Fax: 320-532-5222. [CEM]

Wadena, Wadena Co., St. Ann's, Rev. Albert Holmes.
Res., 514 First St., S.E., 56482. Tel: 218-631-1593; Fax: 218-631-7149. [CEM]
School—Tel: 218-631-2631; Fax: 218-631-7149.
Lay Teachers 9; Students 75.

Wahkon, Mille Lacs Co., Sacred Heart, Rev. Raymond Steffes, O.S.C.
Mailing Address: Crosier Community, P.O. Box 500, Onamia, 56359. Tel: 320-532-3103; Fax: 320-532-3103, Ext. 214. [CEM]

Waite Park, Stearns Co., St. Joseph's, Rev. Ronald Weyrens; Deacon Richard Midas.
Res., 106 Seventh Ave. N., 56387. Tel: 320-251-5231; Fax: 320-251-3010. [CEM]
School—Tel: 320-251-4741, Ext. 1.
Lay Teachers 8; Students 131.

Ward Springs, Todd Co., St. Bernard's. Closed. For inquiries for parish records contact St. Joseph, Grey Eagle.

West Union, Todd Co., St. Alexius, Rev. Joseph Vandeberg.
Res., P.O. Box 4A, 56389. Tel: 320-352-2563. [CEM]

Wheaton, Traverse Co., Ave Maria, Rev. Stanley Wieser.
Res., 201 Ninth St. S., 56296. Tel: 320-563-4421. [JC]

Zimmerman, Sherburne Co., St. Pius X, Rev. Antonio Marfori.
Res., Box 152, 55398. Tel: 763-856-4401; Fax: 763-856-4401. [CEM]

Chaplains of Public Institutions

ST. CLOUD. *Minnesota State Reformatory for Men.* Rev. Joel Kelly, O.S.B., Res., St. John's Abbey, Collegeville, 56321.
U.S. Veteran's Hospital 56301. Rev. Alfred Stangl.

CAMBRIDGE. *Cambridge State School and Hospital.* Vacant. 55008.

FERGUS FALLS. *State Hospital Chapel.* Vacant. 56537.

Special Assignment:
Reverend Fathers—
Belland, David
Eccleston, John
Fehrenbacher, Henry
Garding, William
Stangl, Alfred
Taufen, Daniel, V.G.
Thoennes, James
Trussel, Christopher
Wagner, Donald
Walz, Richard

On Duty Outside the Diocese:
Reverend Fathers—
Kalkman, Richard, 23 Diaz Ave., San Francisco, CA 94132

Retired:
Reverend Fathers—
Bednark, Walter, 23189 State Hwy. 4, Paynesville, MN 56362
Belair, Eugene, 511 S. Fourth Ave, Princeton, MN 55371
Botz, Lawrence, Box 95, Elrosa, MN 56325

Brenny, Kenneth, P.O. Box 608, Buckman, MN 56317
Donnay, Raymond, 808 Ann Marie Cir., # 701, Little Falls, MN 56345
Ebner, Frank, 10339 Parrish Ave., N.E., Elk River, MN 55330
Fadrowski, Stanislaus, 1934 Michigan Ave., Englewood, FL 34224
Finnegan, Roscoe L., 715 Farney Rd., Las Cruces, NM 88005
Furlan, William, 320 Fourth Ave. S., Sauk Rapids, MN 56379
Gall, Sylvester, 520 First St., N.E., Apt. 80, Sartell, MN 56377
Haupt, Lloyd, 929 Brenda Lee Dr., St. Cloud, MN 56303
Heid, Richard J., Box 256, Brandon, MN 56315
Hoppe, Arthur, 28905 County Rd. 17, Freeport, MN 56331
Illies, Wilfred, 2000 15th Ave., S.E. #338, St. Cloud, MN 56304
Kinzer, Victor, 321 Jefferson St., Apt. 6, Alexandria, MN 56308
Kleinschmidt, Sylvester, 412 First St. S., Apt. 1, Sauk Centre, MN 56378
Kloeckner, William, 10540 County Rd. 34, N.W., Alexandria, MN 56308
Kraemer, Edwin, 828 Village Ave., Sartell, MN 56377
Lang, Raymond, 1615 15th Ave., S.E. #342, St. Cloud, MN 56304
MaJerus, Daniel, 8722 Timberbriar, San Antonio, TX 78250
Maus, Le Roy, 25-8th Ave., S., St. Cloud, MN 56301
Meyer, Thomas, 30325 Pan Drive, Cushing, MN 56443
Minette, James, 101 Enterprise Dr., Apt. 163, Rohnert Park, CA 94928
Otto, Leo, R.R. 3, Box 118, Perham, MN 56573
Pavelis, Harold, Box 88, Concord, CA 94522
Pecovnik, Karel, RR #1, Box 211A, Parkers Prairie, MN 56361
Podrosky, Alfred, 117 Bechwood Dr., Monongahela, PA 15063
Poncelet, Frank, Institute of Christ the King, P.O. Box 12, Glenwood, MN 56334
Ramacher, Edward, 102 St. Michael Ave. N. Spring Hill, Melrose, MN 56352
Rieder, Donald, 1615 15th Ave., S.E., Apt. 328, St. Cloud, MN 56304
Riley, Patrick, 3034 Fulton Cir., Clearwater, MN 55320
Santo, Vincent, Das Goldene Wohnheim, 632 Main St., New Munich, MN 56356
Sauer, Alban, 1120 11th Ave. N., St. Cloud, MN 56303
Schmelzer, Paul, 213 Third St. S., St. Cloud, MN 56301
Schmitt, Silverius, 5290-175th St., N.W., Box 353, Royalton, MN 56373
Schwieters, Severin, 207-3rd. St. S., St. Cloud, MN 56301
Schwinghammer, Claude, Park Gardens, 114 First St. N., Apt. 219, Waite Park, MN 56387
Speiser, Allan, 101 Riverside Dr. S.E. Apt. 224, St. Cloud, MN 56304
Thielman, Kenneth, Park View Center, 125 N. Fifth Ave. W., Melrose, MN 56352
Torborg, Elmer, P.O. Box 1248, St. Cloud, MN 56302
Vogel, Arthur, 617 Pinecone Rd., Apt. 308, Sartell, MN 56377
Vogrin, Joseph, RR # 1, Box 211A, Parkers Prairie, MN 56361
Wey, Richard, 30325 Pan Dr., Cushing, MN 56443
Wiersgalla, Joseph, St. Benedict's Senior Community, 1810 S.E. Minnesota Blvd., St. Cloud, MN 56304
Zylla, Paul, 1615-15th Ave., S.E. #251, St. Cloud, MN 56304

Permanent Deacons:
Adams, Cecil, St. Henry's Monticello
Anderberg, George, Owatonna
Bates, Kenneth, Country Manor, Sartell
Bobertz, Charles, Holy Spirit, St. Cloud
Eichers, Elmer, (Retired)
Fromm, Jeffrey, St. Mary's, Holdingford
Geyer, Bruce, Our Lady of Lourdes, Little Falls
Hackett, Russell, Immaculate Conception, Rice
Hennen, Stanley, Assumption, Morris
Hennes, James C., St. Augustine, St. Cloud
Kaas, Lawrence, Our Lady of the Angels, Sauk Centre
Keable, Michael, St. Paul, St. Cloud
Kedrowski, Kurt, Sacred Heart, Sauk Rapids
Kosiba, Leo, St. Mary, St. Cloud
Krebs, Brian
Kruchten, Kenneth R., (Retired)
Kunkel, Andrew, Holy Cross, Pearl Lake
Leisen, Vincent, St. Joseph, Grey Eagle
Lindmeier, David, St. Paul, St. Cloud
Maltzen, Bruce, Mary of the Immaculate Conception, Rockville
Midas, Richard, St. Joseph, Waite Park
Murray, Thomas, St. Joseph, St. Joseph.
Nord, Carl, St. Anthony, St. Cloud
Reker, Fred, St. John Cantius, St. Cloud
Roth, Jerome
Salchert, John, St. Boniface, Cold Spring
Schmainda, Frank, Sacred Heart, Glenwood
Schmitz, Vernon, Holy Spirit, St. Cloud
Schwarzbauer, Jerome, St. Mary's, Holdingford
Scott, John W., (Retired)
Shaffer, Robert, St. Isidore, Moran
St. Jean, Fred, St. Andrew, Elk River
Steele, Gregory J., Immaculate Conception, Becker
Tzinski, Donald, Elko, NV
Warren, Todd, St. Paul, St. Cloud
Woods, John, St. Peter, St. Cloud
Yanish, Stephen
Zenner, Mark, Mary of Mt. Carmel, Long Prairie

INSTITUTIONS LOCATED IN THE DIOCESE

[A] SEMINARIES, RELIGIOUS OR SCHOLASTICATES

COLLEGEVILLE. *St. John's Seminary*, 56321. Tel: 320-363-2100; Fax: 320-363-3145.
E-mail: mbanken@csbsju.edu
Web site: www.csbsju.edu/sot
Rev. Luke Steiner, O.S.B., Rector. Legal Title: *St. John's Seminary.*

[B] COLLEGES AND UNIVERSITIES

COLLEGEVILLE. *St. John's University*, (1857), 56321-2000. Tel: 320-363-2011; Fax: 320-363-2504.
E-mail: nthorburn@csbsju.edu
Web site: www.csbsju.edu
For a complete listing, refer to the Colleges and Universities section.

ST. JOSEPH. *College of St. Benedict*, (1913) 37 S. College Ave., 56374-2099. Tel: 320-363-5407 (Inst. Mktg. & Communications); Fax: 320-363-5136 (Inst. Mktg. & Comm.).
E-mail: cms@csbsju.edu
Web site: www.csbsju.edu
For a complete listing, refer to the Colleges and Universities section.

[C] HIGH SCHOOLS, DIOCESAN

ST. CLOUD. *Cathedral High and John XXIII Middle School*, P.O. Box 1579, 56302. Tel: 320-251-3421; Fax: 320-253-5576. Mr. Robert Stewart, Pres.; Mr. Raymond Aafedt, Prin.; Rev. Christopher Trussel. Priests 1; Sisters 1; Lay Teachers 55; Students 756.
Cathedral High School Education Foundation, P.O. Box 1579, 56302. Tel: 320-251-3421. Jim Marrer, Chm.

[D] HIGH SCHOOLS, PRIVATE

COLLEGEVILLE. *St. John's Preparatory School*. College Preparatory. P.O. Box 4000, 56321. Tel: 320-363-3315; Fax: 320-363-3513.
E-mail: gtavis@csbsju.edu
Web site: www.csbsju.edu
Rev. Gordon Tavis, O.S.B., Pres. Priests 1; Students 292(Grades 7-12); Brothers 2; Lay Teachers 17.

[E] INTER-PAROCHIAL SCHOOLS

ST. CLOUD. *St. Elizabeth Ann Seton School*. (Grades K-3), Primary: 1615 Eleventh Ave. S., 56301. Tel: 320-251-1988. Bonnie Massmann, Prin. Lay Teachers 12; Students 160. Middle: (Grades 4-6), 2410 First St. N., 56303. Tel: 320-251-6231. Dan Hollenhorst, Prin. Lay Teachers 7; Students 103. Consolidation of schools of the following parishes: Holy Spirit & St. Anthony, St. Cloud.

Sts. Peter, Paul and Michael School. (Grades K-4), Primary: 925 N. 30th Ave., 56303. Tel: 320-251-4737; Fax: 320-253-7110.
E-mail: stcsppmssc@impresso.com
Principals: Mrs. Sharon Bichler; Gary Heineman. Lay Teachers 20. Middle: (Grades 5-8), 1215 N. 11th Ave., 56303. Tel: 320-251-5295. Lay Teachers 19; Students 644. Consolidation of the following parishes: St. Michael; St. Paul; St. Peter, St. Cloud.

FOLEY. *St. John's Area School*. (Grades K-6), 215 7 Ave. S., 56329. Tel: 320-968-7972; Fax: 320-968-9956. Mary Sahin, Prin. Consolidation of the following parishes: St. John of Foley; St. Lawrence, Duelm; St. Elizabeth, Brennyville; St. Joseph, Morrill; SS. Peter and Paul, Gilman; St Louis, Foreston; St. Patrick of Minden Township. Lay Teachers 9; Students 100.

LITTLE FALLS. *Mary of Lourdes Elementary and Middle School*. (Grades K-4), Primary: 307 Fourth St., S.E., 56345. Tel: 320-632-5408; Fax: 320-632-5409.
E-mail: moles@uslink.net
Web site: www.molschool.org
Janet Stone, Prin. Benedictine Sister 1; Lay Teachers 12; Students 182; Preschool Students 40. Middle: (Grades 5-8), 205 N.W. Third St., 56345. Tel: 320-632-6742; Fax: 320-632-3556. Debra J. Meyer, Prin. Lay Teachers 10; Students 130. Consolidation of following parishes: St. Mary and Our Lady of Lourdes, Little Falls.

PIERZ. *Holy Trinity School*, Box 427, 56364. Tel: 320-468-6446; Fax: 320-468-6446.
E-mail: holytrinity@pierznet.com
Sr. Joyce Willenbring, O.S.B.; Rev. Gerald Dalseth, Pres. Corporate Board. Lay Teachers 13; Students 173. Consolidation of the following parishes: St. Michael's, Buckman; Holy Cross, Harding; St. John Nepomuk, Lastrup; St. Joseph, Pierz.

SAUK CENTRE. *Holy Family School*. (Grades K-6), 231 Sinclair Lewis Ave., 56378. Tel: 320-352-6535; Fax: 320-352-6537.
E-mail: hfs@isd743.k12.mn.us
Web site: www.rc.net/stcloud/hfs
Lynn Peterson, Prin. Consolidation of the following parishes: St. Paul's and Our Lady of the Angels, Sauk Centre. Lay Teachers 17; Students 279.

[F] HOMES FOR EMOTIONALLY DISTURBED AND HANDICAPPED

ST. CLOUD. *Caritas Family Services, Catholic Charities Community Services*, 305 N. Seventh Ave., 56303. Tel: 320-650-1660; Fax: 320-252-4508.
Web site: www.stcdio.org/cc/
For a complete listing, refer to the Special Care Facilities section.

Community Services of Catholic Charities, 205 Seventh Ave. N., 56303. Tel: 320-650-3337; Fax: 320-240-3339.
Web site: www.stcdio.org/cc/
For a complete listing, refer to the Special Care Facilities section.

Day Programs Services, 1726 Seventh Ave. S., 56301. Tel: 320-650-1590; Fax: 320-203-1173.
E-mail: nwebster@gw.stcdio.org
For a complete listing, refer to the Special Care Facilities section.

In-Home Family Services, Catholic Charities Community Services, 700 Mall Germain, 56302. Tel: 320-251-1404; Fax: 320-252-8180.
Web site: www.stcdio.org/cc/
For a complete listing, refer to the Special Care Facilities section.

LaPaz Community Inc., 1730 Seventh Ave. S., 56301. Tel: 320-253-9470; Fax: 320-253-7464
For a complete listing, refer to the Special Care Facilities section.

St. Cloud Children's Home of the Diocese of St. Cloud, 1726 Seventh Ave. S., 56301. Tel: 320-650-1500; Fax: 320-251-3198
For a complete listing, refer to the Special Care Facilities section.

St. Elizabeth Home, 306 15th Ave. N., 56303. Tel: 320-252-8350; Fax: 320-252-8350.
E-mail: dtupy@gw.stcdio.org
For a complete listing, refer to the Special Care Facilities section.

COLD SPRING. *Bethany Home*, 13 Eighth Ave. S., 56320. Tel: 320-685-7899
For a complete listing, refer to the Special Care Facilities section.

Mother Teresa Home, 101 Tenth Ave., 56320. Tel: 320-685-8626; Fax: 320-685-8626
For a complete listing, refer to the Special Care Facilities section.

St. Ann's Home, 103 10th Ave. N., 56320. Tel: 320-685-7898; Fax: 320-685-8626
For a complete listing, refer to the Special Care Facilities section.

St. Luke's Home, 411 Eighth Ave. N., 56320. Tel: 320-685-7750
For a complete listing, refer to the Special Care Facilities section.

FERGUS FALLS. *Catholic Charities Intensive Treatment Unit*, P.O. Box 1006, 56538-1006. Tel: 218-739-9325; Fax: 218-739-2242
For a complete listing, refer to the Special Care Facilities section.

LITTLE FALLS. *St. Camillus Place*, 1100 S.E. Fourth St., 56345. Tel: 320-632-1212; Fax: 320-632-1383
For a complete listing, refer to the Special Care Facilities section.

WAITE PARK. *St. Francis Home*, 25 Second St. N., 56387. Tel: 320-251-7630
For a complete listing, refer to the Special Care Facilities section.

[G] GENERAL HOSPITALS

ST. CLOUD. *St. Cloud Hospital*, 1406 Sixth Ave. N., 56303. Tel: 320-251-2700; Fax: 320-255-5711.
Web site: www.stcloudhospital.com
For a complete listing, refer to the Hospitals section.

ALBANY. *Albany Area Hospital*, 300 Third Ave., 56307. Tel: 320-845-2121; Fax: 320-845-4707
For a complete listing, refer to the Hospitals section.

BRECKENRIDGE. *St. Francis Medical Center*, 415 Oak St., 56520. Tel: 218-643-3000; Fax: 218-643-7502.
E-mail: nancywhitney@chi-midwest.org
For a complete listing, refer to the Hospitals section.

LITTLE FALLS. *St. Gabriel's Hospital*, 815 S.E. Second St., 56345. Tel: 320-632-5441; Fax: 320-632-1190
For a complete listing, refer to the Hospitals section.

[H] HOMES FOR AGED

ST. CLOUD. *St. Benedict's Senior Community*, 1810 Minnesota Blvd., S.E., 56304. Tel: 320-252-0010; Fax: 320-654-2351
For a complete listing, refer to the Special Care Facilities section.

ALBANY. *Mother of Mercy Nursing Home and Retirement Center*, Box 676, 56307. Tel: 320-845-2195; Fax: 320-845-7092.
E-mail: mother@albanytel.com
For a complete listing, refer to the Special Care Facilities section.

BRECKENRIDGE. *St. Francis Home*, 56520. Tel: 218-643-7661.
E-mail: davidnelson@chi-midwest.org
For a complete listing, refer to the Special Care Facilities section.

COLD SPRING. *Assumption Court*, 615 First St. N., 56320. Tel: 320-685-4110; Fax: 320-685-7044
For a complete listing, refer to the Special Care Facilities section.

Assumption Home, 715 First St. N., 56320. Tel: 320-685-3693; Fax: 320-685-7044
For a complete listing, refer to the Special Care Facilities section.

John Paul Apartments, 200 Eighth Ave. N., 56320. Tel: 320-685-4429; Fax: 320-685-7044.
E-mail: jpa@cloudnet.com
For a complete listing, refer to the Special Care Facilities section.

LITTLE FALLS. *Alverna Apartments*, 300 Eighth Ave., S.E., 56345. Tel: 320-632-1246; Fax: 320-632-1190
For a complete listing, refer to the Special Care Facilities section.

St. Otto's Care Center, 920 S.E. 4th St., 56345. Tel: 320-632-9281; Fax: 320-632-1120
For a complete listing, refer to the Special Care Facilities section.

MORRIS. *Villa of St. Francis Nursing Home*, 1001 Scott Ave., 56267. Tel: 320-589-1133; Fax: 320-589-3005.
E-mail: vosf@info.link.net
For a complete listing, refer to the Special Care Facilities section.

PARKERS PRAIRIE. *St. William's Living Center*, P.O. Box 30, 56361. Tel: 218-338-4671; Fax: 218-338-5917.
E-mail: pbaer@midwestinfo.net
For a complete listing, refer to the Special Care Facilities section.

PIERZ. *St. Mary's Villa Inc.*, 56364. Tel: 320-468-6405
For a complete listing, refer to the Special Care Facilities section.

STAPLES. *Mary Rondorf Retirement Home of Sacred Heart Parish*, 56479. Tel: 218-894-2124; Fax: 218-894-3067
For a complete listing, refer to the Special Care Facilities section.

[I] MONASTERIES AND RESIDENCES OF PRIESTS AND BROTHERS

COLLEGEVILLE. *St. John's Abbey, of the Order of St. Benedict.* and St. John's University, School of Theology, Seminary, Preparatory School and Novitiate. P.O. Box 2015, 56321-2015. Tel: 320-363-2011; Fax: 320-363-2504.
Web site: www.sja.osb.org
Rt. Rev. John Klassen, O.S.B., Abbot and Chancellor; Very Revs. Geoffrey Fecht, O.S.B., Prior; Douglas Mullin, O.S.B., Subprior; Revs. Henry Anderl, O.S.B.; Knute Anderson, O.S.B.; Thomas Andert, O.S.B.; Alexander Andrews, O.S.B.; Burkard Arnheiter, O.S.B.; Timothy Backous, O.S.B., College Chap.; Stephen Beauclair, O.S.B.; Michael Bik, O.S.B.; Simon Bischof, O.S.B.; Burton Blums, O.S.B.; Roger Botz, O.S.B.; Allan Bouley, O.S.B.; Silvan Bromenshenkel, O.S.B.; Alto Butkowski, O.S.B.; Jerome Coller, O.S.B.; Corwin Collins, O.S.B.; Cletus Connors, O.S.B.; David Cotter, O.S.B.; Alberic Culhane, O.S.B.; Cosmas Dahlheimer, O.S.B.; Godfrey Diekmann, O.S.B.; Meinrad Dindorf, O.S.B.; Ian Dommer, O.S.B.; Nicholas Doub, O.S.B.; Daniel Durken, O.S.B.; John Patrick Earls, O.S.B.; Richard Eckroth, O.S.B.; John Eidenschenk, O.S.B.; Joseph Feders, O.S.B.; Gall Fell, O.S.B.; Jonathon Fischer, O.S.B.; Melchior Freund, O.S.B.; Athanase Fuchs, O.S.B.; Thomas Gillespie, O.S.B.; Cyril Gorman, O.S.B.; Thomas Hallsten, O.S.B., Leave of Absence; Nathanael Hauser, O.S.B.; Henry Bryan Hays, O.S.B.; Francis Hoefgen, O.S.B., Guestmaster; Eric Hollas, O.S.B., HMML Dir.; Roger Kasprick, O.S.B.; Philip Kaufman, O.S.B.; Joel Kelly, O.S.B.; Timothy Kelly, O.S.B.; Chrysostom Kim, O.S.B.; Roger Klassen, O.S.B.; Robert Koopmann, O.S.B.; John Kulas, O.S.B.; Michael Kwatera, O.S.B.; Nathan Libaire, O.S.B.; Dale Launderville, O.S.B.; Donald LeMay, O.S.B.; Jonathan Licari, O.S.B.; Brennan Maiers, O.S.B.; Luke Mancuso, O.S.B.; Paul Marx, O.S.B.; Omer Maus, O.S.B.; J. Patrick McDarby, O.S.B.; Finian McDonald, O.S.B.; Kilian McDonnell, O.S.B.; Eugene J. McGlothlin, O.S.B.; Rene McGraw, O.S.B.; Gregory Miller, O.S.B.; Vernon Miller, O.S.B.; Dustan Moorse, O.S.B.; Florian Muggli, O.S.B.; Michael Naughton, O.S.B., Dir. Liturgical Press; Benedict Nordick, O.S.B.; Virgil O'Neill, O.S.B.; Michael Patella, O.S.B.; Roman Paur, O.S.B.; Raymond Pedrizetti, O.S.B.; Robert Pierson, O.S.B.; Martin Rath, O.S.B.; James Reichert, O.S.B.; Berthold Ricker, O.S.B.; Stanley Roche, O.S.B.; Landelin A. Robling, O.S.B.; Anthony Ruff, O.S.B.; Dominic Ruiz, O.S.B.; Bartholomew Sayles, O.S.B.; Julian Schmiesing, O.S.B.; Mark Schneider, O.S.B.; Francisco Schulte, O.S.B.; Kevin Seasoltz, O.S.B.; Gregory Sebastian, O.S.B.; Cyprian Seitz, O.S.B.; Gervase Soukup, O.S.B.; Gregory Soukup, O.S.B.; Mathias Spier, O.S.B.; Benjamin Stein, O.S.B.; Luke Steiner, O.S.B., Seminary Rector; Columba Stewart, O.S.B., Formation Dir.; Edwin Stueber, O.S.B.; Don Talafous, O.S.B.; Allen Tarlton, O.S.B.; Donald Tauscher, O.S.B.; Gordon Tavis, O.S.B., Pres., St. John's Preparatory School; Vincent Tegeder, O.S.B.; Aelred Tegels, O.S.B.; Mark Thamert, O.S.B.; Wilfred Theisen, O.S.B.; Hilary Thimmesh, O.S.B.; Thomas Thole, O.S.B.; James Tingerthal, O.S.B.; Jerome Tupa, O.S.B.; Stephen Wagman, O.S.B.; Arnold Weber, O.S.B.; Magnus Wenninger, O.S.B.; Robert Wieber, O.S.B.; Hugh Witzmann, O.S.B.; Bruce Wollmering, O.S.B.; Angelo Zankl, O.S.B.
On Special Assignments: Very Rev. Simeon J. Thole, O.S.B., Admin., St. Leo Abbey, Saint Leo, FL, 33574-9999. Tel: 352-588-8623. Rev. Luigi Bertocchi, O.S.B., Sant' Anselmo, Piazza Cavalieri di Malta, 5, Rome, Italy, 1-00153. Tel: 3906-5791-264. Rev. Daniel Ward, O.S.B., 3095 Chesterwood Dr., Silver Springs, MD, 20906. Tel: 301-460-4688. Rev. Barnabas Laubach, O.S.B., St. Bernardine Hospital, 2101 N. Waterman Ave., San Bernardino, CA, 92404. Tel: 909-883-8711. Rev. Blane Wasnie, O.S.B., Duluth, MN.
Priests of the Abbey Serving Abroad: Rev. George Wolf, O.S.B., St. Augustine Monastery, Box N-3940, Nassau, Bahamas. Tel: 242-364-1331; Fax: 242-364-8929. Very Rev. Mel Taylor, O.S.B.; Rev. Fintan Bromenshenkel, O.S.B., St. Augustine Monastery, Box N-3940, Nassau, Bahamas. Tel: 242-364-1511; Fax: 242-364-8929. Revs. Neal Henry Lawrence, O.S.B.; Aloysius Michels, O.S.B.; Thomas Wahl, O.S.B.; Very Revs. Peter Kawamura, O.S.B.; Kieran Nolan, O.S.B., Prior; Rev. William Skudlarek, O.S.B. Japan, Holy Trinity Benedictine Monastery, 3110 Fujimi-Fujimi Machi, Nagano Ken, Japan, 399-0211. Tel: 011-81-266-62-8770; Fax: 011-81-266-62-8765. Rev. Cyprian Weaver, O.S.B., Benedictine Wimmer Priory, 1 Lane 96, Ming Chih Rd., Sec. 3, Taishan, Taipei, Hsien Republic of China, Taiwan, 24302. Tel: 011-886-2901-8343. Community Priests 130; Professed Brothers 63; Novices 1; Claustral Oblate 1.

ONAMIA. *Crosier Monastery*, 56359. Tel: 320-532-3103; Fax: 320-532-5222.
E-mail: jremmers@aol.com
Web site: www.crosiers.org
Legal Title: *Crosier Fathers of Onamia.* Very Rev. James Remmerswaal, O.S.C., Prior.; Revs. Joseph Brennan, O.S.C.; Charles Kunkel, O.S.C.; William T. McNiff, O.S.C.; Henry Miller, O.S.C.; Bernard Mischke, O.S.C.; James Moeglein, O.S.C.; Raymond Steffes, O.S.C.
Priests Elsewhere: Revs. Clement N. Gustin, O.S.C., Hibbing; James Cashman, O.S.C., Foreston; John J. Fleischhacker, O.S.C., McGregor; Richard T. John, O.S.C., Milaca.
The National Shrine of St. Odilia is sponsored and maintained by the Crosier Fathers of Onamia. Priests in Residence 8; Priests Elsewhere 4; Brothers in Residence 13.

[J] CONVENTS AND RESIDENCES FOR SISTERS

LITTLE FALLS. *St. Francis Convent*, 116 Eighth Ave., S.E., 56345. Tel: 320-632-2981; Fax: 320-632-6313.
E-mail: info@fslf.org
Web site: www.fslf.org
Motherhouse of Franciscan Sisters of Little Falls, MN. Sr. Rose Margaret Schneider, Community Min.; Rev. John Eccleston, Chap. Sisters 79; Total in Community 238.

ST. JOSEPH. *St. Benedict's Monastery*, 104 Chapel Ln., 56374-0220. Tel: 320-363-7100; Fax: 320-363-7130.
E-mail: bkort@csbsju.edu
Web site: www.sbm.osb.org
Motherhouse and Formation House for Sisters of the Order of Saint Benedict. Sr. Ephrem Hollermann, O.S.B., Prioress; Sr. Elaine Schroeder, O.S.B., Coord. Eucharistic Presiders. Sisters 191; Total in Community 390.

SAUK RAPIDS. *St. Clare's Monastery.* Major Papal Cloister, 421-S. 4th St., 56379. Tel: 320-251-3556. Franciscan Poor Clare Nuns. Mother Mary Peter, O.S.C, Abbess. Cloistered Nuns: Solemn Professed 14; Simple Professed 1; Extern Sisters: Perpetual Professed 3; Novices 1.

[K] RETREAT HOUSES

ST. FRANCIS. *Pacem in Terris Center for Spirituality*, Hermitage Retreats, P.O. Box 418, 55070. Tel: 763-444-6408; Fax: 763-444-9649.
E-mail: jeffrey@paceminterris.org
Jeffrey Wanchena, Dir.

[L] NEWMAN CENTERS

ST. CLOUD. *Newman Center, Inc.*, 396 First Ave. S., 56301. Tel: 320-251-3260; 251-2712 (Home); Fax: 320-252-3930.
E-mail: newman@stcloudstate.edu
Web site: www.stclouldstate.edu/~newman/
Rev. Kevin Anderson.

MORRIS. *Newman Catholic Student Center*, 306 E. Fourth St., 56267. Tel: 320-589-1947.
E-mail: newmanha@info-link.net
Web site: www.mrs.umn.edu/~catholic/
Directors of Campus Ministry: Jeff Schaffer; Carol Schaffer.

[M] MISCELLANEOUS

ST. CLOUD. *Domus Transitional Housing of Catholic Charities*, 17-19 1/2 Ave., S., 56301. Tel: 320-259-9270; Fax: 320-259-4967.
E-mail: domusthp@cloudnet.com
321 & 323 Fourteenth Ave. S.E., 56301. Tel: 320-259-9270; Fax: 320-259-4967. Mr. Steven P. Bresnahan; Harvey Schmitt.

Key Row Community, Inc.; Key Row-Little Falls, Inc.; Key Row-Milaca, Inc., 157 Roosevelt Rd., Ste. 200, 56301. Tel: 320-253-9470. Organizations providing low-cost housing to Elderly and Families Little Falls, Milaca, Morris, and St. Cloud. Mr. Steven P. Bresnahan, Exec. Dir.; Harvey Schmitt, Dir. Housing Svcs.

Sacred Music Inc. of the Diocese of St. Cloud, Box 1248, 56302.

St. Joseph's Apartment, Inc. Located in St. Joseph and Sauk Centre, MN. 1730 Seventh Ave. S., 56301. Tel: 320-253-9470. Mr. Steven P. Bresnahan, Exec. Dir.; Harvey Schmitt, Dir. Housing Svcs.

St. Therese Center for Special Ministry, 216 N. 6th Ave., 56303. Tel: 320-251-8064. Rev. John H. McManus, O.M.I.; Sr. Georganne Burr, O.S.B.; Nan Figge; Bernadette Stein.

Services to Aging of Catholic Charities, 157 Roosevelt Rd., Ste. 2000, 56301. Tel: 320-252-2048; Fax: 320-253-7464.
E-mail: gdonovan@gw.studio.org
Mr. Steven P. Bresnahan, Exec. Dir.; Sr. Grace Donovan, O.S.B., Dir. Aging Svcs. Legal Title: *Services to Aging of Catholic Charities: Senior Dining / Meals on Wheels, Share-A-Home, Foster Grandparent Program.*

The Society of the Homeless Orphan of the Diocese of St. Cloud, 1730 Seventh Ave. S., 56301. Tel: 320-252-0412.

Valley Vista Apartments of Browns Valley Inc., 1730 Seventh Ave. S., 56301. Tel: 320-253-9470. Mr. Steven P. Bresnahan, Exec. Dir.; Harvey Schmitt, Dir. Housing Svcs.

ALEXANDRIA. *Carmelite Hermits of Adoration, Inc.*, 7005 E. State Hwy. 27, 56308. Tel: 320-762-0341. Sr. Angela, Prioress. Sisters 2.

Central Minnesota Residents Encountering Christ, 1209 Jefferson St., 56308. Tel: 320-763-4580.
E-mail: cmrec@rea-alp.com
Jim Stroot, Coord. Tel: 320-763-4580.

BROWNS VALLEY.
Browns Valley Health Center, 114 Jefferson St. S., 56219. Tel: 320-695-2165; Fax: 320-695-2166.
E-mail: bvhc@info-link.net

CAMBRIDGE. *Benedictine Health Dimensions, Inc.*, 1995 E. Rum River Dr. S., 55008. Tel: 763-689-1162; Fax: 612-689-1197.
E-mail: dmthompson@bhshealth.org
Web site: www.bhshealth.org
Dale Thompson, Pres. & CEO.

LITTLE FALLS. *Franciscan Sisters Health Care, Inc.*, 116 Eighth Ave., S.E., 56345-2981. Tel: 320-632-3601; Fax: 320-632-6313. Sr. Rose Margaret Schneider, O.S.F., Pres.

Franciscan Sisters of Little Falls, MN Charitable Trust, 116 Eighth Ave., S.E., 56345. Tel: 320-632-2981; Fax: 320-632-6313.
E-mail: info@fslf.org
Web site: www.fslf.org

MORRIS. *St. Francis Health Services*, 801 Nevada, Ste. 100, 56267. Tel: 320-589-2004; Fax: 320-589-1270.
E-mail: lhoffman@sfhs.org
Web site: www.sfhs.org

Prairie Community Services, 801 Nevada Ave., P.O. Box 468, 56267. Tel: 320-589-3077; Fax: 320-589-2543.

ONAMIA. *National Shrine of St. Odilia*, 56359. Tel: 320-532-3103; Fax: 320-532-5222.
E-mail: info@crosiers.org
Web site: www.crosiers.org
Sponsored and maintained by The Crosiers of Onamia. Bro. Albert Becker, O.S.C., Contact Person.

ST. JOSEPH. *Monastic Interreligious Dialogue*, St. Benedict's Monastery, 104 Chapel Ln., 56374-2020. Tel: 320-363-7187; Fax: 320-363-7173.
E-mail: khoward@csbsju.edu
Web site: www.monasticdialog.org
Sr. Katherine Howard, O.S.B., Contact Person.

RELIGIOUS INSTITUTES OF MEN REPRESENTED IN THE DIOCESE

For further details refer to the corresponding bracketed number in the Religious Institutes of Men or Women section.

[0200]—*Benedictine Monks.* (Collegeville, MN).—O.S.B.

[0400]—*Canons Regular of the Order of the Holy Cross.* (Province of St. Odilia).—O.S.C.

RELIGIOUS INSTITUTES OF WOMEN REPRESENTED IN THE DIOCESE

[0230]—*Benedictine Sisters of Pontifical Jurisdiction.*—O.S.B.

[1920]—*Congregation of the Sisters of the Holy Cross.*—C.S.C.

[1310]—*Franciscan Sisters of Little Falls, Minnesota.*—O.S.F.

[3760]—*Order of St. Clare.*—O.S.C.

[2970]—*School Sisters of Notre Dame.* (Northwestern Prov.).—S.S.N.D.

[1710]—*Sisters of St. Francis of Mary Immaculate.*—O.S.F.

NECROLOGY

† Kost, Harold J, Belle Prairie, MN Holy Family Church. —Died Aug. 20, 2000.

Archdiocese of St. Louis

(Archidioecesis S. Ludovici)

Most Reverend

JUSTIN F. RIGALI, J.C.D.

Archbishop of St. Louis; ordained April 25, 1961; appointed Titular Archbishop of Bolsena June 8, 1985; ordained Bishop September 14, 1985; appointed Archbishop of St. Louis January 25, 1994; installed March 15, 1994.

The Catholic Center: 4445 Lindell Blvd., St. Louis, MO, 63108-2497. Tel.: 314-633-2222; Fax: 314-633-2333.

Web site address: www.archstl.org

E-mail address: stika@archstl.org

Most Reverend

GEORGE J. GOTTWALD, D.D.

Former Auxiliary Bishop of St. Louis; ordained June 9, 1940; appointed Titular Bishop of Cedamusa and Auxiliary Bishop of St. Louis June 10, 1961; consecrated August 8, 1961; retired August 1, 1988. *All communications should be addressed to: The Catholic Center, 4445 Lindell Blvd., St. Louis, MO, 63108-2497.*

Most Reverend

JOSEPH F. NAUMANN, D.D.

Auxiliary Bishop of St. Louis; ordained May 24, 1975; appointed Titular Bishop of Caput Cilla and Auxiliary Bishop of St. Louis July 9, 1997; consecrated September 3, 1997. *Res., 8900 Clayton Rd., Richmond Heights, MO, 63117.*

Most Reverend

MICHAEL J. SHERIDAN, D.D.

Auxiliary Bishop of St. Louis; ordained May 29, 1971; appointed Titular Bishop of Thibiuca and Auxiliary Bishop of St. Louis July 9, 1997; consecrated September 3, 1997. *Res., 6047 Bishops Place, St. Louis, MO, 63109.*

DIOCESE JULY 18, 1826; ARCHDIOCESE JULY 20, 1847.

Square Miles 5,968.

Comprises that portion of the State of Missouri bounded on the north by the northern line of the County of Lincoln; on the west by the western lines of the Counties of Lincoln, Warren, Franklin and Washington; on the south by the southern lines of the Counties of Washington, St. Francois and Perry; on the east by the Mississippi River.

Heavenly Patrons—Saint Louis, King, Saint Vincent de Paul and Saint Rose Philippine Duchesne.

For legal titles of parishes and archdiocesan institutions, consult the Catholic Center.

STATISTICAL OVERVIEW

Personnel	
Archbishop	1
Auxiliary Bishops	2
Retired Bishops	1
Abbots	1
Retired Abbots	1
Priests: Diocesan Active in Diocese	333
Priests: Active Outside Diocese	18
Priests: Diocesan in Foreign Missions	7
Priests: Retired, Sick or Absent	98
Number of Diocesan Priests	456
Religious Priests in Diocese	381
Extern Priests in Diocese	13
Ordinations:	
Diocesan Priests	6
Religious Priests	2
Permanent Deacons	15
Permanent Deacons in Diocese	225
Total Brothers	157
Total Sisters	2,106
Parishes	
Parishes	228
With Resident Pastor:	
Resident Diocesan Priests	195
Resident Religious Priests	26
Without Resident Pastor:	
Administered by Priests	7
Missions	8
Closed Parishes	2

Welfare	
Catholic Hospitals	10
Total Assisted	1,180,000
Homes for the Aged	34
Total Assisted	30,000
Residential Care of Children	9
Total Assisted	1,200
Day Care and Extended Day Care Centers	16
Total Assisted	1,700
Specialized Homes	17
Total Assisted	4,000
Special Centers for Social Services	35
Total Assisted	124,043
Educational	
Seminaries, Diocesan	2
Students from This Diocese	43
Students from Other Diocese	60
Seminaries, Religious	5
Students Religious	55
Total Seminarians	98
Colleges and Universities	2
Total Students	13,172
High Schools, Diocesan and Parish	14
Total Students	6,649
High Schools, Private	15
Total Students	9,052
Elementary Schools, Diocesan and Parish	139

Total Students	41,469
Elementary Schools, Private	8
Total Students	1,842
Non-residential Schools for the Disabled	9
Total Students	328
Catechesis/Religious Education:	
High School Students	970
Elementary Students	24,327
Total Students Under Catholic Instruction	97,907
Teachers in the Diocese:	
Priests	39
Scholastics	1
Brothers	12
Sisters	174
Lay Teachers	3,569
Vital Statistics	
Receptions into the Church:	
Infant Baptism Totals	6,940
Adult Baptism Totals	1,568
Received into Full Communion	8,669
First Communions	8,454
Confirmations	7,908
Marriages:	
Catholic	1,717
Interfaith	945
Total Marriages	2,662
Deaths	4,413
Total Catholic Population	555,621
Total Population	2,089,000

Former Bishops—Rt. Rev. JOSEPH ROSATI, C.M., Bishop of St. Louis; cons. Bishop of the Titular See of Tenagra and constituted Coadjutor of Bishop DuBourg of Louisiana at Donaldsville, LA, March 25, 1824. When the See of Louisiana was divided Bishop Rosati was made Bishop of St. Louis and Administrator of New Orleans. He died while on business in Rome on September 25, 1843.—Most Rev. LOUIS WILLIAM VALENTINE DUBOURG, Archbishop of the Cardinalatial See of Besancon; cons. in Rome, Sept. 24, 1815, Bishop of Louisiana, Upper and Lower, took his first residential seat in St. Louis, Jan. 6, 1818. On July 18, 1826, the Diocese of Louisiana was divided and the Sees of St. Louis and New Orleans erected. Bishop DuBourg, having resigned the See of Louisiana, was transferred to the Diocese of Montauban in France, Aug. 13, 1826, and made Archbishop of the Cardinalatial See of Besancon, Feb. 15, 1833, where he died Dec. 12 of the same year.—Most Rev. PETER RICHARD KENRICK, D.D., Archbishop of St. Louis; cons. Nov. 30, 1841, Bishop of Drasa and Coadjutor to.—Rt. Rev. BISHOP ROSATI, Bishop of St. Louis, 1843; Archbishop, 1847; Titular Archbishop of Marcianopolis, May 21, 1895; died March 4, 1896.—Most Rev. JOHN JOSEPH KAIN, D.D., Archbishop of St. Louis; cons. Bishop of Wheeling, WV on May 23, 1875; Titular Archbishop of Oxyrynchia and Coadjutor "cum jure successionis" of Archbishop of St. Louis, 1893; Administrator of Archdiocese of St. Louis, Dec. 14, 1893; created Archbishop of St. Louis on May 21, 1895; died Oct. 13, 1903.—His Eminence JOHN CARDINAL GLENNON, D.D., Archbishop of St. Louis; born June 14, 1862; ord. Dec. 20, 1884; appt. Titular Bishop of Pinara and Coadjutor to the Bishop of Kansas City, March 14, 1896; cons. June 29, 1896; transferred to St. Louis, April 27, 1903, as Coadjutor to the Archbishop of St. Louis "cum jure successionis"; Archbishop of St. Louis, Oct. 13, 1903; Pallium received May 14, 1905; Assistant at the Pontifical Throne, June 21, 1921; created Cardinal Priest, Feb. 18, 1946; died March 9, 1946.—His Eminence JOSEPH CARDINAL RITTER, D.D., Archbishop of St. Louis; born July 20, 1892; ord. May 30, 1917; appt. Titular Bishop of Hippo, Feb. 3, 1933 and Auxiliary Bishop of Indianapolis; cons. March 28, 1933; appt. Archbishop of Indianapolis, Nov. 11, 1944; appt. Archbishop of St. Louis, July 20, 1946 assistant at the Pontifical Throne, Oct. 5, 1956; created Cardinal, Priest Jan. 16, 1961; died June 10, 1967.—His Eminence JOHN JOSEPH CARDINAL CARBERRY, D.D.,

S.T.D., J.C.D., Ph.D., Archbishop of St. Louis; ord. July 28, 1929; appt. Titular Bishop of Elis and Coadjutor of Lafayette in Indiana, May 3, 1956; cons. July 25, 1956; succeeded to See, Nov. 20, 1957; transferred to Columbus, Jan. 16, 1965; appt. Archbishop of St. Louis, Feb. 17, 1968; installed March 25, 1968; created Cardinal, April 28, 1969; retired July 31, 1979; died June 17, 1998.—Most Rev. JOHN L. MAY, D.D., Archbishop of St. Louis; ord. May 3, 1947; appt. Auxiliary Bishop of Chicago, June 21, 1967; cons. Aug. 24, 1967; transferred to Mobile, Oct. 8, 1969; installed as Bishop of Mobile, Dec. 10, 1969; appt. Archbishop of St. Louis, Jan. 29, 1980; installed March 25, 1980; resigned Dec. 9, 1992; died March 24, 1994.

The Catholic Center—4445 Lindell Blvd., St. Louis, 63108-2498. Tel: 314-633-2222; Fax: 314-633-2333. Office Hours: Mon.-Fri. 8:30-4.

Vicars General—Most Rev. EDWARD K. BRAXTON, Ph.D., S.T.D., V.G.; Most Rev. JOSEPH F. NAUMANN, V.G.; Most Rev. MICHAEL J. SHERIDAN, V.G.; Rev. Msgr. RICHARD F. STIKA, V.G.

Moderator of the Curia—Rev. Msgr. RICHARD F. STIKA, V.G.

Chancellor—Rev. Msgr. RICHARD F. STIKA, V.G., *4445 Lindell Blvd., St. Louis, 63108.* Tel: 314-633-2273; Fax: 314-633-2306.

Secretary to the Archbishop—Rev. HENRY J. BREIER.

Masters of Ceremonies to the Archbishop—Revs. HENRY J. BREIER; MARK S. RIVITUSO.

Master of Ceremonies to the Cathedral of St. Louis—Rev. PAUL J. NIEMANN.

Chief Financial Officer—Deacon C. FRANK CHAUVIN.

Metropolitan Tribunal—4445 Lindell Blvd., St. Louis, 63108. Tel: 314-633-2280; Fax: 314-633-2301.

Judicial Vicar—Rev. JOHN B. SHAMLEFFER, J.C.L., M.C.L., M.Div.

Adjutant Judicial Vicar—Revs. MARK S. RIVITUSO, J.C.L., M.C.L., M.A., M.Div.; JOHN A. BROCKLAND, J.C.L., M.A., M.Div.

Judges—Rev. JAMES J. RAMACCIOTTI, J.C.L.; Sr. CHARLOTTE RIGALI, C.S.J., J.C.D.; Deacon J. GERARD QUINN, J.C.L.

Defenders of the Bond—Revs. JAMES J. RAMACCIOTTI, J.C.L.; JEROME D. BILLING, J.C.L.

Director of Advocate Services—Rev. JOHN A. BROCKLAND, J.C.L.

Auditors—Rev. CHARLES C. DEISTER; Deacon ROBERT REIGEL.

Promoter of Justice—Rev. JEROME D. BILLING, J.C.L.

Notaries—Mrs. JOYCE KOETTING; Mrs. PATRICIA LANASA; Mrs. JOAN HENSLEY.

Archdiocesan Consultors—Most Rev. EDWARD K. BRAXTON, Ph.D., S.T.D., V.G.; Most Rev. JOSEPH F. NAUMANN, V.G.; Most Rev. MICHAEL J. SHERIDAN, V.G.; Rev. Msgr. DENNIS DELANEY; Rev. Msgr. RICHARD F. STIKA, V.G.; Revs. PETER BLAKE; MICHAEL DIECKMANN; NORBERT A. ERNST; JOHN G. DEMPSEY.

Deaneries/Deans—Very Rev. CARL J. SCHEBLE, V.F., North St. Louis; Very Rev. DENNIS E. DOERHOFF, V.F., South St. Louis; Very Rev. DONALD R. WESTER, V.F., Northeast County; Very Rev. ROBERT J. HERMANN, V.F., Northwest County; Rev. Msgr. JAMES E. PIEPER, V.F., Southwest County; Very Rev. DENNIS STEHLY, V.F., Southeast County; Very Rev. RONALD HOPMEIR, V.F., Festus; Very Rev. JAMES P. CALLAHAN, V.F., St. Charles; Rev. Msgr. JAMES E. HANSON, V.F., Ste. Genevieve; Very Rev. RICHARD COERVER, V.F., Washington.

Vicar for Administration—Rev. Msgr. JOHN R. MAGUIRE.

Vicar for Pastoral Planning and Evangelization—Rev. Msgr. TED WOJCICKI.

Co-Vicar for Religious—Sr. EVA MARIA ACKERMAN, O.S.F.

Archdiocesan Offices and Directors

Archdiocesan Archives—Rev. Msgr. RICHARD F. STIKA, V.G., Chancellor; Mr. ROBERT FAHEY, Archivist; Sr. TERESA MARIA EGAN, C.S.J.; ELAINE SNYDER, *7800 Kenrick Rd., St. Louis, 63119.* Tel: 314-961-4320, Ext. 101; Fax: 314-961-0901.

Archdiocesan Building and Boundary Commission—Rev. Msgr. RICHARD J. GALLAGHER, Exec. Sec.

Catholic Family Service—Dr. JERRY MARKS, D.S.W., A.C.S.W., Exec. Dir., *7800 Kenrick Rd., St. Louis, 63119.* Tel: 314-968-8010. See MISCELLANEOUS section for more information.

Archdiocesan Development Appeal—See MISCELLANEOUS section for more information; Mr. FRANK COGNATA, JR., Chief Devel. Officer; TERESA MANNA, Dir., *4140 Lindell Blvd., St. Louis, 63108.* Tel: 314-371-0165.

Catholic Information Center—Rev. VALENTINE YOUNG, O.F.M.Cap., Dir. Tel: 314-621-6555; 231-9991. See MISCELLANEOUS section for more information.

Catholic Office of Disability Ministry—LORRAINE FAHEY, Dir., *7800 Kenrick Rd., St. Louis, 63119.* Tel: 314-961-4320, Ext. 110; Fax: 314-961-5817. Also see MISCELLANEOUS section.

Catholic Relief Services—Rev. Msgr. BERNARD H. SANDHEINRICH, Dir., *4140 Lindell Blvd., St. Louis, 63108.* Tel: 314-371-4980.

Catholic Cemeteries of St. Louis—Rev. Msgr. ROBERT MCCARTHY, Dir., *6901 Mackenzie Rd., St. Louis, 63123.* Tel: 314-381-1313. See CEMETERIES section for more information.

Central Purchasing—Mrs. EDITH TIERNEY, Dir., *7800 Kenrick Rd., St. Louis, 63119.* Tel: 314-961-4320, Ext. 163; Fax: 314-961-0901.

Catholic Charities—Mr. RICHARD VEHIGE, Pres. NETTA KOWALSKI, Dir., Finance, *4532 Lindell Blvd., St. Louis, 63108.* Tel: 314-367-5500; Fax: 314-367-2982. See MISCELLANEOUS section for more information.

Cardinal Ritter Institute-Archdiocesan Office for Services to the Elderly—ARTHUR J. KORTE, COO-Svcs. MICHAEL J. LALLY, COO-Residences, *4483 Lindell Blvd., St. Louis, 63108.* Tel: 314-652-3600; Fax: 314-652-8840. See SERVICES FOR THE ELDERLY section for more information.

Catholic Commission on Housing—KAREN WALLENSAK, Exec. Dir., *4140 Lindell Blvd., St. Louis, 63108.* Tel: 314-371-4980; Fax: 314-371-0058. See MISCELLANEOUS section for more information.

Catholic Community Services—Sr. BETTY BRUCKER, F.S.M., Exec. Dir., *325 N. Newstead, St. Louis, 63108-2707.* Tel: 314-531-0511; Fax: 314-531-2328. See MISCELLANEOUS section for more information.

Archdiocesan Deaf Ministry—Rev. VICTOR A. BARNHART, Dir.; See MISCELLANEOUS section for more information.

Archdiocesan Orphan Board-(Managers of the Roman Catholic Orphan Asylums)—Mr. THOMAS LOWTHER, Pres., *4753 S. Grand Blvd., St. Louis, 63111-1459.* Tel: 314-367-5500; Fax: 314-367-2982.

Catholic Services for Children and Youth—Mr. JOHN W. MCCARTHY, Admin., *4140 Lindell Blvd., St. Louis, 63108.* Tel: 314-371-4980; Fax: 314-371-0271. See MISCELLANEOUS section for more information.

Archdiocesan Data Center—Mr. GERALD F. LAWLER, Dir. Mgmt. Information Systems, *4140 Lindell Blvd., St. Louis, 63108.* Tel: 314-371-0124; Fax: 314-371-2385.

Office for Ecumenical & Interreligious Affairs—Rev. VINCENT A. HEIER, Dir., *7800 Kenrick Rd., St. Louis, 63119.* Tel: 314-961-4320, Ext. 429; Fax: 314-961-0796.

Archdiocesan Office of Worship—Rev. PAUL J. NIEMANN, *7800 Kenrick Rd., St. Louis, 63119.* Tel: 314-961-4320, Ext. 117; Fax: 314-961-0901.

Archdiocesan Commission for Sacred Liturgy—Sr. CATHY DOHERTY, S.S.N.D., Chm.; Mrs. ANA ANITA ATOK; Deacon GEORGE BEINKE; Dr. GLENN BYER; Rev. DONALD CAREY; Mrs. ELIZABETH COFFMAN; Deacon RICHARD COFFMAN; Mr. JIM COMBS; Ms. RUBY DOUTHET; Mrs. KATHY GIBLER; Mrs. SHARON MCGINNIS; Mrs. MARGE MEYER.

Archdiocesan Commission for Sacred Music—Mr. JEFF BUSH, Chm.; Mrs. MARY KAY CHRISTIAN; Mr. PHIL BARRECA; Mr. CHRISTOPHER ORF; Mr. DAVID BRINKER; Dr. JOHN A. ROMERI; Dr. MARIE KREMER.

Archdiocesan Commission for Sacred Art and Architecture—Mr. ROBERT BARRINGER, Chm.; Ms. BETH PILLARSKI; Sr. GABRIELLA ROGENSKI, C.D.P.; Mr. DARREN STROSS; Sr. JOSEPHINE NIEMANN.

Archdiocesan Human Rights Office/HRO System—Mr. EDWARD R. MARTIN, JR., Dir.; Rev. Msgr. JOHN A. SHOCKLEE, M.A., Dir., Emeritus, *462 N. Taylor Ave., St. Louis, 63108.* Tel: 314-652-6100; Fax: 314-535-2874.

Commission on Human Rights—

Capitol Punishment Opposition—

Black & Native American Missions Program—

Catholic Campaign for Human Development—

Committee on Women in the Church—

National Black Catholic Congress—

Catholic Legal Assistance Ministry—Tel: 314-454-6964.

Immigration Law Project—Tel: 314-454-6867.

Council of Catholic Youth—Mr. MICHAEL P. KALIST, Exec. Dir., *4140 Lindell Blvd., St. Louis, 63108.* Tel: 314-371-4980, Ext. 110; Fax: 314-371-0055.

Holy Childhood, Pontifical Association—Rev. Msgr. BERNARD H. SANDHEINRICH, Dir., *4140 Lindell Blvd., St. Louis, 63108.* Tel: 314-371-4980.

Holy Name Society—Rev. MARVIN C. KOPFF, Spiritual Dir.; Mr. JOSEPH A. RYAN, SR., Pres., *Mailing Address: Holy Name Society, P.O. Box 190435, St. Louis, 63119-6435.* Tel: 314-968-2240.

Latin American Apostolate, Archdiocese of St. Louis—Rev. Msgr. BERNARD H. SANDHEINRICH, Dir., *4140 Lindell Blvd., St. Louis, 63108.* Tel: 314-371-4980; Fax: 314-371-0002.

The Legion of Mary—Mrs. MARY BUDDE, Pres., *P.O. Box 1313, St. Louis, 63188.* Tel: 314-631-3447. Spiritual Directors: Revs. ROBERT C. LISS; EDWARD HILGEMAN; JOSEPH CAMPBELL.

Pan y Amor—Rev. Msgr. BERNARD H. SANDHEINRICH, Dir., *4140 Lindell Blvd., St. Louis, 63108.* Tel: 314-371-4980; Fax: 314-371-0002.

Archdiocesan Newspaper "The St. Louis Review"—Rev. ROBERT W. FINN, Editor; Mr. PAUL P. PENNICK, Mng. Editor; Mr. THOMAS L. COURTAWAY, Business Mgr., *462 N. Taylor, St. Louis, 63108.* Tel: 314-531-9700; Fax: 314-531-2269.

Archdiocesan Office of Stewardship & Development—Mr. FRANK J. COGNATA, JR., Chief Devel. Officer, *4445 Lindell Blvd., St. Louis, 63108.* Tel: 314-633-2288; Fax: 314-633-2313.

Archdiocesan Charitable Bequest Council—See MISCELLANEOUS section for more information.

Office for the Continuing Formation of Priests—Rev. MICHAEL J. WITT, Dir., *7800 Kenrick Rd., St. Louis, 63119.* Tel: 314-961-4320, Ext. 428; Fax: 314-918-0878.

Priests' Mutual Benefit Society—Rev. Msgr. JOHN R. MAGUIRE, Pres.; Rev. CHARLES BARTHEL, Exec. Sec.; Rev. MARVIN KOPFF, Archbishop's Rep.- Retired Priests, *7800 Kenrick Rd., St. Louis, 63119.* Tel: 314-961-4320, Ext. 450; Fax: 314-968-5486.

Priests' Purgatorial Society—Rev. Msgr. RICHARD F. STIKA, V.G., Pres.

Pro-Life—Mrs. MOLLY CORCORAN KERTZ, Dir. & Coord., *462 N. Taylor Ave., St. Louis, 63108.* Tel: 314-531-5565; Fax: 314-531-5509.

Regina Cleri—Sr. GERALDINE VOGEL, Admin.; Rev. MARVIN KOPFF, Archbishop's Rep., *7850 Kenrick Rd., St. Louis, 63119.* Tel: 314-968-2240; Fax: 314-968-1049.

Society for the Propagation of the Faith—Rev. Msgr. BERNARD H. SANDHEINRICH, Dir., *4140 Lindell Blvd., St. Louis, 63108.* Tel: 314-371-4980, Ext. 004; Fax: 314-371-0267.

Today and Tomorrow Education Foundation—JULIE TURNER, Exec. Dir., *4140 Lindell Blvd., St. Louis, 63108.* Tel: 314-371-0269; Fax: 314-371-0027.

Criminal Justice Ministry—1408 S. Tenth St., St. Louis, 63104. Tel: 314-241-8062; Fax: 314-241-1307.

Office of Communications—Mr. STEVE MAMANELLA, Dir., *462 N. Taylor Ave., St. Louis, 63108.* Tel: 314-531-9700, Ext. 220; Fax: 314-531-2944.

Society of St. Vincent de Paul, Council of St. Louis—Rev. JAMES CORMACK, C.M., Spiritual Advisor; RICHARD J. KLOHR, III, Pres. LAURA ELLER, Acting Interim Exec. Dir., *4141 Forest Park Ave., St. Louis, 63108.* Tel: 314-521-2183; Fax: 314-531-6712. See MISCELLANEOUS section for more information.

Society of St. Vincent de Paul, Council of the United States—(Territory: United States)—Most Rev. EDWIN M. CONWAY, D.D., Auxiliary Bishop of Chicago, Spiritual Advisor; EUGENE B. SMITH, Pres. RICHARD E. HENNICKE, Exec. Dir., *58 Progress Pkwy., St. Louis, 63043-3706.* Tel: 314-576-3993; Fax: 314-576-6755. See MISCELLANEOUS section for more information.

Schools/Catholic Education Office—Mr. GEORGE HENRY, Supt., *4140 Lindell Blvd., St. Louis, 63108.* Tel: 314-371-4980, Ext. 207; Fax: 314-371-0267. See SCHOOLS section for more information.

St. Louis Roman Catholic Theological Seminaries, Inc.—Rev. Msgr. RICHARD F. STIKA, V.G., Sec., *4445 Lindell Blvd., St. Louis, 63108.* Tel: 314-533-1887.

Kenrick-Glennon Seminary (St. Louis Roman Catholic Theological Seminary-Kenrick School of Theology)—Rev. Msgr. DENNIS M. DELANEY, Pres. & Rector.

Cardinal Glennon College—Rev. JEFFREY G. VOMUND, Dir., *5200 Glennon Dr., St. Louis, 63119.* Tel: 314-792-6100; Fax: 314-792-6500. See SEMINARIES section for more information.

Office of Vocations—Rev. MICHAEL T. BUTLER, Dir.; Rev. BRYAN KUCHAR, Assoc. Dir., *5200 Glennon Dr., St. Louis, 63119.* Tel: 314-792-6460; Fax: 314-792-6502.

Archdiocesan Pastoral Council—Most Rev. JUSTIN RIGALI. Vicars General: Most Rev. EDWARD K. BRAXTON, V.G.; Most Rev. JOSEPH F. NAUMANN, V.G.; Most Rev. MICHAEL J. SHERIDAN, V.G.; Rev. Msgr. RICHARD F. STIKA, V.G.; Rev. Msgr. TED WOJCICKI, Vicar for Pastoral Planning.

Deaneries—North Deanery: Very Rev. CARL SCHEBLE, V.F.; Ms. CAROLE JOHNSON, Deanery Representative. South Deanery: Very Rev. DENNIS DOERHOFF, V.F.; Mrs. BARBARA LOEB, Deanery Representative. Northeast Deanery: Very Rev. DONALD WESTER, V.F.; Mrs. DENISE SAUSER, Deanery Representative. Northwest Deanery: Very Rev. ROBERT HERMANN, V.F.; Ms. ROSEMARY JOST, Deanery Representative. Southwest Deanery: Rev. Msgr. JAMES PIEPER, V.F.; Mrs. PATRICIA KOZARITIS, Deanery Representative. Southeast Deanery: Very Rev. DENNIS STEHLY, V.F.; Mr. PAUL GOLDAK, Deanery Representative. Festus Deanery: Very Rev. RONALD HOPMEIR, V.F.; Judge TIMOTHY PATTERSON, Deanery Representative. St. Charles Deanery: Very Rev. JAMES CALLAHAN, V.F.; Mr. KEVIN KAST, Deanery Representative. Ste. Genevieve Deanery: Rev. Msgr. JAMES HANSON, V.F.; Mrs.

JANET ABTS, Deanery Representative. Washington Deanery: Very Rev. RICHARD COERVER, V.F.; Mr. JOSEPH SOETE, Deanery Representative. Religious Representatives: Sr. DORETTA D'ALBERO, A.S.C.J.; Bro. LAWRENCE HUMPHREY, F.S.C.; Sr. HELEN NEGRI, D.C. Deacon: Deacon JOSEPH KENNEDY, Representative.

Archdiocesan Council of Priests—Most Rev. JUSTIN RIGALI, Pres.; Most Rev. EDWARD K. BRAXTON, V.G.; Most Rev. JOSEPH F. NAUMANN, V.G.; Most Rev. MICHAEL J. SHERIDAN, V.G.; Rev. Msgr. RICHARD F. STIKA, V.G., Chancellor Ex Officio; Revs. PATRICK CHRISTOPHER, Chm., Washington Deanery; STEPHEN G. JOYCE, Northwest County Deanery; MICHAEL BOEHM, Chm., Southwest County Deanery; JOHN G. DEMPSEY, Dir., Priests' Personnel Ex Officio; ROBERT SUIT, Festus Deanery; MICHAEL WITT, Dir., Continuing Formation of Priests Ex Officio; KEVIN J. MAHONEY, St. Charles Deanery; EUGENE G. ROBERTSON, Ste. Genevieve Deanery; ERIC FECHNER, Sec., Northeast County Deanery; KEVIN G. CALLAHAN, Southeast County Deanery; Rev. Msgr. DENNIS DELANEY, Ex Officio, Kenrick-Glennon Seminary; Revs. MARK C. ULLRICH, North City Deanery; MICHAEL J. LYDON, South City Deanery; HARRY BYRNE, O.P., Religious-Teaching; BENET FONCK, O.F.M., Religious-Parish; RICHARD BUHLER, S.J., Religious-Other.

Office of Priests' Personnel—Rev. JOHN G. DEMPSEY, Dir., *4532 Lindell Blvd., St. Louis, 63108.* Tel: 314-367-5530; Fax: 314-367-5128.

Archdiocesan Priests' Personnel Board—Most Rev. JUSTIN RIGALI; Most Rev. EDWARD K. BRAXTON, V.G.; Most Rev. JOSEPH F. NAUMANN, V.G.; Most Rev. MICHAEL J. SHERIDAN, V.G.; Rev. Msgr. RICHARD F. STIKA, V.G.; Rev. JOHN G. DEMPSEY, Personnel Dir.; Rev. Msgr. EDWARD W. REILLY; Rev. Msgr. JAMES E. PIEPER; Rev. Msgr. JOHN T. RONQUEST; Revs. H. JOHN REIKER; KEVIN G. CALLAHAN; NORBERT A. ERNST, Ex Officio - Vicars General.

Archdiocesan Office of Urban and Community Affairs—Rev. Msgr. SALVATORE E. POLIZZI, Dir. LOUIS G. BERRA, Consultor, *6052 Waterman, St. Louis, 63112.* Tel: 314-721-6340; Fax: 314-721-1656.

Archdiocesan Office of the Permanent Diaconate—Deacon GEORGE MILLER, Dir., *7800 Kenrick Rd., St. Louis, 63119.* Tel: 314-961-4320, Ext. 401; Fax: 314-961-5046. Associate Directors: Deacon THOMAS FORSTER; Rev. JAMES SWIFT, C.M.; Mrs. PATRICIA MCVEY, Sec.

Archdiocesan Office of Laity and Family Life—Mrs. SUSAN EDWARDS, Exec. Dir., *7800 Kenrick Rd., St. Louis, 63119.* Tel: 314-961-4320, Ext. 404; Fax: 314-918-0544.

Catholic Services Agencies Building—Mr. ROBERT J. FAHEY, Admin. & Bldg. Mgr., *4140 Lindell Blvd., St. Louis, 63108.* Tel: 314-371-4980.

Archdiocesan Pastoral Center—Deacon ROBERT SNYDER, Admin., *7800 Kenrick Rd., St. Louis, 63119.* Tel: 314-961-4320, Ext. 114; Fax: 314-961-0901.

CLERGY, PARISHES, MISSIONS AND PAROCHIAL SCHOOLS

CITY OF ST. LOUIS
(St. Louis County)

1—CATHEDRAL BASILICA OF SAINT LOUIS (1896), Rev. Msgr. James T. Telthorst; Deacons Maurice Grant; T. Michael Kenney; Anne Carleton, Business Mgr.; Mary Wainscott, Ph.D., Pastoral Assoc. In res., Most Rev. Edward K. Braxton, V.G.; Revs. Bryan M. Kuchar; Paul J. Niemann.
Res., 4431 Lindell Blvd., 63108. Tel: 314-533-2824; Fax: 314-533-2844.
School—Tel: 314-531-3375. Michel Wendell, Prin.
Lay Teachers 12; Students 207.

2—EPIPHANY OF OUR LORD (1911), Rev. Dale P. Wunderlich; Deacon Chris Winkelmann; Terry Signaigo, Bus. Mgr.
Res., 6596 Smiley Ave., 63139. Tel: 314-781-1199; Fax: 314-645-8760.
School—Tel: 314-781-5626. Mr. Tom Archer, Prin.
Lay Teachers 22; Students 400.
Catechesis/Religious Programs—Students 427.

3—HOLY FAMILY (1898), Rev. R. John Schwaig; Deacon Robert Keeney.
Res., 4125 Humphrey St., 63116. Tel: 314-772-8292; Fax: 314-773-2283.
School—Tel: 314-771-2007. Mary Ann Kauffman, Prin.
Lay Teachers 13; Students 250; Preschool 55.
Catechesis/Religious Programs—Students 3.

4—HOLY GUARDIAN ANGELS. Closed. For inquiries for parish records contact the Chancery.

5—HOLY INNOCENTS (1893), Rev. George P. Brennan; Deacon Fred Hummel.
Res., 4923 Odell St., 63139. Tel: 314-776-6440; Fax: 314-776-6441.
School—Tel: 314-771-2188.
Lay Teachers 5; Students 70.
Catechesis/Religious Programs—Students 100.

6—IMMACULATE CONCEPTION-ST. HENRY (1865), Rev. John Gavin, O.S.A. In res., Rev. Francis Lawlor, O.S.A.
Res., 3120 Lafayette Ave., 63104. Tel: 314-776-1333; Fax: 314-776-0642.
Catechesis/Religious Programs—Students 170.

7—IMMACULATE HEART OF MARY (1951), Revs. John Reiker; Mark Whitman.
Res., 4092 Blow St., 63116. Tel: 314-481-7543; Fax: 314-481-6316.
School—4070 Blow St., 63116. Tel: 314-832-1678; Fax: 314-832-1627. Mrs. Pam Brown, Prin.
Lay Teachers 23; Students 350.
Catechesis/Religious Programs—Students 40.

8—MOST BLESSED SACRAMENT (1907). Closed. For inquiries for parish records contact the Chancery.

9—MOST HOLY NAME OF JESUS. Merged with Most Holy Trinity.

10—MOST HOLY ROSARY (1891). Closed. See St. Elizabeth, Mother of John the Baptist.

11—MOST HOLY TRINITY (1848), Rev. Richard H. Creason; Deacon Robert S. Smerek; Sr. Joyelle Proot, S.S.N.D., Pastoral Assoc.
Res., 3519 N. Fourteenth St., 63107-3796. Tel: 314-241-9165; Fax: 314-436-9291.
School—1435 Mallinckrodt St., 63107-3796. Tel: 314-231-9014. Sr. Janet McCann, A.S.C., Prin.
Sisters 2; Lay Teachers 6; Students 106.
Convent—Tel: 314-621-6835.
Sisters 1.

12—OUR LADY OF MOUNT CARMEL. Closed. For inquiries for parish records contact the Chancery.

13—OUR LADY OF PERPETUAL HELP. Merged with Most Holy Trinity.

14—OUR LADY OF SORROWS (1907), Revs. Michael Campbell; Bradley E. Modde; Gary P. Wolken; Deacons Robert Wertz; Robert H. Schnable; Ed Auer.
Res., 5020 Rhodes Ave., 63109. Tel: 314-351-1600; Fax: 314-351-1602.
School—5831 S. Kingshighway, 63109. Tel: 314-353-1451; Fax: 314-351-8464.
Sisters of Notre Dame 2; Lay Teachers 45; Students 510.
Catechesis/Religious Programs—Students 510.

15—OUR LADY OF THE HOLY CROSS (1864), Rev. Mark C. Ullrich, M.Div., M.S.W.; Deacon Donald Driscoll.
Res., 8115 Church Rd., 63147. Tel: 314-381-0323; Fax: 314-381-4828.
School—1018 Baden Ave., 63147. Tel: 314-383-4782; Fax: 314-383-5982.
Sisters 3; Lay Teachers 8; Students 145.

16—RESURRECTION OF OUR LORD (1930), Revs. Thomas W. Wyrsch; Robert W. Argent.
3900 Meramec St., 63116. Tel: 314-832-7023; Fax: 314-832-7024.
School—3880 Meramec St., 63116. Tel: 314-772-6745; Fax: 314-772-6745. Sr. Louise Schmid, Prin.
Sisters 2; Lay Teachers 8; Students 146.

17—VISITATION-ST. ANN'S SHRINE (1881) (African American), Rev. Timothy R. Cook.
Res., 4515 Evans Ave., 63113. Tel: 314-535-8804; Fax: 314-531-8486.
School—Bishop Healy at Blessed Sacrament, Tel: 314-367-5696.

18—ST. ADALBERT/ST. PHILIP NERI. See St. Simon of Cyrene.

19—ST. AGATHA (1871), Rev. James Rodis.
Res., 3239 S. 9th St., 63118. Tel: 314-772-1603; Fax: 314-772-3979.

20—ST. AGNES. Closed. For inquiries for parish records contact the Chancery.

21—ST. ALOYSIUS GONZAGA (1892) (Italian), Rev. John Blomberg; Deacon Richard C. Lake.
Res., 5608 N. Magnolia Ave., 63139. Tel: 314-647-2541; Fax: 314-647-2011. [JC]
School—5628 N. Magnolia Ave., 63139. Tel: 314-647-7056. Sr. Michele Intravia, O.S.U., Prin.
Sisters 1; Lay Teachers 10; Students 130.
Preschool—5625 S. Magnolia, 63139. Tel: 314-645-2363.
Extended Day Care—.
Lay Teachers 4; Students 50.
Catechesis/Religious Programs—Students 130.

22—ST. ALPHONSUS LIGUORI (1867) (African American), Revs. Maurice Nutt, C.SS.R.; Richard Potts, C.SS.R.; Deacons Leslie A. Johnson; Henry Buckner. In res., Rev. Gary Ziuraitis, C.SS.R.; Bro. Terrance Burke, C.SS.R.
Res., 1118 N. Grand Blvd., 63106. Tel: 314-533-0304; Fax: 314-533-4260.
Catechesis/Religious Programs—Students 274.

23—ST. AMBROSE (1903) (Italian), Revs. Vincent R. Bommarito; James J. Ramacciotti; Sr. Patricia Kofron, A.S.C.J., Pastoral Assoc.; Deacons John J. Stoverink; Daniel J. Tracy, Sr.
Res., 5130 Wilson Ave., 63110. Tel: 314-771-1228; Fax: 314-771-0454.
School—5110 Wilson Ave., 63110. Tel: 314-772-1437; Fax: 314-771-4560. Sr. Patricia Brady, A.S.C.J., Prin.
Apostles of the Sacred Heart of Jesus 4; Lay Teachers 16; Students 294.
Catechesis/Religious Programs—Tel: 314-771-5298.
Students 294.

24—ST. ANN, MOTHER B.V.M. Closed. For inquiries for parish records contact the Chancery.

25—ST. ANTHONY OF PADUA (1863), Revs. Robert C. Sieg, O.F.M.; James A. Lause, O.F.M.; Lisa Sieve, Parish Mgr.
Res., 3140 Meramec St., 63118. Tel: 314-353-7470; Fax: 314-655-0573.
School—4235 Compton Ave., 63118. Tel: 314-752-3397; Fax: 314-752-4384. Ms. Joan Feldmann, Prin.
Lay Teachers 14; Students 160.

26—ST. BARBARA. Closed. See St. Augustine for details.

27—ST. AUGUSTINE (1992) (African American), Rev. Robert J. Gettinger.
1371 Hamilton Ave., 63112. Tel: 314-385-1934; Fax: 314-385-2949. Consolidation of St. Barbara, St. Rose of Lima, St. Edward, St. Mark and Notre Dame de Lourdes (Wellston).

28—ST. BONIFACE (1859) (German), Rev. Thomas M. Begley; Deacons Earl Tresch; Richard Stevens.
Res., 7622 Michigan Ave., 63111. Tel: 314-638-1438; Fax: 314-638-1460.
Catechesis/Religious Programs—(Clustered with St. Andrew, Lemay).

29—ST. BRIDGET OF ERIN (1853) (African American), Rev. Msgr. Richard A. Buchheit.
Res., 2401 Carr St., 63106. Tel: 314-231-8870; Fax: 314-231-3780.
School—Central Catholic/St. Nicholas School, 1106 N. Jefferson Ave., 63106. Tel: 314-231-6254.
Sisters 1; Lay Teachers 18; Students 350.

30—ST. CECILIA (1906), Rev. Francis X. Blood; Deacons Michael Suden; John Curtin. In res., Rev. Cletus Nwabuzo, O.P.
Res., 5418 Louisiana Ave., 63111. Tel: 314-351-1318; Fax: 314-351-3372.
Church—Eiler & Alaska Ave., 63111.
School—906 Eichelberger Ave., 63111. Tel: 314-353-2455. Jim Ford, Prin.
Lay Teachers 11; Students 210.

31—ST. CRONAN (1878), Revs. Joseph D. Ross; James A. Krings.
Res., 1203 S. Boyle Ave., 63110. Tel: 314-289-9545; Fax: 314-289-9546.
Catechesis/Religious Programs—Students 22.

32—ST. EDWARD, KING. Closed. See St. Augustine for details.

33—ST. ELIZABETH, MOTHER OF JOHN THE BAPTIST (1891) (African American), Revs. Carl J. Scheble; Mike Freymuth; Deacons Nathaniel E. Shipp; Jesse Bell; Allen Conley.
Res., 4330 Shreve Ave., 63115. Tel: 314-381-4145; Fax: 314-381-2212.
School—St. Engelbert "FOCUS" Consolidated School, 4720 Carter Ave., 63115. Tel: 314-389-0401; Fax: 314-389-7042. Mrs. Sybill Selfe, Prin.
Religious 2; Lay Teachers 12; Students 206.
St. Engelbert "FOCUS" Day Care Center—4746 Carter Ave., 63115. Tel: 314-389-0720. Ms. Belinda Palmer, Dir.
Lay Teachers 18; Students 105.

34—ST. FRANCIS DE SALES (1867) (German), Revs. Michael P. Joyce, C.M.; David G. Nations, C.M.; Deacon Thomas A. Buhr. In res., Rev. Romain G. Morales, C.M.
Res., 2653 Ohio Ave., 63118. Tel: 314-771-3100; Fax: 314-771-3295.
School—Notre Dame Elementary, 3022 Oregon, 63118. Tel: 314-776-0883; Fax: 314-776-4912.
Catechesis/Religious Programs—Students 76.

35—ST. FRANCIS XAVIER (1841). (College). Revs. Leonard E. Kraus, S.J.; Richard J. Vogt, S.J.
3628 Lindell Blvd., 63108. Tel: 314-977-7300; Fax: 314-977-7315.
Catechesis/Religious Programs—Tel: 314-977-7302.
Students 86.

36—ST. GABRIEL THE ARCHANGEL (1934), Revs. Charles E. Burgoon; Gary M. Meier; Edwin J. Burmester; Deacons Phillip Gerdes; James Volansky.
Res., 6303 Nottingham Ave., 63109. Tel: 314-353-6303; Fax: 314-353-7704.

School—4700 Tamm Ave., 63109. Tel: 314-353-1229; Fax: 314-353-6303.
Lay Teachers 39; Students 533.
Catechesis/Religious Programs—Students 835.

37—St. Hedwig (1904), Rev. Msgr. Joseph W. Baker.
Res., 3202 Pulaski St., 63111. Tel: 314-481-2486; Fax: 314-353-2454.

38—St. James the Greater (1860) (Irish), Rev. David E. Rauch.
Res., 6401 Wade Ave., 63139. Tel: 314-645-0167; Fax: 314-645-0168.
School—1360 Tamm Ave., 63139. Tel: 314-647-5244; Fax: 314-647-8237. Ms. Karen Battaglia, Prin.
Lay Teachers 11; Students 152.

39—St. Joan of Arc (1941), Rev. Msgr. Lawrence J. Walsh; Rev. Kenneth J. Etter; Deacon Daniel H. Henroid. In res., Rev. Msgr. Richard J. Gallagher; Rev. John G. Dempsey.
Res., 5800 Oleatha St., 63139. Tel: 314-832-2838; Fax: 314-352-9350.
School—Tel: 314-752-4171. Mrs. Debra Dalay, Prin.
Lay Teachers 30; Students 450.

40—St. John the Apostle and Evangelist (1847), Rev. John J. Johnson.
Res., 15 Plaza Sq., 63103. Tel: 314-421-3467; Fax: 314-588-9544.
Catechesis/Religious Programs—Students 4.

41—St. John the Baptist (1914) (German), Revs. Edward M. Rice; Edward R. Goldian, S.J.; Leo J. Spezia.
4200 Delor St., 63116. Tel: 314-353-1255; Fax: 314-752-3154.
School—4170 Delor St., 63116. Tel: 314-481-6654; Fax: 314-481-3179.
Sisters of the Most Precious Blood, O'Fallon 1; Lay Teachers 19; Students 315.
High School—5021 Adkins St., 63116. Tel: 314-351-5604; Fax: 314-351-3050. Mrs. Sandra Brady, Prin.
Sisters 1; Lay Teachers 28; Students 425.
Catechesis/Religious Programs—Students 740.

42—St. John Nepomuk (1854) (Czech), Rev. Paul Spielmann.
Res., 1625 S. 11th St., 63104. Tel: 314-231-0141.

43—Shrine of St. Joseph, Capuchin Fathers (1844) (German). Unassigned.
Res., 1220 N. 11th St., 63106. Tel: 314-231-9407; Fax: 314-231-0802.

44—St. Joseph (1904) (Croatian), Revs. Joseph M. Abramovic, O.F.M.; Robert Galinac, O.F.M.
Res., 2112 S. 12th St., 63104. Tel: 314-771-0958; Fax: 314-771-0958.
Catechesis/Religious Programs—Students 34.

45—St. Liborius. Closed. For inquiries for parish records contact the Chancery.

46—Basilica of St. Louis, King of France (1770), Rev. Msgr. Bernard H. Sandheinrich; Rev. Richard J. Quirk.
Res., 209 Walnut St., 63102. Tel: 314-231-3250; Fax: 314-231-4280.

47—St. Margaret of Scotland (1899), Rev. Kenneth Brown.
Res., 3854 Flad Ave., 63110. Tel: 314-776-0363; Fax: 314-776-0364.
School—3964 Castlemen, 63110. Tel: 314-776-7837.
Sisters 2; Lay Teachers 11; Students 257.
Catechesis/Religious Programs—Students 257.

48—St. Mark, Evangelist. Closed. See St. Augustine for details.

49—St. Mary Magdalen (1919), Very Rev. Dennis E. Doerhoff, V.F.; Rev. Thomas C. Bryon. In res., Rev. Mark Rivituso.
Res., 4924 Bancroft Ave., 63109. Tel: 314-352-2111; Fax: 314-481-7661.
School—4911 Sutherland Ave., 63109. Tel: 314-832-3360; Fax: 314-481-7661.
Lay Teachers 15; Students 207.
Catechesis/Religious Programs—Southside Regional Parish School of Religion, Tel: 314-752-9908. Students 70.

50—Sts. Mary and Joseph (1821), Rev. Robert L. Szydlowski; Rev. Msgr. Fenton J. Runge, Senior Priest.
Res., 6304 Minnesota Ave., 63111. Tel: 314-481-6304; Fax: 314-481-6337.
Catechesis/Religious Programs—Students 10.

51—St. Mary of Victories (Hungarian), Rev. Paul E. Spielman.
Res., 744 S. 3rd St., 63102. Tel: 314-231-8101.

52—St. Matthew, Apostle (1893) (African American), Revs. Matthew D. Ruhl, S.J.; Jeffrey D. Harrison, S.J.; William J. Hutchison, S.J.; Stephen M. Belt, S.J.; Chad Thilburger, S.J.
Res., 2715 N. Sarah St., 63113. Tel: 314-531-6443; Fax: 314-533-7318. [CEM]
Catechesis/Religious Programs—Students 39.

53—St. Nicholas (1865) (African American), Revs. Stephen Brown, S.V.D.; Thomas Potts, S.V.D.; Deacon Stanley Peterson. Pastoral Assocs.: Sr. Antona Ebo, F.S.M.; Ms. Ella L. Scott.
Res., 701 N. 18th St., 63103. Tel: 314-231-2860; Fax: 314-231-9823.
School—Central Catholic/St. Nicholas School, 1805 Lucas St., 63103. Tel: 314-421-1822.
Lay Teachers 40; Students 300.
Catechesis/Religious Programs—Students 9.
Chapel—Christ the King.

54—St. Patrick (1981), Revs. Valentine Young, O.F.M.Cap.; Simon R. Conrad, O.F.M.Cap.; Canice Froelich, O.F.M.Cap.; Simeon Gallagher, O.F.M.Cap.; Julian Haas.
Res., 1000 N. 7th St., 63101. Tel: 314-231-9991; Fax: 314-231-9289.
Shrine—Shrine of St. Joseph, Tel: 314-231-9407.

55—Sts. Peter and Paul (1849), Rev. Bruce H. Forman; Deacons Joseph T. Haefner; Thomas Gorski.
Res., 1919 S. 7th Blvd., 63104. Tel: 314-231-9923; Fax: 314-231-7464.

56—St. Simon of Cyrene (1993) (African American), Rev. Stephen P. Robeson; Deacons Raymond V. Mroczkowski, (Retired); Fred Dodson; Ralph Hayes.
Res., 5076 Durant Ave., 63115. Tel: 314-385-0068; Fax: 314-385-5339.
Catechesis/Religious Programs—Students 4.

57—St. Pius the Fifth (1905), Rev. Michael J. Lydon; Sr. Dianne Kaimann, O.S.F., Business Mgr.; Deacons Walter W. Christ; Bill Casseau. Pastoral Assocs.: Sr. Paulette Weindell, C.PP.S.; Sr. Dorothy Ann Katke, C.PP.S. In res., Rev. Joseph Kaberia (Kenya).
Res., 3310 S. Grand Blvd., 63118. Tel: 314-772-1525; Fax: 314-772-5615.
School—3530 Utah, 63118. Tel: 314-773-8770. Sr. Barbara Siderewicz, O.S.F., Prin.
Sisters 4; Lay Teachers 14; Students 180.

58—St. Raphael the Archangel (1950), Rev. Msgr. William A. Drennan; Rev. Matthew L. O'Toole. In res., Most Rev. Michael J. Sheridan, V.G.; Deacon Gerald Geiser.
Res., 6047 Bishops Pl., 63109. Tel: 314-352-8100; Fax: 314-353-6603.
School—Tel: 314-352-9474; Fax: 314-352-7285. Mrs. Susan Brown, Prin.
Sisters 1; Lay Teachers 12; Students 190.
Catechesis/Religious Programs—Students 301.

59—St. Roch (1911), Rev. Msgr. Salvatore E. Polizzi; Rev. Lawrence A. Herzog. In res., Rev. Msgr. Adrian I. Dwyer.
Res., 6052 Waterman Ave., 63112. Tel: 314-721-6340; Fax: 314-721-1656.
School—6040 Waterman Ave., 63112. Tel: 314-721-2595. Mrs. Gloria Openlander, Prin.
Lay Teachers 15; Students 204.

60—St. Rose of Lima. Closed. See St. Augustine for details.

61—St. Sebastian (1953), Rev. Robert L. Banken; Deacon Herbert L. Ehrhard.
Res., 9950 Glen Owen Dr., 63136. Tel: 314-868-0730; Fax: 314-868-0731.
School—1826 Chambers Rd., 63136. Tel: 314-869-1923.
Lay Teachers 16; Students 200.
Catechesis/Religious Programs—Students 235.

62—St. Stanislaus Kostka (1880) (Polish), Rev. Msgr. Ted L. Wojcicki.
Res., 1413 N. 20th St., 63106. Tel: 314-421-5948; Fax: 314-421-5948.

63—St. Stephen, Protomartyr (1926), Revs. Charles Barthel; Ronald Chochol, Senior Assoc.
Res., 3949 Wilmington Ave., 63116. Tel: 314-481-1133; Fax: 314-481-6036.
School—3923 Wilmington Ave., 63116. Tel: 314-752-4700. Sr. Mary Eschbacher, C.S.J., Prin.
Lay Teachers 12; Students 205.

64—St. Teresa of Avila (1865), Rev. Robert E. Zinser.
Res., 3636 N. Market St., 63113. Tel: 314-371-1190; Fax: 314-531-1047.
Missionaries of Charity—3629 Cottage, 63113. Tel: 314-533-2777.
Catechesis/Religious Programs—Students 35.

65—St. Thomas of Aquin (1882), Revs. Chau Pham, S.V.D.; Edward Waid, S.V.D.; Hien Pham, S.V.D.
Res., 3949 Iowa Ave., 63118. Tel: 314-772-2644; Fax: 314-776-4639.
Catechesis/Religious Programs—Students 117.

66—St. Vincent de Paul (1841), Rev. James B. Cormack, C.M.; Deacon Joe Cox. Pastoral Assocs.: Sr. Jackie Tben, S.S.N.D.; Sr. Joanne Vasa, D.C.; Mr. Dennis Wells; Mrs. Tanya Parker. In res., Rev. William E. Hartenbach, C.M.
Res., 1408 S. Tenth St., 63104. Tel: 314-231-9328; Fax: 314-621-2232.
Catechesis/Religious Programs—Jenny Kwolek, D.R.E.
Students 24.

67—St. Wenceslaus (1895) (Bohemian), Very Rev. Joseph Paul Roelke, M.S.F.; Rev. John Carl Lombardi, M.S.F.; Deacon George W. Miller.
Res., 3014 Oregon Ave., 63118-1498. Tel: 314-865-1020; Fax: 314-664-8260.
Catechesis/Religious Programs—Notre Dame Elementary School, 3022 Oregon Ave., 63118-1498. Tel: 314-776-0883; Fax: 314-776-4912.
Students 132.

CHURCHES IN ST. LOUIS COUNTY

Affton, St. Dominic Savio (1956), Revs. James R. Michler; Richard J. Heman; Deacon James L. Murphy.
Res., 6120 Pebble Hill Dr., 63123. Tel: 314-353-7629; Fax: 314-481-2908.
Church—7748 MacKenzie Rd., 63123.
School—Tel: 314-832-4161. Mrs. Susan E. Hooker, Prin.
Lay Teachers 16; Students 250.
Catechesis/Religious Programs—Students 83.

St. Timothy (1958), Rev. Patrick K. Hambrough; Jane Brown, Pastoral Assoc.; Deacons Philip Caruana; Gene Hoffmann. In res., Rev. John D. Corrigan, S.J.
Res., 816 Union Rd., St. Louis, 63123. Tel: 314-631-4244; Fax: 314-631-4250.
School—824 Union Rd., St. Louis, 63123. Tel: 314-631-0991; 638-4557. Margaret Kenny, Prin.
Lay Teachers 12; Students 205.
Catechesis/Religious Programs—Tel: 314-631-4557.
Students 265.

Seven Holy Founders (1927), Revs. Michael Doyle, O.S.M.; Joseph Chamblain, O.S.M.; John Fontana, O.S.M.; Deacons Charles Lombardo; Ted Rodis.
Office: 6820 Aliceton Ave., St. Louis, 63123. Tel: 314-638-3938; Fax: 314-638-0613.
Church—6741 Rock Hill Rd., St. Louis, 63123. Tel: 314-631-3938.
School—6737 Rock Hill Rd., St. Louis, 63123. Tel: 314-631-8149. Mrs. Peggy Hogan, Prin.
Lay Teachers 35; Students 495.
Catechesis/Religious Programs—Tel: 314-631-2333.
Students 175.

Ballwin, Holy Infant (1954), Rev. Msgr. Jerome J. Buchheit; Revs. Michael P. Boehm; Joseph R. Monahan; Deacon Kenneth C. Clemens.
Res., 627 Dennison Dr., 63021. Tel: 636-227-7440; Fax: 636-227-4548.
School—Tel: 636-227-0802; Fax: 636-227-9184. Sr. Rosario Delaney, R.S.M., Prin.
Sisters of Mercy (Meath Mercy Generalate, Ireland) 4; Lay Teachers 36; Students 900.
Catechesis/Religious Programs—Tel: 636-227-0802; Fax: 636-227-9184.
Students 695.

Bellefontaine Neighbors, Our Lady of Good Counsel (1951), Rev. Donald R. Wester.
Res., 1160 St. Cyr Rd., St. Louis, 63137. Tel: 314-867-1441; Fax: 314-867-1442.
School—1134 St. Cyr Rd., St. Louis, 63137. Tel: 314-867-2400; Fax: 314-867-3776. Sr. Barbara Thomas, A.S.C.J., Prin.
Sisters 4; Lay Teachers 8; Students 186.
Convent—1142 St. Cyr Rd., St. Louis, 63137. Tel: 314-868-3067.

Bel-Ridge, St. Thomas More (1955). Closed. For inquiries for parish records contact the Chancery.

Berkeley, Holy Ghost (1923). Closed. For inquiries for parish records please see St. Bartholomew, Hazelwood.

Bissell Hills, St. Jerome (1952), Rev. Mark A. Dolan.
Res., 10235 Ashbrook Dr., St. Louis, 63137. Tel: 314-868-2310; Fax: 314-868-3919.
School—Tel: 314-867-2100; Fax: 314-388-1350.
Lay Teachers 17; Students 221.

Brentwood, St. Mary Magdalen (1912), Revs. Bernard J. Wilkins; Michael Witt; Deacon Leroy Martin.
Res., 2618 Brentwood Blvd., 63144. Tel: 314-961-8400; Fax: 314-961-7019.
School—8762 Magdalen Ave., 63144. Tel: 314-961-0149; Fax: 314-961-7208. Ms. Julie Hesed, Prin.
Sisters 1; Lay Teachers 12; Students 180.
Catechesis/Religious Programs—Students 180.

Bridgeton, St. Mary (1852), Rev. William J. Baier.
Res., 4605 Long Rd., 63044-2388. Tel: 314-731-0593; Fax: 314-731-3613. [CEM]
Catechesis/Religious Programs—Students 20.

St. Lawrence the Martyr (1960), Rev. Msgr. Donald E. Rau; Deacons Wm. Walbridge; R. Fielding Harrison.
Res., 4335 DuPage Dr., 63044. Tel: 314-739-0496; Fax: 314-739-2768.

School—4329 DuPage Dr., 63044. Tel: 314-739-3123.
Catechesis/Religious Programs—Students 200.

Chesterfield, Ascension (1923), Rev. Msgr. Joseph Pins; Revs. Richard Nelke; Christopher F. Holtmann; Deacons Larry Hutti; Frank Chauvin; William P. Wunderlich.
Res., 230 Santa Maria Dr., 63005. Tel: 636-532-3304; Fax: 636-532-3518.
Preschool: Ascension Early Childhood Center—238 Santa Maria Dr., 63005. Tel: 636-532-3375.
School—238 Santa Maria Dr., 63005. Tel: 636-532-1151; Fax: 636-532-6502. Mrs. Carol Flaherty, Prin.
Lay Teachers 31; Students 650.
Catechesis/Religious Programs—Tel: 636-532-1136; 532-9344 (Adult Education).
Students 836.

Incarnate Word (1965), Revs. Robert J. Hermann; Eugene E. Utrup; Clark M. Maes.
Res., 13416 Olive Blvd., 63017. Tel: 314-576-5366; Fax: 314-576-2046.
School—Tel: 314-576-5366, Ext. 11. C. Michael Welling, Prin.
Lay Teachers 23; Students 448.
Catechesis/Religious Programs—Tel: 314-576-5366, Ext. 26. Mrs. Denise DeFord, D.R.E.
Students 205.

Clayton, St. Joseph (1842), Rev. Msgr. Vernon E. Gardin, Ph.D.; Rev. John S. Siefert; Deacon Albert Williams.
Res., 106 N. Meramec Ave., 63105. Tel: 314-726-1221; Fax: 314-721-5110.
Catechesis/Religious Programs—Tel: 314-727-9059. Mrs. Terri Venneman, D.R.E.
Students 190.

Concord Village, St. Simon the Apostle (1959), Revs. William B. Ahrens; James B. Wilke; Rev. Msgr. John T. Ronquest; Deacon Carl Beckman.
Res., 11011 Mueller Rd., St. Louis, 63123. Tel: 314-842-3848; Fax: 314-842-9829.
Preschool—11015 Mueller Rd., St. Louis, 63123. Tel: 314-842-3435.
School—11019 Mueller Rd., St. Louis, 63123. Tel: 314-842-0181; Fax: 414-849-6355.
Lay Teachers 25; Students 488.
Catechesis/Religious Programs—Students 130.

Crestwood, St. Elizabeth of Hungary (1956), Rev. Thomas J. Haley; Deacons Robert Snyder; Robert Kiechlin. In res., Revs. Donald J. Hoffman; John P. Cormer.
Res., 1420 S. Sappington Rd., 63126. Tel: 314-968-0760; Fax: 314-968-8023.
School—1414 S. Sappington Rd., 63126. Tel: 314-962-9698; Fax: 314-918-1976. Mr. Kenneth Weis, Prin.
Sisters 1; Lay Teachers 13; Students 199.
Catechesis/Religious Programs—Tel: 314-962-0834.
Students 80.
Convent—1405 S. Sappington Rd., 63126. Tel: 314-961-2630.

Creve Coeur

1—St. Anselm (1966), Revs. Gerard Garrigan, O.S.B.; R. Benedict Allin, O.S.B.; Deacons William J. McKenna; Steven H. Wohlert, Pastoral Assoc.
Res., 530 S. Mason Rd., St. Louis, 63141. Tel: 314-878-2120; Fax: 314-878-2199.
Catechesis/Religious Programs—Students 200.

2—St. John Bosco (1972), Rev. Gerard R. Welsch. In res., Rev. Msgr. Jerome F. Wilkerson, Ph.D.; Rev. David T. Thomas; Deacon Charles W. Georges.
Res., 12934 Marine Ave., St. Louis, 63146. Tel: 314-434-1312; Fax: 314-434-1315.
Catechesis/Religious Programs—Tel: 314-878-6492.
Students 190.

3—St. Monica (1872), Rev. Msgr. Nicholas A. Schneider; Rev. Raymond D. Hager; Deacons Robert K. Gamache; Millard R. Miller; James P. Martin; Thomas K. Coeruer, Dir. Business Admin. In res., Rev. Kenneth Sleyman, M.M.
Res., 12136 Olive Blvd., 63141-6629. Tel: 314-434-4211; Fax: 314-434-5978. [CEM]
School—12132 Olive Blvd., 63141-6698. Tel: 314-434-2173; Fax: 314-434-7689. Mr. James J. Spies, Prin.
Lay Teachers 26; Students 394.
Catechesis/Religious Programs—Students 113.

4—Our Lady of the Pillar (1938), Rev. James M. Tobin, S.M.; Deacon Norman B. Werner. In res., Rev. J. Donald Cahill, S.M.
Res., 401 S. Lindbergh Blvd., St. Louis, 63131. Tel: 314-993-2280; Fax: 314-993-6462.
School—Tel: 314-993-3353; Fax: 314-993-2172.
Franciscan Sisters of Our Lady of Perpetual Help 4; Lay Teachers 21; Students 222.
Catechesis/Religious Programs—Students 85.
Convent—403 S. Lindbergh Blvd., 63131. Tel: 314-993-3666.

5—St. Richard (1963), Rev. C. Robert Dorhauer. In res., Rev. Phil Krahman; Deacon Jerry N. McGuire.
Res., 11223 Schuetz Rd., St. Louis, 63146. Tel: 314-432-6224; Fax: 314-432-6030.
School—11211 Schuetz Rd., St. Louis, 63146. Tel: 314-872-3152; Fax: 314-872-7326. Mrs. Julie Blow, Prin.
Sisters 1; Lay Teachers 16; Students 171.
Catechesis/Religious Programs—Students 105.

Des Peres, St. Clement (1951), Rev. Msgr. James E. Pieper; Rev. Msgr. Robert McCarthy; Rev. William C. Thess.
Res., 1510 Bopp Rd., St. Louis, 63131. Tel: 314-965-0709; Fax: 314-965-1486.
School—1508 Bopp Rd., St. Louis, 63131. Tel: 314-822-1903; Fax: 314-822-8371. Mary Christina Reichardt, Prin.
Lay Teachers 35; Students 450.
Catechesis/Religious Programs—Students 140.

Ellisville, St. Clare of Assisi (1963), Revs. Richard E. Hanneke; Michael J. Esswein; James Dyer.
Res., 15642 Clayton Rd., 63011. Tel: 636-394-7307; Fax: 636-394-6264.
School—Tel: 636-227-8654; Fax: 636-394-0359. Mrs. Marie Sinnett, Prin.
Sisters 1; Lay Teachers 23; Students 450.
Catechesis/Religious Programs—Tel: 636-394-4368; Fax: 636-394-4397.
Students 825.

Eureka, Sacred Heart (1889), Rev. Alexander R. Anderson.
Res., 350 E. Fourth St., 63025. Tel: 636-938-5048; Fax: 636-587-2736.
School—Tel: 636-938-4602. Sharon Morgenthaler, Prin.
Lay Teachers 13; Students 275.
Catechesis/Religious Programs—Students 315.

Fenton, St. Paul (1878), Rev. Michael Dieckmann; Rev. Msgr. Robert J. Muesenfechter; Rev. Joseph J. Welschmeyer; Deacons John Weatherholt; Paul Crafts.
Res., 15 Forest Knoll, 63026. Tel: 636-343-1234; Fax: 636-343-4809. [CEM]
School—465 New Smizer Mill Rd., 63026. Tel: 636-343-4333.
Religious 2; Lay Teachers 22; Students 498.
Catechesis/Religious Programs—Tel: 636-343-1678.
Students 510.

Ferguson, Good Shepherd (1958), Rev. Gregory R. Mikesch.
Res., 921 Smith Ave., 63135. Tel: 314-521-1008; Fax: 314-521-1034.
School—1050 Smith Ave., 63135. Tel: 314-524-4332.
Sisters 1; Lay Teachers 13; Students 185.

Sts. John and James (1882), Rev. Timothy M. Foley; Deacon L. Jerome Marren.
Res., 140 N. Elizabeth Ave., 63135. Tel: 314-522-0275; Fax: 314-522-9404.
School—150 N. Elizabeth Ave., 63135. Tel: 314-522-3888; Fax: 314-595-9274.
Catechesis/Religious Programs—Students 239.

Our Lady of Guadalupe (1954), Revs. A. John Schuler; Dick Vogt, S.J.; Sr. Cathy Doherty, Pastoral Assoc.
Res., 17 Hawkesbury Dr., 63121. Tel: 314-522-9264; Fax: 314-522-8461.
School—1115 S. Florissant Rd., 63121. Tel: 314-524-1948. Kathryn Sedlacek, Prin.
Lay Teachers 10; Students 160.
Catechesis/Religious Programs—Students 10.

Florissant

1—North American Martyrs (1954), Rev. James J. Byrnes; Deacons Robert J. Powers; Peter Gounis.
Res., 1400 S. Lafayette St., 63031-7997. Tel: 314-837-9304; Fax: 314-837-9305.
Catechesis/Religious Programs—63033. Tel: 314-837-0369, Ext. 3.
Students 84.

2—Our Lady of Fatima (1950), Rev. Donald L. Buhr; Deacon Andrew Neimeyer, (Retired).
Res., 4550 Washington St., 63033. Tel: 314-837-9366; Fax: 314-837-9367.
School—4500 Washington St., 63033. Tel: 314-921-0437.
Lay Teachers 12; Students 207.
Catechesis/Religious Programs—Tel: 314-921-9814.
Students 220.

3—St. Angela Merici (1962), Revs. Ferdinand J. Wesloh; Erich A. Fechner.
Res., 14005 Davey Dr., 63034. Tel: 314-838-6565; Fax: 314-838-6566.
School—3860 N. Hwy. 67, 63034. Tel: 314-831-8012.
Lay Teachers 24; Students 330.
Catechesis/Religious Programs—Students 75.

4—St. Christopher (1967), Rev. Donald L. Dyer; Deacons Kenneth M. Potzman; George A. Graham; George Blase.
Res., 11575 Old Halls Ferry Rd., 63033. Tel: 314-839-2427; Fax: 314-839-2428.

5—St. Dismas (1956), Revs. Robert W. Burkemper; Timothy P. Cronin; Deacon Herbert B. Gettemeier.
Res., 2650 Parker Rd., 63033. Tel: 314-837-3410; Fax: 314-837-6628.
School—1220 Paddock Dr., 63033. Tel: 314-837-0369.
Lay Teachers 14; Students 246.
Catechesis/Religious Programs—St. Dismas School, 2650 Parker Rd., 63033. Tel: 314-837-0369.
Students 116.

6—St. Ferdinand (1788), Revs. Gary Gebelein; Richard Rath; Glennon Goellner; Deacons Raymond C. Hennicke; Joseph Kroutil.
Res., 1765 Charbonier Rd., 63031. Tel: 314-837-3165; Fax: 314-837-3166.
School—Tel: 314-921-2201; Fax: 314-921-2253.
Sisters of the Most Precious Blood 1; Lay Teachers 19; Students 297.
Catechesis/Religious Programs—Students 330.

7—Sacred Heart (1866) (German), Revs. John Paul Hess; Thomas C. Miller.
Res., 751 N. Jefferson St., 63031. Tel: 314-837-3757; Fax: 314-837-8897.
School—501 St. Louis St., 63031. Tel: 314-831-3372. Ms. Clare Ortmeier, Prin.
Religious 2; Lay Teachers 24; Students 397.
Catechesis/Religious Programs—Tel: 314-837-3757, Ext. 232.
Students 100.

8—St. Norbert (1965), Revs. Michael E. Turek; Brian P. Smith; Deacon Robert Klostermann.
Res., 16455 New Halls Ferry Rd., 63031. Tel: 314-831-3874; Fax: 314-831-3875.
School—Tel: 314-839-0948; Fax: 314-839-0948. Mrs. Pam Gilbert, Prin.
Sisters 1; Lay Teachers 25; Students 470.
Catechesis/Religious Programs—Tel: 314-830-0841. Deacon Leonard Sisul, D.R.E.
Students 223.

9—St. Sabina (1960), Rev. Robert J. Samson; Deacons Harold A. Strauss; Joseph Marcinkiewicz, Jr.; Alvin Dietz; Paul Porterfield.
Res., 1365 Harkee Dr., 63031. Tel: 314-837-1365; Fax: 314-837-7680.
School—1625 Swallow Dr., 63031. Tel: 314-837-6524; Fax: 314-837-3162. Sr. Joan Galli, C.S.J., Prin.
Sisters 2; Lay Teachers 15; Students 235.
Catechesis/Religious Programs—Tel: 314-837-6524.
Students 280.

10—St. Thomas the Apostle (1960), Revs. Henry J. Garavaglia; Leroy A. Valentine; Deacons Joseph Morris; Charles Holmes.
Res., 500 Clemens Dr., 63033. Tel: 314-838-4017; Fax: 314-921-6724.
School—3500 St. Catherine St., 63033. Tel: 314-921-7313. Colleen Mackin, Prin.
Religious 1; Lay Teachers 17; Students 297.

11—Transfiguration (1965), Rev. Joseph W. Banden.
Res., 6685 Lakeside Hills Dr., 63033. Tel: 314-741-2309; Fax: 314-355-7527.
School—12555 Partridge Run Dr., 63033. Tel: 314-741-0413. Carol Werner, Prin.
Lay Teachers 9; Students 160.
Convent—12613 Partridge Run Dr., 63033. Tel: 314-741-6568.

Gardenville, St. George (1915), Revs. Harold H. Voelker; Joseph J. Adragna; Ralph E. Stroot; Deacons Roy E. Schulze; Robert Penberthy.
Res., 4980 Heege Rd., St. Louis, 63123. Tel: 314-352-3544; Fax: 314-832-6916.
School—4974 Heege Rd., St. Louis, 63123. Tel: 314-832-6432.
Lay Teachers 12; Students 187.
Catechesis/Religious Programs—Students 230.

Glasgow Village, St. Pius X (1954), Rev. James C. Marshall.
Res., 335 Shepley Dr., St. Louis, 63137. Tel: 314-867-1139; Fax: 314-867-7083.

Glen Owen, St. Sebastian. See St. Sebastian, St. Louis County.

Grantwood, Our Lady of Providence (1954), Revs. Robert F. Johnston; Glennon C. Doherty, Pastoral Assoc.; Deacons Gerald Prives; David Amelotti. In res., Rev. John P. Heil.
Res., 8866 Pardee Rd., St. Louis, 63123. Tel: 314-843-3570; Fax: 314-843-8033.
School—8874 Pardee Rd., St. Louis, 63123. Tel: 314-842-2073. Mary Jo Masterson, Prin.
Lay Teachers 13; Students 242.
Catechesis/Religious Programs—Students 67.

Hathaway Manor, St. Casimir. Closed. For inquiries for parish records contact the Chancery.

Hazelwood, St. Bartholomew (1959), Rev. John Brockland, J.C.L., Admin.; Deacon Charles Davanzo.
Res., 8370 Latty Ave., 63042. Tel: 314-524-4422; Fax: 314-524-7036.

Our Lady of Mercy (1964), Rev. James M. Sullivan.
Res., 1607 VilleMaura Ln., 63042. Tel: 314-739-9369; Fax: 314-739-1242.
Catechesis/Religious Programs—Students 60.

St. Martin de Porres (1962), Revs. G. Timothy Vowels; Martin J. Mulvihill.
Res., 615 Dunn Rd., 63042-1799. Tel: 314-895-1100; Fax: 314-895-5992.
School—631 Undercliff, 63042. Tel: 314-895-3600; Fax: 314-895-3601.
Lay Teachers 13; Students 218.
Kinderhaus—627 Undercliff, 63042.
Catechesis/Religious Programs—Tel: 314-895-4631.
Students 100.

Jennings

1—Corpus Christi (1915), Revs. James J. Foster; William J. Wigand; Deacon Raymond Audrain.
Res., 8449 Jennings Station Rd., St. Louis, 63136. Tel: 314-388-0123; Fax: 314-868-2401.
School—2120 Switzer Ave., St. Louis, 63136. Tel: 314-388-0468; Fax: 314-388-3855.
Lay Teachers 13; Students 188.

2—St. Frances Xavier Cabrini (1965). Merged with Coprus Christi, Jennings.

3—St. Louise de Marillac (1935). Merged with Corpus Christi to form Corpus Christi, Jennings.

4—St. Lucy. See Corpus Christi for details.

Kinloch, Holy Angels (1931) (African American), Rev. Edward J. Schramm; Deacon Frank Nesbitt; Judy Brown, Pastoral Assoc.
Res., 8122 Scott St., 63140. Tel: 314-522-0863; Fax: 314-521-3208.
School—Tel: 314-521-0877.
Lay Teachers 10; Students 135.

Kirkwood, St. Peter (1832), Revs. John J. Brennell; John Rogers Vien; Deacon Joseph Sulze. In res., Rev. Theodore Burghoff.
Res., 243 W. Argonne Dr., 63122. Tel: 314-966-8600; Fax: 314-966-5721. [CEM]
School—215 N. Clay St., 63122. Tel: 314-821-0460.
Lay Teachers 25; Students 428.
Catechesis/Religious Programs—Tel: 314-822-1347. Linda Doyle, D.R.E.
Students 284.

St. Gerard Majella (1955), Revs. Herbert C. Hauck; Frank D'Amico; Deacons Timothy Dolan; James Burton; Donald Denham.
Res., 1969 Dougherty Ferry Rd., 63122. Tel: 314-965-3985; Fax: 314-965-7650.
School—2005 Dougherty Ferry Rd., 63122. Tel: 314-822-8844. Jane Koberlein, Prin.
Lay Teachers 17; Students 336.
Catechesis/Religious Programs—Tel: 314-965-8077.
Students 295.

Ladue, Church of the Annunziata (1929), Rev. Msgr. Robert M. Krawinkel; Christie Murphy, Pastoral Assoc.
Res., 925 Cella Rd., St. Louis, 63124. Tel: 314-993-4422; Fax: 314-994-7877.
Catechesis/Religious Programs—Students 165.

Lemay

1—Mary, Queen of the Universe (1955), Rev. William W. McCumber; Deacon Eugene Czarnecki.
Res., 4230 Ripa Ave., St. Louis, 63125. Tel: 314-638-3030; Fax: 314-638-5353.
School—4220 Ripa Ave., St. Louis, 63125. Tel: 314-638-2520.
Lay Teachers 14; Students 146.
Catechesis/Religious Programs—Twinned with St. Martin of Tours, St. Louis.

2—Most Precious Blood (1961), Rev. Msgr. Charles Forst; Rev. Richard F. Everding; Sr. Rose Dobelman, C.P.P.S.; Deacons Allen Boedeker; Kenneth Inman.
Res., 3635 Union Rd., St. Louis, 63125. Tel: 314-487-6456; Fax: 314-487-5358.
School—Tel: 314-892-5349. Roseanne Burgoon, Prin.
Lay Teachers 12; Students 184.
Catechesis/Religious Programs—Sr. Rose Dobelman, C.P.P.S., D.R.E.
Students 74.

3—St. Andrew (1905), Rev. Edward J. Hilgeman; Deacon Robert Karsznia.
Res., 309 Hoffmeister Ave., St. Louis, 63125-1609. Tel: 314-631-0691; Fax: 314-631-0692.
School—Sisters of Notre Dame, 317 Hoffmeister Ave., St. Louis, 63125. Tel: 314-631-5135; 631-2010; Fax: 314-631-5633. Robert S. Cowell, Prin.
Catechesis/Religious Programs—317 Hoffmeister Ave., St. Louis, 63125. Tel: 314-631-5135.
Students 171.
Convent—232 Hoffmeister Ave., St. Louis, 63125. Sisters of Notre Dame

4—St. Bernadette (1947), Rev. Mark S. Ebert; Deacons Wayne Bryant, Pastoral Assoc.; Michael Coppage.
Res., 68 Sherman Rd., Jefferson Barracks, 63125. Tel: 314-892-6882; Fax: 314-892-7716.
Catechesis/Religious Programs—Students 108.

5—St. Martin of Tours (1939), Revs. Kevin G. Callahan; Norbert A. Mersinger, (Retired); Nicholas W. Smith; Deacons Terry McNamee; Ed Fronick; Ms. Leslie Walrath, Pastoral Assoc.
Res., 610 W. Ripa Ave., 63125. Tel: 314-544-5664; Fax: 314-631-3118.
School—618 W. Ripa Ave., 63125. Tel: 314-544-5793; Fax: 314-544-1892. Mrs. Mary Chrapek, Prin.
Lay Teachers 12; Students 250.
Catechesis/Religious Programs—Students 75.

6—St. Matthias (1959), Rev. William J. Kester; Deacon Joseph Hercules.
Res., 796 Buckley Rd., St. Louis, 63125. Tel: 314-892-5109; Fax: 314-892-0629.
School—800 Buckley Rd., St. Louis, 63125. Tel: 314-892-7500.
Lay Teachers 17; Students 158.
Convent—798 Buckley Rd., St. Louis, 63125.

Manchester, St. Joseph (1865), Revs. Thomas J. Santen; John J. Wetmore; Robert A. Marshall.
Res., 567 St. Joseph Ln., 63021. Tel: 636-227-5247; Fax: 636-391-8393. [CEM]
School—555 St. Joseph Ln., 63021. Tel: 636-391-1253; Fax: 636-391-1462. Phyllis Fredrickson, Prin.; Greg Sturgill, Asst. Prin.
Sisters of Notre Dame 1; Lay Teachers 36; Students 567.
Catechesis/Religious Programs—Tel: 636-391-1404.
Students 508.

Christ, Prince of Peace (1971), Revs. Joseph E. Wormek; Robert Corbett.
Res., 415 Weidman Rd., 63011. Tel: 636-391-1307; Fax: 636-391-1319.
School—417 Weidman Rd., 63011. Tel: 636-394-6840. Mrs. Chris Einig, Prin.
Dominican Sisters 1; Lay Teachers 27; Students 365.
Catechesis/Religious Programs—Tel: 636-391-1560.
Students 202.

Maplewood, Immaculate Conception (1904), Rev. Thomas J. Ripper, M.S.; Sr. Georgeann Hanson, S.L., Pastoral Assoc.; Deacon Clyde McEntire.
Res., 2900 Marshall Ave., 63143. Tel: 314-645-3307; Fax: 314-645-0672. [JC]
Additional Residence for Priests—2900 Marshall, 63143. Tel: 314-645-5904; Fax: 314-781-8907. Revs. Joseph C. Shea, M.S.; Peter D. Kohler.
Catechesis/Religious Programs—Students 10.

Maryland Heights, St. Blaise (1961), Revs. Richard J. Bockskopf; Tom Kirchhoefer; Deacons Jacob W. Dorhauer; Eugene Naumann. In res., Rev. Fred Lens (JOL).
Res., 3130 Parkwood Ln., 63043. Tel: 314-739-0230; Fax: 314-739-0237.
School—Tel: 314-739-1934; Fax: 314-739-7703.
Sisters 3; Lay Teachers 12; Students 252.
Catechesis/Religious Programs—Tel: 314-739-9796. D.R.E.: Ree Gerdes; Donna Wright.
Students 281.

Mattese, Assumption (1839), Rev. Msgr. Thomas J. Dempsey, V.F.; Revs. Terry J. Borgerding; Richard J. Schilli; Deacons Frederick J. Mueller, Jr.; Richard B. Levac.
Res., 4725 Mattis Rd., St. Louis, 63128. Tel: 314-487-7970; Fax: 314-892-5513. [CEM]
School—Tel: 314-487-6520; Fax: 314-487-3598. Margaret Adams, Prin.
Lay Teachers 24; Students 503.
Catechesis/Religious Programs—Tel: 314-487-2149. Evelyn Tucker, D.R.E.
Students 204.

Mary, Mother of the Church (1971), Rev. Msgr. Edward Reilly; Rev. Msgr. Edward Deutschmann; Deacon Richard Coffman.
Res., 5901 Kerth Rd., St. Louis, 63128. Tel: 314-894-1373; Fax: 314-894-3801.
Catechesis/Religious Programs—Ed Lewandowski, D.R.E.
Students 372.

Mehlville, St. Margaret Mary Alacoque (1962), Very Rev. Dennis R. Stehly, V.F.; Rev. Thomas G. Keller. In res., Rev. Alan J. Knaup, (Retired).
4900 Ringer Rd., St. Louis, 63129. Fax: 314-487-4475.
Res., 5056 Faust Ct., St. Louis, 63129. Tel: 314-487-2522.
School—Tel: 314-487-1666.
Lay Teachers 35; Students 696.
Catechesis/Religious Programs—Students 400.

Normandy, Ascension-St. Paul (1955), Rev. Stephen G. Joyce; Deacon Albert Bernsen.
Res., 7005 Ascension Dr., 63121. Tel: 314-385-6750; Fax: 314-385-6965.
School—3801 Nelson Dr., 63121. Tel: 314-261-1592; Fax: 314-385-9095. Merl Mountain, Prin.
Lay Teachers 14; Students 176.

St. Ann (1856), Rev. James T. Edwards; Deacon Norman Janson.
Res., 7530 Natural Bridge Rd., 63121. Tel: 314-385-5090; Fax: 314-385-6527. [CEM]
School—Tel: 314-381-0113; Fax: 314-381-1367. Sr. Dawn Achs, Prin.
Lay Teachers 13; Students 215.

Oakville, St. Francis of Assisi (1927), Revs. Robert Behnen, O.F.M.; David Eckelkamp, O.F.M.; Gary Bernhardt, O.F.M.; Deacons Alan Ecker; George R. Fink; Lawrence Kelly. In res., Revs. Valerian Schott, O.F.M.; Ermin Micka, O.F.M.; Bernardine Hahn, O.F.M.; Benet Fonck, O.F.M.; Bro. Gregory Bumm, O.F.M.
Res., 4556 Telegraph Rd., St. Louis, 63129. Tel: 314-487-5736; Fax: 314-487-3701.
School—4550 Telegraph Rd., St. Louis, 63129. Tel: 314-892-3918; Fax: 314-892-3918. Barbara Danner, Prin.
Franciscan Sisters of Our Lady of Perpetual Help 1; Lay Teachers 20; Students 460.
Catechesis/Religious Programs—Tel: 314-487-5736, Ext. 125.
Students 225.

Queen of All Saints (1972), Rev. Msgr. Robert P. Jovanovic, M.Ed.; Revs. John L. Hallemann, Senior Assoc.; Edward J. Stanger.
Res., 6603 Christopher Dr., 63129-4919. Tel: 314-846-8207; Fax: 314-846-0636.
School—6611 Christopher Dr., 63129-4919. Tel: 314-846-0506; Fax: 314-846-4939. Sr. JoDonna Grimes, S.S.N.D., Prin.
Students 740.
Catechesis/Religious Programs—Tel: 314-846-8126. Marge Schumer, D.R.E.
Students 475.

Overland, All Souls (1906), Rev. Paul J. Rothschild; Deacon Arnold Krieger.
Res., 9550 Tennyson Ave., 63114. Tel: 314-427-0442; Fax: 314-427-3872.
School—2543 Hood, 63114. Tel: 314-429-5319; Fax: 314-423-4248. Sr. Linda Markway, C.S.J., Prin.
Lay Teachers 8; Students 140.
Catechesis/Religious Programs—Students 60.

Our Lady of the Presentation (1915), Rev. Dennis R. Port; Deacons Singleton Harris; Gerry Lauternwasser.
Res., 8860 Tudor Ave., St. Louis, 63114. Tel: 314-427-0486; Fax: 314-423-3020.
School—8840 Tudor Ave., St. Louis, 63114. Tel: 314-428-8191; Fax: 314-423-1213.
Lay Teachers 19; Students 224.
Catechesis/Religious Programs—Students 58.

Pagedale, St. Catherine of Siena (1909), Rev. Victor A. Barnhart.
Res., 6815 Page Ave., St. Louis, 63133-1505. Tel: 314-721-3069 (Voice); 727-2747 (TDD); Fax: 314-727-2747.
Catechesis/Religious Programs—Students 1.

Pine Lawn, St. Paul the Apostle. Merged to form Ascension-St. Paul, Normandy.

Richmond Heights, Immacolata (1945), Revs. John M. Seper; Gary J. Faust; Robert L. Roedig. In res., Most Rev. Joseph F. Naumann, V.G.
Church—8900 Clayton Rd., 63117. Tel: 314-991-5700; Fax: 314-991-4769.
School—8910 Clayton Rd., 63117. Tel: 314-991-1924. Mr. Salvatore Latragna, Prin.
Lay Teachers 20; Students 285.
Catechesis/Religious Programs—Tel: 314-991-1832.
Students 117.

Little Flower, St. Teresa of the Infant Jesus (1925), Rev. James J. Benz; Deacons Stephen Murray; William G. Weiss.
Res., 1264 Arch Terrace, 63117. Tel: 314-645-1445; Fax: 314-645-3258.
School—1275 Boland Pl., 63117. Tel: 314-781-4995; Fax: 314-781-9177. Mrs. Deborah Marino, Prin.
Sisters 2; Lay Teachers 11; Students 240.

St. Luke the Evangelist (1914), Rev. Richard L. Stoltz. In res., Rev. K. Robert Smoot.
Res., 7230 Dale Ave., St. Louis, 63117. Tel: 314-644-2144; Fax: 314-644-4624.
School—1414 Bellevue Ave., St. Louis, 63177. Tel: 314-781-2072; Fax: 314-781-7411.
Lay Teachers 15; Students 125.

Riverview Gardens, St. Catherine of Alexandria (1921), Rev. Thomas M. Robertson; Deacon Edwin Schulte.
Res., 351 Chambers Rd., St. Louis, 63137. Tel: 314-867-8515; Fax: 314-867-3751.
School—10014 Diamond Dr., St. Louis, 63137. Tel: 314-869-0515. Mrs. Nancy Frese, Prin.
Sisters 1; Lay Teachers 11; Students 153.

St. Ann, St. Gregory (1942), Rev. John I. Caffe; Deacon William F. Priesmeyer.
Res., 3500 St. Luke Ln., 63074. Tel: 314-428-3346; Fax: 314-429-5177.
School—3400 St. Gregory Ln., 63074. Tel: 314-429-0964; Fax: 314-429-3238.
Lay Teachers 9; Students 89.

St. Kevin (1953) (Irish), Revs. John J. Leykam; Andrew J. O'Connor.
Res., 10909 St. Henry Ln., 63074. Tel: 314-427-6336; Fax: 314-427-5333.
School—10901 St. Henry Ln., 63074. Tel: 312-427-7074. Margaret Ahle, Prin.
Lay Teachers 16; Students 265.
Catechesis/Religious Programs—Students 69.

Sappington, St. Catherine Laboure (1953), Revs. Patrick J. Keeley, C.M.; Ignatius M. Melito, C.M.; Raymond Ross, C.M.; Deacon George Tichacek.
Res., 9740 Sappington Rd., St. Louis, 63128. Tel: 314-843-3245; Fax: 314-843-3196.
School—9750 Sappington Rd., St. Louis, 63128. Tel: 314-843-2819; Fax: 314-843-7687. Mrs. Christina Cheak, Prin.
Lay Teachers 26; Students 492.
Catechesis/Religious Programs—Tel: 314-843-2996.
Students 485.

Shrewsbury, Cure' of Ars (1966), Rev. Clarence P. Good. In res., Rev. Msgr. John R. Maguire.
Res., 670 S. Laclede Station Rd., St. Louis, 63119. Tel: 314-962-5883; Fax: 314-968-3554.
Catechesis/Religious Programs—Students 10.

St. Michael (1895), Revs. Edmond J. Fitzgibbon; Jerome D. Billing, J.C.L.; Bernard A. Suellentrop; Deacons Stephen Arnold; Thomas O. Murphy.
Res., 7622 Sutherland Ave., St. Louis, 63119. Tel: 314-647-5611; Fax: 314-781-9211.
School—7630 Sutherland Ave., St. Louis, 63119. Tel: 314-647-7159; Fax: 314-644-1433.
Lay Teachers 18; Students 212.
Catechesis/Religious Programs—Students 78.

Spanish Lake, St. Aloysius (1871), Rev. Gerald T. Nienhaus; Deacon Walter J. Ruegg.
Res., 12110 Larimore Rd., St. Louis, 63138. Tel: 314-741-3690; Fax: 314-741-6468.
School—St. John Neumann, 1650 Redman Rd., St. Louis, 63138. Tel: 314-741-0400. Sr. Mary Lawrence, S.S.N.D., Prin.
Sisters 1; Lay Teachers 12; Students 265.
Catechesis/Religious Programs—Trinity School of Religion (Combined with Our Lady of Loretto and Transfiguration). Fax: 314-741-0400.
Students 100.

Our Lady of Loretto (1959), Rev. Stephen M. Gira, C.R.; Deacons Francis Droesch; James Michael Buckley.
Res., 11725 Bellefontaine Rd., St. Louis, 63138. Tel: 314-741-7700; Fax: 314-741-7700.
School—St. John Neumann, 1650 Redman Ave., St. Louis, 63138. Tel: 314-741-0400. Sr. Mary Lawrence, S.S.N.D., Prin.
Lay Teachers 16; Students 257.
Catechesis/Religious Programs—Tel: 314-741-2583.
Students 100.

Sunset Hills, St. Justin Martyr (1964), Revs. Bernard J. Schloemer; Thomas J. Schaab.
Res., 11962 Bardmont Dr., St. Louis, 63126. Tel: 314-843-8482; Fax: 314-843-8507.
School—11914 Eddie and Park Rd., St. Louis, 63126. Tel: 314-843-6447; Fax: 314-843-9257. Mrs. Judy Talleur, Prin.
Lay Teachers 12; Students 229.
Catechesis/Religious Programs—Students 78.

University City

1—ALL SAINTS (1901), Rev. Donald Molitor.
Res., 6403 Clemens Ave., 63130. Tel: 314-721-6403.

2—CHRIST THE KING (1927), Rev. John A. Ditenhafer. In res., Rev. John Jay Hughes; Deacon E. Ray Kiely.
Res., 7316 Balson Ave., 63130. Tel: 314-721-8737; Fax: 314-721-8738.
School—7324 Balson Ave., 63130. Tel: 314-725-5855; Fax: 314-725-5981. Sr. Rosella McNamee, R.S.M., Prin.
Sisters of Mercy 1; Lay Teachers 14; Students 210.

3—OUR LADY OF LOURDES (1916), Rev. Msgr. Edward J. Sudekum; Rev. Msgr. Norbert J. Dietz; Rev. David A. Novak; Deacon Albert X. Vaughn.
Res., 7148 Forsyth Blvd., 63105. Tel: 314-726-6200; 6201; Fax: 314-726-1602.
School—7157 Northmoor Dr., 63105. Tel: 314-726-3352; Fax: 314-726-0503.
Lay Teachers 20; Students 245.

4—ST. PATRICK (1940), Rev. Eugene Bendel.
Res., 8665 Olive Blvd., 63132. Tel: 314-993-1277; Fax: 314-993-2031.

Valley Park, Sacred Heart (1903), Revs. Robert T. Rosebrough; Rickey J. Valleroy; Sr. Donna Fischer, S.S.N.D., Pastoral Assoc.; Deacons Ewald Winker; Larry Damato; Allen F. Love.
Res., 17 Ann Ave., 63088. Tel: 636-225-5268; Fax: 636-225-6969. [CEM]
School—12 Ann Ave., 63088. Tel: 636-225-3824; Fax: 636-225-8941. Sharon Baumgartner, Prin.
Lay Teachers 24; Students 364.
Catechesis/Religious Programs—Tel: 636-225-0341. Sr. Lynne Schmidt, S.S.N.D., D.R.E.
Students 475.

Vinita Park, St. Rita (1919), Rev. David L. Wichlan; Deacon Louis J. Reynoso.
Res., 8240 Washington St., St. Louis, 63114. Tel: 314-428-4845; Fax: 314-428-4845.

Warson Woods, Ste. Genevieve Du Bois (1956), Rev. Msgr. Paul G. Anthony; Rev. John B. Shamleffer. In res., Rev. Msgr. John P. Holland, Senior Priest.
Res., 1575 N. Woodlawn Ave., 63122. Tel: 314-966-3780; Fax: 314-966-4687.
School—Tel: 314-821-4245; Fax: 314-821-1241. Mrs. Tozia George, Prin.
Lay Teachers 13; Students 206.
Catechesis/Religious Programs—Tel: 314-822-1347.
Students 17.

Webster Groves, Annunciation (1950), Revs. Denny M. Schaab; John G. Klocker, Senior Priest; Deacon Tom Forster Tel: 314-631-5440. In res., Rev. Mark Fuller.
Res., 12 W. Glendale Rd., 63119. Tel: 314-962-5955; Fax: 314-961-0643.
School—16 W. Glendale, 63119. Tel: 314-961-7712. Mrs. Ann Cleeland, Prin.
Lay Teachers 15; Students 244.
Catechesis/Religious Programs—Students 113.

Holy Redeemer (1886), Rev. Joseph M. Simon; Deacon Richard Wessels. In res., Rev. Robert W. Finn.
Res., 17 Joy Ave., 63119. Tel: 314-962-0038; Fax: 314-962-2084.
School—341 E. Lockwood, 63119. Tel: 314-962-8989. Cynthia Hasten, Prin.
Lay Teachers 13; Students 204.
Catechesis/Religious Programs—Tel: 314-962-1487.
Students 178.

Mary, Queen of Peace (1922), Rev. Gerald A. Meier; Rev. Msgr. Richard J. Lubeley, Senior Priest; Rev. John J. Borcic; Deacons Robert C. Riegel; Paul McKee; William Kieffer.
Res., 676 W. Lockwood Blvd., 63119. Tel: 314-962-2311; Fax: 314-968-9885.
School—680 W. Lockwood Ave., 63119. Tel: 314-961-2891. Mr. Michael Biggs, Prin.
Dominican Sisters 1; Sisters of Loretto at the Foot of the Cross 1; Lay Teachers 24; Students 590.
Catechesis/Religious Programs—Sr. Charlotte Flarlong, D.R.E.
Students 155.

Wellston, Notre Dame De Lourdes. Closed. See St. Augustine, St. Louis for details.

West Overland, St. Jude (1953), Rev. Joseph L. Parisi.
Res., 2218 N. Warson Rd., St. Louis, 63114. Tel: 314-428-2262; Fax: 314-890-2257.
Catechesis/Religious Programs—Students 62.

Wildwood, St. Alban Roe (1980), Rev. Msgr. Edmund O. Griesedieck; Rev. C. Robert Manning. In res., Rev. Robert D. Boisaubin.
Res., 2001 Shepard Rd., 63038. Tel: 636-458-2977; Fax: 636-405-1276.
School—2005 Shepard Rd., 63038. Tel: 636-458-6084. Marie Moritz, Prin.
Catechesis/Religious Programs—Tel: 636-458-2460; Fax: 636-405-3026. Susan Gibbar, D.R.E.
Students 1,112.

Woodson Terrace, St. William (1953), Rev. Eugene P. Selzer; Deacon Dave Bolderson.
Res., 9311 Stansberry Ave., 63134. Tel: 314-428-7371; Fax: 314-428-1158.
School—9330 Stansberry Ave., 63134. Tel: 314-427-6444.
Lay Teachers 7; Students 88.

CHURCHES OUTSIDE ST. LOUIS CITY AND ST. LOUIS COUNTY

Apple Creek, Perry Co., St. Joseph (1828) (German), Rev. Mark S. Bozada.
Res., 138 St. Joseph Ln., 63775. Tel: 573-788-2330; Fax: 573-788-2351. [CEM][JC 2]
School—(Grades K-8). Tel: 573-788-2320. Kathy First, Prin.
Lay Teachers 3; Students 43.

Arnold, Jefferson Co., Immaculate Conception (1840), Revs. Earl R. Meyer, O.F.M.Cap.; Gilmary Tallman, O.F.M.Cap.; Deacons Joseph C. Streckfuss; Bradford M. Buchek. In res., Rev. John Schmeidler, O.F.M.Cap.
Res., 2300 Church Rd., P.O. Box 217, 63010. Tel: 636-296-5289. [CEM]
School—Holy Child School. Consolidated with St. David, Arnold. Tel: 636-296-0055; Fax: 636-296-5639. Mrs. Marlene DiMaggio, Prin.
Lay Teachers 25; Students 372.
Catechesis/Religious Programs—Tel: 636-296-5598. Joyce Ott, D.R.E.
Students 422.

St. David (1963), Rev. Thomas Schmidt; Deacons Thomas G. Politte; Diosdado Maranan, M.D.
Res., 2334 Tenbrook Rd., 63010. Tel: 636-296-5485; Fax: 636-296-5526.
School—Holy Child Consolidated School. See Immaculate Conception for details. Tel: 636-296-0055.
Catechesis/Religious Programs—Students 220.

Augusta, St. Charles Co., Immaculate Conception (1851), Rev. Edward L. Heim.
Res., 5912 Hwy. 94 S., 63332. Tel: 636-482-4455; Fax: 636-228-4529. [CEM]
Catechesis/Religious Programs—Students 29.

Belgique, Perry Co., Nativity of the Blessed Virgin Mary. Closed. For inquiries for parish records contact the Chancery.

Berger, Franklin Co., St. Paul (1853) (German), Rev. Daniel E. Mosley.
Res., 603 Miller St., New Haven, 63068. Tel: 573-237-3372; Fax: 573-237-3372. [CEM]
Catechesis/Religious Programs—Students 1.

Biehle, Perry Co., St. Maurus (1870) (German), Rev. Mark S. Bozada.
Res., 10198 Hwy. B, Perryville, 63775. Tel: 573-788-2330; Fax: 573-788-2351. [CEM][JC]

Bloomsdale, Ste. Genevieve Co., St. Agnes (1835), Rev. Raymond J. Oge.
Res., P.O. Box 124, 63627. Tel: 573-483-2555; Fax: 573-483-9497. [CEM]
School—Tel: 573-483-2506. Sr. Donna Marie Kist, C.PP.S., Prin.
Sisters of the Most Precious Blood (O'Fallon, MO) 1; Lay Teachers 13; Students 189.
Catechesis/Religious Programs—Students 26.

Bonne Terre, St. Francois Co., St. Joseph's (1872), Rev. John H. Schneider; Deacon Ronald Kreff.
Res., 15 St. Joseph St., 63628. Tel: 573-358-2112; Fax: 573-358-4233. [CEM]
School—(Grades K-6). Tel: 573-358-5947. Barbara Monahan, Admin.
Lay Teachers 4; Students 40.
Mission—French Village, St. Francois Co., St. Anne, 5425 Brickey Rd., P.O. Box 307, French Village, 63036. Tel: 573-358-2112.

Brewer, Perry Co., Christ the Savior (1907), Rev. Felipe J. Martinez, C.M.
Res., 57 Shady Ln., Perryville, 63775. Tel: 573-547-2677; Fax: 573-547-7556. [CEM]
Catechesis/Religious Programs—Students 50.

Catawissa, Franklin Co., St. James (1913), Rev. Hubert E. Creason.
Res., 1107 Summit Dr., 63015. Tel: 636-271-6038; Fax: 636-257-2235. [CEM]
Catechesis/Religious Programs—Students 30.
Mission—Armagh, Franklin Co., St. Patrick, Hwy. NN & Rock Church Rd., 63015. [CEM]

Clover Bottom, Franklin Co., St. Ann's (1883) (Polish-German), Rev. Timothy J. Toohey.
Res., Clover Bottom, 7851 State Rd. YY, Washington, 63090-9627. Tel: 636-239-3222; Fax: 636-390-2849. [CEM]

Coffman, Ste. Genevieve Co., St. Catherine of Alexandria (1929). Attended by River Aux Vases. Rev. F. Joseph Reilly.
Res., 18411 RAV Church Rd., Ste. Genevieve, 63670. Tel: 573-883-2923; Fax: 573-883-9605. [CEM]

Concord Hill, Warren Co., St. Ignatius (1857) (German), Rev. Finbarr Dowling, O.S.B.
Res., 701 Mill Rd., Marthasville, 63357. Tel: 636-932-4445; Fax: 636-932-4032. [CEM 3]
School—691 Mill Rd., 63357. Tel: 636-932-4444. Cynthia Newman, Prin.
Lay Teachers 5; Students 69.

Cottleville, St. Charles Co., St. Joseph (1873), Rev. Msgr. Walter M. Whited; Revs. Brian A. Kennebeck; Frances F. Koeninger. Pastoral Assocs.: Sr. Mary Pezold, C.C.V.I.; Judy Powers; Deacons Ronald Bachista; George A. Beinke; Gary Meyerkord; Glennon Schultheis.
Res., 1355 Motherhead Rd., St. Charles, 63304. Tel: 636-441-0055; Fax: 636-926-7341. [CEM]
School—1351 Motherhead Rd., St. Charles, 63304. Fax: 636-441-9932. Ms. Mary Ellen Schraeder, Prin.; Mrs. Charlotte Litzinger, Asst. Prin.
Lay Teachers 42; Students 781.
Catechesis/Religious Programs—Tel: 636-441-0055, Ext. 104. D.R.E.: Mrs. Barbara Blackburn; Mrs. Laura Lucas Tel: 314-441-0055, Ext. 105.
Students 1,158.

Crystal City, Jefferson Co., Sacred Heart (1881), Revs. Michael L. Donald; Anthony A. Dattilo; Deacon Gerard G. Stoverink.
Res., 555 Bailey Rd., 63019-1798. Tel: 636-937-4662; Fax: 636-931-5507. [CEM]
School—Tel: 636-931-5701;937-5298; Fax: 636-931-0422.
Lay Teachers 11; Students 143.
Catechesis/Religious Programs—Tel: 636-937-5298; Fax: 636-931-0422.
Students 201.

Dardenne, St. Charles Co., Immaculate Conception (1880), Revs. Robert J. Reiker; Gregory S. Klump; Deacons Don Schiffman; Charles Drayton.
Res., 7701 Hwy. N, O'Fallon, 63366. Tel: 636-561-4459; Fax: 636-561-3883. [CEM]
School—Tel: 636-561-4450.
Lay Teachers 13; Students 281.
Catechesis/Religious Programs—Tel: 636-561-1974.
Students 920.

De Soto, Jefferson Co., St. Rose of Lima (1885), Revs. Ronald J. Hopmeir; Robert J. Suit; Deacon Edward J. Boyer.
Res., 504 S. Third St., 63020. Tel: 636-337-2212; Fax: 636-337-2394. [CEM]
School—Tel: 636-586-3594; 337-7855. Sr. Margaret Schmidt, S.N.D., Prin.
Sisters 2; Lay Teachers 8; Students 177.
Catechesis/Religious Programs—Students 135.

Dutzow, Warren Co., St. Vincent de Paul (1856), Rev. Stephen F. Bauer.
Res., 7602 S. Hwy. 94, Marthasville, 63357. Tel: 636-433-2678; Fax: 636-433-2924. [CEM]
School—Tel: 636-433-2466.
Lay Teachers 10; Students 147.

Elsberry, Lincoln Co., Sacred Heart (1905), Rev. James P. Grady.
Res., 714 Lincoln St., 63343. Tel: 573-898-2202; Fax: 573-898-2652.
Catechesis/Religious Programs—Students 84.

Farmington, St. Francois Co., St. Joseph (1890), Revs. Eugene Robertson; Thomas J. Wissler; Deacons William J. Greif; Albin A. Gegg.
Res., 5 S. Carleton, 63640. Tel: 573-756-4250; Fax: 573-756-6938. [JC 2]
School—501 Ste. Genevieve Ave., 63640. Tel: 573-756-6312; Fax: 573-756-0783.
Students 167.
Catechesis/Religious Programs—Students 72.

Festus, Jefferson Co., Our Lady (1957), Rev. John V. Kerber; Sr. Pat Murray, O.S.F., Pastoral Min.
Res., 1550 St. Mary Ln., 63028. Tel: 636-937-5513; 931-4702 (toll-free); Fax: 636-931-5875.
School—Tel: 636-937-5008.
Lay Teachers 11; Students 210.
Catechesis/Religious Programs—Students 159.

Flint Hill, St. Charles Co., St. Theodore (1883), Rev. Albert A. Mattler.
Res., P.O. Box 246, 63346. Tel: 636-332-9269; Fax: 636-639-1385. [CEM]
School—Tel: 636-332-9465; Fax: 636-332-9465.
Lay Teachers 8; Students 117.

Gildehaus, Franklin Co., St. John the Baptist (1839), Rev. William J. Leach.
Res., 5567 Gildehaus Rd., Villa Ridge, 63089. Tel: 636-583-2488; Fax: 636-583-6114. [CEM]
School—Tel: 636-583-2392; Fax: 636-583-6112. Marian Schelich, Prin.
Lay Teachers 12; Students 190.
Catechesis/Religious Programs—Students 54.

Hawk Point, Lincoln Co., St. Mary (1919) (Bohemian), Rev. Bernard Nienhaus.
Res., P.O. Box 205, 63349. Tel: 636-338-4331; Fax: 636-338-4007. [CEM 2]
Catechesis/Religious Programs—Students 60.

Herculaneum, Jefferson Co., Church of the Assumption of B.V.M. (1916), Rev. Robert V. Fleiter.
Res., 329 Station St., 63048-1328. Tel: 636-475-5305; Fax: 636-475-5305. [CEM]

High Ridge, Jefferson Co., St. Anthony of Padua (1921), Revs. Eugene R. Sinz; Richard H. Suren; Deacons Bill Gearon; David Camden; Dick Shelby.
Res., 3009 High Ridge Blvd., 63049. Tel: 636-677-4868; Fax: 636-677-2781.
School—3005 High Ridge Blvd., 63049. Tel: 636-677-3585. Mrs. Pat Kohn, Prin.
Lay Teachers 11; Students 156.
Catechesis/Religious Programs—Students 156.

Hillsboro, Jefferson Co., Church of the Good Shepherd (1934), Rev. Dennis C. Schmidt.
Res., 703 Third St., 63050-4342. Tel: 636-789-3356; Fax: 636-789-9986. [CEM]
School—Tel: 636-797-2300; Fax: 636-789-5798. Mrs. Peggy Visconti, Prin.
Lay Teachers 11; Students 96.
Catechesis/Religious Programs—Students 114.

House Springs, Jefferson Co., Our Lady, Queen of Peace (1961), Revs. Norbert A. Ernst; Larry T. Huber, Jr.; Deacons Thomas Gerling; Paul Turek.
Res., 4696 Notre Dame Ln., 63051. Tel: 636-671-3062; Fax: 636-671-0003. [CEM 2]
School—Tel: 636-671-0247. Mrs. Debbi Clark, Admin.
Sisters 1; Lay Teachers 12; Students 220.
Catechesis/Religious Programs—Students 286.

Imperial, Jefferson Co., St. John Lateran (1869), Rev. Michael G. Murphy; Deacon Norbert Gawedzinski.
Res., 4525 Old Hwy. 21, 63052. Tel: 636-296-8061; Fax: 636-296-8067. [CEM]
School—Tel: 636-296-8112. Mrs. Vicky Meadows Yochum, Prin.
Lay Teachers 9; Students 150.
Catechesis/Religious Programs—Students 160.

Josephville, St. Charles Co., St. Joseph (1852), Rev. Timothy P. Elliott.
Res., 1390 Josephville Rd., Wentzville, 63385. Tel: 636-332-6676; Fax: 636-332-8648. [CEM]
School—1410 Josephville Rd., Wentzville, 63385. Tel: 636-327-7174. Barbara Rygelski, Prin.
Lay Teachers 6; Students 102.

Kimmswick, Jefferson Co., St. Joseph (1905), Revs. Andrew J. Sigmund; Charles C. Deister, Senior Assoc.; Deacons Kenneth A. Henning; Glennon P. Politte, Sr.
Res., 6020 Old Antonia Rd., Imperial, 63052-0968. Tel: 636-464-1013; Fax: 636-461-0411. [CEM]
School—6024 Old Antonia Rd., Imperial, 63052. Tel: 636-464-9027. Pat Kirk, Prin.
Students 245.
Catechesis/Religious Programs—Students 240.

Krakow, Franklin Co., St. Gertrude (1845), Rev. Dennis B. Zacheis; Deacons Charles Gildehaus; Gary Kuenz.
Res., 6535 Hwy. YY, Washington, 63090. Tel: 636-239-4216; Fax: 636-451-0220. [CEM]
School—Tel: 636-239-2347; Fax: 636-239-3550. Mike Newbanks, Prin.
Lay Teachers 22; Students 317.
Catechesis/Religious Programs—Students 229.

Lawrenceton, Ste. Genevieve Co., St. Lawrence (1872). Attended by St. Agnes Rectory. Rev. Raymond J. Oge.
Bloomsdale, 63627. Tel: 573-483-2555; Fax: 573-483-9497. [CEM]
Catechesis/Religious Programs—Students 11.

Luebbering, Franklin Co., St. Francis of Assisi (1874), Rev. John B. McEntee.
Res., 1000 Luebbering Rd., 63061-9705. Tel: 636-629-1717. [CEM]
Catechesis/Religious Programs—Students 69.

Millwood, Lincoln Co., St. Alphonsus (1850), Rev. John L. Mayer.
Res., 29 St. Alphonsus Rd., Silex, 63377. Tel: 573-384-6223. [CEM]
School—Tel: 573-384-5305.
Lay Teachers 5; Students 70.
Catechesis/Religious Programs—Students 35.

Moselle, Franklin Co., St. Mary's (1905), Rev. Lawrence J. Schieber.
Res., 1587 Hwy. AM, Villa Ridge, 63089. Tel: 636-451-4685. [CEM]

Neier, Franklin Co., St. Joseph (1881), Rev. Kevin V. Schmittgens.
Res., 2401 Neier Rd., Union, 63084. Tel: 636-583-2806; Fax: 636-583-0627. [CEM]
Catechesis/Religious Programs—Students 70.

New Haven, Franklin Co., Assumption (1892) (German), Rev. Daniel E. Mosley.
Res., 603 Miller St., 63068. Tel: 573-237-3372; Fax: 573-237-3372. [CEM]
Catechesis/Religious Programs—Students 113.

New Melle, St. Charles Co., Immaculate Heart of Mary (1945), Rev. Joseph A. Weber; Deacon Lonnie Weishaar; Shawn Mueller, Pastoral Assoc.
Res., 26 W. Hwy. D, Box 100, 63365-0100. Tel: 636-398-5270; Fax: 636-398-5577. [CEM]
Catechesis/Religious Programs—Sandra Robor, D.R.E.
Students 200.

O'Fallon, St. Charles Co., Assumption (1871) (German), Revs. Joseph G. Kempf; Ronald J. Rubbelke; Jeffrey N. Knight; Deacon Fred Volansky.
Res., 115 W. Third St., 63366. Tel: 636-240-3721; Fax: 636-240-3722. [CEM]
School—Tel: 636-240-4474. Sr. Patricia Cody, O.P., Prin.
Lay Teachers 22; Students 455.
Catechesis/Religious Programs—Tel: 636-978-3857.
Students 419.

St. Barnabas (1961), Rev. Daniel M. Hogan.
Res., 1400 N. Main St., 63366. Tel: 636-240-4556; Fax: 636-978-3358.
Catechesis/Religious Programs—Students 95.

Old Mines, Washington Co., St. Joachim (1723), Rev. Theodore X. Pieper; Deacon Steven Politte.
Res., Rte. 1, Box 1110, Cadet, 63630. Tel: 573-438-6181; Fax: 573-438-6181. [CEM]
School—Tel: 573-438-3973; Fax: 573-438-3161. Joyce Politte, Prin.
Lay Teachers 7; Students 75.
Catechesis/Religious Programs—Students 40.

Old Monroe, Lincoln Co., Immaculate Conception (1857), Rev. Gregory L. Schmidt; Deacon Anthony Trautman.
Res., 110 Maryknoll Rd., 63369. Tel: 636-661-5002. [CEM]
School—120 Maryknoll Rd., 63369. Tel: 636-661-5156. Susan Stewart, Prin.
Sisters of the Third Order Regular of St. Francis (Oldenburg, IN) 1; Lay Teachers 9; Students 170.
Catechesis/Religious Programs—Students 55.
Convent—122 Maryknoll Rd., Tel: 636-661-5177.

Ozora, Ste. Genevieve Co., Sacred Heart (1898), Rev. James W. Schaefer.
Res., 17742 State Rte. N., St. Mary, 63673. Tel: 573-543-2209; Fax: 573-543-2209. [CEM]
School—Tel: 573-543-2997. Sr. Agnes Keena, B.V.M., Prin.
Sisters of Charity 1; Lay Teachers 2; Students 24.
Catechesis/Religious Programs—Students 29.

Pacific, Franklin Co., St. Bridget Church (1841) (Irish), Rev. Richard V. Coerver.
Res., 111 W. Union St., 63069. Tel: 636-271-3993; Fax: 636-271-3993. [CEM]
School—Tel: 636-257-4533; Fax: 636-257-2504.
Lay Teachers 8; Students 120.
Catechesis/Religious Programs—Students 105.

Park Hills, St. Francois Co., Immaculate Conception (1903), Rev. James R. French; Deacon Walter Roderick.
Res., 1020 W. Main St., Box 66, 63601-0066. Tel: 573-431-2427; Fax: 573-431-4060. [CEM][JC]
Catechesis/Religious Programs—Students 107.
Mission—Bismarck, St. Francois Co., St. John, (1879) Maple St. & Walnut St., Bismarck, 63624. [CEM][JC]

Perryville, Perry Co., St. Vincent De Paul (1818), Rev. Kevin P. Fausz, C.M.
Res., 1000 Rosati Court, 63775. Tel: 573-547-4591; Fax: 573-547-4145. [CEM 4]
Parish Center—1010 Rosati Ct., 63775.
School—Tel: 573-547-6503. Robert Rousseau, Prin.
Daughters of Charity of St. Vincent de Paul 1; Lay Teachers 20; Students 342.
Junior-Senior High School—Tel: 573-547-2560. Richard Wibbenmeyer, Prin.
Daughters of Charity of St. Vincent de Paul 1; Lay Teachers 23; Students 276.
Catechesis/Religious Programs—Parish School of Religion.
Students 231.
Missions—Highland, Perry Co., St. Joseph, 1701 W. St. Joseph, Perryville, 63775. Tel: 314-547-6533; Fax: 573-547-2204; Crosstown, Perry Co., St. James, c/o St. Vincent De Paul Parish, Perryville, 63775.

Portage Des Sioux, St. Charles Co., St. Francis of Assisi (1799) (French-German), Rev. Michael J. Sandweg.
Res., P.O. Box 128, 63373. Tel: 636-899-0906; Fax: 636-899-0909. [CEM 2][JC]
Mission—West Alton, St. Charles Co., Immaculate Conception, 14060 Hwy. 94 N., West Alton, 63386.

Port Hudson, Franklin Co., Holy Family (1872), Rev. Robert G. Leibrecht.
Res., 124 Holy Family Church Rd., New Haven, 63068. Tel: 573-459-6441; Fax: 573-459-2257. [CEM]
Catechesis/Religious Programs—Tel: 573-459-6594; 764-3292.
Students 38.
Mission—New Haven, Franklin Co., St. Gerald, 124 Holy Family Church Rd., New Haven, 63068.

Potosi, Washington Co., St. James (1829), Rev. George Galovich.
Res., 201 N. Missouri Ave., 63664. Tel: 573-438-4686; 1-888-868-8188 (toll-free); Fax: 573-438-2100. [CEM 2]
Catechesis/Religious Programs—Students 120.

Richwoods, Washington Co., St. Stephen's (1841), Rev. Robert C. Liss.
Res., H.C.R. 63, Box 1, 63071-9701. Tel: 573-678-2207; 678-2203 (Hall); Fax: 573-678-2380. [CEM]

River Aux Vases, Ste. Genevieve Co., SS. Philip and James (1840), Rev. F. Joseph Reilly.
Res., 18411 RAV Church Rd., Ste. Genevieve, 63670. Tel: 573-883-2923; Fax: 573-883-9605. [CEM]
Catechesis/Religious Programs—Students 32.

St. Charles, St. Charles Co.,

1—ST. CHARLES BORROMEO, (1792), Revs. Richard J. Tillman; John A. Keenoy; Deacon Charles E. Drayton.
Res., 601 N. 4th St., 63301. Tel: 636-946-6370; 946-1893; Fax: 636-946-1893.
School—431 Decatur, 63301. Tel: 636-946-2713; Fax: 636-946-3096.
Sisters of Notre Dame 1; Lay Teachers 25; Students 339.
Catechesis/Religious Programs—Tel: 636-946-2916.
Students 140.
Chapel—Convent of the Sacred Heart, Regis Hall, Tel: 636-946-6456.

2—ST. CLETUS, (1965), Very Rev. James P. Callahan; Revs. Dennis M. Doyle; Donald E. Henke; Deacons Frank Prideaux; Frank Olmsted.
Res., 2705 Zumbehl Rd., 63301. Tel: 6364-946-6327; Fax: 636-946-6466.
School—Tel: 636-946-7756.
Lay Teachers 24; Students 295.
Catechesis/Religious Programs—Tel: 636-946-5936.
Students 165.

3—ST. ELIZABETH ANN SETON, (1975), Revs. Kevin J. Mahoney; Vincent R. Nyman; Donald L. Neuner.
Res., 2 Seton Ct., 63303. Tel: 636-946-6717; Fax: 636-946-9263.
School—Tel: 636-946-6716; Fax: 636-946-2670.
Sisters 1; Lay Teachers 36; Students 710.
Catechesis/Religious Programs—Tel: 314-949-3833. Nancy Burian, D.R.E.
Students 548.

4—STS. JOACHIM AND ANN, (1981), Revs. Dennis J. Doyle; James L. Gahan; Jeffrey A. Maassen.
Mailing Address: 4112 McClay Rd., 63304. Tel: 636-441-7503; Fax: 636-441-6574.
School—(Grades K-8) 4110 McClay Rd., 63304-7915. Tel: 636-441-4835; Fax: 636-441-9534. Sr. Kathleen Eilers, C.S.J., Prin.
Sisters 2; Lay Teachers 29; Students 580.
Catechesis/Religious Programs—Tel: 314-926-0021.
Students 735.

5—ST. PETER, (1850), Revs. John J. Ghio; Donald D. Carey; Deacons Thomas J. Willbrand; Donald A. Wussler. In res., Rev. Msgr. Raymond A. Hampe.
Res., 324 S. Third St., 63301-3413. Tel: 636-946-6641; Fax: 636-946-9789. [CEM]
School—222 Jackson St., 63301. Tel: 636-947-9669.
Lay Teachers 22; Students 321.
Catechesis/Religious Programs—Students 141.

6—ST. ROBERT BELLARMINE, (1964), Revs. Fred A. Meyer; John Patrick Day, C.P.
Res., 1424 First Capitol Dr. S., 63303. Tel: 636-946-6799; Fax: 636-946-0380.
School—Tel: 636-946-1474. Ken Morr, Prin.; Ann Madden, Asst. Prin.
Lay Teachers 8; Students 203.
Catechesis/Religious Programs—Students 180.

St. Clair, Franklin Co., St. Clare (1916), Rev. Paul E. Telken.
Res., Box 526, 63077. Tel: 636-629-0315; Fax: 636-629-2327. [CEM]
School—Tel: 636-629-0413.
Lay Teachers 6; Students 60.
Catechesis/Religious Programs—Students 57.

Ste. Genevieve, Ste. Genevieve Co., Ste. Genevieve (1759), Revs. John C. Deken; Matthew M. Mitas.
Res., 49 Du Bourg Pl., 63670. Tel: 573-883-2731; Fax: 573-883-2907. [CEM]
School—40 N. Fourth St., 63670. Tel: 573-883-2403.
Lay Teachers 20; Students 316.
High School—Valle High School, Tel: 573-883-7496; Fax: 573-883-9142.
Lay Teachers 16; Students 158.
Catechesis/Religious Programs—Students 85.

St. Mary, Ste. Genevieve Co., Immaculate Conception (1869), Rev. Richard C. Kasznel.
Res., P.O. Box 27, 63673. Tel: 573-543-2536. [CEM]

St. Paul, St. Charles Co., St. Paul (1850), Rev. Msgr. John J. Hickel.
Res., P.O. Box 66069, 63366. Tel: 636-978-1400 (Rectory); 978-1900 (Parish Center Offices); Fax: 636-980-2722 (Parish Center Offices). [CEM]
School—P.O. Box 66070, 63366. Tel: 636-978-1900, Ext. 230. Mary Price, Prin.
Lay Teachers 17; Students 227.
Catechesis/Religious Programs—Students 140.

St. Peters, St. Charles Co., All Saints (1815), Revs. Michael L. Henning; James M. Mitulski; Robert C. Lane; Deacon Gerald Knobbe.
Res., 7 McMenamy Rd., 63376. Tel: 636-397-1440; Fax: 636-397-1421. [CEM]
School—Tel: 636-397-1477; Fax: 636-970-3735. Rae Ann Kielty, Prin.
Lay Teachers 22; Students 443.
Catechesis/Religious Programs—Tel: 636-397-6995. Ms. Marya Pohlmeier, D.R.E.
Students 571.

Sereno, Perry Co., Our Lady of Victory (1908), Rev. Francis H. Agnew, C.M.
Res., 172 PCR 920, Perryville, 63775. Tel: 573-547-6812; Fax: 573-547-6812. [JC]
Catechesis/Religious Programs—Students 58.

Silver Lake, Perry Co., St. Rose of Lima (1885), Rev. Kevin P. Fausz, C.M.
Res., 1010 Rosati Ct., Perryville, 63775. Tel: 573-547-4591; Fax: 573-547-4145. [CEM]

Sullivan, Franklin Co., St. Anthony (1891), Rev. Theodore J. Brunnert.
Res., 201 W. Springfield Ave., 63080. Tel: 573-468-6101; Fax: 573-468-8584. [CEM]
School—101 W. Springfield Ave., 63080. Tel: 573-468-4423. E. Anne Hanneken, Prin.
Lay Teachers 6; Students 80.
Church of the Holy Martyrs of Japan (1879), Rev. James J. Pavlik.
Church—8244 Hwy. AE, 63080-3229. Tel: 573-627-3378. [CEM 2]
Catechesis/Religious Programs—Students 20.

Tiff, Washington Co., St. Joseph (1723), Rev. Theodore X. Pieper, Admin.
Res., R.R.I. Box 1110, Cadet, 63630. Tel: 573-438-6181; Fax: 573-438-6181. [CEM]

Troy, Lincoln Co., Sacred Heart (1891), Rev. Donald C. Schramm; Sr. Mary Ann Fisher, C.S.J., Pastoral Min.; Deacon Thomas Burkemper.
Res., 100 Thompson Dr., 63379. Tel: 636-528-8219; Fax: 636-528-3983. [CEM]
School—Tel: 636-528-6684; Fax: 636-528-3923. Sr. Jeannette Fennewald, S.S.N.D., Prin.
Lay Teachers 11; Students 264.
Catechesis/Religious Programs—Students 215.

Union, Franklin Co., Immaculate Conception (1866), Revs. Peter M. Blake; Gerald T. Simpson.
Res., 100 N. Washington Ave., 63084. Tel: 636-583-5144; Fax: 636-583-7784. [CEM]
School—6 W. State St., 63084. Tel: 636-583-2641.
Sisters 1; Lay Teachers 12; Students 276.
Catechesis/Religious Programs—Students 151.

Warrenton, Warren Co., Holy Rosary (1868), Rev. Eugene P. Brennan.
Res., 724 E. Booneslick Rd., 63383. Tel: 636-456-3698; Fax: 636-456-5560. [CEM]
School—Tel: 636-456-2882. Sr. Mary Ann Boes, Prin.
Sisters of St. Joseph of Carondelet 1; Lay Teachers 8; Students 183.
Catechesis/Religious Programs—Students 130.

Washington, Franklin Co., St. Francis Borgia (1834) (German), Revs. John M. Costello; Patrick Christopher; Deacons Gilbert Holtmeyer; Leon Noelker.
Res., 311 W. Second St., 63090. Tel: 636-239-6701; Fax: 636-239-9499. [CEM]
School—225 Cedar St., 63090. Tel: 636-239-2590; Fax: 636-316-9384.
Lay Teachers 27; Students 397.
Catechesis/Religious Programs—Students 145.
Our Lady of Lourdes (1958), Rev. Robert L. Heimos; Deacon Richard J. Boland.
Res., 1014 Madison Ave., 63090. Tel: 636-239-3520; Fax: 636-239-7682.
School—950 Madison Ave., 63090. Tel: 636-239-5292; Fax: 636-239-7682.
Lay Teachers 21; Students 297.
Catechesis/Religious Programs—Students 95.

Weingarten, Ste. Genevieve Co., Our Lady Help of Christians (1872), Rev. John Suren.
Res., 13370 Hwy. 32, Ste. Genevieve, 63670-9402. Tel: 573-883-3796; Fax: 573-883-8871. [CEM]

Wentzville, St. Charles Co., St. Patrick (1905), Revs. Patrick J. O'Laughlin; Donald A. Glastetter; Deacons Paul H. Chavaux; Bernard A. Buckman.
Res., 405 S. Church St., 63385. Tel: 636-332-9225; Fax: 636-332-6998. [CEM]
School—701 Church St., 63385. Tel: 636-332-9913. Mrs. Janice Ward, Prin.
Lay Teachers 17; Students 277.
Catechesis/Religious Programs—Tel: 636-332-9036.
Students 300.

West Alton, St. Charles Co., Immaculate Conception. Closed. See St. Francis, Portage des Sioux.

Zell, Ste. Genevieve Co., St. Joseph (1845), Rev. Msgr. James E. Hanson.
Res., 11824 Zell Rd., Ste. Genevieve, 63670. Tel: 573-883-3481; Fax: 573-883-7829. [CEM]
School—Tel: 573-883-5097.
Adorers of the Blood of Christ (Ruma, IL) 1; Lay Teachers 4; Students 57.
Catechesis/Religious Programs—Students 82.

Korean Ministry

Ellisville, St. Andrew Kim Korean Catholic Community Church (1970) (Korean), Rev. Seung Sik Hong, Admin.
Res., P.O. Box 3953, Ballwin, 63011. Tel: 636-230-9601; Fax: 636-537-8547.
82 Henry Ave., Ballwin, 63011.

Chaplains of Public Institutions

ST. LOUIS. *Barnes Hospital*. Rev. James C. Gray.
Christian Hospital Northeast-Northwest. (Vacant) 11133 Dunn Rd., 63136. Tel: 314-355-2300.
DePaul Health Center. Revs. Fred Lens; Lawrence Asma, C.M.
Lammert International Airport. Deacon Arnold Krieger Tel: 314-427-8787.
Regional Hospital 5535 Delmar Blvd., 63112. Tel: 314-361-2273. Rev. Francis J. Shine, C.M., Chap.
St. John's Mercy Medical Center Tel: 314-569-6470. Rev. Philip G. Krahman.
Saint Louis University Hospital Tel: 314-577-8066. Rev. Gregory G. Kirsch.
St. Mary's Health Center Tel: 314-768-8000. Revs. Hernando J. Ramirez, S.J.; James A. Krings Tel: 314-289-9545.

KIRKWOOD. *St. Joseph Hospital* Tel: 314-966-1596. Rev. Mark L. Fuller Tel: 314-962-0038.

ST. CHARLES. *St. Joseph Health Center* Tel: 636-946-6641. Rev. Msgr. Raymond H. Hampe Tel: 636-946-5487.

WASHINGTON. *St. John's Hospital* Tel: 636-239-3222. Rev. Timothy J. Toohey; Sr. Louise Eggen, O.S.B., Chap.

Special Assignment:
Reverend Monsignors—
O'Brien, Joseph M., Mktg. & Devel., Catholic Family Services, 7800 Kenrick Rd., St. Louis, MO 63119. Tel: 314-968-8010; Fax: 314-968-5478
Stika, Richard F., V.G., Chancellor, 4510 Lindell, St. Louis, MO 63108. Tel: 314-367-4437
Reverend Fathers—
Aten, Robert L., Heart of Mary Hermitage, Lesterville, MO. Tel: 573-648-2467
Breier, Henry, Secretary to the Bishop
Dalton, Donald T., Ursuline Provincialate, 210 Glennon Heights Rd., Crystal City, MO 63019. Tel: 636-937-6206;Fax: 636-937-7627

On Duty Outside the Archdiocese:
Reverend Monsignors—
Dolan, Timothy M., Rome, Italy
Ratermann, David A., Cochabamba, Bolivia
Reverend Fathers—
Blattner, Joseph H., Burlington, VT
Bolderson, John D., Kansas City, MO
Hayden, Patrick T., La Paz, Bolivia
Hederman, Kevin F., Belmopan, Belize
Kopfensteiner, Thomas R., Fordham University, Bronx, NY
Lampert, Robert E., Christus Health, Irving, TX
Lockwood, Gregory, Cincinnati, OH
Mannion, Martin K., Yuma, AZ
Means, David A., Anchorage, AK
Menner, Robert J., La Paz, Bolivia
Rutkowski, James, San Antonio, TX
Ryan, Patrick, Owensboro, KY
Siebert, Anthony G., Belize, Central America
Stretch, Daniel P., La Paz, Bolivia
Tichacek, Charles P., La Paz, Bolivia
Vollmer, Gary L., Las Vegas, NV

Graduate Studies:
Reverend Fathers—
Bene, Philip J., M.A., M.Div., Rome, Italy
Morris, C. Eugene, Rome, Italy
Teater, Kristian C., Rome, Italy

Military Chaplains:
Reverend Fathers—
Breig, Gary R.
Kovalcin, John A.
Swetnam, R. William
Zinzer, Walter A.

On Medical Leave:
Reverend Monsignors—
Clavenna, Charles G.
Reverend Fathers—
Babka, Robert H.
Christian, Norman H.
Fitzgerald, Alfred J.
Haberkern, Thomas A.
Heck, Donald
McGrath, Michael S.
Palmer, Michael J.
Schaab, Thomas J.
Seidel, Michael J.
Walter, David A.

Retired:
Reverend Monsignors—
Behrmann, Elmer H., 2012 Clermont Crossing Dr., Apt. G, St. Louis, MO 63146
Boessen, Bernard H., 1815 Albert Pl., Apt. B1, Jefferson City, MO 65101
Byrne, Henry L., Regina Cleri, 7850 Kenrick Rd., St. Louis, MO 63119
Chiodini, Jasper J., Regina Cleri, 7850 Kenrick Rd., St. Louis, MO 63119
Dietz, Norbert J., 7148 Forsyth, St. Louis, MO 63105
Dwyer, Adrian I., 6052 Waterman, St. Louis, MO 63112
Forst, Charles J., 3635 Union Rd., St. Louis, MO 63125
Gannon, Rowland E., Regina Cleri, 7950 Kenrick, St. Louis, MO 63119
Glynn, Gerard N., Regina Cleri, 7850 Kenrick Rd., St. Louis, MO 63119
Hartnett, James R., 2013 Trailcrest Ln., St. Louis, MO 63122
Holland, John P., 1575 N. Woodland Ave., St. Louis, MO 63122-1462
Kennedy, John J., 665 S. Skinker #10E, St. Louis, MO 63105
Krieger, Wilfred L., 4286 Putting Green Dr., San Antonio, TX 78217
Lubeley, Richard J., 676 W. Lockwood Blvd., St. Louis, MO 63119
Marschner, Aloysius J., Mother Good Counsel Home, 6825 Natural Bridge Rd., St. Louis, MO 63121
Meyer, Louis F., 4908 Sutherland, St. Louis, MO 63109
Molloy, Patrick J., Regina Cleri, 7850 Kenrick Rd., St. Louis, MO 63119
Muesenfechter, Robert J., 9401 Easy St., Hillsboro, MO 63050
O'Brien, Joseph T., 5005 Coquina Key Dr., S.E., Apt. C, St. Petersburg, FL 33739
O'Connell, James P., #60 Plaza Sq., Apt. 1207, St. Louis, MO 63103
Overman, Robert F., 1711 Parhaven, San Antonio, TX 78232
Peet, Arthur V., Mother of Good Counsel, 6825 Natural Bridge, St. Louis, MO 63121
Regan, Michael F., Mother of Good Counsel, 6825 Natural Bridge, St. Louis, MO 63121
Ronquest, John T., St. Simon Rectory, 11011 Mueller Rd., St. Louis, MO 63123
Shocklee, John A., 3225 N. Florissant Ave., St. Louis, MO 63107
Sommer, Jerome, Regina Cleri, 7850 Kenrick Rd., St. Louis, MO 63119
Sullivan, Leo F., 6825 Natural Bridge Rd., St. Louis, MO 63121
Wilkerson, Jerome F., St. John Bosco, 12934 Marine Ave., St. Louis, MO 63146
Woracek, Thomas J., Regina Cleri, 7850 Kenrick Rd., St. Louis, MO 63119
Reverend Fathers—
Althoff, Arthur J., Regina Cleri, 7850 Kenrick Rd., St. Louis, MO 63119
Bell, Ira J., Regina Cleri, 7850 Kenrick Rd., St. Louis, MO 63119
Boisaubin, Robert D., 2001 Shepard Rd. 10, Wildwood, MO 63038
Britt, William J., Regina Cleri, 7850 Kenrick Rd., St. Louis, MO 63119
Bromschwig, Arthur F., 6825 Natural Bridge Rd., St. Louis, MO 63121
Bukauskas, Anthony, 7850 Kenrick Rd., St. Louis, MO 63119
Burghoff, Theodore H., 243 W. Aragonne Dr., St. Louis, MO 63122
Burmester, Edwin J., St. Gabriel, 6303 Nottingham, St. Louis, MO 63109
Campbell, John R., 5375 Kenrick Park Dr., #301, St. Louis, MO 63119
Cooper, Thomas T., Regina Cleri, 7850 Kenrick Rd., St. Louis, MO 63119
Deutsch, Bernard F., 101 Winter Harbor Rd., Ocean City, MD 21842
Ditch, Robert G., Regina Cleri, 7850 Kenrick Rd., St. Louis, MO 63119
Eilers, Joseph B., Regina Cleri, 7850 Kenrick Rd., St. Louis, MO 63119
Feuerbacher, Edward F., 5076 Durant Ave., St. Louis, MO 63115
Forst, Aloysius A., 4141 Germania, Apt. 2B, St. Louis, MO 63116
Gambon, John A., 300 E. Lane Dr., Washington, MO 63090
Geoghegan, John F., Regina Cleri, 7850 Kenrick Rd., St. Louis, MO 63119
Gibson, Michael P., 665 S. Skinker Blvd., St. Louis, MO 63105
Goellner, Glennon J., 1765 Charbonier Rd., Florissant, MO 63031
Gummersbach, James L., 4445 Lindell Blvd., St. Louis, MO 63108
Haar, George B., Regina Cleri, 7850 Kenrick Rd., St. Louis, MO 63119
Hemkens, Edward B., 6825 Natural Bridge Rd., St. Louis, MO 63121
Hoffman, Donald J., 1420 S. Sappington Rd., St. Louis, MO 63126
Hrdlicka, Lambert A., 4243 LaSalette Dr., St. Louis, MO 63123
Huhn, Donald W., Regina Cleri, 7850 Kenrick Rd., St. Louis, MO 63119
Julius, James A., 1800 Beach Dr., Gulf Port, MS 39507
Kersgieter, Paul J., 2605 Mullanphy Ln., Florissant, MO 63031
Keutzer, Walter J., P.O. Box 348, Osage Beach, MO 65065
Knaup, Alan J., 4900 Ringer Rd., St. Louis, MO 63129
Knoll, Urban H., 629 S. Fourth St., St. Charles, MO 63301
Komaska, James R., 60 Shawnee Valley Rd., Marthasville, MO 63357
Kraus, Robert J., 1306 W. Main, #214, Jefferson City, MO 65109
Lessard, Joseph P., P.O. Box 322, Prairie DuRocher, IL 62277
Lewis, Leo T.
Liermann, Raymond B., 910 Hackman Rd., St. Paul, MO 63366
Matyas, Francis B., Regina Cleri, 7850 Kenrick Rd., St. Louis, MO 63119
Mersinger, Arthur J., Alexian Bros. Lansdowne Village, 4624 Lansdowne, St. Louis, MO 63116
Mersinger, Norbert A., St. Martin of Tours, 610 W. Ripa Ave., St. Louis, MO 63125
Morse, John A., 525 Mill Rd., Marthasville, MO 63357
Murphy, James E., 16 Tournament Tee Dr., O'Fallon, MO 63366
Noser, J. Homer, Regina Cleri, 7850 Kenrick Rd., St. Louis, MO 63119
Portucheck, Joseph J., Regina Cleri, 7850 Kenrick Rd., St. Louis, MO 63119
Rehme, Albert A., 362 Rue Bonne Terre (TDL), Bonne Terre, MO 63628
Ruff, Charles R., Regina Cleri, 7850 Kenrick Rd., St. Louis, MO 63119
Ryan, Joseph J., 2725 Terra Ceia Bay Blvd., Apt. 104, Palmetto, FL 34221
Scheer, Joseph O., 311 S. Clay, Kirkwood, MO 63122
Schlattmann, Edward B., Regina Cleri, 7850 Kenrick Rd., St. Louis, MO 63119
Schmaltz, Albert F., 7850 Kenrick Rd., St. Louis, MO 63119
Schneider, John G., 1607 Tomkins St., St. Charles, MO 63301
Somos, Joseph, Hungary
Stolzer, Vincent A., 1011A Cy Ann Dr., Town & Country, MO 63017
Stratman, Ambrose F., 8604 W. Shore Dr.-LL, Hillsboro, MO 63050
Stroot, Ralph E., 4980 Heege Rd., St. Louis, MO 63123
Suellentrop, Bernard A., 7622 Sutherland Ave., St. Louis, MO 63119
Thomas, David T., J.C.D., 12934 Marine Ave., St. Louis, MO 63146
Tiefenbrunn, Ronald R., 2403 Albert Rasche Dr., Cape Girardeau, MO 63701
Wetzel, William I., Col., 770 Carolyn Ave., Summerland Key, FL 33042-5646
Wolf, Joseph B., 1970 Greenpoint Dr., Apt. 103, St. Louis, MO 63122

Permanent Deacons:
Amelotti, David
Arnold, Steven J.
Audrain, Raymond J.
Auer, Edward J.
Bachista, Ronald J.
Baker, John H., M.D.
Bansbach, Paul, On Duty Outside the Archdiocese
Basler, James H.
Bauwens, Gerard, On Duty Outside the Archdiocese
Beckman, Carl H.
Beinke, George A.
Bell, Jesse H.
Bernsen, Albert B.
Blase, George A.
Boedeker, C. Allen
Boland, Richard J.
Bolderson, David A.
Bourbon, Glennon L., Sr.
Boyer, Edward J.
Bryant, Wayne T.
Buchek, Bradford M.
Buckley, James Mike
Buckley, John J.
Buckman, Bernard A.
Buhr, Thomas A.
Burkemper, Thomas B.
Burton, James L.
Butler, James R.
Camden, David M.
Caruana, Philip P.
Casseau, William U.
Chauvin, C. Frank
Chavaux, Paul H.
Chitwood, Dennis M.
Christ, Walter W.
Clemens, Kenneth C., Jr.
Coffman, Richard W.
Conley, Allen M.
Coppage, Michael J., Jr.
Cox, Joseph E.
Crafts, R. Paul
Curtin, John A.
Czarnecki, Eugene J.
Damato, Larry (PAT)
Daus, Andrew C.
Davanzo, Charles R.
Denham, Donald C.
DePyper, Robert R.
Dickerson, Raymond A.
Dietz, Alvin J.
Dingman, Edwin H.
Dobelmann, Vernon L.
Dodson, Fred
Dolan, Timothy C.
Dorhauer, Jacob W.
Dowd, Thomas L.
Drayton, Charles E.
Driscoll, Donald L.
Droesch, Francis A.
Ecker, Alan E.
Efken, Donald C.
Ehrhard, Herbert L.
Esswein, Leo F.
Eultgen, Thomas L.
Fink, George Russ
Flint, Edward G.
Forster, Thomas E.
Fronick, Edward C.
Gabbert, William L.
Gamache, Robert K. (DEN)
Gawedzinkski, Norbert L.
Gearon, William A.
Gegg, Albin A.
Geiser, Gerald J.
Georges, Charles W.
Gerdes, Philip J.
Gerling, Thomas J. (JC)
Gettemeier, Herbert B.
Ghiglione, James J.
Gholston, Clifford
Gildehaus, Charles R.
Gorski, Thomas (ARL)
Gounis, Peter E.
Graham, George A.
Grant, Maurice A., Sr.
Greif, William J.
Griffard, James M.
Grotpeter, Edward R.
Gunsaullus, Roland J.
Haefner, Joseph Tom
Hanses, Eugene J.
Harris, Singleton L.
Harrison, R. Fielding
Hayes, Ralph
Heitert, Donald C.
Hengen, Philip R.
Hennicke, Raymond C.
Henning, Kenneth A.
Henroid, Daniel H.
Hercules, Joseph E.
Hoffmann, Eugene A.
Holmes, Charles E.
Holtmeyer, Gilbert C.
Hummel, Fred J.
Hutti, Lawrence J., Jr.
Inman, Kenneth A.
Janson, Norman F.
Johnson, Leslie A.
Jurek, Thomas F., On Duty Outside the Archdiocese
Karsznia, Robert A.
Keeney, Robert J.
Kelly, Lawrence C.
Kennedy, Joseph M.
Kenney, T. Michael, III
Kiechlin, Robert J., Jr.
Kieffer, William A.
Kiely, E. Ray
Klempert, Michael L.
Klostermann, Robert A., Sr.
Knobbe, Gerald E.
Kreft, Ronald J.

Krieger, Arnold F.
Kroutil, Joseph C.
Kuenz, Gary J.
La Martina, Joseph A.
Lake, Richard C.
Lauterwasser, Gerard M.
Levac, Richard B.
Lombardo, Charles W.
Longmeyer, Harold
Love, Allen F.
Luke, Herbert, M.D.
Macauley, Edward C.
Maranan, Diosdado L.
Marcinkiewicz, Joseph, Jr.
Marren, L. Jerome
Martin, James P.
Martin, Leroy A., Jr.
McEntire, Clyde W.
McGuire, Jerry N.
McKee, Paul R., Ph.D.
McKenna, William J., B.B.A., M.S.
McNamee, George W., On Duty Outside the Archdiocese
McNamee, Terrance M.
Menard, Louis A.
Meyerkord, Gary A.
Miller, George W.
Miller, Millard Ray
Morris, Joseph C.
Mroczkowski, R. V.
Mueller, Frederick J.
Murphy, James L.
Murphy, Thomas P.
Murphy, Thomas O.
Murray, Stephen L.
Naumann, Eugene J.
Nesbitt, Frank E.
Niemeyer, Andrew C.
Noelker, Leon R.
O'Leary, John A.
Olmsted, Francis J.
Otzenberger, Joseph M.
Peacock, Joseph C.
Penberthy, Robert S.
Peterson, Stanley M., Jr.
Politte, Glennon P., Sr.
Politte, Stephen A.
Politte, Thomas G.
Porterfield, Paul D.
Potzman, Kenneth M.
Powers, Robert J.
Prideaux, Frank W.
Priesmeyer, W., Jr.
Prives, Gerald J.
Quinn, J. Gerard
Reynoso, Louis J.
Riegel, Robert C.
Roberson, Robert L.
Roderick, Walter L.
Rodis, Theodore J.
Ruegg, Walter J.
Schiffman, Donald J.
Schnable, Robert H.
Schulte, Edwin
Schultheis, Glennon J.
Schulze, Roy E.
Shelby, Richard L.
Sinak, William S.
Sisul, Leonard A.
Smerek, Robert S.
Smith, James R.
Smith, John F.
Snyder, Robert J.
Snyder, Robert C.
Stallings, Larry J.
Stevens, Richard L.
Stigall, Donald R.
Stoverink, Gerard G.
Stoverink, John J.
Strauss, Harold A.
Streckfuss, Joseph C.
Suden, Michael E., D.D.S.
Sulze, Joseph W.
Sutton, Ronald L.
Tichacek, George A.
Toohey, Jerome V.
Towey, Martin G., Ph.D.
Tracy, Daniel J.
Trautman, Anthony G.
Tresch, Earl K.
Turek, Paul J., Sr.
Vaughn, Albert X.
Volansky, Fred N.
Volansky, James M.
Walbridge, William F.
Weatherholt, Harold J.
Weishaar, Lonnie G.
Weiss, William G.
Werner, Norman B.
Wertz, Robert E.
Wessels, Richard H.
White, Otis D.
Willbrand, Thomas J.
Williams, Albert C.
Winkelmann, Christian H.
Winker, Ewald
Wohlert, Steven H.
Wood, George F.
Wunderlich, William P.
Wussler, Donald A.

INSTITUTIONS LOCATED IN THE ARCHDIOCESE

[A] SEMINARIES, ARCHDIOCESAN

ST. LOUIS. *Kenrick-Glennon Seminary.* (St. Louis Roman Catholic Theological Seminary).

Kenrick School of Theology, 5200 Glennon Dr., 63119. Tel: 314-792-6100; Fax: 314-792-6500.
Web site: www.kenrick.edu
Rev. Msgr. Dennis M. Delaney, Rector; Revs. Thomas M. Molini, M.A., Vice Rector & Dean Students; Lawrence C. Brennan, S.T.D., Academic Dean; Rev. Msgr. William J. Lyons, S.T.L., Dir. Pre-Theology; Mr. William J. Matula, B.A., Business Officer; Mr. Peter S. Maher, J.D., LL.M., Dir. Devel.; Revs. John F. Clark, C.M., M.A.; Glennon C. Doherty, M.A.; Damien R. Dougherty, O.F.M., S.T.D.; Matthew J. Gutowski, S.T.L.; John P. Heil, S.S.D.; James J. Ramacciotti, J.C.L.; Edward J. Richard, M.S., D.Th.M.; James E. Swift, C.M., S.T.D.; Michael J. Witt, Ph.D.; Rev. Msgr. Edward C. Eichor, M.A.; Rev. Ted J. Wojcicki, Ed.D.; Sr. Zoe Glenski, D.C., Ph.D.; Sr. Ann McElhatton, R.S.C.J., M.A.; Glenn C.J. Byer, S.L.D.; Susanne M. Harvath, Ph.D.; Peter F. Hesed, M.A.; Anne Marie Kitz, Ph.D.; Germaine Fry Murray, Ph.D.; David A. Murray, Ph.D.; Andrew J. Sopko, Ph.D.; Lucille Trujillo-Tiroch, M.A.; Lawrence J. Welch, Ph.D.; Shawn M. Welch, Ph.D.; Deacon George W. Miller, B.S. Priests 13; Sisters 2; Deacons 1; Students 69; St. Louis Students 20.
Permanent Staff: Priests 13; Sisters 2; Lay Staff 12.

Cardinal Glennon College, 5200 Glennon Dr., 63119. Tel: 314-792-6100; Fax: 314-644-3079. Revs. Jeffrey G. Vomund, Dir.; Mitchell S. Doyen, Assoc. Dir.; Rev. Msgr. William J. Lyons, Spiritual Dir.; Sr. Elizabeth Ann Buscher, S.C.C., Academic Advisor; Sr. Pat Dalton, S.S.N.D.; Mrs. Marion Love, R.N. Priests 3; Sisters 2; Lay Teachers 1; Students 33; St. Louis Students 22; Birmingham, AL Students 1; Omaha, NE Students 5; Peoria, IL Students 2.
Permanent Staff: Priests 3; Sisters 2; Lay Teachers 1.

[B] SEMINARIES, RELIGIOUS, OR SCHOLASTICATES

ST. LOUIS. *Aquinas Institute of Theology*, 3642 Lindell Blvd., 63108. Tel: 314-977-3882; Fax: 314-977-7225.
E-mail: aquinas@slu.edu
Web site: www.ai.edu
Rev. Charles E. Bouchard, O.P., Pres.; Sr. Diane Kennedy, O.P., Dean; Rev. Albert G. Glade, O.P., Business Mgr. & Dir. Student Affairs; Eileen Wickham, Inst. Advancement; Ron Knapp, Admissions; Sara McGinnis, Alumni & Public Rels.; Revs. Richard A. Peddicord, O.P.; Jay Harrington, O.P.; Gregory J. Heille, O.P.; Thomas E. Esselman, C.M.; Harry M. Byrne, O.P.; Michael Mascari, O.P.; Frank C. Quinn, O.P.; George R. Boudreau, O.P.; Sr. Marygrace Peters, O.P.; Sr. Jean deBlois, C.S.J.; Sr. Joan Delaplane, O.P.; Sr. Mary Margaret Pazdan, O.P.; Sr. Carla Mae Streeter, O.P.; Sr. Catherine Vincie, R.S.H.M.; Sr. Patricia Walter, O.P. Priests 10; Sisters 8; Lay Teachers 10; Seminarians 32; Total Enrollment 246.

St. John Neumann House. Redemptorist College Seminary Residence, 3737 Washington Blvd., 63108. Tel: 314-531-2777; Fax: 314-531-5726.
E-mail: cssrinfo@catholic.org
Web site: www.redemptorists-denver.org
Revs. Gary Lauenstein, C.Ss.R., Rector & Supr.; Richard Boever, C.Ss.R., Dir. Formation; David Polek, C.Ss.R., Vocation Dir.; Wm. Emmett Collins, C.Ss.R.; Jack Hacker, C.Ss.R. Priests 5; Seminarians 11.

[C] COLLEGES AND UNIVERSITIES

ST. LOUIS. *Fontbonne College*, 6800 Wydown Blvd., 63105. Tel: 314-862-3456; Fax: 314-889-1451.
E-mail: sking@fontbonne.edu
Web site: www.fontbonne.edu
For a complete listing, refer to the Colleges and Universities section.

Saint Louis University, 221 N. Grand Blvd., DB 351, 63103-2097. Tel: 314-977-2222; Fax: 314-977-3874.
Web site: www.slu.edu
For a complete listing, refer to the Colleges and Universities section.

[D] RELIGIOUS EDUCATION

ST. LOUIS. *Paul VI Institute of Catechetical and Pastoral Studies*, 5200 Glennon Dr., 63119. Tel: 314-792-6450; Fax: 314-792-6455.
E-mail: paul6@archstl.org
Web site: www.archstl.org
Revs. Edward J. Richard, M.S., Dir.; Jeffrey G. Vomund, Assoc. Dir. Priests 18; Brothers 1; Sisters 2; Deacons 3; Lay Teachers 18; Total Enrollment 1,810.

[E] HIGH SCHOOLS, ARCHDIOCESAN

ST. LOUIS. *Bishop DuBourg High School*, 5850 Eichelberger St., 63109. Tel: 314-832-3030; Fax: 314-832-0529.
E-mail: info@dubourg.org
Web site: http://www.dubourg.org
A Co-Educational School Staffed by Diocesan Priests, Religious and Lay Teachers. Mr. Thomas Jokerst, Prin. Associate Principals: Dr. Gerald Gruszka; Mrs. Chris Kwiatkowski. Priests 3; Sisters 5; Lay Teachers 55; Students 840.

Cardinal Ritter College Prep, 5421 Thekla Ave., 63120. Tel: 314-381-7980; Fax: 314-381-8050.
E-mail: crcphs@stlnet.com
Web site: info.csd.org/ritter.htm
Co-Educational High School Staffed by Religious and Laity. Mrs. Carmele U. Hall, Pres. & Prin. Priests 1; Sisters 1; Lay Teachers 14; Students 220.

Rosati-Kain High School, 4389 Lindell Blvd., 63108. Tel: 314-533-8513; Fax: 314-533-1618.
E-mail: archstl808@impresso.com
Web site: www.rosati-kain.org
Conducted for Girls by Diocesan Priests, the Sisters of St. Joseph and the School Sisters of Notre Dame. Sr. Joan Andert, S.S.N.D., Prin.; Nancy P. Lydon, Assoc. Prin. Priests 1; Sisters 4; Lay Teachers 25; Girls 441.

Saint Mary's High School, 4701 S. Grand Blvd., 63111. Tel: 314-481-8400; Fax: 314-481-3670.
E-mail: archstl809@connectinc.com
Web site: www.stmaryshs.com
For Boys, Staffed by Brothers of Mary and Archdiocesan Priests. Mr. Kevin Hacker, B.A., M.Ed., Prin. Priests 2; Lay Teachers 33; Total Enrollment 510.

FESTUS. *St. Pius X High School*, 1030 St. Pius Dr., 63028. Tel: 636-937-3695; 931-7487; Fax: 636-931-7487.
Web site: stpius.com
A Co-Educational High School Conducted by Diocesan Priests and Lay Faculty. Mr. Charles Nolan, Prin.; Ms. Norma Overberg, Assoc. Prin. Priests 1; Lay Teachers 29; Students 438.

FLORISSANT. *St. Thomas Aquinas-Mercy High School*, 845 Dunn Rd., 63031. Tel: 314-837-1144; Fax: 314-837-4255.
E-mail: archstl810@impresso.com
Web site: www.inlink.com/~aquinas
A Co-Educational High School Conducted by One Diocesan Priest, a Vincentian Priest, and Lay Men and Women. Mr. George Pressey, Prin.; Patricia Moore, Asst. Prin. Priests 2; Lay Teachers 28; Students 403.

MANCHESTER. *John F. Kennedy Catholic High School*, 500 Woods Mill Rd., 63011. Tel: 636-227-5900; Fax: 636-227-0298.
E-mail: admin@JFK-Catholic-high.org
Web site: www.jfk-catholic-high.org
A Co-Educational High School Staffed by Lay Faculty. Randy Berzon, Prin. Lay Teachers 47; Students 540.

O'FALLON. *St. Dominic High School*, 31 St. Dominic Dr., 63366. Tel: 636-240-8303; Fax: 636-240-9884.
E-mail: mainoffice@stdominichs.org
Web site: www.stdominichs.org
A Co-Educational High School Conducted by Diocesan Priests and Sisters of the Third Order of St. Dominic and laymen and laywomen. Sr. Mary H. Bender, S.S.N.D., Admin.; Sr. Carolyn, O.P., Prin. Priests 1; Sisters 3; Lay Teachers 36; Students 690.

ST. CHARLES. *Duchesne High School*, 2550 Elm St., 63301-1494. Tel: 636-946-6767; Fax: 636-946-6267.
E-mail: archstl821@impresso.com
Web site: www.duchesne-hs.org
A Co-Educational College Prep High School Conducted by Archdiocesan Priests and Catholic Lay Staff. Under the Auspices of the Catholic Education Office. Sponsored by Seven Parishes in and around St. Charles, MO. Dr. Daniel J. Matusiak, Admin.; Mr. Donald C. Burkhart, Prin.; Revs. James L. Gahan; Donald E. Henke. Priests 2; Brothers 1; Sisters 1; Lay Teachers 44; Students 710.

SPANISH LAKE. *Rosary High School*, 1720 Redman Ave., 63138. Tel: 314-741-1333; Fax: 314-741-1335.
E-mail: archstl807@impresso.com

Web site: www.rosaryhighschool.com
A Co-Educational High School Staffed by Archdiocesan Priests, Religious and Lay Teachers. Sr. Karl Mary Winkelmann, S.S.N.D., Prin.; Mr. Richard Barrett, Asst. Prin. Priests 1; Sisters 1; Lay Teachers 32; Students 431.

WASHINGTON. *St. Francis Borgia Regional High School*, 1000 Borgia Dr., 63090. Tel: 636-239-7871; Fax: 636-239-1198.
E-mail: mtraffas@borgia.com
Web site: www.borgia.com
A Co-Educational High School Staffed by Diocesan Priests and School Sisters of Notre Dame and dedicated lay faculty. Marilyn Traffas, Admin.; Mr. George Wingbermuehle, Prin. Priests 1; Sisters 2; Lay Teachers 43; Students 674.

[F] HIGH SCHOOLS, PRIVATE

ST. LOUIS. *Christian Brothers College High School (C.B.C.)*, 6501 Clayton Rd., 63117. Tel: 314-721-1200; Fax: 314-721-2471.
E-mail: admin@cbc-stl.org
Web site: www.cbc-stl.org
Bro. Lawrence Humphrey, F.S.C., Pres.; Mr. James B. Gerdes, Prin. Brothers 7; Lay Teachers 60; Students 928.

Cor Jesu Academy, 10230 Gravois, 63123. Tel: 314-842-1546; Fax: 314-842-6061.
E-mail: principal@corjesu.pvt.k12.mo.us
Web site: http://www.corjesu.pvt.k12.mo.us
Apostles of the Sacred Heart. Sr. Sheila O'Neill, A.S.C.J., Prin. Priests 1; Sisters 10; Lay Teachers 30; Students 525.

De Smet Jesuit High School, 233 N. New Ballas Rd., 63141. Tel: 314-567-3502; Fax: 314-567-1519.
Web site: www.desmet.org
Dr. Gregory A. Densberger, Ph.D., Prin.; Rev. John D. Arnold, S.J., Pres. Priests 8; Sisters 2; Brothers 1; Lay Teachers 76; Students 1,259.

Incarnate Word Academy, 2788 Normandy Dr., 63121. Tel: 314-725-5850; Fax: 314-725-2308.
E-mail: archstl873@impresso.com
Web site: www.iwacademy.org
Sisters of Charity of Incarnate Word of San Antonio. Mrs. Nancy Repking, Prin. Sisters 1; Lay Teachers 40; Support Staff 14; Students 512.

Notre Dame High School, 320 E. Ripa Ave., 63125. Tel: 314-544-1015; Fax: 314-544-8003.
E-mail: archstl875@connectinc.com
Web site: www.ndhs.net
Sr. Michelle Emmerich, S.S.N.D., Prin. Sisters 3; Lay Teachers 43; Girls 471.

St. Elizabeth Academy, 3401 Arsenal St., 63118. Tel: 314-771-5134; Fax: 314-771-3528.
E-mail: rjhenry@ninenet.com
Sisters of the Most Precious Blood. Mrs. Rosalie Henry, Prin. Sisters 4; Lay Teachers 29; Students 230.

St. Joseph's Academy, 2307 S. Lindbergh Blvd., 63131. Tel: 314-965-7205; Fax: 314-965-9114.
E-mail: archstl877@impresso.com
Web site: www.stjosephacad.com
Sr. Nancy Folkl, C.S.J., Prin. Sisters of St. Joseph of Carondelet 4; Lay Teachers 45; Girls 622.

St. Louis University High School, George H. Backer Memorial, 4970 Oakland Ave., 63110. Tel: 314-531-0330; Fax: 314-534-3441.
Web site: www.sluh.org.
Revs. Richard E. Hadel, S.J.; Paul G. Sheridan, S.J., Pres.; Martin Hagan, S.J.; Jeffrey D. Harrison, S.J.; James G. Knapp, S.J., Supr.; Ralph D. Houlihan, S.J.; Bros. Thomas C. Thornton, S.J.; Richard H. Witzofsky, S.J. In res. Very Rev. Frank E. Reale, S.J. Priests 6; Brothers 2; Scholastics 1; Admin. 5; Lay Teachers 91; Students 1,039.

CREVE COEUR. *Chaminade College Preparatory School Inc.*, 425 S. Lindbergh Blvd., 63131-2799. Tel: 314-993-4400; Fax: 314-993-4403.
E-mail: archstl851@impresso.com
Web site: www.chaminademo.com
Residents and Day Students. Society of Mary. Rev. Ralph A. Siefert, S.M., Pres.; James E. Gerker, Prin.; Michael Thro, Campus Min. Priests 2; Brothers 2; Sisters 1; Lay Teachers 70; Students 600.

St. Louis Priory School, 500 S. Mason Rd., 63141-8500. Tel: 314-434-3690; Fax: 314-576-7088.
Web site: http://www.priory.org.
Rev. J. Gregory Mohrman, O.S.B., Headmaster; Rt. Rev. Thomas Frerking, O.S.B.; Revs. Christopher Hanson, O.S.B.; T. Peter Kessler, O.S.B.; M. Paul Kidner, O.S.B.; J. Laurence Kriegshauser, O.S.B.; Dominic Lenk, O.S.B.; Bede Price, O.S.B.; D. Ralph Wright, O.S.B. Priests 9; Brothers 5; Lay Teachers 37; High School Students 245; Students (Grades 7-8) 138.

FRONTENAC. *Villa Duchesne/Oak Hill*, 801 S. Spoede Rd., 63131. Tel: 314-432-2021; Fax: 314-432-7713.
E-mail: acaire@vddh.org
Web site: www.sofie.org/villa/web
(Girls: PreK-12; Boys: PreK-6). Religious of the Sacred Heart. Mrs. Renee Allen, Prin. (7-12); Dr. Sam Sciortino, Prin. (PreK-6); Sr. Ann Caire, R.S.C.J., Headmistress. Sisters 5; Lay Faculty 65; Elementary School Students (PreK-6) 393; High School Students (7-12) 405.

KIRKWOOD. *St. John Vianney High School*, 1311 S. Kirkwood Rd., 63122. Tel: 314-965-4853; Fax: 314-965-1950.
E-mail: vianneyrich@vianney.com
Web site: www.vianney.com
Conducted for Boys by the Society of Mary (Marianists). Revs. Richard Wosman, S.M., Pres.; J. Donald Cahill, S.M.; William R. Wightman, S.M. Priests 3; Brothers 5; Sisters 1; Lay Teachers 65; Students 838.

Ursuline Academy, 341 S. Sappington Rd., 63122. Tel: 314-966-4556; Fax: 314-965-4443.
Web site: www.ursulinestl.org
Ursuline Nuns of the Roman Union. Sr. Madonna O'Hara, Pres.; Dr. Patricia Hensley, Prin. Sisters 2; Lay Teachers 50; Students 635.

TOWN AND COUNTRY. *Visitation Academy*, 3020 N. Ballas Rd., 63131. Tel: 314-432-5353; Fax: 314-432-7210.
E-mail: madlersfluegel@visitation.com
Web site: www.inlink.com/~viz
Sr. Anne Madeleine Godefroy, V.H.M., Acting Head of School; Maxine Adlersfluegel, Ph.D., Prin. (Grades 7-12); Barbara McMullen, Asst. Prin. Visitation Sisters 2; Lay Teachers 40; Students 411.

WEBSTER GROVES. *Nerinx Hall High School*, 530 E. Lockwood, 63119. Tel: 314-968-1505; Fax: 314-968-0604.
Web site: www.nerinxhs.org
Sr. Barbara Roche, S.L., Pres.; Mrs. Jane W. Kosash, Prin.; Mrs. Teresa R. Corley, Assoc. Prin. Sisters of Loretto at the Foot of the Cross 3; Religious 3; Lay Teachers 46; Students 604.

[G] ELEMENTARY SCHOOLS, PRIVATE

CHESTERFIELD. *Linda Vista Catholic School*, 1633 Kehrs Mill Rd., 63005. Tel: 314-532-3315; Fax: 314-532-2578.
E-mail: archstl512@impresso.com
Web site: www.inlink.com/~lvcs6
Conducted by the Sisters of the Most Precious Blood.
Preschool Classes for 3-6 Year Olds, Grades 1-8. Lay Teachers 40; Students 315.

CREVE COEUR. *Chaminade College Preparatory*. (Middle School), Residents and Day Students, 425 S. Lindbergh Blvd., 63131. Tel: 314-993-4400; Fax: 314-993-4403.
E-mail: archstl851@impresso.com
Web site: www.chaminademo.com
(Boys Grades 7-12). Society of Mary. Rev. Ralph A. Siefert, S.M., Pres.; Mr. Michael T. Bander, Prin. Lay Teachers 17; Students 330.

St. Louis Priory School, 500 S. Mason Rd., 63141-8500. Tel: 314-434-3690; Fax: 314-576-7088.
Web site: www.priory.org
(Boys Grades 7-8).
Corporate Title: The Abbey of St. Mary and St. Louis. Rev. J. Gregory Mohrman, O.S.B., Headmaster. Priests 3; Brothers 3; Lay Teachers 31; Students 138.

FRONTENAC. *Oak Hill School*, 801 S. Spoede Rd., 63131. Tel: 314-432-2021; Fax: 314-432-7713.
E-mail: acaire@vdoh.org
Web site: www.sofie.org/villa/web
(Grades PreK-6) (Coed). Dr. Sam Sciortino, Prin.; Sr. Ann Caire, R.S.C.J., Headmistress. Sisters 2; Lay Teachers 31; Students 393.

Villa Duchesne. (Girls 7-12). Mailing Address: 801 S. Spoede Rd., St. Louis, 63131-2699. Tel: 314-432-2021; Fax: 314-432-7713.
E-mail: rallen@vdoh.org
Web site: www.vdoh.org
Mrs. Renee Allen, Prin.; Sr. Ann Caire, R.S.C.J., Headmistress. Sisters 3; Lay Teachers 41; Girls 406.

ST. CHARLES. *Academy of the Sacred Heart*. (Coed), 619 N. 2nd St., 63301. Tel: 636-946-6127; Fax: 636-949-6659.
E-mail: mcaire@ash1818.org
Web site: www.ash1818.org
Owned and Operated by the Religious of the Sacred Heart and Academy of the Sacred Heart of St. Charles, MO. Sr. Margaret Caire, Headmistress; Mrs. Kathy Hopper, Prin. Sisters 10; Lay Teachers 45; Students 686.

TOWN AND COUNTRY. *Visitation Academy*. (Grades PreK-6), 3020 N. Ballas Rd., 63131. Tel: 314-432-5353.
E-mail: archstl510@impresso.com
Web site: www.inlink.com/~viz
Sr. Anne Madeleine Godefroy, V.H.M., Acting Head of School; Mimi Kueneke, Prin. (PreK-6). Visitation Sisters 2; Lay Teachers 18; Students 250.

[H] DEPARTMENT OF SPECIAL EDUCATION

ST. LOUIS. *Catholic Guidance Center*, 4472 Lindell Blvd., 63108. Tel: 314-533-3454; Fax: 314-533-0140.
E-mail: aspedstl@impresso.com
Psycho-Educational Testing Facility and also Administrative Office for the Archdiocesan Department of Special Education, Serving Children with Developmental Disabilities, Mental Retardation, Learning Disabilities or Attention Deficit Disorder. Rev. Msgr. Vernon E. Gardin, Ph.D., Exec. Dir.
Special Ungraded Day Classes, Schools, Preschool, PSR for Disabled and with Mental Retardation Children or Major Learning Disabilities (ages 5-16). Located in the Following Parish Schools: Holy Innocents (3 LD Classes); Sacred Heart (2 MR Classes); St. Christopher (5 LD Classes); Annunziata (6 LD Classes); St. John the Baptist (3 LD Classes); St. George (3 LD Classes); St. Gregory (2 LD Classes); Ascension, Chesterfield (2 LD Classes). Sisters 3; Teachers 37; Total Number of Children Served 300.

St. Mary's Special Services, 1724 Redman Ave., 63138. Tel: 314-261-8533; Fax: 314-653-2591. Legal Title: *St. Mary's Special School for Exceptional Children*. Rev. Msgr. Vernon E. Gardin, Exec. Dir. Early Intervention therapies and child care for preschool children (ages 6 months-5 years) developmentally disabled in a normalized mainstream setting (capacity 80). Lay Staff 64; Clients 97.

Special Religious Education Ministry, 4472 Lindell Blvd., 63108. Tel: 314-533-3454, Ext. 227; Fax: 314-533-0140.
E-mail: SpecRelEdu@aol.com
Department of Special Education. Mary Beth Schulte, Coord. Provides catholic religious education for children with disabilities in public special programs. (ages 7-21) & for adults with disabilities living in institutions or in their own homes. Priests 1; Lay Teachers 30; Total Enrollment 100.

CHESTERFIELD. *St. Joseph Institute for the Deaf*, 1809 Clarkson Rd., 63017-5065. Tel: 314-532-4560 (Voice/TDD); Fax: 314-532-3211. School for the Deaf (School for Handicapped). J. Michael Keller, Pres.; Marietta Paterson, Ph.D., Prin. Sisters 12; Lay Teachers 27; Students 110. Audio/oral day & residential school for hearing-impaired children from birth-8th grade. Early intervention therapy for children 0-5; pre- & elementary school offering intense speech & academic prog.

[I] SERVICES FOR THE ELDERLY

ST. LOUIS. *Cardinal Ritter Institute*, 4483 Lindell Blvd., 63108. Tel: 314-652-3600; Fax: 314-652-8840.
E-mail: akorte@archstl.org
Archdiocesan Office Provides Social Services, Health Services and Housing Services, Employment & Volunteer Services for the Elderly. Legal Title: *Cardinal Ritter Institute, Inc.* Arthur J. Korte, Exec. Dir. Total Clients Served 29,851.

Cardinal Ritter Institute Residential Services, Inc., 4483 Lindell Blvd., 63108. Tel: 314-652-3600; Fax: 314-652-8840. Provides housing Mgmt. & other svcs. for residential facilities for the elderly. Michael J. Lally, Assoc. Exec. Dir.

Alexian Court Apartments. (Legal Title: Alexian Brothers Services, Inc.), 2636 Chippewa St., 63118. Tel: 314-771-5604; Fax: 314-771-7629.
Sponsored by Alexian Brothers of Missouri, Inc., Managed by Cardinal Ritter Institute.

St. John Neumann Apartments, Inc., 8424 Lucas Hunt Rd., 63136. Tel: 314-385-0707; Fax: 314-385-5299.

St. Joseph Apartments, Inc., 7677 Watson Rd., 63119. Tel: 314-962-0969; Fax: 314-962-1393.

St. Patrick Apartments, Inc., 555 Bluff Parks Dr., 63031. Tel: 314-839-3212; Fax: 314-839-7537.

San Luis Apartments, Inc., 4483 Lindell Blvd., 63108. Tel: 314-534-4730; Fax: 314-652-0312.

Santa Ana Apartments, Inc., 3737 Ashby Rd., 63074. Tel: 314-428-7385; Fax: 314-428-6541.

Visitation Senior Apartments, Inc., 1911 N. Taylor Ave., 63113. Tel: 314-652-3600; Fax: 314-652-8840.

Holy Infant Apartments, Inc., 7663 Watson Rd., 63119. Tel: 314-962-7878; Fax: 314-962-1393.

St. Agnes Apartments, Inc., 2840 Wisconsin, 63118. Tel: 314-664-1255; Fax: 314-664-1192. St. Peter Residence for Seniors, 333 S. Second St., St. Charles, 63301-6401. Tel: 314-947-7004. Property of St. Peter Parish, Managed by Cardinal Ritter Institute. Santa Maria Apartments, 12565 Santa Maria Ct., Hazelwood, 63042. Tel: 314-739-7220; Fax: 314-739-2950.

Pope John Paul II Apartments, Inc., 6325 Waterways Dr., 63033. Tel: 314-653-0400, Ext. 294; Fax: 314-652-8840.

Cardinal Carberry Senior Living Center. Tel: 314-961-8000; Fax: 314-961-1934. Sr. Suzanne Wesley, C.S.J., Dir.

Our Lady of Life Apartments, 7655 Watson Rd., 63119. Tel: 314-968-9447; Fax: 314-968-9533.

Mother of Perpetual Help Residence, 7609 Watson Rd., 63119. Tel: 314-961-8000; Fax: 314-961-1934.

Mary, Queen and Mother Center, 7601 Watson Rd., 63119. Tel: 314-961-8000; Fax: 314-961-1548. Total Staff 338; Total Housing Units 1,933.

Corporate Action for the Care of the Elderly, Inc., 7400 Christopher Dr., 63129-5799. Tel: 314-846-2575, Ext. 204; Fax: 314-846-2575. Association Composed of Representatives of 14 Religious Communities. Corporal Work of Mercy in the Metro St. Louis Area. Sr. Cathy Vetter, O.C.V.I., Pres.

St. Elizabeth Adult Day Care Center, 3401 Arsenal St., 63118. Tel: 314-772-5107; Fax: 314-772-3674. E-mail: sjamiller@juno.com
Web site: www.cpps-ofallon.org
Conducted by the Sisters of the Most Precious Blood to Provide Day Care for the Elderly and handicapped. Sr. John Antonio Miller, C.PP.S., Dir.

St. Elizabeth East Adult Day Care Center, 3227 S. Ninth St., 63118. Tel: 314-771-1591.

St. Elizabeth West Adult Day Care Center, 7240 Anna, 63143. Tel: 314-644-6585; Fax: 314-644-6585.

St. Elizabeth North Adult Day Care Center, 2142 Switzer, 63136. Tel: 314-867-6511; Fax: 314-867-6511.

St. Elizabeth/Visitation Adult Day Care Center, 1421 N. Taylor, 63113. Tel: 314-531-2985; Fax: 314-531-2985.

St. Elizabeth/Visitation Adult Day Care Center, 2000 El Lago, Arnold, 63010. Tel: 314-461-0730; Fax: 314-461-0730. For all: Total Assisted 219; Total Staff 48.

[J] CHILD GUIDANCE

ST. LOUIS. *Central Intake*, 4140 Lindell Blvd., 63108. Tel: 314-371-0047; 371-0053; Fax: 314-371-0271.
E-mail: snelson@archstl.org
Sally Nelson, A.C.S.W., L.C.S.W., Dir. of Central Intake. Provides evaluation & referral svcs. for Catholic Charities Children's Network & handles managed care referrals for entire Catholic Charities Federation of St. Louis. Total Assisted 3,494; Total Staff 2.

Child Center of Our Lady, 7900 Natural Bridge Rd., 63121. Tel: 314-383-0200; Fax: 314-383-6334. Psychiatric Treatment Center. Edward S. Koszykowski, Exec. Dir. Legal Title: *Child Center of Our Lady of Grace, Inc.* Patients assisted annually 139 (Children, Parents and Families); Total Staff 48.

[K] GENERAL HOSPITALS

ST. LOUIS. *Alexian Brothers Hospital*, 3933 S. Broadway, 63118. Tel: 314-865-3333; Fax: 314-865-7938
For a complete listing, refer to the Hospitals section.

St. Anthony's Medical Center, 10010 Kennerly Rd., 63128. Tel: 314-525-1000; Fax: 314-525-4485.
Web site: www.stanthonymedcenter.com
For a complete listing, refer to the Hospitals section.

SSM St. Mary's Health Center, 6420 Clayton Rd., 63117. Tel: 314-768-8000; Fax: 314-768-8011
For a complete listing, refer to the Hospitals section.

BRIDGETON. *SSM De Paul Health Center*, 12303 De Paul Dr., 63044. Tel: 314-344-6000
For a complete listing, refer to the Hospitals section.

CREVE COEUR. *St. John's Mercy Medical Center*, 615 S. New Ballas Rd., 63141. Tel: 314-569-6000; Fax: 314-569-6910
For a complete listing, refer to the Hospitals section.

KIRKWOOD. *SSM St. Joseph Hospital of Kirkwood*, 525 Couch Ave., 63122. Tel: 314-966-1601; Fax: 314-966-1681
For a complete listing, refer to the Hospitals section.

LAKE ST. LOUIS. *SSM St. Joseph Hospital West*, 100 Medical Plaza, 63367. Tel: 314-625-5200; Fax: 314-625-5314
For a complete listing, refer to the Hospitals section.

ST. CHARLES. *SSM St. Joseph Health Center*, 300 First Capitol Dr., 63301. Tel: 314-947-5000; Fax: 314-947-5090
For a complete listing, refer to the Hospitals section.

WASHINGTON. *St. John's Mercy Hospital*, 200 Madison Ave., 63090. Tel: 314-239-8000; Fax: 314-569-6733
For a complete listing, refer to the Hospitals section.

[L] SPECIAL HOSPITALS

ST. LOUIS. *SSM Cardinal Glennon Children's Hospital*, 1465 S. Grand Blvd., 63104. Tel: 314-577-5600; Fax: 314-268-6468.
E-mail: Doug_Ries@ssmhc.com
Web site: www.cardinalglennon.com
For a complete listing, refer to the Special Care Facilities section.

SSM Rehab, 6420 Clayton Rd., Exec. Offices, 63117-1861. Tel: 314-768-5300; Fax: 314-768-5355.
Web site: www.ssmrehab.com
For a complete listing, refer to the Special Care Facilities section.

[M] PROTECTIVE INSTITUTIONS

Day Care Centers

ST. LOUIS. *Guardian Angel Settlement Association*, Mailing Address: P.O. Box 2055, 63158. Tel: 314-231-3188; Fax: 314-231-3188, Ext. 17. Fonda Fantroy, Exec. Dir. Founded by the Daughters of Charity of St. Vincent de Paul.
Child Day Care Services.

DeSales Day Care, 2652 Ohio, 63118. Tel: 314-771-6417; Fax: 314-231-3188, Ext. 17.

St. Patrick's Day Care, 1200 N. 6th St., 63106. Tel: 314-421-2816; Fax: 314-231-3188, Ext. 17.

Social Services, 1401 La Salle St., 63104. Tel: 314-231-3188; Fax: 314-231-3188, Ext. 17. Casework & Case Mgmt.; Emergency Svcs.; Senior Prog., Summer Youth Employment Prog.; Neighborhood Activities; Art, Gardening & Environmental Prog.; Paralegal on staff. For all: Total Assisted 14,964; Total Staff 50.

Sacred Heart Villa, 2108 Macklind Ave., 63110. Tel: 314-771-2224; Fax: 314-771-1262.
E-mail: SHVilla@aol.com
Web site: hometown.aol.com/shvilla
Sr. Barbara Ann Matazzaro, A.S.C.J., Dir. Full-Time Care From 6:30-5:30 for children 3-5 years old. Conducted by the Apostles of the Sacred Heart of Jesus. Total Assisted 125; Total Staff 22.

Stella Maris Child Center, 5654 Delmar Blvd., 63112. Tel: 314-367-7950; Fax: 314-367-8849.
E-mail: stellamaris_2000@yahoo.com
Bonnie Shearin, Exec. Dir. Conducted by a Board of Directors and Staff of Lay Teachers. Licensed Capacity 132; Total Assisted 163; Total Staff 40.

Visitation Child Development Center, 1421 N. Taylor, 63113. Tel: 314-533-8411. E. Nancy Norman, Dir. Learning Center and Day Care Service for children 2-6 years old; Kindergarten Included. Conducted by Visitation Parish. Total Assisted 2; Total Staff 5.

BERKELEY. *St. Martin's Child Center*, 6315 Garfield, P.O. Box 34103, 63134. Tel: 314-524-4719; Fax: 314-524-5969.
E-mail: lbstallings@hotmail.com
Web site: www.stmccinc.org
Ms. Lula Stallings, Exec. Dir. Day care for children 6 weeks-14 years old. Legal Title: *St. Martin Child Center, Inc.* Bed Capacity 99; Infant Daycare 16; Total Assisted 100; Total Staff 21.

IMPERIAL. *Queen of Apostles Center*, 800 Montebello Camp Rd., 63052. Tel: 636-464-0163; Fax: 636-464-1136.
E-mail: som1916@aol.com
Apostles of the Sacred Heart of Jesus 3; Total Staff 12; Children 65.

KIRKWOOD. *Carmelite Child Development Center*, 1111 N. Woodlawn Ave., 63122. Tel: 314-822-0058; Fax: 314-822-3573.
E-mail: vocations@carmelitedcj.org
Web site: www.carmelitedcj.org
Sr. Mary Joseph, D.C.J., Dir. Operated by the Carmelite Sisters of the Divine Heart of Jesus. Provides child development, child care and services. Full Day 106; Kindergarten 25; Total Staff 15.

St. Joseph Educational Child Care Center, 1132 S. Glenwood Ave., 63122. Tel: 314-821-6636; Fax: 314-965-8146. Operated by the St. Joseph Hospital in Kirkwood. Total Staff 22.

[N] HOMES FOR CHILDREN

ST. LOUIS. *Boys Hope/Girls Hope of St. Louis, Inc.*, 755 S. New Ballas Rd., Ste. 120, 63141. Tel: 314-692-7477; Fax: 314-692-7810.
E-mail: sbrock@bhgh.org
Web site: www.boyshopegirlshope.org/stlouis.htm
For a complete listing, refer to the Special Care Facilities section.

Marian Hall Agencies, 1340 Partridge Ave., 63130. Tel: 314-726-3339; Fax: 314-726-3470.
E-mail: srclarke@archstl.org
For a complete listing, refer to the Special Care Facilities section.

Marian Hall Emergency Shelter, 325 N. Newstead, 63108. Tel: 314-531-0511; Fax: 314-531-2993
For a complete listing, refer to the Special Care Facilities section.

St. Joseph's Home for Boys, 4753 S. Grand Blvd., 63111-1459. Tel: 314-481-9121; Fax: 314-481-5605.
E-mail: bbradley@archstl.org
Web site: www.stjosephhome.org
For a complete listing, refer to the Special Care Facilities section.

FLORISSANT. *Father Dunne's News Boys Home*, 853 Dunn Rd., 63031. Tel: 314-837-0513; Fax: 314-837-0883.
E-mail: cblake@archstl.org
For a complete listing, refer to the Special Care Facilities section.

Marygrove Services, Inc., 2705 Mullanphy Ln., 63031. Tel: 314-837-1702; Fax: 314-830-6263.
E-mail: mgrove@swb.net
For a complete listing, refer to the Special Care Facilities section.

NORMANDY. *St. Vincent Home for Children*, 7401 Florissant Rd., 63121. Tel: 314-261-6011; Fax: 314-385-1467
For a complete listing, refer to the Special Care Facilities section.

[O] HOMES FOR AGED

ST. LOUIS. *Alexian Brothers Lansdowne Village*, 4624 Lansdowne, 63116. Tel: 314-351-6888; Fax: 314-351-5825
For a complete listing, refer to the Special Care Facilities section.

Alexian Brothers Sherbrooke Village, 4005 Ripa Ave., 63125. Tel: 314-544-1111; Fax: 314-544-5134
For a complete listing, refer to the Special Care Facilities section.

Chariton Apartments, 4249 Michigan Ave., 63111. Tel: 314-352-7600; Fax: 314-352-0022
For a complete listing, refer to the Special Care Facilities section.

Fusz Pavilion, 3601 Lindell Blvd., 63108. Tel: 314-534-1201; Fax: 314-977-7211
For a complete listing, refer to the Special Care Facilities section.

Little Sisters of the Poor, Home for the Aged, 3225 N. Florissant Ave., 63107. Tel: 314-421-6022; Fax: 314-436-9069
For a complete listing, refer to the Special Care Facilities section.

Mary, Queen and Mother Center, 7601 Watson Rd., 63119. Tel: 314-961-8000; Fax: 314-961-1548.
E-mail: rmantia@archstl.org
Web site: cardinalcarberry.org
For a complete listing, refer to the Special Care Facilities section.

Mother of Good Counsel Home, 6825 Natural Bridge Rd., (St. Louis Co.), 63121. Tel: 314-383-4765
For a complete listing, refer to the Special Care Facilities section.

Mother of Perpetual Help Residence, 7609 Watson Rd., 63119. Tel: 314-961-8000; Fax: 314-961-1934.
E-mail: swesley@archstl.org
For a complete listing, refer to the Special Care Facilities section.

Nazareth Living Center, 2 Nazareth Ln., 63129. Tel: 314-487-3950; Fax: 314-487-8001.
E-mail: lwesthoff@nlccsj.com
For a complete listing, refer to the Special Care Facilities section.

Our Lady of Life Apartments, Inc., 7655 Watson Rd., 63119. Tel: 314-968-9447.
E-mail: jschwaegel@archstl.org
For a complete listing, refer to the Special Care Facilities section.

Regina Cleri Residence, 7850 Kenrick Rd., 63119. Tel: 314-968-2240; Fax: 314-968-1049.
E-mail: reginacleri@earthlink.net
For a complete listing, refer to the Special Care Facilities section.

EUREKA. *Price Memorial*, Forby Rd., P.O. Box 476, 63025. Tel: 636-587-3200; Fax: 636-938-2266
For a complete listing, refer to the Special Care Facilities section.

St. Joseph Hill Infirmary, Inc. dba St. Joseph Hill Infirmary, St. Joseph Rd., 63025. Tel: 636-587-3661; Fax: 636-938-6398
For a complete listing, refer to the Special Care Facilities section.

KIRKWOOD. *St. Agnes Home for the Elderly*, 10341 Manchester Rd., 63122. Tel: 314-965-7616; Fax: 314-965-3179
For a complete listing, refer to the Special Care Facilities section.

ST. CHARLES. *St. Joseph Carmelite Home*, 723 First Capitol Dr., 63301. Tel: 314-946-4140; Fax: 314-218-1104.
E-mail: stjoseph@carmelitedcj.org
Web site: carmelitedcj.org
For a complete listing, refer to the Special Care Facilities section.

[P] MONASTERIES AND RESIDENCES OF PRIESTS AND BROTHERS

ST. LOUIS. *The Abbey of St. Mary and St. Louis*, 500 S. Mason Rd., 63141-8500. Tel: 314-434-2557; Fax: 314-434-0795.
Web site: www.priory.org.
Benedictines of the English Congregation. Rt. Rev. Thomas Frerking, O.S.B., Abbot; Very Rev. M. Paul Kidner, O.S.B., Prior; Rt. Rev. J. Luke Rigby, O.S.B.; Very Rev. Timothy Horner, O.S.B.; Revs. D. Ralph Wright, O.S.B.; R. Benedict Allin, O.S.B.; P. Finbarr Dowling, O.S.B.; J. Laurence Kriegshauser, O.S.B.; J. Gregory Mohrman, O.S.B.; Gerard Garrigan, O.S.B.; Christopher Hanson, O.S.B.; Peter Kessler, O.S.B.; Dominic Lenk, O.S.B.; Bede Price, O.S.B. Priests 14; Brother Monks 9; Oblates 1; Total Staff 24.

Bellarmine House of Studies, 3737 Westminster Pl., 63108-3407. Tel: 314-652-8862; Fax: 314-535-4597. Jesuit Residence for Students in the College of Philosophy and Letters of St. Louis University. Rev. Ralph G. Huse, S.J., Rector; Bro. Pablo Hernandez, S.J., Treas.; Revs. John A. Apel, S.J.; William T. Oulvey, S.J.; Bro. Thomas Naughton, S.J., Asst. Rector. Priests 3; Brothers 3; Students 16; Total Staff 3.

De Smet Jesuit High School Community, 233 N. New Ballas Rd., 63141. Tel: 314-567-3500; Fax: 314-567-1519. Revs. Michael H. Durso, S.J., Supr.; John D. Arnold, S.J.; Richard L. Bailey, S.J.; John J. Bergin, S.J.; Robert E. Bosken, S.J.; John V. Craig, S.J.; Bro. Donald E. Lee, S.J.; Revs. Michael A. Marchlewski, S.J.; Thomas F. McQueeny, S.J.; William J. Snyders, S.J.; Bro. Henry E. Welch, S.J. Jesuits 11.

Dominican Community of St. Louis. St. Louis Bertrand Priory - Province of St. Albert the Great. 97 Waterman St., 63112-1820. Tel: 314-361-4445; Fax: 314-977-7225. Revs. Frank C. Quinn, O.P., Prior; Jay M. Harrington, O.P., Subprior; Benedict M. Ashley, O.P.; Ralph A. Powell, O.P.; Eric A. Reiran, O.P.

Assigned but living elsewhere: Revs. Charles E. Bouchard, O.P.; Harry M. Byrne, O.P., Dominicans, 4116 Westminster Pl., 63108-3131. Tel: 314-535-9817.

Franciscan Friary of St. Anthony of Padua. (Franciscan Province of the Sacred Heart-Provincial Headquarters), 3140 Meramec St., 63118-4339. Tel: 314-353-7470; Fax: 314-353-0935.
E-mail: provoff@aol.com
Web site: www.thefriars.org
Legal Title: *The Franciscan Friars of the State of Missouri.* Co-sponsor of the 8th Day Center for Justice in Chicago. Very Rev. John Doctor, O.F.M., Prov. Minister; Revs. Maynard Billig, O.F.M., Priest's Confessor; Kenneth Capalbo, O.F.M., Provincial Vicar; Allan DaCorte, O.F.M., Prov. Treas.; Bro. Patrick Darnell, O.F.M.; Rev. Thomas Gardner, O.F.M., Prov. Promotor for Missions, Commissary of the Holy Land & Exec. Dir. Franciscan O.F.M. Conference; Bros. Loyola Freightman, O.F.M.; Leo Geurts, O.F.M., Dir. Franciscan Connection; Patrick Hanrahan, O.F.M., (Sabbatical); James Hickey, O.F.M., Devel. Office; Herman Joseph James, Cord Machine; Rev. James Kelly, O.F.M., Internal Ministry; Bros. Donald Lachowicz, O.F.M.; Christopher Lambert, O.F.M., Province Sec.; Revs. James Lause, O.F.M.; Andrew Lewandowski, O.F.M., Chap. for Franciscan Sisters of Mary; Elvan Maschmann, O.F.M., (Retired); Bro. Damian Pfeifer, O.F.M.; Rev. John Rausch, O.F.M., Chap., St. Louis University Hospital; Bros. Joseph Rogenski, O.F.M., Assoc. Dir. Franciscan Missionary Union, Holy Land Commissariat; David Schulte, O.F.M.; William Schulte, O.F.M., Dir. Office of Public Rels. & Devel., St. Anthony Bread for the Poor & Franciscan Charities; Revs. Robert Sieg, O.F.M.; Henry Willenborg, O.F.M., Dir. Office Friar Formation; Martin Wolter, O.F.M., Chap. Little Portion, Eureka Springs, AR. Priests 20; Brothers 12.

Military Chaplains: Revs. Richard Bendorf, O.F.M., Ft. Bragg, NC; Joseph Carlos, CHC, USNR, St. James Church, 134 North Ave., Highwood, IL, 60040-1522. Tel: 847-926-2670.

Friars of Sacred Heart Province Serving Abroad: Rev. Albert Haase, China World Century Towers, Chao Yang District, No. 18, Guangqumenwai Ave., West Lodge, Apt. 8D, Beijing 100022. Tel: 86-10-135-0136-1146. Bro. Jeffrey Haller, O.F.M., Guangzhou Universtiy Guangdog Province, Jiefang Beilu Guihuagang, Guangzhou, PRC, 519405. Tel: 86-020-86237632. Rev. Basil Tsung-Li-Chuen, O.F.M., Catholic Mission Church, Kanchuang Rd. 305, Tashi Taoyuan, Taiwan, ROC. Rev. James Perluzzi, O.F.M., Curia Generalizia dei Frati Minori, Via Santa Maria Mediatrice, 25, Rome, Italy, 00165. Tel: 3906-68491-9. Rev. Jesus Aguirre-Garza, O.F.M., 51 Rue Driba, Meknes-Median, Morocco, 50004.

Friars Attached to the Province but Residing Elsewhere: Rev. Ambrose German, O.F.M., St. George Church, Hermann. Rev. Charles E. Gunti, O.F.M., 319 Dawnbridge Dr., San Antonio, TX, 78213-3107. Tel: 210-979-6506. Rev. Kenneth Kieffer, O.F.M., 1782 Troy Ln., Oceanside, CA, 92054. Revs. Edmund Mundwiller, O.F.M.; Leon Reuter, O.F.M., St. Joseph, 125 E. Broadway, Shelbyville, IN, 46176. Rev. Raymond Rickles, O.F.M., 422 S. Moody Rd., St. Croix Falls, WI, 54024. Revs. Luis Runde, O.F.M., (Sabbatical); Conran Schneider, O.F.M., Talheim Apartments, 407 Oak St. N., #304, Chaska, MN, 55318. Rev. Steve Suding, O.F.M., International Fraternity, Brussels, Belgium. Rev. Allan Wolter, O.F.M., St. Bonaventure University, St. Bonaventure, NY, 14778. Rev. Eric Kahn, O.F.M., Cordis House, 648 S. Assisi Way, Republic, 65738. Rev. Theodosius A. Schelich, O.F.M., Chap. St. Francis Hospital, 1215 E. Union, Litchfield, IL, 62056. Rev. Gary German, O.F.M., 2165 Central Ave., #1, Alameda, CA, 94501.

Friars Associated with the Friary but Residing Elsewhere: Revs. Thomas Gardner, O.F.M., Dir. Franciscan Missionary Union; Prov. Sec., Missionary Evangelization & Commissary of the Holy Land; Larry Nickels, O.F.M., Prov. Councilor & Interim Dir, Office of Ministries.

Hallahan House, 4511 W. Pine Blvd., 63108-2191. Tel: 314-361-7765 (day); 758-7125 (night); Fax: 314-758-7166.
E-mail: treasurer@jesuits-mis.org
Web site: www.jesuits-mis.org
Revs. Robert F. Weiss, S.J., Supr.; William K. Kellett, S.J., Min.; J. David Corrigan, S.J.; James J. Dougherty, S.J.; Thomas J. Hogan, S.J.; Gregory H. Jacobsmeyer, S.J.; L. Gene Martens, S.J.; Walter G. Nesbit, S.J.; Raymond M. Tully, S.J.; Ralph E. Vonderhaar, S.J.; Bro. Julius F. Petrk, S.J. Total in Residence 11; Total Staff 4.

Jesuit Community Corporation at St. Louis University - Jesuit Hall, 3601 Lindell Blvd., 63108-3393. Tel: 314-658-2588; Fax: 314-535-0402.
E-mail: obrienec@slu.edu
Revs. John W. Padberg, S.J., Rector; James H. Baker, S.J.; Lawrence H. Biondi, S.J.; A. James Blumeyer, S.J.; Francis C. Brennan, S.J.; Joseph E. Brown, S.J.; Robert A. Brungs, S.J.; J. Richard Burtschi, S.J.; Lucius F. Cervantes, S.J.; Francis X. Cleary, S.J.; J. Eugene Coomes, S.J.; Anthony C. Daly, S.J.; Denis E. Daly, S.J.; Terrence E. Dempsey, S.J.; Everett A. Diederich, S.J.; Michael J. Doody, S.J.; William B. Faherty, S.J.; Philip C. Fischer, S.J.; Robert S. Flack, S.J.; David L. Fleming, S.J.; John B. Foley, S.J.; William B. Foley; Ignatius Y. Futo, S.J.; Eugene E. Grollmes, S.J.; Francis J. Guentner, S.J.; Martin Hagan, S.J.; Garth L. Hallett, S.J.; Marcus A. Haworth, S.J.; W. Charles Heiser, S.J.; Harry H. Hoormann, S.J.; John F. Kavanaugh, S.J.; Joseph A. Kemme, S.J.; George V. Kennard, S.J.; John J. Killoren; Eugene C. Kollasch, S.J.; Leonard E. Kraus, S.J.; Thomas N. Lay, S.J.; Gerhardt B. Lehmkuhl, S.J.; Daniel P. Lidebach, S.J.; Edwin Lisson, S.J.; Michael W. Maher, S.J.; Michael K. May, S.J.; John L. McCarthy, S.J.; J. Barry McGannon, S.J.; Frederick G. McLeod, S.J.; Maurice B. McNamee, S.J.; Gregory L. Miller, S.J.; John J. Mueller, S.J.; William L. Mugan, S.J.; Joseph Tuoc Trong, S.J.; Edward C. O'Brien, S.J.; Martin D. O'Keefe, S.J.; Claude N. Pavur, S.J.; Frank L. Pedrotti, S.J.; Robert L. Phillips, S.J.; Hernando J. Ramirez, S.J.; Donald F. Rauscher, S.J.; Paul C. Reinert, S.J.; Raymond H. Reis, S.J.; Ralph C. Renner, S.J.; Isidoro Ribas, S.J.; Anthony J. Rochel, S.J.; John C. Ruoff, S.J.; John A. Schwantes, S.J.; James A. Sebesta, S.J.; John F.X. Sheehan, S.J.; John F. Snyder, S.J.; Carl F. Starkloff, S.J.; William V. Stauder, S.J.; David J. Suwalsky, S.J.; Linus J. Thro, S.J.; John G. Valenta; James V. Veltrie, S.J.; Richard J. Vogt, S.J.; James K. Voiss, S.J.; Raymond L. Windle, S.J. Priests 75; Brothers 3; Scholastics 1.

The Jesuits of the Missouri Province, 4511 W. Pine Blvd., 63108-2191. Tel: 314-361-7765; Fax: 314-758-7164.
E-mail: moprov@jesuits-mis.org
Web site: jesuits-mis.org
Missouri Province of the Society of Jesus. Very Rev. Frank E. Reale, S.J., Prov.; Revs. Philip G. Steele, S.J., Socius & Asst. Secondary Educ.; Robert F. Weiss, S.J., Treas. & Asst. Higher Educ.; John A. Apel, S.J., Asst. for Jesuits in Pastoral & Intl. Apostolates; Thomas G. Cwik, S.J., Asst. for Social Ministries; William T. Oulvey, S.J., Asst. for Vocations & Province Planning; Walter G. Nesbit, S.J., Data Mgr.; L. Gene Martens, S.J., Assoc. Dir. Jesuit Devel. Office; David L. Fleming, S.J., Dir. Publications & Editor of the Jesuit Bulletin; William L. Mugan, S.J., Archivist; William B. Faherty, S.J., Archivist Emeritus; William V. Stauder, S.J., Asst. Dir. Devel. Priests 262; Students in Major Seminary 23; Novices 6; Brothers 28.

Missouri Province Jesuit Priests Not Listed Elsewhere: Rev. John R. Daly, S.J., 2426 Alto Cerro Cir., San Diego, CA, 92109-1501. Tel: 858-274-0057; Fax: 858-274-0055. Rev. Carl A. Dehne, S.J., Mother of Good Counsel Home, 6825 Natural Bridge Rd., 63121-5397. Tel: 314-385-9387; Fax: 314-383-7256. Rev. Joseph L. Hebert, S.J., 1085 Zang, Golden, CO, 80401-4250. Tel: 303-233-3046. Revs. Charles F. Ferrara, S.J., Awaiting Assignment; Gerald J. Guida, S.J., The Argyle, 4115 W. 38th Ave., Denver, CO, 80212-1900. Tel: 303-455-9513. Rev. Randall C. Hall, S.J., P.O. Box 246, Grand Junction, CO, 81502. Revs. Tuan Quoc Le, S.J., Awaiting Assignment; Curtis E. Van Del, S.J., Nazareth Motherhouse, P.O. Box 279, Concordia, KS, 66901-0279. Tel: 785-243-2113; Fax: 785-243-2239. Rev. James J. White, S.J., 12600 Hollingsworth, Kansas City, KS, 66109-3821. Tel: 913-721-3966.

La Salette Missionaries, 4650 S. Broadway, 63111-1398. Tel: 314-353-5000; Fax: 314-353-4582.
Web site: www.lasalette.org
Missionaries of Our Lady of La Salette, Province of Mary Queen. Very Rev. Dennis J. Meyer, M.S., Prov. Supr.; Rev. Peter D. Kohler.

Provincial Vocation Office. Tel: 314-353-5000; Fax: 314-353-4582.
Web site: lasalette.8m.com/

La Salette Ministries Development Center. Tel: 314-752-0760; Fax: 314-481-1896. Very Rev. Dennis J. Meyer, M.S., Dir.

La Salette Spirituality Center. Tel: 314-752-0760; Fax: 314-481-1896. Revs. James R. Dunphy, M.S.; Dennis J. Meyer, M.S.; Thomas Mcnamara; Edward Richard, M.S.; Dennis Meyer; Louis L. VanDane, M.S.; Alan McGuirk; Patrick McCarthy; Bros. Roman Wilbers, M.S.; Thomas Murphy, M.S. Priests and Brothers of the Province Serving in the Foreign Missions:
Diocese of Morondava, Madagascar: Revs. Arthur A. Lueckenotto, M.S.; Joseph Shea.
Diocese of Cordoba, Argentina: Revs. John M. Garvey, M.S.; John M. McCarthy, M.S.
Rome, Italy: Generalate, Missionari di N.S. de La Salette, Piazza Madonna della Salette, 3. Tel: (06) 53-04-51; Fax: 06-39-06-534-62-18. Very Rev. Isidro Perin, M.S.; Revs. Roland Nadeau, Vicar Gen.; James Staijkowski, Gen. Councillor; Andre Ravelojaona, Gen. Councillor & Treas.; Henry Kuman, Gen. Councillor; Rene Butler, Procurator to Holy See & Gen. Sec. Priests 32; Brothers 4; Oblates 2; Total Staff 3.

Lazarist Residence, 13245 Tesson Ferry Rd., 63128-3888. Tel: 314-843-0108; Fax: 314-849-1267. Revs. John F. Clark, C.M., Supr.; Joseph E. Begue, C.M.; Wilbert H. Bruns, C.M.; Robert F. Coerver, C.M.; Bro. F. Joseph Hess, C.M.; Revs. Martin J. Culligan, C.M.; Anthony J. Falanga, C.M.; Glennon E. Figge, C.M.; Henry W. Grodecki, C.M.; Richard L. Lause, C.M.; J. Dennis Martin, C.M.; Ronald W. Ramson, C.M.; Paul Otto Schneebeck, C.M.; James E. Swift, C.M.; Jules G. Yallaly, C.M. Priests 10; Brothers 1.

Leo Brown Jesuit Community, 5047 Washington Pl., 63108. Tel: 314-367-8013; Fax: 314-367-1478.
E-mail: kellyt@slu.edu
Revs. Philip G. Steele, S.J.; Michael D. Barber, S.J.; Thomas E.J. Kelly, S.J., Supr.; James Goeke, S.J.; Donald W. Reck, S.J.; Bro. Donald R. Schlichter. Total in Residence 6.

Marianist Community. P.O. Box 718, Eureka, 63025. Tel: 636-938-5470; Fax: 636-938-3493.
E-mail: macmrcc@aol.com
Bro. Richard Thompson, S.M., Dir.; Revs. Herbert Pieper, S.M.; Jose Ramirez, S.M.; Bros. James Droste, S.M.; Fred Hausch, S.M.; Robert Massa, S.M.; Edmund Schiermeier, S.M. Priests 2; Brothers 5.

Maryknoll House, 4542 W. Pine Blvd., 63108. Tel: 314-361-7729.
E-mail: mklstl@igc.org
Web site: maryknoll.org
Revs. Stephen L. Schroeppel, M.M.; John C. Ganly, M.M.

Provincialate of the Society of Mary, Province of St. Louis, P.O. Box 23130, 63156-3130. Tel: 314-367-0390; Fax: 314-361-3131.
E-mail: tdwyer@smstl.org
Web site: www.neosoft.com/~csjga
4538 Maryland Ave., 63108-1911. Tel: 314-367-0390; Fax: 314-361-3131. Rev. Timothy Dwyer, S.M., Prov.; Bros. Jerome Bommer, S.M., Asst. Prov.; Richard Dix, S.M., Temporalities; Rev. Alvin McMenamy, S.M., Rel. Life. Total in Residence 7; Total Staff 11.

Priests of the Province on Special Assignment: Rev. Edward M. Jach, S.M., 1600 Madison Rd., Cincinnati, OH, 45206-1815. Tel: 513-961-1945; Fax: 513-221-4907. Rev. Bernard M. Rochon, S.M., St. Timothy Parish, 1515 Saltillo St., San Antonio, TX, 78207-6898. Tel: 210-434-2391. Rev. Adolf M. Windisch, S.M., 300 College Park, Dayton, OH, 45469-0300. Tel: 937-229-4663. Rev. David Paul, S.M., 2012 Hickory St., 63104-2413. Tel: 314-367-0390; Fax: 314-367-3131. Rev. George Montague, S.M., 1701 Alametos, San Antonio, TX, 78201-3500. Tel: 210-734-6727.

Priests of the Province Serving Outside the USA: Rev. David Fleming, S.M., Supr. Gen., Marianisti, Via Latina 22, Rome, Italy, 00179. Tel: 011-39-06-704-75-892; Fax: 011-39-06-700-0406.

Priests of the Province Serving in the Missions: Rev. William A. Christensen, S.M., IIRD, House #5/10, Rd. Number 48, Block-E, Lalmatia, Bangladesh, Dhaka-1207. Tel: 011-88-02-817435; Fax: 011-88-02-815770. Rev. Charles Miller, S.M., Pontifical Biblical Institute, P.O. Box 497, Jerusalem, Israel, 91004. Rev. Michael Barber, S.M., Comunidad Marianista Sagrado Corazon, Apartado 839,

96400 Coatzacoalcos, Veracruz, Mexico. Tel: 011-52-921-41399; Fax: 011-52-921-41399. Rev. Paul Neumann, S.M., Noviciado Marianista, Apartado 180, Corregidora Queretaro, Mexico, 76900. Tel: 011-52-422-52005. Rev. Quentin Hakenewerth, S.M., Noviciado Marianista, Apartado 180, Queretaro, QRO, Mexico, 76900. Tel: 011-52-4-2252005. Rev. Sylverius Kerketta, S.M., St. Mary's Training Centre, Alaknath Rd., Barh P.O., Patna Dt., 803 213, Bihar, India. Tel: 011-91-6132-42-238.

Special Status: Revs. Anthony Pogorelc, S.M.; John Moder, S.M.; Paul Donoghue, S.M.

Priests and Brothers of the Province Living Elsewhere: Bro. Chester Burnog, S.M.; Rev. J. Donald Cahill, S.M.; Bros. Arthur Dofing, S.M.; Walter Ebbesmeyer, S.M.; James Eppy, S.M.; Louis Fornier, S.M.; Augustin Guzman, S.M.; Francis Haug, S.M.; Gerald Hyland, S.M.; Kenneth Jung, S.M.; Melvin Meyer, S.M.; Richard Middleton, S.M.; Robert Minges, S.M.; Urban Naal, S.M.; William O'Leary, S.M.; Joseph O'Meara, S.M.; Revs. Richard O'Shaughnessy, S.M.; Robert Osborne, S.M.; Bros. Louis Pinckert, S.M.; Robert Riemann, S.M.; Leonard Rudy, S.M.; Rev. Ralph Siefert, S.M.; Bros. Leo Slay, S.M.; Gerald Sullivan, S.M.; Revs. James Tobin, S.M.; Daniel Triulzi, S.M.; Joseph Uvietta, S.M.; William Wightman, S.M.; Richard Wosman, S.M.

St. Alphonsus Rectory of the Redemptorist, 1118 N. Grand Blvd., 63106. Tel: 314-533-0304; Fax: 314-533-4260.
E-mail: the-rock@saintly.com
Web site: www.stalphonsusrock.org
Revs. Maurice Nutt, C.SS.R.; Richard Potts, C.SS.R. In res. Revs. Paul Coury, C.SS.R.; Gary Ziuraitis, C.SS.R.; Bro. Terrance Burke, C.SS.R. Total Staff 4.

St. Crispin's Friary, 3731 Westminster Pl., 63108. Tel: 314-531-4506; Fax: 314-531-4506 (Call first).
E-mail: blaineb@slu.edu
Web site: www.midamcaps.org
Revs. Blaine Burkey, O.F.M.Cap., Guardian; Jeff Ernst, O.F.M.Cap., Vicar; Didacus Joseph Dunn, O.F.M.Cap.; Bros. Benignus Scarry, O.F.M.Cap.; Conrad Coleman, O.F.M.Cap. Priests 3; Lay Brothers 2; Postulants 1.

St. Dominic Priory, 3601 Lindell Blvd., 63108. Tel: 314-977-2588; Fax: 314-977-7225.
E-mail: philibp@slu.edu
Web site: www.op.org/stlouis
Revs. Paul J. Philibert, O.P., Prior; Arthur L. Kinsella, O.P.; Philip J. Lamberty, O.P.; Albert G. Glade, O.P.; Gregory J. Heille, O.P., Subprior; George R. Boudreau, O.P.; Richard A. Peddicord, O.P.; Michael A. Mascari, O.P.; Andrew Carl Wisdom, O.P.; David Carol, O.P. Total in Residence 40.

St. Louis University High School Jesuit Community, #3 Lawn Pl., 63110. Tel: 314-652-5425; Fax: 314-652-7028. Revs. James G. Knapp, S.J., Supr.; Richard E. Hadel, S.J.; Ralph D. Houlihan, S.J.; Frank E. Reale, S.J.; Paul G. Sheridan, S.J.; Bros. C. Thomas Thornton, S.J.; Richard H. Witzofsky, S.J. Priests 5; Brothers 2; Scholastics 1.

St. Matthew Jesuit Community, 2715 N. Sarah St., 63113-2940. Tel: 314-531-6443; Fax: 314-533-7318.
E-mail: stmatt@nothnbut.net
Revs. Matthew D. Ruhl, S.J., Supr.; Jeffrey D. Harrison, S.J.; William Hutchison, S.J.

St. Patrick Friary, 1000 N. 7th St., 63101. Tel: 314-231-9991; Fax: 314-231-9289. Revs. Valentine Young, O.F.M.Cap., Supr.; Simon R. Conrad, O.F.M.Cap.; Canice Froehlich, O.F.M.Cap.; Simeon Gallagher, O.F.M.Cap.; Julian Haas; Bro. Eugene Pellegrino. Priests 5.

Servants of the Paraclete, St. Michael's Community, 13270 Maple Dr., 63127. Tel: 314-965-0860; Fax: 314-965-7202.
E-mail: manilasp@aol.com
Web site: www.theservants.org
Revs. Mario D'Agostini, S.P.; Joseph McNamara, S.P., Vianney Renewal Center, 6476 Eime Rd., 63023. Tel: 314-274-5226; Fax: 314-274-1430.

Vincentian Community, St. Francis de Sales Rectory, 2653 Ohio Ave., 63118. Tel: 314-771-3100; Fax: 314-771-3295. Revs. Michael P. Joyce, C.M., Supr.; Romain G. Morales, C.M.; David G. Nations, C.M. Attached But Not In Residence: Rev. Daniel P. Kearns, C.M., Cahokia, IL.

Vincentian Residence, 10336 Corbeil Dr., 63146-5928. Tel: 314-997-5645; 872-2990. Revs. Lawrence F. Asma, C.M.; James T. Beighlie, C.M.

Vincentian Residence, 2904 Arsenal St., 63118. Tel: 314-773-7633; Fax: 314-773-0882. Revs. Daniel A. Ricci, C.M.; Edward F. Murphy, C.M.; Bro. David P. Goodman, C.M. Priests 2; Brothers 1.
Attached But Not In Residence: Revs. John V. Farris, C.M., St. Louis, MO; Daniel E. Harris, C.M., St. John's Seminary Theologate, Camarillo, CA 93012; Patrick J. McDevitt, C.M., Colorado Springs, CO; John E. Rybolt, C.M., Paris, France; P. Vincent Aherne, C.M., Carlsbad, CA; Philip M. Floersh, C.M., Flagstaff, AZ; Bro. Stanley J. Connor, C.M., St. Louis, MO.

Vincentian Residence, 2912 Arsenal St., 63118. Tel: 314-771-1869; Fax: 314-771-2410. Bro. James E. Donlevy, C.M.; Revs. Francis J. Shine, C.M.; Thomas E. Esselman, C.M.

White House Retreat Jesuit Community, 7400 Christopher Dr., 63129-5799. Tel: 314-846-2575; Fax: 314-846-2575.
E-mail: whthouse@i-plex.net
Web site: www.gabrielmedia.org/whr
Office, 3601 Lindell Blvd., 63108-3393. Tel: 314-533-8903; 800-643-1003; Fax: 314-533-8428. Rev. Richard O. Buhler, S.J., Dir. & Supr.; Bro. George R. Hale, S.J., Min. & Treas. Associate Directors: Revs. Donald M. Cunningham, S.J.; Robert A. Doyle, S.J.; David W. Koesterer, S.J.; Paul C. Pilgram, S.J.; William H. Runde, S.J.

ARNOLD. *Immaculate Conception Friary*, 2300 Church Rd., P.O. Box 217, 63010. Tel: 314-296-5301.
E-mail: icerl@juno.com
Revs. Gilmary Tallman, O.F.M.Cap., Vicar; Earl R. Meyer, O.F.M.Cap., Supr. In res. Rev. John Schmeidler, O.F.M.Cap.

CENTERVILLE. *Contemplative Heart of Mary Hermitage*. Tel: 573-648-2467. Rev. Robert L. Aten, Mailing Address: R.R. #1 309-C, Lesterville, 63654. Tel: 573-648-2467.

EARTH CITY. *Congregation of the Mission Midwest Province (Vincentians)*, 13663 Rider Tr. N., 63045-1512. Tel: 314-344-1184; Fax: 314-344-2989.
E-mail: cmstlouis@aol.com
Web site: www.vincentian.org
Very Rev. William E. Hartenbach, C.M., Prov.; Rev. Christopher S. Robinson, C.M.; Bro. F. Joseph Hess, C.M., Treas.

Vincentian Foreign Mission Society, 13663 Rider Tr. N., 63045-1512. Tel: 314-344-1184; Fax: 314-344-2989. Office for Vincentian Foreign Missions' Personnel and Projects. Rev. James P. Graham, C.M., Dir.

EUREKA. *Franciscan Brothers House of Studies*, Forby Rd., P.O. Box 129, 63025. Tel: 636-938-5539. House of Studies of Franciscan Missionary Brothers of the Sacred Heart of Jesus. Bro. John Spila, O.S.F., Dir. Total in Residence 2; Total Staff 1.

Our Lady of the Angels Monastery, St. Joseph Rd., 63025. Tel: 636-587-3661; Fax: 636-938-4960.
E-mail: shrinelolc@aol.com
Web site: www.blackmadonnashrine.org
Generalate of Franciscan Missionary Brothers of the Sacred Heart of Jesus. Bros. Matthew Gallagher, O.S.F., Dir. General; Damien DeBraekeleer, O.S.F., Asst. Dir.; Rev. Josef Lukaszczyk, Chap. Professed Brothers 13.
Apostolate: Price Memorial Nursing Home and St. Joseph's Hill Infirmary/Black Madonna Shrine, Adult Boarding Facility at Camilus Hall Boarding Home, Merkle Knipprath Nursing home, Joliet Diocese and Countryside Villas Retirement Center, Clifton, IL 60927.

HIGH RIDGE. *Society of Our Mother of Peace*, Sons of Our Mother of Peace, Maria Fonte Solitude, 6150 Antire Rd., 63049-2135. Tel: 636-677-3235. Rev. Placid Guste, S.M.P., Supr. Priests 2; Brothers 7; Total in Residence 9; Total Staff 4.

LIGUORI. *Alphonsian Foundation Office*, One Liguori Dr., 63057-9999. Tel: 636-464-2500; Fax: 636-464-8449.
E-mail: alph_foundation@compuserve.com
Web site: www.alfonsiana.edu
Purpose: to provide public relations and financial support for the Alphonsian Academy of Moral Theology in Rome. Victor L. Ottenlips, Devel. Dir.; Rev. John C. Vargas, C.SS.R., Exec. Dir.

Foundation Office - Redemptorists/New Orleans Vice-Province, One Liguori Dr., 63057-9999. Tel: 636-464-2500; Fax: 636-464-8449.
E-mail: liguori21@stlnet.com
Victor L. Ottenlips, Exec. Dir.

Liguori Mission House/Redemptorists, Ten Liguori Dr., 63057. Tel: 314-464-6999; Fax: 314-464-6765.
E-mail: william@jcnl.com
Web site: www.jcnl.com/william
Very Rev. Daniel L. Lowery, C.SS.R.; Revs. Charles C. Bueche, C.SS.R.; Thomas Cosgrove, C.SS.R.; Thomas Duggan, C.SS.R.; Paul Farrell, C.SS.R.; James Gleason; James J. Higgins, C.SS.R.; William Hogan, C.SS.R.; Victor Karls, C.SS.R.; William McKee, C.SS.R.; Bro. Gabriel Medic, C.SS.R.; Revs. Norman J. Muckerman, C.SS.R.; James Patterson, C.SS.R.; Allan Weinert, C.SS.R.; Henry McKeever, C.SS.R. Priests 14; Brothers 1.

Redemptorists Foundation Office, One Liguori Dr., 63057-9999. Tel: 636-464-2500; Fax: 636-464-8449.
E-mail: 75424.1416@compuserve.com
Web site: www.redemptorists-denver.org
Conducted by the Redemptorist/Denver Province in the Archdiocese of St. Louis. Purpose: supports the religious and charitable purposes of the Redemptorists. Victor L. Ottenlips, Exec. Dir.

St. Clement Health Care Center, 300 Liguori Dr., 63057. Tel: 636-464-3666; Fax: 636-464-4717. The Redemptorists. Revs. Gary L. Heinecke, C.Ss.R., Rector & Admin.; Clarence A. Bodden, C.Ss.R.; Norbert E. Delort, C.Ss.R.; Robert M. Gaydos, C.Ss.R.; Wallis W. George, C.Ss.R.; Milton F. Girse, C.Ss.R.; Harry A. Grile, C.Ss.R.; Bernard J. Guenther, C.Ss.R.; Gerald B. Heim, C.Ss.R.; Harry G. Korte, C.Ss.R.; Bruno V. Lischwe, C.Ss.R.; Francis G. Novak, C.Ss.R.; Robert M. Oelerich, C.Ss.R.; Stephen A. Plei, C.Ss.R.; Gerard F. Resch, C.Ss.R.; J. Robert Rossbach, C.Ss.R.; Francis J. Ryan, C.Ss.R.; Carl V. Schwarz, C.Ss.R.; John H. Shaughnessy, C.Ss.R.; Anthony A. Stuebben, C.Ss.R.; Raymond F. Walter, C.Ss.R.; Bros. Damian Bronson, C.Ss.R.; Gerard Clark, C.Ss.R.; Marvin Hamann, C.Ss.R.; Harry Jadczak, C.Ss.R.; Oliver Koehler, C.Ss.R.; Daniel Korn, C.Ss.R.; Martin Shields, C.Ss.R.; Martin Temple, C.Ss.R. Total in Residence 29; Total Staff 4.

OAKVILLE. *St. Francis Friary*, 4556 Telegraph Rd., 63129. Tel: 314-487-5736; Fax: 314-487-3701. Franciscan Friars. Revs. David Eckelkamp, O.F.M., Sr. Priest in Residence; Robert Behnen, O.F.M.; Bernardine Hahn, O.F.M., Chap. Poor Clare Monastery; Valerian Schott, O.F.M., (Retired); Ermin Micka, O.F.M., (Retired); Benet Fonck, O.F.M.; Gary Bernhardt, O.F.M.; Bro. Gregory Bumm, O.F.M., Franciscan Connection.

PERRYVILLE. *Congregation of The Mission*, St. Mary's Seminary, 63775-1599. Tel: 573-547-6533; Fax: 573-547-2204. U.S. Motherhouse of the Congregation of the Mission (Vincentian Fathers, Prov. of the Midwest). Very Rev. John F. Gagnepain, C.M., Supr.; Revs. Charles T. Herbst, C.M.; Robert J. Brockland, C.M.; Clarence J. Bogetto, C.M.; Francis A. Byrne, C.M.; John P. Tackaberry, C.M.; Alphonse X. Hoernig, C.M.; Charles F. Shelby, C.M.; Gilmore H. Guyot, C.M.; Charles D. Saunders, C.M.; Kenneth E. Grass, C.M.; Francis Germovnik, C.M.; Nicholas E. Persich, C.M.; Robert J. Zimney, C.M.; Louis J. Derbes, C.M.; James P. Graham, C.M.; John F. Zimmerman, C.M.; Oscar Lukefahr, C.M.; C. William Stein, C.M.; Edward J. Mullin, C.M.; Arthur L. Trapp, C.M.; Patrick V. Harrity, C.M.; Bros. Peter Baxter, C.M.; Harvey Goertz, C.M.; Richard A. Hermann, C.M.; Mark Howard Argus, C.M.; John Mangogna, C.M.; Matthew J. Teel, C.M.; Raymond J. Tochtrop, C.M.; Richard Zoellner, C.M. Fathers 21; Professed Brothers 8; Total Staff 4.

[Q] PERSONAL PRELATURES

KIRKWOOD. *Prelature of the Holy Cross and Opus Dei*, Wespine Study Center, 100 E. Essex Ave., 63122. Tel: 314-821-1608; Fax: 314-821-4722.
E-mail: WespineSTL@aol.com

Prelature of the Holy Cross and Opus Dei, 100 E. Essex Ave., 63122.
E-mail: info@opusdei.org
Web site: www.opusdei.org
Revs. Mark S. Mannion; John J. Alvarez.

[R] CONVENTS AND RESIDENCES FOR SISTERS

ST. LOUIS. *Adorers of the Blood of Christ, United States Province*, 721 Emerson Rd., Ste. 685, 63141. Sr. Cecilia M. Hellmann, A.S.C., Acting Prov.

Benedictine Convent of Perpetual Adoration, 8300 Morganford Rd., 63123. Tel: 314-638-6427; Fax: 314-638-2028 (Community); 638-7360.
E-mail: cathleen@benedictinesisters.org
Web site: www.benedictinesisters.org
Generalate and Healthcare Community of Benedictine Sisters of Perpetual Adoration, under Pontifical Jurisdiction. Sr. Mary Jane Romero, Prioress Gen.
Four other interdependent monasteries: Clyde, MO; Tucson, AZ; Sand Springs, OK; and Dayton, WY. Membership in St. Louis Community 52; Total in Congregation 122; Postulants 1; Novices 3.

Congregation of Mary, Queen of the World Community, 4540 Lindell Blvd., 63108. Tel: 314-361-8211; Fax: 314-361-8211.
E-mail: Dongtrinhvuong@juno.com
Web site: www.trinhvuong.org
Sr. Irene Dinh, C.M.R., Local Supr. Sisters 15.

Daughters of Our Mother of Peace, 5587 Page Blvd., 63112. Tel: 314-382-2592. Sr. Maryjoy Lambert, S.M.P., Supr. Sisters 3.

Daughters of St. Paul Convent, 9804 Watson Rd., 63126. Tel: 314-965-3512; Fax: 314-821-8401.
E-mail: FSPLouis@aol.com
Web site: www.Pauline.org
Sisters 8.

Eucharistic Missionaries of St. Theresa, 4440 Maryland, 63108-2496. Tel: 314-534-1826. Sr. Noemi Martinez, M.E.S.T.

Franciscan Sisters of Mary Administration, 1100 Bellevue Ave., 63117-1883. Tel: 314-768-1824; Fax: 314-768-1880.
E-mail: jmotzel@fsmonline.org
Web site: www.fsmonline.org
Offices of the Franciscan Sisters of Mary & Convent. Jacqueline Motzel, Pres.; Rev. Andrew Lewandowski, O.F.M., Chap. Professed Sisters in Archdiocese 143; In Residence 97.

Franciscan Sisters of Mary Novitiate, 1100 Bellevue Ave., 63117-1883. Tel: 314-768-1703; Fax: 314-768-1744.
E-mail: sschwartz@fsmonline.org
Web site: www.fsmonline.org

Franciscan Sisters of Mary, Sabbath Home, 909-B Madison St., 63301-2754. Tel: 636-916-0771; Fax: 636-947-5090.

Franciscan Sisters of Our Lady of Perpetual Help, 335 S. Kirkwood Rd., 63122. Tel: 314-965-3700; Fax: 314-965-3710.
E-mail: srmonica@postnet.com
Web site: www.franciscansisters-olph.org
Motherhouse and Novitate of Franciscan Sisters of Our Lady of Perpetual Help. Sr. Monica Marie Laws, O.S.F., Supr. Gen. Total Sisters in the Community 135; Total Staff 4.

Heart of Mary Center, 5431 Vicar Ct., 63119. Tel: 314-962-8498; Fax: 314-962-5714. Sr. Loretta Elfrink, D.H.M., Supr. Daughters of the Heart of Mary 4.

Incarnate Word Sisters, 3264 Sulphur, #2, 63139. Tel: 314-351-6916.
E-mail: mary.seeker@prodigy.net
Regional House of the St. Louis Province of the Sisters of Charity of the Incarnate Word of San Antonio. Sr. Helena Monahan, C.C.V.I., Prov. Supr.; Sr. Mary Ann Seeker, C.C.V.I., Contact. Sisters 18.

Loretto Center, 590 E. Lockwood, 63119-3279. Tel: 314-968-1887; Fax: 314-968-0164. Sisters 30; Total Staff 24.

Medical Mission Sisters, 2800 Olive St. #3C, 63103. Tel: 314-535-4383. Sr. Joan Coughlin, Local Contact.

Missionaries of Charity, 3629 Cottage Ave., 63113-3539. Tel: 314-533-2777. Sr. M. Marcella, M.C., Supr. Sisters 6; Total Assisted 24,737.
Missionaries of Charity also in: Peoria, IL; Chicago, IL; Detroit, MI; Memphis, TN; Dallas, TX; Little Rock, AR; Baton Rouge, LA; Lafayette, LA; Jenkins, KY; Atlanta, GA; Charlotte, NC; Gary, IN; Indianapolis, IN.

Monastery of St. Clare of the Immaculate Conception, 200 Marycrest Dr., 63129-4813. Tel: 314-846-2618. Poor Clare Nuns. Mother Mary Leo Hoffman, O.S.C., Abbess. Cloistered Nuns 9.

Mount Grace Convent and Chapel of Perpetual Adoration, 1438 E. Warne Ave., 63107. Tel: 314-381-2654; Fax: 314-381-8869.
E-mail: sspsap@inlink.com
Web site: www.mountgraceconvent.org
Sister Servants of the Holy Spirit of Perpetual Adoration (Generalate, Bad Driburg, Germany). Sr. Mary Gemma, Supr., 1438 E. Warne Ave., 63107. Tel: 314-381-2654; Fax: 314-381-8869. Attended by Divine Word Fathers. 1446 E. Warne Ave., 63107. Tel: 314-381-0219; Fax: 314-381-8521. Sisters 25.

Provincial House, Society of the Sacred Heart-United States Province, 4389 W. Pine Blvd., 63108. Tel: 314-652-1500; Fax: 314-534-6800.
E-mail: provincialhouse@rscj.org
Web site: www.rscj.org
Total in Residence 8; Total Staff 4. Province Corporations: California Province of the Society of the Sacred Heart, Inc.; Ladies of the Sacred Heart of St. Louis, Missouri; Society of the Sacred Heart, Chicago Province, Inc.; Religious of the Sacred Heart, Washington Province, Inc.; Religious of the Sacred Heart, New York Province, Inc.; Religious of the Sacred Heart in Massachusetts, Inc.

St. Joseph's Convent of Mercy, 611 S. New Ballas Rd., 63141. Tel: 314-569-6800; Fax: 314-569-6910.
E-mail: cacallahan@rsm-stl.org
Sr. Carol Ann Callahan, R.S.M., Coord. Sisters of Mercy of the Americas. Sisters 40.

St. Joseph's Provincial House, 6400 Minnesota Ave., 63111-2899. Tel: 314-481-8800; Fax: 314-481-2366; 351-3111.
E-mail: bldreher@aol.com
Web site: www.fontbonne.edu/csjsl.html
Prov. House of the Sisters of St. Joseph of Carondelet. Sr. Barbara Dreher, C.S.J., Prov. Dir.; Sr. Marion Renkens, C.S.J., Admin. Sisters in Province 563; In Archdiocese 374.

School Sisters of Notre Dame, Sancta Maria in Ripa, 320 E. Ripa Ave., 63125-2897. Tel: 314-544-0455; Fax: 314-544-6754.
Web site: www.ssnd.org
Motherhouse of the School Sisters of Notre Dame, St. Louis Province. Sr. Joanne Hanrahan, Prov. Leader; Rev. John M. Unger, Chap. Sisters in Diocese 380.

Interprovincial Novitiate for School Sisters of Notre Dame, 4950 Heege Rd., 63123. Tel: 314-481-8634; Fax: 314-481-8643. Sisters 3.

Liturgical Fabric Arts. Tel: 314-544-0455; 633-7030; Fax: 314-544-6754.

Maria Center. Tel: 314-544-6757; 633-7030; Fax: 314-544-6754.

Resource Development. Tel: 314-631-3530; Fax: 314-544-6754.

Sisters of Good Shepherd Province of Mid North America, 7654 Natural Bridge Rd., 63121. Tel: 301-384-1192. Sr. Mary Brigid Lawlor, R.G.S., Contact Person.

Sisters of Mercy of the Americas, Regional Community of St. Louis, 2039 N. Geyer Rd., 63131-3399. Tel: 314-966-4313; Fax: 314-909-4600.
E-mail: jarvin@corp.smhs.com
Web site: www.sistersofmercy.org
Sr. Richard Mary Burke, R.S.M., Regl. Pres. Regional Sisters in Archdiocese 80.
Convent Corporations:
Sisters of Mercy of the St. Louis Regional Community, Inc. Tel: 314-966-4313; Fax: 314-909-4600.
St. Joseph's Convent of Mercy of St. Louis. Tel: 314-569-5800; Fax: 314-569-6910.
Education Institutions:
Sisters of Mercy Education System, St. Louis, Inc., Begin Literacy Program. Tel: 601-362-9024; Fax: 601-206-1271.
Health Institutions:
Sisters of Mercy Health System, St. Louis, Inc. Tel: 314-965-6100; Fax: 314-984-6160.
Other: Mercy Center, Conference/Retreat Ministry.

Sisters of St. Francis of the Martyr St. George. Mother of Good Counsel Home, 6825 Natural Bridge Rd., 63121. Tel: 314-383-4765; Fax: 314-383-7256. Sisters 13.

Society of Helpers, 3432A Crittenden, 63118. Tel: 314-771-7482.
E-mail: hottingp@slu.edu
Web site: www.helpers.org
Legal Title: *Society of the Helpers of the Holy Souls.* Sr. Patricia A. Hottinger, S.H., Contact; Sr. Mary Funge, S.H., 3817 McDonald Ave., 63116. Tel: 314-776-6917.
E-mail: Mary_Funge@claret.org
Spiritual direction, Parish Weeks of Guided Prayer.

Villa Gesu, 11755 Riverview Dr., 63138. Tel: 314-741-6830.
E-mail: villagesu@juno.com
School Sisters of Notre Dame. Meeting Center for Sisters of the St. Louis Province. Sr. Joan DiProspere, S.S.N.D., Admin. Sisters 3.

BRIDGETON. *Providence Center,* 3415 Bridgeland Dr., 63044. Tel: 314-209-9181; Fax: 314-209-9207.
E-mail: jfolklcdp@juno.com
Web site: www.divineprovidence-cdpmo.org
Provincial Offices of the Sisters of Divine Providence of the St. Louis Prov. Sr. Janet Folkl, C.D.P., Prov. Legal Titles: *Sisters of Divine Providence of Missouri.; Sisters of Divine Providence of Missouri Charitable Trust.* Sisters 52.

CHESTERFIELD. *Missionary Sisters of St. Peter Claver,* 667 Woods Mill Rd. S., P.O. Box 401, 63006-0401. Tel: 314-434-8084; Fax: 314-469-0869.
E-mail: Chesclaver@aol.com
Sr. M. Irene Brahmakulath, S.S.P.C., Supr. Sisters 8.

CRYSTAL CITY. *Ursuline Provincialate,* 210 Glennon Heights Rd., 63019. Tel: 636-937-6206; Fax: 636-937-7627.
E-mail: centralosu@aol.com
Web site: www.osucentral.org
Central Province of the Ursuline Nuns of the Roman Union. Sr. Pauline Lorch, O.S.U., Prov. Prioress. Sisters: In Province 190; In the Archdiocese 39; In residence 12.
Other Locations: 512 S. Third St., DeSoto, 63020. Tel: 636-337-2854. Sisters 3. 353 S. Sappington Rd., St. Louis, 63122. Tel: 314-821-2150; Fax: 314-821-5827. Sr. Julie Hickey, O.S.U., Prioress, Sisters 11. 4900 Reber Pl., St. Louis, 63139. Tel: 314-773-4829; Fax: 314-773-3982. Sr. Marietta Boyd, O.S.U., Prioress. Sisters 8.

ELLISVILLE. *Passionist Nuns Monastery,* 15700 Clayton Rd., 63011-2300. Tel: 636-227-3550. Mother Mary Veronica, C.P., Supr. Professed Religious 10. Cloistered Contemplatives.

FLORISSANT. *Contemplative Sisters of the Good Shepherd,* 2711 Mullanphy Ln., 63031. Tel: 314-837-1719; Fax: 314-837-5925.
E-mail: cgsflo@primary.net
Web site: www.archstl.org
Sr. Sharon Rose Authorson, C.G.S., Supr. Sisters 21.

Pallottine Missionary Sisters-Queen of Apostles Province, 15270 Old Halls Ferry Rd., 63034-1661. Tel: 314-837-7100; Fax: 314-837-1041.
E-mail: Pall4@juno.com
Web site: members.aol.com/PRCRenewal/Home.html/
Provincialate, novitiate & renewal center of the Missionary Sisters of the Catholic Apostolate. Sr. Elisabeth Heptner, S.A.C., Prov. Professed Sisters 6; Total Staff 15. Convent Frascati, 1932 W. Linda Ln., Lonedell, 63060-9739. Tel: 314-629-5610. Professed Sisters 3; Total Staff 3.

FRONTENAC. *Congregational Office of the Sisters of St. Joseph of Carondelet,* 2307 S. Lindbergh Blvd., 63131. Tel: 314-966-4048; Fax: 314-966-5041.
E-mail: congctrcsj@aol.com
Web site: www.csjcongregation.org
Congregational Leadership Team: Sr. Marie Damien Adams, C.S.J.; Sr. Maureen Freeman, C.S.J.; Sr. Mary McGlone, C.S.J.; Sr. Virginia Webb, C.S.J.; Sr. Helene Wilson, C.S.J. Sisters 5.

Religious of the Sacred Heart Convent, Villa Duchesne, 801 S. Spoede Rd., 63131. Tel: 314-432-2021; Fax: 314-432-7713. Sisters 5.

HIGH RIDGE. *Society of Our Mother of Peace, Daughters of Our Mother of Peace,* Maria Fonte Solitude, 6150 Antire Rd., 63049-2135. Tel: 636-677-3235. Sr. Mary Catherine Snyder, S.M.P., Supr. Sisters 18; Total in Residence 7.

KIRKWOOD. *Carmelite Sisters of the Divine Heart of Jesus Provincial House and Novitiate,* 10341 Manchester Rd., 63122. Tel: 314-965-1638; Fax: 314-822-3154.
E-mail: stagnes@primary.net
Web site: carmelitedcj.org
Sr. M. Lydia Braun, Prov. Supr. Sisters 11; Novices 9; Postulants 12. We are a house of formation where young women are taught to be religious. Besides our child care center we have St. Agnes Home, a nursing home.

LADUE. *Carmel of St. Joseph,* 9150 Clayton Rd., 63124-1898. Tel: 314-993-6899; Fax: 314-993-5039.
E-mail: peace@carmelofstlouis.org
Discalced Carmelites.
Chapel of the Precious Blood. Mother Mary Joseph, O.C.D., Prioress; Rev. Kevin D. Horrigan, Res. Chap. Professed 8; Extern Sisters 1; Novices 4; Postulants 1.

LIGUORI. *Monastery of St. Alphonsus,* 200 Liguori Dr., 63057-9999. Tel: 636-464-1093; Fax: 636-464-9446.
E-mail: rednun@jcnl.com
Order of the Most Holy Redeemer (Redemptoristine Nuns). Professed 16.

LONEDELL. *Pallottine Missionary Sisters-Frascati Community,* 1932 W. Linda Ln., 63060-9739. Tel: 636-629-5610; Fax: 636-629-5610.
E-mail: pallotti@mail.usmo.com
Sr. Carolyn Callahan, Supr. Sisters 3.

NORMANDY. *Convent of the Immaculate Heart,* 7626 Natural Bridge Rd., 63121. Tel: 314-383-0300; Fax: 314-383-6523. A residence for aged & infirm Good Shepherd Sisters of the St. Louis Prov. Total Staff 45; Total in Residence 31.

Good Shepherd Provincialate, 7654 Natural Bridge Rd., 63121. Tel: 314-381-3400; Fax: 314-381-6449.
E-mail: norapatof@aol.com
Sr. Barbara Beasley, R.G.S., Prov. Sisters 12; Total Staff 8.

Pelletier Trust, a Charitable Trust of the Sisters of the Good Shepherd. Tel: 314-381-3400; Fax: 314-381-6449.

Marillac Provincial House. 4328 Westminster Pl., St. Louis, 63108. Tel: 314-533-3004. Provincial Offices, 7800 Natural Bridge Rd., St. Louis, 63121-4694. Tel: 314-382-2800; Fax: 314-382-8392.
E-mail: rdowney@dcwcp.org
Daughters of Charity of St. Vincent de Paul. Provincial House for Daughters of Charity. Sr. Marie Therese Sedgwick, D.C., Visitatrix; Very Rev. J. Dennis Martin, C.M., Dir. Sisters in Archdiocese 90.

O'FALLON. *St. Mary's Institute,* 204 N. Main St., 63366-2299. Tel: 636-240-3420; 240-6010; Fax: 636-272-5031.
E-mail: susanb@cpps-ofallon.org
Web site: www.cpps-ofallon.org
Motherhouse of the Sisters of the Most Precious Blood.
Chapel of St. Joseph. Sr. Susan Borgel, C.PP.S., Supr. Gen. Sisters in Archdiocese 238.

ST. CHARLES. *Franciscan Sisters of Mary,* 567 Jackson St., 63301-2667. Tel: 636-946-7258; Fax: 636-947-5090.
E-mail: mvehige@accessus.net
Sisters 2.

Religious of the Sacred Heart, 301 Decatur St., 63301-2089. Tel: 636-946-7276; Fax: 636-949-6659.
E-mail: mmmunch@rscj.org
Sisters 4.

Religious of the Sacred Heart, 800 N. 5th St., 63301. Tel: 636-946-6148.
Web site: www.rscj.org
Sisters 4.

Religious of the Sacred Heart-Regis, 221 Decatur St., 63301. Tel: 636-946-6456; Fax: 636-946-4425.
E-mail: regis211@aol.com
Sisters 6.

ST. LOUIS COUNTY. *Religious of the Sacred Heart*, 13644 Conway Rd., 63141. Tel: 314-434-7687.
E-mail: hpadberg@rscj.org
Sisters 2. 13648 Conway Rd., 63141. Tel: 314-878-1882. Sisters 4.

Religious of the Sacred Heart, 541 S. Mason Rd., 63141-8550. Tel: 314-878-6705.
Web site: www.rscj.org
Sisters 4.

TOWN AND COUNTRY. *Monastery of the Visitation, St. Louis*, 3020 N. Ballas Rd., 63131. Tel: 314-432-5353; Fax: 314-432-5354.
E-mail: verhar42@lycos.com
Web site: www.inlink.com/~vhmstl/
Sr. M. Veronica Haronik, V.H.M., Supr. Residence of Visitation Nuns Teaching or Living at the Monastery of the Visitation. Sisters 24.

[S] HOMES FOR MEN AND WOMEN

ST. LOUIS. *Cathedral Tower*, 325 N. Newstead Ave., 63108. Tel: 314-531-0511, Ext. 114; Fax: 314-533-6073.
E-mail: nrichter@archstl.org
For a complete listing, refer to the Special Care Facilities section.

Father Dempsey's Hotel, Inc., 3427 Washington Ave., 63103. Tel: 314-535-7221
For a complete listing, refer to the Special Care Facilities section.

Father Jim's Home, 3427 Washington Ave., 63103. Tel: 314-535-7221
For a complete listing, refer to the Special Care Facilities section.

Queen of Peace Center, 325 N. Newstead Ave., 63108. Tel: 314-531-0511; Fax: 314-531-1458.
E-mail: cneumann@archstl.org
For a complete listing, refer to the Special Care Facilities section.

Rosati Group Home, Inc., 4532 Lindell Blvd., 63108. Tel: 314-367-5500; Fax: 314-367-2982
For a complete listing, refer to the Special Care Facilities section.

Rosati Stabilization Center, 4224 N. Grand Ave., 63107. Tel: 314-534-6624; Fax: 314-535-4394
For a complete listing, refer to the Special Care Facilities section.

St. Martha's Hall, P.O. Box 4950, 63108. Tel: 314-533-1313; Fax: 314-533-2035
For a complete listing, refer to the Special Care Facilities section.

St. Philippine Duchesne Shelter, 1015 Goodfellow Blvd., 63112. Tel: 314-454-1012; Fax: 314-367-7455
For a complete listing, refer to the Special Care Facilities section.

Villa Maria Center, 2647 Ohio Ave., 63118. Tel: 314-664-4715; Fax: 314-664-4970
For a complete listing, refer to the Special Care Facilities section.

NORMANDY. *Maria Droste Residence*, 7660 Natural Bridge Rd., 63121. Tel: 314-383-5553; Fax: 314-382-5294
For a complete listing, refer to the Special Care Facilities section.

[T] RETREAT HOUSES

ST. LOUIS. *The Cenacle*, 7654 Natural Bridge Rd., 63121-4989. Tel: 314-381-7070; Fax: 314-381-2370. Congregation of Our Lady of the Retreat in the Cenacle. Sr. Mary Westhues, R.C., Supr. Sisters 6.

Mercy Center, 2039 N. Geyer Rd., 63131. Tel: 314-966-4686; Fax: 314-909-4631.
E-mail: mkaletta@somh.smhs.com
Mary Ann Kaletta, Admin. Conference and Renewal Ministry. Operated by the Sisters of Mercy of the Americas, Province St. Louis.

White House Retreat, Office: 3601 Lindell Blvd., Ste. 204, 63108. Tel: 314-533-8903; Fax: 314-533-8428.
E-mail: whthouse@i-plex.net
Web site: www.gabrielmedia.org/whr
Retreat House, 7400 Christopher Dr., 63129. Tel: 314-846-2575; Fax: 314-846-2575. Rev. Richard O. Buhler, S.J., Dir. Associate Directors: Revs. William H. Runde, S.J.; Robert A. Doyle, S.J.; David W. Koesterer, S.J.; Paul C. Pilgram, S.J.; Bro. George R. Hale, S.J.; Rev. Donald M. Cunningham, S.J. Total in Residence 7; Total Staff 7.

DITTMER. *Il Ritiro-The Little Retreat*, Eime Rd., P.O. Box 38, 63023. Tel: 636-285-3759; Toll Free from St. Louis: 636-274-0554; Fax: 636-274-2380.
E-mail: gpeter@nightowl.net
7935 St. Francis Lane, 63023. Operated by the Franciscan Friars. Revs. Bertin Miller, O.F.M., Exec. Dir.; Nathan McNally, O.F.M., Retreat Dir.; Dismas Bonner, O.F.M.; Gavin Griffith, O.F.M.; Damien R. Dougherty, O.F.M.; Leonard Paskert, O.F.M.; Michael Crosby, O.F.M. Total in Residence 11; Total Staff 6.

Vianney Renewal Center, 6476 Eime Rd., P.O. Box 130, 63023. Tel: 636-274-5226; 677-1828; Fax: 636-274-1430.
Web site: www.theservants.org
Operated by the Servants of the Paraclete. Rev. Peter Lechner, S.P., Dir. of Prog. Total in Residence 15; Total Staff 5.

EUREKA. *Marianist Retreat & Conference Center*, P.O. Box 718, 63025. Tel: 636-938-5390; Fax: 636-938-3493.
E-mail: macmrc@aol.com
Center for Formation and Growth in the Christian Life. Conducted by the Society of Mary. Revs. Joseph Uvietta, S.M., Dir.; Jose Ramirez, S.M.; Herbert Pieper, S.M. Total in Residence 6; Total Staff 18.

FLORISSANT. *Pallottine Renewal Center*, 15270 Old Halls Ferry Rd., 63034. Tel: 314-837-7100; Fax: 314-837-1041.
E-mail: Pall4@juno.com
Web site: members.aol.com/PRCRenewal/Home.html/
Pallottine Missionary Sisters. Sr. Bernadita Peterson, S.A.C., Admin. Total in Residence 7; Total Staff 15.

HIGH RIDGE. *Society of Our Mother of Peace-Maria Fonte Solitude*, 6150 Antire Rd., 63049-2135. Tel: 636-677-3235. Sr. Mary Perpetua, S.M.P.; Rev. Placid Guste, S.M.P.

WILDWOOD. *La Salle Institute - Retreat and Conference Center*, 2101 Rue De La Salle, 63038-2299. Tel: 636-938-5374; Fax: 636-587-9792.
E-mail: CBLaSalle@aol.com
Community: De La Salle Christian Brothers (FSC). Tel: 636-938-6142; Fax: 636-587-9792. Bro. Joseph Zastrow, Dir. Community 4; Total in Residence 4; Total Staff 5.

[U] NEWMAN CENTERS

ST. LOUIS. *University of Missouri, St. Louis, Newman House*, 8200 Natural Bridge Rd., 63121. Tel: 314-385-3455; Fax: 314-385-1523.
E-mail: cncumsl@aol.com
Web site: www.umsl.edu/~newman
Rev. William Kempf, Dir.

Washington University Newman Centers. Washington University Newman Chapel, 6352 Forsyth Blvd., 63105-2269. Tel: 314-935-9191; Fax: 314-727-6053.
E-mail: newman@rescomp.wustl.edu
Web site: www.rescomp.wustl.edu/~newman/
Rev. Gary G. Braun, Archdiocesan Dir. of Campus Ministries. In res. Rev. Msgr. William J. Lyons. Total in Residence 2; Total Staff 15.

[V] MISCELLANEOUS

ST. LOUIS. *Alexian Brothers of Missouri, Inc.*

Alexian Brothers of St. Louis, Inc.

Alexian Brothers Salus Place, 2703 Keokuk Ave., 63118. Tel: 314-771-5400; Fax: 314-771-5454. Patrick Kerwin, Exec. Dir. Established to Serve Persons with Dual Diagnosis of HIV and Substance Abuse.

Alexian Brothers Services, Inc.

Almost Home, 3200 St. Vincent Ave., 63104-1336. Tel: 314-771-4663; Fax: 314-865-4692.
E-mail: almost_home@alhome.org
Transitional living program for teenage mothers and their children who are homeless. Sr. Jacinta Marie Elmendorf, F.S.M., Exec. Dir. Total Assisted 200; Total Staff 15.

Anna Trust, 6400 Minnesota Ave., 63111. Tel: 314-481-8800; Fax: 314-481-2366. A Charitable Trust Fund Established to Support the Religious and Charitable Purposes of the Sisters of St. Joseph of Carondelet, St. Louis Province.

Archdiocesan Charitable Bequest Council, 4445 Lindell Blvd., 63108. Tel: 314-533-1887; Fax: 314-533-1889.
E-mail: www.archstl.org
Mr. Frank J. Cognata, Jr., Chief Devel. Officer; Mr. Dennis Kempf, Dir. Planned Giving; Mr. Rudy Beck; Mr. Joseph R. Beckerle; Christine Burghoff; Angela M. Dalton; Mr. William Drennan; Rosemary Fairhead; Thomas Keeline; Mr. Michael Niemann; William O'Connor; Mr. Matthew G. Perlow; Sharon Sanders; Ms. Teresa Schlafly; Michael Weisbrod.

Archdiocesan Development Appeal, 4140 Lindell Blvd., 63108. Tel: 314-371-4980, Ext. 166; Fax: 314-371-0277.
E-mail: manna@archstl.org
Web site: www.archstl.org
Teresa Manna, Dir.

Archdiocesan Stewardship Education Committee, 4445 Lindell Blvd., 63108. Tel: 314-533-1887; Fax: 314-533-1889.
E-mail: erschen@arstl.org
Web site: www.archstl.org/stewardship
Mr. Frank J. Cognata, Chief Devel. Officer; Susan Erschen, Dir. Stewardship Education; Kassandra Bufford; Anne Carleton; Mr. Jim Richter; Mr. Kevin Conway; Mr. Tom Coerver; Timothy P. Killion; Craig L. Wentworth; Revs. Michael P. Boehm; Robert Hermann; Michael L. Henning; Thomas W. Wyrsch.

Ascension Health, 4600 Edmundson Rd., 63134. Tel: 314-253-6700; Fax: 314-253-6807.
E-mail: dbrennan@ascensionhealth.org
Web site: www.ascensionhealth.org
Donald A. Brennan, Pres. & CEO.
Co-sponsored by four of the United States Provinces of the Daughters of Charity: Northeast Prov., Albany, NY; Southeast Prov., Emmitsburg, MD; East Central Prov., Evansville, IN; West Central Prov., St. Louis, MO and by the Congregation of the Sisters of St. Joseph of Nazareth, Nazareth, MI.

Aware, Inc., St. Anthony's Medical Center, 10016 Kennerly Rd., 63128. Tel: 314-525-1622. Merrilee Underhill, Pres.

B.R.E.M. Catholic Social Ministry, 1371 Hamilton Ave., 63112. Tel: 314-383-4666; Fax: 314-383-5366. Ms. Dorothy Kastigar, Dir. Provides Employment Counseling and Referrals, Health Outreach, and Referrals for Food, Clothing and Housing. Also Provides Community Education, Leadership Development, Family Support and Community Development Services. Total Assisted 3,000; Total Staff 2.

Birthright, 2206 S. Brentwood Blvd., 63144. Tel: 314-962-5300; Fax: 314-962-7606.
Web site: www.birthright.org
Shirley E. Ducey, Admin. Dir. Total Assisted 7,000; Total Staff 13.
Branch Offices: 215 Clarkson Exec. Pkwy., 63011. Tel: 636-227-2266; Fax: 636-227-2012. 6680 Chippewa, 63109. Tel: 314-962-3653; Fax: 314-351-4531. 3435A Bridgeland, 63044. Tel: 636-227-8775; Fax: 314-298-0813. 205 N. 5th St., St. Charles, 63301. Tel: 636-724-1200; Fax: 636-946-0447. 4144 Lindell, 63108. Tel: 636-946-4900; Fax: 314-531-3051.

Cardinal Carberry Senior Living Center, 7609 Watson Rd., 63119. Tel: 314-961-8000; Fax: 314-961-1548.
E-mail: swesley@archstl.og
Sr. Suzanne Wesley, Contact Person.

Cardinal Glennon Children's Hospital Foundation, 1465 S. Grand Blvd., 63104. Tel: 314-577-5605; Fax: 314-268-6416.
E-mail: info@glennon.org
Web site: www.glennon.org
Member of SSM Health Care.

Caritas. Ladies of Charity Service Center, 7500 Natural Bridge Rd., 63121. Tel: 314-383-4207; Fax: 314-383-0605. Legal Title: *Ladies of Charity Service Center*. Thrift Store & Food Pantry. Cindy Barry, Coord. Total Assisted 28,910; Total Staff 58.

The Caroline Trust, 320 E. Ripa Ave., 63125-2897. Tel: 314-633-7021; Fax: 314-544-6754. Supports the Religious and Charitable Purposes of the School Sisters of Notre Dame and Provides Support for the Aged, Infirm and Disabled Sisters of the Province.

Carondelet Health System, 13801 Riverport Dr., Ste. 300, 63043-4810. Tel: 314-770-0333; Fax: 314-770-0444.
E-mail: gchristiansen@chs-stl.com
Web site: chs-stl.com
Andrew W. Allen, Pres. Tel: 314-770-0333.

Catholic Charities Dial Help, 325 N. Newstead, 63108. Tel: 314-371-4357; 800-666-9990; Fax: 314-533-6073.
E-mail: nrichter@archstl.org
Nancy A. Richter, Admin., Exec. Opers. Total Assisted 23,009; Total Staff 2. Information and Referral Service Operated by Catholic Charities.

Catholic Charities Foundation, 4532 Lindell Blvd., 63108. Tel: 314-367-5500; Fax: 314-367-2983.
Web site: www.ccstl.org
Mr. Richard J. Vehige, Pres. A Charitable Fund Established to Support the Activities of Catholic Charities.

Catholic Charities Refugee Services, 2840 Wisconsin Ave., 63118. Tel: 314-771-2570; Fax: 314-771-6406.
E-mail: ccrs@lida.net
To Facilitate the Resettlement of Refugees. Total Staff 9; Total Assisted 910.

Catholic Charities Volunteer Department, 4532 Lindell Blvd., 63108. Tel: 314-367-5500, Ext. 128; Fax: 314-367-2982.
E-mail: jsmith@archstl.org
Web site: www.ccstl.org
The Recruiting and Referral Office for Volunteers Serving the Needs of the Various Programs Affiliated with Catholic Charities in Conjunction with the St. Vincent Pallotti Center for Apostolic Development which Develops and Enhances Lay Volunteer Ministry by Bringing Together Clergy, Religious and Laity.

Catholic Commission on Housing, 4140 Lindell Blvd., 63108. Tel: 314-371-4980; Fax: 314-371-0058.
E-mail: cch@archstl.org
Web site: ccstl.org
Karen Wallensak, Exec. Dir. An Agency of the Catholic Charities Federation that assists low and moderate-income families purchase their first home; maintain and repair their property; and avoid foreclosure through achieving financial stability. Total Staff 9; Total Assisted 750.

Catholic Community Services Administration, 325 N. Newstead, 63108-2728. Tel: 314-531-0511, Ext. 132; Fax: 314-531-2328.
E-mail: bettyfsm@aol.com
Sr. Betty Brucker, F.S.M., Exec. Dir. An Agency of the Catholic Charities Federation. A Consolidation of Catholic Charities Outreach Services, Catholic Health Outreach Program and the Archbishop's Commission on Community Health.

Midtown Catholic Community Services, 1202 S. Boyle Ave., 63110-3814. Tel: 314-534-1180; Fax: 314-534-3727.

Jefferson County Catholic Community Services, P.O. Box 668, Festus, 63028-0668. Tel: 636-931-5859; Fax: 636-933-5148.

Father Tolton Catholic Community Services, 2011 E. Linton Ave., 63107-1134. Tel: 314-534-5323; Fax: 314-534-3958.

St. Jane Catholic Community Services, 7005 Ascension Dr., 63121-3427. Tel: 314-383-6539; Fax: 314-383-6591.

St. Joseph Catholic Community Services, 6322 Minnestoa, 63111-2553. Tel: 314-351-6407; Fax: 314-752-3896.

Southside Catholic Community Services, 2647 Ohio, 63118. Tel: 314-773-6100; Fax: 314-773-2346.

St. Charles County Catholic Community Services, 1101 S. Service Rd. (E. Hwy. 40), Ste. 255, Wentzville, 63385-4845. Tel: 636-332-6889; Fax: 636-332-5285.

Catholic Community Services-Vietnamese Center, 2901 Cherokee St., 63118-2901. Tel: 314-664-8990; Fax: 314-664-8991.

Catholic Community Services - Friends of Moms. At Joint Neighborhood Ministry, 2911 McNair Ave., 63118-1632. Tel: 314-771-3987; Fax: 314-383-6591.

Catholic AIDS Outreach, 1420 S. Sappington Rd., 63126-1699. Tel: 314-962-9757; Fax: 314-968-8023.

Language Access Metro Project (LAMP), 2647 Ohio Ave., 63118-1533. Tel: 314-962-6477; Fax: 314-773-2346.

Catholic Charities Physician Referral Services/ LAMP, 2647 Ohio Ave., 63118-1533. Tel: 314-865-5267; Fax: 314-773-2346.

Northside Community Center/St. Matthew, 4120 Maffitt St., 63113-2933. Tel: 314-531-1971; Fax: 314-531-2791.

Catholic Charities Refugee Services, 2840 Wisconsin Ave., 63118-1656. Tel: 314-771-2570; Fax: 314-771-6406. For all: Total Families Assisted 24,000; Total Staff 81.

Catholic Deaf Ministry, 6815 Page Ave., 63133-1505. Tel: 314-721-3069; 727-2747 (TDD); Fax: 314-727-2747. Provides Services for Deaf and Hearing Impaired Persons.

Catholic Family Services dba Catholic Family Counseling, 7800 Kenrick Rd., 63119. Tel: 314-968-8010; Fax: 314-968-5478.
E-mail: jmarks@archstl.org
Dr. Jerry Marks, D.S.W., Exec. Dir. Provides professional counseling (individual & small groups) to individuals, couples & families experiencing stress. Family Life Education and Outreach available. Fees based on ability to pay.
District Offices:

South, 7800 Kenrick Rd., 63119. Tel: 314-968-8010; Fax: 314-968-5478.

Northwest, 4450 Washington, Florissant, 63033. Tel: 314-831-1533; Fax: 314-831-1391.

West County, 498 Woods Mill Rd., Manchester, 63011. Tel: 636-391-9966; Fax: 636-391-9966.

Lincoln County, 911 Turnbull Tr., Ste. E, Troy, 63379. Tel: 636-528-2248.

St. Charles, 1360 S. Fifth, St. Charles, 63301. Tel: 636-946-6014; Fax: 636-946-3005.

North City, 2405 N. Grand, 63113. Tel: 314-535-0017; Fax: 314-535-3155.

Crystal City/Festus, 109 N. Mill, Festus, 63028. Tel: 636-937-2157; 937-2163; 1-800-652-8055; Fax: 636-937-3172.

Franklin Warren Counties, 119 W. Locust, Union, 63084. Tel: 636-583-1800; 1-800-583-8355; Fax: 636-583-0836.

St. Vincent Church, De Paul Bldg., 1010 Rosati Ct., Perryville, 63775. Tel: 573-547-4591; 1-800-652-8055. For all: Total Assisted 9,615; Total Staff 46.

The Catholic Health Association of the United States, 4455 Woodson Rd., 63134-3797. Tel: 314-427-2500; Fax: 314-427-0029.
Web site: www.chausa.org
Established June 24, 1915. Rev. Michael D. Place, S.T.D., Pres. & CEO.

Catholic High School Association, 4140 Lindell Blvd., 63108. Tel: 314-371-4980; Fax: 314-371-0206.
E-mail: stlsupt@impresso.com
Web site: www.archstl.org/education/
Mr. George Henry, Supt.

FOCUS Foundation (Federation of Catholic Urban Schools), 4140 Lindell Blvd., 63108. Tel: 314-371-4980; Fax: 314-371-0267. Sr. Margaret McCulloch, B.V.M., Dir.

Today and Tomorrow Educational Foundation, 4140 Lindell Blvd., 63108. Tel: 314-371-4980; Fax: 314-371-0027. Julie Turner, Dir.

Catholic Education Office, 4140 Lindell Blvd., 63108. Tel: 314-371-4980; Fax: 314-371-0206. George Henry, Superintendent.

Catholic Information Center, 1000 N. Seventh St., 63101. Tel: 314-621-6555; 231-9991; Fax: 314-231-9289. Rev. Valentine Young, O.F.M.Cap., Dir.

Catholic Kolping Society of America, 4035 Keokuk St., 63116. Tel: 314-776-5312. Otto J. Eichhorn, Treas.

Catholic Office of Disability Ministry, 7800 Kenrick Rd., 63119-5004. Tel: 314-961-4320, Ext. 110; Fax: 314-918-5817.
E-mail: codm@networkusa.net
Web site: www.archstl.org
Lorraine Fahey, Dir.

Catholic Services for Children and Youth, 4140 Lindell Blvd., 63108. Tel: 314-371-4980; Fax: 314-371-0271.
E-mail: RKing@archstlouis.org
Richard L. King, A.C.S.W., Exec. Dir. Child Welfare Agency Providing Adoption, Foster Family Care, Outreach Counseling in Own Home, Social Services for Residential Treatment Centers and Services for Unmarried and Single Parents. Total in Residence 3,400; Total Staff 60.

Central Bureau of the CCUA, 3835 Westminster Pl., 63108-3472. Tel: 314-371-1653.
E-mail: centbur@juno.com
Rev. John H. Miller, C.S.C., Dir. and Editor of the Social Justice Review.

Chiara Corporation, 1100 Bellevue Ave., 63117-1883. Tel: 314-768-1817; Fax: 314-768-1803.
E-mail: joshaughnessy@fsmonline.org
Mr. John O'Shaughnessy, Contact Person. Ministries that promote, enhance and provide for the spiritual, religious, physical or mental well-being of members of society in accordance with the religious and charitable purposes of the Franciscan Sisters of Mary.

Child Center Foundation, 7900 Natural Bridge Rd., 63121. Tel: 314-383-0200; Fax: 314-383-6334.
E-mail: edward@archstl.org
Karen D. Roebuck, Pres., Bd. of Directors.
Child Center Foundation provides financial support to the Child Center of Our Lady, a residential and day treatment facility serving severely emotionally disturbed children and their families.

CSJ Ministries, 6400 Minnesota Ave., 63111. Tel: 314-481-8800; Fax: 314-481-2366.

Daughters of Charity Healthcare Foundation of St. Louis, 231 S. Bemiston, Ste. 350, 63105. Tel: 314-802-2060; Fax: 314-802-2051.
Web site: www.daughtersofcharityfdn.org
Sr. Joan Kuester, D.C., Exec. Dir.

Daughters of Charity National Health System, Inc., 4600 Edmundson Rd., 63134. Tel: 314-253-6700; Fax: 314-253-6407.
E-mail: dbrennan@ascensionhealth.org
Donald A. Brennan, Pres. & CEO.

Daughters of Charity West Central Region Foundation, 231 S. Bemiston, Ste. 350, 63105. Tel: 314-802-2060; Fax: 314-802-2051.
Web site: www.daughtersofcharityfdn.org
Sr. Joan Kuester, D.C., Exec. Dir. Provides funds for the poor & underserved; will fund projects related to health education & wellness primary/ preventive medical svcs. & social svcs.

Dismas House of St. Louis, 5025 Cote Brilliante Ave., 63113. Tel: 314-361-2802; Fax: 314-361-8780. Rev. Joseph M. Kohler, Exec. Dir. Total in Residence 170; Total Staff 60.

Equestrian Order of the Holy Sepulchre of Jerusalem-Northern Lieutenancy, 6 Southcote Rd., 63144. Tel: 314-993-4658; Fax: 314-994-0586.
E-mail: mgguyol@aol.com
Mr. William B. Guyol, Lieutenant.

Franciscan Sisters of Mary, 1100 Bellevue Ave., 63117-1883. Tel: 314-768-1824; Fax: 314-768-1880.
E-mail: jmotzel@fsmonline.org
Web site: www.fsmonline.org

Friends of the Archbishop, 4445 Lindell Blvd., 63108. Tel: 314-633-2273; Fax: 314-633-2306. F. Gilbert Bickel, Chm.; Rev. Msgr. Richard F. Stika, Incorporator. Purpose: To Raise Funds to Support the Roman Catholic Archdiocese of St. Louis.

Good Shepherd Programs, Inc., 7654 Natural Bridge Rd., 63121. Tel: 314-381-3400; Fax: 314-382-5294. Operates the Maria Droste Residence. Total Staff 6; Total Assisted 70.

Hispanic Ministry of the Archdiocese of St. Louis, 5418 Louisiana, 63111. Tel: 314-351-7009; Fax: 314-351-2611.
E-mail: lapastoral@yahoo.com
Mr. Juan Escarfuller, Dir.; Sr. Concepcion De La Cruz, S.L., Asst. Dir.; Rev. Michael P. Joyce, C.M., Moderator. Total Staff 3.

Incarnate Word Foundation, 710 N. Second St., Ste. 400 S., 63102. Tel: 314-621-4090; Fax: 314-621-7971.
E-mail: iwfdn@swbell.net
Web site: www.incarnatewordfund.com
Bridget McDermott Flood, Exec. Dir. Provides Grants to Health and Social Service Agencies.

Incarnate Word Foundation, Missouri, 710 N. Second St., Ste. 400 S., 63102. Tel: 314-621-4090; Fax: 314-621-7971.
E-mail: iwfdn@swbell.net
Web site: www.incarnatewordfund.com
Bridget M. Flood, Exec. Dir.

Institute for Theological Encounter with Science & Technology (ITEST), 221 N. Grand Blvd., 63103. Tel: 314-977-2703; Fax: 314-977-7264.
E-mail: postigm@slu.edu
Web site: ITEST.slu.edu
Rev. Robert A. Brungs, S.J., Dir.

Institute of Jesuit Sources, 3601 Lindell Blvd., 63108. Tel: 314-977-7257; Fax: 314-977-7263.
E-mail: ijs@slu.edu
Rev. John W. Padberg, S.J., Dir.

Intercommunity Housing Association, 3407 Lafayette Ave., Ste. 204, 63104-1313. Tel: 314-664-6811; Fax: 314-664-7189.
E-mail: IHAstlouis@aol.com
Provides safe, affordable housing & supportive svcs. for economically disadvantaged & working poor families in St. Louis. Total Staff 3; Total Assisted 126.

Jesuit Community - Ministries, 3601 Lindell Blvd., 63108. Tel: 314-977-2598; Fax: 314-977-7211. Rev. John F. Snyder, S.J., Past Pres. - Gregorian University Foundation. Total in Residence 75.

The Jesuits of the Missouri Province, Office of Development: 4517 W. Pine Blvd., 63108. Tel: 314-361-7765; Fax: 314-758-7163.
E-mail: development@jesuits-mis.org
Web site: www.jesuit-mis.org
Mr. Ray Markham, Dir.; Rev. L. Gene Martens, S.J., Assoc. Dir. Legal Title: *The Jesuits of the Missouri Prov.*

Ladies of Charity of St. Catherine Laboure, 12160 Leelaine Dr., 63126. Affiliate with Ladies of Charity of the United States & the Assoc. of Intl. Charities of St. Vincent de Paul. Susan Tumminia, Pres.

Ladies of Charity of St. Vincent-Guardian Angel. St. Vincent's Church, 1408 S. Tenth St., 63104. Affiliate with Ladies of Charity of the United States & the Assoc. of Intl. Charities of St. Vincent de Paul. Natalie Cox, Pres.

Ladies of Charity of the United States of America, P.O. Box 31697, 63131-1697. Tel: 314-821-1296; Fax: 314-344-2989. Charleen Brain, Pres.
LCUSA continues, expands, and improves the charitable works of the local associations of the LCUSA, which number 79.

Mary and Joseph Trust, 1100 Bellevue Ave., 63117-1883. Tel: 314-768-1817; Fax: 314-768-1803.
E-mail: joshaughnessy@fsmonline.org

McAuley Charitable Trust, 2039 N. Geyer Rd., 63131-3399. Tel: 314-909-4617; Fax: 314-909-4622.
E-mail: kglosenger@corp.smhs.com
The Sisters of Mercy of the Americas, Regional Community of St. Louis. Sr. Katherine Marie Glosenger, R.S.M., Contact Person.

The Missionaries of Our Lady of La Salette, Provincialate, 4650 S. Broadway, 63111-1398. Tel: 314-353-5000; Fax: 314-353-4582.
Web site: www.lasalette.org
Total in Residence 11; Total Staff 3.

Missionaries of the Kingship of Christ, P.O. Box 2234, 63109. Tel: 314-353-2446; Fax: 314-351-8662.
E-mail: clmaley@inlink.com
Web site: www.simkc.org
Rev. Msgr. Louis F. Meyer, Spiritual Dir. Total in Residence 1. Madonna House, 4908 Sutherland Ave., 63109. Tel: 314-352-5822.
A Pontifical Secular Institute.

The Museum of Western Jesuit Missions, 700 Howdershell Rd., Box 1095, 63031. Tel: 314-361-5122; Fax: 314-758-7166.
E-mail: pastoral@jesuits-mis.org
Rev. William B. Faherty, S.J., Curator. Total in Residence 1; Total Staff 10.

National Christian Life Community of the United States of America (CLC), 3601 Lindell Blvd., Rm. 202 (Jesuit Hall), 63108-3393. Tel: 314-977-7370; Fax: 314-977-7371.
Web site: www.clc-usa.org
Patricia Carter, Pres. Founded c. 1540 & approved 1584, a public, intl. assn. of the Faithful of Pontifical Right which builds small Faith-Communities for mission & Svc. to the church. It uses the Spiritual Exercises of Saint Ignatius of Loyola as its specific source & characteristic instrument for its spirituality. Membership equally open to primarily catholic christian men, women, youth & young adults, clergy, brothers & sisters.

Network of Sacred Heart Schools, Inc., 4389 W. Pine Blvd., 63108. Tel: 314-652-1500; Fax: 314-534-6800.
E-mail: nshoffice@sofie.org
Web site: www.sofie.org
Sr. Kathleen Hughes, Prov.

Notre Dame Ministry Corporation, 320 Ripa Ave., 63125. Tel: 314-544-0455; Fax: 314-544-6754. Sr. Barbara Marie McInturff, S.S.N.D. Includes: Notre Dame High School, Notre Dame Preschool, Notre Dame Travel & Notre Dame Tutorial Center.

Our Lady's Inn, 4223 S. Compton, 63111. Tel: 314-351-4590; Fax: 314-351-2119.
E-mail: olidirector@misi.org
Web site: www.ourladysinn.org
Gloria Lee, Contact Person. Total Assisted 350; Total Staff 18. A residential shelter for pregnant women who have no home, who are being abused, who have no one who cares, and/or who are being pressured to abort their baby. We provide living facilities, food, clothing, counseling, vocational guidance and followup care.

Papal Visit 1999, St. Louis, 4445 Lindell Blvd., 63108. Tel: 314-633-2222; Fax: 314-633-2306.
Web site: archstl.org
Provided arrangements for religious services and related activities in conjunction with the January 1999 visit to St. Louis, MO of Pope John Paul II.

Pediatric Research Institute Foundation, 3662 Park Ave., 63104. Tel: 314-577-5606; Fax: 314-577-5379.
E-mail: raycg@slu.edu
Web site: prifoundation.org
C. George Ray, M.D.

Perpetual Help Charitable Trust, 335 S. Kirkwood Rd., 63122. Tel: 314-965-3700; Fax: 314-965-3710.
E-mail: srmonica@postnet.com
Web site: www.franciscansister-olph.org
Established by the Franciscan Sisters of Our Lady of Perpetual Help to Support the Religious and Charitable Purposes of the Franciscan Sisters of Our Lady of Perpetual Help.

Review for Religious, 3601 Lindell Blvd., Rm. 428, 63108. Tel: 314-977-7363; Fax: 314-977-7362.
E-mail: review@slu.edu
Web site: www.reviewforreligious.org
Rev. David L. Fleming, S.J., Editor. Total Staff 6.

Sacred Heart Program, Inc., 3900 Westminster Pl., 63108. Tel: 314-533-0320; Fax: 314-533-0335.
E-mail: gkolarcik@sacredheartprogram.org
Web site: www.sacredheartprogram.org
Gary Kolarcik, Exec. Dir. Total Staff 8. The Sacred Heart Program produces "Contact," an international broadcast designed to help society's "strugglers" - the spiritually, physically or financially impoverished. It also produces "Pathways" a series of one-minute radio spots dealing with basic human needs and family issues. The organization also offers Sacred Heart devotional items.

St. Charles Lwanga Center, 5021 Northland Ave., 63113-1014. Tel: 314-367-7929; Fax: 314-367-4134.
E-mail: lwangacenter@postnet.com
Provides spiritual formation and leadership development with evangelization and youth outreach for the Black Catholic Community, those working in the community and all interested persons in the Archdiocese of St. Louis and throughout the United States. Jane W. Brown, Dir. Total Staff 5.

St. Francis de Sales Association, 228 Chestnut Ave., 63119. Tel: 314-962-4941.
E-mail: mmmarthakie@aol.com
Mrs. Martha Smith, Western Regl. Dir. A call to the laity to live thier individual vocation in the spirit of Jesus, using the writings of St. Francis de Sales as a means to see and do God's will and grow in holiness.

St. John's Mission, 4517 W. Pine Blvd., 63108. Tel: 314-361-7765; Fax: 314-758-7163.
E-mail: development@jesuits-mis.org

St. Louis Catholic Charismatic Renewal, 7800 Kenrick Rd., 63119. Tel: 314-961-3420, Ext. 418; Fax: 314-961-4320, Ext. 444.
E-mail: hs@stlcharismatic.org
Web site: stlcharismatic.org
Deacon Dennis Chitwood, Liaison & Dir.; Robert Gleason, Admin., Healing & Deliverance Ministry. Tel: 314-961-3420, Ext. 416. Overflowing Joy Ministry. Tel: 314-961-3420, Ext. 410. Tree House Healing Ministry. Tel: 314-961-3420, Ext. 413. Theotokos Ministry, 4311 S. Compton, 63111. Tel: 314-351-6061. Center with books & tapes, prayer time, ministry times, retreats for parishes, leaders training, small faith groups, conferences, special events & days of renewal.

St. Martha's Hall, P.O. Box 4950, 63108. Tel: 314-533-1313; Fax: 314-715-6670. Provides Emergency Shelter, Counseling, Advocacy to Abused Women and their Children. Michelle Schiller-Baker, Dir. Total Assisted 340; Total Staff 10.

St. Mary's Health Center Foundation, 6420 Clayton Rd., 63117. Tel: 314-768-8067; Fax: 314-768-8011.
E-mail: Tony_Pisciotta@ssmhc
Member of SSM Health Care.

St. Patrick Center, 614 N. 11th, 63101. Tel: 314-436-1283; Fax: 314-436-5483. An Agency in Downtown St. Louis, Housing a Wide Range of Social Services for Mentally Ill and/or Chemically Dependent Homeless Persons and for Residents in the Area at Risk of Becoming Homeless. Total Assisted 10,000; Total Staff 87.

St. Paul Books and Media, 9804 Watson Rd., 63126. Tel: 314-965-3512; Fax: 314-821-8401.
E-mail: FSPLouis@aol.com
Web site: www.Pauline.org
Daughters of St. Paul. Total in Residence 5.

St. Vincent Pallotti Center for Apostolic Development, 4532 Lindell Blvd., 63108. Tel: 314-367-5500, Ext. 128; Fax: 314-367-2982.
E-mail: volsvcs@swbell.net
Web site: pallotti.cua.edu
Support for lay volunteers in full-time service. (See Catholic Charities Volunteer Department).

The Sarah Community, 1100 Bellevue Ave., 63117-1883. Tel: 314-768-1833; Fax: 314-768-1880.
E-mail: jmotzel@fsmonline.org
Purpose: provides retirement housing and services to members of religious congregations and laity. Operates the following: Anna House, a skilled nursing facility; Veronica House, a residential care facility; Naomi House, an independent living facility.

The Sarah Community Foundation, 1100 Bellevue Ave., 63117-1883. Tel: 314-768-1833; Fax: 314-768-1880.
E-mail: jmotzel@fsmonline.org
Jacqueline Motzel, Contact Person.

Seminar on Jesuit Spirituality, 3601 Lindell Blvd., 63108. Tel: 314-977-7257; Fax: 314-977-7263.
E-mail: ijs@slu.edu
Rev. John W. Padberg, S.J., Chm. Total Staff 7.

Sisters of Mercy Education System, Inc., 2039 N. Geyer Rd., 63131. Tel: 314-909-4604; Fax: 314-909-4600.
E-mail: mkoorie@corp.smhs.com
Serves the Mission of the Sisters of Mercy in its Charitable Ministry and Education Services.

Society of St. Vincent De Paul, Council of St. Louis, 4141 Forest Park Ave., 63108-2808. Tel: 314-531-2183; Fax: 314-531-6712.
Lay-based volunteer organization which provides both direct aid and program services to all eleven counties of the Archdiocese. Affiliated with 167 parishes. Total Assisted 245,000; Total Staff 29. Cars For A Cause, 4141 Forest Park Ave., 63108-2808. Tel: 800-240-4225. Car donation program whose proceeds benefit agency programs and services. Criminal Justice Ministry, 1408 S. 10th St., 63104. Tel: 314-241-8062. Serves the incarcerated, their familites, and victims through a three-fold approach of direct service, public education, and advocacy for systemic change within the judicial and corrections systems. 1st STEP Job Ministry, 4127 Forest Park Ave., 63108. Tel: 314-531-2183. Provides job acquisition skill training, assessment, and job placement assistance to applicants sponsored by Vincentians (members). Food and Fuel for Life, 4141 Forest Park Ave., 63108-2808. Tel: 314-531-2183. Archdiocesan outreach program targeting hunger and utility relief, administered by the Society of St. Vincent De Paul. Richard J. Klohr, III, Chm., Susanna Family Violence Ministry, 4141 Forest Park Ave., 63108-2808. Tel: 314-531-2183. Provides direct assistance to domestic abuse victims treated by St. Martha's Hall and Kathy J. Weinman Shelter. St. Vincent De Paul Thrift Store, 4127 Forest Park Ave., 63108. Tel: 314-531-2183. Provides household resources to members attempting to help needy individuals. Offers low-cost items for sale to the public. Proceeds benefit agency programs and services.

Society of St. Vincent DePaul, Council of the United States, 58 Progress Pkwy., 63043-3706. Tel: 314-576-3993; Fax: 314-576-6755.
E-mail: svdpus@aol.com
Web site: www.svdpuscouncil.org
Most Rev. Edwin M. Conway, D.D., Auxiliary Bishop of Chicago, Episcopal Advisor; Eugene B. Smith, Pres.; Richard E. Hennicke, Exec. Sec. & Dir., Tel: 314-576-3993; Fax: 314-576-6755.

SSM Health Businesses, 477 N. Lindbergh, 63141. Tel: 314-994-7800. Member of SSM Health Care.

SSM Health Care Corporation, 477 N. Lindbergh, 63141. Tel: 314-994-7800. Member of SSM Health Care.

SSM Health Care Portfolio Management Company, 447 N. Lindbergh Blvd., 63141. Tel: 314-994-7800. Sr. Mary Jean Ryan, F.S.M., Contact Person.

SSM Health Care St. Louis, 1173 Corporate Lake Dr., 63141. Tel: 314-989-2025. Member of SSM Health Care.

SSM Regional Health Services, 477 N. Lindbergh Blvd., 63141. Tel: 314-994-7800. Member of SSM Health Care.

SSM Rehab Foundation, 6420 Clayton Rd., Exec. Offices, 63117. Tel: 314-768-5358; Fax: 314-768-5355.
E-mail: Nicole_C_Slavens@ssmhc.com
Web site: www.ssmrehab.com
Member of SSM Health Care.

Theology Digest, 3800 Lindell Blvd., 63156-0907. Tel: 314-977-3410; Fax: 314-977-1602. Total Staff 3.

The Vincentian Press Religious Supply, 1405 S. Ninth St., 63104. Tel: 314-421-2834. Rev. Joseph E. Begue, C.M., Dir. Total Staff 3.

We & God Spirituality Center, 3601 Lindell Blvd., 63108. Tel: 314-977-2696; Fax: 314-977-7211.
E-mail: wgsc@slu.edu

Woman's Place, 2716 Sutton Blvd., 63143-3036. Tel: 314-645-4848; Fax: 314-645-4683.
E-mail: womanplace@wanlab.com
Co-Directors: Sr. Irma Kennebeck, F.S.M.; Sr. Jeanne Marie Meurer, F.S.M.
A Drop-In Center of Hospitality for Adult Women.

Women for Faith and Family, P.O. Box 8326, 63132. Tel: 314-863-8385; Fax: 314-863-5858.
E-mail: 72223.3601@compuserve.com
Web site: www.wf-f.org
Mrs. Helen Hull Hitchock, Pres.

BRIDGETON. *Boys Hope Girls Hope*, 12120 Bridgeton Square Dr., 63044. Tel: 314-298-1250; Fax: 314-298-1251.
E-mail: hope@bhgh.org
Web site: www.boyshopegirlshope.org
John L. Doman, Pres. & CEO. A College Preparatory Residential Child Care Agency Serving Abandoned, Abused and Neglected Children. Founded in 1977. Total Assisted 3,600; Total Staff 130.
With affiliated programs in: Baton Rouge; Chicago; Cincinnati; Denver; Detroit; Jacksonville; Nevada; New Orleans; New York; Northeast Ohio; Orange County, CA; Phoenix; Pittsburgh; St. Louis; San Antonio; San Francisco.

DePaul Health Center Foundation, 12303 DePaul Dr., 63044. Tel: 314-344-7477; Fax: 314-344-6840.
E-mail: cbell@ssmhc.com
Member of SSM Health Care.

Providence Ministry Corporation, 3415 Bridgeland Dr., 63044. Tel: 314-209-9181; Fax: 314-209-9207.
E-mail: jfolklcdp@juno.com
Web site: www.divineprovidence-cdpmo.org
Sr. Janel Folkl, C.D.P., Contact Person.

CADET. *Rural Parish Workers of Christ the King*, R.R. 1, Box 1667, 63630. Tel: 636-586-5171; Fax: 636-586-5918.
E-mail: rpwck@jcn.net
Web site: web.jcn.net/rpwck
Miss Natalie Villmer, Gen. Dir. A Secular Institute of the Archdiocese of St. Louis. Workers 4; Total Assisted 2,500; Total in Residence 7; Total Staff 7.

CHESTERFIELD. *Saint Louis LaSalle Leadership, Inc.*, 645 Clovertrail Dr., 63017-2612. Tel: 314-434-8789; Fax: 314-434-8789.
E-mail: stl3i@aol.com
Waldemar E. Bode, Pres.; John J. Hall, Sec.; Staunton E. Boudreau, Treas.

CRYSTAL CITY. *St. Louis Area Women Religious Collaborative Ministries*, 210 Glennon Heights Rd., 63019. Tel: 636-937-6206; Fax: 636-937-7627. Sr. Margaret Mary Moore, O.S.U., Contact Person.

Ursuline Sisters Trust Fund, 210 Glennon Heights Rd., 63019. Tel: 636-937-6206; Fax: 636-937-7627. Sr. Margaret Mary Moore, O.S.U., Contact Person.

EARTH CITY. *Congregation of the Mission International Fund*, 13663 Rider Tr. N., 63045-1512. Tel: 314-344-1184; Fax: 314-344-2989.
E-mail: cmstlouis@aol.com
Bro. F. Joseph Hess, C.M.

Lazarist Trust Fund, 13663 Rider Tr. N., 63045-1512. Tel: 314-344-1184; Fax: 314-344-2989.
E-mail: cmstlouis@aol.com

EUREKA. *Providence Trust*, Our Lady of the Angels Monastery, St. Joseph Rd., 63025; Fax: 636-938-4960.
E-mail: shrinelolc@aol.com
Web site: www.blackmadonnashrine.org
Purpose: To support the religious and charitable purposes of the Franciscan Missionary Brothers of the Sacred Heart.

FLORISSANT. *Marygrove, Inc.*, 2705 Mullanphy, 63031. Tel: 314-837-1702; Fax: 314-830-6263.
E-mail: mgrove@swb.net
Total Assisted 91; Total Staff 10.

Pope John Paul II Apartments, Inc., 6325 Waterways Dr., 63033. Tel: 314-653-0400; Fax: 314-653-2840. Purpose: to provide facilities and services specifically designed to meet the physical, social, spiritual and psychological needs of elderly persons.

GRANITE CITY, IL. *Women of Providence in Collaboration*, 3341 Village Ln., 62040. Sr. Barbara McMullen, C.D.P., Contact Person.

KIRKWOOD. *St. Joseph Hospital of Kirkwood Foundation.* 525 Couch Ave., St. Louis, 63122. Tel: 314-966-1644.
E-mail: mbcook@ssmhc.com
Member of SSM Health Care.

LIGUORI. *Redemptorist Fathers dba Liguori Publications,* One Liguori Dr., 63057. Tel: 636-464-2500; Fax: 636-464-8449.
E-mail: hgrile@liguori.org
Web site: www.liguori.org
Rev. Harry A. Grile, C.SS.R.

O'FALLON. *Centers for Professional and Pastoral Services,* 204 N. Main St., 63366. Tel: 636-240-6010; Fax: 636-272-5031.
E-mail: ruthk@cpps-ofallon.org
Sponsored by Sisters of the Most Precious Blood of O'Fallon, MO. Sr. Susan Borgel, C.PP.S. Centers 4; Total Assisted 435; Total Staff 4.

Charitable Trust, Sisters of the Most Precious Blood of O'Fallon, MO, 204 N. Main St., 63366-2299. Tel: 636-240-6010; Fax: 636-272-5031.
E-mail: ginnyj@cpps-ofallon.org
Web site: www.cpps-ofallon.org
Trust fund for support of retired Sisters of the Most Precious Blood.

St. Dominic Endowment Fund, St. Dominic High School, 31 St. Dominic Dr., 63366. Tel: 314-240-8303; Fax: 314-240-9884.
E-mail: mainoffice@stdominichs.org
Web site: www.stdominichs.org
Sr. Mary H. Bender, S.S.N.D., Treas.

PERRYVILLE. *Association of the Miraculous Medal,* 1811 W. St. Joseph St., 63775. Tel: 573-547-8343; Fax: 573-547-1389.
E-mail: amm1@amm.org
Web site: www.amm.org
Rev. Charles F. Shelby, C.M., Pres.

Catholic Home Study Service, P.O. Box 363, 63775. Tel: 573-547-4084; Fax: 573-547-4085.
E-mail: chss@ldd.net
Web site: http://www.amm.org/chss.htm
Rev. Oscar Lukefahr, C.M., Dir.
Offers free correspondence courses on the Catholic Faith.

Ladies of Charity of St. Vincent de Paul Parish, 1010 Rosati Ct., 63775. Tel: 573-547-4591. Affiliate with Ladies of Charity of the United States & the Assoc. of Intl. Charities of St. Vincent de Paul. Dorothy Barry, Pres. Total Assisted 600; Total Staff 25.

St. Vincent De Paul Educational Foundation Perryville, 1010 A Rosati Ct., 63775. Tel: 573-547-4591. Develops, Promotes and Sustains Catholic Education in Perry County. Rev. Kevin P. Fausz, C.M., Mod.

PEVELY. *Vision of Peace Ministries,* Abby Ln., P.O. Box 69, 63070. Tel: 636-475-3697; Fax: 636-475-3697.
E-mail: visofpeace@juno.com
Web site: www.dogbird.com/vision_of_peace
Mrs. James Ruth Muskopf. Total in Residence 2; Total Staff 2.

ST. CHARLES. *Academy of the Sacred Heart of St. Charles, Missouri Endowment Trust Fund,* 619 N. 2nd St., 63301. Tel: 636-946-5632.

Duchesne High School Endowment Fund Inc., 2550 Elm St., 63301. Tel: 636-946-6767; Fax: 636-946-6267.
E-mail: archstl82@impresso.com
Web site: www.duchesne-hs.org
Dr. Daniel Matusiak, Admin. Receives Bequests and Gifts from Various Donors for the Express Purpose of Aiding and Benefitting Duchesne High School, St. Charles, and by Investment and Use of Such Bequests and Gifts and Income therefrom Aids and Benefits the High School in Fulfilling its Educational Purposes.

St. Joseph Health Center and St. Joseph Hospital West Foundation, 300 First Capitol Dr., 63301. Tel: 314-947-5612; Fax: 314-947-5090. Member of SSM Health Care.

RELIGIOUS INSTITUTES OF MEN REPRESENTED IN THE ARCHDIOCESE

For further details refer to the corresponding bracketed number in the Religious Institutes of Men or Women section.

[0120]—*Alexian Brothers.* (Chicago).—C.F.A.
[0140]—*The Augustinians. (Prov. of Our Mother of Good Counsel).*—O.S.A.
[0200]—*Benedictine Monks. (English, Swiss American Congregation).*—O.S.B.
[]—*Brothers of St. Charles Lawanga.*—B.S.C.L.
[0330]—*Brothers of the Christian Schools. (St. Louis Prov.).*—F.S.C.
[0600]—*Brothers of the Congregation of Holy Cross.*—C.S.C.
[0470]—*The Capuchin Friars.* (Kansas City, MO).—O.F.M.Cap.
[]—*Claretian Missionaries.*—C.M.F.
[1330]—*Congregation of the Mission. (Midwest Prov.).*—C.M.
[0630]—*Congregation of the Missionaries of the Holy Family.* (Europe).—M.S.F.
[1000]—*Congregation of the Passion. (Western Prov. of Holy Cross).*—M.S.F.
[1130]—*Congregation of the Priests of the Sacred Heart.*—S.C.J.
[1080]—*Congregation of the Resurrection.* (Rome, Italy).—C.R.
[0480]—*Conventual Franciscans. (Our Lady of Consolation Prov.).*—O.F.M.Conv.
[0520]—*Franciscan Friars. (Croatian Franciscan Commissariat, Sacred Heart Prov.).*—O.F.M.
[0540]—*Franciscan Missionary Brothers of the Sacred Heart of Jesus.* (Eureka, MO).—O.S.F.
[]—*Franciscans.*—O.F.M.
[0690]—*Jesuit Fathers and Brothers.* (Missouri Prov.).—S.J.
[0800]—*Maryknoll.*—M.M.
[0720]—*The Missionaries of Our Lady of La Salette.*—M.S.
[0870]—*Monfort Missionaries.*—S.M.M.
[0910]—*Oblates of Mary Immaculate.*—O.M.I.
[0430]—*Order of Preachers.*—O.P.
[0610]—*Priests of the Congregation of Holy Cross.*—C.S.C.
[1070]—*Redemptorist Fathers.* (St. Louis Prov.).—C.SS.R.
[1230]—*Servants of the Paraclete.*—s.P.
[1240]—*Servites.* (Chicago).—O.S.M.
[]—*Society of Christ.*—S.Ch.
[0760]—*Society of Mary.* (St. Louis Prov.).—S.M.
[0420]—*Society of the Divine Word.* (Northern Prov.).—S.V.D.
[]—*Society of the Precious Blood.*—C.PP.S.
[]—*Sons of Our Mother.*—S.M.P.

RELIGIOUS INSTITUTES OF WOMEN REPRESENTED IN THE ARCHDIOCESE

[0100]—*Adorers of the Blood of Christ.* (Ruma, IL; Wichita, KS).—A.S.C.
[]—*Adorers of the Blood of Christ.* (Columbia).—A.S.C.
[0130]—*Apostles of the Sacred Heart of Jesus.*—A.S.C.J.
[0160]—*Augustinian Cloistered Nuns.*—O.S.A.
[0230]—*Benedictine Sisters of Pontifical Jurisdiction.* (Atchison; Columbia; Fort Smith; Olivetan; Yankton).—O.S.B.
[0360]—*Carmelite Sisters of the Divine Heart of Jesus.* (Carmel).—D.C.J.
[3110]—*Congregation of Our Lady of the Retreat in the Cenacle.*—R.C.
[0220]—*Congregation of the Benedictine Sisters of Perpetual Adoration of Pontifical Jurisdiction.*—O.S.B.
[0460]—*Congregation of the Sisters of Charity of the Incarnate Word.*—C.C.V.I.
[1830]—*Contemplatives of the Good Shepherd.*—C.G.S.
[]—*Daughters of Calvary.*—C.M.F.C.
[0760]—*Daughters of Charity of St. Vincent de Paul.*—D.C.
[]—*Daughters of Our Mother of Peace.*—S.M.P.
[0810]—*Daughters of the Heart of Mary.*—D.H.M.
[0420]—*Discalced Carmelite Nuns.*—O.C.D.
[1070-01]—*Dominican Sisters.*—O.P.
[1070-11]—*Dominican Sisters.* (Sparkill).—O.P.
[1070-13]—*Dominican Sisters.* (Akron).—O.P.
[1070-28]—*Dominican Sisters.* (Akron).—O.P.
[1070-05]—*Dominican Sisters.* (Amityville, NY).—O.P.
[1070-24]—*Dominican Sisters.* (Great Bend, KS).—O.P.
[1070-19]—*Dominican Sisters.* (Houston, TX).—O.P.
[1070-09]—*Dominican Sisters.* (Racine, WI).—O.P.
[1070-03]—*Dominican Sisters.* (Sinsinawa, WI).—O.P.
[]—*Dominican Sisters of Hope.*—O.P.
[]—*Dominican Sisters of St. Catherine of Siena, KY.*—O.P.
[]—*Eucharist Missionaries of St. Theresa.*—M.E.S.T.
[1370]—*Franciscan Missionaries of Mary.*—F.M.M.
[]—*Franciscan Sisters.* (Oldenburg, IN).—O.S.F.
[]—*Franciscan Sisters.* (Wheaton).—O.S.F.
[1310]—*Franciscan Sisters of Little Falls, Minnesota.*—O.S.F.
[1415]—*Franciscan Sisters of Mary.*—F.S.M.
[]—*Franciscan Sisters of Mary Immaculate.*—O.S.F.
[1430]—*Franciscan Sisters of Our Lady of Perpetual Help.*—O.S.F.
[2340]—*Little Sisters of the Poor.*—L.S.P.
[2490]—*Medical Mission Sisters.*—M.M.S.
[2710]—*Missionaries of Charity.*—M.C.
[0390]—*Missionary Carmelites of St. Teresa.*—C.M.S.T.
[3990]—*Missionary Sisters of St. Peter Claver.*—S.S.P.C.
[3760]—*Order of St. Clare.*—O.S.C.
[2010]—*Order of the Most Holy Redeemer.*—O.SS.R.
[0950]—*Pius Society Daughters of St. Paul.*—F.S.P.
[3170]—*Religious of the Passion of Jesus Christ.*—C.P.
[3465]—*Religious of the Sacred Heart of Mary.*—R.S.H.M.
[]—*Rural Parish Workers of Christ the King.*—R.P.W.C.
[2970]—*School Sisters of Notre Dame.*—S.S.N.D.
[]—*School Sisters of St. Francis.* (Milwaukee, WI).—O.S.F.
[0630]—*Sisters of Charity of St. Vincent de Paul.*—S.V.Z.
[0430]—*Sisters of Charity of the Blessed Virgin Mary.*—B.V.M.
[]—*Sisters of Charity of the Incarnate Word.* (San Antonio, TX).—C.C.V.I.
[0660]—*Sisters of Christian Charity.*—S.C.C.
[]—*Sisters of Christian Community.*—S.F.C.C.
[0990]—*Sisters of Divine Providence.*—C.D.P.
[2360]—*Sisters of Loretto at the Foot of the Cross.* (St. Louis Prov.).—S.L.
[2570]—*Sisters of Mercy.*—R.S.M.
[2580]—*Sisters of Mercy of the Americas.*—R.S.M.
[2630]—*Sisters of Mercy of the Holy Cross.*—S.C.S.C.
[3000]—*Sisters of Notre Dame de Namur.*—S.N.D.deN.
[1540]—*Sisters of Saint Francis, Clinton, Iowa.*—O.S.F.
[1600]—*Sisters of St. Francis of the Martyr St. George.*—O.S.F.
[3830]—*Sisters of St. Joseph.*—C.S.J.
[1830]—*Sisters of the Good Shepherd.*—R.G.S.-C.G.S.
[2350]—*Sisters of the Living Word.*—S.L.W.
[3270]—*Sisters of the Most Precious Blood.* (O'Fallon, MO).—C.PP.S.
[3150]—*Sisters of the Pallottine Missionary Society.*—S.A.C.
[3320]—*Sisters of the Presentation of the Blessed Virgin.*—P.V.B.M.
[3540]—*Sisters Servants of the Holy Spirit of Perpetual Adoration.*—S.Sp.S.deA.P.
[2150]—*Sisters, Servants of the Immaculate Heart of Mary.*—I.H.M.
[1890]—*Society of Helpers of the Holy Souls.*—S.H.
[4070]—*Society of the Sacred Heart.*—R.S.C.J.
[4110]—*Ursuline Nuns.*—O.S.U.
[4120-05]—*Ursuline Nuns, of the Congregation of Paris.* (Maple Mount).—O.S.U.
[4190]—*Visitation Nuns.*—V.H.M.

ARCHDIOCESAN CEMETERIES

ST. LOUIS. *Calvary,* 5239 W. Florissant Ave., 63115. Tel: 314-381-1313.

Resurrection, 6901 Mackenzie Rd., 63123. Tel: 314-352-5300.

SS. Peter and Paul, 7030 Gravois Ave., 63116. Tel: 314-352-5300.

CREVE COEUR. *St. Monica,* Olive Street Rd., 63141. Tel: 314-352-5300.

DARDENNE. *Our Lady of the Miraculous Medal,* Freymuth & Orf Rd., 63366. Tel: 314-381-1313.

FLORISSANT. *Sacred Heart,* Graham Rd., 63033. Tel: 314-381-1313.

GLENCOE. *Holy Cross,* 16200 Manchester Rd., 63038. Tel: 314-352-5300.

HAZELWOOD. *St. Ferdinand,* Graham Rd., 63042. Tel: 314-381-1313.

KIRKWOOD. *St. Peter,* Geyer & W. Monroe Ave., 63122. Tel: 314-381-1313.

LEMAY. *Mount Olive,* 3906 Mount Olive St., 63125. Tel: 314-352-5300.

ST. CHARLES. *St. Charles Borromeo,* Randolph St., 63301. Tel: 314-381-1313.

NECROLOGY

† Boul, Walter M., (Retired). —Died July 14, 2000.

† Hesseldenz, Rev. Msgr. Clarence H., (Retired). —Died Oct. 25, 1999.

† Huhn, Bernard F., (Retired). —Died March 7, 2000.

† Lippert, Alexander W., Ozora, MO Sacred Heart. —Died April 16, 2000.

† Nienhaus, Bernard J., Hawk Point, MO St. Mary. —Died Nov. 8, 2000.

† Obmann, Rev. Msgr. Russell J., (Retired). —Died Sept. 21, 2000.

† Schilly, Rev. Msgr. Adolph M., (Retired). —Died Jan. 12, 2000.

† Sullivan, Rev. Msgr. Donald E., (Retired). —Died July 1, 2000.

Archdiocese of St. Paul and Minneapolis

(Archidioecesis Paulopolitana et Minneapolitana)

Most Reverend

HARRY J. FLYNN, D.D.

Archbishop of Saint Paul and Minneapolis; ordained May 28, 1960; appointed Coadjutor of Lafayette April 19, 1986; consecrated June 24, 1986; appointed Bishop of Lafayette May 13, 1989; appointed Coadjutor Archbishop of Saint Paul and Minneapolis February 22, 1994; appointed Archbishop of Saint Paul and Minneapolis September 8, 1995.

Most Reverend

FREDERICK F. CAMPBELL, D.D.

Auxiliary Bishop of Saint Paul and Minneapolis; ordained May 31, 1980; appointed Titular Bishop of Afufenia and Auxiliary Bishop of St. Paul and Minneapolis March 2, 1999; consecrated May 14, 1999. 226 Summit Ave., St. Paul, MN, 55102. Tel.: 651-291-4400.

Most Reverend

J. RICHARD HAM, M.M., D.D.

Retired Auxiliary Bishop of Saint Paul and Minneapolis; ordained June 12, 1948; appointed Titular Bishop of Putzia of Numidia and Auxiliary Bishop of Guatemala November 28, 1967; consecrated January 6, 1968; appointed Auxiliary Bishop of Saint Paul and Minneapolis October 7, 1980; resigned October 30, 1990. *Res., St. Teresa Residence, Maryknoll, NY, 10545.*

Most Reverend

JOHN R. ROACH, D.D.

Retired Archbishop of Saint Paul and Minneapolis; ordained June 8, 1946; appointed Titular Bishop of Cenae and Auxiliary Bishop of Saint Paul and Minneapolis July 12, 1971; consecrated September 8, 1971; appointed Archbishop of Saint Paul and Minneapolis May 21, 1975; installed July 16, 1975; resigned September 8, 1995. *Office: 226 Summit Ave., St. Paul, MN, 55102.* Tel.: 651-291-4400.

Most Reverend

RICHARD E. PATES

Auxiliary Bishop of Saint Paul and Minneapolis; ordained December 20, 1968; appointed Titular Bishop of Suacia and Auxiliary Bishop of Saint Paul and Minneapolis December 22, 2000; ordained March 26, 2001. *2441 Ventura Dr., Woodbury, MN, 55125-3930.*

DIOCESE ESTABLISHED, JULY 19, 1850. ARCHDIOCESE ESTABLISHED, MAY 4, 1888.

Square Miles 6,187.

Comprises the following twelve Counties of the State of Minnesota: Ramsey, Hennepin, Anoka, Carver, Chisago, Dakota, Goodhue, Le Sueur, Rice, Scott, Washington and Wright.

Corporate Title: The Archdiocese of Saint Paul and Minneapolis.

For legal titles of parishes and archdiocesan institutions, consult the Chancery.

Chancery: 226 Summit Ave., St. Paul, MN, 55102. Tel.: 651-291-4400; Fax: 651-290-1629.

Web site address: www.archspm.org

E-mail address: archcom@archspm

STATISTICAL OVERVIEW

Personnel	
Archbishop	1
Retired Archbishops	1
Auxiliary Bishops	2
Retired Bishop	1
Priests: Diocesan Active in Diocese	226
Priests: Active Outside Diocese	11
Priests: Diocesan in Foreign Missions	3
Priests: Retired, Sick or Absent	103
Number of Diocesan Priests	343
Religious Priests in Diocese	160
Extern Priests in Diocese	42
Ordinations:	
Diocesan Priests	8
Permanent Deacons	12
Permanent Deacons in Diocese	173
Total Brothers	52
Total Sisters	1,090
Parishes	
Parishes	222
With Resident Pastor:	
Resident Diocesan Priests	177
Resident Religious Priests	29
Without Resident Pastor:	
Administered by Priests	15
Administered by Deacons	1
Missions	5
Pastoral Centers	4
Professional Ministry Personnel:	
Brothers	1
Sisters	70
Lay Ministers	620
Welfare	
Catholic Hospitals	3
Total Assisted	94,685
Homes for the Aged	4
Total Assisted	1,025
Residential Care of Children	1
Total Assisted	4,100
Specialized Homes	4
Special Centers for Social Services	5
Educational	
Seminaries, Diocesan	2
Students from This Diocese	69
Students from Other Diocese	111
Total Seminarians	69
Colleges and Universities	3
Total Students	17,305
High Schools, Diocesan and Parish	10
Total Students	7,228
High Schools, Private	2
Total Students	429
Elementary Schools, Diocesan and Parish	91
Total Students	28,017
Elementary Schools, Private	1
Total Students	264
Catechesis/Religious Education:	
Elementary Students	65,422
Total Students Under Catholic Instruction	118,734
Teachers in the Diocese:	
Priests	22
Brothers	14
Sisters	57
Lay Teachers	2,031
Vital Statistics	
Receptions into the Church:	
Infant Baptism Totals	11,202
Adult Baptism Totals	480
Received into Full Communion	1,702
First Communions	10,869
Confirmations	7,887
Marriages:	
Catholic	2,372
Interfaith	1,318
Total Marriages	3,690
Deaths	4,967
Total Catholic Population	769,135
Total Population	2,831,931

Former Bishops—Rt. Rev. JOSEPH CRETIN, D.D., cons. Jan. 26, 1851; died Feb. 22, 1857.—Most Rev. THOMAS L. GRACE, O.P., D.D., cons. July 24, 1859; resigned July 31, 1884; named Titular Bishop of Menith, and later, Titular Archbishop of Siunia; died Feb. 22, 1897.—Most Rev. JOHN IRELAND, D.D., cons. Dec. 21, 1875; Bishop of Maronea, and Coadjutor to.—Most Rev. THOMAS L. GRACE, O.P., D.D., succeeded to the See of St. Paul, July 31, 1884; appt. Archbishop, May 15, 1888; died Sept. 25, 1918.—Most Rev. AUSTIN DOWLING, D.D., Archbishop of St. Paul; ord. June 24, 1891; appt. Bishop of Des Moines, Iowa, Jan. 31, 1912; cons. April 25, 1912 Nominated Archbishop of St. Paul, Feb. 1, 1919; died Nov. 29, 1930.—Most Rev. JOHN GREGORY MURRAY, S.T.D., ord. April 14, 1900; appt. Titular Bishop of Flavias, Auxiliary to the Bishop of Hartford, Nov. 15, 1919; cons. April 28, 1920; transferred to the Diocese of Portland, May 29, 1925; appt. Archbishop of St. Paul, Oct. 29, 1931; died Oct. 11, 1956.—Most Rev. WILLIAM O. BRADY, D.D., Archbishop of St. Paul; ord. Dec. 21, 1923; appt. Bishop of Sioux Falls, June 10, 1939; cons. Aug. 24, 1939; appt. Titular Archbishop of Selymbria and Coadjutor "cum jure successionis" of St. Paul, June 16, 1956; succeeded to See, Oct. 11, 1956; died Oct. 1, 1961.—Most Rev. LEO C. BYRNE, D.D., Coadjutor Archbishop "cum jure successionis" of Saint Paul and Minneapolis; ord. June 10, 1933; appt. titular Bishop of Sabidia and Auxiliary of St. Louis, May 21, 1954; cons. June 29, 1954; transferred to Wichita, "cum jure successionis" 1961; appt. Apostolic Administrator of Wichita, Feb. 25, 1963; promoted to St. Paul and Minneapolis, Aug. 2, 1967; died Oct. 21, 1974.—Most Rev. LEO BINZ, D.D., ord. March 15, 1924; appt. Titular Bishop of Pinara and Coadjutor Bishop of Winona, Nov. 21, 1942; cons. Dec. 21, 1942; Titular Archbishop of Silyum and Coadjutor to the Archbishop of Dubuque "cum jure successionis," Oct. 15, 1949; Archbishop of Dubuque, Dec. 2, 1954; appt. Archbishop of Saint Paul, Dec. 16, 1961; resigned May 21, 1975; died Oct. 9, 1979.—Most Rev. JOHN R. ROACH, D.D., Archbishop of St. Paul and Minneapolis; ord. June 8, 1946; appt. Titular Bishop of Cenae and Auxiliary Bishop of St. Paul and Minneapolis, July 12, 1971; cons. Sept. 8, 1971; appt. Archbishop of St. Paul and Minneapolis, May 21, 1975; resigned Sept. 8, 1995.

Chancery—226 Summit Ave., St. Paul, 55102. Tel: 651-291-4400; Fax: 651-290-1629. Office Hours: Mon.-Fri. 9-5 All Official business should be directed to this office.

Vicar General and Moderator of the Curia—Rev. KEVIN M. MCDONOUGH, J.C.D.

Chancellor for Civil Affairs—Mr. WILLIAM S. FALLON, J.D.
Chancellor for Canonical Affairs—Sr. M. DOMINICA BRENNAN, O.P., J.C.L.
Vice Chancellor—Rev. AUSTIN T. WARD.
Assistant Chancellor—Bro. VINCENT H. CHAMPINE, O.P.
Delegate for Marriage Dispensations—Bro. VINCENT H. CHAMPINE, O.P.
Episcopal Vicars—
For Eastern Vicariate—Rev. KEVIN M. MCDONOUGH, J.C.D.
For Western Vicariate—Vacant.
For Southern Vicariate—Most Rev. HARRY J. FLYNN.
For Hispanic Vicariate—Vacant.
For Canonical Affairs—Rev. KEVIN M. MCDONOUGH, J.C.D.
For African-American Catholics—Rev. KEVIN M. MCDONOUGH, J.C.D.
For Retired Priests—Rev. CHARLES M. EGGERT.
For Marriages—Revs. KEVIN M. MCDONOUGH, J.C.D.; AUSTIN T. WARD.
Co-Vicars for Religious—Sr. DOMINICA BRENNAN, O.P.; Sr. FRAN DONNELLY, B.V.M.
Archdiocesan Divisions—
Administration and Financial Services—Rev. AUSTIN T. WARD, Dir.
Christian Formation and Education—THOMAS MCCARVER, Dir.
Ministry Personnel—Sr. FRAN DONNELLY, B.V.M., Dir.
Outreach—Mrs. JANET KROCHESKI, Dir.
Community Services—Rev. LARRY J. SNYDER, Dir.
Resource Development—JAMES MULLIN, Dir.
Due Process Dir.—Sr. M. DOMINICA BRENNAN, O.P., J.C.L.
Administrative Asst. to the Vicar General and to the Moderator of the Curia—Mrs. JUDY DELANEY.
Special Asst. to Archbishop Flynn—Sr. ANN GANLEY, S.S.N.D.
Archivist—Mr. STEVEN T. GRANGER; Mr. PATRICK ANZELC, Asst.
Controller—Mr. THOMAS J. BAKER.
Assistant Controller—Mr. SCOTT J. DOMEIER.
Department of Human Resources, Pension Plan, General Insurance Program and Personnel Director—Vacant.
Metropolitan Tribunal—*328 W. Kellogg Blvd., St. Paul, 55102-1997.* Tel: 651-291-4466.
Judicial Vicar—Rev. JOSEPH L. WAJDA, J.C.L.
Adjutant Judicial Vicars—Revs. RONALD J. BOWERS, J.C.D; KEVIN M. MCDONOUGH, J.C.D.
Associate Judges—Rev. Msgr. ELLSWORTH KNEAL, J.C.D.; Revs. LEO J. TIBESAR, M.A.; MICHAEL V. TEGEDER; THOMAS J. WALKER, J.D.; Deacon PAUL W. CARLSON; Sr. DOMINICA BRENNAN, O.P., J.C.L.; Mrs. RUTH DUHAMEL, J.C.L.; Mrs. MARILIES YOUNG, J.U.D; Mr. MICHAEL D. REISBIG, J.D.; Ms. M. JEAN KWIATOWSKI, J.C.L.
Defenders of the Bond—Revs. JEROME W. FEHN; JAMES P. BURNS; Bro. VINCENT H. CHAMPINE, O.P.
Auditors—Deacon GERALD A. SCHERKENBACH, M.A.; Mr. MERLIN N. ROERS, M.Div.; Mr. EUGENE E. BURKE, M.A.
Ecclesiastical Notaries—Mrs. LINDA BOTKIN; Mrs. MARJE BRUSTAD; Ms. LOIS ECKSTEIN; Mrs. MICHELLE GERLACH; Ms. EILEEN PEARSON.
Archdiocesan Consultors—Most Rev. FREDERICK F. CAMPBELL; Revs. SEBASTIEN BAKATU, C.I.C.M.; KEVIN M. MCDONOUGH, J.C.D.; JOHN P. ECHERT; CHARLES LACHOWITZER; RICHARD J. MAHONEY; MICHAEL C. SKLUZACEK; GREGORY T. WELCH.
Presbyteral Council—Most Rev. HARRY J. FLYNN; Revs. GREGORY T. WELCH, Exec. Dir. JONATHAN P. SHELLEY; MICHAEL L. PAPESH; JOSEPH G. GALLATIN; CHARLES LACHOWITZER; JAMES M. GROGAN; RICHARD J. MAHONEY; THOMAS J. GARVEY; ROBERT E. JOHNSON; PATRICK J. HIPWELL; GREGORY TOLAAS; ROBERT M. SCHWARTZ; BRADLEY C. BALDWIN, T.O.R.; LEO J. TIBESAR; A. MICHAEL SAUBER; JAMES C. NOTEBAART; JOHN M. SIEBENALER; JOHN P. ECHERT; SEBASTIEN BAKATU, C.I.C.M.; PETER E. FELDMEIER; PAUL A. LAFONTAINE; Rev. Msgr. STANLEY R. SRNEC; Revs. BRIAN J. FIER; MICHAEL C. SKLUZACEK.
Provincial Councilors—Revs. STEVEN HENRICH, O.S.C.; MICHAEL VAN SLOUN, O.S.C.; TIMOTHY CONLON, O.S.C.
Corporate Board—Most Rev. HARRY J. FLYNN; Most Rev. RICHARD E. PATES; Revs. KEVIN M. MCDONOUGH, J.C.D.; AUSTIN T. WARD; THOMAS HOLLORAN; MARY FREY; CHERYL O'SHAUGHNESSY; JERRY HALLORAN; WILLIAM S. FALLON.
Censores Librorum—Rev. GEORGE A. WELZBACHER, Chm. Bd., *Church of St. Nicholas, P.O. Box 9, New Market, 55054.* Rev. Msgr. RICHARD J. SCHULER; Revs. DENNIS J. DEASE; CHARLES L. FROEHLE; JAMES A. LAVIN; DAVID W. SMITH; ARTHUR L. KENNEDY; MARK B. DOSH; JOSEPH R. JOHNSON; Dr. DON J. BRIEL.

Archdiocesan Offices and Directors

Advisory Board on Natural Family Planning—Deacon JAMES F. BASKFIELD, Liaison, *328 W. Kellogg Blvd., St. Paul, 55102.* Tel: 612-291-4438.
Allocations Committee—Rev. AUSTIN T. WARD, Dir., *226 Summit Ave., St. Paul, 55102.* Tel: 612-291-4400.
Archbishop Ireland Educational Fund, Inc.—Most Rev. HARRY J. FLYNN, D.D., Pres., *226 Summit Ave., St. Paul, 55102.*
Archdiocesan AIDS Ministry Office—Sr. JOANNE LUCID, B.V.M., Dir., *Riverside Medical Center, Riverside at 25th Ave. S., Minneapolis, 55454.* Tel: 612-672-4345.
Archdiocesan Council of Catholic Women—Rev. Msgr. JAMES D. HABIGER, Moderator; ELAINE MONITOR, Pres., *328 W. Kellogg Blvd., St. Paul, 55102.* Tel: 651-291-4545.
Archdiocesan Finance Council—Mr. ROBERT REGAN, Chm., *7600 Parklawn Ave., Ste. 300, Edina, 55435.* Tel: 612-835-1185.
Building Commission—Rev. AUSTIN T. WARD, Coord., *226 Summit Ave., St. Paul, 55102.*
Campus Ministry—Rev. JEFFREY H. HUARD, Dir., *University of St. Thomas, 2115 Summit Ave., P.O. Box 5028, St. Paul, 55105.*
Catholic Center for the Separated and Divorced—STEVE KING, Dir., *215 Old Sixth St., St. Paul, 55102.* Tel: 651-222-3001.
Catholic Charities—Rev. LARRY SNYDER, Dir., *1200 2nd Ave., S., Minneapolis, 55403.* Tel: 612-664-8500.
Catholic Commission on Social Justice—JULIE SMENDZIOL-O'BRIEN, Chm. RON KRIETEMEYER, Dir., *328 W. Kellogg Blvd., St. Paul, 55102.* Tel: 651-291-4477.
Catholic Committee on Scouting—Deacon DONALD RINKENBERGER, Church of St. Joseph the Worker: *Maple Grove, 55369.* Tel: 612-559-9178.
Catholic Education and Formation Ministries—THOMAS MCCARVER, Dir., *328 W. Kellogg Blvd., St. Paul, 55102.* Tel: 651-291-4500.
Cemeteries—Mr. JOHN CHEREK, Dir., *400 Selby Ave., St. Paul, 55102.* Tel: 651-228-9991.
Center for Ministry—Sr. FRAN DONNELLY, B.V.M., Dir., *244 Dayton Ave., St. Paul, 55102.* Tel: 651-290-1616.
Charismatic Renewal Office—COLIN LAVERGNE, Dir., *3927 E. Lake, Minneapolis, 55406.* Tel: 612-721-2543.
Christ Child Services, Inc.—*226 Summit Ave., St. Paul, 55102.* Tel: 612-291-4400.
Christian Sharing Fund—SARA MCGRATH JOHNSON, *328 W. Kellogg Blvd., St. Paul, 55102.* Tel: 651-291-4477.
Commission on Bio-Medical Ethics—Dr. RICHARD BERQUIST, Chm., *University of St. Thomas, 2115 Summit Ave., St. Paul, 55105.* Tel: 651-647-5000.
Commission on Chemical Health—Rev. BRYAN O'ROURKE, Chm., *Church of St. Mary of the Lake, 105 N. Forestview Ln., Plymouth, 55441.* Tel: 612-545-1447.
Commission on Women—PHYLLIS A. WILLERSCHEIDT, Exec. Coord., *328 W. Kellogg Blvd., St. Paul, 55102.* Tel: 651-291-4495.
Commission for Black Catholics—HERBERT GIBBS, Chm.; Sr. SHARON M. HOWELL, C.S.J., Exec. Sec., *2115 Summit Ave., Mail #5006, St. Paul, 55105.* Tel: 651-962-6462.
Commission for Ecumenism and Interreligious Affairs—Rev. ARTHUR L. KENNEDY, Chm., *University of St. Thomas, 2115 Summit Ave., P.O. Box 5022, St. Paul, 55105.* Tel: 651-647-5300.
Commission on Pastoral Health Care—Sr. MARY HEINEN, C.S.J., Chm., *1884 Randolph Ave., St. Paul, 55105.* Tel: 651-690-7028.
Commission on Ministry—CHRIS ZIRKER, Chm., *244 Dayton Ave., St. Paul, 55102.* Tel: 651-290-1616.
Common Bond Communities—Mr. JOSEPH A.L. ERRIGO, JR., Pres., *328 W. Kellogg Blvd., St.Paul, 55102.* Tel: 651-291-1750.
Communications Office—NICOLE SELLECK, Dir., *226 Summit Ave., St. Paul, 55102.* Tel: 651-291-4411.
Council of Religious—Sr. FRAN DONNELLY, B.V.M., Ex Officio, *244 Dayton Ave., St. Paul, 55102.* Tel: 651-290-1616.
Cursillo—Rev. EUGENE POULIOT, Spiritual Advisor. Lay Directors: ED LUCAS; BETTY LUCAS, *6534 Aster Ter., Excelsior, 55331.* Tel: 612-474-5075.
Holy Childhood, Pontifical Association, Society for the Propagation of the Faith—ALICIA KELLY, Dir., *328 W. Kellogg Blvd., St. Paul, 55102.*
Institute of Christian Life & Ministry—Mr. SCOTT HIPPERT, Exec. Coord., *2260 Summit Ave., St. Paul, 55104.* Tel: 651-962-6876.
Legion of Mary—St. Paul Curia and Comitium, Rev. Msgr. RICHARD J. SCHULER, *548 Lafond Ave., St. Paul, 55103.* Tel: 651-293-1710. North Minneapolis Curia, Rev. FRANCIS L. FRIED, *1315 2nd St., N.E., Minneapolis, 55413.* Tel: 612-379-9736. South Minneapolis Curia, Rev. MICHAEL SAUBER, *535 S. Lewis St., Shakopee, 55379.* Tel: 612-445-1319.
Marriage Encounter—JEANNE STOESSEL, Exec. Dir., *953 Lake Dr., St. Paul, 55120.* Tel: 651-454-3238.
Marriage and Family Life Office—KATHLEEN M. LAIRD, Dir., *328 W. Kellogg Blvd., St. Paul, 55102.* Tel: 651-291-4438.
Migration and Refugee Services—Mr. THOMAS KOSEL, Admin., *215 Old Sixth St., St. Paul, 55102.* Tel: 651-222-3001.
Ministry to Hmong—Rev. ROBERT B. WELLISCH; Deacon VA THAI LO, *Twin Cities Hmong Catholic Community, 68 W. Exchange St., St. Paul, 55102.* Tel: 651-771-4644.
Ministry to Koreans—Rev. ANDREW LIM, *Church of St. Andrew Kim, 1449 Cleveland Ave., St. Paul, 55108.* Tel: 651-642-9822.
Ministry to Vietnamese—Rev. MATTHIAS CHUONG, C.M.C., *Church of St. Joseph Hien, 1800 Dupont Ave. N., Minneapolis, 55411.* Tel: 612-522-5006.
Nazareth Hall College and Seminary, Inc.—Most Rev. HARRY J. FLYNN, D.D., Pres.
Newman Centers—Rev. JOHN J. BEHNKE, C.S.P., Dir., *1201 5th St., S.E., Minneapolis, 55414.* Tel: 612-331-7941. Macalester College; Rev. PETER ETZEL, S.J., Campus Min., *1550 Summit Ave., St. Paul, 55105.* Tel: 651-644-9041.
Newspaper—*"The Catholic Spirit"*; Mr. ROBERT ZYSKOWSKI, Assoc. Publisher; Mr. MIKE KROKOS, Editor, *244 Dayton Ave., St. Paul, 55102.* Tel: 651-291-4444.
Office of the Deaf—CAROL JOHNSON, *701 Fillmore St., N.E., Minneapolis, 55413.* Tel: 612-623-4019; 378-1344 (TTD).
Office of Indian Ministry—Rev. JAMES C. NOTEBAART, Dir., *3045 Park Ave., Minneapolis, 55407.* Tel: 612-824-7616.
Office for Social Justice—Mr. RON KRIETEMEYER, Admin., *328 W. Kellogg Blvd., St. Paul, 55102.* Tel: 651-291-4477.
Office of Due Process—Sr. M. DOMINICA BRENNAN, O.P., J.C.L., Dir., *226 Summit Ave., St. Paul, 55102.* Tel: 651-291-4437.
Office of Ecumenism—Rev. ARTHUR L. KENNEDY, Ecumenical Officer, *University of St. Thomas, 2115 Summit Ave., P.O. Box 5022, St. Paul, 55105.* Tel: 651-962-5050.
Office of Evangelization—JANET KROSHESKI, Sec., *328 W. Kellogg Blvd., St. Paul, 55102.* Tel: 651-291-4488.
Office of Human Resources—LARRY VANDENPLAS, *328 W. Kellogg Blvd., St. Paul, 55102.* Tel: 651-291-4499.
Office of Pastoral Planning—Mr. ROBERT J. BURKE, Dir., *328 W. Kellogg Blvd., St. Paul, 55102.* Tel: 651-291-4544.
Office of Presbyteral Personnel Resources—Revs. PAUL JAROSZESKI, Exec. Sec. LAWRENCE BLAKE, *226 Summit Ave., St. Paul, 55102.* Tel: 651-291-4430.
Parish Pastoral Council Assistance Center—Mr. ROBERT J. BURKE, Dir., *328 W. Kellogg Blvd., St. Paul, 55102.* Tel: 651-291-4544.
Pastoral Council—Most Rev. HARRY J. FLYNN, D.D., Chm.; Mr. ROBERT J. BURKE, Exec. Sec., *328 W. Kellogg Blvd., St. Paul, 55102.* Tel: 651-291-4544.
Permanent Deacon Assembly—Deacon DANIEL D. KIRCHOFFNER, Pres., *2220 Summit Ave., St. Paul, 55105.* Tel: 651-962-6875.
Permanent Deacon Office—Deacon PETER A. D'HEILLY, Dir., *2220 Summit Ave., St. Paul, 55105.* Tel: 651-962-6875.
Presbyteral Council—Rev. JOHN R. ESTREM, Exec. Dir., *226 Summit Ave., St. Paul, 55102.* Tel: 651-291-4400.
Propagation of the Faith—ALICIA KELLY, Dir., *328 W. Kellogg Blvd., St. Paul, 55102.* Tel: 651-222-6556.
Resource Development Office—Mr. JAMES MULLIN, Dir., *328 W. Kellogg Blvd., St. Paul, 55102.* Tel: 651-290-1610.
Annual Catholic Appeal—MARY NICHOLSON, Dir.
Endowment Campaign—Mr. JAMES MULLIN, Consultant.
Respect Life—Mrs. SHARON SODERLUND, Dir., *328 W. Kellogg Blvd., St. Paul, 55102.* Tel: 651-291-4505.
Rural Life Conference—Mr. DALE R. HENNEN, *105 3rd St., N.W., Montgomery, 56069.* Tel: 612-364-7323.
Sacerdotal Union of Daily Adoration—Rev. ALBERT F. BYRNE, *2590 Margaret St., North St. Paul, 55109.*
Seton Center—MICHELLE BAILEY, Admin., *Spruce Tree Center, Ste. 400, 1600 University Ave., St. Paul, 55104.* Tel: 651-641-1180. Outpatient social and medical services for unwed women and young couples.
Society of St. Vincent De Paul, Archdiocesan Council—Ms. BERNICE MARUSKA, Pres., *1008 Arcade St., St. Paul, 55102.* Tel: 651-771-0358.

To Encounter Christ (TEC)—PAM GEEMSCHEID DEMORETT, Coord., *1201 S.E. 5th St., Minneapolis, 55414.* Tel: 612-331-3644.

Venezuelan Missions—Revs. PATRICK J. RYAN; GREGORY J. SCHAFFER, *El Buen Pastor Parroquia San Francisco de Asis, Apartado 272, Puerto Ordaz, Estado Bolivar, Venezuela, 8015.*

Vocation Office—Rev. WILLIAM E. PELANT, Dir., Vocations, *2260 Summit Ave., St. Paul, 55105.* Tel: 651-962-6890.

Worship Board—Ms. ANNA OTTO, Chm., *244 Dayton Ave., St. Paul, 55102.* Tel: 651-290-1625.

Worship Center—VICKI KLIMA, Dir.; Mr. MICHAEL SILHAVY, Assoc. Dir., Music, *244 Dayton Ave., St. Paul, 55102.* Tel: 651-290-1625.

CLERGY, PARISHES, MISSIONS AND PAROCHIAL SCHOOLS

METROPOLITAN ST. PAUL
(Ramsey County)

1—CATHEDRAL OF ST. PAUL (1850), Revs. John Estrem, Rector; Robert Hart; Deacons Rip Riordan; Nathan Allen.
Res., 239 Selby Ave., 55102. Tel: 651-228-1766; Fax: 651-228-9942.

2—ASSUMPTION (1856) (German), Rev. John M. Malone.
Res., 51 W. Seventh St., 55102. Tel: 651-224-7536; Fax: 651-224-8514.

3—BLESSED SACRAMENT (1916), Revs. Thomas R. McDonough; Orlando Tatel.
Res., 1801 La Crosse Ave., 55119. Tel: 651-735-3707; Fax: 651-578-1125. [CEM]
School—1800 Ames Ave., 55119. Tel: 651-735-3676; Fax: 651-264-0647.
Lay Teachers 10; Students 130.
Catechesis/Religious Programs—Students 91.

4—HOLY CHILDHOOD (1946), Rev. James G. Wolnik.
Res., 1435 Midway Pkwy., 55108. Tel: 651-644-7495.
School—1435 Midway Pkwy., 55108. Tel: 651-644-2791; Fax: 651-917-8797. Raymond Aresenault, Prin.
Sisters 6; Lay Teachers 11; Students 140.
Catechesis/Religious Programs—Tel: 651-644-5645. Gregory Deacy, D.R.E.
Students 15.

5—HOLY SPIRIT (1936), Rev. Michael L. Papesh; Deacons William Umphress; W. Richard Barrett.
Res., 515 S. Albert St., 55105. Tel: 651-698-3353; Fax: 651-698-1605.
School—Joy Biedrzycki, Pastoral Assoc.
Catechesis/Religious Programs—Tel: 651-698-3353; Fax: 651-698-1605.
Students 50.

6—THE IMMACULATE HEART OF MARY (1949), Rev. Charles F. Burns, S.J.; Sr. Mary Claire Inhofer, O.S.B., Pastoral Assoc. In res., Revs. Richard C. Burbach, S.J. Tel: 651-644-9018; Richard M. Rice, S.J.; Peter J. Etzel, S.J. Tel: 651-644-9041; Philip Dreckman, S.J. Tel: 651-646-2938.
Mailing Address: 1550 Summit Ave., Saint Paul, 55105-2290.
Res., 1543 Summit Ave., 55105. Tel: 651-699-7722 (Office); Fax: 651-642-5103.
School—IHM-St. Luke. See St. Luke, St. Paul for details. Tel: 651-224-4836; Fax: 651-224-0097.
Catechesis/Religious Programs—Students 34.

7—MATERNITY OF THE BLESSED VIRGIN (1949), Rev. Paul D. Sirba.
Res., 1414 N. Dale St., 55117. Tel: 651-489-8825; Fax: 651-488-4055.
School—Maternity of Mary-St. Andrew, 592 Arlington Ave., 55117. Tel: 651-489-1459; Fax: 651-489-3560.
Sisters 2; Lay Teachers 23; Students 365.
Catechesis/Religious Programs—Tel: 651-489-8827; Fax: 651-488-4055. Mary Weyandt, D.R.E.
Students 165.

8—THE NATIVITY OF OUR LORD (1922), Revs. Peter Christensen; John W. Kelley, (Retired); Thomas S. Margevicius.
Office: 1900 Wellesley, 55105. Tel: 651-698-0309; Fax: 651-696-5458.
School—1900 Stanford Ave., 55105. Tel: 651-699-1311; Fax: 651-696-5420.
Sisters of St. Joseph 1; Lay Teachers 41; Students 776. Principals: Mrs. Margo Weiberg; Ms. Kate Wollan.
Catechesis/Religious Programs—Tel: 651-696-5454; Fax: 651-696-5458.
Students 200.

9—OUR LADY OF GUADALUPE (1931) (Hispanic), Rev. Hugo L. Montero (Ecuador).
Res., 401 Concord Street, 55107. Tel: 651-228-0506; Fax: 651-224-5162.
Catechesis/Religious Programs—Students 190.

10—SACRED HEART (1881) (German), Revs. John Dombrowski, O.F.M.; Paul Pare, O.F.M.; Deacons Wayne Wittman; Martin Jaques, Jr. In res., Revs. Fabian F. Burdiek, O.F.M.; Nicholas W. Meyer, O.F.M.; Salvador Valdez, O.F.M.; Bro. Lester Kochlin, O.F.M.
Res., 840 E. Sixth St., 55106. Tel: 651-776-2741; Fax: 651-776-2759.
School—Trinity Catholic School. Collaborative School with St. Patrick & St. Casimir Parishes in St. Paul. 835 E. Fifth St., 55106. Tel: 651-776-2763; Fax: 651-776-2764.
Catechesis/Religious Programs—Tel: 651-774-7505. Kim Roering, D.R.E.
Students 236.

11—ST. ADALBERT (1881), Revs. Timothy J. Kernan; Vincent The Nguyen, S.D.D.; Deacons Kao Yang; Bill Falvey; Dominic Dieu Tran. In res., Rev. Michael J. Stevens.
Res., 265 Charles Ave., 55103. Tel: 651-228-9002.
Catechesis/Religious Programs—Students 85.

12—ST. AGNES (1887) (German), Rev. Msgr. Richard J. Schuler; Revs. Robert J. Altier; Robert Clark; Deacons Harold Hughesdon; Bernard Pedersen.
Res., 548 Lafond Ave., 55103. Tel: 651-293-1710; Fax: 651-227-4229.
School—530 Lafond Ave., 55103. Tel: 651-227-1886; Fax: 651-228-1158. Mr. John Boone, Prin.
Sisters of Notre Dame 2; Lay Teachers 15; Students 227.
High School—Tel: 651-228-1161. Mr. William Peper, Prin.
Sisters of Notre Dame 1; Lay Teachers 23; Students 327.
Catechesis/Religious Programs—Students 72.

13—ST. ANDREW (1895), Rev. Roger F. Carroll.
Res., 1051 Como Ave., 55103. Tel: 651-488-6775; Fax: 651-488-4461.
School—Maternity of Mary/St. Andrew. Consolidated. See Maternity of the Blessed Virgin for details. Tel: 651-489-1459; Fax: 651-489-3560.
Catechesis/Religious Programs—Twinned with Maternity of Mary, St. Paul. Tel: 651-489-8827; Fax: 651-488-4055.
Students 30.

14—ST. ANDREW KIM (1990) (Korean), Rev. Dong Chun John Kim (Korea).
Res., 1449 N. Cleveland Ave., 55108. Tel: 651-642-9822 (Rectory); Fax: 651-642-0140. [JC]
Catechesis/Religious Programs—Tel: 651-644-1605.
Students 76.

15—ST. BERNARD (1890) (German), Revs. Michael F. Anderson; Joseph G. Gallatin; Deacon Sonny Laqui.
Mailing Address: 1160 Woodbridge St., 55117-4491. Tel: 651-488-6733; Fax: 651-489-9203.
Res., 197 W. Geranium Ave., 55117-4437. Tel: 651-488-6733.
School—(Grades PreK-8) 170 W. Rose Ave., 55117-4437. Fax: 651-488-9466.
Lay Teachers 17; Students 217.
High School—170 W. Rose Ave., 55117-4437. Tel: 651-489-1338. Jennifer Cassidy, Pres. (PreK-12); Mark Lenihan, Prin. (PreK-12).
Lay Teachers 23; Students 228.
Catechesis/Religious Programs—Students 79.

16—ST. CASIMIR (1892) (Polish), Rev. Chester Cappucci, O.M.I.; Tony Schreiner, Business Mgr.
Res., 934 E. Geranium Ave., 55106. Tel: 651-774-0365; Fax: 651-774-0508.
School—Trinity Catholic School. Collaborative School with St. Patrick & Sacred Heart Parishes in St. Paul. 835 E. Fifth St., Tel: 651-776-2763; Fax: 651-776-2764.
Students 270; Preschool 45.
Catechesis/Religious Programs—Tel: 651-776-5641.
Students 113.

17—ST. CECILIA (1912), Rev. Paul A. Jaroszeski.
Res., 2357 Bayless Pl., 55114. Tel: 651-644-4502; Fax: 651-647-1445.
Catechesis/Religious Programs—Students 102.

18—ST. COLUMBA, Revs. Paul A. LaFontaine; Thomas Tam (Vietnam); Deacon Thomas Stiles.
Res., 1327 Lafond Ave., 55104. Tel: 651-645-9179; Fax: 651-645-9170.
School—1330 Blair Ave., 55104. Tel: 651-644-1807.
Lay Teachers 15; Students 191.
Catechesis/Religious Programs—Tel: 651-644-9078.
Students 200.

19—ST. FRANCIS DE SALES (1884) (German), Rev. Dennis Dempsey.
Res., 650 Palace Ave., 55102-3593. Tel: 651-228-1169; Fax: 651-224-7744.
School—St. Francis-St. James United School, 426 S. Osceola St., 55102. Tel: 651-228-1167; Fax: 651-228-0169.
Sisters of Notre Dame 3; Lay Teachers 17; Students 219.

20—ST. GREGORY THE GREAT (HIGHLAND CATHOLIC COMMUNITY) (1951). (A formation of the following: St. Gregory the Great, St. Paul; St. Leo, St. Paul and St. Therese, St. Paul). Revs. John M. Bauer; Thomas P. Hunstiger; Deacon Gerald Scherkenbach.
Mailing Address: 2055 Bohland Ave., 55116.
Church—1668 Montreal Ave., 55116-2499. Tel: 651-698-3767.
Parish Center: Tel: 651-698-5581; Fax: 651-698-9526.
School—Highland Catholic School. See listing under Institutions located in the Archdiocese for details. Tel: 651-690-2477; Fax: 651-699-1869.
Catechesis/Religious Programs—Highland Catholic Community, Tel: 651-698-5583.
Students 282.

21—ST. JAMES (1887), Rev. Dennis Dempsey.
Res., 650 Palace Ave., 55102. Tel: 651-227-7029.
School—St. Francis-St. James United School, (Grades K-8). See St. Francis De Sales for details. Tel: 651-228-1167; Fax: 651-228-0169.
Catechesis/Religious Programs—Tel: 651-228-1169; Fax: 651-224-7744.
Students 233.

22—ST. JOHN OF ST. PAUL (1886) (Irish), Rev. Thomas Pingatore. In res., Rev. Richard M. Hogan.
Res., 977 E. Fifth St., 55106. Tel: 651-771-3690; Fax: 651-771-7919.
Catechesis/Religious Programs—Students 44.

23—ST. LEO (HIGHLAND CATHOLIC COMMUNITY) (1945). (A formation of the following: St. Gregory the Great, St. Paul; St. Leo, St. Paul; St. Therese, St. Paul). Revs. John M. Bauer; Thomas P. Hunstiger; Deacon Gerald Scherkenbach.
Office: 2055 Bohland Ave., 55116. Tel: 651-698-5581; Fax: 651-698-9526.
School—Highland Catholic School. See listing under Institutions located in the Archdiocese for details. Tel: 651-690-2477; Fax: 651-699-1869.
Catechesis/Religious Programs—Highland Catholic Community, Tel: 651-698-5583; Fax: 651-698-9526.
Students 282.

24—ST. LOUIS KING OF FRANCE (1868) (French), Revs. Paul F. Morrissey, S.M.; Merle J. Fisher, S.M.
Res., 506 Cedar St., 55101-2280. Tel: 651-224-3379; Fax: 651-224-0017.

25—ST. LUKE (1888), Rev. Richard C. Burbach, S.J.; Deacon Thomas Dzik.
Center: 1079 Summit Ave., 55105. Tel: 651-227-7669; Fax: 651-227-0847.
School—IHM-St. Luke, 1065 Summit Ave., 55105. Tel: 651-224-4836; Fax: 651-224-0097.
Sisters 2; Lay Teachers 27; Students 416.
Catechesis/Religious Programs—Students 176.

26—ST. MARK (1889), Rev. Jerome F. Keiser; Deacon Scott Wright. In res., Rev. Anthony Andrade, O.S.B.
Res., 2001 Dayton Ave., 55104. Tel: 651-645-5717; Fax: 651-644-0011.
School—1983 Dayton Ave., 55104. Tel: 651-644-3380; Fax: 651-644-1923.
Sisters 2; Lay Teachers 22; Students 367.
Catechesis/Religious Programs—Fax: 651-645-5717.
Students 100.

27—ST. MARY (1865), Revs. Marek Stroba, O.M.I.; Daniel Taillez, O.M.I., (France) Hmong Chap.; Donald Dummer, O.M.I., Chap., Regions Hospital; Joseph Menker, O.M.I., Chap., Regions Hospital. In res., Rev. Robert Allie, O.M.I.
Res., 261 E. 8th St., 55101. Tel: 651-222-2619; Fax: 651-224-1190.

28—ST. MATTHEW (1886) (German), Revs. Stephen J. Adrian; Martin L. Warren (England); Deacon John Murphy.
Office: 490 Hall Ave., 55107.
Church—510 Hall Ave, 55107. Tel: 651-224-9793; Fax: 651-228-9448.
Res., 507 Hall Ave., 55107. Tel: 651-224-1037; Fax: 651-292-0925.
School—497 Humboldt Ave., 55107. Tel: 651-224-6912. Sr. Leonius Skarr, O.P., Prin.
Sisters 1; Lay Teachers 12; Students 206.
Catechesis/Religious Programs—Students 125.

29—ST. PASCAL BAYLON (1946), Rev. Thomas H. Brioschi; Deacons Joseph Schmitz; Richard Pashby.
Res., 1757 Conway St., 55106. Tel: 651-774-1585; Fax: 651-774-9152.
School—1770 E. 3rd St., 55106. Tel: 651-776-0092; Fax: 651-776-2365.
Sisters 1; Lay Teachers 24; Students 382.
Catechesis/Religious Programs—Tel: 651-774-0655.
Students 130.

30—St. Patrick (1884) (Irish), Rev. Jerome B. Hackenmueller.
Res., 1095 De Soto St., 55101. Tel: 651-774-8675; Fax: 651-774-9106.
School—Trinity Catholic School. Collaborative School with St. Patrick, St. Casimir & Sacred Heart Parishes in St. Paul. Tel: 651-776-2763; Fax: 651-774-9943.
Catechesis/Religious Programs—Tel: 651-776-7686.
Students 110.

31—St. Peter Claver (1892) (African American), Rev. Kevin M. McDonough; Deacon Fred L. Johnson.
Res., 375 N. Oxford St., 55104. Tel: 651-646-1797; Fax: 651-646-3021.
Catechesis/Religious Programs—Students 162.

32—St. Stanislaus (1872) (Czech), Rev. John C. Clay.
Res., 398 Superior St., 55102. Tel: 651-292-0303; Fax: 651-292-1098.
Catechesis/Religious Programs—395 Superior St., 55102. Tel: 651-292-1913.
Students 130.

33—St. Therese (Highland Catholic Community) (1926). (A consolidation of the following: St. Gregory the Great, St. Paul; St. Leo, St. Paul; and St. Therese, St. Paul). Revs. John M. Bauer; Gerald G. Grieman; Thomas P. Hunstiger; Deacon Gerald Scherkenbach.
Mailing Address: & Office:—2055 Bohland Ave., 55116.
Parish Center—Tel: 651-698-5581; Fax: 651-698-9526.
School—Highland Catholic School. See listing under Institutions located in the Archdiocese for details. Tel: 651-690-2477; Fax: 651-699-1869.
Catechesis/Religious Programs—Highland Catholic Community, Tel: 651-698-5583.
Students 274.

34—St. Thomas The Apostle (1954), Rev. Joseph Anthony Andrade; Deacon Ervin Barrett.
Res., 2119 Stillwater Ave., 55119. Tel: 651-738-0677; Fax: 651-738-6492.
Catechesis/Religious Programs—Tel: 651-738-2995.
Students 90.

35—St. Vincent de Paul (1888), Rev. Chue Ying Vang; Deacon Va Thai Lo.
Res., 651 Virginia St., 55103. Tel: 651-488-6737; Fax: 651-487-6790. [CEM]

OUTSIDE METROPOLITAN ST. PAUL

Cottage Grove, Washington Co., St. Rita (1966), Rev. James M. Grogan; Deacons Jack Nicklay; Steve Koop.
8694 80th St. S., 55016. Tel: 651-459-4596; Fax: 651-459-5364.
Catechesis/Religious Programs—Students 700.

Little Canada, Ramsey Co., St. John the Evangelist (1851), Revs. Robert J. Fitzpatrick; Michael I. Kueber (P); Marie Winn, Pastoral Assoc.; Suzanne Laddusire, Dir. Pastoral Ministry; Deacon R. Thomas Keyes.
Res., 380 Little Canada Rd., 55117. Tel: 651-484-2708; Fax: 651-484-0567. [CEM]
Preschool:—Tel: 651-484-8913.
Lay Teachers 2; Students 40.
School—2621 McMenemy St., 55117. Tel: 651-484-3038; Fax: 651-481-1355. Mary Kay Rowan, Prin.
Lay Teachers 18; Students 254.
Catechesis/Religious Programs—Tel: 651-484-0048. Jean Conant Winter, D.R.E.
Students 560.

Mahtomedi, Washington Co., St. Jude of the Lake (1939), Rev. Jon P. Shelley.
Res., 700 Mahtomedi Ave., 55115. Tel: 651-426-3245; Fax: 651-653-3554.
School—600 Mahtomedi Ave., 55115. Tel: 651-426-2562; Fax: 651-653-3662. Ann Austin McCormick, Prin.
Lay Teachers 15; Students 250.
Catechesis/Religious Programs—Students 641.

Maplewood, Ramsey Co., Holy Redeemer (1880) (Italian), Rev. Austin T. Ward.
Res., 2555 Hazelwood Ave., 55109. Tel: 651-777-1321.

Presentation of the Blessed Virgin Mary (1946), Revs. Charles V. Lachowitzer; Scott M. Carl; Deacon Jack Veiman.
Res., 1725 Kennard St., 55109. Tel: 651-777-8116; Fax: 651-777-8743.
School—1695 Kennard St., 55109. Tel: 651-777-5877.
Lay Teachers 21; Students 366.
Catechesis/Religious Programs—Tel: 651-777-6041; Fax: 651-777-8743.
Students 260.

St. Jerome (1940), Rev. Kenneth F. Ludescher.
1894 McMenemy Rd., 55117. Tel: 651-771-1928.
Church—380 Roselawn Ave. E., 55117. Tel: 651-771-1209; Fax: 651-771-3623.
School—384 E. Roselawn Ave., 55117. Tel: 651-771-8494.
Lay Teachers 13; Students 225.
Catechesis/Religious Programs—Students 110.

Mendota, Dakota Co., St. Peter (1840) (Native American-French-English), Revs. Kevin I. Clinton; Joel Cycenas. In res., Rev. Gilbert J. Gustafson.
Res., P.O. Box 50679, 55150. Tel: 651-452-4030; Fax: 651-456-0646. [CEM]
Catechesis/Religious Programs—Tel: 651-452-4550, Ext. 3; Fax: 651-456-0646. Ellen Casey, D.R.E.
Students 383.

New Brighton, Ramsey Co., St. John the Baptist (1906) (Polish), Revs. William Murtaugh; Michael C. Becker; Deacons Joseph McPherson; Joseph Kenney.
Parish Center:—835 2nd Ave., N.W., 55112. Tel: 651-633-8333; Fax: 651-633-7404.
Res., 812 1st Ave., N.W., 55112. [CEM]
School—845 2nd Ave., N.W., 55112. Tel: 651-633-1522; Fax: 651-633-1522.
Sisters 1; Lay Teachers 22; Students 424.
Catechesis/Religious Programs—Tel: 651-633-1540; Fax: 651-633-7404.
Students 1,140.

North St. Paul, Ramsey Co., St. Peter (1888), Revs. James McConville; George Kolath (India); Deacon James Hepp.
Res., 2590 N. Margaret St., 55109. Tel: 651-777-8304; Fax: 651-777-0497. [CEM]
Preschool:—Tel: 651-777-5282.
Lay Teachers 2; Students 80.
School—2602 N. Margaret St., 55109. Tel: 651-777-3091; Fax: 651-777-7750.
Lay Teachers 22; Students 476.
Catechesis/Religious Programs—Students 483.

Oakdale, Washington Co., Guardian Angels (1885), Revs. William F. Martin; Stanley Maslowski; Sr. Dorothy Mrock, O.S.F.
Res., 8260 Hudson Blvd., 55128. Tel: 651-738-2223; Fax: 651-738-2453. [CEM]
Catechesis/Religious Programs—Students 967.

Transfiguration (1939), Rev. James D. Smith; Deacon Dan Kirchoffner.
Res., 6133 15th St. N., 55128. Tel: 651-738-2646; Fax: 651-501-2230.
School—935 Ferndale Ave., Maplewood, 55119. Tel: 651-501-2220; Fax: 651-501-2258. Ted Zarembski, Prin.
Lay Teachers 17; Students 354.
Catechesis/Religious Programs—Tel: 651-501-2204. Carole Zempel, D.R.E.
Students 670.

Roseville, Ramsey Co., Corpus Christi (1939), Rev. Robert C. Nygaard.
Res., 2131 N. Fairview Ave., 55113-5499. Tel: 651-639-8888; Fax: 651-639-8288.
Catechesis/Religious Programs—D.R.E.: Colleen Ciaccio; Alisa Weber.
Students 80.

St. Rose of Lima (1939), Rev. Walter L. Sochacki.
Res., 2048 N. Hamline Ave., 55113. Tel: 651-645-9389; Fax: 651-646-4187.
School—2072 Hamline Ave. N., 55113. Tel: 651-646-3832; Fax: 651-647-6437.
Sisters 3; Lay Teachers 25; Students 434.
Catechesis/Religious Programs—Tel: 651-646-8029. Deb McPherson, D.R.E.
Students 130.

Shoreview, Ramsey Co., St. Odilia (1960), Revs. Richard McGuire, O.S.C.; Jerome Schik, O.S.C.; Marven Tellers, O.S.C.; Deacons John Flood; Jerome Ciresi.
3495 N. Victoria St., 55126. Tel: 651-484-6681; Fax: 651-484-0780.
School—(Grades K-8). Tel: 651-484-3364; Fax: 651-415-3395. Mr. Robert Grose, Prin.
Lay Teachers 35; Students 711.
Catechesis/Religious Programs—Tel: 651-484-2777. Sr. Penny Dunn, O.S.F., D.R.E.
Students 1,534.

West St. Paul, Dakota Co., St. Joseph (1942), Revs. Lee A. Piche; Michael J. Miller.
Res., 1154 Seminole Ave., 55118. Tel: 651-457-2781; Fax: 651-451-1272.
School—1138 Seminole Ave., 55118. Tel: 651-457-8550; Fax: 651-451-1272.
Lay Teachers 44; Students 730.
Catechesis/Religious Programs—Tel: 651-457-8841.
Students 315.

St. Michael (1879), Rev. Gerald L. Dvorak.
Res., 337 E. Hurley, 55118. Tel: 651-457-2334; Fax: 651-451-1668.
School—E. Haskell & Sperl, 55118. Tel: 651-457-2510.
Sisters 4; Lay Teachers 11; Students 200.
Catechesis/Religious Programs—Tel: 651-457-0172.
Students 85.

White Bear Lake, Ramsey Co., St. Mary of the Lake (1881), Rev. Roger P. Pierre; Deacon Sherm Stromen.
Res., 4690 Bald Eagle Ave., 55110. Tel: 651-429-7771; Fax: 651-429-9539. [CEM]
School—4690 Bald Eagle Ave., 55110. Tel: 651-429-5378.
Lay Teachers 10; Students 304.
Catechesis/Religious Programs—Tel: 651-429-8001. D.R.E.: Helen Welter; Mary Beth Jambor.
Students 900.

St. Pius X (1954), Revs. Michael J. Krenik; Jerry F. Fenton; Deacon Thomas L. Semlak.
Mailing Address: 3878 Highland Ave., 55110. Tel: 651-429-5337; Fax: 651-429-9359.
School—Tel: 651-429-5338.
Lay Teachers 21; Students 357.
Catechesis/Religious Programs—Tel: 651-429-5994.
Students 221.

Woodbury, Saint Ambrose of Woodbury (1998), Rev. Msgr. Richard E. Pates; Deacon Steve Moses.
Mailing Address: 4125 Woodbury Dr., 55129-9627. Tel: 651-714-1058; Fax: 651-714-9257.
Catechesis/Religious Programs—Students 984.

METROPOLITAN MINNEAPOLIS
(Hennepin County)

1—The Basilica of St. Mary Co-Cathedral (1907), Revs. Michael O'Connell, Rector; Joseph P. Gillespie; Joseph E. Whalen; Deacons David Ingwell; Del Ferguson; Roger Carlson; George Babcock.
Mailing Address: P.O. Box 50010, 55405-0010.
Res., 88 N. 17th St., 55403-1295. Tel: 612-333-1381; Fax: 612-333-7230.
Catechesis/Religious Programs—Tel: 612-317-3473.
Students 325.

2—All Saints (1916) (Polish), Rev. George J. Kovalik.
Res., 435 4th St., N.E., 55413. Tel: 612-379-4996.
School—Northeast Regional Catholic School. See Elementary Schools, Consolidated, Parochial under Institutions located in the Archdiocese for details. Tel: 612-789-8851.

3—Annunciation (1922), Rev. Kenneth J. Pierre.
Res., 509 W. 54th St., 55419. Tel: 612-824-0787; Fax: 612-823-8467.
School—525 W. 54th St., 55419. Tel: 612-823-4394; Fax: 612-824-9915.
Sisters 1; Lay Teachers 25; Students 450.
Catechesis/Religious Programs—Students 180.

4—Ascension (1890), Rev. Michael O'Connell; Deacon John Winkleman.
Res., 1723 Bryant Ave. N., 55411. Tel: 612-529-9684; Fax: 612-529-7618.
School—1726 Dupont Ave. N., 55411. Tel: 612-521-3609; Fax: 612-522-3862.
Sisters 1; Lay Teachers 13; Students 270.
Catechesis/Religious Programs—Students 25.

5—Christ the King (1938), Rev. John M. Hofstede.
5029 Zenith Ave. S., 55410. Tel: 612-920-5030; Fax: 612-920-1179. [JC]
School—Cooperative program with St. Thomas the Apostle, Minneapolis. Tel: 612-927-8673; 920-9075; Fax: 612-927-7426.

6—Holy Cross (1886) (Polish), Revs. David T. Ostrowski, O.S.B.; Andrzej Gallant, S.Ch. (Poland).
Res., 1621 University Ave., N.E., 55413. Tel: 612-789-7238; Fax: 612-789-5769.
School—Northeast Regional Catholic School. See Elementary Schools, Consolidated, Parochial under Institutions located in the Archdiocese for details. Tel: 612-789-8851; Fax: 612-789-8773.
Catechesis/Religious Programs—Students 82.

7—Holy Name (1916), Rev. Leo J. Schneider; Deacon Don Fidler.
Res., 3637 11th Ave. S., 55407. Tel: 612-724-5465; Fax: 612-724-5466.
School—Risen Christ Catholic School. See Elementary Schools, Consolidated, Parochial under Institutions located in the Archdiocese for details. Tel: 612-822-5329; Fax: 612-822-5903.
Catechesis/Religious Programs—Students 35.

8—Holy Rosary (1878) (Hispanic), Revs. Charles M. Santoro, O.P.; Jacob Joerger, O.P.; Sr. Martha Wiegand, O.P., Pastoral Assoc.
Res., 2424 18th Ave. S., 55404. Tel: 612-724-3651; Fax: 612-728-8944.
School—Risen Christ Catholic School. See Elementary Schools, Consolidated, Parochial under Institutions located in the Archdiocese for details. Tel: 612-822-5329.
Catechesis/Religious Programs—Students 225.

Convent—1614 E. 24th St., 55404. Tel: 612-724-2620.
Dominican Sisters (Sinsinawa, WI) 4.

9—INCARNATION (1909), Rev. Robert Monaghan.
Res., 3817 Pleasant Ave., 55409-1296. Tel: 612-822-2101; Fax: 612-822-7928.
School—Risen Christ Catholic School. See Elementary Schools, Consolidated, Parochial under Institutions located in the Archdiocese for details. Tel: 612-822-5329; Fax: 612-822-5903.
Catechesis/Religious Programs—Students 87.

10—OUR LADY OF LOURDES (1877) (French-Canadian). Unassigned.
Res., One Lourdes Pl., 55414. Tel: 612-379-2259; Fax: 612-379-0165.
Catechesis/Religious Programs—Students 84.

11—OUR LADY OF MOUNT CARMEL (1938) (Italian), Rev. William J. Kenney, (Retired); Carol L. Johnson, Parish Life Admin.
Res., 701 Fillmore St., N.E., 55413. Tel: 612-623-4019; Fax: 612-331-3407.
School—Northeast Regional Catholic School. See Elementary Schools, Consolidated, Parochial under the Institutions located in the Archdiocese for details. Tel: 612-789-8851.
Catechesis/Religious Programs—Students 14.

12—OUR LADY OF PEACE (1991), Rev. Kevin T. Kenney.
Res., 5425 11th Ave. S., 55417. Tel: 612-823-8253; Fax: 612-823-5102.
School—5435 11th Ave. S., 55417. Tel: 612-824-3455; Fax: 612-824-7328.
Lay Teachers 23; Students 430.
Catechesis/Religious Programs—Students 178.

13—OUR LADY OF PERPETUAL HELP. Closed. For inquiries for parish records contact the Chancery.

14—OUR LADY OF VICTORY (1945), Rev. Terrence M. Hayes.
Res., 5155 Emerson Ave. N., 55430. Tel: 612-529-7788; Fax: 612-529-3343.
Church—52nd and Fremont Aves., 55430.
School—St. Elizabeth Seton, 5140 Fremont Ave. N., 55430. Tel: 612-529-7781.
Lay Teachers 22; Students 231.
Catechesis/Religious Programs—Tel: 612-521-7454.
Students 44.

15—ST. ALBERT THE GREAT (1935), Rev. Thomas R. Poulsen, O.P. In res., Revs. Brendan J. McMullen, O.P.; James R. Motl, O.P.; John G. O'Connell, O.P.; C. A. Kilroy, O.P.; Joseph P. Gillespie, O.P.; Jacob Joerger, O.P.; Joseph E. Bidwill, O.P.; Charles M. Santoro, O.P.; Cletus J. Wessels, O.P.; Bro. Vincent H. Champine, O.P.
Mailing Address: & Parish Center: 2836-33rd Ave. S., 55406. Tel: 612-724-3643; Fax: 612-722-9726.
Res., 2833 32nd Ave. S., 55406. Tel: 612-724-3644; Fax: 612-724-5057.
Catechesis/Religious Programs—Students 30.

16—ST. ANNE (1884) (French), Rev. Michael G. Monogue.
Res., 2627 Queen Ave. N., 55411. Tel: 612-529-0503; Fax: 612-529-5860.
School—St. Elizabeth Seton. (Consolidated). 5140 Fremont Ave. N., 55430-3496. Tel: 612-529-7781; Fax: 612-529-3343.
Catechesis/Religious Programs—Students 5.

17—ST. ANTHONY OF PADUA (1849), Rev. Joseph G. Kivel.
Res., 804 Second St., N.E., 55413. Tel: 612-379-2324; Fax: 612-379-2325.
School—Northeast Regional Catholic School. See Elementary Schools, Consolidated, Parochial under the Institutions located in the Archdiocese for details. Tel: 612-789-8851.
Catechesis/Religious Programs—Students 6.

18—ST. AUSTIN (1937), Rev. Gregory T. Welch; Sr. Anne Becker, S.S.N.D., Pastoral Assoc.
Res., 4050 Upton Ave. N., 55412. Tel: 612-529-9561; Fax: 612-529-8787.
School—St. Elizabeth Seton, 5140 Fremont Ave. N., 55430. Tel: 612-529-7781; Fax: 612-529-3343.
Lay Teachers 14; Students 230.
Catechesis/Religious Programs—Students 38.

19—ST. BONIFACE (1858) (German), Rev. Mark S. Wasinger.
Res., 629 Second St., N.E., 55413. Tel: 612-379-2761; Fax: 612-676-1532.
School—Northeast Regional Catholic School. See Elementary Schools, Consolidated, Parochial under the Institutions located in the Archdiocese for details. Tel: 612-789-8851.
Catechesis/Religious Programs—Students 23.

20—ST. BRIDGET (1915), Rev. Cyprian Mercieca, T.O.R. In res., Revs. Vincent J. Spinos, T.O.R.; J. Patrick Quinn, T.O.R.; John O'Hara (MIA).
Res., 3811 Emerson Ave. N., 55412. Tel: 612-529-7779; Fax: 612-529-8451.
School—(Consolidated) 5140 Fremont Ave. N., 55430-3497. Tel: 612-529-7781; Fax: 612-529-3343.
Joyce Klevens, Prin.
Sisters 1; Lay Teachers 20; Students 360.
Catechesis/Religious Programs—555 Emerson Ave., N. Minneapolis, 55430. Tel: 612-521-7454.
Students 45.

21—ST. CHARLES BORROMEO (1938), Revs. Paul A. LaFontaine; Mark A. Huberty.
Res., 2420 St. Anthony Blvd., 55418. Tel: 612-781-6529; Fax: 612-781-9723.
School—2727 Stinson Blvd., 55418. Tel: 612-781-2643; Fax: 612-788-7768.
Lay Teachers 24; Students 358.
Catechesis/Religious Programs—Students 133.

22—ST. CLEMENT (1902), Rev. Earl C. Simonson.
Res., 911 24th Ave., N.E., 55418. Tel: 612-789-3533.
School—Northeast Regional Catholic School. See Elementary Schools, Consolidated, Parochial under the Institutions located in the Archdiocese for details. Tel: 612-789-8851.

23—SS. CYRIL & METHODIUS (1891) (Slovak), Rev. Mark S. Wasinger. In res., Rev. David A. Barrett.
Res., 1315 2nd St., N.E., 55413. Tel: 612-379-9736; Fax: 612-676-1532.
School—Northeast Regional Catholic School. See Elementary Schools, Consolidated, Parochial under the Institutions located in the Archdiocese for details. Tel: 612-789-8851.
Catechesis/Religious Programs—629 2nd St., N.E., Tel: 612-379-2761.
Students 30.

24—ST. FRANCES CABRINI (1946), Rev. Leo J. Tibesar; Marie Rossa, Admin.
Res., 1500 Franklin Ave., S.E., 55414-3697. Tel: 612-339-3023; Fax: 612-339-0734.
Catechesis/Religious Programs—Students 120.

25—ST. HEDWIG (1914) (Polish), Rev. Theodore C. Guminga, Admin.
Res., 129 29th Ave., N.E., 55418. Tel: 612-789-4830; Fax: 612-789-1985.
School—Northeast Regional Catholic School. See Elementary Schools, Consolidated, Parochial under the Institutions located in the Archdiocese for details.

26—ST. HELENA (1913), Rev. Richard R. Villano.
3204 E. 43rd St., 55406. Tel: 612-729-7344.
Res., 4320 33rd Ave. S., 55406. Tel: 612-729-2252; Fax: 612-724-8695.
School—3200 E. 44th St., 55406. Tel: 612-729-9301.
Lay Teachers 13; Students 192.
Catechesis/Religious Programs—Students 60.

27—ST. JOAN OF ARC (1946), Rev. George P. Wertin.
Res., 4537 3rd Ave. S., 55409. Tel: 612-823-8205; Fax: 612-825-7028.
Catechesis/Religious Programs—Kathy Itzin, D.R.E.
Students 803.

28—ST. JOSEPH HIEN (1987) (Vietnamese), Revs. Jim N. Khoi, C.M.C.; Andrew Dolinh Sang, C.M.C. (Vietnam).
Res., 1814 Dupont Ave. N., 55411. Tel: 612-522-5006; Fax: 612-522-5006. [JC]
Catechesis/Religious Programs—Tel: 612-513-9112.
Students 450.
Mission—St. Paul, Mission of the Mother-Coredemptrix.

29—ST. LAWRENCE (1887), Revs. John J. Behnke, C.S.P.; James DiLuzio, C.S.P.; Donald A. Andrie, C.S.P.; Deacon Paul Carlson. In res., Rev. Wilfred A. Brimley, C.S.P.
Res., 1201 5th St., S.E., 55414. Tel: 612-331-7941; 331-3437; Fax: 612-378-1771.

30—ST. LEONARD OF PORT MAURICE (1941) (African American), Rev. James R. DeBruycker.
Res., 3949 Clinton Ave., 55409. Tel: 612-825-5811; 347-2260; Fax: 612-825-5811.
Catechesis/Religious Programs—Students 16.

31—ST. OLAF (1941), Revs. John E. Forliti; Joseph R. Johnson; John A. Klockeman; Leon F. Klimczyk, S.J.; Deacon Stephen Boatwright.
Res., 215 S. 8th St., 55402. Tel: 612-332-7471; Fax: 612-332-3412. [JC]

32—ST. PHILIP (1906) (Polish), Rev. Gregory Tolaas.
Res., 2507 Bryant Ave. N., 55411. Tel: 612-529-3125; Fax: 612-287-9133.

33—ST. STEPHEN (1885), Revs. Patrick E. Griffin; Lawrence E. Hubbard.
Parish Center—2211 Clinton Ave., 55404. Tel: 612-874-0311; Fax: 612-874-0313.
School—Risen Christ Catholic School. See Elementary Schools, Consolidated, Parochial under Institutions located in the Archdiocese for details. Tel: 612-822-5329.

34—ST. THOMAS THE APOSTLE (1908), Rev. Stephen R. O'Gara.
Res., 2914 W. 44th St., 55410. Tel: 612-922-0041; Fax: 612-922-1921.
School—Combined program with Christ the King, Minneapolis. 2900 W. 44th St., 55410. Tel: 612-920-9075; Fax: 612-927-7426.
Lay Teachers, Both Campuses; 32; Students 450.
Catechesis/Religious Programs—Students 60.

35—VISITATION (1946), Rev. Francis A. Pouliot; Deacon Peter A. D'Heilly.
Res., 4500 Lyndale Ave. S., 55409. Tel: 612-822-3139.
School—4530 Lyndale Ave. S., 55409. Tel: 612-827-3861; Fax: 612-824-3515.
Lay Teachers 11; Students 110.
Catechesis/Religious Programs—Students 7.

OUTSIDE METROPOLITAN MINNEAPOLIS

Blaine, Anoka Co., St. Timothy's (1943), Rev. Harold J. Tasto; Deacons Bernie Dols; Kevin Jents.
Res., 707 89th Ave., N.E., 55434. Tel: 763-784-1329; Fax: 763-784-0652.
Catechesis/Religious Programs—Fax: 612-784-0654.
Students 799.

Bloomington, Hennepin Co., Nativity of the Blessed Virgin Mary (1949), Rev. Robert E. Johnson; Deacons James McLaughlin; Rob Warhol.
Office: 9900 Lyndale Ave. S., 55420. Tel: 612-881-8671; Fax: 612-881-8692.
School—9901 Bloomington Fwy., 55420. Tel: 612-881-8160; Fax: 612-881-3032.
Lay Teachers 22; Students 445.
Catechesis/Religious Programs—Tel: 612-881-1451; Fax: 612-881-8671. Rose Ann Stans, D.R.E.
Students 200.

St. Bonaventure (1959), Revs. Bernard Zajdel, O.F.M.Conv.; Thomas Merrill, O.F.M.Conv.; Deacons Jack Herzog; Jon DeLuney. In res., Rev. Urban S. Wagner, O.F.M.Conv.; Bro. Steve McMichael.
Res., 901 E. 90th St. S., 55420. Tel: 612-854-4733; Fax: 612-851-9690.
Catechesis/Religious Programs—Tel: 612-854-7062.
Students 246.

St. Edward (1967), Rev. Michael Tegeder; Deacon Willard F. Dornfeld.
Res., 9401 Nesbitt Ave. S., 55437. Tel: 952-835-7101; Fax: 952-835-0156.
Catechesis/Religious Programs—Students 845.

Brooklyn Center, Hennepin Co., St. Alphonsus (1959), Revs. Patrick Grile, C.SS.R.; Arthur Rossie, C.SS.R., (Retired); Martin Stillmock, C.SS.R.; Joseph The Pham, C.SS.R.; Wil Lowery, C.SS.R.; Deacons Jerome H. Bisek; Bobby May; David Holst; Rick Fischer, C.SS.R.; Bro. Raymond Bowersox, C.SS.R. In res., Rev. David Shannon, C.SS.R.
Res., 7025 Halifax Ave. N., 55429. Tel: 763-561-5100; Fax: 763-561-0336.
School—7031 Halifax Ave., N., 55429. Tel: 763-561-5101.
Lay Teachers 18; Students 302.
Catechesis/Religious Programs—4111 71st Ave. N., 55429. Tel: 612-561-5102. Barbara Walhood, D.R.E.
Students 761.

Brooklyn Park, Hennepin Co., St. Gerard (1970), Revs. Anthony Criscitelli, T.O.R.; Bradley Baldwin, T.O.R.
Res., 9600 Regent Ave. N., 55443. Tel: 612-424-8770; Fax: 612-424-4327. [JC]
Catechesis/Religious Programs—Tel: 612-424-8600; Fax: 612-424-4327.
Students 751.

Burnsville, Dakota Co., Mary, Mother of the Church (1965), Revs. James C. Zappa, Jr.; Peter M. Richards; Deacon Peter Huberty; Barry Haller, Business Admin.
Church—3333 Cliff Rd., 55337. Tel: 612-890-0045; Fax: 612-890-0789.
Catechesis/Religious Programs—Al Rocklage, D.R.E.
Students 1013.

Church of the Risen Savior (1970), Revs. Tim Wozniak; James Gorman; Deacon Richard Stevens; Tim Dornfeld, Admin.
Office: 1501 E. County Rd. 42, 55306. Tel: 952-431-5222; Fax: 952-431-5221.
Catechesis/Religious Programs—D.R.E.: Karen Fitzpatrick; Barbara Skierecki; Suzan Ford.
Students 1017.

Columbia Heights, Anoka Co., Immaculate Conception (1923), Rev. Paul G. Moudry; Deacon Larry Palkert.
Res., 4030 Jackson St., N.E., 55421. Tel: 763-788-9062; Fax: 763-788-0202.
School—4030 Jackson Street NE, 55421. Tel: 763-788-9065.
Sisters of St. Francis 2; Lay Teachers 16; Students 254.
Catechesis/Religious Programs—Tel: 763-788-9067.
Students 234.

Coon Rapids, Anoka Co., Church of the Epiphany (1964), Revs. Bernard A. Reiser; Thomas W. Wilson; James E. Holl; James L. Lamm, Admin.
Res., 1900 111th Ave., N.W., 55433. Tel: 763-755-1020; Fax: 763-862-4303. [CEM]

School—11001 Hanson Blvd., 55433. Tel: 763-754-1750; Fax: 763-862-4350. Michael Strauss, Prin.
Lay Teachers 45; Students 823.
Catechesis/Religious Programs—11001 Hanson Blvd., 55433. Tel: 763-755-5010; Fax: 763-862-4354.
Students 1,826.

Crystal, Hennepin Co., St. Raphael (1951), Revs. Mark R. Juettner; Timothy Deutsch; Timothy D. Cloutier.
Res., 7301 Bass Lake Rd., 55428. Tel: 612-537-8401; Fax: 612-537-4878.
School—Tel: 612-504-9450; Fax: 612-504-9460.
Sisters 1; Lay Teachers 30; Students 466.
Catechesis/Religious Programs—Tel: 612-537-8401, Ext. 211; Fax: 612-537-4878. Paulette Schatz, D.R.E.
Students 259.

Eagan, Dakota Co., St. Thomas Becket (1989), Rev. Thomas M. Kommers; Deacon Paul Tatone.
Res., 4455 S. Robert Tr., 55123. Tel: 651-683-0689; 683-9808 (Parish Center); Fax: 651-683-0361.
Catechesis/Religious Programs—Students 394.

St. John Neumann (1977), Revs. Robert M. Schwartz; Albert P. Backmann; Deacon Michael F. Friesen.
Res., 4030 Pilot Knob Rd., 55122. Tel: 651-454-2079; Fax: 651-454-0860.
Catechesis/Religious Programs—Students 2,217.

Eden Prairie, Hennepin Co., Pax Christi (1981), Rev. J. Timothy Power; Deacons Mike Gerdts; Al Schroeder.
Res., 12100 Pioneer Tr., 55347. Tel: 612-941-3150; Fax: 612-941-7942.
Catechesis/Religious Programs—Tel: 612-941-6007; Fax: 612-941-7942.
Students 1,676.

Edina, Hennepin Co., Our Lady of Grace (1946), Revs. Robert T. Cassidy; Robert L. Valit; Christopher J. Beaudet; Deacons Donald Pendergast; Anthony Pasko. In res., Rev. Jerome W. Fehn.
Res., 5071 Eden Ave., 55436. Tel: 952-929-3317; Fax: 952-929-4612.
School—5051 Eden Ave., 55436. Tel: 952-929-5463; Fax: 952-929-8170.
Lay Teachers 32; Students 623.
Catechesis/Religious Programs—Students 730.

St. Patrick (1857) (Irish), Rev. Thomas H. Sieg; Deacon Byron Rudolphi.
Res., 6820 St. Patrick's Ln., 55439. Tel: 952-941-3164; Fax: 952-941-7371.
Catechesis/Religious Programs—Tel: 612-941-1407. D.R.E.: Patricia Brady; Cheryl Wood; Brenda Latterell.
Students 609.

Fridley, Anoka Co., St. William (1963), Rev. Patrick A. Kennedy, Admin.; Deacon Jim Wagner.
Res. and Admin. Center: 6120 5th St., N.E., 55432. Tel: 763-571-5600; Fax: 763-571-6924.
Catechesis/Religious Programs—Students 221.

Golden Valley, Hennepin Co., Good Shepherd (1946), Rev. Theodore C. Campbell; Deacon Thomas Kasbohm.
Res., 145 Jersey Ave. S., 55426. Tel: 763-544-0649; Fax: 763-544-9896. [JC]
School—Tel: 763-545-4285; Fax: 763-545-1896.
Lay Teachers 20; Students 330.
Catechesis/Religious Programs—Students 130.

St. Margaret Mary (1946), Rev. Jose Gutierrez.
Res., 2301 Zenith Ave., N., 55422. Tel: 612-588-9466; Fax: 612-588-0190.
Catechesis/Religious Programs—Students 131.

Ham Lake, Anoka Co., Saint Paul (1981), Rev. Timothy F. Nolan; Deacon Bill Beck.
Res., 1740 Bunker Lake Blvd., N.E., 55304. Tel: 612-757-6910; Fax: 612-757-6920.
Catechesis/Religious Programs—Trudy Swanson, D.R.E.
Students 775.

Lino Lakes, Anoka Co., St. Joseph (1891), Revs. Timothy Morin; Minh Vu.
Office: 171 Elm St., 55014. Tel: 651-784-3015; Fax: 651-784-3699. [CEM]
Catechesis/Religious Programs—D.R.E.: Deacon Thomas Konkel; Shirley Gormley; Christine Olson; Denise Walsh; Jeanne Degerstrom; Dorie Thul; Jerry Hendrickson.
Students 1,428.

New Hope, Hennepin Co., St. Joseph (1858), Rev. Robert Hazel.
Res., 8701 36th Ave. N., 55427. Tel: 763-544-3352. [CEM]
Parish Center & Office—Fax: 763-544-3435.
Catechesis/Religious Programs—D.R.E.: Mary Greving, (Catechetics); Christopher Briggs, (High School); Larry Thomas, (Middle School).
Students 652.

Plymouth, Hennepin Co., St. Mary of the Lake (1935), Rev. Bryan A. O'Rourke.
Res., 105 Forestview Ln. N., 55441. Tel: 763-545-1443; Fax: 763-797-0996.
Catechesis/Religious Programs—Students 203.

Richfield, Hennepin Co., Assumption of the B.V.M. (1876) (German), Rev. Michael Tix; Deacon Robert Smith.
Res., 305 E. 77th St., 55423. Tel: 612-866-5019; Fax: 612-866-5274. [CEM]
School—Blessed Trinity Nicollet & Penn Campus, Tel: 612-869-5200 (Trinity); 866-6906 (Penn); Fax: 612-869-0277;866-5080.
Students 480.
Catechesis/Religious Programs—Students 200.

St. Peter (1943), Rev. Rodger R. Bauman; Deacon Ed Janes.
Res., 6740 Nicollet Ave. S., 55423. Tel: 612-866-5089; Fax: 612-866-5080.
School—Consolidation of Assumption, St. Peter & St. Richard. 6720 Nicollet Ave. S., 55423. Tel: 612-869-5200.
Lay Teachers 23; Students 488.
Catechesis/Religious Programs—Tel: 612-866-3257.
Students 165.

St. Richard (1952), Rev. Thomas Krenik; Deacon William J. Berghoff.
Office: 7540 Penn Ave. S., 55423. Tel: 612-869-2426; Fax: 612-869-0277.
School—Blessed Trinity Catholic School. Consolidation of Assumption, St. Peter & St. Richard. Tel: 612-866-6906.
Lay Teachers 23; Students 480.
Catechesis/Religious Programs—Students 380.

Robbinsdale, Hennepin Co., Sacred Heart (1911), Rev. Robert E. Zasacki; Deacons Thomas Coleman; James Ramsey.
Office: 4087 W. Broadway, 55422. Tel: 763-537-4561; Fax: 763-537-5426.
Res., 4510 40-1/2 Ave. N., 55422.
School—4050 Hubbard, 55422. Tel: 763-537-1329; Fax: 763-537-1486.
Lay Teachers 20; Students 262.
Catechesis/Religious Programs—Cyrilene Brouillard, D.R.E.
Students 143.

St. Louis Park, Hennepin Co., Most Holy Trinity (1943), Rev. Dennis Thompson.
Parish Center: 4017 Utica Ave., 55416. Tel: 952-926-7516; Fax: 952-926-6069.
School—3946 Wooddale Ave., 55416. Tel: 952-926-2222; Fax: 952-926-2222.
Lay Teachers 9; Students 104.
Catechesis/Religious Programs—Students 103.

Holy Family (1926), Rev. Thomas W. Dufner.
Res., 5900 W. Lake St., 55416. Tel: 612-929-0113; Fax: 612-915-1474.
Catechesis/Religious Programs—Tel: 612-929-0113.
Students 200.

OUTSIDE TWIN-CITY METROPOLITAN AREA

Albertville, Wright Co., St. Albert (1902), Rev. Ronald R. Harrer, O.M.I.
Mailing Address: P.O. Box 127, 55301. Tel: 612-497-2474. [CEM]
Catechesis/Religious Programs—P.O. Box 67, 55301. Tel: 612-497-3782.
Students 218.

Annandale, Wright Co., St. Ignatius (1882), Rev. Stanley Kozlak.
Res., 55302. Tel: 320-274-8828. [CEM]
Catechesis/Religious Programs—Tel: 320-274-5064; Fax: 320-274-3961.
Students 264.

Anoka, Anoka Co., St. Stephen (1856), Revs. Michael Paquet, O.S.C.; Michael Van Sloun, O.S.C.; William Deziel; Adrian Piotrowski, O.S.C.; Deacons Peter Bednarczyk; Dominic Ehrmantraut; Daniel Nalezny; Charles Waugh. In res., Revs. Edward Greiwe, O.S.C.; Ignatius Lempart, O.S.C.; Kenneth Opat, O.S.C.; Eugene D. Plaisted, O.S.C.; Oscar Schoenberg, O.S.C.
Office: 525 Jackson St., 55303. Tel: 763-421-2471; Fax: 763-421-4230. [CEM]
Rectory: 516 School St., Tel: 763-421-7115 (Res.).
School—506 Jackson St., 55303. Tel: 763-421-3236; Fax: 763-712-7433.
Lay Teachers 22; Students 448.
Catechesis/Religious Programs—Students 1,003.

Bayport, Washington Co., St. Charles (1943), Rev. Mark J. Underdahl; Deacon Roger B. Carlson.
Res., 409 N. 3rd St., 55003. Tel: 651-439-4511; Fax: 651-430-9717. [CEM]
School—St. Croix Catholic School. See Elementary Schools, Consolidated, Parochial under Institutions located in the Archdiocese for details. 621 S. 3rd St., Stillwater, 55082. Tel: 651-439-5581; Fax: 651-439-8360.
Catechesis/Religious Programs—Tel: 651-439-7142; Fax: 651-439-7705.
Students 75.

Bellechester, Goodhue Co., St. Mary (1859) (Luxembourgian), Rev. Peter Njoku (Nigeria) Admin.
Res., 223 Chester Ave., 55027. Tel: 651-923-4305. [CEM]

Belle Creek, Goodhue Co., St. Columbkill (1860) (Irish), Rev. Bruce Peterson.
Res., 311 N. 6th St., Goodhue, 55027. Fax: 651-923-4184. [JC]
Catechesis/Religious Programs—Tel: 612-923-4472.
Students 148.
Mission—Goodhue, Goodhue Co., Holy Trinity, 308 4th St. N., 55027. Tel: 651-923-4472.

Belle Plaine, Scott Co., Our Lady of the Prairie (1972), Rev. Thomas McCabe.
Res., 215 N. Chestnut St., 56011. Tel: 952-873-2323; Fax: 952-873-6717. [CEM 2]
School—Tel: 612-873-6564.
Lay Teachers 5; Students 45.
Catechesis/Religious Programs—Mrs. Donna Woodard, D.R.E.
Students 193.

Buffalo, Wright Co., St. Francis Xavier (1888), Rev. Charles L. Froehle; Deacons Richard Boisclair; Greg Elsenpeter.
Res., 9 N.W. 3rd St., 55313. Tel: 763-682-1183; Fax: 763-682-0485. [CEM 2]
School—Tel: 763-682-1295; Fax: 763-684-5377. Robert Ligday, Prin.
Lay Teachers 16; Students 218.
Catechesis/Religious Programs—Tel: 763-684-5326. D.R.E.: Sharon Kelly; Amanda Busse; Sara Jo Heutinck.
Students 630.

Cannon Falls, Goodhue Co., St. Pius V (1856), Rev. Roger J. Hessian, Admin.; Deacon Patrick Evans.
Res., 410 W. Colvill Ave., P.O. Box 367, 55009-0367. Tel: 507-263-2578; Fax: 507-263-8005. [CEM]
Catechesis/Religious Programs—Tel: 507-263-4800 (Grades PreK-8); 263-4680 (Grades 9-12).
Students 333.

Carver, Carver Co., St. Nicholas (1868) (German), Rev. William J. Paron.
Res., 412 W. Fourth St., Box 133, 55315. Tel: 952-448-2345. [CEM 2]
Catechesis/Religious Programs—Tel: 952-448-7015.
Students 127.

Cedar, Anoka Co., St. Patrick (1894), Rev. Michael J. Kennedy; Thomas Patricia Orzechowski, Parish Admin.; Deacon Terry Scherer.
Res., 19921 Nightingale St., N.W., Oak Grove, 55011-9243. Tel: 763-753-2011; Fax: 763-753-9803. [CEM]
Catechesis/Religious Programs—Tel: 763-753-2036. Emilie Bauer, D.R.E.
Students 708.

Cedar Lake, Scott Co., St. Patrick (1856) (Irish), Rev. Sebastien Bakatuinamina, C.I.C.M.
Res., Cedar Lake Twp., 24425 Old Hwy. 13 Blvd., Jordan, 55352. Tel: 612-492-6276; Fax: 612-492-6276. [CEM]
Catechesis/Religious Programs—Tel: 612-492-6290.
Students 221.
Mission—Spring Lake Twp., Scott Co., St. Catherine, (1865) 4500 E. 220th St., Prior Lake, 55372. Tel: 612-447-2180. [CEM]

Centerville, Anoka Co., St. Genevieve (1854) (French Canadian), Rev. Thomas Fitzgerald.
Res., 7087 Goiffon Ave., 55038. Tel: 651-429-7937; Fax: 651-653-0071. [CEM]
Catechesis/Religious Programs—Tel: 612-426-1818.
Students 230.

Chanhassen, Carver Co., St. Hubert (1865) (German), Revs. Stephen D. Ulrick; Lawrence R. Blake; Deacons Timothy Helmeke; Robert Wagner.
Res., 8201 Main St., 55317. Tel: 952-934-9106; Fax: 952-934-8209. [CEM]
School—Tel: 952-934-6003; Fax: 952-906-1229.
Lay Teachers 35; Students 465.
Catechesis/Religious Programs—Students 1,019.

Chaska, Carver Co., Guardian Angels (1858), Rev. Lawrence R. Johnson.
Res., 215 W. 2nd St., 55318. Tel: 612-448-4100; Fax: 612-448-3076. [CEM]
School—Tel: 612-448-2562; Fax: 612-448-3281.
Lay Teachers 22; Students 305.
Catechesis/Religious Programs—Tel: 612-448-3478.
Students 265.

Clearwater, Wright Co., St. Luke (1870), Rev. Thomas Rayar.
Mailing Address: P.O. Box 249, 55320-0249. Tel: 320-558-2124; Fax: 320-558-2875.
Res., 425 Spring St., 55320. [CEM]
Catechesis/Religious Programs—Students 130.

Cleveland, Le Sueur Co., Church of the Nativity of the Blessed Virgin Mary (1865) (Irish-German), Rev. Glen T. Jenson.
Mailing Address: P.O. Box 187, 56017-0187.
Res., 56017-0187. Tel: 507-931-5409. [CEM]
Catechesis/Religious Programs—Students 67.

Coates, Dakota Co., St. Agatha (1870), Rev. James W. Whalen, Temp. Admin.
Res., University of St. Thomas, 2115 Summit Ave., St. Paul, 55105. Tel: 651-645-2400; Fax: 651-962-6360. [CEM]
Catechesis/Religious Programs—Students 58.

Cologne, Carver Co., St. Bernard (1859), Rev. George Thoomkuzhy (India) (Ujjain).
Res., 212 Church St. E., 55322. Tel: 952-466-2031; Fax: 952-466-2031. [CEM]
School—300 Church St. E., 55322. Tel: 952-466-5917.
Sisters of Notre Dame 1; Lay Teachers 4; Students 55.

Corcoran, Hennepin Co., St. Thomas the Apostle (1896), Rev. George R. Kinney.
Res., 20,000 County Rd. 10, Hamel, 55340. Tel: 612-420-2385; Fax: 612-420-4710. [CEM 4][JC 4]
Catechesis/Religious Programs—Tel: 612-420-2385; Fax: 612-420-4710. D.R.E.: Lori Palmode; Pam Dombeck; Linda Stanton.
Students 313.

Dayton, Hennepin Co., St. John the Baptist (1862) (French Canadian), Revs. Dale Ettel, O.S.C.; David Gallus, O.S.C.
Res., P.O. Box 201, 55327. Tel: 763-428-2828; Fax: 763-428-6462. [CEM 2]
Catechesis/Religious Programs—Tel: 763-856-3122.
Students 157.

Deephaven, Hennepin Co., St. Therese (1946), Rev. Martin Shaiibetter; Deacon James F. McDonald.
Res., 18323 Minnetonka Blvd., 55391. Tel: 612-473-4422; Fax: 612-473-2685.
School—18325 Minnetonka Blvd., 55391. Tel: 952-473-4355.
Sisters 4; Lay Teachers 20; Students 329; Pre-School 47.
Catechesis/Religious Programs—Tel: 612-473-2891; 473-5455. Margaret Stimmler, D.R.E.
Students 827.

Delano, Wright Co., St. Joseph (1902) (Polish), Rev. Thomas G. Boedy, S.J.; Deacons Joseph Frederick; Joseph Kittok.
Church—401 River St., P.O. Box 470, 55328-0470. Tel: 763-972-2077; Fax: 763-972-6177. [CEM]
School—St. Peter School, Tel: 763-972-2528.
Catechesis/Religious Programs—Clustered with St. Peter, Delano. Tel: 763-972-2976.

St. Mary of Czestochowa (1884) (Polish), Rev. James T. Livingston.
Office & Res.: 1867 95th St., S.E., 55328. Tel: 952-955-1139. [CEM]
Catechesis/Religious Programs—Students 63.

St. Peter (1865) (German), Rev. Thomas G. Boedy, S.J.; Deacons Joseph Frederick; Joseph Kittok.
Offices: 204 River St., P.O. Box 470, 55328. Tel: 763-972-2077; Fax: 763-972-6177. [CEM 2]
School—St. Peter, Tel: 763-972-2528.
Lay Teachers 10; Students 131.
Catechesis/Religious Programs—Clustered with St. Joseph, Delano. 235 S. 2nd St., 55328. Tel: 763-972-2976; Fax: 763-972-6177.
Students 300.

Elysian, Le Sueur Co., St. Andrew, Waterville, MN (1894), Rev. Michael W. Ince, Admin.
Church—Box 261, 56028. Tel: 507-267-4928.
Catechesis/Religious Programs—Students 54.

Excelsior, Lake Minnetonka, Hennepin Co., St. John the Baptist (1903), Rev. Mark B. Dosh; Deacons John MacKenzie; Gary Hoffman.
Res., 680 Mill St., 55331. Tel: 952-474-8868; Fax: 952-474-5962. [CEM]
School—Tel: 952-474-5812.
Lay Teachers 14; Students 178.
Catechesis/Religious Programs—Students 42.

Faribault, Rice Co.,

1—IMMACULATE CONCEPTION, (1856), Revs. Kevin Finnegan; Andrew Cozzens; Deacon R. Daniel Wesley.
Res., 4 Second Ave., S.W., 55021-6029. Tel: 507-334-2266; Fax: 507-334-3895. [CEM]
School—Catholic School of Faribault. See Elementary Schools, Consolidated, Parochial under Institutions located in the Archdiocese for details. Tel: 507-334-7704.
Catechesis/Religious Programs—Tel: 507-334-9142.
Students 310.

2—SACRED HEART, (French-German). Merged with St. Lawrence, Faribault, and renamed Sacred Heart - St. Lawrence of Faribault in 1996.

3—ST. LAWRENCE, (1869) (German). Merged with Sacred Heart, Faribault, and renamed Sacred Heart - St. Lawrence of Faribault in 1996.

4—SACRED HEART - ST. LAWRENCE OF FARIBAULT. Sacred Heart, Faribault, and St. Lawrence, Faribault, were merged and renamed in 1996. Rev. David W. Kohner.
Res., 520 4th Ave., N.W., 55021-4227. Tel: 507-334-7175. [CEM]
Catechesis/Religious Programs—Tel: 507-334-1615.
Students 320.

Farmington, Dakota Co., St. Michael (1854), Rev. Eugene A. Pouliot.
Res., 622 5th St., 55024-0227. Tel: 651-463-3360; Fax: 651-463-2339.
Church and Center: 22120 Denmark Ave., P.O. Box 227, 55024. [CEM]
Catechesis/Religious Programs—Students 421.

Forest Lake, Washington Co., St. Peter (1904), Revs. Robert J. Sipe; Jerome C. Kern; Deacons Gary Houle; Ralph L'Allier, Pastoral Min.; Mylo Shoberg.
Res., 1250 S. Shore Dr., 55025. Tel: 651-982-2200; Fax: 651-982-2220. [CEM]
School—Tel: 651-982-2215. Sharon Tomlin, Prin.
Lay Teachers 18; Students 320.
Catechesis/Religious Programs—Tel: 651-464-7557. D.R.E.: Judy Foster; Susan Fast.
Students 664.

Hamel, Hennepin Co., St. Anne (1879), Rev. Robert A. Patterson.
Res., 200 Hamel Rd., Box 256, 55340-0256. Tel: 763-478-6644; Fax: 763-478-9141. [CEM]
Catechesis/Religious Programs—Students 117.

Hampton, Dakota Co., St. Mathias (1900), Rev. Valerius U. Messerich, O.F.M.
Res., 23315 Northfield Blvd., 55031-9701. Tel: 612-437-9030; Fax: 612-437-3427. [CEM]
School—(Grades K-5). Tel: 612-437-5282.
Lay Teachers 4; Students 57.
Catechesis/Religious Programs—Students 145.

Hancock Township, Carver Co., Assumption. Closed. For inquiries for parish records contact the Chancery.

Hassan Township, Hennepin Co., St. Walburga (1857), Deacon Dominic Ehrmentrant.
Res., 12020 Fletcher Ln., Rogers, 55374. Tel: 612-428-2081; Fax: 612-428-4032. [CEM 2]
Catechesis/Religious Programs—Students 89.

Hastings, Dakota Co., St. Elizabeth Ann Seton (1987), Revs. Eugene J. McGlothlin, O.S.B.; Landelin A. Robling, O.S.B.; Stephen G. Beauclair, O.S.B.
Res., 2035 W. Fifteenth St., 55033. Tel: 651-437-4254; Fax: 651-438-2948. [CEM][JC]
School—Tel: 651-437-3098; Fax: 651-438-3377. Rita Humbert, Prin.
Lay Teachers 34; Students 389.
Catechesis/Religious Programs—Tel: 651-437-9191; Fax: 651-437-9785.
Students 391.

Hazelwood, Rice Co., Annunciation of the B.V.M. (1863), Rev. Dennis D. Evenson.
Res., 4996 Hazelwood Ave., Northfield, 55057. Tel: 612-652-2625. [CEM]
Catechesis/Religious Programs—Students 85.

Heidelberg, Le Sueur Co., St. Scholastica (1856) (German-Czech), Rev. Richard P. Roedel.
Res., Rte. 1, Box 218, New Prague, 56071. Tel: 612-758-4292. [CEM]
Catechesis/Religious Programs—Students 4.

Hopkins, Hennepin Co., St. John the Evangelist (1950), Rev. Ralph J. Goman.
Res., 6 Interlachen Rd., 55343. Tel: 952-935-5536; Fax: 952-938-2724.
School—John Ireland Schools. See Elementary Schools, Consolidated, Parochial under Institutions located in the Archdiocese for details. Tel: 952-938-3442.
Catechesis/Religious Programs—Tel: 952-935-4696.
Students 84.

St. Joseph's (1926), Rev. John M. Long; Deacon Francis J. Tangney. In res., Rev. Gerald E. Keefe.
Res., 1310 Main St., 55343. Tel: 952-935-0111; Fax: 952-935-4539. [CEM]
School—John Ireland Schools. See Elementary Schools, Consolidated, Parochial under Institutions located in the Archdiocese for details. Tel: 952-938-3442; Fax: 952-938-3457.
Catechesis/Religious Programs—Tel: 952-935-7004; 935-5059.
Students 268.

Hugo, Washington Co., St. John the Baptist (1902), Rev. Daniel W. Friberg.
Res., 14383 N. Forest Blvd., 55038. Tel: 651426-1004; Fax: 651-429-3190. [CEM]
Catechesis/Religious Programs—Tel: 651-429-9170. Alice Christiansen, D.R.E.
Students 231.

Inver Grove Heights, Dakota Co., St. Patrick (1856) (Irish), Rev. Michael M. Arms; Deacon Harlan Christensen.
Res., 3535 72nd St. E., 55076. Tel: 651-455-6624; Fax: 651-455-8984. [CEM]
Catechesis/Religious Programs—Tel: 651-455-5900.
Students 563.

Jordan, Scott Co., St. John the Baptist (1858), Rev. John J. Mitchell.
Res., 313 E. 2nd St., 55352. Tel: 952-492-2640; Fax: 952-492-5683. [CEM][JC]
School—215 E. 2nd St., 55352. Tel: 612-492-2030; Fax: 612-492-3211.
Lay Teachers 15; Students 155.
Catechesis/Religious Programs—Tel: 952-492-5827.
Students 359.

Kenyon, Goodhue Co., St. Michael (1944), Rev. Dennis C. Kampa, Admin.
Church & Mailing Address: 108 Bullis St., 55946. Tel: 507-789-6120.
Res., 451 5th St., S.W., Box 368, Pine Island, 55963. Tel: 507-356-4944; Fax: 507-356-2080. [CEM]
Catechesis/Religious Programs—Students 145.

Kilkenny, Le Sueur Co., St. Canice (1858) (Irish), Rev. Ronald W. Dahlheimer.
Res., 56052. Tel: 507-595-2561. [CEM]
Catechesis/Religious Programs—Students 126.

Lake St. Croix Beach, Washington Co., St. Francis Of Assisi (1938), Rev. James Kolb, C.S.P.
Res., 16770 13th St., 55043. Tel: 651-436-7817; Fax: 651-436-6524.
Catechesis/Religious Programs—Students 290.

Lakeville, Dakota Co., All Saints (1889), Revs. Eugene W. Tiffany; Robert Grabner; Deacons James Marschall; George Nugent.
Res., 19795 Holyoke Ave., 55044. Tel: 952-469-4481; Fax: 952-469-5752. [CEM]
School—Tel: 952-469-3332. Jan Heuman, Prin.
Lay Teachers 13; Students 307.
Catechesis/Religious Programs—19795 Holyoke Ave., 55044. Tel: 952-469-6461. Mary Brezinski, D.R.E.
Students 1,907.

Le Center, Le Sueur Co., St. Mary (1899), Rev. Raymond G. Monsour.
Res., 165 N. Waterville Ave., 56057. Tel: 507-357-4838; Fax: 507-357-4838. [CEM]
Catechesis/Religious Programs—Tel: 507-357-6633.
Students 234.

Le Sueur, Le Sueur Co., St. Anne (1852), Rev. Kenneth L. O'Hotto.
Res., 217 N. 3rd St., 56058. Tel: 507-665-2047; Fax: 507-665-3811. [CEM 2]
School—Tel: 507-665-2489.
Lay Teachers 9; Students 103.
Catechesis/Religious Programs—503 N. 4th St., 56058. Tel: 507-665-3811.
Students 164.

Lexington, Le Sueur Co., St. Joseph (1903) (Polish), Rev. Richard P. Roedel.
Res., Rte. 1, Box 218, New Prague, 56071. Tel: 952-758-4292. [CEM]
Catechesis/Religious Programs—Students 10.

Lindstrom, Chisago Co., St. Bridget of Sweden (1948), Rev. Charles A. Brambilla.
Res., Box 754, 55045. Tel: 651-257-2474; Fax: 651-257-1498.
Catechesis/Religious Programs—Tel: 651-257-8346.
Students 450.

Long Lake, Hennepin Co., St. George (1917), Rev. Timothy Dolan; Deacon Walter Haselhuhn.
Church—133 N. Brown Rd., 55356-9560. Tel: 952-473-1247. [CEM]
Res., Tel: 952-4476-0170; Fax: 952-404-0129.
Catechesis/Religious Programs—Students 130.

Lonsdale, Rice Co., Immaculate Conception (1903), Rev. A. Michael Sauber.
Res., 55046-0169. Tel: 507-744-2829. [CEM 2]
School—Lonsdale, New Market, Veseli Area School. See Elementary Schools, Consolidated, Parochial under Institutions located in the Archdiocese for details. Tel: 507-744-2394.
Catechesis/Religious Programs—Students 72.

Loretto, Hennepin Co., SS. Peter and Paul (1867). Unassigned.
Mailing Address: P.O. Box 96, 55357. Tel: 763-479-0535; Fax: 763-479-4383.
Res., 145 Railway St., E., 55357. Tel: 763-479-0537. [CEM]
School—Tel: 763-479-0540; Fax: 763-479-4046.
Lay Teachers 13; Students 174.
Catechesis/Religious Programs—Tel: 763-479-0538.
Students 150.

Maple Grove, Hennepin Co., St. Joseph the Worker (1870), Rev. Michael Sullivan; Deacon Donald S. Rinkenberger.
Church—7180 Hemlock Ln., 55369-5597. Tel: 763-425-6505; Fax: 763-425-6587.
Catechesis/Religious Programs—763. Tel: 763-425-9801. Stephen R. Robach, D.R.E.
Students 1,056.

Maple Lake, Wright Co., St. Timothy (1882), Rev. Michael J. McGlauchlin; Deacon Ron Freeman.
Res., 8 N. Oak Ave., Box 281, 55358. Tel: 320-963-3726; Fax: 320-963-2008. [CEM 3]
School—Tel: 320-963-3417. Mr. Frank Mazzuca, Sr., Prin.
Lay Teachers 6; Students 80.
Catechesis/Religious Programs—Students 251.

Marysburg, Le Sueur Co., Immaculate Conception (1857) (Irish), Rev. Glen T. Jenson.
Res., Rte. 1, Box 196, Madison Lake, 56063. Tel: 507-243-4157. [CEM]
Catechesis/Religious Programs—Students 67.

Marystown, Scott Co., St. Mary of the Purification (1855), Rev. John R. Gilbert, (Retired); Deacon Jack Weiland, Parish Life Admin.
15850 Marystown Rd., Shakopee, 55379-9556. [CEM]
Parish Center: Tel: 612-445-2647; Fax: 612-403-9330.
School—Shakopee Area Catholic School. See Elementary Schools, Consolidated, Parochial under Institutions located in the Archdiocese for details.

Miesville, Dakota Co., St. Joseph (1873) (German-Irish), Rev. Marvin J. Klaers. In res., Rev. Michael F. O'Connor, (Retired).
Mailing Address: Office, 23955 Nicolai Ave. E., 55033-9650. Fax: 651-437-3526.
Res., 8433 239th St. E., New Trier, 55031. Tel: 651-437-5520. [CEM]
Church—55033. Tel: 651-437-3526.
Catechesis/Religious Programs—Tel: 651-437-3506.
Students 171.

Minnetonka, Hennepin Co., Immaculate Heart of Mary (1946), Revs. Patrick J. Hipwell; Eugene J. Theisen; Deacon David Huibregtse.
Res., 13505 Excelsior Blvd., 55345. Tel: 952-935-1432; Fax: 952-935-0474.
Catechesis/Religious Programs—Tel: 612-935-7077.
Students 292.

Montgomery, Le Sueur Co., Holy Redeemer (1881), Revs. George J. Grafsky; Clarence J. Vavra.
Res., 206 Vine Ave. W., 56069. Tel: 507-364-7981; Fax: 507-364-8660. [CEM 2]
School—205 Vine Ave. W., 56069. Tel: 507-364-7383.
Sisters of St. Benedict 1; Lay Teachers 12; Students 131.
Catechesis/Religious Programs—Students 160.

Monticello, Wright Co., St. Henry (1904), Rev. Timothy C. Rudolphi; Deacons Cecil Adams; Greg Woznick.
Office: 1001 E. 7th St., 55362. Tel: 763-295-2402; Fax: 763-295-6333. [CEM]
Catechesis/Religious Programs—D.R.E.: Renee Logeais; Karen Jendro.
Students 698.
Convent—Sisters of the Presentation.

Mound, Hennepin Co., Our Lady of the Lake (1909), Rev. Stan P. Mader.
Res., 2385 Commerce Blvd., 55364. Tel: 952-472-1284; Fax: 952-472-1216. [CEM]
Preschool:—.
Students 65.
School—Tel: 952-472-3400; Fax: 952-472-3400. Susan Harries, Prin.
Lay Teachers 18; Students 209.
Catechesis/Religious Programs—Tel: 952-472-4848.
Students 300.

New Market, Scott Co., St. Nicholas (1893) (German), Rev. George A. Welzbacher.
Res., 51 Church St., P.O. Box 9, 55054-0009. Tel: 952-461-2403; Fax: 952-461-2403. [CEM]
School—Lonsdale, New Market, Veseli Area School. See Elementary Schools, Consolidated, Parochial under Institutions located in the Archdiocese for details. Tel: 507-744-2394; Fax: 507-744-4117.

New Prague, Scott Co., St. Wenceslaus (1857), Rev. George J. Freeman; Deacons Leonard J. Shanbour; Robert Raleigh.
Res., 215 Main St. E., 56071-1837. Tel: 612-758-3225; Fax: 612-758-2960. [CEM]
School—Tel: 612-758-3133; Fax: 612-758-2958. Sarah Mueller, Prin.
Lay Teachers 20; Students 339.
Catechesis/Religious Programs—Tel: 612-758-2276. Margaret Benson, D.R.E.
Students 263.

New Trier, Dakota Co., St. Mary (1856), Rev. Marvin J. Klaers.
Res., 8433 239th St. E., Hampton, 55031. Tel: 651-437-5520. [CEM]
School—Tel: 651-437-5546; Fax: 651-437-5546.
Lay Teachers 3; Students 29.
Catechesis/Religious Programs—Students 40.

North Branch, Chisago Co., St. Gregory (1874), Revs. John F. Parkos; James T. Schoenberger, (Retired); Deacon Thomas P. Langlois; Elizabeth R. Langlois, Pastoral Min.
Res., P.O. Box 609, 55056. Tel: 612-674-4056. [CEM]
Catechesis/Religious Programs—Tel: 612-674-7382.
Students 349.

Northfield, Rice Co., St. Dominic (1869), Rev. Francis L. Fried; Deacon Len Gruber.
Office & Mailing Address: 216 N. Spring St., 55057-1431. Tel: 507-645-8816; Fax: 507-645-8818.
Res., 116 N. Linden St., 55057. Tel: 507-663-0154. [CEM]
School—Tel: 507-645-8136.
School Sisters of Notre Dame 1; Students 209.
Catechesis/Religious Programs—Students 373.

Norwood, Carver Co., Ascension (1859) (German), Rev. Paul C. Ardolf.
Res., 323 Reform St., N., 55368. Tel: 612-467-3351. [CEM 2]
Catechesis/Religious Programs—Students 140.

Brooklyn Park, Hennepin Co., St. Vincent de Paul (1855) (French), Revs. Curtis F. Lybarger; Mark Maus; Deacon Sherman H. Otto.
Res., 9100 93rd Ave. N., 55445-1407. Tel: 763-425-2210; Fax: 763-425-7898. [CEM]
School—Tel: 763-425-3970; Fax: 763-425-2674.
Lay Teachers 15; Students 335.
Catechesis/Religious Programs—D.R.E.: Arlys Lingen; Renee Paske, (Elementary); Bruce Baumann, (Jr. & Sr. High School); Kathleen Pommerlau, (Preschool).
Students 1,480.

Pine Island, Goodhue Co., St. Michael (1878), Rev. Dennis C. Kampa.
Res., P.O. Box 368, 55963-0368. Tel: 507-356-4944; Fax: 507-356-2080. [CEM]
Catechesis/Religious Programs—Tel: 507-356-4280.
Students 239.
Mission—Kenyon, Goodhue Co., St. Michael, 108 Bullis St., Kenyon, 55946. Tel: 507-789-6120.

Prior Lake, Scott Co., St. Michael (1912), Rev. Richard A. Banker; Deacon Russell D. Shupe.
Res., 16311 Duluth Ave., S.E., 55372. Tel: 952-447-2491; Fax: 952-447-2489. [CEM 2]
Preschool:—Tel: 952-447-2483; Fax: 952-447-2182.
Lay Teachers 2; Students 80.
School—(Grades K-8). Tel: 952-447-2124.
Sisters 1; Lay Teachers 29; Students 486.
Catechesis/Religious Programs—Tel: 612-447-2486; Fax: 612-447-2489. D.R.E.: Janel Boegeman, (Elementary); Gina Tupy, (Senior High).
Students 605.

Red Wing, Goodhue Co., St. Joseph (1865), Rev. Thomas J. Walker.
Res., 426 8th St., 55066. Tel: 651-388-1133; Fax: 651-388-5294. [CEM]
School—Tel: 651-388-9493. Marion Willis, Prin.
Religious 1; Lay Teachers 8; Students 111.
Catechesis/Religious Programs—Tel: 651-388-6000.
Students 580.

Rogers, Hennepin Co., St. Martin (1912), Rev. Lawrence R. Johnson.
Office: 21304 Church Ave., 55374-9445. Tel: 763-428-2585; Fax: 763-428-3460. [CEM]
School—Tel: 763-428-2355; Fax: 763-428-2062.
Lay Teachers 10; Students 154.
Catechesis/Religious Programs—Tel: 763-428-2427; Fax: 763-428-2427.
Students 215.

Rosemount, Dakota Co., St. Joseph (1865), Rev. Thomas F. Hill, O.F.M.Cap.
Res., 14375 S. Robert Tr., 55068. Tel: 651-423-4402; Fax: 651-423-6616. [CEM 2]
School—Tel: 651-423-1658.
Sisters 1; Lay Teachers 9; Students 234.
Catechesis/Religious Programs—Tel: 651-423-3131; Fax: 651-423-1855. Sr. Mary Louise McKenna, D.R.E.
Students 765.

Rush City, Chisago Co., Sacred Heart (1872) (Irish), Rev. Ralph F. Huar.
Res., P.O. Box 45, 55069. Tel: 320-358-4370. [CEM]
Catechesis/Religious Programs—Students 115.

St. Benedict, Scott Co., St. Benedict (German), Rev. Elgar Bockenfeld, O.F.M.
Res., Rte. 1, P.O. Box 93, New Prague, 56071. Tel: 612-738-4642. [CEM][JC]
Catechesis/Religious Programs—Students 39.

St. Bonifacius, Hennepin Co., St. Boniface (1859) (German), Rev. James T. Livingston.
Res., 4025 Main St., P.O. Box 68, 55375. Tel: 612-446-1054; Fax: 612-446-1158. [CEM]
Catechesis/Religious Programs—8801 Wildwood Ave., P.O. Box 276, 55375. Tel: 952-446-1224.
Students 106.

St. Henry, Le Sueur Co., Church of St. Henry, Rev. Frederick C. Meyer.
Mailing Address: P.O. Le Sueur, R.R. No. 1, Box 52, 56058. Tel: 507-357-4990. [CEM]
Catechesis/Religious Programs—Students 57.

St. Michael, Wright Co., St. Michael (1857), Rev. Leonard Siebenaler; Deacons Maynard Warne; Donald Becker.
Res., P.O. Box 180, 55376. Tel: 612-497-2745; Fax: 612-497-2745. [CEM]
School—Tel: 612-497-3887.
Lay Teachers 18; Students 239.
Catechesis/Religious Programs—Students 760.

St. Paul Park, Washington Co., St. Thomas Aquinas (1885), Rev. Gregory L. Esty.
Res., 920 Holly Ave., 55071. Tel: 651-459-2131; Fax: 651-459-8765. [CEM]
Catechesis/Religious Programs—Fax: 651-459-8756.
Students 440.

St. Thomas, Le Sueur Co., St. Thomas (1858) (Irish), Rev. Richard P. Ruedel.
Res., Rte. 1, Box 218, New Prague, 56071. Tel: 612-758-4292. [CEM]
Catechesis/Religious Programs—Students 16.

Savage, Scott Co., St. John the Baptist (1854), Revs. Peter C. Wittman; Rinaldo B. Custodio; Deacon Tom Michaud.
Res., 55378. Tel: 952-890-9465; Fax: 952-890-3006. [CEM]
School—Tel: 952-890-6604; Fax: 952-890-9465.
Lay Teachers 34; Students 829.
Catechesis/Religious Programs—Tel: 952-890-9434; Fax: 952-890-9481. D.R.E.: Amy Kusber; Andi Little; Jan Jirik; Tracy Tredinnick.
Students 952.

Shakopee, Scott Co., St. Mark (1856) (German), Rev. William F. Stolzman; Deacon William Beckfield.
Res., 350 S. Atwood St., 55379-1238. Tel: 952-445-1229; Fax: 952-445-9639. [JC 2]
School—Shakopee Area Catholic School. See Elementary Schools, Consolidated, Parochial under Institutions located in the Archdiocese for details. Tel: 952-445-3387; Fax: 952-445-7256.
Catechesis/Religious Programs—305 S. Scott St., 55379. Tel: 952-445-3488; Fax: 952-402-9210.
Students 565.

St. Mary (1865) (Irish), Rev. Joseph Fink; Deacon James L. Thornton.
Res., 535 S. Lewis St., 55379. Tel: 952-445-1319; Fax: 952-445-0511. [CEM][JC]
School—Shakopee Area Catholic School. See Elementary Schools, Consolidated, Parochial under Institutions located in the Archdiocese for details. Tel: 952-445-3387; 445-3159; Fax: 952-445-7256.
Catechesis/Religious Programs—Shakopee Area Religious Education. This is a consolidation of three parish programs. 305 S. Scott St., 55379. Tel: 952-445-3488. D.R.E.: Carol Hauser; Karen Martin.
Students 567.

Shieldsville, Rice Co., St. Patrick (1856) (Irish-Czech), Revs. Clarence Vavra; George J. Grafsky.
Res., 7525 Dodd Rd., Faribault, 55021. Tel: 507-334-6002. [CEM]
Catechesis/Religious Programs—Students 108.

South St. Paul, Dakota Co., Holy Trinity (1918) (Polish), Revs. John M. LeVoir; Mark D. Moriarty.
Res., 752 5th Ave. S., 55075. Tel: 651-455-1228.
Office: 749 6th Ave. S., 55075. Tel: 651-455-1302; Fax: 651-455-6004.
School—745 6th Ave. S., 55075. Tel: 651-455-8557.
Lay Teachers 24; Students 386.
Catechesis/Religious Programs—Tel: 651-455-6004.
Students 223.

St. Augustine (1896), Revs. John M. LeVoir; Mark D. Moriarty.
Res., 302 5th Ave. N., 55075. Tel: 651-451-1212.
Catechesis/Religious Programs—Tel: 651-451-1560; 451-0685; Fax: 651-451-1560. Sr. Bernadine Frischmon, O.S.B., D.R.E.
Students 190.

St. John Vianney (1946), Rev. Thadeus Aravindathu; Deacon Fred de los Reyes.
Res., 789 17th Ave. N., 55075. Tel: 651-451-1863; Fax: 651-451-1864. [CEM]
School—1815 Bromley, 55075. Tel: 651-451-8395.
Lay Teachers 12; Students 310.
Catechesis/Religious Programs—Students 285.

Stillwater, Washington Co., St. Mary (1865), Revs. Michael C. Skluzacek; Michael S. Creagan; Deacon Russell J. Evans, Pastoral Admin.

Church & Mailing Address: 423 S. Fifth St., 55082. Res., 407 S. 5th St., 55082. Tel: 651-439-1270; Fax: 651-439-7705. [JC]
School—St. Croix Catholic School. See Elementary Schools, Consolidated, Parochial under Institutions located in the Archdiocese for details. Tel: 651 439-5581; Fax: 651-439-8360.
Catechesis/Religious Programs—Tel: 651-439-7142.
Students 128.

St. Michael (1853), Revs. Michael C. Skluzacek; Michael S. Creagan; Deacon Roger Carlson.
Res., 407 S. 5th St., 55082. Tel: 651-439-4400; Fax: 651-430-3271. [JC]
School—St. Croix Catholic School. See Elementary Schools, Consolidated, Parochial under Institutions located in the Archdiocese for details. Tel: 651-439-5581; Fax: 651-439-8360. Cressy Epperly, Prin.
Catechesis/Religious Programs—Tel: 651-439-7142; Fax: 651-439-7705. William Klein, D.R.E.
Students 386.

Taylors Falls, Chisago Co., St. Joseph's (1873), Rev. Albert J. Shanley, M.S.; Deacon Kevin Madden.
Res., 500 River St., 55084. Tel: 651-465-7345. [CEM][JC]
Catechesis/Religious Programs—Students 220.
Mission—Franconia, Chisago Co., St. Francis Xavier, 55084.

Union Hill, Le Sueur Co., St. John the Evangelist, Rev. Elgar Bockenfeld, O.F.M.
Res., Rte. 1, P.O. Box 93, New Prague, 56071. Tel: 612-758-4642. [CEM]
Catechesis/Religious Programs—Students 136.

Vermillion, Dakota Co., St. John the Baptist (1881), Rev. Joseph J. Arackal, V.C.
Res., 106 W. Main St., 55085. Tel: 651-437-5652; Fax: 651-437-1933. [CEM]
School—111 W. Main St., 55085. Tel: 651-437-2644; Fax: 651-437-2644.
Franciscan Clarist Sisters 2; Lay Teachers 6; Students 89.
Catechesis/Religious Programs—Students 121.

Veseli, Rice Co., Most Holy Trinity (1874) (Czech), Rev. John G. Lapensky.
Res., 9845 Main St., 55046. Tel: 507-744-2823; Fax: 507-744-2823. [CEM 2]
School—Lonsdale, New Market, Veseli Area School. See Elementary Schools, Consolidated, Parochial under Institutions located in the Archdiocese for details. Tel: 507-744-2394; Fax: 507-744-2395.
Catechesis/Religious Programs—Students 174.

Victoria, Carver Co., St. Victoria (1856) (German), Rev. Robert L. White; Deacons Allan Schroeder; James Huber.
Res., 8228 Victoria Dr., 55386. Tel: 612-443-2661; Fax: 612-443-3866. [CEM]
Catechesis/Religious Programs—Tel: 612-443-3536.
Students 145.

Waconia, Carver Co., St. Joseph (1859), Rev. Martin J. Siebenaler.
Res., 32 E. 1st St., 55387. Tel: 952-442-2384; Fax: 952-442-2538. [CEM]
School—Tel: 952-442-4500; Fax: 952-442-4671.
Lay Teachers 12; Students 192.
Catechesis/Religious Programs—Tel: 952-442-4871.
Students 199.

Watertown, Carver Co., Immaculate Conception (1863) (German-Irish), Rev. Frank J. Wampach.
Res., 109 Angel Ave., N.W., P.O. Box 548, 55388. Tel: 612-955-1458; Fax: 612-955-1777. [CEM]
Catechesis/Religious Programs—113 Angel Ave., N.W., Tel: 612-955-1777. Patti Pokorney, D.R.E.
Students 300.

Waterville, Le Sueur Co., Holy Trinity (1892), Rev. Michael W. Ince.
Res., 506 Common St., 56096. Tel: 507-362-4311. [CEM]
Catechesis/Religious Programs—Tel: 507-362-8396.
Students 103.

Waverly, Wright Co., St. Mary (1884), Rev. Robert Wiley, S.M.
Res., P.O. Box 278, 55390. Tel: 763-658-4319; Fax: 763-658-3519. [CEM][JC 3]
Catechesis/Religious Programs—Tel: 763-658-4118.
Students 260.

Wayzata, Hennepin Co., Holy Name (1865), Rev. Arnold Weber, O.S.B.; Deacons Joe Wierschem; Nelson Hickman; Terry Schneider; Mike Winn.
Res., 155 County Rd., 24, 55391. Fax: 612-473-3488. [CEM]
School—Tel: 763-473-3675; Fax: 763-745-3499.
Lay Teachers 22; Students 363.
Catechesis/Religious Programs—Tel: 763-473-7901.
Students 1463.

St. Bartholomew (1916), Rev. Michael A. Reding.
Office: 630 E. Wayzata Blvd., 55391. Tel: 952-473-6601; Fax: 952-473-0980.
School—(Grades PreK-6). Tel: 952-473-6189.
Lay Teachers 17; Students 294.
Catechesis/Religious Programs—Students 390.

Zumbrota, Goodhue Co., St. Paul (1900), Rev. Peter Njoku (Nigeria).
Office & Mailing Address: 749 S. Main St., 55992-1608. Tel: 507-732-5324; Fax: 507-732-5324.
Res., 590 Sequoia Ln., 55992. Tel: 507-732-4396. [CEM][JC]
Catechesis/Religious Programs—Tel: 507-732-5501; Fax: 507-732-5501.
Students 122.

Chaplains of Public Institutions

ST. PAUL. *Bethesda Medical Center*. Rev. Jonathan Fischer, O.S.B, Chap.
Gillette Children's Hospital. Revs. Joseph Menker, O.M.I.; Robert Allie, O.M.I.
HealthEast, Inc. Rev. Gerald K. Foley (CR).
Ramsey County Correctional Facilities. Rev. Edward J. Flahavan.
Ramsey County Home. Vacant. 1735 Kennard St., 55109.
St. Joseph's Hospital. Rev. Michael Erlander, Chap.
St. Paul-Ramsey Hospital 261 E. 8th St., 55101. Revs. Joseph Menker, O.M.I.; Robert Allie, O.M.I.
United Hospitals, Inc. Rev. Joseph A. Andrade, Chap.

MINNEAPOLIS. *Abbot-Northwestern Hospital* 3617 38th Ave. S., 55066. Rev. Clement J. Burke (DUB).
Hennepin County Courts. Rev. James W. Jackson, 2055 Bohland Ave., St. Paul, 55116.
Hennepin County Medical Center 2421 Third Ave. S., 55404. Rev. James R. DeBruycker.
Metropolitan Medical Center. Rev. James Cassidy, Chap.
Minneapolis Children's Medical Center 3617 38th Ave. S., 55406. Rev. Robert A. Patterson.
Minnesota Soldiers' Home. Rev. Eugene J. Abbott.
Riverside Medical Center 2450 Riverside Ave., 55454. Rev. Leo J. Tibesar.
University of Minnesota Hospitals. Rev. Joseph N. Pershe, S.J., Chap.
Veterans Administration Medical Center. Rev. Joseph Safraniec, Chap.

ANOKA. *Anoka State Hospital*. Vacant. 516 School St., 55303.

EDINA. *Fairview-Southdale Hospital*. Rev. Jerome W. Fehn, Chap.

FARIBAULT. *Faribault State School and Hospital*. Attended by Immaculate Conception Parish. Braille and Sight Saving School, Minnesota School for the Deaf, (Retardation).

GOLDEN VALLEY. *North Memorial Hospital*. Rev. Leo D. Krautkremer, 4003 Bryant Ave. N., Minneapolis, 55412.

LINO LAKES. *Minnesota Correctional Facility*. Rev. Msgr. J. Jerome Boxleitner, Chap., 1121 E. 46th St., Minneapolis, 55407.

MAPLEWOOD. *St. John's Hospital*. (Lutheran) 1575 Beam Ave., 55109. Rev. Fabian F. Burdiek, O.F.M.

ST. LOUIS PARK. *Methodist Hospital*. Rev. Jerome W. Fehn, Chap.

SHAKOPEE. *Women's State Reformatory*. Rev. James T. Schoenberger, Church of St. Gregory, North Branch.

STILLWATER. *Minnesota State Prison*. Rev. Gregory A. Skrypek.

Special Assignment:
Reverend Fathers—
Gamber, William K., Chap., V.A. Medical Center
Hubbard, Lawrence E., Hispanic Ministry
Jackson, James W., Chap., Hennepin County Courts
Jeub, Richard H., Chancery Pro Tem
Kapoun, Robert E., Chancery Pro Tem
Lepak, Roy C., Hermit, Cotton, MN
Notebaart, James C., Office of Indian Ministry
Snyder, Larry J., Catholic Charities
Stevens, Michael J., Catholic Education Center
Wajda, Joseph L., Tribunal
Walsh, Harry A., Chancery Pro Tem

On Duty Outside the Archdiocese:
Reverend Monsignors—
Namie, James B., Maronite Chancery, P.O. Box 280036 - Dyker Heights Station, Brooklyn, NY 11228-0002
Reverend Fathers—
Brandes, John F., Parroquia San Lucas Toliman, Dept. Solola 07013 Guatemala
Bury, Harold J., P.O. Box 20310, Cleveland, OH 44120
Magee, Paul L., El Buen Pastor Parroquia San Francisco de Asis, Apartado 272, Puerto Ordaz, Estado Bolivar, 8015 Venezuela
O'Connell, Marvin R., University of Notre Dame, IN
Schaffer, Gregory J., El Buen Pastor Parraquia San Francisco de Asis, Apartado 22, Puerto Ordaz, Estado Bolivar 8015 Venezuala
Slusser, Michael S., Dept. of Theology, Duquesne Univ., Pittsburgh, PA 15282

Military Chaplains:
Reverend Fathers—
Himmelsbach, James R., U.S. Army
Smith, John B., U.S. Army
Vakoc, Henry T., U.S. Army

Graduate Studies:
Reverend Fathers—
Byron, J. Michael
Conlin, Daniel C.

Retired:
Reverend Monsignors—
Baumgaertner, William L., 2190 Summit Ave., St. Paul, MN 55105
Boxleitner, J. Jerome, 1011 E. 46th St., Minneapolis, MN 55407
DuLac, Henri J., 1011 Feltl Ct., No. 628, Hopkins, MN 55343
Fleming, Francis J., 2115 Summit Ave., Mail #4337, St. Paul, MN 55105
Hessian, Patrick J., 8066 Timber Lake Dr., Eden Prairie, MN 55347
Kneal, Ellsworth, 2260 Summit Ave., St. Paul, MN 55105
Lavin, James M., 2115 Summit Ave., St. Paul, MN 55105
Murphy, Terrance J., 2115 Summit Ave., St. Paul, MN 55105
Probst, Robert L., College of St. Thomas, 2115 Summit Ave., St. Paul, MN 55105
Sankovitz, John P., 2115 Summit Ave., St. Paul, MN 55105
Srnec, Stanley J., Leo Byrne Residence, St. Paul, MN
Sweeney, John A., 60 S. Mississippi River Blvd., #227, St. Paul, MN 55105
Reverend Fathers—
Abbott, Eugene J., 1241 Edgcumbe Rd., St. Paul, MN 55105
Beckman, Martin A., P.O. Box 1751, Minnetonka, MN 55345
Berg, Richard V., 60 S. Mississippi River Blvd., St. Paul, MN 55105
Blais, Melvin J., Gallery Towers-Unit 1606, 26 W. 10th St., St. Paul, MN 55102
Boller, Robert J., 1435 Hampshire S., St. Louis Park, MN 55426
Brandes, John F., Parroquia San Lucas Toliman, DeptoSola La, 07013 Guatemala
Brown, John T., Box 10, Cannon Falls, MN 55009
Burns, Donald W., 2067 Sheperd Rd. #205, St. Paul, MN 55116
Clubb, Ronald E., St. Benedict, Honaunau, HI 96726
Cody, Nicholas A., P.O. Box 22, Cross Lake, MN 56442
Colon, Vincent A., 2350 Springside Dr., Maplewood, MN 55119
Conroy, Thomas J., 2115 Summit Ave., Mail 4042, St. Paul, MN 55105
DeSutter, Gilbert J., 24571 W. Cedar Lake Dr., Jordan, MN 55352
Dobihal, Robert F., 2067 Shepard Rd., Apt. 202, St. Paul, MN 55116
Dolan, Leo A., 2190 Summit Ave., St. Paul, MN 55105
Donahue, John G., Maternity of Mary, St. Paul, MN
Dufresne, Oliver J., 26262 Hwy. 65, N.E., Isanti, MN 55040
Dunn, John P., 1926 Norfolk Ave., St. Paul, MN 55116
Egan, Harvey F., 121 S. Washington, No. 512, Minneapolis, MN 55401
Eggert, Charles M., 2190 Summit Ave., St. Paul, MN 55105
Endres, Gilbert J., 13100 318th St., Lot 158, Lindstrom, MN 55045
Fitzpatrick, John P., Rte. 1, P.O. Box 825, Ogilvie, MN 56358
Flahavan, Edward J., 811 Portland Ave., St. Paul, MN 55104
Fleming, Martin M.P., 383 Portland Ave., St. Paul, MN 55104
Gamber, William K.
Gannon, Joseph T., 2190 Summit Ave., St. Paul, MN 55105
Garvey, Thomas J., 1041 16th Ave., S.E., Minneapolis, MN 55414
Gilbert, John R., St. Mary of the Purification, Shakopee, MN 55379
Grieman, Gerald G., 264 Ashurst Dr., Phoenix, AZ
Grzeskowiak, Edward S.

Guminga, Theodore C., St. Hedwig, Minneapolis, MN 55418
Hamel, Robert F., 2136 Reaney, St. Paul, MN 55119
Hermes, Roger J., 2329 N. Recker Rd., #117, Mesa, AZ
Holl, James E., 1800-111th Ave., N.W., Coon Rapids, MN 55433
Huber, Leo R., 2260 Summit Ave., Box 325, St. Paul, MN 55105
Janski, Jerome J., 16551 S. Temple Dr., St. Paul, MN 55345
Jenniges, Leonard J., R.R. 2, Sanborn, MN 56083
Jude, Robert J., P.O. Box 219, Maple Lake, MN 55358
Kapoun, Robert E., 17135 Fisher Rd., Cold Spring, MN 56320-9706
Karels, Agdus S., 513 N.W. 4th St., Ortonville, MN 56278
Keane, Robert E., 5921 14th Ave. S., Minneapolis, MN 55417
Keefe, Gerald E.
Keller, Lawrence E., 1212 Larpenteur Ave. E., St. Paul, MN 55109
Kelly, John W., 1900 Wellesley Ave., St. Paul, MN 55105
Kenney, William J., Our Lady of Mount Carmel, Minneapolis, MN 55413
Kittock, Francis R., Leo Byrne Residence, St. Paul, MN
Klein, Bernard C., 86 Wilkin St., #203, St. Paul, MN 55102
Kolar, Thomas F., 2750 N. Victoria St., Room 225, Roseville, MN 55113
Kubat, Alphonse M., 2190 Summit Ave., St. Paul, MN 55105
Larkin, Richard
LaVan, Kenneth G., St. Joseph, Lino Lakes, MN 55014
Mahon, Ambrose J., 1010 Coventry Pl., Edina, MN 55435
Mahoney, Richard J.
McIntyre, Allen J., Leo Byrne Residence, St. Paul, MN
Mertz, Frederick A., 391 Laurel Ave., #102, St. Paul, MN 55102
Mertz, William H., 4115 Beaver Dam Rd., Eagan, MN 55152
Mitchell, John E., 1824 Eleanor Ave., St. Paul, MN 55116
Moorman, Raymond J., 3220 S. Yosemite Ave. S., St. Louis Park, MN 55416
Moudry, Richard P., 11113 Hyland Ter., Eden Prairie, MN 55344
Mycue, Gordon E., 5805 Winnetka Ave. N., New Hope, MN 55428
Namie, James B., 9701 Shore Rd. #4A, Brooklyn, NY 11209
Payant, Remi J., 2190 Summit Ave., St. Paul, MN 55105
Pingatore, Thomas J., Pastor Emeritus, St. Ambrose, Woodbury, MN
Reidy, James E., University of St. Thomas, C301, Mail 4066, St. Paul, MN
Riley, John F., 2190 Summit Ave., St. Paul, MN 55105
Roach, Francis J., 2132 Bard Ct., P.O. Box 1064, Faribault, MN 55021
Russell, J. Christopher, Leo Byrne Residence, St. Paul, MN
Schoenberger, James T., Leo Byrne Residence, St. Paul, MN
Seefeldt, Wilbert T., 15442 Red Oaks Rd., S.E., Prior Lake, MN 55372
Siebenaler, John M., Leo Byrne Residence, St. Paul, MN
Skluzacek, Richard F., 1903 Silver Bell Rd., Eagan, MN 55122
Stromberg, James S., University of St. Thomas, St. Paul, MN
Thurner, Robert M., Chancery Pro Tem, 2190 Summit Ave., St. Paul, MN 55105
Vrana, Francis R., 14840 62nd St. N., No. 205, Stillwater, MN 55082
Wagner, Alfred S., 2190 Summit Ave., St. Paul, MN 55105
Whalen, James W., University of St. Thomas
Whittier, William O., St. Mary of the Lake, White Bear Lake, MN 55110
Wirth, John J., 330 S. Exchange, St. Paul, MN 55102
Wirth, Richard P., 2350 Stillwater Ave. #212, St. Paul, MN 55117
Wittman, Karl M., Leo Byrne Residence, St. Paul, MN
Wolter, Richard J., Leo Byrne Residence, St. Paul, MN
Zweber, Clement J., P.O. Box 962, Lakeville, MN 55044
Zweber, Raymond J., 330 S. Exchance St. #422, St. Paul, MN 55102

Permanent Deacons:
Allen, Nathan, Cathedral of St. Paul
Asenbrenner, Francis, Maternity of Mary, St. Paul
Babcock, George H., (Retired)
Backmann, Howard, St. Anthony of Padua, MN
Barrett, Ervin F., (Retired)
Barrett, Thomas F., St. John the Baptist, Hugo
Barrett, W. Richard, Holy Spirit, St. Paul
Baskfield, James F., Diocese of Duluth
Beck, William E., St. Paul, Ham Lake
Becker, Donald L., St. Michael, St. Michael
Beckfeld, William F., St. Mark, Shakopee
Bednarczyk, Peter, St. Stephen, Anoka
Bellavance, Peter G., St. Mary, Stillwater
Berghoff, William J., St. Richard, Richfield
Bernard, Charles V., Risen Savior, Burnsville
Bilder, Jerome J., (Retired)
Bisek, Jerome H., St. Alphonsus, Brooklyn Center and AIDS Ministry
Blissenbach, Gerald, (Retired)
Boatwright, Stephen, St. Olaf, Minneapolis
Boisclair, A. Richard, St. Francis, Buffalo
Bramwell, Robert, St. Thomas, Corcoran
Broich, Richard, St. Edward, Bloomington
Brown, Fredrick L., (Retired)
Campbell, Kevin A., On Leave of Absence
Carlson, Paul, St. Lawrence, Minneapolis and Metropolitan Tribunal
Carlson, Roger B., St. Mary, Stillwater
Christensen, Harlan L., St. Patrick, Inver Grove Heights
Ciresi, Jerome D., St. Odilia, Shoreview
Coleman, Thomas F., Sacred Heart, Robbinsdale
Conlin, Robert E., (Retired)
D'Heilly, Peter, Dir., Center for Diaconate and Visitation, Minneapolis
DeLosReyes, Alfredo L., St. John Vianney, South St. Paul
DeLuney, Jon, St. Bonaventure, Bloomington; Minneapolis Police Dept.
Devine, Gerald L., St. Peter, North St. Paul
DeVinney, Charles A., Unassigned
Dinzeo, Anthony J., Sabbatical
Dolan, Thomas E., Holy Rosary, Minneapolis
Dols, Bernard R., St. Timothy, Blaine
Dondelinger, James, St. Austin, Minneapolis
Donnelly, Patrick T., (Retired)
Dornfeld, Willard, St. Edward, Bloomington
Dubay, Frank X., Diocese of Venice, FL
Dzik, Thomas W., St. Luke, St. Paul
Ehrmantraut, Dominic, St. Stephen, Anoka and St. Walburga, Fletcher
Elsenpeter, Gregory, St. Francis, Buffalo
Erpenbach, William L., Sacred Heart, St. Lawrence, Faribault
Evans, Patrick, St. Pius V, Cannon Falls
Evans, Russell, St. Mary, Stillwater
Falvey, William E., St. Adalbert, St. Paul
Feffer, Edward F., (Retired)
Ferguson, Delmar F., (Retired)
Fidler, Donald, Holy Name, Minneapolis
Flood, John J., St. Odilia, Shoreview
Frederick, Joseph J., Delano Catholic Community
Freeman, Ronald, St. Timothy, Maple Lake
Friesen, Michael, St. John Neumann, Eagan
Gerdts, Michael G., Pax Christi, Eden Prairie
Getz, Ronald L., Retired
Glover, Guy, St. Michael/St. Mary, Stillwater
Gruber, Leonard L., St. Dominic, Northfield
Hamilton, Donald, St. Rose of Lima, Roseville
Hanson, Dennis, Holy Name, Medina
Harrer, Timothy, St. Joseph, Waconia
Haselhuhn, Walter, St. George, Long Lake
Hathaway, Donald F., (Retired)
Heidenreich, Michael, Diocese of Las Vegas, NV
Helmeke, Timothy, St. Hubert, Chanhassen
Hepp, James E., Cathedral of St. Paul, St. Paul
Hickman, Nelson, Holy Name, Medina
Hoffman, Gary, St. John Excelsior
Holst, David, St. Alphonsus, Brooklyn Park
Houle, Gary J., St. Peter, Forest Lake
Huber, James, St. Victoria, Victoria
Huberty, Peter J., (Retired)
Hughesdon, Harold, St. Agnes, St. Paul
Huibregtse, David, Immaculate Heart of Mary, Minnetonka, AIDS Ministry
Humbert, Michael, St. Elizabeth Ann Seaton, Hastings
Ingwell, David, Basilica of St. Mary, Minneapolis
Janes, Edward, St. Peter, Richfield
Jaques, Martin, Sacred Heart, St Paul
Jents, Kevin, St. Timothy, Blaine
Johnson, Fred, St. Peter Claver, St. Paul
Kasbohm, Thomas F., (Retired)
Kenney, Joseph G., St. John the Baptist, New Brighton
Keyes, Thomas, St. John the Evangelist, Little Canada
Kirchoffner, Daniel D., Transfiguration, Maplewood & St. Genevieve, Centerville
Kittok, Joseph, St. Peter/St. Joseph, Delano
Klish, Richard, St. John Neumann, Eagan
Konkel, Thomas A., St. Joseph, Lino Lakes
Koop, Steven E., St. Rita, Cottage Grove
Kuebler, Myon, St. Michael, Pine Island
L'Allier, Ralph, St. Peter, Forest Lake
Langlois, Thomas, St. Gregory the Great, North Branch
Laqui, Marciano I., St. Bernard, St. Paul
Lee, Joseph, Office of Indian Ministry, National Korean Evangelization
Lo, Va Thai, Hmong Community, St. Vincent de Paul, St. Paul
Lukach, George, Diocese of Spokane
MacKenzie, John M., St. John the Baptist, Excelsior
Madden, Kevin, St. Joseph, Taylors Falls; St. Francis, Franconia
Mangan, John T., Minnesota Veteran's Home
Mann, George A., On Leave of Absence
Mantel, James F., On Leave of Absence
Marshall, James, All Saints, Lakeville
May, Bobby, St. Alphonsus, Brooklyn Center
McDonald, James F., St. Therese, Deephaven
McLaughlin, James, Nativity, Bloomington
McPherson, Joseph T., Office of Indian Ministry
Medley, Michael, St. Ignatius, Annandale
Medlicott, James V., (Retired)
Michaud, Thomas P., St. John, Savage
Moses, Steven, St. Ambrose, Woodbury/St. Paul Police Dept.
Murphy, James W., St. John, Hopkins
Murphy, John L., St. Matthew, St. Paul
Murphy, Lawrence J., Guardian Angels, Lake Elmo, Diocese of Superior
Nalezny, Daniel, St. Stephen, Anoka
Nelson, Ronald, Sacred Heart/St. Lawrence, Faribault
Neumann, Dennis J., (Retired)
Nicklay, John, St. Rita, Cottage Grove
Nicolosi, Dr. Charles, On Leave of Absence
Nugent, George J., All Saints, Lakeville
O'Connor, Robert, (Retired)
O'Keefe, Clyde, (Retired)
Otto, Sherman H., St. Vincent de Paul, Osseo
Palkert, Lawrence, Immaculate Conception, Columbia Heights
Palmer, Rodney, St. John the Baptist, New Brighton
Pashby, Richard E., St. Pascal, St. Paul
Pasko, Anthony, Our Lady of Grace, Edina
Pederson, Bernard A., St. Agnes, St. Paul
Pendergast, Donald, Our Lady of Grace, Edina
Quayle, Thomas, St. John the Baptist, New Brighton & Hennepin County Juvenile Center
Rajcich, G. Michael, St. Bridget, Lindstrom
Raleigh, Robert, St. Wenceslaus, New Prague/ Minnesota Correctional Facility
Ramsey, James, Sacred Heart, Robbinsdale
Reed, John A., Diocese of Duluth
Rinkenberger, Donald, St. Joseph the Worker, Maple Grove
Riordan, William, Cathedral, St. Paul
Rollings, Virgil, (Retired)
Rudolphi, Byron W., Jr., St. Patrick, Edina
Saumweber, James, St Peter, North St. Paul
Scherer, Terrance P., St. Patrick, Cedar
Scherkenbach, Gerald A., St. Leo, St. Paul; Tribunal
Schmitz, Joseph, Woodbury Health Care Center
Schneider, Frank J., St. Jerome, Maplewood
Schneider, Terrence, Holy Name, Medina
Schramer, Joseph J., Campus Ministry, University of St. Thomas
Schroeder, Allan, St. Victoria, Victoria
Schroeder, Alphonse, Pax Christi, Eden Prairie
Seaton, James B., (Retired)
Semlak, Thomas L., St. Pius X, White Bear Lake
Shambour, Leonard, St. Wenceslaus, New Prague
Shoberg, Mylo, St. Peter, Forest Lake
Shupe, Russell, St. Michael, Prior Lake
Smith, James, (Retired)
Smith, Robert B., Assumption, Richfield
Stickney, Stephen S., St. Cyril, Minneapolis
Stiles, Thomas G., St. Columba, St. Paul
Stromen, Sherman, St. Mary of the Lake, White Bear Lake
Swirtz, Lawrence, (Retired)
Tangney, Francis J., St. Joseph, Hopkins
Tatone, Paul M., St. Thomas Becket, Eagan
Thell, Frank J., St. Paul Police Chap.
Thornton, James, St. Mary, Shakopee
Tift, J. Neil, Archdiocese of Washington, DC
Timmerman, Dale, St. Peter, Forest Lake
Umphress, William G., Holy Spirit, St. Paul
Urbanski, Roger G., (Retired)
Valdez, Carl R., Hispanic Ministry
Veiman, John, Presentation, Maplewood
Wagner, James M., St. William, Fridley
Wagner, Robert C., St. Hubert, Chanhassen
Warhol, Robert W., Nativity of B.V.M., Bloomington

Warne, Maynard E., St. Michael, St. Michael
Waugh, Charles, St. Stephen, Anoka
Weiland, John D., St. Mary, Marystown
Wesley, R. Daniel, Immaculate Conception, Faribault
Wierschem, Joseph G., Holy Name, Medina
Williams, Merlin J., Nation Association of Native American Deacons
Winkelman, John W., Ascension, Minneapolis
Winn, Luther E., (Retired)
Winn, Michael, Holy Name, Medina
Wirtz, Howard, Archdiocese of Milwaukee
Wittman, Wayne C., Sacred Heart, St. Paul
Witucki, Richard P., St. Bartholomew, Wayzata
Wright, Scott, St. Mark & St. Paul
Yaeger, Loren, (Retired)
Yang, Naokao, St. Adalbert, St. Paul

INSTITUTIONS LOCATED IN THE ARCHDIOCESE

[A] SEMINARIES, ARCHDIOCESAN

ST. PAUL. *St. John Vianney Seminary*, 2115 Summit Ave., 55105. Tel: 651-962-6825; Fax: 651-962-6835.
E-mail: sjv@stthomas.edu
Web site: www.stthomas.edu/sjv
Rev. William J. Baer, Rector. Spiritual Directors-Counselors: Revs. James M. Perkl; Donald E. DeGrood; Xavier Thelakkatt; Mrs. Theresa Thurmes, Apostolic Life Coord.; John Daniewicz, D.R.E. Priests 4; Lay Teachers 2; Students 97.

The Saint Paul Seminary, School of Divinity of the University of St. Thomas, 2260 Summit Ave., 55105. Tel: 651-962-5050; Fax: 651-962-5790.
E-mail: jpmclean@stth
Web site: department.stthomas.edu/sod
Legal Title: *The Saint Paul Seminary*. Rev. Phillip J. Rask, Ph.D., Rector; Mrs. Jan Viktora, M.A., Asst. Academic Dean; Revs. Dominic Serra, S.L.D., (On leave); David W. Kohner, Dir. Spiritual Formation; Jerome M. Dittberner, S.T.D.; Paul F. Feela, M.A., Dir. Worship; Peter E. Feldmeier, Ph.D.; Ms. Mary Martin, M.A., Theological Librarian; Revs. James R. Motl, O.P., Ph.D.; J. Patrick Quinn, T.O.R., S.T.D.; Ronald Bowers, J.C.D., Vice Rector; J. Michael Byron; Thomas Fisch, Ph.D.; Jeanne P. McLean, Ph.D., Academic Dean; Rev. John Echert, S.S.L.; Sr. Christine Athans, B.V.M., Ph.D.; Gene Scapanski, S.T.D.; Charlotte Berres, D.Min., Dir. Field Educ.; David Jenkins, D.Mus., Dir. Liturgical Music; Sr. Paul Therese Saiko, S.S.N.D., M.A.; Sr. Katarina Schuth, O.S.F., Ph.D.; Rev. Douglas E. Dandurand; Walter D. Ray, Ph.D. M.Div./Seminarians 78; M.Div./non-Sems 4; Pastoral Studies Division 49; Pastoral Studies (non-degree) 11; Doctor of Ministry 19; Priests 12; Sisters 4; Lay Staff 9.

[B] SEMINARIES, RELIGIOUS, OR SCHOLASTICATES

ST. PAUL. *Jesuit Novitiate*, 1035 Summit Ave., 55105-3034. Tel: 651-224-5593; Fax: 651-224-4734.
E-mail: sjatpaul@aol.com
Revs. Michael G. Harter, S.J., Supr. and Novice Director; Matthew L. Linn, S.J., Retreat Dir.; John M. Paul, S.J., Novice Dir.; Bro. John J. Masterson, S.J., Asst. to Novice Dir. Priests 3; Brothers 1; Novices 12.

[C] COLLEGES AND UNIVERSITIES

ST. PAUL. *College of St. Catherine*, 2004 Randolph Ave., 55105. Tel: 651-690-6000; Fax: 651-690-6024.
E-mail: admissions@stkate.edu
Web site: www.stkate.edu
For a complete listing, refer to the Colleges and Universities section.

University of St. Thomas, 2115 Summit Ave., 55105. Tel: 651-962-5000; Fax: 651-962-6504.
Web site: www.stthomas.edu
For a complete listing, refer to the Colleges and Universities section.

MINNEAPOLIS. *The College of St. Catherine-Minneapolis*, 601 25th Ave. S., 55454. Tel: 651-690-7702; Fax: 651-690-7849.
E-mail: mkmclaughlin@stkate.edu
Web site: www.stkate.edu
For a complete listing, refer to the Colleges and Universities section.

[D] HIGH SCHOOLS, PAROCHIAL

ST. PAUL. High Schools are maintained in the following parishes (for particulars refer to the individual parish). City of St. Paul: St. Agnes, St. Bernard.

[E] HIGH SCHOOLS, ARCHDIOCESAN

ST. PAUL. *Hill-Murray School*. (Grades 7-12). Tel: 651-777-1376; Fax: 651-748-2444.
Web site: www.hill-murray.org
2625 Larpenteur Ave., E., Maplewood, 55109-5098; Fax: 612-770-5262. Joseph M. Peschges, Pres. Lay Teachers 66; Students 917.

The Saint Thomas Academy. (Boys). 949 Mendota Heights Rd., Mendota Heights, 55120-1496. Tel: 651-454-4570; Fax: 651-454-4574.
E-mail: sta@cadets.com
Web site: www.cadets.com
Mr. John B. Greving, Headmaster; Rev. John L. Ubel, Chap. Lay Teachers 56; Students 708.

MINNEAPOLIS. *DeLaSalle High School*, Christian Brothers, One De La Salle Dr., 55401.
E-mail: info@delasalle.com
Web site: www.delasalle.com
Bro. Michael Collins, F.S.C., Pres.; Barry C. Lieske, Prin. Priests 1; Brothers 6; Sisters 1; Lay Teachers 27; Students 480.

Totino-Grace High School. Tel: 763-571-9116; Fax: 763-571-9118.
Web site: www.totinograce.org
1350 Gardena Ave., N.E., Fridley, 55432-5899. Tel: 763-571-9116; Fax: 912-571-9118. Bro. Milton Barker, F.S.C., Pres.; Kathleen M. Murphy, Prin. Brothers 2; Lay Teachers 69; Students 1,087.

ST. LOUIS PARK. *Benilde-St. Margaret's School*, 2501 Hwy. 100 S., 55416. Tel: 612-927-4176; Fax: 612-920-8889.
E-mail: jhamburge@bsm-online.org
Web site: http:www.bsm.pvt.k12.mn.us
Mr. James F. Hamburge, Pres.; Mr. Robert C. Tift, Prin.; Mary Andersen, Asst. Prin. Priests 1; Sisters 1; Lay Teachers 83; Students 1,067.

[F] HIGH SCHOOLS, PRIVATE

ST. PAUL. *Cretin-Derham Hall*, 550 S. Albert St., 55116. Tel: 651-690-2443; Fax: 651-696-3394.
E-mail: rengler@cretin-derhamhall.org
Web site: www.cretin-derhamhall.org
Co-Sponsors: Brothers of the Christian Schools and Sisters of St. Joseph of Carondelet. Richard Engler, Pres. & Prin. Sisters 4; Brothers 3; Lay Teachers 97; Students 1,290.

FARIBAULT. *Bethlehem Academy*, 55021. Tel: 507-334-3948; Fax: 507-334-3949.
E-mail: principal@bacards.pvt.k12.mn.us
Web site: www.bacards.pvt.k12.mn.us
Sisters 1; Lay Teachers 13; Students 208.

Faribault B.A., Inc., 55021. Tel: 507-334-3948; Fax: 507-334-3949.
E-mail: principal@bacards.pvt.k12.mn.us
Web site: www.bacards.pvt.k12.mn.us
Sisters of St. Dominic (Sinsinawa, WI). Sisters 1; Lay Teachers 13; Students 208.

MENDOTA HEIGHTS. *Convent of the Visitation School*. Day School for Girls grades 7-12; coed grades PreK-6. 2455 Visitation Dr., 55120. Tel: 651-683-1700; Fax: 651-454-7144.
E-mail: adoffice@mneta.net
Web site: www.visitation.net
Dawn Nichols, Head of School. Sisters 19; Lay Teachers 60; Students 586.

RICHFIELD. *Academy of Holy Angels*, 6600 Nicollet Ave. S., 55423-2498. Tel: 612-798-2600; Fax: 612-798-2610.
E-mail: jreilly@ahastars.org
Web site: www.ahastars.org
Dr. Jill M. Reilly, Pres. & Prin. Priests 1; Sisters 1; Lay Teachers 56; Students 772.

VICTORIA. *Holy Family Catholic High School*, 8101 Kochia Ln., 55386. Tel: 952-443-4659; Fax: 952-443-1822.
E-mail: communications@holyfamilycatholichs.org
Web site: www.holyfamilycatholichs.org
Robert J. Roy, Chm.; Theo Chalgren, Vice Chm.; Dianna Goebel, Sec.; Paul Stauffacher, Pres. Lay Teachers 11; Students 147.

[G] ELEMENTARY SCHOOLS, PRIVATE

MENDOTA HEIGHTS. *Convent of the Visitation School*. (Montessori-Grade 12), 2455 Visitation Dr., 55120. Tel: 651-683-1700; Fax: 651-454-7144.
E-mail: vischool@mneta.net
Web site: www.visitation.net
Dawn Nichols, Head of School. Sisters of The Visitation of Holy Mary 19; Lay Teachers 60; Students 586.

[H] ELEMENTARY SCHOOLS, CONSOLIDATED, PAROCHIAL

ST. PAUL. *Highland Catholic School*. (Grades K-8), 2017 Bohland Ave., 55116. Tel: 651-690-2477; Fax: 651-699-1869.
E-mail: highland@winternet.com
Lay Teachers 30; Students 473. Serving the parishes of Highland Catholic Community.

IHM-St. Luke's School. (Grades K-8), 1065 Summit Ave., 55105. Tel: 651-224-4836; Fax: 651-224-0097.
E-mail: 0999ihms@infomns.k12.mn.us
Web site: www.ties.k12.mn.us/~ihmstluk/
Sisters 2; Lay Teachers 26; Students 429. Serving the parishes of Immaculate Heart of Mary and St. Luke.

Maternity of Mary / St. Andrew School, 592 Arlington Ave. W., 55117. Tel: 651-489-1459; Fax: 651-489-3560.
E-mail: florence@cpinternet.com
Web site: www.mmsaschool.org
Sisters 2; Lay Teachers 25; Students 425. Serving the parishes of Maternity of Mary and St. Andrew.

Trinity Catholic School, 835 E. Fifth St., 55106. Tel: 651-776-2763; Fax: 651-772-4847.
Web site: www.trinity-catholic.org
Sisters 5; Lay Teachers 18; Students 277. Serving the parishes of Sacred Heart, St. Casimir and St. Patrick.

MINNEAPOLIS. *Northeast Regional Catholic School*, 1630 Fourth St, N.E., 55413. Tel: 612-789-8851; Fax: 612-789-8773. Sisters 2; Lay Teachers 12; Students 192. Serving the parishes of St. Cyril & Methodius, Holy Cross, St. Anthony, All Saints, Our Lady of Lourdes, St. Hedwig, St. Clement, St. Boniface, St. Maron, St. Constantine, Our Lady of Mt. Carmel and St. Lawrence.

Risen Christ Catholic School. (Grades K-2), East Campus: 1120 E. 37th St., 53407. Tel: 612-729-2336.
E-mail: risenchrist@hes.k12.mn.us
Lay Teachers 7; Students 150. (Grades 3-8), West Campus: 3800 Pleasant Ave., 55409. Tel: 612-822-5329; Fax: 612-822-5903. Lay Teachers 16; Students 250. Serving the parishes of Holy Name, Holy Rosary, Incarnation, St. Albert the Great and St. Stephen.

EAGAN. *Faithful Shepherd Catholic School*, 4030 Pilot Knob Rd., 55122. Tel: 651-452-0929; Fax: 651-454-0860. Revs. Kevin I. Clinton; Robert M. Schwartz, Pres.; Thomas Kommers, Vice Pres.; Robert Cass, Treas. Serving the parishes of St. Peter, St. John Neumann and St. Thomas Becket.

FARIBAULT. *Consolidated Catholic School of Faribault*. (Grades PreK-6), 15 S.W. Third Ave., 55021. Tel: 507-334-7706; Fax: 507-332-2669.
E-mail: bbehnke@faribaultcatholics.com
Lay Teachers 25; Students 450. Serving the parishes of Immaculate Conception, St. Lawrence and Sacred Heart.

HASTINGS. *St. Elizabeth Ann Seton School*, 600 Tyler St., 55033. Tel: 651-437-3098; Fax: 651-437-3377.
Web site: www.seasparish.org
Mrs. Rita Humbert, Admin. Lay Teachers 22; Students 397.

HOPKINS. *John Ireland Schools*. (Grades PreK-8), 1320 Main Street, 55343. Tel: 612-938-3442; Fax: 612-938-0642.
E-mail: principal@johnireland.org
Web site: www.johnireland.org
Lay Teachers 48; Students 540. Serving the parishes of St. John the Evangelist, St. Joseph and Immaculate Heart of Mary.

LONSDALE. *Lonsdale, New Market, Veseli Area Catholic School*, 108 First Ave., S.E., P.O. Box 10, 55046. Tel: 507-744-2394; Fax: 507-744-4117.
E-mail: lnmvschool@excite.com
Sisters 1; Lay Teachers 11; Students 198. Serving the parishes of Veseli, New Market and Lonsdale.

RICHFIELD. *Blessed Trinity Catholic School of Richfield, Minnesota*, 7540 Penn Ave. S., 55423. Tel: 612-866-6906. Rev. Gregory L. Esty, Pres. Lay Teachers 20; Students 450. Serving the parishes of Assumption, St. Peter's and St. Richard's.

SHAKOPEE. *Shakopee Area Catholic School*. (Grades PreK-8), 305 S. Scott, 55379. Tel: 612-445-3387; Fax: 612-445-7256.
E-mail: sacselem@ties.k12.mn.us
Notre Dame Sisters 1; Lay Teachers 28; Students 715. Serving the parishes of St. Mark, St. Mary, St. Mary of the Purification.

STILLWATER. *St. Croix Catholic Educational Programs*, 611 S. 3rd St., 55082. Tel: 651-439-4400; Fax: 651-439-8360.
E-mail: cepperly@stccs.com
Rev. Michael C. Skluzacek, Pres. Lay Teachers 26; Students 427. Serving the parishes of St. Michael's, St. Mary's, and St. Charles.

St. Croix Catholic School. (Grades K-8), 621 S. Third St., 55082. Tel: 612-439-5581. Mr. Marty Weisbeck, Prin. Lay Teachers 21; Students 397. Serving the parishes of St. Charles, Bayport; St. Mary, Stillwater; St. Michael, Stillwater.

[I] HOMES FOR CHILDREN

MINNEAPOLIS. *St. Joseph's Home for Children*, 1121 E. 46th St., 55407. Tel: 612-827-6241
For a complete listing, refer to the Special Care Facilities section.

[J] GENERAL HOSPITALS

FARMINGTON. *Trinity Hospital*, 3410 - 213th St., West, 55024. Tel: 651-460-1169
For a complete listing, refer to the Hospitals section.

HASTINGS. *Regina Medical Center*, 1175 Nininger Rd., 55033. Tel: 651-480-4100; Fax: 651-480-4212.
Web site: www.reginamedical.com
For a complete listing, refer to the Hospitals section.

NEW PRAGUE. *Queen of Peace Hospital*, 302 Second St., N.E., 56071. Tel: 612-758-4431; Fax: 612-758-5009.
E-mail: sjean@qofp.org
Web site: www.np.k12.mn.us/~qofp.htm
For a complete listing, refer to the Hospitals section.

SHAKOPEE. *St. Francis Regional Medical Center*, 1455 St. Francis Ave., 55379-3380. Tel: 612-403-3000; Fax: 612-403-3820
For a complete listing, refer to the Hospitals section.

[K] SPECIAL HOSPITALS AND SANATORIA FOR INVALIDS

ST. PAUL. *Our Lady of Good Counsel Home*, 2076 St. Anthony Ave., 55104. Tel: 651-646-2797; Fax: 651-646-7884
For a complete listing, refer to the Special Care Facilities section.

[L] SOCIAL SERVICE AGENCIES

ST. PAUL. *Home of the Good Shepherd*, 5100 Hodgson Rd., 55126. Tel: 651-484-0221; Fax: 651-486-1616.
E-mail: marge@goodshepherdsisters.org
Margaret Cashman, Admin. Transitional housing and case-management services for at-risk, homeless women. Sisters 5; Lay Staff 19.

[M] HOMES FOR AGED

ST. PAUL. *Bethany Convent for Retired Sisters*, 1870 Randolph, 55105. Tel: 651-696-2500; Fax: 651-696-2501
For a complete listing, refer to the Special Care Facilities section.

Franciscan Health Community, 1925 Norfolk Ave., 55116. Tel: 651-696-8400
For a complete listing, refer to the Special Care Facilities section.

Good Shepherd Care Center, Inc., 324 Johnson Pkwy., 55106. Tel: 651-774-9737; Fax: 651-774-9641
For a complete listing, refer to the Special Care Facilities section.

Holy Family Residence, 330 S. Exchange St., 55102. Tel: 651-227-0336; Fax: 651-227-7321
For a complete listing, refer to the Special Care Facilities section.

MINNEAPOLIS. *City of Lakes Care Center*, 110 E. 18th St., 55403. Tel: 612-879-2800
For a complete listing, refer to the Special Care Facilities section.

CANNON FALLS. *Our Lady of the Angels Care Center*, 300 N. Dow St., 55009-1899. Tel: 507-263-4658; Fax: 507-263-4127.
E-mail: angel@cannon.net
For a complete listing, refer to the Special Care Facilities section.

HASTINGS. *Regina Convalescent and Nursing Care and Retirement Center*, 55033. Tel: 651-480-4336; Fax: 651-480-4212.
Web site: www.reginamedical.com
For a complete listing, refer to the Special Care Facilities section.

SHAKOPEE. *St. Gertrude's Health Center*, 1850 Sarazin St., 55379. Tel: 612-403-3499
For a complete listing, refer to the Special Care Facilities section.

[N] MONASTERIES AND RESIDENCES OF PRIESTS AND BROTHERS

ST. PAUL. *Franciscan Brothers of Peace*, Queen of Peace Friary, 1289 Lafond Ave., 55104-2035. Tel: 651-646-8586. Bros. Paul J. O'Donnell, F.B.P., Guardian Overall; Anthony J. Sweere, F.B.P., Vicar; Michael A. Gaworski, F.B.P.; Hilary McGee, F.B.P.; Conrad Richardson, F.B.P.; Joseph Katzmarek, F.B.P.; John Mary Kaspari, F.B.P.; Pio King, F.B.P; James Voeller, F.B.P.

Oblate Residence, 104 N. Mississippi River Blvd., 55104-2374. Tel: 651-645-3560; Fax: 651-645-3704. Rev. Joseph H. Hitpas, O.M.I., Dir. of House. In res. Revs. Paul Ischler, O.M.I.; William Mason, O.M.I.; John E. Pilaczynski, O.M.I.

MINNEAPOLIS. *Franciscan Brothers of Peace*, St. Francis Friary, 2002 Penn Ave. N., 55411. Tel: 612-521-7560. Bros. John Mary Kaspari, F.B.P.; Joseph Katzmarek, F.B.P.; Pio King, F.B.P.

La Storta Jesuit Community, 2201 Pillsbury Ave. S., 55404. Tel: 612-871-1612; Fax: 612-871-0947. Revs. Dennis R. Karamitis, S.J.; Michael J. Vjecha, S.J.; Eugene L. Donahue, Supr.; Robert P. Neenan, S.J.; Joseph N. Pershe, S.J.; Aloysius F. Schmitz, S.J.; Francis J. Burke, S.J.; Thomas G. Boedy, S.J.; Leon F. Klimczyk, S.J.; John M. Ginsterblum, S.J.; Bro. Lee A. McNamee, S.J.

Paulist Fathers, 1201 5th St., S.E., 55414. Tel: 612-331-7941; Fax: 612-378-1771.
E-mail: nccampus@stlawrencenewman.org
Web site: www.stlawrencenewman.org/~mccampus
Revs. John J. Behnke, C.S.P.; Wilfred A. Brimley, C.S.P., (Retired); Donald A. Andrie, C.S.P.; James DiLuzio, C.S.P. Total in Residence 4.

St. Albert the Great Priory, 2833 32nd Ave. S., 55406. Tel: 612-724-3644; Fax: 612-724-5057.
E-mail: domcom@mn.uswest.com
Rev. Charles M. Santoro, O.P., Prior. Order of Preachers (Dominicans). Province of St. Albert the Great. Total in Residence 11.

ANOKA. *Crosier Community of Anoka*, 516 School St., 55303-2349. Tel: 612-421-7115; Fax: 612-323-2974. In res. Revs. William Deziel, O.S.C.; Dale Ettel, O.S.C.; David E. Gallus, O.S.C.; Edward Greiwe, O.S.C.; Kenneth Opat, O.S.C., Supr.; Michael Paquet, O.S.C.; Eugene D. Plaisted, O.S.C.; Michael Van Sloun, O.S.C., Rector; Ignatius Lempart, O.S.C.; Adrian Piotrowski, O.S.C.; Oscar Schoenberg, O.S.C., 48, St. Mary's International School, 1-6-19, Seta Setagaya-Ku, Tokyo, 158-8668, Japan. Tel: 81-3-709-3416. In res. Revs. Lyle Ehmke, O.S.C.; Jim Herrmann, O.S.C. Total in Residence 7; Total Staff 10.

BLOOMINGTON. *Maryknoll Fathers and Brothers, Catholic Foreign Mission Society of America*, 10345 Portland Ave. S., 55420-5433. Tel: 612-884-7743; Fax: 612-884-7744. Rev. Dennis T. Dunne, Dir.

SHOREVIEW. *Crosier Community of Shoreview*, 3500 Vivian Ave., 55126-3852. Tel: 651-486-7456; Fax: 651-287-1130.
E-mail: shoreview@crosier.org
Revs. Jerome Schik, O.S.C.; Dale Ehrman, O.S.C.; Marven Tellers, O.S.C.; Richard McGuire, O.S.C.; Thomas O'Brien, O.S.C.; Kermit Holl, O.S.C., Prior; Stephan Bauer, O.S.C.; Steven Henrich, O.S.C.; Bros. Timothy Tomczak, O.S.C.; Jim Kewandowski, O.S.C.; Greg Madigan, O.S.C.; Bob Mandernach, O.S.C.

Crosier Provincial House Province of St. Odilia, 3470 Vivian Ave., 55126-3853. Tel: 651-486-7456; Fax: 651-287-1130.
E-mail: provincial@crosier.org
Web site: www.crosier.org
In res. Very Rev. Thomas R. Carkhuff, O.S.C., Prov.; Revs. Philip Suehr, O.S.C.; Joseph Hennen, O.S.C; Michael Cotone, O.S.C.

[O] CONVENTS AND RESIDENCES FOR SISTERS

ST. PAUL. *Contemplative Sisters of the Good Shepherd*, 5104 Hodgson Rd., 55126-1229. Tel: 651-482-5240; Fax: 651-486-1600. Sr. Ann J. Dye, Coord. Sisters 19.

Convent of the Good Shepherd, 5100 Hodgson Rd., 55126-1297. Tel: 651-484-0221; Fax: 651-486-1600. Sisters of the Good Shepherd 33. Contemplative Sisters of the Good Shepherd, 5104 Hodgson Rd., 55126-1229. Tel: 651-482-5240; Fax: 651-486-1600. Sisters 18.

Franciscan Sisters of Little Falls, MN (O.S.F.), 727 E. Margaret St., 55106. Tel: 651-772-1740; Fax: 651-793-0086.
E-mail: fslformatn@aol.com
Professed 4.

Franciscan Sisters of St. Paul, Franciscan Regional Center, 1388 Prior Ave. S., 55116. Tel: 651-690-1501; Fax: 651-690-2509.
E-mail: spfrancis@isd.net
Web site: http://askmotherrose.org
Sr. Mary Wolfe, O.S.F., Reg. Dir. Sisters 12.

Monastery of the Visitation, 2455 Visitation Dr., 55120. Tel: 651-683-1700; Fax: 651-454-0602. Sr. Marie Therese Conaty, Supr. Visitation Nuns 19.

St. Mary's Mission House, 265 Century Ave., 55125. Tel: 651-738-9704; Fax: 651-738-9704. Missionary Sisters of St. Peter Claver. Sr. Maria Moryl, S.S.P.C., Supr. Sisters 13; Novices 1.

St. Paul's Monastery, 2675 Larpenteur Ave. E., 55109-5097. Tel: 651-777-8181; Fax: 651-777-4442.
E-mail: mfujan@usinternet.com
Benedictine Sisters of Pontifical Jurisdiction. Sr. Marie Fujan, O.S.B., Prioress; Sr. Annette Esboldt, O.S.B., Subprioress. Sisters 76.

Sisters of St. Joseph of Carondelet, 1884 Randolph Ave., 55105. Tel: 651-690-7000; Fax: 651-690-7039.
Web site: www.csj-carondelet-sp.org
Province Leadership Team: Sr. Christine Ludwig, C.S.J.; Sr. Susan Oefling, C.S.J.; Sr. Dolere Rochon, C.S.J. Sisters of Province 410; Total Staff 91.
Carondelet Center; St. Joseph School of Music; Suzuki Talent Education School for Strings; Editorial Development Associates; Project One-Fifty; Sisters Care; Sarah's; Vineyard; Carondelet LifeCare Ministries/St. Mary's Health Clinics; Youth & Family Center, Inc.; Holy Family Hospital; Sisters of St. Joseph of Carondelet Ministries Foundation, St. Paul Province; Learning in Style; Women at the Well; Adult Literacy; The College of St. Catherine; Minnesota Center for Health Care Ethics; Wisdom Ways: A Resource Center for Spirituality; St. Joseph's Hospital, Inc.

MINNEAPOLIS. *Congregation of the Handmaids of the Holy Child Jesus*, 1707 Bryant Ave. S., 55411. Tel: 612-521-3127. Sr. Mary Angela Itiat, Pres.; Sr. Rosemary I. Essien, Vice Pres.; Sr. Regina Nworah, Treas.; Sr. Theresa Essienuko, Sec.; Sr. Anne Egem. Total in Residence 5.

St. Clare's Monastery of the Infant Jesus, 8650 Russell Ave. S., 55431-1998. Tel: 612-881-4766; Fax: 612-881-0358.
E-mail: mplsclares@juno.com
Sr. Frances Getchell, O.S.C., Abbess. Franciscan Poor Clare Nuns. Professed Nuns 12.

Visitation Monastery of Minneapolis, 1527 Fremont Ave. N., 55411. Tel: 612-521-6113; Fax: 612-521-4020.
E-mail: vmonastery@aol.com
Sr. Mary Francis Reis, V.H.M., Supr.

LAKE ELMO. *Carmel of Our Lady of Divine Providence*, 8251 De Montreville Tr. N., 55042-9547. Tel: 651-777-3882. Sr. Rose of the Sacred Heart, O.C.D., Prioress; Rev. John M. Burns, Chap. Discalced Carmelite Nuns. Professed 11; Novices 1; Postulants 1.

WAYZATA. *Franciscan Clarist Congregation, F.C.C.*, Vimala Province, Convent of St. Therese House, 17931 Minnetonka Blvd., 55391. Tel: 612-473-4771.
E-mail: tresajose@yahoo.com
Total in Residence 9.

[P] SECULAR INSTITUTES

ST. PAUL. *Missionaries of the Kingship of Christ*, The Chancery, 226 Summit Ave., 55102. Tel: 612-291-4400. Sr. M. Dominica Brennan, O.P. Secular Institute of Pontifical Right for women and men founded in Italy in 1919.

[Q] RETREAT HOUSES AND CENTERS OF SPIRITUALITY

ST. PAUL. *Benedictine Center - St. Paul's Monastery*, 2675 E. Larpenteur Ave., 55109. Tel: 651-777-7251; Fax: 651-773-5124.
E-mail: info@benedictctr.org
Web site: www.osb.org/spm
Carol Rennie, Dir. Total Staff 7.

Loyola, 389 N. Oxford St., 55104. Tel: 612-641-0008; Fax: 651-641-0554.
E-mail: loyolasrr@aol.com
Web site: loyolasp.faithweb.com
Revs. Richard M. Rice, S.J.; Frederic A. Maples, S.J.; Sr. Elizabeth Kerwin, C.S.J., Dir. Total Staff 8.

Maryhill, 1988 Summit Ave., 55105. Tel: 651-696-2970; Fax: 651-696-1190.
E-mail: maryhillsd@earthlink.net
Daughters of the Heart of Mary Sisters 9; Total in Residence 3; Total Staff 4.

BUFFALO. *Christ the King Retreat Center*, 621 First Ave. S., 55313. Tel: 612-682-3453.
E-mail: christtheking@kingshouse.com
Revs. Aloysius Svobodny, O.M.I.; John H. McManus, O.M.I.; Raymond R. Kirtz, O.M.I.; James D. Deegan, O.M.I., Dir.; Mark Dean, O.M.I.; Bro. Anthony Szklarski, O.M.I., Bus. Mgr. Total in Residence 6; Total Staff 25.

FRONTENAC. *Villa Maria Center*, 29847 County Blvd. 2, 55026. Tel: 651-345-4582; Fax: 651-345-3457.
E-mail: micoth@hotmail.com
Web site: villamariaretreats.org
Sr. Carolyn Marie Brockland, O.S.U., Prioress; Sr. Mary Ann Koth, O.S.U., Dir. Ursuline Sisters of the Roman Union 11.

LAKE ELMO. *Jesuit Retreat House*, 8243 Demontreville Tr. N., 55042-9546. Tel: 651-777-1311. Revs. Gerald E. Goetz, S.J., Dir.; Edward S. Sthokal, S.J., Asst.; James M. Kubicki, S.J. Total in Residence 3; Total Staff 6.

MARINE ON ST. CROIX. *Christian Brothers Retreat Center*, 15525 St. Croix Tr. N., 55047. Tel: 651-433-2486; Fax: 651-433-5755.
E-mail: dunrovincbrc@juno.com
Web site: www.dunrovin.org
Jerome Meeds, Dir. Total in Residence 12; Total Staff 11.

PRIOR LAKE. *Franciscan Retreat House*, 16385 Saint Francis Ln., 55372. Tel: 612-447-2182; Fax: 612-447-2170.
E-mail: franciscan-retreats@juno.com
Revs. Ken Bartsch, O.F.M.Conv., Guardian & Retreat Dir.; Mark F. Mindrup, O.F.M.Conv.; Ambrose Finnegan, O.F.M.Conv.; Camillus Gott; Thomas Smith, O.F.M.Conv.

[R] HOMES FOR DISABLED

ST. PAUL. *Our House of Minnesota, Inc. I*, 1846 Dayton Ave., 55104. Tel: 651-644-6650; Fax: 651-646-1104
For a complete listing, refer to the Special Care Facilities section.

Our House of Minnesota, Inc. II, 1846 Portland, 55104. Tel: 651-644-2411; Fax: 651-646-1104
For a complete listing, refer to the Special Care Facilities section.

WEST ST. PAUL. *Guild Incorporated*, 1025 Dodd Rd., 55118. Tel: 612-450-2220
For a complete listing, refer to the Special Care Facilities section.

[S] MINNESOTA CATHOLIC CONFERENCE (M.C.C.)

ST. PAUL. *Minnesota Catholic Conference*, 475 University Ave. W., Ste. B, 55103. Tel: 651-227-8777; Fax: 651-227-2675.
E-mail: info@mncc.org
Web site: www.mncc.org
Rev. David F. McCauley (FAR), Exec. Dir.; Thomas J. Pearson, Dir. Social Concerns; Peter A. Noll, DIr. Educ.; Patrick D. Menke, Dir. MN Nonpublic School Accrediting Assn. Total Staff 7. The M.C.C. is a Minnesota Corporation, the purpose of which is to promote the general welfare of the people of the State of Minnesota. All Catholic Bishops of the State of Minnesota constitute Ex Officio the Board of Directors.

[T] ASSOCIATIONS OF THE FAITHFUL

ST. PAUL. *The Companions of Christ*, 2137 Marshall Ave., 55104. Tel: 651-642-5933.
E-mail: tominstpaul@msn.com
Jeffrey Huard, Mod. Total in Residence 16.

Franciscan Brothers of Peace, Queen of Peace Friary, 1289 Lafond Ave., 55104-2035. Tel: 651-646-8586; Fax: 651-646-9083. Bros. Paul O'Donnell, F.B.P., Guardian Overall; Anthony J. Sweere, F.B.P., Vicar; Michael Gaworski, F.B.P.; Hilary McGee, F.B.P.; Conrad Richardson, F.B.P.; James Voeller, F.B.P. Total in Residence 9; Total Staff 1.

LAKE ELMO. *Hermits of the Most Blessed Virgin Mary of Mount Carmel*, 8249 De Montreville Tr. N., 55042-9545. Tel: 651-779-7351; Fax: 651-779-7351.
E-mail: carmelus@mn.uswest.net
Carmel of the Blessed Virgin Mary. Revs. John M. Burns, Prior; Daniel M. Schneider; Joseph V. Vaccaro. Priests 3; Brothers 5.

WEST ST. PAUL. *Community of Christ the Redeemer*, 110 Crusader Ave., 55118. Tel: 651-451-6114; Fax: 651-453-0810.
E-mail: ccrspo@juno.com
Mr. James C. Kolar, Pres.

NET Ministries, Inc., 110 Crusader Ave. W., 55118-4427. Tel: 651-450-6833; Fax: 651-450-9984.
E-mail: ministry@netusa.org
Web site: www.netusa.org
Mr. Mark Berchem, Exec. Dir. Total Staff 26.

[U] CAMPS AND COMMUNITY CENTERS

MCGREGOR. *Catholic Youth Camps, Inc.* Mailing Address: Administrative Office: 2131 Fairview Ave. N., Ste. 200, Roseville, 55113. Tel: 651-636-1645; Fax: 651-628-9323.
E-mail: campcyc@earthlink.net
Web site: catholicyouthcamp.org
Bob Bruan, Co-Exec. Dir.; Maggie Bruan, Co-Exec. Dir., Location: 19590 520th Ln., 55760. Tel: 218-426-3383; Fax: 218-426-4675. Total Assisted 1,535; Total Staff 55.

[V] NEWMAN CENTERS

MINNEAPOLIS. *Newman Center at St. Lawrence*, 1201 5th St., S.E., 55414. Tel: 612-331-7941; Fax: 612-378-1771.
E-mail: nccampus@stlawrencenewman.org
Web site: www.stlawrencenewman.org/~nccampus
Revs. John J. Behnke, C.S.P., Dir.; Charles A. Martin, C.S.P.; Donald A. Andrie, C.S.P.; James DiLuzio. Total Staff 4.

[W] MISCELLANEOUS LISTINGS

ST. PAUL. *Carondelet LifeCare Ministries/St. Mary's Health Clinics*, 1884 Randolph Ave., 55105-1700. Tel: 651-690-7020; Fax: 651-690-7075.
E-mail: bdickie@stmarysclinics.org
Barbara L. Dickie, Exec. Dir. Neighborhood Clinics 11; Patients assisted annually 4,741; Total Staff 11.

Catholic Community Foundation, 328 W. Kellogg Blvd., 55102. Tel: 651-290-1613; Fax: 651-291-4547.
E-mail: ccfendow@archspm.org
Web site: www.catholiccommunityfoundation.org
Mr. James Mullin, Exec. Dir.

Catholic Finance Corporation, 226 Summit Ave., 55102-2197. Tel: 651-291-4400. Michael P. Schaefer, Contact.

Christian Brothers Youth Home, 1540 Lincoln Ave., 55105. Tel: 651-699-0736. Bro. Michael Lee Anderson, F.S.C., Dir.; Mr. Bob Paradise, Pres. Total Assisted 8; Total Staff 1.

Growing in Faith Capitol Campaign, 328 W. Kellogg Blvd., 55102. Tel: 651-290-1613. James A. Mullin, Dir.

The Highland Catholic Community, 2055 Bohland Ave., 55116. Tel: 651-698-5581; Fax: 651-698-9526. Revs. John M. Bauer, Pres.; Thomas P. Hunstiger, Vice Pres.; Mr. John Hannahan, Sec.; Sr. Janet Wermerskirchen, Pastoral Min.; Deacon Gerald Scherkenbach; Lynn Johnson, D.R.E.; Chuck Lenz, Liturgist.

Highland Catholic School. (Grades K-8).

Mary Mother of God Mission Society, 1854 Jefferson Ave., 55105-1662. Tel: 651-690-5139; Fax: 651-690-5139.
E-mail: russianmission@juno.com
Web site: www.vladmission.org
Sandra Sonnen, Contact Person.

Minnesota Catholic Education Association, 475 University Ave., 55103-1996. Tel: 651-277-8777; Fax: 651-227-2675.
E-mail: pnoll@mncc.org
Dr. Peter Noll, Exec. Dir.

Missionary Oblates of Mary Immaculate, 104 N. Mississippi River Blvd., 55104-5698. Tel: 651-645-3560; Fax: 651-645-3702. Rev. Joseph H. Hitpas, O.M.I., Area Supr. Members Attached to the Office of the Area Superior: Rev. James Pillar, O.M.I., 5245 Zachary Grove, Apt. 202, Colorado Springs, CO, 80919. Tel: 719-531-0113. Rev. Charles Press, O.M.I., Little Sisters of the Poor, 86 Wilkin St., #112, 55102. Tel: 651-227-0336. Rev. Raymond Quesnel, O.M.I., Madonna Towers, 4001 19th Ave., N.W. #810, Rochester, 55901. Tel: 507-285-0781. Rev. Eugene Tremblay, O.M.I., 1614 S. 17th St., Manitowoc, WI, 54220. Tel: 920-683-9860. Legal Title: *Missionary Oblates of Mary Immaculate U.S. Prov.*

Nativity of Our Lord Endowment Fund, 1900 Wellesley Ave., 55105. Tel: 612-699-0309; Fax: 612-696-5458.
E-mail: info@nativity-mn.org
Web site: nativity-mn.org
Total Assisted 5,000; Total Staff 15.

Oblate Media and Communication Corporation, 104 N. Mississippi River Blvd., 55104. Tel: 651-645-3560. Rev. David A. Kalert, O.M.I., Pres. Oblates of Mary Immaculate, U.S. Province.

Safe Place for Newborns, P.O. Box 16092, 55116. Tel: 612-317-2895; Fax: 612-317-2899.
E-mail: safeplace@safeplacefor newborns.com
Office, 120 S. 6th St., Ste1250, Minneapolis, 55402. Tel: 612-317-2890; Fax: 612-317-2899. Lillian C. Riordan, Pres.

St. Joseph's Hospital Sponsor, Inc., 1884 Randolph Ave., 55105. Tel: 651-690-7000; Fax: 651-690-7039. Sr. Mary Heinen, C.S.J., Chair.

Sisters of St. Joseph of Carondelet Ministries Foundation, St. Paul Province, 1884 Randolph Ave., 55105. Tel: 651-690-7026.
E-mail: ioneill@mtn.org
Sr. Irene O'Neill, C.S.J., Exec. Dir.

To Encounter Christ of the Archdiocese of St. Paul-Minneapolis, Minnesota, Inc., 1079 Summit Ave., 55105. Tel: 651-281-0085; Fax: 651-225-1885.
E-mail: smtec@juno.com
Web site: www.serve.com/smtec
Caroline Metzinger, Admin. Coord.; Nathan Metzinger, Prog. Coord. Total Staff 2.

Trinity Catholic School, 835 E. 5th St., 55106. Tel: 651-776-2763; Fax: 651-772-4847.
E-mail: sferrin@trinity-catholic.org
Web site: www.trinity-catholic.org

MINNEAPOLIS. *Catholic Eldercare, Inc.*, 817 Main St., N.E., 55413. Tel: 612-379-1370. Mary Broderick, Pres. & CEO.
Skilled Nursing Facility, 150 Beds; Assisted Living Apartments for Elderly Adults, 52 Units; Home Health Care for the Elderly, 250 Assisted. Total Assisted 500; Total Staff 300.

The Legion of Christ, Inc., 405 Second Ave., South, 55401. Anthony Bannon, Pres.; Anthony Bailleres, Vice Pres.

Sagrado Corazon de Jesus, 2211 Clinton Ave., S., 55404. Tel: 612-870-2268. Rev. Lawrence E. Hubbard, Pres.; Bradley Capouch, Vice Pres.; Hugo Artola, Sec.; Armando Blas Garcia, Treas.

Twin Cities Catholic Alumni Club, Mailing Address: P.O. Box 581321, 55458-1321. Tel: 612-338-1288. Teddi Tri, Club Pres.

Youth and Family Center Inc., 4405 E. Lake St., 55406. Tel: 612-722-9612. Sr. Martha Merriman, C.S.J., Dir.; Sr. Betty Wurm, C.S.J., Dir. Counseling Center. Total Assisted 45; Total Staff 3.

MAPLEWOOD. *Maple Tree: Priory Childcare Center*, 1695 Century Ave. N., 55109. Tel: 651-770-0766. Sr. Marie Fujan, Prioress - St. Paul Priory; Sr. Annette Esboldt, Vice Pres. Total Assisted 67; Total Staff 21.

SHOREVIEW. *Crosier Missions*, 3510 Vivian Ave., 55126-3852. Tel: 651-486-7456; Fax: 651-287-1130.
E-mail: dgallus@crosier.org
Web site: oscgeneral.org
Rev. David E. Gallus, O.S.C., Mission Coord. Total Staff 1.

WEST ST. PAUL. *St. Paul's Outreach, Inc.*, 110 Crusader Ave., 55118. Tel: 651-451-6114; Fax: 651-453-0810.
E-mail: ccrspo@juno.com
Web site: www.spo.org
Mr. Gordon C. DeMarais, Pres.; Dr. James C. Kolar, Vice Pres.; Patrick D. Menke, Sec. & Treas.

RELIGIOUS INSTITUTES OF MEN REPRESENTED IN THE ARCHDIOCESE

For further details refer to the corresponding bracketed number in the Religious Institutes of Men or Women section.

[0200]—*Benedictine Monks.* (St. John's Abbey).—O.S.B.
[0330]—*Brothers of the Christian Schools.* (Winona Province).—F.S.C.
[0400]—*Canons Regular of the Order of the Holy Cross.*—O.S.C.
[0470]—*The Capuchin Fathers.* (Prov. of St. Joseph).—O.F.M.Cap.
[0480]—*Conventual Franciscans.* (Prov. of Our Lady of Consolation).—O.F.M.Conv.
[0520]—*Franciscan Friars.* (Prov. of Sacred Heart).—O.F.M.
[0690]—*Jesuit Fathers and Brothers.* (Wisconsin Prov.).—S.J.
[0780]—*Marist Fathers.* (American Prov.).—S.M.
[0800]—*Maryknoll.*—M.M.
[0720]—*The Missionaries of Our Lady of La Salette.*—M.S.
[0910]—*Oblate Fathers of Mary Immaculate.* (Central Prov.).—O.M.I.
[0430]—*Order of Preachers (Dominicans).* (Prov. of St. Albert the Great).—O.P.
[1030]—*Paulist Fathers.*—C.S.P.
[1070]—*Redemptorist Fathers.* (St. Louis Prov.).—C.SS.R.
[1060]—*Society of the Precious Blood.* (Cincinnati Prov.).—C.PP.S.
[0560]—*Third Order Regular of St. Francis.* (Prov. of the Immaculate Conception).—T.O.R.
[]—*Vincentian Congregation.* (India).—V.C.

RELIGIOUS INSTITUTES OF WOMEN REPRESENTED IN THE ARCHDIOCESE

[0230]—*Benedictine Sisters of Pontifical Jurisdiction.* (Crookston, St. Paul, St. Joseph, Duluth, MN).—O.S.B.
[3110]—*Congregation of Our Lady of the Retreat in the Cenacle.*—R.C.
[3710]—*Congregation of the Sisters of St. Agnes.*—C.S.A.
[1780]—*Congregation of the Sisters of the Third Order of St. Francis of Perpetual Adoration.* (Eastern Region).—F.S.P.A.
[0810]—*Daughters of the Heart of Mary.*—D.H.M.
[0420]—*Discalced Carmelite Nuns.*—O.C.D.
[1070-03]—*Dominican Sisters.*—O.P.
[1070-10]—*Dominican Sisters.*—O.P.
[1070-23]—*Dominican Sisters.*—O.P.
[1170]—*Felician Sisters.*—C.S.S.F.
[1310]—*Franciscan Sisters of Little Falls, Minnesota.*—O.S.F.
[1485]—*Franciscan Sisters of St. Paul, MN.*—O.S.F.
[2575]—*Institute of the Sisters of Mercy of the Americas.* (Dubuque, IA; Detroit, MI; Omaha, NE).—R.S.M.
[2340]—*Little Sisters of the Poor.*—L.S.P.
[3990]—*Missionary Sisters of St. Peter Claver.*—S.S.P.C.
[3760]—*Order of St. Clare.*—O.S.C.
[3230]—*Poor Handmaids of Jesus Christ.*—P.H.J.C.
[2970]—*School Sisters of Notre Dame.*—S.S.N.D.
[1680]—*Schools Sisters of St. Francis.*—O.S.F.
[3590]—*Servants of Mary (Servite Sisters).*—O.S.M.
[3520]—*Servants of the Holy Heart of Mary.*—S.S.C.M.
[0520]—*Sisters of Charity of Our Lady, Mother of Mercy.*—S.C.M.M.
[0430]—*Sisters of Charity of the Blessed Virgin Mary.*—B.V.M.
[0660]—*Sisters of Christian Charity.*—S.C.C.
[1705]—*The Sisters of St. Francis of Assisi.*—O.S.F.
[1530]—*Sisters of St. Francis of the Congregation of Our Lady of Lourdes, Sylvania, Ohio.*—O.S.F.
[1570]—*Sisters of St. Francis of the Holy Family.*—O.S.F.
[3840]—*Sisters of St. Joseph of Carondelet.*—C.S.J.
[3880]—*Sisters of St. Joseph of Medaille.*—C.S.J.
[3930]—*Sisters of St. Joseph of the Third Order of St. Francis.*—S.S.J.-T.O.S.F.
[1020]—*Sisters of the Divine Redeemer.*—S.D.R.
[1830]—*The Sisters of the Good Shepherd.*—R.G.S.
[3320]—*Sisters of the Presentation of the B.V.M.* (Dubuque, IA; Sioux Falls, SD).—P.B.V.M.
[1720]—*Sisters of the Third Order Regular of St. Francis of the Congregation of Our Lady of Lourdes.*—O.S.F.

[2150]—*Sisters, Servants of the Immaculate Heart of Mary.*—I.H.M.
[4110]—*Ursuline Nuns (Roman Union).*—O.S.U.
[4190]—*Visitation Nuns.*—V.H.M.

ARCHDIOCESAN CEMETERIES

ST. PAUL. *Calvery.*
The Catholic Cemeteries, 400 Selby Ave., Ste. S, 55102. Tel: 612-228-9991.

MINNEAPOLIS. *St. Anthony & St. Mary.*

MENDOTA HEIGHTS. *Resurrection.*

NEW HOPE. *Assumption & Gethsemane.*

PARISH CEMETERIES

SHAKOPEE, MN. *Catholic Cemeteries of Shakapee, Minnesota, Inc.* A corporation formed by the Church of St. Mark and the Church of St. Mary, both of Shakopee, to consolidate separate cemeteries. 535 S. Lewis St., 55379.

NECROLOGY

† Dudley, Francis R., (Retired). —Died Jan. 26, 2000.
† Dynes, Leo, (Retired). —Died Jan. 1, 2000.
† Houle, Cecil, (Retired). —Died April 25, 2000.
† Howley, Leo W., (Retired). —Died Aug. 17, 2000.
† Joyce, John, (Retired). —Died Oct. 15, 2000.
† Ryan, Kenneth T., (Retired). —Died April 25, 2000.
† Schnitzius, Donald, (Retired). —Died Jan. 12, 2000.
† Streff, Joseph, (Retired). —Died April 26, 2000.
† Ward, William J., Minneapolis, MN Our Lady of Lourdes. —Died Nov. 17, 2000.

Diocese of St. Petersburg

(Dioecesis Sancti Petri in Florida)

Most Reverend

ROBERT N. LYNCH

Fourth Bishop of St. Petersburg; ordained May 13, 1978; appointed Fourth Bishop of St. Petersburg December 5, 1995; consecrated and installed January 26, 1996. *Office: P.O. Box 40200, St. Petersburg, FL, 33743-0200.*

Most Reverend

W. THOMAS LARKIN, D.D.

Retired Bishop of St. Petersburg; ordained May 15, 1947; appointed Second Bishop of St. Petersburg April 24, 1979; ordained Bishop May 27, 1979; installed June 28, 1979; retired November 28, 1988.

ESTABLISHED JUNE 17, 1968.

Square Miles 3,177.

Comprises the Counties of Citrus, Hernando, Hillsborough, Pasco and Pinellas in the State of Florida.

For legal titles of parishes and diocesan institutions, consult the Chancery.

Chancery: P.O. Box 40200, St. Petersburg, FL, 33743-0200. Tel.: 727-344-1611; Fax: 727-345-2143.

Web site address: www.dioceseofstpete.org

E-mail address: comdosp@aol.com

STATISTICAL OVERVIEW

Personnel	
Bishop	1
Retired Bishops	2
Priests: Diocesan Active in Diocese	92
Priests: Active Outside Diocese	4
Priests: Retired, Sick or Absent	35
Number of Diocesan Priests	131
Religious Priests in Diocese	134
Extern Priests in Diocese	117
Ordinations:	
Diocesan Priests	2
Religious Priests	1
Permanent Deacons in Diocese	93
Total Brothers	50
Total Sisters	341
Parishes	
Parishes	73
With Resident Pastor:	
Resident Diocesan Priests	61
Resident Religious Priests	12
Without Resident Pastor:	
Administered by Priests	2
Missions	4
Pastoral Centers	1
Welfare	
Catholic Hospitals	2
Total Assisted	182,875
Health Care Centers	7
Total Assisted	35,000
Homes for the Aged	8
Total Assisted	874
Residential Care of Children	5
Total Assisted	11,000
Day Care and Extended Day Care Centers	14
Total Assisted	1,500
Specialized Homes	3
Total Assisted	1,225
Special Centers for Social Services	10
Total Assisted	15,000
Educational	
Diocesan Students in Other Seminaries	19
Total Seminarians	19
Colleges and Universities	1
Total Students	2,708
High Schools, Diocesan and Parish	3
Total Students	2,110
High Schools, Private	2
Total Students	960
Elementary Schools, Diocesan and Parish	29
Total Students	11,200
Elementary Schools, Private	4
Total Students	1,190
Non-residential Schools for the Disabled	2
Total Students	145
Catechesis/Religious Education:	
High School Students	2,400
Elementary Students	19,000
Total Students Under Catholic Instruction	39,732
Teachers in the Diocese:	
Priests	11
Scholastics	2
Brothers	5
Sisters	60
Lay Teachers	841
Vital Statistics	
Receptions into the Church:	
Infant Baptism Totals	4,869
Adult Baptism Totals	741
Received into Full Communion	623
First Communions	5,329
Confirmations	3,684
Marriages:	
Catholic	973
Interfaith	673
Total Marriages	1,646
Deaths	4,258
Total Catholic Population	371,714
Total Population	2,478,095

Former Bishops—Most Rev. CHARLES B. MCLAUGHLIN, D.D., ord. June 6, 1941; appt. Titular Bishop of Risinium and Auxiliary of Raleigh, Jan. 13, 1964; appt. First Bishop of St. Petersburg, May 8, 1968; installed June 17, 1968; died in Office, Dec 14, 1978.—Most Rev. W. THOMAS LARKIN, D.D., ord. May 15, 1947; Second Bishop of St. Petersburg; appt. April 24, 1979; ord. Bishop, May 27, 1979; installed June 28, 1979; retired Nov. 28, 1988.—Most Rev. JOHN C. FAVALORA, D.D., Third Bishop of St. Petersburg; ord. Dec. 20, 1961; appt. Bishop of Alexandria, June 16, 1986; ord. and installed July 29, 1986; appt. Third Bishop of St. Petersburg, March 7, 1989; installed May 16, 1989; installed Third Archbishop of Miami, Dec. 20, 1994.

Diocesan Offices

Pastoral Center—6363 Ninth Ave. N., St. Petersburg, 33710. Tel: 727-344-1611; Fax: 727-345-2143., *Mailing Address: P.O. Box 40200, St. Petersburg, 33743-0200.*

Tribunal—905 S. Prospect Ave., Clearwater, 33756. Tel: 727-446-2326; 442-8884; Fax: 727-446-4287.

Catholic Media Center—2816 Morrison Ave., Tampa, 33629. Tel: 813-289-4562., *Mailing Address: P.O. Box 18081, Tampa, 33679.*

WBVM Radio—Tampa. Tel: 813-289-8040.

Office of the Bishop

Office of the Bishop—Most. Rev. ROBERT N. LYNCH.

Executive Secretary—Mrs. SUE TULLY, Notary.

Diocesan Curia

Vicar General and Moderator of the Curia—Rev. Msgr. BRENDAN MULDOON, V.G.

Chancellor—Rev. ROBERT C. GIBBONS, J.C.L.; Mrs. CATHERINE OUELLETTE, Exec. Sec. & Notary; Mrs. LISA MOBLEY, Archivist & Notary.

Vice Chancellor—Mrs. JOAN MORGAN, Notary.

Director of Priest Personnel—Rev. ROBERT MORRIS.

Secretary for Pastoral Programs—Rev. Msgr. FRANK MOUCH.

Secretary for Administration—Mrs. ELIZABETH DEPTULA; Miss BARBARA STUTTS, Exec. Sec. & Notary.

The Tribunal—

Judicial Vicar—Rev. Msgr. DACIAN DEE, J.C.D.

Tribunal Staff—

Judges—Rev. Msgr. DACIAN DEE, J.C.D.; Revs. ROBERT GIBBONS, J.C.L.; RONALD AUBIN, J.C.L.; Mr. ANTHONY ELLUL, J.C.D.; Rev. WALTER BUECHE, C.SS.R.

Promoter of Justice—Rev. WILLIAM SWENGROS, J.C.L.

Defenders of the Bond—Rev. STEPHEN DAMBRAUSKAS, J.C.L.; Mr. DAVID RIDENOUR, J.C.L.

Auditor—Mr. KAZ MIELCAREK, Ph.D.

Notaries—Mrs. SARAH DURST; Mrs. LOUISE KNOCHELMANN; Mrs. MARY SUE OLIVER; Ms. ANA RIVERA.

Priests Personnel Board—Revs. ARTHUR PROULX, Chm. DENNIS HUGHES; ROBERT MORRIS; Rev. Msgr. J. BERNARD CAVERLY. Ex Officio: Rev. Msgr. JOHN NEFF; Rev. Msgr. BRENDAN MULDOON; Rev. ROBERT

C. GIBBONS, J.C.L.; Mrs. ELIZABETH DEPTULA; Mrs. JOAN MORGAN; Rev. Msgr. FRANK MOUCH.

Incardination Commission—Rev. Msgr. JOHN NEFF, Chm.; Rev. ROBERT C. GIBBONS, J.C.L., Exec. Sec.; Very Rev. JOSEPH PELLEGRINO, V.F.; Rev. Msgr. BRENDAN MULDOON, V.G.; Revs. MICHAEL LYDON; AUSTIN MULLEN.

Vocations Office—Rev. LEONARD PLAZEWSKI, Dir. Vocations; Sr. PHYLLIS SHAUGHNESSY, O.S.C., Asst. Dir. for Rel. Communities; Mrs. GAIL LINKOGLE, Admin. Asst.

Permanent Diaconate Office—Rev. ALAN WEBER, Dir.; Deacon VINCENT ALTERIO, Admin. Asst.; Mrs. HEIDI SUMNER, Sec.

Vicar for Religious—Sr. GERMAINE BEVANS, O.S.B.; Sr. EUGENE MARIE SCHNEIDER, O.S.F., Sec.

Department of Pastoral Programs

Worship, Office of—Rev. JOHN TAPP, Sec. for Worship; Mr. DOUGLAS REATINI, Dir.; Mrs. KATHY PROEFKE, Admin. Asst.

Our Lady of Good Counsel Camp—Very Rev. JAMES JOHNSON, Dir., *8888 E. Gobbler Dr., Floral City, 32636.* Tel: 352-726-2198.

Black Catholics, Office of—Rev. Msgr. AUGUSTINE NDEUKOYA, Dir.; Ms. YVONNE NELLUM, Coord.

Charismatic Renewal, Office of—Dr. RONALD NOVOTNY, Coord., *709 Bayview Ave., Clearwater, 33759.* Tel: 727-797-3311. Rev. ANTONIO DIEZ, Spanish Speaking Spiritual Moderator, *6819 Krycul Ave., P.O. Box 418, Riverview, 33569.* Tel: 813-677-2175.

Cursillo—Vacant.

Spanish Cursillo—Deacon JOHN SIERRA, Dir., *St. Paul Church, 12708 N. Dale Mabry Hwy., Tampa, 33624.* Tel: 813-961-3023.

Cursillo Center—1706 11th Ave., Tampa, 33675. Tel: 813-248-3942.

Ecumenical and Inter-Religious Affairs—Rev. Msgr. J. BERNARD CAVERLY, *St. Raphael Church, 1376 Snell Isle Blvd., N.E., St. Petersburg, 33704.* Tel: 727-821-7989.

Evangelization, Office of—Rev. Msgr. JOHN SCULLY, P.A., Dir.

Hispanic Apostolate—Mrs. SANDRA BONILLA, Dir.; Rev. RAMON HERNANDEZ, Spiritual Moderator.

St. Casimir Lithuanian Apostolate—Rev. ANTONAS GRABNICKAS, O.F.M., Dir., *555 68th Ave., St. Petersburg Beach, 33706.* Tel: 727-367-2408.

Miserere Guild, Inc.—Rev. Msgr. J. BERNARD CAVERLY, Dir., *St. Raphael Church, 1376 Snell Isle Blvd. N.E., St. Petersburg, 33704.* Tel: 727-821-7989.

Calvary Catholic Cemetery—Rev. Msgr. NORMAN BALTHAZAR, Dir. Cemeteries; Mr. JEFFREY R. STEPHANZ, Gen. Mgr., *11801 U.S. Hwy. 19 N., Clearwater, 34624-7407.* Tel: 727-572-4355; Fax: 727-592-9241.

Prison and Jail Ministry—Rev. JOSE FURTADO, Dir.

Propagation of the Faith—Rev. Msgr. JOHN SCULLY, P.A., Diocesan Dir.

Sea, Apostleship of the—

Port of St. Petersburg—Rev. BERNARDINE SMITH, T.O.R., Chap., *515 4th St., St. Petersburg, 33701.* Tel: 727-896-2191.

Port of Tampa—Deacon MAXIMO MONTAYRE, *2514 E. Hanna Ave., Tampa, 33610.* Tel: 813-234-8693.

Department of Catholic Formation and Education

Executive Director—BARBARA MCCONVILLE, Ph.D.

Catholic Schools Office—Bro. JOHN CUMMINGS, F.M.S., Supt.; Ms. MARY BRYAN, Assoc. Supt. for Administrative Svcs.; Ms. KAY RIZZO, Assoc. Supt. for Curriculum.

Family Life Office—Deacon JOSEPH GROTE, Dir.

Father William F. Balfe Memorial Library—Mrs. CLARA BLOWERS, Dir.

Religious Education Office—Mr. BRIAN A. LEMOI, Dir.

Respect Life Office—Mrs. SHARON ILER, Dir.

Scouting Office—Rev. Msgr. ANTON DECHERING, Dir., *1600 54th Ave. S., St. Petersburg, 33712.* Tel: 727-867-3663. Rev. ED PALKA, Assoc. Dir. Tel: 727-733-3606.

Youth Ministry Office—Bro. GERALD D. MEEGAN, S.D.B., Dir.

Department of Communications

Executive Director—Mr. WILLIAM J. URBANSKI.

Catholic Television Mass—MARY JO MURPHY, Producer.

Diocesan Radio - WBVM 90.5 FM & WLMS 88.3 FM—Mr. JOHN MORRIS, Station Mgr., *Media Center, Tampa.* Tel: 813-289-8040; 800-223-WBVM.

"The Florida Catholic" Newspaper—JANET SHELTON, Editor.

Circulation & Subscription—P.O. Box 3551, Orlando, 32802. Tel: 407-423-3438.

Department of Temporal Affairs

Department of Temporal Affairs—Rev. Msgr. BRENDAN MULDOON, V.G., Chief Fin. Officer; Mrs. ELIZABETH DEPTULA, Sec. for Admin.; Mr. PAUL A. WARD, JR., Exec. Dir.; Mr. JOSEPH CORSETTI, Asst. to Exec. Dir.

Diocesan Finance Council—Mrs. LAURA KRUEGER BROCK, Chm.; Mr. C. DAVID CARLEY; Rev. Msgr. BRENDAN MULDOON; Mr. JAMES QUINLAN, SR.; Rev. ROBERT C. GIBBONS; Mr. FRED DOBBINS; Mr. GREGORY C. JEWELL; Mr. WILLIAM G. TAPP; Mr. PATRICK WALSH; Rev. Msgr. FRANK MOUCH; Rev. GREGG TOTTLE; Mrs. ELIZABETH DEPTULA; Rev. COLMAN COOKE.

Insurance, Health & Welfare Administration—Mr. DONALD BRASIER, Dir.; Mrs. KAE YAUCHLER, Admin. Asst.

Real Estate—Mr. RONALD G. BENTO, Real Estate Mgr.; Mr. STEVE B. ZIENTEK, Real Estate Planning.

Department of Construction Management

Office of Construction Management—Mrs. DENISE DIGRUCCIO, Exec. Dir.

Pastoral Offices and Consultative Bodies to the Diocesan Curia

Presbyteral Council—Most Rev. ROBERT N. LYNCH, Pres.; Rev. Msgr. BRENDAN MULDOON, V.G., Vice Pres.; Very Rev. RALPH ARGENTINO, V.F., Chm.; Rev. Msgr. JOHN NEFF; Rev. ROBERT GIBBONS, J.C.L.; Rev. Msgr. DACIAN DEE, J.C.D.; Very Revs. ROBERT DONLAN, V.F.; JAMES JOHNSON, V.F.; ROBERT SCHNEIDER, V.F.; JOSEPH PELLEGRINO, V.F.; GERARD POWERS, V.F.; Rev. Msgr. JOHN CIPPEL; Revs. JOSEPH DOYLE, S.J.; THOMAS MADDEN; JACOB MONTELEONE; ROBERT MORRIS; Very Rev. MICHAEL MUHR, V.F.; Revs. LEONARD PLAZEWSKI; ARTHUR PROULX; RICHARD JANKOWSKI; GREGG TOTTLE; KEN MALLEY; DAVID TOUPS; TIM SHERWOOD; LOUIS MOLINELLI, S.D.B.; Rev. Msgr. FRANK MOUCH.

College of Consultors—Rev. Msgr. BRENDAN MULDOON, V.G.; Rev. ROBERT C. GIBBONS, J.C.L., Sec.; Rev. Msgr. JOHN NEFF; Rev. Msgr. DACIAN DEE, J.C.D.; Very Revs. RALPH ARGENTINO, V.F.; ROBERT DONLAN, V.F.; JAMES JOHNSON, V.F.; ROBERT SCHNEIDER, V.F.; MICHAEL MUHR, V.F.; JOSEPH PELLEGRINO, V.F.; GERARD POWERS, V.F.; Rev. GREGG TOTTLE.

Vicars Forane—Very Revs. RALPH ARGENTINO, V.F., East Hillsborough Deanery; JOSEPH PELLEGRINO, V.F., Upper Pinellas Deanery; ROBERT SCHNEIDER, V.F., Lower Pinellas Deanery; MICHAEL MUHR, V.F., West Hillsborough Deanery; GERARD POWERS, V.F., Pasco Deanery; ROBERT DONLAN, V.F., Hernando Deanery; JAMES JOHNSON, V.F., Citrus Deanery.

Organizations Serving the Diocese

Archdiocese of Miami, Diocese of St. Petersburg, and Diocese of Venice Pension Plan—

Pension Plan Administrator—Gabriel, Roeder, Smith & Co., 301 E. Las Olas Blvd., Ste. 200, Fort Lauderdale, 33301. Tel: 954-527-1616; Fax: 954-525-0083.

Catholic Charities, Diocese of St. Petersburg, Inc.

Central Services—1213 16th St., N., St. Petersburg, 33705. Tel: 727-893-1314; Fax: 727-893-1307. Mr. ARNOLD ANDREWS, Exec. Dir.

Pious Foundations

Catholic Education Foundation, Inc.—6363 Ninth Ave. N., St. Petersburg, 33710. Tel: 727-344-1611., *Mailing Address: P.O. Box 40200, St. Petersburg, 33743.*

Organizations of the Catholic Faithful

Catholic Daughters of America—Mrs. ROSE TOMASSI, Natl. Dir. Tel: 727-360-8508. Mrs. ROSE MONCHECOURT, State Regent. Tel: 813-934-6209.

Diocesan Council of Catholic Women—Rev. Msgr. HAROLD BUMPUS, Diocesan Moderator. Tel: 813-634-2328.

Family of St. Jerome, "Familian Sancti Hieronymi"—Mr. JAN G. HALISKY, P.A., Praeses Generalis, *507 S. Prospect Ave., Clearwater, 33756.*

Knights of Columbus—Rev. PAUL HERVEY, Diocesan Chap. Tel: 813-885-7861.

Society of St. Vincent de Paul—

Council of St. Petersburg Diocese—P.O. Box 13938, Tampa, 33681-0938. Tel: 813-832-5486. Mr. MARVIN ROPERT, Pres.

Hernando/Citrus St. Vincent de Paul Society District Council—Mr. CESAR LANDAETA, Pres. Tel: 904-688-9070.

Hillsborough District Council—Mr. JOSEPH LATINA, Pres. Tel: 813-985-1012.

Ozanam District Council (Pasco Deanery)—Mr. DENNIS HOLT, Pres. Tel: 813-966-2046.

Lower Pinellas District Council—Mr. WILLIAM REAGOR, Pres. Tel: 727-345-0212.

Upper Pinellas District Council—Mr. WALTER HAINS, Pres. Tel: 727-442-7370.

CLERGY, PARISHES, MISSIONS AND PAROCHIAL SCHOOLS

CITY OF ST. PETERSBURG
(Pinellas County)

1—CATHEDRAL OF ST. JUDE THE APOSTLE (1950), Very Rev. David T. DeJulio, Rector; Revs. Joel M. Kovanis; Robert Gately; Jerome P. Laubacker, O.de.M.; Deacon David Sirrianna.
Tel: 727-347-9702; Fax: 727-343-8370.
School—Tel: 727-347-8622; Fax: 727-343-0305. Larry Lopez, Prin.
Lay Teachers 31; Students 535.
Catechesis/Religious Programs—Fax: 727-343-8370. Ms. Dorothy Sanderson, D.R.E.
Students 334.

2—BLESSED TRINITY (1960), Rev. Msgr. Anton Dechering; Revs. J. Frederick McGuire (CIN); Paul Bondi (ALB) (Retired); Sr. Jean Barrett, O.S.F., Pastoral Assoc.
Res., 1600 54th Ave. S., 33712. Tel: 727-867-3663; Fax: 727-864-2679.
School—St. Paul Interparochial School. See Elementary Schools, Interparochial under Institutions Located in the Diocese. Tel: 727-823-6144; Fax: 727-896-0609.
Catechesis/Religious Programs—Tel: 727-867-2421; Fax: 727-864-2679. Mrs. Sonya Adkins, D.R.E.
Students 156.

3—HOLY CROSS (1965), Revs. Robert L. Schaeufele; Gerald Hendry; Thomas Dieter (JOL); Deacons Richard Brady; Richard Nagle, Jr.; Gene Powell.
Res., 7851 54th Ave. N., 33709. Tel: 727-546-3315; 541-2242; Fax: 727-547-2005.
Catechesis/Religious Programs—Tel: 727-547-2004; Fax: 727-547-2005.
Students 230.

4—HOLY FAMILY (1959), Revs. Robert J. Schneider; Jerome E. Diffley, Pastor Emeritus; Timothy H. Sherwood; Sr. Jamesann McCue, I.H.M., Dir., Pastoral Assoc.; Deacon Michael Columbus; David J. Koval, Admin.
Res., 200 78th Ave., N.E., 33702. Tel: 727-526-5783; Fax: 727-521-2545.
School—250 78th Ave., N.E., 33702. Tel: 813-526-8194; Fax: 813-527-6567. Sr. Florence Ann Marino, I.H.M.; Sr. Electa Schmidt, I.H.M.
Sisters 1; Lay Teachers 15; Students 240.
Catechesis/Religious Programs—Anne P. Perez, D.R.E. (Adult and Elementary).
Students 327.

5—ST. JOSEPH (1926), Rev. Callist N. Nyambo. In res., Rev. Pierre Pham Van Chinh (Vietnam).
Res., 2624 Union St. S., 33712. Tel: 727-822-2153; Fax: 727-823-5820.
Preschool—Immaculate Conception, Tel: 727-822-2156; Fax: 727-553-9133.
Lay Teachers 17; Students 171.
Catechesis/Religious Programs—Tel: 727-822-8427.
Students 61.
Mission—St. Petersburg, Pinellas Co., Vietnamese Martyrs Mission, Tel: 727-822-7344.

6—ST. MARY OUR LADY OF GRACE (1921), Revs. Bernardine J. Smith, T.O.R.; Brian J. Miller, T.O.R.; Deacon Julio Morales.
Res., 515 Fourth St. S., 33701. Tel: 727-896-2191; Fax: 727-895-6279.
St. Mary's Center—.

7—ST. PAUL (1929), Revs. Robert C. Gibbons; Michael Robert Cormier.
Res., 1800 12th St. N., 33704. Tel: 727-822-3481; Fax: 727-822-1754.
School—St. Paul Interparochial School. See Elementary Schools, Interparochial under Institutions Located in the Diocese. Tel: 727-823-6144; Fax: 727-896-0609.
Catechesis/Religious Programs—Tel: 727-822-3481; Fax: 727-822-1754.
Students 55.
Mission—St. Petersburg, The Mercy of God Polish Mission, 1358 20th Ave. N., 33704. Tel: 813-823-6997; Fax: 813-821-8242. Rev. Janusz Burzawa (Poland).

8—ST. RAPHAEL (1961), Rev. Msgr. J. Bernard Caverly; Rev. Michel Robert Smith; Deacon Joseph Grote. In res., Rev. Jose Gonzalez.
Res., 1376 Snell Isle Blvd., N.E., 33704. Tel: 727-821-7989; Fax: 727-896-9619.
School—Tel: 727-821-9663; Fax: 727-821-9665. Mr. Harry Plummer, Prin.
Lay Teachers 19; Students 272.
Catechesis/Religious Programs—Tel: 727-821-7989. Rhona Beettam, D.R.E.
Students 265.

9—TRANSFIGURATION (1959), Rev. Steven M. Roszczewski, O.deM.; Rev. Msgr. John F. Bolger,., Pastor Emeritus; Revs. Anthony M. Fortunato, O.de.M.; Oscar Z. Kozyra, O.deM.
Res., 4000-43 St. N., 33714-4335. Tel: 727-525-0262; Fax: 727-526-7794.
School—Tel: 727-527-2880; Fax: 727-522-1328. Mrs. Joanne Clarie, Prin.
Religious 1; Lay Teachers 15; Students 268.
Catechesis/Religious Programs—Mrs. Kathryn Brasseur, D.R.E.
Students 98.

OUTSIDE THE CITY OF ST. PETERSBURG

Beverly Hills, Citrus Co., Our Lady of Grace (1966), Rev. Paul Mizener. In res., Rev. Jorge Gonzalez.
Res., 6 Roosevelt Blvd., 34465. Tel: 352-746-2144; Fax: 352-746-6892.
School—Pope John Paul II, Lecanto. See Elementary Schools, Interparochial under Institutions Located in the Diocese. Tel: 352-746-2020; Fax: 352-746-3448.
Catechesis/Religious Programs—Tel: 352-746-2144; Fax: 352-746-6892. Maryann Gajos, D.R.E.
Students 114.

Brandon, Hillsborough Co., Church of the Nativity (1960), Rev. Msgr. James C. Lara, Pastor Emeritus; Very Rev. Ralph J. Argentino, V.F.; Rev. Ybain Ramirez (Venezuela); Deacons Jim Pescatore; Luis Zayas.
Church—705 E. Brandon Blvd., 33511. Tel: 813-681-4608; Fax: 813-653-9482.
Res., 805 Westbrook, 33511. Tel: 813-684-0256. [JC]
School—Tel: 813-689-3395; Fax: 813-681-5406. Sr. Irene St. Jean, C.S.C., Prin.
Sisters of Holy Cross (Pittsfield, NH) 2; Lay Teachers 33; Students 754.
Catechesis/Religious Programs—Tel: 813-689-3395; Fax: 813-681-5406. Thomas Neal, D.R.E.
Students 1300.

Brooksville, Hernando Co., St. Anthony (1892), Rev. Robert R. Donlan; Deacon Manuel Carreiro. In res., Sr. Loretta Lonsdorf, O.S.M.
Res., 20428 Cortez Blvd., 34601-5601. Tel: 352-796-2096; Fax: 352-796-7144.
School—Notre Dame Interparochial School. See Elementary Schools, Interparochial under Institutions Located in the Diocese. Tel: 352-683-0755; Fax: 352-683-3924.
Catechesis/Religious Programs—Fax: 352-796-7144. Sr. Patricia Saunders, O.P., D.R.E.
Students 198.

Citrus Springs, Citrus Co., St. Elizabeth Ann Seton (1976), Rev. Raymond A. Lettre; Rev. Msgr. George Cummings, Pastor Emeritus. In res., Rev. William Kearney.
Office: 1460 W. St. Elizabeth Pl., 34434. Tel: 352-489-4889; Fax: 352-489-4770.
School—Pope John Paul II. See Elementary Schools, Interparochial under Institutions Located in the Diocese. Lecanto, Tel: 352-746-2020; Fax: 352-746-3448.
Catechesis/Religious Programs—Tel: 352-489-4889. Mrs. Claire Giordano, D.R.E.
Students 35.

Clearwater, Pinellas Co.,

1—ALL SAINTS, (1987), Rev. Gregory J. Andrews.
Office: 2801 Curlew Rd., 33761. Tel: 727-789-1025; Fax: 727-784-8025.
School—Guardian Angels Interparochial School. See Elementary Schools, Interparochial under Institutions Located in the Diocese. Tel: 727-799-6724; Fax: 727-724-9018.
Catechesis/Religious Programs—Students 36.

2—LIGHT OF CHRIST, (1966), Revs. Jacob Monteleone; John Gerth; Peter Pathikattil (India); Deacon James Hassett.
Res., 2176 Marilyn St., 33765. Tel: 727-441-4545; Fax: 727-441-8771.
School—St. Cecelia Interparochial School. See Elementary Schools, Interparochial under Institutions Located in the Diocese. Tel: 727-461-1200; Fax: 727-446-9140.
Pre-School—Tel: 727-442-4797; Fax: 727-441-8771. Mrs. Rebecca Daschbach, Dir.
Lay Teachers 4; Students 65.
Catechesis/Religious Programs—Tel: 727-442-7081. William Woodard, D.R.E.
Students 394.

3—ST. BRENDAN, (1978), Rev. Msgr. Michael F. Devine.
Res., 245 Dory Passage, 33767. Tel: 727-443-5485; Fax: 727-442-5896.
School—St. Cecelia Interparochial School. See Elementary Schools, Interparochial Under Institutions Located in the Diocese. Tel: 727-447-3494; Fax: 727-442-4810.

4—ST. CECELIA, (1924), Revs. Aiden Foynes; Merrell T. Dickey; Francis X. Sarjeant, S.J. In res., Rev. Eduardo Wal.
Res., 820 Jasmine Way, 33756. Tel: 727-447-3494; Fax: 727-442-4810.
School—St. Cecelia Interparochial School. See Elementary Schools, Interparochial under Institutions Located in the Diocese. Tel: 727-461-1200; Fax: 727-446-9140.
Catechesis/Religious Programs—Mrs. Mary M. Thomas, D.R.E.
Students 375.

5—ST. MICHAEL THE ARCHANGEL, (1980), Revs. Colman M. Cooke; Ted Costello; Ronald Marecki; Sr. Theresa Betz, S.N.D., Pastoral Assoc.
Res., 2281 State Rd. 580, 33763. Tel: 727-797-2375; Fax: 727-791-8287.
Catechesis/Religious Programs—Tel: 727-797-7083. Mrs. Katie White, D.R.E.
Students 207.

Crystal River, Citrus Co., St. Benedict (1953), Rev. Vincent R. Morton; Deacon James Pullar.
Mailing Address: 455 S. Suncoast Blvd., 34429. Tel: 352-795-4478; 4479; Fax: 352-795-4160.
School—Pope John Paul II. See Elementary Schools, Interparochial under Institutions Located in the Diocese. Lecanto, Tel: 352-746-2020; Fax: 352-746-3448.
Catechesis/Religious Programs—Tel: 352-795-4050. Suzanne Cummins, D.R.E.
Students 123.

Dade City, Pasco Co., St. Rita (1912) (Hispanic), Rev. Ramon Hernandez. In res., Rev. Anselm Harry Morrison, A.A.
Office & Mailing Address: 14404 14th St., 33523. Tel: 352-567-2894; Fax: 352-567-2777.
Res., 14325 13th St., 33523. Tel: 352-521-3145.
School—St. Anthony Interparochial School. See Elementary Schools, Interparochial under Institutions Located in the Diocese. San Antonio, Tel: 352-588-3041; Fax: 352-588-3142.
Catechesis/Religious Programs—Sr. Eugenia Aguilar, O.P., D.R.E.
Students 247.

Dunedin, Pinellas Co., Our Lady of Lourdes (1958), Revs. Thomas L. Madden; Thomas M. Conmy, C.S.C.; Edwin Palka. In res., Rev. Denis Kitenge (Zaire).
Res., 750 San Salvador Dr., 34698. Tel: 727-733-3606; Fax: 727-733-8305.
School—Tel: 727-733-3776; Fax: 727-733-3776. Mrs. Janice Metz.
Sisters of Notre Dame (Chardon Ohio) 3; Lay Teachers 15; Students 335.
Catechesis/Religious Programs—Tel: 813-733-0872; Fax: 813-733-8305. Sr. Kathleen Dede, S.P., D.R.E.
Students 560.

Gulfport, Pinellas Co., Most Holy Name of Jesus (1960), Revs. Raymond O'Neill; Paul Kochu (West Indies); Deacon Glenn Pickart.
Res., 5800 15th Ave. S., 33707. Tel: 727-347-9989; Fax: 727-343-6420.
School—Tel: 727-347-1774; Fax: 727-381-7225. Karen L. Evjue, Prin.
Lay Teachers 14; Students 125.
Catechesis/Religious Programs—Lyn Folsom, D.R.E.
Students 172.

Holiday, Pasco Co., St. Vincent De Paul (1969), Revs. Paul Goudreau; Emil Styczen; Sr. Josephine Rooney, O.S.C., Pastoral Assoc.; Deacons Frank Longo; Gerard White; Sr. Madeleine Donnelly, O.S.C.
Res., 4843 Mile Stretch Dr., P.O. Box 3865, 34690. Tel: 727-938-1974; Fax: 727-938-1975.
School—Bishop Larkin Interparochial School. See Elementary Schools, Interparochial under Institutions Located in the Diocese. Hudson, Tel: 727-862-6981.
Catechesis/Religious Programs—Tel: 727-934-8035. Jane Etzel, D.R.E.
Students 240.

Homosassa, Citrus Co., St. Thomas the Apostle (1987), Rev. David A. Banks; Deacon Richard Meyer.
Res., 7040 S. Suncoast Blvd., 34446. Tel: 352-628-7000; Fax: 352-628-4723.
School—Pope John Paul II. See Elementary Schools, Interparochial under Institutions Located in the Diocese. Lecanto.
Catechesis/Religious Programs—Students 63.

Hudson, Pasco Co., St. Michael (1971), Revs. Desmond Daly; John McEvoy; Seamus Collins, O.P.; Deacons Robert Simpson; Howard Page.
Res., 8014 State Rd. #52, 34667. Tel: 727-868-5276; Fax: 727-862-9187.
Catechesis/Religious Programs—Tel: 727-863-9742. Mary Alber, D.R.E.
Students 502.

Indian Rocks Beach, Pinellas Co., St. Jerome (1956), Very Rev. Msgr. Brendan Muldoon, V.G.; Revs. Kenneth Malley; Sean O'Sullivan, I.C.; Deacon William Mahood; Cathie Darnauer, Admin. Pastoral Assocs.: Sr. Lucia Brady, O.S.C.; Sr. Cecilia McDonnell, O.S.C. In res., Very Rev. Msgr. Dacian Dee, J.C.D., V.E.; Rev. Msgr. John McCall.
Mailing Address: P.O. Box 100, 33785.
Res., 10895 Hamlin Blvd., Largo, 33774. Tel: 727-595-4610; Fax: 727-596-6792.
Early Childhood Center: Tel: 727-596-9491. Denise Roach, Dir.
Catechesis/Religious Programs—Tel: 727-595-3100. Tamara Gildea, D.R.E.
Students 843.

Inverness, Citrus Co., Our Lady of Fatima (1955), Revs. James B. Johnson; Charles Leke; Desmond Gill, Pastor Emeritus; Deacon Steve Kurylowicz.
Mailing Address: 550 U.S. Hwy. 41 S., 34450. Tel: 352-726-1670; Fax: 352-344-8384.
Res., 518 Desota Ave., 34450. Tel: 352-726-1670.
School—Pope John Paul II. See Elementary Schools, Interparochial under Institutions Located in the Diocese. Tel: 352-746-2020; Fax: 352-746-3448.
Catechesis/Religious Programs—D.R.E.: Rebecca Pound; Annette Tremante.
Students 247.

Land O'Lakes, Pasco Co., Our Lady of the Rosary (1952), Rev. Ronald B. Aubin; Deacons Augustin Ortiz; Eric Wells.
2348 Collier Pkwy., 34639.
Res., P.O. Box 1229, 34639. Tel: 813-949-4565; Fax: 813-948-1981.
School—Most Holy Redeemer Interparochial School. See Elementary Schools, Interparochial under Institutions Located in the Diocese. Tampa, Tel: 813-933-4750; Fax: 813-933-3181.
Catechesis/Religious Programs—Tel: 813-949-2699; Fax: 813-948-1981.
Students 403.

Largo, Pinellas Co.,

1—ST. CATHERINE OF SIENA, (1976), Revs. Michael J. Finnegan; John O'Donovan (Ireland). Pastoral Assocs.: Tel: 727-531-1690. Sr. Ann Gertrude, S.S.J.; Sr. Therese Ganly, S.S.J.
Res., 1955 S. Belcher Rd., Clearwater, 33764. Tel: 727-531-7721; Fax: 727-531-7723.
School—St. Cecelia Interparochial School. See Elementary Schools, Interparochial under Institutions Located in the Diocese. Tel: 727-461-1200; Fax: 727-442-4810.
Catechesis/Religious Programs—Paula Sikora, D.R.E.
Students 262.

2—ST. JUSTIN MARTYR, (1987), Rev. Michael O'Brien.
Res., 10725 Ridge Rd., Seminole, 33778. Tel: 727-397-3312; Fax: 727-392-6653.
Catechesis/Religious Programs—Tel: 727-397-3312, Ext. 311. JIm Rood, D.R.E.
Students 184.

3—ST. MATTHEW, (1985), Rev. Richard J. Allen.
Mailing Address: P.O. Box 10097, 33773-0097.
Office: 9111 90th Ave. N., 33777. Tel: 727-393-1288; Fax: 727-398-2683.
Catechesis/Religious Programs—Tel: 727-398-6618, Ext. 207. Ruth Appel, D.R.E.
Students 300.

4—ST. PATRICK, (1958), Revs. Arthur J. Proulx; John D'Antonio, O.Praem.; Deacon John DiVito.
Res., 2121 16th Ave. S.W., P.O. Box 167, 33779. Tel: 727-584-2318; Fax: 727-586-5413.
School—Tel: 727-581-4865; Fax: 727-581-7842. Edward F. Andrade, Prin.
Lay Teachers 17; Students 239.
Catechesis/Religious Programs—Tel: 727-584-6697. Kathy Filippelli, D.R.E.
Students 345.

Lecanto, Citrus Co., St. Scholastica (1987), Rev. Richard Jankowski; Deacons Terrence E. Knox; Stephen Sablone. In res., Rev. James Hoge, O.S.B.
Res., 4301 W. Homosassa Tr., 34461-9106. Tel: 352-746-9422; 563-2296; Fax: 352-746-2335.
School—Pope John Paul II. See Elementary Schools, Interparochial under Institutions Located in the Diocese. Tel: 352-746-2020; Fax: 352-746-3448.
Catechesis/Religious Programs—Tel: 352-746-9422; Fax: 352-746-2335. Judi Bescher, D.R.E.
Students 406.

Masaryktown, Pasco Co., St. Mary, Our Lady of Sorrows (1931), Rev. James A. Bucaria.
Mailing Address: P.O. Box 9250, 34604. Tel: 352-796-2792; Fax: 352-544-0398.
School—Notre Dame Interparochial School. See Elementary Schools, Interparochial under Institutions Located in the Diocese. Spring Hill, Tel: 352-683-0755; Fax: 352-683-3924.
Catechesis/Religious Programs—Students 20.

New Port Richey, Pasco Co., Our Lady Queen of Peace (1913) (Hispanic), Revs. Gerard E. Powers, V.F.; Kenneth Slattery; Jairo Atehortua; John Anoia (SPR); Joseph A. Pastick, (Retired); Deacons Roger F. Lind (RVC); John Liggan (NY); Antonio Morales.

Administrators: Carol Passenti; Ed Wenger.
Res., 5340 High St., 34652. Tel: 727-849-7521; Fax: 727-849-4814.
School—Bishop Larkin Interparochial School. See Elementary Schools, Interparochial under Institutions Located in the Diocese. Hudson, Tel: 727-862-6981; Fax: 727-869-9893.
Catechesis/Religious Programs—Tel: 727-842-9396. Abad Perez, D.R.E.
Students 236.

St. Thomas Aquinas (1980), Revs. Michael Lydon; Francis Dionne.
Res., 8320 Old C.R. #54, 34653. Tel: 727-372-8600; Fax: 727-376-7204.
St. Thomas Early Childhood Development Center—Tel: 727-376-2330; Fax: 727-372-5712.
School—Bishop Larkin Interparochial School. See Elementary Schools, Interparochial under Institutions Located in the Diocese. Hudson, Tel: 727-862-6981; Fax: 727-862-9187.
Catechesis/Religious Programs—Tel: 727-376-1622. Jeanne Schneider, D.R.E.
Students 825.

Palm Harbor, Pinellas Co., St. Luke the Evangelist (1985), Rev. Ronald J. Poirier. Pastoral Assocs.: Sr. Bridget Mulligan, O.S.C.; Deacons James Blaney; John Edgerton.
Res., 2757 Alderman Rd., 34684. Tel: 727-786-3648; Fax: 727-789-9556.
St. Luke Early Childhood Center—Tel: 727-787-2914.
School—Guardian Angels Interparochial School. See Elementary Schools, Interparochial under Institutions Located in the Diocese. Clearwater, Tel: 727-799-6724.
Students 171.
Catechesis/Religious Programs—Tel: 727-787-2845. Paula Matta, D.R.E.
Students 600.

Pinellas Park, Pinellas Co., Sacred Heart (1910), Revs. James Merkel; Thomas Anastasia; Deacons Louis Izzo; L. Roger Cartier.
Res., 8001 46th St. N., 33781. Tel: 727-541-4447; Fax: 727-541-2073.
School—7951 46th Way N., 34665. Tel: 727-544-1106; Fax: 727-541-2073. Mrs. JoEllen Caldwell, Prin.
Lay Teachers 16; Students 233.
Catechesis/Religious Programs—Ms. Lynn Edmonds, D.R.E.
Students 108.

Plant City, Hillsborough Co., St. Clement (1912), Revs. Thomas Spillett; Luis A. Soler.
Res., 1104 Alexander St., 33566. Tel: 813-752-8251; Fax: 813-759-2721.
Catechesis/Religious Programs—Jo Ann Parolini, D.R.E.
Students 410.

Port Richey, Pasco Co., St. James the Apostle (1984), Rev. Dennis E. Hughes; Deacon Paul G. Metilly.
Res., 8400 Monarch Dr., 34668. Tel: 727-869-3130; Fax: 727-869-8886.
School—Bishop Larkin Interparochial School. See Elementary Schools, Interparochial under Institutions Located in the Diocese. Hudson, Tel: 727-862-6981; Fax: 727-869-9893.
Catechesis/Religious Programs—Tel: 727-869-3132. Sr. M. Bernadette Wyman, O.S.F., D.R.E.
Students 328.

Ridge Manor, Hernando Co., St. Anne (1960,
Res., 4142 Tremain Blvd., Hwy. 301, 33525. Tel: 352-583-2550; Fax: 352-583-0300. Rev. Gerard Murphy.
Catechesis/Religious Programs—Students 14.

Riverview, Hillsborough Co., Resurrection (1983), Rev. Msgr. Antonio Diez.
Mailing Address: P.O. Box 418, 33568.
Res., 6819 Krycul Ave., 33569. Tel: 813-677-2175; Fax: 813-671-7844.
Catechesis/Religious Programs—Students 73.

Ruskin, Hillsborough Co., St. Anne (1956), Rev. Norman Choate, C.R.
Office: 106 11th Ave., N.E., 33570. Tel: 813-645-1714; Fax: 813-645-5570.
Catechesis/Religious Programs—D.R.E.: Sr. Marian Stenken, S.C.N.; Mrs. Cindy Cyman.
Students 218.

Safety Harbor, Pinellas Co., Espiritu Santo (1960), Revs. Gregg Tottle; Thomas Morgan. Pastoral Assocs.: Sr. Phyllis Shaughnessy, O.S.C.; Sr. Paulamarie Lacy, S.N.D.; Sr. Nanette Herman, S.N.D.; Deacons Dominic P. Friscia, D.R.E.; Vincent Alterio.
Res., 2405 Philippe Pkwy., P.O. Box 176, 34695. Tel: 727-726-8477; Fax: 727-799-2062.
School—St. Cecelia Interparochial School. See Elementary Schools, Interparochial under Institutions Located in the Diocese. Clearwater, Tel: 813-461-1200.
Catechesis/Religious Programs—Tel: 727-726-6742.
Students 950.

St. Joseph, Pasco Co., Sacred Heart (1888), Rev. Patrick M. Rebel; Deacon William Connors.
Res., 32145 St. Joe Rd., Dade City, 33525. Tel: 352-588-3641; Fax: 352-588-5299. [CEM]
School—St. Anthony Interparochial School. See Elementary Schools, Interparochial under Institutions Located in the Diocese. San Antonio, Tel: 352-588-3041; Fax: 352-588-3142.
Catechesis/Religious Programs—Tel: 352-588-3641; Fax: 352-588-5299.
Students 90.
Sacred Heart Child Care Center—32245 St. Joe Rd., Dade City, 33525. Tel: 352-588-4060; Fax: 352-588-4871. Mrs. Toni Watkins.

St. Pete Beach, Pinellas Co., St. John (1939), Revs. John C. Murphy; Julio B. Rivero, T.O.R.; Deacon Karl A. Boehme. In res., Rev. Msgr. Patrick Trainor, P.A.; Revs. George A. Reskey; Elmer J. McDonald.
Res., 445 82nd Ave., 33706. Tel: 727-360-1147; Fax: 727-360-5267 (Rectory) 367-4418 (Office).
School—500 84th Ave., 33706. Tel: 727-360-1113; Fax: 727-367-8734. Sr. Joan Brennan, S.C., Prin.
Sisters 1; Lay Teachers 14; Students 226.
Catechesis/Religious Programs—Tel: 727-360-1147, Ext. 101. Sr. Elizabeth Moran.
Students 151.

San Antonio, Pasco Co., St. Anthony of Padua (1884), Rev. Henry J. Riffle; Deacon Barry Wallace.
Res., 32832 Massachusetts Ave., P.O. Box 578, 33576. Tel: 352-588-3081; Fax: 352-588-5070. [CEM]
School—St. Anthony Interparochial School. See Elementary Schools, Interparochial under Institutions Located in the Diocese. Tel: 352-588-3041; Fax: 352-588-3142.
Catechesis/Religious Programs—Tel: 352-588-3081.
Students 94.

Seffner, Hillsborough Co., St. Francis of Assisi (1987), Very Rev. Christopher Fitzgerald, I.C., V.F.; Rev. Msgr. John Scully; Deacon Jerome Thomas.
Res., P.O. Box 1218, 33583. Tel: 813-681-9115; Fax: 813-689-4148.
Catechesis/Religious Programs—Joan McCollum, D.R.E.
Students 310.

Seminole, Pinellas Co., Blessed Sacrament (1959), Revs. James Gordon, I.C.; G. Richard Pilger, I.C.
Res., 11565 66th Ave. N., 33772. Tel: 727-391-4661.
School—Tel: 727-391-4060; Fax: 727-391-5638. Jane Moerschbacher, Prin.
Lay Teachers 21; Students 305.
Catechesis/Religious Programs—Students 192.

Spring Hill, Hernando Co., St. Theresa (1969), Revs. James McAteer, I.C.; Frank Oman, I.C.; Deacon Gerard Uzzi.
Res., 1107 Commercial Way, 34606. Tel: 352-683-2849; Fax: 352-683-3437.
School—Notre Dame Interparochial School. See Elementary Schools, Interparochial under Institutions Located in the Diocese.
Catechesis/Religious Programs—Margaret Uhl, D.R.E.
Students 225.

St. Frances Xavier Cabrini (1980), Rev. Msgr. John A. Cippel; Rev. David L. Toups. In res., Rev. Andrew Beaudoin, S.S.S.
Mailing Address: 5030 Mariner Blvd., 34609. Tel: 352-683-9666; Fax: 352-688-2660.
School—Notre Dame Interparochial School. See Elementary Schools, Interparochial under Institutions Located in the Diocese. Tel: 352-683-0755.
Catechesis/Religious Programs—Linda Spenceley, D.R.E.
Students 929.

Saint Joan of Arc (1988), Rev. Marciano G. Martin, C.PP.S.
Res., 13485 Spring Hill Dr., 34609. Tel: 352-688-0663; Fax: 352-686-7937.
School—Notre Dame Interparochial School. See Elementary Schools, Interparochial under Institutions Located in the Diocese.
Catechesis/Religious Programs—Students 230.

Sun City Center, Hillsborough Co., Prince of Peace (1970), Rev. Msgr. Harold Bumpus; Deacon Angelo Pignataro. In res., Rev. Desmond Gill.
Res., 1002 Fordham Dr., 33573. Tel: 813-634-2328; Fax: 813-633-9244.
Mailing Address: 702 Valley Forge Blvd., 33573-5353. Tel: 813-634-2328.
Catechesis/Religious Programs—Students 20.

Tampa, Hillsborough Co.,

1—Blessed Sacrament, (1959) (Spanish), Rev. Jose Furtado, Admin.
Res., 1205 Windermere Way, 33619-4601. Tel: 813-626-2984; Fax: 813-626-2842.
Church—7001 12th Ave. S., 33619-4649.
Catechesis/Religious Programs—1603 Carnegie Cir., 33619. Tel: 813-626-9564.
Students 70.

2—Christ the King, (1941), Revs. Michael Muhr; John Blum; Timothy Moffatt, T.O.R.; Deacons William E. Diaz; Michael Solomon.
Res., 821 S. Dale Mabry Hwy., P.O. Box 10395, 33679-0395. Tel: 813-876-5841; Fax: 813-873-2426.
School—Tel: 813-876-8770; Fax: 813-879-0315. Sr. Patricia Roche, F.M.A., Prin.
Daughters of Mary Help of Christians 4; Lay Teachers 28; Students 529.
Catechesis/Religious Programs—Tel: 813-870-2509. D.R.E.: Linda A. Waggoner; Linda B. Edge, (Adult).
Students 529.

3—Epiphany, (1963), Rev. Ignatius Tuoc; Deacons Richard McIntosh; Maximo E. Montayre.
Mailing Address: P.O. Box 11246, 33680. Fax: 813-238-5060.
Res., 2510 E. Hanna Ave., 33610. Tel: 813-238-5060; 234-8693.
Catechesis/Religious Programs—Tel: 813-238-1751. Nancy Perkins, D.R.E.
Students 44.
Mission—Tampa, Hillsborough Co., St. Joseph Vietnamese Mission, 2510 E. Hanna Ave., 33610. Tel: 813-238-5060.

4—Good Shepherd, (1966), Rev. William F. Keane, S.D.B.; Deacon Edmond Anctil.
Res., 6410 E. Hillsborough Ave., 33610. Tel: 813-626-7588; Fax: 813-626-5882.
Catechesis/Religious Programs—Tel: 813-626-9991 (Sundays).
Students 40.

5—Incarnation, (1962), Revs. Eric Hunter; Paul Hervey; Luis Uribe-Villa; Deacon Joseph Krzanowski.
Res., 5124 Gateway Dr., 33615. Tel: 813-885-7861; Fax: 813-884-3624.
School—Tel: 813-884-4502; Fax: 813-885-3743. Mrs. Carolyn Goslee, Prin.
Lay Teachers 31; Students 575.
Catechesis/Religious Programs—Tel: 813-887-5110; Fax: 813-884-3624. Barbara Catineau, D.R.E.
Students 572.

6—Most Holy Redeemer, (1937), Revs. Peter Nicosia, O.F.M.Cap.; Alfonso D. Pagliara, O.F.M.Cap. Pastoral Assocs.: Bro. John Paul Russo, O.F.M.Cap.; Deacons Lowell L. Hecht, Jr.; J. Manuel Rodriguez.
Res., 10110 Central Ave., 33612. Tel: 813-933-2859; Fax: 813-933-8258.
School—See Elementary Schools, Interparochial under Institutions Located in the Diocese. Tel: 813-933-4750; Fax: 813-933-3181.
Catechesis/Religious Programs—Fax: 813-931-8258. Bro. John Paul Russo, O.F.M.Cap., D.R.E.
Students 150.

7—Our Lady of Perpetual Help, (1890) (Hispanic-Haitian), Revs. Thomas A. Stokes, S.M.; Robert Fahey, S.M., (Retired); Richard Colbert, S.M.; John Jazwiecki, S.M., (Retired).
Res., 1711 11th Ave., 33605. Tel: 813-248-5701; Fax: 813-241-4128. [JC]
Catechesis/Religious Programs—Debbie Toth, D.R.E.
Students 80.

8—Sacred Heart, (1860), Revs. Clair M. Cazayoux, S.J.; Paul V. Osterle, S.J., Parochial Vicar; Robert Nilon, S.J., Chap., Tampa General Hospital.
P.O. Box 1524, 33601. Tel: 813-229-1595; Fax: 813-221-2350.
School—Tel: 813-229-0618; Fax: 813-223-7667. Mr. Richard T. Moran, Prin.
Lay Teachers 20; Students 225.
Catechesis/Religious Programs—Students 44.

9—St. Joseph, (1896), Rev. Felix Sanchez; Rev. Msgr. Augustine Ndeukoya.
Mailing Address: P.O. Box 4298, 33677.
Res., 3012 Cherry St., 33607. Tel: 813-877-5729; Fax: 813-877-5720.
School—Tel: 813-879-7720; Fax: 813-873-0804.
Daughters of Mary Help of Christians (Paterson, NJ) 3; Lay Teachers 15; Students 250.
Catechesis/Religious Programs—Students 118.

10—St. Lawrence, (1959), Rev. Msgr. Laurence E. Higgins, P.A.; Rev. Edward C. Keating, O.F.M.
Mailing Address: 5225 N. Himes Ave., 33614.
Res., 3407 W. Caracas Ave., 33614. Tel: 813-875-4040; Fax: 813-876-0491.
School—Tel: 813-879-5090; Fax: 813-879-6886.
Lay Teachers 33; Students 643.
Catechesis/Religious Programs—Tel: 813-875-4040, Ext. 206; Fax: 813-876-0491.
Students 243.

11—St. Mark the Evangelist, (1996), Revs. Austin M. Mullen; Eric Peters.
Res., 9724 Cross Creek Blvd., 33647-7556. Tel: 813-907-9717; Fax: 813-907-9617.

Catechesis/Religious Programs—Tel: 813-615-1866; Fax: 813-615-1860.
Students 301.

12—St. Mary, (1966), Rev. Robert Morris; Sr. Nancy Christopher, O.S.F., Pastoral Care.
Res., 15520 North Blvd., 33613. Tel: 813-961-1061; Fax: 813-961-3782.
School—Most Holy Redeemer Interparochial School. See Elementary Schools, Interparochial under Institutions Located in the Diocese. Tel: 813-933-4750; Fax: 813-933-3181.
Catechesis/Religious Programs—Tel: 813-963-2079. Sabrina Burton, D.R.E.
Students 322.

13—St. Patrick, (1958), Revs. Colman McGarrill, T.O.R.; Angelus Migliore, T.O.R.; Joseph Chancler, T.O.R.; Bro. Edward Bennett, T.O.R.; Mrs. Maureen Connelly, Parish Mgr.
Parish Office: 4212 Fair Oaks Ave., 33611. Tel: 813-839-5337; Fax: 813-831-2778. [JC]
School—4518 S. Manhattan Ave., 33611. Tel: 813-839-5056; Fax: 813-832-5907. Mr. Robert Kenel, Prin.
Lay Teachers 18; Students 323.
Catechesis/Religious Programs—Tel: 813-839-4958. Mrs. Vicki Hawkins, D.R.E., Tel: 813-839-4958.
Students 240.

14—St. Paul, (1963), Rev. Msgr. John F. Neff; Revs. Leonard Piotrowski; Hugh Chikawe; Deacons John Alvarez; Greg Lambert; Greg Kovalesky, Pastoral Assoc.; Juan Sierra; Ron Rojas; Winston McDonald.
Mailing Address: 12708 N. Dale Mabry, 33618. Tel: 813-961-3023; Fax: 813-962-8780.
School—Most Holy Redeemer Interparochial School. See Elementary Schools, Interparochial under Institutions Located in the Diocese. Tel: 813-933-4750; Fax: 813-933-3181.
Catechesis/Religious Programs—Tel: 813-961-3023, Ext. 230. Sr. Barbara Jean Rosswurm, D.R.E.
Students 951.

15—St. Peter Claver, (1893) (African American), Rev. Edward Lamp.
Res., 1203 N. Nebraska Ave., 33602. Tel: 813-223-7098; Fax: 813-223-6520.
School—(Grades PreK-8). Tel: 813-224-0865; Fax: 813-223-1982. Sr. Catherine Bitzer, S.S.J., Prin.
Lay Teachers 10; Students 159.
Catechesis/Religious Programs—Students 50.

16—St. Timothy, (1985), Revs. John G. Tapp; Patrick Kennedy; Deacon Jerry L. Crall.
Res., 4015 Ragg Rd., 33624. Tel: 813-968-1077; Fax: 813-961-9429.
School—Most Holy Redeemer Interparochial School. See Elementary Schools, Interparochial under Institutions Located in the Diocese. Tel: 813-933-4750; Fax: 813-933-3181.
Catechesis/Religious Programs—Tel: 813-961-1716; Fax: 813-961-9429. Mary Olson, D.R.E.
Students 773.

Tarpon Springs, Pinellas Co., St. Ignatius (1956), Very Rev. Joseph A. Pellegrino, V.F.; Revs. Jaroslaw Sztybel; Louis DeTommaso, O.F.M. In res., Rev. John P. Henry (RVC).
Mailing Address: P.O. Box 1306, 34688-1306.
Res., 715 E. Orange St., 34689. Tel: 727-937-4050; Fax: 727-943-0676.
School—Guardian Angels Interparochial School, Clearwater. See Elementary Schools, Interparochial under Institutions Located in the Diocese. Tel: 727-799-6724; Fax: 727-724-9018.
Catechesis/Religious Programs—Tel: 727-934-4163; Fax: 727-942-2331. Diane Magoulis, D.R.E.
Students 750.

Temple Terrace, Hillsborough Co., Corpus Christi (1958), Revs. Joseph L. Waters; Peter A. Plourde; Ryszard Stradomski (Poland); Deacon Thomas Shiel.
Res., 9715 N. 56th St., 33617. Tel: 813-988-1593; Fax: 813-985-3583.
School—Tel: 813-988-1722; Fax: 813-989-2665. Margaret A. Penn, Prin.
Lay Teachers 16; Students 297.
Catechesis/Religious Programs—Paul F. Archer, D.R.E.
Students 415.

Valrico, Hillsborough Co., St. Stephen (1987), Revs. Patrick Irwin; Paul Pecchie.
Church—5049 Bell Shoals Rd., 33594. Tel: 813-689-4900; Fax: 813-689-7492.
Catechesis/Religious Programs—Tel: 813-689-7174; Fax: 813-661-9619. Joyce Morgan, D.R.E.
Students 1,130.

Zephyrhills, Pasco Co., St. Joseph (1912), Revs. George Rozycki; John Hays; Mrs. Patricia Young, Business Admin. In res., Rev. Msgr. Norman Balthazar; Deacon Raymond A. Haberle; Rev. Robert Young.
Church—5316 11th St., 33540. Tel: 813-782-2813; Fax: 813-788-1036.
School—St. Anthony Interparochial School, San Antonio. See Elementary Schools, Interparochial under Institutions Located in the Diocese. Tel: 352-588-3041; Fax: 352-588-3142.
Catechesis/Religious Programs—Tel: 813-788-2510. Mrs. Annetta Wallace, D.R.E.
Students 220.

On Duty Outside the Diocese:
Reverend Fathers—
Galan, Juan Cerro
Garcia, Avelino
McDonough, Donat Michael
Swengros, William

Absent on Leave:
Reverend Fathers—
Lau, William

Military Chaplains:
Reverend Fathers—
McCahon, Joseph F.S., U.S.A.F.

Retired:
Reverend Monsignors—
Bolger, John F.
Conesa, Diego
Cummings, George
DuBois, William
Lara, Jaime C.
McCall, John
McNulty, John
Mulligan, Edward
Scully, John
Trainor, Patrick
Reverend Fathers—
Colgan, John
Cottrell, James
D'Angelo, Rocco
Dambrauskas, Stephen
Dauss, Francis
Diffley, Jerome E.
Earner, Thomas
Estibalez, Inocencio
Gardner, Simeon
Gill, Desmond
Goodman, Frank
Kearney, William
Lagan, Hugh
Leininger, Donald
Mahony, John
Malin, George
Obert, Martin
Rittmeyer, Robert
Szymusiak, Bruno
Villemaire, Arthur

Permanent Deacons:
Alterio, Vincent
Alvarez, John
Anctil, Edmond
Andre, Peter
Beaudry, Richard
Bevvino, Frank, On Duty Outside of Diocese
Blaney, James (RVC)
Boehme, Karl
Boutros, Peter (NTN)
Brady, Richard
Brennan, Lee
Breznak, Charles
Brown, Joseph
Carreiro, Manuel
Cartier, Roger L. (NOR)
Ciarciaglino, Joseph (PSC)
Coccia, Christopher, O.F.M.
Cole, Robert (SFE)
Columbus, Michael
Connors, William
Crall, Jerry
D'argis, Leo (DET)
Desjardins, Roland (ORL)
Diaz, William
DiVito, John
Dunphy, Melvin (WOR)
Edgerton, John (NY)
Evans, Forrest, On Duty Outside the Diocese
Friscia, Dominic
Gould, Stanley, On Duty Outside of Diocese
Grote, Joseph
Haberle, Raymond
Hassett, James
Hecht, Lowell, Jr.
Hewitt, Wesley (GR)
Horan, Francis (VEN)
Iadanza, John (TR)
Izzo, Louis
Knox, Terrence (MIA)
Koppenaal, John, On Duty Outside of Diocese
Kovalesky, George
Krzanowski, Joseph
Kurylowicz, Stephen
Lambert, Greg
Lamothe, Allan
Liggan, John (NY)
Lind, Roger F. (RVC)
Loffredo, Eugene E. (HRT)
Longo, Frank (SY)
Lyczak, Edward (FTW)
Lyons, John
Mahood, William
Mathias, James (LAN)
McDonald, Winston
McGory, Gerald
McIntosh, Richard
Metilly, Paul (FR)
Meyer, Richard (TR)
Montayre, Maximo
Morales, Julio (BRK)
Moschetto, Samuel (BO)
Nagle, Richard
Ortiz, Augustin
Page, Howard (SCR)
Pescatore, James (RVC)
Pickart, Glenn
Pignatoro, Angelo
Polcari, Joseph (MIA)
Powell, Eugene
Pullar, James
Quiles, Rafael (CLV)
Rodriguez, Manuel
Rojas, Ronald (PCE)
Rosa, Abraham (CHI)
Sablone, Stephen
Schott, Thomas (OKL)
Shiel, Thomas (NY)
Sierra, John
Simpson, Robert C. (RVC)
Sirrianna, David
Solomon, Michael
Thomas, Jerome
Thompson, Alfred (NY)
Tibbetts, Albert
Uzzi, Gerard (PAT)
Vance, Ronald, On Duty Outside the Diocese
Vasquez, Julio (HRT)
Wallace, Barry
Wells, Eric
White, Gerard (ORL)
Yarawsky, William
Zayas, Luis (MIA)
Zeitler, Richard

INSTITUTIONS LOCATED IN THE DIOCESE

[A] COLLEGES

Saint Leo. *Saint Leo University, University Ministry*, P.O. Box 6665, MC 2186, 33574-6665. Tel: 352-588-8200; 8331; Fax: 352-588-8885.
E-mail: michael.coopersj@saintleo.edu
Web site: www.saintleo.edu
For a complete listing, refer to the Colleges and Universities section.

[B] HIGH SCHOOLS, DIOCESAN

St. Petersburg. *St. Petersburg Catholic High School*, 6333 Ninth Ave. N., 33710. Tel: 727-344-4065; Fax: 727-343-9311.
E-mail: info@spchs.org
Web site: spchs.org
Revs. Richard J. McCormick, S.D.B., Dir.; Louis J. Molinelli, S.D.B., Prin.; Ms. Barbara A. Rusin, Asst. Prin. for Academics; Mr. Michael Shelby, Asst. Prin. for Student Life; Rev. Michael Conway, S.D.B., Coord. Youth Ministry; Bro. William Hanna, S.D.B. Salesians of St. John Bosco (New Rochelle, NY) 4; Sisters of the Holy Names of Jesus & Mary (FL) 1; Brothers 1; Lay Teachers 44; Students 620.

Clearwater. *Clearwater Central Catholic High School*, 2750 Haines Bayshore Rd., 33760. Tel: 727-531-1449; Fax: 727-535-7034.
E-mail: DionCCC@Hotmail.com
Web site: www.cchs.org
Sr. Mary Dion Horrigan, S.N.D., Prin. Sisters of Notre Dame (Chardon, Ohio) 2; Lay Teachers 48; Students 611.

Tampa. *Tampa Catholic High School*, 4630 N. Rome Ave., 33603. Tel: 813-870-0860; Fax: 813-877-9136.
E-mail: contactperson@tampacatholic.com
Web site: www.tampacatholic.com
Bro. David M. McMahon, C.F.C., Prin. Priests 1; Congregation of Christian Brothers (New Rochelle, NY) 2; Sisters 1; Lay Teachers 59; Students 810.

[C] HIGH SCHOOLS, PRIVATE

TAMPA. *Academy of the Holy Names High School*, 3319 Bayshore Blvd., 33629. Tel: 813-839-5371; Fax: 813-839-1486.
E-mail: sregan@holynamestpa.org
Web site: holynamestpa.org
Ms. Colleen Brady, Pres.; Ms. Sarah Regan, Prin.; Mrs. Janet Blackburn, Asst. Prin. Academics; John Crumbley, Dean of Students. Legal Titles: *Academy of the Holy Names of Florida, Inc.*; *Academy of the Holy Names Foundation, Inc.* Sisters 3; Lay Teachers 28; Students 311.

Jesuit High School, 4701 N. Himes Ave., 33614. Tel: 813-877-5344; Fax: 813-872-1853.
E-mail: jhscomm@aol.com
Web site: www.jesuittampa.org
Revs. Peter J. Callery, S.J., Rector; Joseph Doyle, S.J., Chap. & Pres.; Donald E. Saunders, S.J., Prin.; Michael E. Chesney, S.J.; Brian Garry, S.J.; Michael F. Kennelly, S.J.; Rodney T. Kissinger, S.J.; Vincent A. Orlando, S.J.; Bros. A. Joseph Martin, S.J., Minister; Lawrence J. Huck, S.J.; Mr. Anthony G. Rauschuber, S.J. Legal Titles: *Jesuit High School of Tampa, Inc., FKA.*; *St. Louis Catholic, Benevolent and Educational Association, Inc.*; *Jesuit High School Foundation, Inc.* Priests 3; Brothers 1; Scholastics 1; Sisters 1; Lay Teachers 43; Students 679.

[D] ELEMENTARY SCHOOLS, INTERPAROCHIAL

ST. PETERSBURG. *St. Paul Interparochial School.* (Grades PreK-8), 1900 12th St. N., 33704. Tel: 727-823-6144; Fax: 727-896-0609.
E-mail: Lcusumano@mail.stpaulcatholicschool.org
Web site: www.webcoast.com/stpaulcs
Louise Cusumano, Prin. Serving Blessed Trinity and St. Paul. Sisters 2; Lay Teachers 18; Students 324.

CLEARWATER. *Guardian Angels Catholic School.* (Grades K-8), 2270 Evans Rd., 33763. Tel: 727-799-6724; Fax: 727-724-9018.
E-mail: gacs@gte.net
Web site: www.gacsfl.com
Robert Yarnell, Prin. Serving All Saints, St. Ignatius, St. Luke and St. Michael the Archangel. Sisters 1; Lay Teachers 28; Students 440.

St. Cecelia Interparochial School. (Grades K-8), 400 S. Hillcrest Ave., 34616. Tel: 727-461-1200; Fax: 724-446-9140. Mrs. Helen S. Marston, Prin. Serving Espiritu Santo, Light of Christ, St. Brendan, St. Catherine of Siena and St. Cecelia. Sisters 1; Deacons 1; Lay Teachers 44; Students 805.

LECANTO. *Pope John Paul II Catholic School*, 4341 W. Homosassa Tr., 34461. Tel: 352-746-2020; Fax: 352-746-3448. Penelope N. Howell, Prin. Serving Our Lady of Fatima, Our Lady of Grace, St. Benedict, St. Elizabeth Ann Seton, St. Scholastica and St. Thomas the Apostle. Lay Teachers 18; Students 239.

PORT RICHEY. *Bishop Larkin Interparochial School* oodo. (Grades PreK-8), 8408 Monarch Dr., 34668. Tel: 727-862-6981; Fax: 727-869-9893.
E-mail: bishop4@microd.com
Serving Our Lady Queen of Peace, St. James, St. Michael the Archangel, St. Thomas Aquinas and St. Vincent de Paul. Lay Teachers 15; Sisters 3; Students 315.

SAN ANTONIO. *St. Anthony Interparochial Catholic School.* (Grades K-8), 32902 Massachusetts Ave., P.O. Box 847, 33576-0847. Tel: 352-588-3041; Fax: 352-588-3142.
E-mail: sasadmin@saintleo.edu
Serving Sacred Heart, St. Anthony, St. Joseph and St. Rita. Sisters 1; Lay Teachers 10; Students 230.

SPRING HILL. *Notre Dame Interparochial School.* (Grades PreK-8), 1117 Suzanne Dr., 34607. Tel: 352-683-0755; Fax: 352-683-3924.
Web site: http://home.imsweb.net/~notredmei
Maureen Wickert, Prin. Serving St. Anne, St. Anthony, St. Frances Xavier Cabrini, St. Joan of Arc, St. Mary and St. Theresa. Lay Teachers 24; Students 366.

TAMPA. *Most Holy Redeemer Interparochial School.* (Grades K-8), 302 E. Linebaugh Ave., 33612. Tel: 813-933-4750; Fax: 813-933-3181.
E-mail: mhrtampa@dosp.org
Fred Coffaro, Prin.; Dr. Jo Ann Quinn, Asst. Prin. Serving Most Holy Redeemer, Our Lady of the Rosary, St. Mary, St. Paul and St. Timothy. Lay Teachers 26; Students 527.

[E] ELEMENTARY SCHOOLS, PRIVATE

TAMPA. *Academy of the Holy Names Elementary.* (Grades PreK-12), 3319 Bayshore Blvd., 33629. Tel: 813-839-5371; Fax: 813-837-5710.
E-mail: webmaster@holynamestpa.org
Web site: www.holynamestpa.org
Colleen K. Brady, Pres. Principals: Ms. Caryl Nolan, Lower School; Dr. Carmen Caltagirone, Middle School; Ms. Sarah Regan, High School. Legal Titles: *Academy of the Holy Names of Florida, Inc.*; *Academy of the Holy Names Foundation, Inc.* Sisters of the Holy Names of Jesus and Mary (Albany) 7; Lay Teachers 73; Students 838.

Mary Help of Christians School. (Grades 6-8). (Boys), 6400 E. Chelsea St., 33610-5699. Tel: 813-626-6191; Fax: 813-621-5251.
E-mail: sf9tof@scfn.thpl.lib.fl.us
Salesians of St. John Bosco. (Day School). Revs. William F. Keane, S.D.B., Dir.; Kenneth Germaine, S.D.B., Admin.; Lawrence Urban, S.D.B., Youth Dir.; Mr. Paul Bosco, Prin.; Revs. August Bruce Craig, S.D.B.; Bernard Justen, S.D.B.; Thinh Nguyen, S.D.B.; Gerard Pellegrino, S.D.B.; Bros. Joseph Ackroyd, S.D.B.; George Marquis, S.B.D.; John Versaggi, S.D.B.; Jorge Barraza, S.D.B. Legal Title: *Salesian Society, Inc.* Priests 5; Brothers 2; Lay Teachers 7; Students 120.

Villa Madonna School, 315 W. Columbus Dr., 33602. Tel: 813-229-1322; Fax: 813-223-4812.
E-mail: fmavilla@aol.com
Sr. Liz Ryan, F.M.A., Prin. Legal Title: *Salesian Sisters of Tampa, Inc.* Daughters of Mary Help of Christians 6; Lay Teachers 22; Students 528.

[F] PRESCHOOLS AND DAY CARE CENTERS

ST. PETERSBURG. *Immaculate Conception Early Childhood Center.* Ages 2-5, Extended Care. Lower Pinellas Deanery, 2100 26th Ave. S., 33712. Tel: 727-822-2156; Fax: 727-553-9133. Mrs. Rita A. Jackson, Dir.; Mrs. Mary Calloway, Asst. Dir.; Rev. Callist N. Nyambo. Lay Teachers 17; Children 165; Total Staff 24.

CLEARWATER. *Light of Christ Preschool.* Ages 2-5, Extended Care. Upper Pinellas Deanery, 2176 Marilyn St., 33765. Tel: 727-442-4797; Fax: 727-441-8771.
E-mail: locecc@is.net
Ms. Rebecca Daschbach, Preschool Dir. Lay Teachers 10; Students 60.

Little Nazareth Early Childhood Center. Ages 3-4. Upper Pinellas Deanery, 820 Jasmine Way, 33756. Tel: 727-447-3494; Fax: 727-442-4810.
E-mail: cecelia820@aol.com
Web site: www.stceceliachurch.org
Mrs. Sandra A. Barbeau, Dir.; Very Rev. Aiden Foynes. Lay Teachers 2; Children 35.

DADE CITY. *Sacred Heart Child Care Center.* Infant-PreK, Extended Care. Pasco Deanery, 32245 Saint Joe Rd., 33525. Tel: 904-588-4060; Fax: 904-588-4871.
E-mail: sheccstjoe@aol.com
Mrs. Toni Watkins, Dir. Lay Teachers 9; Children 187.

LARGO. *St. Jerome Early Childhood Center.* Ages 3-4. 10895 Hamlin Blvd., 33774. Tel: 727-596-9491; Fax: 727-596-8953.
E-mail: Deniseecc@aol.com
Denise Roach, Dir.; Rev. Msgr. Brendan Muldoon, V.G. Lay Teachers 1; Children 110.

NEW PORT RICHEY. *St. Thomas Aquinas Early Childhood Center*, 8320 State Rd. 54, 34653. Tel: 727-376-2330; Fax: 727-376-7204.
E-mail: staecc@aol.com
Mrs. Cindy McKallip, Dir.; Rev. Michael Lydon; Pamela Bruno, Sec. Lay Teachers 6; assistants 6; Children 104.

PALM HARBOR. *St. Luke Early Childhood Center.* Ages 2-4, Extended Care. 2757 Alderman Rd., 34684. Tel: 813-787-2914; Fax: 813-789-9556.
E-mail: stlecc@gte.net
Ms. Carol Hussin, Dir.; Rev. Ronald Poirier. Full-time Lay Teachers 2; Children 160; Total Staff 24.

SAN ANTONIO. *Holy Name Academy Child Care Center dba Bendictine Sisters of Florida.* (aka Holy Name Academy, Inc.) Ages 2-5, Extended Care. 12117 Wichers Rd., 33576. Tel: 352-588-8325; Fax: 352-588-3331.
E-mail: cmsrichter@aol.com
Mrs. Carol M. Richter, Dir. Lay Teachers 6; Children 52.

TAMPA. *St. Paul Preschool.* Ages 3-4. 12708 N. Dale Mabry Hwy., 33618-2802. Tel: 813-961-3023, Ext. 241; Fax: 813-962-8780.
E-mail: mmiller@stpaulchurch.com
Mrs. Maureen Miller, Dir.; Rev. Msgr. John F. Neff. Lay Teachers 16; Children 164.

St. Timothy Catholic Early Childhood Learning Center, 4015 Ragg Rd., 33694-0129. Tel: 813-960-4857. Ms. Daisy Cintron, Dir.; Rev. John G. Tapp. Students 76.

TARPON SPRINGS. *St. Ignatius Early Childhood Center.* Ages 2-6. 725 E. Orange St., P.O. Box 1306, 34688-1306. Tel: 813-934-4163; Fax: 727-937-5427.
E-mail: ecenter123@aol.com
Mrs. Nancy Gorby, Dir.; Rev. Joseph A. Pellegrino, V.F. Full-time Lay Teacher 1; Children 95.

[G] SCHOOLS FOR EXCEPTIONAL CHILDREN

PINELLAS PARK. *Morning Star School*, 4661 80th Ave. N., 33781. Tel: 813-544-6036; Fax: 813-546-9058.
E-mail: mschool2@tampabay.rrcom
Web site: morningstarschool.com
Ms. Mary Lou Giacobbe, Prin. Lay Teachers 9; Students 55.

TAMPA. *Morning Star School*, 210 E. Linebaugh Ave., 33612. Tel: 813-935-0232; 932-2321; Fax: 813-932-2321.
E-mail: tampamstar@empresso.com
Web site: www.tampa-morningstar.org
Miss Jeanette Friedheim, Prin. Lay Teachers 11; Students 85.

[H] SCHOOLS FOR THEOLOGICAL AND SPIRITUAL TRAINING

ST. PETERSBURG. *St. Petersburg Diocesan Library*, 6533 Ninth Ave. N., 33710. Tel: 727-345-3338; Fax: 727-347-6508.
E-mail: cmb@dosp.org
Mailing Address: P.O. Box 43022, 33743-3022. Tel: 727-345-3338. Rev. Msgr. Frank Mouch, Exec. Dir.; Ms. Clara Blowers, Dir. Diocesan Library.

CLEARWATER. *The Cenacle of Our Lady of Divine Providence.* School of Spirituality. 702 S. Bayview Ave., 33759. Tel: 727-724-9505; Fax: 727-724-9421.
E-mail: cenacleofourlady@aol.com
Web site: http://www.divineprovidence.org
Ronald W. Novotny, S.T.L., Ph.D., Dir. Lay Teachers 3; Total Staff 9; Total Enrollment 500.

[I] DAY CARE CENTERS

TAMPA. *Peter Claver Day Care Center, Inc.*, 1431 Tampa Park Plaza, 33605. Tel: 813-229-7632; Fax: 813-259-9082.
E-mail: vlwithers@aol.com
Total Staff 13; Total Assisted 75.

[J] CATHOLIC CHARITIES

ST. PETERSBURG. *Catholic Charities, Diocese of St. Petersburg, Inc.* Tel: 727-893-1314; Fax: 727-893-1307.
E-mail: aandrews@ccdosp.org
Web site: www.ccdosp.org
Mailing Address: 6533 Ninth Ave. N., Ste. 1 E., 33710. Tel: 727-893-1314; Fax: 727-893-1307. Provides Counseling Services to Individuals, Families and Children; Pregnancy Related Services; Adoption Placement; Foster Home Placement; Elderly Services; Refugee and Immigration Services; Emergency CareServices; AIDS Volunteer; Catholic Campaign for Human Development; Catholic Relief Services; Disabilities Services; Housing Counseling.Services; AIDS Volunteer; Catholic Campaign for Human Development; Catholic Relief Services; Disabilities Services; Housing Counseling.

Central Services, 6533 Ninth Ave. N., 33710. Tel: 727-893-1314, Ext. 210; Fax: 727-893-1307. Mr. Arnold Andrews, Exec. Dir.

[K] GENERAL HOSPITALS

ST. PETERSBURG. *St. Anthony's Hospital, Inc.*, 1200 Seventh Ave. N., 33705. Tel: 727-825-1100; Fax: 727-825-1704.
E-mail: al.hall@baycare.org /terry.fleming@baycare.org
Web site: www.bsahealth.org
For a complete listing, refer to the Hospitals section.

TAMPA. *St. Joseph's Hospital, Inc.*, 3001 W. Martin Luther King Blvd., 33607
For a complete listing, refer to the Hospitals section.

[L] RETIREMENT AND HEALTH CARE CENTERS

ST. PETERSBURG. *Bon Secours-Maria Manor Nursing Care Center, Inc.*, 10300 Fourth St. N., 33716. Tel: 727-576-1025; Fax: 727-576-1447
For a complete listing, refer to the Hospitals section.

CLEARWATER. *The Tepeyac Corporation dba La Clinica Guadalupana*, 1215 Drew St., Ste. 7B, 33755. Tel: 727-461-7730; Fax: 727-462-8117.
E-mail: laclinica@compuserve.com
For a complete listing, refer to the Hospitals section.

[M] RETIREMENT HOUSING

ST. PETERSBURG. *Bethlehem Housing, Inc.*, c/o Diocese of St. Petersburg, P.O. Box 40200, 33743-0200. Tel: 727-344-1611; Fax: 727-345-2143
For a complete listing, refer to the Hospitals section.

Blessed Trinity Housing, Inc., c/o Diocese of St. Petersburg, 33743-0200. Tel: 727-344-1611; Fax: 727-345-2143
For a complete listing, refer to the Hospitals section.

Holy Cross Housing dba Casa Santa Cruz, 7825 54th Ave. N., 33709. Tel: 727-541-2631; Fax: 727-547-6741.
E-mail: barb0113@aol.com
For a complete listing, refer to the Hospitals section.

CLEARWATER. *St. Michael's Housing, Inc. dba Casa Miguel*, 2285 State Rd. #580, 33763. Tel: 727-797-8551
For a complete listing, refer to the Hospitals section.

TAMPA. *Christ the King Housing II, Inc. dba Kings Manor*, 2946 W. Columbus Dr., 33607. Tel: 813-875-0139; Fax: 813-875-6061.
E-mail: Betsy0545@aol.com
For a complete listing, refer to the Hospitals section.
Christ the King Housing, Inc. dba Kings Arms, 4125 N. Lincoln Ave., 33607. Tel: 813-873-0234
For a complete listing, refer to the Hospitals section.
Epiphany Housing of Tampa, Inc. dba Epiphany Arms, 2508 E. Hanna Ave., 33610. Tel: 813-232-2693; Fax: 813-232-2984.
E-mail: epiparms@aol.com
For a complete listing, refer to the Hospitals section.
St. Patrick's Housing Corporation dba Patrician Arms, 4516 S. Manhattan Ave., 33611. Tel: 813-835-8227
For a complete listing, refer to the Hospitals section.

[N] SENIOR CENTERS

LARGO. *Bethlehem Centre, Inc.*, 10895 Hamlin Blvd., 34644. Tel: 727-596-9394. Senior Center Offering Daily Programming of a Fitness Aerobics, Social, Educational, Remedial, and Religious Nature; Luncheon on Tuesday and Friday, Counseling; Computer, Classical Music. William J. Galloway, Dir. Total Staff 2; Total Assisted 400.

[O] MONASTERIES AND RESIDENCES OF PRIESTS AND BROTHERS

ST. PETERSBURG. *Missionaries of Africa*, 5757 Seventh Ave. N., 33710. Tel: 727-343-1001; Fax: 727-343-4395.
E-mail: jolmet@gte.net
Revs. Joseph E. Hebert, M.Afr., Coord.; Jean C. Robitaille, M.Afr., Coord.; John J. Braun, M.Afr.; Paul J. Heon, M.Afr.; Joseph Kay, M.Afr.; Aime F. Lacasse, M.Afr.; Charles E. Lebel, M.Afr.; Joseph Sys, M.Afr.; Bros. Charles Feldmann, M.Afr.; Philip J. Nadeau, M.Afr. Total in Residence 10.
Notre Dame Residence, 1101 66th St. N., 33710. Tel: 727-384-0546.
St. Anthony Friary. Franciscan Residence and Retirement Community. 357 Second St. N., 33701. Tel: 727-822-7917; Fax: 727-821-8067.
E-mail: St.AnthonyFriary@worldnet.att.net
Revs. Christopher A. Coccia, O.F.M., Guardian; Roy Gasnick, O.F.M., Vicar; Cornelius Conti, O.F.M.; Venard Murphy, O.F.M.; Bros. Richard James, O.F.M.; Michael Madden, O.F.M.; Valerian Vaverchack, O.F.M.
Full-time Active Ministry: Revs. James Jones, O.F.M.; Arthur Murray, O.F.M.; Thomas K. Murphy, O.F.M.
Retirement Community: Revs. Charles F. Adams, O.F.M.; Patrick Adams, O.F.M.; Theodore A. Blackowski, O.F.M.; Arnold Brown, O.F.M.; Edward Burke, O.F.M.; Simeon Capizzi, O.F.M.; Peter Carr, O.F.M.; Martin A. Hanhauser, O.F.M.; Clement Healy, O.F.M.; Joseph Kiernan, O.F.M.; Vincent McCann, O.F.M.; Guy Morgan, O.F.M.; Alexis P. Morris, O.F.M.; James P. Mulhern, O.F.M.; Columba Murphy, O.F.M.; Anthony Schneider, O.F.M.; James Schwantner, O.F.M.; Bro. Marion Ressel, O.F.M. Total in Residence 27; Total Staff 7.
St. Peter Nolasco Residence, 5650 Seventh Ave. N., 33710-7112. Tel: 813-345-4766; Fax: 813-347-5345. Revs. Jerome Laubacker, O.de.M., Local Supr.; Benedict Ptacek, O.de.M.; Michael E. Perry, O.de.M.; Bro. Richard Henry, O.de.M. Total Staff 4; Total in Residence 4.

BELLEAIR BLUFFS. *St. James Friary*, 2433 Indian Ave., 33770-2032. Tel: 727-585-2521; Fax: 727-585-2460.
Web site: FRANMOW.ORG
Franciscan Friars Ministry of the Word (New York). Revs. Roch Coogan, O.F.M.; Edward Flanagan, O.F.M.

CLEARWATER BEACH. *St. Paul Friary*, 50 Somerset St., 33767. Tel: 727-443-7351. Rev. Edmond Ansaloni, O.F.M., Guardian.

PINELLAS PARK. *Priests of the Sacred Heart*, 6701 82nd Ave. N., 34665. Tel: 813-541-2661; Fax: 813-547-0408.
E-mail: dmurphy@ij.net
Bro. Timothy Murphy, S.C.J., Coord.; Most Rev. Joseph A. DePalma, S.C.J., Retired Bishop of DeAar, S.Africa; Revs. Joseph Poirier, S.C.J., (Staff); Joseph Doscher, S.C.J., (Retired); John Kevin McInnis, S.C.J., (Retired); Kenneth Mitchell, S.C.J., (Retired); Leonard Tadyszak, S.C.J., (Retired); Raymond Vega, S.C.J., (Retired); Richard Zelonis, S.C.J., (Retired); Bro. Gabriel Kersting, S.C.J., (Retired). Total Staff 2; Total in Residence 10.

ST. LEO. *St. Leo Abbey*, P.O. Box 2350, 33574. Tel: 352-588-8624; Fax: 352-588-5217. Very Rev. Simeon J. Thole, O.S.B., Apostolic Admin.; Revs. Robert Velten, O.S.B., Prior; Gregory Traeger, O.S.B.; Damian DuQuesnay, O.S.B.; Andrew Metzger, O.S.B.; Paul Romfh, O.S.B.; Jude Krogol, O.S.B.; Boniface Steinwachs, O.S.B.; Jonathan Zingales, O.S.B.
On Duty Outside the Monastery: Rt. Rev. Patrick Shelton, O.S.B., Retired Abbot; Revs. James Hoge, O.S.B.; David Draim, O.S.B.; Richard Hugli, O.S.B. Priests 13; Brothers 16; Internal Oblates 1.

ST. PETE BEACH. *Franciscan Friary*, 555 - 68th Ave., 33706. Tel: 727-367-2408.

SEMINOLE. *Capuchin Franciscan Residence*, 7171 128th St. N., 33776. Tel: 727-397-0011; Fax: 727-392-7183.
E-mail: floridacaps@juno.com
Revs. Joseph Testagrossa, O.F.M.Cap., Admin.; Anthony Donahue, O.F.M.Cap.

[P] CONVENTS AND RESIDENCES FOR SISTERS

ST. PETERSBURG. *St. Anthony Hospital Convent*, 631 11th St. N., 33705. Tel: 727-825-1142; Fax: 727-825-1184.
Web site: www.fsalleg.org
Franciscan Sisters of Allegany (Allegany, NY). Total in Residence 10.

HOLIDAY. *St. Clare's Convent*, 2109 Tilogia Ct., 34690. Tel: 727-938-0868.
E-mail: FALTE_JO@YAHOO.COM
Sr. Lucia Brady, O.S.C., Regl. Supr.
St. Clare Sisters Retreat Ministry. Tel: 813-786-3821.

ST. LEO. *Holy Name Monastery*, P.O. Box 2450, 33574-2450. Tel: 352-588-8320; Fax: 352-588-8319.
E-mail: holyname@saintleo.edu
Mailing Address: P.O. Box 2450, 33574-2450. Tel: 352-588-8320; Fax: 352-588-8319.
E-mail: holyname@saintleo.edu
Motherhouse and Novitiate of the Benedictine Sisters of Florida. Legal Title: *Holy Name Academy, Inc.* Sr. Mary Clare Neuhofer, O.S.B., Prioress. Professed Sisters 27.

TAMPA. *St. Clare Convent*, 2924 Curtis St., 33614. Tel: 813-870-4272. Franciscan Sisters of Allegany (Allegany, NY).
St. Elizabeth Convent, 3000 Perry Ave., 33603. Tel: 813-229-1978; Fax: 813-228-9066. Franciscan Sisters of Allegany. Total Staff 3; Total in Residence 24.
Villa Madonna Convent, 2611 N. Massachusetts Ave., 33602. Tel: 813-229-1322, Ext. 393; Fax: 813-223-4812.
E-mail: fmavilla@aol.com
Daughters of Mary Help of Christians (Haledon, NJ). Total Staff 9; Total in Residence 9.

[Q] RETREAT CENTERS

ST. LEO. *St. Leo Abbey Retreat Center*, P.O. Box 2350, 33574. Tel: 352-588-2009. Mrs. Donna Cooper, Dir. Total Staff 4.

TAMPA. *Franciscan Center, Retreat House*, 3010 Perry Ave., 33603. Tel: 813-229-2695; Fax: 813-228-0748.
E-mail: FranCntr@AOL.com
Web site: www.fsalleg.org/franciscancenter.htm
Franciscan Sisters of Allegany. Sr. Catherine Cahill, O.S.F., Dir.; Sr. Kay Aherne, O.S.F.; Sr. Sean Fitzsimmons; Sr. Regina Kane, O.S.F.; Sr. Margaret Rumsey, O.S.F.; Sr. Candice Tucci, O.S.F. Total Staff 15.

[R] PRIVATE ASSOCIATIONS OF THE CHRISTIAN FAITHFUL

CLEARWATER. *Community of the Marian Servants of Divine Providence*, 702 S. Bayview Ave., 33759. Tel: 727-797-7412; Fax: 727-726-1631.
E-mail: marianservants@juno.com
Web site: www.divineprovidence.org
Our Lady of Divine Providence House of Prayer.

[S] SUMMER CAMPS

ST. PETERSBURG. *Our Lady of Good Counsel Camp*.
E-mail: gcccamp@citrus.infi.net
Mailing Address: 8888 E. Gobbler Dr., Floral City, 34436. Tel: 352-726-2198; Fax: 352-726-3212.
E-mail: gcccamp@citrus.infi.net
Rev. James B. Johnson, Dir., Our Lady of Fatima Church, 550 U.S. Hwy. 41 S., Inverness, 34450. Tel: 352-726-1910; Fax: 352-344-8384.

[T] CAMPUS MINISTRY

ST. PETERSBURG. *Eckerd College - Campus Ministry*, c/o 5650 7th Ave. N., 33710-7112. Tel: 727-864-8470; Fax: 727-384-9073. Bro. Richard Henry, O.de.M., Chap. Total in Residence 1.

TAMPA. *Catholic Student Center, University of South Florida*, 13005 N. 50th St., 33617. Tel: 813-988-3727; Fax: 813-988-3727.
E-mail: director@catholicusf.org
Web site: www.catholicusf.org
Rev. Alan Weber, Chap.
University of Tampa, 401 West Kennedy St., 33606-1490. Tel: 813-253-6211; Fax: 813-258-7398.
E-mail: admissions@alpha.utampa.edu
Web site: www.utampa.edu
Rev. C. Kirk Mansell, S.J.

[U] MISCELLANEOUS

ST. PETERSBURG. *Catholic Charities Housing, Inc.*, 1213 16th St. N., 33705. Tel: 727-893-1314; Fax: 727-893-1307.
E-mail: aandrews@ccdusp.org
Web site: www.ccdosp.org
Chancery Office, 6363 Ninth St., 33743. For detailed information on the following listings contact the Chancery Office.
Allegany Community Out Reach Grant Fund, Inc.
Catholic Charities Housing, Inc.
Catholic Education Foundation, Inc.
Catholic Media Ministry, Inc.
Christopher Assurance, Inc.
The Congregation of the Sisters of St. Clare (Florida), Inc., 625 Court St. 2nd Floor, Clearwater, 33756.
Franciscan Sisters of Allegany Health System, Inc.
Regis Manor, Inc.
WBVM, 90.5 FM, Inc., Clearwater.
Catholic Charities Foundation of Tampa Bay, Inc.
The Greater Tampa Catholic Lawyers Guild, Inc., P.O. Box 1816, Tampa, 33601.
St. Francis Residence, Inc.
Franciscan Center of Tampa, FL, Inc., 3000 Perry Ave., Tampa, 33603. Tel: 813-229-1978; Fax: 813-228-9066.
Magnificat Inc., Lower Pinellas Deanery Chapter of the Diocese of St. Petersburg, Florida, 1448 83rd Ave. N., 33702. Tel: 727-576-4988; Fax: abdiaco@msn.com.

ST. LEO, FL. *St. Leo Abbey Foundation, Inc.*, P.O. Box 2350, 33574. Tel: 352-588-8679; Fax: 352-588-5217.
E-mail: frpaul@saintleo.edu
Web site: saintleoabbey.org

VAL RICO.
Knanya Catholic Congress of Central Florida, Inc., 2620 Washington, 33594.

RELIGIOUS INSTITUTES OF MEN REPRESENTED IN THE DIOCESE

For further details refer to the corresponding bracketed number in the Religious Institutes of Men or Women section.

[0140]—*The Augustinians.* (Villanova, PA).—O.S.A.
[0190]—*Basilian Salvatorian Fathers.* (Methuen, MA).—B.S.O.
[0200]—*Benedictine Monks.* (St. Leo, FL).—O.S.B.
[1350]—*Brothers of St. Francis Xavier.* (Ellicott City, MD).—C.F.X.
[0470]—*The Capuchin Friars.* (White Plains, NY; Union City, NJ).—O.F.M.Cap.
[0350]—*Cistercians Order of the Strict Observance (Trappists).* (Spencer, MA).—O.C.S.O.
[0310]—*Congregation of Christian Brothers.* (New Rochelle, NY).—C.F.C.
[0220]—*Congregation of the Blessed Sacrament.* (Cleveland, OH).—S.S.S.
[1130]—*Congregation of the Priests of the Sacred Heart.* (Hales Corner, WI).—S.C.J.
[0520]—*Franciscan Friars.* (New York, NY; Pulaski, WI; Kennebunkport, ME; Dublin, Ireland).—O.F.M.
[0530]—*Franciscan Friars of the Atonement.* (Garrison, NY).—S.A.
[0650]—*Holy Ghost Fathers.* (Dublin, Ireland).—C.S.Sp.
[0300]—*Institute of Charity.* (Peoria, IL).—I.C.
[0690]—*Jesuit Fathers and Brothers.* (New Orleans, LA; Baltimore, MD;Chicago, IL).—S.J.
[0780]—*Marist Brothers.* (New York, NY).—F.M.S.
[0780]—*Marist Fathers.* (Washington, DC).—S.M.
[0800]—*Maryknoll.*—M.M.
[0850]—*Missionaries of Africa.* (Washington, DC).—M.Afr.
[0970]—*Order of Our Lady of Mercy.* (Cleveland, OH).—O.deM.
[0430]—*Order of Preachers (Dominicans).* (Dublin, Ireland).—O.P.
[0610]—*Priests of the Congregation of the Holy Cross.* (Notre Dame, IN; Bridgeport, CT).—C.S.C.
[1190]—*Salesians of Don Bosco.* (New Rochelle, NY).—S.D.B.
[]—*Scarboro Foreign Missions.* (Scarboro, Ontario, Canada).—S.F.M.
[1060]—*Society of the Precious Blood.* (Dayton, OH).—C.PP.S.
[0560]—*Third Order Regular of Saint Francis.* (Pittsburgh, PA;Etlers, PA).—T.O.R.

RELIGIOUS INSTITUTES OF WOMEN REPRESENTED IN THE DIOCESE

[0230]—*Benedictine Sisters of Pontifical Jurisdiction.* (St. Leo, FL).—O.S.B.

[0270]—*Congregation of Bon Secours.* (Marriottsville,MD).—C.B.S.
[1010]—*Congregation of Divine Providence.* (San Antonio,TX).—C.D.P.
[3110]—*Congregation of Our Lady of Retreat in the Cenacle.* (Lake Ronkonkoma, NY).—R.C.
[3710]—*Congregation of the Sisters of St. Agnes.*—C.S.A.
[1920]—*Congregation of the Sisters of the Holy Cross.* (Notre Dame, IN).—C.S.C.
[1930]—*Congregation of the Sisters of the Holy Cross.* (Montreal;Quebec).—C.S.C.
[1730]—*Congregation of the Sisters of the Third Order of St. Francis, Oldenburg, IN.*—O.S.F.
[0760]—*Daughters of Charity of St. Vincent de Paul.* (Emmitsburg, MD).—D.C.
[0850]—*Daughters of Mary Help of Christians.* (Haledon, NJ).—F.M.A.
[]—*Daughters of Mary Immaculate.* (Vietnam).—F.M.I.
[0960]—*Daughters of Wisdom.* (Islip, NY).—D.W.
[1070-01]—*Dominican Sisters.*—O.P.
[1070-02]—*Dominican Sisters.* (Columbus,OH).—O.P.
[1070-05]—*Dominican Sisters.*—O.P.
[1070-11]—*Dominican Sisters.* (Sparkill, NY).—O.P.
[1070-13]—*Dominican Sisters.* (Adrian, MI).—O.P.
[1070-03]—*Dominican Sisters.* (Sinsinawa, WI).—O.P.
[1070-15]—*Dominican Sisters.* (Blauvelt, NY).—O.P.
[1070-17]—*Dominican Sisters.* (Elkins Park, PA).—O.P.
[1070-28]—*Dominican Sisters.* (Akron,OH).—O.P.
[]—*Dominican Sisters of the Immaculate Conception.* (Ecuador).
[1120]—*Dominican Sisters of the Roman Congregation.*—O.P.
[1140]—*Eucharistic Missionaries of St. Dominic.*—O.P.
[1180]—*Franciscan Sisters of Allegany, New York.*—O.S.F.
[1310]—*Franciscan Sisters of Little Falls, Minnesota.*—O.S.F.
[1370]—*Franciscan Sisters of Mary.* (Bronx, NY).—F.M.M.
[1430]—*Franciscan Sisters of Our Lady of P.H.* (St. Louis, MO).
[]—*Handmaids of the Holy Child Jesus.* (Nigeria).—H.H.C.J.
[2420]—*Marist Missionary Sisters (Missionary Sisters of the Society of Mary).*—S.M.S.M.
[2490]—*Medical Mission Sisters.* (Philadelphia, PA).—S.C.M.M./M.M.S.
[2480]—*Medical Missionaries of Mary.* (City Island, NY).—M.M.M.
[2720]—*Mission Helpers of the Sacred Heart.* (Baltimore, MD).—M.H.S.H.
[3760]—*Order of St. Clare.* (Evansville, IN).—O.S.C.
[4180]—*Religious Venerini Sisters.* (Worcester,MA).—M.P.V.
[2970]—*School Sisters of Notre Dame.* (Baltimore, MD; Wilton, CT).—S.S.N.D.
[1680]—*School Sisters of St. Francis.* (Milwaukee, WI).—S.S.S.F.
[3590]—*Servants of Mary (Servite Sisters).* (Ladysmith, WI).—O.S.M.
[0140]—*Sisters Auxillaries of the Apostolate .*—S.A.A.
[()]—*Sisters for Christian Community.*—S.F.C.C.
[0440]—*Sisters of Charity of Cincinnati, Ohio.* (Mt. St. Joseph, OH).—S.C.
[0500]—*Sisters of Charity of Nazareth.*—S.C.N.
[0590]—*Sisters of Charity of Saint Elizabeth, Convent Station.*—S.C.
[0570]—*Sisters of Charity of Seton Hill.* (Greensberg, PA).—S.C.
[0650]—*Sisters of Charity of St. Vincent de Paul.*—S.C.
[1930]—*Sisters of Holy Cross.* (Pittsfield, NH).—C.S.C.
[]—*Sisters of Mary, Mother of God.* (Tampa, FL).—S.M.M.G.
[2575]—*Sisters of Mercy of The Americas.* (Chicago, IL; Cumberland, RI; Dobbs Ferry, NY; Rochester, NY; Erie, PA; Windhaur, NH).—R.S.M.
[2990]—*Sisters of Notre Dame.* (Chardon, OH).—S.N.D.
[3000]—*Sisters of Notre Dame de Namur.* (Boston, MA).—S.N.D.deN.
[]—*Sisters of Our Lady of Charity.* (WI).—S.O.L.C.
[3360]—*Sisters of Providence.* (St. Mary of the Woods, IN.).—S.P.
[3893]—*Sisters of Saint Joseph of Chestnut Hill, Philadelphia.*—S.S.J.
[3720]—*Sisters of St. Anne.*—S.S.A.
[]—*Sisters of St. Anne Bangalone.*—S.A.B.
[3750]—*Sisters of St. Chretienne.* (Wrentham, MA).—S.S.Ch.
[3770]—*Sisters of St. Clare.* (Dublin, Ireland).—O.S.C.
[1510]—*Sisters of St. Francis.*—O.S.F.
[1710]—*Sisters of St. Francis of Mary Immaculate.* (Joliet, IL).—O.S.F.
[1630]—*Sisters of St. Francis of Penance and Christian Charity.* (Stella Niagara,NY).—O.S.F.
[1650]—*Sisters of St. Francis of Philadelphia.*—O.S.F.
[1570]—*Sisters of St. Francis of the Holy Family.* (Dubuque,IA).—O.S.F.
[]—*Sisters of St. Francis of the Mission of the Immaculate Virgin.* (Hastings, NY).—O.S.F.
[3830-11]—*Sisters of St. Joseph.* (Nazareth).—S.S.J.
[3830-14]—*Sisters of St. Joseph.*—S.S.J.
[3840]—*Sisters of St. Joseph of Carondelet.* (St. Louis, MO).—C.S.J.
[3880]—*Sisters of St. Joseph of Medaille.*—C.S.J.
[3890]—*Sisters of St. Joseph of Peace.* (Englewood Cliffs, NJ).—C.S.J.P.
[3900]—*Sisters of St. Joseph of St. Augustine, Florida.* (Chestnut Hill, PA).—S.S.J.
[1990]—*Sisters of the Holy Names of Jesus and Mary.* (Albany, NY).—S.N.J.M.
[3730]—*Sisters of the Order St. Basil the Great.* (Uniontown, PA).—O.S.B.M.
[1490]—*Sisters of the Third Franciscan Order.*—O.S.F.
[]—*Society of the Sisters of the Church.* (Patterson,NJ).—S.S.C.
[4120-03]—*Ursuline Nuns of the Congregation of Paris.* (Louisville, KY).—O.S.U.

DIOCESAN CEMETERIES

CLEARWATER. *Calvary Catholic,* 11801 U.S. Hwy. 19 N., 33764-7407.

NECROLOGY

† Jozwiak, Zygmunt, (Retired). —Died Nov. 12, 2000.

Diocese of Salina

(Dioecesis Salinensis)

Most Reverend

GEORGE K. FITZSIMONS, D.D.

Bishop of Salina; ordained March 18, 1961; appointed Titular Bishop of Pertusa and Auxiliary Bishop of Kansas City-St. Joseph May 27, 1975; Episcopal ordination July 3, 1975; appointed Bishop of Salina March 22, 1984; installed May 29, 1984. *Address all official communications to: P.O. Box 980, Salina, KS, 67402.*

Chancery Office: 103 N. Ninth, P.O. Box 980, Salina, KS, 67402-0980. Tel.: 785-827-8746; Fax: 785-827-6133.

E-mail address: chancery@midusa.net

FORMERLY DIOCESE OF CONCORDIA.

ESTABLISHED AUGUST 2, 1887.

SEE TRANSFERRED TO SALINA DECEMBER 23, 1944.

Square Miles 26,685.

(New boundaries established by Apostolic Letters dated July 1, 1897).

Bounded on the west by Colorado, on the north by Nebraska, on the east by the east lines of Washington, Riley, Geary and Dickinson Counties, and on the south by the south lines of Dickinson, Saline, Ellsworth, Russell, Ellis, Trego, Gove, Logan and Wallace Counties in the State of Kansas.

For legal titles of parishes and diocesan institutions, consult the Chancery Office.

STATISTICAL OVERVIEW

Personnel	
Bishop	1
Retired Bishops	1
Priests: Diocesan Active in Diocese	48
Priests: Active Outside Diocese	1
Priests: Diocesan in Foreign Missions	1
Priests: Retired, Sick or Absent	17
Number of Diocesan Priests	67
Religious Priests in Diocese	11
Extern Priests in Diocese	3
Ordinations:	
Diocesan Priests	2
Total Brothers	1
Total Sisters	222
Parishes	
Parishes	92
With Resident Pastor:	
Resident Diocesan Priests	39
Resident Religious Priests	4
Without Resident Pastor:	
Administered by Priests	43
Administered by Women Religious	4
Administered by Lay People	2
Professional Ministry Personnel:	
Brothers	1
Sisters	20
Lay Ministers	21
Welfare	
Homes for the Aged	4
Total Assisted	297
Educational	
Diocesan Students in Other Seminaries	8
Total Seminarians	8
High Schools, Diocesan and Parish	4
Total Students	468
High Schools, Private	1
Total Students	441
Elementary Schools, Diocesan and Parish	12
Total Students	2,023
Catechesis/Religious Education:	
High School Students	2,090
Elementary Students	5,316
Total Students Under Catholic Instruction	10,346
Teachers in the Diocese:	
Priests	3
Sisters	4
Lay Teachers	202
Vital Statistics	
Receptions into the Church:	
Infant Baptism Totals	999
Adult Baptism Totals	90
Received into Full Communion	185
First Communions	822
Confirmations	896
Marriages:	
Catholic	193
Interfaith	199
Total Marriages	392
Deaths	603
Total Catholic Population	50,113
Total Population	318,359

Former Bishops—Rt. Rev. RICHARD SCANNELL, D.D., cons. in Nashville, Tenn., Nov. 30, 1887; transferred to Omaha, Jan. 30, 1891; died Jan. 8, 1916.—Rt. Rev. JOHN J. HENNESSY, D.D., Apostolic Administrator, 1891-98, Bishop of Wichita.—Rt. Rev. THADDEUS BUTLER, D.D., Bishop-elect; died July 17, 1897.—Rt. Rev. JOHN F. CUNNINGHAM, D.D., cons. Sept. 21, 1898; died June 23, 1919.—Most Rev. FRANCIS J. TIEF, D.D., cons. March 30, 1921; retired and appointed Titular Bishop of Nisa, June 11, 1938; died Sept. 22, 1965.—Most Rev. FRANK A. THILL, D.D., cons. Oct. 28, 1938; transferred to Salina, Dec. 23, 1944; died May 21, 1957.—Most Rev. FREDERICK W. FREKING, D.D., cons. Nov. 30, 1957; transferred to LaCrosse, Dec. 30, 1964.—Most Rev. CYRIL J. VOGEL, D.D., ord. Bishop, June 17, 1965; died Oct. 4, 1979.—Most Rev. DANIEL W. KUCERA, O.S.B., Ph.D., D.D., ord. May 26, 1949; appt. Titular Bishop of Natchez and Auxiliary Bishop of Joliet, June 6, 1977; cons. July 21, 1977; appt. Bishop of Salina, March 11, 1980; installed May 7, 1980; transferred to Archbishop of Archdiocese of Dubuque, Feb. 23, 1984; retired Oct. 16, 1995.

Chancery Office—103 N. Ninth, P.O. Box 980, Salina, 67402-0980. Tel: 785-827-8746; Fax: 785-827-6133.

Vicar General and Chancellor—Rev. Msgr. JAMES E. HAKE, J.C.L., *Res., Sacred Heart Cathedral, 118 N. 9th, Salina, 67401.*

Vice Chancellor—Rev. BARRY BRINKMAN, J.C.L., *Res., St. Mary's Church, 230 E. Cloud, Salina, 67401.*

Diocesan Finance Officer—Rev. JEROME L. MORGAN, *Res., St. Wenceslaus, P.O. Box 528, Wilson, 67490.* Mr. GREG LUST, Asst. Finance Officer & Business Mgr., *P.O. Box 980, Salina, 67402-0980.*

Diocesan Office of Planning—ARVILLA JUENEMANN, Dir.

Diocesan Tribunal—103 N. Ninth, P.O. Box 980, Salina, 67402-0980. Tel: 785-827-8746; Fax: 785-827-6133.

Judicial Vicar-Officialis—Rev. KENNETH LOHRMEYER, J.C.L.

Associate Judges—Revs. KENNETH P. LOHRMEYER, J.C.L.; BARRY BRINKMAN, J.C.L.

Defender of the Bond—Rev. Msgr. JAMES E. HAKE, J.C.L.

Auditor-Notary—EDITH M. PIERCE.

Promoter of Justice and Guardian—Rev. DANIEL SCHEETZ, J.C.L.

Procurator and Advocate—Rev. RALPH ASCHENBRENNER.

Diocesan Finance Council—Most Rev. GEORGE K. FITZSIMONS, D.D.; Rev. JEROME L. MORGAN; BILL BECKMEYER; DONALD P. DIEDERICH; JOHN GRAHAM; GREG LUST; ROBERT SCHMIDT.

College of Consultors—Rev. Msgr. JAMES E. HAKE, J.C.L.; Revs. MELVIN LONG; JEROME L. MORGAN; DONALD D. ZIMMERMAN; FRANK COADY; JAMES HOOVER.

Episcopal Vicars—Rev. ROGER MEITL, Western District; Rev. DONALD D. ZIMMERMAN, West Central District; Rev. JEROME L. MORGAN, East Central District; Rev. MELVIN LONG, Eastern District.

Council of Priests—Revs. DONALD D. ZIMMERMAN, Chm. JOSEPH POPELKA, Vice Chm. RANDALL WEBER, Sec. ALLEN SCHEER, Treas. KENNETH LOHRMEYER; Rev. Msgr. JAMES E. HAKE, J.C.L.; Revs. FRANK COADY; FRANK GRINKO, O.F.M.Cap.; MELVIN LONG; JEROME L. MORGAN; BARRY BRINKMAN; JAMES HOOVER; DARYL OLMSTEAD.

Diocesan Pastoral Council—Most Rev. GEORGE K. FITZSIMONS, D.D.; ARVILLA JUENEMANN, Moderator; Revs. JEROME L. MORGAN; JAMES HOOVER; DAVID METZ; MARK WESELY; Sr. CAROLYN JUENEMANN, C.S.J.; Sr. MARY CATHERINE GRIEF, C.S.A.; Sr. KENNETH STRUCKHOFF, C.S.A.; Sr. MARY JO THUMMEL, C.S.J. Laity: STANLEY KRIER, Vice Chm. ROXANNA MARTIN, Sec. TERRY CHAPUT; ROSANN FELDER; VERNA FLAX; RANDY HUSER; RON LAGER; MARLENE MONTGOMERY; DENNIS PAHLS, Chm. LEE PLOUSSARD; JOAN WESSEL; ESTHER TOUSLEE; MIKE STALLINGS; RICHARD KRAMER; DOLORES JUENEMANN; FRANCIS SWEAT; ANN THORNTON.

Personnel Board—Most Rev. GEORGE K. FITZSIMONS, D.D.; Revs. HENRY BAXA, Sec. AL BRUNGARDT; FRANK COADY, Chm. ROGER MEITL; JEROME MORGAN; Rev. Msgr. JAMES E. HAKE, J.C.L., Ex Officio.

Vocation Ministry Committee—Most Rev. GEORGE K. FITZSIMONS, D.D. Co-Directors: Revs. ALLEN SCHEER; JOSEPH POPELKA; Revs. KEVIN WEBER; MARK WESELY; DAVID METZ; KEITH WEBER; FRED GATSCHET; GALEN LONG; Bro. AUGUSTINE ROHDE, O.F.M.Cap.; Sr. BARBARA ELLEN APACELLER, C.S.J.

Diocesan Offices and Directors

Art and Architecture Commission—Rev. JEROME L. MORGAN, Chm.; Rev. Msgr. JAMES E. HAKE, J.C.L., Vice Chm.; Rev. Msgr. JOHN GEORGE WEBER; Revs. FRANK COADY; DONALD D. ZIMMERMAN; KEVIN WEBER; Mr. GILBERT URBAN; Mr. GREG LUST.

Priests' Continuing Formation Committee—Revs. MELVIN LONG, Chm. RANDALL WEBER; FRANK COADY; BARRY BRINKMAN. Ex Officio: Most Rev. GEORGE K. FITZSIMONS, D.D.; Rev. Msgr. JAMES HAKE, J.C.L.

Catholic Charities Board—Dr. KAREN S. HAUSER, CEO; LARRY CURRAN, Pres.; Rev. DAMIAN RICHARDS; STEVE BROWN, Treas.; Rev. ALLEN SCHEER, Sec. JIM LEDUC; SUSAN LEDUC; RON RIPPE; DEBI RIPPE, Vice Pres. GUY STEIER; JULIE STEIER; ROSIE RUNDELL; Most

Rev. GEORGE K. FITZSIMONS, D.D., Ex Officio.

Catholic Charities of Salina, Inc.—Dr. KAREN S. HAUSER, Ed.D., CEO; LILLIAN ANDROES, L.B., Adoption; JOSEPHINE HERNANDEZ, L.S.C.S.W., Counseling; BONNIE OTEY, Office Mgr., *425 W. Iron, P.O. Box 1366, Salina, 67401.* Tel: 785-825-0208. Tel: 888-468-6909; Fax: 785-826-9708.

Family Life—SHEILA MARCOTTE, Exec. Sec.

Immigration—BEATRICE ZAPATA; Sr. JUDY STEPHENS, C.S.J.; MARIA LUZ RODRIGUEZ.

Catholic Charities Outreach Office - Hays—JOAN PERKINS, Office Mgr. JANET RUSSELL, L.S.C.S.W., Adoption & Counseling; Rev. BILL SURMEIER, M.S., Counseling, *2707 Vine, #17, P.O. Box 811, Hays, 67601.* Tel: 785-625-2644; Fax: 785-625-6497.

Catholic Charities Outreach Office - Manhattan—IRIS CURLEY-ROARK, L.M.S.W., Adoption, *1105 Sunset Ave., Manhattan, 66502.* Tel: 785-587-4227.

Catholic Community Annual Appeal—*P.O. Box 980, Salina, 67402-0980;* Fax: 785-827-6133.

Office of Catholic Formation—Rev. Msgr. JAMES E. HAKE, J.C.L., Dir., *103 N. Ninth, P.O. Box 825, Salina, 67402.* Tel: 785-827-8746; Fax: 785-827-6133.

Coordinator of Office of Catholic Formation—Sr. BARBARA ELLEN APACELLER, C.S.J.

Director of Religious Education—Sr. BARBARA ELLEN APACELLER, C.S.J.

Superintendent of Schools—Dr. NICK COMPAGNONE.

Consultant for Religious Education & Media—(Grades K-8), PEGGY HERBERT.

Consultant for Religious Education—(Grades 9-12), Sr. BARBARA ELLEN APACELLER, C.S.J.

Director of Religious Studies/School of Pastoral Leadership—Rev. FRANK COADY.

Valuing Your Sexuality—PEGGY HEBERT, Dir.

Audio-Visual—PEGGY HEBERT.

Catholic Youth Organization and Youth Ministry—Sr. BARBARA ELLEN APACELLER, C.S.J., *P.O. Box 980, Salina, 67402.*

Office of Communications—*P.O. Box 980, Salina, 67402.*

Diocesan Council of Education—NADINE KARLIN, Pres. PEGGY HEBERT; MARTHA BRUNGARDT; TOM SCHMITZ; JEAN ROSS; PAT LEGLEITER; VERNA FLAX; DOROTHY JACOBS; Revs. HENRY BAXA; CHARLES STEIER; ALBERT DESANCTIS; KEVIN WEBER. Ex Officio from Chancery Staff: Rev. Msgr. JAMES E. HAKE, J.C.L.; Sr. BARBARA APACELLER, C.S.J.; Dr. NICK COMPAGNONE.

Due Process Board—Rev. KENNETH P. LOHRMEYER, J.C.L., Chm.; Sr. BETH STOVER, C.S.J.; Dr. NICK COMPAGNONE; MARY JO HEATH; Mr. LEROY HERRMAN; Rev. Msgr. JAMES E. HAKE, J.C.L., Clerk.

Holy Childhood, Pontifical Association—Rev. Msgr. JAMES E. HAKE, J.C.L., Dir., *P.O. Box 980, Salina, 67402.*

Office of Liturgy—Rev. FRANK COADY, Dir., *P.O. Box 980, Salina, 67402.* Tel: 785-827-8746; Fax: 785-827-6133.

Newspaper—*"The Register, Northwestern Kansas Edition";* Rev. Msgr. RAYMOND MENARD, Editor; Mr. GREG LUST, Business Mgr., *P.O. Box 1038, Salina, 67402.*

Propagation of the Faith—Rev. Msgr. JAMES E. HAKE, J.C.L., Dir., *P.O. Box 980, Salina, 67402.* Tel: 785-827-8746.

Rural Life Conference—Rev. Msgr. JOHN GEORGE WEBER, Dir., *926 E. Republic, Salina, 67432.* Tel: 785-823-1322.

Salina Diocesan Clergy Health and Retirement Association, Inc.—Board of Trustees: Most Rev. GEORGE K. FITZSIMONS, D.D., Pres., *103 N. Ninth, P.O. Box 980, Salina, 67402-0980.* Revs. DONALD MCCARTHY; ROGER HOUGH; LOREN WERTH; LOUIS MATTAS; RALPH ASCHENBRENNER; FRED GATSCHET. Ex Officio: Rev. JEROME MORGAN; Mr. GREG LUST.

Salina Diocesan Council of Catholic Women (S.D.CC.W.)—DOLORES JUENEMANN, Pres., *2422 Sunflower Rd., Washington, 66968.* Rev. KEVIN WEBER, Moderator, *St. Mary's Church, 703 Monroe St., Ellis, 67637.*

Boy Scouts—Rev. DONALD P. MCCARTHY, *625 Freeman Ave., Oakley, 67748.*

Girl Scouts—Sr. BARBARA ELLEN, C.S.J., Dir., *P.O. Box 825, Salina, 67402-0825.*

Vocations—

Diocesan Director of Vocations—Co-Directors: Revs. ALLEN SCHEER; JOSEPH POPELKA.

CLERGY, PARISHES, MISSIONS AND PAROCHIAL SCHOOLS

CITY OF SALINA
(Saline County)

1—CATHEDRAL OF THE SACRED HEART (1876), Rev. Msgr. James E. Hake; Revs. Larry Letourneau; Francisco Montoya; Sr. Mary Augustine, C.S.J., Pastoral Assoc. In res., Rev. Msgr. Raymond Menard; Rev. Richard Lutgen.
Res., 118 N. Ninth St., 67401. Tel: 785-823-7221; Fax: 785-820-8063. [JC]
School—(Grades PreK-6) 406 W. Iron Ave., 67401. Tel: 785-825-4798. Pat Breckunitch, Prin.
Lay Teachers 9; Students 131.
Catechesis/Religious Programs—Tel: 785-823-2713. Sherry Headlee, D.R.E.
Students 125.

2—ST. ELIZABETH ANN SETON (1982), Rev. Frank Coady, Priest Supvr.; Sr. Rose Walters, C.S.A., Parish Dir. & Pastoral Admin.
Res., 1000 Burr Oak Ln., 67401. Tel: 785-825-5282; Fax: 785-825-1140. [JC]
Catechesis/Religious Programs—D.R.E.: Melanie Melander; Lucy Larson.
Students 150.

3—ST. MARY'S (1959), Revs. Kerry Ninemire; Barry Brinkman.
Res., 230 E. Cloud St., 67401. Tel: 785-827-5575; Fax: 785-827-8997. [JC]
School—(Grades PreK-6) 304 E. Cloud St., 67401. Tel: 785-827-4200; Fax: 785-827-7765. Mr. Nick Compagnone, Prin.
Lay Teachers 36; Students 405.
Catechesis/Religious Programs—D.R.E.: Mrs. Nancy Main; Nancy Sherffius.
Students 290.

OUTSIDE THE CITY OF SALINA

Abilene, Dickinson Co., St. Andrew's (1874), Rev. Randall Weber.
Res., 311 S. Buckeye Ave., P.O. Box 429, 67410. Tel: 785-263-1570; Fax: 785-263-3570. [CEM]
School—(Grades PreK-5). Tel: 785-263-2453. Dennis McCall, Prin.
Lay Teachers 7; Students 96.
Catechesis/Religious Programs—Tel: 785-263-1570. Theresa Brierton, D.R.E.
Students 165.

Angelus, Sheridan Co., St. Paul's (German). Attended by St. Joseph's Church, Oakley.
Mailing Address: 625 Freeman Ave., Oakley, 67748. Tel: 785-672-3828.
Church—Tel: 785-824-3256. [CEM]
Catechesis/Religious Programs—Students 58.

Antonino, Ellis Co., Our Lady Help of Christians (1905). Attended by St. Joseph, Hays.
Mailing Address: P.O. Drawer 1000, Hays, 67601. Tel: 785-625-7356; Fax: 785-625-7394.

Atwood, Rawlins Co., Sacred Heart (1879), Rev. Damian Richards.
Res., Sacred Heart, 508 N. Railroad Ave., 67730. Tel: 785-626-3335; Fax: 785-626-3335. [CEM][JC 3]
Catechesis/Religious Programs—Tel: 785-626-3431. Loretta A. Studer, D.R.E.
Students 109.

Aurora, Cloud Co., St. Peter's (1884). Attended by St. John the Baptist, Clyde.
Church—. [CEM][JC]
Catechesis/Religious Programs—Tel: 785-464-3461.
Students 34.

Beardsley, Rawlins Co., St. John's (1910) Czechoslovak, Rev. Beryl Gibson.
Mailing Address: P.O. Box 1170, St. Francis, 67756.
Church—Atwood, 67730. [CEM]
Catechesis/Religious Programs—Students 43.

Belleville, Republic Co., St. Edward's (1901), Rev. John A. Moeder.
Res., 1827 Q St., P.O. Box 99, 66935. Tel: 785-527-5559. [CEM]
Catechesis/Religious Programs—Sacred Hearts Center, 1813 Q St., 66935. Tel: 785-527-5819. Bev Lapo, D.R.E.
Students 127.

Beloit, Mitchell Co., St. John the Baptist (1869), Rev. Henry R. Baxa; Sr. Mary Stanislaus Porter, C.S.J., Pastoral Assoc.
Res., 701 E. Court St., 67420. Tel: 785-738-2851; Fax: 785-738-3410. [CEM]
School—(Grades PreK-6). Tel: 785-738-3941. Charlotte Scheckel, Prin.
Lay Teachers 9; Students 109.
High School—(Grades 7-12). Tel: 785-738-2942; Fax: 785-738-4462. Charlotte Scheckel, Prin.
Priests 1; Lay Teachers 11; Students 93.
Catechesis/Religious Programs—Tel: 785-738-2851.
Students 103.

Bird City, Cheyenne Co., St. Joseph's (1911). Attended by St. Francis, St. Francis. Rev. Beryl Gibson.
Mailing Address: 625 River St., P.O. Box 1170, St. Francis, 67756.
Church—67731. Tel: 785-332-2680.
Catechesis/Religious Programs—Students 33.

Brookville, Saline Co., St. Joseph's (1884). Attended by Sacred Heart Cathedral, Salina.
Mailing Address: 118 N. 9th, Salina, 67401. Tel: 785-823-7221.
Church—67425. [CEM]

Catharine, Ellis Co., St. Catherine's (1892). Attended by St. Joseph's, Hays.
Mailing Address: 1681 St. Joseph St., P.O. Box 18, 67627. Tel: 785-625-5091. [CEM 2]

Cawker City, Mitchell Co., SS. Peter and Paul (1878) (German). Attended by St. Boniface, Tipton.
Church—Tel: 785-781-4319; 373-4455. [CEM]
Catechesis/Religious Programs—1202 Holly, 67430. Tel: 785-781-4835.
Students 42.

Chapman, Dickinson Co., St. Michael's (1883), Carolyn Juenemann, C.S.J., Parish Dir. & Pastoral Admin.; Rev. Richard E. Lutgen; Marita Campbell, Pastoral Admin.
Res., P.O. Box 217, 67431. Tel: 785-922-6509. [CEM]
Catechesis/Religious Programs—Tel: 785-922-6509. Julie Hamel, D.R.E.
Students 91.

Claudell, Smith Co., St. Francis (1914). Attended by SS. Philip & James, Phillipsburg.
Mailing Address: 690 S. 7th, Phillipsburg, 67661. Tel: 785-543-5367.

Clay Center, Clay Co., SS. Peter and Paul (1879), Rev. Merlin Kieffer.
Res., 730 Court St., 67432. Tel: 785-632-5011; Fax: 785-632-3914. [CEM]
Catechesis/Religious Programs—Tel: 913-632-3204. Cyndy Schwensen, D.R.E.
Students 100.

Clifton, Washington Co., St. Mary's (French-German). Attended by St. John the Baptist, Clyde.
Mailing Address: 204 N. High, Clyde, 66938. Tel: 785-446-3474; Fax: 785-446-3669.
Church—Tel: 913-455-3384. [CEM]
Catechesis/Religious Programs—Tel: 913-455-2291. Mrs. Linda Kantack, D.R.E.
Students 72.

Clyde, Cloud Co., St. John the Baptist's (1880) (French-German), Rev. LeRoy Metro; Brenda Koch, D.R.E.
Res., 204 N. High, 66938. Tel: 785-446-3474; Fax: 785-446-3669. [CEM]
Catechesis/Religious Programs—Students 102.

Colby, Thomas Co., Sacred Heart, Rev. Galen Long; Sr. Donna Marie Kleinsorge, C.S.A., Pastoral Assoc. & D.R.E.
Res., 585 N. French Ave., 67701. Tel: 785-462-2179; Fax: 785-462-6613. [CEM]
School—(Grades PreK-5). Tel: 785-462-2813; Fax: 785-462-9688. Mr. David Everet, Prin.
Lay Teachers 9; Students 160.
Catechesis/Religious Programs—Tel: 785-462-3890.
Students 221.

Collyer, Trego Co., St. Michael's (1893) (German). Attended by Christ the King, Wakeeney.
Mailing Address: Ainsie Ave., Box 174, 67631. Tel: 785-769-5272. [CEM][JC]
Catechesis/Religious Programs—Laura Walt, D.R.E.
Students 60.

Concordia, Cloud Co., Our Lady of Perpetual Help (1887) (French), Rev. Steven Heina.
Office: 307 E. Fifth, P.O. Box 608, 66901. Tel: 785-243-1099; Fax: 785-243-1939.
Res., 420 Kansas, P.O. Box 608, 66901. Tel: 785-243-4658. [CEM]
Catechesis/Religious Programs—Tel: 785-243-1410. Laura Jo Meyer, D.R.E.
Students 247.

Cuba, Republic Co., St. Isidore's (1873) (Czech). Attended by St. Edward, Belleville.
Mailing Address: P.O. Box 99, Belleville, 66935. [CEM]

Damar, Rooks Co., St. Joseph's (1912) (French). Attended by Immaculate Heart of Mary, Hill City. In res., Rev. Bill Kilian, (Retired).
Mailing Address: 10 N. 10th Ave., Hill City, 67642. Tel: 785-839-4343. [CEM]
Catechesis/Religious Programs—Tel: 785-839-4360. Gil Berland, D.R.E.
Students 66.

Delphos, Ottawa Co., St. Paul's. Attended by Immaculate Conception, Minneapolis. Rev. Kenneth Lohrmeyer.
Res., 216 Cherry St., Box 167, Minneapolis, 67467.

Tel: 785-392-2079. [CEM]

Densmore, Norton Co., St. Mary's. Closed. For inquiries for parish records contact the Chancery.

Dorrance, Russell Co., St. Joseph's (1902) (German-Irish). Attended by St. Wenceslaus, Wilson. Rev. Jerome Morgan.
Mailing Address: P.O. Box 528, Wilson, 67490. Tel: 785-658-3361. [CEM]
Catechesis/Religious Programs—Students 22.

Downs, Osborne Co., St. Mary's (1903). Attended by St. Aloysius, Osborne.
Mailing Address: P.O. Box 267, Osborne, 67473.
Church—1312 Prentice, 67437. Tel: 785-454-3551.
Catechesis/Religious Programs—Students 46.

Ellis, Ellis Co., St. Mary's (1870), Rev. Kevin Weber; Sr. Doris M. Flax, Pastoral Assoc.
Church—703 Monroe, 67637. Tel: 785-726-4522.
School—(Grades PreK-6). Tel: 913-726-3185. Dale James Koerner, Prin.
Sisters of St. Joseph 2; Lay Teachers 9; Students 62.
Catechesis/Religious Programs—Sr. Donna Otter, D.R.E.
Students 112.

Ellsworth, Ellsworth Co., St. Bernard's (1909), Rev. Daniel L. Scheetz.
Res., 911 Kansas St., 67439. Tel: 785-472-3136.
Catechesis/Religious Programs—Students 97.

Elmo, Dickinson Co., St. Columba's. Attended by St. John the Evangelist, Herington. Rev. Mark Wesely. 712 N. Broadway, Herington, 67449. Tel: 785-258-2013. [CEM]

Esbon, Jewell Co., Sacred Heart (1887). Attended by St. Theresa's, Mankato.
Mailing Address: P.O. Box 265, Mankato, 66956.
Church—Tel: 785-378-3939. [CEM]

Fort Riley, Riley Co., Fort Riley Catholic Community. Attended by Archdiocese for the Military Services.

Glasco, Cloud Co., St. Mary's (1878). Attended by St. Patrick, Lincoln.
Mailing Address: P.O. Box 327, Lincoln, 67455. Tel: 785-524-4823.
Church—301 E. First St., P.O. Box 554, 67445. [CEM]

Goodland, Sherman Co., Our Lady of Perpetual Help (1887), Rev. Daryl Olmstead.
Church—307 W. 13th, 67735. Tel: 785-899-7205.
Catechesis/Religious Programs—Mary Ann Weishapl, D.R.E.
Students 200.

Gorham, Russell Co., St. Mary's (1984), Rev. Charles Steier, Supvr.; Sr. Mary Jo Thummel, C.S.J., Admin.
Res., Box 135, 67640. Tel: 785-637-5241. [CEM]
Catechesis/Religious Programs—St. Mary's Parish Center, 161 Chicago, 67640.
Students 22.

Grainfield, Gove Co., St. Agnes (1910) (German). Attended by Sacred Heart, Park. Rev. Mark Berland.
Mailing Address: P.O. Box 78, Park, 67751-0078. Tel: 785-673-4684. [JC]
Catechesis/Religious Programs—Tel: 785-673-5510. Janice Manhart, D.R.E.
Students 68.

Greenleaf, Washington Co., Sacred Heart (1890). Attended by St. John the Baptist, Hanover. Rev. Edward J. Oen, C.PP.S. Pastoral Assocs.: Lawrence Hogan; James Donigan.
Mailing Address: P.O. Box 395, Hanover, 66945. Tel: 785-337-2207.
Church—Tel: 785-747-2862. [CEM]

Grinnell, Gove Co., Immaculate Conception (1888) (German). Attended by St. Joseph's Oakley. Rev. Roger K. Meitl, Parish Dir. & Pastoral Admin.
Mailing Address: 625 Freeman Ave., Oakley, 67748. Tel: 785-672-3828. [CEM]
Catechesis/Religious Programs—Fax: 785-824-3388. Sr. Kenneth Struckhoff, D.R.E.
Students 63.

Gypsum, Saline Co., St. Patrick's. Attended by Immaculate Conception, Solomon. Rev. John Wolesky. Parish Directors/Pastoral Administrators: Mr. James Karber; Mrs. Alan (Debie) Martin.

Hanover, Washington Co., St. John the Baptist (1868) (Bohemian), Rev. Edward J. Oen, C.PP.S.
Res., Box 395, 66945. Tel: 785-337-2207. [CEM]
School—(Grades 1-8). Tel: 785-337-2782. Mr. Timothy Rundle, Prin.
Lay Teachers 7; Students 94.
Catechesis/Religious Programs—Students 53.

Hays, Ellis Co., Immaculate Heart of Mary (1967), Revs. Donald D. Zimmerman; David Metz; Sr. Rosalia Costello, C.S.A., Pastoral Assoc.
Res., 1805 Vine, 67601. Tel: 785-625-7339; Fax: 785-625-7643. [JC]
Catechesis/Religious Programs—D.R.E.: Dorothy Jacobs; Pat Legleiter.
Students 636.

St. Joseph's (1885), Revs. Michael Scully, O.F.M.Cap.; Michael Suchnicki, O.F.M.Cap.; Earl Befort, O.F.M.Cap.; Paulinus I. Karlin, O.F.M.Cap. In res., Most Rev. Firmin Schmidt, O.F.M.Cap., (Retired); Rev. Bennett Collucci.
Res., P.O. Drawer 1000, 67601. Tel: 785-625-7356; Fax: 785-625-7394. [JC]
School—(Grades K-6). Tel: 785-625-3131. Dolores McKibbin, Prin.
Lay Teachers 16; Students 308.
Catechesis/Religious Programs—Tel: 785-628-2311. D.R.E.: Martha A. Brungardt; Jerry Michaud; Renee Michaud.
Students 210.

St. Nicholas of Myra (1983), Jeanie Munsch, Pastoral Admin.; Rev. William J. Surmeier.
Office: 2901 E. 13th, P.O. Box 932, 67601. Tel: 785-628-1446; Fax: 785-628-6627.
Res., 2405 A Henry Dr., 67601. Tel: 785-628-6658.
Catechesis/Religious Programs—Tel: 785-628-2188. Sr. Martina Stegman, O.P., D.R.E.
Students 169.

Herington, Dickinson Co., St. John the Evangelist, Res Rev. Mark Wesely.; Res., 712 N. Broadway, 67449. Tel: 785-258-2013. [CEM]
Catechesis/Religious Programs—Judy Zimmer, D.R.E.
Students 92.

Herndon, Rawlins Co., Assumption (1880) (German). Attended by Sacred Heart, Atwood. Rev. Damian Richards.
Mailing Address: 508 N. Railroad Ave., Atwood, 67730. Tel: 785-626-3335; Fax: 785-626-3431.
Church—Box 247, 67739. Tel: 785-322-5560. [CEM]
Catechesis/Religious Programs—Students 34.

Hill City, Graham Co., Immaculate Heart of Mary (1958), Rev. Donald P. McCarthy.
Res., 10 N. 10th Ave., 67642. Tel: 785-421-2535.
Catechesis/Religious Programs—Tel: 785-421-2665. Joyce Tauber, D.R.E.
Students 111.

Holyrood, Ellsworth Co., St. Mary's (1886). Attended by St. Bernard's, Ellsworth. Rev. Daniel L. Scheetz.
Mailing Address: 911 Kansas, Ellsworth, 67439. Tel: 785-472-3136.

Hope, Dickinson Co., St. Phillip's. Attended by St. John's, Herington. Rev. Mark Wesely.
Mailing Address: 712 N. Broadway, Herington, 67449. Tel: 785-258-2013.
Church—67451. Tel: 785-366-7353.
Catechesis/Religious Programs—Esther Dillon, D.R.E.
Students 46.

Hoxie, Sheridan Co., St. Frances Xavier Cabrini (1948), Revs. Benjamin Saw (Burma); Roger Meitl; Arvilla Juenemann, Pastoral Admin.
Res., 924 N. 17th, Box 38, 67740. Tel: 785-675-3300; Fax: 785-675-2235. [CEM]
Catechesis/Religious Programs—Twinned with St. Martin's, Seguin, Hoxie, KS. Verlene Feldt, D.R.E.
Students 144.

Jamestown, Cloud Co., St. Mary's (1873). Closed. For sacramental records contact Our Lady of Perpetual Help, Concordia.

Junction City, Geary Co., St. Francis Xavier's, Rev. Aloysius Brungardt.
Res., 218 N. Washington, P.O. Box 399, 66441. Tel: 785-238-2998; Fax: 785-238-4731. [CEM]
School—(Grades PreK-8) 280 N. Jefferson St., 66441. Tel: 785-238-3867. Mr. John Rodriguez, Prin.
Lay Teachers 11; Students 173.
High School—Mr. Mike Schrant, Prin. Lay Teachers 12; Students 100.
Catechesis/Religious Programs—Tel: 785-238-2841; Fax: 785-238-5021.
Students 118.

Kanopolis, Ellsworth Co., St. Ignatius Loyola (1947) (Mexican). Attended by St. Bernard's, Ellsworth. Rev. Daniel L. Scheetz.
Mailing Address: 911 Kansas, Ellsworth, 67439. Tel: 785-472-3136.
Church—Tel: 785-472-4628. [JC]

Kimeo, Washington Co., St. Michael's. Closed. For inquiries for parish records contact St. John's, Hanover.

Leoville, Decatur Co., Immaculate Conception (1885). Attended by Sacred Heart Parish, Selden.
Mailing Address: P.O. Box 57, Selden, 67757. Tel: 785-386-4496; Fax: 785-386-4445.
Church—Tel: 785-386-4409. [CEM]
Catechesis/Religious Programs—Jill Reichert, D.R.E.
Students 51.

Lincoln, Lincoln Co., St. Patrick's (1870), Rev. Ralph L. Aschenbrenner.
Res., 206 N. Fifth, Box 327, 67455. Tel: 785-524-4823. [CEM 2]
Catechesis/Religious Programs—Tel: 785-524-3043. Mary Byarlay, D.R.E.
Students 77.

Logan, Phillips Co., St. John's (1888). Attended by St. Thomas, Stockton. Rev. James P. Grennan.
Mailing Address: 722 Main St., Stockton, 67669. Tel: 785-425-6656. [CEM]
Catechesis/Religious Programs—Tel: 785-689-4299. Joan Long, D.R.E.
Students 52.

Manhattan, Riley Co., Seven Dolors (1880), Revs. Lawrence E. Grennan; Urbano Tin (Burma).
Res., 731 Pierre St., Box 844, 66502. Tel: 785-565-5000; Fax: 785-565-5003.
School—(Grades PreK-8) 306 S. Juliette, 66502. Tel: 785-565-5050; Fax: 785-565-5055. Tom Schmitz, Prin.
Lay Teachers 20; Students 270.
Catechesis/Religious Programs—D.R.E. Rosie Rundell, Pastoral Assoc.; Maggie Haag.
Students 207.

St. Isidore (1963), Rev. Keith Weber.
Res., 711 Denison St., 66502. Tel: 785-539-7496; Fax: 785-539-0220.

St. Thomas More Parish (1981), Rev. Melvin T. Long.
Church Office—2900 Kimball Ave., 66502. Tel: 785-776-5151; Fax: 785-776-5219.
Catechesis/Religious Programs—Tel: 785-776-1398.
Students 372.

Mankato, Jewell Co., St. Theresa of Infant Jesus (1949), Rev. Allen Scheer.
Res., 422 N. Commercial, Box 265, 66956. Tel: 785-378-3939; Fax: 785-378-3913. [CEM]

McDowell, Geary Co., St. Joseph. Closed. For inquiries for parish records contact the Chancery.

Meredith, Cloud Co., St. Peter's. Closed. Sacramental records are located at St. Peter.

Miltonvale, Cloud Co., St. Anthony's (1910). Attended by SS. Peter and Paul, Clay Center.
Mailing Address: 730 Court St., Clay Center, 67432. Tel: 785-632-5011; Fax: 785-632-3914.
Church—Tel: 785-427-2253.

Minneapolis, Ottawa Co., Immaculate Conception of the Blessed Virgin Mary, Rev. Kenneth Lohrmeyer.
Res., 216 Cherry St., Box 167, 67467. Tel: 785-392-2079; 392-2013 (Church Hall).
Catechesis/Religious Programs—Students 70.

Morrowville, Washington Co., SS. Peter and Paul (1887). Attended by St. Augustine's, Washington. 410 B St., Washington, 66968. Tel: 785-325-2346. [CEM]

Munden, Republic Co., St. George's (1887) (Czech). Attended by St. Edward's, Belleville.
Mailing Address: P.O. Box 99, Belleville, 66935. [CEM]

Munjor, Ellis Co., St. Francis of Assisi (1876), Rev. William J. Surmeier.
Church—883 Moscow, 67601. Tel: 785-625-5314. [CEM]

New Almelo, Norton Co., St. Joseph's (1878). Attended by St. Francis of Assisi, Norton. Deacon Stan Chapin.
Res., 67645-9742. Tel: 785-567-4875. [CEM]

Niles, Ottawa Co., Sacred Heart. Closed. Sacramental records are located at Immaculate Conception.

Norton, Norton Co., St. Francis of Assisi (1878), Rev. John Walsh.
Res., 108 S. Wabash, Box 148, 67654. Tel: 785-877-2234.
Catechesis/Religious Programs—Jennifer Terrell, D.R.E.
Students 131.
Mission—New Almelo, Norton Co., St. Joseph's Church, HC-1 Box 175, New Almelo, 67652. Tel: 785-567-4875.

Oakley, Logan Co., St. Joseph's (1890), Rev. Roger K. Meitl.
Res., 625 Freeman Ave., 67748. Tel: 785-672-3828. [CEM]
School—(Grades K-5) 725 Freeman Ave., 67748. Tel: 785-672-4451. Mr. Robert Sattler, Prin.
Priests 1; Lay Teachers 7; Students 75.
Catechesis/Religious Programs—St. Joseph Parish Annex, 405 E. Seventh, 67748. Tel: 785-672-4443. Phyllis Temaat, D.R.E.
Students 118.

Oberlin, Decatur Co., Sacred Heart (1888), Rev. James F. Hoover; Sr. Marilyn Wall, C.S.J., Pastoral Admin. & Dir.
Res., 210 E. Washington, 67749. Tel: 785-475-3103. [JC]
Catechesis/Religious Programs—Doris Pahls, D.R.E.
Students 71.

Ogden, Riley Co., St. Patrick's (1866). Attended by Seven Dolors, Manhattan.
Res., P.O. Box A, 66517. Tel: 785-565-5090. [CEM]

Osborne, Osborne Co., St. Aloysius (1881), Rev. Roger W. Hough.
Res., Box 267, 67437. Tel: 785-346-5582. [CEM]
Catechesis/Religious Programs—Rhonda Reed, D.R.E.
Students 124.
Mission—Downs, Osborne Co., St. Mary's, 1312 Prentice, 67437. Tel: 785-454-3551.

Park, Gove Co., Sacred Heart (1898) (German), Rev. Mark Berland.
Res., P.O. Box 78, 67751. Tel: 785-673-4684. [CEM]
Catechesis/Religious Programs—D.R.E.: Tonia Couse; Pam Nemechek.
Students 105.

Pfeifer, Ellis Co., Holy Cross. Closed. For sacramental records contact St. Fidelis, Victoria.

Phillipsburg, Phillips Co., SS. Philip and James (1875), Rev. Alvin Werth.
Res., R.R. #3, Box 144A, 67661. Tel: 785-543-5577; 543-5367.
Catechesis/Religious Programs—Monica Blair, D.R.E.
Students 102.
Mission—Claudell, Smith Co., St. Francis.

Plainville, Rooks Co., Sacred Heart (1890), Rev. Joseph Popelka.
Res., 206 N. Washington, P.O. Box 100, 67663. Tel: 785-434-4658; Fax: 785-434-2480. [CEM]
School—Tel: 785-434-2157.
Sisters 1; Lay Teachers 6; Students 140.
Catechesis/Religious Programs—Students 101.

Russell, Russell Co., St. Mary's (1886), Rev. Charles Steier.
Res., 28 N. Kansas St., 67665. Tel: 785-483-2871; Fax: 785-483-2871. [CEM]
Catechesis/Religious Programs—Tel: 785-483-2871. Gladys Leiker, D.R.E.
Students 160.

St. Francis, Cheyenne Co., St. Francis (1912) (German), Rev. Beryl Gibson.
Res., 625 S. River St., P.O. Box 1170, 67756. Tel: 785-332-2680.
Catechesis/Religious Programs—Myra Douthit, D.R.E.
Students 38.
Missions—Bird City, Cheyenne Co., St. Joseph's, 203 N. Bird, Bird City, 67731. Tel: 785-734-2287; Beardsley, Rawlins Co., St. John's, Rte. 2, 67756. Tel: 785-626-3946. [JC]

St. Joseph, Cloud Co., St. Joseph's. Closed. For sacramental records contact St. John the Baptist, Clyde.

St. Peter, Graham Co., St. Anthony's (1894) (German). Closed. For inquiries for parish records contact Christ the King, WaKeeney.

Schoenchen, Ellis Co., St. Anthony's (1877). Attended by St. Joseph's, Hays.
Res., 215 W. 13th, P.O. Drawer 1000, Hays, 67601. Tel: 785-625-7356; Fax: 785-625-7394. [CEM]

Seguin, Sheridan Co., St. Martin's (1910). Attended by St. Frances Xavier Cabrini, Hoxie. Religious education twinned with St. Francis Xavier Cabrini, Hoxie, KS.
Mailing Address: P.O. Box 38, Hoxie, 67740. Tel: 785-675-3300; Fax: 785-675-2235. [CEM]

Selden, Sheridan Co., Sacred Heart (1906), Rev. James F. Hoover.
Res., Box 57, 67757. Tel: 785-386-4496; Fax: 785-386-4445. [CEM]
Catechesis/Religious Programs—Students 65.

Sharon Springs, Wallace Co., Holy Ghost (1907), Rev. Francis Stuart, O.S.B.
Res., 403 N. Main St., 67758. Tel: 785-852-4984.
Catechesis/Religious Programs—Shirley Blaesi, D.R.E.
Students 58.
Mission—Wallace, Wallace Co., St. Peter.

Smith Center, Smith Co., St. Mary's (1959). Attended by St. Theresa, Mankato.
403 W. Hwy. 6, Box 263, 66967. Tel: 785-282-6888.
Catechesis/Religious Programs—Mrs. Stacey Rempe, D.R.E.
Students 86.

Solomon, Dickinson Co., Immaculate Conception (1886), Daylene Tracy, Pastoral Assoc. In res., Rev. John Wolesky.
Res., 3599 N. Field Rd., P.O. Box 337, 67480. Tel: 785-655-2221. [CEM]
Catechesis/Religious Programs—Robin Daniels, D.R.E.
Students 67.

Stockton, Rooks Co., St. Thomas (1878), Rev. James P. Grennan.
Res., 722 Main St., 67669. Tel: 785-425-6656. [CEM]
Catechesis/Religious Programs—Cindy Kriley, D.R.E.
Students 81.

Tipton, Mitchell Co., St. Boniface's (1874), Rev. Albert DeSanctis.
Res., Box 87, 67485. Tel: 785-373-4455. [CEM]
High School—Tel: 785-373-5635.
Priests 1; Lay Teachers 6; Students 32.
Catechesis/Religious Programs—Students 93.

Victoria, Ellis Co., St. Fidelis (1876), Rev. Frank X. Grinko, O.F.M.Cap.
Church Office—601 10th St., 67671. Tel: 785-735-2777.
Res., 900 Cathedral Ave., 67671. Tel: 785-735-2777; 735-9456; Fax: 785-735-9455. [CEM]
Catechesis/Religious Programs—Tel: 785-735-9244. D.R.E.: Shirley Brungardt; Yvonne Braun.
Students 222.

Vincent, Ellis Co., St. Boniface (1904) (German-Russian). Attended by St. Fidelis, Victoria. Rev. Frank X. Grinko, O.F.M.Cap.
601 10th St., Victoria, 67671. Tel: 785-735-2777; 735-9456. [CEM]

WaKeeney, Trego Co., Christ the King (1933), Rev. Donald F. Pfannenstiel.
Res., 412 N. Ninth St., 67672. Tel: 785-743-2330. [CEM]
Catechesis/Religious Programs—Tel: 785-743-2339. Verna Flax, D.R.E.
Students 147.

Walker, Ellis Co., St. Ann's (1904) (German-Russian). Attended by St. Fidelis, Victoria.
Mailing Address: 601 10th St., Victoria, 67671. Tel: 785-735-2777. [CEM]
Catechesis/Religious Programs—Twinned with St. Fidelis, Victoria.

Wallace, Wallace Co., St. Peter's (1877). Attended by Holy Ghost Church, Sharon Springs.
Mailing Address: P.O. Box 190, 67761.

Washington, Washington Co., St. Augustine's (1946), Revs. Vincent Thu Laing; Merlin Kieffer.
Res., 410 B St., 66968. Tel: 785-325-2346. [JC]
Catechesis/Religious Programs—Twinned with SS. Peter & Paul, Morrowville, Washington, KS., and Sacred Heart, Greenleaf, Hanover, KS. Donna Baker, Contact Person.
Students 64.

Wilson, Ellsworth Co., St. Wenceslaus (1882) (Slovak), Rev. Jerome Morgan.
Res., P.O. Box 528, 67490. Tel: 785-658-3361; Fax: 785-658-3364. [CEM]
Catechesis/Religious Programs—Tel: 785-658-3474. Mrs. Mary Ellen Stoppel, D.R.E.
Students 60.
Mission—Dorrance, Russell Co., St. Joseph, P.O. Box 528, Wilson 67490.

Zurich, Rooks Co., St. Ann's (1886). Attended by Sacred Heart, Plainville. Rev. Joseph Popelka.
Res., P.O. Box 8, 67676. Fax: 785-434-2480. [CEM]

On Duty Outside the Diocese:
Reverend Fathers—
Dallen, James, W. 818 21st Ave., Spokane, WA 99203
Dlabal, Norbert F., In Mission in Peru, Parroquia San Juan Bautista, Correo Central, Marcona-Nasca, Peru

---

Retired:
Reverend Monsignors—
Girard, Armand, 2150 Westchester, #3, Manhattan, KS 66503
Kruse, Clement, 205 E. 25th St. Terrace, Hays, KS 67601
Lemoine, Vincent P., 1605 W. 80th Dr., Osborne, KS 67473
Sinner, Emil E., 209 24th St., Box 549, Wilson, KS 67490
Wasinger, Alfred J., Nazareth Motherhouse, Box 279, Concordia, KS 66901
Weber, John George, 926 E. Republic, Salina, KS 67401
Reverend Fathers—
Conklin, Christopher J., P.O. Box 454, Concordia, KS 66901
Dion, Maurice B., 214 E. North St., Hanover, KS 66945
Kilian, William T., St. Joseph Church, P.O. Box 68, Damar, KS 67632
Kramer, Carl, 513 E. 19th, Hays, KS 67601
Lahey, John, 124A S. Second, Salina, KS 67401
Mattas, Louis, 410 Jefferson, Abilene, KS 67410
Moeder, August L., P.O. Box 74, 217 Grant, Quinter, KS 67752
Pierce, Larry E., P.O. Box 237, Oakley, KS 67748
Scheetz, Joseph, 510 Easter Ave., Wakeeney, KS 67672
Torrez, Basil, P.O. Box 214, Collyer, KS 67631
Werth, Loren, 1725 Winne Dr., Manhattan, KS 66502

INSTITUTIONS LOCATED IN THE DIOCESE

[A] HIGH SCHOOLS, INTER-PAROCHIAL

SALINA. *Sacred Heart Junior-Senior High School*, 230 E. Cloud, 67401. Tel: 785-827-4422; Fax: 785-827-8648. John Krajicek, Prin. Sisters 1; Lay Teachers 19; Total 243.

[B] HIGH SCHOOLS, PRIVATE

HAYS. *Thomas More Prep-Marian*, 1701 Hall, 67601. Tel: 785-625-6577; Fax: 785-625-3912. Jean Ross, Pres. Legal Title: *Thomas More Prep-Marian High Inc.* Four-year Catholic High School, with college preparatory programs conducted by Capuchin Friars and Sisters of St. Agnes; residency programs for boys and girls; special program for candidates for Priesthood and Religious Life. Capuchin Friars 2; Lay Teachers 29; Students 308.
Endowment Foundation of Thomas More Prep-Marian, Inc. Dennis Bieker, Pres.

[C] HOMES FOR AGED

CONCORDIA. *Mount Joseph Senior Community*, 1110 West 11th St., 66901. Tel: 785-243-1347; Fax: 785-243-1907
For a complete listing, refer to the Special Care Facilities section.

HAYS. *St. John's New Horizons*, 2225 Canterbury, 67601. Tel: 785-628-8742
For a complete listing, refer to the Special Care Facilities section.

MANHATTAN. *St. Joseph Senior Community, Inc.*, 2423 Kimball Ave., 66502. Tel: 785-539-7671; Fax: 785-539-9125.
E-mail: dfrihart@via.christi.org
Web site: www.manhattan-ks.org/sjsc
For a complete listing, refer to the Special Care Facilities section.

VICTORIA. *St. John's Rest Home*, 701 Seventh St., 67671. Tel: 785-735-2208
For a complete listing, refer to the Special Care Facilities section.

[D] MONASTERIES AND RESIDENCES OF PRIESTS AND BROTHERS

HAYS. *St. Joseph's Friary*, P.O. Drawer 1000, 67601. Tel: 785-625-7356; Fax: 785-625-7394. Revs. Michael Scully, O.F.M.Cap.; Michael Suchnicki, O.F.M.Cap.; Earl Befort, O.F.M.Cap. In res. Most Rev. Firmin Schmidt, O.F.M.Cap., (Retired); Revs. Bennett Collucci, O.F.M.Cap.; Paulinus I. Karlin, O.F.M.Cap.

VICTORIA. *St. Fidelis Friary*, 67671. Tel: 785-735-9456; Fax: 785-735-9455. Revs. Christian Fey, O.F.M.Cap.; Felix Petrovsky, O.F.M.Cap.; Berard Tomassetti, O.F.M.Cap.; Frank X. Grinko, O.F.M.Cap., Pastor & Guardian; Maris Goetz, O.F.M.Cap.; Bro. Augustine Rohde, O.F.M.Cap. Total in Residence 7.

[E] CONVENTS AND RESIDENCES FOR SISTERS

SALINA. *Medaille Center*, 148 N. Oakdale St., 67401. Tel: 785-827-3685.
E-mail: medaille@midusa.net
Sisters of St. Joseph. Sr. Therese Richstatter, C.S.J., Coord. Sisters 18.

CONCORDIA. *Nazareth Convent & Academy Coporation Sisters of St. Joseph of Concordia*, Administration Offices, 215 Court St., P.O. Box 279, 66901. Tel: 785-243-2149; Fax: 785-243-4741.
E-mail: csjcenter@dustdevil.com
Web site: www.csj.kansas.org
Sr. Patricia McLennon, C.S.J., Pres., Nazareth Motherhouse for the Sisters of St. Joseph; Rev. Curtis E. Van Del, S.J., Chap. Professed Sisters 219; Postulants 1; Novices 2; In Community 222.
Saint Joseph Foundation for Apostolic and Charitable Purposes. Tel: 785-243-2149; Fax: 785-243-4741.

[F] RETREAT CENTERS

CONCORDIA. *Manna House of Prayer*, 323 E. Fifth St., Box 675, 66901. Tel: 785-243-4428.
E-mail: mannahse@dustdevil.com
Web site: www.mannahouse.org
Sr. Bette Suther, C.S.J., Admin. Total Staff 10; Total in Residence 6.

VICTORIA. *Capuchin Center for Spiritual Life*, 900 Cathedral Ave., 67671. Tel: 913-735-9393; Fax: 913-735-9455.
E-mail: ccsl@ruraltel.net

[G] CAMPUS MINISTRY

HAYS. *Comeau Catholic Campus Center at Fort Hays State University*, Office: 506 W. Sixth, 67601. Tel: 785-625-7396.
E-mail: comeauccc@ruraltel.net
Rev. Fred Gatschet, Chap. Total Staff 2.

MANHATTAN. *St. Isidore's Catholic Student Center*. Kansas State University. 711 Denison, 66502. Tel: 785-539-7496.
E-mail: stisidor@flinthills.com
Web site: www.flinthills.com/~st.isidor
In res. Rev. Keith Weber, Chap. Total Staff 4; Total in Residence 1.

[H] MISCELLANEOUS

SALINA. *Marymount Memorial Educational Trust Fund*, P.O. Box 980, 67402-0980. Tel: 785-827-8746; Fax: 785-827-6133.
E-mail: chancery@midusa.net
Most Rev. George K. Fitzsimons, D.D., Trustee.

Sacred Heart Junior-Senior School Endowment Fund, P.O. Box 6318, 67401. Tel: 785-825-4011.
E-mail: heart@sacredheartknights.org
Web site: www.sacredheartknights.org

Salina Catholic Diocese Education Endowment, Inc., 103 N. Ninth St., P.O. Box 980, 67402-0980. Tel: 785-827-8746; Fax: 785-827-6133.
E-mail: chancery@midusa.net

Salina Catholic Diocese Gift & Annuity Fund, Inc., 103 N. Ninth St., P.O. Box 980, 67402-0980. Tel: 785-827-8746; Fax: 785-827-6133.
E-mail: chancery@midusa.net

Salina Catholic Diocese Seminary Burses, Inc., 103 N. Ninth St., P.O. Box 980, 67402-0980. Tel: 785-827-8746; Fax: 785-827-6133.
E-mail: chancery@midusa.net

Salina Diocesan Clergy Health and Retirement Association, Inc., Diocese of Salina, P.O. Box 980, 67402-0980. Tel: 785-827-8746; Fax: 785-827-6133. Most Rev. George K. Fitzsimons, Pres.

RELIGIOUS INSTITUTES OF MEN REPRESENTED IN THE DIOCESE

For further details refer to the corresponding bracketed number in the Religious Institutes of Men or Women section.

[0470]—*The Capuchin Friars.* (Province of Mid-America).—O.F.M.Cap.

[]—*Jesuits.* (Missouri Prov. of Jesuits. St. Louis, MO).—S.J.

[0200]—*Monks of St. Benedict.* (Conception, MO).—O.S.B.

[1060]—*Society of the Precious Blood.* (Kansas City Prov.).—C.PP.S.

RELIGIOUS INSTITUTES OF WOMEN REPRESENTED IN THE DIOCESE

[3710]—*Congregation of the Sisters of Saint Agnes.*—C.S.A.

[1070-24]—*Dominican Sisters.*—O.P.

[]—*Missionary Sisters of the Holy Spirit & the Holy Family.*

[3830-15]—*Sisters of St. Joseph.*—C.S.J.

NECROLOGY

† Dwyer, Albert, Junction City, KS St. Francis Xavier. —Died Feb. 29, 2000.

† Landoll, Rev. Msgr. Gilbert J., Solomon, KS Immaculate Conception. —Died Sept. 1, 2000.

Diocese of Salt Lake City

(Dioecesis Civitatis Lacus Salsi)

Most Reverend

GEORGE H. NIEDERAUER, D.D., PH.D.

Bishop of Salt Lake City; ordained April 30, 1962; appointed Bishop of Salt Lake City November 3, 1994; ordained January 25, 1995. *Office: 27 C St., Salt Lake City, UT, 84103-2397.* Tel.: 801-328-8641, Ext. 304; Fax: 801-328-0324.

Diocesan Offices and Organizations: 27 C St., Salt Lake City, UT, 84103-2397. Tel.: 801-328-8641; Fax: 801-328-9680.

Web site address: www.utahcatholicdiocese.org

E-mail address: dioslc@xmission.com

ESTABLISHED AS A VICARIATE-APOSTOLIC ON NOV. 23, 1886.

ERECTED A DIOCESE ON JANUARY 27, 1891.

Square Miles 84,990.

Originally comprised all Utah and the Counties of Eureka, Lander, Lincoln, White Pine, Nye, Elko and Clark in the State of Nevada. By Apostolic Constitution dated March 27, 1931, the Nevada section was separated from the Salt Lake Diocese and incorporated in the Reno Diocese. The name was changed to Diocese of Salt Lake City on March 31, 1951.

Comprises the State of Utah.

Patron of the Diocese of Salt Lake City: St. Mary Magdalene.

For legal titles of parishes and diocesan institutions, consult the Chancery Office.

STATISTICAL OVERVIEW

Personnel	
Bishop	1
Retired Abbots	1
Priests: Diocesan Active in Diocese	43
Priests: Active Outside Diocese	5
Priests: Diocesan in Foreign Missions	1
Priests: Retired, Sick or Absent	8
Number of Diocesan Priests	57
Religious Priests in Diocese	27
Extern Priests in Diocese	7
Ordinations:	
Diocesan Priests	2
Transitional Deacons	2
Permanent Deacons in Diocese	39
Total Brothers	12
Total Sisters	52
Parishes	
Parishes	47
With Resident Pastor:	
Resident Diocesan Priests	35
Resident Religious Priests	8
Without Resident Pastor:	
Administered by Priests	3
Administered by Lay People	1
Missions	15
New Parishes Created	3
Professional Ministry Personnel:	
Sisters	10
Lay Ministers	35
Welfare	
Homes for the Aged	1
Total Assisted	750
Day Care and Extended Day Care Centers	9
Total Assisted	387
Special Centers for Social Services	3
Total Assisted	289,191
Educational	
Diocesan Students in Other Seminaries	10
Total Seminarians	10
High Schools, Diocesan and Parish	3
Total Students	1,479
Elementary Schools, Diocesan and Parish	10
Total Students	3,690
Catechesis/Religious Education:	
High School Students	1,507
Elementary Students	6,905
Total Students Under Catholic Instruction	13,591
Teachers in the Diocese:	
Priests	6
Sisters	2
Lay Teachers	310
Vital Statistics	
Receptions into the Church:	
Infant Baptism Totals	3,308
Adult Baptism Totals	439
Received into Full Communion	269
First Communions	2,031
Confirmations	1,162
Marriages:	
Catholic	405
Interfaith	231
Total Marriages	636
Deaths	580
Total Catholic Population	107,000
Total Population	2,130,000

Former Bishops—Rt. Rev. LAWRENCE SCANLAN, D.D., ord. June 24, 1868; appt. Vicar-Apostolic of Utah, Jan. 25, 1887; cons. Titular Bishop of Larandum, June 29, 1887; named first Bishop of Salt Lake, Jan. 30, 1891; died May 10, 1915.—Rt. Rev. JOSEPH S. GLASS, C.M., D.D., LL.D., ord. Aug. 15, 1897; cons. Aug. 24, 1915; died Jan. 26, 1926.—Most Rev. JOHN J. MITTY, D.D., ord. Dec. 22, 1906; cons. Sept. 8, 1926; made Coadjutor Archbishop of San Francisco, cum jure successionis, Feb. 4, 1932; Titular Archbishop of Egina; succeeded to the See, March 5, 1935; died Oct. 15, 1961.—Most Rev. JAMES E. KEARNEY, D.D., ord. Sept. 19, 1908; appt. July 4, 1932; cons. Oct. 28, 1932; appt. Bishop of Rochester, July 31, 1937; installed Nov. 11, 1937; died Jan. 12, 1977.—Most Rev. LEO J. STECK, D.D., ord. June 8, 1924; appt. Auxiliary Bishop of Salt Lake, March 3, 1948; cons. Titular Bishop of Ilium, May 20, 1948; died June 19, 1950.—Most Rev. DUANE G. HUNT, D.D., LL.D., ord. June 27, 1920; appt. Aug. 6, 1937; cons. Oct. 28, 1937; appt. assistant at the Pontifical Throne; appt. May 25, 1946; died March 31, 1960.—Most Rev. JOSEPH LENNOX FEDERAL, D.D., ord. Dec. 8, 1934; appt. Auxiliary Bishop of Salt Lake City, Feb. 5, 1951; cons. April 11, 1951; made Coadjutor Bishop of Salt Lake City, May 8, 1958; succeeded to the See, March 31, 1960; retired April 1980; died Aug. 31, 2000.—Most Rev. WILLIAM KEITH WEIGAND, D.D., ord. May 25, 1963; appt. Sept. 3, 1980; ord. Bishop, Nov. 17, 1980; transferred to the See of Sacramento; installed Jan. 27, 1994.

Diocesan Pastoral Center—27 C. St., Salt Lake City, 84103-2397. Tel: 801-328-8641; Fax: 801-328-9680.

Office of the Bishop—SHIRLEY MARES, Sec. Tel: 801-328-8641, Ext. 304; Fax: 801-328-0324.

Vicar General and Moderator of the Curia—Rev. Msgr. J. TERRENCE FITZGERALD, Ext. 305.

Chancellor—Deacon SILVIO MAYO, Ext. 315.

Vice Chancellor—Rev. LANGES J. SILVA, , Ext. 312.

Diocesan Offices

Apostleship of Prayer—Rev. MATTHEW O. WIXTED, Dir., *15 S. 7th St., Tooele, 84074.* Tel: 435-882-3860.

Archives—BERNICE MOONEY, Dir., Ext. 346. Rev. Msgr. JEROME STOFFEL, Dir., Emeritus.

Campus Ministry—Sr. MARILYN MARK, O.S.B., *484 North 300 E. Basement Apt., Logan, 84321.* Tel: 435-753-7445.

Catholic Community Services—RON PIERRE, Exec. Dir., *2570 W. 1700 S., Salt Lake City, 84104.* Tel: 801-977-9119; Fax: 801-977-8227. FRANK LEONARD, Bd. Pres.

Catholic Foundation of Utah—IRENE C. SWEENEY, Pres. KURT SIMPSON, Exec. Dir., Ext. 306.

Catholic Relief Services—Deacon SILVIO MAYO, Ext. 315.

Catholic Schools Offices—Sr. CATHERINE KAMPHAUS, C.S.C., Supt., Ext. 330. MARY MONTANO, Sec., Ext. 329.

Cemetery—Mount Calvary—JENNINGS H. MEASE, Dir. Tel: 801-355-2476. HARRIET MALLOY, Sec.

Chancery—ALANA LENDVAY, Sec., Ext. 317.

College of Consultors—Rev. Msgr. ROBERT J. BUSSEN; Rev. Msgr. J. TERRENCE FITZGERALD; Rev. Msgr. JOHN J. HEDDERMAN; Rev. Msgr. ROBERT R. SERVATIUS; Rev. Msgr. JOHN J. SULLIVAN; Rev. VICTOR G. BONNELL.

Communications Media Office—Vacant, , Ext. 344. MARY MAYO, Volunteer, Ext. 333.

Deans—Revs. WILLIAM FLEGGE, Wasatch Deanery; JOSEPH W. MORRIS, S.J., Southeastern Deanery; VICTOR G. BONNELL, Northern Deanery; RUDOLPH DAZ, Salt Lake Deanery; MICHAEL WINTERER, Southwestern Deanery.

Development Office—KURT SIMPSON, Dir., Ext. 306.

Diaconate Formation—Sr. JEREMIA JANUSCHKA, O.S.B., Dir., Ext. 327.

Diaconate Training—Deacon OWEN CUMMINGS, Dir., Ext. 320.

Diocesan Development Drive—KURT SIMPSON, Dir., Ext. 306.

Diocesan Lay Volunteers—Deacon OWEN CUMMINGS, Dir., Ext. 320.

Diocesan Office for Persons with Disabilities—Vacant, Ext. 345.

Diocesan Pastoral Council—JESS SHACKELFORD, Pres.

Ecumenical Commission—Revs. VICTOR G. BONNELL; LANGES J. SILVA.

Ethnic Ministry—Sr. M. GEORGITA CUNNINGHAM, R.S.M., Dir., Ext. 335.

Engaged Encounter—RICHARD FERRONE; JOYCE FERRONE. Tel: 801-942-8241.

Family Life-Natural Family Planning—VEOLA MARTINEZ-BURCHETT, Ext. 337.

Finance Council—Most Rev. GEORGE H. NIEDERAUER, Ex Officio; Rev. Msgr. J. TERRENCE FITZGERALD; Rev.

Msgr. JOHN J. HEDDERMAN; Rev. COLIN F. BIRCUMSHAW; MARY KAY GRIFFIN; O. YOGI GILLILAND; MICHAEL JOSEPH; MICHAEL LEE; JILL MORBY; JOE PACHECO; JOAN LOFFREDO; GEORGE BEATON.

Finance Office—JOAN LOFFREDO, Dir., Ext. 309. DEBRA CANDELARIA, Sec., Ext. 310.

Government Liaison—DEE ROWLAND, Ext. 336.

Hispanic Ministry—MISAEL MAYORGA, Ext. 338. MARIA-CRUZ GRAY, Sec., Ext. 361.

Holy Childhood Association—Deacon SILVIO MAYO, Dir., Ext. 315.

Lay Ministries—Deacon OWEN CUMMINGS, Ext. 320.

Liturgy Office—MAXINE KAISER, Ext. 321. LYNDE HOOPES, Sec., Ext. 322.

Liturgical Commission—Rev. COLIN F. BIRCUMSHAW, Chm. Tel: 801-399-5627.

Marriage Encounter—GARY IVERSON; MARY IVERSON. Tel: 801-546-9943.

Ministry to Correctional Institutions—Rev. JAMES E. BLAINE, Dir., *P.O. Box 142, American Fork, 84003.* Tel: 801-756-7771. Rev. THOMAS J. KAISER. Tel: 801-272-9216. Rev. FRANCISCO PIRES. Tel: 435-896-5539. Deacon OTTO JOHANSSON. Tel: 801-328-1112. Deacon MICK SPENCER. Tel: 801-968-2369. Rev. REYES G. RODRIGUEZ. Tel: 801-486-4231.

Ministry to Priests Team—Clergy Continuing Education, Rev. WILLIAM H. FLEGGE, Dir., *172 North 500 West, Provo, 84601.* Tel: 801-374-5001. Team: Revs. JOSEPH ROY, S.S.S.; DAVID BITTMENN; ANDRZEJ SKRZYPIEC.

Newspaper—"Intermountain Catholic", BARBARA S. LEE, Editor, Ext. 340. Vacant, Staff Writer, Ext. 342. CRIS PAULSEN, Business Mgr., Ext. 339.

Peace and Justice Commission—DEE ROWLAND, Dir., Ext. 336.

People's Eucharistic League—Blessed Sacrament Fathers.

Presbyteral Council—Revs. JOSEPH M. MAYO, Pres. ANDREW SKRZPIEC, Vice Pres. KENNETH VIALPANDO, Sec.

Priests' Mutual Benefit Society (Retirement)—Most Rev. GEORGE H. NIEDERAUER, Chm. Ex Officio; Bd. of Dirs.: Rev. Msgr. J. TERRENCE FITZGERALD, Vice Chm.; Rev. Msgr. JOHN J. HEDDERMAN, Sec. & Treas.; Rev. Msgr. JOHN J. SULLIVAN; Revs. JOSEPH M. MAYO; DONALD E. HOPE; COLIN F. BIRCUMSHAW.

Priests' Personnel Board—Most Rev. GEORGE H. NIEDERAUER; Rev. Msgr. JOHN J. HEDDERMAN; Rev. Msgr. J. TERRENCE FITZGERALD; Revs. JOSEPH MAYO; WILLIAM WHEATON; DONALD E. HOPE; EUGENIO YARCE.

Real Estate Office—RICHARD SALVITTI, Ext. 360.

Religious Education—DANIEL JOHN, Dir., Ext. 326.

Retreat House—Sr. DANILE KNIGHT, O.S.B., Dir., *1794 Lake St., Ogden, 84401.* Tel: 801-392-9231.

Retrouvaille—MIKE BEDARD; SUE BEDARD. Tel: 800-470-2230.

Sisters' Council—Executive Team: Sr. JEREMIA JANUSCHKA, O.S.B.; Sr. M. GEORGITA CUNNINGHAM, R.S.M.; Sr. CATHERINE KAMPHAUS, C.S.C.; Sr. LINDA WILMER, D.C.; Sr. ROSE FRANCES GILMORE, O.L.V.M.

Society for the Propagation of the Faith—Deacon SILVIO MAYO, Dir., Ext. 315.

Pastoral Operations—MICHAEL LEE, Dir., Ext. 364.

Special Needs Program Scholarship Assistance—Sr. STELLA MARIE ZAHNER, D.C., Ext. 334.

Spirituality Center—Sr. BRIDGET CLARE MCKEEVER, S.S.L., Ph.D., Dir., *2570 West 1700 South, Salt Lake City, Utah, 84104.* Tel: 801-975-7440.

Tribunal—

Judicial Vicar—Rev. Msgr. JOHN J. HEDDERMAN, J.C.L., Ext. 318.

Secretary & Notary—VIOLA SMITH, Ext. 316.

Adjutant Judicial Vicars—Rev. ROBERT T. MORIARTY, , Ext. 319. Rev. GERALD P. LYNCH. Tel: 801-596-7233. Rev. LANGES SILVA, Ext. 312.

Promoter of Justice—Rev. COLIN F. BIRCUMSHAW.

Defenders of the Bond—Rev. Msgr. ROBERT R. SERVATIUS; Rev. Msgr. JOHN J. SULLIVAN; Revs. J. TERENCE MOORE; JOSEPH M. MAYO.

Judges—Rev. Msgr. JOHN J. HEDDERMAN; Revs. GERALD P. LYNCH; ROBERT T. MORIARTY; WALTER RIENDEAU, S.S.S.; LANGES SILVA.

Vocation Office—Rev. WILLIAM WHEATON, Dir., Ext. 324.

Youth and Young Adult Ministry—MARY FASIG, Dir., Ext. 313.

CLERGY, PARISHES, MISSIONS AND PAROCHIAL SCHOOLS

SALT LAKE CITY (Salt Lake County)

1—CATHEDRAL OF THE MADELEINE (1866), Very Rev. Joseph M. Mayo, Rector; Rev. Patrick H. Elliott; Deacons Owen Cummings; Silvio Mayo. In res., Rev. Langes J. Silva.
Res., 331 E. S. Temple St., 84111. Tel: 801-328-8941; Fax: 801-364-6504.
School—Madeleine Choir School, Tel: 801-323-9850; Fax: 801-323-0581. Betsy Hunt, Prin.
Lay Teachers 19; Students 110.
Catechesis/Religious Programs—Tel: 801-328-1241; Fax: 801-364-6504.
Students 59.

2—OUR LADY OF GUADALUPE (1944) (Hispanic), Rev. Kenneth L. Vialpando; Deacons Hector Mota; Mario Rodriguez.
Res., 715 W. 300 N., 84116. Tel: 801-364-2019.
Catechesis/Religious Programs—Tel: 801-596-2469.
Students 255.

3—OUR LADY OF LOURDES (1913), Rev. John E. Norman.
Res., 1085 E. 700 S. St., 84102. Tel: 801-322-3330; Fax: 801-363-6007. [CEM]
School—1065 E. 700 S. St., 84102. Tel: 801-364-5624; Fax: 801-364-0925. Cathy Moore, Prin.
Lay Teachers 13; Students 264.
Catechesis/Religious Programs—Tel: 801-322-3330; Fax: 801-363-6007.
Students 264.

4—OUR LADY OF PERPETUAL HELP (1994) (Vietnamese). (Vietnamese Catholic Community and Center). Rev. Thuy Dang Ha.
Mailing Address: P.O. Box 18306, 84118-0306. Tel: 801-968-8981.
Church and Res.: 5415 S. 4360 W., Kearns, 84118. Tel: 801-968-8981.
Catechesis/Religious Programs—Students 114.

5—SACRED HEART (1917) (Hispanic), Rev. Hernando Diaz; Deacon Fernando Godina.
Res., 948 S. 2nd East St., 84111. Tel: 801-363-8632; Fax: 801-363-1539.
Catechesis/Religious Programs—174 E. 900 S., 84111.
Students 7.

6—ST. AMBROSE (1948), Rev. Msgr. John J. Hedderman; Rev. David J. Bittmenn.
Res., 2315 Redondo Ave., 84108. Tel: 801-485-5610; 484-3642.
School—J. E. Cosgriff Memorial School, 2335 Redondo Ave., 84108. Tel: 801-486-3197; Fax: 801-484-8270. Mrs. Judith Puhr, Prin.
Lay Teachers 19; Students 305.
Catechesis/Religious Programs—Tel: 801-485-9324; Fax: 801-484-1065.
Students 242.

7—ST. ANN (1917), Rev. Msgr. John J. Sullivan; Rev. Robert Moriarty; Deacon Mansueto Flaim. In res., Rev. Reyes G. Rodriguez.
Res., 2119 S. 400 E., 84115. Tel: 801-487-1000.
School—430 E. 2100 S., 84105. Tel: 801-486-0741; Fax: 801-486-0742. Kathleen Hood, Prin.
Lay Teachers 18; Students 350.
Catechesis/Religious Programs—Tel: 801-261-5943.
Students 125.

8—ST. CATHERINE OF SIENA (1981), Revs. Denis Reilly, O.P.; Bartholomew Hutcherson, O.P.
Res., 170 S. University, 84102. Tel: 801-359-6066; Fax: 801-359-4547.
Catechesis/Religious Programs—Students 140.

9—ST. PATRICK'S (1892) (Hispanic-Tongan-Korean), Rev. Gerald P. Lynch; Deacons Otto Johansson; Sefo Manu; Dan Herron.
Res., 1058 W. 400 S., 84104-1261. Tel: 801-596-7233; Fax: 801-363-3743.
Catechesis/Religious Programs—Tel: 801-596-7255. Mary A. Hutchings, D.R.E.
Students 94.

10—ST. THOMAS MORE (1981), Rev. James Semple; Deacon Steve Kirts.
Res. & Parish Center: 3015 E. Creek Rd., Sandy, 84093-6575. Tel: 801-942-5285 (Office); 942-7678 (Rectory); Fax: 801-942-5287.
Catechesis/Religious Programs—Tel: 801-942-5285.
Students 288.

11—ST. VINCENT DE PAUL (1925), Rev. George F. Davich. In res., Rev. Thomas J. Kaiser.
Res., 1375 E. Spring Ln., 84117. Tel: 801-272-9216; Fax: 801-273-1156.
School—(Grades PreK-8) 1385 E. Spring Ln., 84117. Tel: 801-277-6702; Fax: 801-424-0450. Mark Longe, Prin.
Lay Teachers 21; Students 333.
Catechesis/Religious Programs—Tel: 801-272-2132.
Students 220.

SUBURBAN SALT LAKE CITY

1—IMMACULATE CONCEPTION, Salt Lake Co., (1890). Unassigned.
Res., P.O. Box 151, Copperton, Bingham Canyon, 84006. Tel: 801-569-2706.
Catechesis/Religious Programs—Students 70.

2—ST. FRANCIS XAVIER, Salt Lake Co., (1955), Revs. William F. Wheaton; Francisco Gomez.
Res., P.O. Box 18631, 84118. Tel: 801-968-2123; Fax: 801-966-1639.
School—See separate listing under Elementary Schools, Regional in the Diocese. Fax: 801-966-1369.
Catechesis/Religious Programs—Tel: 801-968-2123, Ext. 413.
Students 550.

3—OUR LADY OF LOURDES, Salt Lake Co., (1916) (English), Rev. Andrzej Skrzypiec (Poland); Deacon Robert Carranza.
Res., P.O. Box 38, 84044. Tel: 801-250-6349; Fax: 801-250-3860. [CEM]
Catechesis/Religious Programs—8585 W. 3010 S., 84044. Tel: 801-250-6052.
Students 145.

4—ST. THERESE OF THE CHILD JESUS, Salt Lake Co., (1925), Revs. Stanislaw Herba; Javier G. Virgen; Deacons Stanley Stott; Rubel Salaz.
Office: 7832 S. Allen St., 84047. Tel: 801-255-3721; Fax: 801-256-9692.
Res., 7860 S. Allen St., 84047. Tel: 801-255-0340.
Catechesis/Religious Programs—Tel: 801-561-2495.
Students 225.

5—ST. JUDE, Salt Lake Co., (1975) (Maronite Rite), Rev. Gebran Bou-Merhi.
Res., 4893 Wasatch St., 84107. Tel: 801-268-2820. [CEM]
Catechesis/Religious Programs—Students 10.

6—BLESSED SACRAMENT, Salt Lake Co., (1972), Rev. Msgr. Robert R. Servatius; Rev. James A. Janda; Deacon Russell Langner.
Res., 9757 S. 1700 E., 84092. Tel: 801-571-5517 (Office); 576-1644 (Rectory); Fax: 801-571-2071.
School—1745 E. 9800 S., 84092. Tel: 801-572-5311; Fax: 801-572-0251. Mr. James Markosian, Prin.
Lay Teachers 24; Students 314.
Catechesis/Religious Programs—1745 E. 9800 S., 84092. Tel: 801-571-2071.
Students 223.
Station—Alta, Our Lady of the Snows.

7—ST. MARTIN DE PORRES, Salt Lake Co., (1982), Rev. Michael P. Noreika, S.S.S.; Bro. David Phelan, S.S.S.; Deacon Noel W. Spencer, Jr. In res., Rev. Joe Roy, S.S.S.
Mailing Address: 4976 Valois Cir., 84118. Tel: 801-969-8857; Fax: 801-966-9675.
Church—4914 S. 2200 W., 84118. Tel: 801-968-2369.
Catechesis/Religious Programs—Students 115.

8—ST. JOSEPH THE WORKER, Salt Lake Co., (1969), Rev. Patrick F. Carley; Deacon Mel Sanchez.
Res., P.O. Box 98, 84084. Tel: 801-255-8902; Fax: 801-255-5003.
Catechesis/Religious Programs—Tel: 801-561-4062.
Students 248.

9—SS. PETER AND PAUL, Salt Lake Co., (1972), Rev. Francis B. Pellegrino; Deacon Rick Huffman.
Res., P.O. Box 70308, 84170. Tel: 801-966-5111; 966-5119.
Catechesis/Religious Programs—Tel: 801-969-7116; Fax: 801-966-2114.
Students 170.

OUTSIDE SALT LAKE CITY

American Fork, Utah Co., St. Peter's (1969), Rev. James E. Blaine; Deacon Kevin Crowell.
Res., 622 N. 600 East, 84003. Tel: 801-756-7771; Fax: 801-756-7768.
Catechesis/Religious Programs—Tel: 801-756-2747.
Students 98.

Bountiful, Davis Co., St. Olaf (1944), Rev. Rudolph A. Daz; Deacon Thomas J. Stewart.
Res., 276 E. 1700 South, 84010. Tel: 801-295-3621; Fax: 801-295-8261.
School—1793 S. Orchard Dr., 84010. Tel: 801-295-5341; Fax: 801-295-5915.
Lay Teachers 13; Students 246.
Catechesis/Religious Programs—Students 126.

Brigham City, Box Elder Co., St. Henry (1950), Revs. F. Warren Schoeppe, S.J.; Jesus Montoya (Colombia); Deacons Bob Bambrick; Dick Werling.
Res., P.O. Box 872, 84302. Tel: 435-723-2941.
Catechesis/Religious Programs—Tel: 801-723-1215.
Students 150.
Mission—Tremonton, Box Elder Co., Santa Ana, 760 W. 600 N., Tremonton, 84337.

Cedar City, Iron Co., Christ the King (1934), Rev. Michael J. Winterer.
Res., 61 N. 100 West, P.O. Box 626, 84721. Tel: 435-586-8298; Fax: 435-865-5960.
Catechesis/Religious Programs—Students 122.
Missions—Panguitch, Garfield Co., St. Gertrude, S. Main St., Panguitch, 84759.; Escalalute, Wayne Co., St. Sylvester.
Stations—St. Dominic, Bryce Canyon.; Beryl Junction.; Brian Head. (Winter).

Draper, Salt Lake Co., St. John the Baptist (1999), Rev. Terence M. Moore.
300 E. 11800 S., 84020. Tel: 801-984-7101; Fax: 801-984-7122.
School—Tel: 801-984-7115. Sr. Karla McKinnie, C.S.C., Prin.
Priests 1; Sisters 2; Lay Teachers 40; Students 914.
Catechesis/Religious Programs—Students 340.

East Carbon, Carbon Co., Good Shepherd (1947), Rev. Joseph W. Morris, S.J.
Res., P.O. Box 99, 84520. Tel: 435-888-3306.
Catechesis/Religious Programs—Students 25.
Mission—Green River, Emery Co., St. Michael, 140 N. Long St., Green River, 84525. Tel: 801-564-3320.

Eureka, Juab Co., St. Patrick's (1885) (Irish), Rev. Walter A. Riendeau, S.S.S.
Res., P.O. Box 387, Payson, 84651. Tel: 801-465-4782.

Helper, Carbon Co., St. Anthony's (1944), Rev. Erik J. Richtsteig.
Res., 5 S. Main, 84526. Tel: 435-472-5661; Fax: 435-472-3235. [JC]
Catechesis/Religious Programs—Students 110.

Huntsville, Weber Co., St. Florence Catholic Community (1990), Rev. Charles T. Cummins, Admin.
Mailing Address: 514-24th St., Ogden, 84401-1594. Tel: 801-399-9531.
Church: Tel: 801-745-5673.
Catechesis/Religious Programs—Students 47.

Kanab, Kane Co., St. Christopher's (1953), Rev. Wayne Epperly, C.S.Sp., Admin.
Res., 39 W. 200 S., 84741. Tel: 801-644-5652; Fax: 801-644-3413.
Catechesis/Religious Programs—Students 33.
Station—North Rim, Grand Canyon.

Layton, Davis Co., St. Rose of Lima (1948), Revs. Victor G. Bonnell; Reyes G. Rodriquez; Deacons Robert Quintana, (Retired); John Weis.
Mailing Address: 210 South Chapel St., P.O. Box 557, 84041. Tel: 801-544-4269; Fax: 801-593-0808.
Res., 321 Whitesides St., 84041. Tel: 801-546-2541.
Catechesis/Religious Programs—448 N. Constitution Cir., 84041. Tel: 801-544-5425.
Students 330.

Logan, Cache Co., St. Thomas Aquinas (1941), Rev. Clarence J. Sandoval; Sr. Marilyn Mark, O.S.B., Pastoral Assoc.
Res., 795 N. 800 E., 84321. Tel: 435-752-1478; Fax: 435-792-3792.
Catechesis/Religious Programs—Students 159.

Milford, Beaver Co., St. Bridget (1948), Rev. Fawaz Ayoub, Admin.
Res., 210 S. 1st West, P.O. Box 785, 84751. Tel: 435-387-2732.
Catechesis/Religious Programs—Students 20.
Missions—Delta, Millard Co., St. John Bosco, P.O. Box 924, Delta, 84624. Tel: 435-864-3710; Fillmore, Millard Co., Holy Family, 390 N. Main St., Fillmore, 84631.

Moab, Grand Co., St. Pius X (1955), Rev. Joseph S. Rooney, S.J.
Res., 122 W. 400 North, P.O. Box 357, 84532. Tel: 435-259-5211; Fax: 435-259-3984.
Catechesis/Religious Programs—Students 48.
Mission—LaSal, San Juan Co., Sacred Heart, Hwy. 46/Main, 84530. Tel: 435-686-2255.

Monroe, Sevier Co., St. Elizabeth's (1947), Rev. Francisco Pires; Deacon James McElfresh.
Res., 840 Sunset Dr., Richfield, 84701. Tel: 435-896-5539.
Catechesis/Religious Programs—Students 10.
Missions—Torrey, Wayne Co., St. Anthony of the Desert, North on Sandcreek Rd., Torrey, 84775. Tel: 435-425-3319; Ephraim, Sanpete Co., St. Jude, 160 E. Center St., Ephraim, 84627. Tel: 435-283-6242.
Station—Central Utah Correctional Facility, Gunnison, Tel: 801-528-6000; Fax: 801-528-6259. [JC]

Monticello, San Juan Co., St. Joseph (1935) (Spanish), Rev. Joseph S. Rooney, S.J.
Res., P.O. Box 518, 84535. Tel: 435-587-2322. [JC]
Catechesis/Religious Programs—Students 61.
Station—Blanding.

Ogden, Weber Co.,

1—HOLY FAMILY, (1979), Rev. Lawrence P. Sweeney.
Res., P.O. Box 3070, 84409. Tel: 801-479-1112; Fax: 801-479-1126. [JC]
Catechesis/Religious Programs—Students 185.

2—ST. JAMES, (1966), Rev. Donald E. Hope; Deacon Bud J. Wardle.
Res., 495 N. Harrison Blvd., 84404. Tel: 801-782-5393.
Catechesis/Religious Programs—Tel: 801-782-7372; Fax: 801-479-4909.
Students 270.

3—ST. JOSEPH'S, (1875), Revs. Colin F. Bircumshaw; Richard T. Sherman; Charles E. Cummins; Deacons John Conniff; Thomas Buller; Michael Bulson; Tony Lopez.
Res., 514 24th St., 84401. Tel: 801-399-5627; Fax: 801-399-5918.
School—See separate listing under Elementary Schools, Regional located in the Diocese. Tel: 801-393-6051; Fax: 801-393-6086. R. Louise Price, Prin.
Catechesis/Religious Programs—Tel: 801-621-3602.
Students 408.
Mission—Huntsville, Weber Co., St. Florence, 6481 E. Hwy. 39, 84317. Tel: 801-745-5673.

4—ST. MARY'S, (1957), Revs. Martin Rock, S.J.; John Ferguson, S.J.
Res., P.O. Box 9196, 84409. Tel: 801-621-7961; Fax: 801-394-1244.
Catechesis/Religious Programs—Tel: 801-621-2274.
Students 341.

Park City, Summit Co., St. Mary of the Assumption (1881), Revs. Robert J. Bussen; David J. Bittmenn; Deacon Reynaldo Merino.
Res., P.O. Box 669, 84060. Tel: 435-649-9676; Fax: 435-647-9678.
Catechesis/Religious Programs—Tel: 435-649-1447.
Students 355.
Mission—Heber City, Wasatch Co., St. Lawrence, 1st West Center, Heber City, 84032. Tel: 435-654-4035; Fax: 435-654-4035.

Payson, Utah Co., San Andres (1986), Rev. Walter A. Riendeau, S.S.S.
Mailing Address: P.O. Box 387, 84651. Tel: 801-465-4782.
Church—315 E. 100 N., 84651.
Catechesis/Religious Programs—Students 65.
Missions—Nephi, Utah Co., Our Lady of Victory Mission, c/o San Andres, 84651.; Eureka, Utah Co., St. Patrick Parish, c/o San Andres, 84651.

Price, Carbon Co., Notre Dame de Lourdes (1918), Rev. Michael R. Sciumbato.
Res., 160 N. Carbon Ave., 84501. Tel: 435-637-1846; Fax: 435-637-6338. [JC 2]
Catechesis/Religious Programs—Tel: 435-637-1207.
Students 155.
Mission—Huntington, Emery Co., San Rafael, 1716 S. Hwy. 10, Huntington, 84528. Tel: 435-687-2116; Fax: 435-384-3215.

Provo, Utah Co., St. Francis of Assisi (1892), Revs. William Flegge; Gustavo A. Vidal; Deacons Tranquilino Otero; Andres Montoya.
Res., 65 E. 500 N., Orem, 84057-4030. Tel: 801-221-1307.
Catechesis/Religious Programs—Tel: 801-221-0750, Ext. 16; Fax: 801-221-0759.
Students 337.
Mission—Elberta, Utah Co., San Isidro, 12537 W. Hwy. 6, Elberta, 84626.

Roosevelt, Duchesne Co., St. Helen's (1940) (Native American), Rev. Thomas L. Culleton.
Res., 433 E. 200 North, P.O. Box 415, 84066. Tel: 801-722-2975; Fax: 801-722-0525. [CEM]
Catechesis/Religious Programs—Students 23.
Missions—Duchesne, Duchesne Co., Holy Spirit; Fort Duchesne, Uintah Co., Blessed Kateri Tekakwitha, P.O. Box 533, 84026. Tel: 801-722-4734.

St. George, Washington Co., St. George's (1955), Rev. Wayne Epperley, C.S.Sp.; Deacons John O'Brien; Mark Bourget, Sr. In res., Rev. Henry Planinsek, C.S.Sp.
Mailing Address: P.O. Box 188, 84771. Tel: 435-673-2604; Fax: 435-688-2704.
Res., 165 N. 200 West, 84770. Tel: 435-673-7354.
Catechesis/Religious Programs—Students 140.
Station—Zion National Park. (Lodge). Tel: 435-772-3256.

Tooele, Tooele Co., St. Marguerite's (1910), Revs. Matthew O. Wixted; Eugenio Yarce; Deacons Joseph Cormier, Pastoral Assoc.; James Garcia.
Res., 15 S. 7th St., 84074. Tel: 435-882-3860; Fax: 435-882-3866.
Pre-School—Tel: 801-882-0081. Mrs. Janet Barbiero, Coord.
Catechesis/Religious Programs—Tel: 435-882-0082.
Students 298.

Vernal, Uintah Co., St. James the Greater (1923), Rev. Jan Bednarz.
Res., 138 N. 100 West St., 84078. Tel: 801-789-3016; Fax: 801-789-3016. [JC]
Catechesis/Religious Programs—Tel: 801-789-3034.
Students 160.

Wendover, Tooele Co., San Felipe (2000), Rev. Eugenio Yance.
Res., 606 E. Aria Blvd., P.O. Box 1270, 84083. Fax: 435-665-0368.
Catechesis/Religious Programs—Tel: 801-665-2339; Fax: 801-665-2339.
Students 425.

Chaplains of Public Institutions

SALT LAKE CITY. *County Youth Detention Center*. Deacon Mick Spencer.
Decker Lake Youth Center. Rev. Thomas J. Kaiser.
Oxbow Correctional Facility. Deacon Otto Johansson.
Salt Lake County Jail. Rev. Reyes G. Rodriguez.
Veterans Administration Hospital 500 Foothill Dr., 84113. Tel: 801-581-2121. Rev. Reyes G. Rodriguez; Sr. Julie Maher.

DRAPER. *State Penitentiary*. Rev. James E. Blaine, P.O. Box 142, American Fork, 84003. Tel: 801-756-7771.

GUNNISON. *State Penitentiary*. Rev. Francisco Pires.

On Duty Outside the Diocese:
Reverend Fathers—
Bauer, Rick, Mary Knoll Fathers & Brothers, P.O. Box 867, Daressalam, Tanzania
Curran, Patrick J., 872 Farmington Ave., Hartford, CT 06119
Gaeta, David R., 1225 E. Bennington St., Boston, MA 02128
Govorchin, Vincent, 240 Nice Ln. #203, Newport Beach, CA 92663
Tkach, Norman A., 40958 Cypress Point Dr., Cherry Valley, CA 92223

Retired:
Reverend Monsignors—
Kenny, James T.
Pollock, Robert C.
Stoffel, Jerome C.
Reverend Fathers—
Curnutte, William G.
Fischer, Louis A.
Fogarty, James
Kaiser, Thomas J.
Spellen, Lawrence M.

Permanent Deacons:
Bambrick, Robert W., St. Henry's, Brigham City
Bourget, Mark A., Sr., St. George
Buller, Thomas M., St. Joseph's, Ogden
Bulson, Michael E., St. Joseph's, Ogden
Carranza, Robert, Our Lady of Lourdes, Magna
Conniff, John J., St. Joseph's, Ogden
Cormier, Joe H., St. Marguerite, Tooele
Crowell, Kevin, St. Peters, American Fork
Flaim, Mansueto, St. Ann's, Salt Lake City
Foote, Deane L., (Retired)
Garcia, James D., St. Marguerite's, Tooele
Glodowski, Robert J., On Duty Outside the Diocese
Godina, Fernando L., Sacred Heart, Salt Lake City
Herron, Dan, St. Patrick, Salt Lake City
Huffman, Rick C., St. Peter & Paul, West Valley City
Januszewski, William A., On Duty Outside the Diocese
Johansson, Otto, St. Patrick, Salt Lake City
Johnson, Lynn R., (Unassigned)
Kirts, Steven W., St. Thomas More, Sandy
Langner, Russell R., Blessed Sacrament, Sandy
Lopez, Anthony J., St. Joseph, Ogden
Manu, Sefo A., St. Patrick, Salt Lake City
Mayo, Silvio, Chancellor, Cathedral, Salt Lake
McElfresh, James L., St. Elizabeth, Richfield
Merino, Reynaldo Q., St. Mary of the Assumption, Park City
Montoya, Andres C., (Unassigned)
Mota, Hector, Our Lady of Guadalupe, Salt Lake City
O'Brien, John P., St. George, St. George
Otero, Tranquilino, St. Francis Assisi, Provo
Palm, Lowell L., Our Lady of Lourdes, Salt Lake City
Quintana, Robert J., (Retired)
Reed, Joseph W., On Duty Outside the Diocese
Rodriguez, Mario A., Our Lady of Guadalupe, Salt Lake City
Salaz, Rubel J., St. Therese, Midvale
Sanchez, Mel J., St. Joseph the Worker, West Jordan
Sliger, Douglas R., Hill Air Force Base, Ogden
Spencer, Noel W., St. Martin de Porres, Taylorsville

Stewart, Thomas J., St. Joseph, Ogden
Stott, Stanley L., St. Therese, Midvale
Toro, German A., On Duty Outside the Diocese
Wardle, Bud J., St. James, Ogden
Weis, John C., St. Rose of Lima, Layton
Werling, Richard E., St. Henry, Brigham City

INSTITUTIONS LOCATED IN THE DIOCESE

[A] SEMINARIES, RELIGIOUS, OR SCHOLASTICATES

HUNTSVILLE. *Abbey of Our Lady of the Holy Trinity*, 1250 S. 9500 E., 84317. Tel: 801-745-3784; Fax: 801-745-6430.
E-mail: hta@xmission.com
Web site: www.xmission.com/~hta
Revs. Alan Hohl, O.C.S.O., Supr. and Dir. of Studies; Charles J. Cummini, O.C.S.O., Novice Master. Priests 11; Brothers 10; Oblates 1.

[B] HIGH SCHOOLS, DIOCESAN

SALT LAKE CITY. *Judge Memorial Catholic High School*, 650 S. 11th E., 84102. Tel: 801-363-8895; Fax: 801-521-3920.
E-mail: jmchs5@softsolutions.com
Web site: www.judgememorial.com
Day School. (Coed). Rev. John Norman, Pres.; Robert Jackson, Prin.; Revs. James P. McHugh, O.S.F.S.; Marc Clifford, O.S.F.S. Priests 3; Lay Teachers 55; Students 871; Total Staff 115.

DRAPER. *Juan Diego Catholic High School*, 300 E. 11800 S., 84020. Tel: 801-984-7600; Fax: 801-984-7601.
E-mail: Dr.GaleyColosimo@SkaggsCatholicCenter.org
Web site: www.skaggscatholiccenter.org
Dr. Gabriel Colosimo, Prin. Priests 3; Sisters 1; Lay Teachers 34.

OGDEN. *St. Joseph Catholic High School*, 1790 Lake St., 84401. Tel: 801-394-1515; Fax: 801-394-6428.
E-mail: stjosephcatholic@home.com
Web site: www.myplanet.net/ourcoine
David A. Lang, Admin. & Prin. Lay Teachers 17; Students 171; Total Staff 24.

[C] ELEMENTARY SCHOOLS, REGIONAL

KEARNS. *St. Francis Xavier Regional School*, 4501 W. 5215 S., 84118. Tel: 801-966-1571; Fax: 801-966-1639.
E-mail: slcxavier@impresso.com
Revs. William F. Wheaton; Francisco Gomez; Nancy Essary, Prin. Lay Teachers 9; Students 266.

OGDEN. *St. Joseph Regional School*. (Grades PreK-8), 2980 Quincy Ave., 84403. Tel: 801-393-6051; Fax: 801-393-6086. Revs. Colin F. Bircumshaw; Richard Sherman; R. Louise Price, Prin. Lay Teachers 28; Students 545.

[D] FOUNDATIONS

SALT LAKE CITY. *Catholic Foundation of Utah*, 27 C St., 84103. Tel: 801-328-8641; Fax: 801-328-9680.
E-mail: Kurt.Simpson.mail.dioslc.org
Web site: www.utahcatholicdiocese.org
Kurt Simpson, Exec. Dir.; Irene C. Sweeney, Pres.

OGDEN. *St. Benedict's Foundation*, 6000 S., 1075 E., Ste. 100, 84405-4945. Tel: 801-479-1800; Fax: 801-479-4997.
E-mail: stbenedictsfdn@dellnet.com
Estelle G. Dahlkemper, Exec. Dir.; Steve Spurlock, Foundation Bd. Chm.

[E] HOMES FOR AGED

SALT LAKE CITY. *Christus Halth Utah d.b.a. Christus St. Joseph Villa*, 451 Bishop Federal Ave., 84115. Tel: 801-487-7557; Fax: 801-487-1112.
Web site: www.stjosephvilla.com
For a complete listing, refer to the Special Care Facilities section.
CHRISTUS St. Joseph Villa, 451 Bishop Federal Ln., 84115-2295. Tel: 801-487-7557; Fax: 801-487-1112.
Web site: www.stjosephvilla.com
For a complete listing, refer to the Special Care Facilities section.

[F] MONASTERIES AND RESIDENCES OF PRIESTS AND BROTHERS

SALT LAKE CITY. *Oblate House*, 554 E St., 84103. Tel: 801-359-8201.
E-mail: jmosfs@softsolutions.com
Oblates of St. Francis de Sales. Rev. James P. McHugh, O.S.F.S., Contact Person. Total in Residence 4.

HUNTSVILLE. *Abbey of Our Lady of the Holy Trinity of the Order of Cistercians*, 1250 S. 9500 E., 84317. Tel: 801-745-3784; Fax: 801-745-6430.
E-mail: hta@xmission.com
Web site: www.xmission.com/~hta
Revs. Alan Hohl, O.C.S.O., Supr. Ad Nutum; David Altman, O.C.S.O.; Casimir Bernas, O.C.S.O.; Patrick Boyle, O.C.S.O.; Charles Cummings, O.C.S.O., Novice Master; Malachy Flaherty, O.C.S.O.; Bartholomew Gottemoller, O.C.S.O.; Brendan Hanratty, O.C.S.O.; Joseph Schroer, O.C.S.O.; Baldwin Shea, O.C.S.O.; Emmanuel Spillane, O.C.S.O. Priests 11; Brothers 10; Oblates 1; Total in Community 22.
Legal Title: *Abbey of Our Lady of the Holy Trinity of the Order of Cistercians of the Strict Observance.*
Residing Elsewhere: Revs. Cletus Dollinger, O.C.S.O.; Gregory Santos, O.C.S.O.; Leander Dosch, O.C.S.O.

[G] CONVENTS, MONASTERIES AND RESIDENCES FOR SISTERS

SALT LAKE CITY.
Carmel of the Immaculate Heart of Mary Monastery, 5714 Holladay Blvd., 84121. Tel: 801-277-6075; Fax: 801-277-4263.
E-mail: carmelslc@worldnet.att.net
Web site: www.carmelslc.org
Mother Margaret Mary Miller, O.C.D., Prioress. Professed Cloistered Sisters 6; Professed Out-Sisters 1.
Our Lady of Lourdes Convent, 675 S. 1100 E., 84102. Tel: 801-583-1204. Sisters of the Holy Cross 4.
St. Joseph Villa Convent, 451 Bishop Federal Ln., 84115-2295. Tel: 801-487-7557, Ext. 3064. Congregation of Sisters of Charity of the Incarnate Word 5.
St. Vincent de Paul Convent, 1385 E. Spring Ln., 84117-6797. Tel: 801-277-7890. Sisters of the Holy Family 1; Sisters of the Holy Cross 2.

DRAPER. *Sisters of the Holy Cross, Vivian Skaggs Armstrong Convent*, 554 E. 11800 S., 84020. Tel: 801-501-8349; Fax: 801-984-7601. Sisters 3.

HELPER. *St. Anthony Convent*, 30 S. Main St., 84526. Tel: 435-472-5468; Fax: 801-472-5468. Total Assisted 2,000.

MURRAY. *Sisters of the Holy Cross Convent*, 1238 W. Bullion St., 84123. Tel: 801-313-9611. Legal Title: *Sisters of the Holy Cross, Inc.* Sisters 4.

OGDEN. *Mount Benedict Monastery*, 6000 S. 1075 E., 84405-4945. Tel: 801-479-6030; Fax: 801-479-2091.
E-mail: mbmutah@hotmail.com
Sisters of St. Benedict 8. St. Benedict's Convent, 665 S. 1100 E., Salt Lake City, 84102. Tel: 801-582-1042; Fax: 801-328-9680. 484 N. 300 E., Logan, 84321. Tel: 435-753-7445; Fax: 435-792-3792.

WEST JORDAN. *St. Joseph the Worker Convent*, 7405 S. Redwood Rd., 84084. Tel: 801-561-4090.

[H] NEWMAN CENTERS

SALT LAKE CITY. *University of Utah, Newman Center*. (St. Catherine of Siena University Parish), 170 S. University, 84102. Tel: 801-359-6066; Fax: 801-359-4547.
E-mail: uunewman@hotmail.com
Web site: www.newman.utah.edu
Revs. Denis Reilly, O.P.; Bartholomew Hutcherson, O.P. Total Students in Residence 9; Total Staff 5.

EPHRAIM. *St. Jude Catholic Center*, 160 E. Center, 84627. Tel: 435-283-6242. Rev. Francisco Pires, Pastor. Total Staff 1.

LOGAN. *St. Thomas Aquinas, Newman Center*. (Utah State University), 795 N. 800 E., 84321. Tel: 435-752-1478; Fax: 435-792-3792. Rev. Clarence J. Sandoval; Sr. Marilyn Mark, O.S.B., Campus Min. Total in Residence 1; Total Staff 2.

OGDEN. *Weber State University, Newman Center*, 3738 Custer Ave., 84403. Tel: 801-399-9531. Rev. Charles T. Cummins, Dir. Total in Residence 3; Total Staff 1.

PRICE. *College of Eastern Utah, Newman Club*, 454 E. 400 North, 84501. Tel: 801-637-6785.
E-mail: dremom@hotmail.com
Rev. Mike Sciumbato. Total Staff 1.

ST. GEORGE. *Dixie College, Newman Center*. Tel: 435-673-2604; 673-7354; Fax: 435-688-2704.
E-mail: frleo@sginet.com
Mailing Address: St. George Church, P.O. Box 188, 84771. Rev. Wayne Epperley, C.S.S.P., 165 N. 200 W., 84770. Tel: 435-673-7354.

[I] RETREAT HOUSES

OGDEN. *Our Lady of the Mountains*, 1794 Lake St., 84401. Tel: 801-392-9231; Fax: 801-392-9231 (Call First).
E-mail: olmrh@juno.com
Sr. Danile Knight, O.S.B., Dir. Total Staff 4; Total in Residence 1.

[J] CATHOLIC SOCIAL SERVICES

SALT LAKE CITY. *Catholic Community Services*, 2570 W. 1700 S., 84104. Tel: 801-977-9119; Fax: 801-977-8227; 977-9224.
E-mail: rpierre@ccsutah.org
Web site: www.ccsutah.org
Richard Etter, Board Pres.; Ronald L. Pierre, Exec. Dir. Total Assisted 25,224; in addition 143,967 meals were served at the St. Vincent de Paul Center; Total Staff 75.
Northern Utah Office, 622 23rd St., Ogden, 84401. Tel: 801-394-5944; Fax: 801-394-5948. Sharon Downing, Admin. Dir.
Marillac House, 2570 W. 1700 S., 84104. Tel: 801-363-3621; Fax: 801-359-0830. Danielle Winther, Program Dir. Tel: 801-359-0830.
St. Mary's Home For Men, 1206 W. 200 S., Box 941, 84110. Tel: 801-328-1894; Fax: 801-328-1895. Three daily family style meals. 40 beds for homeless, fundless, sober men. Work Obligation, Inc., nonprofit organization, 1972. Robert Doren, C.S.W., Program Dir.
St. Vincent de Paul Center, 437 W. 200 S., 84101. Tel: 801-534-1500; Fax: 801-363-7647. Mr. Robert D. Mayo, Admin. Dir.
Marillac Transitional Housing Services, Inc., 2570 W. 1700 S., 84104. Tel: 801-977-9119, Ext. 222.
Weigand Homeless Day Center, 235 Rio Grande St., 84101. Tel: 801-363-7710; Fax: 801-363-7647. Kathie Caldwell, Program Dir.
Villa Maria, 2570 W. 1700 S., 84104. Home for Single Pregnant Women.
Shelter Plus Housing, 622 23rd St., Ogden, 84401. Tel: 801-359-5944; Fax: 801-394-5948. Sharon Downing, Admin. Dir. Housing for people with AIDS/HIV.
Additional Programs:
Refugee Resettlement and Immigration Services, 2570 W. 1700 S., 84104; Fax: 801-977-9224. Sharon Young, Admin. Dir. Tel: 801-977-9119 Ext. 203.
Family and Counseling Services, 2570 W. 1700 S., 84104. Pam Sanders, Admin. Dir. Tel: 801-977-9119.
Adoption Services, 2570 W. 1700 S., 84104. Laura Crosetti, Admin. Dir. Tel: 801-977-9119.
Holy Cross Ministries, 2570 W. 1700 S., 84102. Tel: 801-908-0293; Fax: 801-908-8854.
E-mail: suz@ccsutah.org
Sr. Suzanne Brennan, C.S.C. Outreach Program, Literacy Programs, Seniors, Children, Women. Total Staff 32; Total Annually Assisted 12,000.

RELIGIOUS INSTITUTES OF MEN REPRESENTED IN THE DIOCESE

For further details refer to the corresponding bracketed number in the Religious Institutes of Men or Women section.

[0220]—*Congregation of the Blessed Sacrament.*—S.S.S.
[0650]—*Holy Ghost Fathers.*—C.S.Sp.
[0690]—*Jesuit Fathers.* (California Prov.).—S.J.
[0920]—*Oblates of St. Francis de Sales.*—O.S.F.S.
[0350]—*Order of Cistercians of the Strict Observance (Trappists).*—O.C.S.O.
[0430]—*Order of Preachers (Dominicans).* (Western Province).—O.P.
[1060]—*Society of the Precious Blood.*—C.PP.S.

RELIGIOUS INSTITUTES OF WOMEN REPRESENTED IN THE DIOCESE

[2575] —*Sisters of Mercy of the America's* —R.S.M.
[0230]—*Benedictine Sisters of Pontifical Jurisdiction.*—O.S.B.
[0470]—*Congregation of the Sisters of Charity of the Incarnate Word, Houston, Texas.*—C.C.V.I.
[3935]—*The Congregation of the Sisters of St. Louis, Juilly-Monaghan.*—S.S.L.
[3935]—*The Congregation of the Sisters of St. Louis, Juilly-Monaghan.* (California Region).—S.S.L.
[1920]—*Congregation of the Sisters of the Holy Cross.*—C.S.C.
[0760]—*Daughters of Charity of St. Vincent de Paul.* (Province of the West).—D.C.
[0760]—*Daughters of Charity of St. Vincent De Paul.*—D.C.
[0420]—*Discalced Carmelite Nuns.*—O.C.D.
[1190]—*Franciscan Sisters of the Atonement.*—S.A.
[2575]—*Institute of the Sisters of Mercy of the Americas.*—R.S.M.
[3130]—*Our Lady of Victory Missionary Sisters.*—O.L.V.M.
[]—*Sisters for Christian Community.*—S.F.C.C.
[1960]—*Sisters of the Holy Family.*—S.H.F.

DIOCESAN CEMETERIES

SALT LAKE CITY. *Mount Calvary Catholic*, Office, 275 U St., 84103. Tel: 801-355-2476. Mr. Jennings H. Mease, Dir.; Harriet Malloy, Sec.

NECROLOGY

† Federal, Most Rev. Joseph Lennox, (Retired). —Died Aug. 31, 2000.

Diocese of San Angelo

(Dioecesis Angeliana)

Most Reverend

MICHAEL D. PFEIFER, O.M.I.

Bishop of San Angelo; ordained December 21, 1964; consecrated and installed Bishop of San Angelo July 26, 1985. *Res., P.O. Box 1829, San Angelo, TX, 76902.*

The Chancery: P.O. Box 1829, San Angelo, TX, 76902. Tel.: 915-651-7500; Fax: 915-651-6688.

Web site address: www.san-angelo-diocese.org

E-mail address: mdpomi@aol.com

ESTABLISHED OCTOBER 16, 1961.

Square Miles 37,433.

Comprises 29 Counties in the State of Texas as follows: Andrews, Brown, Callahan, Coke, Coleman, Concho, Crane, Crockett, Ector, Glasscock, Howard, Irion, Kimble, McCulloch, Martin, Menard, Midland, Mitchell, Nolan, Pecos, Reagan, Runnells, Schleicher, Sterling, Sutton, Taylor, Terrell, Tom Green and Upton.

For legal title of parishes and diocesan institutions, consult the Chancery Office.

STATISTICAL OVERVIEW

Personnel	
Bishop	1
Priests: Diocesan Active in Diocese	26
Priests: Active Outside Diocese	4
Priests: Retired, Sick or Absent	9
Number of Diocesan Priests	39
Religious Priests in Diocese	16
Extern Priests in Diocese	7
Permanent Deacons in Diocese	40
Total Sisters	30
Parishes	
Parishes	49
With Resident Pastor:	
Resident Diocesan Priests	25
Resident Religious Priests	9
Without Resident Pastor:	
Administered by Priests	12
Administered by Deacons	1
Administered by Women Religious	2
Missions	24
Professional Ministry Personnel:	
Sisters	13
Lay Ministers	9
Educational	
Diocesan Students in Other Seminaries	7
Total Seminarians	7
Elementary Schools, Diocesan and Parish	3
Total Students	818
Catechesis/Religious Education:	
High School Students	4,078
Elementary Students	9,068
Total Students Under Catholic Instruction	13,971
Teachers in the Diocese:	
Sisters	1
Lay Teachers	60
Vital Statistics	
Receptions into the Church:	
Infant Baptism Totals	2,143
Adult Baptism Totals	186
Received into Full Communion	343
First Communions	2,046
Confirmations	1,595
Marriages:	
Catholic	368
Interfaith	142
Total Marriages	510
Deaths	679
Total Catholic Population	78,557
Total Population	687,730

Former Bishops—Most Rev. THOMAS J. DRURY, D.D., LL.D., ord. June 2, 1935; appt. Oct. 16, 1961; cons. and installed Jan. 24, 1962; transferred to Corpus Christi, July 19, 1965; died July 22, 1992.—Most Rev. THOMAS TSCHOEPE, D.D., ord. May 30, 1943; appt. Bishop Jan. 12, 1966; cons. March 9, 1966; transferred to Dallas, Aug. 27, 1969.—Most Rev. STEPHEN A. LEVEN, D.D., ord. June 10, 1928; cons. Feb. 8, 1956, Auxiliary of San Antonio; appt. to San Angelo Oct. 22, 1969; retired April 16, 1979; died June 28, 1983.—Most Rev. JOSEPH A. FIORENZA, ord. May 29, 1954; appt. Sept. 4, 1979; ord. and installed October 25, 1979; transferred to Galveston-Houston, Dec. 18, 1984.

Vicar General—Rev. Msgr. TIMOTHY J. MURPHY, J.C.L.

Chancery Office—804 Ford, San Angelo, 76905. Tel: 915-651-7500; Fax: 915-651-6688. Office Hours: Mon.-Fri. 9-5, *Mailing Address: Box 1829, San Angelo, 76902.*

Chancellor—Rev. Msgr. LARRY J. DROLL, J.C.L.

Diocesan Tribunal—P.O. Box 1829, San Angelo, 76902.

Judicial Vicar—Rev. Msgr. TIMOTHY J. MURPHY, J.C.L., *P.O. Box 1829, San Angelo, 76902.*

Judges—Revs. WILLIAM DUBUISSON, O.M.I., J.C.L., Adjutant Judicial Vicar; TOM BARLEY, J.C.L.

Promoter Justitiae—Rev. JAMES PLAGENS.

Defensores Vinculi—Rev. Msgr. LARRY J. DROLL, J.C.L.; Revs. CHARLES GREENWELL; MARK WOODRUFF.

Diocesan Consultors—Rev. Msgr. LARRY J. DROLL, J.C.L.; Revs. MICHAEL GOODE, C.PP.S.; MARK WOODRUFF; Rev. Msgr. TIMOTHY J. MURPHY; Revs. WILLIAM DU BUISSON, O.M.I.; TOM BARLEY.

Priests' Personnel Committee—Rev. Msgr. LARRY J. DROLL, J.C.L., Chm.

Presbyteral Council—Rev. TOM BARLEY, J.C.L.; Rev. Msgr. TIMOTHY J. MURPHY; Rev. Msgr. LARRY J. DROLL, J.C.L.; Revs. HUBERT WADE; MICHAEL GOODE, C.PP.S; TOM KELLEY; GEORGE VARAKUKALA; JOE VASQUEZ; WILLIAM DU BUISSON, O.M.I.

Vicar for Women Religious—Sr. MALACHY GRIFFIN, O.P.

Diocesan Offices and Directors

Diocesan Finance Officer—Mr. LES MAIMAN.

Campaign for Human Development—Mr. LES MAIMAN.

Catholic Relief Services—Mr. LES MAIMAN.

Catholic University, Friends of—Rev. Msgr. TIMOTHY J. MURPHY.

Communications Office—Mr. PETE MICALE.

Continuing Education of the Clergy—Rev. JAMES PLAGENS.

Cursillos de Cristiandad—Rev. BERNARD GULLY.

Deans—Revs. HUBERT WADE, San Angelo Deanery; MARK WOODRUFF, Midland-Odessa Deanery; FRED NAWARSKAS, Abilene Deanery.

Diocesan Liturgical Commission—Rev. JAMES PLAGENS.

Holy Childhood, Pontifical Association—Miss MARY SUE BREWER.

Newspaper—"West Texas Angelus"; Mr. PETE MICALE, Editor.

Office of Education and Formation—Sr. JOAN MARKUS, S.S.N.D.

Permanent Deacon Director—Deacon ALAN NEFF.

Permanent Deacon Formation—Rev. TOM KELLEY.

Pro-Life—Rev. JOE VASQUEZ.

Priests' Pension Plan—Board of Directors: Rev. Msgr. TIMOTHY J. MURPHY; Rev. Msgr. LARRY J. DROLL, J.C.L.; Very Rev. CHARLES GREENWELL; Rev. Msgr. FRED NAWARSKAS; Rev. BENEDICT ZIENTEK.

Propagation of the Faith—Rev. Msgr. TIMOTHY J. MURPHY.

Rural Life—Deacon LEROY BEACH, Dir.

Schools—Sr. ELIZABETH ANN SWARTZ, S.S.N.D., Supt.

Vocations—Rev. TOM BARLEY, Dir.

CLERGY, PARISHES, MISSIONS AND PAROCHIAL SCHOOLS

CITY OF SAN ANGELO
(Tom Green County)

1—CATHEDRAL OF THE SACRED HEART (1884), Very Rev. Maurice Voity, Rector; Deacon Jerry Trevino, Pastoral Assoc.

Office: 19 S. Oakes St., 76903. Tel: 915-658-6567; Fax: 915-659-0588.

School—Angelo Catholic School, Sacred Heart Campus, (Grades 2-7). Tel: 915-655-3325; Fax: 915-655-1286. Mr. Charles Guenat, Prin.

Lay Teachers 10; Students 170.

Catechesis/Religious Programs—Mr. Charles Guenat, D.R.E.

Students 290.

Sacred Heart Cathedral-Parish Educational Endowment Fund, Inc.—Tel: 915-658-6567.

2—HOLY ANGELS (1961), Rev. Charles C. Greenwell; Mr. Ed Bendinelli, Business Mgr.

Parish Office: 2202 Rutgers Ave., 76904. Tel: 915-949-3308; 944-8967; Fax: 915-944-3633.

School—Angelo Catholic School, (Grades PreK-1). Holy Angels Campus 2315 A & M Ave., Tel: 915-655-3325; Fax: 915-942-1547. Mr. Charles Guenat, Prin.

Lay Teachers 4; Students 64.

Catechesis/Religious Programs—Tel: 915-942-8192; Fax: 915-659-0588. Mrs. Judy Feist, D.R.E., (Grades PreK-6).

Students 465.

3—St. Margaret (1967), Rev. Joseph Vathalloor, C.M.I.; Deacon Ray Smith, Pastoral Coord.
Office: 2619 Era St., 76905. Tel: 915-651-4633; Fax: 915-651-4366.
Catechesis/Religious Programs—D.R.E.: Dorothy Holguinn, (Grades PreK-6); Becky Torres, (Grades PreK-6); Andy Gonzalez, (Grades 7-12).
Students 45.

4—St. Mary's (1930) (Hispanic), Rev. Terence Brenon; Deacons Lazaro Sevier; Mario Torres; Roy Ibarra. In res., Rev. George Fey, C.PP.S.
Res., 7 West Ave. N., 76903. Tel: 915-655-6278; Fax: 915-655-1524.
Catechesis/Religious Programs—Minnie Ibarra, D.R.E.
Students 361.

5—St. Joseph (1942) (Hispanic), Rev. Joe S. Vasquez; Deacon John Munoz. In res., Revs. Joseph Vathalloor Tel: 915-234-3557 (Cellular); Miguel Dinio, O.P. Tel: 915-482-8438.
Res., 301 W. 17th, 76903. Tel: 915-653-5006; Fax: 915-659-2795.
Catechesis/Religious Programs—Tel: 915-658-8759. Michael R. Wyse, D.R.E.
Students 468.

OUTSIDE THE CITY OF SAN ANGELO

Abilene, Taylor Co.,

1—Sacred Heart, (1891), Revs. Robert Bush; Romanus A. Akamike (Nigeria); Deacon William Smith.
Res., 837 Jeanette St., 79602. Tel: 915-677-7951; Fax: 915-677-7710.
Catechesis/Religious Programs—Tel: 915-673-0697. Pam Carlson, D.R.E.
Students 327.
Mission—Clyde, Callahan Co., Sts. Joachim and Ann, N. 1st St. & Cherry St., Clyde 79510. [CEM] Deacon Peter Ballaro.

2—Holy Family, (1976), Rev. Msgr. Frederick Nawarskas; Sr. Regina Decker, C.D.P., Pastoral Assoc.; Deacons Paul Klein; Gerald Schwalb.
Res., 5410 Buffalo Gap Rd., P.O. Box 5970, 79606. Tel: 915-692-1820; Fax: 915-698-5131.
Catechesis/Religious Programs—Sr. Marie de Lourdes Unterreiner, S.S.N.D., D.R.E.
Students 426.

3—St. Francis of Assisi, (1906) (Hispanic), Revs. Joseph H. Uecker, C.PP.S.; Nilo Nalugon; Deacon Jose Sanchez.
Office: 826 Cottonwood St., 79601. Tel: 915-672-6695.
Catechesis/Religious Programs—Tel: 915-695-7233. D.R.E.: Melinda C. Stone; Elena Hernandez.
Students 147.

4—St. Vincent Pallotti, (1963) (Mexican-American), Revs. Joseph H. Uecker, C.PP.S. Tel: 915-673-7048; Nilo Nalugon; Sr. Rebecca Otter, O.P., Pastoral Assoc., Tel: 915-672-5933.
Res., 2525 Westview, 79603. Tel: 915-672-1794 (Office); Fax: 915-672-8780.
Catechesis/Religious Programs—Minerva Garcia, D.R.E.
Students 269.

Andrews, Andrews Co., Our Lady of Lourdes (1958), Rev. Bernard L. Gully.
Res., 201 N.E. Ave. K, 79714. Tel: 915-523-4215; Fax: 915-523-5070.
Catechesis/Religious Programs—Tel: 915-524-2789. Carol Garcia, D.R.E.
Students 441.

Ballinger, Runnels Co., St. Mary Star of the Sea (1885), Rev. Hubert Wade, Jr.; Deacons Henry Martinez; D.J. Goetz.
Res., 608 Sixth St., 76821. Tel: 915-365-2687; Fax: 915-365-2455. [JC]
Catechesis/Religious Programs—Marta Arteaga, D.R.E.
Students 270.
Missions—Bronte, Coke Co., St. James, 215 N. Washington, Bronte, 76933.; Robert Lee, Coke Co., Our Lady of Guadalupe, 601 W. 10th, Robert Lee, 76945.

Big Lake, Reagan Co., St. Margaret of Cortona (1949), Rev. Barry McLean, O.F.M.
107 First St., 76932. Tel: 915-652-8216; Fax: 915-652-3219.
Res., Drawer G, McCamey, 79752. Tel: 915-652-8214. [JC]
Catechesis/Religious Programs—Tel: 915-884-6874. Linda Lozano, D.R.E.
Students 190.
Mission—Rankin, Upton Co., St. Thomas.

Big Spring, Howard Co., Immaculate Heart of Mary (1961), Revs. Richard Regan; Jeremiah McCarthy, M.S.C.; Deacons Wayne Rock; David King, (Retired).
Res., 1009 Hearn St., 79720. Tel: 915-267-4124; Fax: 915-267-7844.
Catechesis/Religious Programs—Mrs. Isabel Villarreal, D.R.E.
Students 156.
Mission—Big Spring, Howard Co., St. Joseph.

Sacred Heart (1948) (Hispanic), Revs. James A. Plagens; Cornelius J. Scanlan, O.M.I., (Retired).
Res., 508 N. Aylford, 79720. Tel: 915-263-7884; Fax: 915-263-3621.
Mailing Address: P.O. Box 2101, 79721-2101.
Catechesis/Religious Programs—Tel: 915-263-0648. Linda Olivas, D.R.E.
Students 245.

St. Thomas (1887) (Hispanic), Revs. Cornelius J. Scanlan, O.M.I.; James A. Plagens.
Res., 605 N. Main St., P.O. Box 627, 79721. Tel: 915-263-2864; Fax: 915-263-3621.
Catechesis/Religious Programs—Sacred Heart/St. Thomas combined. Miss Mary Chavez, D.R.E.
Students 320.

Brady, McCulloch Co., St. Patrick's (1876), Revs. George Thirumangalam, C.M.I.; Quirino Cornejo.
Res., P.O. Box 1188, 76825. Tel: 915-597-2324; Fax: 915-597-2991.
Catechesis/Religious Programs—Lisa Fible, D.R.E.
Students 189.
Mission—Melvin, McCullogh Co., St. Francis Xavier.

Brownwood, Brown Co., St. Mary's (1896), Rev. Msgr. Benedict Zientek; Deacon John Specht.
Res., 1105 Main Ave., 76801. Tel: 915-646-7455.
Catechesis/Religious Programs—Tel: 915-646-9630; Fax: 915-646-9630. Carol Bludau, D.R.E.
Students 304.

Carlsbad, Tom Green Co., St. Therese of the Child Jesus (1957), Revs. Miguel Dinio, O.P. (Phillippines); Terry Brenon; Sr. Mary Kay Bailey, Pastoral Coord.
Mailing Address: P.O. Box 416, 76934-0416. Tel: 915-465-8062.
Catechesis/Religious Programs—Students 56.
Mission—Sterling City, Sterling Co., St. Paschal Baylon, P.O. Box 271, Sterling City, 76951-0271.
Station—San Angelo State School for the Mentally Retarded, Tel: 915-465-4391.

Coleman, Coleman Co., Sacred Heart (1950) (Anglo-Hispanic), Rev. Lawrence S. Cyr, C.PP.S.; Sr. Esperanza Razura, A.S.C., Pastoral Assoc. In res., Rev. Austin C. Herrmann, C.PP.S.
Rectory: 303 E. Elm, 76834. Tel: 915-625-5773; Fax: 915-625-3320.
Catechesis/Religious Programs—201 San Saba, 76834. Tel: 915-625-3893.
Students 131.

Colorado City, Mitchell Co., St. Ann's (1943), Rev. David Espitia.
Res., 2005 Walnut, 79512. Tel: 915-728-3252; Fax: 915-728-3252.
Catechesis/Religious Programs—Tel: 915-728-5865. Sr. Barbara Potthast, S.S.S.F., D.R.E.
Students 285.
Mission—Loraine, Mitchell Co., San Jose, (1924) 403 S. Hinson, Loraine 79532.

Crane, Crane Co., Good Shepherd, Rev. Barry McLean; Deacons Julio Carrasco; Apolonio Gutierrez.
Mailing Address: P.O. Box 1294, 79731. Fax: 915-652-3219.
Res., 1109 S. Virginia St., 79731. Tel: 915-558-2718.
Church—9th & S. Virginia St., 79731.
Catechesis/Religious Programs—D.R.E.: Minerva Garza; Theresa Figuora.
Students 197.

Eden, Concho Co., St. Charles (1927) (Mexican), Rev. Michael A. Rodriguez; Deacons Leroy Beach; Joe Lopez.
Res., P.O. Box 575, 76837. Tel: 915-869-8311.
Catechesis/Religious Programs—Tel: 915-869-5283.
Students 47.
Missions—Millersview, Concho Co., Our Lady of Guadalupe, P.O. Box 123, Millersview, 76862.; Eola, Concho Co., St. Philip, P.O. Box 711, Eola, 76937.

Eldorado, Schleicher Co., Our Lady of Guadalupe (1924) (Hispanic-Anglo), Rev. George Varakukala.
Res., P.O. Box 211, 76936. Tel: 915-853-2663; Fax: 915-853-2663.
Catechesis/Religious Programs—Tel: 915-853-3366. D.R.E.: Sylvia Belman; Martha Acosta; Muriel Emerson.
Students 189.
Missions—Knickerbocker, Tom Green Co., Immaculate Conception, P.O. Box 36, Knickerbocker, 76939. Tel: 915-944-2820; Mertzon, Irion Co., St. Peter's, 324 N. Commerce, P.O. Box 772, Mertzon 76941. Tel: 915-835-2000.

Fort Stockton, Pecos Co., St. Joseph's (1875) (Hispanic), Rev. David Herrera; Deacon Cosme Ureta, Jr.
Res., 403 S. Main, 79735. Tel: 915-336-5027; Fax: 915-336-6668. [CEM]
Catechesis/Religious Programs—Tel: 915-336-5037. Elizabeth C. Rojo, D.R.E.
Students 292.

St. Agnes (1953) (Hispanic), Rev. David Herrera; Deacon Simon Franco.
Mailing Address: Rte. 1, Box 105, 79735. Tel: 915-336-2724; Fax: 915-336-6950. [CEM]
Catechesis/Religious Programs—D.R.E.: Lillian Subia; Arabella Granado.
Students 221.
Missions—Coyanosa, Pecos Co., St. Isidore; Imperial, Pecos Co., Our Lady of Lourdes.

Junction, Kimble Co., St. Theresa of the Child Jesus (1959), Rev. Quirino H. Cornejo; Deacon Tim Graham.
Res., P.O. Box 486, 76849. Tel: 915-446-3393; Fax: 915-446-3393.
Catechesis/Religious Programs—Students 66.

McCamey, Upton Co., Sacred Heart (1935), Rev. Barry L. McLean.
Res., Drawer G, 79752. Tel: 915-652-8216; Fax: 915-652-3219.
Catechesis/Religious Programs—Students 130.
Mission—Iraan, Pecos Co., St. Francis of Assisi, Tel: 915-652-8216. Deacon James Bacon.

Menard, Menard Co., Sacred Heart (1873), Rev. Quirino H. Cornejo.
Res., P.O. Box 788, 76859. Tel: 915-396-4906; Fax: 915-396-2076.
Catechesis/Religious Programs—Students 101.

Midland, Midland Co.,

1—St. Ann's, (1896) (Anglo), Rev. Msgr. Timothy J. Murphy; Rev. Arturo P. Pestin, O.P. Pastoral Assocs.: Sr. Mary Brian Overfield, S.S.N.D.; Sr. Denise DuPlessis, D.C.
Res., 1908 W. Texas Ave., 79701. Tel: 915-682-6303; 6304; 682-6694; 682-8905; Fax: 915-684-4528.
School—(Grades PreK-8) 2000 W. Texas Ave., Tel: 915-684-4563; Fax: 915-687-2468. Mrs. Barbara Ransbottom, Prin.
Lay Teachers 26; Students 409.
Catechesis/Religious Programs—Tel: 915-687-0941. Carol Ann Hunt, D.R.E.
Students 544.

2—Our Lady of Guadalupe, (1960) (Hispanic), Revs. Jerome Burnet, O.M.I.; Ray Wilhelm, O.M.I.; Deacon Jesse Guajardo, Pastoral Assoc.
Res., 1401 E. Garden Ln., P.O. Box 7, 79702. Tel: 915-682-2581; Fax: 915-682-9364.
Catechesis/Religious Programs—Tel: 915-683-8908. D.R.E.: Sr. Rita Marie Cuevas, O.N.D.; Sr. Lily Oliver, O.N.D.; Sr. Marietta Alo, O.N.D.
Students 826.

3—Our Lady of San Juan de Los Lagos, (1984) (Hispanic), Rev. Thomas Kelley.
Res., 1008 W. New Jersey, 79701. Tel: 915-570-0952.
Catechesis/Religious Programs—Tel: 915-570-0349; Fax: 915-687-5082. Elidia Padilla, D.R.E.
Students 543.

4—St. Stephen's, (1982), Rev. James P. Bridges.
Res. & Mailing Address: 4601 Neely Ave., 79707. Tel: 915-520-7394; Fax: 915-520-7395.
Catechesis/Religious Programs—Tel: 915-520-3065. Gregg Elsner, D.R.E.
Students 384.

Miles, Runnels Co., St. Thomas (1962), Rev. Stephen Kennelly (Ireland); Sr. Helen Rivas, C.D.P., Pastoral Assoc.
Res., P.O. Box 306, 76861. Tel: 915-468-3171.
Catechesis/Religious Programs—Tel: 915-442-4021.
Students 160.

Odessa, Ector Co.,

1—Holy Redeemer, (1961) (Hispanic), Rev. Frank Chavez; Deacons Ignacio Cisneros; Antonio Gonzales.
Res., 2633 Conover, 79763. Tel: 915-580-4295; Fax: 915-332-6631.
Catechesis/Religious Programs—Tel: 915-332-9231. D.R.E.: Anita Diaz; Steven D. Rojo, (Elementary & RCIA).
Students 963.

2—St. Anthony, (1948) (Mexican), Revs. Gilbert Rodriguez; Fidelo Lugo; Deacon Barney Rodriguez.
Office: 1321 W. Monahans St., 79763. Tel: 915-337-6314; Fax: 915-333-3631.
Catechesis/Religious Programs—Tel: 915-337-0241. D.R.E.: Sr. Regina Javiea; Belinda Urias; Yolanda Chavarria; Irene Nunez.
Students 213.

3—St. Elizabeth Ann Seton, (1982), Rev. Mark Woodruff. Pastoral Assocs.: Deacon Alan Neff, Business Mgr.; Tom Burke; Deacon Manuel Luevano.
Office: 7601 N. Grandview, 79765. Tel: 915-367-4657; Fax: 915-367-0700.

Catechesis/Religious Programs—Tel: 915-367-4668. D.R.E.: Nancy Cardona; Maria Isela Carrasco. Students 512.

Mission—Odessa, Ector Co., Our Lady of San Juan, 905 Edgeport, Odessa, 79765. Deacon Pedro Santoya.

4—ST. JOSEPH, (1948), Revs. Gilbert Rodriguez; Fidelo Lugo; Deacon Abel Campos.

Res., 907 S. Dixie St., 79761. Tel: 915-337-2213; Fax: 915-333-3631.

Catechesis/Religious Programs—Tel: 915-337-4734. D.R.E.: Sr. Regina Javier; Terry Gutierrez; Mary Rivas; Debra Jimenez; Virginia Salazar. Students 465.

Mission—Odessa, Ector Co., St. Martin de Porres, 2821 E. Hammett, 79766.

5—ST. MARY'S, (1938), Revs. Francis Frey; Mathews Chackalackal, C.M.I.

Res., 612 E. 18th St., 79761. Tel: 915-332-5334; Fax: 915-332-1844.

School—(Grades PreK-8) 1703 N. Adams, 79761. Tel: 915-337-6052; Fax: 915-337-6052. Mrs. Lupe Molina, Prin.

Sisters 2; Lay Teachers 10; Students 175.

Catechesis/Religious Programs—Nan Goodwin, D.R.E. Students 233.

Olfen, Runnels Co., St. Boniface (1901), Rev. Stephen Kennelly.

Res., P.O. Box 96, Rowena, 76875-0096. Tel: 915-442-2893. [CEM]

Church—1118 County Rd. 234, Rowena, 76875. Tel: 915-442-2893.

Catechesis/Religious Programs—Students 24.

Ozona, Crockett Co., Our Lady of Perpetual Help (1929), Rev. Henry Laenen, O.M.I.

Res., P.O. Box 1069, 76943. Tel: 915-392-3063; Fax: 915-392-3353.

Catechesis/Religious Programs—Tel: 915-392-3429. Fannie Sanchez, D.R.E. Students 324.

Mission—Sheffield, Pecos Co., Good Shepherd, 79781.

Rowena, Runnels Co., St. Joseph's (1906) (German-Czech), Rev. Stephen Kennelly; Sr. Helen Louise Rivas, C.D.P., Pastoral Assoc.

Res., P.O. Box 96, 76875. Tel: 915-442-3521; Fax: 915-442-4602. [CEM]

Catechesis/Religious Programs—Mrs. Ina Albarado, D.R.E. Students 145.

St. Lawrence, Glasscock Co., St. Lawrence (1948) (German), Rev. Bernardito Getigan.

Res., 2400 FM 2401, Garden City, 79739. Tel: 915-397-2300; Fax: 915-397-2300. [CEM]

Catechesis/Religious Programs—Tel: 915-397-2777. Kay Donna Machicek, D.R.E. Students 201.

Mission—Midkiff, Upton Co., St. Thomas, Tel: 915-535-2266.

Sanderson, Terrell Co., St. James (1916) (Hispanic), Rev. David Herrera.

Res., 209 E. Hackberry, P.O. Box 520, 79848. Tel: 915-345-2354.

Catechesis/Religious Programs—Tel: 915-345-2354. Gina Garza, D.R.E. Students 65.

Sonora, Sutton Co., St. Ann's (1927), Very Rev. William Du Buisson, O.M.I.

Office: 311 W. Plum St., P.O. Box 1397, 76950. Tel: 915-387-2278; Fax: 915-387-2278.

Res., 105 Oakwood, Box 1397, 76950. Tel: 915-387-5966.

Catechesis/Religious Programs—Students 285.

Stanton, Martin Co., St. Joseph's (1882) (Mexican-American), Rev. Msgr. Timothy Murphy; Rev. Arturo Pestin, O.P.; Sr. Laureana Perez, D.C., Pastoral Coord.; Deacon Ernie Sanchez.

Res., P.O. Box 846, 405 N. Convent St., 79782-0846. Tel: 915-756-3743; Fax: 915-756-3756.

Catechesis/Religious Programs—Tel: 915-756-3743. Sr. Laureana Perez, D.R.E. Students 198.

Mission—Lenorah, Martin Co., St. Isidore, P.O. Box 846, 79782. [JC]

Sweetwater, Nolan Co., Holy Family (1885) (Hispanic), Revs. Michael Goode, C.PP.S.; Sam Homsey, C.PP.S.

Mailing Address: P.O. Box 847, 79556.

Res., 507 Crane St., 79556. Tel: 915-235-2694; Fax: 915-235-3483.

Catechesis/Religious Programs—Tel: 915-235-3529. Laura Jones, D.R.E. Students 90.

Mission—Merkel, Taylor Co., Our Mother of Mercy, P.O. Box 206, Merkel, 79536. Tel: 915-928-5239; Fax: 915-928-3739.

Immaculate Heart of Mary (1962), Revs. Michael Goode, C.P.P.S.; Sam Homsey, C.P.P.S.

Res., 511 W. Alabama, 79556. Tel: 235-3318 (Office); Fax: 915-235-0258.

Catechesis/Religious Programs—Students 218.

Mission—Roscoe, Nolan Co., St. Albert the Great, 511 W. Alabama Ave., Rosco 79556.

Wall, Tom Green Co., St. Ambrose (1941), Rev. Msgr. Larry J. Droll.

Res., P.O. Box 228, 76957. Tel: 915-651-7551; Fax: 915-651-6605. [CEM]

Catechesis/Religious Programs—D.R.E.: Dolores Gully; Amy Fuchs; Sherry Sefcik; Sylvia Chappa. Students 293.

Mission—Mereta, Tom Green Co., Holy Family, P.O. Box 228, Mereta 76957. Tel: 915-468-3101.

Winters, Runnels Co., Our Lady of Mt. Carmel (1962) (Anglo-Hispanic), Rev. Obioma Desmond Obi.

Res., 119 W. College, 79567. Tel: 915-754-4626.

Catechesis/Religious Programs—Tel: 915-754-4893. Dinell Jacob, D.R.E. Students 92.

On Special or Other Diocesan Assignment:
Reverend Fathers—
Barley, Tom, Box 1829, San Angelo, TX 76902
Prasad, Gallela, Box 1829, San Angelo, TX 76902

On Duty Outside the Diocese:
Reverend Fathers—
Esquivez, Miguel

Military Chaplains:
Reverend Fathers—
Diab, Thomas, 2 BW/HC, 275 Barksdale Blvd. E., Barksdale AFB, LA 71710-2121
Hicks, Steven, USNR, Naval Sup. Activity, 2300 General Meyer Ave., New Orleans, LA 70142

Retired:
Reverend Fathers—
Colacicco, Frank L., St. Isidore Church, 445 LaGanda, CA 94526
Coleman, James, Padua Place, 80 Peter Baque Rd., San Antonio, TX 78209
Droll, Louis J., 132 Retama Dr., Georgetown, TX 78626
Gallagher, Raymond, 1352 Ford Rd., Lyndhurst, OH 44124
Heyburn, Kevin, Padua Place, 80 Peter Baque Rd., San Antonio, TX 78209
Larue, Charles, Padua Place, 80 Peter Baque Rd., San Antonio, TX 78209
Schultz, Russell, 209 S. 3rd St., Kenedy, TX 78119-0359
Vergauwen, Peter, 80 Peter Baque, San Antonio, TX 78209

Permanent Deacons:
Bacon, James, Sacred Heart, McCamey
Ballero, Peter, Sts. Joachim & Ann Mission, Clyde
Beach, Leroy, Our Lady of Guadalupe, Millersview
Camacho, Isaac, Holy Family, Abilene
Campos, Abel, San Jose, Odessa
Carrasco, Julio, Good Shepherd, Crane
Cisneros, Ignacio, Holy Redeemer, Odessa
Crochet, Larry, Austin
Esparza, Jose, Our Lady Of Lourdes, Imperial
Franco, Simon, St. Agnes, Ft. Stockton
Giovannitti, Thomas, On Duty Outside the Diocese
Goetz, D. J., St. Mary's, Ballinger
Gonzales, Antonio, Holy Redeemer, Odessa
Graham, Tim, St. Theresa, Junction
Guajardo, Jesse, Our Lady of Guadalupe, Midland
Gutierrez, Apolonio, Good Shepherd, Crane
Hernandez, Andres, St. Agnes, Ft. Stockton
Ibarra, Roy, St. Mary, San Angelo
King, David, Immaculate Heart of Mary, Big Spring
Klein, Paul, Holy Family, Abilene
Lopez, Joseph, St. Philip's, Eola
Luevano, Manuel, St. Elizabeth, Odessa
Maldonado, Manuel, St. Joseph, San Angelo
Martinez, Enrique, St. James, Bronte
Mercado, Jesus, St. Joseph, Odessa
Munoz, John, St. Joseph, San Angelo
Neff, Alan, St. Elizabeth Ann Seton, Odessa
Pena, Daniel, On Duty Outside the Diocese
Rock, Wayne, Immaculate Heart of Mary, Big Spring
Rodriguez, Barney, St. Anthony's, Odessa
Samaniego, Enemencio, St. Ann, Sonora
Sanchez, Ernie, St. Joseph, Stanton
Sanchez, Pedro, St. Francis, Abilene
Santoya, Pedro, St. Elizabeth, Odessa
Schwalb, Gerald, Holy Family, Abilene
Sevier, Lazaro, St. Mary, San Angelo
Smith, Raymond, St. Margaret, San Angelo
Smith, William, Sacred Heart, Abilene
Specht, John, St. Mary, Brownwood
Torres, Mario, St. Mary, San Angelo
Trevino, Jerry, Sacred Heart, San Angelo
Ureta, Cosme, St. Joseph, Fort Stockton
Yanez, Horacio, St. Thomas, Big Spring

INSTITUTIONS LOCATED IN THE DIOCESE

[A] MONASTERIES AND RESIDENCES OF PRIESTS & BROTHERS

CHRISTOVAL. *Mount Carmel Hermitage*, Box 337, 76935-0337. Tel: 915-896-2249; Fax: 915-896-2249.
E-mail: fatherfabian@juno.com
Web site: www.carmelitehermits.org
Hermits of the Most Blessed Virgin Mary of Mt. Carmel. Rev. Fabian Maria Rosette, H.O.Carm., Prior. Hermits 4.

[B] CONVENTS AND RESIDENCES FOR SISTERS

SAN ANGELO. *School Sisters of Notre Dame*, 2627 Era St., 76905.

CHRISTOVAL. *Carmelite Nuns of the Ancient Observance*, Monastery of Our Lady of Grace, 1 Via Maria, 76935. Tel: 915-853-1722; Fax: 915-853-1722.
E-mail: prayeris@msn.com
Sr. Marie Hoffarth, O.Carm., Supr.

MIDLAND. *Oblates of Notre Dame*, 1400 Garden Ln., 79701. Tel: 915-684-8318; Fax: 915-682-9364.
E-mail: rcjavierond@prodigy.net
1321 W. Monahans, Odessa, 79763. Tel: 915-580-8872; Fax: 915-333-3631.

ROWENA. *Sisters of Divine Providence*, Mailing Address: P.O. Box 132, 76875. Tel: 915-442-4021.

[C] ST. VINCENT DE PAUL SOCIETY

SAN ANGELO. *Catholic Outreach Services*, 102 N. Chadbourne, 76903. Tel: 915-658-4124; Fax: 915-481-0315.
E-mail: cos@wcc.net
Thrift Store Social Services.

ABILENE. *St. Vincent De Paul Society*, 1241 Walnut, 79601. Tel: 915-677-6871.
St. Vincent De Paul Thrift Store. Total Assisted 12,000; Total Staff 4.

BIG SPRING. *St. Vincent De Paul Society*, 1009 Hearn, 79720. Tel: 915-267-4124.
Food Distribution. Families 1,022; People 2,815.

MIDLAND. *St. Vincent De Paul Society*. Mailing Address: P.O. Box 711, 79702-0711. Total Staff 2.

ODESSA. *Catholic Charities Community Services Odessa, Inc.*, 606 W. 10th, 79761. Tel: 915-332-1387.

STANTON. *St. Vincent De Paul Society*. Mailing Address: P.O. Box 158, 79782.

[D] CAMPUS MINISTRY

SAN ANGELO. *Catholic Newman Center*, 2451 Dena Dr., 76904. Tel: 915-949-8033. Sr. Marie Malachy Griffin, O.P., Campus Min. Total Staff 1.

[E] MISCELLANEOUS

SAN ANGELO. *Christ the King Retreat Center*, 802 Ford, 76905. Tel: 915-651-5352; 651-5358; Fax: 915-651-5667.
E-mail: ckrc@wcc.net
Rev. John Castro, O.M.I., Dir. Tel: 915-651-5472..Total in Residence 1; Total Staff 10.

RELIGIOUS INSTITUTES OF MEN REPRESENTED IN THE DIOCESE

For further details refer to the corresponding bracketed number in the Religious Institutes of Men or Women section.

[1110]—*Missionaries of the Sacred Heart.* (Cork Ireland Prov.).—M.S.C.

[0910]—*Oblates of Mary Immaculate.* (Southern American Prov.).—O.M.I.

[]—*Order of Preachers (Dominicans).* (Philippines).—O.P.

[1060]—*Society of the Precious Blood.* (Kansas City Prov.).—C.PP.S.

RELIGIOUS INSTITUTES OF WOMEN REPRESENTED IN THE DIOCESE

[0100]—*Adorers of the Blood of Christ.*—A.S.C.

[0320]—*Carmelite Nuns of the Ancient Observance.*—O.Carm.
[1010]—*Congregation of Divine Providence of San Antonio, Texas.*—C.D.P.
[0460]—*Congregation of Sisters of Charity of the Incarnate Word.*—C.C.V.I.
[]—*Congregation of the Humility of Mary.*—C.H.M.
[0760]—*Daughters of Charity of St. Vincent De Paul.*—D.C.
[1070-24]—*Dominican Sisters of Great Bend, Kansas.*—O.P.
[1070-19]—*Dominican Sisters, Houston.*—O.P.
[1070-03]—*Dominican Sisters, Sinsinawa.*—O.P.
[2730]—*Missionary Sisters of Our Lady of the Holy Rosary.*—M.S.H.R.
[2960]—*Oblates of Notre Dame.*—O.N.D.
[]—*Oblates of Notre Dame.* (Midland, TX).
[]—*Oblates of Notre Dame, Philippines.*
[2970]—*School Sisters of Notre Dame.* (St. Louis & Dallas Provinces).—S.S.N.D.
[1680]—*School Sisters of St. Francis.*—S.S.S.F.
[1570]—*Sisters of St. Francis of the Holy Family.*—O.S.F.
[2350]—*Sisters of the Living Word.*—S.L.W.

NECROLOGY

† Aaron, James, (Retired). —Died Dec. 12, 1999.
† Femenia, Nicholas, (Retired). —Died Dec. 28, 1999.

Archdiocese of San Antonio

(Archidioecesis Sancti Antonii)

Most Reverend

PATRICK F. FLORES, D.D.

Archbishop of San Antonio; ordained May 26, 1956; appointed Titular Bishop of Italica and Auxiliary of San Antonio March 18, 1970; consecrated May 5, 1970; appointed Bishop of El Paso April 4, 1978; installed May 29, 1978; promoted Archiepiscopal See of San Antonio August 28, 1979; installed October 13, 1979. *Res., 2600 W. Woodlawn Ave., San Antonio, TX, 78228.All official communications to the Most Reverend Archbishop should be addressed to the Chancery Office. P.O. Box 28410, San Antonio, TX, 78228-0410.* Tel.: 210-734-2620.

Most Reverend

BERNARD F. POPP, D.D.

Retired Auxiliary Bishop of San Antonio; ordained February 24, 1943; appointed Titular Bishop of Capsus and Auxiliary Bishop of San Antonio June 7, 1983; consecrated July 25, 1983. *Res., 4535 Lord Rd., San Antonio, TX, 78220. Mailing Address: P.O. Box 28410, San Antonio, TX, 78228-0410.* Tel.: 210-734-2620.

Most Reverend

THOMAS J. FLANAGAN, D.D.

Auxiliary Bishop of San Antonio and Titular Bishop of Bavagaliana; ordained June 10, 1956; appointed January 15, 1998; consecrated February 16, 1998. *Res., Oblate Madonna House, 5722 Blanco Rd., San Antonio, TX, 78216-6615. Mailing Address: P.O. Box 28410, San Antonio, TX, 78228-0410.* Tel.: 210-734-2620.

Most Reverend

PATRICK J. ZUREK, D.D.

Auxiliary Bishop of San Antonio and Titular Bishop of Tamugadi; ordained June 29, 1975; appointed January 5, 1998; consecrated February 16, 1998. *Res., 5015 Bayonne, San Antonio, TX, 78228. Mailing Address: P.O. Box 28410, San Antonio, TX, 78228-0410.* Tel.: 210-734-2620.

ESTABLISHED AUGUST 28, 1874.

CREATED AN ARCHBISHOPRIC, AUGUST 3, 1926.

Square Miles 23,180.

The San Antonio Archdiocese comprises Atascosa, Bandera, Bexar, Comal, Edwards, Frio, Gillespie, Gonzales, Guadalupe, Karnes, Kendall, Kerr, Kinney, McMullen (that part of McMullen County north of the Nueces River), Medina, Real, Uvalde, Val Verde and Wilson.

For legal titles of parishes and archdiocesan institutions, consult the Chancery Office.

Chancery Office: 2718 W. Woodlawn Ave., P.O. Box 28410, San Antonio, TX, 78228-0410. Tel.: 210-734-2620; Fax: 210-734-0231.

Web site address: www.archdiosa.org

E-mail address: Administrator@archdiosa.org

STATISTICAL OVERVIEW

Personnel	
Archbishop	1
Auxiliary Bishops	2
Retired Bishops	1
Priests: Diocesan Active in Diocese	102
Priests: Active Outside Diocese	11
Priests: Retired, Sick or Absent	38
Number of Diocesan Priests	151
Religious Priests in Diocese	207
Extern Priests in Diocese	41
Ordinations:	
Diocesan Priests	4
Religious Priests	2
Transitional Deacons	1
Permanent Deacons in Diocese	284
Total Brothers	91
Total Sisters	919
Parishes	
Parishes	144
With Resident Pastor:	
Resident Diocesan Priests	88
Resident Religious Priests	51
Without Resident Pastor:	
Administered by Priests	4
Administered by Deacons	1
Missions	32
Pastoral Centers	3
Professional Ministry Personnel:	
Brothers	7
Sisters	37
Lay Ministers	137
Welfare	
Catholic Hospitals	4
Total Assisted	158,309
Health Care Centers	3
Homes for the Aged	8
Total Assisted	497
Residential Care of Children	3
Total Assisted	131
Day Care and Extended Day Care Centers	19
Specialized Homes	4
Total Assisted	520
Special Centers for Social Services	8
Other Institutions	1
Total Assisted	139
Educational	
Seminaries, Diocesan	1
Students from This Diocese	6
Students from Other Diocese	30
Diocesan Students in Other Seminaries	5
Seminaries, Religious	9
Students Religious	43
Total Seminarians	54
Colleges and Universities	4
Total Students	11,458
High Schools, Diocesan and Parish	2
Total Students	775
High Schools, Private	8
Total Students	3,222
Elementary Schools, Diocesan and Parish	38
Total Students	11,199
Elementary Schools, Private	4
Total Students	1,745
Catechesis/Religious Education:	
High School Students	11,885
Elementary Students	37,191
Total Students Under Catholic Instruction	77,529
Teachers in the Diocese:	
Priests	37
Scholastics	2
Brothers	28
Sisters	129
Lay Teachers	1,379
Vital Statistics	
Receptions into the Church:	
Infant Baptism Totals	13,307
Adult Baptism Totals	538
Received into Full Communion	636
First Communions	10,554
Confirmations	6,350
Marriages:	
Catholic	2,058
Interfaith	620
Total Marriages	2,678
Deaths	5,209
Total Catholic Population	679,712
Total Population	1,949,506

Former Bishops—Rt. Rev. ANTHONY DOMINIC PELLICER, D.D., cons. Dec. 8, 1874; died April 14, 1880.—Rt. Rev. JOHN C. NERAZ, D.D., cons. May 8, 1881; died Nov. 15, 1894.—Rt. Rev. JOHN ANTHONY FOREST, D.D., cons. Oct. 28, 1895; died March 11, 1911.—Most Rev. JOHN W. SHAW, D.D., Coadjutor Bishop of San Antonio; appt. Feb. 7, 1910; cons. Titular Bishop of Castabala, April 14, 1910; succeeded to the See of San Antonio, March 11, 1911; made assistant at the Pontifical Throne, Sept., 1916; promoted to the See of New Orleans, Jan. 25, 1918; died Nov. 2, 1934.—Most Rev. ARTHUR JEROME DROSSAERTS, D.D., LL.D., Bishop of San Antonio; appt. July 18, 1918; cons. Dec. 8, 1918; named Archbishop, Aug. 3, 1926; assistant at the Pontifical Throne, Aug. 19, 1934; died Sept. 8, 1940.—Most Rev. ROBERT E. LUCEY, S.T.D., Bishop of Amarillo; appt. Feb. 10, 1934; cons. May 1, 1934; promoted to the Archiepiscopal See of San Antonio, Jan. 23, 1941; died Aug. 1, 1977.—Most Rev. FRANCIS J. FUREY, Titular Bishop of Temnus and Auxiliary of Philadelphia; appt. Aug. 24, 1960; cons. Dec. 22, 1960; promoted to Coadjutor and Apostolic Administrator "sede plena" of San Diego, July 25, 1963; promoted to Archiepiscopal See of San Antonio, June 4, 1969; Pallium conferred, Dec. 15, 1969; died April 23, 1979.

Vicar General and Moderator of the Curia—Rev. Msgr. LAWRENCE STUEBBEN, V.G.

Chancery Office—2718 W. Woodlawn Ave., P.O. Box 28410, San Antonio, 78228-0410. Tel: 210-734-2620; Fax: 210-734-0231. Office Hours: Mon.-Fri. 8:30-5:00.

Chancellor and Judicial Vicar—Rev. Msgr. TERENCE NOLAN, J.C.L.

Archives—Bro. EDWARD J. LOCH, S.M., Archivist.

Administrative Asst. to the Archbishop—Rev. Msgr. LAWRENCE J. STUEBBEN, V.G.

Office of the Archbishop—Secretaries to the Archbishop: MYRTLE G. SANCHEZ; CARMEN IRUEGAS, *2718 W. Woodlawn Ave., P.O. Box 28410, San Antonio, 78228-0410.*

Office of the Synod—Sr. JANET MARIE ABBACCHI, S.S.N.D., Coord., *P.O. Box 28410, San Antonio, 78228-0410.* Tel: 210-734-2620; Texas: 1-800-SYNOD-98.

College of Consultors—Most Rev. BERNARD F. POPP, D.D., V.G.; Most Rev. THOMAS FLANAGAN, D.D., V.G.; Most Rev. PATRICK ZUREK, D.D., V.G.; Rev. Msgr. LAWRENCE STUEBBEN, V.G.; Rev. Msgr. TERENCE NOLAN, J.C.L.; Rev. Msgr. BALTHASAR JANACEK, V.U.; Rev. Msgr. MICHAEL YARBROUGH; Very Rev. MICHAEL BOULETTE, V.F.; Revs. DAVID GARCIA; WILLIAM MCNAMARA.

Deans—In Metropolitan Area: Very Rev. GERALD HAMMEL, S.M., V.U., North; Rev. Msgr. BALTHASAR JANACEK, V.U., Central; Very Rev. WALTER D'HEEDENE, C.I.C.M., V.U., Northwest; Very Rev. SAMUEL HEITKAMP, V.U., Northeast; Very Rev. DENNIS DARILEK, V.U., Western; Very Rev. JEFFREY SALWACH, O.F.M., V.U., Southwest; Very Rev. LAWRENCE BRUMMER, O.F.M., V.U., Southeast; In Rural Area: Very Rev. JOHN FLANAGAN, V.F., Floresville; Very Rev. MICHAEL BOULETTE, V.F., Fredericksburg; Very Rev. WALLIS STILES, V.F., Hondo; Rev. CARLOS DAVALOS, V.F., Pleasanton; Very Rev. GERALD HUBERTUS, V.F., Seguin; Very Rev. KENNETH DAKIN, V.F., Uvalde.

Vicars for Religious—Rev. Msgr. THOMAS FRENCH, *Incarnate Word Residence, 4515 Broadway, San Antonio, 78209.* Tel: 210-822-0385. Sr. CHARLENE WEDELICH, C.D.P., *P.O. Box 28410, San Antonio, 78228-0410.* Tel: 210-734-2620.

Vicar for Priests—Vacant.

Vicar for Retired Priests—Rev. Msgr. ALEXANDER WANGLER.

Archdiocesan Presbyteral Council—Most Rev. PATRICK F. FLORES, D.D.; Most Rev. BERNARD POPP, D.D., V.G.; Most Rev. THOMAS FLANAGAN, D.D., V.G.; Most Rev. PATRICK ZUREK, D.D., V.G.; Rev. Msgr. TERENCE NOLAN, J.C.L.; Rev. Msgr. BALTHASAR JANACEK, V.U., Chm.; Rev. Msgr. LAWRENCE STUEBBEN, V.G.; Very Revs. SAMUEL HEITKAMP, V.U.; GERALD HAMMEL, S.M., V.U.; WALLIS STILES, V.F.; Rev. WALTER D'HEEDENE, C.I.C.M., V.F.; Very Revs. GERALD HUBERTUS, V.F.; DENNIS DARILEK, V.U.; JEFFREY SALWACH, O.F.M., V.U.; LAWRENCE BRUMMER, O.F.M., V.U.; MICHAEL BOULETTE, V.F.; JOHN FLANAGAN, V.F.; Revs. CARLOS DAVALOS, V.F.; KENNETH DAKIN, V.F.; Rev. Msgr. ALEX WANGLER; Rev. Msgr. MICHAEL YARBROUGH; Revs. MICHAEL DEGEROLAMI; DAVID GARCIA; J. WILLIS LANGLINAIS, S.M.

Women's Commission—Mrs. MARTHA BRINKMANN, Chm., *P.O. Box 28410, San Antonio, 78228-0410.*

Archdiocesan Tribunal—*P.O. Box 28410, San Antonio, 78228-0410.* Tel: 210-734-2620, Ext. 135.

Judicial Vicar—Rev. Msgr. TERENCE NOLAN, J.C.L.

Assistant Director—Ms. MARGARITA M. PARRA.

Judges—Rev. Msgr. JOHN FLYNN; Rev. Msgr. BERNARD MULLANEY; Rev. Msgr. TERENCE NOLAN, J.C.L.; Rev. Msgr. JAMES HENKE; Rev. Msgr. JAMES JANISH; Revs. EMMET CAROLAN; MICHAEL KENNY; JOSEPH LOPEZ.

Promoter Justitiae—Rev. Msgr. J. L. MANNING, J.C.D., P.A.

Defenders of the Bond—Rev. KEVIN RYAN; Rev. Msgr. PATRICK CRONIN; Revs. PAUL CLEARY; JOHN MAKOTHAKAT, J.C.D.; Rev. Msgr. ADOLFO VALDIVIA, J.C.L.; Rev. Msgr. THOMAS MURPHY; Revs. RAY WILHELM, O.M.I., J.C.L.; WARREN A. BROWN, O.M.I., J.C.L.; ANH Q. TRAN, J.C.L. (FTW); JAMES M. KOTARA; EDWARD RODEN-LUCERO, J.C.L. (ELP); MICHAEL P. CALWELL, J.C.L.; Sr. MARGARET A. RAMSDEN, S.F.C.C., J.C.L.; Ms. DENISE J. DOYLE, J.C.D., Ph.D.; Ms. LAURA L. LEFAVE, J.C.L.

Approved Advocates—Rev. Msgr. LAMBERT BILY, V.U.; Rev. JOHN O'DONOGHUE, M.Ed.; STEVE GENGENBACHER; Mrs. CARMEN MASON; Sr. BERNICE A. LINDSEY, O.S.B.; Mrs. ADRIANA FERRARO SEAWRIGHT; Mrs. EDNA BONO, M.S.W.; Mrs. JACQUIE NACEWSKI.

Notaries—Ms. MARGARITA M. PARRA; Mrs. SUE FORBRICH; Mrs. ANNA FOLLIS; Mrs. LORETTA REYES; Mrs. JANENE TIJERINA; MARTIN LEOPOLD.

Interdiocesan Appellate Court—*P.O. Box 28410, San Antonio, 78228-0410.* Tel: 210-736-9444; 736-2620, Ext. 145, 147.

Moderator—Most Rev. PATRICK F. FLORES, D.D.

Judicial Vicar—Rev. FRED SACKETT, O.M.I., J.C.D.

Judges—Revs. LESLIE A. VANCE, J.C.L.; ALBERT HUBERTUS; TIMOTHY A. GOLLOB (DAL); DAVID-MARIE A. JAEGER, O.F.M., J.C.D.; JOHN MAKOTHAKAT, J.C.D.

Due Process: Councils of Conciliation and Arbitration—*Chancery Office, 2718 W. Woodlawn Ave., San Antonio, 78228-5195.* Tel: 210-734-2620.

Diocesan Administration

Administrative Services Department—Rev. Msgr. LAWRENCE J. STUEBBEN, V.G., Dir., *P.O. Box 28410, San Antonio, 78228-0410.* Tel: 210-734-2620.

Archives—Bro. EDWARD J. LOCH, S.M., *P.O. Box 28410, San Antonio, 78228-0410.* Tel: 210-734-2620.

Archdiocesan Business Manager and Finance Officer—Mr. DAVID CASTILLEJA, *P.O. Box 28410, San Antonio, 78228-0410.* Tel: 210-734-2620; Fax: 210-734-2774.

Archdiocesan Office of Stewardship and Development—Mr. CHRISTOPHER A. GRASSO, Dir., *P.O. Box 28410, San Antonio, 78228-0410.* Tel: 210-734-2620; Fax: 210-734-0231.

Archdiocesan Finance Council—Ms. VELIA GUERRA; Mr. THOMAS TARRILLION; Mr. GERARDO GONZALES; Mr. JOHNNY LAMBARIA; Mr. JOHN POERNER; Mrs. MARY LOU BENAVIDES; Deacon ROBERT KUSENBERGER; Mr. ALAN CROSBY; Mr. ALTON PETSCH; Mr. DARRELL GRECO; Mrs. ELVIRA O. NANEZ.

Archdiocesan Debt Review Committee—Mr. DAVID CASTILLEJA, Sec.; Mr. ALEX HINOJOSA; Mr. LOUIS SANCHEZ; Mr. GEORGE VOLZ; Mr. ALEX STEWART; Mr. JOHN D. SPECIA; Mr. S. F. DANYSH; Mrs. JENNITA POSTON; Mrs. DORA ANN VERDE; Mr. JOHN F. KRAMER.

Building Board—Mr. ROBERT ZEPEDA; Mr. COSMO F. GUIDO; Mr. JIM RODRIGUEZ; Mr. DAN CERNA; Mr. STEVE PERSYN.

Lay Pension Plan—Mr. RENE WILKES, Mgr., *P.O. Box 28410, San Antonio, 78228-0410.* Tel: 210-734-2620.

Archdiocesan Cemeteries Office—Most Rev. THOMAS J. FLANAGAN, D.D., V.G., Dir.; Mr. ALBERT J. SANCHEZ, Supt., *746 Castroville Rd., San Antonio, 78207.* Tel: 210-432-2303.

Computer Center—CARLETON BROWN, *P.O. Box 28410, San Antonio, 78228-0410.* Tel: 210-734-2620.

Director of Accounting—DELIA THOMAS, *P.O. Box 28410, San Antonio, 78228-0410.* Tel: 210-734-2620.

Parish Accounting System—Ms. ROSE RODRIGUEZ. Tel: 210-734-2420.

Print/Mail Room—MARIA HINJOSA. Tel: 210-734-2620; Fax: 210-734-0231.

Department of Educational Services—Sr. THERESE SAN MIGUEL, O.S.F., Dir., *P.O. Box 28410, San Antonio, 78228-0410.* Tel: 210-734-2620.

Archdiocesan Schools Office—Mr. DALE HOYT, Supt., *P.O. Box 28410, San Antonio, 78228-0410.* Tel: 210-734-2620.

Archdiocesan Catechetical-Religious Education Center—BONNIE LE MELLE ABADIE, Dir., *P.O. Box 28410, San Antonio, 78228-0410.* Tel: 210-734-2620.

Office of Catholic Youth Ministry-CYO—Mr. PAT PERILLO, Dir., *P.O. Box 28410, San Antonio, 78228-0410.* Tel: 210-734-2620.

Catholic Committee on Scouting (Boys)—Sr. ANN CASSIDY, F.M.A., Chm., *2718 W. Woodlawn, San Antonio, 78228.* Tel: 210-734-2620, Ext. 157.

Catholic Committee on Girl Scouting—Sr. ANN CASSIDY, F.M.A., Chm., *2718 W. Woodlawn, San Antonio, 78228.* Tel: 210-734-2620, Ext. 157.

Campus Ministry (Newman Apostolate)—Mrs. CAROL WHITE, Dir. SAC, St. Philip's, UTSA, UTSA Downtown, Palo Alto, Northwest Vista, Texas Lutheran, Schreiner College, Kerrville, Trinity, UT Health Science Center, S.W. Texas Junior College-Uvalde. *Catholic Student Center, 312 Courtland, San Antonio, 78212.* Tel: 210-736-3752; Fax: 210-736-5365. Sr. IMELDA PHELAN, C.S.B., *St. Anthony Catholic Student Center at U.T.S.A. 14523 Roadrunner Way, San Antonio, 78249.* Tel: 210-699-9594.

Family Life Office—Mr. STEVE GENGENBACHER, Dir., *P.O. Box 28140, San Antonio, 78228-0410.* Tel: 210-734-2620.

Natural Family Planning Office—Mrs. HENRIETTA O'CONNOR, Dir., *P.O. Box 28410, San Antonio, 78228.* Tel: 210-734-2620.

Office of Worship—Rev. Msgr. JAMES HENKE, Chm., Liturgy Commission; DOLORES MARTINEZ, Dir., *P.O. Box 28410, San Antonio, 78228-0410.* Tel: 210-734-2620.

Missions Awareness Office—(Holy Childhood Pontifical Assn.; Propagation of the Faith). MARY WISNIEWSKI, Dir., *P.O. Box 28410, San Antonio, 78228-0410.* Tel: 210-734-2620.

Young Adult Ministry—Mr. STEVE GENGENBACHER, Contact, *Family Life Office, P.O. Box 28140, San Antonio, 78228-0410.*

Department of Personnel Services—Most Rev. THOMAS J. FLANAGAN, D.D., V.G.

Priests Personnel Board—Rev. Msgr. MICHAEL YARBROUGH, Chm.; Rev. Msgr. MICHAEL O'GORMAN; Rev. Msgr. EMIL WESSELSKY; Rev. Msgr. ALOIS GOERTZ; Revs. WILLIAM MCNAMARA; CONOR MCGRATH; ANTHONY VILANO; FRANK MACIAS; JAMES KOTARA; RUDY CARROLA.

Office for Priests—Most Rev. THOMAS J. FLANAGAN, D.D., V.G.

Catholic Counseling and Consultation Center—LILLIAN YONKERS, Exec. Dir.; Rev. JAMES RUTKOWSKI, S.T.L., *Northside Center, 1840 Lockhill Selma, Ste. 102, San Antonio, 78213.* Tel: 210-377-1133; Fax: 210-377-1230.

Assumption-St. John's Seminary—Rev. GERALD L. BROWN, S.S., *P.O. Box 28240, San Antonio, 78284-2701.* Tel: 210-734-5137.

Permanent Diaconate Program—Rev. JOHN O'DONOGHUE, Dir., *114 Shannon Lee, San Antonio, 78216-7316.* Tel: 210-930-8118; Fax: 210-930-8377.

Vocation Office—Rev. JOE AVILES, Dir.; Sr. MARY FAGAN, S.H.S.P., Assoc. Dir., *2600 W. Woodlawn Ave., P.O. Box 28240, San Antonio, 78284-2701.* Tel: 210-735-0553.

Catholic Television of San Antonio—(CTSA) Channel 15. Mr. RICHARD YZAGUIRRE, *2718 W. Woodlawn, San Antonio, 78228.* Tel: 210-734-2620; Fax: 210-734-2939.

Today's Catholic Newspaper—Mrs. MARTHA PACK BRINKMAN, Editor, *2718 W. Woodlawn, San Antonio, 78228.* Tel: 210-734-2620; Fax: 210-734-2939.

Department of Social and Community Services—Mr. PETER MONOD DE FROIDEVILLE, Dir., *P.O. Box 28410, San Antonio, 78228-0410.* Tel: 210-734-2620; Fax: 210-734-0231.

Office of Social Concerns—Mr. PETER MONOD DE FROIDEVILLE.

Campaign for Human Development—Mr. PETER MONOD DE FROIDEVILLE.

Ministry to Hearing Impaired—CHERYL VAN LEEUWEN RIOS, *223 E. Summit, San Antonio, 78212.* Tel: 210-731-8404 (Voice); 731-9208 (TDD).

Ministry to Persons with Disabilities—BECKY VILLARREAL, *815 McDougal, San Antonio, 78223.* Tel: 210-533-3120.

Bexar County Detention Ministries—Sr. MARGARET CAREW, C.C.V.I. Tel: 210-270-6328. Sr. TERESA CARTER, C.S.B. Tel: 210-270-6329. Deacon GILBERT PRATT. Tel: 210-270-6457. Rev. CARL SCHINDLER, C.SS.R. Tel: 210-270-6320., *200 N. Comal, San Antonio, 78207.* Sr. JOYCE DES JARDINS, S.S.N.D., *Juvenile Detention, 600 Mission Rd., San Antonio, 78210.* Tel: 210-531-1040. Each works in a different area of the system.

St. Peter and Joseph's Home—(See Protective Institutions).

Seton Home—(See Protective Institutions).

Health Ministry Committee—Vacant.

Catholic Charities, Archdiocese of San Antonio—Mr. STEVEN SALDANA, Pres., *1405 N. Main Ave., Ste. 222, San Antonio, 78212-4315.* Tel: 210-222-1294; Fax: 210-227-0217.

Refugee Resettlement Services—PAM CURRIER, *2903 W. Salinas, San Antonio, 78207.* Tel: 210-433-3256; Fax: 210-433-0851.

Director Immigration Services—TERESA COLES-DAVILA, *2903 W. Salinas St., San Antonio, 78207.* Tel: 210-433-3256; Fax: 210-433-0851.

Pastoral Center, Archdiocese of San Antonio, Western District—*Catholic Pastoral Center, Western District, 420 South Getty, Ste. B, Uvalde, 78801.* Tel: 830-278-9680; Fax: 830-278-9628.

Diocesan Offices And Directors

Apostleship of Prayer—Vacant.

Archdiocesan Council of Catholic Women—Mrs. EMMA CANNON, *4803 Bill Anders, San Antonio, 78219.* Tel: 210-661-7145. Rev. JOE AVILES, Spiritual Moderator, *2600 W. Woodlawn, San Antonio, 78228.* Tel: 210-735-0553.

Catholic Center for Charismatic Renewal—Most Rev. THOMAS FLANAGAN, D.D., Dir., Liaison, *1707 S. Flores, San Antonio, 78204.* Tel: 210-226-7545; Fax: 210-212-9330.

Catholic Lawyers Guild—Rev. Msgr. TERENCE NOLAN, J.C.L., Spiritual Moderator, *P.O. Box 28410, San Antonio, 78228-0410.* Tel: 210-734-2620.

Catholic Physicians Guild—Rev. JOHN A. LEIES, S.M., S.T.D.; MIGUEL BEDOLLA, M.D., Ph.D., Pres., *520 Fordham Ln., San Antonio, 78228.* Tel: 210-436-3227.

Censores Librorum—Rev. FRED SACKETT, O.M.I.

Movimiento de Apostolado Familiar & Marriage Encounter (Rural)—Rev. ABRAHAM LA TORRE, (Colombia), *3107 N. St. Mary's St., San Antonio, 78212.* Tel: 210-732-6295.

Movimiento Familiar Cristano (Urban)—Presidents: CHELO MEDINA; JOSE MEDINA, *9215 Brink, San Antonio, 78221.* Tel: 210-924-2972.

Christian Life Communities—Vacant.

Black Catholic Apostolate—Deacon THOMAS WHITE, Dir., *1819 Nevada, San Antonio, 78203.* Tel: 210-532-5358.

Cursillo Movement (Spanish)—Rev. ABRAHAM LA TORRE,

602 Urban Loop, San Antonio, 78207. Tel: 210-224-2796.

Cursillo Movement (English)—Sr. BERNICE LINDSEY, O.S.B., *9303 Whitehall, San Antonio, 78216.* Tel: 210-816-8504.

Ecumenical Affairs—Rev. J. WILLIS LANGLINAIS, S.M., Dir., *One Camino Santa Maria, P.O. Box 18, San Antonio, 78228-8518.* Tel: 210-436-3092.

Holy Childhood, Pontifical Association—MARY WISNIEWSKI, *P.O. Box 28410, San Antonio, 78228-0410.* Tel: 210-734-2620.

Holy Name Society—HENRY ALMAGUER, JR., *306 Beryl Dr., San Antonio, 78213.* Tel: 210-340-2914.

Pre-Seminary Program—Rev. JOE AVILES, Dir., *Assumption Seminary, P.O. Box 28240, San Antonio, 78284-2701.* Tel: 210-735-0553.

Priests Eucharistic League—Most Rev. THOMAS J. FLANAGAN, D.D., V.G., Dir., *P.O. Box 28410, San Antonio, 78228-0410.* Tel: 210-734-2620.

Propagation of the Faith—MARY WISNIEWSKI, *P.O. Box 28410, San Antonio, 78228-0410.*

Public Relations Council—Col. JOSEPH B. MCSHANE, *1410 Treasure Way, San Antonio, 78209.* Tel: 210-826-3361.

Retreats, Men—Rev. KEVIN COLLINS, O.M.I., Dir., *Oblate Renewal Center, 127 Oblate Dr., San Antonio, 78216.* Tel: 210-349-4173.

Respect Life Program—Rev. Msgr. SHERRILL SMITH, Moderator, *8520 Cross Mountain Tr., #201, San Antonio, 78255.* Tel: 210-698-8819.

Rural Life Conference—Vacant.

St. Vincent de Paul Society—Mr. HOMER CADENA, Pres., Mailing Address: *928 W. Commerce, San Antonio, 78207.* Tel: 210-225-7837.

CLERGY, PARISHES, MISSIONS AND PAROCHIAL SCHOOLS

CITY OF SAN ANTONIO

1—CATHEDRAL OF SAN FERNANDO (1731) (Hispanic), Revs. David Garcia; James L. Emperur, S.J.; Dennis Arechiga; Deacons Albert Garza; Doroteo E. Pedroza; Enrique Barrera; Pedro Garza.
Res., 115 Main Plaza, 78205. Tel: 210-227-1297; Fax: 210-271-0149.
Catechesis/Religious Programs—Sr. Willie Ontiveros, M.C.D.P., D.R.E.
Students 825.
Mission—San Antonio, Bexar Co., San Francesco di Paola (Italian), 205 Piazza Italia, 78207. Tel: 210-227-0548; Fax: 210-226-5086. Rev. Msgr. Balthasar J. Janacek.

2—BLESSED SACRAMENT (1956), Rev. John O'Donoghue; Deacons Joe Fertitta; Joseph Jorgensen; Bruce Bellg.
Office: 600 Oblate Dr., 78216. Tel: 210-824-7231; Fax: 210-822-2144.
School—Tel: 210-824-3381; Fax: 210-826-6147. Mrs. Lucy Williams, Prin.
Lay Teachers 18; Students 275; Day Care 114.
Catechesis/Religious Programs—Students 300.

3—CHRIST THE KING (1928) (Hispanic), Rev. Richard Pena; Esther Rodriguez, Admin.
Res., 2623 Perez St., 78207. Tel: 210-433-6301; Fax: 210-435-2736.
Catechesis/Religious Programs—Tel: 210-433-3640. Joseph Liedecke, D.R.E.
Students 350.

4—DIVINE PROVIDENCE (1981) (Hispanic), Rev. P. John Mannion; Deacons Jose Suniga; Juan G. Martinez.
Church—5667 Old Pearsall Rd., 78242-2335. Tel: 210-623-3970; Fax: 210-623-3978.
Catechesis/Religious Programs—Diane Garza-Valdez, D.R.E.
Students 715.

5—HOLY FAMILY (1963) (Hispanic), Rev. James Kotara; Deacons Manuel Carranza; Javier Tamez; Roman Soto; Pedro Castillo.
Res., 152 Florencia, 78228-5899. Tel: 210-433-8216; Fax: 210-433-8216. [CEM]
Catechesis/Religious Programs—Tel: 210-433-3006. Ester Mango, D.R.E.
Students 281.

6—HOLY NAME (1961) (Polish/Hispanic), Rev. Msgr. Franciszek Kurzaj; Deacons David L. Herbert; Reynaldo Hinojosa, Sr.
Res., 3814 Nash Blvd., 78223. Tel: 210-333-5020; 5021.
School—Tel: 210-333-7356; Fax: 210-333-7642. Mrs. Kimberly Lubianski, Prin.
Lay Teachers 19; Students 288.
Catechesis/Religious Programs—Tel: 210-333-3613; Fax: 210-333-5021. Margaret Miksch, D.R.E.
Students 244.

7—HOLY REDEEMER (1901) (African American), Rev. Celestin Tongatani, C.I.C.M. (Zaire); Deacon Thomas White.
Res., 1819 Nevada, 78203. Tel: 210-532-5358; Fax: 210-532-3699. [CEM]
Catechesis/Religious Programs—Students 68.

8—HOLY ROSARY (1948) (Hispanic), Revs. John J. Manahan, S.M.; Bernard Meyer, S.M.; James Russell, S.M.; James Schimelpfening, S.M. Pastoral Assocs.: Bros. Richard Schrader, S.M.; Robert Hatesohl, S.M.; Deacons Felipe Barajas; Earl Colley.
Res., 159 Camino Santa Maria, 78228. Tel: 210-433-3241; Fax: 210-433-2133.
School—155 Camino Santa Maria, 78228. Tel: 210-433-4312; Fax: 210-433-7055. Sr. Gretchen Trautman, F.M.I., Prin.
Sisters 2; Lay Teachers 12; Students 164.
Catechesis/Religious Programs—Tel: 210-433-2133. Sr. Marcy Loehrlein, F.M.I., D.R.E.
Students 235.

9—HOLY SPIRIT (1964), Revs. Anthony Pesek; Gregory Nevlud; Deacons Joe Krupa; Sonny Staudt; Jesse Greer.
Res., 758 W. Ramsey Rd., 78216. Tel: 210-341-1395; Fax: 210-341-8438.
School—770 W. Ramsey Rd., 78216. Tel: 210-349-1169; Fax: 210-349-1247. Mrs. Joann Gawlik, Prin.
Lay Teachers 58; Students 488.
Catechesis/Religious Programs—Tel: 210-341-1397; Fax: 210-341-2287. Pat Keene, D.R.E.
Students 723.

10—HOLY TRINITY (1987), Rev. Msgr. Douglas Fater; Deacons Jerry Micek; Norbert Laskowski.
Res., 20523 Huebner Rd., 78258. Tel: 210-497-4200; Fax: 210-497-4285.
Catechesis/Religious Programs—Tel: 210-497-4145. Veronica Benson, D.R.E.
Students 787.

11—IMMACULATE CONCEPTION (1933) (Hispanic), Rev. William Collins, M.S.C.; Deacons Jose Hernandez; Marcos Criado.
Res., 314 Merida St., 78207. Tel: 210-225-2986; Fax: 210-225-2987.
Catechesis/Religious Programs—Students 110.

12—IMMACULATE HEART OF MARY (1912) (Hispanic), Revs. Ignacio Blanco, C.M.F.; Robert Alvarado, C.M.F.; Deacon Jorge Bonilla-Valentin. In res., Revs. Michael Cecere, C.M.F.; George Sturm, C.M.F.; Martin Sanz.
Res., 617 S. Santa Rosa Blvd., 78204. Tel: 210-226-8268; 8269; Fax: 210-222-1479.
Catechesis/Religious Programs—Tel: 210-224-8829. Alfonso Cervantes, D.R.E.
Students 115.

13—OUR LADY OF THE ANGELS (1947) (Hispanic), Rev. Mauricio A. Lopez (Colombia); Deacons Albert Ramirez; Jose F. Moreno.
Res., 1214 Stonewall St., 78211. Tel: 210-924-6591; Fax: 210-924-6593.
Catechesis/Religious Programs—Tel: 210-924-8046. Alicia Q. Gutierrez, D.R.E.
Students 394.

14—OUR LADY OF THE ATONEMENT CATHOLIC (1983). (A Personal Parish for the Anglican Use). Rev. Christopher G. Phillips; Deacon James P. Orr.
Res., 8015 Shady Hollow Ln., 78255. Tel: 210-695-3332.
Church—15415 Red Robin Rd., 78255. Tel: 210-695-2944; Fax: 210-695-9679.
School—Atonement Academy, Tel: 210-695-2240.
Lay Teachers 10; Students 206.
Catechesis/Religious Programs—Students 329.

15—OUR LADY OF GOOD COUNSEL (1952) (Hispanic), Rev. Dennis Darilek.
Res., 1204 Castroville Rd., 78237. Tel: 210-432-0873; Fax: 210-432-7576.
Catechesis/Religious Programs—Fax: 210-432-7571.
Students 275.

16—OUR LADY OF GRACE (1938), Rev. Msgr. Lawrence Walsh; Deacon Robert Schonhoff.
Res., 223 E. Summit Ave., 78212. Tel: 210-734-7285; Fax: 210-734-8334.
Catechesis/Religious Programs—Students 127.

17—OUR LADY OF GUADALUPE (1911) (Hispanic), Revs. Martin L. Elsner, S.J.; James L. Lambert, S.J.; Samuel Rosales, S.J.; Bro. Alexander Gussio, S.J.; Deacons Joe Camero; Robert Galvan; John Huttinger; Carlos Sandoval.
Res., 1321 El Paso St., 78207. Tel: 210-226-4064; Fax: 210-226-4973.
Catechesis/Religious Programs—R. Lee Thielen, D.R.E.
Students 200.

18—BASILICA OF THE NATIONAL SHRINE OF OUR LADY OF MT. CARMEL AND ST. THERESE, DISCALCED CARMELITE FATHERS (1926) (Hispanic), Revs. Ralph Reyes, O.C.D.; Michael Okuroski, O.C.D.; Christopher Timoney, O.C.D.; James Anthony Curiel, O.C.D.; Mary Philip Wurth, O.C.D.; Jerome Earley, O.C.D.; Deacon Dan Cisneros.
Res., 906 Kentucky Ave., 78201-6097. Tel: 210-735-9126; 9127 (Res.); Fax: 210-735-1389 (Parish); 738-0818 (Res.).
School—905 Kentucky Ave., 78201. Tel: 210-732-9207; Fax: 210-732-3214. Sr. Eileen Mannion, S.H.Sp., Prin.
Sisters of the Holy Spirit 4; Franciscan Sisters 1; Lay Teachers 14; Students 287.
Catechesis/Religious Programs—Tel: 210-734-4893. Irene Luevano, D.R.E.
Students 274.

19—OUR LADY OF PERPETUAL HELP (1913) (Hispanic), Rev. Gilbert A. Enderle, C.SS.R. Pastoral Assocs.: Sr. Eva Coper, M.P.S.; Sr. Alma Sevilla, M.P.S.
Res., 618 S. Grimes St., 78203. Tel: 210-532-7031; Fax: 210-534-1280.
Catechesis/Religious Programs—Tel: 210-534-7193.
Students 90.

20—OUR LADY OF SORROWS (1915) (Hispanic), Rev. Lambert S. Bily; Deacon Jesse Fraga. In res., Revs. Abraham LaTorre; Marian Piekarczyk, S.D.S., (Poland) Dir. Polish Catholic Mission.
Res., 3107 N. St. Mary's St., 78212. Tel: 210-732-6295; 736-6719 (Polish); Fax: 210-732-6295.
Catechesis/Religious Programs—Tel: 210-732-9249. Donna Salas, D.R.E.
Students 145.

21—PRINCE OF PEACE (1980), Rev. Msgr. Patrick Cronin; Deacons Robert Garza; Scott Imburgia; Pino Sanabria; Tom Neal; William Thornberry; Robert Caldwell.
Res., 7893 N. Grissom Rd., 78251. Tel: 210-681-8330; Fax: 210-681-2286.
Catechesis/Religious Programs—Tel: 210-681-5063. D.R.E.: Deborah Ruiz; Lydia Pena.
Students 1,439.

22—RESURRECTION OF THE LORD (1981), Rev. Paul A. Raaz; Deacon Thomas Swift.
Offices & Mailing Address: 7990 W. Military Dr., 78227. Tel: 210-675-1470; Fax: 210-675-8203.
Res., 7151 Cypress Grove, 78227.
Catechesis/Religious Programs—Tel: 210-675-8360.
Students 720.

23—SACRED HEART (1899) (Hispanic), Rev. Walter O. D'heedene, C.I.C.M. (Belgium); Deacon Valentine Gallegos.
Res., 2114 W. Houston St., 78207-3496. Tel: 210-227-5059; Fax: 210-227-6209.
Catechesis/Religious Programs—Tel: 210-227-9763. Sr. Juanita Ramirez, D.R.E.
Students 230.

24—ST. AGNES (1923) (Hispanic), Rev. Msgr. Peter O'Callaghan; Deacon Leon Guerrero. In res., Very Rev. Lawrence Stuebben, V.G.
Office: 814 Ruiz St., 78207. Tel: 210-227-8255; Fax: 210-212-7757.
Res., 804 Ruiz St., 78207. Tel: 210-227-8258.
Catechesis/Religious Programs—Sr. Margaret Mary Barrett, D.R.E.
Students 590.

25—ST. ALPHONSUS (1925) (Hispanic), Friar Arturo M. O'Campo, O.F.M.; Sr. Adele Massaro, Pastoral Assoc.
Res., 2004 Chihuahua St., 78207. Tel: 210-433-9365; Fax: 210-433-9365.
Catechesis/Religious Programs—Tel: 210-432-3176.
Students 124.

26—ST. ANN (1912) (Hispanic), Revs. Emiliano Zapata, O.P.; Cayet Mangiaracina, O.P.; Vincente M. Pena, O.P.; John Raymond Corr, O.P.; Marcelo Solorzano, O.P.; Bruce B. Schultz, O.P.
Res., 210 St. Ann St., 78201. Tel: 210-734-6687; Fax: 210-738-1755.
Catechesis/Religious Programs—Tel: 210-733-9681.
Students 335.

27—ST. ANTHONY MARY CLARET (1988), Rev. Jan Klak.
Res., 6150 Roft Rd., 78253. Tel: 210-688-9033; Fax: 210-688-3575.
Catechesis/Religious Programs—Sr. Marian Sturm, I.W.B.S., D.R.E.
Students 545.

28—ST. ANTHONY OF PADUA (1957), Rev. Patrick O'Shea, M.S.C.; Deacon Gilbert Wiessler.
Res., 102 Lorenz Rd., 78209. Tel: 210-824-1743; Fax: 210-824-3283.
Catechesis/Religious Programs—Tel: 210-824-6740. Mrs. Carmen Ortiz, D.R.E.
Students 371.

29—ST. BENEDICT (1958) (Polish/Hispanic), Rev. Edward A. Pavlicek, Jr.; Most Rev. Bernard F. Popp, D.D.; Deacon Dan Kearns.

Res., 4535 Lord Rd., 78220. Tel: 210-648-0123; Fax: 210-648-1722.
School—Tel: 210-648-1611. Mrs. Frances Grams, Prin.
Lay Teachers 15; Students 155.
Catechesis/Religious Programs—Tel: 210-648-4632. Deborah Desjean, D.R.E.
Students 152.

30—St. Bonaventure (1959) (Hispanic), Rev. Raymond Schuster; Deacons Fidel Hinojosa; Amador Gonzalez; Edward Patino.
Res., 1918 Palo Alto Rd., 78211. Tel: 210-922-1685; Fax: 210-922-7821.
Catechesis/Religious Programs—Tel: 210-922-1882. Mrs. Diane Guerra, D.R.E.
Students 495.

31—St. Brigid (1972), Rev. Leslie A. Vance; Deacons Thomas Billimek; Pasquale M. Benigno; Patrick F. Frisina; Paul Heye.
Res., 6907 Kitchener Rd., 78240. Tel: 210-696-0896; Fax: 210-696-7319.
Catechesis/Religious Programs—Charlene Staedtler, D.R.E.
Students 390.

32—St. Cecilia (1919) (Hispanic), Revs. Francis M. Landwermeyer, S.J.; Ubaldo Santos.
Res., 125 W. Whittier St., 78210-2897. Tel: 210-533-7109; Fax: 210-532-2599.
School—Tel: 210-534-2711; Fax: 210-533-8284. Mrs. Mary I. Crow, Prin.
Sisters 5; Lay Teachers 9; Students 217.
Catechesis/Religious Programs—Tel: 210-532-1994. Mrs. Limba Reyes, D.R.E.
Students 380.
Mission—San Antonio, Bexar Co., Purisima Concepcion, 807 Mission Rd., 78210.

33—St. Clare (1959) (Hispanic), Rev. Jeffery Salwach, O.F.M.
Res., 7701 Somerset Rd., 78211. Tel: 210-924-5252.
Catechesis/Religious Programs—Tel: 210-922-6458. Maria Delores M. Marek, D.R.E.
Students 285.

34—St. Dominic (1971), Rev. Paul Cleary; Deacons Lionel Garza; Alan Fitzpatrick; Jimmie Trevino; Bert Stewart.
Res., 5919 Ingram Rd., 78228. Tel: 210-435-6211; Fax: 210-435-1732.
Catechesis/Religious Programs—Tel: 210-435-9267. Sue Graves, D.R.E.
Students 689.

35—St. Francis of Assisi (1980), Rev. Msgr. James Henke; Sr. Frances Briseno, O.S.B., Pastoral Assoc.; Deacons Tom Franklin; Gilbert Pratt.
Res., 4201 De Zavala Rd., 78249-2000. Tel: 210-492-4600; Fax: 210-492-8128.
Education Office—Tel: 210-492-4683.
Catechesis/Religious Programs—Gloria Clayton, D.R.E.
Students 450.

36—St. Gabriel (1958) (Hispanic), Rev. Louis Jaspers, C.I.C.M. (Belgium); Deacon Frank Castellano.
Res., 747 S.W. 39th St., 78237. Tel: 210-433-3689; Fax: 210-433-0546.
Catechesis/Religious Programs—Tel: 210-433-3354. D.R.E.: Mavis Montemayor; Nickie Cantu.
Students 188.

37—St. Gerard Majella (1911), Revs. Alton Carr, C.SS.R.; John Farnik, C.SS.R. In res., Revs. Francis Pham, C.SS.R.; Monroe Perrier, C.SS.R.
Res., 1523 Iowa St., 78203. Tel: 210-533-0161 (Church Office); Fax: 210-533-0558.
School—1619 Iowa St., 78203. Tel: 210-533-9541; Fax: 210-533-4196. Mrs. Catherine Tynan, Prin.
Sisters 1; Lay Teachers 9; Students 171.
High School—Archdiocesan Regional, 521 S. New Braunfels Ave., 78203. Tel: 210-533-8061; Fax: 210-533-3697. Maurice Abadie, Pres.; Theresa Skloss, Prin.
Sisters 2; Brothers 2; Lay Teachers 15; Students 204.
Catechesis/Religious Programs—Students 137.

38—St. Gregory's (1955), Rev. Msgr. Michael B. O'Gorman (Ireland). Pastoral Assocs.: Sr. M. Carmel O'Callaghan, P.B.V.M.; Sr. Luz Valdez, M.C.M.; Sr. Clare Conway, P.B.V.M.; Deacon Fred Campos, Jr.
Res., 700 Dewhurst, 78213. Tel: 210-342-5271; Fax: 210-342-0542.
School—Tel: 210-342-0281; Fax: 210-308-7177. Martha Gomez, Prin.
Lay Teachers 51; Students 647.
Catechesis/Religious Programs—Tel: 210-342-3826. Gloria Silva, D.R.E.
Students 323.

39—St. Helena (1974), Rev. Msgr. Leo M. Dolan; Deacons Leonard Standcombe; Paul Gustowski; Joseph De Leon; Rose Marden, Pastoral Asst.
Office: 14714 Edgemont, 78247. Tel: 210-653-3316; Fax: 210-653-3163.
Res., 14527 Angora, 78247. Tel: 210-653-3850.
Catechesis/Religious Programs—Tel: 210-653-3316. D.R.E.: Suzan Roy; Joan Martinez.
Students 852.

40—St. Henry (1904) (Hispanic), Rev. Msgr. Emil J. Wesselsky.
Res., 1619 S. Flores St., 78204. Tel: 210-225-6877; Fax: 210-225-6878.
Catechesis/Religious Programs—Tel: 210-227-1585. Sr. Clara Ruiz, H.C.G., D.R.E.
Students 225.

41—St. James the Apostle (1954) (Hispanic), Revs. Emmet Carolan; Michael McManus; Onofre Toscano, Pastoral Assoc.
Res., 907 W. Theo Ave., 78225. Tel: 210-922-2136; Fax: 210-923-0940.
School—Tel: 210-924-1201; Fax: 210-924-0201. Sr. Cecilia Henry, F.M.A., Prin.
Daughters of Mary Help of Christians 2; Lay Teachers 20; Students 377.
Catechesis/Religious Programs—Tel: 210-922-4061. Mary Toscano, D.R.E.
Students 517.

42—St. John, The Evangelist (1956), Rev. Stuart Juleen; Deacons Rosendo Urrabazo; Evan Wittig; Hugo Chavez; Edward Lopez.
Res., 102 S. Audubon Dr., 78212. Tel: 210-738-2201; Fax: 210-738-0599.
School—128 S. Audubon Dr., 78212. Tel: 210-735-3526; Fax: 210-735-3526. Mrs. Linda Murphy, Prin.
Sisters 1; Lay Teachers 15; Students 225.
Catechesis/Religious Programs—Sr. Luz, D.R.E.
Students 90.

43—St. John Berchmans (1910) (Hispanic), Rev. Carlos B. Velazquez; Deacons Jose Diaz; Librado Cena.
Res., 1147 Cupples Rd., 78226. Tel: 210-434-3247; Fax: 210-432-0431.
School—Tel: 210-433-0411; Fax: 210-433-2335. Ms. Deborah Goering, Prin.
Lay Teachers 23; Students 475.
Catechesis/Religious Programs—Tel: 210-433-2121. Marta Lucia Garcia, D.R.E.
Students 270.

44—St. John Neumann (1977), Rev. Msgr. Robert Silverman.
Church—6680 Crestway Dr., 78239. Tel: 210-654-1643; Fax: 210-654-8031.
Catechesis/Religious Programs—Tel: 210-654-3707.
Students 360.

45—St. Joseph (Downtown) (1868) (German), Rev. Thomas J. Fitzgerald, S.S.S. In res., Revs. Dominic Luong, S.S.S.; Roger C. Prefontaine, S.S.S.; Bro. Martin Hayes, S.S.S.
Res., 623 E. Commerce St., 78205. Tel: 210-227-0126; Fax: 210-227-7690. [CEM]

46—St. Joseph (South San) (1935) (Hispanic), Revs. Antonio Posadas, O.F.M.; Blane O'Neil, O.F.M.; Deacon Genaro Herrera. In res., Rev. Jeffery Salwach, O.F.M.
Res., 535 New Laredo Hwy., 78211-1900. Tel: 210-924-4383; Fax: 210-928-9020.
School—Tel: 210-922-0193; Fax: 210-927-4229. Mrs. Margaret Schlueter, Prin.
Lay Teachers 16; Students 201.
Catechesis/Religious Programs—Tel: 210-924-4383. D.R.E.: Carmen Sanchez; Cindy Machado.
Students 505.

47—St. Jude (1954) (Hispanic), Rev. Jose A. Giganto, O.S.A. In res., Rev. Leonidas Fresno, O.S.A.
Res., 130 S. San Augustine Ave., 78237. Tel: 210-432-8044; Fax: 210-432-1760.
Catechesis/Religious Programs—Tel: 210-432-5786. Rosalinda F. Rodriguez, D.R.E.
Students 600.
Mission—San Antonio, Santa Maria Goretti.

48—St. Lawrence (1959) (Hispanic), Rev. Msgr. Adolfo A. Valdivia; Deacons Alois Keller; Richard Gonzalez; Ernest Leal.
Res., 236 E. Petaluma, 78221. Tel: 210-924-4401; Fax: 210-924-4401.
Catechesis/Religious Programs—Tel: 210-924-7231.
Students 700.

49—St. Leo (1919) (Hispanic), Rev. Msgr. Enda McKenna; Rev. Edward Bernal. Pastoral Assocs.: Deacons John Landez; Alvino Pacheco; Ramon Gutierrez; Lupe Sielski.
Res., 4401 S. Flores, 78214. Tel: 210-533-9108; Fax: 210-533-0643.
School—119 Octavia Pl., 78214. Tel: 210-532-3166; Fax: 210-532-5997. Carol Johnson, Prin.
Lay Teachers 12; Students 146.
Catechesis/Religious Programs—Gilda Castano, D.R.E.
Students 295.

50—St. Leonard's (1966) (Hispanic), Rev. Amando Trujillo-Cano, T.O.R. (Mexico); Deacons Carlos Salinas, (Retired); Rey Ybarra.
Res., 8510 S. Zarzamora, 78224-2099. Tel: 210-924-6000; Fax: 210-924-5552.
Catechesis/Religious Programs—Tel: 210-924-6000, Ext. 19.
Students 465.

51—St. Luke (1959), Rev. Patrick J. Ragsdale.
Office: 4603 Manitou, 78228-1889. Tel: 210-433-2777; Fax: 210-433-2778.
Res., 6014 Horizon, 78228.
School—Tel: 210-433-2777; Fax: 210-432-2419. Kathy Schaub, Acting Prin.
Lay Teachers 29; Students 575.
Catechesis/Religious Programs—Fax: 210-433-2778. Kathy Hill, D.R.E.
Students 502.

52—St. Margaret Mary (1955) (Hispanic), Revs. Dennis A. Jarzombek; Mario S. Cardenas; Deacons Gerardo Mechler; Zeke Moczygemba; Jose Almanza.
Res., 1314 Fair Ave., 78223. Tel: 210-532-6309; Fax: 210-532-6333.
School—Tel: 210-534-6137; Fax: 210-534-2225. Miss Susan Bukala, Prin.
Felician Sisters 2; Lay Teachers 15; Students 241.
Catechesis/Religious Programs—Theresa Pawelek, Prin.
Students 310.
Mission—San Antonio, Bexar Co., St. Catherine, 2202 Hicks, 78210.

53—St. Mark the Evangelist (1976), Rev. Kevin E. Ryan; Dorothea G. Hamlin, Pastoral Admin.; Deacons Ernest Zepeda; Steven Marques; Larry Stallings.
Res., 1602 Thousand Oaks Dr., 78232-2398. Tel: 210-494-1606; 1607; Fax: 210-494-4957.
Catechesis/Religious Programs—Tel: 210-494-7434.
Students 1,414.

54—St. Martin de Porres (1964) (Hispanic), Rev. Gilbert Obin, C.I.C.M.; Deacons Jose Menchaca; Anthony Patlan.
Res., 1730 Dahlgreen St., 78237. Tel: 210-432-5203; Fax: 210-436-1187.
Catechesis/Religious Programs—Tel: 210-436-2071.
Students 190.

55—St. Mary (1852) (Irish), Rev. Michael Levy, O.M.I.
Res., 202 N. St. Mary's St., 78205. Tel: 210-226-8381; Fax: 210-226-8440. [CEM]
School—207 N. St. Mary's St., 78205. Tel: 210-223-8581; Fax: 210-223-5672. Sr. Agnes Pawelek, C.S.S.F., Prin.
Sisters 1; Lay Teachers 12; Students 153.

56—St. Mary Magdalen (1940) (Hispanic), Rev. Robert E. Hogan, S.M.; Deacons Gerald Campa; Ismael Casanova.
Res., 1710 Clower St., 78201. Tel: 210-735-5269; Fax: 210-738-0698.
School—Tel: 210-735-1381; Fax: 210-735-2406. Sr. Patricia O'Sullivan, Prin.
Sisters 2; Lay Teachers 9; Students 220.
Catechesis/Religious Programs—Tel: 210-735-5284. Linda Froboese, D.R.E.
Students 569.

57—St. Matthew's (1968), Rev. Msgr. Michael H. Yarbrough; Revs. John A. Wagner; Don C. Shepanski; Michael Horan; Jose Franciso Puente; Jersy Sieczynski; Deacons Tom Fox; Wilbur Hoelschler; Horacio Tudon; Keith Werner; William Ziske, (Retired); Albert Hollstein, (Retired).
Res., 10703 Wurzbach Rd., 78230. Tel: 210-696-4161; Fax: 210-696-8858.
School—Tel: 210-696-7433; Fax: 210-696-7624. Cynthia Salinas, Prin.
Sisters 1; Lay Teachers 43; Students 700.
Catechesis/Religious Programs—Fax: 210-696-8858. Sr. Therese Gleitz, D.R.E.
Students 1,197.

58—St. Michael (1866) (Hispanic), Rev. Jesus Murugarren, O.S.A. (Spain); Lillie P. Ramirez, Admin. Pastoral Assocs.: Juan Garcia; Alice Olivera; Nicholas Farley.
Res., 418 Indiana, 78210. Tel: 210-532-3707; Fax: 210-532-3707. [CEM]
Catechesis/Religious Programs—Students 96.

59—St. Patrick (1895) (Hispanic), Rev. Walter E. Ebarb (SHP). In res., Rev. Thomas McSwiggan.
Res., 1114 Willow St., 78208. Tel: 210-226-5223; Fax: 210-227-8616.
Catechesis/Religious Programs—Tel: 210-227-5478. Sr. Alicia Drone, A.S.C., D.R.E.
Students 346.

60—St. Paul (1954) (Hispanic), Revs. Jimmy D. Drennan; Florencio Rodriguez, T.O.R.; Deacons Clayton Mangold; Daniel Muriada; Agustin Arismendez; Joseph Richard. In res., Rev. Joe Aviles.
Res., 350 Sutton Dr., 78228-3199. Tel: 210-733-7152; Fax: 210-733-0929.

School—307 John Adams, 78228. Tel: 210-732-2741; Fax: 210-732-7702. Sr. Virginia Huser, C.D.P., Prin.
Religious Sisters 2; Lay Teachers 26; Students 433.
Ministry & Service Office: 1201 Donaldson, 78228. Tel: 210-732-8735; Fax: 210-732-6279. Jesus Suarez, Coord.; Elsa Davis, Dir. Senior Svs.; Community Center: Tel: 210-736-0055; Fax: 210-738-9600.
Learning Center—(Daycare). Tel: 210-738-8715. Dolores Lozano, Dir.
Children 70.
Catechesis/Religious Programs—Virginia Valenzuela, D.R.E.
Students 460.

61—St. Peter Prince of the Apostles (1923), Rev. Msgr. Thomas Murphy; Teresa Berg, Admin.; Deacons John Dunn; John L. Spitzer, (Retired); Raymond Cross; Richard De Hoyos.
Res., 111 Barilla Pl., 78209. Tel: 210-822-3367; Fax: 210-828-5826.
School—112 Marcia Pl., 78209. Tel: 210-824-3171; Fax: 210-822-4504. Leslie Kvapil, Prin.
Lay Teachers 39; Students 441.
Catechesis/Religious Programs—Tel: 210-822-1605. Alma Small, D.R.E.
Students 295.

62—St. Philip of Jesus (1914) (Hispanic), Rev. Michael DeGerolami; Deacons G. T. Zapata; Jose Sanchez.
Res., 131 Bank St., 78204. Tel: 210-226-5024; Fax: 210-226-9005.
School—134 E. Lambert St., 78204. Tel: 210-222-2872; Fax: 210-229-1829. Sr. Celly Ann Amparano, S.S.N.D., Prin.
Sisters 2; Lay Teachers 14; Aides 5; Students 276.
Catechesis/Religious Programs—Tel: 210-225-6622. Christina Harris, D.R.E.
Students 276.

63—St. Pius X (1957), Rev. Msgr. Liam P. Brosnan; Rev. Francis McHugh; Deacons Thomas Crowley; Eugene Townsend.
Office: 3303 Urban Crest, 78209. Tel: 210-824-0139; Fax: 210-829-5125.
Res., 654 Cave Ln., 78209. Tel: 210-826-4064.
School—(Grades PreK-8) 7734 Robin Rest Dr., 78209. Tel: 210-824-6431; Fax: 210-824-7454. Celeste Bonsignore, Prin.
Lay Teachers 29; Students 442.
Catechesis/Religious Programs—Tel: 210-824-4533. Chris Henderson, D.R.E.
Students 442.

64—St. Rose of Lima (1981), Revs. Juan Alfaro; Virgil Elizondo; Deacons Rey Jasso; Antonio Lira; Chester Ostaszewski.
Res., 9883 Marbach Rd., 78245. Tel: 210-675-1920; Fax: 210-675-6067.
Catechesis/Religious Programs—Students 1,000.

65—St. Stephen (1965) (Hispanic), Rev. Luis Ruiz.
Res., 2127 S. Zarzamora St., 78207. Tel: 210-224-8474; Fax: 210-224-8474.
Catechesis/Religious Programs—Tel: 210-224-7116.
Students 250.

66—St. Thomas More (1964), Rev. John M. Makothakat; Deacon Jerome Ciarrocchi.
Res., 4411 Moana, 78218. Tel: 210-655-5070; Fax: 210-655-8446.
School—4427 Moana, 78218. Tel: 210-655-2882; Fax: 210-655-9603. Mrs. Mary Jane Regel, Prin.
Lay Teachers 12; Students 210.
Catechesis/Religious Programs—Tel: 210-654-6824.
Students 200.

67—St. Timothy's (1953) (Hispanic), Rev. Bernard M. Rochon, S.M.; Deacons Pedro M. Soriano; Rudy Medrano; Antonio Caballero; Tomas Alvarado.
Res., 1515 Saltillo St., 78207. Tel: 210-434-2391; Fax: 210-434-4828.
Catechesis/Religious Programs—Students 105.

68—St. Vincent de Paul (1961), Rev. Jose Luis De La Rosa; Sr. Katrina Ruane, S.H.Sp., Pastoral Assoc.; Deacon Leobardo Longoria.
Res., 4222 S.W. Loop 410, 78227-4495. Tel: 210-674-1200; Fax: 210-674-1640.
Catechesis/Religious Programs—Tel: 210-674-4291. Maricella Salazar, D.R.E.
Students 361.

69—San Francisco de la Espada (1731) (Hispanic), Rev. Lawrence Brummer, O.F.M.
Res., 10040 Espada Rd., 78214. Tel: 210-627-2064; Fax: 210-627-2064.
Catechesis/Religious Programs—Tel: 210-627-2962. Juan Manuel Trevinto, D.R.E.
Students 80.
Mission—San Antonio, Bexar Co., St. Frances Cabrini, 1606 San Casimiro, 78214. Tel: 210-627-9263.

70—San Jose y San Miguel (1720) (Hispanic), Revs. Herbert Jones, O.F.M.; Thomas Shaughnessy, O.F.M.; John Abts, O.F.M.; Sr. Immaculata Kelly, P.B.V.M., Pastoral Assoc.; Deacons Santiago Rodriguez; Tomas Torres. In res., Revs. Maury Smith, O.F.M.; Charles Gunti, O.F.M.; Bros. Thomas Eisenmenger, O.F.M.; Dionisio Flores, O.F.M.
Res., 701 E. Pyron Ave., 78214. Tel: 210-922-0543; Fax: 210-932-2271.
Catechesis/Religious Programs—Tel: 210-923-8681. Kathleen Rollow, D.R.E.
Students 200.

71—San Juan Capistrano (1731) (Hispanic), Rev. James G. Galvin (Ireland).
Mailing Address: P.O. Box 14308, 78214-0308.
Res., 9101 Graf Rd., 78214.
Church—78214. Tel: 210-534-3161; Fax: 210-534-2426.
Mission—Southton, Bexar Co., St. Ann.

72—San Juan De Los Lagos (1952) (Hispanic), Rev. Tom Ovalle, O.M.I.; Deacons Albert Salinas; Eleodoro Vasquez.
Res., 3231 El Paso St., 78207. Tel: 210-433-9722; Fax: 210-433-9526.
Catechesis/Religious Programs—Tel: 210-433-2411.
Students 300.

73—Santo Nino de Cebu (1993) (Filipino), Rev. Martin Parayno, O.S.B. (Philippines); Dr. Salvador Baylan, Parish Council Chair, Tel: 210-731-4105.
Mailing Address: 5655 Rigsby Ave., 78222. Tel: 210-648-1705; Fax: 210-648-5365.
Catechesis/Religious Programs—Students 79.

74—Vietnamese Martyrs Catholic Center (1976), Rev. Dominic Luong, S.S.S.
Centers—1208 S. W.W. White, P.O. Box 111, 78291. Tel: 210-359-9523.

OUTSIDE THE CITY OF SAN ANTONIO

Bandera, Bandera Co., St. Stanislaus (1855) (Polish), Rev. Stanislaw Oleksy, S.D.S.
Res., Box 757, 78003-0757. Tel: 830-460-4712; Fax: 830-796-7641. [CEM][JC]
Catechesis/Religious Programs—Tel: 210-796-3573. Elouise Mangold, D.R.E.
Students 240.
Mission—Medina Lake, Bandera Co., St. Victor's Chapel, Park Rd. 37, Lakehills, 78063. Tel: 830-612-3012.

Boerne, Kendall Co., St. Peter the Apostle (1866) (German), Rev. Anthony O. Cummins; Mary Ann Chandler, Admin.
Mailing Address: 202 W. Kronkosky St., 78006. Tel: 830-816-2233; Fax: 830-249-6175.
Catechesis/Religious Programs—D.R.E.: Valerie Vogel; Donna Oats; Jeanette Belter; Michelle Pechacek.
Students 750.

Brackettville, Kinney Co., St. Mary Magdalen (1875), Rev. Msgr. James Cashin.
Res., Box 95, 78832. Tel: 830-563-2487. [CEM]
Catechesis/Religious Programs—Candace O'Neill, D.R.E.
Students 150.
Mission—Spofford Junction, Kinney Co., St. Blaise.

Canyon Lake, Comal Co., St. Thomas the Apostle (1967), Rev. Msgr. Marvin G. Doerfler.
Res., 180 St. Thomas Dr., 78133-4131. Tel: 830-964-3497; Fax: 830-964-2574.
Catechesis/Religious Programs—Students 150.

Castroville, Medina Co., St. Louis (1844) (Alsatian), Rev. James Conway; Deacon Gene Ebner.
Res., 610 Madrid, 78009. Tel: 830-931-2826; Fax: 830-931-9016. [CEM]
School—Tel: 830-931-3544. Sr. Marie Elise VanDijik, C.D.P., Prin.
Lay Teachers 11; Students 228.
Catechesis/Religious Programs—Tel: 830-931-2556. Barbara Robbins, D.R.E.
Students 381.
Mission—Mico, Medina Co., St. Francis of Assisi (Medina Lake Chapel).

Cestohowa, Karnes Co., Nativity of the Blessed Virgin Mary (1873) (Polish), Rev. Gregory Sawicki, S.D.S.
Res., 300 FM 3191 Cestohowa, Falls City, 78113. Tel: 830-745-2633. [CEM]
Catechesis/Religious Programs—Students 80.

Charlotte, Atascosa Co., St. Rose of Lima (1909) (Hispanic), Rev. Anthony Vilano.
Mailing Address: P.O. Box 69, 78011. Tel: 830-277-1242; Fax: 830-277-1242.
Catechesis/Religious Programs—Students 104.
Mission—Tilden, McMullen Co., St. Joseph, 703 Congress St., P.O. Box 297, Tilden, 78072. Tel: 361-274-3374.

Comfort, Kendall Co., Sacred Heart (1949), Rev. Eduardo D. Morales.
Mailing Address: P.O. Box 599, 78013-0599. Tel: 830-995-3708.
Church—510 Broadway, 78013. Tel: 830-995-3708; Fax: 830-995-2952.
Res., 104 Daniel St., 78013. Tel: 830-995-3501.
Catechesis/Religious Programs—Students 203.

Converse, Bexar Co., St. Monica (1959), Rev. Msgr. Patrick J. Flanagan (Ireland).
Res., 501 North St., P.O. Box 429, 78109. Tel: 210-658-3816; Fax: 210-566-3821.
School—Tel: 210-658-6701; Fax: 210-658-6945. James Mollicone, Prin.
Lay Teachers 24; Students 543; Day Care 280.
Catechesis/Religious Programs—Tel: 210-658-7920. Janice Van Slambrouck, D.R.E.
Students 402.

Del Rio, Val Verde Co., Our Lady of Guadalupe (1906) (Hispanic), Rev. Jose de la Cruz Longoria Gomez, M.N.M. (Mexico); Deacons Eliesar Hernandez; Adrian Falcon; Juan Padilla.
Res., 509 Garza St., 78840. Tel: 830-775-3713; Fax: 830-775-9161.
Catechesis/Religious Programs—Tel: 830-775-2178.
Students 650.
Mission—Del Rio, San Juan Diego Chapel, 523 Jeffery Dr., V V Park Estates, 78840.

Sacred Heart (1895), Revs. James Fichler, C.I.C.M.; Carl Sadsoeitoeboen, C.I.C.M.; Deacons John C. Graf; Robert C. Kusenberger; David B. Scarbo; Roger Rodriguez.
Mailing Address: P.O. Box 1503, 78841.
Office: 307 E. Losoya, 78840. Tel: 830-775-2143; Fax: 830-775-9902. [CEM]
Res., 411 Spring St., 78840. Tel: 830-775-4240.
School—209 E. Greenwood, 78840. Tel: 830-775-3274; Fax: 830-774-2836. Mr. Billy Guerra, Prin.
Lay Teachers 14; Students 220.
Catechesis/Religious Programs—Tel: 830-775-9230. Sr. Luisita Iglesias, O.N.D., D.R.E.
Students 212.
Mission—Comstock, Valverde Co., Mary, Queen of the Universe, P.O. Box 1455, 78841.

St. Joseph's (1927) (Hispanic), Revs. Ramiro Cortez, O.M.I.; Charles Moran, O.M.I.; Deacons Filomeno Salazar; Efrain Santana; Raymundo Mendoza; Ronnie Van Dyke.
Res., 510 Wernett St., P.O. Box 1455, 78840. Tel: 830-775-4753; Fax: 830-774-7128. [CEM]
Catechesis/Religious Programs—Tel: 830-775-5200. D.R.E.: Esther G. Cardenas; Mr. Evaristo Patino; Mrs. Blanca Patino.
Students 829.

Devine, Medina Co., St. Joseph's (1897), Rev. Clement De Meersman, C.I.C.M.
Res., 108 S. Washington Dr., 78016. Tel: 830-663-2244; Fax: 830-663-2244. [CEM]
Catechesis/Religious Programs—Janie Saucedo, D.R.E.
Students 211.

D'Hanis, Medina Co., Holy Cross (1847) (Hispanic), Rev. Wallis Stiles.
Res., P.O. Box 426, 78850. Tel: 830-363-7268. [CEM]
Catechesis/Religious Programs—Students 150.
Mission—Yancy, Medina Co., Immaculate Heart of Mary.

Dilley, Frio Co., St. Joseph's (1899) (Hispanic), Rev. Msgr. Pablo Sicilia; Deacons Bernard Carroll; Salvador Tijerina.
Res., 114 E. Frio, P.O. Box N, 78017. Tel: 830-965-1926; Fax: 830-965-2125.
Catechesis/Religious Programs—Diana Carpenter, D.R.E.
Students 124.
Mission—Dilley, Frio Co., St. Mary.

Elmendorf, Bexar Co., St. Anthony (1896) (Hispanic), Rev. William McNamara; Deacons John K. Miller; Armando J. Scott; Robert Thayer.
Res., P.O. Box 248, 78112. Tel: 210-635-8539; Fax: 210-635-8644. [CEM]
Catechesis/Religious Programs—Tel: 210-635-8570. Anita Casillas, D.R.E.
Students 255.
Mission—Saspamco, Bexar Co., Our Lady of Perpetual Help. [CEM]

Falls City, Karnes Co., Holy Trinity (1902) (Polish), Rev. Walter Mushalla; Deacon Stanley Kolodzie.
Res., Box 158, 78113. Tel: 830-254-3539; Fax: 830-254-3530. [CEM]
Catechesis/Religious Programs—Rose Lee Moczygemba, D.R.E.
Students 151.

Floresville, Wilson Co., Sacred Heart (1882), Rev. Victor Carrillo; Rose Marie Pennartz, Admin.; Deacons Scott Donaho; Mike Perez.
Res., 1009 Trail St., 78114. Tel: 830-393-6117. [CEM]
School—Tel: 830-393-2117. Ms. Lilia Holt, Prin.
Sisters 2; Lay Teachers 11; Students 101.
Catechesis/Religious Programs—Debbie Leal, D.R.E.
Students 330.

Fredericksburg, Gillespie Co., St. Mary's (1846) (German), Revs. Phillip D. Henning; Edwin B. Metzger (ROC); Deacons Gregorio Martinez, Jr.; Francisco De La Torre; Louis Loth.
Res., 306 W. San Antonio St., 78624. Tel: 830-997-9523; Fax: 830-997-1037. [CEM]
School—Tel: 830-997-3914; 997-2203; Fax: 830-997-2382. Billy Pahl, Prin.
Lay Teachers 20; Students 323.
Catechesis/Religious Programs—Tel: 830-997-7487.
Students 337.
Mission—Fredericksburg, Gillespie Co., Our Lady of Guadalupe.

Gonzales, Gonzales Co., St. James (1885), Revs. Francisco A. Macias; Lenin E. Naffate; Deacon Alfonso Moreno.
Res., 417 N. College St., 78629. Tel: 830-672-2945; Fax: 830-672-1058. [CEM]
Catechesis/Religious Programs—Tel: 830-672-6291.
Students 522.
Missions—Gonzales, Gonzales Co., Sacred Heart, 426 St. John, 78629.; Waelder, Gonzales Co., St. Patrick, U.S. Hwy. 90 A, 78959.
Stations—Gonzales, Care Inn of Gonzales, Tel: 830-672-2867; Cartwheel Lodge, Tel: 830-672-2887; Ottine, Warm Springs Rehabilitation Hospital, Tel: 830-672-6592.

Harper, Gillespie Co., St. Anthony's (1909), Deacon Curtis Klein.
Res., Box 318, 78631. Tel: 830-864-4026. [CEM]

Helotes, Bexar Co., Our Lady of Guadalupe (1942), Revs. Gerald Hammel, S.M.; Gerald Pleva, S.M.; John Klobuka, S.M.; Deacon Timothy Houlihan.
Res., P.O. Box 639, 78023. Tel: 210-695-8791; Fax: 210-695-9957. [CEM]
Catechesis/Religious Programs—D.R.E.: Nancy Drymala; Jan Growney; Cindy Tejeda; Mary Shrader.
Students 1,015.

Hobson, Karnes Co., St. Boniface (1901), Rev. Gregory Sawicki, S.D.S. (Poland).
Res., US Hwy. 181, 78117. Tel: 830-780-3559. [CEM]
Catechesis/Religious Programs—Students 36.

Hondo, Medina Co., St. John the Evangelist (1892), Rev. Jeffrey Pehl; Deacon Albert Villa; Vangie Pimentel, Admin.
Res., 2102 Avenue J, 78861. Tel: 830-741-2236; Fax: 830-426-3339. [CEM]
Catechesis/Religious Programs—Tel: 830-426-2565. Norma Villa, D.R.E.
Students 618.

Jourdanton, Atascosa Co., St. Matthew's (1912) (Hispanic), Rev. Lawrence J. Christian, C.M.F., Admin.; Deacons Eusebio Guevara; Welton Fiedler, Jr.
Mailing Address: Box 670, 78026.
Res., 1700 Campbell, 78026. Tel: 830-769-3687; Fax: 830-769-2861. [CEM]
Catechesis/Religious Programs—Mrs. Diane Tymrak.
Students 157.
Mission—Christine, Atascosa Co., St. Ignatius.

Karnes City, Karnes Co., St. Cornelius (1917), Revs. Robert Ploch (Poland); Adrian Adamik (Poland).
Res., 605 E. Calvert St., 78118. Tel: 830-780-3947.
Catechesis/Religious Programs—Tel: 830-780-3949. Deacon Cesar Ponce, D.R.E.
Students 267.
Mission—Fashing, Atascosa Co., St. Elizabeth.

Kenedy, Karnes Co., Our Lady of Peace (1959), Revs. Patrick P. Bergin (CC); John Flanagan, M.S.F.
Mailing Address: P.O. Box 89, 78119.
Res., One Notre Dame Pl., 78119. Tel: 830-583-2417; Fax: 830-583-2410. [CEM]
Catechesis/Religious Programs—Tel: 830-583-2247. Janie Hernandez, D.R.E.
Students 240.

Kerrville, Kerr Co., Notre Dame (1889), Revs. Michael J. Boulette; Joselyn Mendiveloso; Deacons Daniel Arriaga; Charles Domingues; Juan A. Martinez; Denis Link.
Res., 909 Main St., 78028. Tel: 830-257-5961; Fax: 830-257-5961.
School—907 Main St., 78028. Tel: 830-257-6707; Fax: 830-792-4370. Sr. Conchessa Johnston, C.C.V.I., Prin.
Sisters of Charity of the Incarnate Word 3; Lay Teachers 11; Students 231.
Catechesis/Religious Programs—Tel: 830-896-4233.
Students 431.

Kirby, Bexar Co., St. Joan of Arc (1971), Rev. Samuel Heitkamp; Deacons John Buchanan; Robert Galan, Jr.; Joseph P. Nash; Gilbert P. Rivera.
Res., 2829 Ackermann Rd., San Antonio, 78219-2100. Tel: 210-661-5277; Fax: 210-661-5735.
Catechesis/Religious Programs—Tel: 210-661-2220. Mrs. Paulette Petron, D.R.E.
Students 360.

Kosciuszko, Wilson Co., St. Ann's (1898) (Polish), Rev. Bill Zadora, S.D.S. (Poland).
Res., 8161 FM 541-E, Stockdale, 78160-6554. Tel: 830-745-2541; Fax: 830-745-2434. [CEM]
Catechesis/Religious Programs—Students 65.

LaCoste, Medina Co., Our Lady of Grace (1911), Rev. Msgr. Thomas M. Palmer.
Res., P.O. Box 39, 78039. Tel: 830-985-3357 (Office): 985-3346 (Rectory); Fax: 830-985-3357 [*]51. [CEM]
Catechesis/Religious Programs—Tel: 830-985-3355. Mr. Martin Cerda, D.R.E.
Students 267.
Mission—Meadow Wood Acres, Bexar Co., St. John Vianney.

La Vernia, Wilson Co., St. Ann (1917), Rev. Peter McKenna.
Res., 14151 U.S. Hwy. 87 W., LaVernia, 78121. Tel: 830-779-3131; Fax: 830-779-1749. [CEM]
Catechesis/Religious Programs—D.R.E.: Gloria Bocanegra; Irene Martinez; Patti King.
Students 215.

Leon Springs, Bexar Co., St. Elizabeth Ann Seton (1961), Rev. Patrick L. Marron.
Res., 8500 Cross Mountain Tr., San Antonio, 78255. Tel: 210-698-1941; Fax: 210-698-1983.
Catechesis/Religious Programs—Students 200.

Losoya, Bexar Co., El Carmen Catholic Church (1898) (Hispanic). (Our Lady of Mt. Carmel). Rev. Richard J. McCarthy, C.M., Admin. In res., Revs. Oscar J. Miller, C.M., (Retired); Thomas Kavanaugh, C.M., (Retired).
Res., 18555 Leal Rd. (Losoya), San Antonio, 78221. Tel: 210-626-2333; Fax: 210-626-1874. [CEM]
Catechesis/Religious Programs—Tel: 210-626-1063. D.R.E.: Emily Ortiz; Mary Esther Rodriguez.
Students 233.

Lytle, Atascosa Co., St. Andrew (1904), Rev. Romeo D. Olivares, C.I.C.M.
Res., P.O. Box 326, 78052. Tel: 830-709-4287. [CEM]
Catechesis/Religious Programs—Tel: 830-709-0069.
Students 221.
Missions—Natalia, Medina Co., St. John Bosco; Coal Mine, Atascosa Co., Immaculate Conception, P.O. Box 326, Coal Mine, 78052.

Macdona, Bexar Co., Our Lady Queen of Heaven (1994) (Hispanic), Rev. Rudolph T. Carrola, Jr.
Res., 9961 Aliann, 78054.
Mailing Address: P.O. Box 94, 78054-0094. Tel: 210-622-3282; Fax: 210-622-3282.
Catechesis/Religious Programs—Students 77.

Martinez, Bexar Co., St. Jerome (1925), Rev. Thomas J. O'Brien; Deacons Joe Champagne; George Valenta.
Res., 7955 Real Rd., San Antonio, 78263. Tel: 210-648-2694; Fax: 210-648-3690. [CEM]
Catechesis/Religious Programs—Tel: 210-648-0336. Shirley Bordovsky, D.R.E.
Students 241.

New Braunfels, Comal Co., Holy Family (1964) (Hispanic), Rev. James Wasser, M.S.F.; Amelia Lankford, Pastoral Assoc.
Res., 245 S. Hidalgo, 78130. Tel: 830-609-5320; Fax: 830-609-5322.
Catechesis/Religious Programs—Tel: 210-608-9615. Angie Gomez, D.R.E.
Students 408.

Our Lady of Perpetual Help (1926), Rev. Richard Oberstar, M.S.F.; Deacons Cayetano Morales; Ramond Ybarra.
Res., 138 W. Austin St., 78130. Tel: 830-625-3534; Fax: 830-625-3566.
Catechesis/Religious Programs—Marcia Brock, D.R.E.
Students 200.
Mission—Hunter, Comal Co., St. John, 210 House St., Hunter, 78132. [CEM]

SS. Peter and Paul (1845), Rev. Msgr. Eugene O'Callaghan, V.F.; Rev. Msgr. Edward Bily; Deacons Fred Fey; Ray Kaufman; Ben Wehman; Frank Fikac; William Schroeder; James Behling; Michael Peinemann; Robert Gorman.
Res., 386 N. Castell St., 78130. Tel: 830-625-4531; Fax: 830-606-5461. [CEM 2]
School—Tel: 830-625-4531, Ext. 3; Fax: 830-606-6916. Sr. Geraldine Bienek, Prin.
Lay Teachers 17; Students 299.
Catechesis/Religious Programs—386 N. Castell, 78130. Tel: 830-625-4531, Ext. 201. Bill Smith, D.R.E.
Students 850.
Mission—Comal, Comal Co., St. Joseph.

Nixon, Gonzales Co., St. Joseph's (1915), Rev. David Tarlizzo, O.M.I.; Deacons Dimas Medina; Daniel Medina, Sr.
Res., 207 S. Washington Ave., 78140-2920. Tel: 830-582-1127. [CEM]
Catechesis/Religious Programs—Students 97.

Panna Maria, Karnes Co., Immaculate Conception of the Blessed Virgin Mary (1854) (Polish), Revs. Robert Ploch (Poland); Adrian Adamik (Poland).
Res., P.O. Box 9, 78144. Tel: 830-780-2748; Fax: 830-780-4564. [CEM]
Mission—Helena, Karnes Co., St. Helena.

Pearsall, Frio Co., Immaculate Heart of Mary (1891), Rev. Andrew Kafara (Poland); Deacon Manuel Carrizales.
Res., 422 W. Brazos, P.O. Box AK, 78061. Tel: 830-334-2382. [CEM][JC]
Catechesis/Religious Programs—Tel: 210-334-4879. Esther Martinez, D.R.E.
Students 460.

Pleasanton, Atascosa Co., St. Andrew (1913) (Hispanic), Rev. Carlos Davalos; Deacons Norman Phillips; Jose Valenzuela; Bennie Garcia, Jr.
Res., 626 Market St., 78064-2747. Tel: 830-569-3356; 281-4902 (Metro). [CEM][JC 3]
Catechesis/Religious Programs—Sr. Dorothy Moczygemba, C.S.S.F., D.R.E.
Students 460.
Mission—Campbellton, Atascosa Co., Sacred Heart, Campbell and St. Francis St., Campbellton, 78008.

St. Luke-Loire (1859), Rev. James Hoelscher; Deacons Jose Trevino; Richard Gonzalez.
Res., 3930 FM 536, 78064. Tel: 830-393-6021; Fax: 830-216-4286.
Catechesis/Religious Programs—Students 141.
Mission—Leming, Atascosa Co., Our Lady of Guadalupe, P. O. Box 110, Leming, 78050. [CEM][JC 2]

Poteet, Atascosa Co., St. Philip Benizi (1897) (Hispanic), Rev. Felix A. Avau, C.I.C.M.
Res., P.O. Box 348, 78065. Tel: 830-742-3796. [CEM]
Catechesis/Religious Programs—Beatrice Bermudez, D.R.E.
Students 250.

Poth, Wilson Co., Blessed Sacrament (1910), Rev. Thaddeus Tabak, S.D.S. (Poland); Deacon Alan Crosby.
Res., P.O. Box 339, 78147. Tel: 830-484-3302; Fax: 830-484-2903. [CEM]
Catechesis/Religious Programs—Tel: 830-484-3303.
Students 229.

Rocksprings, Edwards Co., Sacred Heart of Mary (1900) (Hispanic), Rev. Jose A. Villanueva.
Res., P.O. Box 887, 78880. Tel: 830-683-6165; Fax: 830-683-6165. [JC]
Catechesis/Religious Programs—Students 81.
Missions—Camp Wood, Real Co., St. Mary Magdalen, P.O. Box 610, Camp Wood, 78833. Tel: 830-597-5165; Leakey, Real Co., St. Raymond of Pennafort, P.O. Box 989, Leakey, 78873. Tel: 830-232-5852. Deacons Reuben Navarro; Warren Seymour.

Runge, Karnes Co., St. Anthony's (1901) (Polish), Revs. Paschal Bergin (CC) Admin.; John Flanagan, M.S.F.
Mailing Address: P.O. Box 188, 78151.
Res., Arsenso St., 78151. Tel: 830-239-4146. [CEM 2]
Catechesis/Religious Programs—Students 75.

Sabinal, Uvalde Co., St. Patrick's (1884) (Hispanic), Rev. Einer R. Ochoa.
Res., Box 117, 78881. Tel: 830-988-2255; Fax: 830-988-2255. [CEM]
Catechesis/Religious Programs—Students 89.
Missions—Knippa, Uvalde Co., St. Joseph; Vanderpool, Bandera Co., St. Mary.

St. Hedwig, Bexar Co., Annunciation of the Blessed Virgin Mary (1857) (Polish), Revs. Damien Tomiczek, S.D.S.; Martin Kaminski, S.D.S.
Res., P.O. Box 100, 78152. Tel: 210-667-1232; Fax: 210-667-9088. [CEM]
Catechesis/Religious Programs—Students 255.

Schertz, Guadalupe Co., Church of the Good Shepherd (1972), Rev. Msgr. Roger P. Robbins; Mrs. Micki Christy, Admin.; Deacons John J. Gorman; Paul La Combe; George Vick, Jr.
Res., P.O. Box 929, 78154. Tel: 210-658-4350; Fax: 210-658-7051.
Catechesis/Religious Programs—Tel: 210-658-6188. D.R.E.: Mrs. Gerry Stift; Mrs. Jean Smith.
Students 460.
Mission—Marion, Guadalupe Co., Immaculate Conception, Santa Clara and Klein, Marion, 78124.

Seguin, Guadalupe Co., Our Lady of Guadalupe (1908) (Hispanic), Revs. Alberto T. Trevino, M.S.F.; James E. Wuerth, M.S.F.; Deacons Nick Carillo; Juan Garza.
Res., 409 W. Krezdorn, 78155-4429. Tel: 830-379-4338; Fax: 830-303-1002. [CEM]
Catechesis/Religious Programs—Tel: 830-379-2818. Mr. George Oliva, D.R.E.
Students 830.

Mission—Redwood, Guadalupe Co., St. Joseph.
St. James (1873), Rev. Msgr. Gerald Hubertus.
Res., 510 S. Camp St., 78155. Tel: 830-379-1796; Fax: 830-379-1797. [CEM]
School—507 S. Camp St., 78155. Tel: 830-379-2878; Fax: 830-379-2878. Janice Jessen, Prin.
Sisters 3; Lay Teachers 12; Students 204.
Catechesis/Religious Programs—Tel: 830-379-7684. Sr. Pat Crehan, S.H.Sp., D.R.E.
Students 209.

Selma, Bexar Co., Our Lady of Perpetual Help (1897) (German), Revs. Conor McGrath; Edward Kelly; Deacons Clifford Friesenhahn; Donald Lauer.
Res., 16075 N. Evans Rd., 78154-3824. Tel: 210-651-6913; Fax: 210-651-5516. [CEM]
School—Tel: 210-651-6811; Fax: 210-651-6811. Mr. Terry Taubert, Prin.
Sisters of Incarnate Word and Blessed Sacrament 2; Lay Teachers 25; Students 417.
Catechesis/Religious Programs—Tel: 210-651-6747; Fax: 210-651-6952. Verneanne Wong, D.R.E.
Students 800.

Smiley, Gonzales Co., St. Philip Benizi (1963) (Hispanic), Rev. David Tarlizzo, O.M.I.; Deacons Frank Rojas Pastoral Admin.; John J. Moreno.
Res., P.O. Box 32, 78159-0032. Tel: 830-587-6258.
Catechesis/Religious Programs—Students 50.

Somerset, Bexar Co., St. Mary's (1920), Rev. Paul M. Newhouse, C.I.C.M. (Belgium).
Res., Box 295, 78069. Tel: 830-429-3645. [CEM]
Catechesis/Religious Programs—Mrs. Sylvia Cruz, D.R.E.
Students 204.

Spring Branch, Comal Co. (Honey Creek), St. Joseph (1876), Rev. James Janish; Sandy Strange, Pastoral Assoc.; Deacons Johnny Gass; James Legendre. In res., Rev. Mark A. Garrett, O.S.A.
Res., 25781 Hwy. 46 W., 78070-3613. Tel: 830-980-2268; Fax: 830-980-3184. [CEM]
Catechesis/Religious Programs—Sandy Strange, D.R.E.
Students 312.

Stockdale, Wilson Co., St. Mary (1895) (Polish), Rev. Wieslaw Iwaniec; Deacon Jack Karam.
Res., Box 535, 78160. Tel: 830-996-3415; Fax: 830-996-3415. [CEM]
Catechesis/Religious Programs—Students 170.

Stonewall, Gillespie Co., St. Francis Xavier (1945) (German-Hispanic), Rev. Joseph G. De La Garza.
Res., 404 St. Francis St., 78671-3717. Tel: 830-644-2368. [CEM]

Uvalde, Uvalde Co., Sacred Heart (1883), Revs. Kenneth M. Dakin; Roy Milton Quioque, C.I.C.M.; Deacons Hector V. Garcia; Antonio Hinojosa; Fortunato Hinojosa; Gonzalo Uriegas.
Res., 408 Fort Clark St., 78801. Tel: 830-278-3448; Fax: 830-278-2835. [CEM]
School—Tel: 830-278-2661. Ms. Cheryl Elledge, Prin.
Teresian Sisters 3; Lay Teachers 11; Students 168.
Catechesis/Religious Programs—Tel: 830-278-3060. Linda Milam, D.R.E.
Students 1,204.

Von Ormy, Bexar Co., Sacred Heart (1935) (Hispanic), Rev. Rudolph T. Carrola, Jr.; Deacons Ricardo de la Garza; Carlos Rodriguez.
13466 IH 35 S., 78073-3302. Tel: 210-622-3457; 622-3282; Fax: 210-622-3282.
Res., P.O. Box 94, Macdona, 78054-0094. Tel: 210-622-3282; Fax: 210-622-3282.
Catechesis/Religious Programs—Denise Barker, D.R.E.
Students 99.
St. Peter the Fisherman (1990) (Hispanic), Rev. Miguel Arango (Colombia); Deacons Richard Wells; Ernesto Bravo.
Office: 17534 N. State Hwy. 16, 78073. Tel: 830-276-8778; 276-4985 (Res.); Fax: 830-276-8778.
Catechesis/Religious Programs—Students 300.
Missions—Moore, Frio Co., St. Augustine, P.O. Box 252, Moore, 78057-0252.; Bigfoot, Frio Co., Our Lady of Mt. Carmel, P.O. Box 68, Bigfoot, 78065-0068.

KOREAN APOSTOLATE

Boerne, Korean Martyrs Catholic Church (1982) (Korean), Rev. David H. Kim (Korea); Deacon Philip Kim.
Res., 7655 Curres Cir., 78015. Tel: 210-698-3877; Fax: 210-655-1838.

OLD SPANISH MISSIONS

San Antonio, Old Spanish Missions, Rev. Msgr. Balthasar J. Janacek, Dir.
Mailing Address: c/o Catholic Chancery, P.O. Box 28410, 78228.
Purisima Concepcion—807 Mission Rd., 78210.
San Francisco de la Espada—10040 Espada Rd., 78214.
San Juan Capistrano—9101 Graf Rd., 78214.
San Jose—701 E. Pyron Rd., 78214.

Chaplains of Public Institutions

SAN ANTONIO. *Audie Murphy VA Hospital* 7400 Merton Minter, 78229. Tel: 210-617-5308. Revs. Harry Martin; Richard R. Benonis.
Baptist Memorial Hospital 111 Dallas St., 78205. Tel: 210-222-8431. Mrs. Pat Sammis.
Brooke Army Medical Center Tel: 210-916-1105; 916-2172; Fax: 210-916-1169. Rev. James Schellenberg, D.Min. Tel: 210-916-4141 (After 4:30 pm & Weekends), Res., Bldg. 3600, 3851 Roger Brooke Blvd., Fort Sam Houston, 78234. Tel: 210-916-4141 (After 4:30pm & Weekends).
Methodist Hospital 7700 Floyd Curl, 78229. Tel: 210-692-4030. Rev. Marian Piekarczyk.
St. Luke's Baptist Hospital; University Hospital 4502 Medical Dr., 78229. Tel: 210-680-2635 (Residence). Rev. Nicholas Brown, S.C.J.
San Antonio State Hospital 6711 S. New Braunfels, 78223. Tel: 210-532-8811. Rev. Augustine Amanzeh.
Santa Rosa Hospital System 519 W. Houston, 78207. Tel: 210-704-2021. Revs. Mark Scheffler, C.Ss.R.; Michael Norton, C.PP.S.; Palmer Maxwell; Mr. Richard Woodley.
Southwest General Hospital Tel: 210-921-2000. Deacon Leon Mueller.

KERRVILLE. *Veterans' Administration Hospital*. Vacant. Tel: 210-896-2020.

Special Assignment:
Reverend Fathers—
Baistra, Jorge, In Charge of Big Foot and Moore, TX
Cepeda, Jose Arturo, Rome
Cowan, Anthony, Hospital Min., New York
Horan, Michael
Martinez, Leo

On Duty Outside the Archdiocese:
Reverend Monsignors—
Martinez, Leo, Mexico
Reverend Fathers—
Dillane, Maurice, Ireland
Garret, Sean, 110 St. Mary St., S.W., Fort Walton Beach, FL 32548. Tel: 904-243-3742
Kenny, Michael, All Hallows College, Grace Park Rd., Drumcondra, Dublin 9, Ireland
Kownacki, Robert, 7224 Balmoral, Chicago, IL 60656. Tel: 312-775-7315
Martinez, Manuel, Federal Correctional Institute, P.O. Box 1000 La Tuna, Anthony, NM 88021
Rubaj, Leon, Incarnate Word Sister's Convent, 1101 N.E. Water St., Victoria, TX 77901

Military Chaplains:
Reverend Fathers—
Barlow, James P., Chaplain Major, 8539 Odyssey Dr., Universal City, TX 78148
Gonzalez, George G., Chap. Major, 6726 Widgeon Dr., Midland, GA 31820
Hernandez, Alfred Ricardo, Col. Catholic Chap., 3240 Old Lawley Toll Rd., Calistoga, CA 94515
Nee, Eugene O., A.P.O., PFE 50, Box RET 667, APO, AE 09494
Tellez, Jairo, Major, U.S.A.F., HAD 2930 Support Battallion, USAREUR, APO AE, 09086

On Leave:
Reverend Fathers—
Crane, Jeff
Currie, Donald
Davila, Johnny
De La Rosa, Vincent
Dietz, Xavier Ortiz
Duran, Jorge
Hernandez, Antonio
Kammerer, James
O'Sullivan, Michael
Ruiz, Enrique
Sandoval, Luis

Retired:
Reverend Monsignors—
Costantino, Anthony J., 80 Peter Baque Rd., San Antonio, TX 78209. Tel: 210-826-7721
Fecher, Vincent, 8520 Cross Mountain Trail #302, San Antonio, TX 78255. Tel: 210-698-3923
Garcia, Raymond, 8520 Cross Mountain Tr., #202, San Antonio, TX 78255. Tel: 210-698-9079
Goertz, Alois J., 8520 Cross Mountain Tr., #100, San Antonio, TX 78255. Tel: 210-698-9067
Hubertus, Albert, Casa de Padres, San Antonio, TX
Manning, J. Leroy, 8520 Cross Mountain Tr. #1102, San Antonio, TX 78255. Tel: 210-698-3183
Matocha, John L., Box 158B, Mathis, TX 78368. Tel: 512-547-9859
Meurer, David, 8520 Cross Mountain Tr., #1001, San Antonio, TX 78255. Tel: 210-698-0175
Palmer, Patrick, Cross Mountain Tr., #1101, San Antonio, TX 78255. Tel: 210-698-3276
Petsch, Joseph, Casa de Padres, 8520 Cross Mountain Tr. #702, San Antonio, TX 78255. Tel: 210-698-7055
Pugh, Charles, Padua Place, San Antonio, TX
Rihn, Roy, 8520 Cross Mountain Tr. #301, San Antonio, TX 78255. Tel: 210-698-0287
Smith, Sherrill, 8520 Cross Mountain Tr., #201, San Antonio, TX 78255. Tel: 210-698-8819
Stuebben, George, 314 Cave Ln., San Antonio, TX 78209. Tel: 210-829-0238
Wangler, Alex, 6701 Blanco Rd., Apt. 110, San Antonio, TX 78216-6111. Tel: 210-342-6063
Reverend Fathers—
Evans, George J., O.C.S.O., 6061 Dezavala Rd., Apt. 113, San Antonio, TX 78249. Tel: 210-694-0452
Goebel, Bernard M., 150 Beethoven St., San Antonio, TX 78210. Tel: 210-359-9034
Johnston, Robert F., 601 Van Ness Ave., #1052, San Francisco, CA 94102. Tel: 415-674-3572
Kavanaugh, Thomas, C.M., El Camen Parish, 18555 Leal Rd., San Antonio, TX 78221. Tel: 210-626-2333
Maus, Jasper, O.F.M., St. Francis Nursing Home, San Antonio, TX
O'Callaghan, Patrick, Mailing Address: P.O. Box 34413, San Antonio, TX 78265
Paniagua, Pablo, 8520 Cross Mountain Tr., #401, San Antonio, TX 78255. Tel: 210-698-8036
Wagner, John, St. Matthews, 10703 Warzbach, San Antonio, TX 78230. Tel: 210-696-4161
Zumaya, David, Mexico

Permanent Deacons:
Almanza, Jose M., St. Margaret Mary, San Antonio
Alvarado, Thomas, St. Timothy's, San Antonio
Amo, Ernest Roy, St. Brigid, San Antonio
Arismendez, Agustin, St. Paul, San Antonio
Arriaga, Dan, Notre Dame, Kerrville
Baker, Robert L., Colonial Beach, VA
Barajas, Felipe, Holy Rosary, San Antonio
Barrera, Enrique, San Fernando, San Antonio
Bautista, Teofilo, Annunciation of BVM, St. Hedwig
Behling, James, Ss. Peter and Paul, New Braunfels
Bellg, Bruce J., Blessed Sacrament, San Antonio
Bemrich, Richard, (Retired)
Benigno, Pasquale, St. Brigid's, San Antonio
Billimek, Thomas E., St. Brigid's, San Antonio
Bonilla-Valentin, Jorge, Immaculate Heart of Mary, San Antonio
Bozek, Edwin J., Jr., San Francesco di Paola, San Antonio
Bravo, Ernesto G., St. Peter the Fisherman, Von Ormy
Breck, Ralph, Our Lady of Perpetual Help, New Braunfels
Brumley, Denson C., On Leave
Buchanan, John, (Retired)
Caballero, Antonio, St. Timothy, San Antonio
Caldwell, Robert M., Jr., Prince of Peace, San Antonio
Callaway, George, Jr., St. Anthony Mary Claret, San Antonio
Camero, A. C., Our Lady of Guadalupe & Jail Ministry, San Antonio
Campa, Gerard, St. Mary Magdalen, San Antonio
Campos, Fred, Jr., St. Gregory the Great, San Antonio
Carranza, Manuel G., Jr., Holy Family, San Antonio
Carrillo, Nick L., Our Lady of Guadalupe, Seguin
Carrillo, Victor, Jr., Bremen, IN
Carrizales, Manuel, Immaculate Heart of Mary, Pearsall
Carroll, Bernard, St. Joseph, Dilley
Casanova, Ismael G., St. Mary Magdalen, San Antonio
Castellano, Frank V., St. Gabriel, San Antonio
Castillo, Pedro C., Holy Family, San Antonio
Cena, Librado, St. John Berchmans, San Antonio
Champagne, Joseph, St. Jerome, Martinez
Chavez, Hugo V., St. John the Evangelist, San Antonio
Ciarrochi, Jerome, St. Thomas More, San Antonio
Cisneros, Daniel, Basilica of Our Lady of Mt. Carmel & St. Therese (aka Little Flower), San Antonio
Clancey, Patrick, The Patrician Movement, San Antonio
Colley, Earl M., Holy Rosary, San Antonio
Criado, Marcos, Imaculate Conception, San Antonio
Crosby, Alan, Blessed Sacrament, Poth
Cross, Raymond, St. Peter Prince of Apostles, San Antonio
Crowley, Thomas, St. Pius X, San Antonio
Cruz, Robert, Our Lady of Good Counsel, San Antonio

Cuellar, Federico, (Retired)
D'Agostino, Michael, St. Helena, San Antonio
De Hoyos, Richard, St. Peter Prince, San Antonio
De la Torre, Francisco, St. Mary's, Fredericksburg
DeCuir, Harold, St. Helena, San Antonio
DeLaGarza, Gustavo, On Leave
DeLaGarza, Ricardo, Sacred Heart, Von Ormy
DeLauter, Paul, (Retired)
DeLeon, Joseph L., El Cerito, CA
Diaz, Jose G., St. John Berchman, San Antonio
Dillard, Henry, St. Stephen, San Antonio
Domingues, Charles, Notre Dame, Kerrville
Donaho, Scott, Jr., Sacred Heart, Floresville
Donias, Justo, Jr., Catholic Charities, Fort Wayne, IN
Droll, Victor, St. Elizabeth's, Pflugerville
Dunn, John N., St. Peter Prince of Apostles, San Antonio
Ebner, Eugene, St. Louis, Castroville
Elliot, Robert R., St. James, Seguin
Enriquez, Marcos, On Leave
Espinosa, Jose R., On Leave
Estrada, Melchor, On Leave
Falcon, Adrian, Our Lady of Guadalupe, Del Rio
Fertitta, J. V., Sr., Blessed Sacrament, San Antonio
Fey, Fred, Sts. Peter & Paul, New Braunfels
Fiedler, Welton J., St. Matthew, Jourdanton, TX
Fikac, Frank J., Sts. Peter & Paul, New Braunfels
Fitzpatrick, Alan, St. Dominic, San Antonio
Fox, Thomas J., St. Matthew's, San Antonio
Fraga, Jesse, Our Lady of Sorrows, San Antonio
Franklin, Thomas M., St. Francis of Assisi, San Antonio
Friesenhahn, Clifford, Our Lady of Perpetual Help, Selma
Frisina, Patrick, St. Brigid, San Antonio
Galan, Roberto L., Jr., St. Joan of Arc, Kirby
Gallegos, Valentine, Sacred Heart, San Antonio
Galvan, Robert, Our Lady of Guadalupe, San Antonio
Garcia, Bennie, St. Andrew, Pleasanton
Garcia, Hector, Sacred Heart, Uvalde
Garcia, Roberto, Austin
Garza, Albert G., San Fernando Cathedral, San Antonio
Garza, Juan, Our Lady of Guadalupe, Seguin
Garza, Lionel, Jr., St. Dominic, San Antonio
Garza, Pedro F., San Fernando Cathedral, San Antonio
Garza, Robert M., Prince of Peace, San Antonio
Gass, Johnny J., St. Joseph, Honey Creek, Spring Branch
Gonzalez, Amador, St. Bonaventure, San Antonio
Gonzalez, Richard, St. Luke-Loire, Pleasanton
Gorman, John J., Good Shepherd, Schertz
Gorton, Everett D., San Fernando Cathedral, San Antonio
Graf, John E., Sacred Heart, Del Rio
Greer, Jesse R., Church of the Holy Spirit, san Antonio
Guerrero, Leon, St. Agnes, San Antonio
Guevara, Eusebio, St. Matthew's, Jourdanton
Gutierrez, Pedro, Fresno, CA
Gutierrez, Ramon, St. Leo, San Antonio
Hansbauer, Eugene, St. Luke, San Antonio
Henson, Archibald, St. Louis, Castroville
Herbert, David L., Holy Name, San Antonio
Hernandez, Elieser, Our Lady of Guadalupe, Del Rio
Hernandez, Jose D., St. Lawrence, San Antonio
Herrera, Genaro M., St. Joseph's (South San), San Antonio
Herrera, Ramon, On Leave
Heye, Paul F., St. Brigid, San Antonio
Hinojosa, Antonio, Sacred Heart, Uvalde
Hinojosa, Fidel, St. Bonaventure, San Antonio
Hinojosa, Fortunado, Sacred Heart, Uvalde
Hinojosa, Reynaldo G., Sr., Holy Name, San Antonio
Hobbs, John R., San Francisco di Paola, San Antonio
Hoelscher, Wilbur L., St. Matthew's, San Antonio
Hollstein, Albert, (Retired)
Holmstrom, Joseph, On Leave
Houlihan, Timothy, Our Lady of Guadalupe, Helotes, TX
Hunsucker, Paul, St. Thomas the Apostle, Canyon Lake
Huttinger, John X., Our Lady of Guadalupe, San Antonio
Imburgia, Scott, Permanent Diaconate Office, San Antonio
Jasso, Reynaldo, St. Rose of Lima, San Antonio
Jorgensen, J. D., Blessed Sacrament, San Antonio
Joslin, Wayne L., March A.F.B., Moreno Valley, CA
Karam, Jack, St. Mary's, Stockdale
Kasavage, Richard, (Retired)
Kaufman, Raymond, (Retired)
Kearns, W. Daniel, St. Benedict, San Antonio
Keller, Alois, Jr., St. Lawrence, San Antonio
Kim, Philip C., Korean Community, San Antonio
Klein, Curtis, St. Anthony, Harper
Knopp, Kenneth P., (Retired)
Kolodzie, Stanley, Holy Trinity, Falls City
Krupa, Joseph, Church of the Holy Spirit, San Antonio
Kusenberger, Robert, Sacred Heart, Del Rio
La Combe, Paul B., Church of Good Shepherd, Schertz, TX
Lamm, Wilfred, St. Margaret Mary, San Antonio
Lammons, Charles, St. Benedict, San Antonio
Landez, John, St. Leo & Permanent Diaconate Office, San Antonio
Laskowski, Norbert C., Holy Trinity, San Antonio
Lauer, Donald E., Our Lady of Perpetual Help, Selma
Leal, Ernesto T., St. Lawrence, San Antonio
Legendre, James F., St. Joseph, Honey Creek, Spring Branch
Link, John Dennis, Notre Dame, Kerrville
Lira, Antonio, St. Rose of Lima, San Antonio
Lira, Rodolfo, Toledo, OH
Longoria, Leobardo, St. Vincent De Paul, San Antonio
Lopez, Edward V., St. John the Evangelist, San Antonio
Loth, Louis E., St. Mary's, Fredricksburg
Ludolph, Anthony, Hardy, AR
Mangold, Clayton, St. Paul, San Antonio
Marin, Arturo, San Bernardino, CA
Marques, Steven J., St. Mark the Evangelist, San Antonio
Martinez, Gregorio, Jr., St. Mary, Fredricksburg
Martinez, Ignacio, (Retired)
Martinez, Juan G., Divine Providence, San Antonio
Martinez, Juan A., Notre Dame, Kerrville
McDonald, John, St. James, San Antonio
Mechler, Gerardo A., St. Margaret Mary, San Antonio
Medina, Damacio, St. Joseph, Nixon
Medina, Daniel G., St. Joseph, Nixon
Medina, Henry, St. Dominic, San Antonio
Medina, Ricardo, III, Goshen, IN
Medrano, Rudy C., St. Timothy, San Antonio
Menchaca, Jose, St. Martin De Porres, San Antonio
Mendoza, Raymundo V., St. Joseph, Del Rio
Merlin, Joseph, On Leave
Meyers, Joseph L., Austin, TX
Micek, Jerome, Holy Trinity, San Antonio
Michel, John A., St. Pius X, San Antonio
Miller, John K., St. Anthony, Elmendorf
Miller, Mark C., Indianapolis, IN
Miller, Myles, St. Luke, San Antonio
Moczygemba, Zafirin, St. Margaret Mary, San Antonio
Morales, Cayetano, Our Lady of Perpetual Help, New Braunfels
Moreno, Alfonso, Sacred Heart, Gonzales
Moreno, Florencio, Diocese of El Paso, TX
Moreno, John J., St. Philip's, Smiley
Moreno, Jose F., Our Lady of Angels, San Antonio
Mueller, Leon, (Retired)
Munoz, Antonio, Immaculate Conception, San Antonio
Muraida, Daniel, St. Paul's, San Antonio
Nash, Joseph, St. Joan of Arc, Kirby, TX
Navarro, Ruben W., St. Raymond Pennafort, Leakey
Neal, Thomas R., Prince of Peace, San Antonio
Nelson, Robert W., Fort Worth
Neville, Richard F., Jr., Randolph, A.F.B., San Antonio
Novian, Donald, On Leave
Olivares, Jesse, On Leave
Orr, James, Our Lady of Atonement, San Antonio
Ortega, Sylvester, St. Jude, San Antonio
Ortiz, Antonio H., St. Jude, San Antonio
Ostaszewski, Chester R., St. Rose of Lima, San Antonio
Pacheco, Alvino, St. Leo, San Antonio
Padilla, Juan R., O.L., Guadalupe, Del Rio
Paiz, Gabriel, (Retired)
Patino, Edward, St. Agnes, San Antonio
Patlan, Antonio, St. Martin de Porres, San Antonio
Patlan, Pedro, St.Paul, San Antonio
Pedroza, Doroteo E., San Fernando, San Antonio
Peinemann, Michael E., Sts. Peter & Paul, New Braunfels
Perez, Julio T., On Assignment, U.S. State Dept.
Perez, Miguel, Jr., Sacred Heart, Floresville
Perez, Oscar, Mission San Francisco de la Espada, San Antonio
Phillips, Norman D., St. Andrew, Pleasanton
Ponce, Cesar, St. Cornelius, Karnes City
Pope, Charles F., Sr., St. Clare, San Antonio
Pratt, Gilbert, St. Francis of Assisi & Jail Ministry, San Antonio
Prevott, Raymond, (Retired)
Pruneda, Esmeraldo, St. Jude, San Antonio
Quarles, Fred J., On Leave
Ramirez, Albert, Our Lady of Angels, San Antonio
Ramirez, Victor, (Retired)
Raso, James, On Leave
Reyes, Ramiro, Ligonier, IN
Richard, Joseph N., St. Paul, San Antonio
Riojas, Francisco, St. Philip, Smiley
Rivera, Gilbert, St. Joan of Arc, Kirby
Rodriguez, Carlos, Sacred Heart, Von Ormy
Rodriguez, Roger, Elkhart, IN
Rodriguez, Santiago, San Jose Mission, San Antonio
Rodriguez, Severo, Jr., On Leave
Rondon-Martinez, Angel, Unassigned
Ruiz, Roberto R., Espada Mission, San Antonio
Salazar, Filomeno, St. Joseph, Del Rio
Salinas, Alberto, San Juan DeLos Lagos, San Antonio
Salinas, Carlos, (Retired)
Sanabria, Agripino, Prince of Peace, San Antonio
Sanchez, Jose H., St. Philip of Jesus, San Antonio
Sandoval, Carlos, Our Lady of Guadalupe, San Antonio
Santana, Efrain, St. Joseph, Del Rio
Scarbo, David B., Sacred Heart, Del Rio
Schonhoff, Robert L., Our Lady of Grace, San Antonio
Schroeder, William, Sts. Peter and Paul, New Braunfels
Scott, Armando, St. Anthony, Elmendorf
Sekinger, Eugene, Military Parochial, Brooks Air Force Base
Seymour, Warren V., (Retired)
Shockley, Gordon F., Unassigned
Shoemake, William, Christ the King, Belton
Soriano, Pedro, St. Timothy, San Antonio
Soto, Roman, Holy Family, San Antonio
Spitzer, John L., On Leave
Stallings, Larry, St. Mark, San Antonio
Staudt, Milton N., Church of the Holy Spirit, San Antonio
Stewart, Wilbert, St. Dominic, San Antonio
Stockton, Ree, St. Dominic, San Antonio
Stokes, Leslie, Federal Way, WA
Suniga, Jose A., Divine Providence, San Antonio
Svatek, Anton, (Retired)
Swift, Thomas N., Resurrection of the Lord, San Antonio
Tamez, Javier, Holy Family, San Antonio
Terry, Frank, St. Anthony Mary Claret, San Antonio
Thayer, Robert, St. Anthony, Elmendorf
Thornberry, William, Prince of Peace, San Antonio
Tijerina, Salvador, St. Joseph, Dilley
Torres, Thomas, San Jose Mission, San Antonio
Townsend, Eugene, St. Pius X, San Antonio
Trevino, Jimmie, St. Dominic, San Antonio
Trevino, Jose S., St. Luke Loire, Pleasanton
Trujillo, Jose M., Galveston-Houston
Tudon, Horacio R., St. Matthew's, San Antonio
Uriegas, Gonzalo, Sacred Heart, Uvalde
Urrabazo, Rosendo, St. John the Evangelist, San Antonio
Valenta, George, St. Jerome, San Antonio
Valenzuela, Jose J., On Leave
Van Dyke, Ronnie, St. Joseph, Del Rio
Vasquez, Eleodore, San Juan de Los Lagos, San Antonio
Vick, George, Jr., Good Shepherd, Schertz
Villa, Albert G., St. John the Evangelist, Hondo
Villareal, Ricardo, St. Brigid, San Antonio
Wasniewski, Michael, On Leave
Wehman, Ben, Sts. Peter and Paul, New Braunfels
Weissler, Gilbert, St. Anthony of Padua, San Antonio
Wells, Richard, St. Peter The Fisherman, Von Ormy
Werner, Keith N., St. Matthew's, San Antonio
White, George, St. Matthew, San Antonio
White, Thomas, St. Clair, Holy Redeemer, San Antonio
Wittig, Evan, St. John Evangelist, San Antonio
Wright, Michael, O.F.M.Conv., Brunswick, GA
Ybarra, Hermengildo Rey, St. Leonard, San Antonio
Ybarra, Raymond, Our Lady of Perpetual Help, New Braunfels
Zapata, Gumercindo, St. Philip of Jesus, San Antonio
Zapata, Thomas, On Leave
Zepeda, Ernest, (Retired)
Zizke, William, St. Matthew's, San Antonio

INSTITUTIONS LOCATED IN THE ARCHDIOCESE

[A] SEMINARIES, ARCHDIOCESAN

SAN ANTONIO. *The Assumption-St. John's Seminary,* 2600 W. Woodlawn Ave., P.O. Box 28240, 78228. Tel: 210-734-5137; Fax: 210-734-2324. Legal Title: *The Seminary of the Assumption of the Blessed Virgin Mary-St. John of San Antonio, TX.* Revs. Gerald L. Brown, Rector, Admissions & Devel. & Admin.; Norman Ermis, Vice Rector & Assoc. Dir. Internship, Admissions & Community Life; Thomas H. Dymowski, O.SS.T., Dir. Spiritual Formation; Sr. Patricia E. Casey, O.P., Dir. Pastoral Formation & Coord. Cultural Prog.; Sr. Addie Walker, S.S.N.D., Dir. Liturgical Formation & Co-Coord. Cultural Program; Sr. Carmen Terese Lazo, M.C.D.P., Dir. Multicultural Formation; Revs. John Kemper, S.S., Dir. Internship Prog. & Spiritual Dir. In Residence; Anthony F. Lobo, S.S., Spiritual Dir. In Res. Priests 5; Sisters 3; Seminarians 36; Domestic Dept.: Josephine Sisters (Mexico City, Mexico) 9.

Diaconate Program, 114 Shannon Ln., 78216-7316. Tel: 210-930-8118; Fax: 210-930-8377.
E-mail: diacprog@swbell.net
Rev. John O'Donoghue, Dir. Assistant Directors: Deacons John Landez; George White; Joe Fertitta.

[B] SEMINARIES, RELIGIOUS OR SCHOLASTICATES

SAN ANTONIO. *Congregation of Holy Cross - Formation Community,* Bro. Charles Andersen Residence, 320 Brahan Blvd., 78215-1020. Tel: 210-233-9117; Fax: 210-223-2081. Bro. Donald Blauvelt, C.S.C., Co-Dir.; Rev. Lawrence A. LeVasseur, C.S.C., Co-Dir. Brothers 2; Seminarians 2.

Dominican Priory of San Juan Macias, 210 St. Ann St., 78201-6393. Tel: 210-734-6688; Fax: 210-738-1755.
E-mail: st-ann@juno.com
Revs. John Raymond Corr, O.P.; Joseph Determan, O.P.; John E. Keefer, O.P.; Cayet Mangiaracina, O.P.; Vincente M. Pena, O.P.; Bruce B. Schutz, O.P.; Marcelo Solorzano, O.P.; Emiliano Zapata, O.P. Novices 13.

Franciscan Formation Program in San Jose Friary (Casa Juan Diego), 701 E. Pyron Ave., 78214. Tel: 210-922-4976; Fax: 210-932-2271.
E-mail: casavo@aol.com
Rev. Herbert Jones, O.F.M., Dir.; Bro. John Abts, O.F.M., Asst. Dir. Seminarians 3.

George Sexton House of Studies. (Theology), 314 E. King's Hwy., 78212. Tel: 210-735-7318; Fax: 210-734-3150.
E-mail: demazenod1@aol.com
Missionary Oblates of Mary Immaculate, United States Region. Revs. James Brobst, O.M.I.; Joseph T. La Belle, O.M.I. Scholastics 9.

Immaculate Heart Claretian Seminary, 617 S. Santa Rosa Blvd., 78204. Tel: 210-222-9510; Fax: 210-222-1479. Rev. Stephen K. Sherwood, C.M.F., Admin. Brothers 1.

Missionhurst Formation Community, 1147-A Cupples Rd., 78226. Tel: 210-434-5347; Fax: 210-432-2621.
E-mail: MCIcm49085@aol.com
Revs. Anselme Malonda, C.I.C.M., Dir. Formation; David Curran, C.I.C.M. Theology 4.

MSF Formation Community, 104 Cas-Hills Dr., 78213-3322. Tel: 210-344-9145; Fax: 210-344-9146.
E-mail: jbeegan@hotmail.com
Web site: www.catholic-forum.com/msf
Rev. James Beegan, M.S.F. Seminarians 1; Brothers 1.

Priests of the Sacred Heart-House of Formation, 133 Thelma Dr., 78212-2517. Tel: 210-826-6091; 6092; Fax: 210-826-8019.
E-mail: huffscj@yahoo.com
Revs. Stephen Huffstetter, S.C.J., Dir. Formation; Nicholas Brown, S.C.J.; Bro. Peter Mankins, S.C.J., Dir. In res. Bro. Francis Snider, S.C.J. Students 5.

Redemptorist Formation Program, 1523 Iowa, 78203-1817. Tel: 210-533-0442, 0443; Fax: 210-533-0558.
E-mail: monper@compuserve.com
Web site: www.redemptorists-denver.org
Revs. Monroe Perrier, C.Ss.R., Dir.; Francis Pham, C.SS.R., Vice-Prov. of New Orleans. Students 7.

St. Anthony Mary Claret Formation House, 402 John Adams Dr., 78228-4231. Tel: 210-734-2678; Fax: 210-733-8732.
E-mail: aclaretsem@aol.com
Web site: home.earthlink.net/~cmfftex/
Rev. Steven Niskanen, C.M.F., Prefect. Seminarians 6.

San Damiano Friary, Prenovitiate House of Formation, 1104 Kentucky Ave., 78201. Tel: 210-734-4962; Fax: 210-734-6322. Conventual Franciscan Friars. Revs. Miguel Briseno, O.F.M.Conv.; James Oberhausen, O.F.M.Conv., Guardian & Dir. House of Formation; Bros. Timothy Unser, O.F.M.Conv.; Paul Clark, O.F.M. Conv. Seminarians 6.

[C] COLLEGES AND UNIVERSITIES

SAN ANTONIO. *Oblate School of Theology,* (1903) 285 Oblate Dr., 78216-6693. Tel: 210-341-1366; Fax: 210-341-4519.
Web site: www.ost.edu
For a complete listing, refer to the Colleges and Universities section.

Our Lady of the Lake University, 411 S.W. 24th, 78207-4689. Tel: 210-434-6711; Fax: 210-436-0824.
E-mail: mahos@lake.OLLUSA.edu
Web site: www.ollusa.edu
For a complete listing, refer to the Colleges and Universities section.

St. Mary's University of San Antonio, Texas, (1852) One Camino Santa Maria, 78228-8572. Tel: 210-436-3011; Fax: 210-436-3500.
E-mail: jmoder@alvin.stmarytx.edu
Web site: www.stmarytx.edu
For a complete listing, refer to the Colleges and Universities section.

The United Colleges of San Antonio, 285 Oblate Dr., 78216. Tel: 210-341-1366; Fax: 210-341-4519
For a complete listing, refer to the Colleges and Universities section.

University of the Incarnate Word, 4301 Broadway, 78209. Tel: 210-829-6000; Fax: 210-829-3901.
E-mail: douge@universe.uiwtx.edu
Web site: www.uiw.edu
For a complete listing, refer to the Colleges and Universities section.

[D] HIGH SCHOOLS, ARCHDIOCESAN

SAN ANTONIO. *Antonian College Preparatory High School.* (Coed), 6425 West Ave., 78213. Tel: 210-344-9265; Fax: 210-344-9267.
E-mail: gsaenz@prodigy.net
Web site: Antonian.org
Dr. Gilbert L. Saenz, Prin. Deacons 1; Lay Teachers 37; Students 570.

[E] HIGH SCHOOLS, REGIONAL

SAN ANTONIO. *St. Gerard Catholic High School,* 521 S. New Braunfels Ave., 78203. Tel: 210-533-8061; Fax: 210-533-3697. Maurice Abadie, Pres.; Teresa Skloss, Prin. Sisters 2; Brothers 2; Lay Teachers 20; Students 205.

[F] HIGH SCHOOLS, PRIVATE

SAN ANTONIO. *Blessed Sacrament Academy,* 1135 Mission Rd., 78210. Tel: 210-532-4731; Fax: 210-534-6568.
E-mail: odilia@texas.net
Web site: sticky-wickets.org
Sr. M. Odilia Korenek, I.W.B.S., Dir. & Supr.

Second Chance High School, Texas Charter School. Tel: 210-532-9161; Fax: 210-533-5612. Sisters of the Incarnate Word and Blessed Sacrament 2; Lay Teachers 11; Other Sisters 1; Students 180; Support Staff 17.

Child Development Center. Tel: 210-532-5363; Fax: 210-532-6698. Sisters of the Incarnate Word and Blessed Sacrament 2; Lay Teachers 11; Students 145; Support Staff 17.

Parents Academy. Tel: 210-534-0894; Fax: 210-532-6698. Sisters 1; Lay Teachers 1; Support Staff 7; Students 250.

Central Catholic High School, 1403 N. St. Mary's St., 78215-1785. Tel: 210-225-6794; Fax: 210-227-9353.
E-mail: admissions@cchs-satx.org
Web site: www.cchs-satx.org
Rev. Joseph A. Tarrillion, S.M., Pres.; Dr. Paul M. Sullivan, Ed.D., Prin.; Revs. Donald Cowie, S.M.; Joseph G. Rasky, S.M. Priests 3; Brothers 6; Sisters 2; Lay Teachers 33; Students 513.

Healy-Murphy Center, Inc., 618 Live Oak St., 78202. Tel: 210-223-2944; Fax: 210-224-1033. Douglas J. Watson, Prin. & Exec. Dir. Day School for High School Students. Provides an alternative to the Regular School System. Sisters 1; Lay Teachers 45; Counselors 2; Nurses 1; Students 300; Child Development Department: Ages 6 wks. - 5 yrs 110; On Campus Clinic: Nurse 1.

Holy Cross High School, 426 N. San Felipe, 78228. Tel: 210-433-9395; Fax: 210-433-1666.
E-mail: SAHCMAN@hotmail.com
Web site: www.holycross-sa.org
Brothers of the Holy Cross. Bro. Stanley Culotta, C.S.C., Prin. Brothers 4; Sisters 1; Lay Teachers 38; Students 500.

Incarnate Word High School, 727 E. Hildebrand Ave., 78212-2598. Tel: 210-829-3100; Fax: 210-829-3120. Mr. Roger Labat, Prin. Sisters 7; Brothers 2; Lay Teachers 50; Students 590.

Providence High School, 1215 N. St. Mary's St., 78215-1787. Tel: 210-224-6651; Fax: 210-224-6214.
Web site: www.providencehs.com
Anne Bristol, Prin. Sisters 2; Lay Teachers 32; Students 477.

St. Anthony Catholic High School, 3200 McCullough Ave., 78212-3099. Tel: 210-832-5600; Fax: 210-832-5615.
Boys boarding department. Michael J. Trodden, Prin.; Rev. Arturo Flores, O.M.I. Priests 1; Sisters 2; Lay Teachers 25; Students 270.

St. Francis Academy, 1807 Centennial Ave., 78211. Tel: 210-923-1421; Fax: 210-921-4948. Sr. Jeanne Marie Ulica, O.S.F., Prin. School Sisters of St. Francis 6; Lay Teachers 16; Students 142.

[G] ELEMENTARY SCHOOLS, PRIVATE

SAN ANTONIO. *Mount Sacred Heart School.* (Grades PreK-8), 619 Mount Sacred Heart Rd., 78216. Tel: 210-342-6711; Fax: 210-342-4032.
E-mail: asacsmsheart@impresso.com
Web site: nsheagles.com
Mrs. Sylvia D. Herrera, Prin.; Rev. Stefan Wiera, Chap. Sisters 4; Lay Teachers 27; Students 454.

Our Lady of Peace, aka, Westside Catholic Interparish School. (Grades K-8), Mailing Address: P.O. Box 830513, 78283-0513. Tel: 210-224-2450; Fax: 210-224-1101. 314 Merida St., 78207. Tel: 210-224-2450; Fax: 210-224-1101.
E-mail: guangels@intx.net
Mrs. Marianne Mongiello. Sisters 1; Lay Teachers 8; Students 133.

St. Anthony's School, 205 W. Huisache St., 78212. Tel: 210-732-8801; Fax: 210-732-5968.
E-mail: asacstanthel@impresso.com
John P. Kennedy, Ed.D., Prin.; Rev. Vincent Fecher. Priests 1; Sisters 1; Lay Teachers 20; Students 333.

St. John Bosco School. (Grades K-8), 5630 W. Commerce St., 78237. Tel: 210-432-8011; Fax: 210-432-5168. Day School. Institute of the Daughters of Mary Help of Christians (Salesian Sisters of St. John Bosco). Sr. Theresa Sironi, F.M.A., Supr.; Sr. Josephine Ochoa, F.M.A., Prin. Sisters 18; Lay Teachers 26; Students 665.

St. Martin Hall, Our Lady of the Lake University of San Antonio, 411 S.W. 24th St., 78207. Tel: 210-434-6711, Ext. 308; Fax: 210-432-8526.
E-mail: ramiro@lake.ollusa.edu
Web site: education.ollusa.edu/stmartinhall/
Robert Ramirez, Prin. Campus Laboratory School, Preschool Kindergarten and Elementary. Sisters 1; Deacons 1; Lay Teachers 22; Students 335.

[H] GENERAL HOSPITALS

SAN ANTONIO. *Christus Santa Rosa Children's Hospital,* 519 W. Houston St., 78207-3198. Tel: 210-704-2011; Fax: 210-704-3632
For a complete listing, refer to the Hospitals section.

Christus Santa Rosa Health Care Corporation, 519 W. Houston St., 78207-3198. Tel: 210-704-2011; Fax: 210-704-3632.
Web site: www.santarosahealth.org
For a complete listing, refer to the Hospitals section.

Christus Santa Rosa Hospital, 519 W. Houston St., 78207-3198. Tel: 210-704-2011
For a complete listing, refer to the Hospitals section.

Christus Santa Rosa Medical Center, 2827 Babcock Rd., 78229. Tel: 210-705-6300
For a complete listing, refer to the Hospitals section.

Incarnate Word Health System, 4500 Broadway, 78209. Tel: 210-828-2224
For a complete listing, refer to the Hospitals section.

[I] PROTECTIVE INSTITUTIONS

SAN ANTONIO. *Father Flanagan's Boys' and Girls' Town of San Antonio,* 503 Urban Loop, 78204. Tel: 210-271-1010; Fax: 210-271-3333.
E-mail: morales@boystown.org
Web site: www.boystown.org
For a complete listing, refer to the Special Care Facilities section.

Providence Home & Family Services, Inc., 2650 Castroville Rd., 78237. Tel: 210-434-2111; Fax: 210-433-2806.
E-mail: cbovarice@compuserve.com
For a complete listing, refer to the Special Care Facilities section.

St. Peter & Joseph Childrens Home, 919 Mission Rd., 78210. Tel: 210-533-1203; Fax: 210-533-6177.
E-mail: sbomlaski@stpjhom.org
For a complete listing, refer to the Special Care Facilities section.

Seton Home for Homeless, Pregnant Young Women, 1115 Mission Rd., 78210. Tel: 210-533-3504; Fax: 210-533-3467
For a complete listing, refer to the Special Care Facilities section.

Visitation Hospitality House of San Antonio, Texas and Interconnections, 945 W. Huisache, 78201. Tel: 210-735-6910; Fax: 210-738-8794.
E-mail: visitprog@aol.com
Web site: www.visitationhouseministries.org
For a complete listing, refer to the Special Care Facilities section.

BOERNE. *Childrens' Inn*, 216 W. Highland Dr., 78006. Tel: 830-249-9456; Fax: 830-249-3327.
E-mail: childrensinn@netscape.net
For a complete listing, refer to the Special Care Facilities section.

[J] DAY CARE CENTERS AND KINDERGARTENS

SAN ANTONIO. *Blessed Sacrament Learning Center*, 222 W. Cevallos St., 78204. Tel: 210-223-5013; Fax: 210-223-5013. Mercedarian Sisters of the Blessed Sacrament. Sr. Bernadette Gomez, H.M.S.S., Admin. Sisters 3; Children 30.

Carmelite Learning Center, 2006 Martin Luther King Dr., 78203. Tel: 210-533-0651; Fax: 210-533-3910. Sr. Angela Therese Lovato, D.C.J., Dir. Carmelite Sisters of the Divine Heart of Jesus 5; Lay Staff 15; In Day Care 120.
Attended from St. Patrick's Church.

Immaculate Conception Kindergarten and Nursery, 2407 W. Travis St., 78207. Tel: 210-226-3934; Fax: 210-226-3934. Sr. Maria Del Carmen Sanchez, A.P.G., Dir. Sisters 5; Lay Staff 14; Kindergarten & Nursery Children 53.

St. Anthony Day Care Learning Center; Infant and Toddler Center, 1707 Centennial Blvd., 78211. Tel: 210-924-4443; Fax: 210-924-4469.
E-mail: salc@aol.com
Sr. Mary Ann Domagalski, M.S.S.A., Admin.; Sr. Lucelia Sanchez, M.S.S.A., Dir. Sisters 2; Lay Staff 25; Children 140.

St. Brigid's Kindergarten, 5118 Loma Linda Dr., 78201. Tel: 210-733-0037; Fax: 210-785-2820. Sr. Stephenie Deegan, C.S.B., Dir. Children 30.

BOERNE. *St. Albert Hall dba St. Albert Early Learning Center*, 216 W. Highland Dr., 78006. Tel: 210-816-2059; 2060; Fax: 210-816-2060. Dolores Zapata, Min. Dir. Children 200; Staff 31.

[K] HOMES FOR AGED

SAN ANTONIO. *Casa De Padres*, 8520 Cross Mountain Tr., P.O. Box 100, 78255 Fax: 830-981-9192.
E-mail: jengberg@gvtc.com
For a complete listing, refer to the Special Care Facilities section.

Incarnate Word Retirement Community, 4707 Broadway, 78209. Tel: 210-829-7561; Fax: 210-828-0020
For a complete listing, refer to the Special Care Facilities section.

Marianist Residence: Skilled Nursing, 520 Fordham Ln., 78228-4821. Tel: 210-436-3771 (Nurses' Station); Fax: 210-431-4240.
E-mail: jjaeckle@stmarytx.edu
For a complete listing, refer to the Special Care Facilities section.

Oblate Madonna Residence, 5722 Blanco Rd., 78216. Tel: 210-341-2350
For a complete listing, refer to the Special Care Facilities section.

Padua Place, 80 Peter Baque Rd., 78209. Tel: 210-826-7721; Fax: 210-824-4554.
E-mail: paduaplace@aol.com.
For a complete listing, refer to the Special Care Facilities section.

St. Francis Nursing Home, 630 W. Woodlawn, 78212. Tel: 210-736-3177; Fax: 210-783-2221
For a complete listing, refer to the Special Care Facilities section.

The South Texas Catholic Retirement Center, Inc., P.O. Box 15378, 78212-8578. Tel: 210-734-8310; Fax: 210-734-8369.
E-mail: coughlin@universe.uiwtx.edu
For a complete listing, refer to the Special Care Facilities section.

KENEDY. *John Paul II Nursing Home*, 209 S. 3rd St., P.O. Box 359, 78119. Tel: 830-583-9841; Fax: 830-583-9458
For a complete listing, refer to the Special Care Facilities section.

[L] BOARDING HOMES

SAN ANTONIO. *Seraphic Sisters Boarding Home for the Aged*, 619 W. Craig Pl., 78212. Tel: 210-736-3177. Mailing Address: c/o St. Francis Nursing Home, 630 W. Woodlawn, 78212. Sr. Agnes Bochenek, S.O.L.S., Dir. Guests 2.

[M] MONASTERIES AND RESIDENCES OF PRIESTS AND BROTHERS

SAN ANTONIO. *Casa Maria Marianist Community*, St. Mary's University, One Camino Santa Maria #18, 78228-8518. Tel: 210-436-3066; Fax: 210-431-4216. Rev. Christian Janson, S.M. Tel: 210-436-3273; Bros. Joseph Barrett, S.M. Tel: 210-436-3228; Roger Bau, S.M. Tel: 210-431-2269; Terrence O'Connor, S.M. Tel: 210-436-3246; Fred A.R. Stovall, S.M., Dir. Tel: 210-436-3242; Michael Sullivan, S.M. Tel: 210-436-3258.

Casa Pasionista Guadalupe, 700 Waverly, 78201. Tel: 210-736-5228; Fax: 210-737-6549.
E-mail: clementecp@cs.com
Web site: www.passionist.org
Rev. Clemente Barron, C.P.

Casa San Juan Marianist Community, 1701 Alametos, 78201. Tel: 210-734-6727; Fax: 210-431-6884.
E-mail: gmontag@stmarytx.edu
Revs. George T. Montague, S.M., Dir.; Robert E. Hogan, S.M.

Central Catholic Marianist Community, 1403 N. St. Mary's St., 78215-1785. Tel: 210-225-1112; Fax: 210-227-9353. Revs. Donald Cowie, S.M., Dir.; Joseph G. Rasky, S.M. Brothers 10.

Chaminade Community House, 10910 Wild Grape, 78230-3459. Tel: 210-641-6354.
E-mail: ckaczkowski@stmarytx.edu
Marianists. Revs. Conrad J. Kaczkowski, S.M.; Joseph A. Tarrillion, S.M., Supr.; Charles H. Miller, S.M.

De Mazenod House. (Faculty Residence), 7707 Madonna Dr., 78216. Tel: 210-349-8572; Fax: 210-979-0240. Missionary Oblates of Mary Immaculate. Revs. Ken Hannon, O.M.I., Supr.; Jan Heemrood, O.M.I.; Donald J. Joyce, O.M.I.; Ray John Marek, O.M.I.; Leopoldo G. Perez, O.M.I., S.T.D.; Frederick Sackett, O.M.I.; Ronald W. Young, O.M.I. Priests 7.

Discalced Carmelites (Prov. of St. Therese), 906 Kentucky Ave., 78201-6097. Tel: 210-735-9126; Fax: 210-735-1389.
E-mail: satfriar@aol.com
Web site: www.2.dcci.com/ocdokla/
Revs. Ralph Reyes, O.C.D.; James Anthony Curiel, O.C.D.; Jerome Earley, O.C.D., Supr.; Michael Okuroski, O.C.D.; Christopher Timoney, O.C.D.; Mary Philip Wurth, O.C.D. Priests 6; Scholastics 3; Postulants 2.

Holy Cross Community, 426 N. San Felipe St., 78228. Tel: 210-434-9100; Fax: 210-433-1666.
E-mail: SAHCMAN@hotmail.com
Web site: www.holycross-sa.org
Bro. Stanley Culotta, C.S.C., Dir.; Revs. John W. Lubbers, C.S.C.; Bernard Foley, C.S.C. Priests 2; Brothers 5.

Bro. Charles Andersen Residence, 320 Brahan Blvd., 78215. Tel: 210-223-9117. Rev. Lawrence A. LeVasseur, C.S.C., Dir.; Bro. Donald Blauvelt, C.S.C., Co-Dir. Priests 1; Brothers 2; Seminarians 2.

Holy Rosary Marianist Community, 159 Camino Santa Maria, 78228-4997. Tel: 210-433-6137; Fax: 210-433-2133. Revs. John J. Manahan, S.M.; James Russell, S.M.; Bros. Daniel Calvo, S.M.; Richard Schrader, S.M.; Robert Hatesohl, S.M., Dir.

Hospital Ministry House, 6111 Walking Gait, 78240. Tel: 210-680-3685. Rev. Nicholas Brown, S.C.J.

Joseph Gerard House, 302 Oblate Dr., 78216. Rev. Robert Wright, O.M.I. Tel: 210-348-0545.

Marianist Residence, St. Mary's University, 520 Fordham Ave., 78228-4821. Tel: 210-436-3744; Fax: 210-436-3747. Bro. Joseph Grieshaber, S.M., Dir. Tel: 210-436-3745; Revs. J. Willis Langlinais, S.M. Tel: 210-431-4362; John A. Leies, S.M. Tel: 210-436-3227; Bernard Meyer, S.M. Tel: 210-436-3761; John Rechtein, S.M. Tel: 210-431-2092; Paul Ryan, S.M. Tel: 210-436-3766; W. Franz Schorp, S.M. Tel: 210-431-2259. Priests 6; Brothers 17.

Marianist Vocation Ministry, One Camino Santa Maria, 78228-8556. Tel: 210-431-2193; Fax: 210-436-3724.
E-mail: mumike@stmarytx.edu
Web site: marianist.udayton.edu
Bro. Michael Sullivan, S.M., Dir.; Rev. Christian Janson, S.M.

Marianist Woodlawn Community, 3303 W. Woodlawn Ave., 78228. Tel: 210-436-0182; Fax: 210-436-0188. Revs. Lawrence Doersching, S.M., Dir.; Norbert Brockman, S.M. Priests 2; Brothers 6.

Missionaries of the Sacred Heart. Sectional Headquarters of the Irish Province for California and Southern States. 237 W. Magnolia, 78212-2916. Tel: 210-737-6394; Fax: 210-737-0327. Revs. James Dudley, M.S.C., Supr.; James Harnan, M.S.C.; Colm Mulligan, M.S.C.
Miscellaneous: Rev. Patrick J. Stenson, M.S.C., Religious Activities Office, 3700 N. Capitol St. N.W., Washington, DC, 20317. Tel: 202-882-1888.

Missionary Oblates of Mary Immaculate, 327 Oblate Dr., 78216-6698. Tel: 210-349-1475; Fax: 210-349-7411.
E-mail: t-singer@pcn.net
Web site: www.omiusa.org
Revs. Thomas Singer, O.M.I., Reg. Councillor; Galeb Mokarzel, O.M.I. Tel: 210-342-1951; Salvatore F. DeGeorge, O.M.I., Southwest Area Supr. & Dir. Vocations. Tel: 210-349-1475; Charles Breault, O.M.I. Tel: 210-348-9045, 214 Oblate Dr., 78216. Revs. William Morell, O.M.I. Tel: 210-342-3476; Thomas Singer, O.M.I. Tel: 210-342-3492, 218 Oblate Dr., 78216. Rev. Patrick Guidon, O.M.I. Tel: 210-826-8501, 527 Thelma, 78212.

Missionhurst Community Residence, 1746 Donaldson, 78228. Revs. Francis Loos, C.I.C.M. Tel: 210-432-6062; Pieter Van Der Paalen, C.I.C.M. Tel: 210-435-4210; Paul Van Coillie, C.I.C.M. Tel: 210-432-1034.
Other Addresses: 7600 Blanco Rd., Apt. 1605, 78216. Tel: 210-344-3813. Rev. Ralph Nuytten, C.I.C.M.

MSF Center & Provincialate, 210 El Rancho Way, 78209. Tel: 210-826-9815; Fax: 210-826-3339.
E-mail: msfroh@netscape.net
Web site: www.catholic-forum.com
Congregation of the Missionaries of the Holy Family. Very Rev. Robert E. O'Hara, M.S.F., Prov. In res. Rev. Gary Perret, M.S.F.; Bros. John Griffin, M.S.F.; James J. Beegan, M.S.F.

Oblate Benson Residence (Southwest Area), 334 W. Kings Hwy., 78212. Tel: 210-732-5162; Fax: 210-732-6143. Missionary Oblates of Mary Immaculate - Southwest Area. Revs. Gerard Weber, O.M.I. Tel: 210-732-8024; J. C. Cain, O.M.I. Tel: 210-732-5162; Salvatore DeGeorge, O.M.I. Tel: 210-732-8771; Arturo Flores, O.M.I. Tel: 210-735-6773; Andrew Wueste, O.M.I. Tel: 210-732-5162. Priests 5.

Redemptorists of Texas-San Antonio #1, 1617 Iowa St., 78203. Tel: 210-534-4351; Fax: 210-534-1280.
E-mail: RUHNKE@flash.net
Web site: www.marriagepreparation.com
(Vice Province of New Orleans). Revs. Robert A. Ruhnke, C.SS.R., Supr.; Jose Chavez, C.SS.R.; Gilbert A. Enderle, C.SS.R.; Carl Schindler, C.SS.R.; Mark Sheffler, C.SS.R.; Bro. Charles Fucik, C.SS.R.

San Damiano Friary, 1104 Kentucky Ave., 78201. Tel: 210-734-4962; Fax: 210-734-6322.
E-mail: miguelb@aol.com
Conventual Franciscan Friars. Revs. Miguel Briseno, O.F.M.Conv.; James Oberhausen; Bros. Tim Unser, O.F.M.Conv.; Paul Clark, O.F.M. Conv.

NEW BRAUNFELS. *Congregation of the Holy Ghost*, 19440 IH 35 N., 78132-4839. Tel: 830-609-1200; Fax: 830-609-4738. Rev. Joseph Gaglione, C.S.Sp.

[N] CONVENTS AND RESIDENCES FOR SISTERS

SAN ANTONIO. *Blessed Sacrament Convent*, 222 W. Cevallos St., 78204. Tel: 210-223-5013; Fax: 210-223-5013. Mercedarian Sisters of the Blessed Sacrament. Sr. Dolores Munoz, H.M.S.S., Supr. Sisters 9.

Blessed Sacrament Convent, 118 Melba, 78216. Tel: 210-828-0155. Sr. Terese Fritz, I.W.B.S., Supr. Sisters of the Incarnate Word and Blessed Sacrament. Sisters 2.

Carmelite Convent, 2006 Martin Luther King Dr., 78203. Tel: 210-533-0651; Fax: 210-533-3910. Carmelite Sisters of the Divine Heart of Jesus. Sr. Pauline Therese, D.C.J., Supr.

Cordi-Marian Missionary Sisters, Cordi-Marian Villa, 11624 FM 471, 78253. Tel: 210-688-3099; 688-3889; Fax: 210-688-3564. Convent, Provincial House and Retreat Center. Sr. Celestine Castro, M.C.M., Prov. Supr.; Sr. Celina Martin, M.C.M., Supr.; Rev. Jeremiah Murphy, M.S.C., Chap. Sisters 21.

Cordi-Marian Missionary Sisters Convent, 2902 Morales St., 78207. Tel: 210-433-5064. Sr. Mary Elia Jaime, M.C.M., Supr. Sisters 4.

Daughters of Charity Convent, 7603 Somerset Rd., 78211. Tel: 210-927-2795; Fax: 210-922-0332.
E-mail: sanglim@dessa.org
Daughters of Charity of St. Vincent de Paul. Sr. Suzanne Anglim, D.C., Supr. Sisters 4.

The Daughters of St. Paul Convent. (Pontifical F.S.P.), 114 Main Plaza, 78205. Tel: 210-224-8101; Fax: 210-224-0938.
E-mail: saantonio@pauline.org
Web site: www.pauline.org
Sr. Maria Teresa Meza, F.S.P., Supr. Sisters 5.

El Carmen Sister's Residence, 1835-1 Martinez-Losoya Rd., 78221. Tel: 210-626-2024; Fax: 210-626-1849.
E-mail: dclcarmen@ibm.net
Daughters of Charity of St. Vincent de Paul. Sr. Constance Hummel, D.C., Supr. Sisters 4.

Eucharistic Franciscan Missionary Sisters, 558 Cumberland, 78204. Tel: 210-224-7993. Sr. Flora Ramirez, M.E.F., Supr. Sisters 4.

Felician Sisters, 3910 Meadow Ridge, 78210-5720. Tel: 210-532-3433.
E-mail: felsister@aol.com
Sr. Martha Janysek, C.S.S.F., Supr. Sisters 3.

Hermanas Catequistas Guadalupanas Convent, 4110 S. Flores St., 78214. Tel: 210-532-9344. Sr. Martha Ruiz, H.C.G., Supr. Sisters 5.

Holy Rosary Convent, 543 Westminister, 78228. Tel: 210-433-1108. Sr. Joyce des Jardins, S.S.N.D., Correspondent. Sisters 4.

Holy Spirit Motherhouse, 301 Yucca St., 78203. Tel: 210-533-5149; Fax: 210-533-3434.
E-mail: holyspirit@shsp.org
Web site: www.shsp.org
Motherhouse of the Sisters of the Holy Spirit and Mary Immaculate. Sr. Veronica Cahill, S.H.Sp., Gen. Supr. Sisters 51.

Incarnate Word and Blessed Sacrament Convent, 1135 Mission Rd., 78210. Tel: 210-534-8005; Fax: 210-534-6568.
E-mail: odilia@texas.net
Web site: sticky-wickets.com
Sisters of the Incarnate Word and Blessed Sacrament. Sr. M. Odilia Korenek, Supr. Sisters 9.

Incarnate Word Generalate (1869), 4503 Broadway, 78209-6297. Tel: 210-828-2224; Fax: 210-828-9741.
E-mail: iwg011@ccvisanantonio.org
Web site: www.ccvisanantonio.org
General Administration of the Congregation of Sisters of Charity of the Incarnate Word. Sr. Teresa Stanley, C.C.V.I., Gen. Supr., U.S. Province, P.O. Box 15378, 78212-8578. Tel: 210-734-8310; Fax: 210-734-8369. Sr. Helena Monahan, C.C.V.I., Prov. Coord. Total in Congregation 491; Total in U.S. Province 285.

Incarnate Word Retirement Community, U.S. Province, 4707 Broadway, 78209-6200. Tel: 210-829-7561 (Retirement Center); Fax: 210-828-0020.
E-mail: helenam@universe.uiwtx.edu
Mr. Richard Boyd, Exec. Dir.; Sr. Margaret Nugent, C.C.V.I., Admin. Extended Care; Sr. Philomena Birmingham, C.C.V.I., Coord. for Sisters; Sr. Agnes Moloney, C.C.V.I., Asst. Coord. Extended Care; Michelle Todd, Dir. Admissions & Mktg.; Rev. Msgr. Thomas A. French, Chap. Sisters in Extended Care 39; Sisters Independent Living 68; Sisters in Assisted Living 16; Lay Independent Living 40; Lay Assisted Living 16; Lay Extended Care 21.

Institute of the Daughters of Mary Help of Christians, Province of Mary Immaculate, 6019 Buena Vista St., 78237. Tel: 210-432-0089; 0090; Fax: 210-432-4016.
E-mail: fmasuopr@aol.com
Salesian Sisters of St. John Bosco. Sr. Phyllis Neves, F.M.A., Prov. Supr.

Missionary Catechists of Divine Providence. Central House and Admin. Offices, St. Andrew's Convent, 2318 Castroville Rd., 78237. Tel: 210-432-0113; Fax: 210-432-1709.
E-mail: micadipr@aol.com
Sr. Guadalupe Ramirez, M.C.D.P., Supr., Casa Benitia - House of Initial Formation, 2318 Castroville Rd., 78237. Tel: 210-431-3207. Sisters 2; Students 2. Casa Juan Diego, 147 School, 78210. Tel: 210-533-1238. Sisters 3. Casa Providencia, 203 Tansyl Dr., 78213. Tel: 210-348-6534. Sisters 2. Casa Santa Cruz, 111 Tampico, 78207. Tel: 210-226-5054. Sisters 2. Sisters 9.

Monastery of the Discalced Carmelite Nuns, 6301 Culebra & St. Joseph Way, 78238-4909. Tel: 210-680-1834; Fax: 210-680-3106.
E-mail: saocdnun@dcci.com
Rev. Mother Therese Leonard, O.C.D., Prioress. Sisters 9.

North American Union, Sisters of Our Lady of Charity, 1900 Montana, P.O. Box 10443, 78210. Tel: 210-475-9390; Fax: 210-475-9373. Sr. Agnes O'Mahoney, O.L.C., Supr. Sisters 8.

Our Lady of the Lake Convent, 515 S.W. 24th St., 78207. Tel: 210-434-1866; Fax: 210-431-9965. Sisters of Divine Providence. Sr. Eugenia Ann Stell, C.D.P., Coord. Professed Sisters 41. O.L.L. Convent Home for retired Sisters of Divine Providence. Coordinators: Sr. Madonna Sangalli, C.D.P.; Sr. Anna-Lee Prather, C.D.P.; Sr. Roberta Haby, C.D.P., McCullough Hall Nursing Center and Regan Hall, 603 S.W. 24th St., 78207. Tel: 210-433-6011. Home for retired Sisters of Divine Providence. Sisters 77.

Our Lady of the Pillar Convent, 251 W. Ligustrum Dr., 78228. Tel: 210-433-5501; Fax: 210-431-9611.
E-mail: escobarFMI@ad.com
Centralhouse of the Congregation of the Daughters of Mary Immaculate. Marianist Sisters. Sr. Evangeline Escobar, F.M.I., Prov.; Sr. Eileen Cehyra, F.M.I., Dir. of Sisters. Sisters 13.

Our Lady of Victory Missionary Sisters Convent, 1114 San Carlos, 78207-6727. Tel: 210-433-3296. Sr. Connie Lewandowski, O.L.V.M. Sisters 2.

Presentation Convent, 8931 Callaghan Rd., 78230-4570. Tel: 210-342-2503; Fax: 210-349-4772.
E-mail: pbvmsat@juno.com
Residence of the Community of the Union of the Sisters of the Presentation of the B.V.M. Sr. Mary F. O'Driscoll, P.B.V.M., Supr. Sisters 13.

Provincial Offices of the Sisters of the Sacred Heart of St. Jacut, 11931 Radium St., 78216-2714. Tel: 210-344-7203; Fax: 210-341-0721.
E-mail: jnlv@juno.com
Sr. Juana O. Villescas, S.S.C.J., Prov., 7014 Spent Wing, 78213. Sisters 5. 818 Firefly, 78216. Sisters 4. 7112 Hagy Cir., 78216. Sisters 5. 919 Briarcliff, 78213. Sisters 5.

Sacred Heart Sisters' Convent, 2318 Castroville Rd., 78237. Tel: 210-432-6830. Sisters 11. Novitiate, 1203 Viewridge, 78213. Sisters 4. Sisters 61 in Province.

Religious of Mary Immaculate Convent, 719 Augusta St., 78215. Tel: 210-226-0025; Fax: 210-226-3305.
E-mail: villamaria@stic.net
Religious of Mary Immaculate Sisters. Sr. Ada Marie Mier, R.M.I., Local Supr. Sisters 12.

St. Anthony Convent, 100 Peter Baque Rd., 78209. Tel: 210-824-4553; Fax: 210-824-4554.
E-mail: mssa@aol.com
Motherhouse and Novitiate of the Missionary Servants of St. Anthony. Sr. Mary Ann Domagalski, M.S.S.A., Supr. Sisters 5.

St. Brigid's Convent, 5118 Loma Linda Dr., 78201. Tel: 210-733-0701; 736-1671; Fax: 210-785-2820; 737-3683.
E-mail: Txbrigidines@juno.com
Regional House. Sr. Teresa Carter, C.S.B., Regional Coord.
Address matters connected with congregation to the Regional Coord. Sisters 16.

St. James Convent, 402 Nunes, 78225. Tel: 210-533-9659; Fax: 210-924-0201.
E-mail: fmasuosj@stic.net
Daughters of Mary Help of Christians (Salesian Sisters of St. John Bosco). Sr. Cecilia Henry, F.M.A., Supr. Sisters 6.

St. John Bosco Convent, 5630 W. Commerce St., 78237. Tel: 210-432-8011; Fax: 210-434-8559.
E-mail: fmasuojb@stic.net
Daughters of Mary Help of Christians. Sr. Theresa Sironi, F.M.A., Supr. Sisters 18.

St. Joseph's Convent - S.S.N.D. House of Formation, 2372 W. Southcross, 78211-1898. Tel: 210-923-2364.
E-mail: sjsassnd@aol.com
Sr. Marcell Stos, S.S.N.D., Coord. Sisters 2.

St. Teresa's Convent, 138 Fair Ave., 78223-1014. Tel: 210-533-5330; Fax: 210-533-2532.
E-mail: carmestj@aol.com
Web site: www.teresians.org
Sr. Carmelina Guzman, S.T.J., Coord. Society of St. Teresa of Jesus 15.

School Sisters of Notre Dame, Convents: Caroline House, 3415 W. Woodlawn, 78228. Tel: 210-435-3234. Sr. Ann Semel, S.S.N.D., Correspondent. Sisters 2.

Seraphic Sisters of Our Lady of Sorrows Convent, 621 W. Woodlawn Ave., 78212. Tel: 210-734-3364. Sr. Sancja Panek, S.O.L., Supr. Sisters 6.

The Sisters of Perpetual Adoration Convent, 2403 W. Travis St., 78207. Tel: 210-227-5546; Fax: 210-226-3934. Sr. Maria Del Carmen Sanchez, A.P.G., Supr. Sisters 9.

Stella Maris Convent, 2702 Castroville Rd., 78237-3341. Tel: 210-434-1314. Congregation of Divine Providence, Inc. Sisters 4.

Ursuline Residences, 4812 Vance Jackson Rd., 78230. Tel: 210-344-1800; Fax: 210-344-6673. Sr. Marianne Mullen, Prioress. Sisters 6.

BIG WELLS. *Carmelitas del Sagrado Corazon - OCD*, P.O. Box 276, 78830. Tel: 830-457-2693. Sr. Ma Guadalupe Esparza, O.C.D., Supvr. Sisters 2.

BOERNE. *St. Scholastica Monastery*, 416 W. Highland, 78006. Tel: 830-249-2645; 830-816-8504; Fax: 830-249-4728.
E-mail: benstrs@tex.net
Web site: www.boernebenedictines.com
Congregation of Benedictine Sisters, Monastery, Novitiate and Omega Retreat Center. Sr. Mary Agnes Zinni, O.S.B., Prioress. Sisters 21.

HELOTES. *Generalate of the Congregation of Divine Providence*, P.O. Box 197, 78023. Tel: 210-695-8721; Fax: 210-695-6033.
E-mail: glate@lake.ollusa.edu
Sr. Antoinette Billeaud, C.D.P., Supr. Gen. Sisters 3.

UVALDE. *Society of St. Teresa of Jesus*. (Teresian Sisters), Mailing Address: 343 N. Crisp St., 78801. Tel: 830-278-6724; Fax: 830-278-5170.
E-mail: teresians@aol.com
Web site: teresians.org
Sisters 3.

[O] RETREAT HOUSES

SAN ANTONIO. *Oblate Renewal Center*, Mailing Address: 5700 Blanco Rd., 78216-6615. Tel: 210-349-4173; Fax: 210-349-4281.
E-mail: orcsa@express-news.net
Rev. Kevin Collins, O.M.I.; Bro. Patrick McGee, O.M.I.; Sr. Theresa O'Toole, S.H.Sp.; Ms. Shirley Russell, Hospitality Dir.

BOERNE. *Omega Retreat Center*, 216 W. Highland Dr., 78006. Tel: 830-816-8471 (San Antonio); 249-3894 (Boerne); Fax: 830-249-3327.
E-mail: omegactr@boernenet.com
Web site: www.bornebenedictines.com
Mr. Andrew Anderson, Dir.

CASTROVILLE. *Moye Center*, 600 London, 78009. Tel: 830-931-2233; Fax: 830-931-2227.
E-mail: moyecenter@aol.com
Linda Follis, Dir. Center for Retreats, Renewal, and Conferences. Under the direction of the Sisters of Divine Providence. Sisters 3.

[P] CATHOLIC CHARITABLE ORGANIZATIONS AND CLINICS

SAN ANTONIO. *Catholic Charities, Archdiocese of San Antonio*. Administration, 1405 N. Main Ave., Ste. 222, 78212-4351. Tel: 210-222-1294; Fax: 210-227-0217.
E-mail: ccaosa@flashnet.net
Adolescent Pregnancy Prog., Adoption, Counseling, Childrens' Health Insurance Programs. Office, 1405 N. Main Ave., Ste.222, 78212-4351. Tel: 210-475-9011; Fax: 210-475-0436. Refugee Resettlement, Family Support Immigration Services. 2903 W.Salinas St., 78207. Tel: 210-433-3256; Fax: 210-433-0851. Senior community services, Foster Grandparents, RSVP, Older Worker Program. 1405 N. Main Ave., Ste. 222, 78212-4351. Tel: 210-222-1294; Fax: 210-222-9326.
See Curia Section - Department of Social & Community Services.

Daughters of Charity Services of San Antonio, 7607 Somerset Rd., 78211-3752. Tel: 210-921-0071; Fax: 210-922-0332.
E-mail: lmejia@dcssa.org
Mr. Larry Mejia, Exec. Dir. Daughters of Charity Svcs.
This corporation operates centers at three locations: De Paul Family Center, 7603 Somerset, 78211. Tel: 210-924-5903; Fax: 210-922-0332. El Carmen Center, 18555-1 Leal Rd., 78221. Tel: 210-626-2121; Fax: 210-626-1848. Sisters 3. LA Mission Family Health Care, 19780 U.S. Hwy. 281 S., 78221. Tel: 210-626-3854; Fax: 210-626-1174.

Society of St. Vincent de Paul, 928 W. Commerce, 78207. Tel: 210-225-7837; Fax: 210-225-8878. Homer Cadena, Pres.; Mary M. Armstrong, Exec. Dir.

[Q] NEWMAN CENTERS

SAN ANTONIO. *Catholic Campus Ministry*, Catholic Student Center, 312 W. Courtland Pl., 78212-3906. Tel: 210-736-3752; Fax: 210-736-5365.
E-mail: whitecccm@juno.com
Carol White, Dir.
Archdiocesan Campus Ministry: Martin Martinez, San Antonio College; Imelda Morales, Palo Alto College & UTSA Downtown Campus; Gloria M. Keller, St. Phillip's College. Tel: 210-533-9819; Sr. Imelda Phelan, C.S.B., University of Texas at San Antonio.

St. Anthony Catholic Student Center, 14523 Roadrunner Way, 78249. Tel: 210-699-9594; Fax: 210-699-9572. Mrs. Beatriz M. Garcia; Imelda Ramirez.

Trinity University, c/o 312 Courtland Pl, 78212. Tel: 210-736-3752. Rev. John Keefer, O.P.

Southwest Texas Junior College, 2401 Garner Field Rd., Uvalde, 78801-6297. Tel: 830-278-4401; Fax: 830-951-7354. Dr. Lawrence Lewis.

Texas Lutheran University, 1000 W. Court St., Seguin, 78155-5999. Tel: 830-372-6047.
E-mail: llewis@tlu.edu

Schreiner College, 2100 Memorial Blvd., Kerrville, 78028-5697. Tel: 830-792-7401.
E-mail: csullivan@shreiner.edu
Dr. Claudia Sullivan.

[R] PERSONAL PRELATURES

SAN ANTONIO. *Opus Dei Prelature of the Holy Cross and Opus Dei*, 345 E. Summit, 78212. Tel: 210-732-3065; Fax: 210-732-8613.
E-mail: info@opusdei.org
Web site: www.opusdei.org
Rev. George Crafts.

[S] FOUNDATIONS, ENDOWMENTS AND TRUSTS

SAN ANTONIO. *The Archbishop Charity Fund*, P.O. Box 28410, 78228. Tel: 210-734-2620; Fax: 210-734-0708.

Archbishop Flores Charity Fund, P.O. Box 28410, 78228. Tel: 210-734-2620; Fax: 210-734-0708.

Archdiocesan Endowment Fund, P.O. Box 28410, 78228-0410. Tel: 210-734-2620; Fax: 210-734-0708. Most Rev. Patrick Flores.

Assumption Seminary Endowment Fund, P.O. Box 28410, 78228-0410. Tel: 210-734-2620; Fax: 210-734-0708. Most Rev. Patrick Flores.

Casa de Padres Endowment Fund, P.O. Box 28410, 78228-0410. Tel: 210-734-2620; Fax: 210-734-0708. Most Rev. Patrick Flores.

Foundation for Christian Education, STJ, 138 Fair Ave., 78223-1014. Tel: 210-532-5272; Fax: 210-533-2532.
E-mail: stjfce@aol.com
Sr. Hortense Ricca, S.T.J., Contact Person; Sr. Isabel Ordono, S.T.J., Pres.

Historical Centre Foundation, 115 Main Ave., 78205. Tel: 210-227-1297; Fax: 210-271-0149. Rev. David Garcia.

Holy Spirit Sisters' Trust, 301 Yucca St., 78203. Tel: 210-533-8142; Fax: 210-533-3434.
E-mail: holyspirit@shsp.org
Sisters of the Holy Spirit. Sr. Veronica Cahill, S.H.Sp., Pres.

National Foundation for Mexican-American Vocations, P.O. Box 7367, 78207-0367. Tel: 210-227-0548; Fax: 210-226-5086. A nonprofit organization to help financially Mexican American Seminarians. Rev. Msgr. Balthasar J. Janacek, Chm.

Sts. Peter and Joseph Childrens' Home Endowment Fund, P.O. Box 28410, 78228-0410. Tel: 210-734-2620; Fax: 210-734-0708. Most Rev. Patrick Flores.

Seton Home Endowment Fund, P.O. Box 28410, 78228-0410. Tel: 210-734-2620; Fax: 210-734-0708. Most Rev. Patrick Flores.

BOERNE. *Benedictine Sisters Charitable Trust One*, 416 W. Highland Dr., 78006. Tel: 210-735-4988; Fax: 210-735-2615.
E-mail: srmika@texas.net
Sr. Susan Mika, O.S.B., Contact Person.

Benedictine Sisters Charitable Trust Two, 416 W. Highland, 78006. Tel: 830-816-8504; Fax: 830-249-4728. Sr. Sylvia Ahr, O.S.B., Trustee.

HELOTES. *Providence Trust*, P.O. Box 197, 78023. Tel: 210-695-8721; Fax: 210-695-6033.
Congregation of Divine Providence, Inc. Charitable Trust. Trustees: Sr. Imelda Gonzalez, C.D.P.; Sr. Christine Stephens, C.D.P.; Sr. Madonna Sangalli, C.D.P.

[T] SHRINES

SAN ANTONIO. *Basilica of the National Shrine of the Little Flower*, 906 Kentucky, 78201. Tel: 210-735-9127; Fax: 210-738-0818.
E-mail: lfbasilica@msn.com
Web site: www2.dcci.com/ocdokla
Rev. Jerome Early, O.C.D., Supr. of Discalced Carmelites of San Antonio.

Oblate Lourdes Grotto Shrine of the Southwest, Tepeyac de San Antonio. Mailing Address: P.O. Box 96, 78291-0096. 5722 Blanco Rd., 78216-6615. Tel: 210-342-9864; Fax: 210-342-7144.
E-mail: omsa@oblatemissions.org
Web site: www.oblatemissions.org
Revs. Richard A. Houlahan, O.M.I., Grotto Dir.; Gerard Weber, O.M.I., Ministries Dir.

Our Lady of Czestochowa, Grotto Shrine and Convent, 138 Beethoven St., 78210. Tel: 210-333-4582; 337-8193 (Convent). Seraphic Sisters of Our Lady of Sorrows. Sr. Helen Haladyna, S.O.L.S., Supr.; Rev. Bernard M. Goebel, Chap. Sisters 7.

[U] MISCELLANEOUS

SAN ANTONIO. *"Today's Catholic"*, Mailing Address: P.O. Box 28410, 78228-0410. 2718 W. Woodlawn Ave., 78228. Tel: 210-734-2620; Fax: 210-734-2939.
E-mail: tcpaper@aol.com
Official Catholic newspaper of the Archdiocese of San Antonio. Owned and operated by the San Antonio Archdiocesan Publishing Society. Most Rev. Patrick F. Flores, Publisher; Mrs. Martha Pack Brinkmann, Editor.

Archdiocesan Union of Holy Name Societies, 2610 Perez St., 78207. Tel: 210-433-6301; Fax: 210-432-2271. Rev. Richard Pena, Spiritual Mod. and Dir.

Benedictine Resource Center, 530 Bandera Rd., 78228-5525. Tel: 210-735-4988; Fax: 210-735-2615.
E-mail: snmika@texas.net
Sr. Mary Agnes Zinni, O.S.B., Pres.; Susan Mika, O.S.B., Ministry Dir.

Benitia Family Center, 4650 Eldridge Ave., 78237-2600. Tel: 210-433-9300; Fax: 210-432-6739.
E-mail: benitiafamilycenter@yahoo.com
Sr. Carmen M. Sanchez, M.C.D.P., Dir. Sisters 2.

The Blue Army, 6680 Crestway, 78239. Tel: 210-654-1643; Fax: 210-654-8031.
E-mail: IJNS@swbell.net
Rev. Robert Silverman, Archdiocesan Chap.

Brothers of the Beloved Disciplel. A private association of the faithful. 1701 Alametos, 78201. Tel: 210-734-6727; Fax: 210-431-6884.
E-mail: gmontag@stmarytx.edu
Web site: geocities.com/brothersbeloveddisciple
Revs. George Montague, S.M.; Robert E. Hogan, S.M.

Christus Santa Rosa Family Health Center, 519 W. Houston St., 78207. Tel: 210-704-2535; Fax: 210-704-3632. Dr. James Martin, M.D., Dir.

Christus Santa Rosa Home Care, 4415 Centerview Dr., 78228. Tel: 210-581-5200; Fax: 210-581-5291.
E-mail: pamela-steding@csrh.1whs.org
Pamela Steding, Pres.

Daughters of Mary Help Development Office, 6019 Buena Vista St., 78237-1700. Tel: 210-436-1424; Fax: 210-436-1424.
E-mail: fmasuodv@progidy.net
Sr. Katherine Keane, F.M.A., Dir. Promotes the apostolic works of both the Daughters of Mary Help of Christians (Salesian Sisters) and VIDES-USA (Volunteers Internationally Dedicated to Education and Service, especially socially at-risk youth and women).

Eucharistic Adoration of San Antonio, Inc., P.O. Box 691006, 78269-1006. Tel: 210-558-8802; Fax: 210-558-4477.
E-mail: adore24@aol.com
Web site: www.adore24.org
Mary Therese Corcoran, Pres.

Federation of Catholic Parent Teacher Clubs of the Archdiocese of San Antonio, 8208 Lynbrook Manor, 78250. Tel: 210-820-5951 (Work); 680-3500 (Home). Mrs. Edith G. Montez, Pres.

Focolare Movement, Mailing Address: P.O. Box 15726, 78212.
Web site: www.focolare.org
(Work of Mary) (Men and Women), Founded in Trent, Italy, in 1943. International Headquarters is in Rome. Women's Branch, Texas, 10714 Mt. Tipton, 78213. Tel: 210-341-8445; Fax: 210-341-4160. Marigen Lohla, Dir., Men's Branch, Texas, 9315 Overton Rd., 78217. Tel: 210-590-8812; Fax: 210-590-8921. Mr. Claudio Amato, Dir.

Friends of Santa Rosa Foundation dba Friends of Christus Santa Rosa Foundation, 519 W. Houston St., 78207. Tel: 210-704-2541; Fax: 210-704-2384. Stuart Turgel, CEO.

Friends of the Patrician Movement, 222 E. Mitchell St., 78210. Tel: 210-532-3216; Fax: 210-534-3779.
E-mail: pclancey@netexpress.com
Patrick Clancey, Ed.D., Exec. Dir.

Hispanic Telecommunications Network, Inc., 7711 Madonna Dr., 78216. Tel: 210-227-5959; Fax: 210-554-0822. Mr. Jose Roberto Gutierrez, Pres.
Principal Activity is the production of Nuestra Familia, the National Catholic evangelization television series for U.S. Hispanics.

Ladies of Charity of El Carmen, 18555 Leal Rd., 78221. Tel: 210-626-1432. Agapita Lopez, Pres.

Madonna Neighborhood Center, 1906 Castroville Rd., 78237. Tel: 210-432-2374; Fax: 210-432-2389. Norma J. Funari, Dir. Casework, Day Care, After School Care, Social Services, Adult & Youth Socialization Programs. Emergency Food Pantry, Clothing, Furniture, Counseling, Evening Meal, Summer Recreation, Case Management.

Marian Center of San Antonio, P.O. Box 831001, 78283-1001. Tel: 210-225-6279; Fax: 210-225-0044.
E-mail: mariancenterofsa@hotmail.com
Ms. Therese H. Palacios, Pres.

Mary Help Network (ADMA), 6019 Buena Vista St., 78234-1700. Tel: 210-432-0089; 0090; Fax: 210-432-4016. Sr. Mary Gloria del Mar, F.M.A., Dir.

Merced Housing Texas, 212 W. Laurel St., 78212. Tel: 210-281-0234; Fax: 210-281-0238.
E-mail: merced@netxpress.com
Web site: www.mercedhousingtexas.org
Susan R. Sheeran, Pres. Founded by a consortium of religious orders to provide quality, affordable, service enriched housing for the economically poor, to strengthen families and promote healthy communities.

Missionaries of Pastoral Charity Society, 1135 Mission Rd., 78210-4598. Tel: 210-534-7115; Fax: 210-534-6568.
E-mail: mcp@navegante.com
Rev. Kenneth C. Myers (El Salvador), Dir.; Sr. Claudia Klesel, I.W.B.S., Office Mgr.

Oblate Missions, 323 Oblate Dr., 78216-0096. Tel: 210-736-1685; Fax: 210-736-1314.
E-mail: omsa@oblatemissions.org
Web site: www.oblatemissions.org
Mailing Address: P.O. Box 96, 78291. Tel: 210-736-1685; Fax: 210-736-1314. Mailing Address: P.O. Box 2904, 78299-2904. Missionary Association of Mary Immaculate; Island of Lepers; Isles of Hope; Children of the Mountain. Most Rev. Philip F. Smith, O.M.I., D.D. (Philippines); Revs. Richard A. Houlahan, O.M.I., Dir.; Saturnino Lajo, O.M.I., Spanish Consultant.

The Patrician Movement, 222 E. Mitchell St., 78210. Tel: 210-532-3126; Fax: 210-534-3779.
E-mail: pclancey@netexpress.com
Field Offices: 1249 S. St. Mary St., 78210. Tel: 210-533-9191; Fax: 210-533-9194. 278 E. Mitchell, 78210. Tel: 210-533-2507. 528 S. Polaris, 78203. Tel: 210-534-4029; Fax: 210-534-4835. 215 Claudia, 78210. Tel: 210-533-0226; Fax: 210-533-8847. A non-profit corporation chartered under the laws of the State of Texas. Rev. Msgr. Dermot N. Brosnan, Pastoral Counseling; Deacon Patrick M. Clancey, Ed.D., Exec. Dir. & Contact Person. Provides comprehensive, Residential and Outpatient Substance Abuse Treatment Services. Accredited by the Joint Commission on Accreditation of Healthcare Organizations. Licenced by the Texas Commission on Alcohol and Drug Abuse. 222 E. Mitchell, 78210. Total Assisted 2,732.

Pauline Book and Media Center, 114 Main Plaza, 78205. Tel: 210-224-8101; Fax: 210-224-0938.
E-mail: sanantonio@pauline.org
Web site: www.pauline.org
Sr. Maria Teresa Meza, F.S.P., Supr. Daughters of St. Paul 5.

Pilgrim Center of Hope - Evangelization Center, 7680 Joe Newton, 78251. Tel: 210-521-3377; Fax: 210-521-0288.
E-mail: DTMJFOX@netxpress.com
Web site: www.pilgrimcenter.catholicweb.com
Directors: Deacon Tom Fox; Mrs. Mary Jane Fox.

Pillars of San Fernando Cathedral, 115 Main Plaza, 78205. Tel: 210-734-2620. An organization of benefactors that promotes and helps finance the oldest cathedral-sanctuary in the United States. Rev. Msgr. Balthasar J. Janacek.

Polish American Priest Association (P.A.P.A.), 5035 Bernadine, 78220. Tel: 210-648-1991; Fax: 210-648-8252[*]51. Rev. Thomas Michalski (BRK), Pres.

Religious of Mary Immaculate. (Pontifical), Villa Maria, 719 Augusta St., 78215. Tel: 210-226-0025; Fax: 210-226-3305.
E-mail: villamar@stic.net
Sr. Ada Mabel Meir, R.M.I., Local Supr. Apostolic Work: Counseling & guidance of young women of good moral conduct of any race or religion. Sisters 12; Girls 139.

St. Monica's Guild (1929), 6515 Broadway, 78209. Tel: 210-828-9266; Fax: 210-824-6110.
E-mail: mcbarron@worldwidenet.net
Mrs. Celeste Barron, Contact Person.
A social, civic, and charitable group.

San Antonio Community Law Center, 322 W. Woodlawn Ave., 78212. Tel: 210-271-9595; Fax: 210-734-4410. Provides legal assistance to the working poor. Attorneys: Bro. William Dooling, C.S.C.; Charles E. Montemayor.

San Antonio Inter-Community Finance Office, 11931 Radium Dr., 78216. Tel: 210-341-8884; Fax: 210-341-0721.
E-mail: saifo@juno.com
Sr. Susan Welsby, A.S.C., Dir.

Secular Franciscan Order, 10040 Espada Rd., 78214. Tel: 210-627-2507. Deacon Oscar Perez, S.F.O.

Serra Club of San Antonio, Inc., 8204 Sterling Green Dr., 78254-5672. Tel: 210-522-9052.
E-mail: mother@juno.com
Marilyn Edelen, Pres.

Socially Responsible Investment Coalition, P.O. Box 90238, 78209. Tel: 210-344-6778; Fax: 210-344-6805.
E-mail: sric@flashnet.net
Web site: www.flash.net/~sric
James W. Donovan, Exec. Dir.

Teleton Navideno, 2903 W. Salinas, 78207. Tel: 210-433-3256. Christmas Telethon-Branch of Catholic Charities of San Antonio, Inc. Mr. Olegario G. Tijerina, Volunteer Admin. Coord.

BOERNE. *Benedictine Ministries Corporation*, 416 Highland Dr., 78006. Tel: 830-816-8504; Fax: 830-249-3327.
E-mail: srmichl@texas.net
Sr. Michael Brandt, O.S.B., Contact Person.

HELOTES. *Marianist Lay Network of North America*, 18803 Lookout Mountain Tr., 78023. Tel: 210-695-3483; Fax: 210-436-3300.
E-mail: ahill@alvin.stmarytx.edu
Web site: www.mlnna.com
Andy Hill, Pres.

MOUNTAIN HOME. *Tecaboca - A Center For Spiritual Renewal*, P.O. Box 69, 78058. Tel: 830-866-3425; Fax: 830-866-3781.
E-mail: tecaboca@maverickbbs.com
Web site: www.tecaboca.org
Texas Catholic Boy's Camp (mid-June to mid-August). Operated by the Society of Mary, Province of St. Louis. Timothy Kelly, Apostolic Dir.

RELIGIOUS INSTITUTES OF MEN REPRESENTED IN THE ARCHDIOCESE

For further details refer to the corresponding bracketed number in the Religious Institutes of Men or Women section.

[0140]—*The Augustinians.* (Prov. of Castile).—O.S.A.

[0200]—*Benedictine Monks.*—O.S.B.

[0600]—*Brothers of the Congregation of Holy Cross.*—C.S.C.

[0350]—*Cistercian Order of the Strict Observance.*—O.C.S.O.

[0360]—*Claretian Missionaries.* (Western Prov.).—C.M.F.

[0220]—*Congregation of the Blessed Sacrament.*—S.S.S.

[1330]—*Congregation of the Mission.* (Southern Prov.).—C.M.

[0630]—*Congregation of the Missionaries of the Holy Family.*—M.S.F.

[1000]—*Congregation of the Passion.*—C.P.

[1130]—*Congregation of the Priests of the Sacred Heart.*—S.C.J.
[0480]—*Conventual Franciscans.*—O.F.M.Conv.
[0260]—*Discalced Carmelite Fathers.*—O.C.D.
[0520]—*Franciscan Friars.* (Sacred Heart Prov.).—O.F.M.
[0650]—*Holy Ghost Fathers.* (Western Prov.).—C.S.Sp.
[0690]—*Jesuit Fathers and Brothers.* (New Orleans Prov.).—S.J.
[]—*Missionaries of the Nativity of Mary.* (Mexico).—M.N.M.
[1110]—*Missionaries of the Sacred Heart.*—M.S.C.
[0860]—*Missionhurst Congregation of the Immaculate Heart of Mary.*—C.I.C.M.
[0910]—*Oblates of Mary Immaculate.*—O.M.I.
[0430]—*Order of Preachers (Dominican).* (New Orleans Prov.).—O.P.
[1310]—*Order of the Holy Trinity.*—O.SS.T.
[0610]—*Priests of the Congregation of Holy Cross.*—C.S.C.
[1070]—*Redemptorist Fathers.*—C.SS.R.
[0760]—*Society of Mary (Marianists).*—S.M.
[1200]—*Society of the Divine Savior.*—S.D.S.
[1060]—*Society of the Precious Blood.*—C.PP.S.
[1290]—*Society of the Priests of St. Sulpice.*—S.S.
[0560]—*Third Order Regular of St. Francis.*—T.O.R.

RELIGIOUS INSTITUTES OF WOMEN REPRESENTED IN THE ARCHDIOCESE

[0100]—*Adorers of the Blood of Christ.*—A.S.C.
[0230]—*Benedictine Sisters of the Pontifical Jurisdiction.*—O.S.B.
[1810]—*Bernardine Sisters of the Third Order of St. Francis.*—O.S.F.
[]—*Carmelitas del Sagrado Corazon.*—O.C.D.
[0360]—*Carmelite Sisters of the Divine Heart of Jesus.*—Carmel.D.C.J.
[0460]—*Congregation of Sisters of Charity of the Incarnate Word.*—C.C.V.I.
[3735]—*Congregation of St. Brigid.*—C.S.B.
[0870]—*Congregation of the Daughters of Mary Immaculate (Marianist Sisters).*—F.M.I.
[2200]—*Congregation of the Incarnate Word and Blessed Sacrament.*—I.W.B.S.
[0725]—*Cordi-Marian Sisters.*—M.C-M.
[0760]—*Daughters of Charity of St. Vincent de Paul.*—D.C.
[0850]—*Daughters of Mary Help of Christians.*—F.M.A.
[0420]—*Discalced Carmelite Nuns.*—O.C.D.
[1070-13]—*Dominican Sisters.*—O.P.
[1070-19]—*Dominican Sisters.*—O.P.
[1150]—*Eucharistic Franciscan Missionary Sisters.*—E.F.M.S.
[1170]—*Felician Sisters.*—C.S.S.F. [1310]—*Franciscan Sisters of Little Falls, MN.*
[1430]—*Franciscan Sisters of Our Lady of Perpetual Help.*—O.S.F.
[1900]—*Hermanas Catequistas Guadalupanas.*—H.C.G.
[1910]—*Hermanas Josefinas.*—H.J.
[2590]—*Hermanas Mercedarias Del Santisimo Sacramento.*—H.M.S.S.
[2720]—*Mission Helpers of the Sacred Heart.*—M.H.S.H.
[2770]—*Missionaries of Jesus, Mary and Joseph.*—M.J.M.J.
[2690]—*Missionary Catechists of Divine Providence, San Antonio, Texas.*—M.C.D.P.
[2890]—*Missionary Servants of St. Anthony.*—M.S.S.A.
[]—*Missionary Sisters of Our Lady of Perpetual Help.*—M.P.S.
[2760]—*Missionary Sisters of the Immaculate Conception of the Mother of God.*—S.M.I.C.
[3070]—*North American Union of the Sisters of Our Lady of Charity.*—O.L.C.
[]—*Oblate Missionaries of Mary Immaculate.*—O.M.M.I.
[3130]—*Our Lady of Victory Missionary Sisters.*—O.L.V.M.
[0950]—*Pious Society Daughters of St. Paul.*—F.S.P.
[3460]—*Religious of Mary Immaculate.*—R.M.I.
[2970]—*School Sisters of Notre Dame.*—S.S.N.D.
[1680]—*School Sisters of St. Francis. WI.*—S.S.S.F.
[1690]—*School Sisters of the Third Order of St. Francis.*—O.S.F.
[]—*Seraphic Franciscan Sisters of Our Lady of Sorrows.* (Poland).—O.L.S.
[0480]—*Sisters of Charity of Leavenworth, KS.*—S.C.L.
[1010]—*Sisters of Divine Providence of San Antonio, Texas.*—C.D.P.
[2360]—*Sisters of Loretto At the Foot of the Cross.*—S.L.
[3000]—*Sisters of Notre Dame de Namur.*—S.N.D.deN.
[3195]—*Sisters of Perpetual Adoration.*—A.P.G.
[3460]—*Sisters of Providence of Saint Mary-of-the-Woods, Indiana.*—S.P.
[1570]—*Sisters of St. Francis of the Holy Family.*—O.S.F.
[3840]—*Sisters of St. Joseph of Carondolet.*—C.S.J.
[1930]—*Sisters of the Holy Cross.*—C.S.C.
[1960]—*Sisters of the Holy Family.*—S.H.F.
[2050]—*Sisters of the Holy Spirit and Mary Immaculate.*—S.H.Sp.
[2110]—*Sisters of the Humility of Mary.*—H.M.
[3320]—*Sisters of the Presentation of the B.V.M.*—P.B.V.M.
[3670]—*Sisters of the Sacred Heart of Jesus.*—S.S.C.J.
[2150]—*Sisters, Servants of the Immaculate Heart of Mary.*—I.H.M.
[4020]—*Society of St. Theresa of Jesus.*—S.T.J.
[4110]—*Ursuline Nuns (Roman Union).*—O.S.U.

ARCHDIOCESAN CEMETERIES

SAN ANTONIO. *Holy Cross.*
San Fernando No. 1.
San Fernando No. 2.
San Fernando No. 3 (Roselawn).

NECROLOGY

† Keane, John F., On Leave.

Diocese of San Bernardino

Most Reverend

GERALD R. BARNES

Bishop of San Bernardino; ordained December 20, 1975; appointed Titular Bishop of Montefiascone and Auxiliary of San Bernardino January 27, 1992; succeeded to the See, December 28, 1995; installed as Second Bishop of San Bernadino March 12, 1996. *Office: 1201 E. Highland Ave., San Bernardino, CA, 92404.*

Most Reverend

DENNIS P. O'NEIL

Auxiliary Bishop of San Bernardino; ordained April 30, 1966; appointed January 16, 2001; ordained March 27, 2001.

Chancery: 1201 E. Highland Ave., San Bernardino, CA, 92404. Tel.: 909-475-5300; Fax: 909-475-5155.

Web site address: www.sbdiocese.org

E-mail address: sbdiocese@sbdiocese.org

Diocese Established November 6, 1978.

Square Miles 27,293.

Comprises the Counties of San Bernardino and Riverside.

Legal Titles:

The Roman Catholic Bishop of San Bernardino, a Corporation Sole (Churches, Rectories, Halls, Catechetical Centers, etc.).

Diocese of San Bernardino Education and Welfare Corporation (Schools, Convents, Newman Facilities, etc.).

Diocese of San Bernardino Catholic Charities.

St. Bernardine Plaza.

La Paz Dev. Corp. (Senior Citizens Housing).

San Gorgonio Villa.

Caritas Telecommunications.

A California Non-profit Corporation.

STATISTICAL OVERVIEW

Personnel	
Bishop	1
Auxiliary Bishop	1
Priests: Diocesan Active in Diocese	71
Priests: Active Outside Diocese	7
Priests: Retired, Sick or Absent	55
Number of Diocesan Priests	133
Religious Priests in Diocese	111
Extern Priests in Diocese	12
Ordinations:	
Diocesan Priests	1
Religious Priests	2
Transitional Deacons	1
Permanent Deacons in Diocese	89
Total Brothers	19
Total Sisters	154
Parishes	
Parishes	97
With Resident Pastor:	
Resident Diocesan Priests	49
Resident Religious Priests	29
Without Resident Pastor:	
Administered by Priests	11
Administered by Deacons	3
Administered by Women Religious	4
Administered by Lay People	1
Missions	13
Professional Ministry Personnel:	
Brothers	1
Sisters	18
Lay Ministers	130
Welfare	
Catholic Hospitals	2
Total Assisted	185,174
Specialized Homes	3
Total Assisted	3,100
Special Centers for Social Services	67
Total Assisted	68,000
Residential Care of Disabled	1
Total Assisted	6,500
Educational	
Seminaries, Diocesan	1
Students from This Diocese	10
Diocesan Students in Other Seminaries	11
Total Seminarians	21
High Schools, Diocesan and Parish	2
Total Students	942
Elementary Schools, Diocesan and Parish	34
Total Students	8,117
Elementary Schools, Private	1
Total Students	343
Catechesis/Religious Education:	
High School Students	16,030
Elementary Students	39,928
Total Students Under Catholic Instruction	65,381
Teachers in the Diocese:	
Priests	3
Sisters	21
Lay Teachers	480
Vital Statistics	
Receptions into the Church:	
Infant Baptism Totals	12,691
Adult Baptism Totals	2,490
Received into Full Communion	2,040
First Communions	13,564
Confirmations	6,799
Marriages:	
Catholic	2,235
Interfaith	305
Total Marriages	2,540
Deaths	3,706
Total Catholic Population	899,416
Total Population	3,212,000

Former Bishop—Most. Rev. PHILLIP F. STRALING D.D., Bishop of San Bernardino; ord. March 19, 1959; appt. July 18, 1978; cons. Nov. 16, 1978; transferred to See of Reno, June 29, 1995.

Chancellor—Sr. MARY FRANCES COLEMAN, R.S.M., *1201 E. Highland Ave., San Bernardino, 92404.* Tel: 909-475-5100.

Moderator of the Curia/Director of Priest Personnel—Rev. GERARD M. LOPEZ, S.T.L., *1201 E. Highland Ave., San Bernardino, 92404.* Tel: 909-475-5120; Fax: 909-475-5109.

Liturgy Coordinator—Rev. PAUL GRANILLO, *1201 E. Highland Ave., San Bernardino, 92404.* Tel: 909-475-5344.

Bishop's Secretary—Mrs. MARIA ECHEVERRIA, *1201 E. Highland Ave., San Bernardino, 92404.* Tel: 909-475-5110; Fax: 909-475-5109.

Director of Pastoral Planning—DOUGLAS RODRIGUES, *1201 E. Highland Ave., San Bernardino, 92404.* Tel: 909-475-5147.

Chancery—*1201 E. Highland Ave., San Bernardino, 92404.* Tel: 909-475-5300; Fax: 909-475-5155. Office Hours: Mon.-Fri. 8:30-4:30.

The Ministry of Administrative Services—Deacon JOHN SKORA, Dir. Tel: 909-475-5100.

Human Resources (Personnel/Payroll)—Deacon JOHN SKORA, Interim Dir. Tel: 909-475-5177. SHERYL BURNHAM, Coord. Tel: 909-475-5172. BETH ANDERSON, Benefits Admin. Tel: 909-475-5174. CHRISTINE GLASS, Recruitment Coord. Tel: 909-475-5175., *1201 E. Highland Ave., San Bernardino, 92404-4607.* Tel: 909-475-5170; Fax: 909-475-5189.

Presbyteral Council—Ex Officio Members: Most Rev. GERALD R. BARNES; Very Rev. THOMAS WALLACE, V.G.; Rev. GERALD LOPEZ, S.T.L., Moderator of the Curia. Appointed Members: Very Revs. JACK BARKER, V.F.; RENO AIARD, I.M.C., V.F.; ANTHONY FERRERO, V.F.; TIM KEPPEL, C.R., V.F.; STEVE PORTER, V.F.; ROMEO SELECCION, M.S., V.F. Elected Members: Revs. TIMOTHY JERNEJCIC; PETER COVAS; VINCENT CONNOR; Very Rev. ROBERT MILLER.

Pastoral Practices Committee—Rev. MICHAEL MAHER, SS.CC., Chm., *St. Paul the Apostle Church, 14085 Peyton Dr., Chino Hills, 91709.*

Pastoral Status and Pastoral Relations Committee—Rev. GEORGE GONZALES, Chm., *St. Francis of Assisi Church, P.O. Box 1503, LaQuinta, 92253-1503.*

Education Committee—Rev. DAVID GEIB, O.P., Chm., *St. Andrew Newman Center, 105 W. Big Springs Rd., Riverside, 92507.*

Priestly Life Committee—Rev. GERALD LEONARD, S.V.D., *St. Anne Church, 6885 Del Rosa Ave., San Bernardino, 92404.*

Peace and Justice Committee—Rev. MIGUEL CEJA, *Our Lady of Solitude, 151 W. Alejo Rd., Palm Springs, 92262.*

Finance Committee—Rev. HOWARD LINCOLN, *St. Catherine of Siena Church, 339 N. Sycamore Ave., Rialto, 92376.*

Diocesan Curia—Most Rev. GERALD R. BARNES; Rev. GERARD M. LOPEZ, S.T.L.; Sr. MARY FRANCIS COLEMAN; MARY ROSE WALLACE; Rev. RONALD LARKIN, M.S.C.; PETER BRADLEY; Sr. CARMEL CRIMMINS, R.S.M.; Sr. THERESA PHAN, L.H.C.; Sr. CECILIA CALVA, S.N.J.M.; Sr. ALICE MOLINA, R.S.H.M.;

Deacon JOHN SKORA; DOUGLAS RODRIGUES; Rev. Msgr. DONALD S. WEBBER, J.C.L.

College of Consultors—Rev. Msgr. PHILIP BEHAN; Rev. Msgr. PETER LUQUE; Rev. Msgr. DONALD S. WEBBER, J.C.L.; Very Rev. RENO AIARDI, I.M.C.; Rev. MICHAEL BROOKS, SS.CC.; Very Rev. VINCENT CONNOR; Rev. GEORGE GONZALES; Very Rev. STEPHEN PORTER; Rev. ARTURO BALAGAT.

Council of Religious—Council Members: Sr. LOUISE BOND, S.N.J.M.; Sr. ANA MORALES, F.S.J.; Sr. SARAH SHREWSBURY, O.S.C.

Finance Council—MARY ROSE WALLACE, Chm., *1201 E. Highland Ave., San Bernardino, 92404-4607.* Tel: 909-475-5150.

Finance Council Members—Most Rev. GERALD R. BARNES; Rev. GERARD LOPEZ, S.T.L.; Very Rev. STEVEN C. PORTER, S.T.L., V.F.; Revs. HOWARD LINCOLN; CHARLES PATRON; Sr. MARY FRANCES COLEMAN, R.S.M.; MARY ROSE WALLACE; LINDA BORBA; WILLIAM J. BRUNICK; PHILLIP BURBACH; DON CAVAZOS; RICHARD GRANILLO; WILFRID C. LEMANN; MARTIN MATICH; MICHAEL V. MCINTIRE; JEFFERY G. ROLLERT; JOHN VAN DAELE; EDWARD I. TALLEN; BRUCE SATZGER; STEVE OSBORN, Canonical Council.

Diocesan Boards and Committees

Priests' Personnel Board—1201 E. Highland Ave., San Bernardino, 92404-4607. Tel: 909-475-5120. Personnel Board Members: Most Rev. GERALD R. BARNES; Rev. GERARD M. LOPEZ, S.T.L.; Rev. Msgr. PETER LUQUE; PATRICK KIRSCH; MICHAEL STURN; CIRO LIBANATI.

Building Committee—Deacon JOHN SKORA, Construction Project Mgr. & Committee Coord., *1201 E. Highland Ave., San Bernardino, 92404.* Tel: 909-475-5305. Committee Members: Rev. GERALD DELUNEY; Very Rev. TIMOTHY KEPPEL, C.R.; Rev. Msgr. DONALD S. WEBBER, S.T.L.; Mr. MICHAEL PODEGRACZ; Mr. BURRELL R. HANDY, III; KRISTI HANSON; DON GARDNER; DALE KLEIN; RAY KENZ; JAN ZUPPARDO. Staff Members: JOHN SKORA, Dir. Office of Construction & Real Estate; MARY ROSE WALLACE, Chief Financial Officer; JUDY FLORES, Oper. Project Mgr.

Parish Staffing Committee—Rev. ARTURO BALAGAT; Sr. LUCILLE MARTINEZ, O.L.V.M.; Sr. MAUREEN CHICOINE, R.S.C.J.; PETER BRADLEY, Chm. KATHY JEFFRIES; PAT WOODS; Rev. GERARD M. LOPEZ, S.T.L.

Diocesan Tribunal—1201 E. Highland Ave., San Bernardino, 92404-4607. Tel: 909-475-5320; Fax: 909-475-5330.

Judicial Vicar—Rev. Msgr. DONALD S. WEBBER, J.C.L.

Adjutant Judicial Vicars—Rev. Msgr. ROBERT E. LAWRENCE, J.C.L.; Rev. ANTHONY T. FERRERO, J.C.L.

Defenders of the Bond—Rev. FRANCIS WIESER, J.C.D.; Rev. Msgr. ROBERT E. LAWRENCE, J.C.L.

Judges—Mr. STEPHEN H. OSBORN, J.C.L.; Rev. ANTHONY T. FERRERO, J.C.L.

Pro-Synodal Judges—Revs. ROBERT ERICKSON; GEORGE GONZALEZ; ADRIAN BRINN; Rev. Msgr. CORNELIUS O'LEARY, Ph.D., Col./Chap.

Lay Advocates—(Please refer to your parish).

Administrator—GWENDOLYN GIFFORD.

Secretaries—GINA GRADIAS; IRENE MARTINEZ.

Notaries—GWENDOLYN GIFFORD; GINA GRADIAS; IRENE MARTINEZ.

Vicar for Deacons—Rev. RONALD LARKIN, M.S.C. Tel: 909-475-5458.

Vicar General—Very Rev. THOMAS WALLACE, *St. Martha Church, 37200 Whitewood Rd., Murrieta, 92563.* Tel: 909-698-8180.

Judicial Vicar—Rev. Msgr. DONALD S. WEBBER, J.C.L., *1201 E. Highland Ave., San Bernardino, 92404-4607.* Tel: 909-475-5320.

Vicar for African-Americans—Very Rev. RICHARD MCGEE, C.R., *St. Joseph Church, 17080 Arrow Blvd., Fontana, 92335.* Tel: 909-822-0566.

Vicar for Clergy—Rev. RON LARKIN, M.S.C., *1201 E. Highland Ave., San Bernardino, 92404-4607.* Tel: 909-475-5455; 5458.

Office of Hispanic Affairs—Sr. CECILIA CALVA, S.N.J.M., Dir., *1201 E. Highland Ave., San Bernardino, 92404-4607.* Tel: 909-475-5360; Fax: 909-475-5457.

Vicar for Native Americans—Very Rev. RAFAEL PARTIDA, *Our Lady of Perpetual Help Church, P.O. Box BB, Indio, 92201-2527.* Tel: 760-347-3507.

Vicar for Priests in Special Works—Very Rev. VINCENT CONNOR, *1201 E. Highland Ave., San Bernardino, 92404-4607.* Tel: 909-475-5341.

Office for Men and Women Religious—Sr. LOUISE BOND, S.N.J.M., Dir., *1201 E. Highland Ave., San Bernardino, 92404-4607.* Tel: 909-475-5345; Fax: 909-475-5354.

Vicar for Retired Priests—Rev. Msgr. THOMAS MEAGHER, *1011 St. Andrew St., Upland, 91766.*

Vicars Forane—Very Rev. ANTHONY FERRERO, Hemet Vicariate. Tel: 909-657-2380. Very Rev. ROMEO SELECCION, M.S., V.F., High Desert Vicariate. Tel: 760-242-4427. Very Rev. JACK BARKER, V.F., Lower Desert Vicariate. Tel: 760-564-1255. Very Rev. RENO AIARDI, I.M.C., V.F., Riverside Vicariate. Tel: 909-475-5130. Very Rev. TIMOTHY KEPPEL, C.R., V.F., San Bernardino Vicariate. Tel: 909-337-2333. Very Rev. STEVEN PORTER, V.F., West End Vicariate. Tel: 909-899-1049.

The Ministry of Communications—Rev. HOWARD LINCOLN, Diocesan Spokesperson. Tel: 909-875-1360., *1201 E. Highland Ave., San Bernardino, 92404-4607.* Tel: 909-475-5350; Fax: 909-475-5357.

Caritas Telecommunications—1201 E. Highland Ave., San Bernardino, 92404-4607. Tel: 909-475-5350; Fax: 909-475-5357. CLARE COLELLA, Dir. Tel: 909-475-5351.

Information Services—1201 E. Highland Ave., San Bernardino, 92404-4607. Tel: 909-475-5400. DALE JONASSON, Dir. Tel: 909-475-5401.

Office of Construction and Real Estate—1201 E. Highland Ave., San Bernardino, 92404-4607. Tel: 909-475-5310. Deacon JOHN SKORA, Dir., *909-475-5312,* JUDY A. JUAREZ-FLORES, Oper. Mgr. Tel: 909-475-5313.

Diocesan Archivist—JOHN DEGANO, *1201 E. Highland Ave., San Bernardino, 92404-4607.* Tel: 909-475-5399.

The Ministry of Ecclesial Services—

Vicar for Clergy—Rev. RON LARKIN, M.S.C., *1201 E. Highland Ave., San Bernardino, 92404-4607.* Tel: 909-475-5458; Fax: 909-475-5343.

Committee for the Continuing Education of Priests—Rev. RON LARKIN, M.S.C., *1201 E. Highland Ave., San Bernardino, 92404-4607.* Tel: 909-475-5458; Fax: 909-475-5343.

Seminarains—Rev. JOSE SANZ, D.L.P., Dir. Tel: 909-788-9931; Fax: 909-781-9031.

Office for Men and Women Religious—Sr. CAROLYN GRIES, O.S.B., Dir., *1201 E. Highland Ave., San Bernardino, 92404-4607.* Tel: 909-475-5345; Fax: 909-475-5354.

Office of Vocations—1201 E. Highland Ave., San Bernardino, 92404-4607. Tel: 909-475-5470; Fax: 909-475-5475. Sr. SARAH SHREWSBURY, O.S.C., Vocations Dir. Tel: 909-475-5471. Rev. PAUL GRANILLO, Assoc. Dir.

Serra International, District 157, San Bernardino—LORRAINE SPONSLER, Governor, *3171 Valencia Ave., San Bernardino, 92404.* Tel: 909-883-9324.

Palm Springs Chapter—BOB COYNE, Pres., *69558 Cimarron Ct., Cathedral City, 92234.* Tel: 760-324-8498.

Riverside Chapter—WYLIE HOFFMAN, Pres., *2057 Bronson Way, Riverside, 92506.* Tel: 909-683-2319.

San Bernardino Chapter—RICH HERBST, Pres., *28795 Canyon Oak Dr., Highland, 92346.* Tel: 909-862-7773.

Blessed Junipero Serra House of Formation—Revs. JOSE SANZ, D.L.P., Rector; PEDRO ARRIBAS, D.L.P., Spiritual Dir., *3325 13th St., Riverside, 92501.* Tel: 909-788-9931; Fax: 909-781-9031., For seminarians call:: Tel: 909-683-8749.

Permanent Diaconate Office—Rev. ROBERT NOGOSEK, C.S.C., Dir., *1201 E. Highland Ave., San Bernardino, 92404-4607.* Tel: 909-475-5160; Fax: 909-475-5155.

The Ministry of Educational Services—Sr. ALICE MOLINA, R.S.H.M., Dir., *1201 E. Highland Ave., San Bernardino, 92404-4607.* Tel: 909-475-5450; Fax: 909-475-5457.

The Office of Catholic Schools—Dr. JAMES BRENNAN, Supt. of Catholic Schools; STEPHEN KRUP, Asst. Supt. Schools; Sr. SARA KANE, C.S.J., Asst. Supt. Schools, *1201 E. Highland Ave., San Bernardino, 92404-4607.* Tel: 909-475-5437; Fax: 909-475-5477.

Campus Ministry—Rev. JACK MCGINNIS, *Christ of the Desert Newman Center, 73-441 Fred Waring Dr., Palm Desert, 92260.* Tel: 760-346-0089; Fax: 760-340-2245.

Missions Office of the Diocese of San Bernardino—Very Rev. RENO AIARDI, I.M.C., V.F., Dir.; Sr. ROSALINE O'CONNOR, R.S.M., Coord., Holy Childhood Association, Offices: *1201 E. Highland Ave., San Bernardino, 92404-4607.* Tel: 909-475-5130; Fax: 909-475-5135., *Mailing Address: P.O. Box 1416, San Bernardino, 92402-1416.*

Diocesan Media Center—LEE ALLARD, Dir. Tel: 909-475-5391.

The Office of Religious Education and Formation—Sr. ALICE MOLINA, R.S.H.M., Dir., *1201 E. Highland Ave., San Bernardino, 92404-4607.* Tel: 909-475-5450; Fax: 909-475-5457.

Vicariate Pastoral Centers—

Center A: San Bernardino/High Desert—MARIA COVARRUBIAS, Consultant, High Desert, *1201 E. Highland Ave., San Bernardino, 92404-4607.* Tel: 760-843-0597; 909-475-5354.

Center B: Hemet/Low Desert—BOB MELEVIN, Consultant, *1612 First St., Coachella, 92236.* Tel: 760-398-0606; 219-9398; 909-679-7707.

Center C: Riverside/West End—1201 E. Highland Ave., San Bernardino, 92404. ROLANDO ROSALES, Consultant. Tel: 909-475-5384; Fax: 909-475-5457.

Youth Programming & Field Consultant for Youth Ministry—EVELIA CENTENO, Consultant for Youth Ministry. Tel: 909-475-5380; Fax: 909-475-5457.

Ministry Formation Institute—

Evangelization & Catechesis—Sr. NADINE MCGUINNESS, C.S.J., Program Coord. Tel: 909-475-4385.

Leadership Formation—STEVE VALENZUELA, Program Coord. Tel: 909-475-5382.

The Ministry of Ethnic Affairs—

Diocesan African-American Catholic Commission and Assembly—1201 E. Highland Ave., San Bernardino, 92404-4607. Tel: 909-475-5194. JOE BANKS, Chm. MAUDRY OWINGS, Coord.; Very Rev. RICHARD MCGEE, C.R., Vicar, *St. Joseph Church, 17080 Arrow Blvd., Fontana, 92335.* Tel: 909-822-0566.

Arab-American Ministry—Rev. LABIB KOBTI, *St. Joseph Church, 1150 W. Holt Ave., Pomona, 91768.* Tel: 909-865-6895.

Asian-Pacific Islander Ministry—Sr. THERESA PHAN, L.H.C., Dir., *1201 E. Highland Ave., San Bernardino, 92404.* Tel: 909-475-5348.

Filipino Ministry—Rev. ARTURO BALAGAT, Diocesan Dir., *St. George Church, 325 W. E St., Ontario, 91762.* Tel: 909-983-2637.

Hmong Ministry—JOHN YING YANG, *248 Allview Dr., Banning, 92220.* Tel: 909-849-7908.

Indonesian Ministry—LANI FUKUMOTO, Dir., *33785 Date Palm Dr., Cathedral City, 92234.* Tel: 760-324-7740.

Korean Ministry—PETER CHUNG, Diocesan Liaison, *5405 Via Cervantes, Yorba Linda, 92887.* Tel: 909-787-3906. Rev. BERNARD YOUN, *St. Andrew Kim Korean Catholic Community, 4110 Corona Ave., Norco, 91760.* Tel: 909-372-9932.

Native American Ministry—Rev. EARL HENLEY, M.S.C., *23600 Soboba Rd., P.O. Box 1027, San Jacinto, 92581.* Tel: 909-654-2086.

Tongan Ministry—KAPILILI POMEE; NITA POMEE, *7752 Trey Ave., Riverside, 92503.* Tel: 909-351-8140., *St. Joseph Church, Upland, 91786.*

Vietnamese Ministry—Rev. PIUS M. NGUYEN QUANG DAM, C.M.C., *Congregation of the Mother Coredemptrix, Shrine of Presentation, 1775 S. Main St., Corona, 91720.* Tel: 909-737-4125; Fax: 909-340-9880.

The Ministry of Hispanic Affairs—Sr. CECILIA CALVA, S.N.J.M., Dir., Office of Hispanic Affairs, *1201 E. Highland Ave., San Bernardino, 92404-4607.* Tel: 909-475-5451; Fax: 909-475-5457.

Valley Missionary Program, Shrine of Our Lady of Guadalupe—Rev. JOSE MARTELLI, C.S.C., Dir. DAVID FAJARDO, Retreats Coord., *52-565 Oasis Palm, Coachella, 92236.* Tel: 760-398-9277; Fax: 760-398-9281.

The Ministry of Financial Affairs—1201 E. Highland Ave., San Bernardino, 92404-4607. Tel: 909-475-5150. MARY ROSE WALLACE, Chief Fin. Officer. Tel: 909-475-5150.

Accounting Services—1201 E. Highland Ave., San Bernardino, 92404-4607. Tel: 909-475-5480. PEGGY KOSTER, Dir. Tel: 909-475-5482.

Payroll Services—TRANG PHAM, Dir. Tel: 909-475-5188.

Parish Assistance Program—BARB LOGGINS, Dir. & Internal Auditor. Tel: 909-475-5491.

Development Office—1201 E. Highland Ave., San Bernardino, 92404-4607. Tel: 909-475-5460. PETER ROELL, Dir. Tel: 909-475-5461. MARICELA SANDOVAL, Assoc. Dir. Tel: 909-475-5462.

Catholic Mutual Insurance Group—1201 E. Highland Ave., San Bernardino, 92404-4607. Tel: 909-475-5140; Fax: 909-475-5144. TAMAR BRINKERHOFF, Claims & Risk Mgr. Tel: 909-475-5141.

The Ministry of Pastoral Services—1201 E. Highland Ave., San Bernardino, 92404-4607. Tel: 909-475-5340; Fax: 909-475-5155. PETER BRADLEY, Dir.

Office of Worship—Sr. MARILU COVANI, S.P., Dir. Tel: 909-475-5336.

Office of Renew 2000—Sr. SUSAN DEGUIDE, R.S.M., Dir., *1201 E. Highland Ave., San Bernardino, 92404.* Tel: 909-475-5193.

Charismatic Renewal—Vacant, Dir., *1201 E. Highland Ave., San Bernardino, 92404.* Tel: 909-475-5365; Fax: 909-824-5481.

Ministry of Social/Community Services—Sr. CARMEL CRIMMINS, R.S.M., Dir., *1201 E. Highland Ave., San Bernardino, 92404.* Tel: 909-475-5474.

Catholic Charities San Bernardino/Riverside—Administrative Offices, 1450 N. D St., San Bernardino, 92405. Tel: 909-388-1239; Fax: 909-384-1130. Sr. GEORGIANNA CAHILL, L.C.S.W., Exec. Dir. KEN SAWA, M.S.W., A.C.S.W., L.C.S.W., Exec. Asst.

Cathedral City Regional Center—Vacant, Assoc. Dir. for Riverside County, *35-325 E. Date Palm Dr., Ste. 153-A, Cathedral City, 92234.* Tel: 760-202-1222; Fax: 760-202-1230.

West End Regional Center—635 Taylor St., Ontario, 91761. Tel: 909-391-1617; Fax: 909-391-2466. LORRAINE MEDINA, Program Coord.

High Desert Regional Center—16051 Kasota Rd., Ste. 700, Apple Valley, 92307. Tel: 760-242-2311, Ext. 8454; Fax: 760-242-1801. MARTA MELENDEZ, Program Coord.

Riverside County, Moreno Valley Regional Center—12540 Heacock, Moreno Valley, 92556. Tel: 909-485-2185; Fax: 909-485-2188. BELINDA MARQUEZ, Program Mgr.

Morongo Basin Regional Center—WALTER FLEWELLEN, Program Coord., *56300 29 Palms Hwy., Yucca Valley, 92284.* Tel: 760-369-7444; Fax: 760-369-0622.

San Bernardino Regional Center—1800 Western Ave., Ste. 107, San Bernardino, 92411. Tel: 909-880-3635; Fax: 909-880-9847. BEVERLY EARL, Regl. Dir.

Caritas Counseling Services—1265 N. LaCadena Dr., Ste. 4, Colton, 92324. Tel: 909-370-1293; Fax: 909-370-4679. KEN SAWA, M.S.W., A.C.S.W., L.C.S.W., Program Admin. SHARI LOWDER, M.S., M.F.T., Clinical Dir.

Farm Worker Resource Program—Contact Moreno Valley Regional Center.

HIV/AIDS Programs—Contact Regional Centers.

Nightengale Manor Homeless Shelter—Contact Cathedral City Regional Center.

Refugee and Immigration Services—MY HANH LUU, Program Dir. Contact Administrative Office:Tel: 909-388-1243; Fax: 909-384-1130.

Office of Social Concerns—1450 N. D St., San Bernardino, 92405. Tel: 909-885-7101; Fax: 909-885-6621. JEANETTE ARNQUIST, Dir.

Affiliated Programs—

Children and Family Council—1441 N. D St., Ste. 208, San Bernardino, 92405. Tel: 909-885-7107; Fax: 909-885-6621. JEANETTE ARNQUIST, Dir.

Detention Ministry—Contact Administrative Office-:Tel: 909-388-1239.

Natural Family Planning—P.O. Box 133325, Big Bear Lake, 92315-8920. Tel: 909-866-4767. Deacon RALPH PARTIDA.

Respect for Life Ministries—2879 Burnt Oak Dr., Chino Hills, 91709. Tel: 909-393-9498; Fax: 909-393-3165. MARIE WIDMANN, Coord.

Commissions/Committees—

Children and Family Council—JEANETTE ARNQUIST, Coord., *1441 N. D St., San Bernardino, 92405.* Tel: 909-885-7101.

Pro-Life Catholic Ministries—MARIE WIDMANN, Coord., *2879 Burnt Oak Dr., Chino Hills, 91709.* Tel: 909-393-9498.

Catholic Organizations in the Diocese—

Catholic Daughters of America—MARY ANN AARSET, *1821 S. Ethel St., Alhambra, 91803.* Tel: 323-283-6956.

Cursillo—AL AUSTIN, English Language Dir.; Rev. ARTURO BALAGAT, Filipino Dir. Tel: 909-983-2637. DAVID CHUNG, Korean Dir. Tel: 909-883-0880. JUAN ARREDONDO, Spanish Dir. Tel: 760-241-2907. TAM VAN DO, Vietnamese Dir. Tel: 909-272-3446.

Council of Catholic Women—JOAN MERRIMAN, *225 Elk St., Sp. 1, Hemet, 92542.* Tel: 909-658-5911.

Diocesan Marian Council—HOWARD C. LITTLEFIELD, Chm., *758 W. 24th St., San Bernardino, 92405.* Tel: 909-882-7146.

Equestrian Order of Holy Sepulchre of Jerusalem—MARY HUMANN, *1605 Laurel Ave., Upland, 91784.* Tel: 909-982-7206.

Italian Catholic Federation—MARGUERITE HALSTED, Corresponding Office Sec., *4159 Largewood Pl., Riverside, 92506.* Tel: 909-683-1994.

Knights of Columbus—DIETRICH RUBELIUS, *36204 Golden Gate Dr., Yucaipa, 92399.*

World Apostolate of Fatima (Blue Army)-San Bernardino Division—FERNE C. SCHMITT, Pres., *P.O. Box 361, Rialto, 92377-0361.* Tel: 909-875-2894.

Ministry for Special Needs—

Engaged Encounter (English)—Coords.: JOE SANTANGLEO; DOLLY SANTANGLEO. Tel: 909-689-6314.

Engaged Encounter (Spanish)—Coords.: ALBERTO SANTANA; MONICA SANTANA. Tel: 909-872-0738.

Pre-Cana Marriage Preparation—Deacon JAMES DALE, *St. Frances de Sales Church, 4268 Lime St., Riverside, 92501.* Tel: 909-686-4004 (Church); 689-4411 (Work); 684-4623 (Residence).

Pre-Marital Instruction in Spanish—Deacon RALPH PARTIDA. Tel: 909-866-4767.

Marriage Ministry—

Marriage Encounter (English)—DAN QUAM; THERESA QUAM, *1421 Francine Ct., San Jacinto, 92583.* Tel: 909-487-9325.

Marriage Encounter (Spanish)—GUILLERMO MENDEZ; SOCCORO MENDEZ, *5686 Deodar St., Montclair, 91763.* Tel: 909-986-9838.

Marriage Enrichment—Regl. Coordinators: CEECEE TERJO; CLAYTON TERJO, *1473 E. 13th St., Upland, 91786.* Tel: 909-985-7864. JIM RAU; JOYCE RAU, *15677 Live Oak Rd., Chino Hills, 91709.* Tel: 909-393-9310.

Catholic Committee on Scouting—(Boy Scouts and Girl Scouts); PHILIP COLELLA, Chm., *4862 Pershing Ave., San Bernardino, 92407.* Tel: 909-882-6372.

CLERGY, PARISHES, MISSIONS AND PAROCHIAL SCHOOLS

CITY OF SAN BERNARDINO
(San Bernardino County)

1—OUR LADY OF THE ROSARY CATHEDRAL (1927), Revs. Robert Miller; Bill Paiz.
Office: 265 W. 25th St., 92405. Tel: 909-883-8991; Fax: 909-882-2061.
Res., 2525 Arrowhead Ave., 92405. Tel: 909-881-1588; Fax: 909-882-2061.
School—2620 Arrowhead Ave., 92405. Tel: 909-886-1088; Fax: 909-475-5263.
Lay Teachers 9; Students 219.
Catechesis/Religious Programs—Tel: 909-883-8991.
Students 550.

2—CHRIST THE KING (1934), Rev. Miguel Urrea.
Res., 272 E. Rialto Ave., 92408. Tel: 909-885-1476; Fax: 909-885-3926.

3—OUR LADY OF THE ASSUMPTION (1954), Rev. Joseph E. Krah.
Res., 796 W. 48th St., 92407. Tel: 909-882-2931; Fax: 909-883-4851.
School—Tel: 909-881-2416. Sr. Maura Redington, Prin.
Sisters of Mercy 2; Lay Teachers 13; Students 304.
Catechesis/Religious Programs—Tel: 909-883-4731.
Students 275.

4—OUR LADY OF FATIMA (1952), Rev. Edward J. Molumby, S.T.; Sr. Lucille Martinez, O.L.V.M., Pastoral Coord.
Office: 1000 N. Valencia Ave., 92410. Tel: 909-885-0948; Fax: 909-384-0576.
Catechesis/Religious Programs—Students 250.

5—OUR LADY OF GUADALUPE (1925) (Hispanic), Revs. Eliseo Hernandez, O.R.C.; Jose Varela, O.R.C.; Rev. Msgr. Adolphus Chavez.
Res., 1430 W. Fifth St., 92411. Tel: 909-888-0044; 884-8010; Fax: 909-888-4428.
Catechesis/Religious Programs—1475 W. 7th St., 92411. Tel: 909-381-1628.
Students 1,286.

6—ST. ANNE (1938), Revs. Gerald Leonard, S.V.D.; Matthias Nguyen H. Chuong.
Res., 6885 Del Rosa Ave., 92404. Tel: 909-884-6375; Fax: 909-884-8976.
School—6886 Del Rosa Ave., 92404. Tel: 909-885-7472; Fax: 909-884-5870.
Lay Teachers 9; Students 128.
Catechesis/Religious Programs—Tel: 909-884-5400.
Students 368.

7—ST. ANTHONY (1948), Revs. Roberto Villao, S.V.D.; Paul Vung Le, S.V.D.
Res., 1640 Western Ave., 92411. Tel: 909-887-3810; Fax: 909-880-0982.
School—1510 W. 16th St., 92411. Tel: 909-887-5413; Fax: 909-887-5413.
Sisters of Mercy 5; Lay Teachers 7; Students 270.
Catechesis/Religious Programs—Tel: 909-887-3210.
Students 210.

8—ST. BERNARDINE (1862), Rev. Edward Molumby, S.T.; Sr. Marita Beumer, C.PP.S., Pastoral Coord.
Res., 531 North F St., 92410. Tel: 909-884-0104; Fax: 909-885-4634.
Catechesis/Religious Programs—Tel: 909-884-5463.
Students 225.

9—ST. PHILLIP THE APOSTLE (1989). (Melkite-Greek Catholic Mission). Rev. Justin Rose.
Res., 923 W. Congress, 92410. Tel: 909-889-3579; Fax: 909-889-5461.
Catechesis/Religious Programs—Students 45.

10—ST. THERESA. Closed. For inquiries for parish records contact the Chancery.

OUTSIDE THE CITY OF SAN BERNARDINO

Adelanto, San Bernardino Co., Christ the Good Shepherd (1962), Rev. Antonio Das Neves.
Res., 17900 Jonathan, P.O. Box 577, 92301. Tel: 760-246-7083; Fax: 760-246-4603.
Catechesis/Religious Programs—Students 201.

Alta Loma, San Bernardino Co., St. Peter & St. Paul (1970), Rev. Peter Covas.
Mailing Address: P.O. Box 248, 91701. Tel: 909-987-9312; Fax: 909-980-9404.
School—9135 Banyan Ave., 91701. Tel: 909-987-7908.
Lay Teachers 9; Aides 5; Students 116.
Catechesis/Religious Programs—Tel: 909-980-9423. Dot Flagg, D.R.E.
Students 1,700.
Youth Ministry—Tel: 909-944-8483. Olivia Obregon.
Students 300.

Anza, Riverside Co., Sacred Heart (1993), Rev. Bernard J. Carr.
Mailing Address: P.O. Box 390118, 92539.
Res., 56250 Cahuilla Rd., Hwy. 371, 92539. Tel: 909-763-5636; Fax: 909-763-0236.
Catechesis/Religious Programs—Ms. Linda Bahash, D.R.E.
Students 130.
Missions—Anza, Riverside Co., Our Lady of the Snows, Cahuilla Indian Reservation, 92539. Tel: 909-763-5549; Anza, Riverside Co., Cahuilla Indian Reservation, Hwy. 371, 92539.; Riverside Co., Santa Rosa Indian Mission, Santa Rosa Reservation, 92539. Tel: 909-659-2708; Anza, Riverside Co., Santa Rosa Reservation, Hwy. 74, 92539.

Apple Valley, San Bernardino Co., Our Lady of the Desert (1974), Revs. Romeo N. Seleccion, M.S.; Antonio Quijano, M.S.; Deacons Carlos Reyes; Robert Rittman.
Office: 18386 Corwin Rd., 92307. Tel: 760-242-4427; Fax: 760-242-1195.
Catechesis/Religious Programs—Tel: 760-242-5819.
Students 465.

Banning, Riverside Co., Precious Blood (1890), Rev. Michael Lama; Ms. Monica A. Gomez, Pastoral Assoc.
Res., 157 W. Nicolet St., 92220. Tel: 909-849-2434; Fax: 909-849-8698.
School—P.O. Box 458, 92220. Tel: 909-849-2433; Fax: 909-849-0843.
Lay Teachers 9; Students 198.
Mission—Banning, Riverside Co., St. Mary, 11231 N. Mission Rd., 92220. Tel: 909-849-6170.
Catechesis/Religious Programs—Tel: 909-849-1897.
Students 173.

Barstow, San Bernardino Co., St. Joseph (1914), Revs. Charles Patron; Mark Lander; Deacons Francis Roman; Margarito Saenz; Donald Burgett.
Res., 505 E. Mountain View Ave., 92311. Tel: 760-256-6818; Fax: 760-256-8307.
School—555 E. Mountain View Ave., 92311. Tel: 760-256-2397; Fax: 760-256-5328.
Sisters of Mercy of the Blessed Sacrament 3; Lay Teachers 9; Students 150.
Mission—Baker, San Bernardino Co., Our Lady of the Desert, 92311.
Catechesis/Religious Programs—Tel: 760-256-1801.
Students 368.
St. Philip Neri Church (1979). Unassigned.
Mailing Address: 909 Armory, #409, 92311. Tel: 760-253-5412; Fax: 760-253-2021. [JC]
Catechesis/Religious Programs—Students 75.

Beaumont, Riverside Co., San Gorgonio (1908), Rev. Frank T. Dicristina.
Res., P.O. Box 155, 92223. Tel: 909-845-2849; Fax: 909-845-9259.
Catechesis/Religious Programs—Students 220.

Big Bear Lake, San Bernardino Co., St. Joseph (1931), Rev. John Hindman.
Res., 42242 N. Shore Dr., P.O. Box 1709, 92315. Tel: 909-866-3030; Fax: 909-866-5087. [JC]
Catechesis/Religious Programs—Tel: 909-866-4581; Fax: 909-866-4581.
Students 125.

Bloomington, San Bernardino Co., St. Charles Borromeo (1939) (Hispanic), Rev. Richard Humphrys.
Mailing Address: P.O. Box 248, 92316.
Office: 11342 Spruce St., 92316. Tel: 909-877-0792; Fax: 909-877-4304.
Res., 11368 Spruce St., 92316.
Catechesis/Religious Programs—Tel: 909-421-1494.
Students 317.

Blythe, Riverside Co., St. Joan of Arc (1920), Rev. Paul Schmidt, S.V.D.
Res., 875 E. Chanslorway, 92225. Tel: 760-922-3261; Fax: 760-922-5279.

Catechesis/Religious Programs—Tel: 760-922-8934.
Students 255.
Mission—Ripley, Riverside Co., Our Lady of Guadalupe.

Cathedral City, Riverside Co., St. Louis (1948), Rev. Michael J. Brooks, SS.CC.
Res., 68633 C St., 92234. Tel: 760-328-2398; Fax: 760-770-4598.
Catechesis/Religious Programs—Students 235.

Chino, San Bernardino Co., Our Lady of Guadalupe (1902) (Hispanic), Rev. Ramon Rosales.
Res., 5048 D St., 91710. Tel: 909-591-9402; Fax: 909-591-9404. [JC]
Catechesis/Religious Programs—Tel: 909-628-3615.
Students 639.

St. Margaret Mary (1947), Revs. Michael Sturn; Omer-Luzolo Lwa-Lu Zombe, O.P. (Zaire).
Res., 12686 Central Ave., 91710. Tel: 909-627-8466; Fax: 909-627-8049. [JC]
School—12664 Central Ave., 91710. Tel: 909-591-8419.
Sisters of St. Francis 1; Lay Teachers 8; Students 357.
Catechesis/Religious Programs—Tel: 909-591-7408.
Students 676.

Chino Hills, San Bernardino Co., St. Paul the Apostle (1986), Rev. Michael N. Maher, SS.CC.; Deacon Pat Martinez, Pastoral Assoc. In res., Rev. William Moore, SS.CC.
Office: 14085 Peyton Dr., 91709. Tel: 909-465-5503; Fax: 909-465-1683.
Res., 14860 Cherry Dr., 91709. Tel: 909-597-6154.
Catechesis/Religious Programs—Tel: 909-465-5503, Ext. 16. Lori Muniz, D.R.E.
Students 1,650.

Coachella, Riverside Co., Our Lady of Soledad (1923) (Hispanic), Revs. Bruce Cecil, C.S.C.; John S. Connor, C.S.C. In res., Revs. Jose M. Martelli, C.S.C.; Daniel Groody, C.S.C.
Res., 52-525 Oasis Palm, 92236. Tel: 760-398-5577; Fax: 760-398-1783.
Catechesis/Religious Programs—Tel: 760-398-1790. Judy Hoy, D.R.E.
Students 500.
Missions—Thermal, Riverside Co., El Senor de la Misericordia, Kokell St., Thermal, 92274.; One Hundred Palms, Riverside Co., San Felipe de Jesus, Hwy. 86, Thermal, 92274.
Chapel—Torres-Martinez Reservation, Sacred Heart.

Colton, San Bernardino Co., Immaculate Conception (1943) (Spanish), Revs. Edmund Gomez; Christopher Soupos; Deacon Wayne Joslin.
Office: 1106 N. La Cadena Dr., 92324. Tel: 909-825-5110; Fax: 909-825-0912.
Res., 1090 N. La Cadena Dr., 92324. Tel: 909-825-3004. [CEM 2][JC]
Catechesis/Religious Programs—Students 573.

San Salvador (1893) (Hispanic), Rev. Pierre Deglaire, C.S.Sp.
Parish Center: 178 W. K St., 92324. Tel: 909-825-3481; Fax: 909-825-4473.
Church—Seventh St. & L St., 92324.
Catechesis/Religious Programs—Students 430.

Corona, Riverside Co.,

1—CORPUS CHRISTI CHURCH, (1994), Rev. Gerald C. Deluney.
Office: 3670 McKinley, 92879. Tel: 909-272-9043; Fax: 909-272-6821.
Catechesis/Religious Programs—Students 635.

2—ST. EDWARD, (1896), Rev. Msgr. Peter Luque; Rev. John S. Vieira.
Res., 605 W. Fifth St., 91720. Tel: 909-737-6432; Fax: 909-737-7259.
School—500 S. Merrill St., 91720. Tel: 737-2530.
Lay Teachers 20; Students 550.
Catechesis/Religious Programs—Tel: 909-737-5060.
Students 895.

3—ST. MARY MAGDALENE, (1989), Sr. Maureen Chicoine, R.S.C.J., Pastoral Coord.; Rev. John McHenry, S.V.D.; Deacon Martin Filipek.
Church—8540 Weirick Rd., 92883. Tel: 909-277-1801; Fax: 909-277-2513.
Catechesis/Religious Programs—Tel: 909-277-3038.
Students 400.

4—ST. MATTHEW, (1973), Sandra Boyd, Pastoral Coord.
Res., 2140 W. Ontario, 92882. Tel: 909-737-1621; Fax: 909-737-9715.
Catechesis/Religious Programs—Lou Ann Tannaz, D.R.E.
Students 960.

Crestline, San Bernardino Co., St. Frances Xavier Cabrini (1946), Rev. Amaro Saumell, Admin.
Res., 23079 Crest Forest Dr., P.O. Box 3817, 92325. Tel: 909-338-2303; Fax: 909-338-2383.
Catechesis/Religious Programs—Tel: 909-338-4381.
Students 60.

Desert Hot Springs, Riverside Co., St. Elizabeth of Hungary (1946), Rev. Edward McGuiness.
Res., 66700 E. Pierson Blvd., 92240. Tel: 760-329-8794; Fax: 760-329-6760.
Catechesis/Religious Programs—Tel: 760-251-9268.
Students 235.

Fontana, San Bernardino Co.,

1—CHURCH OF THE RESURRECTION, (1953), Rev. Leonard Krzywda, C.R. In res., Rev. Humphrey Ruszel, C.R.
Res., 7650 Tamarind, 92336. Tel: 909-822-4732; Fax: 909-822-0620.
School—17434 Miller Ave., 92335. Tel: 909-822-4431; Fax: 909-822-0617.
Lay Teachers 10; Students 248.
Catechesis/Religious Programs—Tel: 909-822-2502.
Students 698.

2—ST. GEORGE, (1954), Rev. Philip A. O'Carroll.
Res., 17895 San Bernardino Ave., 92335. Tel: 909-877-1531; Fax: 909-877-6531.
Catechesis/Religious Programs—Tel: 909-877-3935; 877-1070 (Spanish).
Students 380.

3—ST. JOSEPH, (1930), Revs. Richard F. McGee, C.R.; Henry Ruszel, C.R.; Casmir Tadia, C.R.; Deacon Michael Juback.
Office: 17080 Arrow Blvd., 92335. Tel: 909-822-0566; Fax: 909-829-1739.
School—8460 Mango Ave., 92335. Tel: 909-822-5423; Fax: 909-349-2488.
Lay Teachers 10; Students 215.
Catechesis/Religious Programs—Tel: 909-822-3411.
Students 505.

4—ST. MARY, (1939), Rev. Peter Balili; Deacon Mario Gutierrez, Pastoral Admin.
Church—16550 Jurupa Ave., 92337. Tel: 909-822-5670 (English); 357-4682 (Spanish); Fax: 909-357-4688.
Catechesis/Religious Programs—Tel: 909-357-4683 (English); 357-4684 (Spanish).
Students 450.

5—ST. NICHOLAS, (Byzantine Rite), Rev. Joseph Hutsko.
Res., 9112 Oleander Ave., 92335-5599. Tel: 909-822-9917.

Grand Terrace, San Bernardino Co., Christ the Redeemer (1980), Sr. Deanna O'Neill, O.S.B., Pastoral Coord.
Res., 12745 Oriole, 92313. Tel: 909-783-3811; Fax: 909-783-4689.
Catechesis/Religious Programs—Tel: 909-783-3800.
Students 160.

Guasti, San Bernardino Co., San Secondo d'Asti (1926) (Italian), Rev. Louis Marx.
Res., 250 N. Turner Ave., P.O. Box 1056, 91743. Tel: 909-390-0011; Fax: 909-390-9919.
Catechesis/Religious Programs—Students 158.

Hemet, Riverside Co., Holy Spirit Parish (1991), Rev. Silvio D'Ostilio, C.S.Sp.; Joyce Frichtel, Pastoral Assoc.
Res., 26340 Soboba Ave., Box 5268, 92544. Tel: 909-927-8544; Fax: 909-927-8546.
Catechesis/Religious Programs—Students 165.

Our Lady of the Valley (1946), Revs. James H. Burnie, C.S.Sp.; Clement Lachowsky, C.S.Sp.; George Healy, C.S.Sp.; John vanDyk, C.S.Sp.; Deacon Jack Henke.
Mailing Address: P.O. Box 2446, 92546.
Res., Parish Office, 780 S. State St., 92543. Tel: 909-929-6131; Fax: 909-929-8009.
Catechesis/Religious Programs—Tel: 909-658-7436. Tim Smith, D.R.E.
Students 650.

Hesperia, San Bernardino Co., Holy Family, Revs. Charles E. Miller; John S. Vieira.
Res., 9974 I Ave., 92345. Tel: 760-244-9180; Fax: 760-244-1959.
Catechesis/Religious Programs—Tel: 760-244-0269.
Students 962.

Highland, San Bernardino Co., St. Adelaide (1956), Rev. John Ryan; Sr. Maura Feeley, Admin. Assoc.
Res., 27457 E. Baseline, 92346. Tel: 909-862-8669; Fax: 909-862-1603.
School—27487 E. Baseline, 92346. Tel: 909-862-5851; Fax: 909-862-2877.
Lay Teachers 11; Students 270.
Catechesis/Religious Programs—Tel: 909-862-8184.
Students 492.
Mission—East Highlands, San Bernardino Co., St. John Bosco, 28991 Merris St., Highland, 92346. Tel: 909-425-0931. Rev. John Ryan.

Idyllwild, Riverside Co., Queen of Angels (1942), Rev. Charles Devine.
Res., 54525 N. Circle Dr., P.O. Box 1106, 92549. Tel: 909-659-2708; Fax: 909-659-0208.
Catechesis/Religious Programs—Students 39.

Indio, Riverside Co., Our Lady of Perpetual Help (1937), Revs. Rafael A. Partida; Ramon Pedrosa, Jr., O.S.A.
Office: 82-450 Bliss St., 92201. Tel: 760-347-3507; Fax: 760-347-8367.
Res., 45-173 Park St., 92201. Tel: 760-347-5661 (Rectory).
School—82-470 Bliss St., 92201. Tel: 760-347-3786; Fax: 760-347-7207.
Lay Teachers 11; Students 165.
Catechesis/Religious Programs—Tel: 760-347-0594.
Students 1,000.

Joshua Tree, San Bernardino Co., St. Christopher of the Desert (1960), Rev. Ignatius Rasquinha, Admin.
Res., 61350 Wahl Terr., 92252. Tel: 760-366-8710; Fax: 760-366-2690. [JC]
Church—Parish Center, 61261 Sunburst Dr., 92252. Tel: 760-366-8810.
Catechesis/Religious Programs—Students 28.

Lake Arrowhead, San Bernardino Co., Our Lady of the Lake (1938), Very Rev. Timothy F. Keppel, C.R., V.F.
Res., 27627 Rim of the World Dr., P.O. Box 7, Crest Park, 92326. Tel: 909-337-2333; Fax: 909-337-5041. [CEM]
Catechesis/Religious Programs—Tel: 909-336-1605.
Students 270.

Lake Elsinore, Riverside Co., St. Frances of Rome (1887), Revs. Robert Guerrero; Martin Tharakan, O.I.C.; Deacon Bud Burris.
Res., 21591 Lemon St., Wildomar, 92595. Tel: 909-674-6881; Fax: 909-674-6443. [JC]
Catechesis/Religious Programs—Students 610.

Lake Tamarisk, Riverside Co., St. Augustine. Unassigned.
Mailing Address: P.O. Box 768, Desert Center, 92239. Tel: 619-227-3191; Fax: 619-328-8392.

La Quinta, Riverside Co., St. Francis of Assisi (1974), Very Rev. Jack D. Barker, Vicar Forane; Rev. George Gonzales.
Res., 47-225 Washington, P.O. Box 1503, 92253. Tel: 760-564-1255; Fax: 760-564-0763.
Catechesis/Religious Programs—Tel: 760-564-2069.
Students 378.

Loma Linda, San Bernardino Co., St. Joseph the Worker (1944), Rev. Ignatius Rodrigues.
Res., 10816 Mt. View Ave., 92354. Tel: 909-796-2605; Fax: 909-796-0755.
Catechesis/Religious Programs—Tel: 909-796-4308.
Students 160.

Lucerne Valley, San Bernardino Co., St. Paul (1963), Very Rev. Romeo N. Seleccion, M.S., Admin.
Res., 8973 Mesa Rd., P.O. Box 588, 92356. Tel: 760-248-7410; Fax: 760-248-2559.
Catechesis/Religious Programs—Students 35.

Mecca, Riverside Co., Our Lady of Guadalupe Shrine (1927) (Hispanic), Rev. Martin S. Rodriguez, O.R.C.
Mailing Address: 2858 Ninth Street, Riverside, 92507. Tel: 909-684-0279.
Church—65-100 Dale Killer Rd., 92254.
Res., 91-110 5th St., 92254.
Catechesis/Religious Programs—Tel: 909-684-0279; Fax: 909-684-0390.
Students 500.

Montclair, San Bernardino Co., Our Lady of Lourdes (1956), Rev. Robert J. Donat.
Res., 10191 Central Ave., 91763. Tel: 909-626-7278; Fax: 909-626-0562.
School—5303 Orchard St., 91763. Tel: 909-621-4418; 624-5164; Fax: 909-626-0318.
Sisters of the Presentation 3; Lay Teachers 9; Students 310.
Catechesis/Religious Programs—Tel: 909-626-0318. Sr. Angela Callanan, D.R.E.
Students 790.

Moreno Valley, Riverside Co., St. Christopher (1959), Revs. Efren Musngi, M.S.; Antonio Abuan, M.S.; Wilfredo Iminga, M.S.; Deacon Samual Sanchez.
Res., 25075 Cottonwood Ave., 92553. Tel: 909-924-1968; Fax: 909-247-6477.
Catechesis/Religious Programs—D.R.E.: Elizabeth Scretchings, (English); Mirca Sanchez, (Spanish).
Students 2,192.

Murrieta, Riverside Co., St. Martha (1992), Very Rev. Thomas Wallace; Rev. Santos Ortega; Mr. H. Ronald Eldridge, Pastoral Assoc.; Deacons Harold Melton; George Paulicivic; Richard Ward.

Church—37200 Whitewood Rd., 92563. Tel: 909-698-8180; Fax: 909-698-7353.
Catechesis/Religious Programs—Tel: 909-698-8180, Ext. 14.
Students 1,160.

Needles, San Bernardino Co., St. Ann (1888), Rev. William M. Brunner, S.S.C.
Res., 218 D St., P.O. Box 175, 92363. Tel: 760-326-2721; Fax: 760-326-3068. [JC 2]
Catechesis/Religious Programs—Elaine Blake, D.R.E.
Students 100.

Norco, Riverside Co., St. Mel (1959), Rev. Timothy Jernejcic; Deacon Joe Garcia.
Res., 4200 Corona Ave., P.O. Box 700, 92860. Tel: 909-737-7144; Fax: 909-735-8332.
Catechesis/Religious Programs—Students 486.

Ontario, San Bernardino Co., Our Lady of Guadalupe (1948) (Hispanic), Revs. Sacramento Perez, O.de.M.; Adrian Ochoa, O.de.M.
Res., 710 S. Sultana St., 91761. Tel: 909-986-6154; Fax: 909-984-1541.
Catechesis/Religious Programs—Tel: 909-983-2904.
Students 885.

St. George (1905), Revs. Arturo Balagat; Lorenzo Paz. In res., Rev. Msgr. Timothy Lawlor; Rev. Joseph Yim (South Korea).
Res., 325 W. E St., 91762. Tel: 909-983-2637; Fax: 909-395-9707. [CEM][JC]
School—322 W. D St., 91762. Tel: 909-984-9123; Fax: 909-984-0921.
Lay Teachers 10; Students 252.
Catechesis/Religious Programs—Tel: 909-460-1578.
Students 252.

St. Elizabeth Ann Seton (1980), Rev. Charles F. Schultz, S.T.D.
Res., 2713 S. Grove Ave., 91761. Tel: 909-947-2956; Fax: 909-947-2946.
Catechesis/Religious Programs—Students 578.

Palm Desert, Riverside Co., Christ of the Desert (1986). (Newman Center). Rev. Jack P. McGinnis.
Res., 73441 Fred Waring Dr., 92260. Tel: 760-346-0089; Fax: 760-340-2245.
Catechesis/Religious Programs—Students 75.

Sacred Heart (1956), Revs. Anthony J. Timlin; Jean Lenoir (Spain).
Res., 43-775 N. Deep Canyon Rd., 92260. Tel: 760-346-6502; Fax: 760-773-4873.
School—Tel: 760-346-3513; Fax: 760-773-0673. Sr. Joan Griffin, O.S.F., Prin.
Lay Teachers 10; Students 286.
Catechesis/Religious Programs—Tel: 760-340-0143.
Students 201.

Palm Springs, Riverside Co., Our Lady of Guadalupe (1912) (Cahuilla Indian), Rev. Adrian Brinn.
Res., 204 S. El Segundo, P.O. Box 1947, 92263. Tel: 760-325-5809; Fax: 760-327-2049.

Our Lady of Solitude (1929) (Hispanic), Rev. Miguel Ceja; Deacon John Skora.
Res., 151 W. Alejo Rd., 92262. Tel: 760-325-3816; Fax: 760-325-5316. [JC]
Catechesis/Religious Programs—Students 225.

St. Theresa (1948), Rev. Msgr. Philip A. Behan.
Res., 2800 E. Ramon Rd., 92264. Tel: 760-323-2669; Fax: 760-322-8581.
School—455 S. Compadre, 92262. Tel: 760-327-4919.
Lay Teachers 19; Students 334.
Catechesis/Religious Programs—Tel: 760-323-4351 (English); 323-8862 (Spanish).
Students 480.

Perris, Riverside Co., St. James (1907), Very Rev. Anthony Ferrero, V.F., J.C.L. In res., Rev. John Niessen, S.V.D.
Office: 269 W. Third St., 92570. Tel: 909-657-2380; Fax: 909-943-7290.
School—250 W. Third St., 92570. Tel: 909-657-5226; Fax: 909-657-1793.
Irish Sisters of Mercy 3; Lay Teachers 10; Students 300.
Catechesis/Religious Programs—Tel: 909-657-8809. D.R.E.: Sr. Noreen O'Connor; Martha Ascencio, (Spanish).
Students 1,125.

Phelan, San Bernardino Co., Blessed Junipero Serra Church (1989), Rev. Patrick V. Kirsch.
Mailing Address: P.O. Box 292570, 92329-2570. Fax: 760-868-2171.
Rectory Office: 4471 Sunrise Blvd., 92371. Tel: 760-868-4342; Fax: 760-249-3438.
Catechesis/Religious Programs—Students 172.

Rancho Cucamonga, San Bernardino Co., Our Lady of Mount Carmel (1905), Rev. Francisco Cabarello, O.de.M.
Res., 10079 Eighth St., P.O. Box 303, 91729-0303. Tel: 909-987-2717; Fax: 909-987-3818.
Catechesis/Religious Programs—Students 410.

Sacred Heart (1953), Very Rev. Stephen C. Porter; Rev. Michael Krelovich.
Church Office: 12704 Foothill Blvd., 91739. Tel: 909-899-1084, Ext. 10; Fax: 909-899-3229.
School—12676 Foothill Blvd., 91739. Fax: 909-899-0413.
Lay Teachers 12; Students 285.
Catechesis/Religious Programs—Tel: 909-899-1049, Ext. 17; Fax: 909-899-3229.
Students 500.

Redlands, San Bernardino Co., Sacred Heart (1894), Revs. Thomas Burdick; Paul Johnson, O.P.; Deacons William Keough, (Retired); Richard Cover.
Res., 115 W. Olive Ave., 92373. Tel: 909-793-2469; Fax: 909-335-1719. [JC]
School—215 S. Eureka St., 92373. Tel: 909-792-3958; Fax: 909-792-7292.
Lay Teachers 13; Students 295.
Catechesis/Religious Programs—Tel: 909-798-4167.
Students 308.

St. Mary (1941) (Latino), Rev. Miguel A. Urrea.
Res., 1214 Columbia St., 92374. Tel: 909-792-3695; Fax: 909-798-2665. [JC]
Catechesis/Religious Programs—Tel: 909-335-0096.
Students 380.

Rialto, San Bernardino Co., St. Catherine of Siena (1949), Rev. Howard A. Lincoln; Deacons Edwin Chamberlayne; Gonzalo Sotelo. Pastoral Assocs.: Kay Halder; Horacio Cortez.
Res., 339 N. Sycamore, 92376-3517. Tel: 909-875-1360; Fax: 909-875-2822.
School—335 N. Sycamore Ave., 92376. Tel: 909-875-7821.
Lay Teachers 9; Students 300.
Catechesis/Religious Programs—Students 1,200.

St. Thomas More (1961), Rev. Edward A. Dubel, C.R.
Res., 222 E. Easton, P.O. Box 367, 92376. Tel: 909-421-7030; Fax: 909-421-1374.

Riverside, Riverside Co.,

1—Our Lady of Guadalupe Shrine, (1929) (Hispanic), Rev. Martin S. Rodriguez, O.R.C.; Deacon Rudy Ybarra.
Res., 2858 Ninth St., 92507. Tel: 909-684-0279; Fax: 909-684-0390.
Catechesis/Religious Programs—Tel: 909-683-1123.
Students 608.

2—Our Lady of Perpetual Help, (1955), Revs. Rutilio J. del Riego, D.L.P.; Pedro Arribas, D.L.P.; Leo Vu Dinh Huyen, C.M.C.; Deacons Joe Gomeck; Ysidro, Gurrola; Larry Quilliam.
Res., 5250 Central Ave., 92504. Tel: 909-689-8921; Fax: 909-689-3619.
School—6686 Streeter Ave., 92504. Tel: 909-689-2125; Fax: 909-689-9354.
Lay Teachers 11; Students 290.
Catechesis/Religious Programs—Students 636.

3—Queen of Angels, (1949), Revs. Ronald Rocky, O.F.M.Conv.; Anthony Howard, O.F.M.Conv.; Jesus Manuel Galvez, O.F.M. Conv.
Res., 4824 Jones Ave., 92505. Tel: 909-689-3674; Fax: 909-687-6146.
School—Tel: 909-689-1992.
Lay Teachers 9; Students 142.
Catechesis/Religious Programs—Tel: 909-687-5407.
Students 809.

4—Sacred Heart, (1945), Rev. Edward J. Connolly.
Res., 9935 Mission Blvd., 92509. Tel: 909-685-5058; Fax: 909-685-1056. [JC]
Catechesis/Religious Programs—Tel: 909-685-8510.
Students 1,183.

5—St. Anthony, (1923), Rev. Eloy Trujillo, O.R.C.
Res., 3074 Madison St., 92504. Tel: 909-352-8393; Fax: 909-352-8816.
Catechesis/Religious Programs—Tel: 909-785-4908.
Students 373.

6—St. Catherine of Alexandria, (1946), Revs. Joseph Kuehner; Jerimiah Roche; Deacon Paul Von Ins, Jr.
Res., 7050 Brockton Ave., 92506. Tel: 909-683-0800; Fax: 909-683-4114.
School—3728 Arlington Ave., 92506. Tel: 909-684-1091; Fax: 909-684-4936.
Lay Teachers 17; Students 360.
Catechesis/Religious Programs—Tel: 909-781-9855. Kathleen Serra, D.R.E.
Students 686.

7—St. Francis de Sales, (1886), Revs. Robert Viscardi, I.M.C., Admin.; Louis Abdoo, I.M.C.; Deacon James Dale. In res., Revs. Reno Aiardi, I.M.C.; Giovanni Saffario, I.M.C.
Res., 4268 Lime St., 92501. Tel: 909-686-4004; Fax: 909-686-3948. [JC]
School—Tel: 909-683-5083; Fax: 909-683-0249.
Religious 1; Lay Teachers 12; Students 343.
Catechesis/Religious Programs—Tel: 909-784-0987.
Students 220.

8—St. John the Evangelist, (1956), Rev. Michael Fredericks.
Res., 3980 Opal St., 92519. Tel: 909-684-6864; Fax: 909-684-3115.
Catechesis/Religious Programs—Tel: 909-686-5181.
Students 582.
Mission—Rubidoux, Riverside Co., Our Lady of Guadalupe, 2518 Hall Ave., P.O. Box 3024, Riverside, CA 92519. Tel: 909-788-1464.

9—St. Patrick, (1989), Rev. James McLaughlin.
Mailing Address: 10915 Pigeon Pass Rd., Moreno Valley, 92557. Tel: 909-485-6673; Fax: 909-485-3834.
Church—6296 Rivercrest Dr., 92507.
Catechesis/Religious Programs—Students 616.

10—St. Andrew's Newman Center, (1971). Serving Riverside Community College & UCR. Revs. David Geib, O.P.; Martin Diaz, O.P.
Mailing Address: 105 W. Big Springs Rd., 92507. Tel: 909-682-8751; Fax: 909-682-3513.
Res., 872 Spruce St., 92507. Tel: 909-784-0160.
Catechesis/Religious Programs—Frances Hodgkinson, D.R.E.
Students 200.

11—St. Thomas the Apostle, (1903), Revs. Joseph Felker; Joseph Borba; Deacon Paul Myers.
Office: 3774 Jackson St., 92503. Tel: 909-689-1131; Fax: 909-354-7402.
School—9136 Magnolia Ave., 92503. Tel: 909-689-1981; Fax: 909-689-1985.
Lay Teachers 11; Students 320.
Catechesis/Religious Programs—Tel: 909-689-7180. Nancy Corbitt, D.R.E.
Students 471.
Mission—Riverside, Riverside Co., Our Lady of Guadalupe, 9398 Indiana Ave., 92503. Rev. Robert M. Herbst, O.F.M.Conv.

Running Springs, San Bernardino Co., St. Anne in the Mountains (1963), Very Rev. Timothy F. Keppel, C.R., V.F.
Res., 30480 Fredalba Rd., P.O. Box 2400, 92382. Tel: 909-867-2832; Fax: 909-867-2832.

San Jacinto, Riverside Co., St. Anthony (1890), Rev. Ciro Libanati.
Res., 630 S. Santa Fe Ave., 92583. Tel: 909-654-7911; Fax: 909-654-2309.
School—St. Hyacinth Academy, Tel: 909-654-2013.
Sisters 2; Lay Teachers 11; Students 224.
Catechesis/Religious Programs—Tel: 909-654-3311.
Students 285.

Soboba Indian Reservation, Riverside Co., St. Joseph (1888) (American Indian), Rev. Earl Henley, M.S.C.
Mailing Address: P.O. Box 1027, San Jacinto, 92581. Tel: 909-654-2086; Fax: 909-654-2086. [CEM]

Sun City, Riverside Co., St. Vincent Ferrer (1965), Rev. Gerard J. McGuinness; Deacon Ronald Rehaume. In res., Rev. Michael O'Day.
Res., 27931 Murrieta Rd., 92586-2320. Tel: 909-679-4531; Fax: 909-679-7521. [JC]
Catechesis/Religious Programs—Tel: 909-672-4019.
Students 351.

Temecula, Riverside Co., St. Catherine (1979), Rev. John Wagner; Deacons John Barth; Robert Phillips.
Res., 41875 C St., 92592. Tel: 909-676-4403; Fax: 909-695-6659.
Catechesis/Religious Programs—Tel: 909-695-6656. D.R.E.: Kathleen Igo; Maria Barth, Spanish Min., Tel: 909-587-0023.
Students 108.

Thermal, San Bernardino Co., San Felipe de Jesus, Revs. Bruce Cecil, C.S.C.; John S. Connor, C.S.C.
Church—67-305 Hwy. 86, 92274. Tel: 760-398-5577; Fax: 760-398-1783.

Trona, San Bernardino Co., St. Madeleine Sophie Barat, Rev. William J. Kiefer.
Res., 83395 Trona Rd., 93562. Tel: 760-372-4717.

Thousand Palms, San Bernardino, St. Philip the Apostle (1991), Rev. Joseph Mawicke.
Res., 31-525 Via Pared, P.O. Box 405, 92276. Tel: 760-343-1911; Fax: 760-343-3211.
Catechesis/Religious Programs—Students 14.

Twentynine Palms, San Bernardino Co., Blessed Sacrament, Rev. James Moore.
Office: 6785 Sage Ave., 92277. Tel: 760-367-3343; Fax: 760-367-0543.
School—6755 Sage Ave., 92277. Tel: 760-367-3341.
Lay Teachers 8; Students 122.
Catechesis/Religious Programs—Tel: 760-367-3347. Alice-Ann Patu, D.R.E.
Lay Teachers 9; Students 140.

Upland, San Bernardino Co., St. Joseph (1922), Revs. Tom Burns, M.S.C.; Angel Garcia, M.S.C.; John Schweikert, M.S.C.; Deacons Charles Pobjoy, (Retired); Frank Simoni; John Kim; George Schmit; Greg Moore.
Res., 877 N. Campus Ave., 91786. Tel: 909-981-8110; Fax: 909-949-8090. [JC]
School—905 Campus Ave., 91786. Tel: 909-920-5185; Fax: 909-920-5190.
Sisters of the Presentation 3; Lay Teachers 12; Students 352.
Catechesis/Religious Programs—Tel: 909-982-9518. Liliana Moore, D.R.E.
Students 816.

St. Anthony (1974), Rev. Edmond G. O'Donnell; Deacon Eugene Bello.
Res., 2110 N. San Antonio Ave., P.O. Box 608, 91785. Tel: 909-985-2803; Fax: 909-982-8643.
Church—2110 N. San Antonio Ave., 91785.
Catechesis/Religious Programs—Tel: 909-981-7080. Susan Breen, D.R.E.
Students 450.

Victorville, San Bernardino Co., Holy Innocents (1992), Rev. Mark E. Kotlarczyk.
Mailing Address: 15384 Tamarack Rd., 92392. Tel: 760-955-6010; Fax: 760-955-2100.
Catechesis/Religious Programs—Tel: 760-955-6262.
Students 485.

St. Joan of Arc (1922), Revs. Gerardo Mendoza; John Fahnestock.
Res., 15512 Sixth St., 92392. Tel: 760-245-7674; Fax: 760-245-7077.
Catechesis/Religious Programs—15503 5th St., 92392. Tel: 760-245-4904.
Students 404.

Wrightwood, San Bernardino Co., Our Lady of the Snows (1946), Rev. Patrick V. Kirsch.
Mailing Address: P.O. Box 292570, Phelan, 92329. Tel: 760-868-4342; Fax: 760-868-2171.
Rectory Office: 4471 Sunrise Blvd., Phelan, 92371.
Catechesis/Religious Programs—Students 74.

Yucaipa, San Bernardino Co., St. Frances Xavier Cabrini (1953), Revs. Kenneth Jenkins; Joseph Quattropane, O.F.M. Cap.
Res., 12687 California St., 92399. Tel: 909-797-2533; Fax: 909-790-5803.
Catechesis/Religious Programs—Students 150.

Yucca Valley, San Bernardino Co., St. Mary of the Valley (1953), Revs. Ponciano M. Ramos, S.V.D.; Luc Tran, S.V.D.
Res., 7495 Church St., 92284-3247. Tel: 760-365-2287; Fax: 760-369-0622.
Catechesis/Religious Programs—Tel: 760-365-7937.
Students 150.

Chaplains of Public Institutions

SAN BERNARDINO. *Arrowhead Regional Medical Center* 805 Medical Center Dr., 92404. Tel: 909-387-8111. Rev. Robert Marzullo, O.P.
San Bernardino City and County Jails. Vacant.
San Bernardino Community Hospital 805 Medical Center Dr., 92411. Tel: 909-887-6333; 881-4053. Rev. Peter Balili.
San Bernardino Juvenile Hall & Verdemont Boys Ranch. Vacant. Catholic Charities, 1450 N. D St., 92405. Tel: 909-388-1239.
San Bernardino Medical Center 2101 N. Waterman Ave., 92404. Tel: 909-883-8711. Rev. Barnabas Laubach, O.S.B.

BLYTHE. *Chuckawalla Valley State Prison* P.O. Box 2289, 92226. Tel: 760-243-7243. Rev. John Rusk.

CHINO. *California Institute for Men* P.O. Box 128, 91710. Tel: 909-681-6497; 597-1821, Ext. 2289; 2689. Rev. Chester Kopec, O.P.
California Youth Authority. Vacant.
Camp Prado. Vacant.
Southern Conservation Center P.O. Box 128, 91710. Tel: 909-597-1821, Ext. 2289. Rev. Michael Bucaro.

FONTANA. *Kaiser Permanente Hospital* 9961 Sierra Ave., 92335. Tel: 909-829-5850; 829-5000 (Emergency). Rev. William Marcotte.

FRONTERA. *California Institute for Women* 16756 Chino-Corona Rd., 91720. Tel: 909-597-1771. Rev. Neil D. Fuller, S.V.D., Chap.

LOMA LINDA. *Jerry Pettis Memorial Hospital* 11201 Benton St., 92354. Tel: 909-825-7084. Rev. Msgr. Adolphus Chavez, (Hispanics).
Loma Linda Community Hospital 25333 Barton Rd., 92354. Tel: 909-796-7311, Ext. 4367. Rev. Leonard Mestas.
Loma Linda University Medical Center Barton Rd. and Anderson St., 92354. Tel: 909-824-0800. Rev. Leonard Mestas.

MORENA VALLEY. *Riverside County Regional Medical Center* 56520 Cactus Ave., 92555. Tel: 909-486-4000; 486-4334. Rev. Arturo Chavez.

NORCO. *California Rehabilitation Center* Western & Fifth Sts., P.O. Box 1841, 91760. Tel: 909-737-2683, Ext. 4305. Rev. Msgr. Cosimo Corciulo.

PATTON. *Patton State Hospital*. Rev. Bernard Donaghey.

PILOT ROCK. *Crestline*. Vacant. Tel: 909-338-2303.

RIVERSIDE. *Riverside General Hospital* 9851 Magnolia Ave., 92503. Tel: 909-358-7100; 689-3674. Bro. Dario Garcia, O.F.M.Conv.
Riverside Juvenile Hall. Vacant.

Special or Other Diocesan Assignment:
Reverend Monsignors—
Lawrence, Robert E., J.C.L., Adjutant Judicial Vicar, Canonical Svcs.
Webber, Donald S., J.C.L., Judicial Vicar, Canonical Svcs.
Reverend Fathers—
Balili, Peter, Hospital Chap., San Bernardino Community Hospital
Granillo, Paul, Bishop's Liturgy Coord. & Assoc. Dir., Vocations
Larkin, Ronald, M.S.C., Vicar for Clergy
Lopez, Gerard M., S.T.L., Mod. Curia & Dir. Priest Personnel
Nogosek, Robert, C.S.C., Dir. Diaconate Formation
Very Rev.—
Aiardi, Reno, I.M.C., Dir. Missions Office

On Duty Outside the Diocese:
Reverend Fathers—
Andel, David, North American College, Vatican City, 00120 Italy
Buchanan, Robert E., Our Lady of Snows, 1138 Wright St., Las Vegas, NV 89509
Frankovich, Frank, Companions of the Cross, 100 Young St., Ottawa, Ontario, Canada KIY 3P7
Gaglia, Fred, 1730 W. Guadalupe Rd., Mesa, AZ 85202
Kurilec, Robert, USN, 3908 Roebling Ln., Virginia Beach, VA 23452
Lowe, Frank, Capt., Chap., 1245 Jefferson Ridge #3, Manhattan, KS 66502
Tomkin, Robert, Immaculate Heart of Mary, 719 Ferry St., Sedro Wooley, WA 98284

Military Chaplains:
Reverend Fathers—
Serban, Ron, Captain, National Training Center, Center Chapel, P.O. Box 105053, Fort Irwin, CA 92310. Tel: 760-380-4211; 380-4212

On Leave:
Reverend Fathers—
Soupos, Christopher

Retired:
Reverend Monsignors—
Andreatta, Tullio, 2245 Fort Stockton Rd., San Diego, CA 92103
Lawlor, Timothy, 325 W. E St., Ontario, CA 91762
Meagher, Thomas, 1011 St. Andrews #4, Upland, CA 91786
O'Leary, Cornelius, 25098 Jaclyn Ave., Moreno Valley, CA 92543
Reverend Fathers—
Baseford, Paul, 485 Foxenwood Dr., Santa Maria, CA 92355
Battle, Lawrence, 73450 Country Club Dr. #190, Palm Desert, CA 92260
Bonacum, Thomas, 124 Box Garner Valley Rd., Mountain Center, CA 92561
Cardoza, Edward, 21267 George Brown, Riverside, CA 92518
Casey, Donald A., 546 Reliance Ave., Henderson, NV 89015-9690
Cerezo, Alfonso, 865 E. Yale, Ontario, CA 91764
Cima, Jose, 23505 Evening Snow, Moreno Valley, CA 92557
Coslowsky, Marion, 733 Belinda Ave., Barstow, CA 92311
DePasquale, Dominic, 4673 Braemar Pl., Riverside, CA 92501
DiLeo, Anthony, 43981 Northgate, Temecula, CA 92592
Domas, John, 800 Pennslyvania Ave. #15, Beaumont, CA 92223
Downey, Robert, P.O. Box 292629, Phelan, CA 92329
Erickson, Robert, P.O. Box 460, Rim Forest, CA 92378
Erstad, William, 9600 19th St. Apt. 81, Alta Loma, CA 91737
Fitzwilliam, Ivan, 388 Reposo St., San Jacinto, CA 92582
Ganahl, James, 15767 Tuscola Rd., Apt. 1, Apple Valley, CA 92307
Gill, Paul, 39335 Vineland, Sp. 66, Cherry Valley, CA 92223
Gillespie, Thomas, 1201 E. Highland, San Bernardino, CA 92404
Gorman, John, Nazareth House, 6333 Rancho Mission Rd., San Diego, CA 92108
Grajek, Lawrence, P.O. Box 2077, Big Bear City, CA 92314
Greiner, Lawrence, 197 Via Lola, Apt. 10, Palm Springs, CA 92262
Guillen, Manuel R., 1535 Third Ave., San Diego, CA 92101
Guillen, Patricio, 2002 S. Magnolia Ave., Ontario, CA 91762
Jalbert, Marcel, 25714 Mesa Ct., San Bernardino, CA 92404
Kiefer, William J., 83395 Trona Rd., Trona, CA 93562
Leahy, Anthony, P.O. Box 4027, Oceanside, CA 92051
Leissler, Joseph L., 45-803 Hwy. 74, Palm Desert, CA 92260
McNally, Michael R., P.O. Box 3685, San Bernardino, CA 92413
Morquillas, Fructuoso, 23883 Copper Hill Pl., Moreno Valley, CA 92557
O'Day, Michael, 28710 Olympia Way, Sun City, CA 92586
O'Keeffe, Patrick, 1201 E. Highland Ave., San Bernardino, CA 92404
O'Sullivan, Brendan, 1001 Encinitas Blvd., San Diego, CA 92024
Roach, Joseph, 9466 Navajo Tr., Morongo Valley, CA 92256
Rogan, Brian, 819 Sherwood St., Redlands, CA 92373
Schilly, Joseph, Nazareth House, 6333 Rancho Mission Rd., San Diego, CA 92108
Speno, Eugene, 1201 E. Highland, San Bernardino, CA 92404
Stauber, James, 4967 Chicago Ave., Riverside, CA 92507
Trong, Joseph, 12772 Louise Cir., Garden Grove, CA 92643
Valdes, Luis, 1201 E. Highland, San Bernardino, CA 92404
Vehovec, Valentine, 6333 Rancho Mission Rd., #104, San Diego, CA 92108
Wadell, John, Cl. Fra. Pere Fornes, 13, Muro, Mallorca, Spain 07440
Walters, Vincent, 4651 Braemer Pl. #26, Riverside, CA 92501-3040
Waterfall, Richard A., P.O. Box 409, Palm Springs, CA 92263
White, Kris, 11171 Oakwood Dr., I-305, Loma Linda, CA 92354
Wieser, Francis, 10831 Deerfield Dr., Cherry Valley, CA 92223

Permanent Deacons:
Acosta, Joseph, Highland
Aguilera, Santos, Hesperia
Alaniz, Frank, Hesperia
Amador, Robert, Colton
Ampuero, Marcial, Adelanto
Avila, Robert, Indio
Barth, John, Temecula
Bello, Eugene, Upland
Borne, Edward, Moreno Valley
Brannick, Thomas, Rialto
Burgett, Donald, Barstow
Burns, Charles, La Quinta
Burris, Bud, Lake Elsinore
Campbell, Gerald, Desert Hot Springs
Cardenas, Roberto, San Bernardino
Carroll, Christopher, Alto Loma
Chamberlayne, Edwin, Rialto
Clinton, Jack, Upland
Cover, Richard, Redlands
Dale, James R., Riverside
Fausto, Juan, Palm Springs
Filipek, Marlin, Corona
Fultz, Charles, Upland
Garcia, Jose Israel, Coachella
Garcia, Joseph, Norco
Gomeck, Joseph, Riverside
Gomez, Manuel, Apple Valley
Gonzalez, Victor, Coachella
Gurrola, Ysidro, Riverside
Gutierrez, Mario, Fontana
Haproff, David, Corona
Henke, Jack, San Jacinto
Heredia, Juan, Palm Desert
Hodnick, Mark, Alta Loma
Hoy, Wayne, Coachella
Hunsicker, Scott, Hesperia
Hunt, Sam, La Quinta
Jelley, Michael, Reche Canyon
Joslin, Wayne, Moreno Valley
Juback, Michael, Fontana
Kafka, Gene, San Bernardino
Keough, William, Redlands
Kermott, Philip P., Banning
Key, Joseph, San Bernardino
Kilbourn, Austin, Moreno Valley

Kim, John, Upland
Marin, Arturo, Cathedral City
Martinez, M. Pat, Chino
Melton, Harold, Murrieta
Mirci, Philip, Redlands
Moore, Greg, Ontario
Murvin, Royal, Banning
Myers, Paul, Riverside
Neufell, James, Riverside
Olivas, Manuel, Riverside
Ortiz, Joseph, Riverside
Partida, Ralph, Jr., Big Bear, Murrieta
Paulicivic, George, Sr., Temecula
Phillips, Robert, Temecula
Pimental, Simon, Victorville
Pobjoy, Charles, Cucamonga
Quilliam, Lawrence, Riverside
Ramirez, Victor, Rialto
Rehaume, Ronald J., Sun City
Reyes, Carlos, Apple Valley
Rios, Joseph, Redlands
Rittman, Robert, Apple Valley
Rodriguez, Brijido, Indio
Roman, Francis, Barstow
Salinas, Arcadio, Jr., Coachella
Sanchez, Samuel, Moreno Valley
Schlemer, Jon, Chino Hills
Schmit, George, San Bernardino
Sepulveda, Ralph, Banning
Shalhoub, William J., Loma Linda
Silva, Francisco, Coachella
Simoni, Frank, Upland
Simpson, Jerome, Running Springs
Skora, John, Palm Springs
Sotelo, Gonzalo, Rialto
Taylor, Daniel, East Highland
Vasquez, Sergio, Coachella
Vela, Joe, Corona
Von Ins, Paul, Alta Loma
Ward, Richard, Murrieta
Ybarra, Rudy, Riverside
Zambrano, Jose, Corona

INSTITUTIONS LOCATED IN THE DIOCESE

[A] SEMINARIES, RELIGIOUS OR SCHOLASTICATES

RIVERSIDE. *Blessed Junipero Serra House of Formation*, 3325 13th St., 92501. Tel: 909-788-9931; Fax: 909-781-9031. Revs. Jose Sanz, D.L.P., Rector; Pedro Arribas, D.L.P., Spiritual Dir. Priests 2; Seminarians 10.

Divine Word Seminary, 11316 Cypress Ave., 92505. Tel: 909-689-4858; Fax: 909-785-0327.
E-mail: wjcaffrey@aol.com
Revs. William Caffrey, S.V.D., Rector; Alexander Hoefler, S.V.D.; Joseph Fertal, S.V.D.; Charles Burns, S.V.D.; Marek Kalwak; Michael Manning; John McHenry, S.V.D.; John Shevlin, S.V.D.; Richard Winters, S.V.D.; Francis Mihalic, S.V.D.; Henry Noga, S.V.D.; William Adams, S.V.D.; Bros. Bernard Dorade, S.V.D.; Daniel Yunck, S.V.D.

[B] HIGH SCHOOLS, DIOCESAN

SAN BERNARDINO. *Aquinas High School*. (Coed), 2772 Sterling Ave., 92404. Tel: 909-886-4659; Fax: 909-886-7717.
E-mail: Aquinas@Aquinashs.net
Web site: www.aquinashs.net
Rev. Andrew Sotelo, S.J., Prin. Priests 2; Sisters 1; Lay Teachers 19; Students 315.

RIVERSIDE. *Notre Dame High School*. (Coed), 7085 Brockton Ave., 92506. Tel: 909-369-2810; Fax: 909-781-9020.
Web site: www.notrehs.com
Dr. Jo Dean Salley, Prin. Priests 2; Sisters 1; Lay Teachers 37; Students 620.

[C] HOMES FOR SENIOR CITIZENS

SAN BERNARDINO. *St. Bernardine Plaza*, 550 W. Fifth St., 92401. Tel: 909-888-0153; Fax: 909-381-1589
For a complete listing, refer to the Special Care Facilities section.

PALM DESERT. *La Paz Villas*, P.O. Box 1962, 92261. Tel: 760-772-1382; Fax: 760-360-6638.
E-mail: brallo@aol.com
For a complete listing, refer to the Special Care Facilities section.

[D] GENERAL HOSPITALS AND CLINICS

SAN BERNARDINO. *St. Bernardine Medical Center*, 2101 N. Waterman Ave., 92404. Tel: 909-883-8711; Fax: 909-881-4546
For a complete listing, refer to the Hospitals section.

APPLE VALLEY. *St. Mary Medical Center*, 18300 Hwy. 18, 92307. Tel: 760-946-8195; Fax: 760-242-2994
For a complete listing, refer to the Hospitals section.

VICTORVILLE. *St. John of God Health Care Services*, P.O. Box 2457, 92392. Tel: 760-241-4917; Fax: 760-241-8911
For a complete listing, refer to the Hospitals section.

[E] MONASTERIES AND RESIDENCES OF PRIESTS AND BROTHERS

APPLE VALLEY. *Hospitaller Brothers St. John of God*, P.O. Box 1664, 92307. Tel: 760-242-2783; Fax: 760-241-8911. Bro. Richard Gaule, O.H., Prior. Brothers 6.

BURLINGTON. *Capuchin Franciscans*, 1345 Cortez Ave., 94010. Tel: 650-342-4550. Rev. Ronald Talbot, O.F.M.Cap.

CHINO HILLS. *Congregation of the Sacred Hearts, SS.CC.*, Western U.S. Province, St. Paul the Apostle Rectory, 14860 Cherry Dr., 91709. Tel: 909-597-6154; Fax: 909-465-1683. Rev. Michael N. Maher, SS.CC., Diocesan Contact.

CORONA. *Congregation of the Mother Coredemptrix*, 1775 S. Main St., 91720-4961. Tel: 909-737-4125; 340-9880.
E-mail: corona@doncong.org
Web site: corona.dongcong.org
Shrine of Presentation (Den Thanh Duc Me Dang Con). Revs. Pius M. Nguyen Dan, C.M.C., Dir.; Leo M. Vu Dinh Huyen, C.M.C.; Matthias M. Nguyen Huy Chuong, C.M.C.; Aloysius M. Tran Ngoc Thoai, C.M.C.; Luke M. Do Binh Dinh, C.M.C.

HEMET. *Holy Ghost Fathers*, Casa Laval, 309 E. Whitter Ave., 92546-3509. Tel: 909-658-6851; Fax: 909-765-3137.
E-mail: spiritan@pc.net
Web site: www.spiritan.org
Revs. Edmond J. Leonard, C.S.Sp.; Edward Bernacki, C.S.Sp.; James Burke, C.S.Sp.; Richard Kissane, C.S.Sp., Holy Spirit, P.O. Box 5268, 92544-0268. Tel: 909-927-4478; Fax: 909-927-8546. Rev. Silvio D'Ostilio, C.S.Sp., Our Lady of the Valley, P.O. Box 2446, 92546-0414. Tel: 909-929-6131. Revs. John van Dyk, C.S.Sp.; James H. Burnie, C.S.Sp., Admin.; Clement Lachowsky, C.S.Sp.

MORONGO VALLEY. *St. Michael's of Morongo Valley, Inc.*, 9466 Navajo Tr., 92256. Tel: 760-363-6617. Retirement Facility. In res. Revs. Gerald F. Clune (ALB), (Retired); Aloysius A. Lucking, (Retired); Joseph Buttimer (LOA); Gino G. Rive, (Retired); Joseph W. Roach, S.A.G., (Retired).

RIVERSIDE. *Operarios Del Reino De Cristo, O.R.C.*, 2858 Ninth St., 92507. Tel: 909-684-0279; Fax: 909-684-0309. Revs. Jose Varela, O.R.C., Local Contact; Edwardo Carmona (Mexico), Regl. Dir.; Eliseo Hernandez, O.R.C.; Martin S. Rodriguez, O.R.C.; Eloy Trujillo Contreras.

St. Vincent Ferrer House, 872 Spruce St., 92507. Tel: 909-784-0160; Fax: 909-682-3513.
E-mail: catholicucr@earthlink.net
Dominicans. Revs. David Geib, O.P.; Lawrence Farrell, O.P.; Martin Diaz, O.P.; Robert Marzullo, O.P.

[F] CONVENTS AND RESIDENCES FOR SISTERS

SAN BERNARDINO. *Daughters of St. Joseph of California, F.S.J.*, 6677 Del Rosa Ave., 02404. Tel: 909-888-4877; Fax: 909-888-4387. Sr. Rosario Rodriguez, F.S.J., Major Supr.

CALIMESA. *Missionary Sisters of the Immaculate Conception*, 1271 Nugget Ct., 92320; Fax: 909-795-8128.
E-mail: judinefran@aol.com
Sr. Judine Jacobs, S.M.I.C.; Sr. Frances Karovic, S.M.I.C. Madonna of Desert Community 2.

GRAND TERRACE. *Sisters of St. Benedict, Holy Spirit Monastery*, 22791 Pico St., 92313-5750. Tel: 909-783-4446; Fax: 909-783-3525.
E-mail: hsmonastery@prodigy.net
Web site: www.re.net/sanbernardino.hsmonastery
Sr. Mary Ann Schepers, O.S.B., Prioress. Sisters 12.

REDLANDS. *Congregation of the Sisters of Mercy*, Provincial House, 10175 Bermuda Dr., 92374. Tel: 909-798-4747.

Sisters of Mercy, U.S. Province, 1075 Bermuda Dr., 92374. Tel: 909-798-4747; Fax: 909-798-5300.
E-mail: tess1075@aol.com
Sr. Teresa O'Connell, R.S.M., Prov.; Sr. Carmel Crimmins. Total in Residence 143.

TUSTIN. *Sisters of the Company of Mary (O.D.N.)*, 16791 E. Main St., 92780. Tel: 714-541-3125; Fax: 714-835-0648.
E-mail: odn@ocweb.com
Web site: www.ocweb.com/odnusa
Sr. Mary Salud Estrada, O.D.N., Maj. Sup.; Sr. Doris Louise, O.D.N. Total in Residence 16; Total Staff 4.

Vina de Lestonnac Ministry Center-Convent, 39300 De Portola Rd., Temecula, 92592. Tel: 909-302-2800. Total in Residence 11.

Vina de Lestonnac Ministry Center-Retreat, 39300 De Portola Rd., Temecula, 92592. Tel: 909-302-5571; Fax: 909-302-2830. Total Staff 8.

Lestonnac Chalet, 24719 San Moritz Dr., Lake Gregory, 92325. Tel: 909-338-1525; Fax: 714-835-0648.

St. Jeanne de Lestonnac School, 32650 Avenida Lestonnac, Temecula, 92592. Tel: 909-587-2505; Fax: 909-587-2515.
E-mail: sjdltem@earthlink.com

YUCAIPA. *Our Lady of Victory Missionary Sisters*, 12755 California St., 92399. Tel: 909-381-3095. Sr. Mary Matilda Spetter, O.L.V.M., D.R.E.; Sr. Elizabeth Hann, O.L.V.M., Ministry to Elderly. Sisters 2.

[G] CAMPS & RETREATS

BIG BEAR LAKE. *Sacred Heart Retreat Camp*, 896 Cienega Rd., P.O. Box 1795, 92315. Tel: 909-866-5696; Fax: 909-866-5650. Total in Residence 5; Total Staff 12.

CHERRY VALLEY. *Servants of the Paraclete Guadalupe Retreat Center*, 39100 Orchard Ave., 92223-3797. Tel: 909-845-7777; Fax: 909-845-6271. Rev. Gregory McCormick, s.P., Supr. Total in Residence 13; Total Staff 3.

LOS ANGELES. *Camp Mariastella, Inc.* Camp for girls. 2303 S. Figueroa Way, 90007. Tel: 213-745-7870; Fax: 213-745-7871. P.O. Box 99, Wrightwood, 92394. Founded by the Sisters of Social Service. Total Staff 3; Summer Staff 30.

REDLANDS. *El Carmelo Retreat House*, 926 E. Highland Ave., P.O. Box 446, 92373. Tel: 909-792-1047. Revs. Patrick Sugrue, O.C.D., Supr.; Dominic O'Callaghan, O.C.D.; Charles Garrity, O.C.D.; Albert Bunsic, O.C.D.; Bros. Boniface Scheerer, O.C.D.; Fernando Pinto. Priests 4; Brothers 2; Sisters 4; Total in Residence 10; Total Staff 10.

RIVERSIDE. *Divine Word Retreat Center*, 11316 Cypress Ave., 92505. Tel: 909-689-4858.

RUNNING SPRINGS. *St. Joachin & St. Anne Retreat Center*, P.O. Box 1760, 92382. Tel: 909-867-7362.

[H] NEWMAN CENTERS

SAN BERNARDINO. *Newman Catholic Fellowship*, 265 W. 25th St., 92405. Tel: 909-883-8991; Fax: 909-882-2061.

PALM DESERT. *Christ of the Desert Newman Center*, 73441 Fred Waring Dr., 92260. Tel: 760-346-0089; Fax: 760-340-2245. Rev. Jack P. McGinnis, Dir. Total in Residence 2; Total Staff 5.

REDLANDS. *University of Redlands Newman Community*, 1200 E. Colton Ave., P.O. Box 3080, 92373-0999; Fax: 909-475-5457. Sr. Alice Molina, R.S.H.M.

RIVERSIDE. *St. Andrews Newman Center*, 105 W. Big Springs Rd., 92507. Tel: 909-682-8751; Fax: 909-682-3513.
E-mail: catholictuer@earthlink.net
Rev. David Geib, O.P., Dir.
Serving Riverside Community College and University of California at Riverside.

[I] MISCELLANEOUS

SAN BERNARDINO.

Caritas Telecommunications, 1201 E. Highland Ave., 92404. Tel: 909-475-5350; Fax: 909-475-5357.
E-mail: caritas@sbdiocese.org
Web site: www.caritastelecommunications.org
Clare Colella, Dir.

Mary's Mercy Center, Inc., 641 Roberds Ave., P.O. Box 7563, 92411. Tel: 909-889-2558; Fax: 909-386-7704.
E-mail: mmcinc@earthlink.net
Adrienne Schubert, Contact Person.

INDIO.

Martha's Kitchen, Inc., 83-791 Date Ave., 92201. Tel: 760-347-4741; Fax: 760-347-9551.
E-mail: marthaskit@aol.com
Claudio E. Castorena, Contact Person.

RIVERSIDE.

Wordnet, Inc., Divine Word Seminary, 11316 Cypress Ave., Ste. 9, 92505. Tel: 909-689-4885. Rev. Michael Manning, S.V.D.

VICTORVILLE. *Casa Venegas*, 16694 Allen St., 92392-3511. Tel: 760-241-6607. Home for homeless. Bro. Gerard Cole, O.H., Contact Person.

St. John of God Health Care Services, 13333 Palmdale Rd., P.O. Box 2457, 92393. Tel: 760-241-4917; Fax: 760-241-8911.
E-mail: sjghcs@aol.com
Sponsored by the Brothers of St. John of God. Alcohol & Drug Rehabilitation Program.
Board of Trustees: Bro. Richard Gaule, O.H., Pres. & CEO; Gerald Farber, Chm.; Bros. Edward Francis McEnroe; Stephen De La Rosa, O.H.; Richard Janzer; Marion Harris, Sec.; Debbie Proper, Recording Sec.; Jim McManus, Treas.
Advisory Council: Gerald Farber, Chm.; Rick Ewaniszyk; Elizabeth Grinstead; Don Butterworth; Flo Drobnick.

RELIGIOUS INSTITUTUES OF MEN REPRESENTED IN THE DIOCESE

For further details refer to the corresponding bracketed number in the Religious Institutes of Men or Women section.

[0140]—*Augustinians*.—O.S.A.
[]—*Byzantine Brothers of St. Francis*.—B.B.S.F.
[0470]—*Capuchin Friars*.—O.F.M.Cap.
[0360]—*Claretian Missionaries*.—C.M.F.
[0610]—*Congregation of Holy Cross*.—C.S.C.
[]—*Congregation of Mother Coredemptrix*.—C.M.C.
[1080]—*Congregation of the Resurrection*.—C.R.
[1140]—*Congregation of the Sacred Hearts of Jesus and Mary*. (Western Prov.).—SS.CC.
[0390]—*Consolata Missionaries*.—I.M.C.
[]—*Diocesan Laborer Priests*.—D.L.P.
[0260]—*Discalced Carmelite Friars*. (Western Prov.).—O.C.D.
[0650]—*Holy Ghost Fathers*.—C.S.Sp.
[0670]—*Hospitaller Brothers of St. John of God*.—O.H.
[0720]—*Missionaries of Our Lady of La Salette*.—M.S.
[1110]—*Missionaries of the Sacred Heart*.—M.S.C.
[0840]—*Missionary Servants of the Most Holy Trinity*.
[]—*Operarios del Reino de Cristo*.—O.R.C.
[0200]—*Order of Benedict*.—O.S.B.
[0970]—*Order of Our Lady of Mercy*.—O.de.M.
[]—*Order of Preachers*.—O.P.
[0430]—*Order of Preachers (Dominicans)*. (Holy Name Prov.).—O.P.
[0480]—*Order of the Friars Minor, Conventual*.—O.F.M.Conv.
[]—*Order of the Imitation of Christ*.—O.I.C.
[1230]—*Servants of the Paraclete*.—s.P.
[0690]—*Society of Jesus*.—S.J.
[0760]—*Society of Mary*.—S.M.
[0370]—*Society of St. Columbian*.—S.S.C.
[0420]—*Society of the Divine Word*. (Western Prov.).—S.V.D.

RELIGIOUS INSTITUTES OF WOMEN REPRESENTED IN THE DIOCESE

[]—*Adrian Dominican Sisters*.—O.P.
[0230]—*Benedictine Sisters of Pontifical Jurisdiction*. (Grand Terrace, CA).—O.S.B.
[3260]—*Congregation of Sisters of the Precious Blood*.—C.PP.S.
[2549]—*Congregation of the Sisters of Mary*. (U.S. Prov.).—R.S.M.
[0790]—*Daughters of Divine Charity*.—F.D.C.
[0880]—*Daughters of Mary and Joseph*.—D.M.J.
[1070-13]—*Dominican Sisters*. (Adrian).—O.P.
[1070-15]—*Dominican Sisters*. (Baurelt).—O.P.
[1070-19]—*Dominican Sisters*. (Houston).—O.P.
[1070-20]—*Dominican Sisters*. (Tacoma).—O.P.
[1170]—*Felician Sisters of the Southwest*.—C.S.S.F.
[1230]—*Franciscan Sisters of Christian Charity*.—O.S.F.
[]—*Immaculate Heart Community*.—I.H.M.
[2370]—*Institute of the Blessed Virgin Mary (Loretto Sisters)*.—I.B.V.M.
[2760]—*Missionary Sisters of the Immaculate Conception of the Mother of God*.—S.M.I.C.
[]—*Oblates of Santa Marta*.—O.S.M.
[3130]—*Our Lady of Victory Missionary Sisters*.—O.L.V.M.
[3465]—*Religious of the Good Shepherd*.—R.G.S.
[1680]—*School Sisters of St. Francis*.—O.S.F.
[]—*Servants of Holiness*.—S.O.H.
[]—*Sisters for Christian Community*.—S.F.C.C.
[0430]—*Sisters of Charity of the Blessed Virgin Mary*.—B.V.M.
[]—*Sisters of Charity of the Incarnate Word*.—C.C.V.I.
[2360]—*Sisters of Loretto at the Foot of the Cross*.—S.L.
[2549]—*Sisters of Mercy*. (Sligo, Ireland).—R.S.M.
[2590]—*Sisters of Mercy of the Blessed Sacrament*.—H.M.S.S.
[3360]—*Sisters of Providence of St. Mary of-the-Woods*.—S.P.
[1540]—*Sisters of Saint Francis*. Clinton, Iowa.—O.S.F.
[4080]—*Sisters of Social Service*.—S.S.S.
[]—*Sisters of St. Benedict*.—O.S.B.
[3770]—*Sisters of St. Clare*.—O.S.C.
[1720]—*Sisters of St. Francis*.—O.S.F.
[1650]—*The Sisters of St. Francis of Philadelphia*.—O.S.F.
[1550]—*Sisters of St. Francis of the Holy Cross*.—O.S.F.
[3830-03]—*Sisters of St. Joseph*.—C.S.J.
[3840]—*Sisters of St. Joseph of Carondolet*.—C.S.J.
[0700]—*Sisters of the Company of Mary Our Lady*.—O.D.N.
[1990]—*Sisters of the Holy Names of Jesus and Mary*.—S.N.J.M.
[3320]—*Sisters of the Presentation of the B.V.M.*—P.B.V.M.
[3330]—*Sisters of the Presentation of the B.V.M.* (Phoenix, AZ).—P.B.V.M.
[4050]—*Sisters of the Society Devoted to the Sacred Heart*.—S.D.S.H.
[2150]—*Sisters, Servants of the Immaculate Heart of Mary*.—I.H.M.
[4070]—*Society of the Sacred Heart*.—R.S.C.J.

NECROLOGY

† Avila, Lourenco, Onatrio, CA St. Elizabeth Ann Seton. —Died Feb. 11, 2000.
† Diezel, Joseph, (Retired). —Died Aug. 9, 2000.
† Nagler, Robert, San Diego, CA St. Michael's. —Died May 18, 2000.
† Zaratti, Elio, San Diego, CA Nazareth House. —Died June 11, 2000.

Diocese of San Diego

(Dioecesis Sancti Didaci)

Most Reverend

ROBERT H. BROM, D.D.

Bishop of San Diego; ordained December 18, 1963; appointed Bishop of Duluth March 25, 1983; consecrated and installed May 23, 1983; appointed Coadjutor Bishop of San Diego April 22, 1989; appointed Bishop of San Diego July 10, 1990. *Office: P.O. Box 85728, San Diego, CA, 92186-5728.* Tel.: 858-490-8200.

Most Reverend

GILBERT E. CHAVEZ, D.D.

Auxiliary Bishop of San Diego and Titular Bishop of Magarmel; ordained March 19, 1960; appointed April 19, 1974; Episcopal ordination June 21, 1974. *Res., 1535 Third Ave., San Diego, CA, 92101.*

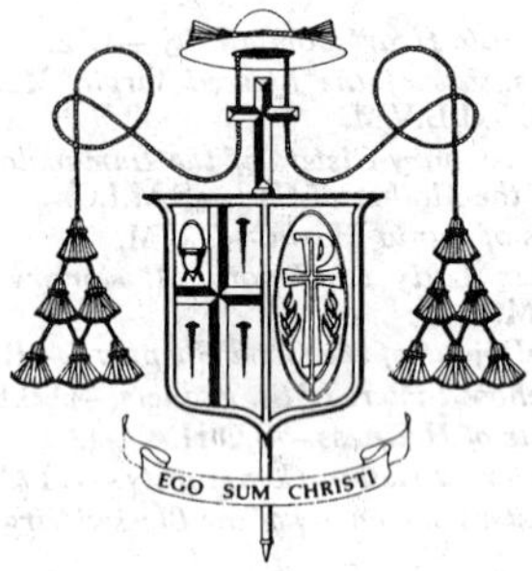

ESTABLISHED JULY 11, 1936.

Square Miles 8,852.

Legal Titles: *The Roman Catholic Bishop of San Diego, a Corporation Sole*—(Churches, Rectories, Halls, Catechetical Centers, etc.) Diocese of San Diego.

Comprises the Counties of Imperial and San Diego in the State of California.

For legal titles of parishes and diocesan institutions, consult the Diocesan Office.

Pastoral Center: P.O. Box 85728, San Diego, CA, 92186-5728. Tel.: 858-490-8200; Fax: 858-490-8272.

Web site address: www.diocese-sdiego.org

E-mail address: scallaha@diocese-sdiego.org

STATISTICAL OVERVIEW

Personnel	
Bishop	1
Auxiliary Bishops	1
Abbots	1
Retired Abbots	1
Priests: Diocesan Active in Diocese	118
Priests: Active Outside Diocese	9
Priests: Diocesan in Foreign Missions	1
Priests: Retired, Sick or Absent	74
Number of Diocesan Priests	202
Religious Priests in Diocese	102
Extern Priests in Diocese	94
Ordinations:	
Permanent Deacons	5
Permanent Deacons in Diocese	105
Total Brothers	20
Total Sisters	355
Parishes	
Parishes	98
With Resident Pastor:	
Resident Diocesan Priests	85
Resident Religious Priests	11
Without Resident Pastor:	
Administered by Priests	2
Missions	17
Pastoral Centers	2
Closed Parishes	1
Professional Ministry Personnel:	
Brothers	3
Sisters	49
Lay Ministers	165
Welfare	
Catholic Hospitals	1
Total Assisted	20,000
Health Care Centers	1
Total Assisted	17,000
Homes for the Aged	5
Total Assisted	624
Residential Care of Children	3
Total Assisted	428
Day Care and Extended Day Care Centers	1
Total Assisted	594
Specialized Homes	11
Total Assisted	78,533
Special Centers for Social Services	10
Total Assisted	88,845
Residential Care of Disabled	1
Total Assisted	61
Other Institutions	3
Total Assisted	471
Educational	
Seminaries, Diocesan	1
Students from This Diocese	6
Students from Other Diocese	12
Diocesan Students in Other Seminaries	7
Total Seminarians	13
Colleges and Universities	1
Total Students	6,806
High Schools, Diocesan and Parish	3
Total Students	2,118
High Schools, Private	2
Total Students	1,374
Elementary Schools, Diocesan and Parish	43
Total Students	13,872
Elementary Schools, Private	1
Total Students	359
Non-residential Schools for the Disabled	1
Total Students	220
Catechesis/Religious Education:	
High School Students	9,039
Elementary Students	31,473
Total Students Under Catholic Instruction	65,274
Teachers in the Diocese:	
Priests	23
Brothers	1
Sisters	52
Lay Teachers	1,450
Vital Statistics	
Receptions into the Church:	
Infant Baptism Totals	11,488
Adult Baptism Totals	1,145
Received into Full Communion	982
First Communions	9,495
Confirmations	4,456
Marriages:	
Catholic	1,842
Interfaith	580
Total Marriages	2,422
Deaths	2,994
Total Catholic Population	896,105
Total Population	3,056,800

Former Bishops—Most Rev. CHARLES F. BUDDY, D.D., S.T.D., Ph.D., ord. Sept. 19, 1914; appt. Oct. 31, 1936; cons. Dec. 21, 1936; named Asst. at Pontifical Throne, Jan. 12, 1964; died March 6, 1966.—Most Rev. FRANCIS J. FUREY, D.D., Ph.D., LL.D., ord. March 15, 1930; appt. Auxiliary Bishop of Philadelphia, Aug. 24, 1960; cons. Dec. 22, 1960; succeeded to the See of San Diego, March 6, 1966; translated to Archbishop of San Antonio, June 4, 1969; died April 23, 1979.—Most Rev. LEO T. MAHER, D.D., Bishop of San Diego; ord. Dec. 18, 1943; First Bishop of Santa Rosa; appt. Feb. 21, 1962; cons. April 5, 1962; translated to San Diego, Aug. 27, 1969; retired July 10, 1990; died Feb. 23, 1991.

Pastoral Center—3888 Paducah Dr., San Diego, 92117., Mailing Address: P.O. Box 85728, San Diego, 92186-5728. Tel: 858-490-8200; Fax: 858-490-8272. Office Hours: Mon.-Fri. 8:30-4:30.

Auxiliary Bishop and Vicar General—Most Rev. GILBERT E. CHAVEZ, D.D., *1535 Third Ave., San Diego, 92101-3192.* Tel: 619-239-0229.

Chancellor—Rev. Msgr. STEVEN CALLAHAN, J.C.L. Tel: 858-490-8310.

Vice Chancellor—RODRIGO VALDIVIA, J.C.L. Tel: 858-490-8310.

Assistants to Bishop Robert H. Brom—Rev. EDWARD P. MCNULTY. Tel: 858-490-8306. NARCISCO GUZMAN. Tel: 858-490-8315.

Diocesan Tribunal

Judicial Vicar—Very Rev. Msgr. MARK A. CAMPBELL, B.A., M.Ed., J.C.L.

Promoter of Justice—Rev. Msgr. DANIEL J. DILLABOUGH, S.T.D., J.C.L.

Defenders of the Bond—Rev. Msgr. DANIEL J. DILLABOUGH; Rev. Msgr. STEVEN CALLAHAN, J.C.L.; Revs. JOHN PROCTOR, JR.; DIONISIO MACALINTAL.

Diocesan Judges—Very Rev. Msgr. MARK A. CAMPBELL, B.A., M.Ed., J.C.L.; Revs. DAVID CROISETIERE, J.C.L., M.C.L.; BRIAN HAYES, J.C.L.; MARY JO GRETSINGER, S.T.L., J.C.L.; EDWARD PETERS, J.D., J.C.D.

Auditor—Rev. LOUIS I. NEWMAN, B.A.

Notaries—CONNIE NOEL; INES ANDREWS.

Consultants—Rev. JOHN HOWARD, C.J.M., Ph.D.; PETER McDADE, Ph.D.

Diocesan Offices and Directors

Archivist—Contact, *Chancellor's Office*. Tel: 858-490-8208.

Canonical Affairs—EDWARD PETERS, J.D., J.C.D., Dir. Tel: 858-490-8314.

Catholic Charities—Sr. RAYMONDA DUVALL, C.H.S., Exec. Dir., *349 Cedar St., San Diego, 92101*. Tel: 619-231-2828.

Cemetery Committee—Rev. Msgr. W. FRANCIS PATTISON, Dir., *Holy Cross Cemetery, 4470 Hilltop Dr., San Diego, 92102*. Tel: 619-264-3127.

Censores Librorum—Rev. Msgr. RICHARD F. DUNCANSON, S.T.D.; Revs. DENNIS W. KROUSE, S.T.D.; NORBERT J. RIGALI, S.J., Ph.D.; BERNADEANE CARR, S.T.L.; TERENCE MCGOLDRICK, S.T.D.

Civil Affairs—ALEXANDRA KELLY, Esq., Dir. Tel: 858-490-8277. EDWARD PETERS, Esq. of Counsel.

Clergy Counseling and Spiritual Direction—Rev. JOHN FLANNERY, O.P., Dir. Tel: 619-291-7584.

Communications—BERNADEANE CARR, Dir. Tel: 858-490-8370.

Computer Services—JOHN ELLIS, Information Systems Admin. Tel: 858-490-8329.

Construction Services—JOEL KING, Dir. Tel: 858-490-8215.

Ecumenical and Interreligious Affairs—Rev. Msgr. DENNIS MIKULANIS, S.T.D., Vicar, *990 Saturn Blvd., San Diego, 92154*. Tel: 619-423-0242.

Education—

San Diego Diocesan Institute for Adult Education and Formation for Ministry—TERENCE MCGOLDRICK, S.T.D., Dir. Tel: 858-490-8212.

Evangelization & Catechetical Ministry—GINGER INFANTINO, Dir. Tel: 858-490-8232. MARYJO WAGGONER, Asst. Dir. for Hispanic Catechesis. Tel: 858-490-8233.

Schools—THOMAS BEECHER, Dir. Tel: 858-490-8240. Sr. BREEGE BOYLE, S.S.L., Assoc. Dir. Tel: 858-490-8240. PATRICIA BANNON, Assoc. Dir. Tel: 858-490-8244.

Youth and Young Adult Ministry—ANGELA HAMMER, Dir. ERIKA TORAYA, Assoc. Dir. SANTIAGO ROBLES, Asst. Dir. Tel: 619-490-8260.

Hispanic Evangelization—Sr. GLORIA GALVAN, S.F.C.C., Assoc. Dir. for Hispanic Evangelization. Tel: 858-490-8214.

Facilities and Related Services—RODRIGO VALDIVIA, J.C.L., Dir. Tel: 858-490-8301.

Finance—H.L. "HAL" GARDNER, Finance Officer. Tel: 858-490-8284. KAREN TISI, Dir., Accounting. Tel: 858-490-8207.

Hispanic Affairs—ENRIQUE MENDEZ, Dir.; Sr. MARIA ESPINOZA, M.F.P., Asst. Dir. Tel: 858-490-8248.

Human Resources—MICHAEL CROLL, Dir. Tel: 858-490-8282.

Liturgy and Spirituality—MARY ANN FALLON, Dir. Tel: 858-490-8290. JENSINE NOLAN, Asst. Dir. Liturgical Music. Tel: 858-490-8294. Rev. PHILLIP SESSIONS, Pastoral Coord. Diocesan Liturgies. Tel: 858-490-8271.

Marriage and Family Life—JEANNENE FALLER, Dir. Tel: 858-490-8295.

Missions—Rev. Msgr. RAYMOND C. KIRK, Dir.; Sr. KATHY SCHMITTGENS, S.S.N.D., Assoc. Dir. Tel: 858-490-8250.

Multicultural Affairs—RODRIGO VALDIVIA, J.C.L., Dir. Tel: 858-490-8301.

Permanent Diaconate—Sr. CARLOTTA DI LORENZO, C.S.J.; Deacon JOSE ERNESTO GONZALEZ, Assoc. Tel: 858-490-8239.

Priests—Rev. MICHAEL MURPHY, Dir., *1667 Santa Paula Dr., San Diego, 92111*. Tel: 619-291-9539.

Seminary—St. Francis—Rev. Msgr. STEVEN CALLAHAN, J.C.L., Rector, *1667 Santa Paula Dr., San Diego, 92111*. Tel: 619-291-7446. Rev. JOHN FLANNERY, O.P., Dir. Spiritual Formation. Tel: 619-291-7584. Rev. PATRICK MURPHY, Dir., Admissions & Student Life. Tel: 619-291-5042.

Social Ministry—KENT PETERS, Dir.; Deacon LOUIS ROCHA, Assoc. Dir. LINDA ARREOLA, Asst. Dir. Tel: 858-490-8323.

"Southern Cross"—(Diocesan Newspaper)—CYRIL JONES-KELLETT, Editor. Tel: 858-490-8268.

Special Events—JO-ELLEN LARUE, Dir. Tel: 858-490-8334.

Stewardship and Development—ERIN JONES, Dir. Tel: 858-490-8280.

Vocations—Deacon RAY ARNOLD, Dir. Tel: 858-490-8351.

Women Religious—Sr. NANCY KANE, R.S.C.J. Tel: 858-490-8289.

Advisory Bodies

Clergy Personnel Board—Rev. Msgr. STEVEN CALLAHAN, J.C.L., Chm. Tel: 858-490-8310.

College of Consultors—Most Rev. GILBERT E. CHAVEZ; Rev. Msgr. DANIEL J. DILLABOUGH; Rev. Msgr. JOHN A. DICKIE; Rev. Msgr. W. FRANCIS PATTISON; Rev. Msgr. LAWRENCE PURCELL; Rev. Msgr. STEVEN CALLAHAN, J.C.L.

Diocesan Pastoral Council—NARCISO GUZMAN, Exec. Coord. Tel: 858-490-8315.

Finance Council—Most Rev. ROBERT H. BROM, Chm.; Mr. THOMAS BLAKE; Very Rev. Msgr. STEVEN CALLAHAN, J.C.L.; Dr. CONSTANCE CARROLL; Mrs. SUSAN CARTER; Mr. DEAN DWYER; Mr. MICHAEL EYER; Mr. DAVID GARDNER; Rev. PETER MCGUINE; Mr. MICHAEL MAHER; Mr. TIMOTHY MEISSNER; Mr. FRANK MERCARDANTE; Mr. RICHARD MIRANDO; Mr. RALPH RUBIO; Rev. Msgr. DONAL SHEAHAN; Mr. RICHARD VANDERHOFF.

Presbyteral Council—Most Rev. ROBERT H. BROM; Most Rev. GILBERT E. CHAVEZ; Rev. Msgr. W. FRANCIS PATTISON; Rev. EDWARD P. MCNULTY, Exec. Sec.; Rev. Msgr. JOHN DICKIE; Rev. Msgr. DANIEL DILLABOUGH; Rev. Msgr. ROGER LECHNER; Rev. Msgr. LAWRENCE PURCELL; Rev. Msgr. STEVEN CALLAHAN, J.C.L.; Revs. MICHAEL BAUMGARDNER; BEN DAVISON; JOHN DOLAN; BRIAN HAYES; MICHAEL KLARER; MICHAEL MURPHY; BRUCE ORSBORN, Chm. JAMES POULSEN; JOHN PROCTOR, JR.; CHARLES SHESLO; MATTHEW SPAHR; CAVANA WALLACE.

Vicars Forane—Very Rev. KENNETH DEL PRIORE, Cathedral; Very Rev. RAYMOND O'DONNELL, El Cajon; Very Rev. JAMES RAFFERTY, Escondido; Very Rev. NICHOLAS DEMPSEY, La Jolla; Very Rev. RAMON MARRUFO, Oceanside; Very Rev. Msgr. MARK CAMPBELL, University; Very Rev. EDMUNDO ZARATE-SUAREZ, El Centro; Very Rev. Msgr. RICHARD DUNCANSON, South Bay.

Miscellaneous

Apostleship of the Sea—Rev. DANIEL WALSH, C.S.Sp., Port Chap., *1140 Evergreen St., San Diego, 92106*. Tel: 619-223-2200.

Charismatic Renewal—SHAWN QUINN, Admin., *2725 55th St., San Diego, 92105-5094*. Tel: 619-263-1700.

Hispanic Charismatic Renewal Center—JOSE MACIAS, Coord. Tel: 619-640-2723.

Christ Child Society—Rev. ANTON KOLLAR, Spiritual Advisor. Tel: 619-523-1375.

Cursillo—Rev. LOUIS LEVESQUE, Spiritual Advisor. Lay Directors: FREDRICK FREY; GLORIA FREY. Tel: 760-729-2991.

Filipino—MARIE DELA CRUZ, Lay Dir.; Deacon SAM MARTINEZ, Spiritual Dir. Tel: 858-484-6131.

Hispanic—MARGARITA SANDOVAL, Pres. Secretariat. Tel: 619-232-6681.

Vietnamese—Rev. BIEN QUANG DO, Spiritual Adv. NGHI VU, Lay Dir. Tel: 858-272-9356.

Holy Childhood Association—Rev. Msgr. RAYMOND KIRK, Dir., *P.O. Box 82386, San Diego, 92138-2386*. Tel: 858-490-8250.

Propagation of the Faith—Rev. Msgr. RAYMOND KIRK, Dir.; Sr. KATHY SCHMITTGENS, S.S.N.D., Assoc. Dir., *P.O. Box 82386, San Diego, 92186-2386*. Tel: 858-490-8250.

CLERGY, PARISHES, MISSIONS AND PAROCHIAL SCHOOLS

CITY OF SAN DIEGO
(San Diego County)

1—ST. JOSEPH CATHEDRAL (1874), Most Rev. Gilbert E. Chavez, D.D. In res., Rev. Paul Balio (Philippines).
Res., 1535 Third Ave., 92101-3192. Tel: 619-239-0229; Fax: 619-239-3788.
Catechesis/Religious Programs—Students 105.

2—ASCENSION (1980), Rev. Scott J. McColl; Deacon Jim Scull.
Res., 11292 Clairemont Mesa Blvd., 92124-1524. Tel: 858-279-2735; Fax: 858-279-1023.
Catechesis/Religious Programs—Tel: 858-279-2752. Susan Paul, D.R.E.
Students 240.

3—BLESSED SACRAMENT (1938), Revs. William F. Rowland, C.J.M.; Louis Levesque, C.J.M.; James Burson, C.J.M.; Deacons Louis Principe; Alfred Albers; James Ribbeck. In res., Rev. Jerry Hamperzonian.
Res., 4540 El Cerrito Dr., 92115. Tel: 619-582-5722; Fax: 619-582-2505.
School—Tel: 619-582-3862; Fax: 619-265-9310. Ms. Theodora Furtado, Prin.
Lay Teachers 26; Students 413.
Catechesis/Religious Programs—Tel: 619-582-4633.
Students 122.
Mission—San Diego, San Diego Co., SDSU Newman Center, 5855 Hardy Ave., 92115. Tel: 619-583-9181; Fax: 619-583-8925.

4—CHRIST THE KING (1938), Revs. Eduardo A. Samaniego, S.J.; Gregory Baumann, S.J. In res., Revs. Gilbert J. Gentile, S.J.; Michael Agliardo, S.J.
Res., 29 N. 32nd St., 92102. Tel: 619-231-8906; Fax: 619-238-7060.
Catechesis/Religious Programs—Students 180.

5—GOOD SHEPHERD (1970), Revs. Fernando Ramirez; Michael Baumgardner; Richard Huston; Deacons Manny Carpizo; Alberto Paras.
Res., 8200 Gold Coast Dr., 92126-3699. Tel: 858-271-0207; Fax: 858-271-0748.
School—8180 Gold Coast Dr., 92126. Tel: 858-693-1522; Fax: 858-271-3439. Mrs. Chris Corpora, Prin.
Lay Teachers 14; Students 314.
Catechesis/Religious Programs—Tel: 858-271-8769; Fax: 858-271-0207. Sr. Teresa Boland, O.S.F., D.R.E.
Lay Teachers 108; Students 1,186.

6—HOLY FAMILY (Linda Vista) (1942), Revs. Mike Ortiz; Joseph Khuyen Van Lai; Deacons Thomas Dougherty; Paul Davidson; John A. Ellis.
Res., 1957 Coolidge St., 92111-7098. Tel: 858-277-0404; Fax: 858-277-6414.
School—Tel: 858-277-0222; Fax: 858-277-0224.
Lay Teachers 12; Students 254.
Catechesis/Religious Programs—Tel: 619-268-0557.
Students 155.

7—HOLY SPIRIT (1952), Rev. Msgr. Roger A. Lechner; Rev. Doan Van Lai; Deacons Marvin Threatt; Manny Robles. In res., Rev. Robert Golish, M.M.
Res., 2725-55th St., 92105-5094. Tel: 619-262-2435; Fax: 619-262-8718.
Catechesis/Religious Programs—Tel: 619-263-9307.
Students 490.

8—IMMACULATA (1958), Most Rev. Robert H. Brom; Rev. Edward P. McNulty.
Res., University of San Diego Campus, 5998 Alcala Park, 92110-2492. Tel: 619-574-5700; Fax: 619-574-5707.
Catechesis/Religious Programs—Tel: 619-574-5702; 5703.
Students 102.

9—IMMACULATE CONCEPTION (1849), Rev. Msgr. Alphonsus Moloney.
Res., 2540 San Diego Ave., 92110-2840. Tel: 619-295-4148; Fax: 619-297-6916.

10—MISSION BASILICA SAN DIEGO DE ALCALA (1769). (California's First Mission). Rev. Msgr. Thomas Prendergast; Rev. William A. Springer; Deacons Bill Vasquez; Ernest Grosso. In res., Rev. Msgr. Mark A. Campbell.
Res., 10818 San Diego Mission Rd., 92108-2498. Tel: 619-283-7319; Fax: 619-283-7762.
Catechesis/Religious Programs—Tel: 619-624-0900.
Students 232.

11—OUR LADY OF ANGELS (1906) (Hispanic), Rev. Kenneth Del Priore.
Res., 656 24th St., 92102-2911. Tel: 619-239-1231; Fax: 619-234-5520.
School—Our Lady's School-North Campus, Tel: 619-233-8888; Fax: 619-234-5520.
Sisters 3; Lay Teachers 11; Students 314.
Catechesis/Religious Programs—Sr. Dina Marie Garcia, D.R.E.
Students 626.

12—OUR LADY OF GUADALUPE (1919) (Mexican), Revs. Richard H. Brown, S.J.; James I. Rasura, S.J.; Augusto Berrio, S.J.; John P. Auther, S.J.; Gilbert Chacon, S.J.
Res., 1770 Kearny Ave., 92113-1128. Tel: 619-233-3838; Fax: 619-233-3252.
School—Our Lady's School-South Campus, 744 Beardsley, 92113. Tel: 619-233-8888; Fax: 619-233-0982.
Religious 2; Lay Teachers 2; Students 133.
Catechesis/Religious Programs—Tel: 619-233-3838; Fax: 619-233-3252.
Students 300.

13—OUR LADY OF MT. CARMEL (Rancho Penasquitos) (1976), Rev. Msgr. Henry F. Fawcett; Rev. Joselito Tiongson; Deacons Bernard Yeatts; John Phelps; H. Thomas Jones; Manuel Porciuncula.
Res., 13541 Stoney Creek Rd., 92129. Tel: 858-566-3550; 484-1070; Fax: 858-484-6157.
Catechesis/Religious Programs—Students 750.

14—OUR LADY OF REFUGE (Pacific Beach) (1977), Rev. David N. Croisetiere.
Res., 4226 Jewell St., 92109. Tel: 858-274-9670; Fax: 858-274-7486.
Catechesis/Religious Programs—Tel: 858-274-2959. Jose Ferrer, D.R.E.
Students 150.

15—OUR LADY OF THE ROSARY (1925) (Italian), Revs. Steven M. Grancini, C.R.S.P.; Louis M. Solcia, C.R.S.P.
Res., 1659 Columbia St., 92101-2584. Tel: 619-234-4820; Fax: 619-234-3559.
Catechesis/Religious Programs—Tel: 619-234-4820. Esther Leuzzi, D.R.E.
Students 222.

16—OUR LADY OF THE SACRED HEART (1911), Revs. Richard L. Perozich; Joseph Phen Van Pham; Deacon Gustavo Magana.
Res., 4177 Marlborough Ave., 92105-1412. Tel: 619-280-0515; Fax: 619-280-0517.
School—Tel: 619-284-1715; Fax: 619-284-8332. Sr. Linda Lutz, Prin.
Lay Teachers 12; Students 240.
Catechesis/Religious Programs—Tel: 619-283-9262; Fax: 619-283-0159. Mrs. Toni Guerrero, D.R.E.
Students 660.

17—OUR MOTHER OF CONFIDENCE (University City) (1964), Rev. Msgr. Donal C. Sheahan; Rev. Brian Hayes; Deacons William Klopchin; Arnold Hess.
Res., 3131 Governor Dr., 92122. Tel: 858-453-0222; Fax: 858-453-2547.
Catechesis/Religious Programs—Tel: 858-453-3554. D.R.E.: Cathy Whelan; Sr. Frances Franey, S.N.J.M.
Students 354.

18—SACRED HEART (Ocean Beach) (1911), Rev. Ronald Hebert; Deacon Giles Schmitt.
Res., 4776 Saratoga, 92107-9990. Tel: 619-224-2746; Fax: 619-224-0459.
School—Tel: 619-222-7252; Fax: 619-222-2836. Mr. Robert Hamm, Prin.
Lay Teachers 12; Students 300.
Catechesis/Religious Programs—Tel: 619-223-4594. Cathleen Hornsby, D.R.E.
Students 62.

19—ST. AGNES (Pt. Loma) (1932), Revs. Joseph Mel Collier; Daniel Walsh, C.S.Sp.
Res., 1140 Evergreen St., 92106. Tel: 619-223-2200; Fax: 619-223-7568.
Catechesis/Religious Programs—Tel: 619-223-9748. Mrs. Elise Spondike, D.R.E.
Students 160.

20—ST. ANNE (1921), Rev. Robert D. Nikliborc.
Res., 621 Sicard St., 92113-2334. Tel: 619-239-8253.
Catechesis/Religious Programs—Tel: 619-263-5913.
Students 200.

21—ST. BRIGID (Pacific Beach) (1940), Rev. Peter Escalante; Rev. Msgr. Sean Murray, Pastor Emeritus. In res., Rev. Msgr. Raymond Kirk.
Res., 4735 Cass St., 92109-2698. Tel: 858-483-3030; Fax: 858-483-7131.
Catechesis/Religious Programs—Tel: 858-483-3032. D.R.E.: Sr. Hilda McDonagh, R.S.M.; Sr. Josephine Breen.
Students 200.

22—ST. CATHERINE LABOURE (1964), Rev. Joseph Brady.
Mailing Address: 4124 Mt. Abraham Ave., 92111.
Res., 4026 Mt. Abraham Ave., 92111. Tel: 858-277-3133; Fax: 858-277-9181.
Catechesis/Religious Programs—Tel: 619-279-0587. Sandra Welch, D.R.E.
Students 300.

23—ST. CHARLES (1946), Rev. Msgr. Dennis Mikulanis; Rev. Dennis J. O'Connor; Deacon Seodello Martinez. In res., Rev. Aurelio P. Crisologo, (Retired).
Res., 990 Saturn Blvd., 92154. Tel: 619-423-0242; Fax: 619-423-1966.
School—Tel: 619-423-3701; Fax: 619-423-5331.
Sisters of Mercy 1; Lay Teachers 14; Students 298.
Catechesis/Religious Programs—Tel: 619-575-2240.
Students 508.

24—ST. CHARLES BORROMEO (1946), Rev. Cavana Wallace.
Res., 2802 Cadiz St., 92110-4813. Tel: 619-225-8157; Fax: 619-225-2288.
School—Tel: 619-223-8271.
Sisters 2; Lay Teachers 13; Students 266.

25—ST. COLUMBA (1955), Rev. Msgr. Patrick J. Mullarkey; Deacons Louis X. Ball; Nick Santiago. In res., Rev. Louis Newman.
Res., 3327 Glencolum Dr., 92123. Tel: 858-277-3863; Fax: 858-279-9053.
School—(Grades PreK-8). Tel: 858-279-1882; Fax: 858-279-1653.
Lay Teachers 16; Students 340.
Catechesis/Religious Programs—Tel: 858-277-3861.
Students 150.

26—ST. DIDACUS (1926), Rev. Michael Robinson; Deacon Peter Nguyen. In res., Rev. William Ortmann.
Res., 4772 Felton St., 92116. Tel: 619-284-3472; Fax: 619-284-3484.
School—4630 34th St., 92116. Tel: 619-284-8730; Fax: 619-284-1764.
Lay Teachers 16; Students 315.
Catechesis/Religious Programs—Tel: 619-284-7050. Michael Molino, D.R.E.
Students 68.

27—ST. GREGORY THE GREAT (1985), Rev. James N. Poulsen; Deacons L. Ferris Bell; Ronald H. Diem.
Mailing Address: 11451 Blue Cypress Dr., 92131. Tel: 858-653-3540; Fax: 858-653-3550.
Catechesis/Religious Programs—Tel: 858-653-3594.
Students 811.

28—ST. JEROME (1985), Rev. Bruce J. Osborn; Deacon Raul Hernandez.
Office: 2515 Beyer Blvd., 92154-1502. Tel: 619-423-0405; Fax: 619-423-9363.
Res., 4485 Murrieta Cir., 92154-1713. Tel: 619-428-7978.
Catechesis/Religious Programs—Tel: 619-423-5302. Sr. Roberta Collins, C.S.J.P., D.R.E.
Students 299.

29—ST. JOHN THE EVANGELIST (1913), Rev. Phillip D. Sessions, Admin. In res., Rev. Manuel Ediza (Philippines); Deacon Carl Shelton.
Res., 1638 Polk Ave., 92103. Tel: 619-291-1660; Fax: 619-291-4597.
Catechesis/Religious Programs—Tel: 619-460-0340.
Students 70.

30—ST. JUDE (1946) (Hispanic), Revs. Henry Rodriguez; Joseph Lal.
Res., 1129 S. 38th St., 92113-3210. Tel: 619-264-2195; Fax: 619-264-8528. [CEM]
School—1228 S. 38th St., 92113. Tel: 619-264-3154; Fax: 619-264-8050.
Lay Teachers 12; Students 310.
St. Jude's Child Care and Development Center—1129 S. 38th St., 92113. Tel: 619-264-8256; Fax: 619-264-8256.
St. Jude's Senior Nutrition Program—Tel: 619-264-4771; Fax: 619-264-9175.
Catechesis/Religious Programs—Fax: 619-264-2195. D.R.E.: Javier Maldonado, (Spanish); Eddie Johnson, (English).
Students 962.

31—ST. MARY MAGDALENE (Clairemont) (1953), Rev. Msgr. John A. Dickie; Rev. Anthony C. May; Deacon Robert H. Fitzmorris.
Res., 1945 Illion St., 92110. Tel: 619-276-1041; Fax: 619-276-0144.
School—Tel: 619-276-6545; Fax: 619-276-5359.
Lay Teachers 32; Students 600.
Catechesis/Religious Programs—Tel: 619-276-1248. Mrs. Margaret Mansur, D.R.E.
Students 137.

32—ST. MAXIMILIAN KOLBE MISSION (1971) (Polish). Unassigned. (Quasi Parish).
Res., 1735 Grand Ave., 92109. Tel: 858-272-7655; Fax: 858-668-0485.
Catechesis/Religious Programs—Students 56.

33—ST. MICHAEL (1957) (Filipino), Rev. Msgr. Fernando Gutierrez (Philippines); Rev. Michael Albano (Philippines).
Res., 2643 Homedale St., 92139. Tel: 619-470-1977; Fax: 619-470-6357.
Preschool—6285 Seascape Dr., Tel: 619-472-5437.
School—2637 Homedale St., 92139. Tel: 619-470-4880; Fax: 619-470-4881.
Sisters 1; Lay Teachers 17; Students 384.
Catechesis/Religious Programs—Tel: 619-470-2291. Mr. Louis Costa, D.R.E.
Students 1,105.

34—ST. PATRICK (1921), Rev. Anthony J. Wasko, O.S.A. In res., Rev. James P. Retzner, O.S.A.
Res., 3585 30th St., 92104. Tel: 619-295-2157; Fax: 619-688-1225.
School—Tel: 619-297-1314; Fax: 619-297-3346.
Lay Teachers 10; Students 233.
Catechesis/Religious Programs—Tel: 619-284-5063. Lisa Laughter, D.R.E.
Students 60.
Chapel—St. Augustine, 3266 Nutmeg St., 92104. Tel: 619-282-2028; Fax: 619-282-1203.

35—ST. RITA (1941), Rev. Msgr. Francis Pattison; Rev. Juvencio D. Ricafort. In res., Rev. Msgr. Joseph A. Carroll.
Res., 5124 Churchward St., 92114-3797. Tel: 619-264-3165; Fax: 619-264-2907.
School—Tel: 619-264-0109.
Lay Teachers 16; Students 260.
Catechesis/Religious Programs—Tel: 619-264-4399. Margaret Castro, D.R.E.
Students 477.

36—ST. THERESE (1956), Rev. Msgr. Frederick J. Florek; Rev. John Cuddigan, S.J.; Deacons Leo Dube; Robert Ekhaml.
Res., 6016 Camino Rico, 92120-3099. Tel: 619-582-3716; Fax: 619-582-2535.
School—St. Therese Academy, Tel: 619-583-6270; Fax: 619-583-5721.
Sisters 4; Lay Teachers 14; Students 335.
Catechesis/Religious Programs—Tel: 619-582-2585. Sr. Damien Peters, F.D.C., D.R.E.
Students 325.

37—ST. VINCENT DE PAUL (1910), Revs. Nicholas P. Clavin; James Rankin, (Retired).
Res., 4077 Ibis St., 92103-1899. Tel: 619-299-3881; Fax: 619-299-9509.
School—Tel: 619-296-2222; Fax: 619-296-2763.
Sisters of Mercy 2; Lay Teachers 8; Students 256.
Catechesis/Religious Programs—Tel: 619-295-9672.
Students 105.

38—SAN RAFAEL (Rancho Bernardo) (1974), Rev. Msgr. Lloyd V. Bourgeois.
Res., 17252 Bernardo Center, 92128. Tel: 858-487-4314; Fax: 858-487-1498.
Catechesis/Religious Programs—Tel: 858-674-1145. D.R.E.: Mary Jane Heggeness; Sr. Joan Derry, S.H.F.
Students 950.

OUTSIDE THE CITY OF SAN DIEGO

Alpine, San Diego Co., Queen of Angels (1950), Rev. Matthew D. Spahr.
Res., 2569 Victoria Dr., 91901-3662. Tel: 619-445-2145; Fax: 619-445-9682.
Catechesis/Religious Programs—Students 310.

Bonita, San Diego Co., Corpus Christi (1984), Rev. John G. Proctor, Jr.; Deacon James H. Hitch.
Mailing Address: P.O. Box 1349, 91908.
Res., 2934 Degen Dr., 91902. Tel: 619-482-3954; Fax: 619-482-7236.
Church—450 Corral Canyon Rd., 91902.
Catechesis/Religious Programs—Tel: 619-482-3957; Fax: 619-482-7236. Deacon James H. Hitch, D.R.E.
Students 460.

Borrego Springs, San Diego Co., St. Richard (1954), Rev. Simon Lefebvre, C.S.V.
Res., P.O. Box 1128, 92004-1128. Tel: 760-767-5701. [CEM]
Catechesis/Religious Programs—Students 118.
Mission—Salton City, Imperial Co., 92275.

Brawley, Imperial Co., Our Lady of Perpetual Help (1956) (Hispanic), Rev. Jorge Moreno.
Res., 1250 B St., P.O. Box 1283, 92227. Tel: 760-344-2226; Fax: 760-344-1557.
Catechesis/Religious Programs—Tel: 760-344-5787. Jenny Benavides, D.R.E.
Students 250.

Sacred Heart (1908), Rev. Ben Davison; Deacon Donald L. Spinney.
Res., 402 S. Imperial St., 92227. Tel: 760-344-3171; Fax: 760-344-3174.
School—(Grades K-8). Tel: 760-344-2662; Fax: 760-344-1910.
Lay Teachers 9; Students 138.
Catechesis/Religious Programs—Sr. Dawnna Spinney, D.C.M., D.R.E.
Students 145.

St. Margaret Mary (1934) (Hispanic), Rev. Roque P. Vano.
Res., 620 Cesar Chavez St., 92227. Tel: 760-344-3571; Fax: 760-344-3598.
Catechesis/Religious Programs—Tel: 760-344-6515; Fax: 760-344-7598.
Students 540.

Calexico, Imperial Co., Our Lady of Guadalupe (1907), Revs. Jose Edmundo Zarate-Suarez; Gerardo Fernandez.
Res., 124 E. Fifth St., 92231. Tel: 760-357-1822; Fax: 760-357-0115.
School—Our Lady of Guadalupe Academy, Tel: 760-357-1986; Fax: 760-357-3282.
Sisters, Servants of the Blessed Sacrament 5; Lay Teachers 21; Students 618.
Catechesis/Religious Programs—Tel: 760-357-2532. Sr. Maria Teresa Bandera, C.V.I., D.R.E.
Students 596.

Calipatria, Imperial Co., St. Patrick (1919), Revs. Amador Lopez, O.M.I.; James Kernan, O.M.I.
Res., 133 E. Church St., P.O. Box 238, 92233. Tel: 760-348-2733; Fax: 760-348-7070.
Catechesis/Religious Programs—Tel: 760-348-2454.
Students 200.

Carlsbad, San Diego Co., St. Elizabeth Seton (1997), Rev. Donald E. Coleman; Deacon Henry Chia.
Res., 6628 Santa Isabel St., 92009-5148. Tel: 760-438-3393; Fax: 760-438-7739.
Catechesis/Religious Programs—Tel: 760-438-3438. Larry Broding, D.R.E.
Students 525.

St. Patrick (1943) (Spanish), Revs. Stephen P. McCall; Joseph E. Mullen, S.J.; Higinio Garcia; Deacons Michael Frazee; Richard Mather.
Res., 3821 Adams St., 92008-0249. Tel: 760-729-2866; Fax: 760-434-3325.

School—3820 Pio Pico, 92008. Tel: 760-729-1333; Fax: 760-729-4643. Mrs. Kathleen Taylor, Prin.
Lay Teachers 19; Students 398.
Catechesis/Religious Programs—Tel: 760-729-8442.
Students 955.

Chula Vista, San Diego Co.,

1—MOST PRECIOUS BLOOD, (1957), Rev. Frank Wagner, O.M.I.
Res., 1245 4th Ave., 91911-3012. Tel: 619-422-2100; Fax: 619-422-1375.
Catechesis/Religious Programs—Tel: 619-422-2159. Sr. Camille Crabbe, C.V.I., D.R.E.
Students 462.

2—OUR LADY OF GUADALUPE, (1945) (Hispanic), Rev. Mario Vesga; Deacons Daniel Parra; Margarito Lozoya.
Res., 345 Anita St., 91911-4198. Tel: 619-422-3977; Fax: 619-422-1056.
Catechesis/Religious Programs—Tel: 619-427-2774.
Students 389.

3—ST. PIUS X, (1955), Revs. Joseph G. Masar; Donald R. Kulleck, Pastor Emeritus; Victor T. Maristela; Deacons Dan De Pozo; Glenn Vecchitto.
Res., 1120 Cuyamaca Ave., 91911-3506. Tel: 619-420-9193; Fax: 619-420-9353.
School—37 E. Emerson, 91911. Tel: 619-422-2015; Fax: 619-422-0048. Eileen Hanson, Prin.
Lay Teachers 14; Students 312.
Catechesis/Religious Programs—Tel: 619-426-2263. Lois Richards, D.R.E.
Students 503.

4—ST. ROSE OF LIMA, (1913), Rev. Msgr. Richard F. Duncanson; Revs. Michael X. Tran; Andre Ramos; Deacons Gerardo Marquez; Gregory Smyth.
Res., 293 H St., 91910-4703. Tel: 619-427-0230; Fax: 619-427-5786.
School—473 Third Ave., 91910. Tel: 619-422-1121; Fax: 619-422-8007.
Religious 1; Lay Teachers 13; Students 340.
Catechesis/Religious Programs—Tel: 619-426-6717. Sr. Margaret Ann Altmiller, O.L.V.M., D.R.E.
Students 1,454.

Coronado, San Diego Co., Sacred Heart (1897), Rev. Michael F. Murphy; Rev. Msgr. John R. Portman, Pastor Emeritus; Deacon Robert E. Griffin, Jr. In res., Rev. Msgr. Jeremiah O'Sullivan, Pastor Emeritus; Rev. John Wheeler.
Res., 655 C Ave., 92118-2299. Tel: 619-435-3167; Fax: 619-437-1572.
School—Tel: 619-437-4431; Fax: 619-437-1559.
Benedictine Sisters 1; Lay Teachers 9; Students 252.
Catechesis/Religious Programs—Tel: 619-435-4858; Fax: 619-437-3167.
Students 310.

Del Mar, San Diego Co., St. William of York (1985), Rev. Nicholas Dempsey.
Res., 4343 Del Mar Trails Rd., San Diego, 92130. Tel: 858-481-3232; Fax: 858-481-3289.
Catechesis/Religious Programs—Tel: 858-481-4061. Ann Marie Moznett, D.R.E.
Students 500.

Descanso, San Diego Co., Our Lady of Light (1935), Rev. Gerald F. Palcheck.
Res., 9136 Riverside Dr., P.O. Box 219, 91916. Tel: 619-445-3620; Fax: 619-445-3620.
Catechesis/Religious Programs—Eleanor Denton, D.R.E.
Students 50.

El Cajon, San Diego Co.,

1—HOLY TRINITY, (1903), Revs. Brian M. Corcoran; Eddie Ruiz; Deacon Louis Rocha.
Res., 405 Ballard St., 92019. Tel: 619-444-9425; Fax: 619-444-9426.
School—Tel: 619-444-7529; Fax: 619-444-3721.
Lay Teachers 19; Students 328.
Catechesis/Religious Programs—Tel: 619-444-5043.
Students 558.

2—OUR LADY OF GRACE, (1954), Rev. Msgr. Michael J. Gallagher; Revs. Ralph Poirier, C.S.Sp.; Joseph Bien Quang Do; Omer LeBlanc, C.J.M.; Deacons George Shea; Ray Arnold; Bill Korty; Sr. Carmel Lohan, S.M., Pastoral Asst.
Res., 2766 Navajo Rd., 92020-2183. Tel: 619-469-0133; Fax: 619-469-0575.
School—Tel: 619-466-0055; Fax: 619-466-8994.
Lay Teachers 14; Students 308.
Catechesis/Religious Programs—Tel: 619-466-5656.
Students 500.
Mission—Jacumba, San Diego Co., St. Mary Magdalene, P.O. Box 406, Jacumba, 91934-0406.

3—ST. KIERAN, (1958), Rev. Francis G. Penko; Deacon John Trumble.
Mailing Address: P.O. Box 2428, 92021-0428.
Office: 1510 Greenfield Dr., 92021-0428. Tel: 619-588-6881; Fax: 619-588-5274.
School—1347 Camillo Way, Tel: 619-588-6398; Fax: 619-588-6382. Ms. Michaele Durant, Prin.
Lay Teachers 15; Students 245.
Catechesis/Religious Programs—Tel: 619-447-2424.
Students 205.

4—ST. LOUISE DE MARILLAC, (1944), Rev. Louis A. Salca.
Res., 2005 Crest Dr., 92021-4309. Tel: 619-444-3076.
Catechesis/Religious Programs—Students 21.

5—ST. LUKE, (1985), Rev. Raymond G. O'Donnell; Deacon John Snyder.
Res., 1980 Hillsdale Rd., 92019. Tel: 619-442-1697; Fax: 619-442-2293.
Catechesis/Religious Programs—Tel: 619-442-2515. D.R.E.: Rosalie Camacho, (K-5); Jane Alfano, (6-12).
Students 357.

El Centro, Imperial Co., Our Lady of Guadalupe (1946), Rev. Jaime Escobedo.
Res., 153 E. Brighton Ave., 92243. Tel: 760-352-5535; Fax: 760-352-8003.
Catechesis/Religious Programs—Tel: 760-352-5554. Victor Hernandez, D.R.E.
Students 564.

St. Mary (1907), Rev. Msgr. Thomas J. Vidra; Deacon Luciano Arias.
Res., 795 LaBrucherie, P.O. Box 3425, 92244. Tel: 760-352-4211; Fax: 760-352-7397. [JC]
School—Tel: 760-352-7285; Fax: 760-352-9726.
Sister Servants of the Blessed Sacrament 5; Lay Teachers 17; Students 288.
Catechesis/Religious Programs—Tel: 760-353-8260.
Students 234.

Encinitas, San Diego Co., St. John the Evangelist (1946), Rev. Msgr. Timothy Harnett; Rev. Earl Eggleston.
Res., 1001 Encinitas Blvd., 92024-0457. Tel: 760-753-6254; Fax: 760-753-7118.
School—Tel: 760-944-8227.
Lay Teachers 18; Students 488.
Catechesis/Religious Programs—Tel: 760-436-0664.
Students 908.

Escondido, San Diego Co., Church of the Resurrection (1970), Revs. Charles Fuld; David A. Sereno; Deacons James Kostick; Leopoldo Valdivia.
Res., 1445 Conway Dr., 92027. Tel: 760-747-2322; Fax: 760-747-7079. [JC]
Catechesis/Religious Programs—Tel: 760-747-4550. Margaret Butkis, D.R.E.
Students 1,500.
Comunidad Hispana—.

Church of St. Timothy (1985), Rev. James E. Rafferty.
Church and Administration Center: 2960 Canyon Rd., 92025-7402. Tel: 760-489-1200; Fax: 760-489-2731.
Catechesis/Religious Programs—Tel: 760-489-0482. Christopher O'Donnell, D.R.E.
Students 340.

St. Mary (1890), Rev. Peter Navarra.
Res., 1160 S. Broadway Ave., 92025-5815. Tel: 760-745-1611; Fax: 760-745-1238.
School—Tel: 760-743-3431; Fax: 760-743-6808.
Lay Teachers 13; Students 309.
Catechesis/Religious Programs—130 E. 13th Ave., 92025. Tel: 760-745-8255. Sharon Twilliger, D.R.E.
Students 969.

Fallbrook, San Diego Co., St. Peter (1946), Revs. Edward Kaicher; Bernard A. Rapp; Deacons James Cooper; Manuel Villarreal.
Res., 450 S. Stage Coach Ln., 92028. Tel: 760-728-7034; Fax: 760-723-4050.
School—St. Peter's Catholic School, Tel: 760-728-6961; Fax: 760-723-4050.
Lay Teachers 9; Students 206.
Catechesis/Religious Programs—Tel: 760-728-3412.
Students 790.

Holtville, Imperial Co., St. Joseph (1911), Rev. Cecilio T. Moraga.
Res., 560 Maple Ave., 92250. Tel: 760-356-2147; Fax: 760-356-1985.
Catechesis/Religious Programs—Tel: 760-356-5738. Eleanor Valenzuela, D.O.M., D.R.E.
Students 355.

Imperial, Imperial Co., St. Anthony of Padua (1948), Revs. Gianantonio Baggio, C.S. (Italy); Angelo Risoli, C.S.
Res., 210 W. Seventh St., 92251. Tel: 760-355-1347; Fax: 760-355-1226.
Catechesis/Religious Programs—Tel: 760-355-1304. Maria Fugett, D.R.E.
Students 540.
Missions—Heber, Imperial Co., Sacred Heart, 46 E. Main St., Heber, 92249. Tel: 760-353-6987; Seeley, Imperial Co., Holy Spirit, 1798 Rio Vista, 92273. Tel: 760-352-3811.

Jacumba, San Diego Co., St. Mary Magdalene (1947). A mission of Our Lady of Grace, El Cajon.

Jamul, San Diego Co., St. Pius X (1956), Rev. Scott A. Burnia.
Res., 14107 Lyons Valley Rd., P.O. Box 369, 91935-0369. Tel: 619-669-0085; Fax: 619-669-0087.
Catechesis/Religious Programs—Tel: 619-669-0086. Agnes McKnight, D.R.E.
Students 108.

Julian, San Diego Co., St. Elizabeth (1949), Rev. Donal C. Walsh.
Res., P.O. Box 366, 92036-0366. Tel: 760-765-0613; Fax: 760-765-0552.
Catechesis/Religious Programs—Students 50.

La Jolla, San Diego Co., All Hallows (1959), Rev. Msgr. Patrick Fox. In res., Rev. Thomas Thompson.
Res., 6602 La Jolla Scenic Dr. S., 92037-5799. Tel: 858-459-2975; Fax: 858-459-9712.
School—2390 Nautilus, 92037. Tel: 619-459-6074; Fax: 619-459-4602.
Sisters 1; Lay Teachers 21; Students 287.
Catechesis/Religious Programs—Karen Downs, D.R.E.
Students 80.

Mary, Star of the Sea (1906), Rev. Msgr. Eamonn F. Lyng; Rev. Msgr. James M. Gilfillan, Pastor Emeritus; Rev. Eduardo Gudino; Deacon William Dalzell.
Res., 7727 Girard Ave., 92037-4480. Tel: 858-454-2631; Fax: 858-454-5968.
School—Stella Maris Academy, 7654 Herschel Ave., 92037. Tel: 858-454-2461; Fax: 858-454-4913.
Lay Teachers 15; Students 274.
Catechesis/Religious Programs—Tel: 858-454-1714. D.R.E.: Donna Widmer; Martin Magana.
Students 363.

Lakeside, San Diego Co., Blessed Kateri Tekakwitha (1982) (Native American), Rev. Joseph Viet Hoang; Deacon Bill Clarke.
Res., 1054 Barona Rd., 92040-1502. Tel: 619-443-3412; Fax: 619-443-3018. [CEM]
Catechesis/Religious Programs—Tel: 619-445-8333. Edward Nolan, D.R.E.
Students 56.
Missions—Lakeside, Assumption of BVM, 1054 Barona Rd., 92040-1502. Tel: 619-443-3412; Alpine, Nativity of BVM; El Cajon, Immaculate Conception of BVM.

Our Lady of Perpetual Help (1947), Rev. Msgr. Neal T. Dolan.
Res., 13208 Lakeshore Dr., 92040. Tel: 619-443-1412; Fax: 619-443-1733.
School—Tel: 619-443-1440. Ms. Jane Pflaum, Prin.
St. Joseph of Carondelet Sisters 1; Lay Teachers 12; Students 235.
Catechesis/Religious Programs—Tel: 619-443-5018. D.R.E.: Joan Lopez, (Jr. High School); Joe Hamilton, (High School); Connie Finney, (Adult Ed.).
Students 482.

La Mesa, San Diego Co., St. Martin of Tours (1921), Revs. John M. Sproul; Walter H. Halloran, S.J. In res., Rev. Msgr. Patrick O'Neill; Deacon Timothy Treadwell.
Res., 7710 El Cajon Blvd., 91941. Tel: 619-465-5334; Fax: 619-465-7297.
School—Tel: 619-466-3241; Fax: 619-466-0285.
Lay Teachers 16; Students 311.
Catechesis/Religious Programs—Tel: 619-698-8434. Christine Davis, D.R.E.
Students 364.

Lemon Grove, San Diego Co., St. John of the Cross (1939), Rev. Msgr. Edward Brockhaus; Revs. James J. Bahash; Ruben Fuentes, O.F.M.; Deacons Frank Santoyo; Martin Villafana.
Res., 8086 Broadway, 91945-2598. Tel: 619-466-3209; Fax: 619-466-9276.
School—8175 Lemon Grove Way, 91945. Tel: 619-466-8624; Fax: 619-466-3732. Sr. Guadalupe Mier Y Teran, H.M.S.S., Prin.
Sisters 3; Lay Teachers 16; Students 371.
Catechesis/Religious Programs—Tel: 619-461-2681. Karen Dey, D.R.E.
Students 725.
Convent—8171 Lemon Grove Way, 91945. Tel: 619-460-4271.
Sisters of Mercy of the Blessed Sacrament 5.

National City, San Diego Co., St. Anthony of Padua (1910) (Hispanic), Rev. Willaim T. Lawson; Deacon Joe Arismendez. In res., Rev. Peter Borda.
410 W. 18th St., 91951.
Res., 1816 Harding Ave., P.O. Box 1507, 91951-1507. Tel: 619-477-4520; Fax: 619-477-8708.
Catechesis/Religious Programs—Angelina Sampo, D.R.E.
Students 224.

St. Mary (1926), Revs. Dionisio Macalintal (PH); Luis C. Valenciano (PH); Deacon Daniel Prado.
Mailing Address: 426 E. Seventh St., 91950-2322.
Res., 1310 "L" Ave., 91950-4811. Tel: 619-474-1501; Fax: 619-474-1502.
Catechesis/Religious Programs—Tel: 619-474-5777; Fax: 619-474-5777.
Students 650.

Oceanside, San Diego Co.,

1—MISSION SAN LUIS REY, (1798), Revs. Michel Gagnon, O.F.M.; Jorge Hernandez, O.F.M.; Garrett Galvin, O.F.M.; Deacon Jesse Pagliaro.
Res., 4070 Mission Ave., 92057-6497. Tel: 760-757-3250; Fax: 760-757-3299.
Catechesis/Religious Programs—Tel: 760-757-3250, Ext. 334.
Students 788.
Mission—San Luis Rey, San Diego Co., San Luis Rey de Francia, (1798) 4050 Mission Ave., San Luis Rey, 92068. Tel: 760-757-3651; Fax: 760-757-4613. [CEM]

2—ST. MARGARET, (1977), Rev. William F. Gold; Deacon Lewis Beatty.
Res., 4300 Oceanside Blvd., 92056-2999. Tel: 760-941-5560; Fax: 760-941-1857.
Catechesis/Religious Programs—Tel: 760-941-5561. Sr. Yvonne Hawker, O.S.F., D.R.E.
Students 297.

3—ST. MARY, STAR OF THE SEA, (1937) (Hispanic), Revs. John P. Dolan; Michael M. Pham. In res., Rev. Humberto C. Zanetti, O.F.M. (Italy).
Res., 609 Pier View Way, 92054-2861. Tel: 760-722-1688; Fax: 760-722-2653.
School—Tel: 760-722-7259; Fax: 760-722-0862.
Lay Teachers 19; Students 387.
Catechesis/Religious Programs—Tel: 760-722-1000.
Students 774.

4—ST. THOMAS MORE, (1985), Rev. Peter M. McGuine; Deacon Thomas A. Goeltz.
Church & Mailing Address: 1450 S. Melrose Dr., 92056. Tel: 760-758-4100; Fax: 760-758-4165.
Res., 1945 Pinewood Rd., Vista, 92083.
Catechesis/Religious Programs—Students 262.

Pala, San Diego Co., Mission San Antonio de Pala (1816) (Native American), Rev. Paul Marconi, C.R.S.P.
Res., P.O. Box 70, 92059-0070. Tel: 760-742-3317; Fax: 760-742-3040.
Catechesis/Religious Programs—Tel: 760-742-1714; Fax: 760-742-1600.
Students 204.
Convent—Tel: 760-742-1714.
Franciscan Sisters of Philadelphia 3.
Chapels—Rincon Indian Reservation, St. Bartholomew.; Pauma, El Centro Guadalupano, Tel: 760-742-4559; La Jolla Indian Reservation, Our Lady of Refuge.; Pauma Indian Reservation, St. James.

Poway, San Diego Co., St. Gabriel (1973), Rev. Michael Froidurot.
Res., 13734 Twin Peaks Rd., P.O. Box 867, 92074-0867. Tel: 858-748-5348; Fax: 858-748-5764.
Catechesis/Religious Programs—Tel: 858-748-7475. Martha Lyles, D.R.E.
Students 560.

St. Michael (1959), Rev. Msgr. Joseph L. Finnerty; Rev. William Mooney; Deacon Franz Scholz.
Res., 15546 Pomerado Rd., 92064-2404. Tel: 858-487-4755; Fax: 858-487-5937.
School—15542 Pomerado Rd., 92064. Tel: 858-485-1303; Fax: 858-485-5059.
Sisters of Mercy of Sligo 2; Lay Teachers 18; Students 385.
Catechesis/Religious Programs—Tel: 858-487-0360. Kathy Wood, D.R.E.
Students 1,250.

Ramona, San Diego Co., Immaculate Heart of Mary (1947), Rev. Michael J. Sinor; Deacon A. R. McDaniel.
Res., 537 E St., 92065. Tel: 760-789-0583; Fax: 760-789-3875.
Catechesis/Religious Programs—Tel: 760-789-6151. Eileen Morgan, D.R.E.
Students 596.

Rancho Santa Fe, San Diego Co., Church of the Nativity (1985), Rev. Msgr. Dennis R. Clark.
Mailing Address: P.O. Box 8770, 92067-8770.
Res., 6309 El Apajo Rd., 92067. Tel: 858-756-1911; Fax: 858-756-9562.
School—(Grades K-8) P.O. Box 9180, 92067. Tel: 858-756-6763; Fax: 858-756-9128.
Students 175.
Catechesis/Religious Programs—Tel: 858-756-0937. Mrs. Anne Lonnecker, D.R.E.
Students 375.

San Marcos, San Diego Co., St. Mark (1963), Revs. George Dunkley; Burt Boudion; Deacons Dick Jansing; Joseph Wisocky.
Res., 1147 Discovery, 92069. Tel: 760-744-1540; Fax: 760-744-3828. [CEM]
Catechesis/Religious Programs—Tel: 760-744-1130.
Students 991.

Santa Ysabel, San Diego Co., Santa Ysabel Indian Mission (1818) (Native American), Rev. William P. Stevenson.
Res., 23013 Hwy. 79, P.O. Box 129, 92070-1010. Tel: 760-765-0810; Fax: 760-765-3494. [CEM]
Mission—Warner Springs, San Diego Co., St. Francis, Hwy. 79, Warner Springs, 92086.

Santee, San Diego Co., Guardian Angels (1962), Rev. Michael A. Cunnane; Deacon Ronald Schmitz.
Res., 9310 Dalehurst Rd., 92071-1010. Tel: 619-448-1213; Fax: 619-448-2980.
Catechesis/Religious Programs—9310 Dalehurst, 92071. Tel: 619-448-1213, Ext. 312. Sr. Mary Potter, R.S.M., D.R.E.
Students 475.

San Ysidro, San Diego Co., Our Lady of Mt. Carmel (1927) (Hispanic), Revs. Emmet L. Farrell; Jose Castillo.
Res., 2020 Alaquinas Dr., 92173-2107. Tel: 619-428-1415; Fax: 619-428-5626.
School—Tel: 619-428-2091; Fax: 619-428-8324. Sr. Ana Rosa Aceves, Prin.
Sisters of the Most Blessed Sacrament 11; Lay Teachers 6; Students 349.
Catechesis/Religious Programs—109 Seaward Ave., 92173. Tel: 619-428-3686.
Students 400.

Solana Beach, San Diego Co., St. James (Del Mar) (1911), Rev. Msgr. Lawrence M. Purcell; Deacons John Brice; Ted Bear; Joseph R. Santen. In res., Rev. John Howard, C.J.M.
Office: 625 S. Nardo Ave., 92075-2398. Tel: 858-755-2545; Fax: 858-755-3845.
School—Tel: 858-755-1777; Fax: 858-755-3124. Principals: Jodee Ann Moore, (School Rel.); Donna Kruszona, (St. James Academy).
Lay Teachers 15; Students 392.
Catechesis/Religious Programs—Tel: 858-755-2545. Robert Kidd, D.R.E.
Students 600.
Mission—Solana Beach, San Diego Co., St. Leo, 936 Genevieve, 92075. Tel: 858-481-6788; Fax: 858-481-5832.

Spring Valley, San Diego Co., Santa Sophia (1956), Revs. Michael Ratajczak; Gary Holtey; Deacon James Keeley.
Res., 9800 San Juan St., 91977. Tel: 619-463-6629; Fax: 619-463-8101.
School—Tel: 619-463-0488; Fax: 619-668-5469.
Lay Teachers 18; Students 324.
Catechesis/Religious Programs—Tel: 619-463-6011. Sr. Alyce Waters, D.R.E.
Students 388.

Valley Center, San Diego Co., St. Stephen (1981), Rev. William A. Kernan.
Res., P.O. Box 1015, 31020 Cole Grade Rd., 92082. Tel: 760-749-3324; Fax: 760-749-6684.
Catechesis/Religious Programs—Tel: 760-749-3352; Fax: 760-749-6608. Penny Phillips, D.R.E.
Students 260.

Vista, San Diego Co., St. Francis of Assisi (1941), Revs. Ramon R. Marrufo; Patrick J. Mulcahy; Peter Nguyen (Vietnamese); Deacons Robert P. Mueller; Michael Collins; Frank Mercardante; Ronald Arnold; Pedro Enciso.
Res., 525 W. Vista Way, 92083-5974. Tel: 760-945-8000; Fax: 760-945-8036.
School—Tel: 760-630-7960; Fax: 760-726-2910. Linda McCotter, Prin.
Lay Teachers 19; Students 345.
Catechesis/Religious Programs—Tel: 760-945-8010. Susan Ferraris, D.R.E.
Students 1,077.

Westmorland, St. Joseph (1939) (Mexican-American). Administered by St. Patrick, Calipatria.
Res., 300 N. Center St., 92281. Tel: 760-348-2733.
Catechesis/Religious Programs—Students 95.

Winterhaven, Imperial Co., St. Thomas (1780). (Indian Mission). Rev. Duncan W. Monohan.
Res., P.O. Box 1176, 92283-1176. Tel: 760-572-0283; Fax: 760-572-0283.
Catechesis/Religious Programs—Students 8.
Mission—Winterhaven, Imperial Co., St. Mary, 92283.

Eastern Churches

San Diego, San Diego Co., Our Lady of Perpetual Help (1960). (Ukrainian Catholic). Rev. Myron Mykyta.
Res., 4061 Winona Ave., 92105. Tel: 619-282-9538; Fax: 619-282-9538.

El Cajon, San Diego Co., St. Peter (1973). (Chaldean Eastern Catholic). Rev. Michael J. Bazzi.
Res., 1627 Jamacha Way, 92019. Tel: 619-579-7913; 588-9921; Fax: 619-588-8281.
Catechesis/Religious Programs—Khelood Allos, D.R.E.
Students 710.
Convent—1591 Jamacha Way, 92019. Tel: 619-447-4842. Chaldean Sisters

Chaplains of Public Institutions

Hospitals

SAN DIEGO. *Alvarado, Grossmont and Kaiser Hospitals.* Revs. James Burson, C.J.M. Tel: 619-287-3270; James P. Retzner, O.S.A.
Children's Hospital Tel: 858-541-3475. Rev. Manuel Ediza.
Scripps Hospital. Rev. Thomas Thompson Tel: 858-457-4123.
Scripps Mercy Hospital. Revs. Benjamin Bachmeier; Frank Hoffmann Tel: 619-260-7020.
Sharp Memorial Hospital. Revs. Manuel Ediza Tel: 858-541-3475; James V. Corrigan, O.S.A., Clinical Pastoral Ed.
UCSD Medical Center. Rev. Paul Balio Tel: 619-543-6737.

LA JOLLA. *Thornton Hospital.* Rev. Thomas Thompson Tel: 858-657-7000.
Veterans Administration Hospital Tel: 858-552-8585. Rev. Jerry Hamperzonian.

Retirement Homes

SAN DIEGO. *Nazareth House.* Rev. George Byrne Tel: 619-563-0480.

LA MESA. *Little Flower Haven.* Rev. Philip Bronk, S.T. Tel: 619-466-3163.

Detention Ministries

SAN DIEGO. *Central Detention Facility and San Diego City Jail.* Rev. James I. Rasura, S.J. Tel: 619-236-3011.
East Mesa Detention Facility Tel: 619-661-2608. Deacon Manny Carpizo.
George F. Bailey Maximum Security Facility Tel: 619-661-2620. Rev. John P. Auther, S.J.
Juvenile Hall. (Vacant) Office for Social Ministry, Tel: 858-490-8323.
Metropolitan Correction Center. Jesuit Fathers. Tel: 619-232-4311.
R.J. Donovan Correctional Facility. Rev. Walter P. Vogel, O.S.A. Tel: 619-661-6500.
San Diego Detention Center. (Vacant) Office for Social Ministry, Tel: 858-490-8323.
Wackenhut Detention Facility. (Vacant) Office for Social Ministry, Tel: 858-490-8323.

BRAWLEY. *Calipatria State Prison* Tel: 760-348-7000. Rev. Thomas Dermody.

CHULA VISTA. *South Bay Detention Facility.* Rev. James V. Caldwell.

EL CENTRO. *El Centro Juvenile Hall.* (Vacant) Office for Social Ministry, Tel: 858-490-8323.
Imperial County Jail. Julia Ulloa Tel: 760-339-6367.

IMPERIAL. *Centinela State Prison.* Rev. Romeo Supnet Tel: 760-337-7900.

SANTEE. *Las Colinas Women's Detention Facility.* Deacon George Shea Tel: 619-258-3176.

VISTA. *Vista Detention Facility.* Deacon Jim Kostick Tel: 760-940-4473.

State Conservation Camps

SAN DIEGO. *Rainbow Work Camp.* Rev. Bud Kaicher Tel: 760-728-7034.

On Duty Outside the Diocese:
Reverend Monsignors—
Cordileone, Salvatore
Reverend Fathers—
Conwill, Giles
Cribbin, James
Flynn, Edward R.
Huggins, Michael
Mejia, Ricardo
Parrales, Napoleon J.
Reilly, John (Ireland)
Stanonik, Anthony
White, Robert

Military Chaplains:
Reverend Fathers—
Buchmiller, Ronald J., Ch.C., USN
Diaz, Michael, CHC, USN
Jennings, Tommie, CHC, USNR
Merris, Christopher

Unassigned:
Reverend Fathers—
Bauer, Paul
Dunn, Stephen
Foley, Patrick
Gomes-Kelly, John R.
Langille, Justin
Polizzi, Daniel

Retired:
Reverend Monsignors—
Aldasoro, Francisco
Balderas, Luis G.
Bolger, William
Brennan, Joseph F.
Briody, Thomas
Campion, John J.
Chylewski, Anthony
Coughlan, Michael J.
Creighton, Edward
Cuddihy, William
Elliott, William
Galindo, Rudolph
Giesing, Anthony
Gilfillan, James M.
Hanley, Andrew W.
Kearney, Patrick J.
Kraft, William A.
Kulleck, Donald
McDermott, Thomas J.
Mimnagh, Peter F.
Moore, J. Raymond
Murray, Sean
O'Donoghue, James P.
O'Neill, Patrick J.
O'Sullivan, Jeremiah
Portman, John R.
Topping, Joseph
Reverend Fathers—
Borda, Peter Paul
Buchanan, Donald
Buttimer, Joseph
Caldwell, James
Chase, Maurice
Crisologo, Aurelio
Fischer, Eugene
Holland, Kilian
Houck, Richard
Keenan, John J.
Keith, John C.
Lorenz, Vincent E.
Lucev, John
McDonnell, Francis
Nesbitt, John B.
Nguyen, Peter
Ortmann, William
Palmitessa, Paul
Quinn, John T.
Rankin, James
Roll, David H.
Russell, Richard J.
Ryan, Alphonsus
Ryland, Raymond
Salada, Urbano
Sheslo, Charles
Sierra, Francis A.
Smith, Aquinas
Sostrich, John L.
Thompson, J. Noel
Tindall, Harold
Twarog, Theodore S.
Uboldi, Victor
Ullman, Earl L.
Wheeler, John

Permanent Deacons:
Albers, Tony, Blessed Sacrament, San Diego
Arias, Luciano, St. Mary, El Centro
Arismendez, Joe, St. Anthony, National City
Arnold, Ray, Our Lady of Grace, El Cajon
Arnold, Ron, St. Francis, Vista
Ball, Lou, St. Columba, San Diego
Bear, Ted, St. James, Solana Beach
Beatty, Lewis, St. Margaret, Oceanside
Bell, L. Ferris, St. Gregory the Great, San Diego
Brice, John, St. James, Solona Beach
Carpizo, Manuel, Good Shepherd, San Diego
Chia, Henry, St. Elizabeth Seton, Carlsbad
Clarke, William G., Blessed Kateri Tekakwitha, Jamul
Collins, Michael, Saint Francis, Vista
Cooper, Jim, St. Peter, Fallbrook
Corder, Richard G., St. John the Evangelist, Encinitas
Corrao, Jack P., (Retired)
Costello, John M., (Retired)
Dalzell, William, (Retired)
Davidson, Paul, Holy Family, San Diego
Dean, Ben, On Leave
Delano, Joe, On Leave
DePozo, Daniel, St. Pius X, Chula Vista
Diem, Ronald H., St. Gregory the Great, San Diego
Dougherty, Thomas P., Holy Family, San Diego
Dube, Leo, (Retired)
Early, John M., St. Timothy, Escondido
Ekhaml, Robert T., St. Therese, San Diego
Ellis, John A., Holy Family, San Diego
Enciso, Pedro, St. Francis, Vista
Finn, Kenneth, (Retired)
Fitzmorris, Robert H., St. Mary Magdalene, San Diego
Frazee, Mike, St. Patrick, Carlsbad
Gallagher, John V., (Retired)
Gasparovic, Anthony L., Our Lady of Perpetual Help, Lakeside
Goeltz, Thomas A., St. Thomas More, Vista
Graff, Albert P., (Retired)
Griffin, Robert E., Jr., Sacred Heart, Coronado
Grosso, Ernest, Mission San Diego de Alcala, San Diego
Gullotta, Daniel, Lakeside, MT
Hernandez, Raul, St. Jerome, San Diego
Hess, Arnie, Our Mother of Confidence, San Diego
Hitch, James, Corpus Christi, Bonita
Hunt, Sam, Seal Beach, CA
Jansing, Dick, St. Mark, San Marcos
Jones, Thom, Our Lady of Mt. Carmel, San Diego
Keeley, Jim, Santa Sophia, Spring Valley
Klopchin, Bill, Our Mother of Confidence, San Diego
Korty, Bill, Our Lady of Grace, El Cajon
Kostick, Jim, Resurrection, Escondido
Kutler, Harold, Mary, Star of the Sea, Oceanside
Leach, Dave, San Luis Obispo
Lozoya, Margarito, Our Lady of Guadalupe, Chula Vista
Mackey, Bob, (Retired)
Magana, Gustavo, Unassigned
Maher, Thomas M., Jr., St. Mary, Escondido
Marquez, Gerardo, St. Rose of Lima, Chula Vista
Martinez, Seodello A., St. Charles, San Diego
Mather, Dick, St. Patrick, Carlsbad
McDaniel, Al, Immaculate Heart of Mary, Ramona
Mercardante, F., St. Francis, Vista
Michaels, Larry, Unassigned
Montoya, Ken, Unassigned
Mueller, Robert, St. Francis, Vista
Nevins, William J., (Retired)
Nguyen, Peter Can, St. Didacus, San Diego
Nunez, Manuel, St. Jude, San Diego
Osgood, Franklin B., (Retired)
Pagliaro, Jesse, Mission San Luis Rey, Oceanside
Parra, Daniel, Our Lady of Guadalupe, Chula Vista
Paulicivic, George, Sr., Murrieta, CA
Perez, Modesto, (Retired)
Phelps, John, (Retired)
Pollock, William, (Retired)
Porciuncula, Manny, Our Lady of Mt. Carmel, San Diego
Prado, Daniel, St. Mary, National City
Principe, Louis, Blessed Sacrament, San Diego
Robbins, Ralph, (Retired)
Robles, Manny, Holy Spirit, San Diego
Rocha, Louis, Holy Trinity, El Cajon
Roy, James, Klamath Falls, OR
Santen, Joseph R., St. James, Solana Beach
Santiago, Nicholas M., St. Columba, San Diego
Santoyo, Juan, St. John of the Cross, Lemon Grove
Schmitt, Giles V., Sacred Heart, San Diego
Schmitz, Ron, Guardian Angels, Santee
Scull, James, Ascension, San Diego
Shea, George, (Retired)
Shelton, Carl, St. John the Evangelist, San Diego
Shockley, Gordon E., San Antonio, TX
Skupnik, Ray, Long Beach, CA
Smyth, Greg, St. Rose of Lima, Chula Vista
Snyder, John A., St. Luke, El Cajun
Threatt, Marvin, Holy Spirit, San Diego
Treadwell, Timothy, St. Martin of Tours, La Mesa
Trumble, John, St. Kieran, El Cajon
Valdivia, Leopoldo, Resurrection, Escondido
Vasquez, Bill, Mission San Diego de Alcala, San Diego
Vecchitto, Glenn, St. Pius X, Chula Vista
Villafana, Martin, St. John of the Cross, Lemon Grove
Villarreal, Manuel, St. Peter, Fallbrook
Vivio, Bill, Phoenix, AZ
Walling, Robert, Bend, OR
Wisocky, Joe, St. Mark, San Marcos
Wood, Joseph, All Hallows, La Jolla
Yeatts, Bernard, Our Lady of Mt. Carmel, San Diego

INSTITUTIONS LOCATED IN THE DIOCESE

[A] SEMINARIES, DIOCESAN

SAN DIEGO. *St. Francis Seminary*, 1667 Santa Paula Dr., 92111. Tel: 619-291-7446; Fax: 619-291-7011. Rev. Msgr. Steven Callahan, J.C.L., Rector; Revs. Patrick Murphy; John Flannery, O.P. Priests 3; Sisters 1; Students 17.

[B] COLLEGES AND UNIVERSITIES

SAN DIEGO. *Austin House*, 1605 28th St., 92102-1417. Tel: 619-233-9141.
E-mail: osa-west@k-online.com
For a complete listing, refer to the Colleges and Universities section.

University of San Diego, 5998 Alcala Park, 92110-2492. Tel: 619-260-4600
For a complete listing, refer to the Colleges and Universities section.

[C] HIGH SCHOOLS, DIOCESAN

SAN DIEGO. *Academy of Our Lady of Peace.* (Grades 9-12), 4860 Oregon St., 92116. Tel: 619-297-2266; Fax: 619-297-2473.
E-mail: aolpadmin@excite.com
(Girls). Sr. Dolores Anchondo, C.S.J., Prin. Sisters of St. Joseph of Carondelet 2; Lay Teachers 40; Students 710.

Marian Catholic High School, 1002 18th St., 92154. Tel: 619-423-2121; Fax: 619-423-6910.
E-mail: mchs@home.com
Web site: www.mariancatholic.org
(Coed). Mrs. Estelle Kassebaum, Prin. Religious 1; Lay Teachers 34; Students 463.

St. Augustine High School, 3266 Nutmeg St., 92104-5199. Tel: 619-282-2184; Fax: 619-282-1203.
E-mail: kteven@sahs.org
Web site: www.sahs.org
Conducted by The Augustinians. (Boys). Revs. John R. Sanders, O.S.A., Prin.; Tom Verber, O.S.A., Campus Min.; Bro. Stephen McKenna, O.S.A.; Deacon Richard Hardick, O.S.A.
(For information concerning the monastery see separate listing under Monasteries). Priests 2; Brothers 1; Deacons 1; Lay Teachers 30; Students 664.

University of San Diego High School. (Coed), 5961 Linda Vista Rd., 92110-1947. Tel: 619-298-8277; Fax: 619-260-1696.
E-mail: rkelly@usdhs.org
Web site: usdhs.org
Richard E. Kelly, Ph.D., Prin.; Rev. Michael White, C.S.Sp. Priests 1; Lay Teachers 90; Students 1,457.

CALEXICO. *Vincent Memorial High.* (Grades 9-12), 525 W. Sheridan, 92231. Tel: 760-357-3461; Fax: 760-357-0902. (Coed). Conducted by Sisters Servants of the Blessed Sacrament. Sisters 2; Lay Teachers 14; Students 203.

[D] SPECIAL SCHOOLS

EL CAJON. *St. Madeleine Sophie's Center for Developmentally Disabled Adults*, 2119 E. Madison Ave., 92019-1111. Tel: 619-442-5129; Fax: 619-442-2590.
E-mail: stmsc01@stmsc.org
Debra Turner, Exec. Dir. Lay Teachers 80; Enrollment 220.

[E] PROTECTIVE INSTITUTIONS

SPRING VALLEY. *Noah Homes*, 12526 Campo Rd., 91978. Tel: 619-660-6200; Fax: 619-660-1481.
E-mail: NoahHomesSKJ@aol.com
For a complete listing, refer to the Special Care Facilities section.

[F] HOSPITALS

SAN DIEGO. *Scripps Mercy Hospital*, 4077 Fifth Ave., 92103. Tel: 619-294-8111; Fax: 619-686-3530.
Web site: www.scrippshealth.com
Tom Gammiere, Senior Vice Pres. Admin.; Sr. JoCeal Young, Dir. Mission Svcs.; Revs. Frank Hoffmann; Benjamin Bachmeier. Chaplains: Sr. Barbara Checkhart; John Gillman, Supvr. C.P.E.; Michael Harkay; Rev. Loran Long; Sr. Mary Sutherland; Rev. John Whitacre. Bed Capacity 520; Total Staff 2,099; Patients assisted annually 20,000.

[G] HOMES FOR SENIOR CITIZENS

SAN DIEGO. *Cathedral Plaza*, 1551 Third Ave., 92101. Tel: 619-234-0093; Fax: 619-234-5168.
E-mail: cathplaza@aol.com
For a complete listing, refer to the Special Care Facilities section.

Guadalupe Plaza, 4142 42nd St., 92105. Tel: 619-584-2414; Fax: 619-584-2886.
E-mail: GDplaza@aol.com
For a complete listing, refer to the Special Care Facilities section.

Nazareth House Retirement Home, 6333 Rancho Mission Rd., 92108. Tel: 619-563-0480; Fax: 619-624-9215.
E-mail: fmack@cts.com
For a complete listing, refer to the Special Care Facilities section.

St. John's Plaza 8150 Broadway Lemon Grove, 91945. Tel: 619-466-5354; Fax: 619-466-6643.
For a complete listing, refer to the Special Care Facilities section.

LA MESA. *Little Flower Haven*, 8585 La Mesa Blvd., 91941. Tel: 619-466-3163; Fax: 619-466-9642
For a complete listing, refer to the Special Care Facilities section.

[H] MONASTERIES AND RESIDENCES OF PRIESTS AND BROTHERS

SAN DIEGO. *Augustinian Community*, 3266 Nutmeg St., 92104. Tel: 619-282-2028; Fax: 619-282-2233. Revs. Harry M. Neely, O.S.A., Prior; John R. Sanders, O.S.A., Prin.; Thomas P. Garrett, O.S.A.; James E. Hannan, O.S.A.; John D. Keller, O.S.A.; Thomas Verber, O.S.A.; Bro. Michael Bube, O.S.A., Procurator, Augustinian Community, St. Patrick's Parish, 3585 30th St., 92104-4196. Tel: 619-295-2157. Revs. James O. Mott, O.S.A.; Anthony J. Wasko, O.S.A.; James P. Retzner, O.S.A.; John Blethen, O.S.A., 1605 28th St., 92102. Tel: 619-233-9141. Revs. Walter P. Vogel, O.S.A., Prior; Stephen Ochoa, O.S.A., Prov.; Jerome Bevilacqua, O.S.A.; Bro. J. Stephen McKenna, O.S.A.; Deacon Richard Hardick.

Monica House - Augustinian Community, 1621 28th St., 92102-1417. Tel: 619-235-0247; Fax: 619-231-2814.
E-mail: osa-west@k-online.com
Mailing Address: 1605 28th St., 92102-1417. Total in Residence 2.

BOULEVARD. *Cedar Pines - Augustinian Community*, 1371 Tierra del Sol Rd., 91905-4694. Tel: 619-766-4101.
E-mail: cleos@wwdb.org
Mailing Address: Provencial Office, 1605 28th St., San Diego, 92102-1417.

OCEANSIDE. *Mission San Luis Rey*, 4050 Mission Ave., 92057-6402. Tel: 760-757-3651; Fax: 760-757-4613.
E-mail: ben@sanluisrey.org
Web site: www.sanluisrey.org
Franciscan Friars. Rev. Ben R. Innes, O.F.M., Guardian; Bros. Maurice Peltier, O.F.M.; Roch Schwab, O.F.M.; Martin Soto, O.F.M.; Revs. Mel Bucher, O.F.M.; Abraham Chiu, O.F.M.; Michel Gagnon, O.F.M.; Garrett Galvin, O.F.M.; Anthony Garibaldi, O.F.M.; William Haney, O.F.M.; Jorge Hernandez, O.F.M.; Vincent Hughes, O.F.M.; David Johnson, O.F.M., Casa San Diego, 630 East 2nd St., National City, 91950. Tel: 619-474-6640; Fax: 619-474-4869. Bros. Ed Dunn, O.F.M.; Tom Thing, O.F.M.; Revs. Paul Lee, O.F.M.; Andres Rivero, O.F.M. Priests 9; Brothers 5.

Prince of Peace Abbey, Benet Hill, 92054. Tel: 760-430-1305; 1306; Fax: 760-967-8711.
E-mail: princeabby@aol.com
Benedictine Fathers. Rt. Revs. Charles Wright, O.S.B., Abbot; Claude Ehringer, O.S.B., (Retired), Abbot; Revs. David Carvalho, O.S.B.; Luke Dougherty, O.S.B.; Sharbel Ewen, O.S.B.; Angelus Ferrara, O.S.B.; Anselm Fister, O.S.B. Oregon; Alexis Foyo, O.S.B.; Basil Mattingly, O.S.B.; Aquinas Nichols, O.S.B. Rome; Herbert Palmer, O.S.B.; Stephanos Pedrano, O.S.B.; Bros. Peter Aslin, O.S.B.; Timothy Balk, O.S.B., Bro. Oblate; Joseph Black, O.S.B.; Anselm Clark, O.S.B.; Blaise Heuke, O.S.B.; Clement Kennedy, O.S.B.; Benedict Menezes, O.S.B.; Raphael Meyer, O.S.B.; Michel Pham, O.S.B.; Mario Quizon, O.S.B.; Daniel Sokol, O.S.B.; Mathias Strass, O.S.B., Bro. Oblate; Meinrad Taylor, O.S.B. Priests 12; Brothers 13.

[I] CONVENTS AND RESIDENCES FOR SISTERS

SAN DIEGO. *Carmelite Monastery of San Diego, California*. (Discalced), 5158 Hawley Blvd., 92116-1934. Tel: 619-280-5425; Fax: 619-283-2121. Sr. Yvonne Hanke, O.C.D., Prioress. Sisters 14.

Community of the Holy Spirit, 6151 Rancho Mission Rd., #205, 92108. Tel: 619-584-0809.
E-mail: glayva@transport.com
Sr. Emily Weir, C.H.S., Gen. Coord. Sisters 17.

Daughters of Divine Charity, 6036 Camino Rico, 92120. Tel: 619-287-1320. Sisters 5.

Maryknoll Sisters, 2227 31st St., 92104. Tel: 619-283-5678. Sisters 4.

Missionaries of Charity, 3877 Boston Ave., 92113. Tel: 619-263-9566. Sisters 7.

Poor Sisters of Nazareth, 6330 Rancho Mission Rd., 92108. Tel: 619-563-0480; Fax: 619-624-9215.
E-mail: fmack@cts.com
Sisters 8.

Religious of Jesus and Mary, 1510 Third Ave., 92101. Tel: 619-234-0556; Fax: 619-234-0202.
E-mail: agnesjofa@juno.com
Sisters 9.

Religious of the Sacred Heart. Tel: 619-299-3639; Fax: 619-291-4207.
E-mail: shaffer@acusd.edu
Casa Maria Community, Univ. of San Diego, 5998 Alcala Park, F.H. 115, 92110-2492. Tel: 619-299-3639; Fax: 619-291-4207.

School Sisters of Notre Dame, 1997 Magdalene Way, 92110. Tel: 619-276-5830.
E-mail: jweisma1@san.rr.com
Sisters 5.

Sisters of Loretto, 6528 Bradford St., 92115. Tel: 619-287-8388. Sisters 2.

Sisters of Mercy (Ireland & South Africa), 10726 Caminito Cascara, #15, 92108. Tel: 619-284-1027; Fax: 619-284-1027. Sisters 2.

Sisters of Mercy of the Americas (Burlingame), 4216 Albatross Dr., 92103. Tel: 619-260-8047. Sisters 2.

Sisters of Social Service, 3525 Third Ave., 92103-4908. Tel: 619-295-1896. Sisters 5.

Sisters of St. Joseph Brentwood, NY, 4158 Utah St., 92104. Tel: 619-528-1531.

Sisters of St. Joseph of Carondelet, 4860 Oregon St., 92116. Tel: 619-295-2891; 295-2887; Fax: 619-297-2473.
E-mail: aolpadmin@excite.com
Sisters 2.

Sisters of St. Joseph of Peace, 2880 Caulfield Dr., 92154. Tel: 619-423-7360. Sisters 2.

Sisters of St. Louis, 5824 Kantor Ct., 92122. Tel: 858-625-8370.

Sisters of the Holy Family, 6333 College Grove Way, B9, 92115. Tel: 619-286-3371.

Sisters of the Precious Blood, 4202 58th St., 92115. Tel: 619-229-1817.
E-mail: kateandellie@juno.com
Sisters 2.

Society of the Holy Child Jesus, 6243 Caminito Telmo, 92111. Tel: 858-277-0309.
E-mail: corneliasd@aol.com
Sisters 2.

CALEXICO. *Sister Servants of the Blessed Sacrament*, 536 Rockwood, 92231. Tel: 760-357-1046. Sisters 8.

CARLSBAD. *Sisters of Charity of the Blessed Virgin Mary*, 7238 Santa Barbara, 92009. Tel: 760-804-0841. Sr. Mary Kay Dum, Reg. Supr. Sisters 2.

CHULA VISTA. *Benedictine Sisters of Glendora*, 236 Alvarado, 91910-3610. Tel: 619-422-3610.
E-mail: auxilia2@aol.com
Sisters 2.

Franciscan Missionaries of Our Lady of Peace, 575 E. St., #120, 91910. Tel: 619-691-9008.

Religious of Jesus and Mary, 1354 Hilltop Dr., 91911. Tel: 619-427-5834; Fax: 619-427-6803.
E-mail: rosienicholson@juno.com
Sr. Rosemary Nicholson, R.J.M., Reg. Supr. Sisters 6.

Religious of the Incarnate Word, 153 Rainier Ct., 91911. Tel: 619-420-0231; Fax: 619-691-5939.
E-mail: iwsisters@aol.com
Sisters 6.

EL CAJON. *Sisters of Mercy (Ireland & South Africa)*, 2766 Navajo Rd., 92020. Tel: 619-465-2233; Fax: 619-463-4421. Sisters 3.

EL CENTRO. *Our Lady of Victory Convent*, 604 El Centro Ave., 92243. Tel: 760-352-8407.
E-mail: licha@thegrid.net
Sisters 3.

Religious of the Incarnate Word, 102 W. Holt, 92243-2730. Tel: 760-353-4146. Sisters 4.

IMPERIAL BEACH. *Sisters of the Holy Cross*, 1197 Boulevard Ave., 91932-1707. Tel: 619-424-8895.

LA JOLLA. *Dominican Sisters of Adrian*, 6570 La Jolla Scenic Dr., 92037. Tel: 619-459-3681; Fax: 619-459-4602.
E-mail: kathleen@allhallows.com
Web site: allhallows.com
Sisters 2.

LA MESA. *Carmelite Sisters of the Divine Heart of Jesus*, 8585 La Mesa Blvd., 91941. Tel: 619-466-3163; Fax: 619-462-8261.
E-mail: carmeldcj2000@att.net
Sr. M. Fatima Cardoza, Prov. Supr.; Sr. Mary Alice Prieto, Supr. Sisters 14; Novices 4; Postulants 5.

Franciscan Sisters of Little Falls, MN, 8681 Lemon Ave., #1, 91941. Tel: 619-698-5301.

Medical Mission Sisters. (Western District). Mailing Address: 7808 El Cajon Blvd., Ste. Q, 91941. Tel: 619-589-7000; Fax: 619-698-2815.
E-mail: mmscalsd@juno.com
Web site: www.libertynet.org/~mmsl
Legal Title: *Society of Catholic Medical Missionaries, Inc.* Sr. D. Jeanette McDermott, M.M.S., Western Dist. Coord., 5673 Marne Ave., San Diego, 92120. Tel: 619-286-6880. Sisters 3. 4300 Echo Court, Apt. D, 91941-6658. Tel: 619-337-1364. Sisters 2. 636 Mariposa Cir., Chula Vista, 91911-2511. Tel: 619-482-3109. Sisters 4. 2250 Tampa Ave., #1, El Cajon, 92020. Tel: 619-466-7100. 8585 La Mesa Blvd., 91941. Tel: 619-466-3163. Sisters 6. 369 K St., #49, Chula Vista, 91911. Tel: 619-425-3829. 4142 42nd St. #501, San Diego, 92105. Tel: 619-584-8221. 8150 Broadway #127, Lemon Grove, 91945. Tel: 619-462-3888.

LAKE SAN MARCOS. *Daughters of Mary and Joseph*, 1545 Via Brisa del Lago, 92069. Tel: 760-744-6578.

LEMON GROVE. *Mercedarian Sisters of the Blessed Sacrament*, 8171 Lemon Grove Way, 91945. Tel: 619-460-4271; Fax: 619-460-1060.
E-mail: smarilup@stjohncross.org
Sisters 5.

OCEANSIDE. *Sisters of the Precious Blood*, 4070 Mission Ave., 92057. Tel: 760-757-3250, Ext. 313.

PALA. *Sisters of St. Francis (Philadelphia)*, P.O. Box M, 92059. Tel: 760-742-1714. Sisters 3.

SAN YSIDRO. *Medical Missionaries of Mary*, 438 Blackshaw Ln., 92173. Tel: 619-690-9237; Fax: 619-428-9551.
E-mail: mmmsy@aol.com
Web site: www.mmmusa.org
Sisters 5.

Sister Servants of the Blessed Sacrament, 333 W. Park Ave., 92173. Tel: 619-428-1314. Sisters 11.

SPRING VALLEY. *Sisters of St. Joseph of Orange*, 10771 Del Rio Rd., 91978. Tel: 619-670-9663. Sisters 4.

VISTA. *Sisters of St. Clare*, Santa Clara, 1974 Cherrywood St., 92083. Tel: 760-597-0981; Fax: 760-597-0986. Sisters 2.

[J] SOCIAL SERVICES

SAN DIEGO.

Bayside Settlement House, 2202 Comstock St., 92111-6502. Tel: 858-278-0771; Fax: 858-278-6193. Grover Diemert, Exec. Dir. Total Assisted 8,200; Total Staff 15.

Catholic Charities, 349 Cedar St., 92101. Tel: 619-231-2828; Fax: 619-234-2272.
E-mail: srmduvall@ccdsd.org
Web site: www.ccdsd.org
Sr. RayMonda DuVall, C.H.S., Exec. Dir.
Emergency Services—Main Office: Tel: 619-231-2828. Michele Dunne, Dir., St. Francis Center—Vista. Tel: 760-631-2819.
Counseling Services. Peter McDade, Ph.D., Dir. Tel: 619-231-2828, Pregnancy, Parenting, and Adoption. Tel: 619-231-2828. Delia Sables, Dir., Refugee & Immigrant Services—San Diego. Tel: 619-287-9454. Dr. Robert Moser, Deputy Dir., La Posada de Guadalupe de Carlsbad. Tel: 619-929-2322. El Centro—Imperial Valley Services, 250 W. Orange, El Centro, 92243. Tel: 760-353-6822. Joe Silva, Deputy Dir., House of Hope—Imperial Valley, Emergency Shelter. Tel: 760-352-1182. Our Lady of Guadalupe Shelter. Tel: 760-357-2894.
Homeless Women's Services. Martha Ranson, Dir.

Rachel's Women's Center—San Diego. Tel: 619-696-0873. Women's Bean Project. Tel: 619-230-1151. Barbara Sage, Dir.

Joan of Arc Residence, 1510 Third Ave., 92101. Tel: 619-239-2663; Fax: 619-234-0202.
E-mail: agnesjofa@juno.com
Residence for Employed Young Women and College Students 18-60 Years. Sr. Agnes Bell, R.J.M., Supr. Religious 9; Permanent Residents 60; Capacity 71.

S.V.D.P. Management Inc., 3350 E St., 92102. Tel: 619-687-1000; Fax: 619-687-1010. Rev. Msgr. Joseph A. Carroll, Pres. Total Staff 85. Owns and manages the property for St. Vincent de Paul Village, Inc.; Fr. Joe's M.A.S.H. Village in Las Vegas, NV; Martha's Village & Kitchen in Indio, CA, and Toussaint Youth Villages in San Diego.

St. Vincent de Paul Village, 3350 E St., 92102-3332. Tel: 619-687-1000; Fax: 619-687-1010. Rev. Msgr. Joseph A. Carroll, Pres. Total Staff 400; Total Assisted Annually 162,540.

Joan Kroc Homeless Center, 1501 Imperial Ave., 92101. Tel: 619-687-1000; Fax: 619-687-1010. Mary Case, Vice Pres.

Bishop Maher Men's Center, 1501 Imperial Ave., 92101. Tel: 619-687-1000.

Josue AIDS Centers, 3350 E St., 92102. Tel: 619-466-4827.

Paul Mirabile Center—Mirabile Housing Inc., 1501 Imperial Ave., 92101. Tel: 619-233-8500.

Toussaint Teen Centers, 1404-5th St., 92101. Tel: 619-687-1080, Ext. 3399. Village Place, 32-17th St., 92102. Tel: 619-687-1000; Fax: 619-687-1010. 54 unit low to moderate apartments.

Thrift Stores, 815 33rd St., 92102. Tel: 619-687-1021; Fax: 619-687-1010. Keith MacKay, Vice Pres., Tom Dyke Ranch, Campo. Tel: 619-687-1315; Fax: 619-687-1010. Rev. Bill Metzdorf, Development Dir., 3350 E St., 92102. Tel: 619-687-1315; Fax: 619-687-1010.

[K] RETREATS

SAN DIEGO. *Spiritual Ministry Center*, 4822 Del Mar Ave., 92107-3407. Tel: 619-224-9444.

Whispering Winds Catholic Conference Center. 8186 Commercial St., La Mesa, 91942-2926. Tel: 619-464-1479; Fax: 619-464-4491.
E-mail: wwccc@aol.com
Don Kojis, Exec. Dir.

ALPINE. *La Providencia Spiritual Renewal Center*, 1510 Peutz Valley Rd., 91901-1223. Tel: 619-445-4570; Fax: 619-445-8289.
E-mail: laprovda@flash.net
Web site: www.laprov.org
Sr. Patricia Hanson, C.S.J.O.

DESCANSO. *Camp Oliver*. Summer Resident Camp for Girls & Boys, ages 6-16. Directed by Sisters of Social Service. (June-Aug.; Available Sept.-June for

rental groups). P.O. Box 712525, 2202 Comstock St., Ste. 2, San Diego, 92171. Tel: 858-492-9171; Fax: 858-874-2939.
E-mail: camp_oliver@yahoo.com
Web site: www.campoliver.com
David L. Kaplan, Exec. Dir.

OCEANSIDE. *Mission San Luis Rey Retreat*, 4050 Mission Ave., 92057-6402. Tel: 760-757-3659; Fax: 760-757-8025.
E-mail: slretreat@sanluisrey.org
Web site: www.sanluisrey.org
Revs. Ben R. Innes, O.F.M., Retreat Dir.; William Haney, O.F.M., Retreat Master & Guardian; Mel Bucher, O.F.M., Retreat Mgr.; Abraham Chiu, O.F.M., Assoc. Retreat Min.

Prince of Peace Retreat Center, 650 Benet Hill Rd., 92054. Tel: 760-430-1305; 1306; Fax: 760-967-8711.
E-mail: princeabby@aol.com
Web site: hometown.aol.com/princeabby/princeofpeaceabbey.html
Benedictine Fathers-Benet Hill. Bro. Meinrad Taylor, O.S.B., Guest Master.

PALA. *Pala Rey Youth Camp & Retreat Center*, 10779 Pala Rd., 92059. Tel: 760-742-8767. Mr. Roy Alvarado, Contact Person.

[L] NEWMAN CENTERS

SAN DIEGO. *Newman Center - SDSU*, 5855 Hardy Ave., 92115. Tel: 619-583-9181; Fax: 619-583-8925.
E-mail: cardnc1967@aol.com
Revs. Cesar Rubiano, C.J.M., Dir.; Ricardo Chinchilla, C.J.M.

University of California at San Diego (Campus Ministry). 9595 La Jolla Shores Dr., La Jolla, 92037. Tel: 858-452-1957 (Office); 455-6862 (Res.); Fax: 858-452-1957.
E-mail: cathcom@ucsd.edu
Web site: orpheus.ucsd.edu/csa
Revs. Cassian Lewinski, O.P., Dir.; Mark Padrez, O.P.

[M] MISCELLANEOUS

SAN DIEGO. *Catholic Committee on Scouting*, 3350 E St., 92102. Tel: 619-687-1000; Fax: 619-687-1010. Rev. Msgr. Joseph A. Carroll, Scout Chap.; Steve Rostart, Chm.

Central San Diego Magnificat, 5592 Gala St., 92120. Tel: 619-583-3389. Barbara Faucher, Coord.

Mercy Hospital Foundation, San Diego, 4077 Fifth Ave., 92103. Tel: 619-686-3836. Karen Stone, Exec. Vice Pres.

Pauline Book and Media Center, 5945 Balboa Ave., 92111. Tel: 858-565-9181; Fax: 858-565-9295.
E-mail: sandiego@pauline.org
Web site: www.pauline.org
Daughters of St. Paul. Sr. Armanda Santos, F.S.P., Supvr. Sisters 2.

SVDP Management, Inc., c/o Msgr. Joseph Carroll, 3350 E. St., 92102-1332. Tel: 619-687-1000; Fax: 619-687-1010.

EL CAJON.
Catholic Answers, Inc., 2020 Gillespie Way, 92020. Tel: 619-387-7200; Fax: 619-387-0042.
Web site: www.catholic.com
Karl Keating, Pres.

Kraemer Endowment Foundation, Inc., 2119 E. Madison Ave., 92019-1111. Tel: 619-584-4101; Fax: 858-292-2040.
E-mail: pavila@kraemerendowment.org
Web site: www.kraemerendowment.org

ESCONDIDO.
Benedictus, 8975-76 Lawrence Welk Dr., 92026. Tel: 760-751-8541; Fax: 760-751-8505.
E-mail: bendictus1@aol.com
Web site: www.stdismas.org
Deacon Kenneth J. Finn, Contact Person.

NILAND. *Immaculate Heart of Mary*, 19 Sixth St., 92257. Tel: 760-359-0464. Mailing Address: P.O. Box 238, Calipatria, 92233-0238.

RELIGIOUS INSTITUTES OF MEN REPRESENTED IN THE DIOCESE

For further details refer to the corresponding bracketed number in the Religious Institutes of Men or Women section.

[0140]—*The Augustinians*.—O.S.A.
[0200]—*Benedictine Monks*.—O.S.B.
[0270]—*Carmelite Fathers*.—O.Carm.
[1320]—*Clerics of St. Viator*.—C.S.V.
[0160]—*Clerics Regular of St. Paul*.—C.R.S.P.
[0450]—*Congregation of Jesus and Mary*.—C.J.M.
[1330]—*Congregation of the Mission*.—C.M.
[0520]—*Franciscan Friars*.—O.F.M.
[0650]—*Holy Ghost Fathers*.—C.S.Sp.
[]—*Holy Ghost Fathers of Ireland*.—C.S.Sp.
[0690]—*Jesuit Fathers and Brothers*.—S.J.
[0800]—*Maryknoll Fathers*.—M.M.
[1210]—*Missionaries of St. Charles (Scalabrinians)*.—C.S.
[0840]—*Missionary Servants of the Most Holy Trinity*.—S.T.
[0910]—*Oblates of Mary Immaculate*.—O.M.I.
[0430]—*Order of Preachers (Dominicans)*.—O.P.
[1030]—*Paulist Fathers*.—C.S.P.
[1260]—*Society of Christ*.—S.Ch.
[0370]—*Society of St. Columban*.—S.S.C.

RELIGIOUS INSTITUTES OF WOMEN REPRESENTED IN THE DIOCESE

[0100]—*Adorers of the Blood of Christ*.
[0230]—*Benedictine Sisters of Pontifical Jurisdiction*. (Glendora, CA; St. Joseph, MN).—O.S.B.
[0360]—*Carmelite Sisters of the Divine Heart of Jesus*.—Carmel.D.C.J.
[2020]—*Community of the Holy Spirit*.—C.H.S.
[1920]—*Congregation of the Sisters of the Holy Cross*.—C.S.C.
[1710]—*Congregation of the Third Order of St. Francis of Mary Immaculate, Joliet, IL*.—O.S.F.
[0790]—*Daughters of Divine Charity*.—F.D.C.
[0880]—*Daughters of Mary and Joseph*.—D.M.J.
[0420]—*Discalced Carmelite Nuns*.—O.C.D.
[1070-03]—*Dominican Sisters*.—O.P.
[1070-11]—*Dominican Sisters*.—O.P.
[1070-13]—*Dominican Sisters*.—O.P.
[1070-20]—*Dominican Sisters*.—O.P.
[1070-21]—*Dominican Sisters*.—O.P.
[]—*Franciscan Missionaries of Our Lady of Peace*.—M.F.P.
[1310]—*Franciscan Sisters of Little Falls, MN*.—O.S.F.
[1845]—*Guadalupan Missionaries of the Holy Spirit*.—M.G.Sp.S.
[2470]—*Maryknoll Sisters of St. Dominic*.—M.M.
[2490]—*Medical Mission Sisters*.—M.M.S.
[2480]—*Medical Missionaries of Mary*.—M.M.M.
[2590]—*Mercedarian Sisters of the Blessed Sacrament*.—H.M.S.S.
[2710]—*Missionaries of Charity*.—M.C.
[3070]—*North American Unions of Sisters of Our Lady of Charity*.—N.A.U.-O.L.C.
[3130]—*Our Lady of Victory Missionary Sisters*.—O.L.V.M.
[0950]—*Pious Society Daughters of St. Paul*.—F.S.P.
[3242]—*Poor Sisters of Nazareth*.—P.S.N.
[3450]—*Religious of Jesus and Mary*.—R.J.M.
[3449]—*Religious of the Incarnate Word*.—C.V.I.
[3465]—*Religious of the Sacred Heart of Mary*.—R.S.H.M.
[2970]—*School Sisters of Notre Dame*.—S.S.N.D.
[1680]—*School Sisters of St. Francis*.—O.S.F.
[0480]—*Sisters of Charity of Leavenworth, KS*.
[0520]—*Sisters of Charity of Our Lady, Mother of Mercy*.—S.C.M.M.
[0430]—*Sisters of Charity of the Blessed Virgin Mary*.—B.V.M.
[2360]—*Sisters of Loretto At the Foot of the Cross*.—S.L.
[2549]—*Sisters of Mercy of Ireland & U.S. Province*.—R.S.M.
[2575]—*Sisters of Mercy of The Americas*. (Burlingame, CA; Omaha, NE,).—R.S.M.
[1540]—*Sisters of Saint Francis, Clinton, Iowa*.—O.S.F.
[4080]—*Sisters of Social Service of Los Angeles, Inc*.—S.S.S.
[3770]—*Sisters of St. Clare*.—O.S.C.
[1705]—*The Sisters of St. Francis of Assisi*.—O.S.F.
[1630]—*Sisters of St. Francis of Penance and Christian Charity*.—O.S.F.
[1650]—*Sisters of St. Francis of Philadelphia*.—O.S.F.
[3830-03]—*Sisters of St. Joseph*. (Orange).—C.S.J.
[]—*Sisters of St. Joseph*. (Brentwood, NY).—C.S.J.
[3840]—*Sisters of St. Joseph of Carondelet*. (Los Angeles, CA; St. Louis, MO).—C.S.J.
[3890]—*Sisters of St. Joseph of Peace*. (Bellevue, WA).—C.S.J.P.
[]—*Sisters of St. Louis*.—S.S.L.
[1960]—*Sisters of the Holy Family*.—S.H.F.
[1990]—*Sisters of the Holy Names of Jesus and Mary*.—S.N.J.M.
[3260]—*Sisters of the Precious Blood (Dayton, Ohio)*.—C.PP.S.
[]—*Sisters of the Sacramental Heart of Jesus*.—H.C.J.S.
[1720]—*Sisters of the Third Order Regular of St. Francis of The Congregation of Our Lady of Lourdes*.—O.S.F.
[1490]—*Sisters of Third Franciscan Order*.—O.S.F.
[3499]—*Sisters Servants of the Blessed Sacrament*.—S.J.S.
[4060]—*Society of the Holy Child Jesus*.—S.H.C.J.
[4070]—*Society of the Sacred Heart*.—R.S.C.J.

DIOCESAN CEMETERIES

SAN DIEGO. *Holy Cross, El Campo, Mission San Diego de Alcala*.
DEL MAR. *Calvary*.
JACUMBA. 3 Indian Reservation cemeteries.
PALA INDIAN MISSIONS. 6 separate Indian burial grounds.
SAN LUIS REY. *Mission San Luis Rey*.
SANTA YSABEL INDIAN MISSIONS. 15 separate Indian burial grounds.

NECROLOGY

† Bauer, Paul, Chula Vista, CA St. Pius X. —Died March 30, 2000.
† Goce, Lauro, (Retired). —Died Sept. 8, 2000.
† McManus, Martin, (Retired). —Died March 28, 2000.
† O'Curneen, Hugh, (Retired). —Died April 19, 2000.
† Rhatigan, Rev. Msgr. John, (Retired). —Died Sept. 19, 2000.
† Smith, Michael, (Retired). —Died April 28, 2000.

Archdiocese of San Francisco

(Archidioecesis Sancti Francisci)

Most Reverend

WILLIAM J. LEVADA, S.T.D.

Archbishop of San Francisco; ordained December 20, 1961; appointed Titular Bishop of Capri and Auxiliary Bishop of Los Angeles March 29, 1983; Episcopal ordination May 12, 1983; appointed Archbishop of Portland in Oregon July 1, 1986; installed as Archbishop of Portland in Oregon September 21, 1986; appointed Coadjutor Archbishop of San Francisco August 17, 1995; succeeded to See December 27, 1995. *Office: 1 Peter Yorke Way, San Francisco, CA, 94109-6602.*

Most Reverend

JOHN R. QUINN, D.D.

Archbishop Emeritus of San Francisco; ordained July 19, 1953; appointed Auxiliary Bishop of San Diego and Titular Bishop of Thisiduo October 21, 1967; Episcopal ordination December 12, 1967; transferred to Oklahoma City and Tulsa November 18, 1971; appointed as Archbishop of the Archdiocese of Oklahoma City on February 6, 1973; appointed Archbishop of San Francisco February 22, 1977; installed as Archbishop of San Francisco April 26, 1977; resigned December 27, 1995.

Most Reverend

JOHN C. WESTER, D.D.

Auxiliary Bishop of San Francisco and Titular Bishop of Lamiggiga; ordained May 15, 1976; appointed June 30, 1998; Episcopal ordination September 18, 1998. *Office: 1 Peter Yorke Way, San Francisco, CA, 94109-6602.*

ESTABLISHED JULY 29, 1853.

Square Miles 1,012.

Legal Title: *The Roman Catholic Archbishop of San Francisco, a Corporation Sole.*

Code Address: *Roman, San Francisco.*

Comprises the Counties of San Francisco, San Mateo and Marin in the State of California.

PATRONS OF THE ARCHDIOCESE OF SAN FRANCISCO: St. Francis of Assisi, October 4; St. Patrick, March 17.

For legal titles of parishes and archdiocesan institutions, consult the Chancery Office.

The Chancery Office: 1 Peter Yorke Way, San Francisco, CA, 94109-6602. Tel.: 415-565-3600; Fax: 415-565-3678.

Web site address: www.sfarchdiocese.org

E-mail address: ezappia@sfarchdiocese.org

STATISTICAL OVERVIEW

Personnel	
Archbishop	1
Retired Archbishops	1
Auxiliary Bishops	1
Retired Bishops	1
Priests: Diocesan Active in Diocese	136
Priests: Active Outside Diocese	7
Priests: Diocesan in Foreign Missions	2
Priests: Retired, Sick or Absent	70
Number of Diocesan Priests	215
Religious Priests in Diocese	185
Extern Priests in Diocese	52
Ordinations:	
Diocesan Priests	1
Religious Priests	2
Permanent Deacons in Diocese	72
Total Brothers	45
Total Sisters	801
Parishes	
Parishes	90
With Resident Pastor:	
Resident Diocesan Priests	76
Resident Religious Priests	14
Missions	11
Pastoral Centers	5
Welfare	
Catholic Hospitals	3
Total Assisted	513,000
Homes for the Aged	13
Total Assisted	3,000
Residential Care of Children	16
Total Assisted	15,000
Day Care and Extended Day Care Centers	5
Total Assisted	363
Special Centers for Social Services	8
Total Assisted	16,500
Other Institutions	35
Total Assisted	788,000
Educational	
Seminaries, Diocesan	1
Students from This Diocese	8
Students from Other Diocese	95
Diocesan Students in Other Seminaries	6
Students Religious	4
Total Seminarians	14
Colleges and Universities	3
Total Students	11,098
High Schools, Diocesan and Parish	4
Total Students	3,666
High Schools, Private	10
Total Students	4,538
Elementary Schools, Diocesan and Parish	60
Total Students	18,004
Elementary Schools, Private	5
Total Students	1,849
Catechesis/Religious Education:	
High School Students	1,733
Elementary Students	15,572
Total Students Under Catholic Instruction	56,474
Teachers in the Diocese:	
Priests	43
Scholastics	1
Brothers	18
Sisters	39
Lay Teachers	1,436
Vital Statistics	
Receptions into the Church:	
Infant Baptism Totals	7,831
Adult Baptism Totals	611
Received into Full Communion	527
First Communions	5,312
Confirmations	3,245
Marriages:	
Catholic	1,347
Interfaith	522
Total Marriages	1,869
Deaths	3,063
Total Catholic Population	422,500
Total Population	1,760,000

Former Bishops—Rt. Rev. FRANCIS GARCIA DIEGO Y MORENO, O.F.M., D.D., cons. Bishop of both Californias, Oct. 4, 1840; died in Santa Barbara, April 30, 1846.—Most Rev. JOSEPH SADOC ALEMANY, O.P., D.D., cons. Bishop of Monterey, June 30, 1850; appt. first Archbishop of San Francisco, July 29, 1853; resigned and appt. Titular Archbishop of Pelusio, Dec. 28, 1884; died in Valencia, Spain, April 14, 1888.—Most Rev. PATRICK WILLIAM RIORDAN, D.D., cons. Titular Archbishop of Cabasa and appt. Coadjutor Archbishop of San Francisco *cum jure successionis* Sept. 16, 1883; succeeded to Dec. 28, 1884; died in San Francisco, Dec. 27, 1914.—Most Rev. GEORGE MONTGOMERY, D.D., cons. Titular Bishop of Tmui and appt. Coadjutor Bishop of Monterey and Los Angeles *cum jure successionis* April 8, 1894; succeeded to May 6, 1896; appt. Titular Archbishop of Osimo and Coadjutor Archbishop of San Francisco *cum jure successionis* March 27, 1903; died in San Francisco, Jan. 10, 1907.—Most Rev. EDWARD J. HANNA, D.D., cons. Titular Bishop of Titopolis and appt. Auxiliary Bishop of San Francisco Dec. 4, 1912; appt. Archbishop of San Francisco, June 1, 1915; resigned and appt. Titular Archbishop of Gortyna, March 2, 1935; died July 10, 1944.—Most Rev. JOHN JOSEPH MITTY, D.D., cons. Bishop of Salt Lake City, June 21, 1926; appt. Coadjutor Archbishop of San Francisco *cum jure successionis,* Jan. 29, 1932; succeeded to March 2, 1935; died Oct. 15, 1961.—Most Rev. JOSEPH T. MCGUCKEN, S.T.D., appt. Auxiliary of Los Angeles, Feb. 4, 1941; cons. Titular Bishop of Sanavo March 19, 1941; appt. Coadjutor Bishop of Sacramento *cum jure successionis,* Oct. 26, 1955; succeeded to Jan. 14, 1957; appt. Archbishop of San Francisco, Feb. 21, 1962; appt. Assistant at the Pontifical Throne, March 19, 1966; retired Feb. 22, 1977; died Oct. 26, 1983.—Most Rev. JOHN R. QUINN, appt. Auxiliary Bishop of San Diego, Oct. 21, 1967; cons.

Titular Bishop of Thisiduo, Dec. 12, 1967; transferred to Oklahoma City and Tulsa, Nov. 18, 1971; appt. Archbishop of the Archdiocese of Oklahoma City, Feb. 6, 1973; appt. Archbishop of San Francisco, April 26, 1977; resigned Dec. 27, 1995.

Chancery and Pastoral Center—One Peter Yorke Way, San Francisco, 94109-6602. Tel: 415-614-5500; Fax: 415-614-5555. Open Mon.-Fri. All applications for dispensations, faculties, etc., and all correspondence should be addressed: Chancery and Pastoral Center.

Vicar General, Vicar for Clergy and Moderator of the Curia—Most Rev. JOHN C. WESTER, V.G.

Administrative Assistant to the Bishop—ANNABELLE GROH. Tel: 415-614-5500; Fax: 415-614-5555.

Assistant to the Moderator of the Curia—Rev. DAVID M. PETTINGILL.

Director for Pastoral Ministry—Sr. M. ANTONIO HEAPHY, P.B.V.M.

Vicar for Administration—Rev. Msgr. HARRY G. SCHLITT. Tel: 415-614-5500; Fax: 415-614-5555.

Chancellor—Rev. Msgr. IGNATIUS C. WANG, J.C.D. Tel: 415-614-5500; Fax: 415-614-5555.

Vice Chancellor—Very Rev. MICHAEL PADAZINSKI, J.C.D.

Administrative Assistant to the Archbishop—Rev. Msgr. THOMAS S. MERSON.

College of Consultors—Most Rev. WILLIAM J. LEVADA; Most Rev. JOHN C. WESTER; Rev. Msgr. ROBERT W. MCELROY, V.G.; Rev. Msgr. JAMES P. MCKAY; Rev. Msgr. MAURICE M. MCCORMICK; Rev. ALBERT C. VUCINOVICH.

Deans—Rev. LAWRENCE GOODE, Deanery 1 (San Francisco); Rev. BRUCE A. DREIER, Deanery 2 (San Francisco); Rev. Msgr. JOHN O'CONNOR, Deanery 3 (San Francisco); Rev. DANIEL MCCOTTER, C.S.P., Deanery 4 (San Francisco); Rev. PETER J. SAMMON, Deanery 5 (San Francisco); Rev. RICHARD S. DEITCH, Deanery 6 (Marin County); Rev. THOMAS DALY, Deanery 7 (Marin County); Rev. EUGENE D. TUNGOL, Deanery 8 (San Mateo Co.); Rev. RENE GOMEZ, Deanery 9 (San Mateo Co.); Rev. ALBERT VUCINOVICH, Deanery 10 (San Mateo Co.); Rev. RANDOLPH R. CALVO, Deanery 11 (San Mateo Co.).

Council of Priests—Rev. LOUIS VITALE, O.F.M., Chm.; Mrs. MARY ELLEN HOFFMAN, Admin. Asst.

Censores Librorum—Rev. Msgr. WARREN HOLLERAN, S.T.D.; Revs. GERALD D. COLEMAN, S.S., S.T.L., Ph.D.; MILTON T. WALSH, S.T.D.

Metropolitan Tribunal

San Francisco Metropolitan Tribunal—One Peter Yorke Way, San Francisco, 94109-6602. Tel: 415-614-5500; Fax: 415-614-5555.

Judicial Vicar and Director—Very Rev. C. MICHAEL PADAZINSKI, J.C.D.

Adjutant Judicial Vicars—Revs. JOSE CHAVARIN, J.C.L.; STEPHEN A. MERIWETHER, J.C.L.

Associate Director of Tribunal—Sr. NANCY REYNOLDS, S.P., J.C.L.

Promoter of Justice—Rev. Msgr. RICHARD S. KNAPP.

Defenders of the Bond—Rev. GREGORY INGELS, J.C.D.

Judges—Sr. NANCY REYNOLDS, S.P., J.C.L.; Rev. Msgr. IGNATIUS WANG, J.C.D.; Revs. RANDOLPH R. CALVO, J.C.D.; WILLIAM E. DUGGAN, J.C.L.

Tribunal Auditors—Sr. RAYA HANLON, O.P.; Sr. BERNADETTE HESLIN, R.S.M.

Notaries and Secretaries to the Tribunal—REINA A. PARADA; MAUREEN DUNNE; SARAH B. GLEASON.

Department of the Moderator of the Curia

Moderator of the Curia—Most Rev. JOHN C. WESTER, V.G. Tel: 415-614-5500; Fax: 415-614-5555.

Archives—JEFFREY BURNS, Ph.D., Dir.; Rev. JOHN J. REILLY, Assoc. Dir.; Sr. CATHERINE ANN CURRY, P.B.V.M., Asst. Archivist, *320 Middlefield Rd., Menlo Park, 94025.* Tel: 650-328-6502; Fax: 650-322-0997.

Cemeteries, Office of—Mrs. KATHERINE ATKINSON, Dir., *P.O. Box 1577, Colma, 94014.* Tel: 650-756-2060; Fax: 650-994-8147.

Communications, Office of—Mr. MAURICE HEALY, Dir.

Ecumenism and Interreligious Affairs, Office of—Rev. P. GERARD O'ROURKE, Dir.

Mission Office—(San Francisco Society for the Propagation of the Faith and Holy Childhood Association); Rev. Msgr. IGNATIUS C. WANG, Dir.

Newspaper: "Catholic San Francisco"—Mr. PATRICK JOYCE, Editor.

Public Policy and Social Concerns, Office of—Mr. GEORGE WESOLEK, Dir.

Respect Life—KATHLEEN BUCKLEY.

Detention Ministry—Mr. RAY MCKEON.

Campaign for Human Development—GEORGE WESOLEK.

Department of the Vicar for Clergy

Vicar for Clergy—Most Rev. JOHN C. WESTER, V.G.; ANNABELLE GROH, Exec. Asst. EILEEN WAGNER, Admin. Asst. Tel: 415-614-5500; Fax: 415-614-5555.

Priests Personnel, Office of—Most Rev. JOHN C. WESTER, V.G.

Priests Personnel Board—Most Rev. JOHN C. WESTER, V.G., Chm.; Most Rev. WILLIAM J. LEVADA.

Vicar for Spanish Speaking—Rev. Msgr. JOSE RODRIGUEZ.

Clergy Education, Office of—Most Rev. JOHN C. WESTER, V.G.; ANDRITA TOSTANOSKI, Admin. Asst.

Permanent Diaconate, Office of—Deacon LEON KORTENKAMP, Dir.

Office of Formation for the Permanent Diaconate—Rev. GREGORY INGELS, J.C.D., Dir., *St. Patrick's Seminary, 320 Middlefield Rd., Menlo Park, 94025-3509.* Tel: 650-323-1703; Fax: 650-326-6870.

Vocations, Office of—Rev. CRAIG FORNER, Dir.

Vicar for Religious—Rev. ANDREW F. MAGINNIS, S.J.

Priests Retirement Board—Most Rev. JOHN C. WESTER, V.G., Chm.

Archbishop's Liaison to Retired Priests—

San Francisco County—Rev. Msgr. JAMES FLYNN, *St. Mary's Cathedral Rectory, 1111 Gough St., San Francisco, 94109.* Tel: 415-567-2020.

Marin County—Rev. WARREN WOODS, *Nazareth House, 245 Nova Albion Way, San Rafael, 94903.* Tel: 415-507-9497.

San Mateo County—Rev. WILLIAM WORNER, *Serra Clergy House, 455 W. 20th Ave., San Mateo, 94403.* Tel: 415-358-1572.

Department of the Vicar for Administration

Vicar for Administration—Rev. Msgr. HARRY G. SCHLITT. Tel: 415-614-5500; Fax: 415-614-5555.

Director of Finance / Chief Finance Officer—Mr. RICHARD P. HANNON.

Director of Real Estate—Mr. LES MCDONALD.

Director of Stewardship / Development—Mrs. JOANNE MAHER, Dir.

Director of Human Resources—Mr. CARL FEIL.

Legal Counsel—Mr. JACK M. HAMMEL, Esq.

Legal Counsel—Mr. JACK M. HAMMEL, Esq.

Pastoral Center Facilities Manager—Mr. LES MCDONALD.

Finance Council—Rev. Msgr. HARRY G. SCHLITT, V.G., Chm.; Mr. DONALD BAIRD; Mr. JAMES M. CORISTON; Rev. Msgr. BRUCE DREIER; Mr. ERNEST GO; Mrs. CECILIA HERBERT; Mr. RICHARD HANNON; Mr. JOHN HITCHCOCK, JR.; Deacon HENRY JACQUEMET, JR.; Mr. RAYMOND MARINO; Mr. DENNIS MCQUAID; Mr. JAMES P. MISCOLL; Deacon GARY WEST.

Investment Committee—Mrs. CECILIA HERBERT, Chm.; Rev. JACQUES DIDIER, M.E.P.; Mr. VICTOR BARRIOS; Mr. JOHN KELLER; Mr. PETER MAIER; Mr. I. P. SICOTTE, JR.; Mr. JAMES BUCKLEY; Mr. ROBERT C. BARRETT; Mr. RICHARD HANNON.

Building and Maintenance Committee—Rev. Msgr. JAMES P. MCKAY, Chm.; Rev. Msgr. HARRY G. SCHLITT; Mr. JAMES HAGEN; Mr. RICHARD HANNON; Mr. DONALD JUNKIN; Mr. BEN MURPHY; Mr. LES MCDONALD; Mr. STEVE KALPAKOFF; Ms. KATIE HALEY.

Real Estate Committee—Rev. Msgr. HARRY G. SCHLITT; Mr. DONALD BAIRD; Mr. JOHN A. CATTALINI; Mr. BILL HALEY; Mr. RICK HANNON; Mr. TERRENCE E. O'BRIEN; Mr. RALPH MARCHESE; Ms. KATIE HALEY; Mr. LES MCDONALD; Mr. JOHN WEINGARTNER.

Department of Pastoral Ministry

Director—Sr. M. ANTONIO HEAPHY, P.B.V.M. Tel: 415-614-5500; Fax: 415-614-5555.

Ethnic Ministries, Office of—Ms. NOEMI CASTILLO, Dir.

Chinese Ministry—Sr. MARIA HSU, Fd.CC., Coord.

Hispanic Ministry—Mrs. CECILIA ARIAS-RIVAS, Coord.

Japanese Mission—Mr. HARRY YASUMURA, Liaison, *St. Francis Xavier Church, 1801 Octavia St., San Francisco, 94109.* Tel: 415-346-7309.

Arab-American Roman Catholic Ministry—Rev. LABIB KOBTI, *St. Anne Church, 850 Judah St., San Francisco, 94122.* Tel: 415-564-3211; Fax: 415-665-1603.

Polish Mission and Croatian-Slovene Mission—Rev. CZESLAW RYBACKI, S.Ch., Coord., *245 Linden St., San Francisco, 94102.* Tel: 415-252-5799.

Korean Catholic Ministry—Rev. BARTHOLOMEO JAE IK YOON, Pastor, *32 Broad St., San Francisco, 94112.* Tel: 415-333-1194; Fax: 415-333-1196.

Tongan Ministry—Rev. SAIMONE MOALA, Coord., *St. Timothy Church, 1515 Dolan Ave., San Mateo, 94401.* Tel: 650-342-2470; Fax: 650-342-8156.

Vietnamese Catholic Ministry—Rev. TE VAN NGUYEN, Coord., *3240 Lawton St., San Francisco, 94122.* Tel: 415-759-4293; Fax: 415-664-9775.

Evangelization / Renew, Office of—Sr. ANTONIO HEAPHY, P.B.V.M., Dir.

Marriage and Family Life, Office of—CHRISTOPHER LYFORD, Dir.

Parish Life, Office of—Rev. DAVID M. PETTINGILL, Dir.

Religious Education & Youth Ministry, Office of—Sr. CELESTE ARBUCKLE, S.S.S., Dir. GRACE C. CASSETTA, Youth Ministry.

School of Pastoral Leadership—Rev. MICHAEL C. BARBER, S.J., Dir., *475 Eucalyptus Dr., San Francisco, 94132.* Tel: 415-242-9087; Fax: 415-242-9089.

Worship, Office of—Rev. JOHN TALESFORE, Dir.

Young Adult Ministry, Office of—Sr. CHRISTINE WILCOX, O.P.

Department of Catholic Schools

Superintendent—Sr. GLENN ANNE MCPHEE, O.P.; Mr. PAUL BERGEZ, Assoc. Supt. Devel. & Finance; Sr. MARIANNE VIANI, S.N.J.M., Assoc. Supt. Curriculum/School Improvement; LOIS BAUER, Asst. Supt. Administrative/Student Svcs. LARS LUND, Asst. Supt. for Faith Formation & Religion Curriculum; MARILYN LYNCH, Asst. Supt. for Personnel & Staff Devel. Tel: 415-614-5500; Fax: 415-614-5555.

Archdiocesan Board of Education—Most Rev. WILLIAM J. LEVADA. Chairmen: GERALYN O'MAHONEY; JOSEPH CRIVELLO; EDWARD CUNNINGHAM; GREGORY MYALL; DELIA PEREZ-SOLIS; RICHARD C. GIARDINA, Ph.D.; DEBRA RAMOS; ROBERT SULLIVAN; Rev. MARK TAHENY; JANET CASTAGNOLA SHAPIRO.

The Roman Catholic Welfare Corporation of San Francisco—Board of Directors: Most Rev. WILLIAM J. LEVADA, Pres.; Most Rev. JOHN C. WESTER, V.G.; Rev. Msgr. HARRY G. SCHLITT; Rev. Msgr. FRED A. BITANGA, SR.; Rev. Msgr. JOSE A. RODRIGUEZ; Rev. Msgr. JAMES H. MACDONALD; Rev. Msgr. IGNATIUS C. WANG, J.C.D.; Rev. RANDOLPH R. CALVO, J.C.D.; Mr. PAUL BERGEZ; Sr. GLENN ANNE MCPHEE, O.P.; Mr. RICHARD P. HANNON. Tel: 415-614-5500; Fax: 415-614-5555.

CLERGY, PARISHES, MISSIONS AND PAROCHIAL SCHOOLS

CITY OF SAN FRANCISCO
(San Francisco County)

1—CATHEDRAL OF ST. MARY (ASSUMPTION) (1891), Rev. Msgr. John J. O'Connor; Revs. Agnel De Heredia; Jean Pierre Boncilla; Rev. Msgr. James B. Flynn, (Retired); Deacon Peter Boulware. In res., Rev. Jose Chavarin.
Cathedral Office: 1111 Gough St., 94109. Tel: 415-567-2020; Fax: 415-567-2040.

2—ST. AGNES (1893), Revs. Russell J. Roide, S.J.; John Chandler, S.J.
Res., 1025 Masonic Ave., 94117. Tel: 415-487-8560; Fax: 415-487-8575.

3—ALL HALLOWS (1886). Closed. For sacramental records please contact Our Lady of Lourdes, San Francisco.

4—ST. ANNE (1904), Revs. Eduardo Dura; Dominic Savio Lee; Deacon John Dupre. In res., Rev. Msgr. Thomas S. Merson; Revs. Fidel Palisoc; Antonio Claudio.
Res., 850 Judah St., 94122. Tel: 415-665-1600; Fax: 415-665-1603.
School—1320 14th Ave., 94122. Tel: 415-664-7977; Fax: 415-661-6904.
Sisters 1; Lay Teachers 20; Students 575.
Catechesis / Religious Programs—Students 53.

5—ST. ANTHONY OF PADUA (1893), Revs. Ignatius DeGroot, O.F.M.; Robert Pfisterer, O.F.M.; Salvador Parisi, O.F.M.; Guglielmo Lauriola, O.F.M. In res., Revs. Floyd A. Lotito, O.F.M., Guardian; Anthony Baumann, O.F.M.; Finian McGinn, O.F.M.; Francisco Reyes, O.F.M.
Res., 3215 Cesar Chavez St., 94110. Tel: 415-647-2704; Fax: 415-647-7282.
School—St. Anthony-Immaculate Conception, 299 Precita Ave., 94110. Tel: 415-648-2008; Fax: 415-648-1825. Sr. Carol Ward, O.P., Prin.
Sisters 4; Lay Teachers 23; Students 515.
Chapel—Immaculate Conception Chapel. Under the care and administration of the pastor of St. Anthony of Padua parish. 3255 Folsom St., 94110. Tel: 415-824-1762; Fax: 415-824-0129.
Catechesis / Religious Programs—Tel: 415-641-2704.
Students 100.

6—ST. BENEDICT PARISH AT ST. FRANCIS XAVIER CHURCH (1913) (Japanese). (Founded 1962 for Deaf and Hearing Impaired). Rev. Daniel Adams.
Res., 1801 Octavia, 94109. Tel: 415-567-9855; 567-0438 (TDD); Fax: 415-567-0916.
Masses for the Hearing Impaired:—.
St. Anthony: 3500 Middlefield Rd., Menlo Park, 94025. Tel: 650-366-4692.; Marin Catholic High School: 675 Sir Francis Drake Blvd., Kentfield, 94904. Tel: 415-461-8844.
Catechesis / Religious Programs—Students 22.

7—ST. FRANCIS OF ASSISI CHURCH (1997). Closed. For sacramental records, please contact SS. Peter and Paul, San Francisco.

8—ST. BONIFACE (1860) (German), Rev. Louis Vitale, O.F.M.; Kate McMichael, Pastoral Assoc.; John-Francis Pepka, Admin. Pastoral Assocs.: Revs. Sergio Santos; Damian Gamboa, O.F.M.; John Luat Nguyen, O.F.M. In res., Revs. Joaquin Moreno, O.F.M., (Retired); Stephen Tan Nguyen, O.F.M.; Stephen Kain, O.F.M.; Richard Purcell, O.F.M.; Bros. Robert Brady, O.F.M.; Regan Chapman, O.F.M.; David Cobian, O.F.M.; Kelly Cullen, O.F.M.; Dennis Duffy, O.F.M.; Stephen Gillis, O.F.M.; Nicholas Ronalter, O.F.M.
Res., 133 Golden Gate Ave., 94102. Tel: 415-863-0111; Fax: 415-863-7602.
Catechesis/Religious Programs—Students 80.

9—ST. BRENDAN (1929), Revs. Thomas M. Parenti; William P. Crowley, C.S.Sp.; Gaudence Milambo, A.L.C.P. In res., Rev. John J. Talesfore.
Res., 29 Rockaway Ave., 94127. Tel: 415-681-4225; Fax: 415-681-3976.
School—234 Ulloa St., 94127. Tel: 415-731-2665; Fax: 415-731-7207.
Sisters of St. Dominic, Adrian, MI 2; Lay Teachers 21; Students 340.
Catechesis/Religious Programs—Tel: 415-664-8481.
Students 10.

10—ST. BRIGID (1863). Closed. For sacramental records please contact St. Vincent de Paul, San Francisco.

11—ST. CECILIA (1917), Revs. Michael D. Harriman; Lodovico Joseph Landi; Thuan Van Hoang. In res., Rev. Msgr. John T. Foudy; Rev. Heribert Duquet, M.E.P.
Res., 2555 17th Ave., 94116. Tel: 415-664-8481; Fax: 415-661-2957.
School—660 Vicente St., 94116. Tel: 415-731-8400; Fax: 415-731-5686.
Sisters of the Holy Names 4; Lay Teachers 17; Students 580.
Catechesis/Religious Programs—Students 100.

12—ST. CHARLES BORROMEO (1887), Rev. Msgr. Jose A. Rodriguez; Revs. Victorio Balagapo; Moises Agudo.
Res., 713 S. Van Ness Ave., 94110. Tel: 415-824-1700; Fax: 415-824-0844.
School—3250 18th St., 94110. Tel: 415-861-7652; Fax: 415-861-0221.
Dominican Sisters of the Most Holy Rosary (Philippines) 6; Lay Teachers 9; Students 298.
Catechesis/Religious Programs—Students 269.

13—CORPUS CHRISTI (1898), Revs. Thomas L. Juarez, S.D.B.; Armand Oliveri, S.D.B.; John O'Brien, S.D.B.; Aloysius Pestun, S.D.B.
Res., 62 Santa Rosa Ave., 94112. Tel: 415-585-2291; Fax: 415-585-0773.
School—75 Francis St., 94112. Tel: 415-587-7014; Fax: 415-587-1575.
Salesian Sisters of St. John Bosco (Daughters of Mary Help of Christians) 6; Lay Teachers 10; Students 307.
Catechesis/Religious Programs—Tel: 415-585-3240.
Students 250.

14—ST. DOMINIC (1873), Revs. Dominic R. Briese, O.P., Dir., Shrine of St. Jude; Xavier M. Lavagetto, O.P.; Steven Maekawa, O.P.; Bro. Mark Gorski, O.P., Pastoral Assoc.; Deacon Fred Swanson. In res., Very Rev. Thomas J. Hayes, O.P., Prior; Revs. Gregory H. Anderson, O.P.; Felix F. Cassidy, O.P.; Brian T. Mullady, O.P.; Samuel R. Parsons, O.P.; Paul Chrysostom Raftery, O.P.; Terence J. Reilly, O.P.; Gregory T. Tatum, O.P.; Bros. Gregory Lira, O.P.; Peter Yost, O.P.
Res., 2390 Bush St., 94115. Tel: 415-567-7824; Fax: 415-567-1608.
School—2445 Pine St., 94115. Tel: 415-346-9500; Fax: 415-346-8001.
Sisters of the Third Order of St. Dominic, Congregation of the Most Holy Name 4; Sisters of the Holy Names of Jesus and Mary 1; Lay Teachers 7; Students 274.
Catechesis/Religious Programs—Students 80.

15—ST. EDWARD (1916). Closed. For sacramental records please contact Star of the Sea, San Francisco.

16—ST. ELIZABETH (1912), Revs. Edwin W. Farrugia; Toan X. Nguyen; Edward Phelan.
Res., 449 Holyoke Ave., 94134. Tel: 415-468-0820; Fax: 415-468-1457.
School—450 Somerset St., 94134. Tel: 415-468-3247; Fax: 415-468-1804.
Lay Teachers 9; Students 295.
Catechesis/Religious Programs—Tel: 415-468-0423.
Students 103.

17—ST. EMYDIUS (1913), Revs. William J. Brady; David M. Pettingill; Deacon Noel Santillan.
Res., 286 Ashton Ave., 94112. Tel: 415-587-7066; Fax: 415-587-6690.
School—301 DeMontfort Ave., 94112. Tel: 415-333-4877; Fax: 415-333-3040. Miss Nell Jeffrey, Prin.
Lay Teachers 12; Students 183.
Catechesis/Religious Programs—Students 25.

18—CHURCH OF THE EPIPHANY (1914), Rev. Msgr. Bruce A. Dreier; Revs. Manuel Estrada; Charito Suan; Deacons Manuel Ocon; Ding Viray.
Res., 827 Vienna St., 94112. Tel: 415-333-7630; Fax: 415-333-1803.
School—600 Italy Ave., 94112. Tel: 415-337-4030; Fax: 415-337-8583.
Sisters 1; Lay Teachers 23; Students 625.
Catechesis/Religious Programs—Tel: 415-333-5051.
Students 89.

19—ST. FINN BARR (1926), Revs. Lawrence C. Goode; Anthony P. La Torre.
Res., 415 Edna St., 94112. Tel: 415-333-3627; Fax: 415-333-4090.
School—419 Hearst Ave., 94112. Tel: 415-333-1800; Fax: 415-452-0177.
Dominican Sisters of the Holy Rosary (Philippines) 6; Lay Teachers 12; Students 309.
Catechesis/Religious Programs—Students 37.

20—ST. FRANCIS OF ASSISI CHURCH. Closed. For sacramental records please contact SS. Peter and Paul, San Francisco.

21—ST. GABRIEL (1941), Revs. John A. Ryan; W. Paul O'Dell. In res., Rev. P. Gerard O'Rourke.
Res., 2559 40th Ave., 94116. Tel: 415-731-6161; Fax: 415-731-1270.
School—2550 41st Ave., 94116. Tel: 415-566-0314; Fax: 415-566-3223.
Lay Teachers 20; Students 479.
Catechesis/Religious Programs—Students 168.

22—HOLY CROSS (1887) (Korean). Closed. For sacramental records please contact St. Michael, San Francisco.

23—HOLY FAMILY CHINESE MISSION (1921) (Chinese). (aka St. Mary's Chinese Catholic Center—1903). Rev. Daniel E. McCotter, C.S.P.; Sr. Paulette Yueng, M.M., Pastoral Assoc., Teahouse Ministry; Ms. Lisa Tom French, Admin.
Res., 660 California St., 94108. Tel: 415-421-5636; Fax: 415-929-4698.
School—St. Mary Chinese Day School, 910 Broadway, 94133. Tel: 415-929-4690; Fax: 415-929-4699. Jerry DiNoto, Prin.
Sisters 4; Lay Teachers 16; Students 300.
Chinese Language School—Tel: 415-929-4694. Stephen Woon Wah Tang, Prin.
Chinese Teachers 15; Elementary Students 600; High School Students 50; Total Students 650.
Holy Family Association—Fax: 415-929-4698. Lance Hall, Pres.; Frances Hall, Pres.
Catechesis/Religious Programs—Students 40.

24—HOLY NAME OF JESUS (1925), Revs. Donald S. D'Angelo; Jesus Labor. In res., Rev. Msgr. Ignatius Wang; Rev. Te Van Nuyen; Deacon Dennis Rivera.
Res., 3240 Lawton St., 94122. Tel: 415-664-8590; Fax: 415-664-9775.
School—1560 40th Ave., 94122. Tel: 415-731-4077; Fax: 415-731-3328.
Sisters 2; Lay Teachers 30; Students 543.
Catechesis/Religious Programs—Students 41.

25—ST. IGNATIUS (1855), Revs. Charles R. Gagan, S.J.; Albert A. Grosskopf, S.J.; Thomas G. Piquado, S.J.; Robert McDevitt, S.J.
Res., 2170 Hayes St., 94117. Tel: 415-422-2188; Fax: 415-387-1867.

26—IMMACULATE CONCEPTION (1912) (Italian). Closed. For sacramental records please contact St. Anthony of Padua, San Francisco.

27—ST. JAMES (1888), Revs. Daniel E. Carter; Michael Greenwell, O.Carm.
Res., 1086 Guerrero St., 94110. Tel: 415-824-4232; Fax: 415-824-0605.
School—321 Fair Oaks St., 94110. Tel: 415-647-8972; Fax: 415-647-0166.
Lay Teachers 9; Students 225.
Catechesis/Religious Programs—Students 107.

28—ST. JOHN THE EVANGELIST (1893), Revs. James E. Myers, S.S.; Agustin M. Escalante; Sr. Louise O'Reilly, S.N.D., Pastoral Assoc.
Res., 19 St. Mary's Ave., 94112-1098. Tel: 415-334-4646; Fax: 415-334-0891.
Parish Center: 98 Bosworth St., 94112. Tel: 415-334-4646; Fax: 415-334-0891.
School—925 Chenery St., 94131. Tel: 415-584-8383; Fax: 415-584-8359.
Lay Teachers 8; Students 240.
Catechesis/Religious Programs—Students 85.

29—ST. JOHN OF GOD (1967), Rev. Labib Kobti; Deacon John Hutzler.
Res., 1290 Fifth Ave., 94122. Tel: 415-566-5610; Fax: 415-566-5073.
Catechesis/Religious Programs—Tel: 415-334-5655. Anne Donjacour, D.R.E.
Students 40.

30—ST. JOSEPH (1861). Closed. For sacramental records please contact St. Patrick, San Francisco.

31—ST. KEVIN (1922), Rev. Antonio Petilla.
Res., 704 Cortland Ave., 94110. Tel: 415-648-5751; Fax: 415-648-4441.
Catechesis/Religious Programs—Tel: 415-282-0277.
Students 134.

32—OLD ST. MARY'S CATHEDRAL (1854), Revs. Robert L. Pinkston, C.S.P.; Peter G. Shea, C.S.P. In res., Revs. Charles W. Albright, C.S.P., (Retired); Philip Cunningham, C.S.P., (Retired); Charles A. Donovan, C.S.P., (Retired); Thomas J. Dove, C.S.P., (Retired); Daniel E. McCotter, C.S.P.; John A. Carr, C.S.P., (Retired); Joseph M. Hanly, C.S.P., (Retired); Edward A. Maher, C.S.P., (Retired).
Res., 660 California St., 94108. Tel: 415-288-3800; Fax: 415-288-3838.

33—ST. MICHAEL KOREAN CHURCH (1898) (Korean), Rev. Bartholomeo Jae Ik Yoon.
Res., 32 Broad St., 94112. Tel: 415-333-1194; Fax: 415-333-1196.

34—MISSION DOLORES BASILICA (1776). (San Francisco de Asis). Rev. Msgr. Maurice M. McCormick; Rev. Gabriel Flores. In res., Revs. Ronald A. Burke, (Retired); Charles Onubogu; Deacon Vicente Cervantes.
Res., 3321 16th St., 94114. Tel: 415-621-8203; Fax: 415-621-2294. [CEM]
School—3371 16th St., 94114. Tel: 415-861-7673; Fax: 415-861-7620. Andreina Gualco, Prin.
Sisters 1; Lay Teachers 10; Students 259.
Catechesis/Religious Programs—Students 91.

35—ST. MONICA (1911), Rev. John L. Greene. In res., Revs. John Kavanaugh, (Retired); Didacus W. Ma, (Retired); Simeon Chang, (Retired); Paul Duggan, (Retired); Deacon John Carpenter.
Res., 470 24th Ave., 94121. Tel: 415-751-5275; Fax: 415-751-0440.
School—5920 Geary Blvd., 94121. Tel: 415-751-9564; Fax: 415-751-0781.
Sisters of the Blessed Virgin Mary 2; Lay Teachers 7; Students 261.
Catechesis/Religious Programs—Students 50.

36—MOST HOLY REDEEMER (1900), Rev. Zachary J. Shore. In res., Rev. William W. Young.
Res., 100 Diamond St., 94114-2414. Tel: 415-863-6259; Fax: 415-552-8786.

37—NATIVITY (1902) (Polish and Croatian-Slovene), Rev. Czeslaw Rybacki, S.Ch.
Res., 245 Linden St., 94102. Tel: 415-252-5799; Fax: 415-252-5799, Ext. 11.

38—NOTRE DAME DES VICTOIRES (1856) (French), Revs. Etienne Siffert, S.M.; Phillip d'Auby, S.M.; Bro. Joseph Grima, S.M., Pastoral Assoc.
Res., 566 Bush St., 94108. Tel: 415-397-0113; Fax: 415-397-3217.
School—659 Pine St., 94108. Tel: 415-421-0069; Fax: 415-421-1440. Mary K. Ghisolfo, Prin.
Sisters of St. Joseph of Orange 1; Lay Teachers 17; Students 275.
Catechesis/Religious Programs—Tel: 415-397-0113; Fax: 415-397-3217.
Students 45.

39—OUR LADY OF FATIMA BYZANTINE CATHOLIC CHURCH (1954). (The Eastern Catholic Center of San Francisco). Rev. Steven A. Armstrong, S.J.; Deacon Gerald F. Sondergaard.
Res., 101 20th Ave., 94121-1398. Tel: 415-752-2052; Fax: 415-752-6073.

40—OUR LADY OF GUADALUPE. Closed. For sacramental records please contact Church of the Visitation, San Francisco.

41—OUR LADY OF LOURDES (1942), Rev. Kirk Ullery.
Res., 1715 Oakdale Ave., 94124. Tel: 415-285-3377; Fax: 415-285-2191.
Catechesis/Religious Programs—Joint program with St. Paul of the Shipwreck.
Students 30.
Mission—San Francisco, San Francisco Co., All Hallows Chapel, 1400 Newhall St., 94124.

42—ST. PATRICK (1851), Rev. Msgr. Fred A. Bitanga; Revs. Henry J. Trainor; Raymund M. Reyes; Deacon Virgil Capati.
Res., 756 Mission St., 94103. Tel: 415-421-3730; Fax: 415-512-9730.
Catechesis/Religious Programs—Students 84.

43—ST. PAUL (1880), Revs. Mario P. Farana; Mamerto Sigaran; Mary Tan, Pastoral Assoc. In res., Rev. Msgr. Daniel R. Cahill, (Retired).
Res., 221 Valley St., 94131. Tel: 415-648-7538; Fax: 415-648-4740.
St. Paul Littlest Angel Pre-School—Tel: 415-824-5437; Fax: 415-824-5430. Ms. Peg Kayser, Prin.
Students 40.
School—St. Paul, 1690 Church St., 94131. Tel: 415-648-2055; Fax: 415-648-1920. Sr. Ann Cronin, B.V.M., Prin.
Sisters 1; Lay Teachers 9; Students 240.

Catechesis/Religious Programs—Tel: 415-826-4484.
Students 45.
Convent—312 29th St., 94131. Tel: 415-647-1889. Novitiate of the Missionaries of Charity

44—ST. PAUL OF THE SHIPWRECK (1915), Revs. John Heinz, O.F.M. Conv.; Paul Gawlowski, O.F.M.Conv.; Bros. Kevin Cushing, O.F.M.Conv.; George Cherrie, O.F.M.Conv.
Res., 3350 Jennings St., 94124. Tel: 415-468-3434; Fax: 415-468-1400.
School—St. Paul of the Shipwreck Catholic School, 1060 Key Ave. at Third St., 94124. Tel: 415-467-1798; Fax: 415-467-0569.
Lay Teachers 12; Students 190.
Catechesis/Religious Programs—Students 38.

45—ST. PETER (1867), Revs. Daniel J. Maguire; Francis MacPeck, S.J.; Jose Eduardo Mendoza; Deacons Roger Hernandez; David Gamarra; Nate Bacon. In res., Revs. Edmund M. Shipp; Zosimo C. Alvar, Jr.
Res., 1200 Florida St., 94110. Tel: 415-282-1652; Fax: 415-282-6097.
School—1266 Florida St., 94110. Tel: 415-647-8662; Fax: 415-647-4618. Vicki Butler, Prin.
Sisters 3; Lay Teachers 18; Students 530.
Catechesis/Religious Programs—Tel: 414-643-9885.
Students 375.

46—SS. PETER AND PAUL (1884) (Italian), Revs. David T. Purdy, S.D.B.; Salvatore Giacomini, S.D.B.; John Lam, S.D.B.; Jerry Bonjean, S.D.B.; Steve Whelan, S.D.B. In res., Revs. Austin Conterno, S.D.B.; Paul Maniscalco, S.D.B.; Michael Ribotta, S.D.B.; Gabriel J. Zavattaro, S.D.B.
Res., 666 Filbert St., 94133. Tel: 415-421-0809; Fax: 415-421-0217.
School—632 Filbert St., 94133. Tel: 415-421-5219; Fax: 415-421-1831. Sr. Sandra Neaves, F.M.A., Prin.
Salesian Sisters 5; Lay Teachers 15; Students 300.
Catechesis/Religious Programs—Students 45.

47—ST. PHILIP THE APOSTLE (1910), Rev. Michael J. Healy. In res., Revs. Brendan McBride; John P. Conley.
Res., 725 Diamond St., 94114. Tel: 415-282-0141; Fax: 415-282-8962.
School—665 Elizabeth St., 94114. Tel: 415-824-8467; Fax: 415-282-5746. Steven Farren, Prin.
Lay Teachers 10; Students 250.
Catechesis/Religious Programs—Students 250.

48—SACRED HEART (1885), Rev. Paulinus M. Mangesho, A.L.C.P.
Res., 546 Fillmore St., 94117. Tel: 415-861-5460; Fax: 415-861-7839.
School—735 Fell St., 94117. Tel: 415-621-8035; Fax: 415-861-7039. Mrs. Reese Fernandes, Prin.
Religious 1; Lay Teachers 8; Students 109.
Catechesis/Religious Programs—Students 16.

49—STAR OF THE SEA (1894), Rev. Msgr. Charles J. Durkin; Revs. Benedict Chang; Greg Aherne, S.J.
Res., 4420 Geary Blvd., 94118. Tel: 415-751-0450; Fax: 415-368-5651.
School—360 Ninth Ave., 94118. Tel: 415-221-8558; Fax: 415-221-7118. Sr. Rosemarie Carroll, C.S.J., Prin.
Sisters 4; Lay Teachers 6; Students 312.
Catechesis/Religious Programs—Tel: 415-831-6047.
Students 307.
Convent—4350 Geary Blvd., 94118. Tel: 415-752-6050. Sisters of St. Joseph of Carondelet

50—ST. STEPHEN (1950), Revs. Joseph R. Walsh; Paul F. Warren; Deacon Gary West. In res., Rev. Joseph P. O'Reilly.
Res., 601 Eucalyptus Dr., 94132.
Office: 451 Eucalyptus Dr., 94132. Tel: 415-681-2444; Fax: 415-681-7843.
School—401 Eucalyptus Dr., 94132. Tel: 415-664-8331; Fax: 415-242-5608. Sr. Paulina Simms, R.S.M., Prin.
Sisters of Mercy 2; Lay Teachers 10; Students 310.
Catechesis/Religious Programs—Cathy Collins, D.R.E.
Students 54.

51—ST. TERESA (1880), Rev. Peter J. Sammon. Pastoral Assocs.: Sr. Kathleen Healy, P.B.V.M.; Sr. Lucia Lodolo, P.B.V.M.; Deacon Charles Allen. In res., Rev. Edward K. Murray.
Res., 390 Missouri St., 94107. Tel: 415-285-5272; Fax: 415-285-8510.
Church—19th & Connecticut Sts., 94107.
Catechesis/Religious Programs—Students 47.

52—ST. THOMAS THE APOSTLE (1922), Revs. Kirby C. Hanson; Stanley Wu. In res., Rev. Francis Filice, (Retired).
Res., 3835 Balboa St., 94121. Tel: 415-387-5545; Fax: 415-221-0868.
School—3801 Balboa St., 94121. Tel: 415-221-2711; Fax: 415-221-8611.
Lay Teachers 10; Students 295.
Catechesis/Religious Programs—Students 5.

53—ST. THOMAS MORE (1950), Rev. Jerome P. Foley, Chap.
Res., 1300 Junipero Serra Blvd., 94132. Tel: 415-452-9634; Fax: 415-452-9653.

54—ST. VINCENT DE PAUL (1901), Revs. John K. Ring; William S. Myers; Benjamin A. Nombrado; Sr. M. Sheila Donegan, P.B.V.M., Pastoral Assoc., Dir. of Religious Formation.
Res., 2320 Green St., 94123. Tel: 415-922-1010; Fax: 415-922-7203.
School—2350 Green St., 94123. Tel: 415-346-0970; Fax: 415-346-0970. Ms. Barbara Harvey, Prin.
Lay Teachers 10; Students 253.

55—VISITACION, CHURCH OF THE (1907), Revs. Thomas L. Seagrave; Gabriel R. Flores, M.C.C.J.
Res., 655 Sunnydale Ave., 94134. Tel: 415-239-5950; Fax: 415-239-0538.
School—Our Lady of the Visitacion, 785 Sunnydale Ave., 94134. Tel: 415-239-7840. Sr. Lois Lapeyre, D.C., Prin.
Daughters of Charity of St. Vincent de Paul 4; Lay Teachers 7; Students 278.
Catechesis/Religious Programs—Tel: 415-239-6723.
Students 280.
Mission—Brisbane, San Mateo Co., Our Lady of Guadalupe, 285 Alvarado St., Brisbane, 94005.

OUTSIDE THE CITY OF SAN FRANCISCO

Belmont, San Mateo Co., Immaculate Heart of Mary (1947), Revs. James H. MacDonald; Joseph Healy. In res., Rev. Stephen H. Howell; Deacons Steven Hackett; Henry Jacquemet; Robert Kahn.
Res., 1040 Alameda de las Pulgas, 94002. Tel: 650-593-6157; Fax: 650-593-1665.
School—1000 Alameda de las Pulgas, 94002. Tel: 650-593-4265. Dr. Margaret Purcell, Prin.
Lay Teachers 12; Students 312.
Catechesis/Religious Programs—Mrs. Genny Pereira, D.R.E.
Students 356.

St. Mark (1965), Rev. Msgr. Floro B. Arcamo. In res., Revs. Miles O'Brien Riley; William J. Flanagan, Pastor Emeritus.
Res., 325 Marine View Ave., 94002. Tel: 650-591-5937; Fax: 650-591-7645.
Catechesis/Religious Programs—Tel: 650-591-7072.
Students 175.

Burlingame, San Mateo Co., St. Catherine of Siena (1908), Revs. Albert P. Vucinovich; Daniel Nascimento. In res., Revs. Frank Murray, (Retired); Joseph Bradley.
Res., 1310 Bayswater Ave., 94010. Tel: 650-344-6884; Fax: 650-344-1022.
School—1300 Bayswater Ave., 94010. Tel: 650-344-7176; Fax: 650-344-7426. Sr. Teresa J. Pallitto, M.S.C., Prin.
Sisters of the Sacred Side of Jesus 3; Lay Teachers 19; Students 322.
Catechesis/Religious Programs—Students 190.

Our Lady of Angels (1926), Revs. Gerald Barron, O.F.M.Cap.; Gregory Coiro, O.F.M.Cap.; John De La Riva, O.F.M.Cap.; Hung Nguyen, O.F.M.Cap. In res., Revs. Emilian Meade, O.F.M.Cap.; Eugene Ludwig, O.F.M.Cap.
Res., 1721 Hillside Dr., 94010. Tel: 650-347-7768; Fax: 650-347-3550.
School—1328 Cabrillo Ave., 94010. Tel: 650-343-9200; Fax: 650-343-5260. Carol Meshinsky, Prin.
Lay Teachers 18; Students 317.
Preschool—1341 Cortez Ave., 94010. Tel: 650-343-3115. Co-Directors: Theresa DeBarbrie; Sandy Sterling.
Lay Teachers 8; Students 95.
Catechesis/Religious Programs—Tel: 650-347-3671. Mrs. Kathryn Jones, D.R.E.
Students 490.

Colma, San Mateo Co., Holy Angels (1914), Revs. John J. Cloherty; Arturo Albano; Deacons John Ruiz; Lernito Prudenciado; Tony Paulino.
Res., 107 San Pedro Rd., 94014. Tel: 650-755-0478; Fax: 650-755-7653.
School—20 Reiner St., 94014. Tel: 650-755-0220.
Sisters 4; Lay Teachers 9; Students 311.
Catechesis/Religious Programs—Tel: 650-992-5539.
Students 487.

Daly City, San Mateo Co., St. Andrew (1968) (Filipino), Revs. Alex L. Legaspi; Francis Mark Ma. Garbo, M.M.H.C.
Church—1571 Southgate Ave., 94015. Tel: 650-756-3223; Fax: 650-756-0251.
Rectory: One Ridgefield Ave., 94015. Tel: 650-756-3223; Fax: 650-756-0251.
Catechesis/Religious Programs—Tel: 650-991-2937. Michele Bussey, D.R.E.
Students 390.

Our Lady of Mercy (Westlake) (1954), Revs. William E. Brown; William L. Vaughan.
Res., One Elmwood Dr., 94015. Tel: 650-755-2727; Fax: 650-755-6704.
School—7 Elmwood Dr., 94015. Tel: 650-756-3395; Fax: 650-756-5872. Arlene Fife, Prin.
Sisters 3; Lay Teachers 24; Students 620.
Catechesis/Religious Programs—Tel: 650-992-5769. Sr. Margie Aguilar, R.V.M., D.R.E.
Students 195.
Convent—15 Elmwood Dr., 94015. Religious of the Virgin Mary, Our Lady of Mercy

Our Lady of Perpetual Help (Westlake) (1925), Rev. Msgr. John R. Pernia; Rev. Aquino D. Padilla, Parochial Vicor; Deacon William Bruening.
Res., 60 Wellington Ave., 94014. Tel: 650-755-9786; Fax: 650-756-2268.
School—80 Wellington Ave., 94014. Tel: 650-755-4438. James Costello, Prin.
Religious 1; Lay Teachers 8; Students 320.
Catechesis/Religious Programs—Tel: 650-755-4010.
Students 312.

East Palo Alto, San Mateo Co., St. Francis of Assisi (1951), Rev. Joseph A. Gordon; Deacon Louis Dixon.
Res., 1425 Bay Rd., 94303. Tel: 650-322-2152; Fax: 650-322-7319.
Catechesis/Religious Programs—Tel: 650-325-6236.
Students 300.

Fairfax, Marin Co., St. Rita (1930), Rev. Robert P. Cipriano; Deacons Peter Kehrlein; William Turrentine. In res., Rev. Paul A. Perlite, (Retired).
Res., 100 Marinda Dr., 94930. Tel: 415-456-4815; Fax: 415-456-3677.
School—102 Marinda Dr., 94930. Tel: 415-456-1003; Fax: 415-456-7946. Jan Lovette, Prin.
Lay Teachers 12; Students 253.
Catechesis/Religious Programs—Tel: 415-456-1489.
Students 75.

Foster City, San Mateo Co., St. Luke (1970), Revs. John P. Penebsky; Jonathan Paala; Deacons Mar Tano; Paul Lucia.
Res., 1111 Beach Park Blvd., 94404. Tel: 650-345-6660; Fax: 650-345-8167.
Catechesis/Religious Programs—Tel: 650-574-9191; 650-573-7409.
Students 359.

Greenbrae, Marin Co., St. Sebastian (1951), Revs. Kenneth M. Westray; Paul E. Perry.
Res., 373 Bon Air Rd., 94904. Tel: 415-461-0704; Fax: 415-461-2018.
Catechesis/Religious Programs—Students 98.

Half Moon Bay, San Mateo Co., Our Lady of the Pillar (1868), Revs. Domingo Orimaco; Fabio Medina; John Bohrer; Deacon John McGhee.
Res., 400 Church St., 94019. Tel: 650-726-4674; Fax: 650-726-0980. [CEM]
Rectory: 696 North St., Pescadero, 94060.
Catechesis/Religious Programs—Tel: 650-726-5587. Sr. Teresa Walsh, C.S.J., D.R.E.
Students 494.
Mission—Pescadero, San Mateo Co., St. Anthony, P.O. Box 277, Pescadero, 94060. Tel: 650-879-0750. [CEM]
Mission—La Honda, San Mateo Co., Our Lady of Refuge, 146 Sears Ranch Rd., La Honda, 94060. Tel: 650-879-0750.

Lagunitas, Marin Co., St. Cecilia (1937), Rev. Joseph E. Richard.
Rectory: 450 West Cintura Ave., 94938.
Mailing Address: Box 289, 94938. Tel: 415-488-9799; Fax: 415-488-1963.
High School—Marin Catholic, 675 Sir Francis Drake Blvd., Kentfield, 94904. Tel: 415-461-8844; Fax: 415-461-7161.
Catechesis/Religious Programs—Students 20.
Mission—Nicasio, Marin Co., St. Mary, (1867) Town Square, 94946.

Larkspur, Marin Co., St. Patrick (1915), Rev. John D. Shanahan. In res., Rev. Joseph Eagan, S.J., (Retired).
Res., 114 King St., 94939. Tel: 415-924-0600; Fax: 415-924-3617.
School—120 King St., 94939. Tel: 415-924-0501; Fax: 415-924-3554. Ann Kalayjian, Prin.
Lay Teachers 9; Students 270.
Catechesis/Religious Programs—Students 150.

Menlo Park, San Mateo Co.,
1—ST. ANTHONY, (1951), Revs. James L. Garcia; Jose M. Corral; Rafael DeAvila, M.G.
Res., 3500 Middlefield Rd., 94025. Tel: 650-366-4692; Fax: 650-366-4135.
Catechesis/Religious Programs—Tel: 650-365-6071. Gladys Fields, D.R.E.
Students 750.
Mission—Redwood City, San Mateo Co., San Jose

Obrero (St. Joseph the Workman), 400 Heller St., Redwood City, 94063.

2—ST. DENIS, (1853; Restored 1961), Rev. Msgr. John F. Rodriguez.
Res., 2250 Avy Ave., 94025. Tel: 650-854-5976; Fax: 650-854-3754.
Mission—Portola Valley, San Mateo Co., Our Lady of the Wayside, (1902) 930 Portola Rd., 94028. Tel: 650-851-5085; Fax: 650-851-1019. Rev. George L. Thomas, Pastor Emeritus.
Catechesis/Religious Programs—Tel: 650-854-3754.
Students 452.

3—THE CHURCH OF THE NATIVITY, (1877), Revs. Stephen A. Meriwether; Steven E. Davies.
Res., 210 Oak Grove Ave., 94025. Tel: 650-323-7914; Fax: 650-323-3231.
School—1250 Laurel St., 94025. Tel: 650-325-7304; Fax: 650-325-3841.
Lay Teachers 11; Students 292.
Catechesis/Religious Programs—Tel: 650-327-2319. Sr. Carmel Silva, P.B.V.M., D.R.E.
Students 120.

4—ST. RAYMOND, (1950), Revs. Patrick T. Michaels; Edward A. Bohnert.
Office: 1100 Santa Cruz Ave., 94025. Tel: 650-323-1755; Fax: 650-323-3206.
Res., 1231 Arbor Rd., 94025. Tel: 650-321-1339.
School—1211 Arbor Rd., 94025. Tel: 650-322-2312; Fax: 650-322-2910. Sr. Ann Bernard O'Shea, C.S.J., Prin.
Sisters 3; Lay Teachers 15; Students 268.
Catechesis/Religious Programs—Tel: 650-323-6353; Fax: 650-323-3206. Sr. Rita McCloskey, D.R.E.
Students 110.

Millbrae, San Mateo Co., St. Dunstan (1940), Revs. Dermon Kavanagh, C.S.Sp.; Francis Mulloy, C.S.Sp.; Joseph Glynn, C.S.Sp. In res., Rev. William Doolin, C.S.Sp.
Res., 1133 Broadway, 94030. Tel: 650-697-4730; 650-697-4736; Fax: 650-697-5203.
School—1150 Magnolia Ave., 94030. Tel: 650-697-8119; Fax: 650-697-9295.
Lay Teachers 14; Students 311. Principals: Shirley Nussbaum; Sue Pallari.
Catechesis/Religious Programs—Tel: 650-697-7451. Sherre Leone, D.R.E.
Students 390.

Mill Valley, Marin Co., Our Lady of Mt. Carmel (1910), Revs. Joseph O'Connell; Francis Vi Tiso; Deacons Bruce Hall; Dick Enos. In res., Rev. Feliciano T. Mofan.
Res., 3 Oakdale Ave., 94941. Tel: 415-388-4190; Fax: 415-388-4197.

Novato, Marin Co., St. Anthony of Padua (1968), Revs. Kevin P. Gaffey; Brian L. Costello; Deacon Joseph Brumbaugh. In res., Rev. James E. O'Malley, (Retired).
Res., 1000 Cambridge St., 94947. Tel: 415-883-2177; Fax: 415-883-4049.
Catechesis/Religious Programs—Tel: 415-883-9000. D.R.E.: Judith Ann Ross; Marianne Iacobucci.
Students 450.

Our Lady of Loretto (1892), Revs. William McCain; Carlos Castillo (Costa Rica) Parochial Vicar; Deacon William Mitchell; Sr. Jeanette Lombardi, Pastoral Assoc. In res., Rev. Msgr. Richard Knapp, (Retired).
Res., 1806 Novato Blvd., 94947. Tel: 415-897-2171; Fax: 415-897-8251.
School—1811 Virginia Ave., 94947. Tel: 415-892-8621; Fax: 415-892-9631. Ms. Clare Menezes, Prin.
Lay Teachers 13; Students 260.
Catechesis/Religious Programs—Tel: 415-897-6714. D.R.E.: Betty McDonald; Michel Mangini.
Students 275.

Olema, Marin Co., Sacred Heart (1867), Rev. Richard C. Bain.
Res., 10189 State Route # 1, 94950.
Mailing Address: P.O. Box 70, 94950. Tel: 415-663-1139; Fax: 415-663-9660. [CEM]
Mission—Bolinas, Marin Co., St. Mary Magdalen.

Pacifica, San Mateo Co., Good Shepherd (1951), Rev. Piers M. Lahey; Sr. Carol Fleitz, S.N.J.M., Pastoral Assoc.
Res., 901 Oceana Blvd., 94044. Tel: 650-355-2593; Fax: 650-355-1832.
School—909 Oceana Blvd., 94044. Tel: 650-359-4544. Patricia Volan, Prin.
Lay Teachers 14; Students 341.
Catechesis/Religious Programs—Sr. Eleanor Maloney, S.N.J.M., D.R.E.
Students 369.

St. Peter (1956), Rev. Leonard J. Calegari; Deacon Peter Solan. In res., Most Rev. John C. Webster.
Res., 700 Oddstad Blvd., 94044. Tel: 650-359-6313; Fax: 650-359-2262.
Catechesis/Religious Programs—Tel: 650-359-5000. Mrs. Barbara Malone, D.R.E.
Students 584.

Portola Valley, San Mateo Co., Our Lady of the Wayside (1941). See St. Denis, Menlo Park.

Redwood City, San Mateo Co., Our Lady of Mount Carmel (1887), Revs. Randolph Calvo; David Ghiorso; Deacons Paul Moriarty; Thomas Boyle. In res., Rev. Msgr. William M. Roche, (Retired); Rev. Msgr. Dominique Desjardins (Ottawa) (Retired).
Res., 347 Grand St., 94062.
Parish Center—300 Fulton St., 94062. Tel: 650-366-3802; Fax: 650-366-1421.
School—301 Grand St., 94062. Tel: 650-366-6127; Fax: 650-366-0902.
Lay Teachers 12; Students 306.
Catechesis/Religious Programs—Tel: 650-368-8237.
Students 315.

St. Matthias (1961), Rev. John Glogowski; Deacon George Salinger.
Res., 1685 Cordilleras Rd., 94062. Tel: 650-366-9544; Fax: 650-366-4817.
St. Matthias Day Care Center—533 Canyon Rd., 94062. Tel: 650-367-1320; Fax: 650-366-1049.
Students 90.
Catechesis/Religious Programs—Tel: 650-366-7085.
Students 145.

St. Pius (1951), Rev. Msgr. Peter G. Armstrong; Rev. Ireneo Ramoso. In res., Rev. Msgr. James J. Haggarty; Revs. Anthony Chung; William Scanlon; Deacon Steve Michaelson.
Res., 1100 Woodside Rd., 94061. Tel: 650-361-1411; Fax: 650-369-3641.
School—Tel: 650-368-8327; Fax: 650-368-7031. Rita Carroll, Prin.
Lay Teachers 13; Students 313.
Catechesis/Religious Programs—Tel: 650-368-0429. Sr. Mary Keefe, D.R.E.
Students 195.

San Anselmo, Marin Co., St. Anselm (1907), Revs. Peter McDonald; Neal Healy; Deacons Bernard O'Halloran; Edward Cunningham. In res., Rev. Dennis McManus, C.S.Sp.
Res., Shady Ln. & Bolinas Ave., Ross, 94957. Tel: 415-453-2342; Fax: 415-453-8713.
Mailing Address: P.O. Box 1061, Ross, 94957.
School—40 Belle Ave., 94960. Tel: 415-454-8667; Fax: 415-454-4730. Odile Steel, Prin.
Lay Teachers 20; Students 264.
Catechesis/Religious Programs—Tel: 415-457-5910. Tom Kavanaugh, D.R.E.
Students 180.

San Bruno, San Mateo Co., St. Bruno (1912), Rev. Rene J. Gomez; Deacons Ramon De La Rosa; Joseph Lavulo. In res., Rev. Thomas Matthew.
Res., 555 San Bruno Ave. W., 94066. Tel: 650-588-2121; Fax: 650-588-6087.
Catechesis/Religious Programs—Tel: 650-588-4509. Mrs. Gloria Flores, D.R.E.
Students 316.

St. Robert (1958), Revs. Vincent D. Ring; James H. Morris; Mark V. Taheny; Deacon Rusty Duffey. In res., Rev. Joseph J. Marini, (Retired).
Res., 1380 Crystal Springs Rd., 94066. Tel: 650-589-2800; Fax: 650-588-3628.
School—345 Oak Ave., 94066. Tel: 650-583-5065; Fax: 650-583-1418.
Lay Teachers 14; Students 315.
Catechesis/Religious Programs—Tel: 650-588-0477.
Students 452.

San Carlos, San Mateo Co., St. Charles (1928), Revs. Kieran D. McCormick; Alwyn Furtado, C.S.Sp.; Sr. Pat Hunter, S.N.J.M., Pastoral Assoc.; Deacon Michael Young.
Res., 880 Tamarack Ave., 94070. Tel: 650-591-7349; Fax: 650-637-1968.
School—850 Tamarack Ave., 94070. Tel: 650-593-1629; Fax: 650-593-9723. Arlene B. Weidner, Prin.
Lay Teachers 15; Students 309.
Catechesis/Religious Programs—D.R.E.: Joanne Thompson; Georgia Moye.
Students 591.

San Mateo, San Mateo Co.,

1—ST. BARTHOLOMEW, (1955), Revs. Daniel T. Keohane; Tom Moran; Deacon John Sequeira. In res., Rev. George R. Meyer.
Res., 600 Columbia Dr., 94402. Tel: 650-347-0701; Fax: 650-347-2429.
Catechesis/Religious Programs—Fax: 650-347-3429. Karen Melko, D.R.E.
Students 490.

2—ST. GREGORY, (1941), Rev. Msgr. Robert W. McElroy; Revs. Joseph Pham Hung; Kevin Kennedy; Deacon Fred Iskander. In res., Rev. Msgr. Edward P. McTaggart, (Retired).
Res., 2715 Hacienda St., 94403. Tel: 650-345-8506; Fax: 650-345-9329.
School—2701 Hacienda St., 94403. Tel: 650-573-0111; Fax: 650-573-6548. Linda Grund, Prin.
Lay Teachers 10; Students 304.
Catechesis/Religious Programs—Tel: 650-574-8716.
Students 455.

3—ST. MATTHEW, (1863), Rev. Msgr. James McKay; Revs. William J. Ahlbach; Terence J. Horan; Lester Lezama.
Res., One Notre Dame Ave., 94402. Tel: 650-344-7622; Fax: 650-344-4830.
School—910 S. El Camino Real, 94402. Tel: 650-343-1373; Fax: 650-343-2046. Mr. Kenneth F. Boegel, Prin.
Lay Teachers 24; Students 545.
Catechesis/Religious Programs—Tel: 650-344-7622.
Students 378.

4—ST. TIMOTHY, (1954), Revs. Clifford A. Martin, Admin.; Jorge Roman del Real; Deacons Angel Aguilar; Nicolas Rodriguez; Faira Po'oi. In res., Revs. Craig Forner; Saimone Moala.
Res., 1515 Dolan Ave., 94401. Tel: 650-342-2468; Fax: 650-342-8156.
School—Tel: 650-342-6567; Fax: 650-342-5913. Mrs. Evelyn Nordberg, Prin.
Lay Teachers 10; Students 291.
Catechesis/Religious Programs—Tel: 650-579-0901. Mrs. Irl Bolin, D.R.E.
Students 275.

San Rafael, Marin Co.,

1—BLESSED SACRAMENT, (1951). Closed. For sacramental records please contact St. Isabella, San Rafael.

2—ST. ISABELLA, (Terra Linda) (1961), Revs. Michael J. Keane; Cyril O'Sullivan; Deacons Jerry Friedman, (Retired); James Myers. In res., Rev. William L. Knapp, (Retired).
Res., One Trinity Way, 94903.
Mailing Address: P.O. Box 6166, 94903. Tel: 415-479-1560; Fax: 415-479-8303. [CEM]
School—P.O. Box 6188, 94903. Tel: 415-479-3727. Cynthia Bergez, Prin.
Sisters 1; Lay Teachers 18; Students 275.
Catechesis/Religious Programs—Tel: 415-479-1222. Sharon Grant, D.R.E.
Students 483.

3—ST. RAPHAEL, (1817), Revs. Paul J. Rossi; Honesto DeGuzman Gile, Jr.; Julio Recio, O.P.
Res., 1104 Fifth Ave., 94901. Tel: 415-454-8141; Fax: 415-454-8193.
School—1100 Fifth Ave., 94901. Tel: 415-454-4455; Fax: 415-454-5927. Sr. Anne Marie Mullin, O.P., Prin.
Lay Teachers 20; Students 247.
Catechesis/Religious Programs—Tel: 415-459-7331; Fax: 415-454-8193.
Students 247.
Mission—San Rafael, Marin Co., St. Sylvester, 1115 Point San Pedro Rd., 94901.
Station—San Quentin, State Prison, Tel: 415-456-8161.

4—ST. SYLVESTER, (1961). Closed. For sacramental records please contact St. Raphael, San Rafael.

Sausalito, Marin Co., St. Mary Star of the Sea (1881), Rev. Richard S. Deitch. In res., Rev. Eugene F. Duggan, (Retired).
Res., 180 Harrison Ave., 94965. Tel: 415-332-1765; Fax: 415-332-4962.
Catechesis/Religious Programs—Students 15.

South San Francisco, San Mateo Co.,

1—ALL SOULS, (1913), Revs. William J. Justice; Santos Rodriguez; Deacon Alex Aragon.
Res., 315 Walnut Ave., 94080. Tel: 650-871-8944; Fax: 650-871-5806.
School—479 Miller Ave., 94080. Tel: 650-583-3562; Fax: 650-952-1167. Eileen Gorman, Prin.
Lay Teachers 11; Students 324.
Catechesis/Religious Programs—Tel: 650-873-5356. Dr. Alex Aragon, D.R.E.
Students 310.

2—MATER DOLOROSA, (1961), Revs. Hugh O'Donnell; Rolando A. Caverte. In res., Rev. C. Michael Padazinski.
Res., 307 Willow Ave., 94080. Tel: 650-583-4131; Fax: 650-761-2232.
School—1040 Miller Ave., 94080. Tel: 650-588-8175; Fax: 650-588-0426. William Kovacich, Prin.
Sisters 2; Lay Teachers 8; Students 268.
Catechesis/Religious Programs—Tel: 650-589-4448; Fax: 650-589-4448. Sr. Bernard Joseph, P.B.V.M., D.R.E.
Students 150.

3—ST. AUGUSTINE, (1970), Revs. Eugene D. Tungol; Jed Sumampong; Roberto Andrey; Deacons Robert Bertolani; Frank Almeida.
Res., 3700 Callan Blvd., 94080. Tel: 650-873-2282; Fax: 650-873-1356.

Catechesis/Religious Programs—Tel: 650-873-2878. Sr. Nona Barairo, D.R.E. Students 595.

4—St. Veronica, (1951), Revs. Wilton S. Smith; Lawrence Finegan; Deacons Roger Beaudry; Joseph LeBlanc. In res., Rev. Edward Cleary, (Retired).
Res., 434 Alida Way, 94080. Tel: 650-588-1455; Fax: 650-588-1481.
School—Tel: 650-589-3909; Fax: 650-589-2826. Joan Coleman, Prin.
Lay Teachers 13; Students 334.
Catechesis/Religious Programs—Tel: 650-871-5607. Sr. M. Julie O'Neill, B.V.M., D.R.E. Students 410.

Tiburon, Marin Co., St. Hilary (1951), Rev. James Tarantino; Deacon Joseph Borg. In res., Rev. Msgr. Francis A. Lacey, P.A., Pastor Emeritus.
Res., 761 Hilary Dr., 94920-1498. Tel: 415-435-1122; Fax: 415-435-1862.
School—765 Hilary Dr., 94920. Tel: 415-435-2224; Fax: 415-435-5895. Mrs. Theresa Canizzaro, Prin.
Lay Teachers 16; Students 278.
Catechesis/Religious Programs—Tel: 415-435-1639; Fax: 415-435-1639. Maryann Sztaba, D.R.E. Students 150.

Tomales, Marin Co., Church of the Assumption (1860), Rev. Robert K. White.
Res., 26825 Shoreline Hwy., 94971-0082. Tel: 707-878-2208; Fax: 707-878-2208. [CEM]
Mailing Address: P.O. Box 82, 94971-0082.
Catechesis/Religious Programs—Students 20.
Mission—Tomales, Marin Co., St. Helen, (1902) P.O. Box 82, 94971-0082.

Woodside, San Mateo Co., St. Marcella Mission. Closed. For sacramental records please contact St. Denis, Menlo Park.

Chaplains of Public Institutions

San Francisco. *Catholic Healthcare West/Bay Area Region*. Rev. Edward Smink, O.H., Dir. of Spiritual Care.
Kaiser Hospital San Francisco. Rev. Michael Greenwell, O.Carm.
Knights of Malta. The Sovereign Military Order of Malta (Western U.S.A. Association of the Sovereign Military Hospitaller Order of St. John of Jerusalem of Rhodes and of Malta—a Nonprofit Corporation). Rev. Msgr. Steven D. Otellini; Revs. Egon J. Javor, O.S.B.; John P. Kavanaugh; Milton T. Walsh.
Laguna Honda Home. Rev. Timothy Enright, C.S.Sp.; Deacon Pete Palimiano.
St. Anne's Home. Rev. Michael Strange, S.S.
St. Francis Hospital. Rev. Louis Vitale, O.F.M.
St. Mary's Medical Center. Revs. Michael Greenwell, O.Carm., Contact; Edward K. Murray.
St. Thomas More Society. (Lawyers). Rev. Jose Chavarin.
San Francisco Fire Department. Revs. John L. Greene; Geroge M. Twigg-Porter, S.J.
San Francisco General Hospital. Revs. Edmund M. Shipp; Zosimo C. Alvar, Jr.
San Francisco Police Department. Rev. Msgr. John P. Heaney; Rev. Msgr. Thomas A. Daly.
San Francisco State Univ., Newman Center. Rev. Jerome Foley.
Serra Club of San Francisco (Downtown). Rev. Craig Forner.
Serra Club of San Francisco (Golden Gate). Rev. Msgr. Edward P. McTaggart.
Young Ladies' Institute. Rev. Msgr. Edward P. McTaggart, Moderator-ACCW.
Youth Guidance Center. Rev. Daniel E. Carter.

Marin. *Serra Club of Marin*. Rev. Paul J. Rossi.

San Mateo. *Serra Club of San Mateo*. Rev. Msgr. James McKay.
Seton Medical Center. Deacon Richard J. Olsen.
Sheriff's Honor Camp and Medium Security Facility. Served by St. Vincent de Paul volunteers, Redwood City.

San Quentin. *California State Prison*. Rev. Denis McManus, C.S.Sp.

Special Assignment:
Most Rev.—
Wester, John C., Vicar General, Vicar for Clergy and Moderator of the Curia
Reverend Monsignors—
Holleran, J. Warren, St. Patrick Seminary
Merson, Thomas S., Admin. Asst. to the Archbishop
Otellini, Steven D., Pres., Marin Catholic High School
Schlitt, Harry G., Vicar for Adminstration
Wang, Ignatius, Dir. Propagation of the Faith & Chancellor
Reverend Fathers—
Bain, Richard C., Dir. Healing Ministry
Barber, Michael C., Dir. School of Pastoral Leadership
Bradley, Joseph, Chap. Junipero Serra High School, San Mateo
Brennan, Bernard, Chap. Ft. Mason
Chung, Anthony, Chap., Kaiser and Sequoia Hospitals, Redwood City
Daly, Thomas A., Marin Catholic High School, Kentfield & St. Vincent School for Boys, San Rafael
Foley, Jerome, Chap., San Francisco State University Newman Club
Forner, Craig, Vocations
Howell, Stephen H., Junipero Serra High School, San Mateo
Ingels, Gregory G., J.C.D., Dir. of Formation/Permanent Diaconate, Defender of the Bond
Madden, Thomas, Vallombrosa Center, Menlo Park
Murray, Edward K., Chap. St. Mary's Hospital, San Francisco
Murray, Francis, Chap. Kaiser and Sequoia Hospitals, Redwood City
Nguyen, Te Van, Coord., Vietnamese Ministry
O'Rourke, P. Gerard, Ecumenical & Interreligious Affairs
Padazinski, C. Michael, Judicial Vicar, Metropolitan Tribunal, San Francisco, Vice Chancellor
Pettingill, David M., Asst. to Moderator of the Curia
Riley, Miles O'Brien, Communications
Shipp, Edmund M., San Francisco General Hospital
Smith, Raymond K., Silver Penny Farm
Talesfore, John J., Dir., Office of Worship
Woods, Warren L., Nazareth House, San Rafael
Worner, William H., Serra Clergy House

On Duty Outside the Archdiocese:
Reverend Fathers—
Bravo, Joseph A., San Jose
Coleman, John, VA Hospital, Palo Alto
Ervin, Thomas, Los Angeles
Fredericks, James L., Loyola-Marymount, Los Angeles
Hagan, James, Mexico
Maguire, Anthony, NCCB
Ochylski, Ronald S., Society of St. Sulpice, Madrid, Spain
Smith, Raymond K., Silver Penny Farm, Petaluma
Trong, Joseph Nguyen, Diocese of Las Vegas

Absent on Leave:
Reverend Monsignors—
O'Shea, Patrick J.
Reverend Fathers—
Aylward, James W.
Balleza, John
Ervin, Thomas
Hoenisch, Richard
Kaylor, Lee
Leach, Jerome
Ludeman, Edward J.
Marks, Mark
Shipper, Carl A.

Retired:
Most Rev.—
Hurley, Mark J.
Quinn, John R.
Reverend Monsignors—
Cahill, Daniel R.
Flynn, James B.
Foudy, John T.
Gallagher, Eugene A.
Heaney, John P.
Keane, James P.
Kennedy, Edwin J.
Kennedy, Thomas I.
Kenny, John J.
Knapp, Richard
Lacey, Francis A., P.A.
McTaggart, Edward P.
Sullivan, Joseph P.
Reverend Fathers—
Atkins, James
Avila, Martin C.
Bitangjol, Albert P.
Burke, Ronald A.
Burns, Thomas J.
Chang, Simeon
Cleary, Edward M.
Davenport, Clement A.
Decker, Raymond G.
Duggan, Eugene F.
Duggan, Paul E.
Duggan, William E.
Filice, Francis P.
Flanagan, William J.
Greenlaw, Martin
Jaszovsky, Joseph
Jocson, Salvador
Kavanaugh, John P.
Keane, Patrick J.
Knapp, William L.
Lee, Anthony
Ma, Didacus W.
Marini, Joseph J.
McCarthy, Patrick P.
McDonnell, Donald C.
McElligott, Thomas J., Berkeley
Meyer, George R.
Mihovilovich, John B.
Murray, Francis
O'Connell, William A.
O'Malley, James E.
O'Reilly, Joseph P.
Ojeda, Filemon G.
Perlite, Paul A.
Piro, Frank R.
Pyne, Donald E.
Quinn, William P.
Raimondi, Michele
Reilly, John
Robello, Louis J.
Rodriguez, Guillermo
Stadler, Robert G.
Thomas, George L.
Ward, John J.
Worner, William H.
Wu, Stanley
Zohlen, Ray J.
Zoph, John L.

Permanent Deacons:
Aguilar, Angel, St. Timothy, San Mateo
Allen, Charles, St. Teresa, San Francisco
Almeida, Frank, St. Augustine, South San Francisco
Aragon, Alex, All Souls, South San Francisco
Ayalin, Romeo, St. Andrew, Daly City
Bacon, Nate, St. Peter, San Francisco
Beaudry, Roger, St. Veronica, South San Francisco
Bertolani, Robert, St. Augustine, South San Francisco
Borg, Joseph, St. Hilary Church, Tiburon
Boulware, Peter, St. Mary's Cathedral, San Francisco
Boyle, Thomas J., Our Lady of Mount Carmel, Redwood City
Bruening, William, Our Lady of Perpetual Help, Daly City
Brumbaugh, Joseph, St. Anthony of Padua, Novato
Buenavista, Tom
Capati, Virgil, St. Patrick, San Francisco
Carpenter, John, St. Monica, San Francisco
Cervantes, Vicente, Mission Dolores, San Francisco
Cunningham, Ed, St. Anselm, San Anselmo
DeLaRosa, Ramon, St. Bruno, San Bruno
Dixon, Louis, St. Francis of Assisi, East Palo Alto
Duffey, Rusty, St. Robert, San Bruno
Dupre, John, St. Anne, San Francisco
Enos, Richard, Our Lady of Mt. Carmel, Mill Valley
Friedman, Jerome, Nazareth House/St. Isabella, San Rafael
Gamarra, David, St. Peter, San Francisco
Hackett, Steven, Immaculate Heart of Mary, Belmont
Hall, J. Bruce, Our Lady of Mt. Carmel, Mill Valley
Hernandez, Roger, St. Peter, San Francisco
Holm, Russell, (Retired)
Hutzler, John, St. John of God, San Francisco
Ilao, Thomas, St. Finn Barr, San Francisco
Iskander, Fred, St. Gregory, San Mateo
Jacquemet, Henry, Immaculate Heart of Mary, Belmont
Kahn, Robert, Immaculate Heart of Mary, Belmont
Karp, Robert, (Retired)
Kehrlein, Peter, St. Rita, Fairfax
Kortenkamp, Leon, Dir., Permanent Diaconate
Lavulo, Joseph, St. Bruno, San Bruno
LeBlanc, Joseph, St. Veronica, South San Francisco
Lucia, Paul, St. Luke, Foster City
McGhee, John, Our Lady of Pillar, Half Moon Bay; Our Lady of Refuge, La Honda; St. Anthony Mission, Pescadero
McNeil, Chuck, Sacred Heart, San Francisco
Michaelson, Steven, St. Pius, Redwood City
Mitchell, William, Our Lady of Loretto, Novato
Moriarty, Paul K. (RIC), St. Vincent de Paul, San Francisco; Detention Ministry, San Mateo County
Myers, Jim, St. Isabella, San Rafael
O'Halloran, Bernard, St. Anselm, San Anselmo
Ocon, Manuel, Epiphany, San Francisco
Paulino, Tony, Holy Angels, Colma
Pelimiano, Pete, St. Augustine, South San Francisco
Peloso, Dominick, Church of the Nativity, Menlo Park
Po'oi, Faiva, St. Timothy, San Mateo
Prudenciado, Lernito, Holy Angels, Colma
Rivera, Dennis, Holy Name of Jesus, San Francisco
Rodriguez, Nicolas, St. Timothy, San Mateo

Rosen, Dan, St. Vincent de Paul, San Francisco
Ruiz, Juan, Holy Angels, Colma
Salinger, George, St. Matthias, Redwood City
Santillan, Noel, St. Emydius, San Francisco
Sequeira, John, St. Bartholomew, San Mateo
Solan, Peter, St. Peter, Pacifica
Solano, Jose, St. John the Evangelist, San Francisco
Sondergaard, Gerald, Our Lady of Fatima Byzantine Catholic, San Francisco
Swanson, Fred, St. Dominic, San Francisco
Tano, Mar, St. Luke, Foster City
Turrentine, William, St. Rita, Fairfax
Twitty, Roy, St. Catherine, Burlingame
Viray, Ricardo, Epiphany, San Francisco
West, Gary, St. Stephen, San Francisco
Young, Michael, St. Charles, San Carlos

INSTITUTIONS LOCATED IN THE ARCHDIOCESE

[A] SEMINARIES, ARCHDIOCESAN

MENLO PARK. *St. Patrick Seminary* (1898), 320 Middlefield Rd., 94025. Tel: 650-325-5621; 321-5655 (Library); Fax: 650-322-0997.
E-mail: info@stpatricksseminary.org
Web site: www.stpatricksseminary.org
Major Seminary of the Archdiocese of San Francisco, under the direction of the Society of St. Sulpice. Legal Title: *(1891, 1944): The Roman Catholic Seminary of San Francisco.* Most Rev. William J. Levada, Chancellor; Revs. Gerald D. Coleman, S.S., Ph.D., Pres. & Rector; James P. Oberle, S.S., Ph.D., Vice Rector; Milton T. Walsh, S.T.D., Academic Dean; James L. McKearney, S.S., Dean of Students; Thomas K. Diaz, M.A., Dir. Field Educ. & Pastoral Year; Dr. Cecil White, Ph.D., Librarian; Ms. Dorothy Tully, D.A., Registrar.
Faculty in Residence: Rev. Msgr. J. Warren Holleran, S.T.D.; Revs. Gerald D. Coleman, S.S., Ph.D.; Frederick J. Cwiekowski, S.S., S.T.D.; Robert V. Gavin, S.S.; James L. McKearney, S.S., M.S.; James P. Oberle, S.S., S.T.D., Dir. Spiritual Life Prog. & Dir. Recruitment; Martin D. Tran, S.S., S.T.D.; Milton T. Walsh, S.T.D. Priests 10; Religious 2; Lay Teachers 3; Students 102.

[B] SEMINARIES, RELIGIOUS OR SCHOLASTICATES

SAN FRANCISCO. *Capuchin House of Studies*, San Buenavista Friary, 750 Anza St., 94118. Tel: 415-387-7005. Revs. Julian Gonzalez-Montenegro, O.F.M.Cap., Guardian Instructor; James Stump, O.F.M.Cap; Bros. Francis Driscoll, O.F.M.Cap., Hospital Chap.; Mark Ortega, Instructor. Priests 4; Brothers 2.

[C] COLLEGES AND UNIVERSITIES

SAN FRANCISCO. *University of San Francisco*, 2130 Fulton St., 94117-1080. Tel: 415-422-5555; Fax: 415-422-2303
For a complete listing, refer to the Colleges and Universities section.

BELMONT. *College of Notre Dame*, 1500 Ralston Ave., 94002. Tel: 650-593-1601; Fax: 650-508-3736.
E-mail: gwhite@cnd.edu
Web site: www.cnd.edu
For a complete listing, refer to the Colleges and Universities section.

SAN RAFAEL. *Dominican University of California*, 50 Acacia Ave., 94901-2298. Tel: 415-457-4440; Fax: 415-485-3205.
E-mail: enroll@dominican.edu
Web site: www.dominican.edu
For a complete listing, refer to the Colleges and Universities section.

[D] HIGH SCHOOLS, ARCHDIOCESAN

SAN FRANCISCO. *Archbishop Riordan High School (Boys)*, 175 Phelan Ave., 94112. Tel: 415-586-8200; Fax: 415-587-1310.
E-mail: fr.tim.kenney@riordan.pvt.k12.ca.us
Web site: www.riordan.pvt.k12.ca.us
Rev. Timothy M. Kenney, S.M., Prin. Priests 3; Brothers 8; Lay Teachers 45; Students 700.

Sacred Heart Cathedral Preparatory (Coed), 1055 Ellis St., 94109. Tel: 415-775-6626; Fax: 415-931-6941.
E-mail: shcp.edu
John Scudder, Prin. Brothers 4; Sisters 2; Lay Teachers 76; Students 1,231.

KENTFIELD. *Marin Catholic College Preparatory (Coed)*, 675 Sir Francis Drake Blvd., 94904. Tel: 415-461-8844; Fax: 415-461-7161.
Web site: www.marincatholic.marin.k12.ca.us
Dr. Milton Werner, Prin.; Rev. Msgr. Steven D. Otellini, Pres.; Rev. Thomas A. Daly, Chap. In res. Rev. John J. Ward, (Retired). Priests 3; Franciscan Sisters 1; Lay Teachers 52; Students 760.

SAN MATEO. *Junipero Serra High School (Boys)*, 451 W. 20th Ave., 94403-1385. Tel: 650-345-8207; Fax: 650-573-6638.
E-mail: PADRES@SERRAHS.COM
Web site: www.serrahs.com
Rev. Stephen H. Howell, Pres.; Mr. C. Michael Peterson, Prin.; Rev. Joseph Bradley, Chap. Priests 2; Sisters 1; Lay Teachers 63; Students 975.

[E] HIGH SCHOOLS, PRIVATE

SAN FRANCISCO. *Immaculate Conception Academy, (Girls)*, 3625 24th St., 94110. Tel: 415-824-2052; Fax: 415-821-4677.
E-mail: ICA@ICACADEMY.ORG
Sr. Janice Therese Willington, O.P., Prin. Sisters 6; Lay Teachers 23; Students 244.

Mercy High School (Girls), 3250 19th Ave., 94132. Tel: 415-334-0525; Fax: 415-334-9726.
E-mail: DMcCrea138@aol.com
Web site: www.mercysf@mercyhs.org
Ms. Dorothy McCrea, Prin. Sisters 3; Lay Teachers 41; Students 580.

St. Ignatius College Preparatory (Coed), 2001 37th Ave., 94116. Tel: 415-731-7500; Fax: 415-731-9704.
Web site: www.siprep.org
Revs. Gregory M. Goethals, S.J., Supr.; Anthony P. Sauer, S.J., Pres.; Michael C. Barber, S.J.; Samuel P. Bellino, S.J.; Paul F. Capitolo, S.J.; Harry V. Carlin, S.J., Exec. Vice Pres.; Edward S. Fassett, S.J.; Charles A. Hofmann, S.J.; Gerald F. Hudson, S.J.; Michael J. Kotlanger, S.J.; Andrew F. Maginnis, S.J.; Gregory L. Miller, S.J.; Michael R. Moodie, S.J.; Ronald J. Sanfilippo, S.J.; Peter Kin Chung Siu, S.J.; A. Francis Stiegeler, S.J.; Theodore T. Taheny, S.J.; Warren J. Wright, S.J. Priests 18; Scholastics 1; Brothers 4; Lay Teachers 91; Students 1,414.

Schools of the Sacred Heart, Convent of the Sacred Heart High School (Girls), 2222 Broadway, 94115. Tel: 415-563-2900; Fax: 415-929-0553.
E-mail: heart@sacred.sf.ca.us
Web site: www.sacred.sf.ca.us
Pamela Hayes, Dir.; Mr. Douglas Grant, Head. Religious 1; Lay Teachers 32; Students 199.

Schools of the Sacred Heart, Stuart Hall High School. (Boys), 1715 Octavia St., 94109. Tel: 415-292-3193; Fax: 415-563-3005.
E-mail: heart@sacred.sf.ca.us
Web site: www.sacred.sf.ca.us
Pamela Hayes, Dir.; Mr. Gordon Sharafinski, Head. Lay Teachers 6; Students 44.

ATHERTON. *Sacred Heart Preparatory (Schools of the Sacred Heart Atherton) (Co-Ed)*, 150 Valparaiso, 94027. Tel: 650-322-1866; Fax: 650-322-7151.
Web site: www.shschools.org
Religious of the Sacred Heart. Joseph J. Ciancaglini, Ed.D., Dir. Schools; Mr. Richard Dioli, Prin. Religious 1; Lay Teachers 59; Students 448.

BELMONT. *Notre Dame High School (Girls)*, 1540 Ralston Ave., 94002. Tel: 650-595-1913; Fax: 650-595-2116.
E-mail: rgleason@ndhsb.org
Ms. Rita Gleason, Prin. Lay Teachers 53; Students 770.

BURLINGAME. *Mercy High School (Girls)*, 2750 Adeline Dr., 94010-5597. Tel: 650-343-3631; Fax: 650-343-2316.
E-mail: mercyhsb@aol.com
Sr. Rosann Fraher, R.S.M., Prin. Sisters 2; Lay Teachers 29; Students 446.

PORTOLA VALLEY. *Woodside Priory School.* (Coed, Boarding). 302 Portola Rd., 94028. Tel: 650-851-8221; Fax: 650-851-2839.
E-mail: woodsidepriory.com
Web site: www.woodsidepriory.com
Mr. Tim Molak, Headmaster. Priests 4; Brothers 1; Lay Teachers 41; Students 250. Legal Title: *Benedictine Fathers of the Priory, Inc.*

SAN ANSELMO. *San Domenico School.* (Grades 1-8, Coed; Grades 9-12, Girls. Boarding and Day Students.), 1500 Butterfield Rd., 94960-1099. Tel: 415-258-1990; Fax: 415-258-9197.
E-mail: mheersche@sandomenico.org
Web site: www.sandomenico.org
Mathew Heersche, Head of School; John Bowermaster, Upper School Prin. Chaplains 1; Lay Teachers 36; Students 143.

[F] ELEMENTARY SCHOOLS, ARCHDIOCESAN

SAN FRANCISCO. *St. Brigid Elementary School.* (Grades K-8), 2250 Franklin St., 94109. Tel: 415-673-4523; Fax: 415-674-4187.
E-mail: stbrigid@aimnet.com
Web site: www.stbrigidschool@best.com
Sr. Encarnacion Ortega, R.C.M., Prin. Sisters 4; Lay Teachers 14; Students 326.

St. Thomas More School. (Grades K-8), 50 St. Thomas More Way, 94132. Tel: 415-337-0100.
E-mail: StThomasMore@impresso.com
Web site: www.StThomasMore.com
Joseph T. Elsbernd, Prin. Lay Teachers 11; Students 325.

[G] ELEMENTARY SCHOOLS, PRIVATE

SAN FRANCISCO. *DeMarillac Middle School of San Francisco*, 133 Golden Gate Ave., 94102. Tel: 707-252-0222.
E-mail: staylor@dlso.org
Steve Taylor, Dir. Finance.

Schools of the Sacred Heart, Convent of the Sacred Heart Elementary School. (Grades K-8), 2222 Broadway, 94115. Tel: 415-563-2900; Fax: 415-563-0438.
E-mail: heart@sacred.sf.ca.us
Web site: www.sacred.sf.ca.us
Pamela Hayes, Dir.; Sr. Anne Wachter, R.S.C.J., Head..Sisters 1; Lay Teachers 37; Students 326.

Schools of the Sacred Heart, Stuart Hall For Boys. (Grades K-8), 2222 Broadway, 94115. Tel: 415-563-2900; Fax: 415-292-3165.
E-mail: heart@sacred.sf.ca.us
Web site: www.sacred.sf.ca.us
Schools of the Sacred Heart. Pamela Hayes, Dir.; Mr. Gerald Grossman, Headmaster. Sisters 1; Lay Teachers 51; Students 325.

ATHERTON. *St. Joseph's School.* (Grades PreK-8), 50 Emilie Ave., 94027. Tel: 650-322-9931; Fax: 650-322-7656.
Web site: www.shschools.org
Dr. Joseph Ciancaglini, Dir.; Mr. John Miller, Prin. Sisters 1; Lay Teachers 61; Students 518.

BELMONT. *C.N.D. Early Learning Center.* (Preschool), 1500 Ralston Ave., 94002. Tel: 650-508-3519; Fax: 650-508-3519. Sisters of Notre Dame de Namur. Antonia Werner, Dir. Lay Teachers 8; Children 81.

Notre Dame Elementary School, 1500 Ralston Ave., 94002. Tel: 650-591-2209; Fax: 650-591-4798.
Web site: www.belmont.gov/educ/ndes
Sr. Dolores Quigg, S.N.D.deN., Prin. Sisters 4; Lay Teachers 20; Students 261.

SAN ANSELMO. *San Domenico Early Education (PK-5) and Middle School (6-8)*, 1500 Butterfield Rd., 94960-1099. Tel: 415-258-1900; Fax: 415-258-1901.
E-mail: mheersche@sandomenico.org
Web site: www.sandomenico.org
Matthew Heersche, Head of School; Carole Chase, Primary School Prin. (PreK-5); Robert Lewis, Prin. Middle School (6-8). Sisters 2; Chaplains 1; Lay Teachers (Middle and Lower School) 38; (Early Education) 7; Students 419.

[H] ST. VINCENT DE PAUL SOCIETY

SAN FRANCISCO. *Society of St. Vincent de Paul Archdiocesan Council*, 1825 Mission St., 94103. Tel: 415-621-5314; Fax: 415-340-8568.
E-mail: vincent@vincent.org
Web site: www.vincent.org/
Deborah Payne, Pres.

San Francisco District Council of the St. Vincent de Paul Society, 425 Fourth St., 94107. Tel: 415-977-1270; Fax: 415-977-1271. Edward Dollard, Pres.; Louis Alessandria, Jr., Exec. Dir.

Thrift Store Pickups. Tel: 415-908-3656.

Vehicle Donations. Tel: 1-800-YES-SVDP.

Vehicle Donor Program. Tel: 415-977-1270, Ext. 3011. Jim Vlantis, Gift Admin.

Vincentian Villa, 1825 Mission St., 94103. Tel: 415-621-5305. Housing project for fixed income seniors and handicapped. Capacity 124.

Arlington Residence, 480 Ellis St., 94102. Tel: 415-673-9600. A safe and sober residential, low cost hotel for men and women in recovery. Rooms 171.

Ozanam Center, 1175 Howard St., 94103. Tel: 415-864-3057. Detox and counseling services for drop-in clients and 3-day stay.

Rosalie House, 3543 18th St. #4, 94110. Tel: 415-255-2894. An eight week emergency shelter for victims of domestic violence. Beds 20.

San Francisco Vincentian Life, 425 Fourth St., 94107. Tel: 415-977-1270, Ext. 3003. Steve Maraccini, Dir. Vincentian Life. Supports and develops membership of the Society through parish conferences and involvement in the programs.

South of Market Multi-Service Center, 525 Fifth St., 94107. Tel: 415-597-7970. A 24-hour shelter for homeless men, offering social, physical and counseling services. Beds 345.

Brennan House. Tel: 415-255-2894; 415-831-3535 (Crisis Hotline). Transitional housing program for the survivors of domestic violence. Program provides in-depth counseling, job rehabilitation, education, children's programs, and support groups. Beds 30.

Riley Center Community Office, 3543 18th St., #4, 94110. Tel: 415-552-2943. Provides drop-in counseling and follow up services for survivors of domestic abuse. Community outreach available.

San Francisco Vincentian Desk, 411 Fourth St., 94107. Tel: 415-977-1270, Ext. 3005. Sr. Mary Loretta, Contact. Homeless help desk.

SAN MATEO. *San Mateo County District Council*. Main Office, St. Vincent de Paul Society. 50 N. B St., 94401. Tel: 650-343-4405; Fax: 650-343-9495.
E-mail: svdpLM@yahoo.com
Web site: www.svdp.org
Joe Marchetti, Pres.; Lorraine Moriarty, Exec. Dir.; Loretta Pehanich, Dir. of Development & Pub. Rels.
Thrift Stores:
113 S. B St., 94401. Tel: 650-347-5101.
344 Grand Ave., South San Francisco, 94080. Tel: 650-589-8445; Fax: 650-244-0543.
6298 Mission St., Daly City, 94014. Tel: 650-992-9271.
2406 El Camino Real, Redwood City, 94063. Tel: 650-366-6367.
Thrift Store Pickups:
South San Francisco. Tel: 650-871-6844; Fax: 650-244-0543.
Tel: 650-342-1860.
Redwood City. Tel: 650-369-2837.

Vehicle Donation & Sales. Tel: 650-871-6844; Fax: 650-598-9150.

St. Vincent de Paul Dining Room at St. Francis of Assisi Church. Monday evenings 5-6:30pm, 1425 Bay Rd., East Palo Alto, 94303. Tel: 650-322-2152; Fax: 650-322-7319.

Services for the Incarcerated - Hope in Action Ministry, 50 N. B St., 94401. Tel: 650-366-9847; Fax: 650-343-9495. Deacon Paul Moriarty, Chap.

Homeless Services: Tel: 650-343-4405; Fax: 650-343-9495.

Central County. M-F, 10am-12noon, 50 N. B St., 94401. Tel: 650-343-4403; 650-343-9251; Fax: 650-343-9495.

North County. M-F, 10am-12noon, 344 Grand Ave., South San Francisco, 94080. Tel: 650-589-9039; Fax: 650-244-0543.

South County. M-F, 1:00pm-2:00pm, 2600 Middlefield Rd., Redwood City, 94063. Tel: 650-343-4403.

SAN RAFAEL. *St. Vincent de Paul Society Marin County District Council*, 820 B St., P.O. Box 150527, 94915. Tel: 415-454-3303; Fax: 415-454-3406. John R. Maurer, Pres.; Sr. Dorothea Ross, C.S.J., Exec. Dir.

St. Vincent de Paul Dining Room, 820 B St., 94901-3003. Tel: 415-454-0366; Fax: 415-454-3406.

Marin County Vincentian Desk, 820 B. St., 94915. Tel: 415-454-3303; Fax: 415-454-3406.

[I] DAY NURSERIES

SAN FRANCISCO. *Holy Family Day Home*, 299 Dolores St., 94103. Tel: 415-861-5361; Fax: 415-398-1925.
E-mail: ADMIN@holyfamilydayhome.org
Web site: www.holyfamilydayhome.org
Legal Title: *Holy Family Day Homes of San Francisco*. Donna M. Cahill, Exec. Dir. Religious 1; Lay Staff 27; Capacity 100.

[J] GENERAL HOSPITALS

SAN FRANCISCO. *St. Mary's Medical Center*, 450 Stanyan St., 94117. Tel: 415-668-1000; Fax: 415-750-5608
For a complete listing, refer to the Hospitals section.

DALY CITY. *Seton Medical Center*, 1900 Sullivan Ave., 94015-2229. Tel: 650-992-4000; Fax: 650-991-6024.
E-mail: MBaez@chw.edu
For a complete listing, refer to the Hospitals section.

MOSS BEACH. *Seton Medical Center Coastside*, 600 Marine Blvd., 94038. Tel: 650-563-7100; Fax: 650-728-5314.
E-mail: kinnerst@cww.edu
For a complete listing, refer to the Hospitals section.

[K] SENIOR CITIZEN RESIDENCES

SAN FRANCISCO. *Alexis Apartments of St. Patrick's Parish*, 390 Clementina St., 94103. Tel: 415-495-3690; Fax: 415-495-3629.
E-mail: alexisapts@aol.com
For a complete listing, refer to the Special Care Facilities section.

Home for the Aged of the Little Sisters of the Poor, St. Anne's Home, 300 Lake St., 94118. Tel: 415-751-6510; Fax: 415-751-0650
For a complete listing, refer to the Special Care Facilities section.

Madonna Residence, 350 Golden Gate Ave., 94102. Tel: 415-592-2864; Fax: 415-928-5867.
E-mail: CKoger@St.AnthonySF.org
For a complete listing, refer to the Special Care Facilities section.

Mercy Terrace Corporation Apartments, 333 Baker St., 94117. Tel: 415-931-2325; Fax: 415-931-7206.
E-mail: mercyterrace@msn.com
For a complete listing, refer to the Special Care Facilities section.

SAN RAFAEL. *Nazareth House*, 245 Nova Albion Way, 94903. Tel: 415-479-8282; Fax: 415-479-8824
For a complete listing, refer to the Special Care Facilities section.

[L] RESIDENTIAL GROUP HOMES

SAN FRANCISCO. *The Good Shepherd Gracenter*, 1310 Bacon St., 94134. Tel: 415-337-1938; Fax: 415-586-0355
For a complete listing, refer to the Special Care Facilities section.

Mount St. Joseph-St. Elizabeth, (1976) 100 Masonic Ave., 94118. Tel: 415-567-8370; Fax: 415-351-5531.
E-mail: sreileendc@aol.com
Web site: www.mountsjse.org
For a complete listing, refer to the Special Care Facilities section.

[M] RETREAT HOUSES

BURLINGAME. *Mercy Center, Spirituality and Conference Center*, 2300 Adeline Dr., 94010. Tel: 650-340-7474; Fax: 650-340-1299.
E-mail: mc@mercy-center.org
Web site: mercy-center.org
H. William Goehring, Exec. Dir.; Sr. Lorita Moffatt, R.S.M., Prog. Dir.; Rita Moser, Coord. of Guest Svcs.; Sue Thourson, Reservation Coord. Staff 21; Overnight capacity 90; Daytime use 300.

MENLO PARK. *Vallombrosa Center* (1946), 250 Oak Grove Ave., 94025. Tel: 650-325-5614; Fax: 650-325-0908.
E-mail: host@vallombrosa.org
Web site: www.vallombrosa.org
Rev. J. Thomas Madden, Live-in Dir. Legal Title: *Vallombrosa Center, Conference and Retreat Center of the Archdiocese of San Francisco*.

PETALUMA. *Silver Penny Farm Retreat Center*, 5215 Old Lakeville Rd., No. 1, 94954. Tel: 707-762-1498. Rev. Raymond K. Smith, Dir.

REDWOOD CITY. *Mount Alverno Conference and Retreat Center*, 3910 Bret Harte Dr., 94064-1028. Tel: 650-369-0798; Fax: 650-369-9358.
E-mail: info@mountalverno.com
Web site: www.mountalverno.com

SAN RAFAEL. *Santa Sabina Center*, 25 Magnolia, 94901. Tel: 415-457-7727; Fax: 415-457-2310.
E-mail: sntasabina@aol.com
Sr. Susannah Malarkey, O.P., Dir. Dominican Sisters Retreat and Conference Center.

[N] MONASTERIES AND RESIDENCES OF PRIESTS AND BROTHERS

SAN FRANCISCO. *Jesuit Community at St. Ignatius College Preparatory*, 2001 37th Ave., 94116-1165. Tel: 415-731-7500; Fax: 415-731-9408.
E-mail: postmaster@siprep.org
Revs. Michael C. Barber, S.J.; Samuel P. Bellino, S.J.; Paul F. Capitolo; Harry V. Carlin; Edward S. Fassett; Gregory M. Goethals; Charles A. Hofmann, S.J.; Gerald F. Hudson; Michael J. Kotlanger; Andrew Maginnis, S.J.; Michael R. Moodie, S.J.; Ronald J. Sanfilippo, S.J.; Anthony P. Sauer; Peter Kin Chung Siu, S.J.; A. Francis Stiegeler, S.J.; Theodore Tahney, S.J.; Warren J. Wright; Bros. Douglas E. Draper; Thomas J. Koller; Arthur W. Lee; John E. Maloney. Scholastics: Mr. Tien Nam, S.J. Priests 17; Brothers 4; Scholastics 1.

Jesuit Community at University of San Francisco. (Corporate Title: Jesuit Community at University of San Francisco), 2600 Turk Blvd., 94118-4347. Tel: 415-422-4200; Fax: 415-422-5651.
E-mail: treacyj@usfca.edu
Web site: www.usfca.edu/jesuit
Revs. John R. Treacy, S.J., Rector; Edward V. Stackpoole, S.J.; Joseph T. Angilella, S.J.; Francis J. Buckley, S.J.; Michael P. Caruso, S.J.; Albert Chan, S.J. (China); Denis E. Collins, S.J.; Geoffrey R. Dillon, S.J. (NO); Charles R. Gagan, S.J.; Donal Godfrey, S.J. (Ireland); Albert A. Grosskopf, S.J.; R. Daniel Kendall, S.J.; John P. Koeplin, S.J.; Fouis Libbey, S.J.; John J. Lo Schiavo, S.J.; Thomas M. Lucas, S.J.; Edwin J. McDermott, S.J.; Robert L. McDevitt, S.J.; Robert L. Niehoff, S.J. (ORE); Thomas G. Piquado, S.J.; Stephen A. Privett, S.J., Pres. University of San Francisco; David C. Robinson, S.J.; Vernon J. Ruland, S.J.; John D. Savard, S.J.; George E. Schultze, S.J.; Peter J. Togni, S.J.; Marioalberto A. Torres, S.J. (Puerto Rico); Bro. John Keck, S.J. Priests 27; Brothers 1.

Marianist Community, 175 Phelan Ave., 94112. Tel: 415-586-8082. Revs. Thomas French, S.M., Supr.; Timothy M. Kenney, S.M.; Joseph Hartzler, S.M.; Bros. Thomas Deasy, S.M.; Paul Fennelly, S.M.; John Haster, S.M.; Thomas Jalbert, S.M.; James Leahy, S.M.; Patrick McMahon, S.M.; Richard Olsen, S.M. Priests 2; Brothers 7.

Marist Center of the West. Atlanta Province of the Society of Mary (Marist), 625 Pine St., 94108-3210. Tel: 415-398-3543; Fax: 415-781-4937. Revs. James L. Pratt, S.M.; Patrick J. Coyle, S.M.; Francis Springer, S.M.; Nicholas Kutulas, S.M.; Edward C. Blee, S.M.; Juan Carranco, S.M.; Bros. Patrick Souza, S.M., Admin.; John Hunt, S.M. Priests 6; Brothers 2.

Maryknoll Fathers and Brothers, Catholic Foreign Mission Society of America, Inc., 2555 Webster St., 94115. Tel: 415-921-1100; Fax: 415-775-8261.
E-mail: mklsanfran@aol.com
Web site: www.maryknoll.org
Revs. Manuel J. Mejia, M.M., Dir.; Ralph F. Christman, M.M. Priests 2.

Paris Foreign Mission Society Residence, 930 Ashbury St., 94117. Tel: 415-664-6747; Fax: 415-564-5335. Revs. Jacques R. Didier, M.E.P., Dir.; Heribert Duquet, M.E.P. Priests 2.

St. Dominic Priory, 2390 Bush St., 94115-3124. Tel: 415-567-7824; Fax: 415-567-3360; 415-567-1608 (Parish).
Web site: www.stdominics.org
Very Rev. Thomas Hayes, O.P., Prior; Revs. Xavier Lavagetto, O.P., Pastor & Sub-Prior; Gregory H. Anderson, O.P.; Dominic R. Briese, O.P., Dir. Shrine of St. Jude; Felix F. Cassidy, O.P., Vicar of Prior; Steven Maekawa, O.P.; Samuel R. Parsons, O.P.; Paul Chrysostom Raftery, O.P.; Terence J. Reilly, O.P.; Gregory T. Tatum, O.P.; Bros. Mark A. Gorski, O.P.; Gregory R. Lira, O.P.; Peter A. Yost, O.P. In res. Rev. Brian T. Mullady, O.P. Priests 11; Brothers 3.

Salesian Provincial Residence, 1100 Franklin St., 94109. Tel: 415-441-7144; Fax: 415-563-5394.
E-mail: suosec@aol.com
Revs. Nicholas J. Reina, S.D.B., Prov.; Thomas Prendiville, S.D.B., Dir.; Bro. Richard Presenti, S.D.B., Prov. Treas.; Rev. Ralph Murphy, S.D.B. In res. Revs. Joseph Scanagatta, S.D.B.; Larry Lorenzoni, S.D.B.; Bernard Dabbene, S.D.B. Priests 7.
Military Chaplain: Rev. Robert Delis, S.D.B., 2172 S. Coast Hwy, Oceanside, 92054.

BURLINGAME. *Capuchin Provincial House*, 1345 Cortez Ave., 94010. Tel: 650-342-1489; Fax: 650-342-5664.
E-mail: ofmcap@aol.com
Revs. Ronald Talbott, O.F.M.Cap., Prov.; Enda Heffernan, O.F.M.Cap.; Richard Lopes, O.F.M.Cap.; Bertram Mulligan, O.F.M.Cap.; Miguel Angel Ortiz, O.F.M.Cap.; Camillus MacRory, O.F.M.Cap.; Flavian Welstead, O.F.M.Cap.; Bro. Peter Ciolino, O.F.M.Cap. Priests 7; Brothers 1.

DALY CITY. *Verbum Dei Missionary Fraternity*, 59 Risel St., 94014. Tel: 415-585-8804; Fax: 415-334-1593. Rev. Gerardo Flores, V.D.M.F. Priests 1.

PORTOLA VALLEY. *Woodside Priory*, 302 Portola Rd., 94028. Tel: 650-851-8220; Fax: 650-851-2839.
E-mail: mmager@woodsidepriory.com
Web site: www.woodsidepriory.com
Very Rev. Martin J. Mager, O.S.B., Supr.; Revs. Pius L. Horvath, O.S.B.; Egon J. Javor, O.S.B.; Maurus B. Nemeth, O.S.B.; Bro. Edward Englund. Priests 4; Brothers 1. Legal Title: *Benedictine Fathers of the Priory, Inc.*

[O] CONVENTS AND RESIDENCES FOR SISTERS

SAN FRANCISCO. *Carmelite Monastery of Cristo Rey, Discalced Carmelite Nuns*, 721 Parker Ave., 94118-4297. Tel: 415-387-2640; Fax: 415-751-5330. Mother Mary Joseph Chavez, O.C.D., Prioress. Professed Nuns 17.

Daughters of St. Paul, 46 Geary St., 94108. Tel: 415-781-5180; Fax: 415-781-1905.
E-mail: fspsanfran@aol.com
Web site: www.pauline.org
Sr. Mary Bernardine Sattler, F.S.P., Supr..Sisters 4.

Franciscan Missionaries of Our Lady of Peace, Our Lady of Guadalupe Convent, 46 Harrington St., 94112. Tel: 415-587-3729; Fax: 415-824-0605. Sr. Hilda Sandoval, Supr.

Monastery of Perpetual Adoration, Nuns of Perpetual Adoration, 771 Ashbury St., 94117. Tel: 415-566-2743; Fax: 415-564-4469. Mother Rosalba Vargas, A.P., Supr. Cloistered Nuns 20.

Presentation Convent, Motherhouse of the Sisters of the Presentation of B.V.M., 2340 Turk Blvd., 94118. Tel: 415-751-0406; Fax: 415-751-1932.
E-mail: admoffice@aol.com
Web site: www.presentationsistersf.org
Sr. Ann Therese Lynch, P.B.V.M., Acting Pres. Sisters in Archdiocese 65; Total in congregation 133.

St. Francis Convent of Mercy (Sisters of Mercy-Burlingame), 826 30th Ave., 94121. Sisters 3.

Sisters of Social Service, 1850 Ulloa St., 94116. Tel: 415-681-9219; Fax: 415-665-2471.
E-mail: SSSSF@earthlink.net
Web site: www.socialservicesisters.org
Sisters 3.

Sisters of St. Joseph of Orange, 544 Bush St., 94108. Tel: 415-398-7383.
E-mail: ndvsf@earthlink.net
Sisters 3.

Sisters of St. Joseph of Orange, 1737 Silliman St., 94134. Tel: 415-585-0159.
E-mail: csjsf@earthlink.net
Sisters 3.

Sisters of the Good Shepherd, 1310 Bacon St., 94134. Tel: 415-586-2822; Fax: 415-586-0355.
E-mail: rgssfca@aol.com
Sisters 8.

Sisters of the Holy Family, 174 Stanyan St. #2, 94118. Tel: 415-221-7704. Sisters 4.

Sisters of the Precious Blood, 326 Ewing Ter., 94118. Sisters 2.

Sisters of the Visitation of Japan, 604 Cabrillo St., 94118. Tel: 415-751-5067. Sisters 3. Serving the Archdiocese in Japanese Bible Study and visiting the elderly and sick.

Society of Helpers (Helpers of the Holy Souls), 855 Lincoln Way, 94122. Tel: 415-661-6316; Fax: 415-664-6827.
E-mail: VDONLON@JPS.NET
Sr. Veronica Donlon, Local Supr..Sisters 6.

Verbum Dei Missionary Fraternity. (Apostolic Institute: Instituto Apostolico Verbum Dei, Loeches, Madrid), 1239 Howard St., 94103. Tel: 415-863-4469; Fax: 415-863-4911.
E-mail: mverbumdei@aol.com
Prayer and ministry of the Word, working with youth, young adults & adults. Sr. Ellen Hess, V.D.M.F., Supr.; Sr. Raquel Mora, V.D.M.F.; Sr. Guadalupe Medrano, V.D.M.F.; Sr. Bella Rodas, V.D.M.F.; Sr. Julia Prinz, V.D.M.F.; Sr. Amelisa Hernandez, V.D.M.F.; Sr. Maria del Pilar Rodriguez, V.D.M.F.; Sr. Brenda Cerda, V.D.M.F.; Sr. Graciela Soto, V.D.M.F.; Sr. Cathriona O'Mahony, V.D.M.F.; Sr. Teresa Quirino, V.D.M.F.; Sr. Rose Marie Hastings, V.D.M.F.

ATHERTON. *Religious of the Sacred Heart Oakwood*, 140 Valparaiso Ave., 94027. Tel: 650-323-8343; Fax: 650-326-2251. Sr. Catherine Baxter, R.S.C.J., Dir. Sisters 37. Infirmary for elderly Religious of the Sacred Heart.

BURLINGAME. *Regional Community of the Sisters of Mercy of the Americas*, 2300 Adeline Dr., 94010-5599. Tel: 650-340-7410; Fax: 650-347-2550.
E-mail: sombur@aol.com
Web site: www.mercy.org.sisters
Sisters 56; Total in congregation 198; Total in Archdiocese 130.

DALY CITY. *Daughters of Charity of St. Vincent de Paul*, 2000 Sullivan Ave., 94015-2202. Sr. William Eileen Dunn, Supr.

Quinhon Missionary Sisters of the Holy Cross, 298 Southgate Ave., 94015. Tel: 650-992-1560.
E-mail: hocviendaly@hotmail.com
Sisters 17; Novices 10; Postulants & Aspirants 6.

Religious of the Virgin Mary, Our Lady of Mercy Convent, 15 Elmwood Dr., 94015. Tel: 650-992-5769; Fax: 650-756-3457. Sr. Olive Kingsbury, R.V.M., Contact Person.

MENLO PARK. *Corpus Christi Monastery*, 215 Oak Grove Ave., 94025-3249. Tel: 650-322-1801; Fax: 650-322-6816.
E-mail: nunsmenlo@aol.com
Web site: www.op/nunsmenlo
Nuns of the Order of Preachers. Sr. Mary of the Holy Family, Prioress. Cloistered Religious 18; Extern Sisters 2.

PACIFICA. *Missionaries of Charity*. (India), 164 Milagra Dr., 94044. Tel: 650-355-3091. Sisters 7. Noviciate, 312 29th St., San Francisco, 94131. Tel: 415-647-1889. Sisters 4; Novices 32. 55 Sadowa St., San Francisco, 94117. Tel: 415-566-3449; Fax: 415-586-3449. Sisters 4.

REDWOOD CITY. *Casa Chiara Community*, 3910 Bret Harte Dr., Box 685, 94064-0685. Tel: 650-366-3968.
E-mail: casachiara@juno.com
Mailing Address: P.O. Box 685, 94064-0685. Franciscan Sisters. Sisters 5.

Provincial House of the Sisters of St. Francis of Penance and Christian Charity, 3910 Bret Harte Dr., 94064. Tel: 650-369-1725; Fax: 650-369-0845.
E-mail: jamsie@juno.com
Mailing Address: P.O. Box 1028, 94064. Legal Titles: *Sisters of St. Francis-Mount Alverno.*; *Sisters of St. Francis Charitable Trust.* Sr. Maria Elena Martinez, O.S.F., Prov. Min. Sisters 18; Total in Province 100.

SAN RAFAEL. *Carmelite Monastery of the Mother of God, Discalced Carmelite Nuns*, 530 Blackstone Dr., 94093. Tel: 415-479-6872; Fax: 415-491-4964. Mother Anna Marie Vanni, O.C.D., Prioress. Sisters 6.

Dominican Sisters of San Rafael Generalate & Convent, 1520 Grand Ave., 94901-2236. Tel: 415-453-8303; Fax: 415-453-8367.
E-mail: patsimpsonop@juno.com
Web site: sanrafaelop.org
Sr. Patricia Simpson, O.P., Prioress Gen. Total in Community 147; Total in Archdiocese 88.

Dominican Convent, 1540 Grand Ave., 94901. Tel: 415-454-9221. Sisters 21.

Our Lady of Lourdes Convent (Infirmary), 77 Locust Ave., 94901. Tel: 415-457-3171. Sisters 25.

Our Lady of Mt. Carmel Convent, 34 Buena Vista Ave., Mill Valley, 94941. Tel: 415-389-0328. Sisters 6.

San Domenico Convent, 1500 Butterfield Rd., San Anselmo, 94960. Tel: 415-453-9172. Sisters 7.

St. Catherine of Siena Convent, 14 Roger Dr., 94901. Tel: 415-453-4330; Fax: 415-453-0844.

St. Margaret Convent, 40 Locust Ave., 94901. Tel: 415-458-2952. Sisters 8.

St. Dominic Convent, 2517 Pine St., San Francisco, 94115. Tel: 415-567-8282. Sisters 8.

St. Rose Convent, 2515 Pine St., San Francisco, 94115. Tel: 415-441-2685. Sisters 7.

SOUTH SAN FRANCISCO. *Holy Family Convent*, 381 Avalon Dr., 94080. Tel: 650-588-3471. Sisters 3.

TIBURON. *Society of the Holy Child Jesus*, 263 Diviso St., 94920. Sr. Sheila McNiff, S.H.C.J., Contact Person.

[P] CATHOLIC CHARITIES

SAN FRANCISCO. *Catholic Charities of the Archdiocese of San Francisco*, 2255 Hayes St., 94117. Tel: 415-592-9200; Fax: 415-592-9201.
Web site: www.ccasf.org
Mr. Brian Cahill, Interim Exec. Dir.; Mr. Terry Fuetsch, Interim Dir., Finance; Ms. D. Dooley, Interim Dir. Development; Ms. Rose Brown, Interim Dir., Human Resources.
MARIN BEHAVIORAL HEALTH CARE SERVICES.

Marin Counseling, 179 Los Ranchitos Rd., San Rafael, 94903. Tel: 415-499-1470, Ext. 24; Fax: 415-479-2667.
SAN MATEO BEHAVIORAL HEALTH CARE SERVICES. Tel: 650-579-0277.

Pregnancy Counseling / Adoption Services / Foster Care, 94103. Tel: 1-800-CARE-002 Hotline (statewide).

Grief Care, 2559 40th Ave., 94116. Tel: 415-564-7882; Fax: 415-731-1270.
CHILDREN AND FAMILY SERVICES. Bonita Davenport, Svc. Dir.

San Francisco Family Services, 240 Golden Gate Ave., 3rd Fl., 94102. Tel: 415-345-1290; Fax: 415-345-1280. Hearing Impaired, 1801 Octavia St., 94109. Tel: 415-749-3812; Fax: 415-567-0916.

Richmond Hills Family Center, 6324 Geary Blvd., 94121. Tel: 415-750-5080; Fax: 415-750-5085.

Guerrero House, 899 Guerrero St., 94110. Tel: 415-550-4478; Fax: 415-550-4481.

West Marin Social Services, 11315 State Rte. 1, Point Reyes Station, 94956. Tel: 415-663-1252; Fax: 415-663-1319.

Marin Family Services, 179 Los Ranchitos Rd., San Rafael, 94903. Tel: 415-499-1470, Ext. 14; Fax: 415-479-2667.
SOCIAL MINISTRY AND COMMUNITY OUTREACH:

Citizenship Services, 179 Los Ranchitos Rd., San Rafael, 94903. Tel: 415-499-1470; Fax: 415-479-2667.

St. Joseph's Village, 220 10th St., 94103. Tel: 415-575-4920; Fax: 415-575-4925.
HIV Community Housing and Services: Ms. Tiffany Mock-Goeman, Svc. Dir.

HIV Direct Services, 240 Golden Gate Ave., 3rd Fl., 94102. Tel: 415-345-9112; Fax: 415-345-1269.

Leland Avenue Project, 141 Leland Ave., 94134. Tel: 415-405-2000.

HIV Money Management, 240 Golden Gate Ave., 3rd Fl., 94102. Tel: 415-345-9112; Fax: 415-345-1269.

HIV Housing Services, 240 Golden Gate Ave., 3rd Fl., 94102. Tel: 415-345-9112; Fax: 415-345-1269.

Peter Claver Community, 1340 Golden Gate Ave., 94115. Tel: 415-749-3800; Fax: 415-563-3153.

Derek Silva Community, 1594 Market St., 94102. Tel: 415-553-8700; Fax: 415-575-3729.

HIV Food & Emergency Services, 600 Columbia Dr., San Mateo, 94402. Tel: 650-579-7490; Fax: 650-343-0413. 36 37th Ave., San Mateo, 94403. Tel: 650-295-2160.
AGING SERVICES: Bea Lopez, Dir.

San Francisco Senior Services, 2255 Hayes St., 4th Fl., 94117. Tel: 415-592-9200; Fax: 415-592-9201.

Meals on Wheels, 600 Columbia Dr., San Mateo, 94002. Tel: 650-295-2160.

Ombudsman, 600 Columbia Dr., San Mateo, 94402. Tel: 650-579-0277, Ext. 3312; Fax: 650-343-0413.

San Carlos Adult Day Care, 787 Walnut St., San Carlos, 94070. Tel: 650-595-9325; Fax: 650-593-2316.

Noriega Adult Day Support Center, 3601 Noriega St., 94122. Tel: 415-242-8015; Fax: 415-242-8017.

OMI Senior Center, 446 Randolph St., 94132. Tel: 415-587-1443; Fax: 415-586-7960.

Marin Senior Services, 179 Los Ranchitos, San Rafael, 94903. Tel: 415-499-1470, Ext. 16; Fax: 415-479-2667.

[Q] CATHOLIC YOUTH ORGANIZATIONS

SAN RAFAEL. *Catholic Youth Organization of the Archdiocese of San Francisco*. 98 Bosworth St., San Francisco, 94112. Tel: 415-406-2360; Fax: 415-406-2361. Mr. Brian Cahill, Exec. Dir.; Terry Fuetsch, CFO; Geraldine Dooley, Dir. of Devel.; Kent Eagleson, Dir. of Residential Svcs.; Steve Grant, Dir. of Facilities; Paula Raia, Dir. Outdoor Programs; Marie de Porres Taylor, Dir. of Community Based Svcs.; Marty Rea, Dir. of Transportation. Board of Trustees: Most Rev. William J. Levada, Pres.; Charles I. Daniels, Jr., Vice Pres.; Catherine J. Knopf, Sec.; Rev. Michael Harriman, Treas.; Deacon Henry Jacquemet, Asst. Treas.

CYO Archbishop McGucken Youth Retreat and Conference Center. Location of CYO Camp Armstrong, and CYO Caritas Creek Environmental Education Program, 2136 Bohemian Hwy., Occidental, 95465. Tel: 707-874-0210. Steve Grant, Dir. A 225 acre multi-use year-round facility providing the building and grounds for youth retreats, residential camping & environmental programs.

CYO Sports & Recreation. San Francisco Program: 98 Bosworth St., San Francisco, 94112. Tel: 415-406-2360; Fax: 415-406-2361.
Marin Program: 1 St. Vincent Dr., 94903. Tel: 415-507-4237. Provides a variety of organized team sports programs throughout the year for elementary school age children.

CYO Camp Armstrong, P.O. Box 188, Occidental, 95465. Tel: 707-874-0200. Paula Raia, Dir. Summer residential camp located at Archbishop McGucken Youth Center, serving children and youth 7-18 years of age.

CYO Creek Environmental Education Program, P.O. Box 188, Occidental, 95465. Tel: 707-874-0200. Paula Raia, Dir. A spiritually based environmental education program located at Archbishop McGucken Youth Center, serving children grades 5-8 from schools throughout the bay area. High School Juniors & Seniors participate in a teen leadership development program.

CYO Mission Day Care, 180 Fair Oaks St., San Francisco, 94110. Tel: 415-826-6880. Liliana Carnero-Rossi, Dir. Provides before and after-school care, summer day camps, and holiday recess camps for elementary school age children.

CYO San Francisco Boys and Girls Home, 1 St. Vincent Dr., 94903. Tel: 415-507-2000. Kent Eagleson, Exec. Dir. Since 1915, residential group homes located in San Francisco providing residential treatment, shelter care, transition care, special education and home-based services for emotionally, behaviorally, and educationally disadvantaged children ages 12-18. Referrals are made by juvenile courts through the Dept. of Social Services, Mental Health & school districts.

St. Vincent's School for Boys, 1 St. Vincent Dr., 94903. Tel: 415-507-2000. Mr. Kent Eagleson, Exec. Dir. Since 1855, residential group homes on a campus setting providing residential treatment, transition care, special education, and home-based services for emotionally, behaviorally, and educationally disadvantaged children ages 7-18. Referrals are made through Juvenile Courts through the Dept. of Social Services, Mental Health, and school districts.

CYO Transportation Services, 699 Serramonte Blvd., Ste. 210, Daly City, 94015. Tel: 650-757-2110. Martin Rea, Dir. Provides school bus transportation services for all CYO-related programs, parishes, and for other non-profit school and community organizations.

CYO / St. Vincent's Foster Family Agency, 1 St. Vincent Dr., 94903. Tel: 415-507-4387. Megan Chesnut, Dir. State licensed program recruits and supervises therapeutic foster homes for abused boys and girls ages 3-18. Homes are located in the North and East Bay Area. Children are served from throughout Northern California Specializes in children with behavior problems and in foster parent support.

CYO Family Based Crisis and Support Program, 1 St. Vincent Dr., 94903. Tel: 415-507-4269. Marie de Porres Taylor. Intensive in-home therapy to families where there is a risk of out of home placement for at least one child in the family due to a myriad of factors including abuse/neglect, delinquency, chemical dependency and other mental health issues. The goal of the program is to help families remain intact and to become empowered to more effectively confront their challenges, thus avoiding the profoundly traumatic effects of placement on children and families.

[R] NEWMAN CENTERS

SAN FRANCISCO. *Newman Center, San Francisco State University*, St. Thomas More Church, 1300 Junipero Serra Blvd., 94123. Tel: 415-452-9634; Fax: 415-452-9653.
E-mail: stmchurch@hotmail.com
Web site: www.rc.net/sanfrancisco/stm
Rev. Jerome P. Foley, Chap.; Sr. Christine Le, L.H.C., Admin.; Sr. Jacqueline Golden, S.N.D.deN., Pastoral Assoc.

Newman Center, University of California Medical Center, 1290 Fifth Ave., 94122. Tel: 415-566-5610; Fax: 415-566-5073.
E-mail: labibkobti@aol.com
Web site: www.sjog.org
Revs. Labib Kobti; James Stump, O.F.M.Cap.

[S] PERSONAL PRELATURES

SAN FRANCISCO. *Prelature of the Holy Cross and Opus Dei*, 765 14th Ave., 94118. Tel: 415-386-0431; Fax: 415-752-7177.
Web site: www.opusdei.org
Very Rev. George M. Rossman, Vicar for California; Revs. Torlach C. Delargy; John R. Meyer.
Other Priests in the Archdiocese: Rev. Matthew Bloomer.
Menlough Study Center, 1835 Bay Laurel, Menlo Park, 94025. Tel: 650-327-1675. Rev. Jose P. Ruisanchez.
Westwood Study Center, 108 Kipling Dr., Mill Valley, 94941. Tel: 415-388-4531.

[T] MISCELLANEOUS LISTINGS

SAN FRANCISCO.
All Hallows Community, Inc., c/o Mercy Services Corp., 1038 Howard St., 94103. Tel: 415-550-1637; Fax: 415-550-0306.
Apostleship of Prayer, 300 Lake St., 94118-1357. Tel: 415-831-0941; Fax: 415-751-1423. Rev. George M. Twigg-Porter, S.J., Dir.
Archdiocesan Council of Catholic Women, One Peter Yorke Way, 94109-6602. Tel: 415-614-5500; Fax: 415-353-5555. Rosemary Phelps, Pres.
Association of Ladies of Charity of St. Vincent de Paul, 2570 Ocean Ave., P.O. Box 194, 94132. Tel: 650-369-6287; Fax: 650-639-6290. Lauren Santucci, Pres. Tel: 650-592-2160; Linda Ramelot, Vice-Pres.; Nina Smith, Sec.; Hilda Barradas, Recording Sec.; Marilyn Christen, Treas.; Charlotte Kiesel, Founding Pres. The purpose of the Association is to make known the spirit of St. Vincent de Paul, St. Louise de Marillac and St. Elizabeth Ann Seton by performing corporal works of mercy for the poor and needy of the San Francisco Archdiocese.
California Handicapables, Inc. (1965), 1311 Montgomery St., 94133-3521. Tel: 415-781-1311; Fax: 415-576-1826.
E-mail: saltooley@aol.com
Miss Nadine Calligiuri, Founder; Sally Tooley, Treas. To give shut-ins and handicapped people of all faiths an opportunity for monthly Mass, lunch and general fellowship. We generally meet the third Saturday of every month at St. Mary's Cathedral, San Francisco. Please call for more information.
Catholic Healthcare West, 1700 Montgomery St., Ste. 300, 94111. Tel: 415-438-5500; Fax: 415-438-5726.
E-mail: cfinley@chw.edu
Web site: www.chw.edu
A nonprofit corporation. CHW is a multi-congregational Health System co-sponsored by the Auburn Regional Community of the Sisters of Mercy; the Burlingame Regional Community of the Sisters of Mercy; the Sisters of St. Dominic of the Congregation of the Most Holy Rosary, Adrian, MI; the Daughters of Charity of St. Vincent de Paul, Province of the West; the Sisters of the Third Order of St. Dominic, Congregation of the Most Holy Name, San Rafael, CA; the Congregation of the Sisters of St. Catherine of Siena of Kenosha, WI; Franciscan Sisters of the Sacred Heart of Frankfurt, IL; Sisters of St. Francis of Penance and Christian Charity of Redwood City, CA. There are several affiliated hospitals, retirement homes, long-term care facilities, and related corporations, located in California, Arizona, and Nevada. This organization provides centralized management and support functions for the following affiliated nonprofit organizations in the Archdiocese of San Francisco (other affiliates are listed in their respective dioceses): Catholic Healthcare West-Bay Area, which includes St. Mary's Medical Center, San Francisco; Seton Medical Center, Daly City; Seton Medical Center, Coastside, Moss Beach; Seton Health Services Foundation; St. Mary's Medical Center Foundation; Mercy Terrace Corporation; MSC Psychiatric Services Corporation; San Francisco Heart Institute.
Catholic Kolping Society, 440 Taraval St., 94116. William Taylor, Pres.; Catherine Vennemeyer, Treas.
Catholics for Truth & Justice, P.O. Box 26756, 94126-0756. Tel: 415-693-2TRU. Rev. John P. Penebsky, Chap.; Rev. Msgr. Harry Schlitt.
Charismatic Movement, Advisory Board, 2555 - 17th Ave., 94116. Tel: 415-664-8481; Fax: 415-661-2957.
E-mail: sfccr@sfspirit.com
Web site: sfspirit.com
Rev. L. Joseph Landi, Liason.
Equestrian Order of the Holy Sepulchre of Jerusalem - Northwest Lieutenancy, 3050 24th Ave., 94132. Tel: 415-664-6565; Fax: 415-664-5069. Albert E. Maggio, Honorary Lieutenant, 312 Clark Dr., San Mateo, 94107. Tel: 650-344-4452; Fax: 415-391-6070. Robert F. Begley, Lieutenant.
Father Raphael Piperni Charitable Trust, 1100 Franklin St., 94109. Tel: 415-441-7144; Fax: 415-441-7155.
E-mail: suosec@aol.com
(The FRPC (R) Trust).
Filipino Cursillo Secretariat, P.O. Box 881601, 94188-1601. Deacon Mar Tano, Spiritual Advisor.
Franciscan Friars of California, Provincial Office of Communications, 121 Golden Gate Ave., 94102-3809. Tel: 415-592-2740; Fax: 415-863-8240.
E-mail: falfonso@aol.com
Rev. Floyd A. Lotito, O.F.M., Dir.
Guadalupe Associates, Inc., 2515 McAllister St., 94118. Tel: 415-387-2324; Fax: 415-387-0896.
E-mail: info@ignatius.com
Web site: www.ignatius.com
Carolyn Lemon, Pres.; Anthony Ryan, CFO; Roxanne Mei Lum, Sec.
Italian Catholic Federation, 4420 Geary Blvd., 94118-3095. Tel: 415-751-0450. Rev. Msgr. Charles Durkin, Chap.
Jesuit Volunteer Corps: Southwest, 474 Valencia St. #230, 94103. Mailing Address: P.O. Box 40039, 94140. Tel: 415-522-1599; Fax: 415-522-1633.
E-mail: jvcsw@JesuitVolunteers.org
Web site: www.JesuitVolunteers.org
Mary Ashley, Exec. Dir.
Legion of Mary, 415 Edna St., 94112. Tel: 415-333-3627; Fax: 415-333-4090. Rev. Lawrence C. Goode, Dir.
Mercy / Charities Housing California, 1038 Howard St., 94103. Housing development for low-income families, elderly, and singles.
Mercy Family Plaza, c/o Mercy/Charities Housing California, 1038 Howard St., 94103. Thirty-six affordable units for families.
MSC Psychiatric Services. Provides certain psychiatric patient care services.
Mercy Terrace Corporation. Housing project for low- and moderate-income persons and families; also multi-services for residents and community.
Pauline Books & Media, 46 Geary St., 94108. Tel: 415-781-5180; Fax: 415-781-1905.
E-mail: fspsanfran@aol.com
Web site: www.pauline.org
Daughters of St. Paul. Sr. Mary Bernardine Sattler, F.S.P., Supr. Sisters 4.
Philip Rinaldi Charitable Trust, P.O. Box 640009, 94164-0009. Tel: 415-441-7144; Fax: 415-441-7155.
E-mail: suosec@aol.com
For the care of needy youth and for the formation needs of Salesians of St. John Bosco. Thomas Prendiville, Sec.
Religious Trust (RETA), Box 7443, 94120. Tel: 415-456-9300; Fax: 415-536-4002. A nonprofit multiple, religious employer health plan.
The Ricci Institute for Chinese-Western Cultural History at the Center for the Pacific Rim, University of San Francisco, 2130 Fulton St., 94117-1080. Tel: 415-422-6401; Fax: 415-422-2291.
E-mail: ricci@usfca.edu
Web site: www.usfca.edu/ricci
Xiaoxin Wu, Ed.D., Dir.; Rev. Albert Chan, S.J., Ph.D., Senior Research Fellow; Monica Chang, Asst. Dir.; Mark Mir, Research Fellow and Chinese Library Cataloguer; May Lee, Sec.
St. Anthony Foundation, 121 Golden Gate Ave., 94102. Tel: 415-241-2600; Fax: 415-252-1635.
E-mail: info@stanthonysf.org
Web site: www.stanthonysf.org
Sr. Patrick Curran, R.S.M., Exec. Dir.; Revs. Dan Lackie, O.F.M., Chap.; Floyd Lotito, O.F.M., Consultant. A nonprofit, charitable corporation assisting the homeless and low-income.
St. Benedict Center for Deaf and Hearing Impaired at St. Francis Xavier Church. Res., 1801 Octavia, 94109. Tel: 415-567-9855; 415-567-0438 (TDD); Fax: 415-567-0916.
Masses for the Hearing Impaired. Tel: 415-567-0438 (TDD); Fax: 415-567-0916.
St. Anthony. 3500 Middlefield Rd., Menlo Park, 94025. Tel: 650-366-4692.
Marin Catholic High School. 675 Sir Francis Drake Blvd., Kentfield, 94904.
St. Rose Academy Corporation, Rose Court, 2501 Pine St., 94115. Tel: 415-440-9568.
E-mail: patsimpsonop@juno.com
Officers of the Board: Sr. Patricia Simpson, O.P., Pres.; Thomas Bertelsen, Jr., CFO & Sec.; Sr. Katherine Hamilton, O.P., Sec. Directors: Sr. Patricia Simpson, O.P.; Sr. Ann Bertain, O.P.; Sr. Carla Kovack, O.P.; Sandy Mori; Valerie Street; Thomas Bertelsen, Jr.
Shrine of St. Francis of Assisi, 610 Vallejo St., 94133. Tel: 415-983-0405; Fax: 415-983-0407.
E-mail: shrinesf@flash.net
Web site: www.shrinesf.org
Rev. Robert Ouellette, O.F.M.Conv.
Shrine of St. Jude Thaddeus, 2390 Bush St., 94115. Tel: 415-931-5919; Fax: 415-771-3612.
Sisters of the Presentation Community Support Trust Fund, 2340 Turk Blvd., 94118. Tel: 415-751-0406; Fax: 415-731-3071.
E-mail: admoffice@aol.com
Trust used for the religious and charitable needs of the Sisters of the Presentation of the Blessed Virgin Mary. Trustees: Sr. Pamela Chiesa, P.B.V.M.; Sr. Patricia Anne Cloherty, P.B.V.M.; Sr. Roberta Green, P.B.V.M.; Sr. Patricia Marie Mulpeters, P.B.V.M.; Sr. Rose Therese Sousa, P.B.V.M.
The Ordinary Mutual, RRG, P.O. Box 191867, 94119-4002. Tel: 415-536-8440; Fax: 415-536-4002.
E-mail: dennis_o'hara@ajg.com
Dennis O'Hara, Underwriting Mgr.; Randolph E. Steiner, Pres. A Risk Retention Group Corporation, incorporated in Vermont, serving the Dioceses of Boise, Tucson, Fresno, Monterey, Oakland, Orange, Sacramento, San Jose, Santa Rosa, and Stockton, and the Archdioceses of Los Angeles and San Francisco.
Together in the Mission of Education (T.I.M.E.), 301 DeMontfort Ave., 94112. Tel: 415-334-4334; Fax: 415-334-4334.
E-mail: TIME2000@juno.com
Nell Jeffrey, Exec. Dir.; Arleen Guaraglia, Treas.; Caitlan Jeffrey, Devel. Dir.

BURLINGAME. *Music at Kohl Mansion, Inc.*, 2750 Adeline Dr., 94010. Tel: 650-343-8463; Fax: 650-343-2316.
E-mail: info@musicatkohlmansion.org
Web site: www.musicatkohlmansion.org
To develop and promote public knowledge and appreciation of musical arts by sponsoring chamber music concerts and other public performances of music, as well as music education activities.

DALY CITY. *Association of Catholic Student Councils*, 86 Cityview Dr., 94014. Tel: 415-584-9877; Fax: 415-584-9877.
E-mail: The ACSC@aol.com
Marilyn Thickett, Exec. Dir.

HOLLYWOOD. *Christian Life Communities*, 6657 Sunset Blvd., 90028. Tel: 323-462-6311, Ext. 314; Fax: 323-462-0113.
E-mail: jlevecke@aol.com
Rev. John LeVecke, S.J., Ecclesial Asst. for CLC.

MENLO PARK. *Hospital and Health Services Liaison*, St. Patrick Seminary, 320 Middlefiled Rd., 94025. Tel: 650-325-5621; Fax: 650-322-0997.
E-mail: coleman@stpatricksseminary.org
Rev. Gerald D. Coleman, S.S., Ph.D.
St. Joseph's-St. Patrick's College Alumni Association, St. Patrick's Seminary, 320 Middlefield Rd., 94025. Tel: 650-325-5621; Fax: 650-654-3503. Mr. James P. Murphy, Contact.
Vatican II Institute for Clergy Formation, 320 Middlefield Rd., 94025. Tel: 650-325-9122; Fax: 650-325-6765.
E-mail: vat2ins@aol.com
Rev. Eugene J. Konkel, S.S., Dir.

PACIFICA. *Cursillo*. 3321 16th St., San Francisco, 94114. Tel: 415-621-8203; Fax: 415-621-2294.
E-mail: mdolores@earthlink.net
Rev. Msgr. Maurice M. McCormick, Chap., Gen. Secretariat.

REDWOOD CITY. *The Catholic Worker Community*, 545 Cassia St., 94063. Tel: 650-366-4415. Lawrence P. Purcell, Dir. A foster home for teenagers.
St. Francis Center of Redwood City, 101 Buckingham Ave., 94064. Tel: 650-365-7829.
E-mail: SCristina@aol.com
Mailing Address: P.O. Box 7134, 94064. Sr. Christina Heltsley, O.P., Exec. Dir.

SAN RAFAEL. *Catholic Scouting*, 1 St. Vincent Dr., 94903. Tel: 415-507-2000; Fax: 415-491-0842. Rev. David A. Ghiorso.
Center Interfaith Housing, 164 N. San Pedro Rd., 94903; Fax: 415-453-8367.
Mission Holding Corporation, 1520 Grand Ave., 94901. Tel: 415-453-8303; Fax: 415-453-8367.
E-mail: patsimpsonop@juno.com
Web site: sanrafaelop.org
Governing Board: Sr. Sharon Cross, O.P.; Sr. Patricia Simpson, O.P.; Sr. Anne Bertain, O.P.; Sr. Katherine Hamilton, O.P.; Sr. Abby Newton, O.P.
Third Order of St. Dominic Support and Charitable Trust Fund, 1520 Grand Ave., 94901. Tel: 415-453-8303; Fax: 415-453-8367.
E-mail: patsimpsonop@juno.com
Web site: sanrafaelop.org
Legal Title: *Third Order of St. Dominic, Congregation of the Most Holy Name, Support and Charitable Trust Fund.* Trust used for the religious and charitable needs of the Sisters of the Third Order of St. Dominic, Congregation of the Most Holy Name. Trustees: Sr. Patricia Boss, O.P.; Sr. Patricia Simpson, O.P.; Sr. Sharon Cross, O.P.; Sr. Pamela Chiesa, O.P.; Sr. Katherine Hamilton, O.P.; Rev. Msgr. Richard Knapp; Dr. Dennis Burke; Mr. Thomas Bertelsen.

[U] CLOSED INSTITUTIONS

SAN FRANCISCO. *All Hallows Church.* For sacramental records please contact Our Lady of Lourdes, 1715 Oakdale Ave., San Francisco 94124. Tel: 415-285-3377; Fax: 415-285-2191.

Holy Cross Korean Church. For sacramental records please contact St. Michael, 32 Broad St., San Francisco, 94112. Tel: 415-333-1194; Fax: 415-333-1196.

Immaculate Conception Church. For sacramental records please contact St. Anthony of Padua, 3215 Cesar Chavez St., San Francisco, 94110. Tel: 415-647-2704; Fax: 415-647-7282.

Our Lady of Guadalupe Church. For sacramental records please contact SS. Peter and Paul, 666 Filbert St., San Francisco, 94133. Tel: 415-421-0809; Fax: 415-421-0217.

St. Brigid Church. For sacramental records please contact St. Vincent de Paul, 2320 Green St., San Francisco 94123. Tel: 415-992-1010; Fax: 415-922-7203.

St. Edward the Confessor Church. For sacramental records please contact Star of the Sea, 4420 Geary Blvd., San Francisco, 94118. Tel: 415-751-0450; Fax: 415-368-5651.

St. Francis of Assisi Church. For sacramental records please contact SS. Peter and Paul, 666 Filbert St., San Francisco, 94133. Tel: 415-421-0809; Fax: 415-421-0217.

St. Joseph Church. For sacramental records please contact St. Patrick, 756 Mission St., San Francisco, 94103. Tel: 415-421-0547; 415-512-9730.

SAN RAFAEL. *Blessed Sacrament Church.* For sacramental records please contact St. Isabella, One Trinity Way, San Rafael, 94901. Tel: 415-479-1560; Fax: 415-479-8303.

St. Sylvester Church. For sacramental records please contact St. Raphael, 1104 Fifth Ave., San Rafael, 94901. Tel: 415-453-2314; Fax: 415-453-5402.

WOODSIDE. *St. Marcella Mission.* For sacramental records please contact St. Denis, 2250 Avy Ave., Menlo Park, 94025. Tel: 650-854-5976; Fax: 650-854-3754.

RELIGIOUS INSTITUTES OF MEN REPRESENTED IN THE ARCHDIOCESE

For further details refer to the corresponding bracketed number in the Religious Institutes of Men or Women section.

[0140]—*The Augustinians.*—O.S.A.
[0200]—*Benedictine Monks.* (Hungary).—O.S.B.
[0330]—*Brothers of the Christian Schools.* (Prov. of San Francisco).—F.S.C.
[0470]—*The Capuchin Franciscans.* (Irish Prov.).—O.F.M.Cap.
[0310]—*Congregation of Christian Brothers.*—C.F.C.
[0480]—*Conventual Franciscans.*—O.F.M.Conv.
[0520]—*Franciscan Friars.* (Santa Barbara Prov.).—O.F.M.
[0650]—*Holy Ghost Fathers.*—C.S.Sp.
[0690]—*Jesuit Fathers and Brothers.* (California Prov.).—S.J.
[0780]—*Marist Fathers.* (American Prov.).—S.M.
[0800]—*Maryknoll.*—M.M.
[0430]—*Order of Preachers (Dominicans).* (Western Prov.).—O.P.
[0897]—*Paris Foreign Mission Society.*—M.E.P.
[1030]—*Paulist Fathers.*—C.S.P.
[]—*Pilgrim Brothers.*—P.B.S.F.
[1170]—*St. Patrick Missionary Society.*—S.P.S.
[1190]—*Salesian Don Bosco.*—S.D.B.
[1260]—*Society of Christ.* (Chicago Prov.).—S.Ch.
[0760]—*Society of Mary (Marianists).* (Prov. of the Pacific).—S.M.
[1200]—*Society of the Divine Savior.*—S.D.S.
[1290]—*Society of the Priests of Saint Sulpice.* (American Prov.).—S.S.
[]—*Verbum Dei Missionary Fraternity.*—V.D.M.F.

RELIGIOUS INSTITUTES OF WOMEN REPRESENTED IN THE ARCHDIOCESE

[]—*Apostolic Society, Society of the Divine Will.*—D.D.W.
[]—*Congregation of Divine Providence.*—C.D.P.
[1920]—*Congregation of the Sisters of the Holy Cross.* (Notre Dame, IN).—C.S.C.
[1940]—*Congregation of the Sisters of the Holy Faith.*—C.H.F.
[1710]—*Congregation of the Third Order of St. Francis of Mary Immaculate, Joliet, IL.*—O.S.F.
[0730]—*Daughters of Charity of Canossa.*—F.D.C.C.
[0760]—*Daughters of Charity of St. Vincent de Paul.* (Prov. of the West).—D.C.
[0880]—*Daughters of Mary and Joseph.*—D.M.J.
[0850]—*Daughters of Mary Help of Christians.*—F.M.A.
[0420]—*Discalced Carmelite Nuns.*—O.C.D.
[]—*Dominican Sisters of the Philippines.*
[1050]—*Dominican Contemplative Nuns.*—O.P.
[1070-03]—*Dominican Sisters.*—O.P.
[1070-13]—*Dominican Sisters.*—O.P.
[1070-19]—*Dominican Sisters of Houston.*—O.S.F.
[1070-04]—*Dominican Sisters of San Rafael.*—O.P.
[]—*Franciscan Missionaries, Our Lady of Peace.*—M.F.P.
[]—*Las Hermanas Misioneras.*—M.S.C.Gpe.
[2340]—*Little Sisters of the Poor.*—l.s.p.
[2390]—*Lovers of the Holy Cross Sisters.*—L.H.C.
[2420]—*Marist Missionary Sisters, Society of Mary.*—S.M.S.M.
[2470]—*Maryknoll Sisters of St. Dominc.*—M.M.
[2720]—*Mission Helpers of the Sacred Heart.*—M.H.S.H.
[2710]—*Missionary Sisters of Charity.*—M.C.
[]—*Missionary Sisters of the Sacred Side.*—M.C.S.
[3190]—*Nuns of the Perpetual Adoration of the Blessed Sacrament.*—A.P.
[]—*Oblates Sisters of Jesus the Priest.*—O.S.J.
[]—*Order of Preachers (Dominican Nuns).*—O.P.
[0950]—*Pious Society Daughters of St. Paul.*—F.S.P.
[3242]—*Poor Sisters of Nazareth.*—P.S.N.
[]—*Religious of the Sacred Heart of Jesus.*—R.S.C.J.
[3465]—*Religious of the Sacred Heart of Mary.*—R.S.H.M.
[]—*Religious of the Virgin Mary.*—R.V.M.
[0440]—*Sisters of Charity of Cincinnati, Ohio.*—S.C.
[0430]—*Sisters of Charity of the Blessed Virgin Mary.*—B.V.M.
[2575]—*Sisters of Mercy of the Americas.* (Burlingame, CA).—R.S.M.
[2580]—*Sisters of Mercy of the United States of America.*—R.S.M.
[3000]—*Sisters of Notre Dame de Namur.* (Prov. of CA).—S.N.D.deN.
[3360]—*Sisters of Providence of Saint Mary-of-the-Woods, Indiana.*—S.P.
[4080]—*Sisters of Social Service of Los Angeles, Inc.*—S.S.S.
[]—*Sisters of St. Dominic of Mission San Jose.*—O.P.
[1570]—*Sisters of St. Francis of Holy Family.*—O.S.F.
[1630]—*Sisters of St. Francis of Penance and Christian Charity.*—O.S.F.
[]—*Sisters of St. Joseph.* Nazareth, MI.
[3840]—*Sisters of St. Joseph of Carondelet.* (Los Angeles Prov.).—C.S.J.
[3930-03]—*Sisters of St. Joseph of Orange.*—C.S.J.O.
[3890]—*Sisters of St. Joseph of Peace.*—C.S.J.P.
[1830]—*The Sisters of the Good Shepherd.*—R.G.S.
[1960]—*Sisters of the Holy Family.* (San Francisco, CA).—S.H.F.
[1990]—*Sisters of the Holy Names of Jesus and Mary.* (Provs. of CA; Oregon; Washington).—S.N.J.M.
[2130]—*Sisters of the Immaculate Conception.* (Prov. of Madrid).—R.C.M.
[3260]—*Sisters of the Precious Blood (Dayton, Ohio).*—C.PP.S.
[3320]—*Sisters of the Presentation of the B.V.M.*—P.B.V.M.
[1720]—*Sisters of the Third Order Regular of St. Francis of the Congregation of Our Lady of Lourdes.*—O.S.F.
[1890]—*Society of Helpers.*—H.H.S.
[4060]—*Society of the Holy Child of Jesus.*—S.H.C.J.
[3330]—*Union Sisters of the Presentation of the Blessed Virgin Mary.*—P.B.V.M.
[4110]—*Ursuline Nuns (Roman Union).*—O.S.U.
[]—*Ursuline Sisters of the Immaculate Conception.* (Louisville,KY).—O.S.U.
[]—*Verbum Dei Missionary Fraternity.*
[4190]—*Visitation Nuns.*—V.H.M.

ARCHDIOCESAN CEMETERIES AND MAUSOLEUMS

SAN FRANCISCO. *Holy Cross Cemetery and Mausoleum.* Mailing Address: P.O. Box 1577, Colma, 94014. Tel: 650-756-2060; Fax: 650-994-8147.
E-mail: suemhcc@aol.com

MENLO PARK. *Holy Cross.* Mailing Address: P.O. Box 1577, Colma, 94014. Tel: 650-756-2060; Fax: 650-994-8147.
E-mail: suemhcc@aol.com

SAN RAFAEL. *Mount Olivet.* Mailing Address: P.O. Box 4368, 94903.
E-mail: suemhcc@aol.com

NECROLOGY

† Lacey, Thomas E., Redwood City, CA St. Matthias Church. —Died Aug. 13, 2000.

† Lowery, William R., San Mateo, CA St. Bartholomew Church. —Died May 15, 2000.

Diocese of San Jose in California

(Dioecesis Sancti Josephi in California)

Most Reverend

PATRICK J. MCGRATH, D.D., J.C.D.

Bishop of San Jose; ordained June 7, 1970; appointed Auxiliary Bishop of San Francisco and Titular Bishop of Allegheny December 6, 1988; Episcopal ordination January 25, 1989; appointed Coadjutor Bishop of San Jose June 29, 1998.

Most Reverend

PIERRE DUMAINE, D.D., PH.D.

Bishop Emeritus of San Jose; ordained June 15, 1957; appointed Auxiliary Bishop of San Francisco and Titular Bishop of Sarda April 28, 1978; Episcopal ordination June 29, 1978; appointed Bishop of San Jose January 27, 1981; installed as Bishop of San Jose March 18, 1981. *Office: Diocese of San Jose, 900 Lafayette St., Ste. 301, Santa Clara, CA, 95050-4966.*

ESTABLISHED JANUARY 27, 1981.

Square Miles 1,300.

Legal Title: The Roman Catholic Bishop of San Jose, a Corporation Sole.

The Diocese of San Jose comprises the County of Santa Clara in the State of California.

PATRONS OF THE DIOCESE OF SAN JOSE: St. Joseph, Husband of Mary, March 19; St. Clare of Assisi, August 11.

For legal titles of parishes and diocesan institutions, consult the Chancery Office.

Diocese of San Jose: 900 Lafayette St., Ste. 301, Santa Clara, CA, 95050-4966. Tel.: 408-983-0100; Fax: 408-983-0295.

Web site address: www.dsj.org

E-mail address: chancellor@dsj.org

STATISTICAL OVERVIEW

Personnel	
Bishop	1
Retired Bishops	1
Priests: Diocesan Active in Diocese	79
Priests: Active Outside Diocese	6
Priests: Retired, Sick or Absent	31
Number of Diocesan Priests	116
Religious Priests in Diocese	169
Extern Priests in Diocese	30
Ordinations:	
Diocesan Priests	2
Permanent Deacons in Diocese	8
Total Brothers	68
Total Sisters	401
Parishes	
Parishes	48
With Resident Pastor:	
Resident Diocesan Priests	39
Resident Religious Priests	8
Without Resident Pastor:	
Administered by Priests	1
Missions	3
Pastoral Centers	1
Professional Ministry Personnel:	
Brothers	5
Sisters	35
Lay Ministers	95
Welfare	
Catholic Hospitals	2
Total Assisted	195,438
Homes for the Aged	2
Total Assisted	143
Day Care and Extended Day Care Centers	1
Total Assisted	215
Other Institutions	2
Total Assisted	185
Educational	
Diocesan Students in Other Seminaries	14
Total Seminarians	14
Colleges and Universities	1
Total Students	7,668
High Schools, Diocesan and Parish	2
Total Students	1,828
High Schools, Private	4
Total Students	4,136
Elementary Schools, Diocesan and Parish	29
Total Students	10,392
Catechesis/Religious Education:	
High School Students	3,067
Elementary Students	15,878
Total Students Under Catholic Instruction	42,983
Teachers in the Diocese:	
Priests	1
Brothers	1
Sisters	26
Lay Teachers	492
Vital Statistics	
Receptions into the Church:	
Infant Baptism Totals	9,977
Adult Baptism Totals	752
Received into Full Communion	493
First Communions	5,720
Confirmations	2,879
Marriages:	
Catholic	1,306
Interfaith	435
Total Marriages	1,741
Deaths	1,918
Total Catholic Population	411,855
Total Population	1,647,419

Diocese of San Jose—900 Lafayette St., Ste. 301, Santa Clara, 95050-4966. Tel: 408-983-0100; Fax: 408-983-0295.

Vicar General and Moderator of the Curia—Rev. Msgr. MICHAEL J. MITCHELL, V.G., Moderator, *Diocese of San Jose, 900 Lafayette St., Ste. 301, Santa Clara, 95050-4966.* Tel: 408-983-0240.

Episcopal Vicar for Clergy—Rev. FRANCIS V. CILIA. Tel: 408-983-0154.

Chancellor—LINDA BEARIE. Tel: 408-983-0160.

Vicar for Religious—Rev. DAVID H. SCHUYLER, S.M., S.T.L., J.C.D. Tel: 408-983-0219.

Episcopal Director for Pastoral Ministry—TERRIE IACINO. Tel: 408-983-0122.

Bishop's Executive Committee—Most. Rev. PATRICK J. MCGRATH, D.D., J.C.D.; Rev. Msgr. MICHAEL J. MITCHELL, V.G.; Rev. FRANCIS V. CILIA, Vicar for Clergy; Sr. PATRICIA MITCHELL, Dir., Office of Parish & Planning; MARIAN STUCKEY, Supt., Education; TERRIE IACINO, Episcopal Dir., Pastoral Ministry; LINDA BEARIE, Chancellor; DIANE PELOSI SAIGN, CEO, Catholic Charities; ROBERTA WARD, Editor, "The Valley Catholic".

Diocesan Consultors—Rev. Msgr. MICHAEL J. MITCHELL, V.G.; Rev. Msgr. J. PATRICK BROWNE; Revs. BERNARD K. FREYNE; FRANCIS CILIA; V. WARWICK JAMES; EUGENE P. O'DONNELL; LAWRENCE HENDEL; Rev. Msgr. ALEXANDER C. LARKIN.

Council of Priests—Most. Rev. PATRICK J. MCGRATH, D.D., J.C.D.; Rev. Msgr. MICHAEL J. MITCHELL, V.G.; Rev. Msgr. J. PATRICK BROWNE; Rev. Msgr. ALEXANDER C. LARKIN; Revs. BARRY FREYNE; NORMAN SEGOVIA; FRANCIS V. CILIA; WARWICK JAMES; THOMAS AHERN; PETER LUC PHAN; ROLANDO BEHAS; LAWRENCE HENDEL; GERALD WADE, S.J.; RAYMOND KENNY; STEVEN BROWN; RICK RODONI; JOSEPH BENEDICT; EUGENE P. O'DONNELL; JOSEPH V. HALEY, C.M.; FRANCISCO RIOS, I.V.E.

Council of Religious—Revs. DAVID H. SCHUYLER, S.M., S.T.L., J.C.D., Liaison; Revs. PETER FILICE, S.J.; RAYMOND ALLENDER, S.J.; Sr. DORIS CAVANAUGH, P.B.V.M.; Sr. AILEEN DONOHUE, S.N.D.deN.; Sr. PAULE FREEBURG, D.C.; Sr. MARY PETER MCCUSKER, R.S.M.; Sr. MARGARET MCGRAW, C.S.J.; Bro. THOMAS FREY, C.S.C.

Deans—Rev. BERNARD FREYNE, Northern Deanery; Rev. Msgr. ALEXANDER LARKIN, Northwestern Deanery; Rev. WARWICK JAMES, Northeastern Deanery; Rev. EUGENE P. O'DONNELL, Southwestern Deanery; Rev. J. PATRICK BROWNE, Central Deanery; Rev. JEFFREY T. LABELLE, S.J., Southeastern Deanery.

Ecumenical and Interreligious Affairs—Rev. JOSE ANTONIO RUBIO, Dir. & Delegate to Eastern Rite Churches.

Chinese Catholic Community—Rev. MATTHEW KOO, Chap. KATHERINE NIE, Sec., *900 Lafayette St., Ste. 301, Santa Clara, 95050.* Tel: 408-983-0211; Fax: 408-983-0212.

Catholic Charities—Catholic Charities of Santa Clara County. DIANE PELOSI SAIGN, CEO, *2625 Zanker Rd., Ste. 200, San Jose, 95134.* Tel: 408-468-0100; Fax: 408-944-0275.

Catholic Telemedia Network—SHIRLEY CONNOLLY, Gen. Mgr., *324 Middlefield Rd., Menlo Park, 94025.* Tel: 650-326-7850; Fax: 650-326-4605.

Propagation of the Faith-Holy Childhood Association-Catholic Relief Service—MELISSA BOSE, Rep. Tel: 408-983-0167.

Roman Catholic Welfare Corporation—

"The Valley Catholic" (Diocesan Newspaper)—ROBERTA WARD, Editor; MICHAEL HAWKINS, Business Mgr., *Diocese of San Jose, 900 Lafayette St., Ste. 301, Santa Clara, 95050-4966.* Tel: 408-983-0260.

Diocesan Tribunal—Diocese of San Jose, 900 Lafayette St., Ste. 301, Santa Clara, 95050-4966. Tel: 408-983-0219.

Judicial Vicar—Rev. DAVID H. SCHUYLER, S.M., S.T.L., J.C.D.

Adjutant—Rev. HIEN MINH NGUYEN, J.C.D.

Judges—Revs. DAVID H. SCHUYLER, S.M., S.T.L., J.C.D.; ABEL LOPEZ, J.C.L.; HEIN MINH NGUYEN, J.C.D.; Sr. MARIE GERTRUDE ROLDAN, C.S.J., J.C.L.

Defenders of the Bond—Revs. FRANCIS V. CILIA; MICHAEL R. MOODIE, S.J., J.C.D.; RANDOLPH CALVO, J.C.D.; ANDRES LIGOT, J.C.D.

Case Instructors—Sr. M. JUDE RISTEY, P.B.V.M. Tel: 408-983-0221. Sr. MICHELE MANGAN, O.S.F. Tel: 408-983-0224.

Administrative Assistant—Mrs. BELVA M. DICAROLIS. Tel: 408-983-0219.

Finance Office—Rev. Msgr. MICHAEL J. MITCHELL, V.G., Dir.; Mr. CHARLES TULLY, Controller & Assoc. Dir.

Finance Council—Most Rev. PATRICK J. MCGRATH, D.D., J.C.D.; Rev. Msgr. MICHAEL J. MITCHELL, V.G.; ROBERT MCADAMS; MATTHEW O'ROURKE; EUGENE TOOMEY; DONALD WAITE; DIANE S. GIANNINI.

Building Committee—Rev. Msgr. MICHAEL J. MITCHELL, V.G.; Revs. FRANCIS V. CILIA; MARK CATALANA; DANIEL DERRY; ROBERT GRAY; STEPHEN E. PERATA; JUSTIN ZAWADZKI; Mr. CHARLES F. BUCKLEY, Consultant.

Development Office—Tel: 408-983-0245.

Department of Cemeteries—Rev. ROBERT GRAY, Dir.

Office of the Vicar for Clergy—Rev. FRANCIS V. CILIA, Episcopal Vicar for Clergy. Tel: 408-983-0154.

Diocesan Clergy Personnel Board—Most Rev. PATRICK J. MCGRATH, D.D., J.C.D., Ex Officio; Revs. FRANCIS V. CILIA, Chm. MARK CATALANA; ROBERT MORAN; RICK RODONI; EUGENE P. O'DONNELL; FRANCIS V. CILIA; Rev. Msgr. JOSEPH MILANI; ENRICO HERNANDEZ.

Ongoing Formation of Clergy Committee—Revs. JACK BONSOR, Chm. GEORGE MANCHA; DAVID MERCER; RICK RODONI; ROBERT HAYES; ENRICO HERNANDEZ; FRANCIS V. CILIA; ANTHONY MANCUSO; TIMOTHY KIDNEY.

Clergy Retirement Board—Rev. ARTHUR HARRISON, Chm.; Rev. Msgr. MICHAEL J. MITCHELL, V.G.; Revs. FRANCIS V. CILIA; GARY THOMAS; STEPHEN PERATA; THOMAS AHERN; GREGORY KIMM; MATTHEW O'ROURKE; Mr. GEORGE DELUCCHI.

Vocation Office—Rev. MARK CATALANA, Dir. Tel: 408-983-0255.

Permanent Diaconate—Rev. JACK BONSOR, Dir. Tel: 408-983-0156.

Department of the Chancellor—LINDA BEARIE, Chancellor. Tel: 408-983-0160.

Archives—Mr. BAYNE BENTLEY, Records Management, *Diocese of San Jose, 1068 The Alameda Suite 4, San Jose, 95126.* Tel: 408-292-7128.

Personnel Office—LINDA BEARIE, Dir. PATRICIA WEIS, Associate for Personnel. Tel: 408-983-0149.

Education Department—MARIAN STUCKEY, Supt. of Schools; PRISCILLA MURPHY, Asst. Supt. of Schools; CHARLENE LEMANN, Curriculum Consultant; Sr. CLAUDE POWER, P.B.V.M., Consultant to the Dept. of Education, *Diocese of San Jose, 900 Lafayette St., Ste. 301, Santa Clara, 95050-4966.* Tel: 408-983-0185.

Office of Pastoral Ministry—

Episcopal Director of Pastoral Ministry—TERRIE IACINO.

Associate for Catechetics—JEANNINE LEICHNER.

Associate for Hispanic Catechetics—LUPITA VITAL. Tel: 408-983-0133.

Associate for Hispanic Youth and Young Adults—ANTONIO OJEDA.

Associate for Human Concerns—Sr. ELIZABETH AVALOS, B.V.M.

Associate for Liturgy—Sr. BETTE GAMBONINI, B.V.M.

Associate for Pastoral Care and Special Ministries—LORETTA PFAFF. Tel: 408-983-0141.

Associate for Pastoral Care of Families—LINDA BATTON.

Small Christian Communities—DIANA COUCH, Coord. Tel: 408-983-0133.

Detention Ministry—MARILU EDER.

Human Concerns Commission—Sr. ELIZABETH AVALOS, B.V.M., Liaison. Tel: 408-983-0137.

Liturgical Commission—Sr. BETTE GAMBONINI, B.V.M., Liaison. Tel: 408-983-0136.

Pastoral Care Advisory Committee—LORETTA PFAFF, Liaison. Tel: 408-983-0141.

Pastoral Resource Committee for Ministry to Gay and Lesbian Catholics—TERRIE IACINO, Chm. Tel: 408-983-0122.

Respect Life Program—Sr. ELIZABETH AVALOS, B.V.M., Assoc. Dir. Tel: 408-983-0137.

Advisory Committee for Ministry with the Deaf and Persons with Disabilities—LORETTA PFAFF, Liaison. Tel: 408-983-0141.

Institute for Leadership in Ministry—ANNE GRYCZ, Dir. Tel: 408-983-0111. SANDRA TORRES, Asst. Dir. Tel: 408-983-0174.

Office for Parish & Planning—Sr. PATRICIA MITCHELL, Dir. Tel: 408-983-0143.

CLERGY, PARISHES, MISSIONS AND PAROCHIAL SCHOOLS

CITY OF SAN JOSE

1—CATHEDRAL BASILICA OF ST. JOSEPH (1849), Rev. Msgr. J. Patrick Browne; Revs. Jon Pedigo; Luis Gerardo Menchaca (Mexico).
Res. and Church—80 S. Market St., 95113. Tel: 408-283-8100; Fax: 408-283-8110.
Catechesis/Religious Programs—Susan Olsen, D.R.E.
Students 274.

2—ST. FRANCIS OF ASSISI (1997), Rev. Msgr. John Sandersfeld; Deacon Salvador Alvarez.
Res., 5111 San Felipe Rd., 95135. Tel: 408-223-1562; Fax: 408-223-1759.
Catechesis/Religious Programs—Ginny Hinkle, D.R.E.
Students 380.

3—CHRIST THE KING (1997), Rev. Norman Segovia.
Res., 5278 B Monterey Rd., 95111. Tel: 408-362-9958; Fax: 408-362-9695.
Catechesis/Religious Programs—Students 145.

4—FIVE WOUNDS PORTUGUESE NATIONAL CHURCH (1914) (Portuguese), Rev. Leonel C. Noia. In res., Revs. Jack La Rocca; Robert Gray.
Res., 1375 E. Santa Clara St., 95116. Tel: 408-292-2123; Fax: 408-292-0201.
School—1390 Five Wounds Ln., 95116. Tel: 408-293-0425; Fax: 408-971-7607. Sandra Jewett-Ramirez, Prin.
Priests 1; Sisters 1; Lay Teachers 18; Students 279.
Catechesis/Religious Programs—Tel: 408-293-3938; Fax: 408-292-0201. Joanne Dobrzynski, D.R.E.
Students 668.

5—ST. FRANCES CABRINI (1955), Revs. Robert Kiefer; Eamonn O'Brien (Great Britian); Dominic Joseph (India). In res., Rev. Don D. Flickinger (FRS).
Res., 15333 Woodard Rd., 95124. Tel: 408-879-1120; Fax: 408-377-3587.
School—15325 Woodard Rd., 95124. Tel: 408-377-6545; Fax: 408-377-8491. Yvonne Gomez, Prin.
Sisters 1; Lay Teachers 31; Students 685.
Catechesis/Religious Programs—Susan Clingingsmith, D.R.E.
Students 173.

6—HOLY CROSS (1911) (Italian), Revs. Antonio DeAngelis, C.S.; Rafael Surmay, C.S.
Res., 580 E. Jackson St., 95112. Tel: 408-294-2440; Fax: 408-294-8609.
Catechesis/Religious Programs—Tel: 408-294-1310; Fax: 408-294-8609. Bro. Charles Muscat, C.S., D.R.E.
Students 510.

7—HOLY FAMILY (1905), Revs. Matthew D. Stanley; Anthony Nguyen.
Res., 4848 Pearl Ave., 95136. Tel: 408-265-4040; Fax: 408-978-9979.
School—4850 Pearl Ave., Tel: 408-978-1355; Fax: 408-978-0290. Gail Harrell, Prin.
Lay Teachers 24; Students 635.
Catechesis/Religious Programs—Tel: 408-265-6201. Virginia Silvers, D.R.E.
Students 260.

8—HOLY SPIRIT (1963), Rev. Paul P. Weisbeck.
Res., 1200 Redmond Ave., 95120. Tel: 408-997-5101; Fax: 408-997-5102.
School—1198 Redmond Ave., 95120. Tel: 408-268-0794; Fax: 408-268-5281. Eileen Beck, Prin.
Lay Teachers 13; Students 215.
Catechesis/Religious Programs—Tel: 408-997-5115. Joy Hill, D.R.E.
Students 339.

9—ST. ANTHONY (1982), Rev. George Mancha.
Mailing Address: 20101 McKean Rd., 95120. Tel: 408-997-4800; Fax: 408-997-4801.
Catechesis/Religious Programs—Tel: 408-997-4808. Joann Maier, D.R.E.
Students 208.

10—ST. BROTHER ALBERT CHMIELOWSKI POLISH CATHOLIC PASTORAL MISSION (1986) (Polish), Rev. Pawel Bandurski, S.Chr. (Poland).
Res., 10250 Clayton Rd., 95127-4336. Tel: 408-251-8490; Fax: 408-251-8960.
Catechesis/Religious Programs—Students 50.

11—ST. CHRISTOPHER (1951), Revs. James Walsh; Christopher Bennett (Ireland); William Pegnam (Ireland).
Office: 2278 Booksin Ave., 95125. Tel: 408-269-2226; Fax: 408-269-2784.
School—Tel: 408-723-7223; Fax: 408-978-5458. Arlene Ernst, Prin.
Sisters of the Presentation 2; Lay Teachers 34; Students 617.
Catechesis/Religious Programs—Tel: 408-264-8764; Fax: 408-978-5458. Sr. Felicia Gross, O.S.F., D.R.E.
Students 395.

12—ST. JOHN VIANNEY (1952), Revs. Lawrence Hendel; Michael Carson; Arthur Yabes, S.V.D. (Philippines); Deacon Joseph Alvarez. In res., Rev. Jon Pedigo.
Res., 4609 Alum Rock Ave., 95127.
Church—4600 Hyland Ave., 95127. Tel: 408-258-7832 (Office); Fax: 408-258-6152 (Office).
School—4601 Hyland Ave., 95127. Tel: 408-258-7677; Fax: 408-258-5997. Sr. Michele Anne Murphy, P.B.V.M., Prin.
Sisters of the Presentation B.V.M. 2; Lay Teachers 28; Students 621.
Catechesis/Religious Programs—Fax: 408-272-1045. Victor Valdez, D.R.E.
Students 365.

13—ST. JULIE BILLIART (1974), Rev. Richard C. Fry; Rev. Msgr. Jose V. Suarez (Philippines).
Res., 366 St. Julie Dr., 95119. Tel: 408-629-3030; Fax: 408-629-3343.
Catechesis/Religious Programs—Tel: 408-226-3595. Sandy Zangara, D.R.E.
Students 282.

14—ST. LEO THE GREAT (1923), Rev. Francisco Rios, I.V.E. In res., Revs. Matthew Koo (China); Luis Atencio, I.V.E. (Argentina); Walter Suarez, I.V.E. (Argentina).
Res., 88 Race St., 95126. Tel: 408-293-3503; Fax: 408-293-3516.
School—Tel: 408-293-4846; Fax: 408-293-5855. Phyllis Taurosa, Prin.
Lay Teachers 11; Students 277.
Catechesis/Religious Programs—Tel: 408-293-1662. Gayle Morrissette, D.R.E.
Students 252.

15—ST. MARIA GORETTI (1961), Revs. Kevin Joyce; Luis Vargas; Peter LucThePhan; Antonio Isidro Martin-Rono (Mexico).
Res., 2980 Senter Rd., 95111. Tel: 408-363-2300; Fax: 408-363-2305.
Catechesis/Religious Programs—Tel: 408-363-2310. Jeanne Gaffney, D.R.E.
Students 1,227.

16—ST. MARTIN OF TOURS (1914), Revs. David Mercer; Joseph Pacquina (Philippines).
Res., 200 O'Connor Dr., 95128. Tel: 408-294-8953; Fax: 408-294-2624.
School—300 O'Connor Dr., 95128. Tel: 408-287-3630; Fax: 408-287-4313. Karen DeMonner, Prin.
Lay Teachers 33; Students 354.
Catechesis/Religious Programs—Tel: 408-289-9608. Paula Liu-Smith, D.R.E.
Students 105.

17—MOST HOLY TRINITY (1961) (Hispanic-Filipino), Revs. Michael Ravenkamp, S.J.; Doan Hoang, S.J.; Kevin Ballard, S.J.; Deacon Vicente R. Perez.
Res., 2040 Nassau Dr., 95122. Tel: 408-729-0101; Fax: 408-258-4131.
School—Tel: 408-729-3431; Fax: 408-729-3432. Susan Barry, O.S.U., Prin.
Priests 4; Brothers 1; Lay Teachers 10; Students 226.
Catechesis/Religious Programs—Clara R. Morales, D.R.E.
Students 800.

18—OUR LADY OF GUADALUPE (1962) (Hispanic), Revs. Rene Juarez, O.F.M.; Joseph Zermeno, O.F.M.; Deacon Eloy Chavez. In res., Revs. Javier Alvarez, O.F.M.; Miguel Obregon, O.F.M.
Office: 2020 E. San Antonio St., 95116. Tel: 408-258-7057; Fax: 408-258-8249.

Catechesis/Religious Programs—Tel: 408-258-0544. Connie Torres, D.R.E.
Students 735.

19—St. Patrick (1999) (Vietnamese). (Personal Parish). Rev. Msgr. Dominic Dinh Do. Parochial Vicars: Revs. Hao Dinh; Lieu Vu; Jose Antonio Medina, M.G. (Mexico).
Res., 389 E. Santa Clara St., 95113. Tel: 408-294-8120; Fax: 408-283-5852.
Vietnamese Ministry:—Tel: 408-291-6280; Fax: 408-291-6289.
School—51 N. 9th St., 95112. Tel: 408-283-5858; Fax: 408-291-6277. John Bracco, Prin.
Lay Teachers 11; Students 320.
Catechesis/Religious Programs—Tel: 408-239-1039; Fax: 408-239-1039. Bro. Fortunat Tran Trong An Phong, F.S.C., Vietnamese D.R.E.
Students 1,870.

20—St. Thomas of Canterbury (1967), Rev. Walter M. McMahon.
Res., 1522 McCoy Ave., 95130. Tel: 408-378-1595; Fax: 408-378-1215.
Catechesis/Religious Programs—Students 120.

21—Queen of Apostles (1960), Rev. James J. Mifsud, S.M.; Bro. T. William Bolts, S.M.
Res., 4911 Moorpark Ave., 95129. Tel: 408-253-7560; Fax: 408-253-9530.
School—Tel: 408-252-3659; Fax: 408-873-2645. Marianna Willis, Prin.
Sisters 1; Lay Teachers 15; Students 316.
Catechesis/Religious Programs—Patricia Sarria, D.R.E.
Students 316.

22—Sacred Heart of Jesus (1920), Revs. Jose Antonio Rubio; Luis Varga; Abel Lopez.
Res., 325 Willow St., 95110. Tel: 408-292-0146; Fax: 408-292-0172.
School—Sacred Heart Nativity School, 310 Edwards, 95110. Tel: 408-287-2029. Rev. Peter Pabst, S.J., Pres.
Catechesis/Religious Programs—Students 200.

23—Santa Teresa (1967), Rev. Raymond G. Kenny.
Res., 794 Calero Ave., 95123. Tel: 408-629-7777; Fax: 408-629-5260.
Catechesis/Religious Programs—Tel: 408-227-5915; Fax: 408-629-5260. Sandy Mory, D.R.E.
Students 149.

24—Church of the Transfiguration (1965), Rev. George Aranha.
Mailing Address: 4325 Jarvis Ave., 95118. Tel: 408-264-3600; Fax: 408-266-2745.
Catechesis/Religious Programs—Tel: 408-266-2743. Paula Ramos, D.R.E.
Students 186.

25—St. Victor (1961), Revs. Stephen F. Perata; Robert R. Taheny, S.J.; Candido O. Lim, S.J. (Philippines).
Res., 3108 Sierra Rd., 95132. Tel: 408-251-7055; Fax: 408-251-5528.
School—Tel: 408-251-1740; Fax: 408-251-1492. Sr. Sharon Breden, C.S.J., Prin.
Sisters of St. Joseph of Carondelet 1; Lay Teachers 17; Students 317.
Catechesis/Religious Programs—Tel: 408-251-0154; Fax: 408-251-5528. Angela Giampaoli, D.R.E.
Students 519.

26—St. Mary of the Assumption (1975). (Croatian Mission). Rev. Dujo Boban, O.F.M.
Res., 901 Lincoln Ave., 95126. Tel: 408-279-0279; Fax: 408-292-5868.
Catechesis/Religious Programs—Students 47.
Croatian Franciscan Fathers Corporation—Tel: 408-279-0279; Fax: 408-292-5868.
Franciscan Fathers—Tel: 408-276-0279; Fax: 408-292-5868.

OUTSIDE THE CITY OF SAN JOSE

Alviso, Santa Clara Co., Our Lady, Star of the Sea (1985) (Mexican-American), Rev. Steven P. Brown.
Mailing Address: P.O. Box 426, 95002.
Res., 1385 Michigan Ave., 95002. Tel: 408-263-2121; Fax: 408-263-1182.
Catechesis/Religious Programs—Tel: 408-263-6637; Fax: 408-263-1182. Sr. Josefina Montalvo, R.S.C.J., D.R.E.
Students 145.

Campbell, Santa Clara Co., St. Lucy (1947), Rev. Msgr. Terrence J. Sullivan; Rev. Joseph M. Benedict. In res., Rev. Robert Passalacqua.
Res., 2350 Winchester Blvd., 95008. Tel: 408-378-2464; Fax: 408-378-5548.
School—76 Kennedy Ave., 95008. Tel: 408-871-8023; Fax: 408-378-4945. Sr. Jolene Schmitz, C.H.S., Prin.
Sisters 2; Lay Teachers 15; Students 319.
Catechesis/Religious Programs—Tel: 408-379-5900; Fax: 408-378-5548. Sr. Fidelma Heeran, R.S.M., D.R.E.
Students 348.

Cupertino, Santa Clara Co., St. Joseph of Cupertino (1913), Revs. Robert Hayes; Paul-Cuong Q. Murphy Phan; Anthony Mancuso. In res., Rev. Msgr. Joseph J. Milani.
Res., 10110 N. DeAnza Blvd., 95014. Tel: 408-252-7653; Fax: 408-252-5263.
School—10120 N. DeAnza Blvd., 95014. Tel: 408-252-6441. Mary Lyons, Prin.
Lay Teachers 15; Students 313.
Catechesis/Religious Programs—Tel: 408-253-0660. Donna Brock, D.R.E.
Students 344.

Gilroy, Santa Clara Co., St. Mary (1865), Revs. Daniel Derry; Jeronimo Guitierrez (Mexico). In res., Rev. John Coleman.
Res., 11 First St., 95020. Tel: 408-847-5151; Fax: 408-847-4851. [CEM]
School—7900 Church St., 95020-4499. Tel: 408-842-2827; Fax: 408-847-7679. Christa Hanson, Prin.
Religious 1; Lay Teachers 15; Students 310.
Catechesis/Religious Programs—7950 Church St., 95020. Tel: 408-847-2652; Fax: 408-847-4851. D.R.E.: Carrie Rauch; Hilda Porcella.
Students 1,160.

Los Altos, Santa Clara Co., St. Nicholas (1947), Rev. Gary R. Thomas.
Res., 473 Lincoln Ave., 94022. Tel: 650-948-2158; Fax: 408-948-8566.
School—12816 S. El Monte Ave., Los Altos Hills, 94022. Tel: 650-941-4056; Fax: 650-941-3682. Mary Williams, Prin.
Lay Teachers 14; Students 271.
Catechesis/Religious Programs—Tel: 650-941-7622. Jan Cicoletti, D.R.E.
Students 257.
Station—Seven Oaks, Residential Park for the Aged, 1174 Los Altos Ave., 94022. Tel: 650-948-7337.

St. Simon (1955), Rev. Msgr. Ludwig M. Andre; Revs. Alexander Affonso; Joseph Thannickal, S.D.B. In res., Rev. Thomas Murray.
Res., 1860 Grant Rd., 94024. Tel: 650-967-8311; Fax: 650-967-8876.
School—1840 Grant Rd., 94024. Tel: 650-968-9952; Fax: 650-988-9308. Sr. Margaret Rose Adams, I.H.M., Prin.
Sisters, Servants of the Immaculate Heart of Mary (Immaculata, PA) 3; Lay Teachers 29; Students 614.
Catechesis/Religious Programs—Tel: 650-968-9552, Ext. 38. Sr. Pauline Komrska, C.S.J., D.R.E.
Students 201.

St. William (1959) (South African), Rev. Michael J. Burns. In res., Rev. Robert McKay (South Africa).
Res., 611 S. El Monte Ave., 94022-4058. Tel: 650-948-8169; Fax: 650-948-8508.
Catechesis/Religious Programs—Tel: 650-941-1460; Fax: 650-948-8508. Anne Piazzon, D.R.E.
Students 125.

Los Gatos, Santa Clara Co., St. Mary of the Immaculate Conception (1912), Revs. Justin Zawadzki; Christopher Bransfield.
Res., 219 Bean Ave., 95030. Tel: 408-354-3726; Fax: 408-354-9302.
School—30 Lyndon Ave., 95030. Tel: 408-354-3944; Fax: 408-395-9151. Sr. Nicki Thomas, S.N.J.M., Prin.
Sisters of the Holy Names of Jesus and Mary 5; Lay Teachers 21; Students 310.
Catechesis/Religious Programs—Tel: 408-354-4061; Fax: 408-354-9302. Terri Trotter, D.R.E.
Students 490.

Milpitas, Santa Clara Co., St. Elizabeth (1968), Revs. Edward Samy; Leonard Traverso, Parochial Vicar. In res., Rev. Hien Minh Nguyen.
Res., 750 Sequoia Dr., 95035. Tel: 408-262-8100; Fax: 408-946-8703.
Catechesis/Religious Programs—Tel: 408-263-1995. Sr. John Bosco Crivello, S.H.F., D.R.E.
Students 295.

St. John the Baptist (1877), Revs. G. Robert Leger; Daniel C. Urcia, C.R.S.; Deacon Eugene O'Sullivan.
Res., 279 S. Main St., 95035. Tel: 408-262-2546; Fax: 408-263-2564.
School—360 S. Abel St., 95035. Tel: 408-262-8110; Fax: 408-262-0814. Judy Perkowski, Prin.
Augustinian Recollect Sisters 2; Lay Teachers 10; Students 341.
Catechesis/Religious Programs—Tel: 408-262-7726; Fax: 408-262-3955. Sr. Edora Clotilde, A.R., D.R.E.
Students 380.

Morgan Hill, Santa Clara Co., St. Catherine of Alexandria (1909), Revs. Eugene P. O'Donnell; Francisco Miramontes; Gil-Romeo Abesamis.
Res., 17400 Peak Ave., 95037. Tel: 408-779-3959; Fax: 408-779-0289.
School—Tel: 408-779-9950. Suzanne Rich, Prin.; Judy Cory, Vice Prin.
Lay Teachers 13; Students 306.
Catechesis/Religious Programs—Tel: 408-779-9604. Mrs. Wendy Scherbart, D.R.E.
Students 958.

Mountain View, Santa Clara Co., St. Athanasius (1959), Revs. Diarmuid Casey, C.S.Sp. (Ireland); Kevin B. Corrigan, C.S.Sp. (Ireland). In res., Rev. Desmond McGlade, C.S.Sp. (Ireland).
Res., 160 N. Rengstorff Ave., 94043. Tel: 650-961-8600; Fax: 650-968-5633.
Catechesis/Religious Programs—Tel: 650-967-7900; Fax: 650-968-5633. Margery Ryan, D.R.E.
Students 285.

St. Joseph (1901), Revs. Oscar D. Tabujara (Philippines); Robert B. Moran. In res., Rev. Enrico Hernandez.
Res., 582 Hope St., 94041. Tel: 650-967-3831; Fax: 650-691-1522.
School—1120 Miramonte Ave., 94040. Tel: 650-967-1839; Fax: 650-691-1530. Stephanie Mirenda-Knight, Prin.
Lay Teachers 18; Students 282.
Catechesis/Religious Programs—Tel: 650-691-1525. Sr. Elizabeth Daly, O.P., D.R.E.
Students 110.

Palo Alto, Santa Clara Co., St. Thomas Aquinas (1901), Revs. Barry Freyne; Jose Antonio Medina; Gregory Kimm; Deacon Carl Bunje. In res., Rev. John Hester; Rev. Msgr. William Lenane; Revs. James Woolever; Charles Macedo.
Office: 3290 Middlefield Rd., 94306. Tel: 650-494-2496; Fax: 650-494-3780.
School—St. Elizabeth Seton Catholic Community School, 1095 Channing Ave., 94306. Tel: 650-326-9004; Fax: 650-326-2949. Kevin Eagleson, Prin.
Priests 1; Sisters 2; Lay Teachers 10; Students 269.
Catechesis/Religious Programs—Tel: 650-494-3097; Fax: 650-494-3780.
Students 275.

St. Albert the Great (1961). Merged with St. Thomas Aquinas Parish.

Our Lady of the Rosary (1959). Merged with St. Thomas Aquinas Parish.

Santa Clara, Santa Clara Co.,

1—Chinese Catholic Community, (1983), Rev. Matthew Koo.
Res., 900 Layfayette St., Ste. 301, 95050-4966. Tel: 408-983-0211; Fax: 408-983-0212.
Catechesis/Religious Programs—Students 179.

2—St. Clare, (1777), Revs. Rick Rodoni, S.J.; Paul Devot, S.J.
Mailing Address: 725 Washington St., 95050-4935. Tel: 408-248-7786; Fax: 408-248-8150.
Church—941 Lexington St., 95050.
School—Tel: 408-246-6797. Kathy Almazol, Prin.
Sisters 1; Lay Teachers 14; Students 294.
Catechesis/Religious Programs—Tel: 408-248-7786; Fax: 408-248-1589. Mrs. Diane Madruga, D.R.E.
Lay Teachers 19; Aides 5; Students 160.
Station—Convalescent Hospital. (Mission skilled Nursing Home). Tel: 408-248-3736.

3—St. Justin, (1951), Revs. Jose Galang; Francis Chiawa (Nigeria); Joseph Prendergast.
Res., 2655 Homestead Rd., 95051. Tel: 408-296-1193; Fax: 408-244-9437.
School—Tel: 408-248-1094. Sandra Colombo Hodges, Prin.
Lay Teachers 10; Students 300.
Catechesis/Religious Programs—Dorothy Carlson, D.R.E.
Students 210.

4—St. Lawrence the Martyr, (1959), Revs. V. Warwick James (South Africa); Brendan P. McGuire. In res., Rev. Victor L. Wilkiemeyer, Pastor Emeritus.
Res., 1971 St. Lawrence Dr., 95051. Tel: 408-296-3000; Fax: 408-296-3100.
Schools—(Grades PreK-5) 1977 St. Lawrence Dr., 95051. Tel: 408-296-2260; Fax: 408-296-1068.
Lay Teachers 8; Students 201; (Grades 6-8). Tel: 408-296-3013. Arlene Cimino, Prin.
Sisters 1; Lay Teachers 10; Students 189; (Grades 9-12) 2000 Lawrence Ct., 95051. Tel: 408-296-3013; Fax: 408-296-3794. Ron Modeste, Prin.
Priests 1; Sisters 2; Lay Teachers 24; Students 371.
Catechesis/Religious Programs—Sr. Kathleen Hanley, R.S.M., D.R.E.
Students 101.

5—Our Lady of Peace, (1961), Rev. Msgr. John J. Sweeny. In res., Rev. Msgr. Edgar P. McCarren (RVC); Rev. Dominic DeDomenico, O.P.
Res., 2800 Mission College Blvd., 95054. Tel: 408-988-4585; Fax: 408-988-0679.
School—Sisters 1; Students 36.
Catechesis/Religious Programs—Tel: 408-988-7543.
Students 638.

Saratoga, Santa Clara Co., Sacred Heart (1951), Rev. Msgr. Alexander C. Larkin. In res., Rev. Msgr. Michael J. Mitchell; Deacon Thomas Combellick.
Res., 13724 Saratoga Ave., 95070. Tel: 408-867-3634; Fax: 408-867-5339.

Schools—13718 Saratoga Ave., 95070. Tel: 408-867-9241; Fax: 408-867-9242. Jane Daigle, Prin.
Lay Teachers 15; Students 305; Pre-School.
Lay Teachers 3.
Catechesis/Religious Programs—Tel: 408-867-1530. Maureen Wright, D.R.E.
Students 321.

Church of the Ascension (1964), Rev. Paul Duong. In res., Revs. Raymund Field, C.S.V.; Charles Dougherty.
Res., 12033 Miller Ave., 95070. Tel: 408-725-3939.
Catechesis/Religious Programs—Tel: 408-725-3930; Fax: 408-725-3932. Ann Liebmann, D.R.E.
Students 190.

Stanford, Catholic Community at Stanford (1977), Revs. Patrick LaBelle, O.P.; John Paul Forte, O.P.
P.O. Box 2031, 94309. Tel: 650-725-0080; Fax: 650-723-6797.
Catechesis/Religious Programs—Students 20.

Sunnyvale, Santa Clara Co.,

1—STS. ANDREW AND PAUL KOREAN CATHOLIC MISSION OF SAN JOSE, (1981), Rev. Andrew Kyeng-Kuk Min (Korea).
Res., 531 E. Weddell Dr., 94089-2162. Tel: 408-734-9721; Fax: 408-734-9723.
Catechesis/Religious Programs—John Choi, D.R.E.
Students 220.

2—ST. CYPRIAN, (1961), Rev. Timothy Kidney.
Res., 1133 W. Washington, 94086. Tel: 408-739-8506; Fax: 408-739-2815.
School—195 Leota Ave., 94086. Tel: 408-738-3444; Fax: 408-733-3730. Kay Ingalls, Prin.
Lay Teachers 9; Students 258.
Catechesis/Religious Programs—Tel: 408-739-9417. Sr. Ruth Ella, S.N.D.deN., D.R.E.
Students 82.

3—ST. MARTIN, (1916), Revs. Benito O. Manding; Anthony Pereira.
Res., 590 Central Ave., 94086. Tel: 408-736-3725; Fax: 408-736-4968.
School—597 Central Ave., 94086. Tel: 408-736-5534. Eugenie Florczyk, Prin.
Lay Teachers 13; Students 325.
Catechesis/Religious Programs—Tel: 408-736-0967. Judy Kelch, D.R.E.
Students 302.

4—CHURCH OF THE RESURRECTION, (1963), Rev. Michael J. O'Connor. Parochial Vicars: Revs. Joseph N. Vanthu; Rolando T. Benas.
Res., 725 Cascade Dr., 94087. Tel: 408-245-5554; Fax: 408-245-5589.
Church—1399 Hollenbeck Ave., 94087.
School—1395 Hollenbeck Ave., 94087. Tel: 408-245-4571; Fax: 408-733-7301. Virginia Mirrione, Prin.
Religious 1; Lay Teachers 12; Students 285.
Catechesis/Religious Programs—Tel: 908-746-0172.
Students 260.

Chaplains of Public Institutions

SAN JOSE. *Agnews State Hospital*. Rev. Thomas J. Byrne, S.J. Tel: 408-294-9224.
Archbishop Mitty High School. Rev. Enrico Hernandez.
Catholic Scouting. Rev. Paul A. Soukup, S.J. Tel: 408-554-4124.
Columbia Regional Hospital. Rev. Arturo Mateo, M.S.C. Tel: 408-259-5000.
Detention Ministry for Juveniles. Rev. Jack LaRocca Tel: 408-280-7744.
O'Connor Hospital. Revs. Basil Royston; Rory Murphy, Capetown, South Africa.
Presentation High School. Rev. George Aranha.
St. Francis High School. Rev. Mark Catalana.
San Jose State University Catholic Campus. Rev. Charles Dougherty.
Santa Clara County Jail. Revs. Miguel Obregon; Andrew Skotnicki, O.Carm.
Santa Clara County Women's Facility. Ms. Marilu Eder.
Villa Siena. Rev. Salvatore M. DiNardo, O.P.

LOS GATOS. *Presentation Center*. Rev. Jack Bonsor Tel: 408-354-2346.

MILPITAS. *Stanford Medical Center*. Rev. John Hester Tel: 650-723-4000.

Special Assignment:
Reverend Monsignors—
Do, Dominic Dinh, Vicar Vietnamese Ministry
Mitchell, Michael J., Vicar General
Reverend Fathers—
Bonsor, Jack, Permanent Deacon Formation
Brown, Steven P., Dir. Seminarians
Catalana, Mark, Dir. Vocations
Cilia, Francis V., Vicar for Clergy
Galang, Jose, Vicar for Filipino Ministry
Gray, Robert, Dir. Cemeteries
Menchaca, Luis Gerardo, Vicar Hispanic Min.
Nguyen, Hien Minh, Adjutant Judicial Vicar
Rubio, Jose Antonio, Dir. Ecumenical & Interreligious Affairs & Delegate Eastern Rite Churches
Schuyler, David, S.M., Judicial Vicar & Vicar for Religious
Tucker, James, S.S., Pastoral Services

On Duty Outside the Diocese:
Reverend Fathers—
Keulman, Kenneth P., New Orleans, LA
Rich, Joseph, Newport Beach, CA
Saso, Michael, Carmel, CA
Tinh, Joseph Nguyen, Heimback-Vlatten, Germany

Graduate Studies:
Reverend Fathers—
Brocato, Robert, Mexico
Manrique, Wilfredo, Rome

Military Chaplains:
Reverend Fathers—
Hendel, Lawrence, Army National Guard. Tel: 408-252-7653

On Leave of Absence:
Reverend Fathers—
Arnone, A.
Browne, Dennis
Delgado, Joseph
Hilliard, Richard
Lagututta, Nunzio J.
Marx, Robert
Nabbefeld, Grant
Smith, Brian
Sullivan, Mervyn

Absent on Sick Leave:
Reverend Fathers—
Kilcoyne, Patrick
McCrillis, Philip
Neary, Mark

Retired:
Reverend Monsignors—
Boyle, Eugene
Coleman, John
Cottrell, Frank
Lenane, William
Maher, James
McCarren, Edgar P.
Milani, Joseph J.
Reverend Fathers—
Ahern, Thomas
Baltazar, Ayala
Blandino, Salvatore
Davis, Terrence
Field, Raymund, C.S.V.
Harrison, Arthur
Hlebs, Milan
Hofmann, Arthur
Largente, Laurent
Leininger, William
Lopez, Fausto
Macedo, Charles
Maher, Raymond
Murray, Thomas
O'Connor, William
Passalacqua, Robert
Peace, John
Re, Angelo
Shea, Thomas
Wilkiemeyer, Victor L.

Permanent Deacons:
Alvarez, Jose, St. John Vianney & St. Patrick
Alvarez, Salvador, St. Francis of Assisi
Bunje, Carl, St. Thomas Aquinas
Chavez, Eloy, Our Lady of Guadalupe
Combellick, Thomas, Sacred Heart, Saratoga
O'Sullivan, Eugene, St. John the Baptist
Perez, Vicente, Most Holy Trinity
Sweeney, Thomas, Saint Martin

INSTITUTIONS LOCATED IN THE DIOCESE

[A] SHRINES

SANTA CLARA. *Shrine of Our Lady of Peace*, 2800 Mission College Blvd., 95054. Tel: 408-988-4585; Fax: 408-988-0679. Rev. John J. Sweeny, Dir.; Mary Jean Kula, Staff.
Our Lady of Peace Gift Shop. Tel: 408-980-9825.

[B] COLLEGES AND UNIVERSITIES

SANTA CLARA. *Santa Clara University*, 500 El Camino Real, 95053-0001. Tel: 408-554-4000; Fax: 408-554-2700.
E-mail: username@scu.edu
Web site: www.scu.edu
For a complete listing, refer to the Colleges and Universities section.

[C] HIGH SCHOOLS, DIOCESAN

SAN JOSE. *Archbishop Mitty High School*. (Coed), 5000 Mitty Ave., 95129. Tel: 408-252-6610; Fax: 408-252-0518.
E-mail: brosnan@mitty.com
Web site: Mitty.com
Mr. Timothy Brosnan, Prin.; Rev. Enrico Hernandez, Campus Chap. Priests 1; Sisters 1; Lay Teachers 83; Students 1,458; Total Staff 136.

SANTA CLARA. *Saint Lawrence Academy*, 2000 Lawrence Ct., 95051. Tel: 408-296-3013.
E-mail: slhighschool@yahoo.com
Web site: www.saintlawrence.org/academys
College Prep Coed. Ron Modeste, Prin.; Ruth Benz, Assoc. Prin. Sisters 2; Lay Teachers 22; Students 343.

[D] HIGH SCHOOLS, PRIVATE

SAN JOSE. *Bellarmine College Preparatory*, 850 Elm St., 95126-1899. Tel: 408-294-9224; Fax: 408-294-1894.
Web site: www.bcp.org
Society of Jesus.
Non-Resident Students: Mark Pierroti, Prin.; Revs. Gerald T. Wade, S.J., Chancellor; William H. Muller, S.J., Pres.; James E. Morse, S.J.; Raymond P. Allender, S.J., Supr. & Contact; Mario L. Capitolo, S.J.; Ronald M. Clemo, S.J.; Eugene J. Corbett, S.J.; Paul D. Devot, S.J.; Carlo A. Farina, S.J.; John L. Flynn, S.J.; Gerald J. Lentz, S.J.; Robert B. Mathewson, S.J.; Edward J. McFadden, S.J.; Leo P. Prengaman, S.J.; Michael G. Scully, S.J.; Robert J. Shinney, S.J.; Daniel J. Sullivan; Bros. Raymond P. Koeplin, S.J.; Edmund W. Ryan, S.J. Priests 17; Lay Teachers 92; Students 1,390.

Notre Dame High School, 596 S. Second St., 95112. Tel: 408-294-1113; Fax: 408-293-9779.
Web site: www.ndsj.org
Sisters of Notre Dame de Namur.
Non-Resident Students. Mary Lou Schoone, Prin. Sisters 3; Lay Teachers 24; Total Staff 54; Students 560.

Presentation High School, 2281 Plummer Ave., 95125. Tel: 408-264-1664; Fax: 408-266-3028.
Web site: www.Pres-Net.com
Sisters of the Presentation. Mary Miller, Prin.; Rev. George Aranha, Chap. Priests 1; Lay Teachers 60; Students 710; Total Staff 70.

MOUNTAIN VIEW. *St. Francis High School*, 1885 Miramonte Ave., 94040. Tel: 650-968-1213; Fax: 650-968-3241.
E-mail: kemaklev@sfhs.com
Web site: www.sfhs.com
Brothers of Holy Cross. Mr. Kevin Makley, Pres.; Ms. Christie Filios, Dir. Activities; Mrs. Patty Tennant, Prin.; Angelo Aguiar, Exec. Dir. Devel.; Rev. Mark Catalana, Chap. Brothers 2; Sisters 1; Lay Teachers 83; Students 1,476; Total Staff 136.

[E] THE CATHOLIC CHARITIES OF THE DIOCESE OF SAN JOSE

SAN JOSE. *Catholic Charities of Santa Clara County*, 2625 Zanker Rd., 95134. Tel: 408-468-0100; Fax: 408-944-0275.
Web site: www.ccsj.org
Diane Pelosi Saign, CEO; Michael Veuve, CFO; Leslie Arioto, Community/Parish Relations; Marilou Cristina, Dir. Family Svcs.; Jennifer Yuan, Annual Giving Mgr.; Sr. Marilyn Lacey, R.S.M., Dir. Immigration, Refugee & Employment Svcs.; Buu Thai, Dir. Youth Svcs.; Kitty Mason, Dir., Behavioral Health Svcs.; Ron Ober, Assoc. Dir. Clinical Svcs.
Children's Counseling Center. Tel: 408-944-0469; Fax: 408-468-0147.
Community Counseling & Education Svcs. Tel: 408-944-0469; Fax: 408-468-0147.
Focus for Work. Tel: 408-944-0591; Fax: 408-944-0468.
Oasis. (Older Adult Mental Health Team). Tel: 408-955-9170; Fax: 408-949-0275.
Substance Abuse Services. Tel: 408-468-0100; Fax: 408-949-0275.
FAMILY SERVICES:
Foster Grandparent Program. Tel: 408-325-5132; Fax: 408-949-0275.
Independent Aging Program. Tel: 408-282-8608; Fax: 408-280-1026.

Day Break Respite Services. Tel: 408-270-4900.
Long Term Care Ombudsman Program. Tel: 408-944-0567; Fax: 408-944-0776.
Multi-Service Senior Center Programming, Eastside Neighborhood Ctr., 2150 Alum Rock Ave., 95112. Tel: 408-251-0215; Fax: 408-280-1026.
John XXIII Multiservice Center, 195 E. San Fernando St., 95112. Tel: 408-282-8600; Fax: 408-280-1026.
HOUSING DEVELOPMENT & SERVICE: 195 E. San Fernando St., 95112. Tel: 408-282-1129; Fax: 408-280-1311.
Shared Housing Program. Tel: 408-282-1144; Fax: 408-280-1311.
Housing Development. Tel: 408-282-1129; Fax: 408-280-1311.
IMMIGRATION, REFUGEE & EMPLOYMENT SERVICES: Sr. Marilyn Lacey, R.S.M., Dir.
Immigration Legal Services, 2625 Zanker Rd., 95134. Tel: 408-944-0691; Fax: 408-944-0347.
Second Immigration Legal Services Site, 7950 Church St., Gilroy, 95020. Tel: 408-842-4808; Fax: 408-842-9768.
Employment Services. Tel: 408-325-5150; Fax: 408-944-0275.
Parish Partnership Program. Tel: 408-325-5159; Fax: 408-944-0347.
USCC Refugee Resettlement. Tel: 408-468-0100; Fax: 408-944-0347.
E-mail: res@ccsj.org
SENIOR NUTRITION SERVICES: Tel: 408-944-0282; Fax: 408-944-0275.
Eastside Nutrition Site, 2150 Alum Rock Ave., 95116. Tel: 408-251-0215; Fax: 408-251-0218.
Gilroy Nutrition Site, 7371 Hanna St., Gilroy, 95020. Tel: 408-842-4200.
John XXIII Nutrition Site, 195 E. San Fernando, 95112. Tel: 408-282-8607; Fax: 408-280-1026.
Martha's Kitchen, 311 Willow St., 95110. Tel: 408-293-6111; Fax: 408-292-0172.
Morgan Hill Nutrition Site, 17666 Crest Ave., Morgan Hill, 95037. Tel: 408-776-0111.
Volunteer Services, Program Manager. Tel: 408-944-0282; Fax: 408-944-0275. All Nutrition Sites: Number Assisted 2,665; Meals 116,367.
YOUTH SERVICES:
Y.E.S. Youth Empowered for Success. Tel: 408-283-6150; Fax: 408-283-6152.
Washington Youth Center. Tel: 408-938-6731; Fax: 408-947-1107.
Teen Intervention Services. Tel: 408-283-6150; Fax: 408-283-6152.
Teen Leadership/Prevention Services. Tel: 408-283-6150; Fax: 408-283-6152.
HANDICAPABLES PROGRAM:
Handicapables Program, 2625 Zanker Rd., 95134. Tel: 408-325-5179; Fax: 408-944-0275. Sid Dunbar, Program Coord.
PALO ALTO/LOS ALTOS AUXILIARY:
Palo Alto/Los Altos Auxiliary, 1849 Mark Twain, Palo Alto, 94303. Tel: 650-948-3425.

[F] DAY CARE CENTERS

SAN JOSE. *St. Elizabeth's Day Home,* 1544 McKinley Ave., 95126. Tel: 408-295-3456; Fax: 408-295-5917.
E-mail: sedhd@kepnet.com
Web site: www.stelizabethsdayhome.org
Robert Freiri, Dir. Lay Staff 50; Children 215.

[G] GENERAL HOSPITALS

SAN JOSE. *O'Connor Hospital,* 2105 Forest Ave., 95218. Tel: 408-947-2500; Fax: 408-947-2819.
Web site: www.chwbay.org
For a complete listing, refer to the Hospitals section.

GILROY. *St. Louise Regional Hospital,* Admin. Office, 9400 N. Name Uno, 95020. Tel: 408-848-2000; Fax: 408-842-2155.
E-mail: tfox@chw.edu
Web site: www.chw.edu
For a complete listing, refer to the Hospitals section.

[H] SPECIAL SANATORIUM AND HOSPITALS

SARATOGA. *Our Lady of Fatima Villa,* 20400 Saratoga-Los Gatos Rd., 95070. Tel: 408-741-2950; Fax: 408-741-4930.
E-mail: ourlady@earthlink.com
For a complete listing, refer to the Special Care Facilities section.

[I] HOTEL, SENIOR CITIZENS RESIDENCE

SAN JOSE. *Giovanni Center, Inc.,* 85 S. Fifth St., 95112. Tel: 408-288-7436; Fax: 408-288-7264.
E-mail: alaujdm@aol.com
Web site: hometown.aol.com/alaujdm/myhomepage/business.html
For a complete listing, refer to the Special Care Facilities section.

Jeanne d'Arc Manor, 85 S. Fifth St., 95112. Tel: 408-288-7421; Fax: 408-288-7264.
E-mail: alaujdm@aol.com
Web site: hometown@aol.com/alaujdm/myhomepage/business-html
For a complete listing, refer to the Special Care Facilities section.

[J] HOMES FOR THE AGED

MOUNTAIN VIEW. *Villa Siena,* 1855 Miramonte Ave., 94040. Tel: 650-961-6484; Fax: 650-961-6254
For a complete listing, refer to the Special Care Facilities section.

[K] RETREATS

LOS ALTOS. *Jesuit Retreat House,* 300 Manresa Way, 94022. Tel: 650-948-4491; Fax: 650-948-0640.
E-mail: retreat@elretiro.org
Web site: www.elretiro.org
Revs. William J. Rewak, S.J., Supr. & Contact; Gerald P. McCourt, S.J.; Bernard J. Bush, S.J.; Robert J. Fabing, S.J.; Joseph J. Fice, S.J.; Jerrold W. Lindner, S.J.; Dare J. Morgan, S.J.; James R. Hanley, S.J.; Bro. Lawrence Thoo, S.J. Priests 8; Brothers 1.

LOS GATOS. *Presentation Retreat & Conference Center,* 19480 Bear Creek Rd., 95033-9519. Tel: 408-354-2346; Fax: 408-354-5226. Retreat and Conference Center for Religious and Laity. Sr. Patricia Marie Mulpeters, P.B.V.M., Dir. & Contact. Capacity 109; Staff 20; In Residence: Religious 8; Lay People 2.
Villa Holy Names, 82 Prospect Ave., 95032. Tel: 408-354-2312. Sr. Dorothy Clare Klingler, S.N.J.M. Total Staff 2.

[L] MONASTERIES AND RESIDENCES OF PRIESTS AND BROTHERS

SAN JOSE. *Carmelite Monastery, Novitiate,* P.O. Box 3420, 95156-3420. Tel: 408-251-1361; Fax: 408-251-1854. Very Rev. Gerald Werner, O.C.D., Prior & Contact; Revs. Ailbe Doolan, O.C.D.; Chrostopher La Rocca, O.C.D.; Richard Mandoli, O.C.D.; Pascal Pierini, O.C.D.; Jan Lundberg, O.C.D. Novices: Robert Barcelos; Brian Prince; Thomas Reeves; Kenneth Sampson. Postulants: Kevin Alexy; William Cesolini; David Guzman; Paul Jussen; John Marshall; Mark Moran; Salvador Roman. Postulants 7.
Marianist Community, 10381 Singleton Rd., 95111. Tel: 408-972-2716.
E-mail: wmjoseph@IX.netcom.com
Bros. Ronald Allen, S.M.; William Farrell, S.M., Contact. Priests 2.

CUPERTINO. *Marianist Provincial Residence.*
E-mail: pacprov@aol.com
Web site: www.marianistspacific.com
Legal Title: *Marianist Province of the Pacific.* Mailing Address: P.O. Box 1775, 95015-1775. Res., 22825 San Juan Rd., 95014. Tel: 408-253-4841; Fax: 408-253-5280. Rev. John Russi, S.M., Prov.; Bro. Gary E. Morris, S.M., Asst. Prov. & Dir. Education & Community Dir. In res. Rev. John Rielly, S.M.; Bros. Stanley Murakami, S.M.; James Riley, S.M. Priests 2; Brothers 3.
Priests of the Pacific Province Working at Other Locations: Rev. James Mifsud, S.M., Queen of Apostles, 4911 Moorpark Ave., San Jose, 95111. Bro. William Bolts, S.M., Queen of Apostles, 4911 Moorpark Ave., San Jose, 95111. Rev. Jorge da Silva, 461 Monterey Ave., Los Gatos, 95030-5302. Rev. Francis Nakagawa, S.M., 1184 Bishop St., Honolulu, HI, 96813-2857. Retreat Center 1; Lay Staff Only 22.
Marianist Community: 319 Pineview Dr., Santa Clara, 95050. Tel: 408-241-7110. Rev. David Schuyler, S.M.; Bros. Stephen Johnson, S.M.; Joseph Nuuanu, S.M.; Robert Hoppe, S.M., Supr.
Avila House, 618 Crestmoor Dr., San Jose, 95129-2102. Bros. Joseph Aspell, S.M.; Robert Juenemann, S.M.
Marianist Novitiate Corporation, P.O. Box 1775, 95015-1775.
Marianist Retreat Center, 22622 Marianist Way, 95014. Tel: 408-253-6279; Fax: 408-253-1834.
E-mail: marcenter@aol.com
Web site: www.homepages.go.com/~marcenter/main.html
Kevin Dincher, Dir.; Ann Repanich, Business Mgr. Retreat Center 2; Staff 10; Total Assisted 15,000 Adults.
Villa Saint Joseph, 22840 Mercedes Rd., 95014-3920. Tel: 408-257-4427; Fax: 408-255-9006.
E-mail: stutas@aol.com
Marianist Retirement Home. Revs. Joseph Stefanelli, S.M.; Stephen Tutds, S.M. In res. Bros. Robert Wade, S.M.; James Wipfield, S.M.; Leo Rausch, S.M.; Charles Ehrenfeld, S.M.; Anthony Beyer, S.M.; Charles Boglitz, S.M.; Eugene Frank, S.M.; John Samaha, S.M.; Xavier Schultz, S.M.; John O'Donnell, S.M. Priests 2; Brothers 10; Total in Residence 12.

LOS ALTOS. *Maryknoll,* 23000 Cristo Rey Dr., 94024. Tel: 650-967-3822; Fax: 650-965-3473. Retirement House for Priests and Brothers. In res. Revs. Daniel P. Jensen, M.M., Admin.; Richard A. Bell, M.M.; James A. Bodenstedt, M.M.; Clyde F. Davis, M.M.; Gilbert J. DeRitis, M.M.; John J. Drew, M.M.; John M. Breen, M.M.; Thomas F. Foley, M.M.; Francis J. Garvey, M.M.; Donald J. Haren, M.M.; Leon A. Harter, M.M.; Walter W. Johnson; Joseph A. Klecha, M.M.; Joseph J. O'Neill, M.M.; Richard T. Ouellette, M.M.; John J. Ridyard, M.M.; Michael J. Ruck, M.M.; Philip F. Sheerin, M.M.; Norbert M. Verhagen, M.M.; John J. Vinsko, M.M.; James R. Whitmore, M.M.; Bros. Thomas A. Hickey, Asst. Admin.; Luke R. Baldwin, M.M.; John Brown, M.M.; Duane S. Crockett, M.M.; Gordon M. Burns, M.M.; Conrad Fleisch, M.M.; Charles A. Heschele, M.M. Priests 20; Brothers 7.

LOS GATOS. *California Province of the Society of Jesus, Jesuit Provincial Office,* P.O. Box 519, 95031. Tel: 408-354-6143.
E-mail: calprovsj@aol.com
Very Rev. Thomas H. Smolich, S.J., Regl. Prov.; Revs. Alfred E. Naucke, S.J., Exec. Asst. & Contact; Anthony E. Sholander, S.J.; Thomas H. Smolich, S.J.; Robert L. St. Clair, S.J.
Sacred Heart Jesuit Center, Box 128, 95031. Tel: 408-354-9240; Fax: 408-354-1773. Legal Title: *California Province of the Society of Jesus dba Sacred Heart Jesuit Center.* Revs. Richard E. Cobb, S.J., Supr. & Contact; Joseph G Azadian, S.J.; Bro. Joseph Avila; Revs. James R. Blaettler, S.J.; Philip L. Bourret, S.J. (China); Thomas H. Byrne, S.J.; J. Ripley Caldwell; James N. Chevedden, S.J.; Joseph M. Costa, S.J.; Eugene J. Colosimo; George L. Crain, S.J.; Robert F. Curran, S.J.; Lenox C. Day, S.J.; Raymond A. Devlin, S.J.; Patrick D. Doherty, S.J.; Charles W. Dullea, S.J.; Bro. Howard C. Ellis, S.J.; Revs. Thomas P. Finsterbach, S.J.; David Fitch, S.J.; Thomas W. Foster, S.J.; Francis A. Frugoli, S.J.; Francis J. Gallagher, S.J.; John C. Geary, S.J.; Daniel V. Germann, S.J.; Bro. John F. Graham, S.J.; Revs. Neale W. Herrlich, S.J.; John E. Huesman, S.J.; Bro. Jack Hughes, S.J.; Revs. Pierre P. Jacobs, S.J.; Charles J. Kavanagh, S.J.; Bro. Raymond F. Keefe, S.J.; Revs. George J. Koch, S.J.; Terrence E. Koch, S.J.; Bro. Norbert J. Korte, S.J.; Revs. George E. Krivanek, S.J.; William F. Lester, S.J.; Robert L. Maloney, S.J.; Angelo Mariano, S.J.; William J. Maring, S.J.; Bro. Thomas A. Marshall, S.J.; Rev. Roger D. McAuliffe, S.J.; Bro. Paul I. McElligott, S.J.; Revs. Joseph F. Meehan, S.J.; James R. Menard, S.J.; Everett J. Mibach, S.J.; Cornelius J. Monacell, S.J.; James Monaghan, S.J.; Richard Mulcahy, S.J.; Stephen G. Olivo, S.J.; Bro. Daniel J. Peterson, S.J.; Revs. Gerald J. Phelan; Alfred G. Playoust, S.J.; Thomas A. Reed; Bro. Theodore C. Rohrer, S.J.; Revs. Arthur F. Rutledge, S.J.; Arthur J. Schenk, S.J.; Francis J. Silva, S.J.; Thomas H. Smolich, S.J.; Donald F. St. Sure, S.J.; Alden F. Stevenson, S.J.; Bro. Leonard J. Sullivan, S.J.; Revs. William V. Thom, S.J.; Salvano P. Votto, S.J.; Francis X. Wang, S.J. (China); Ronald D. Wolf, S.J.; George Wong, S.J. (China); Eugene R. Zimmers, S.J.; Michael J. Zimmers, S.J.
Priests of the Province residing elsewhere: Revs. Thomas G. Allender, S.J., San Francisco; Ernesto Arbelaez, S.J. (COL); Mark C. Ciccone, S.J.; Thomas G. Hand, S.J.; Stephen M. Kelly, S.J., PA; Candido O. Lim, S.J. (PHI); Francis D. Mac Peck, S.J. (SF); James P. McCauley, S.J., (Nevada); Robert R. Taheny, S.J.; Bro. John Moniz, S.J., Dittmer, MO. Priests 38; Brothers 12.

SANTA CLARA. *Marianist Community,* 319 Pineview Dr., 95050. Tel: 408-241-7110. Bro. Robert G. Hoppe, S.M., Dir. Priests 1; Brothers 3.

SARATOGA. *St. Patrick's Missionary Society.* (St. Patrick Fathers), 19536 Eric Dr., 95070. Tel: 408-253-3135; Fax: 408-253-5433.
E-mail: spsca@earthlink.net
Revs. Michael Moore, S.P.S.; Steven Donohue, S.P.S., Supr. Priests 2.

[M] CONVENTS AND RESIDENCES FOR SISTERS

SAN JOSE. *Community of the Holy Spirit,* 1275 Naglee Ave., 95126. Tel: 408-275-1710. Sr. Jolene M. Schmitz, C.H.S., Contact.
Daughters of Charity of St. Vincent de Paul, O'Connor Hospital, Sisters' Residence, 350 O'Connor Dr., 95128. Tel: 408-289-9215.
E-mail: dococon@aol.com
Sr. Rachela Silvestri, D.C., Contact. Sisters 9.
Dominican Sisters, Congregation of the Sacred Heart, Houston, 1092 W. San Fernando St., 95126. Tel: 408-294-7151.
E-mail: srclar@aol.com
Sr. Clarice Sparkman, O.P., Contact.

Eucharistic Missionaries of the Most Holy Trinity, 815 S. Daniel Way, 95128. Tel: 408-243-3157.
E-mail: sjosemesst@aol.com
Sr. Maria Luisa Chapa, M.E.S.S.T., Supr. Sisters 6.

LaSallian Sisters, 3867 Silver Creek Rd., 95121-1969. Tel: 408-238-9351; Fax: 408-258-4870.
E-mail: lasankirk@aol.com
Web site: saigon.com/-vietedu
Sr. Anne Julienne Bui, Supr. Sisters 18.

Pious Disciples of the Divine Master, 2076 Lincoln Ave., 95125. Tel: 408-265-8105. Sr. M. Michelle Hernandez, P.D.D.M., Local Contact. Sisters 3.

Quinhon Missionary Sisters of the Holy Cross. 1295 Eldamar Ct., 95121. Tel: 408-362-9719. Sr. Josephine Dao Vu, L.H.C., Local Contact. Sisters 6.

Sinsinawa Dominican Congregation of the Most Holy Rosary, 952 Carrabelle Way, 95120. Tel: 408-997-1713. Sr. Rita Claire Dorner, O.P. Sisters 4.

Sisters of Charity of Nazareth, 3208 Neal Ave., 95117. Tel: 408-244-4206.
E-mail: rmmaguire@juno.com
Sr. Rose Mary Maguire, S.C.N., Contact. Sisters 2.

Sisters of St. Joseph of Carondelet, 3383 Whitman Way, 95132. Sr. Margaret Gregg, Contact Person (St. Louis); Sr. Francis Marie Hansen, Contact Person (Los Angeles). Sisters 12.

Sisters of the Holy Family, Holy Family Convent, 1050 St. Elizabeth Dr., 95126. Tel: 408-287-8385; Fax: 408-287-8383. Sisters 8. St. Elizabeth's Day Home Day Care Center. Children 250.

Society of the Sacred Heart, 195 E. San Fernando, 95112. Tel: 408-282-1126; Fax: 408-280-1311.
E-mail: rstatt@rscj.org
Web site: www.sofie.org/rscj/
Sr. Rosemary Statt, R.S.C.J., Contact. Sisters 3.

CUPERTINO. *Blessed Virgin Missionaries of Carmel (B.V.M.C.)*, 10130 N. Deanza Blvd., 95014. Tel: 408-257-1022. Sr. Adelpha Luminate, B.V.M.C., Supr. Sisters 3.

Intercommunity Convent, 10351 S. Blaney Ave., 95014-3122. Tel: 408-725-0898; Fax: 408-252-4848.
E-mail: J96write@aol.com
Web site: www.nsyte-inc.com
Sr. Harriet Dow, O.S.F. Sisters 2.

Medical Mission Sisters, 10150 Torre Ave., Apt. 236, 95014-2156; Fax: 408-446-4913.
Web site: www.Libertynet.org/mms/
Sr. Marie Boniface Lischwe, M.M.S., Area Contact.

LOS ALTOS HILLS. *Daughters of Charity of St. Vincent de Paul (Laboure Residence), Seton Provincialate*, 26000 Altamont Rd., 94022. Tel: 650-941-4490; Fax: 650-949-3874.
E-mail: doc-psec@aol.com
Sr. Margaret Keavney, D.C., Prov.; Rev. Joseph V. Haley, C.M., Dir. Sisters 40; Total in Province 148; Total in Diocese 49.

Immaculate Heart Monastery of the Poor Clares, 28210 Natoma Rd., 94022. Tel: 650-948-2947. Mother Maura, P.C.C., Abbess. Sisters 15.

LOS GATOS. *Sisters of the Holy Names of Jesus & Mary*, Provincial Administration, P.O. Box 907, 95031. Tel: 408-395-5150; Fax: 408-354-8305.
E-mail: snjmcddsm@impresso.com
Sr. Margaret Spiller, S.N.J.M., Prov. Supr. & Contact; Sr. Sally Gunn, S.N.J.M., Northern Regl.; Sr. Barbara Boundreau, S.N.J.M., Southern Regl. Leadership Team: Sr. Marguerite Kirk, S.N.J.M.; Sr. Mary Ondreyco. Total in Province 250; Total in Diocese 93. Convent of the Holy Names, P.O. Box 1906, 95031. Tel: 408-354-1730; Fax: 408-395-6447. Ms. Julie Harrigan, Admin.; Sr. Joan Doyle, S.N.J.M., Community Life Coord. Total in Convent 65. Other sisters reside in communities in Santa Clara, Los Gatos, and San Jose.

MILPITAS. *Sisters of Mercy of Americas (Burlingame)*, 186 Beresford Ct. #F303, 95035. Tel: 408-946-5946. Sr. Maria Juanita Van Bommel, R.S.M., Local Contact. Sisters 8.

REDWOOD CITY. *Sisters of the Third Order of St. Francis of Penance and of Christian Charity*, P.O. Box 685, 94064. Sr. Felicia Gross, O.S.F., Contact Person. Sisters 3.

SANTA CLARA. *Carmelite Monastery of the Infant Jesus, Discalced Carmelite Nuns*, 1000 Lincoln St., 95050. Tel: 408-296-8412; Fax: 408-248-4846.
E-mail: santaclaracarmel@aol.com
Sr. Emmanuel, O.C.D., Prioress. Sisters 18; Novices 3.

Dominican Sisters of San Rafael. Congregation of the Most Holy Name, 1156 Main St., #11, 95050. Tel: 408-554-6431. Sisters 2.

Sisters of Charity of the Blessed Virgin Mary, 444 Saratoga Ave. Apt. 7A, 95050. Tel: 408-249-0773. Sr. Ann Marie Dress, B.V.M., Contact. Sisters 9.

SARATOGA. *Sisters of Notre Dame de Namur*, 14800 Bohlman Rd., 95070. Tel: 408-741-0324; Fax: 408-741-5809.
E-mail: calsnd@aol.com
Web site: www.sndden-ca.org
Sr. Nancy O'Shea, S.N.D.deN., Team Liaison for Diocese. Sisters in Province 154; Sisters in Diocese 48.

[N] NEWMAN CENTERS

SAN JOSE. *The Newman Center/Catholic Campus Ministry*, San Jose State University, 300 S. 10th St., 95112. Tel: 408-938-1610; Fax: 408-938-1612.
Web site: www.sjsuccm.org
Mailing Address: Catholic Campus Ministry/SJSU, The Newman Community, 300 S. 10th St., 95112. Rev. Charles Dougherty, Chap.; Sr. Marcia Krause, O.P., Dir.

[O] MISCELLANEOUS LISTINGS

SAN JOSE. *Caritas Housing Corporation*, 195 E. San Fernando St., 95112. Tel: 408-280-1311. Dan Wu, Dir.

Charities Housing Development Corporation of Santa Clara County, 195 E. San Fernando St., 95112. Tel: 408-282-1125; Fax: 408-280-1311. Dan Wu, Exec. Dir. Units 54; Total in Residence 92; Total Staff 2.

Hope Charities Housing Corporation, 195 E. San Fernando St., 95112. Tel: 408-285-1125; Fax: 408-280-1311. Dan Wu, Contact Person.

St. Vincent de Paul Society, District Council of Santa Clara County, 2040 S. 7th St., 95112. Tel: 408-298-7290; Fax: 408-993-0885.
E-mail: help@svdp.org
Web site: www.svdp.org
Mr. Stephen J. Pehanich, Exec. Dir. Total Assisted 70,000; Total Staff 50.

San Tomas/Charities Housing Corporation, 195 E. San Fernando St., 95112. Tel: 408-282-1125; Fax: 408-280-1311. Dan Wu, Exec. Dir. Units 100; In Residence 300; Total Staff 3.

Sierra Vista I/Charities Housing Corporation, 195 E. San Fernando St., 95112. Tel: 408-285-1125; Fax: 408-280-1311. Dan Wu, Contact Person.

Stoney Pine Charities Housing Corporation, 195 E. San Fernando St., 95112. Tel: 408-285-1125; Fax: 408-280-1311. Dan Wu, Contact Person.

Vietnamese Youth and Culture Association, La Salle Vietnam House, 1103 Maxey Ct., 95132. Tel: 408-926-4665; Fax: 408-254-3379.
E-mail: lasanvnsj@aol.com
Web site: www.lasan.org
Brothers of the Christian Schools (San Francisco Prov.). Bro. Valery Nguyen Van An, F.S.C., Dir.

LOS ALTOS. *Jesuit Institute for Family Life*, 300 Manresa Way, 94022. Tel: 650-948-4854. Rev. Robert J. Fabing, S.J., Dir.

St. Joseph the Worker Center, 4898 El Camino Real, Ste. 300, 94022. Tel: 650-962-1902; Fax: 650-962-1819.
Additional Center: 1664 Alum Rock Ave., San Jose, 95116. Tel: 408-923-9019; Fax: 408-923-8091. A service of St. Vincent dePaul of Santa Clara County. Day Worker Center. Mary Martinez, Dir. Total Assisted 3,500; Total Staff 9.

Serra Clubs District 31, 1515 Oakhurst Ave., 94024. Tel: 650-968-5155; Fax: 650-254-1174. Laurence Schott, Contact.

LYNWOOD. *Daughters of Charity Ministry Sevices Corporation*, 3663 Martin Luther King, Jr. Blvd., 90262. Tel: 310-638-0075; Fax: 310-603-6007. Robert Issai, CFO.

MENLO PARK. *Roman Catholic Communications Corp*. The Catholic Telemedia Network. 324 Middlefield Rd., 94025. Tel: 650-326-7850; Fax: 650-326-4605. Legal Title: *Roman Catholic Communications Corporation of the Bay Area*. Most Revs. John S. Cummins, Chm.; Patrick J. McGrath, Vice Chm.; Shirley Connolly, Gen. Mgr.

MOUNTAIN VIEW. *Villa Siena Foundation*, 1885 Miramonte Ave., 94040. Tel: 650-961-6484. Corine Bernard, Exec. Dir.

SANTA CLARA. *The Roman Catholic Welfare Corporation of San Jose*, 900 Lafayette St., Ste. 301, 95050-4966. Tel: 408-983-0240; Fax: 408-983-0296.
E-mail: mitchell@dsj.org
Rev. Msgr. Michael J. Mitchell, Contact Person. Total Staff 4.

St. Joseph Seminary Corporation, 900 Lafayette St., Ste. 301, 95050-4966. Tel: 408-983-0237; Fax: 408-983-0296.
E-mail: mitchell@dsj.org
Rev. Msgr. Michael J. Mitchell, Contact Person.

San Jose Cathedral Foundation. (A nonprofit, charitable, public-benefit California corporation.), 900 Lafayette St., Ste. 301, 95050-4966. Tel: 408-983-0100; Fax: 408-983-0295.
E-mail: mitchell@dsj.org
Most Rev. Patrick J. McGrath, Chm. of Bd. & Pres.

SARATOGA. *Our Lady of Fatima Villa Foundation*, 20400 Saratoga-Los Gatos Rd., 95070. Tel: 408-741-2968. Preston Wisner, Contact Person.

RELIGIOUS INSTITUTES OF MEN REPRESENTED IN THE DIOCESE

For further details refer to the corresponding bracketed number in the Religious Institutes of Men or Women section.

[0330]—*Brothers of the Christian Schools*.—F.S.C.
[0600]—*Brothers of the Congregation of the Holy Cross (Southwest Province)*.—C.S.C.
[1320]—*Clerics of St. Viator*.—C.S.V.
[1330]—*Congregation of the Mission (Vincentians)*.—C.M.
[0260]—*Discalced Carmelite Friars*.—O.C.D.
[]—*Franciscan Friars*. (Croatia).—O.F.M.
[]—*Guadalupe Missionaries*. (Mexico).—M.G.
[0650]—*Holy Ghost Fathers*.—C.S.Sp.
[]—*Institute of Incarnate Word*. (Argentina).—I.V.E.
[0690]—*Jesuit Fathers and Brothers, Society of Jesus (California Province)*.—S.J.
[0760]—*Marianists (Society of Mary)*.—S.M.
[0780]—*Marist Fathers*.—S.M.
[0800]—*Maryknoll (Catholic Foreign Mission Society of America, Inc.)*.—M.M.
[1210]—*Missionaries of St. Charles - Scalabrinians (Province of St. John Baptist)*.—C.S.
[1110]—*Missionaries of the Sacred Heart*.—M.S.C.
[0520]—*Order of Friars Minor (Province of St. Barbara)*.—O.F.M.
[]—*Franciscan Friars*. (Croatia).—O.F.M.
[0430]—*Order of Preachers (Province of the Most Holy Name of Jesus-Western Dominican Province)*.—O.P.
[1250]—*Order of the Clerics Regular of Somasca*. (Phillipines).—C.R.S.
[0610]—*Priests of the Congregation of Holy Cross (Eastern Province)*.—C.S.C.
[1170]—*St. Patrick's Missionary Society*.—S.P.S.
[1190]—*Salesians of Don Bosco*.—S.D.B.
[1260]—*Society of Christ*.—S.Ch.
[0420]—*Society of the Divine Word*.—S.V.D.
[1290]—*Society of the Priests of St. Sulpice*.—S.S.
[1250]—*Somascan Fathers, Order of the Clerics Regular of Somasca*.—C.R.S.

RELIGIOUS INSTITUTES OF WOMEN REPRESENTED IN THE DIOCESE

[]—*Blessed Virgin Missionaries of Carmel*.—B.V.M.C.
[]—*Caritas Sisters of Miyazaki*.—C.S.M.
[2020]—*Community of the Holy Spirit*.—C.H.S.
[]—*Congregation of the Augustinian Recollects*.—A.R.
[1070-25]—*Congregation of the Dominican Sisters of Saint Catherine of Siena of Kenosha*.—O.P.
[2100]—*Congregation of the Humility of Mary*.—C.H.M.
[]—*Congregation of the Most Holy Name*.
[1070-13]—*Congregation of the Most Holy Rosary (Dominican Sisters)*.—O.P.
[1070-12]—*Congregation of the Queen of the Holy Rosary (Dominican Sisters)*.—O.P.
[0760]—*Daughters of Charity of St. Vincent De Paul*.—D.C.
[0420]—*Discalced Carmelite Nuns*.—O.C.D.
[1070-19]—*Dominican Sisters of Houston, Texas (Congregation of the Sacred Heart)*.—O.P.
[1070-30]—*Dominican Sisters of Oakford*.—O.P.
[]—*Dominican Sisters of San Rafael*.
[]—*Eucharistic Missionaries of the Most Holy Trinity*. (Mexico).—M.E.S.S.T.
[]—*LaSallian Sisters*. (Vietnam).—L.S.
[2470]—*Maryknoll Sisters of St. Dominic*.—M.M.
[2490]—*Medical Mission Sisters*.—M.M.S.
[]—*Missionary Sisters Oblates of the Holy Family*. (Taiwan).—O.H.F.
[2715]—*Missionary Sisters of Christ the King*.—M.S.C.K.
[3760]—*Order of St. Clare (Immaculate Heart Monastery of Poor Clares)*.—M.Chr.
[0980]—*Pious Disciples of the Divine Master*.—P.D.D.M.
[]—*Quinhon Missionary Sisters of the Holy Cross*. (Vietnam).—Q.M.H.C.
[1070-03]—*Sinsinawa Dominican Congregation of the Most Holy Rosary*.—O.P.
[0500]—*Sisters of Charity of Nazareth (Southern Region)*.—S.C.N.
[0430]—*Sisters of Charity of the Blessed Virgin Mary*.—B.V.M.
[2516]—*Sisters of Mercy (Ireland)*.—R.S.M.
[2570]—*Sisters of Mercy of the Americas (Regional Community of Burlingame)*.—R.S.M.
[3000]—*Sisters of Notre Dame de Namur (California Province)*.—S.N.D.deN.

[3840]—*Sisters of St. Joseph of Carondelet (Province of Los Angeles).*—C.S.J.

[3840]—*Sisters of St. Joseph of Carondelet (Province of St. Louis).*—C.S.J.

[1960]—*Sisters of the Holy Family.*—S.H.F.

[1990]—*Sisters of the Holy Names of Jesus and Mary (California Province).*—S.N.J.M.

[3320]—*Sisters of the Presentation of the Blessed Virgin Mary.*—P.B.V.M.

[1630]—*Sisters of the Third Order of Saint Francis of Penance and Christian Charity.*—O.S.F.

[2170]—*Sisters, Servants of the Immaculate Heart of Mary.*—I.H.M.

[2150]—*Sisters, Servants of the Immaculate Heart of Mary, Monroe, Michigan.*—I.H.M.

[1890]—*Society of Helpers (American Province).*—H.H.S.

[4070]—*Society of the Sacred Heart.*—R.S.C.J.

DIOCESAN CEMETERIES AND MAUSOLEUMS

San Jose. *Calvary.* (Santa Clara Co.), 2655A Madden Ave., 95126. Tel: 408-258-2940; Fax: 408-258-5614.

Los Altos. *Gate of Heaven,* 22555 Cristo Rey Dr., 94024. Tel: 415-428-3730; Fax: 415-428-3733.

NECROLOGY

† Sheedy, Rev. Msgr. Mateo E., San Jose, Sacred Heart of Jesus. —Died Oct. 20, 2000.

Archdiocese of Santa Fe

(Archidioecesis Sanctae Fidei)

Most Reverend

MICHAEL J. SHEEHAN, S.T.L., J.C.D.

Archbishop of Santa Fe; ordained July 12, 1964; consecrated and installed as First Bishop of Lubbock June 17, 1983; appointed Apostolic Administrator of Santa Fe April 6, 1993; installed as Eleventh Archbishop of Santa Fe September 21, 1993. *Res., Catholic Center, 4000 St. Joseph Pl., N.W., Albuquerque, NM, 87120.*

Archdiocese of Santa Fe Catholic Center: 4000 St. Joseph Pl., N.W., Albuquerque, NM, 87120. Tel.: 505-831-8100.

ESTABLISHED IN 1850.

CREATED AN ARCHBISHOPRIC IN 1875.

Solemnly consecrated to the Immaculate Heart of Mary on October 7, 1945.

Square Miles 61,142.

Comprises the Counties of Colfax, Curry, DeBaca, Guadalupe, Harding, Los Alamos, Mora, Quay, Roosevelt, San Miguel, Santa Fe, Socorro, Taos, Torrance and Union with a part of Bernalillo, Sandoval, Rio Arriba and Valencia Counties.

PATRON OF THE ARCHDIOCESE: St. Francis of Assisi.

For legal titles of parishes and archdiocesan institutions, consult the Chancery Office.

STATISTICAL OVERVIEW

Personnel	
Archbishop	1
Retired Archbishops	1
Abbots	2
Priests: Diocesan Active in Diocese	71
Priests: Active Outside Diocese	3
Priests: Retired, Sick or Absent	37
Number of Diocesan Priests	111
Religious Priests in Diocese	92
Extern Priests in Diocese	9
Ordinations:	
Diocesan Priests	4
Permanent Deacons	2
Permanent Deacons in Diocese	146
Total Brothers	86
Total Sisters	254
Parishes	
Parishes	92
With Resident Pastor:	
Resident Diocesan Priests	65
Resident Religious Priests	24
Without Resident Pastor:	
Administered by Deacons	1
Administered by Women Religious	2
Missions	217
Pastoral Centers	4
Professional Ministry Personnel:	
Brothers	1
Sisters	34
Lay Ministers	175
Welfare	
Catholic Hospitals	4
Total Assisted	13,806
Health Care Centers	1
Total Assisted	6,646
Homes for the Aged	3
Total Assisted	152
Day Care and Extended Day Care Centers	1
Total Assisted	274
Specialized Homes	4
Total Assisted	1,402
Special Centers for Social Services	5
Total Assisted	281,412
Residential Care of Disabled	1
Total Assisted	16
Educational	
Diocesan Students in Other Seminaries	25
Students Religious	18
Total Seminarians	43
Colleges and Universities	1
Total Students	1,774
High Schools, Diocesan and Parish	1
Total Students	1,041
High Schools, Private	1
Total Students	758
Elementary Schools, Diocesan and Parish	16
Total Students	4,187
Catechesis/Religious Education:	
High School Students	5,694
Elementary Students	18,729
Total Students Under Catholic Instruction	32,226
Teachers in the Diocese:	
Brothers	5
Sisters	25
Lay Teachers	346
Vital Statistics	
Receptions into the Church:	
Infant Baptism Totals	7,136
Adult Baptism Totals	391
Received into Full Communion	675
First Communions	5,891
Confirmations	3,443
Marriages:	
Catholic	1,253
Interfaith	246
Total Marriages	1,499
Deaths	2,939
Total Catholic Population	286,155
Total Population	1,071,238

Former Archbishops—Most Rev. J. B. LAMY, cons. Nov. 24, 1850; created first Archbishop, 1875; resigned July 18, 1885; died Feb. 13, 1888.—Most Rev. J. B. SALPOINTE, D.D., second Archbishop; cons. Bishop of Doryla and Vicar Apostolic of Arizona, June 20, 1869; appt. Coadjutor of Santa Fe "cum jure successionis", April, 22, 1884; promoted to the Titular Archiepiscopal See of Anazarba, Oct. 11 of same year; succeeded to the See of Santa Fe, July 18, 1885; resigned Jan. 7, 1894; Titular Archbishop of Tomi; died July 15, 1898.—Most Rev. P. L. CHAPELLE, cons. Nov. 1, 1891; Archbishop of Santa Fe, Jan. 7, 1894; transferred to New Orleans, Dec. 1, 1897; died Aug. 9, 1905.—Most Rev. PETER BOURGADE, D.D., cons. May 1, 1885; Bishop of Thaumacum and Vic. Ap. of Arizona; Bishop of Tucson, May 8, 1897; transferred to Santa Fe, Jan. 7, 1899; died May 17, 1908.—Most Rev. J. B. PITAVAL, D.D., cons. Titular Bishop of Sora and Auxiliary of Santa Fe, July 25, 1902; promoted to the See of Santa Fe, Jan. 3, 1909; resigned Feb., 1918; appt. Titular Archbishop of Amida, July 29, 1918; died May 23, 1928.—Most Rev. ALBERT T. DAEGER, O.F.M., D.D., cons. May 7, 1919; died Dec. 2, 1932.—Most Rev. RUDOLPH ALOYSIUS GERKEN, D.D., cons. Bishop of Amarillo, April 26, 1927; appt. Archbishop of Santa Fe, June 2, 1933; installed as Archbishop of Santa Fe, Aug. 23, 1933; died March 2, 1943.—Most Rev. EDWIN V. BYRNE, D.D., cons. Bishop of Ponce, P.R. transferred to Diocese of San Juan, P.R. promoted to Archbishop of Santa Fe, June 15, 1943; died July 25, 1963.—Most Rev. JAMES P. DAVIS, D.D., cons. Bishop of San Juan, P.R., Oct. 6, 1943; promoted to Archbishop, April 30, 1960; transferred to Archdiocese of Santa Fe, Jan. 3, 1964; retired Oct. 1974; died March 4, 1988.—Most Rev. ROBERT F. SANCHEZ, cons. 10th Archbishop of Santa Fe, July 25, 1974; resigned April 6, 1993.—

All offices are located at the *Archdiocese of Santa Fe Catholic Center, 4000 Saint Joseph Pl., N.W., Albuquerque, NM 87120. Tel. 505-831-8100, unless otherwise indicated.*

Office of the Archbishop

Vicar-General—Rev. Msgr. LEO LUCERO, V.G., *P.O. Box 7007, Albuquerque, 87194.*

Secretary to the Archbishop—Ms. DOLORES CORDOVA. Tel: 505-831-8120.

Office of the Chancellor

Chancellor—Rev. Msgr. JOSEPH A. PEPE, J.C.D. Tel: 505-831-8158. Vice Chancellors: Sr. NANCY KAZIK, O.S.F. Tel: 505-831-8188. Rev. DONALD STARKEY. Tel: 505-831-8348.

Archivist and Artistic Patrimony—Mrs. MARINA OCHOA, *213 Cathedral Pl., Santa Fe, 87501.* Tel: 505-983-3811., *Albuquerque Office at the Catholic Center.* Tel: 505-831-8174.

Attorney for the Archdiocese—Mr. CHARLES P. REYNOLDS, *201 12th St., N.W., Albuquerque, 87102.* Tel: 505-842-8177.

Communications-Media—Mrs. CELINE RADIGAN, Dir. Tel: 505-831-8180.

Ecumenical Commission and Inter-Religious Affairs—Rev. ERNEST FALARDEAU, S.S.S., Dir., *St. Charles Borromeo Church, 1818 Coal, S.E., Albuquerque, 87106.* Tel: 505-242-3462.

Madonna Retreat and Conference Center—Mr. DOMINIC KOLLASCH, Dir., *4040 St. Joseph Pl., N.W., Albuquerque, 87120.* Tel: 505-831-8196.

Newspaper, Archdiocesan "People of God"—Most Rev. MICHAEL J. SHEEHAN, Publisher; Sr. NANCY KAZIK, O.S.F., Editor, *4000 St. Joseph Pl., N.W., Albuquerque, 87120.* Tel: 505-831-8188.

Parish Bulletin Service, "The Catholic Communicator"—JENNY CHILSON, *P.O. Box 93244, Albuquerque, 87199-3244.* Tel: 505-856-0333; Fax: 505-822-5589.

Human Resources—Mr. WALTER DUGUAY, Dir. Tel: 505-831-8130.

Immaculate Heart of Mary Retreat and Conference Center—BEN ARMIJO, Dir. Tel: 505-988-1975.

Canonical Services Division

Judicial Vicar—Rev. JEROME PLOTKOWSKI, J.C.L. Tel: 505-831-8177.

College of Consultors—Very Revs. LEO LUCERO, V.G.; LARRY DUNHAM, O.F.M.; Revs. JUAN MENDEZ; RICHARD OLONA; FRANCIS EGGERT; MIKE SHEA; LAMBERT LUNA; DOUGLAS RAUN.

Council of Men & Women Religious—Vacant.

Holy Childhood Association—See Mission Office.

Mission Office—Rev. ARKAD BICZAK, Dir. Propagation of

the Faith; Holy Childhood; Catholic Relief Svcs., *John XXIII Catholic Community, 4831 Tramway Ridge Dr., N.E., Albuquerque, 87111.* Tel: 505-293-0088.

Office of Religious—Sr. NANCY KAZIK, O.S.F., Dir. Tel: 505-831-8188.

Permanent Diaconate Program—Deacon DONATO LUCERO, Dir., *Immaculate Heart of Mary, 3700 Canyon Rd., Los Alamos, 87544.* Tel: 505-662-6193.

Pilgrimage for Vocations—Rev. EDMOND SAVILLA, Dir., *P.O. Box 888, Taos, 87571.* Tel: 505-758-9208.

Presbyteral Council of the Archdiocese of Santa Fe—Most Rev. MICHAEL J. SHEEHAN, Pres.; Rev. Msgr. JOSEPH A. PEPE, Ex Officio; Very Rev. LEO LUCERO, V.G., Ex Officio; Vacant, Chm.; Vacant, Sec. Exec. Committee. Exec. Board Members: Rev. LAMBERT LUNA; Rev. Msgr. DOUG RAUN.

Propagation of the Faith—See Mission Office.

Vicars Forane (Deans)—Very Revs. JEROME MARTINEZ Y ALIRE, Santa Fe Deanery; FRANK PRIETO, Albuquerque-Deanery A; RONALD BRUCKNER, Albuquerque-Deanery B; Rev. EDMOND SAVILLA, Albuquerque-Deanery C; Very Revs. ANTHONY MARTINEZ, Southwest Deanery; CHARLES BROWN, Northwest Deanery; VINCENT DEFAZIO, Northeast Deanery; JOHN DANIEL, Southeast Deanery.

Tribunal—Tel: 505-831-8177.
Judicial Vicar—Rev. JEROME PLOTKOWSKI, J.C.L.
Adjutant Judicial Vicar—Vacant.
Promoter of Justice—Rev. JEROME MARTINEZ Y ALIRE, J.C.L.
Defenders of the Bond—Revs. SOTERO SENA; ADAM ORTEGA Y ORTIZ; RICK ZERWAS; JOHN RODRIQUEZ.
Associate Judges—Revs. RAMON ARAGON; C. JOHN BRASHER; CRISPIN C. BUTZ, O.F.M.; JOHN R. CONWAY; NORMAN R. FALARDEAU, S.S.S.
Notaries—Mrs. LEDIA APODACA; Ms. JULIANA JARAMILLO; Ms. HELEN WILLS.
Delegate for Matrimonial Dispensations—Revs. JEROME PLOTKOWSKI, J.C.L.; DONALD J. STARKEY.

Appeal Court—Tel: 505-831-8177.

Vocation Director—Rev. JOHN CARNEY, Dir. Tel: 505-831-8143. Rev. RICK ZERWAS, Assoc. Dir.; Deacon RUDY ZAMORA, Asst. Dir.

Finance Division

Executive Director of Finance—Mr. TONY SALGADO, C.P.A. Tel: 505-831-8132.

Annual Catholic Appeal Foundation—Archdiocesan Annual Appeal Program, Mrs. LINDA J. GARCIA, C.F.R.E., Exec. Dir. Tel: 505-831-8155.

Archdiocese of Santa Fe Catholic Foundation—MARY P. DUNN, Exec. Dir., *2201 San Pedro, N.E., Bldg. 2, Ste. 211, Albuquerque, 87110.* Tel: 505-872-2901. Non-profit corporation for financial support of Archdiocese of Santa Fe.

Finance Council—Most Rev. MICHAEL J. SHEEHAN, Pres.; Mr. WILLIAM GRADY, Chm.; Very Revs. LARRY DUNHAM, O.F.M.; LEO LUCERO, V.G.; Rev. Msgr. JOSEPH A. PEPE; Rev. JOHN CONWAY; Mr. GIG BRUMMEL; Mr. TONY SALGADO, C.P.A.; Mr. TIM SHEEHAN; Ms. JENNIFER CANTRELL; Sr. NANCY KAZIK, O.S.F.

Property Managers and Construction Contract Coord.—Mr. JOHN HUCHMALA. Tel: 505-831-8136.

Pastoral Ministries

Executive Director—Ms. FRANCES VOGEL-MONTANO, *4000 St. Joseph Pl., N.W., Albuquerque, 87120.* Tel: 505-831-8151.

AIDS/HIV Ministry of the Archdiocese of Santa Fe—JEFF STROBEL, Dir., *P.O. Box 4231, Albuquerque, 87196.* Tel: 505-243-3203; 800-497-2450.

Campaign for Human Development—Mrs. JOAN LEAHIGH, Coord., *4000 St. Joseph Pl., N.W., Albuquerque, 87120.* Tel: 505-831-8167.

Catholic Committee on Scouting—(Boy Scouts and Girl Scouts). Deacon DONALD BRUCKNER, Dir. Scouting.

Catholic Schools Office—Sr. MICHELLE MICEK, O.S.F., Supt. Tel: 505-831-8173.

Catholic Charities of Albuquerque—GREGORY R. KEPFERLE, M.A., M.Div., Exec. Dir., *2010 Bridge, S.W., Albuquerque, 87105., Mailing Address: P.O. Box 25405, Albuquerque, 87125.* Tel: 505-247-9521.

Catholic Charities of Santa Fe, Inc.—GREGORY R. KEPFERLE, M.A., M.Div., Exec. Dir., *138 Park Ave., Santa Fe, 87501., Mailing Address: P.O. Box 443, Santa Fe, 87504.* Tel: 505-982-0441.

Cursillo Movement—Rev. CHRYSOSTOM PARTEE, O.F.M., Coord., *San Diego Friary, P.O. Box 79, Jemez Pueblo, 87024.* Tel: 505-834-7300.

Ministry to the Disabled—Ms. PATRICIA STEFFES, Dir.

Ministry to the Deaf—Mrs. ARDITH MONTANO, Coord. Tel: 505-831-8174.

Evangelization—Deacon JUAN BARAJAS. Tel: 505-831-8152.

Formation for Christian Service—FRANCES VOGEL-MONTANO, Dir. Tel: 505-831-8151.

Hospital Ministry—Ms. PATRICIA STEFFES, Coord. Tel: 505-831-8174.

Prison & Detention Ministry—PATRICIA STEFFES, Dir. Tel: 505-831-8174.

Archdiocesan Network for Catholic Legislative Advocacy—Mrs. JOAN LEAHIGH. Tel: 505-831-8167.

Liturgical Commission—Most Rev. MICHAEL J. SHEEHAN, Pres. LUIS CASTILLO, Chm., *4000 St. Joseph Pl., N.W., Albuquerque, 87120.* Tel: 505-831-8194.

Marriage and Family Life Office—Mrs. REMEDIOS (HEDDY) LONG, Dir. Tel: 505-831-8117.

Ministry to Spanish Speaking—Deacon JUAN BARAJAS. Tel: 505-831-8152.

African American Ministry—Ms. BRENDA DABNEY. Tel: 505-831-8167.

Native American Ministry—Mr. MIKE VALDO. Tel: 505-831-8243.

Newman Centers—
ALBQ: Aquinas Newman Center—Rev. ROBERT KELLER, O.P., Dir., *Univ. of New Mexico, 1815 Las Lomas Rd., N.E., Albuquerque, 87106.* Tel: 505-247-1095.
LAS VEGAS: Newman Center—Rev. VINCENT CHAVEZ, Coord., *Highlands University, 811 Sixth St., Las Vegas, 87701.* Tel: 505-425-9295.
PORTALES: St. Thomas Moore Newman Center—Very Rev. TOBIN HITT, Chap., *Eastern New Mexico University, P.O. Box 2253, Portales, 88130.* Tel: 505-356-5615.
SANTE FE: College of Santa Fe—Rev. JAMES CRONIN, Dir., *St. Michael's Dr., Santa Fe, 87501.* Tel: 505-473-6011.
Santa Fe Community College—Bro. JAMES BROWN, Campus Min. Tel: 505-473-6587.

Office of Worship—Mrs. DOLORES SOKOL. Tel: 505-831-8194.

Peace Pilgrimage—Deacon JOHN LEAHIGH, Coord. Tel: 505-831-8167.

Pro Life Commission—JOAN LEAHIGH, Dir., *4000 St. Joseph Pl., N.W., Albuquerque, 87120.* Tel: 505-831-8167.

RCIA—Rev. THOMAS MAYEFSKE. Tel: 505-831-8194.

Religious Education—Ms. CATHERINE ABEYTA, Dir. Tel: 505-831-8127. Ms. MARYANN HOLLAND, Dir. Catechetical Support, *4000 St. Joseph Pl., N.W., Albuquerque, 87120.* Tel: 505-831-8128.

Schools of Lay Ministry Formation—
Albuquerque Deanery A,B,C, "Emmaus Journey"—FRANCES VOGEL-MONTANO, Coord., *4000 St. Joseph Pl., N.W., Albuquerque, 87120.* Tel: 505-831-8151.
Northwest Deanery—Ms. MARY ANN HOLLAND, Coord., *Ojo Sarco, 87550.* Tel: 505-689-2457.
Santa Fe Deanery—(Jornada de Fe). JUANITA MONTOYA, Coord., *St. John the Baptist, 1301 Osage Ave., Santa Fe, 87505.* Tel: 505-983-5034.

St. Vincent de Paul Council—Deacon SANTOS ABEYTA, Spiritual Dir., *Holy Family Parish, P.O. Box 12127, Albuquerque, 87195.* Tel: 505-842-5426.

Social Justice—Mrs. JOAN LEAHIGH. Tel: 505-831-8167.

Stewardship—Deacon JUAN BARAJAS, Dir. Tel: 505-831-8152.

Youth and Young Adult Ministry—Mrs. BERNADETTE JARAMILLO, Dir. Tel: 505-831-8145.

Ministry Resource Center—Mrs. PATRICIA MCINTIRE, Dir. Tel: 505-831-8187.

CLERGY, PARISHES, MISSIONS AND PAROCHIAL SCHOOLS

CITY OF SANTA FE
(Santa Fe County)

1—THE CATHEDRAL OF SAN FRANCISCO DE ASIS (1610), Revs. Jerome Martinez y Alire, J.C.L., Rector; Jose Superiaso, M.T.S.; Lawrence R. Brito, M.Div.; Deacons William Kollasch; Juan Martinez. In res., Rev. Robert Lussier, O.S.B.
Res., P.O. Box 2127, 87504. Tel: 505-982-5619; Fax: 505-989-1952. [CEM]
School—Tel: 505-982-0331; Fax: 505-982-0667. Sr. Josephine Macias, C.D.P., Admin.; Sr. Phyllis Stowell, S.C.L., Prin.
Sisters 2; Lay Teachers 17; Students 236.
Catechesis/Religious Programs—Tel: 505-982-3625. Juanita Montoya, D.R.E.
Students 193.
Missions—Santa Clara, Rio Arriba Co., Indian Pueblo; San Ildefonso, Sante Fe Co., Indian Pueblo; Tesuque, Sante Fe Co., Indian Pueblo.

2—OUR LADY OF GUADALUPE (1882) (Hispanic), Rev. Michael J. Shea; Deacons Anthony Trujillo; Carlos F. Pacheco.
Res., 417 Agua Fria St., 87501. Tel: 505-983-8868; Fax: 505-983-4304. [CEM][JC]
Catechesis/Religious Programs—Tel: 505-988-3336. Theresa Montez, D.R.E.
Students 265.
Missions—Tesuque, Santa Fe Co., San Ysidro, P.O. Box 65, Tesuque, 87574. Tel: 505-984-2930; Rio en Medio, Sante Fe Co., Our Lady of Sorrows, Tel: 505-982-5588.

3—CRISTO REY (1940), Rev. Lambert Joseph Luna; Deacon Randy Rodriguez.
Office: 1120 Canyon Rd., 87501. Tel: 505-983-8528; Fax: 505-992-6836. [JC]
School—Tel: 505-983-8411; Fax: 505-983-8411 (Call first). Terry Lopez, Prin.
Lay Teachers 8; Students 156.
Mission—Santa Fe, Santa Fe Co., Old Guadalupe, La Canada de los Alamos, Santa Fe, 87501.
Catechesis/Religious Programs—Students 95.

4—ST. ANNE'S (1942) (Spanish), Rev. Clarence Maes.
Res., 511 Alicia, 87501. Tel: 505-983-4430; Fax: 505-983-7483. [JC]
Catechesis/Religious Programs—Students 247.

5—ST. JOHN THE BAPTIST (1953), Revs. John A. Flaska, Jr.; John C. Rodriguez; Deacons Andres Carrillo; Tony Rodriguez.
Res., 1301 Osage Ave., 87505. Tel: 505-983-5034; Fax: 505-983-1861.
Catechesis/Religious Programs—Connie C. Smith, D.R.E.
Students 310.

6—SAN ISIDRO (1835) (Hispanic), Rev. Franklin D. Pretto.
Res., 3552 Agua Fria St., 87501. Tel: 505-471-0710; Fax: 505-471-9034. [CEM 2]
Catechesis/Religious Programs—Sr. Lorraine Delisle, S.C., D.R.E.
Students 221.
Mission—La Cienega, Santa Fe Co.

7—SANTA MARIA DE LA PAZ CATHOLIC COMMUNITY (1990), Rev. Adam Lee Ortega y Ortiz. Pastoral Assocs.: Felipe R. Mirabal; Paul Lujan; Sr. Paula Gallagher, I.H.M.; Sr. Colleen Shanahan, O.S.F.; Deacons Facundo R. Rodriguez; Tom Van Volkenburgh.
Res., 11 College Ave., 87505. Tel: 473-4200 (Office); Fax: 505-473-1602.
Catechesis/Religious Programs—Mrs. Patricia Lopez, D.R.E.
Students 799.

OUTSIDE THE CITY OF SANTA FE

Abiquiu, Rio Arriba Co., St. Thomas Apostle (1745) (Hispanic), Rev. Mark E. Granito.
Res., P.O. Box 117, 87510. Tel: 505-685-4462. [CEM 5]
Catechesis/Religious Programs—Tel: 505-685-4462 (All Missions).
Students 150.
Missions—Canones, Rio Arriba Co.; Medanales, Rio Arriba Co.; Youngsville, Rio Arriba Co.; Coyote, Rio Arriba Co.; Mesa de Poleo, Rio Arriba Co.; Capulin, Rio Arriba Co.; Gallina, Rio Arriba Co.

Albuquerque, Bernalillo Co.,

1—ANNUNCIATION, (1959), Rev. Ronald L. Bruckner; Deacons Harry Gogan; Victor J. Bachechi.
Res., 2600 Vermont N.E., 87110. Tel: 505-293-5462; 298-7553.
Office: 2532 Vermont N.E., 87110. Tel: 505-298-7553; Fax: 505-294-7418.
School—2610 Utah N.E., 87110. Tel: 505-299-6783; Fax: 505-299-2182. Sr. Rose Therese Wich, S.C., Prin.
Lay Teachers 34; Students 475.
Catechesis/Religious Programs—Tel: 505-296-0411. Sr. Necy Guan, Fd.C.C., D.R.E.
Students 216.

2—ASCENSION, (1962), Rev. Edmund Savilla; Deacon Bill Hoefler.
Res., 2150 Raymac Rd., S.W., 87105. Tel: 505-877-8550; Fax: 508-877-8508. [CEM 2]
Catechesis/Religious Programs—Tel: 505-877-8144. Sr. Josie Peralta, Fd.C.C., D.R.E.
Students 306.

3—COMMUNITY OF THE RISEN SAVIOR, (1979), Rev. Msgr. Joaquin Bazan; Revs. Richard Olona; Dennis M. Garcia; Sr. Marie Luisa Vasquez, O.P., Pastoral Assoc.
Church—7701 Wyoming, N.E., 87109. Tel: 505-821-1571; Fax: 505-857-0065.
Catechesis/Religious Programs—D.R.E.: Gerry Wood; Susan Pilcher.
Students 1,248.

4—HOLY FAMILY, (1953) (Hispanic), Rev. Manuel Viera, O.F.M.; Don Conklin, Pastoral Assoc.; Deacons Santos Abeyta; Robert Paiz; Eddie Blea; Enrique

Padilla. In res., Rev. Lawrence Schreiber, O.F.M.; Bros. Peter Forton, O.F.M.; Bruce Michalek, O.F.M. Res., 562 Atrisco Dr., S.W., P.O. Box 12127, 87105. Tel: 505-842-5426; Fax: 505-842-9767.
Catechesis/Religious Programs—D.R.E.: Marta Sanchez; Karen Mitchell; Mary Ann Gutierrez; Susan Frost; Don Conklin.
Students 460.

5—HOLY GHOST, (1953), Rev. Thomas J. Mayefske; Deacons Pat Kneafsey; Robert Stromberg; Ubaldo Chavez.
Res., 833 Arizona Ave., S.E., 87108. Tel: 505-265-5957; Fax: 505-265-5958.
School—Tel: 505-256-1563; Fax: 505-262-9635. Noreen Copeland, Prin.
Sisters 2; Lay Teachers 20; Students 227.
Catechesis/Religious Programs—Tel: 505-265-1975. Sr. Connie Martinez, Fd.CC., D.R.E.
Students 192.

6—IMMACULATE CONCEPTION, (1883) (Hispanic), Revs. Edmundo Rodriguez, S.J.; Richard W. McGowan, S.J.; Louis J. Lambert, S.J.; Thomas J. Steele, S.J.; William M. King, S.J.; Deacons Gilbert Valverde; George Sandoval.
Res., 619 Copper Ave., N.W., 87102. Tel: 505-247-4272; Fax: 505-243-0402.
School—St. Mary, 227 Seventh St., 87102. Tel: 505-242-6271; Fax: 505-242-4837. Sr. Marianella Domenici, S.C., Prin.
Sisters 1; Lay Teachers 36; Students 606.
Catechesis/Religious Programs—Tel: 505-247-2555.
Students 155.

7—NATIVITY OF THE BLESSED VIRGIN MARY, (1911), Revs. Juan Mendez; Nathan Libaire, O.S.B.; Deacon Robert Contreras.
Res., 9502 Fourth St., N.W., 87114. Tel: 505-898-5253; Fax: 505-898-0496. [CEM][JC 2]
Catechesis/Religious Programs—Tel: 505-898-1441. Mary Duneman, D.R.E.
Students 495.
Mission—Albuquerque, Bernalillo Co., Our Lady of Mount Carmel, 7807 Edith, 87114.

8—OUR LADY OF FATIMA, (1949), Rev. Francis X. Eggert; Deacons Thomas Jones; Frank See; Hugh Hackett; Sandy Hall; Rudy Baca. In res., Rev. Vidal M. Martinez.
Res., 4020 Lomas, N.E., 87110. Tel: 505-265-5868; Fax: 505-268-0680. [JC]
School—Tel: 505-255-6391. Linda Honeyfield, Prin.
Lay Teachers 23; Students 299.
Catechesis/Religious Programs—Students 299.

9—OUR LADY OF GUADALUPE, (1954) (Hispanic), Rev. Joe Vigil; Deacons Manuel Facio, Pastoral Assoc. & Bus. Mgr.; Jim Delgado; George Valverde. In res., Rev. Ramon Aragon.
Res., 1860 Griegos, N.W., 87107. Tel: 505-345-4596; Fax: 505-342-2984.
Catechesis/Religious Programs—Tel: 505-344-7153. Molly C. De Baca, D.R.E.
Students 380.

10—OUR LADY OF LAVANG, (1986) (Vietnamese), Rev. Tin Mahn Bui.
Mailing Address: 2115 Inez, N.E., 87110. Tel: 505-275-3079.
Church—8600 Gonzales Rd., S.W., 87105. Tel: 505-839-4738. [JC]

11—OUR LADY OF THE ASSUMPTION, (1954), Revs. Luis D. Jaramillo; Michael Cimino; Deacons James Baca; Rue White.
Office & Mailing Address: 811 Guaymas, N.E., 87108-2398. Tel: 505-256-9818; 256-9877; Fax: 505-256-3131.
Res., 8030 Fruit, N.E., 87108. Tel: 505-255-5727.
School—817 Guaymas, N.E., 87108. Tel: 505-256-3167; Fax: 505-256-3167 (Call first). Robert M. Kaiser, Prin.
Lay Teachers 16; Students 200.
Catechesis/Religious Programs—Robert Shields, D.R.E.
Students 330.

12—OUR LADY OF MOST HOLY ROSARY, (1950) (Hispanic), Revs. Joel P. Garner, O.Praem.; Eugene Gries, O.Praem.; Deacons Juan Barajas; Harry Beare; Charles Johnson; Frank Perez; Gene Tuma.
Office: 5415 Fortuna Rd., N.W., 87105. Tel: 505-836-5011; Fax: 505-836-7562.
Res., Santa Maria de la Vid Priory, 5825 Coors S.W., 87121. Tel: 505-873-4399; Fax: 505-873-4667.
Catechesis/Religious Programs—Tel: 505-831-2525. D.R.E.: Christina Spahn; Sr. Evangeline Salazar, O.S.B.
Students 579.

13—PRINCE OF PEACE CATHOLIC COMMUNITY,
Office: 12500 Carmel, N.E., 87122. Tel: 505-856-7657; Fax: 505-856-2560. Rev. Antonio Mondragon.

14—QUEEN OF ANGELS NATIVE AMERICAN CENTER AND ARCHDIOCESAN SHRINE TO KATERI TEKAKWITHA, (1952) (Native American), Rev. Paul Juniet, O.F.M.
Res., I 40 & 12 St., N.W., P.O. Box 6881, 87197. Tel: 505-243-0835.
Catechesis/Religious Programs—Students 50.

15—QUEEN OF HEAVEN, (1952), Rev. Johnny Lee Chavez; Deacons Ruben Barela; Larry Cleveland; Pilar Garcia; Dan Lopez; Julian Padilla. In res., Rev. Stephen A. Sanchez.
Office: 5311 Phoenix, N.E., 87110. Tel: 505-881-1772; Fax: 505-883-5222.
School—Tel: 505-881-2484; Fax: 505-837-1123. Mary Cunning, Prin.
Lay Teachers 35; Students 375.
Catechesis/Religious Programs—Tel: 505-881-0715. Donna Duran, D.R.E.
Students 466.

16—SACRED HEART, (1903), Rev. James Moore; Deacon Thomas Perez.
Res., 412 Stover Ave., S.W., 87102. Tel: 505-242-0561; Fax: 505-243-7857. [JC]
Catechesis/Religious Programs—Tel: 505-247-8930.
Students 115.

17—SAINT JOSEPH ON THE RIO GRANDE, (1986), Rev. Frank Prieto; Deacons Don Bruckner; Frank Lucero; Jerry Hietpas.
Office: 5901 St. Joseph's Dr., N.W., 87120. Tel: 505-839-7952; Fax: 505-839-7955.
Catechesis/Religious Programs—Tel: 505-831-8346. Harv Weakland, D.R.E.
Students 446.

18—SAN FELIPE DE NERI, (1706) (Hispanic), Rev. Msgr. Leo Lucero; Deacons Jose Lucero; James Robert (Bob) Lewis.
Res., P.O. Box 7007, 87194. Tel: 505-243-4628; Fax: 505-224-9495.
School—2000 Lomas Blvd., N.W., 87104. Tel: 505-242-2411; Fax: 505-242-7355. Nancy A. Suedkamp, Prin.
Sisters 1; Lay Teachers 15; Students 210.
Catechesis/Religious Programs—Tel: 505-247-2041. Sr. Rosina Sandoval, D.R.E.
Students 118.
Mission—Albuquerque, Bernalillo Co., San Jose de los Duranes, 2110 Los Luceros Rd., N.W., 87104.

19—SAN IGNACIO, (1916) (Hispanic), Deacon Merce Villareal, Admin.
Res., 1300 Walter, N.E., 87102. Tel: 505-243-4287; Fax: 505-243-7346.
Catechesis/Religious Programs—Students 47.

20—SAN JOSE, (1938), Revs. Joseph A. Farias, S.D.B.; Sergio Abreu, S.D.B.; Manual Fernandez, S.D.B.; Deacon Charles Lucero; Evelyn Quintana Maritnez, Bus. Admin.
Res., 2401 Broadway, S.E., 87102-5009. Tel: 505-242-3658; Fax: 505-248-0810. [CEM]
Catechesis/Religious Programs—Tel: 505-243-7130. Sr. Teresa Aparicio, O.L.V.M., D.R.E.
Students 489.

21—SANTUARIO SAN MARTIN DE PORRES, (1979), Rev. Daniel L. Farris; Deacon Patricio Santistevan.
Res., 8321 Camino San Martin, S.W., 87121. Tel: 505-836-4676.
Catechesis/Religious Programs—Renee Ortiz, D.R.E.
Students 227.

22—SANGRE DE CRISTO, (1972), Rev. Albert J. Podvin; Deacon Lloyd Martinez.
Res., 8901 Candelaria, N.E., 87112. Tel: 505-293-2327; Fax: 505-292-0590.
Catechesis/Religious Programs—Tel: 505-293-2328.
Students 231.

23—ST. ANNE, (1929) (Armijo), Rev. Daniel M. Balizan; Deacons Tibo Chavez; Rene Greivel.
Res., 1400 Arenal Rd., S.W., 87105. Tel: 505-877-3121; Fax: 505-877-0084.
Catechesis/Religious Programs—Tel: 505-873-2188. D.R.E.: Sr. Marcella Campos, C.S.J.; Sr. Gemella Casey, C.S.J.
Students 405.
Mission—Albuquerque, Bernalillo Co., Monada de San Jose, 2100 La Vega Rd., S.W., 87105.

24—ST. BERNADETTE, (1959), Revs. Thomas A. Zotter; Domingo Gumpal, M.S.; Deacons Alfred McLane; J. Robert Martinez; Byron Wicker.
Res., 1800 Martha, N.E., 87112. Tel: 505-298-7557; Fax: 505-271-8099.
Catechesis/Religious Programs—Tel: 505-293-7779; Fax: 505-298-2412.
Students 380.

25—ST. CHARLES BORROMEO, (1934), Revs. Robert Chabot, S.S.S.; Normand R. Falardeau, S.S.S.; Ernest Falardeau, S.S.S.; Julian Rousseau, S.S.S.; Robert Stark, S.S.S.; Joseph Thai Minh Tran, S.S.S.; Bro. Peter Mahady, S.S.S.; Deacons Lorenzo Castillo; John Leahigh; Ron Schultz; Paul Dung Van Nguyen.
Res., 1818 Coal Pl., S.E., 87106. Tel: 505-242-3462; Fax: 505-247-1292. [JC]
School—Tel: 505-243-5788; Fax: 505-764-8842. Ms. Barbara Rossow, Prin.
Sisters 1; Lay Teachers 24; Students 380.
Catechesis/Religious Programs—Tel: 505-242-3462, Ext. 42. Elisa Zachery, D.R.E.
Students 232.

26—ST. EDWIN, (1965) (Hispanic), Rev. Jose Hernandez; Deacons Nestor Garcia; Desiderio Luna.
Res., 2105 Barcelona, S.W., 87105. Tel: 505-877-2967; Fax: 505-877-6810. [CEM]
Catechesis/Religious Programs—Tel: 505-877-3727.
Students 332.

27—ST. FRANCIS XAVIER, (1928) (Hispanic), Revs. Joseph Farias; Manuel Fernandez, S.D.B.
Res., 2401 Broadway S.E., 87102. Tel: 505-243-5201; Fax: 505-243-1179. [JC]
Catechesis/Religious Programs—817 Arno, S.E., 87102. Tel: 505-766-9379.
Students 126.

28—ST. JOHN THE APOSTLE, (1984). (John XXIII Catholic Community). Rev. Arkad Biczak; Deacons John Russo; John Wertz; Alex Trujillo; Clara Maestas, Bus. Mgr.
Res., 4831 Tramway Ridge Dr., N.E., 87111. Tel: 505-293-0088; Fax: 505-293-7276.
Catechesis/Religious Programs—Tel: 505-293-7756. Kyle Kemp, D.R.E.
Students 452.

29—ST. JUDE THADDEUS, (Paradise Hills) (1968), Rev. John R. Conway; Deacon Robert Aragon.
Mailing Address: P.O. Box 67710, 87193. Tel: 505-898-0826 (Church); 897-0391 (Res.); Fax: 505-799-9810.
Catechesis/Religious Programs—Tel: 505-897-4006.
Students 412.

30—ST. THERESE OF THE INFANT JESUS OF THE LITTLE FLOWER, (1947), Revs. John Plans, S.F.; Charles L Stoeber, S.F., (Retired); Deacons Esequiel Torres, (Retired); Manuel Montoya.
Res., 300 Mildred, N.W., 87107. Tel: 505-344-8050.
School—Tel: 505-344-4479; Fax: 505-344-3349. Antoinette Crump, Prin.
Lay Teachers 16; Students 248.
Catechesis/Religious Programs—Tel: 505-344-7643.
Students 245.

31—ST. THOMAS AQUINAS UNIVERSITY PARISH, (1954). (Serving the University of New Mexico). Revs. Robert J. Keller, O.P.; Matthew T. Strabala, O.P.; Melanie Ahern, Campus Min.; Deacon Bruce Eklund. In res., Revs. John Vincent Blake, O.P.; Michael T. Demkovich, O.P.; Patrick F. Norris, O.P.; Kevin W. Niehoff, O.P.
Res., 1815 Las Lomas Rd., N.E., 87106-3803. Tel: 505-247-1094; Fax: 505-247-2933.
Catechesis/Religious Programs—Carole A. Everton, D.R.E.
Students 237.

Anton Chico, Guadalupe Co., San Jose (1857) (Hispanic), Rev. Patrick S. Duffy, O.C.S.O.
Res., Box 99, 87711. Tel: 505-427-1164. [CEM][JC 5]
Catechesis/Religious Programs—Tel: 505-427-1211.
Students 24.
Missions—Dilia, Guadalupe Co.; Dahlia, Guadalupe Co.; Tecolotito, San Miguel Co.

Arroyo Seco, Taos Co., La Santisima Trinidad (1834) (Spanish), Rev. Vincent P. Chavez; Deacon Michael L. Kittredge.
Res., Box 189, 87514. Tel: 505-776-2273; Fax: 505-776-1543. [CEM][JC 4]
Catechesis/Religious Programs—Tel: 505-770-7688.
Students 95.
Missions—Arroyo Hondo, Taos Co., Nuestra Senora de Dolores, Upper Plaza, Arroyo Hondo, 87513.; Valdez, Taos Co., San Antonio de Padua, Valdez Plaza, Valdez, 87580.; Las Colonias, Taos Co., Santo Nino de Atocha, Santo Nino Rd., Las Colonias, 87529.; San Cristobal, Taos Co., San Cristobal.

Belen, Valencia Co., Our Lady of Belen (1793), Revs. David Gallegos, O.S.M.; Thomas Greaney, O.S.M.; Bro. Chris Moran, O.S.M.; Deacons Felix Barela; Manuel Gallegos; Norbert C. Sanchez; Robert Sanchez; Rudy Zamora.
Res., 101-A N. 10th St., 87002. Tel: 505-864-8043; Fax: 505-861-0969. [CEM][JC]
School—Tel: 505-864-0484. Rudy Chavez, Prin.
Sisters 1; Lay Teachers 7; Students 207.
Catechesis/Religious Programs—Tel: 505-864-7869. Judith Quintana, D.R.E.
Students 700.
Missions—Los Chavez, Valencia Co.; Jarales, Valencia Co.; Pueblitos, Valencia Co.; Bosque, Valencia Co.

Bernalillo, Sandoval Co., Our Lady of Sorrows (1699) (Indio-Hispanic), Rev. Virgil Furfaro; Deacon Paul Maestas.
Office: P.O. Box 607, 87004. Tel: 505-867-5252; Fax: 505-867-0267.
Res., 301 Camino del Pueblo, P.O. Box 607, 87004. Tel: 505-867-0585. [CEM 3]
Catechesis/Religious Programs—Ursulita Perez, D.R.E.
Students 487.
Missions—Placitas, Sandoval Co.; Algodones, Sandoval Co.; Sandia Indian Pueblo, Sandoval Co.

Cerrillos, Santa Fe Co., St. Joseph (1850), Rev. Donnan Herbe, O.F.M.
Res., Box 98, 87010. Tel: 505-471-1562; Fax: 505-471-1562. [CEM 4]
Catechesis/Religious Programs—Students 51.
Missions—Golden, Santa Fe Co.; Galisteo, Santa Fe Co.

Chama, Rio Arriba Co., St. Patrick (1963), Rev. Florian U. Renaud.
Res., 247 Pine St., Box 36, 87520-0036. Tel: 505-756-2926; Fax: 505-756-2926. [JC]
Catechesis/Religious Programs—Students 107.
Missions—Cebolla, Rio Arriba Co., Santo Nino; Canjilon, Rio Arriba Co., St. Juan Nepumoceno.

Chimayo, Rio Arriba Co., Holy Family (1955) (Hispanic), Revs. Jose Maria Conde, S.F.; Casimiro Roca, S.F.; Lazaro Cuesta-Padilla, S.F.; Deacon Jose Lopez.
Res., P.O. Box 235, 87522. Tel: 505-351-4360; Fax: 505-351-4698. [CEM][JC 2]
Catechesis/Religious Programs—Tel: 505-351-4131.
Students 345.
Missions—Truchas, Rio Arriba Co., Holy Rosary; Trampas, Taos Co., San Jose de Gracia; Cundiyo, Rio Arriba Co., Santo Domingo; Cordova, Rio Arriba Co., San Antonio; Rio Chiquito, Rio Arriba Co., Sagrado Corazon; Ojo Sarco, Rio Arriba Co., Santo Tomas; El Valle, Taos Co., San Miguel Archangel; El Santuario, Santa Fe Co., El Santuario Shrine, Tel: 505-351-4889.

Cimarron, Colfax Co., Immaculate Conception Church (1864) (Hispanic-Mexican), Rev. C. John Bresler; Sr. Hildegard Smith, S.C.C., Pastoral Assoc.
Res., Rte. 1, Box 11, 87714. Tel: 505-376-2553; Fax: 505-376-2553. [JC]
Catechesis/Religious Programs—D.R.E.: Sr. Hildegarde Smith, S.C.C.; Mrs. Linda Pavletick; Maria Sedillo.
Students 91.
Convent—Tel: 505-376-2553; Fax: 505-376-2553. Sisters of Christian Charity
Missions—Eagle Nest, Colfax Co., St. Mel, 200 Willow Creek, Eagle Nest, 87718. Tel: 505-376-2553; Black Lake, Colfax Co., St. Anthony.

Clayton, Union Co., St. Francis Xavier (1937), Rev. George Silva; Deacon P. Louis Montoya.
Res., 115 N. First St., 88415. Tel: 505-374-9500; Fax: 505-374-9500.
Catechesis/Religious Programs—Students 107.
Missions—Des Moines, Union Co., Our Lady of Guadalupe; Folsom, Union Co., St. Joseph; Moses, Union Co., Sacred Heart; Hayden, Quay Co., Holy Trinity.

Clovis, Curry Co., Sacred Heart (1908), Rev. Carlos Chavez; Deacons Juan A. Rodriguez; Michael A. Rowley.
Res., 921 Merriwether St., 88101. Tel: 505-763-6947; Fax: 505-762-5557.
Catechesis/Religious Programs—Students 287.
Mission—Melrose, Curry Co., 88124.

Our Lady of Guadalupe (1945), Rev. Sotero A. Sena; Sr. Rose Urban, Pastoral Assoc.; Deacons Bob Pullings; Daniel Chavez.
Res., 108 Davis St., 88101. Tel: 505-763-4445; Fax: 505-763-0261. [JC 2]
Catechesis/Religious Programs—Tel: 505-762-7343. D.R.E.: Sally Romero, (Grades K-6); Rachel Page, (RCIA Prog.); Manuela Torres, (Grade K-6); Elena Vigil, (Grades 7-12).
Students 375.
Mission—Texico, Curry Co., Box 122, Texico, 88135.

Corrales, Sandoval Co., San Ysidro (1966), Rev. Clarence F. Galli; Deacon Faustin Archuleta.
Res., 5005 Corrales Rd., Box 182, 87048. Tel: 505-898-1779; Fax: 505-897-6967. [CEM]
Catechesis/Religious Programs—Tel: 505-899-0276. Kathy M. Carr, D.R.E.
Students 163.

Dixon, Rio Arriba Co., St. Anthony (1929), Rev. Robert Lancaster.
Res., 1114 Private Dr. #5, P.O. Box 39, 87527-0039. Tel: 505-579-4389; Fax: 505-579-4389. [CEM 3]
Catechesis/Religious Programs—Students 112.
Missions—Velarde, Rio Arriba Co., Nuestra Senora de Guadalupe; Pilar, Taos Co., Nuestra Senora de los Dolores; Lyden, Rio Arriba Co., San Jose.

El Rito, Rio Arriba Co., San Juan Nepomuceno (1832) (Spanish), Rev. Patrick J. Chavez; Deacon Fabian Garcia.
Res., P.O. Box 7, 87530. Tel: 505-581-4714. [CEM][JC 9]
Catechesis/Religious Programs—Students 83.
Missions—La Madera, Rio Arriba Co., Gen. Del., La Madera, 87539.; Las Tablas, Taos Co., Gen. Del., Las Tablas, 87539.; Ojo Caliente, Rio Arriba Co., Gen. Del., Ojo Caliente, 87549.; Petaca, Taos Co., Gen. Del., Petaca, 87539.; Servilleta, Taos Co., Gen. Del., Servilleta, 87539.; Vallecitos, Rio Arriba Co., Gen. Del., Vallecitos, 87581.; Canon de Vallecitos, Rio Arriba Co., Gen. Del., Canon de Vallecitos, 87581.; Tres Piedras, Taos Co., Gen. Del., Tres Piedras, 87579.; Placitas, Rio Arriba Co., P.O. Box 7, Placitas, 87530.

Espanola, Rio Arriba Co., Sacred Heart (1950) (Hispanic), Rev. Augustine J. Moore, Ph.D.; Sr. Carol Ghionzoli, S.C.C.; Deacons Diego Herrera; Benjie Lopez.
Res., P.O. Box 69, 87532. Tel: 505-753-4225. [CEM 2]
Catechesis/Religious Programs—Tel: 505-753-9413; 753-1695; Fax: 505-753-9413.
Students 175.
Missions—Hernandez, Rio Arriba Co.; El Guache, Rio Arriba Co.; Guachupanque, Rio Arriba Co.; El Duende, Rio Arriba Co.

Fort Sumner, De Baca Co., St. Anthony (1958) (Hispanic). Attended by St. Rose of Lima, Santa Rosa. Rev. Stephen Schultz; Sr. Teresita Garcia, O.P., Parish Life Coord.
Res., 439 S. Third St., Santa Rosa, 88435.
Church—114 W. Richard Ave., P.O. Box 370, 88119. Tel: 505-355-2320. [CEM]
Catechesis/Religious Programs—Students 60.

Isleta, Pueblo Bernalillo Co., St. Augustine (1613) (Native American), Rev. Nicholas E. Nirschl, O.Praem.
Res., P.O. Box 463, 87022. Tel: 505-869-3398; 873-4399.
Catechesis/Religious Programs—Sr. Lisa Doty, D.R.E.
Students 160.

Jemez Pueblo, Sandoval Co., San Diego Indian Missions (1608) (Native American-Spanish), Revs. Chrysostom Partee, O.F.M.; Larry Gosselin, O.F.M.
Res., P.O. Box 79, 87024. Tel: 505-834-7300; Fax: 505-834-9167. [CEM][JC 4]
School—Indian Mission School, Tel: 505-834-7419. Sr. Barbara Tylkowski, O.S.F., Prin.
Sisters 2; Lay Teachers 7; Students 85.
Catechesis/Religious Programs—Verna Tosa, D.R.E.
Students 45.
Missions—Canyon, Sandoval Co.; Ponderosa, Sandoval Co.; San Ysidro, Sandoval Co.; Santa Ana, Sandoval Co.; Zia, Sandoval Co.

Jemez Springs, Sandoval Co., Our Lady of the Assumption (1947), Rev. James Sampson, s.P.
Res., Tel: 505-829-3586; Fax: 505-829-3592. [CEM]

La Joya, Socorro Co., Our Lady of Sorrows (1930) (Spanish), Rev. Vincent A. Nicosia, S.O.L.T.; Deacon Alfred Edwin Esquibel.
Mailing Address: 19 Calle de la Iglesia, P.O. Box 32, 87028. Tel: 505-864-4461; Fax: 505-861-3552.
Res., 1249 Hwy. 304, Veguita, 87062. Tel: 505-864-0745. [CEM 6]
Catechesis/Religious Programs—Students 70.
Missions—Abeytas, Socorro Co., San Antonio; Contreras, Socorro Co., San Jose; Las Nutrias, Socorro Co., San Isidro; Veguita, Socorro Co., San Juan; Sabinal, Socorro Co., San Antonio.

Las Vegas, San Miguel Co., Immaculate Conception (1885), Rev. George V. Salazar.
Res., 811 Sixth St., 87701. Tel: 505-425-7791; Fax: 505-425-6991. [CEM]
Catechesis/Religious Programs—Tel: 505-454-0685. D.R.E.: Rosa de Aragon; Jay Moore; Maricela Hidalgo; Steve Montano.
Students 511.
Mission—San Antonio, San Miguel Co., Los Vigiles (Our Lady of Refuge), 811 6th, San Antonio, 87701.

Our Lady of Sorrows Church (1851) (Hispanic), Rev. Vincent G. DeFazio; Deacons Jose Leroy Martinez; Macedon Montoya, Jr.
Res., 403 Valencia St., 87701. Tel: 505-454-1469; Fax: 505-425-0949. [CEM][JC 2]
Catechesis/Religious Programs—Tel: 505-425-6823. Mrs. Rosa de Aragon, D.R.E.
Students 350.
Missions—Sapello, San Miguel Co., Our Lady of Guadalupe, HC 68, Box 11, Sapello, 87745. Tel: 505-425-8084; Trujillo, San Miguel Co., San Isidro, HC 32 Box 26, Trujilllo, 87701. Tel: 505-641-5367; Variadero, San Miguel Co., Holy Family, Box 1020, Garita, 88421. Tel: 505-641-5339; Rociada Abajo, San Miguel Co., Santo Nino, HC 69 Box 4, Rociada, 87742. Tel: 505-425-8251; Gallinas, San Miguel Co., Santo Nino, Box 63 El Porvenir Rte., Montezuma, 87731. Tel: 505-425-6015.
Chapels—Christ the King, 2609 Encino St., 87701. Tel: 505-425-6894; San Jose, Hot Springs.; San Antonio, Rte. Box 90, El Porvenir, 87731. Tel: 505-425-8010; San Ignacio, HC 68 Box 15, Sapello, 87745. Tel: 505-425-3092; 454-1139; Our Lady of Sorrows, Box 39 Anton Chico Rte., 87701. Tel: 505-421-5599; San Geronimo, Box 310 Mineral Hill Rte., 87701. Tel: 505-425-3011; San Antonio, P.O. Box 85, 87701. Tel: 505-425-3405; Lourdes.; San Jose, HC 69 Box 12A, Rociada, 87742. Tel: 505-425-2809; San Rafael, c/o Al Sanchez Jr., General Delivery, Trementina, 88439. Tel: 505-641-5384; Santo Nino de Atocha, Anton Chico Rte., Box 20, 87701. Tel: 505-425-8014; Ojitos Frios.; Manuelitas.; Santo Nino, Tel: 505-454-0409.

Los Alamos, Los Alamos Co., Immaculate Heart of Mary (1946), Rev. Charles C. Brown; Deacons Gerald Langner; Don Lucero; Ray Alcouffe; Roberto Villareal.
Mailing Address: 3700 Canyon Rd., 87544.
Res., 3694 Canyon Rd., 87544. Tel: 505-662-6193; Fax: 505-662-5191.
Catechesis/Religious Programs—Tel: 505-662-7773. Karen McLoughlin, D.R.E.
Students 505.
Mission—White Rock, Los Alamos Co., 196 Meadow, White Rock, 87544. Tel: 505-672-1270.

Los Lunas, Valencia Co., St. Clement (1961), Rev. Rick Zerwas; Deacons Edward Espinosa; John O'Hare.
Res., P.O. Box 147, 87031. Tel: 505-865-7385; Fax: 505-865-8323. [CEM][JC]
Catechesis/Religious Programs—Tel: 505-865-3018. Sr. Charlotte Moser, O.P., D.R.E.
Students 535.
Mission—Los Lentes, Valencia Co., San Antonio.

Los Ojos, Rio Arriba Co., San Jose (1883) (Spanish), Rev. Salvador Aragon, O.F.M.
Res., Box 6, 87551. Tel: 505-588-7473. [CEM][JC 2]
Catechesis/Religious Programs—Twinned with Santo Nino, Tierra Amarilla.
Students 64.
Missions—Ensenada, Rio Arriba Co.; La Puente, Rio Arriba Co.; Plaza Blanca, Rio Arriba Co.

Mora, Mora Co., St. Gertrude (1851) (Hispanic), Rev. Tien-Tri Nguyen; Bercy Espinoza, Pastoral Assoc.
Res., P.O. Box 599, 87732. Tel: 505-387-2336; Fax: 505-387-5786. [CEM][JC 9]
Catechesis/Religious Programs—Mary Romero, D.R.E.
Students 296.
Missions—Le Doux, Mora Co.; El Carmen, Mora Co.; Lucero, Mora Co.; Santiago-Talco, Mora Co.; Ojo Feliz, Mora Co.; Buenavista, Mora Co.; Golondrinas, Mora Co.; Rainsville, Mora Co.; Chacon, Mora Co.; Holman, Mora Co.; Cleveland, Mora Co.; Guadalupita, Mora Co.; Monte Aplanado, Mora Co.; Turquillo, Mora Co.; La Cueva, Mora Co.; Holman, Mora Co.; Canoncito, Mora Co.

Moriarty, Torrance Co., Estancia Valley Catholic Parish (1972), Rev. Anthony L. Martinez; Deacon Juan S. Lucero.
Res., P.O. Box 129, 87035. Tel: 505-832-6655; Fax: 505-832-6057. [CEM 3]
Catechesis/Religious Programs—Corriene Lucero, D.R.E.
Students 610.
Missions—Estancia, Torrance Co., Sts. Peter & Paul, St. Joseph St. & Third St., Estancia 87016.; San Antonio, P.Sandia Park Co., Hwy. 55, San Antonio 87047.; Edgewood, Santa Fe Co., St. Elizabeth, Hwy. 344, Edgewood 87015.

Mountainair, Torrance Co., St. Alice (1946) (Hispanic), Rev. Edward Domme.
Res., P.O. Box 206, 87036. Tel: 505-847-2264. [CEM 5][JC]
Catechesis/Religious Programs—Tel: 505-847-0803. Prescilla Quintana, D.R.E.
Students 131.
Missions—Abo, Torrance Co.; Punta de Agua, Torrance Co.; Manzano, Torrance Co.; Torreon, Torrance Co.; Willard, Torrance Co.

Pecos, San Miguel Co., St. Anthony (1862), Rev. Bennett J. Voorhies.
Res., HC 70, Box 23, 87552. Tel: 505-757-6345; Fax: 505-757-6377. [CEM 5]
Catechesis/Religious Programs—Tel: 505-757-6305.
Students 322.
Missions—Canoncito, Santa Fe Co.; Las Colonias, San Miguel Co.; Glorieta, Santa Fe Co.; Rowe, San Miguel Co.; El Macho, San Miguel Co.

Pena Blanca, Sandoval Co., Nuestra Senora De Guadalupe (1877) (Hispanic-Native American), Revs. Hilaire Valiquette, O.F.M.; Joseph Redinbo, O.F.M.; Deacon Albert Arquero.
Res., P.O. Box 1270, 87041. Tel: 505-465-2226. [CEM 3]

Catechesis/Religious Programs—Tel: 505-465-3011. Sr. Jeanne Tranel, O.P., D.R.E.
Students 265.
Missions—Cochiti, Sandoval Co., Indian Pueblo; San Felipe, Sandoval Co., Indian Pueblo; Santo Domingo, Sandoval Co., Indian Pueblo; Sile, Sandoval Co.; La Bajada, Sandoval Co.

Penasco, Taos Co., San Antonio de Padua (1866), Rev. Robert Lancaster Tel: 505-579-4389; Deacon Alberto Sandoval Tel: 505-587-0447.
Res., 14079 N. Hwy. 75, P.O. Box 460, 87553-0460. Tel: 505-587-2188 (Res); 587-0399 (Office); Fax: 505-587-2188. [CEM]
Catechesis/Religious Programs—Tel: 505-587-2216. Joyce Kilgore, D.R.E.
Students 209.
Missions—Chamisal, Taos Co., Santa Cruz Mission; Llano Largo, Taos Co., San Acacio Mission; Rio Lucio, Taos Co., Sagrado Corazon Mission; Vadito, Taos Co., Nuestra Senora de los Dolores Mission; Picuris Indian Pueblo, Taos Co., San Lorenzo Mission; Llano San Juan, Taos Co., San Juan Nepomuceno Mission; Placita, Taos Co., Nuestra Senora de la Asuncion Mission; Rodarte, Taos Co., Santa Barbara Mission.

Peralta, Valencia Co., Our Lady of Guadalupe (1970), Rev. Albert Gallegos, O.S.M.; Deacon Joe Trujillo, (Retired).
Res., P.O. Box 288, 87042. Tel: 505-869-2189; Fax: 505-869-5850. [CEM]
Catechesis/Religious Programs—Tel: 505-869-6993. Betty Mascarena, D.R.E.
Students 377.
Station—Peralta, Valencia.

Pojoaque, Santa Fe Co., N.S. de Guadalupe del Valle de Pojoaque (1959) (Spanish-Native American), Rev. Jose Flavio Santillanes; Deacons John Archuleta; Pedro Garcia.
Res., 9 Grazing Elk, Santa Fe, 87501-7140. Tel: 505-455-2472; Fax: 505-455-3849. [CEM 2]
Catechesis/Religious Programs—Tel: 505-455-2267. Donna Martinez, D.R.E.
Students 259.
Missions—Nambe, Santa Fe Co.; El Rancho, Santa Fe Co.; Nambe Indian Pueblo, Sante Fe Co.

Portales, Roosevelt Co., St. Helen (1952), Rev. Tobin E. Hitt.
Office: Tel: 505-356-4241; Fax: 505-359-1721.
Res., 1600 S. Avenue O, 88130.
Catechesis/Religious Programs—Tel: 505-356-4241. D.R.E.: Tom Sullivan; Cathy Sullivan.
Students 291.
Mission—Portales, Roosevelt Co., University Catholic Center, P.O. Box 2253, 88130. Tel: 505-356-5615.

Questa, Taos Co., St. Anthony (1841), Rev. William E. Young (NY).
Res., Box 200, 87556. Tel: 505-586-0470; 0471; Fax: 505-586-1755. [CEM 6]
Catechesis/Religious Programs—Tel: 505-586-0388.
Students 207.
Missions—Cerro, Taos Co.; Red River, Taos Co.; Costilla, Taos Co.; Amalia, Taos Co.

Ranchos De Taos, Taos Co., San Francisco de Asis (1936) (Hispanic), Rev. Tim Martinez; Deacon Pat Delozier.
Res., P.O. Box 72, 87557-0072. Tel: 505-758-2754; Fax: 505-751-3923. [CEM]
School—(Grades K-5) P.O. Box 463, 87557. Tel: 505-758-1236. Sr. Grace Aufderbeck, Prin.
Sisters of Charity of Cincinnati 2; Lay Teachers 5; Students 103.
Catechesis/Religious Programs—Students 225.
Missions—Talpa, Taos Co., N.S. de San Juan de Los Lagos; Llano Quemado, Taos Co., N.S. del Carmel; Los Cordovas, Taos Co., San Isidro.

Raton, Colfax Co., St. Patrick/St. Joseph (1891), Rev. James L. Vance; Deacon Thomas Alderette.
Res., 105 Buena Vista St., Box 278, 87740. Tel: 505-445-9763; Fax: 505-445-9763. [CEM][JC]
School—401 S. Fourth St., 87740. Tel: 505-445-3862; Fax: 505-445-3862.
Sisters 2; Lay Teachers 5; Students 94.
Catechesis/Religious Programs—104 Buena Vista St., 87740. Tel: 505-445-9563.
Students 199.

Ribera, San Miguel Co., San Miguel Del Vado (1804) (Hispanic-Native American), Rev. Gary P. Ortiz.
Res., P.O. Box 507, 87560. Tel: 505-421-2405; 421-2780 (Office); Fax: 505-421-2779. [CEM]
Catechesis/Religious Programs—Students 120.
Missions—San Isidro Norte, San Miguel Co. [CEM][JC]
San Jose, San Miguel Co. [CEM][JC]
San Juan, San Miguel Co. [CEM][JC]
Santa Rita, San Miguel Co. [CEM][JC]
El Pueblo, San Miguel Co., San Antonio de Padua. [CEM][JC]
La Lagunita, San Miguel Co. [CEM][JC]
San Isidro Sur, San Miguel Co. [CEM][JC]

Rio Rancho, Sandoval Co., St. Thomas Aquinas (1974), Rev. Msgr. Douglas A. Raun; Revs. Leo W. Ortiz; Scott D. Mandfield; Deacons Aston Bailey; Kenneth Hill.
Res., 1502 Sara Rd., S.E., 87124. Tel: 505-892-1511; Fax: 505-891-3044.
School—1100 Hood Rd., S.E., 87124. Tel: 505-892-3221; Fax: 505-892-3350. Sr. Mary Klersy, M.P.F., Prin.
Religious 3; Lay Teachers 6; Students 144.
Catechesis/Religious Programs—Tel: 505-892-1497.
Students 1,605.
Missions—Rio Rancho, Sandoval Co., Church of the Incarnation, 2309 Monterrey, 87124. Tel: 505-771-8331; Rio Rancho, Sandoval Co., St. John Vianney, 100123 Ave., N.E., 87124.

Roy, Harding Co., Holy Family-St. Joseph (1918) (Hispanic), Rev. Guy R. Roberts.
Res., P.O. Box 37, 87743. Tel: 505-485-9633. [CEM 4]
Catechesis/Religious Programs—Students 16.
Missions—Bueyeros, Harding Co.; Gallegos, Harding Co.; Sabinoso, San Miguel Co.; Mosquero, Harding Co.

San Juan Pueblo, Rio Arriba Co. (Indian Pueblo), St. John the Baptist (1598) (Hispanic-Native American), Deacon Eloy E. Martinez.
Res., P.O. Box 1075, 87566. Tel: 505-852-4179; Fax: 505-852-9719.
Catechesis/Religious Programs—Tel: 505-852-2270. Sr. Clarita Trujillo, D.R.E. & Pastoral Assoc.
Students 358.
Missions—Alcalde, Rio Arriba Co.; Chamita, Rio Arriba Co.; El Guique, Rio Arriba Co.; Ranchitos, Rio Arriba Co.; Estaca, Rio Arriba Co. [CEM]
Shrine—Our Lady of Lourdes. Pilgrimage shrine.

Santa Cruz, Santa Fe Co., Holy Cross (1695) (Hispanic), Revs. Ron Carrillo, S.F.; Jose Maria Blanch, S.F.; Julio Gonzalez, S.F.
Res., P.O. Box 1228, 87567. Tel: 505-753-3345; Fax: 505-753-3787. [CEM]
School—Tel: 505-753-4644; Fax: 505-753-7401. Mrs. Cordelia Garcia, Prin.
Sisters 3; Lay Teachers 10; Students 178.
Catechesis/Religious Programs—Tel: 505-753-4567; Fax: 505-753-7401. D.R.E.: Sr. Angelina Gonzales, O.P., (Elementary); Mrs. Lynda Martinez, (Junior & Senior High).
Students 1,177.
Convent—Box 1137, 87567. Tel: 505-753-3340.

Santa Rosa, Guadalupe Co., St. Rose of Lima (1907) (Hispanic), Rev. Stephen C. Schultz; Deacon Arsenio C. Sanchez.
Res., 439 Third St., 88435. Tel: 505-472-3724; Fax: 505-472-3724. [CEM]
Catechesis/Religious Programs—Tel: 505-472-3992. D.R.E.: Sr. Helen Halligan; Sr. Ann Kaufmann.
Students 275.
Missions—Puerto de Luna, Guadalupe Co.; San Ignacio, Guadalupe Co.; Borica, Guadalupe Co.; Cuervo, Guadalupe Co.; Colonias, Guadalupe Co.; Pintada, Guadalupe Co.; Milagro, Guadalupe Co.

Socorro, Socorro Co., San Miguel (1615) (Native American-Hispanic), Rev. William E. Sanchez; Deacon Alfred Gilbert.
Res., 403 El Camino Real, N.W., 87801. Tel: 505-835-1620; Fax: 505-835-2750. [CEM 8][JC]
Catechesis/Religious Programs—Tel: 505-835-2891. Stella C. Castillo, D.R.E.
Students 309.
Missions—Lemitar, Socorro Co.; Polvadera, Socorro Co.; Luis Lopez, Socorro Co.; San Antonio, Socorro Co.; Alamillo, Socorro Co.; Magdalena, Socorro Co.; Kelly, Socorro Co.; Riley, Socorro Co.

Springer, Colfax Co., St. Joseph (1882) (Hispanic), Rev. C. John Brasher; Deacon Edward Olona.
Res., 605 Fifth St., P.O. Box 516, 87747. Tel: 505-483-2775. [JC]
Catechesis/Religious Programs—Martha Lopez, D.R.E.
Students 65.
Missions—Palo Blanco, Colfax Co.; Maxwell, Colfax Co.; Tinaja, Colfax Co.
Station—New Mexico Boys' School. (Detention Facility). Tel: 505-483-2775. Rev. Jacob McLeroy, Chap.

Taos, Taos Co., Nuestra Senora De Guadalupe (1801) (Spanish), Rev. George Salazar; Deacon Donald Martinez.
Res., P.O. Box 888, 87571. Tel: 505-758-2095; Fax: 505-758-2745. [CEM]
Catechesis/Religious Programs—Tel: 505-770-7688. Patricia Kessler, D.R.E.
Students 380.
Missions—Taos, Taos Co., St. Jerome, Taos Pueblo, 87571.; Taos Pueblo.
Chapels—El Prado, St. Theresa.; Canon, Our Lady of Sorrows.; Ranchitos, Immaculate Conception.; La Loma, San Antonio.

Tierra Amarilla, Rio Arriba Co., Santo Nino (1966) (Spanish), Rev. Salvador Aragon, O.F.M.
Mailing Address: Box 193, 87575. Tel: 505-588-7463. [JC]
Catechesis/Religious Programs—Twinned with San Jose, Los Ojos.

Tijeras, Bernalillo Co., Holy Child (1962), Rev. John F. Carney; Deacon Jose Escandon.
Res., Box 130, 87059. Tel: 505-281-1502; 281-2297 (Office); Fax: 505-281-0355. [CEM 9][JC 2]
Catechesis/Religious Programs—Students 328.
Missions—Carnuel, Bernalillo Co., Holy Child; Chilili, Bernalillo Co., San Juan de Nepumoceno; Escobosa, Bernalillo Co., San Isidro; San Antonio, Bernalillo Co.; Sedillo, Bernalillo Co., San Isidro; Canoncito, Bernalillo Co.; Tijeras, Bernalillo Co.

Tome, Valencia Co., Immaculate Conception (1750) (Spanish), Rev. Carl Feil, O.S.M.
Res., P.O. Box 100, 87060-0100. Tel: 505-865-7497; Fax: 505-865-7497. [CEM]
Catechesis/Religious Programs—7 Church Loop, Juan Diego Hall.
Students 208.
Mission—Casa Colorada, Valencia Co., State Hwy. 304 S., Casa Colorada, 87002.

Tucumcari, Quay Co., St. Anne (1910), Rev. John C. Daniel; Deacon Robert Welch.
Res., 306 W. High St., 88401. Tel: 505-461-2515; Fax: 505-461-3058. [JC]
Catechesis/Religious Programs—Tel: 505-461-3568. Nancy Arias, D.R.E.
Students 400.
Missions—Logan, Quay Co., San Antonio; Nara Visa, Quay Co., Sacred Heart; San Jon, Quay Co., Our Lady of Guadalupe.

Vaughn, Guadalupe Co., St. Mary (1936) (Hispanic), Rev. Christopher J. Pieroni.
Res., P.O. Box 276, 88353. Tel: 505-584-2954. [CEM][JC]
Catechesis/Religious Programs—Students 69.
Missions—Encino, Torrance Co.; Duran, Torrance Co.; Pastura, Guadalupe Co.; Pinos Wells, Torrance Co.

Villanueva, Our Lady of Guadalupe (1830) (Hispanic), Rev. Gary P. Ortiz; Sr. Helen Carney, O.L.V.M., Parish Life Coord.
Mailing Address: P.O. Box 39, 87583. Tel: 505-421-2548; Fax: 505-421-2779. [CEM]
Catechesis/Religious Programs—Students 60.
Missions—Sena, San Miguel Co.; Cerrito, San Miguel Co.; Gonzales Ranch, San Miguel Co.; Leyba, San Miguel Co.; Aurora, San Miguel Co.

Wagon Mound, Mora Co., Santa Clara (1882) (Hispanic). Attended by Holy Family, Roy. Rev. Guy R. Roberts.
Res., P.O. Box 186, 87752. Tel: 505-666-2478. [CEM]
Catechesis/Religious Programs—Students 41.
Missions—Ocate, Mora Co.; Los Hueros, Mora Co.,; Los Le Febres, Mora Co.; Watrous, Mora Co.

Priests Serving Private and Public Institutions

SANTA FE. *Hospital & Prison Ministry*. Rev. John Shedlock.
New Mexico State Penitentiary. Rev. Ricardo Russo, O.F.M.
St. Vincent's Hospital. Rev. Arthur Jakobiak, Chap.

ALBUQUERQUE. *Lovelace Hospital*. Revs. Mark E. Granito; Florian U. Renaud.
Presbyterian Hospital. Rev. Stephen A. Sanchez.
Prison Ministry. Rev. Millan Garcia.
St. Joseph Medical Center. Revs. Christian T. O'Brien, O.Praem.; James P. Huth, O.Praem.
University Hospital. Rev. Vidal Martinez.
Veterans Administration Medical Center. Rev. Julian Rousseau, S.S.S.

LAS VEGAS. *State Hospital*. Attended by Immaculate Conception Parish.

LOS LUNAS. *Correctional Facility (State)*. Deacon Lorenzo Castillo.

SPRINGER. *New Mexico Boys School*. Attended by St. Joseph Parish, Springer.

On Duty Outside the Archdiocese:
Reverend Fathers—
Berg, Timothy

Absent on Leave:
Reverend Fathers—
Ortega, Eduardo

Retired:
Reverend Monsignors—
Hill, Peter J.
McNiff, James

Salas, Sipio
Stadtmueller, Fred
Reverend Fathers—
Amiro, Raymond M.
Anstiss, Arthur
Aragon, Ramon
Auman, Robert
Bayer, Leonard
Bolman, Anthony P.
Coughlan, Robert
Cuesta, Benedicto
Cushing, Alan
Debaenst, Emmanuel
Falbo, Samuel
Fitzgerald, John W.
Galli, Clarence
Hendren, Lucien
Hendriks, Boniface
Homola, William B.
Kapitz, Donald
LaVoie, Joseph
Montoya, Ernest
Rebold, John
Rivera, Guadalupe
Runnebaum, Conrad
Savard, Wilfred

Permanent Deacons:
Abeyta, Santos, Holy Family, Albuquerque
Aguilar, Gregory, Santa Clara, Pueblo
Aird, Gordon, Community of the Risen Savior, Albuquerque
Alcouffe, Raymond, Immaculate Heart of Mary, Los Alamos
Alderette, Thomas, St. Joseph-St. Patrick, Raton
Allen, Charles, John XXIII, Albuquerque
Aragon, Raphael, Cannon A.F.B.
Aragon, Robert, St. Jude Thaddeus, Paradise Hills
Archuleta, Faustin, Our Lady of Fatima, Albuquerque
Archuleta, John, Our Lady of Guadalupe, Pojoaque
Arquero, Albert, Nuestra Senora de Guadalupe, Pene Blanca
Baca, James, Estancia Valley Parish, Moriarty
Baca, Rudolph, Our Lady of Fatima, Albuquerque
Baca, Tomas, St. Michael's School
Bachechi, Victor, Annunciation, Albuquerque
Bailey, Aston, St. Thomas Aquinas, Rio Rancho
Ballard, Alphonse L., (Retired)
Barajas, Juan, Holy Rosary, Albuquerque, Stewardship, Evangelization
Barela, Felix, Our Lady of Belen, Belen
Barela, Ruben, Queen of Heaven, Albuquerque
Bates, Charles, St. Francis Cathedral, Santa Fe
Beare, Harry, St. Thomas Aquinas, Rio Rancho
Black, Joseph, NM National Guard, Santa Fe
Blea, Edward, Holy Family, Albuquerque
Bruckner, Donald G., St. Joseph on the Rio Grande, Albuquerque
Bussemeier, Mark, Risen Savior, Albuquerque
Carrillo, Andres, St. John the Baptist, Santa Fe
Casaus, Luis, Immaculate Conception, Las Vegas
Castillo, Lorenzo, St. Charles, Albuquerque
Chavez, Andrew, St. Francis Xavier, Albuquerque
Chavez, Daniel, Our Lady of Guadalupe, Clovis
Chavez, Tiburci, St. Anne, Albuquerque
Chavez, Ubaldo, Holy Ghost, Albuquerque
Cleveland, Larry, Queen of Heaven, Albuquerque; Ministry to Deaf, Santa Fe
Contreras, Robert, Nativity of Blessed Virgin Mary, Alameda
Cordova, Raynaldo A., Our Lady of Sorrows, Las Vegas
Cullen, Charles, Queen of Heaven, Albuquerque
Delgado, James P., Our Lady of Guadalupe, Albuquerque
Delozier, Patrick, Holy Trinity, Arroyo Seco
Dimas, Claudio, New Mexico State Penitentiary
Doherty, James, St. Joseph, Springer
Duran, Charles, Our Lady of Fatima, Albuquerque
Eklund, Bruce, St. Thomas Aquinas Newman Center, Albuquerque
Elsberg, Alexander, San Miguel, Socorro
Escandon, Jose, St. Bernadette, Albuquerque
Espinosa, Edward, San Clemente, Los Lunas
Esquibel, A. Edwin, Our Lady of Sorrows, La Joya
Facio, Manuel, Our Lady of Guadalupe, Albuquerque
Gagnon, Fabian, Lovelace Medical Center, Albuquerque
Gallegos, Manuel A., Our Lady of Belen, Belen
Garcia, David, Holy Trinity, Arroyo Seco
Garcia, Fabian A., San Juan Nepomuceno, El Rito
Garcia, Nestor, St. Edwin, Albuquerque
Garcia, Pedro, Our Lady of Guadalupe, Pojoaque
Garcia, Pilar, Queen of Heaven, Albuquerque
Gilbert, Alfred, San Miguel, Socorro
Gogan, Harry L., Annunciation, Albuquerque
Greivel, Rene, St. Anne, Albuquerque
Grossman, William L., St. Edwin, Albuquerque
Hackett, Hugh, Our Lady of Fatima, Albuquerque
Hall, Sandy, Our Lady of Fatima, Albuquerque
Herrera, Diego A., Sacred Heart, Espanola
Hietpas, Gerald M., San Felipe de Neri, Albuquerque
Hill, Kenneth, St. Thomas, Rio Rancho
Hoefler, William C., Ascension, Albuquerque
Johnson, Charles V., Holy Rosary, Albuquerque
Jones, Thomas E., Our Lady of Fatima, Albuquerque
Kazek, Chester, Leave of Absence
Kittredge, Michael, Holy Trinity, Arroyo Seco
Kneafsey, John, Holy Ghost, Albuquerque
Kollasch, William, St. Francis Cathedral, Santa Fe
Langner, Gerald, Immaculate Heart of Mary, Los Alamos
Leahigh, John, St. Charles, Albuquerque
Lewis, Bob, San Felipe de Neri, Albuquerque
Lopez, Benjamin, Sacred Heart, Espanola
Lopez, Demetrio, Queen of Heaven, Albuquerque
Lopez, Jose O., Holy Family, Chimayo
Lovato, Frank, (Retired)
Lucero, Charles, San Jose, Albuquerque
Lucero, Donato, Dir. of Deacons; Immaculate Heart of Mary, Los Alamos
Lucero, Frank, St. Joseph on the Rio Grande, Albuquerque
Lucero, Jose E., San Felipe de Neri, Albuquerque
Lucero, Juan S., Estancia Valley Parish, Estancia
Luna, Desiderio, St. Edwin, Albuquerque
Maestas, Pablo, Our Lady of Sorrows, Bernalillo
Martinez, Donald J., Our Lady of Guadalupe, Taos
Martinez, Eloy, San Juan, San Juan Pueblo
Martinez, J. Robert, St. Bernadette, Albuquerque
Martinez, Jose Leroy, Our Lady of Sorrows, Las Vegas
Martinez, Lloyd, Sangre de Cristo, Albuquerque
McLane, Alfred, St. Bernadette, Albuquerque
Medina, Jesus, San Jose, Albuquerque
Meyrick, Earl, John XXIII, Albuquerque
Mishler, Richard, Holy Rosary, Albuquerque
Moffett, Stephen, Estancia Valley Parish, Estancia
Montoya, Macedon, Jr., Our Lady of Sorrows, Las Vegas
Montoya, P. Louis, St. Francis Xavier, Clayton
Nguyen, Dung (Paul), San Jose, Albuquerque
O'Hare, John J., Our Lady of Belen, Belen
Olona, Edward, St. Joseph, Springer
Pacheco, Carlos Felix, Our Lady of Guadalupe, Santa Fe
Pacheco, Charles, Immaculate Heart of Mary, Los Alamos
Padilla, Enrique, Our Lady of Sorrows, Bernalillo
Padilla, Julian, Queen of Heaven, Albuquerque
Paiz, Robert, Holy Family, Albuquerque
Perez, Frank, Holy Rosary, Albuquerque
Perez, Tomas, Sacred Heart, Albuquerque
Porto, Tony, (Retired)
Pullings, Harold, Our Lady of Guadalupe, Clovis
Rodriguez, Antonio, St. John the Baptist, Santa Fe
Rodriguez, Facundo, Santa Maria de la Paz, Santa Fe
Rodriguez, Juan, Santa Maria de la Paz, Santa Fe
Rodriguez, Juan A., Sacred Heart, Clovis
Rodriguez, Randall, Cristo Rey, Santa Fe
Rowley, Michael, Sacred Heart, Clovis
Russo, John L., John XXIII Catholic Community, Albuquerque
Sanchez, Arsenio, St. Rose of Lima, Santa Rosa
Sanchez, Norbert C., Our Lady of Belen, Belen
Sanchez, Robert, Our Lady of Belen, Belen
Sandoval, Alberto, San Antonio de Padua, Penasco
Sandoval, George, Immaculate Conception, Albuquerque
Santistevan, Patrick, San Martin de Porres, Albuquerque
Santistevan, Peter, Our Lady of Sorrows, Bernalillo
Schultz, Ronald, St. Charles, Albuquerque
Schwenn, Charles E., St. Joseph, Cerrillos
See, Frank C., Our Lady of Fatima, Albuquerque
Stromberg, Robert, Holy Ghost, Albuquerque
Torres, H. Esequiel, St. Therese, Albuquerque
Tourville, John, St. Edwin, Albuquerque
Toya, Patrick, San Diego Mission, Jemez Pueblo
Trujillo, Alex, John XXIII, Albuquerque
Trujillo, Anthony, Our Lady of Guadalupe, Santa Fe
Trujillo, Joseph, Our Lady of Guadalupe, Peralta
Tuma, Eugene, St. Jude Thaddeus, Albuquerque
Valkenburgh, Thomas Van, Santa Maria de Paz, Santa Fe
Valverde, George, Our Lady of Guadalupe, Albuquerque
Valverde, Gilbert, Immaculate Conception, Albuquerque
Vigil, Ralph, Sacred Heart, Espanola
Villareal, Merce A., Admin., Sacred Heart, Espanola
Villarreal, Robert, Immaculate Heart of Mary, Los Alamos
Welch, Robert, St. Anne, Tucumcari
Wertz, John, John XXIII Catholic Community, Albuquerque
White, Rue, Our Lady of the Assumption, Albuquerque
Wicker, Byron, St. Bernadette, Albuquerque
Zamora, Rudy R., Our Lady of Belen, Belen; Vocations Office, Santa Fe

PILGRIMAGE SHRINES

CHIMAYO. *Santuario de Chimayo.* Attended by Holy Family, Chimayo. 87522.

SAN JUAN. *Our Lady of Lourdes.* (San Juan Pueblo P.O.) P.O. Box 1075, 87566.

INSTITUTIONS LOCATED IN THE ARCHDIOCESE

[A] SEMINARIES, RELIGIOUS OR SCHOLASTICATES

SANTA FE. *Sangre de Cristo Center,* 410 State Rd. 592, 87501-9804. Tel: 505-983-7291; Fax: 505-983-6963.
E-mail: SANGRE@cybermesa.com
Web site: www.sangredecristo.org
Bro. William Clarey, F.S.C., Dir. Associate Directors: Bros. Joseph Schmidt, F.S.C.; Tim Wentworth, F.S.C.; Sr. Helen Collier, C.C.V.I.; Sr. Julie McCole, O.S.F. Program of refoundation for religious and priests, under the administration of the Christian Brothers. Participants 68 annually. Brothers 3; Sisters 2; Total Staff 5.

[B] COLLEGES AND UNIVERSITIES

SANTA FE. *College of Santa Fe,* (1947) 1600 St. Michaels Dr., 87505. Tel: 505-473-6011
For a complete listing, refer to the Colleges and Universities section.

[C] HIGH SCHOOLS, ARCHDIOCESAN AND PAROCHIAL

ALBUQUERQUE. *St. Pius X High School,* 5301 St. Joseph Dr., N.W., 87120. Tel: 505-831-8400. Lay Teachers 69; Students 1,041.

[D] HIGH SCHOOLS, PRIVATE

SANTA FE. *St. Michael's High School.* (Grades 7-12). (Coed Day School), 100 Siringo Rd., 87505. Tel: 505-983-7353; Fax: 505-982-8722.
E-mail: mainoffice@stmikes.k12.nm.us
Bro. Richard Kovatch, F.S.C., Prin..Brothers of the Christian Schools 6; Deacons 1; Lay Teachers 37; Students 758.

[E] GENERAL HOSPITALS

ALBUQUERQUE. *St. Joseph Healthcare Foundation,* 500 Walter, N.E., 87102. Tel: 505-727-2709; Fax: 505-727-7034.
E-mail: conem@sjhs.org
For a complete listing, refer to the Hospitals section.

St. Joseph Healthcare System. Tel: 505-727-2709; Fax: 505-727-7034.
E-mail: ConeM@SJHS.ORG Mailing Address: P.O. Box 25555, 87125-0555.
For a complete listing, refer to the Hospitals section.

St. Joseph Medical Center. Tel: 505-727-2709; Fax: 505-727-7034.
E-mail: ConeM@SJHS.ORG Mailing Address: P.O. Box 25555, 87125-0555.
For a complete listing, refer to the Hospitals section.

St. Joseph Northeast Heights Hospital. Tel: 505-727-2709; Fax: 505-727-7034.
E-mail: ConeM@SJHS.ORG Mailing Address: P.O. Box 25555, 87125-0555.
For a complete listing, refer to the Hospitals section.

St. Joseph Physician Group, 7850 Jefferson, N.E., Ste. 100, 87109. Tel: 505-727-2709; Fax: 505-727-7034.
E-mail: conem@sjhs.org
For a complete listing, refer to the Hospitals section.

St. Joseph Rehabilitation Hospital. Tel: 505-727-2709; Fax: 505-727-7034.
E-mail: ConeM@SJHS.ORG Mailing Address: P.O. Box 25555, 87125-0555.
For a complete listing, refer to the Hospitals section.

St. Joseph West Mesa Hospital. Tel: 505-727-2709; Fax: 505-727-7034.
E-mail: ConeM@SJHS.ORG Mailing Address: P.O. Box 25555, 87125-0555.
For a complete listing, refer to the Hospitals section.

[F] SPECIAL HOSPITALS AND SANATORIA FOR INVALIDS

SANTA FE. *Villa Therese Catholic Clinic,* 219 Cathedral Pl., 87501. Tel: 505-983-8561; Fax: 505-983-8561.
E-mail: vtcc@juno.com
For a complete listing, refer to the Special Care Facilities section.

[G] SHELTER CARE HOMES

ALBUQUERQUE. *Good Shepherd Center, Inc.*, 218 Iron St., S.W., P.O. Box 749, 87103. Tel: 505-243-2527; Fax: 505-243-2207
For a complete listing, refer to the Special Care Facilities section.

Good Shepherd Manor, 10127 Guadalupe Tr., N.W., P.O. Box 10248, 87184. Tel: 505-898-0177; Fax: 505-898-9756
For a complete listing, refer to the Special Care Facilities section.

Marie Amadea Shelter for Unwed Mothers, P.O. Box 708, 87103. Tel: 505-242-1516; Fax: 505-243-0402
For a complete listing, refer to the Special Care Facilities section.

[H] CARE HOMES FOR PHYSICALLY AND MENTALLY HANDICAPPED

ALBUQUERQUE. *Casa Angelica*, 5629 Isleta Blvd., S.W., 87105. Tel: 505-877-5763; Fax: 505-873-2786
For a complete listing, refer to the Special Care Facilities section.

[I] MONASTERIES AND RESIDENCES OF PRIESTS AND BROTHERS

ABIQUIU. *Monastery of Christ in the Desert*, 87510. Tel: 801-545-8567; Fax: 801-545-8567.
E-mail: porter@christdesert.org
Web site: www.christdesert.org
Subiaco Congregation. Rt. Rev. Philip Lawrence, O.S.B., Abbot; Revs. Christian Leisy, O.S.B., Sub Prior; Bernard Cranor, O.S.B.; Ezequiel Bas Luna, O.S.B.; Luis Regalado, O.S.B.; Fernando Hool, O.S.B.; Tomas Mitchell, O.S.B.; Odon Nguyen, O.S.B. Monks 50.

ALBUQUERQUE. *Little Brothers of the Good Shepherd*, Villa Mathias-Foundation House, 901 Bro. Mathias Pl., N.W., P.O. Box 389, 87103. Tel: 505-243-4238; Fax: 505-764-9721. Brothers 9; Total Staff 2.

San Antonio Provincial Friary, 1350 Lakeview Rd., S.W., 87105. Tel: 505-877-5425; Fax: 505-877-1440.
E-mail: ofmprovsec@aol.com
Web site: www.olgofm.org
Very Rev. Larry C. Dunham, O.F.M., Minister Prov.; Revs. Gino Correa, O.F.M., Vicar Prov.; George Ward, O.F.M., Treas. of Prov.; Bro. Duane Torisky, O.F.M., Sec. of Prov. Priests 54; Brothers 16; Postulants 1. Legal Titles: *Franciscan Indian Missions.*; *Franciscan Mission Center.*; *The Province of Our Lady of Guadalupe of the Order of Friars Minor, Inc.*; *Southwest Franciscan Services, Inc.*; *Southwest Franciscan Missions, Inc.*

Santa Maria de la Vid Priory, 5825 Coors Rd., S.W., 87121-6700. Tel: 505-873-4399; Fax: 505-873-4667.
E-mail: jedwa25382@aol.com
Web site: www.norbertines.org
Canons Regular of Premontre (Norbertine Community). Very Rev. Joel P. Garner, O.Praem., Prior & Vocation Dir.; Revs. Vincent J. DeLeers, O.Praem.; Eugene Gries; James P. Huth, O.Praem.; Nicholas E. Nirschl, O.Praem.; Francis W. Dorff, O.Praem; Christian T. O'Brien, O.Praem.; Laurence A. Mayer; Bro. Dennis Butler. Priests 8.
Sponsor of "Center for Spiritual Life.".

JEMEZ SPRINGS. *Our Lady of Lourdes Novitiate*, P.O. Box 10, 87025-0010. Tel: 505-829-3586; Fax: 505-829-3706.
E-mail: servants@theservants.org
Web site: www.theservants.org
Very Rev. Peter Lechner, s.P., Servant Gen.; Rev. Paul Valley, s.P., Dir. Formation, Formation House. Priests 1.

PECOS. *Our Lady of Guadalupe Abbey.* (Olivetan Benedictine Monks), P.O. Box 1080, 87552-1080. Tel: 505-757-6415; Fax: 505-757-2285. Rt. Rev. James Liprie, O.S.B., Abbot; Revs. Paul Meaden, O.S.B., Prior; Sam Dennis, O.S.B.; Colman Heffern, O.S.B.; Bernard Lebiedz, O.S.B.; Michael Leek, O.S.B.; Robert Lussier, O.S.B.; Andrew Miles, O.S.B.; Wilfrid Tunink, O.S.B. Priests 9; Brothers 8.

[J] CONVENTS AND RESIDENCES FOR SISTERS

SANTA FE. *Discalced Carmelite Monastery*, 49 Mount Carmel Rd., 87501-4597. Tel: 505-983-7232. Mother Rose Teresa, O.C.D., Prioress; Revs. Crispin Bietz, O.F.M., Chap.; Ricardo Russo, O.F.M., Chap.; Solemn Professed Nuns 7; Simple Professed 2; Extern Sisters 3.

ABIQUIU. *Monastery of Our Lady of the Desert*, P.O. Box 1040, 87510. Tel: 505-470-3407.
E-mail: soeurjulie@aol.com
Benedictine Nuns. Sr. Julianne Allen, Prioress; Sr. Benedicta Serna, Sub. Prioress.

ALBUQUERQUE. *Cristo Rey Provincial House*, 5625 Isleta Blvd., S.W., 87105. Tel: 505-873-2854; Fax: 505-873-0678.
E-mail: fdccalb@aol.com
Canossian Daughters of Charity. Sr. Elizabeth Chambers, Prov. Supr. Sisters 43.

JEMEZ SPRINGS. *Cor Jesu Monastery*, 87025. Tel: 505-829-3906; Fax: 505-829-3423. Motherhouse and Novitiate of the Handmaids of the Precious Blood. Rev. Mother John Paul, H.P.B., Mother Prioress. Perpetually Professed Sisters 33; First Professed Sisters 1.

RIO RANCHO. *Felician Sisters*, Provincial House & Novitiate, 4210 Meadowlark Ln., S.E., 87124-1021. Tel: 505-892-8862; Fax: 505-891-3893.
E-mail: cssfrrnm@nm.net
Assumption of the Blessed Virgin Mary. Sr. Rosemarie Goins, C.S.S.F., Prov. Min. In res. Rev. Cecil Kleber, O.F.M., Chap. Residents 38; Professed Sisters of Province 74; Total Assisted per Month 400; Total Staff 17; Postulants 2.

[K] RETREAT HOUSES

ALBUQUERQUE. *Madonna Retreat and Conference Center*, 4040 St. Joseph Pl., N.W., 87120. Tel: 505-831-8196; Fax: 505-831-8103.
E-mail: asfmod@flash.net
Web site: www.archdiocesesantafe.org
Dominic G. Kallasch, Dir..Total in Residence 2; Total Staff 4.

The Spiritual Renewal Center, Inc., 2348 Pajarito Rd., S.W., 87105-6642. Tel: 505-877-4211; Fax: 505-877-1413.
E-mail: domreths@swcp.com
Web site: www.christdesert.org/dominican
Center for Retreats. Dominican Sisters (Elkins Park, PA). Sisters 2; Total Staff 3.

PECOS. *Our Lady of Guadalupe Olivetan Benedictine Abbey*, P.O. Box 1080, 87552. Tel: 505-757-6415; Fax: 505-757-2285.
E-mail: guestmaster@juno.com
Web site: www.pecosabbey.org
Monastery. Rt. Rev. James Liprie, O.S.B., Abbot; Revs. Paul Meaden, O.S.B., Claustral Prior; Samuel Dennis, O.S.B.; Robert Lussier, O.S.B.; Bernard Lebiedz, O.S.B.; Andrew Miles, O.S.B.; Colman Heffern, O.S.B.; Michael Leek, O.S.B.; Wilfrid Tunink, O.S.B. Priests 9; Brothers 5; Monastic Oblate Sisters 11; Novices 2; Total in Residence 27.

SANTE FE. *Immaculate Heart of Mary Retreat and Conference Center*, Mt. Carmel Rd., 87501. Tel: 505-988-1975; Fax: 505-988-3963. Ben Armijo, Dir.

[L] NEWMAN CENTERS

ALBUQUERQUE. *St. Thomas Aquinas (Newman Center) University Parish*, 1815 Las Lomas Rd., N.E., 87106. Tel: 505-247-1094; Fax: 505-247-2933.
E-mail: aquinasnew@aol.com
Web site: www.swcp.com/newmancenter
Revs. Robert Keller, O.P.; Matthew T. Strabala..Total in Residence 5; Total Staff 10.

LAS VEGAS. *Highlands University Newman Center*, 909 Eighth St., 87701. Tel: 505-454-6050.
E-mail: s_lopez_c@hotmail.com
Attended by Immaculate Conception Parish, Las Vegas. Rev. George V. Salazar, Chap.

PORTALES. *University Catholic Center - St. Thomas More Chapel*, P.O. Box 2253, E.N.M.U., 88130. Tel: 505-356-5615.
E-mail: Tony.Martinez@ENMU.Edu
Web site: www.std.ENMU.EDU/Cathcntr/Home.htm
Rev. Tobin Hitt, Chap..Total Staff 3.

[M] MISCELLANEOUS LISTINGS

SANTA FE. *Medjugorje Group*, 1010 A Calle Hermosa, 87505. Tel: 505-992-8207. Rosie Sweeney.

St. Michael's High School Foundation, 100 Siringo Rd., 87505. Tel: 505-988-2264; Fax: 505-988-2264. Mrs. Clarice Pick, Pres.

ALBUQUERQUE. *Annual Catholic Appeal Foundation of the Archdiocese of Santa Fe*, 4000 St. Joseph Pl., N.W., 87120. Tel: 505-831-8155; Fax: 505-831-8111.
E-mail: asfaca@flash.net
Web site: www.flash.net/~astaca
Linda J. Garcia, C.F.R.E., Exec. Dir.

Archbishop's School Fund, 4000 St. Joseph Pl., N.W., 87120. Tel: 505-831-8173; Fax: 505-831-8173.
E-mail: cathsch@nedcomm.nm.org
Web site: www.nm.org/catholicschools
Carol Zonski, Pres.

Archdiocese of Santa Fe Catholic Foundation, 2201 San Pedro, N.E., Bldg. 2, Ste. 211, 87110. Tel: 505-872-2901; Fax: 505-872-2905.
E-mail: cathfdn@aol.com
Mary P. Dunn, Contact Person..Total Staff 3.

Brother Mathias Barrett, Inc., dba Good Shepherd Manor, P.O. Box 10248, 87184. Tel: 505-898-0177; Fax: 505-898-9756. Charles D. Milligan, Pres. Total Assisted 40; Total Staff 21.

Brothers of the Good Shepherd Inc. of New Mexico, 901 Brother Mathias Pl., N.W., P.O. Box 389, 87102-7103. Tel: 505-243-4238; Fax: 505-764-9721. Total in Residence 9; Total Staff 2.

Caritas Deus Inc., P.O. Box 389, 87103. Tel: 505-243-2527; Fax: 505-247-2207. Property management nonprofit corporation.

Catholic Charismatic Center, 1412 Fifth St., N.W., 87102. Tel: 505-247-0398; Fax: 505-843-9147.
E-mail: mcgarrysmjccc@aol.com
Web site: sites.netscape.net/smjccc/swccc
Sr. Martha Jean McGarry, I.H.M., Dir..Total in Residence 1; Total Staff 5.

Center for Action and Contemplation, P.O. Box 12464, 87195. Tel: 505-242-9588; Fax: 505-242-9518.
E-mail: cacforprophet@juno.com
Web site: cacradicalgrace.org
Rev. Richard Rohr, O.F.M., Founder & Animator; Kathleen O'Malley, Dir. Total in Residence 2; Total Staff 7.

Charity Unlimited, Inc., P.O. Box 389, 87103. Tel: 505-243-4238; Fax: 505-764-9721. Property management nonprofit corporation.

Community of Damien of Molokai, Inc., P.O. Box 4231, 87196. Tel: 505-243-3203; 800-497-2540. HIV/AIDS Ministry.

Dominican Ecclesial Institute, 1815 Las Lomas, N.E., 87106. Tel: 505-243-0525; Fax: 505-247-2933.
E-mail: lumen@sprynet.com
Web site: www.op.org/dei
Rev. Michael T. Demkovich, O.P..Total in Residence 1; Total Staff 2.

Fraternidad Piadosa de Nuestro Padre Jesus Nazareno, 4000 St. Joseph Pl., N.W., 87120. Rev. Jerome J. Martinez y Alire, Chap.

Good Shepherd Center, Inc. of New Mexico, 218 Iron St., N.W., P.O. Box 749, 87103. Tel: 505-243-2527; Fax: 505-247-2207. Total Staff 8; Total Assisted 190,000.

Good Shepherd Formation Center, Inc. of New Mexico, 1323 Espanola, N.E., 87110. Tel: 505-232-4546. Bro. Savio Charron.

Norbertine Community of New Mexico, Inc., 5825 Coors Rd., N.W., 87121-6700. Tel: 505-873-4399.
E-mail: jedwa25382@aol.com
Web site: www.norbertine.org
Rev. Joel P. Garner, O.Praem..Total in Residence 17; Total Staff 5.

St. Francis Gardens Nursing Home. Tel: 505-727-2709; Fax: 505-727-7034.
E-mail: ConeM@SJHS.ORG
Mailing Address: P.O. Box 25555, 87125-0555. 904 Las Lomas Rd., NE, 87102. Tel: 505-727-2804; Fax: 505-727-2814.
Affiliate of Catholic Health Initiatives. Lynne Anker-Unnever, Admin.; Sr. Marie Raphael Morell, O.P., Dir. Spiritual Care. Chaplains/Priests Available 2; Beds 90; Total Staff 116.

St. Pius X High School Foundation, Inc., 5301 St. Joseph Dr., N.W., 87120. Tel: 505-831-8406; Fax: 505-831-8413.
Web site: www.saintpiusx.com
Nonprofit corporation for the financial support of St. Pius X High School. Rev. Albert R. Gaelens, C.S.B.

SPX Towers, 3009 Louisiana Blvd., N.E., 87110. Tel: 505-884-1309; Fax: 505-889-2720. Thomas P. Macken, Esq., Contact Person. To generate funds for use as financial aid for economically disadvantaged children to attend St. Puis X High School.

St. Bernadette Institute of Sacred Art, P.O. Box 8249, 87198. Tel: 505-265-9126; Fax: 505-266-4678.
E-mail: bernadet@iex.net
Web site: www.stbernadette-abq.org/
Dan Paulos, Contact Person. Sponsors and supports Catholic art and artists.

Villa Mathias Inc., P.O. Box 389, 87103. Tel: 505-243-4238; Fax: 505-764-9721.

JEMEZ SPRINGS. *EDSA Charitable Trust*, P.O. Box 10, 87025. Tel: 505-829-3586.
E-mail: linda@jemez.com
Linda Soroos, Contact Person.

Fitzgerald Charitable Trust, P.O. Box 10, 87025. Tel: 505-829-3586; Fax: 505-829-3706.
E-mail: manilasp@aol.com
Web site: www.theservants.org
Very Rev. Peter Lechner, s.P.

RIO RANCHO. *St. Felix Pantry, Inc.*, 4020 Barbara Loop, 87124-1023. Tel: 505-891-8075. Sr. Seraphine Moynier, Contact Person. Total Assisted per Month 8,000; Total Staff 65.

RELIGIOUS INSTITUTES OF MEN REPRESENTED IN THE ARCHDIOCESE

For further details refer to the corresponding bracketed number in the Religious Institutes of Men or Women section.

[0350]—*Abbey of Our Lady of New Melleray.* (Peosta, PA).—O.C.S.O.

[0170]—*Basilian Fathers.*—C.S.B.

[0200]—*Benedictine Monks.* (Our Lady of Guadalupe Abbey, Pecos; Abbey of Christ in the Desert, Abiquiu; St. John Abbey, Collegeville, MN).—O.S.B.

[1350]—*Brothers of St. Francis Xavier.*—C.F.X.

[0330]—*Brothers of the Christian Schools.* (Baltimore, Midwest & De La Salle Provinces).—F.S.C.

[0580]—*Brothers of the Good Shepherd.*—B.G.S.

[0900]—*Canons Regular of Premontre.* (Norbertine Fathers and Brothers of De Pere, Wisconsin).—O.Praem.
[0220]—*Congregation of the Blessed Sacrament.*—S.S.S.
[0610]—*Congregation of the Holy Cross.* (Midwest Province).—C.S.C.
[0520]—*Franciscan Friars.* (Our Lady of Guadalupe, St. John the Baptist & St. Barbara Provinces).—O.F.M.
[0720]—*Missionaries of Our Lady of La Salette.*—M.S.
[]—*Order of Friar Servants of Mary.* (U.S.A. Prov.)(Chicago, IL).
[0430]—*Order of Preachers-Dominicans.* (St. Albert the Great Province).—O.P.
[1190]—*Salesians of Don Bosco.* (San Francisco Province).—S.D.B.
[1230]—*Servants of the Paraclete.*—s.P.
[0690]—*Society of Jesus.* (New Orleans Prov., Missouri Prov.).—S.J.
[0975]—*Society of Our Lady of the Most Holy Trinity.*—S.O.L.T.
[0640]—*Sons of the Holy Family.* (Silver Spring, MD).—S.F.

RELIGIOUS INSTITUTES OF WOMEN REPRESENTED IN THE ARCHDIOCESE

[0200]—*Benedictine Sisters.* (Pecos and Abiquiu, NM).—O.S.B.
[0730]—*Canossian Daughters of Charity.* (Albuquerque, NM).—Fd.C.C.
[1780]—*Congregation of the Sisters of the Third Order of St. Francis of Perpetual Adoration.* (La Crosse, WI).—F.S.P.A.
[0760]—*Daughters of Charity of St. Vincent de Paul.* (St. Louis, MO).—D.C.
[0420]—*Discalced Carmelite Nuns.* (Santa Fe, NM).—O.C.D.
[1070-02]—*Dominican Sisters.* (Columbus, OH).—O.P.
[1070-03]—*Dominican Sisters.* (Sinsinawa, WI).—O.P.
[1070-09]—*Dominican Sisters.* (Racine, WI).—O.P.
[1070-13]—*Dominican Sisters.* (Adrian, MI).—O.P.
[1070-14]—*Dominican Sisters.* (Grand Rapids, MI).—O.P.
[1070-17]—*Dominican Sisters.* (Elkins Park, PA).—O.P.
[1070-21]—*Dominican Sisters.* (Edmonds, WA).—O.P.
[1170]—*Felician Sisters.* (Congregation of Sisters of St. Felix of Cantalice).—C.S.S.F.
[1310]—*Franciscan Sisters of Little Falls.* (MN).—O.S.F.
[1500]—*Franciscan Sisters of Mary Immaculate of the Third Order of St. Francis of Assisi.* (Amarillo, TX).—F.M.I.
[1430]—*Franciscan Sisters of Our Lady of Perpetual Help.* (St. Louis, MO).—O.S.F.
[1860]—*Handmaids of the Precious Blood.* (Jemez Springs, NM).—H.P.B.
[2470]—*Maryknoll Sisters of St. Dominic.* (Maryknoll, NY).—M.M.
[3130]—*Our Lady of Victory Missionary Sisters.* (Huntington, IN).—O.L.V.M.
[3430]—*Religious Teahers Filippine.* (St. Lucy Filippine Province, Morristown, NJ).—M.P.F.
[1680]—*School Sisters of St. Francis.* (Milwaukee, WI).—O.S.F.
[]—*Sisters for Christian Community.* (Cincinnati).—S.F.C.C.
[0440]—*Sisters of Charity of Cincinnati, Ohio.* (Mt. St. Joseph, OH).—S.C.
[0480]—*Sisters of Charity of Leavenworth, Kansas.*—S.C.L.
[0460]—*Sisters of Charity of the Incarnate Word.* (San Antonio, TX).—C.C.V.I.
[0660]—*Sisters of Christian Charity.* (Wilmette, IL).—S.C.C.
[0990]—*Sisters of Divine Providence.* (Allison Park, PA).—C.D.P.
[2360]—*Sisters of Loretto at the Foot of the Cross.* (Denver, CO).—S.L.
[2575]—*Sisters of Mercy of the Americas.* (Omaha, NE).—R.S.M.
[0230]—*Sisters of Pontifical Jurisdiction.* (Colorado Springs, CO).—O.S.B.
[1705]—*The Sisters of St. Francis of Assisi.* (Milwaukee, WI).—O.S.F.
[1620]—*Sisters of St. Francis of Millvale, PA.*—O.S.F.
[1630]—*Sisters of St. Francis of Penance and Christian Charity.* (Sacred Heart & Holy Name Provinces).—O.S.F.
[1640]—*Sisters of St. Francis of Perpetual Adoration.* (St. Joseph Province, Colorado Springs, CO).—O.S.F.
[1650]—*Sisters of St. Francis of Philadelphia.* (Aston, PA).—O.S.F.
[1530]—*Sisters of St. Francis of the Congregation of Our Lady of Lourdes, Sylvania, Ohio.*—O.S.F.
[1570]—*Sisters of St. Francis of the Holy Family.* (Dubuque, IA).—O.S.F.
[3830-01]—*Sisters of St. Joseph.* (Boston, MA).—C.S.J.
[3830-11]—*Sisters of St. Joseph.* (Kalamazoo, MI).—S.S.J.
[0260]—*Sisters of the Blessed Sacrament for Indians and Colored People.* (Bensalem, PA).—S.B.S.
[3320]—*Sisters of the Presentation of B.V.M..* (Aberdeen, SD).—P.B.V.M.
[3670]—*Sisters of the Sacred Heart of Jesus.* (San Antonio, TX).—S.S.C.J.
[1760]—*Sisters of the Third Order of St. Francis of Penance and Charity.* (Tiffin, OH).—O.S.F.
[1720]—*Sisters of the Third Order Regular of St. Francis of the Congregation of Our Lady of Lourdes.* (Rochester, MN).—O.S.F.
[2150-60]—*Sisters, Servants of the Immaculate Heart of Mary.* (Monroe, MI; Scranton, PA).—I.H.M.
[3105]—*Society of Our Lady of the Most Holy Trinity.* (Robstown, TX).—S.O.L.T.
[4120]—*Ursuline Nuns, of the Congregation of Paris.* (Maple Mount, KY).—O.S.U.

ARCHDIOCESAN CEMETERIES

ALBUQUERQUE. *Archdiocesan Cemetery Association,* 4000 St. Joseph Pl., N.W., 87120. Tel: 505-831-8100. Operates Rosario Cemetery, Santa Fe; Mount Calvary & Gate of Heaven, Albuquerque.
Catholic Cemetery Association, 4000 St. Joseph Pl., N.W., 87120. Tel: 505-831-8100.

NECROLOGY

† Dennis, Henry Clay, (Retired). —Died Oct. 27, 2000.
† Hunt, Ted J, Espanola, NM Sacred Heart. —Died July 26, 2000.

Diocese of Santa Rosa in California

(Dioecesis Sanctae Rosae in California)

Most Reverend

DANIEL F. WALSH, D.D.

Bishop of Santa Rosa in California; ordained March 30, 1963; appointed Titular Bishop of Tigia and Auxiliary of San Francisco September 24, 1981; appointed Bishop of Reno-Las Vegas June 9, 1987; installed August 6, 1987; appointed Bishop of Santa Rosa in California on April 4, 2000; installed May 22, 2000. *Res., 3336 Hermit Way, Santa Rosa, CA, 95405.*

Most Reverend

G. PATRICK ZIEMANN, D.D.

Resigned Bishop of Santa Rosa; ordained April 29, 1967; appointed Titular Bishop of Obba and Auxiliary of Los Angeles on December 29, 1986; ordained Bishop on February 23, 1987; appointed Bishop of Santa Rosa July 14, 1992.

ESTABLISHED FEBRUARY 21, 1962.

Square Miles 11,711.

Comprises six Counties in the State of California-viz., Del Norte, Humboldt, Lake, Mendocino, Napa and Sonoma.

Legal Titles: "The Roman Catholic Bishop of Santa Rosa, a Corporation Sole" and "The Roman Catholic Welfare Corporation of Santa Rosa."

For legal titles of parishes and diocesan institutions, consult the Chancery Office.

Chancery Office: 320 Tenth St., P.O. Box 1297, Santa Rosa, CA, 95402-1297. Tel.: 707-545-7610; Fax: 707-542-9702.

Web site address: www.santarosacatholic.org

STATISTICAL OVERVIEW

Personnel	
Bishop	1
Retired Bishops	2
Priests: Diocesan Active in Diocese	58
Priests: Active Outside Diocese	5
Priests: Retired, Sick or Absent	20
Number of Diocesan Priests	83
Religious Priests in Diocese	17
Extern Priests in Diocese	13
Ordinations:	
Diocesan Priests	1
Transitional Deacons	1
Permanent Deacons	22
Permanent Deacons in Diocese	38
Total Brothers	38
Total Sisters	78
Parishes	
Parishes	42
With Resident Pastor:	
Resident Diocesan Priests	40
Resident Religious Priests	2
Without Resident Pastor:	
Administered by Priests	1
Missions	21
Pastoral Centers	13
Closed Parishes	1
Professional Ministry Personnel:	
Sisters	7
Lay Ministers	26
Welfare	
Catholic Hospitals	5
Total Assisted	563,975
Homes for the Aged	1
Total Assisted	53
Residential Care of Children	1
Total Assisted	107
Day Care and Extended Day Care Centers	2
Total Assisted	80
Special Centers for Social Services	12
Total Assisted	26,237
Residential Care of Disabled	2
Total Assisted	12
Educational	
Diocesan Students in Other Seminaries	6
Total Seminarians	6
High Schools, Diocesan and Parish	3
Total Students	998
High Schools, Private	3
Total Students	1,015
Elementary Schools, Diocesan and Parish	12
Total Students	2,850
Elementary Schools, Private	1
Total Students	31
Catechesis/Religious Education:	
High School Students	1,053
Elementary Students	6,709
Total Students Under Catholic Instruction	12,662
Teachers in the Diocese:	
Priests	4
Sisters	8
Lay Teachers	290
Vital Statistics	
Receptions into the Church:	
Infant Baptism Totals	3,065
Adult Baptism Totals	104
Received into Full Communion	189
First Communions	1,976
Confirmations	741
Marriages:	
Catholic	654
Interfaith	215
Total Marriages	869
Deaths	989
Total Catholic Population	146,024
Total Population	751,312

Former Bishops—Most Rev. LEO T. MAHER, D.D., ord. Dec. 18, 1943; appt. First Bishop of Santa Rosa, Feb. 21, 1962; cons. April 5, 1962; translated San Diego, Aug. 27, 1969; died Feb. 23, 1991.—Most Rev. MARK J. HURLEY, D.D., Ph.D., J.C.B., L.L.D., ord. Sept. 23, 1944; appt. Titular Bishop of Thunusuda and Auxiliary of San Francisco, Oct. 12, 1967; cons. Jan. 4, 1968; translated Santa Rosa, Nov. 9, 1969; appt. member of the Vatican Secretariat for Non-Believers, consultor to the Congregation for Catholic Education; resigned as Bishop of Santa Rosa, April 15, 1986.—Most Rev. JOHN T. STEINBOCK, D.D., ord. May 1, 1963; Titular Bishop of Midila and Auxiliary Bishop of Orange; appt. May 29, 1984; translated Santa Rosa, March 31, 1987; translated Fresno, Nov. 25, 1991.—Most Rev. G. PATRICK ZIEMANN, D.D., ord. April 29, 1967; appt. Titular Bishop of Obba and Auxiliary Bishop of Los Angeles, Dec. 29, 1986; ord. Bishop, Feb. 23, 1987; appt. Bishop of Santa Rosa, July 14, 1992; resigned as Bishop of Santa Rosa, July 21, 1999.

Chancery Office—320 Tenth St., P.O. Box 1297, Santa Rosa, 95402. Tel: 707-545-7610; Fax: 707-542-9702. Office Hours: Mon.-Fri. 9-5 All applications for dispensations, faculties, etc., and all correspondence should be addressed to the Chancery Office.

Vicar General—Rev. Msgr. JAMES E. PULSKAMP, V.G.

Members of the Curia—Rev. Msgr. JOHN J. BRENKLE, J.C.D.; Rev. Msgr. JAMES E. PULSKAMP, V.G.; Revs. DANIEL P. WHELTON, J.C.L.; STEPHEN MACPHERSON; GARY LOMBARDI; TED OSWALD; DAVID SHAW; PATRICK STEPHENSON; LOREN ALLEN.

Deans—Rev. DAVID SHAW, Sonoma-North; Rev. PATRICK STEPHENSON, Napa; Rev. GARY LOMBARDI, Sonoma-South; Rev. TED OSWALD, Mendocino-Lake; Rev. STEPHEN MACPHERSON, Humboldt-Del Norte.

Chancellor—Rev. Msgr. JAMES E. PULSKAMP, V.G.

Director of Clergy Personnel—Rev. Msgr. JAMES E. PULSKAMP, V.G.

Vicar for Priests—Rev. DANIEL P. WHELTON, J.C.L.

Vicar of Finance—Rev. Msgr. JOHN J. BRENKLE, J.C.D.

Business Manager—Mr. THOMAS CUNEO.

Secretary to the Bishop—PAM HAWKINS. Tel: 707-566-3310.

Diocesan Tribunal—P.O. Box 1297, Santa Rosa, 95402. Tel: 707-542-9014; Fax: 707-542-9015.

Judicial Vicar—Rev. DANIEL P. WHELTON, J.C.L.

Adjutant Judicial Vicar—Rev. Msgr. JOHN J. BRENKLE, J.C.D.

Promoter of Justice—Rev. STEPHEN J. CANNY.

Defender of the Bond—Rev. DAVID SHAW.

Diocesan Judges—Rev. Msgr. JOHN J. BRENKLE, J.C.D.; Rev. Msgr. JAMES P. GAFFEY; Revs. JOHN CREWS;

WILLIAM E. DUGGAN; DANIEL P. WHELTON, J.C.L.; Mrs. MARGUERITE B. STEIN, J.C.L., J.D.

Advocates—Revs. MICHAEL M. KELLY; FERGAL MCGUINNESS; WALTER ROGINA; Sr. MAURA MURPHY, O.S.U.; Deacon RODRIGO AGUDELO; STELLA AGUDELO.

Auditor—Sr. ROSE MARY KUKLOK, O.S.B.

Notary—Rev. Msgr. JAMES E. PULSKAMP, V.G.

Board of Consultors—Rev. Msgr. JOHN J. BRENKLE, J.C.D.; Rev. Msgr. JAMES E. PULSKAMP, V.G.; Revs. LOREN ALLEN; STEPHEN MACPHERSON; GARY LOMBARDI; TED OSWALD; DAVID SHAW; PATRICK STEPHENSON; DANIEL P. WHELTON, J.C.L.

Priests' Council—Rev. Msgr. JAMES E. PULSKAMP, V.G.; Rev. Msgr. JOHN J. BRENKLE, J.C.D.; Revs. LOREN ALLEN; GARY LOMBARDI; DAVID SHAW; PATRICK STEPHENSON; TED OSWALD; STEPHEN MACPHERSON; DANIEL P. WHELTON, J.C.L.; RAMON PONS, O.A.R.; Rev. Msgr. GERARD BRADY; Revs. JOHN MARTIN; THOMAS DEVERAUX; OSCAR DIAZ.

Finance Committee—Rev. Msgr. JOHN J. BRENKLE, J.C.D.; Rev. Msgr. JAMES P. GAFFEY; Rev. Msgr. JAMES E. PULSKAMP, V.G.; Deacon JIM HERCHER; Sr. MARY ANN BREIDENICH, O.P.; ROBERT ARMANINO; CLEM CARINALLI; WILLIAM CORNELISON; JAMES DILLON; PEGGY FURTH; JOHN KLEIN; JOHN MOYNIER; DON RAMATICI; DAVID ROBINSON; DIRK ROPER; RICK ROSA; JOSEPH SCHUNK; HENRY TRIONE; RAY WOOD.

Diocesan Building Committee—WILLIAM CORNELISON, Chm.; Rev. Msgr. JAMES E. PULSKAMP, V.G.; Rev. Msgr. JOHN J. BRENKLE, J.C.D.; Rev. MICHAEL CLEARY; ANTHONY BATTAGLIA; LOWELL ALLEN; TOM CUNEO; PAUL DIXON; TOM FELLENZ; ED RONCHELLI; DIRK ROPER.

Diocesan Communications Committee—DEIRDRE FRONTCZAK, Chm. JUDY BARRETT; JEFF SCHARFEN; VALERIE PRESTON; EILEEN LIMBERG; PETER ROSS.

Sensitive Issues Committee—MARGARET BUTLER, Chm.; Rev. Msgr. JAMES E. PULSKAMP, V.G.; Rev. Msgr. JOHN J. BRENKLE, J.C.D.; ELAINE HAMLIN, Ph.D.; LEONARD SCHWARTZBURD, Ph.D.

Diocesan Offices and Directors

AIDS Ministry Outreach—Rev. RODNEY DEMARTINI, *P.O. Box 960, Occidental, 95465.* Tel: 707-874-1344.

Archivist—Rev. Msgr. JAMES E. PULSKAMP, V.G., *320 Tenth St., P.O. Box 1297, Santa Rosa, 95402.* Tel: 707-566-3312.

Attorney for the Diocese—Mr. JOHN KLEIN, *P.O. Box 1845, Santa Rosa, 95402.* Tel: 707-546-6767.

Boy Scouts—320 Tenth St., P.O. Box 11574, Santa Rosa, 95406. Tel: 707-566-3330; Fax: 707-566-3350.

Catholic Charities, Central Admin. Office—MAUREEN E. SHAW, A.C.S.W., Diocesan Dir., *2325 Montgomery Dr., P.O. Box 4900, Santa Rosa, 95402.* Tel: 707-528-8712.

Catholic Community Foundation—JAMES DILLON, Acting Exec. Dir., *320 Tenth St., P.O. Box 1297, Santa Rosa, 95402.* Tel: 707-545-2311; 566-3357; Fax: 707-566-3310.

Catholic Youth Organization—Rev. Msgr. THOMAS J. KEYS, Dir., Office: *545 White Oak Fr., Santa Rosa, 95409.* Tel: 707-539-6262; Fax: 707-539-8620.

Cemeteries—Rev. Msgr. GERARD FAHEY, Dir., Office: *P.O. Box 2098, 2930 Bennett Valley Rd., Santa Rosa, 95404.* Tel: 707-546-6290.

Clergy Formation—Rev. DANIEL P. WHELTON, J.C.L., *320 Tenth St., P.O. Box 1297, Santa Rosa, 95402.* Tel: 707-542-9014; Fax: 707-542-9015.

Detention Ministry, Adult & Juvenile—24A Ursuline Rd., Santa Rosa, 95403. Tel: 707-544-9080.

Development—Rev. Msgr. JOHN J. BRENKLE, J.C.D., Dir., *320 Tenth St., P.O. Box 1297, Santa Rosa, 95402.* Tel: 707-545-7610.

Disabled—Chancery Office, 320 Tenth St., P.O. Box 1297, Santa Rosa, 95402. Tel: 707-545-7610.

Ecumenical and Interreligious Affairs—Rev. THOMAS W. DEVEREAUX, Dir., *208 Matheson St., Healdsburg, 95448.* Tel: 707-433-5536.

Hispanic Ministry—

Cursillos De Cristiandad—Rev. MANUEL CHAVEZ, Spiritual Dir., *8460 Alden Ln., Windsor, 95492.* Tel: 707-837-8962.

Movimiento Familiar Cristiano—Deacon RODRIGO AGUDELO, Spiritual Dir., *3727 View Ct., Santa Rosa, 95403.* Tel: 707-526-4892.

Renovacion Carismatica Catolica—Rev. JOSE GONZALEZ, Dir., *303 Stony Point Rd., Santa Rosa, 95401.* Tel: 707-544-7272.

National Council of Catholic Women—Sr. ANTONIA KILLIAN, S.M., Spiritual Dir., *320 Tenth St., P.O. Box 1297, Santa Rosa, 95402.* Tel: 707-545-7610; Fax: 707-542-9702.

Native American Affairs—Rev. RALPH MONTEIRO, O.S.A., Liaison, *P.O. Box 429, Hoopa, 95546.* Tel: 530-625-4415.

Newspaper—"Redwood Crozier", Rev. ALLAN BOHNER, Editor, *320 Tenth St., P.O. Box 1297, Santa Rosa, 95402.* Tel: 707-545-7610.

Parish Priest Consultors—Rev. Msgr. WILLIAM HYNES; Rev. Msgr. GERARD FAHEY; Revs. MICHAEL J. CLEARY; THOMAS W. DEVEREAUX.

Permanent Diaconate—Directors: Deacon JOSEPH REMLEY; LINDA REMLEY, *24-A Ursuline Rd., Santa Rosa, 95403.* Tel: 707-525-0531.

Pontifical Association of Holy Childhood—Deacon W. EVERETT WOODRUFF, *320 Tenth St., P.O. Box 1297, Santa Rosa, 95402.* Tel: 707-579-9599.

Priests' Personnel Committee—Rev. Msgr. JAMES E. PULSKAMP, V.G.; Rev. Msgr. JAMES P. GAFFEY; Revs. OSCAR DIAZ; GORDON KALIL; DENIS O'SULLIVAN.

Propagation of the Faith—Deacon W. EVERETT WOODRUFF, *320 Tenth St., P.O. Box 1297, Santa Rosa, 95402.* Tel: 707-579-9599.

Council of Religious—Sr. JEAN HOPMAN, O.S.U.; Sr. ANTONIA KILLIAN, S.M.; Sr. JOYCE POESCHL, O.P.; Bros. THOMAS JONES, F.S.C.; BEDE VAN DUREN, F.S.C.

Religious Education—Sr. OLIVE MURPHY, S.M., Dir., *320 Tenth St., P.O. Box 11574, Santa Rosa, 95406.* Tel: 707-566-3366; Fax: 707-566-3320.

Schools—Dr. JOHN COLLINS, Acting Supt. of Schools, Office: *320 Tenth St., P.O. Box 6654, Santa Rosa, 95406.* Tel: 707-566-3311.

Serra Club—Rev. WALTER ROGINA, Chap., *P.O. Box 339, Occidental, 95465.* Tel: 707-874-3812.

Vocations—Chancery Office, 320 Tenth St., P.O. Box 1297, Santa Rosa, 95402. Tel: 707-545-7610.

CLERGY, PARISHES, MISSIONS AND PAROCHIAL SCHOOLS

CITY OF SANTA ROSA
(Sonoma County)

1—CATHEDRAL OF ST. EUGENE (1950), Rev. Msgr. James P. Gaffey; Rev. Daniel Kassis (Gallup); Deacon W. Everett Woodruff. In res., Rev. Msgr. Patrick McCoy (England); Deacon Michael Heinzelman.
Res., 2323 Montgomery Dr., 95405. Tel: 707-542-6984; Fax: 707-542-1621. [CEM]
School—300 Farmers Ln., 95405. Tel: 707-545-7252; Fax: 707-545-2594. Mrs. Barbara Gasparini, Prin.
Lay Teachers 13; Students 350.
Catechesis/Religious Programs—Tel: 707-542-1525. Diane Drew, D.R.E.
Students 325.

2—HOLY SPIRIT (1964), Rev. Msgr. James E. Pulskamp; Rev. Roger Lamoureux.
Res., 1244 St. Francis Rd., 95409. Tel: 707-539-4495; Fax: 707-539-3343.
Catechesis/Religious Programs—Bernard Ciernick, D.R.E.
Students 150.

3—ST. ROSE OF LIMA (1877), Revs. Denis A. O'Sullivan; Gerard Gormley; David Villalobos; Deacons Stepehn Ellis; Jesus Fernandez. In res., Rev. Alvin Villaruel.
Res., 398 10th St., 95401. Tel: 707-542-6448; Fax: 707-542-3359.
School—4300 Old Redwood Hwy., 95403. Tel: 707-545-0379; Fax: 707-545-7150. Kathy Ryan, Prin.
Lay Teachers 13; Students 360.
Catechesis/Religious Programs—Tel: 707-542-3080; Fax: 707-542-3359. Sr. Shelia Coffey, S.M., D.R.E.
Students 296.

4—RESURRECTION (1967), Revs. David Shaw; Jose Gonzalez; Deacon Rodrigo Agudelo.
Res., 303 Stony Point Rd., 95401. Tel: 707-544-7272; Fax: 707-544-2901.
Catechesis/Religious Programs—Tel: 707-544-0708. Betty Kovanis, D.R.E.
Students 350.

5—STAR OF THE VALLEY (1981), Rev. Msgr. Thomas J. Keys; Rev. Msgr. Gerard Fahey, Pastor Emeritus; Rev. Msgr. Patrick McCoy (England). In res., Rev. Patrick J. Leslie (SAC).
Parish Center: 545 White Oak Dr., 95409. Tel: 707-539-6262; Fax: 707-539-8620.

OUTSIDE CITY OF SANTA ROSA

American Canyon, Holy Family, Rev. Patrick Stephenson; Deacon Michael Simmons.
Res., 402 Donaldson Way, 94589. Tel: 707-645-9331.
Catechesis/Religious Programs—Tel: 707-544-1183. Lia Estupin, D.R.E.
Students 91.

Arcata, Humboldt Co., St. Mary's (1883), Rev. Michael M. Kelly; Deacon John Gai.
Res., 1690 Janes Rd., 95521. Tel: 707-822-7696; Fax: 707-822-6931. [CEM]
School—1730 Janes Rd., 95521. Tel: 707-822-3877; Fax: 707-822-6931. Susan Buchanan, Prin.
Lay Teachers 5; Students 75.
Catechesis/Religious Programs—Tel: 707-822-7696. Patricia Heavilin, D.R.E.
Students 153.
Mission—Blue Lake, St. Joseph.

Boyes Hot Springs, Sonoma Co., St. Leo (1966), Revs. J. Lawrence Carolan; Aurelio Villa, O.F.M.
Res., 601 Agua Caliente Rd., Sonoma, 95476. Tel: 707-996-8422; Fax: 707-996-3984.
Church—P.O. Box 666, 95416.
Catechesis/Religious Programs—Tel: 707-996-7503. Cindy Vrooman, D.R.E.
Students 318.

Calistoga, Napa Co., Our Lady of Perpetual Help (1915), Rev. Andrew Metcalf.
Res., 901 Washington St., 94515. Tel: 707-942-6894; Fax: 707-942-1091.
Catechesis/Religious Programs—Tel: 707-942-4769; Fax: 707-942-4681. D.R.E.: Veronica Donald; Teresa Olguin.
Students 145.

Clearlake, Lake Co., Our Lady, Queen of Peace (1967), Rev. Louis J. Nichols (SY) Admin.; Deacon Ruben De Los Santos.
Res., P.O. Box 460, 95422. Tel: 707-994-6618; Fax: 707-994-2223.
Catechesis/Religious Programs—D.R.E.: Helen Layne; Carol Combs.
Students 195.
Mission—Lucerne, Queen of the Rosary.

Cloverdale, Sonoma Co., St. Peter's (1917), Rev. Robert Blake; Deacon Harry Martin.
Res., 491 S. Franklin St., 95425. Tel: 707-894-2535; Fax: 707-894-9603.
Catechesis/Religious Programs—Fax: 707-894-9603. Kendall Galvez, D.R.E.
Students 100.
Mission—Asti, Our Lady of Mt. Carmel.

Cotati, Sonoma Co., St. Joseph (1913), Revs. Stephen J. Canny; Eric Freed; Deacon Joseph Remley.
Res., 150 St. Joseph Way, 94931-4117. Tel: 707-795-4807; Fax: 707-795-7851.
Catechesis/Religious Programs—Tel: 707-795-7678. Georgette Parry, D.R.E.
Students 471.

Crescent City, Del Norte Co., St. Joseph (1869), Rev. George Risden.
Res., 319 E St., 95531. Tel: 707-465-1762; Fax: 707-465-1763. [CEM]
School—300 E St., 95531. Tel: 707-464-3477. Sr. Phyllis Manternach, O.S.F., Prin.
Sisters 1; Lay Teachers 5; Students 86.
Catechesis/Religious Programs—Tere Darby, D.R.E.
Students 22.
Mission—Klamath, St. Robert and Ann. Closed.

Eureka, Humboldt Co., St. Bernard (1864), Revs. Loren Allen; Robert Benjamin; Deacons Jim Hercher; Frank Weber; Edie Young, Pastoral Assoc.
Res., P.O. Box 169, 95502. Tel: 707-442-6466; Fax: 707-443-0914. [CEM]
Catechesis/Religious Programs—Suanna Rowell, D.R.E.
Students 270.
Mission—Eureka, St. Joseph.

Sacred Heart (1963), Rev. Donald W. Eagleson; Ann Lynch, Pastoral Assoc.; Deacons Steven Justus; Anthony Viegas.
Res., 2085 Myrtle Ave., 95501. Tel: 707-443-8429; Fax: 707-443-8420.
Catechesis/Religious Programs—Larry McNeil, D.R.E.
Students 85.

Ferndale, Humboldt Co., Church of the Assumption (1878), Rev. Allan G. Bohner.
Res., 546 Berding St., P.O. Box 1097, 95536. Tel: 707-786-9551. [CEM]
Catechesis/Religious Programs—Maura Eastman, D.R.E.
Students 76.
Mission—Petrolia, St. Patrick.

Fort Bragg, Mendocino Co., Our Lady of Good Counsel (1890), Rev. Michaelraj Philominsamy.
Res., 255 S. Harold St., 95437. Tel: 707-964-0229; Fax: 707-964-0728.
Catechesis/Religious Programs—Tel: 707-964-5727. Lucresha Rentonci, D.R.E.
Students 174.

Fortuna, Humboldt Co., St. Joseph (1909), Rev. James Trent (DET) Admin.; Deacons Thomas Silva; Francisco Nunez.
Res., P.O. Box 430, 95540. Tel: 707-725-1148; Fax: 707-725-5678. [CEM]

Catechesis/Religious Programs—2292 Newburg Rd., 95540. Tel: 707-725-1216.
Students 150.
Mission—Loleta, St. Patrick.

Garberville, Humboldt Co., Our Lady of the Redwoods (1950), Rev. Thomas Gowing, Admin.
Mailing Address: P.O. Box 115, 95542.
Res., 515 Maple Ln., 95542. Tel: 707-923-7864.
Catechesis/Religious Programs—Students 14.
Mission—Leggett, St. Cecilia, (1954).

Guerneville, Sonoma Co., St. Elizabeth (1916), Rev. Philip J. Ryan, Admin.
Res., 14095 Woodland Dr., 95446-9553. Tel: 707-869-2107.
Catechesis/Religious Programs—Tel: 707-923-7864.
Students 34.
Missions—Monte Rio, St. Catherine; Cazadero, St. Colman.

Healdsburg, Sonoma Co., St. John the Baptist (1884), Revs. Thomas W. Devereaux; Hans Ruygt; Deacon Juventino Vera; Rose Marie Woodruff, Pastoral Asst. & D.R.E. In res., Rev. Daniel P. Whelton.
Res., 208 Matheson St., 95448. Tel: 707-433-5536; Fax: 707-433-1813.
School—217 Fitch St., 95448. Tel: 707-433-2758; Fax: 707-433-0353. Janet Suzio, Prin.
Lay Teachers 13; Students 271.
Catechesis/Religious Programs—Tel: 707-433-5112.
Students 265.

Hoopa, Humboldt Co., Mission of Blessed Kateri Tekakwitha (1986), Rev. Ralph Monteiro, O.S.A., Admin.
Res., P.O. Box 429, 95546. Tel: 530-625-4415; Fax: 530-625-4530.
Tekakwitha Center—P.O. Box 845, 95546. Tel: 530-625-4464. Sr. Patricia Carson, R.S.M., Dir.

Lakeport, Lake Co., St. Mary (1871), Rev. Ted Oswald; Deacon David Robinson.
Res., 801 N. Main St., 95453. Tel: 707-263-4401; Fax: 707-263-6325. [CEM]
Catechesis/Religious Programs—Tel: 707-263-0606. Terri Denton, D.R.E.
Students 114.
Mission—Kelseyville, St. Peter. [CEM]

McKinleyville, Humboldt County, Christ the King (1967), Rev. Stephen MacPherson; Deacon Robert Shell.
Res., P.O. Box 2367, 95519. Tel: 707-839-2911; Fax: 707-839-9823.
Catechesis/Religious Programs—Eva Adams, D.R.E.
Students 80.
Mission—Trinidad, Holy Trinity.

Mendocino, Mendocino Co., St. Anthony (1864), Rev. John J. Martin, M.M., Admin.
Res., P.O. Box 665, 95460. Tel: 707-937-5808. [CEM]

Middletown, Lake Co., St. Joseph (1894), Rev. Ray Rioux, Admin.
Res., P.O. Box 1350, 95461. Tel: 707-987-3676; Fax: 707-987-2792.
Catechesis/Religious Programs—Students 110.
Mission—Loch Lomond, Our Lady of the Lake.
Station—Forest Lake, Our Lady of the Pines.

Napa, Napa Co., St. Apollinaris (1957), Revs. Michael J. Cleary; John McCormick; Deacons Francis Dahl; Joel Momsen.
Res., 3700 Lassen St., 94558. Tel: 707-257-2555; Fax: 707-257-3552.
School—Tel: 707-224-6525. Patricia Granucci, Prin.
Sisters 1; Lay Teachers 16; Students 320.
Catechesis/Religious Programs—Tel: 707-255-7200. Sr. Peggy Cruise, S.M., D.R.E.
Students 320.

St. John the Baptist (1859), Revs. Timothy J. O'Sullivan; Oscar Diaz; Deacon Charles Stanton.
Res., Box 178, 94559. Tel: 707-226-9379; Fax: 707-254-9262.
School—983 Napa St., 94559. Tel: 707-224-8388; Fax: 707-224-0236.
Sisters 1; Lay Teachers 14; Students 278. Principals: Charles Stanton; Judy Stanton.
Catechesis/Religious Programs—Tel: 707-255-3533. D.R.E.: Charles Stanton; Judy Stanton.
Students 354.
Station—Imola, State Hospital, St. Luke's Chapel.

St. Thomas Aquinas (1964), Rev. Msgr. Gerard J. Brady. In res., Rev. Gary Sumpter.
Res., 2725 Elm St., 94558. Tel: 707-255-2949.
Catechesis/Religious Programs—Students 123.

Occidental, Sonoma Co., St. Philip (1964), Rev. Walter Rogina; Deacon William Moody.
Res., P.O. Box 339, 95465. Tel: 707-874-3812; Fax: 707-874-9201.
Catechesis/Religious Programs—Judy Van Gorder, D.R.E.
Students 60.
Mission—Bodega, St. Teresa. [CEM]

Petaluma, Sonoma Co., St. James (1964), Rev. Michael A. Culligan; Deacons Ray Noll; Ken Manz; Kenneth Begin. In res., Rev. Msgr. Joseph Alzugaray.
Res., 125 Sonoma Mt. Pky., 94954. Tel: 707-762-4256; Fax: 707-762-4044.
Catechesis/Religious Programs—Tel: 707-762-9063.
Students 695.

St. Vincent de Paul (1857), Revs. Gary Lombardi; Ramon Pons, O.A.R.; Luis Penaloza; Deacons James Carr; Armando Lemos; John Norris.
Res., 35 Liberty St., 94952. Tel: 707-762-4278; Fax: 707-763-8188.
School—Howard & Union Sts., 94952. Tel: 707-762-6426; Fax: 707-762-6791. Susan Roffmann, Prin.
Lay Teachers 12; Students 300.
High School—849 Keokuk, P.O. Box 517, 94953. Tel: 707-763-1032; Fax: 707-763-9448. Mr. Edward Kavanaugh, Prin.
Priests 1; Lay Teachers 29; Students 390.
Catechesis/Religious Programs—Camilla Edwards, D.R.E.
Students 620.

Point Arena, Mendocino Co., St. Aloysius (1950), Rev. Thomas P. O'Sullivan (SAC) Admin.; Deacon Arturo Ramirez.
Res., P.O. Box 66, 95468. Tel: 707-884-4920; Fax: 707-884-4920. [CEM]
Catechesis/Religious Programs—Students 42.
Mission—Gualala, Mary, Star of the Sea.

Rohnert Park, Sonoma Co., St. Elizabeth Seton (1981), Rev. John Griffin; Deacons Paul Bromham; Bradley Andrews; Joseph Olsen, Jr.
Res., 4595 Snyder Ln., 94928. Tel: 707-585-3708; Fax: 707-585-1201.
Catechesis/Religious Programs—Tel: 707-585-8821; Fax: 707-585-1202. Moira Bromham, D.R.E.
Students 170.

Saint Helena, Napa Co., St. Helena (1887), Rev. Msgr. John J. Brenkle; Revs. Gordon Kalil; Carlos Ortega; Deacon Robert Little.
Res., 1340 Tainter St., 94574. Tel: 707-963-1228; Fax: 707-963-2894. [CEM]
School—1255 Oak Ave., 94574. Tel: 707-963-4677; Fax: 707-963-4677. Tom Giugni, Prin.
Sisters 1; Lay Teachers 8; Students 140.
Catechesis/Religious Programs—Tel: 707-963-8290. Maria Conroy Phelps, D.R.E.
Students 114.

Scotia, Humboldt Co., St. Patrick (1930). Unassigned.
Res., P.O. Box 98, 95565. Tel: 707-764-5446.
Catechesis/Religious Programs—Students 10.

Sebastopol, Sonoma Co., St. Sebastian (1898), Rev. Msgr. William Hynes; Rev. George Aziz, S.J.
Res., 7983 Covert Ln., 95472. Tel: 707-823-2208; Fax: 707-823-1098.
Catechesis/Religious Programs—Barbara Schliemann, D.R.E.
Students 158.

Sonoma, Sonoma Co., St. Francis Solano (1878), Revs. James McSweeney; Robert Castro; Xavier Ochoa.
Res., 469 Third St., W., 95476. Tel: 707-996-6759; Fax: 707-939-8128. [CEM]
School—342 W. Napa St., 95476. Tel: 707-996-4994. Dr. Lydia Treadwell-Blecksmith, Prin.
Lay Teachers 25; Students 360.
Catechesis/Religious Programs—Tel: 707-996-1578. Will Roll, D.R.E.
Students 275.

Ukiah, Mendocino Co., St. Mary of the Angels (1887), Revs. Michael Cloney; Perfecto Nacional (Philippines); Mary Leittem-Thomas, Pastoral Assoc.
Res., 900 S. Oak St., 95482. Tel: 707-462-1431; Fax: 707-462-2879.
School—991 S. Dora St., 95482. Tel: 707-462-3888; Fax: 707-462-6014. Thomas Rooney, Prin.
Lay Teachers 16; Students 235.
Catechesis/Religious Programs—Tel: 707-462-1131. Leslie Loopstra, D.R.E.
Students 243.
Missions—Hopland, St. Francis; Booneville, Sonoma Co., St. Elizabeth Seton.

Willits, Mendocino Co., St. Anthony (1923), Rev. Bruce Lamb.
Res., 61 W. San Francisco Ave., 95490. Tel: 707-459-2252.
Catechesis/Religious Programs—Robyn Carter, D.R.E.
Students 95.
Mission—Covelo, Queen of Peace. [CEM]

Windsor, Sonoma Co., Our Lady of Guadalupe (1969), Revs. Angelito Peries, C.Ss.R., Admin.; Manuel Chavez.
Mailing Address: 8460 Alden Ln., 95492. Tel: 707-837-8962; Fax: 707-837-9157.
Catechesis/Religious Programs—D.R.E.: Rita Agius; Dawn Graverson.
Students 600.

Yountville, Napa Co., St. Joan of Arc (1920), Rev. Mathew Ittiyappara; Deacon Jerry Cain.
Res., Box 2009, 94599. Tel: 707-944-2461; Fax: 707-944-2202.
Catechesis/Religious Programs—Students 52.
Mission—Rutherford, Holy Family.

Chaplains Of Public Institutions

CRESCENT CITY. *Pelican Bay State Prison*. Rev. Joseph Vallooran.

ELDRIDGE. *Sonoma Developmental Center*. Rev. Patrick J. Leslie (SAC) Chap.

IMOLA. *Napa State Hospital* 94558. Rev. James Lantsberger, O.M.I., Chap.

PETALUMA. *U.S. Coast Guard Training Center*. Rev. Keith Shuley, C.C.

YOUNTVILLE. *Veterans Administration Home*. Rev. Paul F. Ledermann (OG) Chap.

Special Assignment:
Reverend Fathers—
Kilianski, Edward, S.J.C.

Military Chaplains:
Reverend Fathers—
Serban, Ron

Unassigned:
Reverend Fathers—
Talcott, Peter

On Duty Outside the Diocese:
Reverend Fathers—
Baptista, Diego
Diaz, Thomas K.

Graduate Studies:
Reverend Fathers—
McGuinness, Fergal

On Leave:
Reverend Fathers—
Bernard, Andre
Boettcher, John
Logan, Gary
Martinez, Luis

Retired:
Reverend Monsignors—
Fleming, Vincent A.
Monaghan, George D.
Serado, William
Tournier, Andre
Reverend Fathers—
Faucher, Henry L.
Hanratty, Brendan
Healy, John
Keffer, Thomas
Keogh, Thomas
McAllister, Alex
McIntyre, Justin
Munari, Mario
Sheehy, Wilfred
Thomas, Jerald
Tracy, Charles

Permanent Deacons:
Agudelo, Rodrigo, Santa Rosa
Andrews, Bradley, Rohnert Park
Begin, Kenneth, Petaluma
Bond, Ken, Arcata
Bromham, Paul, Rohnert Park
Cain, Jerry B., Yountville
Carr, James, Petaluma
Dahl, Francis, Napa
De Los Santos, Ruben, Clearlake
Ellis, Stephen, Santa Rosa
Fernandez, Jesus, Santa Rosa
Gai, John, Aracata
Heinzelman, Michael, Santa Rosa
Hercher, James, Eureka
Justus, Steven, Eureka
Lemos, Armando, Petaluma
Little, Robert, St. Helena
Manz, Kenneth, Petaluma
Martin, Harry, Sebastopol
Momsen, Joel, Napa
Moody, William, Occidental
Noll, Ray, Petaluma
Norris, John, Petaluma
Nunez, Francisco, Fortuna
Olsen, Joseph, Rohnert Park
Ramirez, Arturo, Point Arena

Remley, Joseph, Rohnert Park
Robinson, David, Lakeport
Ross, Norman, Santa Rosa
Seagraves, Skip (HON), Eureka
Shell, Robert, McKinleyville
Silva, Thomas, Fortuna
Simmons, Michael, American Canyon
Stanton, Charles, Napa
Vera, Juventino, Healdsburg
Viegas, Anthony, Eureka
Weber, Frank
Woodruff, W. Everett, Santa Rosa

INSTITUTIONS LOCATED IN THE DIOCESE

[A] SEMINARIES, RELIGIOUS, OR SCHOLASTICATES

NAPA. *Mont La Salle Novitiate*, 4405 Redwood Dr., 94558. Tel: 707-252-3821; Fax: 707-252-3731.
E-mail: novitiate@dlsi.org
Web site: www.delasalle.org
Brothers of the Christian Schools. Bro. Richard Moratto, F.S.C., Dir. Brothers 2; Novices 4.

[B] HIGH SCHOOLS, DIOCESAN

SANTA ROSA. *Cardinal Newman High School*, 50 Ursuline Rd., 95403. Tel: 707-546-6470; Fax: 707-544-8502.
E-mail: cnhsinfo@yahoo.com
Web site: cardinalnewman.org
Dennis Krandall, Interim Prin.; Rev. Alvin M. Villaruel. Priests 1; Lay Teachers 27; Students 402.

EUREKA. *St. Bernard Catholic School*, 222 Dollison St., 95501. Patrick W. Daly, Prin.; Craig Brown, Campus Min. Sisters 1; Brothers 1; Lay Teachers 27; Students 281.
High School Campus. Tel: 707-443-2735; Fax: 707-443-4723.
Elementary School Campus. Tel: 707-443-2226; Fax: 707-443-2227.

[C] HIGH SCHOOLS, PRIVATE

SANTA ROSA.
Ursuline High School, 90 Ursuline Rd., 95403. Tel: 707-524-1130; Fax: 707-542-0131.
E-mail: fdelaforest@ursulinehs.org
Web site: www.ursulinehs.org
Ursuline Sisters of the Roman Union. Legal Title: *Santa Rosa Ursuline Corporation*. Carole Ellis, Interim Prin. Sisters 1; Lay Teachers 31; Students 358.
Ursuline Parent Association of Santa Rosa.
Ursuline Memorial Scholarship Fund.

NAPA. *Justin-Siena High School*, 4026 Maher St., 94558. Tel: 707-255-0950; Fax: 707-255-0334.
Web site: Justin-siena.com
Joseph W. Bracco, Pres. & CEO; Gregory J. Schmitz, Prin.; Bruce Halverson, Chair Guidance Dept. Sisters 1; Lay Teachers 50; Students 649.
Justin-Siena High School Corporation, Inc.
Justin-Siena High School Foundation, Inc.
Kolbe Academy for Boys and Girls, 1600 F St., 94559. Tel: 707-256-4306; Fax: 707-255-1581.
E-mail: KOLBEACAD@EARTHLINK.NET
Web site: www.KOLBE.ORG
John Kamprath, Admin. Lay Teachers 3; Students 8.

[D] ELEMENTARY SCHOOLS, PRIVATE

NAPA.
Kolbe Academy for Boys and Girls, 1600 F St., 94559. Tel: 707-256-4306.
E-mail: KOLBEACAD@earthlink.net
Web site: www.KOLBE.ORG
John Kamprath, Admin. Lay Teachers 4; Students 31.

[E] CATHOLIC CHARITIES

SANTA ROSA.
Diocese of Santa Rosa, Catholic Charities.
Central Administrative Offices, 2325 Montgomery Dr., P.O. Box 4900, 95402. Tel: 707-528-8712; Fax: 707-575-4910. Maureen E. Shaw, A.C.S.W., Diocesan Dir.; Mary Ann McGee, R.N., Regl. Dir. of Sonoma, Mendocino & Lake Counties; Sharon McCarty, Dir. Admin. Svcs. & Human Resources; Lia Boatman, Dir. Accounting Svcs. & Finance; Frances Caballo, Dir. Devel. & Communication.
Family Support Center, 465 A St., 95401. Tel: 707-542-5426; Fax: 707-542-3148. Mailing Address: P.O. Box 4900, 95402. David Hinkley, Prog. Dir.
Homeless Service Center, 600 Morgan St., 95401. Tel: 707-525-0226; Fax: 707-545-1920. Mailing Address: P.O. Box 4900, 95402. Nick Baker, Program Dir.
Professional Foster Care, 3295 Claremont Way, Ste. #1, Napa, 94558. Tel: 707-224-3191; Fax: 707-224-2889. Danda Winford, Regl. Dir., Napa; Judy Bell, Prog. Mgr.
Immigration and Resettlement Services, 2325 Montgomery Dr., 95405. Tel: 707-578-6000; Fax: 707-575-4910. Mailing Address: P.O. Box 4900, 95402. Vicki Mayster, Program Dir.
Interfaith Volunteer Caregiver Program, 9470 Mendenhall Ave., Upper Lake, 95485. Tel: 707-275-9161; Fax: 707-275-3514. Mailing Address: P.O. Box 925, Upper Lake, 95485. Sr. Marti McCarthy, Prog. Coord.
Rural Food Program, 465 A St., 95401. Tel: 707-542-5426; Fax: 707-542-3148. Mailing Address: P.O. Box 4900, 95402. Sr. Kathleen McGrath, B.V.M., Program Dir., Mailing Address: P.O. Box 4900, 95402. Michele Osmon, Program Dir.
Alzheimer's Respite / Resource Center, 320 Tenth St., 95401. Tel: 707-528-8712; Fax: 707-575-4910. 1000 N. Gravenstein Hwy., Sebastopol, 95472. Tel: 707-528-8712; Fax: 707-575-4910. Mailing Address: P.O. Box 4900, 95402. Scott Hale, Program Dir.
Professional Counseling Services of Humboldt / Del Norte, 2936 J St., Eureka, 95501. Tel: 707-444-9611; Fax: 707-444-9613. 1151 Main St., Fortuna, 95540. Tel: 707-725-3389. Charlie Herbelin, Regl. Dir., Humboldt.
Housing Options, 3295 Claremont Way, Ste. #1, Napa, 94558. Tel: 707-224-4403; Fax: 707-224-2889. Danda Winford, M.A., Regl. Dir.; Sheila Edridge, Prog. Mgr.
Teen Mom Program, 3295 Claremont Way, Ste. #1, Napa, 94558. Tel: 707-224-3191; Fax: 707-224-2889. Danda Winford, M.A., Regl. Dir., Napa; Marjorie Lewis, Mgr.
Free-To-Be, 1180 Montgomery Dr., 95405. Tel: 707-526-3819; Fax: 707-526-3851. Mailing Address: P.O. Box 4900, 95402. Sue Bisbee, Program Dir.
Rainbow House, 1209 Jefferson St., Napa, 94559. Tel: 707-258-0260; Fax: 707-258-0442. Dandra Winford, Regl. Dir., Napa; Sabrina Bucklin, House Coord.
Parish / Community Services, 2325 Montgomery Dr., 95405. Tel: 707-528-8712; Fax: 707-575-4910. Mailing Address: P.O. Box 4900, 95402. Michele Osmon, Prog. Dir.
Phase Two - Housing Development, 2325 Montgomery Dr., 95405. Tel: 707-528-8712; Fax: 707-575-4910. Mailing Address: P.O. Box 4900, 95402. Sr. Teresita Poulin, B.V.M., Prog. Dir.
Phase Two - Supportive Services, 516 Morgan St., 95401. Tel: 707-577-7696; Fax: 707-578-6046. Gary Pierce, Prog. Dir.
Drug and Alcohol Prevention Services, 3295 Claremont Way, Ste. 1, Napa, 94558. Tel: 707-224-4403; Fax: 707-224-2889. Danda Winford, Regl. Dir., Napa; Karen Valentine, Prog. Mgr.
PYRAMID, 2936 J St., Eureka, 95501. Tel: 707-444-9611; Fax: 707-444-9613. Christopher Evans, Coord.
Representative Payee, 516 Morgan St., 95401. Tel: 707-525-1231; Fax: 707-578-6046. Mailing Address: P.O. Box 4900, 95402. Gary Pierce, Prog. Dir.
Housing Counseling, 516 Morgan St., 95401. Tel: 707-542-1554; Fax: 707-578-6046. Mailing Address: P.O. Box 4900, 95402. Gary Pierce, Prog. Dir.
Bereavement Counseling, 2736 J St., Eureka, 95501. Tel: 707-444-9611; Fax: 707-444-9613. Charles Herbelin, Regl. Dir., Humboldt; Sally Orchard, Coord.
DeMeo House, 310 Ridgeway Ave., 95401. Tel: 707-525-1554; Fax: 707-578-6046. Mailing Address: P.O. Box 4900, 95402. Gary Pierce, Prog. Dir.
HomeBase, 3295 Claremont Way, Ste. 1, Napa, 94558. Tel: 707-224-4403; Fax: 707-224-2889. Danda Winford, Regl. Dir., Napa.

[F] VOLUNTEER SERVICES

EUREKA. *Society of St. Vincent de Paul, District Council of the Redwood Region*, 528 Second St., P.O. Box 1386, 95502. Tel: 707-443-8676; Fax: 707-443-6321.
E-mail: dj-heinen@yahoo.com
C. M. Weisel, Pres.; Dan Heinen, Ex. Dir.

NAPA. *Society of St. Vincent de Paul, District Council of Napa County*, 1250 Sweetbriar Dr., 94558. Tel: 707-253-0445. Hillman Brooks, Pres.

ROHNERT PARK. *Society of St. Vincent de Paul, District Council of Sonoma County*, P.O. Box 1095, 94957. Tel: 800-584-1579; Fax: 707-586-8128.
E-mail: SVPAUL@PACBEL.NET
Mr. Bob Solak, Pres.; Deacon Paul Bromham, Exec. Dir.; Rev. Msgr. Thomas J. Keys, Spiritual Dir.

[G] GENERAL HOSPITALS

SANTA ROSA. *Santa Rosa Memorial Hospital*, 1165 Montgomery Dr., 95405. Tel: 707-546-3210
For a complete listing, refer to the Hospitals section.

EUREKA. *St. Joseph Hospital of Eureka*, 2700 Dolbeer St., 95501. Tel: 707-445-8121; Fax: 707-269-3897.
Web site: www.sjhshumboldtcounty.org
For a complete listing, refer to the Hospitals section.

FORTUNA. *Redwood Memorial Hospital*, 3300 Renner Dr., 95540. Tel: 707-725-3361; Fax: 707-725-7212
For a complete listing, refer to the Hospitals section.

NAPA. *Queen of the Valley Hospital of Napa*, 1000 Trancas St., 94558. Tel: 707-252-4411; Fax: 707-257-4173.
E-mail: PHaley@qvh.stjoe.org
Web site: www.thequeen.org
For a complete listing, refer to the Hospitals section.

PETALUMA. *Petaluma Valley Hospital*, 400 N. McDowell Blvd., 94954. Tel: 707-778-1111
For a complete listing, refer to the Hospitals section.

[H] RESIDENTIAL TREATMENT CENTERS

ARCATA.
Butler Valley, Inc.
Butler Valley #1: Administrative Office, 380 12th St., 95521. Tel: 707-822-0301; Fax: 707-822-3589. Staff 15; Residents 6.
Butler Valley #2: 3971 F St., Eureka, 95501. Tel: 707-442-7313. Robert Clayton, Exec. Dir. Residents 6; Staff 15.

SONOMA. *Hanna Boys Center*, P.O. Box 100, 95476. Tel: 707-996-6767; Fax: 707-996-4742.
E-mail: www.hannacenter.org
Legal Title: *Hanna Boys Center*. For underprivileged, emotionally disturbed and pre-delinquent boys, ages 9 to 18 years. Revs. John S. Crews, Ed.D., Exec. Dir.; Gregory Klaas; Chinh Nguyen. Priests 3; Sisters 1; Staff 136; Students 107.

[I] HOMES FOR SENIOR CITIZENS

SANTA ROSA. *Vigil Light Apartments (The Vigil Light, Inc.)*, 1945 Long Dr., 95405. Tel: 707-544-2810; Fax: 707-544-1219.
E-mail: VIGILLIGHT@MINSPRING.COM
For a complete listing, refer to the Special Care Facilities section.

[J] CAMPS AND COMMUNITY CENTERS

DUNCAN MILLS. *St. Joseph Camp*. Brothers of the Christian Schools. Mailing Address: P.O. Box 198, 95430-0198. Tel: 707-865-2135; Fax: 707-865-1025. Bro. Raphael-Philip, F.S.C., Dir. Tel: 707-865-9804.

LEGGETT. *Camp St. Michael*. (Boys - Girls). Tel: 707-984-6877; 546-5289.
E-mail: campwizard@aol.com
Web site: www.camp-st-michael.org
Mailing Address: P.O. Box 9557, Santa Rosa, 95405. Mrs. Agnes J. Bailey, Dir.

MIDDLETOWN. *Camp Salesian*, 95461. Office, Salesian Provincial Residence, 1100 Franklin St., P.O. Box 640009, San Francisco, 94164-0009. Tel: 415-441-7144, Ext. 13; Fax: 415-441-7155.
Conducted by the Salesians of St. John Bosco.

[K] NEWMAN CENTERS

ARCATA. *Newman Community, Humboldt State University*, 700 Union St., 95521. Tel: 707-822-6057; Fax: 707-822-6057.
E-mail: Newman@ave.humboldT.edu
Web site: www.humboldT.edu/newman
Rev. Louis Coddaire, O.S.B.Cam.; Deacon Kenneth M. Bond.

PENNGROVE. *Newman Hall, Sonoma State University, Intercollegiate Catholic Ministries*, 1798 E. Cotati Ave., 94951. Tel: 707-794-7957. Rev. Eric Freed; Deacon Bradley Andrews.

[L] HOUSES OF PRAYER AND RETREAT HOUSES

SANTA ROSA. *Angela Center*, 535 Angela Dr., 95403. Tel: 707-528-8578; Fax: 707-528-0144.
E-mail: ANGELACENTER@juno.com
Web site: www.ANGELACENTER.com
Sr. Christine Van Swearingen, O.S.U., Dir.
Cardinal Newman Retreat Center, 24 A Ursuline Rd., 95403. Tel: 707-568-6822; Fax: 707-566-3360. Richard Boyer, Mgr.

NAPA. *Christian Brothers Retreat and Conference Center*. Mailing Address: 4401 Redwood Rd., P.O. Box 3720, 94558. Tel: 707-252-3810; 3811; Fax: 707-252-3818.
E-mail: lbausch@dlsi.org
Web site: www.christianbrosretreat.com
Ronald R. Tapper, Dir.

OAKVILLE. *Carmelite House of Prayer*, P.O. Box 347, 94562. Tel: 707-944-2454; Fax: 707-944-8533.
E-mail: CARMELOAKVILLE@aol.com
Rev. John Reginald McSweeney, O.C.D., Dir.

[M] MONASTERIES AND RESIDENCES FOR PRIESTS AND BROTHERS

MONTE RIO. *St. Benilde Community*, 22410 Moscow Rd., 95462-0367. Tel: 707-865-3061; Fax: 707-865-3064. Mailing Address: P.O. Box 367, 95462-0367. Brothers of the Christian Schools. Bro. Raphael-Philip, F.S.C., Dir. Brothers 2.

NAPA. *De La Salle Institute/Provincial Office*, 4401 Redwood Rd., 94558-0372. Tel: 707-252-0222; Fax: 707-252-0407.
E-mail: bsokol@dlsi.org
Web site: www.delasalle.org
Mailing Address: P.O. Box 3720, 94558. Brothers of the Christian Schools. Bro. David Brennan, F.S.C., Pres.
Lasallian Education Corporation.
District of San Francisco Christian Brothers Charitable Trust.
De La Salle Institute Foundation.
Holy Family Community, 4405 Redwood Rd., 94558-9708. Tel: 707-252-3768; Fax: 707-252-3842.
E-mail: astewart@dlsi.org
Brothers of the Christian Schools. Bro. Arnold Stewart, F.S.C., Dir. Brothers 16.
Justin Community, 4026 Maher St., 94558-2297. Tel: 707-256-4450; Fax: 707-258-9341. Brothers of the Christian Schools. Bro. James Riordan, F.S.C., Dir. Brothers 11.
Provincialate Community, 4403 Redwood Rd., 94558. Tel: 707-252-0802; Fax: 707-252-7046. Brothers of the Christian Schools. Bros. David Brennan, F.S.C., Prov.; Stanislaus Campbell, F.S.C., Asst. Prov.; Raphael Willeke, F.S.C., Dir.; Rev. David L. Deibel, Chap. Brothers 7.

OAKVILLE. *Carmelite House of Prayer*. Mailing Address: P.O. Box 347, 94562. Tel: 707-944-2454; 944-2460; Fax: 707-944-8533.
E-mail: CARMELOAKVILLE@aol.com
Discalced Carmelite Friars. Revs. John R. McSweeney, O.C.D., Supr.; Mark Kristy, O.C.D.; Michael Buckley, O.C.D.; John Melka, O.C.D.; Bro. Roger Larre, O.C.D. Priests 4; Brothers 1.

[N] CONVENTS AND RESIDENCES FOR SISTERS

SANTA ROSA. *Memorial Hospital Convent*, 271 Doyle Park Dr., 95405. Tel: 707-525-5235; Fax: 707-522-1558.
E-mail: srmconvent@srm.stejoe.org
Sister St. Joseph of Orange. Sisters 5.
Provincialate of Ursuline Nuns, 639 Angela Dr., 95403. Tel: 707-545-6811; Fax: 707-579-8571.
E-mail: fxporter@juno.com
Ursulines of the Roman Union - Western Province. Sr. Francis Xavier Porter, O.S.U., Prov.

CRESCENT CITY. *Holy Family Convent*, 440 Third St., 95531. Tel: 707-464-3450. Sisters St. Francis of Holy Family.

FORTUNA. *Redwood Memorial Hospital Convent*, 3300 Renner Dr., 95540. Tel: 707-725-3361; Fax: 707-725-7212.
E-mail: glaroche@sje.stjoe.org
Web site: www.sjhshumboldtcounty.org
Sisters St. Joseph of Orange. Sisters 2.

NAPA. *Queen of the Valley Convent*, 1000 Trancas St., 94558. Tel: 707-255-6169; Fax: 707-257-4192.
E-mail: sisters@qvh.stjoe.org
Sisters St. Joseph of Orange. Sisters 5.
St. Apollinaris Convent, 3700 Lassen St., P.O. Box 3012, 94558. Tel: 707-255-2185; Fax: 707-251-0621. Congregation of the Sisters of Mercy - The United States Province. Sisters 3.
Siena Convent, 4038 Maher St., 94558. Tel: 707-255-6110. Dominican Sisters of San Rafael; Franciscan Sisters. Sisters 9.

ROHNERT PARK. *Hermitage of Christ the King*, 1326 E. Cotati Ave., #127, 94928-4583. Tel: 707-795-8555. Sisters of Christ the King. Sr. Michael Bird, S.C.K., Supr. Sisters 2; Assoc. Sisters 5.

WHITETHORN. *Our Lady of the Redwoods Abbey*, 18104 Briceland-Thorn Rd., 95589. Tel: 707-986-7419; Fax: 707-986-1176. Cistercian Nuns of the Strict Observance. Sr. Kathy De Vico, O.C.S.O., Abbess; Rev. Maurice Flood, O.C.S.O., Chap. Priests 1; Sisters 9.

WINDSOR. *Ursuline Residence*, 9248 Lakewood Dr., 95492. Tel: 707-838-4973.
E-mail: jhopman@juno.com
Ursuline Nuns. Sisters 2.

[O] MISCELLANEOUS

SANTA ROSA. *Apostolic Endowment Trust*, P.O. Box 1297, 95402. Tel: 707-545-7610. Rev. Msgr. John J. Brenkle, Dir.
Catholic Community Foundation, 320 Tenth St., P.O. Box 1297, 95402. Tel: 707-545-2311; 566-3357; Fax: 707-566-3310. James Dillon, Acting Exec. Dir.
Hand of Help Christian Service Program, 320 Tenth St., 95401. Tel: 415-606-6260. Mailing Address: P.O. Box 14307, San Francisco, 94114-0307. Bro. Fred Buerman, S.M., Exec. Dir.
Loyola Counseling Institute, 24 A Ursuline Rd., 95403. Tel: 707-526-1167. Robert Dalzell, Dir.

SEBASTOPOL. *National Catholic AIDS Network*, 12500 Dupont Rd., 95472. Tel: 707-874-3031; Fax: 707-874-1433.
E-mail: ncan@SONIC.NET
Web site: www.ncan.org
Rev. Rodney J. DeMartini, Exec. Dir.

RELIGIOUS INSTITUTES OF MEN REPRESENTED IN THE DIOCESE

For further details refer to the corresponding bracketed number in the Religious Institutes of Men or Women section.

[0140]—*Augustinians.*—O.S.A.
[0330]—*Brothers of the Christian Schools.* (San Francisco Prov.).—F.S.C.
[]—*Camaldolese Hermits.*—O.S.B.Cam.
[1130]—*Congregation of the Priests of the Sacred Heart.*—S.C.J.
[0260]—*Discalced Carmelite Friars.* (Anglo-Irish Prov.).—O.C.D.
[0520]—*Franciscan Friars.*—O.F.M.
[0690]—*Jesuit Fathers.*—S.J.
[0910]—*Oblates of Mary Immaculate.*—O.M.I.
[0150]—*Order of Augustinian Recollects.*—O.A.R.
[0430]—*Order of Preachers.*—O.P.
[1070]—*Redemptorist Fathers.*—C.SS.R.

RELIGIOUS INSTITUTES OF WOMEN REPRESENTED IN THE DIOCESE

[0670]—*Cistercian Nuns of the Strict Observance.*—O.C.S.O.
[1070-03]—*Dominican Sisters.*—O.P.
[1070-04]—*Dominican Sisters.*—O.P.
[1070-13]—*Dominican Sisters.*—O.P.
[2575]—*Institute of the Sisters of Mercy of the Americas.*—R.S.M.
[1680]—*School Sisters of St. Francis.* (Holy Name Prov.).—O.S.F.
[0430]—*Sisters of Charity of the Blessed Virgin Mary.* (Dubuque, IA).—B.V.M.
[]—*Sisters of Christ the King.*—S.C.K.
[2516]—*Sisters of Mercy.*—S.M.
[0230]—*Sisters of St. Benedict.*—O.S.B.
[3740]—*Sisters of St. Casimir.*—S.S.C.
[1570]—*Sisters of St. Francis of the Holy Family.* (Dubuque, IA).—O.S.F.
[3830-03]—*Sisters of St. Joseph.*—C.S.J.
[3840]—*Sisters of St. Joseph of Carondelet.*—C.S.J.
[1990]—*Sisters of the Holy Names of Jesus and Mary.*—S.N.J.M.
[3320]—*Sisters of the Presentation of the B.V.M.*—P.B.V.M.
[1705]—*Sisters of the Third Order of St. Francis of Assisi.*—O.S.F.
[4110]—*Ursuline Nuns.* (Western Prov.).—O.S.U.

DIOCESAN CEMETERIES

SANTA ROSA. *Calvary Catholic.*
EUREKA. *St. Bernard.*
PETALUMA. *Calvary Catholic.*
ST. HELENA. *Holy Cross.*
SONOMA. *St. Francis Solano.*

NECROLOGY

† Doyle, Denis, Ferndale, CA Assumption of Blessed Virgin Mary. —Died Sept. 18, 2000.

Diocese of Savannah

(Dioecesis Savannensis)

Most Reverend

J. KEVIN BOLAND, D.D.

Bishop of Savannah; ordained June 14, 1959; appointed Bishop of Savannah February 7, 1995; ordained and installed April 18, 1995.

Most Reverend

RAYMOND W. LESSARD, D.D.

Retired Bishop of Savannah; ordained December 16, 1956; appointed March 5, 1973; consecrated and installed April 27, 1973. *Catholic Pastoral Center: 601 E. Liberty St., Savannah, GA, 31401-5196.* Tel.: 912-238-2320.

ESTABLISHED AS DIOCESE OF SAVANNAH JULY 19, 1850. NAME CHANGED TO DIOCESE OF SAVANNAH-ATLANTA JAN. 5, 1937; REDESIGNATED NOV. 8, 1956.

Square Miles 37,038.

Comprises 90 Counties in the southern part of the State of Georgia.

PATRONS OF THE DIOCESE: I. ST. JOHN THE BAPTIST; II. OUR LADY OF PERPETUAL HELP. This diocese was solemnly consecrated to the Sacred Heart of Jesus, May 7, 1872, and on Dec. 8, 1943, it was solemnly consecrated to the Immaculate Heart of Mary.

For legal titles of parishes and diocesan institutions, consult the Chancery.

Chancery: Catholic Pastoral Center, 601 E. Liberty St., Savannah, GA, 31401-5196. Tel.: 912-238-2320; Fax: 912-238-2335.

Web site address: www.dioceseofsavannah.org

E-mail address: Diosav@msn.com

STATISTICAL OVERVIEW

Personnel	
Bishop	1
Retired Bishops	1
Priests: Diocesan Active in Diocese	43
Priests: Active Outside Diocese	9
Priests: Retired, Sick or Absent	11
Number of Diocesan Priests	63
Religious Priests in Diocese	29
Extern Priests in Diocese	10
Ordinations:	
Diocesan Priests	1
Transitional Deacons	3
Permanent Deacons in Diocese	31
Total Brothers	15
Total Sisters	129
Parishes	
Parishes	51
With Resident Pastor:	
Resident Diocesan Priests	36
Resident Religious Priests	15
Missions	27
New Parishes Created	1
Closed Parishes	2
Professional Ministry Personnel:	
Brothers	15
Sisters	129
Lay Ministers	22
Welfare	
Catholic Hospitals	3
Total Assisted	300,000
Residential Care of Children	1
Total Assisted	51
Specialized Homes	1
Total Assisted	20
Special Centers for Social Services	20
Total Assisted	117,875
Educational	
Diocesan Students in Other Seminaries	21
Total Seminarians	21
High Schools, Diocesan and Parish	2
Total Students	495
High Schools, Private	3
Total Students	1,385
Elementary Schools, Diocesan and Parish	16
Total Students	4,608
Catechesis/Religious Education:	
High School Students	1,142
Elementary Students	5,223
Total Students Under Catholic Instruction	12,874
Teachers in the Diocese:	
Brothers	3
Sisters	15
Lay Teachers	254
Vital Statistics	
Receptions into the Church:	
Infant Baptism Totals	1,742
Adult Baptism Totals	251
Received into Full Communion	703
First Communions	1,456
Confirmations	1,251
Marriages:	
Catholic	237
Interfaith	266
Total Marriages	503
Deaths	656
Total Catholic Population	76,048
Total Population	3,385,646

Former Bishops—Rt. Rev. FRANCIS X. GARTLAND, D.D., first bishop; cons. Nov. 10, 1850; died Sept. 20, 1854.—Rt. Rev. JOHN BARRY, D.D., second bishop; cons. Aug. 2, 1857; died Nov. 21, 1859.—Rt. Rev. AUGUSTIN VEROT, S.S., D.D., cons. April 25, 1858; Vic. Ap. of Florida; transferred to Savannah, July 14, 1861; returned to Florida as first Bishop of St. Augustine, 1870; died June 10, 1876.—His Eminence IGNATIUS CARDINAL PERSICO, D.D., transferred to this See March 11, 1870; resigned 1872; created Cardinal Jan. 16, 1893; died Dec. 7, 1895.—Rt. Rev. W. H. GROSS, C.SS.R., D.D., cons. April 27, 1873; promoted to Oregon 1885; died Nov. 14, 1898.—Rt. Rev. THOMAS A. BECKER, D.D., cons. Bishop of Wilmington, Aug. 16, 1868; transferred to Savannah, March 26, 1886; died July 29, 1899.—Rt. Rev. BENJAMIN J. KEILEY, D.D., cons. June 3, 1900; resigned Feb. 13, 1922; appt. Titular Bishop of Scillium, March 24, 1922; died June 17, 1925.—Most Rev. MICHAEL J. KEYES, S.M., D.D., appt. July 8, 1922; cons. Oct. 18, 1922; resigned Sept. 23, 1935; appt. Titular Bishop of Areopolis and Assistant at the Pontifical Throne; died July 31, 1959.—Most. Rev. GERALD P. O'HARA, D.D., J.U.D., appt. Titular Bishop of Heliopolis and Auxiliary Bishop of Philadelphia, April 26, 1929; cons. May 20, 1929; transferred to See of Savannah, Nov. 16, 1935 received personal title of Archbishop July 12, 1950; appt. Apostolic Nuncio to Ireland, 1951; appt. Apostolic Delegate to Great Britain, 1954; resigned Nov. 11, 1959; died July 16, 1963.—Most Rev. THOMAS J. MCDONOUGH, D.D., J.C.D., appt. Titular Bishop of Thaenae and Auxiliary Bishop of St. Augustine, March 10, 1947; cons. April 30, 1947; transferred to Savannah, Jan. 2, 1957; succeeded to See, March 2, 1960; promoted to Archbishop of Louisville, March 1, 1967; resigned Sept. 29, 1981; died Aug. 4, 1998.—Most Rev. GERARD L. FREY, D.D., appt. May 31, 1967; cons. Aug. 8, 1967; transferred to Bishop of Lafayette, Nov. 7, 1972; retired May 13, 1989.—Most Rev. RAYMOND W. LESSARD, D.D., appt. March 5, 1973; cons. April 27, 1973; resigned Feb. 7, 1995.

Vicar General—Rev. FRANCIS J. NELSON, J.C.L., *Catholic Pastoral Center, 601 E. Liberty St., Savannah, 31401-5196.* Tel: 912-238-2338.

Chancery—Catholic Pastoral Center, 601 E. Liberty St., Savannah, 31401-5196. Tel: 912-238-2320; Fax: 912-238-2335.

Chancellor and Coordinator of the Curia—Sr. MARY FAITH MCKEAN, R.S.M.

Chief Finance Officer—JOHN F. BENWARE, *Catholic Pastoral Center, 601 E. Liberty St., Savannah, 31401-5196.* Tel: 912-238-2324.

Diocesan Tribunal—Catholic Pastoral Center, 601 E. Liberty St., Savannah, 31401-5196. Tel: 912-238-2320.

Officialis—Rev. JEREMIAH J. MCCARTHY, J.C.L.

Director of the Tribunal—CATHERINE A. GILLIGAN, J.C.L.

Tribunal Judges—Revs. FRANCIS J. NELSON, J.C.L.; HERBERT J. WELLMEIER; CATHERINE A. GILLIGAN, J.C.L.

Defender of the Bond—Rev. J. GERARD SCHRECK, J.C.D.

Notaries—CAROLE BARRAS; KATHLEEN TRAHAN.

Promoter of Justice—Rev. HERBERT J. WELLMEIER.

Censor Librorum—Rev. DOUGLAS K. CLARK, S.T.L.

Archivist—Ms. GILLIAN BROWN, *Catholic Pastoral Center, 601 E. Liberty St., Savannah, 31401-5196.* Tel: 912-238-2320.

Legal Counsel—JOHN M. BRENNAN; JOSEPH P. BRENNAN, *Catholic Pastoral Center, 601 E. Liberty St., Savannah, 31401-5196.* Tel: 912-238-2320.

Finance Board—Mr. S. SCOTT VOYNICH, Chm.; Most Rev. J. KEVIN BOLAND; Revs. FRANCIS J. NELSON, V.G.; P. JAMES COSTIGAN; Mr. E. J. MADDOCKS; Mr. EMMETT T. BOYD; Mr. FRED MILLER; Mr. J. TOM COLEMAN, JR.; Mr. EDWARD C. MIZELLE; Mr. KENNETH R. THOMPSON, JR.; Mrs. JULIE FORTUNATO; Mr. JAMES M. PIETTE; Mr. JOHN F. BENWARE; Mr. JOHN M. BRENNAN; Mr. JOSEPH P. BRENNAN; Sr. MARY FAITH MCKEAN.

Investment Committee—Most Rev. J. KEVIN BOLAND; Rev. P. JAMES COSTIGAN; Mr. EMMETT T. BOYD; Mr. FRED MILLER; Mr. KEN THOMPSON; Mr. JOHN F. BENWARE.

Clergy Personnel—Rev. JOHN A. KENNEALLY, V.F., Advisor.

Deans—

Savannah Deanery: Rev. JOHN A. KENNEALLY, V.F., *8412 Whitfield Ave., Savannah, 31406-6198.* Tel: 912-355-1523.

Augusta Deanery: Rev. JOHN J. LYONS, V.F., *2607 Lumpkin Rd., Augusta, 30906-3222.* Tel: 706-798-1920.

Albany Deanery: Rev. FINBARR P. STANTON, V.F., *421 Edgewood Ln., Albany, 31707-3910.* Tel: 229-439-2302.

Columbus Deanery: Rev. LAWRENCE A. LUCREE, V.F., *1953 Torch Hill Rd., Columbus, 31903-2745.* Tel: 706-689-5720.

Macon Deanery: Rev. FRED J. NIJEM, V.F., *P.O. Box 5052, Warner Robins, 31099-5052.* Tel: 478-923-0124.

Statesboro Deanery: Rev. MICHAEL SMITH, V.F., *P.O. Box 4304, Eastman, 31023-4241.* Tel: 478-374-4031.

Valdosta-Brunswick Deanery: Rev. JOHN O'BRIEN, V.F., *800 Gornto Rd., Valdosta, 31602-1699.* Tel: 229-244-2430.

College of Consultors—Revs. JOHN J. FITZPATRICK; BRETT A. BRANNEN; DOUGLAS K. CLARK; JEREMIAH MCCARTHY; FRANCIS J. NELSON, V.G.; DANIEL P. O'CONNELL; J. GERARD SCHRECK.

Council of Priests—Revs. BRETT A. BRANNEN, Pres. PAUL BRICK, S.D.S.; DOUGLAS K. CLARK; LORENZO GARCIA; MICHAEL J. KAVANAUGH; BRIAN LABURT; JEREMIAH MCCARTHY; FRANCIS J. NELSON, V.G.; J. GERARD SCHRECK; JOSEPH A. SMITH; JAMES KIRCHNER; DANIEL P. O'CONNELL; TIMOTHY C. DONAHUE; THOMAS J. PEYTON.

Temporal Affairs Vicar—Rev. P. JAMES COSTIGAN, *1420 Monte Sano Ave., Augusta, 30904-5394.* Tel: 706-733-6627.

Diocesan Offices and Directors

Newspaper—"The Southern Cross"; Rev. DOUGLAS K. CLARK, Editor, Business Office: *Catholic Pastoral Center, 601 E. Liberty St., Savannah, 31401-5196.* Tel: 912-238-2320; Fax: 912-238-2339., Printing Office: *601 E. 6th St., Waynesboro, 30830.* Tel: 706-554-7888.

Director of Communications—Mrs. BARBARA KING, *Catholic Pastoral Center, 601 E. Liberty St., Savannah, 31401-5196.* Tel: 912-238-2320; Fax: 912-238-2335.

Superintendent of Schools—Sr. ROSE MARY COLLINS, S.S.J., *Catholic Pastoral Center, 601 E. Liberty St., Savannah, 31401-5196.* Tel: 912-238-2320; Fax: 912-238-2339.

Director of African American Ministry—Vacant, *Catholic Pastoral Center, 601 E. Liberty St., Savannah, 31401-5196.* Tel: 912-238-2320; Fax: 912-238-2339.

Director of Campus Ministry—Ms. JANE HALL, *221 John Paul Ave., Statesboro, 30458-5016.* Tel: 912-681-6726.

Director of Catholic Social Services—Sr. JACQUELINE GRIFFITH, S.S.J., *601 E. Liberty St., Savannah, 31401-5196.* Tel: 912-238-2326; Fax: 912-238-2339.

Director of Family Life—Sr. PATRICIA BROWN, S.S.M.N., *Catholic Pastoral Center, 601 E. Liberty St., Savannah, 31401-5196.* Tel: 912-238-2320.

Director of Hispanic/Migrant Ministry—Rev. MICHAEL H. SMITH, *P.O. Box 4304, Eastman, 31023-4241.* Tel: 478-374-4031.

Director of Permanent Diaconate—Deacon GEORGE H. FOSTER, *4568 Betty's Branch Way, Evans, 30809.* Tel: 404-860-2379.

Director of Religious Education—Ms. ANN PINCKNEY, *Catholic Pastoral Center, 601 E. Liberty St., Savannah, 31401-5196.* Tel: 912-238-2320; Fax: 912-238-2339.

Director of Stewardship and Development—Ms. PATRICIA SIGNS, *Catholic Pastoral Center, 601 E. Liberty St., Savannah, 31401-5196.* Tel: 912-238-2320.

Director of Vocations—Rev. BRETT A. BRANNEN, *131 Ward St., Macon, 31204-3193.* Tel: 912-743-1454; Fax: 912-741-8899.

Director of Vocations—Irish Seminarians: Rev. JOHN O'BRIEN, V.F., *800 Gornto Rd., Valdosta, 31602-1699.* Tel: 912-244-2430; Fax: 912-244-5352.

Director of Youth Ministry—Vacant, *Catholic Pastoral Center, 601 E. Liberty St., Savannah, 31401-5196.* Tel: 912-238-2320.

Apostleship of the Sea—Rev. K. D. XAVIER, *112 Fell St., Savannah, 31401-1828.* Tel: 912-236-7716.

Campaign for Human Development—Sr. JACQUELINE GRIFFITH, S.S.J., *Catholic Pastoral Center, 601 E. Liberty St., Savannah, 31401-5196.* Tel: 912-238-2326; Fax: 912-238-2339.

Catholic Cemetery Advisory Board—Board Members: Rev. JAMES M. MAYO; Mrs. GERALDINE WILLIAMS; Mr. JOHN F. BENWARE; Mr. M. SCOTT CLARK, *601 E. Liberty St., Savannah, 31401-5196.* Tel: 912-238-2320.

Catholic Relief Services—Sr. MARY FAITH MCKEAN, Dir., *Catholic Pastoral Center, 601 E. Liberty St., Savannah, 31401-5196.* Tel: 912-238-2328.

Council of Catholic Women—Rev. ALLAN J. MCDONALD, Chap., *P.O. Box 2446, Augusta, 30903-2446.* Tel: 706-722-4944. Mrs. HELEN JENKINS, Pres., *1575 15th St., Augusta, 30901-3481.*

Diocesan Worship Commission—Rev. JOHN J. FITZPATRICK, Chm., *P.O. Box 38, Tybee Island, 31328.* Tel: 912-786-4505; Fax: 912-786-6653.

Diocesan Scout Chairman—Vacant, *Catholic Pastoral Center, 601 E. Liberty St., Savannah, 31401-5196.* Tel: 912-238-2320.

Ecumenism and Interreligious Affairs—Rev. MICHAEL J. KAVANAUGH, Dir., *P.O. Box 4056, Port Wentworth, 31407-4056.* Tel: 912-964-0219; Fax: 912-966-5468.

Georgia Catholic Conference—Mr. CHEATHAM HODGES, Exec. Sec., *3200 Deans Bridge Rd., Augusta, 30906.* Tel: 706-798-1719.

Holy Childhood Association—Sr. ROSE MARY COLLINS, S.S.J., Dir., *Catholic Pastoral Center, 601 E. Liberty St., Savannah, 31401-5196.* Tel: 912-238-2346.

Home Missions—Rev. LAWRENCE A. LUCREE, Dir., *1953 Torch Hill Rd., Columbus, 31903-2745.* Tel: 706-689-5720.

Natural Family Planning—Mrs. SALLY KENNEDY, Dir.; Mrs. KATE PAYNE, Asst. JAMES ROUTON, M.D., Medical Consultant, *601 E. Liberty St., Savannah, 31401-5196.* Tel: 912-238-2320.

Propagation of the Faith—Ms. ANN PINCKNEY, *Catholic Pastoral Center, 601 E. Liberty St., Savannah, 31401-5196.* Tel: 912-238-2320.

CLERGY, PARISHES, MISSIONS AND PAROCHIAL SCHOOLS

CITY OF SAVANNAH
(Chatham County)

1—CATHEDRAL OF ST. JOHN THE BAPTIST (1873), Revs. William O. O'Neill; Douglas K. Clark; Bro. Robert Sokolowski, S.M., Pastoral Assoc.; Deacon Dewain Smith.
Res., 222 E. Harris St., 31401-4699. Tel: 912-233-4709; Fax: 912-233-8229.

2—ST. ANTHONY OF PADUA (1909). Closed.

3—ST. BENEDICT THE MOOR (1874) (African American), Rev. Desmond Ohankwere, M.S.P.
Res., 556 E. Gordon St., 31401-5000. Tel: 912-232-7147; Fax: 912-238-0184.
School—Notre Dame Academy, Tel: 912-232-5473; Fax: 912-232-3352. Ms. Patricia Ratcliffe, Prin.
Lay Teachers 10; Sisters 2; Students 159.

4—MOST BLESSED SACRAMENT (1920), Revs. Jeremiah J. McCarthy; Robert T. Hand; Deacon Michael F. Daly; Sr. Anna Gaffney, S.S.M.N., Pastoral Assoc.
Res., 1003 E. Victory Dr., 31405-2499. Tel: 912-356-6980; Fax: 912-692-0010.
School—Tel: 912-356-6987; Fax: 912-356-6988. Ms. Marci Arling, Prin.
Lay Teachers 28; Students 427.

5—MOST PURE HEART OF MARY (1907). Closed.

6—RESURRECTION OF OUR LORD, Rev. Robert E. Chaney. In res., Rev. Xavier Kumbalaparampil.
112 Fell St., GA 31415-1828. Tel: 912-232-5258.

7—SACRED HEART OF JESUS (1880), Rev. Francis C. Higgins. Pastoral Assocs.: Sr. Lida Bulf, M.F.I.C.; Sr. Isabella Lohan, M.F.I.C.
Res., 1707 Bull St., 31415-7422. Tel: 912-232-0792; Fax: 912-236-0065.

8—ST. FRANCES XAVIER CABRINI (1968), Rev. Francis J. Nelson; Deacons Louis J. Andruzzi; John F. Benware. In res., Rev. Joseph F. Ware.
Res., 11500 Middleground Rd., 31419-1227. Tel: 912-925-4725; Fax: 912-925-1379.
School—Tel: 912-925-1379. Ms. Nina Delk, Prin.
Lay Teachers 5; Students 30.

9—ST. JAMES (1956), Revs. John A. Kenneally, V.F.; Joseph A. Smith; Sr. Ann Lyons, F.S.S.J., Pastoral Assoc.
Res., 8412 Whitfield Ave., 31406-6198. Tel: 912-355-1523; Fax: 912-353-7226.
School—Tel: 912-355-3132; Fax: 912-355-1996. Sr. Joan Felicia, I.H.M., Prin.
Sisters 4; Lay Teachers 25; Students 576.
Mission—Isle of Hope, Our Lady of Good Hope.

10—ST. PETER THE APOSTLE CHURCH (1993), Revs. Patrick O'Brien; Gabriel Cummings.
Mailing Address: 7020 Concord Rd., P.O. Box 30859, 31410.
Res., 302 Bryson Dr., 31410. Tel: 912-897-5156; Fax: 912-897-7924.
School—Tel: 912-897-5224; Fax: 912-897-0801. Dr. James Gibson, Prin.
Lay Teachers 22; Sisters 1; Students 368.

11—STS. PETER AND PAUL (1980) (Vietnamese), Rev. Kim Son Nguyen.
Res., 3115 Victory Dr., 31404-4598. Tel: 912-354-4014.

OUTSIDE THE CITY OF SAVANNAH

Albany, Dougherty Co., St. Teresa (1875), Revs. Finbarr P. Stanton, V.F.; James P. Dalton (Ireland).
Res., 421 Edgewood Ln., 31707. Tel: 229-432-0891; 439-2302 (Office); Fax: 229-439-0516.
School—417 Edgewood Ln., 31707-3991. Tel: 912-436-0134; Fax: 912-436-0135. Mrs. Grace Ledwitch, Prin.
Lay Teachers 28; Students 359.

Americus, Sumter Co., St. Mary (1891), Revs. George A. Gonzalez; Michael O'Keeffe.
Res., 332 S. Lee St., 31709-3916. Tel: 229-924-3495; Fax: 229-924-7124.
Mission—Montezuma, Macon Co., St. Michael, N. Dooly St., Montezuma, 31063-1507. Tel: 478-472-5124; Fax: 478-924-7124.

Augusta, Richmond Co.,

1—CHURCH OF THE MOST HOLY TRINITY, Revs. Allan J. McDonald; Andrew T. Doris; Daniel M. Munn; Deacons Donald R. McArdle; Ephraim J. Williams. Pastoral Assocs.: Sr. Bernadette Quinlan, M.F.I.C.; Dr. Christopher Welch; Mr. William H. Harper.
Mailing Address: P.O. Box 2446, 30903-2446. Tel: 706-722-4944; Fax: 706-722-7774.
Res., 303 Broad St., 30901. Tel: 706-724-4367.
School—Immaculate Conception School, Tel: 706-722-9964. Sr. Margaret Mary Mohr, M.F.I.C., Prin.
Sisters 3; Lay Teachers 10; Students 175. Missionary Franciscan Sisters of the Immaculate Conception.
Convent & Chapel—Immaculate Conception, 1018 Laney Walker Blvd., 30901. Tel: 706-722-2380.

2—ST. JOSEPH, (1954), Rev. John Lyons, V.F.; Deacon Gregory L. Bernard.
Res., 2607 Lumpkin Rd., 30906-3222. Tel: 706-798-1920; Fax: 706-798-8594.

3—ST. MARY ON THE HILL, (1917), Revs. P. James Costigan; Robert A. Girardeau; Gaspar Hegedus; Deacons Donald G. Cisick; George Foster.
Res., 1420 Monte Sano Ave., 30904-5394. Tel: 706-733-6627; Fax: 706-733-4887.
School—1220 Monte Sano Ave., 30904-5394. Tel: 706-733-6193; Fax: 706-737-7985. Mr. Charles McCormack, Prin.
Lay Teachers 44; Students 507.
Chapels—St. Joseph Hospital.; Aquinas High School.

4—ST. TERESA OF AVILA, (1968), Rev. Thomas J. Peyton; Deacon William L. Johnson; Mr. Michael Roverse, Pastoral Assoc.
Res., 117 Pleasant Home Rd., 30907-3517. Tel: 706-863-4956; Fax: 706-863-5001.

Bainbridge, Decatur Co., St. Joseph's, Rev. Joel S. Bladt, S.T.
Res., 822 Ramsey St., P.O. Box 192, 31717-0151. Tel: 229-248-0030.
Mission—Donalsonville, Seminole Co., Church of the Incarnation.

Blakely, Early Co., Holy Family (1965), Rev. Walter O'Donnell, S.T. In res., Rev. Luke Mikschl, S.T.
Mailing Address: Box 425, 31723-0425.
Res., 109 Arlington St., P.O. Box 425, 31723-0425. Tel: 229-723-3339; Fax: 229-723-6358.
Mission—Cuthbert, Randolph Co., St. Luke.

Brunswick, Glynn Co., St. Francis Xavier, Revs. Wilfrid Logsdon, O.F.M.Conv.; Cletus Pifher, O.F.M.Conv.; Bro. Michael Wright, O.F.M.Conv.; Deacons Ntungwa Maasha; George F. Ruehling, III.
Res., 729 Union St., 31520-8018. Tel: 912-265-3249; Fax: 912-265-6797.

School—Tel: 912-265-9470; Fax: 912-265-9471. Ms. Jane O'Day, Prin.
Lay Teachers 19; Students 250.
Mission—Darien, McIntosh Co., Nativity of Our Lady.

Claxton, Evans Co., St. Christopher (1958), Revs. Brian LaBurt, Glmy.; Robert Healy, Glmy.; Sr. Janet Fischer, F.S.P.A., Pastoral Assoc.
Res., 400 S. River St., P.O. Box 890, 30417-2150. Tel: 912-739-3913.
Convent—402 S. River St., 30417-2150. Tel: 912-739-2275. Franciscan Sisters of Perpetual Adoration
Missions—Glennville, Tattnall Co., St. Jude, P.O. Box 772, Glennville, 30427-0772. Tel: 912-654-1908; Pembroke, Bryan Co., Holy Cross, P.O. Box 890, 30417-0890.

Columbus, Muscogee Co.,

1—HOLY FAMILY, (1835), Revs. Frank Patterson, V.F.; Arthur Weltzer, Pastor Emeritus.
Res., 320 12th St., 31901-2454. Tel: 706-323-6908; Fax: 706-323-2043.

2—OUR LADY OF LOURDES, (1958), Rev. Lawrence A. Lucree, V.F.; Deacon Francis P. Benyo.
Res., 1953 Torch Hill Rd., 31903-2745. Tel: 706-689-5720; Fax: 706-687-9579.
School—1973 Torch Hill Rd., 31903. Tel: 706-689-5644; Fax: 706-689-5644. Mr. Charles Kraft, Prin.
Lay Teachers 13; Students 156.
Mission—Buena Vista, Marion Co., St. Mary Magdalen.

3—ST. ANNE, (1961), Revs. J. Gerard Schreck; John R. Madden; Timothy C. Donahue; Mrs. Margo Truett, Pastoral Assoc.
Mailing Address: 2000 Kay Circle, 31907-3229.
Res., 3544 Trinity Dr., 31907-3229. Tel: 706-561-8678; Fax: 706-568-0179.
School—3550 Trinity Dr., 31907. Tel: 706-561-8232; Fax: 706-563-0211. Mrs. Patricia Nobes, Prin.
Lay Teachers 25; Students 412.
High School—Pacelli High School.
Mission—Pine Mountain, Harris Co., Christ the King, P.O. Box 32, Hamilton, 31811-0066. Tel: 706-628-5158. Sr. Philomena Fogarty, F.M.M., Pastoral Assoc.
Chapels—St. Francis Hospital.; Pacelli High School.

4—ST. BENEDICT THE MOOR, (1958) (African American), Rev. Paul T. Brick, S.D.S.
Church—2935 Ninth St., P.O. Box 5705, 31906-0714. Tel: 706-323-1749; Fax: 706-324-2641.
Res., 2939 Ninth St., 31906. Tel: 706-323-8300; Fax: 706-324-7099.

Cordele, Crisp Co., St. Theresa (1993), Rev. Raul Perez, Admin.
Res., 807 Third St. S., 31015-1705. Tel: 912-273-3446.

Douglas, Coffee Co., St. Paul's (1938), Rev. Daniel O'Connell. Pastoral Assocs.: Sr. Bertha Capetillo, C.S.S.; Sr. Elisa Bonano, O.S.F.; Sr. Suzanne Susany, O.S.F.
Res., 523 E. Ward St., 31533-3912. Tel: 912-384-3560; Fax: 912-383-0779.
Missions—Fitzgerald, Ben Hill Co., St. William, 807 S. Merrimac, Fitzgerald, 31750-0801. Tel: 229-423-5076; Willacoochee, Atkinson Co., Holy Family, Tel: 912-384-3560.

Dublin, Laurens Co., Immaculate Conception (1911), Revs. Gerald P. Ragan; Charles Hughes, Glmy.
Res., 204 N. Church St., 31021-6152. Tel: 478-272-0266; Fax: 478-275-8806.
Chapel—Dublin, VA Hospital, Tel: 912-272-1210.
Mission—Sandersville, Washington Co., St. William, 301 S. Smith St., Sandersville, 31082.

Hazlehurst, Jeff Davis Co., Good Shepherd (1967), Rev. Herbert Graf, O.F.M.Conv.
Mailing Address: P.O. Box 1468, 31539-1381. Tel: 912-375-5948.
Mission—Baxley, Appling Co., St. Rose of Lima, N. City Circle Rd., Baxley, 31513.

Hinesville, Liberty Co., St. Stephen, First Martyr (1980), Rev. James M. Mayo.
Res., 399 Woodland Ave., 31313-2719. Tel: 912-876-4364; Fax: 912-876-4368.

Jesup, Wayne Co., St. Joseph, Rev. Weston J. Lamb, O.SS.T., Admin.
Res., 1048 E. Cherry St., 31546-3114. Tel: 912-427-9239; Fax: 912-427-9238.

Lakeland, Lanier Co., Queen of Peace (1940), Rev. Christian LeFrois, O.S.B, Admin.; Bro. Walter Gluhm, C.S.C., Pastoral Assoc.
Res., 1332 S. Mill St., P.O. Box 26, 31635-0087. Tel: 229-482-3555.
Missions—Nashville, Berrien Co., St. Mary, 1145 Laurel, Nashville, 31639. Tel: 229-686-2752; Adel, Cook Co., St. Margaret Mary, 1706 S. Hutchinson, Adel, 31620. Tel: 229-896-4555.

Macon, Bibb Co., St. Joseph (1841), Revs. John Cuddy; Timothy P. McKeown.
Res., 830 Poplar St., 31201-2093. Tel: 478-745-1631; Fax: 478-745-2254.
School—Tel: 478-742-0636; Fax: 478-746-7685. Ms. Nancy Gillespie, Prin.
Lay Teachers 22; Students 351.
Holy Spirit (1968), Rev. Sam Zebron, O.F.M. Conv.; Deacon Daniel W. Bish, Jr.
Res., 4074 Chambers Rd., 31206-4702. Tel: 478-788-6386; Fax: 478-788-2837.
Parish Center—4074 Chambers Rd., 31206-4702. Tel: 478-788-6386.
St. Peter Claver, Rev. Brett A. Brannen; Sr. Carmel Tursi, S.B.S., Pastoral Assoc.
Res., 131 Ward St., 31204-3193. Tel: 478-743-1454, Ext. 478; Fax: 478-743-9868.
School—133 Ward St., 31204-3193. Tel: 478-743-3985. Sr. Joanne Goecke, D.C., Prin.
Sisters 2; Lay Teachers 15; Students 145.

McRae, Telfair Co., Holy Redeemer (1968), Rev. Michael H. Smith, V.F.
201 Telfair, 31055-1625. Tel: 478-868-2002; Fax: 478-868-2939.
Res., 105 Plaza Dr. J-59, Eastman, 31023. Tel: 478-374-4031.
Mission—Eastman, Dodge Co., St. Mark, P.O. Box 4304, Eastman, 31023-4241. Tel: 478-374-0238; Fax: 478-374-4454.

Moultrie, Colquitt Co., Immaculate Conception (1978), Revs. Edward R. Frank; Lorenzo Garcia; Deacon Philip J. Walsh.
Res., 202 Hillcrest Ave., S.E., 31768-5932. Tel: 229-985-6550.
Mission—Camilla, Mitchell Co., St. John Vianney, P.O. Box 391, Camilla, 31730-0394. Tel: 229-336-8685.

Perry, Houston Co., St. Patrick (1969), Rev. Charles Roland, Admin.; Deacons Ralph H. McAtee; Ken Hutnick.
Res., 1041 St. Patrick Dr., 31069-0611. Tel: 478-987-4213.
Mission—Fort Valley, Peach Co., St. Juliana.

Port Wentworth, Chatham Co., Our Lady of Lourdes (1940), Rev. Michael J. Kavanaugh; Sr. Georgette Cunniff, M.F.I.C., Pastoral Assoc.
Res., 501 S. Coastal Hwy., (GA Hwy. 25), P.O. Box 4056, 31407-4056. Tel: 912-964-0219; Fax: 912-966-5468.
Mission—Springfield, St. Boniface, P.O. Box 941, Springfield, 31329-5207. Tel: 912-754-7473. Sr. Elizabeth Mannion, M.F.I.C., Pastoral Assoc.

Richmond Hill, Bryan Co., St. Anne (1951), Rev. Herbert J. Wellmeier.
Res., P.O. Box 648, 31324-0601. Tel: 912-756-3338.

St. Marys, Camden Co., Our Lady Star of the Sea (1969), Rev. William J. Leahy; Deacon Edward C. Stives.
Res., P.O. Box 290, 31558-0221. Tel: 912-882-4718.
Mission—Folkston, Charlton Co., St. Francis of Assisi, 1609 N. 2nd St., Folkston, 31537-0151. Tel: 912-496-3219.

St. Simons Island, Glynn Co., St. Williams (1968), Revs. Gerard Herman, O.F.M.Conv.; Germain Belen, O.F.M.Conv.; George Schroeder, O.F.M.Conv.
Res. & Mailing Address: 2300 Frederica, 31522-1965. Tel: 912-638-2647; Fax: 912-638-2743.

Statesboro, Bulloch Co., St. Matthew (1944), Rev. David Stachurski, O.F.M.Conv.
Res., 221 John Paul Ave., 30458-5016. Tel: 912-681-6726; Fax: 912-681-6727.

Swainsboro, Emanuel Co., Holy Trinity (1957), Rev. Victor Subb, Glmy.
Res., 928 W. Main St., 30401-5502. Tel: 478-237-8722.
Mission—Metter, Candler Co., Holy Family, P.O. Box 231, Metter, 30439-0231. Tel: 912-685-5811. Sr. Paul Marie Westlake, R.S.M., Pastoral Assoc.

Sylvania, Screven Co., Our Lady of the Assumption (1957), Rev. Edward V. Gorny, Glmy.; Sr. Mary Ellen Barrette, Glmy, Pastoral Assoc.
Res., 121 Ridgecrest Dr., 30467-1840. Tel: 912-564-2312.
Mission—Millen, Jenkins Co., St. Bernadette, P.O. Box 616, Millen, 30442-0501. Tel: 478-982-1445.
Chapel—Bay Branch, St. Joseph.

Thomasville, Thomas Co., St. Augustine (1936), Rev. Thomas J. Murphy; Deacon Howard G. Halladay.
Res., 211 N. Pinetree Blvd., 31792-3973. Tel: 229-226-3624; Fax: 229-226-8808.
Mission—Cairo, Grady Co., St. Elizabeth Ann Seton, 11th Ave. N.W., Cairo, 31728-4007. Tel: 229-377-6996.

Thunderbolt, Chatham Co., Nativity of Our Lord. Closed. For inquiries for parish records contact the Chancery.

Tifton, Tift Co., Our Divine Saviour (1953), Rev. Juan J. Lopez; Mrs. Margo Martin, Pastoral Assoc.
Res., P.O. Box 212, 31793-0201. Tel: 229-382-4600; Fax: 229-382-7611.
Mission—Alapaha, Berrien Co., St. Ann, Hwy. 82 E., 31622.

Tybee Island, Chatham Co., St. Michael, Rev. John J. Fitzpatrick; Deacons Charles J. Hosti; Fretwell G. Crider.
Res., 802 Lovell Ave., P.O. Box 38, 31328-0001. Tel: 912-786-4505; Fax: 912-786-6653.
School—808 Lovell Ave., P.O. Box 740, 31328-0001. Tel: 912-786-4507; Fax: 912-786-4551. Ms. Glynn M. Poole, Prin.
Lay Teachers 11; Students 105.

Valdosta, Lowndes Co., St. John the Evangelist, Rev. John O'Brien.
Church Office: 800 Gornto Rd., 31602-1699. Tel: 229-244-2430; Fax: 229-244-5352.
Res., 2402 Berkley Dr., 31602-1699. Tel: 229-244-9920.
Newman Center—412 Baytree Rd., 31602. Tel: 229-247-6707. Dr. Carl Hand, Campus Minister.
School—Sisters of St. Joseph, Tel: 229-244-2556; 244-0055 (Convent); Fax: 229-244-0865. Sr. Pauline Oetgen, C.S.J., Prin.
Sisters 4; Lay Teachers 24; Students 306.

Vidalia, Toombs Co., Sacred Heart (1979), Rev. Mark J. Ross; Deacon Joseph P. Claroni.
Mailing Address: P.O. Box 1086, 30474-1086. Tel: 912-537-7709; Fax: 912-537-4691.
Res., 3119 E. North St., 30474. Tel: 912-537-7709.
Mission—Reidsville, Tattnall Co., St. Andrew the Apostle.

Warner Robins, Houston Co., Sacred Heart (1945), Revs. Fred J. Nijem; Michael C. Lubinsky; Sr. Teresa Baugh, P.B.V.M., Pastoral Assoc.; Deacons Harold P. Kimball; Dennis A. Arcand.
Mailing Address: P.O. Box 5052, 31099-5052. Tel: 478-923-0124; Fax: 478-328-3078.
School—Sisters of Presentation, Tel: 912-923-9668; Fax: 912-923-5822. Mrs. Bonnie Solinsky, Prin.
Sisters 2; Lay Teachers 20; Students 282.

Waycross, Ware Co., St. Joseph's (1960), Rev. James Kirchner, Admin.
Res., 2011 Darling Ave., P.O. Box 1846, 31501-1846. Tel: 912-283-7700; Fax: 912-283-1944.
Mission—Alma, Bacon Co., St. Raymond.

Waynesboro, Burke Co., Sacred Heart (1961), Rev. Laurence Goulding, Glmy.
Res., 115 S. Liberty St., 30830-4548. Tel: 706-554-2535; Fax: 706-554-1448.
Mission—Louisville, Jefferson Co., St. Joan of Arc, Tel: 478-625-3433.

Special Assignment:
Reverend Fathers—
Canty, Richard J., Memorial Medical Center & Candler General Hospital
Cushing, Robert A., 3890 Russell St., S.W., Smyrna, GA 30082-3533. Tel: 770-436-4730
Ryan, Timothy K., 1310 Primrose Dr., Roswell, GA 30076. Tel: 404-667-1313; 667-6305 (Fax)

On Duty Outside the Diocese:
Reverend Fathers—
Healy, Thomas, c/o Catholic Pastoral Center, 601 E. Liberty St., Savannah, GA 31401-5196
Keohane, Donal
Pachence, Ronald A., University of San Diego, San Diego, CA 92110
Schreck, Christopher J., St. Charles Borromeo Seminary, 1000 E. Wynnewood Rd., Wynnewood, PA 19096-3099. Tel: 215-667-3394

Military Chaplains:
Reverend Fathers—
Cerrone, Michael J., U.S.A.
Minch, Richard, U.S.A.
Quang, John, U.S.N.

Unassigned:
Reverend Fathers—
Brown, Wayland Y., Old Montgomery Rd., Savannah, GA 31406

Retired:
Reverend Monsignors—
Donnelly, Felix G., Cathedral of St. John the Baptist, P.O. Box 8307, Savannah, GA 31412. Tel: 912-233-4709
LeFrois, Marvin J., 800 Gornto Rd., Valdosta, GA 31602-1699. Tel: 912-253-0041
Reverend Fathers—
Barry, Francis, St. James Apts., Knock, Co. Mayo, Ireland
Campbell, Thomas E., 206 W. Gen. Stewart Way, Hinesville, GA 31313. Tel: 912-876-3731

Doris, Andrew T., 2346 McDowell St., Augusta, GA 30904. Tel: 706-736-0593
Dowling, William P.
Payne, Thomas H., P.O. Box 24683, St. Simons Island, GA 31522. Tel: 912-634-9189
Weltzer, Arthur, 320 12th St., Columbus, GA 31901

Permanent Deacons:
Andruzzi, Louis J., St. Frances Cabrini, Savannah
Arcand, Dennis A., Sacred Heart, Warner Robins
Benware, John F., St. Francis Cabrini, Savannah
Benyo, Francis P., Our Lady of Lourdes, Columbus
Bernard, Gregory L., St. Joseph's, Augusta
Bish, Daniel W., Jr., Holy Spirit, Macon
Burke, Clayton J., Jr., 5835 Medlock Bridge Pkwy., Alpharetta, GA 30022
Cisick, Donald G., St. Mary's on the Hill, Augusta
Claroni, Joseph P., Sacred Heart, Vidalia
Crider, Fretwell G., St. Michael's, Tybee Island
Daly, Michael F., Blessed Sacrament, Savannah
Fleury, Philippe D., 3659 N.W. 44th Ln., Gainesville, FL 32605
Foley, Michael F., P.O. Box 324, Tybee Island, GA 31328
Foster, George H., St. Michael, Fort Gordon
Halladay, Howard G., St. Augustine, Thomasville
Hosti, Charles J., St. Michael, Tybee Island
Houghton, Arthur A., 88 Miner Dr., Richmond Hill, GA 31324
Hutnick, Kenneth P., St. Juliana Church, Perry
Jackson, Prince A., Jr., 1215 E. Duffy St., Savannah, GA 31404
Johnson, William L., St. Teresa of Avila, Augusta
Kimball, Harold P., Sacred Heart, Warner Robins
Maasha, Ntungwa, St. Francis Xavier, Brunswick
McArdle, Donald R., Holy Trinity, Augusta
McAtee, Ralph H., St. Patrick, Perry
O'Neill, Robert, Unassigned
Pierce, Raymond G., (Retired)
Rowe, John A., Unassigned
Ruehling, George F., III, St. Francis Xavier, Brunswick
Sanchez, Aurelio, Holy Trinity Church, Swainsboro
Smith, Dewain E., Cathedral of St. John the Baptist, Savannah
Stives, Edward C., St. Francis Of Assisi, Folkston
Walsh, Philip J., Immaculate Conception, Moultrie
West, James L., St. Anne, Columbus
White, George H., 4 Dolan Dr., Savannah, GA 31406
Williams, Ephraim J., Holy Trinity, Augusta

INSTITUTIONS LOCATED IN THE DIOCESE

[A] HIGH SCHOOLS, DIOCESAN

AUGUSTA. *Aquinas High School*, 1920 Highland Ave., 30904-5305. Tel: 706-736-5516; Fax: 706-736-2678.
Web site: www.aquinas@aquinashigh.org
Mr. John Albert, Prin.; Mrs. Penny Jackson, Asst. Prin. Sisters 1; Lay Teachers 28; Students 303.

COLUMBUS. *Pacelli Catholic High School*, 3556 Trinity Dr., 31907. Tel: 706-561-8243; Fax: 706-561-3243.
E-mail: Pacelli@fiac.net
Web site: www.pacelli.net
Ms. Barbara Perryman, Prin.; Rev. J. Gerard Schreck, Diocesan Moderator. Sisters 1; Lay Teachers 22; Students 192.

[B] HIGH SCHOOLS, PRIVATE

SAVANNAH. *Benedictine Military School.* (Grades 9-12), 6502 Seawright Dr., P.O. Drawer 13577, 31416-3577. Tel: 912-356-3500; Fax: 912-356-3527.
Web site: bccadets.org
Secondary school conducted by the Dependent Priory of Benedictine Monks of St. Vincent Archabbey, Latrobe, PA. Very Rev. Jude W. Brady, O.S.B., Pres.; Ms. Kelly Burke, Prin.; Revs. Wilfred M. Dumm, O.S.B.; Albert Bickerstaff, O.S.B.; Ronald P. Gatman, O.S.B.; Anthony P. Wesolowski, O.S.B.; Meinrad J. Lawson, O.S.B.; Jeffrey S. Nyardy, O.S.B.; Bros. Gerard J. Klaric, O.S.B.; Timothy J. Brown, O.S.B.; Francis G. Ehnat, O.S.B. Priests 4; Brothers 1; Lay Teachers 25; Boys 442.

Convent and Academy of St. Vincent de Paul, 207 E. Liberty St., 31401-3577. Tel: 912-236-9541; Fax: 912-236-7877.
E-mail: svapri@bellsouth.net
Web site: www.asd.com#114491
Sisters of Mercy of the Americas. Sr. Helen Marie Buttimer, R.S.M., Prin. Sisters 7; Lay Teachers 24; Girls 370.

MACON. *Mount de Sales Academy.* (Grades 7-12), 851 Orange St., 31201-6136. Tel: 478-751-3240; Fax: 478-751-3241.
E-mail: srosina@mds.macon.ga.us
Web site: www.mds.macon.ga.us
Sisters of Mercy of the Americas. Sr. Mary Rosina Bayliss, R.S.M., Pres.& Prin. Sisters 2; Lay Teachers 43; Students 578.

[C] CHILD CARE HOMES

SAVANNAH. *St. Mary's Home*, 2170 E. Victory Dr., P.O. Box 3627-B, 31414. Tel: 912-236-7164; Fax: 912-236-9699.
E-mail: STMARYHOME@aol.com
For a complete listing, refer to the Special Care Facilities section.

[D] RESIDENCES FOR SINGLE PREGNANT WOMEN

MACON. *Nazareth Home, Residence for Single Pregnant Women*, 538 Orange St., P.O. Box 204, 31202-0204. Tel: 478-746-9803; Fax: 478-746-9803.
E-mail: Nazareth@hom.net
Web site: www.hom.net/~nazareth
Sr. Mary Shea, D.C., Dir.

[E] GENERAL HOSPITALS

SAVANNAH. *St. Joseph's Hospital*, 11705 Mercy Blvd., P.O. Box 60129, 31419-1791. Tel: 912-925-4100
For a complete listing, refer to the Hospitals section.

AUGUSTA. *St. Joseph Center For Life, Inc.*, 2260 Wrightsboro Rd., 30904-4726
For a complete listing, refer to the Hospitals section.

St. Joseph Hospital, Augusta, GA, Inc., 2260 Wrightsboro Rd., 30904-4726. Tel: 706-481-7400; Fax: 706-481-7599
For a complete listing, refer to the Hospitals section.

COLUMBUS. *St. Francis Hospital*, 2122 Manchester Expwy., P.O. Box 7000, 31908-7000. Tel: 706-596-4000
For a complete listing, refer to the Hospitals section.

[F] MONASTERIES AND RESIDENCES OF PRIESTS

SAVANNAH. *The Benedictine Priory*, 6502 Seawright Dr., P.O. Drawer 13577, 31416-3577. Tel: 912-356-3520; Fax: 912-356-3527.
Web site: bccadets.org
Dependent Priory of St. Vincent Archabbey, Latrobe, PA. Very Rev. Jude W. Brady, O.S.B., Prior; Revs. Wilfred M. Dumm, O.S.B.; Anthony P. Wesolowski, O.S.B.; Ronald P. Gatman, O.S.B.; Jeffrey S. Nyardy, O.S.B.; Albert Bickerstaff, O.S.B.; Meinrad J. Lawson, O.S.B.; Bros. Gerard J. Klaric, O.S.B.; Timothy Brown, O.S.B.; Francis Ehnat, O.S.B.

[G] CONVENTS AND RESIDENCES FOR SISTERS

SAVANNAH. *Carmelite Monastery*, 11 W. Back St., 31419-3219. Tel: 912-925-8505; Fax: 912-925-0797.
E-mail: terjonthe@juno.com
Sr. Carmela Marolda, O.C.D., Prioress. Professed Nuns 5; Postulants 1.

Mercy Convent. Retired Sisters of Mercy, 11801 McAuley Dr., 31419-1709. Tel: 912-925-3800; Fax: 912-925-3823.
E-mail: mercyconv@aol.com
Mrs. Gina McNamara, Admin. Sisters 7.

[H] NEWMAN CENTERS

SAVANNAH. *Savannah State University Newman Group*, 4 Indigo Ct., 31406. Tel: 912-925-5477. Mrs. Ann Lipsey, Campus Min.

MACON. *Mercer University, Wesleyan College Newman Center*, c/o St. Joseph Church, 830 Poplar St., 31201-2093. Tel: 478-745-1631. Aaron Killips, Campus Min.

STATESBORO. *St. Matthew Newman Center at Georgia Southern University*, 221 John Paul Ave., 30458-5016. Tel: 912-681-6726; Fax: 912-681-6727.
E-mail: jchall@gsaix2.cc.gasou.edu
Ms. Jane Hall, Campus Min.

VALDOSTA. *Valdosta State College Newman Center.* Mailing Address: 800 Gornto Rd., 31602. 412 Baytree Rd., 31602. Tel: 229-247-6707. Dr. Carl Hand, Campus Min.

[I] RETREAT HOUSES

SAVANNAH. *Dominican Friars*, 112 Palmetto Dr., Wilmington Island, 31410.
E-mail: HGrooverOP@aol.com

[J] MISCELLANEOUS

SAVANNAH. *Catholic Social Services*, 601 E. Liberty St., 31401-5196. Tel: 912-238-2320; Fax: 912-238-2339.
E-mail: csssav246@aol.com
Sr. Jacqueline Griffith, S.S.J., Dir.

Social Apostolate of Savannah, 502 E. Liberty St., P.O. Box 8703, 31412. Tel: 912-233-1877; Fax: 912-651-3638.
E-mail: socapsa@aol.com
Sr. Pauline O'Brien, M.F.I.C., Dir.

ALBANY. *Neighbors in Need*, 2005 Martin Luther King Dr., P.O. Box 3032, 31706-3001. Tel: 229-883-2872; Fax: 229-883-9116.
E-mail: nin3032@juno.com
Mrs. Rosemary Baughman, Dir.

St. Clare's Evangelization-Community Center, 2005 Martin Luther King Dr., P.O. Box 4123, 31706-4194. Tel: 912-883-2566; Fax: 912-883-9116. Co-Directors: Sr. Noelle Hart; Sr. Cecilia Ridge, M.F.I.C.

AUGUSTA. *Catholic Social Services*, 811 12th St., 30901-2749. Tel: 706-722-4390; Fax: 706-722-4758. Mr. Richard Tuchscherer, Dir.

BRUNSWICK. *Society of St. Vincent de Paul*, 1217 Newcastle St., 31520-7534. Tel: 912-262-6027; Fax: 912-265-6797. Marilee Williamson, Pres.

CLAXTON. *Clothesbasket*, 402 S. River St., 30417-2150. Tel: 912-739-2275. Sr. Janet Fischer, F.S.P.A., Dir.

COLUMBUS. *Holy Family Soup Kitchen*, 320 12th St., 31901-2454. Tel: 706-322-0098; Fax: 706-327-8191. Mrs. Frances Cummings, Dir.

Our Lady of Lourdes, 1953 Torch Hill Rd., 31903-2754. Tel: 706-689-5720; Fax: 706-687-9579. Mrs. Judie Huff, Dir.

St. Benedict Social Concerns, 2935 Ninth St., 31906-6354. Tel: 706-323-8300. Mrs. Helen Linton, Dir.

St. Vincent de Paul, St. Anne Conference, 3502 Kay Cir., 31907-3254. Tel: 706-568-1592; Fax: 706-568-0179. Paul and Claire Arrington, Dirs.

HAMILTON. *Christ the King (FOCUS)*, Hwy. 27, Box 32, 31811-0066. Tel: 706-628-5158; Fax: 706-628-5158. Sr. Philomena Fogarty, F.M.M., Dir.

MACON. *Mother & Child Ministries, Inc.*, 570 High Pl., 31201-2073. Tel: 478-745-7165; Fax: 478-745-9662.
E-mail: anninascharper@juno.com
Sr. Annina Scharper, D.C., Dir.

MILLEN. *Catholic Thrift Shop*, 706 Bay St., 30442. Tel: 478-982-8361. Sr. Mary Ellen Barrette, Dir.

VALDOSTA. *St. Francis Center*, P.O. Box 1331, 31601-1321. Tel: 229-242-8656; Fax: 229-244-5352.
E-mail: jcarver@datasys.net
Mr. Dwight Carver, Dir.

WARNER ROBINS. *Sacred Heart Christian Service Center*, P.O. Box 5052, 31099-5052. Tel: 478-929-3897; Fax: 478-328-3078.
E-mail: sheart@hom.net
Web site: www.hom.net/~sheart
Mr. Ermal Sirmans, Dir.

RELIGIOUS INSTITUTES OF MEN REPRESENTED IN THE DIOCESE

For further details refer to the corresponding bracketed number in the Religious Institutes of Men or Women section.

[0200]—*Benedictine Monks.* (St. Vincent Archabbey).—O.S.B.
[0600]—*Brothers of the Congregation of Holy Cross.*—C.S.C.
[0480]—*Conventual Franciscans.* (Provs. of Our Lady of Consolation & St. Anthony of Padua).—O.F.M.Conv.
[0570]—*Glenmary Home Missioners.* (Glendale, OH).—Glmy.
[0770]—*The Marist Brothers.* (Poughkeepsie, NY).—F.M.S.
[0780]—*Marist Fathers.* (Washington Prov.).—S.M.
[0840]—*Missionary Servants of Most Holy Trinity.* (Dublin).—S.T.
[1310]—*Order of the Most Holy Trinity.*—O.SS.T.
[1200]—*Society of the Divine Savior.* (American Prov.).—S.D.S.

RELIGIOUS INSTITUTES OF WOMEN REPRESENTED IN THE DIOCESE

[1780]—*Congregation of the Sisters of the Third Order of St. Francis of Perpetual Adoration.*—F.S.P.A.
[0760]—*Daughters of Charity of St. Vincent De Paul.* (Emmitsburg, MD).—D.C.
[0420]—*Discalced Carmelite Nuns.*—O.C.D.
[1370]—*Franciscan Missionaries of Mary.*—F.M.M.
[1470]—*Franciscan Sisters of St. Joseph.*—F.S.S.J.
[1845]—*Guadalupan Missionaries of the Holy Spirit.*—M.G.Sp.S.
[2080]—*Home Mission Sisters of America.*
[1360]—*Missionary Franciscan Sisters of the Immaculate Conception.*—M.F.I.C.
[3230]—*Poor Handmaids of Jesus Christ.* (Indiana).—P.H.J.C.
[0440]—*Sisters of Charity of Cincinnati.*—S.C.
[2575]—*Sisters of Mercy of the Americas.* (Baltimore, Burlingame, Chicago, Erie).—R.S.M.
[3950]—*Sisters of Saint Mary of Namur.*—S.S.M.N.
[1070-18]—*Sisters of St. Dominic of the American Congregation of the Sacred Heart of Jesus.*—O.P.

[1620]—*Sisters of St. Francis of Millvale, PA.*—O.S.F.

[3893]—*Sisters of St. Joseph.* (Chestnut Hill, PA).—S.S.J.

[3840]—*Sisters of St. Joseph of Carondelet.* (St. Louis, MO).—C.S.J.

[0260]—*Sisters of the Blessed Sacrament for Indians and Colored People.*—S.B.S.

[2170]—*Sisters, Servants of the Immaculate Heart of Mary.*—I.H.M.

[3330]—*Union of the Sisters of the Presentation of the Blessed Virgin Mary.*—P.B.V.M.

DIOCESAN CEMETERIES

SAVANNAH. *Catholic Cemetery and Properties.* Catholic Pastoral Center, 601 E. Liberty St., 31401-5196. Tel: 912-238-2320. Mr. John Benware, Dir.

AUGUSTA. *Catholic Cemetery.* Holy Trinity Church, 720 Telfair St., P.O. Box 2446, 30903. Tel: 706-722-4944. Rev. Allan J. McDonald.

DOUGLAS. *St. Paul's,* c/o 523 Ward St., 31533. Tel: 912-384-3560.

SYLVANIA. *Catholic Cemetery.* Our Lady of the Assumption Church, 121 Ridgecrest Dr., 30467. Tel: 912-564-2312. Rev. Edward V. Gorny, Glmy.

WILLACOOCHEE. *Catholic Cemetery.* Rev. Daniel P. O'Connell.

NECROLOGY

† Walker, James B., (Retired). —Died Sept. 23, 2000.

Diocese of Scranton

(Dioecesis Scrantonensis)

Most Reverend

JAMES C. TIMLIN, D.D.

Bishop of Scranton; ordained July 16, 1951; appointed Titular Bishop of Gunugo and Auxiliary Bishop of Scranton August 3, 1976; consecrated September 21, 1976; succeeded to See of Scranton April 24, 1984; installed June 7, 1984. *Office: 300 Wyoming Ave., Scranton, PA, 18503.* Tel.: 570-207-2216.

Most Reverend

JOHN M. DOUGHERTY, D.D., V.G.

Auxiliary Bishop of Scranton; ordained June 15, 1957; appointed Titular Bishop of Sufetula and Auxiliary Bishop of Scranton February 7, 1995; Episcopal ordination received March 7, 1995. *Office: 300 Wyoming Ave., Scranton, PA, 18503.* Tel.: 570-207-2216.

ESTABLISHED MARCH 3, 1868.

Square Miles 8,847.

Comprises the Counties of Luzerne, Lackawanna, Bradford, Susquehanna, Wayne, Tioga, Sullivan, Wyoming, Lycoming, Pike and Monroe in Pennsylvania.

For legal titles of parishes and diocesan institutions, consult the Chancery Office.

Chancery Office: 300 Wyoming Ave., Scranton, PA, 18503. Tel.: 570-207-2216; Fax: 570-207-2236.

Web site address: www.dioceseofscranton.org

STATISTICAL OVERVIEW

Personnel	
Bishop	1
Auxiliary Bishops	1
Priests: Diocesan Active in Diocese	251
Priests: Active Outside Diocese	19
Priests: Retired, Sick or Absent	77
Number of Diocesan Priests	347
Religious Priests in Diocese	96
Extern Priests in Diocese	7
Ordinations:	
Diocesan Priests	3
Transitional Deacons	4
Permanent Deacons in Diocese	51
Total Brothers	11
Total Sisters	760
Parishes	
Parishes	198
With Resident Pastor:	
Resident Diocesan Priests	191
Resident Religious Priests	7
Missions	85
Pastoral Centers	25
Professional Ministry Personnel:	
Sisters	64
Lay Ministers	19
Welfare	
Catholic Hospitals	7
Total Assisted	916,372
Health Care Centers	3
Total Assisted	96,832
Homes for the Aged	4
Total Assisted	768
Residential Care of Children	5
Total Assisted	983
Day Care and Extended Day Care Centers	9
Total Assisted	438
Specialized Homes	9
Total Assisted	1,576
Special Centers for Social Services	13
Total Assisted	198,763
Residential Care of Disabled	1
Total Assisted	159
Educational	
Seminaries, Diocesan	1
Students from This Diocese	10
Students from Other Diocese	7
Diocesan Students in Other Seminaries	16
Seminaries, Religious	1
Total Seminarians	26
Colleges and Universities	4
Total Students	11,365
High Schools, Diocesan and Parish	9
Total Students	3,455
High Schools, Private	2
Total Students	779
Elementary Schools, Diocesan and Parish	50
Total Students	12,044
Non-residential Schools for the Disabled	1
Total Students	19
Catechesis/Religious Education:	
High School Students	10,835
Elementary Students	23,123
Total Students Under Catholic Instruction	61,646
Teachers in the Diocese:	
Priests	14
Sisters	94
Lay Teachers	884
Vital Statistics	
Receptions into the Church:	
Infant Baptism Totals	4,131
Adult Baptism Totals	435
Received into Full Communion	395
First Communions	5,573
Confirmations	8,225
Marriages:	
Catholic	1,304
Interfaith	528
Total Marriages	1,832
Deaths	5,408
Total Catholic Population	337,454
Total Population	1,032,536

Former Bishops—First Bishop: Rt. Rev. WILLIAM O'HARA, D.D., cons. July 12, 1868; died Feb. 3, 1899.—*Second Bishop:* Rt. Rev. MICHAEL J. HOBAN, D.D., cons. Coadjutor, March 22, 1896; succeeded to See, Feb. 3, 1899; died Nov. 13, 1926.—*Third Bishop:* Most Rev. THOMAS C. O'REILLY, D.D., ord. June 4, 1898 elected Dec. 19, 1927, cons. Feb. 16, 1928; installed March 8, 1928; died March 25, 1938.—*Fourth Bishop:* Most Rev. WILLIAM J. HAFEY, D.D., ord. June 16, 1914; appt. First Bishop of Raleigh, April 6, 1925; cons. June 24, 1925; transferred to Scranton as Coadjutor *cum jure successionis* and Apostolic Administrator, Oct. 2, 1937; succeeded to See, March 25, 1938; died May 12, 1954.—*Fifth Bishop:* Most Rev. JEROME D. HANNAN, D.D., ord. May 22, 1921; appt. August 17, 1954; cons. Sept. 21, 1954; died Dec. 15, 1965.—*Sixth Bishop:* Most Rev. J. CARROLL M. MCCORMICK, D.D., ord. July 10, 1932; appt. Titular Bishop of Ruspae and Auxiliary of Philadelphia, Jan. 11, 1947; cons. April 23, 1947; appt. Bishop of Altoona-Johnstown, June 25, 1960; transferred to the See of Scranton, March 4, 1966; installed May 25, 1966; retired Feb. 15, 1983; died Nov. 2, 1996.—*Seventh Bishop:* Most Rev. JOHN J. O'CONNOR, D.D., ord. Dec. 15, 1945; appt. Titular Bishop of Cuzola and Auxiliary Bishop to the Military Vicar April 24, 1979; cons. May 27, 1979; appt. Bishop of Scranton, May 10, 1983; installed June 29, 1983; transferred to the See of New York, Jan. 31, 1984; died May 3, 2000.

Vicar General—Most Rev. JOHN M. DOUGHERTY, D.D., V.G., *300 Wyoming Ave., Scranton, 18503-1279.* Tel: 570-207-2216.

Chancery Office—300 Wyoming Ave., Scranton, 18503-1279. Tel: 570-207-2216; Fax: 570-207-2236.

Moderator of the Curia—Most Rev. JOHN M. DOUGHERTY, D.D., V.G. Tel: 570-207-2216.

Chancellor—Mr. JAMES B. EARLEY. Tel: 570-207-2216; 207-2225; Fax: 570-207-2236.

Secretary to Bishop Timlin—Rev. JOHN J. CHMIL. Tel: 570-207-2216; 207-2241; 344-7231 (After 5 P.M.).

Diocesan Financial Office—JAMES M. QUINN, Dir. Tel: 570-207-2239.

Diocesan Tribunal—300 Wyoming Ave., Scranton, 18503-1279. Tel: 570-207-2246; Fax: 570-207-2274. Direct all inquiries concerning marriage nullity, dispensations and permissions to this office.

Judicial Vicar—Rev. Msgr. PATRICK J. PRATICO, J.C.D.

Coordinator—JOSEPH V. FOX.

Judges—Rev. Msgr. JOSEPH C. BAMBERA, J.C.L.; CHARLES J. REID, J.D., J.C.L.; Rev. Msgr. PATRICK J. PRATICO, J.C.D.; LINDA E. PRICE, J.C.L.; Rev. JOHN L. SULLIVAN, J.C.L.

Defenders of the Bond—Rev. Msgr. JOSEPH G. QUINN, J.D., J.C.L.; Rev. Msgr. JOHN A. BERGAMO, J.C.L.; Very Rev. JAMES J. WALSH, J.C.L., V.F.

Promoter of Justice—Rev. Msgr. JOHN A. BERGAMO, J.C.L.

Auditors—JOSEPH A. BARRETT, Ph.D.; JOSEPH V. FOX; Rev. Msgr. JOHN A. BERGAMO, J.C.L.; Very Rev. CYRIL D. EDWARDS, M.Div., V.F.; Revs. BERNARD P. EVANOFSKI; JOSEPH ELSTON; MICHAEL J. SULLIVAN.

Procurator/Advocates—JOSEPH V. FOX; Revs. PHILIP A. ALTAVILLA; DAVID R. BETTS; BERNARD P. EVANOFSKI.

Psychological Expert—JOSEPH A. BARRETT, Ph.D.

Notaries—ANN WALSH; PATRICIA WALTON; JOSETTE JORDAN.

Diocesan Finance Council—Most Rev. JOHN M. DOUGHERTY, D.D., V.G.; Rev. Msgr. JOHN J. BENDIK; Mrs. ELLEN DERMODY; JOHN D. MCCARTHY; JAMES E. O'BRIEN, JR., ESQ.; MARY THERESA PATERSON, ESQ.; Rev. Msgr. NEIL J. VAN LOON, V.F.; JAMES M. QUINN; JAMES B. EARLEY; THOMAS MEDICO.

Diocesan Consultors—Most Rev. JOHN M. DOUGHERTY, D.D., V.G.; Rev. Msgr. JOSEPH C. BAMBERA; Rev. Msgr. VINCENT J. GRIMALIA, V.F.; Rev. Msgr. STEPHEN D. MCGOUGH; Very Rev. RICHARD J. LOCH, V.F.; Revs. JOHN J. KILPATRICK; ALBERT M. LIBERATORE; RICHARD J. POLMOUNTER; CHARLES W. ROKOSZ; EDWARD R. SCOTT; PHILLIP J. SLADICKA; JOHN J. TURI.

Ex Officio—Rev. JOHN J. CHMIL, Sec.

Diocesan Pastoral Council—Contact: ELLEN C. DERMODY, Diocesan Dir., Pastoral Planning, *300 Wyoming Ave., Scranton, 18503-1279.* Tel: 570-207-2267.

Deans—Very Rev. RICHARD J. LOCH, V.F., Scranton-South; Very Rev. EDWARD J. SHOBACK, V.F., Scranton-West; Rev. Msgr. DALE R. RUPERT, V.F., Scranton-North; Rev. Msgr. PAUL J. PURCELL, V.F., Scranton-Central; Very Rev. JAMES J. WALSH, V.F., Carbondale; Very Rev. JOSEPH M. BOLES, V.F., Abingtons; Very Rev. JOHN A. DORIS, V.F., Dunmore; Very Rev. CYRIL D. EDWARDS, V.F., Freeland; Very Rev. GIRARD F. ANGELO, V.F., Hazleton; Rev. Msgr. NEIL J. VAN LOON, V.F., Kingston; Very Rev. JAMES E. MCGAHAGAN, V.F., Nanticoke; Very Rev. CYRIL J. RABLE, V.F., Old Forge; Very Rev. WILLIAM B. BLAKE, V.F., Olyphant; Very Rev. JAMES J. PAISLEY, V.F., Pittston; Rev. Msgr. VINCENT J. GRIMALIA, V.F., Plymouth; Very Rev. GREGORY T. FINN, O.S.J., V.F., West Pittston; Very Rev. J. DUANE GAVITT, V.F., Wilkes-Barre Central/South; Very Rev. E. FRANCIS KELLY, V.F., Wilkes-Barre Plains; Very Rev. RONALD J. HUGHES, V.F., Bradford and Sullivan; Rev. Msgr. FRANCIS J. CASTELLANO, V.F., Lycoming; Rev. Msgr. KEVIN P. O'NEILL, V.F., Monroe; Rev. Msgr. WILLIAM P. WARD, V.F., Pike; Very Rev. THOMAS A. CAPPELLONI, V.F., Susquehanna; Very Rev. BERT S. KOZEN, V.F., Tioga; Very Rev. KEVIN P. MULHERN, V.F., Wayne; Very Rev. JOHN S. TERRY, V.F., Ashley-Mountain Top.

Presbyteral Council—Most Rev. JAMES C. TIMLIN, D.D., Pres.; Rev. Msgr. JOSEPH C. BAMBERA, Chm.; Rev. PAUL M. MULLEN, Vice Chm.; Rev. JOSEPH O. WEBER, Sec.; Rev. Msgr. JOHN J. BENDIK; Rev. Msgr. JOHN A. BERGAMO; Rev. Msgr. WILLIAM L. DONOVAN; Rev. Msgr. VINCENT J. GRIMALIA, V.F.; Rev. Msgr. DONALD A. MCANDREWS; Rev. Msgr. JAMES J. MCGARRY; Rev. Msgr. STEPHEN D. MCGOUGH; Rev. Msgr. NEIL J. VAN LOON, V.F.; Very Revs. CYRIL D. EDWARDS, V.F.; RICHARD J. LOCH, V.F.; Revs. PHILIP A. ALTAVILLA; JOHN J. BEGLEY, S.J.; JOHN J. CHMIL; JOSEPH ELSTON; JOSEPH J. EVANKO; WILLIAM J. FLYNN, S.S.; LOUIS T. KAMINSKI; JOHN J. KILPATRICK; ANDREW KUROVSKY; ALBERT M. LIBERATORE; JOHN K. MANNO; FRANCIS MCHUGH, O.F.M.; THOMAS D. MCLAUGHLIN; RICHARD J. POLMOUNTER; CHARLES W. ROKOSZ; EDWARD R. SCOTT; THOMAS P. SHOBACK; PHILLIP J. SLADICKA; JOHN J. TURI; JEFFREY J. WALSH. Ex Officio: Most Rev. JOHN M. DOUGHERTY, D.D., V.G.; Rev. JOSEPH R. KOPACZ.

Diocesan Building Commission—All plans for building should be sent to Chancery Office, *300 Wyoming Ave., Scranton, 18503-1279.* MICHAEL A. BARBETTI; Rev. Msgr. JOHN J. BENDIK; WILLIAM J. BURKAVAGE, JR.; Rev. Msgr. ANTHONY C. MARRA; JOSEPH M. O'CONNOR; PAUL S. ROTELLA, ESQ.; Rev. Msgr. NEIL J. VAN LOON, V.F. Ex Officio: Most Rev. JOHN M. DOUGHERTY, D.D., V.G.; JAMES B. EARLEY.

Vicar for Canonical Services—Rev. Msgr. PATRICK J. PRATICO, J.C.D., *300 Wyoming Ave., Scranton, 18503-1279.* Tel: 570-207-2246.

Vicar for Priests—Rev. JOSEPH R. KOPACZ, *300 Wyoming Ave., Scranton, 18503-1279.* Tel: 570-207-2269.

Vicars for Religious—Most Rev. JOHN M. DOUGHERTY, D.D., V.G., *300 Wyoming Ave., Scranton, 18503-1279.* Tel: 570-207-2216. Sr. M. GABRIEL KANE, I.H.M., *300 Wyoming Ave., Scranton, 18503-1279.* Tel: 570-207-2243.

Diocesan Offices and Directors

Blue Army of Our Lady of Fatima—Rev. DAVID W. CRAMER, Diocesan Spiritual Dir., *St. Ann's Rectory, P.O. Box 86, Richardson St., Shohola, 18458.* Tel: 570-559-7642.

Catholic Campaign for Human Development Director—Rev. WILLIAM B. PICKARD, *2010 Adams Ave., Scranton, 18509.* Tel: 570-207-8713; Fax: 570-207-6875.

Campus Ministry—Sr. CATHERINE ANN GILVARY, I.H.M., Dir., *Lycoming College, 700 College Pl., Box 149, Williamsport, 17701.* Tel: 570-321-4111; Fax: 570-321-4337.

Catholic Charismatic Renewal—Very Rev. RICHARD J. LOCH, V.F., Spiritual Advisor; ROBERT VALIANTE, Coord., *P.O. Box 3306, Scranton, 18505.* Tel: 570-344-2214.

Catholic Health Care Facilities Director and Representative to Catholic Institutions of Higher Learning—Rev. Msgr. ANDREW J. MCGOWAN, *Mercy Hospital, Scranton, 18501.* Tel: 570-348-7010.

Catholic Relief Services—JAMES B. EARLEY, Chancellor, *300 Wyoming Ave., Scranton, 18503-1279.* Tel: 570-207-2216.

Catholic Social Services—Mr. NED DELANEY, M.A., Diocesan Dir., *400 Wyoming Ave., Scranton, 18503-1272.* Tel: 570-207-2287.

Lackawanna County Branch—

Scranton Office—Mr. STEPHEN R. NOCILLA, M.A., Exec. Dir., *400 Wyoming Ave., Scranton, 18503-1272.* Tel: 570-207-2283; Fax: 570-207-2206.

Carbondale Office—39 S. Main St., Carbondale, 18407. Tel: 570-282-0460.

Luzerne County Branch—

Wilkes-Barre Office—Mr. NED DELANEY, M.A., Exec. Dir., *33 E. Northampton St., Wilkes-Barre, 18701.* Tel: 570-822-7118; Fax: 570-829-7781.

Hazleton Office—Mr. NEIL OBERTO, M.A., Exec. Dir., *81 S. Church St., Hazleton, 18201.* Tel: 570-455-1521; Fax: 570-455-2707.

Lycoming County Branch—

Williamsport Office—Mr. ROBERT MAKOS, L.S.W., Exec. Dir., *1201 Grampian Blvd., Ste. 2G, Williamsport, 17701.* Tel: 570-322-4220; Fax: 570-322-4276.

Wyoming County Branch—

Tunkhannock Office—Ms. JOANNE DONATO, L.S.W., *102 Warren Ave., Tunkhannock, 18657-0704.* Tel: 570-836-1101; Fax: 570-836-3765.

Monroe County Branch—

Stroudsburg Office—Mrs. MARY LOU MALLOY, L.S.W., Exec. Dir., *411 1/2 Main St., Stroudsburg, 18360.* Tel: 570-476-6460; Fax: 570-476-6466.

Pike County Branch—

Milford Office—Ms. ERIN BUSTELOS, *Rte. 6, P.O. Box 1195, Milford, 18337.* Tel: 800-916-1913; 570-296-1054; Fax: 570-296-9227.

Tioga County Branch—

Wellsboro Office—Mr. BERN MAKOS, L.S.W., *109 East Ave., Wellsboro, 16901.* Tel: 570-724-2734; Fax: 570-724-5855.

Natural Family Planning Coordinator—ELLEN DERMODY, Diocesan Coord., *300 Wyoming Ave., Scranton, 18503-1279.* Tel: 570-207-2267.

Diocesan Board of Education—Rev. SANTINO J. FANUCCI, Pres.; Rev. Msgr. VINCENT J. GRIMALIA, V.F., Vice Pres. JANE QUINN, Sec.

Cemeteries—Mr. WALTER BENNETT, Dir., *1708 Oram St., Scranton, 18504.* Tel: 570-207-2209.

Censor Librorum—Rev. Msgr. DAVID A. BOHR, S.T.D., *St. Pius X Seminary, Dalton, 18414.* Tel: 570-563-1131.

Continuing Education of Priests—Rev. JOSEPH R. KOPACZ, Dir., *300 Wyoming Ave., Scranton, 18503-1279.* Tel: 570-207-2269; 563-8515.

Cursillo Movement—Rev. JAMES R. NASH, Spiritual Moderator, *60 S. Main St., Montrose, 18801.* Tel: 570-278-1504.

Diocesan Commission on Ethics for Catholic Health Care Facilities—Rev. Msgr. DAVID A. BOHR, S.T.D., Chm. LYNN MARIE BUSCH, O.C.V.; JOSEPH CASCIANO; Deacon THOMAS M. CESARINI; Sr. KATHRYN CLAUSS, I.H.M.; Sr. VINCENTIA DORSEY, I.H.M.; Rev. JAMES J. DOYLE, C.S.C.; JAMES MCKENNA, M.D.; JOANNE ORLOSKI, M.D.; Rev. JAMES A. RAFFERTY, S.T.L.; WILLIAM P. SMEDLEY, M.D.; Rev. JOSEPH B. WILSON, Ph.D.; GLEN YANIK, ESQ.

Diocesan Commission on Ecumenism and Inter-Faith Matters—Rev. PHILIP A. ALTAVILLA, Diocesan Dir., *St. John the Baptist Rectory, 408 N. Main St., Taylor, 18517-1108.* Tel: 570-562-1341.

Diocesan Director of Public Relations—Sr. MARIANNE ADDY, I.H.M., Dir., *300 Wyoming Ave., Scranton, 18503-1279.* Tel: 570-207-1452.

Diocesan Engineer—Mr. TERRY K. STEPHENS, *300 Wyoming Ave., Scranton, 18503-1279.* Tel: 570-207-2232; 207-2240; Fax: 570-207-2273.

Diocesan Historian—Rev. CHARLES P. CONNOR, Ph.D., *St. John the Evangelist Rectory, 101 Jackson Ave., Susquehanna, 18847-1543.* Tel: 570-853-4634.

Diocesan Office for Communications—Mrs. MARIA ORZEL, Exec. Dir., *400 Wyoming Ave., Scranton, 18503-1272.* Tel: 570-207-2219; 800-246-0288; Fax: 570-207-2281.

Diocesan Office of Development—ERNEST PAPPA, Dir., *300 Wyoming Ave., Scranton, 18503-1279.* Tel: 570-207-2250.

Diocese of Scranton Catholic Community Foundation—ERNEST PAPPA, Dir., *300 Wyoming Ave., Scranton, 18503-1279.* Tel: 570-207-2250; Fax: 570-207-1459.

Diocesan Office of Ecumenism—Rev. PHILIP A. ALTAVILLA, Dir., *St. John the Baptist Rectory, 408 N. Main St., Taylor, 18517-1108.* Tel: 570-562-1341.

Diocesan Office of Parish Ministries—JOSEPH CASCIANO, Exec. Dir. JOAN TUREL, Worship Dir. SARAH MOUNTAIN, Youth & Young Adult Ministry Dir. CHRISTOPHER TIGUE, Dir, C.Y.O. MARY ANN PAULUKONIS, Family Life Dir. MARTIN A. KEARNEY, Social Concerns Dir., *300 Wyoming Ave., Scranton, 18503-1279.* Tel: 570-207-2213.

Ministry for Persons with Disabilities—Sr. MARY BETH MAKUCH, SS.C.M., Dir., *400 Wyoming Ave., Scranton, 18503-1272.* Tel: 570-207-2286.

Ministry with Deaf and Hard of Hearing—Sr. MARY BETH MAKUCH, SS.C.M., Dir., *400 Wyoming Ave., Scranton, 18503-1272.* Tel: 570-207-2286., Audio-Visual Resource Center. Tel: 570-207-2284.

Diocesan Pro-Life Office—JOSEPH CASCIANO, Diocesan Dir., *300 Wyoming Ave., Scranton, 18503-1279.* Tel: 570-207-2228.

Holy Childhood Association—Rev. Msgr. JOHN A. ESSEFF, Dir., *300 Wyoming Ave., Scranton, 18503-1279.* Tel: 570-207-2259.

Holy Name Society—Rev. SCOTT P. STEROWSKI, Spiritual Moderator, *St. Patrick's Rectory, 200 Delaware Ave., Olyphant, 18447-1535.* Tel: 570-489-0752.

Legion of Mary—Vacant.

Liturgical Commission—Rev. JOHN GERACCI, C.S.C., Chm. MARION EAGEN, Vice Chm. JOAN TUREL, Diocesan Worship Dir.

Marriage Encounter—Very Rev. RICHARD J. LOCH, V.F., Spiritual Advisor, *St. Mary of the Assumption Rectory, 430 Pittston Ave., Scranton, 18505.* Tel: 570-961-2297.

D.C.C.M.—Rev. SCOTT P. STEROWSKI, Spiritual Moderator, *St. Patrick's Rectory, 200 Delaware Ave., Olyphant, 18447.* Tel: 570-489-0752.

D.C.C.W.—Rev. Msgr. FRANCIS J. CALLAHAN, Spiritual Moderator, *St. Therese's Rectory, 25 Old River St., Wilkes-Barre, 18702.* Tel: 570-822-1075.

Newspaper—"The Catholic Light"; Mr. WILLIAM R. GENELLO, Editor, *300 Wyoming Ave., Scranton, 18503-1279.* Tel: 570-207-2229; 207-2272; Fax: 570-207-2271.

Office of Pastoral Planning—ELLEN C. DERMODY, Exec. Dir., *300 Wyoming Ave., Scranton, 18503-1279.* Tel: 570-207-2267.

Diocesan Television Station-CTV—Mrs. MARIA ORZEL, Exec. Dir. JAMES BRENNAN, Mgr., *400 Wyoming Ave., Scranton, 18503-1272.* Tel: 570-207-2219; Fax: 570-207-2281.

Permanent Diaconate Office—Rev. Msgr. DAVID A. BOHR, Dir., *St. Pius X Seminary, 1000 Seminary Rd., Dalton, 18414.* Tel: 570-563-1131.

Pilgrimages—Rev. ANDREW S. HVOZDOVIC, Diocesan Dir., *118 Kendall Ave., Jersey Shore, 18705.* Tel: 570-398-2557.

Priests' Purgatorial Society—Rev. JOSEPH R. KOPACZ, Sec., *300 Wyoming Ave., Scranton, 18503-1279.* Tel: 570-207-2269; 563-8515.

Priests' Retirement Advisory Board—Most Rev. JOHN M. DOUGHERTY, D.D., V.G.; Rev. Msgr. WILLIAM J. PAKUTKA; JAMES M. QUINN; Rev. JOHN J. KILPATRICK; Very Rev. RICHARD J. LOCH, V.F.; Revs. RICHARD J. POLMOUNTER; JOSEPH R. KOPACZ; Mr. JAMES B. EARLEY.

Propagation of the Faith—Rev. Msgr. JOHN A. ESSEFF, Dir., *300 Wyoming Ave., Scranton, 18503-1279.* Tel: 570-207-2259; Fax: 570-207-2268.

Pastoral Formation Institute—Rev. Msgr. DAVID A. BOHR, S.T.D., Dir. LYNN MARIE BUSCH, O.C.V., Coord., *St. Pius X Seminary, 1000 Seminary Rd., Dalton, 18414.* Tel: 570-563-8501.

Renewal—Fatima Center—Sr. ROBERTA PETERS, I.H.M., *1000 Seminary Rd., Dalton, 18414.* Tel: 570-563-8500; Fax: 570-563-1857.

Retirement Fund for Religious—Directors: Sr. MARIANNE ADDY, I.H.M.; Sr. M. GABRIEL KANE, I.H.M. Tel: 570-207-1452; 207-2243.

Schools—RUTH A. CONNOLLY, Ed.D., Supt., *300 Wyoming Ave., Scranton, 18503-1279.* Tel: 570-207-2253. PATRICK G. CAWLEY, Asst. Supt. Curriculum & Staff Devel. Tel: 570-207-2254. DANIEL F. DONOVAN, Asst. Supt., Personnel. Tel: 570-207-2252. Rev. JAMES A. RAFFERTY, Asst. Supt., Christian Formation. Tel: 570-282-2991; 282-2790. JOSEPH S. HAGGERTY, Fiscal Mgr.

Scouts of America—Rev. BRYAN B. WRIGHT, Diocesan Chap., *St. John the Evangelist Rectory, 35 William St., Pittston, 18640-2597.* Tel: 570-654-0053.

Council of Women Religious—Contact: Sr. M. GABRIEL KANE, I.H.M., Vicar for Religious, *300 Wyoming Ave., Scranton, 18503-1279.* Tel: 570-207-2243.

Christian Life Communities—Sr. MARYLA FARFOUR, I.H.M., Coord., *333 Wyoming Ave., Scranton, 18503.* Tel: 570-344-9725. Rev. ROBERT J. SIMON, Spiritual Advisor, *2523 Jackson St., Scranton, 18504.* Tel: 570-344-9745.

Vocations—Rev. DONALD J. WILLIAMS, Dir.; Sr. MINNETTE WELDING, I.H.M., Assoc. Dir., *St. Pius X Seminary, 1000 Seminary Rd., Dalton, 18414.* Tel: 570-563-8504.

CLERGY, PARISHES, MISSIONS AND PAROCHIAL SCHOOLS

CITY OF SCRANTON
(Lackawanna County)

1—ST. PETER'S CATHEDRAL (1853), Rev. Msgr. Joseph G. Quinn, J.D., J.C.L.; Revs. John J. Chmil; Thomas G. Sinnott. In res., Most Rev. James C. Timlin, D.D.
Res., 315 Wyoming Ave., 18503. Tel: 570-344-7231; Fax: 570-344-4749.

2—ST. ANN'S BASILICA PARISH (1901), Revs. Roger Elliott, C.P.; Kenneth Walsh, C.P.
Res., 1250 St. Ann St., 18504. Tel: 570-342-5166; Fax: 570-348-3750.
School—1228 St. Ann St., 18504. Tel: 570-348-3753; Fax: 570-348-3758.
Lay Teachers 12; Students 201.

3—ST. ANTHONY OF PADUA (1913) (Italian), Rev. Michael A. Penn. In res., Rev. Robert J. Barone.
Res., 1402 Short Ave., 18508. Tel: 570-342-4190.

4—ST. DAVID'S (1946), Rev. Robert J. Simon.
Res., 2523 Jackson St., 18504. Tel: 570-344-9745; Fax: 570-344-4176.

5—ST. FRANCIS (1920) (Italian), Rev. Msgr. Philip A. Gray.
Res., 630 Genet St., 18505. Tel: 570-346-0797; Fax: 570-346-7187.

6—HOLY CROSS (1897). Merged with St. Patrick's, Scranton.

7—HOLY FAMILY (1891), Rev. Msgr. Constantine V. Siconolfi.
Res., 510 Gibson St., 18509. Tel: 570-342-8548; Fax: 570-342-2581. [CEM]

8—HOLY NAME (1938), Rev. John J. Kilpatrick.
Res., 1414 E. Elm St., 18505. Tel: 570-346-3859; Fax: 570-346-3859.

9—HOLY ROSARY (1871), Rev. Msgr. Dale R. Rupert, V.F.; Rev. Arbogaste Satoun; Deacon Edward Protzman.
Res., 316 William St., 18508. Tel: 570-342-4881; Fax: 570-344-2130.
School—312 William St., 18508. Tel: 570-344-7565.
Priests 1; Sisters of the I.H.M. 4; Lay Teachers 11; Students 241. (Merged with St. Stanislaus and its mission, St. Stephen's Church, Scranton.).

10—IMMACULATE CONCEPTION (1967), Revs. William D. Campbell; Edward F. Barrett; Glenn E. McCreary.
Res., 801 Taylor Ave., 18510. Tel: 570-961-5211.

11—ST. CLARE (1967), Rev. Msgr. Joseph A. Fadden.
Res., 2301 N. Washington Ave., 18509. Tel: 570-344-9884.
School—2215 N. Washington Ave., 18509. Tel: 570-343-2790.
Sisters of the I.H.M. 5; Lay Teachers 18; Students 281.

12—ST. JOHN THE BAPTIST (1885) (German). Merged with St. Patrick's, Scranton.

13—ST. JOHN THE EVANGELIST (1886), Rev. Eugene L. Gunning.
Res., 516 Fig St., 18505. Tel: 570-343-6026.

14—ST. JOSEPH'S (1894) (Lithuanian), Rev. Msgr. Peter P. Madus.
Res., 116 Theodore St., 18508. Tel: 570-342-4339; Fax: 570-342-4245. [CEM]

15—ST. JOSEPH'S (1875), Rev. John M. Lapera. In res., Rev. Conan Conaboy, C.P.
Res., 312 Davis St., 18505. Tel: 570-344-1724; Fax: 570-344-1787. [CEM]

16—ST. LUCY'S (1901) (Italian), Revs. Paul P. Cottone; Salvatore A. Bentivegna, O.S.J.
Res., 949 Scranton St., 18504. Tel: 570-347-9421.

17—ST. MARY OF THE ASSUMPTION (1854) (German), Very Rev. Richard J. Loch, V.F. In res., Revs. Patrick D. Healey; Thomas Pulickal, O.C.D.
Res., 430 Pittston Ave., 18505. Tel: 570-961-2297; Fax: 570-961-1468. [CEM 2]
School—Please see Marian Catholic Interparochial School in the Institute section located under Inter-Parochial Elementary Schools.

18—ST. MARY'S (1904) (Polish), Rev. Albert E. Oldfield.
Res., 3335 Greenwood Ave., Moosic, 18507. Tel: 570-343-4024; Fax: 570-343-8323. [CEM]

19—ST. MICHAEL'S (1914) (Lithuanian), Rev. Carlos S. Casavantes, F.S.S.P.
Res., 1703 Jackson St., 18504. Tel: 570-961-1205; Fax: 570-961-2284.

20—NATIVITY OF OUR LORD (1903), Rev. Msgr. Joseph P. Kelly. In res., Rev. John C. Ruth.
Res., 633 Orchard St., 18505. Tel: 570-344-6159; Fax: 570-207-4932.
School—Please see Marian Catholic Interparochial School in the Institute section located under Inter-Parochial Elementary Schools.

21—ST. PATRICK'S (1870), Rev. Msgr. Paul F. Leonard; Revs. Thomas Yuen; Paul E. Miller. In res., Rev. Michael P. Litcheck.
Res., 1403 Jackson St., 18504. Tel: 570-344-2679; 343-4353; Fax: 570-343-2835. (Merged with Holy Cross and St. John the Baptist, Scranton).
School—115 S. Lincoln Ave., 18504. Tel: 570-343-8114.
Sisters of the I.H.M. 1; Lay Teachers 16; Students 289.
Chapel—Scranton, Immaculate Heart of Mary.

22—ST. PAUL'S (1887), Rev. Msgr. Paul J. Purcell, V.F. In res., Rev. Gerard F. Lupa.
Res., 1510 Penn Ave., 18509. Tel: 570-961-1549; Fax: 570-343-0069.
School—1527 Penn Ave., 18509. Tel: 570-343-7880; Fax: 570-343-0069.
Lay Teachers 14; Students 235.

23—SS. PETER AND PAUL (1910) (Polish), Very Rev. Edward J. Shoback, V.F.
Res., 1309 W. Locust St., 18504. Tel: 570-343-7015; Fax: 570-343-7023. [CEM]

24—SACRED HEARTS OF JESUS AND MARY (1885) (Polish), Rev. Msgr. Leonard J. Novak. In res., Revs. Emil M. Hussack; Walter L. Ferrett.
Res., 1217 Prospect Ave., 18505. Tel: 570-343-6420. [CEM]

25—ST. STANISLAUS (1915) (Polish). Merged with Holy Rosary, Scranton and its mission, St. Stephen's Church, Scranton.

26—ST. VINCENT DE PAUL (1925), Rev. Richard J. Cirba.
Res., 1201 Providence Rd., 18508. Tel: 570-346-9739; Fax: 570-347-3250.

OUTSIDE THE CITY OF SCRANTON

Archbald, Lackawanna Co., St. Thomas Aquinas (1858), Revs. Gerard M. Gannon; Edward P. Lyman.
Res., 411 Church St., 18403. Tel: 570-876-1701; Fax: 570-876-3617. [CEM]

Ashley, Luzerne Co., Holy Rosary (1900) (Slovak), Rev. John F. Samson.
Res., 60 Charles St., 18706. Tel: 570-822-7543.
St. Leo's (1887), Rev. Thomas J. O'Malley.
Res., 33 Manhattan St., 18706. Tel: 570-825-6669; Fax: 570-823-3714.

Athens, Bradford Co., St. Joseph (1852). Merged with St. John the Evangelist, South Waverly.

Avoca, Luzerne Co., St. Mary's (1871), Rev. Joseph Elston.
Res., 715 Hawthorne St., 18641. Tel: 570-655-8218; 457-3412; Fax: 570-655-8218. [CEM]
School—742 Spring St., 18641. Tel: 570-457-9700; 457-9600.
Lay Teachers 10; Students 184.
SS. Peter and Paul (1909) (Polish), Rev. Mark J. Bochinski.
Res., 912 Vine St., 18641. Tel: 570-457-2483; 457-9806. [CEM]

Bastress, Lycoming Co., Immaculate Conception (1838) (German), Rev. Robert T. Busteed.
Res., 5973 Jacks Hollow Rd., Williamsport, 17702. Tel: 570-745-3301. [CEM]
School—6101 Jacks Hollow Rd., Williamsport, 17702. Tel: 570-745-3320; Fax: 570-745-3723.
Sisters of Christian Charity 1; Lay Teachers 7; Students 92.

Bear Creek Township, Luzerne Co., St. Christopher (1962). Merged with Holy Saviour, Wilkes-Barre.
St. Elizabeth (1938), Rev. Anthony M. Urban.
Res., P.O. Box 25, 18602. Tel: 570-472-3061; Fax: 570-472-3061.
Mission—Thornhurst, Luzerne Co., St. Mark.

Bentley Creek, Bradford Co., St. Ann's (1843), Rev. John C. O'Bell.
Res., R.R. No. 3, Box 138A, Gillett, 16925. Tel: 570-596-2109; Fax: 570-596-2107. [CEM]
Mission—Ridgebury, Bradford Co., Our Lady of Perpetual Help.

Blakeslee, Monroe Co., Christ the King (1976), Rev. Raymond L. Deviney.
Res., P.O. Box 171, 18610. Tel: 570-646-8990.

Blossburg, Tioga Co., St. Andrew's. Merged with St. Mary, Blossburg.
St. Mary's (1874) (Polish), Rev. Richard E. Fox.
Res., 138 St. Mary's St., 16912. Tel: 570-638-3241; Fax: 570-638-2952. [CEM 3]
(Merged with St. Andrew, Blossburg).
Missions—Arnot, Tioga Co., St. Stanislaus Kostka; Morris Run, Tioga Co., St. Joseph.

Brodheadsville, Monroe Co., Our Lady Queen of Peace (1968), Rev. William J. McCawley.
Res., P.O. Box 38, 18322. Tel: 610-681-6137; Fax: 610-681-6139.

Buttonwood, Luzerne Co., Exaltation of the Holy Cross (1917) (Polish), Very Rev. James E. McGahagan, V.F.
Res., 420 Main Rd., Buttonwood, Wilkes-Barre, 18702. Tel: 570-823-6242; Fax: 570-829-4732. [CEM]

Canadensis, Monroe Co., St. Bernadette (1967), Rev. Alfred J. Vito; Deacon Ronald P. Verkon.
Res., P.O. Box 14, 18325. Tel: 570-595-2139; 595-7622 (Maloney Hall); Fax: 570-595-6235.
Mission—Promised Land, Monroe Co., Our Lady of Fatima.

Canton, Bradford Co., St. Michael (1853), Very Rev. Bert S. Kozen, V.F.; Deacon William H. Graham.
Res., 24 N. Washington St., 17724. Tel: 570-673-5253; Fax: 570-673-5630. [CEM]
Missions—Troy, Bradford Co., St. John Nepomucene, Tel: 570-297-4405. [CEM]
Ralston, Lycoming Co., St. Aloysius.

Carbondale, Lackawanna Co., Our Lady of Mt. Carmel (1882) (Italian), Rev. Russell E. Motsay.
Res., 15 Fallbrook St., 18407. Tel: 570-282-5172. [CEM]
St. Rose of Lima (1830), Rev. Msgr. William J. Feldcamp; Revs. Thomas J. McDermott; James A. Rafferty. In res., Rev. Samuel T. Perrins.
Res., 6 N. Church St., 18407. Tel: 570-282-2991; Fax: 570-282-7580. [CEM 2]

Carverton, Luzerne Co., St. Frances Cabrini (1947), Rev. Joseph O. Weber.
Res., 585 Mt. Olivet Rd., Kingston Twp., Wyoming, 18644-9333. Tel: 570-696-3737; Fax: 570-696-9767.
Mission—Centermoreland, Luzerne Co., Blessed Sacrament.

Clarks Green, Lackawanna Co., St. Gregory (1974), Rev. Msgr. John H. Louis.
Res., 330 N. Abington Rd., 18411. Tel: 570-587-4808; Fax: 570-587-0276.

Clarks Summit, Lackawanna Co., Our Lady of the Snows (1911), Rev. Msgr. James J. McGarry; Rev. Joseph F. Sica.
Res., 301 S. State St., 18411. Tel: 570-586-1741; Fax: 570-586-2504.
Mission—Newton, Lackawanna Co., St. Benedict.

Conyngham, Luzerne Co., St. John Bosco (1964), Rev. Msgr. Joseph C. Bambera; Rev. Albert P. Leonard.
Res., 2 Charles Ave. P.O. Box 919, 18219. Tel: 570-788-1997; Fax: 570-788-6667.
Parish Center—Tel: 570-788-9933.

Dallas, Luzerne Co., Gate of Heaven (1951), Rev. John C. Lambert; Deacon Thomas M. Cesarini.
Res., Machell Ave., 18612. Tel: 570-675-2121; Fax: 570-675-7143.

Dalton, Lackawanna Co., Our Lady of the Abingtons (1967), Very Rev. Joseph M. Boles, V.F.
Res., W. Main St., 18414. Tel: 570-563-1622; Fax: 570-563-1622.

Dickson City, Lackawanna Co., St. Thomas the Apostle. Merged with Visitation of the Blessed Virgin Mary (Polish), Dickson City.
Visitation of the Blessed Virgin Mary (1890) (Polish), Rev. Msgr. Stanley W. Piorkowski; Rev. John Peter Swaminathan.
Res., St. Mary's Square, P.O. Box 9038, 18519. Tel: 570-489-2091; Fax: 570-489-0349. [CEM]
(Merged with St. Thomas the Apostle, Dickson City).
School—Tel: 570-489-0061; Fax: 570-489-0157.
Bernardine Sisters of St. Francis 2; Lay Teachers 10; Students 213.

Dorrance, Luzerne Co., Our Lady Help of Christians (1948) (Polish), Rev. Mark G. Balczeniuk.
Res., R.R. No. 1, Box 263, (Dorrance), Wapwallopen, 18660-9765. Tel: 570-868-5855; Fax: 570-868-5876. [CEM]

Drums, Luzerne Co., Church of the Good Shepherd (1940), Rev. Gerard F. Safko.
Res., 87 South Hunter Hwy., 18222. Tel: 570-788-3141; Fax: 570-788-2916.

Dunmore, Lackawanna Co.,
1—ALL SAINTS, (1905) (Slovak). Merged with St. Mary of Mount Carmel, Dunmore.
2—CHRIST THE KING, (1949), Rev. John F. Poplawski.
Res., 1214 Quincy Ave., 18510. Tel: 570-343-2777.
3—ST. ANTHONY OF PADUA, (1894) (Italian), Rev. Msgr. Anthony C. Marra; Deacon Carmine Mendicino.
Res., 303 Smith St., 18512. Tel: 570-344-1209; Fax: 570-344-1200.
School—208 Smith St., 18512. Tel: 570-342-1182. Sisters 2; Lay Teachers 9; Students 189.
Convent—215 Franklin St., 18512. Tel: 570-343-1422. Religious Teachers Filippini
4—ST. CASIMIR, (Polish). Merged with St. Mary of Mount Carmel, Dunmore.
5—ST. MARY OF MOUNT CARMEL, (1856), Very Rev. John A. Doris, V.F.; Rev. David R. Betts. In res., Rev. Joseph J. Evanko.
Res., 322 Chestnut St., 18512. Tel: 570-346-7429; Fax: 570-346-0523. [CEM 2]
School—325 Chestnut St., 18512. Tel: 570-346-4429.
Sisters of the I.H.M. 2; Priests 1; Lay Teachers 14; Students 280. (Merged with All Saints and St. Casimir, Dunmore.).
6—ST. ROCCO'S, (1905) (Italian), Rev. Anthony R. Tombasco.
Res., 118 Kurtz St., 18510-1539. Tel: 570-344-1239.

Dupont, Luzerne Co., Sacred Heart of Jesus (1902) (Polish), Rev. Joseph D. Verespy.
Res., 215 Lackawanna Ave., 18641. Tel: 570-654-3713; Fax: 570-654-8827. [CEM]
School—217 Lackawanna Ave., 18641. Tel: 570-654-8822; Fax: 570-654-8822.
Lay Teachers 10; Students 170.

Duryea, Luzerne Co., Holy Rosary (1893) (Polish), Rev. Charles W. Rokosz.
Res., 127 Stephenson St., 18642. Tel: 570-457-3502. [CEM]
School—110 1/2 Stephenson St., 18642. Tel: 570-457-2553; Fax: 570-457-3537.
Bernardine Sisters 1; Lay Teachers 10; Students 271.
Sacred Heart of Jesus (1889) (German), Rev. Albert M. Liberatore.
Res., 529 Stephenson St., 18642. Tel: 570-457-2253; Fax: 570-451-2633.
St. Joseph's (1909) (Lithuanian). Merged with Sacred Heart of Jesus, Duryea.

Dushore, Sullivan Co., St. Basil's (1838), Rev. Michael B. Harris.
Res., 101 Churchill St., P.O. Box 307, 18614. Tel: 570-928-8865; Fax: 570-928-7972. [CEM]
Missions—Cummiskey, Sullivan Co., St. Francis of Assisi; Overton, Sullivan Co., St. Francis Xavier; Laporte, Sullivan Co., Sacred Heart; Eagles Mere, Sullivan Co., St. Francis of Assisi.
Shrine—Sugar Ridge, SS. Philip and James Church-St. John Neumann Shrine.

East Stroudsburg, Monroe Co., St. John (1986), Rev. Msgr. Kevin P. O'Neill, V.F.
Mailing Address: 5171 Milford Rd., 18301. Tel: 570-223-9144; Fax: 570-223-9146.
St. Matthew's (1902), Rev. Msgr. John A. Bergamo; Revs. Thomas J. Sokolowski; Daniel J. Yenkevich.
Res., 200 Brodhead Ave., 18301. Tel: 570-421-2342; Fax: 570-421-8414.

Edwardsville, Luzerne Co., SS. Cyril and Methodius (1900) (Slovak). Merged with St. Anthony's, Larksville.

Elkland, Tioga Co., St. Thomas the Apostle (1907), Rev. Joseph P. Kutch.
Res., 111 First St., 16920. Tel: 814-258-5121; Fax: 814-258-5122.
Mission—Westfield, Tioga Co., St. Catherine, Lincoln St., Westfield 16950.

Elmhurst, Lackawanna Co., St. Eulalia (1950), Rev. Msgr. F. Allan Conlan, Ph.D. In res., Rev. Donald J. Williams.
Res., P.O. Box 143, 18416. Tel: 570-842-7656; Fax: 570-842-7193.

Exeter, Luzerne Co., St. Anthony of Padua (1928) (Italian), Very Rev. Gregory T. Finn, O.S.J., V.F.; Rev. Raymond Tabon, O.S.J. In res., Rev. Silvio Chini, O.S.J.
Res., 28 Memorial Ave., Exeter Boro, Pittston, 18643. Tel: 570-654-2103; Fax: 570-655-3313.
St. Cecilia (1900), Rev. Daniel D. Hitchko.
Res., 1700 Wyoming Ave., 18643. Tel: 570-654-2133; Fax: 570-654-3449. [CEM]
Convent—1690 Wyoming Ave., 18643. Tel: 570-655-8119. (Merged with St. John the Baptist, Exter.).
St. John the Baptist (1898) (Polish). Merged with St. Cecilia, Exeter.

Eynon, Lackawanna Co., St. Mary's Czestochowa (1915) (Polish), Rev. Msgr. Patrick J. Pratico.
Res., 417 Main St., 18403. Tel: 570-876-2223; Fax: 570-876-3081. (Merged with St. Mary of Vilna, Eynon.).
St. Mary of Vilna (Lithuanian). Merged with St. Mary's Czestochowa, Eynon.

Fairmount Springs, Luzerne Co., St. Martha's (1966). Merged with Our Lady of Mt. Carmel, Lake Silkworth.

Forest City, Susquehanna Co., Sacred Heart of Jesus (1904) (Polish), Rev. Patrick L. Albert.
Res., 612 Hudson St., 18421. Tel: 570-785-3838. (Merged with St. Agnes, Forest City).
St. Joseph's (1904) (Slovenian). Merged with Sacred Heart of Jesus, Forest City.

Freeland, Luzerne Co.,
1—ST. ANN'S, (1862), Very Rev. Cyril D. Edwards, V.F.; Rev. Joseph J. Mattey; Deacon Cyril J. Kowalchick.
Office: 898 Centre St., 18224. Tel: 570-636-3035; Fax: 570-636-1743. [CEM]
Res., 420 Vine St., 18224.
2—ST. ANTHONY'S. Merged with St. Ann's, Freeland.
3—ST. CASIMIR'S. Merged with St. Ann's, Freeland.
4—ST. JOHN NEPOMUCENE. Merged with St. Ann's, Freeland.

Friendsville, Susquehanna Co., St. Francis Xavier's (1831), Rev. W. Jeffrey Paulish.
Res., P.O. Box 50, 18818. Tel: 570-553-2288; Fax: 570-553-2975. [CEM 3]
(Merged with St. Thomas the Apostle, Little Meadows.).
Mission—Middletown, Susquehanna Co., St. Patrick.
St. Joseph's (1829), Rev. Richard G. Ghezzi.
Res., Quinn Rd., R.R. #1, Box 1402, 18818. Tel: 570-553-2300; Fax: 570-553-2958. [CEM 2][JC]
Mission—Silver Lake, Susquehanna Co., St. Augustine.

Glen Lyon, Luzerne Co., St. Adalbert's (1889) (Polish), Rev. Carl T. Prushinski.
Res., 31 S. Market St., 18617. Tel: 570-736-6372. [CEM]
(Merged with St. Denis and St. Michael, Glen Lyon and St. Mary, Wanamie).
St. Michael's. Merged with St. Adalbert's and St. Denis, Glen Lyon and St. Mary's, Wanamie.

Gouldsboro, Wayne Co., St. Rita (1975), Rev. Martin M. Boylan, Ph.D.
Res., P.O. Box 537, 18424. Tel: 570-842-4995; Fax: 570-842-5429.
Missions—South Sterling, Wayne Co., St. Mary Magdalene; Newfoundland, Wayne Co., St. Anthony of Padua.

Great Bend, Susquehanna Co., St. Lawrence's (1872), Rev. John J. Kulavich.
Res., 506 Franklin St., 18821. Tel: 570-879-2392. [CEM]
Mission—New Milford, Susquehanna Co., St. John. [CEM]

Harding, Luzerne Co., Church of the Holy Redeemer (1952), Rev. Thomas E. McCann.
Res., R.D. 1, Pittston, 18643. Tel: 570-388-6300.

Harleigh, Luzerne Co., Sacred Heart of Jesus (1903), Very Rev. Girard F. Angelo, V.F.
Res., One Church Pl., 18225. Tel: 570-455-1162; Fax: 570-455-0306.
Shrines—National Shrine of the Sacred Heart, (1975).; Men of the Sacred Heart, National Office, (1977), Tel: 570-455-1162.

Harveys Lake, Luzerne Co., Our Lady of Victory (1969), Rev. Joseph P. Rafferty.
Res., R.D. #1, Box 309, 18618. Tel: 570-639-1535; Fax: 570-639-1294.

Hawley, Wayne Co., Blessed Virgin Mary, Queen of Peace (1852), Rev. William B. Healey.
Res., 314 Chestnut Ave., 18428. Tel: 570-226-3183; Fax: 570-226-2126. [CEM]
Mission—Lake Wallenpaupack, Pike Co., St. Veronica.

Hazleton, Luzerne Co.,
1—ST. GABRIEL'S, (1855), Rev. Msgr. Michael J. Delaney; Rev. John E. Melnick.
Res., 122 S. Wyoming St., 18201. Tel: 570-454-0212; Fax: 570-459-5187. [CEM]
2—CHURCH OF THE MOST PRECIOUS BLOOD, (1885) (Italian), Revs. Maurice L. Raymond; Wieslaw M. Ziebacz.
Res., 131 E. Fourth St., 18201. Tel: 570-454-8714; Fax: 570-454-8754.
3—HOLY ROSARY, (1916) (Italian), Rev. Patrick J. Genello.
Res., 240 S. Poplar St., 18201. Tel: 570-454-6693.
4—HOLY TRINITY, (1887) (German), Rev. Patrick J. McLaughlin.
Res., 123 W. Oak St., 18201. Tel: 570-454-5394; Fax: 570-454-0767. [CEM 2]
School—35 N. Church St., 18201. Tel: 570-455-9645; Fax: 570-454-9776.
Lay Teachers 10; Students 197. (Merged with Our Lady of Mount Carmel, Tyrolese.).
5—HOLY TRINITY, (1907) (Slovak), Rev. Leonard M. Butcavage; Deacon Louis Smolinsky.
Res., 178 N. Wyoming St., 18201. Tel: 570-454-3233; Fax: 570-454-0237. [CEM]
6—ST. JOSEPH'S, (1882) (Slovak), Rev. Msgr. Francis J. Beeda; Rev. Stephen A. Krawontka; Deacon Leonard G. Kassick.
Res., 604 N. Laurel St., 18201. Tel: 570-454-0881; Fax: 570-454-1285. [CEM]
School—600 N. Laurel St., 18201. Tel: 570-454-4411; Fax: 570-454-4411.
Sisters of SS. Cyril and Methodius 4; Lay Teachers 8; Students 195.
Mission—Hazleton, Luzerne Co., St. Ladislaus.
7—OUR LADY OF GRACE, (1910) (Italian), Rev. Msgr. Neil O. Gugliemelli.
Res., 750 N. Vine St., 18201. Tel: 570-454-8797. [CEM]
8—OUR LADY OF MOUNT CARMEL, (1905) (Tyrolese). Merged with Holy Trinity (German), Hazleton.
9—SS. PETER AND PAUL, (1887) (Lithuanian). Merged with Transfiguration, West Hazleton.
10—ST. STANISLAUS, (1893) (Polish), Rev. Louis S. Garbacik.
Res., 652 Carson St., 18201-4423. Tel: 570 454-0662; Fax: 570-454-0662. [CEM]

Honesdale, Wayne Co., St. John the Evangelist (1842), Very Rev. Kevin P. Mulhern, V.F.; Rev. Andrew R. Sinnott; Deacon Mark S. Jennings.
Res., 150 Terrace St., 18431. Tel: 570-253-4561; Fax: 570-253-1058. [CEM 3]
Mission—Rileyville, Wayne Co., St. Joseph.
Chapel—Honesdale, St. Mary Magdalene, (1853).

Hudson, Luzerne Co., St. Joseph's (1889) (Polish), Rev. Msgr. David L. Tressler.
Res., 25 Oak St., (Hudson), Wilkes-Barre, 18705. Tel: 570-823-0238; Fax: 570-822-0394. [CEM]
(Merged with Sacred Heart, Plains.).

Hughestown, Luzerne Co., Blessed Sacrament (1945), Rev. Thomas J. Maloney.
Res., 65 Rock St., 18640. Tel: 570-654-6553; Fax: 570-654-0466.

Inkerman, Luzerne Co., St. Mark's (1900), Rev. Edward M. Masakowski.
Res., 1 St. Mark Ln., 18640. Tel: 570-654-0033.

Jackson, Susquehanna Co., St. Martin of Tours (1940), Very Rev. Thomas A. Cappelloni, V.F.
Res., P.O. Box 20, 18825. Tel: 570-756-2541; Fax: 570-756-2105.
Mission—Starrucca, Wayne Co., St. Paul.

Jermyn, Lackawanna Co., Sacred Heart of Mary (1889), Very Rev. James J. Walsh, V.F.
Res., 624 Madison Ave., 18433. Tel: 570-876-1061; Fax: 570-876-2493. [CEM]

Jersey Shore, Lycoming Co., St. Luke's (1902), Rev. Andrew S. Hvozdovic.
Res., 118 Kendall Ave., 17740. Tel: 570-398-2557; Fax: 570-398-0126.

Jessup, Lackawanna Co., St. Mary's Assumption (1904) (Italian), Rev. Andrew R. Gallia.
Res., 516 Third Ave., 18434. Tel: 570-489-4726. [CEM]
St. James (1899), Very Rev. William B. Blake, V.F. In res., Rev. Joseph A. Matz; Deacon John Hatala.
Res., 605 Church St., 18434. Tel: 570-489-2252; Fax: 570-489-2527. [CEM]
(Merged with St. Michael, Jessup).
Mission—Jessup, Lackawanna Co., St. Stanislaus.

Kingston, Luzerne Co., St. Hedwig's (1901) (Polish), Rev. Richard A. Zavacki.
Res., 207 Zerbey Ave., 18704. Tel: 570-287-5634; Fax: 570-287-8566. [CEM]
School—16 Pulaski St., 18704. Tel: 570-288-6051.
Lay Teachers 8; Students 110.
St. Ignatius (1885), Rev. Msgr. Neil J. VanLoon, V.F.; Rev. Thomas J. Petro; Deacon John E. O'Connor.
Res., 339 N. Maple Ave., 18704. Tel: 570-288-6446; Fax: 570-288-0463. [CEM]
Chapel—St. Ann's, Tel: 570-288-5919.
St. Mary's Annunciation (1902) (Lithuanian), Rev. Msgr. Joseph J. Lasky.
Res., 258 Zerbey Ave., 18704. Tel: 570-287-5096; Fax: 570-283-0162.

Laflin, Luzerne Co., St. Maria Goretti (1967), Very Rev. James J. Paisley, V.F.
Res., 42 Redwood Dr., 18702. Tel: 570-655-8956; Fax: 570-655-1746.

Lake Ariel, Wayne Co., St. Thomas More (1941). Merged with St. Martha's, Fairmount Springs. Rev. Edward R. Scott.
Mailing Address: Box 188, 18436. Tel: 570-698-5584; Fax: 570-698-8468. [CEM]
Mission—Ledgedale, Wayne Co., St. Mary.

Lake Silkworth, Luzerne Co., Our Lady of Mount Carmel (1923), Rev. Thomas R. Hudak; Deacon Frank J. Sehn.
Res., R.R. 2, Box 265, Lake Silkworth, Hunlock Creek, 18621. Tel: 570-477-5040. [CEM]
(Merged with St. Martha's, Fairmount Springs.).

Lake Winola, Wyoming Co., St. Mary of the Lake (1986), Rev. Jeffrey J. Walsh; Deacon Raymond A. Pieretti.
Res., P.O. Box 1, Fairview Rd., 18625. Tel: 570-378-2181; Fax: 570-378-3948.

Larksville, Luzerne Co., St. Anthony of Padua (1908) (Slovak), Rev. Bernard P. Evanofski.
Res., 1 Wilson St., 18704. Tel: 570-287-4018. [CEM]
(Merged with SS. Cyril and Methodius, Edwardsville).

Lattimer Mines, Luzerne Co., St. Mary's (1903) (Italian). Merged with St. Nazarius, Pardeesville.

Little Meadows, Susquehanna Co., St. Thomas the Apostle (1887). Merged with St. Francis Xavier, Friendsville.

Lords Valley, Pike Co., St. John Neumann (1976), Rev. Gerard L. Hawley; Deacons John Nash; Philip Bouwmann.
Res., Lords Valley, HC8, Box 8390, Hawley, 18428. Tel: 570-775-6791; Fax: 570-775-1527.
Mission—Blooming Grove, Good Shepherd.

Luzerne, Luzerne Co.,

1—HOLY FAMILY, (1999), Rev. Robert P. Arnold.
Res., Rear 574 Bennett St., P.O. Box 125, 18709. Tel: 570-287-6600.
School—469 Miller St., 18709. Tel: 570-287-3431.
Sisters of Christian Charity 2; Lay Teachers 6; Students 156.

2—SACRED HEART CHURCH, (1893) (German). Closed. For inquiries for parish records contact Holy Family, Luzerne.

3—ST. ANN'S, (1924) (Lithuanian). Merged with Holy Family, Luzerne.

4—ST. JOHN NEPOMUCENE, (1907) (Slovak). Merged with Holy Family, Luzerne.

Mansfield, Tioga Co., Holy Child (1953), Rev. Louis T. Kaminski.
Res., 237 S. Main St., 16933. Tel: 570-662-3568; Fax: 570-662-2113.
Mission—Tioga, Tioga Co., St. Mary, Center St., Tioga 16946. Tel: 570-835-9697.

Matamoras, Pike Co., St. Joseph's (1892), Rev. John J. Turi.
Res., 309 Ave. F, 18336. Tel: 570-491-2618; Fax: 570-491-4404.
Mission—Mill Rift, Pike Co., Holy Family, Cemetery Rd., Mill Rift 18340.

Mayfield, Lackawanna Co., Sacred Heart of Jesus (1904) (Polish), Rev. Joseph S. Sitko.
Res., 420 Hudson St., 18433. Tel: 570-876-1950. [CEM]

Meshoppen, Wyoming Co., St. Joachim's (1873), Rev. Joseph J. Manarchuck.
Res., P.O. Box 67, 18630. Tel: 570-833-2114; Fax: 570-833-2115. [CEM]
Mission—Auburn, Susquehanna Co., St. Bonaventure. [CEM]

Mildred, Sullivan Co., St. Francis of Assisi (1894). Merged with St. Basil, Dushore.
Missions—Eagles Mere, Sullivan Co., St. Francis of Assisi; Laporte, Sullivan Co., Sacred Heart.

Milford, Pike Co., St. Patrick's (1946), Rev. Gerald F. Mullally.
Res., 111 E. High St., P.O. Box W, 18337. Tel: 570-296-7451; Fax: 570-296-7451.
St. Vincent de Paul (1976), Rev. Msgr. William P. Ward; Deacons Albert W. Perreault; Joseph A. LaCorte.
Res., 101 St. Vincent Dr., 18337-9672. Tel: 570-686-4545; Fax: 1-800-565-1762.

Mocanaqua, Luzerne Co., St. Mary, Our Lady of Perpetual Help (1904) (Polish), Rev. Thomas D. Skotek.
Res., 150 Main St., 18655. Tel: 570-542-4157; Fax: 570-542-4158. [CEM]

Montdale, Lackawanna Co., Corpus Christi (1942), Rev. William J. Flynn, S.S.
Res., R.R. 1, Box 389, Olyphant, 18447. Tel: 570-254-9502; Fax: 570-254-6233.

Montoursville, Lycoming Co., Our Lady of Lourdes (1942), Rev. Thomas P. Shoback.
Res., 800 Mulberry St., 17754. Tel: 570-368-8598; Fax: 570-368-2912.

Montrose, Susquehanna Co., Holy Name of Mary (1898), Rev. James R. Nash.
Res., 60 S. Main St., 18801. Tel: 570-278-1504; Fax: 570-278-1504. [CEM]

Moscow, Lackawanna Co., St. Catherine of Siena (1861), Rev. Michael E. Finn; Deacon John J. Franceschelli.
Res., 220 Church St., P.O. Box 250, 18444. Tel: 570-842-4561; Fax: 570-842-6648.

Mount Pocono, Monroe Co., St. Mary of the Mount (1909), Rev. Msgr. Arthur J. Kaschenbach.
Res., 27 Fairview Ave., 18344. Tel: 570-839-7138.
Mission—Pocono Summit, Monroe Co., St. Joan of Arc.

Mountaintop, Luzerne Co., St. Jude's (1953), Rev. Paul M. Mullen; Deacon Eugene J. Kovatch.
Res., 420 S. Mountain Blvd., 18707. Tel: 570-474-6315; Fax: 570-474-0775.
School—Tel: 570-474-5803.
Lay Teachers 24; Students 426.

Muncy, Lycoming Co., Resurrection (1941), Rev. David P. Cappelloni.
Res., 526 S. Main St., 17756. Tel: 570-546-3900; Fax: 570-546-5272.

Nanticoke, Luzerne Co.,

1—HOLY CHILD, (1942) (Polish). Merged with Holy Trinity (Polish), Nanticoke.

2—HOLY TRINITY, (1894) (Polish), Rev. Msgr. Bernard A. Toloczko; Rev. Joseph F. Orloski.
Res., 520 S. Hanover St., 18634-2799. Tel: 570-735-4834; Fax: 570-735-2281. [CEM]

3—ST. FRANCIS OF ASSISI, (1872), Rev. William J.P. Langan.
Res., 173 E. Green St., 18634. Tel: 570-735-6903; 735-7011; Fax: 570-735-6903. [CEM]

4—ST. JOSEPH'S, (1888) (Slovak), Rev. Leo M. Gardzalla.
Res., 107 E. Noble St., 18634. Tel: 570-735-0331. [CEM]

5—ST. MARY OF CZESTOCHOWA, (1901) (Polish), Rev. John S. Krafchak.
Res., 1030 S. Hanover St., 18634. Tel: 570-735-6911. [CEM]

6—ST. STANISLAUS, (1875) (Polish), Rev. Joseph R. Kakareka.
Res., 38 W. Church St., 18634. Tel: 570-735-0313; Fax: 570-735-2123. [CEM]

Nicholson, Wyoming Co., St. Patrick's (1888), Rev. John V. Polednak.
Res., 100 Main St., 18446. Tel: 570-942-6602. [CEM]

Old Forge, Lackawanna Co.,

1—ST. LAWRENCE O'TOOLE, (1895), Rev. Michael J. Kirwin.
Res., 620 S. Main St., 18518. Tel: 570-457-2032.

2—ST. MARY'S, (1897) (Italian), Revs. Joseph F. Cipriano; Stanley J. Kurash.
Res., 123 W. Grace St., 18518. Tel: 570-457-5900.
School—216 W. Grace St., 18518. Tel: 570-457-6750.
Sisters 2; Lay Teachers 10; Students 180.

3—ST. MICHAEL'S, (1905) (Polish), Rev. Joseph M. Brozena.
Res., 236 Vine St., 18518. Tel: 570-457-3353.

4—ST. STANISLAUS, (1903) (Polish), Very Rev. Cyril J. Rable, V.F.
Res., 1267 Franklin St., 18518. Tel: 570-457-5103. [CEM]

Olyphant, Lackawanna Co., Holy Ghost (1888) (Slovak). Merged with St. Patrick's Church, Olyphant.
Convent—126 Willow Ave., 18447. Tel: 570-489-0792. Sisters of SS. Cyril and Methodius
St. Michael the Archangel (1909) (Polish), Rev. Kenneth G. Kizis.
Res., 132 Lincoln St., 18447. Tel: 570-489-0623. [CEM]
St. Patrick's (1875). Merged with Holy Ghost (Slovak), Olyphant. Revs. Phillip J. Sladicka; Scott P. Sterowski.
Res., 200 Delaware Ave., 18447. Tel: 570-489-0752; Fax: 570-489-0225. [CEM]

Pardeesville, Luzerne Co., St. Nazarius (1966) (Italian), Rev. Joseph W. Bucolo.
Res., R.D. 2, P3D3, Hazleton, 18201. Tel: 570-454-2469; Fax: 570-454-4296. (Merged with St. Mary, Lattimer Mines).

Peckville, Lackawanna Co., Sacred Heart of Jesus (1946), Revs. Santino J. Fanucci; Joseph J. Fanti.
Res., 1101 Willow St., 18452. Tel: 570-383-3244; Fax: 570-383-8697.

Pittston, Luzerne Co.,

1—OUR LADY OF MT. CARMEL, (1904) (Italian), Rev. Paul A. McDonnell, O.S.J.
Res., 237 William St., 18640. Tel: 570-654-6902.

2—ST. CASIMIR'S, (1890) (Lithuanian). Merged with St. John the Evangelist, Pittston.

3—ST. JOHN THE BAPTIST, (1892) (Slovak), Rev. Andrew F. Strish.
Res., 16 William St., 18640. Tel: 570-654-2112; Fax: 570-654-4210. [CEM 2]
School—12 William St., 18640. Tel: 570-654-0845. Robert Kaluzavich, Prin.
Lay Teachers 9; Students 225.

4—ST. JOHN THE EVANGELIST, (1854), Rev. Msgr. John J. Bendik; Revs. Frank S. Homets; Bryan B. Wright. In res., Rev. Hugh H. McGroarty.
Res., 35 William St., 18640. Tel: 570-654-0053; Fax: 570-654-3751. [CEM]
(Merged with St. Casimir and St. Joseph, Pittston).

5—ST. JOSEPH'S, (1909) (Polish). Merged with St. John the Evangelist, Pittston.

6—ST. MARY, HELP OF CHRISTIANS, (1851), Rev. Richard J. Polmounter.
Res., 535 N. Main St., 18640. Tel: 570-654-0263; Fax: 570-654-0195. [CEM]

7—ST. MARY'S ASSUMPTION, (1863) (German). Merged with St. Mary, Help of Christians, Pittson.
School—41 Carroll St., 18640. Tel: 570-654-8313; Fax: 570-654-8320.
Sisters of Christian Charity 2; Lay Teachers 10; Students 267.

8—ST. ROCCO, (1919) (Italian), Rev. Joseph D. Sibilano, O.S.J.
Res., 62 W. Oak St., 18640. Tel: 570-654-2914; Fax: 570-654-1614. [CEM]

Plains, Luzerne Co., Sacred Heart (1883), Rev. Msgr. David L. Tressler.
Res., 25 Oak St., Hudson, 18705-3499. Tel: 570-823-0238. (Merged with St. Joseph's, Hudson.).
SS. Peter and Paul (1898) (Polish), Rev. Joseph A. Greskiewicz.
Res., 13 Hudson Rd., 18705. Tel: 570-825-6663; Fax: 570-823-4556. [CEM]
School—15 Hudson St., 18705. Tel: 570-824-9433.
Lay Teachers 10; Students 204.

Pleasant Mount, Wayne Co., St. James (1887), Rev. Richard W. Beck.
Res., P.O. Box 53, 18453. Tel: 570-448-2211.
Missions—Hill Top, Wayne Co., St. Cecilia; Lake Como, Wayne Co., Assumption of the B.V.M.

Plymouth, Luzerne Co.,

1—NATIVITY OF THE BLESSED VIRGIN MARY, (1885) (Polish), Rev. Msgr. Vincent J. Grimalia, V.F.; Rev. Anthony J. Generose; Deacons Leo R. Thompson; Peter Smith.
Res., 66 Willow St., 18651. Tel: 570-779-5324; Fax: 570-779-4921. [CEM 2]

2—ST. JOHN THE BAPTIST, (1899) (Polish), Rev. Gerald J. Gurka.
Res., 126 Nesbitt St., (Larksville), 18651. Tel: 570-779-9620. [CEM]

3—ST. STEPHEN'S, (1886) (Slovak). Merged with Nativity of the Blessed Virgin Mary, Plymouth.

4—ST. VINCENT DE PAUL, (1872), Rev. Joseph F. Houston; Deacon Peter G. Smith.
Res., 101 Church St., 18651. Tel: 570-779-9508; Fax: 570-779-2332. [CEM]

Pocono Pines, Monroe Co., Our Lady of the Lake (1985), Rev. John B. Boyle.
Res., P.O. Box 0, 18350. Tel: 570-646-6424; Fax: 570-646-1047.

Rock Lake, Wayne Co., St. Juliana's (1838). Merged with St. James, Pleasant Mount.
P.O. Box 53, Pleasant Mount, 18453. Tel: 570-448-2211.

Royal, Susquehanna Co., St. Pius X (1967), Rev. Peter V. Herhenreader.
Res., Box 64, Clifford, 18413. Tel: 570-222-4209.

Sayre, Bradford Co., Church of the Epiphany (1888), Revs. William J. Karle; Jacek Bialkowski.
Res., 304 S. Elmer Ave., 18840. Tel: 570-888-9641.
School—627 Stevenson St., 18840. Tel: 570-888-5802.
Sisters of I.H.M. 2; Lay Teachers 10; Students 186.

Shavertown, Luzerne Co., St. Therese (1926), Rev. Msgr. J. Peter Crynes.
Res., 64 Davis St., 18708. Tel: 570-696-1144; Fax: 570-696-1210.

Shohola, Pike Co., St. Ann's (1928), Rev. David W. Cramer.
Res., P.O. Box 86, 18458. Tel: 570-559-7642; Fax: 570-559-7499. [CEM]
Missions—Lackawaxen, Pike Co., St. Mary; Greeley, Pike Co., Sacred Heart.

Simpson, Lackawanna Co., St. Michael's (1903), Rev. Hilary L. Malinowski.
Res., 46 Midland St., 18407. Tel: 570-282-2161. [CEM]

South Waverly, Bradford Co., St. John the Evangelist (1902), Rev. Vincent F. Langan.
Res., 85 Division St., 18840-2847. Tel: 570-888-2123.

South Williamsport, Lycoming Co., St. Lawrence's (1931), Rev. Francis L. Pauselli.
Res., 344 Winthrop St., 17701. Tel: 570-322-0403; Fax: 570-322-4335.

Stroudsburg, Monroe Co., St. Luke's (1968), Revs. Thomas D. McLaughlin; Carmen J. Perry.
Office: 818 Main St., 18360. Tel: 570-421-9097; 421-9863; Fax: 570-421-6015.
Res., 906 Main St., 18360. Tel: 570-421-8460; Fax: 570-421-6015.

Sugar Notch, Luzerne Co., Holy Family (1901) (Polish), Very Rev. John S. Terry, V.F.; Deacon Philip Harris.
Office: 828 Main St., 18706. Tel: 570-822-8983; Fax: 570-822-6016. [CEM]
(Merged with St. Charles, Borromeo.).
SS. Peter and Paul (1847) (Lithuanian). Merged with Holy Family, Sugar Notch.

Susquehanna, Susquehanna Co., St. John the Evangelist (1847), Rev. Charles P. Connor.
Res., 101 Jackson Ave., 18847. Tel: 570-853-4634; Fax: 570-853-3356. [CEM]

Swoyersville, Luzerne Co.,

1—Holy Name of Jesus, (1905). Merged with St. Mary of Czestochowa, Swoyersville.

2—Holy Name/St. Mary's, Rev. Louis A. Grippe; Deacon George Mochin.
Res., 283 Shoemaker St. (P.O. Kingston), 18704. Tel: 570-287-2139; Fax: 570-287-6474. [CEM]

3—Holy Trinity, (1895) (Slovak), Rev. Michael J. Zipay.
Res., 116 Hughes St. (P.O. Kingston), 18704. Tel: 570-287-6624. [CEM]

4—St. Mary of Czestochowa, (1909). Merged with Holy Name of Jesus, Swoyersville.

Tannersville, Monroe Co., Our Lady of Victory (1968), Rev. Richard E. Czachor.
Res., Rte. 611, 18372. Tel: 570-629-4572; Fax: 570-629-5325.

Taylor, Lackawanna Co., Immaculate Conception (1898), Rev. Philip A. Altavilla.
Mailing Address: 408 N. Main St., 18517.
202 Church St., 18517. Tel: 570-562-2390; 562-1341; Fax: 570-562-2807. (Merged with St. John the Baptist, Taylor.).
St. John the Baptist (1904) (Slovak),
408 N. Main St., 18517. Tel: 570-562-1341; Fax: 570-562-2807. (Merged with Immaculate Conception, Taylor.).

Throop, Lackawanna Co., St. Anthony's (1911) (Polish). Merged with St. Bridget's and St. John the Baptist, Throop. Rev. August A. Ricciardi.
Office: 215 Rebecca St., 18519. Tel: 570-489-1963. [CEM]
Res., 520 Charles St., 18512. Tel: 570-489-1682.
St. Bridget's (1916). Merged with St. John the Baptist & St. Anthony's, Throop. Rev. August A. Ricciardi.
Office: 520 Sanderson St., 18512. Tel: 570-489-1682.
Res., 520 Charles St., 18512.
St. John the Baptist (1905) (Slovak). Merged with St. Bridget's and St. Anthony's, Throop. Rev. August A. Ricciardi.
Office: 520 Sanderson St., 18512. Tel: 570-489-1822. [CEM]
Res., 520 Charles St., 18512. Tel: 570-489-1682.

Tobyhanna, Monroe Co., St. Ann (1923), Rev. Michael J. Kloton; Deacon Michael Squillante.
Res., Main St., P.O. Box 188, 18466-0188. Tel: 570-894-8018; Fax: 570-894-9619. [CEM 2]

Towanda, Bradford Co., SS. Peter and Paul (1841), Very Rev. Ronald J. Hughes, V.F.
Res., 106 Third St., 18848. Tel: 570-265-2113; Fax: 570-265-2114. [CEM 3]
School—St. Agnes, 102 Third St., 18848. Tel: 570-265-6803; Fax: 570-265-3065.
Lay Teachers 10; Students 203.
Mission—Ulster, Bradford Co., Immaculate Conception, Tel: 570-358-3558.

Tunkhannock, Wyoming Co., Nativity of Blessed Virgin Mary (1884), Rev. Joseph M. Ziobro; Deacon Patrick Cooney.
Res., 99 E. Tioga St., 18657. Tel: 570-836-3275; Fax: 570-836-4268. [CEM 2]

Wanamie, Luzerne Co., St. Mary's (1906) (Lithuanian), Rev. Carl T. Prushinski.
Res., c/o 31 S. Market St., Glen Lyon, 18617. Tel: 570-736-6372. [CEM]
(Merged with St. Adalbert, St. Denis and St. Michael, Glen Lyon).
Mission—Nanticoke, Luzerne Co., St. Joseph.

Waymart, Wayne Co., St. Mary's (1915), Rev. John T. Albosta.
Res., 242 Carbondale Rd., P.O. Box 160, 18472. Tel: 570-488-6440; Fax: 570-488-7440. [CEM]
Mission—Canaan, Wayne Co., St. Patrick.

Wellsboro, Tioga Co., St. Peter's (1879), Rev. Michael J. Sullivan.
Res., 38 Central Ave., 16901. Tel: 570-724-3371; Fax: 570-724-6322. [CEM 2]
Mission—Morris, Tioga Co., Sacred Heart.

West Hazleton, Luzerne Co., St. Francis of Assisi (1940), Rev. Connell A. McHugh.
Res., 544 N. Broad St., 18201. Tel: 570-454-3072.
Mission—Harwood, Luzerne Co., St. Michael.
Transfiguration (1907) (Polish), Rev. Robert M. Timchak.
Res., 213 W. Green St., 18201. Tel: 570-454-3933; Fax: 570-454-8326. [CEM]
School—217 W. Green St., 18201. Tel: 570-454-6131.
Bernardine Sisters of St. Francis 4; Lay Teachers 9; Students 160.

Weston, Luzerne Co., Sacred Heart (1888), Rev. Patrick D. McDowell.
Res., P.O. Box A, 18256. Tel: 570-384-4121; Fax: 570-384-3976. [CEM]
Mission—Nuremberg, Luzerne Co., St. Joseph.

West Pittston, Luzerne Co., Immaculate Conception (1910), Rev. Michael J. Piccola.
Res., 605 Luzerne Ave., 18643. Tel: 570-654-2753; Fax: 570-654-9244.

West Wyoming, Luzerne Co., Our Lady of Sorrows (1953), Rev. Michael J. Rafferty.
Res., 363 W. 8th St., 18644. Tel: 570-693-1991.

White Haven, Luzerne Co., St. Patrick's (1874), Rev. Stephen J. Stavoy.
Res., 580 Elmira St., 18661. Tel: 570-443-9944; Fax: 570-443-9777. [CEM]
Station—White Haven Center, Tel: 570-453-9564.

White Mills, Wayne Co., St. Joseph's (1968), Rev. Michael H. Marchetti.
Mailing Address: Box 153, 18473. Tel: 570-253-0307; Fax: 570-253-0314.
Mission—Beach Lake, Wayne Co., St. Bernard, Tel: 570-729-7247.

Wilkes-Barre, Luzerne Co.,

1—St. Aloysius, (1899), Rev. Msgr. Donald A. McAndrews; Revs. Thomas J. Major; Paul Eruva; Deacon James Calderone.
Res., 143 W. Division St., 18702. Tel: 570-823-3791; Fax: 570-826-0233.
School—321 Barney St., 18702. Tel: 570-824-6131; Fax: 570-824-1643.
Lay Teachers 14; Students 210.

2—Blessed Sacrament, (1917), Rev. Joseph A. Kearney.
Res., 213 E. Main St., 18705. Tel: 570-822-9561; Fax: 570-822-4347. [CEM]
Station—Wilkes-Barre, Geisinger Wyoming Valley Hospital, Tel: 570-826-7300. (Merged with St. Francis of Assisi and St. John the Baptist.).

3—St. Boniface, (1896) (German), Rev. Msgr. Bernard E. Yarrish; Deacon Francis J. Bradigan.
Res., 225 Blackman St., 18702. Tel: 570-822-8330; Fax: 570-819-4125.

4—St. Casimir's, (1889) (Lithuanian), Rev. James F. Boyle, C.S.C. In res., Bro. Richard Kyle, C.S.C.
Res., 301 Delaney St., Lyndwood, Wilkes-Barre, 18702. Tel: 570-825-2598. [CEM]

5—St. Dominic, (1882), Rev. William R. Culnane.
Res., 155 Austin Ave., 18705. Tel: 570-822-8871.

6—St. Francis of Assisi, (1913) (Lithuanian). Merged with St. John the Baptist and Blessed Sacrament, Wilkes-Barre.

7—Holy Rosary, (1906) (Italian), Rev. Peter D. Menghini.
Res., 363 Park Ave., 18702. Tel: 570-822-1183.

8—Holy Saviour, (1895), Very Rev. E. Francis Kelly, V.F.; Deacon Carl J. Orbon.
Res., 54 Hillard St., 18702. Tel: 570-822-1186; Fax: 570-822-1074.

9—Holy Trinity, (1893) (Lithuanian), Rev. Theodore L. Obaza.
Res., 416 E. South St., 18702. Tel: 570-823-1081. [CEM 2]

10—St. John the Evangelist, (1927). Merged with Sacred Heart of Jesus, Wilkes-Barre.

11—St. John the Baptist, (1924) (Slovak). Merged with Blessed Sacrament and St. Francis of Assisi, Wilkes-Barre.

12—St. Joseph, (Georgetown) (1898), Revs. Francis M. McHugh, O.F.M.; Raymond J. Lynch, O.F.M. In res., Rev. Benjamin J. Foerch, O.F.M.
Res., St. Joseph's Friary, 783 E. Northampton St., 18702. Tel: 570-822-8023; Fax: 570-822-2891.

13—St. Joseph's, (1927) (Slovak). Merged with St. Mary's Church of the Immaculate Conception, Wilkes-Barre.

14—St. Mary's Church of the Immaculate Conception, (1845), Rev. Msgr. Thomas V. Banick; Rev. Vincent Dang.
Res., P.O. Box 348, 134 S. Washington St., 18703-0348. Tel: 570-823-4168; Fax: 570-822-3477. [CEM]

15—Maternity of the Blessed Virgin Mary, (1885) (Polish), Rev. Msgr. Alexander T. Kulik; Deacon Andrew F. Stoshak.
Res., 40 Park Ave., 18702. Tel: 570-824-7832. [CEM 2]

16—St. Nicholas, (1856) (German), Rev. Msgr. Joseph G. Rauscher; Rev. Peter J. O'Rourke. In res., Rev. Francis P. Skitski.
Res., 226 S. Washington St., 18701-2897. Tel: 570-823-7736; 823-5842; Fax: 570-823-0256. [CEM 2]

17—St. Patrick's, (1920), Very Rev. J. Duane Gavitt, V.F.
Res., 316 Parrish St., 18702. Tel: 570-823-1948.

18—Sacred Heart-St. John, (1896) (Slovak), Rev. Msgr. John J. Sempa; Rev. Joseph T. Gilbert; Deacons Joseph F. DeVizia; Pete Hoegen; Sr. Therese Marie, Pastoral Assoc.
Res., 601 N. Main St., 18705-1794. Tel: 570-823-4988; Fax: 570-823-5932. [CEM]
(merged with St. John the Evangelist, Wilkes-Barre).
School—607 N. Main St., 18705. Tel: 570-824-0818.
Sisters of SS. Cyril and Methodius 3; Lay Teachers 12; Students 232.

19—St. Stanislaus Kostka, (1908) (Polish), Rev. Joseph M. Horanzy.
Res., 666 N. Main St., 18705. Tel: 570-822-8026. [CEM]

20—St. Therese's, (1929), Rev. Msgr. Francis J. Callahan; Rev. James J. Alco. In res., Rev. George A. Jeffrey.
Res., 25 Old River Rd., 18702. Tel: 570-822-1075; 824-3052; Fax: 570-829-4147.

Williamsport, Lycoming Co.,

1—Annunciation, (1865), Revs. John K. Manno; Nicholas E. Nnabuaku, C.S.Sp.; John M. Kita; Deacon J. Morris Smith.
Res., 410 Walnut St., 17701. Tel: 570-323-9456; Fax: 570-323-3728. [CEM]
School—711 W. Edwin St., 17701. Tel: 570-322-6036, 322-2754; Fax: 570-322-1479.
Sisters of I.H.M. 3; Lay Teachers 8; Students 161.

2—Ascension, (1907), Rev. Charles J. Cummings.
Office: 2100 Linn St., 17701. Tel: 570-326-4922.
Res., 2111 Linn St., 17701. Tel: 570-326-4922; Fax: 570-327-1196.

3—St. Boniface's, (1853) (German), Rev. Msgr. Stephen D. McGough; Rev. Paul Ines, S.D.B.; Deacon Clair J. Raisch.
Res., 326 Washington Blvd., 17701. Tel: 570-326-1544; Fax: 570-326-6746.
School—710 Franklin St., 17701. Tel: 570-326-3738; Fax: 570-326-7385.
Sisters of Christian Charity 1; Lay Teachers 11; Students 187.

4—Holy Rosary, (1915) (Polish), Rev. Andrew J. Krusinski.
Res., 313 Arch St., 17701. Tel: 570-323-6316.

5—Mater Dolorosa, (1908) (Italian), Rev. Msgr. Francis J. Castellano, V.F.
Res., 635 Hepburn St., 17701. Tel: 570-326-9769; Fax: 570-327-8141.

6—St. Ann's, (1959), Rev. Andrew Kurovsky.
Res., 1220 Northway Rd., 17701. Tel: 570-322-5935; Fax: 570-322-2451.
School—1225 Northway Rd., 17701. Tel: 570-323-0500.
Sisters of Christian Charity 1; Lay Teachers 8; Students 200.
Mission—Cascade, Lycoming Co., Assumption of the B.V.M.

Wyalusing, Bradford Co., St. Mary's Assumption (1950), Rev. Kenneth M. Seegar.
Parish Office & Mailing Address: R.R. 4, Box 4003, 18853. Tel: 570-746-1006.
Res., 200 Front St., 18853.
Mission—Stowell, Wyoming Co., St. Anthony.

Wyoming, Luzerne Co., St. Joseph's (1914) (Polish), Rev. Walter F. Skiba.
Res., 97 E. Sixth St., 18644. Tel: 570-693-0510. [CEM]

Chaplains of Public Institutions

Clarks Summit. *Clarks Summit State Hospital*. Attended by Our Lady of the Snows, Clarks Summit. Tel: 570-586-1741. 18411.

Dallas. *State Correctional Institution* 18612. Tel: 570-675-1101. Deacon Jose A. Munoz.

East Stroudsburg. *East Stroudsburg State University* P.O. Box 331, 18301. Tel: 570-476-0321; Fax: 570-422-3777. Joan Fabian, Campus Min.

La Plume. *Keystone Junior College*. Rev. Joseph F. Sica, Clarks Summit. Tel: 570-586-1741.

Muncy. *Muncy Prison* Tel: 570-546-3900. Rev. David P. Cappelloni, Chap., Res., Resurrection Rectory, 526 S. Main St., 17756.

WILKES-BARRE. *Geisinger Wyoming Valley Hospital* Tel: 570-822-9561. Rev. Joseph A. Kearney, Res., Blessed Sacrament Rectory, 213 E. Main St., 18705.
Veteran's Administration Hospital Tel: 570-824-3521. Rev. Benjamin J. Foerch, O.F.M., Chap., Res., St. Joseph's Friary, 783 E. Northampton St., 18702.

WILLIAMSPORT. *Lycoming College* 700 College Pl., Box 149, 17701. Tel: 570-321-4111. Sr. Catherine Ann Gilvary, I.H.M., Campus Min.

On Special or Other Diocesan Assignment:
Reverend Monsignors—
McGowan, Andrew J., Dir., Catholic Health Care Facilities & Rep., Catholic Institutions of Higher Learning, Mercy Hospital, Scranton, PA 18501. Tel: 570-348-7010
Reverend Fathers—
Finn, Edward S., Chap., R.D. #1, Box 310A, Equinunk, PA 18417. Tel: 717-224-4380
Quinnan, Michael F., Sabbatical Leave
Yaszcz, Thomas A., 52 W. Grove St., Nanticoke, PA 18634. Tel: 570-735-8754, Ext. 315

On Duty Outside the Diocese:
Reverend Monsignors—
Jordan, John J., Save Our Schools, Inc., NCEA, 1077 30th St., N.W., Washington, D.C. 20007-3852. Tel: 202-378-5767
Reverend Fathers—
Doherty, Daniel J., Society of St. Sulpice, St. Mary's Seminary & University, 5400 Roland Ave., Baltimore, MD 21210-1994. Tel: 410-864-4258
Fives, Carl J., Mt. St. Mary's College, Emmitsburg, MD 21727. Tel: 301-447-6122
Gabuzda, Richard J., Dir., Institute for Priestly Formation, Kenefick #1208, 320 N. 20th St., Omaha, NE 68178. Tel: 402-546-6384
Gregoris, Nicholas L., North American College, Vatican City, 00120 Italy. Tel: 011-39-06-690-011
Kilpatrick, Andrew W., North American College, Vatican City, Italy 00120. Tel: 011-39-06-690-011
McGlone, Gerard M., Congregation of the Passion
McKernan, Leo J., Chap., Gonzaga University, c/o Bp. White Seminary, 429 E. Sharp Ave., Spokane, WA 99202-1837. Tel: 509-323-4243 (office); 509-325-6471 (residence)
Rossetti, Mark T., St. Paul's Church, 82 Lake Rd. W., Congers, NY 10920. Tel: 914-268-4464
Rossi, Walter R., Assoc. Rector & Dir., Pilgrimages, Basilica of the National Shrine of the Immaculate Conception, 400 Michigan Ave., N.E., Washington, DC, 20017. Tel: 202-526-8300
Walsh, John A., 14710 County Rd. 561A, Clermont, FL 34711-8789
Waznak, Robert J., S.S., Society of St. Sulpice
Wysocki, Joseph A., 5424 Burling Rd., Bethesda, MD 20014

Military Chaplains:
Reverend Fathers—
Dormer, David J., Chap. Major, U.S. Army, 9081 A Nancy Rd., Ft. Drum, NY 13603
Ferretti, Samuel J., Chap., U.S. Navy, PSG 482, Box 2441, FPO AP, 96362-2441
Hochreiter, Robert S., Chap., Lt. Col., U.S.A.F., 1755 Chennault Circle, Apt. B, San Antonio, TX 78226. Tel: 210-925-7874
Kelly, Brian F., Chap., U.S.N., USN Dept., USS Carl Vinson (CVN 70), FPO AP, 96629-2840. Tel: 360-476-3917
Motsay, Joseph R., Chap. Major, U.S.A.F., PSC 50, Box 778, APO AE, 09490
Petruska, William M., CHC, U.S.N., 307 Saddle Ridge Rd., Annapolis, MD 21403. Tel: 410-267-0073

Unassigned or Leave of Absence:
Reverend Fathers—
Gibson, Robert J.
Homer, Lawrence P.
Kringe, Charles J., 708 N. Broad St. W., West Hazleton, PA 18201. Tel: 717-454-1380
Kulik, Francis J.
McGee, James J., S.S.
McGlone, Gerard M.
Schaal, John K.

Retired:
Reverend Monsignors—
Casey, George T., P.O. Box 1578, Hollywood, FL 33022. Tel: 954-920-0681
Cawley, Thomas J., Villa St. Joseph, Dunmore, PA 18509. Tel: 570-343-2254
Clarke, James T., Villa St. Joseph, Dunmore, PA 18509. Tel: 570-969-1235
Demuth, George R., Holy Family Pavilion, 2510 Adams Ave., Apt. 303, Scranton, PA 18509-1597. Tel: 570-344-3719
Donovan, William L., Villa St. Joseph, Dunmore, PA 18509. Tel: 570-963-9383
Gajewski, Chester A., Villa St. Joseph, Dunmore, PA 18509. Tel: 570-347-1851
Gallagher, John P., Ph.D., 1026 Wheeler Ave., Scranton, PA 18510. Tel: 570-342-1991
Law, Joseph A., Hemlock Farms, Box 2170, Hawley, PA 18428. Tel: 570-775-0912
Masakowski, John C., 157 W. Church St., Nanticoke, PA 18634
Mecca, Mark A., St. Mary's Villa, Elmhurst, PA 18416. Tel: 570-842-7621
Meier, Joseph F., Villa St. Joseph, Dunmore, PA 18509. Tel: 570-346-3887
Norkunas, Anthony J., 253 S. Meade St., Wilkes-Barre, PA 18702. Tel: 570-824-6490
O'Brien, John J., Villa St. Joseph, Dunmore, PA 18509. Tel: 570-961-1865
Pakutka, William J., Villa St. Joseph, Dunmore, PA 18509. Tel: 570-341-9168
Penkala, Edmund S., Villa St. Joseph, Dunmore, PA 18509. Tel: 570-344-6288
Reverend Fathers—
Adonizio, Joseph J., 154 Rock St., Pittston, PA 18640. Tel: 570-654-8032
Alisauskas, Peter J., 366 Indian Lake Tr., White Haven, PA 18661. Tel: 570-472-3360
Bonner, Joseph P., 1077 Valley of the Lakes, Hazleton, PA 18201. Tel: 570-384-2575
Breslin, Joseph W., Villa St. Joseph, Dunmore, PA 18509. Tel: 570-341-3315
Brogus, Albert G., 43 James St., Plains, PA 18705
Burnett, Robert E., 158 Wyoming St., Carbondale, PA 18407. Tel: 570-282-1600
Carr, Eugene R., P.O.Box 1063, Killington, VT 05751. Tel: 802-422-3589
Casey, John W., P.O. Box 1578, Hollywood, FL 33022. Tel: 954-920-0681
Conboy, Joseph T., Villa St. Joseph, Dunmore, PA 18509. Tel: 570-941-9405
Cortese, Patrick S., 1007 Crossroad Ln., Hazleton, PA 18201. Tel: 570-459-5929
Delaney, T. Timothy, 180 Madison St., Wilkes-Barre, PA 18702. Tel: 570-824-5552
Domnick, Alphonsus M., T.O.R., Villa St. Joseph, Dunmore, PA 18509. Tel: 570-341-9176
Everling, Robert M., Villa St. Joseph, Dumore, PA 18509. Tel: 570-343-4925
Fabian, John L., Villa St. Joseph, Dunmore, PA 18509. Tel: 570-348-0728
Ferrara, Joseph J., 320 W. Mine St., Hazleton, PA 18201. Tel: 570-450-8355
Flannery, Joseph D., Villa St. Joseph, Dunmore, PA 18509. Tel: 570-347-8019
Flynn, Thomas A., Villa St. Joseph, Dunmore, PA 18509. Tel: 570-348-0589
Fox, Joseph F., 1706 Delaware St., Dunmore, PA 18509. Tel: 570-343-5522
Gaiardo, Martin J., Mulberry Tower, 499 Mulberry St., Apt. 1216, Scranton, PA 18503. Tel: 570-347-4826
Gallagher, Edward F., Villa St. Joseph, Dunmore, PA 18509. Tel: 570-348-6873
Hines, William F., 2461 S.W. 82nd Ave., Bldg. 2-Apt. 105, Ft. Lauderdale, FL 33324. Tel: 305-423-9301
Hlopko, John J., Lake Rd., P.O. Box 67, Bear Creek, PA 18602. Tel: 570-472-3483
Kalinowski, Stainslaus J., 3020 Cedar Ave., Scranton, PA 18505
Kelley, John J., Candlewood Park, 12 Hunter Rd., Hazleton, PA 18201. Tel: 570-450-0131
Langan, James J., 2420 S.W. 81st Ave., Arrowhead Condominium, Bldg. 7, Apt. 402, Davie, FL 33324
Lewis, Harry J., Villa St. Joseph, Dunmore, PA 18509. Tel: 570-343-5499
Maloney, Andrew P., P.O. Box 583, Mountainhome, PA 18342. Tel: 570-595-7679
Marinko, John S., Villa St. Joseph, Dunmore, PA 18509. Tel: 570-941-3446
Markowski, Clement A., Villa St. Joseph, Dunmore, PA 18509. Tel: 570-343-0555
Mulrooney, Charles F., Villa St. Joseph, Dunmore, PA 18509. Tel: 570-969-1305
Mulrooney, F. Harold, 1203 Schlager St., Scranton, PA 18504. Tel: 570-343-8704
Noviello, Anthony A., 301 Tallman Ave., South Williamsport, PA 17702. Tel: 570-323-6552
O'Haire, John A., Villa St. Joseph, Dunmore, PA 18509. Tel: 570-342-6865
Olszewski, Daniel D., 74 Pinewood Dr., Laflin, PA 18702. Tel: 570-655-2165
Pace, William J., Villa St. Joseph, Dunmore, PA 18509. Tel: 570-961-5856
Plevyak, Valentine R., Villa St. Joseph, Dunmore, PA 18509. Tel: 570-969-9109
Purcell, William F., Villa St. Joseph, Dunmore, PA 18509. Tel: 570-348-0695
Rusin, Joseph C., St. Mary's Rectory, P.O.Box 9038, Dickson City, PA 18519-0038. Tel: 570-489-2091
Ryan, Joseph F., P.O. Box 77, Pocono Summit, PA 18346. Tel: 570-839-9260
Sokolowski, Edward V., 3 Regina Dr., Mountaintop, PA 18707. Tel: 570-474-2269
Stalavicz, George P., Little Flower Manor, 200 S. Meade St., Wilkes-Barre, PA 18702
Ulrich, Carl G., Villa St. Joseph, Dunmore, PA 18509. Tel: 570-341-5898
Wayda, Henry A., St. Mary's Villa, Elmhurst, PA 18416. Tel: 570-842-7621
Zapotocki, Henry E., P.O. Box 847, Tannersville, PA 18372. Tel: 570-629-1235
Zawadzki, Victor C., 5 O'Donnell St., Wilkes-Barre, PA 18702. Tel: 570-819-1629
Zawodniak, Edward J., 25 Hickory Tree Rd., Loyalville, Dallas, PA 18612. Tel: 570-477-2086

INSTITUTIONS LOCATED IN THE DIOCESE

[A] SEMINARIES, DIOCESAN

DALTON. *Saint Pius X Seminary.* (Collaborative College/Pre-Theology Seminary), 1000 Seminary Rd., 18414. Tel: 570-563-1131; Fax: 570-563-8520. Rev. Msgr. David A. Bohr, S.T.D., Rector; Rev. Msgr. John A. Esseff, D.Min., M.A., S.T.L., Dir., Apostolic Formation; Revs. Jeffrey J. Walsh, M.A., Spiritual Dir. & Dir., Liturgical Formation; Joseph R. Kopacz, M.Div., M.A. Ph.D., Formation Advisor.
Non-Resident Faculty: Revs. Robert J. Barone, S.T.D.; Albert M. Liberatore, S.T.L.; James A. Rafferty, S.T.L., Academic Dean; Mr. Edward G. Mathews, Jr., M.A., M.Phil., Ph.D. Seminarians 17.

[B] SEMINARIES, RELIGIOUS

PITTSTON. *St. Joseph's Oblate Seminary*, 1880 Hwy. 315, 18640. Tel: 570-654-7542; Fax: 570-654-8621. Revs. Paul J. Pavese, O.S.J., Rector; Mario Buttini, O.S.J., Vice Rector; Joseph D. Sibilano, O.S.J.

[C] COLLEGES AND UNIVERSITIES

SCRANTON. *Marywood University*, 18509. Tel: 570-348-6211; Fax: 570-340-6014.
E-mail: mreap@ac.marywood.edu
Web site: www.marywood.edu
For a complete listing, refer to the Colleges and Universities section.
University of Scranton, 18510. Tel: 570-941-7533; Fax: 570-941-6340.
Web site: www.scranton.edu
For a complete listing, refer to the Colleges and Universities section.

DALLAS. *College Misericordia*, 18612. Tel: 570-674-6400; Fax: 570-675-2441.
Web site: www.miseri.edu
For a complete listing, refer to the Colleges and Universities section.

WILKES-BARRE. *Kings College*, 18711. Tel: 570-208-5900; Fax: 570-825-9046.
Web site: www.kings.edu
For a complete listing, refer to the Colleges and Universities section.

[D] HIGH SCHOOLS, DIOCESAN

SCRANTON. *Bishop Hannan High School*, 330 Wyoming Ave., 18503. Tel: 570-346-4643; Fax: 570-346-0048. Mr. James P. Marcks, Prin.; Rev. Thomas Sinnott, Dir., Religious Formation; Mr. Steve Coviello, Dean Students; Miss Christina Royce, Dean Academic Affairs. Priests 2; Sisters Servants of the Immaculate Heart of Mary 5; Lay Teachers 32; Students 417.

CARBONDALE. *Sacred Heart Junior / Senior High School*, 44 S. Church St., 18407. Tel: 570-282-2790; Fax: 570-282-2380.
Web site: superbrainiac.com
Sr. Margo McCormick, I.H.M., Prin.; Rev. James A. Rafferty, Dir., Religious Formation; Mr. Charles Barlow, Dean of Students. Priests 1; Sisters 5; Lay Teachers 14; Students 202.

DUNMORE. *Bishop O'Hara High School*, 501 E. Drinker St., 18512. Tel: 570-346-7541; Fax: 570-348-1070.
E-mail: bishop-ohara@intiques.com
Web site: www.superbrainiac.com
Mrs. Anita M. Sirak, Prin.; Mr. Charles J. Buzad, Vice Prin.; Rev. Scott P. Sterowski, Dir., Religious Formation. Sisters, Servants of the Immaculate Heart of Mary. Priests 1; Sisters 1; Lay Teachers 23; Students 408.

EAST STROUDSBURG. *Notre Dame Junior / Senior High School*, 60 Spangenburg Ave., 18301. Tel: 570-421-0466; Fax: 570-476-0629.
E-mail: notredame@usnetway.com
Jeffrey N. Lyons, Prin.; Rev. Msgr. John A. Bergamo, Dir., Religious Formation; John D. Gormley, Dean of Students. Priests 2; Sisters, Servants of

the Immaculate Heart of Mary 1; Lay Teachers 24; Students 356.

HAZLETON. *Bishop Hafey Junior/Senior High School*, 1700 W. 22nd St., 18201. Tel: 570-455-9431; Fax: 570-455-2847.
E-mail: bhafey@ptd.net
Web site: www.homework-central.com/schools/bishophafey
Mr. Michael S. Reese, Prin.; Rev. Christopher Clay, Chap.; Mr. Michael Stofko, Dir. Public Rels., Student Activities, Technological Svcs, Academic Dean of Studies; Mr. Joseph Clark, Athletic Dir.; Mr. Thomas A. Kostic, Dir., Religious Formation; Sr. Barbara Sable, SS.CM., Dir., Guidance; Mrs. Miriam Jamelli, Jr. High Guidance Counselor; Mr. William J. Phillips, Business Mgr. Priests 1; Religious 1; Lay Teachers 43; Students 601.

KINGSTON. *Bishop O'Reilly High School*, 316 N. Maple Ave., P.O. Box 1346, 18704. Tel: 570-288-1404; Fax: 570-288-6634.
E-mail: boreilly@liul8.K12.pa.us
Web site: www.liul8.K12.pa.us:80/~oreilly4
Miss Susan Dennen, Prin.; Mr. Alfred T. Kozlek, Asst.Prin.; Rev. Anthony J. Generose, Dir. Rel. Formation; Mrs. Linda Prawdzik, Dir., Guidance; Mr. Ralph Mancuso, Business Mgr. Priests 1; Sisters 2; Lay Teachers 29; Students 393.

PITTSTON. *Seton Catholic High School*, 37 William St., 18640. Tel: 570-654-4831; 655-0208; Fax: 570-654-2599. James J. Redington, Prin.; Rev. Frank S. Homets, Dir., Religious Formation. Sisters 3; Lay Teachers 21; Students 277.

WILKES-BARRE. *Bishop Hoban High School*, 159 S. Penna Blvd., 18701-3394. Tel: 570-829-2424; Fax: 570-829-4412.
E-mail: libhoban@ptd.net
Rev. Msgr. David L. Tressler, Prin.; Sr. Leonita Duhoski, R.S.M., Dir. of Devel.; Sr. Catherine Ann Morris, SS.C.M., Dir. of Guidance; Sr. Ellen Maroney, I.H.M., Dean of Students; Mrs. Anne Thomas, Dean of Academic Studies. Priests 3; Sisters 10; Lay Teachers 42; Students 580.

WILLIAMSPORT. *Bishop Neumann Junior/Senior High School*, 901 Penn St., 17701. Tel: 570-323-9953; Fax: 570-321-7146. Mr. Paul Ward, Prin.; Ms. Judith Folmar, Asst. Prin.; Revs. Andrew S. Hvozdovic, Dir., Religious Formation; Andrew Kurovsky, Chap. Priests 1; Sisters 1; Lay Teachers 20; Students 224.

[E] HIGH SCHOOLS, PRIVATE

SCRANTON.
Scranton Preparatory School, 1000 Wyoming Ave., 18509. Tel: 570-941-7737; Fax: 570-941-6118.
E-mail: hhewitt@scrantonprep.com
Web site: www.scrantonprep.com
Society of Jesus. Revs. Herbert B. Keller, S.J., Pres.; Brendan G. Lally, S.J., Rector.
Faculty: Revs. Michael A. Hricko, S.J.; Leonard A. Martin, S.J.; William J. McGrath, S.J.; Bros. James C. Lemon, S.J.; Darrell Burns, S.J., Chap. Priests 4; Brothers 2; Sisters 1; Lay Teachers 50; Students 719; Scholastics 1.

MOSCOW. *St. Gregory's Academy*, R.R. 8, Box 8214, 18444. Tel: 570-842-8112; Fax: 570-842-4513. Priestly Fraternity of St. Peter. Rev. Bruno Stemler, F.S.S.P., Chap.; Alan Hicks, Headmaster. Lay Teachers 7; Students 61.

[F] INTER-PAROCHIAL ELEMENTARY SCHOOLS

SCRANTON. *Marin Catholic Interparochial School*, 430 River St., 18505-1157. Tel: 570-342-9700.
Nativity of Our Lord Campus. (Grades PreK-8), 638 Hemlock St., 18505. Tel: 570-346-9922; Fax: 570-346-9482.
Web site: www.northeastweb.com/nativity/index.html
Karen DeSandis, Prin. Sisters of the I.H.M. 1; Lay Teachers 21; Students 406.
St. Mary of the Assumption Campus. (Grades PreK-8), 430 River St., 18505-1157. Tel: 570-342-9700; Fax: 570-341-7664.
E-mail: stmary1@ns.neiu.k12.pa.us
Web site: www.ns.neiu.k12.pa.us/www/sma
Sr. Felice Donelin, S.C.C., Prin. Sisters of Christian Charity 3; Lay Teachers 15; Students 254.
Saint Mary Czestochowa Campus. (Grades PreK-6), 3357 Greenwood Ave., Moosic, 18507. Tel: 570-342-2215; Fax: 570-342-0260.
Web site: www.rpmwebworx.com/stmarys
Vincent M. Montoro, Prin. Lay Teachers 7; Students 70.

CARBONDALE. *Sacred Heart Elementary School Primary Center*, 27-33 Fairview St., 18407. Tel: 570-282-0340; Fax: 570-281-3677. Mrs. Ellen M. Murphy, Prin. Sisters 2; Lay Teachers 10; Students 210.
Sacred Heart Intermediate Center, 7th Ave. & Church St. Tel: 570-282-7930. Sr. Karen Steinberg, I.H.M., Prin. Sisters 2; Lay Teachers 7; Students 77.

CLARKS GREEN. *Our Lady of Peace Elementary School*, 410 N. Abington Rd., 18411. Tel: 570-587-4152; Fax: 570-586-5393.
E-mail: OLP@epix.net
Web site: www.nvds.com/olp.html
Mrs. Jane Quinn, Prin. I.H.M. Sisters 1; Lay Teachers 20; Students 440.
Saint Gregory Early Childhood Center, 330 N. Abington Rd., 18411. Tel: 570-587-4808; Fax: 570-586-4515.
E-mail: jlouis3662@aol
Web site: www.NVDS.com.STGREGORY.html
Rev. Msgr. John H. Louis, Acting Prin. Lay Teachers 3; Students 65.

CRESCO. *Monsignor McHugh Elementary School*, R.R. 1, Box 567, 18326. Tel: 570-595-7463; Fax: 570-595-9639.
E-mail: msgrmchugh@enter.net
Kathleen A. Serafin, Prin. Sisters, Servants of the Immaculate Heart of Mary 3; Lay Teachers 19; Students 470.
Immaculate Heart of Mary Convent, R.R. 1, Box 568, 18326. Tel: 570-595-7548.

DALLAS. *Gate of Heaven Elementary School*, 40 Machell Ave., 18612. Tel: 570-675-6566; Fax: 570-674-0198.
E-mail: gohtiguem@hotmail.com
Web site: www.gateofheaven.dalla.pa.us
Mrs. Mary Tigue, Prin. Lay Teachers 24; Students 515.

EAST STROUDSBURG. *Notre Dame Elementary School*, 78 Ridgeway St., 18301. Tel: 570-421-3651; Fax: 570-422-6935.
E-mail: ndelem@usnetway.com
Sr. Mary Alice Kane, I.H.M., Prin. I.H.M. Sisters 3; Lay Teachers 17; Students 420.

EXETER. *Wyoming Area Catholic Elementary School*, 1690 Wyoming Ave., 18643. Tel: 570-654-7982; Fax: 570-654-0605.
E-mail: wacs@microserve.net
Web site: www.wacsh.com
Sr. Dorothy Kibler, I.H.M., Prin. I.H.M. Sisters 3; Lay Teachers 10; Students 242.

FORTY FORT. *Regis Elementary School*, 1133 Wyoming Ave., 18704. Tel: 570-288-5558; Fax: 570-288-5560. Ms. Kathleen Hanlon, Prin. Lay Teachers 12; Students 224.

HAZLETON. *Holy Spirit Academy*, 225 E. Fourth St., 18201. Tel: 570-459-0054; Fax: 570-459-2567.
E-mail: holysprt@intergrafix.net
Mrs. Alice Flynn, Prin. Priests 5; Sisters 2; Lay Teachers 15; Students 312.

HONESDALE. *Saint Vincent Elementary School*, 329 Cliff St., 18431. Tel: 570-253-1074; Fax: 570-253-2014.
Web site: www.myschoolonline.com/PA/stvincentsschool
Mrs. Sue Delling, Prin. Lay Teachers 10; Students 249.

JESSUP. *La Salle Academy*, 309 First Ave., 18434. Tel: 570-489-2010. Dr. James Tarity, Jr., Prin. Sisters 2; Lay Teachers 23; Students 460.

NANTICOKE. *Pope John Paul II Elementary School*, 518 S. Hanover St., 18634. Tel: 570-735-7935; Fax: 570-735-2281. Mr. James A. Jones, Prin. Lay Teachers 16; Students 370.

PLYMOUTH. *Holy Child Elementary School*, 119 Willow St., 18651. Tel: 570-779-2843; Fax: 570-779-3119.
E-mail: scrluhc@impresso.com
Web site: school-zone.net
Sr. Carole Griffin, I.H.M., Prin. Sisters 4; Lay Teachers 9; Students 133.

SWOYERSVILLE. *Regis Academy*, 112 Hughes St., 18704. Tel: 570-287-3133; Fax: 570-287-1453.
E-mail: regisaca@epix.net
Joseph A. Triano, Prin. Lay Teachers 14; Students 183.

WILKES-BARRE. *Saint Boniface Interparochial School*, 221 Blackman St., 18702-4576. Tel: 570-823-0939; Fax: 570-823-2856.
E-mail: stbon@epix.net
Sr. John Marie Hickl, S.C.C., Prin. S.C.C. Sisters 2; Lay Teachers 9; Students 212.
Saint Nicholas-Saint Mary Elementary School, 242 S. Washington St., 18701. Tel: 570-823-8089; Fax: 570-823-1402.
E-mail: snsm46@hotmail.com
Sr. Mary Catherine Slattery, S.C.C., Prin. S.C.C. Sisters 4; Lay Teachers 22; Students 481.

[G] PRESCHOOLS AND CHILD CARE CENTERS

SCRANTON. *Immaculate Care Preschool*, 800 Taylor Ave., 18510. Tel: 570-344-4380. Ann Marie McDonald, Dir./Head Teacher.
Marywood-Tony Domiano Early Childhood Center. Marywood University, 2300 Adams Ave., 18509. Tel: 570-340-6085.
E-mail: muro@ac.marywood.edu
Sr. Marilyn Muro, I.H.M., Dir.

MILFORD. *St. Patrick Preschool*, 111 E. High St., P.O. Box W, 18337. Tel: 570-296-4721; Fax: 570-296-7451. Rita Straka, Teacher.
St. Vincent de Paul Preschool, 101 St. Vincent Dr., 18337. Tel: 570-686-1867; Fax: 1-800-565-1762.
E-mail: stvincentdepaul@pikeonline.net
Web site: members.xoom.com/saintvincent
Diane C. Quintiliani, Teacher.

MOSCOW. *St. Catherine Preschool*, Church St., P.O. Box 250, 18444. Tel: 570-848-1258; Fax: 570-842-6648. Kathy LoRusso, Dir.

MUNCY. *Resurrection Early Childhood Center*, 526 S. Main St., 17756. Tel: 570-546-5272; Fax: 570-546-5272. Rev. David P. Cappelloni, Dir.

PITTSTON. *St. Mary's Early Childhood Learning Center*, 535 N. Main Ave., 18640-2244. Tel: 570-654-8188; Fax: 570-654-8320.
E-mail: srestherfalzone@aol.com
Sr. Esther Falzone, S.C.C., Prin.

[H] RENEWAL CENTERS

CRESCO. *The Immaculate Heart of Mary Spiritual Renewal Center*, R.R. 1, Box 568, 18326. Tel: 570-595-7548; 7549. Sr. Anne Mary Boslett, I.H.M., Dir.

DALTON. *Fatima Renewal Center*, 1000 Seminary Rd., 18414. Tel: 570-563-8500; Fax: 570-563-1857. Diocesan Renewal Center. Tel: 570-563-8510; Fax: 570-563-1857. Sr. Roberta Peters, I.H.M., Retreat & Prog.Coord.

NANTICOKE. *Holy Family Spiritual Renewal Center*, 151 Old Newport St., 18634-1300. Tel: 570-735-2599; Fax: 570-735-2679.
E-mail: marhudak@voicenet.com
Co-Directors: Martin J. Hudak; Louise V. Hudak.

[I] GENERAL HOSPITALS

SCRANTON. *Mercy Hospital*, 746 Jefferson Ave., 18501. Tel: 570-348-7100; Fax: 570-348-7639.
E-mail: spetula@mhs.nepa.com
For a complete listing, refer to the Hospitals section.
Mercy Med-Care, Inc., 746 Jefferson Ave., 18501. Tel: 570-348-7074; Fax: 570-348-7021
For a complete listing, refer to the Hospitals section.

CARBONDALE. *Marian Community Hospital*, 100 Lincoln Ave., 18407. Tel: 570-281-1000; Fax: 570-282-7177.
E-mail: Prdept@marian.hcrn.com
For a complete listing, refer to the Hospitals section.
Maxis Foundation, 100 Lincoln Ave., 18407. Tel: 570-281-1000; Fax: 570-282-4730
For a complete listing, refer to the Hospitals section.
Maxis Medical Services, 100 Lincoln Ave., 18407. Tel: 570-281-1000
For a complete listing, refer to the Hospitals section.

HAZLETON. *Hazleton-Saint Joseph Medical Center*, 687 N. Church St., 18201. Tel: 570-501-6000; Fax: 570-501-6203.
E-mail: brudegair@ghha.org
Web site: www.ghha.org
For a complete listing, refer to the Hospitals section.

MUNCY. *Muncy Valley Hospital*, 215 E. Water St., 17756. Tel: 570-546-8282; Fax: 570-546-4150.
E-mail: Lcioffi:@shscares.org
For a complete listing, refer to the Hospitals section.

NANTICOKE. *Mercy Special Care Hospital*, 128 W. Washington St., 18634. Tel: 570-735-5000; Fax: 570-740-5220
For a complete listing, refer to the Hospitals section.

WILKES-BARRE. *Mercy Hospital*, 25 Church St., 18765. Tel: 570-826-3100; Fax: 570-831-8989
For a complete listing, refer to the Hospitals section.

WILLIAMSPORT. *Divine Providence Hospital of the Sisters of Christian Charity*, 1100 Grampian Blvd., 17701. Tel: 570-326-8000; Fax: 570-326-8902.
E-mail: Lcioffi@shscares.org
Web site: shscarcs.org
For a complete listing, refer to the Hospitals section.
Providence Health System Foundation, Inc., 1100 Grampian Blvd., 17701. Tel: 570-320-7010; Fax: 570-326-8902.
E-mail: Lcioffi@shscares.org
Web site: www.shscares.org
For a complete listing, refer to the Hospitals section.
Sisters of Christian Charity Healthcare Corporation, 1100 Grampian Blvd., 17701. Tel: 570-326-8181; Fax: 570-326-8902.
E-mail: Lcioffi@shscares.org
Web site: www.shscares.org
For a complete listing, refer to the Hospitals section.
Susquehanna Regional Home Health Services, 1100 Grampian Blvd., 17701. Tel: 570-320-7690; Fax: 570-323-0716.
E-mail: Lcioffi@shscares.org
Web site: www.shscares.org
For a complete listing, refer to the Hospitals section.

[J] SPECIAL HOSPITALS

SCRANTON. *St. Joseph's Center*, 2010 Adams Ave., 18509. Tel: 570-342-8379; Fax: 570-342-6080.
E-mail: wecare@stjosephscenter.org
Web site: www.stjosephcenter.org
For a complete listing, refer to the Special Care Facilities section.

NANTICOKE. *Mercy Health Care Center*, Newport St., 18634. Tel: 570-735-7300
For a complete listing, refer to the Special Care Facilities section.

[K] SPECIAL EDUCATION SCHOOLS

CLARKS GREEN. *Lourdesmont*, 537 Venard Rd., 18411. Tel: 570-587-4741; Fax: 570-586-0030. Legal Title: *Good Shepherd Corporation of Clarks Summit, PA.* Sr. Mary Pauline Bilbrough, R.G.S., Coord.; John Bishop, Prin.; John A. Antognoli, Ed.D., CEO. Sisters of the Good Shepherd 5; Staff 108; Total Assisted 508.

PINE GROVE. *St. Michael's Group Home*, 25 Oak Grove Rd., 17963. Tel: 570-345-1160; Fax: 570-345-6307. Total Assisted 8; Total Staff 8.

TUNKHANNOCK. *St. Michael's School*, Box 370, 18657. Tel: 570-388-6155; Fax: 570-388-6979.
E-mail: stmikes@epix.net
Mr. Andrew M. Varzaly, M.S.W., L.S.W., Exec. Dir. Students Assisted 315; Total Staff 170.

WILLIAMSPORT. *St. Michael's Group Home*, 119 E. Fourth St., 17701. Tel: 570-322-0561; Fax: 570-322-8901. Total Assisted 8; Total Staff 7.

[L] HOMES FOR AGED

SCRANTON. *Home for Aged of the Little Sisters of the Poor, Holy Family Residence*, 2500 Adams Ave., 18509. Tel: 570-343-4065; 346-5788; Fax: 570-346-1196.*For a complete listing, refer to the Special Care Facilities section.*

DALLAS. *Mercy Center Nursing Unit, Inc.*, Lake St., Box 370, 18612. Tel: 570-675-2131; Fax: 570-674-7606
For a complete listing, refer to the Special Care Facilities section.

ELMHURST. *St. Mary's Villa Nursing Home*, 18416. Tel: 570-842-7621; Fax: 570-842-2953
For a complete listing, refer to the Special Care Facilities section.

WILKES-BARRE. *Little Flower Manor of the Diocese of Scranton*, 200 S. Meade St., 18702. Tel: 570-823-6131; Fax: 570-823-5171
For a complete listing, refer to the Special Care Facilities section.

[M] MONASTERIES AND RESIDENCES OF PRIESTS AND BROTHERS

SCRANTON. *Saint Ann's Passionist Monastery*, 1233 St. Ann St., 18504. Tel: 570-347-5691; Fax: 570-347-9387.
E-mail: cyuhaus@aol.com
Congregation of the Passion.
Chaplaincies: St. Gabriel's Convent, Clarks Summit, 18411. Tel: 570-586-9099; Fax: 570-586-9203. Very Rev. Cassian J. Yuhaus, C.P., Rector, Monastery & Shrine-Basilica; Exec. Dir., Ministry for Rel. Research & Consultancy. Tel: 570-586-9099;9203; Revs. Richard Nalepa, C.P., Vice Rector; Berard Tierney, C.P.; Kenneth Walsh, C.P.; Benedict Berlo, C.P.; Vincent Boney, C.P.; Alphonsus Coen, C.P.; Conan Conaboy, C.P.; John Connor, C.P.; Roger Elliott, C.P.; Peter A. Grace, C.P.; James McHugh, C.P.; Bros. Daniel Turner, C.P.; Jerome Cowan, C.P. Priests 12; Brothers 2.

Servants Minor of St. Francis, 1124 Jackson St., 18504. Tel: 570-344-7442. Bro. Gabriel Francis, Guardian.

BRODHEADSVILLE. *Salesian Monastery*, HC 1, Frantz Rd., Box 455, 18322-9630. Tel: 570-992-0230 (Monastery); 992-3448 (Abbot's Office); Fax: 570-992-3448 (Monastery); 570-992-3448.
E-mail: monk@epix.net
Web site: gentlestrength.org.
Bro. Bernard Seif, S.M.C., Abbot.

ELMHURST. *Priestly Fraternity of St. Peter (F.S.S.P.), North American District Headquarters*, Griffin Rd., P.O. Box 196, 18416. Tel: 570-842-4000; Fax: 570-842-4001.
E-mail: info@fssp.com
Web site: www.fssp.com
Revs. Paul J. Carr, F.S.S.P.; James Mercer, F.S.S.P.; Bruno Stemler, F.S.S.P., Chap., St. Gregory's Academy; Deacons Joseph R. Howard; Neal A. Nichols; Philip Wolfe.
On Duty Outside the Diocese: Revs. Hubert Bizard, F.S.S.P.; James B. Buckley, F.S.S.P.; Louis J. Campbell, F.S.S.P.; Calvin Goodwin, F.S.S.P.; James Jackson, F.S.S.P.; Robert Novokowsky, F.S.S.P.; Joseph Poisson, F.S.S.P.; Chad Ripperger, F.S.S.P.; Charles Van Vliet, F.S.S.P. Priests 39; Seminarians 62.
Priests Working Elsewhere: Rev. Carlos S. Casavantes, F.S.S.P., St. Michael's Church, 1703 Jackson St., Scranton, 18504. Tel: 570-961-1205; Fax: 570-961-2284. Rev. Paul, Roman, F.S.S.P., Chap., St. Michael the Archangel Latin Mass Community, 3036 Saratoga Blvd., Apt. E, Corpus Christi, TX, 78415. Tel: 361-855-8244. Rev. Joseph Portzer, F.S.S.P., Chap., Community of St. John the Baptist, 1418 W. 20th St., N. Little Rock, AR, 72114. Tel: 501-812-9155; Fax: 501-812-9225. Revs. Gary Dilley, F.S.S.P. (Y); Howard Remski, F.S.S.P., Asst. Pastor, Queen of the Holy Rosary Parish, 291 Scoville Dr., Vienna, OH, 44473. Tel: 330-856-4204; Fax: 330-856-9587. Rev. Mark Fischer, F.S.S.P. (ATL), Chap., St. Francis de Sales Latin Mass Community, 587 Landers Dr., Mableton, GA, 30126. Tel: 770-948-6888 (Church); 745-3464 (Rectory); Fax: 917-477-6274. Rev. Valentine Young, O.F.M., Asst. Pastor, St. Michael the Archangel Latin Mass Community, 522 Columbus St., Rapid City, SD, 57701. Tel: 605-341-1578; Fax: 605-341-8751. Rev. George Gabet, F.S.S.P., Community of St. Peter. (St. Augustine Church), 1720 E. Apache, Tulsa, OK, 74148. Tel: 918-425-0486; Fax: 918-425-2077. Rev. Edouard de Mentque, F.S.S.P. (KCK), Chap., Community of St. Peter, 5049 Canterbury Rd., Roeland Park, KS, 66205. Tel: 913-362-5677; Fax: 913-362-5808. Rev. Dennis Duvelius, F.S.S.P. (IND), Assoc. Pastor, SS. Peter and Paul Cathedral, 137 N. Meridian St., Indianapolis, IN, 46202. Tel: 317-634-4519; Fax: 317-634-0151. Revs. Joseph Terra, F.S.S.P., Chap.; John Berg, F.S.S.P., Asst. Chap., P.O. Box 5382, Sacramento, CA, 95817. Tel: 916-457-7824; Fax: 916-737-8930. Revs. Jose Salgado, F.S.S.P. (DEN), Chap.; Thomas Fritschen, F.S.S.P., Asst. Chap., Our Lady of Mount Carmel Community, P.O. Box 1063, Wheat Ridge, CO, 80034-1063. Tel: 303-657-8495; Fax: 303-657-8496. Revs. Denis Bouchard, F.S.S.P., Admin.; Nicholas Zolnerowicz, F.S.S.P., Asst., Our Lady of Fatima Chapel, 32 W. Franklin Ave., Pequannock, NJ, 07440. Tel: 973-694-6727; Fax: 973-694-7629. Rev. Joseph R. Valentine, F.S.S.P. (DAL), Chap., Mater Dei Community, 6228 Winton St., Dallas, TX, 75214. Tel: 214-887-8696; Fax: 214-887-8717. Rev. Eric Flood, F.S.S.P., Asst. Pastor, St. Patrick, 1404 Castelar St., Omaha, NE, 68180. Tel: 402-341-1305; Fax: 402-342-5510. Rev. Michael T. Irwin, F.S.S.P., Chap., Community of St. John-Mary Vianney, 208 Sunset Ln., P.O. Box 98, Maple Hill, KS, 66507. Tel: 785-256-4727; Fax: 785-256-4115. Rev. S. William Allen, F.S.S.P., Shrine of Our Lady of the Prairies, P.O. Box 216, Powers Lake, ND, 58773. Tel: 701-464-5458; Fax: 701-464-5674. Rev. Karl Pikus, F.S.S.P. (LN), Rector, St. Francis of Assisi, 3400 S. 17th St., Lincoln, NE, 68502. Tel: 402-477-5145; Fax: 402-477-5159. Rev. Anthony Tyrrell, F.S.S.P., Chap., Archdiocesan Pastoral Center, Oklahoma City. Tel: 405-720-2801.
Working Outside of the Fraternity of St. Peter. Revs. Daniel Oppenheimer; Mario Portella; Nathan Vail.

LACEYVILLE. *Franciscan Missionary Hermits of St. Joseph*, R.R. 1, Box 1590, 18623. Tel: 570-869-2918. Rev. Pio Mandato, F.M.H.J.

LITTLE MEADOWS. *St. Joseph's House*, R.R. 1, Box 1454, 18830. Rev. Vincent J. Young, Dir.

MOUNT POCONO. *Newman House*, 21 Fairview Ave., 18344. Tel: 570-839-2185; Fax: 570-839-0405. Very Rev. Peter M.J. Stravinskas, Ph.D., S.T.D., Provost; Revs. Christopher R. Clay; Nicholas L. Gregoris. Priests 3; Seminarians 3.

PITTSTON. *Eastern Province of the Oblates of St. Joseph*, 1880 Hwy. 315, 18640. Tel: 570-654-7542; Fax: 717-654-8621. Very Rev. Gregory T. Finn, O.S.J., Prov.; Revs. Paul A. McDonnell, O.S.J., 1st Councilor; Daniel L. Schwebs, O.S.J., 2nd Councilor. Priests 10.

SHOHOLA. *Society of Saint John*, Drummond House, 702 Rte. 434, 18458-9979. Tel: 570-685-5151; Fax: 570-685-5152.
E-mail: info@ssjohn.org
Web site: www.ssjohn.org
Revs. Carlos Urrutigoity, Supr. Gen.; Dominic A. Carey; Eric S. Ensey; Daniel J. Fullerton; Marshall M. Roberts; Basel R. Sarweh; C. Bernardo Terrera.

WILKES-BARRE. *Moreau House*. (House of Formation for the Congregation of Holy Cross - C.S.C.), 847 Scott St., 18705. Tel: 570-824-2622. Revs. Robert E. de Leon, C.S.C.; Thomas P. Looney, C.S.C.

St. Joseph's Friary, 783 E. Northampton St., 18702. Tel: 570-822-8023; Fax: 570-822-2891.
E-mail: frankofm@epix.net
Revs. Francis M. McHugh, O.F.M., Pastor/ Guardian; Raymond J. Lynch, O.F.M., Sr. Friar Assoc.; Benjamin J. Foerch, O.F.M. Priests 3.

[N] DIOCESAN RESIDENCE FOR RETIRED PRIESTS

DUNMORE. *Villa St. Joseph*, 1600 Green Ridge St., 18509. Tel: 570-343-4791. Most Rev. John M. Dougherty, D.D., V.G., Rector. Tel: 570-344-3272. In res. Rev. Msgr. Thomas J. Cawley. Tel: 570-343-2254; Rev. Msgr. James T. Clarke. Tel: 570-969-1235; Rev. Msgr. William L. Donovan. Tel: 570-963-9383; Rev. Msgr. Chester A. Gajewski. Tel: 570-347-1851; Rev. Msgr. Joseph F. Meier. Tel: 570-346-3887; Rev. Msgr. John J. O'Brien. Tel: 570-961-1865; Rev. Msgr. William J. Pakutka. Tel: 570-341-9168; Rev. Msgr. Edmund S. Penkala. Tel: 570-344-6288; Revs. Joseph W. Breslin. Tel: 570-341-3315; Joseph T. Conboy. Tel: 570-941-9405; Alphonsus M. Domnick, T.O.R. Tel: 570-341-9176; Robert M. Everling. Tel: 570-343-4925; John L. Fabian. Tel: 570-348-0728; Joseph D. Flannery. Tel: 570-347-8019; Thomas A. Flynn. Tel: 570-348-0589; Edward F. Gallagher. Tel: 570-348-6873; Alex J. Hazzouri. Tel: 570-343-2859; Harry J. Lewis. Tel: 570-343-5499; John S. Marinko. Tel: 570-941-3446; Clement A. Markowski. Tel: 570-343-0555; Joseph F. Meighan. Tel: 570-941-0509; Charles F. Mulrooney. Tel: 570-969-1305; John A. O'Haire. Tel: 570-342-6865; William J. Pace. Tel: 570-961-5856; Valentine R. Plevyak. Tel: 570-969-9109; William F. Purcell. Tel: 570-969-0695; Carl G. Ulrich. Tel: 570-341-5898.

[O] CONVENTS AND RESIDENCES FOR SISTERS

SCRANTON. *Immaculate Heart of Mary Center, Marywood*, 2300 Adams Ave., 18509. Tel: 570-342-6850; Fax: 570-342-6850.
E-mail: sandersihm@aol.com
Web site: www.marywood.edu.ww2/ihmpage/
Sisters, Servants of the Immaculate Heart of Mary. Sr. Anne Munley, I.H.M., Pres. Tel: 570-346-5425; Rev. Robert J. Barone, S.T.D., Chap.; Sr. Jane Snyder, I.H.M., Vice Pres.; Councilor, Missioning & Community Life. Tel: 570-346-5409; Sr. Catherine Luxner, I.H.M., Councilor, Spiritual Devel. Tel: 570-346-5402; Sr. Mary Persico, I.H.M., Councilor, Temporal Resources. Tel: 570-346-5405; Sr. Theresa Jordan, I.H.M., Business Mgr. Tel: 570-346-5406; Sr. Annmarie Sanders, I.H.M., Dir. Communications. Tel: 570-346-5404 Ext. 508; Sr. Maria del Rey Shevlin, I.H.M., Dir. Office of Missioning Resources. Tel: 570-346-5401; Sr. Patricia Tippen, I.H.M., Dir. Novices & Candidates. Tel: 570-346-5414; Sr. Rosemarie Mozzachio, I.H.M., Dir. Vocations. Tel: 570-346-5413; Sr. Kathleen Mary Lunsman, I.H.M., Dir. Devel. Tel: 570-346-5431 Ext. 599.
Councilors, Missioning & Community Life: Sr. Eleanor Mary Marconi, I.H.M. Tel: 570-346-5407; Sr. Ellen Smith, I.H.M. Tel: 570-346-5410; Sr. Eileen Coleman, I.H.M., Dir. Volunteers. Tel: 570-963-2480; Sr. Joan Coyne, I.H.M., Dir. Assoc. Tel: 570-346-5411. Professed Sisters 617.

Marian Convent, Marywood, 18509. Tel: 570-346-1752; Fax: 570-346-5418.
E-mail: marian@ac.marywood.edu
Sr. St. Mel Wright, I.H.M., Coord. Tel: 570-346-1752; Sr. Rosemary Goulet, I.H.M., Admin. Tel: 570-346-5423; Rev. Gerard F. Lupa, Chap. Sisters, Servants of the Immaculate Heart of Mary 140.

Parish Visitors of Mary Immaculate, 410 S. Main Ave., 18504. Tel: 570-343-7841; Fax: 570-343-7841. Sr. Mary Remias, P.V.M.I., Supr. Sisters 5.

CLARKS SUMMIT. *St. Gabriel's Monastery*, 631 Griffin Pond Rd., 18411. Tel: 570-586-2791; Fax: 570-586-8210.
E-mail: cpnuns@intiques.com
Web site: www.intiques.con/cpnuns/
Religious of the Passion of Jesus Christ; Passionist Nuns (Contemplative). Sr. Mary Regina, C.P., Pres.; Sr. Paul Colette, C.P., Vicar; Sr. Teresita, C.P., Councilor. Professed Sisters 10.

DALLAS. *Sisters of Mercy of the Americas Regional Community of Dallas*, P.O. Box 369, 18612-0369. Tel: 570-675-1966; Fax: 570-675-9051.
E-mail: srcatherinem@somdallasreg.org
Web site: www.somdallasreg.org
Sr. Catherine McGroarty, R.S.M., Pres.; Sr. Mary Ellen Fuhrman, R.S.M., Vice Pres. Tel: 717-675-2048. Sisters 323.

GREELEY. *Oblates of Mary, Queen of Apostles*, Priory of Our Lady, 897 Rte. 434, 18425. Tel: 570-685-5154. Mailing Address: 702 Rte. 434, Shohola, 18458. Sr. Therese McNamara, Prioress. Oblates of Mary, Queen of Apostles 5; Novices 2; Postulants 2.

[P] RETREAT HOUSES

CLARKS SUMMIT. *St. Gabriel's Retreat Center*, 631 Griffin Pond Rd., 18411. Tel: 570-586-4957; Fax: 570-586-8210.
E-mail: cpnuns@intiques.com
Web site: http://www.intiques.com/cpnuns/
Religious of the Passion of Jesus Christ; Passionist Nuns (Contemplative).

MOUNT POCONO. *Villa Our Lady Retreat House*, HCR 1, Box 41, 18344-9714. Tel: 570-839-7217; Fax: 570-839-7553.
E-mail: sbona@ptdprolog.net
Sr. M. Bonaventa, O.S.F., Supr. & Dir. Retreat. Bernadine Sisters 8.

[Q] CAMPS AND COMMUNITY CENTERS

SCRANTON. *Catholic Youth Center*, 500 Jefferson Ave., 18510. Tel: 570-347-3311; Fax: 570-347-1165.
E-mail: cycscr@epix.net
Web site: www.cyc-scranton.org
Deacon Albert W. Perreault, Exec. Dir.

TUNKHANNOCK. *Camp St. Andrew*, P.O. Box 679, 18657. Tel: 570-836-2975.
E-mail: jjpkel@aol.com
Off-Season Mailing Address: P.O. Box 189, Hawley, 18428. Tel: 570-226-4606. Rev. Msgr. Joseph P. Kelly, Exec. Dir. Regular Camp, Basketball Clinics 1,000 children.

WILKES-BARRE. *Catholic Youth Center*, 36 S. Washington St., 18702. Tel: 570-823-6121. Very Rev. John S. Terry, V.F., Dir.; Mr. Anthony D. English, Jr., Exec. Dir.

[R] MISCELLANEOUS LISTINGS

SCRANTON.
Aid to the Church in Russia, 300 Wyoming Ave., 18503-1279. Tel: 570-207-2216. James B. Earley, Dir., Scranton Office.

The Catherine McAuley Center, 709 Madison Ave., 18510. Tel: 570-342-1342; Fax: 570-341-8108.
E-mail: mcauleyscranton@yahoo.com
Sr. Therese Marie Marques, R.S.M., Exec. Dir.

The Catherine McAuley Center - Bridge Program, 709 Madison Ave., 18510. Tel: 570-342-1342; Fax: 570-341-8108.
E-mail: mcauleyscranton@yahoo.com
Sr. Therese Marie Marques, R.S.M., Exec. Dir.

The Catherine McAuley Center - Maple Street House, 1030 Maple St., 18505. Tel: 570-342-1342; Fax: 570-341-8108. Sr. Therese Marie Marques, R.S.M., Exec. Dir.

The Catherine McAuley Center - Swetland Street House, 709 Madison Ave., 18510. Tel: 570-342-1342; Fax: 570-341-8108.
E-mail: mcauleyscranton@yahoo.com
Sr. Therese Marie Marques, R.S.M., Exec. Dir.

The Catherine McAuley House Annex, 115 Ferdinand St., 18508. Tel: 570-342-1342; Fax: 570-341-8108.
E-mail: mcauleyscranton@yahoo.com
Sr. Therese Marie Marques, R.S.M., Exec. Dir.

Cross Apartments, 507 Broadway, 18505. Tel: 570-342-1342; Fax: 570-341-8108. Sr. Therese Marie Marques, R.S.M., Exec. Dir.; Sr. Marise Fabie, R.S.M., Dir. Housing.

Frances Warde House, 1646 Capouse Ave., 18509. Tel: 570-342-6962; Fax: 570-341-8108.
E-mail: mcauleyscranton@yahoo.com
Sr. Therese Marie Marques, R.S.M., Exec. Dir.; Sr. Marise Fabie, R.S.M., Dir. Housing.

The Guild Studios, 400 Wyoming Ave., 18503. Tel: 800-367-6610; 570-342-8246; Fax: 570-342-5940.
E-mail: guilds@aol.com; guild01@aol.com
Trish Morrow, Gen. Mgr., Religious Store, 400 Wyoming Ave., 18503. Tel: 800-367-6610; 570-342-8246; Fax: 570-342-5940.
E-mail: guild01@aol.com
Joseph McGuire, Store Mgr., Religious Store, 670 Union Blvd., Allentown, 18103. Tel: 610-437-1894; Fax: 610-437-1895. Patrick Keating, Store Mgr., Religious Store, Rte. 611, Tannersville Plaza, Tannersville, 18372. Tel: 570-619-5411; Fax: 570-619-5412. Patricia Valentine, Store Mgr., Religious Store, 102 S. Main St., Wilkes-Barre, 18701. Tel: 570-822-6045; Fax: 570-822-6045. Mary Swirbel, Store Mgr.

I.H.M. Congregation Charitable Trust, 2300 Adams Ave., 18509. Tel: 570-342-6850; Fax: 570-346-5439.
E-mail: ihmmap@aol.com
Web site: www.ihm.marywood.edu
Congregation of the Sisters, Servants of the Immaculate Heart of Mary.

ISECP, Inc., 1105 Cornell St., 18504-3008. Tel: 570-344-7295; Fax: 570-941-6340.
E-mail: jroemer/@email.msn.com
Web site: www.isecp.org
Sr. Judith A. Roemer, Pres.

Saint Ann's Media, Inc., Box 111, 1230 St. Ann St., 18504-0111. Tel: 570-941-0100; Fax: 570-941-0185.
E-mail: frpeter@themass.com
Web site: www.theMass.com or www.prayerline.org
Rev. Peter A. Grace, C.P., Dir.; Mr. Sid Michaels, Gen. Mgr.; Mrs. Regina Hanlon, Coord.; Mrs. Vera Kowal Krewsun, Mktg. Dir. Sponsored by the Passionist Community.

St. Anthony's Haven, 409 Olive St., 18509. Tel: 570-342-1295; Fax: 570-341-6623. St. James Manor, 600 Wyoming Ave., 18509. Tel: 570-342-1295; Fax: 570-341-6623.

St. Francis of Assisi Kitchen, 500 Penn Ave., 18509. Tel: 570-342-5556; Fax: 570-963-8832. Rev. Msgr. Constantine V. Siconolfi, M.S., Dir.

CLARKS SUMMIT. *Ministry for Religious Research and Consultancy*, 631 Griffin Pond Rd., 18411. Tel: 570-586-9099; Fax: 570-586-9203.
E-mail: cyuhaus@aol.com
Very Rev. Cassian J. Yuhaus, C.P., Exec. Dir.
VMR Charitable Trust (Vehicle Management for Religious). Tel: 570-586-9099; Fax: 570-586-9203.

DALLAS. *Studio I*, Mercy Center, Box 370, 18612. Tel: 570-675-2131; 675-3281.
E-mail: srkiel@aol.com
Designing and handcrafting fine jewelry and sculpture. Workshops in jewelry making using the lost wax casting technique: A. Couples - wedding bands/ engagement rings. B. All ages interested in learning the art of jewelry making. Sr. Regina Kiel, R.S.M., Designer & Artist.

HARLEIGH. *National Shrine of the Sacred Heart*, 1 Church Pl., 18225. Tel: 570-455-1162; Fax: 570-455-0306. National Office: Men of the Sacred Heart, P.O. Box 500, 18225. Tel: 570-455-1162.

NANTICOKE. *People of God Community of Northeastern PA*, 151 Old Newport St., 18634-1300. Tel: 570-735-2599; Fax: 570-735-2679.
E-mail: marhudak@voicenet.com
Martin J. Hudak, Pres.

PITTSTON. *The Gabriel House*, 13 William St., 18640. Tel: 570-654-7157. Anne Marie McCawley, Project Coord.
Residence for low income women and women with children.

PLYMOUTH. *The Catherine McAuley House*, 121 Church St., 18651. Tel: 570-779-2801; Fax: 570-779-5240.
E-mail: kittymca@juno.com
Sr. Therese Marie Marques, R.S.M., Exec. Dir.; Sr. Marie Larkin, P.B.V.M., Mgr.

WILKES-BARRE. *Project REMAIN*. Service for the elderly and the needy residents in the High Rises. Valley View Terrace, 215 High St., Apt. 100, 18702. Tel: 570-829-5373. Sr. Miriam Francis Stadulis, R.S.M., Dir.; Sr. Gertrude Marie Bogdon, R.S.M., Dir., McGlynn Learning Center. Outreach to low income families in the housing projects. 72 Midland Ct., 18701. Tel: 570-824-8891. Sr. Miriam Francis Stadulis, R.S.M., Dir.

St. Vincent De Paul Kitchen, 39 E. Jackson St., 18701. Tel: 570-829-7796; Fax: 570-829-7721.
E-mail: kitchenwb@aol.com
Ned Delaney, M.A., Exec. Dir.

RELIGIOUS INSTITUTES OF MEN REPRESENTED IN THE DIOCESE

For further details refer to the corresponding bracketed number in the Religious Institutes of Men or Women section.

[0470]—*The Capuchin Friars.*—O.F.M.Cap.
[1000]—*Congregation of the Passion.* (Union City, NJ).—C.P.
[0520]—*Franciscan Friars.* (Prov. of the Most Holy Name of Jesus).—O.F.M.
[0690]—*Jesuit Fathers and Brothers.* (Maryland Prov.).—S.J.
[0920]—*Oblates of St. Francis de Sales.*—O.S.F.S.
[0930]—*Oblates of St. Joseph.* (Asti, Italy).—O.S.J.
[1065]—*Priestly Fraternity of St. Peter.*—F.S.S.P.
[0610]—*Priests of the Congregation of Holy Cross.* (Wilkes-Barre, PA).—C.S.C.
[]—*Society of St. John.*—S.S.I.
[1290]—*Society of the Priests of St. Sulpice.*—S.S.
[0560]—*Third Order Regular of St. Francis.*—T.O.R.

RELIGIOUS INSTITUTES OF WOMEN REPRESENTED IN THE DIOCESE

[1810]—*Bernardine Sisters of the Third Order of St. Francis.*—O.S.F.
[0330]—*Carmelite Sisters of the Aged and Infirm.*—O.Carm.
[2980]—*Congregation of Notre Dame.*—C.N.D.
[3830-05]—*Congregation of the Sisters of St. Joseph.* (Brentwood).—C.S.J.
[0890]—*Daughters of Our Lady of Mercy.*—D.M.
[]—*Dominican Sisters of St. Catherine de Ricci.*—O.P.
[1180]—*Franciscan Sisters of Allegany, N.Y.*—O.S.F.
[1310]—*Franciscan Sisters of Little Falls, Minnesota.*—O.S.F.
[2575]—*Institute of the Sisters of Mercy of the Americas.*—R.S.M.
[2340]—*Little Sisters of the Poor.*—P.S.D.P.
[]—*Oblates of Mary, Queen of Apostles.*—O.M.R.A.
[3160]—*Parish Visitors of Mary Immaculate.*—P.V.M.I.
[3240]—*Poor Sisters of Jesus Crucified and the Sorrowful Mother.*—C.J.C.
[3170]—*Religious of the Passion of Jesus Christ.*—C.P.
[3430]—*Religious Teachers Filippini.*—M.P.F.
[1700]—*School Sisters of the Third Order of St. Francis.* (Bethlehem, PA).—O.S.F.
[0570]—*Sisters of Charity of Seton Hill, Greensburg, PA.*—S.C.
[0660]—*Sisters of Christian Charity.*—S.C.C.
[2990]—*Sisters of Notre Dame.* (Ohio).—S.N.D.
[3780]—*Sisters of Saints Cyril and Methodius.*—SS.C.M.
[3840]—*Sisters of St. Joseph of Carondelet.*—C.S.J.
[3893]—*Sisters of St. Joseph of Chestnut Hill.*—S.S.J.
[1830]—*Sisters of the Good Shepherd.*—R.G.S.
[1970]—*Sisters of the Holy Family of Nazareth.*—C.S.F.N.
[2160]—*Sisters, Servants of the Immaculate Heart of Mary.*—I.H.M.

DIOCESAN CEMETERIES

SCRANTON. *Cathedral*, 1708 Oram St., 18504. Tel: 570-347-9251; Fax: 570-347-4354.
Diocesan Cemeteries Office, 1708 Oram St., 18504. Tel: 570-207-2209; Fax: 570-347-4354. Walter Bennett, Dir.

CARVERTON. *Mount Olivet*, P.O. Box 257, 18644. Tel: 570-696-3636.

DRUMS. *Calvary*, P.O. Box 485, 18222. Tel: 570-788-2150.

MOSCOW. *St. Catherine's*, Main St., P.O. Box 114, 18444. Tel: 570-842-8411; Fax: 570-842-8406.

OLD FORGE. *Holy Cross*, 18518. Tel: 570-347-9251; Fax: 570-347-4354.

WILLIAMSPORT. *Resurrection*, P.O. Box 12, 17754. Tel: 570-368-2727.

NECROLOGY

† Kvedrovicz, Richard J. —Died July 18, 2000.

† Sammons, Joseph F., Athens, GA St. Joseph's. —Died Dec. 30, 1999.

† Silvestri, Luke A., (On Duty Outside the Diocese). —Died July 18, 2000.

Archdiocese of Seattle

Archidioecesis Seattlensis

Most Reverend

ALEXANDER J. BRUNETT, PH.D.

Archbishop of Seattle; ordained July 13, 1958; appointed Bishop of Helena April 19, 1994; consecrated and installed July 6, 1994; appointed Archbishop of Seattle October 28, 1997; installed December 18, 1997. *Res., Connolly House, 1104 Spring St., Seattle, WA, 98104.* Tel.: 206-623-2625; Fax: 206-682-9661.

Most Reverend

RAYMOND G. HUNTHAUSEN, D.D.

Retired Archbishop of Seattle; ordained June 1, 1946; appointed Bishop of Helena, Montana July 8, 1962; consecrated August 30, 1962; appointed Archbishop of Seattle February 25, 1975; installed May 22, 1975; retired August 21, 1991. *Office: 910 Marion St., Seattle, WA, 98104.* Tel.: 206-382-4884; Fax: 206-382-3495.

Most Reverend

GEORGE L. THOMAS, D.D., PH.D.

Auxiliary Bishop of Seattle; ordained May 22, 1976; appointed November 19, 1999. *Office: 910 Marion St., Seattle, WA, 98104.* Tel.: 206-382-4888; Fax: 206-382-3495.

Chancery Office: 910 Marion St., Seattle, WA, 98104. Tel.: 206-382-4560; Fax: 206-382-4840.

Web site address: www.seattlearch.org

E-mail address: kathyj@seattlearch.org

Legal Title: *"Corporation of the Catholic Archbishop of Seattle".*

ESTABLISHED MAY 31, 1850. NAME CHANGED TO SEATTLE, SEPTEMBER 11, 1907.

CREATED ARCHDIOCESE, JUNE 23, 1951.

Square Miles 24,834.

Comprises the Counties of Clallam, Clark, Cowlitz, Grays Harbor, Island, Jefferson, King, Kitsap, Lewis, Mason, Pacific, Pierce, San Juan, Skagit, Skamania, Snohomish, Thurston, Wahkiakum and Whatcom in the State of Washington.

For legal titles of parishes and archdiocesan institutions, consult The Chancery.

STATISTICAL OVERVIEW

Personnel	
Archbishop	1
Retired Archbishops	1
Auxiliary Bishops	1
Abbots	1
Retired Abbots	1
Priests: Diocesan Active in Diocese	126
Priests: Active Outside Diocese	6
Priests: Retired, Sick or Absent	47
Number of Diocesan Priests	179
Religious Priests in Diocese	117
Extern Priests in Diocese	16
Ordinations:	
Diocesan Priests	2
Religious Priests	1
Transitional Deacons	1
Permanent Deacons in Diocese	74
Total Brothers	13
Total Sisters	495
Parishes	
Parishes	139
With Resident Pastor:	
Resident Diocesan Priests	104
Resident Religious Priests	15
Without Resident Pastor:	
Administered by Priests	10
Administered by Women Religious	5
Administered by Lay People	5
Missions	30
New Parishes Created	1
Welfare	
Catholic Hospitals	8
Total Assisted	1,500,000
Health Care Centers	11
Total Assisted	310,000
Homes for the Aged	15
Day Care and Extended Day Care Centers	7
Total Assisted	675
Specialized Homes	3
Total Assisted	61
Special Centers for Social Services	24
Total Assisted	51,608
Residential Care of Disabled	1
Total Assisted	45
Educational	
Diocesan Students in Other Seminaries	26
Total Seminarians	26
Colleges and Universities	2
Total Students	7,408
High Schools, Diocesan and Parish	3
Total Students	2,358
High Schools, Private	6
Total Students	3,165
Elementary Schools, Diocesan and Parish	53
Total Students	15,275
Elementary Schools, Private	3
Total Students	855
Catechesis/Religious Education:	
High School Students	5,451
Elementary Students	34,744
Total Students Under Catholic Instruction	69,282
Vital Statistics	
Receptions into the Church:	
Infant Baptism Totals	6,794
Adult Baptism Totals	1,268
Received into Full Communion	773
First Communions	6,238
Confirmations	4,714
Marriages:	
Catholic	931
Interfaith	827
Total Marriages	1,758
Deaths	2,914
Total Catholic Population	525,040
Total Population	4,526,200

Former Bishops—Rt. Rev. A. M. A. BLANCHET, cons. Bishop of Walla Walla, Sept. 27, 1846; transferred to Nesqually, May 31, 1850; resigned 1879 made Bishop of Ibora; died Feb. 25, 1887.—Rt. Rev. AEGIDIUS JUNGER, D.D., cons. Oct. 28, 1879; died Dec. 26, 1895.—Most Rev. EDWARD JOHN O'DEA, D.D., cons. Bishop of Nesqually, Sept. 8, 1896 See transferred to Seattle, Sept. 11, 1907; died Dec. 25, 1932.—Most Rev. GERALD SHAUGHNESSY, S.M., S.T.D., Bishop of Seattle; appt. July 1, 1933; cons. Sept. 19, 1933; died May 18, 1950.—Most Rev. THOMAS A. CONNOLLY, D.D., cons. Aug. 24, 1939 succeeded, May 18, 1950; retired Feb. 25, 1975; died April 18, 1991.—Most Rev. RAYMOND G. HUNTHAUSEN, D.D., ord. June 1, 1946; appt. Bishop of Helena, Montana, July 8, 1962; cons. Aug. 30, 1962; appt. Archbishop of Seattle, Feb. 25, 1975; installed May 22, 1975; retired Aug. 21, 1991.—Most Rev. THOMAS J. MURPHY, D.D., S.T.D., ord. April 12, 1958; appt. Bishop of Great Falls, July 5, 1978; appt. Coadjutor Archbishop of Seattle, May 26, 1987; succeeded to See Aug. 21, 1991; died June 26, 1997.

Chancery Office—Office of the Archbishop, 910 Marion St., Seattle, 98104. Tel: 206-382-4560; Fax: 206-382-3495.

Auxiliary Bishop and Vicar General—Most Rev. GEORGE L. THOMAS, Ph.D., V.G., D.D., *910 Marion St., Seattle, 98104.* Tel: 204-382-4888.

Chancellor—CHRISTINE M. TAYLOR, *910 Marion St., Seattle, 98104.* Tel: 206-382-4857.

Executive Assistant to the Archbishop—Ms. ANGELA KISON. Tel: 206-382-4525.

Presbyteral Council—Most Rev. GEORGE L. THOMAS; Very Revs. JAMES D. PICTON, J.D.; K. SCOTT CONNOLLY; KENNETH HAYDOCK; DAVID JAEGER; MICHAEL J. MCDERMOTT; JOHN E. MCMULLAN; Revs. LAWRENCE MINDER, O.S.B.; JOSEPH MITCHELL; Very Revs. HUNG NGUYEN; TUAN NGUYEN; Revs. JAMES NORTHROP; HANS OLSON; JOSEPH PETOSA; PATRICK RITTER; Very Revs. MICHAEL J. RYAN; STEVEN SALLIS; TIMOTHY SAUER; TERENCE WAGER, O.S.B.

College of Consultors—Most Rev. GEORGE L. THOMAS, Ph.D., V.G., D.D.; Very Rev. JAMES D. PICTON, J.D.; Very Rev. OLIVER DUGGAN; Rev. WILLIAM LANE; Very Rev. MICHAEL J. MCDERMOTT; Revs. JOSEPH MITCHELL; HANS M. OLSON; PATRICK RITTER; Very Rev. TIMOTHY SAUER.

Deans—Very Rev. TIMOTHY SAUER, Northern; Very Rev. KENNETH HAYDOCK, Snohomish; Very Rev. HUNG NGUYEN, Olympic; Very Rev. JOHN MCMULLAN, North Seattle; Very Rev. STEVEN SALLIS, Eastside; Very Rev. DAVID JAEGER, South Seattle; Very Rev. MICHAEL J. RYAN, South King; Very Rev. MICHAEL J. MCDERMOTT, Pierce; Very Rev. TUAN NGUYEN, South Sound; Very Rev. K. SCOTT CONNOLLY, Southern.

Metropolitan Tribunal

Judicial Vicar—Very Rev. ANTHONY E. BAWYN, J.C.D., *910 Marion St., Seattle, 98104.* Tel: 206-382-4830; Fax: 206-382-2071.

Adjunct Judicial Vicar—Very Rev. JOSEPH H. DOOGAN, J.C.L.

Judges—Rev. ANTHONY BAWYN, J.C.D.; JAMES L. BROOKS, M.Ed.; CHARLENE CRAM, J.C.L.; Rev. Msgr. JOHN P. DOOGAN, M.Ed.; Very Rev. JOSEPH H. DOOGAN, J.C.L.; Rev. JAMES EBLEN, S.T.L., Ph.D.; DONALD R. ESPEN, J.C.D.; Deacon JOHN LARUSSA; Rev. PHILIP LUCID, S.J., J.D.; Deacon LAWRENCE J. SULLIVAN; Rev. JAMES A. WILLIAMS, J.C.L.

Defenders of the Bond—CHARLOTTE S. EDMAN; KAREN GIFFIN; Sr. ANNE HERKENRATH, S.N.J.M.; Sr. GAIL MILHOLLAND, S.N.J.M.; Very Rev. JAMES D. PICTON, J.D.; Hon. JOHN F. WILSON, J.D.

Notaries—VALERIE BLESENER; IRENE DELVILLAR.

Archdiocesan Offices and Directors

African American/Black Catholic Affairs—SHARON PITRE-WILLIAMS, Dir., *910 Marion St., Seattle, 98104.* Tel: 206-382-2061; Fax: 206-382-2069.

AIDS Ministry—Very Rev. DAVID JAEGER, Chap., *910 Marion St., Seattle, 98104.* Tel: 206-382-4885.

Archbishop's Delegate for Religious Communities/ Ecumenism—Sr. JOYCE COX, B.V.M., *910 Marion St., Seattle, 98104.* Tel: 206-382-4829; Fax: 206-382-4840.

Archdiocesan Liturgical Commission—Ms. CAROLYN LASSEK, *910 Marion St., Seattle, 98104.* Tel: 206-382-4838.

Administration and Finance—Mr. PATRICK SURSELY, Archbishop's Delegate, *910 Marion St., Seattle, 98104.* Tel: 206-382-4529; Fax: 206-382-4266.

Archdiocesan Finance Council—Mr. PATRICK SURSELY, Staff; Mr. GERALD ALFERS, Chm., *910 Marion St., Seattle, 98104.* Tel: 206-382-4529; Fax: 206-382-4266.

Archdiocesan Pastoral Council—Mr. DENNIS O'LEARY, Exec. Sec., *910 Marion St., Seattle, 98104.* Tel: 206-382-4289; Fax: 206-382-4840.

Archdiocesan Women's Commission—Ms. CARLA CALDWELL, Liaison, *910 Marion St., Seattle, 98104.* Tel: 206-382-4268.

Archdiocesan Housing Authority—Mr. MICHAEL KEICHERT, Pres., *1902 2nd Ave., Seattle, 98101.* Tel: 206-448-3360; Fax: 206-448-8495.

Archives—Ms. CHRISTINE TAYLOR, *910 Marion St., Seattle, 98104.* Tel: 206-382-4857; Fax: 206-382-4840.

Asian/Pacific American Affairs—VERONICA LEASIOLAGI BARBER, Dir., *910 Marion St., Seattle, 98104.* Tel: 206-382-4828.

Campaign for Human Development—Mr. J. L. DROUHARD, Dir., *910 Marion St., Seattle, 98104.* Tel: 206-382-4869; Fax: 206-382-3487.

Campus Ministry—Rev. THOMAS DEMAN, O.P., *Newman Center, U of W, 4502 20th Ave., N.E., Seattle, 98105.* Tel: 206-527-5072.

Canonical Services—Very Rev. ANTHONY E. BAWYN, J.C.D., Judicial Vicar, *910 Marion St., Seattle, 98104.* Tel: 206-382-4565.

Catholic Community Services of Western Washington—Mr. MICHAEL REICHERT, Pres., *100 23rd Ave. S., Seattle, 98144-2302.* Tel: 206-328-5696; Fax: 206-328-5699.

Office of Cahtolic Faith Formation—Dr. MARY CROSS, Archbishop's Delegate for Catholic Faith Formation. Tel: 206-382-4835. Ms. CARLA CALDWELL, Dir. Lay Ecclesial Ministry. Tel: 206-382-4268. Dr. JUDY FORD, Dir. Religious Educ. Tel: 206-382-4614. Mr. JOSE RAMIREZ-LOMELI, Dir. Pastoral Formation Programs for Cultural & Ethnic Faith Communities. Tel: 206-654-4644.

Catholic Relief Services—J.L. DROUHARD, Dir., *910 Marion St., Seattle, 98104.* Tel: 206-382-4869.

Catholic Schools—Dr. HARRY PURPUR, Ph.D., Supt., *910 Marion St., Seattle, 98104.* Tel: 206-382-4855.

Catholic Youth Organization—Mr. PATRICK D'AMELIO, Dir., *814 N.E. 85th St., Seattle, 98115.* Tel: 206-382-4562; Fax: 206-903-4627.

Associated Catholic Cemeteries—Mr. RICHARD PETERSON, Dir., *910 Marion St., Seattle, 98104.* Tel: 206-382-9281; 253-838-2240.

Censores Librorum—Revs. PETER CHIRICO, S.S., S.T.D.; WILLIAM TREACY; MICHAEL RASCHKO, Ph.D.

Chancery Operations—Mr. DENNIS J. O'LEARY, Dir., *910 Marion St., Seattle, 98104.* Tel: 206-382-4289.

Chinese, Ministry to—Rev. Msgr. JOHN CHI, Chap., *1531 Bradner Pl., S., Seattle, 98144.* Tel: 206-324-8521.

Communications Office—Mr. WILLIAM GALLANT, Archbishop's Delegate, *910 Marion St., Seattle, 98104.* Tel: 206-382-4862; Fax: 206-382-3487.

Broadcast Division—Ms. TERRY MURPHY, Producer.

Web Division—Ms. KATHY JOHNSON, Mgr.

Newspaper "The Catholic Northwest Progress"—Mr. STEPHEN M. KENT, Exec. Editor. Tel: 206-382-4850.

Detention Ministry—KEVIN GLACKIN-COLEY, *910 Marion St., Seattle, 98104.* Tel: 206-382-4868.

Due Process Program—Ms. JESSIE DYE, Admin., *910 Marion St., Seattle, 98104.* Tel: 206-382-4592.

Ecumenical and Interfaith Commission—Sr. JOYCE COX, B.V.M., Archbishop's Delegate for Religious Communities & Ecumenism, *910 Marion St., Seattle, 98104.* Tel: 206-382-4829; Fax: 206-382-4840.

Events Planning—Ms. KATHLEEN NELSON, Dir., *910 Marion St., Seattle, 98104.* Tel: 206-382-4879; Fax: 206-382-4840.

Hispanic/Latino Affairs—MARIA ESTHER BAZAN-MYRICK, Dir., *910 Marion St., Seattle, 98104.* Tel: 206-382-4825.

Holy Childhood, Pontifical Association of the—J.L. DROUHARD, Dir., *910 Marion St., Seattle, 98104.* Tel: 206-382-4583.

Hospital Ministry, Tacoma—Rev. MICHAEL WALSH, S.J., Dir., *911 S. 5th, Tacoma, 98405.* Tel: 253-591-9474.

Hospital Ministry, Seattle—*910 Marion St., Seattle, 98104.* Tel: 206-382-3492.

Hospital Ministry, Eastside—Rev. WILLIAM HERIC, Chap., *9460 N.E. 14th St., Bellevue, 98004.* Tel: 206-361-4015.

Human Resources—Ms. MARY SANTI, Archbishop's Delegate, *910 Marion St., Seattle, 98104.* Tel: 206-264-2089; Fax: 206-382-4267.

Benefits Services—GERALYN MIRANTE-MARLEY, Admin. Tel: 206-382-4566; Fax: 206-382-3493.

Inclusion Ministry—KATHY SMALLEY, Dir., *910 Marion St., Seattle, 98104.* Tel: 206-382-2014.

Information Services Group—Mr. RICHARD CARDWELL, Dir., *910 Marion St., Seattle, 98104.* Tel: 206-382-3483.

Justice and Peace Office—Mr. J. L. DROUHARD, Dir., *910 Marion St., Seattle, 98104.* Tel: 206-382-4869; Fax: 206-382-3487.

Koreans, Ministry to—Rev. MICHAEL AHN, *11700 1st Ave., N.E., Seattle, 98125.* Tel: 206-362-2492; 362-2278.

Library Media Center—*910 Marion St., Seattle, 98104.* Tel: 206-382-4883; Fax: 206-382-3487.

Liturgy Office—Ms. CAROLYN LASSEK, *910 Marion St., Seattle, 98104.* Tel: 206-382-4838.

Missions Office—Mr. J. L. DROUHARD, Dir., *910 Marion St., Seattle, 98104.* Tel: 206-382-4580; Fax: 206-382-3487.

Native American Affairs—FRANCES FARWELL, Contact, *910 Marion St., Seattle, 98104.* Tel: 206-382-4833.

Parish Financial Services—Mr. ED WILLIAMS, Dir., *910 Marion St., Seattle, 98104.* Tel: 206-382-7316; Fax: 206-382-4840.

Parishes and Faith Communities, Office of—Mr. STEPHEN HUEFFED, Archbishop's Delegate. Tel: 206-382-2016. Very Rev. JAMES D. PICTON, J.D., Vicar. Tel: 206-382-4852., *910 Marion St., Seattle, 98104.*

Planned Giving—Mr. PAUL LEBLANC, Dir., *910 Marion St., Seattle, 98104.* Tel: 206-382-4865.

Planning & Research—Mr. DENNIS J. O'LEARY, Dir., *910 Marion St., Seattle, 98104.* Tel: 206-382-4832. Ms. MARY BETH CELIO, Dir. Research. Tel: 206-382-4272.

Polish Speaking, Ministry to—Revs. PIOTR DZIKOWSKI, S.Ch., *3422 Portland Ave., Tacoma, 98404.* Tel: 206-272-5232. JOZEF CALIK, S.Ch., *3221 14th Ave., W., Seattle, 98119.* Tel: 206-282-1804.

Priests' Health Plan—Most Rev. ALEXANDER J. BRUNETT, D.D., Ph.D., Pres.; Rev. SEAN FOX, Chm.

Priests' Pension Plan—Most Rev. ALEXANDER J. BRUNETT, D.D., Ph.D.; Rev. SEAN FOX, Chm.

Propagation of the Faith, Society for the—J.L. DROUHARD, Dir., *910 Marion St., Seattle, Wa, 98104.* Tel: 206-382-4869.

Property and Construction Office—Mr. EDWARD FOSTER, Dir., *910 Marion St., Seattle, 98104.* Tel: 206-382-4851; Fax: 206-382-4266.

Sisters' Council—Sr. SHARON PARK, O.P., *22010 S.E. 35th St., Issaquah, 98027.* Tel: 206-391-4493.

Stewardship and Development Office—Mr. ROGER JAROCH, Dir., *910 Marion St., Seattle, 98104.* Tel: 206-382-4562; Fax: 206-382-4266.

Theological Resources—Rev. PETER CHIRICO, S.S., S.T.D., *804 9th Ave., Seattle, 98104.* Tel: 206-628-3920. Rev. JAMES EBLEN, S.T.L., Ph.D., *408 Bellevue Ave. E., Seattle, 98102.* Tel: 206-329-5692. Rev. MICHAEL RASCHKO, Ph.D., *1614 Summit Ave., #502, Seattle, 98122.* Tel: 206-296-5311.

Vicar for Clergy, Office of—Very Rev. PAUL MAGNANO, Vicar for Clergy, *910 Marion St., Seattle, 98104.* Tel: 206-382-7317; Fax: 206-654-4654. Vacant, Dir. Office of Clergy Formation; Mr. RICH SHIVELY, Dir. Office of Permanent Diaconate & Office of Vocations. Tel: 206-382-4595. Very Rev. TIMOTHY SAUER, Dir. Office of Seminarians. Tel: 206-382-4880.

Vietnamese, Representative for—Rev. ANTHONY TON, Chap., *Church of the Vietnamese Martyrs, 1230 E. Fir, Seattle, 98122.* Tel: 206-325-5626.

CLERGY, PARISHES, MISSIONS AND PAROCHIAL SCHOOLS

CITY OF SEATTLE
(King County)

1—ST. JAMES CATHEDRAL, Very Rev. Michael G. Ryan; Rev. David A. Brant. In res., Rev. Peter F. Chirico, S.S.
Res., 804 Ninth Ave., 98104. Tel: 206-622-3559; Fax: 206-622-5303.
Convent—907 Columbia St., 98104. Tel: 206-682-1308.
Sisters 8.

2—ST. ALPHONSUS, Rev. James Gandrau. In res., Rev. George Limbani (Malawi, Africa).
Res., 5816 15th Ave., N.W., 98107. Tel: 206-784-6464; Fax: 206-789-5709.
School—Tel: 206-782-4363. Dr. Robert Scripko, Prin.
Lay Teachers 17; Students 188.
Catechesis/Religious Programs—Students 71.

3—ST. ANNE (1908), Rev. Robert Camuso.
Res., 1411 1st Ave. W., 98119. Tel: 206-282-0223; Fax: 206-217-9541.
School—101 W. Lee St., 98119. Tel: 206-282-3538; Fax: 206-284-4191. Mrs. Pat Durand, Prin.
Sisters of the Holy Names of Jesus and Mary 1; Lay Teachers 15; Students 212.

4—ST. BENEDICT (1906), Rev. Paul Waldie, O.M.I. In res., Revs. Gerard Clenaghan, O.M.I.; Edward T. McHugh, O.M.I.
Res., 1805 N. 49th St., 98103. Tel: 206-632-1475; Fax: 206-632-2167.
School—4811 Wallingford N., 98103. Tel: 206-633-3375; Fax: 206-632-3236. Dr. Fred McCarthy, Prin.
Lay Teachers 17; Students 170.
Catechesis/Religious Programs—Tel: 206-632-0843.
Students 60.

5—ST. BERNADETTE (1958), Rev. James A. Williams; Deacon Joseph Kvempl.
Res., 861 S.W. 126th St., 98146. Tel: 206-242-7370; Fax: 206-242-7371.
School—1028 S.W. 128th St., 98146. Tel: 206-244-4934; Fax: 206-244-4943. Sr. Marie Colarossi, S.N.J.M., Prin.
Sisters 2; Lay Teachers 16; Students 257.
Catechesis/Religious Programs—Students 70.

6—ST. BRIDGET (1968), Rev. Marlin Connole; Deacon Dennis Duffell.
Res., 4900 N.E. 50th, 98105. Tel: 206-523-8787; Fax: 206-528-7511. [CEM]
Catechesis/Religious Programs—Tel: 206-523-4760.
Students 224.

7—ST. CATHERINE (1929), Rev. Lyle Konen, C.Ss. R.; Very Rev. Paul Magnano, Mod.; Victoria Ries, Pastoral Life Dir.
Res., 8610 8th Ave., N.E., 98115. Tel: 206-524-8800; Fax: 206-527-6339.
School—8524 8th Ave., N.E., 98115. Tel: 206-525-0581. Steve Mezich, Prin.
Lay Teachers 20; Students 192.
Catechesis/Religious Programs—Tel: 206-525-5852.
Students 50.

8—ST. EDWARD (1906), Revs. Joseph J. Tyson; James Eblen; Joseph R. Stocking, S.J.; Poao Saena.
Res., 4250 S. Mead St., 98118. Tel: 206-722-7888; Fax: 206-722-7895.
School—Tel: 206-725-1774; Fax: 206-725-4569. Sr. Nancy Anderson, S.N.J.M., Prin.
Sisters 3; Lay Teachers 6; Students 133.
Catechesis/Religious Programs—Students 38.

9—ST. GEORGE (1903), Revs. Joseph J. Tyson; James Eblen; Joseph R. Stocking, S.J.; Poao Saena.
Res., 5306 13th Ave. S., 98108. Tel: 206-762-7744; Fax: 206-762-4207.
School—5117 13th Ave. S., 98108. Tel: 206-762-0656; Fax: 206-763-3220. Bernadette Mahoney, Prin.
Lay Teachers 17; Students 219.
Catechesis/Religious Programs—Students 135.

10—ST. JOHN (1917), Rev. William A. McKee.
Office: 121 N. 80th St., 98103. Tel: 206-782-2810; Fax: 206-706-2704.
School—(Grades PreK-8). Tel: 206-706-2704. Agnes Jacobson, Prin.
Lay Teachers 29; Students 376.
Catechesis/Religious Programs—Students 146.

11—ST. JOSEPH (1907), Revs. Craig Boly, S.J.; Lee Kapfer, S.J.
Res., 732 18th Ave., E., 98112. Tel: 206-324-2522; Fax: 206-329-5698.
School—700 18th Ave., E., Tel: 206-329-3260; Fax: 206-324-7773. George Hofbauer, Prin.
Sisters 1; Lay Teachers 41; Students 610.
Catechesis/Religious Programs—Students 350.

12—ST. LUKE (1955), Rev. Roger O'Brien.
Res., 322 N. 175th St., Shoreline, 98133. Tel: 206-546-2451; Fax: 206-546-0328.
School—17533 St. Luke Pl. N., Shoreline, 98133. Tel: 206-542-1133; Fax: 206-546-8693. Mr. John Allen, Prin.
Sisters of St. Dominic 2; Lay Teachers 20; Students 395.
Catechesis/Religious Programs—Students 285.

13—ST. MARGARET OF SCOTLAND (1910), Rev. Robert Camuso. In res., Rev. Joseph Calik, S.Ch., Polish Ministry.
Res., 3221 14th Ave., W., 98119. Tel: 206-282-1804; Fax: 206-282-6461.

14—ST. MARK (1954), Rev. Dennis Kemp. In res., Rev. Msgr. John P. Doogan; Very Rev. Anthony Bawyn.
Res., 18033 15th Pl., N.E., Shoreline, 98155. Tel: 206-364-7900; Fax: 206-367-3919.
School—Tel: 206-364-1633. Kathryn Palmquist-Keck, Prin.
Lay Teachers 14; Students 229.
Catechesis/Religious Programs—Students 210.

15—ST. MARY (1899), Rev. Anthony J. Haycock.
Res., 611 20th Ave., S., 98144. Tel: 206-324-7100; Fax: 206-329-4596.
Catechesis/Religious Programs—Students 73.
Convent—2021 S. Weller St., 98144. Tel: 206-324-1535. Religious of the Sacred Heart of Jesus.

16—ST. MATTHEW (1954), Rev. Clarence Jones, C.O.; Very Rev. Paul Magnano; Sr. Kathleen Buzard, S.N.J.M., Pastoral Life Dir.
Res., 1240 N.E. 127th St., 98125. Tel: 206-363-6767; Fax: 206-362-4863.
School—1230 N.E. 127th St., 98125. Tel: 206-362-2785. Maureen Reid, Prin.
Lay Teachers 15; Students 236.
Catechesis/Religious Programs—Students 177.

17—ST. PATRICK (1918), Rev. C. Vincent Peterson.
Res., 2702 Broadway E., 98102. Tel: 206-329-2960; Fax & TTY: 206-329-2961.
Catechesis/Religious Programs—Students 86.

18—ST. PAUL (1953), Revs. Joseph J. Tyson; Joseph R. Stocking, S.J.; James Eblen; Poao Saena.
Res., 5600 S. Ryan St., 98178. Tel: 206-725-2050; Fax: 206-725-7476.
School—10001 57th Ave., S., 98178. Tel: 206-725-0780; Fax: 206-722-5732. Wayne Melonson, Prin.
Lay Teachers 16; Students 197.
Catechesis/Religious Programs—Students 40.

19—ST. PETER (1931), Rev. Peter Duggan.
Res., 2807 15th Ave., S., 98144. Tel: 206-324-2290.
Catechesis/Religious Programs—Students 37.

20—ST. THERESE (1926), Very Rev. Paul Magnano.
Res., 3416 E. Marion St., 98122. Tel: 206-325-2711; Fax: 206-329-8373.
School—900-35th Ave., 98122. Tel: 206-324-0460; Fax: 206-324-8464. Mrs. Eileen Gray, Prin.
Sisters 2; Lay Teachers 14; Students 224.
Catechesis/Religious Programs—Students 118.

21—ASSUMPTION, Rev. Oliver Duggan.
Office: 3214 N.E. 62nd St., 98115. Tel: 206-522-7674; Fax: 206-522-6308.
School—Tel: 206-524-7452; Fax: 206-524-6757. Michael Foy, Prin.
Sisters 1; Lay Teachers 30; Students 536.

22—BLESSED SACRAMENT, Rev. Reginald Martin, O.P. In res., Revs. Thomas DeMan, O.P.; John Adams, O.P.; Michael Sweeney, O.P.; James Jenner, O.P.
Res., 5041 Ninth Ave., N.E., 98105. Tel: 206-547-3020; Fax: 206-547-6371.
Catechesis/Religious Programs—Students 50.

23—CHRIST THE KING, Rev. Ward Oakshott, Parochial Vicar; Very Rev. Paul Magnano; Rev. Alberto Cerezo; Ms. Patty Repikoff, Pastoral Life Dir.
Res., 405 N. 117th St., 98133. Tel: 206-362-1545; Fax: 206-364-8325.
School—415 N. 117th, 98133. Tel: 206-364-6890. Sheila Harrison, Prin.
Lay Teachers 16; Students 201.

24—HOLY FAMILY (1921), Rev. Phillip Bloom; Deacon Ted Wiese.
Res., 9622 20th Ave., S.W., 98106. Tel: 206-767-6220; Fax: 206-767-0374.
School—Tel: 206-767-6640; Fax: 206-767-0374. Stephen Morissette, Prin.
Sisters 2; Lay Teachers 14; Students 237.
Catechesis/Religious Programs—Students 87.

25—HOLY ROSARY (1907), Rev. Jeffery L. Sarkies.
Res., 4139 42nd Ave., S.W., 98116. Tel: 206-935-8353; Fax: 206-935-4303.
School—Tel: 206-937-7255; Fax: 206-937-2610. Kristi Brown, Prin.
Lay Teachers 34; Students 470.
Catechesis/Religious Programs—Students 120.

26—IMMACULATE CONCEPTION (1891), Rev. Fabian MacDonald, Parochial Vicar; Very Rev. James Picton; Rev. Jaime Tolang; Mrs. Joan McGuire, Pastoral Coord.
Res., 820 18th Ave., 98122. Tel: 206-322-5970; Fax: 206-322-9417.
Catechesis/Religious Programs—Students 48.

27—OUR LADY OF FATIMA, Rev. Thomas Quinn; Deacon Walter Shields. In res., Very Rev. Joseph H. Doogan.
Res., 3218 W. Barrett, 98199. Tel: 206-283-1456; Fax: 206-283-5788.
School—3301 W. Dravus St., 98199. Tel: 206-283-7031; Fax: 206-283-7696. Susan Burdett, Prin.
Sisters 1; Lay Teachers 19; Students 278.
Catechesis/Religious Programs—Students 278.

28—OUR LADY OF GUADALUPE (1960), Rev. William Hallahan, O.M.I.
Res., 7000-35th Ave. S.W., 98126. Tel: 206-935-0358; Fax: 206-935-1230.
School—3401 S.W. Myrtle, 98126. Tel: 206-935-0651; Fax: 206-938-3695. Kristin Dixon, Prin.
Lay Teachers 16; Students 233.
Catechesis/Religious Programs—Students 65.

29—OUR LADY OF THE LAKE (1929), Very Rev. John E. McMullan.
Res., 8900 35th Ave., N.E., 98115. Tel: 206-523-6776; Fax: 206-524-0848.
School—3520 N.E. 89th St., 98115. Tel: 206-525-9980; Fax: 206-523-2858. Mrs. Maureen Blum, Prin.
Lay Teachers 16; Students 209.
Catechesis/Religious Programs—Tel: 206-522-0848.
Students 160.

30—OUR LADY OF LOURDES, Rev. Gerald L. Mayovsky.
Res., 10240 12th Ave. S, 98168. Tel: 206-762-3343; Fax: 206-768-1507.

31—OUR LADY OF MOUNT VIRGIN (1911), Very Rev. James Picton; Rev. Pasquale M. Spoletini, S.J. Pastoral Coord.: Charlene P. Collora; Joua Pao Yang. In res., Rev. James Elliott.
Res., 1531 Bradner Pl. S., 98144. Tel: 206-324-8521; Fax: 206-322-6406.
Catechesis/Religious Programs—Students 63.

32—SACRED HEART OF JESUS (1889), Revs. Gregory Schmitt, C.SS.R., Admin.; Brian Johnson, C.SS.R.; Bro. David Werthmann, C.SS.R. In res., Revs. Bernard Mulligan, C.SS.R.; Anthony Slane, C.SS.R.; Michael Logan, C.SS.R.; Joseph Nuttman, C.SS.R.
Res., 205 2nd Ave. N., 98109. Tel: 206-284-4680; Fax: 206-284-3161.

OUTSIDE THE CITY OF SEATTLE

Aberdeen, Grays Harbor Co., St. Mary (1885), Sr. Deanna Carr, B.V.M., Pastoral Life Dir.; Revs. Patrick McDermott; Stephen Roman; Very Rev. Paul Magnano; Rev. Derek Lappe.
Res., 306 E. Third St., 98520. Tel: 360-532-8300; Fax: 360-538-9987.
School—518 N. H St., 98520. Tel: 360-532-1230; Fax: 360-532-1209. Joanne Lott, Prin.
Lay Teachers 11; Students 142.
Mission—Westport, Grays Harbor Co., St. Paul, P.O. Box 332, Westport, 98585. Tel: 206-268-0665. In res., Rev. Stephen Roman.

SS. Peter and Paul (1907) (Polish), Sr. Deanna Carr, B.V.M., Pastoral Life Dir.; Revs. Patrick McDermott; Stephen Roman; Very Rev. Paul Magnano; Rev. Derek Lappe.
Res., 306 E. Third St., 98520. Tel: 360-532-8300; Fax: 360-538-9987.

Anacortes, Skagit Co., St. Mary (1910), Rev. William R. Harris.
Res., 4001 St. Mary's Dr., 98221. Tel: 360-293-2101; Fax: 360-293-6396.
Catechesis/Religious Programs—Tel: 360-293-6882; Fax: 360-293-2102.
Students 153.

Arlington, Snohomish Co., Immaculate Conception (1890), Rev. Richard J. Spicer.
Res., 1200 E. Fifth, P.O. Box 69, 98223. Tel: 360-435-8565; Fax: 360-435-3781.
Catechesis/Religious Programs—Tel: 360-435-8519.
Students 146.
Mission—Darrington, Snohomish Co., St. John Mary Vianney, 1150 Riddle St., Darrington, 98241.

Auburn, King Co., Holy Family (1904), Rev. Phuong Hoang.
Res., 505 17th St., S.E., P.O. Box 290, 98071. Tel: 253-833-5130; Fax: 253-833-3421.
School—(Grades K-8) 505 17th St., S.E., 98002. Tel: 253-833-8688; Fax: 253-833-9311. Kathleen Cowin, Prin.
Lay Teachers 17; Students 247.
Catechesis/Religious Programs—Tel: 253-833-8506.
Students 422.

Bainbridge Island, Kitsap Co., St. Cecilia (1950), Rev. Dennis Sevilla.
Res., 1310 Madison Ave. N., 98110. Tel: 206-842-3594; Fax: 206-842-6988.

Battle Ground, Clark Co., Sacred Heart (1877), Rev. Franklin Lott.
Mailing Address: P.O. Box 38, 23505 N.E. 132nd Ave., 98604. Tel: 360-687-4515; Fax: 360-687-3322. [CEM]
Catechesis/Religious Programs—Tel: 360-687-4515; Fax: 360-687-3322.
Students 144.
Missions—Yacolt, Clark Co., St. Joseph the Workman, 200 Jones St., Yacolt, 98675.; Ridgefield, Clark Co., St. Mary of Guadalupe, (1888) 28309 N.W. 11th, Ridgefield, 98642.

Bellevue, King Co., Sacred Heart (1946), Rev. Patrick Ritter.
Res., 9460 N.E. 14th St., 98004. Tel: 425-454-9536; Fax: 425-450-3909.
School—9450 N.E. 14th St., 98004. Tel: 425-451-1773; Fax: 425-454-9538. Dr. Karen Matthews, Prin.
Lay Teachers 30; Students 469.
Catechesis/Religious Programs—Tel: 425-451-1775.
Students 290.

St. Louise (1960), Revs. Philip D. Wallace; Emilio Gonzalez, Parochial Vicar.
Res., 141 156th Ave., S.E., 98007. Tel: 425-747-4450; Fax: 425-644-3678.
School—133 156th Ave., S.E., 98007. Tel: 425-746-4220; Fax: 425-644-3294. Dan Fitzpatrick, Prin.
Lay Teachers 27; Students 468.
Catechesis/Religious Programs—Students 280.

St. Madeleine Sophie (1968), Very Rev. James D. Picton; Rev. Emmanuel Iweh; Deacon Eugene R. Vanderzanden.
Res., 4400 130th Pl., S.E., 98006-2014. Tel: 425-747-6770; Fax: 425-747-6349.
Catechesis/Religious Programs—Tel: 425-747-6771.
Students 392.

Bellingham, Whatcom Co., Assumption B.V.M., Revs. Joseph A. De Folco; Reynaldo Yu.
Res., 2116 Cornwall Ave., 98225. Tel: 360-733-1380; Fax: 360-733-5644.
School—Tel: 360-733-6133; Fax: 360-733-3601. Ms. Anne Brand, Prin.
Lay Teachers 18; Students 305.
Catechesis/Religious Programs—Students 182.

Sacred Heart (1905), Revs. Joseph A. De Folco; Reynaldo Yu. In res., Rev. Franklin R. Schuster.
Res., 1110 14th St., 98225. Tel: 360-734-2850; Fax: 360-734-0947. [JC]
Catechesis/Religious Programs—Students 110.

Black Diamond, King Co., St. Barbara (1912), Rev. M. Charles Palluck.
Res., Sixth Ave. near Baker, P.O. Box 189, 98010. Tel: 360-886-2229.
Catechesis/Religious Programs—Students 472.

Bothell, King Co., St. Brendan (1949), Very Rev. Steven Sallis; Deacons Eamon Parsons; Hank Fraczek.
Res., 10051 N.E. 195th, 98011-2931. Tel: 425-483-9400; Fax: 425-486-9735.
School—Tel: 425-483-8300; Fax: 425-483-2839. Arlene Sullivan, Prin.
Sisters 2; Lay Teachers 12; Students 265.
Catechesis/Religious Programs—Students 152.

St. Elizabeth Ann Seton, Snohomish Co., (1983), Revs. Eusebio Elizondo, M.Sp.S.; Jorge Gomez del Valle, M.Sp.S.
Res., P.O. Box 12429, Mill Creek, 98082-0429. Tel: 425-481-0303; Fax: 425-485-8510.
Catechesis/Religious Programs—Tel: 425-481-9358. Mavis Kalbrener, D.R.E.
Students 715.

Bremerton, Kitsap Co., Our Lady, Star of the Sea (1902), Rev. Patrick W. Freitag; Deacon James Bemis.
Office: 1513-6th St., 98337. Tel: 360-479-3777; Fax: 360-479-1468.
School—1516-5th St., 98337. Tel: 360-373-5162. Jill Metcalf, Prin.
Lay Teachers 12; Students 195.
Catechesis/Religious Programs—Students 293.

Holy Trinity (1964), Rev. Jack Buckalew.
Mailing Address: P.O. Box 910, Tracyton, 98393.
Res., 4215 Pine Rd., 98310. Tel: 360-377-7674; Fax: 360-377-6181.
Catechesis/Religious Programs—Tel: 360-479-9525.
Students 362.

Buckley, Pierce Co., St. Aloysius (1892), Rev. Hervey Vanasse.
Res., 211 W. Mason St., P.O. Box H, 98321. Tel: 360-862-6014.
Mission—Wilkeson, Pierce Co., Our Lady of Lourdes, (1894).

Burlington, Skagit Co., St. Charles, Revs. Lawrence Minder, O.S.B., Admin.; Gilberto Mora Tapia; Robert Tomkins; William Treacy.
Res., 935 Peterson Rd., 98233. Tel: 360-757-0128; Fax: 360-757-0418.

Camas, Clark Co., St. Thomas Aquinas (1870), Rev. Ronald H. Belisle; Deacon William Townsend.
Res., 324 N.E. Oak, 98607. Tel: 360-834-2126; Fax: 360-834-5106. [CEM]
Catechesis/Religious Programs—Students 252.
Mission—Stevenson, Skamania Co., Star of the Sea, P.O. Box 901, Stevenson, 98648. Tel: 509-427-8478.

Castle Rock, Cowlitz Co., St. Mary, Rev. Michael H. Wright.
Mailing Address: P.O. Box 960, 98611-0960.
Rectory—635 Buland Ave., 98611-0960. Tel: 360-274-7404; Fax: 360-274-7404.
Church—120 Powell Rd., 98611-0960.

Centralia, Lewis Co., St. Mary (1910), Very Rev. Tuan Nguyen.
Res., 225 N. Washington Ave., 98531. Tel: 360-736-4356; Fax: 360-807-0758.
Catechesis/Religious Programs—Students 80.

Chehalis, Lewis Co., St. Joseph (1888), Very Rev. Tuan Nguyen; Rev. Gerald Woodman; Deacon Loren Lane.
Mailing Address: 157 S.W. 6th St., 98532.
Res., 682 S.W. Cascade Ave., 98532. Tel: 360-748-4953; Fax: 360-748-3149.
School—123 S.W. 6th St., 98532. Tel: 360-748-0961; Fax: 360-748-3149. Susan Bergman, Prin.
Lay Teachers 11; Students 125.
Catechesis/Religious Programs—Tel: 360-748-4161.
Students 135.

Covington, King Co., St. John the Baptist (1991), Rev. Jack Walmesley; Deacon Ted Childs.
Church—25810 156th Ave., S.E., 98042. Tel: 253-630-0701; Fax: 253-630-3174.
Catechesis/Religious Programs—Sr. Carol Ann McMullen, S.N.J.M., D.R.E.
Students 350.

Des Moines, King Co., St. Philomena (1927), Rev. Martin Bourke.
Res., 1790 S. 222nd St., 98198. Tel: 206-878-8709; Fax: 206-824-3480.
School—1815 S. 220th, 98198. Tel: 206-824-4051; Fax: 206-878-4664. Karen Tarabochia, Prin.
Lay Teachers 20; Students 250.
Catechesis/Religious Programs—Tel: 206-878-1761. Monesa Grant, D.R.E.
Students 107.

Edmonds, Snohomish Co., Holy Rosary (1940), Very Rev. Kenneth Haydock.
Res., 630 7th Ave. N., P.O. Box 206, 98020. Tel: 425-778-3122; Fax: 425-672-4909.
School—770 Aloha St., 98020. Tel: 425-778-3197; Fax: 425-771-8144. Kathy Carr, Prin.
Sisters 1; Lay Teachers 17; Students 288.
Catechesis/Religious Programs—Students 241.

Elma, Grays Harbor Co., St. Joseph (1890), Rev. David Gese; Deacons Joseph Pellegrino; Frank Hawkins.
Res., 510 W. Waldrip St., P.O. Box AA, 98541. Tel: 360-482-3190; Fax: 360-482-6490. [CEM]
Catechesis/Religious Programs—Students 130.
Mission—Montesano, Grays Harbor Co., St. John, Broadway and Church St., Montesano, 98563. Tel: 360-249-5766.

Enumclaw, King Co., Sacred Heart of Jesus (1888), Rev. James Northrop.
Res., 1614 Farrelly St., 98022. Tel: 360-825-3759; Fax: 360-825-6832. [CEM]
Catechesis/Religious Programs—Tel: 360-825-2333.
Students 343.
Station—Crystal Springs, Crystal Mountain Chapel.

Everett, Snohomish Co., Immaculate Conception (1904), Revs. Dennis E. Robb; John Cornelius; Deacon Matt Zuanich.
Mailing Address: 2619 Cedar St., 98201.
Res., 2430 Hoyt Ave., 98201. Tel: 425-349-7014; Fax: 425-349-7015.
School—2508 Hoyt Ave., 98201. Tel: 425-349-7777; Fax: 425-349-7048. Pat Green, Prin.
Lay Teachers 27; Students 424.
Catechesis/Religious Programs—Students 150.

Our Lady of Perpetual Help, Revs. Dennis E. Robb; John Cornelius; Deacon Matt Zuanich.
Res., 2619 Cedar St., 98201. Tel: 425-349-7014; Fax: 425-349-7015. [JC]

St. Mary Magdalen (1957), Revs. Joseph M. Marquart; Reynaldo Yu.
Res., 8717 7th Ave., S.E., 98208. Tel: 206-353-1211; Fax: 206-348-0458.
School—8615 7th Ave., S.E., 98208. Tel: 206-353-7559; Fax: 206-356-2687. Dr. Joanne McCauley, O.P., Prin.
Sisters 2; Lay Teachers 22; Students 426.
Catechesis/Religious Programs—Tel: 425-353-3133.
Students 271.
Mission—Mukilteo, Snohomish Co., St. John.

Federal Way, King & Pierce Cos., St. Theresa (1924), Rev. Kevin Moran.
Res., 3939 S.W. 331st, 98023. Tel: 253-838-5924; Fax: 253-838-0300.
Catechesis/Religious Programs—Students 373.

St. Vincent De Paul, King Co., (1961), Revs. Thomas L. Vandenberg; David Mayovsky.
Res., 30525 8th Ave., S., 98003. Tel: 253-839-2320; Fax: 253-839-1819.
School—30527 8th Ave., S., 98003. Tel: 253-839-3532; Fax: 253-839-1819. Wanda Stewart, Prin.
Lay Teachers 19; Students 286.
Catechesis/Religious Programs—Tel: 253-839-4333.
Students 420.

Ferndale, Whatcom Co., St. Joseph (1893), Very Rev. Timothy J. Sauer; Deacon George Ficken.
Res., 5781 Hendrickson Ave., 98248. Tel: 360-384-3651; Fax: 360-384-1879.
Catechesis/Religious Programs—Tel: 360-384-8818.
Students 226.
Missions—Blaine, Whatcom Co., St. Anne, 98230. Tel: 360-332-3651; Lummi, Whatcom Co., St. Joachim (Indian Reservation), 98226. Tel: 360-734-3651.

Fife, Lakewood Co., St. Martin of Tours, Rev. Patrick K. O'Brien.
Res., 2303-54th Ave., E., 98424. Tel: 253-922-7882.
School—All Saints, 2323 54th Ave., E., 98424. Tel: 253-922-5360. Alice Milam, Prin.
Lay Teachers 10; Students 195.
Catechesis/Religious Programs—Students 95.

Forks, Clallam Co., St. Anne Parish (1992), Rev. Gerald O. Brunet, O.M.I.
Res., 511-5th Ave., P.O. Box 2359, 98331. Tel: 360-374-9184.
Catechesis/Religious Programs—Tel: 360-374-6405.
Students 75.
Mission—Clallam Bay, Clallam Co., St. Thomas the Apostle.

Friday Harbor, San Juan Co., St. Francis (1860), Rev. Robert L. Evenson.
Res., 425 Price St., P.O. Box 1489, 98250. Tel: 360-378-2910 (Office); 378-6603 (Rectory); Fax: 360-378-1608. [CEM]
Catechesis/Religious Programs—Students 121.
Stations—Eastsound, St. Francis, 956 N Beach Rd., Eastsound, 98245. Tel: 360-376-6301; 378-2910; Lopez Island.; San Juan Island, Roche Harbor.

Gig Harbor, Pierce Co., St. Nicholas (1931), Rev. Gary Weisenberger; Deacon John Ricciardi.
Res., 3510 Rosedale St., P.O. Box 220, 98335. Tel: 253-851-8850; Fax: 253-851-8823.
School—7701 Skanskie Ave., 98335. Tel: 253-858-7632. Dr. Carola Wittmann, Prin.
Lay Teachers 13; Students 124.
Catechesis/Religious Programs—Tel: 253-851-9040.
Students 415.

Hoquiam, Grays Harbor Co., Our Lady of Good Help (1906), Sr. Deanna Carr, B.V.M., Pastoral Life Dir.; Revs. Patrick McDermott; Stephen Roman; Very Rev. Paul Magnano; Rev. Derek Lappe.
Mailing Address: 611 2nd St., 98550.
Res., 200 L St., 98550. Tel: 360-532-6103; Fax: 360-533-9012.
Catechesis/Religious Programs—Students 26.
Mission—Quinault, Grays Harbor & Jefferson Cos., Our Lady of the Olympics, Box 165, Quinault, 98575. Tel: 360-288-2802.

Issaquah, King Co., St. Joseph (1962), Rev. Patrick S. Clark; Deacon Patrick Moynihan.
Res., 220 Mt. Park Blvd., S.W., P.O. Box 200, 98027. Tel: 425-392-5516; Fax: 425-392-2722.
School—(Grades (K-5)). Tel: 425-313-9129. Jackie Olund, Prin.
Lay Teachers 19; Students 80.
Catechesis/Religious Programs—Students 150.

Kelso, Cowlitz Co., Immaculate Heart of Mary (1910), Rev. Michael H. Wright.
Res., 2200 Allen St., 98626. Tel: 360-423-3650; Fax: 360-423-4165.
Catechesis/Religious Programs—Tel: 360-423-3653.
Students 126.

Kent, King Co., Holy Spirit Parish (1890), Very Rev. Michael J. Ryan; Rev. Michael A. Tyrell, S.J.
Res., 310 3rd Ave., S., 98032. Tel: 253-859-0444; Fax: 253-859-5974. [CEM]
Catechesis/Religious Programs—Students 256.

Kirkland, King Co., Holy Family (1915), Revs. Gary Morelli; Stephen Szeman.
Res., 7355 120th Ave., N.E., 98033. Tel: 425-822-0295; Fax: 425-827-0648.
School—Tel: 425-827-0444; Fax: 425-827-0150. Sue Ford Clausen, Prin.
Lay Teachers 16; Students 259.

St. John Mary Vianney (1971), Rev. Kevin F.X. Duggan.
Res., 12600 84th Ave., N.E., 98034. Tel: 425-823-0787; Fax: 425-814-2115.
Catechesis/Religious Programs—Students 485.

LaConner, Skagit Co., Sacred Heart (1875), Revs. Lawrence Minder, O.S.B., Admin.; Robert Tomkins; Gilberto Mora Tapia; William Treacy; Deacon George Peterson.
Res., P.O. Box 757, 98257-0757. Tel: 360-466-3967; Fax: 360-466-3942.
Catechesis/Religious Programs—410 Douglas St., 98257.
Students 42.

St. Paul (Swinomish) (1867) (Native American), Revs. Lawrence Minder, O.S.B., Admin.; Patrick Twohy, S.J., Parochial Vicar.
Mailing Address: P.O. Box 2100, 98257. Tel: 360-466-5737; Fax: 360-466-4039.
Church—17456 Pioneer Pkwy. Rd., 98257.

Lacey, Thurston Co., Sacred Heart of Jesus (1923), Rev. Richard Parle.
Res., P.O. Box 3805, 98509-3805. Tel: 360-491-0890; Fax: 360-456-1028.
Catechesis/Religious Programs—Students 590.

Lakewood, Pierce Co., St. Francis Cabrini (1952), Rev. James P. Coyne.
Res., 5505 108th St., S.W., 98499. Tel: 253-588-2141; Fax: 253-582-5351.
School—Tel: 253-584-3850; Fax: 253-582-5351. Stephanie Van Leuven, Prin.
Sisters 1; Lay Teachers 13; Students 230.
Catechesis/Religious Programs—Students 201.

St. John Bosco (1968), Rev. Dennis V. Champagne.
Res., 10508 112 St., S.W., 98498. Tel: 253-582-1028; Fax: 253-584-0633.
Catechesis/Religious Programs—Students 296.
Mission—Steilacoom, Pierce Co., Immaculate Conception, Nisqually & Main, 98388.

Langley, Island Co., St. Hubert (1938), Rev. Gerald Moffat; Deacon Ed Read.
Mailing Address: P.O. Box 388, 98260-0388.
Res., 815 Saratoga Ave., 98260. Tel: 360-221-5383; Fax: 360-221-2011. [CEM]
Catechesis/Religious Programs—Tel: 360-221-5030.
Students 125.

Longview, Cowlitz Co., St. Rose de Viterbo (1928), Very Rev. K. Scott Connolly.
Mailing Address: 701-26th, 98632.
Res., 2571 Nichols Blvd., 98632. Tel: 360-425-4660; Fax: 360-577-5820.
School—727 25th Ave., 98632. Tel: 360-577-6760; Fax: 360-577-3689. Kay Purcell, Prin.
Sisters 2; Lay Teachers 14; Students 205.
Catechesis/Religious Programs—Tel: 360-577-7346.
Students 245.
Mission—Cathlamet, Wahkiakum Co., St. Catherine, 400 Columbia St., Cathlamet, 98612. Tel: 360-795-8725.

Lynden, Whatcom Co., St. Joseph, Rev. Richard McCallister.
Res., 205 Twelfth St., 98264. Tel: 360-354-2334; Fax: 360-354-5889.
Catechesis/Religious Programs—Students 214.
Mission—Deming, Whatcom Co., St. Peter, 6210 Mt. Baker Hwy., Deming, 98244. [CEM 3]

Lynnwood, Snohomish Co., St. Thomas More (1962), Rev. James Dalton.
Res., 6511-176th S.W., Lynwood, 98037. Tel: 425-743-2929; Fax: 425-743-3652.
School—Tel: 425-743-4242; Fax: 425-745-8367. Patrick White, Prin.
Sisters 1; Lay Teachers 15; Students 242.
Catechesis/Religious Programs—Tel: 425-743-5780.
Students 301.

Marysville, Snohomish Co., St. Mary (1888), Rev. Horacio Yanez.
Res., 4200 88th St, N.E., 98270. Tel: 360-653-9400; Fax: 360-658-7439. [CEM]
Catechesis/Religious Programs—Students 476.
Mission—Tulalip, Snohomish Co., Tulalip Indian Reservation, St. Anne, 7213 Totem Beach Rd., Tulalip, 98271.

Mercer Island, King Co., St. Monica (1958), Rev. John Bowman; Deacon Jack Warfield. In res., Rev. John Horan.

Res., 4301 88th S.E., P.O. Box 730, 98040. Tel: 206-232-2900; Fax: 206-232-7875.
School—4320 87th S.E., 98040. Tel: 206-232-5432; Fax: 206-275-2874. Mrs. Pamela Dellino, Prin.
Lay Teachers 12; Students 239.
Catechesis/Religious Programs—Tel: 206-232-9829; Fax: 206-232-3321.
Students 275.

Monroe, Snohomish Co., St. Mary of the Valley (1902), Rev. Michael C. O'Brien.
Res., 601 W. Columbia, P.O. Box 279, 98272. Tel: 360-794-8945; Fax: 360-805-0201.
Catechesis/Religious Programs—Students 208.

Morton, Lewis Co., Sacred Heart, Rev. Roger J. Smith.
Res., 7th and W. Adams Sts., P.O. Box 880, 98356. Tel: 360-496-5456; Fax: 360-496-5616.
Mission—Harmony, Lewis Co., St. Yves. [CEM]
Station—Packwood.

Mountlake Terrace, Snohomish Co., St. Pius X (1955), Revs. Sean P. Fox; Ronald Knudsen.
Res., 22106 56th W., 98043. Tel: 425-775-7545; Fax: 425-775-8744.
School—22105 58th W., 98043. Tel: 425-778-9861. Mrs. Terri McDermott, Prin.
Lay Teachers 13; Students 230.
Catechesis/Religious Programs—Students 115.

Mount Vernon, Skagit Co., Immaculate Conception (1899), Revs. Lawrence Minder, O.S.B., Admin.; Robert Tomkins; Gilberto Mora Tapia; William Treacy.
Res., 215 N. 15th St., 98273. Tel: 360-336-6622; Fax: 360-336-5203.
School—1321 E. Division St., 98273. Tel: 360-428-3912; Fax: 360-424-8838. Sally Merriwether, Prin.
Lay Teachers 21; Students 315.

Oak Harbor, Island Co., St. Augustine, Rev. John J. O'Leary, S.J., Admin.
Res., 185 N. Oak Harbor St., 98277. Tel: 360-675-2303; Fax: 360-675-9490.
Catechesis/Religious Programs—Students 342.
Mission—Coupeville, Island Co., St. Mary, 207 N. Main, 98239. Tel: 360-678-6536.

Ocean Shores, Grays Harbor Co., St. Jerome (1969), Sr. Deanna Carr, B.V.M., Pastoral Life Dir.; Revs. Patrick McDermott; Stephen Roman; Very Rev. Paul Magnano; Rev. Derek Lappe; Deacon Bruce MacPherson.
Res., P.O. Box 190, 98569. Tel: 360-289-2838; Fax: 360-289-0163.

Olympia, Thurston Co., St. Michael (1848), Revs. James Lee; Don Perea; Paul Weckert, O.S.B.
Res., 1021 Boundary St. S.E., P.O. Box 766, 98507. Tel: 360-754-4667; Fax: 360-754-0628. [CEM]
School—1203 E. 10th, 98501. Tel: 360-754-5131; Fax: 360-753-6090. Thomas Ward, Prin.
Lay Teachers 19; Students 252.
Catechesis/Religious Programs—1010 Eastside St. SE, 98507. Tel: 360-754-4077.
Students 476.

Pe Ell, Lewis Co., St. Joseph (1894), Very Rev. Tuan Nguyen.
Res., 417 N Main, P.O. Box 235, 98572. Tel: 360-291-3434. [CEM 2]
Catechesis/Religious Programs—Students 16.
Mission—Frances, Pacific Co., Holy Family. State Hwy. 6.

Port Angeles, Clallam Co., Queen of Angels (1891), Rev. Kurt Nagel.
Res., 209 W. 11th St., 98362. Tel: 360-452-2351; Fax: 360-452-1447.
School—1107 S. Oak, 98362. Tel: 360-457-6903; Fax: 360-457-6866. Mrs. Theresa Sekac, Prin.
Lay Teachers 15; Students 168.

Port Orchard, Kitsap Co., St. Gabriel (1942), Rev. Lester McCloskey.
Res., 1150 Mitchell Ave., 98366-4416. Tel: 360-876-2762; Fax: 360-876-6085.
Catechesis/Religious Programs—Tel: 360-876-2834.
Students 457.
Mission—Belfair, Mason Co., Prince of Peace, (1970) N.E. 1171 Sand Hill Rd., P.O. Box 517, Belfair, 98528. Tel: 360-275-8760; Fax: 360-275-4418.
Catechesis/Religious Programs—Students 51.

Port Townsend, Jefferson Co., St. Mary's, Star of the Sea (1859), Rev. Raymond J. Heffernan.
Res., 1335 Blaine St., 98368. Tel: 360-385-3700; Fax: 360-379-1989. [CEM]
Catechesis/Religious Programs—Tel: 360-385-1662.
Students 84.

Poulsbo, Kitsap Co., St. Olaf (1968), Very Rev. Hung Nguyen; Deacon Carl Moyer.
Res., 18943 Caldart Ave., N.E., 98370. Tel: 360-779-4291; Fax: 360-779-1240.
Catechesis/Religious Programs—Tel: 360-779-9510.
Students 402.
Mission—Suquamish, Kitsap Co., St. Peter.

Puyallup, Pierce Co., All Saints (1899), Rev. Richard Basso, Admin.; Deacon Michael McGillicuddy.
Res., 204 6th S.W., 98371. Tel: 253-845-7521; Fax: 253-845-3105.
Schools—504 2nd S.W., 98371. Tel: 206-845-5025; Fax: 253-435-9841.
Lay Teachers 9; Students 154; St. Martin of Tours School (Satellite School), (Grades PreK-2) 2323 54th Ave., E., Fife, 98424. Tel: 253-922-5360. Jack Nelson, Prin.
Lay Teachers 10; Students 149.
Catechesis/Religious Programs—Students 412.

Holy Disciples (1996), Rev. Gary Southerton.
Res., 15012 Meridian Ave., E., Ste. 4, 98375. Tel: 253-845-0828; Fax: 253-845-0930.
Catechesis/Religious Programs—Fax: 253-845-0828.
Students 390.
Mission—Eatonville, Pierce Co., Our Lady of Good Counsel, 229 Antonie Ave. N., Eatonville, 98328. Tel: 360-832-6363; Fax: 360-832-6363.

Raymond, Pacific Co., St. Lawrence, Rev. Victor A. Olvida.
1112 Blake St., P.O. Box 31, 98577. Tel: 360-942-3000; Fax: 360-942-3000.
Catechesis/Religious Programs—Students 49.

Redmond, King Co., St. Jude (1978), Revs. Gerald F. Lovett; Daniel Madigan.
Res., 10526 166th N.E., 98052. Tel: 425-883-7685; Fax: 425-881-2207. [CEM]
Catechesis/Religious Programs—Students 872.

Renton, King Co., St. Anthony (1901), Revs. Gary Zender; James Elliott; Deacon Richard Combs.
Res., 314 S. 4th St., 98055. Tel: 425-255-3132; Fax: 425-271-4729.
School—336 Shattuck Ave., S., 98055. Tel: 425-255-0059; Fax: 425-235-6555. Gary Teale, Prin.
Sisters 2; Lay Teachers 30; Students 527.
Catechesis/Religious Programs—Students 476.

St. Stephen the Martyr (1966), Rev. John C. Madigan.
Res., 13055 S.E. 192nd St., 98058. Tel: 253-631-1940; Fax: 425-255-2943.
Catechesis/Religious Programs—Tel: 253-631-6175.
Students 380.

Sammamish, King Co., Mary, Queen of Peace (1987), Revs. J. Paul Dalton; Michael Raschko; Deacon William Taube.
Res., 1121 228th Ave., S.E., 98075. Tel: 435-391-1178; Fax: 425-391-3797.
Catechesis/Religious Programs—Students 593.

Seahurst, King Co., St. Francis of Assisi (1929), Revs. Richahrd K. Hayatsu; Michael Angelovic.
Res., 15236 21st Ave., S.W., P.O. Box 929, 98062. Tel: 206-242-4575; Fax: 206-242-1957.
School—P.O. Box 870, 98062. Tel: 206-243-5690; Fax: 206-433-8593. Sheila Keaton, Prin.
Lay Teachers 25; Students 434.
Catechesis/Religious Programs—Tel: 206-246-1230.
Students 135.

Seaview, Pacific Co., St. Mary (1965), Rev. Victor A. Olvida; Deacon Glenn Clifton.
Res., P.O. Box 274, 98644. Tel: 360-642-2002.
Station—McGowan.

Sedro Woolley, Skagit Co., Immaculate Heart of Mary (1890), Revs. Lawrence Minder, O.S.B., Admin.; Robert Tompkins; Gilberto Mora Tapia; William Treacy.
Res., 719 Ferry St., 98284. Tel: 360-855-0077; 855-2282; Fax: 360-855-2282.
Mission—Concrete, Skagit Co., St. Catherine, 239 Limestone, Concrete, 98237. Tel: 360-853-8941.

Sequim, Clallam Co., St. Joseph (1916), Rev. Thomas Beattie.
Res., 121 E. Maple, P.O. Box 1209, 98382. Tel: 360-683-6076; Fax: 360-683-4674.
Catechesis/Religious Programs—Tel: 360-683-1640.
Students 150.

Shelton, Mason Co., St. Edward (1892), Revs. Dominic D. Hahn, O.S.B.; Alberto Cerezo.
Res., 321 N. 3rd St., P.O. Box 758, 98584. Tel: 360-426-6134; Fax: 360-426-6231. [JC]
Catechesis/Religious Programs—Students 116.

Snohomish, Snohomish Co., St. Michael (1886), Rev. Richard Ward; Deacon Ed White.
Res., 1512 Pine Ave., 98290. Tel: 360-568-0821; Fax: 360-568-6426.
Mission—Granite Falls, Snohomish Co., Holy Cross, Tel: 360-691-5945.

Snoqualmie, King Co., Our Lady of Sorrows (1929), Revs. Jan Larson; Ross Fewing.
Res., 39025 S.E. Alpha St., P.O. Box 909, 98065. Tel: 425-888-2974; Fax: 425-888-7098.
Catechesis/Religious Programs—Students 262.
Missions—Carnation, King Co., St. Anthony, P.O. Box 175, Carnation, 98014. Tel: 425-333-4930; Duvall, King Co., Holy Innocents, P.O. Box 850, Duvall, 98019. Tel: 425-788-1400; Fax: 425-844-2384.
Station—Snoqualmie Summit, St. Bernard's Chapel, Tel: 206-454-6161.

Stanwood, Snohomish Co., St. Cecilia (1908), Rev. Paul Koenig, O.C.D. In res., Revs. Colm Stone, O.C.D.; David Centner, O.C.D.
Res., 26900 78th Ave., N.W., P.O. Box 1002, 98292. Tel: 360-629-3737; Fax: 360-629-6127.
Catechesis/Religious Programs—Tel: 360-629-4425.
Students 203.

Sumner, Pierce Co., St. Andrew (1921), Rev. Thomas A. Belleque.
Res., 704 Kincaid Ave., 98390. Tel: 253-863-2253; Fax: 253-863-3567.
Catechesis/Religious Programs—Tel: 253-863-4394.
Students 410.
Mission—Orting, Pierce Co., SS. Cosmas and Damian, 213 W. Leber St., Orting, 98360. Tel: 360-893-3154.

Tacoma, Pierce Co.,

1—St. Ann, (1924), Revs. Vincent Pastro; John Nwanze, O.P. (Nigeria); Daniel Chiezey, O.P. (Nigeria).
Res., 7001 S. Park Ave., 98408. Tel: 253-472-1360; Fax: 253-475-6335.
Catechesis/Religious Programs—Students 101.

2—St. Charles Borromeo, (1956), Very Rev. Michael J. McDermott; Rev. James O. Johnson, Jr.
Res., 7112 S. 12th St., 98465. Tel: 253-564-5185; Fax: 253-565-0936.
School—Tel: 253-581-2908. Patrick Feist, Prin.
Sisters of St. Francis of Philadelphia 1; Lay Teachers 23; Students 508.
Catechesis/Religious Programs—Tel: 253-564-5185, Ext. 3036.
Students 232.

3—St. John of the Woods, (1924), Revs. Vincent Pastro; John Nwanze, O.P. (Nigeria); Daniel Chiezey, O.P. (Nigeria).
Res., 9903 24th Ave., E., 98445. Tel: 253-537-8551; Fax: 253-537-0459.
Catechesis/Religious Programs—Tel: 253-531-7110.
Students 93.

4—St. Joseph, (1911) (Slovak), Rev. John J. Wilkie.
Res., 608 S. 34th St., 98418. Tel: 253-472-2489.

5—St. Leo the Great, (1879), Revs. John D. Fuchs, S.J.; Dominic Nguyen, S.J.
Res., 710 S. 13th St., 98405. Tel: 253-272-5136; Fax: 253-272-6285.
Catechesis/Religious Programs—Students 135.

6—St. Patrick, (1891), Rev. Seamus Laverty.
Res., 1001 N. J St., 98403. Tel: 253-383-2783; Fax: 253-627-5396.
School—1112 N. G St., 98403. Tel: 253-272-2297; Fax: 253-383-2003. Larry Di Palma, Prin.
Sisters 3; Lay Teachers 26; Students 401.
Catechesis/Religious Programs—Students 165.

7—SS. Peter & Paul, (1892) (Polish), Rev. Piotr Dzikowski, S.Ch.
Res., 3422 Portland Ave., 98404. Tel: 253-272-5232; Fax: 253-627-7848.

8—St. Rita, (1922) (Italian), Rev. Carmine J. Sacco, S.J.
Res., 1403 S. Ainsworth, 98405. Tel: 253-627-4851; Fax: 253-274-0436.
Catechesis/Religious Programs—Students 70.

9—Holy Cross, (1915), Rev. Robert Rekofke, S.J.
Res., 5510 N. 44th St., 98407. Tel: 253-759-3368; Fax: 253-759-6126.
Catechesis/Religious Programs—Students 40.

10—Holy Rosary, (1891), Rev. John J. Wilkie.
Res., 512 S. 30th St., 98402. Tel: 253-383-4549; Fax: 253-779-0622.
School—504 S. 30th, 98402. Tel: 253-272-7012. Mrs. Catherine Lendosky, Prin.
Lay Teachers 24; Students 200.

11—Our Lady, Queen of Heaven, (1893), Rev. John Renggli.
Parish Office: 14601 A St. S., 98444. Tel: 253-537-3252; Fax: 253-536-2662.
Catechesis/Religious Programs—Students 202.

12—Sacred Heart, (1912), Revs. Vincent Pastro; John Nwanze, O.P. (Nigeria); Daniel Chiezey, O.P. (Nigeria).
Res., 4520 McKinley Ave., 98404. Tel: 253-472-7738.
Catechesis/Religious Programs—Students 147.

13—Visitation, (1892), Rev. David Gese.
Res., 3314 S. 58th St., 98409. Tel: 253-473-4960; Fax: 253-474-8378.
School—3306 S. 58th St., 98409. Tel: 253-474-6425; Fax: 253-474-6718. Imelda Mead, Prin.
Lay Teachers 13; Students 181.

Catechesis/Religious Programs—Students 78.

Toledo, Lewis Co., St. Francis Xavier (1838), Very Rev. Tuan Nguyen; Rev. Gerald Woodman.
Res., 139 Spencer Rd., 98591. Tel: 360-864-4126; Fax: 360-864-4126. [CEM]

Tukwila, King Co., St. Thomas, Rev. Gerald L. Mayovsky.
Res., 4415 S. 140th St., 98168. Tel: 206-242-5501; Fax: 206-244-9387.
Catechesis/Religious Programs—Tel: 206-242-8189.
Students 122.

Vancouver, Clark Co.,

1—HOLY REDEEMER, (2000), Rev. Joseph P. Mitchell.
Mailing Address: P.O. Box 871417, 98687-1417. Tel: 360-885-7780.
Church—Mill Plain Center, Ste. A-100, 705 S.E. Parkcrest Ave., 98687.

2—OUR LADY OF LOURDES, (1958), Rev. John J. Ludvik, Admin.; Deacon Robert Tomich.
Res., 4723 Franklin St., N.W., 98663. Tel: 360-695-1366; Fax: 360-695-7966.
School—Tel: 360-696-2301; Fax: 360-696-6700. Ms. Shirley Loesch, Prin.
Lay Teachers 18; Students 270.
Catechesis/Religious Programs—Students 222.

3—ST. JAMES, (1836), Revs. Clay Meyer; Anthony Lan Tran.
Res., 218 W. 12th St., 98660. Tel: 360-693-3052; Fax: 360-693-3077. [CEM]
Catechesis/Religious Programs—Students 73.

4—ST. JOHN, Rev. Philip Fitzsimons (Ireland) Admin.
Res., 8701 N.E. 119 St., 98662. Tel: 360-573-3325; Fax: 360-573-3344. [CEM]
Catechesis/Religious Programs—Students 275.
Station—Larch Mountain Corrections Center.

5—ST. JOSEPH, (1952), Revs. Hans Olson; Bryan Hersey.
Res., 6600 Highland Dr., 98661. Tel: 360-696-4407; Fax: 360-696-3959.
School—6500 Highland Dr., 98661. Tel: 360-696-2586; Fax: 360-696-3959. Dr. Leslie McDaniel, Prin.
Lay Teachers 26; Students 409.
Catechesis/Religious Programs—Students 596.

Vashon, King Co., St. John Vianney (1964), Rev. Richard R. Roach, S.J.
Res., P.O. Box 308, 98070. Tel: 206-567-4149; Fax: 206-567-4198.
Mission—Dockton, King Co., St. Patrick, 26100 99th Ave. SW, Dockton, 98070.

Winlock, Lewis Co., Sacred Heart (1909), Rev. Gerald Woodman.
Res., P.O. Box 69, 98596. Tel: 360-785-3653. [CEM]
Station—St. Urban.

Woodland, Cowlitz Co., St. Philip (1950), Rev. Joseph P. O'Shea.
Res., 430 Bozarth, Box 2169, 98674. Tel: 360-225-8308; Fax: 360-225-8866. [CEM]
Catechesis/Religious Programs—Students 164.
Mission—Kalama, Cowlitz Co., St. Joseph, 4th & Elm, Kalama, 98625. Tel: 360-673-4682 (Hall).

Yelm, Thurston Co., St. Columban (1960), Rev. Terence J. Wager, O.S.B.
Res., 506 1st St. S., 98597. Tel: 360-458-3031; Fax: 360-458-4094.
Mission—Tenino, Thurston Co., St. Peter, P.O. Box 744, Sussex & Keithan St., Tenino, 98589. Tel: 360-264-2124; Fax: 360-264-2666.
Catechesis/Religious Programs—Students 139.

Chaplains of Public Institutions

SEATTLE. *Callum Bay Correction Center*. Rev. Gerald O. Brunet, O.M.I.
Federal Detention Center SEA-TAC. Sr. Joan Campbell, S.P., Pastoral Min.
Olympic/Clearwater Correction Center. Rev. Gerald O. Brunet, O.M.I.
U.S. Public Health Hospital. Attended by St. Peter Church, Seattle.
Veterans Administration Medical Center. Rev. Thomas R. Park, O.S.B.

BUCKLEY. *Rainier School*. Rev. James Boyle.
Western State Custodial School. Attended from St. Aloysius Church, Buckley.

CHEHALIS. *Green Hill School*. Very Rev. Tuan Nguyen; Deacon Loren Lane, Pastoral Min.

GIG HARBOR. *Washington Corrections Center for Women*. Mary Bradford, Pastoral Min.

LITTLE ROCK. *Cedar Creek Correction Center*. Joenne Hibbelin, Pastoral Min.

MCNEIL ISLAND. *McNeil Island Correction Center*. Rev. Thomas Suss.

MONROE. *Monroe Correctional Complex*.
Minimum Security Unit, Sr. Renee Kittleson, M.S.C., Pastoral Min.
Special Offenders Center, Sr. Renee Kittleson, M.S.C., Pastoral Min.,
Twin Rivers Correction Center, Rev. Lyle Konen, C.Ss.R.; Linda Haptonstall, Pastoral Min.
Washington State Reformatory. Pastoral Ministers: Rev. Lyle Konen, C.Ss.R.; Linda Haptonstall.

ORTING. *U.S. Soldiers' Home*. Rev. Thomas A. Belleque.

PORT ORCHARD. *Washington Veterans Home Hospital*. Rev. Lester McCloskey.

SHELTON. *Washington Corrections Center*. Vacant. P.O. Box 900, 98584. Shannon O'Donnell, Pastoral Min.

SNOQUALMIE. *Echo Glen Children's Center*. Betsy Staal, Pastoral Min.

STEILACOOM. *Western State Hospital*. Rev. Robert Tino.

TACOMA. *Veterans Admin. Medical Center*. Rev. David W. Prebula, O.S.B.

VANCOUVER. *Veterans Administration Hospital*. Attended from Archdiocese of Portland in Oregon.
Washington State School for the Blind. Attended from St. James Church, Vancouver.
Washington State School for the Deaf. Attended from St. Joseph Church, Vancouver.

YACOLT. *Larch Mountain Correction Center*. Vacant.

Special Assignment:
Reverend Fathers—
Eblen, James, Theologian, 910 Marion St., Seattle, WA 98104. Tel: 206-382-4593
Fewing, Ross, Swedish Hospital Ministry
Jaeger, David, AIDS Ministry, 910 Marion St., Seattle, WA 98104
Magnano, Paul, Vicar for Clergy, 910 Marion St., Seattle, WA 98104
Picton, James, Vicar for Parishes & Faith Communities, 910 Marion St., Seattle, WA 98104
Raschko, Michael, Theologian, 1614 Summit, #602, Seattle, WA 98122
Sauer, Timothy J., Dir. Seminarians, 910 Marion St., Seattle, WA 98104
Snyder, Brian, Seattle Hospital Ministry, 910 Marion, Seattle, WA 98104
Stehly, Mark, Seattle Hospital Ministry, 910 Marion St., Seattle, WA 98104

On Duty Outside the Archdiocese:
Reverend Fathers—
Larrivee, Leo J., S.S., 4210 N. Charles St. #3, Baltimore, MD 21218
Pins, Herbert J., Diocese of Helena
Rogerson, Daniel, Mount Angel Abbey, St. Benedict, OR 97373
Rowan, Stephen, Interim Pres., Carroll College, Helena, MT

Military Chaplains:
Reverend Fathers—
Bailey, Lawrence, 9041 A McConnell, Laughlin AFB, TX 78840-2745
McKenna, Timothy J., 5435B Sundog Ct., Eielson AFB, AR 99702

Unassigned:
Reverend Fathers—
Ashwell, Barry G., 910 Marion St., Seattle, WA 98104
Guzman, Armando, 910 Marion St., Seattle, WA 98104
Hart, Brian, 910 Marion St., Seattle, WA 98104
Lesnick, Richard, 910 Marion St., Seattle, WA 98104
Tucker, Michael, 910 Marion St., Seattle, WA 98104

Retired:
Reverend Monsignors—
Doogan, John P., 18033-15th Pl., N.E., Shoreline, WA 98155
Reverend Fathers—
Aspiras, Jose, Station Rita East, Agoo, La Union Philippines
Bulger, John, 54 Mitchell St., Pittson, PA 18640
Chivico, Peter, S.S., 804 9th Ave., Seattle, WA 98104
Cloquet, Victor, P.O. Box 1232, Allyn, WA 98524-1232
Cody, Michael, 910 Marion St., Seattle, WA 98104
Crosse, Charles, 8539 Zircon Dr. S.W., Tacoma, WA 98498
Delahunty, Thomas, 7320C 142nd Ave., E., Summer, WA 98390
Domandich, Anthony, P.O. Box 2169, Woodland, WA 98674-0002
Doogan, Joseph H., 3218 W. Barrett, Seattle, WA 98199
Gallagher, Richard, 5809 S. 234th Pl., Kent, WA 98032
Gallagher, William E., 6108 N. Park, Tacoma, WA 98407
Godley, Patrick, 15892 West Arrowhead Dr., Surprise, AR 85374
Harrington, Cornelius, 1156 Alki Ave. S.W., Seattle, WA 98116
Heneghan, Jarlath, 17833 W. Arizona Dr., Surprise, AZ 85374
Heneghan, Sean, 12450 20th Ave., S., Seattle, WA 98168
Horan, John, P.O. Box 730, Mercer Island, WA 98040
Jennings, John A., 6041 California Ave. S.W., #403, Seattle, WA 98136-1651
Jonientz, Bernard, 4231 S. Juneau, Seattle, WA 98118
Koehler, John, Harborview Apartments #14, 2902 - N. Carr St., Tacoma, WA 98403
Kramis, Joseph, 2009 Walker Park Rd., Shelton, WA 98584
Lane, William, 20826 70th Ave. W., #6, Lynnwood, WA 98036
Linehan, David, 515 S. 136th St., Seattle, WA 98168
Lynch, Ibar, 1427 3rd Ave. W., #19, Seattle, WA 98119
Mallahan, James, 949 N. 35th St., #103, Seattle, WA 98103
McEnnis, Thomas, 10343 W. Cameo Dr., Sun City, AZ 85351
McGreal, James, 910 Marion St., Seattle, WA 98104
McLaughlin, John, 1930 S.E. Oakview Dr., Chehalis, WA 98532
McMahon, Desmond, 1115 N. "I." St., Apt. 305, Tacoma, WA 98403
Moore, Gerald T., 2810 W. Hayes, Seattle, WA 98199
Moynihan, Timothy, Arbor Square, 11039 17th N.E., Seattle, WA 98125
Naumes, Matthew, 5212 70th W., Tacoma, WA 98467
O'Callaghan, Thomas, P.O. Box 346, Suquamish, WA 98392
O'Neil, Michael, 1065 N. American Ln., Coupeville, WA 98239
O'Neill, Patrick, 16351 W. Labrynth Ln., Surprise, AZ 85374
Petosa, Joseph, 1120 Spring St., #11, Seattle, WA 98104
Phelan, Thomas, 512 S.E. 169th Ave., Vancouver, WA 98684-8413
Quigg, Harold, 910 Marion St., Seattle, WA 98104
Rice, John A., 1208-6455 Willingdon Ave., Burnaby, B.C. V5H 4E4
Rink, George, 1828 S.W. 318th Pl., Unit D, Federal Way, WA 98023
Slate, William, P.O. Box 4258, Kent, WA 98032
Sondergeld, Theodore, 2627 S. 310th, Federal Way, WA 98003
Szeman, Stephen, 4814 N.E. 5th Ct., Renton, WA 98059
Tolang, Jaime, 820 18th Ave., Seattle, WA 98122
Treacy, William, Camp Brotherhood, 2301 Legge Rd., Mount Vernon, WA 98273
White, David, 10501 8th Ave. N., Seattle, WA 98125

Permanent Deacons:
Alexander, Richard, Indio, CA
Allen, Daniel
Anderson, Carl
Anderson, David
Bemis, James
Benedict, Nathan
Bentley, Ernest
Burkholder, Thomas, On Leave
Cavanaugh, Robert
Cliffton, Glenn
Crandall, Charles
Curtis, Joseph
Dardis, Robert
Denby, Marshall
Dodson, Arthur, On Leave
Dolan, Robert
Dorr, LuVerne
Duffell, Denny
Dunne, Joseph
Edtl, Lee
Ellis, Rolland
Erskine, Thomas
Ficken, George
Frost, Harold
Hanika, Donald
Hartzell, Clay
Hawkins, Tom
Henn, Thomas, Sun City West, AZ
Ho, Bernard, San Jose, CA
Hoover, Delbert
Huelett, William
Kim, Duk
Krempl, Joseph
La Russa, John
Lane, Loren
MacPherson, Bruce

Magnuson, John
Maher, Dean, Connell, WA
Majeau, Henrie, On Leave
Marcell, Terrance
Marshall, Norman, On Leave
McGary, Fred, On Leave
McGary, Robert, On Leave
McGillicuddy, Michael
Michalak, William, On Leave
Minetti, Bernard, Tucson, AZ
Monuteaux, Lawrence
Moyer, Carlton
Moynihan, Patrick
Murdy, Don, Inactive
Myer, Philip
O'Loane, Phil
O'Neill, Richard, Inactive
Olsen, Richard, Daly City, CA
Origenes, Maurice
Parsons, Eamon D.
Pellegrino, Joseph
Peterson, George
Pioli, Albert, On Leave
Ricciardi, John
Ruiz, Nehemias, Thornton, CO
Rupno, Robert
Sarver, Richard, Las Vegas, NV
Shields, Walter J.
Snider, Lloyd
Stenson, Mark
Stromberg, Alton L., Seaside, OR
Tanasse, William
Taube, William
Tomich, Robert
Townsend, William
Vanderzanden, Gene
Warfield, Jack
Warmuth, David
Wiese, Ted
Wilson, Howard
Zuanich, Matthew

INSTITUTIONS LOCATED IN THE ARCHDIOCESE

[A] COLLEGES AND UNIVERSITIES

SEATTLE. *Seattle University*, 900 Broadway, 98122. Tel: 206-296-6000; Fax: 206-296-6200.
E-mail: mafcseattleu.edu
Web site: www.seattleu.edu
For a complete listing, refer to the Colleges and Universities section.

LACEY. *St. Martin's College*, 5300 Pacific Ave., S.E., 98503. Tel: 360-438-4311; Fax: 360-459-4124.
E-mail: admissions@stmartin.edu
Web site: www.stmartin.edu
For a complete listing, refer to the Colleges and Universities section.

[B] HIGH SCHOOLS, ARCHDIOCESAN

SEATTLE. *Bishop Blanchet High School*. (Coed), 8200 Wallingford Ave. N., 98103. Tel: 206-527-7711; Fax: 206-527-7712.
E-mail: info@blanchet.k12.wa.us
Web site: www.blanchet.k12.wa.us
Mr. Kent P. Hickey, Prin.; Rev. Gordon Douglas. Sisters 1; Lay Teachers 68; Students 1,006.

John F. Kennedy Memorial High School. (Coed), 140 S. 140th, 98168. Tel: 206-246-0500; Fax: 206-242-0831.
E-mail: info@jfk-hs.pvt.k12.wa.us
Web site: www.kennedyhs.org
Mr. John Schuster, Prin.; Rev. Michael J. Batterberry. Priests 1; Sisters 1; Lay Teachers 58; Students 874.

O'Dea High School. (Boys), 802 Terry Ave., 98104. Tel: 206-622-6596; Fax: 206-340-4110.
Conducted by the Congregation of Christian Brothers. Bro. Dominic Murray, C.F.C., Prin. Priests 1; Brothers 9; Lay Teachers 25; Students 478.

[C] HIGH SCHOOLS, PRIVATE

SEATTLE. *Holy Names Academy*. (Girls), 728 21st Ave. E., 98112. Tel: 206-323-4272; Fax: 206-323-5254.
E-mail: eswift@holynames-sea.org
Web site: www.holyname-sea.org
Sisters of the Congregation of the Holy Names of Jesus and Mary. Ms. Elizabeth Swift, Prin. Sisters 5; Lay Teachers 36; Students 548.

Seattle Preparatory School, 2400 - 11th Ave., E., 98102. Tel: 206-324-0400; Fax: 206-323-6509.
E-mail: tfields@seaprep.org
Web site: www.seaprep.org
Dr. Robert P. Graby, Ed.D., Pres.; Matt Barmore, Prin. Priests 4; Lay Teachers 86; Students 654.

BELLEVUE. *Eastside Catholic High School*. (Coed), 11650 S.E. 60th, 98006. Tel: 206-644-7737. Bruce Shoup, Pres.; Glen T. Lutz, Prin.; Rev. Richard Basso. Priests 1; Sisters 1; Lay Teachers 48; Students 545.

Forest Ridge School of the Sacred Heart. (Grades 5-12). (Girls), 4800 139th Ave. S.E., 98006. Tel: 425-641-0700; Fax: 425-643-3881.
E-mail: firstinitiallastname@forestridge.org
Web site: www.forestridge.org
Dr. Mary M. Smith, Head of School. Religious of the Sacred Heart 1; Lay Teachers 51; Students 363.

EVERETT. *Archbishop Thomas J. Murphy High School*. (Coed), 12911 39th Ave., S.E., 98208-6159. Tel: 425-379-6363; Fax: 425-385-2875.
Web site: www.holycross-hs.org
Dr. Kristine Brynildsen-Smith, Prin. Sisters 1; Students 283; Lay Teachers 21.

TACOMA. *Bellarmine Preparatory School*. (Coed), 2300 S. Washington, 98405. Tel: 253-752-7701; Fax: 253-756-3887.
Web site: www.bellarmineprep.org
Owned by the Jesuit Fathers. Board of Directors: 4 members of the Jesuit order and 16 others. Very Rev. Michael A. Tyrrell, S.J., Rector; Mr. Jack Peterson, Pres. In res. Revs. Gerard E. Chapdelaine, S.J.; Frederick P. Mayovsky, S.J.; Dominic Nguyen, S.J.; James E. Poole, S.J.; Thomas Sexton, S.J.; Francis Walsh, S.J.; Daniel C. Weber, S.J.; Gregory D. Vance, S.J.; Thomas G. Williams, S.J.; Bros. Patrick Flannigan, S.J.; Michael Richards, S.J.; Mr. Craig Hightower, S.J., Scholastic; Mr. Bryan Viet-Hung Pham, S.J., Scholastic, Ministry to Street People, 1419 1/2 G St., 98405. Tel: 206-627-4347. Priests 9; Brothers 2; Sisters 1; Scholastics 2; Lay Teachers 77; Students 988.

[D] ELEMENTARY SCHOOLS, PRIVATE

SEATTLE. *Villa Academy*. (Grades PreK-8). (Coed), 5001 N.E. 50th St., 98105. Tel: 206-524-8885; Fax: 206-523-7131.
Web site: www.thevilla.org
Pauline Skinner, Head of School. Lay Teachers 53; Students 574.

LACEY. *Holy Family School*. (Grades PreK-8), 2606 Carpenter Rd., S.E., P.O. Box 3700, 98503. Tel: 360-491-7060; Fax: 360-456-3725.
E-mail: hfslacey@ixlnet.com.com
Mr. Daniel Millar, Prin. Lay Teachers 21; Students 187.

[E] CATHOLIC SOCIAL SERVICES OF THE ARCHDIOCESE OF SEATTLE

SEATTLE. *Catholic Community Services of Western Washington*, 100 23rd Ave. S., 98144-2302. Tel: 206-328-5696; 328-5646 (TTY); Fax: 206-328-5699.
Web site: www.catholiccharitiesseattlearch.org
Michael L. Reichert, Pres.

Josephinum Housing Institute, 1902 Second Ave., 98102. Tel: 206-448-8500. Michael L. Reichert, Pres.

Catholic Community Services Northwest. Tel: 360-676-2164; Fax: 360-676-2144. Thomas MacIntyre, Agency Dir., Whatcom Family Center, 1133 Railroad Ave., Ste. 100, Bellingham, 98225-5054. Tel: 360-676-2187; Fax: 360-676-2144. Everett Family Center, 1918 Everett Ave., Everett, 98201. Tel: 425-257-2111; Fax: 425-257-2120.

Catholic Community Services of King County, 100-23rd Ave. S., 98144-2302. Tel: 206-323-6336; TDD: 206-328-5646; Fax: 206-324-4835. Josephine Tamayo Murray, Agency Dir. Tel: 206-328-5701.

Catholic Community Services Southwest, 1323 S. Yakima St., Tacoma, 98405. Tel: 253-383-3697; Fax: 253-502-2750. Denny Hunthausen, Agency Dir.

Archdiocesan Housing Authority (AHA), 1902 Second Ave., 98101. Tel: 206-448-3360; Fax: 206-448-8495. Michael L. Reichert, Pres.

Redmond Elderly Housing Association, 7960-169th Ave, N.E., Redmond, 98053. Tel: 425-869-2424. Michael L. Reichert, Pres.

AHA-Pierce County Association, 112 S. 127th, Tacoma, 98444. Tel: 253-845-3557. Michael L. Reichert, Pres.

St. Martin's Housing Institute, 2008 Westlake Ave., 98121. Tel: 206-340-0410. Michael L. Reichert, Pres.

Halcyon Foundation, 1200 134th Ave. N.E., Bellevue, 98005. Tel: 425-643-7806.

Catholic Community Services of Western Washington Long Term Care System. Tel: 253-502-2729; Fax: 253-272-6356. Tacoma Office, 1323 S. Yakima St., Tacoma, 98405. Tel: 253-502-2716; Fax: 253-272-6356. Olympia Office, P.O. Box 7845, Olympia, 98507. Tel: 425-704-3394; Fax: 425-357-8823. Gary Church, CCSWW Long Term Care Dir.

[F] DAY CARE CENTERS

SEATTLE. *Martin Luther King. Jr., Day Home Center*, 1855 S Ln., 98144. Tel: 206-328-5670; Fax: 206-328-6314.
E-mail: mkoetje@ccsww.org
Mr. Michael L. Koetje, Dir. Total Staff 9; Total Assisted 72.

Our Place Day Care, 1307 E. Spring St., 98122. Tel: 206-328-5724. Christine Coe, Dir.

BELLENGHAM. *CCS Children's Center*, 1200 Indian Center, 98225. Tel: 360-715-6412. Maria Scott, Dir.

EVERETT. *Tree of Life Program*, 10110 19th Ave. S.E., #R100, 98208. Tel: 425-337-7817; Fax: 425-337-6586.

OLYMPIA. *St. Mike's Tikes*, 1010 Eastside St., S.E., 98501. Tel: 360-943-3080; Fax: 360-943-1125.

POULSBO. *St. Olaf's Daycare*, 18943 Caldart Ave., N.E., 98370. Tel: 360-779-5791; Fax: 360-598-5888.

TACOMA. *Childcare System Coordinator*, 1323 S. Yakima St., 98405. Tel: 253-502-2686; Fax: 253-502-2750. Dawn Larsen, Coord.

Kids' Place Child Care Center, 1411 S. Yakima St., 98405. Tel: 253-305-0836.

[G] HOSPITALS

BELLINGHAM. *The Martin Center*, 2806 Douglas Ave., 98225. Tel: 206-733-5804
For a complete listing, refer to the Hospitals section.

St. Joseph Hospital, 2901 Squalicum Pkwy., 98225. Tel: 360-734-5400; Fax: 360-738-6393
For a complete listing, refer to the Hospitals section.

CENTRALIA. *Providence Centralia Hospital*, 914 S. Scheuber Rd., 98531. Tel: 360-736-2803; Fax: 360-330-8614.
E-mail: burdick@psph.providence.org
Web site: providence. org
For a complete listing, refer to the Hospitals section.

EVERETT. *Providence Everett Medical Center*, 1321 Colby Ave., P.O. Box 1147, 98206. Tel: 425-261-2000.
Web site: www.providence.org/everett/
For a complete listing, refer to the Hospitals section.

FEDERAL WAY. *St. Francis Hospital of Federal Way*, 34515 9th Ave. S., 98003-6761. Tel: 253-927-9700; 838-9700; Fax: 253-952-7988.
Web site: fhshealth.org
For a complete listing, refer to the Hospitals section.

LAKEWOOD. *St. Clare Hospital*, 11315 Bridgeport Way S.W., 98499. Tel: 253-588-1711; Fax: 253-584-3001.
Web site: www.fhshealth.org
For a complete listing, refer to the Hospitals section.

LONGVIEW. *PeaceHealth, St. John Medical Center*, 1615 Delaware St., P.O. Box 3002, 98632. Tel: 360-414-2000; Fax: 360-414-7550.
Web site: www.peacehealth.org
For a complete listing, refer to the Hospitals section.

OLYMPIA. *Providence St. Peter Hospital*, 413 Lilly Rd., N.E., 98506. Tel: 360-491-9480
For a complete listing, refer to the Hospitals section.

TACOMA. *St. Joseph Medical Center*, 1717 S. J St., P.O. Box 2197, 98405-2197. Tel: 253-627-4101; Fax: 253-591-6880.
E-mail: annemcnamara@chiwest.com
For a complete listing, refer to the Hospitals section.

[H] NURSING HOMES

SEATTLE. *Providence Mount St. Vincent*, 4831 35th Ave. S.W., 98126. Tel: 206-937-3700; Fax: 206-938-8999.
E-mail: cboyd@providence.org
For a complete listing, refer to the Special Care Facilities section.

ISSAQUAH. *Providence Marianwood*, 3725 Providence Point Dr., S.E., 98029. Tel: 425-391-2800; Fax: 425-391-5440.
E-mail: leedaniels@providence.org
Web site: www.providencemarianwood.org
For a complete listing, refer to the Special Care Facilities section.

[I] HOSPICES

EVERETT. *Providence Home Care and Hospice of Snohomish County*, 2731 Wetmore Ave., #520, 98201. Tel: 425-261-4800
For a complete listing, refer to the Special Care Facilities section.

OLYMPIA. *Providence Mother Joseph Care Center*, 3333 Ensign Rd., N.E., 98506. Tel: 360-493-4900; Fax: 360-493-4948.
E-mail: wildenhausb@psph.providence.org
For a complete listing, refer to the Special Care Facilities section.

Providence Sound Home Care and Hospice, 3706 Griffin Ln., S.E., 98501. Tel: 800-869-7062; 360-459-8311
For a complete listing, refer to the Special Care Facilities section.

[J] RESIDENCES FOR ELDERLY, DISABLED, OR LOW INCOME

SEATTLE. *Broadway House*, 2609 Broadway Ave. E., 98102. Tel: 206-860-4272
For a complete listing, refer to the Special Care Facilities section.

Chancery Place, 910 Marion, 98104. Tel: 206-343-9415
For a complete listing, refer to the Special Care Facilities section.

The Franciscan, 15237 21st Ave. S.W., 98166. Tel: 206-431-8001
For a complete listing, refer to the Special Care Facilities section.

Providence Mount St. Vincent, 4831 35th Ave. S., 98126. Tel: 206-937-3700
For a complete listing, refer to the Special Care Facilities section.

Spruce Park Apartments, 155 21st Ave., 98122. Tel: 206-322-0450
For a complete listing, refer to the Special Care Facilities section.

Vincent House, 1423 First Ave., 98101. Tel: 206-682-9307; Fax: 206-682-0548
For a complete listing, refer to the Special Care Facilities section.

The Westlake, 2008 Westlake Ave., 98121. Tel: 206-340-0410; Fax: 206-682-8843
For a complete listing, refer to the Special Care Facilities section.

BELLEVUE. *Champion House*, 1800 145th Pl. S.E., 98007-6209. Tel: 425-644-4477; Fax: 425-746-0438.
E-mail: championhse@aol.com
For a complete listing, refer to the Special Care Facilities section.

Elbert House, 16000 N.E. 8th St., 98008. Tel: 206-747-5111
For a complete listing, refer to the Special Care Facilities section.

Halcyon, 1200 134th Ave. N.E., 98005. Tel: 206-643-7806; Fax: 206-746-0438
For a complete listing, refer to the Special Care Facilities section.

BOTHELL. *Franciscan Health System, Care Center at Bothell*, 10909 N.E. 185th St., 98011. Tel: 425-486-7174; 483-9905; Fax: 425-486-4962
For a complete listing, refer to the Special Care Facilities section.

CHEHALIS. *Providence Place*, 350 S.E. Washington Ave., 98532. Tel: 360-740-8389; Fax: 360-740-6504
For a complete listing, refer to the Special Care Facilities section.

REDMOND. *Emma McRedmond Manor*, 7960 169th N.E., 98052. Tel: 206-869-2424
For a complete listing, refer to the Special Care Facilities section.

SPANAWAY. *Norm Fournier Court*, 112 S. 127th, 98444. Tel: 253-531-5087
For a complete listing, refer to the Special Care Facilities section.

TACOMA. *Franciscan Health System, Care Center at Tacoma*, 6220 S. Alaska, 98408. Tel: 253-473-2273; Fax: 253-475-2921
For a complete listing, refer to the Special Care Facilities section.

TUMWATER. *Tumwater Apartments*, 5701 6th Ave., S.W., 98501. Tel: 360-352-4321; Fax: 360-352-3557.
E-mail: tumwater@bilbo.w.linknet
For a complete listing, refer to the Special Care Facilities section.

[K] SOCIAL SERVICES

SEATTLE. *Association for Catholic Childhood*, 3701 Magnolia Blvd. N.W., 98199. Tel: 206-328-5973. Pat Dixon, Pres.

Catholic Seamen's Club, 2330 1st Ave., 98121. Tel: 206-441-4773; Fax: 206-441-8059.
E-mail: apostleshipofseaseattle@juno.com
Rev. Anthony J. Haycock, Chap., St. Mary Church, 611 20th Ave. S., 98144. Tel: 206-324-7100, Ext. 14. Total Assisted 21,450.

Providence Hospitality House, P.O. Box 22382, 98122. Tel: 206-322-2107; Fax: 206-322-2107.
E-mail: PHHTeam@aol.com
Sisters of Providence - Mother Joseph Province. Total Staff 3; Total Assisted 124.

St. Francis House, 169 12th Ave., 98122. Tel: 206-621-0945. Third Order of St. Francis, Sponsor. Mary Lou Newman, Dir.

Society of St. Vincent de Paul - Archdiocesan Council, 8239 - 43rd, N.E., 98115. Tel: 206-525-4833. Robert M. Klima, Pres.

Society of St. Vincent de Paul District - Council of Seattle Area, 5950 4th Ave. S., 98108-3208. Tel: 206-767-6449. Mrs. Barbara Carver, Pres.

Society of St. Vincent de Paul - Stores. No. 1, 13555 Aurora Ave. N., 98133. Tel: 206-364-8495. No. 2, 9835 16th Ave., S.W., 98106. Tel: 206-763-2130. No. 3, 13445 1st Ave., S., 98166. Tel: 206-243-6370. No. 4, 2825 Sunset Blvd., N.E., Renton, 98056. Tel: 425-226-9426. No. 5, 5950 4th Ave. S., 98108-3208. Tel: 206-767-3835. Mr. David Koenigs, Exec. Dir., No. 6, 4501 Tolt Ave., S., Carnation, 98014.

Sojourner Place, P.O. Box 95892, 98105. Tel: 206-545-4200; Fax: 206-633-3525. Sisters of Providence - Pariseau Association. Staff 2; Residents 8.

AUBURN. *Society of St. Vincent de Paul - Mother Joseph Council Store*, 926 Auburn Way N., 98002. Tel: 253-833-0400. Total Staff 20; Total Assisted 2,215.

BREMERTON. *St. Vincent de Paul Assistance Office*, 1137 N. Callow, 98312. Tel: 360-479-7017; Fax: 360-479-2182. Thrift Store, 1117 N. Callow, 98312. Tel: 360-377-2929; Fax: 360-479-2182. Total Staff 4; Total Assisted 12,635.

EVERETT. *Society of St. Vincent de Paul*. Council of Snohomish County, 6424 Broadway, 98203. Tel: 425-355-3504; Fax: 425-513-6051. Mrs. Dorothy Trinen, Pres.

OLYMPIA. *Sunshine House*, 413 N. Lilly Rd., 98506. Tel: 360-493-7900. Legal Title: *Sisters of Providence in Washington*. Total Staff 5; Total Assisted 2,800.

SEQUIM. *Society of St. Vincent de Paul and Related Stores*. District Council of Olympic Peninsula. 232 Turnstone Ln., 98382. Tel: 360-683-6097.
E-mail: billrita@olypen.com
Mr. William Cunningham, Pres.

TACOMA. *Society of St. Vincent de Paul - Particular Council of Tacoma*, 4009 S. 56th, 98409. Tel: 253-474-0519; Fax: 253-473-2176. Joan Christnacht, Pres.

Society of St. Vincent de Paul Stores- District Council of Tacoma Stores and Workshop. No. 1, 4009 S. 56th St., 98409. Tel: 253-474-0519; Fax: 253-473-2176. No. 2, 3805-07 S. Yakima Ave., 98408. Tel: 253-472-7334. No. 3, 113 Meeker W., 98371. Tel: 253-848-5637. St. Vincent de Paul Emergency Office, 4009 S. 56th St., 98409. Tel: 253-472-1783; Fax: 253-473-2176.

[L] MONASTERIES AND RESIDENCES OF PRIESTS AND BROTHERS

SEATTLE. *Congregation of Christian Brothers*. (Irish Christian Brothers), 1021 Columbia St., 98104-2018. Tel: 206-622-2639; Fax: 206-340-4110. Bros. J. Hugh Greenan, C.F.C., Comm. Leader; James R. McDonald, C.F.C.; Jerome A. Heustis, C.F.C.; Robert A. Koppes, C.F.C.; D. Peter Ryan, C.F.C.; G. Gregory Lindeman, C.F.C.; D Dominic Murray, C.F.C., Prin.; John A. Pettit, C.F.C.; D. Thomas LeJeune, C.F.C. Brothers 9.

Jesuit Community, 2838 Broadway E., 98102. Tel: 206-324-0329. Revs. L. Paul Fitterer, S.J.; Richard D. Perry, S.J.; Joseph W. Conyard, S.J.; Robert Jones, S.J.; John D. Whitney, S.J., Supr.

Jesuit House, Seattle, 621 17th Ave. E., 98112. Tel: 206-324-7496. Revs. Robert J. Egan, S.J., Supr.; Alexander F. McDonald, S.J.; Joseph P. O'Connell, S.J.; Pasquale M. Spoletini, S.J.; Armand M. Nigro, S.J.

Maryknoll Fathers & Brothers, 958 - 16th Ave. E., 98112. Tel: 206-322-8831; Fax: 206-324-6909.
E-mail: mklseatl@aol.com
Web site: www.maryknoll.org
Bro. W. Timothy Raible, M.M.

LACEY. *St. Martin's Abbey*. Order of St. Benedict, College, and Novitiate. 5300 Pacific Ave, S.E., 98503-1297. Tel: 360-491-4700; Fax: 360-438-4441.
E-mail: thabbot@stmartin.edu
Web site: www.stmartin.edu
Rt. Revs. Neal G. Roth, O.S.B., Abbot; Conrad R. Rausch, O.S.B., Resigned Abbot; Adrian J. Parcher, O.S.B., Resigned Abbot; Very Revs. Alfred J. Hulscher, O.S.B., Prior, Treas. & Dir. Fiscal Affairs; Nicholas Rausch, O.S.B., Subprior; Revs. Edward R. Receconi, O.S.B., Junior Master; Thaddaeus R. Arledge, O.S.B.; Benedict L. Auer, O.S.B.; Richard S. Cebula, O.S.B.; Kieran P. Cunningham, O.S.B.; Urban C. Feucht; Dominic D. Hahn, O.S.B.; Gerard D. Kirsch, O.S.B.; Timothy J. Lamm, O.S.B.; William A. Maat, O.S.B.; Killian Malvey, O.S.B.; Sean R. Malvey, O.S.B.; Justin D. McCreedy, O.S.B.; Luke N. O'Donnell, O.S.B.; Clement H. Pangratz, O.S.B.; Thomas R. Park, O.S.B.; David W. Prebula, O.S.B.; George J. Seidel, O.S.B.; John Scott, O.S.B.; Terence Wagner, O.S.B.; Harvey J. Wingfield, O.S.B.; Paul M. Weckert, O.S.B. Priests 26; Brothers 11.

[M] CONVENTS AND RESIDENCES FOR SISTERS

SEATTLE. *St. Joseph's Carmelite Monastery*. 2215 N.E. 147th, Shoreline, 98155. Tel: 206-363-7150; Fax: 206-365-7335.
E-mail: seattlecarmel@att.net
Sr. Marie Therese, O.C.D., Prioress. Discalced Carmelites 8; In Formation 1.

St. Joseph's Residence, 4800 37th Ave. S.W., 98126. Tel: 206-937-4600; Fax: 206-938-6193 (8:30am-8:30pm). Sr. Anita Butler, S.P., Supr.; Rev. John A. Jennings, Chap. Sisters of Providence 60; Dominican Sisters 7; Daughters of Mary 2; Benedictines 1; Carmelites 1; Sisters of St. Joseph of Peace 1.

Sisters of St. Joseph of Peace, 1104 21st Ave., E., 98112. Tel: 206-324-1529. Sisters 4.

BELLEVUE. *St. Mary's Provincialate*, 1663 Killarney Way, Box 248, 98009-0248. Tel: 425-451-1770; Fax: 425-462-9760.
E-mail: kpruitt@csjp.ojp.org
Sr. Kathleen Pruitt, C.S.J.P., Prov. Sisters of St. Joseph of Peace, Our Lady Province.

St. Mary's Residence and Novitiate, 1663 Killarney Way, P.O. Box 1763, 98009. Tel: 425-451-1833; Fax: 425-462-9760.
E-mail: eabrennan@csjp.olp.org
Web site: www.csjp.org/olp
Sr. Elizabeth Ann Brennan. Sisters of St. Joseph of Peace 30.
Our Lady Province.

EDMONDS. *Rosary Heights*. (Motherhouse of the Dominican Sisters Congregation of Holy Cross), 23120 Woodway Park Rd., P.O. Box 280, 98020-0280. Tel: 206-542-7511; Fax: 206-546-9490.
E-mail: opedmonds@netos.com
Web site: www.opedmonds.org
Sr. Michele Kopp, O.P., Prioress, Holy Angels Alumnae Assoc., 942 N.W. 60th, Seattle, 98107. Tel: 206-782-1181.

LACEY. *St. Placid Priory*, 500 College St., N.E., 98516. Tel: 360-438-1771; Fax: 360-438-9236.
E-mail: stplacid@stplacid.org
Web site: www.stplacid.org
Sr. Laura Swan, O.S.B., Prioress. Sisters of St. Benedict 25; Novices 1. Includes The Priory Spirituality Center and The Priory Store.

SHAW ISLAND. *Franciscan Sisters of the Eucharist*, P.O. Box 455, 98286. Tel: 360-468-2288; Fax: 360-468-3766. Mother Helen Jean Brinkman, F.S.E., Supr. Sisters 4.

Our Lady of the Rock Priory. (Cloistered), P.O. Box 425, 98286. Tel: 360-468-2321; Fax: 360-468-2319. Benedictine Nuns. Rev. Mother Therese Critchley, O.S.B., Supr. Professed Nuns 8; Novices 1.

TACOMA. *III Order of St. Dominic*, Tacoma Dominican Center, 935 Fawcett Ave., S., 98402. Tel: 253-272-9688; Fax: 253-272-8790.
E-mail: dominicans@tacoma-op.org
Sr. Kathleen Reilly, O.P., Pres.
(Congregation of St. Thomas Aquinas), Sisters of Saint Dominic of Tacoma Charitable Trust - Tacoma Dominican Center.

Sister of St. Francis of Philadelphia, St. Ann Retirement Convent, 6602 S. Alaska St., 98408. Tel: 253-474-8319; 475-0791; Fax: 253-474-0734.
E-mail: saintann@worldnet.att.net
Serra House, 6602 S. Alaska St., 98408. Tel: 253-474-8026. Evergreen House, 6602 S. Alaska St., 98408. Tel: 253-474-9803. Olympus House, 6602 S. Alaska St., 98408. Tel: 253-474-8573. Marian House, 6802 47th St. W., 98466. Tel: 253-564-1816. La-Verna, 701 North K St. #12, 98403. Tel: 253-272-2232. St. Charles Borromeo Convent, 7114 S. 12th St., 98465. Tel: 253-564-3880. St. Marguerite Convent, 4019 S. Thompson, 98408. Tel: 253-472-9702.

[N] RETREAT HOUSES, CONFERENCE CENTERS AND CAMPS

SEATTLE. *Camp Don Bosco*, Contact C.Y.O., 814 N.E. 85th St., 98115. Tel: 206-382-4350; Fax: 206-903-4627.
E-mail: cyo@seattlearch.org

Still Point, 1111 Harvard Ave., 98122-4205. Tel: 206-322-8006; Fax: 209-322-9266.
E-mail: stillpt@nwnexus.com
Donna Kamos, Dir.

EDMONDS. *Dominican Reflection Center*, 23120 Woodway Park Rd., P.O. Box 280, 98020. Tel: 206-542-3740; 546-6561; Fax: 206-546-9490.
E-mail: drc@netos.com
Sr. Mary White, O.P., Dir.

FEDERAL WAY. *Palisades Retreat Center*. (Owned by Archdiocese of Seattle), P.O. Box 3739, 98063. Tel: 206-838-9583; 927-9621 (Tacoma); Fax: 206-927-9624.
E-mail: palisades @seattlesearch.org
David Jones, Dir.

MONROE. *Camp Hamilton*, 25405 Lake Fontal Rd., 98272. Contact C.Y.O., 814 N.E. 85th St., Seattle, 98115. Tel: 206-382-4350.

TOLEDO. *St. Mary Conference Center*, 107 Spencer Rd., 98591. Tel: 360-864-6464; Fax: 360-864-6465.
E-mail: sstmarys@toledotel.com
Web site: toledotel.com/~stmarys

[O] NEWMAN CENTERS

SEATTLE. *Campus Ministry*. Rev. Thomas De Man, O.P., Archdiocesan Coord. Tel: 206-527-5072.

Seattle University Campus Ministry, E. Colombia & 12th Ave., 98122. Tel: 206-296-6075. Mary Romer Cline, Dir.

University of Washington, Catholic Newman Center, 4502 20th Ave. N.E., 98105. Tel: 206-527-5072. Rev. Thomas De Man, O.P., Dir.

Western Washington University (Bellingham). Catholic Campus Ministry. 102 Highland Dr., Bellingham, 98225. Tel: 206-733-3400. Rev. Frank Schuster, Chap.

St. Martin's College (Lacey). Campus Ministry. 5300 Pacific Ave. S.E., Lacey, 98503. Tel: 360-491-4700. Susan Leyster, Dir.; Fred Finnegan, Assoc. Dir.

[P] MISCELLANEOUS

SEATTLE. *Cursillo Movement,* 14712 Bothell Way, N.E., 98155. Tel: 206-361-9901. Mr. Ed Schaefer. Tel: 206-361-5579.

The Food Bank at St. Mary's, 611 20th Ave., S., 98144. Tel: 206-324-7100, Ext. 18. Sue Mana, Dir.

Intercommunity Housing, 1920 E. Madison, 98122. Tel: 206-223-1051; Fax: 206-860-2094.
E-mail: intercommunity@mercyhousing.org
Jane Graf, Reg. Pres.

Intercommunity Housing Ferndale, 1920 E. Madison, 98122. Tel: 206-223-1051; Fax: 206-860-2094.
E-mail: intercommunity@mercyhousing.org
Jane Graf, Reg. Pres.

Intercommunity Ministry Volunteer Program, 1216 N.E. 65th St., Ste. 200, 98115. Tel: 206-442-4268; Fax: 206-621-7046.
E-mail: imvpcnetos.com
Web site: www.imvp.org
Sr. Mary Medved, S.N.J.M., Dir.

Intercommunity Peace & Justice Center, 1216 N.E. 65th St., 98115. Tel: 206-223-1138; Fax: 206-621-7046.
E-mail: ipjc@igc.org
Web site: www.ipjc.org
Sr. Linda Haydock, S.N.J.M., Exec. Dir.

Larche Noah Sealth of Seattle, P.O. Box 22023, 98122-0023. Tel: 206-325-9434.
E-mail: info@larche.com
Web site: www.larche.com

Oratorian Community, 226 N.E. 91st St., 98115. Tel: 206-268-0043. Revs. Robert Dell, C.O.; Clarence Edward Jones, C.O.

The Rosary, P.O. Box 33762, 98133. Tel: 206-525-3045.
E-mail: hjcoveny@juno.com
Mrs. Pauline Coveny, Pres.

Seattle, Vietnamese Catholic Center, 1230 E. Fir St., 98122. Tel: 206-325-5626; Fax: 206-329-0196. Rev. Anthony Ton (Vietnam).

Sisters of Providence, Mother Joseph Province, 506 2nd Ave., Ste. 1200, 98104. Tel: 206-464-3394; Fax: 206-464-3984.
E-mail: bschamber@providence.org
Web site: For Seattle Health Systems Only: www-.providence.org
Sr. Barbara Schamber, S.P., Prov. Supr.
For detailed information on corporate holdings for the Sisters of Providence, Mother Joseph Province, please refer to Religious Institutes of Women in the back of the directory. Providence Health System-Oregon. Tel: 503-215-4700; Fax: 503-215-4703. Providence Health System-Washington. Tel: 206-464-2698; Fax: 206-464-4686. Providence Health System-California. Tel: 818-843-5111; Fax: 818-843-0641.

Washington State Catholic Conference, 508-2nd Ave. W., 98119-3928. Tel: 206-301-0556; Fax: 206-301-0558.
E-mail: wscc99@aol.com
Sr. Sharon Park, O.P., Exec. Dir.

BELLEVUE. *Sisters of St. Joseph of Peace, Our Lady Province, Charitable Trust,* 1663 Killarney Way, P.O. Box 248, 98009-0248. Tel: 425-451-1770; Fax: 425-462-9760.
E-mail: cmcinnes@csjp-olp.org
Web site: www.csjp.org/olp
Sr. Kathleen Pruitt, C.S.J.P., Prov. Leader.

Sisters of St. Joseph of Peace, PeaceHealth, Corporate Center, 15325 S.E. 30th Pl., Ste. 300, 98007. Tel: 206-747-1711; Fax: 206-649-3825. John Hayward, Pres. & CEO.

EDMONDS. *Edmonds Dominicans, Holy Angels Alumnae Assoc.* Tel: 425-546-6561. 942 N.W. 60th, Seattle, 98107. Tel: 206-782-1181; Fax: 206-789-2498.

MOUNT VERNON. *Skagit Valley Regional Ministry,* 110 S. 5th St., 98273. Tel: 360-336-6622; Fax: 360-416-0428. Rev. Lawrence Minder, O.S.B.

TACOMA. *Catholic Pastoral Care-Hospital Tacoma Ministry,* 911 S. Fifth St., 98405. Tel: 253-591-9474. Rev. Michael E. Walsh, S.J., Dir.

Pierce County Association for Catholic Education (PACE), 2300 S. Washington, 98405. Tel: 253-756-7830; Fax: 253-756-0296.

Pierce County Deanery, 1001 N. J St., 98403. Tel: 253-383-3496; Fax: 253-627-5396.
E-mail: pcdeanery@juno.com
Mary DeForrest, Admin.

RELIGIOUS INSTITUTES OF MEN REPRESENTED IN THE ARCHDIOCESE

For further details refer to the corresponding bracketed number in the Religious Institutes of Men or Women section.

[0200]—*Benedictine Monks.* (Olympia, WA).—O.S.B.
[0310]—*Congregation of Christian Brothers.* (Western U.S.).—C.F.C.
[0260]—*Discalced Carmelites Friars.* (California Prov.).—O.C.D.
[0690]—*Jesuit Fathers and Brothers.* (Oregon Province).—S.J.
[0800]—*Maryknoll.*—M.M.
[0910]—*Oblates of Mary Immaculate.* (Western Province).—O.M.I.
[]—*Oratorian Community.*
[0430]—*Order of Preachers (Dominicans).* (San Francisco, CA).—O.P.
[1070]—*Redemptorist Fathers.* (Oakland Province).—C.SS.R.
[1250]—*Society of Christ.* (American-Canadian Prov.).—S.Ch.
[1290]—*Society of the Priests of Saint Sulpice.*—S.S.

RELIGIOUS INSTITUTES OF WOMEN REPRESENTED IN THE ARCHDIOCESE

[0180]—*Benedictine Nuns of the Primitive Observance.*—O.S.B.
[0230]—*Benedictine Sisters of Pontifical Jurisdiction.* (Lacey, WA; Duluth, MN).—O.S.B.
[]—*Carmelite.*—O.L.
[2100]—*Congregation of the Humility of Mary.*—C.H.M.
[1920]—*Congregation of the Sisters of the Holy Cross.*—C.S.C.
[1780]—*Congregation of the Sisters of the Third Order of St. Francis of Perpetual Adoration.* (Western Region).—F.S.P.A.
[0420]—*Discalced Carmelite Nuns.*—O.C.D.
[1070-03]—*Dominican Sisters.* (Edmonds).—O.P.
[1070-04]—*Dominican Sisters.* (Tacoma).—O.P.
[1070-19]—*Dominican Sisters.* (Sinsinawa).—O.P.
[1070-21]—*Dominican Sisters.* (Houston).—O.P.
[]—*Eucharistic Heart of Jesus.*
[]—*Franciscan Sisters of Rochester.*—O.S.F.
[1250]—*The Institute of the Franciscan Sisters of the Eucharist.*—F.S.E.
[]—*Missionary Sisters of the Rosary of Fatima.*—M.R.F.
[2860]—*Missionary Sisters of the Sacred Heart.*—M.S.C.
[]—*Our Lady of Perpetual Help (Korean).*
[1830]—*Religious of the Good Shepherd.*—R.G.S.
[4070]—*Religious of the Sacred Heart.*—R.S.C.J.
[]—*Religious Sisters of Mercy.*—R.S.M.
[2970]—*School Sisters of Notre Dame.*—S.S.N.D.
[]—*Sisters for Christian Community.*—S.F.C.C.
[0480]—*Sisters of Charity of Leavenworth, Kansas.*—S.C.L.
[0430]—*Sisters of Charity of the Blessed Virgin Mary.*—B.V.M.
[3000]—*Sisters of Notre Dame De Namur.*—S.N.D.deN.
[3350]—*Sisters of Providence.*—S.P.
[1650]—*The Sisters of St. Francis of Philadelphia.*—O.S.F.
[3840]—*Sisters of St. Joseph of Carondelet.* (California Prov.).—C.S.J.
[3890]—*Sisters of St. Joseph of Peace.*—C.S.J.P.
[1990]—*Sisters of the Holy Names of Jesus and Mary.*—S.N.J.M.
[]—*Sisters of the Holy Names of Jesus and Mary.* (Oregon Prov.).—S.N.J.M.
[]—*Sisters of the Holy Names of Jesus and Mary.* (California Prov.).—S.N.J.M.

ARCHDIOCESAN CEMETERIES

Central Office: 910 Marion, 98104. Tel: 206-382-9281

SEATTLE. *Calvary,* 5041 35th Ave. N.E., 98105. Tel: 206-522-0996.

Holyrood, 205 N.E. 205th, 98155. Tel: 206-363-8404.

FEDERAL WAY. *Gethsemane,* 37600 Pacific Hwy. S., 98003. Tel: 206-838-2240.

NECROLOGY

† Auer, Paul A., (Retired). —Died Sept. 26, 2000.
† Lukas, Michael, (Retired). —Died May 7, 2000.
† Manning, Joseph. —Died Feb. 22, 2000.
† Murray, Maximillian, (Retired). —Died March 29, 2000.
† Rafalowski, Leonard, (Retired). —Died Dec. 13, 1999.

Diocese of Shreveport

(Dioecesis Sreveportuensis in Louisiana)

Most Reverend

WILLIAM B. FRIEND, D.D.

Bishop of Shreveport; ordained May 7, 1959; appointed Titular Bishop of Pomaria and Auxiliary Bishop of Alexandria-Shreveport August 31, 1979; ordained Bishop October 30, 1979; appointed Bishop of Alexandria-Shreveport November 23, 1982; installed January 11, 1983; appointed Bishop of Shreveport June 16, 1986. *Address all communications to: Catholic Center, 3500 Fairfield Ave., Shreveport, LA, 71104.* Tel.: 318-868-4441; Fax: 318-868-4605.

Chancery Office: 3500 Fairfield Ave., Shreveport, LA, 71104. Tel.: 318-868-4441; Fax: 318-868-4605.

Web site address: www.dioshpt.org

ESTABLISHED AND CREATED A DIOCESE JUNE 16, 1986.

Comprises the Counties (parishes) of Bienville, Bossier, Caddo, Claiborne, DeSoto, East Carroll, Jackson, Lincoln, Morehouse, Ouachita, Red River, Richland, Sabine, Union, Webster and West Carroll.

For legal titles of parishes and diocesan institutions, consult the Chancery Office.

STATISTICAL OVERVIEW

Personnel	
Bishop	1
Priests: Diocesan Active in Diocese	30
Priests: Active Outside Diocese	2
Priests: Retired, Sick or Absent	11
Number of Diocesan Priests	43
Religious Priests in Diocese	16
Extern Priests in Diocese	2
Ordinations:	
Diocesan Priests	1
Transitional Deacons	1
Permanent Deacons	1
Permanent Deacons in Diocese	6
Total Brothers	5
Total Sisters	51
Parishes	
Parishes	32
With Resident Pastor:	
Resident Diocesan Priests	22
Resident Religious Priests	9
Without Resident Pastor:	
Administered by Priests	1
Missions	13
Pastoral Centers	2
Professional Ministry Personnel:	
Sisters	1
Lay Ministers	18
Welfare	
Catholic Hospitals	2
Total Assisted	938
Health Care Centers	3
Total Assisted	705,884
Homes for the Aged	1
Total Assisted	192
Day Care and Extended Day Care Centers	2
Total Assisted	80
Specialized Homes	2
Total Assisted	280
Special Centers for Social Services	21
Total Assisted	13,400
Residential Care of Disabled	1
Total Assisted	184
Other Institutions	2
Total Assisted	2,864
Educational	
Diocesan Students in Other Seminaries	2
Total Seminarians	2
High Schools, Diocesan and Parish	2
Total Students	700
Elementary Schools, Diocesan and Parish	8
Total Students	2,046
Catechesis/Religious Education:	
High School Students	681
Elementary Students	2,091
Total Students Under Catholic Instruction	5,520
Teachers in the Diocese:	
Brothers	1
Sisters	8
Lay Teachers	213
Vital Statistics	
Receptions into the Church:	
Infant Baptism Totals	567
Adult Baptism Totals	74
Received into Full Communion	231
First Communions	457
Confirmations	597
Marriages:	
Catholic	119
Interfaith	138
Total Marriages	257
Deaths	336
Total Catholic Population	38,929
Total Population	778,633

Vicar General—Rev. Msgr. J. CARSON LACAZE, V.G.

Vicars Forane—Rev. Msgr. EARL V. PROVENZA, V.F., Western Deanery; Very Rev. J. ROBERT INZINA, V.F., Eastern Deanery; Very Rev. DAVID T. RICHTER, V.F., Southern Deanery.

Chancery Office—Catholic Center, 3500 Fairfield Ave., Shreveport, 71104. Tel: 318-868-4441; Fax: 318-868-4605.

Chancellor—Sr. MARGARET DAUES, C.S.J., Ph.D.

Archives—Mrs. CHRISTINE RIVERS.

Diocesan Tribunal—3500 Fairfield Ave., Shreveport, 71104. Tel: 318-868-4441; Fax: 318-868-4605.

Judicial Vicar—Rev. PETER B. MANGUM, J.C.L.

Associate Judge—Rev. ROTHELL PRICE, J.C.L.

Director of the Tribunal—Sr. MARILYN R. VASSALLO, C.S.J., J.C.L.

Auditor/Secretary—RICOLE WILLIAMS.

Judges—Rev. PETER B. MANGUM, J.C.L., J.V.; Rev. Msgr. FRANZ GRAEF, S.T.D.; Revs. EDMUND A. NIEHOFF; ROTHELL PRICE, J.C.L.; Sr. MARILYN R. VASSALLO, C.S.J., J.C.L.; Rev. CURTIS WOODS.

Defenders of the Bond—Revs. PHILIP F. MICHIELS; WILLIAM H. CAREY.

Promoter of Justice—Rev. WILLIAM H. CAREY.

Advocates—Rev. Msgr. EDMUND J. MOORE; Revs. KARL DAIGLE; RICHARD LOMBARD; Very Rev. DAVID T. RICHTER; Rev. MARK WATSON.

Notaries—RICOLE WILLIAMS; DEBBY SMITH.

Corporate Council—Most Rev. WILLIAM B. FRIEND, D.D.; Rev. Msgr. J. CARSON LACAZE, V.G.; Sr. MARGARET DAUES, C.S.J., Ph.D.

College of Consultors—Revs. WILLIAM H. CAREY; CHARLES GLORIOSO; TIMOTHY C. HURD; JOHN D. KENNEDY; PATRICK J. MADDEN; PETER B. MANGUM, J.C.L., J.V.; EDMUND A. (LARRY) NIEHOFF; WILLIAM SPENCER, O.F.M.; LAVERNE (PIKE) THOMAS; Very Revs. J. ROBERT INZINA, V.F.; DAVID T. RICHTER, V.F.; Rev. Msgr. J. CARSON LACAZE, V.G.; Very Rev. EARL V. PROVENZA, V.F.; Rev. Msgr. FRANZ GRAEF, S.T.D.

Finance Council—Most Rev. WILLIAM B. FRIEND, D.D.; Rev. Msgr. J. CARSON LACAZE, V.G., Ex Officio; Sr. MARGARET DAUES, C.S.J., Ex Officio; Rev. Msgr. WILLIAM O'HANLON; REGINALD W. ABRAMS; MARY A. BROWN; DAVID CATTAR; NONA DAILEY; JOAN FISHER; MARGARET GREEN; JOHN HUSSEY, Chm. GLENN KINSEY; Dr. JAMES ROBERT MICHAEL; PHYLLIS MURDOCK; LYNN ROOS; NICHOLAS ROPPOLO; LAWRENCE H. RUSSO, III; WILLIAM STAAB.

Presbyteral Council—Most Rev. WILLIAM B. FRIEND, D.D.; Rev. Msgr. J. CARSON LACAZE, V.G.; Rev. Msgr. EARL V. PROVENZA, V.F.; Revs. WILLIAM H. CAREY; CHARLES GLORIOSO, Vice Chm. TIMOTHY C. HURD; JOHN D. KENNEDY; PATRICK J. MADDEN; PETER B. MANGUM, J.C.L., J.V., Sec. EDMUND A. (LARRY) NIEHOFF; WILLIAM SPENCER, O.F.M.; LAVERNE (PIKE) THOMAS; Very Revs. J. ROBERT INZINA, V.F.; DAVID T. RICHTER, V.F., Chm.; Rev. Msgr. FRANZ GRAEF, S.T.D.

Diocesan Pastoral Council—Dr. JOSEPH FELDHAUS, Monroe; Mr. DAVID FOLEY, Shreveport; Mr. TOM GUANELLA, Bossier City; Mrs. LINDA HOLYFIELD, Monroe; Mrs. BESSIE MCKINNEY, Grambling; Mrs. ALICE PRUDHOMME, Mansfield; Mrs. LUCY A. RIVERO, Shreveport; Mr. CHARLES SCOTT, Monroe; Mr. STEVE VASKO, Shreveport; Ms. ELIZABETH LIPPI, Shreveport; Mrs. ROSE MARIE CLARKE, Shreveport; Sr. MARGARET DAUES, Shreveport.

Priests' Retirement Board—Rev. Msgr. J. CARSON LACAZE, V.G., Chm. WADE DUPUIS; Very Rev. J. ROBERT INZINA, V.F.; Rev. EDMUND A. (LARRY) NIEHOFF; NICHOLAS ROPPOLO; Rev. Msgr. EARL V. PROVENZA, V.F.; Rev. DANIEL M. WALSH.

The Catholic Foundation of North-Central Louisiana, Inc.—Contact the Catholic Center for information. Tel: 318-868-4441; Fax: 318-868-4605.

Diocesan Offices and Directors

Black Catholic Commission—Rev. ROTHELL PRICE, Chap., *St. Jude Church, 3800 Viking Dr. E., Bossier City, 71111-7403.* Tel: 318-746-2508.

Business Affairs—Mr. E. MICHAEL SCHOFIELD, C.P.A., *Catholic Center, 3500 Fairfield Ave., Shreveport, 71104.* Tel: 318-868-4441; Fax: 318-868-4605.

Campaign for Human Development—Address Communications to: Office of Special Ministries. *Catholic Center, 3500 Fairfield Ave., Shreveport, 71104.* Tel: 318-868-4441; Fax: 318-868-4605.

Campus Ministry—Mrs. TAMMY YATCKO, Coord., *Catholic Center, 3500 Fairfield Ave., Shreveport, 71104.* Tel: 318-868-4441; Fax: 318-868-4605.

Catechetics and Worship—Mrs. MARY MCGILL, M.A., *Catholic Center, 3500 Fairfield Ave., Shreveport, 71104.* Tel: 318-868-4441; Fax: 318-868-4605.

Catholic Charities—Address Communications to: Office of Special Ministries. *Catholic Center, 3500 Fairfield Ave., Shreveport, 71104.* Tel: 318-868-4441; Fax: 318-868-4605.

Catholic Relief Services—Rev. Msgr. J. CARSON LACAZE, V.G., *Catholic Center, 3500 Fairfield Ave., Shreveport, 71104.* Tel: 318-868-4441; Fax: 318-868-4605.

Cemeteries—Mr. E. MICHAEL SCHOFIELD, C.P.A., *Catholic Center, 3500 Fairfield Ave., Shreveport, 71104.* Tel: 318-868-4441; Fax: 318-868-4605.

Censor of Books—Rev. Msgr. FRANZ GRAEF, S.T.D.

Charismatic Movement—Mr. JOHN J. GUERRIERO, JR., *2316 Sauvelle Dr., Monroe, 71201-2953.* Mr. THOMAS HARLAN, *9536 Pitch Pine, Shreveport, 71118-4527.*

Church Vocations—Rev. MARK WATSON, Dir., *3500 Fairfield Ave., Shreveport, 71104.* Tel: 318-868-4441; Fax: 318-868-4605.

Church Vocations Board—Mr. LAWRENCE W. PETTIETTE, JR., Chm.; Revs. MARK WATSON, Dir. CHARLES GLORIOSO; Sr. EILEEN MCGRORY, S.C.; Sr. SANDRA NORSWORTHY, O.L.S.; Sr. SHARON RAMBIN, O.L.S.; Mrs. ANNE JONES; Mr. DON ANZELMO; Mr. SAM GILLIAM; Mr. BRIAN D. LANDRY. Ex Officio Members: Most Rev. WILLIAM B. FRIEND; Rev. Msgr. J. CARSON LACAZE, V.G.

Continuing Education for the Clergy—Rev. CHARLES GLORIOSO, Dir., *St. Pius X Church, 4300 N. Market St., Shreveport, 71107.* Tel: 318-222-2165.

Development and Public Relations—Mr. JOHN MARK WILLCOX, Dir., *Catholic Center, 3500 Fairfield Ave., Shreveport, 71104.* Tel: 318-868-4441; Fax: 318-868-4605.

Diocesan Publications—Mrs. POLLY V. MACIULSKI, Editor, *Catholic Center, 3500 Fairfield Ave., Shreveport, 71104.* Tel: 318-868-4441; Fax: 318-868-4605.

Ecumenism and Interreligious Affairs—Rev. Msgr. CARSON J. LACAZE, V.G., *Our Lady of the Holy Rosary Church, 1755 Corbitt St., Shreveport, 71108-3098.* Tel: 318-636-3530.

Facility Director, Catholic Center—Mr. EUGENE BARATTINI, *Catholic Center, 3500 Fairfield Ave., Shreveport, 71104.* Tel: 318-868-4441; Fax: 318-868-4605.

Fairview House (Residence for Clergy)—1000 Fairview, Shreveport, 71104. Contact Person: Mr. EUGENE BARATTINI, Dir. Facilities, Catholic Center. Tel: 318-868-4441; Fax: 318-868-4605.

Greco Institute—Mr. BRIAN SCHMISEK, M.A., A.B.D., Ph.D.(Cand.), *Catholic Center, 3500 Fairfield Ave., Shreveport, 71104.* Tel: 318-868-4441; Fax: 318-868-4605.

Health Ministry—Rev. WILLIAM H. CAREY, Ph.D., KCHS, Coord., *St. Francis Medical Center, P.O. Box 1901, Monroe, 71201-1901.*

Hispanic Community—Mrs. ELISA MILAZZO, Coord., *Catholic Center, 3500 Fairfield Ave., Shreveport, 71104.* Tel: 318-868-4441; Fax: 318-868-4605. Rev. RIGOBERTO BETANCURT, Chap.

Holy Childhood—Sr. CAROL SHIVELY, O.S.U., Contact Person, *Catholic Center, 3500 Fairfield Ave., Shreveport, 71104.* Tel: 318-868-4441; Fax: 318-868-4605.

Human Resources—Mrs. CHRISTIE WEEKS, Dir., *Catholic Center, 3500 Fairfield Ave., Shreveport, 71104.* Tel: 318-868-4441; Fax: 318-868-4605.

Information Systems Management—Ms. PATRICIA PILLORS, Dir., *Catholic Center, 3500 Fairfield Ave., Shreveport, 71104.* Tel: 318-868-4441; Fax: 318-868-4605.

Jail-Prison Ministry—Rev. DANIEL WALSH, Coord., *Cathedral of St. John Berchmans, 939 Jordan St., Shreveport, 71101-4391.* Tel: 318-221-5296. Rev. RICHARD PUSCH, Chap., Forcht Wade Correctional Center, *3538 Eastlake Dr., Shreveport, 71105.*

Diocesan Liturgy Commission—JODI TOLIVER; MICHAEL KENNEY; Very Rev. DAVID RICHTER, V.F.; MARY CUNNINGHAM; ARCHIE PERRY; Rev. PHILIP F. MICHIELS; PAM FOWLER; Deacon RON MORRIS; JOE JARZABEK; MARY MCGILL, Ex Officio.

Mission Director—Rev. Msgr. J. CARSON LACAZE, V.G., *Catholic Center, 3500 Fairfield Ave., Shreveport, 71104.* Tel: 318-868-4441; Fax: 318-868-4605.

Permanent Deacon Formation Program—Mr. CLARY NASH, Dir., *Catholic Center, 3500 Fairfield Ave., Shreveport, 71104.* Tel: 318-868-4441; Fax: 318-868-4605.

Permanent Deacon Coordinator—Rev. PHILIP F. MICHIELS, *St. Joseph Church, P.O. Box 760, Mansfield, 71052.* Tel: 318-872-1158.

Dean Permanent Deacons—Deacon CLARY NASH, *St. John Berchmans Cathedral, 939 Jordan St., Shreveport, 71101-4391.* Tel: 318-221-5296.

Propagation of the Faith—Rev. Msgr. J. CARSON LACAZE, V.G., *Catholic Center, 3500 Fairfield Ave., Shreveport, 71104.* Tel: 318-868-4441; Fax: 318-868-4605.

Religious Education—Mrs. MARY MCGILL, M.A., Dir., *Catholic Center, 3500 Fairfield Ave., Shreveport, 71104.* Tel: 318-868-4441; Fax: 318-868-4605.

Resource Center (Library)—Sr. EILEEN MCGRORY, Dir., *Catholic Center, 3500 Fairfield Ave., Shreveport, 71104.* Tel: 318-868-4441; Fax: 318-868-4605.

Schools—Sr. CAROL SHIVELY, O.S.U., Supt.; Sr. ANN MIDDLEBROOKS, S.E.C., School Planning Consultant, *Catholic Center, 3500 Fairfield Ave., Shreveport, 71104.* Tel: 318-868-4441; Fax: 318-868-4605.
Child Nutrition Program—3500 Fairfield Ave., Shreveport, 71104. Tel: 318-868-4441; Fax: 318-868-4605.

Scouting—Very Rev. DAVID RICHTER, V.F., Coord., *St. Joseph Church, P.O. Box 8, Zwolle, 71486-0008.* Tel: 318-645-9852; 645-6155.

Spanish-Speaking Ministers—Rev. Msgr. C. MURRAY CLAYTON, *Sacred Heart of Jesus Church, P.O. Box 19467, Shreveport, 71149-0467.* Rev. RIGOBERTO BETANCURT, *Cathedral of St. John Berchmans, 939 Jordan St., Shreveport, 71101-4391.*

St. Catherine Community Center—Mr. ROBERT ALFORD, Dir., *331 E. 71st St., Shreveport, 71106-4305.* Tel: 318-865-9817.

St. Vincent de Paul Society—DOROTHY JARZABEK, Contact Person, *Catholic Center, 3500 Fairfield Ave., Shreveport, 71104.* Tel: 318-868-4441; Fax: 318-868-4605.

Special Ministries—Mr. DONALD EMGE, Ph.D., Dir., *Catholic Center, 3500 Fairfield Ave., Shreveport, 71104.* Tel: 318-868-4441; Fax: 318-868-4605.

The Beginning Experience—MILDRED COLLINS, Shreveport. Tel: 318-797-5960.

Youth and Young Adult Ministry—Mrs. TAMMY YATCKO, Dir., *Catholic Center, 3500 Fairfield Ave., Shreveport, 71104.* Tel: 318-868-4441; Fax: 318-868-4605.

CLERGY, PARISHES, MISSIONS AND PAROCHIAL SCHOOLS

CITY OF SHREVEPORT
(Caddo Parish)

1—ST. JOHN BERCHMANS CATHEDRAL (1902), Revs. Curtis W. Woods, Rector; Daniel M. Walsh; Rigoberto Betancourt; Deacon Clary Nash.
Office: 939 Jordan St., 71101-4391. Tel: 318-221-5296; Fax: 318-221-8076.
School—Tel: 318-221-6005; Fax: 318-425-0648. Miss Marie R. Rinaudo, Prin.
Lay Teachers 22; Students 317.
Catechesis/Religious Programs—947 Jordan St., 71101. Tel: 318-424-2317.
Students 109.

2—HOLY TRINITY (1856), Rev. Msgr. Franz Graef.
Res., 315 Marshall St., P.O. Box 144, 71161-0144. Tel: 318-221-5990; Fax: 318-221-3545.

3—OUR LADY OF THE BLESSED SACRAMENT (1923) (African American), Revs. Andre McGrath, O.F.M.; Francis Ngumi Kamau, F.M.H.
Res., 1558 Buena Vista St., 71101-2448. Tel: 318-222-3790; Fax: 318-222-3793.
School—2932 Murphy St., 71103-2241. Tel: 318-222-5051; Fax: 318-222-5840. Winnie Vance-Antoine, Prin.
Franciscan Missionaries of Hope 1; Lay Teachers 14; Students 208.

4—OUR LADY OF THE HOLY ROSARY (1952), Rev. Msgr. J. Carson LaCaze.
Res., 1755 Corbitt St., 71108-3098. Tel: 318-636-3530; Fax: 318-632-4955.
School—1730 Cox St., 71108. Tel: 318-636-3826; Fax: 318-636-9123. Lou Ann Rainey, Prin.
Sisters of Our Lady of Sorrows 2; Lay Teachers 22; Students 195.
Catechesis/Religious Programs—Students 14.

5—SACRED HEART OF JESUS (1966), Rev. Msgr. C. Murray Clayton.
Res., 4736 Lyba St., P.O. Box 19467, 71149-0467. Tel: 318-635-2121; Fax: 318-635-5226.
Catechesis/Religious Programs—Tel: 318-635-5446.
Students 46.

6—ST. CATHERINE OF SIENA (1938), Rev. William Spencer, O.F.M.
Res., 331 E. 71st St., 71106-4305. Tel: 318-868-6506; Fax: 318-861-6177.

7—ST. ELIZABETH ANN SETON (1984), Rev. LaVerne Thomas, III; Deacon William Long.
Res., 522 E. Flournoy-Lucas Rd., 71115-2073. Tel: 318-798-1887; Fax: 318-797-7302.
Catechesis/Religious Programs—Students 260.

8—ST. JOSEPH (1949), Revs. Peter B. Mangum, J.C.L., J.V.; Richard J. Lombard.
Res., 228 Patton Ave., 71105. Tel: 318-865-3581; Fax: 318-865-5125.
School—1210 Anniston Ave., 71105. Tel: 318-865-3585; Fax: 318-868-1859. Mr. David Schommer, Prin.; Mrs. Mary Cacioppo, Asst. Prin.
Lay Teachers 37; Students 581.
Catechesis/Religious Programs—Students 281.

9—ST. MARY OF THE PINES (1973), Rev. Edmund A. Niehoff.
Res., 1050 Bert Kouns Industrial Loop, 71118-3499. Tel: 318-687-5121; Fax: 318-687-5124.
Catechesis/Religious Programs—Students 170.

10—ST. PIUS X (1955), Rev. Charles Glorioso; Susan R. Lanier, Pastoral Assoc.
Res., 4300 N. Market St., 71107-2953. Tel: 318-222-2165; Fax: 318-222-9160.
Catechesis/Religious Programs—Students 114.

11—ST. THERESA. Consolidated with St. John Berchmans Cathedral.

OUTSIDE THE CITY OF SHREVEPORT

Bastrop, Morehouse Parish, St. Joseph (1943), Rev. Joseph Robert Inzina.
Res., 217 Harrington Ave., 71220-3025. Tel: 318-281-4327; Fax: 318-281-0982. [CEM]
School—Tel: 318-281-5894; Fax: 318-281-5890. Angie Druhan, Prin.
Lay Teachers 12; Students 156.
Catechesis/Religious Programs—Students 28.
Our Lady Help of Christians. Consolidated with St. Joseph, Bastrop.

Bossier City, Bossier Parish, Christ the King (1939), Rev. Joseph Martina, Jr.
Res., 425 McCormick St., 71111-4692. Tel: 318-221-0238; Fax: 318-425-0011.
Catechesis/Religious Programs—Tel: 318-221-0730; Fax: 318-425-0211.
Students 46.
Mission—Doyline, Webster Parish, Mary, Queen of the Holy Rosary, Tel: 318-747-9496.
St. Jude (1964), Revs. Rothell Price; James R. McLelland; Deacon John J. Finnorn, Jr.
Res., 3800 Viking Dr., E., 71111-7403. Tel: 318-746-2508; Fax: 318-742-4526.
Catechesis/Religious Programs—Students 438.
Mission—Benton, Bossier Parish, Mary, Queen of Heaven.
Mary, Queen of Peace (1999), Rev. Msgr. Earl V. Provenza, V.F.
Res., 2101 Hope St., 71112. Tel: 318-752-5971; Fax: 318-752-5973.
Catechesis/Religious Programs—Students 124.
Mission—Coushatta, Red River Parish, St. George, P.O. Box 937, Coushatta, 71019-0937. Tel: 318-932-3733.

Grambling, Lincoln Parish, St. Benedict the Black (1966) (African American), Rev. John Eaton, O.F.M.
Res., 471 Main St., 71245-3088. Tel: 318-247-6734; Fax: 318-247-6288.

Hodge, Jackson Parish, St. Lucy (1935), Rev. Robert A. Leonhardt, O.F.M.
Res., 1104 S. 2nd St., P.O. Drawer 100, 71247-0100. Tel: 318-259-2326. [CEM]
Catechesis/Religious Programs—Students 21.

Lake Providence, East Carroll Parish, St. Patrick (1870), Rev. Zacharias Prakuzhy, C.M.I. (India).
Res., P.O. Box 351, 71254-0351. Tel: 318-559-1276; Fax: 318-559-7733. [CEM]
Catechesis/Religious Programs—Students 23.

Mansfield, DeSoto Parish, St. Joseph (1907), Rev. Philip F. Michiels.
Res., 305 Jefferson St., P.O. Box 760, 71052-0760. Tel: 318-872-1158; Fax: 318-872-1161. [CEM 4]
Catechesis/Religious Programs—Tel: 318-872-2313.
Students 58.
Mission—Stonewall, DeSoto Parish, St. Ann's Chapel, 2260 Hwy. 171, P.O. Box 271, Stonewall, 71078. Tel: 318-858-3976.

Many, Sabine Parish, St. John the Baptist (1871), Rev. John Pardue.
Res., 1130 E. San Antonio Ave., 71449-3226. Tel: 318-256-5680; 256-5689; Fax: 318-256-9177. [CEM]
Catechesis/Religious Programs—Students 101.
Mission—Many, Sabine Parish, St. Terence, Hwy. 191 & 476, 1130 E. San Antonio Ave., 71449. Tel: 318-586-7444.

Minden, Webster Parish, St. Paul (1942), Revs. Karl J. Daigle; Phillip Pazhayakari, C.M.I. (India).
Res., 414 Fincher Rd., P.O. Box 799, 71058-0799. Tel: 318-377-5364; Fax: 318-377-5119.
Catechesis/Religious Programs—Students 80.
Missions—Ringgold, Bienville Parish, Blessed Sacrament, Hwy. 7 at Hwy. 4, Ringgold, 71068.; Homer, Claiborne Parish, St. Margaret, 600 E. 2nd St., Homer, 71040.; Springhill, Webster Parish, Sacred Heart, 304 Gaisser St., Springhill, 71075.

Monroe, Ouachita Parish,
1—JESUS THE GOOD SHEPHERD, (1958), Rev. Timothy C. Hurd. In res., Rev. Msgr. Edmund J. Moore, (Retired).
Office: 2510 Emerson St., 71201-2699. Tel: 318-325-7549; Fax: 318-322-6969.; Priest's Residence: 800 Marquette St., 71201. Tel: 318-325-6956.

School—900 Good Shepherd Ln., 71201. Tel: 318-325-8569; Fax: 318-325-9730.
Lay Teachers 20; Students 300.
Catechesis/Religious Programs—Students 52.

2—LITTLE FLOWER OF JESUS, (1940) (African American), Rev. Carroll Mizicko, O.F.M.
Res., 616 S. 16th St., 71201. Tel: 318-324-9706.
Church Office: 600 S. 16th St., 71201. Tel: 318-322-1224; Fax: 318-322-1261.
School—610 S. 16th St., 71201. Tel: 318-322-7379. Mrs. Ida P. Jackson, Dir. Preschool.
Lay Teachers 4; Students 30.
Catechesis/Religious Programs—Students 50.

3—OUR LADY OF FATIMA, (1952), Revs. Richard Norsworthy; Patrick J. Madden.
Res., 3205 Concordia, P.O. Box 4136, 71211-4136. Tel: 318-325-7595; Fax: 318-325-7595. [JC]
School—3202 Franklin St., 71211. Tel: 318-387-1851; Fax: 318-387-7593. Sherry Fontana, Prin.
Lay Teachers 15; Students 186.
Catechesis/Religious Programs—Students 75.
Mission—Swartz, Ouachita Parish, St. Lawrence, 357 Swartz School Rd., Swartz, 71281. Tel: 318-343-1618.

4—ST. JOSEPH, (1956), Rev. Boby Mannamplackal Alex (India).
Res., 506 Benton Ave., P.O. Box 1203, 71210-1203. Tel: 318-325-4527; Fax: 318-322-8445.
Catechesis/Religious Programs—Students 21.

5—ST. MATTHEW, (1856), Rev. Joseph Puthuppally.
Res., 121 Jackson St., 71201. Tel: 318-323-8878; 8879; Fax: 318-323-2537. [CEM]
Catechesis/Religious Programs—Students 22.

Noble, Sabine Parish, St. Ann (1955), Rev. Kenneth Williams.
Res., 5272 Hwy. 482, 71462. Tel: 318-645-9419; Fax: 318-645-9419. [CEM]
Catechesis/Religious Programs—Tel: 318-645-7033.
Students 55.
Mission—Noble, Sabine Parish, St. Catherine, 5272 Hwy. 482, 71462. Tel: 318-645-2711. [CEM]

Oak Grove, West Carroll Parish, Sacred Heart (1947), Rev. Zacharias Prakuzhy, C.M.I. (India).
Church—203 Purvis St., P.O. Box 419, 71263-0419. Tel: 318-428-2683.

Rambin, DeSoto Parish, St. Mary. Consolidated with St. Joseph, Mansfield.

Rayville, Richland Parish, Sacred Heart (1920), Rev. Thomas J. Flynn, C.S.Sp.
Res., 716 Francis St., P.O. Box 717, 71269-0717. Tel: 318-728-2445; Fax: 318-728-0009.
Catechesis/Religious Programs—Students 16.
Mission—Delhi, Richland Parish, St. Theresa, 420 Main St., P.O. Box 363, Delhi, 71232-0363. Tel: 318-878-3484. [JC]

Ruston, Lincoln Parish, St. Thomas Aquinas (1941), Rev. Jerome Thelen, O.F.M.; Deacon John J. Serio.
Res., 810 Carey Ave., 71270-4915. Tel: 318-255-2870; Fax: 318-254-8319.
Catechesis/Religious Programs—Students 172.

Vivian, Caddo Parish, St. Clement (1945), Rev. Patrick A. Scully.
Office: 819 N. Pine, 71082-3354. Tel: 318-375-2789; Fax: 318-375-5919.

West Monroe, Ouachita Parish, St. Paschal (1940), Rev. Michael Haney, O.F.M. In res., Rev. Donatus Grunloh, O.F.M.; Bro. Claver Boerner, O.F.M.
Res., 711 N. Seventh St., 71291-4211. Tel: 318-323-1631; Fax: 318-361-0527. [CEM]
School—102 Wilson St., 71291. Tel: 318-322-8246; Fax: 318-322-8477. Peggy Buffington, Prin.
Lay Teachers 11; Students 105.
Catechesis/Religious Programs—Students 140.
Missions—Calhoun, Ouachita Parish, St. Francis of Assisi, Tel: 318-322-1487; Farmerville, Union Parish, Our Lady of Perpetual Help, Tel: 318-368-9239. Rev. John Eaton, O.F.M., Admin.
Res., 471 Main St., Grambling, 71245-3088. Tel: 318-247-6734.

Zwolle, Sabine Parish, St. Joseph (1881), Revs. David T. Richter; Tej Lal, I.M.S. (India).
Res., P.O. Box 8, 71486-0008. Tel: 318-645-6155; Fax: 318-645-9852. [CEM 2]
Catechesis/Religious Programs—Students 264.

Chaplains of Public Institutions

SHREVEPORT. *Forcht Wade Correctional Center*. Rev. Richard Pusch, Chap., Res., 3538 Eastlake Dr., 71105.
Overton Brooks Veteran's Administration Medical Center 510 E. Stoner Ave., 71101. Rev. Philip F. Michiels, Chap. Emergencies, Res., St. Joseph Church, P.O. Box 760, Mansfield, 71052-0760. Tel: 318-872-1158.

MONROE. *Swanson Correctional Center for Youth*. (Formerly Louisiana Training Institute) 4701 S. Grand, 71202-6499. Tel: 318-323-4406. Rev. Carroll Mizicko, O.F.M., Chap.

On Special Assignment:
Reverend Fathers—
Watson, Mark, Dir. Church Vocations

On Duty Outside the Diocese:
Reverend Fathers—
Ebarb, Walter E.
Howard, Joseph, Jr.

Retired:
Reverend Monsignors—
Buvens, Norman C.
Moore, Edmund J.
O'Hanlon, William
Reverend Fathers—
Beaulieu, Earl G.
Binh, John Phan Cong
Fuoco, Armando
Germain, Jean M.
McMullen, Roger
Moraus, Govie
Tremblay, Leger

On Leave:
Reverend Fathers—
Garcia, Juan F.

Permanent Deacons:
Finnorn, John J., Jr.
Long, William R.
Morris, Ronald J.
Nash, Clary
Serio, John J.
Wisdom, Clarence, Inactive

INSTITUTIONS LOCATED IN THE DIOCESE

[A] HIGH SCHOOLS, DIOCESAN

SHREVEPORT. *Loyola College Prep*, 921 Jordan St., 71101-4390. Tel: 318-221-2675; Fax: 318-221-2678.
E-mail: flyers@loyolaprep.org
Web site: www.loyolaprep.org
Mrs. Mary Ann Whited, Prin. Sisters 1; Lay Teachers 37; Students 395.

MONROE. *St. Frederick High School*, 3300 Westminster, 71201-3299. Tel: 318-323-9636; Fax: 318-323-7456.
E-mail: sfsimon@bayou.com
Franciscan Sisters of Our Lady of Perpetual Help. Mr. William Simon, Prin. Sisters 1; Lay Teachers 24; Students 303.

[B] GENERAL HOSPITALS

SHREVEPORT. *Christus Schumpert Health System*, (1907) One St. Mary Pl., P.O. Box 21976, 71120-1976. Tel: 318-681-4500; Fax: 318-681-4177 (Administration)
For a complete listing, refer to the Hospitals section.

COUSHATTA. *Christus Coushatta Health Care Center*, 1635 Marvel St., 71019. Tel: 318-932-2000; Fax: 318-932-2198
For a complete listing, refer to the Hospitals section.

MONROE. *St. Francis Medical Center*, P.O. Box 1901, 71210-1901. Tel: 318-327-4000; Fax: 318-327-4142.
E-mail: hoganr@stfran.com
Web site: www.stfran.com
For a complete listing, refer to the Hospitals section.

St. Francis Specialty Hospital, (1995) 309 Jackson St., P.O. Box 1532, 71210. Tel: 318-327-4600; Fax: 318-327-4082.
E-mail: hightob@stfran.com
Web site: www.specialtyhospital.com
For a complete listing, refer to the Hospitals section.

St. Patrick Psychiatric Hospital, Inc., 309 Jackson St., P.O. Box 1901, 71210-1901. Tel: 318-327-4686; Fax: 318-327-4951.
E-mail: rogersc@stfran
Web site: www.stpatricks.net
For a complete listing, refer to the Hospitals section.

[C] PROTECTIVE INSTITUTIONS

SHREVEPORT. *Holy Angels Residential Facility*, 10450 Ellerbe Rd., 71106-7712. Tel: 318-797-8500; 797-9070; Fax: 318-798-0159.
E-mail: scrider@prysm.net
For a complete listing, refer to the Special Care Facilities section.

[D] HOMES FOR AGED

MONROE. *Christus St. Joseph Home*, 2301 Sterlington Rd., P.O. Box 6057, 71211-6057. Tel: 318-323-3426; Fax: 318-387-7157
For a complete listing, refer to the Special Care Facilities section.

[E] SPECIAL CENTERS FOR SOCIAL SERVICES & ASSISTANCE

SHREVEPORT. *St. Catherine Community Center*, 331 E. 71st St., 71106-4305. Tel: 318-865-9817; Fax: 318-861-6177.
E-mail: RAlford318@aol.com
Afterschool Enrichment, Summer Day Camp, Parenting, Literacy, Arts. Mr. Robert Alford, Dir. Total Assisted 1,500; Total Staff 40.

[F] CONVENTS AND RESIDENCES FOR SISTERS

SHREVEPORT. *Motherhouse of the Daughters of the Cross in America*, 411 E. Flournoy-Lucas Rd., 71115-3901. Tel: 318-797-0887; Fax: 318-797-7102.
E-mail: dcsrs@bayou.com
Sr. Mary Louise Parisy, D.C., Supr. Sisters 6.
Religious House of Formation and Retirement-Our Lady of Sorrows, 9894 Norris Ferry Rd., 71106-7724. Tel: 318-797-0213; Fax: 318-797-7003.
E-mail: olscon@softdisk.com
Web site: www.ols.org
Sr. Seraphine Ricci, O.L.S., Supr. Sisters 10; Novices 5.

[G] NEWMAN CENTERS

GRAMBLING. *Student Center*, 471 S. Main St., 71245-3088. Tel: 318-247-6734 (Office); Fax: 318-247-6288.
E-mail: eatonofm@aol.com
Friar John Eaton, O.F.M., Dir.

MONROE. *Catholic Campus Ministry at the University of Louisana at Monroe*. (formerly Northeast Louisiana University), 911 University Ave., P.O. Box 7250, 71211-7250. Tel: 318-343-4897; Fax: 318-325-7595.
E-mail: ccm@bayou.com
Rev. Patrick J. Madden, Campus Min.

RUSTON. *E. Donn Piatt Catholic Student Center at Louisiana Tech University*, 600 S. Thornton St., 71270-4946. Tel: 318-251-0793; Fax: 318-254-8319.
E-mail: trason@bayou.com
Web site: www.members.tripod.com~aquinas/
Rev. Jerome Thelen, O.F.M.

RELIGIOUS INSTITUTES OF MEN REPRESENTED IN THE DIOCESE

For further details refer to the corresponding bracketed number in the Religious Institutes of Men or Women section.

[0275]—*Carmelites of Mary Immaculate (India)*.—C.M.I.
[0520]—*Franciscan Friars*. (Sacred Heart Prov.).—O.F.M.
[0520]—*Franciscan Friars*. (Prov. of St. John the Baptist).—O.F.M.
[]—*Franciscan Missionaries of Hope*. (Nairobi, Kenya).—F.M.H.
[0650]—*Holy Ghost Fathers of Ireland*. (Louisiana Prov.).—C.S.Sp.
[]—*Indian Missionary Society*. (India).—I.M.S.
[0560]—*Third Order Regular of St. Francis (Spanish Province of Immaculate Conception)*.—T.O.R.

RELIGIOUS INSTITUTES OF WOMEN REPRESENTED IN THE DIOCESE

[]—*Congregation of the Mother of Carmel*. (India).—C.M.F.
[0470]—*Congregation of the Sisters of Charity of the Incarnate Word, Houston, Texas*.—C.C.V.I.
[0770]—*Daughters of the Cross*.—D.C.
[1380]—*Franciscan Missionaries of Our Lady*.—O.S.F.
[1430]—*Franciscan Sisters of Our Lady of Perpetual Help*.—O.S.F.
[1530]—*Franciscan Sisters of Sylvania*. Ohio.—O.S.F.
[2970]—*School Sisters of Notre Dame, St. Louis Province*.—S.S.N.D.
[0650]—*Sisters of Charity of St. Vincent de Paul of New York*.—S.C.
[3120]—*Sisters of Our Lady of Sorrows*.—O.L.S.
[3840]—*Sisters of St. Joseph of Carondelet*.—C.S.J.
[]—Sisters of the Eucharistic Covenant.—S.E.C.
[4120-03]—*Ursuline Nuns of the Congregation of Paris*.—O.S.U.

DIOCESAN CEMETERIES

SHREVEPORT, LA. *St. Joseph*, Catholic Center, 3500 Fairfield Ave., 71104. Tel: 318-868-4441; Fax: 318-868-4605. Mr. E. Michael Schofield, C.P.A., Contact Person.

NECROLOGY

(No Deaths)

Diocese of Sioux City

(Dioecesis Siopolitana)

Most Reverend

DANIEL N. DINARDO, D.D.

Bishop of Sioux City; ordained July 16, 1977; appointed Coadjutor Bishop of Sioux City August 19, 1997; consecrated October 7, 1997; appointed Bishop of Sioux City November 28, 1998. *Address all correspondence to: P.O. Box 3379, Sioux City, IA, 51102-3379; Fax: 712-233-7557.*

Most Reverend

LAWRENCE D. SOENS, D.D.

Retired Bishop of Sioux City; ordained May 6, 1950; appointed Bishop of Sioux City June 15, 1983; consecrated and installed August 17, 1983; retired November 28, 1998. *Address all correspondence to: P.O. Box 3379, Sioux City, IA, 51102-3379; Fax: 712-233-7598.*

Corporate Title: *"The Diocese of Sioux City."*

ESTABLISHED JANUARY 15, 1902.

Square Miles 14,518.

Comprises 24 Counties in the northwest part of Iowa, west of Winnebago, Hancock, Wright, Hamilton and Story Counties, and north of Harrison, Shelby, Audubon, Guthrie and Dallas Counties.

For legal titles of parishes and diocesan institutions, consult the Chancery.

Chancery: Administrative Offices, 1821 Jackson St., P.O. Box 3379, Sioux City, IA, 51102-3379. Tel.: 712-255-7933; Fax: 712-233-7598.

Web site address: www.scdiocese.org

E-mail address: sernett@scdiocese.org

STATISTICAL OVERVIEW

Personnel	
Bishop	1
Retired Bishops	1
Priests: Diocesan Active in Diocese	109
Priests: Active Outside Diocese	10
Priests: Retired, Sick or Absent	49
Number of Diocesan Priests	168
Ordinations:	
Diocesan Priests	1
Permanent Deacons	38
Permanent Deacons in Diocese	38
Total Sisters	96
Parishes	
Parishes	124
With Resident Pastor:	
Resident Diocesan Priests	89
Without Resident Pastor:	
Administered by Priests	35
Pastoral Centers	1
Professional Ministry Personnel:	
Sisters	9
Lay Ministers	13
Welfare	
Catholic Hospitals	3
Total Assisted	405,780
Homes for the Aged	3
Total Assisted	313
Specialized Homes	1
Special Centers for Social Services	4
Total Assisted	5,874
Educational	
Diocesan Students in Other Seminaries	13
Total Seminarians	13
Colleges and Universities	1
Total Students	937
High Schools, Diocesan and Parish	8
Total Students	2,413
Elementary Schools, Diocesan and Parish	26
Total Students	5,369
Catechesis/Religious Education:	
High School Students	4,233
Elementary Students	7,871
Total Students Under Catholic Instruction	20,836
Teachers in the Diocese:	
Priests	7
Sisters	19
Lay Teachers	546
Vital Statistics	
Receptions into the Church:	
Infant Baptism Totals	1,868
Adult Baptism Totals	107
Received into Full Communion	272
First Communions	1,670
Confirmations	1,564
Marriages:	
Catholic	359
Interfaith	333
Total Marriages	692
Deaths	1,201
Total Catholic Population	97,413
Total Population	468,549

Former Bishops—Most Rev. PHILIP J. GARRIGAN, D.D., ord. June 11, 1870; appt. March 21, 1902; cons. May 25, 1902; died Oct. 14, 1919.—Most Rev. EDMOND HEELAN, D.D., ord. June 24, 1890; cons. April 8, 1919; died Sept. 20, 1948.—Most Rev. JOSEPH M. MUELLER, D.D., ord. June 14, 1919; cons. Oct. 16, 1947; died Aug. 9, 1981.—Most Rev. FRANK H. GRETEMAN, D.D., ord. Dec. 8, 1932; appt. Titular Bishop of Vissalsa April 14, 1965; cons. May 26, 1965; appt. Bishop of Sioux City Oct. 20, 1970; installed Dec. 9, 1970; retired Aug. 17, 1983; died March 21, 1987.

Vicars General—Rev. Msgr. ROGER J. AUGUSTINE, V.G., *Immaculate Conception Church, 419 Jones St., P.O. Box C, Moville, 51039-0802.* Tel: 712-873-3745. Rev. Msgr. MICHAEL D. SERNETT, V.G., *1821 Jackson St., P.O. Box 3379, Sioux City, 51102-3379.*

Episcopal Vicar for Canonical Affairs—Rev. Msgr. R. MARK DUCHAINE, J.C.L., *P.O. Box 3379, Sioux City, 51102.* Tel: 712-255-7933.

Chancery—Administrative Offices, 1821 Jackson St., P.O. Box 3379, Sioux City, 51102-3379. Tel: 712-255-7933; Fax: 712-233-7598.

Chancellor—Rev. Msgr. MICHAEL D. SERNETT, *Res., 1821 Jackson St., P.O. Box 3379, Sioux City, 51104.* Tel: 712-277-1606.

Vice Chancellors—Rev. MARK J. STOLL, J.C.L., *St. Joseph Church, 28174 Nature Ave., Hinton, 51024.* Tel: 712-233-7537. Mrs. KAY MORRISSEY, *P.O. Box 3379, Sioux City, 51102.* Tel: 712-233-7532.

Diocesan Tribunal—Address all marriage related materials to: *Diocesan Tribunal, P.O. Box 3379, Sioux City, 51102-3379.* Tel: 712-233-7533; Fax: 712-233-7588.

Judicial Vicar—Rev. Msgr. R. MARK DUCHAINE, J.C.L., *1821 Jackson St., P.O. Box 3379, Sioux City, 51102-3379., Res., Our Lady of Good Counsel Church, 513 Mueller St., Holstein, 51025-9802.* Tel: 712-368-4755.

Promoter of Justice—Rev. Msgr. RICHARD E. ZENK, J.C.D.

Defender of the Bond—Rev. ROBERT P. BROWN, S.T.L.; Rev. Msgr. RICHARD E. ZENK, J.C.D.; Rev. EUGENE ULSES, J.C.L.

Judges—Rev. Msgr. MICHAEL D. SERNETT, J.C.D.; Rev. Msgr. ROGER AUGUSTINE, V.G.; Revs. PAUL-LOUIS ARTS; JEROME COSGROVE; MARK J. STOLL, J.C.L.; DONALD J. SLAVEN, J.C.L.

Notary—JUDY E. PUETZ.

Diocesan Corporate Board—Most Rev. DANIEL N. DINARDO, Pres.; Rev. Msgr. ROGER J. AUGUSTINE, V.G., Vice Pres.; Rev. Msgr. MICHAEL D. SERNETT, Sec. Directors: Most Rev. LAWRENCE D. SOENS; Revs. THOMAS E. GEELAN; ROGER J. LINNAN; Mr. MICHAEL J. MOELLER; Mr. JEFFREY R. MOHRHAUSER; Mrs. SUSAN H. PIERCE; Dr. DANIEL J. SHEY; Mrs. BEVERLY WHARTON; Dr. JACK CALARESO.

Diocesan Legal Counsel—Mr. MAURICE NIELAND,(Rawlings, Nieland, Probasco, Killinger, Ellenwanger, Jacobs, Mohrhauser, Law Firm, Sioux City). Refer all legal matters to The Chancery.

Presbyteral Council—Most Rev. DANIEL N. DINARDO; Rev. Msgr. ROGER J. AUGUSTINE, V.G.; Rev. Msgr. KENNETH A. SEIFRIED; Rev. Msgr. MERVIN J. HOOD; Revs. PAUL-LOUIS ARTS; PAUL D. BORMANN; ARMAND J. BERTRAND; THOMAS E. GEELAN; EDWARD M. GIRRES; DANIEL GUENTHER; STEVEN J. MCLOUD; ALFRED MCCOY; KEVIN M. RICHTER; ROBERT J.

SCHIMMER; JOHN M. THOMAS; TIMOTHY J. HOGAN; Rev. Msgr. MICHAEL D. SERNETT.

Diocesan Consultors—Rev. Msgr. ROGER J. AUGUSTINE, V.G.; Rev. Msgr. MICHAEL D. SERNETT; Rev. Msgr. MERVIN J. HOOD; Revs. PAUL-LOUIS ARTS; TIMOTHY J. HOGAN; THOMAS E. GEELAN; VICTOR F. RAMAEKER; A. E. MCCOY; ROBERT J. SCHIMMER.

Deans—Very Rev. GARY B. SNYDER, V.F., Southwestern Deanery; Very Rev. ROBERT J. SCHIMMER, V.F., Central Deanery; Very Rev. JAMES C. MCALPIN, V.F., South Central Deanery; Very Rev. LAURENCE J. BURNS, V.F., Southeastern Deanery; Very Rev. DANIEL C. GUENTHER, V.F., Northeastern Deanery; Very Rev. Msgr. KENNETH A. SEIFRIED, V.F., Northwestern Deanery.

Diocesan Offices and Directors

Board of Education—Most Rev. DANIEL DINARDO, Ex Officio Chm.; Revs. PAUL-LOUIS ARTS; PATRICK WALSH; TERRY RODER; Mrs. MARY GERBER; Mr. JOE DANIEL; Sr. MARY CLARENITA FROEHLICH, P.B.V.M.; Sr. RUTH SCHOCK, O.S.F.; Sr. JOAN STOFFEL, O.S.F.; Mr. KEN HAJEK; Mrs. MAUREEN ELBERT; Mr. JAMES SCHALL; Mrs. SHERRY NILLES; Mr. PATRICK RINKER; Sr. KATHY KNIPPER, O.S.F.; Ms. MARY JANE SPIRK; Mrs. KATHEE FROEHLICH; Mrs. MARIBETH NIDAY.

Building Commission—Most Rev. DANIEL N. DINARDO, Chm.; Revs. CLAIR L. BOES; JEROME DEGEN; BRIAN C. HUGHES; ANDREW LANGE.

Catholic School Foundation of the Diocese of Sioux City—Most Rev. DANIEL N. DINARDO, Pres., *1821 Jackson St., P.O. Box 3379, Sioux City, 51102.*

Archives—Sr. KEVIN CUMMINGS, P.B.V.M., *1821 Jackson St., P.O. Box 3379, Sioux City, 51102-3379.* Tel: 712-233-7525.

Catholic Youth Organization—Rev. RANDY L. SCHON, *St. Catherine Church, P.O. Box 538, Oyens, 51045-0538.* Tel: 712-546-4588.

Office of Religious Education and Youth Ministry—Mr. PATRICK RINKER, Dir., *1821 Jackson St., P.O. Box 3379, Sioux City, 51102-3379.*

Censor Librorum—Rev. Msgr. JAMES K. LAFFERTY, Ph.D., *St. Joseph Church, 408 S. Main, Schaller, 51053.* Tel: 712-275-4238.

Catholic Charities—Mr. JERRY EATON, Dir., *1601 Military Rd., Sioux City, 51103.* Tel: 712-252-4547. Fort Dodge Office: *3 N. 16th, Fort Dodge, 50501.* Tel: 515-576-4156. Carroll Office: *409 1/2 W. 7th St., P.O. Box 13, Carroll, 51401.* Tel: 712-792-9597.

Office of Youth Ministry and Catechesis—Directors: Mr. PATRICK RINKER; MARY JANE SPIRK, *1821 Jackson St., P.O. Box 3379, Sioux City, 51102-3379.* Tel: 712-233-7520.

Continuing Education for Priests—Rev. ROGER J. LINNAN, Ph.D., Dir., *Sacred Heart Church, 111 14th Ave. W., Spencer, 51301.*

Council of Catholic Women—Rev. BENJAMIN JENSEN, Moderator, *Sacred Heart Church, P.O. Box 400, Ruthven, 51358-0400.* Tel: 712-837-5240.

Ecumenical Commission—Rev. Msgr. FRANK J. BRADY, Chm.; Revs. ROBERT W. GRALAPP; JAMES C. MCALPIN; ALFRED E. MCCOY.

Episcopal Representative for Religious—Sr. ROSALIE ERDMANN, S.L.W., *1812 Jackson St., Sioux City, 51105-1054.* Tel: 712-258-2579.

Episcopal Representative for Hospitals and Health Care—Vacant, *1821 Jackson St., P.O. Box 3379, Sioux City, 51102-3379.*

Family Life Office And Adult Ministries—Mrs. KAY MORRISSEY, Dir., *1821 Jackson St., P.O. Box 3379, Sioux City, 51102-3379.* Tel: 712-233-7530.

Holy Childhood Association—Rev. Msgr. RICHARD E. ZENK, J.C.D., Dir., *P.O. Box 3379, Sioux City, 51102-3379.*

Liturgy Commission—Rev. TIM FITZGERALD, Chm.; Mrs. MONICA PEARSON; Revs. STEVE BRODERSEN; BRIAN DANNER; BRUCE LAWLER; TIM SCHOTT; Sr. MARGE STAUDT, O.S.F.; Sr. JANICE HOFFMAN, O.S.F.; Sr. M. ARNOLD STAUDT, O.S.F.; Mr. LARRY GEISLER; Mrs. MARLENE FITZPATRICK; Mr. BERNARD KENINGER; Rev. DAVE HERMANN; Deacon LEROY RUPP; Mr. ANDY LANG.

Office Of Communications—"The Globe"—Deacon JOSEPH F. MAHER, Mgr., *1825 Jackson St., P.O. Box 5079, Sioux City, 51102-5079.* Tel: 712-255-2550. Editorial Office; Circulation.

Office of Catholic Education—Tel: 712-233-7589. Sr. JOAN STOFFEL, Supt., *1821 Jackson, P.O. Box 3379, Sioux City, 51102-3379.*

Permanent Diaconate—Rev. ARMAND J. BERTRAND, Co-Dir., *Immaculate Conception Church, P.O. Box 658, Cherokee, 51012-0658.* Tel: 712-225-4606. Deacon RONALD M. FORREST, Co-Dir., *1821 Jackson St., P.O. Box 3379, Sioux City, 51102-3379.*

Priests' Personnel Board—Rev. Msgr. ROGER J. AUGUSTINE, V.G., Bishop's Liaison; Revs. PAUL EISELE; EDWARD M. GIRRES; ANDREW W. HOFFMAN; PAUL J. KELLY.

Priests' Pension Plan - Board of Trustees—Most Rev. DANIEL N. DINARDO; Rev. Msgr. MICHAEL SERNETT; Revs. GARY B. SNYDER; ROGER LINNAN; DANIEL LYNCH; BRUCE A. LAWLER; Mr. RICHARD L. BILLINGS, Chm.; Mr. PATRICK D. KUEHL; Mr. MICHAEL J. MOELLER; Mr. JEFFREY R. MOHRHAUSER; Mr. ROBERT V. WILLIAMS.

Propagation of the Faith, Association of the Holy Childhood, Catholic Students' Mission Crusade—Rev. Msgr. RICHARD E. ZENK, J.C.D., Dir., *1821 Jackson St., P.O. Box 3379, Sioux City, 51102-3379.*

Radio and Television—Deacon JOSEPH F. MAHER, Dir., *P.O. Box 5079, Sioux City, 51102-5079.*

Rural Life Conference—MARILYN MURPHY, Dir., *1601 Military Rd., Sioux City, 51103.* Tel: 712-252-4547.

St. Joseph Education Society—(Diocesan Seminarian Board). Rev. PAUL-LOUIS ARTS, Exec. Sec., *P.O. Box 2817, Sioux City, 51106-2817.* Tel: 712-276-4821.

Vocations—Rev. BRIAN C. HUGHES, *5000 Military Rd., Sioux City, 51103-1564.* Tel: 712-233-7523; 233-1652.

CLERGY, PARISHES, MISSIONS AND PAROCHIAL SCHOOLS

CITY OF SIOUX CITY
(Woodbury County)

1—CATHEDRAL OF THE EPIPHANY (1867), Revs. Paul J. Kelly; Randy J. Guerdet; Hieu Nguyen (Vietnam); Verne P. Stapenhorst.
Res., 1011 Douglas St., 51105-1399. Tel: 712-255-1637; Fax: 712-255-4194.
School—Holy Family Epiphany Center. See separate listing under Inter-Parochial Schools in Institution section.
Catechesis/Religious Programs—Tel: 712-258-5944.
Students 90.

2—BLESSED SACRAMENT (1922), Revs. Thomas E. Geelan; Jeffrey A. Schleisman; Deacons John Hefferman; Fred Karpuk; George Spellman; Ronald C. Pietz, Business Mgr.
Res., 3012 Jackson St., 51104-2799. Tel: 712-277-2949; Fax: 712-277-2963.
School—See separate listing under Inter-Parochial Schools in Institution Section.
Catechesis/Religious Programs—Tel: 712-277-4155; Fax: 712-258-3698. Patricia Walsh, D.R.E.
Students 166.

3—ST. BONIFACE (1906) (German), Rev. Kevin M. Richter; Deacon James Sands. In res., Rev. Richard A. Sitzmann.
Res., 703 W. Fifth St., 51103-3799. Tel: 712-255-3577; Fax: 712-279-0751. [JC]
School—Holy Family. See separate listing under Inter-Parochial Schools in Institution Section.
Catechesis/Religious Programs—Students 81.

4—ST. CASIMIR (1915) (Lithuanian). Closed. For inquiries for parish records contact the Chancery.

5—ST. FRANCIS OF ASSISI (1907) (Polish). Closed. For inquiries for parish records contact the Chancery.

6—IMMACULATE CONCEPTION (1905), Revs. Paul-Louis Arts; Daniel M. Greving; Brian J. Danner.
Res., P.O. Box 2817, 51106-2817. Tel: 712-276-4821; Fax: 712-276-1321. [JC]
School—See separate listing under Inter-Parochial Schools in Institution Section.
Catechesis/Religious Programs—Tel: 712-276-4571; Fax: 712-276-1321.
Students 206.

7—ST. JOSEPH (1887), Rev. Gary B. Snyder; Deacons Jerome Reicks; Ronald Pietz.
Res., 1112 Eighth St., 51105-1899. Tel: 712-258-3813; Fax: 712-258-7101. [JC]
School—Holy Family. See separate listing under Inter-Parochial Schools in Institution Section.
Catechesis/Religious Programs—Tel: 712-258-5944.
Students 46.

8—ST. MICHAEL (1907), Rev. Timothy J. Hogan; Deacons Larry Sitzman; William Berger, (Retired); Sr. Jean Ann Rausch, F.S.P.A., Pastoral Min.
Res., 2223 Indian Hills Dr., 51104-1605. Tel: 712-239-2411; Fax: 712-239-4710. [JC]
School—See separate listing under Inter-Parochial Schools in Institution Section.
Catechesis/Religious Programs—Tel: 712-258-2977.
Students 126.

9—NATIVITY OF OUR LORD JESUS CHRIST (1966), Rev. Gerald Feierfeil.
Res., 4242 Natalia Way, 51106-4099. Tel: 712-276-3022; Fax: 712-274-2703.
School—Mater Dei School. See separate listing under Inter-Parochial Schools in Institution Section.
Catechesis/Religious Programs—Tel: 712-274-0497.
Students 372.

10—SACRED HEART (1907), Rev. Bruce Lawler. In res., Rev. Brian Hughes.
Res., 5000 Military Rd., 51103-1564. Tel: 712-233-1652; Fax: 712-255-3056. [JC]
School—See separate listing under Inter-Parochial Schools in Institution Section.
Catechesis/Religious Programs—Students 118.

OUTSIDE SIOUX CITY

Akron, Plymouth Co., St. Patrick, Rev. Msgr. Richard E. Zenk.
Res., 650 Dakota St., P.O. Box 317, 51001-0317. Tel: 712-568-3292. [CEM]
Catechesis/Religious Programs—Students 110.

Algona, Kossuth Co., St. Cecelia (1892), Rev. Steven W. Brodersen; Deacon Bob Larsen.
Res., P.O. Box 633, 50511-0633. Tel: 515-295-3435; Fax: 515-295-9290. [CEM]
School—Seton Elementary. Consolidation of St. Cecelia, Algona, St. Benedict, St. Joseph, Wesley, St. Joseph, Bode. Tel: 515-295-3509; Fax: 515-295-7739.
Presentation Sisters 3; Lay Teachers 22; Students 243.
Catechesis/Religious Programs—Students 204.

Alton, Sioux Co., St. Mary's (1870) (German), Rev. James Tigges.
Res., 609 10th St., 51003. Tel: 712-756-4224. [CEM]
School—Spalding Catholic, (Grades 4-6). Consolidation of Alton, Hospers and Granville. Tel: 712-756-4532.
Lay Teachers 3; Students 72.
Catechesis/Religious Programs—Cluster of St. Mary, St. Anthony's, and St. Joseph's.
Students 60.

Anthon, Woodbury Co., St. Joseph's (1890), Rev. Mark Harrington; Sr. Mary Clare Walling, Pastoral Min.
Res., P.O. Box 285, 51004-0285. Tel: 712-373-5573. [CEM]
Catechesis/Religious Programs—Tel: 712-373-5573.
Students 114.

Arcadia, Carroll Co., St. John the Baptist (1875), Rev. William Schreiber.
Res., P.O. Box 23, 51430-0023. Tel: 712-689-2595; Fax: 712-689-2282. [CEM]
Catechesis/Religious Programs—Tel: 712-689-1491.
Students 63.

Armstrong, Emmet Co., St. Mary's (1892), Rev. Jerome P. Cosgrove.
Office: 404 Fifth Ave., P.O. Box 437, 50514-9301. Tel: 712-864-3160. [CEM][JC]
Catechesis/Religious Programs—Tel: 712-362-4172.
Students 39.

Ashton, Osceola Co., St. Mary's Catholic Church (1880), Rev. Clair L. Boes.
Res., P.O. Box 157, 51232-0157. Tel: 712-724-6411. [CEM]
Catechesis/Religious Programs—2191 Nettle Ave., 51232. Tel: 712-724-6297. Mrs. Nancy Marnach, D.R.E.
Students 35.

Auburn, Sac Co., St. Mary's (1893) (German), Rev. Lawrence L. McCarty.
Res., P.O. Box H, 51433. Tel: 712-688-2845. [JC]
Catechesis/Religious Programs—Students 49.

Bancroft, Kossuth Co., St. John the Baptist's (1891), Rev. Paul D. Bormann; Deacon Philip Doocy.
Res., P.O. Box 195, 50517-0195. Tel: 515-885-2462; Fax: 515-885-2424. [CEM]
School—St. John's Elementary School, Tel: 515-885-2580.
Lay Teachers 5; Students 53.
Catechesis/Religious Programs—Tel: 515-885-2580. Lori Geitzenauer, D.R.E.
Students 183.

Barnum, Webster Co., St. Joseph's (1891). Unassigned.
Area Catholic Office: P.O. Box 994, Fort Dodge, 50501. Tel: 515-573-3616; Fax: 515-573-4556.
Res., P.O. Box 105, Clare, 50524-0105. Tel: 515-546-4505. [CEM]
Catechesis/Religious Programs—Students 51.

Bode, Kossuth Co., St. Joseph's (1876), Rev. Paul F. Eisele.
Res., 1023 Hwy. 169, 50519. Tel: 515-379-1470; Fax: 515-379-1811. [CEM]
Catechesis/Religious Programs—Students 79.

Boone, Boone Co., Sacred Heart (1868), Rev. Clem W. Currans.
Res., 921 12th St., 50036-2295. Tel: 515-432-1971; Fax: 515-432-7150. [CEM]
School—Sacred Heart Elementary, Tel: 515-432-4124; Fax: 515-433-9927.
Lay Teachers 13; Students 178.
Catechesis/Religious Programs—Tel: 515-432-2884.
Students 227.

Breda, Carroll Co., St. Bernard's (1880), Rev. James R. Smith.
Res., P.O. Box 39, 51436-0031. Tel: 712-673-2351. [CEM]
School—Christ the King Elementary. Consolidation of Breda, Lidderdale, Maple River and Mt. Carmel. Tel: 712-673-2582.
Lay Teachers 12; Students 145.
High School—Kuemper High School, Tel: 712-792-3596.
Students 38.
Catechesis/Religious Programs—Tel: 712-792-0513.
Students 19.

Carroll, Carroll Co., St. Lawrence (1914), Revs. Timothy R. Schott; Joseph A. Dillinger; Deacons Robert Bruner; Louis Westendorf; Tim Murphy. In res., Rev. Robert M. Fangman.
Res., 1607 N. West St., 51401-4198. Tel: 712-792-9244; Fax: 712-792-9245. [JC]
School—Kuemper Catholic Grade Schools, (Grades K-8) 1519 N. West St., 51401. Tel: 712-792-2123; Fax: 712-792-3365.
Franciscan Sisters of Perpetual Adoration 1; Lay Teachers 55; Students 658.
Catechesis/Religious Programs—Shared with Holy Spirit and surrounding parishes. Tel: 712-792-0513.
Students 472.

Holy Spirit (1964). SS Peter / Paul, and St. Joseph-,Carroll merged to form Holy Spirit, Carroll. Revs. James D. McCormick; Peter Duc Hung Nguyen; Deacons Anthony Reuter; William Schroeder.
Res., 421 E. Bluff St., 51401-3099. Tel: 712-792-4386; Fax: 712-792-8038. [JC]
School—Kuemper Catholic Grade Schools, Tel: 712-792-3610; Fax: 712-792-8072.
Franciscan Sisters of Perpetual Adoration 1; Opus Spiritus Sisters 1; Lay Teachers 48; Students 229.
Catechesis/Religious Programs—Tel: 712-792-0513; Fax: 712-792-9245. Deacon Timothy Murphy, D.R.E.
Students 159.

Charter Oak, Crawford Co., St. Boniface (1883) (German-Irish), Rev. Richard D. Ball.
Res., P.O. Box 317, Dow City, 51528. Tel: 712-678-3449. [CEM]
Mission—Ute, Monona Co., St. Mary's, c/o Box 317, 51528. [CEM]
Catechesis/Religious Programs—Tel: 712-674-3329.
Students 77.

Cherokee, Cherokee Co., Immaculate Conception (1870), Rev. Armand J. Bertrand; Deacon Leroy Rupp.
Res., 709 W. Cedar St., P.O. Box 658, 51012-0658. Tel: 712-225-4606. [CEM]
Catechesis/Religious Programs—7th & Willow, 51012. Tel: 712-225-4466.
Students 302.

St. Dymphna Chapel (1960). (Chapel for Patients). Rev. Eugene E. Sitzmann.
Mailing Address: 1251 W. Cedar Loop, 51012.
Res., 975 540th St., 51012. Tel: 712-225-6929; Fax: 712-225-6925.

Churdan, Greene Co., St. Columbkille's (1886) (German-Irish), Rev. Steven J. McLoud; Deacon Donald Kunecke.
Res., 807 Head St., P.O. Box 128, 50050-0128. Tel: 515-389-3625; Fax: 515-389-3795. [JC]
Catechesis/Religious Programs—Tel: 515-389-3156.
Students 65.

Clare, Webster Co., St. Matthew's (1886), Rev. Lawrence Burns.
Area Catholic Office: P.O. Box 994, Fort Dodge, 50501. Tel: 515-573-3616; Fax: 515-573-4556.
Res., P.O. Box 105, 50524-0105. Tel: 515-546-4505. [CEM]
Catechesis/Religious Programs—Students 65.

Coon Rapids, Carroll Co., Annunciation (1891), Rev. Anthony Pick.
Res., P.O. Box 76, 50058-0076. Tel: 712-999-2823; Fax: 712-999-2823. [CEM]
Catechesis/Religious Programs—Tel: 712-999-5235.
Students 133.

Danbury, Woodbury Co., St. Mary's (1897), Rev. Mark Harrington.
Res., P.O. Box 318, 51019-0318. Tel: 712-883-2406; Fax: 712-883-2458. [CEM]
School—Danbury Elementary, Tel: 712-883-2244.
Priests 1; Sisters 2; Lay Teachers 4; Students 41.
Catechesis/Religious Programs—Students 90.

Dayton, Webster Co., Christ the King (1950), Rev. Timothy J. Boekelman. Pastoral Ministers: Sr. Mary Lois Lehmann, P.B.V.M.; Sr. Mary Bernard Mauss, P.B.V.M.
Res., P.O. Box 135, Moorland, 50566. Tel: 515-549-3556. [CEM]
Catechesis/Religious Programs—Tel: 515-547-2743.
Students 34.

Dedham, Carroll Co., St. Joseph's (1892), Rev. Anthony Pick.
Res., P.O. Box 47, 51440-0047. Tel: 712-683-5744. [CEM]
School—Kuemper Catholic Grade Schools. Consolidation of Dedham, Willey Elementary, Holy Spirit and St. Lawrence. Tel: 712-792-3610; Fax: 712-792-3365.

Denison, Crawford Co., St. Rose of Lima (1872), Rev. Edward G. Murray.
Res., 1008 2nd Ave. S., P.O. Box 280, 51442-0280. Tel: 712-263-2152; Fax: 712-263-2153. [CEM]
School—Tel: 712-263-5408.
Lay Teachers 10; Students 84.
Catechesis/Religious Programs—Tel: 712-263-5408.
Students 241.

Dow City, Crawford Co., St. Mary's (1947) (German-Irish), Rev. Richard D. Ball.
Res., 215 Clark St., P.O. Box 317, 51528-0317. Tel: 712-674-3329.
Catechesis/Religious Programs—Students 46.

Duncombe, Webster Co., St. Joseph's (1880), Rev. Timothy J. Boekelman.
Res., P.O. Box 135, Moorland, 50566-0135. Tel: 515-549-3556. [CEM]
Catechesis/Religious Programs—Students 90.

Early, Sac Co., Sacred Heart (1882), Rev. Patrick J. O'Kane.
Res., P.O. Box 378, 50535-0378. Tel: 712-273-5482; Fax: 712-273-5798. [CEM]
Catechesis/Religious Programs—Tel: 712-273-5577.
Students 84.

Emmetsburg, Palo Alto Co., Holy Family (1870) (Irish), Rev. Daniel C. Guenther.
Res., 2001 S. Broadway, P.O. Box 322, 50536-0322. Tel: 712-852-3187; Fax: 712-852-3464. [CEM]
School—Emmetsburg Catholic School, (Grades 1-8). Tel: 712-852-3464. Mrs. Jean Hyslop, O.S.F., Prin.
Lay Teachers 11; Students 114.
Catechesis/Religious Programs—Tel: 712-852-3187. Mary Freeman, D.R.E.
Students 100.

St. Thomas. Closed. For sacramental records contact Holy Family, Emmetsburg.

Estherville, Emmet Co., St. Patrick's (1891), Rev. Jerome P. Cosgrove.
Res., P.O. Box 383, 51334-0383. Tel: 712-362-5851; Fax: 712-362-5852. [CEM]
Catechesis/Religious Programs—Duhigg Center, 902 Central Ave., 51334. Tel: 712-362-4172.
Students 335.

Fonda, Pocahontas Co., Our Lady of Good Counsel (1884), Rev. Harry D. McAlpine; Deacons J. R. Hogan; Eldon Sullivan.
Res., P.O. Box 306, 50540-0306. Tel: 712-288-6480. [CEM]
School—Tel: 712-288-4465.
Sisters 1; Lay Teachers 5; Students 64.
Catechesis/Religious Programs—Students 53.

Fort Dodge, Webster Co., Corpus Christi (1856), Revs. Christian J. Van Oosbree; Michael Erpelding.
Area Catholic Office: P.O. Box 994, 50501-0994.
Res., 416 N. 8th St., 50501. Tel: 515-573-3616; Fax: 515-573-4556. [JC]
School—School relocated to Sacred Heart, Holy Rosary, St. Edmond. Tel: 515-576-0522.
Lay Teachers 15; Students 304.
Catechesis/Religious Programs—Students 144.

Holy Rosary (1946), Rev. Lynn Bruch.
Area Catholic Office: P.O. Box 994, 50501. Tel: 515-573-3616; Fax: 515-573-4556.
Res., 2401 9th Ave. S., 50501-6246. Tel: 515-573-3162 (Res.); 573-2018 (Church). [JC]
School—See separate listing under Inter-Parochial Schools in Institution Section.
Catechesis/Religious Programs—Students 64.

Sacred Heart (1897), Rev. Edward M. Girres.
Area Catholic Office: P.O. Box 994, 50501. Tel: 515-573-3616; Fax: 515-573-4556.
Res., 1321 Second Ave. S., 50501-4925. Tel: 515-573-7617. [JC]
Catechesis/Religious Programs—Students 107.

Gilmore City, Pocahontas Co., St. John's (1889), Rev. Eugene J. Ulses.
Res., 311 4th St. N., Humboldt, 50548. Tel: 515-332-2856; Fax: 515-373-6016. [CEM]
Catechesis/Religious Programs—Students 26.

Graettinger, Palo Alto Co., Immaculate Conception (1891), Rev. Msgr. Thomas M. Donahoe.
Res., P.O. Box 448, 51342-0448. Tel: 712-859-3327; Fax: 712-859-3327. [CEM]
Catechesis/Religious Programs—Tel: 712-859-3990.
Students 96.

Grand Junction, Greene Co., St. Brigid's (1873) (Irish), Rev. Daniel C. Guenther.
Res., Jefferson, 50129. Tel: 515-738-2684. [CEM]
Catechesis/Religious Programs—St. Brigid Parish Center, 602 Hager St. E., 50107. Tel: 515-738-2254.
Students 59.

Granville, Sioux Co., St. Joseph (1886), Rev. Msgr. Kenneth A. Seifried.
Res., P.O. Box 127, 51022-0127. Tel: 712-727-3551. [CEM]
School—Spalding Catholic School, (Grades 7-8). Consolidation of Alton, Hospers and Granville. Tel: 712-727-3451; Fax: 712-727-3455.
Lay Teachers 2; Students 47.
High School—Spalding Catholic High School.
Priests 1; Lay Teachers 18; Students 90.
Catechesis/Religious Programs—Pilgrim cluster held at St. Mary's, Alton.

Halbur, Carroll Co., St. Augustine's (1904), Rev. Dale E. Reiff.
Res., P.O. Box 13, 51444-0013. Tel: 712-658-2464. [CEM]
School—Holy Trinity Elementary. Consolidation of Halbur, Templeton and Roselle. Tel: 712-669-3346.
Lay Teachers 4; Students 53.
High School—Kuemper High School, Tel: 712-792-3596.
Students 24.
Catechesis/Religious Programs—Tel: 712-792-0513 (Carroll); 653-2131 (Mannina).
Students 18.

Hawarden, Sioux Co., St. Mary's (1887), Rev. LeRoy L. Seuntjens.
Res., P.O. Box 271, 51023-0271. Tel: 712-551-1501. [JC]
Catechesis/Religious Programs—Students 124.

Holstein, Ida Co., Our Lady of Good Counsel (1884), Rev. Msgr. R. Mark Duchaine.
Res., 513 Mueller St., 51025-9802. Tel: 712-368-4755; Fax: 712-368-2470. [CEM]
Catechesis/Religious Programs—Tel: 712-368-2504.
Students 148.
Mission—Quimby, Cherokee Co., St. John the Baptist, 208 E. Railway, Quimby, 51049. Tel: 712-445-2256.

Hornick, Woodbury Co., St. Philip's (1900). Closed. For inquiries for parish records contact the Chancery.

Hospers, Sioux Co., St. Anthony's (1877), Rev. James Tigges.
Res., 506 Elm, P.O. Box 86, 51238-0086. Tel: 712-752-8784. [CEM]
School—Spalding Elementary, (Grades K-3). Consolidation of Alton, Hospers and Granville. Tel: 712-752-8286.
Lay Teachers 4; Students 80.
Catechesis/Religious Programs—Clustered with St. Mary, Alton, and St. Joseph, Granville.

Humboldt, Humboldt Co., St. Mary's (1878), Rev. Eugene J. Ulses.
Res., 311 Fourth St. N., 50548-1647. Tel: 515-332-2856. [CEM]
School—Tel: 515-332-2134.
Sisters 2; Lay Teachers 12; Students 125.
Catechesis/Religious Programs—Tel: 515-332-2784.
Students 145.

Ida Grove, Ida Co., Sacred Heart (1878), Rev. Gerald M. Fisch.
Res., 800 N. Main, P.O. Box 244, 51445-1297. Tel: 712-364-2718. [CEM]
Catechesis/Religious Programs—Tel: 712-364-3628.
Students 163.

Jefferson, Greene Co., St. Joseph's (1875), Rev. Donald C. Ries.
Res., 503 N. Chestnut St., 50129-1507. Tel: 515-386-2638; Fax: 515-386-3672.
Catechesis/Religious Programs—501 N. Locust, 50129. Tel: 515-386-4010.
Students 265.

Mission—Grand Junction, Greene Co., St. Brigid, Tel: 515-738-2254. [CEM]

Kingsley, Plymouth Co., St. Michael's (1888), Rev. James E. Fangman.
Res., P.O. Box 99, 51028-0099. Tel: 712-378-2722. [CEM]
Catechesis/Religious Programs—Tel: 712-378-2021.
Students 160.

Lake City, Calhoun Co., St. Mary's (1894), Rev. Dennis L. Sefcik; Deacon Don Kunecke.
Res., P.O. Box 131, 51449-0131. Tel: 712-464-3395; Fax: 712-464-7669. [CEM][JC]
Catechesis/Religious Programs—Students 143.

Larchwood, Lyon Co., St. Mary (1898) (German-Dutch), Rev. John A. Vakulskas, Jr.; Deacon Jeffrey F. Gallagher.
Res., P.O. Box 37, 51241-0037. Tel: 712-477-2273; Fax: 712-477-2162. [JC]
Catechesis/Religious Programs—Tel: 712-477-2803; Fax: 712-477-2403.
Students 111.

Laurens, Pocahontas Co., Sacred Heart (1893), Rev. Msgr. Leonard M. Ziegmann.
Res., P.O. Box 171, 50554-0171. Tel: 712-845-4596. [CEM]
Catechesis/Religious Programs—Tel: 712-289-6481.
Students 112.

Ledyard, Kossuth Co., Sacred Heart (1887), Rev. Paul D. Bormann.
Mailing Address: P.O. Box 67, 50556-0067. Tel: 515-646-2525.
Res., 204 S. Summit Ave., P.O. Box 195, Bancroft, 50517. Tel: 515-885-2462; Fax: 515-885-2424. [CEM]
Catechesis/Religious Programs—Twinned with St. John's, Bancroft.

Le Mars, Plymouth Co., St. Joseph's (1875) (German), Rev. Andrew W. Hoffmann; Rev. Msgr. Gerald F. Lyon, (Retired).
Res., 20 Sixth Ave., N.E., 51031-3714. Tel: 712-546-5223; Fax: 712-546-8346. [CEM][JC]
School—Gehlen Catholic School, Plymouth St., S.E., 51031. Tel: 712-546-4181; Fax: 712-546-9384.
Catechesis/Religious Programs—Tel: 712-546-6038.
Students 166.

St. James (1883), Rev. Richard S. Ries; Deacon Donald Kunkel.
Res., 109 Sixth Ave., S.W., 51031-3434. Tel: 712-546-5201; Fax: 712-546-8696. [JC]
School—Gehlen Catholic Elementary, Tel: 712-546-5126.
Lay Teachers 25; Students 357.
High School—Gehlen Catholic High School, Tel: 712-546-4181.
Lay Teachers 30; Students 198.
Catechesis/Religious Programs—20 Sixth Ave., N.E., 51031. Tel: 712-546-6038.
Students 230.

Lidderdale, Carroll Co., Holy Family (1914) (German), Rev. Merlin J. Schrad.
Res., P.O. Box 160, 51452-0160. Tel: 712-822-5522. [CEM]
High School—Kuemper Catholic High School, Tel: 712-742-3596; Fax: 712-792-7080.
School—Christ the King Elementary. Consolidation of Breda, Lidderdale, Maple River and Mt. Carmel. Tel: 712-673-2582.
Catechesis/Religious Programs—Tel: 712-792-0513.
Students 216.
Mission—Glidden, Carroll Co., St. Elizabeth Seton Church.

Livermore, Humboldt Co., Sacred Heart (1881), Rev. Dan Greving.
Res., 403 East St. S., P.O. Box 38, Wesley, 50483-0038. Tel: 515-679-4279. [CEM]
Catechesis/Religious Programs—Tel: 515-379-2508.
Students 77.

Lohrville, Calhoun Co., St. Joseph's (1885) (Irish), Rev. Dennis L. Sefcik.
Res., N. Lloyd St., P.O. Box 131, Lake City, 51449. Tel: 712-464-3395; Fax: 712-464-7669. [CEM]
Catechesis/Religious Programs—Students 59.

Madrid, Boone Co., St. Malachy's (1923), Rev. Marvin J. Boes; Deacon Frank Milani.
Res., 207 Gerald St., 50156-1464. Tel: 515-795-2731; Fax: 515-795-2731. [JC]
Church—405 Gerald St., 50156. Tel: 515-795-2613.
Catechesis/Religious Programs—Students 154.
Mission—Woodward, Dallas Co., St. John of God.

Mallard, Palo Alto Co., St. Mary's (1889), Rev. Bruce A. Lefebvre.
Res., P.O. Box 236, 50562-0236. Tel: 712-425-3359. [CEM]
Catechesis/Religious Programs—Tel: 515-887-3333; Fax: 515-887-3334.
Students 47.

Manilla, Crawford Co., Sacred Heart (1887), Rev. Robert W. Gralapp.
Res., 269 6th St., P.O. Box 339, 51454-0339. Tel: 712-654-9511. [CEM]
Catechesis/Religious Programs—Students 123.

Manning, Carroll Co., Sacred Heart (1916) (German), Rev. James C. McAlpin.
Res., 203 Sue St., 51455-1399. Tel: 712-653-3804. [CEM]
Catechesis/Religious Programs—Tel: 712-653-2933.
Students 260.

Manson, Calhoun Co., St. Thomas (1885), Rev. Jerome A. Degen.
Res., P.O. Box 99, 50563-0099. Tel: 712-469-3743. [CEM 2]
Catechesis/Religious Programs—Tel: 712-469-3334.
Students 124.

Maple River, Carroll Co., St. Francis of Assisi (1907) (German), Rev. Robert Brown.
Res., 19481 140th St., Carroll, 51401-9499. Tel: 712-792-3934; Fax: 712-792-3977. [CEM]
School—Christ the King Elementary. Consolidation of Breda, Lidderdale, Maple River and Mt. Carmel. Tel: 712-792-3977.
Lay Teachers 9.
Catechesis/Religious Programs—Tel: 712-792-9422.
Students 40.

Mapleton, Monona Co., St. Mary's (1894), Rev. Edmund Tiedeman. In res., Rev. Gerald Zensen.
Res., 703 Heisler St., 51034-1222. Tel: 712-827-4467. [CEM][JC]
Catechesis/Religious Programs—Tel: 712-882-1780.
Students 114.
Mission—Oto, Woodbury Co., St. Mary's, 620 State St., Box 67, Oto, 51044-6007.

Marcus, Cherokee Co., Holy Name (1877), Rev. Richard R. Remmes.
Res., 110 N. Elm St., P.O. Box 366, 51035-0366. Tel: 712-376-2628. [CEM]
Catechesis/Religious Programs—Tel: 712-376-2625.
Students 176.

Maryhill, Cherokee Co., Visitation of the B.V.M. (1895), Rev. Eugene E. Sitzmann.
Res., 975-540th St., Cherokee, 51012-7151. Tel: 712-225-2131; Fax: 712-225-2742. [CEM]
Catechesis/Religious Programs—Tel: 712-225-2131.
Students 48.

Merrill, Plymouth Co., Assumption Church (1890), Rev. Robert J. Waters.
Res., 527 Center St., P.O. Box 175, 51038-0175. Tel: 712-938-2236.
Catechesis/Religious Programs—Tel: 712-938-2596. Vicki Hemmelman, D.R.E.
Students 70.
Mission—Merrill, Plymouth Co., St. Joseph at Ellendale. [CEM 2]
Catechesis/Religious Programs—Students 95.

Milford, Dickinson Co., St. Joseph's (1884), Rev. James A. Bruch.
1413 Okoboji Ave., 51351-1232.
Res., 1014 13th St., 51351. Tel: 712-338-2274; Fax: 712-338-2191. [CEM]
Catechesis/Religious Programs—Students 213.

Moorland, Webster Co., Our Lady of Good Counsel (1902), Rev. Timothy J. Boekelman.
Res., P.O. Box 135, 50566-0135. Tel: 515-549-3556. [CEM]
Catechesis/Religious Programs—Students 18.

Mount Carmel, Carroll Co., Our Lady of Mt. Carmel (1869) (German), Rev. Robert Brown.
Res., 19481 140th St., Carroll, 51401-9499. Tel: 712-792-3934; Fax: 712-792-3977. [CEM]
School—Christ the King Elementary. Consolidation of Breda, Lidderdale, Maple River and Mt. Carmel. Tel: 712-792-3977.
Lay Teachers 10; Students 147.
Catechesis/Religious Programs—Tel: 712-792-9244.
Students 46.

Moville, Woodbury Co., Immaculate Conception (1892), Rev. Msgr. Roger J. Augustine, V.G.
Res., 419 Jones St., P.O. Box C, 51039-0802. Tel: 712-873-3745.
Catechesis/Religious Programs—Tel: 712-873-3644.
Students 223.

Neptune, Plymouth, St. Joseph (Hinton) (1884) (German), Rev. Mark J. Stoll.
Res., 28172 Nature Ave., Hinton, 51024-8553. Tel: 712-546-8228; Fax: 712-546-8228. [CEM]
Catechesis/Religious Programs—LeMars Religious Education Program, 20 6th Ave., N.E., LeMars, 51031. Tel: 712-546-6038; Fax: 712-546-8346.
Students 58.

Odebolt, Sac Co., St. Martin's (1877), Rev. Allan Reicks.
Res., P.O. Box 500, 51458-0500. Tel: 712-668-2690. [CEM]
Catechesis/Religious Programs—Students 126.

Ogden, Boone Co., St. John's (1896), Rev. Msgr. James K. Lafferty.
Res., 801 West Division St., 50212-0810. Tel: 515-275-2580; Fax: 515-275-3245. [CEM]
Catechesis/Religious Programs—Tel: 515-275-4095.
Students 89.

Onawa, Monona Co., St. John (1900), Rev. Francis J. Nemmers.
Res., 1009 13th St., 51040-1508. Tel: 712-423-2656.
Catechesis/Religious Programs—Tel: 712-423-3555.
Students 150.
Mission—Blencoe, Monona Co., St. Bernard.

Oyens, Plymouth Co., St. Catherine's (1900), Rev. Randy L. Schon.
Res., P.O. Box 538, 51045-0538. Tel: 712-546-4588. [CEM]
School—St. Catherine-St. Mary's Elementary. (Oyens-Remsen). Tel: 712-786-2764.
Lay Teachers 11; Students 204.
Catechesis/Religious Programs—321 Fulton St., Remsen, 51050. Tel: 712-786-1160.
Students 180.

Pocahontas, Pocahontas Co., Church of the Resurrection (1973), Rev. Merle F. Kollasch.
Res., 21 3rd St., S.W., 50574-0157. Tel: 712-335-3242; Fax: 712-335-3919. [CEM]
School—Pocahontas Catholic Elementary, Tel: 712-335-3603; Fax: 712-335-3603.
Sisters 5; Lay Teachers 7; Students 85.
Catechesis/Religious Programs—Students 85.

Pomeroy, Calhoun Co., St. Mary's (1881), Rev. Jerome A. Degen; Deacon Robert Lenz.
Mailing Address: P.O. Box 99, Manson, 50563-0099.
Res., 1076 8th St., Manson, 50563. Tel: 712-469-3743. [CEM]
Catechesis/Religious Programs—Tel: 712-468-2248.
Students 43.

Remsen, Plymouth Co., St. Mary's (1889), Rev. Thomas J. Hart; Deacon Allan Wieler.
Res., Box #509, 51050. Tel: 712-786-1437; 786-1444. [CEM]
School—St. Catherine-St. Mary's Elementary. (Oyens-Remsen). Tel: 712-786-1160; Fax: 712-786-1167.
Sisters 1; Lay Teachers 17; Students 198.
High School—Tel: 712-786-1433; Fax: 712-786-2499.
Priests 1; Lay Teachers 12; Students 110.
Catechesis/Religious Programs—Tel: 712-786-2376; Fax: 712-786-1167.
Students 198.

Rock Rapids, Lyon Co., Holy Name (1871) (Irish), Rev. J. Charles Yetmar.
Res., 1108 S. Carroll St., 51246-9529. Tel: 712-472-3248. [CEM]
Catechesis/Religious Programs—Students 81.

Rock Valley, Sioux Co., St. Mary's (1895), Rev. Eugene Murray.
Res., 1821 14th St., 51247-0098. Tel: 712-476-2060; Fax: 712-476-9074. [CEM]
Catechesis/Religious Programs—Totals include Sacred Heart and Christ the King, Sioux Center.
Students 133.
Missions—Alvord, Lyon Co., Sacred Heart, 301 Seefield St., Alvord, 51230. Tel: 712-473-2215. [CEM]
Sioux Center, Sioux Co., Christ the King, 501 2nd Ave. S.W., Sioux Center, 51250. Tel: 712-722-3011.

Rockwell City, Calhoun Co., St. Francis of Assisi (1899) (German), Rev. Richard Kielbasa.
Res., 744 Main St., 50579-1399. Tel: 712-297-8263. [CEM]
Catechesis/Religious Programs—Tel: 712-297-7183.
Students 105.

Rolfe, Pocahontas Co., St. Margaret's (1895), Rev. Merle Kollasch.
Res., 21 S.W. 3, Pocahontas, 50574. Tel: 712-335-3242. [CEM]
Catechesis/Religious Programs—Tel: 712-848-3301. Lori Pedersen, D.R.E.
Students 46.

Roselle, Carroll Co., Holy Angels (1874), Rev. Dale E. Reiff.
Res., Box 13, Halbur, 51444-0013. Tel: 712-658-2464. [CEM]
School—Holy Trinity Elementary, Tel: 712-669-3346.
Students 10.

High School—Kuemper Catholic High School, Tel: 712-792-3596.
Students 12.
Catechesis/Religious Programs—Tel: 712-792-0513 (Carroll); 653-2131 (Mennina).
Students 10.

Royal, Clay Co., St. Louis (1923) (French-German), Rev. Timothy J. Fitzgerald.
Res., P.O. Box 49, 51357-0049. Tel: 712-933-2667; Fax: 712-933-2356.
Catechesis/Religious Programs—Tel: 712-933-2356.
Students 90.
Mission—Everly, Clay Co., St. Mary's, P.O. Box 49, 51357. Tel: 712-834-2681.

Ruthven, Palo Alto Co., Sacred Heart (1888), Rev. Benjamin E. Jensen.
Church—P.O. Box 400, 51358-0400. Tel: 712-837-5240. [CEM]
Catechesis/Religious Programs—Students 70.
Mission—Ayrshire, Palo Alto Co., Sacred Heart, P.O. Box 207, Ayrshire, 50515. Tel: 515-426-3260.

Sac City, Sac Co., St. Mary's (1892) (German-Irish), Rev. Lawrence L. McCarty.
Res., P.O. Box 324, 50583-0324. Tel: 712-662-7240; Fax: 712-662-4371. [CEM]
Catechesis/Religious Programs—Students 148.

St. Benedict, Kossuth Co., St. Benedict's (1877), Rev. Daniel M. Greving.
Res., P.O. Box 38, Wesley, 50483. Tel: 515-679-4165. [CEM]
School—Seton Elementary. Consolidation of St. Cecelia, Algona, St. Benedict and St. Joseph, Wesley. Tel: 515-295-3509; Fax: 515-295-7739.
Students 18.
High School—Bishop Garrigan, Tel: 515-295-3521.
Students 12.
Catechesis/Religious Programs—St. Cecelia, 715 E. North St., Algona, 50511.
Students 2.

Salix, Woodbury Co., St. Joseph's (1869), Rev. Donald J. Slaven; Deacon Ronald Forrest.
Res., P.O. Box 270, 51052-0270. Tel: 712-946-5635. [CEM][JC]
Catechesis/Religious Programs—Students 202.

Sanborn, O'Brien Co., St. Cecilia's (1882), Rev. Timothy A. Johnson.
Res., P.O. Box 326, 51248-0326. Tel: 712-729-3423. [CEM]
Catechesis/Religious Programs—Tel: 712-728-2626. Melody Hilbert, D.R.E.
Students 135.
Mission—Hartley, O'Brien Co., St. Joseph's, 260 N. 4th Ave. W., 51346. Tel: 712-728-2626.

Schaller, Sac Co., St. Joseph's (1891), Rev. Thomas J. Topf.
Res., P.O. Box 457, 51053-0457. Tel: 712-275-4238. [CEM]
Catechesis/Religious Programs—Students 52.

Scranton, Greene Co., St. Paul's (1926) (German-Irish), Rev. Steven J. McLoud.
Res., 807 Head St., Chordan, 50050. Tel: 712-652-3448 (Church). [JC]
Catechesis/Religious Programs—Tel: 515-389-3625; Fax: 515-389-3795.
Students 37.

Sheldon, O'Brien Co., St. Patrick's (1873) (Irish), Rev. John McGuirk.
Res., 310 10th St., 51201-1530. Tel: 712-324-3220. [CEM]
School—Tel: 712-324-3181.
Sisters 1; Lay Teachers 11; Students 107.
Catechesis/Religious Programs—Tel: 712-324-4588.
Students 168.

Sibley, Osceola Co., St. Andrew's (1896), Rev. Clair L. Boes.
Res., 716 Eighth St., 51249-0130. Tel: 712-754-3311. [CEM]
Catechesis/Religious Programs—Tel: 712-754-2739.
Students 158.

Sioux Rapids, Buena Vista Co., St. Joseph (1886), Rev. John F. Cain.
Res., 708 Thomas Street, P.O. Box 450, 50585-0450. Tel: 712-283-2765; Fax: 712-283-2332. [CEM]
Catechesis/Religious Programs—Students 90.

Spencer, Clay Co., Sacred Heart (1883), Rev. Roger Linnan.
Res., 1111 4th Ave. W., P.O. Box 817, 51301-0817. Tel: 712-262-3047; Fax: 712-262-4067.
School—Tel: 712-262-6428.
Lay Teachers 13; Students 174.
Catechesis/Religious Programs—Tel: 712-262-4486.
Students 253.

Spirit Lake, Dickinson Co., St. Mary's (1914), Rev. Albert O. Grendler.
Res., P.O. Box 354, 51360-0354. Tel: 712-336-1742; Fax: 712-336-0546. [CEM]
Catechesis/Religious Programs—Students 252.

Storm Lake, Buena Vista Co., St. Mary's (1872), Revs. Robert J. Schimmer; Douglas M. Klein; Eriberto DaCosta.
Res., Third & Seneca Sts., P.O. Box 1106, 50588-1106. Tel: 712-732-3110; Fax: 712-732-8173. [CEM]
Elementary & High School—Tel: 712-732-1856 (Elementary); 732-4166 (High School); Fax: 712-732-4590.
Sisters of the Presentation 2; Lay Teachers 32; Students 319.
Catechesis/Religious Programs—Tel: 712-732-4585.
Students 207.

Struble, Plymouth Co., St. Joseph's (1903), Rev. Terry Roder.
Res., 430 Main St., Lemars, 51031-1015. Tel: 712-562-6401. [CEM 2]
Catechesis/Religious Programs—Tel: 712-546-5223.
Students 43.

Sutherland, O'Brien Co., Sacred Heart (1883), Rev. Gerald L. Zeman.
Res., P.O. Box 70, 51058-0070. Tel: 712-446-3742. [CEM]
Catechesis/Religious Programs—Students 100.
Mission—Primghar, O'Brien Co., St. Anthony of Padua, 375 S. Green St., Primghar, 51245. Tel: 712-757-3735. [CEM]

Templeton, Carroll Co., Sacred Heart (1882), Rev. Dale C. Reiff.
Res., Box 13, Halbur, 51444. Tel: 712-658-2464. [CEM]
School—Holy Trinity Elementary. Consolidation of Halbur, Templeton and Roselle. Tel: 712-669-3341.
Lay Teachers 5; Students 54.
High School—Kuemper Catholic High School, Tel: 712-792-3596.
Students 27.
Catechesis/Religious Programs—Tel: 712-792-0513 (Carroll); 653-2131 (Mannina).
Students 22.

Vail, Crawford Co., St. Ann's (1878), Rev. John M. Thomas.
Res., P.O. Box 158, 51465-0158. Tel: 712-677-5556. [CEM]
School—Holy Cross Elementary, Tel: 712-677-5555.
High School—Interparochial Catholic High School, Tel: 712-792-3596; Fax: 712-792-8070.
Students 14. Sisters of St. Francis of Clinton, Tel: 712-677-2398.
Lay Teachers 2; Students 22.
Catechesis/Religious Programs—Tel: 712-677-2783.
Students 88.

Varina, Pocahontas Co., St. Columbkille's (1882), Rev. Harry D. McAlpine.
Res., Box 306, Fonda, 50540-0306. Tel: 712-288-6480. [CEM]

Wall Lake, Sac Co., St. Joseph's (1878), Rev. Leo L. Riesberg.
Res., P.O. Box 130, 51466-0130. Tel: 712-664-2915.
Catechesis/Religious Programs—Tel: 712-664-2910.
Students 141.

Wesley, Kossuth Co., St. Joseph's (1891), Rev. Daniel M. Greving.
Res., P.O. Box 38, 50483-0038. Tel: 515-679-4279; 679-4135. [CEM]
School—Seton Elementary. Consolidation of St. Cecelia, Algona, St. Benedict, St. Joseph, Wesley, St. Michael's, Whittemore, and St. Joseph, Bode. Tel: 515-295-3509.
Students 62.
High School—Bishop Garrigan High School, Tel: 515-295-3521.
Students 31.
Catechesis/Religious Programs—Students 18.

West Bend, Palo Alto Co., SS. Peter and Paul (1888), Rev. Bruce A. Lefebvre; Deacon Gerald Streit.
Res., P.O. Box 316, 50597-0316. Tel: 515-887-3333; Fax: 515-887-3334. [CEM]
School—Tel: 515-887-4542; Fax: 515-887-3334.
Lay Teachers 8; Students 70.
Catechesis/Religious Programs—Students 102.

Whittemore, Kossuth Co., St. Michael's (1889), Rev. Victor F. Ramaeker; Deacon Joseph Straub.
Res., P.O. Box 337, 50598-0337. Tel: 515-884-2669; Fax: 515-884-2618. [CEM]

Willey, Carroll Co., St. Mary's (1882), Rev. Craig A. Collison.
Res., 201 Olympic Ave., Carroll, 51401-9726. Tel: 712-792-4516; Fax: 712-792-2549. [CEM]
School—Consolidation of Holy Spirit, Dedham, Willey and St. Lawrence Elementary. Tel: 712-792-3610.
Students 48.
High School—Kuemper Catholic High School, Tel: 712-792-3596; Fax: 712-792-8070.
Students 30.
Catechesis/Religious Programs—Tel: 712-792-4386.
Students 2.

Woodward, Boone Co., St. John of God (1965). (State Hospital and School). Rev. Marvin J. Boes; Deacon Frank Milani.
Res., 207 Gerald St., Madrid, 50156-1464. Tel: 515-795-2731; Fax: 515-795-2731.

Chaplains of Public Institutions

SIOUX CITY. *Mercy Medical Center*. Rev. Richard A. Sitzmann.

CARROLL. *St. Anthony Regional Hospital*. Rev. Thomas J. Munn.

CHEROKEE. *State Mental Health Institute*. Rev. Eugene E. Sitzmann.

FORT DODGE. *Trinity Regional Hospital*. Revs. P. Joseph Nooney; Eugene F. Walding.

ROCKWELL CITY. *Calhoun County State Reformatory, Minimum Security for Men*. Rev. Richard A. Keilbasa.

WOODWARD. *Woodward State Hospital and School*. Rev. Marvin Boes Madrid.

Special Assignment:
Reverend Fathers—
Guredet, Randy J., Co-Dir., Minorities & Human Development, 1011 Douglas St., Sioux City, IA 51105-1399
Hartz, Gerald A., Chap., Holy Spirit Retirement Home, 1701 W. 25th St., Sioux City, IA 51103-1799. Tel: 712-255-6022
Larkin, Michael T., Sioux City Nursing Homes, 1122 Grandview Blvd., Apt. 7, Sioux City, IA 51103-4398. Tel: 712-258-5202
Meinen, Dennis W., Ministry to People with Disabilities, 1122 Grandview Blvd., Apt. 1, Sioux City, IA 51103-1472. Tel: 712-258-9120

On Duty Outside the Diocese:
Reverend Monsignors—
McCoy, Kevin C., North American College, 00120 Vatican City State, Europe
Schnurr, Dennis M., Gen. Sec., National Conference of Catholic Bishops, St. John's Hall, 4001 14th St., N.E., Washington, DC 20017
Reverend Fathers—
Barrett, Miles J., USS Kitty Hawk (CV-63), Chaplain's Office, FPO AP, 96634-2770
Dale, George
Dandurand, Douglas E., Archdiocese of St. Paul and Minneapolis, MN
Farrell, Emmett L., 2020 Alaquinas Dr., San Ysidro, CA 92173
Flanagan, Thomas J., Pfarrer-Bendel-Weg 2, D-61462 Koenigstein-Mammolshain, Germany. Tel: 011-496-1734-169
Friedrichsen, Timothy A., 10690 Weymouth St.#102, Bethesda, MD 20814-4245
Higgins, Francis E., CMR 149, Box 294, APO AE, 09102
Kurzak, John, USAF, P.O. Box 16152, Beverly Hills, CA 90209-2152

Absent on Leave:
Reverend Fathers—
Adam, Richard A.

Retired:
Reverend Monsignors—
Behrens, A.W., P.O. Box 94, Marcus, IA 51035-0094. Tel: 712-376-4788
Brady, Frank J., 1703 W. 25th St., Apt. B208, Sioux City, IA 51103-1799. Tel: 712-255-9343
Hood, Mervin J., 458 N. 26th Pl. Portside, Apt. 9, Fort Dodge, IA. Tel: 515-576-3268
Lilly, E. C., 1701 W. 25th St., Bldg. B, Apt. 205, Sioux City, IA 51103-1799. Tel: 712-255-5423
Lyon, Gerald F., 20-6th Ave., N.E., LeMars, IA 51031. Tel: 712-546-3714
Quinn, Robert J., P.O. Box 1346, Imperial Beach, CA 91933-1346. Tel: 619-437-0180
Ruba, Nicholas J., 403 Cleveland Ct., Remsen, IA 51050. Tel: 712-786-2719
Reverend Fathers—
Adams, Edmond F., Sacred Heart Church, 1321 2nd Ave. S., Fort Dodge, IA 50501-4925. Tel: 515-573-7617
Alvey, J. Paul, 7791 E. Via Del Futuro, Scottsdale, AZ 85258
Beacom, Vincent L., R.R. 3, Arnolds Park, IA 51331-9803
Becker, Nicholas J., January thru March: 10360 N. 76th Dr., Peoria, AZ, P.O. Box 633, Algona, IA 50511-0633
Brennan, C. John, 1703 W. 25th, Apt. 204, Sioux City, IA 51103-1799. Tel: 712-277-8981

Bruch, Walter L., 110 Peeble Ln., Apt. 16, Carroll, IA 51401. Tel: 712-792-6251
Cain, John F., St. Joseph Church, P.O. Box 450, Sioux Rapids, 50585-0450. Tel: 712-283-2765
Calkins, Raymond J., 326 Green Chase Cir., Montgomery, AL 36117. Tel: 334-215-1813
Carpenter, Edward V., 1122 Grandview Blvd., Apt. #5, Sioux City, IA 51105-4398. Tel: 712-252-2338
Ceperley, Eugene F., Marian Village, Apt. 102, 2320 6th Ave. N., Fort Dodge, IA 50501
Condon, Robert M., 2300 Indian Hills Dr., Apt. 2-201, Sioux City, IA 51104
Cooper, Harold V., 2507-33rd. St., Sioux City, IA 51105. Tel: 712-239-2880
Devine, William B., 1703 W. 25th St., Apt. 212, Sioux City, IA 51103. Tel: 712-234-0857
Fangman, Robert M., 422 E. 7th St., Apt. 23, Carroll, IA 51401
Fransco, Peter J., 1803 Bruce St., Ruthven, IA 51358. Tel: 712-837-4323
Friedman, Cecil H., 1021 E. Call St., Algona, IA 50511
Greving, Louis H., Grotto of the Redemption, P.O. Box 376, West Bend, IA 50597-0376. Tel: 515-887-2371
Holland, Thomas D., 4050 Pacific Harbors Dr., #244, Las Vegas, NV 89121
Kollasch, Louis, Marian Village, Apt. 113, 2320 6th Ave. N., Fort Dodge, IA 50501. Tel: 515-573-8500
Koster, Dale F., P.O. Box 264 W. 1st St., Apt. 8, Auburn, IA 51433
Leiting, Robert L., 604 S. Sivision St., Apt. A4, Arcadia, IA. Tel: 712-689-2616
Lisowski, Jan, 1122 Grandview Blvd., Apt. 3, Sioux City, IA 51103-4398. Tel: 716-549-0372
Lynch, Daniel C., 407 S. 13th St., Sac City, IA 50583. Tel: 712-662-4801
Macke, Richard J., 100 Circle Dr., Lake City, IA 51449
McFadden, George B., 1122 Grandview Blvd., Apt. 2, Sioux City, IA 51105-4398. Tel: 712-255-0827
Montag, Bernard J., P.O. Box 73, West Bend, IA 50597-0073. Tel: 515-887-6874
Munn, Thomas J., 421 S. Clark St., Carroll, IA 51401. Tel: 712-792-5546
Nooney, Patrick J., Trinity Regional Hospital, S. Kenyond Rd., Fort Dodge, IA 50501-5795
O'Rourke, Gabriel A., Holy Spirit Retirement Home, 1701 W. 25th St., Sioux City, IA 51103-1798
Reinhart, Ralph W., 312 Elm St., Apt. 2, Manning, IA 51455
Schumacher, Eugene T., 303 S. Portland St., Bancroft, IA. Tel: 515-885-2231
Smith, Donald R., 3929 Winona Way, Apt. 4, Sioux City, IA 51104-4447. Tel: 712-239-5865
Thiele, Robert A., 101 N. Earl, Lake City, IA 51449
Thom, Elmer D., 1122 Grandview Blvd., Apt. 9, Sioux City, IA 51103-4398. Tel: 712-277-3954
Waite, Patrick J., 5682 Tulane St., San Diego, CA 92122-3244
White, Lloyd W., 130 Peeble Ln., Apt. 6, Carroll, IA 51401-3020. Tel: 712-792-5633
Wieling, Raymond P., 3015 Chicago Ave., Sioux City, IA 51106-1259. Tel: 712-276-7065
Wingert, D. William, 4014 Yellow Ave., Hartley, IA 51346-7606
Wingert, Gerald R., 216 W. Nebraska, Algona, IA 50511-2608. Tel: 515-295-3123
Young, Edward J., 1122 Grandview Blvd., Apt. 1, Sioux City, IA 51103-4398. Tel: 712-277-4638
Zensen, Gerald F., P.O. Box 67, Oto, IA 51044-0067

Permanent Deacons:
Berger, William J., St. Michael's, Sioux City
Bertrand, Gerald L., Holy Name, Marcus
Bruner, Robert S., St. Lawrence, Carroll
Doocy, Philip F., St. John the Baptist, Bancroft
Easter, Jack L., Sacred Heart, Spencer
Forrest, Ronald M., Associate Dir., Permanent Diaconate, Sioux City
Gallagher, Jeffrey F., Holy Name,Larchwood
Hand, Michael J., Church of the Nativity, Sioux City
Hart, M. Peter, St. Joseph, Milford
Heffernan, John J., Blessed Sacrament Church, Sioux City
Hogan, Joseph R., Our Lady of Good Counsel Church, Fonda
Karpuk, Fred P., Blessed Sacrament Church, Sioux City
Kunecke, Donald L., St. Mary's Church, Lake City
Kunkel, Donald M., St. Joseph Church, LeMars
Larson, Robert, Algona
Lenz, Robert D., St. Mary's Church, Pomeroy
Lester, Jary, Sioux City
MacDonald, W. B., St. Cecelia Church, Algona
Maher, F. Joseph, St. Mary's Church, Hawarden
Milani, Frank J., St. Malachy's Church, Madrid
Morgan, Tom, St. John's, Onawa
Murphy, Tim, Carroll
Pietz, Ronald C., St. Joseph Church, Sioux City
Portz, Ray, St. Patrick, Sheldon
Reicks, Jerome A., St. Joseph Church, Sioux City
Reuter, Anthony C., Holy Spirit Church, Carroll
Rupp, J. LeRoy, Immaculate Conception Church, Cherokee
Sands, James H., Sioux City
Sitzman, Larry K., St. Michael's Church, Sioux City
Spellman, George G., Ph.D., Mercy Medical Center & Blessed Sacrament Church, Sioux City
Straub, Joseph J., St. Michael's Church, Whittmore
Streit, Gerald B., Sts. Peter & Paul Church, West Bend
Sullivan, Eldon, Our Lady of Good Counsel, Fonda
Weiler, Allan A., St. Mary's Church, Remsen
Westendorf, Louis B., M.D., St. Lawrence Church, Carroll
Wiskus, Robert A., Sacred Heart Church, Sioux City

INSTITUTIONS LOCATED IN THE DIOCESE

[A] COLLEGES AND UNIVERSITIES

SIOUX CITY. *Briar Cliff College*, 3303 Rebecca St., P.O. Box 2100, 51104-2100. Tel: 712-279-5405; Fax: 712-279-5410.
E-mail: wielandt@briarcliff.edu
Web site: www.briarcliff.edu
For a complete listing, refer to the Colleges and Universities section.

[B] INTER-PAROCHIAL SCHOOLS

SIOUX CITY. *Blessed Sacrament*, 3030 Jackson St., 51104. Tel: 712-277-4739; Fax: 712-258-3698. Priests 1; Lay Teachers 26; Students 405.
Catholic Schools of Sioux City, 1021 Douglas, 51105. Tel: 712-252-0573; Fax: 712-252-4897.
E-mail: heelan.pvt.k12.ia.us
Web site: www.siouxlan.com/heelan
Serving the parishes of the Siouxland area. Dr. James Rouse, Supt.; Richard A. Bancke, Prin.; Revs. Paul A. Deyo; Verne P. Stapenhorst; Alfred E. McCoy. Priests 3; Sisters 1; Lay Teachers 46; Students 664.
Catholic Schools of Sioux City, 1018 Grandview Blvd., 51102. Tel: 712-252-1350; Fax: 712-252-9086. James Rouse, Supt.
Holy Family Epiphany Center. (Grades 6-8), 1000 Douglas St., 51105. Tel: 712-252-3181; Fax: 712-252-3181. Sisters 1; Lay Teachers 8; Students 97.
Holy Family St. Boniface Center. (Grades K-2), 700 W. Sixth St., 51103. Tel: 712-258-9464. Lay Teachers 8; Students 119.
Holy Family St. Joseph Center. (Grades 3-5). Consolidated with Cathedral of the Epiphany and St. Boniface. 709 Iowa St., 51105. Tel: 712-258-7101; Fax: 712-258-7101. Lay Teachers 5; Students 86.
Mater Dei School Immaculate Conception Center, 3719 Ridge Ave., 51106. Tel: 712-276-6216; Fax: 712-274-1221. Priests 2; Lay Teachers 23; Students 236.
Mater Dei School Nativity Center. (Grades 6-8). Consolidated with Immaculate Conception Parish. 4242 Natalia Way, 51106-4099. Tel: 712-276-3022; Fax: 712-274-2703.
Sacred Heart, 5010 Military Rd., 51103. Tel: 712-233-1624; Fax: 712-233-1469. Sisters 2; Lay Teachers 17; Students 249.
St. Michael, 4106 Van Buren St., 51104. Tel: 712-239-1090; Fax: 712-239-8546. Sisters of the Blessed Virgin Mary 2; Lay Teachers 11; Students 218.

ALGONA. *Bishop Garrigan Catholic High School*, 1224 N. McCoy St., 50511. Tel: 515-295-3521; Fax: 515-295-7739.
Serving the parishes at Algona, St. Benedict, Bode, Wesley, and Whittemore. Mr. Eugene Meister, Pres. Priests 1; Sisters 1; Deacons 1; Lay Teachers 25; Students 250.

CARROLL. *Keumper Catholic Grade School*, 201 S. Clark St., 51401. Tel: 712-792-2123. Mary Dobson, Prin.
St. Lawrence Center, 1519 N. West St., 51401. Tel: 712-792-2123; Fax: 712-792-2123.
Holy Spirit Center, 201 S. Clark St., 51401. Tel: 712-792-2123.
Kuemper Catholic High School, 109 S. Clark St., 51401. Tel: 712-792-3596; Fax: 712-792-8070.
E-mail: cmconradt@kuemper.pvt.K12.ia.us
Web site: www.kuemper.pvt.K12.ia.us
Serving the thirteen parishes of Carroll-Holy Spirit and St. Lawrence Parishes; Arcadia; Dedham; Halbur; Lidderdale-Glidden; Maple River; Mount Carmel; Roselle; Templeton; Vail; Willey and Breda. Rev. Merlin J. Schrad, Pres.; Candace Conradt, Prin.; Rev. Craig A. Collison. Priests 3; Lay Teachers 41; Students 477.

FORT DODGE. *Fort Dodge Catholic Grade School Holy Rosary*, 2406 9 1/2 Ave., S., 50501. Tel: 515-576-0574; Fax: 515-576-2243. Lay Teachers 8; Students 108.
Fort Dodge Catholic Schools, Inc., 501 N. 22nd St., 50501. Tel: 515-955-5850; Fax: 515-955-3569. Rev. Patrick R. Walsh, Pres.; Mr. Chuck Elbert, Prin.; Mr. Thomas Mikio, Dir. Devel.; Sr. Dominic Church, P.B.V.M.; Rev. Michael Erpelding, Spiritual Life Dir. Priests 2; Sisters 1; Lay Teachers 27; Students 393.

GRANVILLE. *Spalding Catholic High School*, 51022. Tel: 712-727-3451; Fax: 712-727-3455.
E-mail: rkozak@mtcnet.net
Web site: spalding-catholic.pvt.k12.ia.us
Serving the parishes of Granville; Alton and Hospers. Rev. Msgr. Kenneth A. Seifried, Pres.; Rev. Tim Johnson, Religion Teacher. Priests 3; Lay Teachers 7; Students 90.

LE MARS. *Gehlen Catholic School*, 709 Plymouth St. N.E., 51031. Tel: 712-546-4181; Fax: 712-546-9384.
E-mail: gehlen@pionet.net
Web site: www.pionet.net/~gehlen
Serving St. James & St. Joseph, LeMars; Assumption, Merrill; St. Joseph's, Ellendale; St. Joseph's, Neptune; St. Joseph's, Struble. Rev. Andrew Hoffman, Pres.; Thomas Jastram, Prin. (Gr. 7-12); Lorie A. Nussbaum, Prin. (Gr. K-6). Priests 1; Sisters 1; Lay Teachers 45; Students 605.

REMSEN. *St. Mary's High School*, 523 Madison, 51050. Tel: 712-786-1433; Fax: 712-786-2499.
E-mail: stmarys@nwidt.com
Ken Hajek, Prin. Priests 1; Lay Teachers 13; Students 109.

STORM LAKE. *St. Mary's High School*, 50588. Tel: 712-732-4166; Fax: 712-732-4590.
E-mail: gadrus@main.stmarys-storm.pvt.k12.ia.us
Serving St. Mary's. Sisters 1; Lay Teachers 17; Students 97.

[C] GENERAL HOSPITALS

SIOUX CITY. *Mercy Medical Center - Sioux City*, 801 Fifth St., 51101. Tel: 712-279-2010; Fax: 712-279-2034.
E-mail: brehanyj@trinity-health.org
Web site: www.mercy-siouxcity.com
For a complete listing, refer to the Hospitals section.

CARROLL. *St. Anthony Regional Hospital*, 51401. Tel: 712-792-3581; Fax: 712-792-2124.
E-mail: stanthony@netins.net
Web site: stanthonyhospital.org
For a complete listing, refer to the Hospitals section.

ESTHERVILLE. *Holy Family Hospital*, 826 N. Eighth St., 51334. Tel: 712-362-2631; Fax: 712-362-2636.
E-mail: info@avera-holyfamily.org
For a complete listing, refer to the Hospitals section.

[D] HOMES FOR THE AGED

SIOUX CITY. *Holy Spirit Retirement Home*, 1701 W. 25th St., 51103. Tel: 712-252-2726
For a complete listing, refer to the Special Care Facilities section.

CARROLL. *St. Anthony Nursing Home*, 406 E. Anthony St., 51401. Tel: 712-792-3581; Fax: 712-792-8288.
E-mail: stanthony@netins.net
Web site: www.netins.net/showcase/sarh/
For a complete listing, refer to the Special Care Facilities section.

FORT DODGE. *The Marian Home*, 2400 Sixth Ave. N., 50501. Tel: 515-576-1138; Fax: 515-576-5009
For a complete listing, refer to the Special Care Facilities section.

[E] CONVENTS AND RESIDENCES FOR SISTERS

SIOUX CITY. *Monastery of the Discalced Carmelite Nuns*, 2901 S. Cecelia St., 51106-3299. Tel: 712-276-1680; Fax: 712-276-5966.
E-mail: SrTherese@aol.com
Web site: members.aol.com/srtherese/
Mother Therese of the Spirit of Love, O.C.D., Prioress. Solemn Professed 9; Temporary Professed 2.

[F] SECULAR INSTITUTES

POCAHONTAS. *Opus Spiritus Sancti*, 21 S.W. 3rd St., 50574. Tel: 712-335-3242. Rev. Merle F. Kollasch, Regl. Coord. Community Activities & Member Secular Institute of Priests.

[G] MISCELLANEOUS

SIOUX CITY. *Cathedral Arts Guild*, 1018 Grandview Blvd., 51104. Tel: 712-255-1637.
The Catholic Schools Foundation of the Diocese of Sioux City, 1821 Jackson St., 51105. Tel: 712-255-7933; Fax: 712-233-7598.
E-mail: srjoan@scdiocese.org
Web site: www.scdiocese.org

Holy Spirit Retirement Home Foundation, Inc., 1701 W. 25th St., 51103. Tel: 712-252-2726. Daniel DiNardo, Pres. Directors: Roger J. Augustine; Patrick J. Tomscha.

CARROLL. *Carroll Area Catholic Schools Foundation, Inc.*, 1st St. & Clark St., 50511. Tel: 712-792-3596. Rev. Merlin J. Schrad, Pres.

Orchard View, Inc., S. Clark St., 51401. Tel: 712-792-2042; Fax: 712-792-2124.
E-mail: stantony@netins.net
Web site: stanthonyhospital.org
Franciscan Sisters of Perpetual Adoration. Gary P. Riedmann, Admin. Total in Residence 45.

St. Anthony Foundation, S. Clark St., 51401. Tel: 712-792-3581; Fax: 712-792-2124.
E-mail: stantony@netins.net
Web site: stanthonyhospital.org
Mr. Gary P. Reidmann.

FORT DODGE. *Fort Dodge Catholic Grade System Foundation*, 2220 4th Ave., N., 50501. Tel: 515-955-5850. Rev. Patrick Walsh, Pres.

Fort Dodge Catholic Schools Foundation, 2220 4th Ave., N., 50501. Tel: 515-955-5850. Rev. Patrick Walsh, Pres.

St. Edmund High School Foundation, 2220 4th Ave., N., 50501. Tel: 515-955-5850. Rev. Patrick Walsh, Pres.

WEST BEND. *Grotto of the Redemption.*
E-mail: grotto@ncn.net
Web site: www.nw-cybermall.com/grotto.htm
Mailing Address: P.O. Box 376, 50597. Tel: 515-887-2371; Fax: 515-887-2372. Deacon Gerald Streit, Dir.

RELIGIOUS INSTITUTES OF WOMEN REPRESENTED IN THE DIOCESE

For further details refer to the corresponding bracketed number in the Religious Institutes of Women section.

[0230]—*Benedictine Sisters of the Pontifical Jurisdiction.*—O.S.B.
[1780]—*Congregation of the Sisters of the Third Order of St. Francis of Perpetual Adoration.* (Central Prov.).—F.S.P.A.
[0420]—*Discalced Carmelite Nuns.*—O.C.D.
[]—*Opus Spiritus Sancti.*—O.S.S.
[2970]—*School Sisters of Notre Dame.* (Mankato Province).—S.S.N.D.
[2970]—*School Sisters of Notre Dame.* (Milwaukee Province).—S.S.N.D.
[2970]—*School Sisters of Notre Dame.* (St. Louis Province).—S.S.N.D.
[3580]—*Servants of Mary.* (American Province).—O.S.M.
[]—*Sisters For Christian Community.*—S.F.C.C.
[0430]—*Sisters of Charity of the Blessed Virgin Mary.*—B.V.M.
[2575]—*Sisters of Mercy of the Americas.* (Cedar Rapids Regional Community).—R.S.M.
[]—Sisters of St. Benedict. (Taegu, Korea).—O.S.B.
[1540]—*Sisters of St. Francis, Clinton, Iowa.*—O.S.F.
[1570]—*Sisters of St. Francis of the Holy Family.*—O.S.F.
[2350]—*Sisters of the Living Word.*—S.L.W.
[3270]—*Sisters of the Most Precious Blood (O'Fallon, MO).*—C.PP.S.
[3320]—*Sisters of the Presentation of the B.V.M.*—P.B.V.M.
[1720]—*Sisters of the Third Order Regular of St. Francis of the Congregation of Our Lady of Lourdes.*—O.S.F.

DIOCESAN CEMETERIES

SIOUX CITY. *Calvary*, Office, 1821 Jackson St., P.O. Box 3379, 51102-3379. Tel: 712-233-7511.

NECROLOGY

(No Deaths)

Diocese of Sioux Falls

(Dioecesis Siouxormensis)

Most Reverend

ROBERT J. CARLSON

Bishop of Sioux Falls; ordained May 22, 1970; appointed Titular Bishop of Aviocala and Auxiliary Bishop of Saint Paul and Minneapolis November 22, 1983; consecrated January 11, 1984; appointed Coadjutor Bishop of Sioux Falls, 1994; succeeded to the See, March 21, 1995.

Most Reverend

PAUL V. DUDLEY, D.D.

Retired Bishop of Sioux Falls; ordained June 2, 1951; appointed Titular Bishop of Ursona and Auxiliary Bishop of St. Paul and Minneapolis November 16, 1976; Episcopal ordination January 25, 1977; appointed Bishop of Sioux Falls September 26, 1978; installed December 13, 1978; retired March 21, 1995. *Res., 2500 W. 320th St., Northfield, MN, 55057.* Tel.: 507-663-1145; Fax: 507-645-0558.

"Jesus is Lord"

ESTABLISHED NOVEMBER 12, 1889.

Square Miles 35,091.

Comprises that part of the State of South Dakota East of the Missouri River.

For legal titles of parishes and diocesan institutions, consult the Chancery Office.

Chancery Office: 523 N. Duluth Ave., Sioux Falls, SD, 57104. Tel.: 605-334-9861; Fax: 605-334-2092.

Web site address: SFCatholic.org

E-mail address: jklein@SFCatholic.org

STATISTICAL OVERVIEW

Personnel	
Bishop	1
Retired Bishops	1
Abbots	1
Retired Abbots	2
Priests: Diocesan Active in Diocese	81
Priests: Active Outside Diocese	3
Priests: Retired, Sick or Absent	42
Number of Diocesan Priests	126
Religious Priests in Diocese	38
Extern Priests in Diocese	12
Ordinations:	
Diocesan Priests	1
Transitional Deacons	8
Permanent Deacons	3
Permanent Deacons in Diocese	25
Total Brothers	12
Total Sisters	404
Parishes	
Parishes	151
With Resident Pastor:	
Resident Diocesan Priests	62
Resident Religious Priests	13
Without Resident Pastor:	
Administered by Priests	64
Administered by Deacons	4
Administered by Professed Men Religious	2
Administered by Women Religious	1
Administered by Pastoral Teams, etc.	3
Completely Vacant	2
Professional Ministry Personnel:	
Brothers	1
Sisters	33
Lay Ministers	47
Welfare	
Catholic Hospitals	9
Total Assisted	485,000
Homes for the Aged	9
Total Assisted	1,500
Specialized Homes	2
Total Assisted	145
Special Centers for Social Services	5
Total Assisted	112,000
Residential Care of Disabled	1
Total Assisted	15
Educational	
Diocesan Students in Other Seminaries	33
Total Seminarians	33
Colleges and Universities	2
Total Students	1,912
High Schools, Diocesan and Parish	3
Total Students	1,043
Elementary Schools, Diocesan and Parish	22
Total Students	4,640
Catechesis/Religious Education:	
High School Students	6,426
Elementary Students	9,828
Total Students Under Catholic Instruction	23,882
Teachers in the Diocese:	
Priests	2
Brothers	1
Sisters	9
Lay Teachers	324
Vital Statistics	
Receptions into the Church:	
Infant Baptism Totals	1,845
Adult Baptism Totals	95
Received into Full Communion	284
First Communions	1,951
Confirmations	1,848
Marriages:	
Catholic	376
Interfaith	348
Total Marriages	724
Deaths	1,042
Total Catholic Population	125,120
Total Population	503,000

Former Bishops—Rt. Rev. MARTIN MARTY, O.S.B., D.D., appt. Bishop of Tiberias, Aug. 8, 1879; appt. Vicar Apostolic of Dakota, Aug. 12, 1879; cons. Feb. 1, 1880; Bishop of Sioux Falls, 1889; transferred to St. Cloud, MN, 1894; died Sept. 19, 1896.—Rt. Rev. THOMAS O'GORMAN, D.D., appt. Jan. 24, 1896; cons. April 19, 1896; died Sept. 18, 1921.—Most Rev. BERNARD J. MAHONEY, D.D., appt. May 22, 1922; cons. June 29, 1922; died March 20, 1939.—Most Rev. WILLIAM O. BRADY, S.T.D., D.D., appt. Bishop of Sioux Falls, June 10, 1939; cons. Aug. 24, 1939; appt. Coadjutor of St. Paul, June 21, 1956; succeeded to the See, Oct. 11, 1956; died Oct. 1, 1961.—Most Rev. LAMBERT A. HOCH, D.D., Former Bishop of Sioux Falls; ord. May 30, 1928; Bishop of Bismarck; appt. Jan. 23, 1952; cons. March 25, 1952; transferred to Sioux Falls, Nov. 27, 1956; retired June 13, 1978; died June 27, 1990.—Most Rev. PAUL V. DUDLEY, D.D., Bishop of Sioux Falls; ord. June 2, 1951; appt. Sept. 26, 1978; installed Dec. 13, 1978; retired March 21, 1995.

Vicar General—Rev. Msgr. MARVIN MCPHEE, V.G., *523 N. Duluth Ave., Sioux Falls, 57104.*

Episcopal Vicar for Clergy—Rev Msgr. MARVIN MCPHEE.

Chancery Office—523 N. Duluth Ave., Sioux Falls, 57104. Tel: 605-334-9861; Fax: 605-334-2092. Refer all official business to this address.

Chancellor—Mr. JEROME KLEIN, *523 N. Duluth Ave., Sioux Falls, 57104.* Tel: 605-988-3745.

Vice Chancellor—Mr. JAY CONZEMIUS, J.C.L., *523 N. Duluth Ave., Sioux Falls, 57104.*

Diocesan Theologian—Dr. STEPHEN A. HIPP, S.T.D., *523 N. Duluth Ave., Sioux Falls, 57104.*

Diocesan Tribunal—523 N. Duluth Ave., Sioux Falls, 57104. Tel: 605-988-3757. (Address all marriage papers and rogatory commissions to this address).

Tribunal Judges—Revs. AL KRZYZOPOLSKI; RODNEY FARKE; DONALD IMMING; THOMAS RYAN, Presiding Judge; GARY TERNES, J.C.L.; JORDAN HITE, T.O.R., J.C.D.; SCOTT TRAYNOR; Mr. JAY CONZEMIUS, J.C.L.

Defender of the Matrimonial Bond—Rev. GREGORY TSCHAKERT, J.C.L.

Promoter of Justice—Rev. GREGORY TSCHAKERT, J.C.L.

Defender of the Bond-Appellate Tribunal—Sr. LYNN MARIE WELBIG, P.B.V.M., J.C.L.

Judicial Vicar—Rev. Msgr. DONALD KETTLER, J.C.L.

Executive Coordinator of Matrimonial Tribunal—Ms. VICKIE BEACH, Ecclesiastical Notary.

Diocesan Consultors—Rev. Msgr. MARVIN MCPHEE, V.G.; Rev. Msgr. STEVEN BARNETT; Revs. ROBERT KRANTZ; LARRY REGYNSKI; RODNEY FARKE; GARI RUTHENBERG, O.M.I.; DANIEL MANNING; AL KRZYZOPOLSKI; THOMAS HECK.

Consilium Administrationis—Most Rev. Bishop, Vicar General, Chancellor.

Deans—Rev. Msgr. STEVEN BARNETT; Revs. LARRY REGYNSKI; RODNEY FARKE; GARI RUTHENBERG, O.M.I.; THOMAS HECK; DANIEL MANNING; ROBERT KRANTZ; AL KRZYZOPOLSKI.

Presbyteral Council—Most Rev. ROBERT J. CARLSON; Rev. Msgr. MARVIN MCPHEE, V.G.; Rev. Msgr. STEVEN BARNETT; Revs. LARRY REGYNSKI; RODNEY FARKE; GARI RUTHENBERG, O.M.I.; THOMAS HILLENBRAND, O.S.B.; DANIEL MANNING; ROBERT KRANTZ; AL KRZYZOPOLSKI; DAVID STEVENS.

Diocesan Offices and Directors

Apostleship of Prayer—523 N. Duluth Ave., Sioux Falls, 57105.

Bishop's Bulletin—Rev. MICHAEL GRIFFIN, Exec. Editor; Mr. GENE YOUNG, Mgr. Editor, *523 N. Duluth Ave., Sioux Falls, 57104.* Tel: 605-988-3789.

Building Commission—JEROME KLEIN, Chancellor, *Catholic Chancery Office, 523 N. Duluth Ave., Sioux Falls, 57104.*

Catholic Charities—523 N. Duluth Ave., Sioux Falls, 57104.

Catholic Foundation for Eastern South Dakota—MARK CONZEMIUS, Exec. Dir. ELIZABETH THEOBALD, Dir., Planned Giving, *523 N. Duluth Ave., Sioux Falls, 57104.* Tel: 605-988-3788.

Catholic Relief Services—JEROME KLEIN, Chancellor, *523 N. Duluth Ave., Sioux Falls, 57104.*

Catholic Family Services—Sr. MARY CAROLE CURRAN, O.S.B., Exec. Dir., *523 N. Duluth Ave., Sioux Falls, 57104.* Tel: 605-988-3775.

Catholic Family Sharing Appeal—Mr. KEVIN MILES, Dir., *523 N. Duluth Ave., Sioux Falls, 57104.* Tel: 605-988-3788.

Censor Librorum—Dr. STEPHEN HIPP, S.T.D., *523 N. Duluth Ave., Sioux Falls, 57104.*

Communications Office—DARYL THURINGER, *523 N. Duluth Ave., Sioux Falls, 57104.* Tel: 605-988-3789.

Cursillo—Rev. RODNEY FARKE, *P.O. Box 689, Yankton, 57078.* Tel: 605-664-6214.

Development Office—MARK CONZEMIUS, Dir., *523 N. Duluth Ave., Sioux Falls, 57104.* Tel: 605-988-3788.

Diocesan Archivist—JEROME KLEIN, Chancellor, *523 N. Duluth Ave., Sioux Falls, 57104.* Tel: 605-334-9861.

Diocesan Office of Education—Sr. NATHALIE MEYER, O.P., Ph.D., Supt. of Schools; KEITH BORCHERS, Dir. Religious Educ., *523 N. Duluth Ave., Sioux Falls, 57104.* Tel: 605-988-3766.

Ecumenical Commission—Rev. Msgr. JAMES ANDRASCHKO, *3601 E. Dudley Ln., Sioux Falls, 57103.* Tel: 605-371-2320.

Family Life Ministry—JEAN LORANG, *523 N. Duluth Ave., Sioux Falls, 57104.* Tel: 605-988-3767.

Finance Officer—MICHAEL BANNWARTH, *523 N. Duluth Ave., Sioux Falls, 57104.* Tel: 605-988-3759; Fax: 605-988-3746.

Good Shepherd Center—Sr. GABRIELLA CROWLEY, P.B.V.M., *300 N. Main Ave., Sioux Falls, 57102.* Tel: 605-335-3321.

Worldwide Marriage Encounter—Rev. JAMES M. JOYCE, *900 E. 14th St., Apt. 112, Sioux Falls, 57104.* Tel: 605-978-1592.

Newman Apostolate—Rev. MICHAEL GRIFFIN, Coord., *P.O. Box 7019, Brookings, 57007.* Tel: 605-692-9461.

Office of Worship—Vacant, *523 N. Duluth Ave., Sioux Falls, 57104.* Tel: 605-988-3751.

Permanent Diaconate Formation—Dr. STEPHEN HIPP, S.T.D., *523 N. Duluth Ave., Sioux Falls, 57104.* Tel: 605-334-9861.

Permanent Diaconate Council—Deacon JAMES WALDEN, *4301 Vista Ln., Sioux Falls, 57105.* Tel: 605-336-1381.

Personnel Board—Most Rev. ROBERT J. CARLSON, Chm.

Propagation of the Faith—Rev. JEROME RANEK, Dir., *St. Joseph Parish, 514 2nd Ave. W., Mobridge, 57601.*

Respect Life Office—KENYON GLEASON, Dir., *523 N. Duluth Ave., Sioux Falls, 57104.* Tel: 605-988-3755.

Search—523 N. Duluth Ave., Sioux Falls, 57104. Tel: 605-334-9861.

Spanish-Speaking Apostolate—Rev. JOHN RADER, *1220 E. 8th St., Sioux Falls, 57103.* Tel: 605-338-8126.

Special Events and Planning—NANCY WERNER, Dir., *523 N. Duluth Ave., Sioux Falls, 57104.* Tel: 605-988-3798.

Teens Encounter Christ—523 N. Duluth Ave., Sioux Falls, 57104. Tel: 605-334-9861.

Vocations—WAYNE RZIHA, Assoc. Dir., *523 N. Duluth Ave., Sioux Falls, 57104.* Tel: 605-988-3772.

Youth Ministry—SEAN DALTON, *523 N. Duluth Ave., Sioux Falls, 57104.* Tel: 605-988-3785.

CLERGY, PARISHES, MISSIONS AND PAROCHIAL SCHOOLS

CITY OF SIOUX FALLS
(Minnehaha County)

1—ST. JOSEPH CATHEDRAL, Most Rev. Robert J. Carlson; Rev. Scott Traynor.
Res., 521 Duluth Ave., 57104. Tel: 605-336-7390; Fax: 605-330-0416. [JC]
School—See separate listing under Inter-Parochial Schools in the Institution section. Tel: 605-338-3159; Fax: 605-338-2647.
Catechesis/Religious Programs—Students 168.

2—CHRIST THE KING (1949), Rev. Msgr. Donald Kettler; Deacon James J. Walden.
Res., 1501 W. 26th St., 57105. Tel: 605-332-5477; Fax: 605-332-0552.
School—See separate listing under Inter-Parochial Schools in the Institution section. Tel: 605-338-5103; Fax: 605-335-1231.
Catechesis/Religious Programs—Students 115.

3—HOLY SPIRIT (1988), Rev. Msgr. James F. Andraschko; Rev. David Stevens; Deacon John Cole.
Res., 3601 E. Dudley Ln., 57103. Tel: 605-371-2320; Fax: 605-371-1957.
Catechesis/Religious Programs—Students 621.

4—OUR LADY OF GUADALUPE (1996), Rev. John S. Rader. In res., Rev. Bernard Ashfeld.
Res., 1220 E. 8th St., 57103-1702. Tel: 605-338-8126; Fax: 605-338-0419. [JC]
Catechesis/Religious Programs—Students 113.

5—ST. LAMBERT (1957), Revs. Mark Lichter; Stanley Stanizewski; Deacons Ralph C. Counter; Jerome F. Wathen; James Boorman.
Res., 1000 S. Bahnson Ave., 57103. Tel: 605-336-8808; Fax: 605-339-4389.
School—See separate listing under Inter-Parochial Schools in the Institution section. Tel: 605-338-7042; Fax: 605-336-8727.
Catechesis/Religious Programs—Tel: 605-338-4728.
Students 400.

6—ST. MARY (1947), Revs. David Krogman; Gary Ternes; Deacon Henry Knapp.
Res., 2109 S. Fifth Ave., 57105. Tel: 605-332-6391; Fax: 605-338-2953.
School—See separate listing under Inter-Parochial Schools in the Institution section. Tel: 605-334-9881; Fax: 605-334-9224.
Catechesis/Religious Programs—Tel: 605-334-1912.
Students 187.

7—ST. MICHAEL (1979), Revs. Joseph Vogel; Daniel Wolfgram.
Res., 1600 S. Marion Rd., 57106. Tel: 605-361-1600; Fax: 605-361-4350. [JC]
School—See separate listing under Inter-Parochial Schools in the Institution section. Tel: 605-361-0021; Fax: 605-361-0094.
Catechesis/Religious Programs—Tel: 605-361-1317.
Students 1,040.

8—ST. THERESE (1917), Rev. Charles L. Cimpl; Deacon Michael Conrads.
Res., 1301 N. Dubuque Ave., 57110-6450. Tel: 605-338-2433; Fax: 605-339-2203.
Catechesis/Religious Programs—Students 211.

OUTSIDE THE CITY OF SIOUX FALLS

Aberdeen, Brown Co., Sacred Heart (1882), Revs. Terry Anderson; Christopher Hughes; Deacon Peter Mehlhaff.
Res., 409 3rd Ave., S.E., 57401. Tel: 605-225-7065; Fax: 605-226-5992. [CEM]
School—See separate listing under Inter-Parochial Schools in the Institution section.
Catechesis/Religious Programs—Tel: 605-229-4100.
Students 398.

St. Mary, Revs. Gregory Tschakert; Douglas Binsfeld.
Res., 215 N. Arch St., 57401. Tel: 605-229-4422; Fax: 605-226-4908. [CEM]
School—See separate listing under Inter-Parochial Schools in the Institution section.
Catechesis/Religious Programs—Students 198.

Alexandria, Hanson Co., St. Mary of Mercy (1880), Rev. Robert J. Fox.
Res., P.O. Box 158, 57331. Tel: 605-239-4532; Fax: 605-239-4532. [CEM]
Catechesis/Religious Programs—Students 115.

Andover, Day Co., All Saints (1880). Closed. For inquiries for parish records contact the Chancery.

Arlington, Kingsbury Co., St. John the Evangelist. Served from Ramona. Rev. Darrell Lamberty.
P.O. Box 128, Ramona, 57054. Tel: 605-482-8214.
Catechesis/Religious Programs—Tel: 605-983-4704.
Students 54.

Armour, Douglas Co., St. Paul the Apostle (1886), Rev. William Hamak.
Res., Box 400, 57313. Tel: 605-724-2191.
Catechesis/Religious Programs—Tel: 605-724-2121.
Students 69.

Artesian, Sanborn Co., St. Charles (1908). Attended by St. Wilfrid, Woonsocket.
Mailing Address: Box 266, Woonsocket, 57385. Tel: 605-796-4666. [JC]
Catechesis/Religious Programs—Students 53.

Athol, Spink Co., St. Mary (1885). Closed. For inquiries for parish records contact All Saints, Mellette.

Aurora, Brookings Co., St. William (1881), Deacon Edwin Gruhot, Admin.
Mailing Address: 47483 215th St., 57002-6535. Tel: 605-693-3910. [CEM]
Catechesis/Religious Programs—Students 21.

Beresford, Union Co., St. Teresa of Avila (1885), Rev. Denis Meier.
Res., 903 S. Third, P.O. Box 472, 57004. Tel: 605-763-2028; 763-5159 (Church). [CEM]
Catechesis/Religious Programs—Students 117.

Big Bend, Hughes Co., St. Catherine (1950). Attended by Fort Thompson.
Box 47, Fort Thompson, 57339. Tel: 605-245-2350. [CEM]
Catechesis/Religious Programs—Students 36.

Big Stone City, Grant Co., St. Charles (1882), Rev. Raymond Otto, O.S.B.
Res., P.O. Box 68, 57216. Tel: 605-862-8485; Fax: 605-862-8319. [CEM]
Catechesis/Religious Programs—Students 58.

Blunt, Hughes Co., Holy Spirit. Closed. For inquiries for parish records contact the Chancery.

Bowdle, Edmunds Co., St. Augustine (1894), Rev. Brian Simon. Box 310, 57428. Tel: 605-285-6466. [CEM]
Catechesis/Religious Programs—Students 38.

Brandon, Minnehaha Co., Risen Savior (1979), Rev. Anthony Imberi.
Res., 301 N. Splitrock Blvd., P.O. Box 80, 57005-0080. Tel: 605-582-2947; 582-6902 (Church); Fax: 605-582-3993. [JC]
Catechesis/Religious Programs—Tel: 605-582-2292.
Students 439.

Bridgewater, McCook Co., St. Stephen (1880), Rev. Paul Offerman.
Res., Box 49, 57319. Tel: 605-729-2505. [CEM]
Catechesis/Religious Programs—Students 72.

Bristol, Day Co., St. Anthony (1885). Served from Groton. Rev. David Janes.
Res., Box 336, 57219. Tel: 605-492-3135. [CEM]
Catechesis/Religious Programs—Students 35.

Britton, Marshall Co., St. John de Britto (1888), Rev. Msgr. Edward Burian.
Res., Box 108, 57430. Tel: 605-448-5379; Fax: 605-448-5388. [JC]
Catechesis/Religious Programs—Students 72.

Brookings, Brookings Co., St. Thomas More (1904), Rev. Thomas A. Heck.
Res., 1700 8th St. S., 57006. Tel: 605-692-4361; Fax: 605-692-6176. [CEM]
Catechesis/Religious Programs—Tel: 605-692-6941.
Students 550.

Bryant, Hamlin Co., St. Mary (1881). Attended by St. Thomas, De Smet.
Res., Box 15, De Smet, 57231. Tel: 605-854-3564. [CEM]

Canton, Lincoln Co., St. Dominic, Rev. Lawrence A. Jonas, S.J.; Deacon Edward B. Oliver.
Res., 809 E. Walnut, 57013. Tel: 605-764-5640; Fax: 605-764-3085.
Catechesis/Religious Programs—Students 143.

Castlewood, Hamlin Co., St. John (1885). Attended by Kranzburg.
Mailing Address: Box 166, Kranzburg, 57245. Tel: 605-886-9166; Fax: 605-886-9166. [JC]
Catechesis/Religious Programs—Students 63.

Cavour, Beadle Co., St. Patrick (1883). Closed. For inquiries for parish records contact Holy Trinity, Huron.

Centerville, Turner Co., Good Shepherd (1888). Attended by Beresford.
P.O. Box 98, 57014. Tel: 605-563-2220. [JC]
Catechesis/Religious Programs—Students 73.

Chamberlain, Brule Co., St. James (1891), Rev. Anthony Kelly, S.C.J.
Res., 400 S. Main, 57325. Tel: 605-734-6122; Fax: 605-734-6729. [JC]
Catechesis/Religious Programs—Tel: 605-734-6122; Fax: 605-734-6729.
Students 229.

Chelsea, Faulk Co., Sacred Heart. Attended by Mellette.
Mailing Address: P.O. Box 46, Mellette, 57461. Tel: 605-887-3414.

Clark, Clark Co., St. Michael (1887), Rev. Ken Bain.
Res., 110 N. Idaho St., 57225. Tel: 605-532-3855; Fax: 605-532-3866. [CEM]
Catechesis/Religious Programs—112 N. Idaho St., 57225. Tel: 605-532-3776.
Students 150.

Clear Lake, Deuel Co., St. Mary (1900), Rev. Msgr. Steven Barnett.
Res., 408 Third St. W., Box 589, 57226. Tel: 605-874-2080.
Catechesis/Religious Programs—Students 103.

Colman, Moody Co., St. Peter (1905), Rev. David Roehrich; Deacon Michael Huntington.
Res., Box J, 57017. Tel: 605-534-3612; Fax: 605-534-3612. [CEM]
Catechesis/Religious Programs—Students 121.

Conde, Spink Co., St. John the Baptist (1906), Rev. Mathew Vazhappilly, C.M.I. (India).
Res., P.O. Box 228, 57434. Tel: 605-382-5902; Fax: 605-382-5257. [CEM]

Dakota Dunes, Union Co., Mother Teresa Catholic Community (1999), Rev. Anthony Opem.
Church—102 Levee Tr., 57049. Tel: 605-235-1942.
Catechesis/Religious Programs—Students 9.

Dante, Charles Mix Co., Assumption B.V.M. (1909), Rev. Jordan Hite, T.O.R.
P.O. Box 36, 57329-0036. Tel: 605-384-5155. [CEM]
Catechesis/Religious Programs—Students 107.

Dell Rapids, Minnehaha Co., St. Mary's (1898), Rev. Chester Murtha.
Res., 608 8th St., 57022. Tel: 605-428-3390; Fax: 605-428-5304. [CEM][JC]
Preschool:—.
Lay Teachers 1; Students 22.
School—Tel: 605-428-3459.
Lay Teachers 7; Students 128.
Middle School:—.
Lay Teachers 4; Students 70.
High School—Tel: 605-428-5591; Fax: 605-428-5377.
Lay Teachers 8; Students 65.
Catechesis/Religious Programs—Tel: 605-428-3597.
Students 195.

De Smet, Kingsbury Co., St. Thomas Aquinas (1901), Rev. Cathal Gallagher.
Res., Box 15, 57231. Tel: 605-854-3564; Fax: 605-854-3564. [CEM]
Catechesis/Religious Programs—Students 73.

Dimock, Hutchinson Co., SS. Peter and Paul (1885), Rev. Joseph Glancy, T.O.R.
Res., 146 W. 1st St., 57331. Tel: 605-928-3883; Fax: 605-928-3498. [CEM]
Catechesis/Religious Programs—Tel: 605-928-3498.
Students 82.

Doland, Spink Co., St. Joseph of Doland (1909). Attended by Conde.
P.O. Box 393, 57436-0393. Tel: 605-635-6301; Fax: 605-635-6411.
Catechesis/Religious Programs—Students 49.

Duncan, Buffalo Co., St. Placidus (1887). Attended by Wessington Springs.
510 N. Wallace, P.O. Box N, Wessington Springs, 57382-0348. Tel: 605-293-3484. [CEM]
Church—HCR 3, Box 17, Gann Valley, 57341.

Eden, Marshall Co., Sacred Heart (1917), Rev. Paul Pathiyamoola.
Res., Box 15, 57232. Tel: 605-486-4702. [CEM]
Catechesis/Religious Programs—Students 85.

Elk Point, Union Co., St. Joseph (1901), Rev. John C. Rasmussen.
Res., Box 340, 605 E. Main St., 57025. Tel: 605-356-2693; Fax: 605-356-3284. [CEM]
Catechesis/Religious Programs—Students 199.

Elkton, Brookings Co., Our Lady of Good Counsel (1879). Attended by Flandreau.
Mailing Address: 105 S. Bates, Flandreau, 57028.
Res., Box E, 57026. Tel: 605-542-8221; Fax: 605-542-8221. [CEM]
Catechesis/Religious Programs—P.O. Box 206, 57026. Tel: 605-542-3121. Diane Baker, D.R.E.
Students 121.

Emery, Hanson Co., St. Martin (1884), Rev. Joseph Thalanany, V.C. (India).
Res., Box 312, 57332. Tel: 605-449-4374. [CEM]
Catechesis/Religious Programs—Students 70.

Epiphany, Hanson Co., Church of the Epiphany (1896). Attended by Howard. In res., Rev. Arnold Petrosky, T.O.R., (Retired).
Mailing Address: Box 100, Howard, 57349. Tel: 605-523-2640. [CEM]
Catechesis/Religious Programs—Students 60.

Estelline, Hamlin Co., St. Francis de Sales (1884). Attended by Clear Lake.
Res., Box B, 57234. Tel: 605-873-2254. [CEM]
Catechesis/Religious Programs—Tel: 605-874-2080.
Students 49.

Ethan, Davison Co., Holy Trinity (1889). Attended by Dimock.
146 W. 1st St., Dimock, 57331. Tel: 605-928-3883. [CEM]
Catechesis/Religious Programs—Tel: 605-227-4666. Mrs. Glen Erpenback, D.R.E.
Students 60.

Eureka, McPherson Co., St. Joseph (1896). Attended by Herreid.
Mailing Address: P.O. Box 37, Herreid, 57632. Tel: 605-437-2614.
Catechesis/Religious Programs—Students 50.

Farmer, Hanson Co., St. Peter (1889). Merged with St. Mary, Spencer to form St. John Neumann, Spencer-Farmer.

Faulkton, Faulk Co., St. Thomas the Apostle (1903), Rev. Randy Phillips; Deacon Arvid Holsing.
Res., P.O. Box 394, 57438. Tel: 605-598-6590; Fax: 605-598-6745. [CEM]
Catechesis/Religious Programs—Deb Clement, D.R.E.
Students 69.

Flandreau, Moody Co., SS. Simon and Jude (1882), Rev. David Roehrich.
Res., 105 S. Bates, 57028. Tel: 605-997-2610; Fax: 605-997-2610. [CEM]
Catechesis/Religious Programs—Students 150.

Florence, Codington Co., Blessed Sacrament (1889), Rev. Albert Cizewski (Poland).
Res., Box 6, 57235. Tel: 605-758-2271; Fax: 605-758-2113. [CEM]
Catechesis/Religious Programs—Students 53.

Fort Thompson, Buffalo Co., St. Joseph (1889), Revs. Yvon Sheehy, S.C.J., Moderator; Jim L. Walters, S.C.J.
Mailing Address: Box 47, 57339. Tel: 605-245-2350. [CEM]
Catechesis/Religious Programs—Students 115.

Frankfort, Spink Co., St. Ann (1884). Attended by Redfield.
Mailing Address: 213 E. 6th Ave., Redfield, 57469. Tel: 605-472-2500; Fax: 605-472-3397.
Catechesis/Religious Programs—Students 48.

Garretson, Minnehaha Co., St. Rose of Lima (1898), Rev. Anthony Imberi; Deacon Pete Cheskie.
Res., Drawer O, 57030. Tel: 605-594-3750. [CEM]
Catechesis/Religious Programs—Tel: 605-594-3560.
Students 103.

Garryowen, Union Co., St. Mary. Closed. For sacramental records contact St. Joseph, Elk Point.

Gary, Deuel Co., St. Peter (1900). Attended by Clear Lake.
408 3rd St. W., Box 589, Clear Lake, 57226. Tel: 605-874-2080.
Catechesis/Religious Programs—Students 34.

Geddes, Charles Mix Co., St. Ann (1902). Attended by Platte.
Mailing Address: P.O. Box 335, Platte, 57369-0335. Tel: 605-337-2465; 337-3710; Fax: 605-337-9717. [CEM][JC]
Catechesis/Religious Programs—Students 52.

Gettysburg, Potter Co., Sacred Heart (1905), Rev. Ken Lulf. In res., Rev. Msgr. Marvin McPhee.
Res., Box 285, 57442. Tel: 605-765-2161. [CEM]
Catechesis/Religious Programs—Tel: 605-765-2359.
Students 113.

Grenville, Day Co., St. Joseph (1885). Attended by Eden.
Res., Box 191, 57239. Tel: 605-947-4540. [CEM]
Catechesis/Religious Programs—Students 39.

Groton, Brown Co., St. Elizabeth Ann Seton (1883). (formerly St. John the Baptist). Rev. David Janes.
Res., 803 1st St. North, P.O. Box 407, 57445. Tel: 605-397-8448. [CEM]
Catechesis/Religious Programs—Students 107.

Grover, Codington Co., St. Peter (1901). Attended by Blessed Sacrament, Florence.
Mailing Address: P.O. Box 6, Florence, 57235. Tel: 605-758-2271; Fax: 605-758-2113.
Catechesis/Religious Programs—Students 17.

Harrold, Hughes Co., St. John the Evangelist. Attended by Highmore.
Box 457, Highmore, 57345. Tel: 605-852-2733. [CEM]
Catechesis/Religious Programs—Students 35.

Hartford, Minnehaha Co., St. George (1882), Rev. Michael D. Kelly; Sr. Muriel Spartz, O.S.B., Pastoral Assoc.
Res., 300 W. Mickelson, 57033.
Catechesis/Religious Programs—St. George Center, 207 S. Main Ave., 57033. Tel: 605-528-3902; Fax: 605-528-3902.
Students 318.
100 N. Mundt, Box 577, 57033. Tel: 605-528-3426; Fax: 605-528-3902. [CEM]

Hecla, Brown Co., St. Anthony (1904). Attended by St. John, Britton.
Box 108, Britton, 57430. Tel: 605-448-5379. [JC]

Henry, Codington Co., St. Henry. Florence.
Mailing Address: P.O. Box 98, 57243. Tel: 605-758-2271.
Catechesis/Religious Programs—Students 51.

Herreid, Campbell Co., St. Michael (1895), Rev. Jim D. Friedrich.
Res., Box 37, 57632. Tel: 605-437-2614; Fax: 605-437-2505. [CEM]
Catechesis/Religious Programs—Students 84.

Highmore, Hyde Co., St. Mary, Rev. John Short.
Res., Box 457, 57345. Tel: 605-852-2733. [CEM]
Catechesis/Religious Programs—Students 80.

Hosmer, Edmunds Co., Holy Trinity (1912). Attended by Bowdle.
Res., P.O. Box 46, 57448. Tel: 605-283-2275. [CEM]

Hoven, Potter Co., St. Anthony of Padua (1887), Rev. Joseph Short.
Res., Box 98, 57450. Tel: 605-948-2451; Fax: 605-948-2245. [CEM]
Catechesis/Religious Programs—Students 133.

Howard, Miner Co., St. Agatha (1882), Rev. Michael Schneider.
Res., Box 100, 57349. Tel: 605-772-5564. [CEM]
Catechesis/Religious Programs—Students 133.

Humboldt, Minnehaha Co., St. Ann (1912), Rev. John Riedman; Deacon Francis Graff; Sr. Mildred Nikolas, O.S.B.
Res., 204 S. Jefferson, 57035. Tel: 605-363-3330. [CEM]
Catechesis/Religious Programs—Tel: 605-363-5068.
Students 111.

Huntimer, Minnehaha Co., St. Joseph the Workman (1889). Attended by Hartford.
Mailing Address: 100 N. Mundt, P.O. Box 577, Hartford, 57033. Tel: 605-528-3426. [CEM]
Catechesis/Religious Programs—Students 136.

Huron, Beadle Co., Holy Trinity (1999). New parish resulted in the merger between Church of the Resurrection, Huron and St. Martin, Huron. Revs. J. Joseph Holzhauser; James Zimmer.
Mailing Address: 133 5th St. S.E., 57350.
Res., 400 20th St. S.W., 57350. Tel: 605-352-2203; Fax: 605-353-0889. [CEM]
School—Tel: 605-352-9344; Fax: 605-352-0988.
Lay Teachers 10; Students 105.
Catechesis/Religious Programs—Students 416.

Idylwilde, Turner Co., St. Boniface (1885). Attended by St. Christina, Parker.
Box 610, Parker, 57053. Tel: 605-297-4983. [CEM]
Catechesis/Religious Programs—Students 74.

Ipswich, Edmunds Co., Holy Cross (1886), Rev. Thomas Clement.
Res., Box 67, 57451. Tel: 605-426-6967; Fax: 605-426-6967. [CEM]
School—Tel: 605-426-6222.
Lay Teachers 6; Students 56.
Catechesis/Religious Programs—Students 132.

Iroquois, Kingsbury Co., St. Paul. Attended by St. Thomas Aquinas, De Smet.
Box 15, De Smet, 57231. Tel: 605-854-3564; Fax: 605-854-3564. [CEM]

Jefferson, Union Co., St. Peter (1867), Rev. Andrew K. Swietochowski.
Res., P.O. Box 188, 57038-0188. Tel: 605-966-5716; Fax: 605-966-5492. [CEM]
School—P.O. Box 98, 57038-0098. Tel: 605-966-5529.
Lay Teachers 7; Students 50.
Catechesis/Religious Programs—Students 88.

Kimball, Brule Co., St. Margaret (1884), Rev. Daniel Manning.
Res., Box 137, 57355. Tel: 605-778-6420. [CEM]
Catechesis/Religious Programs—Tel: 605-778-6487.
Students 167.

Kranzburg, Codington Co., Holy Rosary (1879), Rev. Richard Baumberger.
Res., Box 166, 57245. Tel: 605-886-9166; Fax: 605-886-9166. [CEM]
School—(Grades K-6). Tel: 605-886-8114; Fax: 605-886-9166.
Lay Teachers 4; Students 41.
Catechesis/Religious Programs—Students 111.

Lake Andes, Charles Mix Co., St. Mark (1904), Bro. Martin Zatsick, T.O.R., Admin.
Res., Box 250, 57356. Tel: 605-487-7300. [CEM]

Catechesis/Religious Programs—Tel: 605-487-7056.
Students 35.

Lake City, Marshall Co., St. Joseph (1919). Attended by Eden.
Box 15, Eden, 57232. Tel: 605-486-4702. [CEM]

Lennox, Lincoln Co., St. Magdalen. Attended by St. Nicholas, Tea.
Mailing Address: Box 136, 57039. Tel: 605-647-2187. [CEM]
Catechesis/Religious Programs—Students 156.

Leola, McPherson Co., Our Lady of Perpetual Help (1891), Rev. Thomas Clement.
Res., P.O. Box 67, Ipswich, 57451. Tel: 605-426-6967; Fax: 605-426-6967. [CEM]
Catechesis/Religious Programs—Students 49.

Lesterville, Yankton Co., St. John the Baptist (1904). Attended by St. Wenceslaus, Tabor.
Mailing Address: 205 N. Lidice, Tabor, 57063. Tel: 605-463-2336; Fax: 605-463-2518. [CEM]
Catechesis/Religious Programs—Students 51.

Letcher, Sanborn Co., St. Scholastica. Closed. For inquiries for parish records contact the Chancery.

Lily, Day Co., St. Joseph. Closed. For sacramental records contact St. Anthony, Bristol.

Madison, Lake Co., St. Thomas Aquinas (1881), Rev. Robert B. Vinslauski.
Res., 217 N.W. Fourth St., 57042. Tel: 605-256-2304; Fax: 605-256-3953. [CEM]
School—Tel: 605-256-4419.
Lay Teachers 10; Students 100.
Catechesis/Religious Programs—Students 221.

Marion, Turner Co., Our Lady of Perpetual Help (1880). Attended by St. Christina, Parker.
Res., Box 610, Parker, 57053. Tel: 605-297-4983. [CEM]
Catechesis/Religious Programs—Students 58.

Marty, Charles Mix Co., St. Paul's Church (1913), Rev. David Tickerhoof, T.O.R.; Sr. Miriam Shindelar, O.S.B.S., Admin.; Deacon Edward P. Zephier.
Res., P.O. Box 266, 57361. Tel: 605-384-3234; Fax: 605-384-3575. [CEM]
Catechesis/Religious Programs—Students 90.

Mayfield, Yankton Co., St. Columba (1902), Rev. Leonard Kayser.
1105 W. Eighth St., Yankton, 57078. Tel: 605-668-1236. [CEM]
Catechesis/Religious Programs—Students 46.

Mellette, Spink Co., All Saints, Rev. Joseph Puthenkulan (India).
Box 46, 57461. Tel: 605-887-3414. [CEM]
Catechesis/Religious Programs—Students 70.

Milbank, Grant Co., St. Lawrence (1882), Rev. Denis Quinkert, O.S.B.
Res., 101 6th St. S., 57252. Tel: 605-432-5353. [CEM]
School—Tel: 605-432-5673.
Sisters 1; Lay Teachers 9; Students 127.
Catechesis/Religious Programs—Tel: 605-432-5353.
Students 260.

Miller, Hand Co., St. Ann (1884), Rev. Terry Weber.
Res., 709 E. 4th, P.O. Box 198, 57362. Tel: 605-853-2207; Fax: 605-853-3037. [CEM]
Catechesis/Religious Programs—Tel: 605-853-2735.
Students 172.

Mitchell, Davison Co., Holy Family (1880), Revs. Edward J. Pierce; Thaliyam Joseph Jesudas, C.M.E. (India); Deacon Joseph Graves.
Res., 321 E. 3rd Ave., 57301. Tel: 605-996-3639; Fax: 605-996-9257. [CEM]
School—Holy Family/Holy Spirit-Mitchell Catholic Schools, Tel: 605-996-2365; Fax: 605-995-0378.
Lay Teachers 17; Students 263.
Catechesis/Religious Programs—200 N. Kimball St., 57301. Tel: 605-996-3842.
Students 302.

Holy Spirit (1962), Rev. Richard Fox.
Res., 1412 W. Cedar Ave., 57301. Tel: 605-996-7424; Fax: 605-996-6964.
School—Holy Family/Holy Spirit-Mitchell Catholic Schools. See Holy Family for details. Tel: 605-996-2365; Fax: 605-995-0378.
Catechesis/Religious Programs—Tel: 605-996-3842.
Students 234.

Mobridge, Walworth Co., St. Joseph (1912), Rev. Jerome M. Ranek.
Res., 514 W. Second Ave., 57601. Tel: 605-845-2100. [JC]
Preschool—.
Lay Teachers 1; Students 30.
Catechesis/Religious Programs—614 W. Second Ave., 57601. Tel: 605-845-2646.
Students 157.

Montrose, McCook Co., St. Patrick (1904), Rev. John Reidman.
211 S. Church, P.O. Box 158, 57048. Tel: 605-363-5068; Fax: 605-363-3856. [CEM]
Catechesis/Religious Programs—Students 127.

Mount Vernon, Davison Co., St. Michael. Attended by Plankinton.
Box 430, Plankinton, 57368.
Catechesis/Religious Programs—Students 71.

New Effington, Roberts Co., Sacred Heart (1913). Attended by Rosholt.
P.O. Box 45, Rosholt, 57260. Tel: 605-537-4583.

Oldham, Kingsbury Co., St. Catherine of Sienna. Attended by St. William, Ramona.
P.O. Box 128, Ramona, 57054-0128.

Onaka, Faulk Co., St. John the Baptist (1906). Attended by St. Anthony of Padua, Hoven.
P.O. Box 98, Hoven, 57450. Tel: 605-948-2451. [CEM]

Onida, Sully Co., St. Pius X (1959). Attended by Sacred Heart, Gettysburg. Sr. Veronica Haag, O.S.B., Pastoral Assoc.
P.O. Box 13, 57564. Tel: 605-258-2336. [CEM]
Catechesis/Religious Programs—Students 71.

Orient, Faulk Co., St. Joseph (1884). Attended by Polo.
17985 354th Ave., 57467. Tel: 605-392-2440.
Catechesis/Religious Programs—36.

Parker, Turner Co., St. Christina (1887), Rev. Gregory Frankman; Deacon William Frankman.
Res., P.O. Box 610, 57053. Tel: 605-297-4983. [CEM]
Catechesis/Religious Programs—Students 61.

Parkston, Hutchinson Co., Sacred Heart (1887), Rev. Robert V. Krantz; Deacon Barry Wagner.
Res., Box 460, 57366. Tel: 605-928-3676; Fax: 605-928-3862. [CEM 2]
Catechesis/Religious Programs—Students 209.

Pierre, Hughes Co., SS. Peter and Paul (1882), Revs. Hal Barber; Lipton Mariados (India).
Res., 304 N. Euclid, 57501. Tel: 605-224-2483; Fax: 605-224-1483. [CEM]
School—Tel: 605-224-7185; Fax: 605-224-1014.
Benedictine Sisters 3; Lay Teachers 8; Students 158.
Catechesis/Religious Programs—Students 520.

Plankinton, Aurora Co., St. John, Rev. Alex Bombera, T.O.R.
Res., Box 430, 57368. Tel: 605-942-7125.
Catechesis/Religious Programs—Students 120.

Platte, Charles Mix Co., St. Peter the Apostle (1904), Rev. Paul Josten.
Res., Box 335, 57369. Tel: 605-337-3710, 337-2465; Fax: 605-337-9717. [CEM]
Catechesis/Religious Programs—Students 90.

Polo, Hand Co., St. Liborius (1904), Sr. Mary Myles Schwahn, S.S.N.D., Pastoral Assoc.
Res., 17985 354th Ave., Orient, 57467. Tel: 605-392-2440. [CEM]
Catechesis/Religious Programs—Students 42.

Pukwana, Brule Co., St. Anthony. Attended by Chamberlain.
400 S. Main, Chamberlain, 57325. Tel: 605-734-6122; Fax: 605-734-6729.

Ramona, Lake Co., St. William of Vercelli, Rev. Darrell Lamberty.
Mailing Address: P.O. Box 128, 57054-0128. Tel: 605-482-8234.
Catechesis/Religious Programs—Students 26.

Redfield, Spink Co., St. Bernard (1884), Rev. Roger Geditz.
Res., 213 E. 6th Ave., 57469-1249. Tel: 605-472-2500; Fax: 605-472-3397. [CEM]
Catechesis/Religious Programs—Tel: 605-472-1482.
Students 202.

Revillo, Grant Co., Annunciation, Rev. Ray Otto, O.S.B.
Res., P.O. Box 432, Milbank, 57252-0432. Tel: 605-432-4623; Fax: 605-432-5412. [CEM]
Catechesis/Religious Programs—Students 54.

Roscoe, Edmunds Co., St. Thomas Apostle (1906). Attended by Bowdle.
Res., P.O. Box 257, 57471. Tel: 605-285-6466. [JC]
Catechesis/Religious Programs—Students 43.

Rosholt, Roberts Co., St. John the Baptist (1911), Rev. Dennis Deis, O.M.I.
Res., Box 45, 57260. Tel: 605-537-4583. [CEM]
Catechesis/Religious Programs—Students 66.

Salem, McCook Co., St. Mary (1885), Rev. Joseph Ripp. In res., Rev. Charles J. Duman, (Retired).
Res., Box 308, 340 N. Idaho, 57058. Tel: 605-425-2600; Fax: 605-425-2600. [CEM]
School—Tel: 605-425-2607.
Lay Teachers 10; Students 80.
Catechesis/Religious Programs—Students 111.

Scotland, Bon Homme Co., St. George (1906), Rev. John Maliyekal, V.C. (India).
Res., Box 449, 57059. Tel: 605-583-4318; Fax: 605-583-4318. [CEM]
Catechesis/Religious Programs—Tel: 605-583-4696.
Students 75.

Selby, Walworth Co., St. Anthony. Attended by Herreid.
P.O. Box 37, Herreid, 57632-0037.
Catechesis/Religious Programs—Students 46.

Seneca, Faulk Co., St. Boniface (1903). Attended by St. Thomas the Apostle, Faulkton.
P.O. Box 394, Faulkton, 57438-0094.

Sigel, Yankton Co., St. Agnes (1885), Rev. Leonard Kayser.
1105 W. 8th St., Yankton, 57078-3724. Tel: 605-668-1236. [CEM]
Catechesis/Religious Programs—Students 16.

Sisseton, Roberts Co., St. Catherine (1962), Revs. Randy Oswald, O.M.I.; Gari Ruthenberg, O.M.I.
Office: 120 E. Chestnut, 57262. Tel: 605-698-7414; Fax: 605-698-7236. [CEM 2]

St. Peter (1899), Revs. Randy Oswald, O.M.I.; Gari Ruthenberg, O.M.I.
Office: 120 E. Chestnut, 57262. Tel: 605-698-7414; Fax: 605-698-7236. [CEM]
Catechesis/Religious Programs—Students 130.

Spencer, McCook Co., St. Mary (1906). Merged with St. Peter, Farmer to form St. John Neumann, Spencer-Farmer.

Spencer-Farmer, McCook Co., St. John Neumann. Attended by Bridgewater.
P.O. Box 49, Bridgewater, 57319. Tel: 615-729-2505.

Springfield, Bon Homme Co., St. Vincent. Attended by Tyndall.
P.O. Box 130, 57062-0130.

Stephan, Hyde Co., Immaculate Conception (1886), Revs. Yvon Sheehy, S.C.J., Moderator; James L. Walters, S.C.J.
Res., 57346. Tel: 605-852-2216. [CEM][JC]

Stickney, Aurora Co., St. Mary (1908). Attended by Armour.
Box 400, Armour, 57313. Tel: 605-724-2191. [CEM]
Catechesis/Religious Programs—Students 31.

Tabor, Bon Homme Co., St. Wenceslaus (1872), Rev. William Osborn; Deacon David Kostel.
Res., 205 N. Lidice St., 57063-2005. Tel: 605-463-2336; Fax: 605-463-2518. [CEM]
Catechesis/Religious Programs—Students 72.

Tea, Lincoln Co., St. Nicholas (1905), Rev. Kenneth Koster.
Res., 510 W. Maple, P.O. Box 116, 57064. Tel: 605-498-5449; Fax: 605-498-2110. [JC]
Church—200 Maple St., 57064. Tel: 605-498-5449.
Catechesis/Religious Programs—Students 136.

Tripp, Hutchinson Co., Holy Rosary. Attended by Parkston.
P.O. Box 358, 57376-0358.

Turton, Spink Co., St. Joseph (1888). Attended by Conde.
Mailing Address: P.O. Box 127, 57477. Tel: 605-382-5902. [CEM][JC]

Tyndall, Bon Homme Co., St. Leo (1890), Rev. Jerry Kopel. In res., Rev. Antonio Ramos.
Res., Box 47, 57066. Tel: 605-589-3504; Fax: 605-589-3392. [CEM]
Catechesis/Religious Programs—Students 175.
Station—Springfield Correctional Facility, Tel: 605-369-2201.

Veblen, Marshall Co., St. John Nepomucene. Attended by Catholic Community, Sisseton.
120 Chestnut St. E., Sisseton, 57262-1428.

Vermillion, Clay Co., St. Agnes (1860), Rev. Donald Imming.
Res., 416 Walker St., 57069. Tel: 605-624-4478 (Church); 605-624-4479 (Rec.); Fax: 605-624-4418. [CEM 2][JC 3]
School—909 E. Lewis St., 57069. Tel: 605-624-4144.
Lay Teachers 7; Students 137.
Catechesis/Religious Programs—Tel: 605-624-5161.
Students 218.

Vodnany, Bon Homme Co., SS. Cyril and Methodius (1886). Attended by Scotland.
Mailing Address: P.O. Box 102, Kaylor, 57354. [CEM]

Wagner, Charles Mix Co., St. John the Baptist (1903), Rev. Jordan Hite, T.O.R.; Deacon Albert J. Kocer.
Res., Box 637, 57380. Tel: 605-384-5518; Fax: 605-384-5518. [CEM]
Catechesis/Religious Programs—Tel: 605-384-5314.
Students 176.

Wakonda, Clay Co., St. Patrick (1904). Attended by Newman Center, Vermillion. Rev. Joseph Forcelle, Admin.; Deacon Thomas Vogel.

320 Cherry St., Vermilllion, 57069. Tel: 605-624-2697. [CEM 2]
Catechesis/Religious Programs—Tel: 605-267-2676.
Students 51.

Watertown, Codington Co., Holy Name (1955), Rev. John Lantsberger.
Res., 1009 Skyline Dr., 57201. Tel: 605-886-2628; Fax: 605-886-2142. [JC]
Catechesis/Religious Programs—Tel: 605-886-3368; Fax: 605-886-2141.
Students 475.

Immaculate Conception (1887), Rev. James Bream.
Res., 309 Second Ave., S.E., 57201. Tel: 605-886-4049; Fax: 605-882-2911. [CEM]
School—Tel: 605-886-3883; Fax: 605-886-0199.
Lay Teachers 14; Students 199.
Catechesis/Religious Programs—103 Third St., S.E., 57201. Tel: 605-886-2772.
Students 461.

Waubay, Day Co., Immaculate Conception (1894). Attended by Webster.
Mailing Address: 1101 E. 1st St., Webster, 57274. Tel: 605-345-3447; Fax: 605-345-4871.

Waverly, Codington Co., St. Joseph (1889). Attended by Kranzburg.
Box 166, Kranzburg, 57245. Tel: 605-886-9166; Fax: 605-886-9166. [CEM]

Webster, Day Co., Christ the King, Rev. John M. Garvey.
Res., 1101 E. 1st St., 57274. Tel: 605-345-3447; Fax: 605-345-4871. [CEM]
Catechesis/Religious Programs—Students 204.

Wellington, Minnehaha Co., St. Joseph. Closed. For sacramental records contact St. Ann, Humboldt.

Wessington, Beadle Co., St. Joseph. Attended by Miller.
P.O. Box 198, Miller, 57362-0198.

Wessington Springs, Jerauld Co., St. Joseph (1906), Rev. Augustine Belinda, T.O.R.
Mailing Address: P.O. Box N, 510 N. Wallace, 57382. Tel: 605-539-9569; Fax: 605-539-9569. [JC]
Catechesis/Religious Programs—Students 67.

Westport, Brown Co., Sacred Heart of Westport (1889), Rev. Larry Regynski.
Mailing Address: Aberdeen Aquinas Student Center, 310 15th Ave S.E., Aberdeen, 57401. Tel: 605-229-1011; Fax: 605-226-3274. [CEM]
Catechesis/Religious Programs—Tel: 605-226-3713.
Students 65.

White, Brookings Co., St. Paul (1898), Rev. Michael Griffin.
Mailing Address: Box 7019, University Sta., Brookings, 57007. Tel: 605-692-9461. [JC]
Catechesis/Religious Programs—Students 66.

White Lake, Aurora Co., St. Peter (1883). Attended by Kimball.
Res., Box 277, 57383. Tel: 605-249-2700. [CEM]
Catechesis/Religious Programs—Students 114.

Willow Lake, Clark Co., St. James (1895). Attended by St. Michael, Clark.
110 N. Idaho St., Clark, 57225. Tel: 605-532-3855; Fax: 605-532-3866.

Wilmot, Roberts Co., St. Mary (1886), Rev. John McMullen, O.S.B.
Res., Box 204, 57279. Tel: 605-938-4289; Fax: 605-398-9201. [CEM]
Catechesis/Religious Programs—Students 34.

Woonsocket, Sanborn Co., St. Wilfrid (1884), Rev. Gerald Thury.
Res., Box 266, 57385. Tel: 605-796-4666. [CEM]
Catechesis/Religious Programs—Students 94.

Worthing, Lincoln Co., St. Edward (1908). Attended by St. Dominic, Canton.
800 E. Walnut, Canton, 57013. Tel: 605-764-5640; Fax: 605-764-3085. [CEM]

Yankton, Yankton Co., St. Benedict (1993), Rev. Rodney Farke; Deacon Leon Cantin.
Res., 1500 St. Benedict Dr., 57078. Tel: 605-664-6214; Fax: 605-664-2305. [JC]
Catechesis/Religious Programs—1500 St. Benedict Dr., 57078. Tel: 605-665-6214.
Students 315.

Sacred Heart (1871), Revs. John Fischer; DeWayne Kayser.
Res., 509 Capitol St., 57078. Tel: 605-665-3655; Fax: 605-665-6768. [CEM]
School—Tel: 605-665-5841.
Sisters 1; Lay Teachers 9; Students 268.
Catechesis/Religious Programs—Students 465.

Zell, Hand Co., St. Mary. Attended by Mellette.
P.O. Box 46, Mellette, 57461-0046.
Catechesis/Religious Programs—Students 38.

Chaplains of Public Institutions

SIOUX FALLS. *South Dakota State Penitentiary & Minnehaha County Jail*. Rev. Bernard Ashfeld.
State School for the Deaf. Vacant. 523 N. Duluth Ave., 57104.

FLANDREAU. *Government Indian School*. Attended by SS. Simon & Jude, Flandreau.

PLANKINTON. *State Training School*. Attended by St. John Church, Plankinton.

REDFIELD. *State Hospital and State School, SD*. Attended by St. Bernard Church, Redfield.

SPRINGFIELD. *State Prison*. Rev. Antonio Ramos.

YANKTON. *State Hospital*. Rev. Leonard Kayser.

On Duty Outside the Diocese:
Reverend Monsignors—
Gullickson, Thomas E., Apostolic Nunciature, Postfach 200152, D-53131, Bonn, Germany
Reverend Fathers—
Mangan, Charles M., Casa Santa Maria dell 'Umilta, Via dell 'Umilta, 30, 00187, Roma, Italy

Military Chaplains:
Reverend Fathers—
Wagner, Joseph, 92 ARW/HC, Fairchild AFB, WA 99011

On Leave of Absence:
Reverend Fathers—
Dobitz, Roger
Englert, James
Johnson, Douglas
Marohn, Donald
McCormick, James
McNeil, Frank J.
Sieverding, Dale

Retired:
Reverend Monsignors—
Doyle, James Michael, 2913 Ridgeview Way, Sioux Falls, SD 57105
Duraczynski, Jerome A., 1041 Singer Ln., Norristown, PA 19403
Foley, Andrew E., 1265 4th St., N.W., Watertown, SD 57201-1128
Hermann, Carlton P., 505 Burgess Rd., Yankton, SD 57078-1819
McEneaney, John P.A., 423 N. Duluth Ave., Sioux Falls, SD 57104
McPhee, Marvin, P.O. Box 285, Gettysburg, SD 57442
Zwinger, Leonard, 400 E. 13th St., #120, Sioux Falls, SD 57104
Reverend Fathers—
Brady, John, 509 Broadway, Yankton, SD 57078
Burns, Thomas, 411 Vander Horck, P.O. Box 297, Britton, SD 57430
Carroll, Howard, 4701 S. Oxbow Ave., #320, Sioux Falls, SD 57106
Cashel, Richard, 1020 W. Norway Ave., #302, Mitchell, SD 57301
Connolly, Thomas, 3109 Corona Dr., Holiday, FL 34690
Duman, Charles J., 330 N. Idaho, Salem, SD 57058
Fox, Leo, P.O. Box 1441, Watertown, SD 57201
Fox, Leonard, 4500 Prince of Peace Pl. #A-5, Sioux Falls, SD 57103
Friedrich, Lawrence, 4510 S. Prince of Peace Pl., Apt. #213, Sioux Falls, SD 57103. Tel: 605-371-4537
Holtzman, Jerome, 17 Fourth St. S.E. #5, Watertown, SD 57201
Joyce, James, 900 E. 14th St., #112, Sioux Falls, SD 57104
Keating, David, c/o Ann Lemon, P.O. Box 177, Yankton, SD 57078
Krzyzopolski, Al, 4700 S. Cliff Ave., #210, Sioux Falls, SD 57103
MacArthur, Bruce, P.O. Box 416, Clint, TX 79836
Marbach, Lawrence J., 617 Maple St., Yankton, SD 57078-3823
Mardian, Pius, 4510 Prince of Peace Pl., #120, Sioux Falls, SD 57103
Martini, Ivo, 1615 15th Ave., S.E., #101, St. Cloud, MN 56304
McPhillips, Thomas J., Bishop Hoch Villa, 500 S. Ohlman, Mitchell, SD 57301
Mociun, Casimir T., 3020 Cedar Ave., Scranton, PA 18505
Molumby, Donald, Laurel Oaks, 4510 S. Prince of Peace Pl., #210, Sioux Falls, SD 57103
Morgen, Paul, 4504 S. Prince of Peace Pl. #9, Sioux Falls, SD 57103
Mowry, Raymond G., Aurora-Brule Nursing Home, P.O. Box 217, White Lake, SD 57383
Murphy, Joseph, St. Catharine's, 500 S. Gould Rd., Columbus, OH 43209
Murray, John I., 912 Missoula Ave., Helena, MT 59601
Ortmeier, Richard J., Mother of God Monastery, Benet Place, 100 28th Ave., S.E., #311, Watertown, SD 57201
Petrucci, Dominic, c/o Gloria Cunningham, 102 Christine Ct., Fairmont, WV 26554
Ryan, Thomas J., 609 W 5th St., Sioux Falls, SD 57104-2734
Wolf, James, 215 N. Arch, Aberdeen, SD 57401

Permanent Deacons:
Bierer, Richard B., (Retired), Sioux Falls
Boorman, James
Cantin, Leon, St. Benedict, Yankton
Cheskie, Pete, St. Rose, Garretson
Cole, John M., Holy Spirit, Sioux Falls
Conrads, Michael, St. Therese, Sioux Falls
Counter, Ralph, St. Lambert, Sioux Falls
Frankman, William, Admin., St. Christina, Parker
Graff, Francis, (Retired)
Graves, Joseph, Holy Family, Mitchell
Gruhot, Edward, St. William, Aurora
Healy, Thomas, (Retired), Yankton
Holsing, Arvid, St. Thomas the Apostle, Faulkton
Huntington, Michael, Admin., St. Peter, Colman
Knapp, Henry J., St. Mary's, Sioux Falls
Kocer, Albert, St. John the Baptist, Wagner
Kostel, David, St. Wenceslaus, Tabor
Mehlhaff, Peter, Sacred Heart, Aberdeen
Oliver, Edward B., St. Dominic, Canton
Pardew, Harold, Hospital Chap.
Vogel, Thomas, St. Patrick, Wakonda
Wagner, Barry, Sacred Heart, Parkston
Walden, James I., Christ the King Parish, Sioux Falls
Wathen, Jerome F., St. Lambert, Sioux Falls
Zephier, Edward P., Jr., St. Paul Parish, Marty

INSTITUTIONS LOCATED IN THE DIOCESE

[A] COLLEGES AND UNIVERSITIES

ABERDEEN. *Presentation College*, 57401. Tel: 605-225-1634; Fax: 605-229-8430.
E-mail: lorhale@presentation.edu
Web site: www.presentation.edu
For a complete listing, refer to the Colleges and Universities section.

YANKTON. *Mount Marty College*, 1105 W. 8th St., 57078. Tel: 800-658-4552; Fax: 605-668-1357.
E-mail: bzhang@mtmc.edu
Web site: www.mtmc.edu
For a complete listing, refer to the Colleges and Universities section.

[B] EDUCATION CENTERS, PRIVATE

CHAMBERLAIN. *St. Joseph Indian School*, N. Main, 57326. Tel: 605-734-3300; Fax: 605-734-3480.
Web site: www.stjo.org
Revs. Joseph Haselbauer, S.C.J.; William Pitcavage, S.C.J.; Bro. David Nagel, S.C.J., Exec. Dir. Brothers 1; Lay Teachers 24; Students 224.

WATERTOWN. *Mount Marty College - Watertown Campus*, 1225 Arrow Ave., P.O. Box 1385, 57201. Tel: 605-886-6777. Conducted by Benedictine Sisters. Linda Schurmann, Dir. Lay Teachers 50; Students 325.

[C] INTER-PAROCHIAL SCHOOLS

SIOUX FALLS. *Sioux Falls Catholic School System*, 3100 W. 41st St., 57105. Tel: 605-336-6241; Fax: 605-373-1035.
E-mail: tlorang@sfcss.org
Dr. Thomas Lorang, Supt.

O'Gorman High School. (Grades 9-12), 3201 S. Kiwanis Ave., 57105. Tel: 605-336-3644; Fax: 605-373-1035. Eric Sammons, Prin.; Rev. Michael Kelly, Chap. Priests 1; Sisters 3; Lay Teachers 48; Students 670.

St. Joseph Cathedral Elementary. (Grades PreK-6), 601 W. 4th St., 57104. Tel: 605-338-3159; Fax: 605-338-2647. John Bradbury, Prin. Lay Teachers 9; Students 168.

O'Gorman Catholic Junior High. (Grades 7-8), 3100 W. 41st St., 57105. Tel: 605-988-0546; Fax: 605-336-9839. Colley Broveliet, Prin. Lay Teachers 19; Students 295.

St. Mary - Holy Spirit Elementary. (Grades K-6), 2001 S. 5th Ave., 57105. Tel: 605-334-9881; Fax: 605-334-9224. Courtney Tielke, Prin. Lay Teachers 28; Students 434.

Christ the King Elementary School. (Grades PreK-6), 1801 S. Lake Ave., 57105. Tel: 605-338-5103; Fax: 605-335-1231. Nancy Clarey, Prin. Benedictine Sisters 1; Lay Teachers 13; Students 269.

St. Lambert Elementary School. (Grades PreK-6), 1000 S. Bahnson Ave., 57103. Tel: 605-338-7042; Fax: 605-336-8727. Barbara Lockwood, Prin. Lay Teachers 18; Students 273.

St. Michael Elementary School. (Grades K-6), 1600 S. Marion Rd., 57106. Tel: 605-361-0021; Fax:

605-361-0094. Lisa Huemoeller, Prin. Lay Teachers 15; Students 287.

ABERDEEN. *Aberdeen Catholic Schools Education Office*, 1400 N. Dakota St., S.E., 57401. Tel: 605-226-2100; Fax: 605-226-0616.
E-mail: b.graham@midco.net
Mr. Bob Graham, Supt.

Roncalli Elementary School. (Grades PreK-2), 424 Second Ave. N.E., 57401. Tel: 605-225-3460. Nancy A. Zenk, Prin. Sisters 5; Lay Teachers 7; Students 154.

Roncalli High School. (Grades 7-12), 1400 N. Dakota St., 57401. Tel: 605-225-7440; Fax: 605-226-0616. Bob Graham, Supt. Priests 1; Lay Teachers 25; Students 308.

Roncalli Middle School. (Grades 3-6), 505 Third Ave. S.E., 57401. Tel: 605-229-4100; Fax: 605-229-4104.
E-mail: schwab@midco.net
Mary Schwab, Prin. Lay Teachers 13; Students 222.

YANKTON. *Sacred Heart School*, 504 Capitol, 57078. Tel: 605-665-8931. Barb Rezac, Devel. Dir.

[D] GENERAL HOSPITALS

SIOUX FALLS. *Avera McKennan*, 57110-5045. Tel: 605-322-8000; Fax: 605-322-7822.
Web site: www.mckennan.org
For a complete listing, refer to the Hospitals section.

ABERDEEN. *Avera St. Luke's*, 57401. Tel: 605-622-5000
For a complete listing, refer to the Hospitals section.

GETTYSBURG. *Gettysburg Medical Center*, 57442. Tel: 605-765-2488
For a complete listing, refer to the Hospitals section.

MILBANK. *St. Bernard Providence Hospital*, 901 E. Virgil Ave., 57252. Tel: 605-432-4538; Fax: 605-432-5412
For a complete listing, refer to the Hospitals section.

MITCHELL. *Avera Queen of Peace*, 525 N. Foster, 57301. Tel: 605-995-2000; Fax: 605-995-2441.
E-mail: ron.jacobson@averaqueenofpeace.org
Web site: www.averaqueenofpeace.org
For a complete listing, refer to the Hospitals section.

PARKSTON. *St. Benedict Health Care Center dba Avera St. Benedict Health Center*, 57366. Tel: 605-928-3311; Fax: 605-928-7368.
E-mail: sbhc@santel.net
For a complete listing, refer to the Hospitals section.

PIERRE. *St. Mary's Foundation*, 800 E. Dakota, 57501. Tel: 605-224-3451; Fax: 605-224-3459.
E-mail: ellenlee@chi-midwest.org
Web site: www.St_Marys.com
For a complete listing, refer to the Hospitals section.

St. Mary's Healthcare Center of Pierre, South Dakota, 800 E. Sioux Ave., 57501. Tel: 605-224-3100; Fax: 605-224-3439.
E-mail: jimrussell@chi-midwest.org
Web site: www.St_Mary's.com
For a complete listing, refer to the Hospitals section.

TYNDALL. *St. Michael's Hospital*, 57066. Tel: 605-589-3341
For a complete listing, refer to the Hospitals section.

YANKTON. *Sacred Heart Health Services dba Avera Sacred Heart Hospital*, 501 Summit, 57078. Tel: 605-668-8000; Fax: 605-665-0170
For a complete listing, refer to the Hospitals section.

[E] HOMES FOR AGED

ABERDEEN. *Aberdeen Living Center* 1700 N. Hwy. 281, 57401. Tel: 605-225-7315; Fax: 605-225-0078.
For a complete listing, refer to the Special Care Facilities section.

MILBANK. *St. William Home for the Aged*, 901 E. Virgil Ave., 57252. Tel: 605-432-4538; Fax: 605-432-5412
For a complete listing, refer to the Special Care Facilities section.

SISSETON. *Tekakwitha Nursing Center, Inc.*, 6 E. Chestnut, 57262. Tel: 698-693-7693; Fax: 605-698-3091
For a complete listing, refer to the Special Care Facilities section.

[F] MONASTERIES AND RESIDENCES OF PRIESTS AND BROTHERS

EMERY. *Vincentian Congregation.* North American Headquarters, Vincentian House, P.O. Box 252, 57332-0252. Tel: 605-449-4999; Fax: 605-449-4999.
E-mail: vincentians@yahoo.com
Rev. Joseph Thalanany, V.C., Regl. Coord.

MARVIN. *Blue Cloud Abbey*, 46561 147th St., P.O. Box 98, 57251-0098. Tel: 605-398-9200; Fax: 605-398-9201.
E-mail: abbey@bluecloud.org
Web site: www.bluecloud.org
Rt. Revs. Thomas Hillenbrand, O.S.B.; Alan Berndt, O.S.B., Retired Abbot; Denis Quinkert, O.S.B., Retired Abbot; Revs. George Lyon, O.S.B., Prior; Stanislaus Maudlin, O.S.B.; Julius Armbruster, O.S.B.; Thomas Roznowski, O.S.B.; Guy Gau, O.S.B.; Peter Schwartz, O.S.B.; John McMullen, O.S.B.; Raymond Otto, O.S.B.; Basil Dilger, O.S.B.; Cletus Miller, O.S.B.; Odilo Burkhardt, O.S.B.; Bernardine Ness, O.S.B.; Theophane Gonnelly, O.S.B.; Larry Barnett, O.S.B.; Christopher Uehlein, O.S.B.; Wilfrid Lambertz, O.S.B.; Pedro Choc, O.S.B.; Francisco Arrivillaga Lemus, O.S.B.; Matthew Kowalski; Carlos Antonio Pop, O.S.B. Priests 23; Brothers 21.

[G] CONVENTS AND RESIDENCES FOR SISTERS

ABERDEEN. *Presentation Convent*, 57401. Tel: 605-225-0420; Fax: 605-229-8412.
E-mail: vvetter@nvc.net
Motherhouse and Novitiate of the Sisters of the Presentation of the B.V.M. Sr. Virginia McCall, P.B.V.M., Pres. Final Professed Sisters 146.

ALEXANDRIA. *Monastery of Our Mother of Mercy, Discalced Carmelite Nuns*, 221 5th St. W., P.O. Box 67, 57311-0067. Tel: 605-239-4382; Fax: 605-239-4676. Legal Title: *Discalced Carmelite Nuns of Alexandria, South Dakota, Inc.* Mother Marie Therese of the Child Jesus, O.C.D., Prioress. Solemnly Professed Sisters 5; First Professed 3; Novices 2; Postulants 1.

MARTY. *Motherhouse Oblate Sisters of the Blessed Sacrament.* St. Sylvester's Convent, Box 217, 57361-0217. Tel: 605-384-3305.
E-mail: osbs@charles-mix.com
Sr. Patricia Mylott, O.S.B.S. Professed Sisters 7.

MITCHELL. *Sisters of St. Francis of Our Lady of Guadulupe*, 1417 W. Ash, 57301. Tel: 605-996-1410. Private Association of the Faithful. Sr. M. Loretta Von Rueden, Sister Leader. Professed Sisters 5.

WATERTOWN. *Mother of God Monastery*, 110 28th Ave., S.E., 57201-8418. Tel: 605-882-6600; Fax: 605-882-6658.
E-mail: monastery@dailypost.com
Web site: www.monastery@dailypost.com
Motherhouse and Novitiate of Benedictine Sisters. Sr. Judith Fischer, Prioress. Sisters 72.

YANKTON. *Sacred Heart Monastery*, 1005 W. Eighth St., 57078. Tel: 605-668-6000; Fax: 605-668-6153.
E-mail: jernster@mtmc.edu
Motherhouse and Novitiate of the Benedictine Sisters. Sr. Jacquelyn Ernster, O.S.B., Prioress; Revs. Mel Patton, O.S.B., Chap.; Herbert Schmidt. Sisters 158.

[H] NEWMAN CENTERS

ABERDEEN. *Aquinas Student Center.*
E-mail: nsunewman@dtgnet.com
Northern State University, 310 15th Ave. S.E., 57401. Tel: 605-229-1011; Fax: 605-226-3274.
E-mail: nsunewman@mdex.net
Rev. Larry Regynski, Chap.; Michala Heller, Campus Min.

BROOKINGS. *Diocesan Newman Apostolate*, P.O. Box 7019, 57007-7019. Tel: 605-692-9461. Rev. Michael Griffin, Coord. Total Staff 3.

Pius XII Student Center. Our Lady of Wisdom Chapel. South Dakota State University, Box 7019 University Station, 57007. Tel: 605-692-9461; Fax: 605-692-9461. Rev. Michael Griffin.

MADISON. *Dakota State University Newman Club Office.* Attended by St. Thomas Parish, Madison. Trojan Center #101, 57042. Tel: 606-256-4135.
E-mail: schaefbt@pluto.dsu.edu

VERMILLION. *St. Thomas More Catholic Newman Center.*
E-mail: newmanpc@usd.edu
University of South Dakota, 320 E. Cherry St., 57069. Tel: 605-624-2697; Fax: 605-624-4145. Rev. Joseph Forcelle; Sr. Rosemarie Maly, O.S.B., Assoc. Dir.; Brian Begley, Activities Coord.

[I] MISCELLANEOUS LISTINGS

SIOUX FALLS. *Avera Health*, 3900 W. Avera Dr., 57108-5721. Tel: 605-322-4700; Fax: 605-322-4799.
E-mail: joanne.herman@avera.org
Sponsored by the Sisters of the Presentation of the B.V.M., Aberdeen, SD, and the Benedictine Sisters of Sacred Heart Monastery, Yankton, SD.

Avera Health Foundation, 3900 W. Avera Dr., Ste. 301, 57108-5721. Tel: 605-322-4750.
E-mail: jerry.soholt@avera.org

The Banquet, 300 N. Main Ave., 57104. Tel: 605-335-7066; Fax: 605-335-1091. Carolyn Downs, Exec. Dir. Total Staff 8; Total Assisted 96,958.

The Berakhah House, 400 Western Ave. N., 57104. Tel: 605-332-4017. Rev. Howard Carroll, Dir. Total Assisted 10.

The Catholic Foundation for Eastern South Dakota, 523 N. Duluth Ave., 57104. Tel: 605-988-3788; Fax: 605-988-3746. Mark Conzemius, Exec. Dir.

Community Outreach, 431 N. Cliff Ave., 57103. Tel: 605-331-3935; Fax: 605-336-8924. Jerry Bohnhoff, Dir. Total Staff 2; Total Families Assisted Annually 863.

Good Shepherd Center, 300 N. Main Ave., 57104. Tel: 605-332-3176; Fax: 605-332-3041. Sr. Gabriella Crowley, P.B.V.M., Assoc. Dir.

Holy Family Child Care Center, 217 N. Sherman, 57103. Tel: 605-357-9227; Fax: 605-357-0273. Elsa Johnson, Dir.

Kateri Indian Center, 300 N. Main Ave., 57104. Tel: 605-335-3321; Fax: 605-332-3041.

Little Flower of Jesus School Foundation, Inc., 901 N. Tahoe Tr., 57110-5779. Tel: 605-338-2433; Fax: 605-339-2203.
E-mail: therese@dtgnet.com

St. Francis House, 1301 E. Austin St., 57103. Tel: 605-334-3879; Fax: 605-575-3999.
E-mail: stfranhse@aol.com
Mr. Robin Zimmer, Dir. Bed Capacity 38.

St. Joseph Catholic Housing, Inc., Catholic Chancery Office, 523 N. Duluth Ave., 57104. Tel: 605-334-9861.

St. Mary / Holy Spirit School Endowment Trust, 3601 E. Dudley Ln., 57103. Tel: 605-371-2320; Fax: 605-371-1957. Rev. Msgr. James Andraschko, Trustee.

St. Vincent de Paul Store, 431 N. Cliff Ave., 57103. Tel: 605-335-5823; Fax: 605-336-8924. Mary Beth Piatt, Mgr. Staff 7.

Sioux Falls Catholic School Corporation, 3100 W. 41st St., 57105. Tel: 605-336-6241; Fax: 605-373-1035. Total Staff 12.

ALEXANDRIA. *Fatima Family Apostolate*, St. Mary of Mercy Church, P.O. Box 158, 57311. Tel: 605-239-4532; Fax: 605-239-4532.
E-mail: fatimafambks@basec.net
Web site: www.tot.com
Rev. Robert J. Fox, Dir.

MARVIN. *Blue Cloud Abbey Retirement Trust*, P.O. Box 98, 57251-0098. Tel: 605-398-9200; Fax: 605-398-9201.
E-mail: mcmullen@tnics.com
Rev. John McMullen, O.S.B., Treas.

SISSETON. *Tekakwitha Housing Corp*, 711 Veteran's Ave., 57262. Tel: 605-698-7090; Fax: 605-698-7326.

Tekakwitha Indian Mission, Inc., 120 E. Chestnut, 57262. Tel: 605-698-7414; Fax: 605-698-7236.

WATERTOWN. *Immaculate Conception School Foundation, Inc.*, 309 2nd Ave., S.E., 57201. Tel: 605-886-3883; Fax: 605-886-0199.

Retirement Trust, Mother of God Monastery, 110 28th Ave., S.E., 57201. Tel: 605-882-6654; Fax: 605-882-6658.
E-mail: monastery@dailypost.com

St. Ann's Corporation, Mother of God Monastery, 110 28th Ave., S.E., 57201. Tel: 605-882-6600; Fax: 605-882-6658.
E-mail: monastery@dailypost.com

Benet Place. Independent Living. 100 28th Ave., S.E., 57201. Tel: 605-886-9177; Fax: 605-882-3193. Units 39; Staff 8.

Evergreen Assisted Living, 90 28th Ave., S.E., 57201. Tel: 605-882-8555; Fax: 605-882-8556. Units 10; Staff 10.

YANKTON. *Benedictine Center, Inc.*, 1005 W. 8th, 57078. Tel: 605-668-6000; Fax: 605-668-6153.

Benedictine Health Foundation, Inc., 1017 W. Fifth, 57078. Tel: 605-668-8310. Kelly Kathol, Exec. Dir.

The House of Mary Shrine, Inc., Box 455, Lewis & Clark Lake, 57078-0455. Tel: 605-668-0121. Russell Weller, Pres. Bd. Dirs.; Rev. Rodney Farke, Spiritual Dir.

Yankton Catholic Community Development Office, 509 Capitol, 57078. Tel: 605-665-8931. Barb Rezac, Devel. Dir.

RELIGIOUS INSTITUTES OF MEN REPRESENTED IN THE DIOCESE

For further details refer to the corresponding bracketed number in the Religious Institutes of Men or Women section.

[0200]—*Benedictine Monks.* (Aurora, IL; Marvin, SD).—O.S.B.

[]—*Carmelite.* (India).

[1130]—*Congregation of the Priests of the Sacred Heart.* (Hales Corners, WI).—S.C.J.

[0690]—*Jesuit Fathers and Brothers.* (Wisconsin Prov.).—S.J.

[0910]—*Oblates of Mary Immaculate.* (Central Prov.).—O.M.I.

[0560]—*Third Order Regular of Saint Francis.* (Loretto, PA).—T.O.R.

[1335]—*Vincentian Congregation.* (India).—V.C.

RELIGIOUS INSTITUTES OF WOMEN REPRESENTED IN THE DIOCESE

[0230]—*Benedictine Sisters of Pontifical Jurisdiction.* (Yankton, Watertown, SD).—O.S.B.

[0940]—*Daughters of St. Mary of Providence.*—D.S.M.P.

[0420]—*Discalced Carmelite Nuns of the Monastery of Our Mother of Mercy.* (Alexandria, SD).—O.C.D.

[1070-14]—*Dominican Sisters*. Grand Rapids.—O.P.
[1310]—*Franciscan Sisters of Little Falls, MN*.—O.S.F.
[3010]—*Oblate Sisters of the Blessed Sacrament*.—O.S.B.S.
[2970]—*School Sisters of Notre Dame*. (Mankato Prov.).—S.S.N.D.
[1030]—*Sisters of the Divine Savior*.—S.D.S.
[3320]—*Sisters of the Presentation of the B.V.M.*—P.B.V.M.
[1720]—*Sisters of the Third Order Regular of St. Francis of the Congregation of Our Lady of Lourdes*.—O.S.F.

INTER-PAROCHIAL CEMETERIES

Sioux Falls. *St. Michael*, 3001 N. Cliff, 57104. Tel: 605-338-3376.

NECROLOGY

† Power, Joseph L., (Retired). —Died Jan. 5, 2000.

Diocese of Spokane

(Dioecesis Spokanensis)

Most Reverend

WILLIAM S. SKYLSTAD, D.D.

Bishop of Spokane; ordained May 21, 1960; appointed Bishop of Yakima February 22, 1977; consecrated and installed May 12, 1977; transferred to Spokane April 17, 1990; succeeded to the See April 27, 1990. *Office: W. 1023 Riverside Ave., P.O. Box 1453, Spokane, WA, 99210-1453. Res., W. 1025 Cleveland, Spokane, WA, 99205-3320.*

Catholic Pastoral Center: W. 1023 Riverside Ave., P.O. Box 1453, Spokane, WA, 99210-1453. Tel.: 509-358-7300.

Web site address: www.dioceseofspokane.org

E-mail address: cathdio@gntech.net

Solemnly consecrated to the Immaculate Heart of Mary on December 8, 1948.

ESTABLISHED DECEMBER 17, 1913.

Square Miles 24,356.

Corporate Title: *"The Catholic Bishop of Spokane, a Corporation Sole."*

Comprises the following Counties in the State of Washington: Okanogan, Ferry, Stevens, Pend Oreille, Lincoln, Spokane, Adams, Whitman, Franklin, Walla Walla, Columbia, Garfield and Asotin.

For legal titles of parishes and diocesan institutions, consult the Chancery Office.

STATISTICAL OVERVIEW

Personnel	
Bishop	1
Retired Bishops	1
Retired Abbots	1
Priests: Diocesan Active in Diocese	50
Priests: Active Outside Diocese	5
Priests: Diocesan in Foreign Missions	1
Priests: Retired, Sick or Absent	33
Number of Diocesan Priests	89
Religious Priests in Diocese	99
Extern Priests in Diocese	5
Ordinations:	
Diocesan Priests	6
Transitional Deacons	2
Permanent Deacons in Diocese	48
Total Brothers	12
Total Sisters	299
Parishes	
Parishes	78
With Resident Pastor:	
Resident Diocesan Priests	43
Resident Religious Priests	4
Without Resident Pastor:	
Administered by Priests	28
Administered by Women Religious	2
Missions	3
Pastoral Centers	1
Professional Ministry Personnel:	
Sisters	2
Lay Ministers	1
Welfare	
Catholic Hospitals	7
Total Assisted	368,925
Health Care Centers	2
Total Assisted	18,011
Homes for the Aged	11
Total Assisted	1,704
Day Care and Extended Day Care Centers	14
Total Assisted	993
Specialized Homes	2
Total Assisted	294
Special Centers for Social Services	4
Total Assisted	17,022
Other Institutions	1
Total Assisted	715
Educational	
Seminaries, Diocesan	1
Students from This Diocese	5
Diocesan Students in Other Seminaries	5
Total Seminarians	10
Colleges and Universities	1
Total Students	4,602
High Schools, Diocesan and Parish	1
Total Students	239
High Schools, Private	2
Total Students	1,035
Elementary Schools, Diocesan and Parish	16
Total Students	3,032
Catechesis/Religious Education:	
High School Students	532
Elementary Students	2,074
Total Students Under Catholic Instruction	11,524
Teachers in the Diocese:	
Priests	5
Scholastics	1
Brothers	4
Sisters	2
Lay Teachers	281
Vital Statistics	
Receptions into the Church:	
Infant Baptism Totals	1,241
Adult Baptism Totals	323
Received into Full Communion	208
First Communions	798
Confirmations	329
Marriages:	
Catholic	281
Interfaith	143
Total Marriages	424
Deaths	1,802
Total Catholic Population	76,691
Total Population	720,569

Former Bishops—Most Rev. A. F. SCHINNER, D.D., cons. Bishop of Superior, July 25, 1905; resigned from that See, Jan. 15, 1913; appt. first Bishop of Spokane, March 18, 1914; resigned Dec. 17, 1925, and made Titular Bishop of Sala; died Feb. 7, 1937.—Most Rev. CHARLES D. WHITE, D.D., ord. Sept. 24, 1910; appt. Dec. 20, 1926; cons. Feb. 24, 1927; died Sept. 25, 1955.—Most Rev. BERNARD J. TOPEL, D.D., Ph.D., appt. coadjutor Bishop Aug. 9, 1955; cons. Sept. 21, 1955; succeeded to to the See Sept. 25, 1955; retired April 11, 1978; died Oct. 22, 1986.—Most Rev. LAWRENCE H. WELSH, D.D., ord. May 26, 1962; appt. Bishop of Spokane Nov. 7, 1978; cons. and installed Dec. 14, 1978; resigned April 17, 1990; appt. Auxiliary of St. Paul-Minneapolis, Nov. 5, 1991; died Jan. 13, 1999.

Vicar General—Rev. Msgr. JOHN M. STEINER, *P.O. Box 1453, Spokane, 99210-1453.* Tel: 509-358-7303; 466-0220; 483-4796.

Catholic Pastoral Center—*W. 1023 Riverside Ave., P.O. Box 1453, Spokane, 99210-1453.* Tel: 509-358-7300; Fax: 509-358-7302. Office Hours: Mon.-Fri. 9-5.

Moderator of the Curia—Rev. Msgr. JOHN M. STEINER, *P.O. Box 1453, Spokane, 99210-1453.* Tel: 509-358-7303.

Chancellor—Rev. MARK PAUTLER, *P.O. Box 1453, Spokane, 99210-1453.* Tel: 509-358-7336.

Archivists—Revs. EDWARD J. KOWRACH; THEODORE BRADLEY, *P.O. Box 1453, Spokane, 99210-1453.* Tel: 509-358-7300.

Diocesan Tribunal—*W. 1023 Riverside Ave., P.O. Box 1453, Spokane, 99210-1453.* Tel: 509-358-7336.

Judicial Vicar—Rev. MARK PAUTLER, J.C.L.

Defensor Vinculi—Rev. Msgr. JOHN M. STEINER; Rev. JOSE LUIS MILLAN.

Secretary—JUDY ELLIFRITT.

Diocesan Consultors/Presbyteral Council—Rev. Msgr. JOHN M. STEINER; Rev. Msgr. WILLIAM VAN OMMEREN; Revs. ED CAFFREY; TOM CASWELL; TOM KHUE; MARK PAUTLER; RICHARD POOLE; SCOTT COBLE, S.J.; W. ROY FLOCH; TY SCHAFF; EUGENE GLATT; ERIC ZUCKERMAN, S.J.

Pastoral Council—Rev. Msgr. JOHN M. STEINER; Rev. TERENCE TULLY; Sr. MAUREEN HEALY, O.P.; RON DALLA; LIDWYNA DALLA; AL GILMORE; KATIE GRANT; DONNA GIVENS; JO GOOLEY; JANICE HOUSE; KATHRYN HILL; JESSICA HENDERSON; JANICE LATHROP; TESSA LEACH; DEBRA LINK; MARTY MARKARIAN; JON MCFARLAND; SHIRLEY PANTALEO; DICK PELKIE; JAMES PRINCE; TRACEY RICE; MAGGIE SANCHEZ; ANNIE SMART; PATTI VAN HEEL; ROGER SMART; JOHN VLAHOVICH; MARTY MARKARIAN; Deacon THOMAS BUCKMAN; MARGARET ALBO.

Diocesan Offices and Directors

Administrative Division: Diocesan Business Affairs—Sr. BERNADETTE BOTCH, S.P., Bishop Sec., *Mailing Address: P.O. Box 1453, Spokane, 99210-1453. 1023 W. Riverside Ave., Spokane, 99210.* Tel: 509-358-7333; Fax: 509-358-7302.

Director of Fiscal Services—MERRILIN FULTON, *P.O. Box 1453, Spokane, 99210-1453.* Tel: 509-358-7320.

Catholic Foundation-Development Office—STEVEN C. KOCHARHOOK, Ph.D, *P.O. Box 1453, Spokane, 99210-1453.* Tel: 509-358-4280.

Computer Department—JERRY M. DUFRESNE, *P.O. Box 1453, Spokane, 99210-1453.* Tel: 509-358-7346.

Administrative Division: Catholic Schools—Bishop's Secretary: Mr. DUANE SCHAFER, Supt., *Office of Education, P.O. Box 1453, Spokane, 99210-1453.* Tel: 509-358-7330.

Administrative Division: Evangelization and Ministries Formation—BETTY NEWSTROM, Bishop's Sec., *P.O. Box 1453, Spokane, 99210-1453.* Tel: 509-358-7311.

Parish Services Office—BETTY NEWSTROM, Dir., *P.O. Box 1453, Spokane, 99210-1453.* Tel: 409-358-7311.

Communications Office—Deacon ERIC MEISFJORD, Dir. & Editor, *Inland Register, P.O. Box 1453, Spokane, 99210-1453.* Tel: 509-358-7340. NANCY LOBERG, Advertising Mgr. Tel: 509-358-7343.

Charismatic Renewal—Rev. DANIEL WETZLER, *St. Paschal Parish, 7404 E. Marietta Ave., Spokane, 99212.* Tel: 509-924-4871.

Ecumenical Relations—Rev. THOMAS CASWELL, *St. Rose of Lima Parish, 460 N. 5th St., Cheney, 99004-2210.* Tel: 509-235-6229.

Spanish Speaking Apostolates—Vacant.

Vietnamese Apostolate—Vietnamese Catholic Community of the Diocese of Spokane, Revs. JOACHIM L. HEIN, *St. Charles Parish, 4515 N. Alberta St., Spokane, 99205-1598.* Tel: 509-327-9573. TOM KHUE, *St. Patrick Parish, 5021 N. Nelson St., Spokane, 99207-6161.* Tel: 509-487-1325.

Vocation Director—Very Rev. DARRIN CONNALL, *Bishop White Seminary, 429 E. Sharp Ave., Spokane, 99202.* Tel: 509-487-3761.

Diocesan Liturgical Commission—Rev. STEVE DUBLINSKI, St. Mary Parish: *304 S. Adams Rd., Spokane, 99216-3112.* Tel: 509-928-3210.

Director of Deacon Formation—Rev. MICHAEL KWIATKOWSKI, *St. Joseph Parish, 3720 E. Colbert Rd., Colbert, 99005-9661.* Tel: 509-466-4991.

Director of Deacons—Deacon JOHN SICILIA, *St. Charles Parish, 4515 N. Alberta St., Spokane, 99205-1598.* Tel: 509-327-9573.

Deacon Council—Deacon DICK MALONE, *117 N. Evergreen Rd., Spokane, 99216.* Tel: 509-922-0484.

Catholic Committee on Scouting—Rev. TERENCE TULLY, Chap., *221 E. Rockwood Blvd., Apt.308, Spokane, 99202-1200.* Tel: 509-458-7674.

Bishop White Seminary—Very Rev. DARRIN CONNALL, Dir. Seminarians & Rector, *429 E. Sharp Ave., Spokane, 99202.* Tel: 509-326-3255.

Administrative Division: Social Ministries/Catholic Charities Diocesan Director—Mrs. DONNA HANSON, Bishop's Sec., *W. 1023 Riverside, P.O. Box 1453, Spokane, 99210-1453.* Tel: 509-358-4250.

Catholic Charities Associate Directors—ROB MCCANN; JEAN O'KEEFE, *W. 1023 Riverside, P.O. Box 1453, Spokane, 99210-1453.* Tel: 509-358-4260.

St. Vincent de Paul Society—E. 2901 Trent Ave., Spokane, 99202. Tel: 509-535-2491.

Censor Liborum—Rev. MICHAEL SAVELESKY, Ph.D., *St. Patrick Church Rectory, 408 W. Poplar St., Walla Walla, 99362-2831.* Tel: 509-525-1602.

Continuing Education of Priests—Rev. PAUL VEVIK, *St. Francis Xavier Parish, 3715 N. Standard St., Spokane, 99207.*

Detention Ministry—Sr. MYRTA ITURRIAGA, S.P., *P.O. Box 1453, Spokane, 99210-1453.* Tel: 509-358-7315.

Director of Cemeteries—DENNIS FAIRBANK, *Catholic Cemeteries of Spokane, P.O. Box 18006, Spokane, 99208-0006.* Tel: 509-467-5496.

Holy Childhood, Pontifical Association—Rev. MARK PAUTLER, *W. 1023 Riverside Ave., P.O. Box 1453, Spokane, 99210.* Tel: 509-358-7336.

Immaculate Heart Retreat Center—Deacon JOHN RUSCHEINSKY, Dir., *6910 S. Ben Burr Rd., Spokane, 99223.* Tel: 509-448-1224.

Priests' Personnel Board—Rev. Msgr. ROBERT PEARSON; Rev. Msgr. FRANK BACH; Revs. DARRIN CONNALL; MARK PAUTLER, Sec. AL GRASHER; JAMES KUHNS, *P.O. Box 1453, Spokane, 99210-1453.* Tel: 509-358-7336.

Propagation of the Faith—Rev. MARK PAUTLER, *W. 1023 Riverside Ave., P.O. Box 1453, Spokane, 99210.* Tel: 509-358-7336.

CLERGY, PARISHES, MISSIONS AND PAROCHIAL SCHOOLS

CITY OF SPOKANE
(Spokane County)

1—CATHEDRAL OF OUR LADY OF LOURDES, Rev. Msgr. James M. Ribble, Ph.D.; Deacons J. Andrew Phelps, M.D.; Richard Skok.
Res., 1115 W. Riverside Ave., 99201. Tel: 509-358-4290; Fax: 509-358-4277.

2—ASSUMPTION OF THE BLESSED VIRGIN MARY, Rev. Joseph W. Bell; Deacons John Crow; Kelly Stewart.
Office: 3624 W. Indian Trail Rd., 99208. Tel: 509-326-0144; 326-6951; Fax: 509-326-0537.
School—Tel: 509-328-1115; Fax: 509-328-7872. Sonia Flores-Davis, Prin.
Sisters 1; Lay Teachers 18; Students 300.
Station—Tum Tum, Our Lady of the Lake, Tel: 509-276-6165.

3—MARY QUEEN, Rt. Rev. Adrian Parcher, O.S.B., Abbot.
Res., 3423 E. Carlisle Ave., 99217-7208. Tel: 509-483-4384.

4—OUR LADY OF FATIMA, Revs. James Kuhns; Victor Blazovics; Deacons John Byrne; Walter Weid.
Office: 1517 E. 33rd Ave., 99203. Tel: 509-747-7213; Fax: 509-747-7217.
School—All Saints Interparochial, (Grades 5-8). Tel: 509-624-5712; Fax: 509-624-7752. Ms. Kathy Hicks, Prin.
Lay Teachers 14; Students 160.

5—SACRED HEART, Rev. Michael Krieg; Deacons Dan Ritchie; Jim Blaine, Pastoral Assoc.
Res., 219 E. Rockwood Blvd., 99202. Tel: 509-747-5810; Fax: 509-747-5033.

6—ST. ALOYSIUS, Revs. Erik Zuckerman, S.J.; Christopher Weekly, S.J.; Deacon Jack Back; Mr. Donald Weber, Pastoral Admin.
Res., 330 E. Boone Ave., 99202. Tel: 509-323-5896; Fax: 509-323-5892.
School—611 E. Mission Ave., 99202. Tel: 509-489-7825. Joanne Duffy, Prin.
Montessori Education Center—Marta Schollenberger, Dir.
Lay Teachers 13; Students 300.

7—ST. ANN, Linda Kobe-Smith, Admin.
Church—2120 E. First Ave., 99202. Tel: 509-535-3031.

8—ST. ANTHONY, Rev. Msgr. John Donnelly.
Res., 2320 N. Cedar St., 99205. Tel: 509-327-1162; Fax: 509-328-4128.
School—Trinity Interparochial School. Serving St. Anthony and St. Joseph. Tel: 509-327-9369. Mike Trudeau, Prin.
Lay Teachers 8; Students 143.
Educare Center—.
Lay Teachers 7; Students 40.

9—ST. AUGUSTINE, Rev. Msgr. Robert A. Pearson; Rev. Richard Semple; Deacons Kenneth Dunlap; Gary Cooper, Pastoral Assoc.
Res., 428 W. 19th Ave., 99203. Tel: 509-747-4421; Fax: 509-747-9086.
School—Cataldo Catholic Interparochial, Tel: 509-624-8759; Fax: 509-624-8763.
Lay Teachers 24; Students 379.

10—ST. CHARLES, Rev. Hein Joachim Le Quang; Deacon John F. Sicilia.
Res., 4515 N. Alberta St., 99205. Tel: 509-327-9573; Fax: 509-327-9574.
School—Tel: 509-327-9575; Fax: 509-325-9353. Dr. Marquita Yriarte, Prin.
Lay Teachers 16; Students 240.

11—ST. FRANCIS OF ASSISI, FRIARS, Revs. Brian V. Flynn, O.F.M.; Sebastian Drake, O.F.M.
Res., W. 1104 Heroy Ave., 99205. Tel: 509-325-1321.

12—ST. FRANCIS XAVIER, Rev. Paul Vevik.
Office: 3715 N. Standard St., 99207. Tel: 509-487-6363, Ext. 200; Fax: 509-487-6363.

13—ST. JOHN VIANNEY, Rev. Tyrone J. Schaff; Deacons Derwood Braungardt; David Dudinsky. In res., Rev. Charles D. Skok.
Office: 503 N. Walnut Rd., 99206. Tel: 509-926-5428; Fax: 509-922-5282.
School—(Grades PreK-8) N. 501 Walnut Rd., 99206. Tel: 509-926-7987; Fax: 509-891-9030. Dr. Judith Morbeck, Prin.
Lay Teachers 11; Students 166.

14—ST. JOSEPH, Sr. Irene Knopes, S.N.J.M., Parish Admin.; Rev. Mark Pautler.
Res., 1503 W. Dean Ave., 99201. Tel: 509-328-4841; Fax: 509-328-4841.
School—Trinity Interparochial School. (See listing under St. Anthony).

15—ST. MARY, Revs. Steven L. Dublinski; Thomas Connolly; Deacons Richard Malone; Cary Heth.
Res., 304 S. Adams Rd., 99216. Tel: 509-928-3210; Fax: 509-928-3215.
School—14601 E. 4th Ave., 99216. Tel: 509-924-4300. Mrs. Carol Speltz, Prin.
Lay Teachers 13; Students 242.

16—ST. PASCHAL, Rev. Daniel E. Wetzler; Deacon John Crandall.
Res., 7404 E. Marietta Ave., 99212. Tel: 509-924-4871; Fax: 509-924-8731.
School—N. 2521 Park Rd., 99212. Tel: 509-924-5090; Fax: 509-924-6106. Sr. Loretta Giampietri, F.S.P.A., Prin.
Sisters 1; Lay Teachers 6; Students 83.
Educare Center—Tel: 509-922-7616. Dawn Davis, Dir. & Prog. Supvr.
Lay Teachers 12; Students 100.

17—ST. PATRICK, Rev. Thomas L.T. Khue; Deacons John Gress; Mike Samuels.
Res., 5021 N. Nelson St., 99207. Tel: 509-487-1325; Fax: 509-487-1325.
School—Tel: 509-487-2830. Randy Wallace, Ph.D., Prin.
Lay Teachers 13; Students 206.
Convent—5008 N. Lacey St., 99207. Tel: 509-487-1166.

18—ST. PETER, Rev. Eugene Tracy; Deacons Roy Dahl; John Ruscheinsky.
Res., 3520 E. 18th Ave., 99223-3814. Tel: 509-534-2227; Fax: 509-534-5522.
School—All Saints Interparochial, (Grades K-4). Tel: 509-534-1098; Fax: 509-534-1529. Ms. Kathy Hicks, Prin.
Lay Teachers 10; Students 249.

19—ST. THOMAS MORE, Rev. Msgr. John M. Steiner; Rev. Jose Luis Millan; Don McKenzie, Pastoral Assoc.
Res., N. 8112 Howard Dr., 99208. Tel: 509-466-0220; Fax: 509-466-0220.
School—Doug Banks, Prin. Lay Teachers 10; Students 258.

OUTSIDE THE CITY OF SPOKANE

Brewster, Okanogan Co., Sacred Heart, Rev. Pat Kerst; Deacon Wynn Webster.
Res., P.O. Box 548, 98812. Tel: 509-689-2931; Fax: 509-689-2931.

Cheney, Spokane Co., St. Rose of Lima, Rev. Thomas C. Caswell; Deacon Eric Meisfjord.
Res., 460 N. Fifth St., 99004. Tel: 509-235-6229.

Chewelah, Stevens Co., St. Mary of the Rosary, Rev. Albert Grasher, Jr.
Res., P.O. Box 188, Valley, 99181. Tel: 509-937-2452.
Church—504 E. Main St., P.O. Box 26, 99109. Tel: 509-935-8028; Fax: 509-953-8028. [CEM]

Clarkston, Asotin Co., Holy Family, Rev. Leonard Forsmann.
Res., 917 Chestnut St., 99403. Tel: 509-758-6102; Fax: 509-758-4997. [CEM]
School—(Grades PreK-6). Tel: 509-758-6621; Fax: 509-758-7025. Mrs. Sharon Clizer, Prin.
Lay Teachers 7; Students 140.
Educare Preschool—Tel: 509-758-2737.
Students 30.

Clayton, Stevens Co., St. Joseph, Rev. Edward F. Caffrey.
Mailing Address: 316 N. Main St., P.O. Box 749, Deer Park, 99006. Tel: 509-276-2948.

Colbert, Spokane Co., St. Joseph, Rev. Michael Kwiatkowski; Deacon John Riherd.
Res., 3720 E. Colbert Rd., 99005. Tel: 509-466-4991; Fax: 509-466-4992.

Colfax, Whitman Co., St. Patrick, Rev. Felix P. Lorge.
Res., 1108 S. Main St., 99111. Tel: 509-397-3921.

Colton, Whitman Co., St. Gall, Rev. Patrick MacMahon.
Res., P.O. Box 108, 99113. Tel: 509-229-3548. [CEM]
School—Guardian Angel-St. Boniface Interparochial, Tel: 509-299-3579. Tami Druttel, Prin.
Lay Teachers 4; Students 59.

Colville, Stevens Co., Immaculate Conception, Rev. Robert J. McNeese.
Res., 320 N. Maple St., 99114. Tel: 509-684-6223; Fax: 509-684-8084.

Connell, Franklin Co., St. Vincent, Rev. Richard Poole.
Res., P.O. Box 1030, 99326. Tel: 509-234-2262; Fax: 509-234-0295.

Coulee Dam, Okanogan Co., St. Benedict. Closed. Sacramental records maintained at St. Henry's, Grand Coulee (Diocese of Yakima).

Curlew, Ferry Co., St. Patrick, Rev. George H. Morbeck.
Res., P.O. Box 333, Republic, 99166. Tel: 509-775-3935.

Cusick, Kalispel Indian Reservation, Our Lady of Sorrows, Rev. Edward Marier.
Res., 612 W. First St., Box C, Newport, 99156. Tel: 509-447-4231.

Davenport, Lincoln Co., Immaculate Conception. Unassigned.
Res., 1310 Adams, P.O. Box 910, 99122. Tel: 509-725-1761. [CEM]

Dayton, Columbia Co., St. Joseph, Rev. Fernando Maldonado; Deacon Mike Breier.
Res., R.R. 1, Box 4, Pomeroy, 99347. Tel: 509-843-3801.
Church—112 S. First St., 99328-1307. Tel: 509-382-2311.

Deer Park, Spokane Co., St. Mary's Presentation, Rev. Edward F. Caffrey.
Res., 316 N. Main St., P.O. Box 749, 99006. Tel: 509-276-2948. [CEM]

Eltopia, Franklin Co., St. Paul, Rev. Richard Poole.
Res., 14181 Glade North Rd., 99330. Tel: 509-297-4371.

Ford, Stevens Co., St. Philip Benizi, Rev. Jake Morton, S.J.
Res., Indian-Spokane Reservation, P.O. Box 214, Wellpinit, 99040. Tel: 509-258-7233.

Harrington, Lincoln Co., St. Francis of Assisi. Unassigned.
Res., P.O. Box 166, 99134. Tel: 509-253-4310.

Inchelium, Ferry Co., St. Michael's Mission, Rev. Jake Morton, S.J.; Jenny-Ann Edgen, Admin.; Deacon Alvin Toulou.
Res., P.O. Box 122, 99138. Tel: 509-722-4592.

Ione, Pend Oreille Co., St. Bernard, Rev. Edward Marier.
Mailing Address: Box 731, 99139. Tel: 509-447-4231.
Res., 612 W. First St., P.O. Box C, Newport, 99156. Tel: 509-447-4231.

Keller, Ferry Co., St. Rose of Lima, Rev. Robert Erickson, S.J.
Res., P.O. Box 70, Nespelem, 99155. Tel: 509-634-4249.

Kettle Falls, Stevens Co., Sacred Heart of Jesus, Rev. Robert McNeese.
Mailing Address: P.O. Box 303, 99141. Tel: 509-738-2356.

Lacrosse, Whitman Co., St. Joseph, Rev. Felix P. Lorge.
Res., St. Patrick Parish, 1018 S. Main St., Colfax, 99111. Tel: 509-397-3921.

Lind, Adams Co., St. Ambrose, Rev. James V. McGreevy.
Res., 404 E. Fifth Ave., Ritzville, 99169. Tel: 509-659-0437.

Medical Lake, Spokane Co., St. Anne, Rev. John P. Krier (GF); Deacon Robert King.
Res., 708 E. Lake St., P.O. Box 125, 99022. Tel: 509-299-3585; Fax: 509-299-9219.

Metaline Falls, Pend Oreille Co., St. Joseph, Rev. Edward Marier.
Mailing Address: P.O. Box 417, 99153. Tel: 509-446-2651.
Res., 612 W. First St., P.O. Box C, Newport, 99156. Tel: 509-447-4231.

Nespelem, Okanogan Co., Sacred Heart Mission, Rev. Robert Erickson, S.J.
Res., P.O. Box 70, 99155. Tel: 509-634-4249. [CEM]

Newport, Pend Oreille Co., St. Anthony, Rev. Edward Marier.
Res., 612 W. First St., P.O. Box C, 99156. Tel: 509-447-4231.

Northport, Stevens Co., Pure Heart of Mary, Rev. Robert McNeese.
Res., P.O. Box 29, 99157. Tel: 509-684-6223; Fax: 509-684-6223.

Oakesdale, Whitman Co., St. Catherine of Alexandria, Rev. Eugene Glatt.
Res., P.O. Box 8, Rosalia, 99170. Tel: 509-523-4011.

Odessa, Lincoln Co., St. Joseph, Rev. W. Roy Floch.
Res. & Mailing Address:—P.O. Box 106, Wilbur, 99185. Tel: 509-647-2380.

Okanogan-Omak, Okanogan Co., Our Lady of the Valley, Rev. Rory Pittstick.
Res., Rte. 2, 2511 N. Elmway, Okanogan, 98840. Tel: 509-422-5049; Fax: 509-422-5049.

Omak, Okanogan Co., St. Mary Mission, Rev. Charles Peterson, S.J.; Bettejo Passalaqua, Pastoral Assoc.
Res., Rte. 2, P.O. Box 66A, 98841. Tel: 509-826-6401. [CEM]
St. Joseph, Rev. Charles Peterson, S.J.
Mailing Address: 6th & Jackson, Rte. 2, P.O. Box 12, 98841.
Res., 323 Edmonds, 98841. Tel: 509-826-6401.

Oroville, Okanogan Co., Immaculate Conception, Rev. Steven A. Werner.
Res., 1715 Main St., P.O. Box 2270, 98844. Tel: 509-476-2110; Fax: 509-476-2110.

Othello, Adams Co., Sacred Heart, Rev. Timothy Hays; Deacons Antonio Beraza; Joel Pruneda.
Res., 616 E. Juniper St., 99344. Tel: 509-488-5653.

Otis Orchards, Spokane Co., St. Joseph, Rev. James Mangan; Deacon Tom Heafey.
Res., 4521 N. Arden Rd., 99027-9358. Tel: 509-926-7133; Fax: 509-926-9454.

Pasco, Franklin Co., St. Patrick, Rev. Msgr. Pedro Ramirez-Alejos; Revs. John Birk; Daniel Barnett; Miguel Mejia; Deacons Andres Espinoza; Robert Kalinowski; Gary Franz; Juanita Contreras, Pastoral Assoc.
Res., 1320 W. Henry, 99301. Tel: 509-547-8841; Fax: 509-547-3604, Ext. 22.
School—1016 N. 14th Ave., 99301. Tel: 509-547-7261. Rev. Thomas Burnell, S.J., Prin.
Lay Teachers 9; Students 150.

Pomeroy, Garfield Co., Holy Rosary, Rev. Fernando Maldonada.
Mailing Address: R.R.1, P.O. Box 4, 99347-9702.
Res., 634 High St., 99347. Tel: 509-843-3801. [CEM]

Pullman, Whitman Co., Sacred Heart, Rev. Edgar Borchardt.
Office: 440 N.E. Ash St., 99163. Tel: 509-332-5312; Fax: 509-334-0575.

Reardan, Lincoln Co., St. Michael. Unassigned.
Mailing Address: P.O. Box 451, Rearden, 99029. Tel: 509-725-1761.

Republic, Ferry Co., Immaculate Conception, Rev. George H. Morbeck.
Res., 756 S. Portland, 99166. Tel: 509-775-3935.

Ritzville, Adams Co., St. Agnes, Rev. James V. McGreevy.
Res., 404 E. Fifth Ave., 99169. Tel: 509-659-0437.

Rockford, Spokane Co., St. Joseph, Rev. Steven L. Dublinski; Deacon Donald Bentley.
Res., P.O. Box 54, 99030. Tel: 509-291-3481.

Rosalia, Whitman Co., Holy Rosary, Rev. Eugene Glatt.
Res., 600 N. Whitman Ave., P.O. Box 8, 99170. Tel: 509-523-4011.

St. John, Whitman Co., Our Lady of Perpetual Help, Rev. Eugene Glatt.
Mailing Address: P.O. Box 325, 99171.
Res., P.O. Box 8, Rosalia, 99170. Tel: 509-523-4011.

Sprague, Lincoln Co., Mary Queen of Heaven, Rev. James V. McGreevy.
Res., 404 E. Fifth Ave., Ritzville, 99160. Tel: 509-659-0437. [CEM]

Springdale, Stevens Co., Sacred Heart, Rev. Albert Grasher, Jr.
Res., P.O. Box 188, Valley, 99181. Tel: 509-937-2452.

Tekoa, Whitman Co., Sacred Heart, Rev. Eugene Glatt.
Res., P.O. Box 8, Rosalia, 99170. Tel: 509-523-4011. [CEM]

Tonasket, Okanogan Co., Holy Rosary, Rev. Steven A. Werner.
Res. & Mailing Address: 1715 Main St., P.O. Box 2270, Oroville, 98844. Tel: 509-476-2110; Fax: 509-476-2110.

Twisp, Okanogan Co., St. Genevieve, Rev. Pat Kerst; Deacon Wynn Webster.
Res., P.O. Box 6, 98856. Tel: 509-997-4201.

Uniontown, Whitman Co., St. Boniface, Rev. Patrick MacMahon.
Res., P.O. Box 108, Colton, 99113. Tel: 509-229-3548. [CEM]
School—Guardian Angel-St. Boniface Interparochial. See St. Gall, Colton.

Usk, Pend Oreille Co., St. Jude, Rev. Edward Marier.
Res., 612 W. First St., P.O. Box C, Newport, 99156. Tel: 509-447-4231.

Valley, Stevens Co., Holy Ghost, Rev. Albert Grasher, Jr.
Res., P.O. Box 188, 99181. Tel: 509-937-2452.
Station—Jump-off Joe, Stevens Co., St. Joseph.

Waitsburg, Walla Walla Co., St. Mark, Rev. Fernando Maldonado; Deacon Mike Breier.
Office: 112 S. 1st St., Dayton, 99328-1307. Tel: 509-382-2311.
Res., R.R. 1, Box 4, Pomeroy, 99347. Tel: 509-843-3801.

Walla Walla, Walla Walla Co., Assumption of the Blessed Virgin Mary, Rev. Otto Koltzenburg; Sr. Helen Mason, S.P., Pastoral Assoc.; Deacon Dale Shaeffer.
Res., 2098 E. Alder St., 99362. Tel: 509-525-8163.
School—Assumption Interparochial, Tel: 509-525-9283. Mrs. Michele Acock, Prin.
Lay Teachers 13; Students 204.
St. Francis of Assisi, Revs. Michael Savelesky, Ph.D.; Jose Luis Hernandez; Sr. Sharon Bongiorno, F.S.P.A., Pastoral Min.
Res., 722 W. Alder St., 99362. Tel: 509-525-1663; Fax: 509-529-7849.
Sisters 3.
St. Patrick, Revs. Michael Savelesky, Ph.D.; Jose Luis Hernandez; Deacon Olegario Reyes, Pastoral Assoc.
Office and Res.: 408 W. Poplar St., 99362.

Washtunca, Adams Co., Holy Trinity, Rev. James V. McGreevy.
Res., 404 E. Fifth St., Ritzville, 99169. Tel: 509-659-0437.

Wellpinit, Stevens Co., Sacred Heart, Rev. Jake Morton, S.J.
Res., Indian-Spokane Reservation, P.O. Box 214, 99040. Tel: 509-258-7233. [CEM]

Westend, Stevens Co., Our Lady of Lourdes, Rev. Jake Morton, S.J.
Res., Indian-Spokane Reservation, P.O. Box 214, Wellpinit, 99040. Tel: 509-258-7233.

Wilbur, Lincoln Co., Sacred Heart, Rev. W. Roy Floch.
Res., P.O. Box 106, 99185. Tel: 509-647-2380.

Chaplains of Public Institutions

SPOKANE. *U.S. Veterans Hospital*. Rev. Theodore F.X. Bradley.

WALLA WALLA. *U.S. Veterans Hospital*. Vacant.
Washington State Penitentiary. Served by priests of Walla Walla.

Special Ministry:
Reverend Fathers—
Birk, John, Our Lady of Lourdes Health Center, Pasco
Venneri, Michael D., Sacred Heart Medical Center, Spokane

On Duty Outside the Diocese:
Reverend Fathers—
Baronti, David, Guatamala
Codd, Kevin, American College, Louvain
Lucatero, Heliodoro, University of Notre Dame
McGrann, John E., St. Rose of Lima, Eugene, OR
Turner, Robert D., Mt. Angel Seminary, St. Benedict, OR

Absent on Leave:
Reverend Fathers—
Boulden, Garry
Root, Richard

Retired:
Reverend Monsignors—
Bach, Frank J., 1306 N. Blake Rd., Unit B, Spokane, WA 99216-1149
Mertens, Arthur, 221 E. Rockwood Blvd., No. 320, Spokane, WA 99202
Rosage, David E., 221 E. Rockwood Blvd., No. 222, Spokane, WA 99202
Van Ommeren, William, Immaculate Heart Retreat, 6910 S. Ben Burr Rd., Spokane, WA 99203-1899
Reverend Fathers—
Barry, Bernard J., Colonial Court, 12016 E. Cataldo Ave., Spokane, WA 99206
Beaver, Reinard W., 1101 Powell St., Steilacoon, WA 98388
Bradley, Theodore F.X., 700 W. 7th Ave., Apt. 801, Spokane, WA 99204
Brennan, William J., 2030 Delaware, Walla Walla, WA 99362
Donnelly, Sean, 1 Parkview, Freshford Rd., Kilkenny, Ireland
Dugan, William M., 272 Kennedy St., No. 48, Chula Vista, CA 92011
Eis, Charles, 9202 Irvington Ave., San Diego, CA 92123-3129
Grant, James, 217 W. Spokane Falls, No. 1802, Spokane, WA 99201
Hanley, William, Killula, Newmarket-on-Fergus, Claire Co., Ireland
Haspedis, George, 3916 Salder Cir., Spokane, WA 99228-7300
Helfenstein, Maurice R., 14819 E. Mission, Spokane, WA 99216-1960
Hullings, Clifford, 3110 E. Chattaroy Rd., No. 43, Chattaroy, WA 99003
Kelley, Joseph, 221 E. Rockford Blvd., No. 104, Spokane, WA 99202-1200
Kowrach, Edward, 530 Flora Rd., Veradale, WA 99037
McCabe, George V., 12016 E. Cataldo Ave., Spokane, WA 99206-4963
O'Brien, John P., P.O. Box 1808, Santa Rosa, CA 95402
O'Malley, James J., Kilsallagh, Westport, Mayo Co., Ireland
Pash, Joseph, 221 E. Rockwood Blvd., No. 204, Spokane, WA 99202
Rompa, John, 4423 S. Sunny Creek Dr., Spokane, WA 99204-8460
Sand, John, 634 High St., Pomeroy, WA 99347
Schoffelmeer, Arnold L., N. Findlay Rd., Box 36123, Deer Park, WA 99006
Schwemin, Ralph H., 3915 N. Washington St., Spokane, WA 99205
Tully, Terence, 221 E. Rockwood Blvd., No. 308, Spokane, WA 99202
Verdoon, Cornelius, Colonial Court, 12016 E. Cataldo Ave., Spokane, WA 99206
Wenning, Paul A., 7423 N. Laurelhurst Dr., Spokane, WA 99208
Westbrook, J. Severyn, 221 E. Rockwood Blvd., No. 318, Spokane, WA 99202
Wietensteiner, Joseph M., P.O. Box 8087, Spokane, WA 99203

Permanent Deacons:
Back, Jack, St. Aloysius, Spokane; Prison Ministry
Barnufsky, Stephen, Retirement Residences
Bentley, Donald, St. Joseph, Rockfort
Beraza, Antonio, Sacred Heart, Othello
Blaine, Jim, St. Mary, Spokane
Braungardt, Derwood, St. John Vianney, Spokane
Breier, Michael, St. Joseph, Dayton; St. Mark, Waitsburg
Buckman, Thomas, Kateri Institute
Byrne, John, Our Lady of Fatima, Spokane
Cooper, Gary, St. Augustine, Spokane
Crandall, John, St. Paschal, Spokane
Crow, John, Assumption Parish, Spokane

Dahl, Roy, St. Peter, Spokane
Dalecki, Robert, On Duty Outside the Diocese
Dudinsky, David, St. John Vianney, Spokane
Dunlap, Kenneth, St. Augustine, Spokane
Espinoza, Andres, St. Patrick, Pasco
Farrell, Daniel, St. Henry, Grand Coulee
Franz, Gary, St. Patrick, Pasco
Gerber, Vincent, (Retired)
Gress, John, St. Patrick's Parish, Spokane
Heafy, Thomas, St. Joseph, Ottis Orchards
Heath, Cary, St. Mary, Spokane
Kalinowski, Robert, St. Patrick, Pasco
King, Robert, St. Anne, Medical Lake
Lukach, George, Our Lady of the Lake, Tum Tum
Mackin, Francis, Sitka, AL
Malone, Richard, St. Mary, Spokane
Martinez, Gonzalo, St. Mary's, Spokane
McKenzie, Gerald, (Retired)
Meisfjord, Eric, St. Rose of Lima, Cheney
Murphy, James E., Sacred Heart Medical Center, Spokane
Phelps, J. Andrew, Our Lady of Lourdes, Spokane
Polensky, Hugh, Sacred Heart Medical Center, Spokane
Prawdzik, Stephen, Fairchild AFB; Holy Family, Clarkston
Pruneda, Joel, Sacred Heart, Othello
Reyes, Olegario, St. Patrick, Walla Walla
Riherd, John, St. Joseph, Colbert
Ritchie, Dan, Sacred Heart, Spokane
Ruscheinsky, John, St. Peter, Spokane
Samuel, Mike, St. Patrick's, Spokane
Sando, William, (Retired)
Shaeffer, Dale, Assumption, Walla Walla
Sicilia, John F., St. Charles, Spokane
Skok, Richard, Cathedral of Our Lady of Lourdes, Spokane
Stewart, Kelly, Assumption, Spokane
Toulou, Alvin, St. Michael, Inchelium
Webster, Wynn, Sacred Heart, Brewster
Weid, Walter, Our Lady of Fatima, Spokane
Wilson, Charles, Port Angeles

INSTITUTIONS LOCATED IN THE DIOCESE

[A] SEMINARIES, DIOCESAN

SPOKANE. *Bishop White Seminary*, E. 429 Sharp Ave., 99202. Tel: 509-326-3255; Fax: 509-326-3761.
E-mail: bwsgonzaga.edu
Very Rev. Darrin Connall, Rector; Rev. Leo McKernan (Scranton), Dir. of Spiritual Formation. Students 5.

[B] COLLEGES AND UNIVERSITIES

SPOKANE. *Gonzaga University*, 99258. Tel: 509-328-4220
For a complete listing, refer to the Colleges and Universities section.
The Ministry Institute, E. 405 Sinto Ave., 99202-1849. Tel: 509-328-8332; Fax: 509-325-4011
For a complete listing, refer to the Colleges and Universities section.

[C] HIGH SCHOOLS, INTERPAROCHIAL

WALLA WALLA. *Walla Walla Catholic School System*. (Grades Educare-12), E. 919 Sumach, 99362. Tel: 509-525-3030; Fax: 509-527-0361.
E-mail: desales@wwics.com
Mrs. Michele Acock, Prin. (Grades K-5); John Lesko, Admin & Prin. (Grades 6-12). Lay Teachers 35; Students: Elementary 215; High School 239.

[D] HIGH SCHOOLS, PRIVATE

SPOKANE. *Gonzaga Preparatory School*, E. 1224 Euclid Ave., 99207. Tel: 509-483-7737; Fax: 509-483-3124.
E-mail: gonzaga@mail.gntech.com
Mr. John Traynor, Pres.; Mr. Al Falkner, Prin.; Revs. J.K. Adams, Rector; Robert A. Goebel, S.J.; Richard R. Mercy, S.J.; Joseph Showalter, S.J.; Thomas Lamanna, S.J. Priests 2; Scholastics 1; Lay Teachers 53; Students 984.

TRI CITIES. *Tri Cities Prep, A Catholic High School*. (Grades 9-11), P.O. Box 4744, 99302-4744. Tel: 509-546-2465; Fax: 509-546-2490. Rev. Thomas Burnell, S.J., Prin. & Pres. Priests 1; Lay Teachers 7; Students 51.

[E] INTERPAROCHIAL GRADE SCHOOLS

SPOKANE. *All Saints School*. (Grades 5-8), E. 1428 33rd Ave., 99203. Tel: 509-624-5712.
E-mail: allsaint@spkn.uswest.net
Kathy Hicks, Prin.
All Saints Primary. (Grades K-4), E. 3406 18th Ave., 99223. Tel: 509-534-1098. Kathy Hicks, Prin. Serving St. Peter, St. Ann, and Our Lady of Fatima Parishes. Lay Teachers 24; Students 410.
Cataldo Catholic School. (Grades K-8), W. 455-18th Ave., 99203. Tel: 509-624-8759.
E-mail: cataldoc@spokane.net
Mr. Richard Pelkie, Prin. Serving St. Augustine, Sacred Heart, and Our Lady of Lourdes Parishes. Lay Teachers 24; Students 375.
Trinity School. (Grades K-8), W. 1306 Montgomery Ave., 99205. Tel: 509-327-9369. Mr. Michael S. Trudeau, Prin.
Serving St. Anthony and St. Joseph Parishes. Lay Teachers 8; Students 183.

COLTON. *Guardian Angel-St. Boniface School*, P.O. Box 48, 99113. Tel: 509-229-3579. Tami Druftel, Prin. Serving St. Gall and St. Boniface Parishes. Lay Teachers 4; Students 59.

WALLA WALLA. *Assumption Elementary School*. (Grades PreK-5), E. 2066 Alder St., 99362. Tel: 509-525-9283.
E-mail: assumption@wwics.com
Mrs. Michele Acock, Prin. & Bldg. Admin.
Serving Assumption, St. Francis of Assisi, and St. Patrick Parishes. Lay Teachers 12; Students 255.
Walla Walla Catholic School System. See listing under High Schools, Interparochial.

[F] GENERAL HOSPITALS

SPOKANE. *Holy Family Adult Day Health* 6018 N. Astor, 99207. Tel: 509-482-2475; Fax: 509-482-2490.
For a complete listing, refer to the Hospitals section.
Holy Family Hospital, N. 5633 Lidgerwood St., 99207. Tel: 509-482-0111
For a complete listing, refer to the Hospitals section.
Sacred Heart Medical Center, W. 101 Eighth Ave., TAF-C9, 99220. Tel: 509-455-3131
For a complete listing, refer to the Hospitals section.

CHEWELAH. *St. Joseph's Hospital of Chewelah*, E. 500 Webster, 99109. Tel: 509-935-8211; Fax: 509-935-5257
For a complete listing, refer to the Hospitals section.

COLVILLE. *Mount Carmel Hospital*, 982 E. Columbia, Box 351, 99114. Tel: 509-684-2561
For a complete listing, refer to the Hospitals section.

DEER PARK. *Deer Park Health Center and Hospital* Mailing Address: 5633 N. Lidgerwood Spokane, 99207.
For a complete listing, refer to the Hospitals section.

PASCO. *Lourdes Medical Center*, 520 N. Fourth Ave., P.O. Box 2568, 99302. Tel: 509-547-7704; Fax: 509-546-2291
For a complete listing, refer to the Hospitals section.

WALLA WALLA. *St. Mary Medical Center*, 401 W. Poplar St., 99362. Tel: 509-525-3320; Fax: 509-522-5950
For a complete listing, refer to the Hospitals section.

[G] PROTECTIVE INSTITUTIONS (Catholic Social Service)

SPOKANE. *Catholic Charities, Inc.*, W. 1023 Riverside Ave., P.O. Box 1453, 99210-1453. Tel: 509-358-4250; Fax: 509-358-4259
For a complete listing, refer to the Special Care Facilities section.
Guse Summit View Mailing Address: P.O. Box 1453, 99210-1453.
For a complete listing, refer to the Special Care Facilities section.
House of Charity, 32 W. Pacific, P.O. Box 1453, 99210-1453. Tel: 509-624-7821
For a complete listing, refer to the Special Care Facilities section.
Miryam's House, W. 1805 Ninth St., 99204
For a complete listing, refer to the Special Care Facilities section.
Morning Star Boys' Ranch, Inc., P.O. Box 8087, 99203. Tel: 509-448-1411
For a complete listing, refer to the Special Care Facilities section.
St. Anne's Children's Home, N. 707 Cedar St., 99201-1999. Tel: 509-325-7672
For a complete listing, refer to the Special Care Facilities section.
St. Joseph's Counseling Center, N. 1016 Superior St., 99202. Tel: 509-483-6495.
E-mail: sjfc@icehouse.net
For a complete listing, refer to the Special Care Facilities section.
St. Margaret's Shelter, P.O. Box 1453, 99210. Tel: 509-624-9288; Fax: 509-624-1461
For a complete listing, refer to the Special Care Facilities section.
St. Vincent de Paul Social Service Office, E. 2901 Trent Ave., 99202. Tel: 509-534-2824 (Social Svc.); 535-2491 (Main Store & Office)
For a complete listing, refer to the Special Care Facilities section.
St. Vincent de Paul Society, E. 2901 Trent Ave., 99202. Tel: 509-534-2824
For a complete listing, refer to the Special Care Facilities section.
Transitional Living Center, 3128 N. Hemlock, 92204.
E-mail: tlc@cet.com
For a complete listing, refer to the Special Care Facilities section.
Women's Drop In Center, 218 S. Howard, 92204-1419
For a complete listing, refer to the Special Care Facilities section.

CHEWELAH. *DominiCare*, 303 E. King St., P.O. Box 1070, 99109
For a complete listing, refer to the Special Care Facilities section.

CLARKSTON. *Lewis and Clark District Council of St. Vincent de Paul* Office, 604 Second St., 99403. Tel: 509-758-7061; Fax: 509-758-9545.
For a complete listing, refer to the Special Care Facilities section.

COLVILLE. *The Rhodena, A Washington Non-profit Organization* Mailing Address: P.O. Box 1453 Spokane, 99210-1453.
For a complete listing, refer to the Special Care Facilities section.

DAYTON. *St. Vincent de Paul Store*, 257 E. Main St., 99328. Tel: 509-382-4146
For a complete listing, refer to the Special Care Facilities section.

PASCO. *St. Vincent de Paul Store*, 1120 W. Sylvester, 99301. Tel: 509-547-2341; Fax: 509-547-7804
For a complete listing, refer to the Special Care Facilities section.

WALLA WALLA. *Catholic Children and Family Service*, 5 W. Alder St., Ste. 333, 99362. Tel: 509-525-0572; Fax: 509-525-0576
For a complete listing, refer to the Special Care Facilities section.
St. Vincent de Paul Store, 308 W. Main St., 99362. Tel: 509-525-3903 (Store); 529-6778 (Office)
For a complete listing, refer to the Special Care Facilities section.

[H] SENIOR CITIZEN HOUSING

SPOKANE. *Cathedral Plaza Apartments*, W. 1120 Sprague Ave., 99204
For a complete listing, refer to the Special Care Facilities section.
The Delaney, W. 242 Riverside Ave., 99201
For a complete listing, refer to the Special Care Facilities section.
Fahy Garden Apartments, W. 1403 Dean Ave., 99201
For a complete listing, refer to the Special Care Facilities section.
Fahy West Apartments, W. 1523 Dean Ave., 99201
For a complete listing, refer to the Special Care Facilities section.
The O'Malley, E. 707 Mission Ave., 99202
For a complete listing, refer to the Special Care Facilities section.
Rockwood Lane / Court, E. 221 Rockwood Blvd., 99202
For a complete listing, refer to the Special Care Facilities section.
Senior Citizen Housing, W. 242 Riverside Ave., 99201. Tel: 509-624-6060
For a complete listing, refer to the Special Care Facilities section.

CLARKSTON. *Austen Manor*, 1222 Chestnut St., 99403
For a complete listing, refer to the Special Care Facilities section.

PULLMAN. *Pioneer Square*, S.E. 220 Kamiaken, 99163
For a complete listing, refer to the Special Care Facilities section.

WALLA WALLA. *Garden Court Apartments*, Sixth & Alder Sts., 99362
For a complete listing, refer to the Special Care Facilities section.
Mike Foye Apartments Mailing Address: P.O. Box 1453 Spokane, 99210.
For a complete listing, refer to the Special Care Facilities section.

[I] HOMES FOR AGED

SPOKANE. *St. Joseph Care Center*, E. 17 Eighth Ave., 99202. Tel: 509-474-5678
For a complete listing, refer to the Special Care Facilities section.

[J] MONASTERIES AND RESIDENCES OF PRIESTS AND BROTHERS

SPOKANE. *Regis Community*, N. 1107 Astor St., 99202. Tel: 509-328-4220; Fax: 509-484-2818. Most Rev. Robert L. Whelan, S.J. (Fairbanks), (Retired); Revs. Robert L. Fitts, S.J., Supr.; Thomas Colgan, S.J.; William C. Dibb, S.J.; James P. Goodwin, S.J.; Dominic W. Doyle, S.J.; Anton P. Jahner, S.J.; John S. Harrington, S.J.; Paul P. Luger, S.J.; James McCready, S.J.; William C. Hausmann, S.J.; Edmund J. Robinson, S.J.; Robert J. Schlim, S.J.; Gordon L. Keys, S.J.; Frank D. Masterson, S.J.; John D. McCluskey, S.J.; Eric Zuckerman, S.J.; John Schwarz, S.J.; John R. Thatcher, S.J.; Bros. James J. Lee, S.J.; Fenton J. Melia, S.J.; William L. Yami, S.J.; George A. McMonagle, S.J.

[K] CONVENTS AND RESIDENCES FOR SISTERS

SPOKANE. *Convent of the Holy Names*, 2911 W. Fort George Wright Dr., 99224. Tel: 509-328-4310; Fax: 509-328-9824.
E-mail: snjmchn1@sisna.com
Web site: www.snjm.org
Sisters of the Holy Names of Jesus and Mary. Sr. Ann Pizelo, S.N.J.M., Prov. Dir. Professed Sisters 188.

Dominican Center, Sinsinawa Dominican Sisters, 3102 W. Fort George Wright Dr., 99224-5203. Tel: 509-328-8033; Fax: 509-325-9877. Sisters 19.

Holy Names Foundation, 2911 W. Fort George Wright Dr., 99224. Tel: 509-328-7470; Fax: 509-328-9824. Sr. Ann Pizelo, S.N.J.M., Prov. Dir. Support for educational activities of Sisters of the Holy Names of Jesus and Mary.

Holy Spirit Community, 2416 E. 46th Ave., 99223-6412. Tel: 509-448-6224. Sr. Elisabeth M. Pfeiffer, Pres.

Mary of the Angels Convent, P.O. Box 30250, 99223-3004. Tel: 509-448-0674; Fax: 509-448-5192. Sr. Eileen Neumann, F.S.P.A., Local Community Liaison. Sisters 3.

Monastery of St. Clare, 4419 N. Hawthorne St., 99205-1399. Tel: 509-327-4479. Sr. Mary Rita Dolan, O.S.C., Abbess. Poor Clare Nuns, Solemn Vows.
Papal Enclosure Novitiate. Professed Cloistered Nuns 8.

Mount St. Joseph. Retirement residence and community. 12 W. Ninth Ave., 99204-2394. Tel: 509-838-2594; Fax: 509-838-3220. Sisters of Providence, Mother Joseph, Province. Alice Anderson, Gen. Mgr.; Sr. Ida Mae Marceau, Supr. Sisters 37.

Sisters of Providence, Mother Joseph Province, 12 W. Ninth Ave., 99204-2309. Tel: 509-474-4884; Fax: 509-474-4882. Sr. Barbara Schamber, S.P., Team Leader/Prov. Supr.
Sisters of Providence, Mother Joseph Province (a Washington non-profit corporation). Members of Providence Services (a Washington non-profit corporation). Sisters 7.

NEWPORT. *Carmelite Sisters of Mary*, 2892 State Rte. 211, 99156. Sr. Leslie L. Lund, Prioress. Sisters 2; Hermitages 4.

OMAK. *The Franciscan Sisters of Little Falls, Minnesota*, P.O. Box 3745, 98841-3745. Tel: 509-826-6742. Sr. Maurita Bernet, Contact Person.

PULLMAN. *Sisters of the Humility of Mary*, 223 NW Ann St, 99163-3543. Tel: 509-332-8388. 3410 S. Regal St., Apt.22, Spokane, 99223-4669. Tel: 509-328-4220.

[L] RETREAT HOUSES

SPOKANE. *Immaculate Heart Retreat Center*, 6910 S. Ben Burr Rd., 99223. Tel: 509-448-1224; Fax: 509-448-1623. Deacon John Ruscheinsky, Exec. Dir.; Rev. Msgr. William Van Ommeren.

KAIROS House of Prayer, 1714 W. Stearns Rd., 99208. Tel: 509-466-2187. Sr. M. Florence Leone, Poch, O.S.F., Coord. Provides a place called to a prayerful, reflective environment. Spiritual accompaniment is available.

SPOKENA. *Spiritual Exercise in Everyday Life (SEEL)*, 330 E. Boone, 99202. Sr. Sheila McEvoy, S.N.J.M., Dir.

TUM TUM. *House of the Lord Retreat Center, Inc.*, P.O. Box 1034, 99034. Tel: 509-276-2219. Ramona Salvatore, Dir.

[M] NEWMAN CENTERS

CHENEY. *Catholic Newman Center at Eastern Washington University*, 837 Elm St., 99004. Tel: 509-235-8402. Rev. Thomas C. Caswell, Chap.; Jolie Hagan-Monasterio, Campus Min.

PULLMAN. *Washington State University - St. Thomas More Catholic Newman Center*, N.E. 820 B St., P.O. Box 2070, College Station, 99165. Tel: 509-332-6311. Rev. Thomas Mele, Dir.; Susan Adam, Dir.

[N] MISCELLANEOUS

SPOKANE. *Bernadette Place*, 2901 W. Dean Ave., 99201. Tel: 509-358-4264; Fax: 509-358-4259.
E-mail: jokeeffe@dioceseof spokane.org
Office: 1023 W. Riverside Ave, P.O. Box 1453, 99210-1453. Jean O'Keefe, Assoc. Dir. 6 units of affordable housing for persons with disabilities and special needs. 2819 W. Mallon Ave., 99201. 2925 W. Mallon Ave., 99201.

The Catholic Foundation of the Spokane Diocese, W. 1023 Riverside Ave., P.O. Box 1453, 99210-1453. Tel: 509-358-4280; Fax: 509-358-7302. Steven C. Kocharhook, Ph.D., Exec. Dir.

Dominican Health Services, N. 5633 Lidgerwood, 99207. Tel: 509-482-2576. Tom Corley, Pres. & CEO; Mr. Ronald DeArth, Vice Pres. Finance; Ms. Barbara Savage, Vice Pres. Mission Svcs. Serves as a multi-hospital system which includes Holy Family Hospital in Spokane, Mount Carmel Hospital in Colville, and St. Joseph's Hospital of Chewelah in Chewelah.

Dominican Network, 101 W. 8th Ave., 99220-2555. Tel: 509-482-2576. Ryland (Skip) P. Davis, Pres. Serves as a member of Dominican Health Services, a multi-health care system which includes Dominican Health Services, Holy Family Hospital, Spokane; Mount Carmel Hospital, Colville; St. Joseph's Hospital of Chewelah, Chewelah; and Holy Family Hospital Adult Day Health, Spokane; Deer Park Health Center & Hospital, Deer Park; Domini Care, Chewelah.

Dominican Outreach Foundation, c/o Dominican Center, W. 3102 Fort George Wright Dr., 99224. Tel: 509-328-8033. James G. Falkner, Pres. Supports the Sisters educational, religious, and charitable ministries.

Emilie Court Assisted Living, 34 E. 8th Ave., 99202-1202. Tel: 509-474-2550; Fax: 509-474-2618. Alice Anderson, Admin.; Kathleen Schlicht, Dir.

Holy Names Music Center, 3910 W. Custer Dr., 99224. Dr. Judith L. Myers, Exec. Dir. Sisters 5; Lay Teachers 31; Students 560.
Sponsored by Sisters of the Holy Names, Washington Province.

Immaculate Heart Retreat Center Foundation, S. 6910 Ben Burr Rd., 99223-1819.

Kateri Northwest Ministry Institute, 330 E. Boone, 99202-1778. Tel: 509-324-6305; Fax: 509-324-6305.
E-mail: tcolgan@gntech.com
Directors: Revs. Richard R. Mercy, S.J.; Thomas A. Colgan. Purpose: Evangelization and training of Native Americans in the four Northwestern states and one Canadian province for all ministries in the Catholic Church and service in the native community, with attention to ongoing social analysis and to recovery ministries from Alcoholism and Dysfunctional Families. Goal: The development of fully indigenous Catholic churches in Urban centers and on Reservations.

Providence Services, 9 E. Ninth Ave., 99202-1295. Tel: 509-474-7337.

SEEL Spokane, 330 E. Boone, 99202. Sr. Sheila McEvoy, S.N.J.M., Dir. Spiritual Exercises in Everyday Life.

Serra Club of Spokane, P.O. Box 414, 99220-0414.

SPOKANE CATHOLIC INVESTMENT TRUST, P.O. Box 1453, 99210-1453. Most Rev. William S. Skylstad, Pres. A Washington Non-Profit Corporation established to invest funds on behalf of the charitable organizations organized within the Catholic Diocese of Spokane.

Transitional Programs for Women, W. 3102 Fort George Wright Dr., 99224. Tel: 509-328-6702.
E-mail: transprog@aol.com
Transitions.
Miryam's House of Transition.
Transitional Living Center.
Women's Drop In Center.

DAYTON. *Project Timothy: Christian Service Center*, 238 E. Main St., 99328. Tel: 509-382-2943. Mailing Address: 238 E. Main St., 99328.
Sponsored by St. Joseph's & St. Mark's Churches. Sophie J. Arebalos, Dir. Total Assisted 4,550.

RELIGIOUS INSTITUTES OF MEN REPRESENTED IN THE DIOCESE

For further details refer to the corresponding bracketed number in the Religious Institutes of Men or Women section.

[0520]—*Franciscan Friars.* (Santa Barbara Prov.). —O.F.M.

[0690]—*Jesuit Fathers and Brothers.*—S.J.

RELIGIOUS INSTITUTES OF WOMEN REPRESENTED IN THE DIOCESE

[1780]—*Congregation of the Sisters of the Third Order of St. Francis of Perpetual Adoration.*—F.S.P.A.

[1070-03]—*Dominican Sisters.*—O.P.

[1310]—*Franciscan Sisters of the Little Falls, MN.*—O.S.F.

[3760]—*Order of St. Clare.*—O.S.C.

[2970]—*School Sisters of Notre Dame.*—S.S.N.D.

[3350]—*Sisters of Providence.*—S.P.

[1650]—*The Sisters of St. Francis of Philadelphia.*—O.S.F.

[3840]—*Sisters of St. Joseph of Carondelet.*—C.S.J.

[1990]—*Sisters of the Holy Names of Jesus and Mary.*—S.N.J.M.

[2110]—*Sisters of the Humility of Mary.*—H.M.

DIOCESAN CEMETERIES

SPOKANE. *Catholic Cemeteries of Spokane*, 7200 N. Wall St., 99208. Dennis Fairbank, Dir.

Holy Cross, 7200 N. Wall St., 99208. Tel: 509-328-1070.

St. Joseph, 17825 Trent, 99216. Tel: 509-891-6240.

NECROLOGY

† Flour, Anton, (Retired). —Died March 13, 1999.

† O'Dea, John, (Retired). —Died July 21, 1999.

Diocese of Springfield-Cape Girardeau

(Dioecesis Campifontis-Capitis Girardeauensis)

Most Reverend

JOHN J. LEIBRECHT, D.D., PH.D.

Bishop of Springfield-Cape Girardeau; ordained March 17, 1956; appointed October 23, 1984; consecrated December 12, 1984. *Office: The Catholic Center, 601 S. Jefferson Ave., Springfield, MO, 65806-3143.*

Chancery Office: The Catholic Center, 601 S. Jefferson Ave., Springfield, MO, 65806-3143. Tel.: 417-866-0841; Fax: 417-866-1140.

Web site address: www.diocspfdcape.org

E-mail address: treidy@diocspfdcape.org

ESTABLISHED AUGUST 24, 1956.

Square Miles 25,719.

Comprises the following Counties in the State of Missouri: Barry, Barton, Bollinger, Butler, Cape Girardeau, Carter, Cedar, Christian, Dade, Dallas, Dent, Douglas, Dunklin, Greene, Howell, Iron, Jasper, Laclede, Lawrence, McDonald, Madison, Mississippi, New Madrid, Newton, Oregon, Ozark, Pemiscot, Polk, Reynolds, Ripley, Scott, Shannon, Stoddard, Stone, Taney, Texas, Wayne, Webster and Wright.

For legal titles of parishes and diocesan institutions, consult The Catholic Center.

STATISTICAL OVERVIEW

Personnel	
Bishop	1
Retired Abbots	2
Priests: Diocesan Active in Diocese	57
Priests: Active Outside Diocese	2
Priests: Retired, Sick or Absent	16
Number of Diocesan Priests	75
Religious Priests in Diocese	71
Extern Priests in Diocese	4
Ordinations:	
Diocesan Priests	1
Religious Priests	4
Transitional Deacons	1
Permanent Deacons in Diocese	10
Total Brothers	82
Total Sisters	110
Parishes	
Parishes	65
With Resident Pastor:	
Resident Diocesan Priests	47
Resident Religious Priests	9
Without Resident Pastor:	
Administered by Priests	6
Administered by Deacons	1
Administered by Women Religious	2
Missions	19
Pastoral Centers	2
Professional Ministry Personnel:	
Brothers	1
Sisters	17
Lay Ministers	25
Welfare	
Catholic Hospitals	4
Total Assisted	525,380
Homes for the Aged	2
Total Assisted	368
Day Care and Extended Day Care Centers	1
Total Assisted	45
Special Centers for Social Services	1
Total Assisted	1,187
Other Institutions	1
Total Assisted	44,583
Educational	
Diocesan Students in Other Seminaries	12
Seminaries, Religious	2
Students Religious	30
Total Seminarians	42
High Schools, Diocesan and Parish	3
Total Students	878
Elementary Schools, Diocesan and Parish	23
Total Students	3,793
Catechesis/Religious Education:	
High School Students	1,692
Elementary Students	3,998
Total Students Under Catholic Instruction	10,403
Teachers in the Diocese:	
Priests	1
Brothers	1
Sisters	5
Lay Teachers	266
Vital Statistics	
Receptions into the Church:	
Infant Baptism Totals	734
Adult Baptism Totals	520
Received into Full Communion	219
First Communions	1,205
Confirmations	1,020
Marriages:	
Catholic	189
Interfaith	239
Total Marriages	428
Deaths	590
Total Catholic Population	59,038
Total Population	1,187,339

Former Bishops—Most Rev. CHARLES H. HELMSING, D.D., cons. as Titular Bishop of Axomis and Auxiliary Bishop of Archdiocese of St. Louis, April 19, 1949; appt. Bishop of Springfield-Cape Girardeau, Aug. 24, 1956; transferred to Diocese of Kansas City-St. Joseph, Jan. 27, 1962; died Dec. 20, 1993.—Most Rev. IGNATIUS J. STRECKER, D.D., appt. April 7, 1962; cons. June 20, 1962; transferred to Archdiocese of Kansas City in Kansas, Sept. 10, 1969.—His Eminence WILLIAM CARDINAL BAUM, S.T.D., appt. Feb. 18, 1970; cons. April 6, 1970; transferred to Archdiocese of Washington, May 9, 1973; elevated to Cardinal, May 24, 1976 appointed to the Prefect of the Sacred Congregation Seminaries and Catholic Institutes, Jan. 15, 1980.—His Eminence BERNARD CARDINAL LAW, D.D., ord. May 21, 1961; appt. Bishop of Springfield-Cape Girardeau, Oct. 22, 1973; cons. Dec. 5, 1973; appt. Archbishop of Boston, Jan. 23, 1984; elevated to Cardinal, May 25, 1985.

Vicars General—Rev. Msgr. PHILIP A. BUCHER, V.G.; Rev. Msgr. THOMAS E. REIDY, V.G.; Rev. Msgr. RICHARD C. ROLWING, V.G.

Chancery Office—The Catholic Center, 601 S. Jefferson Ave., Springfield, 65806-3143. Tel: 417-866-0841; Fax: 417-866-1140.

Chancellor—Rev. Msgr. THOMAS E. REIDY, V.G.

Vice Chancellor—Rev. THOMAS P. KIEFER, J.C.L.

Regional Priest Moderators—Region I: Rev. JUSTIN D. MONAGHAN,Region II: Rev. PETER J. MORCINIEC,Region III: Rev. J. PATRICK WISSMAN,Region IV: Rev. MARK C. ERNSTMANN,Region V: Rev. GARY M. CARR,Region VI: Rev. JAMES J. UNTERREINER,Region VII (A): Rev. J. FRIEDEL,Region VII (B): Rev. FREDERICK J. LUTZ,Region VIII: Rev. Msgr. WILLIAM J. STANTON,Region IX: Rev. JOHN SHELEY.

Office of Administration

Catholic Foundation Of The Diocese Of Springfield-Cape Girardeau—Most Rev. JOHN J. LEIBRECHT, D.D., Ph.D., Pres.; Rev. Msgr. THOMAS E. REIDY, V.G., Vice Pres.; Mrs. JANET L. SMITH, Sec. Treas.

Development and Properties—Mr. THOMAS B. WALMSLEY, Dir.

Diocesan Development Fund—Mr. THOMAS B. WALMSLEY, Dir. Devel. & Properties; Revs. MARK J. BINDER; ROGER LEVEILLEE; Mrs. CAROL DEHAVEN; Mr. JOHN SEESING.

Finance—Mrs. JANET L. SMITH, Dir.

Financial Council—Mrs. JANET L. SMITH, Director of Finance; Mr. THOMAS B. WALMSLEY, Diocesan Dir. of Devel. & Properties; Mr. LARRY G. GRINSTEAD; Mrs. PATRICIA HOPKINS; Mr. GEORGE MARINO; Mr. JAMES MOORE; Mr. PETER RAMSOUR; Mr. JAMES P. REINAGEL; Mr. KEVIN FITZGERALD; Mrs. KAY A. VAN PELT.

Planned Giving—Mrs. MAUREEN M. JERSAK, Dir.

Office Of Education

Catholic Schools—Sr. JANE HOSCH, O.S.F. Ph.D., Supt. of Schools.

Communications (Public Relations)—Mrs. MARILYN VYDRA, Dir.

Ecumenism—Rev. JOHN F. GAGNEPAIN, C.M.

Media Library—Mrs. MARILYN VYDRA, Supvr.

"The Mirror", Newspaper, Diocese of Springfield-Cape Girardeau—Rev. MARK G. BOYER, M.A., M.Div., M.R.E., Editor; Mrs. CHRISTINE BALLEW-GONZALES, Staff Asst.; Mrs. KARLA ESSNER, Staff Asst.

Religious Education—Sr. ROSALIE DIGENAN, D.C., M.Ed., Dir.

Office Of Ministry

Campus Ministries—Rev. EDDIE DELEON, C.M.F., Southwest Missouri State Univ. Campus Min. Tel: 417-865-0802. Rev. J. FRIEDEL, Southeast Missouri State Univ. Campus Min. Tel: 573-335-3899.

Diocesan Spiritual Director—Rev. JOHN F. GAGNEPAIN, C.M. Tel: 573-547-7276.

Family Ministries—Mr. TROY CASTEEL, M.S., L.P.C., Dir.

Diocesan Council on Family Ministry—Region I, JIM NEWTON; MARGE NEWTON,Region II, DIANE WHITNEY; Rev. PATRICK A. TETER,Region III, Rev. J. PATRICK WISSMAN,Region IV, ROSIE SAN PAOLO; MARGARET SCHATZ; SHARON WEIDELMAN,Region V,

Rev. ERNEST J. MARQUART,Region VI, Rev. JAMES J. UNTERREINER,Region VII, GREG ILLERS; LINDA ILLERS,Region VIII, JACK JACKOVIC; PAT JACKOVIC; MAGGIE SANDERS,Region IX, Rev. MICHAEL V. MCDEVITT; SHERRY LAMPE.

Natural Family Planning—Mr. TROY CASTEEL, M.S., L.P.C., Dir.

Rite Of Christian Initiation Of Adults—Rev. PAUL J. MCLOUGHLIN, Co-Dir.; Sr. ROSALIE DIGENAN, D.C., M.Ed., Co-Dir.

Hispanic Ministries—Sr. SANDRA STRAUB, C.S.J., Dir.

Social Ministry-Resettlement—Sr. FRAN STEIN, R.S.M., Dir.

Regional Catholic Leadership—Rev. DAVID F. HULSHOF, M.A., Dir.

Regional Leaders—Region I, Ms. ROBBIE ROBINSON; Ms. LINDA ROGERS,Region II, Mr. KENT BOURSHESKI; Mrs. STACIE DURKIN,Region III-A, Mr. GENE CONFALONE; Mrs. PHYLLIS CONFALONE,Region III-B, Mrs. DOROTHY MEZZACAPPA; Mrs. CARYN WULLNER-,Region IV-A, Ms. MAURISA AHLSTRAND; Ms. CATHY CLARK,Region V-A, Mr. HARRY CLARK; Mrs. CONNIE CLARK; Ms. BERNICE GIBSON,Region V-B, Mr. PATRICK STEPHENS; Mrs. LYNN LEWIS; Mr. ED PRATT,Region V-C, Mrs. JEAN HORST,Region VI, Dr. RAYMOND DRONEY; Rev. JAMES UNTERREINER-,Region VII-A, Vacant Region VII-B, Mrs. PAT MOORE,Region VIII, Mrs. KATHY MITCHELL; Ms. JAN STEPHENS,Region IX, Ms. BARBARA BATH; Mr. ROBERT SMITH.

Tribunal—

Judicial Vicar—Rev. Msgr. THOMAS E. REIDY, V.G.

Adjutant Judicial Vicar—Rev. THOMAS P. KIEFER, J.C.L.

Judge—Rev. Msgr. MICHAEL F. SWALINA, S.T.D.; Rev. VINCENT E. BERTRAND, J.C.L.

Auditor—Sr. INEZ HALLINAN, C.S.J., M.A.

Promoter of Justice—Rev. Msgr. PHILIP A. BUCHER, V.G.

Advocate—Rev. Msgr. EDWARD M. EFTINK, Ph.D.; Rev. DAVID F. HULSHOF, M.A.

Defenders of the Bond—Rev. Msgr. PHILIP A. BUCHER, V.G.; Rev. MICHAEL V. MCDEVITT, M.A.

Notary—Mrs. LINDA MURPHY; Mrs. MARIE MEYER.

Vicars For The Religious—Rev. Msgr. THOMAS E. REIDY, V.G.; Rev. ROBERT A. SCHUMACHER.

Vocations-Seminarians—Rev. DAVID F. HULSHOF, M.A., Dir.

Associate Director of Vocations/Seminarians—Rev. THOMAS P. KIEFER, J.C.L.; Sr. BERTHA FRANCO, C.C.V.I.

Youth Ministry—Ms. LEIGH STERTEN, Dir.

Catholic Scouting—Rev. GEFFORD C. LAMPREA, Diocesan Chap. Tel: 573-335-9347. Mrs. JEAN WEISSLER, Assoc. Diocesan Chap. Tel: 417-887-0979.

Camp Re-NEW-All—Miss VIRGINIA SANDER, Camp Dir.; Miss VALERIE ZIMMER, Camp Dir.

Office Of Worship

Office of Worship—Rev. PAUL J. MCLOUGHLIN, Dir. & Coord.

Liturgical Commission—Ms. MARY BETH WITTRY, Chm. Tel: 417-883-0837. Rev. PAUL J. MCLOUGHLIN, Dir. Worship.

Priests' Eucharistic League Confraternity Of The Most Blessed Sacrament—Rev. MICHAEL V. MCDEVITT, M.A., Dir.

Officials And Committees

Catholic Relief Services—Rev. Msgr. THOMAS E. REIDY, V.G.

Cemeteries—Rev. Msgr. THOMAS E. REIDY, V.G.

Censor Of Books—Rev. MARK C. ERNSTMANN, S.T.L., M.Ed. Tel: 417-546-5208.

Health Affairs—Mr. TROY CASTEEL, M.S., L.P.C., Dir.

Holy Childhood Association—Rev. Msgr. MICHAEL F. SWALINA, S.T.D. Tel: 573-748-5183.

Missionary Apostolate—Society for the Propagation of the Faith, Rev. Msgr. MICHAEL F. SWALINA, S.T.D. Tel: 573-748-5183.

Mission of the Laity—Apostleship of Prayer, Rev. Msgr. MICHAEL F. SWALINA, S.T.D. Tel: 573-748-5183.

National Shrine Of The Immaculate Conception—Rev. Msgr. THOMAS E. REIDY, V.G., Dir.

Priests' Mutual Benefit Society—Rev. STEPHEN SCHNEIDER, Pres.; Rev. Msgr. RAYMOND V. ORF; Rev. Msgr. THOMAS E. REIDY, V.G., Exec. Sec.; Rev. Msgr. JOHN H. WESTHUES; Revs. ROBERT. A. LANDEWE; RALPH J. DUFFNER, Vice Pres. NORMAND G. VARONE.

Priests' Purgatorial Society—Rev. MARK C. ERNSTMANN, S.T.L., M.Ed., Dir. Tel: 417-546-5208. BENEDICT W. HARTER, Sec.

Pro-Life Director—Sr. FRAN STEIN R.S.M., Dir.

Rural Life Movement—Rev. SYLVESTER W. BAUER. Tel: 573-744-5913.

Diocesan Consultative Groups

Diocesan Consultors—Rev. JOHN J. FRIEDEL; Rev. Msgr. PHILIP A. BUCHER, V.G.; Rev. Msgr. RICHARD C. ROLWING, V.G.; Rev. Msgr. MICHAEL F. SWALINA; Rev. THOMAS P. KIEFER; Rev. Msgr. THOMAS E. REIDY, V.G.; Rev. JAMES J. UNTERREINER.

Presbyteral Council—Revs. JUSTIN D. MONAGHAN, Pres. EDDIE DELEON, C.M.F., Vice Pres. JAMES J. UNTERREINER, Sec.; Rev. Msgr. RAYMOND V. ORF; Revs. DENIS DOUGHERTY, O.S.B.; JOHN S. BRAUN; THOMAS P. KIEFER; DAVID N. COON; ALLAN L. SAUNDERS. Appointed Members: Rev. Msgr. PHILIP A. BUCHER, V.G.; Rev. Msgr. RICHARD C. ROLWING, V.G.; Rev. Msgr. THOMAS E. REIDY, V.G.

Diocesan Pastoral Council—Rev. DAVID J. DOHOGNE, Exec. Sec.

Diocesan School Board—Sr. JANE HOSCH, O.S.F., Ph.D., Supt.

Diocesan Lay Endowment Board—Rev. DAVID F. HULSHOF, M.A., Chm.

Catholic Organizations And Movements

Cursillo Movement—

Secretariat for Cursillo—Deacon CHARLES R. COSTELLO, Diocesan Chap.; Rev. WILLIAM M. HODGSON, Asst. Diocesan Chap.

Daughters of St. Francis de Sales—Rev. Msgr. JOSEPH E. GOSCHE, Diocesan Chap.; Rev. THOMAS P. KIEFER, J.C.L., Chap.

Diocesan Council Of Catholic Women (DCCW)—Revs. JAMES J. UNTERREINER, Diocesan Spiritual Moderator; DAVID F. HULSHOF, M.A., Assoc. Spiritual Moderator; TESS SABLE, Pres. Tel: 417-753-3422.

St. Vincent De Paul Society—Rev. Msgr. THOMAS E. REIDY, V.G., Diocesan Chap.

Apostolates And Commissions

Apostolate to the Deaf—Rev. DAVID L. MILLER, Dir. Tel: 417-476-2463.

Diocesan Peace and Justice Commission—Sr. FRAN STEIN, R.S.M.; Rev. SYLVESTER BAUER. Tel: 573-744-5913.

State Office

Diocesan Delegates To The Missouri Catholic Conference—

Public Policy Committee—Mr. TROY S. CASTEEL; Mrs. MAURA TAYLOR.

CLERGY, PARISHES, MISSIONS AND PAROCHIAL SCHOOLS

CITY OF SPRINGFIELD
(Greene County)

1—CATHEDRAL OF ST. AGNES (1908), Rev. Thomas P. Kiefer; Rev. Msgr. John H. Westhues; Rev. David F. Hulshof; Deacon Clarence (Bud) McKay.
Res., 533 S. Jefferson Ave., 65806. Tel: 417-831-3565; Fax: 417-865-0367. [CEM][JC]
School—531 S. Jefferson Ave., 65806. Tel: 417-866-5038; Fax: 417-866-2906. Ms. Jeanne Skahan, Prin.
Sisters 1; Lay Teachers 15; Students 285.
Catechesis/Religious Programs—Students 180.

2—HOLY TRINITY (1966), Rev. Msgr. Thomas E. Reidy, V.G. In res., Revs. Frank C. Palermo; David Rabenecker, O.S.B.
Res., 2818 E. Bennett, 65804. Tel: 417-883-3440; Fax: 417-883-0072. [JC]
Catechesis/Religious Programs—Students 187.

3—IMMACULATE CONCEPTION (1868), Revs. Stephen A. Schneider; Randolph Tochtrop; Deacon William McNamee. In res., Rev. Vincent E. Bertrand.
Res., 3535 S. Fremont, 65804. Tel: 417-887-9769. [JC]
Church—3555 S. Fremont, 65804. Tel: 417-887-0600; Fax: 417-881-7087.
School—3555A S. Fremont, 65804. Tel: 417-881-7000. Mrs. Paula Baird, Prin.
Lay Teachers 25; Students 603.
Catechesis/Religious Programs—Students 171.

4—SACRED HEART (1882), Rev. Joseph Peplansky, C.M.F. Mailing Address: 1609 N. Summit Ave., 65803. Tel: 417-869-3646; Fax: 417-869-2218.
Res., Villa Claret, 1530 N. Summit, 65803. Tel: 417-869-0075. [JC]
Catechesis/Religious Programs—Students 111.

5—ST. ELIZABETH ANN SETON (1981), Rev. J. Fergus Monaghan; Sr. Barbara Geers, S.S.N.D.
Church—2200 W. Republic Rd., 65807. Tel: 417-887-6472; Fax: 417-887-7027. [CEM]
Catechesis/Religious Programs—Tel: 417-887-6088. Sr. Helen Therese Nienhaus, D.R.E.
Students 361.

6—ST. JOSEPH'S (1892), Revs. Denis Dougherty, O.S.B.; Anthony Shidler, O.S.B., Chap., St. John's Medical Center.
Res., 1115 N. Campbell Ave., 65802. Tel: 417-865-1112. [JC]
School—515 W. Scott, 65802. Tel: 417-866-0667; Fax: 417-866-2862. Leon Witt, Prin.
Lay Teachers 15; Students 148.
Catechesis/Religious Programs—Students 55.

CITY OF CAPE GIRARDEAU
(Cape Girardeau County)

1—CATHEDRAL OF ST. MARY (1868), Rev. Msgr. Richard C. Rolwing, V.G.; Rev. Gefford C. Lamprea. In res., Rev. Roger L. Leveillee.
Res., 629 William St., 63703. Tel: 573-335-9347; Fax: 573-335-0649. [CEM][JC]
School—210 S. Sprigg, 63703. Tel: 573-335-3840. Mrs. Carol Strattman, Prin.
Lay Teachers 13; Students 212.
Catechesis/Religious Programs—Students 32.
Old St. Vincent's—(Chapel of Ease).

2—ST. VINCENT DE PAUL (1838), Revs. Milton Fleming Ryan, C.M.; Daniel Schulte, C.M.; Bro. Kenneth J. Lund.
Res., 741 Forest, 63701. Tel: 573-335-7667; Fax: 573-335-0034.
School—1919 Ritter Dr., 63701. Tel: 573-334-9594. Mrs. Nancy Haberlie, Prin.
Lay Teachers 22; Students 424.
Catechesis/Religious Programs—Students 149.

OUTSIDE THE CITIES OF SPRINGFIELD AND CAPE GIRARDEAU

Advance, Stoddard Co., St. Joseph (1905), Rev. Frederick J. Lutz.
Res., P.O. Box 640, 63730. Tel: 573-722-3504. [CEM]
Catechesis/Religious Programs—Students 60.
Mission—Glennon, Bollinger Co., St. Anthony. [CEM]

Aurora, Lawrence Co., Holy Trinity (1906), Rev. David F. Hulshof; Sr. Mary Ann Fischer, S.S.N.D., Pastoral Assoc.
Res., Hwy. 60 & Carnation Rd., P.O. Box 533, 65605. Tel: 417-678-2403; Fax: 417-678-3714. [CEM]
Catechesis/Religious Programs—Students 72.

Benton, Scott Co., St. Denis (1840), Rev. Normand G. Varone.
Res., P.O. Box 127, 63736. Tel: 573-545-3864; Fax: 573-545-3017. [CEM]
School—Tel: 573-545-3017. Mrs. Deborah McCann, Prin.
Lay Teachers 6; Students 87.
Catechesis/Religious Programs—Students 30.

Billings, Christian Co., St. Joseph (1879), Rev. Patrick A. Teter.
Res., P.O. Box 100, 65610. Tel: 417-744-2490; Fax: 417-744-2528. [CEM]
Catechesis/Religious Programs—Students 133.

Bolivar, Polk Co., Sacred Heart (1946), Rev. J. Patrick Wissman.
Res., 1405 W. Fair Play St., 65613. Tel: 417-326-5596; Fax: 417-326-5596. [CEM]
Catechesis/Religious Programs—Students 94.
Mission—Humansville, Polk Co., St. Catherine, P.O. Box 42, Humansville, 65674. Tel: 417-754-8825.

Branson, Taney Co., Our Lady of the Lake (1951), Rev. Msgr. Philip A. Bucher, V.G.
Res., 202 Vaughn Dr., 65616. Tel: 417-334-2928; Fax: 417-334-6883.
Catechesis/Religious Programs—Mrs. Pat Hutcheson, D.R.E.
Students 200.

Buffalo, Dallas Co., St. William (1946), Rev. John S. Braun.
Res., P.O. Box 518, 65622. Tel: 417-345-2744.
Catechesis/Religious Programs—Students 30.

Carthage, Jasper Co., St. Ann (1872), Rev. Timothy Mai Vinh Loc, C.M.C.
Res., 908 S. Clinton St., 64836. Tel: 417-358-1841; Fax: 417-358-1841.
School—1156 Grand, 64836. Tel: 417-358-2674; Fax: 417-358-4902. Mrs. Bonnie Schaeffer, Prin.
Lay Teachers 7; Students 113.
Catechesis/Religious Programs—Students 71.

Caruthersville, Pemiscot Co., Sacred Heart (1900), Rev. Joseph Campbell.
Res., 605 Ward Ave., 63830. Tel: 573-333-4301.
Catechesis/Religious Programs—Students 50.

Cassville, Barry Co., St. Edward, Rev. David L. Miller. Mailing Address: 107 W. 17th St., P.O. Box 492, 65625. Tel: 417-847-4948; Fax: 417-847-4948 [*]51.
Res., 1802 Y Hwy., P.O. Box 492, 65625. Tel: 417-847-3569.
Catechesis/Religious Programs—Students 76.

Chaffee, Scott Co., St. Ambrose (1907), Rev. Ralph J. Duffner.
Res., 418 S. Third St., 63740. Tel: 573-887-3953. [CEM]

School—Tel: 573-887-6711. Mrs. Andrea Seabaugh, Prin.
Lay Teachers 8; Students 117.
Catechesis/Religious Programs—Students 56.

Charleston, Mississippi Co., St. Henry (1874), Rev. Gerald J. Brown, C.M.
Res., 304 Court St., 63834. Tel: 573-683-4737; Fax: 573-683-4737.
School—306 Court St., 63834. Tel: 573-683-6218. Mrs. Kay Glastetter, Prin.
Lay Teachers 7; Students 61.
Catechesis/Religious Programs—Students 34.

Conway, Laclede Co., Sacred Heart (1908), Rev. John S. Braun.
Res., Box 8, 65632. Tel: 417-589-6782; Fax: 417-589-6187. [CEM]
Catechesis/Religious Programs—Students 37.

Dexter, Stoddard Co., Sacred Heart (1889), Rev. John Sheley.
Res., 103 E. Market St., 63841. Tel: 573-624-8888.
Church—102 E. Castor, 63841. Tel: 573-624-7333; Fax: 578-624-4076.
Catechesis/Religious Programs—Students 113.

Doniphan, Ripley Co., St. Benedict (1859), Rev. David J. Dohogne.
Res., 306 Kegler, 63935. Tel: 573-996-3301. [CEM]
Catechesis/Religious Programs—Students 25.
Mission—Grandin, Carter Co., St. Anne.

El Dorado Springs, Cedar Co., St. Elizabeth (1946), Rev. William C. Krudwig.
Res., 609 S. Main, 64744. Tel: 417-876-3216. [CEM]
Catechesis/Religious Programs—Students 40.
Mission—Stockton, Cedar Co., St. Peter the Apostle, 308 E. Oak St., P.O. Box 583, Stockton, 65785. Tel: 417-276-5588.

Forsyth, Taney Co., Our Lady of the Ozarks (1980), Rev. Mark C. Ernstmann.
Res., 355 Shadowrock Dr., P.O. Box 639, 65653. Tel: 417-546-5208; Fax: 417-546-6615.
Catechesis/Religious Programs—Students 8.

Fredericktown, Madison Co., St. Michael (1827), Rev. Amel A. Shibley, Admin.
Res., 304 W. Main St., 63645. Tel: 573-783-2182; Fax: 573-783-5230. [CEM]
Catechesis/Religious Programs—Students 74.

Glennonville, Dunklin Co., St. Teresa 1905, Rev. Glenn A. Eftink; Deacon Fred Hirtz.
Res., Rte. No. 1, Box 371, Campbell, 63933. Tel: 573-328-4544; Fax: 578-328-4544. [CEM]
School—Rte. No. 1, Box 369, Campbell, 63933. Tel: 573-328-4197. Janet Kuper, Prin.
Lay Teachers 6; Students 86.
Catechesis/Religious Programs—Students 41.

Houston, Texas Co., St. Mark (1975), Rev. Mark J. Binder.
Res., 117 S. Oak Crest, 65483. Tel: 417-967-3589; Fax: 417-967-3747.
Catechesis/Religious Programs—Students 33.
Missions—Roby, Texas Co., St. Vincent de Paul; Licking, Texas Co., St. John The Baptist.

Ironton, Iron Co., Ste. Marie Du Lac (1878), Rev. James J. Unterreiner. In res., Rev. Anthony M. Gaydos, O.S.M., Senior Priest.
Res., 350 S. Main St., 63650. Tel: 573-546-2611. [CEM]
Catechesis/Religious Programs—Students 40.
Missions—Lesterville, Reynolds Co., Our Lady of Sorrows; Viburnum, Iron Co., St. Philip Benizi.

Jackson, Cape Girardeau Co., Immaculate Conception (1874), Rev. Msgr. Edward M. Eftink.
Res., 208 S. Hope St., Ste. 101, 63755. Tel: 573-243-3182; Fax: 573-243-6833. [CEM]
School—308 S. Hope St., 63755. Tel: 573-243-5013. Mrs. Tracy Dumey, M.A., Prin.
Lay Teachers 12; Students 238.
Catechesis/Religious Programs—Students 326.

Joplin, Jasper Co., St. Mary (1938), Rev. Justin D. Monaghan.
Res., 2415 Moffet Ave., 64804. Tel: 417-623-3333; Fax: 417-623-4015. [JC]
School—505 W. 25th St., 64804. Tel: 417-623-1465. Mrs. Tracey Welch, Prin.
Lay Teachers 19; Students 295.
Catechesis/Religious Programs—Students 55.

St. Peter (1877), Rev. Raymond E. O'Connor, C.M.F.
Res., 812 Pearl Ave., 64801-4396. Tel: 417-623-8643; Fax: 417-623-0866. [JC]
School—802 Byers, 64801-4396. Tel: 417-624-5605. Mrs. Debra Smith, Prin.
Lay Teachers 9; Students 103.
Catechesis/Religious Programs—Students 90.

Kelso, Scott Co., St. Augustine (1878), Rev. M. Oliver Clavin.
Res., 201 S. Messmer, Box 26, 63758. Tel: 573-264-4724.
School—230 S. Messmer, P.O. Box 97, 63758-0097. Tel: 573-264-4644; Fax: 573-264-1475. Mr. Thomas Howard, Prin.
Lay Teachers 8; Students 133.

Kennett, Dunklin Co., St. Cecilia (1923), Rev. James L. Reynolds; Deacon David Vrooman, Parish Life Coord.
Res., College & North Bypass, P.O. Box 306, 63857. Tel: 573-888-2412; Fax: 573-888-0613.
Catechesis/Religious Programs—Students 57.

Kimberling City, Stone Co., Our Lady of the Cove (1979), Rev. John A. Brath.
Res., 20 Kimberling Blvd., P.O. Box 548, 65686. Tel: 417-739-4700; Fax: 417-739-5279.
Catechesis/Religious Programs—Students 149.

Lamar, Barton Co., St. Mary (1904), Rev. Jacob S. Biernacki.
Res., 200 E. 17th St., 64759. Tel: 417-682-2492. [CEM]
Catechesis/Religious Programs—Students 39.

Lebanon, Laclede Co., St. Francis De Sales (1870), Rev. Msgr. Raymond V. Orf.
Res., 345 Grand St., 65536. Tel: 417-532-4811; Fax: 417-532-8847. [CEM]
Catechesis/Religious Programs—Students 205.
Chapel—Bennett Springs, Sportman's Chapel.

Leopold, Bollinger Co., St. John (1856), Rev. William A. Huggins.
Res., 103 Main St., P.O. Box 83, 63760. Tel: 573-238-3300. [CEM]
Catechesis/Religious Programs—Students 193.

Malden, Dunklin Co., St. Ann (1890), Rev. Glenn A. Eftink; Deacon Fred Hirtz.
Mailing Address: c/o St. Teresa Parish, Rte. 1, Box 371, Campbell, 63933.
Church—304 N. Douglas St., 63863.
Catechesis/Religious Programs—Students 13.

Mansfield, Wright Co., Immaculate Heart of Mary (1943), Rev. Paul Wightman, O.M.I.
Res., Rte. 6, Box 6700, Ava, 65608. Tel: 417-924-3779; 683-5249.
Catechesis/Religious Programs—Students 46.
Missions—Ava, Douglas Co., St. Leo the Great, Rte. 6, Box 6700, Ava, 65608. Tel: 417-683-5249; Gainesville, Ozark Co., St. William, P.O. Box 367, Gainesville, 65655. Tel: 417-679-4804; Fax: 417-679-2037. Rev. Gerald Fuller, O.M.I.

Marshfield, Webster Co., Holy Trinity (1892), Rev. Michael J. Casteel.
515 E. Washington, 65706-1865. Tel: 417-859-2228.
Catechesis/Religious Programs—Students 117.

Monett, Barry Co., St. Lawrence (1891), Rev. Allan L. Saunders.
Res., 405 Seventh St., 65708. Tel: 417-235-3286; Fax: 417-235-3721. [CEM]
School—407 Seventh St., 65708. Tel: 417-235-3721. Sr. Dominic Rechtorik, V.S.C., Prin.
Sisters 1; Lay Teachers 5; Students 95.
Catechesis/Religious Programs—Students 88.

Mountain Grove, Wright Co., Sacred Heart (1893), Rev. Justin Huelsing, O.M.I.
Res., 302 E. State St., 65711. Tel: 417-926-3803.
Catechesis/Religious Programs—Students 19.
Mission—Cabool, Texas Co., St. Michael.

Mountain View, Howell Co., St. John Vianney (1951), Rev. Ernest J. Marquart.
Res., 808 State Rd. Y, P.O. Box 38, 65548. Tel: 417-934-2649.
Catechesis/Religious Programs—Students 16.
Mission—Eminence, Shannon Co., St. Sylvester.

Mount Vernon, Lawrence Co., St. Susanne (1939), Rev. Robert A. Landewe.
Res., P.O. Box 126, 65712. Tel: 417-466-4190.
Catechesis/Religious Programs—Students 66.
Mission—Greenfield, Dade Co., St. Patrick.

Neosho, Newton Co., St. Canera (1871), Revs. John M. Harth; Joseph Than Van Liem, C.M.C.
Res., 504 S. Washington St., 64850. Tel: 417-451-3411. [JC]
Catechesis/Religious Programs—Students 92.
Mission—Noel, McDonald Co., Nativity of Our Lord, P.O. Box 555, Noel, 64854.

New Hamburg, Scott Co., St. Lawrence (1847), Rev. Normand G. Varone.
Res., 1017 State Hwy. A, Benton, 63736. Tel: 573-545-3317; Fax: 573-545-9185. [CEM]
Catechesis/Religious Programs—Students 115.

New Madrid, New Madrid Co., Immaculate Conception (1789), Rev. Msgr. Michael F. Swalina.
Res., 605 Davis St., 63869. Tel: 573-748-5183.
School—560 Powell, 63839. Tel: 573-748-5123. Ms. Agnes J. Harrington, Prin.
Lay Teachers 5; Students 44.
Catechesis/Religious Programs—Students 25.

Oran, Scott Co., Guardian Angel (1892), Rev. Lewis E. Hejna.
Res., 604 Church St., P.O. Box 158, 63771. Tel: 573-262-3210; Fax: 573-262-3583. [CEM 2]
School—514 Church St., 63771. Tel: 573-262-3583. Mr. Adrian Eftink, Prin.
Lay Teachers 7; Students 86.
Catechesis/Religious Programs—Students 46.

Ozark, Christian Co., St. Joseph the Worker (1961), Rev. Paul J. McLoughlin.
Res., 1796 N. State Hwy. NN, 65721. Tel: 417-581-6328; Fax: 417-581-4957.
Catechesis/Religious Programs—Students 251.

Piedmont, Wayne Co., St. Catherine of Siena (1873), Rev. Matthew J. Rehrauer.
Res., 109 Piedmont Ave., 63957. Tel: 573-223-4924.
Catechesis/Religious Programs—Students 53.
Missions—Van Buren, Carter Co., St. George, Tel: 573-323-8576; Williamsville, Wayne Co., Our Lady of Sorrows.

Pierce City, Lawrence Co., St. Mary (1883), Rev. Peter J. Morciniec.
Res., 200 Front St., 65723. Tel: 417-476-2827; Fax: 417-476-2824. [CEM 2]
School—202 Front St., 65723. Tel: 417-476-2824. Mrs. Paige Wagner, Prin.
Lay Teachers 5; Students 95.
Catechesis/Religious Programs—Jerri Jasumback, D.R.E.
Students 52.

Poplar Bluff, Butler Co., Sacred Heart (1891), Revs. Michael V. McDevitt; Marayya Pamisetty.
Res., 123 N. Eighth St., 63901. Tel: 573-785-9635; Fax: 573-785-2069. [CEM]
School—Eighth Ave. & Vine, 63901-5034. Tel: 573-785-5836. Ms. Gloria Wilson, Prin.
Sisters 1; Lay Teachers 8; Students 186.
Catechesis/Religious Programs—Students 88.
Station—Poplar Bluff, V.A. Hospital.

Portageville, New Madrid Co., St. Eustachius (1902), Rev. James L. Reynolds.
Res., 200 W. Fourth St., 63873. Tel: 573-379-3401.
School—214 W. Fourth St., 63873. Tel: 573-379-3525; Fax: 573-379-3843. Mrs. Sue Ellen Flynn, Prin.
Sisters 2; Lay Teachers 5; Students 74.
Catechesis/Religious Programs—Students 20.

Pulaskifield, Barry Co., SS. Peter and Paul (1892), Rev. Allan L. Saunders.
Res., P.O. Drawer L, Pierce City, 65723. Tel: 417-476-2463. [CEM]
Catechesis/Religious Programs—Students 29.

Salem, Dent Co., Sacred Heart (1880), Rev. Daniel Hirtz.
Res., 602 W. Butler, 65560. Tel: 573-729-4291; Fax: 573-729-3811.
Catechesis/Religious Programs—Mr. Patrick J. Keefe, D.R.E.
Students 35.
Mission—Bunker, Reynolds Co., Christ the King, P.O. Box 177, Bunker, 63629.
Chapel—Montauk, St. Jude.

Sarcoxie, Newton Co., St. Agnes (1870), Rev. Peter J. Morciniec.
Res., P.O. Box 218, Pierce City, 65723-0218. Tel: 417-548-3540; Fax: 417-548-3540. [CEM]
Catechesis/Religious Programs—Students 20.

Scott City, Scott Co., St. Joseph (1911), Rev. David N. Coon.
Res., 604 Sycamore, 63780. Tel: 573-264-4500; Fax: 573-264-1506. [CEM]
School—606 Sycamore, 63780. Tel: 573-264-2600. Mrs. Michele Huffman, Prin.
Lay Teachers 5; Students 63.
Catechesis/Religious Programs—Students 54.

Seneca, Newton Co., St. Mary (1884), Revs. John M. Harth; Joseph Than Van Liem, C.M.C.
Res., P.O. Box 1169, 64865. Tel: 417-776-3786. [CEM]
Catechesis/Religious Programs—Students 34.

Shell Knob, Barry Co., Holy Family (1978), Rev. David L. Miller.
Res., Lake Rd. 39-30, P.O. Box 229, 65747. Tel: 417-858-2518; Fax: 417-858-2518.

Sikeston, Scott Co., St. Francis Xavier's (1893), Rev. Msgr. William J. Stanton; Rev. Robert A. Schumacher.
Res., 217 W. Center St., 63801. Tel: 573-471-2447; Fax: 573-471-9820.
School—106 N. Stoddard, 63801. Tel: 573-471-0841. Susan Long, Prin.
Sisters 1; Lay Teachers 9; Students 192.
Catechesis/Religious Programs—Students 80.

Verona, Lawrence Co., Sacred Heart (1874), Rev. David F. Hulshof; Sr. Mary Ann Fischer, S.S.N.D., Parish Life Coord. In res., Rev. Bill Hodgson.
Res., Adams & Second St., P.O. Box 533, Aurora, 65605. Tel: 417-678-2403; Fax: 417-678-3714. [CEM]
Catechesis/Religious Programs—Students 44.

Webb City, Jasper Co., Sacred Heart (1908), Rev. Rick L. Jones.
Res., 909 N. Madison, 64870. Tel: 417-673-2044; Fax: 417-673-1944.
Catechesis/Religious Programs—Students 142.

West Plains, Howell Co., St. Mary (1902), Rev. Gary M. Carr, Prin.
Res., 965 S. Thayer Ave., 65775. Tel: 417-256-2556; Fax: 417-256-9251.
School—957 S. Thayer Ave., 65775. Tel: 417-256-8634.
Priests 1; Lay Teachers 9; Students 53.
Catechesis/Religious Programs—Students 62.
Mission—Thayer, Oregon Co., Sacred Heart.

Willow Springs, Howell Co., Sacred Heart (1897), Rev. Sherman B. Wall, O.M.I.
Church—1050 W. Bus Hwy. 60-63, 65793. Tel: 417-469-2447. [CEM]
Catechesis/Religious Programs—Students 39.
Mission—White Church, Howell Co., St. Joseph.

Chaplains of Public Institutions

SPRINGFIELD. *Diocesan Hospital Ministry* 1530 E. Erie, Apt.210H, 65804. Tel: 417-883-9391. Rev. Edward P. Nichols.
U.S. Medical Center 1900 W. Sunshine, 65802. Tel: 417-862-7041, Ext. 255. Rev. David Rabenecker, O.S.B., Chap.

CONWAY. *Ozark Correctional Center* P.O.Box 8, 65632-0008. Tel: 417-767-4491. Rev. John S. Braun.

JOPLIN. *Joplin Hospital Ministry* 1102 W. 32nd St., 64801. Tel: 417-781-2727. Rev. Benedict W. Harter.

POPLAR BLUFF. *Poplar Bluff Hospital Ministry*. Revs. Michael McDevitt Tel: 573-785-9635; Marayya Pamisetty Tel: 573-785-9635.

Special Assignment:
Reverend Fathers—
Boyer, Mark G., Editor of "The Mirror", 1703 S. National, Springfield, MO 65804-1123. Tel: 417-886-0841 (Office)
Hodgson, William M., Hispanic Ministry, P.O. Box 1006, Aurora, MO 65605. Tel: 417-498-6754
Hulshof, David F., Vocation Dir., Dir. Regional Catholic Leadership, 601 S. Jefferson Ave., Springfield, MO 65806. Tel: 417-866-0841 (Office)
Morey, Charles W., P.O. Box 11172, Springfield, MO 65708. Tel: 417-887-8245
Nichols, Edward P., Hospital Ministry, 1530 E. Erie, Apt. 210 H, Springfield, MO 65804. Tel: 417-882-9391
Orthel, Joseph A., 620 W. Scott St., Springfield, MO 65802. Tel: 417-869-5417

On Duty Outside the Diocese:
Reverend Fathers—
Drewelow, David C., St. Mary's Church, P.O. Box 191, Wallace, NE 69169

Military Chaplains:
Reverend Fathers—
Wilk, Mitchell S., Major, U.S. Army Chap., Office of the Chaplain, HHD 410th BSB, CMR 438, Box 733, APO AE 09111. Tel: 011-49-671-792860

Leave of Absence:
Reverend Fathers—
Gregovich, Lawrence B., Mater Dei Bldg., 1900 Grand Ave., Carthage, MO 64836. Tel: 417-358-6586
Zatina, Gregory E.J., 686 Tam O'Shanter Dr., Las Vegas, NV 89119. Tel: 702-734-0949

Retired:
Reverend Monsignors—
Gosche, Joseph E., 303 Albert St. P.O. Box 207, Cape Girardeau, MO 63702-0207. Tel: 573-651-8645
Rynish, John F., 620 W. Scott, Springfield, MO 65802. Tel: 417-869-5417
Reverend Fathers—
Baker, John W., Franciscan Villa, 620 W. Scott, Springfield, MO 65802. Tel: 417-869-5417
Bauer, Sylvester W., Rte. 1, P.O. Box 24B, Freeburg, MO 65035. Tel: 573-744-5913
Boeding, Damian, 725 Ohio Ave., Joplin, MO 64801-4925. Tel: 417-782-3959
Brownfield, Frowin, 526 S. Jefferson, #2, Springfield, MO 65806. Tel: 417-865-3836
Chambers, Leonard R., 2701 Mississippi Court, Joplin, MO 64804
Edwards, Byron H., 35 Air Rd., P.O. Box 422, Higden, AR 72067. Tel: 501-825-8085
Eschbacher, Jerome J., 620 W. Scott, Springfield, MO 65802. Tel: 417-869-5417
Harter, Benedict W., St. John's Medical Center, 2727 McClelland Blvd., Joplin, MO 64804. Tel: 417-781-2727
Holterman, Herbert J., Green Meadow Retirement Home, Room 113, Linn, MO 65051
Palermo, Frank C., 2818 E. Bennett, Springfield, MO 65804-1943. Tel: 417-883-3440
Seyer, James A., 150 S. Silver Springs Rd., #4, Cape Girardeau, MO 63703. Tel: 573-651-3939
Shibley, Amel A., 371 Etherton Dr., Cape Girardeau, MO 63703. Tel: 573-335-0221

Permanent Deacons:
Brewer, Thomas, 180 E. Canterbury, Springfield, MO 65804. Tel: 417-881-4450
Costello, Charles R., 1537-A E. Commercial, Springfield, MO 65803. Tel: 417-831-5776
Ellman, Edward V., 3950 E. Stanford St., Springfield, MO 65809-2241. Tel: 417-887-6508
Ghiglione, James J., 908 S. Clinton, Carthage, MO 64836-2832
Hirtz, Fred, RR 1 Box 72, Campbell, MO 63933-9706
Kurtenbach, Joseph, Rte. 6, Box 6754, Ava, MO 65608. Tel: 417-683-6298
McKay, Clarence, 1010 W. Cherokee, Springfield, MO 65807. Tel: 417-882-6675
McNamee, William, 780 Brook Forest, Nixa, MO 65714. Tel: 417-724-9705
Steele, Mike, Pastoral Services, St. John's Regional Health Center, 1235 E. Cherokee, Springfield, MO 65804. Tel: 417-885-2735
Vrooman, David, P.O. Box 306, Kennett, MO 63857-0306. Tel: 573-888-2412

INSTITUTIONS LOCATED IN THE DIOCESE

[A] SEMINARIES, RELIGIOUS, OR SCHOLASTICATES

AVA. *Assumption Novitiate (Trappists)*, Mailing Address: Rte. 5, Box 1056, 65608. Tel: 417-683-5110; Fax: 417-683-5658. Revs. Alberic Maisog, O.C.S.O., Novice Master; Mark A. Scott, O.C.S.O., Supr.; Rt. Revs. Robert Matter, O.C.S.O., Abbot Emeritus; Cyprian Harrison, O.C.S.O., Abbot Emeritus.

CARTHAGE. *Congregation of the Mother Co-Redemptrix*, 1900 Grand Ave., 64836. Tel: 417-358-7787; Fax: 417-358-9508. Very Rev. Joseph M. Tran Ngoc Diep, C.M.C., Prov.

[B] HIGH SCHOOLS, DIOCESAN

SPRINGFIELD. *Springfield Catholic High School*. (Coed), 2340 S. Eastgate, 65809-2832. Tel: 417-887-8817; Fax: 417-885-1165. Mr. Dean O. Crayton, Prin. Priests 1; Lay Teachers 30; Students 303.
Springfield Catholic School System, 3520 S. Culpepper Cir., Ste C, 65804-4206. Tel: 417-865-5567; Fax: 417-865-5278.

CAPE GIRARDEAU. *Notre Dame Regional High School*, 265 Notre Dame Dr., 63701-8517. Tel: 573-335-6772; Fax: 573-335-3458.
Co-Instructional Regional High School. Bro. David Anthony Migliorino, O.S.F., Prin. Priests 1; Brothers 1; Lay Teachers 32; Students 422.

JOPLIN. *McAuley Regional High School*, 930 Pearl Ave., 64801. Tel: 417-624-9320; Fax: 417-626-8334. Jeanette Stengel, Prin. Lay Teachers 12; Students 155.
St. Mary. (Grades PreK-5), 505 W. 25th St., 64804. Tel: 417-623-1465. Mrs. Tracey Welch, Prin. Lay Teachers 19; Students 295.
St. Peter's Junior High School. (Grades 6-8), 802 Byers, 64801. Tel: 417-624-5605. Mrs. Debra Smith, Prin. Lay Teachers 9; Students 103.

[C] GENERAL HOSPITALS

SPRINGFIELD. *St. John's Regional Health Center*, 1235 E. Cherokee, 65804. Tel: 417-885-2000; Fax: 417-888-8730
For a complete listing, refer to the Hospitals section.

CAPE GIRARDEAU. *Saint Francis' Medical Center*, 211 St. Francis Dr., 63703-8399. Tel: 573-331-5128
For a complete listing, refer to the Hospitals section.

JOPLIN. *St. John's Regional Medical Center; Mercy Lifecare Systems, Inc.*, 2727 McClelland Blvd., 64804-1694. Tel: 417-781-2727; Fax: 417-625-2910
For a complete listing, refer to the Hospitals section.

MOUNTAIN VIEW. *St. Francis Hospital*, P.O. Box 82, 65548. Tel: 417-934-2246; Fax: 417-934-6024
For a complete listing, refer to the Hospitals section.

[D] SPECIAL HOSPITALS

SPRINGFIELD. *St. John's Mercy Villa*, 1100 E. Montclair, 65807. Tel: 417-888-8500; Fax: 417-888-8532
For a complete listing, refer to the Special Care Facilities section.

[E] MONASTERIES AND RESIDENCES OF PRIESTS AND BROTHERS

SPRINGFIELD. *Claretians Missionaries' Residence-Villa Claret*, 1530 N. Summit, 65803. Tel: 417-869-0075. Revs. Wayne J. Barron, C.M.F.; Eddie DeLeon, C.M.F.; Joseph Peplansky; Bro. Thomas Haerle, C.M.F.
Congregation of Mother Co-Redemptrix, Our Lady of the Rosary House, 418 S. Kimbrough, 65806. Tel: 417-869-3822. Rev. Francis M. Luong Minh Tuat, C.M.C., Dir. Priests 1; Brothers 10.

AVA. *Assumption Abbey (Trappist)*, Rte. 5, Box 1056, 65608. Tel: 417-683-5110; Fax: 417-683-5658. Rev. Mark A. Scott, O.C.S.O., Supr.; Rt. Revs. Robert Matter, O.C.S.O., Abbot Emeritus; Cyprian Harrison, O.C.S.O., Abbot Emeritus; Revs. David Blackburn, O.C.S.O., (Mercy Villa); Leon Brockman, O.C.S.O.; Richard Fox, O.C.S.O.; Donald Joseph Hamilton, O.C.S.O.; Theodore Koster, O.C.S.O.; Alberic Maisog, O.C.S.O.; Anthony Menz, O.C.S.O., (Manhattan, KS). Priests 7; Brothers 4.

CARTHAGE. *Congregation of the Mother Co-Redemptrix, United States Assumption Province*, 1900 Grand Ave., 64836. Tel: 417-358-7787; Fax: 417-358-9508. Very Rev. Joseph M. Tran Ngoc Diep, C.M.C., Prov.; Revs. Francis Xavier M. Do Cao Tung, C.M.C., Asst. I; Anselm M. Dinh Vuong Can, C.M.C., Asst. II; Peter M. Ngo Chau Minh, C.M.C., Asst. III; John D.M. Ngo Duc Vuong, C.M.C., Treas.; Francis M. Vu Van Vanh, C.M.C., Sec.; Paul M. Nguyen Mang Cach, C.M.C.; Joseph M. Cao Xuan Canh, C.M.C.; Basil M. Doan Quang Dien, C.M.C.; Raymond M. Nguyen Chau Dien, C.M.C.; John Bosco M. Pham Tien Duc, C.M.C.; Felix M. Dinh Viet Luan, C.M.C.; Bartholomew M. Pham An Su, C.M.C.; Cyril M. Vu Thanh Thien, C.M.C.; Joseph M. Vu Kim Ngan, C.M.C.; Vincent de Paul M. Au Quoc Thanh, C.M.C.; Bartholomew Pham Minh Van, C.M.C.; Francis M. Tran Hung Long, C.M.C.; Aloysius M. Tran Thanh Liem, C.M.C.; James M. Pham Ngoc Bich, C.M.C.; Bernard M. Nguyen Trong Thuong, C.M.C.; Isidore M. Dinh Thanh Bac, C.M.C.; Ephrem M. Vu Khiem Cung, C.M.C.; James M. Vu Dai Luong, C.M.C.; Camillus M. Nguyen Duc Tuan, C.M.C.; Bros. John Vianney M. Do Thanh Nhan, C.M.C.; Francis M. Nguyen Hung Cuong, C.M.C.; Henry M. Nguyen Minh Han, C.M.C.; Anthony M. Nguyen Gia Huu, C.M.C.; Pius V M. Nguyen Trung Thu, C.M.C.; Thomas More M. Nguyen Long Truong, C.M.C.; Bede M. Nguyen Quang Tuyen, C.M.C.; Mathew M. Pham Ngoc Thach, C.M.C.; Joseph C.M. Pham Cong Tho, C.M.C.; Stephen Tran Minh Giac, C.M.C.; Patrick M. Tran The Mac, C.M.C.; Bernardine M. Tran Hien Si, C.M.C.; John Tran Trung Thanh, C.M.C.; Thomas M. Trinh Van Chi, C.M.C.; Anthony M. Vu Dinh Huan, C.M.C.; Matthew Vu Duc Kim, C.M.C.; Alphonsus M. Vu Toan Tri, C.M.C.; Cyprian M. Nguyen Van Hien, C.M.C.; George M. Ngo Trung Hau, C.M.C.; Joachim M. Nguyen Khoa Cu, C.M.C.; Justine M. Nguyen Tri Ky, C.M.C.; John B.M. Nguyen Duc Hien, C.M.C.; Dominic H.M. Nguyen Trung Chanh, C.M.C.; Cyril M. Vu Van Hao, C.M.C.; Polycarp M. Nguyen Long Toan, C.M.C.; Anthony Padua M. Nguyen Huan Du, C.M.C.; Anthony M. Le Dat Chuan, C.M.C.; James M. Do Long Van, C.M.C.; Bernard M. Hoang Thy Pham, C.M.C.; Hilary M. Tran Ha Nhuan, C.M.C.; Augustine M. Truong Truong Ky, C.M.C.; Pius M. Nguyen Hoa Dong, C.M.C.; Maximilian Kolbe M. Nguyen Huan Phong, C.M.C.; John M. Pham Lan Ai, C.M.C.; Thomas M. Nguyen Si Dien, C.M.C.; John M. Do Hoan Anh, C.M.C.; Thomas M. Vu Luu Truyen, C.M.C.; Ambrose M. Nguyen Tam Niem, C.M.C.; Charles Borromeo M. Pham Duc Sinh, C.M.C.; Gregory M. Tran Vi, C.M.C.; Thomas-Thein M. Nguyen Duc Hoc, C.M.C.; Paul-Tinh M. Nguyen Duc Quynh, C.M.C.; Augustine-Huy Do Minh Uoc, C.M.C.; Michael M. Pham Ngoc Trac, C.M.C.; Thomas A. M. Nguyen Huy Chau, C.M.C.; Augustine M. Tran Phung Su, C.M.C.; Josaphat M. Tran Tuan Trinh, C.M.C.; Irenaeus M. Vu Duc Thinh, C.M.C.; John Chrysostom M. Vu Manh Thong, C.M.C.; Peter Chrysologus M. Dinh Tuyen Vien, C.M.C.; Stanislaus M. Nguyen Dinh Luu, C.M.C.; Bonaventure M. Nguyen Tuan Bao, C.M.C.; Raphael M. Pham Vu Tuan Tu, C.M.C.; Jerome M. Doan Hung Chien, C.M.C.; Michael M. Dao Trung Dan, C.M.C.; Martin M. Le Dinh Lam, C.M.C.; Ambrose M. Ngugen Tam Niem, C.M.C.; Justine M. Pham Xuan Binh, C.M.C.; Stephen M. Lam Tuan Vu, C.M.C.; Benedict M. Duong Tri Le, C.M.C.; Ignatius Loyola M. Nguyen Quang Dong, C.M.C.; Pius M. Nguyen Binh Thuan, C.M.C.; John M. Bui Quang Trieu, C.M.C.; John M. Cao Vu Nghi, C.M.C.; Raymond M. Tran Huu Thao, C.M.C.; Titus M. Nguyen Si Hanh, C.M.C.; Albert M. Mai Duc Tinh, C.M.C.; Ignatius Loyola M. Tran Thanh Tien, C.M.C.; Irenaeus M. Tran Tung Bach, C.M.C.; Ephrem M. Tran Le Phi Khan, C.M.C. Priests 24; Brothers 70; Novices 5; Postulants 7; Candidates 32. Mater Dei Building. (Home for retired priests), 1900 Grand Ave., 64836. Tel: 417-358-7787; Fax: 417-358-9508. In res., (Not members of the Congregation of the Mother Co-Redemptrix). Revs. Peter Tran Dien; Joseph Dinh Tuan Ngan; Joseph Cao

Phuong Ky, S.S.; John M. Phan Cong Binh; Dominic Mai Minh Luan; James Do Ba Cong; Anthony Hoang Minh Thu; Jerome Nguyen Thanh Lam, O.S.B.; James Thuc Vam Truong, O.S.B.

MARIONVILLE. *The Society of Our Mother of Peace, Sons of Our Mother of Peace*, Queen of Heaven Solitude, 12494 Hwy. T, 65705. Tel: 417-744-2011. Revs. Placid Guste, S.M.P., Supr.; John R. Hansen, S.M.P. Legal Title: *The Society of Our Mother of Peace, Sons of Our Mother of Peace - Queen of Heaven Solitude*.

[F] CONVENTS AND RESIDENCES FOR SISTERS

SPRINGFIELD. *Congregation of Mary Queen*, 625 S. Jefferson Ave., 65806. Tel: 417-869-9842; Fax: 417-832-0852. Sr. Marguerite A. Tran, Regl. Supr. Sisters 6.
St. Anne Monastery, 424 E. Monastery St., 65807-6099. Tel: 417-881-2115. Mother Mary Charles Nelson, O.C.D., Prioress. Discalced Carmelite Nuns 4.
Sisters of Mercy of the Americas. (St. Louis), 1260 E. Sunshine, 65804. Tel: 417-882-1297. Sisters 6.

AVA. *Nazareth Hermitage*, Rte. 5, Box 1122, 65608. Sisters 5.

MARIONVILLE. *The Society of Our Mother of Peace, Daughters of Our Mother of Peace*, 12494 Hwy. T, 65705. Tel: 417-744-2011. Legal Title: *The Society of Our Mother of Peace, Daughters of Our Mother of Peace, Queen of Heaven Solitude*. Sisters 5.

PILOT KNOB. *Our Lady of the Valley Community*, 320 S. McCure St. Box 545, 63663-0545. Tel: 573-546-7229. Sisters 2.

REPUBLIC. *Little Portion Franciscans*, 645 Assisi Way, 65738. Tel: 417-732-6684; Fax: 417-732-6684. Sisters 3.

[G] RETREAT HOUSES

AVA. *Assumption Abbey*. (Trappist), Rte. 5, Box 1056, 65608. Tel: 417-683-5110; Fax: 417-683-5658. Rev. Theodore Koster, O.C.S.O.

MARIONVILLE. *The Society of Our Mother of Peace, Daughters of Our Mother of Peace*, 12494 Hwy. T, 65705. Tel: 417-744-2011. Legal Title: *The Society of Our Mother of Peace, Daughters of Our Mother of Peace, Queen of Heaven Solitude*.

REPUBLIC. *Cordis House*, 648 S. Assisi Way, 65738-2190. Tel: 417-732-8602. Rev. Eric Kahn, O.F.M.; Sr. Coletta Wrasman, P.H.J.C.
Little Portion Retreat Center, 645 S. Assisi Way, 65738. Tel: 417-732-6684. Sr. Lorraine Biebel, O.S.F., Coord.

[H] SHRINES

CARTHAGE. *Shrine of Immaculate Heart of Mary*, 1900 Grand Ave., 64836. Tel: 417-358-8580; Fax: 417-358-9508. Very Rev. Joseph M Tran Ngoc Diep, C.M.C., Prov.

[I] NEWMAN CENTERS

SPRINGFIELD. *The Nancy McGregor House, Southwest MO State University, Drury College, Ozarks Technical Comm. College*, Catholic Campus Ministry, 847 S. Holland, 65806-3513. Tel: 417-865-0802. Rev. Eddie DeLeon, C.M.F., Dir.

CAPE GIRARDEAU. *Southeast Missouri State University, Newman Center*, 512 N. Pacific, 63701-4712. Tel: 573-335-3899; Fax: 573-334-0088. Rev. John J. Freidel, Chap./Dir.

BRANSON. *Catholic Christian Newman Association*. (College of the Ozarks), 202 Vaughn, 65616. Tel: 417-334-2928; Fax: 417-334-6883. Rita Granden, Campus Min.

JOPLIN. *Newman Club, Missouri Southern State College*, 812 S. Pearl Ave., 64801-4336. Tel: 417-623-8643. Rev. Raymond O'Connor, Chap.

[J] MISCELLANEOUS

SPRINGFIELD. *Franciscan Villa*, 620 W. Scott, 65802. Tel: 417-869-5417. Gary A. Thompson, Admin.
The Kitchen, 1630 N. Jefferson, 65803. Tel: 417-837-1500; Fax: 417-831-6709. Sr. Lorraine Biebel, O.S.F., Coord.
The Kitchen Foundation, 1630 N. Jefferson, 65803.
Queen of Angels DayCare Center, 625 S. Jefferson, 65806. Tel: 417-869-9842; Fax: 417-832-0852.
St. John's Health System, Inc., 1235 E. Cherokee, 65804. Tel: 417-885-2000.
St. John's Regional Health Center. (subsidiary of St. John's Health System, Inc.), 1235 East Cherokee, 65804. Sisters of Mercy Health System (St. Louis). Mr. Jay W. Eckersley, Pres. & CEO; Rev. Anthony Shidler, O.S.B., Chap. Sisters 9; Beds 866; Inpatients 28,419; Outpatients 238,853.
St. John's Regional Medicine of the Ozarks, Inc., 1965 S. Fremont St., Ste. 2900, 65804. Tel: 417-885-2211.
St. John's Physicians & Clinics, Inc., 1965 S. Fremont St., Ste. 2950, 65804. Tel: 417-885-2849.

CARTHAGE. *Office of the Immaculate Heart of Mary Shrine*, 1749 Grand Ave., 64836. Tel: 417-358-8580; Fax: 417-358-9508.

ELLINGTON. *Casa Guadalupe, Family Growth Center*, P.O. Box 417, 63638. Tel: 573-663-2766; 663-7322; Fax: 573-663-2933.

RELIGIOUS INSTITUTES OF MEN REPRESENTED IN THE DIOCESE

For further details refer to the corresponding bracketed number in the Religious Institutes of Men or Women section.

[1330]—*Congregation of the Missions (Vincentians)*.—C.M.
[]—*Congregation of the Mother Coredemptrix*.—C.M.C.
[0520]—*Franciscan Friars*.—O.F.M.
[0360]—*Missionary Sons of the Immaculate Heart of Mary (Claretians)*.—C.M.F.
[0910]—*Oblates of Mary Immaculate (Oblates)*. (Central Prov.).—O.M.I.
[0350]—*Order of Cistercians of the Strict Observance (Trappist)*.—O.C.S.O.
[0200]—*Order of St. Benedict (Benedictines)*.—O.S.B.
[1240]—*Order of the Servants of Mary (Servites)*. (Chicago Prov.).—O.S.M.
[1030]—*Paulist Fathers*.—C.S.P.
[0515]—*Religious Brothers of the Third Order Regular of St. Francis (Generalate, St. Francis Monastery, Brooklyn, NY)*.—O.S.F.
[]—*The Society of Our Mother of Peace*.—S.M.P.

RELIGIOUS INSTITUTES OF WOMEN REPRESENTED IN THE DIOCESE

[0100]—*Adorers of the Blood of Christ*. (Ruma).—A.S.C.
[0230]—*Benedictine Sisters of the Pontifical Jurisdiction*. (Columbia).—O.S.B.
[0230]—*Benedictine Sisters of the Pontifical Jurisdiction*. (Eau Claire, WI).—O.S.B.
[0397]—*Congregation of Mary, Queen*.—C.M.R.
[0460]—*Congregation of the Sisters of Charity of the Incarnate Word*. (San Antonio).—C.C.V.I.
[0725]—*Cordi-Marian Missionary Sisters Congregation*.—M.C.M.
[0760]—*Daughters of Charity of St. Vincent de Paul*. (St. Louis).—D.C.
[0920]—*Daughters of St. Francis of Assisi*. (Lacon, Illinois).—D.S.F.
[0420]—*Discalced Carmelite Nuns*.—O.C.D.
[1415]—*Franciscan Sisters of Mary*.—F.S.M.
[1780]—*Franciscan Sisters of Perpetual Adoration*.—F.S.P.A.
[1240]—*Franciscan Sisters, Daughters of the Sacred Hearts of Jesus and Mary*. (Wheaton).—O.S.F.
[]—*Little Portion Franciscans*.—O.S.F.
[]—*Nazareth Hermitage*.
[2960]—*Notre Dame Sisters*. (Omaha).—N.D.
[3230]—*Poor Handmaids of Jesus Christ*. (Donaldson, IN).—P.H.J.C.
[2970]—*School Sisters of Notre Dame*. (St. Louis).—S.S.N.D.
[0430]—*Sisters of Charity of the Blessed Virgin Mary*. (Dubuque).—B.V.M.
[1010]—*Sisters of Divine Providence of San Antonio, TX*.—C.D.P.
[2575]—*Sisters of Mercy of the Americas*. (Dallas, PA Region).—R.S.M.
[2575]—*Sisters of Mercy of the Americas*. (St. Louis, MO Region).—R.S.M.
[2575]—*Sisters of Mercy of the Americas*. (Omaha, NE Region).—R.S.M.
[1530]—*Sisters of St. Francis*. (Sylvania, OH).—O.S.F.
[1570]—*Sisters of St. Francis of the Holy Family*. (Dubuque).—O.S.F.
[3840]—*Sisters of St. Joseph of Carondelet*. (St. Louis).—C.S.J.
[3830]—*Sisters of St. Joseph of LaGrange, IL*.—C.S.J.
[3270]—*Sisters of the Most Precious Blood*. (O'Fallon, MO).—C.PP.S.
[3320]—*Sisters of the Presentation of the B.V.M*. (Fargo).—P.B.V.M.
[1720]—*Sisters of the Third Order Regular of St. Francis of Our Lady of Lourdes*. (Rochester, MN).—O.S.F.
[]—*The Society of Our Mother of Peace*.—S.M.P.
[4110]—*Ursuline Nuns (Roman Union)*. (Crystal City, MO).—O.S.U.
[4120]—*Ursuline Nuns of the Congregation of Paris*. (Maple Mount, Kentucky).—O.S.U.
[4160]—*Vincentian Sisters of Charity*. (Pittsburgh, PA).—V.S.C.

NECROLOGY

† Allen, Thomas E., Lamar, MO St. Mary. —Died Jan. 29, 2000.
† McGrane, Rev. Msgr. Walter J., (Retired). —Died Nov. 5, 2000.

Diocese of Springfield in Illinois

(Dioecesis Campifontis in Illinois)

Most Reverend

GEORGE J. LUCAS, D.D.

Bishop of Springfield in Illinois; ordained May 24, 1975; appointed Bishop of Springfield in Illinois October 19, 1999; ordained and installed December 14, 1999. *Res., P.O. Box 1667, Springfield, IL, 62705-1667. Office: Catholic Pastoral Center, 1615 W. Washington St., P.O. Box 3187, Springfield, IL, 62708-3187.* Tel.: 217-698-8500; Fax: 217-698-8620.

Most Reverend

DANIEL L. RYAN, D.D., J.C.L.

Retired Bishop of Springfield in Illinois; ordained May 3, 1956; ordained Titular Bishop of Surista in Mauritania and auxiliary to the Bishop of Joliet in Illinois September 30, 1981; appointed Bishop of Springfield in Illinois November 22, 1983; installed January 18, 1984; retired October 19, 1999. *Res., 1625 W. Washington St., Springfield, IL, 62702. Office: Catholic Pastoral Center, 1615 W. Washington St., P.O. Box 3187, Springfield, IL, 62708-3187.* Tel.: 217-698-8500; Fax: 217-698-0802.

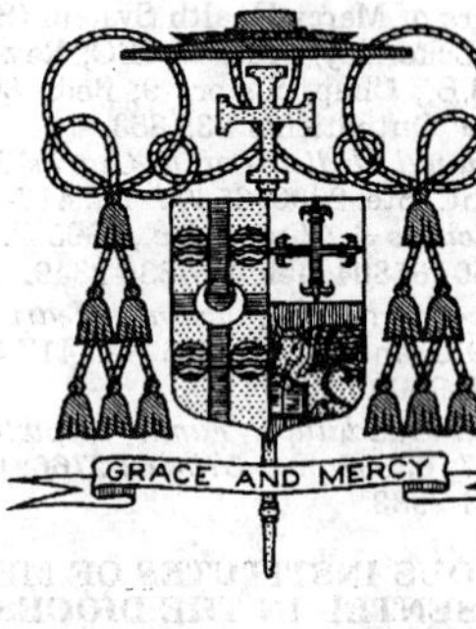

Catholic Pastoral Center: 1615 W. Washington St., P.O. Box 3187, Springfield, IL, 62708-3187. Tel.: 217-698-8500; Fax: 217-698-8620.

FORMERLY DIOCESE OF QUINCY.

ERECTED JULY 29, 1853.

SEE TRANSFERRED TO ALTON, JANUARY 9, 1857. TO SPRINGFIELD, OCTOBER 26, 1923.

Square Miles 15,139.

Comprises the following Counties of Illinois: Adams, Bond, Brown, Calhoun, Cass, Christian, Clark, Coles, Crawford, Cumberland, Douglas, Edgar, Effingham, Fayette, Greene, Jasper, Jersey, Macon, Macoupin, Madison, Menard, Montgomery, Morgan, Moultrie, Pike, Sangamon, Scott and Shelby.

For legal titles of parishes and diocesan institutions, consult the Chancery Office.

STATISTICAL OVERVIEW

Personnel	
Bishop	1
Retired Bishops	1
Priests: Diocesan Active in Diocese	100
Priests: Active Outside Diocese	8
Priests: Diocesan in Foreign Missions	1
Priests: Retired, Sick or Absent	34
Number of Diocesan Priests	143
Religious Priests in Diocese	62
Extern Priests in Diocese	7
Permanent Deacons in Diocese	4
Total Brothers	18
Total Sisters	690
Parishes	
Parishes	164
With Resident Pastor:	
Resident Diocesan Priests	80
Resident Religious Priests	14
Without Resident Pastor:	
Administered by Priests	57
Administered by Women Religious	5
Administered by Lay People	1
Closed Parishes	1
Professional Ministry Personnel:	
Brothers	2
Sisters	31
Lay Ministers	52
Welfare	
Catholic Hospitals	8
Total Assisted	895,689
Homes for the Aged	3
Total Assisted	400
Residential Care of Children	1
Total Assisted	140
Day Care and Extended Day Care Centers	1
Total Assisted	100
Specialized Homes	1
Total Assisted	67
Residential Care of Disabled	1
Total Assisted	93
Educational	
Diocesan Students in Other Seminaries	12
Seminaries, Religious	1
Students Religious	7
Total Seminarians	19
Colleges and Universities	2
Total Students	1,484
High Schools, Diocesan and Parish	2
Total Students	573
High Schools, Private	5
Total Students	2,158
Elementary Schools, Diocesan and Parish	54
Total Students	11,071
Catechesis/Religious Education:	
High School Students	2,573
Elementary Students	8,673
Total Students Under Catholic Instruction	26,551
Teachers in the Diocese:	
Priests	1
Sisters	22
Lay Teachers	668
Vital Statistics	
Receptions into the Church:	
Infant Baptism Totals	2,384
Adult Baptism Totals	353
Received into Full Communion	505
First Communions	2,679
Confirmations	2,805
Marriages:	
Catholic	477
Interfaith	541
Total Marriages	1,018
Deaths	1,862
Total Catholic Population	154,931
Total Population	1,106,124

Former Bishops—Rt. Rev. HENRY DAMIAN JUNCKER, D.D., cons. April 28, 1857; died Oct. 2, 1868.—Rt. Rev. PETER JOSEPH BALTES, D.D., cons. Jan. 23, 1870; died Feb. 15, 1886.—Rt. Rev. JAMES RYAN, D.D., cons. May 1, 1888; died July 2, 1923.—Most Rev. JAMES A. GRIFFIN, D.D., cons. Feb. 25, 1924; died Aug. 5, 1948.—Most Rev. WILLIAM A. O'CONNOR, D.D., cons. March 7, 1949; installed March 17, 1949; retired July 22, 1975; died Nov. 14, 1983.—Most Rev. JOSEPH A. MCNICHOLAS, D.D., cons. March 25, 1969; installed Sept. 3, 1975; died April 17, 1983.—Most Rev. DANIEL L. RYAN, D.D., J.C.L., ord. May 3, 1956; ord. Titular Bishop of Surista in Mauritania and Auxiliary to the Bishop of Joliet in Illinois, Sept. 30, 1981; appt. Bishop of Springfield in Illinois, Nov. 22, 1983; installed Jan. 18, 1984; retired Oct. 19, 1999.

Vicars General—Very Rev. THOMAS P. HOLINGA, M.A., V.G., Dir. Clergy Personnel; Very Rev. JOHN A. RENKEN, S.T.D., J.C.D., M.A., V.G., Moderator of the Curia.

Vicars Forane—

Alton Deanery—Very Rev. VIRGIL W. MANK, V.F.

Decatur Deanery—Very Rev. KEVIN W. VANN, V.F.

Effingham Deanery—Very Rev. LEO J. ENLOW, V.F.

Jacksonville Deanery—Very Rev. JOHN W. SPREEN, V.F.

Litchfield Deanery—Very Rev. LAWRENCE AUDA, V.F.

Quincy Deanery—Very Rev. ROBERT J. JALLAS, V.F.

Springfield Deanery—Very Rev. PATRICK J. WRIGHT, V.F.

Chancellor—Rev. EUGENE E. COSTA, S.T.L.

Tribunal Officers—Very Rev. JOHN A. RENKEN, S.T.D., J.C.D., M.A., V.G., Judicial Vicar; Very Rev. KENNETH C. STEFFEN, J.C.L., M.A., D.Min., Adjutant Judicial Vicar; Bro. PATRICK SHEA, O.F.M., J.D., J.C.L., Defender of the Bond; Rev. ANTHONY THIEMAN, D.Min., Court Expert.

Finance Officer—Mr. JOHN J. MAXWELL, C.P.A.

Episcopal Delegates for Marriage Concerns—Very Rev. KENNETH C. STEFFEN, J.C.L., M.A., D.Min.; Rev. KEVIN LAUGHERY, J.C.L.,

Please send all marriage concerns to Office of the Vicar General.

Diocesan Curia—

All diocesan agencies and councils are located at the Catholic Pastoral Center, unless otherwise indicated., *Catholic Pastoral Center, 1615 W. Washington St., P.O. Box 3187, Springfield, 62708-3187.* Tel: 217-698-8500; Fax: 217-698-0802.

Office of the Bishop—Most Rev. GEORGE LUCAS, D.D.; Mrs. CHERYL KANNALL, Exec. Asst.

Office for Campus Ministry—Mr. ROY LANHAM, Dir., *500 Roosevelt Ave., Charleston, 61920.* Tel: 217-348-0188.

Office for Catholic Charities (Central Administration)—Mr. STEVE ROACH, Exec. Dir., *800 S. Fifth St., Springfield, 62703.* Tel: 217-523-9201; Fax: 217-523-5624.

Office for Catholic Education—Mrs. ROSE MERSINGER, Dir.; Mrs. CHRIS MALMEVICK, Assoc. Dir., Adult Education/Catechist Formation; Ms. BARB BURRIS, Assoc. Dir., Planning; Mrs. JEAN JOHNSON, Assoc.

Dir., Elementary Educ.; Mrs. SHERYL SPEARS, Exec. Sec.; Ms. SUSAN DONNELLY, Statistics & Data Specialist.

Board of Catholic Education—Mr. BOB BERGMAN; Mrs. BARBARA BERNARDI; Revs. PATRICK CAHILL, C.S.V.; GERALD BUNSE; Mr. THOMAS CANTWELL; Mrs. BARBARA COLLINS; Revs. PATRICK CAHILL, C.S.V.; CARL KEMME; Ms. HELEN KLOSTERMANN; Bro. JAMES LEWNARD, C.S.V.; Mr. LEE W. MARTEN; Mrs. MARSHA NARMONT; Sr. KATHERINE O'CONNOR, O.P.; Sr. JOAN SCHWORBUS, C.P.P.S.; Mr. PETER MICHAEL VOELZ; Sr. JOANN VOLK, S.S.N.D.; Mr. GIL WEYHAUPT.

Office for Catholic Times—Ms. KATHIE SASS, Editor; Mrs. LAURIE WEAKLEY, Office Mgr.; Mr. WILLIAM CALLAN, Layout & Design Coord. Reporters: Mrs. CATHERINE LOCHER; Mrs. DIANE SCHLINDWEIN; Ms. PAULA RUOT, Advertising; Mrs. MARIAN GREENAN, Comptroller; Mrs. TAMMY WOLTERS, Sec. & Receptionist, . Fax: 217-698-0619.

Office for Chancellor/Planning Coordinator—Rev. EUGENE E. COSTA, S.T.L.; Mrs. PATRICIA POLONUS, Sec.

Office for Communications—Ms. KATHIE SASS, Dir. Tel: 217-467-5535 (Pager); Fax: 217-698-0619.

Office for Family and Youth Ministry—Mrs. DONNA DAUSMAN, Dir.; Mrs. JANA DOTY, Assoc. Dir.; Mrs. JOAN ANDERSON, Sec.

Office for Finances—Mr. JOHN J. MAXWELL, Dir.; Mr. TOM REISER, Assoc. Dir. Property, Buildings and Cemeteries; Mrs. EDNA MAE BROWN, Assoc. Dir. Insurance-Fire, Extended Coverage, Vandalism, Multi-Peril Liability, Workers Compensation, Boiler, Unemployment, Lay Employee Pension Plan, Priests' Personal Property, Seminarians' Medical Care and Coordinator for Lay Employee Health Insurance; Mr. DAN JAMES, Insurance Asst.; Mr. DAN GAUWITZ, Programmer & Analyst; Mrs. JANET WESTENBERGER, Accounting Mgr. Accountants: Mrs. LAURA MORRELL; Mrs. CHRISTINA DAVIS; Miss BOBBI OZANIC, Coord., Annual Catholic Svcs. Appeal and Sec. Clerks, Annual Catholic Svcs. Appeal: Mrs. KAREN REGAN; Mrs. CLARA FLEISCHACKER.

Diocesan Health Insurance Program Committee—Mrs. EDNA MAE BROWN; PATRICE ARSENEAULT; Rev. GERALD BUNSE; Ms. BARB BURRIS; Mr. LEO LENN; Very Rev. VIRGIL MANK, V.F.; Mr. JOHN MAXWELL; Mrs. JOAN MCKINNEY; Mr. HENRY PETRILLI; Mr. THOMAS REISER; Very Rev. JOHN RENKEN, S.T.D., J.C.D., M.A., V.G.; Mrs. JULIE YOST.

Lay Employees' Pension Plan Administrative Committee—Mrs. EDNA MAE BROWN, Sec.; Mr. THOMAS FRIER; Mr. LEO LENN, Chm.; Mr. JOHN MAXWELL, Treas.; Mrs. ROSE MERSINGER; Mr. HENRY PETRILLI; Very Rev. JOHN RENKEN, S.T.D., J.C.D., M.A., V.G.; Mr. THOMAS REISER; Bro. PATRICK SHEA, O.F.M.; Rev. Msgr. PAUL SHERIDAN; Rev. KENNETH VENVERTLOH.

Commission for Buildings and Property—Rev. DANIEL BERGBOWER; Mr. H. F. BOYLE; Mr. ROBERT BUDNIK, Chm.; Sr. CHAMINADE KELLY, O.S.F.; Very Rev. VIRGIL MANK; Mr. JOHN MAXWELL; Rev. DAVID PETERS; Very Rev. JOHN RENKEN, S.T.D., J.C.D., M.A., V.G. Consultants: Mr. HENRY PETRILLI; Mr. THOMAS REISER.

Office for Lay Ministry—Rev. DAVID LANTZ, Dir.; Mrs. JOAN REED, Sec.

Advisory Board—Sr. JANE BOOS, S.S.N.D.; Mrs. JANA DOTY; Mrs. DONNA DAUSMAN; Mrs. MARY HANDLEY; Mr. ELIOT KAPITAN; Mrs. ROSE MERSINGER; Mrs. CHRISTINE MALMEVICK; Very Rev. JOHN A. RENKEN, S.T.D., J.C.D., M.A., V.G.; Mr. ROBERT J. BUCCINO; Very Rev. KENNETH STEFFEN, J.C.L., M.A., D.Min.

Area Specialization Coordinators—Catechetical Leadership Ministry, Mrs. CHRIS MALMEVICK,*Catholic School Leadership Ministry,* Mrs. ROSE MERSINGER,*Clinical Pastoral Care Ministry,* Mrs. MARY HANDLEY,*Family Life Ministry,* Very Rev. KENNETH C. STEFFEN, J.C.L., M.A., D.Min.; Mrs. DONNA DAUSMAN,*Liturgical Ministry: Christian Initiation of Adult Leadership,* Mr. ELIOT KAPITAN-*Liturgical Ministry: Liturgical Leadership,* Mr. ELIOT KAPITAN,*Parish Life Ministry,* Very Rev. JOHN A. RENKEN, S.T.D., J.C.D., M.A., V.G.,*Social Concerns Ministry,* Sr. JANE BOOS, S.S.N.D.,*Tribunal Advocacy Ministry,* Very Rev. JOHN A. RENKEN, S.T.D., J.C.D., M.A., V.G.,*Youth Ministry,* Mrs. DONNA DAUSMAN; Mrs. JANA DOTY.

Office for Lay Organizations—Rev. JOHN R. OSSOLA, Dir.; Mrs. JOAN ANDERSON, Sec.

Office for the Missions—Vacant, Dir.; Vacant, Assoc. Dir.; Mrs. TERESA BETTIS, Sec., *P.O. Box 7025, Springfield, 62791-7025.*

Office for Social Concerns—Sr. JANE BOOS, S.S.N.D., Dir.; Mr. JOSEPH KAUFMANN, Assoc. Dir. Tel: 217-245-4299 (V/TTY).; Mrs. ELAINE VONDERHEIDE, Assoc. Dir. Spec. Needs. Tel: 217-342-2718. Mrs. MARTHA MAYFIELD, Assoc. Dir. Oper.; Sr. FRANCESCA OKWARA, D.D.L., Sec. Tel: 217-698-9581 (TTY); Fax: 217-698-9581.

Black Catholic Ministry—Mr. LEROY JORDAN.

Campaign for Human Development Advisory Board and Allocation Committee—Sr. JANE BOOS, S.S.N.D., Dir. Deanery Representatives: Mr. HERB REISINGER, Alton Deanery; Mr. WILLIAM JOYNER, Decatur Deanery; Mr. KEN HANDLEY, Decatur Deanery; Ms. RUTH ANN STEWART, Jacksonville Deanery; Mrs. MARGUERITE SCHNEIDER, Quincy Deanery; Mrs. NICOLE WELCH, Quincy Deanery; Mr. LLOYD MOSLEY, Springfield Deanery; Mr. LEROY JORDAN, Springfield Deanery; Mr. KEN STEINER, Member At Large.

Comite Diocesano de Ministerio Hispano - Diocesan Committee for Hispanic Ministry—Revs. JOSEPH ALLEN; CARLOS M. BOHORQUEZ; Sr. JANE BOOS, S.S.N.D.; Rev. CHRIS BREY, Chm. FINA CASTLEMAN; Rev. JAMES EDMINSTON, O.F.M.; BENITA HORN; Sr. MARIA DEL PILAR HINOJOSA, M.A.G.; Sr. RENE LAWLESS, O.P.; Sr. DELGINA MARAVILLA MORALES, M.A.G.; Sr. ANNICE MCCLURE, O.S.F.; Sr. ELIZABETH ROMERO MARTINEZ, M.A.G.; Rev. JOHN O'CONNELL; Sr. ANN PITSENBERGER, O.S.F.; Revs. ROBERT PORTER; ROBERT REBERT; Very Rev. JOHN A. RENKEN, S.T.D., J.C.D., M.A., V.G.; Rev. ANGEL SIERRA; Very Rev. KEVIN VANN, V.F.; Revs. EUGENE WEITZEL, C.S.V.; RICHARD WELTON; Sr. DONNA WOODSON, O.S.F.

Elizabeth Ann Seton Parish Program Board—Sr. JANE BOOS, S.S.N.D., Pres.; Bro. PATRICK SHEA, O.F.M., Vice Pres. CAROLYN BODEWES, Exec. Dir. FRITZIE BELZ, Sec. & Treas. SHELLY HEIDEMAN, Project Coord. AGGIE HAYNOR; ANNE HESSLAN DONDANVILLE; Sr. CHAMINADE KELLEY, O.S.F.; MARY FITZGERALD; ALLISON LAABS; LISA LANZOTTI; Very Rev. VIRGIL MANK, V.F.; MICHELLE MANION; TERRI WOOLBRIGHT.

Hispanic Sacramental Ministry—Sr. RENE LAWLESS, O.P. Tel: 217-243-2815.

Task Force For Racial Justice—JAMES FORSTALL, Chm.

Office for Stewardship and Development—Mrs. MARLENE MULFORD, Dir.; Mrs. CATHY FURKIN, Sec.

Steering Committee—Ms. BARBARA BURRIS; Revs. RICHARD CHIOLA; THOMAS DENNIS; Mrs. CATHY FURKIN; Mrs. CHERYL KANNALL; Mr. JOHN MAXWELL; Mrs. MARLENE MULFORD; Mr. HENRY PETRILLI; Very Rev. JOHN RENKEN, S.T.D., J.C.D., M.A., V.G.; Ms. KATHIE SASS; Very Rev. KENNETH STEFFEN, J.C.L., M.A., D.Min.

Office for the Tribunal—Very Rev. JOHN A. RENKEN, S.T.D., J.C.D., M.A., V.G., Dir., Judicial Vicar; Very Rev. KENNETH C. STEFFEN, J.C.L., M.A., D.Min., Assoc. Dir., Adjutant Judicial Vicar; Bro. PATRICK SHEA, O.F.M., J.C.D., J.D., Defender of the Bond; Rev. ANTHONY THIEMAN, Court Expert; Mrs. JEAN KIRK, Office Mgr. & Notary; Bro. JOEL MARK ROUSSEAU, F.F.S.C., Sec. & Notary.

Office of the Vicar General/Director of Clergy Personnel—Very Rev. THOMAS P. HOLINGA, V.G., *711 S. Sixth St., P.O. Box 234, Petersburg, 62675-0234.* Tel: 217-632-2561 (Rectory); Fax: 217-632-7118.

Commission for the Care of Infirm and Retired Priests—Revs. ROBERT BECKER; GERALD BUNSE; Very Rev. THOMAS P. HOLINGA; Revs. JEFFREY HOLTMAN; VIRGIL MANK; CHARLES MULCRONE; CHARLES NELSON; Very Rev. JOHN RENKEN, S.T.D., J.C.D., M.A., V.G.; Revs. JOHN SPREEN; TERENCE TRACEY.

Office of the Vicar General/Moderator of the Curia—Very Rev. JOHN A. RENKEN, S.T.D., J.C.D., M.A., V.G. Tel: 217-629-9109 (Evenings & Weekends). Bro. PATRICK SHEA, O.F.M., J.C.D., J.D., Exec. Asst. to Vicar General; Legal Counsel; Mrs. CAROL MULLER, Assoc. to Vicar Gen., Records Mgmt. Office Mgr. & Notary; Mrs. JOAN REED, Exec. Sec. Special Projects, Central Purchasing Coord. & Notary; Mrs. TONI COLCLASURE, Receptionist for Catholic Pastoral Center.

Archives—Sr. MARY MATTHIAS CLARKE, O.P., Dir. Tel: 217-522-3986.

CPC Media Resource Center—Mrs. JEAN FORNESS, Dir.; Sr. CHUKWUMA ONYEKWELU, D.D.L., Asst.

Diocesan Historian—Sr. SUSAN KARINA DICKEY, O.P., Ph.D.

Office for Vocations—Revs. R. DEAN PROBST, Dir. CHRISTOPHER BREY; CHRISTOPHER COMERFORD, Assoc. Dir., Fax: 217-854-8119.

Office for Worship—Mr. ELIOT KAPITAN, Dir.; Mrs. JAN GRIGGS, Sec.

Commission for the Liturgy—Mr. JERRY BAUMAN; Revs. BARRY HARMON; ANGEL SIERRA; Mrs. CAROL JOHNSON; Mr. ELIOT KAPITAN; Mrs. MARY KELDERMANS; Rev. JOSEPH RING, Chm.; Mrs. CAROL SEIFERT; Mrs. JUDITH UNGER; Mr. TOM WALKER.

Councils

Diocesan Finance Council—Sr. CHRISTINE BRAMLET, O.S.U.; Mr. WILFRED KALTENBACH; Mr. WILLIAM KESSLER; Mr. LEO LENN, Chm.; Rev. JAMES NEUMAN. Consultants: Very Rev. JOHN RENKEN, S.T.D., J.C.D., M.A., V.G.; Mr. JOHN MAXWELL; Mr. THOMAS REISER.

Presbyteral Council—Most Rev. GEORGE LUCAS, Pres.; Revs. EDWIN ALBERS, O.F.M.; CHRISTOPHER BREY; LARRY BRUNETTE; EUGENE COSTA; ADRIAN FISCHER, O.F.M.; JEFFREY GOECKNER; THOMAS HOLINGA; ROBERT JALLAS; ALLEN KEMME; DONALD KNUFFMAN; MICHAEL KUSE, Vice Chm. WILLIAM MAUL; CHARLES NELSON; MARTIN O'HARA; ROBERT REBERT; Very Rev. JOHN A. RENKEN, S.T.D., J.C.D., M.A., V.G., Sec. & Treas.; Revs. KENNETH STEFFEN, J.C.L., M.A., D.Min., Chm.; KEVIN SULLIVAN; EUGENE WEITZEL, C.S.V.

Catholic Charities Institutions

Area Offices—

Alton. Catholic Charities of Alton and Wood River—Mr. RICK FACCIN, Area Dir., *735 Park Dr., Alton, 62002.* Tel: 618-462-0634; Fax: 618-462-3209.

Carlinville. Catholic Charities—Mrs. PATRICIA A. POPE, Area Dir., *525 W. Second South St., Carlinville, 62626.* Tel: 217-854-4511; Fax: 217-854-8049.

Decatur. Catholic Charities—Mrs. MARIE RADEMACHER, Area Dir., *247 W. Prairie, Decatur, 62523.* Tel: 217-428-3458; Fax: 217-428-4415.

Effingham. Catholic Charities—Sr. BRENDA FRITZ, D.C., Area Dir., *601 W. Fayette, Effingham, 62401.* Tel: 217-342-9800; Fax: 217-342-3873.

Granite City. Catholic Charities—Mr. DAVE DALY, Area Dir., *2105 State St., Granite City, 62040.* Tel: 618-877-1184; Fax: 618-798-4287.

Mattoon. Catholic Charities of Coles, Douglas and Edgar Counties—Vacant, Community Svcs. Dir., *2121 Marshall, Mattoon, 61938.* Tel: 217-235-0420; Fax: 217-235-0423.

Quincy. Catholic Charities—Sr. MARY SHAW, A.S.C., Area Dir., *926 State St., Quincy, 62301.* Tel: 217-222-0958; Fax: 217-222-8737.

Springfield. Catholic Charities—Mrs. DANIELLE K. KELLERS, Area Dir., *120 S. 11th St., Springfield, 62703.* Tel: 217-525-0500; Fax: 217-525-0554.

Institutions—

Alton, Catholic Children's Home—Ms. CANDACE LUMETTA, Admin., *1400 State St., Alton, 62002.* Tel: 618-465-3594; Fax: 618-465-4023.

Springfield. St. Monica's Center—Mr. STEVEN ROACH, Assoc. Dir.; Mr. JOE CAIN, Prog. Dir., *109 E. Lawrence Ave., Springfield, 62704.* Tel: 217-523-7922; Fax: 217-525-8241.

Springfield. St. John's Breadline—Mr. DANIEL FRACHEY, Supvr., *430 N. Fifth St., Springfield, 62701.* Tel: 217-528-6098; Fax: 217-528-3605.

CLERGY, PARISHES, MISSIONS AND PAROCHIAL SCHOOLS

CITY OF SPRINGFIELD

(Sangamon County)

1—CATHEDRAL OF THE IMMACULATE CONCEPTION (1928), Revs. John R. Ossola; Peter C. Harman; Thomas J. Casey, S.J.

Res., 524 E. Lawrence Ave., P.O. Box 1667, 62705. Tel: 217-522-3342; Fax: 217-522-1151. [JC]

School—Tel: 217-523-2652; Fax: 217-523-2750.

Springfield Dominican Sisters 3; Lay Teachers 17; Students 225; Preschool 26.

Catechesis/Religious Programs—Students 70.

2—BLESSED SACRAMENT (1924), Revs. John C. Burnett; William Kessler.

Res., 1725 S. Walnut Ave., 62704. Tel: 217-528-7521; Fax: 217-528-3137.

School—Tel: 217-522-7534; Fax: 217-522-7542.

Lay Teachers 30; Students 436.

Catechesis/Religious Programs—Students 99.

3—CHRIST THE KING (1963), Revs. David S. Lantz; Thom Dennis.

Res., 1930 Barberry Dr., 62704. Tel: 217-546-3527; Fax: 217-793-6393.

School—Tel: 217-546-2159; Fax: 217-546-0291.

Lay Teachers 23; Students 503.

Catechesis/Religious Programs—Elementary, 1920 Barberry Dr., 62704.

Students 83.

4—LITTLE FLOWER (1947), Revs. Henry C. Schmidt; Carlos M. Borhorquez.

800 Stevenson Dr., 62703. Tel: 217-529-1606; Fax: 217-529-1649. [JC]

School—Tel: 217-529-4511; Fax: 217-529-0405.

Sisters 3; Lay Teachers 27; Students 404.

Catechesis/Religious Programs—Students 57.

5—ST. AGNES (1889), Very Rev. Patrick J. Wright, V.F.; Revs. Mark A. Schulte; Robert T. Becker.

Res., 245 N. Amos Ave., 62702. Tel: 217-793-1330; Fax: 217-793-3212.
School—Tel: 217-793-1370; Fax: 217-793-1238.
Lay Teachers 25; Students 500.
Catechesis/Religious Programs—Students 201.

6—ST. ALOYSIUS (1928), Revs. John M. Titus; Donald J. Meehling.
Res., 2119 N. 20th St., 62702. Tel: 217-544-4554; Fax: 217-544-4963.
School—Tel: 217-544-4553; Fax: 217-544-1680.
Lay Teachers 26; Students 409.
Catechesis/Religious Programs—Students 50.

7—ST. FRANCES CABRINI (1948), Rev. Rodney A. Schwartz, Admin.
Res., 1020 N. Milton Ave., 62702. Tel: 217-522-8555; Fax: 217-522-8555.
School—Tel: 217-528-8302.
Lay Teachers 8; Students 66.
Catechesis/Religious Programs—Elementary, 1024 N. Milton, 62702.
Students 66.

8—ST. KATHARINE DREXEL (2001), Very Rev. John A. Renken, Admin.
Office: 700 S. 12th St., P.O. Box 4302, 62708-4302. Tel: 217-744-0578.
Res., P.O. Box 590, Riverton, 62561-0590.
School—St. Patrick, (Grades K-8) 1800 S. Grand Ave. E., P.O. Box 4032, 62703. Tel: 217-523-7670.
Lay Teachers 7; Students 80.

9—ST. JOSEPH (1875), Rev. Patrick W. Render, C.S.V.
Res., 1345 N. Sixth St., 62702. Tel: 217-544-7426; Fax: 217-544-7467.
School—Tel: 217-523-6597.
Ursuline Sisters 1; Lay Teachers 14; Students 195.
Catechesis/Religious Programs—Students 78.

10—ST. PATRICK. Merged with Sacred Heart of Jesus, Springfield to form St. Katharine Drexel, Springfield.

11—SS. PETER AND PAUL (1859) (German), Rev. Frank J. O'Hara.
Res., 426 N. Sixth St., 62702. Tel: 217-523-3681. [JC]

12—SACRED HEART OF JESUS (1884) (German). Merged with St. Patrick, Springfield to form St. Katharine Drexel.

OUTSIDE THE CITY OF SPRINGFIELD

Alexander, Morgan Co., Visitation B.V.M., Rev. Joseph P. Kerber.
Mailing Address: P.O. Box 20, New Berlin, 62670. Tel: 217-488-2410; Fax: 217-488-2410.
Church—Old U.S. 36, 62601. [CEM]

Altamont, Effingham Co., St. Clare (1874) German, Rev. John M. Savoree, Admin.
Res., 216 N. Ninth St., 62411. Tel: 618-483-5346. [CEM]
Catechesis/Religious Programs—Students 145.
Mission—St. Elmo, Fayette Co., St. Mary.

Alton, Madison Co.,

1—SS. PETER AND PAUL, (1855), Revs. Roger Schoenhofen, O.M.I.; Maurice Lange, O.M.I.
Res., 717 State St., 62002. Tel: 618-465-4221; Fax: 618-465-0346. [JC]
School—Tel: 618-465-8711.
Lay Teachers 9; Students 175.
Catechesis/Religious Programs—Students 60.

2—IMMACULATE CONCEPTION-ST. MARY'S, (1858), Revs. John Paul Klein, O.M.V.; Daniel Barron, O.M.V.; James Walther; John Wykes, O.M.V.; Bros. David Guza; Fernando Cuenca.
Mailing Address: 519 E. 4th St., 62002. Tel: 618-465-4284.
Res., 525 E. Fourth St., 62002. Tel: 618-465-4284; Fax: 618-463-4637. [CEM]
School—Tel: 618-465-8523.
Sisters of St. Francis of the Martyr of St. George 5; Lay Teachers 10; Students 219.
Catechesis/Religious Programs—Students 77.

3—ST. PATRICK, (1883). Closed. For inquiries for parish records contact the Chancery.

4—ST. MATTHEW, (1947), Rev. Angel A. Sierra.
Res., 1015 Milton Rd., 62002-3197. Tel: 618-465-8582; Fax: 618-465-5994.
School—Tel: 618-462-6032.
Lay Teachers 11; Students 132.
Catechesis/Religious Programs—Students 27.

Arcola, Douglas Co., St. John the Baptist (1865), Rev. Joseph P. Allen (Chicago) Admin.
Res., 205 S. Locust St., Box 133, 61910. Tel: 217-268-3766; Fax: 217-268-3545. [JC]
Catechesis/Religious Programs—210 S. Pine St., 61910.
Students 106.

Arenzville, Cass Co., St. Fidelis (1853) (German-Irish), Rev. Eugene J. Weitzel, C.S.V.
Res., 215 W. Fifth St., Beardstown, 62618. Tel: 217-323-4345.
Catechesis/Religious Programs—Students 12.

Ashland, Cass Co., St. Augustine (1875), Rev. John W. Spreen.
Res., 320 N. Saratoga, P.O. Box 438, 62612. Tel: 217-476-8856. [CEM]
Catechesis/Religious Programs—Students 46.

Assumption, Christian Co., Assumption B.V.M. (1870), Rev. Alan Hunter.
Res., 301 St. Peter St., 62510. Tel: 217-226-3536; Fax: 217-226-3538. [CEM]
Catechesis/Religious Programs—Tel: 217-226-3205.
Students 63.

Athens, Menard Co., Holy Family (1903), Rev. Eugene E. Costa.
Res., 129 Stardust Dr., Sherman, 62684. Tel: 217-523-3816; Fax: 217-523-3954.
Church—Springfield Rd., 62613. Tel: 217-636-8238.
Catechesis/Religious Programs—Students 52.

Auburn, Sangamon Co., St. Benedict (1903), Rev. Kevin Michael Laughery.
Catechesis/Religious Programs—Students 148.

Barry, Pike Co., Holy Redeemer (1954), Rev. J. Michael Jenkins.
Res., 226 E. Adams, Pittsfield, 62363. Tel: 217-285-4321; Fax: 217-285-9400. [JC]
Catechesis/Religious Programs—Students 24.

Batchtown, Calhoun Co., St. Barbara (1910), Rev. Thomas Hagstrom.
Office: P.O. Box 38, Brussels, 62013. Tel: 618-883-2400; Fax: 618-883-2511.
Res., Meppen Ln., Meppen, 62013. Tel: 618-883-2309. [CEM]

Beardstown, Cass Co., St. Alexius (1838), Rev. Eugene J. Weitzel, C.S.V.
Res., 215 W. 5th St., 62618. Tel: 217-323-4345. [CEM]
Catechesis/Religious Programs—Tel: 217-323-1888.
Students 76.
Mission—Arenzville, Cass Co., St. Fidelis, 100 E. North, 62711. Fax: 217-323-5464.

Belleview, Calhoun Co., St. Agnes (1900) (German), Rev. Thomas Hagstrom.
Res., 404 Main St., P.O. Box C, Hardin, 62047. Tel: 618-576-2228; Fax: 618-576-9448. [CEM]

Beltrees, Jersey Co., St. Michael (1877), Rev. Robert L. Meyer.
Res., 11 N. Evans St., P.O. Box 218, Grafton, 62037. Tel: 618-786-3512; Fax: 618-786-2027. [CEM]
Church—Beltrees Rd., 62022.

Benld, Macoupin Co., St. Joseph (1915), Rev. Lawrence Auda.
Res., 304 N. Macoupin, Gillespie, 62033. Tel: 217-839-3456.
Church—310 W. Central Ave., 62009. Tel: 217-835-4701.
Catechesis/Religious Programs—Students 33.

Bethalto, Madison Co., Our Lady Queen of Peace (1945), Rev. Kevin B. Sullivan.
Res., 132 Butcher St., P.O. Box 100, 62010. Tel: 618-377-6519; Fax: 618-377-9550.
School—Tel: 618-377-6401; Fax: 618-377-6146.
Lay Teachers 13; Students 207.
Catechesis/Religious Programs—Students 99.

Bethany, Moultrie Co., St. Isidore (1864), Rev. James D. O'Shea.
Res., 400 Woodland Ln., Mount Zion, 62549. Tel: 217-864-3467; Fax: 217-864-3091. [CEM]
Catechesis/Religious Programs—Students 14.

Bishop Creek, Effingham Co., St. Aloysius (1865), Rev. Edwin O. Albers, O.F.M.
Res., 19812 E. 1000th Ave., Dieterich, 62424. Tel: 217-925-5579; Fax: 217-925-5578. [CEM]
Catechesis/Religious Programs—Students 248.

Black Jack, Madison Co., St. John the Baptist. Closed. For inquiries for parish records contact the Chancery.

Bluffs, Scott Co., St. Patrick (1871), Rev. Charles T. Nelson.
Res., 108 Pearl St., Winchester, 62694. Tel: 217-742-5224.

Brighton, Macoupin Co., St. Alphonsus (1868) (German), Rev. Raphael Paul.
Res., 918 N. Main St., 62012. Tel: 618-372-3352; Fax: 618-372-8133.
Catechesis/Religious Programs—Students 80.

Brocton, Edgar Co., St. Thomas Aquinas (1899). Closed. For inquiries for parish records contact the Chancery.

Brussels, Calhoun Co., St. Mary (1851), Rev. Thomas Hagstrom.
Office: P.O. Box 38, 62013. Tel: 618-883-2400; Fax: 618-883-2511.
Res., Meppen Ln., Meppen, 62013. Tel: 618-883-2309. [CEM]
School—Tel: 618-883-2124. Mrs. Victoria Klaas, Prin.
Lay Teachers 4; Teacher Aides 1; Students 85.
Catechesis/Religious Programs—Students 20.

Buffalo, Sangamon Co., St. Joseph (1882), Sr. Lois Kikkert, O.P., Parish Life Coord.
Mailing Address: P.O. Box 47, Illiopolis, 62539. Tel: 217-486-3851.
Church—302 W.S. St., Tel: 217-364-4696.
Catechesis/Religious Programs—Students 17.

Bunker Hill, Macoupin Co., St. Mary (1865), Rev. Robert N. Porter.
Res., 300 S. Putnam, P.O. Box A-H, 62014-9512. Tel: 618-585-4700; Fax: 618-585-3449. [CEM]
Catechesis/Religious Programs—Students 43.

Camp Point, Adams Co., St. Thomas (1860), Rev. Charles A. Edwards.
Res., #6 Paradise Acres, P.O. Box 228, Liberty, 62347-0228. Tel: 217-645-3444; Fax: 217-645-3546.
Church—Spring St. & Ohio St., 62320.
Parish Hall: Tel: 217-593-6685.
Catechesis/Religious Programs—Sr. Joan Schnorbus, C.PP.S., D.R.E.
Students 65.

Carlinville, Macoupin Co., St. Mary's of the Immaculate Conception. Closed. For inquiries for parish records contact St. Joseph.
SS. Mary & Joseph (1996). SS. Mary & Joseph was formed by the merger of St. Mary's of the Immaculate Conception & St. Joseph. Rev. R. Dean Probst.
Res., 1011 Ravine, 62626. Tel: 217-854-8034; Fax: 217-854-9228. [JC]
Church—2010 E. First S. St., 62626-0647. Tel: 217-854-7151; Fax: 217-854-9228.
Catechesis/Religious Programs—Holy Family School of Religion, Tel: 217-854-9220.
Students 229.

Carrollton, Greene Co., St. John the Evangelist (1858), Rev. Barry J. Harmon.
Res., 414 Third St., 62016-1319. Tel: 217-942-3551; Fax: 217-942-6767. [CEM]
School—426 Third St., 62016-1319. Tel: 217-942-6814. Mr. Gary E. Miller, Prin.
Lay Teachers 9; Students 145.
Catechesis/Religious Programs—Students 27.

Casey, Clark Co., St. Charles Borromeo (1878), Rev. Jeffery A. Grant.
Church—300 E. Jefferson, P.O. Box 72, 62420.
Res., 110 Lincoln Dr., P.O. Box 156, Greenup, 62428. Tel: 217-923-3523; Fax: 217-923-3523.
Catechesis/Religious Programs—Students 24.

Chandlerville, Cass Co., St. Basil. Merged with St. Luke, Virginia.

Charleston, Coles Co., St. Charles Borromeo (1873), Rev. Joseph G. Ring.
Res., 921 E. Madison St., 61920. Tel: 217-345-3332; Fax: 217-345-4252.
Catechesis/Religious Programs—Students 215.

Chatham, Sangamon Co., St. Joseph (1920), Rev. Robert B. Franzen.
Res., 700 E. Spruce, 62629. Tel: 217-483-3772; Fax: 217-483-4581.
Catechesis/Religious Programs—62629. Tel: 217-483-4514.
Students 509.

Coffeen, Montgomery Co., St. John the Baptist (1898), Rev. Carl Schmidt, Admin.
Res., 400 Jefferson, P.O. Box 278, 62017. Tel: 217-534-2220. [CEM][JC]
Catechesis/Religious Programs—Students 18.

Collinsville, Madison Co., SS. Peter and Paul (1855) (Italian), Revs. John P. Beveridge; Larry H. Brunette; Sr. Mary Magdelen Fearon, O.S.U., Pastoral Assoc.
Res., 207 Vandalia St., 62234. Tel: 618-345-4343; Fax: 618-345-1145. [CEM]
School—Tel: 618-344-5450; Fax: 618-344-5536.
Lay Teachers 23; Students 367.
Catechesis/Religious Programs—Students 180.

Dalton City, Moultrie Co., Sacred Heart (1891). Closed. For inquiries for parish records contact the Chancery.

Decatur, Macon Co.,

1—HOLY FAMILY, (1959), Rev. Carl A. Kemme; Sr. Marianne Nolan, O.P., Pastoral Assoc.
Res., 2400 S. Franklin St., 62521. Tel: 217-423-6223; Fax: 217-423-6237. [JC]
School—Tel: 217-423-7049; Fax: 217-423-7098.
Springfield Dominican Sisters 3; Lay Teachers 17; Students 274; Preschool 30.
Catechesis/Religious Programs—Students 56.

2—OUR LADY OF LOURDES, (1958), Revs. Kevin W. Vann; Jeffrey W. Goeckner; Dominic Anaeto.
Res., 3850 Lourdes Dr., 62526. Tel: 217-877-4404; Fax: 217-877-5257. [JC]
School—3950 Lourdes Dr., 62526-1799. Tel: 217-877-4408; Fax: 217-872-3655.
Lay Teachers 21; Students 348.
Catechesis/Religious Programs—Students 142.

3—ST. PATRICK, (1853), Rev. Donald L. Wolford.
Res., 407 E. Eldorado St., 62523. Tel: 217-429-5363; Fax: 217-429-8206. [JC]
School—Tel: 217-423-4351; Fax: 217-423-7288.
Lay Teachers 12; Students 164.
Catechesis/Religious Programs—Students 44.

4—ST. JAMES, (1877), Sr. Glenda Bourgeois, O.S.U., Parish Life Coord.; Rev. Martin Mangan, Priest Mod.
Res., 742 E. Clay St., 62521. Tel: 217-428-7733; Fax: 217-428-7426. [JC]
School—Tel: 217-422-7031; Fax: 217-422-2121.
Religious 1; Lay Teachers 11; Students 127.
Catechesis/Religious Programs—Students 70.

5—ST. THOMAS THE APOSTLE, (1925), Rev. Dennis D. Kollross.
Res., 2160 N. Edward St., P.O. Box 2697, 62524-2697. Tel: 217-877-4146; Fax: 217-877-4147.
Catechesis/Religious Programs—62524-2697. Students 60.

Dieterich, Effingham Co., Immaculate Conception (1905), Rev. Edwin O. Albers, O.F.M.
Res., 19812 E. 1000th Ave., 62424. Tel: 217-925-5579; Fax: 217-925-5578. [CEM]
Catechesis/Religious Programs—Students 97.

Divernon, Sangamon Co., Sacred Heart (1905), Rev. Kevin Michael Laughery.
Res., 125 E. Washington St., Auburn, 62530. Tel: 217-438-6222; Fax: 217-438-6732. [CEM]
Church—230 S. Lincoln, 62530. Tel: 217-628-3629.
Catechesis/Religious Programs—Students 8.

East Alton, Madison Co., St. Kevin (1959), Rev. Delix Michel, Admin.
Res., 108 Airwood Dr., E., 62024. Tel: 618-259-3363; Fax: 618-259-2276.
School—Tel: 618-259-6040.
Lay Teachers 6; Aides 2; Students 78.
Catechesis/Religious Programs—Students 45.

Edgewood, Effingham Co., St. Anne (1865) (German), Revs. Daniel J. Bergbower; John M. Savoree, Admin.
Res., 216 N. Ninth, Altamont, 62411. Tel: 618-483-5346. [CEM]
Catechesis/Religious Programs—Students 16.

Edwardsville, Madison Co., St. Boniface (1869) (German), Rev. John Corredato, C.S.V.
Res., 110 N. Buchanan St., P.O. Box 423, 62025. Tel: 618-656-6450; Fax: 618-656-7669. [CEM]
Preschool:—Tel: 618-692-9315.
Students 72.
School—Tel: 618-656-6917.
Lay Teachers 12; Students 232; Preschool 72.
Catechesis/Religious Programs—Students 205.

St. Mary (1842), Rev. Gerald L. Bunse.
Res., 1802 Madison, 62025. Tel: 618-656-4857; Fax: 618-656-1715. [JC]
School—Tel: 618-656-1230.
Priests 1; Lay Teachers 19; Students 297.
Catechesis/Religious Programs—Students 70.

Effingham, Effingham Co., Sacred Heart (1892), Rev. Daniel J. Bergbower.
Res., 405 S. Henrietta, P.O. Box 870, 62401. Tel: 217-347-7177; Fax: 217-347-0728. [JC]
School—Tel: 217-342-4060; Fax: 217-342-9251.
Lay Teachers 14; Students 220.
Catechesis/Religious Programs—Students 165.

St. Anthony of Padua (1858), Very Rev. Leo J. Enlow; Rev. Thomas C. Meyer.
Res., 417 N. Third, P.O. Box 764, 62401. Tel: 217-347-7129; Fax: 217-342-6980. [CEM]
School—Tel: 217-347-0419; Fax: 217-347-2749.
Sisters 2; Lay Teachers 27; Students 420.
High School—Tel: 217-342-6969; Fax: 217-342-6997.
Priests 3; Lay Teachers 19; Students 215.
Catechesis/Religious Programs—Fax: 217-347-6980.
Students 92.

Farmersville, Montgomery Co., St. Mary (1876), Rev. David Zimmerman.
Res., 310 Nobbe St., P.O. Box 80, 62533-0080. Tel: 217-227-3349; Fax: 217-227-3324. [CEM][JC]
School—St. Isidore, Tel: 217-227-3359.
Lay Teachers 6; Students 54.

Fieldon, Jersey Co., St. Mary, Rev. William Hembrow.
Res., 306 N. Washington, Jerseyville, 62052. Tel: 618-498-3416. [CEM]
Catechesis/Religious Programs—Clustered with Holy Ghost, Jerseyville.

Franklin, Morgan Co., Sacred Heart of Jesus (1886), Rev. Joseph P. Kerber.
Mailing Address: P.O. Box 20, New Berlin, 62670. Tel: 217-488-2410; Fax: 217-488-2410. [CEM]
Office & Res.—P.O. Box 20, New Berlin, 62670.
Church—62638. Tel: 217-675-2631.
Parish Center—Tel: 217-675-2631.
Catechesis/Religious Programs—Students 65.

Gillespie, Macoupin Co., SS. Simon and Jude (1879), Rev. Lawrence Auda.
Res., 304 N. Macoupin St., 62033. Tel: 217-839-3456. [CEM]
Catechesis/Religious Programs—Students 60.

Girard, Macoupin Co., St. Patrick (1887), Rev. David Zimmerman.
Mailing and Res.: 310 Nobbe St., P.O. Box 80, Farmersville, 62533-0080. Tel: 217-227-3349; Fax: 217-227-3324 (Call First).
Church—745 W. Center, 62640.
Catechesis/Religious Programs—Tel: 217-627-3575.
Students 96.

Glen Carbon, Madison Co., St. Cecilia (1928), Rev. Stephen J. Pohlman.
Res., 155 N. Main St., 62034. Tel: 618-288-3200; Fax: 618-288-3292.
Catechesis/Religious Programs—St. Cecilia Family Life Center, Tel: 618-288-5523.
Students 131.

Godfrey, Madison Co., St. Ambrose (1947), Very Rev. Virgil Mank, V.F.; Mr. Darren Eultgen, M.Div., Pastoral Assoc.; Mr. Patrick Fitzgerald, Pastoral Min.
Church—820 W. Homer Adams Pkwy., 62035. Tel: 618-466-2921; Fax: 618-466-2959.
Res., 3307 Morkel Dr., 62035. Tel: 618-466-6408. [JC]
School—Tel: 618-466-4216; Fax: 618-466-4575. Mary Jo Jacobs, Prin.
Lay Teachers 22; Students 382.
Catechesis/Religious Programs—Students 121.

Grafton, Jersey Co., St. Patrick (1871), Rev. Robert L. Meyer.
Res., 11 N. Evans, P.O. Box 218, 62037. Tel: 618-786-3512; Fax: 618-786-2027.

Granite City, Madison Co., Holy Family (1988), Revs. William P. Fisherkeller, C.S.V.; Thomas F. Wise, C.S.V.
Res., 2606 Washington Ave., 62040-4810. Tel: 618-877-7158; Fax: 618-877-7105. [JC]
School—Tel: 618-877-5500; Fax: 618-877-5502.
Springfield Dominican Sisters 1; Lay Teachers 19; Students 323.
Catechesis/Religious Programs—Tel: 618-452-8244.
Students 146.

St. Elizabeth (1871), Rev. Thomas Liebler. In res., Rev. Francis Tebangura (Uganda).
Res., 2301 Pontoon Rd., 62040. Tel: 618-931-2916; Fax: 618-931-2928. [CEM][JC]
School—Tel: 618-931-0125.
Lay Teachers 13; Students 224.
St. Elizabeth Preschool—2300 Pontoon Rd., 62040. Tel: 618-931-0127.
Catechesis/Religious Programs—Students 130.

Grantfork, Madison Co., St. Gertrude (1872), Rev. James A. Flach.
Res., 120 N. Windmill, P.O. Box 457, Marine, 62061. Tel: 618-887-4535. [CEM]
Catechesis/Religious Programs—6555 Dauderman Rd., Alhambra, 62001. Tel: 618-488-2699. Mitzi Plocher, D.R.E.
Students 63.

Green Creek, Effingham Co., St. Mary Help of Christians (1860) (German), Rev. Emil G. Helfrich, O.M.I.
Res., 20057 N. 1525th St., Effingham, 62401. Tel: 217-844-2062; Fax: 217-844-2062. [CEM]
Catechesis/Religious Programs—Tel: 217-347-2634.
Students 108.

Greenfield, Greene Co., St. Michael (1880), Rev. Edward Groesch.
Res., 411 Sheffield, 62044. Tel: 217-368-2176. [CEM]
Catechesis/Religious Programs—Students 41.

Greenup, Cumberland Co., Christ the King (1937), Rev. Jeffery A. Grant.
Res., 110 Lincoln Dr., P.O. Box 156, 62428. Tel: 217-923-3523; Fax: 217-923-3523.
Catechesis/Religious Programs—Students 61.

Greenville, Bond Co., St. Lawrence (1868), Rev. Victor J. Kaltenbach.
Res., 512 S. Prairie St., 62246. Tel: 618-664-3169. [CEM]
Catechesis/Religious Programs—Tel: 618-664-0960.
Students 170.

Griggsville, Pike Co., Holy Family. Closed. For details for parish records see St. Mary, Pittsfield.

Hagaman, Macoupin Co., St. Catherine (1905), Rev. Edward Groesch.
Res., 411 Sheffield, Greenfield, 62044. Tel: 217-368-2176.

Hardin, Calhoun Co., St. Norbert (1872) (German), Rev. Thomas Hagstrom.
Office: 404 Main St., P.O. Box C, 62047. Tel: 618-576-2517; Fax: 618-576-9448. [CEM]
Res., Meppen Ln., Meppen, 62013. Tel: 618-883-2309.
School—(Grades 1-7). Tel: 618-576-2514.
Lay Teachers 4; Aides 3; Students 75.
Catechesis/Religious Programs—Tel: 618-576-2628.
Students 98.

Highland, Madison Co., St. Paul (1846), Revs. David L. Peters; Robert W. Spriggs.
Res., 1412 Ninth St., 62249. Tel: 618-654-2339; Fax: 618-654-9980. [CEM]
School—(Grades PreK-8). Tel: 618-654-7525; Fax: 618-654-8795.
Sisters 1; Lay Teachers 25; Students 381.
Catechesis/Religious Programs—1420 Ninth St., 62249. Tel: 618-654-4313.
Students 410.

Hillsboro, Montgomery Co., St. Agnes (1840), Rev. Dave Schmidt, Admin.
Res., 419 S. State, Litchfield, 62056. Tel: 217-532-5288. [CEM]
Catechesis/Religious Programs—Tel: 217-532-2631.
Students 152.

Hume, Edgar Co., St. Michael (1876), Rev. Paul H. Skelton.
Res., 208 N. Pine, Box 17, Villa Grove, 61956. Tel: 217-832-8352; Fax: 217-832-8352.
Catechesis/Religious Programs—Students 17.

Illiopolis, Sangamon Co., Visitation B.V.M. (1866), Sr. Lois Kikkert, O.P., Parish Life Coord.
Res., 410 Anne St., P.O. Box 47, 62539. Tel: 217-486-3851. [CEM][JC]
Catechesis/Religious Programs—Students 37.

Island Grove, Jasper Co., St. Joseph (1874), Rev. Edwin O. Albers, O.F.M.
Res., 19812 E. 1000th Ave., Dieterich, 62424. Tel: 217-925-5579; Fax: 217-925-5578. [CEM]
Catechesis/Religious Programs—Students 102.

Jacksonville, Morgan Co., Our Saviour (1851), Revs. Ken J. Venvertloh; Christopher Comerford.
Mailing Address: 453 E. State St., 62650. Tel: 217-245-6184; Fax: 217-245-6185. [CEM]
School—62650. Tel: 217-243-8621. Mrs. Peggy Goodwin, Prin.
Lay Teachers 22; Students 360.
High School—Routt Catholic High School, 500 E. College, 62650. Tel: 217-243-8563; Fax: 217-243-3138. Mr. James Woods, Prin.
Lay Teachers 16; Students 140.
Catechesis/Religious Programs—Tel: 217-245-7633.
Students 135.

Jerseyville, Jersey Co., Holy Ghost (German), Rev. William Hembrow.
Res., 306 N. Washington St., 62052. Tel: 618-498-3416. [JC]
School—St. Francis/Holy Ghost School. See St. Francis. Tel: 618-498-4823.
Catechesis/Religious Programs—Students 467.

St. Francis Xavier (1857) (Irish/German), Rev. Donald Patrick Gibbons.
Res., 506 S. State St., P.O. Box 260, 62052-0260. Tel: 618-498-3518. [CEM][JC]
School—St. Francis/Holy Ghost School, Tel: 618-498-4823.
St. Francis: (Grades K & 5-8) 412 S. State St., 62052. Tel: 618-498-4823.; Holy Ghost: (Grades 1-4) 309 N. Washington St., 62052. Tel: 618-498-4910. Sr. Zita Telkamp, C.D.P., Prin.
Sisters 1; Lay Teachers 20; Students 367.
Catechesis/Religious Programs—Tel: 618-498-5497.
Students 29.

Kampsville, Calhoun Co., St. Anselm (1877) (German), Rev. Thomas Hagstrom.
Office: 404 Main St., P.O. Box C, Hardin, 62047. Tel: 618-576-2517; Fax: 618-576-9448. [CEM]
Res., Meppen Ln., Meppen, 62013. Tel: 618-883-2309.
Catechesis/Religious Programs—Clustered with St. Norbert, Hardin.

Kincaid, Christian Co., St. Rita (1920), Rev. Charles G. Dahlby.
Res., 30 St. Rita Ct., P.O. Box 439, 62540. Tel: 217-237-4339; Fax: 217-237-2477.
Catechesis/Religious Programs—Students 51.

Liberty, Adams Co., St. Brigid (1860), Rev. Charles A. Edwards.
Church—P.O. Box 228, 62347. Tel: 217-645-3444; Fax: 217-645-3546. [CEM]
Res., #6 Paradise Acres., P.O. Box 228, 62347-0228.
Catechesis/Religious Programs—Sr. Joan Schnorbus, C.PP.S., D.R.E.
Students 102.

Lillyville, Cumberland Co., Sacred Heart of Jesus (1877) (German), Rev. Emil G. Helfrich, O.M.I.
Mailing Address: 127 County Rd. 100 E., Sigel, 62462.
Res., 20057 N. 1525 St., Effingham, 62401. Tel: 217-844-2062. [CEM]
Catechesis/Religious Programs—Tel: 217-844-3603.
Students 55.

Litchfield, Montgomery Co., Holy Family (1988). Former St. Mary, founded in 1857. Rev. David L. Schmidt.
Res., 419 S. State St., 62056. Tel: 217-324-2776; Fax: 217-324-2868. [CEM]
Catechesis/Religious Programs—211 E. Columbia St., 62056. Tel: 217-324-5834.
Students 102.

Livingston, Madison Co., Sacred Heart (1913), Rev. George Radosevich Tel: 618-635-8490.
Res., 188 Livingston Ave., P.O. Box 458, 62058. Tel: 618-637-2211. [CEM]
Catechesis/Religious Programs—Students 21.

Lovington, Moultrie Co., St. Mary. Closed. Sacramental records are located at Our Lady of the Holy Spirit.

Macon, Macon Co., St. Stanislaus (1866), Rev. Alan Hunter.
Res., 301 St. Peter St., Assumption, 62510. Tel: 217-226-3536; Fax: 217-226-3538. [JC]
Catechesis/Religious Programs—Tel: 217-226-3205.
Students 14.

Madison, Madison Co., Our Lady of Czestochowa (1912) (Polish). (St. Mary). Friar Edmund Mundwiller, O.F.M., Admin.; Sr. Bernadette Meyer, C.D.P., Parish Admin. In res., Rev. Joseph B. Hagen, O.F.M.
Res., 1621 10th St., 62060. Tel: 618-452-5180. [JC]

Marine, Madison Co., St. Elizabeth (1856), Rev. James A. Flach.
Res., 120 N. Windmill St., P.O. Box 457, 62061. Tel: 618-887-4535. [CEM]
Catechesis/Religious Programs—P.O. Box 169, 62061. Tel: 618-887-4262. Mary Dykes, D.R.E.
Students 57.

Marshall, Clark Co., St. Mary (1847), Rev. Jeffery A. Grant, Admin.
Mailing Address: 414 S. Sixth St., 62441. Tel: 217-826-2845; Fax: 217-826-2845.
Res., 110 Lincoln Dr., P.O. Box 156, Greenup, 62428. Tel: 217-923-3523; 826-2845. [CEM]
Catechesis/Religious Programs—Students 95.

Maryville, Madison Co., Mother of Perpetual Help (1938), Rev. W. Jeffrey Holtman, S.F.O.
Res., 200 N. Lange, 62062. Tel: 618-344-6464; Fax: 618-344-6493.
School—St. John Neumann School, Tel: 618-345-7230; Fax: 618-345-4350.
Lay Teachers 15; Students 346.
Catechesis/Religious Programs—Tel: 618-344-9666.
Students 178.

Mattoon, Coles Co., Immaculate Conception (1856), Rev. Herman J. Niebrugge.
Res., 320 N. 21st St., P.O. Box 468, 61938-0468. Tel: 217-235-0539; Fax: 217-235-0593. [CEM]
School—Tel: 217-235-0431.
Lay Teachers 10; Students 161.
Catechesis/Religious Programs—Tel: 217-234-6648.
Students 157.

Medora, Macoupin Co., St. John the Evangelist (1914) (German), Rev. Raphael Paul, Admin.
Res., c/o St. Alphonsus Church, 918 N. Main St., Brighton, 62012. Tel: 217-372-3352; Fax: 618-372-8133.
Catechesis/Religious Programs—Clustered with St. Alphonsus, Brighton.

Mendon, Adams Co., St. Edward (1890), Rev. Louis Schlangen.
Res., R.R. 1, Box 36, 62351. Tel: 217-936-2289. [CEM]
Catechesis/Religious Programs—Students 63.

Meppen, Calhoun Co., St. Joseph (1864), Rev. Thomas Hagstrom.
Office: P.O. Box 38, Brussels, 62013. Tel: 618-883-2400; Fax: 618-883-2511. [CEM]
Res., Meppen Ln., 62013. Tel: 618-883-2309.

Michael, Calhoun Co., St. Michael (1864) (Irish), Rev. Thomas Hagstrom.
Office: 404 Main St., P.O. Box C, Hardin, 62047. Tel: 618-576-2517; Fax: 618-576-9448. [CEM]
Res., Meppen Ln., Meppen, 62013. Tel: 618-883-2309.
Catechesis/Religious Programs—Clustered with St. Norbert, Hardin.

Montrose, Effingham Co., St. Rose of Lima (1879), Revs. Thomas Ess, O.F.M.; Ken Rosswog, O.F.M.
Mailing Address: P.O. Box 68, 62445. Tel: 217-924-4337. [CEM]
Catechesis/Religious Programs—Students 111.

Morrisonville, Christian Co., St. Maurice (1870), Rev. John T. Hannigan (CHI) Admin.
Res., 706 E. Fourth St., P.O. Box 45, 62546-0045. Tel: 217-526-3363; Fax: 217-526-3110. [CEM]
School—(Grades 1-8). Tel: 217-526-3534.
Lay Teachers 4; Students 44.
Catechesis/Religious Programs—Students 60.

Mount Olive, Macoupin Co., Ascension (1886) (Croatian), Rev. Larry Anschutz, Admin.
Res., 705 E. Main St., 62069. Tel: 217-999-4981; Fax: 217-999-4036. [CEM]
Catechesis/Religious Programs—Students 73.

Holy Trinity (1912) (Slovak), Rev. Larry Anschutz, Admin.
Res., 705 E. Main St., 62069. Tel: 217-999-4981; Fax: 217-999-4036. [CEM]
Church—410 Garfield, 62069.
Catechesis/Religious Programs—Students 35.

Mount Sterling, Brown Co., Holy Family (1864), Rev. Thomas Henseler.
Res., 401 W. North St., P.O. Box 252, 62353. Tel: 217-773-3233. [CEM]
School—Tel: 217-773-2825; Fax: 217-773-2825.
Lay Teachers 10; Students 81.
Catechesis/Religious Programs—Students 57.

Mt. Zion, Macon Co., Our Lady of the Holy Spirit (1976), Rev. James D. O'Shea.
Res., 400 Woodland, 62549. Tel: 217-864-3467; Fax: 217-864-3091.
Catechesis/Religious Programs—Tel: 217-864-4941.
Students 116.

Moweaqua, Shelby Co., St. Frances de Sales (1895), Rev. Alan Hunter.
Res., 301 St. Peter St., Assumption, 62510. Tel: 217-226-3536; Fax: 217-226-3538. [JC]
Catechesis/Religious Programs—Tel: 217-226-3205.
Students 34.

Murrayville, Morgan Co., St. Bartholomew (1883), Rev. Charles T. Nelson.
Res., P.O. Box 47, 62668. Tel: 217-882-3781; 742-5224. [CEM]

Neoga, Cumberland Co., St. Mary of the Assumption (1897) (German), Rev. Robert L. DeGrand.
Res., Church St., P.O. Box 68, Sigel, 62462. Tel: 217-844-3371; Fax: 217-844-2309. [CEM]
Church—690 N. Walnut St., 62447. Tel: 217-895-2166.
Catechesis/Religious Programs—Students 95.

New Berlin, Sangamon Co., Sacred Heart of Mary (1858), Rev. Joseph P. Kerber.
Res., 404 E. Birch, P.O. Box 20, 62670. Tel: 217-488-2410; Fax: 217-488-2410. [CEM]
School—Tel: 217-488-3545; Fax: 217-488-3545.
Lay Teachers 6; Students 70.
Catechesis/Religious Programs—Students 85.

New Douglas, Madison Co., St. Ubaldus (1872), Rev. George Radosevich Tel: 618-635-8490.
Res., 322 E. Main St., Staunton, 62088. Tel: 618-635-8590. [CEM]

Newton, Jasper Co., St. Thomas (1873), Rev. Joseph Molloy.
Res., 402 W. Jourdan St., P.O. Box 225, 62448. Tel: 618-783-8741; Fax: 618-783-2224. [CEM 3]
School—Tel: 618-783-3517.
Lay Teachers 9; Students 143.
Catechesis/Religious Programs—Students 150.

Niantic, Macon Co., St. Ann (1889), Sr. Lois Kikkert, O.P., Parish Life Coord.
Mailing Address: P.O. Box 47, Illiopolis, 62539.
Res., 410 Anne St., Illiopolis, 62539. Tel: 217-486-3851. [JC]
Church—North St. & Macon St., 62551.
Catechesis/Religious Programs—Students 12.

Nokomis, Montgomery Co., St. Louis (1870), Rev. Pat G. Jakel.
Res., 311 S. Elm St., 62075-1310. Tel: 217-563-7146; 563-7808 (Personal); Fax: 217-563-8671. [CEM]
School—509 E. Union, 62075. Tel: 217-563-7445; Fax: 217-563-7450.
Lay Teachers 8; Students 115.
Catechesis/Religious Programs—Students 80.

North Arm, Edgar Co., St. Aloysius (1817), Rev. William J. Overmann.
Res., P.O. Box 577, Paris, 61944. Tel: 217-466-3355; Fax: 217-463-3005. [CEM]
Catechesis/Religious Programs—Clustered with St. Mary's, Paris.

Oblong, Crawford Co., Our Lady of Lourdes (1954), Rev. Richard W. Weltin.
Res., 207 E. Walnut St., P.O. Box 428, Robinson, 62454. Tel: 618-544-7526.
Catechesis/Religious Programs—Students 8.

Oconee, Shelby Co., Sacred Heart of Jesus (1872) (German), Rev. Don J. Roberts, Admin.
Res., P.O. Box 45, 62553. Tel: 217-539-4325. [CEM]
Catechesis/Religious Programs—Students 40.

Palmyra, Macoupin Co., Holy Rosary (1954), Rev. August J. Sperl.
c/o Sacred Heart Church: 721 N. Springfield St., Virden, 62690. Tel: 217-965-4545.
Catechesis/Religious Programs—Clustered with St. Patrick Church, Girard.

Pana, Christian Co., St. Patrick (1858), Rev. Don Roberts.
Res., 6 E. Fifth St., P.O. Box 440, 62557. Tel: 217-562-5396; Fax: 217-562-2308. [CEM]
School—Sacred Heart, Tel: 217-562-2425. Mr. Stanley McCormick, Prin.
Lay Teachers 9; Students 154.
Catechesis/Religious Programs—Tel: 217-824-6120.
Students 65.

Panama, Bond Co., Sacred Heart (1916), Rev. Carl Schmidt.
Res., 400 Jefferson, P.O. Box 278, Coffeen, 62017. Tel: 217-534-2220. [JC]
Catechesis/Religious Programs—Students 16.

Paris, Edgar Co., St. Mary (1849), Rev. William J. Overmann.
Res., 110 E. Edgar, P.O. Box 577, 61944. Tel: 217-466-3355; Fax: 217-463-3005. [CEM]
School—Tel: 217-463-3005; Fax: 217-463-3005.
Lay Teachers 6; Students 68.
Catechesis/Religious Programs—Students 101.

Pawnee, Sangamon Co., St. Mary (1899) (German), Rev. Charles G. Dahlby.
Res., c/o St. Rita, P.O. Box 439, Kincaid, 62540. Tel: 217-237-4339. [CEM]
Catechesis/Religious Programs—Tel: 217-625-7540.
Students 86.

Petersburg, Menard Co., St. Peter (1868), Very Rev. Thomas P. Holinga, V.G.
Res., 711 S. Sixth St., 62675. Tel: 217-632-2561; Fax: 217-632-7118. [CEM]
Catechesis/Religious Programs—Tel: 217-632-7118; Fax: 217-632-7118.
Students 156.

Pierron, Madison and Bond Cos., Immaculate Conception (1892), Rev. Msgr. Paul W. Sheridan.
Res., P.O. Box 410, 62273. Tel: 618-654-3604; Fax: 618-654-8764. [CEM]
Catechesis/Religious Programs—Students 74.

Pittsfield, Pike Co., Immaculate Conception (1870), Rev. J. Michael Jenkins.
Res., 226 E. Adams, 62363. Tel: 217-285-4321; Fax: 217-285-9400. [CEM][JC]
Catechesis/Religious Programs—Tel: 217-285-4774.
Students 54.

Pocahontas, Bond Co., St. Nicholas, Rev. Msgr. Paul W. Sheridan.
Res., P.O. Box 410, Pierron, 62273. Tel: 618-654-3604; Fax: 618-654-8764.
Catechesis/Religious Programs—Students 25.

Quincy, Adams Co.,

1—ALL SAINTS, (1999), Very Rev. Robert J. Jallas, V.F.
1019 Cedar St., 62301. Tel: 217-222-4622; Fax: 217-222-5554. [JC]
Preschool Noah's Ark—.
Lay Teachers 2; Aides 2; Students 64.
School—(Grades K-8) 1236 N. 10th, 62301. Tel: 217-228-1477.
Sisters of Nortre Dame 1; Lay Teachers 8; Students 145.
Catechesis/Religious Programs—Students 26.

2—ST. ANTHONY OF PADUA, (1859), Revs. Adrian Fischer, O.F.M.; Irenaeus Kimminau, O.F.M.
Res., 2223 St. Anthony Rd., 62301. Tel: 217-222-5996; Fax: 217-222-5996. [CEM]
Church—2223 St. Anthony Rd., 62301. Tel: 217-222-5996; Fax: 217-222-5996.
School—Tel: 217-224-6477.
Lay Teachers 5; Students 72.
Catechesis/Religious Programs—Students 90.

3—ST. BONIFACE, (1837) (German), Rev. John Carberry.
Res., 117 N. Seventh St., 62301. Tel: 217-222-3000; Fax: 217-223-6999. [JC]
School—Tel: 217-223-6999.
Lay Teachers 7; Students 75.
Catechesis/Religious Programs—Students 26.

4—St. Dominic, (1977), Rev. Donald Knuffman.
Res., 3800 Columbus Rd., P.O. Box 3364, 62301. Tel: 217-224-9102; Fax: 217-224-0042. [JC]
Church—4100 Columbus Rd., 62301.
School—Tel: 217-224-0041.
Lay Teachers 12; Students 222.
Catechesis/Religious Programs—Students 25.

5—St. Francis Solanus, (1860), Revs. Kurt Hartrich, O.F.M.; Eugene Middendorf, O.F.M.; James Wheeler, O.F.M.
Res., 1721 College Ave., 62301. Tel: 217-222-2898; Fax: 217-222-3020. [JC]
School—Fax: 217-222-5049.
Lay Teachers 12; Students 266.
Catechesis/Religious Programs—1721 College Ave., 62301. Tel: 217-222-4077.
Students 81.

6—St. John the Baptist, (1880) (German). Merged with St. Rose of Lima, Quincy to form All Saints, Quincy.

7—St. Joseph, (1868), Revs. Adrian Fischer, O.F.M.; Irenaeus Kimminau, O.F.M.
Church and Mailing: 1435 E. 1500th St., 62301. Tel: 217-434-8442; Fax: 217-434-8442.
Res., 2223 St. Anthony Rd., 62301. Tel: 217-222-5996; Fax: 217-222-5996.
Catechesis/Religious Programs—Tel: 217-434-8442.
Students 106.

8—St. Mary, (1867). (Immaculate Conception). Rev. Michael Kuse.
Res., 1119 S. Seventh St., 62301. Tel: 217-222-2759; Fax: 217-222-6463. [JC]
School—Tel: 217-223-3388.
Lay Teachers 9; Students 189.
Catechesis/Religious Programs—Students 80.

9—St. Peter, (1839) (Irish), Rev. Roy R. Bauer.
Res., 2600 Maine St., 62301. Tel: 217-222-3155; Fax: 217-222-3584. [JC]
School—Tel: 217-223-1120; Fax: 217-223-1173.
Lay Teachers 23; Students 492.
Catechesis/Religious Programs—Students 120.

10—St. Rose of Lima, (1892) (Irish). Merged with St. John the Baptist, Quincy to form All Saints, Quincy.

Ramsey, Fayette Co., St. Joseph (1870) (German-Irish), Rev. Steven Sotiroff.
Res., 118 E. Main, P.O. Box 455, 62080. Tel: 618-423-2424. [CEM]
Catechesis/Religious Programs—Students 24.

Raymond, Montgomery Co., St Raymond (1874), Rev. John T. Hannigan (CHI) Admin.
Res., 306 S. McElroy, P.O. Box 349, 62560. Tel: 217-229-4435. [CEM]
Catechesis/Religious Programs—Tel: 217-229-3655.
Students 72.

Riverton, Sangamon Co., St. James (1871), Co-Pastors: Very Revs. John A. Renken, V.G.; Kenneth C. Steffen.
Res., 112 N. Sixth St., P.O. Box 590, 62561-0590. Tel: 217-629-9109 (Rectory); 629-7717 (Office).
Catechesis/Religious Programs—Tel: 217-629-7717. Mrs. Mary Johnson, D.R.E.
Students 117.

Robinson, Crawford Co., St. Elizabeth (1908), Rev. Richard W. Weltin.
Res., 207 E. Walnut St., 62454. Tel: 618-544-7526.
Catechesis/Religious Programs—Tel: 618-544-9327.
Students 143.

Rochester, Sangamon Co., Church of St. Jude (1976), Rev. Patrick G. Cahill, C.S.V.
Res., 633 S. Walnut St., 62563. Tel: 217-498-9197; Fax: 217-498-7180.
Parish Center: 635 S. Walnut St., 62563. Tel: 217-498-9524.
Catechesis/Religious Programs—Students 202.

St. Elmo, Fayette Co., St. Bonaventure (1843) (Irish-German), Rev. John M. Savoree, Admin.
Res., 216 N. Ninth, Altamont, 62411. Tel: 618-483-5346. [CEM]
Catechesis/Religious Programs—Students 144.
St. Mary (1904), Rev. John M. Savoree, Admin.
Res., 216 N. Ninth, Altamont, 62411. Tel: 618-483-5341. [CEM]
Catechesis/Religious Programs—Students 145.

St. Jacob, Madison Co., St. James (1894), Rev. James A. Flach.
Res., 120 N. Windmill St., Box 457, Marine, 62061. Tel: 618-887-4535.
Catechesis/Religious Programs—Students 50.

Ste. Marie, Jasper Co., St. Mary of the Assumption (1837) (French-German), Rev. Alan McIntosh, O.S.B.
Res., P.O. Box 68, 62459. Tel: 618-455-3155; Fax: 618-455-3665. [CEM][JC]
Catechesis/Religious Programs—112 W. Embarras St., P.O. Box 68, 62459.
Students 91.

Shelbyville, Shelby Co., Immaculate Conception (1879), Sr. Marie Trutter, Parish Life Coord.
Res., N. Rte. 128, P.O. Box 233, 62565. Tel: 217-774-3434; Fax: 217-774-3516.
Catechesis/Religious Programs—Students 62.

Sherman, Sangamon Co., St. John Vianney (1934), Rev. Eugene E. Costa.
Res., 129 Stardust Dr., P.O. Box 229, 62684. Tel: 217-523-3816; Fax: 217-523-3954.
Catechesis/Religious Programs—Students 148.

Shipman, Macoupin Co., St. Denis (1876), Rev. Robert N. Porter.
Res., P.O. Box A H, Bunker Hill, 62014-9512. Tel: 618-585-4700; Fax: 618-585-3449. [CEM]

Shumway, Effingham Co., Church of the Annunciation (1879), Rev. Alexis Pruemer, O.F.M.
Res., P.O. Box 96, 62461. Tel: 217-857-6404. [CEM]
Catechesis/Religious Programs—Tel: 618-487-5711.
Students 95.

Sigel, Shelby Co., St. Michael the Archangel (1867) (German), Rev. Robert L. DeGrand.
Res., Box 68, 62462. Tel: 217-844-3371; Fax: 217-844-2309. [CEM]
School—Tel: 217-844-2231.
Sisters 1; Lay Teachers 9; Students 141.
Catechesis/Religious Programs—Students 64.

Staunton, Macoupin Co., St. Michael (1875), Rev. George Radosevich.
Office: P.O. Box 240, 62088. Fax: 618-635-3140.
Res., 322 E. Main, 62088. Tel: 618-635-8490. [JC 2]
School—419 E. Main, 62088. Tel: 618-635-3210; Fax: 618-635-3210.
Religious 1; Lay Teachers 6; Students 85.
Catechesis/Religious Programs—Students 120.

Stonington, Christian Co., Holy Trinity (1879) (Irish-German), Rev. Martin O'Hara.
Mailing Address: P.O. Box 257, 62567. Tel: 217-325-3697.
Res., 108 N. Elm, P.O. Box 257, 62567.
Church—308 N. Elm St., 62567. Tel: 217-325-3691.
Catechesis/Religious Programs—Students 62.

Sullivan, Moultrie Co., St. Columcille (1905), Rev. John E. Sohm.
Res., 516 W. Jackson, P.O. Box 464, 61951. Tel: 217-728-4040.
Catechesis/Religious Programs—Students 58.

Taylorville, Christian Co., St. Mary (1845), Rev. John O'Connell.
Res., 116 W. Adams St., P.O. Box 470, 62568. Tel: 217-824-8178.
School—(Grades PreK-6). Tel: 217-824-6501; Fax: 217-824-2803.
Lay Teachers 22; Students 210.
Catechesis/Religious Programs—Students 160.

Teutopolis, Effingham Co., St. Francis of Assisi (1839), Revs. Austin Albers, O.F.M.; Kenneth Rosswog, O.F.M.; Bro. Paulinus Johnson, O.F.M.
Res., 203 E. Main St., 62467. Tel: 217-857-6404; Fax: 217-857-1031. [CEM]
Catechesis/Religious Programs—Tel: 217-857-6477; 857-1500. D.R.E.: Sr. Ann Siemer, S.S.N.D.; Lisa Siemer; Pati Jansen.
Students 792.

Troy, Madison Co., St. Jerome (1881), Rev. Steven A. Janoski.
Res., P.O. Box 94, 62294. Tel: 618-667-6571; Fax: 618-667-2697. [CEM 2]
School—St. John Neumann, Maryville, Tel: 618-345-7230; Fax: 618-345-4350.
Catechesis/Religious Programs—107 Wayland, 62294. Tel: 618-667-6571; Fax: 618-667-2697.
Students 231.

Tuscola, Douglas Co., Forty Martyrs (1865), Rev. Allen Kemme.
Res., 201 E. Van Allen St., P.O. Box 352, 61953. Tel: 217-253-4412; Fax: 217-253-5010.
Catechesis/Religious Programs—Students 196.

Vandalia, Fayette Co., Mother of Dolors (1850), Rev. Stephen T. Sotiroff.
Res., 322 N. Seventh St., P.O. Box 377, 62471. Tel: 618-283-0214; Fax: 618-283-0278. [CEM]
Catechesis/Religious Programs—Students 132.

Venice, Madison Co., St. Mark (1871), Rev. Delix Michel (Haiti).
Res., Sixth and Broadway, 62090. Tel: 618-451-1411. [JC]

Villa Grove, Douglas Co., Sacred Heart (1906), Rev. Paul H. Skelton.
Res., 208 N. Pine, Box 17, 61956. Tel: 217-832-8352; Fax: 217-832-8352.
Catechesis/Religious Programs—Students 57.
Mission—Hume, Edgar Co., St. Michael's, Center St., Hume, 61932. Tel: 217-887-2482.

Virden, Macoupin Co., Sacred Heart (1914) (Slovak). St. Catherine's (1866) Merged in 1978. Rev. August J. Sperl.
Res., 721 N. Springfield, 62690. Tel: 217-965-4545.
Catechesis/Religious Programs—Tel: 217-965-5370.
Students 96.

Virginia, Cass Co., St. Luke (1840), Rev. Ken J. Venvertloh.
Res., 240 E. Myrtle St., 62691. Tel: 217-452-7529.
Catechesis/Religious Programs—Students 45.

Waverly, Morgan Co., St. Sebastian (1856), Rev. Kevin Michael Laughery.
Office and Res.: 125 E. Washington St., Auburn, 62615. Tel: 217-438-6222; Fax: 217-438-6732. [CEM]
Catechesis/Religious Programs—Clustered with St. Benedict's, Auburn.

White Hall, Greene Co., All Saints (1883), Rev. Barry J. Harmon.
Res., c/o St. John, 414 Third St., Carrollton, 62016. Tel: 217-942-3551; Fax: 217-942-6767.
Church—S. Main St., 62092.
Catechesis/Religious Programs—Students 41.

Wilsonville, Macoupin Co., Holy Cross (1926), Rev. Robert N. Porter.
Res., 300 S. Putnam, P.O. Box A-H, Bunker Hill, 62014-9512. Tel: 618-585-4700; Fax: 618-585-3449.

Winchester, Scott Co., St. Mark (1860), Rev. Charles T. Nelson.
Res., 108 Pearl St., 62694. Tel: 217-742-5224. [CEM]

Witt, Montgomery Co., St. Barbara (1905), Rev. Pat G. Jakel.
Res., 311 S. Elm St., Nokomis, 62075-1310. Tel: 217-563-7146; 563-7808 (Personal); Fax: 217-563-8671. [CEM]
Catechesis/Religious Programs—Students 12.

Wood River, Madison Co., St. Bernard (1919), Rev. James L. Neuman.
Res., 345 Acton Ave., 62095. Tel: 618-254-0679 (Office); Fax: 618-254-2690.
School—Tel: 618-254-2697; Fax: 618-254-3906.
Lay Teachers 10; Students 151.
Catechesis/Religious Programs—Students 40.

Chaplains of Public Institutions

Alton. *Alton State Hospital.* Vacant. St. Matthew Parish, 1015 Milton Rd., 62002. Tel: 618-465-8582.

Hillsboro. *Graham Correctional Center.* 11132 Catatoga Dr., Plainview, 62685. Tel: 618-836-7447. Rev. George L. Morelock, Chap.

Jacksonville. *Illinois State Hospital.* Attended by Our Savior Parish. 462 E. State St., 62650. Tel: 217-245-6184.
School for the Blind. Attended by Our Savior Parish. 462 E. State St., 62650. Tel: 217-245-6184.
School for the Deaf. Attended by Our Savior Parish. 462 E. State St., 62650. Tel: 217-245-6184.

Mount Sterling. *Western Illinois Correctional Center.* Attended by Holy Family Parish. 401 W. North St., 62353. Tel: 217-773-3233.

Quincy. *Illinois Veterans' Home* 1901 N. 18th, 62301. Tel: 217-224-0591. Rev. Richard M. Jeske, O.F.M.

Taylorville. *Taylorville Correctional Center.* Attended by St. Mary Parish. 116 W. Adams St., P.O. Box 248, 62658. Tel: 217-824-8178.

Vandalia. *Vandalia Correctional Center.* Attended by Mother of Dolors Parish. 322 N. Seventh, 62471. Tel: 618-283-0214.

On Duty Outside the Diocese:
Reverend Fathers—
Gallenbach, Thomas, 7075 Del Ray, Las Vegas, NV 89117. Tel: 540-254-5488 (Home); 363-1902 (Office)
Habing, Paul, Prelatura, Apt. 102, Ayaviri-Puno, Peru
Meyer, Bernard A., 2425 Sage Rd., Apt. 45, Houston, TX 77056. Tel: 713-629-4822
Porter, Robert A., St. Rose of Lima Church, 226 S. Atlantic St., Dillon, MT 59725. Tel: 406-683-4391
Trojcak, Ronald, 525 N. Randolph St., Holy Springs, MS 38635. Tel: 662-252-4790

Military Chaplains:
Reverend Fathers—
Blickhan, Donald, Chap., U.S. Army
Nolan, John, Chap., U.S. Air Force

Special or Other Diocesan Assignment:
Reverend Fathers—
Kraft, Philip, 929 Rickard Rd. Ct., Box 7492, Springfield, IL 62791. Tel: 217-793-3218
Rebert, Robert, Pope John Paul Apartments, One Pope John Paul Plaza, Springfield, IL 62703

Unassigned:
Reverend Fathers—
Simburger, R. Joseph

Absent on Leave:
Reverend Fathers—
Cernich, Joseph
La Count, Daniel
Lichtenberger, Doug
Poterucha, Michael

Retired:
Reverend Monsignors—
Schwartz, Aloysius B., Villa Health Care East, 100 Marian Pkwy., Box 109, Sherman, IL 62184
Toliusis, Casimir, St. Joseph's Home, 3306 S. Sixth St. RD, Springfield, IL 62703. Tel: 217-529-4202
Reverend Fathers—
Campbell, John, 10323 S. Kostner Ave., Oak Lawn, IL 60453-4511. Tel: 708-857-8396
Corrigan, F. J., 1625 W. Washington, Springfield, IL 62702. Tel: 217-793-0515
Damjanov, Zvonimir, c/o Olga Milicic, A.B. Simica 8, 21213 Kastel Gomilica, Croatia-Hruatiska. Tel: 011-385-21-220-239
Davenport, Thomas J., 1625 W. Washington, Springfield, IL 62702. Tel: 217-793-0515
Donohoe, Peter, 714 Douglas Pl., Alton, IL 62002
Gierut, Casimir, P.O. Box 156, Westmont, IL 60559
Heintz, Robert L., 422 Foulds Ave., Alton, IL 62002. Tel: 618-462-9767
Higgins, Patrick O., Fairfield Residential Home, 115 Banbury Rd., Oxford OX2 6 LA, England
Houran, J. William, 3233 N.E. 32nd Ave., Apt. 902, Fort Lauderdale, FL 33308. Tel: 954-566-9802
Keane, Brendan, 9504 Windsor Club Cir., Fort Myers, FL 33905. Tel: 941-693-7172
Kekeisen, William, 934 Capris Isles Blvd., Apt. 208, Venice, FL 34292-4408. Tel: 941-484-1261
Kennedy, John, 411 Spring Lake Dr., Quincy, IL 62301. Tel: 217-224-5288
Kondrath, James A., Bethlehem Woods, 1571 W. Ogden Ave., LaGrange, IL 60526. Tel: 708-579-0078
Mack, Henry J., 38742 N. Drexel Blvd., Antioch, IL 60002. Tel: 847-395-1949
Mascari, Peter, 115 Stardust Dr., Sherman, IL 62684. Tel: 217-789-0611
Maul, William R., 1204 Preis Ln. Apt. 2, Godfrey, IL 62035. Tel: 618-466-2515
McCarthy, Joseph F., 130 Curtis Ave., Burlington, VT 05401. Tel: 802-362-2320
Miller, Joseph, Our Mother of Good Counsel Home, 6825 Natural Bridge Rd., St. Louis, MO 63121-5397
Morris, Robert, 1113 Wickford Dr., Springfield, IL 62704. Tel: 217-793-1118
Mulcrone, Charles P., 1625 W. Washington, Springfield, IL 62702. Tel: 217-698-4857
O'Reilly, Joseph, 1319 Tendick St., #3, Jacksonville, IL 62650-3120. Tel: 217-243-5483
Quilligan, Maurice, 905 Andra Dr., Maryville, IL 62062. Tel: 618-344-5164
Rieck, Raymond, 632 Sheridan Dr., Venice, FL 34292. Tel: 941-492-6676
Schmidt, Anthony, 520 S. Second St., #906, Lincoln Tower Suites, Springfield, IL 62701. Tel: 217-528-6315
Sederwall, Donald, Marian Heights Apartments, 20 Marian Heights Dr., Alton, IL 62002. Tel: 618-462-2579
Sheahan, John F., 816 Randall Dr., Carlinville, IL 62626. Tel: 217-854-6310
Simpson, Roger, 271 E. Myrtle St., Virginia, IL 62691. Tel: 217-452-3168
Sullivan, James, 10311 Mason Ave., Oak Lawn, IL 60453-4335. Tel: 708-499-5442
Tracey, Terence, St. Francis Convent, Sangamon Ave., P.O. Box 19431, Springfield, IL 62794-9431. Tel: 217-522-3386

INSTITUTIONS LOCATED IN THE DIOCESE

[A] SEMINARIES, RELIGIOUS OR SCHOLASTICATES

GODFREY. *Immaculate Heart of Mary Novitiate*, 4563 Levis Ln., 62035. Tel: 618-466-2233; Fax: 618-466-2430.
E-mail: ominov@aol.com
Web site: www.ominov.itgo.com//ominov.htm
Revs. Rudy Nowakowski, O.M.I.; Leo LeBlanc, O.M.I.; Darrell Rupiper, O.M.I. Priests 3; Clerical Novices 7.

[B] COLLEGES AND UNIVERSITIES

QUINCY. *Quincy University*, (1860) 1800 College Ave., 62301. Tel: 217-222-8020; 228-5318.
Web site: www.quincy.edu
For a complete listing, refer to the Colleges and Universities section.

[C] JUNIOR COLLEGES

SPRINGFIELD. *Springfield College in Illinois*, 1500 N. Fifth St., 62702. Tel: 217-525-1420; Fax: 217-789-1698.
E-mail: rappe@sci.edu
Web site: www.sci.edu
For a complete listing, refer to the Colleges and Universities section.

[D] HIGH SCHOOLS, PRIVATE

SPRINGFIELD. *Sacred Heart-Griffin*, 1200 W. Washington St., 62702. Tel: 217-787-1595; Fax: 217-787-9856.
Web site: www.shg.org
Springfield Dominican Sisters. Sr. Marilyn Jean Runkel, O.P., Pres.; Sr. Margaret Joanne Grueter, O.P., Prin.; Mr. Robert Brenneisen, Asst. Prin. Priests 3; Brothers 1; Sisters 7; Lay Teachers 51; Students 882.
Ursuline Academy, 1400 N. Fifth St., 62702. Tel: 217-523-5169; Fax: 217-523-2131. Mr. Carl J. Sabo, Prin. Priests 2; Lay Teachers 18; Students 210.

DECATUR. *St. Teresa High School*, 2710 N. Water St., 62526. Tel: 217-875-2431; Fax: 217-875-2436.
E-mail: stadmin@st-teresahs.org
Web site: www.st-teresahs.org
Mr. Joseph A. McDaniel, Prin. Priests 1; Ursuline Sisters 1; Lay Teachers 26; Students 339.

JACKSONVILLE. *Routt Catholic High School*, 500 E. College, 62650. Tel: 217-243-8564; Fax: 217-243-3138.
E-mail: jwoods@routt.irtc.net
Web site: www.routtcatholic.com
Lay Teachers 15; Students 137.

QUINCY. *Quincy Notre Dame High School*, 1400 S. 11th, 62301-7299. Tel: 217-223-2479; Fax: 217-223-0023.
E-mail: quincynotredame.org
Web site: quincynotredame.org
Ray E. Heilmann, Prin.; Rev. Charles A. Edwards, Dir. Christian Formation. Priests 1; Lay Teachers 31; Students 590.

[E] HIGH SCHOOLS, DIOCESAN AND PAROCHIAL

ALTON. *Marquette Catholic High School*, 219 E. Fourth St., 62002. Tel: 618-463-0580; Fax: 618-463-0582.
E-mail: marquettH.hs@home.com
Web site: alton-marquette.com
John L. Rogers, Prin. Sisters 1; Lay Teachers 28; Students 358.

EFFINGHAM. *St. Anthony High School*, 304 E. Roadway Ave., P.O. Box 545, 62401. Tel: 217-342-6969; Fax: 217-342-6997.
E-mail: sahs@stanthony.com
Web site: www.stanthony.com
Priests 3; Lay Teachers 21; Students 215.

[F] THE CATHOLIC CHARITIES OF THE DIOCESE OF SPRINGFIELD IN ILLINOIS

SPRINGFIELD. *Catholic Charities of Springfield*, 120 S. 11th St., 62703. Tel: 217-525-0500; Fax: 217-525-0554. Danielle K. Zellers, Area Dir. Total Assisted 12,065; Total Staff 65.
Catholic Charities Administrative Office, 800 South Fifth St., 62703. Tel: 217-523-9201; Fax: 217-523-5624. Mr. Steven E. Roach, M.S., Exec. Dir. Total Staff 21.
Crisis Assistance, 1023 E. Washington, 62703. Tel: 217-523-4551; Fax: 217-523-8425.
Clinics For Kids, 500 N. Sixth St., 62702. Tel: 217-523-1474; Fax: 217-523-0194.
St. John's Breadline, 430 N. Fifth St., 62702. Tel: 217-528-6098; Fax: 217-528-3605.
St. John's Breadline, 430 N. Fifth St., 62702. Tel: 217-528-6098; Fax: 217-528-3605. Meals Served Annually 180,000; Total Staff 8.
Society of St. Vincent de Paul (Diocesan Central Council), 800 S. Fifth St., 62703. Tel: 217-523-9201; Fax: 217-523-5624.

ALTON. *Alton Catholic Charities*, 735 Park Dr., 62002. Tel: 618-462-0634; Fax: 618-462-3209. Total Assisted 620; Total Staff 14.

BEARDSTOWN. *St. Francis Community Clinic*, 111 South State St., 62618. Tel: 217-323-5264; Fax: 217-323-4680. Mr. Steven E. Roach, Exec. Dir.

CARLINVILLE. *Carlinville Catholic Charities*, 525 W. Second South, Box 118, 62626. Tel: 217-854-4511; Fax: 217-854-8049. Ms. Patricia Pope, Area Dir. Total Assisted 265; Total Staff 10.

DECATUR. *Catholic Charities Community Services*, 401 N. Martin Luther King, Jr. Dr., 62523. Tel: 217-428-5724; Fax: 217-428-5729. Judy Rogers, On Site Supvr.; Marie Rademacher, Area Dir. Total Assisted 12,949; Total Staff 7.
Decatur Catholic Charities, 247 W. Prairie Ave., 62523. Tel: 217-428-3458; Fax: 217-428-4415. Mrs. Marie Rademacher, Area Dir. Total Assisted 16,000; Total Staff 36.

EFFINGHAM. *Catholic Charities of Effingham*, 601 W. Fayette, 62401. Tel: 217-342-9800; Fax: 217-342-3873. Sr. Brenda Fritz, D.C., Area Dir. Total Assisted 1,536; Total Staff 15.

GRANITE CITY. *Granite City Catholic Charities*, 2105 State St., 62040. Tel: 618-877-1184; Fax: 618-798-4287.
E-mail: ccdaly@peaknet.net
Mr. David Daly, Area Dir. Total Assisted 11,500; Total Staff 12.

MATTOON. *Catholic Charities of Coles, Douglas, and Edgar Counties*, 4217 Dewitt Ave., 61938. Tel: 217-235-0420; Fax: 217-235-0425.

QUINCY. *Catholic Charities of Quincy*, 620 Maine St., 62301. Tel: 217-222-0958; Fax: 217-222-8737. Sr. Mary Shaw, A.S.C., Area Dir. Total Assisted 280; Total Staff 13.

[G] CHILDREN'S HOMES

ALTON. *Catholic Children's Home*, 1400 State St., 62002. Tel: 618-465-3594; Fax: 618-465-4023.
E-mail: cch1400@ezl.com
For a complete listing, refer to the Special Care Facilities section.

[H] GENERAL HOSPITALS

SPRINGFIELD. *St. John's Hospital*, 800 E. Carpenter St., 62769. Tel: 217-544-6464; Fax: 217-535-3989.
E-mail: rcarlson@st-johns.org
For a complete listing, refer to the Hospitals section.

ALTON. *Saint Anthony's Health Center*, Saint Anthony's Way, P.O. Box 340, 62002-0340. Tel: 618-465-2571; Fax: 618-465-4569.
Web site: www.sahc.org
For a complete listing, refer to the Hospitals section.

DECATUR. *St. Mary's Hospital*, 1800 E. Lake Shore Dr., 62521. Tel: 217-464-2966; Fax: 217-464-1616.
Web site: www.stmarys-hospital.com
For a complete listing, refer to the Hospitals section.

EFFINGHAM. *St. Anthony's Memorial Hospital*, 503 N. Maple St., 62401. Tel: 217-342-2121; Fax: 217-347-1563.
E-mail: hospital@effingham.net
Web site: www.stanthonyshospital.org
For a complete listing, refer to the Hospitals section.

GRANITE CITY. *St. Elizabeth Medical Center*, 2100 Madison Ave., 62040. Tel: 618-798-3000; Fax: 618-798-3508
For a complete listing, refer to the Hospitals section.

HIGHLAND. *St. Joseph's Hospital*, 1515 Main St., 62249. Tel: 618-654-7421; Fax: 618-654-2012.
E-mail: mkorte@sjh.hshs.org
Web site: stjosephs-highland.org
For a complete listing, refer to the Hospitals section.

LITCHFIELD. *St. Francis Hospital*, 1215 Franciscan Dr., P.O. Box 1215, 62056. Tel: 217-324-2191
For a complete listing, refer to the Hospitals section.

TAYLORVILLE. *St. Vincent Memorial Hospital*, 201 E. Pleasant St., 62568. Tel: 217-824-3331; Fax: 217-824-2099
For a complete listing, refer to the Hospitals section.

[I] SPECIAL CARE INSTITUTIONS

SPRINGFIELD. *Brother James Court*, 2500 St. James Rd., 62707. Tel: 217-544-4876.
E-mail: bjcicfdd@aol.com
Web site: ffsc.net
For a complete listing, refer to the Special Care Facilities section.
St. Monica's Center, 109 E. Lawrence Ave., 62704. Tel: 217-523-7922; Fax: 217-525-8241
For a complete listing, refer to the Special Care Facilities section.

[J] HOMES FOR AGED

SPRINGFIELD. *Pope John Paul Apartments*, One Pope John Paul Plaza, 62703. Tel: 217-528-1771; Fax: 217-528-5110.
E-mail: polly@dio.org
Web site: www.dio.org
For a complete listing, refer to the Special Care Facilities section.
St. Joseph's Home, 3306 S. Sixth St. Rd., 62703. Tel: 217-529-5596
For a complete listing, refer to the Special Care Facilities section.

ALTON. *Marian Heights Apartments*, 20 Marian Heights Dr., 62002. Tel: 618-462-0363; Fax: 618-462-0366.
E-mail: marianhgtsapt@alton.net
For a complete listing, refer to the Special Care Facilities section.

[K] MONASTERIES AND RESIDENCES OF PRIESTS AND BROTHERS

SPRINGFIELD. *Franciscan Brothers of the Holy Cross*, 2500 St. James Rd., 62707. Tel: 217-544-4876.
E-mail: ffsc@aol.com
Bro. Luke Morin, F.F.S.C., Supr. Total in Residence 5.

Priests' Retirement Facility, Catholic Pastoral Center, 1625 W. Washington, 62702. Tel: 217-793-0515. Most Rev. Daniel L. Ryan; Revs. Thomas J. Davenport; Francis J. Corrigan; Charles P. Mulcrone. Priests 4.

QUINCY. *St. Francis Solanus Friary*, 1721 College Ave., 62301. Tel: 217-222-2898; Fax: 217-222-3020. Revs. Austin Albers, O.F.M., Pastor; Eugene Middendorf, O.F.M.; James Wheeler, O.F.M. Priests 3.

SHERMAN. *Our Lady of Angels Friary*, 59 Woodsmill Dr., 62684. Tel: 217-496-2803; 496-2066; Fax: 217-496-2451.
E-mail: seniorfriars@aol.com; kleni70138@aol.com
Web site: www.quincy.edu/shp-friar/senior-friars/
Retirement Community of Our Lady of Friars Minor (Sacred Heart Province). Bros. Kevin Lenihan, Guardian; Earl Benz, O.F.M., Vicar; Revs. Cecil Koop, O.F.M.; Wilbert Hegener, O.F.M.; Hugolinus Kiener, O.F.M.; Armand Lubanski, O.F.M.; Roger Niemeyer, O.F.M.; John Ostdiek, O.F.M.; Ladislas Siekaniec, O.F.M.; John Sullivan, O.F.M.; Donulus Wunderlich, O.F.M.; Ralph Zetzl; Victorian Haladus, O.F.M.; Floribert Veverka, O.F.M.; Mathias Kiemen, O.F.M; Bros. Daniel Badsing, O.F.M.; Justin Deken, O.F.M.; Kevin O'Connell, O.F.M.; Joseph Sandlin, O.F.M.; Patrick Shea, O.F.M.; Denis Snelling, O.F.M.; Joseph Weithman, O.F.M.; Crispin Koeppl, O.F.M.; Dan Piasecki, O.F.M.; James Finnegan, O.F.M.

TEUTOPOLIS. *St. Francis Assisi Friary*, 203 E. Main St., P.O. Box 730, 62467-0730. Tel: 217-857-6404; Fax: 217-857-1031.
E-mail: parish@advancenet.net
Revs. Thomas Ess, O.F.M.; Alexis Pruemer, O.F.M.; Theodore Bracco, O.F.M.; Edwin O. Albers, O.F.M.; Kenneth Rosswog, O.F.M.; Bro. Paulinus Johnson, O.F.M. Priests 5.

[L] CONVENTS AND RESIDENCES FOR SISTERS

SPRINGFIELD. *Congregation of Daughters of Divine Love*, Priests' Retirement Home, 1625 W. Washington St., 62702. Tel: 217-793-1908.
E-mail: D.D.love@dio.org
Sr. Theodora Agaju, D.D.L., Local Supr. Total Staff 3.

Convent of Our Lady of the Sacred Heart, 1237 W. Monroe St., 62704. Tel: 217-787-0481; Fax: 217-787-8169.
E-mail: smjtraeger@spdom.org
Web site: www.springfieldop.org
Legal Title: *Dominican Sisters of Springfield in Illinois.* Motherhouse of the Springfield Dominican Sisters. Motherhouse and Novitiate of the Dominican Sisters of Springfield in Illinois. Sr. Mary Jean Traeger, O.P., Prioress Gen.; Sr. Judith Hilbing, O.P., Vicaress Gen.; Sr. M. Noel Plummer, O.P., Prioress; Rev. John H. Gerlach, O.P., Chap. Sisters in the Congregation 308; in Motherhouse 108; Novices 2.

Daughters of Divine Love Congregation, 2523 St. James Rd., 62707. Tel: 217-528-2418.
E-mail: coamedu@hotmail.com
Sr. Mary Henry, D.D.L. Sisters 4.

Missionary Sisters of the Sacred Heart of Jesus "Ad Gentes", 260 N. Amos Ave., 62702. Tel: 217-787-2578. Sr. Delfina Maravillla, M.A.G., Local Supr. Sisters 3.

St. Francis Convent, 4849 LaVerna Rd., P.O. Box 19431, 62794-9431. Tel: 217-522-3386. Motherhouse of the Hospital Sisters of the Third Order of St. Francis. Mailing Address: P.O. Box 19431, 62794-9431. Sr. Joan Winkler, O.S.F., Prov. Supr.; Sr. Mary Kelly, O.S.F., Religious Coord. Chaplains: Revs. Terence Tracey; John Ostdiek. Sisters 139.
Other Locations: 2101 Shabbona, 62702. Tel: 217-789-4936. Sisters 3. 2405 Shabbona, 62702. 4145 Sunderland Dr., Decatur, 62526. Tel: 217-877-2278. Sisters 3. 710 St. Anthony Ave., Effingham, 62401. Tel: 217-342-2873. Sisters 3. 52 Fairview, 62704. Tel: 217-529-3050. 75 Sunflower Dr., Highland, 62249. Tel: 618-654-9759. Sisters 2.

Ursuline Convent, 1400 N. Fifth St., 62702. Tel: 217-789-7910; Fax: 217-789-7913. Sr. Darlene Fulgenzi, O.S.U., Prioress. Ursuline Nuns of the Roman Union in Community 19.

ALTON. *St. Francis Convent*, 2120 Central Ave., P.O. Box 9020, 62002-9020. Tel: 618-463-2750; Fax: 618-465-5064. Headquarters of the Province St. Elizabeth and Novitiate of the Sisters of St. Francis of the Martyr St. George. Mother M. Ingeborg, O.S.F., Prov. Final Professed 83 (in US + 33 in Brazil); Junior Professed 19 (in US + 6 in Brazil); Novices 11 (in US + 11 in Brazil); Postulants 6 (in US + 5 in Brazil).

Ursuline Convent of the Holy Family of the Ursuline Nuns of the Roman Union, 845 Danforth St., 62002. Tel: 618-465-9112; Fax: 618-465-0358.
E-mail: tdavey2@juno.com
Sr. Theresa Davey, O.S.U., Prioress. Sisters 14. Ursuline Infirmary, 845 Danforth St., 62002. Tel: 618-465-0791; Fax: 618-465-0792. Sr. Theresa Davey, O.S.U. Sisters 40.

[M] NEWMAN CENTERS

CARLINVILLE. *Blackburn College*, State Rte. 108 E., P.O. Box 647, 62626. Tel: 217-854-7151; Fax: 217-854-9228.
E-mail: rdean@accunet.net
Chaplains 1; Students 200.

CHARLESTON. *Eastern Illinois University Newman Center*, 500 Roosevelt Ave., 61920. Tel: 217-348-0188; Fax: 217-348-8964.
E-mail: newman@eiu-newman.org
Web site: www.eiu-newman.org
Rev. Christopher Brey, Chap.; Mr. Roy Lanham, Dir.; Mrs. Holly Walters, Volunteer Coord.

DECATUR. *Millikin University Newman Catholic Community*, P.O. Box 2697, 62524-2697. Tel: 217-877-4146. Rev. Dennis D. Kollross, Chap.

EDWARDSVILLE. *Southern Illinois University Catholic Campus Ministry*, The Religious Center, P.O. Box 1059, 62026. Tel: 618-650-3205; Fax: 618-650-3264.
E-mail: catholic@siue.edu
Web site: www.siue.edu/religion/catholic
Sr. Claudia Calzetta, Dir. Total Staff 1.

JACKSONVILLE. *Illinois College Newman Center*, 453 E. State St., 62650. Tel: 217-243-8502; Fax: 217-245-6185.
E-mail: frchris@juno.com
Rev. Christopher Comerford, Chap.

MacMurray College Newman Center, c/o 453 E. State St., 62650. Tel: 217-243-8502; Fax: 217-245-6185.
E-mail: frchris@juno.com
Rev. Christopher Comerford, Chap.

[N] MISCELLANEOUS LISTINGS

SPRINGFIELD. *Benincasa Ministries*, 1237 W. Monroe, 62704. Tel: 217-787-0481.
E-mail: benincas@fgi.net
Sr. Sharon Zayac, O.P., Dir. Total in Residence 3; Total Staff 9.

Catholic Care Center, Inc., One Pope John Paul Plaza, 62703. Tel: 217-528-1771; Fax: 217-528-5110.
E-mail: polly@dio.org
Web site: www.dio.org
Mr. Leo A. Lenn, Pres. Directors: Most Rev. George J. Lucas; John Maxwell, Treas.; Ramon Robertson, Vice Pres.; James Forstall, Sec.; Bob Budnik; Hugh Graham, III; Thomas Reiser, Exec. Sec.; Sr. Joan Winkler, D.S.F.; Mrs. Eugena Costa.

Diocesan Care Management, Inc., 1 Pope John Paul Plaza, 62703. Tel: 217-528-1771; Fax: 217-528-5110.
E-mail: polly@dio.org
Web site: www.dio.org
Most Rev. George J. Lucas, Dir.; Mr. Leo Lenn, Pres.

Dominican Sisters of Springfield in Illinois Charitable Trust, Sacred Heart Convent, 1237 W. Monroe, 62704. Tel: 217-787-0481; Fax: 217-787-8169.
E-mail: smjtraeger@spdom.org
Web site: www.springfieldop.org

Foundation for the People of the Diocese of Springfield in Illinois, Catholic Pastoral Center, 1615 W. Washington, 62702. Tel: 217-698-8500, Ext. 108; Fax: 217-698-0802.
E-mail: mmulford@dio.org
Web site: dio.org
Legal Title: *The Foundation for the People of the Roman Catholic Diocese of Springfield in Illinois.*

Hospital Sisters Health System, 4936 LaVerna Rd., P.O. Box 19431, 62794-9431. Tel: 217-523-4747. Sr. Jomary Trstensky, O.S.F., Pres.

Hospital Sisters of St. Francis Foundation, Inc., 4936 LaVerna Rd., P.O. Box 19431, 62794-9431. Tel: 217-523-4747. Sr. Jomary Trstensky, O.S.F., Contact Person.

Hospital Sisters Services, Inc., 4936 LaVerna Rd., P.O. Box 19431, 62794-9431. Tel: 217-523-4747. Sr. Jomary Trstensky, O.S.F., Pres.

Leadership Conference of Women Religious, 1237 W. Monroe, 62704. Tel: 217-787-9914; Fax: 217-787-8106. Sr. Lea Woll, S.L.W., Chm.; Sr. Diane Collins, O.S.F., Vice Chm.; Sr. Ann Flanagan, R.S.M., Sec.; Sr. Rachelle Riley, O.P., Treas. Sponsored Activity: Project IRENE.
E-mail: irene@dio.org
Sr. Marcelline Koch, O.P., Project Dir.

Legion of Mary, 4030 Thornbrook Dr., 62707. Jean Heioux, Comitium Pres.

Priests' Purgatorial Society. Catholic Pastoral Center, 1615 W. Washington, P.O. Box 3187, 62708-3187. Tel: 217-698-8500; Fax: 217-698-0802.

Springfield Developmental Center Ltd., 4595 Laverna Rd., 62707. Tel: 217-525-8271; Fax: 217-525-5801.
E-mail: sdcstjames@aol.com
Developmental Training Program for Developmentally Disabled Adults. Cathy S. Barnett, Dir. Lay Staff 24; Clients 87.

Theresians of the United States, Inc. Theresian World Ministry, 1237 W. Monroe St., 62704. Tel: 217-726-5484; Fax: 217-523-4598.
E-mail: tustwn@cityscape.net
Web site: www.theresians.org
Sacred Heart Convent. Victoria S. Schmidt, Exec. Dir.

Villa Maria - Catholic Life Center, 1903 E. Lake Dr., 62707. Tel: 217-529-2213. Mrs. Martina Kocher, Activities Coord.

Weber House - Weber Care Corporation, 2520 St. James Rd., 62707. Tel: 217-522-8406. Bro. Raphael Kreikemeier, Exec. Dir.; Laura Rape, Dir. Bed capacity 8; Residence capacity 8.

ALTON. *Saint Anthony's Foundation, Inc.*, Saint Anthony's Way, P.O. Box 340, 62002-0340. Tel: 618-465-2571; Fax: 618-465-4569.
Web site: www.sahc.org
Affiliates: Saint Anthony's Health System and Saint Anthony's Health Center. William E. Kessler, Pres.

Saint Anthony's Health System, Inc., St. Anthony's Way, P.O. Box 340, 62002-0340. Tel: 618-465-2571; Fax: 618-465-4569.
Web site: www.sahc.org
Affiliates: Saint Anthony's Health Center and Saint Anthony's Foundation, Inc. William E. Kessler, Pres.; Rev. John Wykes, O.M.V., Chap. Sisters of St. Francis of the Martyr St. George 1.

Saint Clare's Hospital, 915 E. Fifth St., 62002. Tel: 618-463-5150.
Web site: www.sahc.org
A Division of Saint Anthony's Health Center. William E. Kessler, Pres.; Rev. John Wykes, O.M.V., Chap.

St. Francis Day Care Center, 710 College Ave., P.O. Box 9020, 62002-9020. Tel: 618-463-2766; Fax: 618-465-5064. Day Care Center. Sisters of St. Francis of the Martyr St. George 2; Assisted Daily 100; Total Staff 26.

BRIDGETON, MO. *Sisters of Divine Providence*, 3415 Bridgeland Dr., 63044. Tel: 314-209-9181; Fax: 314-209-9207.
E-mail: jfolkcdp@juno.com
Web site: www.divineprovidence-cdpmo.org
Sr. Janet Folkl, C.D.P., Contact Person.

GRANITE CITY. *St. Elizabeth Health Foundation*, 2100 Madison Ave., 62040. Tel: 618-798-3175; Fax: 618-798-3508.
E-mail: tleilerman@aol.com
Ted Eilerman, Contact Person.

SULLIVAN. *Fields-Wright Medical Facility, Inc.*, 2 W. Adams, 61951. Tel: 217-728-8316. Sponsored by Hospital Sisters of St. Francis. Keith L. Callahan, Pres.; Sr. Jomary Trstensky, O.S.F., Contact Person.

RELIGIOUS INSTITUTES OF MEN REPRESENTED IN THE DIOCESE

For further details refer to the corresponding bracketed number in the Religious Institutes of Men or Women section.

[1320]—*Clerics of St. Viator.* (Chicago Prov.).—C.S.V.
[0510]—*Franciscan Brothers of the Holy Cross.*—F.F.S.C.
[0520]—*Franciscan Friars.* (Sacred Heart Province).—O.F.M.
[0690]—*Jesuit Fathers and Brothers.* (Missouri Province).—S.J.
[0910]—*Oblates of Mary Immaculate.* (Central Province).—O.M.I.
[0940]—*Oblates of the Virgin Mary.*—O.M.V.
[0430]—*Order of Preachers (Dominicans).*—O.P.
[]—*Society of Jesus.* (Missouri Prov.).—S.J.

RELIGIOUS INSTITUTES OF WOMEN REPRESENTED IN THE DIOCESE

[0100]—*Adorers of the Blood of Christ.* (Ruma, IL; Wichita, KS).—A.S.C.
[0230]—*Benedictine Sisters of Pontifical Jurisdiction.* (Nauvoo, IL).—O.S.B.
[2100]—*Congregation of the Humility of Mary.*—C.H.M.
[1710]—*Congregation of the Third Order of St. Francis of Mary Immaculate, Joliet, IL.*—O.S.F.

[0760]—*Daughters of Charity of St. Vincent De Paul.* (East Central Prov.).—D.C.

[1070-10]—*Dominican Sisters.*—O.P.

[1070-13]—*Dominican Sisters.*—O.P.

[1440]—*Franciscan Sisters of the Poor.*—S.F.P.

[1770]—*Hospital Sisters of Third Order of St. Francis.*—O.S.F.

[2575]—*Institute of the Sisters of Mercy of the Union of the Americas.* (Chicago, IL).—R.S.M.

[3230]—*Poor Handmaids of Jesus Christ.*—P.H.J.C.

[2970]—*School Sisters of Notre Dame.* (St. Louis, MO).—S.S.N.D.

[1680]—*School Sisters of St. Francis.*—O.S.F.

[3520]—*Servants of the Holy Heart of Mary.*—S.S.C.M.

[0430]—*Sisters of Charity of the Blessed Virgin Mary.*—B.V.M.

[0990]—*Sisters of Divine Providence.* (St. Louis Prov.).—C.D.P.

[3360]—*Sisters of Providence of Saint Mary-of-the-Woods, Indiana.*—S.P.

[1570]—*Sisters of St. Francis of the Holy Family.*—O.S.F.

[1580]—*Sisters of St. Francis of the Immaculate Conception.*—O.S.F.

[1600]—*Sisters of St. Francis of the Martyr St. George.*—O.S.F.

[]—*Sisters of St. Joseph.* (India).

[3270]—*Sisters of the Most Precious Blood (O'Fallon, MO).*—C.PP.S.

[4110]—*Ursuline Nuns (Roman Union).* (Central Prov.).—O.S.U.

DIOCESAN CEMETERIES

SPRINGFIELD. *Calvary Cemetery Association.*
CARLINVILLE. *Calvary Cemetery Association.*
DECATUR. *Calvary Cemetery Association.*
EDWARDSVILLE. *Calvary Cemetery Association.*
LITCHFIELD. *Holy Cross Cemetery Association.*
MOUNT STERLING. *Catholic Cemetery Association.*
QUINCY. *Catholic Cemetery Association.*

NECROLOGY

† Bretz, Rev. Msgr. John W., Chap, Springfield, St. Joseph's Home. —Died Aug. 9, 2000.

† Schwellenbach, Aloysius, On Leave. —Died Sept. 15, 2000.

† Tamulis, Anthony, (Retired). —Died Nov. 23, 2000.

† Will, Rev. Msgr. Irvin Ross, (Retired). —Died March 20, 2000.

Diocese of Springfield in Massachusetts

(Dioecesis Campifontis)

Most Reverend

THOMAS LUDGER DUPRE, D.D., J.C.D.

Bishop of Springfield; ordained May 23, 1959; appointed Auxiliary Bishop of Springfield and Titular Bishop of Hodelm April 19, 1990; consecrated May 31, 1990; appointed Bishop of Springfield March 14, 1995; installed May 8, 1995. *Res., 68 Elliot St., Springfield, MA, 01101. Mailing Address: P.O. Box 1730, Springfield, MA, 01101.*

Most Reverend

JOSEPH F. MAGUIRE, D.D.

Retired Bishop of Springfield; ordained June 29, 1945; appointed Auxiliary Bishop of Boston and Titular Bishop of Mactaris December 1, 1971; consecrated February 2, 1972; appointed Coadjutor Bishop of Springfield with right of succession April 3, 1976; officially installed as Bishop of Springfield on November 4, 1977; resigned December 27, 1991. *Res., 76 Elliot St., P.O. Box 1730, Springfield, MA, 01101.*

ESTABLISHED JUNE 14, 1870.

Square Miles 2,822.

Comprises the Counties of Berkshire, Franklin, Hampden and Hampshire in the State of Massachusetts.

For legal titles of parishes and diocesan institutions, consult the Chancery Office.

Chancery Office: P.O. Box 1730, Springfield, MA, 01101. Tel.: 413-732-3175; Fax: 413-737-2337.

Web site address: www.diospringfield.org

E-mail address: mail@diospringfield.org

STATISTICAL OVERVIEW

Personnel	
Bishop	1
Retired Bishops	1
Priests: Diocesan Active in Diocese	142
Priests: Active Outside Diocese	7
Priests: Diocesan in Foreign Missions	1
Priests: Retired, Sick or Absent	39
Number of Diocesan Priests	189
Religious Priests in Diocese	41
Extern Priests in Diocese	3
Ordinations:	
Diocesan Priests	2
Permanent Deacons in Diocese	49
Total Brothers	9
Total Sisters	580
Parishes	
Parishes	130
With Resident Pastor:	
Resident Diocesan Priests	116
Resident Religious Priests	7
Without Resident Pastor:	
Administered by Priests	7
Administered by Deacons	1
Missions	15
Pastoral Centers	1
Professional Ministry Personnel:	
Sisters	41
Lay Ministers	50
Welfare	
Catholic Hospitals	1
Total Assisted	198,000
Health Care Centers	10
Total Assisted	92,602
Homes for the Aged	11
Total Assisted	1,281
Residential Care of Children	1
Day Care and Extended Day Care Centers	1
Total Assisted	126
Specialized Homes	1
Total Assisted	5,600
Special Centers for Social Services	3
Total Assisted	62,909
Residential Care of Disabled	1
Total Assisted	1,200
Educational	
Diocesan Students in Other Seminaries	13
Total Seminarians	13
Colleges and Universities	2
Total Students	1,075
High Schools, Diocesan and Parish	4
Total Students	1,637
Elementary Schools, Diocesan and Parish	28
Total Students	7,561
Elementary Schools, Private	1
Total Students	51
Catechesis/Religious Education:	
High School Students	8,657
Elementary Students	23,417
Total Students Under Catholic Instruction	42,411
Teachers in the Diocese:	
Priests	1
Sisters	38
Lay Teachers	413
Vital Statistics	
Receptions into the Church:	
Infant Baptism Totals	3,836
Adult Baptism Totals	153
Received into Full Communion	238
First Communions	3,883
Confirmations	2,919
Marriages:	
Catholic	1,104
Interfaith	307
Total Marriages	1,411
Deaths	4,264
Total Catholic Population	275,899
Total Population	792,195

Former Bishops—Most Rev. PATRICK THOMAS O'REILLY, D.D., cons. Sept. 25, 1870; died May 28, 1892.—Most Rev. THOMAS DANIEL BEAVEN, cons. Oct. 18, 1892; died Oct. 5, 1920.—Most Rev. THOMAS M. O'LEARY, D.D., cons. Sept. 8, 1921; died Oct. 10, 1949.—Most Rev. CHRISTOPHER J. WELDON, D.D., cons. March 24, 1950; retired Oct. 15, 1977; died March 19, 1982.—Most Rev. JOHN A. MARSHALL, D.D., cons. Bishop of Burlington, Jan. 25, 1972; installed Bishop of Springfield, Feb. 18, 1992; died July 3, 1994.—Most Rev. JOSEPH F. MAGUIRE, D.D., cons. Auxiliary Bishop of Boston, Feb. 2, 1972; installed Bishop of Springfield, Nov. 4, 1977; retired Dec. 27, 1991.

Vicar General—Rev. Msgr. RICHARD S. SNIEZYK, Vicar General and Moderator of the Curia, *65 Elliot St., P.O. Box 1730, Springfield, 01101.* Rev. Msgr. LEO A. LECLERC, *St. Rose de Lima Rectory, 600 Grattan St., Chicopee, 01020.*

Episcopal Vicars—Vicars for the Clergy: Revs. DAVID JOYCE; GEORGE FARLAND; Sr. JUDITH O'CONNELL, S.S.J., Vicar for Religious, *65 Elliot St., P.O. Box 1730, Springfield, 01101.* Rev. JOHN J. VARLEY, Berkshire Vicariate; Rev. RONALD G. YARGEAU, Franklin-Hampshire Vicariate; Rev. VERNON P. DECOTEAU, Hampden East Vicariate; Rev. HOWARD MCCORMICK, Hampden Central and Hampden West Vicariate.

Chancery Office—76 Elliot St., Springfield, 01105., Mailing Address: P.O. Box 1730, Springfield, 01101. Tel: 413-732-3175; Fax: 413-737-2337.

Chancellor—Rev. DANIEL P. LISTON, J.C.L.

Vice-Chancellors—Rev. ROBERT W. THRASHER, J.C.D.; Sr. CAROL CIFATTE, C.S.J., J.C.L.

Vicar for Canonical Affairs—Rev. DANIEL P. LISTON, J.C.L.

Secretary to the Bishop—Rev. CHRISTOPHER D. CONNELLY.

Judicial Vicar—Rev. JOHN L. SULLIVAN, J.C.L.

Adjutant Judicial Vicars—Rev. Msgr. ROGER VIAU, J.C.D.; Rev. JOHN P. MCDONAGH, J.C.L.

Judges—Rev. Msgr. JOHN F. HARRINGTON, P.A., J.C.L.; Revs. JOHN J. BONZAGNI; EDWARD M. KENNEDY; DANIEL R. FOLEY, J.C.D.; HENRY KARWEL, O.F.M.Conv., J.C.L.; DANIEL P. LISTON, J.C.L.; JOHN J. SHEA, J.C.D.; ROBERT W. THRASHER, J.C.D.; Sr. CAROL CIFATTE, C.S.J., J.C.L.

Promoter of Justice—Rev. JOHN R. BOURQUE, J.C.D.

Defenders of the Bond—Rev. EDWARD M. KENNEDY, J.C.L.; Sr. CLAIRE LAPOINTE, S.A.S.V., J.C.L.

Procurators-Advocate—Revs. JEDDIE P. BROOKS; JUAN GARCIA, C.R.I.C.; DANIEL B. BRUNTON; JOHN J. BONZAGNI, J.C.L.

Psychotherapeutic Counselor—Rev. J. DONALD R. LAPOINTE, L.I.C.S.W.

Psychological Experts—MARTIN J. MARKEY, Ph.D.; ROBERT SAISI, Ph.D., Ed.D.

Notaries—Mrs. CAROL MENDREK; MARGARET COLLINS; Mrs. ELLEN RIVERS; Ms. BARBARA OGONOSKI.

Diocesan Tribunal—65 Elliot St., P.O. Box 1730, Springfield, 01101. Tel: 413-452-0664; Fax: 413-747-8482.

Bishop's Commission for Clergy—Rev. Msgr. RICHARD S. SNIEZYK, Chm.; Revs. CHRISTOPHER CONNELLY; HUGH F. CREAN; GEORGE A. FARLAND; EUGENE HONAN; DAVID JOYCE; GERARD LAFLEUR; LEO A. LECLERC; FRANCIS J. MANNING; RICHARD M. RUNTE; THOMAS M. SHEA; RONALD G. YARGEAU; DANIEL P. LISTON.

Bishop's Cabinet—Rev. Msgr. RICHARD S. SNIEZYK; Rev. Msgr. LEO A. LECLERC; Rev. Msgr. THOMAS F. DEVINE; Rev. DANIEL P. LISTON; Sr. ANNETTE MCDERMOTT, S.S.J.; Sr. JUDITH O'CONNELL, S.S.J.; Sr. JUDITH SMELTZ, S.S.J.; Sr. BETTE GOULD, S.S.J.; Mr. MICHAEL GRAZIANO; Mr. JOHN SHUMAN.

Diocesan Commission for Ecumenism—Vacant, *76 Elliot St., P.O. Box 1730, Springfield, 01101.* Tel: 413-732-3175.

Diocesan Commission for the Liturgy—Rev. WILLIAM J. HAMILTON, Chm., *Christian Education Center, 625 Carew St., Springfield, 01104.* Tel: 413-732-3175.

Diocesan Director of Ceremonies—Rev. CHRISTOPHER D. CONNELLY, *76 Elliot St., P.O. Box 1730, Springfield, 01101.* Tel: 413-732-3175; Fax: 413-737-2337.

Diocesan Consultors—Rev. Msgr. THOMAS F. DEVINE; Rev. Msgr. JOHN F. HARRINGTON, P.A., J.C.L.; Rev. Msgr. RICHARD S. SNIEZYK; Rev. Msgr. LEO A. LECLERC; Revs. HUGH F. CREAN; GEORGE A. FARLAND; DAVID J. JOYCE; GERARD A. LAFLEUR; DANIEL P. LISTON, J.C.L.

Deans—Rev. TIMOTHY J. CAMPOLI, Franklin Deanery; Rev. ROLAND J. GALIPEAU, Greater Holyoke Deanery; Rev. THOMAS M. SHEA, Greater Springfield I Deanery; Rev. GEORGE A. FARLAND, Greater Springfield II Deanery; Rev. GERARD A. LAFLEUR, Hampden Central Deanery; CHARLES KUZMESKI, Hampden East Deanery; Rev. KENNETH J. TATRO, Hampden West Deanery; ROBERT J. COONAN, Hampshire Deanery; Rev. WILLIAM CYR, Northern Berkshire Deanery; Rev. JOHN A. KOONZ, Southern Berkshire Deanery.

Presbyteral Council—Rev. Msgr. THOMAS F. DEVINE; Rev. Msgr. JOHN F. HARRINGTON, P.A., J.C.L.; Rev. Msgr. RICHARD SNIEZYK; Rev. Msgr. LEO LECLERC; Revs. HUGH F. CREAN; VERNON P. DECOTEAU; CHRISTOPHER CONNELLY; RICHARD SCIOLI, C.S.S.; GEORGE FARLAND; DAVID J. JOYCE; GERARD A. LAFLEUR; DANIEL P. LISTON, J.C.L.; MICHAEL SHERSHANOVICH; PAUL E. MANSHIP; HOWARD W. MCCORMICK; CHRISTOPHER MALATESTA; FRANCIS MANNING.

Co-Vicars For Clergy—Revs. GEORGE FARLAND; DAVID JOYCE, *65 Elliot St., P.O. Box 1730, Springfield, 01101.* Tel: 413-732-3175.

Secretary for Financial Affairs—Mr. JOHN SHUMAN, *65 Elliot St., P.O. Box 1730, Springfield, 01101.* Tel: 413-732-3175.

Vicar for Religious—Sr. JUDITH O'CONNELL, S.S.J., Vicar, *65 Elliot St., P.O. Box 1730, Springfield, 01101.* Tel: 413-452-0609.

Diocesan Offices and Directors

Apostolate to the Handicapped—Rev. ROBERT F. WAGNER, Dir., *Bureau for Exceptional Children and Adults, 537 Northampton St., P.O. Box 1039, Holyoke, 01041.* Tel: 413-538-7450 (Voice and TTY); Fax: 413-536-5691.

Apostolate of the Suffering—ROBERT J. LETASZ, Dir., *P.O. Box 535, Chicopee, 01021.* Rev. ADRIEN T. REMY, Chap., *Mont Marie, Holyoke, 01040.*

Blue Army—Rev. ALBERT E. BRETON, *Nativity Rectory, 780 Chicopee St., Chicopee, 01013-2747.* Tel: 413-532-9421.

Building Commission—Rev. JAMES SCAHILL, Chm., *St. Mary Rectory, 840 Page Blvd., Springfield, 01104-2799.* Tel: 413-739-0456.

Building Consultant—Mr. FREDERICK R. PIQUETTE, *65 Elliot St., P.O. Box 1730, Springfield, 01101.* Tel: 413-452-0672; Fax: 413-785-5449.

Campaign for Human Development—Sr. ANNETTE M. MCDERMOTT, S.S.J., Dir., *65 Elliot St., P.O. Box 1730, Springfield, 01101.* Tel: 413-452-0697; Fax: 413-746-3421.

The Catholic Charismatic Renewal of Springfield, Inc.—Rev. GERALD BRADY, *Holy Name Rectory, 323 Dickinson St., Springfield, 01108.* Tel: 413-733-5823. Sr. MARGARET WALSH, S.S.J., Coord., *P.O. Box 4668, Springfield, 01101-4668.* Tel: 413-247-9001; Fax: 413-247-5605.

Catholic Charities—Sr. ANNETTE MCDERMOTT, S.S.J., *65 Elliot St., P.O. Box 1730, Springfield, 01103.* Tel: 413-452-0613.

Annual Catholic Appeal—Mr. JOHN SHUMAN, Exec. Dir. VIRGINIA WEBB, Dir. & Coord. of Admin., *65 Elliot St., Springfield, 01101., Mailing Address: P.O. Box 1730, Springfield, 01101.* Tel: 413-452-0629; Fax: 413-732-4297.

Catholic Nurses Council—Rev. LAWRENCE J. BERNIER, Chap., St. Michael's Rectory, *128 Maple St., East Longmeadow, 01023.* Tel: 413-525-4253.

Catholic Relief Services—Sr. ANNETTE MCDERMOTT, S.S.J., *65 Elliot St., P.O. Box 1730, Springfield, 01101.* Tel: 413-732-3175.

Cemeteries—Mr. JOSEPH M. KOSTEK, Diocesan Dir. of Cemeteries, *65 Elliot St., Springfield, 01101-1730.* Tel: 413-452-0692; Fax: 413-785-5449. *Saint Michael's Cemetery, 1601 State St., Springfield, 01109.* Tel: 413-733-0659. *Gate of Heaven Cemetery, 421 Tinkham Rd., Springfield, 01129.* Tel: 413-782-4731., *St. Aloysius Cemetery, 1601 State St., Springfield, 01109.* Tel: 413-733-0695. *St. Benedict Cemetery, Liberty St., Springfield, 01104.* Tel: 413-782-4731. *St. Matthew Cemetery, 366 Springfield St., Springfield, 01109.* Tel: 413-733-0659. *Calvary Cemetery, Northampton St., Springfield, 01040.* Tel: 413-733-8140.

Censor of Books—Rev. Msgr. THOMAS F. DEVINE, *519 Longmeadow St., Longmeadow, 01106.* Tel: 413-567-3124.

Clergy Counseling Service—Rev. GEORGE A. FARLAND, *Sacred Heart Rectory, 395 Chestnut St., Springfield, 01104.* Tel: 413-732-3721.

Commission on Church Music—Rev. WILLIAM J. HAMILTON, Chm., *Christian Education Center, 625 Carew St., Springfield, 01104.* Tel: 413-732-3175; Fax: 413-732-1944.

Communications Committee—Mr. MICHAEL GRAZIANO, Chm., *65 Elliot St., P.O. Box 1730, Springfield, 01101.* Tel: 413-732-4546; Fax: 413-747-0273.

Communications and Public Relations—

Catholic Communications Corporation—Mr. MICHAEL GRAZIANO, Chm., *65 Elliot St., P.O. Box 1730, Springfield, 01101.* Tel: 413-737-4744; Fax: 413-747-0273.

Services—

Chalice of Salvation (Televised Mass)—Bro. TERRENCE A. SCANLON, C.P., Exec. Dir., *65 Elliot St., P.O. Box 1730, Springfield, 01101.* Tel: 413-452-0642.

Real to Reel (Television News Magazine)—MARK DUPONT, Exec. Producer, *65 Elliot St., P.O. Box 1730, Springfield, 01101.* Tel: 413-452-0648.

The Catholic Observer (Newspaper)—REBECCA DRAKE, Editor, *65 Elliot St., P.O. Box 1730, Springfield, 01101.* Tel: 413-452-0636.

Continuing Education for Priests—Rev. JOHN T. SMEGAL, *North American Martyrs Rectory, 17 Juleann Dr., R.R. 01, Box 37, Lanesboro, 01237-9518.* Tel: 413-442-2063.

Office of Religious Education-CCD—Sr. PAULA ROBILLARD, S.S.J., Dir.; Sr. JOAN CONNELLY, S.S.N.D., Consultant for R.C.I.A. & Adult Education; Sr. CAROL DATZ, S.S.N.D., Evangelization & Adult Education; JAYNE DOUGHTERTY, Consultant for School Age Catechesis, *625 Carew St., Springfield, 01104.* Tel: 413-452-0807; Fax: 413-452-0817. CHARLES CONAGHAN, Berkshire Consultant, *100 Briggs Ave., Pittsfield, 01201.* Tel: 413-443-3187.

Cursillo Movement—Deacon JOHN BLEDSOE, Dir. English-Speaking Cursillo Movement, *84 Bardwell St., South Hadley, 01075.* Tel: 413-532-6671. Vacant, Dir. Spanish-Speaking Cursillo Movement, *445 Plainfield St., Springfield, 01107.* Tel: 413-736-0076.

Diocesan Board of Christian Education—Rev. Msgr. THOMAS F. DEVINE, Chm., *625 Carew St., Springfield, 01104.* Tel: 413-732-3175.

Diocesan Office of Black Catholic Ministry—Rev. PAUL E. MANSHIP, Dir., *Holy Family Rectory, 235 Eastern Ave., Springfield, 01109.* Tel: 413-732-1422.

Diocesan Office for Communications—Mr. MICHAEL A. GRAZIANO, Coord., *65 Elliot St., P.O. Box 1730, Springfield, 01101.* Tel: 413-732-4546; Fax: 413-747-0273.

Personnel—DOROTHY ORR, Office: *65 Elliot St., P.O. Box 1730, Springfield, 01101-1730.* Tel: 413-452-0691.

Education—Sr. BETTE GOULD, S.S.J., Supt. of Schools; ELAINE BERTHIAUME, Coord. Student Svcs.; Sr. MAUREEN TOOMEY, S.N.D., Dir. Personnel, *Christian Education Center, 625 Carew St., Springfield, 01104.* Tel: 413-452-0830; Fax: 413-452-0817.

Director of Pittsfield Catholic Schools—Priests Committee: Revs. JAMES JOYCE, Chm. HENRY DORSCH; GARY DAILEY; MICHAEL SHERSHANOVICH; JOHN VARLEY, *22 Maplewood Ave., Pittsfield, 01201.* Tel: 413-443-9686.

Family Life Bureau—625 Carew St., Springfield, 01104. Tel: 413-732-3175.

Fiscal Affairs—Rev. JOHN P. MCDONAGH, Coord. Special Projects; WILLIAM F. LABROAD, JR., Controller; Miss JEANNE M. DESROSIERS, Treas., *65 Elliot St., P.O. Box 1730, Springfield, 01101.* Tel: 413-452-0696; Fax: 413-785-5449.

Holy Childhood Association—Rev. Msgr. JOHN F. HARRINGTON, P.A., J.C.L., Dir., *65 Elliot St., P.O. Box 1730, Springfield, 01101.* Tel: 413-732-3175.

Holy Family League of Charity—c/o Office of Catholic Charities, P.O. Box 1730, Springfield, 01101. Tel: 413-732-3175.

Marriage Counseling—Rev. JOHN J. JOHNSON, Dir. Counselors: Mr. ALFRED A. D'AMATO; Mrs. ROSEMARY CASTONGUAY, *65 Elliot St., P.O. Box 1730, Springfield, 01101.* Tel: 413-452-0621; Fax: 413-747-0273.

Massachusetts Catholic Conference—Rev. Msgr. LEO A. LECLERC, V.G.; Rev. Msgr. RICHARD S. SNIEZYK, *65 Elliot St., P.O. Box 1730, Springfield, 01101.* Tel: 413-732-3175.

Ministry to the Deaf—Sr. CAROL LAREAU, S.S.J., *34 Nye St., Springfield, 01104.* Tel: 413-736-0020.

Ministry to the Divorced and Separated—Pastoral Ministry Office, Christian Education Center, 625 Carew St., Springfield, 01104. Tel: 413-732-3175.

Ministry to Priests—Rev. JOHN T. SMEGAL, *North American Martyrs Rectory, 17 Juleann Dr., R.R. 01, Box 37, Lanesboro, 01237.* Tel: 413-442-2063.

Newman Apostolate and Campus Ministry—Rev. FRANCIS LAVELLE, *Newman Center, 472 N. Pleasant St., Amherst, 01002.* Tel: 413-549-0300.

Office of Social Concerns—Sr. ANNETTE MCDERMOTT, S.S.J., *65 Elliot St., P.O. Box 1730, Springfield, 01101-1730.* Tel: 413-452-0615.

Parish Councils—

Pastoral Ministry—Sr. JUDITH SMELTZ, S.S.J., *Christian Education Center, 625 Carew St., Springfield, 01104.* Tel: 413-452-0824; Fax: 413-452-0817.

Permanent Diaconate—Rev. TIMOTHY J. MURPHY, Dir.; Deacon JOSEPH GARDE, Co-Dir., *65 Elliot St., P.O. Box 1730, Springfield, 01101.* Tel: 413-452-0674; Fax: 413-747-0273.

Priests' Retirement Program—Rev. Msgr. RICHARD S. SNIEZYK, V.G., Chm., *65 Elliot St., P.O. Box 1730, Springfield, 01101.*

Pro-Life Commission—Rev. JOHN L. SULLIVAN, J.C.L., *65 Elliot St., P.O. Box 1730, Springfield, 01101-1730.* Tel: 413-732-3175.

Propagation of the Faith—Rev. Msgr. JOHN F. HARRINGTON, P.A., J.C.L., *65 Elliot St., P.O. Box 1730, Springfield, 01101.* Tel: 413-452-0675.

Refugee Resettlement Program/Immigration Services—Vacant, *Office of Social Concerns, 65 Elliot St., P.O. Box 1730, Springfield, 01101.* Tel: 413-732-3175.

Representative of the Bishop at—Mercy Hospital, Springfield: Dr. KEVIN SCHMIDT, Mont Marie Health Care Center: Rev. DANIEL P. LISTON, J.C.L., Sisters of Providence Care Centers, Inc.: Rev. JOHN L. SULLIVAN, J.C.L., Our Lady of Providence Children's Center, West Springfield: Rev. J. DONALD R. LAPOINTE, L.I.C.S.W., Sisters of Providence Health System: Mr. WILLIAM COLLINS.

Retired Priests' Service—Rev. EDWARD M. CALLAHAN, *Sacred Heart Rectory, 395 Chestnut St., Springfield, 01104.*

Southeast Asian Apostolate—Rev. QUYNH DINH TRAN, Dir., *Holy Name Rectory, 323 Dickinson St., Springfield, 01108.* Tel: 413-733-5823.

Spanish Apostolate—Rev. PAUL MANSHIP, Dir., *Holy Family Rectory, 235 Eastern Ave., Springfield, 01109.* Tel: 413-732-1422., *Casa Maria, 51 Hamilton St., Holyoke, 01040.* Tel: 413-533-6016.

Springfield Diocesan Council of Catholic Women—Mrs. KATHERINE KUBERA, Pres., *11 Orchard Rd., East Longmeadow, 01028.*

Springfield Catholic Health Care Chaplains—Rev. DAVID M. FARLAND, *St. Michael's Cathedral, 260 State St., Springfield, 01103.* Rev. MARK S. STELZER, *Sacred Heart Rectory, 395 Chestnut St., Springfield, 01104.*

Vigilance, Council of—The Deans.

Vocations—Rev. CHRISTOPHER MALATESTA, *Christian Education Center, 625 Carew St., Springfield, 01104.* Tel: 413-452-0816; Fax: 413-452-0817.

Office of Youth Ministry—Mr. DONALD BOUCHER, Dir. Youth Min., *Christian Education Center, 625 Carew St., Springfield, 01104.* Tel: 413-732-3175; Fax: 413-732-1944.

Western Massachusetts Funding and Resource Center—65 Elliot St., P.O. Box 1730, Springfield, 01101. Tel: 413-452-0615.

CLERGY, PARISHES, MISSIONS AND PAROCHIAL SCHOOLS

CITY OF SPRINGFIELD (Hampden County)

1—ST. MICHAEL'S CATHEDRAL (1847), Rev. John P. McDonagh, Rector; Sr. Margaret McNaughton, S.S.J., Pastoral Assoc. In res., Rev. David M. Farland.
Res., 260 State St., 01103. Tel: 413-781-3656; Fax: 413-788-7752.
Catechesis/Religious Programs—Tel: 413-736-3804.
Students 63.

2—ALL SOULS (1908) (Spanish), Rev. Juan F. Garcia, C.R.I.C., (Peru) Admin. In res., Rev. Paul E. Manship.
Office: 35 Harriet St., 01107. Tel: 413-736-8208; 736-2167.
Res., 445 Plainfield St., 01107. Tel: 413-736-0076; Fax: 413-731-0962.
Catechesis/Religious Programs—Sr. Mary Cronin, D.M., D.R.E.
Students 58.

3—BLESSED SACRAMENT (1953) (Hispanic), Rev. Juan F. Garcia, C.R.I.C., (Peru) Admin.; Silvia Cabrera, Pastoral Min.; Deacon Genaro Medina.
Pastoral Center: 35 Harriet St., 01107. Tel: 413-736-8208; 736-2167; Fax: 413-731-0962.
Res., 445 Plainfield St., 01107. Tel: 413-736-0076.
Catechesis/Religious Programs—Sr. Mary Cronin, D.M., D.R.E.
Students 301.

4—HOLY CROSS (1949), Revs. Thomas M. Shea; John Sheaffer. In res., Rev. Msgr. Robert E. Foudy, Pastor Emeritus.
Res., 221 Plumtree Rd., 01118. Tel: 413-783-4111; Fax: 413-783-4112.
School—153 Eddywood St., 01118. Tel: 413-782-5246; Fax: 413-782-8137. Mrs. Maria Silvestri, Prin.
Sisters of St. Joseph 1; Lay Teachers 27; Students 478.
Catechesis/Religious Programs—175 Eddywood St., 01118. Tel: 413-782-8284.
Students 182.

5—HOLY FAMILY (1901) (African American-Hispanic), Rev. Paul E. Manship; Deacon Raphael Velazquez.
Res., 235 Eastern Ave., 01109. Tel: 413-732-1422.
Catechesis/Religious Programs—Students 90.

6—HOLY NAME (1909), Revs. Gerald Brady; Quynh Tran, Vietnamese Apostolate; Paul C. Laflamme, II; Sr. Patricia Bernier, Pastoral Min.
Res., 323 Dickinson St., 01108. Tel: 413-733-5823; Fax: 413-788-6481.
Center—57 Alderman St., 01108. Tel: 413-734-7113.
School—37 Alderman St., 01108. Tel: 413-736-4235. Martha Kelliher, Prin.
Lay Teachers 24; Students 328.
Catechesis/Religious Programs—Tel: 413-736-4145. Michelle Crean, D.R.E.
Students 175.

7—IMMACULATE CONCEPTION (1905) (Polish), Rev. Adrian J. Benoit; Deacon Rodney Szymczyk.
Res., 25 Parker St. (Indian Orchard), 01151. Tel: 413-543-3627; Fax: 413-543-4301.
School—34 Kopernick St., 01151. Tel: 413-543-2897; Fax: 413-543-8045.
Felician Sisters 2; Lay Teachers 8; Students 180.
Catechesis/Religious Programs—Mrs. Mary Arabik, D.R.E.
Students 122.

8—OUR LADY OF HOPE (1906), Rev. David J. Joyce; Deacon Armand Tourangeau. In res., Rev. George V. Joyce (WDC).
Res., 577 Carew St., 01104. Tel: 413-739-7369; Fax: 413-788-9313.
School—474 Armory St., 01104. Tel: 413-734-4125.
Lay Teachers 26; Students 455.
Catechesis/Religious Programs—Students 122.

9—OUR LADY OF MT. CARMEL (1907) (Italian), Rev. Richard A. Scioli, C.S.S.; Sr. Elizabeth A. Matuszek, S.S.J., Pastoral Assoc.
Res., 123 William St., 01105. Tel: 413-734-5433; Fax: 413-731-0680.
Preschool—56 Margaret St., 01105. Tel: 413-733-7410.
School—36 Margaret St., 01105. Tel: 413-739-3616.
Lay Teachers 16; Students 170.
Catechesis/Religious Programs—Students 473.
Mission—West Springfield, Hampden Co., St. Ann, 576 Memorial Ave., West Springfield, 01089. Tel: 413-736-3101; Fax: 413-732-4614. Rev. Joseph Massaro, C.S.S.

10—OUR LADY OF THE ROSARY (1917) (Polish), Rev. Stanley Sokol.
Res., 28 Underwood St., 01104. Tel: 413-733-0508. [JC]
Catechesis/Religious Programs—Tel: 413-739-2210.
Students 26.

11—OUR LADY OF THE SACRED HEART (1929), Rev. William Tourigny.
Office: 51 Rosewell Ave., 01109. Tel: 413-782-8041; Fax: 413-783-9150.
Res., 417 Boston Rd., 01109. Tel: 413-782-8041; Fax: 4131-783-9150.
School—52 Rosewell Ave., 01109. Tel: 413-782-8021.
Lay Teachers 17; Students 296.
Catechesis/Religious Programs—Cindee Gagnon, D.R.E.
Students 195.

12—SACRED HEART (1872), Rev. George A. Farland. In res., Revs. Edward M. Callahan Tel: 413-772-3721; Mark S. Stelzer; Christopher D. Connelly.
Res., 395 Chestnut St., 01104. Tel: 413-732-3721; Fax: 413-733-5731.
Catechesis/Religious Programs—Students 159.

13—ST. ALOYSIUS (1873) (French). Merged with St. Matthew, Springfield, to form St. Jude, Indian Orchard.

14—ST. CATHERINE OF SIENA (1961), Revs. Charles F. Gonet; Edward F. Howard, S.J.; Deacon Joseph M. Garde.
Res., 1023 Parker St., 01129. Tel: 413-783-8619; Fax: 413-783-2344.
Catechesis/Religious Programs—Students 507.

15—ST. JOSEPH'S (1873) (French), Rev. John L. Sullivan, Admin.
Res., 82 Howard St., 01105. Tel: 413-733-3527; 733-3745.
Catechesis/Religious Programs—Students 8.

16—ST. MARY'S (1948), Revs. James J. Scahill; Steven C. Amo. In res., Rev. Msgr. Richard S. Sniezyk.
Res., 840 Page Blvd., 01104. Tel: 413-739-0456.
Catechesis/Religious Programs—Tel: 413-736-1622.
Students 199.

17—ST. PATRICK'S (1961), Rev. Thomas M. Courtney; Deacon George Kozach Tel: 413-783-2455.
Res., 1900 Allen St., 01118-1820. Tel: 413-783-6201; Fax: 413-783-7787.
Catechesis/Religious Programs—Alan E. O'Dell, D.R.E.
Students 188.

18—ST. PAUL (1960), Rev. Francis H. Crombie.
Res., 51 Fenimore Blvd., 01108. Tel: 413-737-4422 (Rectory); 736-1539 (Church); Fax: 413-736-8378.
Catechesis/Religious Programs—Students 110.
Mission—East Longmeadow, Hampden Co., St. Joseph's, 146 Vineland Ave., East Longmeadow, 01028. Tel: 413-737-8650.

19—ST. THOMAS AQUINAS (1908) (French-Vietnamese). Closed. For inquiries for sacramental records contact Blessed Sacrament, Springfield.

OUTSIDE THE CITY OF SPRINGFIELD

Adams, Berkshire Co.,

1—NOTRE DAME DES SEPT DOULEURS, (1882) (French). Merged with St. Thomas Aquinas, Adams, to form Notre Dame des Douleurs and St. Thomas Aquinas, Adams.

2—ST. STANISLAUS KOSTKA, (1902) (Polish), Rev. John C. Chwalek.
Res., 25 Hoosac St., 01220. Tel: 413-743-0041. [CEM]
School—108 Summer St., 01220. Tel: 413-743-1091.
Felician Sisters 2; Lay Teachers 9; Students 177.
Catechesis/Religious Programs—Students 132.
Convent—23 Hoosac St., 01220. Tel: 413-743-1221.

3—ST. THOMAS AQUINAS, (1875). Merged with Notre Dame des Sept Douleurs, Adams, to form Notre Dame des Sept Douleurs and St. Thomas Aquinas, Adams.

4—NOTRE DAME DES SEPT DOULEURS AND ST. THOMAS AQUINAS, (1998), Rev. Daniel J. Boyle.
Res., P.O. Box 231, 01220-0231. Tel: 413-743-0577; Fax: 413-743-4665.
Catechesis/Religious Programs—Students 591.

Agawam, Hampden Co., All Saints,
Res., 74 Bridge St., 01220-0231. Tel: 413-786-4451.
St. John the Evangelist (1946), Revs. Howard W. McCormick; William Lunney.
Res., 833 Main St., 01001. Tel: 413-786-8105; Fax: 413-789-6266.
Catechesis/Religious Programs—Students 532.
St. Theresa of the Child Jesus, Hamden Co., (1883). Merged with Saint Anthony Mission to form All Saints, Agawam.

Amherst, Hampshire Co., St. Brigid's (1872), Rev. Bruce N. Teague Tel: 413-253-1828.
Res., 122 N. Pleasant St., P.O. Box 424, 01004-0424. Tel: 413-253-2829; Fax: 413-253-7935. [CEM]
Catechesis/Religious Programs—D.R.E.: Jane Bacon; Susan Nagy; Patty Bonsigneur.
Students 227.

Belchertown, Hampshire Co., St. Francis of Assisi (1926), Revs. Vernon Decoteau; Ronald Wamsher.
Res., 10 Park St., 01007. Tel: 413-323-6272; Fax: 413-323-4307.
Catechesis/Religious Programs—Tel: 413-323-7545. D.R.E.: Mrs. Judy Trickey; Mrs. Susan Martens.
Students 803.

Bondsville, Hampden Co., St. Bartholomew's (1878), Rev. Eugene J. Plasse.
Res., 76 Thorndike St., Palmer, 01069. Tel: 413-283-5091; 283-8841 (Church). [JC]
Catechesis/Religious Programs—Students 71.
St. Adalbert's (1910), Rev. Normand F. Mailloux, M.S.
Res., 18 Depot St., P.O. Box 1083, 01009. Tel: 413-283-3000.
Catechesis/Religious Programs—Students 10.

Brimfield, Hampden Co., St. Christopher's (1953), Rev. Walter A. Swift.
Church—20 Sturbridge Rd., Rte. 20, P.O. Box 387, 01010. Tel: 413-245-7274; Fax: 413-245-8376.
Rectory—16 Sturbridge Rd., Rte. 20, 01010.
Catechesis/Religious Programs—Students 188.
Mission—Wales, Hampden Co., St. Monica.
Station—Holland, St. Bernadette's.

Cheshire, Berkshire Co., St. Mary of the Assumption (1926), Rev. Thomas B. Begley; Deacon Robert Hitter.
Res., 159 Church St., 01225. Tel: 413-743-2110.
Catechesis/Religious Programs—Students 251.

Chicopee, Hampden Co.,

1—ASSUMPTION, (1885) (French), Rev. Gerard A. LaFleur, V.F.
Res., 104 Springfield St., 01013. Tel: 413-592-1597; Fax: 413-592-1597.
Catechesis/Religious Programs—Tel: 413-592-9344.
Students 114.

2—HOLY NAME OF JESUS, (1838), Rev. James J. Flahive.
Res., 33 South St., 01013. Tel: 413-592-0122. [CEM]
School—63 South St., 01013. Tel: 413-592-6857.
Sisters of Notre Dame 3; Lay Teachers 11; Students 230.
Catechesis/Religious Programs—Tel: 413-592-7813.
Students 120.

3—NATIVITY OF THE BLESSED VIRGIN MARY, (1897) (French), Rev. Robert H. Riel.
Res., 780 Chicopee St., 01013-2747. Tel: 413-532-9421; Fax: 413-532-1410. [JC]
Catechesis/Religious Programs—Tel: 413-536-3310.
Students 67.

4—ST. ANNE'S, (1912), Rev. J. Victor Carrier; Deacon Edward J. Finnie, (Retired).
Res., 30 College St., 01020. Tel: 413-532-7503; Fax: 413-542-5970.
Catechesis/Religious Programs—Tel: 413-533-8038.
Students 452.

5—ST. ANTHONY'S, (1926) (Polish), Revs. Benedict Fagone, O.F.M.Conv.; Michael Slonecki, O.F.M.Conv.
Res., 56 St. Anthony St., 01013. Tel: 413-538-9475; Fax: 413-538-9859.
Catechesis/Religious Programs—Students 53.

6—ST. GEORGE'S, (1893) (French), Rev. Ronald P. Lussier.
Res., 202 E. Main St., 01020. Tel: 413-598-8622; Fax: 413-592-8353.
School—Consolidated to form St. Joan of Arc/St. George School. 587 Grattan St., 01020. Tel: 413-533-1475.
Catechesis/Religious Programs—Students 240.

7—ST. MARY'S, (1939), Rev. Francis M. Kennedy; Deacon Joseph A. Smith.
Res., 840 Chicopee St., 01013. Tel: 413-532-1854.
Catechesis/Religious Programs—Students 77.

8—ST. PATRICK'S, (1872) (Irish), Rev. J. Donald Lapointe.
Res., 319 Broadway, 01020. Tel: 413-592-4178. [CEM]
School—125 Montgomery St., 01020. Tel: 413-594-8166; Fax: 413-594-8167.
Sisters of Saint Joseph 1; Lay Teachers 13; Students 275.
Catechesis/Religious Programs—Tel: 413-592-4344.
Students 338.

9—ST. ROSE DE LIMA, (1909) (French), Rev. Msgr. Leo A. Leclerc, V.G.; Rev. Christopher Waitekus; Deacon Leon Mireault.
Res., 600 Grattan St., 01020. Tel: 413-536-4558; Fax: 413-536-4559. [CEM]
School—St. Joan of Arc/St. George School, 587 Grattan St., 01020. Tel: 413-533-1475; Fax: 413-533-1418.
Sisters of the Presentation of Mary 2; Sisters of the Assumption 2; Lay Teachers 14; Students 392.
Catechesis/Religious Programs—Tel: 413-536-6038.
Students 348.

10—ST. STANISLAUS BASILICA, (1891) (Polish), Revs. Michael Kolodziej, O.F.M.Conv.; Albert Scherer, O.F.M.Conv.; Adrian Gallagher, O.F.M.Conv.; Lucian Krolikowski, O.F.M.Conv.; Gary Johnson, O.F.M.Conv.; Bro. William Sudyka, O.F.M.Conv. In res., Revs. Placid Kaczorek, O.F.M.Conv.; Herbert C. Baloga, O.F.M.Conv.; Bro. Frank Grimaldi, O.F.M.Conv.
Res., 566 Front St., 01013. Tel: 413-594-6669; Fax: 413-594-5259. [CEM]
School—Tel: 413-592-5135. Sr. Cecilia Haier, F.S.S.J., Prin.
Franciscan Sisters of St. Joseph 2; Lay Teachers 24; Students 430.
Catechesis/Religious Programs—Tel: 413-592-7955; Fax: 413-598-0187.
Students 186.

Dalton, Berkshire Co., St. Agnes (1907), Rev. John A. Koonz; Deacon Pasqual Baldasaro.
Res., 489 Main St., 01226. Tel: 413-684-0125.
School—30 Carson St., 01226. Tel: 413-684-3143.
Sisters of St. Joseph 2; Lay Teachers 16; Students 242.
Catechesis/Religious Programs—35 Deming St., 01226. Tel: 413-684-3879.
Students 495.

Easthampton, Hampshire Co., Immaculate Conception (1871) (Irish), Rev. William J. Hamilton, K.H.S.
Res., 33 Adams St., 01027. Tel: 413-527-9778; Fax: 413-527-9353. [CEM]
School—Notre Dame-Immaculate Conception School, Tel: 413-527-6133. Mrs. Sharon Sarrasin, Prin.
Lay Teachers 12; Students 248.
Catechesis/Religious Programs—11 Clifford St., 01027. Tel: 413-527-1588.
Students 630.

Our Lady of Good Counsel (1906) (French), Rev. Thomas R. Champigny. In res., Rev. Christopher A. Malatesta.
Res., 35 Pleasant St., 01027. Tel: 413-527-9588; Fax: 413-529-0517.
School—Notre Dame-Immaculate Conception, Tel: 413-527-6133; Fax: 413-527-6625.
Lay Teachers 11; Students 249.
Catechesis/Religious Programs—Students 231.

Sacred Heart (1909) (Polish), Rev. James A. Sipitkowski.
Res., 33 Knipfer Ave., 01027. Tel: 413-527-9036; Fax: 413-529-0936. [CEM]
Catechesis/Religious Programs—Students 141.

East Longmeadow, Hampden Co., St. Michael's (1894), Revs. Lawrence J. Bernier, V.F.; Daniel S. Pacholec; Sr. Mary McGeer, S.S.J., Pastoral Assoc.
Res. & Mailing Address: 128 Maple St., 01028. Tel: 413-525-4253; Fax: 413-525-4254.
Catechesis/Religious Programs—Tel: 413-525-0371. Mrs. Shirley Skiffington, D.R.E.
Students 927.

Feeding Hills, Hampden Co., Sacred Heart (1946), Rev. Ronald F. Sadlowski; Deacon James Martone.
Res., 1103 Springfield St., 01030. Tel: 413-786-8200; Fax: 413-786-7802.
Catechesis/Religious Programs—Tel: 413-789-6705. Kathryn Patterson, D.R.E.
Students 1,293.

Granby, Hampshire Co., Immaculate Heart of Mary (1951), Rev. John J. Shea.
Res., 256 State St., 01033. Tel: 413-467-9821; Fax: 413-467-2988.
Catechesis/Religious Programs—Tel: 413-467-3566.
Students 473.

Great Barrington, Berkshire Co., St. Peter's (1864), Rev. William H. Wallis.
Res., 16 Russell St., 01230. Tel: 413-528-1157. [CEM]
Catechesis/Religious Programs—Tel: 413-528-2037.
Students 225.

Greenfield, Franklin Co., Blessed Sacrament (1960), Rev. Timothy J. Campoli, V.F.
Res., 182 High St., 01301. Tel: 413-773-3311; Fax: 413-773-5785. [CEM]
School—Holy Trinity School, 10 Beacon St., 01301. Tel: 413-773-3831. Mrs. Judith Lapointe, Prin.
Lay Teachers 10; Students 143.
Catechesis/Religious Programs—Tel: 413-774-2918.
Students 107.

Holy Trinity (1868), Rev. Ronald G. Yargeau.
Res., 133 Main St., 01301-3209. Tel: 413-774-2884; Fax: 413-774-3852.
Catechesis/Religious Programs—Students 160.

Sacred Heart (1912) (Polish), Rev. Stanley J. Aksamit; Deacon Albert Routhier.
Res., St. Mary's, 90 Seventh St., Turners Falls, 01376. Tel: 413-863-2585; 772-6377; Fax: 413-863-8978. [CEM]
Catechesis/Religious Programs—Students 90.

Hadley, Hampshire Co., Holy Rosary (1916) (Polish). Merged with St. John, Hadley, to form Most Holy Redeemer, Hadley.

St. John's (1915). Merged with Holy Rosary, Hadley, to form Most Holy Redeemer, Hadley.

Most Holy Redeemer (1998), Rev. William P. Murphy.
Res., 120 Russell St., P.O. Box 375, 01035-0375. Tel: 413-584-1326; Fax: 413-587-0224. [CEM]
Catechesis/Religious Programs—Tel: 413-586-6209.
Students 253.

Hampden, Hampden Co., St. Mary's (1951), Rev. Timothy J. Murphy.
Res., 27 Somers Rd., 01036. Tel: 413-566-8843; Fax: 413-566-5845. [CEM]
Catechesis/Religious Programs—Students 350.

Hatfield, Hampshire Co., St. Joseph's (1899), Rev. Robert J. Coonan.
Mailing Address: P.O. Box 34, 01038.
Res., 11 School St., 01038. Tel: 413-247-9079.
Catechesis/Religious Programs—Students 153.

Holy Trinity (1916) (Polish), Rev. Robert J. Coonan. 73 Main St., P.O. Box 110, 01038. Tel: 413-247-3133; Fax: 413-247-5605. [CEM]
Catechesis/Religious Programs—Students 33.

Haydenville, Hampshire Co., St. Mary's (1889), Rev. Michael H. Devlin.
Res., 173 Main St., P.O. Box 277, 01039-0277. Tel: 413-268-7212; Fax: 413-268-8264. [CEM]
Catechesis/Religious Programs—Students 146.

Hinsdale, Berkshire Co., St. Patrick's (1868), Rev. R. Joseph LeVay.
Res., 43 Church St., P.O. Box 428, 01235. Tel: 413-655-2208. [CEM]
Catechesis/Religious Programs—78 Washington St., Becket, 01223.
Students 143.
Mission—Becket, Berkshire Co., St. Matthew, 78 Washington St., Becket, 01223.

Holyoke, Hampden Co.,

1—BLESSED SACRAMENT, (1913), Revs. Norman B. Bolton; Richard A. Riendeau.
Res., 1945 Northampton St., 01040. Tel: 413-532-0713.
School—21 Westfield Rd., 01040. Tel: 413-536-2236; Fax: 413-534-0795.
Sisters of St. Joseph 1; Lay Teachers 26; Students 382.
Catechesis/Religious Programs—15 Westfield Rd., 01040. Tel: 413-532-8647.
Students 221.
Mission—Holyoke, Hampden Co., Holyoke Soldier's Home Chapel, 110 Cherry St., 01040. Tel: 413-532-9475.

2—HOLY CROSS, (1905), Rev. Roland J. Galipeau.
Res., 23 Sycamore St., 01040. Tel: 413-532-5661; Fax: 413-535-1759.
Catechesis/Religious Programs—Tel: 413-536-8832. Maureen P. Callahan, D.R.E.
Students 231.

3—HOLY FAMILY, (1949), Rev. Robert W. Thrasher; Deacon Joseph A. Badame. In res., Rev. James P. Menge.
Res., 15 Holy Family Rd., 01040. Tel: 413-536-6777.
Catechesis/Religious Programs—Tel: 413-536-1665.
Students 89.

4—IMMACULATE CONCEPTION, (1905), Revs. Thomas Reilly, M.S.; Stephen Krisanda, M.S.; Deacon Frederick Pelletier. In res., Rev. William J. Doherty, M.S.
Res., 54 N. Summer St., 01040. Tel: 413-532-5784; Fax: 413-532-8852. [JC]
Catechesis/Religious Programs—Tel: 413-532-0468.
Students 175.

5—MATER DOLOROSA, (1896) (Polish), Revs. Raphael Zwolenkiewicz, O.F.M.Conv.; John Bambol, O.F.M.Conv.; Andrew Skiba, O.F.M.Conv.; Adam Ziolkowski, O.F.M.Conv.; Bro. Stephen Murphy, O.F.M.Conv., Pastoral Assoc.
Offices: Tel: 413-532-7889; Fax: 413-538-6754.
Res., 71 Maple St., 01040. Tel: 413-532-8272. [CEM]
School—25 Maple St., 01040. Tel: 413-532-2831.
Franciscan Sisters of St. Joseph 1; Lay Teachers 18; Students 293.
Catechesis/Religious Programs—Tel: 413-532-8272.
Students 169.

6—OUR LADY OF PERPETUAL HELP, (1890) (French). Merged with Sacred Heart to form Our Lady of Guadalupe, Holyoke.

7—OUR LADY OF THE ROSARY, (1886). Closed. For inquiries for parish records contact the Chancery.

8—PRECIOUS BLOOD, (1869). Closed. For inquiries for parish records contact Our Lady of Perpetual Help, Holyoke.

9—SACRED HEART, (1876). Merged with Our Lady of Perpetual Help to form Our Lady of Guadalupe, Holyoke.

10—OUR LADY OF GUADALUPE,
Res., 435 Maple St., 01040. Tel: 413-532-4282. [JC]

11—ST. JEROME'S, (1854), Rev. Daniel R. Foley, V.F.
Res., 169 Hampden St., 01040. Tel: 413-532-6381. [CEM]

Housatonic, Berkshire Co., Corpus Christi (1899), Rev. Anthony J. Jutt.
Res., 520 Main St., Box 569, 01236. Tel: 413-274-3443. [CEM]
Catechesis/Religious Programs—Students 72.

All Saints (1913) (Polish), Rev. Anthony J. Jutt.
Res., 204 High St., 01236. Tel: 413-274-3443.
Catechesis/Religious Programs—Students 43.

Huntington, Hampshire Co., St. Thomas (1886), Rev. Donald A. Noiseux.
Res., 8 E. Main St., P.O. Box 547, 01050. Tel: 413-667-3350. [CEM]
Catechesis/Religious Programs—Students 126.
Mission—Chester, Hampden Co., St. John, Middlefield St., Chester, 01011.

Indian Orchard, St. Jude (1998), Rev. William A. Pomerleau.
Res., 1326 Worcester St., 01151. Tel: 413-543-3739; Fax: 413-543-5573.
Church—221 Main St.
Catechesis/Religious Programs—Students 45.
Chapel—Pinevale St.

Lanesboro, Berkshire Co., North American Martyrs (1969), Rev. John T. Smegal, Admin.
Res., 17 Juleann Dr., 01237. Tel: 413-442-2063.
Catechesis/Religious Programs—Students 158.

Lee, Berkshire Co., St. Mary's (1857), Revs. Gary M. Dailey; David M. Darcy.
Res., 40 Academy St., 01238. Tel: 413-243-0275; Fax: 413-243-1926. [CEM]
School—115 Orchard St., 01238. Tel: 413-243-1079.
Sisters of St. Joseph 2; Lay Teachers 10; Students 229.
Catechesis/Religious Programs—Students 225.
Missions—Otis, Berkshire Co., St. Mary of the Lakes, Tel: 413-269-4200; South Lee, Berkshire Co., St. Francis of Assisi.

Leeds, Hampshire Co., St. Catherine's (1911), Rev. Vincent M. O'Connor.
Res., 195 Main St., 01053. Tel: 413-584-1726; Fax: 413-584-2208. [JC]
Catechesis/Religious Programs—Students 170.

Lenox, Berkshire Co., St. Ann's (1891), Rev. Daniel B. Brunton; Deacon George Keator.
Res., 134 Main St., 01240. Tel: 413-637-0157. [CEM]
Catechesis/Religious Programs—Tel: 413-637-4027; Fax: 413-637-2945.
Students 337.

Lenox Dale, Berkshire Co., St. Vincent de Paul's (1904), Rev. Daniel B. Brunton. In res., Rev. John J. Bonzagni Tel: 413-637-1085.
Mailing Address: P.O. Box 259, 01242-0259.
Church & Res.: 29 Crystal St., 01242. Tel: 413-637-3525.
Catechesis/Religious Programs—Tel: 413-637-0519.
Students 54.

Longmeadow, Hampden Co., St. Mary's (1936), Rev. Msgr. Thomas F. Devine; Rev. Dariusz P. Wudarski; Deacon Donald Higby.
Res., 519 Longmeadow St., 01106. Tel: 413-567-3124.
School—56 Hopkins Pl., 01106. Tel: 413-567-0907; Fax: 413-567-7695.
Sisters of St. Joseph 2; Lay Teachers 12; Students 212.
Catechesis/Religious Programs—Tel: 413-567-3420.
Students 1,450.

Ludlow, Hampden Co.,

1—CHRIST THE KING, (1948) (Polish), Rev. Raymond A. Soltys.
Res., 41 Warsaw Ave., 01056. Tel: 413-583-2630.
Catechesis/Religious Programs—Students 309.

2—OUR LADY OF FATIMA, (1948) (Portugese), Rev. Vitor Oliveira, Admin.
Res., 438 Winsor St., 01056. Tel: 413-583-2312; Fax: 413-547-0207.
Catechesis/Religious Programs—Students 527.

3—ST. JOHN THE BAPTIST, (1904) (French), Rev. Homer P. Gosselin; Deacon Edward Faber. In res., Rev. Lionel E. Bonneville.
Res., 181 Hubbard St., 01056. Tel: 413-583-3467; Fax: 413-583-2036.
School—217 Hubbard St., 01056. Tel: 413-583-8550; Fax: 413-589-0544.
Sisters of St. Ann 2; Lay Teachers 16; Students 280.
Catechesis/Religious Programs—Tel: 413-583-4258.
Students 355.

4—ST. MARY, (1968), Rev. Francis J. Manning; Deacons Robert L. Duval; Louis Pancotti.
Res., 12 Cedar St., 01056. Tel: 413-583-2691; Fax: 413-589-1868.
Catechesis/Religious Programs—Tel: 413-583-2153.
Students 468.

Millers Falls, Franklin Co., St. John's (1898), Rev. Dennis P. Bombardier.
Res., 5 Church St., 01349. Tel: 413-659-3435.
Catechesis/Religious Programs—Students 28.
Mission—Erving, Franklin Co., St. Blanche, 16 East Prospect, Erving, 01344.

Monson, Hampden Co., St. Patrick's (1878), Rev. Jeddie P. Brooks; Deacon Bernard Pellissier.
Res., 22 Green St., P.O. Box 473, 01057. Tel: 413-267-3622; Fax: 413-267-0272. [CEM]
Catechesis/Religious Programs—Students 305.

North Adams, Berkshire Co.,

1—HOLY FAMILY, (1997). Merged with Our Lady of Incarnation, North Adams, to form Our Lady of Mercy, North Adams.

2—NOTRE DAME, (1875) (French-Canadian), Revs. Michael W.T. Twardzik; Daniel Nolan; Deacon Robert R. Moulton.
Res., 12 Union St., 01247. Tel: 413-663-7131; Fax: 413-663-3938.
Catechesis/Religious Programs—Students 78.

3—OUR LADY OF THE INCARNATION, (1955). Merged with Holy Family, North Adams, to form Our Lady of Mercy, North Adams.

4—OUR LADY OF MERCY, (1997), Revs. Michael W.T. Twardzik; Daniel Nolan; Deacon Robert Moulton.
Church—635 State Rd., 01247. Tel: 413-663-3976; Fax: 413-663-3938.
Catechesis/Religious Programs—Tel: 413-662-2038. Jackie Gould, D.R.E.
Students 47.
Shrine—1288 Massachusetts Ave., 01247.

5—OUR LADY OF MERCY SHRINE, (1997). Consolidation of Holy Family, North Adams, and Our Lady of the Incarnation, North Adams. Revs. Michael W.T. Twardzik; Daniel Nolan; Deacon Robert Moulton. 1288 Massachussetts Ave., 01247. Tel: 413-663-7131; Fax: 413-664-4940.

6—ST. ANTHONY OF PADUA, (1903) (Italian), Rev. Daniel J. O'Hare.
Res., 70 Marshall St., 01247. Tel: 413-663-3112.
Catechesis/Religious Programs—Tel: 413-663-7331.
Students 175.

7—ST. FRANCIS, (1863), Revs. Michael W.T. Twardzik; Daniel Nolan.
Res., 12 Union St., 01247. Tel: 413-663-5316; Fax: 413-663-3938. [CEM]
Catechesis/Religious Programs—Tel: 413-662-2038.
Students 225.

Northampton, Hampshire Co.,

1—ANNUNCIATION, (1878), Revs. Roy H. Duquette; John S. Lis, Parochial Vicar.
Res., 42 Beacon St., P.O. Box 60055, Florence, 01062-0055. Tel: 413-584-1520; Fax: 413-586-7530.
Catechesis/Religious Programs—87 Beacon St., Florence, 01062-0055. Tel: 413-584-2041. Cindy Teynor, D.R.E.
Students 165.

2—BLESSED SACRAMENT, (1899), Rev. Daniel P. Liston; Deacon Francis J. McCarthy.
Res., 336 Elm St., 01060. Tel: 413-584-1280.
Catechesis/Religious Programs—Tel: 413-586-1111.
Students 225.

3—SACRED HEART, (1886) (French), Rev. Merle L. Lavoie.
Res., 101 King St., 01060. Tel: 413-584-7422.
Catechesis/Religious Programs—Tel: 413-584-4339.
Students 73.

4—ST. JOHN CANTIUS, (1904) (Polish), Rev. Merle L. Lavoie.
Res., 10 Hawley St., 01060. Tel: 413-584-1510; Fax: 413-586-5776.
Catechesis/Religious Programs—101 King St., 01060. Tel: 413-584-7422.
Students 18.

5—ST. MARY OF THE ASSUMPTION, (1866) (Irish), Rev. Eugene D. Honan. In res., Rev. Leo James Hoar.
Res., 3 Elm St., P.O. Box 180, 01061. Tel: 413-584-7310; Fax: 413-584-4788. [CEM]
Catechesis/Religious Programs—Tel: 413-586-1111.
Students 148.

Northfield, Franklin Co., St. Patrick (1973), Rev. John J. Ayers; Deacon Arthur E. Ratte.
Res., 80 Main St., 01360-1022. Tel: 413-498-2728. [CEM]
Catechesis/Religious Programs—Students 88.

Orange, Franklin Co., St. Mary (1903), Rev. Brian McGrath; Deacons Joseph S. Bucci, Jr.; James F. Donelan.
Res., 19 Congress St., 01364. Tel: 978-544-2900; Fax: 978-544-2900.
Catechesis/Religious Programs—Tel: 978-544-8105.
Students 185.

Palmer, Hampden Co., St. Thomas the Apostle (1864), Rev. Eugene J. Plasse; Deacon Edward J. Tenczar.
Res., 76 Thorndike St., 01069. Tel: 413-283-5091. [CEM]
Catechesis/Religious Programs—Tel: 413-283-5651.
Students 335.

Pittsfield, Berkshire Co.,

1—HOLY FAMILY, (1912) (Polish), Rev. Eugene A. Suszek, Admin.
Res., 133 Seymour St., 01201. Tel: 413-442-2036.
Catechesis/Religious Programs—21 Danforth St., 01201. Tel: 413-442-4065. John Arasimowiez, D.R.E.
Students 35.

2—NOTRE DAME, (1868) (French), Rev. Earl Hebert; Deacon Ralph R. Cyr.
Res., 50 Melville St., 01201. Tel: 413-499-2736.
Catechesis/Religious Programs—41 Melville St., 01021. Tel: 413-499-9554; Fax: 413-499-9514.
Students 105.

3—OUR LADY OF MT. CARMEL, (1903) (Italian), Rev. Geoffrey J. Deeker, C.S.S.
Res., 359 Fenn St., 01201. Tel: 413-442-4458; Fax: 413-496-9607.
Catechesis/Religious Programs—Tel: 413-445-4856.
Students 120.
Mission—Pittsfield, Berkshire Co., All Souls, 51 Pembroke Ave., 01201. Tel: 413-442-5090.

4—SACRED HEART, (1919), Revs. James K. Joyce; Royal J. Gardner; Deacon James A. Hager. Pastoral Ministers: Sr. Kathryn Flanagan; Deacon James A. Hager.
Res., 191 Elm St., 01201. Tel: 413-443-6960; Fax: 413-442-9649.
School—Regional School, (Grades K-5) One Meadow Lane, 01201. Tel: 413-443-6379.
Sisters of St. Joseph 1; Lay Teachers 19; Students 319.
Catechesis/Religious Programs—Tel: 413-442-5564. D.R.E.: Mr. Robert Esposito; Mrs. Kim Joseph.
Students 715.

5—ST. CHARLES, (1893), Rev. Peter A. Gregory; Sr. Barbara A. Faille, S.S.J., Pastoral Assoc.; Deacon William G. Moesley.
Res., 89 Briggs Ave., 01201. Tel: 413-442-7470; Fax: 413-445-5267.
Catechesis/Religious Programs—100 Briggs Ave., 01201. Tel: 413-442-0591.
Students 79.

6—ST. FRANCIS, (1960), Rev. Paul A. Bombardier.
Res., 80 Morningview Dr., 01201. Tel: 413-499-1955. [CEM]
Catechesis/Religious Programs—Tel: 413-448-2987. Donna Quallen, D.R.E.
Students 101.

7—ST. JOSEPH'S, (1849), Rev. Michael Shershanovich; Deacon Eugene C. Momnie.
Res., 414 North St., 01201. Tel: 413-445-5789; Fax: 413-443-5466. [CEM]
Catechesis/Religious Programs—Students 278.

8—ST. MARK'S, (1913), Rev. Henry L. Dorsch. In res., Rev. William F. Eckert (CAM).
Res., 27 Onota St., 01201. Tel: 413-447-7510.
Catechesis/Religious Programs—400 Columbus Ave. Ext., 01201. Tel: 413-442-8444.
Students 316.

9—ST. MARY THE MORNING STAR, (1915), Rev. Paul A. Bombardier.
Res., 665 Tyler St., 01201. Tel: 413-445-5008.
Catechesis/Religious Programs—Lillian Quinn, D.R.E.
Students 220.
Parish Center—75 Plunkett St., 01201. Tel: 413-447-7533.

10—ST. TERESA, (1926), Rev. John J. Varley.
Res., 290 South St., 01201. Tel: 413-442-2202; Fax: 413-443-9876.
Catechesis/Religious Programs—Tel: 413-443-5366. Sr. Shirleyanne Greene, S.S.J., D.R.E.
Students 159.

Russell, Hampden Co., Our Lady of the Rosary (1969), Rev. Armando C. Russo.
Res., Huntington Rd., 01071. Tel: 413-862-4418. [JC]
Catechesis/Religious Programs—Students 95.

Sheffield, Berkshire Co., Our Lady of the Valley (1901), Rev. Frederick L. Heberle; Deacon Herbert L. Cary.
Res., 99 Maple Ave., P.O. Box 515, 01257. Tel: 413-229-3028. [CEM]
Catechesis/Religious Programs—Students 152.
Missions—Mill River, Berkshire Co., Immaculate Conception; Monterey, Berkshire Co., Our Lady of the Hills.

Shelburne Falls, Franklin Co., St. Joseph's (1883), Rev. John A. Roach.
Res., 34 Monroe Ave., 01370. Tel: 413-625-6405; Fax: 413-625-6405.
Catechesis/Religious Programs—Students 88.
Missions—Colrain, Franklin Co., St. John the Baptist, Church St., Colrain, 01346.; Charlemont, Franklin Co., St. Christopher, Rte. 2, Charlemont, 01339.

South Deerfield, Franklin Co., St. James (1895), Rev. Julius A. Jutt.
Res., 85 Main St., 01373. Tel: 413-665-4535.
Catechesis/Religious Programs—Students 266.
Mission—Conway, Franklin Co., St. Mark, Delabarre Ave., Conway, 01341.

St. Stanislaus B. and M. (1908) (Polish), Rev. Philippe Roux; Deacon Theodore J. Tudryn.
Mailing Address: 29 Sugarloaf St., 01373. Tel: 413-665-3254.
Res., 27 Sugarloaf St., 01373. Tel: 413-665-2417. [CEM]
Catechesis/Religious Programs—33 Sugarloaf St., 01373. Tel: 413-665-4656.
Students 148.

South Hadley, Hampshire Co., St. Theresa of the Infant Jesus (1946), Revs. Richard A. Bondi; C. Lee Gilbertson; Deacon Thomas A. Callahan.
Res., 9 East Parkview Dr., 01075. Tel: 413-532-3228; Fax: 413-540-0964.
Catechesis/Religious Programs—Linda Duggin, D.R.E.
Students 682.

St. Patrick's (1877), Rev. Richard M. Turner; Deacon John Bledsoe. In res., Rev. David R. Raymond.
Res., 30 Main St., 01075. Tel: 413-532-2850; Fax: 413-552-0241. [CEM]
Catechesis/Religious Programs—Tel: 413-534-7080.
Students 740.

Southwick, Hampden Co., Our Lady of the Lake (1951), Rev. Timothy J. Hallahan.
Res., 224 Sheep Pasture Rd., P.O. Box 1150, 01077. Tel: 413-569-0161.
Catechesis/Religious Programs—Nancy Lauer, D.R.E.
Students 376.

Stockbridge, Berkshire Co., St. Joseph's (1922), Rev. Steven F.C. McGuigan Tel: 413-298-3748.
Res. and Mailing Address: 11 Elm St., P.O. Box 863, 01262. Tel: 413-298-3748. [CEM]
Catechesis/Religious Programs—Students 6.

Thorndike, Hampden Co., St. Mary's (1876), Deacon Edward J. Tenczar, Admin.
Mailing Address: 80 Main St., 01079. Tel: 413-283-3501.
Res., 25 Cheney St., Three Rivers, 01080. Tel: 413-283-5776.

Three Rivers, Hampden Co., St. Anne's (1882) (French), Rev. Sylvio E. Levesque.
Res., 2230 Main St., 01080. Tel: 413-283-5041; Fax: 413-863-8978. [CEM]
Catechesis/Religious Programs—Tel: 413-283-7286.
Students 190.

SS. Peter and Paul (1903) (Polish), Rev. Stefan J. Niemczyk.
Res., 2267 Main St., 01080. Tel: 413-283-6030. [CEM]
Catechesis/Religious Programs—Tel: 413-283-8814.
Students 238.
Convent—358 Main St., 01080. Tel: 413-283-7402. The Sisters Minor of Mary Immaculate 2.

Turners Falls, Franklin Co., St. Mary's (1872) (Irish), Rev. Stanley J. Aksamit; Deacon Albert Routhier.

Res., 90 Seventh St., 01376. Tel: 413-863-2585; Fax: 413-863-8978. [CEM]
Catechesis/Religious Programs—Students 154.
Our Lady of Czestochowa (1909) (Polish), Rev. Charles J. DiMascola.
Res., 84 K St., 01376. Tel: 413-863-4748; Fax: 413-863-9263. [CEM]
Catechesis/Religious Programs—Students 142.
St. Anne (1884) (French), Rev. Stanley J. Aksamit; Deacon Albert Routhier.
Mailing Address: 90 Seventh St., 01376. Tel: 413-863-2585; Fax: 413-863-8978. [CEM]
Church—J St., 01376. Tel: 413-863-7729.
Catechesis/Religious Programs—Students 22.

Ware, Hampshire Co., All Saints (1860), Rev. Edward T. Fitzgerald.
Res., 17 North St., 01082. Tel: 413-967-4963. [CEM][JC 2]
Catechesis/Religious Programs—Students 145.
Our Lady of Mt. Carmel (1871) (French). Closed. For inquiries for sacramental records contact All Saints, Ware.
St. Mary's (1905) (Polish), Revs. Charles H. Kuzmeski; Henry Karwel, O.F.M.Conv.
Res., 60 South St., 01082. Tel: 413-967-5913; Fax: 413-967-4679. [CEM]
School—59 South St., 01082. Tel: 413-967-9936; Fax: 413-967-8217.
Sisters of Immaculate Conception 5; Lay Teachers 9; Students 202.
Catechesis/Religious Programs—Tel: 413-967-5914.
Students 253.

Westfield, Hampden Co.,

1—Holy Trinity, (1903) (Polish), Revs. William D. LaFosse, M.S.; Peter Jandaczek, M.S.
Res., 335 Elm St., 01085. Tel: 413-568-1506; Fax: 413-572-2533.
School—(Grades K-8) 331 Elm St., 01085. Tel: 413-568-4352. Mrs. Janet Snow, Prin.
Lay Teachers 13; Students 161.
Catechesis/Religious Programs—Students 231.

2—Our Lady of the Blessed Sacrament, (1910), Rev. Hugh F. Crean. In res., Rev. Anthony J. Creane.
Res., 6 Union St., 01085. Tel: 413-562-3450; Fax: 413-562-0399.
Catechesis/Religious Programs—Tel: 413-568-3615. D.R.E.: Sr. M. Barbara Ebbe; Mrs. Deborah Lanoue.
Students 540.

3—St. Casimir's, (1915) (Lithuanian), Rev. John J. Brennan. In res., Bro. Terrence A. Scanlon, C.P.
Res., 22 State St., 01085. Tel: 413-568-5421; Fax: 413-562-3879.
Catechesis/Religious Programs—Tel: 413-568-6261.
Students 13.

4—St. Mary's, (1862), Revs. Kenneth J. Tatro; John C. Salatino; Deacon Francis D. Rogers.
Res., 30 Bartlett St., 01085. Tel: 413-562-5477; Fax: 413-562-5478. [CEM]
School—Tel: 413-568-2388; Fax: 413-568-2388. Sr. Christine Lavoie, Prin.
Sisters 4; Lay Teachers 14; Students 232.
High School—Tel: 413-568-5692; Fax: 413-562-3501. Mr. Paul E. Romani, Jr., Prin.
Sisters 2; Lay Teachers 16; Students 160.
Catechesis/Religious Programs—Tel: 413-568-1127. D.R.E.: Mrs. Kay Mowatt, Elementary; Mrs. Dona Kane, Elementary; Mrs. Barbara Queenin, High School.
Students 706.
Convent—86 Mechanic St., 01085. Tel: 413-568-8077.
Sisters of St. Joseph 4.

5—St. Peter's, (1913) (Slovak), Rev. John J. Brennan; Sr. Ann Marie Yenca, O.S.F., Pastoral Min. In res., Revs. John T. Dean; Warren J. Savage.
Res., 22 State St., 01085. Tel: 413-568-5421; Fax: 413-562-3879.
Catechesis/Religious Programs—32 State St., 01085. Tel: 413-568-6261. Sr. Marcella Meluch, O.S.F., D.R.E.
Students 231.
Convent—St. Peter's Convent, 33 State St., 01085. Tel: 413-568-7689; Fax: 413-562-3879.
Sisters 3.

West Springfield, Hampden Co., Immaculate Conception (1877), Rev. Michael J. Twohig. In res., Rev. John J. Johnson.
Res., 475 Main St., 01089-3998. Tel: 413-736-4071; Fax: 413-734-5484.
Catechesis/Religious Programs—Students 92.
St. Louis de France (1895) (French), Rev. Michael J. Twohig, Admin.
Mailing Address: 875 Main St., 01089. Tel: 413-736-4071; Fax: 413-734-5484. [CEM]
St. Thomas the Apostle (1904), Revs. Richard M. Runte; Douglas McGonagle.
Res., 47 Pine St., 01089. Tel: 413-739-4779; Fax: 413-739-1608. [CEM]
School—75 Pine St., 01089. Tel: 413-739-4131.
Sisters of St. Joseph 2; Lay Teachers 27; Students 431.
Catechesis/Religious Programs—89 Pine St., 01089. Tel: 413-737-8267.
Students 552.

West Stockbridge, Berkshire Co., St. Patrick's (1871), Rev. Steven F.C. McGuigan, Admin.
Res., Albany Rd., 01266. Tel: 413-232-4427. [CEM]
Catechesis/Religious Programs—Students 75.

Wilbraham, Hampden Co., St. Cecilia's (1951), Revs. Joseph M. Soranno; John J. Gawienowski Tel: 413-596-8304; Sr. Mary McCue, S.N.D., Pastoral Ministry.
Res., 7 Maple St., 01095. Tel: 413-596-4232; Fax: 413-596-6272.
Catechesis/Religious Programs—42 Main St., 01095. Tel: 413-596-9937. Sr. Mary Patrice Mahoney, S.N.D., D.R.E.
Students 1,117.

Williamstown, Berkshire Co., St. Patrick's (1887). Merged with St. Raphael, Williamstown, to form SS. Patrick and Raphael, Williamstown.
SS. Patrick and Raphael (1997), Rev. William F. Cyr.
Mailing Address: P.O. Box 616, 01267-2414.
Res., 54 Southworth St., 01267. Tel: 413-458-4946; Fax: 413-458-4954.
Catechesis/Religious Programs—53 Southworth St., 01267. Tel: 413-458-5443.
Students 285.
St. Raphael (1891). Merged with St. Patrick, Williamstown, to form SS. Patrick and Raphael, Williamstown.

Chaplains of Public Institutions

Springfield. *Baystate Medical Center.* Served by Springfield Catholic Health Care Chaplains.
Olympus Specialty Hospital Sacred Heart Rectory, 395 Chestnut St., 01104. Tel: 413-732-3721. Rev. Edward M. Callahan.

Holyoke. *Soldiers' Home.* Served by Blessed Sacrament Parish. Tel: 413-532-0713.

Monson. *State Hospital.* Bureau for Exceptional Children and Adults. 537 Northampton St., Box 1039, Holyoke, 01041. Tel: 413-538-7450. Rev. Robert F. Wagner; Deacon Rodney Szymczk.

Northampton. *Veterans Administration Hospital* 421 N. Main St., 01060. Tel: 413-584-4040. Rev. Lionel E. Bonneville.

Pittsfield. *Berkshire Medical Center* Tel: 413-447-2000. Rev. Leroy Smith, One County Rte. 13, Chatham Center, N.Y 12184-9639. Tel: 413-392-4516.

Westfield. *Western Massachusetts Hospital.* Served by Our Lady of the Blessed Sacrament Parish. Tel: 413-562-3450.

Sabbatical:
Reverend Fathers—
Giroux, Regis J.

On Duty Outside the Diocese:
Reverend Fathers—
Marchese, Joseph P., Chap., Boston College, Chestnut Hill, MA 02167
Pham, Pierre
Potvin, Raymond H., Professor Emeritas, Catholic University, Box 1264, Washington, DC 20064
Reilly, Francis, North American College, Louvain, Belgium
Schmitt, Thomas F., Pope John XXII National Seminary, 558 S. St., Weston, MA 02493
Tuohey, John F., Providence St. Vincent Medical Center, 9205 S.W. Barnes Rd., Portland, OR 97225

Military Chaplains:
Reverend Fathers—
Walsh, Francis E., Office of the Chap., PSC 476, Box 61, FPO, AP 96322-1102

Absent on Leave:
Reverend Fathers—
Dube, Donald V.
Graves, Alfred C.
Lavigne, Richard R.
Meehan, Richard F.
Savage, Warren J.

Retired:
Reverend Monsignors—
Foudy, Robert E., Holy Cross Rectory, 221 Plumtree Rd., Springfield, MA 01118
Harrington, John F., 86 Wendover St., Springfield, MA 01118
Montcalm, Rosario L.U., 47 Pine Grove Dr., South Hadley, MA 01075-2196
Viau, Roger, St. Michael's Residence, 86 Wendover Rd, Springfield, MA 01118
Reverend Fathers—
Anoia, John, Our Lady Queen of Peace Rectory
Boudreau, Paul, 3020 N.E. 16 Ave. E101, Fort Lauderdale, FL 33334
Bourque, John R., 4991 S. Clinton St., Englewood, CO 80111
Breton, Albert, Nativity Rectory, 780 Chicopee St., Chicopee, MA 01013
Creane, Anthony, Blessed Sacrament Rectory, 6 Union St., Westfield, MA 01085-2494
Cronin, James E., 14 Fairlawn Dr., Worcester, MA 01602
Darling, Franklin, 10 D Elm Terrace, Greenfield, MA 01301. Tel: 413-772-6187
Delehanty, Thomas F., 2C Stonypoint Dr., P.O. Box 425, Ware, MA 01082
Desilets, Donald A., 35 Raymond Rd., Guildrod, CT 06437
Diemand, James E., P.O. Box 141, Turners Falls, MA 01376
Eckert, William F., Saint Mark Rectory, 27 Onota St., Pittsfield, MA 01201
Forand, Clarence W., #293, 281 Chauncey Walker St., Belchertown, MA 01007
Fournier, W. Donald, 474 Grattan St., Chicopee, MA 01020
Gallerini, Philip G., 134 Old Meadow Way, Palm Beach, FL 33418
Gauvreau, Thomas H., 32 Rickards St., North Adams, MA 01247
Greene, Thomas S., St. Michael's Residence, 86 Wendover Rd., Springfield, MA 01118
Greenway, George G., 29 Orchard Rd., East Longmeadow, MA 01028
Loughran, Peter, 86 Wendover Rd., Springfield, MA 01118
Lucey, John P., P.O. Box 636, Norwell, MA 02061
McCarthy, Thomas J., Holyoke Geriatric Center, 45 Lower Westfield Rd., Holyoke, MA 01040
Menge, James P., Holy Family Recory, 15 Holy Family Rd., Holyoke, MA 01040
O'Connor, Matthew J., 69 Beacon St., Holyoke, MA 01040
Ozimek, Eugene F., Mount St. Vincent Nursing Home, 35 Holy Family Rd., Holyoke, MA 01040
Pagano, Peter E., 1215 Massachusetts Ave., North Adams, MA 01247
Perreault, Leonard J., P.O. Box 144, Spencertown, NY 12165
Quigley, J. Joseph, Newman Center, 472 N. Pleasant St., Amherst, MA 1002
Remy, Adrien T., Mont Marie Motherhouse, Holyoke, MA 01040
Rocha, Manuel, 2399 Boston Rd., Wilbraham, MA 01095
Sexton, John J., 217 Westfield St., W., Springfield, MA 01089
Sgueglia, Charles J.M., 44 Dexter St., Methuen, MA 01844
Sullivan, Charles, 1440 Randolf Ave., Apt. 14, St. Paul, MN 55105
Sullivan, Francis J., St. Michael's Residence, 86 Wendover Rd., Springfield, MA 01118
Sullivan, Francis X., 102 Allyn St., Holyoke, MA 01040
Switalksi, Casimir S., Mount St. Vincent Nursing Home, 35 Holy Family Rd., Holyoke, MA 01040
Tokarz, John, St. Michael's Residence, 86 Wendover Rd., Springfield, MA 01118

Permanent Deacons:
Badame, Joseph, Holy Family, Holyoke
Baldasaro, Pasqual, St. Agnes, Dalton
Bledsoe, John, St. Patrick, South Hadley
Bucci, Joseph, St. Mary's, Orange
Callahan, Thomas A., St. Theresa, South Hadley
Cary, Herbert L., Our Lady of the Valley, Sheffield
Chapdelaine, Roland G., Springfield Municipal Hospital
Cyr, Ralph R., Notre Dame, Pittsfield
Diaz, Celso B., On Duty Outside the Diocese
Donelan, James, St. Mary, Orange
Duval, Robert L., St. Mary of the Assumption, Ludlow
Faber, Edward H., St. John the Baptist, Ludlow
Finnie, Edward J., (Retired)
Fleury, Bernard J., Annunciation, Florence, MA
Garde, Joseph, St. Catherine, Springfield
Geary, Coleman P., On Duty Outside the Diocese
Hager, James A., Sacred Heart, Pittsfield
Herrick, Eugene, Burlington, VT
Higby, Donald, St. Mary, Longmeadow
Hitter, Robert, St. Mary, Cheshire
Keator, George, St. Ann, Lenox
Kozach, George, St. Patrick Church, Springfield
Martone, James A., Sacred Heart, Feeding Hills
McCarthy, Francis J., Blessed Sacrament, Northampton
Medina, Genaro, Sr., Spanish Apostolate at Blessed Sacrament, Springfield

Miller, Lucien M., Campus Ministry, University of Massachusetts, Amherst
Mireault, Leon, St. Rose de Lima, Chicopee
Moesley, William C., St. Charles, Pittsfield
Momnie, Eugene C., St. Joseph, Pittsfield
Monat, Noe, 240 Skycrest Loop, Davenport, FL 33837
Moore, Donald E., (Retired)
Moulton, Robert R., Notre Dame, Our Lady of Mercy, St. Francis, North Adams
O'Brien, John P., On Duty Outside the Diocese
Pancotti, Louis, St. Mary, Ludlow
Pelletier, Frederick J., Immaculate Conception, Holyoke
Pellissier, Bernard, St. Patrick, Monson
Przybylowski, David, Our Lady of the Lake, Southwick
Rael, C. Lincoln, Immaculate Conception, Holyoke
Ratte, Arthur E., St. Patrick, Northfield
Rivera, Jose, On Duty Outside the Diocese
Rogers, Francis, St. Mary, Westfield
Routhier, Albert, St. Anne & St. Mary's, Turners Falls
Smith, Joseph, St. Mary's, Chicopee
Szymzyk, Rodney J., Immaculate Conception, Indian Orchard
Tenczar, Edward J., St. Thomas the Apostle, Palmer & St. Mary, Thorndyke
Tourangeau, Armand, Our Lady of Hope, Springfield
Tudryn, Theodore, St. Stanislaus, South Deerfield
Velazquez, Raphael, Holy Family, Springfield
Wallen, Paul, (Retired), Springfield, MA

INSTITUTIONS LOCATED IN THE DIOCESE

[A] SEMINARIES, RELIGIOUS, OR SCHOLASTICATES

GRANBY. *St. Hyacinth College and Seminary*, 01033. Friary. Tel: 413-467-7180; Fax: 413-467-9609. College: Tel: 413-467-7191; Fax: 413-467-9609. Order of Friars Minor Conventual; Liberal Arts and Sciences. Certificates in Lay Ministry, Biblical Studies, and Catholic Spirituality. Revs. Jude Surowiec, O.F.M.Conv., Chief Academic Officer (Pres.) and Registrar, Co-Dir. Lay Ministry Program; James E. McCurry, O.F.M.Conv., Guardian and Dir. of Militia Immaculata. Tel: 413-467-9190; Jeremy Chodacki, O.F.M.Conv., (Retired); Claude Jarmak, O.F.M.Conv.; Stanley Wlodyka, O.F.M.Conv., (Retired). Priests 5; Non-Resident Students 53.

[B] COLLEGES AND UNIVERSITIES

CHICOPEE. *College of Our Lady of the Elms*, 01013. Tel: 413-594-2761; Fax: 413-592-4871.
E-mail: keating@elms.edu
Web site: www.elms.edu
For a complete listing, refer to the Colleges and Universities section.

[C] HIGH SCHOOLS, DIOCESAN

SPRINGFIELD. *Cathedral High School*, 260 Surrey Rd., 01118. Tel: 413-782-5285; Fax: 413-782-5065.
E-mail: cathigh@worldnet.att.net
Sr. Denise Granger, S.S.J., Prin.; Rev. David R. Raymond, Spiritual Dir. Priests 1; Sisters 5; Lay Teachers 52; Students 830.

HOLYOKE. *Holyoke Catholic High School*, 91 Chestnut St., 01040. Tel: 413-533-0347; Fax: 413-535-1987.
E-mail: gaels_hchs@yahoo.com
Sisters of St. Joseph. Rev. David R. Raymond, Chap.; Mr. William Fitzgerald, Prin. Priests 1; Sisters 6; Lay Teachers 28; Students 402.

PITTSFIELD. *St. Joseph Central High School*, 22 Maplewood Ave., 01201. Tel: 413-447-9121; Fax: 413-443-7020.
Web site: bewan.net/~stjoe
Sisters of St. Joseph. Margaret Downing, Prin. Sisters 1; Lay Teachers 27; Students 252.

[D] ELEMENTARY SCHOOLS, DIOCESAN

SPRINGFIELD. *Sacred Heart School*, 370 Stafford St., 01104. Tel: 413-733-3630; Fax: 413-733-2951. Ms. Carol Brown, Prin. Sisters 1; Lay Teachers 10; Students 180.

INDIAN ORCHARD. *St. Matthew* (1902). (Grades PreK-8), 90 Berkshire St., 01151. Tel: 413-543-1066; Fax: 413-543-2330. Ann Dougal, Prin. Lay Teachers 18; Students 174.

[E] PRIVATE SCHOOLS

TURNER FALLS.
Mariamante Academy, P.O. Box 761, 01376. Tel: 413-863-8191.
E-mail: mmacad@mindspring.com
Stephen M. Mawn, Contact Person & Business Mgr.

[F] ORPHANAGES

WEST SPRINGFIELD. *Brightside, Inc.* 2112 Riverdale St. Springfield, 01089. Tel: 413-788-7366; Fax: 413-747-0182.
For a complete listing, refer to the Special Care Facilities section.

[G] GENERAL HOSPITALS

SPRINGFIELD. *CHE - The Mercy Hospital, Inc.*, 271 Carew St., Box 9012, 01102-9012. Tel: 413-748-9000; Fax: 413-781-7217
For a complete listing, refer to the Hospitals section.

TURNERS FALLS. *Farren Care Center, Inc.*, 340 Montague City Rd., 01376. Tel: 413-774-3111; Fax: 413-774-7049
For a complete listing, refer to the Hospitals section.

[H] FAMILY SERVICES

SPRINGFIELD. *Marriage Counseling Service*, 65 Elliot St., P.O. Box 1730, 01101-1730. Tel: 413-732-3175; 452-0621; Fax: 413-747-0273.
Web site: www.diospringfield.org/MC.html
Rev. John J. Johnson, S.T.D., L.M.F.T., Dir. Counselors: Mr. Alfred A. D'Amato, Ed.D., L.M.F.T.; Mrs. Rosemary Castonguay, M.Ed., L.M.H.C. Total Staff 4; Total Assisted 653.

HOLYOKE. *Mont Marie Child Care Center, Inc.*, Mont Marie, 01040. Tel: 413-536-2964; Fax: 413-536-5557.
E-mail: eharrington@ssjspringfield.com
Sr. Eleanor T. Harrington, S.S.J., Dir. Sisters of St. Joseph 2; Total Staff 21; Children 126.

Providence Ministries for the Needy, Inc., 476 Appleton St., P.O. Box 6269, 01041. Tel: 413-536-9109; Fax: 413-536-1137.
E-mail: PMN1@Javanet.com
Web site: www.providenceministries.freeservers.com
Sponsored by the Sisters of Providence of Holyoke, MA. Mr. Robin L. Goshea, Admin. Total Staff 25; Total Assisted 62,909.

Broderick House. An around-the-clock family shelter. 56 Cabot St., P.O. Box 6269, 01041. Tel: 413-534-7610; Fax: 413-536-8536. D. Jean Wright, Mgr. Capacity 56.

Margaret's Pantry. Provides emergency food to families and individuals. Tel: 413-538-8026; Fax: 413-536-8536.

St. Jude's Center. Distributes clothing and household items to the poor. Tel: 413-534-7610; Fax: 413-536-8536.

St. Jude's Furniture & Furnishing Store. Provides new and pre-owned furniture and furnishings to the community. 51 Hamilton St., 01040. Tel: 413-536-9109; Fax: 413-536-1137.

Loreto House. An around-the-clock shelter for homeless men. 51 Hamilton St., 01041. Tel: 413-533-5909; Fax: 413-536-1137. Charles Carter, Mgr. Capacity 18.

Kate's Kitchen. A community kitchen which provides one meal daily to anyone in need - no questions asked. 435 Main St., 01041. Tel: 413-532-0233; Fax: 413-536-1137. Capacity 99.

PITTSFIELD. *Catholic Charities Counseling Office*, 467 North St., Rm. 15, P.O. Box 1372, 01202. Tel: 413-443-3169. 41 Mahaiwe St., Great Barrington, 01230. Tel: 413-528-9006. Thomas A. Duane, L.I.C.S.W., Supr. Counselors: Robert T. Sykes, M.A.; Janet M. O'Brien, M.A. Total Staff 3; Total Assisted 720.

TURNERS FALLS. *Montague Catholic Social Ministries, Inc.*, 41 Third St., 01376. Tel: 413-863-4805; Fax: 413-863-8593. Pat Fettinger, Contact Person.
Purpose: To be a resource to families in the areas of parent education, family literacy, positive conflict resolution, communication skills, and community building; to assist in providing information and referral, the formation of community partnerships and neighborhood development and to facilitate parish concerns and social justice efforts. Total Staff 4; Total Assisted 200.

[I] HOMES FOR AGED

SPRINGFIELD. *St. Michael's Residence*, 86 Wendover Rd., 01118. Tel: 413-783-6773
For a complete listing, refer to the Special Care Facilities section.

HOLYOKE. *Mont Marie Health Care Center, Inc.*, 34 Lower Westfield Rd., 01040. Tel: 413-536-0853; Fax: 413-533-4505.
E-mail: MMHCC92@aol.com
For a complete listing, refer to the Special Care Facilities section.

Providence Place, Inc., 5 Gamelin St., 01040. Tel: 413-534-9700; Fax: 413-534-9782.
Web site: ProvidencePlace.org
For a complete listing, refer to the Special Care Facilities section.

Sisters of Providence Care Centers, Inc., 35 Holy Family Rd., 01040-2758. Tel: 413-532-3246; Fax: 413-532-0309
For a complete listing, refer to the Special Care Facilities section.

[J] MONASTERIES AND RESIDENCES OF PRIESTS AND BROTHERS

STOCKBRIDGE. *Congregation of Marians of The Immaculate Conception of the BVM*, Eden Hill, 2 Prospect Hill Rd., 01262. Tel: 413-298-3931; Fax: 413-298-1146; 298-1212.
E-mail: wadziordz@aol.com
Web site: www.marian.org
Province: Tel: 413-298-1101; Fax: 413-298-0207. Revs. Walter Dziordz, M.I.C., Prov. Supr.; Kazimierz Chwalek, M.I.C., Prov. Econome; Bro. Kenneth Galisa, M.I.C., Prov. Sec., The National Shrine of The Divine Mercy. Tel: 413-298-3931; Fax: 413-298-3910.
E-mail: dmshrine@marian.org
Rev. Daniel Papineau, M.I.C., Shrine Rector, Association of Marian Helpers, Marian Helpers Center. Tel: 413-298-3691; Fax: 413-298-3583.
E-mail: info@marian.org
Bro. Andrew R. Maczynski, M.I.C., Dir., Marian Helpers Center; Mr. Francis Bourdon, Exec. Dir.

John Paul II Institute of Divine Mercy Merciful Mother Association. Tel: 413-298-1184; Fax: 413-298-4559.
E-mail: divinemerc@aol.com
Mr. Robert Stackpole, Dir.; Sr. Isabel Bettwy, Exec. Dir.; Revs. Francis McGerity, Dir. of Evangelization; S. Seraphim Michalenko, M.I.C., Dir.
Lay Outreach Ministry of the Province:

Life Foundation. Eucharistic Apostles of The Divine Mercy. Tel: 813-681-3699; Fax: 813-681-3009.
E-mail: tampa@thedivinemercy.org
Web site: www.thedivinemercy.org
In res. Revs. Larry Dunn, M.I.C.; Richard Drabik, M.I.C.; Walter Dziordz, M.I.C.; Walter Gurgul, M.I.C. (England); Dariusz Mazewski, M.I.C. (Poland); S. Seraphim Michalenko, M.I.C.; Daniel Papineau, M.I.C.; Walter Pelczynski, M.I.C.; Bros. John Bryda, M.I.C.; Ken Galisa, M.I.C.; Andrew Maczynski, M.I.C.; Albin Milewski, M.I.C.; Fred Wells, M.I.C. Priests 8; Brothers 5.
On Duty Outside of House: Revs. Ireneusz Chodakowski, M.I.C. (PRT); Gerald Ornowski, M.I.C (FBK); Donald Van Alstyne, M.I.C. (MO).
On Duty Outside the U.S.A.: Revs. Mark Garrow, M.I.C., Superior General, Rome; Casimir Krzyzanowski, M.I.C., Poland.

[K] CONVENTS AND RESIDENCES FOR SISTERS

HOLYOKE. *Daughters of the Heart of Mary Provincial Residence*, 1339 Northampton St., 01040-1913. Tel: 413-532-7406; Fax: 413-533-4217.
E-mail: mnajimy@aol
Web site: www.SDHM.net
Sr. Miriam Najimy, D.H.M., Prov. Total in Residence 29; Total Staff 3.

Marian Residence, 1365 Northampton St., 01040. Tel: 413-534-4502; Fax: 413-534-7353.
Web site: www.SDHM.net
Sr. Margaret E. Linehan, D.H.M., Supr. Daughters of the Heart of Mary 17.

Marian Center, Inc., 1365 Northampton St., 01040. Tel: 413-534-4502; Fax: 413-534-7353. Sr. M. Jeannette Levangie, D.H.M., Supr. Daughters of the Heart of Mary 15.

Mont Marie, 01040. Tel: 413-536-0853; Fax: 413-533-3275.
E-mail: ssj2@aol.com
Motherhouse of the Sisters of St. Joseph of Springfield. Sr. Jane F. Morrissey, S.S.J., Pres.; Sr. Maureen Broughan, S.S.J., Vice Pres.; Rev. Adrien T. Remy, Chap. Sisters 367; Total Staff 51.

Mont Marie Child Care, Inc. Tel: 413-536-2964; Fax: 413-533-3275. Total Assisted 103; Total Staff 20.

Mont Marie Health Care Center, Inc. Tel: 413-536-0853; Fax: 413-533-4505. Total Assisted 81; Total Staff 105.

Mont Marie Conference Center. Tel: 413-536-0853; Fax: 413-532-0285. Total Staff 8.

Provincial House and Formation House, 1039 Northampton St., 01040. Tel: 413-532-8156; Fax: 413-534-7741. Franciscan Missionary Sisters of Assisi. Sr. Norbert Petrucci, S.F.M.A., Vice Prov. Sisters 6.

Sisters of Providence. Motherhouse of the Sisters of Providence. Providence Place, 5 Gamelin St., 01040. Tel: 413-536-7511; Fax: 413-536-7917.
E-mail: sisters@sisofprov.org
Web site: www.sisofprov.org
Sr. Ruth McGoldrick, S.P., Pres. of Congregation. In res. Revs. Edward M. Kennedy, Chap.; Richard Meehan. Sisters 104.

Sisters of Providence Infirmary, 1233 Main St., 3rd Floor, 01040-5394. Tel: 413-493-2750; Fax: 413-493-2759.

Sisters of Providence Health System, Inc. Includes an array of Health and Social Service Institutions in the Diocese. 271 Carew St., P.O. Box 9012, Springfield, 01102-9012. Tel: 413-748-9316; Fax: 413-781-7217. Mr. Vincent McCorkle, Pres. & CEO.

Providence Ministries for the Needy, Inc., P.O. Box 6269, 01041-6269. Tel: 413-536-9109; Fax: 413-536-1137.

Genesis Spiritual Life Center, 53 Mill St., Westfield, 01085-4253. Tel: 413-562-3627; Fax: 413-572-1060.

Queen of Peace Centennial House, 64 North St., Greenfield, 01301. Tel: 413-772-2000.

TYRINGHAM. *Order of the Visitation of Holy Mary*, Monastery of the Visitation, P.O. Box 432, 01264. Tel: 413-243-3995; Fax: 413-243-3543. Sr. Mary Ruth Dolch, Supr. Order of the Visitation of Holy Mary 16.

WEST SPRINGFIELD. *Monastery of the Mother of God, Dominican Nuns (Contemplative)*, 1430 Riverdale St., 01089-4698. Tel: 413-736-3639; Fax: 413-736-0850. Adoration to the Blessed Sacrament Chapel. Sr. Mary St. John, O.P., Prioress; Rev. Jacob Restrick, O.P., Chap. Solemnly Professed Nuns 23; Temporarily Professed 2.

[L] RETREAT HOUSES AND CHRISTIAN LIFE CENTERS

SPRINGFIELD. *Center for Spiritual Direction.* Memorial House, Mercy Hospital. P.O. Box 9012, 01102-9012. Tel: 413-734-8843; 788-0195; Fax: 413-788-0195. Sisters 3; Total Staff 5; Laystaff 2.

WESTFIELD. *Genesis Spiritual Life Center*, 53 Mill St., 01085. Tel: 413-562-3627; Fax: 413-572-1060.
E-mail: genretc@exit3.com
Web site: www.westfield-ma.com/genesis
Sr. Elizabeth Oleksak, S.P., Admin.; Sr. Ann Horgan, S.P., Asst. Admin; Ms. Ann McGaharn, Program Coord.; Theresa Dubay, Registrar. Total Staff 10; Total in Residence 2.

WILLIAMSTOWN. *Mount Carmel Retreat Center*, Oblong Rd., P.O. Box 613, 01267. Tel: 413-458-3164; Fax: 413-458-9420.
Web site: carmelretreat.org
Rev. Maurice Cummings, O.Carm. Priests 1; Total in Residence 1; Total Staff 5.

[M] INFORMATION CENTERS

CHICOPEE. *Open Window Book and Gift Shop of the Diocese of Springfield, Inc.*, 12-14 Center St., 01013. Tel: 413-594-5111; Fax: 413-594-2862. Mgrs: Mrs. Barbara Y. McMahon; Mrs. Barbara B. Moran.

[N] SPANISH APOSTOLATES

SPRINGFIELD. *Catholic Latino Ministry*, 235 Eastern Ave., 01109. Tel: 413-730-6623; Fax: 413-827-0780.
E-mail: p.e.manship@att.net
Rev. Paul E. Manship, Dir.; Lucy Ramos, Exec. Sec.

HOLYOKE. *Casa Maria*, 51 Hamilton St., 01040. Tel: 413-533-6016. Pastoral Assocs.: Sr. Ninfa Arellano, S.P.; Sr. M. Immaculate Conception, S.P.

[O] BUREAU FOR EXCEPTIONAL CHILDREN AND ADULTS

HOLYOKE. *Bureau for Exceptional Children and Adults Inc.*, 537 Northampton St., Box 1039, 01041. Tel: 413-538-7450; Fax: 413-536-5691.
E-mail: jericho@the-spa
Rev. Robert F. Wagner, Dir.; Sr. Joan Magnani, S.S.J., Assoc. Dir. Sisters 2; Deacons 1; Lay Staff 3.

[P] YOUTH SERVICES

GOSHEN. *Holy Cross Camp Grounds*, Cape St., P.O. Box 501, 01032-0501. Tel: 413-268-7819.
Web site: www.the-spa/campholycross
Rev. Christopher A. Malatesta. Total Staff 3.

PITTSFIELD. *Catholic Youth Center*, 26 Melville St., 01201. Tel: 413-445-5496; Fax: 413-445-5248. Mr. Vincent P. Marinaro, Exec. Dir. Total Assisted 1,200; Total Staff 25.

[Q] NEWMAN APOSTOLATES AND CAMPUS MINISTRIES

SPRINGFIELD. *Newman Apostolates and Campus Ministries.* Tel: 413-549-0300. The Newman Center, 472 N. Pleasant, Amherst, 01002-1739. Rev. Francis P. Lavelle, Diocesan Dir.
Amherst, MA.
Amherst College. Served by St. Brigid's, 122 N. Pleasant St., Amherst, 01004. Tel: 413-253-1828; Fax: 413-253-7935.
Web site: www.stbrigid.org
Rev. Bruce N. Teague, Chap., Center for Religious Life, Box 2277, Amherst, 01002-5000.
E-mail: pastor@stbrigid.org
University of Massachusetts, Newman Center, 472 N. Pleasant St., Amherst, 01002-1739. Tel: 413-549-0300; Fax: 413-548-9182.
Web site: www.umass.edu/catholic
Rev. Francis P. Lavelle, Dir. & Chap.; Sr. Connie Roy, S.S.J., Campus Min.; Sr. Kathleen Keough, S.S.J., Campus Min.; Deacon Lucien Miller, Campus Min.; Mr. Richard Talbot, Campus Min. In res. Rev. J. Joseph Quigley, Emeritus Dir.
Chicopee, MA.
College of Our Lady of the Elms College, 291 Springfield St., Chicopee, 01013. Tel: 413-594-2761; Fax: 413-592-4871.
E-mail: callanm@elms.edu
Mary Sue Callan-Farley, Camp. Min.
Holyoke, MA.
Holyoke Community College. Served by Blessed Sacrament, 1945 Northampton St., Holyoke, 01040-3498. Tel: 413-532-0713.
Longmeadow, MA.
Bay Path College. Served by St. Mary's, 519 Longmeadow St., Longmeadow, 01106-2299. Tel: 413-567-3124. Rev. Dariusz P. Wudarski, Chap.
North Adams, MA.
Massachusetts College of the Liberal Arts. Served by St. Francis of Assisi, 12 Union St., North Adams, 01247-3593. Tel: 413-663-5316; Fax: 413-663-3938.
E-mail: styx@adelphia.net
Rev. David M. Darcy.
Northampton, MA.
Smith College, Helen Hills, Hills Chapel, Northampton, 01063. Tel: 413-585-2750; 585-2752; Fax: 413-585-2794.
E-mail: ecarr@smith.edu
Elizabeth E. Carr, Ph.D., Campus Min.
Pittsfield, MA.
Berkshire Community College. Served by St. Mark's, 27 Onota St., Pittsfield, 01201-3194. Tel: 413-447-7510. Rev. Henry L. Dorsch, Chap.
South Hadley, MA.
Mount Holyoke College. Served by St. Theresa, 9 E. Parkview Dr., South Hadley, 01075-2103. Tel: 413-538-2054.
E-mail: amagovern@mtholyoke.edu
Rev. Richard A. Bondi, Chap., Res., Office of the Chaplain, Eliot House, South Hadley, 01075. Tel: 413-538-2054; Fax: 413-538-2687. Sr. Anita Magovern, M.M., Religious Advisor. Tel: 413-538-2787.
Springfield, MA.
American International College; Springfield College; Springfield Tech. Comm. College. Rev. Leo James Hoar, Chap., Res. St. Mary Rectory, 3 Elm St., P.O. Box 180, Northampton, 01061-0180. Tel: 413-748-3210; Fax: 413-584-4788. Springfield College Campus Ministry Center, Beveridge Center, 263 Alden St., 01109-3797. Tel: 413-748-3210; Fax: 413-748-3764.
E-mail: leohoar@spfldcol.edu
Western New England College, 1215 Wilbraham Rd., 01119-2684. Tel: 413-782-1628. Rev. Norman B. Bolton, Chap., Res. Blessed Sacrament Rectory, 1945 Northampton St., Holyoke, 01040-349801089. Tel: 413-493-6550.
E-mail: nbolton@aol.com
Westfield, MA.
Westfield State College, Interfaith Center, Westfield, 01085. Tel: 413-572-5567; Fax: 413-562-3613. Rev. John T. Dean, Chap., Res. St. Peter's Rectory, 22 State St., Westfield, 01085-3814. Tel: 413-568-5421.
Williamstown, MA.
Williams College. Served by St. Patrick's, 54 Southwoth St., P.O. Box 616, Williamstown, 01267-0616. Tel: 413-458-4946; Fax: 413-458-4954. Rev. William F. Cyr, Chap.; Mr. Peter Feudo, Camp. Min., Res., Baxter Hall, 39 Chapin Hall Dr., Williamstown, 01267-2569. Tel: 413-597-2483; Fax: 413-597-3955.
E-mail: peter.feudo@williams.edu

[R] MISCELLANEOUS

SPRINGFIELD. *The Foundation of the Roman Catholic Diocese of Springfield, Massachusetts, Inc.*, 65 Elliot St., P.O. Box 1730, 01101-1730. Tel: 413-732-3175; Fax: 413-732-4297.
E-mail: v.webb@diospringfield.org
Web site: www.diospringfield.org

Sisters of Providence Health Systems, Inc., 271 Carew St., 01104. Tel: 413-748-9315; Fax: 413-781-7217. Mr. Vincent J. McCorkle, Pres. & CEO.

GRANBY. *Knights of the Immaculata Movement (Militia Immaculatae, M.I.).* (established 1931), St. Hyacinth College-Seminary, 66 School St., 01033. Tel: 413-467-9190; Fax: 413-467-9190. Rev. James E. McCurry, O.F.M.Conv., Dir.

HOLYOKE. *Mont Marie Conference Center*, 34 Lower Westfield Rd., 01040-2739. Tel: 413-536-0853; Fax: 413-532-0285.
E-mail: montconf@ssjspringfield.com
Agnes Fleming, Dir.

RELIGIOUS INSTITUTES OF MEN REPRESENTED IN THE DIOCESE

For further details refer to the corresponding bracketed number in the Religious Institutes of Men or Women section.

[]—*The Association of Marian Helpers of Stockbridge, MA.*

[0470]—*The Capuchin Fathers.* (St. Mary's Prov.).—O.F.M.Cap.

[0270]—*Carmelite Fathers and Brothers.* (St. Elias Prov.).—O.Carm.

[0740]—*Congregation of Marians of the Immaculate Conception.*—M.I.C.

[1000]—*Congregation of the Passion.* (West Hoboken, NJ).—C.P.

[0480]—*Conventual Franciscans.*—O.F.M.Conv.

[0720]—*The Missionaries of Our Lady of La Salette.*—M.S.

[1280]—*Stigmatine Fathers and Brothers.*—C.S.S.

RELIGIOUS INSTITUTES OF WOMEN REPRESENTED IN THE DIOCESE

[1830]—*Contemplative Sisters of the Good Shepherd.*—C.G.S.

[0860]—*Daughters of Mary of the Immaculate Conception.*—D.M.

[0890]—*Daughters of Our Lady of Mercy.*—D.M.

[0810]—*Daughters of the Heart of Mary.*—D.H.M.

[0820]—*Daughters of the Holy Spirit.*—D.H.S.

[1050]—*Dominican Contemplative Nuns.*—O.P.

[1170]—*Felician Sisters.*—C.S.S.F.

[1330]—*Franciscan Missionary Sisters of Assisi.*—S.F.M.A.

[1470]—*Franciscan Sisters of St. Joseph.*—F.S.S.J.

[1180]—*Franciscan Sisters of the Allegany, New York.*—O.S.F.

[]—*Schonestatt Sisters of Mary.*

[1700]—*School Sisters of St. Francis.*—O.S.F.

[]—*Sister of the Most Holy Soul of Christ.*—S.S.Ch.

[]—*Sisters Minor of Mary Immaculate.*—S.M.M.I.

[3000]—*Sisters of Notre Dame de Namur.*—S.N.D.deN.

[3340]—*Sisters of Providence.*—S.P.

[3718]—*Sisters of St. Ann.*—S.S.A.

[3750]—*Sisters of St. Chretienne.*—S.S.Ch.

[3830-16]—*Sisters of St. Joseph.*—S.S.J.

[3850]—*Sisters of St. Joseph of Chambery.*—C.S.J.

[0150]—*Sisters of the Assumption.*—S.A.S.V.

[3320]—*Sisters of the Presentation of the B.V.M.*—P.B.V.M.

[3310]—*Sisters of the Presentation of Mary.*—P.M.

[4190]—*Visitation Nuns.*—V.H.M.

DIOCESAN CEMETERIES

SPRINGFIELD. *Gate of Heaven*, 421 Tinkham Rd., 01129. Tel: 413-782-4731. Mr. Joseph Sankovich, Interim Diocesan Dir. of Cemeteries. Tel: 413-452-0692.

St. Benedict Cemetery, Liberty St., 01104. Tel: 413-782-4731.

St. Matthew Cemetery, 366 Springfield St., 01109. Tel: 413-733-0659.

St. Michael's, 1601 State St., 01109. Tel: 413-733-0659.

HOLYOKE. *Calvary*, Northampton St., 01040. Office, 1601 State St., Springfield, 01109. Tel: 413-733-0695.

INDIAN ORCHARD. *St. Aloysius Cemetary*, Berkshire Ave., 01151. Office, 1601 State St., Springfield, 01109. Tel: 413-733-8140.

NECROLOGY

† Cain, John T, West Springfield, MA St. Thomas the Apostle. —Died April 20, 2000.

† McKenna, James D., (Retired). —Died Oct. 7, 2000.

† Moreau, Ernest P., (Retired). —Died Sept. 5, 2000.

† O'Connor, Francis A., (Retired). —Died Feb. 27, 2000.

† Pollone, Ralph A, Pittsfield, MA St. Mary the Morning Star. —Died Feb. 9, 2000.

† Posco, Raphael A., (Retired). —Died Jan. 14, 2000.

† Renaud, Roland A., (Retired). —Died Feb. 26, 2000.

Diocese of Steubenville

(Dioecesis Steubenvicensis)

Most Reverend

GILBERT I. SHELDON, D.D., D.MIN.

Bishop of Steubenville; ordained February 28, 1953; appointed Auxiliary and Titular Bishop of Taparura April 20, 1976; consecrated June 11, 1976; appointed to Steubenville January 28, 1992; installed April 2, 1992. *Mailing Address: P.O. Box 969, Steubenville, OH, 43952-5969.*

Most Reverend

ALBERT H. OTTENWELLER, D.D., S.T.L.

Bishop of Steubenville; ordained June 19, 1943; appointed Titular Bishop of Perdices and Auxiliary of Toledo April 17, 1974; consecrated May 29, 1974; appointed to Steubenville October 11, 1977; installed November 22, 1977; retired April 2, 1992. *Res., 609 N. Seventh St., Steubenville, OH, 43952.*

ESTABLISHED 1944.

Square Miles 5,913.

Comprises these thirteen Counties in the State of Ohio: Athens, Belmont, Carroll, Gallia, Guernsey, Harrison, Jefferson, Lawrence, Meigs, Morgan, Monroe, Noble and Washington.

For legal titles of parishes and diocesan institutions, consult the Chancery Office.

Chancery Office: 422 Washington St., P.O. Box 969, Steubenville, OH, 43952-5969. Tel.: 740-282-3631; Fax: 740-282-3327.

Web site address: www.diosteub.org

E-mail address: lnichols@diosteub.org

STATISTICAL OVERVIEW

Personnel

Bishop	1
Retired Bishops	1
Priests: Diocesan Active in Diocese	54
Priests: Active Outside Diocese	10
Priests: Retired, Sick or Absent	47
Number of Diocesan Priests	111
Religious Priests in Diocese	18
Extern Priests in Diocese	24
Ordinations:	
Diocesan Priests	3
Transitional Deacons	1
Permanent Deacons in Diocese	7
Total Brothers	8
Total Sisters	82

Parishes

Parishes	73
With Resident Pastor:	
Resident Diocesan Priests	71
Resident Religious Priests	2
Missions	3

Welfare

Catholic Hospitals	2
Total Assisted	256,232
Homes for the Aged	1
Total Assisted	87
Special Centers for Social Services	1
Total Assisted	14,788
Residential Care of Disabled	1
Total Assisted	55

Educational

Diocesan Students in Other Seminaries	8
Total Seminarians	8
Colleges and Universities	1
Total Students	2,154
High Schools, Diocesan and Parish	3
Total Students	733
Elementary Schools, Private	14
Total Students	2,685
Catechesis/Religious Education:	
High School Students	755
Elementary Students	2,778
Total Students Under Catholic Instruction	9,113
Teachers in the Diocese:	
Priests	4
Sisters	13
Lay Teachers	255

Vital Statistics

Receptions into the Church:	
Infant Baptism Totals	596
Adult Baptism Totals	239
Received into Full Communion	119
First Communions	818
Confirmations	904
Marriages:	
Catholic	168
Interfaith	153
Total Marriages	321
Deaths	776
Total Catholic Population	40,541
Total Population	522,253

Former Bishops—Most Rev. JOHN KING MUSSIO, D.D., J.C.D., named First Bishop of Steubenville. ord. for Diocese of Cincinnati Aug. 15, 1935; appt. First Bishop of Steubenville March 16, 1945; cons. May 1, 1945; retired Oct. 11, 1977; died April 15, 1978.

Vicar General—Rev. Msgr. ROGER J. FOYS, V.G., *422 Washington St., P.O. Box 969, Steubenville, 43952-5969.* Tel: 740-282-3631.

Moderator of the Curia—Rev. Msgr. ROGER J. FOYS, V.G., *422 Washington St., P.O. Box 969, Steubenville, 43952-5969.* Tel: 740-282-3631.

Chancellor—Mrs. LINDA A. NICHOLS.

Chancery Office—*422 Washington St., P.O. Box 969, Steubenville, 43952-5969.* Tel: 740-282-3631; Fax: 740-282-3327.

Diocesan Finance Office—Rev. Msgr. ROGER J. FOYS, V.G., Dir.; Mr. DAVID FRANKLIN, Comptroller, *P.O. Box 969, Steubenville, 43952-5969.* Tel: 740-282-3631.

Diocesan/Parish Share Campaign—Rev Msgr. ROGER J. FOYS, V.G., Dir. MARTIN B. THOMPSON, Assoc. Dir. Tel: 740-282-3631.

Diocesan Tribunal—*422 Washington St., P.O. Box 969, Steubenville, 43952-5969.* Tel: 740-282-3631.

Judicial Vicar— Rev. Msgr. KURT H. KEMO, J.C.L.

Adjutant Judicial Vicar—Rev. Msgr. ROGER J. FOYS, V.G.

Auditors—Revs. THOMAS A. CHILLOG; WILLIAM D. CROSS; DANIEL HEUSEL.

Notary—Rev. DANIEL HEUSEL.

Defenders of the Bond—Rev. Msgr. GERALD E. CALOVINI; Revs. THOMAS A. CHILLOG; WILLIAM D. CROSS.

Secretary to the Tribunal & Notary—COLLEEN BAHEN.

Judges—Rev. Msgr. ROGER J. FOYS, V.G.; Rev. Msgr. MARK J. FROEHLICH; Rev. Msgr. ROBERT H. PUNKE, V.F.; Rev. Msgr. GENE W. MULLETT, V.F.; Rev. VINCENT J. HUBER.

Information & Technology—Rev. Msgr. ROGER J. FOYS, V.G., Dir.; Mr. MARTIN B. THOMPSON, Assoc. Dir.; Mr. ANTHONY TARGOSS, Mgr., *422 Washington St., P.O. Box 969, Steubenville, 43952-5969.* Tel: 740-282-3631.

Office of the Permanent Diaconate—Most Rev. GILBERT I. SHELDON; Rev. Msgr. KURT H. KEMO, J.C.L., Dir.; Rev. Msgr. ROGER J. FOYS; Rev. Msgr. ROBERT J. KAWA; Rev. Msgr. THOMAS C. PETRONEK; Revs. WILLIAM D. CROSS; JAMES M. DUNFEE, *P.O. Box 969, Steubenville, 43952-5969.* Tel: 740-282-3631; Fax: 740-282-3327.

Diocesan Deaneries and Deans

Deans—Rev. Msgr. GEORGE W. YONTZ, V.F., Annunciation Deanery; Rev. Msgr. GERALD E. CALOVINI, V.F., Immaculate Heart of Mary Deanery; Rev. Msgr. JOHN C. KOLESAR, V.F., Mother of God Deanery; Rev. Msgr. PATRICK GAUGHAN, V.F., Nativity of Mary Deanery; Rev. Msgr. ROBERT H. PUNKE, V.F., Presentation Deanery; Rev. Msgr. WILLIAM C. YONTZ, V.F., Visitation Deanery; Rev. Msgr. EDWARD J. KAKASI, V.F., Assumption Deanery; Rev. Msgr. J. MICHAEL CAMPBELL, V.F., Coronation Deanery; Rev. Msgr. WILLIAM MYERS, V.F., Immaculate Conception Deanery; Rev. Msgr. GENE W. MULLETT, V.F., Queen of Peace Deanery.

Continuing Education/Alliance of Priests—Rev. Msgr. ROGER J. FOYS, V.G., Dir.; Rev. Msgr. GERALD E. CALOVINI, V.F.; Rev. Msgr. KURT H. KEMO, J.C.L.;

Revs. WILLIAM D. CROSS; THOMAS A. CHILLOG.

Pastoral Staff—Most Rev. GILBERT I. SHELDON, D.D., D.Min.; Rev. Msgr. ROGER J. FOYS, V.G., Chm.; Mrs. PAT DEFRANCIS; Mrs. LINDA A. NICHOLS; Rev. Msgr. KURT H. KEMO, J.C.L.; Rev. THOMAS A. CHILLOG; Rev. Msgr. GERALD E. CALOVINI, V.F.; Sr. MARY ANN CORR, S.C.; Dr. PETER CHILA; Rev. WILLIAM D. CROSS; Mr. BRIAN HARVEY.

Presbyteral Council—Most Rev. GILBERT I. SHELDON, D.D., D.Min., Pres.; Rev. Msgr. GERALD E. CALOVINI, V.F.; Rev. Msgr. WILLIAM R. CORNELIUS; Rev. VINCENT J. HUBER; Rev. Msgr. MARK J. FROEHLICH; Rev. Msgr. FREDERICK A. PASQUINELLI; Revs. THOMAS A. MAGARY; DAVID GAYDOSIK; THOMAS A. CHILLOG, Exec. Sec. MARTIN J. HOLLER; Rev. Msgr. KURT H. KEMO, J.C.L., Vice Chm.; Revs. LEONARD T. CENCULA; JAMES M. BRYANT; JAMES MORMAN, T.O.R.; SAMUEL SAPRANO; Rev. Msgr. ROGER J. FOYS, V.G., Chm.; Mrs. LINDA NICHOLS, Recording Sec.

College of Consultors—Rev. Msgr. GERALD D. CALOVINI, V.F.; Rev. Msgr. WILLIAM R. CORNELIUS; Rev. WALTER HEINZ; Rev. Msgr. KURT H. KEMO, J.C.L.; Rev. JAMES MORMAN, T.O.R.; Rev. Msgr. ROGER J. FOYS, V.G.

Priests Personnel Board—Rev. Msgr. ROBERT KAWA, Southern Area; Rev. Msgr. JOHN C. KOLESAR, Senior Clergy; Rev. Msgr. PATRICK GAUGHAN, V.F., Middle Age Clergy; Rev. Msgr. J. MICHAEL CAMPBELL, Northern Area; Rev. JAMES M. BRYANT, Younger Clergy; Rev. Msgr. THOMAS C. PETRONEK, Central Area; Rev. Msgr. ROGER J. FOYS, V.G., Ex Officio.

Diocesan Offices and Directors

Building Commission—Mr. BRIAN HARVEY, Chm., *P.O. Box 969, Steubenville, 43952-5969.* Tel: 740-282-3631; Fax: 740-282-3327.

Building & Property Director—Mr. BRIAN HARVEY, *P.O. Box 969, Steubenville, 43952-5969.* Tel: 740-282-3631; Fax: 740-282-3327.

Campus Ministry—Rev. MARTIN J. HOLLER, *75 Stewart St., Athens, 45701.* Tel: 740-592-2711.

Office of Christian Formation—Sr. MARY ANN CORR, S.C., Ed.D., Dir., *P.O. Box 969, Steubenville, 43952-5969.* Tel: 740-282-3631; Fax: 740-282-3327.

Diocesan Communications—Rev. Msgr. GERALD E. CALOVINI, V.F., *P.O. Box 969, Steubenville, 43952-5969.* Tel: 740-282-3631; Fax: 740-282-3327.

Continuing Education of Priests—Rev. Msgr. KURT H. KEMO, J.C.L., Dir., *P.O. Box 969, Steubenville, 43952-5969.* Tel: 740-282-3631; Fax: 740-282-3327.

Diocesan Finance Council—Most Rev. GILBERT I. SHELDON, Pres.; Rev. Msgr. ROGER J. FOYS, V.G., Chm. Council Members: Rev. Msgr. FREDERICK A. PASQUINELLI; GREGORY J. AGRESTA; RICHARD DOLAN; PAMELA DUNLAP; ROBERT DYER; DAVID A. FRANKLIN; THOMAS HISRICH, *422 Washington St., P.O. Box 969, Steubenville, 43952-5969.* Tel: 740-282-3631; Fax: 740-282-3327.

Diocesan Director of Cemeteries—Rev. Msgr. JOHN C. KOLESAR, V.F., *221 Hanna Ave., Adena, 43901.* Tel: 740-546-3463.

Diocesan Director of Ecumenism—Rev. Msgr. DONAL O'CARROLL, *P.O. Box 65, Beverly, 45715.* Tel: 740-984-4204.

Diocesan Office of Worship—Rev. Msgr. KURT H. KEMO, J.C.L., Dir., *P.O. Box 969, Steubenville, 43952-5969.* Tel: 740-282-3631; Fax: 740-282-3327.

Health Panel of the Clergy—Rev. Msgr. DONAL O'CARROLL, Contact Person, *P.O. Box 65, Beverly, 45715.* Tel: 740-984-4204.

Holy Childhood Association—Vacant.

Hospitals—Trinity Health System: *Trinity Medical Center, West, 4000 Johnson Rd., Steubenville, 43952.* Tel: 740-264-8000; Fax: 740-264-8620., *Trinity Medical Center, East, 380 Summit Ave., Steubenville, 43952.* Tel: 740-283-7000. FRED B. BROWER, Pres. Tel: 740-283-7390. Tel: 740-264-8303. Rev. JOHN MCCOY, Chap. Tel: 740-264-8133; 8000.

National Catholic Rural Life Conference—Rev. ANTHONY JABLONOWSKI, C.M.M.I., *Res., R.D. 2, P.O. Box 385, Marietta, 45750.* Tel: 740-896-2060.

Central Office of Catholic Charities—Rev. Msgr. GERALD E. CALOVINI, V.F., Dir., *P.O. Box 969, Steubenville, 43952-5969.* Tel: 740-282-3631; 1-800-339-7890; Fax: 740-282-3327. Services: Campaign for Human Development; Respect Life; Information & Referral, Jefferson County RSVP: Tel: 740-282-9232., St. Steubenville, Housing for Elderly: Tel: 740-282-9232., Samaritan House: Tel: 740-282-0563.

Priests' Retirement Board—Rev. Msgr. JAMES C. MARSHALL, *Holy Rosary Church, 200 Rosemont Ave., Steubenville, 43952.* Tel: 740-264-4880.

Propagation of the Faith—Rev. JAMES M. DUNFEE, *St. Pius X Church, 700 Lovers Lane, Steubenville, 43952.* Tel: 740-282-7681.

Publication, "Steubenville Register"—Most Rev. GILBERT I. SHELDON, D.D., D.Min., Pres. & Publisher; Mrs. PAT DEFRANCIS, Editor, *422 Washington St., P.O. Box 160, Steubenville, 43952-5969.* Tel: 740-282-3631; Fax: 740-282-3238.

RCIA—Rev. Msgr. KURT H. KEMO, J.C.L., Dir., *P.O. Box 969, Steubenville, 43952-5969.* Tel: 740-282-3631; Fax: 740-282-3327.

St. Vincent de Paul Society—Rev. Msgr. GERALD E. CALOVINI, V.F., Dir., *422 Washington St., P.O. Box 969, Steubenville, 43952-5969.* Tel: 740-282-3631.

Schools—Dr. PETER CHILA, Ed.D., Supt., *P.O. Box 969, Steubenville, 43952-5969.* Tel: 740-282-3631; Fax: 740-282-3327.

Vicar for Priests—Rev. Msgr. ROGER J. FOYS, V.G., *P.O. Box 969, Steubenville, 43952-5969.* Tel: 740-282-3631.

Vicar for Religious—Rev. Msgr. J. MICHAEL CAMPBELL, V.F., *St. Gabriel, P.O. Box 275, Minerva, 44657.* Tel: 330-868-4498.

Vicar for Retired Priests—Rev. VINCENT J. HUBER, *1225 N. River Ave., Toronto, 43964.* Tel: 740-537-4433.

Vocations—Rev. Msgr. ROGER J. FOYS, V.G., Dir.; Rev. DANIEL HEUSEL, Asst. Dir., *P.O. Box 969, Steubenville, 43952-5969.* Tel: 740-282-3631.

Woman's Club—Rev. Msgr. ROGER J. FOYS, V.G., Moderator; Mrs. BARBARA JEAN APPLEGARTH, Pres., *73911 Pleasant Grove, Adena, 43901.* Tel: 740-546-3913.

CLERGY, PARISHES, MISSIONS AND PAROCHIAL SCHOOLS

CITY OF STEUBENVILLE
(Jefferson County)

1—HOLY NAME CATHEDRAL, Very Rev. Timothy Shannon, Rector.
Rectory: 411 S. Fifth St., 43952. Tel: 740-282-7322; Fax: 740-284-7195. [JC]

2—HOLY FAMILY, Rev. Richard Tuttle; Deacon Dominic Cerrato, Pastoral Assoc.
Res., 2608 Hollywood Blvd., 43952. Tel: 740-264-2825; Fax: 740-264-9348. [JC]

3—HOLY ROSARY, Rev. Msgr. James C. Marshall; Rev. John McCoy.
Res., 200 Rosemont Ave., 43952. Tel: 740-264-4880; Fax: 740-266-2844. [JC]
School—Central Grade School.
Lay Teachers 23; Students 375.

4—IMMACULATE HEART OF MARY CHAPEL. Closed. For inquiries for parish records contact the Chancery.

5—OUR LADY OF NORTH AMERICA MARTYRS, Rev. John Galea.
Res., 1685 Township Rd. 378, 43952-6959. Tel: 740-283-2983; Fax: 740-283-2107. [JC]

6—ST. ANTHONY OF PADUA, Very Rev. Timothy Shannon.
Res., 411 S. 5th St., 43952. Tel: 740-282-0832. [JC]
School—All Saints, Tel: 740-282-4201; Fax: 740-282-7195.

7—ST. PETER'S, Rev. Msgr. George W. Yontz; Rev. Dominic Fosu (Africa); Bro. Patrick Geary, I.H.M., Pastoral Assoc.
Res., 425 N. Fourth St., 43952. Tel: 740-282-7612; 282-9263. [JC]
School—All Saints Central School, Tel: 740-282-4201.
Lay Teachers 12; Students 112.

8—ST. PIUS X, Revs. Leonard T. Cencula; James M. Dunfree.
Res., 700 Lovers Ln., 43953. Tel: 740-264-7681. [JC]
School—Aquinas Central, 625 Lovers Ln., 43953. Tel: 740-264-3651; Fax: 740-264-4277.
Lay Teachers 15; Students 255.

9—ST. STANISLAUS, Rev. Msgr. George W. Yontz; Rev. Dominic Fosu (Africa).
Mailing Address: 425 N. 4th St., 43952. Tel: 740-282-7612. [JC]

10—SERVANTS OF CHRIST THE KING, Jefferson Co., Rev. Msgr. Roger J. Foys.
Res., 1225 N. River Ave., 43964. Tel: 740-537-4433; Fax: 740-537-9305.

OUTSIDE THE CITY OF STEUBENVILLE

Adena, Jefferson Co., St. Casimir's, Rev. Msgr. John C. Kolesar.
Res., 221 Hanna Ave., 43901. Tel: 740-546-3463; Fax: 740-546-3763. [CEM]

Amsterdam, Jefferson Co., St. Joseph, Rev. Msgr. Kenneth Uram.
Res., 7457 State Hwy., Richmond, 43944. Tel: 740-765-4142. [CEM]

Athens, Athens Co., Christ the King University Parish, Rev. Martin J. Holler, Dir. Campus Ministry; Rev. Msgr. Donald E. Horak, (Retired).
Res., 75 Stewart St., 45701. Tel: 740-592-2711; Fax: 740-594-3314.
St. Paul's, Rev. Msgr. Patrick E. Gaughan, V.F. In res., Rev. Msgr. Donald E. Horak, (Retired).
Res., 38 N. College St., 45701. Tel: 740-593-7822; Fax: 740-593-8602. [CEM]
Chapel—Guysville, St. John.

Barnesville, Belmont Co., Assumption, Rev. Virgil Reischman.
Res., 306 W. Main St., 43713. Tel: 740-425-2181. [CEM]

Barton, Belmont Co., Our Lady of Angels, Rev. Michael Rotolo.
Res., P.O. Box 768, 43905. Tel: 740-695-3039.

Bellaire, Belmont Co., St. John, Rev. Msgr. Gene W. Mullett.
Res., 3745 Tallman Ave., 43906. Tel: 740-676-0051. [JC]
School—Central Grade School, Tel: 740-676-2620; Fax: 740-676-8502.
Lay Teachers 17; Students 251.
St. Michael's, Rev. Msgr. Gene W. Mullett.
Res., c/o St. John Church, 415 37th St., 43906. Tel: 740-676-0051. [CEM][JC]

Belle Valley, Noble Co., Corpus Christi, Rev. Dale F. Tornes.
Res., c/o St. Stephen Church, P.O. Box 186, Caldwell, 43724. Tel: 740-732-4129.
Church—Main St., 43717. Tel: 614-732-7202. [CEM]

Belpre, Washington Co., St. Ambrose, Rev. David L. Huffman.
Res., P.O. Box 426, 45714. Tel: 740-423-7422; Fax: 740-423-7422. [CEM]

Beverly, Washington Co., St. Bernard, Rev. Msgr. Robert J. Kawa.
Res., 307 Seventh St., 45715. Tel: 740-984-2555. [CEM]

Blaine, Belmont Co., All Saints, Rev. Michael Rotolo.
Res., 53839 National Rd., P.O. Box 337, 43909. Tel: 740-635-0642.

Bridgeport, Belmont Co., St. Anthony of Padua, Rev. Msgr. Francis Manieri.
Res., 630 Main St., 43912. Tel: 740-635-0283. [JC]
St. Joseph, Rev. Msgr. Mark J. Froehlich.
Res., 68210 Neola Ave., 43912. Tel: 740-635-0408; Fax: 740-635-1166. [JC]
School—Tel: 740-635-3313.
Lay Teachers 13; Students 117.

Brilliant, Jefferson Co., Our Lady of Fatima. Closed. Sacramental records are located at St. Agnes, Mingo Junction.

Buchtel, Athens Co., St. Patrick. Consolidated with St. Andrew to form St. Mary of the Hills, Nelsonville.

Burkhart, Monroe Co., St. Joseph's, Rev. David L. Gaydosik.
Mailing Address: c/o St. Sylvester Church, 330 S. Main St., Woodsfield, 43793. Tel: 740-472-0187; Fax: 740-472-1994.

Byesville, Guernsey Co., Holy Trinity, Rev. Msgr. William C. Yontz.
Res., 222 S. Fifth St., Box 26, 43723. Tel: 740-685-2184. [CEM]

Cadiz, Harrison Co., St. Teresa, Rev. Thomas A. Vennitti.
Res., 143 E. South St., 43907. Tel: 740-942-2211.

Caldwell, Noble Co., St. Stephen, Rev. Dale F. Tornes.
Res., 1036 Belford St., Box 186, 43724. Tel: 740-732-4129. [CEM]

Cambridge, Guernsey Co., St. Benedict, Rev. Robert D. Borer.
Res., 714 Gomber Ave., 43725. Tel: 740-432-7609; Fax: 740-439-0800.
School—Tel: 740-432-6751; Fax: 740-432-4961.
Franciscan Sisters of Christian Charity 4; Lay Teachers 9; Students 140.

Carlisle, Noble Co., St. Michael, Rev. Samuel Saprano.
Res., 43700 Fulda Rd., Caldwell, 43724. Tel: 740-838-4842, 732-4576. [CEM]

Carrollton, Carroll Co., Our Lady of Mercy, Rev. Thomas Marut.
Res., 616 Roswell Rd., N.W., P.O. Box 155, 44615. Tel: 330-627-4664.

Chesapeake, Lawrence Co., St. Ann, Rev. Thomas R. Nau.
310 Third Ave., Box 428, 45619-0428. Tel: 740-867-4434; 532-0561.

Churchtown, Washington Co., St. John the Baptist, Rev. Anthony Jablonowski, C.M.M.I.
Res., R.F.D. 2, Marietta, 45750. Tel: 740-896-2060. [CEM]
School—Central Grade School, Tel: 740-896-2697; Fax: 740-896-2555.
Lay Teachers 10; Students 112.

Colerain, Belmont Co., St. Frances Cabrini, Rev. Msgr. David E. Reasbeck.
Res., Rte. 250, Box 38, 43916. Tel: 740-635-9933.

Dillonvale, Jefferson Co., St. Adalbert, Rev. Msgr. John C. Kolesar.
Res., c/o 221 Hanna Ave., Adena, 43901. Tel: 740-546-3463; Fax: 740-546-3763. [CEM]

Fairpoint, Belmont Co., St. Joseph, Rev. Thomas J. Graven.
Mailing Address: 71793 Church St., P.O. Box 308, Maynard, 43937. Tel: 740-695-2618; Fax: 740-695-2618.
Church—46982 Columbia St., Box 98, 43927. Tel: 740-695-0840.

Flushing, Belmont Co., St. Paul's, Rev. Msgr. John A. Cymbor.
Res., 115 Morristown Rd., Box 45, 43977. Tel: 740-968-4159. [CEM]

Fulda, Noble Co., Immaculate Conception, Rev. Samuel Saprano.
Res., 43700 Fulda Rd., Caldwell, 43724. Tel: 740-732-4576. [CEM]

Gallipolis, Gallia Co., St. Louis, Rev. Msgr. William R. Myers, V.F.
Res., 85 State St., 45631. Tel: 740-446-0669; Fax: 740-446-9858. [CEM]

Glouster, Athens Co., Holy Cross, Rev. John Mucha.
Rectory: 31 Republic Ave., 45732. Tel: 740-767-3068.
Res., 110 E. Washington St., Nelsonville, 45764. Tel: 740-753-1770; Fax: 740-753-4480. [CEM]
Church—Corner of Madison & Republic Avenues, 45732.

Harriettsville, Noble Co., St. Henry, Rev. Victor Cinson, Jr., Admin.
Mailing Address: R.D. 1, Box 90-B, Lowell, 45744. Tel: 740-896-2207; Fax: 740-896-2207.
Church—Rte. 1, 36575 Church St., CR 47, Lower Salem, 45745. Tel: 740-585-2383. [CEM]

Hopedale, Harrison Co., Sacred Heart, Rev. Thomas A. Vennitti; Deacon Mark Miravalle.
Mailing Address: 205 Cross St., P.O. Box 445, 43976-0445. [JC]
Res., 143 E. South St., Cadiz, 43907. Tel: 740-942-2211.

Ironton, Lawrence Co., St. Joseph, Rev. Thomas R. Nau.
Res., 905 S. Fifth St., P.O. Box 499, 45638. Tel: 740-532-0561; 532-0712. [JC]
St. Lawrence, Rev. Thomas R. Nau.
Res., 905 S. Fifth St., P.O. Box 499, 45638-0499. Tel: 740-532-0561. [JC]
School—St. Lawrence Central Grade School, (Grades K-6). Tel: 740-532-5052.
Lay Teachers 9; Students 119.
High School—St. Joseph Central High School, (Grades 7-12). Tel: 740-532-0485; Fax: 740-532-3699.
Lay Teachers 12; Students 83.

Lafferty, Belmont Co., St. Mary, Rev. Chester J. Pabin.
Res., P.O. Box 188, 43951. Tel: 740-968-3200. [CEM]

Lore City, Guernsey Co., SS. Peter and Paul, Rev. Thomas A. Chillog.
Res., P.O. Box 175, 43755. Tel: 740-685-5582; Fax: 740-685-6336. [CEM]

Lowell, Washington Co., Our Lady of Mercy, Rev. Victor Cinson, Jr.
Res., R.D. 1, Box 90-B, 45744. Tel: 740-896-2207; Fax: 740-896-2207. [CEM]

McConnelsville, Morgan Co., St. James, Rev. Paul Walker.
Res., 257 Bell Ave., P.O. Box 539, 43756. Tel: 740-962-2856.

Malvern, Carroll Co., St. Francis Xavier, Rev. Msgr. J. Michael Campbell.
Res., P.O. Box 275, Minerva, 44657. Tel: 330-868-4498. [CEM]

Marietta, Washington Co., St. Mary's, Rev. Msgr. Edward Kakascik; Rev. Paul Hrezo.
Res., 506 Fourth St., 45750. Tel: 740-373-3643; Fax: 740-376-2956. [CEM 2]
School—320 Marion St., 45750. Tel: 740-374-8181; Fax: 740-374-8602.
Lay Teachers 22; Students 226.

Martins Ferry, Belmont Co., St. Mary, Rev. Thomas A. Magary. In res., Rev. Richard L. Battocletti, (Retired).
Res., 20 N. Fourth St., 43935. Tel: 740-633-1416. [CEM]
School—St. Mary Central, 24 N. Fourth St., 43935. Tel: 740-633-5424. Sr. Louise Smith, S.C.N., Prin.
Sisters 1; Lay Teachers 10; Students 167.

Maynard, Belmont Co., St. Stanislaus, Rev. Thomas J. Graven.
Res., 71793 Church St., P.O. Box 308, 43937. Tel: 740-695-2618; Fax: 740-695-2618.

Miltonsburg, Monroe Co., St. John the Baptist, Rev. David L. Gaydosik.
Church: 35560 Miltonsburg-Calais Rd., Woodsfield, 43793. Tel: 740-472-0187. [CEM]
Res., 330 S. Main St., Woodsfield, 43793.

Minerva, Stark Co., St. Gabriel the Archangel, Rev. Msgr. John Michael Campbell. In res., Rev. Msgr. Cronan T. Molloy, (Retired).
Res., 400 West High, P.O. Box 275, 44657. Tel: 330-868-4498; Fax: 330-868-4498.

Mingo Junction, Jefferson Co., Annunciation. Closed. Parish records can be found at St. Agnes Church, Mingo Junction.
St. Agnes, Revs. William D. Cross; Daniel Heusel; Sr. June Smith, O.S.F., Pastoral Assoc.
Mailing Address: 204 St. Clair St., 43938. Tel: 740-535-1491; Fax: 740-535-0039. [JC]
School—Central Grade School, Tel: 740-535-1012; Fax: 740-535-0039.
Franciscan Sisters of Christian Charity 3; Lay Teachers 12; Students 112.
St. Bernadette. Closed. Sacramental records are located at St. Agnes, Mingo Junction.

Morges, Carroll Co., St. Mary, Rev. Thomas Marut.
Res., P.O. Box 690, Waynesburg, 44688. Tel: 330-866-2023. [CEM]

Neffs, Belmont Co., Sacred Heart, Rev. Gary Zalenski.
Res., 54038 St. Mary Ave., P.O. Box 425, 43940-0425. Tel: 740-676-3277; Fax: 740-676-3400.

Nelsonville, Athens Co., St. Mary of the Hills. Consolidated St. Andrew, Nelsonville consolidated with St. Patrick, Buchtel to form St. Mary of the Hills. Rev. John Mucha.
Res., 110 E. Washington St., 45764. Tel: 740-753-1770; Fax: 740-753-4480.

Pine Grove, Lawrence Co., St. Mary, Rev. Francis L. Kinney, C.PP.S.
Res., Box 639, Ironton, 45638. Tel: 740-532-2420. [CEM]

Piney Fork, Jefferson Co., St. Therese, Rev. A. Donald Mantica, Admin.
Res., Box 25, 43941. Tel: 740-733-7820; 733-7595.

Pomeroy, Meigs Co., Sacred Heart, Rev. Walter E. Heinz.
Res., 161 Mulberry Ave., 45769. Tel: 740-992-5898. [CEM]

Powhatan Point, Belmont Co., St. John Vianney, Rev. Frank C. Cronin.
Mailing Address: St. Mary Church, P.O. Box 68, Shadyside, 43947. Tel: 740-676-3282.
Church: 295 Hwy. 7 N., 43942.

Richmond, Jefferson Co., St. John Fisher, Rev. Msgr. Kenneth Uram.
Res., 7457 St. HGY 152, 43944. Tel: 740-765-4142.

St. Clairsville, Belmont Co., St. Mary's, Rev. Msgr. Robert H. Punke.
Res., 230 W. Main St., 43950. Tel: 740-695-9993; Fax: 740-695-6026.
School—Central Grade School, 226 W. Main St., 43950. Tel: 740-695-3189; Fax: 740-695-3851.
Lay Teachers 11; Students 258.

Shadyside, Belmont Co., St. Mary, Rev. Frank C. Cronin.
350 E. 40th St., P.O. Box 68, 43947. Tel: 740-676-3282; Fax: 740-676-1424.

Smithfield, Jefferson Co., Our Lady, Queen of Peace, Rev. A. Donald Mantica.
Res., P.O. Box 453, 43948. Tel: 740-733-7595. [JC]

Temperanceville, Belmont Co., St. Mary's, Rev. Virgil Reischman.
Res., 306 W. Main St., Barnesville, 43713. Tel: 740-425-2181. [CEM]

Tiltonsville, Jefferson Co., St. Joseph, Rev. Msgr. George R. Coyne.
Res., 204 Mound St., 43963. Tel: 740-859-4018; Fax: 740-859-6041.

Toronto, Jefferson Co., St. Francis of Assisi, Rev. Msgr. Roger J. Foys, V.G.; Rev. Msgr. Kurt H. Kemo; Rev. Vincent J. Huber; Bro. Anthony Motto, I.H.M., Pastoral Assoc.
Res., 1225 N. River Ave., 43964. Tel: 740-537-4433; Fax: 740-537-9305. [JC]
School—Tel: 740-537-2151; Fax: 740-537-9380.
Vincentian Sisters of Charity 1; Lay Teachers 7; Students 101.
St. Joseph's, Rev. Msgr. Roger J. Foys, V.G.; Rev. Msgr. Kurt H. Kemo; Rev. Vincent J. Huber; Bro. Anthony Motto, I.H.M., Pastoral Assoc.
Res., 1225 N. River Ave., 43964. Tel: 740-537-4433; Fax: 740-537-9305. [JC]

Vincent, Washington Co., St. Ambrose. Consolidated with St. Ambrose, Belpre.

Wintersville, Jefferson Co., Blessed Sacrament, Rev. Msgr. Gerald E. Calovini; Rev. Frederick C. Kihm.
Res., 852 Main St., 43953-3870. Tel: 740-264-0868; Fax: 740-264-5449. [JC]
School—Aquinas Elementary, (Grades K-8) 625 Lovers Ln., Steubenville, 43953. Tel: 740-264-3651; Fax: 740-264-4277.
Our Lady of Lourdes, Rev. Msgr. Gerald E. Calovini; Rev. Frederick C. Kihm.
Res., P.O. Box 2612, 43953. Tel: 740-264-2798; 282-3631 (Office); Fax: 740-264-5449. [JC]

Woodsfield, Monroe Co., St. Sylvester, Revs. David Gaydosik; Thomas F. Hamm, Jr.
Res., 330 S. Main St., 43793. Tel: 740-472-0187; Fax: 740-472-1994. [CEM]
School—Central Grade School, Tel: 740-472-0321; Fax: 740-472-1994.
Franciscan Sisters of Christian Charity 2; Lay Teachers 9; Students 153.

Yorkville, Jefferson Co., St. Lucy's, Rev. Bernard Krajcovic.
Res., 107 St. Lucy Ave., 43971. Tel: 740-859-2274.

DIOCESAN MISSIONS

Bloomingdale, Jefferson Co., St. Thomas More Mission. Closed. Sacramental records are located at St. John Fisher, Richmond.

Chauncey, Athens Co., St. Jude Mission. Closed. Sacramental records are located at St. Paul Church, Athens.

Crescent, Belmont Co., St. Elizabeth Mission. Closed. Sacramental records are located at St. Stanislaus Church, Maynard.

Freeport, Harrison Co., St. Matthias Mission, Rev. Thomas A. Chillog.
Res., P.O. Box 175, Lore City, 43755. Tel: 740-685-5582; Fax: 740-685-6336.
Church—Main St., Box 195, 43973. Tel: 740-658-3300.

Hammondsville, Jefferson Co., Nativity of Our Lord Mission. Closed. Sacramental records are located at St. Joseph Church, Toronto.

Jewett, Harrison Co., Our Lady of Perpetual Help Mission, Rev. John M. Galea.
Mailing Address: & Res.—1685 Twp. Rd. 378, Steubenville, 43952-6959. Tel: 740-946-2400; Fax: 740-283-2107.

Sardis, Monroe Co., St. John Bosco Mission, Rev. David L. Gaydosik.
Res., c/o St. Sylvester Church, 330 S. Main St., Woodsfield, 43793. Tel: 740-472-0187; Fax: 740-472-1994. [CEM]

Tappan Lake, Harrison Co., Christ the King Summer Mission. Closed. Sacramental records are located at: 143 E. South St., Cadiz 43907. Tel: 740-942-2211.

Tupper Plains, Meigs Co., Our Lady of Loretto Church. Closed. Sacramental records are located at Sacred Heart Church, Pomeroy.

On Duty Outside the Diocese:
Reverend Monsignors—
Wippel, John, 10105 Portland Pl., Silver Springs, MD 20901. Tel: 301-593-9345; 816-942-8400
Reverend Fathers—
Calabrese, Charles L., TCU, Box 297310, Fort Worth, TX 76129-0001. Tel: 817-923-2176; 921-7830
Direnzo, Michael J., U.S.A.F. Chap. (Lt. Col.), 61 ABG/HC 325 Challenger Way, Los Angeles AFB, El Segundo, CA 90245-4677. Tel: 310-831-5857
Gallagher, Robert A., U.S.A.F. Chap., 108 Robin Hood Dr., Yorktown, VA 23693. Tel: 757-867-9326
Massucci, Joseph D., University of Dayton, 324 Chaminade Hall, Dayton, OH 45469-0534
McCarthy, John R., St. Philomena Church, 13824 Euclid Ave., Cleveland, OH 44114. Tel: 216-541-3540
Mellott, David, Society of Sulpice, 800 Peachtree St., Apt. 8331, Atlanta, GA 30308. Tel: 404-875-7397
Pliauplis, Christopher, Sts. Simon & Jude Rectory, 185 Van Sicklen St., Brooklyn, NY 11223-1750
Safraniec, Joseph, Chap., Chaplain's Office (125), Dept. of VAMC, 1 Veteran's Dr., Minneapolis, MN 55417. Tel: 617-725-2027
Smith, Martin D., 4616 W. Mitchell Ave., Cincinnati, OH 45232. Tel: 513-591-2422

Absent on Leave:
Reverend Monsignors—
Gaetano, Lewis F., 4230 Pebblebrook, N. Canton, OH 44709
Petronek, Thomas C., 21254 St. Louis Rd., Middleburg, VA 20017
Reverend Fathers—
Bernas, Elwood S., 30675 Park St., #106, Lindstrom, MN 55045-9618
Greenwood, Kevin L., The Americana Apts., 380 S. 5th St., Apt. 314, Columbus, OH 43215
Holmes, John, 464 S. Powell, Columbus, OH 43204. Tel: 614-276-6176
Huffman, Timothy J., St. Joseph, 2427 W. Tuscarawas St., Canton, OH 44708. Tel: 330-453-2526

Peltz, Carl F., 1628 E. G Ave., Parchment, MI 49004-1702

Absent Without Leave:
Reverend Fathers—
Bielanski, Joseph J., 246 Dorland, #4, San Francisco, CA 94114
Gadzinski, Mark, 363 W. 2nd Ave., Columbus, OH 43201. Tel: 614-546-3741
McLaughlin, Eugene L.
Moran, Charles

Retired:
Reverend Monsignors—
Adams, George J., 785 Broad St., Brockway, PA 15824. Tel: 814-265-8371
Boehm, James A., 124 N. Main St., Hendersonville, NC 28792-5876. Tel: 828-697-8269
Cappelli, Angelo J., 19241 Edgefield, Apt. 101, Harperswoods, MI 48225. Tel: 313-882-6683
Cornelius, William R., 4333 Steuben Woods Dr., Steubenville, OH 43953. Tel: 740-264-0741
Giannamore, Anthony J., 8110 Clyo Rd., Centerville, OH 45458. Tel: 513-435-3626; 433-7224
Horak, Donald E., St. Paul Church, 75 Stewart St., Athens, WV 45701. Tel: 740-592-5745
Maher, Patrick K., Corville, Roscrea Co., Tipperary, Ireland. Tel: 0505-22600
Metzger, Paul E., 428 Cambridge Dr., Middleton, OH 45042
Molloy, Cronan T., St. Gabriel Church, 400 W. High St., P.O. Box 275, Minerva, OH 44657
Nealon, Joseph A., P.O. Box 158, Carrollton, OH 44615-0158
Nugent, James B., 3440 Olentangy River Rd., Apt. 8F, Columbus, OH 43202. Tel: 614-262-0629
O'Carroll, Donal A., P.O. Box 65, Beverly, OH 45715. Tel: 740-984-4204
Pasquinelli, Frederick A., 4337 Steuben Woods Dr., Steubenville, OH 43953. Tel: 740-264-0970
Wadowicz, Joseph M., 106 Via Estrada, #A, Laguna Hills, CA 92653-4077. Tel: 714-770-6691
Zekas, Stanley, 4335 Steuben Woods Dr., Steubenville, OH 43953. Tel: 740-266-6947

Reverend Fathers—
Battocletti, Richard L., St. Mary Church, 20 N. 4th St., Martins Ferry, OH 43935. Tel: 740-633-1416
Belfield, John, P.O. Box 119, Avon Park, FL 33825. Tel: 813-386-0631
Bober, Bernard S., 1711 S. Jefferson, New Castle, PA 16102-1524. Tel: 412-652-4127
Borosh, Carl A., Box 587, Barton, OH 43905. Tel: 740-695-0827
Connelly, Norbert, 4339 Steuben Woods Dr., Steubenville, OH 43953. Tel: 740-264-0699
Connor, Francis J., 10248 Snead Circle N., Sun City, AZ 85351. Tel: 602-977-7141
Deasio, August J., 935 Yellow Mills Rd., Shortsville, NY 14548. Tel: 716-289-9406
Galea, John M., Our Lady of N. American Martyrs Church, 1685 Township Rd. 378, Steubenville, OH 43952. Tel: 740-282-2983
Gallagher, Cornelius F., 10520 Oakmont Ave., Sun City, AZ 85351. Tel: 602-974-5902
Lyden, Dennis P., St. Joseph Church, P.O. Box 98, Fairpoint, OH 43927. Tel: 740-695-0840
Marr, James G., 7529 Walnut Ln., Philadelphia, PA 19138. Tel: 215-424-7409
Martinosky, Joseph A., 603 Franklin Ave., Apt. #1, Columbus, OH 43215. Tel: 614-224-4498
Mascolino, Charles E., 4338 Steuben Woods Dr., Wintersville, OH 43953. Tel: 740-266-9032
Mascolino, Robert A., P.O. Box 4032, Steubenville, OH 43952-8032. Tel: 740-282-7675
Nadzam, John B., 258 Schwab Ave., Munhall, PA 15120-2239. Tel: 412-461-0623
Pandolfo, Anthony, River Bridge-The Island, 1063 Island Manor Dr., West Palm Beach, FL 33413. Tel: 407-439-5685
Patala, William S., Lancia Country Club Manor, 575 Lovers Ln., Steubenville, OH 43952
Rothbauer, Francis J., 3515 Steubenville Rd., S.E., Amsterdam, OH 43903. Tel: 330-739-4564
Stabene, Edmondo, 2063 Bantam Ridge Rd., P.O. Box 2373, Wintersville, OH 43953. Tel: 740-264-9761
Stromski, Adam F.X., 17530 S.W. 90th Ave., Miami, FL 33157-5800. Tel: 305-251-9948
Voytko, Geo., 2341 Shelva Dr., Akron, OH 44321. Tel: 330-745-8424
Zahorchak, Michael, 500 College St., Apt. 112, Terre Haute, IN 47802. Tel: 812-242-9165

Permanent Deacons:
Cerrato, Dominic, 162 Twp. Hwy. 202, Bloomingdale, OH 43910. Tel: 740-944-1846
Helgeson, Ray (SAC), 134 Brady Circle, E., Steubenville, OH 43952-1429. Tel: 740-282-7925
Hickey, Gerald, 1803 Williams Pl., Steubenville, OH 43952. Tel: 740-283-1585
Meagher, Lawrence, 4620 Lexington Dr., Steubenville, OH 43952. Tel: 740-264-3122
Miravalle, Mark, P.O. Box 338, Hopedale, OH 43976. Tel: 740-283-6433 Fax: 740-937-2555
Pettie, Paul, 1591 San Carlos St., St. Augustine, FL 32080-5480. Tel: 904-471-4541
Redington, Randall, Apostolate for Family Consecration, 3375 Co. Rd. 36, Bloomingdale, OH 43910. Tel: 740-765-4301

INSTITUTIONS LOCATED IN THE DIOCESE

[A] COLLEGES AND UNIVERSITIES

STEUBENVILLE. *Franciscan University of Steubenville*, 1235 University Blvd., 43952. Tel: 740-283-3771; Fax: 740-283-6472.
E-mail: admissions@franuniv.edu
Web site: www.franuniv.edu
For a complete listing, refer to the Colleges and Universities section.

[B] HIGH SCHOOLS, CENTRAL

STEUBENVILLE. *Catholic Central High School*, 320 West View, 43952. Tel: 740-264-5538; Fax: 740-264-5443.
E-mail: cchs_tim@omeresa.net
Web site: omeresa.net/schools/cchs
Rev. Timothy P. McGuire, Prin.; Rev. Msgr. Roger J. Foys, Pastoral Admin. Lay Teachers 27; Students 391.

BELLAIRE. *St. John Central High School*, 3625 Guernsey St., 43906. Tel: 740-676-4932; Fax: 740-676-4934.
E-mail: BSJH_gh@omeresa.ohio.gov
Web site: www.bellairestjohn.sbd.pvt.k12.oh.us
Mr. C. Gary Hill, Prin. Sisters 1; Lay Teachers 17; Students 246.

[C] JUNIOR-SENIOR CENTRAL HIGH SCHOOLS

IRONTON. *St. Joseph Central*. (Grades 7-12), 912 S. Sixth St., 45638. Tel: 740-532-0485; Fax: 740-532-3699.
E-mail: jmains@Scoca-k12.org
James J. Mains, III, Prin. Lay Teachers 16; Students 89.

[D] PRIVATE SCHOOLS

CARROLLTON. *St. John Villa*, P.O. Box 457, 44615. Tel: 330-627-9789; Fax: 330-627-4826.
E-mail: sjvinc@raex.com
Residential facility for persons with developmental disabilities. Sr. Elaine Weber, O.S.F., Exec. Dir. Faculty Staff 85; Residents 55.

[E] GENERAL HOSPITALS

STEUBENVILLE. *Trinity Health System*. Tel: 740-283-7212; Fax: 740-283-7104
For a complete listing, refer to the Hospitals section.

[F] MONASTERIES AND RESIDENCES OF PRIESTS AND BROTHERS

STEUBENVILLE. *Diocesan Brotherhood of Immaculate Heart of Mary*. Villa Maria Motherhouse. Villa Maria Motherhouse, 609 N. Seventh St., 43952. Tel: 740-283-2462. Bro. Dominic Carroll, I.H.M., Supr. Gen. Professed Brothers 4.
Holy Spirit Friary, 1235 University Blvd., 43952. Tel: 740-283-3771; Fax: 740-283-6348.
E-mail: hsfriar@ibm.net
Web site: www.franuniv.edu
Revs. Augustine Donegan, T.O.R.; Brian Cavanaugh, T.O.R.; Dennis Gang, T.O.R.; Stanley Holland, T.O.R.; Terence Henry, T.O.R.; James Morman, T.O.R.; Daniel Pattee, T.O.R.; David Pivonka, T.O.R.; Michael Scanlan, T.O.R.; Dominic Scotto, T.O.R.; Samuel Tiesi, T.O.R.; Joseph Yelenc, T.O.R.; Bros. Patrick Calvey, T.O.R.; Francis Haworth, T.O.R. In res. Revs. Bevil Bramwell, O.M.I.; Conrad Harkins, O.F.M. Priests 12; Brothers 2.

BLOOMINGDALE. *Hermits of Mt. Carmel-Mount Carmel Hermitage*, 388 Fairplay Rd., 43910-7914. Tel: 740-944-1048. Sisters 2.
Holy Family Hermitage, 1501 Fairplay Rd., 43910-7971. Tel: 740-765-4511; Fax: 740-765-4511. Revs. Basil Corriere, e.c., Prior; Paul Vankeirsbilck, e.c. Hermits 2.

[G] CONVENTS AND RESIDENCES FOR SISTERS

STEUBENVILLE. *Sacred Heart Villa*, 36 Villa Dr., 43953-7129. Tel: 740-282-3801. Sr. Rosalba Putrino, Supr. Handmaids of Reparation of the Sacred Heart of Jesus, Motherhouse of America Foundation. Engaged in Kindergarten, Pre-Kindergarten and Parish work.
Sisters of the Reparation of the Most Sacred Heart of Jesus, P.O. Box 3, 707 Market St., 43952. Tel: 740-282-2144. Sr. Wendy McMenamy, S.R., Local Supr. Sisters 2.

CARROLLTON. *North American Union Sisters of Our Lady of Charity*, P.O. Box 158, 620 Roswell Rd., N.W., 44615-0158. Tel: 330-627-7647; Fax: 330-627-4415. Sr. Carol Pregno, Local Supr. Professed Sisters 11.

TORONTO. *Franciscan Sisters Third Order Regular of Penance of the Sorrowful Mother*, 170 Little Church Rd., 43964. Tel: 740-544-5542; Fax: 740-544-5543.
E-mail: torsisters@juno.com
Web site: www.torsisters.com
Sr. Jean Daugherty, T.O.R., Supr. Sisters 14; Novices 6; Postulants 2.

[H] SHRINES

FRANKLIN FURNACE. *Our Lady of Fatima Shrine*, Old Rte. 52, 45629. Mailing Address: 2525 S. 12th St., Ironton, 45638. Mr. Lawrence Holtzapfel. Tel: 740-532-7780.

[I] NEWMAN CENTERS

ATHENS. *Christ the King University Parish - Ohio University*, 75 Stewart St., 45701. Tel: 740-592-2711; Fax: 740-594-3314.
E-mail: newman@frognet.net
Web site: www.seorf.ohiou.edu/~ctk
Rev. Msgr. Donald E. Horak, (Retired); Rev. Martin J. Holler, Dir. Campus Ministry.

IRONTON. *Ohio University - Ironton Branch*, c/o St. Joseph, P.O. Box 499, 45638-0499. Tel: 740-532-0712.
E-mail: stjoelaw@wwd.net
Rev. Thomas R. Nau, Contact Person.

MARIETTA. *Marietta College*, c/o St. Mary Church, 506 Fourth St., 45750. Tel: 740-373-3643. Rev. Msgr. Edward Kakascik, Dir.

NELSONVILLE. *Hocking Technical College*, 45764. Rev. John Mucha, Dir., Res., 110 E. Washington St., 45764. Tel: 740-753-1770.

RIO GRANDE. *Rio Grande University*, 91 State St., 45674. Tel: 740-446-0669. Rev. Msgr. William R. Myers, Contact Person.

ST. CLAIRSVILLE. *Ohio University - Eastern*, c/o St. Mary's Church, 230 W. Main St., 43950. Tel: 740-695-9993. Rev. Msgr. Robert H. Punke, Contact Person.

[J] MISCELLANEOUS LISTINGS

STEUBENVILLE. *Campaign for Human Development*, c/o Catholic Charities, P.O. Box 969, 43952. Tel: 740-282-3631; Fax: 740-282-3327.
E-mail: gcalovini@diosteub.org
Web site: www.diosteub.org
Rev. Msgr. Gerald E. Calovini, Diocesan Dir.
Catholic Community Center, P.O. Box 521, 148 S. Fourth St., 43952. Tel: 740-282-7566. Mr. Brian Harvey, Board Chm.; Mr. Michael J. Barber, Exec. Dir.; Mr. Raymond Saccoccia, Business Mgr.
Catholics United for the Faith, Inc., 827 N. Fourth St., 43952. Tel: 740-283-2484; Fax: 740-283-4011.
E-mail: shughes@cuf.org
Web site: www.cuf.org
Leon J. Suprenant, Jr., Pres.
Charismatic Renewal, P.O. Box 969, 43952-5969. Tel: 740-282-3631.
E-mail: rfoys@diosteub.org
Rev. Msgr. Roger J. Foys.
Diocesan Committee of Administrative Review, P.O. Box 969, 43952. Tel: 740-282-3631.
E-mail: rfoys@diosteub.org
Web site: www.diosteub.org
Rev. Msgr. Roger J. Foys, V.G.
F.I.R.E., Franciscan University, 1235 University Blvd., 43952. Tel: 412-951-0306; Fax: 801-459-5861.
E-mail: jrook@fireministry.org
Web site: fireministry.org
Mr. Jack Rook, Admin. A Catholic Alliance for Faith, Intercession, Repentance, and Evangelism.
Fraternity of Priests, Inc., 100 Belleview Blvd., 43952. Tel: 740-283-4400; Fax: 740-283-3622.
E-mail: contact@fraternityofpriests.org
Web site: www.fraternityofpriests.org
Heart of the Church Foundation, 417 Belleview Blvd., P.O. Box 667, 43952. Tel: 740-283-6317.
E-mail: guardian@clover.net
James M. Hostetler, Pres.
Information & Referral, c/o Catholic Charities, P.O. Box 969, 43952. Tel: 740-282-6880; 800-339-7890; Fax: 740-282-3327.
E-mail: djackson@diosteub.org
Web site: www.diosteub.org
Ms. Diana Jackson, Dir.
Lay Employees Pension Plan, P.O. Box 969, 43952. Tel: 740-282-3631. Rev. Msgr. Roger J. Foys.
Marian Manor, Inc., 180 N. Fourth St., 43952. Tel: 740-282-9232; Fax: 740-282-4517.
E-mail: ftsteuben@stratuswave.net
Mary Eileen Palmer, P.H.M., Mgr.

Ohio Conference Advisory Council, P.O. Box 969, 43952. Tel: 740-282-3631. Mrs. Eileen Carpino, Lay Women's Rep.; Rev. David L. Huffman, Priest Rep.; Mr. John Sissler, Laymen Rep.

RCIA, P.O. Box 969, 43952. Tel: 740-282-3631; Fax: 740-282-3327.
E-mail: kkemo@diosteub.org
Web site: www.diosteub.org
Rev. Msgr. Kurt H. Kemo, J.C.L., Dir.

Synod Committee, 422 Washington St., P.O. Box 969, 43952. Tel: 740-282-3631. Rev. Msgr. Roger J. Foys, V.G., Contact Person.

Trinity Time, Inc., Prime Time, One Ross Park, 43952-2671.

BELPRE. *Boy Scouts*, Rte. 2, Box 20 A, 45714. Tel: 740-423-7422.
E-mail: fatherhuffman@ee.net
Web site: www.rc.net/steubenville/st_ambrose
Rev. David L. Huffman, Dir.

BEVERLY. *Marriage Encounter*. Mailing Address: St. Bernard Church, 307 Seventh St., 45715. Tel: 740-984-2555.
E-mail: kawa4@juno.com
Rev. Msgr. Robert J. Kawa, Dir.

BLOOMINGDALE. *Apostolate for Family Consecration*, John Paul II Holy Family Center, 3375 County Rd. 36, 43910-7903. Tel: 740-765-5500; Fax: 740-765-4941.
E-mail: info@familyland.org
Web site: www.familyland.org

BRIDGEPORT. *Cursillo Moderator*, St. Anthony Church, 630 Main St., 43912. Tel: 740-635-0283. Rev. Msgr. Francis Manieri; Mrs. Peggy Cotton, Lay Dir.

RELIGIOUS INSTITUTES OF MEN REPRESENTED IN THE DIOCESE

For further details refer to the corresponding bracketed number in the Religious Institutes of Men or Women section.

[0680]—*Brothers of the Immaculate Heart of Mary.*—I.H.M.

[0230]—*Camaldolese Hermits of the Congregation of Monte Corona.*

[]—*Carmelite Missionaries of Mary Immaculate.*—C.M.M.I.

[0740]—*Marians of the Immaculate Conception (St. Stanislaus Kostka Province).*—M.I.C.

[0910]—*Oblates of Mary Immaculate (St. Paul's Province).*—O.M.I.

[0560]—*Third Order of Saint Francis. (Sacred Heart Prov.).*—T.O.R.

RELIGIOUS INSTITUTES OF WOMEN REPRESENTED IN THE DIOCESE

[]—*Carmelite Hermits of Reparation.*—E.C.R.

[0370]—*Carmelite Sisters of the Most Sacred Heart of Los Angeles.*—O.C.D.

[1070-02]—*Dominican Sisters, Columbus.*—O.P.

[1230]—*Franciscan Sisters of Christian Charity, Manitowac, WI.*—O.S.F.

[]—*Franciscan Third Order Regular Sisters of the Sorrowful Mother.*—T.O.R.

[1880]—*Handmaids of the Sacred Heart of Jesus for Reparation.*—A.R.

[2760]—*Missionary Sisters of the Immaculate Conception.* (Paterson, NJ).—S.M.I.C.

[3073]—*North American Union Sisters of Our Lady of Charity* .—O.L.C.

[0500]—*Sisters of Charity of Nazareth.*—S.C.N.

[0570]—*Sisters of Charity of Seton Hill, Greensburg, PA.*—S.C.

[]—*Sisters of Holy Family of Nazareth.*—C.S.F.N.

[]—*Sisters of St. Francis of Assisi, Milwaukee, WI.*

[1530]—*Sisters of St. Francis of the Congregation of Our Lady of Lourdes, Sylvania, Ohio.*—O.S.F.

[1510]—*Sisters of St. Francis, Pittsburgh, PA.*—O.S.F.

[3840]—*Sisters of St. Joseph of Carondelet.*—C.S.J.

[1720]—*Sisters of the Third Order Regular of St. Francis of the Congregation of Our Lady of Lourdes.*—O.S.F.

[4160]—*Vincentian Sisters of Charity.*—V.S.C.

[2970]—*School Sisters of Notre Dame.*—S.S.N.D.

[1690]—*Sisters of St. Francis, Pittsburgh, PA.* (Mt. Alvernia).—O.S.F.

[]—*Sisters of St. Francis, Stella Niagra, NY.*—O.S.F.

[0360]—*Carmelite Sisters of the Divine Heart of Jesus.*—Carmel.D.C.J.

NECROLOGY

† Highland, Rev. Msgr. Charles F., Churchtown, OH St. John the Baptist. —Died May 30, 2000.

† Maciejewski, Richard J., (Retired). —Died Feb. 24, 2000.

† Welton, Paul D., Shadyside, OH St. Mary. —Died July 27, 2000.

Diocese of Stockton

(Dioecesis Stocktoniensis)

Most Reverend

STEPHEN E. BLAIRE, D.D.

Bishop of Stockton; ordained April 29, 1967; appointed Titular Bishop of Lamzella on March 20, 1990; ordained Auxiliary Bishop of Los Angeles May 31, 1990; appointed Bishop of Stockton January 18, 1999. *Office: 1105 N. Lincoln St., Stockton, CA, 95203.* Tel.: 209-466-0636.

Most Reverend

DONALD W. MONTROSE, D.D.

Retired Bishop of Stockton; ordained May 7, 1949; appointed Titular Bishop of Vescovio and Auxiliary of Los Angeles on March 25, 1983; consecrated May 12, 1983; translated Bishop of Stockton December 19, 1985; installed February 20, 1986; retired January 18, 1999.

ESTABLISHED JANUARY 13, 1962.

Square Miles 10,023.

Legal Title: The Roman Catholic Bishop of Stockton, a Corporation Sole.

Comprises six Counties in the State of California-viz., Alpine, Calaveras, Mono, San Joaquin, Stanislaus and Tuolumne.

For legal titles of parishes and diocesan institutions, consult the Chancery Office.

Chancery Office: 1105 N. Lincoln St., Stockton, CA, 95203. Tel.: 209-466-0636; Fax: 209-941-9722.

STATISTICAL OVERVIEW

Personnel	
Bishop	1
Retired Bishops	1
Priests: Diocesan Active in Diocese	48
Priests: Active Outside Diocese	4
Priests: Retired, Sick or Absent	12
Number of Diocesan Priests	64
Religious Priests in Diocese	12
Extern Priests in Diocese	14
Ordinations:	
Diocesan Priests	2
Transitional Deacons	1
Permanent Deacons in Diocese	33
Total Brothers	4
Total Sisters	64
Parishes	
Parishes	32
With Resident Pastor:	
Resident Diocesan Priests	28
Resident Religious Priests	4
Missions	12
Pastoral Centers	2
Professional Ministry Personnel:	
Brothers	4
Sisters	21
Lay Ministers	27
Welfare	
Catholic Hospitals	3
Total Assisted	647,837
Health Care Centers	1
Total Assisted	2,447
Homes for the Aged	2
Total Assisted	322
Special Centers for Social Services	1
Total Assisted	19,258
Educational	
Diocesan Students in Other Seminaries	9
Total Seminarians	9
High Schools, Diocesan and Parish	2
Total Students	1,484
Elementary Schools, Diocesan and Parish	12
Total Students	3,485
Catechesis/Religious Education:	
High School Students	1,261
Elementary Students	9,514
Total Students Under Catholic Instruction	15,753
Teachers in the Diocese:	
Priests	2
Brothers	2
Sisters	4
Lay Teachers	263
Vital Statistics	
Receptions into the Church:	
Infant Baptism Totals	4,945
Adult Baptism Totals	382
First Communions	4,057
Confirmations	1,984
Marriages:	
Catholic	710
Interfaith	166
Total Marriages	876
Total Catholic Population	205,350
Total Population	1,102,053

Former Bishops—Most Rev. HUGH A. DONOHOE, D.D., ord. June 14, 1930; appt. Titular Bishop of Taium and Auxiliary of San Francisco Aug. 2, 1947; cons. Oct. 7, 1947; appt. to Stockton Feb. 21, 1962; transferred to Fresno Aug. 27, 1969; died Oct. 26, 1987.—Most Rev. MERLIN J. GUILFOYLE, D.D., J.C.D., ord. June 10, 1933; appt. Titular Bishop of Bulla and Auxiliary of San Francisco Aug. 15, 1950; cons. Sept. 21, 1950; translated to Bishop of Stockton Nov. 19, 1969; retired Feb. 26, 1980; died Nov. 20, 1981.—Most Rev. ROGER M. MAHONY, D.D., ord. May 1, 1962; appt. Titular Bishop of Tamascani and Auxiliary of Fresno, Jan. 7, 1975; cons. March 19, 1975; translated Bishop of Stockton Feb. 26, 1980; elevated to Archbishop of Los Angeles July 16, 1985; elevated to Cardinal, June 28, 1991.—Most Rev. DONALD W. MONTROSE, D.D., ord. May 7, 1949; appt. Titular Bishop of Vescovio and Auxiliary of Los Angeles March 25, 1983; cons. May 12, 1983; translated Bishop of Stockton Dec. 19, 1985; installed Feb. 20, 1986; retired Jan. 18, 1999.

Chancery Office—1105 N. Lincoln St., Stockton, 95203. Tel: 209-466-0636; Fax: 209-941-9722.

Vicar General—Rev. Msgr. RICHARD J. RYAN, J.C.D.

Chancellor—Sr. BARBARA THIELLA, S.N.D.deN.

Chief Financial Officer—RICHARD CHAFFEY.

Special Assistant for Administrative Affairs—Rev. ROBERT J. PEREIRA.

Diocesan Tribunal—1105 N. Lincoln St., Stockton, 95203. Tel: 209-466-0636; Fax: 209-941-9722.

Judicial Vicar—Very Rev. JOHN J.M. FOSTER, J.C.L.

Vice-Officialis—Rev. Msgr. RICHARD J. RYAN, J.C.D, V.G.

Judges—Rev. DAVID DEIBEL, J.C.L; Mrs. DEBORAH A. BARTON, J.C.L.; Sr. BEVERLY DUNN, S.P., J.C.D.

Tribunal Personnel—MARY BARTON, Notary.

Defenders of the Bond—Revs. HARMON SKILLIN, J.C.D.; GEORGE F. LACEY.

College of Consultors/Presbyteral Council—Rev. JOHN FALLON, O.S.F.S., Chm.; Rev. Msgr. JOHN ARMISTEAD, Vice Chm.; Revs. LAWRENCE MCGOVERN, Sec. & Treas. PETER CAROTA; EDITHO MASCARDO; MATTHEW O'DONNELL; KHOI PHAM; IVO ROCHA; Rev. Msgr. RICHARD RYAN, J.C.D., V.G.; Rev. HARMON SKILLIN.

Deans—Rev. WILLIAM C. MOORE, Deanery I; Rev. Msgr. JOHN ARMISTEAD, S.T.L., Deanery II; Rev. ALOYS CONRAD GRUBER, Deanery III; Rev. JOHN M. PRUETT, Deanery IV.

The Roman Catholic Welfare Corporation of Stockton—1105 N. Lincoln St., Stockton, 95203. Tel: 209-466-0636; Fax: 209-941-9722.

Diocesan Building Committee—Mr. LEONARD ABBOTT; Mr. RICHARD CHAFFEY; Very Rev. JOHN J.M. FOSTER, J.C.L.; Mr. HARRY MOORE; Revs. WILLIAM MOORE; RICHARD MORSE, O.S.F.S.; IVO ROCHA; Rev. Msgr. RICHARD J. RYAN, J.C.D., V.G.

Diocesan Finance Council—Mr. PAUL SCHAEFER, Chm.; Mr. JOSEPH ARIAS; Mr. RICHARD CHAFFEY; Mr. KEVIN DOUGHERTY; Mr. TOM DRISCOLL; Rev. JOHN P. FALLON, O.S.F.S.; Mr. JOSE LOUIS SOLORIO; Mrs. MARIA STOKMAN.

Personnel Board—Revs. LAWRENCE GUERRERO; JOSEPH ILLO; JOHN PRUETT; HARMON SKILLIN, J.C.D.; LEO SUAREZ; ARMANDO VERGARA; MARK WAGNER.

Diocesan Offices and Directors

Apostleship of the Sea—Deacon HECTOR GARZA, *1105 N. Lincoln St., Stockton, 95203.* Tel: 209-466-0636.

Catholic Charities—Mr. ROBERT ANDERSON, *1106 N. El Dorado, Stockton, 95202.* Tel: 209-948-1501; Fax: 209-948-2559.

Catholic Youth Organization—TOM O'NEILL, Sports Dir., *1105 N. Lincoln St., Stockton, 95203.* Tel: 209-466-0636.

Cemeteries—Rev. Msgr. JAMES E. CAIN, Dir., *1105 N. Lincoln St., Stockton, 95203.* Tel: 209-466-0636.

Censor Librorum—Vacant.

Apostolado Hispano—Mrs. DIGNA RAMIREZ-LOPEZ, Dir., *1125 N. Lincoln St., Stockton, 95203.* Tel: 209-466-0636.

Communications & Development—Mrs. LINDA PHILIPP, Dir.

Newspaper—*"The Catholic Lantern,* PATRICK JOYCE, Editor, *1105 N. Lincoln St., Stockton, 95203.* Tel: 209-466-0636; Fax: 209-941-9722.

Continuing Education of Clergy—Rev. EUGENE TRAINER, *St. Anthony Church, P.O. Box 909, Hughson, 95326-0909.* Tel: 209-883-4310.

Cursillo Movement-English and Spanish—Rev. ARMANDO VERGARA, Dir.

Ecumenism—Vacant.

Office of Religious Education—Sr. GLORIA DEJESUS SANCHEZ, E.F.M.S., Dir., *1125 N. Lincoln St., Stockton, 95203.* Tel: 209-466-0636. Contact this office for various CCD Centers.

Office of Special Education—YVONNE HARROLD, Dir., *1125 N. Lincoln St., Stockton, 95203.* Tel: 209-466-0636. Programs for physically & mentally impaired.

Engaged Encounter—ED MANN; LAURA MANN. Tel: 209-632-3639.

School of Ministry—Sr. DIANE SMITH, Dir., *1125 N. Lincoln St., Stockton, 95203.* Tel: 209-466-0636. JORGE ECHEVERRIA, Hispanic Dir.

Episcopal Liaison of Catholic Charismatic Renewal—WILLIAM BRENNAN, Ph.D., *13 Pardee Ln., Stockton, 95207.* Tel: 209-474-0571.

Liturgical Commission—Mr. DAVID SPRINGER, Chm., *1105 N. Lincoln St., Stockton, 95203.* Tel: 209-466-0636; Fax: 209-941-9722.

Newman Apostolate—The Newman House at University of the Pacific; Rev. DAVID FONTAINE, O.Carm., Dir., *4101 N. Manchester, Stockton, 95207.* Tel: 209-951-0881. Rev. LONACHAN W. AROUJE, *All Saints Newman Community at Stanislaus State University, 4040 McKenna Dr., Turlock, 95382.* Tel: 209-669-0473.

Office of Catechumenate—Mrs. DOTTIE BURDUE, Dir., *1105 North Lincoln St., Stockton, 95203.* Tel: 209-466-0636.

Permanent Diaconate Program—Deacon JOHN RYAN, Dir., *163 W. Eaton Ave., Tracy, 95376.* Tel: 209-835-4560.

Diaconate Formation—Sr. EMILIE SCHENONE, O.P., *1125 N. Lincoln St., Stockton, 95203.* Tel: 209-466-0636.

Pontifical Association of Holy Childhood—Rev. ROBERT J. PEREIRA, *1105 N. Lincoln St., Stockton, 95203.* Tel: 209-466-0636.

Propagation of the Faith—Rev. ROBERT J. PEREIRA, Dir., *1105 N. Lincoln St., Stockton, 95203.* Tel: 209-466-0636.

Respect Life Office—*Community of Caring Program & Natural Family Planning Program*—Mrs. NANCY BONNET, Dir., *1125 N. Lincoln St., Stockton, 95203.* Tel: 209-466-0636.

Vicar for Religious Women—Sr. ANN VENITA BRITTO, F.C., *St. Joseph Convent, 1168 S. Country Club Dr., Stockon, 95204.*

Catholic School Office—Sr. MAUREEN O'BRIEN, F.C., Supt., *1105 N. Lincoln St., Stockton, 95203.* Tel: 209-466-0636; Fax: 209-941-9722.

Child Help - Our Investment - Catholic Education - Scholarship—(CHOICES) A division of the Roman Catholic Welfare Corporation of Stockton; Sr. MARY ANN BISAILLON, D.H.S., Coord., *1105 N. Lincoln St., Stockton, 95203.* Tel: 209-466-0636; Fax: 209-941-9722.

Vocations Director—Rev. JOSEPH P. ILLO, *1105 N. Lincoln St., Stockton, 95203.* Tel: 209-466-0636.

Office for Worship—Very Rev. JOHN J.M. FOSTER, J.C.L., Dir., *1105 N. Lincoln St., Stockton, 95203.*

Office of Youth Ministry—CHRISTIANE ROCELI, English Coord. JOSE LOPEZ CEJA, Spanish Coord., *1125 N. Lincoln St., Stockton, 95203.* Tel: 209-466-0636.

Catholic Committee on Scouting—Ms. JAMIE BURNS, Chm.; Rev. JOHN J.M. FOSTER, J.C.L., Chap., *1105 N. Lincoln St., Stockton, 95203.* Tel: 209-466-0636.

CLERGY, PARISHES, MISSIONS AND PAROCHIAL SCHOOLS

CITY OF STOCKTON
(San Joaquin County)

1—CATHEDRAL OF THE ANNUNCIATION (1955), Revs. Robert J. Silva; Mario Castaneda. In res., Very Rev. John J.M. Foster, J.C.L.
Res., 425 W. Magnolia St., 95203-2412. Tel: 209-463-1305; Fax: 209-463-0807.
School—1110 N. Lincoln St., 95203. Tel: 209-465-0205; Fax: 209-465-1274. Mrs. Carla Donaldson, Prin.
Lay Teachers 14; Students 294.
Catechesis/Religious Programs—Students 385.

2—ST. BERNADETTE (1955), Rev. William C. Moore.
Res., 2544 Plymouth Rd., 95204. Tel: 209-465-3081; Fax: 209-547-1327.
Catechesis/Religious Programs—Tel: 209-465-9547.
Students 157.

3—ST. EDWARD (1967) (Hispanic), Rev. Leo Suarez, Admin.
Res., 731 S. Cardinal Ave., 95215. Tel: 209-466-3020; Fax: 209-466-0719.
Catechesis/Religious Programs—Tel: 209-466-3020.
Students 240.

4—ST. GEORGE (1951), Rev. Msgr. John M. Armistead, V.F.; Revs. Ramon Bejarano; Camilo Garcia; Deacons Jim Janukites; Don Rodgers; Arturo Sanchez; Jesus Aguilar; Kevin Amen; Joe Orzal; Sr. Gladys Guenter, S.H.F., Pastoral Admin.; Sr. Ancila De La O, S.H.F., Pastoral Assoc.
Res., 120 W. Fifth St., 95206-2695. Tel: 209-463-3413; Fax: 209-463-0167.
School—144 W. Fifth St., 95206. Tel: 209-463-1540; Fax: 209-463-2707. Mr. Alan Cook, Prin.
Sisters 1; Lay Teachers 10; Students 236.
St. George REALMS Foundation—.
Catechesis/Religious Programs—Tel: 209-463-7341.
Students 681.
Missions—French Camp, San Joaquin Co., Good Shepherd, P.O. Box 354, French Camp, 95231. Tel: 209-982-0578; Lathrop, San Joaquin Co., Our Lady of Guadalupe, 16019 Cambridge Dr., Lathrop, 95330. Tel: 209-858-4834.

5—ST. GERTRUDE (1913) (Mexican-American), Revs. Alvaro U. Araque; Francisco Campechano; Deacon Hector Garza. In res., Rev. Louis Garcia.
Res., 1663 E. Main St., 95205. Tel: 209-466-0278; Fax: 209-466-1927.
School—1701 E. Main St., 95205. Tel: 209-941-0301; Fax: 209-941-4515. Mrs. Olga Rodriguez, Prin.
Sisters 1; Lay Teachers 9; Students 227.
Catechesis/Religious Programs—Tel: 209-941-0501.
Students 306.

6—ST. LINUS (1965), Rev. Gustavo Quintero V. In res., Rev. Jose Domingo Ruiz.
Res., 2620 S. B St., 95206. Tel: 209-465-1430; Fax: 209-465-0299.
Catechesis/Religious Programs—Students 550.

7—ST. LUKE (1951) (Vietnamese), Revs. Harmon D. Skillin, J.C.D.; Tuan Nguyen, S.D.B. (Vietnam); Francisco Naranjo; Titian A. Miani, (Retired); George F. Lacey, (Retired); Deacon Joseph Artesi; Ms. Victoria Kimball, Parish Admin.
Res., 3847 N. Sutter St., 95204. Tel: 209-948-3450; Fax: 209-948-2841.
School—4005 N. Sutter St., 95204. Tel: 209-464-0801; Fax: 209-466-1150. Mr. Patrick O'Neill, Prin.
Lay Teachers 12; Students 306.
Catechesis/Religious Programs—Tel: 209-462-0410.
Students 306.
Convent—230 E. Atlee St., 95204. Tel: 209-463-6533.

8—ST. MARY OF THE ASSUMPTION (1851), Revs. Editho Mascardo, Admin.; Jairo H. Ramirez; Deacon Julian Sepulveda. In res., Rev. Paul Manzano.
Res., 203 E. Washington St., 95202. Tel: 209-948-0661; Fax: 209-948-0673.
Catechesis/Religious Programs—Tel: 209-946-9536.
Students 217.

9—ST. MICHAEL (1921) (Italian), Rev. J. Patrick Walker. In res., Rev. Msgr. Richard Ryan; Deacon Allen Moznett.
Res., 5882 N. Ashley Ln., 95215-9308. Tel: 209-931-0639; Fax: 209-931-3621.
Catechesis/Religious Programs—Tel: 209-931-2696.
Students 246.

10—PRESENTATION OF B.V.M. (1952), Revs. Lawrence McGovern, S.T.L.; Pablito Arcaba.
Res., 6715 Leesburg Pl., 95207. Tel: 209-472-2150; Fax: 209-472-0541.
Ministry Center—.
School—1635 W. Benjamin Holt Dr., 95207. Tel: 209-472-2140. Mrs. Linda Boragno-Dopp, Prin.
Lay Teachers 16; Students 296.
Catechesis/Religious Programs—Students 871.

OUTSIDE CITY OF STOCKTON

Angels Camp, Calaveras Co., St. Patrick (1856) (Italian), Rev. Henry P. Johnston; Deacon Adam Pietras.
Res., P.O. Box 576, 95222. Tel: 209-736-4575; Fax: 209-736-2217. [CEM][JC]
Catechesis/Religious Programs—820 S. Main, 95222. Tel: 209-736-4458.
Students 110.
Missions—Murphys, Murphys Co., St. Patrick, 619 Sheepranch Rd., Murphys, 95247. Tel: 209-728-2854; Arnold, Arnold Co., Our Lady of the Sierra, 1301 Linebaugh Rd., Arnold, 95223. Tel: 209-795-7625.

Ceres, Stanislaus Co., St. Jude (1962) (Hispanic), Revs. Octavio Escobar; Peter Carota.
Res., 3824 Mitchell Rd., 95307-9422. Tel: 209-537-0516; Fax: 209-537-3412. [CEM]
Catechesis/Religious Programs—Tel: 209-537-7439.
Students 1,100.

Hughson, Stanislaus Co., St. Anthony (1921) (Hispanic), Revs. Ernesto Arbelaez, S.J., Admin.; Eugene Trainer; Deacon Raymond Flanders.
Mailing Address: P.O. Box 909, 95256. Tel: 209-883-4310; Fax: 209-883-2531.
Res., 2020 Euclid Rd., 95256.
Catechesis/Religious Programs—Tel: 209-883-2280.
Students 450.
Mission—La Grange, Stanislaus Co., St. Louis, Floto St., La Grange, 95329. [CEM]

Linden, San Joaquin Co., Holy Cross (1963) (Italian-Hispanic), Rev. Armando Vergara (Colombia).
Res., 18633 E. Front St., P.O. Box 52, 95236. Tel: 209-887-3341.
Catechesis/Religious Programs—Tel: 209-887-2263.
Students 173.

Lockeford, San Joaquin Co., St. Joachim (1882) (Hispanic), Revs. Enda J. Maguire; Jose Domingo Ruiz, Spanish Min.; Deacon Bill Warren.
Mailing Address: P.O. Box 232, 95237. Tel: 209-727-3912. [CEM]
Catechesis/Religious Programs—Tel: 209-334-0743.
Students 75.

Lodi, San Joaquin Co., St. Anne (1904), Revs. Thomas P. Hayes; Murty M. Fahy, O.S.F.S.; Matthew O'Donnell; Jose E. Jaramillo, M.G. (Mexico); Deacons Juan Mendez; Porfirio Cisneros; Don Bo; Karl Welsbacher.
Mailing Address: P.O. Box 480, 95241. Tel: 209-369-1907; Fax: 209-369-1971.
Office: 215 W. Walnut St., 95240.
Res., 150 S. Pleasant St., 95241. [CEM]
School—200 S. Pleasant St., 95241. Tel: 209-333-7580. Mr. Dennis Taricco, Prin.
Lay Teachers 12; Students 287.
Catechesis/Religious Programs—D.R.E.: Sr. Francine M. Zamaudio, E.F.M.S.; Sr. Luz del Carmen, O.F.M.S.
Students 530.
Mission—Thornton, San Joaquin Co., Mater Ecclesiae, 26500 Sacramento Blvd., 95241.

Mammoth Lakes, Mono Co., St. Joseph (1939), Rev. Andrew C. Dachauer, S.J.; Bro. Daniel C. Corona, S.J.; Deacon Eliseo Gutierrez.
Res., P.O. Box 372, 93546. Tel: 760-934-6276; Fax: 760-934-6276.
Missions—Bridgeport, Mono Co., Infant of Prague, Hwy. 395, Bridgeport, 93517.; Lee Vining, Mono Co., Our Savior of the Mountains, 2nd & Mono, Lee Vining, 93541.; Walker, Mono Co., Our Lady of the Valley, Walker Community Center, Walker, 96107.
Catechesis/Religious Programs—Students 122.

Manteca, San Joaquin Co., St. Anthony (1917), Revs. Richard E. Morse, O.S.F.S.; Alexandre Pacheco; Gilberto Arango; Deacons Alfredo Maestas; Jim Kottinger; Harvey Parolari; Jeff Vierra. In res., Rev. Theodore Lambert.
Res., 525 E. North St., 95336. Tel: 209-823-7197; Fax: 209-823-5238.
School—Tel: 209-823-4513; Fax: 209-825-7447. Dr. John Black, Prin.
Lay Teachers 13; Students 248.
Catechesis/Religious Programs—Tel: 209-239-7848.
Students 984.
St. Vincent de Paul Society—Tel: 209-823-8099.
St. Anthony School Educational Foundation—Tel: 209-239-4513.

Modesto, Stanislaus Co., St. Joseph (1967), Revs. Joseph Illo; V. A. Jesudasan; Joseph P. O'Hare, (Retired).
Res., 1813 Oakdale Rd., 95355. Tel: 209-551-4973; Fax: 209-551-3213.
Catechesis/Religious Programs—Tel: 209-551-0593.
Students 810.

Our Lady of Fatima (1951), Revs. John M. Pruett, V.F.; Dean McFalls; Hung Nguyen.
Res., 505 W. Granger Ave., 95350. Tel: 209-524-7421; Fax: 209-524-7713.
School—501 W. Granger Ave., 95350. Tel: 209-524-4170; Fax: 209-524-3960. Linda Partlow, Prin.
Lay Teachers 14; Students 285; Extended Day Care 100.
Catechesis/Religious Programs—Tel: 209-529-0843.
Students 1,000.
The Monsignor William P. Kennedy Education Foundation—.

St. Stanislaus (1881), Revs. Bill McDonald; Eduardo Perez (Colombia); Edmundante Dammay (Philippines).
Res., 709 J St., P.O. Box 292, 95353. Tel: 209-524-4381; Fax: 209-524-1910.
School—1416 Maze Blvd., 95351. Tel: 209-524-9036; Fax: 209-524-4344. Mrs. Cindy Murray, Prin.
Lay Teachers 12; Students 313.
Catechesis/Religious Programs—Tel: 209-522-6534; Fax: 209-523-9128.
Students 862.

Newman, Stanislaus Co., St. Joachim (1909), Rev. Lawrence M. Guerrero.
Res., 1121 Main St., 95360. Tel: 209-862-3528; Fax: 209-862-3528.
Catechesis/Religious Programs—Tel: 209-862-2878.
Students 255.

Oakdale, Stanislaus Co., St. Mary of the Annunciation (1902), Revs. Aloys Conrad Gruber, V.F., Pastor; Bernard J. Mannion, Pastor Emeritus; Deacon Roberto Magdaleno.
Res., 1225 Olive Ave., 95361. Tel: 209-847-2715; Fax: 209-847-7348.
Catechesis/Religious Programs—Tel: 209-847-3498.
Students 220.

Patterson, Stanislaus Co., Sacred Heart (1917), Revs. James Osendorf, C.M.; Minh J. Pham, C.M.; Deacon Arnold Hernandez.
Res., 529 I St., 95363. Tel: 209-892-9321; Fax: 209-892-2102.
School—505 M St., 95363. Tel: 209-892-3544; Fax: 209-892-3544. Marian De Groot, Prin.
Lay Teachers 13; Students 245.
Catechesis/Religious Programs—Tel: 209-892-6381.
Students 336.
Mission—Crows Landing, Stanislaus Co., Immaculate Heart of Mary, H St., Crows Landing, 95313.
Station—Westley, Guadalupe Center, Tel: 209-894-5404.

Ripon, San Joaquin Co., St. Patrick (1878), Rev. Mark Wagner, Admin.
Res., 19399 E St., Rte. 120 Hwy., 95366. Tel: 209-838-2133; Fax: 209-838-1077.
Catechesis/Religious Programs—Tel: 209-838-3101.
Students 406.

Riverbank, Stanislaus Co., St. Frances of Rome (1953), Revs. Thomas M. Rajanayagam (Sri Lanka); Alvaro Lopez (Colombia); Deacon Felipe Vallejo.
Res., 2827 Topeka St., 95367. Tel: 209-869-2996; Fax: 209-863-1004.
Catechesis/Religious Programs—Tel: 209-869-5830.
Students 515.

San Andreas, Calaveras Co., St. Andrew (1963) (Caucasian), Rev. Michael E. Kelly.
Res., 162 Church Hill Rd., P.O. Box 550, 95249. Tel: 209-754-3815; Fax: 209-754-5611. [CEM]
Catechesis/Religious Programs—Tel: 209-754-3714.
Students 149.
Missions—Mokelumne Hill, Calaveras Co., St. Thomas Aquinas, 8398 Lafayette St., Mokelumne Hill, 95245.; West Point, Calaveras Co., Our Lady of Fatima, 22581 Hwy. 26, West Point, 95255.

Sonora, Tuolumne Co., St. Patrick (1851), Revs. William Kraft; John Foley, O.S.F.S.; Sr. Anne Burgard, S.N.J.M., Pastoral Assoc.
Res., 116 W. Bradford Ave., 95370. Tel: 209-532-7139; Fax: 209-532-4389. [CEM 5][JC]
Catechesis/Religious Programs—Students 235.
Missions—Big Oak Flat, Tuolumne Co., Our Lady of Mt. Carmel, Cemetery Rd., Big Oak Flat, 95321. Tel: 209-962-2156; Columbia, Tuolumne Co., St. Anne, 22518 Church Ln., Columbia, 95310.

Tracy, San Joaquin Co., St. Bernard's (1908), Revs. Ivo D. Rocha; Jose Juan Serna; Deacons John Ryan; Ray Whitlock.
Res., 163 W. Eaton Ave., 95376. Tel: 209-835-4560, Ext. 110; Fax: 209-835-4588.
School—165 W. Eaton Ave., 95376. Tel: 209-835-4560, Ext. 130. Mrs. Diane Rothschild, Prin.
Sisters 1; Lay Teachers 12; Students 315.
Catechesis/Religious Programs—Tel: 209-835-4560, Ext. 116.
Students 828.
Convent—165 W. Eaton Ave., 95376. Tel: 209-835-7391. Daughters of the Cross

Turlock, Stanislaus Co., Sacred Heart (1910), Revs. Francis Prendergast; Sigifredo Misael Avila; Khoi Pham.
Res., 1301 Cooper Ave., 95380. Tel: 209-634-8578; 8579; Fax: 209-634-7124.
School—1225 Cooper Ave., 95380. Tel: 209-634-7787; Fax: 209-634-0156. Mrs. Donna Noceti, Prin.
Lay Teachers 13; Students 282.
Preschool—Tel: 209-667-5512; Fax: 209-664-9428. Debra Cannella, Prin.
Lay Teachers 11; Students 88.
Catechesis/Religious Programs—Sacred Heart Religious Education, 1250 Cooper #1, 95380. Tel: 209-634-5111.
Students 1,357.
Convent—674 Oak, 95380. Tel: 209-634-7708.

Our Lady of the Assumption of the Portuguese (1973) (Portuguese), Rev. Manuel F. Sousa.
Mailing Address: P.O. Box 2030, 95381. Fax: 209-634-2360.
Res., 1343 W. Greenway, 95380. Tel: 209-634-2222; 634-3140; Fax: 209-634-2366.
Catechesis/Religious Programs—Tel: 209-634-7644. Connie Madruga, D.R.E.
Students 344.

Twain Harte, Tuolumne Co., All Saints (1962), Rev. John Fitzgerald, Admin.; Deacon Edward Zoma.
Res., 18674 Cherokee Dr., P.O. Box 642, 95383. Tel: 209-586-3161. [JC]
Catechesis/Religious Programs—Students 91.
Mission—Tuolumne, Tuolumne Co., St. Joseph, Gardner St., Tuolumne, 95379.
Stations—Pinecrest. (Summer).; Strawberry. (Winter).

Chaplains of Public Institutions

STOCKTON. *DeWitt Nelson Training Center* 7650 Newcastle Rd., P.O. Box 213003, 95213-9003. Tel: 209-944-6187. Rev. Paul Manzano, Chap.
Karl Holton School 7650 Newcastle Rd., P.O. Box 213002, 95213-9002. Tel: 209-944-6364. Rev. Theodore Lambert, Chap.
Northern California Women's Facility 7150 Arch Rd., P.O. Box 213006, 95213-9006. Tel: 209-943-1600, Ext. 7053. Rev. Randall Rainwater, Chap.
O.H. Close School 7650 Newcastle Rd., P.O. Box 213001, 95213-9001. Tel: 209-944-6135; 944-6349. Rev. Paul Manzano, Chap.
Stockton Developmental Center. Vacant. 510 E. Magnolia St., 95202-3288. Tel: 209-948-7111.

FRENCH CAMP. *San Joaquin County Jail*. Vacant. 999 W. Matthews Rd., 95231. Tel: 209-468-4562.
San Joaquin General Hospital. St. George Church 500 W. Hospital Rd., 95231. Tel: 209-468-6000.

JAMESTOWN. *Sierra Conservation Center*. Mailing Address: P.O. Box 497, 95327-1213. Tel: 209-984-5291. Rev. Ray Abella, O.S.F.S., Chap.

TRACY. *Deuel Vocational Institution*. Vacant. Mailing Address: P.O. Box 400, 95376-3593. Tel: 209-466-8055.

On Special or Other Diocesan Assignment:
Reverend Fathers—
Leslie, Larry B., Lt., U.S.N.R., U.S.M.C.-MWTC, Bridgeport, CA 93517
Pereira, Robert J., Special Asst. for Admin. Affairs

Absent on Leave:
Reverend Fathers—
Pintacura, Michael

Retired:
Reverend Monsignors—
Cain, James E., 1105 N. Lincoln St., Stockton, CA 95203
Doyle, Walter H., Pastor Emeritus, Mailing Address: P.O. Box 1618, Diamond Springs, CA 95619
Kennedy, William P., Pastor Emeritus, Our Lady of Fatima Church, 1635 Sherwood Ave., Modesto, CA 95350-4299
Reverend Fathers—
Coghlan, John A., Pastor Emeritus, 1152 De Haro, San Francisco, CA 94107
Donohoe, Edward, 5835 Cherokee Rd., #69, Stockton, CA 95215
Ford, William A., St. Mary Star of the Sea, 888 Blvd. of the Arts, #1508, Sarasota, FL 34236
Hughes, William C., Casa Manana, 3700 N. Sutter St., #272, Stockton, CA 95204
Lacey, George F., Pastor Emeritus, 3700 N. Sutter St., Stockton, CA 95204
McCaffrey, James Leo, 27 Miramonte Dr., Moraga, CA 94556
Miani, Titian A., Casa Manana, 3700 N. Sutter St., #207, Stockton, CA 95204
O'Dwyer, James, Pastor Emeritus, Casa Santa Fe, 24 Dillon St., Clonmel, Tipperary, Rep. of Ireland

Permanent Deacons:
Aguilar, Jesus, St. George, Stockton
Amen, Kevin, St. George, Stockton
Artesi, Joseph, St. Luke's, Stockton
Bo, Donald, St. Anne, Lodi
Brennan, William, Newman VOP, Stockton
Broderick, Thomas, School of Ministry, Stockton
Cisneros, Porfirio, St. Anne, Lodi
Flanders, Raymond, St. Anthony, Hughson
Garza, Hector, St. Edward, Stockton
Griego, Nick, St. Patrick, Sonora
Gumerlock, Francis, Our Lady of Fatima, Modesto
Hernandez, Arnold, Sacred Heart, Patterson
Janukites, James, St. George, Stockton
Kottinger, Jim, St. Anthony, Manteca
Maestas, Alfredo, St. Anthony, Manteca
Magdaleno, Roberto, St. Mary, Oakdale
Mendez, Juan, St. Anne, Lodi
Moznett, Al, St. Michael, Stockton
Orzal, Joe, St. George, Stockton
Parolari, Harvey, St. Anthony, Manteca
Pietras, Adam, St. Patrick, Angel's Camp
Rodgers, Donald, Good Shepherd, French Camp
Ryan, John G., St. Bernard, Tracy
Sanchez, Arturo, Our Lady of Guadalupe, Lathrop
Schepcoff, Jacques, Annunciation, Stockton
Sepulveda, Julian R., St. Mary of the Assumption, Stockton
Tansaeng, Haet, St. Luke, Stockton
Torres, Jorge, St. Gertrude, Stockton
Vallejo, Felipe, St. Frances of Rome, Riverbank
Vierra, Jeffrey, St. Anthony, Manteca
Warren, William E., St. Joachim, Lockeford
Welsbacher, Karl, St. Anne, Lodi
Whitlock, Ray, St. Bernard, Tracy
Zoma, Edward T., St. Patrick, Sonora

INSTITUTIONS LOCATED IN THE DIOCESE

[A] HIGH SCHOOLS, DIOCESAN

STOCKTON. *St. Mary's High School*, 5648 N. El Dorado St., P.O. Box 7247, 95267-0247. Tel: 209-957-3340; Fax: 209-957-0861.
E-mail: stmarysstock@impresso.com
Web site: www.stmaryshighschool.org
Non-resident students. Rev. John P. Fallon, O.S.F.S., Pres.; Mr. Peter Morelli, Prin.; Revs. John A. Lindsay, O.S.F.S.; Clark T. Kelley, O.S.F.S.; Bros. James Dorazio, O.S.F.S.; Neil McMenamin, O.S.F.S. Priests 3; Brothers 2; Sisters 1; Lay Teachers 64; Students 1023.
St. Mary's High School Foundation. Tel: 209-957-3340; Fax: 209-957-0861.

MODESTO. *Central Catholic High School*, 200 S. Carpenter Rd., 95351. Tel: 209-524-9611; Fax: 209-524-4913.
E-mail: ccadmin@cchigh.nschool.com
Web site: www.cchs_ca.org
Non-resident students. Mr. Jim Pecchenino, Pres.
Lay Teachers 28; Administrators 5; Students 465.
Central Catholic High School Foundation. Tel: 209-524-6818; 524-9611; Fax: 209-524-4913.

[B] CATHOLIC CHARITIES

STOCKTON. *The Catholic Charities of the Diocese of Stockton*, 1106 N. El Dorado St., 95202. Tel: 209-948-1501; Fax: 209-948-2559.
E-mail: BOBCATHOLICCHARITY@msn.com
Robert Anderson, Exec. Dir.; Mr. Bill Habeeb, Chm. Corp. Bd.
The following services and programs are listed according to counties:
SAN JOAQUIN COUNTY:
Friendly Visiting, 1106 N. El Dorado St., 95202. Tel: 209-948-1501; Fax: 209-948-2559. Juliana Homan, Prog. Dir. Friendly Visitors 25; Clients Served 45.
Homemaker-Personal Care, 1106 N. El Dorado, 95202. Tel: 209-948-1582; Fax: 209-948-2559. Juliana Homan, Prog. Mgr. Homemakers 35; Clients Served 355. (See separate listing for Modesto).
Respite Care Program, 1106 N. El Dorado, 95202. Tel: 209-948-1582; Fax: 209-948-2559. Julie Homan, Prog. Mgr. Respite Workers 15; Clients Served 119.

Making the Right Connections, 1106 N. El Dorado, 95202. Tel: 209-948-1501; Fax: 209-948-2559. Gladys Guenther, Prog. Dir. Students per year 1100.

Home Security & Repairs, 1106 N. El Dorado, 95202. Tel: 209-948-1582; Fax: 209-948-2559. Juliana Homan, Prog. Mgr. Part-time Repairman; Seniors Served 200.

Counseling Services, 1106 N. El Dorado, 95202. Tel: 209-948-1501; Fax: 209-948-2559. Marge M. Verner, Dir.

Emergency Food Distribution, 1106 N. El Dorado, 95202. Tel: 209-466-4210; Fax: 209-948-2559. Allen Nesset, Coord. Clients Served 850 per month.

STANISLAUS COUNTY:

Homemaker Program (Modesto), 400 12th St., Modesto, 95354. Tel: 209-529-3784; Fax: 209-529-6083. Jane Weinheimer, Prog. Dir. Homemakers 11; Clients 260.

Long Term Care Ombudsman Program, 400 12th St., Ste. 4, Modesto, 95354. Tel: 209-529-3784; Fax: 209-529-6083. Jane Weinheimer, Prog. Dir. Ombudsman 18; Facilities Monitored 257; Clients served 6,000.

Senior Transportation, 400 12th St., Ste. 4, Modesto, 95354. Tel: 209-529-3784; Fax: 209-529-6083. Jane Weinheimer, Prog. Dir. Part-time Staff 1; Seniors Served 120.

Elder Abuse Program, 400 12th St., Ste. 4, Modesto, 95354. Tel: 209-529-3784; Fax: 209-529-6083. Jane Weinheimer, Prog. Dir. Community-wide education.

Eldercare Management, 400 12th St., Ste. 4, Modesto, 95354. Tel: 209-529-3784; Fax: 209-529-6083. Jane Weinheimer, Prog. Dir. Part-time Staff 2; Seniors Served 125.

Laura's House, 400 12th St., Ste. 4, Modesto, 95354. Tel: 209-523-0393; Fax: 209-523-7536. Residential substance abuse program. Deanna Morris, Prog. Dir. Full-time Staff 4; Part-time Staff 13; Maximum Occupancy 45.

Samaritan House, 219 S. Broadway, Turlock, 95380. Tel: 209-669-9355; Fax: 209-669-9580. Residential Homeless at Risk Program. Kathleen Paxton, Prog. Dir. Full-time Staff 8; Part-time Staff 7; Maximum Occupancy 39.

MOTHER LODE:

Long Term Care Ombudsman Program, 14855 Mono Way, Ste. 105, Sonora, 95370. Tel: 209-532-7632; Fax: 209-532-8448. Vikki Morehead, Dir. Senior Svcs. Ombudsmen 12; Facilities Monitored 14; Clients Served 650.

Legal Advocacy Program, 14844 Mono Way, Ste. 105, Sonora, 95370. Tel: 209-532-8689; Fax: 209-532-7689. Part-time Staff 1; Legal Advisor 1; Clients Served 100.

[C] GENERAL HOSPITALS

STOCKTON. *Catholic Healthcare West System San Joaquin-Sierra Region*, 1800 N. California St., P.O. Box 213008, 95213-9008. Tel: 209-943-2000; Fax: 209-461-5199.
Web site: www.chwanjoaquin.com
For a complete listing, refer to the Hospitals section.

St. Joseph's Behavioral Health Center, 2510 N. California St., 95204. Tel: 209-948-2100; Fax: 209-464-2270.
Web site: www.stjosephscanhelp.org
For a complete listing, refer to the Hospitals section.

St. Joseph's Medical Center of Stockton, 1800 N. California St., P.O. Box 213008, 95213-9008. Tel: 209-943-2000; Fax: 209-461-3299.
Web site: www.stjosephscares.org
For a complete listing, refer to the Hospitals section.

MANTECA. *St. Dominic's Hospital*, 1777 W. Yosemite Ave., P.O. Box 1307, 95337. Tel: 209-825-3500; Fax: 209-825-3524.
Web site: www.chw.edu/manteca
For a complete listing, refer to the Hospitals section.

[D] HOMES FOR AGED

STOCKTON. *Casa Manana Inn*, 3700 N. Sutter St., 95204. Tel: 209-466-4046
For a complete listing, refer to the Special Care Facilities section.

Garden Oaks, 3334 Wagner Heights Rd., 95209. Tel: 209-956-3401; Fax: 209-956-3494.
E-mail: info@oconnorwoods.org
For a complete listing, refer to the Special Care Facilities section.

St. Joseph's Regional Housing Corp., 1805 N. California St., Ste. 407, 95204. Tel: 209-467-6312; Fax: 209-952-6201.
E-mail: info@oconnorwoods.org
For a complete listing, refer to the Special Care Facilities section.

[E] CONVENTS AND RESIDENCES FOR SISTERS

STOCKTON. *Daughters of the Holy Spirit*, St. Gertrude Convent, 1655 E. Main St., 95205. Tel: 209-462-8850. Sisters 3.

Dominican Sisters of San Rafael, California, St. Joseph's Convent, 407-409 E. Walnut St., 95204. Tel: 209-462-8486; 209-465-3780. Sisters 9.

Eucharistic Franciscan Missionary Sisters, Blessed Sacrament Convent, 1205 N. San Joaquin St., 95202. Tel: 209-462-3906; Fax: 209-469-3759. Sisters 7.

Holy Cross Sisters, Casita Esperanza, P.O. Box 9, 95201. Tel: 209-467-8042.

Holy Family Sisters, 4900 N. Hwy. 99, #146, 95212. Tel: 209-931-2949.
E-mail: gladysshf@aol.com
16019 Cambridge Dr., Lathrop, 95330. Tel: 209-858-4834; Fax: 209-858-4834.

Maryknoll Sisters, 25 S. Commerce St., No. 237, 95202. Tel: 209-462-9394.

Sacro Costato Missionary Sisters, St. Luke's Convent, 230 E. Atlee St., 95204. Tel: 209-462-6533; Fax: 209-464-5342.
E-mail: sacroc2000@aol.com
Sisters 4.

Sisters of Charity of the Blessed Virgin Mary, Presentation Convent, 6830 Leesburg Pl., 95207. Tel: 209-951-5373. Sisters 3.

Sisters of St. Joseph of Carondelet, 1639 W. Swain, 95207. Tel: 209-957-7090.

MODESTO. *Sisters of the Cross of the Sacred Heart of Jesus.* Cloistered Convent. 1320 Maze Blvd., 95351. Tel: 209-526-3525; Fax: 209-526-3525.
E-mail: rcscjmodesto@hotmail.com
Sisters 7; Novices 4.

PATTERSON. *Daughters of the Holy Spirit.* Sacred Heart Convent. 503 M St., 95363. Tel: 209-892-3410.
E-mail: samdhs@juno.com
Sisters 3.

TRACY. *The Daughters of the Cross*, St. Bernard Convent, 165 W. Eaton Ave., 95376. Tel: 209-835-7391; Fax: 209-830-6137.
E-mail: fc1833@inreach.com
Sisters 6.

TURLOCK. *Sisters of the Sacred Hearts of Jesus and Mary.* Sacred Heart Convent, 674 Oak St., 95380. Tel: 209-634-7708; Fax: 209-634-7124.

[F] RETREAT CENTERS

COPPEROPOLIS. *Madonna of Peace Renewal Center.* (Youth Facility), 2010 Hunt Rd., P.O. Box 71, 95228. Tel: 209-785-2157 (Office). Total in Residence 2; Total Staff 2.

[G] MISCELLANEOUS

STOCKTON. *The Bishop's Educational Foundation, Diocese of Stockton*, 1105 N. Lincoln St., 95203. Tel: 209-466-0636; Fax: 209-941-9722.

Instituto Fe y Vida, 1737 W. Benjamin Holt Dr., 95207. Tel: 209-951-3483; Fax: 209-478-5357.
E-mail: feyvida@altavista.net
Total Staff 6.

St. Mary's High School Foundation, Box 7247, 95267-0247. Tel: 209-957-3340; Fax: 209-957-0861.
E-mail: stmarysstock@impresso.com

San Lorenzo Ruiz De Manila (1988), Filipino Plaza, 6 West Main St., Ste. 1, 95202. Tel: 209-464-8572; Fax: 209-546-0191.
E-mail: rubanusa@aol.com
Web site: www.rubanusa.com

LODI. *St. Anne's Endowment*, 215 W. Walnut St., 95240. Tel: 209-369-1907; Fax: 209-369-1971.

MANTECA. *St. Vincent de Paul Society*, 525 E. North St., 95336. Tel: 209-823-8099. Mailing Address: P.O. Box 1644, 95336. Total Staff 25; Total Assisted 13,000.

MODESTO. *Central Catholic High School Foundation*, 200 Carpenter Rd., 95351. Tel: 209-524-6822; Fax: 209-524-5646. Volunteer Board Members 25.

Father John C. Silva Education Foundation, P.O. Box 292, 95353. Tel: 209-524-4381; Fax: 209-524-1910.

The Monsignor William P. Kennedy Education Foundation, 501 W. Granger Ave., 95350. Tel: 209-524-4170; Fax: 209-524-7713.

TURLOCK. *The McElligott Sacred Heart School Foundation*, 1301 Cooper Ave., 95380-4113. Tel: 209-634-8578; Fax: 209-634-7124.
E-mail: sheartch@inreach.com
Rev. Francis Prendergast, Dir. Total Staff 26; Total Students 282.

RELIGIOUS INSTITUTES OF MEN REPRESENTED IN THE DIOCESE

For further details refer to the corresponding bracketed number in the Religious Institutes of Men or Women section.

[0270]—*Carmelite Fathers and Brothers.*—O.Carm.
[0690]—*Jesuit Fathers and Brothers.* (California, Columbia Prov.).—S.J.
[0910]—*Oblates of Mary Immaculate.*—O.M.I.
[0920]—*Oblates of St. Francis De Sales.* (Toledo-Detroit Prov.).—O.S.F.S.
[1190]—*Salesians of St. John Bosco.*—S.D.B.
[]—*Vincentian Fathers.*

RELIGIOUS INSTITUTES OF WOMEN REPRESENTED IN THE DIOCESE

[1920]—*Congregation of the Sisters of the Holy Cross.* (Notre Dame, IN).—C.S.C.
[]—*Daughters of the Cross.*
[0780]—*Daughters of the Cross of Liege.*—F.C.
[0820]—*Daughters of the Holy Spirit.* (Putnam, CT).—D.H.S.
[1070-04]—*Dominican Sisters.* (San Rafael).—O.P.
[1150]—*Eucharistic Franciscan Missionary Sisters.*—E.F.M.S.
[2470]—*Maryknoll Sisters of St. Dominic.*—M.M.
[]—*Missionary Sisters of the Sacred Side of Jesus and the Sorrowful Mother.* (Italy).—M.S.C.
[0430]—*Sisters of Charity of the Blessed Virgin Mary.* (Dubuque, IA).—B.V.M.
[3000]—*Sisters of Notre Dame de Namur.*—S.N.D.deN.
[3840]—*Sisters of St. Joseph of Carondelet.*—C.S.J.
[]—*Sisters of the Cross of the Sacred Heart of Jesus.* (Tijuana, Mexico).—R.C.S.C.J.
[1960]—*Sisters of the Holy Family.* (San Francisco).—S.H.F.
[3680]—*Sisters of the Sacred Hearts of Jesus and Mary.*—S.H.J.M.
[]—*Sisters of the Word of God.*
[4070]—*Society of the Sacred Heart.*—R.S.C.J.

DIOCESAN CEMETERIES AND MAUSOLEUMS

STOCKTON. *San Joaquin Cemetery and Mausoleum.* Mr. Al Vigil, Supt.

ESCALON. *St. John Cemetery.* Cynthia A. Rodriguez, Office Mgr.

MODESTO. *St. Stanislaus Cemetery and Chapel Crypts.* Gretchen Storm, Office Mgr.

NECROLOGY

† Sweeny, Louis L., Newman, CA St. Joachim. —Died Feb. 8, 2000.

Diocese of Superior

(Dioecesis Superiorensis)

Most Reverend

RAPHAEL M. FLISS, D.D.

Bishop of Superior; ordained May 26, 1956; appointed Coadjutor Bishop of Superior with right of succession November 6, 1979; ordained December 20, 1979; succeeded to See, June 27, 1985. *Res., Gitchinadji Dr., Superior, WI, 54880. Office: 1201 Hughitt Ave., Superior, WI, 54880. Mailing Address: Box 969, Superior, WI, 54880.*

ESTABLISHED MAY 3, 1905.

Square Miles 15,715.

Comprises the Counties of Ashland, Barron, Bayfield, Burnett, Douglas, Iron, Lincoln, Oneida, Polk, Price, Rusk, Sawyer, St. Croix, Taylor, Vilas and Washburn in the State of Wisconsin.

Incorporated under the laws of the State of Wisconsin as the *Diocese of Superior.*

For legal titles of parishes and diocesan institutions, consult the Chancery.

Chancery Office: 1201 Hughitt Ave., Box 969, Superior, WI, 54880. Tel.: 715-392-2937; Fax: 715-392-2015.

STATISTICAL OVERVIEW

Personnel	
Bishop	1
Priests: Diocesan Active in Diocese	47
Priests: Active Outside Diocese	1
Priests: Retired, Sick or Absent	28
Number of Diocesan Priests	76
Religious Priests in Diocese	15
Extern Priests in Diocese	1
Ordinations:	
Diocesan Priests	1
Permanent Deacons	2
Permanent Deacons in Diocese	48
Total Brothers	1
Total Sisters	111
Parishes	
Parishes	114
With Resident Pastor:	
Resident Diocesan Priests	44
Resident Religious Priests	8
Without Resident Pastor:	
Administered by Priests	57
Administered by Women Religious	1
Administered by Lay People	4
Pastoral Centers	1
Professional Ministry Personnel:	
Sisters	11
Lay Ministers	31
Welfare	
Catholic Hospitals	5
Total Assisted	137,752
Day Care and Extended Day Care Centers	2
Total Assisted	260
Special Centers for Social Services	2
Total Assisted	380
Residential Care of Disabled	16
Total Assisted	110
Other Institutions	14
Total Assisted	2,063
Educational	
Diocesan Students in Other Seminaries	4
Total Seminarians	4
Elementary Schools, Diocesan and Parish	17
Total Students	2,879
Catechesis/Religious Education:	
High School Students	3,125
Elementary Students	7,114
Total Students Under Catholic Instruction	13,122
Teachers in the Diocese:	
Brothers	1
Sisters	7
Lay Teachers	172
Vital Statistics	
Receptions into the Church:	
Infant Baptism Totals	990
Adult Baptism Totals	286
First Communions	1,329
Confirmations	1,006
Marriages:	
Catholic	259
Interfaith	238
Total Marriages	497
Deaths	1,195
Total Catholic Population	88,715
Total Population	401,631

Former Bishops—Rt. Rev. AUGUSTIN FRANCIS SCHINNER, D.D., ord. March 7, 1886; cons. July 25, 1905; resigned Jan. 15, 1913; appt. Bishop of Spokane, WA, March 18, 1914; died Feb. 7, 1937.—Rt. Rev. JOSEPH M. KOUDELKA, D.D., ord. Oct. 8, 1875; cons. Auxiliary Bishop of Cleveland and Titular Bishop of Germanicopolis, Feb. 25, 1908; transferred to Milwaukee as Auxiliary Bishop, Sept. 4, 1911; appt. to the See of Superior, Aug. 6, 1913; died June 24, 1921.—Rt. Rev. JOSEPH G. PINTEN, D.D., ord. Nov. 1, 1890 elected Dec. 3, 1921; cons. May 3, 1922; transferred to the See of Grand Rapids, June 25, 1926; retired Nov. 1, 1940; died Nov. 6, 1945.—Most Rev. THEODORE H. REVERMAN, D.D., ord. July 26, 1901; cons. Nov. 30, 1926; died July 18, 1941.—Most Rev. WILLIAM PATRICK O'CONNOR, D.D., Ph.D., ord. March 10, 1912; cons. March 7, 1942; transferred to the See of Madison, Jan. 15, 1946.—His Eminence ALBERT GREGORY MEYER, D.D., S.S.L., ord. July 11, 1926; appt. Feb. 18, 1946; cons. April 11, 1946; promoted to Archbishop of Milwaukee, July 21, 1953; transferred to Archbishop of Chicago, Sept. 19, 1958; created Cardinal, Dec. 14, 1959; died April 9, 1965.—Most Rev. JOSEPH JOHN ANNABRING, D.D., ord. May 3, 1927; appt. Jan. 27, 1954; cons. March 25, 1954; died Aug. 27, 1959.—Most Rev. GEORGE A. HAMMES, D.D., Bishop Emeritus of Superior; appt. March 28, 1960; cons. May 24, 1960; retired June 27, 1985; died April 11, 1993.

Chancery—1201 Hughitt Ave., Box 969, Superior, 54880. Tel: 715-392-2937; Fax: 715-392-2015.

Vicar General—Very Rev. DANIEL J. DAHLBERG, Office: *1410 Baxter Ave., Superior, 54880.* Tel: 715-392-8511; Fax: 715-392-3457.

Chancellor—Sr. EILEEN LANG, F.S.P.A., D.Min.

Secretary to Bishop—Mrs. PATRICIA WILDENBERG.

Diocesan Tribunal—

Judicial Vicar—Very Rev. JAMES F. TOBOLSKI, J.C.L.

Adjutant Judicial Vicar—Rev. JAMES P. POWERS, J.C.L.

Promoter of Justice—Appointed by case.

Defender of the Bond—Rev. WILLIAM G. HORATH.

Procurator and Advocate—Sr. RITA MARIE SCHNEIDER, S.S.N.D.

Notary and Secretary—Mrs. PATTI J. HOLT.

Vicar for Canonical Affairs—Very Rev. JAMES F. TOBOLSKI, J.C.L.

Vicar for Religious—Sr. EILEEN LANG, F.S.P.A.

Diocesan Pastoral Council—Most Rev. RAPHAEL M. FLISS, D.D., Pres.; South Central Deanery: WARREN WAGNER; EVELYN LOMPA; GLENN HARDER, Eastern Deanery: NANCY LEVANETZ; JOSEPH BENBENEK; ALAN ZYHOWSKI, Northwest Deanery: MARY LU GALLAGHER; JOSEPH FITZGERALD; JEAN CALCAGNO, North Central Deanery: CHERYL ROCKENBACH; DAVID HNATH; MARY JO HOLZHAEUSER, Chm.; Southwest Deanery: BETTY LISKA; TIMOTHY HEFFERNAN; KENNETH SCHAEFER, Vice Chm.; Deacon PHILIP L. MARTINEAU, Bishop's Appointee. Ex Officio Members: Very Revs. DANIEL J. DAHLBERG; PHILIP J. HESLIN; Sr. PAT CORMACK, S.C.S.C.; Sr. THERESA SANDOK, O.S.M.; Sr. EILEEN LANG, F.S.P.A., Liaison.

Deaneries and Deans—Northwest Deanery: Very Rev. DEAN T. BUTTRICK, Southwest Deanery: Very Rev. JOHN A. DRUMMY, North Central Deanery: Very Rev. VERNON J. OLMER, O.F.M., South Central Deanery: Very Rev. JAMES J. JACKSON, East Deanery: Very Rev. JAMES R. HORATH.

Pastoral Consultors—Very Rev. JOHN A. DRUMMY; Revs. GERALD P. HARRIS; DAVID P. OBERTS; WILLIAM H. GREEN.

Presbyteral Council & Diocesan Consultors—Most Rev. RAPHAEL M. FLISS, Pres.; Very Revs. PHILIP J. HESLIN; DANIEL J. DAHLBERG, Vice Chm.; Revs. DENNIS T. MEULEMANS, Chm. PETER F. SZLESZINSKI, Treas.; Very Revs. JAMES F. TOBOLSKI, Sec. JOHN A. DRUMMY; VERNON J. OLMER, O.F.M.; Revs. MICHAEL L. CRISP; GERALD A. HAGEN; MICHAEL J. TUPA; BRENNAN SCHMIEG, O.F.M.

Personnel Placement Board—Revs. DAVID P. OBERTS, Chm. GERALD P. HARRIS; KEVIN M. GORDON, Sec. THOMAS E. THOMPSON; GREGORY J. HOPEFL; JAMES P. POWERS.

Conciliation and Arbitration Board—THOMAS DUFFY, Chm. REBECCA JEAN ECK; Rev. DAVID P. OBERTS; RAYMOND RYNDA; Sr. RITA MARIE SCHNEIDER, S.S.N.D., Sec.

Diocesan Offices and Directors

Apostleship of Prayer—Contact Chancery.

Apostolate of the Sea—Contact Chancery.

Bureau of Information—Mr. SAM LUCERO, Dir., *1512 N. 12th St., P.O. Box 969, Superior, 54880.* Tel: 715-392-8268.

Catholic Charities Bureau—Mr. BRIAN SOLAND, M.A., Exec. Dir., Office: *1416 Cummings Ave., Box 219, Superior, 54880.* Tel: 715-394-6617; Fax: 715-394-5951.

Catholic Boy and Girl Scout—Rev. THOMAS E. THOMPSON, *P.O. Box 399, Osceola, 54020.* Tel: 715-294-2243; Fax: 715-294-2495.

Catholic Mutual Group—PAUL ALTMANN, Claims/Risk Mgr., *1201 Hughitt Ave., P.O. Box 969, Superior, 54880.* Tel: 715-392-2937, Ext. 122.

Catholic Women, Council of—Rev. PHILIP J. JUZA, Moderator, Office: *315 E. Davlin St., Gilman, 54433.* Tel: 715-447-8510. HELEN GEISLER, Pres., *W11820 Buff Creek Trail, Bruce, 54819.* Tel: 715-868-3818.

Charismatic Renewal Liaison—Deacon MICHAEL D. CULLEN, *513 State Rd., P.O. Box 295, Rib Lake, 54470.* Tel: 715-427-5259. Sr. CASIMIRA BENBENEK, O.S.M., Assoc. Liaison, *St. Mary Church, 320 E. Washington Ave., Tomahawk, 54487.* Tel: 715-453-8385.

Christian Formation—Sr. GENEVIEVE SCHILLO, C.S.J., Ph.D., Dir., *1201 Hughitt Ave., P.O. Box 969, Superior, 54880.* Tel: 715-392-1042, Ext. 119., *Res., 404 24th Ave., E., Superior, 54880.* Tel: 715-398-3002.

Cursillo Movement—Rev. BRENNAN SCHMIEG, O.F.M., Spiritual Dir. ED ANDERSON, Lay Dir., *501 Cascade St., Osceola, 54020.* Tel: 715-294-1690.

Diocesan Coordinator of Health Affairs—Rev. KEVIN GORDON, *111 West Marshall St., Rice Lake, 54868.* Tel: 715-234-2032.

Diocesan Sisters Council—Sr. RITA STOEBERL, O.S.M., Pres., *1000 College Ave., W., Ladysmith, 54848.* Tel: 715-532-3364.

Ecumenical Commission—Very Rev. JAMES F. TOBOLSKI, *P.O. Box 969, Superior, 54880.* Tel: 715-392-2937, Ext. 107.

Evangelization, Office of—Sr. EILEEN LANG, F.S.P.A., Dir., *P.O. Box 969, Superior, 54880.* Tel: 715-392-2937, Ext. 104.

Finance, Department of—VIRGIL S. VAVRA, Dir., *1201 Hughitt Ave., P.O. Box 969, Superior, 54880.* Tel: 715-392-7571, Ext. 121.

Holy Childhood Association—Rev. GREGORY J. HOPEFL, Dir., *13891 W. Mission Rd, Stone Lake, 54876.* Tel: 715-865-3669.

Insurance/Employee Benefits and Payroll, Office of—CINDY GRONSKI, Dir., *1201 Hughitt Ave., P.O. Box 969, Superior, 54880.* Tel: 715-392-7571, Ext. 130.

Newman Apostolate—Superior: Newman and Young Adult Ministry Center, University of Wisconsin, Rev. ROBERT L. KRAJEWSKI, Coord. of Ministry, *823 N. 16th Ave., Superior, 54880.* Tel: 715-394-7710. Thomas More Newman Center, *423 E. Cascade, River Falls, 54022.* Rev. NORMAN VOLK, O.M.I., Chap., *Res., 423 E. Cascade, River Falls, 54022.* Tel: 715-425-7234. Ladysmith: Mt. Senario, Newman and Young Adult Ministry Center, CRAIG VOLDBERG, *611 1st St. S., Ladysmith, 54848.* Tel: 715-532-3051.

Catholic Herald, Superior Edition—Mr. SAM LUCERO, Editor, *1512 N. 12th St., P.O. Box 969, Superior, 54880.* Tel: 715-392-8268., *Res., 1413 E. 3rd St., Superior, 54880.* Tel: 715-392-4936.

Parish Accounting, Office of—DANIEL E. ZUCHOWSKI, Accountant, *1201 Hughitt Ave., P.O. Box 969, Superior, 54880.* Tel: 715-392-7571, Ext. 124.

Pastoral Services, Department of—RICHARD W. LYONS, Dir., *1201 Hughitt Ave., P.O. Box 969, Superior, Wi, 54880.* Tel: 715-392-2937, Ext. 103.

Planning, Office of—RICHARD W. LYONS, Dir., *1201 Hughitt Ave., P.O. Box 969, Superior, 54880.* Tel: 715-392-2937, Ext. 103.

Permanent Diaconate—Deacon TIMOTHY J. KUEHN, Dir., *P.O. Box 969, Superior, 54880.* Tel: 715-392-2937, Ext. 117. Rev. DENNIS M. MULLEN, Consultant-Instructor. Tel: 715-822-2948.

Respect Life Office—ALICE MARTIN, *501 E. River Ave., Ladysmith, 54548-1526.* Tel: 715-532-6023.

Propagation of the Faith—Rev. GREGORY J. HOPEFL, *13891 W. Mission Rd., Stone Lake, 54876.* Tel: 715-865-3669.

Radio and Television—Mr. SAM LUCERO, Dir., *1512 N. 12 St., P.O. Box 969, Superior, 54880.* Tel: 715-392-8268., *Res.* Tel: 715-392-4936.

The Bishop George A. Hammes Center for Religious Education and Youth Ministry—Deacon ROGER CADOTTE, Dir., *315 W. Fifth St., P.O. Box 280, Haugen, 54841.* Tel: 715-234-5044; Fax: 715-234-5241.

Branch Office of Religious Education—*1201 Hughitt Ave., P.O. Box 969, Superior, 54880.* Tel: 715-392-1042.

St. Pius Priest Fund—Bd. of Dirs.: Most Rev. RAPHAEL M. FLISS, Pres.; Revs. DENNIS MULLEN, Vice Pres. PETER F. SZLESZINSKI, Treas. JAMES P. POWERS, Sec. JOHN C. ANDERSON; WILLIAM H. GREEN; DENNIS T. MEULEMANS; DAVID P. OBERTS; ANDREW P. RICCI; JOHN J. SPANJERS; GEORGE L. VOTRUBA.

St. Vincent De Paul Society—Mr. JAMES T. TRACY, Pres., *2409 Hammond Ave., Superior, 54880.* Tel: 715-394-3185. Deacon STAN MERCIER, *40 S. Main St., Rice Lake, 54868.* Tel: 715-234-2372., *2811 Pioneer Ave., Rice Lake, 54568.* Tel: 715-234-7003.

Stewardship and Development, Department of—Mr. STEVE TARNOWSKI, Dir., *1201 Hughitt Ave., P.O. Box 969, Superior, 54880.* Tel: 715-392-2937; Fax: 715-392-2015.

Superintendent of Schools—PHYLLIS SCHLAGEL, Office: *1201 Hughitt Ave., Box 969, Superior, 54880.* Tel: 715-392-1042, Ext. 115.

Vocations, Office of—Rev. KEVIN M. GORDON, Dir., *111 W. Marshall St., Rice Lake, 54868.* Tel: 715-234-5083. Sr. BONNIE ALHO, O.S.M., Asst. Dir. Tel: 715-234-5083.

Office of Worship—Rev. GABRIEL BALTES, O.S.B., Dir., *1201 Hughitt Ave., P.O. Box 969, Superior, 54880.* Tel: 715-392-2937, Ext. 145.

CLERGY, PARISHES, MISSIONS AND PAROCHIAL SCHOOLS

CITY OF SUPERIOR
(Douglas County)

1—CATHEDRAL OF CHRIST THE KING (1886), Very Rev. Daniel J. Dahlberg, V.G., Rector; Rev. Robert J. Krajewski; Deacon Arthur Gil de Lamadrid.
Mailing Address: 1410 Baxter Ave., 54880. [CEM]
Church—Belknap Ave. & Grand, 54880. Tel: 715-392-8511; Fax: 715-392-3457.
School—Cathedral School, 1419 Baxter Ave., 54880. Tel: 715-392-2976; Fax: 715-392-2564. Roy Hamlin, Prin.
Lay Teachers 19; Students 360.

2—HOLY ASSUMPTION OF THE B.V.M. (1891). Also serves St. William, Superior. Rev. Ronald Olson, O.F.M.Conv.; Deacon Robert J. Chammings.
Mailing Address: 5601 Tower Ave., 54880.
Church—5601 Tower Ave., 54880. Tel: 715-394-7919; Fax: 715-392-7779.

3—ST. ANTHONY (1870). Also serves St. Anthony, Lake Nebagamon. Very Rev. Dean T. Buttrick; Deacon Timothy J. Kuehn.
Mailing Address: 4315 E. 3rd St., 54880.
Church—4315 E. 3rd St., 54880. Tel: 715-398-3261; Fax: 715-398-3257.

4—SS. CYRIL AND METHODIUS (Slovak). Closed. For inquiries for sacramental records contact Cathedral of Christ the King.

5—ST. FRANCIS XAVIER (1853), Very Rev. James F. Tobolski; Deacon Philip Martineau.
Church and Mailing Address: 2316 E. 4th St., 54880. Tel: 715-398-7174; Fax: 715-398-3074. [CEM]

6—ST. LOUIS. Closed. For inquiries for sacramental records contact Cathedral of Christ the King.

7—ST. PATRICK. Closed. For inquiries for sacramental records contact Cathedral of Christ the King.

8—ST. STANISLAUS (Polish). Closed. For inquiries for sacramental records contact Cathedral of Christ the King.

9—ST. WILLIAM (1908), Rev. Ronald Olson, O.F.M.Conv.; Deacon Jack McKenna.
Mailing Address: 5601 Tower Ave., 54880.
Church—3095 E. County Rd. B, Tel: 715-394-7919. [CEM]

OUTSIDE THE CITY OF SUPERIOR

Almena, Barron Co., Sacred Heart of Jesus Church (1890), Rev. Dennis M. Mullen.
Mailing Address: 900 St. Anthony St., Cumberland, 54829. Tel: 715-822-2948. [CEM]
Church—Soo Ave., 54805.

Amery, Polk Co., St. Joseph (1890), Very Rev. John A. Drummy; Deacon Florian Heiser.
Church and Mailing Address: 404 Wisconsin Ave., 54001. Tel: 715-268-7717; Fax: 715-268-9986.

Ashland, Ashland Co., Our Lady of the Lake Catholic Community (1872), Very Rev. Vernon J. Olmer, O.F.M.; Rev. Conan Mitchell, O.F.M.
Mailing Address: 106 N. 2nd Ave. E., 54806.
Church—201 Lake Shore Dr. E., 54806. Tel: 715-682-7620; Fax: 715-682-7626. [CEM]
School—215 Lake Shore Dr. E., 54806. Tel: 715-682-7622. Mr. David Eaton, Prin.
Brothers 1; Lay Teachers 15; Students 173.
Holy Family (Polish). Closed. For inquiries for sacramental records contact Our Lady of the Lake Catholic Community, Ashland.

Balsam Lake, Polk Co., Our Lady of the Lakes (1875), Rev. Thomas E. Thompson.
Mailing Address: P.O. Box 220, Centuria, 54824.
Church—601 W. Main, 58410. Tel: 715-646-2253.

Barron, Barron Co., St. Joseph (1907). Also serves St. Peter, Cameron and St. Boniface, Chetek. Rev. Gerard I. Willger.
Church and Mailing Address: 827 E. LaSalle Ave., 54812. Tel: 715-637-3255; Fax: 715-637-3252.

Bayfield, Bayfield Co., Holy Family (1878). Also serves St. Joseph, LaPointe, St. Ann, Cornucopia and St. Francis, Red Cliff. Rev. Glenn Phillips, O.F.M.; Deacon Roger L. Cadotte; Sr. Phyllis Wilhelm, O.S.F., Pastoral Assoc.
Mailing Address: P.O. Box 1290, 54814.
Church—232 N. 1st. St., 54814. Tel: 715-779-3316; Fax: 715-779-3316. [CEM 2]

Birchwood, Washburn Co., St. John Evangelist (1908), Rev. David P. Oberts.
Mailing Address: 2411 23rd St., Rice Lake, 54868.
Church—408 S. Main, 54868. Tel: 715-234-2917; Fax: 715-236-7865.

Bloomville, Lincoln Co., St. John the Baptist (1908), Rev. Michael J. Tupa, Pastoral Supr.; Michele Rein, Parish Dir.
Mailing Address: N10090 County B., Tomahawk, 54487.
Church—Hwy. 17 & County J, Gleason, 54487. Tel: 715-453-2561; Fax: 715-453-4813. [CEM]

Boulder Junction, Vilas Co., St. Anne (1938). Also serves St. Mary, Sayner, and St. Rita, Presque Isle. Rev. Michael T. Hayden.
Mailing Address: P.O. Box 110, 54512.
Church—10315 Main St., 54512. Tel: 715-385-2390; Fax: 715-385-2282. [CEM]

Bruce, Rusk Co., St. Mary (1893), Rev. Lewis E. Burden.
Mailing Address: P.O. Box 207, Weyerhaeuser, 54895.
Church—727 N. 2nd St., 58419. Tel: 715-353-2400. [CEM 2]

Butternut, Ashland Co., Immaculate Conception (1880), Very Rev. James J. Jackson.
Mailing Address: 276 S. 5th Ave., Park Falls, 54552.
Church—Hwy. F, 54514. Tel: 715-769-3644. [CEM]

Cable, Bayfield Co., St. Ann (1902), Rev. William H. Green, Pastoral Supr.; Sr. Virginia Schwartz, O.S.M., Parish Dir.
Mailing Address: P.O. Box 37, 54821-0037.
Church—County Hwy. M, 54821. Tel: 715-798-3855; Fax: 715-798-3850.

Cameron, Barron Co., St. Peter (1908), Rev. Gerard I. Willger.
Mailing Address: 827 E. LaSalle Ave., Barron, 54812.
Church—Creamery Rd. & Hwy. 8, 54822. Tel: 715-637-3255.

Catawba, Price Co., St. Paul the Apostle (1907). Also serves St. John the Baptist, Prentice. Rev. Dismas B. Kalcic, O.S.B.
Mailing Address: P.O. Box 137, 54515-0137.
Church—W9485 Hwy. 8, 54515. Tel: 715-474-2223; Fax: 715-474-3409. [CEM]

Centuria, Polk Co., St. Patrick (1856), Rev. Thomas E. Thompson.
Mailing Address: P.O. Box 220, 54824.
Church—116 Sixth St., 54824. Tel: 715-646-2253. [CEM]

Chelsea, Taylor Co., Assumption of the Blessed Virgin Mary (1887), Rev. John R. Long; Deacon Michael D. Cullen, Parish Life Dir.
Mailing Address: P.O. Box 295, Rib Lake, 54470.
Church—100 Hemlock Ave., 54451. Tel: 715-427-5259.

Chetek, Barron Co., St. Boniface (1880), Rev. Gerard I. Willger.
Mailing Address: 419 S. 3rd St., 54728.
Church—425 S. 3rd St., 54812. Tel: 715-924-3514; Fax: 715-637-3252. [CEM]

Clam Lake, Ashland Co., St. George (1890), Rev. John Scheer, S.A.C., Parochial Admin.
Mailing Address: P.O. Box 17, Mellen, 54546.
Church—Hwy. 77 W., 54546. Tel: 715-264-3471.

Clear Lake, Polk Co., St. John (1890). Also serves St. Bridget, Stanton. Rev. Joseph C. Trinka.
Mailing Address: P.O. Box 337, 54005.
Church—811 Fourth St., 54005. Tel: 715-263-2032; Fax: 715-263-2032.

Cornucopia, Bayfield Co., St. Ann (1914), Rev. Glenn Phillips, O.F.M.
Mailing Address: P.O. Box 1290, Bayfield, 54814.
Church—Superior Ave. & Ash St., 54827. Tel: 715-779-3316.

Crescent Lake, Burnett Co., Sacred Hearts of Jesus and Mary (1857), Rev. William J. Murphy.
Mailing Address: P.O. Box 7, Webster, 54893.
Church—County Rd. A & H, Tel: 715-866-7321. [CEM]

Cumberland, Barron Co., St. Anthony Abbot (1883). Also serves Sacred Heart of Jesus, Almena. Rev. Dennis M. Mullen; Deacon Gregory J. Ricci.
Church and Mailing Address: 900 St. Anthony St., 54829. Tel: 715-822-2948; Fax: 715-822-3588. [CEM]

Danbury, Burnett Co., Our Lady of Perpetual Help (1920), Rev. William J. Murphy.
Mailing Address: P.O. Box 7, Webster, 54893.
Church—7586 Main St., 54830. Tel: 715-866-7321.

Dauby, Bayfield Co., St. Peter (1918), Rev. Barry Schneider, O.F.M.
Mailing Address: P.O. Box 97, Iron River, 54847.
Church—Hwy. 2 & County Rd. F, Tel: 715-372-4756. [CEM]

Dobie, Barron Co., Our Lady of Lourdes (1875). Also serves Holy Trinity, Haugen, and St. John the Evangelist, Birchwood. Rev. David P. Oberts.
Church and Mailing Address: 2411 23rd St., Rice Lake, 54868. Tel: 715-234-2917; Fax: 715-236-7865.

Eagle River, Vilas Co., St. Peter the Fisherman (1890). Also serves St. Albert, Land O' Lakes, and St. Mary, Phelps. Rev. Robert J. Koszarek; Sr. Marla Clercx, A.N.G., Pastoral Assoc.; Deacon John "Skip" McCaughn.
Church and Mailing Address: 509 E. Wall St., P.O. Box 728, 54521. Tel: 715-479-8704; Fax: 715-477-2017. [CEM]
School—115 S. 3rd St., P.O. Box 729, 54521. Tel: 715-479-4332. Marie Hafer, Prin.
Lay Teachers 6; Students 52.

Erin, St. Croix Co., St. Patrick (1857), Rev. Allan P. Bradley.
Mailing Address: 151 S. Washington Ave., New Richmond, 54017.
Church—1880 County Rd. G, 54017. Tel: 715-246-4652. [CEM 2]

Farmington, St. Croix Co., Assumption of the Blessed Virgin Mary (1869), Rev. James J. Brinkman.
Mailing Address: P.O. Box 9, Somerset, 54025.
Church—255 State Hwy. 35, 54025. Tel: 715-247-3310; Fax: 715-247-3174. [CEM]

Fifield, Price Co., St. Francis of Assisi (1888), Very Rev. James J. Jackson.
Mailing Address: 276 S. 5th Ave., Park Falls, 54552.
Church—Balsam St., 54524. Tel: 715-762-4494.

Flambeau, Rusk Co., St. Francis of Assisi (1866), Rev. Lewis E. Burden.
Mailing Address: P.O. Box 207, Weyerhaeuser, 54895.
Church—W10193 Lehman Rd., Holcombe, 54745. Tel: 715-868-3475. [CEM]

Frederic, Polk Co., St. Dominic (1904). Also serves Immaculate Conception, Grantsburg. Rev. David R. Lusson, Parochial Admin.; Deacon Stanley J. Marczak.
Mailing Address: P.O. Box 606, 54837.
Rectory/Parish Office: 107 W. Birth St., 54837.
Church—103 W. Birch St., 54837. Tel: 715-327-8119; Fax: 715-327-8125. [CEM]

Georgetown, Polk Co., Our Lady of the Holy Rosary. Closed. For inquiries for sacramental records contact St. Patrick, Centuria.

Gilman, Taylor Co., SS. Peter and Paul (1910). Also serves St. Michael, Jump River; St. John, Sheldon and St. Stanislaus, Lublin. Rev. Philip J. Juza; Sr. Ann Manthey, O.S.F., Pastoral Assoc.
Church and Mailing Address: 315 E. Davlin St., 54433. Tel: 715-447-8510; Fax: 715-447-8615. [CEM]

Glenwood City, St. Croix Co., St. John the Baptist (1886), Rev. Jozef A. Barszcz, Parochial Admin.; Deacon Wesley G. Tuttle.
Church and Mailing Address: 753 1st St., 54013. Tel: 715-265-7133; Fax: 715-265-7399. [CEM]

Glidden, Ashland Co., Most Precious Blood (1884), Rev. John Scheer, S.A.C., Parochial Admin.
Mailing Address: P.O. Box 17, Mellen, 54546. Tel: 715-264-3471; 274-3701. [CEM]
Church—256 E. 2nd St., 54527.

Gordon, Douglas Co., St. Anthony of Padua (1878), Rev. James P. Powers.
Mailing Address: P.O. Box 303, Solon Springs, 54873.
Church—9718 E. County Rd. Y, 54838. Tel: 715-378-4431.

Grantsburg, Burnett Co., Immaculate Conception (1909), Rev. David R. Lusson, Parochial Admin.
Mailing Address: P.O. Box 606, Frederic, 54837.
Church—411 State Rd. 70, 54840. Tel: 715-327-8119.

Hammond, St. Croix Co., Immaculate Conception (1877). Also serves St. Bridget, Wilson. Rev. Alois Gabrus, O.F.M., Parochial Admin.; Deacon Joseph F. Paron.
Mailing Address: P.O. Box 18, 54015-0018.
Church—1265 Ridgeway, 54015. Tel: 715-796-2244; Fax: 715-796-2599. [CEM]

Harrison, Lincoln Co., St. Augustine (1905), Rev. Michael J. Tupa, Pastoral Supr.; Deacon Clarence D. Towle; Michele Rein, Parish Dir.
Mailing Address: Tomahawk N10090 Cty. B, Tomahawk, 54487. Tel: 715-453-2561; Fax: 715-453-4813. [CEM]
Church—Highways B & D, 54435.

Haugen, Barron Co., Holy Trinity (1896), Rev. David P. Oberts; Deacon Harvey G. Drost.
Mailing Address: 2411 23rd St., Rice Lake, 54868.
Church—317 W. 5th St., 54841. Tel: 715-234-2917; Fax: 715-236-7865. [CEM]

Hawkins, Rusk Co., St. Mary of Czestowchowa (1913), Rev. John C. Anderson.
Mailing Address: 611 1st St. S., Ladysmith, 54848.
Church—County Rd. North M, 54530. Tel: 715-532-3051.

Hayward, Sawyer Co., St. Joseph's (1882). Also serves St. Ann, Cable. Rev. William H. Green.
Mailing Address: P.O. Box 32, 54843.
Church—10593 N. Dakota Ave., 54843. Tel: 715-634-2867; Fax: 715-634-9037.

Highbridge, Ashland Co., St. Anthony (1880), Rev. John Scheer, S.A.C., Parochial Admin.
Mailing Address: P.O. Box 17, Mellen, 54546.
Church—Hwy. 13, 54846. Tel: 715-274-3701.

Hudson, St. Croix Co., St. Patrick (1840), Revs. Peter F. Szleszinski; Ryan G. Erickson; Deacons Peter Braum; Bernard Drevnick.
Church and Mailing Address: 1500 Vine St., 54016. Tel: 715-381-5120; Fax: 715-381-5125. [CEM]
School—403 St. Croix St., 54016. Tel: 715-386-3941. Patricia Brandner, Prin.
Lay Teachers 21; Students 374.

Hurley, Iron Co., St. Mary of the Seven Dolors (1885). Also serves Sacred Heart, Montreal; Holy Redeemer, Pence; and St. Ann, Saxon. Rev. Robert E. O'Connell; Deacon Russell J. Lundgren.
Mailing Address: 404 Iron St., 54534.
Church—Iron Street & 5th Ave., 54534. Tel: 715-561-2606; Fax: 715-561-3739. [CEM]

Ino, Bayfield Co., St. Florian (1913), Rev. Gabriel C. Zepczyk, Parochial Admin.
Mailing Address: 23515 Cty. Rd. G, Ashland, 54806.
Church—19315 Keystone Rd., Tel: 715-372-4756. [CEM]

Iron River, Bayfield Co., St. Michael (1892). Also serves St. Peter, Dauby. Rev. Barry Schneider, O.F.M.
Mailing Address: P.O. Box 97, 54847.
Church—22 George St., 54847. Tel: 715-372-4756; Fax: 715-372-4753. [CEM]

Jump River, Taylor Co., St. Michael (1915), Rev. Philip J. Juza; Sr. Ann Manthey, O.S.F., Pastoral Assoc.
Mailing Address: 315 E. Davlin St., Gilman, 54433. Tel: 715-452-5374.
Church—Hwy. 73, 54434.

Lac du Flambeau, Vilas Co., St. Anthony of Padua Catholic Church (1862). Also serves St. Mary, Odanah. Rev. James P. Bartelme; Deacon John J. Bardos.
Mailing Address: P.O. Box 38, 54538.
Church—650 Old Abe Rd., 54538. Tel: 715-588-3148; Fax: 715-588-2278.

Ladysmith, Rusk Co., Our Lady of Sorrows (1906). Also serves St. Mary, Hawkins, and St. Anthony, Tony. Rev. John C. Anderson; Sr. Jovita Winkel, C.S.A., Pastoral Assoc.; Deacons Richard J. Brockbank; Jerome J. Drahos; Richard D. Leonhard.
Church and Mailing Address: 611 1st St. S., 54848. Tel: 715-532-3051; Fax: 715-532-7368.
School—105 E. Washington Ave., 54848. Tel: 715-532-3232. Tami Stewart, Prin.
Lay Teachers 9; Students 105.

Lake Nebagamon, Douglas Co., St. Anthony (1899), Very Rev. Dean T. Buttrick.
Mailing Address: 4315 E. 3rd St., Superior, 54880.
Church—11648 E. County Rd. B, 54849. Tel: 715-398-3261.

Lake Tomahawk, Oneida Co., St. John Vianney (1859), Revs. James A. Hoffman; Edward F. Beutner; Joan Laut, Pastoral Assoc.
Mailing Address: P.O. Box 30, Woodruff, 54568.
Church—7997 Choate Blvd., 54539. Tel: 715-356-6284.

Land-O'-Lakes, Vilas Co., St. Albert (1894). Also serves St. Mary, Phelps. Rev. Robert J. Koszarek, Pastoral Supr.; Patricia Pintens, Parish Dir.
Mailing Address: P.O. Box 237, 54540.
Church—4351 Hwy. B, 54550. Tel: 715-547-3558; Fax: 715-547-3614.

LaPointe, Bayfield Co., St. Joseph (1669), Rev. Glenn Phillips, O.F.M.; Sr. Phyllis Wilhelm, O.S.F., Pastoral Assoc.
Mailing Address: P.O. Box 1290, Bayfield, 54814. [CEM]
Church—266 Airport Rd., 54850. Tel: 715-779-3316.

Lublin, Taylor Co., St. Stanislaus (1907) (Polish), Rev. Philip J. Juza; Sr. Ann Manthey, O.S.F., Pastoral Assoc.
Mailing Address: 315 E. Davlin St., Gilman, 54433. [CEM]
Church—W13381 South St., 54447. Tel: 715-447-8510.

Manitowish Waters, Vilas Co., Our Lady Queen of Peace (1858), Rev. Michael L. Crisp.
Mailing Address: 5214N Lakeview Ave., P.O. Box 575, Mercer, 54547.
Church—Hwy. 51, 54545. Tel: 715-476-2697.

Medford, Taylor Co., Our Lady of the Holy Rosary (1870), Very Rev. Dennis T. Meulemans; Deacon Joseph Stefancin, Pastoral Assoc.
Mailing Address: P.O. Box 503, 54451.
Church—Washington & Cedar Streets, 54451. Tel: 715-748-3288; Fax: 715-748-6643. [CEM]
School—215 S. Washington Ave., P.O. Box 503, 54451. Tel: 715-748-3336. Barbara Bugar, Prin.
Sisters of Mary 1; Lay Teachers 11; Students 136.

Mellen, Ashland Co., Holy Rosary (1886). Also serves St. George, Clam Lake; Most Precious Blood, Glidden and St. Anthony, Highbridge. Rev. John Scheer, S.A.C., Parochial Admin.
Mailing Address: P.O. Box 17, 54546.
Church—203 N. Main St., 54546. Tel: 715-274-3701; Fax: 715-274-3417.

Mercer, Iron Co., St. Isaac Jogues and Companions (1912). Also serves Our Lady Queen of Peace, Manitowish Waters. Rev. Michael L. Crisp; Deacon Norbert G. Brossmer.
Mailing Address: P.O. Box 575, 54547.
Church—2611 W. Garnet St., 54547. Tel: 715-476-2697; Fax: 715-476-2697.

Merrill, Lincoln Co., St. Francis Xavier (1875), Very Rev. James R. Horath; Deacon Richard G. Heckman.
Church and Mailing Address: 1708 E. 10th St., 54452. Tel: 715-536-2803; Fax: 715-536-7536. [CEM]
School—St. Francis, (Grades PreK-8). Tel: 715-536-6083. Ira Rebella, Prin.
Sisters 1; Lay Teachers 19; Students 203.
St. Robert Bellarmine (1886). Closed. For inquiries for sacramental records contact St. Francis Xavier, Merrill.

Minocqua, Oneida Co., St. Patrick (1894), Rev. Joseph N. Miller.
Mailing Address: P.O. Box 107, 54548.
Church—131 Milwaukee St., 54548. Tel: 715-356-3440; Fax: 715-358-6241. [CEM]

Minong, Washburn Co., St. Mary (1904), Rev. James P. Powers; Deacon Peter R. Huntowski.
Mailing Address: P.O. Box 303, Solon Springs, 54873.
Church—11651 Business 53, 54859. Tel: 715-378-4431.

Montreal, Iron Co., Sacred Heart of Jesus (1904), Rev. Robert E. O'Connell.
Mailing Address: 404 Iron St., Hurley, 54534.
Church—Michigan Ave. & Saxon Rd., 54550. Tel: 715-561-2606.

Moquah, Bayfield Co., Ss. Peter and Paul (1912). Also serves St. Florian, Ino. Rev. Gabriel C. Zepczyk, Parochial Admin.
Mailing Address: 23515 Cty. Rd. G., Ashland, 54806.
Church—23505 County Rd. G, 54806. Tel: 715-746-2549. [CEM 2]

New Post, Sawyer Co., St. Ignatius (1884), Rev. Gregory J. Hopefl.
Mailing Address: 13891 W. Mission Rd., Stone Lake, 54876. Tel: 715-865-3669; Fax: 715-865-3669.

New Richmond, St. Croix Co., Immaculate Conception (1883). Also serves St. Patrick, Erin. Rev. Allan P. Bradley; Deacon Hugh C. Mayer.
Church and Office Address: 151 S. Washington Ave., 54017-1523. Tel: 715-246-4652; 246-2294; Fax: 715-246-2526. [CEM]
School—257 S. Washington Ave., 54017. Tel: 715-246-2469. Mari Zarcone-Patterson, Prin.
Lay Teachers 11; Students 139.

Odanah, Ashland Co., St. Mary (1855), Rev. James P. Bartelme.
Mailing Address: P.O. Box 38, Lac du Flambeau, 54538. Tel: 715-588-3148.

Osceola, Polk Co., St. Joseph (1915). Also serves Our Lady of the Lakes, Balsam Lake, St. Patrick, Centuria. Rev. Thomas E. Thompson; Deacon Fred E. Johnson.
Mailing Address: P.O. Box 399, 54020-0399.
Church—255 10th Ave., 54020. Tel: 715-294-2243; Fax: 715-294-2495.

Park Falls, Price Co., St. Anthony (1881). Also serves Immaculate Conception, Butternut and St. Francis of Assisi, Fifield. Very Rev. James J. Jackson; Deacon Chester E. Ball.
Church and Mailing Address: 276 S. 5th Ave., 54552. Tel: 715-762-4494; Fax: 715-762-0079.
School—200 S. 5th Ave., 54552. Tel: 715-762-4494. Beatrice Weiland, Prin.
Lay Teachers 11; Students 154.

Pelican Lake, Oneida Co., St. John (1905), Rev. James J. Kinney, Parochial Admin.
Mailing Address: 110 S. Conro St., Rhinelander, 54501.
Church—Appleton St. Cty. & Hwy. B, 54463. Tel: 715-362-4012. [CEM]

Pence, Iron Co., Holy Redeemer (1908), Rev. Robert E. O'Connell.
Mailing Address: 404 Iron St., Hurley, 54534.
Church—Hibbert & Birch Streets, 54550. Tel: 715-561-2606.

Phelps, Vilas Co., St. Mary (1908), Rev. Robert J. Koszarek, Pastoral Supr.; Patricia Pintens, Parish Dir.

Mailing Address: P.O. Box 237, Land O'Lakes, 54540.
Church—4464 Town Hall Rd., 54554. Tel: 715-547-3558.

Phillips, Price Co., Our Lady of the North (1876), Rev. Gerald A. Hagen; Deacon James J. Celba.
Church and Mailing Address: 125 N. Argyle Ave., 54555. Tel: 715-339-2222; Fax: 715-339-2216. [CEM]

Pier-Willow, Oneida Co., St. Francis of Assisi (1887), Rev. Michael J. Tupa.
Mailing Address: 320 E. Washington Ave., Tomahawk, 54487.
Church—N. Willow Rd., 54487. Tel: 715-453-2878. [CEM]

Prentice, Price Co., St. John the Baptist (1886), Rev. Dismas B. Kalcic, O.S.B.
Mailing Address: W9485 Hwy. 8, P.O. Box 137, Catawba, 54515-0137.
Church—935 Town St., 54556. Tel: 715-474-2223.

Presque Isle, Vilas Co., St. Rita (1950), Rev. Michael T. Hyden.
Mailing Address: P.O. Box 110, Boulder Junction, 54512.
Church—Lake St., 54557. Tel: 715-385-2390.

Radisson, Sawyer Co., Sacred Heart (1919), Rev. Vincent M. Bromley.
Mailing Address: P.O. Box 216, Winter, 54896.
Church—Hwy. 27, 54867. Tel: 715-266-3441.

Red Cliff, Bayfield Co., St. Francis (1861), Rev. Glenn Phillips, O.F.M.; Sr. Phyllis Wilhelm, O.S.F., Pastoral Assoc.
Mailing Address: P.O. Box 1290, Bayfield, 54814.
Church—Church Rd., 54814. Tel: 715-779-3316. [CEM]

Reserve, Sawyer Co., St. Francis of Solanus (1885) (Indian). Also serves St. Ignatius, New Post, and St. Philip, Stone Lake. Rev. Gregory J. Hopefl.
Church and Mailing Address: 13891 W. Mission Rd., Stone Lake, 54876. Tel: 715-865-3669; Fax: 715-865-3669. [CEM]
School—St. Francis Solanus, 13885 W. Mission Rd., Stone Lake, 54876. Tel: 715-865-3662. Sr. Felissa Zander, S.S.S.F., Prin.
Sisters of St. Francis 2; Lay Teachers 3; Students 50.

Rhinelander, Oneida Co., Immaculate Conception (1883). Also serves St. John, Pelican Lake. Rev. James J. Kinney, Admin.; Deacons Michael O. Harvey; Mathew C. Porten.
Mailing Address: 110 S. Conro St., 54501.
Church—125 E. King St., 54501. Tel: 715-362-4012; Fax: 715-362-2385. [CEM]

St. Joseph's (1909), Rev. John R. Gerritts; Deacons Ronald J. Bosi; Richard J. Meier.
Church and Mailing Address: 1350 N. Stevens St., 54501. Tel: 715-362-3169; Fax: 715-362-1811. [CEM]
School—Rhinelander Catholic Central. Mr. David Columbo, Prin.
St. Joseph: 1340 N. Stevens St., 54501. Tel: 715-362-3366.; St. Mary: 103 E. King, 54501. Tel: 715-362-5588.
Franciscan Sisters of Christian Charity 4; Lay Teachers 17; Students 291.

Rib Lake, Taylor Co., St. John the Baptist (1896). Also serves Assumption of the B. V. M., Chelsea; St. Theresa, Westboro and Our Lady of Perpetual Help, Whittlesey. Rev. John R. Long; Deacons Paul M. Ochodnicky; Michael D. Cullen, Parish Life Dir.
Mailing Address: P.O. Box 295, 54470.
Church—513 State Rd., 54470. Tel: 715-427-5259; Fax: 715-427-5266.

Rice Lake, Barron Co., St. Joseph (1878), Rev. Kevin M. Gordon; Sr. Bonnie Alho, O.S.M., Pastoral Assoc.
Church and Mailing Address: 111 W. Marshall St., 54868. Tel: 715-234-2032; Fax: 715-234-7757. [CEM]
School—St. Joseph School, 128 Humbird St., 54868. Tel: 715-234-7721; Fax: 715-234-5062. Sr. Claudine Balio, S.S.J.-T.O.S.F., Prin.
Sisters of St. Joseph of the Third Order of St. Francis 1; Lay Teachers 11; Students 181.

River Falls, St. Croix Co., St. Bridget (1854), Rev. Gerald P. Harris; Deacons Lawrence P. Hennemann; Lawrence Murphy, Pastoral Assoc.
Mailing Address: P.O. Box 86, 54022. Tel: 715-425-1870; Fax: 715-425-1871. [CEM]
Church—211 E. Division St., 54022.
School—135 E. Division St., 54022. Tel: 715-425-1872; Fax: 715-425-1873. Teresa A. Goodier, Prin.
Lay Teachers 15; Students 236.

Sanborn, Ashland Co., St. Anne (1895), Rev. Brennan Schmeig, O.F.M.
Mailing Address: P.O. Box 070, Washburn, 54891.
Church—County Hwy. E, 54806. Tel: 715-274-3701.

Sarona, Washburn Co., St. Catherine (1917), Rev. Andrew P. Ricci, Parochial Admin.
Mailing Address: 409 Summit St., Spooner, 54801.
Church—W5262 County Hwy. D, 54870. Tel: 715-635-3105.

Saxon, Iron Co., St. Ann's (1886), Rev. Robert E. O'Connell; Sr. Caroline Pfeiffer, C.S.J., Pastoral Assoc.
Mailing Address: 404 Iron St., Hurley, 54534.
Church—200 Church St., 54559. Tel: 715-561-2606.

Sayner, Vilas Co., St. Mary (1912), Rev. Michael T. Hayden.
Mailing Address: P.O. Box 110, Boulder Junction, 54512.
Church—2820 Hwy N, 54560. Tel: 715-542-3480.

Sheldon, Rusk Co., St. John the Apostle (1955), Rev. Philip J. Juza; Sr. Ann Manthey, O.S.F., Pastoral Assoc.
Mailing Address: 315 E. Davlin St., Gilman, 54433.
Church—N657 County Rd. VV, 54766. Tel: 715-452-5374.

Shell Lake, Washburn Co., St. Joseph (1880), Rev. Andrew P. Ricci, Parochial Admin.
Mailing Address: 409 Summit St., Spooner, 54801.
Church—502 N. 2nd St., 54871. Tel: 715-635-3105. [CEM]

Solon Springs, Douglas Co., St. Pius X (1878). Also serves St. Anthony of Padua, Gordon; St. Mary, Minong. Rev. James P. Powers.
Mailing Address: Box 303, 54873.
Church—11651 Business 53, 54873. Tel: 715-378-4431; Fax: 715-378-2064. [CEM]

Somerset, St. Croix Co., St. Anne (1851). Also serves Assumption of the Blessed Virgin Mary, Farmington. Rev. James J. Brinkman; Deacon A. Maurice Baillargeon.
Mailing Address: P.O. Box 9, 54025.
Church—141 Church Hill Rd., 54025. Tel: 715-247-3310; Fax: 715-247-3174. [CEM]
School—140 Church Hill Rd., 54025. Tel: 715-247-3762; Fax: 715-247-4335. Ann Mitchell, Prin.
Lay Teachers 9; Students 138.

Spooner, Washburn Co., St. Francis De Sales (1886). Also serves St. Joseph, Shell Lake & St. Catherine, Sarona. Rev. Andrew P. Ricci, Parochial Admin.
Church and Mailing Address: 409 Summit St., 54801. Tel: 715-635-3105; Fax: 715-635-7341. [CEM 2]
School—300 Oak St., 54801. Tel: 715-635-2774. Linda L. Havlicek, Prin.
Lay Teachers 13; Students 94.

Stanton, St. Croix Co., St. Bridget (1875), Rev. Joseph C. Trinka.
Mailing Address: P.O. Box 337, Clear Lake, 54005.
Church—County Rd. T, Tel: 715-263-2032. [CEM]

Stetsonville, Taylor Co., Sacred Heart of Jesus (1884), Rev. Frederick Brost.
Church and Mailing Address: 322 W. CTH A, 54480. Tel: 715-678-2395; Fax: 715-678-2395. [CEM]

Stone Lake, Sawyer Co., St. Philip (1905), Rev. Gregory J. Hopefl.
Mailing Address: 13891 W. Mission Rd., 54876.
Church—5750 Frost Ave., 54876. Tel: 715-865-3669; Fax: 715-865-3669.

Strickland, Rusk Co., Assumption of the Blessed Virgin Mary (1897), Rev. Lewis E. Burden; Deacon James E. Roberge.
Mailing Address: N3739 1st St., P.O. Box 207, Weyerhaeuser, 54895.
Church—Old Hwy. 14, Tel: 715-353-2400. [CEM]

Sugar Camp, Oneida Co., St. Kunegunda (1892), Rev. William G. Horath; Deacon Albert A. Goodrich.
Mailing Address: P.O. Box 8, Three Lakes, 54562.
Church—6895 Hwy. 17 N., Rhinelander, Tel: 715-272-1191. [CEM]

Three Lakes, Oneida Co., St. Theresa (1892). Also serves St. Kunegunda of Poland, Sugar Camp. Rev. William G. Horath.
Church and Mailing Address: 1701 Superior St., P.O. Box 8, 54562. Tel: 715-546-2159; Fax: 715-546-2159.

Tomahawk, Lincoln Co., St. Mary (1887). Also serves St. Francis of Assisi, Pier-Willow, St. Augustine, Harrison and St. John the Baptist, Bloomville. Rev. Michael J. Tupa; Deacons Bernard J. Lyngdal; Darrell P. Smerz; David C. Bablick.
Church and Mailing Address: 320 E. Washington Ave., 54487. Tel: 715-453-2878; Fax: 715-453-6678. [CEM]
School—110 N. 7th St., 54487. Tel: 715-453-3542. Mary A. Cherf, Prin.
Lay Teachers 9; Students 109.

Tony, Rusk Co., St. Anthony de Padua (1901), Rev. John C. Anderson; Sr. Jovita Winkel, C.S.A., Pastoral Assoc.
Mailing Address: 611 1st St. S., Ladysmith, 54848.
Church—N5333 Maple St., 54563. Tel: 715-532-3051. [CEM]

Turtle Lake, Barron Co., St. Ann (1882), Rev. John J. Spanjers; Mary Ann Perga, Pastoral Assoc.; Deacon Timothy J. Byrnes.
Mailing Address: P.O. Box 118, 54889.
Church—300 Pine St. S., 54889. Tel: 715-986-4651; Fax: 715-986-4153. [CEM]

Washburn, Bayfield Co., St. Louis (1882). Also serves St. Anne, Sanborn. Rev. Brennan Schmieg, O.F.M.
Mailing Address: Box 070, 54891. Tel: 715-373-2132; Fax: 715-373-0365.
Church—217 W. 7th St., 54891. [CEM]
School—713 Washington Ave., P.O. Box 70, 54891. Tel: 715-373-5322. Betty Swiston, Prin.
Lay Teachers 5; Students 84.

Webster, Burnett Co., St. John the Baptist (1880). Also serves Sacred Hearts of Jesus and Mary, Crescent Lake, and Our Lady of Perpetual Help, Danbury. Rev. William J. Murphy; Deacon Ralph W. Heffner.
Mailing Address: P.O. Box 7, 54893.
Church—26455 S. Muskey Ave., 54893. Tel: 715-866-7321; Fax: 715-866-7305. [CEM]

Westboro, Taylor Co., St. Theresa (1904), Rev. John R. Long.
Mailing Address: P.O. Box 295, Rib Lake, 54490. Tel: 715-427-5259; Fax: 715-427-5266.
Church—N8855 2nd St., 54490.

Weyerhaeuser, Rusk Co., SS. Peter and Paul (1897). Also serves Assumption B.V.M., Strickland; St. Mary, Bruce and St. Francis of Assisi, Flambeau. Rev. Lewis E. Burden; Deacon James E. Roberge.
Mailing Address: P.O. Box 207, 54895.
Church—251 First St., 54895. Tel: 715-353-2400; Fax: 715-353-2400. [CEM]

Whittlesey, Our Lady of Perpetual Help (1891), Rev. John R. Long; Deacons Paul M. Ochodnicky; Michael D. Cullen, Parish Life Dir.
Mailing Address: P.O. Box 295, Rib Lake, 54470.
Church—W5409 Whittlesey Ave., 54451. Tel: 715-427-5259; Fax: 715-427-5266. [CEM]

Wilson, St. Croix Co., St. Bridget (1886), Rev. Alois Gabrus, O.F.M., Parochial Admin.
Mailing Address: P.O. Box 18, Hammond, 54015-0018.
Church—120 Depot St., 54027. Tel: 715-265-7133. [CEM]

Winter, Sawyer Co., St. Peter (1908). Also serves Sacred Heart, Radisson. Rev. Vincent M. Bromley.
Mailing Address: P.O. Box 216, 54896.
Church—5106 N. Main St., 54896. Tel: 715-266-3441. [CEM]

Woodruff, Oneida Co., Our Lady Queen of the Universe (1955). Also serves St. John Vianney, Lake Tomahawk. Revs. James A. Hoffman; Edward F. Beutner; Joan Laut, Pastoral Assoc.
Mailing Address: Box 30, 54568.
Church—1025 Margaret St., 54568. Tel: 715-356-6284; Fax: 715-356-2940.

Chaplains of Public Institutions

On Special or Other Diocesan Assignment:
Reverend Fathers—
Heslin, Philip J., Moderator of the Curia, Chancery, Box 969, Superior, WI 54880

Military Chaplains:
Reverend Fathers—
Gonia, Raymond L., 2401 Kelly Dr., Unit 360473, Lackland AFB, TX 78236-6004

On Leave:
Reverend Fathers—
Kraker, James J.

Retired:
Reverend Fathers—
Anctil, Leo, 645 Knotty Oak Rd., Coventry, RI 02816-8227. Tel: 401-821-8199
Briody, Hugh J., Woodmount, Ballinasloe, Co. Galway, Ireland. Tel: 353-905-4439
Cary, William J., 113 Tilltag Dr., #64, Balsam Lake, WI 54810. Tel: 715-485-3305
Cyz, Edward T., P.O. Box 1544, Superior, WI 54880. Tel: 715-392-6713
Dabruzzi, James S., 1348 Carriage Dr., Hudson, WI 54016. Tel: 715-381-2815
Fraher, Leonard W., 804 Woodland Ln., New Richmond, WI 54017. Tel: 715-246-7855
Heinen, Virgil O., 206 Wisconsin St. N., Apt. 102, Hudson, WI 54016. Tel: 715-381-9778
Kelchak, Joseph M., 4165 Oakmont Ct., Crown Point, IN 46307. Tel: 219-663-6726
Kleinheinz, Joseph L., 1809 N. 11th Ave., Wausau, WI 54401. Tel: 715-675-5758
Kowalski, Wladyslaw J., St. John the Baptist Parish (Peplin), 3308 Hwy. 153, Mosinee, WI 54455. Tel: 715-693-3604
Krynski, Leo J., 1240 Easthill Dr., Wausau, WI 54403. Tel: 715-848-5545

Kunda, Brendan J., 4090 Mill Lake Rd., Rhinelander, WI 54501. Tel: 715-272-1464
Meulemans, Edward G., Reflections, 2601 E. McKellips Rd, Apt. 2020, Mesa, AZ 85213. Tel: 480-969-3180
Meyett, Irving C., 2528 E. 3rd St., Superior, WI 54880. Tel: 715-398-7196
Pakosta, Francis J., 13207 Hwy. G, Caledonia, WI 53108. Tel: 414-835-9020
Powell, Edward F., W6771 Branch Rd., Tomahawk, WI 54487-9230. Tel: 715-453-1357
Regh, John, W4598 Emery/Hackett Rd., Phillips, WI 54555-8574. Tel: 715-428-2268
Schoone, Raymond L., 1900 New York Ave., Apt.E 410, Superior, WI 54880. Tel: 715-395-0178
Senn, Edward R., 28312 McKenze Rd., Spooner, WI 54801. Tel: 715-635-3295
Slowey, John P., 184 N. Eyder Ave., Phillips, WI 54555-1244. Tel: 715-339-4068
Speerstra, William F., 9896 Morgan Oaks Dr., Minocqua, WI 54548-8713. Tel: 715-358-3424
Stremski, John P., 1820 Estates Ln., Apt. 2, Shawano, WI 54166. Tel: 715-526-1812
Urban, Robert M., 463 W. Spruce St., Chippewa Falls, WI 54729. Tel: 715-723-2092
Verdegan, Albert L., 403 E. Corbett Ave., Apt. # 3, Ladysmith, WI 54848-1954. Tel: 715-532-0861
Votruba, George L., 132 W. Marshall St., Rice Lake, WI 54868. Tel: 715-236-7091
Wenninger, William, P.O. Box 969, Superior, WI 54880
West, Norbert, House of Loreto, 2812 Harvard Ave., N.W., Canton, OH 44709. Tel: 216-492-1240

Permanent Deacons:
Bablick, David C., St. Mary, Tomahawk
Baillargeon, Maurice A., St. Anne, Somerset
Ball, Chester E., St. Anthony, Park Falls
Bardos, John J., St. Anthony of Padua, Lac Du Flambeau
Bosi, Ronald J., St. Joseph, Rhinelander
Braam, Peter R., St. Patrick, Hudson
Brockbank, Richard J., Our Lady of Sorrows, Ladysmith
Brossmer, Norbert G., St. Isaac Joques and Companions, Mercer
Byrnes, Timothy J., St. Ann, Turtle Lake
Cadotte, Roger, Holy Family, Bayfield
Celba, James J., Our Lady of the North, Phillips
Chammings, Robert J., Holy Assumption, Superior
Cullen, Michael D., St. John the Baptist, Rib Lake
Drahos, Jerome J., Our Lady of Sorrows, Ladysmith
Drevnick, Bernard M., St. Patrick, Hudson
Drost, Harvey G., Holy Trinity, Haugen
Gil de Lamadrid, Arthur, Cathedral of Christ the King, Superior
Goodrich, Albert A., St. Kunegunda of Poland, Sugar Camp
Harvey, Michael O., Immaculate Conception, Rhinelander
Heckman, Richard G., St. Francis Xavier, Merrill
Heffner, Ralph W., St. John the Baptist, Webster
Heiser, Florian H., St. Joseph, Amery
Hennemann, Lawrence P., St. Bridget, River Falls
Huntowski, Peter R., St. Mary, Minong
Johnson, Fred E., St. Joseph, Osceola
Kuehn, Timothy J., St. Anthony, Superior
Leonhard, Richard D., Our Lady of Sorrows, Ladysmith
Lundgren, Russell J., St. Mary, Hurley
Lyngdal, Bernard J., St. Mary, Tomahawk
Marczak, Stanley J., St. Dominic, Frederic
Martineau, Philip L., St. Francis Xavier, Superior
Mayer, Hugh C., Immaculate Conception, New Richmond
McCaughn, John "Skip", St. Peter the Fisherman, Eagle River
McKenna, Jack, St. William, Pattison Park
Meier, Richard J., St. Joseph, Rhinelander
Mercier, Stanley J., St. Vincent de Paul Society, Rice Lake
Murphy, Lawrence, St. Bridget, River Falls
Ochodnicky, Paul M., St. John the Baptist, Rib Lake
Paron, Joseph F., Immaculate Conception, Hammond
Porten, Matthew C., Immaculate Conception, Rhinelander
Reuter, Joseph E., St. Joseph, Hayward
Ricci, Gregory J., St. Anthony Abbot, Cumberland
Roberge, James E., Ss. Peter & Paul, Weyerhaeuser
Roe, Joseph F., Our Lady of the Holy Rosary, Medford
Smerz, Darrell P., St. Mary, Tomahawk
Stefancin, Joseph, Our Lady of the Holy Rosary, Medford
Towle, C. Dan, St. Augustine, Harrison
Tuttle, Wesley G., St. John the Baptist, Glenwood City

INSTITUTIONS LOCATED IN THE DIOCESE

[A] GENERAL HOSPITALS

SUPERIOR. *St. Mary's Hospital of Superior*, 3500 Tower Ave., 54880. Tel: 715-392-8281; Fax: 715-392-8395.
E-mail: tjacobson@smdl.org
Web site: www.smdc.org
For a complete listing, refer to the Hospitals section.

MERRILL. *Good Samaritan Health Center of Merrill, Wisconsin, Inc.*, 601 S. Center Ave., 54452. Tel: 715-536-5511; Fax: 715-539-2170
For a complete listing, refer to the Hospitals section.

NEW RICHMOND. *Holy Family Hospital*, 535 Hospital Rd., 54017. Tel: 715-246-2101; Fax: 715-243-7203.
E-mail: hfhjneed@pressenter.com
For a complete listing, refer to the Hospitals section.

RHINELANDER. *Sacred Heart-St. Mary's Hospitals, Inc.*, 1044 Kabel Ave., 54501. Tel: 715-369-6600; Fax: 715-369-6441
For a complete listing, refer to the Hospitals section.

TOMAHAWK. *Sacred Heart-St. Mary's Hospitals, Inc.*, 216 N. 7th St., 54487. Tel: 715-453-7700; Fax: 715-453-7716
For a complete listing, refer to the Hospitals section.

[B] HOMES FOR AGED

SUPERIOR. *St. Francis Home, Inc.*, 1416 Cumming Ave., 54880. Tel: 715-394-5591; Fax: 715-394-6617
For a complete listing, refer to the Special Care Facilities section.

[C] MONASTERIES

FIFIELD. *King of Martyrs Priory*, 54524. Tel: 715-339-2447. Rev. Clement Sobr, O.S.B.

[D] CONVENTS AND RESIDENCES FOR SISTERS

HUDSON. *Carmel of the Sacred Heart*, 430 Laurel Ave., 54016. Tel: 715-386-2156.
E-mail: carmelit@pressenter.com
Web site: www.pressenter.com/~carmelit/
Sr. Mary O'Neill, O.Carm., Prioress..Sisters 5.

LADYSMITH. *Servants of Mary*, 1000 College Ave., W., 54848. Tel: 715-532-3364; 532-3365; Fax: 715-532-6153, Ext. 19.
Web site: servitesisters.org/index.htm
Sr. Theresa Sandock, O.S.M., Pres. Sisters 79.

MERRILL. *Holy Cross Provincial Office*, 501 S. Center Ave., 54452-3402. Tel: 715-539-5000; Fax: 715-539-5012.
E-mail: hcross@pcpros.net
Web site: www.pcpros.net/~hcross
Sr. Pat Cormack, S.C.S.C., Prov.
Bell Tower Residence, Inc., 1500 O'Day St., 54452. Tel: 715-536-5575; Fax: 715-536-1765. Residence for the Elderly. Sisters 9; Lay Residents 68.

[E] CATHOLIC CHARITIES BUREAU

SUPERIOR. *Catholic Charities Bureau, Inc.*, 1416 Cummings Ave., P.O. Box 219, 54880. Tel: 715-394-6617; Fax: 715-394-5951. Brian Soland, M.A., Exec. Dir.; William Anderson, CFO; Beth Carlson, Dir. Housing/Health Services; Terry Hendrick, Dir. Resources & Planning/Community Services; Richard Klun, Dir.Development/Disability Services; Marilyn Christopherson, Coord. Diocesan Rels.; Jennifer LeMone, Admin. Coord.
Catholic Community Services, Inc., 1416 Cumming Ave., 54880. Tel: 715-394-6617; Fax: 715-394-5951. Terry Hendrick, Dir.
Housing Counseling Program, 1416 Cumming Ave., 54880. Tel: 715-394-6617; Fax: 715-394-5951. Terry Hendrick, Dir.
Hudson Day Care Center (Hudson), 816 Fourth St., Hudson, 54016. Tel: 715-386-5912. Barbara Hallquist, Interim Dir.
United Day Care, Inc., 1416 Cumming Ave., 54880. Tel: 715-394-6617; Fax: 715-394-5951. Rick Klun, Dir. Home Health Service.
The Dove Agency, Inc., 1416 Cumming Ave., 54880. Tel: 715-392-3133; Fax: 715-392-3190. Beth Carlson, Dir.
The Dove, Inc., 1416 Cummng Ave., 54880. Tel: 715-392-3133; Fax: 715-392-3190. Beth Carlson, Dir. Housing-Disabled.
Acorn Apartments (Wisconsin Rapids), 2721 Tenth St. S., Wisconsin Rapids, 54494. Tel: 715-369-2550; Fax: 715-369-5857. Carol Pederson, Mgr.
Apple River, Inc. (Amery), Minneapolis and Broadway, Amery, 54001. Tel: 715-236-2366; Fax: 715-236-3161. Robert Heinze, Mgr.
ARC Group Home (Superior), 3105 Cumming Ave., 54880. Tel: 715-392-5427.
Birchwood Group Home (Siren), 7754 Rasmussen St., Siren, 54872. Tel: 715-349-5724; Fax: 715-349-5505. Joe Wacek, Dir.
Blue Valley, Inc. (Rice Lake), 1310 N. Wisconsin Ave., Rice Lake, 54868. Tel: 715-236-2366; Fax: 715-236-3161. Robert Heinze, Mgr.
Cypress House, 1415 Cypress, 54880. Tel: 715-394-2771; Fax: 715-394-2100. Eugene Chuzles, Dir.
Elmwood Apartments, 1020 Weeks Ave., 54880. Tel: 715-392-3447. Bruce Todd, Mgr.
Harborview Group Home-Handicapped, 910 E. 5th St., 54880. Tel: 715-394-2771; Fax: 715-394-2100. Eugene Chuzles, Dir.
Lakewood Apartments, Fourth St., Siren, 54872. Tel: 715-236-2366; Fax: 715-236-3161. Robert Heinze, Mgr.
Maywood Apartments, 521 Lemke Ave., Medford, 54451. Tel: 715-369-2550; Fax: 715-369-5857. Carol Pederson, Mgr.
McKenzie Manor, 3317 N. 21st St., 54880. Tel: 715-394-2771; Fax: 715-394-2100. Eugene Chuzles, Dir.
Oakwood Apartments (Superior), 1112 John Ave., 54880. Tel: 715-392-3447. Bruce Todd, Mgr. Housing for Chronically Disabled.
Phoenix Villa North (Cumberland), 1490 Arcade, Cumberland, 54829. Tel: 715-236-2366; Fax: 715-236-3161. Robert Heinze, Mgr. Housing for Mentally Ill.
Phoenix Villa of Hayward (Hayward), Rt. 10, 430 Muriel St., Hayward, 54843. Tel: 715-236-2366; Fax: 715-236-3161. Robert Heinze, Mgr.
Phoenix Villa North, 1305 N. Wisconsin St., Rice Lake, 54868. Tel: 715-236-2366; Fax: 715-236-3161. Robert Heinze, Mgr.
Sumac Trail Apartments, Inc., Sumac Tr. and Philip St., Rhinelander, 54501. Tel: 715-369-2550; Fax: 715-369-5857. Carol Pederson, Mgr.
Timberlane Apartments, 880 E. Timber Dr., Rhinelander, 54501. Tel: 715-369-2550; Fax: 715-369-5857. Carol Pederson, Mgr.
Westbay, Inc., 1104 John Ave., 54880. Tel: 715-392-3447. Bruce Todd, Mgr.
Woodview Group Home, 6001 E. Third St., 54880. Tel: 715-394-2771; Fax: 715-394-2100. Eugene Chuzles, Dir. Housing-Senior.
Acorn Apartments (Crandon), 508 W. Washington, Crandon, 54520. Tel: 715-369-2550; Fax: 715-369-5857. Carol Pederson, Mgr.
Acorn Apartments (Minong), P.O. Box 438, Minong, 54859. Tel: 715-236-2366; Fax: 715-236-3161. Robert Heinze, Mgr.
Cedarwood Apartments, Olker Rd., Hayward, 54843. Tel: 715-394-6617; Fax: 715-394-5951. Richard Klun, Acting Mgr.
Evergreen Apartments (Chetek), 707 Tainter Ave., Chetek, 54728. Tel: 715-236-2366; Fax: 715-236-3161. Robert Heinze, Mgr.
Evergreen Apartments (Shell Lake), 801 N. Lake Dr., Shell Lake, 54871. Tel: 715-236-2366; Fax: 715-236-3161. Robert Heinze, Mgr.
Maywood Apartments (Plover), 2601 Madison Ave., Plover, 54467. Tel: 715-369-2550; Fax: 715-369-5857. Carol Pederson, Mgr.
Phoenix Villa, 1100 Weeks Ave., 54880. Tel: 715-392-3447. Bruce Todd, Mgr.
Phoenix Villa of Iron River (Iron River), Hwy. H, Iron River, 54847. Tel: 715-394-6617; Fax: 715-394-5951. Anthony Coletta, Mgr.
Phoenix Villa of Lake Nebagamon (Lake Nebagamon), Main St., Lake Nebagamon, 54849. Tel: 715-394-6617; Fax: 715-394-5951. Anthony Coletta, Mgr.
Phoenix Villa of Rhinelander (Rhinelander), 1011 Mason St., Rhinelander, 54501. Tel: 715-369-2550; Fax: 715-369-5857. Carol Pederson, Mgr. Rehabilitation Centers.
Black River Industries, Inc. (Medford), 650 Jensen Dr., Medford, 54451. Tel: 715-748-2950; Fax: 715-748-6363. Bill Hrabe, Dir.
Challenge Center, 39 N. 25th St. E., 54880. Tel: 715-394-2771. Eugene Chuzles, Dir.
Diversified Services, Inc., P.O. Box 501, Siren, 54872. Tel: 715-349-5724; Fax: 715-349-5505. Joe Wacek, Dir.
Headwaters. Inc. (Rhinelander), 1441 E. Timber Dr., Box 618, Rhinelander, 54501. Tel: 715-369-1337; Fax: 715-369-1793. Elio Pascutti, Dir. Senior Programs.
Foster Grandparent Program, 1509 Tower Ave., 54880. Tel: 715-394-5384; Fax: 715-394-9724. Margaret Hogg, Dir.
Retired Senior Volunteer Program, 1509 Tower Ave., 54880. Tel: 715-394-4425; Fax: 715-394-5775. Kendra-Sue Rohde, Dir.
Retired Senior Volunteer Program, 1835 N. Stevens St., Ste. 22, Rhinelander, 54501. Tel: 715-369-1919; Fax: 715-369-3686. Lori Stroede, Dir.

[F] RETREAT HOUSES

AMERY. *Mount Carmel Hermitage*, 897 U.S. Hwy. 8, 54001-2541. Tel: 715-268-9313; Fax: 715-268-7495. Sr. Kristine Haugen, O.C.D.H, Coord.

ARBOR VITAE. *Marywood Franciscan Spirituality Center (FSPA)*, 3560 Hwy. 51 N., 54568-9538. Tel: 715-385-3750; Fax: 715-385-9118.
E-mail: marywood@newnorth.net
Web site: www.fspa.org
Congregation of the Sisters of the Third Order of St. Francis of Perpetual Adoration (Franciscan Sisters of Perpetual Adoration), F.S.P.A. Sr. Jolynn Brehm, F.S.P.A., Dir.

[G] NEWMAN CENTERS

SUPERIOR. *Superior-UW*. Newman Center Ministry to Young Adults. 823 N. 16th Ave., 54880. Tel: 715-394-7710. Rev. Robert J. Krajewski, Coord. Ministry.

LADYSMITH. *Mt. Senario College*. Newman and Young Adult Ministry Center, 1500 W. College Ave., 54848. Tel: 715-532-5511.
E-mail: cvoldberg@msfs.edu
Office, Our Lady of Sorrows Parish, 611 1st St. S., 54848. Tel: 715-532-3051; Fax: 715-532-7368. Craig Voldberg, Dir.

RIVER FALLS. *St. Thomas More Newman Center*, 423 E. Cascade, 54022. Tel: 715-425-7234. Rev. Norman Volk, O.M.I.

[H] ASSOCIATION OF THE FAITHFUL

AMERY. *Hermits of Mt. Carmel*, 897 Hwy. 8, 54001. Tel: 715-268-9313; Fax: 715-268-7495. Sr. Kristine Haugen, O.C.D.H., Coord.

[I] MISCELLANEOUS

LADYSMITH. *Mary Bradley Corporation*, 1000 College Ave., W., 54848. Tel: 715-532-3364; Fax: 715-532-6153, Ext. 19. Sr. Theresa Sandok, O.S.M., Pres.

MERRILL. *Good Samaritan Health Center Foundation of Merrill, Wisconsin, Inc.*, 601 S. Center Ave., 54452. Tel: 715-536-5511; Fax: 715-539-2170. Michael Hammer, Pres. A not for profit corporation for the purpose of soliciting and receiving contributions for the benefit of Good Samaritan Health Center of Merrill, WI, Inc.

Sisters of Mercy of the Holy Cross Community Support Charitable Trust, 501 S. Center Ave., 54452-3402. Tel: 715-539-5000; Fax: 715-539-5012.
E-mail: hcross@pcpros.net
Web site: www.pcpros.net/~hcross
Sr. Pat Cormack, S.C.S.C., Pres.

NEW RICHMOND. *Holy Family Hospital Foundation, Inc.*, 535 Hospital Rd., 54017. Tel: 715-246-2101; Fax: 715-243-7222.
E-mail: hfhjneed@pressenter.com
Jean Needham, Pres.

RHINELANDER,. *[*]Saints, Inc.*, 1044 Kabel Ave., 54501. Tel: 715-369-6787; Fax: 715-369-6779. Jack Sutliff, Pres.

WEBSTER. *Thomas More Center for Preaching and Prayer, Inc.*, 27781 Leef Rd., 54893. Tel: 715-866-7436; Fax: 715-866-4277.
E-mail: tmcmike@attglobal.net
Web site: www.thomasmorecenter.org
Revs. Michael A. Champlin, O.P., Pres.; Nicholas W. Punch, O.P.; Sr. Joan Bukrey, O.S.F., Vice Pres.

WINTER. *Camp We-Ha-Kee*. (Girls), N. 8104 Barker Lake Rd., 54896. Tel: 715-266-3263; Fax: 715-266-2267.
E-mail: wehakee@win.bright.net
Web site: www.camwehakee@.com
Sr. Arturo Cranston, O.P., Dir.

RELIGIOUS INSTITUTES OF MEN REPRESENTED IN THE DIOCESE

For further details refer to the corresponding bracketed number in the Religious Institutes of Men or Women section.

[0200]—*Benedictine Monks*. (Lisle, IL).—O.S.B.

[0480]—*Conventual Franciscans*. (Arroyo Grande, CA).—O.F.M.Conv.

[0520]—*Franciscan Friars*. (St. Louis, MO).—O.F.M.

[0910]—*Oblates of Mary Immaculate*. (St. Paul, MN).—O.M.I.

[0430]—*Order of Preachers-Province of St. Albert the Great*. Chicago.—O.P.

[1990]—*Society of the Catholic Apostolate*. (Milwaukee, WI).—S.A.C.

[1060]—*Society of the Precious Blood*.—C.P.P.S.

RELIGIOUS INSTITUTES OF WOMEN REPRESENTED IN THE DIOCESE

[0320]—*Carmelite Nuns of the Ancient Observance*.—O.Carm.

[3710]—*Congregation of the Sisters of Saint Agnes*.—C.S.A.

[1780]—*Congregation of the Sisters of the Third Order of St. Francis of Perpetual Adoration (Franciscan Sisters of Perpetual Adoration)*.—F.S.P.A.

[1710]—*Congregation of the Third Order of St. Francis of Mary Immaculate*. (Joilet, IL).—O.S.F.

[1230]—*Franciscan Sisters of Christian Charity*.—O.S.F.

[2970]—*School Sisters of Notre Dame*. (Mankato/Milwaukee).—S.S.N.D.

[1680]—*School Sisters of St. Francis*.—S.S.S.F.

[3590]—*Servants of Mary (Servite Sisters)*.—O.S.M.

[1070-03]—*Sinsinawa Dominican Congregation of the Most Holy Rosary*.—O.P.

[2630]—*Sisters of Mercy of the Holy Cross*.—S.C.S.C.

[2990]—*Sisters of Notre Dame*. (Cleveland Province).—S.N.D.

[0230]—*Sisters of St. Benedict*. St. Paul, MN.—O.S.B.

[1705]—*Sisters of St. Francis of Assisi, Milwaukee*.—O.S.F.

[3840]—*Sisters of St. Joseph of Carondelet*. (Prov. of St. Paul).—C.S.J.

[3930]—*Sisters of St. Joseph of the Third Order of St. Francis*. (Prov. of Immaculate Conception; St. Joseph Prov.).—S.S.J.-T.O.S.F.

[4100]—*Sisters of the Sorrowful Mother*. (Third Order of St. Francis).—S.S.M.

[1720]—*Sisters of the Third Order Regular of St. Francis of the Congregation of Our Lady of Lourdes*.—O.S.F.

NECROLOGY

† Canfield, F. Joseph, (Retired). —Died Feb. 10, 2000.

Diocese of Syracuse

(Dioecesis Syracusensis)

Most Reverend

JAMES M. MOYNIHAN, D.D.

Bishop of Syracuse; ordained December 15, 1957; appointed Bishop of Syracuse April 4, 1995; consecrated and installed in See of Syracuse May 29, 1995. *Office: 240 E. Onondaga St., P.O. Box 511, Syracuse, NY, 13201-0511. Res., Cathedral of the Immaculate Conception, 295 E. Onondaga St., Syracuse, NY, 13202.*

Most Reverend

FRANK J. HARRISON, D.D.

Retired Bishop of Syracuse; ordained June 4, 1937; appointed Titular Bishop of Aquae and Auxiliary Bishop of Syracuse March 1, 1971; consecrated April 22, 1971; appointed Bishop of Syracuse November 16, 1976; installed February 6, 1977; retired June 16, 1987. *Res., Bishop Grimes Faculty House, 6655 Kirkville Rd., East Syracuse, NY, 13057.*

Chancery Office: P.O. Box 511, Syracuse, NY, 13201. Tel.: 315-422-7203; Fax: 315-478-4619.

Most Reverend

THOMAS J. COSTELLO, D.D., V.G.

Auxiliary Bishop of Syracuse and Titular Bishop of Perdices; ordained June 5, 1954; appointed January 10, 1978; consecrated March 13, 1978. *Res., 1515 Midland Ave., Syracuse, NY, 13205.*

ESTABLISHED NOVEMBER 26, 1886.

Square Miles 5,749.

Corporate Title: The Roman Catholic Diocese of Syracuse NY.

Comprises the Counties of Broome, Chenango, Cortland, Madison, Oneida, Onondaga and Oswego.

For legal titles of parishes and diocesan institutions, consult the Chancery Office.

STATISTICAL OVERVIEW

Personnel	
Bishop	1
Auxiliary Bishops	1
Retired Bishops	1
Priests: Diocesan Active in Diocese	201
Priests: Active Outside Diocese	14
Priests: Retired, Sick or Absent	71
Number of Diocesan Priests	286
Religious Priests in Diocese	60
Extern Priests in Diocese	8
Ordinations:	
Diocesan Priests	1
Transitional Deacons	2
Permanent Deacons	6
Permanent Deacons in Diocese	73
Total Brothers	16
Total Sisters	497
Parishes	
Parishes	172
With Resident Pastor:	
Resident Diocesan Priests	147
Resident Religious Priests	5
Without Resident Pastor:	
Administered by Priests	20
Missions	15
Pastoral Centers	20
Professional Ministry Personnel:	
Brothers	18
Sisters	472
Welfare	
Catholic Hospitals	3
Total Assisted	670,000
Health Care Centers	1
Total Assisted	300
Homes for the Aged	54
Residential Care of Children	10
Total Assisted	150
Specialized Homes	3
Total Assisted	60
Special Centers for Social Services	8
Total Assisted	62,800
Residential Care of Disabled	13
Total Assisted	125
Educational	
Diocesan Students in Other Seminaries	21
Total Seminarians	21
Colleges and Universities	1
Total Students	2,915
High Schools, Diocesan and Parish	5
Total Students	3,039
High Schools, Private	1
Total Students	737
Elementary Schools, Diocesan and Parish	39
Total Students	7,345
Elementary Schools, Private	1
Total Students	14
Catechesis/Religious Education:	
High School Students	7,777
Elementary Students	31,003
Total Students Under Catholic Instruction	52,851
Teachers in the Diocese:	
Priests	4
Brothers	6
Sisters	63
Lay Teachers	727
Vital Statistics	
Receptions into the Church:	
Infant Baptism Totals	5,522
Adult Baptism Totals	357
Received into Full Communion	655
First Communions	5,293
Confirmations	4,054
Marriages:	
Catholic	1,383
Interfaith	646
Total Marriages	2,029
Deaths	4,717
Total Catholic Population	345,736
Total Population	1,174,887

Former Bishops—Rt. Rev. PATRICK ANTHONY LUDDEN, D.D., ord. June 21, 1864; cons. May 1, 1887; died Aug. 6, 1912.—Rt. Rev. JOHN GRIMES, D.D., ord. Feb. 19, 1882; cons. May 16, 1909; Coadjutor Bishop, 1909-1912; succeeded to the See, Aug. 6, 1912; died July 26, 1922.—Most Rev. DANIEL JOSEPH CURLEY, D.D., ord. May 19, 1894; cons. May 1, 1923; died Aug. 3, 1932.—Most Rev. JOHN ALOYSIUS DUFFY, D.D., ord. June 13, 1908; cons. June 29, 1933; installed July 11, 1933; appt. Bishop of Buffalo, Jan. 9, 1937; installed in See of Buffalo, April 14, 1937; died Sept. 27, 1944.—Most Rev. WALTER A. FOERY, D.D., Ph.D., ord. June 10, 1916; appt. May 26, 1937; cons. Aug. 18, 1937; appt. assistant at the Pontifical Throne, Dec. 11, 1961; retired and named Titular Bishop of Miseno-Cape, Aug. 4, 1970; died May 10, 1978.—Most Rev. DAVID F. CUNNINGHAM, D.D., ord. June 12, 1926; appt. Titular Bishop of Lampsacus and Auxiliary Bishop of Syracuse, April 5, 1950; cons. June 8, 1950; appt. Coadjutor Bishop "Cum jure successiones," June 19, 1967; succeeded to the See, Aug. 4, 1970; died Feb. 22, 1979.—Most Rev. FRANK J. HARRISON, D.D., ord. June 4, 1937; appt. Titular Bishop of Aquae and Auxiliary Bishop of Syracuse, March 1, 1971; cons. April 22, 1971; appt. Bishop of Syracuse, Nov. 16, 1976; retired June 16, 1987.—Most Rev. JOSEPH T. O'KEEFE, D.D., Bishop of Syracuse; ord. April 17, 1948; appt. Titular Bishop of Tre Taverne and Auxiliary Bishop of New York, July 3, 1982; cons. Sept. 8, 1982; appt. Bishop of Syracuse, June 16, 1987; installed in See of Syracuse, Aug. 3, 1987; retired April 4, 1995; died Sept. 2, 1997.

Vicar General/Vicar for Parishes—Most Rev. THOMAS J. COSTELLO, D.D., *1515 Midland Ave., Syracuse, 13205.*

Vicars Forane—Northern Area Vicar: Rev. DAVID J. BAEHR, *103 W. 7th St., Oswego, 13126.* Southern Area Vicar: Rev. THOMAS J. RYAN, *155 Main St., Johnson City, 13790.* Eastern Area Vicars: Rev. PHILIP A. HEARN, *105 E. Liberty St., Rome, 13440.* Rev. DONALD H. KARLEN, *2 Barton Ave., Utica, 13502.* Western Area Vicars: Rev. RICHARD M. KOPP, *47 Syracuse St., Baldwinsville, 13027.* Rev. GEORGE F. SHEEHAN, *6651 Kirkville Rd., East Syracuse, 13057.*

Chancery Office—240 E. Onondaga St., Syracuse, 13202., Mailing Address: P.O. Box 511, Syracuse, 13201. Tel: 315-422-7203; Fax: 315-478-4619. Office Hours: Mon.-Fri. 8:30-4:30 Send official mail, including marriage dispensations, to Chancery.

Chancellor—Rev. MICHAEL P. MINEHAN, *6104 Cherry Valley Rd., LaFayette, 13084.*

Assistant Chancellor/Secretary to Bishop Moynihan—Rev. JOSEPH S. ZARESKI, *3127 James St., Syracuse, 13206.*

Board of Diocesan Consultors—Most Rev. THOMAS J. COSTELLO, D.D.; Revs. DAVID J. BAEHR; PHILIP A. HEARN; DONALD H. KARLEN; RICHARD M. KOPP; JAMES P. LANG; GREGORY C. LESTRANGE; THOMAS J. MCGRATH; THOMAS J. RYAN; GEORGE F. SHEEHAN.

Management Team—Most Rev. JAMES M. MOYNIHAN; Most Rev. THOMAS J. COSTELLO, D.D.; Revs. LOUIS F. AIELLO; JAMES P. LANG; TIMOTHY S. ELMER; MICHAEL P. MINEHAN; JOSEPH H. PHILLIPS; JOSEPH

S. ZARESKI; Friar THOMAS PURCELL, O.F.M.Conv.; Mrs. MARIA TYKSINSKI; Sr. MARY ANNE HEENAN, C.S.J.; Sr. EILEEN MCCANN; Mr. DENNIS J. MANNING; Ms. DANIELLE CUMMINGS.

Pastoral Council—Most Rev. JAMES M. MOYNIHAN, Pres.; Ms. KATHLEEN M. DYER, Exec. Sec., *101 Ridge Rd., Fulton, 13069.* Tel: 315-592-5566.

Pastoral Examiners—Revs. JOHN P. FENLON; MORITZ FUCHS; THOMAS KEATING; JAMES KENNEDY; RICHARD V. O'NEILL; DANIEL G. MURPHY; JOHN F. ROSE; JOSEPH SALERNO; JOSEPH S. ZARESKI.

Presbyteral Council—Most Rev. JAMES M. MOYNIHAN, Pres.; Most Rev. THOMAS J. COSTELLO; Revs. GREGORY C. LESTRANGE, Chm. EDMUND J. DURR, Vice Chm. ROBERT O'HARA, Treas. JAMES F. SMITH, S.J., Sec. THOMAS F. HOBBES; JOHN E. MIKALAJUNAS; DENNIS HAYES; FREDERICK R. MANNARA; CHARLES M. MAJOR; RICHARD R. THOMPSON; PAUL V. CAREY; JOHN J. COSTELLO; EDWARD J. HAYES; CLIFFORD H. AUTH; THOMAS P. KOBUSZEWSKI; THOMAS I. WARD; GARY M. FUKES; JOHN C. SCHOPFER; G. PETER WORN; Rev. Msgr. WILLIAM J. DONOVAN; Rev. Msgr. LAWRENCE E. GIBLIN; Rev. JUSTIN A. BIASE, O.F.M.Conv.

Diocesan Tribunal—

Judicial Vicar—Rev. TIMOTHY S. ELMER, J.C.L. Tel: 315-470-1480.

Judges—Revs. JOHN P. DONOVAN, J.C.L.; MARK J. GANTLEY, J.C.L.; ROBERT P. HYDE, J.C.L.

Defender of the Bond—Rev. MICHAEL P. MINEHAN, J.C.L.

Promoter of Justice—Rev. Msgr. JAMES A. MCCLOSKEY; Rev. PAUL CARMAN.

Notary of the Tribunal—KATHLEEN CUSHING.

Advocates—Sr. ANNA WALTER MOSSDORF, O.S.F.; MARGARET EDGECOMB.

Auditor—Deacon PAUL MULLIN.

Case Coordinators/Staff—KATHLEEN CUSHING.

Vicar for Administration—Rev. MICHAEL P. MINEHAN, *240 E. Onondaga St., P.O. Box 511, Syracuse, 13201.* Tel: 315-422-7203.

Director for Community Services—Mr. DENNIS J. MANNING, A.C.S.W., *240 E. Onondaga St., P.O. Box 511, Syracuse, 13201.* Tel: 315-424-1830.

Vicar for Parishes—Rev. JAMES P. LANG, *240 E. Onondaga St., P.O. Box 511, Syracuse, 13201.* Tel: 315-470-1437.

Vicar for Priests—Most Rev. THOMAS J. COSTELLO, D.D., *240 E. Onondaga St., P.O. Box 511, Syracuse, 13201.* Tel: 315-470-1460.

Vicar for Religious—Friar THOMAS F. PURCELL, O.F.M.Conv., *240 E. Onondaga St., P.O. Box 511, Syracuse, 13201.* Tel: 315-422-7203; 470-1424.

Diocesan Offices

Accounting—Ms. DEBRA SOCHAN, CFO, *P.O. Box 511, Syracuse, 13201.* Tel: 315-470-9045; Fax: 315-422-9139.

Adminstration—Rev. MICHAEL P. MINEHAN, Vicar, *P.O. Box 511, Syracuse, 13201.* Tel: 315-422-7203.

Archives—Mr. CARL ROESCH, Archivist, *P.O. Box 511, Syracuse, 13201.* Tel: 315-470-1493.

Asian Apostolate—Rev. JOHN TINH TRAN, C.M.C.; Sr. JUDITH HOWLEY, C.S.J., *215 N. State St., Syracuse, 13203.* Tel: 315-472-7043.

Benefits—Ms. CAROLYN CAIN, Dir., *P.O. Box 511, Syracuse, 13201.* Tel: 315-422-9091.

Black Catholic Ministry—RUBY RANDALL, *P.O. Box 511, Syracuse, 13201.* Tel: 315-470-1463.

Boy Scouts/Girl Scouts—Rev. JAMES P. LANG, Chap., *240 E. Onondaga St., P.O. Box 511, Syracuse, 13201-0511.* Tel: 315-470-1437.

Building Commission—Most Rev. JAMES M. MOYNIHAN; Most Rev. THOMAS J. COSTELLO, D.D.; Revs. MICHAEL P. MINEHAN; JOSEPH E. SCARDELLA; Mr. THOMAS V. DADEY, Esq.; Mr. EDWARD T. KING; Mr. J. DOUGLAS ROSS; WILLIAM DORAN; JAMES A. MURPHY; EDWARD SAMOLIS; Ms. DEBRA J. SOCHAN.

Catholic Cemeteries—Rev. JAMES C. FRITZEN, Dir.; Mr. MARK LAZAROSKI, Exec. Dir., *2315 South Ave., Syracuse, 13207.* Tel: 315-475-4639; Fax: 315-422-0363.

Catholic Charities—Mr. DENNIS J. MANNING, A.C.S.W., *P.O. Box 511, Syracuse, 13202.* Tel: 315-424-1830; Fax: 315-478-4619.

Onondaga County Director—Mr. BRIAN WALTON, *1654 W. Onondaga St., Syracuse, 13204.* Tel: 315-424-1806.

Downtown Emergency Assistance Office—SANDY SMITH, *264 E. Onondaga St., Syracuse, 13202.* Tel: 315-424-1876.

Broome County Director—Mr. JOSEPH G. SLAVIK, *232 Main St., Binghamton, 13905.* Tel: 607-729-9166.

Chenango County Director—JANE CODDINGTON, Dir., *3 O'Hara Dr., Norwich, 13815.* Tel: 607-334-8244.

Cortland County Director—PAULA CURRIE, *33-35 Central Ave., Cortland, 13045.* Tel: 607-756-5992.

Oneida and Madison Counties Director—KATHLEEN EICHENLAUB, *1408 Genesee St., Utica, 13502.* Tel: 315-724-2150.

Oswego County Director—ANDREA MCCABE, *365 First St., Fulton, 13069.* Tel: 315-598-3980.

Catholic Deaf Community—MARY MARGARET VAN DAMME, Dir., *1119 Elm St., Utica, 13501.* Tel: 315-735-8184 (TTY/Voice).

Catholic Relief Services—Mr. DENNIS J. MANNING, Dir., *P.O. Box 511, Syracuse, 13201.* Tel: 315-424-1830.

Catholic Schools—Sr. MARY ANNE HEENAN, C.S.J., Supt., *P.O. Box 511, Syracuse, 13201.* Tel: 315-470-1450; Fax: 315-470-1470. Rev. CHARLES S. VAVONESE, Asst. Supt.; Mrs. LESLEY HUGHES, Dir. Curriculum; Sr. PATRICIA GIBSON, Dir. Govt. Programs; Sr. ELOISE EMM, Dir. Formation.

Northern & Western Regions—Sr. HELEN ANN CHARLEBOIS, I.H.M., Asst. Supt., *P.O. Box 511, Syracuse, 13201.* Tel: 315-470-1450; Fax: 315-470-1470.

Southern Region—Dr. WILLIAM DAVENPORT, Asst. Supt., *19 Lincoln Ave., P.O. Box 90, Binghamton, 13905.* Tel: 607-723-1547; Fax: 607-723-5697.

Eastern Region—Ms. KATHLEEN COYE, Asst. Supt., *17 Herkimer Rd., Utica, 13502.* Tel: 315-735-2111; Fax: 315-735-3603.

"The Catholic Sun"—Rev. DONALD BOURGEOIS, Editor in Chief & Gen. Mgr., *421 S. Warren St., Syracuse, 13202.* Tel: 315-422-8153; 800-333-0571; Fax: 315-422-7549.

Catholic Television—Mr. JAMES FUNSON, Dir., *1342 Lancaster Ave., Syracuse, 13210.* Tel: 315-472-3584; Fax: 315-472-8409.

Christopher Community—Mr. PETER WHITE, Exec. Dir., *1654 W. Onondaga St., Syracuse, 13204.* Tel: 315-414-1821.

Clerical Fund Society of the Roman Catholic Diocese of Syracuse—Most Rev. JAMES M. MOYNIHAN, Pres.; Most Rev. THOMAS J. COSTELLO, D.D., Vice Pres.; Rev. MICHAEL P. MINEHAN, Sec. & Treas.

Office of Communications—Ms. DANIELLE CUMMINGS, Dir., *P.O. Box 511, Syracuse, 13201.* Tel: 315-470-1476; Fax: 315-478-4619.

Council of Religious—Sr. ROSE GARRAMONE, O.S.F., Pres., *P.O. Box 511, Syracuse, 13201.*

Development Office—Mr. JERRY FARNSWORTH, *1342 Lancaster Ave., Syracuse, 13210.* Tel: 315-472-0203; 472-7902; Fax: 315-472-8409.

Disabilities Office—Mr. THOMAS CUNNINGHAM, JR., Dir., *P.O. Box 511, Syracuse, 13201.* Tel: 315-424-1830; Fax: 315-478-4619.

Ecumenical Commission—Rev. Msgr. RONALD C. BILL, Dir., *8229 S. Main St., Cicero, 13039.* Tel: 315-699-2752.

Family Life Education—Rev. JOSEPH H. PHILLIPS, Dir., *1342 Lancaster Ave., Syracuse, 13210.* Tel: 315-472-6754; Fax: 315-472-8409.

Finance Committee—Most Rev. JAMES M. MOYNIHAN; Revs. MICHAEL P. MINEHAN; J. ROBERT YEAZEL; JOSEPH S. ZARESKI; Mr. JOHN D. BURKE; Mr. JOSEPH MCGLYNN; Mr. JAMES MURPHY; Ms. CAROL PIEKLIK; Ms. DOREEN SIMMONS, Esq.; Ms. DEBRA SOCHAN.

Formation for Ministry—Deacon JOSEPH DANISZEWSKI, Dir., *P.O. Box 511, Syracuse, 13202.* Tel: 315-470-1421; Fax: 315-478-4619.

Health Care—Mr. DENNIS J. MANNING, A.C.S.W., Coord., *P.O. Box 511, Syracuse, 13201.* Tel: 315-424-1830; Fax: 315-478-4619.

HOPE Appeal—Mr. JERRY FARNSWORTH, *1342 Lancaster Ave., Syracuse, 13210.* Tel: 315-472-0203; Fax: 315-472-8409.

Human Life Office—Mrs. CINDY FALISE, Dir., *P.O. Box 511, Syracuse, 13201.* Tel: 315-424-1830; Fax: 315-478-4619.

Liturgy—MARIA TYKSINSKI, Dir. PATRICIA STACEY, Asst. Dir., *P.O. Box 511, Syracuse, 13201.* Tel: 315-470-1425.

Parish Services—Mr. NICK CROSBY, *P.O. Box 511, Syracuse, 13201.* Tel: 315-470-9089; Fax: 315-422-9139.

Permanent Diaconate—Deacon LESLIE F. DISTIN, Dir., *P.O. Box 511, Syracuse, 13201.* Tel: 315-470-1466.

Priest Personnel—Most Rev. THOMAS J. COSTELLO, D.D., Dir., *P.O. Box 511, Syracuse, 13201.* Tel: 315-470-1460; Fax: 315-478-4619.

Priests' Personnel Committee—Most Rev. JAMES M. MOYNIHAN; Most Rev. THOMAS J. COSTELLO, D.D.; Revs. STEPHEN WIRKES; GERALD J. BUCKLEY; MICHAEL J. CARMOLA; DANIEL M. CARUSO; KEVIN J. CORCORAN; ARTHUR R. HAPANOWICZ; MICHAEL P. MINEHAN; WILLIAM R. JONES; DANIEL J. O'HARA; JAMES T. QUEEN; JOSEPH S. ZARESKI.

Project Rachel—Mrs. CINDY FALISE, Dir., *P.O. Box 511, Syracuse, 13201.* Tel: 315-424-3737.

Personal Resource Center—Rev. NEAL QUARTIER, Dir., *420 Montgomery St., Syracuse, 13202.* Tel: 315-470-1462.

Propagation of the Faith—Rev. JOSEPH H. PHILLIPS, Dir.; Sr. JUDITH MARKERT, C.S.J., Coord., *1342 Lancaster Ave., Syracuse, 13210.* Tel: 315-472-3442; Fax: 315-472-8409.

Religious Education—Rev. LOUIS F. AIELLO, Dir.; Sr. KATIE EIFFE, Asst. Dir., *P.O. Box 511, Syracuse, 13202.* Tel: 315-470-1431; Fax: 315-478-4619.

Eastern Region—CATHERINE CORNUE, Dir., *One Sherman St., New Hartford, 13413.* Tel: 315-797-4030.

Northern Region—Sr. GERMANE HILSTON, Dir., *108 E. 6th St., Oswego, 13126.* Tel: 315-343-5557.

Southern Region—Sr. LOIS BARTON, C.S.J., Dir., *705 W. Main St., Endicott, 13760.* Tel: 607-786-9650.

South (Norwich)—ANGIE DIAMOND, *Resource Center, 20 Randall Ave., Norwich, 13815.* Tel: 607-334-2883.

Western Region—THERESA MAY, Dir., *1342 Lancaster Ave., Syracuse, 13210.* Tel: 315-472-6753.

West (Cortland)—ELANA MOSES, Resource Center, *44 N. Main St., Cortland, 13045.* Tel: 607-756-2532.

Respect for Life—Mrs. CINDY FALISE, Dir., *P.O. Box 511, Syracuse, 13201.* Tel: 315-424-1859.

Laymen & Laywomen Retreat Movements—Rev. MICHAEL J. CARMOLA, Dir., *Christ the King Retreat House, 500 Brookford Rd., Syracuse, 13224.* Tel: 315-446-2680.

Spanish Apostolate—Rev. ROBERT D. CHRYST, Dir., *170 Seymour St., Syracuse, 13204.* Tel: 315-442-9390.

Syracuse Catholic Press Association, Inc.—"The Catholic Sun"; Rev. DONALD BOURGEOIS, Editor in Chief & Gen. Mgr.; Most Rev. JAMES M. MOYNIHAN, Pres., *421 S. Warren St., Syracuse, 13202.* Tel: 315-422-2153; 1-800-333-0571; Fax: 315-422-7549.

Vocation Formation—Rev. NEAL E. QUARTIER, Dir., *P.O. Box 511, Syracuse, 13201.* Tel: 315-470-1452; Fax: 315-478-4619.

Vocation Promotion—Rev. JAMES F. QUINN, Dir.; Sr. ROBERTA SOUTHWICK, S.A., Asst. Dir., *P.O. Box 511, Syracuse, 13201.* Tel: 315-470-1468; Fax: 315-478-4619.

Youth Ministry—Sr. EILEEN MCCANN, C.S.J., Dir. DOMINICK VETERE, Assoc. Dir., *P.O. Box 511, Syracuse, 13201.* Tel: 315-470-1419; Fax: 315-478-4619.

CLERGY, PARISHES, MISSIONS AND PAROCHIAL SCHOOLS

CITY OF SYRACUSE

(Onondaga County)

1—THE CATHEDRAL OF THE IMMACULATE CONCEPTION (1841), Rev. Msgr. Joseph M. Champlin, Rector; Most Rev. James M. Moynihan; Revs. Carmelo Malacari, O.F.M.Conv.; John C. Schopfer; Neal E. Quartier; Deacon Pio Peter Carranti.

Res., 259 E. Onondaga St., 13202. Tel: 315-422-4177; Fax: 315-478-4619.

School—420 Montgomery St., 13202. Tel: 315-422-7217. Sr. Mary Jane Wilcox, D.C., Prin.

Daughters of Charity of St. Vincent de Paul 1; Lay Teachers 14; Students 136.

Stations—Vivian Teal Howard, Tel: 315-478-1641; Clinton St. Plaza, Tel: 315-475-2141; McCarthy Manor, Tel: 315-475-6390; Rosewood Heights, Tel: 315-474-4431.

2—ASSUMPTION B.V.M. (1844) (German), Revs. Patrick Gallagher, O.F.M.Conv.; Robert Amrhein, O.F.M.Conv., Pastoral Assoc.; Bartholomew Gaske, O.F.M.Conv.; Jeffrey Keefe, O.F.M.Conv., Ph.D., Prov. Psychologist, Franciscan Counseling; Charles Nelipowitz, O.F.M.Conv.; Regis Rodda, O.F.M.Conv.; Herman Seibert, O.F.M.Conv.; Conrad Sommerville, O.F.M.Conv.; Michael Taylor.

Res., St. Francis Friary, 812 N. Salina St., 13208. Tel: 315-422-4833; Fax: 315-422-4363. [CEM]

Assumption Cemetery Corporation—2401 Court St., 13208. Tel: 315-454-3841; Fax: 315-454-4931.

3—BLESSED SACRAMENT (1921), Revs. James T. O'Brien; Kevin Corcoran. In res., Rev. Joseph S. Zareski.

Res., 3127 James St., 13206. Tel: 315-437-3394; Fax: 315-432-9198.

School—(Grades PreK-6) 3129 James St., 13206. Tel: 315-437-1261; Fax: 315-463-1628. Mrs. Andrea Polcaro, Prin.

Sisters of St. Joseph of Carondelet 1; Lay Teachers 14; Students 350.

Catechesis/Religious Programs—Students 395.

4—HOLY TRINITY (1891) (German), Rev. Edmund J. Durr; Sr. Mary Margaret Singer, C.S.J., Pastoral Assoc.

Res., 501 Park St., 13203. Tel: 315-474-8681; Fax: 315-474-3154.

Catechesis/Religious Programs—Students 95.

5—MOST HOLY ROSARY (1913), Rev. Frederick R. Mannara.

Res., 111 Roberts Ave., 13207-1397. Tel: 315-478-5749; Fax: 315-478-8629.

School—(Grades PreK-6) 1031 Bellevue Ave., 13207. Tel: 315-476-6035; Fax: 315-476-0219. Sr. Mary Gregory Munger, S.S.J., Prin.
Sisters 4; Lay Teachers 10; Students 194.
Catechesis/Religious Programs—Students 190.

6—OUR LADY OF LOURDES (1947), Rev. Thomas P. Fitzpatrick; Deacon Leo Needham.
Res., 300 Valley Dr., 13207. Tel: 315-476-9576.
School—301 Valley Dr., 13207. Tel: 315-476-2296. Mrs. Margie Hart, Prin.
Lay Teachers 7; Students 90.
Catechesis/Religious Programs—Tel: 315-478-6383.
Students 140.

7—OUR LADY OF POMPEI (1924) (Italian), Revs. Joseph E. Scardella; John T. McGraw; Deacon Kenneth Money. In res., Revs. Frederick A. Pompei; John Tinh Tran.
Res., 301 Ash St., 13208. Tel: 315-422-7163; Fax: 315-422-7164.
School—915-917 N. McBride St., 13208. Tel: 315-422-8548.
Lay Teachers 10; Students 155.
Catechesis/Religious Programs—Tel: 315-472-2260.
Students 245.
Convent—920 N. McBride St., 13208. Tel: 315-422-7922. Franciscan Missionary Sisters of the Immaculate Conception

8—OUR LADY OF SOLACE (1926), Rev. William R. Jones. In res., Rev. Alfred J. Bebel.
Res., 516 Salt Springs Rd., 13224. Tel: 315-446-2060; Fax: 315-446-2061.
Catechesis/Religious Programs—Students 70.

9—SACRED HEART (1892) (Polish), Revs. Peter W. Gleba; Stanley Dudkiewicz (Poland); Stanley Matula (Poland); Deacons James L. Morse; Joseph Daniszewski.
Res., 927 Park Ave., 13204. Tel: 315-422-2343; Fax: 315-422-2344. [CEM 2]
School—1001 Park Ave., 13204. Tel: 315-422-7372; Fax: 315-422-7372. Sr. Melanie Jaworski, C.S.S.F., Prin.
Felician Sisters 3; Lay Teachers 17; Students 151.
Catechesis/Religious Programs—Tel: 315-422-8883; Fax: 315-422-7372.
Students 101.

10—ST. ANDREW THE APOSTLE (1953), Rev. Edward J. Reimer; Sr. Patricia Bergan, O.S.F., Pastoral Assoc.
Res., 124 Alden St., 13210. Tel: 315-476-8656.
Catechesis/Religious Programs—Students 38.

11—ST. ANN (1955), Rev. John L. Roark. In res., Rev. Joseph H. Phillips.
Res., 4461 Onondaga Blvd., 13219. Tel: 315-468-1803; Fax: 315-487-6312.
School—Tel: 315-468-6441. Mrs. Nancy Tario, Prin.
Sisters 1; Lay Teachers 7; Students 150.
Catechesis/Religious Programs—Tel: 315-487-6201.
Students 183.

12—ST. ANTHONY OF PADUA (1901), Rev. Robert D. Chryst. In res., Most Rev. Thomas J. Costello.
Res., 1515 Midland Ave., 13205. Tel: 315-475-4114.

13—ST. BRIGID AND ST. JOSEPH (1926 and 1869), Rev. Laurence W. Kennedy; Deacon Leonard S. Monnat.
Res., 318 Herkimer St., 13204. Tel: 315-488-7122; Fax: 315-484-9723.
Catechesis/Religious Programs—Students 65.

14—ST. CHARLES (1929), Revs. James H. Carey; Philip S. Keane, S.S.; Deacon Peter Vanelli; Sr. Jean A. Burns, Parish Min.
Res., 417 S. Orchard Rd., 13219. Tel: 315-468-4122; Fax: 315-468-4122.
School—200 W. High Ter., 13219. Tel: 315-488-7631; Fax: 315-488-0617. Sr. Donna Driscoll, Prin.
Sisters 2; Lay Teachers 14; Students 239.
Catechesis/Religious Programs—Tel: 315-488-7645.
Students 217.
Convent—401 E. Corey Rd., 13219. Tel: 315-468-6041. Missionary Franciscan Sisters of the Immaculate Conception

15—ST. DANIEL (1932), Rev. Msgr. Eugene M. Yennock; Rev. Mark J. Gantley.
Res., 3004 Court St., 13208. Tel: 315-454-4946; Fax: 315-454-0978.
School—Tel: 315-455-7021. Sr. Antonia Segnetto, O.S.F., Prin.
Sisters of the Third Franciscan Order 1; Lay Teachers 8; Students (Grades K-6) 166; Students (Grades PreK-K) 29.
Catechesis/Religious Programs—621 Roxford Rd., S., 13208. Tel: 315-454-4946.
Students 450.

16—ST. JAMES (1925), Rev. Daniel J. O'Hara. In res., Rev. James P. Lang. Pastoral Assocs.: Sr. Carolyn Chmielewski, C.S.J.; Deacon Donald M. McCabe.
Res., 4845 S. Salina St., 13205. Tel: 315-469-7789; Fax: 315-469-7780.
School—(Grades PreK-6) 4837 S. Salina St., 13205. Tel: 315-492-1054. Sr. David Agnes DeForrest, Prin.
Sisters 2; Lay Teachers 11; Students 138.
Catechesis/Religious Programs—Students 191.
Convent—111 Munson Dr., 13205. Tel: 315-492-3654. Sisters of the Third Franciscan Order M.C.
Station—Brighton Towers.

17—ST. JOHN THE BAPTIST (1827), Rev. John R. DeLorenzo. In res., Rev. Daniel C. Muscalino.
Res., 406 Court St., 13208. Tel: 315-478-0916.
School—1406 Park St., 13208. Tel: 315-422-6982. Mrs. Sally Lisi, Prin.
Lay Teachers 14; Students 159.
Catechesis/Religious Programs—Students 100.

18—ST. JOHN THE EVANGELIST (1851), Rev. Neal E. Quartier, Admin.; Deacon John H. Collins.
Res., 259 E. Onondaga St., 13202. Tel: 315-474-2363; Fax: 315-474-1045.

19—ST. LUCY (1872), Rev. James D. Mathews. In res., Rev. Msgr. Charles J. Fahey.
Res., 432 Gifford St., 13204. Tel: 315-475-7273; Fax: 315-475-7273.
School—(Grades K-6) 422 Gifford St., 13204. Tel: 315-478-6312. Ms. Karen McCann, Prin.
Lay Teachers 6; Students 82.
Catechesis/Religious Programs—Tel: 315-478-6312.
Students 74.

20—ST. PATRICK (1870), Rev. E. Peter Reddick.
Res., 216 N. Lowell Ave., 13204. Tel: 315-475-2185; Fax: 315-476-1565.
School—(Grades PreK-6) 210 Schuyler St., 13204. Tel: 315-476-4076; Fax: 315-476-4052. Cheryl Canfield, Prin.
Sisters of St. Joseph of Carondelet 2; Lay Teachers 10; Students 126.
Catechesis/Religious Programs—Students 85.

21—ST. PETER (1890) (Italian), Rev. Tarcisio Bagatin, C.S.
Res., 709 James St., 13203. Tel: 315-472-4451; Fax: 315-422-3441.
Catechesis/Religious Programs—Students 23.

22—ST. STEPHEN (1915) (Slovak), Revs. Peter W. Gleba; Tadeusz Rudnik (Canada).
Res., 305 N. Geddes St., 13204. Tel: 315-422-5224.

23—ST. THERESE THE LITTLE FLOWER OF JESUS (1926), Rev. Edward J. Reimer.
Res., 112 Lancaster Pl., 13210. Tel: 315-472-9934.
Catechesis/Religious Programs—Fax: 315-472-9941.
Students 100.

24—ST. VINCENT DE PAUL (1893), Rev. Alfred E. Nortz. In res., Revs. Wilbur J. Votraw; Theodore C. Sizing.
Res., 342 Vine St., 13203. Tel: 315-479-6689; Fax: 315-479-6689.
Catechesis/Religious Programs—Students 80.
Convent—1101 Burnet Ave., 13203. Tel: 315-479-8012. Sisters of St. Joseph of Carondelet

25—TRANSFIGURATION (1911) (Polish), Rev. Thomas P. Kobuszewski. In res., Rev. Angelo L. Morbita.
Res., 740 Teall Ave., 13206. Tel: 315-479-6129; Fax: 315-426-0684.

OUTSIDE THE CITY OF SYRACUSE

Bainbridge, Chenango Co., St. John the Evangelist (1914), Rev. Donald E. Bourgeois.
Res., 34 S. Main St., 13733. Tel: 607-967-4481.
Catechesis/Religious Programs—Students 121.
Mission—Afton, Chenango Co., St. Agnes, Spring St., 13730. Tel: 607-639-1200.

Baldwinsville, Onondaga Co., St. Augustine (1966), Rev. John Rose.
Res., 7333 O'Brien Rd., 13027. Tel: 315-638-0585.
Catechesis/Religious Programs—Tel: 315-638-0864.
Students 368.

St. Elizabeth Ann Seton (1985), Rev. John P. Wagner.
Res., 3494 NY State Rte. 31, 13027. Tel: 315-652-4300; Fax: 315-622-1761.
Catechesis/Religious Programs—Tel: 315-652-3900.
Students 1,009.

St. Mary (1852), Rev. Richard M. Kopp.
Res., 47 Syracuse St., 13027. Tel: 315-635-5762; Fax: 315-635-8137. [CEM]
School—49 Syracuse St., 13027. Tel: 315-635-3977. Sr. Mary Shanahan, D.C., Prin.
Sisters of the Third Franciscan Order M.C. 1; Lay Teachers 8; Students 209.
Catechesis/Religious Programs—Tel: 315-635-5454.
Students 380.

Binghamton, Broome Co.,

1—ST. ANDREW, (1955), Rev. Michael T. Meagher.
Res. & Parish Center: 356 Conklin Ave., 13903. Tel: 607-722-4049; Fax: 607-651-9140.
Catechesis/Religious Programs—Tel: 607-722-9474.
Students 237.

2—ST. ANN, (1925) (Slovak), Rev. Paul J. Keebler.
Res., 346 Prospect St., 13905. Tel: 607-797-1856; Fax: 607-797-8452. [JC]
Catechesis/Religious Programs—Students 36.

3—ST. CATHERINE OF SIENA, (1929), Rev. Robert B. Stephenson; Deacon Raymond Goskowski; Sr. Karen Gaube, C.S.J., Pastoral Assoc.
Res., 1031 Chenango St., 13901. Tel: 607-722-4388; Fax: 607-722-1336.
Catechesis/Religious Programs—1051 Chenango St., 13901. Tel: 607-722-4177.
Students 545.

4—ST. CHRISTOPHER, (1940), Rev. Donald C. VanAmburgh.
Res., 103 Castle Creek Rd., 13901. Tel: 607-723-0677.
Catechesis/Religious Programs—Tel: 607-723-7010.
Students 328.

5—SS. CYRIL AND METHOD, (1904) (Slovak), Rev. George Sandor, O.F.M.Conv. In res., Revs. Kenan McGowan, O.F.M.Conv.; Simeon Rukstalis, O.F.M.Conv.; Ambrose Hojsik, O.F.M.Conv.; James Fukes; Bro. Edward Falsey, O.F.M.Conv.
Res., 148 Clinton St., 13905. Tel: 607-724-1372; Fax: 607-724-1468.
Catechesis/Religious Programs—Tel: 607-723-2183.
Students 74.

6—ST. JOHN THE EVANGELIST, (1907), Revs. Paul J. Alciati; C. Patrick Keating.
Res., 1263 Vestal Ave., 13903. Tel: 607-722-0493; Fax: 607-722-0493.
Catechesis/Religious Programs—Fax: 607-723-5171.
Students 448.

7—ST. JOSEPH, (1914) (Lithuanian), Rev. John E. Mikalajunas.
Res., One Judson Ave., 13905. Tel: 607-797-5264; Fax: 607-797-5264.
Catechesis/Religious Programs—Tel: 607-797-5264.
Students 117.

8—ST. MARY OF THE ASSUMPTION, (1887; 1913), Rev. Msgr. Paul A. Brigandi; Rev. Clarence J. Cerwonka; Sr. Linda Gaige, C.S.J.
Res., 37 Fayette St., 13901. Tel: 607-723-5383.
Catechesis/Religious Programs—Students 175.

9—ST. PATRICK, (1838), Rev. Laurence J. Lord. In res., Rev. Robert A. Ours.
Res., 9 Leroy St., 13905. Tel: 607-722-1060; Fax: 607-724-1466.
Catechesis/Religious Programs—Students 140.
Convent—46 Oak St., 13905. Tel: 607-722-4745. Sisters of St. Joseph of Carondelet

10—ST. PAUL, (1896), Rev. Corey S. Van Kuren.
Res., 15 Doubleday St., 13901. Tel: 607-722-6492.

11—ST. STANISLAUS KOSTKA, (1914) (Polish), Rev. John E. Mikalajunas.
Res., 368 Prospect St., 13905-1810. Tel: 607-797-3564; Fax: 607-797-3564.
Catechesis/Religious Programs—Tel: 607-797-5264.
Students 57.
Convent—376 Prospect St., 13905.

12—ST. THOMAS AQUINAS, (1927), Rev. James D. Tormey.
Res., One Aquinas St., 13905. Tel: 607-797-4015; Fax: 607-729-9727.
Catechesis/Religious Programs—4 Aquinas St., 13905. Tel: 607-797-3304.
Students 127.

Boonville, Oneida Co., St. Joseph (1875), Rev. David J. Orzel.
Res., 110 Charles St., 13309. Tel: 315-942-4618; Fax: 315-942-4618. [CEM]
Catechesis/Religious Programs—Tel: 315-942-5955.
Students 124.

Brewerton, Onondaga Co., St. Agnes (1958), Rev. William T. Guckert.
Res., 5472 Miller Rd., 13029. Tel: 315-676-7050; Fax: 315-676-7050.
Catechesis/Religious Programs—Tel: 315-676-5662.
Students 102.

Bridgeport, Onondaga Co., St. Francis of Assisi (1952), Rev. Ralph White, O.F.M.Conv.
Res., P.O. Box 550, 13030-0550. Tel: 315-633-2561; Fax: 315-633-0672.
Parish Center—13030-0550. Tel: 315-633-9682.

Camden, Oneida Co., St. John (1852), Rev. Joseph E. Moskal.
Res., 22 Church St., 13316. Tel: 315-245-1603. [CEM]
Catechesis/Religious Programs—Students 121.

Camillus, Onondaga Co., St. Joseph (1852), Revs. John S. Finnegan; Peter A. Williams.
Res., 5600 W. Genesee St., 13031. Tel: 315-488-8490; Fax: 315-488-4214.

Canastota, Madison Co., St. Agatha (1883), Rev. Anthony F. Tosti; Sr. Dorothy Bunal, C.S.J., Pastoral Min.
Res., 329 N. Peterboro St., 13032. Tel: 315-697-7104; Fax: 315-697-7108. [CEM]
Catechesis/Religious Programs—Tel: 315-697-7827.
Students 295.
Convent—406 Spencer St., 13032. Tel: 315-697-7210.

Cazenovia, Madison Co., St. James (1847), Rev. G. Peter Worn.
Res., 6 Green St., 13035. Tel: 315-655-3441; Fax: 315-655-3442. [CEM]
Catechesis/Religious Programs—Tel: 315-655-4871.
Students 529.

Central Square, Oswego Co., St. Michael (1928), Rev. John J. Smegelsky.
Res., 598 S. Main St., P.O. Box 514, 13036. Tel: 315-676-2898; Fax: 315-676-3103.
Catechesis/Religious Programs—Students 320.

Chadwicks, Oneida Co., St. Anthony of Padua (1907), Rev. Edward J. Hayes.
Res., 3364 Oneida St., P.O. Box 310, 13319. Tel: 315-737-8066.
Catechesis/Religious Programs—Tel: 315-737-8692.
Students 276.

Chenango Forks, Broome Co., St. Rita (1946), Rev. Stanley J. Gerlock.
Res., 2530 NY State Rte. 12, 13746. Tel: 607-648-8816.
Catechesis/Religious Programs—Students 100.

Chittenango, Madison Co., St. Patrick (1853), Rev. Timothy Elmer.
Res., 1341 Murray Dr., 13037. Tel: 315-687-6105; Fax: 315-687-0046. [CEM]
Catechesis/Religious Programs—Tel: 315-687-6561.
Students 353.

Cicero, Onondaga Co., Sacred Heart (1888), Rev. Msgr. Ronald Bill; Rev. David J. Jutton.
Res., 8229 S. Main St., 13039. Tel: 315-699-2752; Fax: 315-699-3775.
Catechesis/Religious Programs—Tel: 315-699-7678.
Students 945.

Clark Mills, Oneida Co., Church of the Annunciation (1908), Rev. Albert J. Proud.
Mailing Address: 7616 E. South St., Clinton, 13323.
Res., 25 South St., 13321. Tel: 315-853-6138.
Catechesis/Religious Programs—Tel: 315-853-6139.
Students 178.

Clayville, Oneida Co., St. Patrick (1864), Rev. William S. Baker.
Res., 8 Church St., Box 285, 13322. Tel: 315-839-5483. [CEM]
Catechesis/Religious Programs—Students 310.

Cleveland, Oswego Co., St. Mary of the Assumption (1854), Rev. William C. Esposito.
Res., 148 State Rte. 49, 13042. Tel: 315-675-3542. [CEM]
Catechesis/Religious Programs—Tel: 315-675-3165.
Students 150.
Mission—Constantia, Oswego Co., St. Bernadette, State Rte. 49, Constantia, 13044. Tel: 315-623-9803.

Clinton, Oneida Co., St. Mary (1850), Rev. John P. Croghan.
Res., 13 Marvin St., 13323. Tel: 315-853-2935; Fax: 315-859-1097. [CEM]
School—(Grades K-6) Prospect St., 13323. Tel: 315-853-6196. Mrs. Linda DePhillips, Prin.
Lay Teachers 12; Students 201.
Catechesis/Religious Programs—Tel: 315-853-2492.
Students 417.

Cortland, Cortland Co., St. Anthony (1917) (Italian), Rev. Jerome A. Katz.
Res., 45 Crandall St., 13045. Tel: 607-756-7533; Fax: 607-756-7697.
Catechesis/Religious Programs—Students 110.

St. Mary (1855), Rev. John P. Fenlon; Deacons Richard J. Dwyer; Laurence Brickner; Joseph Caminiti; Stephen Smith.
Res., 44 N. Main St., 13045. Tel: 607-756-9967; Fax: 607-756-9968.
School—61 N. Main St., 13045. Tel: 607-756-5614. Sr. Harriet Hamilton, O.S.F., Prin.
Franciscan Sisters of Allegany 1; Lay Teachers 21; Students 400.
Catechesis/Religious Programs—Tel: 607-753-6489.
Students 240.

Deposit, Broome Co., St. Joseph (1851), Rev. John A. Booth.
Res., 98 Second St., 13754. Tel: 607-467-2291. [CEM]
Parish Center—74 Second St., 13754. Tel: 607-467-2226.

Dewitt, Onondaga Co., Holy Cross (1943), Revs. J. Robert Yeazel; Charles Currie. In res., Rev. Charles S. Vavonese.
Res., 4112 E. Genesee St., 13214. Tel: 315-446-0473; Fax: 315-446-7608.
School—Tel: 315-446-4890; Fax: 315-446-4799. Sr. Rose Alice Carbery, O.S.F., Prin.
Sisters of the Third Franciscan Order M.C. 1; Lay Teachers 13; Students 197.
Catechesis/Religious Programs—Students 420.

Durhamville, Oneida Co., St. Francis (1860) (German), Rev. Joseph F. Kehoe.
Res., 5334 Foster St., 13054. Tel: 315-363-1572. [CEM]
Mission—Irish Ridge, Oneida Co., St. Mary. [CEM]

East Syracuse, Onondaga Co., St. Matthew (1880), Revs. Robert D. Dwyer; Leo J. Heizman. In res., Rev. Msgr. Robert F. Lavin; Rev. Msgr. Francis L. Sammons.
Res., 229 W. Yates St., 13057. Tel: 315-437-8318; Fax: 315-463-6399.
School—214 Kinne St., 13057. Tel: 315-437-1339; Fax: 315-463-6399. Sr. Julienne Brandt, O.S.F., Prin.
Sisters of the Third Franciscan Order M.C. 3; Lay Teachers 20; Students 331.
Catechesis/Religious Programs—Tel: 315-437-3685.
Students 470.

Endicott, Broome Co.,

1—Our Lady of Good Counsel, (1941), Revs. Edward J. Zandy; Brian E. Lang; Deacon Thomas M. Harley.
Res., 701 W. Main St., 13760. Tel: 607-748-7417; Fax: 607-785-6454.
Catechesis/Religious Programs—Tel: 607-754-2213; Fax: 607-754-2213.
Students 436.

2—St. Ambrose, (1908), Rev. Peter M. Creed. In res., Revs. James J. O'Hanlon; Joseph Mattath, C.M.I. (India).
Res., 203 Washington Ave., 13760. Tel: 607-754-2330; Fax: 607-785-6947.

3—St. Anthony of Padua, (1917) (Italian), Revs. Clarence F. Rumble; Simon K. Mugo (Africa); Paul Carman; Deacons Dominic Rossi; Frank Longo.
Res., 306 Odell Ave., 13760. Tel: 607-754-4333; Fax: 607-757-3221.
School—Consolidated. See separate listing under Institutions Located in the Diocese. Tel: 607-754-0875.
Catechesis/Religious Programs—1000 Jenkins St., 13760. Tel: 607-748-5184.
Students 472.

4—St. Casimir, (1928) (Polish), Rev. Matthew S. Wieczorek.
Res., 212 N. McKinley Ave., 13760. Tel: 607-785-3262.
Catechesis/Religious Programs—Students 58.

5—St. Joseph, (1923) (Slovak), Revs. James P. Serowik; Thomas Ward.
Res., 207 Hayes Ave., 13760. Tel: 607-748-0442; Fax: 607-748-7725.
School—210 N. Jackson Ave., 13760. Tel: 607-748-8631; Fax: 607-748-7745. Sr. Denise Marie, S.S.C.M., Prin.
Sisters 4; Lay Teachers 13; Students 220.
Catechesis/Religious Programs—Students 240.

Endwell, Broome Co., Christ the King (1949), Rev. Thomas F. Hobbes; Deacon George Phillips.
Res., 1501 Davis Ave., 13760. Tel: 607-785-3180.
Catechesis/Religious Programs—Students 50.

Our Lady of Angels (1964), Rev. John D. Roock.
Res., 3600 Phyllis St., 13760. Tel: 607-754-1266; Fax: 607-754-1325.
Catechesis/Religious Programs—Tel: 607-785-4581.
Students 321.

Fairmount, Onondaga Co., Holy Family (1935), Revs. Paul F. Angelicchio; Amedeo Guida; Deacon John P. Brody.
Res., 119 Chapel Dr., Syracuse, 13219. Tel: 315-488-3139; Fax: 315-487-1112.
School—130 Chapel Dr., Syracuse, 13219. Tel: 315-487-8515; Fax: 315-487-8515. Linda Shulkin, Prin.
Catechesis/Religious Programs—Tel: 315-488-5884.
Students 976.

Fayetteville, Onondaga Co., Immaculate Conception (1869), Rev. Gregory C. LeStrange; Sr. Monica Zmolek, O.S.F., Pastoral MIn. In res., Rev. Msgr. James A. McCloskey.
Res., 400 Salt Springs St., 13066. Tel: 315-637-9846; Fax: 315-637-9846. [CEM]
School—Tel: 315-637-3961. Sr. Elizabeth John, O.S.F., Prin.
Sisters of the Third Franciscan Order M.C. 2; Lay Teachers 25; Students 336.
Catechesis/Religious Programs—Tel: 315-637-9840.
Students 1,020.

Florence, Oneida Co., St. Mary (1845), Rev. Joseph E. Moskal.
Res., 22 Church St., Camden, 13316. Tel: 315-245-1603. [CEM]

Forestport, Oneida Co., St. Patrick (1848), Rev. Sean Patrick O'Brien.
Mailing Address: P.O. Box 1, 13338. Tel: 315-392-2341; Fax: 315-392-5651. [CEM]
Mission—Otter Lake, Oneida Co., St. Mary of the Snows.
Catechesis/Religious Programs—Students 140.

Fulton, Oswego Co., Holy Family (1930), Rev. Richard R. Thompson. In res., Rev. John J. Daley.
Res., 45 W. Fourth St., 13069. Tel: 315-592-4159.
Catechesis/Religious Programs—300 Hart St., 13069. Tel: 315-593-8150; Fax: 315-592-4159.
Students 270.

Immaculate Conception (1854), Rev. Carlo Stirpe.
Res., 309 Buffalo St., 13069. Tel: 315-598-9094. [CEM]

St. Michael (1924) (Polish), Rev. Richard R. Thompson, Admin.
Res., 301 Beech St., 13069. Tel: 315-592-7632.

Greene, Chenango Co., Immaculate Conception (1889), Rev. Richard Dellos.
Res., 1180 NY Hwy. 206, 13778. Tel: 607-656-9546; Fax: 607-656-9546.
Catechesis/Religious Programs—Tel: 607-656-7667.
Students 130.

Hamilton, Madison Co., St. Mary (1869), Rev. Msgr. John R. Madden.
Res., 16 Wylie St., 13346. Tel: 315-824-2164. [CEM]
Catechesis/Religious Programs—Tel: 315-824-5024.
Students 120.

Hannibal, Oswego Co., Our Lady of the Rosary (1954), Rev. Moritz A. Fuchs.
Office: 923 Cayuga St., P.O. Box 185, 13074-3138. Tel: 315-564-5201.
Catechesis/Religious Programs—Students 246.
Mission—Southwest Oswego, St. Joseph.

Hinckley, Oneida Co., St. Ann (1895), Rev. Vincent P. Long.
Res., 13352. Tel: 315-896-2540. [CEM]

Holland Patent, Oneida Co., St. Leo (1882), Rev. Vincent P. Long; Deacon Donald E. Joslin; Sally Millick, Pastoral Assoc. In res., Rev. Robert C. Weber.
Res., 7937 Elm St., P.O. Box 185, 13354. Tel: 315-865-5371.

Homer, Cortland Co., St. Margaret (1908), Rev. R. Daniel DeLorme.
Res., 14 Copeland Ave., P.O. Box 356, 13077. Tel: 607-749-2542; Fax: 607-749-4623.
Catechesis/Religious Programs—Tel: 607-749-2080.
Students 228.

Jamesville, Onondaga Co., St. Mary (1899), Rev. Raymond B. Wood.
Res., 6437 E. Seneca Tpke., P.O. Box 368, 13078-0368. Tel: 315-469-6949.

Johnson City, Broome Co., Blessed Sacrament (1945), Rev. Msgr. James D. Kane.
Res., Cenacle Plaza, 13790. Tel: 607-797-5151; Fax: 607-766-9875.
Catechesis/Religious Programs—Tel: 607-797-8603.
Students 188.

St. James (1900), Revs. Thomas J. Ryan; Clifford H. Auth. Pastoral Assocs.: Sr. Rose Margaret Noonan, C.S.J.; Sr. Catherine Joseph McDonough, D.C.; Mr. William P. Gallagher. In res., Rev. James J. Fallon.
Res., 155 Main St., 13790. Tel: 607-729-6147; Fax: 607-797-5966.
Catechesis/Religious Programs—Tel: 607-729-4083.
Students 514.
Convent—147 Main St., 13790. Tel: 607-797-5181.

Jordan, Onondaga Co., St. Patrick (1858), Rev. John E. Phelan.
Res., 28 N. Main St., 13080. Tel: 315-689-9051. [CEM]
Catechesis/Religious Programs—Tel: 315-689-1695; Fax: 315-689-6240.
Students 267.

Kirkwood, Broome Co., St. Mary (1888), Rev. Thomas F. Catucci.
Res., 975 NY Rte. 11, 13795. Tel: 607-775-0086.

Lacona, Oswego Co., St. Frances Xavier Cabrini (1946), Rev. John F. Hogan, Jr.
Mailing Address: 23 Niagara St., Pulaski, 13142. Tel: 315-387-3016; Fax: 315-298-3749.
Catechesis/Religious Programs—Tel: 315-298-5350.
Students 62.

Lafayette, Onondaga Co., St. Joseph (1866), Rev. Michael P. Minehan.
Res., 6104 Cherry Valley Rd., Box 169, 13084. Tel: 315-677-3439.
Catechesis/Religious Programs—Students 205.

Lakeland, Onondaga Co., Our Lady of Peace (1935), Rev. John E. Fetcho.
Res., 203 Halcomb St., Syracuse, 13209. Tel: 315-487-6832.
Catechesis/Religious Programs—Students 170.

Lee Center, Oneida Co., St. Joseph (1923), Rev. Paul V. Carey; Sr. Dorothy Root, Pastoral Assoc.
Res., 13363. Tel: 315-336-2661; Fax: 315-336-8418.
Parish Center—Tel: 315-339-1890.

Liverpool, Onondaga Co.,

1—CHRIST THE KING, (1964), Rev. Jon K. Werner.
Res., 21 Cherry Tree Cir., 13090. Tel: 315-652-3233; 315-652-9266 (Parish Center); Fax: 315-652-5680.
Catechesis/Religious Programs—Tel: 315-652-5782.
Students 410.

2—IMMACULATE HEART OF MARY, (1950), Rev. John V. Ahern.
Res., 425 Beechwood Ave., 13088. Tel: 315-457-8060; Fax: 315-457-6078.
Catechesis/Religious Programs—427 Beechwood Ave., 13088. Tel: 315-457-5367.
Students 438.

3—ST. JOHN, (1971), Rev. Gaetano T. Baccaro.
Res., 8290 Soule Rd., 13090. Tel: 315-652-6591; Fax: 315-652-6631.
Catechesis/Religious Programs—Tel: 315-652-1094.
Students 705.

4—ST. JOSEPH THE WORKER, (1890), Rev. Charles M. Major.
Res., 1001 Tulip St., 13088. Tel: 315-457-6060; Fax: 315-457-4119.
Catechesis/Religious Programs—Students 704.

Maine, Broome Co., Most Holy Rosary (1944), Rev. Thomas F. Keating.
Res., 2596 Main St., Box 248, 13802. Tel: 607-862-3216; Fax: 607-862-0096.
Catechesis/Religious Programs—Tel: 607-862-4758.
Students 220.

Manlius, Onondaga Co., St. Ann (1920), Rev. Msgr. Charles H. Eckermann; Deacons John R. Murray; Gerard T. Pittman. In res., Rev. James F. Quinn.
Res., 104 Academy St., 13104. Tel: 315-682-5181; Fax: 315-682-5248.
Catechesis/Religious Programs—Tel: 315-682-9443.
Students 385.

Marathon, Cortland Co., St. Stephen (1870), Rev. Lester E. Smith.
Res., 12 Academy St., P.O. Box 475, 13803. Tel: 607-849-3480.
Mission—Cincinnatus, Our Lady of Perpetual Help.

Marcellus, Onondaga Co., St. Francis Xavier (1873), Rev. J. Michael Donovan.
Res., P.O. Box 177, 1 W. Main St., 13108. Tel: 315-673-2531; Fax: 315-673-9305. [CEM]

Mattydale, Onondaga Co., St. Margaret (1926), Revs. Kevin E. Hannon; Lawrence Mensah (Africa); Deacons Donald R. Whiting; Fred Cholette.
Res., 203 Roxboro Rd., Syracuse, 13211. Tel: 315-455-5534; Fax: 315-454-4102.
School—Tel: 315-455-5791; Fax: 315-455-1250. Sr. Miriam Anthony, Prin.
Sisters of the Third Franciscan Order M.C. 2; Lay Teachers 21; Students 455.
Catechesis/Religious Programs—200 Roxboro Rd., 13211. Tel: 315-455-2203.
Students 677.

Mexico, Oswego Co., St. Mary, Star of the Sea (1914), Rev. Stephen P. Wirkes.
Res., 3352 Main St., P.O. Box 487, 13114. Tel: 315-963-7182; Fax: 315-963-7204.
Catechesis/Religious Programs—Students 220.

Minetto, Oswego Co., Our Lady of Perpetual Help (1932), Rev. Joseph M. Larkin.
Res., West River Rd., P.O. Box 236, 13115. Tel: 315-343-7922.

Minoa, Onondaga Co., St. Mary (1837), Rev. Dominic E. McGee, O.F.M.Conv.
Res., 401 N. Main St., 13116. Tel: 315-633-0712; Fax: 315-633-0672. [CEM]
Office: Tel: 315-656-3441.
Catechesis/Religious Programs—Tel: 315-656-4220.
Students 432.

Morrisville, Madison Co., St. Joan of Arc (1931), Rev. Joseph F. Kehoe.
Parish Office: P.O. Box 1087, 13408. Tel: 315-684-9551.
Res., St. Therese Rectory, P.O. Box 735, Main St., Munnsville, 13409. Tel: 315-495-2424.
Catechesis/Religious Programs—Students 152.

Munnsville, Madison Co., St. Therese of the Infant Jesus (1926), Rev. Msgr. John R. Madden.
Res., St. Therese Rectory, P.O. Box 735, Main St., 13409. Tel: 315-495-2424; 684-9551 (Office).
Catechesis/Religious Programs—Students 52.

New Berlin, Chenango Co., St. Theresa of the Infant Jesus (1955), Rev. Francis J. Case, Admin.
Mailing Address: P.O. Box 780, 13411-0780.
Res., 24 N. Main St., 13411. Tel: 607-847-6851.
Catechesis/Religious Programs—Students 86.

New Hartford, Oneida Co., Our Lady of the Rosary (1949), Rev. Felix R. Colosimo.
Res., 1736 Burrstone Rd., 13413. Tel: 315-724-0402.

St. John the Evangelist (1883), Rev. Darr F. Schoenhofen. In res., Rev. Msgr. Thomas J. Hayes.
Res., 66 Oxford Rd., 13413. Tel: 315-732-8521; Fax: 315-735-1569. [CEM]
Catechesis/Religious Programs—One Sherman St., 13413. Tel: 315-724-4347. Sr. Martha Vincent Larkin, C.S.J., D.R.E.
Students 1,014.

St. Thomas (1957), Rev. Edmund A. Castronovo. In res., Rev. John M. Quinn.
Res., 150 Clinton Rd., 13413. Tel: 315-735-8381.

New London, Oneida Co., Holy Cross (1968), Rev. Joseph F. Kehoe.
Res., 5334 Foster St., Durhamville, 13054. Tel: 315-363-1572.

New York Mills, Oneida Co., St. Mary (1909), Rev. Valentine C. Krul.
Res., 201 Main St., 13417. Tel: 315-736-4432; Fax: 315-736-8079. [CEM]
School—Consolidated. See separate listing under Institutions Located in the Diocese.
Catechesis/Religious Programs—Students 190.

North Bay, Oneida Co., St. John (1843), Rev. Leo J. Wimett.
Res., P.O. Box A, 13123. Tel: 315-245-0853; Fax: 315-675-3213. [CEM]
Mission—Verona Beach, Oneida Co., St. Mary, Verona Beach, 13162.

North Syracuse, Onondaga Co., St. Rose of Lima (1926), Revs. James M. Kennedy; Frank Young; Daniel Heintz, (Retired); Jerome Amaechi; Sr. Corinne Mullen, O.S.F., Pastoral Min.
Parish Office: 409 S. Main St., 13212. Tel: 315-458-0283; Fax: 315-458-1290.
Res., 407 S. Main St., 13212. Tel: 315-458-0283.
Preschool—Tel: 315-458-4161.
Students 68.
School—(Grades K-6) 411 S. Main St., 13212. Tel: 315-458-6036; Fax: 315-458-6038. Sr. Catherine Laboure, Prin.
Sisters of the Third Franciscan Order of Syracuse 6; Lay Teachers 33; Students 691.
Catechesis/Religious Programs—Tel: 315-458-6592; Fax: 315-458-1290.
Students 1,036.

Norwich, Chenango Co., St. Bartholomew the Apostle (1919) (Italian), Rev. Douglas Cunningham. Pastoral Ministers: Sr. Julie Eigo, C.S.J.; Mary Ann Bodiot.
Office: 81 E. Main St., 13815. Tel: 607-336-2222; Fax: 607-334-2229.
Catechesis/Religious Programs—Tel: 607-334-7989.
Students 180.
Convent—79 E. Main St., 13815. Tel: 607-334-2527.

St. Paul (1851), Rev. Douglas Cunningham.
Res., 30 Pleasant St., 13815. Tel: 607-334-4931; Fax: 607-334-6521. [CEM]

Oneida, Madison Co., St. Joseph (1893), Rev. William A. Lorenz; Rev. Msgr. Matthew C. Luczycki.
Res., 121 St. Joseph Pl., 13421. Tel: 315-363-3280.
Parish Center—111 St. Joseph Pl., 13421. Tel: 315-363-5061.
Catechesis/Religious Programs—Students 113.

St. Patrick (1843), Rev. William A. Mesmer.
Res., 347 Main St., 13421. Tel: 315-363-7570; Fax: 315-363-7523. [CEM]
School—354 Elizabeth St., 13421. Tel: 315-363-3620. Sheila Seigel, Prin.
Lay Teachers 10; Students 167.
Catechesis/Religious Programs—Tel: 315-361-1378.
Students 305.

Onondaga Hill, Onondaga Co., St. Michael (1874), Rev. Henry J. Pedzich. Pastoral Assocs.: Rev. James M. Karepin, O.P.; Deacon Jack Mulvey. In res., Rev. James C. Hayes.
Res., 4782 W. Seneca Tpke., Syracuse, 13215. Tel: 315-469-6995.
Catechesis/Religious Programs—Tel: 315-469-6600.
Students 622.
Mission—Split Rock, Onondaga Co., St. Peter, Split Rock Rd., 13031.

Oriskany, Oneida Co., St. Stephen, Protomartyr (1929), Rev. Walter F. Cannan.
Res., 106 Dexter Ave., P.O. Box 780, 13424. Tel: 315-736-9033.
Catechesis/Religious Programs—Students 176.

Oriskany Falls, Oneida Co., St. Joseph (1870), Rev. Vincent J. Kelly.
Res., 229 Main St., 13425. Tel: 315-821-6122. [CEM]
Catechesis/Religious Programs—Students 56.

Oswego, Oswego Co.,

1—ST. JOHN THE EVANGELIST, (1869), Rev. David J. Baehr, Admin.; Deacon Peter F. Benz, Pastoral Assoc. & Bus. Mgr.
Res., 38 Erie St., 13126. Tel: 315-343-4961.

2—ST. JOSEPH, (1915) (Italian), Rev. James M. Cesta; Deacon Joseph Chillemi.
Res., 178 W. Second St., 13126. Tel: 315-343-2160; Fax: 315-343-2164 (call first).
Catechesis/Religious Programs—Students 183.

3—ST. LOUIS, (1870) (French), Rev. George E. Wurz, Admin.
Res., 81 E. Fourth St., 13126. Tel: 315-343-8912.

4—ST. MARY, (1850), Rev. David J. Baehr; Deacon Peter F. Benz, Pastoral Assoc. & Business Mgr.
Res., 103 W. Seventh St., P.O. Box 118, 13126. Tel: 315-343-3953; Fax: 315-342-5538.
School—Regional Catholic School System 76 W. Sixth St., 13126. Tel: 315-343-0700; Fax: 315-342-9471.
Lay Teachers 23; Students 322.
Catechesis/Religious Programs—Tel: 315-343-8560.
Students 300.

5—ST. PAUL, (1830) (Irish), Rev. Eric K. Harer.
Res., 50 E. Mohawk St., 13126. Tel: 315-343-2333; Fax: 315-343-2334.
Church—134 E. Fifth St., 13126. Tel: 315-343-9764.
School—Trinity Catholic School, 115 E. Fifth St., 13126. Tel: 315-343-6700. Mr. David Friedlander, Prin.; Sr. Marianne Baehr, Co-Prin.
Lay Teachers 15; Students 250.
Catechesis/Religious Programs—Students 200.

6—ST. PETER, (1862) (German), Rev. George E. Wurz, Admin.
Res., 83 E. Albany St., 13126. Tel: 315-343-1352.
Mission—Scriba, Sacred Heart.

7—ST. STEPHEN THE KING, (1908) (Polish), Rev. Edmund Wolak.
Res., 138 Niagara St., Box 417, 13126. Tel: 315-343-0350; Fax: 315-343-0350 (call first).

Oxford, Chenango Co., St. Joseph (1849), Rev. Donald D. Cunningham.
Res., 3 Scott St., 13830. Tel: 607-843-7021. [CEM]
Station—New York State Veterans' Home, 13830.

Parish, Oswego Co., St. Ann (1950), Rev. Anthony J. Keeffe.
Res., P.O. Box 27, 13131. Tel: 315-625-7093. [CEM]
Mailing Address: P.O. Box 33, Williamstown, 13493. Tel: 315-964-2400.
Mission—Williamstown, St. Patrick.

Phoenix, Oswego Co., St. Stephen (1880), Rev. Andrew E. Baranski; Deacon Frank Forish.
Res., 469 Main St., 13135. Tel: 315-695-4531; 695-4608.
Catechesis/Religious Programs—Tel: 315-695-4608.
Students 376.

Pompey, Onondaga Co., Immaculate Conception (1850), Rev. David J. James.
Res., 7386 Academy St., 13138. Tel: 315-677-3061; Fax: 315-677-2873. [CEM]
Mission—Fabius, Onondaga Co., St. Paul, Fabius, 13063.

Pulaski, Oswego Co., St. John the Evangelist (1888), Rev. John F. Hogan, Jr.
23 Niagara St., 13142-4425. Tel: 315-298-5350; 298-3863 (Res.); Fax: 315-298-3749.
Catechesis/Religious Programs—Students 127.

Rome, Oneida Co.,

1—St. John the Baptist, (1909) (Italian), Revs. Joseph J. Clemente; John M. Wood; Robert Conrad.
Res., 210 E. Dominick St., 13440. Tel: 315-337-0990; Fax: 315-336-3841. [CEM]
Catechesis/Religious Programs—Students 622.

2—St. Mary of the Assumption, (1848), Rev. R. Paul Mathis. In res., Rev. Msgr. Francis J. Culkin.
Res., 210 W. Liberty St., 13440. Tel: 315-336-4832; Fax: 315-339-2744. [CEM]
Catechesis/Religious Programs—Students 101.
Station—Rome, Betsy Ross HRF.

3—St. Paul, (1954), Rev. James T. Queen; Deacons Nicholas A. Rosher; Edgar Doyle, Jr. In res., Rev. Msgr. William M. Kelly.
Res., 1807 Bedford St., 13440-2199. Tel: 315-336-3082; Fax: 315-336-3083.
Catechesis/Religious Programs—Tel: 315-334-9570.
Students 214.

4—St. Peter, (1837), Rev. Philip A. Hearn. Pastoral Assocs.: Sr. Elizabeth Colby, C.S.J.; Sr. Phyllis Wulforst, C.S.J. In res., Rev. James A. Culver.
Res., 105 E. Liberty St., 13440. Tel: 315-336-5072; 337-8307. [CEM]
Catechesis/Religious Programs—Students 450.

5—Transfiguration, (1909) (Polish), Rev. Mark A. Pasik. In res., Rev. William C. Cahill.
Res., 111 Ridge St., 13440. Tel: 315-336-1152; Fax: 315-339-5931.
School—(Grades K-6) 400 S. James St., 13440. Tel: 315-336-3430; Fax: 315-334-4650. Mrs. Elizabeth Warwick, Prin.
Lay Teachers 7; Students 126.

Sanitaria Springs, Broome Co., St. Joseph (1914), Rev. Kevin J. Bunger, Admin.
Res., 659 New York Rte. 7, P.O. Box 429, Port Crane, 13833. Tel: 607-648-5209; Fax: 607-648-3570.

Sherburne, Chenango Co., St. Malachy of Armach (1858), Rev. Francis J. Case, Admin.
P.O. Box 722, 13460-0722. Tel: 607-674-9625. [CEM]
Catechesis/Religious Programs—Students 93.

Sherrill, Oneida Co., St. Helena (1917), Rev. John J. Costello.
Res., 210 Primo Ave., 13461. Tel: 315-363-3882. [CEM]
Catechesis/Religious Programs—Students 253.

Skaneateles, Onondaga Co., St. Mary of the Lake (1855), Rev. Thomas J. McGrath; Deacon Robert Borchert.
Res., 81 Jordan St., 13152. Tel: 315-685-5083; Fax: 315-685-8327. [CEM]
Catechesis/Religious Programs—Tel: 315-685-6377.
Students 461.

Solvay, Onondaga Co., St. Cecilia (1903) (Italian), Revs. George F. Hartnett; Robert J. Birchmeyer; Deacon Julius Kulak.
Res., 1001 Woods Rd., 13209. Tel: 315-488-3221; Fax: 315-488-3222.
Catechesis/Religious Programs—Students 310.

South Onondaga, Onondaga Co., Corpus Christi (1938), Rev. Dennis J. Hayes.
Res., P.O. Box 288, Marietta, 13110. Tel: 315-492-0814.
Church—3126 Cedarvale Rd., R.D. 1, Nedrow, 13120. Tel: 315-492-0814.
Apostolate—Onondaga Indian Reservation.

Taberg, Oneida Co., St. Patrick (1876), Rev. Francis A. Wapen.
Res., 9168 Main St., 13471. Tel: 315-336-4079. [CEM]
Mission—Glenmore, Oneida Co., St. Anne, (1846).

Truxton, Cortland Co., St. Patrick (1854), Rev. Daniel C. Muscalino, Admin.
Res., 3656 Rte. 13, Box 15, 13158. Tel: 607-842-6326. [CEM]
Mission—DeRuyter, St. Lawrence.

Tully, Onondaga Co., St. Leo (1891), Rev. Louis F. Aiello.
Res., 10 Onondaga St., 13159. Tel: 315-696-5092; Fax: 315-696-5092.
Catechesis/Religious Programs—Students 330.
Mission—Otisco, Onondaga Co., St. Patrick, P.O. Box 574, 13159. Tel: 315-696-8601. [CEM]

Utica, Oneida Co.,

1—Blessed Sacrament, (1924), Rev. Robert L. Kelly; Sr. Teresa Waldron, O.S.F., Pastoral Min.
Res., 1603 St. Agnes Ave., 13501. Tel: 315-724-8131; Fax: 315-724-5024.
School—Consolidated. See separate listing under Institutions Located in the Diocese.
Catechesis/Religious Programs—1627 St. Agnes Ave., 13501. Tel: 315-733-3946.
Students 150.

2—Holy Trinity, (1896) (Polish), Revs. Arthur R. Hapanowicz; Richard J. Wilczynski (Poland); Deacon Wilbur H. Hazard.
Res., 1206 Lincoln Ave., 13502. Tel: 315-724-7238; Fax: 315-732-5448. [CEM]
School—(Grades PreK-6) 1214 Lincoln Ave., 13502. Tel: 315-724-0540; Fax: 315-724-0540. Sr. Mary Beatrice, C.S.F.N., Supr.; Mrs. Judith Hauck, Prin.
Religious 4; Lay Teachers 8; Students 137.
Convent—1218 Lincoln Ave., 13502. Tel: 315-733-5492; Fax: 315-733-5492.

3—Our Lady of Lourdes, (1919), Rev. Donald H. Karlen; Deacons William P. Hotaling; Paul M. Mullin; Sr. Julia Coyle, S.A.; Sr. Rosita Finnerty, C.S.J. In res., Revs. Jerome F. Weber; Donald J. Bauer; J. Michael Carney.
Res., 2 Barton Ave., 13502. Tel: 315-724-3155; 732-3418; Fax: 315-732-3770.
School—Consolidated. See separate listing under Institutions Located in the Diocese. Tel: 315-732-4374; Fax: 315-738-9720.
Catechesis/Religious Programs—Students 450.

4—Sacred Heart, (1926), Rev. John Flanagan. In res., Rev. Hyacinth Seremet; Deacon John Lee.
Res., 2115 Caroline St., 13502. Tel: 315-735-6105; Fax: 315-735-0216.
School—(Grades PreK-6) 1109 Ney Ave., 13502. Tel: 315-724-3612. Sr. Roseann Klosterman, C.S.J., Prin.
Religious 3; Lay Teachers 9; Students 148.
Catechesis/Religious Programs—Tel: 315-735-3611.
Students 120.

5—St. Agnes, (1887), Rev. Msgr. Francis J. Willenburg.
Res., 700 Kossuth Ave., 13501. Tel: 315-735-5273.
Catechesis/Religious Programs—Students 220.
Convent—783 Blandina St., 13501. Tel: 315-732-1078.

6—St. Anthony of Padua, (1911) (Italian), Rev. Anthony LaFache; Deacon William Dischiavo, Sec.
Res., 422 Tilden Ave., 13501. Tel: 315-732-1177.
Catechesis/Religious Programs—1521 Bleeker St., 13501. Tel: 315-724-3324.
Students 430.

7—St. Francis de Sales, (1876), Rev. Frederick D. Daley; Deacon Laurence Brickner.
Res., 1119 Elm St., 13501. Tel: 315-732-6171; Fax: 315-735-3503.

8—St. George, (1911) (Lithuanian), Rev. Donald J. Hebert.
Res., 702 Columbia St., 13502. Tel: 315-735-4429; Fax: 315-735-1691. [CEM]

9—St. John, (1819), Revs. John A. Buehler; Luis Olguin, Spanish Apostolate, Tel: 315-724-0389. Pastoral Assocs.: Sr. Catherine Joseph Croghan, C.S.J.; Sr. Mary Theresa Kobosinski, D.C.; Deacon William R. Dischiavo.
Res., 240 Bleecker St., 13501. Tel: 315-724-6159.
Parish Apostolate Center—520 John St., 13501. Tel: 315-732-2417. Sr. Mary Theresa Kobosinski, D.C.
Catechesis/Religious Programs—Students 285.

10—St. Joseph and St. Patrick, (1841 and 1849), Rev. Donald J. Hebert. In res., Revs. John S. Drozdzal; David R. Sambor.
Res., 702 Columbia St., 13502. Tel: 315-735-4429; Fax: 315-735-1691.
Catechesis/Religious Programs—530 Varick St., 13502.
Students 117.

11—St. Mark, (1963), Rev. Lucian Urbaniak.
Res., 440 Keyes Rd., 13502. Tel: 315-724-1645.

12—St. Mary, (1870) (German), Rev. Richard V. O'Neill.
Res., 421 South St., 13501. Tel: 315-724-0083.

13—St. Mary of Mt. Carmel, (1896) (Italian), Rev. Joseph Salerno. Pastoral Assocs.: Sr. Lois Paciello, C.S.J.; Sr. Elizabeth Paciello, C.S.J.; Deacon Robert Riggalls. In res., Rev. Luis Olguin.
Res., 648 Jay St., 13501. Tel: 315-735-1482; Fax: 315-735-9806.
Catechesis/Religious Programs—Tel: 315-724-3950. Sr. Linda Love, D.R.E.
Students 235.

14—St. Peter, (1872), Rev. Thomas M. Durant. In res., Rev. James A. Quinn.
Res., 422 Coventry Ave., 13502. Tel: 315-724-6310; Fax: 315-724-4942. [CEM]
School—(Grades PreK-6) 19 Herkimer Rd., 13502. Tel: 315-724-4708. Mr. Patrick Del Piano, Prin.
Lay Teachers 9; Students 178.
Catechesis/Religious Programs—Tel: 315-735-7077.
Students 425.

15—St. Stanislaus, (1911) (Polish), Rev. Casimir J. Krzysiak.
Res., 607 Nichols St., 13501. Tel: 315-732-5919. [CEM]

Vernon, Oneida Co., Holy Family (1926; 1976), Rev. Richard P. Morisette.
Res., 4343 Peterboro St., P.O. Box 988, 13476. Tel: 315-829-3295.
Catechesis/Religious Programs—Students 255.

Verona, Oneida Co., Our Lady of Good Counsel (1913), Rev. Edmund J. Morelle.
Res., 5259 Beacon Rd., P.O. Box 135, 13478. Tel: 315-363-7696.
Catechesis/Religious Programs—Students 132.

Vestal, Broome Co., Our Lady of Sorrows (1941), Revs. John P. Putano; Lawrence Mbogo (Africa). In res., Rev. Matthew F. Brown.
Res., 157 Clark St., 13850. Tel: 607-748-8287; Fax: 607-748-8016.
Catechesis/Religious Programs—Tel: 607-748-4766.
Students 492.

St. Vincent de Paul (1965), Revs. Daniel M. Caruso; Richard J. Giblin, Pastoral Assoc.; Deacon James P. Crowley.
Res., 165 Clifton Blvd., 13850. Tel: 607-722-3988; Fax: 607-722-8787.
Catechesis/Religious Programs—465 Clubhouse Rd., 13850. Tel: 607-722-8372.
Students 363.

Warners, Onondaga Co., Our Lady of Good Counsel (1913), Rev. James C. Hayes.
Res., Newport Rd., Box 67, 13164. Tel: 315-672-3725.
Parish Hall—Tel: 315-672-3750.

Waterville, Oneida Co., St. Bernard (1850), Rev. Richard J. Kapral.
Res., 199 Stafford Ave., 13480. Tel: 315-841-4481. [CEM]
Catechesis/Religious Programs—Students 200.
Mission—North Brookfield, Madison Co., St. Mary.

Whitesboro, Oneida Co., St. Anne (1965), Rev. Frederick J. Prevost.
Res., 8539 Clark Mills Rd., 13492-2754. Tel: 315-736-7672.
Catechesis/Religious Programs—Students 380.

St. Paul (1883), Rev. Abraham L. Esper.
Res., 16 Park Ave., 13492. Tel: 315-736-1124; Fax: 315-768-7915.
Catechesis/Religious Programs—Tel: 315-736-4807.
Students 570.

Whitney Point, Broome Co., St. Patrick (1869), Rev. Robert P. Hyde.
Res., Box 711, 13862. Tel: 607-692-3911. [CEM]

Windsor, Broome Co., Our Lady of Lourdes (1947), Rev. John Booth, Jr.
Res., P.O. Box 361, 13865. Tel: 607-655-2116; Fax: 607-655-8118.
Catechesis/Religious Programs—Students 200.

Chaplains of Public Institutions

Hospitals

Syracuse. *Community General Hospital* Broad Rd., 13215. Tel: 315-492-5011. Rev. James C. Hayes; Sr. Mary Ann Kane, O.S.F.

Crouse Irving Memorial Hospital 736 Irving Ave., 13210. Tel: 315-470-7615. Sr. Carmel Rose Nicita; Sr. Antonella Giba, C.S.J.

James Square Nursing Home. Attended from Blessed Sacrament Parish.

Loretto Geriatric Center 700 E. Brighton Ave., 13205. Tel: 315-469-5570. Rev. Wilbur J. Votraw.

Plaza Extended Care Facility Tel: 315-474-4431. Sr. Monica Hogan, C.S.J.

St. Camillus Health & Rehab Center 813 Fay Rd., 13219. Tel: 315-488-2951. Ms. Kathy Falso, Pastoral Care Coord.

St. Joseph's Hospital Health Center 301 Prospect Ave., 13203. Tel: 315-448-5116. Revs. Robert Amrhein, O.F.M.Conv.; Firmin Finn, O.F.M.Conv.; Sr. Marie Therese Nicholson, O.S.F.; Sr. Patrice Ward, O.S.F.; Sr. Mary Louise Williams, O.S.F.; Sr. Jacqueline Spiridlozzi, Dir.; Sr. Frances Agnes Ryan; Sr. Mary Daniel Golmbieski.

University Hospital 750 E. Adams St., 13210. Tel: 315-464-5540. Rev. Alfred J. Bebel; Sr. Mary Francellette.

Van Duyn Home & Hospital Tel: 315-469-5511. Rev. Msgr. Robert B. Davern; Susan Marcoccia.

Veterans Administration Hospital Res: 800 Irving Ave., 13210. Tel: 315-476-7461. Rev. Wilfred F. Evans.

Binghamton. *Binghamton General Hospital* Tel: 607-762-2200. Rev. John Mikalajunas; Sr. Joan Thomas Mcherney, C.S.J.

Binghamton Psychiatric Hospital. Revs. John Booth; Gerald J. Buckley.

Broome Developmental Center Tel: 607-770-0211. Rev. Paul J. Keebler.

Our Lady of Lourdes Memorial Hospital 179 Riverside Dr., 13905. Tel: 607-798-5111. Sr. Ann Molesevick, D.C., Dir.; Rev. Christopher Boretto; Bro. Daniel Gallucci; Sr. Mary Roark; Sr. Catherine Marie McGranary.

JOHNSON CITY. *Wilson Memorial Hospital* 33 Harrison St., 13790. Tel: 607-763-6000. Rev. Timothy J. Taugher.

LIVERPOOL. *Developmental Center* 36 Grampian Rd. #5, 13090. Rev. Charles A. Aho.

ROME. *Central New York Developmental Services Office*. Vacant. P.O. Box 550, Lower South James, 13442-0550. Tel: 315-336-2300, Ext. 251.

UTICA. *Faxton Hospital* 1676 Sunset Ave., 13502. Tel: 315-738-6545. Sr. Maureen Denn, C.S.J.

St. Elizabeth Hospital 2209 Genesee St., 13501. Tel: 315-798-8100. Rev. Matthew Thelly; Sr. Irene Zegarelli, O.S.F.; Sr. Mary Nicholas Amodio, O.S.F.; Sr. Margaret Woods, O.S.F.

St. Luke Champlin Ave., 13503. Tel: 315-798-6000. Sr. Genevieve Ciscek, C.S.J.; Sr. Susanne Bonville, C.S.J.; Rev. Donald J. Hebert.

VESTAL. *Binghamton Nursing Homes* Our Lady of Sorrows, 157 Clark St., 13850. Tel: 607-748-8287. Rev. Matthew F. Brown, Pastoral Care Chap.

Psychiatric Facilities

SYRACUSE. *Hutchings Psychiatric Center* 406 Court St., 13208. Tel: 315-473-4980. Rev. John T. McGraw.

BINGHAMTON. *Binghamton Psychiatric Hospital* Tel: 607-724-1391. Revs. John Booth; Gerald J. Buckley.

MARCY. *Central New York Psychiatric Center* Old River Rd., Box 330, 13403. Tel: 315-736-8271. Rev. Richard V. O'Neill.

UTICA. *Mohawk Valley Psychiatric Center* 1400 Noyes at York, 13502. Rev. Frederick D. Daley.

Jails

SYRACUSE. *Elmcrest Children's Center*. Vacant. Salt Springs Rd., 13224.

Hillbrook Detention Center 4949 Velasko Rd., 13215. Tel: 315-492-1721. Sr. Judith Falk.

Jail Ministry Office. Vacant. 208 Slocum Ave., 13204. Tel: 315-424-1877.

Public Safety Building 342 Vine St., 13203. Tel: 315-424-1877. William M. Cuddy.

BINGHAMTON. *Broome County Jail*. Rev. Stanley J. Gerlock.

CORTLAND. *Cortland County Jail*. Vacant.

GEORGETOWN. *Camp Georgetown* 31 E. State St., Sheburne, 13346. Tel: 315-837-4446. Rev. Edmund A. Castronovo.

JAMESVILLE. *Jamesville Penitentiary* P.O. Box 143, 13078. Tel: 315-469-5581. Rev. Edward J. Reimer; Sr. Maura Rhode.

MARCY. *Mid-State Correctional Facility* 210 W. Liberty St., 13403. Tel: 315-768-8581. Rev. Robert C. Weber.

MOHAWK. *Oneida Correctional Facility I* P.O. Box 8450, Rome, 13440. Tel: 315-339-6880. Rev. William C. Cahill.

Oneida Correctional Facility II 578 Main St., P.O. Box 8450, Oneida, 13421. Deacon James Chappell.

NORWICH. *Norwich County Jail*. Vacant.

ORISKANY. *Oneida County Jail* 120 Dexter Ave., 13424. Tel: 315-736-9033. Rev. Richard J. Stuczko.

OSWEGO. *Oswego County Jail* 178 W. Second St., 13126. Tel: 315-343-2160. Rev. Msgr. Francis J. Furfaro.

ROME. *Walsh Facility* Tel: 315-339-5232. Rev. Luis Olguin.

SOUTH PLYMOUTH. *Camp Pharsalia*. Rev. Edmund A. Castronovo.

UTICA. *Marcy Correctional Facility* 15-8 Rox Pl., 13502. Tel: 315-768-1400. Deacon William Hotaling.

Special Assignment:
Reverend Fathers—
Aho, Charles A.
Bebel, Alfred J.
Brown, Matthew F.
Cahill, William C.
Carmola, Michael J.
Catucci, Thomas F.
Chryst, Robert D.
Costello, Thomas J.
Croghan, John P.
Davern, Robert B.
Donovan, John P.
Evans, Wilfred F.
Hayes, James C.
Lang, James Paul
Mattice, George F.
Minehan, Michael P.
Moynihan, James M.
Muscalino, Daniel C.
Olguin, Luis
Ours, Robert A.
Phillips, Joseph H.
Pompei, Frederick A.
Quartier, Neal E.
Quinn, James F.
Sambor, David R.
Schopfer, John C.
Sullivan, Robert J.
Taugher, Timothy J.
Vavonese, Charles S.
Votraw, William J.
Weber, Robert C.
Williams, Peter A.
Yeazel, J. Robert

On Duty Outside the Diocese:
Reverend Monsignors—
Fahey, Charles J., Fordham University, New York, NY
Reverend Fathers—
Bassano, Michael
Cincotta, Anthony
Harrold, John
Keane, Philip S., S.S.
Nichols, Louis J.
Rossetti, Stephen
Sears, G. David, Staten Island, NY
Wallace, Harry C.
Woolever, James

Military Chaplains:
Reverend Fathers—
Dunn, Richard, U.S. Air Force
Elkin, Fredic F., U.S. Navy
Gryga, Theodore, U.S. Navy
Madej, Paul D., U.S. Navy

Absent on Leave:
Reverend Fathers—
Lupa, Gerard
O'Leary, Patrick C.
Pichette, David

Absent on Sick Leave:
Reverend Fathers—
Fallon, James J.
Florczyk, Walter

Retired:
Reverend Monsignors—
Borgognoni, Charles L.
Casey, Robert A.
Culkin, Francis J.
Denti, Carl J.
Dillon, Robert E.
Doran, Thomas M.
Furfaro, Francis J.
Giblin, Lawrence E.
Hayes, Thomas J.
Kantor, Adolph A.
Lavin, Robert F.
Luczycki, Matthew C.
Lutz, James M.
McCloskey, James A.
O'Brien, Daniel B.
Sammons, Francis L.
Zeder, John M.
Reverend Fathers—
Bauer, Donald J.
Brennan, Robert E.
D'Alessandro, Salvatore
Daley, John J.
Dwyer, William M.
Guyder, Thomas F.
Kiernan, Thomas
Libera, Angelo
Majdanik, Albin J.
Manning, Thomas J.
McKay, Robert J.
Mulranen, John J.
Neary, Thomas E.
Nold, Joseph K.
O'Hanlon, James J.
Pilla, P. Carl
Prozny, Leopold V.
Regan, William P.
Stuczko, Richard J.
Tucker, Richard
Walsh, Bernard
Wright, Robert

Permanent Deacons:
Altmeter, Robert (ROC), Norwich
Ashley, John, Binghamton
Benz, Peter F., Baldwinsville
Blaine, Edward, Endicott
Borchert, Robert, Skaneateles
Brody, John P., Camillus
Brush, Wesley J., Madison, WI, (On Leave)
Busch, Robert L., Syracuse
Carranti, Pio Peter, Syracuse
Castro, Joseph, North Syracuse
Chappell, James C., Oneida
Chiesa, Richard J., Camillus
Chillemi, Joseph, Oswego
Collins, John H., Pennellville
Cretaro, John T., Oswego
Crosby, James P., Syracuse (On Leave)
Crossett, Thomas F., Johnson City (On Leave)
Crowley, James, Vestal
Dischiavo, William R., Utica
Distin, Leslie, Johnson City
Dotterer, William A., Liverpool
Droz, John J., Sr., (Retired), New Hartford
Dwyer, Richard J., Cortland
Forish, Frank M., Baldwinsville
Gallagher, James T., Binghamton (On Leave)
Goskowski, Raymond, Binghamton
Hachey, Thomas, North Syracuse
Harley, Thomas, Sanitaria Springs
Hazard, Wilbur, Utica
Hotaling, William P., Utica
Joslin, Donald E., Holland Patent
Kopec, John
Kotch, Myron, (Eastern Rite), Syracuse
Kulak, Julius F., Solvay
Longo, Frank A., Endicott
Mailloux, William, Baldwinsville
Manzene, Stephen, Liverpool
Matzke, Leo P., Central Square
Maynard, George E., Clay
McGrath, Michael B., Syracuse
Money, Kenneth, Liverpool
Monnat, Leonard S., Syracuse
Morse, James L., Syracuse
Mulvey, John, Syracuse
Murray, John, Manlius
Needham, Leo I., Syracuse
Nelson, John J., Kirkville
O'Connor, Charles, Syracuse
Phillips, George, Endwell
Pittman, Gerard, Fayetteville
Powers, Paul F., Afton
Riggalls, Robert, Sr., Waterville
Rossi, Dominic L., Endicott
Sims, John E., Endwell (On Leave from Diocese)
Sweenie, David, Oswego
Trepa, John, Greene
Vanelli, Peter P., Syracuse
Warren, Franklin, Oswego
Whiting, Donald R., North Syracuse
Wilber, Richard, Chesire, CT, (On Leave)
Winslow, Frank L., Utica
Woeste, James (NOR), Syracuse

INSTITUTIONS LOCATED IN THE DIOCESE

[A] SEMINARIES, RELIGIOUS, OR SCHOLASTICATES

SYRACUSE. *Saint Andrew Hall*, 420 Demong Dr., 13214-1499. Tel: 315-445-3500; Fax: 315-446-9472. Novitiate for the Maryland and New York Provinces, Society of Jesus. Revs. Bruce A. Maivelett, S.J., Rector & Dir. Novices; Frederick J. Pellegrini, Asst. Dir. Novices. Priests 2; Novices 11.

SKANEATELES. *Roosevelt Hall*, 1 Tallcot Ln., 13152. Tel: 315-685-6417. Bro. John Loehr, F.S.C., Dir. Brothers 8.

[B] COLLEGES AND UNIVERSITIES

SYRACUSE. *Le Moyne College*, 1419 Salt Springs Rd., 13214-1399. Tel: 315-445-4100; Fax: 315-445-4540 *For a complete listing, refer to the Colleges and Universities section.*

[C] HIGH SCHOOLS, DIOCESAN

SYRACUSE. *Bishop Ludden Junior/Senior High School*, 815 Fay Rd., 13219. Tel: 315-468-2591; Fax: 315-468-0097. Mr. Dennis J. Meehan, Prin. Priests 1; Sisters 3; Lay Teachers 52; Students 815.

BINGHAMTON. *Seton Catholic Central High School of Broome County*, 70 Seminary Ave., 13905. Tel: 607-723-5307; Fax: 607-723-4811. Ms. Kathleen M. Dwyer, Prin.; Mr. Max Deus, Asst. Prin.; Rev. Robert A. Ours. Priests 1; Sisters 3; Lay Teachers 42; Students 444.

EAST SYRACUSE. *Bishop Grimes Jr./Sr. High School*, 6653 Kirkville Rd., 13057. Tel: 315-437-0356; Fax: 315-437-0358. Rev. George F. Sheehan, Prin. Priests 2; Friar 1; Sisters 4; Lay Teachers 41; Students 600.

ROME. *Rome Catholic Junior-Senior High School*, 800 Cypress St., 13440. Tel: 315-336-6190; Fax: 315-336-6194.

E-mail: rchlibrary@mohawk.moric.org
Rev. James T. Queen. Priests 1; Sisters 2; Lay Teachers 23; Students 272.

UTICA. *Notre Dame Jr./Sr. High School*, 2 Notre Dame Lane, 13502. Tel: 315-724-5118; Fax: 315-724-9460. Miss Kathleen Donovan. Sisters 4; Lay Teachers 48; Students 616.

[D] HIGH SCHOOLS, PRIVATE

SYRACUSE. *Christian Brothers Academy.* (Grades 9-12), 6245 Randall Rd., 13214. Tel: 315-446-5960; Fax: 315-446-3393.
Web site: www.cbasyracuse.org
Bro. Michael Shubnell, F.S.C., Prin. Brothers of the Christian Schools 2; Sisters 2; Lay Teachers 48; Students 489.

[E] JUNIOR HIGH SCHOOLS, DIOCESAN

SYRACUSE. *All Saints Junior High School*, 301 Valley Dr., 13207. Tel: 315-472-7488. Joan Theresa Smith, Prin. Lay Teachers 3; Students 34.

[F] JUNIOR HIGH SCHOOLS, PRIVATE

SYRACUSE. *Christian Brothers Academy.* (Grades 7-8), 6245 Randall Rd., 13214. Tel: 315-446-5960; Fax: 315-446-3393.
Web site: www.cbasyracuse.org
Students 252.

[G] CONSOLIDATED SCHOOLS

BINGHAMTON. *St. Catherine.* (Grades PreK-3), 1051 Chenango St., 13901. Tel: 607-722-2028. Ms. Mary Ellen Meskell, Prin. Lay Teachers 9; Students 141.

St. John the Evangelist. (Grades K-8), 9 Livingston St., 13903. Tel: 607-723-0703; Fax: 607-772-6210. Sr. Albert J. Guzzi, Prin. Religious 5; Lay Teachers 23; Students 355.

St. Patrick Academy. (Grades 5-8), 58 Oak St., 13905. Tel: 607-723-4601. Lay Teachers 8; Students 55.

St. Thomas Aquinas. (Grades PreK-4), 3 Aquinas St., 13905. Tel: 607-797-6528; Fax: 607-797-6541.
E-mail: stthomas@stny.rr.com
Sr. Patricia Coyle, O.S.F., Prin. Religious 1; Lay Teachers 11; Students 200.

ENDICOTT. *St. Anthony.* (Grades Nursery-4), 906 Jenkins St., 13760. Tel: 607-754-0875. Sr. Paul Kathryn Barno, C.S.J., Prin. Religious 1; Lay Teachers 8; Students 237.

Seton Catholic Middle School. (Grades 5-8), 1112 Broad St., 13760. Tel: 607-748-7423.
E-mail: syrsetonmend@connectinc.com
Marguerite DiFulvio, Prin. Lay Teachers 16; Students 227.

JOHNSON CITY. *Blessed Sacrament.* (Grades PreK-3), Cenacle Plaza, 13790. Tel: 607-729-3302; Fax: 607-729-5791.
E-mail: bsacrame@stny.lrun.com
Web site: home.stny.rr.com/bsacrame
Mary Ellen Kelley, Prin. Lay Teachers 16; Students 262.

St. James Middle School, 143 Main St., 13790. Tel: 607-797-5444; Fax: 607-797-6794.
E-mail: syrstjamejoh@connect.com
Mrs. Maria Carucci, Prin. Sisters 2; Lay Teachers 18; Students 227.

NORWICH. *Holy Family School.* (Grades PreK-6), 17 Prospect St., 13815. Tel: 607-334-6934. Sr. Marie Denise Monser, C.S.J., Prin. Sisters 1; Lay Teachers 11; Students 136.

OSWEGO. *Trinity Catholic School*, 74 W. 6th St., 13126. Tel: 315-343-0700. Sr. Marianne Baehr, Admin.; David Freidlander, Admin., St. Mary's Campus. Students 86. St. Paul's Campus. Students 256.

ROME. *St. Peter.* (Grades K-6), 400 Floyd Ave., 13440. Tel: 315-336-2360. Sr. Cheryl Canfield, C.S.S.F., Prin. Religious 1; Lay Teachers 12; Students 166.

UTICA. *Our Lady of Lourdes.* (Grades PreK-6), 11 Barton Ave., 13502. Tel: 315-732-4374; Fax: 315-738-9720.
E-mail: bkloven@mailcity.com
Web site: www.lourdes.school.com
Mrs. Carol Polito, Prin. Lay Teachers 26; Students 443.

VESTAL. *Our Lady of Sorrows.* (Grades PreK-4), 801 Main St., 13850. Tel: 607-785-3214.
E-mail: syrolsves@connect.net
Barbara Vanston, Prin. Lay Teachers 5; Students 187.

[H] CATHOLIC CHARITIES OF SYRACUSE

SYRACUSE. *Bishop Joseph T. O'Keefe, Inc.*, c/o 240 E. Onondaga St., 13202. Tel: 315-424-1830; Fax: 315-478-4619. Most Rev. James M. Moynihan; Rev. Michael P. Minehan, Chancellor; Most Rev. Thomas J. Costello, Vicar Gen.; Rev. Robert B. Stephenson, Sec.

Catholic Charities of the Roman Catholic Diocese of Syracuse, 240 E. Onondaga St., 13202. Tel: 315-424-1830; Fax: 315-478-4619.
E-mail: charity@aiusa.com
Web site: syrdio.org
Mr. Dennis J. Manning, Pres. & CEO.
Onondaga County: Mr. Brian Walton, Area Dir., 1654 W. Onondaga St., 13204. Tel: 315-424-1800; Fax: 315-424-6045. Mr. Paul Welch, Assoc. Dir., 1654 W. Onondaga St., 13204. Tel: 315-424-1800. Kevin Domanico, Exec. Deputy Dir., 1654 W. Onondaga St., 13204. Tel: 315-424-1800. Donna Brownell, Dir. Human Resources; Patricia Walton, Exec. Dir., Toomey Residential & Community Svcs.; Mark Clary, Assoc. Dir.; Joseph O'Hara, Dir. Devel.; Dorothy Condon, Assoc. Dir., Neighborhood & Family Svcs. Div.

Jail Ministry, Slocum House, 208 Slocum Ave., 13204. Mary Czelusniak, Coord.

Keener Seniors, 1654 W. Onondaga St., 13204. Tel: 315-424-1804. Nutrition Program for the Elderly. Mr. Michael Gannon, Dir.

BINGHAMTON. *Associated Catholic Charities*, 232 Main St., 13905. Tel: 607-729-9166. Mr. Joseph G. Slavik, Exec. Admin.

Catholic Charities Adolescent Group Home, 57 Chestnut St., 13905. Tel: 607-723-6355; Fax: 607-231-2755.
E-mail: kcerasaro@ccbc.net
Ms. Karen Cerasaro, Dir.

The Catholic Foundation of Broome County, 232 Main St., 13905. Tel: 607-729-9166; Fax: 607-729-2062. Mr. Robert W. Aber, Pres. Legal Title: *The Bishops Catholic Education and Charities Foundation, Inc.*

Catholic Social Services of Broome County, 232 Main St., 13905. Tel: 607-729-9166; Fax: 607-729-2062.
E-mail: dyeager@ccbc.net
Web site: www.catholiccharitiesbc.org
Mr. Daniel L. Yeager, M.A., Exec. Dir.; Grazia Tonelli, C.S.W., Supvr. of Clinical Svcs.; Kathy Ford, C.S.W., Supvr. Pregnancy, Parenting & Adopting Program.

CORTLAND. *Catholic Charities of Cortland County*, 33-35 Central Ave., 13045. Tel: 607-756-5992; Fax: 607-756-5999.
E-mail: pcurrie@clarityconnect,com
Paula Currie, Exec. Dir.

Case Management Services for Teens. Tel: 607-756-5992; Fax: 607-756-5999. Ann Marie Phelps, Dir.

Case Management Services for Psychiatrically Disabled. Tel: 607-756-5992; Fax: 607-756-5999. Marie Lord Walsh, Dir.

Residential Services. (Lawrence House Community Residence). Tel: 607-753-3550; Fax: 607-756-4697. Mike Pisa, Dir. Supported Housing; Supportive Apartments; Alcohol Halfway House & Recovery Apartments.

Food Pantry. Tel: 607-756-5992; Fax: 607-756-5999. Ann Marie Phelps, Dir. Emergency & Brief Assistance Program. Summer Lunch (feeding) Program for Children.

Catholic Charities-STEPS-TASA, 33-35 Central Ave., 13045. Tel: 607-756-5992; Fax: 607-756-5999. (Supportive Teen Education-Parents Services), TASA; Case Management; Men's Support Group.

FULTON. *Catholic Charities of Oswego County*, 365 W. First St., 13069. Tel: 315-598-3980. 108 E. Sixth St., Oswego, 13126. Tel: 315-343-9540. Andrea McCabe, Area Dir.

NORWICH. *Chenango County Catholic Charities*, 3 O'Hara Dr., 13815. Tel: 607-334-8244.

The Counseling Program. See separate listing.

Chenango House, 49 Fair St., 13815. Tel: 607-336-8939. Supervised by Community Residence Program.

Intensive Supportive Apartment Program. 49 Fair St., 13815. Tel: 607-336-4359.

Supported Housing Program. 49 Fair St., 13815. Tel: 607-336-4492.

Crossbridge Adolescent Home. Granville Hill Rd., 13460. Tel: 607-674-9422.

Community Residence Program. Catholic Charities of Chenango County, 3 O'Hara Dr., 13815. Tel: 607-334-8244; Fax: 607-336-5779. Provides housing for mentally ill adults and adolescent boys.

The Counseling Program. Catholic Charities of Chenango County, 3 O'Hara Dr., 13815. Tel: 607-334-8244; Fax: 607-336-5779. Jane Coddington, Dir. Provides comprehensive counseling for children and adults, also specialized counseling for abused children.

Crime Victims-Witness Assistance Program. Tel: 607-334-3532; Fax: 607-336-5779. Catholic Charities of Chenango County, 3 O'Hara Dr., 13815. Tel: 607-336-1528; Fax: 607-336-5779. Provides 24 hour Hotline at 607-336-1101, Crisis Intervention, Safe Dwelling, Safe Housing; Court accompaniment; filing affidavits and claims with Crime Victims Board; advocacy with law enforcement agencies; information and referrals.

ONEIDA. *Madison County Catholic Charities*, 119 E. Walnut St., 13421. Tel: 315-363-5274. Dennis Manning, Exec. Dir.; Sue Panetta, Assoc. Dir.

ROME. *Catholic Charities of Rome*, 212 W. Liberty St., 13440. Tel: 315-337-8600.
E-mail: ccharity@borg.com
Kathleen C. Eichenlaub, Area Dir.

UTICA. *Catholic Charities, Eastern Region*, 1408 Genesee St., 13502. Tel: 315-724-2158; Fax: 315-724-5318. Kathleen C. Eichenlaub, Area Dir.; Jan Stasaitis, Dir. Admin.; Anthony J. Conestabile, Dir. Finance; Nanette Conney, Dir. Residential Support.

Catholic Social Services of Utica, 1408 Genesee St., 13502. Tel: 315-724-3167; Fax: 315-724-5318.
E-mail: ccharity@borg.com
Kathleen C. Eichenlaub, Area Dir.

[I] OFFICES OF HUMAN DEVELOPMENT

SYRACUSE. *Bishop Foery Foundation*, 416 W. Onondaga St., 13202. Tel: 315-475-8316. Socio-Educational instruction center for racial minorities.

Caseworkers. Elementary program for children ages 6-12. Larry King, Dir.

BINGHAMTON. *Broome County Catholic Charities Office of Social Concerns*, 232 Main St., 13905. Tel: 607-729-9166; Fax: 607-729-2062. Ms. Amy Fleming, Dir.

[J] ST. VINCENT DE PAUL SOCIETY

SYRACUSE. *St. Vincent de Paul Furniture and Clothing, a Catholic Charities Program.* Thrift Shop, 500 Seymour St., 13204. Tel: 315-476-4797. Thrift Shop, Distribution & Processing Center, 755 N. Salina, 13208. Tel: 315-475-4659. Lakeshore Heights Plaza Thrift Shop, 6195 Rte. 31, Cicero, 13039. Tel: 315-699-5365. Mr. Richard Wagoner, Dir.; Kris Craven, Warehouse & Store Mgr.

St. Vincent de Paul Society, 500 Seymour St., 13204. Tel: 315-476-4797.

FULTON. *St. Vincent de Paul Thrift Shop*, 365 W. First St., 13069. Tel: 315-598-3980; Fax: 315-593-8440.
E-mail: judyegan@dreamscape.com

[K] CATHOLIC YOUTH ORGANIZATIONS

SYRACUSE. *Alliance Division, Catholic Charities*, 1654 W. Onondaga St., 13204. Tel: 315-424-1880; Fax: 315-424-6045. Mark Clary, Assoc. Dir.

Brighton Family Center, 100 Edmund Ave., 13205. Tel: 315-424-9378. Ms. Patricia Campany, Dir.

Catholic Charities, 1654 W. Onondaga St., 13204. Tel: 315-424-1800. Brian Walton, Area Dir.

Family Division, Catholic Charities, 1654 W. Onondaga St., 13204. Tel: 315-424-1840.

Hawley Youth Organization, 716 Hawley Ave., 13203. Tel: 315-472-6343. Dotti Barraco Hetnar, Dir.

Near East Side Adventures Program, 1085 E. Genesee St., 13210. Tel: 315-472-6362. Richard Kline, Dir.

Neighborhood Division, Catholic Charities, 1654 W. Onondaga St., 13204. Tel: 315-424-1804; Fax: 315-424-1800.

Northside CYO, 527 N. Salina St., 13208. Tel: 315-474-7428.

Salina Civic Center, 2826 Lemoyne Ave., Mattydale, 13211. Tel: 315-455-7096. Sandra Diefendorf, Dir.

Toomey Residential and Community Services Corp., 1654 W. Onondaga St., 13204. Tel: 315-424-1845; Fax: 315-424-7567. Patricia M. Walton, Exec. Dir.

Vincent House, 514 Seymour St., 13204. Tel: 315-475-9844; Fax: 315-474-3939. Mr. John Graham, Branch Dir.

BINGHAMTON. *Broome County CYO*, 232 Main St., 13905. Tel: 607-729-5190. Kevin McGoff, Exec. Dir.

FULTON. *CYO Fulton*, 365 W. First St., 13069. Tel: 315-598-3980. Mr. James Smiley, Dir.

UTICA. *Catholic Charities, Youth Services Division*, 1408 Genesee St., 13502. Tel: 315-724-6118; Fax: 315-724-5318. Mr. James T. Carroll, Dir.

[L] CHILDREN'S INSTITUTIONS AND DAY CARE CENTERS

SYRACUSE. *DePaul Day Care Corporation*, 1654 W. Onondaga St., 13204. Tel: 315-424-8129; Fax: 315-424-7654. Mrs. Sharon Coulter, Dir.

House of Providence, 1654 W. Onondaga St., 13204. Tel: 315-424-1800. Mr. Brian Walton. Records only.

Sister Patricia Ann's Preschool dba Gingerbread House Preschool, 2500 Grant Blvd., 13208. Tel: 315-471-4198.

Dorn Day Care Center dba Gingerbread House Day Care Center, 2500 Grant Blvd., 13208. Tel: 315-471-4198. Joan Raven, Dir.

[M] DIOCESAN SUMMER CAMPS

SYRACUSE. *Lourdes Camp*, Office: 1654 W. Onondaga St., 13204. Tel: 315-424-1812; 673-2888 (Summer). Camp Address: 10 Mile Point, Skaneateles, 13152. Michael Preston, Dir.

UTICA. *Camp Nazareth*, Office: 1408 Genesee St., 13502. Tel: 315-724-6118. 112 Long Lake Rd., Woodgate, 13494. Tel: 315-392-3791; Fax: 315-392-6545. James T. Carroll, Dir.

[N] FAMILY LIFE BUREAUS

SYRACUSE. *Eastern Region*, c/o 1342 Lancaster Ave., 13210. Tel: 315-472-6754. Sue & Ronald Kielar, Dir.

Family Life Education, 1342 Lancaster Ave., 13210. Tel: 315-472-6754; Fax: 315-472-8409. Rev. Joseph H. Phillips, Dir.; Margaret Dupee, Coord., Family & Marriage Enrichment; Mary Ann Davis, Sec.; Karen Bandoblu, Coord., Marriage Prep. & Speakers Bureau; Patricia Ennis, Coord., Separated/Divorced, The Third Option, and Parenting; Nancy Devine, Coord. Northern Region; Sue & Ronald Kielar, Coordinators Eastern Region; Kathy Colligan, Coord. Southern Region.

Northern Region, 108 E. Sixth St., Oswego, 13126. Tel: 315-342-1463. Nancy Devine, Regl. Dir., Office of Family Life Education.

Northern Region Religious Education Office & Special Education for Catechetics, 108 E. Sixth St., Oswego, 13126. Tel: 315-343-5557. Sr. Germaine Hilston, C.S.J., Dir.; Mary Jackson, Resource Center Admin.

Southern Region Family Life Education, 400 Corey Ave., Endicott, 13760. Tel: 607-786-0828.
E-mail: JColligan@stny.rr.com
Kathleen Colligan, Dir.

[O] GENERAL HOSPITALS

SYRACUSE. *St. Joseph's Hospital Health Center*, 301 Prospect Ave., 13203. Tel: 315-448-5111; Fax: 315-448-6161.
E-mail: lavalt57@sjsyr.org
Web site: www.sjhsyr.org
For a complete listing, refer to the Hospitals section.

BINGHAMTON. *Our Lady of Lourdes Memorial Hospital*, 169 Riverside Dr., 13905. Tel: 607-798-5111; Fax: 607-798-7681.
Web site: lourdes.com
For a complete listing, refer to the Hospitals section.

UTICA. *St. Elizabeth Hospital*, 2209 Genesee St., 13501. Tel: 315-798-8100; Fax: 315-734-3092.
E-mail: svincent@STEMC.org
Web site: www.stemc.org
For a complete listing, refer to the Hospitals section.

[P] FACILITIES FOR THE AGED

SYRACUSE. *Bernardine Apartments, Inc.*, 417 Churchill Ave., 13205. Tel: 315-469-7786
For a complete listing, refer to the Special Care Facilities section.

Loretto, 700 E. Brighton Ave., 13205. Tel: 315-469-5561; Fax: 315-469-6558
For a complete listing, refer to the Special Care Facilities section.

Loretto Geriatric Community Residences, Inc., 5018 S. Salina St., 13205. Tel: 315-492-0896
For a complete listing, refer to the Special Care Facilities section.

Loretto Rest, Inc., 750 E. Brighton Ave., 13205. Tel: 315-469-5061
For a complete listing, refer to the Special Care Facilities section.

St. Camillus Health & Rehabilitation Center, 813 Fay Rd., 13219. Tel: 315-488-2951; Fax: 315-488-3255.
Web site: www.st-camillus.org
For a complete listing, refer to the Special Care Facilities section.

OSWEGO. *Saint Luke's Health Care Services*, 299 E. First St., 13126. Tel: 315-342-3166; Fax: 315-343-6531.
E-mail: stluke@global2000.net
Web site: www.stlukehs.com
For a complete listing, refer to the Special Care Facilities section.

UTICA. *St. Joseph Nursing Home*, 2535 Genesee St., 13501. Tel: 315-797-1230; Fax: 315-797-5171.
E-mail: frank@stjosephnh.org
Web site: www.stjosephnh.org
For a complete listing, refer to the Special Care Facilities section.

[Q] SPECIALTY HOUSING

SYRACUSE. *Christopher Community, Inc.*, 1654 W. Onondaga St., 13204. Tel: 315-424-1821
For a complete listing, refer to the Special Care Facilities section.

Churchill Manor, Inc., 750 E. Brighton Ave., 13205. Tel: 315-492-1329; Fax: 315-492-6076.
E-mail: cahika@lorettosystem.org
For a complete listing, refer to the Special Care Facilities section.

Harbor View Housing Development Fund Co., Inc., c/o 1654 W. Onondaga St., 13204. Tel: 315-424-1822
For a complete listing, refer to the Special Care Facilities section.

Hawley Winton Housing Development Fund, Inc., Walter Ludovico Apts., 340 Winton St., 13203. Tel: 315-422-0475; Fax: 315-471-1554
For a complete listing, refer to the Special Care Facilities section.

Ludden Housing Development Fund Company, Inc., 1654 W. Onondaga St., 13204. Tel: 315-424-1821
For a complete listing, refer to the Special Care Facilities section.

Marcellus Apartments Housing Development Fund Company, Inc. Mailing Address: 1654 W. Onondaga St., 13204. Tel: 315-424-1821.
For a complete listing, refer to the Special Care Facilities section.

Miller Road Housing Development Co., Inc., (Brewerton) Mailing Address: 1654 W. Onondaga St., 13204. Tel: 315-424-1821.
For a complete listing, refer to the Special Care Facilities section.

Mother Marianne Cope Housing Development Fund Co., Inc., 1654 W. Onondaga St., 13204. Tel: 315-424-1821
For a complete listing, refer to the Special Care Facilities section.

Mount St. James Corporation, 1654 W. Onondaga St., 13204. Tel: 315-424-1821
For a complete listing, refer to the Special Care Facilities section.

Pompei Housing Development Fund Company, Inc. c/o Christopher Community, Inc., 1654 W. Onondaga St., 13204. Tel: 315-424-1821.
For a complete listing, refer to the Special Care Facilities section.

Pond St. Housing Development Fund Co., Inc., Bishop Harrison Apartments, Pond St., 13208. Tel: 315-476-8630; Fax: 315-474-0806.
E-mail: slucas@christopher-community.org
For a complete listing, refer to the Special Care Facilities section.

Providence House Apartments, 1700 W. Onondaga St., 13204. Tel: 315-471-8427; Fax: 315-474-1224
For a complete listing, refer to the Special Care Facilities section.

St. Peter's Italian Church Housing Development Fund Co., Inc. Villa Scalabrini Apts., 709 James St., 13203
For a complete listing, refer to the Special Care Facilities section.

Stoneleigh Housing Development Fund Co., Inc., Stoneleigh Apartments, 400 Lamb Ave., Canastota, 13032
For a complete listing, refer to the Special Care Facilities section.

Tyson Place Housing Development Fund Company, Inc. Mailing Address: St. Joseph Manor, 1654 W. Onondaga St., 13204. Tel: 315-424-1821.
For a complete listing, refer to the Special Care Facilities section.

AUBURN. *Mercy Housing Development Fund Co., Inc.*, Mercy Apartments, 1 Thornton Ave., 13021. Tel: 315-253-2015; Fax: 315-258-8516.
E-mail: dmechowski@christopher-community.org
For a complete listing, refer to the Special Care Facilities section.

BALDWINSVILLE. *Smokey Hollow Housing Development Fund Company, Inc* Mailing Address: St. Mary's Apartments c/o Christopher Community, 1654 W. Onondaga St. Syracuse, 13204. Tel: 315-424-1821.
For a complete listing, refer to the Special Care Facilities section.

BREWERTON. *Bartell Road Housing Development Fund Co., Inc.*, Bartell Rd., 13029
For a complete listing, refer to the Special Care Facilities section.

CICERO. *Cicero Housing Development Fund Company Inc.* Mailing Address: 1654 W. Onondaga St. Syracuse, 13204. Tel: 315-424-1821.
For a complete listing, refer to the Special Care Facilities section.

FAYETTEVILLE. *Redfield South Housing Development Fund Co., Inc.*, Redfield Village Apartments, 380 Salt Springs Rd., 13066. Tel: 315-637-8280; Fax: 315-637-2376
For a complete listing, refer to the Special Care Facilities section.

NORTH SYRACUSE. *Pitcher Hill-Christopher Housing Development Fund Co., Inc.*, 114 Elbow Rd., 13212. Tel: 315-454-0697; Fax: 315-454-0053
For a complete listing, refer to the Special Care Facilities section.

OSWEGO. *St. Luke's Housing Development Fund Co., Inc.*, St. Luke's Apartments, W. First St., 13126
For a complete listing, refer to the Special Care Facilities section.

ROME. *C.N.C. Inc.*, W. Thomas St., 13440. Tel: 315-735-7545
For a complete listing, refer to the Special Care Facilities section.

Rome Mall Housing Development Fund Company, Inc. Mailing Address: 1654 W. Onondaga St. Syracuse, 13204. Tel: 315-424-1821.
For a complete listing, refer to the Special Care Facilities section.

TOWN OF GATES. *Steger Housing Development Fund Co., Inc.*, 4100 Lyell Rd 1654 W. Onondaga St. Syracuse, 13204. Tel: 315-424-1821.
For a complete listing, refer to the Special Care Facilities section.

UTICA. *Catherine St. Housing Development Fund Company, Inc.* Mailing Address: Mt. Carmel Apartments, 1654 W. Onondaga St. Syracuse, 13201-0511. Tel: 315-424-1821.
For a complete listing, refer to the Special Care Facilities section.

[R] PROGRAMS FOR THE HANDICAPPED

SYRACUSE. *L'Arche*, Office: 1232 Teall Ave., 13206. Tel: 315-479-8088; 479-8118; Fax: 315-479-8118.
E-mail: larchesyra@aol.com
Sr. Michelle M. Lister, Dir. A Christian Community concerned with life sharing between persons with a developmental disability and persons who assist them. Homes at 1701 James St., 1226 Butternut St., 1240-42 Teall Ave., Syracuse, 197 Hathaway Rd., DeWitt & 140 Highland Ave., Syracuse.

UTICA. *St. John and St. Joseph Home, Inc.*, 1408 Genesee St., 13502. Tel: 315-724-2150; Fax: 315-724-5318. Kathleen C. Eichenlaub, Contact Person.

YORKVILLE. *The Heenan Spiritual Program for the Handicapped, Inc.*, 17 Sixth St., 13495. Tel: 315-736-4858. Mr. Stanley Zima, Dir.

[S] MONASTERIES AND RESIDENCES OF PRIESTS AND BROTHERS

SYRACUSE. *Jesuits at LeMoyne, Inc.*, 1419 Salt Springs Rd., 13214. Tel: 315-445-4100; Fax: 315-445-4722.
E-mail: jesuit@maple.lemoyne.edu
Web site: www.web.lemoyne.edu/jesuit/index.html
Revs. John B. Breslin, S.J., Rector; Michael T. Siconolfi, S.J., Min.; James F. Smith, S.J., Treas.; Charles J. Beirne, S.J., Pres.; William J. Bosch, S.J.; Paul B. Campbell, S.J.; J. Donald Clark, S.J.; Theodore J. Clarkson, S.J.; James H. Dahlinger, S.J.; William S. Dolan, S.J.; Vincent W. Hevern, S.J.; Donald J. Kirby, S.J.; Donald C. Maldari, S.J.; Thomas R. Marciniak, S.J.; Paul S. Naumann, S.J.; Joseph B. Neville, S.J.; Edmund G. Ryan, S.J.; Vincent B. Ryan, S.J.; Robert E. Scully, S.J.; Andrew L. Szebenyi, S.J. (Hungary); M. Donald Zewe, S.J. Priests 22.

St. Pius X Home, Inc., 714 E. Brighton Ave., 13205. Tel: 315-492-1711. Diocesan home for priests. In res. Rev. Msgr. Robert B. Davern; Rev. Msgr. Robert E. Dillon; Rev. Msgr. Daniel O'Brien; Revs. Charles A. Aho; Gary M. Fukes; Robert J. McKay; Chester A. Misercola; Thomas F. Guyder; Robert Barett; P. Carl Pilla; Joseph F. Kane; Joseph McNamara (ROC); William J. Brown; William Regan; John O'Brien.

EAST SYRACUSE. *Bishop Grimes Priests Residence*, 6655 Kirkville Rd., 13057. Tel: 315-437-8385. Vianney House, 6651 Kirkville Rd., 13057. Tel: 315-463-2619. Most Rev. Frank J. Harrison; Rev. George F. Sheehan.

[T] CONVENTS AND RESIDENCES FOR SISTERS

SYRACUSE. *Convent of St. Anthony and Motherhouse of the Third Franciscan Order*, 1024 Court St., 13208. Tel: 315-422-8652.
E-mail: osfsyr@eznet.net
Web site: www.eznet.net/~osfsyr
Sr. Catherine Hoefer, O.S.F., Local Min., Generalate Offices, 2500 Grant Blvd., 13208. Tel: 315-425-0115; Fax: 315-425-0610. Sr. Marion Kikukawa, O.S.F., Gen. Min. Total Sisters in Diocese 205; Total in Community 320.

Dominican Monastery of the Perpetual Rosary, 802 Court St., 13208. Tel: 315-471-6762. Sr. Marion, O.P., Prioress. Cloistered Nuns 10; Extern Sisters 2; Novices 2.

Franciscan Formation House, 112 Michaels Ave., 13208-1718. Tel: 315-471-7893. Sisters of the Third Franciscan Order. Sisters 5.

St. Clare Convent, 1001 Court St., 13208. Tel: 315-422-4937.

WINDSOR. *Transfiguration Monastery*, 701 NY Rte. 79, 13865-2700. Tel: 607-655-2366; Fax: 607-655-4024.
E-mail: bendon@dep.tds.net
Camaldolese Benedictine Nuns. Sisters 4.

[U] RETREAT HOUSES

SYRACUSE. *Christ the King Retreat House*, 500 Brookford Rd., 13224. Tel: 315-446-2680; Fax: 315-446-2689.
Web site: retreats@christthekingretreat.com
Rev. Michael J. Carmola, Dir.; Ann Richter, Asst.; Marianne Carbone, Admin. Asst. General retreat

house for priests, nuns, laity and youth of upstate New York. Priests 1.

SKANEATELES. *Stella Maris Retreat Center*, 13152. Tel: 315-685-6836; Fax: 315-685-6836. Sisters of the Third Franciscan Order, M.C. Geraldine Kaluzny, Dir.; Sr. Rose Raymond, Admin. Team oriented center for renewal.

[V] NEWMAN CENTERS

SYRACUSE. *LeMoyne College Newman Center*, 13214. Tel: 315-445-4110.

Onondaga Community College Newman Center, c/o 204 Alton St., 13210. Tel: 315-476-5857. Deacon John Mulvey, Chap.

Syracuse University, St. Thomas More Foundation, Inc., Alibrandi Catholic Center, 110 Walnut Pl., P.O. Box 0038, 13210-0038. Tel: 315-478-5959; Fax: 315-443-4465.
E-mail: stmfsu@aol.com
Rev. Adam Keltos, O.F.M.Conv., Chap.

BINGHAMTON. *Broome Community College Newman Center*, P.O. Box 1017, 13902. Tel: 607-778-5033; Fax: 607-778-5330.
E-mail: phillips_g@sunybroome.edu

CAZENOVIA. *Cazenovia College Newman Center*, 10 Seminary St., 13035. Tel: 315-655-7375.
E-mail: syoung@cazcollege.edu
Web site: www.cazcollege.edu/zinterfaith.htm
Deacon Steven R. Young, Chap.

CLINTON. *Hamilton College Newman Center*, 198 College Hill Rd., 13323. Tel: 315-859-4129; Fax: 315-859-4041.
E-mail: jcroghan@hamilton.edu
Web site: www.hamilton.edu/college/newman
Rev. John P. Croghan, Chap.

CORTLAND. *Newman Foundation of Cortland, Inc. at the State University College of New York*, 8 Calvert St., 13045. Tel: 607-753-6737. Mary Croucher, Chap.

HAMILTON. *Catholic Newman Community of Colgate University*, 13 Oak Dr., 13346. Tel: 315-228-7680; Fax: 315-228-7996.
E-mail: jDonovan@mail.colgate.edu
Web site: www.kendrick.colgate.edu/newman/
Rev. John P. Donovan.

MORRISVILLE. *Newman Association at SUNY Morrisville*, 202 Lab Classroom, 13408. Tel: 315-620-4684.
E-mail: YoungSR@morrisville.edu
Web site: www.morrisville.edu/pages/newman
Legal Title: *St. Joan of Arc Newman Association at the State University of New York (SUNY) Morrisville Agricultural and Technical College*. Deacon Steven R. Young, Chap.

OSWEGO. *Newman Foundation, Inc., State University of New York*, Hall Newman Center, 36 New St., P.O. Box 207, 13126. Tel: 315-312-7222; Fax: 315-312-7561.
E-mail: mcnally@oswego.edu
Rev. Edward F. McNally.

UTICA. *Mohawk Valley Community College*. Newman Apostolate, 1204 Sherman Dr., 13501. Tel: 315-797-3419; Fax: 315-735-5545. Deacon William Hotaling.

SUNY Institute of Technology at Utica/Rome Newman Center, P.O. Box 8087, 13505-8087. Tel: 315-792-3284. Rev. Paul J. Drobin, Chap. Legal Title: *State University of New York (SUNY) Institute of Technology at Utica/Rome Newman Center*.

Utica College of Syracuse University Newman Center, P.O. Box 8087, 13505-8087. Tel: 315-792-3284. Rev. Paul J. Drobin, Chap., Res., P.O. Box 8087, 13505-8087. Tel: 315-792-3284.

VESTAL. *Binghamton University Newman Center*, 400 Murray Hill Rd., 13850. Tel: 607-798-7202.
E-mail: frbob@binghamton.edu
Web site: www.binghamton.edu/newman/newman.htm
Rev. Robert J. Sullivan, Chap.

[W] MISCELLANEOUS LISTINGS

SYRACUSE.

David W. Barry Foundation, 240 E. Onondaga St., P.O. Box 511, 13201-0511. Tel: 315-422-7203; Fax: 315-478-4619. Most Revs. James M. Moynihan, Pres.; Thomas J. Costello, Vice Pres.; Rev. Michael P. Minehan, Sec. & Treas.

Grimes Foundation. (Incorporated by special act of the New York State Legislature, May 1, 1916), 240 E. Onondaga St., 13202. Corporation created to establish and maintain charitable, religious and educational facilities within the Roman Catholic Diocese of Syracuse, New York. Most Rev. James M. Moynihan, D.D., Pres. Ex-Officio.

Lasalle Syracuse, Inc., 6245 Randall Rd., 13214. Tel: 315-446-5960; Fax: 315-446-3393.
Web site: www.cbasyracuse.org

Loretto Apartments Housing Development Fund Co., Inc., 700 E. Brighton Ave., 13205. Tel: 315-469-5570, Ext. 277; Fax: 315-498-9073.

ONE (Opportunity Network in Economics), 1101 Burnet Ave., 13203. Tel: 315-479-6301. Kenneth Leeb, Dir.

Onondaga County Catholic School Foundation (Western Region Catholic School Foundation), 240 E. Onondaga St., P.O. Box 511, 13201-0511. Tel: 315-470-1450; Fax: 315-478-4619. Sr. Helen Ann Charlebois, I.H.M., Area Supt. Western Region Schools.

St. Francis Social Adult Day Service, 1108 Court St., 13208. Tel: 315-424-1003; 1004. Sr. Christopher Dixon, O.S.F., Admin. A non-residential adult day-service providing holistic care for the frail elderly. Operated by the Sisters of the Third Franciscan Order.

Saint Thomas Preparatory Seminary Fund, P.O. Box 511, 13201. Incorporated under the Laws of the State of New York, 1963, as a Membership Corporation to solicit funds for the construction of a diocesan seminary.

Sisters of the Third Franciscan Order-Retirement Trust Fund, 2500 Grant Blvd., 13208. Tel: 315-425-0132; Fax: 315-425-0610.
E-mail: osfsyr@ez.net
Web site: www.home.eznet.net/~osfsyr/

Spiritual Renewal Center, 1118 Court St., 13208. Tel: 315-472-6546.
E-mail: src@auisa.com
Web site: www.aiusa.com/src

BINGHAMTON. *Ladies of Charity*, 100 Main St., 13905. Tel: 607-723-0194.

Samaritan House, 11 Fayette St., 13901. Tel: 607-724-3969. Sr. Kathleen Duncan, C.S.J., Dir.

CANASTOTA. *Catholic Diocese of Nakuru Mission Office, Inc.*, 406 Spencer St., 13032. Rev. Simon K. Mugo (Africa), Dir.

ENDICOTT. *Bishop Harrison Education Foundation*. Mailing Address: P.O. Box 7158, 13760.

MAINE. *Mount St. Francis Hermitage, Inc.* Tel: 607-754-0001; Fax: 607-754-0001.
E-mail: ffimaine@marymediatrix.com
Web site: www.marymediatrix.com
Mailing Address: P.O. Box 236, 13802. Tel: 607-754-0001. Revs. Thomas Huff, F.I.; Isaac Relyea, F.I.; Bro. Didacus Cortes, F.I.

MT. UPTON. *The Catholic Bible School of America*, Main St., 13809. Tel: 845-255-5917.
E-mail: cathbible#1@aol.com
Mailing Address: Rev. Donald E. Bourgeois, 34 South Main St., Bainbridge, 13733. Peter Shipley, Exec. Vice Pres.

RICHLAND. *Rural & Migrant Ministry of Oswego Co. Inc.*, 15 Stewart St., P.O. Box 192, 13144-0192. Tel: 315-298-1154. Sr. Sylvia Gamberoni, Contact Person. Staffed by the Sisters of St. Francis, Daughters of Charity, and Sisters of St. Joseph of Carondelet.

UTICA. *The Good News Foundation of Central New York*, 2306 Genesee St., 13502. Tel: 315-735-9730. Deacon John Droz, Exec. Dir.

RELIGIOUS INSTITUTES OF MEN REPRESENTED IN THE DIOCESE

For further details refer to the corresponding bracketed number in the Religious Institutes of Men or Women section.

[1350]—*Brothers of St. Francis Xavier*. (St. Joseph Prov., Milton, MA).—C.F.X.

[0330]—*Brothers of the Christian Schools*. (New York Prov.).—F.S.C.

[1330]—*Congregation of the Mission (Vincentian Fathers)*.—C.M.

[1210]—*Congregation of the Missionaries of St. Charles*. (St. Charles Borromeo Prov.).—C.S.

[0480]—*Conventual Franciscans*.—O.F.M.Conv.

[0690]—*Jesuit Fathers and Brothers*. (New York Prov.).—S.J.

RELIGIOUS INSTITUTES OF WOMEN REPRESENTED IN THE DIOCESE

[0230]—*Benedictine Sisters of Pontifical Jurisdiction*. (Erie, PA).—O.S.B.

[]—*Camaldolese Benedictine Sisters*.—O.S.B.Cam.

[0330]—*Carmelite Sisters for the Aged and Infirm*.—O.Carm.

[0760]—*Daughters of Charity of St. Vincent de Paul*.—D.C.

[1050]—*Dominican Contemplative Nuns*.—O.P.

[1070-01]—*Dominican Sisters*.—O.P.

[1170]—*Felician Sisters*.—C.S.S.F.

[1180]—*Franciscan Sisters of Allegany, New York*.—O.S.F.

[1410]—*Franciscan Sisters of St. Joseph (Mill Hill)*.—F.M.S.J.

[2575]—*Institute of the Sisters of Mercy of the Americas*. (New York, NY; Omaha, NE).—R.S.M.

[1360]—*Missionary Franciscan Sisters of the Immaculate Conception*.—O.S.F.

[3160]—*Parish Visitors of Mary Immaculate*.—P.V.M.I.

[0590]—*Sisters of Charity of Saint Elizabeth, Convent Station*.—S.C.

[3340]—*Sisters of Providence (Holyoke)*.—S.P.

[3950]—*Sisters of Saint Mary of Namur*.—S.S.M.N.

[3780]—*Sisters of Saints Cyril and Methodius*.—SS.C.M.

[1800]—*Sisters of St. Francis of the Third Order Regular*. (Williamsville, New York).—O.S.F.

[3830-14]—*Sisters of St. Joseph*. (Rochester, NY).—S.S.J.

[3840]—*Sisters of St. Joseph of Carondelet*.—C.S.J.

[1970]—*Sisters of the Holy Family of Nazareth*.—C.S.F.N.

[1490]—*Sisters of the Third Franciscan Order*.—O.S.F.

[2160]—*Sisters, Servants of the Immaculate Heart of Mary*.—I.H.M.

[4110]—*Ursuline Nuns (Roman Union)*.—O.S.U.

DIOCESAN CEMETERIES

SYRACUSE. *St. Mary-St. Agnes*, 2315 South Ave., 13207. Tel: 315-475-4639. Rev. James C. Fritzen, Dir.; Richard Dadey, Supt.; Daniel Moorhead, Asst. Supt.

CORTLAND. *St. Mary*, 4101 West Road, 13045. Tel: 607-756-8838. Rev. John P. Fenlon, Dir.; Russell Teeter, Supt.

JOHNSON CITY. *Calvary-St. Patrick*, 501 Fairview St., 13790. Tel: 607-797-2906. Daniel Vuille, Supt.; Ann Tesar, Sec.

OSWEGO. *St. Peter & St. Paul*, R.R. 04 Box 4B, Rte. 481, E. River Rd., 13126. Tel: 315-343-5002. Rev. Msgr. Paul A. Brigandi, Dir.; John Taber, Supt.

UTICA. *Calvary*, 2407 Oneida St., 13501. Tel: 315-735-2727. Rev. Msgr. William Donovan, Dir.; Donald Deck, Supt.

Holy Trinity, Chaplain Ave., 13502. Tel: 315-724-0616. Rev. Arthur R. Hapanowicz, Dir.; Daniel Williams, Supt.

St. Agnes, 601 Arthur St., 13501. Tel: 315-732-8588. Lawrence F. Hagan, Coord.; John McCarthy, Supt.

St. Mary, Webster St., 13501. Tel: 315-735-2727. Donald Deck, Supt.

WHITESBORO. *Mount Olivet*, 70 Wood Rd., 13492. Tel: 315-736-4446. Rev. Donald H. Karlen, Dir.; Joseph Usyk, Supt.

NECROLOGY

† Jakubik, Emil, (Retired). —Died Dec. 14, 1999.

† Lembo, Philip, North Syracuse, St. Rose of Lima. —Died April 16, 2000.

† O'Heron, Edward J., Newman Chap, Cortland, NY State University of New York. —Died Nov. 20, 1999.

† Riley, James L., (Retired). —Died June 6, 2000.

† Ryan, Rev. Msgr. Edward J, Liverpool, Immaculate Heart of Mary. —Died Nov. 5, 2000.

† Segrue, Joseph D., Syracuse, Blessed Sacrament. —Died Dec. 20, 1999.

Diocese of Toledo

(Dioecesis Toletana in America)

Most Reverend

JAMES R. HOFFMAN, D.D., J.C.L.

Bishop of Toledo; ordained July 28, 1957; appointed Titular Bishop of Italica and Auxiliary Bishop of Toledo April 18, 1978; ordained Bishop June 23, 1978; appointed to Toledo December 16, 1980. *Res., 2544 Parkwood Ave., Toledo, OH, 43610.*

Most Reverend

ROBERT W. DONNELLY, D.D.

Auxiliary Bishop of Toledo; ordained May 25, 1957; appointed Titular Bishop of Garba and Auxiliary Bishop of Toledo March 20, 1984; ordained Bishop May 3, 1984. *Res., 2544 Parkwood Ave., Toledo, OH, 43610.*

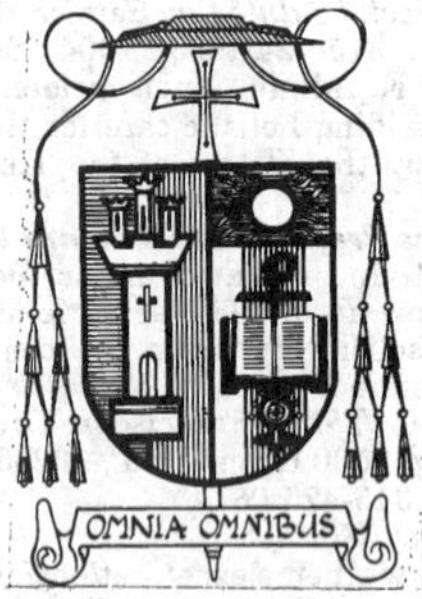

Chancery: P.O. Box 985, Toledo, OH, 43697-0985. Tel.: 419-244-6711; Fax: 419-244-4791.

Web site address: www.toledodiocese.org

E-mail address: chancery@toledodiocese.org

ESTABLISHED APRIL 15, 1910.

Square Miles 8,222.

Comprises the following Counties of northwest Ohio: Williams, Fulton, Lucas, Ottawa, Defiance, Henry, Wood, Sandusky, Erie, Paulding, Putnam, Hancock, Seneca, Huron, Van Wert, Allen, Wyandot, Crawford and Richland.

For legal titles of parishes and diocesan institutions, consult the Chancery.

STATISTICAL OVERVIEW

Personnel	
Bishop	1
Auxiliary Bishops	1
Retired Bishops	1
Priests: Diocesan Active in Diocese	141
Priests: Active Outside Diocese	5
Priests: Diocesan in Foreign Missions	1
Priests: Retired, Sick or Absent	59
Number of Diocesan Priests	206
Religious Priests in Diocese	54
Extern Priests in Diocese	12
Ordinations:	
Diocesan Priests	1
Permanent Deacons	5
Permanent Deacons in Diocese	192
Total Brothers	10
Total Sisters	712
Parishes	
Parishes	162
With Resident Pastor:	
Resident Diocesan Priests	101
Resident Religious Priests	13
Without Resident Pastor:	
Administered by Priests	39
Administered by Women Religious	9
Pastoral Centers	11
Welfare	
Catholic Hospitals	7
Total Assisted	1,012,844
Health Care Centers	2
Total Assisted	717
Homes for the Aged	2
Total Assisted	330
Residential Care of Children	1
Total Assisted	61
Special Centers for Social Services	14
Total Assisted	14,788
Educational	
Diocesan Students in Other Seminaries	18
Total Seminarians	18
Colleges and Universities	2
Total Students	1,513
High Schools, Diocesan and Parish	10
Total Students	3,843
High Schools, Private	4
Total Students	2,726
Elementary Schools, Diocesan and Parish	83
Total Students	21,427
Elementary Schools, Private	3
Total Students	657
Non-residential Schools for the Disabled	1
Total Students	75
Catechesis/Religious Education:	
High School Students	1,981
Elementary Students	10,434
Total Students Under Catholic Instruction	42,674
Teachers in the Diocese:	
Priests	3
Sisters	81
Lay Teachers	1,739
Vital Statistics	
Receptions into the Church:	
Infant Baptism Totals	3,815
Adult Baptism Totals	600
Received into Full Communion	671
First Communions	5,239
Confirmations	7,897
Marriages:	
Catholic	951
Interfaith	852
Total Marriages	1,803
Deaths	3,097
Total Catholic Population	335,909
Total Population	1,481,725

Former Bishops—Most Rev. JOSEPH SCHREMBS, D.D., appt. auxiliary of Grand Rapids, MI Jan. 8, 1911; cons. Feb. 22, 1911; transferred to Toledo, Aug. 11, 1911; transferred to Cleveland, OH, May 11, 1921; died Nov. 2, 1945.—His Eminence SAMUEL CARDINAL STRITCH, D.D., cons. Bishop of Toledo, Nov. 30, 1921; appt. Archbishop of Milwaukee, Aug. 30, 1930; appt. Archbishop of Chicago, Dec. 27, 1939; created Cardinal, Feb. 18, 1946; named Pro-Prefect of the Sacred Congregation of the Propagation of the Faith, March 1, 1958; died in Rome, May 27, 1958.—Most Rev. KARL J. ALTER, D.D., LL.D., appt. Bishop of Toledo, April 17, 1931; cons. June 17, 1931; promoted to Archbishop of Cincinnati, June 14, 1950; died Aug. 23, 1977.—Most Rev. GEORGE REHRING, D.D., cons. Oct. 7, 1937; appt. Bishop of Toledo, July 18, 1950; retired Feb. 25, 1967; died Feb. 29, 1976.—Most Rev. JOHN A. DONOVAN, D.D., ord. Dec. 8, 1935; Titular Bishop of Rhasus and Auxiliary of Detroit, Sept. 6, 1954; ord. Bishop, Oct. 26, 1954; transferred to Toledo, Feb. 25, 1967; retired July 29, 1980; died Sept. 18, 1991.

Chancery—Mailing Address: P.O. Box 985, Toledo, 43697-0985. 1933 Spielbusch, Toledo, 43624. Tel: 419-244-6711; Fax: 419-244-4791. Office Hours: Mon.-Fri. 8:30-5.

Vicar General—Most Rev. ROBERT W. DONNELLY, V.G., *1933 Spielbusch, Toledo, 43624., Mailing Address: P.O. Box 985, Toledo, 43697-0985.* Tel: 419-244-6711.

Chancellor—Rev. MICHAEL R. BILLIAN, *1933 Spielbusch, Toledo, 43624.* Tel: 419-244-6711., *Mailing Address: P.O. Box 985, Toledo, 43697-0985.*

Cabinet—Most Rev. ROBERT W. DONNELLY, V.G., Sec. Personnel & Admin. Svcs. MICHAEL WASSERMAN, Secretariat for Pastoral Leadership; Sr. JANET DOYLE, O.P., Sec. of Catholic Youth & School Svcs. DONALD L. WISLER, L.I.S.W., Sec. Catholic Charities; Rev. MICHAEL R. BILLIAN, Chancellor, *1933 Spielbusch, Toledo, 43624.* Tel: 419-244-6711.

Advisory To Bishop

All Diocesan Offices and Secretaries are located at 1933 Spielbusch, Toledo, OH 43624. Address all mail to: P.O. Box 985, Toledo, OH 43697-0985. Tel: 419-244-6711. unless otherwise indicated

Bishop's Education Council—TOM NOE, Pres.; Mrs. DEBRA SCHAEFER, Vice Pres.; Revs. GREGORY R. HITE; DANIEL J. RING; CLEO S. SCHMENK; HERBERT J. WILLIAM; Sr. MADELEVA KRAUS; Dr. HARRY BASH; MICHAEL BEAZLEY; MARY CONRY; MICHAEL HART; ART JONES; SALLY KOPPINGER; RAYMOND OLSZARK; DIANE SACCONE; DAVID WALROD; THOMAS YOUNG; Mr. JACK ALTENBURGER.

Building Commission—Dr. GEORGE MURNEN, Chm.; Revs. GERALD J. CHMIEL; FRANK K. ECKART; Mr. DAVID BAGGETT; Mr. JAMES CIHAK; Dr. MARK PICKETT.

Consultors—Revs. ALBERT B. CERANOWSKI; GERALD L. CERANOWSKI; GREGORY L. PEATEE; CHRISTOPHER P. VASKO.

Deans—Defiance Deanery: Very Rev. G. ALLAN FILLMAN, V.F., Defiance, Henry and Paulding Counties; Fremont Deanery: Very Rev. RONALD J. LEJEUNE,

V.F., Ottawa and Sandusky Counties; Lima Deanery: Very Rev. DAVID M. ROSS, V.F., S.T.L., J.C.D., Ph.D., Allen, Van Wert and Putnam Counties; Mansfield Deanery: Very Rev. HERBERT F. WEBER, V.F., Richland and Crawford Counties; Tiffin Deanery: Very Rev. FRANCIS A. MURD, V.F., Seneca, Wyandot and Hancock Counties; Toledo Central: Very Rev. RONALD R. WARNIMONT, V.F., Toledo Northwest: Very Rev. ROBERT J. REINHART, V.F., Toledo Southwest: Very Rev. DENNIS M. METZGER, V.F., To-Lu-Wo Deanery: Very Rev. JOSEPH R. STEINBAUER, V.F., Dean for East Lucas and Wood Counties; Sandusky Deanery: Very Rev. FRANKLIN P. KEHRES, V.F., Erie and Huron Counties; Will-Ful-L Deanery: Very Rev. FREDERICK J. DUSCHL, V.F., Williams, Fulton and West Lucas Counties.

Diocesan Pastoral Advisory Council—Vacant, Contact, *P.O. Box 985, Toledo, 43697-0985.*

Finance Council—Most Rev. JAMES R. HOFFMAN; Most Rev. ROBERT W. DONNELLY, V.G.; Mr. RICHARD FAIST; Mr. ROBERT J. KIRK; Mr. THOMAS KRESS.

Priests' Council—Revs. DAVID M. ROSS, Chm. Tel: 419-693-1150. DAVID A. REINHART, Vice Chm., Sec. & Treas. Tel: 419-475-4348.

Secretariat Of Administrative Services

Secretary—Most Rev. ROBERT W. DONNELLY, D.D., *P.O. Box 985, Toledo, 43697-0985.* Tel: 419-244-6711.

Diocesan Department Of Development—RICHARD WARING, Ph.D., Dir.; Mrs. DOROTHY LANGENDERFER, Assoc. Dir.

Financial Services—Mr. JOHN HEINZE, Dir.

Internal Auditor—Ms. SARA G. MARTIN, C.P.A., (Inactive).

Associate Auditor—Ms. SUZANNE STAPLETON.

Information Technology—Mr. FRANK BEIER, Dir.; Ms. SHARON LANDIS, Assoc. Dir.

Cemeteries Office—Mr. JOHN E. CARPENTER, C.C.E., Dir., *5725 Hill Ave., Toledo, 43615-5852.* Tel: 419-531-5747; Fax: 419-531-0946.

Cemeteries—Calvary: *2424 Dorr St., Toledo, 43607.* Tel: 419-536-3751., Mount Carmel: *15 E. Manhattan Blvd., Toledo, 43608.* Tel: 419-536-3751., Resurrection: *5725 Hill Ave., Toledo, 43615.* Tel: 419-531-5747.

Director of Communications—Rev. THOMAS S. QUINN, *P.O. Box 985, Toledo, 43697-0985.* Tel: 419-244-6711; Fax: 419-244-4791.

Diocesan Archives—Sr. LOURDE BEAUREGARD, S.N.D., *c/o 2544 Parkwood Ave., Toledo, 43610.* Tel: 419-255-1890; Fax: 419-244-0471.

"Catholic Chronicle"—PATRICIA L. MORRISON, Mng. Editor, *4913 Harroun Rd., Sylvania, 43560-2102.* Tel: 419-885-6397; Fax: 419-885-6398.

Affiliated:

Diocesan Directory—Mrs. RITA BAUR, Editor.

Catholic Office Building Services—Ms. PATRICIA STEIN, Mgr.

Court of Equity—Mrs. JUDITH GAJDOSTIK, Clerk; FRANK LINK, Presiding Judge, *3250 Hazelton Dr., Oregon, 43616.* Tel: 419-691-7436.

Judges—FRANCIS LANDRY; Sr. EMILY LECHLAK, O.S.F.S.; COLIN MCQUADE; PAULA MINZING; Rev. DANIEL RING; Sr. DOROTHY THUM, R.S.M.; HARRY WELSH; BRUCE WINTERS.

Conciliators—JAMES CARUSO; RICHARD HANUSZ; Sr. THERESE MILNE, I.H.M.; REGINA SCHIMMOELLER; JUDE SUTTER; JOHN F. WETLI.

Intake Officers—ROBERT J. SUTTER; CLARA WESOLEK; ELIZABETH ZEPF.

DCCW (Diocesan Council of Catholic Women)—Mrs. WANDA MILLS, Pres., *1542 Ralston Cir., Ste. 207, Toledo, 43615.* Tel: 419-534-2252.

Secretariat Of Personnel

Secretary—Most Rev. ROBERT W. DONNELLY, D.D.

Vicar for Priests—Vacant.

Director of Ministry to Priests Program—Vacant, Dir.; Sr. MARGARET MCGUINESS, O.P., Assoc. Dir.

Vicar for Deacons—Vacant.

Vicar For Religious—Sr. MARY SUE KENNEDY, O.P.

Diocesan Case Manager—Mr. FRANK DILALLO.

Office of Vocations—Rev. WILLIAM KUBACKI, Dir.; Sr. RITA MARIE SCHROEDER, S.N.D., Assoc. Dir.

Priests' Personnel Board—Rev. KENNETH J. LILL, Chm. Members: Revs. JOHN R. BLASER; RAYMOND E. ENSMAN; KEITH A. STRIPE; JOSEPH R. STEINBAUER, V.F.; ROBERT J. WILHELM, *2544 Parkwood Ave., Toledo, 43610-1317.* Tel: 419-255-1890; Fax: 419-244-0471.

Office of Personnel Services—Mr. MICHAEL CONNELL.

Tribunal—Catholic Office Building, 1933 Spielbusch, Toledo, 43624. Tel: 419-244-6711., *Mailing Address: P.O. Box 985, Toledo, 43697-0985.*

Director—Sr. MARCIA MARIE DESTATTE, S.N.D., J.C.L.

Judicial Vicar—Very Rev. JOHN A. MCCLURE, J.C.L.

Judges—Most Rev. JAMES R. HOFFMAN, D.D., J.C.L.; Revs. JAMES E. AUTH, J.C.L.; MARVIN G. BORGER, J.C.L.; JOSEPH P. JAROS; GEORGE P. MILLER, J.C.L.; WILLIAM C. PARKER; Very Rev. DAVID M. ROSS, S.T.L., J.C.D.; Revs. DENNIS A. SCHROEDER; CHRISTOPHER P. VASKO, J.C.L.; RICHARD T. WURZEL, S.T.D.

Defenders of the Bond—Rev. THOMAS J. BEAUREGARD; Sr. MARCELLA HERMAN, O.S.F/T., J.C.L.; Rev. JOSEPH L. VAMOS; Very Rev. RONALD R. WARNIMONT, J.C.L.

Auditor/Assessor—Sr. MARCIA MARIE DESTATTE, S.N.D., J.C.L.

Notaries—Mrs. PAULA S. BUTLER; Mrs. MARIAN A. KRASNIEWSKI; Mrs. CHARLOTTE A. LAMMERS; Mrs. ANGELA D. WALKER.

Retirement Plan for Lay Employees—Mrs. MARY C. DEPINET, Admin.

Employee Benefit Fund—Mrs. MARY C. DEPINET, Admin.

Secretariat for Pastoral Leadership

Secretary—Mr. MICHAEL WASSERMAN, *Catholic Office Building, 1933 Spielbusch, Toledo, 43624.* Tel: 419-244-6711, Ext. 299; Fax: 419-244-4791., *P.O. Box 985, Toledo, 43697-0985.*

Assistant Secretary—Deacon ALFREDO DIAZ.

Adult Catholic Formation—Sr. MARGARET A. MCGUINESS, O.P., Dir.

Campus Ministry—Rev. NELSON BELIZARIO, O.Carm., Office: *2955 Dorr St., Toledo, 43607.* Tel: 419-534-2023.

Deacon Formation—Deacon LEO T. BISTAK.

Evangelization—Deacon LEO T. BISTAK.

Office of Global Concerns—Deacon RICHARD MISHLER.

Mission of Accompaniment Pastoral Team—Revs. BERNARD J. BOFF, Stateside Dir. THOMAS J. MCQUILLEN, *All Souls Catholic Mission, Box 37, Binga, Zimbabwe, Africa.* Associates: Rev. CHRISTOPHER KARDZIS; Ms. RUTH ANN LEIDORF.

Hispanic Pastoral Ministry—Mrs. ELENA CABALLERO, Dir.

Leadership Formation—

Called and Gifted & Empowering Leadership Programs—Sr. CHRISTINE MATTHEWS, O.P., Dir.

Pastoral Planning—Deacon ALFREDO DIAZ.

Office of Worship—Sr. GEORGETTE ZALEWSKA, R.S.M., Dir.

Toledo Diocesan Liturgical Commission—Sr. GEORGETTE ZALEWSKA, R.S.M., Chm.

Ecumenical & Interreligious Affairs Commission—Rev. DAVID R. BRUNING, Chm., *3030 Tremainsville, Toledo, 43613.* Tel: 419-472-2111.

Secretariat of Catholic Youth & School Services

Secretary—Sr. JANET DOYLE, O.P. Tel: 419-244-6711; 800-926-8277; Fax: 419-255-8269. Team Members: Mr. JACK ALTENBURGER; Ms. SUE SMITH; Mrs. ANNE BURGUNDER; Sr. MARY MARGARET PACHUCKI, O.P.; Ms. ANN SARDESON; Ms. LAURIE GHESQUIERE; Mr. FRANK DILALLO.

Religious Education—

Assistant Superintendent for Religious Education—Sr. MIRIAM EBLE, S.N.D.

Religious Education Consultant—Ms. DONNA THERKELSEN.

Catholic Youth Organization (CYO)—Mr. JEFF MIELCAREK, Dir.

Children's Scholarship Fund—Mr. RIC CERVANTES, Coord.

Catholic Club—Mr. PAUL SZYMANSKI, Dir., *1601 Jefferson Ave., Toledo, 43604.* Tel: 419-243-7255; Fax: 419-243-6337.

Youth & Young Adult Ministry—Rev. RONALD A. SCHOCK, Dir. & Youth Chap. Youth - Area Coordinators: Ms. PATTI TACKETT, Back to Earth, Mansfield Deanery. Tel: 419-347-3910. Ms. LORI KAMELESKY, Beacon, Fremont Deanery. Tel: 419-862-3452. Ms. LORRIE SEIPLE, Crossroads, Defiance & Will-Ful-L Deaneries. Tel: 419-782-5329. Ms. CONNIE CLEEMPUT, Hearthstone, Lima Deanery. Tel: 419-532-3038. Ms. PATTI TACKETT, Heartland, Sandusky Deanery. Tel: 419-347-3910. Ms. LINDA GUTIERREZ, Kaleidoscope, Toledo N & S Deaneries. Tel: 419-868-9971. Ms. PATTI IRONS, Prism, East Toledo. Tel: 419-385-4832. Ms. SUE MORIT, Two Rivers & Tiffin Deanery. Tel: 419-443-1483.

Secretariat of Catholic Charities

Catholic Charities—Mr. DONALD L. WISLER, L.I.S.W., Sec. & Exec. Dir.

Direct Services Division:

Eastern Region—NICOLE CUNNINGHAM, Dir., *Box 288, Norwalk, 44857.* Tel: 419-668-3073; Fax: 419-663-5070.

Western Region—*511 Perry St., Defiance, 43512.* Tel: 419-782-4933; Fax: 419-784-4760.

Equal Access Ministry—Mrs. KITTY KRUSE; Dir. Tel: 419-243-1475 (TTY).

Family Connections—Mr. RICHARD SEVIGNY, Dir.

Family Life/Respect Life Office—Mrs. LUCY ABU-ABSI, Dir.

Mediation Services—Mr. LOUIS COCCHIARELLA, Dir.

Migrant Ministry—Sr. MARY JO TOLL, S.N.D., Dir., *150 Perry St., P.O. Box 548, Fostoria, 44830.* Tel: 419-436-1582.

Out-Patient Counseling Services—Mr. RICHARD SEVIGNY, Dir.

Parish Social Ministry—Mr. LOUIS COCCHIARELLA, Dir.

Rural Life Ministries—Sr. CHRISTINE PRATT, O.S.U., Dir., *1021 W. State St., Fremont, 43420.* Tel: 419-334-1331; Fax: 419-334-9837.

Social Action Office—Sr. JOAN MICHALIK, I.H.M., Dir.

Mareda, Inc. (Vistula Management Co.)—JOHN KIELY, Dir., *P.O. Box 4719, Toledo, 43620.* Tel: 419-242-2300; Fax: 419-246-4703.

Madonna Homes—Ms. BEVERLY THOMAS, Mgr., *722 Huron St., Toledo, 43604.* Tel: 419-244-3758.

Regina Manor—Ms. JODY DOWNEY, Mgr., *3731 N. Erie St., Toledo, 43611.* Tel: 419-246-4731.

Delaware Acres—Ms. MELANIE PARKS-BAYNARD, Mgr., *725 Buchanan, Fremont, 43420.* Tel: 419-334-9558.

Moody Manor—Ms. TRACEY FAILS, Mgr., *2293-1/2 Kent St., Toledo, 43620.* Tel: 419-246-4737.

Hope Manor—Ms. ORA MILTON, Mgr., *4702 Violet Rd., Toledo, 43623.* Tel: 419-246-4733.

Michaelmas Manor—Ms. STEPHANIE DOWNEY, Mgr., *3260 Schneider Rd., Toledo, 43614.* Tel: 419-246-4735.

St. Anthony Villa—Ms. KRIS KAPELA-ALSHEHRI, Ph.D., Regl. Dir., *2740 W. Central Ave., Toledo, 43606.* Tel: 419-473-1353; Fax: 419-473-2963.

St. Vincent De Paul Society—Mr. HAROLD HANLEY, Council Pres.; Ms. SANDRA BLOOMQUIST, Vice Pres.; Mr. WILLIAM MAHONEY, Store Mgr., *1001 Washington St., Toledo, 43624.* Tel: 419-243-6963.

Other Organizations

CCMT (Central City Ministries of Toledo)—Cochairpersons: Rev. RONALD R. WARNIMONT; Mr. EDWARD ALFORS; Miss SUZANNE STAPLETON; SHARON RAPPAPORT, Dir. Devel. & Public Rels. DENNIS PAKULSKI, Business Mgr., *1119 W. Bancroft St., Toledo, 43606.* Tel: 419-244-9516; Fax: 419-244-3676.

Cursillo Movement—Spiritual Directors: Rev. EDWARD J. LITTELMANN, *430 Main St., Huron, 44839.* Tel: 419-433-5725. Rev. JAMES E. BROWN, *802 Barclay St., Marblehead, 43440.* Tel: 419-798-4177. Deacon ALFREDO DIAZ, *1008 Garfield, Fremont, 43420.* Tel: 419-244-6711. Sr. EDNA MICHEL, O.S.F., *P.O. Box 576, Wakeman, 44889-0576.* Tel: 440-839-2023. Lay Directors: SCOTT OTERMAT; KATHY OTERMAT, *1786 C.R. 128, Fremont, 43420.* Tel: 800-929-6080.

Diocesan Attorneys—JOHN HAYWARD; TOM PLETZ, *1000 Jackson St., Toledo, 43624.* Tel: 419-241-4201.

Diocesan Insurance Program—JOSEPH SPENTHOFF, Branch Mgr., *Gallagher-Bassett Insurance Services, 5640 Southwyck Blvd., Toledo, 43614.* Tel: 419-865-8821.

MCCR (Ministry To Catholic Charismatic Renewal)—Mr. ROY HANDY, *550 Clark St., Toledo, 43605-2296.*

Serra International—Mr. MARK HENCH, District Governor, *R1 Mirival Lane, Defiance, 43512.*

Lima Serra Club—RICHARD STOLLY, Pres., *4 Sheffield Lane, Lima, 45805.*

Mansfield Serra Club—FRANK RUSSO, *618 Orchard, Mansfield, 44904.*

Tiffin Serra Club—MARGUERITE BERNARD, *170 Hillcrest, Tiffin, 44883.*

Toledo Serra Club—Mr. TOM WEISENBURGER, *2916 River Rd., Maumee, 43537.*

Defiance Serra Club—DONALD J. MEYER, *19661 S.W. 18W, Defiance, 43512.*

Fremont Serra Club—Ms. JAN HAZEN, *519 Gibson, Fremont, 43420.*

Secular Order of Discalced Carmelites—KENNETH KRASNIEWSKI, Contact Person, *Our Lady of the Holy Rosary Fraternity, 5631 304th St., Toledo, 43611.*

Secular Franciscans—

St. Maximilian Kolbe Region, Ohio—Ms. MARCELLA BINA, S.F.O., Regl. Min., *16820 Brinbourne Ave., Middleburg Heights, 44130-5315.*

St. Anthony of Padua Fraternity, Carey—Ms. ISABELLE BRODMAN, S.F.O., Contact, *420 Clay St., Carey, 43316.*

St. Anthony of Padua Fraternity, Fostoria—Ms. JENNIFER GILLIG, S.F.O., Contact, *1435 N. Union St., Fostoria, 44830.*

St. Maximilian Mary Kolbe Fraternity, Findlay—Mr. ROBERT HILDRETH, S.F.O., Contact, *1020 Hurd Ave., Findlay, 45840.*

St. Joseph Fraternity, Green Springs—Mr. ANDY GOOD, S.F.O., Contact, *528 Glenwood Dr., Fremont, 43420.*

Queen of the Angels Fraternity, Lima—Ms. SHERYL ODENWELLER, S.F.O., Contact, *340 W. 6th St., Delphos, 45833.*

St. Clare Fraternity, Tiffin—Ms. MARY PARADISO, S.F.O., Contact, *141 Oak St., Tiffin, 44883.*

St. Paschal Fraternity—1933 Spielbusch, Toledo, 43624. Ms. DIANE REICHOW, *4811 Wickford Green #4, Sylvania, 43560.*

Worldwide Marriage Encounter—FRED KOPERSKI; CLAUDIA KOPERSKI, *7701 Pope Run, Sylvania, 43560.*

Retrouvaille—Exec. Team Couple: BOB PACER; LAURIE PACER, *5698 County Rd. 9, Delta, 43515.*

CLERGY, PARISHES, MISSIONS AND PAROCHIAL SCHOOLS

CITY OF TOLEDO
(Lucas County)

1—QUEEN OF THE MOST HOLY ROSARY CATHEDRAL (1915), Very Rev. Ronald R. Warnimont, Rector; Deacons Lawrence Adams; Jesus Villagomez. In res., Most Revs. James R. Hoffman; Robert W. Donnelly; Albert H. Ottenweller.
Office: 2535 Collingwood Blvd., 43610. Tel: 419-244-9575; Fax: 419-242-1901.
Res., 2544 Parkwood Ave., 43610-1300. Tel: 419-255-1890; Fax: 419-244-0471.
Church—2561 Collingwood Blvd. and Islington St., 43610. [JC]
School—Tel: 419-243-4396.
Sisters 1; Lay Teachers 14; Students 208.

2—BLESSED SACRAMENT (1924), Rev. Robert J. Reinhart; Deacons Robert Gillen; Zenon Selmek; Harold Welch. In res., Rev. Thomas S. Quinn.
Res., 4227 Bellevue Rd., 43613-3999. Tel: 419-472-2288; Fax: 419-472-0493. [JC]
School—2216 Castlewood Dr., 43613. Tel: 419-472-1121; Fax: 419-472-1679.
Catechesis/Religious Programs—Tel: 419-472-7526.
Students 540.

3—CHRIST THE KING (1953), Revs. Michael O. Brown; Gregory L. Peatee; Deacons Gerald Sortman; Robert Beisser; Mrs. Suzanne Marciniak, Pastoral Assoc.
Office: 4100 Harvest Ln., 43623-4399. Tel: 419-475-4348; Fax: 419-475-4050.
Res., 3727 Woodley Rd., 43606-1160. Tel: 419-474-3643. [JC 3]
School—Tel: 419-475-0909.
Sisters 2; Lay Teachers 22; Students 605.
Catechesis/Religious Programs—Tel: 419-475-1954.
Students 178.

4—COMMUNITY OF THE RISEN CHRIST (1972). Closed. For inquiries for parish records contact the Chancery.

5—CORPUS CHRISTI, UNIVERSITY OF TOLEDO (1970), Rev. James J. Bacik; Deacon James Moncher; Ms. Pam Meseroll, Admin. In res., Rev. Earl A. Loeffer.
Res., 2955 Dorr St., 43607-3023. Tel: 419-531-4992 (Office); Fax: 419-531-1775.

6—GESU (1920), Revs. Joseph B. Kappes, S.J.; Paul A. Woefl, S.J.; David E. Watson, S.J.; Deacons Larry Petersen; Ed Kelley; Richard Warren.
Res., 2049 Parkside Blvd., 43607. Tel: 419-531-1421; Fax: 419-531-0270. [JC]
School—Tel: 419-536-5634; Fax: 419-531-8932.
Sisters of Notre Dame 2; Lay Teachers 26; Students 426.
Catechesis/Religious Programs—Students 150.

7—GOOD SHEPHERD (1873), Revs. John R. Blaser; Jerome F. Nowakowski; Deacon Leon Holmer. In res., Rev. Gerald E. Knueven.
Res., 550 Clark St., 43605. Tel: 419-691-5815. [JC]
Catechesis/Religious Programs—Tel: 419-698-1519; Fax: 419-698-2050.
Students 47.

8—HOLY ROSARY (1906) (Slovak), Revs. Frank E. Eckart; Kenneth G. Morman; Deacon Richard Fazekas.
Res., 821 N. Wheeling St., 43605. Tel: 419-693-2198; Fax: 419-693-2198. [JC]
School—Sacred Heart School, (Grades K-5) 824 Sixth St., NJ 43605. Tel: 419-691-1653.
Religious 2; Lay Teachers 6; Students 116.

9—IMMACULATE CONCEPTION (1868), Rev. Paul M. Kwiatkowski; Deacon Leo T. Bistak.
Res., 434 Western Ave., 43609. Tel: 419-243-1829; Fax: 419-243-0067.
School—Queen of Apostles Consolidated. Also serves St. James Parish and SS. Peter and Paul Parish. 235 Courtland St., 43609. Tel: 419-241-7829; Fax: 419-241-4180. Sr. Brenda Haynes, S.N.D., Prin. Students 177.
Catechesis/Religious Programs—Students 100.

10—LITTLE FLOWER OF JESUS (1928), Rev. Stephen P. Cairns.
Res., 5522 Dorr St., 43615. Tel: 419-537-6997; Fax: 419-537-1469. [JC]
School—Tel: 419-536-1194; Fax: 419-531-5140.
Lay Teachers 17; Students 347.
Catechesis/Religious Programs—Tel: 419-537-6655.
Students 190.

11—OUR LADY OF LOURDES (1926), Rev. Thomas E. Wehinger; Deacons Clifford Kujawa; Robert Pacholski; Steve Veselka.
Res., 6149 Hill Ave., 43615. Tel: 419-865-2345; Fax: 419-865-2545.
School—Tel: 419-866-0736; Fax: 419-866-1351.
Lay Teachers 12; Students 233.
Catechesis/Religious Programs—P.R.E.P. Laurie Skowronski, D.R.E.
Students 78.

12—OUR LADY OF PERPETUAL HELP (1918), Rev. Robert J. Wilhelm; Deacons Victor DeCrane; Daniel Quinn; Robert Lesinski; Michael Learned.
Mailing Address: 2255 Central Grove, 43614. Tel: 419-382-5511; Fax: 419-382-7360.
Res., 3464 Glynn Dr., 43614. Tel: 419-382-4992.
School—(Grades PreK-8). Tel: 419-382-5696.
Lay Teachers 28; Students 515.
Catechesis/Religious Programs—Kathy Dusseau, D.R.E.
Students 103.

13—REGINA COELI (1954), Rev. James E. Auth; Deacons James Dudley; George Mitchell; Larry Schaupp; John Wiciak. In res., Rev. Raymond C. Sheperd.
Res., 530 Regina Pkwy., 43612. Tel: 419-476-0922 (Office); 476-2281 (Home); Fax: 419-478-5846 (Call First).
School—Tel: 419-476-0920.
Lay Teachers 20; Students 350.
Catechesis/Religious Programs—Students 130.

14—SACRED HEART OF JESUS (1883) (German), Revs. Frank K. Eckart; Kenneth G. Morman; Sr. Mary Maxine Young, S.N.D., Pastoral Assoc.
Res., 509 Oswald St., 43605. Tel: 419-698-1664. [JC]
School—Tel: 419-691-0869.
Sisters of Notre Dame 2; Lay Teachers 8; Students 213.
Catechesis/Religious Programs—Students 213.

15—ST. ADALBERT (1907) (Polish), Rev. Marek Ciesla, S.Ch.
Res., 3233 Lagrange St., 43608. Tel: 419-241-4179; Fax: 419-241-1136.
School—Tel: 419-243-5257; Fax: 419-243-6763.
Felician Sisters 2; Lay Teachers 9; Students 170.

16—ST. AGNES (1910), Revs. Joseph L. Vamos; Peter V. Zafe; Deacons John C. Vogel; Clarence Fisher. In res., Rev. Peter Aduba.
Res., 3854 Berkeley Dr., 43612. Tel: 419-478-2384; Fax: 419-478-6556. [JC]
School—Tel: 419-478-7778.
Franciscan Sisters 2; Lay Teachers 8; Students 200.
Catechesis/Religious Programs—Students 64.

17—ST. ANN. Consolidated with St. Teresa to form St. Martin de Porres. See separate listing.

18—ST. ANTHONY (1882) (Polish), Rev. Gerald E. Knueven, Admin.
Res., 1416 Nebraska Ave., 43607. Tel: 419-241-6465.

19—ST. CATHERINE OF SIENA (1930), Rev. Gary R. Walters; Sr. Joyce Hoile, O.S.F., Pastoral Assoc.
Res., 4555 N. Haven Ave., 43612. Tel: 419-478-9558; Fax: 419-478-9434.
School—1155 Corbin Rd., 43612. Tel: 419-478-9900.
Lay Teachers 23; Students 475.
Catechesis/Religious Programs—Students 60.

20—ST. CHARLES BORROMEO (1903), Rev. Thomas J. Extejt. In res., Rev. Bruce L. Farmer.
Res., 1842 Airport Hwy., 43609-2069. Tel: 419-385-7431; Fax: 419-385-9152. [JC]
School—Tel: 419-382-7271; Fax: 419-385-1083.
Lay Teachers 10; Students 206.
Catechesis/Religious Programs—Tel: 419-382-1643.
Students 50.

21—ST. CLEMENT (1947), Revs. Gary R. Miller; David R. Bruning; Deacons Wilbur Moore; Ronald Peeps; Ray Burzynski; LeRoy Houghton.
Res., 3030 Tremainsville Rd., 43613. Tel: 419-472-2111; Fax: 419-479-3215. [JC]
School—Tel: 419-474-9657.
Lay Teachers 20; Students 348.
Catechesis/Religious Programs—Tel: 419-472-1259.
Students 302.

22—ST. FRANCIS DE SALES (1841), Sr. Kathleen Scott, L.C.M., Pastoral Admin.; Revs. Robert Fisher, Chap.; John R. Laudick, Chap.; Sr. Barbara Maunz, O.C.D., Pastoral Assoc.
Office: 501 Cherry St., 43604. Tel: 419-243-4242; Fax: 419-243-4243.
Catechesis/Religious Programs—Students 20.

23—ST. HEDWIG (1875) (Polish), Rev. Joseph J. Przybysz.
Res., 2916 Lagrange St., 43608. Tel: 419-729-3148; Fax: 419-729-0743. [JC]
School—Tel: 419-729-3658; Fax: 419-729-7001.
Franciscan Sisters 1; Lay Teachers 14; Students 260.
Catechesis/Religious Programs—Students 15.

24—ST. HYACINTH (1927) (Polish), Rev. Jonathan C. Wight; Deacon Irvin Gonsiorowski. In res., Rev. Thomas J. Beauregard.
Res., 719 Evesham Ave., 43607. Tel: 419-535-7077; Fax: 419-535-5915. [JC]
School—Tel: 419-535-7078.
Sisters of Notre Dame 2; Lay Teachers 12; Students 207.

25—ST. JAMES (1913), Rev. Paul M. Kwiatkowski; Deacon Bernabe Romo.
Res., 914 Colburn St., 43609. Tel: 419-243-2640; Fax: 419-243-7075.
School—Queen of Apostles. Also serves Immaculate Conception Parish and SS Peter and Paul Parish. Tel: 419-241-7829; Fax: 419-241-4180.
Lay Teachers 9; Students 177.
Catechesis/Religious Programs—Queen of Apostles School, 235 Courtland Ave., 43609.
Students 100.

26—ST. JOAN OF ARC (1978), Rev. Gerald L. Ceranowski; Deacons Stan Przybylek; Larry Lottier; Thomas Sheehan.
Res., 5856 Heatherdowns Blvd., 43614. Tel: 419-866-6181; Fax: 419-866-6142.
School—5850 Heatherdowns Blvd., 43614. Tel: 419-866-6177; Fax: 419-866-4107.
Lay Teachers 27; Students 598.
Catechesis/Religious Programs—Tel: 419-866-6177.
Students 160.

27—ST. JOHN THE BAPTIST (1918), Revs. Francis J. Speier; Richard Eberle, O.S.F.S.
Res., 5153 Summit St., 43611. Tel: 419-726-2034; Fax: 419-726-1447. [JC]
School—Tel: 419-726-7761; Fax: 419-726-1031.
Sisters 2; Lay Teachers 22; Students 407.
Catechesis/Religious Programs—Tel: 419-726-9141.
Students 133.

28—ST. JOSEPH (1854), Rev. Stephen Majoros.
Mailing Address: P.O. Box 790, 43697. Tel: 419-255-5556.
Res., 626 Locust St., 43604.
Church—Erie & 628 Locust Sts., 43604. [JC]

29—ST. JUDE (1955), Rev. Bernard J. Boff. In res., Rev. Nelson Belizario, O.Carm.
Res., 3650 Victory Ave., 43607. Tel: 419-531-1294; Fax: 419-531-5812.
School—Tel: 419-531-4951; Fax: 419-531-5046.
Lay Teachers 8; Students 110.

30—ST. LOUIS (1872) (French), Revs. John R. Blaser; Jerome F. Nowakowski; Sr. Joy Barker, O.S.F., Pastoral Assoc.
Res., 459 6th St., 43605. Tel: 419-691-0422; Fax: 419-691-0422. [JC]
Outreach—Helping Hands Soup Kitchen, Tel: 419-691-0613. Bro. Robert Artman, O.F.M., Program Dir.

31—ST. MARTIN DE PORRES (1990), Rev. P. Martin Donnelly; Deacon John Algee.
Res., 1119 W. Bancroft, 43606. Tel: 419-241-4544; Fax: 419-244-3676.
School—(Grades PreK-8). Tel: 419-241-2892. Mr. Jason Shawberry, Prin.; Mrs. Tamara Matthews, Asst. Prin.
Sisters of Notre Dame 1; Lay Teachers 10; Students 202.

32—ST. MARY OF THE ASSUMPTION (1854), Sr. Phyllis Schenk, O.P.; Revs. Martin Donnelly, Chap.; Ronald R. Warnimont, Chap.; Deacons Stanley Gogol; James Hendricks.
Res., 219 Page St., 43620. Tel: 419-243-9213; Fax: 419-243-5405. [JC]
School—Tel: 419-241-3361; Fax: 419-243-5405. Mr. Mark Sholl, Prin.
Sisters 2; Lay Teachers 12; Students 196.
Convent—217 Page St., 43620. Tel: 419-241-2349.

33—ST. MICHAEL (1900), Rev. Robert J. Fisher.
Res., 420 Sandusky St., 43611. Tel: 419-726-1947; Fax: 419-726-2223.
School—St. Elizabeth Seton School, 1030 Clay St.,

43608. Tel: 419-726-4471; Fax: 419-729-2481.
Sisters 1; Lay Teachers 8; Students 210.

34—St. Patrick Historic (1863) (Irish), Rev. Michael R. Billian. In res., Rev. Ronald Schock; Deacon Thomas S. Carone.
Res., 130 Avondale Ave., 43602. Tel: 419-243-6452; Fax: 419-243-7032.
Catechesis/Religious Programs—Students 6.

35—St. Patrick of Heatherdowns (1956), Revs. Dennis M. Metzger; Kenneth J. Lill; Deacons Joe Kest; Albert Righi; Ms. Germaine Kirk, Pastoral Assoc. In res., Rev. Michael G. Madden, (Retired).
Res., 4201 Heatherdowns Blvd., 43614. Tel: 419-381-1540; Fax: 419-381-2727. [JC]
School—Tel: 419-381-1775; Fax: 419-389-1161.
Sisters 4; Lay Teachers 33; Students 783.
Catechesis/Religious Programs—Tel: 419-381-0240. D.R.E. Ms. Christine Kramer; Mrs. Marla Overholt.
Students 117.

36—SS. Peter and Paul (1866) (Hispanic), Rev. Richard E. Notter.
Office: 728 S. St. Clair St., 43609. Tel: 419-241-5822; Fax: 419-241-5822.
School—Queen of Apostles. (Also serves Immaculate Conception Parish and St. James Parish). 235 Courtland, 43609. Tel: 419-241-7829; Fax: 419-241-4140.
Sisters 2; Lay Teachers 9; Students 194.
Catechesis/Religious Programs—Tel: 419-243-1829.
Students 110.

37—St. Pius X (1953), Rev. Thomas A. Landgraff, O.S.F.S. In res., Rev. John L. Graden, O.S.F.S.
Res., 2929 Ilger Ave., 43606. Tel: 419-535-7672; Fax: 419-535-7810.
School—Tel: 419-535-7688.
Lay Teachers 15; Students 250.
Catechesis/Religious Programs—Students 65.

38—St. Stanislaus (1908) (Polish), Rev. Gerald E. Knueven.
Mailing Address: 1416 Nebraska Ave., 43607. Tel: 419-241-6465.
Church—421 N. Detroit Ave., 43607. Tel: 419-255-6245.

39—St. Stephen (1898) (Hungarian), Revs. Frank K. Eckart; Kenneth G. Morman.
Res., 1880 Genesee St., 43605-1440. Tel: 419-691-1673. [JC]
School—(Grades K-6) 2018 Consaul, 43605. Tel: 419-691-8760.
Lay Teachers 13; Students 155.
Holy Spirit Junior High—.
Students 58.

40—St. Teresa. Consolidated with St. Ann to form St. Martin de Porres. See separate listing.

41—St. Thomas Aquinas (1915), Revs. John R. Blaser; Jerome F. Nowakowski; Sr. Joy Barker, O.S.F., Pastoral Assoc.
Res., 729 White St., 43605-2719. Tel: 419-698-1519; Fax: 419-698-2050.
School—Tel: 419-691-4328; Fax: 419-691-4365.
Lay Teachers 10; Students 245.
Catechesis/Religious Programs—Students 140.

42—St. Vincent de Paul (1928), Rev. John R. Laudick; Deacon Jerry Ignatowski.
Res., 1035 Woodward Ave., 43608. Tel: 419-726-1448; Fax: 419-726-1448. [JC]
School—St. Elizabeth Seton School, 1030 Clay St., 43608. Tel: 419-726-4471; Fax: 419-729-2481.
Sisters 2; Lay Teachers 9; Students 220.
Catechesis/Religious Programs—Students 15.

OUTSIDE THE CITY OF TOLEDO

Alvada, Seneca Co., St. Peter (1854), Revs. Leonard A. Kistler, C.PP.S.; Harry M. Cavanaugh, C.PP.S.; Deacon Lewis E. Reinhart.
Mailing Address: 41 N. Perry St., P.O. Box 89, New Riegel, 44853. Tel: 419-595-2567; Fax: 419-595-2303. [CEM]
Catechesis/Religious Programs—Students 85.

Antwerp, Paulding Co., St. Mary (1868), Rev. Herman F. Scherger; Deacon Robert L. Nighswander, Admin.
Res., 303 S. Monroe St., P.O. Box 1005, 45813. Tel: 419-258-8335. [JC]
Catechesis/Religious Programs—Tel: 419-258-2651.
Students 130.

Archbold, Fulton Co., St. Peter (1846), Rev. Gary M. Ferguson.
Res., 614 N. Defiance St., 43502. Tel: 419-446-9288; Fax: 419-446-9288 (Call first). [CEM]
Catechesis/Religious Programs—Tel: 419-446-2150; Fax: 419-446-0282.
Students 126.

Assumption, Fulton Co., St. Mary of Assumption (1877) (German & Irish), Rev. Lawrence F. Varney; Deacon Joseph Repka.
Res. & Mailing Address: 2649 U.S. 20, Swanton, 43558. Tel: 419-644-4014; Fax: 419-644-2159. [CEM]
School—Holy Trinity, 2639 U.S. 20, Swanton, 43558. Tel: 419-644-3971; Fax: 419-644-5018.
Lay Teachers 14; Students 147; Preschool 23.
Catechesis/Religious Programs—12829 Brint Rd., Berkey, 43504. Tel: 419-829-3717. Rosemary Ott, D.R.E.
Students 61.

Attica, Seneca Co., SS. Peter and Paul (1882), Rev. Joseph P. Szybka.
Res., P.O. Box 461, 44807. Tel: 419-426-3043; Fax: 419-426-3043. [CEM]
Church—14204 E. County Rd. 56, 44807.
Catechesis/Religious Programs—Students 100.

Bascom, Seneca Co., St. Patrick (1864), Rev. Arthur J. Niewiadomski.
Res., 6230 W. Tiffin, Box 226, 44809. Tel: 419-937-2715; Fax: 419-937-2751. [CEM]
Parish Hall: Tel: 419-937-2713.
Catechesis/Religious Programs—Students 134.

Bellevue, Huron Co., Immaculate Conception (1859), Rev. Robert A. Tucceri; Deacon Robert Swartz.
Res., 231 E. Center St., 44811. Tel: 419-483-3417; 419-483-0164 (Parish Center); Fax: 419-483-2585. [CEM]
School—Immaculate Conception School, Tel: 419-483-6066; Fax: 419-483-2736.
Sisters 2; Lay Teachers 24; Students 298.
Catechesis/Religious Programs—Tel: 419-483-8374.
Students 217.

Bethlehem, Richland Co., Sacred Heart of Jesus (1833) (German), Rev. John C. Missler; Deacons Leo Hartings; Stephen R. Keller.
Office: 5742 State Rte. 61 S., Shelby, 44875. Tel: 419-342-2797. [CEM]
School—Tel: 419-683-1697.
Lay Teachers 7; Students 68.
Catechesis/Religious Programs—Students 25.

Bismark, Huron Co., St. Sebastian (1846) (German), Rev. John M. Nagele, C.PP.S.
Res., 16209 E. C. Rd. #46, Bellevue, 44811. Tel: 419-483-3231; Fax: 419-483-4661. [CEM]
Church—5582 Bismark Rd., Bellevue, 44811.
Catechesis/Religious Programs—Students 84.

Blakeslee, Williams Co., St. Joseph (1865) (German), Rev. Frederick J. Duschl.
Res., P.O. Box 196, 43505. Tel: 419-272-2214. [CEM]
School—Tel: 419-272-2914; Fax: 419-272-3400.
Lay Teachers 7; Students 51.
Catechesis/Religious Programs—Tel: 419-485-5914.
Students 80.

Bluffton, Allen Co., St. Mary (1865), Sr. Yvonne Fischer, O.S.F., Pastoral Leader; Revs. David J. Beck, Chap.; Dennis P. Hartigan, Chap.
Mailing Address: 160 N. Spring, 45817. Tel: 419-358-8631; Fax: 419-358-8602.
Catechesis/Religious Programs—Students 186.

Bono, Lucas Co., Our Lady of Mt. Carmel (1917), Sr. Marilyn Gottemoeller, R.S.M., Pastoral Leader; Rev. Charles J. Denny, Chap.
Res., 1105 Elliston Rd., Martin, 43445. Tel: 419-836-7681; Fax: 419-836-7680.
Catechesis/Religious Programs—Students 61.

Bowling Green, Wood Co., St. Aloysius (1862), Rev. Edward J. Schleter; Deacons Jose Bautista; Ramon Llanas.
Res., 150 S. Enterprise, P.O. Box 485, 43402. Tel: 419-352-4195; Fax: 419-352-4738.
School—Tel: 419-352-8614. Mrs. Mary K. Williams, Prin.
Lay Teachers 14; Students 259.
Catechesis/Religious Programs—Tel: 419-352-1139.
Students 179.

St. Thomas More University Parish (1967), Sr. Mary Kuhlman, O.S.F., Pastoral Leader; Rev. Richard J. Saelzler.
Res., 425 Thurstin, 43402. Tel: 419-352-7555; 255-3609; Fax: 419-352-7557.
Catechesis/Religious Programs—Tel: 419-255-3607.
Students 139.

Bryan, Williams Co., St. Patrick (1857), Rev. Charles F. Ritter; Deacons Dennis Jackson; Ignacio Garza; Tom Dominique.
Res., 704 S. Portland, 43506. Tel: 419-636-1044; Fax: 419-636-5054.
School—Tel: 419-636-3592.
Lay Teachers 11; Students 154.
Catechesis/Religious Programs—Tel: 419-636-1044.
Students 188.

Bucyrus, Crawford Co., Holy Trinity (1865) (German), Rev. Dennis A. Schroeder; Deacons Julius Fritz; Jerome Gubernath.
Res., 760 Tiffin Rd., 44820. Tel: 419-562-1346; Fax: 419-562-2784. [CEM]
School—(Grades PreK-8). Tel: 419-562-2741.
Lay Teachers 10; Students 211.
Catechesis/Religious Programs—Tel: 419-562-2645.
Students 140.

Carey, Wyandot Co., Our Lady of Consolation, Basilica-National Shrine (1867), Revs. Peter Damian Massengill, O.F.M.Conv.; Conrad Sutter, O.F.M.Conv.; Benjamin Knopp, O.F.M.Conv.; Ernest Waechter, O.F.M.Conv.; Arthur Young, O.F.M.Conv.; Russan Cole, O.F.M.Conv.; Bros. Andrew Bramanti, O.F.M.Conv.; Bryan Hoban, O.F.M.Conv.; Joseph Candel, O.F.M.Conv.; Hugo Lamm, O.F.M.Conv.; Deacons Arden Harold Nye; Jim Kitzler; Floyd Derr.
Res., 315 W. Clay St., 43316. Tel: 419-396-7107; Fax: 419-396-3355. [CEM]
School—Tel: 419-396-6166.
Lay Teachers 10; Students 195.
Catechesis/Religious Programs—Tel: 419-396-1523.
Students 115.
Mission—Salem Township, Wyandot Co., St. Joseph. [CEM]

Cecil, Paulding Co., Immaculate Conception (1879), Rev. Herman F. Scherger; Deacon David Laker Tel: 419-899-2479.
Res., 21706 State Rte. 114, Cloverdale, 45827. Tel: 419-488-3563. [CEM]
Church—Stratford St., 45821. Tel: 419-399-5644.

Cloverdale, Putnam Co., St. Barbara (1898) (German), Rev. Christopher P. Vasko, J.C.L, Admin.
Res., 160 Main St., P.O. Box 8, 45827. Tel: 419-488-2391; Fax: 419-488-2390. [CEM]
Catechesis/Religious Programs—Students 60.

Clyde, Sandusky Co., St. Mary (1890), Rev. Jeffrey J. Nordhaus; Deacon Tito Ollervides.
Res., 609 Vine St., 43410. Tel: 419-547-9610. [CEM]
School—615 Vine St., 43410. Tel: 419-547-9687; Fax: 419-547-9687. Miss Kathy Holcomb, Prin.
Sisters 1; Lay Teachers 8; Students 147.
Catechesis/Religious Programs—Sr. Bonnie Smith, D.R.E.
Students 108.

Columbus Grove, Putnam Co., St. Anthony of Padua (1912) (German), Rev. Bernard A. Kokocinski.
Res., 512 W. Sycamore St., 45830. Tel: 419-659-2263; Fax: 419-659-5202. [CEM]
School—Tel: 419-659-2103; Fax: 419-659-2974.
Lay Teachers 11; Students 217.
Catechesis/Religious Programs—Students 223.

Continental, Putnam Co., St. John the Baptist (1907), Rev. Christopher P. Vasko, J.C.L., Admin.; Deacon Joseph Heeter.
203 E. Elm St., P.O. Box 368, 45831. Tel: 419-596-4319; Fax: 419-488-2390. [JC]
Catechesis/Religious Programs—Students 105.

Crestline, Crawford Co., St. Joseph (1861) (German), Rev. Michael E. Schelling; Deacons Joseph Burkhart; William Horning; William Rall.
Res., 331 N. Thoman St., 44827. Tel: 419-683-2015; Fax: 419-683-3415. [CEM]
School—333 N. Thoman St., 44827. Tel: 419-683-1284.
Lay Teachers 6; Students 87.
Catechesis/Religious Programs—Students 90.

Cuba, Putnam Co., St. Isidore (1917). Shared with St. Michael, Kalida. Rev. Scott Kramer, C.PP.S.; Deacon Robert Klausing.
Res., 312 N. Broad St., Kalida, 45853. Tel: 419-532-3431; Fax: 419-532-3470. [CEM]

Custar, Wood Co., St. Louis (1864), Rev. Paul A. Fahrbach; Sr. Dionne Sartor, O.S.F., Pastoral Assoc., Tel: 419-669-3920.
Res., 22792 Defiance Pike, 43511. Tel: 419-669-2845. [CEM][JC]
School—22676 Defiance Pike, 43511-9716. Tel: 419-669-2878. Sue Hammer, Prin.
Sisters of St. Francis 1; Lay Teachers 4; Students 75.

Cygnet, Wood Co., Sacred Heart (1890), Sr. Betty Glemboski, O.S.F., Pastoral Leader.
Mailing Address: 115 E. Cherry St., North Baltimore, 45872-1134. Tel: 419-257-2319; Fax: 419-257-3717.
Church—Bradford St., 43413.
Catechesis/Religious Programs—Twinned with Our Lady of the Miraculous Medal, North Baltimore.

Defiance, Defiance Co., St. John the Evangelist (1850), Rev. George E. Wenzinger; Deacons Chris Mendez; Charles Baker; Randall Redington; Donald Meyer.
Res., 510 Jackson St., 43512. Tel: 419-782-7121;

Fax: 419-782-7300. [CEM]
School—Tel: 419-782-2136; Fax: 419-784-5410.
Lay Teachers 12; Students 119.
Catechesis/Religious Programs—Students 275.

St. Mary (1873), Rev. Timothy M. Kummerer; Deacon George Newton.
Res., 707 Jefferson Ave., 43512. Tel: 419-782-2776; Fax: 419-782-1958.
School—(Grades PreK-6). Tel: 419-782-2751; Fax: 419-782-8835.
Lay Teachers 11; Students 203.
Catechesis/Religious Programs—Students 399.

Delphos, Allen Co., St. John the Evangelist (1844) (German), Revs. Thomas J. Gorman; Daniel E. Borgelt.
Res., 331 E. Second St., 45833. Tel: 419-695-4050; Fax: 419-695-4060. [CEM]
School—Tel: 419-692-8561; Fax: 419-692-8561.
Sisters of Notre Dame 2; Lay Teachers 27; Students 715.
High School—Tel: 419-692-5371; Fax: 419-692-5371.
Sisters 1; Lay Teachers 21; Students 309.
Catechesis/Religious Programs—Tel: 419-692-1286.
Students 207.

Deshler, Henry Co., Immaculate Conception (1871), Rev. Paul A. Fahrbach; Sr. Dionne Sartor, O.S.F., Pastoral Assoc., Tel: 419-669-3920.
Mailing Address: 230 Allendale Ave., 43516. Tel: 419-278-3686.
Res., 22767 Defiance Pike, Custar, 43511. Tel: 419-669-3920.
Catechesis/Religious Programs—Students 71.

Edgerton, Williams Co., St. Mary (1865) (German), Rev. Thomas E. Oedy; Deacon Roy Sanders.
Res., 133 Bement St., P.O. Box 355, 43517. Tel: 419-298-2932; Fax: 419-298-3123. [CEM]
School—Tel: 419-298-2531.
Sisters of St. Francis 1; Lay Teachers 6; Students 110.
Catechesis/Religious Programs—Tel: 419-298-3350.
Students 98.

Fayette, Fulton Co., Our Lady of Mercy (1943), Rev. John C. Shiffler; Deacon Guillermo Rodriguez.
Res., Box 429, 43521. Tel: 419-237-2441.
Church—409 E. Main St., 43521.
Catechesis/Religious Programs—14691 E. Camden Rd., Waldron, MI 49288. Tel: 517-286-6496. Linda Higgins, D.R.E.
Students 77.

Findlay, Hancock Co., St. Michael (1834), Revs. Michael G. Hohenbrink; Douglas D. Taylor; Randy P. Giesige; Deacons Robert Billmaier; Dorsey Hazelton; David Sadler; Aggie Hempfling, Business Mgr.
Mailing Address: 422 Western Ave., 45840. Tel: 419-422-2646; Fax: 419-422-2602. [CEM]
School—Tel: 419-422-2512; Fax: 419-422-2517.
Lay Teachers 37; Students 567.
Catechesis/Religious Programs—Tel: 419-423-2123. Geri Leibfarth, D.R.E.
Students 584.

Fort Jennings, Putnam Co., St. Joseph (1848) (German), Rev. Anthony A. Borgia.
Res., 135 Water St., P.O. Box 68, 45844-0068. Tel: 419-286-2132. [CEM]
Catechesis/Religious Programs—Tel: 419-286-2019.
Students 353.

Fostoria, Seneca Co., St. Wendelin (1850), Revs. Daniel J. Ring; Mark R. Bowers; Kent R. Kaufman.
Res., 222 N. Wood St., P.O. Box 836, 44830. Tel: 419-435-1875; Fax: 419-435-7826. [CEM]
School—Tel: 419-435-1809.
Sisters of Notre Dame 1; Lay Teachers 22; Students 396.
High School—Tel: 419-435-8144; Fax: 419-436-4042.
Sisters 1; Lay Teachers 18; Students 200.
Catechesis/Religious Programs—Tel: 419-435-6681. Sr. Elaine Marie Clement, S.N.D., D.R.E.
Students 250.

Fremont, Sandusky Co.,

1—SACRED HEART, (1956), Rev. Mark J. Herzog; Sr. M. Dean Pfahler, S.N.D., Pastoral Assoc.; Deacons Jose Sanchez; Tom Ackerman.
Res., 550 Smith Rd., 43420. Tel: 419-332-7339; Fax: 419-332-9808. [JC]
School—(Grades K-8). Tel: 419-332-7102; Fax: 419-332-1542.
Sisters 1; Lay Teachers 15; Students 302.
Catechesis/Religious Programs—Students 107.

2—ST. ANN, (1843), Rev. Gerald J. Chmiel; Deacons Alfredo Diaz; Norbert Wethington.
Res., 1021 W. State St., 43420. Tel: 419-332-7472; Fax: 419-332-2461. [JC]
School—Tel: 419-332-2461.
Lay Teachers 12; Students 154.
Catechesis/Religious Programs—Students 100.

3—ST. CASIMIR, (1915) (Polish), Rev. Robert J. Weithman.
Res., 537 Lime St., 43420. Tel: 419-332-1157. [JC]

4—ST. JOSEPH, (1857) (German), Very Rev. Ronald J. LeJeune; Revs. James E. Halleron; Todd M. Dominique; Deacons William Snyder; James Hammer; Thomas Mosser, Business Mgr.
Res., 709 Croghan St., 43420. Tel: 419-334-2638; Fax: 419-334-6929. [CEM][JC]
School—Tel: 419-332-5161; Fax: 419-332-7299.
Sisters 2; Lay Teachers 16; Students Grades (K-8) 310; Preschool 24.
Catechesis/Religious Programs—120 N. Clover St., 43420. Tel: 419-332-7367. Susan Kosakowski, D.R.E.
Students 95.

Frenchtown, Seneca Co., St. Nicholas (1856) (German-French), Rev. Conrad Sutter, O.F.M.Conv.; Deacon Floyd Hohman.
Res., 315 W. Clay St., Carey, 43316. Tel: 419-396-7107; Fax: 419-396-3355. [CEM]
Catechesis/Religious Programs—Tel: 419-595-2455.
Students 165.

Galion, Crawford Co., St. Joseph (1853), Rev. Michael E. Schelling; Deacons Kevin Wintersteller; Alfred Sisson; Gregory Kirk; Raymond Lyons, Jr.
Res., 135 N. Liberty St., 44833. Tel: 419-468-2884; Fax: 419-468-9464. [CEM]
School—(Grades PreK-8). Tel: 419-468-5436; Fax: 419-468-3611.
Sisters 2; Lay Teachers 9; Students 201.
Catechesis/Religious Programs—Students 145.

Genoa, Ottawa Co., Our Lady of Lourdes (1856), Rev. James E. Peiffer; Deacons William Perez; Phillip Dazley; Sr. Gemma Fenbert, O.S.F., Pastoral Admin.
Church—204 Main St., 43430. Tel: 419-855-8501; Fax: 419-855-8159.
Catechesis/Religious Programs—Tel: 419-855-7181. Sr. Alice Marie Schmersal, C.D.P., D.R.E.
Students 250.

Gibsonburg, Sandusky Co., St. Michael Church (1892), Rev. Theodore J. Miller; Deacon Rene Gonzalez.
Res., 317 E. Madison St., 43431. Tel: 419-637-2255; Fax: 419-637-2255. [CEM]
Catechesis/Religious Programs—Tel: 419-637-2503.
Students 218.

Glandorf, Putnam Co., St. John the Baptist (1834) (German), Rev. Harold C. Brown, C.PP.S.; Sr. Carol Pothast, Pastoral Assoc.
Res., 109 Main St., Box 48, 45848. Tel: 419-538-6928; Fax: 419-538-6147. [CEM][JC]
Catechesis/Religious Programs—Tel: 419-538-6335.
Students 676.

Hamler, Henry Co., St. Paul (1886), Rev. Robert J. Kill; Deacon Donald Badenhop.
Res., 316 Chicago Ave., Holgate, 43527. Tel: 419-264-3321. [CEM]
Catechesis/Religious Programs—Students 70.

Hicksville, Defiance Co., St. Michael (1878). Attended by Edgerton. Rev. Thomas E. Oedy; Deacon Walter Conkle.
Mailing Address: P.O. Box 52, 43526. Tel: 419-542-8202; Fax: 419-542-8202.
Res., 133 W. Bement St., P.O. Box 355, Edgerton, 43517. Tel: 419-298-2932.
Catechesis/Religious Programs—Students 168.

Holgate, Henry Co., St. Mary (1886), Rev. Robert J. Kill; Deacon LaVon Mack.
Res., 316 Chicago Ave., P.O. Box 487, 43527. Tel: 419-264-3321. [CEM]
Catechesis/Religious Programs—Students 77.

Huron, Erie Co., St. Peter (1888), Rev. Edward J. Littelmann; Deacons John Barrett; Jack Busam.
Res., 430 Main St., 44839. Tel: 419-433-5725; Fax: 419-433-2118. [JC]
School—Tel: 419-433-4640; Fax: 419-433-2118.
Lay Teachers 18; Students 189.
Catechesis/Religious Programs—Students 324.

Junction, Paulding Co., St. Mary (1846), Rev. David D. Tscherne; Deacon Richard Carnahan.
Mailing Address: 05480 Moser Rd., Defiance, 43512. Tel: 419-393-2890.
Catechesis/Religious Programs—Tel: 419-594-2615.
Students 65.

Kalida, Putnam Co., St. Michael (1878), Revs. Scott Kramer, C.PP.S.; John Herber; Deacon Robert Klausing.
Office: 312 N. Broad St., 45853. Tel: 419-532-3474; Fax: 419-532-3470.
Res., 206 N. Broad St., 45853. Tel: 419-532-3431. [CEM]
Catechesis/Religious Programs—Tel: 419-532-3494. Sr. Mary Louisa Heinl, S.N.D., D.R.E.
Students 609.
Mission—Cuba, Putnam Co., St. Isidore. [CEM]

Kansas, Seneca Co., St. James (1890), Rev. Theodore J. Miller.
Res., c/o 875 State Rte. 635, Helena, 43435. Tel: 419-638-3042; Fax: 419-638-3043. [CEM]
Parish Office—Tel: 419-638-3042.
Catechesis/Religious Programs—Students 39.

Kelley's Island, Erie Co., St. Michael (1861), Rev. Nicholas J. Cunningham.
Mailing Address: P.O. Box 490, 43438-0490. Tel: 419-746-2481.

Kirby, Wyandot Co., St. Mary (1861), Rev. James J. Holmer; Sr. Barbara Jean Miller, O.S.F., Pastoral Assoc.
Res., 225 N. Eighth St., Upper Sandusky, 43351. Tel: 419-294-1268; Fax: 419-294-1555. [CEM]
Catechesis/Religious Programs—Students 130.

Landeck, Allen Co., St. John Baptist (1866), Rev. John W. Fleck.
Res., 14755 Landeck Rd., Rte. 1, Delphos, 45833. Tel: 419-692-0636. [CEM]
Catechesis/Religious Programs—Tel: 419-695-2141.
Students 136.
Mission—Spencerville, Allen Co., St. Patrick, 500 S. Canal, Spencerville, 45887. Tel: 419-695-4138.

Leipsic, Putnam Co., St. Mary (1873), Rev. John K. Joseph, C.M.I. (India).
Res., 318 State St., 45856. Tel: 419-943-2952. [CEM]
School—Tel: 419-943-2801.
Sisters of Notre Dame 2; Lay Teachers 8; Students 202.
Catechesis/Religious Programs—Students 270.

Lexington, Richland Co., Resurrection (1969), Rev. Stanley S. Szybka; Deacons James Hostutler; Rudoplh (Rudy) Wolf; Thomas Dubois.
Res., 2600 Lexington Ave., 44904. Tel: 419-884-0060; Fax: 419-884-0261.
Catechesis/Religious Programs—Students 337.

Liberty, Seneca Co., St. Andrew (1834), Rev. Arthur J. Niewiadomski.
Church—3761 State Rte. 635 N., P.O. Box 226, Bascom, 44809. Tel: 419-937-2613; Fax: 419-937-2751.
Res., 6230 W. Tiffin St., Bascom, 44809. Tel: 419-937-2715. [CEM]
Catechesis/Religious Programs—Students 60.

Lima, Allen Co.,

1—ST. CHARLES BORROMEO, (1953), Very Rev. David M. Ross; Rev. William J. Rose. In res., Rev. Arnel Barameda.
Res., 2200 W. Elm, 45805. Tel: 419-228-7635; Fax: 419-229-2835. [JC]
School—Tel: 419-222-2536; Fax: 419-222-8720.
Lay Teachers 41; Students 702.
Catechesis/Religious Programs—Students 392.

2—ST. GERARD, (1916), Very Rev. Henry E. Sattler, C.SS.R.; Revs. Stephen S. Haynes, C.Ss.R.; Thomas Lacey, C.SS.R.; Deacon Elias Pina. In res., Revs. Thomas J. Barrett, C.Ss.R.; Andrew Costello, C.Ss.R.
Res., 240 W. Robb Ave., 45801. Tel: 419-224-3080; Fax: 419-225-2231.
School—(Grades PreK-8). Tel: 419-222-0431; Fax: 419-224-6580.
Lay Teachers 17; Students 202.
Catechesis/Religious Programs—Students 230.
Stations—Plus Health Care, Tel: 419-221-1346; Fax: 419-221-1125; Lima Manor, Tel: 419-227-2611; Fax: 419-224-4755; Allen Correctional Institute, Tel: 419-224-8000; Lima Correctional Institute, Tel: 419-225-8060; Oakwood Correctional Institute, Tel: 419-225-8052.

3—ST. JOHN THE EVANGELIST, (1901), Rev. David J. Beck; Deacon Richard Gleason.
Res., 781 S. Main St., 45804. Tel: 419-223-4476; Fax: 419-228-1825. [JC]
Catechesis/Religious Programs—Students 25.

4—ST. ROSE, (1856), Rev. J. Norbert Howe. In res., Rev. Dennis P. Hartigan.
Res., 479 N. West St., 45801-4294. Tel: 419-222-5521; Fax: 419-228-8439. [JC]
School—Tel: 419-223-6361; Fax: 419-222-2032. Mr. Ronald Huysman, Prin.
Sisters 1; Lay Teachers 10; Students 114.
Catechesis/Religious Programs—Tel: 419-222-2087.
Students 76.

Lyons, Fulton Co., Our Lady of Fatima (1946), Rev. John C. Shiffler; Deacon Gene Betz.
Mailing Address: & Church—P.O. Box 112, 43533. Tel: 419-923-3170.
Res., P.O. Box 429, Fayette, 43521. Tel: 419-237-2441. [CEM]
Catechesis/Religious Programs—236 Kennedry Dr., 43533. Tel: 419-923-7714. Sally Kovar, D.R.E.
Students 130.

Mansfield, Richland Co., St. Mary (1949), Rev. Keith J. McCormack; Deacons Allan D. Kopp; Russell Shoemaker.
Res., 1630 Ashland Rd., 44905. Tel: 419-589-5464; Fax: 419-589-7085. [JC]
School—Tel: 419-589-2114; Fax: 419-589-7085.
Lay Teachers 9; Students 125.
Catechesis/Religious Programs—Students 116.

St. Peter (1844), Revs. Herbert F. Weber; Daniel J. Fraser; Vincente Antonio Vera (Philippines).
Res., 54 S. Mulberry St., 44902. Tel: 419-524-2572; Fax: 419-522-2553. [CEM]
School—63 S. Mulberry St., 44902. Tel: 419-524-3351.
Sisters of St. Francis of Mary Immaculate (Joliet, IL) 1; Lay Teachers 28; Students 523.
High School—104 W. First St., 44903. Tel: 419-524-0979; Fax: 419-524-3336.
Sisters of St. Francis of Mary Immaculate (Joliet, IL) 1; Lay Teachers 23; Students 187.
Catechesis/Religious Programs—Students 121.

Marblehead, Ottawa Co., St. Joseph (1867) (Slovak), Rev. James E. Brown.
Res., 802 Barclay, 43440-2101. Tel: 419-798-4177; Fax: 419-798-4260. [CEM][JC]
Catechesis/Religious Programs—113 James St., 43440. Tel: 419-798-5543.
Students 115.

Marygrove, Lucas Co., Immaculate Conception (1840), Rev. Bruce L. Farmer.
Res., 1842 Airport Hwy., Toledo, 43609. Tel: 419-385-7431. [CEM]
Parish Office: 11383 Sylvania, Berkey, 43504. Tel: 419-829-5421.
Church—1750 Raab Rd., Swanton, 43558.
School—Holy Trinity School (Consolidated), 2639 U.S. Rte. 20, Swanton, 43558. Tel: 419-644-3971.
Students 168.
Catechesis/Religious Programs—Students 120.

Marysdale, Defiance Co., Immaculate Conception (1873), Rev. William J. Martin.
Res., 16166 Speaker Rd., Sherwood, 43556. Tel: 419-899-2549; Fax: 419-899-2549. [CEM]
Catechesis/Religious Programs—Tel: 419-658-2512.
Students 64.

Marywood, Seneca Co., St. Michael's (1839) (German), Rev. John M. Nagele, C.PP.S.
Res., 16209 E.County Rd. 46, Bellevue, 44811. Tel: 419-483-3231; Fax: 419-483-4661. [CEM]
Catechesis/Religious Programs—Students 62.

Maumee, Lucas Co., St. Joseph (1841), Revs. Jeffery P. Sikorski; Mark E. Davis; Deacons John Campbell; Kenneth Dickey; Richard Heban; Edward Irelan; Terry McCauley; Paul Morris; Eileen Williams, Pastoral Assoc.
Res., 104 W. Broadway, 43537. Tel: 419-893-4848; Fax: 419-891-6968. [CEM]
School—Tel: 419-893-3304; Fax: 419-891-6969.
Lay Teachers 21; Students 363.
Catechesis/Religious Programs—Tel: 419-893-7025.
Students 418.

Milan, Erie Co., St. Anthony (1862), Rev. James A. Walsh.
Res., 145 Center St., P.O. Box 1200, 44846-1200. Tel: 419-499-4274; Fax: 419-499-4274, Ext. 51. [CEM]
Catechesis/Religious Programs—Tel: 419-499-4300. Mary Lou Fisher, D.R.E.
Students 170.

Miller City, Putnam Co., St. Nicholas (1888), Rev. A. Robert DeSloover.
Mailing Address: Box 36, 45864. Tel: 419-876-3481; Fax: 419-876-3480. [CEM]
Catechesis/Religious Programs—Deborah Wehri, D.R.E.
Students 378.
Sister Parish—Holy Family, New Cleveland.

Millersville, Sandusky Co., St. Mary (1859), Rev. Theodore J. Miller; Deacon George P. Miller.
Res., 875 State Rte. 635, Helena, 43435. Tel: 419-638-3042; Fax: 419-638-3043. [CEM]
Parish Office—Tel: 419-638-3042.
School—Tel: 419-638-3631.
Lay Teachers 4; Students 54.
Catechesis/Religious Programs—Tel: 419-638-3041.
Students 90.
Mission—Kansas, Seneca Co., St. James, 875 SR635 Helena, 43435.

Monroeville, Huron Co., St. Joseph (1861), Rev. Lawrence C. Scharf.
Res., 66 Chapel St., 44847. Tel: 419-465-4142; Fax: 419-465-2319. [CEM]
School—Tel: 419-465-2625.
Sisters of Notre Dame 2; Lay Teachers 10; Students 172.
Catechesis/Religious Programs—Students 50.

Montpelier, Williams Co., Sacred Heart (1911), Rev. Frederick J. Duschl; Deacon Ralph Dominique.
Mailing Address: P.O. Box 196, Blakeslee, 43505. Tel: 419-485-5914.
Res., 220 S. East Ave., 43543.
Catechesis/Religious Programs—Students 125.

Napoleon, Henry Co., St. Augustine (1856), Rev. T. Patrick Scharf; Deacons Peter Calvillo; Louis Recker; Robert Bost; Bruce Buckmaster.
Office: 210 E. Clinton St., 43545. Tel: 419-592-7656; Fax: 419-592-6316. [CEM]
School—722 Monroe St., 43545. Tel: 419-592-3641.
Lay Teachers 11; Students 128.
Catechesis/Religious Programs—Students 221.

New Bavaria, Henry Co., Sacred Heart of Jesus (1893) (German), Rev. Stephen L. Stanbery; Deacon Kenneth Klear.
Res., 13-779 Road Y, Rte. 1, 43548. Tel: 419-653-4157. [CEM]
Catechesis/Religious Programs—Tel: 419-635-4121.
Students 212.
Mission—North Creek, Putnam Co., St. Joseph, 13-779 Rd. Y, Rte. 1, 43548.

New Cleveland, Putnam Co., Holy Family (1862), Rev. A. Robert DeSloover.
Res., c/o Box 36, Miller City, 45864. Tel: 419-876-3481; Fax: 419-876-3480. [CEM]
Sister Parish—St. Nicholas, Miller City.
Catechesis/Religious Programs—Tel: 419-876-3480.
Students 165.

New London, Huron Co., Our Lady of Lourdes (1853), Rev. Robert L. Haas.
Res., 18 Park Ave., 44851. Tel: 419-929-4401. [CEM]
Catechesis/Religious Programs—Students 128.

New Riegel, Seneca Co., St. Boniface (1834), Revs. Leonard A. Kistler, C.PP.S.; Harry M. Cavanaugh, C.PP.S.; Deacon Lewis E. Reinhart.
Res., 41 N. Perry St., P.O. Box 89, 44853. Tel: 419-595-2567; Fax: 419-595-2303. [CEM]
Catechesis/Religious Programs—Students 179.

New Washington, Crawford Co., St. Bernard (1844), Rev. Robert L. Dendinger; Deacon Eugene L. Wurm.
Res., 422 W. Mansfield, 44854-0337. Tel: 419-492-2295; Fax: 419-492-2604. [CEM]
School—Tel: 419-492-2693.
Sisters 3; Lay Teachers 9; Students 176.
Catechesis/Religious Programs—Tel: 419-492-2973.
Students 72.

North Auburn, Crawford Co., Mother of Sorrows (1879), Rev. Robert L. Dendinger.
Mailing Address: 422 W. Mansfield, New Washington, 44854-0337. Tel: 419-492-2295. [CEM]

North Baltimore, Wood Co., Our Lady of the Miraculous Medal (1891), Sr. Betty Glemboski, O.S.F., Pastoral Leader.
Res., 115 E. Cherry St., 45872-1134. Tel: 419-257-2319; Fax: 419-257-3717.
Catechesis/Religious Programs—Students 63.
Mission—Cygnet, Wood Co., Sacred Heart, Bradford St., Cygnet, 43413.

North Creek, Putnam Co., St. Joseph (1887) (German), Rev. Stephen L. Stanbery; Deacon Kenneth Klear.
Res., c/o 13-779 Road Y, Rte. 1, New Bavaria, 43548. Tel: 419-653-4157. [CEM]
Catechesis/Religious Programs—Students 9.

Norwalk, Huron Co., St. Mary, Mother of the Redeemer (1860) (Irish), Rev. Nelson G. Beaver; Deacon Jack Bleile.
Res., 38 W. League St., 44857. Tel: 419-668-2005; Fax: 419-663-6234. [CEM]
School—Tel: 419-668-8480; Fax: 419-668-3269.
Sisters of Notre Dame 1; Lay Teachers 10; Students 227.
Catechesis/Religious Programs—77 State St., 44857. Tel: 419-668-8480; Fax: 419-668-3269.
Students 42.

St. Paul (1876) (German), Revs. Franklin P. Kehres; William A. Pifher, C.S.C.; David A. Reinhart. In res., Rev. Harvey M. Keller, (Retired).
Res., 91 E. Main St., 44857. Tel: 419-668-6044; Fax: 419-663-5770. [CEM]
School—Tel: 419-668-6091; Fax: 419-663-2420.
Sisters of Notre Dame 1; Lay Teachers 33; Students 606.
High School—Tel: 419-668-3005; Fax: 419-668-6417.
Lay Teachers 24; Students 287.
Catechesis/Religious Programs—Julie Wise, D.R.E.
Students 120.

Oak Harbor, Ottawa Co., St. Boniface (1866), Rev. James E. Peiffer.
Res., 215 Church St., 43449. Tel: 419-898-1389; Fax: 419-898-2212.
School—Tel: 419-898-1340.
Sisters 1; Lay Teachers 4; Students 48.
Catechesis/Religious Programs—Fax: 419-898-4193.
Students 110.

Oregon, Lucas Co., St. Ignatius (1883) (Territorial), Rev. Albert B. Ceranowski.
Res., 212 N. Stadium Rd., 43616. Tel: 419-693-1150; Fax: 419-693-0063. [CEM]
Catechesis/Religious Programs—Tel: 419-693-7662.
Students 405.

Ottawa, Putnam Co., SS. Peter and Paul (1868), Revs. Thomas Hemm, C.PP.S.; Bernard Meiring, C.PP.S.; Deacon Jim Rump.
Res., 307 N. Locust St., 45875. Tel: 419-523-5216; Fax: 419-523-4048. [CEM]
School—Tel: 419-523-3697.
Lay Teachers 18; Students 345.
Catechesis/Religious Programs—320 N. Locust St., Tel: 419-523-5078.
Students 304.

Ottoville, Putnam Co., Immaculate Conception (1848), Rev. Anthony A. Borgia; Deacons Leon Turnwald; Jose Flores; Walter Miller.
Res., 189 Church St., Box 296, 45876. Tel: 419-453-3513; Fax: 419-453-3513. [CEM]
Catechesis/Religious Programs—Tel: 419-453-3702.
Students 531.

Paulding, Paulding Co., St. Joseph (1894), Rev. G. Allan Fillman; Sr. Diane Marie Pfahler, S.N.D., Pastoral Assoc.; Deacons Francis Koenn; Rosalio Martinez; Heather Miller, Business Mgr.
Res., 314 N. Main St., 45879. Tel: 419-399-2576; Fax: 419-399-2577.
Catechesis/Religious Programs—Tel: 419-399-5668. Sr. Lucille Kime, S.N.D., D.R.E.
Students 154.

Payne, Paulding Co., St. John the Baptist (1892), Rev. G. Allan Fillman; Deacons Donald Coughlin; David Jordan.
Res., 203 W. Townline, P.O. Box 38, 45880. Tel: 419-263-2469; Fax: 419-263-2469. [CEM]
School—Tel: 419-263-2114.
Lay Teachers 4; Students 119.
Catechesis/Religious Programs—Students 119.

Perrysburg, Wood Co., St. Rose (1861), Revs. Thomas J. Leyland; Marvin G. Borger; Patrick J. Rohen; Deacons Lawrence Tiefenbach; Ken Cappelletty; Ray Kemer; Victor DeFilippis.
Res., 215 E. Front St., 43551-2254. Tel: 419-874-2217; Fax: 419-874-7462. [CEM]
School—217 E. Front St., 43551-2254. Tel: 419-874-5631; Fax: 419-874-1002.
Lay Teachers 25; Students 613.
Catechesis/Religious Programs—Tel: 419-874-9474. Sr. Jeanne Marie Holtz, O.S.U, D.R.E.
Students 492.

Peru, Huron Co., St. Alphonsus Liguori (1828) (German), Rev. Nelson G. Beaver; Deacon George Stepanic.
Res., 38 W. League St., Norwalk, 44857. Tel: 419-668-2005; Fax: 419-663-6234. [CEM]
Catechesis/Religious Programs—1360 Settlement Dr., Norwalk, 44857. Tel: 419-668-5030; Fax: 419-663-6234.
Students 65.

Plymouth, Huron Co., St. Joseph (1864), Sr. Joann Brodman, O.S.F., Pastoral Leader; Rev. Melvin T. Verhoff, Chap.
Res., 117 Sandusky St., 44865. Tel: 419-687-4611; Fax: 419-687-4611.
Catechesis/Religious Programs—Students 82.

Port Clinton, Ottawa Co., Immaculate Conception (1861), Rev. Raymond E. Ensman; Sr. Mary Jane Fisher, R.S.M., Pastoral Assoc.
414 Madison St., 43452-1922. Tel: 419-734-4004; Fax: 419-734-3477.
School—109 W. Fourth St., 43452. Tel: 419-734-3315; Fax: 419-734-6172.
Sisters of Notre Dame 1; Lay Teachers 9; Students 150.
Catechesis/Religious Programs—Students 142.

Providence, Lucas Co., St. Patrick (1842) (Irish), Rev. F. Anthony Gallagher.
Mailing Address: 14010 U.S. 24, Grand Rapids, 43522-9678. Tel: 419-832-5215; Fax: 419-832-4075. [CEM]
Catechesis/Religious Programs—Students 33.

Put-In-Bay, Ottawa Co., Mother of Sorrows (1866), Rev. Nicholas J. Cunningham, Admin.
Mailing Address: Box 179, 43456. Tel: 419-285-2741.

Reed, Seneca Co., Assumption (1867) (German), Rev. John M. Nagele, C.PP.S.
Res., 16209 E. County Rd. 46, Bellevue, 44811. Tel: 419-483-3231; Fax: 419-483-4661. [CEM]
Church—15030 E. Township Rd. 126, Bellevue, 44811.
Catechesis/Religious Programs—Students 56.

Republic, Seneca Co., St. Aloysius (1879), Rev. Joseph P. Szybka; Deacon Urban Arbogast.
Res., 211 East St., Box 250, 44867. Tel: 419-585-4411; Fax: 419-585-4411.
Catechesis/Religious Programs—Students 107.

Richfield Center, Lucas Co., St. Elizabeth of Hungary (1914), Rev. Bruce L. Farmer.
Mailing Address: 11383 Sylvania Ave., Berkey, 43504. Tel: 419-829-5421.
Res., 1842 Airport Hwy., Toledo, 43609. Tel: 419-385-7431. [CEM]
Holy Trinity School (Consolidated)—See Immaculate Conception, Marygrove for details.
Catechesis/Religious Programs—Students 120.

Rossford, Wood Co., All Saints (1990). Consolidated of SS. Cyril and Methodius and St. Mary Magdalene. Very Rev. Joseph R. Steinbauer; Deacons Jerry Nellett; Rick Vascik; Susan VanHersett, Pastoral Assoc.
Church—721 Dixie Hwy., 43460. Tel: 419-666-1393.
Res., 721 Dixie Hwy., 43460. Tel: 419-666-7499.
School—630 Lime City Rd., 43460. Tel: 419-661-2070; Fax: 419-661-2077.
Sisters 4; Lay Teachers 14; Total Staff 41; Students 288.
Catechesis/Religious Programs—Students 200.

St. Michael's Ridge, Defiance Co., St. Michael (1861), Rev. David D. Tscherne; Sr. Margie Verhoff, C.D.P., Pastoral Assoc. & D.R.E.
Res., 05480 Moser Rd., Defiance, 43512. Tel: 419-497-2161; Fax: 419-497-2058. [CEM]
Catechesis/Religious Programs—Tel: 419-497-3122.
Students 144.

St. Stephen, Seneca Co., St. Stephen (1844), Rev. Joseph P. Szybka; Deacon Robert Felter.
Res., 11658 E. Township Rd. 44, Attica, 44807. Tel: 419-426-1145; Fax: 419-426-1145. [CEM]
Catechesis/Religious Programs—Students 22.

Salem Twp., Wyandot Co., St. Joseph (1849) (English), Revs. Peter Damian Massengill, O.F.M.Conv.; Ernest Waechter, O.F.M.Conv.; Deacon Floyd Derr.
Res., 315 Clay St., Carey, 43316. Tel: 419-396-7107; Fax: 419-396-3355. [CEM]
Catechesis/Religious Programs—Clustered with Our Lady of Consolation, Carey.
Mission—Carey, Wyandot Co., Our Lady of Consolation, 315 Clay St., Carey, 43316.

Sandusky, Erie Co., Holy Angels (1840), Rev. Nicholas Weibl; Sr. Mary de Porres Westrick, S.N.D., Pastoral Assoc. In res., Revs. William L. Richter, (Retired); Philip Suehr, O.S.C.
Res., 1605 W. Jefferson Ave., 44870. Tel: 419-625-3698; Fax: 419-625-5183. [JC]
School—Tel: 419-626-3075.
Lay Teachers 10; Students 117.
Catechesis/Religious Programs—Mary A. Zang, C.R.E.
Students 144.

St. Mary (1855) (German), Revs. Philip S. Feltman; Joseph T. Poggemeyer; Dennis Walsh; Deacon Joseph A. Singler.
Res., 429 Central Ave., 44870. Tel: 419-625-7465; Fax: 419-626-2834. [CEM][JC 3]
School—530 Decatur St., 44870. Tel: 419-626-1648.
Sisters of Notre Dame 1; Lay Teachers 18; Students 349.
High School—410 W. Jefferson St., 44870. Tel: 419-626-1892; Fax: 419-621-2252.
Sisters of Notre Dame 1; Priests 1; Lay Teachers 19; Students 228.
Catechesis/Religious Programs—Tel: 419-621-7456.
Students 222.

SS. Peter and Paul (1866), Revs. Martin B. Nassr; John E. Brennen; Deacons Milton Opper; Raymond Middaugh; John Downey; Sr. Martha Bertke, C.PP.S., Pastoral Assoc.
Res., 510 Columbus Ave., 44870. Tel: 419-625-6655; Fax: 419-625-6576. [CEM][JC]
School—Tel: 419-625-1017.
Sisters of St. Francis of the Congregation of Our Lady of Lourdes 2; Lay Teachers 19; Students 281.
Catechesis/Religious Programs—Cheryl Pawlowski, C.R.E.
Students 244.

Shelby, Richland Co., Most Pure Heart of Mary (1866) (German), Rev. John C. Missler; Deacon Dennis Burkett.
Res., 29 West St., 44875. Tel: 419-347-2381; Fax: 419-347-3934. [CEM]
School—Tel: 419-342-2626; Fax: 419-347-2763.
Sisters 1; Lay Teachers 11; Students 217.
Catechesis/Religious Programs—Sr. Karen Elliott, C.PP.S., D.R.E.
Students 262.

Spencerville, Allen Co., St. Patrick (1858), Rev. John W. Fleck.
Res., 14755 Landeck Rd., Rte. 1, Delphos, 45833. Tel: 419-692-0636. [JC]
Catechesis/Religious Programs—Tel: 419-647-6202.
Students 150.

Stryker, William Co., St. John the Evangelist (1861) (German-Hispanic), Rev. Gary M. Ferguson.
Res., c/o 614 N. Defiance St., Archbold, 43502. Tel: 419-682-1372; 446-9288; Fax: 419-446-9288 (Call first). [JC]
Catechesis/Religious Programs—Tel: 419-446-2150.
Students 30.

Swanton, Fulton Co., St. Richard (1893), Rev. Daniel J. Zak; Deacon Timothy Worline.
Res., 333 Brookside Dr., 43558. Tel: 419-826-2791; Fax: 419-826-7256. [CEM]
School—Tel: 419-826-5041. Kathleen Gallagher, Prin.
Lay Teachers 11; Students 165.
Catechesis/Religious Programs—Kathy Kpupitzer, D.R.E.
Students 132.

Sycamore, Wyandot Co., St. Pius X (1951), Revs. Frank A. Murd; Keith Stripe; Deacon John Daniel.
Res., 1649 T.H. 136, 44882. Tel: 419-447-2087; Fax: 419-927-6062.
Catechesis/Religious Programs—P.O. Box 282, 44882. Tel: 419-927-6062.

Sylvania, Lucas Co., St. Joseph (1873), Revs. Richard T. Wurzel; Joseph P. Cardone; Sr. Patricia Gist, C.PP.S.; Deacons Robert Bodette; William Ulmer.
Res., 5373 S. Main St., 43560. Tel: 419-885-5791; Fax: 419-882-5235. [CEM]
School—5411 S. Main St., 43560. Tel: 419-882-6670; Fax: 419-885-1990.
Sisters 1; Lay Teachers 40; Students 785.
Catechesis/Religious Programs—Tel: 419-885-2181.
Students 400.

The Bend, Defiance Co., St. Stephen (1855), Rev. William J. Martin.
Res., 16166 Speaker Rd., Sherwood, 43556. Tel: 419-899-2549; Fax: 419-899-2549. [CEM]
Catechesis/Religious Programs—Students 65.
Mission—Marysdale, Defiance Co., Immaculate Conception, 16166 Speaker Rd., Marysdale, 43556.

Tiffin, Seneca Co., St. Joseph (1845), Rev. James K. Say; Deacon Daniel Scherger. In res., Rev. Msgr. Edward C. Dunn, (Retired).
Res., 36 Melmore St., 44883-3098. Tel: 419-447-5848; Fax: 419-447-7580. [CEM]
School—357 S. Washington St., 44883. Tel: 419-447-5790.
Sisters 1; Lay Teachers 17; Students 432.
Catechesis/Religious Programs—Students 230.

St. Mary (1831), Very Rev. Francis A. Murd; Rev. Keith A. Stripe; Sr. Maryann Orians, O.S.F., Pastoral Assoc.; Deacons Walter Beat; Robert Hartzell; Donald Worland.
Res., 85 S. Sandusky St., 44883. Tel: 419-447-2087; Fax: 419-447-9940. [CEM]
School—75 S. Sandusky St., 44883. Tel: 419-447-5202; Fax: 419-447-0142.
Lay Teachers 25; Students 315; Preschool 84.
Catechesis/Religious Programs—Tel: 419-448-9341.
Students 322.

Upper Sandusky, Wyandot Co., St. Peter (1857), Rev. James J. Holmer.
Res., 225 N. 8th St., 43351. Tel: 419-294-1268. [CEM][JC]
School—Tel: 419-294-1395; Fax: 419-294-1395.
Sisters of Mercy 2; Lay Teachers 5; Students 197.
Catechesis/Religious Programs—Fax: 419-294-1555.
Students 170.

Van Wert, Van Wert Co., St. Mary (1876), Rev. Joseph M. Schmelzer; Deacons Norbert Reinhart; Andrew McMahon.
Res., 601 Jennings Rd., 45891. Tel: 419-238-3979; Fax: 419-238-3957.
School—Tel: 419-238-5186.
Lay Teachers 7; Students 104.
Catechesis/Religious Programs—611 Jennings Rd., 45891. Tel: 419-238-3079. Mrs. Cherie Freewalt, D.R.E.
Students 186.

Vermilion, Erie Co., St. Mary (1851), Rev. Stephen J. Blum; Deacon John Hartman; Sr. Eve Marie Korzym, O.S.F.S., Pastoral Assoc.
Res., 731 Exchange St., 44089. Tel: 440-967-8711; Fax: 440-967-8712. [JC]
School—5450 Ohio St., 44089. Tel: 440-967-7911.
Lay Teachers 9; Students 170.
Catechesis/Religious Programs—Students 242.

Wakeman, Huron Co., St. Mary (1852), Sr. Edna Michel, O.S.F., Pastoral Leader.
Mailing Address: P.O. Box 576, 44889-0576. Tel: 440-839-2023; Fax: 440-839-2881. [CEM]
Church—46 E. Main St., 44889. Tel: 440-839-2023.
Catechesis/Religious Programs—Students 63.

Walbridge, Wood Co., St. Jerome (1962), Rev. William C. Parker.
Res., 300 Warner St., 43465. Tel: 419-666-2857; Fax: 419-661-2281.
School—(Grades PreK-8). Tel: 419-666-2855.
Sisters of St. Francis 1; Lay Teachers 16; Students 267.
Catechesis/Religious Programs—Students 89.

Wauseon, Fulton Co., St. Caspar (1850), Rev. Robert A. Holden; Deacons Juan Rodriguez; James Dominique; James Schmidt.
Res., 1205 N. Shoop Ave., 43567. Tel: 419-335-3656; Fax: 419-337-2413. [CEM][JC]
Catechesis/Religious Programs—Tel: 419-337-2322.
Students 475.

Willard, Huron Co., St. Francis Xavier (1875), Rev. Melvin T. Verhoff; Deacons Vincent Foos; Russell Niedermeier; Paul Jones.
Res., 21 W. Perry St., 44890. Tel: 419-935-1149; Fax: 419-933-6000. [CEM]
School—Tel: 419-935-4744.
Lay Teachers 9; Students 166.
Catechesis/Religious Programs—Students 151.

Chaplains of Public Institutions

TOLEDO. *St. Vincent Mercy Medical Center* 2213 Cherry St., 43608-2691. Tel: 419-321-3232. Rev. Joel R. Buchman.

LIMA. *St. Rita Hospital and Medical Center* 730 W. Market St., 45801. Rev. Vincent Hoying, C.PP.S.

MANSFIELD. *Mercy Hospital*. Vacant.

OREGON. *St. Charles Mercy Hospital* 2600 Navarre, 43616. Rev. Charles J. Denny.

SANDUSKY. *Soldiers and Sailors Home*. Rev. Tommy Rodrieguez.

Special Assignment:
Reverend Fathers—
Singlar, Charles E., Dir. Field Educ. & Pastoral Internship Program, Mt. St. Mary Seminary, Cincinnati, OH
Weigman, Joseph A., Assoc. Dir. Spiritual Formation, St. Meinrad School of Theology, St. Meinrad, IN
Yeager, Robert J., Diocesan Finance Management Conference

On Duty Outside the Diocese:

Reverend Fathers—
Hiltz, John T., 19767 Yorba Linda Blvd., Yorba Linda, CA 92686
Kardzis, Christopher, All Souls Catholic Mission, P.O. Box 37, Binga, Zimbabwe, Africa
McQuillen, Thomas J., All Saints Catholic Mission, P.O. Box 37, Binga, Zimbabwe

---

Graduate Studies:

Reverend Fathers—
Nuss, David W., Catholic University, Washington, DC

Military Chaplains:
Reverend Fathers—
Kirk, David R., Chap. U.S. Army

Awaiting Assignment:
Reverend Fathers—
Brickner, Ronald J.
Lautermilch, David J.
Lucas, Neal C.

Retired:
Reverend Monsignors—
Dunn, Edward C., 36 Melmore St., Tiffin, OH 44883
Mossing, Lawrence A., 214 S. Munson Rd., Swanton, OH 43558
Smith, Bernard E., 190 St. Francis #107, Tiffin, OH 44883
Yates, Robert J., 4900 Navarre Ave., Oregon, OH 43616-3599
Reverend Fathers—
Ankenbrandt, Thomas W., 75 Tomb St., Tiffin, OH 44883
Badger, Arthur A., 3607 Naples Dr., Toledo, OH 43615
Beauregard, Thomas J., 719 Evesham, Toledo, OH 43607
Bonifas, Roger D., 3651 US Hwy. 27S, Sebring, FL 33870
Caballero, Francisco, P.O. Box 985, Toledo, OH 43697-0985
Curtis, Robert J., 1220 Tiffin Ave., Fremont, OH 43420
Dorley, Paul D., 4811 Estero Pl., Toledo, OH 43623-3734

Downey, Timothy M., 820 S. McDonel St., Lima, OH 45804
Dunn, Richard C., 190 St. Francis Ave., #106, Tiffin, OH 44883
Etzel, Raymond A., 5679 Monroe St., #1015, Sylvania, OH 43560
Gillig, Russell F., 190 St. Francis Ave., Apt. 110, Tiffin, OH 44883
Hanacsek, John, 232 W. Clime St., Delphos, OH 45833
Jaros, Joseph P., 29317 Bates Rd., Perrysburg, OH 43551
Keller, Harvey M., 91 E. Main St., Norwalk, OH 44857
Kirtland, Robert B., P.O. Box 12407, Toledo, OH 43606
Koerber, George M., 2930 W. Lincolnshire, Toledo, OH 43606
Kuhn, Thomas W., 66 Pinecrest Dr., Tiffin, OH 44883
Lamantia, A. Robert, 247 Meadowwood, Perrysburg, OH 42551
Lehmkuhl, John J., 401 N. Broadway, Green Spring, OH 44836-9653
Lester, John E., 1001 N. Byrne Rd., Apt. 321, Toledo, OH 43607
Loeffer, Earl A., 2967 Dorr St., Toledo, OH 43607
Losiewicz, George H., 949-C Tucker Ln., Fremont, OH 43420
Lovisa, Eugene L., 2125 Arlington Ave., # 501, Toledo, OH 43609
Madden, Michael G., 4201 Heatherdowns Blvd., Toledo, OH 43614
McCullen, John L., Box 999, Deerfield Beach, FL 33441
Miller, Richard G., 4900 Navarre Ave., Oregon, OH 43616
Miorin, Albert C., 3423 Blackstone Island, P.O. Box 414, Colon, MI 49040
Mueller, Donald R., 321 E. Madison St., Gibsonburg, OH 43431
Niedermier, Jerome G., 5341 Glendale Dr., Harrison, MI 48625
Nieset, Frank E., 1896 E. Lynwood Dr., Concord, CA 94519-1159
Nietfeld, Fred J., 3521 Environ Blvd. #301, Lauderhill, FL 33311
O'Brien, Joseph L., 2596 Sun Valley #202, Port Clinton, OH 43452
Ollivier, John J., P.O. Box 922, Port Clinton, OH 43452
Ott, Carlton A., 4496 Whittlesey, Norwark, OH 44857-9244
Pitula, Zygmunt J., ul. 22 Lipca 8, 86050 Solec Kujawski, woj. Bydgoszcz, Poland
Radecki, Albin A., 4312 Holland-Sylvania Rd., #323, Toledo, OH 43623
Reichert, Ralph, 3230 Centennial Rd. #31, Sylvania, OH 43560
Rethinger, Omer, 1010 Brush, Apt. A, Fremont, OH 43420
Richter, William L., 1605 W. Jefferson St., Sandusky, OH 44870
Ricker, John Michael, 212 N. Stadium Rd., Oregon, OH 43616-1536
Ringholz, Benedict E., 117 Leisure Ln., Norwalk, OH 44857
Rinkowski, George M., 3409 W. Alexis, #7D, Toledo, OH 43623-1430
Risacher, James E., 8820 Walther Blvd. #4215, Baltimore, MD 21234
Schill, Frederick J., 586 Kaler, Bucyrus, OH 44820
Schreiner, John E., 6488 State Rd., B-14, Parma, OH 44134-4161
Shenk, Bertrand J., 59 Executive Dr., Norwalk, OH 44851
Sherbno, John C., P.O. Box 26378, Fairview Park, OH 44126
Steinle, James, 312 Greenfield St., Tiffin, OH 44883-2427
Thomas, Robert R., 8135 N. Placita Chula, Tuscon, AZ 85704

Permanent Deacons:
Ackerman, Thomas L.
Adams, Lawrence
Algee, John R.
Andrzejewski, Walter S.
Arbogast, Urban
Badenhop, Donald F.
Baker, Charles R.
Barrett, John
Bautista, Jose
Beat, Walter
Beisser, Robert A.
Betz, Eugene N.
Billmaier, Robert C.
Bistak, Leo T.
Bleile, Jack
Bodette, Robert
Bost, Robert
Buckmaster, Bruce
Burkett, Dennis W.
Burkhart, Joseph L.
Burzynski, Raymond
Busam, John
Bussemeier, Mark
Calvillo, Pedro
Campbell, John E.
Cappelletty, Ken
Carnahan, Richard
Carone, Thomas
Conkle, Walter H.
Coughlin, Donald J.
Daniel, John
Dazley, Phil
DeCrane, Victor C.
DeFilippis, Victor
Derr, Floyd
Diaz, Alfredo
Dickey, Kenneth G.
Dominique, Ivan James M.
Dominique, Ralph J.
Dominique, Thomas
Downey, John F.
Dubois, Thomas
Dudley, James M.
Dunn, James
Etue, Timothy W.
Fazekas, Richard S.
Felter, Robert
Fisher, Clarence
Flores, Jose
Foos, Vincent
Frazier, Edward
Fritz, Julius
Garza, Ignacio
Gillen, Robert
Gleason, Richard
Gogol, Stanley S.
Gonsiorowski, Irvin
Gonzalez, Rene S.
Gryczewski, Edward
Gubernath, Jerome
Hall, Maury
Hammer, James E.
Hartings, Leo J.
Hartman, John C.
Hartzell, Robert J.
Hazelton, Dorsey A.
Heban, Richard D.
Heeter, Joseph M.
Hendricks, James
Hohman, Floyd
Holmer, Leon
Horning, William L.
Hostutler, James E.
Houghton, LeRoy H.
Huffman, David A.
Hulderman, Joseph
Ignatowski, Gerald
Irelan, Edgar
Jackson, Dennis
Jones, Gary
Jones, Paul R.
Jordan, David
Karpanty, David J.
Keller, Stephen
Kelley, Edward L.
Kemer, Raymond
Kest, Joseph, Jr.
Kirk, Gregory
Kitzler, James F.
Klausing, Robert R.
Klear, Kenneth
Klein, Frank
Koenn, Francis
Kopp, Allan D.
Kozek, Richard
Krukowski, Timothy K.
Kujawa, Clifford
Lackney, Robert
Laker, David C.
Learned, Michael J., Sr.
Lesinski, Robert J.
Lira, Rudy
Llanos, Ramon
Lochotzki, William
Lopez, Valentin G.
Lottier, Larry
Lyons, Raymond E., Jr.
Mack, La Von L.
Marshall, James
Martinez, Rosalio
McCabe, Patrick
McCauley, Terry L.
McMahon, Andrew P.
Mendez, Chris
Meyer, Donald
Middaugh, Raymond D.
Miller, George
Miller, Walter A.
Mishler, Richard
Mitchell, George R.
Moncher, James
Moore, Wilbur
Morris, Paul J.
Nellett, Gerald L.
Newton, George E.
Niedermeier, Russell
Niese, Thomas B.
Nighswander, Robert L.
Nye, Harold
Ollervides, Tito
Opper, Milton C.
Pacholski, Robert
Peeps, Ronald G.
Pence, Michael W.
Perez, Diego E.A.
Perez, William
Petersen, Laurence
Phillips, Eugene D.
Philpott, Terry B.
Pina, Elias
Przybylek, Stanley
Quinn, Daniel P.
Rall, William
Recker, Louis E.
Redington, Randall
Reinhart, Lewis E.
Reinhart, Norbert
Repka, Joseph
Ricker, David J.
Righi, Albert
Rodriguez, Guillermo
Rodriguez, Juan
Romo, Bernabe
Romo, Jose
Rump, James A.
Sadler, David L.
Sanchez, Jose
Sanchez, Salvador
Sanders, Roy B.
Schaupp, Lawrence
Scherger, Daniel
Schmidt, James
Segura, Alfredo
Selmek, Zenon J.
Sheehan, Thomas M.
Shoemaker, Russell M.
Singler, Joseph A.
Sisson, Alfred N.
Skeldon, Philip
Snyder, William J.
Sortman, Jerome E.
Stepanic, George C.
Swartz, Robert L.
Tiefenbach, Lawrence
Trotter, Lawrence W.
Turnwald, Leon
Ulmer, William A.
Vascik, Richard J.
Veselka, Stephen J.
Villagomez, Jesus
Vogel, Curt
Warren, Richard
Welch, Harold
Westrick, Eugene
Wethington, Norbert A.
White, Paul
White, Richard
Wiciak, John
Winterstellar, Kevin
Wolf, Rudolph
Worland, Donald W.
Worline, Timothy R.
Wurm, Eugene L.
Yakir, Michael D.
Young, James A.
Zalewski, Stanley

INSTITUTIONS LOCATED IN THE DIOCESE

[A] COLLEGES AND UNIVERSITIES

SYLVANIA. *Lourdes College*, 6832 Convent Blvd., 43560. Tel: 419-885-3211; Fax: 419-882-3987.
E-mail: pmazur@lourdes.edu
Web site: www.lourdes.edu
For a complete listing, refer to the Colleges and Universities section.

[B] HIGH SCHOOLS, DIOCESAN

TOLEDO. *Central Catholic High School*, 2550 Cherry St., 43608. Tel: 419-255-2280; Fax: 419-259-2848.
E-mail: fgrh@centralcatholic.org
Web site: www.centralcatholic.org
Conducted by Diocesan Priests, Sisters and Laity. Kathy Hamilton, Prin.; Revs. Gregory R. Hite, Pastor & Pres.; Stephen G. Rogers. Asst. Principals: Mr. William G. Axe; Michael Kaucher. Priests 1; Teaching Sisters 5; Lay Teachers 66; Students 1,311.

FREMONT. *St. Joseph Central Catholic High School*. Consolidated from St. Joseph, Fremont, St. Ann, Fremont, Sacred Heart, Fremont, St. Casimir, Fremont, St. Mary, Clyde, St. Mary, Millersville, & Immaculate Conception, Bellevue. 702 Croghan St., 43420. Tel: 419-332-9947; Fax: 419-332-4945.
E-mail: toledosjhsfr@impresso.com
Web site: www.ed.pvt.k12.oh.us
Michael Gabel. Priests 1; Lay Teachers 29; Students 278.

LIMA. *Central Catholic High School*, 720 S. Cable Rd., 45805. Tel: 419-222-4276; Fax: 419-222-6933.
E-mail: frdenny@lcc.noacsc.org
Web site: www.lcc.noacsc.org
Rev. Dennis P. Hartigan, Prin. Priests 1; Lay Teachers 33; Students 407.

OREGON. *Cardinal Stritch High School*, 3225 Pickle Rd., 43616. Tel: 419-693-0465; Fax: 419-693-0465.
E-mail: tmahoney@cardinalstritch.com
Web site: www.cardinalstritch.com
Serves parishes in Greater Toledo, including Oregon, Rossford, Perrysburg, Bono, Walbridge and Genoa. Rev. John F. Stites, Pastor & Pres.; Mr. Timothy Mahoney, Prin. Priests 1; Sisters 2; Lay Teachers 22; Students 325.

TIFFIN. *Calvert High School*, 152 Madison St., 44883. Tel: 419-447-3844; Fax: 419-447-2922.
E-mail: calv_hs_prin@noeca.esu.k12.oh.us
Web site: www.calvert.tld.pvt.k12.oh.us
Mr. Anthony J. Mass, Prin.; Rev. Michael G. Dandurand, Chap. Priests 1; Sisters 1; Lay Teachers 22; Students 286.

[C] HIGH SCHOOLS, PRIVATE

TOLEDO. *Notre Dame Academy*, 3535 Sylvania Ave., 43623. Tel: 419-475-9359; Fax: 419-475-2558.
E-mail: toledonda@nda.org
Web site: www.nda.org
School for girls. Sisters of Notre Dame. Sr. Mary Carol Gregory, S.N.D., Pres & Prin. Sisters 16; Lay Teachers 38; Lay Staff 31; Students 689.

St. Francis de Sales High School, 2323 W. Bancroft St., 43607. Tel: 419-531-1618; Fax: 419-531-9740.
E-mail: olsz@sfs.utoledo.edu
Web site: www.sfs.utoledo.edu
School for boys. Oblates of St. Francis de Sales. Revs. Ronald W. Olszewski, O.S.F.S., Pres. & Prin.; John I. Extejt, O.S.F.S., Tres. & Network Admin.; Thomas P. O'Neill, O.S.F.S., Academic Dean; James R. Sanford, O.S.F.S.; James H. Roth, O.S.F.S.; John O. Ebenhoeh, O.S.F.S.; Jonathan C. Wight. In res. Revs. John O'Neill, O.S.F.S., (Retired); Daniel J. Earley, O.S.F.S., (Retired); Paul G. Gillespie, O.S.F.S., (Retired); John J. McMenamin, O.S.F.S., (Retired). Priests 7; Lay Teachers 31; Students 658; Total Staff 64.

St. John's Jesuit High School, 5901 Airport Hwy., 43615. Tel: 419-865-5743; Fax: 419-861-5002.
E-mail: rlarcher@stjohns.toledo.oh.us
Web site: www.stjohns.toledo.oh.us
School for boys. Jesuits of the Detroit Province. Revs. Donald Vettese, S.J., Pres.; Thomas J. Pipp, S.J.; Charles J. Sweeney, S.J.; Francis E. Canfield, S.J., Rector; Brian Lehane, S.J.; Patrick Hussey, S.J.; Bros. John Sebian, S.J.; John Moriconi, S.J. Priests 6; Brothers 2; Lay Teachers 46; Students 792; Total Staff 93.

St. Ursula Academy, 4025 Indian Rd., 43606. Tel: 419-531-1693; Fax: 419-534-5777.
E-mail: bjn_stursacd@mavca2.mavca.ohio.gov
Sponsored by Ursuline Sisters of the Sacred Heart. Sr. Kathleen Padden, O.S.U., Pres.; Mrs. Jane Charette, Prin. Lay Teachers 37; Students 579; Total Staff 43.

[D] CONSOLIDATED ELEMENTARY SCHOOLS

TOLEDO. *Queen of Apostles*. Consolidated from Immaculate Conception, St. James and SS. Peter & Paul. 235 Courtland, 43609. Tel: 419-241-7829; Fax: 419-241-4180.
E-mail: toledoquapos@impresso.com
Sr. Mary Brenda Haynes, S.N.D., Prin. Sisters 3; Lay Teachers 9; Total Staff 12; Students 185.

SWANTON. *Holy Trinity*. Consolidated from St. Elizabeth, Richfield Center & Immaculate Conception, Marygrove. 2639 U.S. 20, 43558. Tel: 419-644-3971; Fax: 419-644-5018. Chris Knight, Prin. Lay Teachers 15; Students 202.

[E] ELEMENTARY SCHOOLS, PRIVATE

TOLEDO. *Ladyfield School*, 3837 Secor Rd., 43623. Tel: 419-475-5451; Fax: 419-479-3083.
E-mail: mjszpila@acesstoledo.com
Web site: www.ladyfieldschool.org
Sisters of Notre Dame. Sr. Mary Jo Szpila, S.N.D. Sisters 8; Lay Teachers 8; Students 276.

WHITEHOUSE. *Lial Elementary School*, 5700 Davis Rd., 43571. Tel: 419-877-5167; Fax: 419-877-9385.
E-mail: toledolialw@impresso.com
Sisters of Notre Dame. Sr. Margaret Mary Faist, S.N.D., Prin. Sisters 4; Lay Teachers 14; Students 197.

[F] ELEMENTARY SCHOOLS

TOLEDO. *Mary Immaculate School*, 3837 Secor Rd., 43623. Tel: 419-474-1688; Fax: 419-479-3062.
E-mail: maryim_miller@nwoca.org
Day School for Children with Learning Disabilities, Attention Deficit Disorder and Other Health Impairments. Sr. Mary Alan Miller, S.N.D., Prin. Sisters of Notre Dame 17; Students 80; Lay Teachers 4; Total Staff 21.

SYLVANIA. *St. Francis Education Center*, 6832 Convent Blvd., 43560. Tel: 419-885-3273; Fax: 419-824-3658.
E-mail: toledosfsylv@impresso.com
Web site: www.sev.org/stfrancis
JoAnn Tallarico, Prin. Preschool & Elementary Extended Care. Sisters of St. Francis 2; Lay Teachers 26; Students 300.

[G] CHILD CARE INSTITUTIONS

TOLEDO. *St. Anthony Villa / Boysville of Michigan, Inc.*, 2740 W. Central Ave., 43606. Tel: 419-473-1353; Fax: 419-473-2963.
Web site: www.boysville.org
For a complete listing, refer to the Special Care Facilities section.

[H] GENERAL HOSPITALS

TOLEDO. *Mercy Hospital*, 2200 Jefferson Ave., 43624-9988. Tel: 419-259-1500; Fax: 419-251-1509.
Web site: www.mercyweb.org
For a complete listing, refer to the Hospitals section.

Riverside Mercy Hospital, 1600 N. Superior St., 43604. Tel: 419-729-6074; Fax: 419-729-6031.
E-mail: scott_shook@mhsnr.org
Web site: www.mhsnr.org
For a complete listing, refer to the Hospitals section.

St. Vincent Mercy Medical Center, 2213 Cherry St., 43608-2691. Tel: 419-251-3232; Fax: 419-251-3810.
Web site: www.mercyweb.org
For a complete listing, refer to the Hospitals section.

LIMA. *St. Rita's Medical Center*, 730 W. Market St., 45801. Tel: 419-227-3361; Fax: 419-226-9750.
Web site: www.stritas.org
For a complete listing, refer to the Hospitals section.

OREGON. *St. Charles Mercy Hospital*, 2600 Navarre Ave., 43616. Tel: 419-696-7200; Fax: 419-696-7328.
Web site: www.mercyweb.org
For a complete listing, refer to the Hospitals section.

SANDUSKY. *Providence Hospital Inc.*, 1912 Hayes Ave., 44870. Tel: 419-621-7000; Fax: 419-621-7077.
E-mail: snl@providencehealth.com
For a complete listing, refer to the Hospitals section.

TIFFIN. *Mercy Hospital*, 485 W. Market St., 44883. Tel: 419-447-3130; Fax: 419-448-3138.
Web site: www.mercyweb.org
For a complete listing, refer to the Hospitals section.

WILLARD. *Mercy Hospital of Willard*, 110 E. Howard St., 44890. Tel: 419-933-2931; Fax: 419-935-8966.
Web site: www.mercyweb.org
For a complete listing, refer to the Hospitals section.

[I] SPECIAL HOSPITALS AND SANITORIA FOR INVALIDS

GREEN SPRINGS. *St. Francis Health Care Centre*, 401 N. Broadway St., 44836. Tel: 419-639-2626; Fax: 419-639-6225.
E-mail: emarker@sfhcc.org
For a complete listing, refer to the Special Care Facilities section.

[J] HOMES FOR AGED

OREGON. *Sacred Heart Home*, 4900 Navarre Ave., 43616-3599. Tel: 419-698-4331; Fax: 419-698-1109
For a complete listing, refer to the Special Care Facilities section.

TIFFIN. *St. Francis Home Inc.*, 182 St. Francis Ave., 44883. Tel: 419-447-2723; Fax: 419-448-1337.
E-mail: doretta@bascom.bright.net
For a complete listing, refer to the Special Care Facilities section.

[K] MONASTERIES AND RESIDENCES OF PRIESTS AND BROTHERS

TOLEDO. *Oblate Residences*, 1225 Flaire Dr., 43620-1616. Tel: 419-536-3862; Fax: 419-536-6372. Mailing Address: c/o 2056 Parkwood Ave., 43620-1616. Apartments 100.

Oblates of St. Francis de Sales. Provincial Residence, 2056 Parkwood Ave., 43620-1616. Tel: 419-243-5105; Fax: 419-243-8827. Very Rev. James F. Cryan, O.S.F.S., Prov.; Revs. Martin C. Lukas, O.S.F.S., Vocation Dir.; John I. Extejt, O.S.F.S.; James H. Roth, O.S.F.S., Teacher, St. Francis de Sales H.S. Priests serving elsewhere: Rev. Kenneth N. McKenna, O.S.F.S., Novice Dir., 1124 Ventura, Brooklyn, MI, 49230. Tel: 517-592-8218. Rev. John L. Graden, O.S.F.S., 2929 Ilger, 43606. Tel: 419-535-7672. Rev. David M. Whalen, O.S.F.S., 81 Regal Rd., Toronto, Ontario, M6H-2J6, Canada. Tel: 416-656-3160. Rev. Thomas A. Ribits, O.S.F.S., 152 Plymouth Ave., Buffalo, NY, 14201. Tel: 716-886-6597. Rev. James J. Sottek, O.S.F.S., (Retired), Elizabeth Scott House, Apt. 101, 2720 Albon Rd., Maumee, 43537. Tel: 419-868-6107. Revs. Anthony R. Ceresko, O.S.F.S., Foreign Missions; William G. Auth, O.S.F.S., Mexican Missions; Charles A. LaPenta, O.S.F.S., (Retired), 554 E. Second St., Salt Lake City, UT, 84103. Tel: 801-359-8201. Rev. David A. Kenehan, O.S.F.S., 3812 Vermont Ct., Alexandria, VA, 22304. Tel: 703-370-2040.

St. Francis de Sales High School Faculty House. 2323 W. Bancroft, 43607. Tel: 419-531-1619. Revs. Ronald W. Olszewski, O.S.F.S., Pres.; John J. McMenamin, O.S.F.S., (Retired); Paul G. Gillespie, O.S.F.S., (Retired); Daniel J. Earley, O.S.F.S., (Retired); John O. Ebenhoeh, O.S.F.S.; John P. O'Neill, O.S.F.S., (Retired); Thomas P. O'Neill, O.S.F.S.; James R. Sanford, O.S.F.S.; Bro. Alfred D. Durant, O.S.F.S., 722 N. Huron St., 43604-1754. Tel: 419-242-1352.

St. Francis de Sale High School Endowment Fund, Inc. Rev. Ronald W. Olszewski, O.S.F.S., Pres. Priests 14; Brothers 1.

BELLEVUE.

Mary Lay Center, 4500 State Rte. 269, 44811. Tel: 419-483-0762; Fax: 419-483-6400.
Residence for Staff of Sorrowful Mother Shrine. Rev. James F. McCabe, C.PP.S., Mgr. Total in Residence 6.

[L] CONVENTS AND RESIDENCES FOR SISTERS

TOLEDO. *Monastery of the Visitation*. (Contemplative). Tel: 419-536-1343; Fax: 419-536-0685. Comtemplative Order of the Sisters of the Visitation of Toledo, Ohio. 1745 Parkside Blvd., 43607-1599. Tel: 419-536-1343; Fax: 419-536-0685. Sisters 19; Perpetual Vows 15; In Formation 4. Legal Title: *The Contemplative Order of the Visitation of Toledo, Ohio.* Sr. Jane Frances Rohen, V.H.M., Supr.

Notre Dame Convent, 3535 Sylvania Ave., 43623. Tel: 419-475-4909; Fax: 419-724-2640. Sisters of Notre Dame. Sr. Loretta Marie Borgerding, S.N.D., Supr. Sisters 29.

Notre Dame Provincialate, 3837 Secor Rd., 43623-4484. Tel: 419-474-5485; Fax: 419-474-1336.
E-mail: toledosndsec@impresso.com
Sisters of Notre Dame. Sr. Constance Marie Suchala, S.N.D., Prov.; Sr. Mary Rose Moser, S.N.D., Local Supr.; Rev. WIlliam J. Kubacki, Chap. Sisters 281.

Ursuline Convent of the Sacred Heart. Tel: 419-536-9587; Fax: 419-536-0019.
E-mail: ursulines@accesstoledo.com
Web site: www.toledoursulines.org
Congregational Offices & Novitiate, 4045 Indian Rd., 43606. Tel: 419-536-9587; Fax: 419-536-0019. Sr. Nancy Mathias, O.S.U., Gen. Supr.; Rev. Thomas S. Quinn, Chap. Professed Sisters 90; Associates 134.

FREMONT. *St. Bernardine Home*, 1220 Tiffin St., 43420. Tel: 419-332-8208; Fax: 419-332-4423. Sisters of Mercy of the Americas, Cincinnati Regional Community. Sr. Joan Marie Warnement, R.S.M., Admin.; Sr. Rose Olivieri, R.S.M., Coord.; Mrs. Carolyn Sue Hartenstein, Health Coord. Sisters 30.

SYLVANIA. *Sisters of St. Francis of the Congregation of Our Lady of Lourdes*, 6832 Convent Blvd., 43560-2897. Tel: 419-882-2016; Fax: 419-885-8643.
E-mail: Premley@sistersosf.org
Sr. Carolyn Giera, O.S.F., Min. Gen.; Very Rev. John A. McClure, Chap. Legal Title: *Sisters of St. Francis of the Congregation of Our Lady of Lourdes, Motherhouse and Novitiate.* Professed Sisters 275.

TIFFIN. *St. Francis Convent*, 200 St. Francis Ave., 44883. Tel: 419-447-0435; Fax: 419-447-1612.
E-mail: magersosf@yahoo.com
Web site: www.tiffinohio.com/stfrancis
Motherhouse and Novitiate, Sisters of St. Francis of Tiffin. Sr. Virginia Welsh, Community Min.; Rev. Michael G. Dandurand, Chap. Sisters 136; Total Staff 25.

WHITEHOUSE. *Lial Residence, Sisters of Notre Dame*, 5900 Davis Rd., 43571. Tel: 419-877-0431.
E-mail: mjuliesnd@hotmail.com
Sr. Marie Julie Reineke, S.N.D., Supr. Sisters 36.

[M] RETREAT HOUSES AND CENTERS OF SPIRITUALITY

BELLEVUE. *Sorrowful Mother Shrine*, 4106 State Rte. 269, 44811. Tel: 419-483-3435; Fax: 419-483-6400. Revs. James F. McCabe, C.PP.S., Dir.; Robert Kunisch, C.PP.S.; Donald Shea, C.PP.S.; Emil Dinkel, C.PP.S.; Bro. Charles McCafferty, C.PP.S.

CAREY. *Franciscan Renewal Center/Pilgim House*, 321 Clay St., 43316. Tel: 419-396-7970; Fax: 419-396-3355.
E-mail: spmeyer@juno.com
Web site: www.olcshrine.com
Diocese of Toledo, auspices of Shrine of Our Lady of Consolation, Carey, OH. Lucy Pahl, Admin.

FREMONT. *Our Lady of the Pines Retreat Center*, 1250 Tiffin St., 43420. Tel: 419-332-6522. Sisters of Mercy. Sr. Marianne Longo, R.S.M., Dir. Total in Residence 5; Total Staff 15.

SYLVANIA. *Sophia Counseling Center, Inc.*, 6832 Convent Blvd., 43560. Tel: 419-882-4529; Fax: 419-885-7612.
E-mail: sophiacc@primenet.com
Counselors: Sr. Rachel Marie Nijakowski, O.S.F.S., Psychologist (Ohio 4699); Sr. Sharon Pollnow, C.S.A., M.Ed., M.S.W., L.I.S.W.; Ann Hovest, M.S.Ed., LPC/CR; Bonnie Schrock, M.A., L.S.W.; Joan Dvorak, Learning Disability Specialist; Sr. Mary Thill, O.S.F., Spiritual Eldering; Sr. Mary Ann Szydlowski, O.S.F.S., R.N. Licensed Massage Therapist, Registered Polarity Practitioner: Total Staff 9.

TIFFIN. *St. Joseph Renewal Center*, 200 St. Francis Ave., 44883. Tel: 419-443-1485; Fax: 419-447-1612.
E-mail: sjrc@bright.net
Sisters of St. Francis, Tiffin. Sr. Paulette Schroeder, O.S.F., Dir.

[N] CAMPUS MINISTRY

TOLEDO. *University of Toledo Campus Ministry*. Attended by Corpus Christi University Parish. 2955 Dorr St., 43607. Tel: 419-531-4992; Fax: 419-243-6337.
E-mail: toledocc@impresso.com
Rev. James J. Bacik.

BLUFFTON. *Bluffton College Campus Ministry*, College Ave., 45817. Tel: 419-358-3000. Deacon John Stahl, Campus Min.

BOWLING GREEN. *Bowling Green State University Campus Ministry*. Attended by St. Thomas More University Parish. 425 Thurstin Ave., 43402. Tel: 419-352-7555; Fax: 419-352-7557.
E-mail: mkuhlma@bgnet.bgsu.edu
Web site: www.bgsu.edu/studentlife/organizations/st_toms/
Rev. Richard J. Saelzler; Sr. Mary Kuhlman, O.S.F., Pastoral Leader. Total in Residence 47; Total Staff 6.

DEFIANCE. *Defiance College Newman Campus Ministry*, 701 N. Clinton, 43512. Tel: 419-784-4010, Ext. 444.

FINDLAY. *University of Findlay Campus Ministry*, 422 Western Ave., 45840. Tel: 419-423-2123; Fax: 419-422-2602.
E-mail: dkarch@hotmail.com
Donna Brown, Campus Min.

TIFFIN. *Heidelberg College Campus Ministry*, 310 E. Market St., 44883. Tel: 419-448-2066; Fax: 419-448-2124.
E-mail: mslowick@heidelberg.edu
Web site: www.heidelberg.edu/offices/student/affairs/religion.html
Sr. Margaret Slowick, O.S.F., Campus Min.

[O] MISCELLANEOUS LISTINGS

TOLEDO. *Catholic Club, The*, 1601 Jefferson Ave., 43624. Tel: 419-243-7255; Fax: 419-243-6337.
E-mail: info@catholicclub.org
Web site: www.catholicclub.org
Mr. Paul Szymanski, Dir.

Catholic Foundation of the Diocese of Toledo, P.O. Box 985, 43697-0985. Tel: 419-244-6711; Fax: 419-244-4791. Mr. John Heinze, Contact Person.

Christ Child Society of Toledo, P.O. Box 352254, 43635. Tel: 419-885-1004; Fax: 419-882-3852.
E-mail: bapob@aol.com
Darla Hamstreet, Pres.; Gay Deiger, Treas.; Jo Ansberg, Sec.

Double ARC, 3837 Secor Rd., 43623-4484. Tel: 419-479-3060; Fax: 419-724-1372. Sr. Mary Dianne Rumschlag, S.N.D., Pres.

Farley Health Care Corp., 2200 Jefferson Ave., Sixth Floor, 43624. Tel: 419-251-6501; Fax: 419-241-5441.
Web site: www.familyhealthplan.org
Affiliated with Mercy Health Partners. Mr. Thomas E. Beaty, Pres. & CEO.

Hope Manor, 4702 Violet Rd., 43623. Tel: 419-246-4733. Ora Milton, Mgr. Units 100.

Madonna Homes, Inc., 722 N. Huron St., 43604. Tel: 419-244-3758; Fax: 419-246-4738. Beverly Thomas, Mgr. Units 196.

Mareda, Inc., 1931 Scottwood Ave., Ste. 700, P.O. Box 4719, 43620. Tel: 419-242-2300; Fax: 419-246-4703.
E-mail: jkiely@vmc.org
Housing Agency of the Diocese of Toledo. John Kiely, Dir.

Mercy Health System-Northern Region, dba Mercy Health Partners, 1822 Cherry St., 43608. A. David Jimenez, Pres. Total Staff 41.

Michaelmas Manor, Inc., 3250-3260 Schneider Rd., 46314. Tel: 419-246-4735. Stephanie Downey, Mgr. A corporation organized and operated for the purpose of providing housing facilities and services to elderly persons and handicapped persons. Units for the Elderly 70; Units for the Physically Handicapped 24.

Moody Manor, 2293 1/2 Kent St., 43620. Tel: 419-241-6985. Lydia Lott, Mgr. Family & Elderly Units 119.

Office of Global Concerns, 1933 Spielbusch Ave., 43624. Tel: 419-244-6711; Fax: 419-244-4791.
E-mail: rmishler@toledodiocese.org
Deacon Richard Mishler. Society for the Propagation of the Faith; Holy Childhood Association; Catholic Relief Services; Mission of Accompaniment. Rev. Bernard J. Boff. Mission of Accompaniment Pastoral Team: Rev. Christopher Kardzis, All Souls Catholic Mission Africa, P.O. Box 37, Binga, Zimbabwe. Tel: 011-263-15-215.

Regina Manor, Inc., 3739 N. Erie St., 1B, 43611. Tel: 419-246-4731; Fax: 419-246-4732.
E-mail: jldowney@hotmail.com
Jody Downey, Mgr. Family & Elderly Units 180.

St. Francis de Sales High School Endowment Fund, Inc., 2323 W. Bancroft St., 43607. Tel: 419-531-1618; Fax: 419-531-9740.
E-mail: olsz@sfs.utoledo.edu

Toledo Catholic Charities Corporation, 1933 Spielbusch Ave., 43624. Tel: 419-244-6711; Fax: 419-244-4791. John F. Heinze, Dir., Financial Svcs. The Catholic Charities Corporation is the Diocesan vehicle to collect and distribute endowment funds and bequests for charitable purposes.

U.T. Newman Foundation for Student Education and Development, 2955 Dorr St., 43607-3023. Tel: 419-531-4992; Fax: 419-531-1775. Rev. James J. Bacik.

Women Blessing Women, 534 Lagrange St., 43604. Tel: 419-241-9789; Fax: 419-241-9789.
E-mail: wblessing@toledodiocese.org
Sr. Joyce Marie Bates, S.N.D., Dir.

CAREY. *Franciscan Mission Association*, 322 West St., 43316. Tel: 419-396-6455; Fax: 419-396-6455.
E-mail: CarlosBH@aol.com
Bro. Bryan Hoban, O.F.M.Conv., Dir.

DELPHOS. *St. John Parish Foundation, Inc.* Tel: 419-695-4050; Fax: 419-695-4060. St. John the Evangelist Church, 331 E. Second St., 45833. Tel: 419-695-4050; Fax: 419-695-4060.

FINDLAY. *St. Michael Schools Educational Foundation*, 422 Western Ave., 45840. Tel: 419-422-2646; Fax: 419-422-2602. Michael J. Langevin, Pres.

FREMONT. *Delaware Acres, Inc.*, 725 S. Buchanan St., 43420. Tel: 419-334-9558; Fax: 419-334-9555. Melanie Parks-Baynard, Mgr. Family Units 68.

GREEN SPRINGS. *St. Francis Hospital Foundation*, 401 N. Broadway, 44836. Tel: 419-639-2626; Fax: 419-639-6225.
E-mail: bnovak@sfhcc.org
Sr. Barbara Mary Novak.

LIMA. *Lima Central Catholic Educational Foundation*, 720 S. Cable Rd., 45805. Tel: 419-222-4276; Fax: 419-222-6933.
E-mail: frdenny@lcc.noacsc.org
George T. Scheid, Jr., Chm.

S.R.H.C. Foundation, 730 W. Market St., 45801-4667. Tel: 419-226-9775; Fax: 419-226-9750. Mr. James P. Reber, Pres.; Mr. Kenneth G. Payne, Sec. & Treas.

OREGON. *RSM Creative Services, Inc.* Ambulance & medical transport company. 2600 Navarre Ave., 43616. Tel: 419-696-7200; Fax: 419-696-7328. Gary George, Vice Pres.

St. Charles Mercy Health Foundation, 2600 Navarre Ave., 43616. Tel: 419-676-7200; Fax: 419-676-7328. Tobias Cardone, Foundation Chm.

SANDUSKY. *The Providence Fund*, 1912 Hayes Ave., 44870. Tel: 419-621-7234; Fax: 419-621-7077.
E-mail: scaire@providencehealth.org
Hospital Foundation. George R. Mayer, Chm.; Sandra E. Cairelli, B.A., Dir.

SWANTON. *St. Richard's School Endowment Foundation*, 333 Brookside Dr., 43558-1097.

SYLVANIA. *Franciscan Properties, Inc.*, 6832 Convent Blvd., 43560. Tel: 419-882-8373; Fax: 419-882-7360.
E-mail: rwangler@fscsylvania.org
Sr. Jeanne Stack, O.S.F., Pres. Total in Residence 109; Total Staff 3; Apartments 98.

Franciscan Services Corporation, 6832 Convent Blvd., 43560. Tel: 419-882-8373; Fax: 419-882-7360. Mr. John W. O'Connell, Pres.

Franciscan Shelters-Bethany House, 6832 Convent Blvd., 43560. Tel: 419-729-2017. Michelle Karcher-Clark, Contact Person.

Lourdes College Foundation, 6832 Convent Blvd., 43560. Tel: 419-885-3211; Fax: 419-882-3987.
E-mail: marquett@lourdes.edu
Web site: www.lourdes.edu
Mary Arquette, Vice Pres. Institutional Advancement.

TIFFIN. *Mercy Tiffin Health Foundation*, 485 W. Market St., P.O. Box 727, 44883. Tel: 419-447-3130; Fax: 419-448-3181.
Web site: ww.mercyweb.org
Sr. Marie Catherine Wise, R.S.M., Chm.

St. Francis Home Memorial Foundation, Inc., 182 St. Francis Ave., 44883. Tel: 419-447-2723; Fax: 419-448-1337.
E-mail: doretta@bascom.bright.net
William Booth, Chm.

St. Francis Villas, Inc., 182 St. Francis Ave., 44883. Tel: 419-447-2723; Fax: 419-448-1337.
E-mail: doretta@bascom.bright.net
Sr. Virginia Welsh, O.S.F., Chm.

Tiffin Calvert Foundation, P.O. Box 45, 44883. Tel: 419-447-3844. John Schultz, Pres.

Vision Time, Inc., 200 St. Francis Ave., 44883. Tel: 419-243-6723.
E-mail: nancyw@megsinet.net
Mailing Address: P.O. Box 4887, Toledo, 43620. Sr. Nancy Westmeyer, O.S.F.

VERMILION. *St. Mary's Church Education Endowment Foundation*, 731 Exchange St., 44089-1330. Tel: 440-967-8711; Fax: 440-967-8712.
Web site: www.rthomas@stmaryvermilion.org
Mr. David Nocjar, Pres.

WATERVILLE. *Diocesan Fiscal Management Conference - National Office*, P.O. Box 199, 43566-0199. Tel: 419-878-3146; 877-709-3362; Fax: 419-878-7265.
E-mail: 104227.110@compuserve.com
Web site: www.dfmconf.org
Rev. Robert J. Yeager, Exec. Dir.

RELIGIOUS INSTITUTES OF MEN REPRESENTED IN THE DIOCESE

For further details refer to the corresponding bracketed number in the Religious Institutes of Men or Women section.

[0270]—*Carmelite Fathers and Brothers.*—O.Carm.
[0275]—*Carmelites of Mary Immaculate.*—C.M.I.
[0480]—*Conventual Franciscans.* (Our Lady of Consolation Prov.).—O.F.M.Conv.
[0520]—*Franciscan Friars.* (Immaculate Conception Prov.).—O.F.M.
[0690]—*Jesuit Fathers and Brothers.*—S.J.
[0910]—*Oblates of St. Francis de Sales.*—O.S.F.S.
[1070]—*Redemptorist Fathers.* (Baltimore Prov.).—C.SS.R.
[1260]—*Society of Christ.*—S.Ch.
[1060]—*Society of the Precious Blood.* (Cincinnati Prov.).—C.PP.S.

RELIGIOUS INSTITUTES OF WOMEN REPRESENTED IN THE DIOCESE

[3710]—*Congregation of the Sisters of Saint Agnes.*—C.S.A.
[1710]—*Congregation of the Third Order of St. Francis of Mary Immaculate, Joliet, IL.*—O.S.F.
[4190]—*The Contemplative Order of the Sisters of the Visitation of Toledo, Ohio.*—V.H.M.
[1070-13]—*Dominican Sisters.* (Adrian, MI).—O.P.
[1070-09]—*Dominican Sisters.* (Racine, WI).—O.P.
[1070-28]—*Dominican Sisters.* (Akron, OH).—O.P.
[1070-10]—*Dominican Sisters of Springfield in Illinois.*—O.P.
[1170]—*Felician Sisters.*—C.S.S.F.
[1310]—*Franciscan Sisters of Little Falls, Minnesota.*—O.S.F.
[1430]—*Franciscan Sisters of Our Lady of Perpetual Help.*—O.S.F.
[2575]—*Institute of the Sisters of Mercy of the Americas.* (Cincinnati, OH).—R.S.M.
[2340]—*Little Sisters of the Poor.* (Baltimore Prov.).—L.S.P.

[3130]—*Our Lady of Victory Missionary Sisters.*—O.L.V.M.

[0440]—*Sisters of Charity of Cincinnati, Ohio.*—S.C.

[0490]—*Sisters of Charity of Montreal (Grey Nuns).*—S.G.M.

[1000]—*Sisters of Divine Providence of Kentucky.*—C.D.P.

[2575]—*Sisters of Mercy.* (Brooklyn Regional Community).—R.S.M.

[2990]—*Sisters of Notre Dame.*—S.N.D.

[1530]—*Sisters of St. Francis of the Congregation of Our Lady of Lourdes, Sylvania, Ohio.*—O.S.F.

[3930]—*Sisters of St. Joseph of the Third Order of St. Francis.*—S.S.J.-T.O.S.F.

[2270]—*Sisters of the Little Company of Mary.*—L.C.M.

[3260]—*Sisters of the Precious Blood.* (Dayton, OH).—C.PP.S.

[1760]—*Sisters of the Third Order of St. Francis of Penance and Charity.*—O.S.F.

[2150]—*Sisters, Servants of the Immaculate Heart of Mary.*—I.H.M.

[4120-06]—*Ursuline Nuns of the Congregation of Paris.*—O.S.U.

[4120]—*Ursuline Sisters of the Congregation of Paris.*—O.S.U.-B.C.

DIOCESAN CEMETERIES

TOLEDO. *Calvary*, 2224 Dorr St., 43607. Tel: 419-536-3751. Mr. John O'Connell, Mgr.

Mount Carmel, 15 E. Manhattan Blvd., 43608. Tel: 419-241-2015.

Resurrection, 5725 Hill Ave., 43615.

FREMONT. *St. Joseph.*

LIMA. *Gethsemane.*

SANDUSKY. *Calvary.*

NECROLOGY

† Crowley, Charles E., (Retired). —Died Feb. 15, 2000.

† Heintschel, Rev. Msgr. Donald E., (Retired). —Died Aug. 23, 2000.

† Henady, Martin, (Retired). —Died Jan. 2, 2000.

† Hoshock, Richard J., (Retired). —Died April 2, 2000.

† O'Grady, James W., (Retired). —Died June 1, 2000.

Diocese of Trenton

(Dioecesis Trentonensis)

Most Reverend

JOHN M. SMITH, J.C.D., D.D.

Bishop of Trenton; ordained May 27, 1961; appointed Titular Bishop of Tre Taverne and Auxiliary Bishop of Newark December 1, 1987; consecrated January 25, 1988; appointed Bishop of Pensacola-Tallahassee June 25, 1991; installed July 31, 1991; appointed Coadjutor Bishop of Trenton November 21, 1995; appointed Bishop of Trenton July 1, 1997 901 W. State St., Trenton, NJ, 08618.

Most Reverend

JOHN C. REISS, D.D., J.C.D.

Retired Bishop of Trenton; ordained May 31, 1947; appointed Titular Bishop of Simidicca and Auxiliary of Trenton October 21, 1967; consecrated December 12, 1967; appointed Bishop of Trenton March 4, 1980; installed April 22, 1980; resigned July 1, 1997. *Res., Villa Nianney, 2301 Lawrenceville Rd., Trenton, NJ, 08648.*

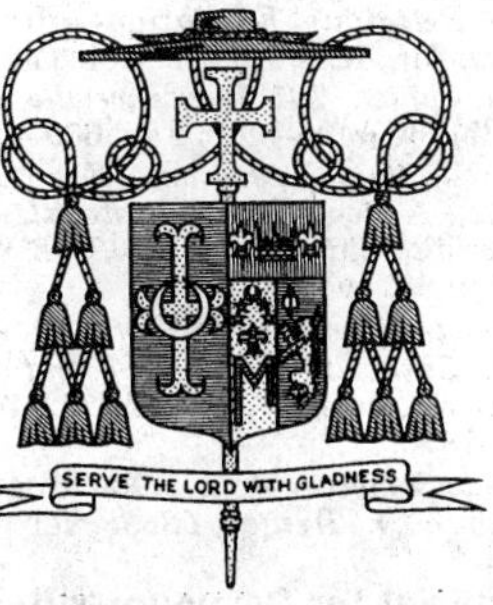

Chancery Office: 701 Lawrenceville Rd., P.O. Box 5147, Trenton, NJ, 08638. Tel.: 609-406-7400; Fax: 609-406-7412.

Legal Corporate Title: "The Diocese of Trenton."

ESTABLISHED AUGUST 11, 1881.

Square Miles 2,155.56.

Comprises four Counties in the State of New Jersey: Burlington, Mercer, Monmouth and Ocean.

For legal titles of parishes and diocesan institutions, consult the Chancery Office.

STATISTICAL OVERVIEW

Personnel	
Bishop	1
Retired Bishops	1
Priests: Diocesan Active in Diocese	151
Priests: Active Outside Diocese	12
Priests: Diocesan in Foreign Missions	1
Priests: Retired, Sick or Absent	71
Number of Diocesan Priests	235
Religious Priests in Diocese	59
Extern Priests in Diocese	41
Ordinations:	
Diocesan Priests	1
Transitional Deacons	1
Permanent Deacons	12
Permanent Deacons in Diocese	268
Total Brothers	66
Total Sisters	440
Parishes	
Parishes	127
With Resident Pastor:	
Resident Diocesan Priests	103
Resident Religious Priests	16
Without Resident Pastor:	
Administered by Priests	7
Completely Vacant	1
Missions	14
Professional Ministry Personnel:	
Brothers	5
Sisters	73
Lay Ministers	140
Welfare	
Catholic Hospitals	1
Total Assisted	139,705
Health Care Centers	1
Total Assisted	3,940
Homes for the Aged	1
Total Assisted	173
Residential Care of Children	1
Total Assisted	15
Day Care and Extended Day Care Centers	5
Total Assisted	475
Specialized Homes	15
Total Assisted	26,670
Special Centers for Social Services	15
Total Assisted	41,320
Residential Care of Disabled	1
Total Assisted	163
Other Institutions	1
Total Assisted	1,700
Educational	
Diocesan Students in Other Seminaries	26
Total Seminarians	26
Colleges and Universities	1
Total Students	2,420
High Schools, Diocesan and Parish	8
Total Students	6,414
High Schools, Private	3
Total Students	1,122
Elementary Schools, Diocesan and Parish	51
Total Students	20,169
Elementary Schools, Private	2
Total Students	584
Non-residential Schools for the Disabled	1
Total Students	17
Catechesis/Religious Education:	
High School Students	962
Elementary Students	65,238
Total Students Under Catholic Instruction	96,952
Teachers in the Diocese:	
Sisters	43
Vital Statistics	
Receptions into the Church:	
Infant Baptism Totals	10,571
Adult Baptism Totals	464
Received into Full Communion	590
First Communions	12,374
Confirmations	9,359
Marriages:	
Catholic	2,141
Interfaith	710
Total Marriages	2,851
Deaths	6,898
Total Catholic Population	728,314
Total Population	1,367,348

Former Bishops—Rt. Rev. MICHAEL J. O'FARRELL, D.D., cons. Nov. 1, 1881; died April 2, 1894.—Rt. Rev. JAMES A. MCFAUL, D.D., LL.D., cons. Oct. 18, 1894; died June 16, 1917.—Most Rev. THOMAS J. WALSH, S.T.D., J.C.D., cons. July 25, 1918; transferred to Newark, NJ, March 2, 1928.—Most Rev. JOHN J. MCMAHON, D.D., cons. April 26, 1928; died Dec. 31, 1932.—Most Rev. MOSES E. KILEY, S.T.D., cons. March 17, 1934; appt. Archbishop of Milwaukee, Jan. 1, 1940.—Most Rev. WILLIAM A. GRIFFIN, D.D., appt. Bishop of Trenton, May 22, 1940; cons. May 1, 1938; died Jan 1, 1950.—Most Rev. GEORGE W. AHR, S.T.D., appt. Bishop of Trenton, Jan. 28, 1950; cons. March 20, 1950; retired June 23, 1979; died May 5, 1993.—Most Rev. JOHN C. REISS, D.D., J.C.D., appt. Bishop of Trenton, March 4, 1980; installed April 22, 1980; retired July 1, 1997.

Chancery Office—701 Lawrenceville Rd., P.O. Box 5147, Trenton, 08638-0147. Tel: 609-406-7400; Fax: 609-406-7412.

Vicar General—Rev. Msgr. WILLIAM F. FITZGERALD, V.G., P.A., J.C.D., *701 Lawrenceville Rd., Trenton, 08648.*

Moderator of the Curia and Chancellor—Very Rev. GREGORY D. VAUGHAN.

Episcopal Vicars—Burlington County and Ocean County: Rev. Msgr. CASIMIR H. LADZINSKI, Monmouth and Mercer County: Very Rev. EUGENE M. REBECK.

Vice Chancellors—Rev. Msgr. EDWARD J. ARNISTER, J.C.L.; Sr. ANNE FULWILER, I.H.M., J.C.L.

Assistant Chancellors—Rev. Msgr. JOHN K. DERMOND, J.C.L.; Rev. Msgr. JAMES G. INNOCENZI.

Secretary to the Bishop—Rev. PABLO T. GADENZ.

Executive Consultant to the Bishop's Office—Sr. AGNES M. GUNN, S.S.J.

Diocesan Tribunal—701 Lawrenceville Rd., Trenton, 08648. Tel: 609-406-7411; Fax: 609-406-7424.

Judicial Vicar—Rev. Msgr. JOHN K. DERMOND, J.C.L.

Associate Judicial Vicar—Rev. Msgr. JAMES G. INNOCENZI.

Defenders of the Bond—Sr. ANNE FULWILER, I.H.M., J.C.L.

Promoter of Justice—Rev. Msgr. LEONARD R. TOOMEY.

Tribunal Judges—Rev. Msgr. EDWARD J. ARNISTER, J.C.L.; Revs. RONALD R. BECKER; THOMAS BRENNAN; Rev. Msgr. ANTHONY L. CAPITANI, J.C.L.; Rev. EMMETT J. CARROLL, O.F.M.Conv.; Rev. Msgr. SAMUEL C. CONSTANCE; Deacon JOSEPH HANNAWACKER; Rev. LOUIS W. KRALOVICH; Rev. Msgr. WILLIAM E. MAGUIRE; Rev. Msgr. WALTER E. NOLAN; Rev. Msgr.

ARMAND A. PEDATA, J.C.D.; Very Rev. EUGENE M. REBECK; Rev. JOHN J. SCULLY; Rev. Msgr. JOSEPH C. SHENROCK, P.A.; Rev. Msgr. ALFRED D. SMITH; Rev. RALPH W. STANSLEY; Rev. Msgr. LEONARD R. TOOMEY; Rev. CHARLES B. WEISER; Rev. Msgr. THADDEUS J. WOJCIEHOWSKI.

Secretary of the Tribunal and Notaries—Ms. PATRICIA ADAMO; Ms. JUDITH MCLAUGHLIN.

Diocesan Consultors—Rev. Msgr. WILLIAM F. FITZGERALD, V.G., P.A., J.C.D.; Very Rev. GREGORY D. VAUGHAN; Rev. Msgr. MANUEL FERNANDEZ; Revs. EDWARD J. GRISWOLD; JAMES J. MCCONNELL; THOMAS J. MULLELLY; Rev. Msgr. WALTER E. NOLAN; Rev. Msgr. HUGH F. RONAN; Revs. JOSEPH S. TEDESCO; KENARD J. TUZENEU; Rev. Msgr. MICHAEL J. WALSH.

Diocesan Council of Priests—Most Rev. JOHN M. SMITH, J.C.D., D.D., Pres.; Rev. Msgr. MICHAEL J. WALSH, Chm.; Revs. EUGENE J. ROBERTS, Vice Chm. RONALD R. BECKER, Sec.; Rev. Msgr. HUGH F. RONAN, At-Large; Rev. RONALD J. BACOVIN, At-Large.

Council of Deacons and Vicariate Rpresentatives—Deacon TOM BAKER, Pres.; Burlington Co.: Deacons JAMES CASA; FRANK GIGLIO, Mercer Co.: Deacon TOM BAKER, Monmouth Co.: Deacons MIKE AULETA; DENNIS SAAKE, Ocean Co.: Deacons RICHARD HAUENSTEIN; EARL LOMBARDO.

Diocesan Pastoral Council—Most Rev. JOHN M. SMITH, J.C.D., D.D., Chm.; Sr. ANNE FULWILER, I.H.M., J.C.L., Liaison; Mr. HOWARD WHITE, Pres.; Ms. JO-ANN D'APOLITO, Past Pres.; Mrs. SHEILA CONWAY, Vice Pres.; Mr. PAUL LAPLANTE, Sec.

Diocesan Finance Council—Most Rev. JOHN M. SMITH, J.C.D., D.D., Pres.; Mr. LAURENCE M. DOWNES, Chm.; Rev. Msgr. WILLIAM F. FITZGERALD, V.G., P.A., J.C.D.; Mr. ALFRED C. KOEPPE; Mr. BERNARD M. MCGLONE; Ms. SUSANNE SVIZENY; Mr. EMIL SCHROTH, JR.; Mr. FRANK T. VANGROFSKI; Very Rev. GREGORY D. VAUGHAN.

Censores Librorum—Rev. Msgr. WILLIAM E. MAGUIRE, S.T.D.; Rev. JOSEPH N. ROSIE, S.T.L.

Diocesan Council of Catholic Women—Sr. ANNE FULWILER, I.H.M., J.C.L., Moderator; Mrs. JILL WHITE, Pres.; Mrs. LORRAINE GERENZA, Vice Pres.; Mrs. SUZANNE MENGES, Sec.; Mrs. FRANCES KELLY, Treas.; Mrs. BARBARA KLEINHAUS, Church Committee.

Secretariat for Temporal Administration

Secretary—Rev. Msgr. WILLIAM F. FITZGERALD, V.G., P.A., J.C.D., *Pastoral Center, 701 Lawrenceville Rd., Trenton, 08648.* Tel: 609-406-7400; Fax: 609-406-7412.

Department of Finance & Resources

Office of Administrative Services—Mr. JOSEPH BIANCHI, Dir., *Pastoral Center, 701 Lawrenceville Rd., Trenton, 08648.* Tel: 609-406-7400; Fax: 609-406-7413.

Office of Human Resources—Mr. NORMAN LEAVER, Dir., *Pastoral Center, 701 Lawrenceville Rd., Trenton, 08648.* Tel: 609-406-7400; Fax: 609-406-7413.

Budget Committee—Very Rev. GREGORY D. VAUGHAN, Chm.; Rev. Msgr. WILLIAM F. FITZGERALD, V.G., P.A., J.C.D.; Mr. BERNARD MCGLONE; Hon. DANIEL O'DONNELL; Ms. DARYL ROWE. Tel: 609-406-7400; Fax: 609-406-7412.

Office of Computer Services—Ms. KATHLEEN MOORE, Dir., *Pastoral Center, 701 Lawrenceville Rd., Trenton, 08648.* Tel: 609-406-7400; Fax: 609-406-7414.

Office of Finance—Ms. DARYL ROWE, Dir., *Pastoral Center, 701 Lawrenceville Rd., Trenton, 08648.* Tel: 609-406-7400; Fax: 609-406-7414.

Department of Marketing & Development

Building Commission—Rev. Msgr. RICHARD C. BRIETSKE, Chm., *Pastoral Center, 701 Lawrenceville Rd., Trenton, 08648.* Tel: 609-406-7400; Fax: 609-406-7415.

Cemeteries—Rev. Msgr. JAMES H. DUBELL, Dir., *St. Paul Church, 223 E. Union St., Burlington, 08016.* Tel: 609-386-0163; Fax: 609-386-0085.

Expansion Commission—Rev. JOSEPH TEDESCO, Chm., *St. Mary of the Lakes Church, 40 Jackson Rd., Medford, 08055.* Tel: 609-654-8208; Fax: 609-654-1734.

Office of Development—Mr. JOHN M. BRADY, Dir., *Pastoral Center, 701 Lawrenceville Rd., Trenton, 08648.* Tel: 609-406-7400; Fax: 609-406-7414.

Secretariat for Catholic Education

Secretary—Sr. MARGO KAVANAUGH, R.S.M., *St. Catharine School, Second St. & Salem Ave., Spring Lake, 07762.* Tel: 732-449-4424; Fax: 732-449-7876.

Department of Catholic Schools

Catholic Education Office—Dr. JUDITH CAVISTON, Supt. of Schools, *Pastoral Center, 701 Lawrenceville Rd., Trenton, 08648.* Tel: 609-406-7400; Fax: 609-406-7416.

Elementary Schools—Sr. DOROTHY PAYNE, S.S.J., Assoc. Supt. for Schools - Mercer & Monmouth Counties, *Pastoral Center, 701 Lawrenceville Rd., Trenton, 08648.* Tel: 609-406-7400; Fax: 609-406-7416. Mrs. MARIANNE FINNEGAN, Assoc. Supt. for Schools - Burlington & Ocean Counties, *Pastoral Center, 701 Lawrenceville Rd., Trenton, 08648.* Tel: 609-406-7400; Fax: 609-406-7416. Dr. MARGARET BOLAND, Assoc. Supt. for Schools - Curriculum & Government Programs, *Pastoral Center, 701 Lawrenceville Rd., Trenton, 08648.* Tel: 609-406-7400; Fax: 609-406-7416.

Secondary Schools—Dr. JUDITH CAVISTON, Supt. of Schools, *Pastoral Center, 701 Lawrenceville Rd., Trenton, 08648.* Tel: 609-406-7400; Fax: 609-406-7416. Dr. MARGARET BOLAND, Assoc. Supt. for Schools Curriculum & Govt. Programs, *Pastoral Center, 701 Lawrenceville Rd., Trenton, 08648.* Tel: 609-406-7400; Fax: 609-406-7416.

Department of Religious Education

Elementary Religious Education—Mrs. ROSEMARIE MCGINTY, Dir.; Mrs. EILEEN HOEFLING, Assoc. Dir., *Pastoral Center, 701 Lawrenceville Rd., Trenton, 08648.* Tel: 609-406-7400; Fax: 609-406-7418.

Secondary Religious Education—Mr. MARTIN J. ARSENAULT, Assoc. Dir., *Pastoral Center, 701 Lawrenceville Rd., Trenton, 08648.* Tel: 609-406-7400; Fax: 609-406-7416.

Campus Ministry—Sr. MARGO KAVANAUGH, R.S.M., Co-ord., *St. Catherine School, Second St. & Salem Ave., Spring Lake, 07762.* Tel: 732-449-4424; Fax: 732-449-7876.

Holy Innocents Society—Mr. ANGELO ROMANELLO, Pres., *5 Shelburne Dr., Trenton, 08638.* Tel: 609-882-4567.

Secretariat for Community Relations

Secretary—Sr. AGNES GUNN, S.S.J., *Pastoral Center, 701 Lawrenceville Rd., Trenton, 08648.* Tel: 609-406-7400; Fax: 609-406-7412.

Department of Mission & Church Relations

Ecumenical / Interreligious Affairs—Rev. JEFFREY E. LEE, Dir., *Pastoral Center, 701 Lawrenceville Rd., Trenton, 08648.* Tel: 609-406-7400; Fax: 609-406-7403.

Pontifical Mission Aid Societies—Rev. Msgr. RICHARD L. TOFANI, Dir., *Pastoral Center, 701 Lawrenceville Rd., Trenton, 08648.* Tel: 609-406-7400; Fax: 609-406-7421.

Department of Media Relations

Office of Media Relations—Mrs. EILEEN MARX, Diocesan Media Spokesperson, *Pastoral Center, 701 Lawrenceville Rd., Trenton, 08648.* Tel: 609-406-7400; Fax: 609-406-7423.

The Monitor—Mr. JAMES A. CASSIDY, Gen. Mgr., *Pastoral Center, 701 Lawrenceville Rd., Trenton, 08648.* Tel: 609-406-7400; Fax: 609-406-7423.

Office of Radio and TV—Mrs. MARIANNE HARTMAN, Sr. Producer of Communications, *Pastoral Center, 701 Lawrenceville Rd., Trenton, 08648.* Tel: 609-406-7400; Fax: 609-406-7423.

Secretariat for Ethnic Ministries

Secretary—Rev. Msgr. MANUEL FERNANDEZ, *St. Mary's Cathedral, 151 N. Warren St., Trenton, 08608.* Tel: 609-396-8447; Fax: 609-396-5624.

The Black Apostolate—Ms. ELLIE ANCRUM, Dir., *34 Pennington Ave., Trenton, 08618.* Tel: 609-394-3500; Fax: 609-394-2225.

The Haitian Apostolate—Rev. Msgr. JOHN K. DERMOND, Dir. (Trenton Area), *St. Francis of Assisi Church, 31 W. Front St., Trenton, 08608.* Tel: 609-393-4851; Fax: 609-393-4555. Rev. LEONARD P. LANG, Dir. (Asbury Park Area), *Holy Spirit Church, 705 Second Ave., P.O. Box 617, Asbury Park, 07712.* Tel: 732-775-0030; Fax: 732-775-7358.

The Hispanic Apostolate—Rev. Msgr. MANUEL FERNANDEZ, Dir., *St. Mary's Cathedral, 151 N. Warren St., Trenton, 08608.* Tel: 609-396-8447; Fax: 609-396-5624.

The Korean Apostolate—Rev. MIN MICHAEL LEE, *Immaculate Conception Church, 64 Broad St., Eatontown, 07724.* Tel: 732-542-0148; Fax: 732-389-2705.

The Portuguese Apostolate—Rev Msgr. MANUEL FERNANDEZ, Dir., *St. Mary's Cathedral, 151 N. Warren St., Trenton, 08608.* Tel: 609-396-8447; Fax: 609-396-5624.

Secretariat for Pastoral Life

Secretary—Rev. RICHARD D. LAVERGHETTA, *St. Gregory the Great Church, 4620 Nottingham Way, Trenton, 08690.* Tel: 609-587-4877; Fax: 609-588-0192.

Department of Parish Life

Office of Parish Services—Directors: Rev. Msgr. RICHARD BRIETSKE; Sr. REGINA WHITE, *Pastoral Center, 701 Lawrenceville Rd., Trenton, 08648.* Tel: 609-406-7400; Fax: 609-406-7415.

Office of Family Life / Respect Life—Rev. JEFFREY E. LEE, Dir., *Pastoral Center, 701 Lawrenceville Rd., Trenton, 08648.* Tel: 609-406-7400; Fax: 609-406-7403.

Scouting—Rev. MICHAEL A. SANTANGELO, Chap., *St. Paul Church, 214 Nassau St., Princeton, 08540.* Tel: 609-924-1743; Fax: 609-924-7980.

Office of Youth / Young Adult Ministry—Sr. DONNA D'ALIA, R.S.M., Dir., *Pastoral Center, 701 Lawrenceville Rd., Trenton, 08648.* Tel: 609-406-7400; Fax: 609-406-7419.

Department of Spiritual Renewal

Charismatic Renewal—Rev. H. BRENDAN WILLIAMS, Liaison, *St. Veronica Church, 4215 Hwy. 9 N., Howell, 08724.* Tel: 732-363-4200; Fax: 732-370-3891.

Cursillo—Rev. JOHN V. BOWDEN, Chap., *Church of Epiphany, 615 Thiele Rd., Brick, 08724.* Tel: 732-458-0220; Fax: 732-458-6921.

Francis House of Prayer—Sr. MARCELLA SPRINGER, S.S.J., Dir., *P.O. Box 392, Rancocas, 08073.* Tel: 609-877-0509; Fax: 609-877-5810.

Legion of Mary—Rev. MICHAEL J. BURNS, Chap., *St. Mary Church, 45 Crosswicks St., Bordentown, 08505.* Tel: 609-298-0261; Fax: 609-298-7178.

Upper Room—Sr. MAUREEN CHRISTENSEN, R.S.M., Dir., *W. Bangs Ave. & Rte. 33, P.O. Box 1104, Neptune, 07754-1104.* Tel: 732-922-0550; Fax: 732-922-3904.

Department of Worship—Rev. SAM A. SIRIANNI, Dir.; Sr. ELEANOR MCCANN, Assoc. Dir., *Pastoral Center, 701 Lawrenceville Rd., Trenton, 08648.* Tel: 609-406-7400; Fax: 609-406-7403.

Secretariat for Personnel in Ministry

Secretary—Rev. KENARD J. TUZENEU, *St. Mary Church, 724 W. Bay Ave., P.O. Box 609, Barnegat, 08005.* Tel: 609-698-5531; Fax: 609-698-6255.

Office of Permanent Deacons—Rev. RALPH W. STANSLEY, Dir., Pastoral Center *701 Lawrenceville Rd., Trenton, 08648.* Tel: 609-406-7400; Fax: 609-406-7417.

Office of Priest Personnel—Rev. RONALD J. BACOVIN, Dir., *Pastoral Center, 701 Lawrenceville Rd., Trenton, 08648.* Tel: 609-406-7400; Fax: 609-406-7422.

Delegate for Religious—Sr. BEATRICE STE. MARIE, S.S.J., Dir., *Pastoral Center, 701 Lawrenceville Rd., Trenton, 08648.* Tel: 609-406-7400; Fax: 609-406-7413.

Office for Vocations—Rev. K. MICHAEL LAMBETH, Dir.; Ms. NANCY MADDEN, Exec. Asst., *Pastoral Center, 701 Lawrenceville Rd., Trenton, 08648.* Tel: 609-406-7400; Fax: 609-406-7413.

Secretariat for Social Justice & Social Services

Secretary—Rev. THOMAS J. MULLELLY, *Aquinas Institute, 65 Stockton St., Princeton, 08540.* Tel: 609-924-1820; Fax: 609-219-9203.

Department of Social Justice

Health Care Facilities—Rev. Msgr. GEORGE ARDOS, *St. George Church, 1370 River Rd., P.O. Box 324, Titusville, 08560.* Tel: 609-737-2015; Fax: 609-737-7863.

Migration & Refugee Services—Sr. JANET YURKANIN, I.H.M., Dir., *33 W. Front St., Trenton, 08608.* Tel: 609-394-8299; Fax: 609-394-0240.

Catholic Persons with Disabilities—Sr. HELEN KLINE, S.S.J., Dir., *Pastoral Center, 701 Lawrenceville Rd., Trenton, 08648.* Tel: 609-406-7400; Fax: 609-406-7420.

Prison Ministry—Rev. ROBERT R. SCHULZE, Dir., *Pastoral Center, 701 Lawrenceville Rd., Trenton, 08648.* Tel: 609-406-7400; Fax: 609-406-7403.

Office of Social Concerns—Rev. RONALD CIOFFI, Dir., *St. Joseph Church, 376 Maple Pl., Keyport, 07735.* Tel: 732-264-0322; Fax: 732-888-3280.

Department of Social Services

Catholic Charities—Mr. FRANCIS E. DOLAN, Dir., *383 W. State St., P.O. Box 1423, Trenton, 08607-1423.* Tel: 609-394-5181; Fax: 609-695-6978.

Catholic Relief Services and Human Development—Rev. BRIAN T. BUTCH, Dir., *Holy Innocents Church, 3455 W. Bangs Ave., P.O. Box 806, Neptune, 07753.* Tel: 732-922-4242; Fax: 732-922-2848.

Martin House—Rev. BRIAN MCCORMICK, Dir., *802 E. State St., P.O. Box 1025, Trenton, 08606.* Tel: 609-989-8143; Fax: 609-989-0933.

Mount Carmel Guild—Sr. LORETTA MAGGIO, O.P., Co-Dir.; Ms. PAULA MAUGANS, Co-Dir., *73 N. Clinton Ave., Trenton, 08609.* Tel: 609-392-5159; Fax: 609-392-5903.

St. Vincent DePaul Society—Rev. ARTHUR F. CONLON, Chap., *Pastoral Center, 701 Lawrenceville Rd., P.O. Box 5147, Trenton, 08638-0147.* Tel: 609-406-7400; Fax: 609-406-7412.

CLERGY, PARISHES, MISSIONS AND PAROCHIAL SCHOOLS

CITY OF TRENTON
(Mercer County)

1—St. Mary Cathedral (1868) (Hispanic), Rev. Msgr. Manuel Fernandez, Rector; Rev. George Berrios; Deacons Emiliano Vazquez; Jose Beauchamps; Juan E. Valentin; Juan A. Rivera, Jr.
Res., 151 N. Warren St., 08608. Tel: 609-396-8447; Fax: 609-396-5624. [CEM]
Catechesis/Religious Programs—D.R.E.: Sr. Pilar Socorro Garcia; Sr. Maria Lorando, Dir.; Mrs. Marisol Rodriguez.
Students 265.
Convent—211 N. Warren St., 08608. Tel: 609-393-4356.
Sisters 2.

2—Blessed Sacrament (1912), Rev. Msgr. Richard L. Tofani; Deacons Joseph A. Hannawacker; Louis F. Slee. In res., Rev. Cesar Anson.
Res., 716 Bellevue Ave., 08618. Tel: 609-396-9231; Fax: 609-396-6432.
Catechesis/Religious Programs—Students 49.
Station—Mercer Hospital, Tel: 609-394-4000.

3—Holy Angels (1921), Revs. Sam A. Sirianni; Albert Ricciardelli.
Res., 1733 S. Broad St., 08610. Tel: 609-396-8316; Fax: 609-393-3747.
School—10 New Cedar Ln., 08610. Tel: 609-396-8916. Ms. Eileen Brett, Prin.
Lay Teachers 12; Students 247.
Catechesis/Religious Programs—Tel: 609-695-1024. Sr. Jane Urban, R.S.M., D.R.E.
Students 250.
Convent—1701 S. Broad St., 08610. Tel: 609-393-2337.

4—Holy Cross (1891) (Polish), Rev. Msgr. Edward J. Arnister; Rev. Henry T. Krajewski, O.F.M.Cap.; Deacon John R. Grussler.
Res., 201 Adeline St., 08611. Tel: 609-393-4826; Fax: 609-278-1192. [CEM]
School—22 Grand St., 08611. Tel: 609-393-8407; Fax: 609-393-5313. Patricia Palinczar, Prin.
Lay Teachers 16; Students 310.
Catechesis/Religious Programs—Students 65.

5—Immaculate Conception (1874), Revs. Raynald Yudin, O.F.M.Conv.; Anthony Kall, O.F.M.Conv.
Res., 540 Chestnut Ave., 08611. Tel: 609-392-5193; Fax: 609-989-1913.
School—Tel: 609-396-8347; Fax: 609-396-0714. Ann Reap, Prin.
Sisters of St. Francis of Philadelphia 2; Lay Teachers 20; Students 261.
Catechesis/Religious Programs—Tel: 609-695-6541.
Students 165.

6—Incarnation (1947), Rev. Msgr. Hugh F. Ronan; Rev. William T. Schneider. In res., Rev. Msgr. Henry S. Bogdan.
Res., 1545 Pennington Rd., 08618. Tel: 609-882-2860; Fax: 609-637-0460.
School—1555 Pennington Rd., 08618. Tel: 609-882-3228; Fax: 609-393-3747. Sr. Margaret Fagan, Prin.
Sisters, Servants of the Immaculate Heart of Mary (West Chester) 2; Lay Teachers 10; Students 260.
Catechesis/Religious Programs—Students 252.

7—Our Lady of the Divine Shepherd (1941) (African American), Rev. Timothy M. Donnelly, S.V.D.
Res., 72 Pennington Ave., 08618. Tel: 609-393-4493; Fax: 609-989-7510.
Catechesis/Religious Programs—Students 54.

8—Our Lady of Good Counsel (1942), Rev. Msgr. William F. Fitzgerald; Rev. John J. Lec; Deacon Robert Brady.
Res., 137 W. Upper Ferry Rd., 08628. Tel: 609-882-3277; Fax: 609-882-4375.
Catechesis/Religious Programs—Students 103.

9—Our Lady of Mount Carmel. Closed. For Sacramental records please contact St. Mary Cathedral, Trenton.

10—Our Lady of Sorrows (1939), Revs. Paul S. Rimassa; Adam Midor; Deacons Joseph Malloy; Anthony J. D'Agostino; Jeffery Pierfy; Tim Moore.
Res., 3816 E. State St. Ext., 08619. Tel: 609-587-4372; Fax: 609-587-7998.
School—3800 E. State St. Ext., 08619. Tel: 609-587-4140; Fax: 609-584-8853. Elizabeth Komar, Prin.
Lay Teachers 34; Students 460.
Catechesis/Religious Programs—3800 E. State St. Ext., 08619. Tel: 609-587-2555; Fax: 609-587-4213. Mrs. Rita Lynn Everist, D.R.E.
Lay Teachers 60; Students 775.
Station—Mercer County Geriatric, Tel: 609-588-5859.

11—Sacred Heart (1814), Rev. Robert M. Tynski.
Res., 343 S. Broad St., 08608. Tel: 609-393-2801; Fax: 609-989-8997.
School—333 S. Broad St., 08608. Tel: 609-396-7316; Fax: 609-396-4757. Jeremiah Kenny, Prin.
Lay Teachers 10; Students 230.
Catechesis/Religious Programs—Students 18.

12—St. Anthony (1921) (Irish-Italian), Rev. Joseph Panthackal (India).
Res., 626 S. Olden Ave., 08629. Tel: 609-586-4181; Fax: 609-586-7206.
School—St. Anthony Grammar School, 530 S. Olden Ave., 08629. Tel: 609-586-5888; Fax: 609-631-9295. Sr. Marie Angela Presenza, Prin.
Sisters 2; Lay Teachers 23; Students 490.
High School—McCorristin High School, 175 Leonard Ave., 08610. Tel: 609-586-3705; Fax: 609-586-6584. Joseph Lemme, Prin.
Priests 2; Sisters 3; Lay Teachers 30; Students 420.
Catechesis/Religious Programs—530 South Olden Ave., 08629. Tel: 609-883-3082.
Students 200.

13—St. Francis of Assisium (1864) (German), Rev. Msgr. John K. Dermond. In res., Revs. Ronald Becker; Charles J. Mehu, C.S.C.
Res., 31 W. Front St., 08608. Tel: 609-393-4851; Fax: 609-393-4555. [CEM 2]
Catechesis/Religious Programs—Students 26.

14—St. Gregory the Great (1953), Revs. Richard D. LaVerghetta; Damian McElroy; Sr. Jean Makovsky, O.S.F., Pastoral Assoc.; Deacons Richard D'Angelo; Joseph Glukowsky; John Groffie; Allan Parr; Neil Pirozzi; William A. Wilson; Ralph LaMachia; Andrew A. Sabados, Sr. In res., Rev. K. Michael Lambeth.
Res., 4620 Nottingham Way, Hamilton, 08690. Tel: 609-587-4877; Fax: 609-588-0192.
School—4680 Nottingham Way, Hamilton, 08690. Tel: 609-587-1131; Fax: 609-587-7704. Regina McIntyre, Prin.
Sisters 1; Lay Teachers 49; Students 531.
Catechesis/Religious Programs—Fax: 609-587-0322. Sr. Alice Gallagher, S.S.J., D.R.E.
Students 1,523.
Convent—13 Stanley Dr., Robbinsville, 08691. Tel: 609-259-3384.

15—St. Hedwig (1904) (Polish), Rev. Henry F. Schabowski.
Res., 872 Brunswick Ave., 08638. Tel: 609-396-9068; Fax: 609-396-3171. [CEM 2]
Catechesis/Religious Programs—Tel: 609-394-1534.
Students 120.

16—St. James (1919), Rev. Boniface Ruzich, O.SS.T.
Res., 29 E. Paul Ave., 08638. Tel: 609-393-4403; Fax: 609-393-6078.
Convent—1016 Princeton Ave., 08638. Tel: 609-695-4088.

17—St. Joachim (1901) (Italian), Rev. Jeffrey E. Lee; Deacon Guido Mattozzi.
Res., 19 Bayard St., 08611. Tel: 609-695-6089; Fax: 609-695-4376.
Convent—25 Bayard St., 08611.

18—St. Joseph (1891) (Spanish), Rev. Msgr. Manuel Fernandez.
Res., 540 N. Olden Ave., 08638. Tel: 609-394-5757; Fax: 609-599-4402.
Catechesis/Religious Programs—Tel: 609-394-3580; Fax: 609-394-3418.
Students 140.
Station—Helene Fuld Hospital, Tel: 609-394-6000.

19—St. Michael (1921) (Slovak), Rev. Msgr. James G. Innocenzi; Rev. Castor G. Sanchez.
Res., 1130 Brunswick Ave., 08638. Tel: 609-393-4050; Fax: 609-393-7335.
Catechesis/Religious Programs—Tel: 609-393-4563.
Students 78.

20—SS. Peter and Paul (1899) (Slovak), Revs. Francis Zalewski; George A. Medina.
Res., 480 Centre St., 08611. Tel: 609-396-2214. [CEM]
Church—480 Second St., 08611.
Catechesis/Religious Programs—Students 49.

21—St. Raphael (1943) (White Horse), Revs. Gregory D. Vaughan; William J.P. Lago; James P. Quinn.
Res., 3500 S. Broad St., 08610. Tel: 609-585-7049; Fax: 609-585-5876.
School—151 Gropp Ave., 08610. Tel: 609-585-7733; Fax: 609-581-8436. Diane M. Kowalewski, Prin.
Sisters 4; Lay Teachers 17; Students 316.
Catechesis/Religious Programs—151 Gropp Ave., 08610. Tel: 609-585-3848.
Students 530.
Convents—3472 Broad St., 08610. Tel: 609-585-8203; Fax: 609-585-5536.
Contemplative Sisters of the Good Shepherd 8; 68 Lakeview Ct., 08620. Tel: 609-585-7041.
Sisters 3.
Station—Robert Wood Johnson University Hospital at Hamilton, Tel: 609-585-7900.

22—St. Stanislaus (1890) (Polish), Rev. Christian Wojciechowski, O.F.M.Conv.
Res., 60 Randall Ave., 08611. Tel: 609-396-9366; Fax: 609-396-3346. [CEM]
Catechesis/Religious Programs—Tel: 609-695-6424.
Students 25.

23—St. Stephen (1903) (Hungarian), Rev. Francis Zalewski.
Mailing Address: P.O. Box 4563, 08611. Tel: 609-394-5965. [CEM]

24—St. Vincent de Paul (1954), Rev. Stanley Krzyston.
Res., 555 Allentown Rd., Yardville, 08620. Tel: 609-585-6470; Fax: 609-585-0137.
Catechesis/Religious Programs—Tel: 609-585-5484.
Students 195.

OUTSIDE THE CITY OF TRENTON

Allentown, Monmouth Co., St. John (1878), Rev. Patrick J. Castles; Sr. Mary Farrell, S.C., Pastoral Assoc., Tel: 609-259-2151.
Res., 1282 Yardville-Allentown Rd., 08501. Tel: 609-259-3391; Fax: 609-259-0313. [CEM]
Catechesis/Religious Programs—Tel: 609-259-3586; Fax: 609-259-0313.
Students 361.

Asbury Park, Monmouth Co., Holy Spirit (1879), Rev. Leonard P. Lang; Deacons Joseph D. Carroll; Edner Andre.
Res., 705 2nd Ave., Box 617, 07712. Tel: 732-775-0030; Fax: 732-775-7358. [CEM]
Catechesis/Religious Programs—Students 10.
Mt. Calvary Cemetery—Rte. 66 and Neptune Blvd., Box 2037, Ocean, 07712. Tel: 732-775-3320.

Our Lady of Mt. Carmel (1905) (Italian), Revs. Gerard F. Lynch, O.SS.T.; Joseph K. Mitko, O.SS.T.; Deacon Kenneth M. McKenna.
Res., 805 Pine St., 07712. Tel: 732-775-1056; Fax: 732-775-8767.
School—First Ave. & Pine St., 07712. Tel: 732-775-8989; Fax: 732-775-0108. Linda Hurley, Prin.
Sisters 2; Lay Teachers 17; Students 233.
Catechesis/Religious Programs—Tel: 732-988-5060.
Students 269.

St. Peter Claver (1943) (African American), Rev. Gerhard Vogel, S.V.D.; Deacon John Cook.
Res., 108 Ridge Ave., 07712. Tel: 732-775-4157; Fax: 732-774-4531.
Catechesis/Religious Programs—Students 35.

Atlantic Highlands, Monmouth Co., St. Agnes (1890), Rev. Leon J. Inverso; Deacon Raymond Rainville.
Res., 103 Center Ave., 07716. Tel: 732-291-0272; Fax: 732-291-4982.
School—55 South Ave., 07716. Tel: 732-291-1050; Fax: 732-872-2293. James Duris, Prin.
Lay Teachers 19; Students 287.
Catechesis/Religious Programs—Students 420.

Avon, Monmouth Co., St. Elizabeth (1907), Rev. Joseph A. Radomski. In res., Rev. Msgr. John J. Endebrock; Rev. Douglas U. Hermansen.
Res., 424 Lincoln Ave., 07717. Tel: 732-774-4089; Fax: 732-774-5848.
Catechesis/Religious Programs—Students 121.

Barnegat, Ocean Co., St. Mary (1942), Revs. Kenard J. Tuzeneu; Vincente Magdaraog.
Res., 747 West Bay Ave., P.O. Box 609, 08005. Tel: 609-698-5531; Fax: 609-698-6255. [CEM]
Catechesis/Religious Programs—Tel: 609-698-7477. Joan Haldenwang, D.R.E.
Students 1,731.

Bay Head, Ocean Co., Sacred Heart (1913), Revs. Thomas Brennan; Dominic A. Marchese, S.S.J.; Deacons John Czarnecki; Jim Tobin.
Res., 751 Main Ave., 08742. Tel: 732-899-1398; Fax: 732-899-2233.
Catechesis/Religious Programs—Students 93.

Bayville, Ocean Co., St. Barnabas (1966), Revs. Michael D. Sullivan; Jack Dwyer; Leon Buni; Deacons Peter M. Clausen; James H. Cummings. Pastoral Assocs.: Sr. Patricia McNiff, O.S.F.; Sr. Patricia Lally, O.P.; Deacon Michael A. Taylor.
Res., 33 Woodland Rd., Box I, 08721. Tel: 732-269-2208; Fax: 732-269-2557.
Catechesis/Religious Programs—Tel: 732-269-3590.
Students 1,660.

Belmar, Monmouth Co., St. Rose (1888), Rev. Msgr. Casmir H. Ladzinski; Rev. Edward M. Jawidzik; Deacons Normand C. Bailey; Eugene G. Malhame.
Res., 603 Seventh Ave., 07719. Tel: 732-681-0512; Fax: 732-681-1693.
School—605 Sixth Ave., 07719. Tel: 732-681-5555; Fax: 732-681-5890. Susan Hillers, Prin.
Sisters 2; Lay Teachers 20; Students 549.

High School—607 Seventh Ave., 07719. Tel: 732-681-2858; Fax: 732-280-2745. Dr. Michelle Campbell, Prin.
Sisters 6; Lay Teachers 42; Students 638.
Catechesis/Religious Programs—Tel: 732-681-6266.
Students 401.

Beverly, Burlington Co., St. Joseph (1864), Rev. Michael J. Lynch; Deacons Herman J. Mosteller; Matthew J. Stap, (Retired); Ronald J. Ulmer; Charles A. Perkins.
Res., 524 Warren St., 08010. Tel: 609-387-0172; Fax: 609-386-8535.
Catechesis/Religious Programs—524 Warren St., 08010. Tel: 609-387-2928.
Students 111.

Bordentown, Burlington Co., St. Mary (1837), Rev. Michael J. Burns; Deacons David M. Harris, Jr.; Harry A. Putnam; Gary T. Richardson; Thomas F. Shea.
Res., 45 Crosswicks St., 08505. Tel: 609-298-0261; Fax: 609-298-7178. [CEM]
School—30 Elizabeth St., 08505. Tel: 609-298-1448; Fax: 609-298-3803. Mary Ellen Moss, Prin.
Lay Teachers 13; Students 115.
Catechesis/Religious Programs—Tel: 609-291-8281; Fax: 609-298-7178.
Students 428.

Bradley Beach, Monmouth Co., Ascension (1907), Rev. David A. Hillier; Deacons John Gerard; James McNulty.
Res., 501 Brinley Ave., 07720. Tel: 732-774-0456; Fax: 732-775-9335.
Catechesis/Religious Programs—Students 100.

Brant Beach, Ocean Co., St. Francis of Assisi (1971), Revs. Andrew J. Reitz, O.F.M.; Kevin Daly, O.F.M.; Francis DiSpigno, O.F.M.; Deacons Albert J. Schwind; James Dougherty; George Walker; Richard Titmas.
Office: 4700 Long Beach Blvd., 08008. Tel: 609-494-8813; Fax: 609-494-1466.
Catechesis/Religious Programs—Sr. Margaret Magee, O.S.F., D.R.E.
Students 800.
Missions—Beach Haven, Ocean Co., St. Thomas Aquinas, 2nd & Atlantic, 08008; Loveladies, Ocean Co., St. Clare, 56th & Long Beach Blvd., 08008; Surf City, Ocean Co., St. Thomas of Villanova, 13th & Long Beach Blvd., 08008.

Brick Town, Ocean Co., Epiphany (1973), Revs. John V. Bowden; Thomas Kunnath (India); Deacons Ron Nowak; Michael Mullarkey; William Heard.
Res., 615 Thiele Rd., 08724. Tel: 732-458-0220; Fax: 732-458-0855.
Catechesis/Religious Programs—Tel: 732-785-0576; 785-0872; Fax: 732-458-0855. Mrs. Janice Santanello, D.R.E.
Students 653.

Visitation (1942), Revs. William M. Dunlap; James J. Sauchelli; Deacons Edward Fischer, III; Salvadore Vicari; Leonard Kruk.
Res., 730 Lynnwood Ave., Brick, 08723-5302. Tel: 732-477-0028; Fax: 732-477-1274.
Catechesis/Religious Programs—Tel: 732-477-5217. Mrs. Nancy Grodberg, D.R.E.
Students 1,310.

St. Dominic (1962), Revs. James J. Brady; Thomas Fesen; Alejandro Gronifilo; Deacon Damian Ayers.
Res., 250 Old Squan Rd., 08724. Tel: 732-840-1410; Fax: 732-840-0522.
School—Tel: 732-840-1412; Fax: 732-840-6457. Robert Zolkiewicz, Prin.
Lay Teachers 33; Students 643.
Catechesis/Religious Programs—Tel: 732-840-1414. Ann M. Cramer, D.R.E.
Students 875.

Browns Mills, Burlington Co., St. Ann (1906), Rev. Edwin J. Mathias; Deacons Daniel Earley; Walter Price; Frank Sherpensky.
Church & Res.—22 Trenton Rd., 08015. Tel: 609-893-3246; Fax: 609-893-8056.
Catechesis/Religious Programs—Students 348.
Stations—Burlington Co. Minimum Security Jail.; Burlington Co. Juvenile Detention Center.; Deborah Heart & Lung Center.; Buttonwood Hall, Evergreen Park.

The Church of the Korean Martyrs (Korean),
Res., 3311 Town Court South, Lawrenceville, 08648. Tel: 609-716-9144; Fax: 609-897-9094.

Burlington, Burlington Co., St. Paul (1864), Rev. Msgr. James H. Dubell; Deacons George Carlin; Francis A. Jones; Alfred Pennise.
Res., 223 E. Union St., 08016. Tel: 609-386-0163; Fax: 609-386-0085.
School—6th & James Sts., 08016. Tel: 609-386-1645; Fax: 609-386-1345. Sr. Peter Damian, Prin.
Sisters of Mercy 1; Lay Teachers 21; Students 406.
Catechesis/Religious Programs—Students 295.

All Saints (1910) (Polish), Rev. Jacek Labinski.
Res., 502 High St., 08016. Tel: 609-386-0152; Fax: 609-386-0190.
School—510 High St., 08016. Tel: 609-387-9207; Fax: 609-387-1358. Maura Kelly, Prin.
Lay Teachers 14; Students 222.
Catechesis/Religious Programs—Students 75.

Cinnaminson, Burlington Co., St. Charles Borromeo (1961), Rev. Thomas J. Triggs; Deacons William S. Sepich; William Gallagher. Pastoral Assocs.: Sr. Jeanne Belli, S.S.J.; Ms. Shana Joy Kruysman.
Res., 2226 Riverton Rd., P.O. Box 2220, 08077. Tel: 856-829-3322; Fax: 856-829-1852.
School—2500 Branch Pike, 08077. Tel: 856-829-2778; Fax: 856-829-3411. Mary Helen Ward, Prin.
Sisters of Mercy 1; Lay Teachers 24; Students 380.
Catechesis/Religious Programs—Tel: 856-829-9119. Kathy Kraemer, D.R.E.
Students 870.

Colts Neck, Monmouth Co., St. Mary (1887), Rev. Edward J. Griswold; Deacons Ralph Imholte; Caleb Weller.
Res., Hwy. 34 & Phalanx Rd., Box H, 07722. Tel: 732-780-2666; Fax: 732-780-0394.
Catechesis/Religious Programs—Tel: 732-294-8841.
Students 1,035.

Deal, Monmouth Co., St. Mary of the Assumption (1901), Revs. John G. DeSandre; Matthew Thelly; Deacon John McCabe.
Res., 46 Richmond Ave., 07723. Tel: 732-531-1409; Fax: 732-531-3931.
School—73 Wickapecko Dr., Ocean, 07712. Tel: 732-531-4433; Fax: 732-531-4054. Marie Busch-Beebe, Prin.
Lay Teachers 17; Students 160.
Catechesis/Religious Programs—Tel: 732-531-1889.
Students 260.

Delran, Burlington Co., Holy Name (1972), Rev. Michael J. O'Connor; Deacons Jim Manaloris; Joseph Barbara. In res., Rev. Joy T. Chacko (India).
Res., 260 Conrow Rd., Box 1038, 08075. Tel: 609-461-6555; Fax: 609-461-1293.
Catechesis/Religious Programs—Students 500.

Eatontown, Monmouth Co., St. Dorothea (1905), Rev. G. William Evans; Deacons Stephen W. Andrews; Edward R. Herr.
Res., 240 Broad St., 07724. Tel: 732-542-0148; Fax: 732-542-1531.
Catechesis/Religious Programs—Tel: 732-542-0303.
Students 573.

Immaculate Conception (1984) (Korean), Rev. Michael Lee.
Res., 64 Broad St., 07724. Tel: 732-389-3830; Fax: 732-389-2705.
Catechesis/Religious Programs—Students 40.

Englishtown, Monmouth Co., Our Lady of Mercy (1948), Rev. Charles R. Valentine.
Res., 58 Main St., 07726. Tel: 732-446-6324; Fax: 732-446-5179.
Catechesis/Religious Programs—Tel: 732-786-1835.
Students 856.
Mission—Perrineville, Monmouth Co., St. Joseph, 58 Main St., 07726. Tel: 732-446-6324. [CEM]

Evesham Township, Burlington Co., St. Isaac Jogues (1996), Rev. Phillip C. Pfleger.
3 Lord Pl., Marlton, 08053. Tel: 856-797-0999; Fax: 856-797-0463.
Catechesis/Religious Programs—St. Joan of Arc Church, 100 WillowBend Rd., Marlton, 08053. Tel: 856-797-1811.
Students 635.

Fair Haven, Monmouth Co., Nativity (1954), Revs. Jerome M. Nolan; Richard R. Sweeny; Deacon John A. Cole.
Res., Ridge Rd. & Hance Rd., P.O. Box 66, 07704-0066. Tel: 732-741-1714; Fax: 732-741-6837.
Catechesis/Religious Programs—Tel: 732-741-4543. Mrs. Jane Shaheen, D.R.E.
Students 871.

Farmingdale, Monmouth Co., St. Catherine of Siena (1912), Rev. Michael S. Vona; Deacon Michael J. Principato.
Res., 31 Asbury Rd., P.O. Box 673, 07727-0673. Tel: 732-938-5375; Fax: 732-938-3260.
Catechesis/Religious Programs—Tel: 732-938-6229.
Students 502.

Florence, Burlington Co., St. Clare (1874) (Irish-Italian), Rev. Felix F. Venza.
Res., 232 E. Front St., 08518. Tel: 609-499-0122. [CEM]
Catechesis/Religious Programs—Duffy House, 306 E. Front St., 08518.
Students 170.

Forked River, Ocean Co., St. Pius X (1961), Rev. Richard Basznianin, Admin.; Sr. Angela Case, S.S.J., Pastoral Assoc.; Deacons James Heller; Ronald Haunss.
Res., 203 W. Lacey Rd., 08731-3598. Tel: 609-693-5107; Fax: 609-693-6829.
Catechesis/Religious Programs—Tel: 609-693-2379. Marge Ferrara, D.R.E.
Students 995.

Freehold, Monmouth Co., St. Rose of Lima (1871), Revs. Richard R. Milewski; Miguel A. Virella, S.V.D., Hispanic Ministry, Tel: 732-303-7800; Fax: 732-303-1228; Norman St. John, S.V.D.; Rocco A. Cuomo; Deacon John Wanat.
Res., 16 McLean St., 07728. Tel: 732-462-0859; Fax: 732-462-8173. [CEM]
School—51 Lincoln Pl., 07728. Tel: 732-462-2646; Fax: 732-462-0331. Sr. Patricia Doyle, Prin.
Sisters 2; Lay Teachers 32; Students 664.
Catechesis/Religious Programs—Tel: 732-308-0215. Mrs. Kathleen Surgent, C.R.E.
Students 907.

St. Robert Bellarmine (1971), Revs. Thomas J. O'Connor; Matthew Adackapara; Deacon Gerald Henwood.
61 Georgia Rd., 07728. Tel: 732-462-7429; Fax: 732-409-3496.
Catechesis/Religious Programs—Tel: 732-431-3404. Mrs. Margo Weber, D.R.E.
Students 1,400.

Hainesport, Burlington Co., Our Lady Queen of Peace (1944), Rev. Daniel Sullivan; Deacon John J. O'Donnell. In res., Rev. Sabinus Nwachukwu (Nigeria).
Res., 1603 Marne Hwy., P.O. Box 188, 08036. Tel: 609-267-0230; Fax: 609-267-0372.
Catechesis/Religious Programs—Tel: 609-267-3641.
Students 440.

Highlands, Monmouth Co., Our Lady of Perpetual Help (1883), Rev. David A. Adams.
Res., 141 Navesink Ave., 07732. Tel: 732-872-1290; Fax: 732-872-2796.
School—121 Miller St., 07732. Tel: 732-872-0281; Fax: 732-291-7907. Sr. Carmelisa Dragoni, Prin.
Franciscan Missionary Sisters of the Infant Jesus 3; Lay Teachers 8; Students 190.
Catechesis/Religious Programs—Students 42.
Convent—159 Navesink Ave., 07732. Tel: 732-872-1420.
Sisters 3.

Hightstown, Mercer Co., St. Anthony of Padua (1885), Revs. Patrick J. McDonnell; Javier Diaz; Deacons Thomas Garvey; Joseph Hepp; Frank Prihoda; Stephen Rasi; Patrick Kennedy.
Res., 251 Franklin St., 08520. Tel: 609-448-0141; Fax: 609-448-8876.
Catechesis/Religious Programs—Tel: 609-443-3318; Fax: 609-443-3390. Sr. Anne McCambley, S.S.J., D.R.E.
Students 850.

Holmdel, Monmouth Co., St. Benedict (1959), Revs. William C. Anderson; Pasquale Papalia; Deacons Herbert J. Schwarz; Raymond R. Pelkowski; Mr. Joseph Bulla, Pastoral Assoc.
Res., 165 Bethany Rd., 07733-1699. Tel: 732-264-4712; Fax: 732-264-9080.
School—Tel: 732-264-5578; Fax: 732-264-8679. Mary Ellen Lilly, Prin.
Lay Teachers 24; Students 472.
Catechesis/Religious Programs—Tel: 732-264-4714.
Students 624.

St. Catharine (1879), Rev. Eugene M. Rebeck; Deacons John P. Flanagan; Peter Fullen; James G. McGrath; Anthony Mustillo; Barbara Gabrielan, Pastoral Assoc. In res., Rev. Joseph McGroarty, O.P.
Res., P.O. Box 655, 07733. Tel: 732-842-3963; Fax: 732-842-9283.
Catechesis/Religious Programs—Tel: 732-758-8568. Sr. Patricia Schladebeck, M.S.C., D.R.E.
Students 1,300.

Hopewell, Mercer Co., St. Alphonsus (1877), Rev. Ralph W. Stansley; Deacons Robert Lafond; John Grant.
Res., 54 E. Prospect St., 08525. Tel: 609-466-0332; Fax: 609-466-2023. [CEM]
Catechesis/Religious Programs—Tel: 609-466-2694. Sr. Rosemary Hendry, O.S.F., D.R.E.
Students 199.

Howell Township, Monmouth Co., St. Veronica (1962), Revs. H. Brendan Williams; Peter Kochery; Donald J. O'Brien; Deacons Richard Eby, Sr.; Gene F. Moir, Sr.; Theodore V. Gularek; James Littlefield; Eugene Genovese; Tomasz Cechulski.
Res., 4215 Hwy. 9 N., Howell, 07731. Tel: 732-363-4200; Fax: 732-370-3891.
School—4219 Hwy. 9 N., Howell, 07731. Tel: 732-364-4130; Fax: 732-363-4932. Sr. Cherree Ann Power, Prin.
Sisters 4; Lay Teachers 36; Students 709.

Catechesis/Religious Programs—Tel: 732-364-4137. Sr. Valerie Paccone, C.R., D.R.E.
Students 2,300.

St. William the Abbot (1985), Rev. Msgr. Leo A. Kelty; Deacon Thomas Noone.
Mailing Address: P.O. Box 500, Allenwood, 08720. Tel: 732-840-3535; Fax: 732-840-3663.
Res., 2400 Lakewood-Allenwood Rd., Wall, 07719. Tel: 732-840-3628.
Catechesis/Religious Programs—Mary Cleary, D.R.E.
Students 480.
Stations—Geraldine Thompson Nursing Home, Tel: 732-938-5250; Brisbane Child Treatment Center.

Jackson, Ocean Co., St. Aloysius Gonzaga (1964), Rev. G. Scott Shaffer; Deacon Rene Perez.
Res., 935 Bennetts Mills Rd., P.O. Box 1285, 08527. Tel: 732-370-0500; Fax: 732-886-9336.
School—Saint Aloysius Grammar School, Tel: 732-370-1515; Fax: 732-370-3555. Mrs. Michele Williams, Prin.
Lay Teachers 22; Students 456.
Catechesis/Religious Programs—Tel: 732-370-1515.
Students 1,302.

Keansburg, Monmouth Co., St. Ann (1924), Revs. Daniel Cahill; Angelo Amaral; Kenneth W. Ekdahl; Deacons Edwin Cook; Robert Vlcej.
Res., 311 Carr Ave., 07734. Tel: 732-787-0315; Fax: 732-787-5254.
School—285 Carr Ave., 07734. Tel: 732-787-1027; Fax: 732-495-3338. Sr. Mary Dora McGrath, R.S.M., Prin.
Sisters 2; Lay Teachers 15; Students 279.
Catechesis/Religious Programs—Tel: 732-787-5744.
Students 570.
St. Ann Child Care Center—121 Main St., 07734. Tel: 732-787-7220; Fax: 732-787-2136.
Sisters 2; Students 80.
Bayshore Senior Day Center—100 Main St., 07734. Tel: 732-495-2454; Fax: 732-495-7897.
Sisters 1; Seniors Serviced 13,500.
Hansel and Gretel Preschool—267 Carr Ave., 07734. Tel: 732-787-9237; Fax: 732-787-9237.
Sisters 1; Children 83.
Project Paul—211 Carr Ave., 07734. Tel: 732-787-4887.

Keyport, Monmouth Co., St. Joseph (1854), Revs. Ronald J. Cioffi; James A. Conover; Miss Kay Hetherington, Pastoral Assoc.; Deacon Christopher O'Brien. In res., Rev. Francis Tam.
Res., 376 Maple Pl., 07735. Tel: 732-264-0322; Fax: 732-888-3280. [CEM]
School—St. Joseph School, Maple Pl., 07735. Tel: 732-264-2114; Fax: 732-264-8696. Ruth Mazzarela, Prin.
Lay Teachers 28; Students 430.
Catechesis/Religious Programs—Students 397.

Jesus the Lord (1978) (Hispanic), Revs. Jack Dwyer, Admin.; Hector Larrea; Randy Guillen.
Res., 123 Broad St., 07735-0673. Tel: 732-739-0323; Fax: 732-264-8276.
Church—120 Broad St., 07735.
Catechesis/Religious Programs—Students 204.

Lakehurst, Ocean Co., St. John (1969), Rev. Bernard Keigher; Deacons Gabriel Gregory; John Gilchrist; Anthony Tarala; Ronald Kerr; Robert Gooden. In res., Rev. James A. Thompson, Pastor Emeritus.
Res., 619 Chestnut St., 08733. Tel: 732-657-6347; Fax: 732-657-8690.
Catechesis/Religious Programs—Tel: 732-657-2348.
Students 400.

Lakewood, Ocean Co., St. Anthony Claret (1977). (Hispanic Parish for Ocean Co.). Revs. Pedro L. Bou, S.V.D.; Rolando Danzine, S.V.D.; Sr. Mary Newett, Pastoral Assoc.
Res., 780 Ocean Ave., 08701-3644. Tel: 732-367-8486; Fax: 732-367-0460.
Catechesis/Religious Programs—Students 240.

St. Mary of the Lake (1890), Rev. Msgr. Michael J. Walsh; Revs. Charles M. Schwartz; Edward Kwoka; Deacons Thomas Cater; Silverius Galvan; John Cullinane; Anthony Martucci. Pastoral Ministers: Sr. Mary Franey, R.S.M.; Sr. Geraldine Contento, M.P.S.; Mrs. Terry Ginther, Pastoral Assoc.
Res., 43 Madison Ave., 08701. Tel: 732-363-0139; Fax: 732-905-1410. [CEM]
School—Holy Family School, 1141 E. County Line Rd., 08701. Tel: 732-363-4771; Fax: 732-363-2914. Sr. Carolyn Houck, P.P.F., Prin.; Sr. Domenica Troiana, M.P.F., Asst. Prin.
Sisters 2; Lay Teachers 32; Students 711.
Catechesis/Religious Programs—Tel: 732-363-3043; Fax: 732-961-0382.
Students 440.
Mission—Lakewood, Ocean Co., Holy Family Church. Fax: 732-905-1410.

Lavallette, Ocean Co., St. Bonaventure (1921), Rev. Msgr. Leonard F. Troiano.
Res., 103 Washington Ave., 08735. Tel: 732-793-7291; Fax: 732-793-8204.
Catechesis/Religious Programs—Students 142.

Lawrenceville, Mercer Co., St. Ann (1937), Revs. R. Vincent Gartland; Pablo Gadenz, Parochial Vicar; Sr. Beth Dempsey, Pastoral Assoc.
Res., 1253 Lawrence Rd., 08648. Tel: 609-882-6491; Fax: 609-882-4366.
School—34 Rossa Ave., 08648. Tel: 609-882-8077; Fax: 609-882-0327. Mr. John McKenna, Prin.
Lay Teachers 28; Students 447.
Catechesis/Religious Programs—Tel: 609-882-1212.
Students 550.

Lincroft, Monmouth Co., St. Leo the Great (1958), Rev. James M. Clark; Deacon Joseph DePaolis. Pastoral Assocs.: Sr. Ann Barry, S.S.J.; Sr. Joan Dreisbach, O.S.F.
Res., 50 Hurley's Ln., 07738. Tel: 732-747-5466; Fax: 732-219-5181.
School—550 Newman-Springs Rd., 07738. Tel: 732-741-3133; Fax: 732-741-2241. Elena Torregrossa, Prin.
Lay Teachers 32; Students 630.
Catechesis/Religious Programs—Tel: 732-530-0717.
Students 909.

Long Branch, Monmouth Co.,

1—Our Lady Star of the Sea, (1878), Rev. M. Joseph Mokrzycki; Deacon Donald A. Young; Sr. Diane Matera, R.S.M., Hospital Pastoral Min.
Res., 101 Chelsea Ave., 07740. Tel: 732-229-0526; Fax: 732-229-2886. [CEM]
Catechesis/Religious Programs—Tel: 732-229-0952.
Students 103.
Station—Long Branch, Long Branch City.

2—Holy Trinity, (1906) (Italian), Rev. Joseph Rosie; Deacon Albert M. Pacitti.
Res., 408 Prospect St., 07740. Tel: 732-222-3216; Fax: 732-222-4313.
School—375 Exchange Pl., 07740. Tel: 732-222-8878; Fax: 732-222-8854. Sr. Roseann Fernandez, Prin.
Religious Teachers Filippni 1; Lay Teachers 12; Students 157.
Catechesis/Religious Programs—Tel: 732-870-1778.
Students 199.
Convent—380 Division St., 07740. Tel: 732-222-8535.

3—St. John the Baptist, (1984) (Spanish), Revs. Victoriano Sandoval; Roman Modino.
Res., 272 Willow Ave., 07740. Tel: 732-229-8527; 229-8905; Fax: 732-571-0280.
Catechesis/Religious Programs—Tel: 732-571-1003.
Students 134.

4—St. Michael, (1885), Rev. Charles B. Weiser; Deacon Eugene A. Somma.
Res., 800 Ocean Ave., West End, 07740. Tel: 732-222-8080; Fax: 732-870-1174.
Catechesis/Religious Programs—Tel: 732-483-0360; Fax: 732-483-0360.
Students 400.

Manalapan, Monmouth Co., St. Thomas More (1970), Revs. John P. Bambrick; Gerald E. McBride; Deacons Keith J. Casey; James Mark Micali; John J. Zebrowski; John J. Walsh.
Res., 186 Gordons Corner Rd., 07726. Tel: 732-446-6661; Fax: 732-446-6507.
Catechesis/Religious Programs—Tel: 732-446-3232.
Students 1,058.

Manasquan, Monmouth Co., St. Denis (1909), Revs. Stanley P. Lukaszewsk; Charles F.X. Dolan, S.J.; William J. Bausch; Rev. Msgr. Harrold Murray.
Res., 90 Union Ave., Box 340, 08736. Tel: 732-223-0287; Fax: 732-528-1901.
School—119 Virginia Ave., 08736. Tel: 732-223-4928; Fax: 732-223-1807. Trudy Bonavita, Prin.
Lay Teachers 14; Students 300.
Catechesis/Religious Programs—Tel: 732-223-1161.
Students 875.
Chapel—Manasquan Beach, Our Lady Star of the Sea. (Summer).

Maple Shade, Burlington Co., Our Lady of Perpetual Help (1920), Revs. John F. Wake; Louis Rayappan (India); Deacons Joseph McHugh; Joseph A. Card; Michael P. Boehm; Lawrence W. Finn, Sr.; Joseph F. Seaman; Ronald S. Meyers.
Res., 236 E. Main St., 08052. Tel: 856-667-8850; Fax: 856-667-3083.
School—Main St. and Fellowship Rd., Tel: 856-779-7526. Mary Ann Figura, Prin.
Sisters 3; Lay Teachers 16; Students 314.
Catechesis/Religious Programs—Tel: 856-779-7529.
Students 509.

Marlboro, Monmouth Co., St. Gabriel (1885), Rev. Eugene J. Roberts; Deacons James C. Russo; Lester Owens; James McKeon; Stephen Sansevere.
Res., 100 N. Main St., 07746. Tel: 732-946-4487; Fax: 732-946-7276.
Catechesis/Religious Programs—Tel: 732-946-2696; Fax: 732-946-2080. James J. Bridges, D.R.E.
Students 1,478.

Marlton, Burlington Co., St. Joan of Arc (1961), Rev. Msgr. Armand A. Pedata; Revs. Andrew V. Jamieson, O.F.M.Cap; Francis Ravi; Sr. Eleanor O'Connell, S.S.J., Pastoral Assoc.; Deacons Barry Tarzy; George Johnston.
Church & Res.—100 Willow Bend Rd., 08053. Tel: 856-983-0077; Fax: 856-983-7716.
School—101 Evans Rd., 08053. Tel: 856-983-0774. Sr. Patricia Pycik, Prin.
Sisters of St. Joseph 2; Lay Teachers 23; Students 501.
Catechesis/Religious Programs—Tel: 856-983-7575. Mrs. Linda Mueller, D.R.E.
Students 1,475.
Convent—99 Evans Rd., 08053. Tel: 856-983-0258.

Matawan, Monmouth Co., St. Clement (1965), Rev. John J. Scully. In res., Rev. Thomas R. Rittenhouse.
Res., 172 Freneau Ave., 07747. Tel: 732-566-3616; Fax: 732-566-9275.
Catechesis/Religious Programs—Tel: 732-591-8090.
Students 900.

Medford, Burlington Co., St. Mary of the Lakes (1943), Revs. Joseph A. Tedesco; Mark Devlin, S.D.B.; Joseph Gnarackatt; Deacons Joseph R. Patton; W. Norman Talbot; Donald P. Doyle; Ronald Little.
Res., 40 Jackson Rd., 08055. Tel: 609-654-8208; Fax: 609-654-1734.
School—196 Rte. 70, 08055. Tel: 609-654-2546; Fax: 609-654-8125. Sr. Justina Marie Miller, Prin.
Sisters of St. Francis of Philadelphia 3; Sisters of St. Joseph 4; Lay Teachers 23; Students 463.
Catechesis/Religious Programs—196 Rte. 70, 08055. Tel: 609-654-8243; Fax: 609-953-8630.
Students 1,102.
Convents—27 Schoolhouse Dr., 08055. Tel: 609-654-5896. Sisters of St. Francis; 24 Summerhill Lane, 08055. Tel: 609-654-1941. Sisters of St. Joseph
St. Vincent DePaul Society-Medford: P.O. Box 1131, 08055. Tel: 609-953-0021; Fax: 609-953-2432. Mr. Paul V. Cannon, Treas.

Middletown, Monmouth Co., St. Catherine (1948), Rev. Daniel C. Hesko.
Res., 5 Shore Acres Ave., 07748. Tel: 732-787-1318; Fax: 732-787-6139.
Catechesis/Religious Programs—Tel: 732-495-7779; Fax: 732-495-7779.
Students 636.

Monmouth Beach, Monmouth Co., Church of the Precious Blood (1947), Rev. John T. Kielb; Deacon William Murray.
Res., 72 Riverdale Ave., 07750. Tel: 732-222-4756; Fax: 732-229-6448.
Catechesis/Religious Programs—Tel: 732-870-1293.
Students 320.

Moorestown, Burlington Co., Our Lady of Good Counsel (1879), Rev. Msgr. James J. McGovern; Rev. Casmir Milewski; Deacons Peter DeLuca, (Retired); Francis P. McGann; Christopher Dixon, Pastoral Assoc.; Joseph A. Paul.
Res., 42 W. Main St., 08057. Tel: 609-235-0181; Fax: 609-235-4987. [CEM]
School—23 W. Prospect St., 08057. Tel: 609-235-7885; Fax: 609-235-2570. Jerome McGowan, Prin.
Dominic Sisters of Hope 1; Lay Teachers 26; Students 514.
Catechesis/Religious Programs—Tel: 609-235-7136. Mrs. Linda M. Dix, D.R.E.
Students 941.

Mount Holly, Burlington Co., Sacred Heart (1848), Rev. Robert J.W. Schecker.
Res., 260 High St., 08060-1404. Tel: 609-702-1848; Fax: 609-267-9293. [CEM]
School—250 High St., 08060. Tel: 609-267-1728; Fax: 609-267-1728. Ronald J. Maniglia, Prin.
Lay Teachers 24; Students 336.
Catechesis/Religious Programs—Tel: 609-267-6319.
Students 800.
Mission—Jobstown, Burlington Co., St. Andrew, 2489 Monmouth Rd., Jobstown, 08041. Tel: 609-702-1848.
Stations—County Jail, Tel: 609-267-3300; Burlington County Hospital Extended Care Center, Tel: 609-367-0700.

Christ the Redeemer (1976) (Hispanic), Rev. Rodolfo Gonzalez Ballesteros, Admin.
Res., 426 Pine St., 08060. Tel: 609-261-0181; Fax: 609-702-0017.
Catechesis/Religious Programs—250 High St., Mt. Holly, 08060. Tel: 609-267-1728.
Students 41.

Mount Laurel, Burlington Co., St. John Neumann (1978), Revs. Lino S. Parente, O.Cist. (Italy); Anselmo M. Florio, O.Cist. (Italy); Teclezghi Ucbaghiorghis, O.Cist.; Maurizio Nicoletti, O.Cist (Italy); Deacons John Hughes; Gene Hoch.
Res., 560 Walton Ave., 08054. Tel: 856-235-1330; Fax: 856-235-9632.
Catechesis/Religious Programs—Students 947.

Neptune, Monmouth Co., Holy Innocents (1959), Rev. Brian T. Butch; Deacon Michael Auleta. In res., Rev. Lawrence Kunnel; Deacons James Walsh; John Klincewicz.
Res., 3455 W. Bangs Ave., P.O. Box 806, 07753. Tel: 732-922-4242; Fax: 732-922-2848.
School—Tel: 732-922-3141; Fax: 732-922-6531. Sr. Elizabeth Calello, Prin.
Religious Teachers Filippini 2; Lay Teachers 14; Students 280.
Catechesis/Religious Programs—Students 283.
Stations—Convacenter Nursing Home, Tel: 732-774-3500; Imperial Nursing Home, Tel: 732-922-3400; Heritage Hall Nursing Home, Tel: 732-922-9330; Medicenter Nursing Home, Tel: 732-774-8300; The Lodge, Kings Manor, Tel: 732-922-1900.

Our Lady of Providence (1981) (Spanish), Revs. Eugene Rochford, S.V.D.; Carlos Paniagua, S.V.D.; Sr. Grace Forker, S.S.J., Pastoral Assoc.; Deacon Victor L. Gomez.
Res., 1228 Fifth Ave., 07753. Tel: 732-776-7164; Fax: 732-776-7164.
Catechesis/Religious Programs—Students 133.

New Egypt, Ocean Co., Assumption (1853), Revs. Joseph J. Farrell; Robert R. Schulze; Deacons Martin Ervin; Raymond W. Staub, Jr.; Fred J. O'Brien.
Res., 76 Evergreen Rd., 08533. Tel: 609-758-2153; Fax: 609-758-6240. [CEM]
Catechesis/Religious Programs—Students 430.
Mission—Jackson, Ocean Co., Church of St. Monica, 679 W. Veteran's Hwy., Jackson, 08527. Tel: 732-928-0279; Fax: 732-928-1853.
Catechesis/Religious Programs—Tel: 732-928-4038.
Students 570.

New Monmouth, Monmouth Co., St. Mary (1878), Revs. John M. Dobrosky; Jeffrey J. Kegley; Sr. Margaret James Curtin, O.P., Pastoral Assoc.; Sr. Catherine Tronolone, O.S.F.; Deacon Henry Ernst.
Res., 26 Leonardville Rd., 07748. Tel: 732-671-0071; Fax: 732-671-6125.
School—538 Church St., 07748. Tel: 732-671-0129; Fax: 732-671-2653. Mr. William V. Smith, Prin.
Lay Teachers 34; Aides 13; Students 611.
High School—Mater Dei High School, Tel: 732-671-9100; Fax: 732-671-9214. Mr. Frank Poleski, Jr., Prin.; Mr. James F. Rochford, Asst. Prin.
Lay Teachers 27; Students 405.
Catechesis/Religious Programs—Tel: 732-671-0124. Mrs. Margaret Krasutsky, D.R.E.
Students 1,340.

Normandy Beach, Ocean Co., Our Lady of Peace (1979), Rev. Gerald J. McCarron.
Residence and Mailing: P.O. Box 728, 7th Ave. & Rte. 35 S., 08739. Tel: 732-793-7803; Fax: 732-793-1808.
Catechesis/Religious Programs—Tel: 732-793-2583.
Students 28.

Pennington, Mercer Co., St. James (1897), Rev. Ronald J. Bacovin; Deacons James W. Palsir; Samuel Sciarrotta; Richard Currie; Kevin Byrne.
Res., 115 E. Delaware Ave., 08534. Tel: 609-737-0122; Fax: 609-737-6912.
Catechesis/Religious Programs—Tel: 609-737-2717.
Students 803.

Point Pleasant, Ocean Co., St. Martha (1972), Revs. Patrick F. Magee; Michael T. Manning; Deacons Edward Maier; John Haney; Francis Groff.
Res. & Mailing Address: 3800 Herbertsville Rd., 08742. Tel: 732-899-7269; 295-3630; Fax: 732-295-9315.
Catechesis/Religious Programs—Tel: 732-295-8252.
Students 780.

Point Pleasant Beach, Ocean Co., St. Peter's (1882), Revs. Richard Rossell, O.F.M.Conv.; Edward Costello, O.F.M.Conv.; Crispin Fuino, O.F.M.Conv.; Deacon Thomas Porter; Bro. Robert Lynch, O.F.M.Conv.
Res., 406 Forman Ave., 08742. Tel: 732-892-0049; Fax: 732-295-9782.
School—415 Atlantic Ave., 08742. Tel: 732-892-1260.
Sisters 3; Lay Teachers 11; Students 257.
Catechesis/Religious Programs—Tel: 732-899-4839.
Students 536.
Convent—401 Atlantic Ave., 08742. Tel: 732-899-2390.

Princeton, Mercer Co., St. Paul (1864), Rev. Msgr. Walter E. Nolan; Rev. Michael Santangelo; Deacons Maurice Benedetti; Paul LaChance; Michael Ross; Joseph Lynch.
Res., 214 Nassau St., 08540. Tel: 609-924-1743; Fax: 609-924-7980. [CEM]
School—218 Nassau St., 08540. Tel: 609-921-7587; Fax: 609-921-0264. Karen Pizarro, Prin.
Sisters 3; Lay Teachers 25; Students 411.
Catechesis/Religious Programs—Tel: 609-924-1743, Ext. 118.
Students 500.

Red Bank, Monmouth Co., St. James (1864), Rev. Msgr. Philip A. Lowery; Revs. Alex Enriquez; John O. Chang; Marianito Ortiz.
Res., 94 Broad St., 07701. Tel: 732-741-0500; Fax: 732-741-1489. [CEM]
(Grades Preschool). Tel: 732-933-1041.
Lay Teachers 4; Students 55.
School—St. James Grammar School, 30 Peters Pl., 07701. Tel: 732-741-3363; Fax: 732-933-4968. Janet Dolan, Prin.
Lay Teachers 34; Preschool 66; Students 520.
High School—Red Bank Catholic High School, 112 Broad St., 07701. Tel: 732-747-1774; Fax: 732-747-1936. Robert Abatemarco, Prin.
Sisters 2; Lay Teachers 77; Students 928.
Catechesis/Religious Programs—Tel: 732-747-6006.
Students 591.
Station—Riverview Hospital, Tel: 732-530-2231; Fax: 732-530-2394.

St. Anthony (1920) (Italian), Rev. Anthony M. Carotenuto.
Res., 121 Bridge Ave., 07701. Tel: 732-747-0813; Fax: 732-224-0059.
Catechesis/Religious Programs—16 Herbert St., 07701. Tel: 732-747-0813. Mrs. Michelle McCue, D.R.E.
Students 244.

Riverside, Burlington Co., St. Peter (1878), Revs. George Sabol, O.F.M.Conv.; Julius Toth, O.F.M.Conv.; Henry Madigan, O.F.M.Conv.; Deacon Joseph Fuoco.
Res., 102 Middleton St., Box 248, 08075. Tel: 856-461-0100; Fax: 856-764-6133.
School—St. Peter, 101 Middleton St., 08075. Tel: 856-461-1087; Fax: 856-461-6983. Joseph Chinnici, Prin.
Sisters 2; Lay Teachers 20; Students 417.
Catechesis/Religious Programs—Tel: 856-461-9343.
Students 312.

St. Casimir (1913) (Polish), Revs. Dennis Mason, O.F.M.Conv.; Stephen King, O.F.M.Conv. In res., Rev. Jude Michael Krill, O.F.M.Conv.
Res., 502 New Jersey Ave., 08075. Tel: 856-461-0532; Fax: 856-461-5781.
School & Preschool—500 New Jersey Ave., 08075. Tel: 856-461-7410; Fax: 856-461-2619. Sr. Lydia Etter, Prin.
Sisters 2; Lay Teachers 13; Students 210.
Catechesis/Religious Programs—Students 95.

Riverton, Burlington Co., Sacred Heart (1878), Rev. John P. Czahur; Deacons Joseph Knipp; Joseph Donadieu.
Res., 400 Thomas Ave., 08077. Tel: 856-829-0090; Fax: 856-829-2087.
Catechesis/Religious Programs—Tel: 609-829-1848; Fax: 609-829-7404.
Students 524.

Roebling, Burlington Co., Holy Assumption (1913), Rev. Francis Walter, O.F.M.; Deacon Robert D. Machion.
Res., 1290 Hornberger Ave., 08554. Tel: 609-499-0161; Fax: 609-499-3074.
School—1238 Hornberger Ave., 08554. Tel: 609-499-0045. Patricia Sacks, Prin.
Lay Teachers 9; Students 188.
Catechesis/Religious Programs—Students 90.

Rumson, Monmouth Co., Holy Cross (1884), Revs. Joseph W. Hughes; Kevin Keelen, O.S.A., Pastoral Assoc.; Deacon Jay C. Harbeck.
Res., 30 Ward Ave., 07760. Tel: 732-842-0348; Fax: 732-842-3226.
School—(Grades PreK-8) 40 Rumson Rd., 07760. Tel: 732-842-0348. Thomas Bugliaro, Prin.
Lay Teachers 26; Students 444.
Catechesis/Religious Programs—Students 680.

Sea Girt, Monmouth Co., St. Mark (1953), Rev. Msgr. William J. Carton. In res., Rev. Msgr. Robert T. Bulman; Deacon Dennis Saake.
Res., 215 Crescent Pkwy., 08750. Tel: 732-449-6364; Fax: 732-449-1646.
Catechesis/Religious Programs—Tel: 732-449-8360.
Students 408.

Seaside Heights, Ocean Co., Our Lady of Perpetual Help (1942), Rev. Emmett Carroll, O.F.M. Conv. In res., Rev. Evan Bucci, O.F.M. Conv.; Bro. Nicholas Lorson.
Res., 100 Grant Ave., 08751. Tel: 732-793-6881; Fax: 732-793-7632.
Catechesis/Religious Programs—Students 70.

Seaside Park, Ocean Co., St. Catharine of Siena (1906), Revs. Brennan Joseph Farleo, O.F.M.Conv., Supr. & Pastor; Eugene Zwahl, O.F.M.Conv.; Eric Fenner, O.F.M.Conv.; Bros. Paul Hardison, O.F.M.Conv.; Kenneth Lucas, O.F.M. Conv.
Res., 50 E. St., 08752. Tel: 732-793-0041; Fax: 732-793-5483.
Catechesis/Religious Programs—Students 200.

Spring Lake, Monmouth Co., St. Catharine (1901), Rev. Msgr. Thomas A. Luebking; Rev. Daniel Gowen; Deacons John P. O'Connor; David Fursman; Edward Jennings.
Res., 215 Essex Ave., 07762. Tel: 732-449-5765; Fax: 732-449-0916. [CEM 2]
School—Second and Salem Ave., Tel: 732-449-4424; Fax: 732-449-7876. Sr. Margo Kavanaugh, Prin.
Sisters 3; Lay Teachers 32; Students 611.
Catechesis/Religious Programs—Students 720.
Convent—211 Essex Ave., 07762. Tel: 732-449-6199.
Mission—Spring Lake, Monmouth Co., St. Margaret, Ludlow Ave., 07762.

Tabernacle, Burlington Co., Holy Eucharist (1982), Rev. Michael P. Lang; Deacon Joseph Lambarski.
Office: 520 Medford Lakes Rd., 08088. Tel: 609-268-8383; Fax: 609-268-3294.
Catechesis/Religious Programs—Tel: 609-268-7742. Dolores Wright, D.R.E.
Students 810.
Stations—New Lisbon Developmental Center, Tel: 609-726-1000; Leisuretown Senior Citizen Community.

Toms River, Ocean Co.,

1—St. Joseph, (Dover Township) (1883), Rev. Msgr. Sean P. Flynn; Revs. William P. Gardner; Roberto Ignacio; Michael B. Figler; Deacons Francis J. Babuschak; Edwin L. Voll, Jr.; Frank J. McKenna; Romeo D. Aquino.
Mailing Address: P.O. Box 387, 509 Hooper Ave., 08754. Tel: 732-349-0018; Fax: 732-286-7064. [CEM]
School—711 Hooper Ave., 08754. Tel: 732-349-2355; Fax: 732-349-1064. Karen Lewis, Prin.
Sisters 1; Lay Teachers 44; Students 944.
High School—Monsignor Donovan High School, Tel: 732-349-8801; Fax: 732-349-8956. Dr. Edward Gere, Prin.
Sisters 5; Lay Teachers 67; Students 926.
Catechesis/Religious Programs—Tel: 732-914-2420.
Students 1,366.
Mission—Island Heights, Ocean Co., St. Gertrude, Ocean & Central Aves., 08732. Tel: 732-288-0036.

2—St. Justin, (Dover Township) (1972), Revs. William J. Nolan; Joseph Halpin; Rainer Herradura; Deacons Gregory Wallack; Richard Hauenstein; David L. Shapiro; Brent McNally; Louis Cartnick; Michael Fullen.
Res., 975 Fischer Blvd., 08753. Tel: 732-270-3980; Fax: 732-929-9411.
Catechesis/Religious Programs—Tel: 732-270-3797. Mrs. Rose Ciallella, D.R.E.
Students 1,062.

3—St. Luke, (Dover Township) (1982), Revs. Louis W. Kralovich; Robert T. Leahy; Deacons Donald G. MacCarrick; Ronald R. Wicks; Stephen F. Delligatti.
Res., 1674 Old Freehold Rd., 08755. Tel: 732-286-2222; Fax: 732-914-1080.
Catechesis/Religious Programs—Tel: 732-505-0108. Mrs. Mary Goss, D.R.E.
Students 1,100.

4—St. Maximilian Kolbe, (Dover Township) (1985), Revs. Francis E. Santitoro; Nilo Apura. In res., Rev. George M. Albano; Deacon Raymond Shea.
Res. & Mailing Address: P.O. Box 4144, 08756. Tel: 732-914-0300; 914-8550 (Res.); Fax: 732-240-9517.

Tuckerton, Ocean Co., St. Teresa (1944), Revs. Terence O. McAlinden; Silvano Amora, Assoc.; Deacons James Petrauskas; Charles Comito; Henry Palan; William Sulzmann; Joseph Vivona.
Res., 128 Cedar St., 08087. Tel: 609-296-2504; Fax: 609-296-4530.
Catechesis/Religious Programs—Tel: 609-296-1940. Mrs. Cathy Mazanek, D.R.E.
Students 659.
Mission—Little Egg Harbor, Ocean Co., St. Michael, 64 W. Calabreeze Way, 08087. Tel: 609-296-3105.

Union Beach, Monmouth Co., Holy Family (1942), Revs. Patrick G. Fitzpatrick; Stanislaus T. Polczyk; Francis Cheruparambil; Deacon John Clymore. Pastoral Ministers: Sr. Rose Mary Malague, R.S.M.; Sr. Gloria Jean Bateman, R.S.M.
Res., Hwy. 36, P.O. Box 56, Keyport, 07735. Tel: 732-264-1484; Fax: 732-264-8369.
School—910 Hwy. 36, Hazlet, 07730. Tel: 732-264-9549; Fax: 732-335-9605. Sr. Mary Nadine Boyle, Prin.
Sisters 2; Lay Teachers 20; Students 420.
Catechesis/Religious Programs—Tel: 732-264-7043. Janet Moisewicz, D.R.E.
Students 822.
Convents—440 Sullivan Pl., 07735. Tel: 732-739-3065. Mercy Convent
Sisters 2; 41 Hemlock St., Hazlet, 07730. Tel: 732-335-9605. Holy Family Convent
Sisters 2.

Washington Crossing, Mercer Co., St. George (1924), Rev. Msgr. George A. Ardos; Sr. Dorothy Jancola, R.S.M., Pastoral Assoc.; Deacons James Toolan; Thomas Daily.
Res., 1370 River Rd., P.O. Box 324, Titusville, 08560. Tel: 609-737-2015; Fax: 609-737-7863.
Catechesis/Religious Programs—Tel: 609-730-1703.
Students 160.
Station—Mercer County Correction Center, Tel: 609-989-6901.

Wayside, Monmouth Co., St. Anselm (1972), Rev. Robert F. Kaeding.
Res., 1028 Wayside Rd., 07712. Tel: 732-493-4411; Fax: 732-493-4272.
Catechesis/Religious Programs—Students 644.

West Long Branch, Monmouth Co., St. Jerome (1956), Revs. Frederick W. Jackiewicz; Michael G. Lankford, Admin.
Res., 254 Wall St., 07764. Tel: 732-222-1424; Fax: 732-222-2291.
School—250 Wall St., 07764. Tel: 732-222-8686; Fax: 732-263-0343. Sr. Angelina Pelliccia, Prin.
Sisters 3; Lay Teachers 16; Students 262.
Catechesis/Religious Programs—250 Wall St., 07764.
Students 175.
Convent—250A Wall St., 07764. Tel: 732-222-2016.

West Windsor, Mercer Co., Church of St. David the King (1988), Rev. Timothy J. Capewell; Deacons Thomas Baker; Roger Dinella.
Res., 517 Village Rd. W., Princeton Jct., 08550.
Church—One New Village Rd., Princeton Jct., 08550-2003. Tel: 609-275-7111; Fax: 609-799-1984.
Catechesis/Religious Programs—Students 900.

Whiting, Ocean Co., St. Elizabeth Ann Seton (1976), Rev. Msgr. Joseph C. Shenrock, P.A.; Rev. Antony P. Poovakulam; Deacons Kyran J. Purcell; Joseph Rider; Robert Wolfe; Russell Alexander; Ralph Cordasco; Thomas White.
Res., 30 Schoolhouse Rd., 08759. Tel: 732-350-5001; Fax: 732-350-0912.
Catechesis/Religious Programs—Tel: 732-350-7391.
Students 195.

Willingboro, Burlington Co., Corpus Christi (1959), Rev. Daniel J. Ryan; Deacons James E. Ayrer; Stanley R. Olshevski; John F. Vassallo, Jr. In res., Rev. Msgr. Richard C. Brietske.
Res., 63 Sylvan Ln., 08046. Tel: 609-877-5322; Fax: 609-877-1695.
School—11 S. Sunset Rd., 08046. Tel: 609-877-2144; Fax: 609-877-3153. Mary O'Donnell, Prin.
Sisters 1; Lay Teachers 21; Students 277.
Catechesis/Religious Programs—Charleston & Sunset Rds., 08046. Tel: 609-871-4680.
Students 156.

Chaplains of Public Institutions

TRENTON. *Donnelly Memorial Hospital of City of Trenton.* Rev. Paul S. Rimassa.
Helene Fuld Hospital St. Joseph Church, 08638.
Katzenbach School for the Deaf. Sr. Helen Kline, S.S.J.,
Pastoral Center, 701 Lawrenceville Rd., P.O. Box 5147, 08648.
Mercer County Correction Center St. George Rectory, Titusville, 08560. Rev. Msgr. George A. Ardos.
New Jersey State Prison CN 861, 08629. Sr. Elizabeth Gnam.
St. Francis Medical Center. Revs. Joel F. Szydlowski, O.F.M.; Linus E. Kopczewski, O.F.M.; Rudolph Wieszczek, O.F.M.

BORDENTOWN. *Bordentown Correction Center, Burlington County.* Vacant.
Edward R. Johnstone Training and Research Center. Attended from St. Mary's Church, Bordentown, NJ.

BURLINGTON. *Burlington County Hospital & Extended Care Center.* 311 High St., Mount Holly, 08060. Rev. Robert J.W. Schecker.
Burlington County Jail. 260 High St., Mount Holly, 08060. Rev. Robert J.W. Schecker.

NEPTUNE. *Jersey Shore Medical Center* Holy Innocents, P.O. Box 806, 07753. Rev. Douglas U. Hermansen.

NEW LISBON. *New Jersey State Colony* Holy Eucharist, Tabernacle, 08088. Tel: 609-726-1000. Rev. Michael Lang.
Ocean County Jail. Attended by St. Joseph, Toms River.

WAYSIDE. *Monmouth County Jail* 1028 Wayside Rd., 07712. Rev. Robert F. Kaeding.

YARDVILLE. *Garden State Correctional Center.*

Military Installations

COLTS NECK. *Naval Weapons Station Earle.* Rev. Anthony Legarski.
FORT DIX. *Fort Dix.* Vacant.
LAKEHURST. *U.S. Naval Air Warfare Center.* Vacant.
LITTLE SILVER *Fort Monmouth.* Rev. Alfonse M. Arminio.
MCGUIRE AIR FORCE BASE. *McGuire Air Force Base.* Vacant.

On Duty Outside the Diocese:
Reverend Monsignors—
Punderson, Joseph R., Villa Stritch, Via Della Nocetta 63, Rome, 00164 Italy
Reverend Fathers—
Bicomong, Sergio, U.S. Penitentiary, Lewisburg, PA
Campoli, John F., His Love Ministry, P.O. Box 433, Allenhurst, NJ 07711
Fahey, Edward J., Wilmington, DE
Hendricks, John J., Society of St. James the Apostle, 24 Clark St., Boston, MA 02109
Krisak, Anthony F., S.S., 618 East St., N.E., #B, Washington, DC 20002
Kselman, John J., S.S., Weston School of Theology, Three Phillips Pl., Cambridge, MA 02138
LaForge, Joseph M., Newark, DE
McKeone, William

Military Chaplains:
Reverend Fathers—
Flood, Peter J., 2603 Dow Dr., Omaha, NE 68123-1736
Inghilterra, Vincent J.
Liguori, Henry A., 7216 Enterprise Dr., Las Vegas, NV 89117

Leave of Absence:
Reverend Fathers—
Brown, Gerard J.
Chester, Thomas
Christian, John S.
Donadio, Vincent J.
Gallagher, Richard
Iazzetta, Frank J.
Keenan, Eugene
McGrath, Francis
McHugh, Joseph F.
Pienciak, Daniel B.
Russo, John W.
Swift, Daniel

Retired:
Most Rev.—
Reiss, John C., Villa Vianney, 2301 Lawrenceville Rd., Lawrenceville, NJ 08648
Reverend Monsignors—
Bogdan, Henry S., Incarnation Church, 1545 Pennington Rd., Trenton, NJ 08618
Bradley, Paul F., 14 Mark Dr., Long Branch, NJ 07740
Bulman, Robert T., St. Mark's Church, 215 Crescent Pkwy., Sea Girt, NJ 08750
Capitani, Anthony L., 1305 Chambers St., Trenton, NJ 08610
Coffey, Thomas A., Villa Vianney, 2301 Lawrenceville Rd., Lawrenceville, NJ 08648
Constance, Samuel C., Villa Vianney, 2301 Lawrenceville Rd., Lawrenceville, NJ 08648
Endebrock, John J., St. Elizabeth's Church, 424 Lincoln Ave., Avon, NJ 07717
Foley, James S., Morris Hall, 1 Bishop's Dr., Lawrenceville, NJ 08648
Maguire, William E., 9-C Lafayette Dr., Whiting, NJ 08759
O'Connor, Joseph A., Villa Vianney, 2301 Lawrenceville Rd., Lawrenceville, NJ 08648
Strano, Edward, 431 S.E. 3rd St, Apt. 403, Dania, FL 33004
Toomey, Leonard R., Villa Vianney, 2301 Lawrenceville Rd., Lawrenceville, NJ 08648
Valentino, Frederick A., 509 Woodland Ave., Brielle, NJ 08730
Wilus, John M., 225 Walnut St., South Amboy, NJ 08879
Wojciehowski, Thaddeus J., Villa Vianney, 2301 Lawrenceville Rd., Lawrenceville, NJ 08648
Reverend Fathers—
Albano, George M., St. Maximillian Kolbe Church, P.O. Box 4144, Toms River, NJ 08756-4144
Atzert, Edward P., St. Joseph Nursing Center, 1 Bishop Dr., Lawrenceville, NJ 08648
Bausch, William J., Box 1068, Point Pleasant Beach, NJ 08742
Bianchi, Raymond S., Italy
Byrnes, John P., 339 Holiday Lake Dr. E., Holiday, FL 33589
Cammisa, James N., 15 Hastings Pl., Monmouth Beach, NJ 07750
Cervenak, Andrew, Janosikova 21, 08001 Presov, Slovak Republic
Coley, James E., Versaille Apt., 224 Sullivan Way, A5B, Trenton, NJ 08628
Conlon, Arthur F., 201 Nottinghill Ln., Trenton, NJ 08619
Cook, John B., 7777 46th Ave. N., Lot 12, St. Petersburg, FL 33709
Delzell, David G., Tower of David, P.O. Box 292, Uniondale, PA 18470
Dougherty, Edward J., Villa Vianney, 2301 Lawrenceville Rd., Lawrenceville, NJ 08648
Eelman, William C., 171 Lakeshore Dr., Southampton, NJ 08088
Farre, Raymond P., Spain
Horvath, Stephen G., P.O. Box 112, Bushkill, PA 18324
Keane, Vincent E., Villa Vianney, 2301 Lawrenceville Rd., Lawrenceville, NJ 08648
Kearns, Adam, Villa Vianney, 2301 Lawrenceville Rd., Lawrenceville, NJ 08648
Matera, Philip T., 750 Estates Blvd., Apt. 254, Mercerville, NJ 08619
McConnell, James J., Villa Vianney, 2301 Lawrenceville Rd., Lawrenceville, NJ 08648
Miele, Joseph J., 388 Cherry Quay Rd., Brick, NJ 08723-6308
Miller, Joseph B., Marcella Nursing & Rehab, 2305 Rancocas Rd., Burlington Twp., NJ 08916
Petri, John C., 259 Squirrel Ridge Rd., Leasburg, NC 27291
Porazzo, Francis J., 61 Foxglove Rd., Pleasant Plains, Toms River, NJ 08753
Rittenhouse, Thomas R., St. Clement's Church, 172 Freneau Ave., Matawan, NJ 07747
Rucinski, Joseph S., 181 N.E. 14th Ave., Hallandale, FL 33009
Siska, Ernest J., Villa Vianney, 2301 Lawrenceville Rd., Lawrenceville, NJ 08648
Sloyan, Gerard S., 6216 41st Ave., Hyattsville, MD 27082
Sullivan, John E., Villa Vianney, 2301 Lawrenceville Rd., Lawrenceville, NJ 08648
Thompson, James A., 49A Cambridge Cir., Leisure Village West, Lakehurst, NJ 08733

Permanent Deacons:
Alexander, Russell, (Retired), St. Elizabeth Ann Seton, Whiting
Allen, John W., (Retired), St. George, Titusville
Amatelli, Nicholas W., (Retired), St. Barnabas, Bayville
Andre, Edner, Holy Spirit, Asbury Park
Andrews, Stephen W., St. Dorothea, Eatontown
Aquino, Romeo D., St. Joseph's, Toms River
Armstrong, Robert B., St. Mary, Barnegat
Auleta, Michael A., Holy Innocents, Neptune
Ayers, Damian, St. Dominic's, Brick
Ayrer, James E., Corpus Christi, Willingboro
Babuschak, Francis J., St. Joseph, Toms River
Bailey, Normand C., St. Rose, Belmar
Baker, Thomas, St. David the King, Princeton Junction
Barbara, Joseph F., Holy Name, Delran
Beauchamps, Jose, St. Mary Cathedral, Trenton
Benedetti, Maurice T., (Retired), St. Paul, Princeton
Billbrough, Joseph C., (Retired), Corpus Christi, Willingboro
Blackwell, M. Darrell, Sacred Heart, Mt. Holly
Boehm, Michael P., Our Lady of Perpetual Help, Maple Shade
Brookes, Edwin H., Jr., St. Peter, Point Pleasant
Byrne, Kevin M., St. James, Pennington
Caponigro, Alfred E., On Duty Outside the Diocese (Arizona)
Card, Joseph A., Our Lady of Perpetual Help, Maple Shade
Carlin, George M., St. Paul, Burlington
Carroll, Joseph D., (Retired), Holy Spirit, Asbury Park
Cartnick, Louis C., St. Justin's, Toms River
Casa, James L., Sacred Heart, Mount Holly
Casey, Keith J., St. Thomas More, Manalapan
Cater, Thomas H., St. Mary of the Lake, Lakewood
Cechulski, Thomas J., St. Veronica, Howell
Chase, Daniel A., Holy Angels, Trenton
Clausen, Peter M., St. Barnabas, Bayville
Clymore, John L., Holy Family, Union Beach

Coccia, Brother Christopher A., On Duty Outside the Diocese (Florida)
Cole, John A., (Retired), Nativity, Fair Haven
Comito, Charles J., St. Theresa, Tuckerton
Cook, Edwin, (Retired), St. Ann, Keansburg
Cook, James P., On Duty Outside the Diocese (Florida)
Cook, John, Sr., St. Peter Claver, Asbury Park
Cortright, William L., On Duty Outside the Diocese (N. Carolina)
Crowley, James, (Retired), St. Agnes Church, Atlantic Highlands
Cummings, James H., St. Barnabas, Bayville
Curria, Richard J., St. James, Pennington
Czarnecki, John W., Sacred Heart, Bay Head
D'Agostino, Anthony J., Our Lady of Sorrows, Mercerville
D'Angelo, Richard V., St. Gregory the Great, Trenton
Daily, Thomas P., St. George, Titusville
DeLuca, Peter J., Our Lady of Good Counsel, Moorestown
DeMauro, Gerald, On Duty Outside the Diocese (New York)
DePaolis, Joseph, St. Leo the Great, Lincroft
Dinella, Roger P., St. David the King, Princeton Junction
Donadieu, Joseph M., Diocesan Office of Communications
Dougherty, James, (Retired), St. Francis of Assisi, Brant Beach
Doyle, Donald P., St. Mary of the Lakes, Medford
Earley, Daniel C., St. Ann, Browns Mills
Eby, Richard, St. Veronica, Howell
Ernst, Henry J., St. Mary, New Monmouth
Ervin, Martin A., Assumption, New Egypt
Finn, Lawrence W., Our Lady of Perpetual Help, Maple Shade
Fiorillo, Joseph A., St. Mary, Barnegat
Fischer, Edward, III, Visitation, Brick
Flanagan, John P., St. Catharine, Holmdel
Fullen, Michael P., Sr., St. Justin, Toms River
Fullen, Peter J., St. Catherine, Holmdel
Fuoco, Joseph R., (Retired), St. Peter, Riverside
Fursman, James David, St. Catherine, Spring Lake
Gallagher, Paul A.
Gallagher, William J., St. Charles Borromeo, Cinnaminson
Galvan, Silverius F., St. Mary of the Lake, Lakewood
Garvey, Thomas J., St. Anthony of Padua, Hightstown
Genovese, Eugene, St. Veronica, Howell
Gerard, John J., (Retired), Ascension, Bradley Beach
Gettlefinger, Robert J., On Duty Outside the Diocese (North Carolina)
Giglio, Frank E., St. Isaac, Jogues, Evesham
Gilchrist, John A., St. John Church, Lakehurst
Glukowsky, Joseph A., St. Gregory the Great, Trenton
Gomez, Victor L., Our Lady of Providence, Neptune
Gooden, Robert, St. John, Lakehurst
Goodrow, Joseph H., On Duty Outside the Diocese (North Carolina)
Grant, John D., St. Alphonsus, Hopewell
Gray, William G., On Duty Outside the Diocese (Indiana)
Gregory, Gabriel, On Duty Outside Diocese (Minnesota)
Gregory, Thomas J., (Retired) Arizona
Groff, Francis W., St. Martha, Point Pleasant
Groffie, John F., St. Gregory the Great, Trenton
Groh, Alfred, On Duty Outside the Diocese (Florida)
Grussler, John R., Holy Cross, Trenton
Gularek, Theodore V., St. Veronica, Howell
Gwiazda, Edward J., St. Isaac Jogues, Marlton
Hambleton, Richard N., St. Mary, Barnegat
Haney, John J., St. Martha, Point Pleasant
Hannawacker, Joseph A., Blessed Sacrament, Trenton
Harbeck, Jay C., Holy Cross, Rumson
Harris, David M., St. Mary, Bordentown
Hauenstein, Richard A., St. Justin, Toms River
Haunes, Ronald J., St. Pius X, Forked River
Hayes, William K., On Duty Outside the Diocese (Virginia)
Heard, William R., Epiphany, Brick Town
Heller, James T., (Retired), St. Pius X, Forked River
Henwood, Gerald V., St. Robert Bellarmine, Freehold
Hepp, Joseph L., St. Anthony of Padua, Hightstown
Herr, Edward R., St. Dorothea, Eatontown
Hilerio, Pedro, Christ the Redeemer, Mount Holly
Hoch, Eugene, St. John Neumann, Mount Laurel
Hoefling, John F., Sacred Heart, Mount Holly
Hooker, George C., (Retired) South Carolina
Hughes, John P., (Retired), St. John Neumann, Mount Laurel
Iadanza, John M., On Duty Outside the Diocese (Florida)
Iglesias, Manuel F., Holy Angels, Trenton
Imholte, Ralph, St. Mary, Colts Neck
Jackson, Frank W., On Duty Outside the Diocese (Florida)
Jennings, Edward F., St. Catharine, Spring Lake
Johnson, George A., St. Mary, Barnegat
Johnston, James G., St. Joan of Arc, Marlton
Jones, Francis A., St. Paul, Burlington
Kelly, James A., Our Lady of Perpetual Help, Highlands
Kennedy, Patrick W., St. Anthony of Padua, Hightstown
Kerr, Ronald J., Sr., St. John, Lakehurst
Kiely, John D., On Duty Outside the Diocese (South Carolina)
Klimaszewski, Norbert J., On Duty Outside the Diocese (Camden)
Klincewicz, John G., Holy Innocents, Neptune
Knipp, Joseph P., Sacred Heart, Riverton
Kole, Gerard J., On Duty Outside the Diocese (Pennsylvania)
Lacey, James A., St. Aloysius, Jackson
Lachance, Paul A., St. Paul, Princeton
Lafond, Robert H., St. Alphonsus, Hopewell
LaMachia, Ralph A., St. Gregory the Great, Hamilton Square
Lambarski, Joseph A., Holy Eucharist, Vincentown
Laurita, Daniel J., On Duty Outside the Diocese (Alabama)
Little, Ronald J., St. Mary of the Lake, Medford
Littlefield, James J., St. Veronica, Howell
Lombardo, Earl H., St. Mary, Barnegat
Lopez, Heriberto, On Duty Outside the Diocese (Florida)
Lydick, Donald E., On Duty Outside the Diocese (Delaware)
Lynch, Joseph A., St. Paul, Princeton
MacCarrick, Donald G., St. Luke, Toms River
MacDonald, Lawrence J., (Retired), On Duty Outside the Diocese (Florida)
Machion, Robert D., Holy Assumption, Roebling
Magee, James D., (Retired)
Maier, Edward, (Retired), St. Martha, Point Pleasant
Malhame, Eugene G., Jr., St. Rose, Belmar
Malloy, Joseph J., Our Lady of Sorrows, Trenton
Manaloris, James A., Holy Name, Delran
Marcello, Salvatore, Holy Angels, Trenton
Martin, Patrick J., St. Mary, Barnegat
Martucci, Anthony R., St. Mary of the Lake, Lakewood
Mattozzi, Guido J., St. Joachim, Trenton
McCabe, John, St. Mary, Deal
McGahran, Andrew R., On Duty Outside the Diocese (North Carolina)
McGann, Francis P., Jr., Our Lady of Good Counsel, Moorestown
McGrath, James, St. Catherine, Holmdel
McHugh, Joseph, Our Lady of Perpetual Help, Maple Shade
McKenna, Francis A., St. Joseph, Toms River
McKenna, Kenneth M., Our Lady of Mt. Carmel, Asbury Park
McKeon, James, St. Gabriel, Marlboro
McNally, Brent G., St. Justin, Toms River
Meyer, Richard G., On Duty Outside the Diocese (Florida)
Meyers, Ronald S., Our Lady of Perpetual Help, Maple Shade
Micali, James Mark, St. Thomas More, Manalapan
Miller, Donald C., (Retired), St. Clement, Matawan
Moir, Gene F., St. Veronica, Howell
Moore, Timothy E., Our Lady of Sorrows, Trenton
Moresco, Edward J., Our Lady of Perpetual Help, Highlands
Mosteller, Herman J., St. Joseph, Beverly
Mullarkey, Michael F., Epiphany, Brick
Murray, William J., Precious Blood Church, Monmouth Beach
Mustillo, Anthony D., St. Catharine, Holmdel
Mylod, Philip J., (Retired), Jersey Shore Medical Center, Neptune
Nimon, Robert R., On Duty Outside the Diocese (Florida)
Nowak, Ronald, Epiphany, Bricktown
O'Brien, Christopher D., St. Joseph, Keyport
O'Brien, Frederick J., Assumption, New Egypt
O'Connor, John P., (Retired), St. Catharine, Spring Lake
O'Donnell, John J., Our Lady Queen of Peace, Hainesport
Olshevski, Stanley R., Corpus Christi, Willingboro
Orkis, Stanley, Holy Eucharist, Vincentown
Owens, Lester J., St. Gabriel's, Marlboro
Pacitti, Albert, Holy Trinity, Long Branch
Palan, Henry N., St. Theresa, Tuckerton
Palsir, James W., St. James, Pennington
Parr, Allan T., Sr., St. Gregory the Great, Trenton
Patton, Joseph R., St. Mary of the Lakes, Medford
Paul, Joseph A., Our Lady of Good Counsel, Moorestown
Pelkowski, Raymond R., St. Benedict, Holmdel
Pennise, Alfred, St. Paul, Burlington
Perez, Rene P., St. Aloysius, Jackson
Perkins, Charles A., St. Joseph, Beverly
Petrauskas, James J., St. Theresa's, Tuckerton
Pierfy, Jeffery, Our Lady of Sorrows, Mercerville
Pirozzi, Neil, St. Gregory the Great, Trenton
Porter, Thomas P., St. Peter, Point Pleasant Beach
Price, Walter L., St. Ann, Browns Mills
Prihoda, Frank J., St. Anthony of Padua, Hightstown
Principato, Michael, St. Catherine, Farmingdale
Provencher, Conrad J., On Duty Outside the Diocese (Pennsylvania)
Purcell, Kyran J., St. Elizabeth Ann Seton, Whiting
Putnam, Harry A., St. Mary, Bordentown
Rainville, Raymond R., St. Agnes, Atlantic Highlands
Ramos, Luis A., St. Mary's Cathedral, Trenton
Rasi, Stephen P., St. Anthony of Padua, Hightstown
Richardson, Gary T., St. Mary, Bordentown
Rider, Joseph H., St. Elizabeth Ann Seton, Whiting
Rivera, Juan A., St. Mary Cathedral, Trenton
Roderique, Raymond O., On Duty Outside the Diocese (Virginia)
Rodriguez, Feliz, On Duty Outside the Diocese (Puerto Rico)
Ross, Michael D., St. Paul's, Princeton
Rowland, James S., On Duty Outside the Diocese (Florida)
Rowley, William R., Sacred Heart, Mt. Holly
Russo, James C., St. Gabriel, Marlboro
Saake, Dennis J., St. Mark, Sea Girt
Sabados, Andrew A., St. Gregory the Great, Hamilton
Sansevere, Stephen A., St. Gabriel, Marlboro
Schwarz, Herbert, St. Benedict, Holmdel
Schwind, Albert, St. Francis of Assisi, Brant Beach
Sciarrotta, Samuel P., St. James Church, Pennington
Seaman, Joseph F., Our Lady of Perpetual Help, Maple Shade
Seaton, George L., On Duty Outside the Diocese (Florida)
Sepich, William S., St. Charles Borromeo, Cinnaminson
Shapiro, David L., St. Justin, Toms River
Shea, Thomas F., St. Mary, Bordentown
Sheehan, Kenneth R., St. Catherine, Middletown
Sherpensky, Frank, St. Ann, Browns Mills
Slavin, Dennis E., Office of Family Life, Trenton
Slee, Louis, Blessed Sacrament, Trenton
Somma, Eugene A., St. Michael, West End
Sowa, Frank J., (Retired), St. Stanislaus, Trenton
Stap, Matthew J., (Retired), St. Joseph, Beverly
Staub, Raymond W., Jr., Assumption, New Egypt
Sulzmann, William P., St. Theresa, Tuckerton
Tarala, Anthony M., (Retired), St. John's, Lakehurst
Tarzy, Barry R., St. Joan of Arc, Marlton
Taylor, Michael A., St. Barnabas, Bayville
Teran, Galo, St. Anthony Claret, Lakewood
Tharp, Robert, Holy Angels, Trenton
Tobin, James R., Sacred Heart, Bay Head
Toolan, James W., St. George, Titusville
Torres, Benito, S.S. Peter & Paul, Trenton
Trani, Eduardo, Christ the Redeemer, Mount Holly
Ulmer, Ronald J., St. Joseph, Beverly
Valentin, Juan E., St. Mary Cathedral, Trenton
Vassallo, John F., Corpus Christi, Willingboro
Vazquez, Emiliano, St. Mary Cathedral, Trenton
Vicari, Salvatore J., Jr., Visitation, Brick Town
Vilches, Arnaldo, Christ the Redeemer, Mount Holly
Vlcej, Robert J., St. Ann's, Keansburg
Vogel, Anthony D., St. Hedwig, Trenton
Voll, Edwin L., Jr., St. Joseph, Toms River
Wallack, Gregory B., St. Justin, Toms River
Walsh, James P., Holy Innocent, Neptune
Walsh, John J., (Retired), St. Thomas More, Manalapan
Wanat, John A., St. Rose of Lima, Freehold
Weller, Caleb J., St. Mary, Colts Neck
White, Edward A., On Duty Outside the Diocese (Washington)
White, Thomas, C. Wagner Youth Correctional Facility, Bordentown
Whitfield, Robert J., On Duty Outside the Diocese (Maryland)
Wilson, William A., St. Gregory the Great, Hamilton Square
Wolfe, Robert A., (Retired), St. Elizabeth Ann Seton, Whiting
Yaccarine, John A., Holy Trinity, Long Branch
Young, Donald A., Our Lady Star of the Sea, Long Branch
Zadworny, Barry J., St. Hedwig, Trenton
Zebrowski, John J., St. Thomas More, Manalapan

INSTITUTIONS LOCATED IN THE DIOCESE

[A] COLLEGES AND UNIVERSITIES

LAKEWOOD. *Georgian Court College*, 900 Lakewood Ave., 08701-2697. Tel: 732-364-2200; Fax: 732-367-3920.
Web site: www.georgian.edu
For a complete listing, refer to the Colleges and Universities section.

[B] HIGH SCHOOLS, DIOCESAN

TRENTON. *Notre Dame High School*, 601 Lawrence Rd., 08648. Tel: 609-882-7900; Fax: 609-882-5723.
E-mail: briley@notredame.k12.nj.us
Web site: www.notredame.k12.nj.us
Mr. Barry Edward Breen, Prin.; Ms. Mary Liz Ivins, Asst. Prin.; Rev. Robert Tynski, Chap..Sisters of Mercy 1; Lay Teachers 76; Students 1,208.

BELMAR. *Saint Rose High School*, 607 Seventh Ave., 07719. Tel: 732-681-2858; Fax: 732-280-2745.
E-mail: mrc@strose.k12.nj.us
Dr. Michele R. Campbell, Ph.D..Students 635; Sisters 6; Lay Teachers 45.

DELRAN. *Holy Cross High School*, 5035 Rte. 130 S., 08075. Tel: 856-461-5400; Fax: 856-764-0806.
E-mail: lyncht@hclance.org
Web site: www.hclance.org
Sisters of I.H.M., Scranton, PA. Mr. Timothy Lynch, Prin. Sisters 2; Lay Teachers 55; Students 943.

HAMILTON. *McCorristin High School*, 175 Leonard Ave., 08610. Tel: 609-586-3705; Fax: 609-586-6584.
E-mail: mchs@mccorristin.pvt.k12.nj.us
Web site: www.mccorristin.pvt.k12.nj.us
Mr. Joseph R. Lemme, Prin..Sisters 2; Brothers 1; Lay Teachers 38; Students 412.

HOLMDEL. *St. John Vianney High School*, 540 Line Rd., 07733. Tel: 732-739-0800; Fax: 732-739-0824.
E-mail: adminoff@sjvhs.com
Web site: www.sjvhs.com
Mr. Joseph F. Deroba, Prin.; Rev. Hector Larrea, Chap..Sisters 1; Lay Teachers 60; Students 935.

NEW MONMOUTH. *Mater Dei High School*, 538 Church St., 07748. Tel: 732-671-9100; Fax: 732-671-9214.
E-mail: mdhstic@aol.com
Web site: www.materdeihs.org
Mr. Frank Poleski, Jr., Prin..Students 402; Lay Teachers 26.

RED BANK. *Red Bank Catholic High School*, 112 Broad St., 07701. Tel: 732-747-1774; Fax: 732-747-1936.
Web site: www.redbankcatholic.com
Mr. Robert Abatemarco, Prin..Sisters 2; Lay Teachers 77; Students 928.

TOMS RIVER. *Monsignor Donovan High School*, 711 Hooper Ave., 08753. Tel: 732-349-8801; Fax: 732-349-8956.
E-mail: egere@mondon.pvt.k12.nj.us
Web site: www.mondon.pvt.k12.nj.us
Mr. Edward Gere, Prin..Priests 1; Sisters 5; Lay Teachers 72; Students 927.

[C] HIGH SCHOOLS, PRIVATE

TRENTON. *Villa Victoria Academy*, 376 W. Upper Ferry Rd., 08628. Tel: 609-882-1700; Fax: 609-882-8421.
E-mail: srlillian@villavictoria.org
Web site: www.villavictoria.org
Upper School, Grades 7-8 (Girls); Grades 9-12 (Girls). Principals: Mrs. Mary Ann Hughes; Sr. Lillian Harrington, M.P.F. Sisters 3; Lay Teachers 16; Students 130.

LINCROFT. *Christian Brothers Academy*, 850 Newman Springs Rd., 07738. Tel: 732-747-1959; Fax: 732-747-1643.
E-mail: adminoff@cbalincroftnj.org
Web site: www.delasalle.org
Bros. Andrew O'Gara, F.S.C., Pres.; Ralph Montedoro, F.S.C., Prin..Priests 1; Brothers 14; Lay Teachers 54; Students 880.

PRINCETON. *Stuart Country Day School of the Sacred Heart.* (Grades 9-12), 1200 Stuart Rd., 08540. Tel: 609-921-2330; Fax: 609-497-0784.
E-mail: asoos@sturat.k12.nj.us
Sr. Francis de la Chapelle, Prin..Lay Teachers 29; Students 134.

[D] INTER-PARISH ELEMENTARY SCHOOLS

TRENTON. *Our Lady's Cathedral Academy*, 31 Chancery Ln., 08618. Tel: 609-393-4493.

MANAHAWKIN. *All Saints Regional Catholic School.* (Grades K-1), 179 S. Main St., 08050. Tel: 609-597-3800; Fax: 609-597-2223.
E-mail: asrc@exit109.com
Sr. Jeanette Daily, Prin..Lay Teachers 8; Total Enrollment 139.

[E] ELEMENTARY SCHOOLS, PRIVATE

TRENTON. *Villa Victoria Academy.* (Grades PreK-6). (Coed), 376 W. Upper Ferry Rd., 08628. Tel: 609-883-5760; Fax: 609-882-8421.
E-mail: mahuges@villavictoria.org
Web site: www.villavictoria.org
Lower School. Mrs. Mary Ann Hughes, Prin. Sisters 1; Lay Teachers 6; Students 140.

PRINCETON. *Stuart County Day School of the Sacred Heart.* (Grades PreK-8), 1200 Stuart Rd., 08540. Tel: 609-921-2330; Fax: 609-497-0784. Mrs. Patricia Schorr, Prin. (PreK-5); Mrs. Tamara Skvir, Prin. (Grades 6-8). Sisters 1; Lay Teachers 55; Students 406.

[F] CATHOLIC CHARITIES, DIOCESE OF TRENTON

TRENTON. *Catholic Charities*, 383 W. State St., P.O. Box 1423, 08607-1423. Tel: 609-394-5181; Fax: 609-695-6978.
E-mail: cctfed@aol.com
Web site: catholiccharitiestrenton.org
Mr. Francis E. Dolan, Exec. Dir.; George Bontcue, Assoc. Exec. Dir., Fiscal Affairs; Barry H. Cole, Ph.D., Assoc. Exec. Dir., Prog. Services; Michael R. Allen, Assoc. Exec. Dir., Community Affairs; Jean Morrow, Dir. Human Resources.

Burlington Behavioral Healthcare Division, 25 Ikea Dr., Westampton, 08060. Tel: 609-267-9339; Fax: 609-267-6655. Frank J. Helverson, Dir.

Mercer Behavioral Healthcare Division, 39 N. Clinton Ave., 08609. Tel: 609-394-9398; Fax: 609-396-8420. Jerome Lindauer, Dir.

Monmouth/Ocean Behavioral Healthcare Division, 36 W. Water St., Toms River, 08753. Tel: 732-505-3113; Fax: 732-747-7590. Robert G. Hodnett, Dir.

Emergency Services Division, P.O. Box 2387, Cinnaminson, 08077. Tel: 856-786-1868; Fax: 856-786-7974. Joyce Campbell, Dir.

Family Development & Child Advocacy Division, 39 N. Clinton Ave., 08609. Tel: 609-394-5157; Fax: 609-394-3010. Services for victims and perpetuators of family violence. Ronald C. Gering, Dir.

Providence House Division, P.O. Box 496, Willingboro, 08046. Tel: 609-871-2003; Fax: 609-835-0774. Services to women and children in danger of physical abuse. Jean Metz, Dir.

Our Lady of Light Chapel, 383 W. State St., Box 1423, 08607-1423. Tel: 609-386-6221; Fax: 609-394-5181.

St. Michael Children's Home, c/o Diocese of Trenton, 701 Lawrenceville Rd., 08648.

[G] DAY CARE CENTERS

LONG BRANCH. *St. John the Baptist Family Center*, 272 Willow Ave., 07740. Tel: 732-229-8905; 229-8527; 571-1003; Fax: 732-571-0280. Day Care and Child Development Center. Children 130.

[H] CARE INSTITUTIONS FOR CHILDREN

TRENTON. *Sister Georgine School*, 544 Chestnut Ave., 08611. Tel: 609-396-5444; Fax: 609-396-0989.
E-mail: srgeorgine@aol.com
Web site: hometown.aol.com/srgeorgine/index.html
For a complete listing, refer to the Special Care Facilities section.

HOPEWELL. *St. Michael's Orphanage and Industrial School* Mailing Address: c/o the Diocese of Trenton, 701 Lawrenceville Rd. Trenton, 08648.
For a complete listing, refer to the Special Care Facilities section.

[I] GENERAL HOSPITALS

TRENTON. *St. Francis Medical Center*, 601 Hamilton Ave., 08629. Tel: 609-599-5000; Fax: 609-695-2744.
E-mail: johnbilik@chi-east.org
Web site: www.sfme-healthytimes.com
For a complete listing, refer to the Hospitals section.

[J] SPECIAL HOSPITALS AND SANATORIA FOR INVALIDS

LAWRENCEVILLE. *Morris Hall/Saint Lawrence, Inc.*, 2381 Lawrenceville Rd., 08648. Tel: 609-896-9500; Fax: 609-895-0242.
E-mail: communityrelations@slrc.org
Web site: www.slrc.org
For a complete listing, refer to the Special Care Facilities section.

Morris Hall/Saint Lawrence, Inc., 1 Bishops' Dr., 08648-2050. Tel: 609-896-0006; Fax: 609-896-8037.
E-mail: info@morrishall.org
Web site: www.morrishall.org
For a complete listing, refer to the Special Care Facilities section.

[K] SPECIALIZED CHILD CARE AGENCIES

RED BANK. *Collier Group Home*, 180 Spring St., 07701. Tel: 732-842-8337; Fax: 732-530-7096.
E-mail: colliersgs@monmouth.com
For a complete listing, refer to the Special Care Facilities section.

WICKATUNK. *Collier Services*, Collier High School, Conover Rd., 07765. Tel: 732-946-4771; Fax: 732-946-3519.
E-mail: info@collierservices.com
Web site: www.collierservices.com
For a complete listing, refer to the Special Care Facilities section.

[L] HOMES FOR AGED

TRENTON. *Cathedral Square Housing, Inc.*, 26 W. Hanover Pl., 08608. Tel: 609-392-1111; Fax: 609-322-4107
For a complete listing, refer to the Special Care Facilities section.

LAWRENCEVILLE. *Morris Hall-Saint Lawrence, Inc.*, 1 Bishops' Dr., 08648-2050. Tel: 609-896-0006; Fax: 609-896-8037.
E-mail: info@morrishall.org
Web site: www.morrishall.org
For a complete listing, refer to the Special Care Facilities section.

[M] MONASTERIES AND RESIDENCES FOR PRIESTS AND BROTHERS

TRENTON. *Villa Vianney* Lawrenceville, 2301 Lawrenceville Rd., P.O. Box 6589, 08648. Tel: 609-219-0177. In res. Most Rev. John C. Reiss; Rev. Msgr. Thomas A. Coffey; Rev. Msgr. Joseph A. O'Connor; Rev. Msgr. Samuel C. Constance; Rev. Msgr. Leonard R. Toomey; Rev. Msgr. Thaddeus J. Wojciehowski; Rev. Msgr. Anthony L. Capitani; Revs. Edward Dougherty; Ernest J. Siska; Adam Kearns; Vincent E. Keane; James J. McConnell; Harry E. Cenefeldt.

BORDENTOWN. *Society of the Divine Word*, 101 Park St., 08505. Tel: 609-298-0549; Fax: 609-298-6014. Very Rev. Martin Padovani, S.V.D., Rector; Revs. Patrick Connor, S.V.D.; Francis Mahon, S.V.D.; Norman R. St. John, S.V.D.; Victor Butler, S.V.D.; Jacques Nyssen, S.V.D.; Joseph Gunning, S.V.D.; Stephen Szmutko, S.V.D.; James Artzer, S.V.D.; Peter Silvester, S.V.D.; Vance Thorne, S.V.D.; Jefferson Pool, S.V.D.; Leo Dusheck, S.V.D.; William Halvey, S.V.D.; Paul Connors, S.V.D.; Bros. Louis Gagnon, S.V.D.; Patrick Hegarty, S.V.D.; James Mullen, S.V.D.; Joseph Hornek, S.V.D.; Robert Zalikowski, S.V.D.

LINCROFT. *Christian Brothers, St. La Salle Auxiliary*, 850 Newman Springs Rd., P.O. Box 238, 07738. Tel: 732-842-4359; Fax: 732-219-1619.
E-mail: cards@dlsaux.org
Web site: dlsaux.org

LaSalle Lincroft, Inc., 850 Newman Springs Rd., 07738. Tel: 732-842-7420. Bro. William Martin, Contact Person. Brothers 3.

De La Salle Hall, Inc., 810 Newman Springs Rd., 07738. Tel: 732-530-9470; Fax: 732-842-6436.
E-mail: bsofsc@hotmail.com
Bro. Stephen Olert, F.S.C., Dir. Brothers Retirement Home. Brothers 3; Lay Staff 40; Patients 25.

La Salle Provincialate Inc., 800 Newman Springs Rd., 07738. Tel: 732-842-7420; Fax: 732-530-3504.
E-mail: bonnielsp@aol.com
Brothers of the Christian Schools. Bro. Michael Corry, F.S.C., Prov.

The Vaugirard Religious & Charitable Trust, 800 Newman Springs Rd., 07738. Tel: 732-842-4359; Fax: 732-219-1619.

MOUNT LAUREL. *Cistercian Monastery of Our Lady of Fatima*, 564 Walton Ave., 08054-9582. Tel: 856-235-1330; Fax: 856-235-9632. Cistercian Fathers. Revs. Lino S. Parente, O.Cist., Prior, (Italy); Anselmo M. Florio, O.Cist.; Maurizio Nicoletti, O.Cist., (Italy); Teclezghi Ucbaghiorghis, O.Cist.

[N] CONVENTS AND RESIDENCES FOR SISTERS

TRENTON. *Monastery of Saint Clare*, 327 S. Broad St., 08608. Tel: 609-392-7673; Fax: 609-392-9233.
Web site: www.poorclare.org/newjersey
Sr. Mary McCourt, O.S.C., Abbess.

Notre Dame Diocesan Convent Lawrenceville. Intercongregational Living, 681 Lawrence Rd., 08648. Tel: 609-406-7437.
E-mail: afulwi@juno.com
Sr. Anne Fulwiler, I.H.M. Tel: 609-406-7400..Sisters 17.

Sisters of St. Francis of Philadelphia, St. Clare Convent, 917 Melrose Ave., 08629. Tel: 609-695-7805; Fax: 609-695-2308.
E-mail: clarecon@bellatlantic.net
Sr. Albert Mary McSwiggin.

HAMILTON SQUARE. *Sisters of St. Francis of Philadelphia*, Franciscan Convent, 24 Shelley Ln., 08690. Tel: 609-588-9076. Sr. Mary Rita Barbernitz.

HARVEY CEDARS. *Maris Stella Retreat House and Summer House*, 7201 Long Beach Blvd., 08008. Tel: 609-494-0499; Fax: 609-494-0499. Sisters of Charity of St. Elizabeth, Convent Station. Sr. Audrey Boettcher, Admin.

HAZLET. *St. Benedict's Convent*, 31 Cresci Blvd., 07730. Tel: 732-264-3553; Fax: 732-264-3553.
E-mail: blarson426@aol.com

WICKATUNK. *Convent of the Sisters of Good Shepherd*, 160 Conover Rd., 07765. Tel: 732-946-7877; 946-7886; Fax: 732-332-1240. Sisters of Good Shepherd of New Jersey. Sisters 11.

[O] CHAPELS

TRENTON. *Our Lady of Light Chapel*, Box 1423, 08607-1423. Tel: 609-386-6221; 394-5181; Fax: 609-695-6978.

LAWRENCEVILLE. *Our Lady of the Rosary Chapel*, 1 Bishops' Dr., 08648-2050. Tel: 609-896-0006; Fax: 609-895-0242.
E-mail: info@morrishall.org
Web site: www.morrishall.org
Located in Morris Hall. Rev. Justin J. Herbst, Chap.

[P] HOUSES OF PRAYER

TRENTON. *Morning Star House of Prayer*, 312 W. Upper Ferry Rd., 08628. Tel: 609-882-2766; Fax: 609-882-2766.
E-mail: psalm106#juno.com
Web site: morningstarprayerhouse.org
Sr. Geraldine Calabrese, M.P.F..Religious Teachers Filippini 2.

MOUNT HOLLY. *Francis House of Prayer*, 39 Springside Rd., 08060.
E-mail: fhop@pics.com
Mailing Address: P.O. Box 392, Rancocas, 08073. Tel: 609-877-0509; Fax: 609-877-5810. Sr. Marcella Springer, S.S.J.

NEPTUNE. *The Upper Room Spiritual Center*, P.O. Box 1104, 07754-1104. Tel: 732-922-0550; Fax: 732-922-3904.
E-mail: upperroom@bytheshore.com
Web site: www.theupper-room.org
Sr. Maureen Christensen, Co-Dir.; Sr. Maureen Conroy, Co-Dir.; Sr. Trudy Ahern, Co-Dir.

[Q] RETREAT HOUSES

ELBERON. *Stella Maris Retreat Center*, 981 Ocean Ave., 07740. Tel: 732-229-0602; Fax: 732-229-8960. Sr. Beatrice Ryan, C.S.J.P., Dir. Sisters of St. Joseph of Peace 2.

HARVEY CEDARS. *Maris Stella*, Sisters Retreat and Vacation Center, 7201 Long Beach Blvd., 08008. Tel: 609-494-0499. Sisters of Charity of St. Elizabeth, Convent Station. Sr. Audrey Boettcher, Admin.

LONG BRANCH. *San Alfonso Retreat House*, 755 Ocean Ave., P.O. Box 3098, 07740. Tel: 732-222-2731; Fax: 732-870-8892.
Web site: www.sanalfonsoretreats.org
Revs. John McGowan, C.SS.R., Rector Dir.; Bernard Power, C.SS.R.; Francis Freel, C.SS.R.; William Collins, C.SS.R.; Dennis Foley, C.SS.R.; Francis Collins, C.SS.R.; Bros. Bernard Colleran, C.SS.R.; Thomas Rochacewicz, C.SS.R.; Sr. Miriam Carmelita Romanelli, S.S.J..Priests 7; Brothers 2; Sisters 1.

SOUTH MANTOLOKING. *St. Joseph by the Sea Retreat House*, 400 Rte. 35 N., 08738. Tel: 732-892-8494.
E-mail: sjbswindy@juno.com
Sr. Donna Gaglioti, M.P.F., Dir..Sisters 2.

[R] PERSONAL PRELATURES

PRINCETON. *Opus Dei*. Prelature of the Holy Cross and Opus Dei, 34 Mercer St., 08540. Tel: 609-497-9448; Fax: 609-497-0906.
Web site: www.opusdei.org
Rev. William G. Shaughnessy.

[S] NEWMAN CENTERS

PRINCETON. *Campus Ministry for the Diocese of Trenton*, Aquinas Institute, Princeton University, 65 Stockton St., 08540. Tel: 609-924-1820; Fax: 609-924-8322.
E-mail: mullelly@princeton.edu
Rev. Thomas J. Mullelly, Dir. & Chap.
Emmaus House, Rider University, 2116 Lawrenceville Rd., Trenton, 08648. Tel: 609-896-0394; Fax: 609-219-9203. Rev. Bruno A. Ugliano, O.S.B., Chap.
Mercer County Community College, 1200 Old Trenton Rd., Hamilton Township, 08690. Tel: 609-896-0394; Fax: 609-219-9203. Rev. Bruno A. Ugliano, O.S.B., Chap.
Bede House, College of New Jersey, 492 Ewingville Rd., Trenton, 08638. Tel: 609-771-9091. Rev. Gabriel Zeis, Chap.
Georgian Court College, Lakewood Ave., Lakewood, 08701. Tel: 732-364-2200. Mrs. Sharon DeSipo, Dir. Campus Ministry.
Monmouth University, Bethlehem House, 16 Beachwood Ave., West Long Branch, 07764. Tel: 732-229-0403. Rev. Frederick W. Jackiewicz, Chap.

[T] MISCELLANEOUS LISTINGS

TRENTON. *The Haitian Community Center*, 31 West Front St., 08608. Tel: 609-394-5693; Fax: 609-394-3276. Rev. Msgr. John K. Dermond, Admin.
Martin House, 802 E. State St., P.O. Box 1025, 08606. Tel: 609-989-1040. Revs. Brian McCormick; William J. McLaughlin.
Martin House Learning Center, 794 E. State St., P.O. Box 1025, 08606. Tel: 609-989-8143; Fax: 609-989-0933.

ASBURY PARK. *Mercy Center, Inc.*, 1106 Main St., 07712. Tel: 732-774-9397; Fax: 732-988-8709.
E-mail: mcyctn@aol.com
Web site: mercycenternj.org
Carol Ann Henry, R.S.M., Dir.

BRICK. *Mid-Life Directions*, 4 Palm Ave., 08723. Tel: 732-255-1239; Fax: 732-255-1239. Sr. Anne Brennan, C.S.J., Contact Person. Purpose: Ministry for personal and spiritual growth specifically for people in midlife and later years.

ELBERON. *Emmaus House*, 80 Norwood Ave., 07740. Tel: 732-229-5834; Fax: 732-870-2538.
E-mail: dwisw1118@aol.com
Sr. Patricia Mary Walsh, O.P., Admin.

LAKEWOOD. *Health and Retirement Planning: Intercommunity Project*, 900 Lakewood Dr., 08701-2697. Tel: 732-364-2200, Ext. 212.
E-mail: jscharf@greynun.org
Web site: www.harpnet.org
Sr. Jean Scharf, G.N.S.H. Purpose: to assist regional participating religious orders in meeting the health care and retirement needs of their members.

LAWRENCEVILLE. *The Foundation of Morris Hall/St. Lawrence, Inc.*, 2381 Lawrenceville Rd., 08648. Tel: 609-896-9500; Fax: 609-895-0242.
Web site: www.slrc.org
Mr. Thomas E. Boyle, CFO & Contact Person.
Morris Hall/St. Lawrence, Inc., 2381 Lawrenceville Rd., 08648. Tel: 609-896-0006. Morris Hall Home for the Aged. Mr. Charles Brennan, Admin.; Rev. Justin J. Herbst, Chap.; Sr. Claire DeStefano, S.S.J., Dir. of Pastoral Care. Bed Capacity 220; Bed Licensure 220.

LINCROFT. *The Bethlehem University Foundation, Inc.*, 800 Newman Springs Rd., 07738. Tel: 212-826-1480. Rev. Msgr. Robert L. Sterns, Chm. Bd.; Bros. David Carroll, F.S.C., Sec.; Gerard Conforti, F.S.C., Treas.
Christian Brothers of Lincroft, NJ, Inc., 850 Newman Springs Rd., 07738. Tel: 732-842-6712. Bro. Edward Cleary, Contact Person & Treas.

MIDDLETOWN. *The Gathering Place*, 130 Bray Ave., 07748. Tel: 732-495-7615; Fax: 732-495-6422.
E-mail: mnoone3161@aol.com
Sr. Margaret Noone, R.S.M., Contact Person. Ministry which promotes systemic change through programs of human development and spiritual growth, with special emphasis on those who are poor.

SWAINTON. *Holy Redeemer Visiting Nurse Agency, Inc.*, 1801 Rte. 9 N., 08210. Tel: 609-465-2082; 800-745-4693; Fax: 609-463-6124.
Web site: www.holyredeemer.com
Terry A. Duncombe, R.N., M.S.H.A., Vice Pres. & Admin. A subsidiary of Holy Redeemer Health System, Inc. Sponsor: Sisters of the Holy Redeemer, C.S.R. A Medicare Certified Home Health Agency serving patients in their own homes. A Medicare Certified Hospice Program providing services for terminally ill patients and their families. Outpatient Rehabilitation.
Atlantic County Office, 701 Rte. 50, Mays Landing, 08330. Tel: 609-625-2200; 800-788-3029; Fax: 609-909-3560.
Ocean County Office, 2214 Rte. 37 E., Toms River, 08753. Tel: 732-288-0868; 800-488-2669; Fax: 732-288-7055.
Holy Redeemer Rehabilitation Center, 1261 Rte. 9 S., Ste. 1, Cape May Court House, 08210. Tel: 609-465-3866; Fax: 609-465-5269.

RELIGIOUS INSTITUTES OF MEN REPRESENTED IN THE DIOCESE

For further details refer to the corresponding bracketed number in the Religious Institutes of Men or Women section.

[0200]—*Benedictine Monks.* (St. Mary's Abbey, Morristown, NJ).—O.S.B.
[0700]—*Saint Joseph's Society of the Sacred Heart.*—S.S.J.
[0030]—*Brothers of the Christian Schools.*—F.S.C.
[0340]—*Cistercian Fathers.* (Cistercian Monastery of Our Lady of Fatima).—O.Cist.
[0480]—*Conventual Franciscans.* (Provs. of the Immaculate Conception & St. Anthony of Padua).—O.F.M.Conv.
[0520]—*Franciscan Friars.* (Prov. of the Most Holy Name of Jesus).—O.F.M.
[0920]—*Oblates of Saint Francis de Sales.* (Wilmington-Philadelphia Prov.).—O.S.F.S.
[0430]—*Order of Preachers (Dominicans).* (Prov. of St. Joseph).—O.P.
[1310]—*Order of the Holy Trinity.*—O.SS.T.
[1070]—*Redemptorist Fathers.* (Baltimore Prov.).—C.SS.R.
[0700]—*Saint Joseph's Society of the Sacred Heart (The Josephites).*—S.S.J.
[0420]—*Society of the Divine Word.*—S.V.D.
[0560]—*Third Order Regular of Saint Francis.* (Prov. of the Most Sacred Heart of Jesus).—T.O.R.

RELIGIOUS INSTITUTES OF WOMEN REPRESENTED IN THE DIOCESE

[1810]—*Bernardine Sisters of Third Order of St. Francis.*—O.S.F.
[2410]—*Congregation of the Marianites of Holy Cross.*—M.S.C.
[1830]—*Contemplative Sisters of the Good Shepherd.*—R.G.S.
[1070-05]—*Dominican Sisters.* (Amityville, NY).—O.P.
[1070-15]—*Dominican Sisters.* (Blauvelt, NY).—O.P.
[1070-18]—*Dominican Sisters.* (Caldwell, NJ).—O.P.
[1070-11]—*Dominican Sisters.* (Sparkhill, NY).—O.P.
[1105]—*Dominican Sisters of Hope.* (Ossining, NY).—O.P.
[1365]—*Franciscan Missionary Sisters of the Infant Jesus.*—F.M.I.J.
[1180]—*Franciscan Sisters of Allegany, NY.*—O.S.F.
[1200]—*Franciscan Sisters of Baltimore.*—O.F.S.
[1470]—*Franciscan Sisters of St. Joseph.* (Hamburg, NY).—F.S.S.J.
[1190]—*Franciscan Sisters of the Atonement (Graymoor).*—S.A.
[1840]—*Grey Nuns of the Sacred Heart.*—G.N.S.H.
[2710]—*Missionaries of Charity.*—M.C.
[3760]—*Order of St. Clare.*—O.S.C.
[]—*Religiose Agostiniane Civitavecchia, Italy.*—A.S.S.E.
[3465]—*Religious of the Sacred Heart of Mary.*—R.S.H.M.
[3430]—*Religious Teachers Filippini.*—M.P.F.
[]—*School Sisters of Notre Dame.* (Wilton, CT).—S.S.N.D.
[2970]—*School Sisters of Notre Dame, Baltimore.* (Province).—S.S.N.D.
[1700]—*School Sisters of the Third Order Regular of St. Francis.* (Bethlehem,PA).—O.S.F.
[]—*Sisters for Christian Community.*—S.F.C.C.
[0590]—*Sisters of Charity of Saint Elizabeth, Convent Station.*—S.C.
[2575]—*Sisters of Mercy of the Americas.* (Merion; New Jersey).—R.S.M.
[3730]—*Sisters of Order of St. Basil the Great.*—O.S.B.M.
[3360]—*Sisters of Providence of Saint Mary of the Woods, IN.*—S.P.
[3830]—*Sisters of Saint Joseph of Brentwood.* (New York).—C.S.J.
[1630]—*Sisters of St. Francis of Penance and Christian Charity.*—O.S.F.
[1650]—*The Sisters of St. Francis of Philadelphia.*—O.S.F.
[3840]—*Sisters of St. Joseph of Carondelet.*—C.S.J.
[3850]—*Sisters of St. Joseph of Chambery.*—C.S.J.
[3893]—*Sisters of St. Joseph of Chestnut Hill, Philadelphia.*—S.S.J.
[3890]—*Sisters of St. Joseph of Peace.*—C.S.J.P.
[1830]—*The Sisters of the Good Shepherd.*—R.G.S.
[1970]—*Sisters of the Holy Family of Nazareth.*—C.S.F.N.
[2110]—*Sisters of the Humility of Mary.*—H.M.
[3480]—*Sisters of the Resurrection.*—C.R.
[1490]—*Sisters of the Third Franciscan Order.* (Syracuse).—O.S.F.
[2170]—*Sisters, Servants of the Immaculate Heart of Mary.* (Philadelphia).—I.H.M.
[2160]—*Sisters, Servants of the Immaculate Heart of Mary.* (Scranton).—I.H.M.
[4060]—*Society of the Holy Child Jesus.*—S.H.C.J.
[4070]—*Society of the Sacred Heart.*—R.S.C.J.

NECROLOGY

† Clancy, Frederick J., (Retired). —Died Jan.4, 2000.

† McManimon, Rev. Msgr. James, Lawrenceville, NJ Morris Hall. —Died Aug. 31, 2000.

† Procaccini, Joseph J., Allentown, NJ St. John. —Died Feb. 17, 2000.

Diocese of Tucson

(Dioecesis Tucsonensis)

ESTABLISHED A VICARIATE-APOSTOLIC 1868.

ERECTED BY HIS HOLINESS POPE LEO XIII, MAY 8, 1897.

Square Miles 42,707.

Comprises the Counties of Cochise, Gila, Greenlee, Graham, La Paz, Pima, Pinal, Santa Cruz and Yuma in the State of Arizona.

For legal titles of parishes and diocesan institutions, consult the Chancery Office.

Most Reverend

MANUEL D. MORENO, D.D.

Bishop of Tucson; ordained April 25, 1961; appointed Titular Bishop of Tanagra and Auxiliary of Los Angeles December 20, 1976; consecrated February 19, 1977; appointed Bishop of Tucson January 12, 1982. *Res., 192 S. Stone Ave., Box 31, Tucson, AZ, 85702.*

Chancery Office: 192 S. Stone Ave., Box 31, Tucson, AZ, 85702. Tel.: 520-792-3410.

Web site address: www.azstarnet.com/~rccdot

E-mail address: rccchan@azstarnet.com

E-mail address: rccdot@azstarnet.com

STATISTICAL OVERVIEW

Personnel	
Bishop	1
Priests: Diocesan Active in Diocese	78
Priests: Active Outside Diocese	7
Priests: Retired, Sick or Absent	30
Number of Diocesan Priests	115
Religious Priests in Diocese	66
Extern Priests in Diocese	30
Ordinations:	
Diocesan Priests	3
Permanent Deacons in Diocese	121
Total Brothers	10
Total Sisters	250
Parishes	
Parishes	71
With Resident Pastor:	
Resident Diocesan Priests	57
Resident Religious Priests	12
Without Resident Pastor:	
Administered by Priests	1
Administered by Women Religious	1
Missions	30
Professional Ministry Personnel:	
Brothers	8
Sisters	106
Welfare	
Catholic Hospitals	3
Total Assisted	363,129
Health Care Centers	1
Total Assisted	36,803
Special Centers for Social Services	1
Total Assisted	400,000
Other Institutions	1
Total Assisted	2,500
Educational	
Diocesan Students in Other Seminaries	13
Total Seminarians	13
High Schools, Diocesan and Parish	4
Total Students	1,664
High Schools, Private	2
Total Students	209
Elementary Schools, Diocesan and Parish	19
Total Students	5,244
Elementary Schools, Private	2
Total Students	241
Catechesis/Religious Education:	
High School Students	3,588
Elementary Students	19,805
Total Students Under Catholic Instruction	30,764
Teachers in the Diocese:	
Priests	4
Brothers	2
Sisters	47
Lay Teachers	400
Vital Statistics	
Receptions into the Church:	
Infant Baptism Totals	7,127
Adult Baptism Totals	366
Received into Full Communion	753
First Communions	6,244
Confirmations	3,021
Marriages:	
Catholic	951
Interfaith	270
Total Marriages	1,221
Deaths	2,535
Total Catholic Population	304,060
Total Population	1,348,371

Former Bishops—Most Rev. JOHN BAPTIST SALPOINTE, D.D., ord. December 21, 1851; appt. Vicar Apostolic of Arizona and Titular Bishop of Doryla Sept. 25, 1868; ord. June 20, 1869; appt. Coadjutor Archbishop of Santa Fe with right of succession April 12, 1884 and Titular Archbishop of Anazarba Oct. 3, 1884; succeeded to the See of Santa Fe July 18, 1885; resigned; appt. titular Archbishop of Tomi Jan. 27, 1894; died Tucson, July 15, 1898.—Most Rev. PETER BOURGADE, D.D., ord. Nov. 30, 1869; appt. Vicar Apostolic of Arizona Jan. 23, 1885 and Titular Bishop of Thaumacum Feb. 7, 1885 and ordained May 1, 1885; appt. first Bishop of Tucson May 10, 1897; appt. fourth Archbishop of Santa Fe Jan. 7, 1899; died Chicago, May 17, 1908.—Most Rev. HENRY REGIS GRANJON, D.D., ord. Dec. 17, 1887; appt. second Bishop of Tucson April 19, 1900; ord. June 17, 1900; died Brignais, France, Nov. 9, 1922.—Most Rev. DANIEL JAMES GERCKE, D.D., ord. June 1, 1901; appt. third Bishop of Tucson June 21, 1923; ord. Nov. 6, 1923; resigned; appt. Titular Archbishop of Cotyaeum Oct. 26, 1960; died Tucson, March 19, 1964.—Most Rev. FRANCIS JOSEPH GREEN, D.D., ord. May 15, 1932; appt. Titular Bishop of Serra in Proconsulari and Auxiliary Bishop of Tucson May 29, 1953; cons. Sept. 17, 1953; appt. Coadjutor "cum jure successionis" May 11, 1960; succeeded to See to become fourth Bishop of Tucson Oct. 26, 1960; retired July 28, 1981; died May 11, 1995.

Vicar General—Rev. Msgr. ARSENIO S. CARRILLO, V.G.

Vicar General/Moderator of the Curia—Rev. VAN A. WAGNER, V.G.

Episcopal Vicar—Vacant.

Chancery Office—*192 S. Stone Ave., P.O. Box 31, Tucson, 85702.* Tel: 520-792-3410.

Secretary and Chancellor—Mrs. JUNE KELLEN, Office: *192 S. Stone Ave., Tucson, 85701.* Tel: 520-792-3410. Rev. ALBERT E. VERBRUGGHE, Vice Chancellor.

Fiscal Manager Office—Mrs. MARY HUERSTEL, CFO; Ms. TERESA POLASHEK, Asst. Mgr. DAVID KNIGHT, Senior Staff Acct., *P.O. Box 31, Tucson, 85702.* Tel: 520-792-3410.

Matrimonial Tribunal—Office: *192 S. Stone Ave., P.O. Box 31, Tucson, 85702.* Tel: 520-792-3410.

Judicial Vicar—Rev. ALBERT E. VERBRUGGHE, M.A., M.B.A., S.T.D., LL.D., J.C.D., Advocate of the Roman Rota.

Adjutant Judicial Vicar—Rev. JOHN P. LYONS, J.D., J.C.L.

Promoter of Justice—Rev. BRYAN SHERRY, J.C.L.

Judges—Rev. Msgr. THOMAS CAHALANE; Revs. RONALD GAGNON; JOSEPH KRAUSE; TODD O'LEARY.

Defenders of the Bond—Revs. MICHAEL BUCCIARELLI; CHARLES KNAPP; MICHAEL STALLINGS.

Advocates and Auditors—Revs. CHARLES CLOUD; JAMES HOBERT; Deacon OSCAR MAGALLANES; Revs. KEVIN ARNOLD; CHARLES ASHLEY; JOHN J. BRADY; DONALD DE GROOD; RICHARD COSGROVE; CHARLES ELLIOTT; JOHN HAAS; LUIS KAME; VINCENT LACSAMANA; THOMAS MCHUGH; MICHAEL MURRAY; GERALD SWEENEY; MORTON SWEENEY.

Auditors, Notaries, Secretaries—CLARA MORENO; HELEN EVANS.

Professional Consultant—STEPHEN J. SCHILTZ, M.S.W.

Finance Council—Ex Officio: Most Rev. MANUEL D. MORENO, D.D.; Rev. Msgr. ARSENIO CARRILLO, V.G.; Rev. VAN A. WAGNER, V.G., Moderator of the Curia; Mrs. MARY HUERSTEL, CFO. O.F.C. Members: ALEX ACOSTA; JOAN DONNELLY; DAVID KNUTTINEN; HUMBERTO LOPEZ; LAWRENCE MCDONOUGH; MARK MISTLER; Revs. JOHN P. LYONS, J.D., J.C.L.; JOSEPH A. LOMBARDO.

Investment Sub-Committee—MARY HUERSTEL; TERESA POLASHEK; DAVID KNUTTINER; THOMAS FEENEY; Rev. JOHN P. LYONS, J.D., J.C.L.

Audit Committee—JOHN GIRVIN, Chm. MARY HUERSTEL.

Catholic Foundation for the Diocese of Tucson—Most Rev. MANUEL D. MORENO, D.D., Chm.; Sr. BARBARA ANN STOWASSER, C.S.J., Past Pres. ELENA B.B. D'AUTREMONT, Pres. DONNA BYERS, Treas. WILLIAM STOUT, Sec.; Hon. JOSEPH HOWARD, Vice Pres. Members: BERNARD J. SULLIVAN, M.D.; Rev. JOSEPH A. LOMBARDO; Sr. JANET BURKHARD, H.M.; MARTIN CAMACHO; GINNY CLEMENTS; BRUNO DISPOTO; ANNE DICKSON; FRANK J. FELIX; CHARLES MAHN; Rev. FLOYD G. STROMBERG; ERNEST NEDDER; DANIEL QUIGLEY; WILLIAM STARR.

Catholic Relief Services—MARGUERITE HARMON, Diocesan Dir., *155 W. Helen, Tucson, 85705.* Tel: 520-623-0344.

Diocesan Consultors—Rev. Msgr. ARSENIO S. CARRILLO, V.G.; Rev. Msgr. RICHARD O'KEEFFE; Revs. VAN A. WAGNER, Vicar Gen. and Moderator of the Curia; MICHAEL BUCCIARELLI; RAUL TREVIZO; JOHN P. LYONS, J.D., J.C.L.

Council of Priests—Most Rev. MANUEL D. MORENO, D.D.; Rev. Msgr. ARSENIO S. CARRILLO, V.G.; Rev. Msgr. THOMAS CAHALANE; Rev. Msgr. RICHARD W. O'KEEFFE; Revs. JOHN P. LYONS, J.D., J.C.L.; RAYMOND RATZENBERGER; MARTIN MARTINEZ; RAUL TREVIZO; DOMENICO C. PINTI; REMIGIO "MIGUEL" MARIANO; MAXIMILIAN HOTLE, O.F.M.; MICHAEL R. BUCCIARELLI; MARCOS VELASQUEZ; EDWARD RYLE; VAN A. WAGNER, V.G., Moderator of the Curia; ALBERT E. VERBRUGGHE, Judicial Vicar & Vice Chancellor.

Vicar for Native Americans—Rev. MAXIMILIAN HOTTLE, O.F.M.

Clergy Health—Rev. EDWARD C. CARSCALLEN.

Ministry to Priests Program—Rev. EDWARD C. CARSCALLEN, Spiritual Dir., *221 C. Paseo Tierra, Green Valley, 85614*. Tel: 520-625-4330. Members: Revs. PAUL H. ROSALES; JAMES M. HOBERT; FLOYD STROMBERG; PAUL LAROCQUE; JEFFREY THUERAUF.

Vicar for Religious—Rev. CYPRIAN KILLACKEY, O.C.D., *Santa Cruz Parish, 1220 S. 6th Ave., P.O. Box 2830, Tucson, 85702*. Tel: 520-623-3833; Fax: 520-624-2833.

Vicar for Priests—Rev. JAMES M. HOBERT, *St. Bernard, P.O. Box 3101, Pirtleville, 85626*. Tel: 520-364-2762.

Vicars Forane—Rev. RAYMOND RATZENBERGER, Cochise Vicariate; Rev. MICHAEL R. BUCCIARELLI, Gila-Pinal East Vicariate; Rev. DOMENICO C. PINTI, Graham-Greenlee Vicariate; Rev. JOHN P. LYONS, J.D., J.C.L., Pima-Central Vicariate; Rev. Msgr. THOMAS CAHALANE, Pima-East Vicariate; Rev. RAUL TREVIZO, Pima-South Vicariate; Rev. STEVEN G. STENCIL, Pima-North Vicariate; Rev. MAXIMILIAN HOTTLE, O.F.M., Pima West Vicariate; Rev. MARTIN MARTINEZ, Pinal-West Vicariate; Rev. MARCOS VELASQUEZ, Santa Cruz Vicariate; Rev. Msgr. RICHARD W. O'KEEFFE, Yuma-La Paz Vicariate.

Diocesan Offices and Directors

Archives—DAN BROSNAN, Archivist, *8800 E. 22nd St., Tucson, 85710*. Tel: 520-886-5201; 886-5223.

Board of Education—Ex Officio Members: Most Rev. MANUEL D. MORENO, D.D.; Sr. ROSA MARIA RUIZ, C.F.M.M., Supt. KAY SULLIVAN, Pres.; Dr. JODY COMSTOCK, Vice Pres. ELIZABETH STAFFORD, Sec.

Diocesan Building Committee—Most Rev. MANUEL D. MORENO, D.D., Honorary Chm.; Rev. VAN A. WAGNER, V.G., Moderator of the Curia; JAMES RONSTADT, Chm. BRIAN MCCARTHY, Vice Chm. MARY HUERSTEL, Fiscal; TERESA POLASHEK, Fiscal; LIZ AGUALLO, Sec. LARRY MCGRATH, Property Mgr.; Rev. TODD O'LEARY; ANDREW B. MARUM; HECTOR MARTINEZ; BOB SUAREZ; CAROL E. SCHRADER; PAUL SWIFT; DANIEL RORBACH; Rev. ROBERT THOMAS; PAUL SWIFT.

Cemeteries—Management Firm: Loewen Group. *Holy Hope Cemetery, 3555 N. Oracle Rd., P.O. Box 5158, Tucson, 85703*. Tel: 520-888-0860.

Catholic Chaplain—Rev. EDWARD C. CARSCALLEN. Tel: 520-888-7459.

Our Lady of the Desert Cemetery—2151 S. Avenida Los Reyes, Tucson, 85703. Tel: 520-885-9173.

Desert Vista Cemetery—2151 S. Avenida Los Reyes, Tucson, 85748. Tel: 520-885-9173.

Censor Librorum—Vacant.

Campaign For Human Development—JOANNE WELTER, Dir., *P.O. Box 31, Tucson, 85702*. Tel: 520-792-3410; Fax: 520-792-0291.

Charismatic Renewal Movement—Deacon RICHARD ORNELAS, Liaison; Rev. FRANK G. CADY, Spiritual Dir. Centro de Renovacion Carismatica: SALVADOR GONZALES, Hispanic Speaking Contact, *1748 S. 4th Ave., Tucson, 85713*. Tel: 520-628-1692.

Catholic Schools—Sr. ROSA MARIA RUIZ, C.F.M.M., Supt. JO ANN SAYRE, Asst. Supt., *8800 E. 22nd St., Tucson, 85710*. Tel: 520-886-5204; Fax: 520-886-6481.

Community Relations—FRED ALLISON, Dir., *P.O. Box 31, Tucson, 85702*. Tel: 520-792-3410.

Cursillo Movement—Deacon JOHN KEATING ACKERLEY, Spiritual Dir., *St. Augustine Cathedral, P.O. Box 324, Cortaro, 85652*. Tel: 520-624-6944.

Detention Ministry—BARBARA MATTUS, Coord., *192 S. Stone Ave., P.O. Box 31, Tucson, 85702*. Tel: 520-792-3410, Ext. 333; 326.

Development Services (Annual Appeal, Parish Stewardship)—MARK CESNIK, Interim Dir., *192 S. Stone Ave., P.O. Box 31, Tucson, 85702*. Tel: 520-792-3410.

Ecumenical Commission—Rev. Msgr. THOMAS F. CAHALANE, *1800 S. Kolb Rd., Tucson, 85710*. Tel: 520-747-1321.

Chief Financial Officer—MARY HUERSTEL, *P.O. Box 31, Tucson, 85702*. Tel: 520-792-3410.

Holy Childhood Association—Rev. VAN A. WAGNER, V.G., Dir., *P.O. Box 31, Tucson, 85702*. Tel: 520-792-3410.

Interfaith Council—LAUVER EDIE. Tel: 520-745-9443.

Legion of Decency—Chancery Office, 192 S. Stone Ave., Tucson, 85702.

Diocesan Liturgical Commission—Rev. REMIGIO "MIGUEL" MARIANO, Dir., *192 S. Stone Ave., Tucson, 85701*. Tel: 520-792-3410.

Diocesan Parish Life and Ministry, Regina Cleri Center—REGINA SASSEEN, Dir. MICHAEL BERGER; RUBEN DAVALOS, *8800 E. 22nd St., Tucson, 85710*. Tel: 520-886-5202; Fax: 520-886-6481.

Ministero Shalom—VIDAL HARO, Treas., *P.O. Box 22378, Tucson, 85734*. Tel: 520-889-0411.

Newspaper—"Catholic Vision", KATE HARRISON, Mng. Editor, *P.O. Box 31, Tucson, 85702*. Tel: 520-792-3410; Fax: 520-792-1179.

Office of Due Process—Chancery Office, P.O. Box 31, Tucson, 85702. Tel: 520-792-3410.

Permanent Diaconate Program—Deacon FRANK LAMBERT, Dir., *P.O. Box 31, Tucson, 85702*. Tel: 520-792-3410; 625-2994.

Deacon Formation—Deacon ALFREDO SILVA, Dir., *8800 E. 22nd Ave., Tucson, 85710*. Tel: 520-886-4645.

Priests' Assurance Association—Most Rev. MANUEL D. MORENO, D.D., Pres. Ex Officio; Rev. VAN A. WAGNER, V.G., Sec. & Treas. Directors: Rev. Msgr. ROBERT D. FULLER; Revs. THOMAS MILLANE; DOMENICO C. PINTI; JOHN F. ALLT.

Priests' Placement Advisory Board—All Vicars Forane: Rev. Msgr. RICHARD W. O'KEEFFE; Rev. Msgr. THOMAS CAHALANE; Revs. DOMENICO C. PINTI; MICHAEL R. BUCCIARELLI; RAYMOND RATZENBERGER; RAUL TREVIZO; REMIGIO "MIGUEL" MARIANO; MAXIMILIAN HOTTLE, O.F.M.; MARTIN MARTINEZ; MARCOS VELASQUEZ; JOHN P. LYONS, J.D., J.C.L.; STEVEN G. STENCIL.

Chancellor—Mrs. JUNE KELLEN; Rev. ALBERT E. VERBRUGGHE, Vice-Chancellor.

Episcopal Vicar—Vacant.

Moderator of the Curia—Rev. VAN A. WAGNER, V.G.

Propagation of the Faith—Rev. Msgr. ARSENIO CARRILLO, V.G., Dir. Pro Tem., *P.O. Box 31, Tucson, 85702*. Tel: 520-792-3410.

Property Manager—LARRY MCGRATH, Mgr., Office: *8800 E. 22nd St., Tucson, 85710*. Tel: 520-886-5223; Fax: 520-751-0547.

Real Estate & Future Parish Sites Committee—CAROL SCHRADER, Chm. DAN RORBACH; HECTOR MARTINEZ; Rev. TODD O'LEARY; MARY HUERSTEL; LARRY MCGRATH; LIZ AGUALLO, Sec.

Rural Life Bureau—Box 31, Tucson, 85702. Tel: 520-792-3410.

Tucson Council of Religious—Sr. JEAN CLARE LITTLE, C.S.C., Leadership Team, *1947 E. Adams, Tucson, 85719*. Tel: 520-325-2234.

Vocations—Rev. REMIGIO "MIGUEL" MARIANO, JR., Dir.; Mrs. MARTY HAMMOND, Administrative Asst., *192, S. Stone Ave., P.O. Box 31, Tucson, 85702-0031*. Tel: 520-792-3410, Ext. 106; Fax: 520-792-0291.

[*]Catholic Commission—JIM DOBRY, Pres., *231 W. Smoot Dr., Tucson, 85705.*

Encuentros de Promocion Juvenile—Rev. FRANCISCO MALDONADO, *P.O. Box 444, Tucson, 85702*. Tel: 520-792-3410.

CLERGY, PARISHES, MISSIONS AND PAROCHIAL SCHOOLS

CITY OF TUCSON
(Pima County)

1—ST. AUGUSTINE'S CATHEDRAL (1863), Rev. Francisco Maldonado, Rector; Rev. Msgr. Arsenio S. Carrillo, Vicar General; Rev. Gilbert Malu Musumbu, M.S.P.
Res., 192 S. Stone Ave., 85701. Tel: 520-623-6351; Fax: 520-792-0291.
Catechesis/Religious Programs—Miss Barbara Valenzuela, D.R.E., Tel: 520-624-8627.
Students 747.

2—BLESSED KATERI TEKAKWITHA (1984) (Native American), Revs. Daniel P. McLaughlin, S.T.; Abram E. Dono, S.T.; Bro. David T. Sommer, S.T.
Res., 101 W. 31st St., 85713. Tel: 520-791-7774; Fax: 520-792-0230.
Offices: 507 W. 29th St., Tuscon, 85713.
Catechesis/Religious Programs—Tel: 520-622-5363.
Students 490.
Missions—South Tucson, Pima Co., St. Nicholas Indian Center, 349 W. 31st St., 85713. Tel: 520-622-1654; Tuscon, Pima Co., San Martin, 418 W. 39th St., 85713.; Tucson, Pima Co., Santa Rosa, 2015 N. Calle Central, 85705. Tel: 520-622-3514; Tucson, Pima Co., Cristo Rey, 7500 S. Camino Benem, 85746. Tel: 520-578-0423; Tucson, Pima Co., El Senor de los Milagros, 3410 S. 16th Ave., 85713.; Tuscon, Pima Co., San Ignacio, 785 W. Sahuaro, 85705.; Marana, Pima Co., San Juan Bautista, Yoem Pueblo Sandario Rd., Marana, 85238.

3—CORPUS CHRISTI (1999), Rev. Richard Kingsley.
Res., 300 Tanque Verde Loop, Tuscon, 85748. Tel: 520-751-4235; Fax: 520-751-1304.
Catechesis/Religious Programs—Joey Perdreauville, D.R.E.
Students 90.

4—HOLY FAMILY (1915), Rev. Joseph M. Baker; Deacon Carl Leinfelder.
Res., 338 W. University Blvd., 85705. Tel: 520-623-6773; Fax: 520-623-3578.
Catechesis/Religious Programs—Students 180.
Mission—Tucson, Pima Co., Santa Rosa, 2015 N. Calle, 85705. Tel: 520-622-3514.

5—MISSION SAN XAVIER DEL BAC (1692) (Native American), Rev. David Gaa, O.F.M.; Bros. Michael Bearce, O.F.M.; Martin Ibarra, O.F.M.; John Gibbons, O.F.M. In res., Rev. Walter Holley, O.F.M.
Res., 1950 W. San Xavier Rd., 85746. Tel: 520-294-2624; Fax: 520-294-3438.
School—1980 W. San Xavier Rd., 85746. Tel: 520-294-0628. Sr. Jacqueline Koenig, O.F.M., Prin. Sisters 5; Students 153.
Catechesis/Religious Programs—Tel: 520-294-0628.
Students 174.
Convent—1996 W. San Xavier Rd., 85746. Tel: 520-746-4779.

6—MOST HOLY TRINITY (1975), Rev. Ronald P. Gagnon.
Res., 1300 N. Greasewood, 85745. Tel: 520-622-1300; Fax: 520-620-0977.
Catechesis/Religious Programs—Tel: 520-884-9021.
Students 308.

7—OUR LADY OF FATIMA (1972), Rev. Peter M. McGloin; Deacons Frank S. Lundgren, Jr.; Robert Negrette.
Res., 5969 S. Sorrel Ln., 85746. Tel: 520-883-1717; Fax: 520-883-4669.
Catechesis/Religious Programs—Tel: 520-883-1717.
Students 375.
Mission—Tucson, Pima Co., St. Mary of the Desert, MSC 55 HC 137, P.O. Box 2000, 85735.

8—OUR LADY OF LA VANG (1999) (Vietnamese), Rev. John Tran Gnoc Bich, C.Ss.R.
Mailing Address: 800 S. Tuscon Blvd., Tuscon, 85716. Tel: 520-903-2895.
Res., 8800 E. 22nd St., Tuscon, 85710. Tel: 520-751-2060.
Catechesis/Religious Programs—Students 55.

9—OUR LADY, QUEEN OF ALL SAINTS (1987) (Hispanic), Rev. Floyd G. Stromberg; Deacons Oscar Magallanes; George Rodriguez. In res., Rev. Martin Atanga Baabuge.
Res., 2915 E. 36th St., 85713-4041. Tel: 520-622-8602; Fax: 520-622-4581.
Catechesis/Religious Programs—Maria Rodriguez, D.R.E.
Students 600.

10—OUR MOTHER OF SORROWS (1958), Rev. Msgr. Thomas P. Cahalane; Rev. Charles D. Knapp; Deacons Robert Speers; Thomas Tighe; Paul J. Welsh; Alfredo Silva.
Res., 1800 S. Kolb Rd., 85710. Tel: 520-747-1321; Fax: 520-790-3308.
School—Tel: 520-747-1027; Fax: 520-747-0797. Jean McKenzie, Ed.S., Prin.
Lay Teachers 37; Students 514.
Catechesis/Religious Programs—Laura Stehle, D.R.E.
Students 481.

11—SACRED HEART (1942), Revs. Joseph F. McGowan, O.Carm.; Bradley Peterson, O.Carm.
Res., 601 E. Fort Lowell Rd., 85705. Tel: 520-888-1530; Fax: 520-888-1227.
Catechesis/Religious Programs—Tel: 520-888-3401.
Students 305.

12—ST. AMBROSE (1946), Revs. Dale A. Branson; Abran R. Tadeo; Deacon Henry M. Gamboa.
Res., 300 S. Tucson Blvd., 85716. Tel: 520-622-6749; Fax: 520-882-3057.
School—Tel: 520-882-8678; Fax: 520-624-6853. Jean-Marie Bushell, Prin.
Lay Teachers 30; Students 465.
Catechesis/Religious Programs—Tel: 520-623-2925.
Students 285.

13—St. Cyril of Alexandria (1948), Revs. James R. McCauley, C.S.P.; Gerard P. Tully, C.S.P. In res., Rev. Edward S. Pietrucha, C.S.P.
Mailing Address: 4725 E. Pima St., Tuscon, 85712. Tel: 520-795-1633; Fax: 520-795-1633.
Res., 1722 N. Mountain View Ave., 85712. Tel: 520-795-7640.
School—Tel: 520-881-4240; Fax: 520-795-0325. Mrs. Peggy Guerrero, Prin.
Lay Teachers 26; Students 395.
Catechesis/Religious Programs—Students 404.

14—St. Frances Cabrini (1961), Rev. Msgr. Robert D. Fuller.
Res., 3201 E. Presidio Rd., 85716. Tel: 520-326-7670; Fax: 520-881-8480.
Catechesis/Religious Programs—Tel: 520-795-1110.
Students 130.

15—St. Francis de Sales (1971), Revs. Robert G. Tamminga; Liam Leahy; Alexander M. Mills, O.S.B.; Deacons Frank J. Collura; Charles Girard; Keith Pavlik; Dennis Scalpone; Alvin Crockette; Robert Nevins; William Vigil.
Res., 1375 S. Camino Seco, 85710. Tel: 520-885-5908; Fax: 520-885-3109.
Catechesis/Religious Programs—Marian Gilbert, D.R.E.
Students 866.

16—St. John the Evangelist (1934), Revs. Raul P. Trevizo; Salvador Cazares Haro; Deacons Ernesto Roche; Bernard Minetti; Jose Ojeda; Don Baker; Jose Duarte; Charles Gallegos, Jr. In res., Rev. Armando Garzon-Blanco.
Res., 602 W. Ajo Way, 85713. Tel: 520-624-7409; Fax: 520-740-1145.
School—Dr. Ernestina Fuentes, Prin. Lay Teachers 5; Students 145.
Catechesis/Religious Programs—Sr. Maria Emmanuel Martinez, D.R.E.
Students 950.

17—St. Joseph (1953), Revs. John F. Allt; Frederic F. Curry, Pastor Emeritus; Deacons George Herrick; Leon Mazza; Philip Garcia; Paul Converse; John Broussard; Efren Medrano. In res., Revs. James A. Freeman; Isaac A. Fynn; William (Guillo) Kohler, C.SS.R.
Res., 215 S. Craycroft Rd., 85711. Tel: 520-747-3100; Fax: 520-745-4606.
School—Tel: 520-747-3060. Mrs. Ellen S. Kwader, Prin.; Mrs. Joan McCormick, Vice Prin.
Lay Teachers 28; Students 518.
Catechesis/Religious Programs—Sharon Takerer, D.R.E.
Students 350.

18—St. Margaret's (1951), Revs. Gilbert Levario, O.C.D.; Bernard Perkins, O.C.D. In res., Rev. Kevin McArdle, O.C.D.; Deacon Carlos Gelabert.
Res., 801 N. Grande Ave., 85745. Tel: 520-622-0168; Fax: 520-882-8022. [CEM]
Catechesis/Religious Programs—Tel: 520-622-5982.
Students 469.

19—St. Mark The Evangelist (1999), Rev. Steven G. Stencil; Deacon Anthony R. Miller.
P.O.Box 68650, Tuscon, 85737-0003. Tel: 520-469-7835; Fax: 520-219-6003.
Catechesis/Religious Programs—Students 58.

20—St. Monica (1964), Revs. Fernando L. Manzo; Viliulfo Valderrama; Deacons John Garcia; Don Fisher; Tomas Morales; Eugene Fernandez. In res., Rev. Rafael Gutierrez.
Res., 212 W. Medina, 85706. Tel: 520-294-2694; Fax: 520-295-0339.
Catechesis/Religious Programs—Tel: 520-889-1944.
Students 1,352.

21—Saint Odilia (1965), Revs. Richard E. Troutman; Christopher Orndorff; Deacon George Scherf.
Res. & Mailing Address—7570 Paseo del Norte, 85704. Tel: 520-297-7271; 7272 (Office); Fax: 520-297-6361.
Catechesis/Religious Programs—Students 520.
Mission—Tucson, Pima Co., Santa Catalina, 14380 N. Oracle, 85739-9599. Tel: 520-825-9611; Fax: 520-825-9866. Sr. Carole Ruland, M.H.S.H., Admin.

22—St. Pius X (1969), Rev. Harry Ledwith; Deacons Michael Ammerman; Tom Wagner.
Res., 1800 N. Camino Pio Decimo, 85715. Tel: 520-885-3573; Fax: 520-885-0945.
Catechesis/Religious Programs—Karen Horton, D.R.E.
Students 792.

23—Saints Peter and Paul (1930), Revs. John P. Lyons, J.C.L.; Donald J. Fiedler. In res., Revs. Van A. Wagner, V.G.; James M. Travis.
Res., 1946 E. Lee St., 85719-4337. Tel: 520-327-6015; Fax: 520-318-3918.
School—Tel: 520-325-2431; Fax: 520-881-4690. Sr. Ann Patrick Adams, S.C., Prin.
Sisters of Charity from Seton Hill 2; Lay Teachers 23; Students 533.
Catechesis/Religious Programs—Tel: 520-321-1892.
Students 265.
Convent—1947 E. Adams St., 85719. Tel: 520-325-2234.

24—Santa Cruz (1919), Revs. Cyprian Killackey, O.C.D.; Ignacio Bach, O.C.D.; Fernando Pinto, O.C.D.
Res., P.O. Box 2830, 85702. Tel: 520-623-3833; Fax: 520-903-2742.
School—Tel: 520-624-2093; Fax: 520-624-2833. Donna Gary, Prin.
Lay Teachers 9; Students 201.
Catechesis/Religious Programs—Tel: 520-882-9687.
Students 435.
Missions—Tucson, Pima Co., Our Lady of Guadalupe, 401 E. 31st St., 85713.; Tucson, Pima Co., St. Anthony's Catholic Instruction Center and Capilla, 225 W. 34th St., 85713. Tel: 520-622-8972.

25—St. Elizabeth Ann Seton (1980), Revs. Thomas J. Millane; Michael Martinez; Deacons James L. Burns; Leo Longoria; Alfred Caponigro; William Krueger; Tom Pintar.
Res., 8650 N. Shannon Rd., 85742. Tel: 520-297-7357; Fax: 520-797-8886.
Catechesis/Religious Programs—Tel: 520-297-8150. Roseanne Skapura, D.R.E.
Students 1,370.

26—St. Thomas the Apostle (1984), Rev. Todd O'Leary (Ireland); Deacon Russell F. Kingery. In res., Rev. Timothy J. Howard, S.J.
Res., 5150 N. Valley View Rd., 85718. Tel: 520-577-8780; Fax: 520-577-0441.
Catechesis/Religious Programs—Tel: 520-577-8782; Fax: 520-577-0441. Leslie Schulz-Crist, D.R.E.
Students 686.

27—St. Thomas More Chapel (1999), Revs. Albert Felice-Pace, O.P.; Daniel J. Rolland, O.P. In res., Rev. Robert A. Burns, O.P.
1615 E. 2nd St., Tuscon, 85719. Tel: 520-327-6662; Fax: 520-327-6559.
Catechesis/Religious Programs—Tel: 520-327-6663.
Students 82.

OUTSIDE THE CITY OF TUCSON

Ajo, Pima Co., Immaculate Conception (1916), Rev. Richard J. Rego.
Office: 101 Rocalla, P.O.Box 550, 85321. Tel: 520-387-7049; Fax: 520-387-5817.
Catechesis/Religious Programs—Students 121.

Apache Junction, Pinal Co., St. George (1968), Rev. Martin S. Martinez, Temp. Admin.; Deacon Bill Hughes. In res., Rev. Msgr. Gerald J. Brynda.
Res., 300 E. 16th Ave., 85219. Tel: 480-982-2929; Fax: 480-982-0036.
Catechesis/Religious Programs—Mrs. Stacy Filewicz-Ross, D.R.E.
Students 352.

Benson, Cochise Co., Our Lady of Lourdes (1895), Rev. Raymond Ratzenberger.
Mailing Address: 244 S. Gila, P.O. Box 2198, 85602. Tel: 520-586-3394; Fax: 520-586-3919.
Res., 210 Eighth St., 85602.
Catechesis/Religious Programs—Students 116.

Bisbee, Cochise Co., St. Patrick (1902), Rev. Stanley Nadolny; Deacons Guillermo Lugo; Joseph L. Delgado.
Res., P.O. Box 164, 85603. Tel: 520-432-5753.
Catechesis/Religious Programs—Tel: 520-432-4012.
Students 259.
Mission—Naco, Cochise Co., St. Michael, 2090 W. Martinez, Naco, 85620.

Casa Grande, Pinal Co., St. Anthony of Padua (1932), Revs. Kevin O. Clinch; Gonzalo J. Villegas; Deacons Bill Kinney; Barnabas Radke; Patrick L. Dugan; Ramon G. Garcia.
Res., P.O. Drawer 12335, 85230-2335. Tel: 520-836-0601; Fax: 520-836-2985.
School—Tel: 520-836-7247; Fax: 520-836-7289. Mrs. Mary People, Prin.
Lay Teachers 13; Students 200.
Catechesis/Religious Programs—Students 230.
Missions—Stanfield, Pinal Co., St. Mary, 85230-2335.; Maricopa, Pinal Co., St. Francis de Sales, P.O. Box 368, Maricopa, 85239-0368. Tel: 520-568-4605.

Clifton, Greenlee Co., Sacred Heart (1899), Rev. Raul H. Rosales, Admin.; Deacon Richard A. Gonzalez. In res., Rev. Bernard A. Konda, M.B.A., J.C.D.
Mailing Address: P.O. Box 938, 85533.
Res., 329 Chase Creek, 85533. Tel: 520-865-2285; Fax: 520-865-1128.
Catechesis/Religious Programs—North Cornado Boulevard Parish Center.
Students 83.
Mission—Clifton, Greenlee Co., St. Mary, Third St., P.O. Box 938, 85533. Tel: 520-359-2343.

Coolidge, Pinal Co., St. James (1947) (Hispanic), Rev. Jeffrey P. Thuerauf; Deacons Florentino Tarango; Viviano Leon.
Parish Center—437 W. Wilson Ave., 85228. Tel: 520-723-3063; Fax: 520-723-5137.
Res., 401 W. Wilson Ave., 85228. Tel: 520-723-4672.
Catechesis/Religious Programs—Tel: 520-723-5137.
Students 204.

Douglas, Cochise Co., Immaculate Conception (1907), Revs. Luis N. Chavez; Jose Manuel Munoz.
Mailing Address: P.O. Box 1176, 85607.
Res., 928 C Ave., 85607. Tel: 520-364-8494.
School—Lestonnac Kindergarten and Day Care Center, Tel: 520-364-3956. Sr. Jean Ramirez, O.D.N., Dir.
Sisters of the Company of Mary 4; Lay Teachers 4; Students 60.
Catechesis/Religious Programs—Students 624.
Convent—Tel: 520-364-7658; Fax: 520-364-3645. Sisters of the Company of Mary

St. Luke (1950), Revs. Robert E. Carney; Marco Antonio Basulto Pitol; Deacons Armando Moulinet; Gabe Saspe.
Res., 1211 15th St., 85607. Tel: 520-364-4411; Fax: 520-364-2397.
School—Loretto Central Catholic, 1200 14th St., 85607. Tel: 520-364-5754; Fax: 520-364-7844. Sr. Caridad Sandoval, O.C.D., Prin.
Sisters 6; Lay Teachers 6; Students 295.
Catechesis/Religious Programs—Tel: 520-364-7109.
Students 523.
Convent—Tel: 520-364-7658; Fax: 520-364-3645. Carmelite Sisters of the Most Sacred Heart of Los Angeles, Loretto Convent

Eloy, Pinal Co., St. Helen (1952) (Hispanic), Rev. Martin S. Martinez.
Res., 205 W. 8th St., 85231. Tel: 520-466-7258; Fax: 520-466-0486.
Catechesis/Religious Programs—Tel: 520-466-9422. Sylvia Diaz, D.R.E.
Students 480.

Florence, Pinal Co., Assumption of the Blessed Virgin Mary (1870), Rev. Charles W. Cloud.
Res., P.O. Box 2550, 85232. Tel: 520-868-5940; Fax: 503-961-9145.
Catechesis/Religious Programs—Tel: 520-868-3075.
Students 245.

Globe, Gila Co., Holy Angels (1905), Rev. Michael Bradley; Deacons Frank Castillo; Jim Gersitz; Richard Le Mieux.
Res., 201 S. Broad St., 85501. Tel: 520-425-3137; Fax: 520-425-3136.
School—1300 E. Cedar St., 85501. Tel: 520-425-5703; Fax: 520-425-5704. Sr. Leonie Bracken, Prin. & Admin.
Presentation Sisters 6; Lay Teachers 8; Students 218.
Catechesis/Religious Programs—Students 167.
Convent—Tel: 520-425-2034.

Green Valley, Pima Co., Our Lady of the Valley (1970), Revs. Joseph A. Lombardo; John K. Wangbu; Deacons Pete Grimaldo; Rudy Norieg; James Stotler.
Res., 505 N. La Canada Dr., 85614. Tel: 520-625-4536; Fax: 520-625-1084.
Catechesis/Religious Programs—Sahuarita, 85629. Tel: 520-625-4536.
Students 140.
Mission—Sahuarita, Pima Co., St. Martin de Porres, 15440 Santarital Rd., Sahuarita, 85629. Tel: 520-625-1154. Rev. Michael Shay, S.D.S., Admin.

Hayden, Gila Co., St. Joseph's (1913), Rev. Larry Kasper; Deacon Arnold Moreno.
Res., P.O. Drawer C, 85235. Tel: 520-356-7223.
Catechesis/Religious Programs—Tel: 520-356-7223.
Students 76.

Kearny, Pinal Co., Infant Jesus of Prague (1961), Rev. William A. Taft, Admin.
Res., 501 Victoria Cir., P.O. Box 459, 85237. Tel: 520-363-7205.
Catechesis/Religious Programs—Tel: 520-363-7428.
Students 70.

Mammoth, Pinal Co., Blessed Sacrament (1970) (Hispanic), Sr. Maria Canez, O.P., Admin.
Res., 122 W. Church Dr., P.O. Box 220, 85618-0220. Tel: 520-487-2451.
Catechesis/Religious Programs—Students 185.
Convent—Mammouth. Blessed Sacrament Convent

Marana, Pima Co., St. Christopher's (1954), Rev. Robert A. Hyman.
Res., 12101 Moore Rd., P.O. Box 188, 85653. Tel: 520-682-3035; Fax: 520-682-3035.
Catechesis/Religious Programs—Students 125.

Miami, Gila Co., Our Lady of the Blessed Sacrament (1915), Rev. Jay R. Luczak.
Res., P.O. Drawer E, 85539. Tel: 520-473-3568; Fax: 520-473-3338.
Catechesis/Religious Programs—Students 171.
Missions—Claypool, Gila Co., St. Joseph, 5678 Pineway St., Claypool, 85532.; Roosevelt Lake, Gila Co., St. Theresa.

Morenci, Greenlee Co., Holy Cross (1913), Rev. Raul H. Rosales; Deacon Samuel Fullen, III.
Res. & Mailing Address: 205 Fairbanks Rd., 85540. Tel: 520-865-3183; Fax: 520-865-3183.
Catechesis/Religious Programs—Tel: 520-865-2285; Fax: 520-865-1228.
Students 419.

Nogales, Santa Cruz Co., Sacred Heart (1897), Revs. Marcos C. Velasquez; Juan Carlos Aguirre. In res., Rev. Willard F. Wiesler.
Res., P.O. Box 968, 85628. Tel: 520-287-9221; Fax: 520-287-9224.
Catechesis/Religious Programs—Tel: 520-397-0963; Fax: 520-397-0909.
Students 701.

San Felipe de Jesus (1987), Revs. Antonio A. Ruiz; Jaime E. Lopez.
Mailing Address: P.O. Box 6600, 85628.
Res., 3272 Villa Hermosa, 85621. Tel: 520-761-3100; Fax: 520-281-4380.
Church—1901 N. Jose Gallego Ln., #1, 85621.
Catechesis/Religious Programs—Students 900.

Parker, La Paz Co., Sacred Heart (1950), Rev. Theodore Lobo; Deacon David Gonzales.
Res., 916 11th St., 85344. Tel: 520-669-2502.
Catechesis/Religious Programs—Students 42.
Missions—Poston, Kateri Tekawitha Indian Mission; Wenden, St. John the Baptist; Quartzsite, Queen of Peace.

Patagonia, Santa Cruz Co., St. Theresa (1955), Rev. Michael W. Stallings.
Res., Box 435, 85624. Tel: 520-394-2954; Fax: 520-394-2831.
Catechesis/Religious Programs—Students 72.
Mission—Sonoita, Santa Cruz Co., Our Lady of Angels, Fire Station, Sonoita, 85637.

Payson, Gila Co., Saint Philip the Apostle (1957), Rev. Joseph A. Krause; Sr. Marilita Michalski, O.S.F., Pastoral Min.
Res., 511 S. St. Philip, 85541-5144. Tel: 520-474-2392; Fax: 520-474-9661.
Catechesis/Religious Programs—Tel: 520-474-1269.
Students 99.

Pirtleville, Cochise Co., St. Bernard's (1914), Revs. James M. Hobert, Jr.; Robert E. Carney.
Res., P.O. Box 3101, 85626. Tel: 520-364-2762; Fax: 520-364-2520.
Catechesis/Religious Programs—Tel: 520-364-5994.
Students 115.
Chapels—Double Adobe, Our Lady of La Salette.; Douglas, Sacred Heart.

Rio Rico, Santa Cruz Co., Nativity of Our Lord Jesus Christ (1987), Rev. Frank G. Cady.
Mailing Address: P.O. Box 4024, 85648.
Res., 384 Cancun Corte, 85648. Tel: 520-281-8702; 281-7414.
Catechesis/Religious Programs—Students 207.

Safford, Graham Co., St. Rose of Lima (1937), Rev. Domenico C. Pinti; Deacons Marcello Arbizo; Ralph Duran.
Res., 311 Central Ave., 85546. Tel: 520-428-4920; Fax: 520-428-7186.
Catechesis/Religious Programs—Tel: 520-428-4922.
Students 506.
Missions—Pima, Graham Co., Pima Mission, 28 S. Main, Pima, 85543.; Thatcher, Graham Co., Neuman Center, 528 4th St., Thatcher, 85552.

San Carlos, Gila Co., San Carlos Catholic Mission (1918) (Apache), Rev. Gino L. Piccoli, O.F.M.
Res., P.O. Box 28, 85550. Tel: 520-475-2210; Fax: 520-475-2210.
School—Tel: 520-475-2449; Fax: 520-475-2449.
Sisters 5; Students 165.
Convent—P.O. Box 338, 85550. Tel: 520-475-2460. St. Charles
Mission—Bylas, Graham Co., Blessed Kateri Tekakwitha, Bylas, 85530.

San Luis, Yuma Co., St. Jude Thaddeus, Rev. Julian Sanz; Deacon Jose Manuel Lopez.
22790 S. Hwy 95, P.O. Box 2888, 85349. Tel: 520-627-8011; Fax: 520-627-3916.

San Manuel, Pinal Co., St. Bartholomew (1954), Rev. Michael R. Bucciarelli; Deacon Flavio Sanchez.
Res., 609 Park Pl., Box 607, 85631. Tel: 520-385-4156.
Catechesis/Religious Programs—Students 130.
Convent—313 Avenue A, P.O. Box 32, 85631. Tel: 520-385-4739. Sisters of Notre Dame de Namur
Mission—Oracle, Pinal Co., St. Helen, HCR 1, Box 2000, Oracle, 85623. Tel: 520-896-2708. Revs. Joseph Nietlong; Paul J. Ranft, Pastor Emeritus.

Sierra Vista, Cochise Co., St. Andrew (1959), Revs. Gregory P. Adolf; German Bartolome Vasquez Johnston, O.S.B.; Deacon Fernando Mezquita.
Res., 800 Taylor Dr., N.W., 85635. Tel: 520-458-2925; Fax: 520-452-0235.
Catechesis/Religious Programs—Students 320.
Mission—Whetstone, Cochise Co., Good Shepherd.

Our Lady of the Mountains (1991), Rev. Robert R. Bryerton; Deacons William Merritt; James Schaff; Robert Sadorf.
Res., 1425 Yaqui St., 85650. Tel: 520-378-2720; Fax: 520-378-6825.
Catechesis/Religious Programs—Tel: 520-378-7012.
Students 289.

Solomon, Graham Co., Our Lady of Guadalupe (1891), Rev. John J. Ancharski; Deacon Gilbert O. Martinez.
Res., P.O. Box 147, 85551. Tel: 520-428-0149.
Catechesis/Religious Programs—Students 55.
Mission—San Jose, Graham Co., San Jose.
Mailing Address: P.O. Box 147, 85551.

Somerton, Yuma Co., Immaculate Heart of Mary (1954), Revs. Javier H. Perez; Felipe A. Martinez.
Res., 310 W. Spring St., P.O. Box 597, 85350. Tel: 520-627-2918; Fax: 520-627-2918.
Catechesis/Religious Programs—Tel: 520-627-2244.
Students 702.

Sunsites, Cochise Co., St. Jude Thaddeus (1983), Rev. Bob Brazaskas.
Res., P.O. Box 328, Pearce, 85625. Tel: 520-826-3869; Fax: 520-826-1166.
Catechesis/Religious Programs—Students 70.
Mission—Elfrida, Cochise Co., St. Francis of Assisi, P.O. Box 587, Elfrida, 85610. Tel: 520-642-3879.

Superior, Pinal Co., St. Francis of Assisi Parish (1930), Rev. Augustine Kattady; Deacon Jesus Yanez.
Res., 11 Church Ave., 85273. Tel: 520-689-2250.
Catechesis/Religious Programs—St. Mary's Center, 100 Sunset Dr., 85273. Tel: 520-689-2116.
Students 150.

Tombstone, Cochise Co., Sacred Heart (1880), Rev. John M. Fahey.
Res., P.O. Box 547, 85638. Tel: 520-457-3364; Fax: 520-457-0017.
Catechesis/Religious Programs—Students 45.

Topawa, Pima Co., San Solano Missions - Tohono O'odham Indian Reservation (1908) (Native American). (For office and sacramental records pertaining to Tohono O'odham Indians and mission churches on the reservation, please refer to San Solano Missions at the P.O. Box 210, Topawa, AZ, 85639 address).
Mailing Address: P.O. Box 210, 85639. Tel: 520-383-2350. Revs. Maximilian Hottle, O.F.M.; Thomas Frost, O.F.M.

Tubac, Santa Cruz Co., St. Ann (1987), Rev. Clarke W. Moore.
Mailing Address: P.O. Box 2911, 85646-2911. Tel: 520-398-2646; Fax: 520-398-0155.
Catechesis/Religious Programs—Students 35.
Missions—Amado, Santa Cruz Co., Assumption Chapel; Arivaca, Pima Co., St. Ferdinand, P.O. Box 2911, 85646.

Vail, Pima Co., Shrine of St. Rita in the Desert (1937), Rev. Robert Wicht, S.D.S. In res., Rev. Alan Wagner, S.D.S.
Res., P.O. Box 400, 85641. Tel: 520-762-5363; Fax: 520-762-5967.
Catechesis/Religious Programs—Tel: 520-762-9688.
Students 111.

Willcox, Cochise Co., Sacred Heart (1936), Rev. John Emanuel.
Res., P.O. Box 490, 85644. Tel: 520-384-3432; Fax: 520-384-2851.
Catechesis/Religious Programs—Tel: 520-384-2194.
Students 87.
Missions—San Simon, Cochise Co., Our Lady of Perpetual Help, San Simon, 85605.; Bowie, Cochise Co., Our Lady of Guadalupe, Bowie, 85605.

Yuma, Yuma Co., Immaculate Conception (1866), Rev. Msgr. Richard W. O'Keeffe; Revs. Martin Mannion; Juan Guillen; John P. Arnold; Deacons Mark Nixen; David Sampson.
Res., 509 Ave. B, 85364. Tel: 520-782-7516; Fax: 520-343-0172.
School—501 Ave. B, 85364. Tel: 520-783-5225. Sr. Theresa Feldkamp, O.S.F., Prin.
Franciscan Sisters of Christian Charity 5; Lay Teachers 11; Students 258.
Catechesis/Religious Programs—Tel: 520-783-1324. Mark Nixen, D.R.E.
Students 983.
Missions—Yuma, Yuma Co., Our Lady of Guadalupe, 417 15th Ave., 85364. Tel: 520-376-6707; Wellton, Yuma Co., St. Joseph the Worker, P.O. Box 157, Wellton, 85356. Tel: 520-785-4275. Rev. Msgr. Richard W. O'Keeffe, Admin.; Rev. Tomas G. Munoz.
Convent—500 24th Ave., 85364. Tel: 520-783-5224. Franciscan Sisters of Christian Charity 11.

St. Francis of Assisi (1948), Revs. Patrick Crino; Jason Thueraf; Deacons Paul Muthart; Gary Pasquinelli; Rick Hernandez; Bill McDonald; Rafael Vidal; Arnulfo Carbajal; Francisco Moreno.
Res., 1815 S. 8th Ave., 85364. Tel: 520-782-1875; Fax: 520-329-9479.
School—700 18th St., 85364. Tel: 520-782-1539; Fax: 520-782-0403. Lydia Mendoza, Prin.
Franciscan Sisters of Christian Charity 2; Lay Teachers 11; Students 202.
Catechesis/Religious Programs—Tel: 520-783-7461. Sr. Nancy Perez, D.R.E.
Students 640.

St. John Neumann (1987), Rev. William J. Parenteau.
Res., 11750 S. Mesa Dr., 85367. Tel: 520-342-3544.

Chaplains of Public Institutions

TUCSON. *Arizona Correctional Training Center*. Sr. Joyce M. Blum, F.S.P.A., Chap., Santa Rita Unit, 10000 S. Wilmot Rd., 85777. Detention Ministry, P.O. Box 31, 85702. Tel: 520-792-3410, Ext. 131. Barbara Mattus, Dir.

Arizona Western College. Attended from St. John Newmann Parish, Yuma. 11750 S. Mesa Dr., 85365. Tel: 520-342-3544.

Christ the King Chapel 836 CSG/HC, Davis Monthan Air Force Base, 85707. Tel: 520-750-5411. Rev. Philip S. Llanos, Chap.

Kino Community Hospital 1220 S. Sixth, 85707. Tel: 520-623-3833. 2800 E. Ajo Way, 85713. Rev. Ignacio Bach, O.C.D.

Metropolitan Correctional Complex 8901 S. Wilmont Rd., 85706. Tel: 520-741-3118. Detention Ministry, P.O. Box 31, 85702. Tel: 520-792-3410, Ext. 131. Barbara Mattus, Dir.

St. Joseph's Hospital 350 N. Wilmot Rd., 85732. Tel: 520-296-3211. Rev. Isaac A. Fynn.

St. Mary's Hospital 1601 W. St. Mary's Rd., 85745. Tel: 520-622-5883. Rev. Joseph Saba.

Tucson Medical Center 5301 E. Grant Rd., 85712. Rev. William (Guillo) Kohler, C.SS.R., Chap., Tel: 520-324-1290; Fax: 520-324-1702.

U.S. Veterans Hospital S. Sixth Ave., 85713. Tel: 520-792-1450. Rev. Armando Garzon-Blanco.

Villa Maria 4310 E. Grant Rd., 85712. Tel: 520-323-9351. Rev. Alexander Mills, Chap.

CATALINA. *Arizona Youth Center*. Attended from St. Odilia Parish. Santa Catalina Mission, Catalina Rural Branch, P.O. Box 8601, 85738. Tel: 520-825-9611.

FLORENCE. *Arizona State Prison*. Vacant St. Dismas Chapel, P.O. Box 550, 85232. Tel: 520-868-5940.

FORT GRANT RURAL STATION. *Fort Grant Training Center* 85632. Revs. John Emanuel; John J. Ancharski.

FORT HUCHUCA. *Fort Huchuca Army Post* 85613. Rev. Patrick H. Mandock, Chap.

SAFFORD. *Conservation Center* Tel: 520-428-0149. Rev. John J. Ancharski.

SOLOMON. *Our Lady of Guadalupe* P.O. Box 147, 85551. Tel: 520-428-1049. Rev. John J. Ancharski.

WILLCOX. *Federal Prison Camp* 85546. Tel: 520-428-6600. Rev. John Emanuel.

YUMA. *MCAS Chapel* Marine Corps Air Station, 85369. Tel: 520-341-2087. Rev. Stephen Donohoe, Chap.

Yuma Regional Medical Center. Attended from St. Francis of Assisi. 1815 8th Ave., 85364. Tel: 520-782-1875.

Special Assignment:
Reverend Monsignors—
Carrillo, Arsenio S., Vicar General & Propagation of the Faith, Dir. Pro-Tem, P.O. Box 31, Tucson, AZ 85702. Tel: 520-792-3410
Reverend Fathers—
Carscallen, Edward C., Spiritual Dir. Ministry to Priests & Catholic Cemeteries Chap. Tel: 520-625-4330
Lyons, John P., J.C.L., Adjutant Judicial Vicar
Sherry, Bryan W., J.C.L., Canonical Consultant, 321 Washington Ave., Florence, AZ 85232. Tel: 520-886-3371
Wagner, Van A., Vicar General/Curia Moderator

On Duty Outside the Diocese:
Reverend Fathers—
Bell, Brian T., 56 FW/HC, 13968 W. Shooting Star St., Lake AFB, AZ 85309-1932
Gonzales, Robert A., Pontifical College Josephinum, 7625 N. High St., Columbus, OH 43085
McCarthy, Jeremiah J., Rector, St. John's Seminary, 5012 E. Seminary Rd., Camarillo, CA 93012
Ryle, Edward J., Exec. Dir., c/o Arizona Catholic Conference, 400 E. Monroe St., Phoenix, AZ 85004
Shuppert, William T.J., U.S.N. Dept. of Religious Ministries, PSC 558 Box 3528, FPO, AP, 96375-3528
Underwood, Gary E., U.S.A.F., 22 ARW/HC, 53150 Kansan St., Ste. 122, McConnel AFB, KS 67221-3602

Absent on Leave:
Reverend Monsignors—
Rosensweig, Walter F.
Trupia, Robert C.
Reverend Fathers—
Cocio, Carlos
Coleman, James G.
Gameros, L. Ignacio
Garzon-Blanco, Armando
Maloney, Charles F.
Noriega, Arnoldo
Taylor, Daniel
Teta, Michael J.

Retired:
Reverend Monsignors—
Brynda, Gerald J., 1724 Minnewawa #53, Clovis, CA 93612
Oliver, John A., 1020 W. 1st St., Yuma, AZ 85364
Reverend Fathers—
Carscallen, Edward C., 221 S. Pas Tera C., Green Valley, AZ 85614
Connelly, George R., 826 N. Bellvedere, Tucson, AZ 85711
Costigan, Richard J., 511 W. Helen St., Tucson, AZ 85705
Cote, Gerald M., 5725 W. Box R St., Tucson, AZ 85713
Curry, Frederic F., 870 Natachee, Tucson, AZ 85710
Diehl, Michael C., 6333 Rancho Mission Rd., San Diego, CA 92109
Graff, Robert L., 5464 E. Boston St., Mesa, AZ 85205
Larocque, Paul M., 392 W. Camino del Sonador, Green Valley, AZ 85614
McGrenra, Cornelius D., Laconnell, Aradra, Co. Donegal, Ireland
O'Flannigan, Thomas L., 409 W. Pontiac Dr. #6, Phoenix, AZ 85027
Padilla, Glibert, 3300 N. Paseo del Los Rios, Apt. #6206, Tucson, AZ 85712
Ranft, Paul J., Villa Maria Care Center, 4310 E. Grant Rd., Apt. #3, Tucson, AZ 85712
Rook, Paul, 3521 N. Flowing Wells Rd., Tucson, AZ 85705
Schlueter, Clemens M., P.O. Box 5886, Phoenix, AZ 85010
Whalen, Norman M., P.O. Box 911, San Marcos, TX 78666
Wiesler, Willard F., P.O.Box 968, Nogales, AZ 85628

Permanent Deacons:
Ackerley, John K., St. Augustine Cathedral, Tucson
Adams, Thomas, Our Lady of Lourdes, Benson
Ammerman, Michael D., St. Pius X, Tucson
Arbizo, Marcello A., St. Rose of Lima, Safford
Baker, Don, St. John the Evangelist, Tuscon
Borquez, Henry S., St. Augustine Cathedral, Tucson
Broussard, John O., St. Joseph, Tucson
Bueno, Oscar L., St. Augustine's, Tucson
Burns, James, St. Elizabeth Ann Seton, Tucson
Callie, Albert, Holy Trinity Monastery, St. David
Caponigro, Alfred E., St. Elizabeth Ann Seton
Carbajal, Arnulfo, St. Francis of Assisi, Yuma
Carmona, Salvador, St. Augustine Cathedral, Tuscon
Castelan, George P., Sacred Heart, Tucson
Castillo, Frank R., Holy Angels, Globe
Collura, Frank J., St. Francis de Sales, Tucson
Converse, Paul E., St. Joseph, Tucson
Crockette, Alvin, St. Francis de Sales, Tucson
Delgado, Joseph, St. Patrick,Bisbee
Desmarais, Ronald, Our Lady of Lourdes, Benson
Duarte, Carlos V., St. Francis of Assisi, Yuma
Duarte, Jose, St. John the Evangelist, Tucson
Dugan, Patrick, St. Anthony of Padua, Casa Grande
Duran, Ralph, St. Rose of Lima, Safford
Fernandez, Eugene, St. Monica, Tucson
Fisher, Donald, St. Monica, Tucson
Force, Richard C., Villa Maria de Guadalupe Geriatric Center, Tucson
Fullen, Samuel, Holy Cross, Morenci
Fuller, Leonard L., Development Office, Associate Director
Gallegos, Charles A., St. John the Evangelist, Tucson
Gamboa, Henry W., St. Ambrose, Tuscon
Garcia, John A., St. Monica, Tucson
Garcia, Marcario, Immaculate Heart of Mary, Somerton
Garcia, Philip, St. Joseph, Tucson
Garcia, Ramon, St. Anthony of Padua, Casa Granade
Gaun, George, St. Andrew the Apostle, Sierra Vista
Gelabert, Carlos G., St. Margaret, Tucson
Gersitz, James M., Holy Angels, Globe
Gibbons, John, O.F.M., Mission San Xavier del Bac
Girard, Charles, St. Francis de Sales, Tucson
Glowdowski, Robert
Gonzales, David, Sacred Heart, Parker Dam, CA
Gonzales, Luciano, Jr., Immaculate Conception, Douglas
Gonzales, Richard A., Sacred Heart, Clifton
Gonzales, Robert J., St. Patrick, Bisbee & St. Michael Mission, Naco
Grimaldo, Pedro, Our Lady of the Valley, Green Valley
Hernandez, Nieves, Office of Catholic Chaplain, Yuma
Hernandez, Richard R., St. Francis of Assisi, Yuma
Herrick, George R., St. Joseph's, Tucson
Hughes, William G., St. George, Apache Junction
Jones, William E.
Kingery, Russell, St. Thomas the Apostle, Tucson
Kinney, William, St. Anthony of Padua, Casa Grande
Krueger, William, St. Elizabeth Ann Seton, Tucson
Lambert, Frank, Dir. Diocesan Permanent Diaconate
LaSalle, James F., St. Thomas More Newman Center, Tucson
Leinfelder, Carl, Holy Family, Tucson
LeMieux, Richard, Holy Angels, Globe
Leon, Viviano, St. James, Coolidge
Longoria, Leopoldo "Leo", St. Elizabeth Ann Seton, Tucson
Lopez, Jose, St. Jude Thaddeus Mission, San Luis
Lugo, Guillermo A. (Bill), St. Patrick's, Bisbee
Lundgren, Frank S., Jr., Our Lady of Fatima, Tucson
Magallanes, Oscar, Our Lady, Queen of All Saints, Tucson
Marion, Kenneth, (Retired), Phoenix
Martinez, Carlos C., St. Augustine Cathedral, Tucson
Martinez, Gilbert O., Our Lady of Guadalupe, Solomon
Mazza, Leon S., St. Joseph, Tucson
McDonald, William, St. Francis of Assisi, Yuma
Medrano, Efren, St. Joseph, Tucson
Merritt, William, Our Lady of the Mountains, Sierra Vista
Mezquita, Fernando, St. Andrew the Apostle, Sierra Vista
Milazzo, Mike, St. Andrew the Apostle, Sierra Vista
Miller, Anthony, St. Mark the Evangelist, Tuscon
Minetti, Bernard, St. John the Evangelist, Tucson
Morales, Tomas, St. Monica, Tucson
Moreno, Arnoldo L., St. Joseph, Hayden
Moreno, Francisco, St. Francis of Assisi, Yuma
Moulinet, Armando A., St. Luke's, Douglas
Muthart, Paul, St. Francis of Assisi, Yuma
Negrette, Robert, Our Lady of Fatima, Tucson
Nevins, Robert, St. Francis de Sales, Tucson
Nixen, Mark, Immaculate Conception, Yuma
Noriega, Rudy, Our Lady of the Valley, Green Valley
Ojeda, Jose, St. John the Evangelist, Tucson
Ornelas, Richard, Santa Cruz, Tucson
Pasquinelli, Gary, St. Francis of Assisi, Yuma
Paulus, Raymond V., Sacred Heart, Tucson
Pavlik, Keith F., St. Francis de Sales, Tucson
Pawloski, Chester E., Saints Peter and Paul, Tucson
Pennington, Charles H., St. Cyril of Alexandria, Tucson
Pintar, Thomas, St. Elizabeth Ann Seton, Tucson
Radke, Robert, St. Francis de Sales Mission, Maricopa
Roche, Ernest C., St. John the Evangelist, Tucson
Rodriguez, George M., Our Lady Queen of All Saints, Tucson
Rombach, Lionel E., St. Joseph, Tucson
Sadorf, Robert G., Our Lady of the Mountains, Sierra Vista; Sacred Heart, Tombstone
Saladon, Jerry, St. John Newmann, Yuma
Sampson, David, Immaculate Conception, Yuma
Sanchez, Falvio, St. Bartholomew, San Manuel
Saspe, Gabriel, St. Luke, Douglas
Scalpone, Dennis R., St. Francis de Sales, Tucson
Schaff, James, Our Lady of the Mountains, Sierra Vista
Scherf, George, St. Odilia, Tucson
Schneider, Paul L., Our Mother of Sorrows, Tucson
Silva, Alfredo A., Our Mother of Sorrows, Tucson
Speers, Robert M., Our Mother of Sorrows, Tucson
Stotler, Jim, Our Lady of the Valley, Green Valley
Tarango, Florentino, St. James, Coolidge
Tellez, Frank J., St. Rose of Lima, Safford
Terry, John, Holy Cross, Morenci
Tighe, Thomas P., Our Mother of Sorrows, Tucson
Valenzuela, Carlos, St. Augustine Cathedral, Tucson
Vega, Rodolfo, Sacred Heart, Nogales
Vidal, Rafael, St. Francis of Assisi, Yuma
Vigil, William, St. Francis de Sales, Tucson
Wagner, Thomas, St. Pius X, Tucson
Welsh, Paul J., Jr., Our Mother of Sorrows, Tucson
Williams, Miguel, Immaculate Conception, Yuma
Yanez, Jesus L. "Chuy", St. Francis of Assisi, Superior
Zapata, Jose S., Immaculate Conception, Douglas

INSTITUTIONS LOCATED IN THE DIOCESE

[A] HIGH SCHOOLS

TUCSON. *Salpointe Catholic High School*, 1545 E. Copper St., 85719. Tel: 520-327-6581; Fax: 520-327-8477.
E-mail: president@salpointe.org
Web site: www.salpointe.org
Priory, 1540 E. Glenn St., 85719. Tel: 520-325-1537; Fax: 520-318-4651.
E-mail: www.salpointe.org
Mrs. Ruth Jenson, Prin. Carmelite Order. Revs. Fred Tillolson, O.Carm., Pres.; Thomas Butler, O.Carm.; Foster Hanley, O.Carm.; Brian Henden, O.Carm.; John Malley, O.Carm. Sisters 6; Lay Teachers 78; Students 1,450.

[B] HIGH SCHOOLS, PRIVATE

TUCSON. *Immaculate Heart High School*, 625 E. Magee Rd., 85704. Tel: 520-297-2851; Fax: 520-797-7374.
E-mail: ihhs@azstarnet.com
Web site: www.azstarnet.com/[]ihhs/
Sr. Luisa Sanchez, I.H.M., Prin. Sisters of the Immaculate Heart of Mary 4; Lay Teachers 10; Students 107.

Yuma Catholic High School, 2100 W. 28th St., 85364. Tel: 520-329-4818; Fax: 520-329-4829.
Web site: yumacatholic.org
Mr. John C. Monnig, Ed.D., Prin.; Rev. John F. Friel, O.S.F.S., Pres. Sisters 2; Lay Teachers 4; Students 73.

NOGALES. *Lourdes Catholic School*. (High School), 555 Patagonia Rd., P.O. Box 1865, 85628. Tel: 520-287-5659; Fax: 520-287-2910.
E-mail: bmcfmm@yahoo.com
Web site: wwwasd.com
Sr. Barbara Monsequr, C.F.F.M., Prin.; Rev. Francis McCarthy, O.Carm., Chap. Priests 1; Minim Daughters of Mary Immaculate 4; Lay Teachers 9; Students 100.

[C] ELEMENTARY SCHOOLS, PRIVATE

TUCSON. *Immaculate Heart Academy*, 410 E. Magee Rd., 85704. Tel: 520-297-6672; Fax: 520-297-9152.
E-mail: IHABeth@aol.com
Web site: www.azstarnet.com/~ihhs/
Mrs. Beth Piekarski, Prin. Sisters of the Immaculate Heart of Mary 2; Lay Teachers 24; Students 440.

NOGALES. *Lourdes Catholic School*. (Elementary School), 207 W. Oak St, 85621. Tel: 520-287-5484; Fax: 520-287-6065.
E-mail: lcel@dakotacom.net
Sr. Esther Hugues, C.F.M.M., Prin. Sisters 3; Lay Teachers 7; Students 260.

[D] CATHOLIC COMMUNITY SERVICES

TUCSON. *Catholic Community Service of Southern Arizona, Inc.*, 155 W. Helen, 85703. Tel: 520-623-0344; Fax: 520-770-8514.
E-mail: peghddp@aol.com
Web site: www.ccs-soaz.org
Mailing Address: P.O. Box 5746, 85703. Nancy Holmes, Corp. Board Pres.; Marguerite Harmon, M.S., CEO.

Social Service Agencies: Pima County. (Including City of Tucson), 155 W. Helen St., Box 5746, 85703. Tel: 520-623-0344; Fax: 520-770-8514.
E-mail: peghddp@aol.com
Web site: ccs-soaz.org

Catholic Community Services of Southern Arizona, Inc. Marquerite Harmon, CEO of CCS; Ronald A. Dankowski, Ph.D., Exec. Dir., Catholic Social Svc. of CSS.
St. Nicholas of Myra Adoption Program, 899 N. Wilmot, No. C-4, 85711. Tel: 520-745-8791; Fax: 520-745-8609. Nancy Larison, C.I.S.W., Prog. Dir.
Catholic Community Services of Cochise County, 19 Howell Ave., Bisbee, 85603. Tel: 520-432-2285; Fax: 520-432-2009.
Migration and Refugee Services, 155 W. Helen, P.O. Box 5746, 85703. Tel: 520-623-0344; Fax: 520-770-8556. Loretta Tracy, M.S.W., Admin.
Santa Cruz Project, 2020 S. Sixth Ave., 85713. Tel: 520-623-0344; Fax: 520-770-8578. Sr. M. Teresa Apalategui, O.P., M.S.W., Admin.
Senior Nutricion; Services, P.O.Box 5746, 85705. Tel: 520-624-1562; Fax: 520-519-1303. Ms. Linda Hutchings, M.S.R.D., Admin.
Merilac Lodge and Casa de Crianza, P.O. Box 5746, 85703. Tel: 520-623-0344; Fax: 520-770-8578. Sr. Mary Ann Bogosoff, C.S.A., Dir.
Immigration Counseling Service, 155 W. Helen St., 85703. Tel: 520-623-0344; Fax: 520-770-8578. Rene Franco, Dir.
Field Offices:
Gila County Case Management, 175 E. Cedar St., Globe, 85501. Tel: 520-425-5130; Fax: 520-425-2888. Sherlyn Harris, M.A., C.O.G.
Catholic Community Services in Western Arizona, 690 E. 32nd St., Yuma, 85365. Tel: 520-341-9400; Fax: 520-341-8428. Patrick Fish, M.S.W., Exec. Dir.
Chaplaincy-Pastoral Ministry to Non-Denominational Nursing Homes, 155 W. Helen, 85703. Tel: 520-623-0344; Fax: 520-770-8514. Sr. Carolyn Nicolai, F.S.P., Coord.; Rev. Angelo Mastria, O.Carm., Chap.
Community Outreach Program for the Deaf, 268 W. Adams, 85705. Tel: 520-792-1906; Fax: 520-770-8544. Anne Levy, M.A., Exec. Dir.
Community Living Program, 268 W. Adams, 85705. Tel: 520-792-1906; Fax: 520-770-8544. Sue Henning-Mitchell, B.A., Dir.
Detention Ministry, 155 W. Helen, Box 5746, 85703-0746. Tel: 520-623-0344; Fax: 520-770-8514. Ms. Barbara Mattus, M.A., Dir.
St. Elizabeth of Hungary Out-Patient Clinic, 140 W. Speedway, 85705. Tel: 520-628-7871; Fax: 520-770-8528. Sr. Barbara Anne Stowasser, C.S.J., Exec. Dir.
Mobile Podiatry, Dentures and Eyeglasses Clinic, 140 W. Speedway Blvd., 85705. Tel: 520-628-7871; Fax: 520-770-8528.
Minority Liaison Agencies:
Pio Decimo Neighborhood Center, 848 S. 7th Ave., 85701. Tel: 520-622-2801; Fax: 520-622-4704. Margaret Kish, M.S.W., Exec. Dir.
Project Ayuda, 155 W. Helen, Box 5746, 85703. Tel: 520-623-0344; Fax: 520-770-8568. Adele Zaccagnini, Project Dir.
Valley Center for the Deaf, 3130 E. Roosevelt, Phoenix, 85008. Tel: 602-267-1921; Fax: 602-273-1872. Debra Schneider, Acting Dir.

[E] GENERAL HOSPITALS

TUCSON. *Carondelet Health Network,* 1601 W. St. Mary's Rd., 85745-2682. Tel: 520-622-5833; Fax: 520-620-5483.
E-mail: srsjwillert@carondelet.org
For a complete listing, refer to the Hospitals section.
St. Elizabeth of Hungary Out-Patient Clinic, 140 W. Speedway Blvd., 85705. Tel: 520-628-7871; Fax: 520-205-8461.
E-mail: stelizccs@aol.com
For a complete listing, refer to the Hospitals section.
NOGALES. *Holy Cross Hospital, Inc.* 1171 W. Target Range Rd., 85621. Tel: 520-287-2771; Fax: 520-287-8015.
For a complete listing, refer to the Hospitals section.

[F] MONASTERIES AND RESIDENCES OF PRIESTS AND BROTHERS

TUCSON. *Carmelite Priory,* 1540 E. Glenn St., 85719. Tel: 520-325-1537; Fax: 520-318-4651. Very Revs. William J. Harry, Western Commissary Prov.; John Malley, O.Carm., Former Prior General; Revs. Angelo Mastria, O. Carm., Prior; Frederick Tillotson, O.Carm., Pres.; Roy Conry, O.Carm.; Foster Hanley, O.Carm.; Vernon Malley, O.Carm.; Brian Henden, O. Carm.; Thomas Butler, O.Carm.; Bros. Thomas Conlon, O.Carm.; Rodolfo Conteras, O.Carm.; Rev. Mario Loya, O.Carm. Fathers and Brothers at Salpointe Catholic High School. Priests 9; Brothers 3.
Discalced Carmelite Friars of St. Margaret's, 801 N. Grande Ave., 85745. Tel: 520-622-0168; Fax: 520-882-8022. Revs. Gilbert Levario, O.C.D.; Bernard Perkins, O.C.D.; Kevin McArdle, O.C.D.
Jesuit Community of the Vatican Observatory, 2017 E. Lee St., 85719. Tel: 520-795-9866; Fax: 520-326-0756. Jesuit Residence. Revs. Richard J. Murphy, S.J., Supr.; Richard P. Boyle, S.J.; George V. Coyne, S.J., Dir. Vatican Observatory; Jose G. Funes, S.J.; William R. Stoeger, S.J.; Andrew P. Whitman, S.J.; Bro. Guy Consolmagno, S.J.
Vatican Observatory Foundation. Tel: 520-621-3225; Fax: 520-621-1532.
Offices of The Vatican Observatory, Steward Observatory, The University of Arizona, 85721. Tel: 520-621-3225; Fax: 520-621-1532.
Kino House-Jesuit Fathers of Southern Arizona, 2844 E. 1st St., 85716. Tel: 520-327-7130; Fax: 520-327-7573.
E-mail: cpolzer@goodnet.com
Steward Observatory, University of Arizona. Tel: 520-621-3225.
Regina Cleri Center, 8800 E. 22nd St, 85710. Tel: 520-886-5223. Revs. John Tran Gnoc Bich, C.Ss.R.; Carlos Cocio; James G. Coleman; James Modeen; David Reinders; Albert E. Verbrugghe; Rev. Msgr. Walter F. Rosenzweig. In res. Most Rev. Francis A. Quinn, Bishop Emeritus of Sacramento, Domestic Department. Sisters of the Oblates of St. Martha 4.
Society of the Divine Word House, Eight Tucson Ter., 85745. Tel: 520-622-6545.
CORTARO. *Desert House of Prayer,* 7350 W. Picture Rocks Rd., P.O. Box 570, 85652. Tel: 520-744-3825; Fax: 520-744-0774.
Web site: desertrenewal.org
Rev. Paul Curtin, C.Ss.R., Dir.
ST. DAVID. *Holy Trinity Monastery,* P.O. Box 298, 85630. Tel: 520-720-4642; 720-4016; Fax: 520-720-4202. Benedictines. Revs. Alcuin M. Almasy, O.S.B.; Lawrence M. Fedor, O.S.B.; Henri Capdeville, O.S.B., Prior; Alexander Mills, O.S.B. Professed 7. Benedictine Sisters of Our Lady of Mount Olivet. Perpetually Professed 2.
SONOITA. *The Benedictine Monastery of Erlac in Sonoita,* P.O. Box 534, 85637. Tel: 520-394-2961; Fax: 520-394-2961. Rt. Rev. James R. Straif.

[G] CONVENTS AND RESIDENCES FOR SISTERS

TUCSON. *Benedictine Monastery,* 800 N. Country Club Rd., 85716-4583. Tel: 520-325-6401; Fax: 520-321-4358.
E-mail: osbtucson@juno.com
Web site: www.benedictinesisters.org
Sr. Dawn Annette Mills, O.S.B., Prioress. Sisters 21.
Carondelet Community, 6571 E. Carondelet Dr., 85710-2156. Tel: 520-721-3832. Sisters 3.
Guadalupe Community, 1833 W. St. Mary's Rd., 85745-2653. Tel: 520-620-4944.
E-mail: conventg2@hotmail.com
Sisters 2.
Immaculate Heart Lodge Convent, 410 E. Magee Rd., 85704. Tel: 520-742-5896. Sr. Alice Marie Martinez, I.H.M., Prov. Supr.; Sr. Barbara Ann Gamboa, I.H.M., Supr. Sisters of the Immaculate Heart of Mary 6.
Masmitja Hall Community, 410 E. Magee Rd., 85704. Tel: 520-297-8961. Sr. Blanche M. Felix, Supr. Sisters of the Immaculate Heart of Mary 4.
Immaculate Heart Novititate, 4100 N. Sabino Canyon Rd., 85750-6503. Tel: 520-885-4981; Fax: 520-886-4273. Sisters of the Immaculate Heart of Mary 2.
Immaculate Heart of Mary Provincial House, 4100 N. Sabino Canyon Rd., 85750. Tel: 520-886-4273. Sr. Alice Marie Martinez, I.H.M., Prov. Supr. Sisters of the Immaculate Heart of Mary 2.
Immaculate Heart Religious Center, 35 E. 15th St., 85701. Tel: 520-624-7221. Sr. Vivian Gallegos, I.H.M., Supr. Sisters of the Immaculate Heart of Mary 2.
Maria Community, 1835 W. St. Mary's Rd., 85745-2653. Tel: 520-620-4940. Sisters 11.
Regina Cleri Convent, 8800 E. 22nd St., 85710. Tel: 520-296-9077. Sisters of the Oblates of St. Martha 4.
St. Ann Convent, 4100 Sabino Canyon Rd., 85750. Tel: 520-298-0064. Sr. Yvonne Marie Flore, Supr. Sisters of the Immaculate Heart of Mary 9.
St. Joseph Community, 6569 E. Carondelet Dr., 85710. Tel: 520-721-3816.
Saints Peter and Paul Convent, 1947 E. Adams St., 85719. Tel: 520-325-2234; Fax: 520-881-4690.
E-mail: smugl@juno.com
Sisters of Charity of Seton Hill.
San Xavier Mission, 1950 W. San Xavier Rd., 85746. Tel: 520-294-2624; Fax: 520-294-3438.
Sisters of the Holy Cross, 1947 E. Adams, 85719-4301. Tel: 520-325-2234.
SS. Peter and Paul Convent.
Saint Charles Convent, 355 San Carlos Ave., San Carlos, 85550. Tel: 520-475-2460.
DOUGLAS. *Loretto Convent,* 1200 - 14th St., 85607. Tel: 520-364-7571; Fax: 520-364-7844.
E-mail: lorettoc@frontier.net
Web site: carmelitegeneralate.homestead.com
Sr. Rita Therese, O.C.D.
FLORENCE. *Chapel of the Gila.* (Historical Site), 255 E. 8th St., 85232. Mailing Address: P.O. Box 2550, 85232-0550.
GLOBE. *Holy Angels Convent,* 1300 E. Cedar, 85501. Tel: 520-425-2034.
E-mail: pbvm@theriver.com
Union of the Sisters of the P.B.V.M. 6.
NOGALES. *Our Lady of Lourdes Convent,* P.O. Box 1865, 85628-1865. Tel: 520-287-3377; Fax: 520-287-2910.
E-mail: lmvaldezcfm@yahoo.com
Minim Daughters of Mary Immaculate C.F.M.M. 13.
St. Joseph Convent, 405 N. Carondelet Dr., 85621-2454. Tel: 520-287-7139. Sr. Celia Ma. Ponce, C.F.M.M., Supr. Minim Daughters of Mary Immaculate C.F.M.M. 9.
SOMERTON. *Immaculate Heart of Mary Convent,* P.O. Box 2888, 85340.
SONOITA. *Santa Rita Abbey,* HC 1, Box 929, 85637-9705. Tel: 520-455-5595; Fax: 520-455-5770.
E-mail: mesamaria@juno.com
Web site: www.cistercian-usa.orgls_rita.htn
Cistercian Nuns of the Strict Observance, O.C.S.O. Mother Miriam Pollard, O.C.S.O., Prioress. Solemn Professed 12; Novices 1.
TOPAWA. *St. Catherine Convent,* P.O. Box 209, 85639.
E-mail: topsis@juno.com
Sr. Georgiana Rank, O.S.F., Contact Person, Village Ministry Services. Sisters 4.
YUMA. *Immaculate Conception Convent,* 500 - 24th Ave., 85364. Tel: 520-783-5224. Sisters 9.

[H] RETREAT HOUSES

TUCSON. *Redemptorist Picture Rocks Retreat,* 7101 W. Picture Rocks Rd., 85743. Tel: 520-744-3400; Fax: 520-744-8021.
Web site: DesertRenewal.org
Mailing Address: P.O. Box 569, Cortaro, 85652. Revs. Thomas Santa, C.SS.R., Rector; Thomas Danielsen, C.SS.R.; Patrick Hawk, C.SS.R.; Anthony Smith, C.SS.R.
CORTARO. *Desert House of Prayer,* 7350 W. Picture Rocks Rd., P.O. Box 570, 85652. Tel: 520-744-3825; Fax: 520-744-0774. In res. Revs. John W. Kane, C.Ss.R.; Paul Curtin, C.Ss.R., Dir.
DOUGLAS. *Joshua Retreat Center of the Saylah Corp.,* 1530 23rd St., 85607. Tel: 520-364-4411; Fax: 520-364-2397. Janet E. Fullen, Contact Person.
ST. DAVID. *Holy Trinity Monastery,* P.O. Box 298, 85630. Tel: 520-720-4642; Fax: 520-720-4016.

[I] NEWMAN CENTERS

TUCSON. *University of Arizona.* St. Thomas More Newman Center, 1615 E. 2nd St., 85719. Tel: 520-327-6662; Fax: 520-327-6559.
E-mail: jhn@az.starnet.com
Web site: w3.arizona.edu
Revs. Albert Felice-Pace, O.P., Supr.; Daniel J. Rolland, O.P.; Sr. Diane Bridenbecher, O.P.; Sr. Eileen Hin. In res. Rev. Robert A. Burns, O.P.
CASA GRANDE. *Central Arizona College, Holy Family Newman Center,* P.O. Box 12335, 85230-2335. Tel: 520-836-0601. Rev. Kevin D. Clinch.
DOUGLAS. *Cochise Community College,* St. Luke, 1211 15th St., 85607. Rev. Robert E. Carney, Jr.; Janet Fullen, Admin.; Ray Nadolny, Dir.
THATCHER. *Eastern Arizona Junior College,* 85552. Rev. Domenico C. Pinti, St. Rose of Lima, 311 Central Ave., Tucson. Tel: 520-428-4920. Cecilia Roudeluesh, Pres., Newman Sustaining Board; Linda Hedges, Dir., Newman Assoc.

[J] MISCELLANEOUS LISTINGS

TUCSON. *Carondelet Foundation,* 120 N. Tuscon Blvd., 85716-4740. Tel: 520-319-5000; Fax: 520-326-3494.
E-mail: jannief@aol.com
Jannie Cox Fernandez, F.A.H.P., CEO.
Casa de los Ninos Crisis Center, 1101 N. 4th Ave., 85705. Tel: 520-624-5600; Fax: 520-623-2443.
E-mail: info@casadelosninos.org
Web site: www.azstarnet.com/~casa
Jeanne Landdeck-Sisco, Exec. Dir.; Sr. Kathleen Clark, C.S.J., Founding Dir. Emeritus.
Casa Maria, 401 E. 26th St., 85713. Tel: 520-624-0312. Mr. Brian Flagg, Coord.
Christ Child Society of Tucson, P.O. Box 36212, 85740-6212. Tel: 520-797-6567.
E-mail: barnaclegr@aol.com
June Roberts, Pres.; Mary Rieder, Vice Pres.; Dolores Christensen, Treas.; Shirley Hollaman, Sec.
Diocese of Tucson Catholic Cemeteries. (Sole Corporation), 3555 N. Oracle Rd., 85705. Tel: 520-888-0860; Fax: 520-887-7360.
Diocese of Tucson Catholic Committee on Scouting, 6401 E. Shepherd Hills Dr., 85710-1124. Tel: 520-886-1823; Fax: 520-886-1823.
E-mail: carlwdasse@vtc.net
Web site: www.azstarnet.com/~rccdot/dotscts.html
Dr. Carl W. Dasse, Chm.

Integrated Auxiliaries The Friends of John Paul II Foundation. Dr. S.F. Poray-Tucholski, Pres., 10121 Prairie Hills Cir., Sun City, 85352. Dr. E.J. Bratkowsha-Kendall, Vice Pres. & Treas., 5611 E. Rochridge Dr., Phoenix, 85018. Czeslaw A. Kozdroj, Esq., 10347 Campana Dr., Sun City, 85351. Mrs. Jacquelina M. Poray-Tucholski, 10121 Prairie Hills Cir., Sun City, 85351.

Knights of Columbus, 9019 E. Palms Park Dr., 85715. Tel: 520-886-7609. Mr. John H. Cardellina, Past State Deputy; Mr. Lawrence G. Costanzo, State Deputy, 4536 W. Bobbie Terrace, Glendale, 85306-1505. Tel: 602-843-4457; Fax: 602-543-7878.

Magnificat - Tucson Chapter, 3560 N. Via San Juanito, 85749. Tel: 520-749-0633.
E-mail: LdSweet@erthlink.net
Mrs. L. J. Elizabeth Celenza, Pres. A ministry to Catholic women.

Ministero Shalom, P.O. Box 22378, 85734. Tel: 520-889-0411. Vidal Haro, Tres.

Redemptorist Community Support Charity Trust. (Western Province), 7101 W. Picture Rocks Rd., 85743. Tel: 520-744-3400; Fax: 520-744-8021. Trustees: Revs. Patrick O'Brien, C.SS.R. Tel: 510-562-9740; Stephen Meyer, C.SS.R.; Raymond Maiser, C.SS.R.

Retorno (Marriage Retorno), 4321 N. Ventana Dr., 85750. Tel: 520-722-2931; Fax: 520-722-2152.
E-mail: stogskk@azstarnet.com
Web site: azstarnet.com/~stogskk/rtrnotuc.html
Prayer Retreat for Couples. Contacts: Rev. Patrick O'Brien, C.SS.R. Tel: 510-562-9740; Kathie & Kevin Stogsdill. Tel: 520-722-2391.

St. Nicholas Indian Center, 349 W. 31st St., 85713. Tel: 520-622-1654; Fax: 520-792-0230. Revs. Daniel P. McLaughlin, S.T.; Abram E. Dono, S.T.; Bro. David T. Sommer, S.T.

Society of St. Vincent de Paul, 829 S. 6th Ave., 85701. Tel: 520-628-7837; Fax: 520-624-9102.

HEREFORD. *Our Lady of the Sierras Foundation*, 10310 Twin Oaks Dr., P.O. Box 269, 85615. Tel: 520-378-2950; Fax: 520-378-2950.
E-mail: ourladysierras@theriver.com
Web site: www.ourladyofthesierras.org
Mr. Gerald A. Chouinard, Pres.

ST. DAVID. *San Pedro Valley Center for the Arts*, Holy Trinity Monastery, Box 160, 85630. Tel: 520-720-4009. Patricia J. Don, Contact Person.

[K] DIOCESAN CEMETERIES

TUCSON. *Holy Hope Cemetery and Mausoleum*, Office, 3555 N. Oracle Rd., P.O. Box 5158, 85703. Tel: 520-888-0860. Lowen Group, Admin.; Rev. Edward C. Carscallen, Catholic Chap.

Our Lady of the Desert Cemetery and Mausoleum, Office, 2151 S. Avenida Los Reyes, P.O. Box 5158, 85703. Tel: 520-885-9173.

RELIGIOUS INSTITUTES OF MEN REPRESENTED IN THE DIOCESE

For further details refer to the corresponding bracketed number in the Religious Institutes of Men or Women sections.

[0200]—*Benedictine Monks*.—O.S.B.
[0470]—*The Capuchin Friars*. (Prov. of St. Joseph).—O.F.M.Cap.
[0270]—*Carmelite Fathers and Brothers*. (Prov. of Most Pure Heart of Mary).—O.Carm.
[0350]—*The Cisterian Order of Strict Observance (Trappists)*.—O.C.S.O.
[0360]—*Claretian Missionaries*.—C.M.F.
[1320]—*Clerics of St. Viator*.—C.S.V.
[1330]—*Congregation of the Mission*.—C.M.
[0260]—*Discalced Carmelites*. (Angol-Irish Prov.).—O.C.D.
[0520]—*Franciscan Friars*.—O.F.M.
[0650]—*Holy Ghost Fathers*. (Western Prov.).—C.S.Sp.
[0300]—*Institute of Charity*.—I.C.
[0690]—*Jesuit Fathers and Brothers*. (Western Prov.).—S.J.
[0800]—*Maryknoll*.—M.M.
[0720]—*The Missionaries of Our Lady La Salette*. (Immaculate Heart of Mary Prov.).—M.S.
[0840]—*Missionary Servants of the Most Holy Trinity*.—S.T.
[0910]—*Oblates of Mary Immaculate*.—O.M.I.
[0430]—*Order of Preachers (Dominicans)*.—O.P.
[1030]—*Paulist Fathers*.—C.S.P.
[1070]—*Redemptorist Fathers*. (Oakland Prov.).—C.SS.R.
[1200]—*Society of the Divine Savior*.—S.D.S.
[0420]—*Society of the Divine Word*.—S.V.D.
[1060]—*Society of the Precious Blood*.—C.PP.S.

RELIGIOUS INSTITUTES OF WOMEN REPRESENTED IN THE DIOCESE

[0100]—*Adorers of the Blood of Christ*.—A.S.C.
[0160]—*Augustine Nuns of Contemplative Life*.—O.S.A.
[0233]—*Benedictine Nuns*.—O.S.B.
[0230]—*Benedictine Sisters of Pontifical Jurisdiction*.—O.S.B.
[0370]—*Carmelite Sisters of the Most Sacred Heart of Los Angeles*.—O.C.D.
[0670]—*Cistercian Nuns of the Strict Observance*.—O.C.S.O.
[0700]—*Company of Mary*.—O.D.N.
[1010]—*Congregation of Divine Providence*.—C.D.P.
[0220]—*Congregation of the Benedictine Sisters of Perpetual Adoration of Pontifical Jurisdiction*.—O.S.B.
[0460]—*Congregation of the Sisters of Charity of the Incarnate Word*.—C.C.V.I.
[3710]—*Congregation of the Sisters of St. Agnes*.—C.S.A.
[1920]—*Congregation of the Sisters of the Holy Cross*.—C.S.C.
[1780]—*Congregation of the Sisters of the Third Order of St. Francis of Perpetual Adoration*.—F.S.P.A.
[1070-03]—*Dominican Sisters*.—O.P.
[1070-09]—*Dominican Sisters*.—O.P.
[1070-12]—*Dominican Sisters*.—O.P.
[1070-13]—*Dominican Sisters*.—O.P.
[1070-30]—*Dominican Sisters*.—O.P.
[1140]—*Eucharistic Missionaries of St. Dominic*.—O.P.
[1230]—*Franciscan Sisters of Christian Charity*.—O.S.F.
[1310]—*Franciscan Sisters of Little Falls, Minnesota*.—O.S.F.
[1425]—*Franciscan Sisters of Peace*.—F.S.P.
[2575]—*Institute of the Sisters of Mercy of the Americas*.—R.S.M.
[2675]—*Minim Daughters of Mary Immaculate*.—C.F.M.M.
[2690]—*Mission Catechists of Divine Providence*.—M.C.D.P.
[2720]—*Mission Helpers of the Sacred Heart*.—M.H.S.H.
[]—*Oblates of St. Martha*.—O.S.M.
[3130]—*Our Lady of Victory Missionary Sisters*.—O.L.V.M.
[2970]—*School Sisters of Notre Dame*.—S.S.N.D.
[1680]—*School Sisters of St. Francis*.—S.S.S.F.-O.S.F.
[3580]—*Servants of Mary*.—O.S.M.
[3590]—*Servants of Mary (Servite Sisters)*.—O.S.M.
[0440]—*Sisters of Charity of Cincinnati, Ohio*.—S.C.
[480]—*Sisters of Charity of Leavenworth, Kansas*.—S.C.L.
[0570]—*Sisters of Charity of Seton Hill, Greensburg, Pennsylvania*.—S.C.
[0660]—*Sisters of Christian Charity*.—S.C.C.
[3720]—*Sisters of Notre Dame de Namur*.—S.N.D.deN.
[1705]—*The Sisters of St. Francis of Assisi*.—O.S.F.
[1800]—*Sisters of St. Francis of the Third Order Regular (Williamsville, New York)*.—O.S.F.
[3830-13]—*Sisters of St. Joseph*.—C.S.J.
[3840]—*Sisters of St. Joseph of Carondelet*.—C.S.J.
[0260]—*The Sisters of the Blessed Sacrament for Indians and Colored People*.—S.B.S.
[1030]—*Sisters of the Divine Savior*.—S.D.S.
[2110]—*Sisters of the Humility of Mary*.—H.M.
[2180]—*Sisters of the Immaculate Heart of Mary*.—I.H.M.
[3270]—*Sisters of the Most Precious Blood*.—C.PP.S.
[3260]—*Sisters of the Precious Blood*. (Dayton, Ohio).—C.PP.S.
[3320]—*Sisters of the Presentation of the Blesssed Virgin Mary*.—P.B.V.M.
[1720]—*Sisters of the Third Order Regular of St. Francis of the Congregation of Our Lady of Lourdes*.—O.S.F.
[2150]—*Sisters, Servants of the Immaculate Heart of Mary*. (Monroe).—I.H.M.

NECROLOGY

† Jackson, Donald F., Oracle, AZ St. Helen Mission. —Died Oct. 17, 2000.

Diocese of Tulsa

(Dioecesis Tulsensis)

Most Reverend

EDWARD J. SLATTERY

Bishop of Tulsa; ordained January 6, 1994 in Rome; installed January 12, 1994.

Chancery Office: 12300 E. 91st St., S., Broken Arrow, OK, 74012. Mailing Address: P.O. Box 690240, Tulsa, OK, 74169. Tel.: 918-294-1904; Fax: 918-294-0920.

E-mail address: chantul@aol.com

ESTABLISHED FEBRUARY 7, 1973.

Square Miles 26,417.

The Diocese of Tulsa comprises the following 31 Counties: Adair, Atoka, Bryan, Cherokee, Choctaw, Coal, Craig, Creek, Delaware, Haskell, Hughes, Latimer, LeFlore, McCurtain, McIntosh, Mayes, Muskogee, Nowata, Okfuskee, Okmulgee, Osage, Ottawa, Pawnee, Payne, Pittsburg, Pushmataha, Rogers, Sequoyah, Tulsa, Wagoner and Washington.

For legal titles of parishes and institutions, consult the Chancery Office.

STATISTICAL OVERVIEW

Personnel	
Bishop	1
Priests: Diocesan Active in Diocese	46
Priests: Active Outside Diocese	4
Priests: Retired, Sick or Absent	25
Number of Diocesan Priests	75
Religious Priests in Diocese	20
Ordinations:	
Diocesan Priests	5
Permanent Deacons	1
Permanent Deacons in Diocese	52
Total Brothers	8
Total Sisters	103
Parishes	
Parishes	80
With Resident Pastor:	
Resident Diocesan Priests	46
Resident Religious Priests	5
Without Resident Pastor:	
Administered by Priests	34
Professional Ministry Personnel:	
Brothers	1
Sisters	12
Lay Ministers	55
Welfare	
Catholic Hospitals	2
Total Assisted	237,045
Homes for the Aged	2
Total Assisted	262
Specialized Homes	2
Special Centers for Social Services	2
Total Assisted	4,555
Educational	
Diocesan Students in Other Seminaries	15
Total Seminarians	15
High Schools, Diocesan and Parish	1
Total Students	953
High Schools, Private	1
Total Students	569
Elementary Schools, Diocesan and Parish	10
Total Students	2,359
Elementary Schools, Private	1
Total Students	1,167
Catechesis/Religious Education:	
High School Students	1,500
Elementary Students	5,000
Total Students Under Catholic Instruction	11,563
Teachers in the Diocese:	
Brothers	1
Sisters	4
Lay Teachers	39
Vital Statistics	
Receptions into the Church:	
Infant Baptism Totals	1,157
Adult Baptism Totals	245
Received into Full Communion	314
First Communions	1,190
Confirmations	828
Marriages:	
Catholic	206
Interfaith	214
Total Marriages	420
Deaths	535
Total Catholic Population	62,673
Total Population	1,500,000

Former Bishops—Most Rev. BERNARD J. GANTER, D.D., ord. May 22, 1952; appt. Bishop of Tulsa, Dec. 19, 1972; ord. Feb. 7, 1973; transferred to Beaumont, Oct. 18, 1977.—Most Rev. EUSEBIUS J. BELTRAN, ord. May 14, 1960; appt. Bishop of Tulsa, Feb. 28, 1978; ord. April 20, 1978; transferred to Archdiocese of Oklahoma City, Nov. 24, 1992.

Vicar General—Rev. Msgr. DENNIS C. DORNEY.

Chancery Office—12300 E. 91st St. S., Broken Arrow, 74012., Mailing Address: P.O. Box 690240, Tulsa, 74169. Tel: 918-294-1904; Fax: 918-294-0920. Office Hours: Mon.-Fri. 9-5.

Chancellor—Dr. HENRY L. HARDER, Ph.D.

Vice Chancellor—Rev. PATRICK J. GAALAAS.

Financial Administrator—Mr. PHILIP J. CREIDER, *P.O. Box 690240, Tulsa, 74169.* Tel: 918-294-1904.

Diocesan Senators—Most Rev. EDWARD J. SLATTERY; Rev. Msgr. DENNIS C. DORNEY, V.G.; Revs. J. RICHARD BRADLEY; PATRICK J. GAALAAS; J. PAUL DONOVAN; PAUL E. EICHHOFF; GREGORY A. GIER; DANIEL H. MUEGGENBORG; TAM N. NGUYEN; MICHAEL R.K. ROONEY; JAMES D. WHITE; KENNETH HARDER; MICHAEL SCHWEIFLER, O.S.A.; JOHN J. WADE.

Ex Officio—Rev. Msgr. DENNIS C. DORNEY.

Diocesan Consultors—Revs. J. RICHARD BRADLEY; PAUL E. EICHHOFF; PATRICK J. GAALAAS; JAMES D. WHITE; Rev. Msgr. DENNIS C. DORNEY; Revs. DANIEL H. MUEGGENBORG; TAM N. NGUYEN; JOHN J. WADE.

Diocesan Marriage Tribunal—

Judicial Vicar—Rev. MICHAEL J. KNIPE, J.C.L.

Defender of the Bond—Rev. TAM N. NGUYEN, J.C.L.

Judges—Revs. JOHN J. WADE; MICHAEL J. KNIPE, J.C.L.; JOHN J. MARQUARDT, J.C.D.; Deacon KASPER E. WEIGANT.

Auditor—HENRY L. HARDER, Ph.D.

Notary—Mrs. MARY JONES.

Priests' Personnel Committee—Rev. Msgr. DENNIS C. DORNEY, V.G.; Revs. J. RICHARD BRADLEY; BRYAN V. BROOKS.

Seminary Board—Rev. Msgr. DENNIS C. DORNEY, V.G.; Mr. ROBERT J. LAFORTUNE; Revs. JACK GLEASON; DANIEL H. MUEGGENBORG; JOE C. TOWNSEND; Ms. ANDREA HYATT.

Federation of Religious of the Diocese of Tulsa—Leadership Team: Sr. MARILYN NORWOOD, O.S.B.; Sr. EUGENIA BROWN, O.S.B., *P.O. Box 3204, Tulsa, 74101.* Tel: 918-582-6247.

Diocesan Offices

Archivist—Mrs. MARY JONES, *P.O. Box 690240, Tulsa, 74169.* Tel: 918-294-1904.

Campaign for Human Development—Dr. HENRY L. HARDER, *P.O. Box 690240, Tulsa, 74169.* Tel: 918-294-1904.

Campus Ministry—Rev. DANIEL H. MUEGGENBORG, Chap.; Mrs. SUZIE CURTIN, Dir. Operations; Mr. STEVE NELSON, Campus Ministry, *St. Philip Neri Newman Center at The University of Tulsa, 440 S. Florence, Tulsa, 74104.* Tel: 918-599-0204. Rev. JOE C. TOWNSEND, *201 N. Knoblock St., Stillwater, 74074.* Tel: 405-372-6408., *Oklahoma State University, 201 N. Knoblock St., Stillwater, 74075.* Tel: 405-372-6408.

Catholic Charities of the Diocese of Tulsa—Deacon TIMOTHY SULLIVAN, Dir., *739 N. Denver, Tulsa, 74106.* Tel: 918-585-8167.

Calvary Cemetery—Mr. JAMES LIICHOW, Supvr., *9101 S. Harvard, Tulsa, 74137.* Tel: 918-299-7348.

Clergy Education—Rev. DANIEL H. MUEGGENBORG, *P.O. Box 690240, Tulsa, 74169.* Tel: 918-294-1904.

Diocesan Catholic Committee on Scouting—Mr. GREGG SLIEF, Dir. Tel: 918-588-7379.

Diocesan Council of Catholic Women—PATTY SOMMERHAUSER, *9989 S. 592 Rd., Miami, 74354.* Tel: 918-540-1481.

Ecumenism—Rev. PATRICK J. GAALAAS, Dir., *2200 W. Ithica, Broken Arrow, 74012.*

Education—Ms. MONICA SKRZYPCZAK, Dir. Religious Formation, *P.O. Box 690240, Tulsa, 74169.* Tel: 918-294-1904.

Family Life Office—Deacon TIMOTHY J. SULLIVAN, Dir., *P.O. Box 6429, Tulsa, 74148.*

Parochial Schools—Mrs. ARDEN GLENN, Supt. Catholic Schools, *820 S. Boulder, Tulsa, 74119.* Tel: 918-582-9177; Fax: 918-582-1851.

Health Affairs—Rev. DENIS CASEY, Dir. Pastoral Care & Health Affairs, *6161 S. Yale Ave., Tulsa, 74136.* Tel: 918-494-1140.

Prison and Social Ministry—Rev. BRYAN V. BROOKS, Dir., *P.O. Box 698, Okmulgee, 74447.*

Hispanic Ministry—Revs. PATRICK BRANKIN, Dir. ROBERT M. DYE, Assoc. Dir., *1541 E. Newton Pl., Tulsa, 74106.* Tel: 918-584-2424.

Historian—Rev. JAMES D. WHITE, *P.O. Box 690240, Tulsa, 74169.*

Pastoral Studies Institute—Ms. MONICA SKRZYPCZAK, Coord., *P.O. Box 690240, Tulsa, 74169.* Tel: 918-294-1904.

Office of Divine Worship—Rev. MATTHEW J. GERLACH, Dir., *P.O. Box 690240, Tulsa, 74169.* Tel: 918-294-1904.

Newspaper "Eastern Oklahoma Catholic"—Mr. JAMES SELLARS, Editor, *P.O. Box 690240, Tulsa, 74169.* Tel: 918-294-1904.

Office of Permanent Diaconate—Rev. J. RICHARD BRADLEY, Vicar of Deacons; Sr. MARIE AMANDA ALLARD, O.P., Dir. Formation, *P.O. Box 690240, Tulsa, 74169.* Tel: 918-294-1904.

Propagation of Faith—Rev. MATTHEW J. GERLACH, Co-ord., *P.O. Box 3204, Tulsa, 74101.* Tel: 918-582-6247.

Guatemala Mission—Mikatokla, Santiago Atitlan, Dept. Sololá, Guatemala, Central America; Rev. TOM MC SHERRY.

Stewardship and Development—Mr. CHARLES R. GISLER, Dir., *P.O. Box 690240, Tulsa, 74169.* Tel: 918-294-1904.

Vocations—Rev. JACK GLEASON; Mrs. THERESA WITCHER, Asst., *P.O. Box 690240, Tulsa, 74169.* Tel: 918-294-1904.

Catholic Student Ministries—440 South Florence, Tulsa, 74104. Tel: 918-599-0204.

Young Adult Ministry—Mr. CHARLES MICHIE, *P.O. Box 690240, Tulsa, 74169.* Tel: 918-294-1904.

Youth Ministry—Mr. CHARLES MICHIE, *P.O. Box 690240, Tulsa, 74169.* Tel: 918-294-1904.

CLERGY, PARISHES, MISSIONS AND PAROCHIAL SCHOOLS

CITY OF TULSA
(Tulsa County)

1—HOLY FAMILY CATHEDRAL (1899), Rev. Gregory A. Gier, Rector; Rev. Msgr. James F. Halpine, Rector Emeritus; Rev. Matthew J. Gerlach; Deacon Millard Kizzia.
Res., 122 W. 8th St., P.O. Box 3204, 74101. Tel: 918-582-6247; Fax: 918-599-8334. [JC]
School—820 S. Boulder St., 74119. Tel: 918-582-0422; Fax: 918-582-9705. Mrs. Holly Goodwin, Prin.
Lay Teachers 18; Students 178.
Catechesis/Religious Programs—Monica Skrzypczak, D.R.E.
Students 88.

2—ST. AUGUSTINE'S (1955) (African American), Rev. Desmond Okpogba (Nigeria); Deacon Steve Litwack.
Church—1720 E. Apache, 74110. Tel: 918-428-3280.

3—ST. BERNARD OF CLAIRVAUX (1978), Revs. Bernard C. Jewitt; Patrick W. Eastman; Deacons Richard Campbell; Alan Mikell; Robert Martin.
Res., 4001 E. 101st St., 74137. Tel: 918-299-9406; Fax: 918-299-7796.
Catechesis/Religious Programs—Sharon Lechtenberg, D.R.E.
Students 746.

4—ST. CATHERINE (1925), Rev. Gary Sherman, Admin.; Deacons Sid Starr; Ned Doty.
Res., 4532 S. 25th Ave., 74107. Tel: 918-446-8124; Fax: 918-446-4506. [JC]
School—2515 W. 46th St., 74107. Tel: 918-446-9756.
Sisters of St. Francis of the Martyr St. George 3; Lay Teachers 8; Students 152.
Catechesis/Religious Programs—Students 58.

5—CHRIST THE KING (1917), Revs. Tam Nguyen; Joshua E. Litwack; Sr. Connie Lennartz, O.P.; Deacon Loren F. Luschen. In res., Rev. William A. Hammil, O.S.A.
Office: 1520 S. Rockford Ave., 74120. Tel: 918-584-4788; 4789; Fax: 918-584-0055.
Res., 1530 S. Rockford Ave., 74120. Tel: 918-584-6693. [JC]
Christ the King Board of Education Endowment Trust—.
School—Marquette School, 1519 S. Quincy, 74120. Tel: 918-584-4631; Fax: 918-584-0055. James J. Pohlman, Prin.
Lay Teachers 25; Students 355.
Catechesis/Religious Programs—Students 85.

6—ST. FRANCIS XAVIER (1926) (Hispanic), Revs. Timothy L. Davison; Jose Maria Briones.
Mailing Address: 2434 E. Admiral Blvd., 74110.
Res. and Church: 2515 E. 1st St., 74110. Tel: 918-592-6770 (Res.); Fax: 918-592-2208 (Res.). [JC]
Catechesis/Religious Programs—Teresa Sotelo, D.R.E.
Students 280.

7—IMMACULATE CONCEPTION (1923). Unassigned.

8—ST. JOSEPH CHURCH (1977) (Vietnamese), Rev. Hoang Viet Le.
Res., 14905 E. 21st St., 74134. Tel: 918-438-1380.
Catechesis/Religious Programs—Tel: 918-438-6325.
Students 79.

9—CHURCH OF THE MADALENE (1946), Rev. Daniel H. Mueggenborg; Sr. Marie Pierre Fleming, O.S.B., Pastoral Assoc.; Deacon Robert DeWeese.
Res., 3188 E. 22nd St., 74114. Tel: 918-744-0023; Fax: 918-744-0024. [JC]
Catechesis/Religious Programs—Tel: 918-744-9417. Mrs. Kay Bashaw, D.R.E.
Students 104.

10—CHURCH OF ST. MARY (1954), Rev. Msgr. Dennis C. Dorney, V.G.; Revs. William J. Swift; Jack A. Gleason; Deacon Richard Bender. In res., Rev. Richard Cristler.
Office: 1347 E. 49th Pl., 74105. Tel: 918-749-1423; Fax: 918-747-9532. [JC]
School—1365 E. 49th Pl., 74105. Tel: 918-749-9361; Fax: 918-712-9604. Todd Goldsmith, Prin.
Lay Teachers 33; Students 340.
Catechesis/Religious Programs—Linda Schoonover, D.R.E.
Students 308.

11—ST. MONICA'S (1926) (African American), Rev. Desmond Okpogba (Nigeria).
Church—633 Marshall Pl., 74106. Tel: 918-587-2965 (Office); Fax: 918-582-0699.
Catechesis/Religious Programs—Students 23.

12—OUR LADY OF GUADALUPE. Closed. For inquiries for sacramental records contact St. Francis Xavier, Tulsa.

13—PARISH OF SAINT PETER (1996), Rev. George G. Gabet, F.S.S.P.
Mailing Address: 1720 E. Apache, 74110. Tel: 918-425-0486; Fax: 918-425-2077.
Res., 1728 E. Apache, 74110.
Catechesis/Religious Programs—Students 51.

14—SS. PETER AND PAUL (1950), Rev. Chi Peter Phung; Deacon Tommy Young.
Res., 1436 N. 67th E. Ave., 74115. Tel: 918-836-2596; Fax: 918-836-2597. [JC]
School—1428 N. 67th E. Ave., 74115. Tel: 918-836-2165; Fax: 918-836-2596. John Kraus, Prin.
Lay Teachers 17; Students 185.
Catechesis/Religious Programs—Karen Campbell, D.R.E.
Students 61.

15—ST. PIUS X (1955), Rev. Thomas M. Hildebrand; Deacons Kasper Weigant; Anthony H. Tran.
Office: 1727 S. 75 E. Ave., 74112. Tel: 918-622-4488; Fax: 918-622-1239. [JC]
Res., 7628 E. 17th St., 74112. Tel: 918-664-9723.
School—1717 S. 75 E. Ave., 74112. Tel: 918-627-5367. Karen Arras, Prin.
Lay Teachers 27; Students 423.
Catechesis/Religious Programs—Adam Barzellone, D.R.E.
Students 107.

16—RESURRECTION (1968), Rev. Michael J. Knipe; Deacon Kenneth Schumacher.
Office: P.O. Box 33169, 74153. Tel: 918-663-1907; Fax: 918-663-2533.
Res., 4338 S. Braden Pl., 74135. Tel: 918-664-8319.
Church—4804 S. Fulton, 74135. Tel: 918-663-1907.
Catechesis/Religious Programs—Sandra Shea, D.R.E.
Students 165.

17—ST. THOMAS MORE (1972), Rev. Gerald J. Coleman; Maria Swindell, Pastoral Assoc.
Res., 3204 S. 124th E. Ave., 74146-2233. Tel: 918-809-0168.
Church—2720 S. 129 E. Ave., 74134. Tel: 918-437-0168; Fax: 918-437-0681.
School—Students 241.
Catechesis/Religious Programs—Becky Bryant, D.R.E.
Students 245.

OUTSIDE CITY OF TULSA

Antlers, Pushmataha Co., St. Agnes (1897), Rev. John J. Marquardt.
Res., 402 N.E. 2nd, P.O. Box 206, 74523. Tel: 580-298-6113.
Mission—Clayton, Pushmataha Co., Holy Trinity, P.O. Box 747, 74523. Tel: 918-569-4767.
Station—Farris, McLeod Correctional Center, Tel: 405-889-6651; Fax: 405-889-2264.

Bartlesville, Washington Co., St. John's (1906), Revs. Stephen E. Austin; W. Gregg Elliott; Deacons Joseph Richard; Dan Willis.
Res., 715 S. Johnstone Ave., 74003. Tel: 918-336-4353; Fax: 918-336-4354. [CEM]
School—Tel: 918-336-0603; Fax: 918-336-0603. Kurt Nelson, Prin.
Lay Teachers 9; Students 109.
Catechesis/Religious Programs—Tonja Senn, D.R.E.
Students 163.

The Community of St. James (1965), Rev. William K. Skeehan.
Res., 5510 Douglas Ln., 74006. Tel: 918-333-5307.
Church—5500 Douglas Ln., 74006.
Catechesis/Religious Programs—Tel: 918-335-0844; Fax: 918-335-0856. Jeanette Pearson, D.R.E.
Students 192.
Mission—Nowata, Nowata Co., St. Catherine, 217 W. Modoc, Nowata, 74048. Tel: 918-273-0737.

Bixby, Tulsa Co., St. Clement's (1958), Rev. Thomas K. Melton.
Mailing Address: P.O. Box 8, 74008.
Res., 21 W. Stadium Rd., 74008. Tel: 918-366-3164; 366-3166.
Catechesis/Religious Programs—Tel: 918-366-3166.
Students 140.

Broken Arrow, Tulsa Co., St. Anne (1936), Rev. Dovan Nguyen.
Res., 301 S. 9th St., 74012. Tel: 918-251-4000; Fax: 918-251-8719. [JC]
Catechesis/Religious Programs—Tel: 918-251-5414. Dayna Cotter, M.T.S., D.R.E.
Students 150.

St. Benedict (1980), Revs. Patrick J. Gaalaas; Paul O. Amaliri; Deacons John Donnelly; Lee Ellis.
Res., 2305 S. Chestnut, 74102. Tel: 918-455-7353.
Church—2200 W. Ithica St., 74012. Tel: 918-455-4451; Fax: 918-451-2199.
Catechesis/Religious Programs—Students 770.

Claremore, Roger Co., St. Cecilia (1911), Rev. Paul E. Eichhoff; Deacons Vincent Mrasek; Peter Schmidt.
Res., 1304 N. Dorothy, 74017. Tel: 918-341-2343; Fax: 918-343-2893.
Catechesis/Religious Programs—Tel: 918-341-4238.
Students 267.

Cleveland, Osage, St. Joseph (1905),
Mailing Address: 333 S. 8th St., Fairfax, 74637. Tel: 918-642-5053.
Church—Osage & C Ave., 74020.
Mission—Hominy, Osage Co., 421 S. Petit, Hominy, 74035.

Coalgate, Coal Co., Blessed Sacrament (1889), Rev. Raymond K. Ackerman.
Res., 1300 E. Beverly, Ada, 74820. Tel: 405-332-2450; Fax: 405-436-1226. [CEM 2][JC]
Catechesis/Religious Programs—Students 16.

Collinsville, Tulsa Co., St. Therese (1906), Rev. Patrick M. Brankin; Deacon Edmundo Martinez, Jr.
Res., 1007 N. 19th St., Box 297, 74021. Tel: 918-371-2704; Fax: 918-371-3895.
Catechesis/Religious Programs—Jane Webb, D.R.E.
Students 128.

Coweta, Wagoner Co., St. Vincent de Paul (1981), Rev. Michael Schweifler, O.S.A, Admin.; Deacon James A. Pierret, Admin.
Res., 1100 S. G St., P.O. Box 771, 74429-0771. Tel: 918-486-4757.
Catechesis/Religious Programs—Students 30.

Cushing, Payne Co., SS. Peter and Paul (1894), Rev. M.E. Cashen; Deacons Jack Berry; Alfonso A. Cardenas.
Res., 214 N. Steele St., Box 828, 74023. Tel: 918-225-0644; Fax: 918-225-6569. [CEM]
Catechesis/Religious Programs—Students 50.
Mission—Drumright, Creek Co., St. Mary, Cimarron & Wood, Drumright, 74030. Tel: 918-352-9327 (Parish Hall).

Dewey, Washington Co., Our Lady of Guadalupe (1955), Rev. Stephen E. Austin; Deacon Richard Chamberlain, Parish Admin.
Res., 400 W. Ninth St., 74029. Tel: 918-534-3420; Fax: 918-534-3013.
Catechesis/Religious Programs—Students 77.

Durant, Bryan Co., St. William, Rev. Valerian Gonsalves, O.S.B. (India); Deacon Albert Miller.
Res., 802 University Blvd., 74701. Tel: 580-924-1989; Fax: 580-931-3044.
Catechesis/Religious Programs—Students 30.
Mission—Atoka, Atoka Co., St. Patrick Church.

Fairfax, Osage Co., Sacred Heart (Osage Indian), Rev. Kenneth W. Lewis; Deacon Vernon Butler.
Mailing Address: 333 S. 8th St., 74637. Tel: 918-642-5053.

Grove, Delaware Co., St. Elizabeth (1949), Rev. Alex Kennedy. In res., Rev. Kenneth A. King.
Office: Tel: 918-256-2281.
Catechesis/Religious Programs—Students 54.

Hartshorne, Pittsburg Co., Holy Rosary (1895), Rev. Chris Daigle.
Res., 102 Center Point Rd., Wilburton, 74548. Tel: 918-465-3996.
Church—912 Cherokee, 74547. [CEM][JC]
Catechesis/Religious Programs—Students 38.
Missions—Talihina, Leflore Co., St. Catherine of Siena, Second & Gann Sts., Talihina, 74571. Tel: 918-567-2587; Wilburton, Latimer Co., Sacred Heart, 102 Center Point Rd., Wilburton, 74578. Deacon Clement Bradley.

Henryetta, Okmulgee Co., St. Michael (1912), Rev. Joseph Vadake Chirayath.
1004 W. Gentry St., P.O. Box 148, 74437. Tel: 918-652-3445. [JC]
Mission—Eufaula, McIntosh Co., St. Paul's, 6th & Forest, Eufaula, 74554.

Holdenville, Hughes Co., St. Stephen's (1905), Rev. Christopher Fernando.
Res., 515 E. Highway, 74848. Tel: 405-379-2512; Fax: 405-379-2512.
Catechesis/Religious Programs—Students 22.
Mission—Okemah, Okfuska Co., St. Teresa, (1927) 8th and Broadway, Okemah, 74859.

Hugo, Choctaw Co., Immaculate Conception (1903), Rev. Robert F. Poandl, Glmy.
Res., HC69, Box 36-1, 74743. Tel: 580-326-7300.
Catechesis/Religious Programs—Students 41.
Mission—Boswell, Choctaw Co., St. Jude, 511 11th St., Boswell, 74727.

Idabel, McCurtain Co., St. Francis De Sales (1945), Rev. John T. Brown, Glmy.
Res., 13 S.E. Jefferson, 74745. Tel: 580-286-3275.
Catechesis/Religious Programs—Students 80.
Mission—Valiant, McCurtain Co., Good Shepherd, P.O. Box 1016, Valiant, 74764. Tel: 580-933-4742. In res., Rev. John Buzga, Glmy (E).
Mission—Plunketville, McCurtain Co., St. Henry, HC 15, P.O. Box 1250, Watson, 74963. Tel: 580-244-3157. [CEM]
In res., Rev. Francisco Schenk, Glmy.

Krebs, Pittsburg Co., St. Joseph's (1886), Revs. Amalorpavam Vima (India); John Dias (India); Deacon Bill Anderson.
Res., P.O. Box 621, 74554. Tel: 918-423-6695; Fax: 918-426-4255. [CEM]
Catechesis/Religious Programs—Tel: 918-423-7130. Sharon Dunbar, D.R.E.
Students 115.
Stations—Krebs, Jackie Brannon Correctional Center, Tel: 918-426-4470; Fax: 918-426-0004; McAlester, Oklahoma State Penitentiary, Tel: 918-423-4700; Fax: 918-423-3862.

Langley, Mayes Co., St. Frances of Rome (1950), Rev. Alex Kennedy, Admin.; Deacon Charles Toppins, Coord. Parish Life.
Res., Hwy. 28, P.O. Box 267, 74350-0267. Tel: 918-782-2248. [CEM][JC]

McAlester, Pittsburg Co., St. John (1895), Revs. Amalor Vima (India); Soccoro John Dias (India).
Res., 300 E. Washington Ave., Box 220, 74502. Tel: 918-423-0810; Fax: 918-429-0098. [CEM]
Catechesis/Religious Programs—Tel: 918-423-1458. Cathy Swope, D.R.E.
Students 127.
Mission—Pittsburg, Pittsburg Co., St. Edwards, Hwy. 63, Pittsburg, 74560.

Miami, Ottawa Co., Sacred Heart (1900), Rev. Michael R. Rooney; Deacon Marvin Morris.
Res., 2515 N. Main, 74354. Tel: 918-542-5281; Fax: 918-542-7591.
Catechesis/Religious Programs—Tel: 918-542-5898. Karen Painter, D.R.E.
Students 73.
Mission—Welch, Craig Co., St. Ann, P.O. Box 25, Welch, 74369. Tel: 918-788-3771.

Muskogee, Muskogee Co., Assumption. Closed. For inquiries for sacramental records contact Saint Joseph Church, Muskogee.
Sacred Heart. Closed. For inquiries for sacramental records contact Saint Joseph Church, Muskogee.
Saint Joseph Church (1992), Rev. J. Richard Bradley; Deacons William Miller; Edwin Falleur, Pastoral Assoc. In res., Revs. Herman J. Foken; Robert M. Dye.
Mailing Address: P.O. Box 189, 74402. Tel: 918-687-1351; Fax: 918-687-5541.
Church—321 N. Virginia, 74402. [CEM]
Res. & Parish Office: 2310 W. Broadway, 74402. Tel: 918-687-1351; 683-2098 (Rectory).
School—(Grades PreK-8) 323 N. Virginia, 74403. Tel: 918-683-1291; Fax: 918-682-5374. Beth Stafford, Prin.
Lay Teachers 13; Students 133.
Catechesis/Religious Programs—Carleen Falleur, D.R.E.
Students 186.
Chapel—Sacred Heart, 74402.

Okmulgee, Okmulgee Co., St. Anthony's (1910), Rev. Bryan V. Brooks. Pastoral Assocs.: Sr. Mary Fox, O.P.; Sr. Loretta McIluenna, O.P.
Res., 515 S. Morton Ave., P.O. Box 698, 74447. Tel: 918-756-4385; Fax: 918-756-3719. [JC]
School—Marian Academy, (Grades PreK-5). Tel: 918-756-9042; Fax: 918-756-6578. Sr. Loretta McIluenna, O.P., Prin.
Catechesis/Religious Programs—Students 58.
Mission—Okmulgee, Okmulgee Co., Uganda Martyrs, 808 E. 3rd, 74447.

Owasso, Tulsa Co., St. Henry (1957), Rev. J. Paul Donovan; Deacons Vernon Foltz; Donald LeMieux.
Mailing Address: P.O. Box 181, 74055-0181. Tel: 918-272-3710; Fax: 918-272-1966.
Res., 903 N. Elm, 74055. Tel: 918-272-7387.
Church—8500 Owasso Expy., 74055.
Catechesis/Religious Programs—Tel: 918-272-3740. Elizabeth Gagner, D.R.E.
Students 370.

Pawhuska, Osage Co., Immaculate Conception (1887) (Osage Indian), Rev. Leonard H. Higgins.
Res., 1314 N. Lynn Ave., 74056. Tel: 918-287-1414. [JC]
Catechesis/Religious Programs—Students 58.
Missions—Barnsdall, Osage Co., St. Mary, 3rd and Chestnut, Barnsdall, 74002.; Shidler, Osage Co., St. Ann, Gypsy St. & Taylor St., Shidler, 74652.

Pawnee, Pawnee Co., St. John (1907), Rev. Joe C. Townsend.
Mailing Address: 201 N. Knoblock, Stillwater, 74075. Tel: 405-372-6408.
Church—8th St. & Oak, 74058.
Catechesis/Religious Programs—Tel: 405-372-7987.
Students 189.

Poteau, Leflore Co., Immaculate Conception (1903), Rev. Khiet T. Nguyen.
Mailing Address: P.O. Box 237, 74953.
Res., 502 N. Bagwell St., 74953. Tel: 918-647-3475.
Church—410 Bagwell St., 74953. Tel: 918-647-3475.
Catechesis/Religious Programs—Students 37.
Missions—Stigler, Haskell Co., St. Joseph, 126 S. Broadway, Stigler, 74462.; Spiro, Leflore Co., St. Elizabeth Seton, Hwy. 9, Spiro, 74959.
Station—Hodgens, Ouachita Correctional Training Center. [JC]
Catechesis/Religious Programs—Students 37.

Pryor, Mayes Co., St. Mark's (1942), Rev. Ken Harder.
Res., 1507 S. Vann, P.O. Box 576, 74362. Tel: 918-824-4470; Fax: 918-825-2338.
Catechesis/Religious Programs—Tel: 918-825-4186. Lissa Rosebrough, D.R.E.
Students 75.

Sallisaw, Sequoyah Co., St. Francis Xavier (1952), Rev. Jeffrey S. Polasek; Deacon Robert Barnes.
Church—2110 N. Dogwood, 74955. Tel: 918-775-6217; Fax: 918-775-6217.
Catechesis/Religious Programs—Students 42.
Missions—Cookson, Cherokee Co., St. John the Evangelist, P.O. Box 4, Cookson, 74427.; Webbers Falls, Muskogee Co., St. Joseph, P.O. Box 53, Webber Falls, 74470. Tel: 918-464-2422; Roland, Sequoyah Co., Blessed Kateri Tekakwitha, P.O. Box 17, Roland, 74954.

Sand Springs, Tulsa Co., St. Patrick's (1919), Rev. Martin Morgan; Deacons Bob Garrett; Noel Hollingshead.
Res., 204 E. Fourth, 74063. Tel: 918-245-5254; Fax: 918-245-5840. [JC]
Catechesis/Religious Programs—Students 114.
Mission—Mannford, Creek Co., Our Lady of the Lake.

Sapulpa, Creek Co., Sacred Heart (1907), Rev. Charles Hewawasam (India); Deacon Francis Decker.
Church—1777 E. Grayson Ave., 74066. Tel: 918-224-0944; Fax: 918-248-4935. [JC]
Catechesis/Religious Programs—Students 91.
Mission—Bristow, Creek Co., St. Joseph, P.O. Box 603, Bristow, 74010. Deacon Tom Loney.

Skiatook, Osage Co., Sacred Heart (1921). (Formerly St. William). Rev. James D. White; Deacon Don Tucker.
Res., 109 W. 5th St., 74070. Tel: 918-396-1179; Fax: 918-396-0267.
Catechesis/Religious Programs—Students 56.
St. Joseph's (1928). Closed. For inquiries for parish records contact the Chancery.

Stillwater, Payne Co., St. Francis Xavier (1895), Rev. Robert T. Schlitt; Deacon Paul Govek.
Res., 623 S. West St., Box 909, 74076. Tel: 405-372-6886. [JC]
Catechesis/Religious Programs—Tel: 405-372-7987. D.R.E.: Cecilia Crane; Barbara Stalzer; Shirley Lewis.
Students 113.

St. John University Parish and Catholic Student Center (1965), Rev. Joe C. Townsend; Deacons Bill Moler; Tom Haan; Richard Berberet.
Res., 201 N. Knoblock, 74075. Tel: 405-372-6408; Fax: 405-372-6409.
Catechesis/Religious Programs—Tel: 405-372-7987. D.R.E.: Rhonda Fulton, (Grades PreK-12); Glen Collum, (Confirmation); Shirley Lewis, (Grades 7-12).
Students 189.

Tahlequah, Cherokee Co., St. Brigid (1966), Rev. Kenneth Iheanaho; Deacon Joseph Faulds.
Res., 807 Crafton St., 74464. Tel: 918-456-8388.
Catechesis/Religious Programs—Tel: 918-456-4204. Donna Ballew, D.R.E.
Students 60.

Vinita, Craig Co., Holy Ghost (1892), Rev. Alex Kennedy.
Res., 120 W. Sequoyah Ave., 74301. Tel: 918-256-2281.
Catechesis/Religious Programs—Tel: 918-256-3118. Sr. Mary Grace Sieben, D.R.E.
Students 66.
Stations—Eastern State Hospital.; Vinita, Northeastern Correctional Facility.

Wagoner, Wagoner Co., Holy Cross (1895), Rev. Kenneth Harder.
Mailing Address: P.O. Box 710, 74477. Tel: 918-485-5145; Fax: 918-485-0656.
Church—S.W. 15th & Pierce, 74477.
Catechesis/Religious Programs—Sherry Ruyle, D.R.E.
Students 33.

Special Assignment:
Reverend Fathers—
Daley, Timothy J.
Dye, Robert M., Hispanic Ministry

On Duty Outside the Diocese:
Reverend Fathers—
Cain, Robert K.C., U.S. Navy
Minh, Vu Duc, U.S. Air Force
Wells, Peter B., Vatican Diplomatic Corps, assigned to Nigeria

Retired:
Reverend Monsignors—
Halpine, James F., P.O. Box 3204, Tulsa, OK 74101
Maszkiewicz, Mark, 1767-A S. Wheeling, Tulsa, OK 74104
Reverend Fathers—
Bartnik, Harry S., Franciscan Villa, 17110 E. 51st St. S., Broken Arrow, OK 74012
Brogan, Neal E., 1212 W. Trudgeon, Henryetta, OK 74437
Dally, Peter F., 1608 S. Victor, Tulsa, OK 74104
Foken, Herman J., P.O. Box 189, Muskogee, OK 74402-0189
Fulton, Kenneth S.
King, Kenneth A., P.O. Box 7206, Grove, OK 74344
Lange, Lawrence P., 12537 E. 41st St., Tulsa, OK 74146
Lundberg, John W., 43 California Ave., Middletown, NY 10940
MacAuley, Stephen A., Franciscan Villa, 17110 E. 51st St. S., Apt. 2, Broken Arrow, OK 74012
Mazaika, Joseph J., 1710 Walnut, Grand Prairie, TX 75050
McCarthy, Jerry, Franciscan Villa, 17110 E. 51st St. S., Broken Arrow, OK 74012
McGlinchey, James J., 1767 S. Wheeling, Tulsa, OK 74104
O'Neil, Lee E., P.O. Box 515, Gulf Shores, AL 36542
Perlinski, Daniel A., 1735 S. Wheeling Ave., Tulsa, OK 74104
Pickett, Robert T., 1414 E. 49th St., Tulsa, OK 74105-4798
Richard, Edward, 1594 S. Chamberlain Blvd., North Port, FL 34286
Swett, Charles J., 2009 Xanthus, Tulsa, OK 74104
Swift, William V., 1779 S. Wheeling, Tulsa, OK 74104

Permanent Deacons:
Anderson, Bill, St. Joseph, Krebs
Barnes, Robert, Blessed Kateri Tekakwitha, Roland
Bender, Richard F., Church of St. Mary, Tulsa
Berberet, Richard, St. John University Parish, Stillwater
Berry, Jack L., Sts. Peter & Paul, Cushing
Bradley, Clement W., Sacred Heart, Wilburton
Breazille, James E., Unassigned
Butler, Vernon, Sacred Heart, Fairfax
Campbell, Richard, St. Bernard, Tulsa
Cardenas, Alfonso, SS. Peter & Paul, Cushing
Chamberlain, Richard, Our Lady of Guadalupe, Dewey
Decker, Francis I., Sacred Heart, Sapulpa
DeLeon, Felix, St. Francis, Tulsa

DeWeese, Robert, Church of the Madalene, Tulsa
Donnelly, John E., St. Benedict, Broken Arrow
Doty, Edward, St. Catherine
Ellis, Lee, St. Benedict, Broken Arrow
Falleur, Edwin E., St. Joseph, Muskogee
Faulds, Joseph M., St. Brigid, Tahlequah
Foltz, Vernon, St. Henry, Owasso
Garrett, James R., St. Patrick, Sand Springs
Gerrior, Joseph A., On Medical Leave
Govek, Paul, St. Francis Xavier, Stillwater
Haan, Tom, St. John University Parish, Stillwater
Hollingshead, Noel, St. Patrick, Sand Springs
Kizzia, Millard H., Holy Family Cathedral, Tulsa
LeMieux, Donald J., St. Henry, Owasso
Litwack, Stephen J., St. Augustine, Tulsa
Loney, Tom, St. Joseph, Bristow
Luschen, Loren F., Christ the King, Tulsa
Martin, Robert, St. Bernard of Clairvaux, Tulsa
Martinez, Edmundo S., St. Therese, Collinsville
Mikell, Alan G., St. Bernard, Tulsa
Miller, Albert J., St. William, Durant
Miller, Bill, St. Joseph, Muskogee
Moler, William J., St. John University Parish, Stillwater
Morris, Marvin D., Sacred Heart, Miami
Mrasek, Vincent J., St. Cecilia, Claremore
Perez, Jose, (Retired)
Pierret, James A., St. Vincent de Paul, Coweta
Richard, Joseph N., St. John, Bartlesville
Schmidt, Peter, St. Cecilia, Claremore
Schumacher, Kenneth, St. Benedict, Broken Arrow
Starr, Sid, St. Catherine, Tulsa
Sullivan, Timothy, Dir. Catholic Charities
Tindall, Billie D.
Toppins, Charles A., St. Frances of Rome, Langley
Tran, Anthony, St. Pius X, Tulsa
Tucker, Donel, Sacred Heart, Skiatook
Walsh, Gary D., Unassigned
Weigant, Kasper E., St. Pius X, Tulsa
Willis, Daniel H., St. John, Bartlesville
Young, Thomas, SS. Peter & Paul, Tulsa

INSTITUTIONS LOCATED IN THE DIOCESE

[A] HIGH SCHOOLS, DIOCESAN

TULSA. *Bishop Kelley High School*, 3905 S. Hudson, 74135-5699. Tel: 918-627-3390; Fax: 918-664-2134.
E-mail: aweyland@bkelleyhs.org
Web site: www.bkelleyhs.org
Alan V. Weyland, H.S. Prin.; Bro. David Poos, F.S.C., Dir.; Marianne Stich, Campus Min. Brothers 3; Lay Teachers 84; Students 953.

[B] HIGH SCHOOLS, PRIVATE

TULSA. *Cascia Hall Preparatory School*. (Grades 6-12), Mailing Address: Box 52247, 74152. Tel: 918-746-2600; Fax: 918-746-2636.
E-mail: info@casciahall.org
Web site: www.casciahall.org
2520 S. Yorktown Ave., 74114. Tel: 918-746-2600; Fax: 918-746-2636. Augustinians (Order of St. Augustine). Coed College Preparatory School. Revs. Bernard C. Scianna, O.S.A., Headmaster; James J. Sheridan, O.S.A.; John H. Gaffney, O.S.A.; Philip C. Cook, O.S.A.; Henry V. Spielmann, O.S.A.; Theodore E. Tack, O.S.A.; Michael Schweifler, O.S.A., Chap.; John J. Sotak, O.S.A.; William A. Perez, O.S.A.; Bro. Paul L. Koscielniak, O.S.A. Priests 9; Brothers 1; Sisters 1; Lay Teachers 44; Students 575.

[C] ELEMENTARY SCHOOLS, DIOCESAN

BROKEN ARROW. *All Saints School*, 299 S. 9th St., 74012. Tel: 918-251-3000; Fax: 918-258-9879.
E-mail: office@allsaints.okschools.net
Deacon Robert Martin, Prin. Deacons 1; Lay Teachers 15; Students 235.

[D] ELEMENTARY SCHOOLS, PRIVATE

TULSA. *Monte Cassino School*. (Grades PreK-8), 2206 S. Lewis, 74114. Tel: 918-743-4471; Fax: 918-742-5206. Sr. Mary Clare Buthod, O.S.B., Dir. & Prin. Sisters 4; Lay Teachers 80; Students 1,167.

[E] GENERAL HOSPITALS

TULSA. *Marian Health System, Inc.*, P.O. Box 4753, 74159-0753. Tel: 918-742-9988; Fax: 918-744-2716
For a complete listing, refer to the Hospitals section.
Saint Francis Hospital, Inc., 6161 S. Yale Ave., 74136. Tel: 918-494-2200; Fax: 918-494-7175
For a complete listing, refer to the Hospitals section.
St. John Health System, Inc., 1923 S. Utica, 74104. Tel: 918-744-2180; Fax: 918-744-2716
For a complete listing, refer to the Hospitals section.
St. John Medical Center, Inc., 1923 S. Utica Ave., 74104. Tel: 918-744-2345; Fax: 918-744-2716.
Web site: www.sjmc.org
For a complete listing, refer to the Hospitals section.

[F] HOMES FOR THE AGED

TULSA. *Frances Streitel Senior Care Corporation*, 1923 S. Utica Ave., 74104. Tel: 918-744-2471
For a complete listing, refer to the Special Care Facilities section.
St. John Villas, Inc., 1923 S. Utica, 74104. Tel: 918-744-2180; Fax: 918-744-2716
For a complete listing, refer to the Special Care Facilities section.

[G] CONVENTS AND RESIDENCES FOR SISTERS

TULSA. *St. Joseph Monastery*, 2200 S. Lewis, 74114-3100. Tel: 918-742-4989; Fax: 918-744-1374.
E-mail: oklaosb@aol.com
Web site: www.rc.net/tulsa/sjm
Motherhouse of Benedictine Sisters (Federation of St. Scholastica). Sr. Barbara Austin, O.S.B., Prioress. Sisters in Community 33.
Sisters of Saint Joseph, 3942 S. Trenton, 74105. Tel: 918-749-8954. Sisters in Community 2.

BROKEN ARROW. *St. Clare Convent*, 17600 E. 51st St., 74012. Tel: 918-355-5581; Fax: 918-355-3534. Sisters in Community 16.
Sisters of the Sorrowful Mother - Our Lady of Sorrows Convent, 17600 E. 51st St., 74012. Tel: 918-355-5581; Fax: 918-355-3534.
E-mail: dirkx@busprod.com
Sr. Paula Jacobs, Coord. Sisters 19.
Sisters of the Sorrowful Mother - U.S./Caribbean Province, Inc., 17600 E. 51st St., 74012. Tel: 918-355-1148; Fax: 918-355-3534.
E-mail: dirkx@busprod.com
Sr. Dorothy Ann M. Dirkx, U.S./Caribbean Prov. Sisters 184.

SAND SPRINGS. *Benedictine Sisters of Perpetual Adoration*, 18701 W. Monastery Rd., 74063. Tel: 918-245-2734; Fax: 918-245-9360.
E-mail: josettaosb@juno.com
Web site: www.benedictinesisters.org
Osage Monastery, OM Forest of Peace Benedictine Convent of Perpetual Adoration in Oklahoma, Inc. Sr. Josetta Grant, O.S.B., Supr. Sisters 4.

[H] NEWMAN CENTERS

TULSA. *St. Philip Neri Newman Center at The University of Tulsa*, 440 S. Florence, 74104. Tel: 918-599-0204; Fax: 918-587-0115.
E-mail: tunewman@webzone.net
Web site: www.webzone.net/tunewman/
Rev. Daniel H. Mueggenborg; Steve Nelson, Campus Min.; Suzanne Curtin, Dir. Opers.

MIAMI. *Northeastern Oklahoma A & M College Newman Center*. Tel: 918-542-5281; Fax: 918-542-7591.
E-mail: mrrooney@rectec.net
Mailing Address: 2515 N. Main, 74354. 200 I N.E. St., 74354. Tel: 918-542-8441; Fax: 918-540-6946. Rev. Michael R. Rooney, Chap.

STILLWATER. *St. John's University Parish and Catholic Student Center*, 201 N. Knoblock, 74075. Tel: 405-372-6408; Fax: 405-372-6409.
E-mail: bishnik2@aol.com
Web site: www.stjohn.stillwater.org
Rev. Joe C. Townsend; Cathy Perry, Campus Min.; Deacons Bill Moler; Thomas Haan; Richard Berberet.

TAHLEQUAH. *Northeastern State University Catholic Student Organization*, 807 Crafton St., 74464. Tel: 918-456-8388. Rev. Kenneth Iheanaho.

[I] MISCELLANEOUS

TULSA. *Bishop Kelley High School Endowment Trust*, 3905 S. Hudson Ave., 74135. Tel: 918-627-3390; Fax: 918-664-2134.
E-mail: dpoos@bkelleyhs.org
Web site: bkelleyhs.org
Bro. David Poos, F.S.C., Dir.
Catholic Foundation of Eastern Oklahoma, Inc., Mailing Address: P.O. Box 690240, 74169. Tel: 918-294-1904.
St. John Medical Center Foundation, Inc., 1923 S. Utica, 74104. Tel: 918-749-3553; Fax: 918-744-2716.
St. Joseph Residence, Inc., P.O. Box 6429, 74148. Tel: 918-587-6456; Fax: 918-587-3560. Total Assisted 36; Total Staff 6.

CLAREMORE. *Apostolate for the Most Holy Rosary and the Brown Scapular Association*, 9155 E. 496 Rd., 74017. Tel: 918-341-5612.
E-mail: Twohtsrsry@aol.com
Mr. Robert C. Tayrien, Pres. & Contact Person.

HULBERT. *Foundation for the Annunciation Monastery of Clear Creek*, 5804 W. Monastery Rd., 74441. Tel: 918-772-2454; Fax: 918-772-1044.

MUSKOGEE. *St. Joseph School Endowment Trust*, P.O. Box 189, 74402. Tel: 918-687-1351.

RELIGIOUS INSTITUTES OF MEN REPRESENTED IN THE DIOCESE

For further details refer to the corresponding bracketed number in the Religious Institutes of Men or Women section.

[0140]—*The Augustinians (Province of Our Mother of Good Counsel)*.—O.S.A.
[0330]—*Brothers of the Christian Schools*. (Province of St. Louis).—F.S.C.
[0570]—*Glenmary Home Missioners*.—Glmy.
[0690]—*Jesuit Fathers and Brothers*. (Province of St. Louis).—S.J.

RELIGIOUS INSTITUTES OF WOMEN REPRESENTED IN THE DIOCESE

[0230]—*Benedictine Sisters of Pontifical Jurisdiction*. (Atchison, KS).—O.S.B.
[0220]—*Congregation of the Benedictine Sisters of Perpetual Adoration of Pontifical Jurisdiction*.—O.S.B.
[]—*Congregation of the Benedictine Sisters of the Sacred Hearts*.—O.S.B.
[1070-03]—*Dominican Sisters*.—O.P.
[]—*Religious Sisters of Mercy*.—R.S.M.
[1510]—*Sisters of Saint Francis*.—O.S.F.
[1570]—*Sisters of St. Francis of the Holy Family*.—O.S.F.
[1600]—*Sisters of St. Francis of the Martyr St. George*.—O.S.F.
[3830]—*Sisters of St. Joseph*.—S.S.J.
[4100]—*Sisters of the Sorrowful Mother (Third Order of St. Francis)*.—S.S.M.

CEMETERIES

TULSA. *Calvary*. Mailing Address: P.O. Box 2009, 74101. Tel: 918-587-3115. 9101 S. Harvard, 74136. Tel: 918-743-5571. James S. Liichow, Suprv.

NECROLOGY

† O'Hara, Arthur T., Pryor, OK St. Mark. —Died Jan. 17, 2000.

Diocese of Tyler

(Dioecesis Tylerensis)

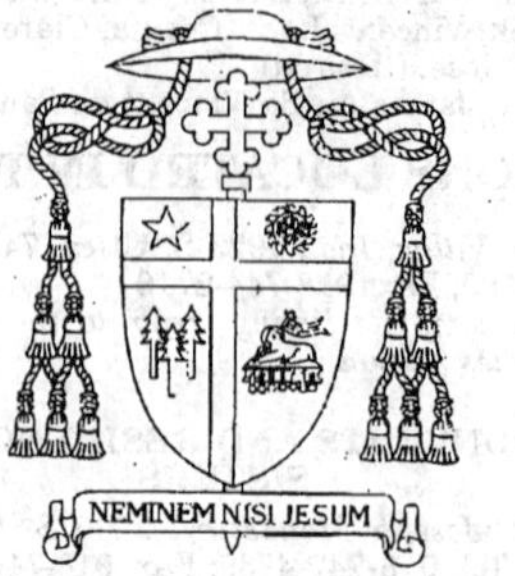

Most Reverend

ALVARO CORRADA DEL RIO, S.J., D.D.,

Bishop of Tyler; ordained July 6, 1974; consecrated August 4, 1985; on assignemnt, as Apostolic Administrator, Diocese of Caguas; appointed Bishop of Tyler December 5, 2000; installed January 30, 2001. *Office: Diocese of Tyler, 1015 E.S.E. Loop 323, Tyler, TX, 75701-9663.* Tel.: 903-534-1077; Fax: 903-534-1370.

Chancery: 1015 E.S.E. Loop 323, Tyler, TX, 75701-9663. Tel.: 903-534-1077; Fax: 903-534-1370.

ESTABLISHED DIOCESE OF TYLER ON DECEMBER 12, 1986.

Square Miles 23,443.

Comprises the following Counties in the State of Texas: Anderson, Angelina, Bowie, Camp, Cass, Cherokee, Delta, Franklin, Freestone, Gregg, Harrison, Henderson, Hopkins, Houston, Lamar, Leon, Madison, Marion, Morris, Nacogdoches, Panola, Rains, Red River, Rusk, Sabine, San Augustine, Shelby, Smith, Titus, Trinity, Upshur, Van Zandt, and Wood.

For legal titles of parishes and diocesan institutions, consult the Chancery Office.

STATISTICAL OVERVIEW

Personnel	
Bishop	1
Priests: Diocesan Active in Diocese	26
Priests: Active Outside Diocese	2
Priests: Retired, Sick or Absent	3
Number of Diocesan Priests	32
Religious Priests in Diocese	20
Extern Priests in Diocese	34
Ordinations:	
Diocesan Priests	2
Transitional Deacons	3
Permanent Deacons	13
Permanent Deacons in Diocese	47
Total Brothers	4
Total Sisters	60
Parishes	
Parishes	40
With Resident Pastor:	
Resident Diocesan Priests	34
Resident Religious Priests	6
Missions	28
Pastoral Centers	2
New Parishes Created	5
Professional Ministry Personnel:	
Brothers	4
Sisters	12
Lay Ministers	16
Welfare	
Catholic Hospitals	4
Total Assisted	310,264
Health Care Centers	42
Total Assisted	639,894
Special Centers for Social Services	1
Total Assisted	120
Educational	
Diocesan Students in Other Seminaries	13
Total Seminarians	13
High Schools, Diocesan and Parish	1
Total Students	176
Elementary Schools, Diocesan and Parish	4
Total Students	938
Catechesis/Religious Education:	
High School Students	1,259
Elementary Students	5,373
Total Students Under Catholic Instruction	7,759
Teachers in the Diocese:	
Brothers	1
Sisters	4
Lay Teachers	90
Vital Statistics	
Receptions into the Church:	
Infant Baptism Totals	1,758
Adult Baptism Totals	188
Received into Full Communion	321
First Communions	1,402
Confirmations	800
Marriages:	
Catholic	256
Interfaith	101
Total Marriages	357
Deaths	316
Total Catholic Population	53,776
Total Population	1,215,918

Former Bishops—Most Rev. CHARLES E. HERZIG, D.D., First Bishop of Tyler; ord. May 31, 1955; Bishop of Tyler; appt. Dec. 12, 1986; cons. Feb. 24, 1987; died Sept. 7, 1991.—Most Rev. EDMOND CARMODY, D.D., Second Bishop of Tyler; ord. June 8, 1957; appt. Auxiliary Bishop of San Antonio, Nov. 8, 1988; cons. Dec. 15, 1988; appt. Bishop of Tyler, March 24, 1992; installed May 25, 1992; transferred Diocese of Corpus Christi, March 17, 2000.

Vicar General—Rev. JOHN A. BRENNAN, *Chancery, 1015 E.S.E. Loop 323, Tyler, 75701-9663.* Tel: 903-534-1077; Fax: 903-534-1370.

Chancery—1015 E.S.E. Loop 323, Tyler, 75701-9663. Tel: 903-534-1077; Fax: 903-534-1370. Office Hours: Mon.-Fri. 8:30-5.

Chancellor—Rev. GAVIN N. VAVEREK, J.C.L., *1015 E.S.E. Loop 323, Tyler, 75701-9663.* Tel: 903-534-1077.

Archivist—Vacant. Tel: 903-534-1077.

College of Consultors—Rev. Msgr. JOHN A. BRENNAN, V.G.; Rev. Msgr. JOSEPH E. STRICKLAND, J.C.L.; Rev. Msgr. GERALD A. PRIEST; Rev. Msgr. JAMES E. YOUNG; Revs. ALPHONSE ANTHONY; RONALD DIEGEL; ZACHARIAS S. KUNNAKKATTUTHARA; LUIS E. LARREA, M.F.E.; GAVIN N. VAVEREK, J.C.L.

Deans—Rev. RONALD DIEGEL, East Central Deanery; Rev. Msgr. GERALD PRIEST, Northeast Deanery; Rev. BERNARD BOTEJU, Northwest Deanery; Rev. Msgr. JAMES E. YOUNG, Southeast Deanery; Rev. ZACHARIAS S. KUNNAKKATTUTHARA, Southwest Deanery; Rev. Msgr. JOSEPH E. STRICKLAND, J.C.L., West Central Deanery.

Tribunal Office—1015 E.S.E. Loop 323, Tyler, 75701-9663. Tel: 903-534-1077; Fax: 903-534-1370.

Judicial Vicar—Rev. Msgr. JOSEPH E. STRICKLAND, J.C.L.

Defender of the Bond—Rev. GAVIN N. VAVEREK, J.C.L.

Administrator/Notary—Mrs. MARGARET OPPENHEIMER. Tel: 903-534-1077.

DIOCESAN ADMINISTRATION

Finance Officer—Mr. JAMES R. SMITH, *1015 E.S.E. Loop 323, Tyler, 75701-9663.* Tel: 903-534-1077.

Diocesan Finance Council—Mr. BILL SULLIVAN, Chm.; Rev. Msgr. JOHN A. BRENNAN; Mr. JAMES CHIARIZIO; Mrs. JANET HUNT; Mr. JAMES KENNEDY; Mr. WESLEY RIVERS; JAMES R. SMITH.

Diocesan Building Board—Mr. BILLY CORDOVA, Chm.; Mr. TOM DEIBEL; Mrs. CHERYL FLOOD; Mr. JAMES R. SMITH; Rev. GAVIN N. VAVEREK.

East Texas Catholic Foundation—JAMES R. SMITH, Dir., *1015 E.S.E. Loop 323, Tyler, 75701-9663.* Mr. DAVID CARLILE; Mrs. SUZIE HAIR; Mr. VINCE RICHBOURG; Mr. WALTER VOLZ; Mr. PAUL WALSH; Mr. TOM WOLF.

Priests' Pension Board—Rev. Msgr. JAMES E. YOUNG; Mr. JAMES R. SMITH, Treas.; Revs. ZACHARIAS S. KUNNAKKATTUTHARA; BERNARD BOTEJU; RONALD DIEGEL; Rev. Msgr. GERALD A. PRIEST; Rev. Msgr. JOSEPH E. STRICKLAND, J.C.L.; GAVIN N. VAVEREK, J.C.L.

Campaign for Human Development—Vacant. Tel: 903-534-1077.

Catholic School Superintendent—Deacon VIC BO, *1015 E.S.E. Loop 323, Tyler, 75701-9663.*

Diocesan School Board—Mrs. SUE PLATZER, Chm.; Mr. WILLIAM BARTUSH; Mrs. THELMA CLANCY, Sec.; Dr. JAMES STOCKS; Mr. PAUL WALKER; Mr. GEORGE WING; Mr. MICHAEL MOORE.

Director of Religious Education—Mrs. LINDA PORTER.

Pastoral Ministries—Rev. LUIS E. LARREA, M.F.E., Dir., *1015 E.S.E. Loop 323, Tyler, 75701-9663.* Tel: 903-534-1077.

Family Life/Youth Ministry—Mr. EDWARD RUESEWALD, Dir., *1015 E.S.E. Loop 323, Tyler, 75701-9663.* Tel: 903-534-1077.

Tyler Catholic Committee on Scouting—Rev. MICHAEL DOYLE, Chap., *1113 S. Main St., Lindale, 75771-1078.* Tel: 903-228-4079. Mr. JERRY STOCK, Chm., *905 Happiness St., Longview, 75601.* Tel: 903-757-7524.

Campus Ministries—Mr. EDWARD RUESEWALD, Dir.

Missions Office—Vacant. Tel: 903-534-1077.

Priests' Personnel Board—Rev. Msgr. JAMES E. YOUNG, Chm.; Rev. Msgr. GERALD A. PRIEST; Rev. Msgr. JOSEPH E. STRICKLAND, J.C.L., Sec.; Revs. BERNARD BOTEJU; RONALD DIEGEL; RUBEN FIGUEROA; LUIS E. LARREA, M.F.E.; ZACHARIAS S. KUNNAKKATTUTHARA; DEVARAJ ARULAPPA.

Presbyteral Council—Rev. LUIS E. LARREA, M.F.E.; Rev. Msgr. JOHN A. BRENNAN; Rev. Msgr. JOSEPH E. STRICKLAND, J.C.L.; Rev. Msgr. GERALD PRIEST, Vice Chm.; Rev. Msgr. JAMES E. YOUNG; Revs. BERNARD BOTEJU; RONALD DIEGEL, Chm. GAVIN N. VAVEREK, J.C.L.; ZACHARIAS S. KUNNAKKATTUTHARA.

Office of Clergy Development/Continuing Education—Rev. LUIS E. LARREA, M.F.E., *1015 E.S.E. Loop 323, Tyler, 75701-9663.* Tel: 903-534-1077.

Permanent Diaconate Director—Deacon JOHN K. SHAFFER, *2108 Ridgewood, Longview, 75605-5199.* Tel: 903-757-5855.

Vocations Director—Rev. GAVIN N. VAVEREK, J.C.L., *1015 E.S.E. Loop 323, Tyler, 75701-9663.* Tel: 903-534-1077. Mr. JIM FINEGAN, Chm., Vocations Awareness Board.

Communications Director—Mr. JAMES H. D'AVIGNON, *1015 E.S.E. Loop 323, Tyler, 75701-9663.* Tel: 903-534-1077.

Bishop's Annual Appeal—Mrs. JUDY GREEN, Dir., *1015 E.S.E. Loop 323, Tyler, 75701-9663.* Tel: 903-534-1077.

Newspaper "Catholic East Texas"—Mr. JAMES H. D'AVIGNON, Editor. Reporters: Mrs. SUSAN DEMATTEO NECESSARY; Mrs. JOANNE FLORES EMBLETON, *1015 E.S.E. Loop 323, Tyler, 75701-9663.* Tel: 903-534-1077; Fax: 903-534-1370.

DIOCESAN OFFICES

Diocesan Council of Catholic Women—Mrs. DOROTHY BONICK, Pres., *P.O. Box 1449, Mount Pleasant, 75456-1449.* Tel: 903-572-0767. Rev. GAVIN N. VAVEREK, J.C.L., Moderator, *2108 Ridgewood, Longview, 75605-5199.* Tel: 903-757-5855.

Respect Life Program—Rev. GAVIN N. VAVEREK, J.C.L., *2108 Ridgewood, Longview, 75605-5199.* Tel: 903-757-5855. Co-Directors: JOE DUDAS; MARGE DUDAS, *1605 H.G. Mosley, Longview, 75604.* Tel: 903-297-3767.

Disaster Relief Director—Mr. ROY SHEAR, *621 Bentley Ct., Tyler, 75703.* Tel: 903-561-0425.

CLERGY, PARISHES, MISSIONS AND PAROCHIAL SCHOOLS

CITY OF TYLER
(Smith County)

1—CATHEDRAL OF THE IMMACULATE CONCEPTION (1987), Rev. Msgr. Joseph E. Strickland, J.C.L.; Revs. Timothy J. Kelly (Ireland); Augustine Tharappel (India); Raymundo Chavez Vasquez; Sr. Susan Seitz, O.S.F., Pastoral Assoc.; Deacon Ramiro Martinez. Social Services:
Office: 423 S. Broadway, 75702. Tel: 903-592-1617; Fax: 903-593-7326.
Res., 114 W. Front St., 75702. Tel: 903-592-5462.
Schools—St. Gregory School, 500 S. College St., 75702. Tel: 903-595-4109; Fax: 903-592-8626. Mrs. Kathy Shieldes Harry, Prin.
Lay Teachers 25; Students 339; Bishop T. K. Gorman Middle School, 1405 E.S.E. Loop 323, 75701. Tel: 903-561-2424; Fax: 903-561-2645. Mr. Jim Franz, Prin.
Students 188.
Bishop Gorman High School—Tel: 903-561-2424.
Priests 1; Lay Teachers 32; Students 183.
Catechesis/Religious Programs—Tel: 903-592-1317.
Lay Teachers 61; Students 551.
Chapel—St. Paul, 1015 E.S.E. Loop 323, 75702.
Station—St. Mary Magdalene, Flint.

2—ST. PETER CLAVER (1936), Rev. Luis Eduardo Larrea, M.F.E.
Res., 1403 N. Tenneha Ave., 75702. Tel: 903-595-2612; Fax: 903-595-2612. [JC]
Catechesis/Religious Programs—Fax: 903-596-9659.
Students 151.

OUTSIDE THE CITY OF TYLER

Athens, Henderson Co., St. Edward Church (1947), Rev. Pancras Savarimuthu (India).
Res., 800 E. Tyler, 75751-2140. Tel: 903-675-2509; Fax: 903-675-8805. [JC]
Catechesis/Religious Programs—Don Andress, D.R.E., Tel: 903-675-6610.
Students 229.

Atlanta, Cass Co., St. Catherine of Siena Church (1965). Unassigned. Vacant.
Res., 309 N. Louise St., P.O. Box 985, 75551-0985. Tel: 903-796-4494; Fax: 903-796-9990. [JC]
Catechesis/Religious Programs—Tel: 903-756-5723. Irene Webster, D.R.E.
Students 45.

Buffalo, Leon Co., Blessed Kateri Tekakwitha Church (1979), Rev. Theodore F. Rydelek.
Mailing Address: 208 N. Merrill, P.O. Box 878, 75831. Tel: 903-322-3705; Fax: 903-322-3155.
Catechesis/Religious Programs—Students 50.

Canton, Van Zandt Co., St. Therese (1980), Rev. Mathew Edassery (India) Admin.
Mailing Address: 14786 FM 859, 75103-3676. Tel: 903-567-4286.
Catechesis/Religious Programs—Students 91.
Mission—Wills Point, Van Zandt Co., St. Luke, 450 E. James St., Wills Point, 75169. Tel: 903-873-1238. Rev. Ouseph Thekumthala.

Carthage, Panola Co., St. William of Vercelli (1948), Rev. D. Stanislaus Perera (Sri Lanka).
Mailing Address: P.O. Drawer F, 75633. Tel: 903-693-3776; Fax: 903-693-3759. [JC]
Res., 202 W. Loop 436, 75633-0240. Tel: 903-693-5586.
Catechesis/Religious Programs—Students 65.

Center, Shelby Co., St. Therese (1951) (Spanish), Rev. Luke Kalarickal.
Res., 717 FM 2974, 75935-6006. Tel: 936-598-8458; Fax: 936-598-5599.
Catechesis/Religious Programs—Students 30.
Mission—Timpson, Shelby Co., Epiphany, 3072 US Hwy. 59 S., Timpson, 75975. Tel: 936-254-9662.

Clarksville, Red River Co., St. Joseph (1870), Rev. John Peter Stanialus.
Res., 406 E. Broadway, 75426-3110. Tel: 903-427-5044; Fax: 903-427-5044. [CEM]

Crockett, Houston Co., St. Francis of the Tejas (1931), Rev. Sales T. (Ranjan) Cletus, I.M.S. (India).
Res., 609 N. Fourth, 75835-4001. Tel: 409-544-5338; Fax: 409-544-7914.
Catechesis/Religious Programs—Amy Reed, D.R.E.
Students 72.
Mission—Centerville, Leon Co., St. Leo the Great, P.O. Box 356, Centerville, 75833-0356. Tel: 903-536-5012.
Station—St. Thomas More, Leon Co.

Daingerfield, Morris Co., Our Lady of Fatima (1951) (Hispanic), Rev. Jose George.
Mailing Address: Rte. 1, Box 4B, 75638-9704.
Res., Bert & Tiger Streets, 75638. Tel: 903-645-5637. [CEM]
Catechesis/Religious Programs—Students 88.

Diboll, Angelina Co., Our Lady of Guadalupe (1971) (Hispanic), Rev. Alirio Corrales; Deacon Jesus Reyes.
Mailing Address: P.O. Box 310, 75941-0310. Tel: 409-829-3650; Fax: 409-829-3650. [CEM]
Res., 100 Maynard St., 75941. Tel: 409-829-2690.
Catechesis/Religious Programs—Tel: 409-829-2981. Mrs. Valerie Maynard, D.R.E.
Students 92.

Fairfield, Freestone Co., St. Bernard of Clairvaux (1976), Rev. Msgr. Samuel Metzger, Admin.
Res., 630 W. Main, 75840-1418. Tel: 903-389-4616.
Catechesis/Religious Programs—Tel: 903-389-2444.
Students 40.
Mission—Teague, Freestone Co., St. Mary, 609 Cedar, 75840-1617. Tel: 254-739-3692. Rev. Jose Cortez (France).

Gilmer, Upshur Co., St. Francis of Assisi (1994), Rev. Daniel Gonzalez.
Mailing Address: P.O. Box 704, 75644-0704. Tel: 903-797-3303.
Res., 208 S. Montgomery, 75644. Tel: 903-843-9030.
Catechesis/Religious Programs—Tel: 903-797-3303.
Students 125.

Gun Barrel City, Henderson Co., St. Jude (1975), Rev. Andrew Melel, O.I.C., (India) Admin.; Deacons A. Howard Palms; Richard Sykora.
Res., 172 Luther Ln., 75147-9358. Tel: 903-887-1452 (Office); 887-5803 (Res.); Fax: 903-887-4906 (Office). [JC]
Catechesis/Religious Programs—Tel: 903-887-5252; 887-9795 (Office). Mrs. Edna Beltz, D.R.E.
Students 105.
Mission—Malakoff, Henderson Co., Mary Queen of Heaven, P.O. Box 508, 2269 CR 1703, Malakoff, 75148-4905. Tel: 903-489-2366. Rev. Joseph Kallookalam, C.M.I.

Hemphill, Sabine Co., St. Pius I (1939), Rev. Basil P. Hoan.
Corner Hwy. 184 & Barber St., P.O. Box 1925, 75948-1925. Tel: 409-787-3287; 787-4189 (Res.). [CEM]
Mission—St. Augustine, San Augustine Co., San Augustine, Hwy. 21, St. Augustine, 75972.

Henderson, Rusk Co., St. Jude (1934), Rev. Dariusz Pawlowski (Poland) Admin.
Res., 200 Morningside, 75652. Tel: 903-657-4398; Fax: 903-657-8958. [JC]
Catechesis/Religious Programs—Tel: 903-895-4655. Gina Juarez, D.R.E.
Students 137.

Jacksonville, Cherokee Co., Our Lady of Sorrows (1954), Rev. Efren Nano (Philippines).
Res., 1023 Corinth Rd., 75766-9801. Tel: 903-586-4538; Fax: 903-586-4996.
Catechesis/Religious Programs—Tel: 903-586-1559. Grace Traylor, D.R.E.
Students 192.
Missions—Rusk, Cherokee Co., Sacred Heart, P.O. Box 947, Rusk, 75785. Tel: 903-683-1862. Rev. Ambrose Chanappa.; New Summerfield, Cherokee Co., Our Lady of Guadalupe, Rt. 5, P.O. Box 357, New Summerfield, 75780-9351. Tel: 903-726-7272. Rev. Rubin Figueroa, O.F.M.

Jefferson, Marion Co., Immaculate Conception (1867), Revs. Henry Lorenc (Poland) Admin.; Joseph Kurian, C.M.I. (India).
Res., 201 N. Vale St., 75657-2143. Tel: 903-665-2869; Fax: 903-665-8778. [CEM]
Catechesis/Religious Programs—Tel: 903-665-8805.
Students 22.
Mission—Waskom, Harrison Co., St. Lawrence Brindisi, P.O. Box 928, Waskom, 75292-0928. Tel: 903-687-2385; Fax: 903-687-4503.
Catechesis/Religious Programs—Tel: 903-687-3532.
Students 42.

Kilgore, Gregg Co., Christ the King (1936), Revs. Mark Kusmirek; Jose Marin; John Whitsell; Deacons Dennis Gilchrist; Alejandro Cisneros; William Holda.
Res., 1407 Broadway, 75662-3209. Tel: 903-984-3716; Fax: 903-984-1426. [JC]
Catechesis/Religious Programs—Tel: 903-986-3573. Sr. Ines Arquello, E.F.M.S., D.R.E.
Students 186.
Mission—Overton, Rusk Co., Our Lady Queen of Angels, 221 State Hwy. East, P.O. Box 322, Overton, 75684. Tel: 903-984-0537.

Lindale, Smith Co., Holy Family (1994), Rev. Michael A. Doyle.
Mailing Address: 16314 FM 849, P.O. Box 1071, 75771. Tel: 903-882-4079; Fax: 903-882-8382.
Res., 113 S. Main St., 75771.
Catechesis/Religious Programs—Students 71.

Longview, Gregg Co., St. Anthony (1880) (Hispanic), Revs. Benjamin Smylie; Roger Appuhamy, Parochial Vicar; Mathias Rodriguez, Parochial Vicar; Deacon Joseph Pipak.
Mailing Address: 908 E. Olive St., 75601-6535. Tel: 903-758-0116; Fax: 903-758-9066.
Res., 908 E. Olive, 75601. Tel: 903-758-9550.
Church—506 N. 6th St., 75601.
Catechesis/Religious Programs—Students 116.
Mission—Big Sandy, Upshur Co., Holy Spirit, Rte. 1, Box 902, Big Sandy, 75755-9604. Deacon Sam Mullen.

St. Mary (1982), Revs. Gavin Vaverek, J.C.L.; Denzil Vithanage, S.S.S.; Deacons John Borens; John Shaffer; William H. Bridwell.
Res., 2108 Ridgewood Dr., 75605-5199. Tel: 903-757-5855.
School—405 Hollybrook Dr., 75605-2464. Tel: 903-753-1657; Fax: 903-758-7347. Mrs. Janel Garner, Prin.
Lay Teachers 20; Students 260.
Catechesis/Religious Programs—Tel: 903-757-5891; Fax: 903-758-5074.
Students 167.
Mission—Hallsville, Harrison Co., Our Lady of Grace, P.O. Box 782, Hallsville, 75650-0782. Tel: 903-668-1876; Fax: 903-668-5219. Rev. Jose Kannampuzha (India).

Lufkin, Angelina Co., St. Andrew (1998),
Mailing Address: P.O. Box 490, 75902.
Res., 1611 Feagin Dr., 75904. Tel: 936-632-9100; Fax: 936-632-0627.
Catechesis/Religious Programs—Students 93.

St. Patrick (1928), Revs. Eduardo Nevares, M.S.; Thomas M. Vellappellil, M.S.; Thomas J. Huhn, M.S.
Res., 2118 Lowry St., 75901-1316. Tel: 409-634-6833; Fax: 409-634-6891.
School—St. Patrick School, (Grades PreK-6). Tel: 409-634-6719. Larry Gaudet, Prin.
Lay Teachers 11; Students 170.
Catechesis/Religious Programs—Tel: 409-639-3676. D.R.E.: Rosie Vasquez, (PreK-6); Barbara Klimpt, (7-12).
Students 262.

Madisonville, Madison Co., St. Elizabeth Ann Seton (1978), Rev. S. Nicholas Perera (Sri Lanka).
Mailing Address: 209 S. Tammye Lane, 77864. Tel: 409-348-5570; Fax: 409-348-6599. [JC]
Catechesis/Religious Programs—Tel: 409-348-6368.
Students 105.

Marshall, Harrison Co., St. Joseph (1874), Rev. Ron Diegel; Deacons Adrian Roden; Santiago Suarez; Felipe Pena.
Res., 410 N. Alamo Blvd., 75670-3450. Tel: 903-935-2536; Fax: 903-938-1591. [CEM]
School—St. Joseph School, (Grades PreK-7) 2307 S. Garrett, 75670. Tel: 903-935-5502; Fax: 903-935-5502. Dean Karns, Prin.
Lay Teachers 8; Students 56.
Catechesis/Religious Programs—Students 171.
Mission—Tatum, Panola Co., San Pedro the Fisherman, Hwy. 43, P.O. Box 430, Tatum, 75691-0430. Tel: 903-947-6358; Fax: 903-947-2876.

Mineola, Wood Co., St. Peter the Apostle (1937), Rev. Bernard Boteju (Sri Lanka).
Res., 1520 N. Newsom, P.O. Box 1022, 75773-7022. Tel: 903-569-3665; Fax: 903-569-6961. [JC]
Catechesis/Religious Programs—Students 80.
Mission—Grand Saline, Van Zandt Co., St. Celestine, 116 W. Frank, Grand Saline, 75140. Rev. Lionel Fernando (Sri Lanka).

Mount Pleasant, Titus Co., St. Michael (1917), Revs. Stephen Joseph Duyka, Admin.; Cristobal de Jesus Puertos Hernandez (Colombia) Parochial Vicar.
Mailing Address: 1403 E. First St., 75455-4715. Tel: 903-572-5227; Fax: 903-572-9659.
Res., 310 Denman Dr., 75455-4157. Tel: 903-572-5611.
Catechesis/Religious Programs—Ofelia Valdez, D.R.E.
Students 241.

Mount Vernon, Franklin Co., Sacred Heart (1986), Rev. Lawrence Chellaian (India).
Mailing Address: P.O. Box 918, Mt. Vernon, 75457-0918. Tel: 903-537-2174; Fax: 903-537-2174.
Church—307 Rutherford St., 75457. [JC]
Catechesis/Religious Programs—Tel: 903-537-7280.
Students 70.

Nacogdoches, Nacogdoches Co., Sacred Heart (1716), Rev. Msgr. James E. Young; Revs. Octavio Suarez; Benedict J. Comisky; Victor Homan; Michael Barone.
Mailing Address: 2508 Appleby Sand Rd., 75961-3632. Tel: 409-564-7807; Fax: 409-564-8777.
Res., 504 North St., 75961. Tel: 409-564-7134. [CEM]
Catechesis/Religious Programs—Sr. Mary Ann Aman, C.H.M., D.R.E.
Students 369.
Missions—Chireno, Nacogdoches Co., Our Lady of Lourdes, 75961. Tel: 409-598-8458. Rev. Jerzy Debosz (Poland).; Moral, Nacogdoches Co., Immaculate Conception, Hwy. 7 West, Moral, 75964. [CEM]
Nacogdoches, Nacogdoches Co., Our Lady of Guadalupe, Hwy. 59 S., Nacogdoches, 75964.
Chapel—Nacogdoches, St. Mary's Chapel, Stephen F. Austin State University, 211 E. College, 75961. Tel: 409-564-0661. Rev. John W. Logan, O.P.

New Boston, Bowie Co., St. Mary of the Cenacle (1918), Rev. Varghese P. Varkey (India).
Mailing Address: P.O. Box 914, 75570-0914. Tel: 903-628-2323; Fax: 903-628-6186. [JC]
Res., 216 Magnolia St., 75570. Tel: 903-628-6186.
Catechesis/Religious Programs—Tel: 903-628-2323.
Students 40.
Mission—New Boston, Bowie Co., Hooks Catholic Community, Main St., 75570-0914.

Palestine, Anderson Co., Sacred Heart (1893), Revs. Zacharias S. Kunnakkattuthara (India); Ruben D. Bedoya (Colombia); Deacons Alex Kobar; Daniel Rose, Prison Chap.
Res., 503 N. Queen St., 75801-2718. Tel: 903-729-2463; Fax: 903-723-9799. [CEM]
Sacred Heart Preschool—503 N. Queen St., 75801-2718. Tel: 903-729-5375. Vivian Hollingsworth, Dir.
Catechesis/Religious Programs—Tel: 903-729-5375. David Bunch, D.R.E.
Students 401.
Missions—Frankston, Anderson Co., St. Charles Borromeo, 1101 Hwy. 155 N., Frankston, 75763. Tel: 903-876-3309; Fax: 903-876-3309. Rev. Zacharias S. Kunnakkattuthara.; Grapeland, Houston Co., St. Stephen, Hwy. 19 N., Grapeland, 75844.

Paris, Lamar Co., Our Lady of Victory (1880), Rev. Anthony Alphonse (India).
Res., 3300 Clarksville St., 75460. Tel: 903-784-1000; Fax: 903-784-3946. [JC]
Catechesis/Religious Programs—Paula Shoffeitt, D.R.E.
Students 239.

Pittsburg, Camp Co., Holy Cross (1987), Rev. Augustine J. Mailadiyil (India).
501 Hill Ave., 75686-1810. Tel: 903-856-7609. [JC]
Catechesis/Religious Programs—Students 90.

Sulphur Springs, Hopkins Co., St. James (1880), Rev. P. Kingsley Nonis (Sri Lanka) Admin.; Deacons Donald R. Brown; Jose Hernandez; William O'Brien; Loren Seely.
Mailing Address: P.O. Box 93, 75483-0093.
297 Texas St., 75483. Tel: 903-885-1222; Fax: 903-885-5855.
Res., 303 Texas St., 75483. Tel: 903-885-2873.
Catechesis/Religious Programs—Tel: 903-885-0157. Susie Thesing, D.R.E.
Students 242.
Missions—Emory, Rains Co., St. John the Evangelist, P.O. Box 93, Emory, 75482.; Winnsboro, Wood Co., St. Ann, P.O. Box 733, Winnsboro, 75494-0733. Tel: 903-629-7884. Rev. Jose G. Kumblumkal (India).; Cooper, Delta Co., St. Clare Mission, 10 E. Side Sq., Cooper, 75432.

Texarkana, Bowie Co., Sacred Heart (1874), Rev. Msgr. Gerald Priest; Rev. Anthony McLaughlin; Deacon Keith A. Woods.
Res., 4505 Elizabeth St., 75503-2998. Tel: 903-794-4444; Fax: 903-792-1529. [CEM 2]
Catechesis/Religious Programs—Tel: 903-792-6846.
Students 260.

Trinity, Trinity Co., Most Holy Trinity (1972), Rev. Felix Chirapurathel, O.Praem., (India) Admin.
Res., Rte. 1, Box 61-X, 75862-9801. Tel: 936-594-6664; Fax: 936-594-5244. [JC]

Tyler, Smith Co., Our Lady of Guadalupe Church (1996) (Hispanic), Rev. Said Duran.
Church & Mailing Address: 922 Old Omen Rd., 75701-3709. Tel: 903-593-2006; Fax: 903-593-6033.
Catechesis/Religious Programs—Tel: 903-877-2380.
Students 240.

Union Grove-Gladewater, Upshur Co., St. Theresa of the Infant Jesus (1945), Rev. Xavier Pappu; Deacon Guy Blasingame.
Mailing Address: P.O. Box 967, Gladewater, 75647-0967. Tel: 903-845-2306.
Old Hwy. 271 & Point Pleasant Rd., Union Grove, Tel: 903-845-2306.
Catechesis/Religious Programs—Students 90.

Whitehouse, Smith Co., Prince of Peace (1996), Rev. Daniel L. Daugherty.
Mailing Address: P.O. Box 456, 75791-0456. Tel: 903-581-9600; Fax: 903-561-4946.
Res., 508 Cottage Ln., 75791. Tel: 903-839-7599.
Catechesis/Religious Programs—Students 96.

Chaplains of Public Institutions

FAIRFIELD. *Boyd Unit, Texas Department of Criminal Justice.* Rev. Msgr. Samuel Metzer, Mailing Address: 630 W. Main, 75840-1418.

LOVELADY. *Eastham Unit, Texas Department of Corrections* Rte. 1, Box 93, 75851. Tel: 409-636-7147. Rev. Virginio C. Vazquez (CC) Chap., Mailing Address: P.O. Box 16, 75851-0016.

NEW BOSTON. *Telford Unit.* Deacon Donald R. Brown Tel: 903-628-2706.

PALESTINE. *Beto I Unit and Louie C. Powledge Unit, Texas Department of Corrections.* Deacon Daniel Rose, Chap., Mailing Address: Beto I Unit & Louie C. Powledge Unit, Texas Department of Corrections, Rte. 2, Box 2250, 75801-9612. Tel: 903-723-5074, Ext: 342 (Beto I Unit); 723-5074 (Louie C. Powledge Unit).

RUSK. *Jerry H. Hodge Unit, TDCC.* Deacon Bryan Carey, P.O. Box 999, 75785-0999. Tel: 903-683-5781.
Rusk State Hospital and Skyview Unit, Texas Dept. of Corrections. Deacon Bryan Carey.

TENNESSEE COLONY. *Michael Unit, Texas Department of Corrections.* Rev. Harold P. Paulsen, Chap., Michael Unit, Box 4500, 75886-4500. Tel: 903-928-2311.

Special Assignment:
Reverend Monsignors—
Joseph, Milam, Pres., University of Dallas, 1845 E. Northgate, Irving, TX 75062. Tel: 214-721-4047

Retired:
Reverend Fathers—
Lenz, Henry J., M.S.
O'Donnell, Robert Patrick, 1106 S. Merritt St., Mount Pleasant, TX 75455. Tel: 903-572-2529
Whitney, Peter A., Queen of Peace, 1224 Cedar Dr., LaMarque, TX 77568-3932

Absent on Sick Leave:
Reverend Fathers—
Zakshesky, Francis, 8409 CR 31, Sinton, TX 78387

Permanent Deacons:
Blasingame, Guylan, St. Theresa, Union Grove
Borens, John, St. Mary, Longview
Bridwell, William H., St. Mary, Longview
Brown, Donald R., Telford Unit, New Boston
Calonge, Elie P., Michael Unit, Tennessee Colony, TDC
Carey, Thomas B., Michael Unit, TDC, Tennessee Colony
Cisneros, Alejandro, Christ the King, Kilgore
Cordero, Abelino, St. Patrick, Lufkin
Flores, William, St. Edward, Athens
Garcia, Edwin, St. James, Sulphur Spring
George, Anthony, (Retired), Cathedral of the Immaculate Conception, Tyler
Germann, Joseph, St. Ann, Winnsboro
Gilchrist, Dennis S., Christ the King, Kilgore
Gonzales, Pedro, Sacred Heart, Nacogdoches
Gutting, Justin, St. Jude, Gun Barrel City
Hall, Dwight S., (Inactive), Cathedral of the Immaculate Conception, Tyler
Hernandez, Jose, St. James, Sulphur Springs
Holda, William M., Christ the King, Kilgore
Kennedy, William C., III, Sacred Heart, Nacodoches
Kobar, Alex, Sacred Heart, Palestine
Martinez, Ramiro, Cathedral of the Immaculate Conception, Tyler
Mijares, Juan, St. Patrick, Lufkin
Milton, John, Assignment Outside Diocese
Mireles, Jose Luis, San Pedro the Fisherman, Tatum
Moreno, Joe Ibarra, St. Michael, Mt. Pleasant
Mullen, Sam, Sacred Heart, Mt. Vernon
O'Brien, William E., St. James, Sulphur Springs
O'Sullivan, William H., (Retired), Cathedral of the Immaculate Conception, Tyler
Palms, Howard A., St. Jude, Gun Barrel City
Panuco, Ignacio, Sacred Heart, Rusk
Pena, Felipe, St. Joseph, Marshall
Perez, Catarino, Jr., Our Lady of Guadalupe,Diboll
Pipak, Joseph, St. Anthony, Longview
Ramos, Manuel, St. Patrick, Lufkin
Reyes, Jesus, Our Lady of Guadalupe, Diboll
Roden, John Adrian, St. Joseph, Marshall
Rojas, Gonzalo, St. Anthony, Longview
Rose, Daniel, Beto I & Powledge Unit, TDC, Palestine
Seely, Loren G., St. James, Sulphur Springs
Shaffer, John K., St. Mary, Longview
Sosa, Librado Cruz, Sacred Heart, Nacogdoches
Suarez, Santiago, St. Joseph, Marshall
Sykora, Richard L., St. Jude, Gun Barrel City
Tapia, Ezequiel, Sacred Heart, Nacogdoches
Torres, Juventino, Our Lady of Sorrows, Jacksonville
Trevino, Gerardo, St. Patrick, Lufkin
Villalobos, Manuel, St. Anthony, Longview
Woods, Keith A., Sacred Heart, Texarkana

INSTITUTIONS LOCATED IN THE DIOCESE

[A] GENERAL HOSPITALS

TYLER. *Trinity Mother Frances Health System,* 800 E. Dawson St., 75701. Tel: 903-593-8441; Fax: 903-531-4067
For a complete listing, refer to the Hospitals section.

MADISON. *Madison Acquisition Company dba Madison St. Joseph Health Center,* P.O. Box 698 - 100 W. Cross St., 77864-0698
For a complete listing, refer to the Hospitals section.

PARIS. *Christus Home Health Services of North Texas,* 165 S.E. 6th St., 75460. Tel: 903-737-3622
For a complete listing, refer to the Hospitals section.
Christus St. Joseph Health Sytstem, 820 Clarksville St., P.O. Box 9070, 75461. Tel: 903-785-4521; Fax: 903-737-3848.
E-mail: monty_mclaurin@iwhs.org
For a complete listing, refer to the Hospitals section.

TEXARKANA. *Christus St. Michael Health System,* 2600 St. Michael Dr., 75503. Tel: 903-614-1000; Fax: 903-614-2541.
E-mail: whited@smit.sch.org
Web site: www.christusstmichael.org
For a complete listing, refer to the Hospitals section.
St. Michael Rehabilitation Hospital, 2400 St. Michael Dr., 75503. Tel: 903-614-4000; Fax: 903-614-4064.
Web site: www.christusstmichael.org
For a complete listing, refer to the Hospitals section.

[B] MONASTERIES AND RESIDENCES OF PRIESTS

PALESTINE. *Hermitage,* Rte. 3, Box 3575, 75801.
E-mail: dhpvcsl@hotmail.com
Revs. Denis Walsh; David Verhalin, C.S.C. Other Institutions: Houses of Religious Men 1; Total in Residence 2; Total Staff 2.
Prayer Mountain Hermitage, Rte. 3, Box 3574, 75801. Sr. Mary Vogel, H.S.S.R.

[C] CONVENTS AND RESIDENCES FOR SISTERS

LUFKIN. *Monastery of the Infant Jesus*, 1501 Lotus Ln., 75904-2699. Tel: 409-634-4233; Fax: 409-634-2156. Cloistered Dominican Nuns. Sr. Mary John, O.P., Prioress; Rev. John Dominic Tamburello, O.P. Professed Sisters 20.

[D] CAMPUS MINISTRY

TYLER. *Tyler Junior College and The University of Texas at Tyler Newman Center*, 423 S. Broadway, 75702. Tel: 903-592-1617. Attended from the Cathedral of the Immaculate Conception.

NACOGDOCHES. *Stephen F. Austin University Catholic Student Center*, P.O. Box 7051, SFASU, 75962. Tel: 936-564-0661. Rev. John D. Logan, O.P., Chap. Other Institutions: Newman Centers; Total in Residence 1; Total Staff 1.

[E] MISCELLANEOUS

TYLER.

Tyler Catholic School Foundation, 1015 E.S.E. Loop 323, 75701-9663. Tel: 903-534-8807; Fax: 903-534-8807. Mailing Address: P.O. Box 131175, 75713. D. V. Emery, Exec. Dir.

LONGVIEW.

Longview Catholic School Endowment Fund, 405 Hollybrook, 75605.

LUFKIN.

St. Patrick School Foundation, 2118 Lowry, 75901. Tel: 409-634-6833; Fax: 409-634-6891. E-mail: stpat@lcc.com

St. Patrick School Fund, 2118 Lowry, 75901. Tel: 409-634-6833; Fax: 409-634-6891. E-mail: stpat@lcc.com

RELIGIOUS INSTITUTES OF MEN REPRESENTED IN THE DIOCESE

For further details refer to the corresponding bracketed number in the Religious Institutes of Men or Women section.

[0600]—*Brothers of the Congregation of the Holy Cross.*—C.S.C.

[]—*Carmelite of Mary Immaculate.*—C.M.I.

[0360]—*Claretian Missionaries.*—C.M.F.

[0220]—*Congregation of the Blessed Sacrament.*—S.S.S.

[]—*Franciscan.*—O.F.M.

[0570]—*Glenmary Home Missioners.*—Glmy.

[]—*Holy Cross of Notre Dame.*—C.S.C.

[]—*Indian Missionary Society.*—I.M.S.

[0720]—*The Missionaries of Our Lady of La Salette.*—M.S.

[]—*Missionaries of St. Francis de Sales.*—M.S.F.S.

[]—*Missionary Franciscans of the Eucharist.*—M.F.E.

[]—*Norbertine Fathers.*—O.Praem.

[0430]—*Order of Preachers - Dominicans.*—O.P.

[]—*Order of the Imitation of Christ.*—O.I.C.

RELIGIOUS INSTITUTES OF WOMEN REPRESENTED IN THE DIOCESE

[0230]—*Benedictine Sisters of Pontifical Jurisdiction.*—O.S.B.

[2100]—*Congregation of the Humility of Mary.*—C.H.M.

[]—*Congregation of the Mother of Carmel.*—C.M.C.

[0470]—*Congregation of the Sisters of Charity of the Incarnate Word. Houston, Texas.* (San Antonio, TX).—C.C.V.I.

[1050]—*Dominican Contemplative Nuns.*—O.P.

[1070-19]—*Dominican Sisters of Houston, Texas (Congregation of the Sacred Heart).*—O.P.

[]—*Eucharistic Franciscan Sisters of Los Angeles.*—E.F.M.S.

[]—*Hermit Sisters of St. Romuald.*—H.S.S.R.

[2970]—*School Sisters of Notre Dame.*—S.S.N.D.

[0990]—*Sisters of Divine Providence.*—C.D.P.

[1570]—*Sisters of St. Francis of the Holy Family.*—O.S.F.

[1970]—*Sisters of the Holy Family of Nazareth.*—C.S.F.N.

NECROLOGY

(No Deaths)

Diocese of Venice

(Diocesis Venetiae in Florida)

Most Reverend

JOHN J. NEVINS, D.D.

Bishop of Venice; ordained June 6, 1959; appointed Titular Bishop of Rusticiana and Auxiliary of Miami February 6, 1979; consecrated March 24, 1979; appointed First Bishop of Venice July 17, 1984; installed October 25, 1984. *Res., P.O. Box 2006, Venice, FL, 34284.*

To Serve with Mercy

ESTABLISHED OCTOBER 25, 1984.

Square Miles 9,035.

Comprises the Counties of Charlotte, Collier, DeSoto, Glades, Hardee, Hendry, Highlands, Lee, Manatee and Sarasota in the State of Florida.

For legal titles of parishes and diocesan institutions, consult the Chancellor.

Catholic Center: P.O. Box 2006, Venice, FL, 34284. Tel.: 941-484-9543; Fax: 941-484-1121.

Web site address: dioceseofvenice.org

E-mail address: info@dioceseofvenice.org

STATISTICAL OVERVIEW

Personnel	
Bishop	1
Priests: Diocesan Active in Diocese	65
Priests: Active Outside Diocese	7
Priests: Retired, Sick or Absent	24
Number of Diocesan Priests	96
Religious Priests in Diocese	73
Extern Priests in Diocese	81
Ordinations:	
Diocesan Priests	1
Religious Priests	1
Transitional Deacons	4
Permanent Deacons in Diocese	78
Total Brothers	24
Total Sisters	120
Parishes	
Parishes	51
With Resident Pastor:	
Resident Diocesan Priests	40
Resident Religious Priests	11
Missions	5
Pastoral Centers	8
New Parishes Created	1
Professional Ministry Personnel:	
Brothers	2
Sisters	22
Lay Ministers	73
Welfare	
Catholic Hospitals	2
Total Assisted	441,499
Health Care Centers	8
Total Assisted	44,455
Homes for the Aged	9
Total Assisted	38,614
Day Care and Extended Day Care Centers	2
Total Assisted	73
Specialized Homes	2
Total Assisted	286
Special Centers for Social Services	17
Total Assisted	48,000
Other Institutions	1
Total Assisted	5,352
Educational	
Diocesan Students in Other Seminaries	11
Total Seminarians	11
High Schools, Diocesan and Parish	3
Total Students	1,652
Elementary Schools, Diocesan and Parish	9
Total Students	3,664
Catechesis/Religious Education:	
High School Students	621
Elementary Students	9,979
Total Students Under Catholic Instruction	15,927
Teachers in the Diocese:	
Priests	5
Brothers	2
Sisters	13
Lay Teachers	318
Vital Statistics	
Receptions into the Church:	
Infant Baptism Totals	4,597
Adult Baptism Totals	215
Received into Full Communion	343
First Communions	2,756
Confirmations	2,311
Marriages:	
Catholic	496
Interfaith	305
Total Marriages	801
Deaths	2,512
Total Catholic Population	181,941
Total Population	1,453,244

Catholic Center—1000 Pinebrook Rd., Venice, 34292. Tel: 941-484-9543; Fax: 941-484-1121., *Mailing Address: P.O. Box 2006, Venice, 34284.*

Office of the Bishop—Rev. JACEK KOWALIK, Asst. to the Bishop; Mrs. JOHANNA MARONE, Exec. Sec.; Ms. DOROTHY VIEIRA, Receptionist & Sec.

Vicar General—Very Rev. THOMAS G. ANGLIM, V.G.

Chancellor and Moderator of the Curia—Very Rev. JEROME A. CAROSELLA.

Administrative Assistant to the Chancellor/Notary—Miss JEANNE C. HICKEY.

Treasurer—Very Rev. NEIL FLEMMING.

College of Consultors—Very Revs. THOMAS G. ANGLIM, V.G.; JEROME A. CAROSELLA, Chancellor; EDWARD D. MORETTI, V.E.; NEIL FLEMMING; JOSEPH STEARNS, V.F.; Revs. GERARD FINEGAN; NICANOR LOBATO; VINCENT SHEEHY; ROBERT D. TABBERT.

Episcopal Vicars and Deans—Very Rev. EDWARD D. MORETTI, V.E., Northern and Eastern Deaneries; Vacant; Southern and Central Deaneries; Very Rev. JOSE H. RUIZ, V.F., Eastern Deanery; Vacant, Central Deanery; Very Rev. JOSEPH STEARNS, V.F., Southern Deanery; Very Rev. FAUSTO STAMPIGLIA, S.A.C., V.F., Northern Deanery.

Presbyteral Council—Very Revs. THOMAS G. ANGLIM, V.G.; JEROME A. CAROSELLA, Chancellor; EDWARD D. MORETTI, V.E.; JOSE H. RUIZ, V.F.; NEIL FLEMMING; FAUSTO STAMPIGLIA, S.A.C., V.F.; JOSEPH STEARNS, V.F.; Revs. CLAUDE BRUBAKER; JOSEPH CLIFFORD; JOHN DEARY, O.S.A.; VICENTE LLARIA; ROBERT MATTINGLY; STEPHEN E. MCNAMARA; ROBERT MONGIELLO; EDWARD PICK; GEORGE RATZMANN; THOMAS ZEDAR.

Theologian to the Bishop—Rev. FAUSTO STAMPIGLIA, S.A.C., V.F.

Censor Librorum—Rev. Msgr. ANTHONY A. LAFEMINA, S.T.L., J.C.D.

Vicar for Priests—Very Rev. EDWARD D. MORETTI, V.E.

Vicar for Deacons—Deacon EDWARD LUNDY.

Vicar for Religious—Sr. CHRYSTA LERHINAN, I.H.M.

Priest Personnel Board—Rev. STEPHEN E. MCNAMARA, Chm.

Continuing Education of Clergy—Rev. MARK HEUBERGER.

Official Archivist—Very Rev. JEROME A. CAROSELLA.

Historical Archivist—Mrs. GAIL M. MCGRATH.

Delegate of the Bishop for Sexual Misconduct Cases—Dr. TERRY REILLY, D.Min., M.A., Case Mgr.

Diocesan Tribunal—All Pastoral Center searches for information prior to October 25, 1984 should be directed to the Diocese of St. Petersburg for Manatee, Hardee, Sarasota, DeSoto, Glades, Charlotte and Lee Counties; to the Diocese of Orlando for Highlands Co. and to the Archdiocese of Miami for Hendry and Collier Counties.

Judicial Vicar—Very Rev. ROBERT R. CANNON, M.Th., J.C.L.

Adjutant Judicial Vicars—Revs. JOSEPH AMATO, J.C.L.; JOHN V. DOLCIAMORE, S.T.L., J.C.L.

Auditor—Rev. MICHAEL A. SCHEIP.

Defender of the Bond—Rev. JOEL SCHEVERS, O.Carm., M.A., Th.M.

Promoter of Justice—Vacant.

Judges—Very Rev. ROBERT R. CANNON, M.Th., J.C.L.; Revs. JOSEPH S. AMATO, J.C.L.; JOHN V. DOLCIAMORE, S.T.L., J.C.L.; DENNIS C. KLEMME, J.C.D.; Rev. Msgr. ELLSWORTH KNEAL, J.C.D.

Ecclesiastical Notaries—Mrs. ANN MANRODT; Mrs. MARIANA BARTOLILLO; Mrs. ZONIA HERRERA.

Vicar for Marriage Matters—Very Rev. ROBERT R. CANNON, M.Th., J.C.L.

Diocesan Offices

Building Department—Mr. RAYMOND HADDAD, Dir.

Campaign for Human Development—Mrs. BRIDGET SHEEHAN, Dir.

Campus Ministry (Pastoral Ministries Department)—Rev. RICHARD WOJNICKI, O.S.F.S., Dir., Mailing Address: *9404 Windlake Dr., Fort Myers, 33912.* Tel: 941-267-2509; Fax: 413-502-3041. Campuses served: Florida Gulf Coast Universtiy, Edison Community College (Lee, Collier and Charlotte Counties). Rev. ALBERTO BUENO, T.O.R., *524 58th St., Sarasota, 34243.* Tel: 941-355-6952. Campuses served: New College (at USF-Sarasota), Ringling School of Art and Design, Manatee Community College.

[*]Catholic Charities of the Diocese of Venice, Inc.—Mrs. ROSEMARY WINDER STRANGE, A.C.S.W., Exec. Dir.

Catholic Relief Services/Operation Rice Bowl—Mrs. BRIDGET SHEEHAN, Dir.

Communications Department—Mrs. GAIL M. MCGRATH, Dir. Tel: 941-486-4702; Fax: 941-486-4761. Mrs. NAOMI ZOELLER, Exec. Asst.

The Florida Catholic, Venice Edition—Most Rev. JOHN J. NEVINS, D.D., Publisher; Mr. JOSHUA NOEM, Editor/Reporter. Tel: 941-486-4701; Fax: 941-486-4763.

The Florida Catholic of Venice, Inc.—Very Rev. JEROME A. CAROSELLA, Pres. & Dir.; Mrs. GAIL M. MCGRATH, Sec. & Dir.; Mr. JOHN G. BAUER, Treas. & Dir.

Catholic Mass on Television—Mrs. GAIL M. MCGRATH, Exec. Producer; Mrs. NAOMI ZOELLER, Production Coord.; Mrs. HEATHER MCBRAYER, Production Asst.

Venice Catholic Communications, Inc.—1000 Pinebrook Rd., Venice, 34292. Most Rev. JOHN J. NEVINS, D.D., Pres. & Dir.; Very Rev. JEROME A. CAROSELLA, Vice Pres. & Dir.; Mrs. GAIL M. MCGRATH, Sec. & Treas. & Dir.

Web Site—Mrs. JUDY PIPER, Internet/Intranet Coord.

Information Technology Services—Ms. PAMELA BURKE, Mgr.; Mr. FRAN STETSON, Technology Coord.

Development Office / Annual Bishop's Appeal—Mr. WILLIAM MCCARTHY, Dir.

Diaconate—Very Rev. FAUSTO STAMPIGLIA, S.A.C., V.F., Dir.

Ecumenical and Interreligious Affairs—Revs. WILLIAM ADAMS; JOEL SCHEVERS, O.Carm.; Ms. JOANNE WEBER.

Education—Sr. ROBERTA SCHMIDT, C.S.J., Dir.; Sr. REGIS KRUSNIEWSKI, S.S.N.D., Dir., Catechetical Ministry; Mrs. ROSEMARY BRATTON, Supt. of Schools; Bros. PAUL HENNESSY, C.F.C., Pres., School for Pastoral Ministry; E. THOMAS HEWITT, C.F.C., Coord., Migrant Education Apostolate, Los Hermanos.

Finance Department—Very Rev. NEIL FLEMMING, V.F., Diocesan Treas.; Mr. JOHN BAUER, Dir.; Mrs. MARY MOORE, Controller.

Insurance—Mr. DAN DURKIN, Mgr.; Ms. JOANNE COYNE, Admin.

Internal Financial Services—Mrs. LEIGH MORROW, Dir.; Ms. JANET FLAGG, Accounting Asst.

Legal—Ms. VICTORIA H. PFLUG, Esq.; Mrs. LORRAINE CARRIERE, Legal Sec.

Ministry to Cultural Groups—

African Caribbean American Ministry (Pastoral Ministries Department) (AFCAAM)—Mr. ISMAEL HERNANDEZ, M.A., Dir.

Hispanic, Migrant and Spanish Speaking Apostolates / National Migration Week—Rev. NICANOR LOBATO, Dir.

Juventud Hispana (Hispanic Youth Ministry)—Rev. JOSE GONZALEZ, Dir. Espiritual. Coord. Laicos: Mr. JUVENCIO ILDEFONSO; Mrs. BLANCA ILDEFONSO.

Office of Black Catholic Ministry (Pastoral Ministries Department)—Ms. CRYSTAL ABRAHAM-HERNANDEZ, Dir. Tel: 941-344-0570.

Ministry to Haitian People in Charlotte, DeSoto, Glades, Highlands and Hardee Counties (Pastoral Ministries Department)—Rev. ANTONIO JEAN.

Ministry to Haitian People in Manatee and Sarasota Counties (Pastoral Ministries Department)—Rev. JEAN RONALD JOSEPH.

Ministry to People with HIV / AIDS—Most Rev. PRIAMO ROSARIO-TEJEDA; Sr. FRANCES NEVOLO, O.L.C., Sarasota County; Sr. JUDY H. SIMONIS, C.S.J., Charlotte County; Sr. MARY JOHN FRANEY, O.L.C., Lee County.

Pastoral Ministries—Directors: Dr. MIMI REILLY, D.Min.; Dr. TERRY H. REILLY, D.Min.

Bishop's Critical Concerns Committee—Mr. JAMES HANKS, Chm. Executive Directors: Dr. MIMI REILLY, D.Min.; Dr. TERRY REILLY, D.Min.

Domestic Violence Task Force—Chairmen: Mrs. PAT HINES; Mrs. SHARON KABEL.

Victim's Assistance Task Force—Ms. MARINA KOPKO, Chm.

Anti-Pornography Task Force—Mrs. ESTHER RACHWAL, Chm.

Charismatic Renewal—Very Rev. ROBERT R. CANNON, M.Th., J.C.L., Spiritual Dir.; Rev. MICHAEL SCHEIP, Asst. Spiritual Dir.; Mrs. EM WEIS, Dir.

Contemplative Prayer—Rev. ROBERT MATTINGLY, Spiritual Moderator; Dr. MIMI REILLY, D.Min., Exec. Dir.

Evangelization—Directors: Dr. MIMI REILLY, D.Min.; Dr. TERRY H. REILLY, D.Min.

Families with Loved Ones in Prison—Ms. CRISSIE CARTER, M.S.W., Dir.

Family Life Office—(includes Parenting and all Marriage Enrichment and Marriage Preparation programs). Directors: Mrs. PATRICIA HINES; Mrs. SHARON KABEL, M.A.

Divorced and Separated Ministry—Rev. GERARD BENSON, O.Carm., Coord.

Lay Ministry Office—Directors: Dr. MIMI REILLY, D.Min.; Dr. TERRY H. REILLY, D.Min.

Older Catholics, Apostolate for—Dr. ANNE SWING, D.Min., Dir.

Parish Pastoral Ministers—Dr. MIMI REILLY, D.Min., Coord.

Peace and Social Justice—Mr. NEIL MICHAUD, Dir.

Persons with Disabilities, Apostolate for—Ms. DAWN MCPARTLAND, Dir.

Respect Life—Rev. NICHOLAS MCLOUGHLIN, Moderator; Very Rev. ROBERT R. CANNON, M.Th., J.C.L., Assoc. Moderator; Mrs. JEANNE BERDEAUX, Dir.; Ms. MARINA KOPKO, Assoc. Dir.

Project Rachel—Tel: 800-329-4787.

Youth Ministry Office—Mrs. LORRAINE SMITH, Exec. Dir.

Teens Encounter Christ—Rev. JOSEPH CLIFFORD, Spiritual Moderator.

Scouting—Rev. TIMOTHY NAVIN, Spiritual Dir.; Deacon FRANCIS COLE, Dir.

Prison Ministry—Priests of the Diocese; Deacon EDWARD D. LUNDY.

Rural Life—Very Rev. JOSE J. RUIZ, V.F., Dir.

Vocations / Seminarian Formation—Revs. ROBERT KANTOR; CELESTINO GUTIERREZ; MARK HEUBERGER.

Other Offices

Propagation of the Faith / Mission Cooperative Program—Rev. EDWARD PICK, Dir.

Organizations

Cursillo Movement—Rev. CHARLES MALLEN, C.SS.R., Spiritual Dir.; Mr. DAVE HARTING, Lay Dir.

Secretariado Hispano de Cursillos—Rev. AURELIANO SANTA OLAYA, Dir. Espiritual; Mr. CARMELO ORTEGA, Dir. Laico.

Holy Childhood Association—Rev. EUGENE MCCARTHY, Dir.

International Order of Alhambra, La Mancha Caravan 250—Mr. WILLIAM LEYDEN, Grand Commander.

Legion of Mary—Revs. VINCENT CLEMENTE, Manasota Curia; RAFAEL PADILLA, Southwest Florida Curia.

Serra International—Mr. FRANKLIN THEN.

St. Vincent DePaul Society—Dr. THOMAS F. FERRARA, Ph.D., Diocesan Trustee.

Venice Diocesan Council of Catholic Women—Rev. CLAUDE BRUBAKER, Spiritual Dir.; Mrs. PATRICIA CONSOLMAGNO, Pres.

Advisory Groups to the Bishop

Audit Committee—Mr. ERNEST SKINNER, Chm.

Finance Advisory Board—Mr. THOMAS OWENS, Chm.

Executive Investment Committee—Mr. THOMAS OWENS, Chm.

Insurance Committee—Very Rev. THOMAS G. ANGLIM, V.G., Chm.

Pension Plan Board of Trustees (Archdiocese of Miami / Dioceses of St. Petersburg and Venice)—Very Rev. THOMAS G. ANGLIM, V.G., Co-Vice Chm.

Planning and Development Committee—Very Rev. THOMAS G. ANGLIM, V.G., Chm.

Priest Personnel Board—Rev. STEPHEN E. MCNAMARA, Chm.

Real Estate Board—Revs. JEROME A. CAROSELLA, Co-Chm. NEIL FLEMMING, Co-Chm.

Resource Team—Dr. TERRY REILLY, D.Min., Case Mgr., *St. Peter Claver Chapel, 3681 Michigan Ave., Fort Myers, 33916.*

CLERGY, PARISHES, MISSIONS AND PAROCHIAL SCHOOLS

CITY OF VENICE
(Sarasota County)

1—EPIPHANY CATHEDRAL (1958), Very Rev. Robert R. Cannon, J.C.L., Rector; Revs. Michael A. Scheip; Lukas Schmidt, O.Carm; Joel Schevers, O.Carm., (Retired); Peter F. Brudzynski, (Retired); Piotr Zawadzki; Deacons John L. Blackburn, (Retired); Richard Nowak; Terry Farrell; Coleman Geary; Robert Tomasso; Francis Cole. In res., Revs. Jack Cosentino; Normando Feliz.
Res., 310 Sarasota St., 34285. Tel: 941-484-3505; Fax: 941-488-9333.
School—316 Sarasota St., 34285. Tel: 941-488-2215; Fax: 941-488-2216. Dewayne Byrnes, Prin. Lay Teachers 27; Students 458.
Catechesis / Religious Programs—Tel: 941-485-2325. Sr. Frances Lalor, R.S.M., D.R.E. Students 406.

2—OUR LADY OF LOURDES (1986), Rev. Vincent J. Sheehy; Deacon James Cooper.
Res., 1301 Center Rd., 34292. Tel: 941-497-2931; Fax: 941-497-5849.
Catechesis / Religious Programs—Students 127.

OUTSIDE THE CITY OF VENICE

Arcadia, De Soto Co., St. Paul (1885), Rev. William Adams, S.T.L.
Res., 1208 E. Oak St., 34266. Tel: 863-494-2611; Fax: 863-494-6385.
Catechesis / Religious Programs—Tel: 863-494-2835.
Students 300.
Mission—Nocatee, De Soto Co., Blessed Juan Diego, 52417 S.W. Hwy. 17, Nocatee, 34266. Tel: 863-993-4095.

Avon Park, Highlands Co., Our Lady of Grace (1956), Rev. Gerald P. Grogan.
Res., 595 E. Main St., 33825. Tel: 863-453-4757; Fax: 863-453-2620.
Catechesis / Religious Programs—Tel: 863-453-7537. Patricia A. White, D.R.E.
Students 172.

Boca Grande, Lee Co., Our Lady of Mercy (1988), Very Rev. Jerome A. Carosella.
Res., P.O. Box 181, 33921. Tel: 941-964-2254; Fax: 941-964-1124.

Bokeelia, Lee Co., Our Lady of the Miraculous Medal (1965), Rev. J. Thomas Pohto, O.S.A.; Deacon Frank Urrico.
Res., 12175 H. Stringfellow Rd., 33922. Tel: 941-283-0456; Fax: 941-283-1118.
Catechesis / Religious Programs—Students 75.

Bonita Springs, Lee Co., St. Leo (1962), Revs. Thaddeus Kloc; Ernest Fears.
Res., 28290 Beaumont Rd., 34134. Tel: 941-992-0901; Fax: 941-992-5282.
Catechesis / Religious Programs—Karen Skrapits, D.R.E.
Students 123.
Mission—Bonita Springs, Lee Co., Hispanic Mission.

Bradenton, Manatee Co., Sacred Heart (1969), Revs. Joseph G. Clifford; Gerard F. Critch; Thomas P. Sharkey, C.S.Sp.
Res., 1220 15th St. W., 34205. Tel: 941-748-2221; Fax: 941-748-1744.
Catechesis / Religious Programs—Tel: 941-746-3650.
Students 293.

St. Joseph (1927), Rev. Robert G. Tierney; Deacon Robert R. Nimon.
Res., 2704 33rd Ave. W., 34205. Tel: 941-756-3732; Fax: 941-758-1244.
School—Tel: 941-755-2611; Fax: 941-755-2611. Sr. Christine Patrick, S.P., Prin.
Sisters 1; Lay Teachers 27; Students 465.
Catechesis / Religious Programs—Tel: 941-755-4335; Fax: 941-753-5634. Luci Hartman, D.R.E.
Students 250.

SS. Peter and Paul the Apostles (1987), Very Rev. Edward D. Moretti, V.E.; Rev. Robert Kantor.
Office: 2850 75th St. W., 34209. Tel: 941-795-1228; Fax: 941-794-0127. [CEM]
Catechesis / Religious Programs—Tel: 941-798-9705; Fax: 941-794-3012. AnnaLuisa Huffman, D.R.E.
Students 471.

Cape Coral, Lee Co., St. Andrew (1964), Revs. James K. Flemming; Arnold Zebrowski; Edward Gibbons; Anthony Hewitt; Deacon Dennis Hedge. In res., Rev. Msgr. John O'Dowd, (Retired); Rev. Marc Lussier, M.S.A.
Res., 2628 Del Prado Blvd., 33904. Tel: 941-574-4545; Fax: 941-574-2450.
School—(Grades K-8). Tel: 941-772-3922; Fax: 941-772-7182. Peg Horan, Prin.
Sinsinawa Dominicans 1; Lay Teachers 26; Students 528.
Catechesis / Religious Programs—Tel: 941-574-2411. Mr. Carmine Macedonio, D.R.E.
Students 910.

Blessed Katharine Drexel (1990), Revs. John F. Deary, O.S.A.; Francis X. Gallogly, O.S.A.
Office: 1922 S.W. 20th Ave., 33991. Tel: 941-283-9501; Fax: 941-283-9502.
Catechesis / Religious Programs—Theresa Idler, D.R.E.
Students 350.

Clewiston, Hendry Co., St. Margaret (1932) (Spanish), Revs. Patrick Farrell; Sofonias Ortez.
Res., 208 N. Deane Duff Ave., 33440. Tel: 863-983-8585; Fax: 863-983-9673.
315 E. Pasadena Ave.
Catechesis / Religious Programs—Tel: 863-983-8844.
Students 280.

Englewood, Sarasota Co., St. Raphael (1957), Rev. Morris F. Wells, O.Carm.
Res., 770 Kilbourne Ave., 34223. Tel: 941-474-9595; Fax: 941-475-5697.

Catechesis/Religious Programs—Tel: 941-473-2359. Kathy Kleinlein, M.A., D.R.E.
Students 130.

Fort Myers, Lee Co.,

1—ST. VINCENT DE PAUL, (1986), Rev. David Arle.
Church & Mailing Address—13031 State Rd. 80, 33905. Tel: 941-693-0818; Fax: 941-693-8459.
Catechesis/Religious Programs—Students 145.

2—CHURCH OF THE RESURRECTION OF OUR LORD, (1974), Revs. Stephen E. McNamara; Oliver Toner; Michael Cremin, O.Carm. (Ireland).
Parish Center & Mailing Address: 8121 Cypress Lake Dr., 33919. Tel: 941-481-7172; Fax: 941-481-8007.
Church—8051 Cypress Lake Dr., 33919.
Catechesis/Religious Programs—Tel: 941-481-6863. Joan Kamm, D.R.E.
Students 225.

3—ST. CECILIA, (1965), Revs. Thomas E. Murphy, O.S.F.S.; Stanley J. Dombrowski, O.S.F.S. In res., Rev. John T. Doyle, O.S.F.S., (Retired); Deacons Bill Brodeur; Lorin Fortier.
Res., 5632 Sunrise Dr., 33919. Tel: 941-936-3635; Fax: 941-936-2108. [CEM]
Catechesis/Religious Programs—Caroline Keys, D.R.E.
Students 215.

4—ST. COLUMBKILLE, (1993), Revs. Charles K. Sullivan; Thomas J. Palko, O.S.F.S.
Church—12171 Iona Rd., 33908. Tel: 941-489-3973; Fax: 941-432-0066.
Catechesis/Religious Programs—Tel: 941-466-5020.
Students 125.

5—ST. FRANCIS XAVIER, (1910), Very Rev. Thomas M. Anglim; Revs. Stanislaus Pierog (Poland); Marian Konobrocki; Tony Cheimel (Haiti).
Res., P.O. Box 912, 2133 Heitman St., 33902. Tel: 941-334-2161; Fax: 941-332-4178.
School—Tel: 941-334-7707; Fax: 941-334-8605. Sr. Elaine Mahoney, O.S.F., Prin.
Franciscan Sisters of Allegany 2; Lay Teachers 29; Students 655.
Catechesis/Religious Programs—2048 Heitman St., 33902. Tel: 941-334-7636.
Students 163.
Mission—Fort Myers, Lee Co., Our Lady of Perpetual Help, 2063 Lafayette St., 33901. Tel: 941-334-2234.

6—JESUS THE WORKER MISSION (JESUS OBRERO), Rev. Aureliano Santa-Olaya.
4235 Michigan Link, 33916. Tel: 941-332-2829.

7—OUR LADY OF LIGHT, (1990), Rev. Angelo F. Maraldo, O.S.F.S.; Bro. Harry McGovern, O.S.F.S.
Office: 19680 Cypress View Dr., 33912. Tel: 941-267-7088; Fax: 941-267-5481.
Res., 9404 Windlake Dr., 33912. Tel: 941-267-2228. [CEM]
Catechesis/Religious Programs—Students 368.

8—SAN JOSE MISSION, Rev. Aureliano Santa-Olaya.
10750 Gladiolus Dr., 33908. Tel: 941-481-1143.

9—ST. PETER CLAVER MISSION, (1999), Rev. Remigious Ssekiranda.
Mailing Address: P.O. Box 50004, 33994.
3681 Michigan Ave., 33994. Tel: 941-461-0233; Fax: 941-461-0236.

Fort Myers Beach, Lee Co., Ascension (1962), Revs. Thomas J. Goggin; Robert Murphy; Deacon Charles Kiesel.
Res., 6025 Estero Blvd., 33931. Tel: 941-463-6754; Fax: 941-765-1923.
Catechesis/Religious Programs—Students 15.

Golden Gate, Collier Co., St. Elizabeth Seton (1975), Revs. Joseph A. Spinelli, O.S.A.; James V. Vitali, O.S.A.
Res., 2760 52 Ter., S.W., 34116. Tel: 941-455-3900; Fax: 941-455-6895.
School—Tel: 941-455-2262; Fax: 941-455-0549. Mrs. Judy Mankowski, Prin.
Lay Teachers 13; Students 290.
Catechesis/Religious Programs—Tel: 941-455-9598. Cecelia Andretta, D.R.E.
Students 398.

Grove City, Charlotte Co., St. Francis of Assisi (1978), Revs. Bartholomew Larkin, O.Carm.; Benedict Hogan, O.Carm.
Res., 80 Oakland Hills Pl., Rotanda West, 33947. Tel: 941-697-4899; Fax: 941-697-0602.
Church—5265 Placida Rd., 34224. [CEM]
Catechesis/Religious Programs—Mary Sedonic, D.R.E.
Students 120.

Holmes Beach, Manatee Co., St. Bernard's (1956), Revs. John H.R. Ellis; Aloysius Hribsek (BGP); O. Tom Jackson.
Res., 248 S. Harbor Dr., 34217, P.O. Box 1036, 34218. Tel: 941-778-4769; Fax: 941-778-4644.
Catechesis/Religious Programs—Tel: 941-778-0277. Alice White, D.R.E.
Students 111.

Immokalee, Collier Co., Our Lady of Guadalupe (1957), Revs. Ettore Rubin, C.S.; Onorio Benacchio, C.S.; Jean Woady Louis.
Res., 207 S. 9th St., 34142. Tel: 941-657-2666; Fax: 941-657-3431.
Catechesis/Religious Programs—Mrs. Maria Marquez, D.R.E.
Students 185.

LaBelle, Hendry Co., Our Lady Queen of Heaven (1975), Revs. Chester Domaszewicz, Admin.; Victor Caviedes.
Res., 355 S. Bridge St., P.O. Box 357, 33935. Tel: 863-675-0030; Fax: 863-675-0756.
Catechesis/Religious Programs—Tel: 863-675-7447. Rita Schoene, D.R.E.
Students 264.

Lake Placid, Highland Co., Communidad Catolica Hispana Santiago Apostol (Santiago Mission) (1991), Rev. Jose Gonzalez.
P.O. Box 899, 33862. Tel: 863-385-6762; Fax: 863-385-3337.
St. James (1962), Revs. Vincent Llaria (Spain); John J. Koros (OM) (Retired).
Mailing Address: 3380 Placid View Dr., 33852. Tel: 863-465-3215; Fax: 863-465-0649. [JC]
779 Hawk Ave., 33852.
Catechesis/Religious Programs—Students 60.

Lehigh Acres, Lee Co., St. Raphael (1962), Revs. Dennis J. Cooney, Admin.; Walter Swietek (Poland); Deacons James Jacob; Lambert Kuhr; Armindo Guzman; Dean Tucker.
Res., 2514 Lee Blvd., 33971. Tel: 941-369-1831; Fax: 941-369-1039. [JC]
Catechesis/Religious Programs—Tel: 941-369-6424.
Students 317.

Longboat Key, Manatee Co., St. Mary Star of the Sea (1973), Rev. Edward Pick.
Res., 4280 Gulf of Mexico Dr., Box 60, 34228. Tel: 941-383-1255; Fax: 941-383-8758.

Marco Island, Collier Co., San Marco (1971), Rev. Eugene J. McCarthy.
Res., 851 San Marco Rd., 33937. Tel: 941-394-5181; Fax: 941-394-1385.
Catechesis/Religious Programs—Tel: 941-394-4068. David Swierczek, D.R.E.
Students 169.
Mission—Everglades City, Collier Co., Holy Family Mission, 200 Datura St., Everglades City, 33929.

Moore Haven, Glades Co., St. Joseph the Worker (1960) (Spanish), Rev. Emilian Swiatecki.
Res., 1800 N. Hwy. 27 NW, P.O. Box 1109, 33471. Tel: 863-946-0696; Fax: 863-946-3444. [JC]
Catechesis/Religious Programs—Students 148.
Mission—Buckhead Ridge, Glades Co., St. Theresa of the Child Jesus, Hwy. 78 & Chobee Loop, Box 1109, Buckhead Ridge, 33471. Tel: 863-946-0696.

Murdock, Charlotte Co., St. Maximilian Kolbe (1988), Rev. Robert Mattingly; Deacons Louis Cosentino; Robert Godlewsky.
Office: 1441 Spear St., Port Charlotte, 33948. Tel: 941-743-6877; Fax: 941-743-9176.
Catechesis/Religious Programs—Sr. Delores Wehle, S.N.J.M., D.R.E.
Students 86.

Naples, Collier Co.,

1—ST. ANN, (1935), Revs. Robert D. Tabbert; John Cashman, C.P.; Joseph Moffatt, C.S.B.; Julius Lang.
Res., 475 Ninth Ave. S., 34102. Tel: 941-262-4256; Fax: 941-262-4296.
School—542 Eighth Ave. S., 34102. Tel: 941-262-4110; Fax: 941-262-3991. Sr. George Francis Riseling, S.N.J.M., Prin.
Sisters 1; Lay Teachers 22; Students 312.
Catechesis/Religious Programs—Students 312.

2—ST. JOHN THE EVANGELIST, (1988), Revs. Thomas J. Glackin; Donald H. Henry; George F. Hazler.
Res., 625 111th Ave. N., 34108. Tel: 941-566-8740; Fax: 941-566-9117. [CEM]
Catechesis/Religious Programs—Tel: 941-514-2927; Fax: 941-566-9117. Dr. Roberta Horton, D.R.E.
Students 610.

3—ST. PETER THE APOSTLE, (1974), Revs. Timothy M. Navin; Richard J. Mueller (PIT); William J. Penn; Deacons David Nolan; Larry McDonald; Robert L. Tetrault; Robert Stone; Michael Salerno; Norman Hunneyman.
Res., 5130 Rattlesnake Hammock Rd., 34113. Tel: 941-774-3337; Fax: 941-774-3077. [CEM]
Catechesis/Religious Programs—Students 241.

4—ST. WILLIAM, (1973), Revs. Joseph E. Stearns; John F. Costello.
Res., 750 Seagate Dr., 34103-2886. Tel: 941-261-4883; Fax: 941-261-8729. [JC]
Catechesis/Religious Programs—Tel: 941-263-5429. Debra Mahr, D.R.E.
Students 320.

North Port, Sarasota Co., San Pedro (1964), Rev. Patrick C. Organ.
Res., 14380 Tamiami Tr., 34287. Tel: 941-426-2500; 426-6810; Fax: 941-423-8710.
Catechesis/Religious Programs—Tel: 941-426-2893.
Students 301.

Palmetto, Manatee Co., Holy Cross (1956), Revs. Nicanor Lobato; Teofilo Useche; Absalom Coutinho.
Res., 506-26th St. W., 34221. Tel: 941-729-3891; Fax: 941-721-9402. [JC 2]
Catechesis/Religious Programs—Tel: 941-729-1558. Sr. Solidad Tun Fuentes, D.R.E.
Students 306.

Parrish, Manatee Co., St. Frances Xavier Cabrini (1992), Rev. Janusz Jancarz, S.T.L.; Deacon Eugene Egendoerfer.
Res., 12001 69th St. E., 34219. Tel: 941-776-9097; Fax: 941-776-1307.
Catechesis/Religious Programs—Students 72.

Port Charlotte, Charlotte Co., St. Charles Borromeo (1959), Revs. Nicholas McLoughlin; William Penn; Thomas Wantland; Antonio Jean; Jaroslav Sniosek.
Office and Church: 21505 Augusta Ave., Ste. 4, 33952. Tel: 941-625-4754; Fax: 941-625-0256. [JC]
School—Tel: 941-625-5533; Fax: 941-625-7359. Dr. Mary Santini, Prin.
Lay Teachers 16; Students 274.
Catechesis/Religious Programs—21505 Augusta Ave., Ste. 5, 33952. Tel: 941-625-5407. Mrs. Elizabeth Hinks, D.R.E.
Students 350.
San Antonio (1993), Revs. Thomas J. Zedar; Christopher L. Senk, O.S.B.; M. Colleen McGinnity, Pastoral Assoc.
24445 Rampart Blvd., 33980. Tel: 941-624-3799; Fax: 941-624-6184.
Catechesis/Religious Programs—Tel: 941-624-5156.
Students 162.

Punta Gorda, Charlotte Co., Sacred Heart (1954), Revs. Robert Mongiello; Vicente Martin; Leszek Sikorski; Tomasz Ochej; Deacons Edward D. Lundy; Anthony Zammett.
Res., 211 W. Charlotte Ave., 33950-5546. Tel: 941-639-3957; Fax: 941-639-2061.
Catechesis/Religious Programs—Tel: 941-639-9545. Sr. Josine Perez, D.R.E.
Students 128.

Sanibel, Lee Co., St. Isabel (1973), Revs. George Ratzmann; Carmen A. Caruso (JOL).
Res., 3559 Sanibel-Captiva Rd., 33957. Tel: 941-472-2763; Fax: 941-472-5351.
Catechesis/Religious Programs—Tel: 941-395-0070.
Students 106.

Sarasota, Sarasota Co.,

1—INCARNATION, (1958), Revs. Gerard Finegan; John J. Ludden; Deacons Joseph Cirieco; John Crescitelli.
Res., 2929 Bee Ridge Rd., P.O. Box 5516, 34277-5516. Tel: 941-921-6631; Fax: 941-927-2521.
School—Tel: 941-924-8588; Fax: 941-925-1248. Sr. Monica Paul Fraser, Prin.
Sisters 1; Lay Teachers 21; Students 309.
Catechesis/Religious Programs—Tel: 941-924-9566. John Garisto, D.R.E.
Students 574.

2—OUR LADY OF THE ANGELS MISSION, Manatee Co., SR 70, 34243. Tel: 941-752-5731; Fax: 941-752-9851.

3—OUR LADY QUEEN OF MARTYRS, Manatee Co., (1959), Revs. Joseph Connolly, T.O.R.; Louis McIntyre, T.O.R.; Thomas Stabile, T.O.R.; Deacon Jesse E. Pipher. In res., Rev. Sean Sullivan, T.O.R., (Retired).
Res., 833 Magellan Dr., 34243. Tel: 941-755-1826; Fax: 941-753-1654. [CEM 2]
Catechesis/Religious Programs—34243. Tel: 941-755-3497. Nina Powell, D.R.E.
Students 344.

4—ST. MARTHA, (1912), Revs. Fausto Stampiglia, S.A.C.; Benedict Abraham, S.A.C.; Carl Bartholomew, S.A.C.; Gangolu Bob Babu, S.A.C.; Vincent L. Clemente, Hospital Min.; Carl A. Birarelli; Celestino Gutierrez, Spanish Min.; George Hogan, Circus Min.; Deacons John D. Wren, Jr., (Retired); William Ladroga; George Blake.
Res., 235 Adelia St., P.O. Box 1706, 34230. Tel: 941-366-4210; Fax: 941-954-8434.
School—801 N. Orange Ave., 34236. Tel: 941-953-4181; Fax: 941-366-5580. Dr. Rosemarie Gilbert.
Religious 2; Lay Teachers 19; Students 294.
Catechesis/Religious Programs—Bro. R. Patrick Wilson, D.R.E.
Students 385.

5—ST. MICHAEL THE ARCHANGEL, (1958), Revs. Claude E. Brubaker; John C. Rourke.
Res., 5394 Midnight Pass Rd., 34242. Tel: 941-349-4174; Fax: 941-349-6388.
Catechesis/Religious Programs—Sr. Luke Crawford, S.P., D.R.E.
Students 115.

6—ST. PATRICK, (1988), Revs. Arthur W. Hannaway; George Brennan.
Res., 7900 Bee Ridge Rd., 34241. Tel: 941-378-1703; Fax: 941-378-2153.
Catechesis/Religious Programs—Tel: 941-378-1521.
Students 424.

7—ST. THOMAS MORE, (1979), Rev. Jerome Callahan, O.Carm. Tel: 941-923-1691; Deacon Robert Horvath.
Mailing Address: 2506 Gulf Gate Dr., 34231. Tel: 941-923-1691; Fax: 941-923-1692.
Res., 2612 Regatta Dr., 34231. [CEM]
Catechesis/Religious Programs—Tel: 941-921-6334; Fax: 941-926-9541.
Students 75.

Sebring, Highlands Co., St. Catherine (1929), Very Rev. Jose H. Ruiz, V.F.
Res., 882 Bay St., P.O. Box 389, 33870. Tel: 863-385-0049; Fax: 863-385-5169. [CEM 2][JC]
Catechesis/Religious Programs—Tel: 863-385-7844. Sr. Julia Zilka, V.S.C., D.R.E.
Students 184.

Wauchula, Hardee Co., St. Michael (1969) (Spanish-Creole), Revs. Michael Koncik, C.SS.R.; Edmund Regensburger, C.SS.R.; George H. Bridge, C.SS.R.; James J. Burke, C.SS.R.
Res., 408 Heard Bridge Rd., 33873. Tel: 863-773-4089; Fax: 863-773-5641.
Catechesis/Religious Programs—Tel: 863-773-4215.
Students 466.
Convent—409 Alice St., 33873. Vincentian Sisters of Charity
Sisters 3.
Missions—Bowling Green, Hardee Co., Holy Child, Chester Ave., Bowling Green, 33834. Tel: 863-375-4881; Zolfo Springs, Hardee Co., San Alfonso Catholic Center, Schoolhouse Rd., Zolfo Springs, 33890.

Military Chaplains:
Reverend Fathers—
McLaughlin, Paul E., U.S. Navy, PSC 819, Box 12, FPO AE, 09645-1900

Absent on Leave:
Reverend Fathers—
Ryan, Eugene
Walk, Donald J.

Absent on Sick Leave:
Reverend Fathers—
Morillo, Jose
Noboa, Origines

Graduate Studies:
Reverend Fathers—
Menzies, Scott
Reverend Fathers—
Strycharz, Stanley
Reverend Fathers—
Zawadzki, Piotr

Retired:
Reverend Monsignors—
Mouch, Frank M.
O'Dowd, John
Schiefen, Robert
Reverend Fathers—
Baier, Donald
Dittman, Bernard F.
Duggan, Joseph P.
Gonzalez, Mario
Gorr, Benjamin
Hickey, Michael
Loncar, Sebastian
Moran, Joseph P.
Murphy, Thomas
Murphy, Timothy
O' Connell, William
Romero, William
Soy, Esteban

Permanent Deacons:
Allen, Eugene (Rockville Centre)
Anderson, John (NY)
Attridge, James (NY)
Blackburn, John L. (VEN)
Blake, George (NY)
Brodeur, Wilfred (CIN)
Cabrera, Crescencio (BO)
Camacho, Francis (FR)
Catanese, Ralph (PH)
Cirieco, Joseph (VEN)
Cobett, Edgar (VEN), Leave of Absence
Cole, Francis (HRT)
Coniglio, Philip (MIA)
Cook, James (TR)
Cooper, James (VEN)
Cosentino, Louis A. (Y)
Crant, Ellis (PHX)
Crescitelli, John (Tulsa)
DiMeglio, Michael (VEN)
DiSalvo, Aldo (HRT)
Dubay, Frank (STP)
Egendoerfer, Eugene (Fort Wayne and South Bend)
Farrell, Terry (Canada)
Fathauer, Ronald (MIA)
Fortier, W. Lorin (VEN)
Fox, Leonard (TOL)
Geary, Coleman (SFD)
Gilbert, John (VEN)
Godlewsky, Robert (HRT)
Grant, Russ (WH)
Gratkowski, Daniel (PEO)
Groh, Al (TR)
Guzman, Armindo (MIL)
Harkin, John (VEN)
Hedge, Dennis (VEN), Leave of Absence
Horan, Francis (VEN)
Horvath, Robert (NY)
Hunneyman, Norman (Ogdensburg)
Jackson, Frank (TR)
Jackson, Thomas O. (BUF)
Jacob, James (HRT)
Jolin, Joseph (NOR)
Kiesel, Charles (VEN)
King, Loren (WOR)
Kuhr, Lambert (SAG)
Ladroga, William (WOR)
Lalone, Norman (DET)
Loafman, Frank (DET)
Lundy, Edward (VEN)
MacDonald, Lawrence (TR)
McCarthy, Charles (Canada)
McGreen, Michael (RVC), Leave of Absence
Mercurio, Joseph (BUF)
Minicozzi, John (PAT)
Moncsko, Walter (MIA)
Mullin, Paul (SY)
Nimon, Robert (TR)
Nolan, David W. (VEN)
Nowak, Richard (JOL)
O'Grady, Lowell (VEN), Serving Outside of the Diocese
Ochner, Ronald (PAT)
Pipher, Jessie (NY)
Rowland, James (TR)
Salerno, Michael (JOL)
Schaupp, Larry (TOL)
Stevens, Robert (KAL)
Tetrault, Robert (JOL)
Tholl, James (TOL)
Thoresen, Norman (MIL)
Tirelli, Raymond (RVC)
Tomasso, Robert (CHI)
Tucker, Dean H. (Ft. Wayne and South Bend)
Urrico, Francis (PRO)
Walsh, Vincent (FR), Serving Outside of the Diocese
Walton, Gilbert Jr. (HRT)
Wendell, Max (LAN)
Wren, John Jr. (VEN)
Zammett, Antony (HRT)

INSTITUTIONS LOCATED IN THE DIOCESE

[A] HIGH SCHOOLS

FORT MYERS. *Bishop Verot High School*, 5598 Sunrise Dr., 33919. Tel: 941-936-6700; Fax: 941-936-1753.
Web site: www.bvhs.org
Oblates of St. Francis de Sales. Revs. Hugh McGuigan, O.S.F.S., Prin.; Joseph A. Beattie, O.S.F.S.; John A. Beattie, O.S.F.S.; J. Christian Beretta, O.S.F.S; Thomas J. McGee, O.S.F.S., Supr. Priests 5; Lay Teachers 43; Students 759; Total Staff 24.

NAPLES. *St. John Neumann High School*, 3000 53rd St., S.W., 34116. Tel: 941-455-3044; Fax: 941-455-2966.
Web site: www.sjnceltics.com
Congregation of Christian Brothers. Laura J. Campbell, Prin.; Bros. Christopher Burns, C.F.C.; Francis Gammaro, C.F.C.; John C. O'Neill, C.F.C., (Retired). Sisters 1; Brothers 2; Lay Teachers 19; Students 294.

SARASOTA. *Cardinal Mooney High School*, 4171 Fruitville Rd., 34232. Tel: 941-371-4917; Fax: 941-371-6924.
E-mail: pridmore@cmhs-sarasota.org
Web site: www.cmhs-sarasota.org
Sisters of Notre Dame of Chardon, OH. Sr. Mary Lucia Haas, S.N.D., Pres.; Mr. Stephen J. Christie, Prin. Sisters 4; Lay Teachers 41; Total Staff 62; Students 610.

[B] SCHOOLS FOR THEOLOGICAL, SPIRITUAL, PASTORAL AND PERSONAL FORMATION

ARCADIA. *Blessed Edmund Rice School for Pastoral Ministry*, 10299 S.W. Peace River St., 34266-4068. Tel: 863-766-7334; Fax: 863-629-8555.
E-mail: riceschool@juno.com
Web site: www.riceschool.org
Bro. Paul K. Hennessy, C.F.C., Pres.; Rev. C. Gerard Austin, O.P. Priests 2; Sisters 3; Brothers 1; Total Staff 9; Students 116.

[C] MIGRANT EDUCATION

BONITA SPRINGS. *Migrant Education Apostolate, Los Hermanos*, P.O. Box 716, 34133. Tel: 941-947-9098; Fax: 941-947-9098. Brothers 3.

[D] GENERAL HOSPITALS

VENICE. *Bon Secours-Venice Healthcare Corp.*, 540 The Rialto, 34285. Tel: 941-483-7773; Fax: 941-483-7699.
E-mail: Michael_Guley@bshsi.com
Web site: www.bshsi-florida.com
For a complete listing, refer to the Hospitals section.

PORT CHARLOTTE. *Bon Secours-St. Joseph Hospital*, 2500 Harbor Blvd., 33952. Tel: 941-766-4122; Fax: 941-766-4140.
E-mail: art_schute@bshsi.com
Web site: www.bonsecours.org/florida
For a complete listing, refer to the Hospitals section.

[E] NURSING AND CONVALESCENT HOMES

PORT CHARLOTTE. *Bon Secours-St. Joseph Nursing Care Center, Inc.*, 2370 Harbor Blvd., 33952. Tel: 941-624-5966; Fax: 941-624-3963
For a complete listing, refer to the Special Care Facilities section.

[F] RESIDENCES FOR THE AGED

FORT MYERS. *Villa Francisco*, 2140 Cottage St., 33901. Tel: 941-332-3229; Fax: 941-332-4178
For a complete listing, refer to the Special Care Facilities section.

PORT CHARLOTTE. *St. Charles Housing I, Inc.*, 2550 Easy St., 33952. Tel: 941-624-2266; Fax: 941-624-2283.
E-mail: dixie0940@aol.com
For a complete listing, refer to the Special Care Facilities section.
St. Charles Housing II, Inc., 22250 Vick St., 33980. Tel: 941-624-4404; Fax: 941-624-5556.
E-mail: fran0941@aol.com
For a complete listing, refer to the Special Care Facilities section.

SARASOTA. *St. Martha's Housing II, Inc.*, 800 N. Lemon Ave., 34236. Tel: 941-365-7913; Fax: 941-365-8887.
E-mail: corab0116@aol.com
For a complete listing, refer to the Special Care Facilities section.
St. Martha's Housing, Inc., 1576 Eighth St., 34236. Tel: 941-366-4448; Fax: 941-366-2544.
E-mail: dorth0115@aol.com
For a complete listing, refer to the Special Care Facilities section.

[G] MONASTERIES AND RESIDENCES OF PRIESTS AND BROTHERS

VENICE. *Carmel in Venice*, 244 Harbor Dr. S., 34285. Tel: 941-485-0606. Revs. Gerard Benson, O.Carm., Prior; Clyde Ozminkowski, O.Carm.; Joel Schevers, O.Carm. Priests 3.
St. Alphonsus Residence, 1230 Schooner Ln., 34292. Tel: 941-485-3673; Fax: 941-486-1524.
E-mail: olphmallen@aol.com
Rev. Charles Mallen, C.Ss.R., Supr.
Xavieran Brothers, 609 Cornwell on the Gulf, 34285. Tel: 941-484-9641. Brothers of St. Francis Xavier - House of Prayer. Brothers 5.

ENGLEWOOD. *Society of St. Edmund Residence*, 617 W. Harvard St., 34223. Tel: 941-473-9526. Revs. Casimir Cichanowicz, S.S.E.; Gerard Grace, S.S.E., Facilitator; Joseph L. Hart, S.S.E.; Edward Leary, S.S.E.; Francis Moriarty, S.S.E.; Maurice F. Ouellet, S.S.E.; Thomas D. Sullivan, S.S.E.; Bro. George Francis Huyer, S.S.E.

FORT MYERS. *Oblates of St. Francis de Sales*, 5598 Sunrise Dr., 33919. Tel: 941-939-5334. Priests 5.

NAPLES. *St. John Neumann High School Faculty Residence*, 3180 53rd St., S.W., 34116. Tel: 941-455-2255; Fax: 941-455-2966.
E-mail: derfsnrub2645@aol.com
Congregation of Christian Brothers. Brothers 3.

Voluntas Dei Institute, 370 Emerald Bay Cir., N-7, 34110. Tel: 941-514-3282; Fax: 941-514-4587.
E-mail: ivdusa@cs.com
Rev. George F. Hazler, Regl. DIr.

NOKOMIS. *Carmel at Mission Valley*, 955 Laurel Rd. E., 34275-4507. Tel: 941-412-0678; Fax: 941-485-5716.
E-mail: franktask@earthlink.net
Revs. John C. Fogarty, O.Carm.; Francis E. McCarthy, O.Carm; Sean O'Leary, O.Carm.; Franklin R. Tasker, O.Carm.; Thomas J. Walsh, O.Carm; Eamon Carroll, O.Carm.

SARASOTA. *Congregation of the Holy Ghost*, 438-464 Golden Gate Pt., 34236. Tel: 941-362-8389; Fax: 941-362-3599. Revs. Timothy T. McDonough, C.S.Sp., Supr.; Stephen J. Lasko, C.S.Sp.; William J. Jackson, C.S.Sp.; David C. Marshall, C.S.Sp.; Anthony A. Bacher, C.S.Sp.; Louis F. Dolan, C.S.Sp.; W. Robert Graves, C.S.Sp.; Eugene H. Hillman, C.S.Sp. Total in Residence 8.

Holy Cross Florida Regional Center, 1635 4th St., 34236. Tel: 941-365-0722.
E-mail: sarasotacsc@aol.com
Holy Cross Brothers Residence.

[H] CONVENTS AND RESIDENCES FOR SISTERS

FORT MYERS BEACH. *San Damiano Monastery of St. Clare.* (Solemn Vows, Papal Enclosure), 6029 Estero Blvd., 33931-4325. Tel: 941-463-5599; Fax: 941-463-4993.
E-mail: bellachair@aol.com
Web site: www.poorclare.org/fmb
Poor Clares. Sr. Mary Emmanuel Kilkenny, O.S.C., Abbess. Cloistered Sisters 4.

[I] RETREAT CENTERS

VENICE. *Our Lady of Perpetual Help Retreat and Spirituality Center*, 3989 S. Moon Dr., 34292. Tel: 941-486-0233; Fax: 941-486-1524.
E-mail: olphsct@aol.com
Web site: www.olphretreat.org
Rev. Charles Mallen, C.SS.R., Dir.; Sr. Carmella T. DeCosty, S.N.J.M., Admin.

ALVA.
Mother of God House of Prayer, 17880 Cypress Creek Rd., 33920. Tel: 941-728-3614; Fax: 941-728-3760.
E-mail: moghop@horizonnet.net
Web site: www.moghop.com
Co-Directors: Sr. Jamesine Riley, S.S.J.; Patricia Ross. Total in Residence 2; Total Staff 3.

LAKE PLACID. *Campo San Jose*, P.O. Box 899, 33862-0899. 70 Sun 'n' Lake Blvd., 33852. Tel: 863-385-6762; Fax: 863-699-1561.
E-mail: antonio@digital.net
Web site: www.camposanjose.com
Rev. Jose Gonzalez, Dir.

[J] CATHOLIC CHARITIES

VENICE. *Catholic Charities of the Diocese of Venice, Inc.*, 1000 Pinebrook Rd., 34292. Tel: 941-488-5581. Rosemary Winder Strange, Exec. Dir.

Our Mother's House, 405 Manatee Ct., 34285. Tel: 941-485-6264; Fax: 941-488-2289.
E-mail: catchristensen@juno.com
Web site: www.ymnetwork.net/omh.
Catherine Christensen, Dir. Total Assisted 60; Total in Residence 6 families. Social housing program for single mothers offering free child care. Adult residents must attend full-time educational or vocational training. Food pantry serves the working poor.

ARCADIA. *Catholic Charities of De Soto County*, 1210 E. Oak St., 33821. Tel: 863-494-1068; Fax: 863-494-1671.
E-mail: arcadiacharities@juno.com

FORT MYERS. *Catholic Hispanic Social Services*, 4235 Michigan Ave. Link, P.O. Box 50301, 33994. Tel: 941-337-4193; Fax: 941-332-2799.
E-mail: ledeckymd@juno.com
Dr. Peter J. Ledecky, M.D., Dir. Total Assisted 7,000; Total Staff 11.

IMMOKALEE. *Guadalupe Social Services*, 211 S. Ninth St., P.O. Box 5034, 34143. Tel: 941-657-6242; Fax: 941-657-7761.
E-mail: brjim@juno.com or gsscc@juno.com
Total Assisted 4,100; Total Staff 8.

NAPLES. *Catholic Charities of Collier County*, Counseling Services, 2210 Santa Barbara Blvd., 34116. Tel: 941-455-2655; Fax: 941-455-7235.
E-mail: drobinski@naples.net
Web site: www.catholiccharitiesdov.coolsite.com

Emergency Assistance, Family Resource Center, 2408 Linwood Ave., Ste. #1, 34112. Tel: 941-793-0059; Fax: 941-774-0523.
E-mail: ccresource@naples.net

PALMETTO. *Palmetto Catholic Charities*, 506 26 St. W., 34221. Tel: 941-721-0924; Fax: 941-722-1063.
E-mail: cathchar@gte.net
Total Assisted 1,900; Total Staff 3.

SARASOTA. *Catholic Charities District I.* Counseling Services. 1900 Main St., Ste. 204, 34236. Tel: 941-957-4496; Fax: 941-951-0223.
E-mail: saracath@cathcharsrq@netzero.net
Emergency Assistance. Tel: 941-955-6597; Fax: 941-955-6597.

Refugees Employed & Productive (REAP), 4029 N. Washington Blvd., Ste. K, 32434. Tel: 941-359-0352; Fax: 941-359-1605.

[K] FOUNDATIONS

VENICE. *Cardinal Mooney High School Foundation*, Catholic Center, 1000 Pinebrook Rd., 34292. Mailing Address: P.O. Box 2006, 34284. Tel: 941-484-9543.

Foundation for the Care of the Migrant Poor, 1000 Pinebrook Rd., 34292. Tel: 941-484-9543; Fax: 941-484-2611.
E-mail: inof@dioceseofvenice.org
Web site: www.dioceseofvenice.org

FORT MYERS. *The Bishop Verot High School Foundation*, 5598 Sunrise Dr., 33919. Tel: 941-274-6700; Fax: 941-939-4904.
Web site: www.buhs.org
Rev. Hugh J. McGuigan, O.S.F.S.

St. Francis Xavier School Foundation, 2133 Heitman St., 33901. Tel: 941-334-2161; Fax: 941-332-4178. Very Rev. Thomas M. Anglim, V.G., Pres.; Dr. Michael Kyle, Chm.

NAPLES.
St. Ann School Foundation, Inc., 475 Ninth Ave. S., 34102. Tel: 941-262-4256; Fax: 941-262-4296.
E-mail: debrubaker@aol.com
Dr. James R. Rehak, Pres.; Rev. Robert D. Tabbert.

SARASOTA. *Incarnation School Foundation*, 2911 Bee Ridge Rd., 34239. Tel: 941-924-8588; Fax: 941-925-1248.

St. Martha School Foundation, 200 N. Orange Ave., 34230. Tel: 941-366-4210; Fax: 941-954-8434.
E-mail: marthacc@aol.com
Mailing Address: P.O. Box 1706, 34230.

[L] MISCELLANEOUS LISTINGS

VENICE. *St. Mark's Housing of Venice, Inc.*, c/o The Diocese of Venice, P.O. Box 2006, 34284-2006.

FORT MYERS. *Societies of St. Vincent de Paul*, 2200 First St., 33901. Tel: 941-334-2736. Mr. Thomas F. Ferrara, Ph.D., Trustee.
District Council of Fort Myers, District Council of Manasota, District Council of Naples.

SARASOTA. *Bethesda House.* (AIDS Ministry), P.O. Box 1706, 34230. Tel: 941-366-1886; Fax: 941-362-9733.
E-mail: bethesdahouse@excite.com
Sr. Frances Nevolo, O.L.C. Total Assisted 5,352; Total Staff 4.

RELIGIOUS INSTITUTES OF MEN REPRESENTED IN THE DIOCESE

For further details refer to the corresponding bracketed number in the Religious Institutes of Men or Women section.

[0140]—*The Augustinians.*—O.S.A.
[0200]—*Benedictine Monks.*—O.S.B.
[1350]—*Brothers of St. Francis Xavier.*—C.F.X.
[0600]—*Brothers of the Congregation of Holy Cross.*—C.S.C.
[0270]—*Carmelite Fathers & Brothers.*—O.Carm.
[0310]—*Congregation of Christian Brothers.*—C.F.C.
[0480]—*Conventual Franciscans.*—O.F.M.Conv.
[0430]—*Dominican Fathers.*—O.P.
[0650]—*Holy Ghost Fathers.*—C.S.Sp.
[0690]—*Jesuit Fathers.*—S.J.
[0720]—*Missionaries of Our Lady of La Salette.*—M.S.
[1210]—*Missionaries of St. Charles Scalabrians.*—C.S.
[0590]—*Missionaries of the Holy Apostles.*—M.Ss.A.
[0920]—*Oblates of St. Francis de Sales.*—O.S.F.S.
[1000]—*Passionist Fathers.*—C.P.
[1070]—*Redemptorist Fathers.*—C.SS.R.
[0700]—*St. Joseph's Society of the Sacred Heart.*—S.S.J.
[0110]—*Society of African Missions.*—S.M.A.
[0440]—*Society of St. Edmund.*—S.S.E.
[0990]—*Society of the Catholic Apostolate.*—S.A.C.
[1200]—*Society of the Divine Savior.*—S.D.S.
[0560]—*Third Order Regular of St. Francis.*—T.O.R.

RELIGIOUS INSTITUTES OF WOMEN REPRESENTED IN THE DIOCESE

[0270]—*Congregation of Bon Secours.* (Marriotsville, MD).—C.B.S.
[1070-15]—*Congregation of St. Dominic (Sisters of St. Dominic of Blauvelt, NY).*—O.P.
[1070-06]—*Dominican Sisters of Hope.*—O.P.
[1070-02]—*Dominican Sisters of St. Mary of the Springs.*—O.P.
[1070-13]—*Dominican Sisters / Congregation of the Most Holy Rosary (Adrian Dominicans).*—O.P.
[1070-03]—*Dominican Sisters / Sinsinawa Dominican Congregation of the Most Holy Rosary.*—O.P.
[1370]—*Franciscan Missionareis of Mary.*—F.M.M.
[1180]—*Franciscan Sisters of Allegheny, NY.*—O.S.F.
[1820]—*Institute of the Blessed Virgin Mary (Sisters of Loretto).*—I.B.V.M.
[2420]—*Marist Missionary Sisters.*—S.M.S.M.
[]—*Missionaries Daughters of Our Blessed Lady of the Light, Yucatan, Mexico.*—M.H.M.L.
[1360]—*Missionary Franciscan Sisters of the Immaculate Conception.* (Newton, MA).—O.S.F.
[2800]—*Missionary Sisters of the Most Sacred Heart of Jesus of Hilltrup.*—M.S.C.
[3070]—*North American Union of Sisters of Our Lady of Charity.*—N.A.U.-O.L.C.
[3760]—*Order of St. Clare.*—O.S.C.
[3465]—*Religious of the Sacred Heart of Mary.* (Eastern North American Province).—R.S.H.M.
[2970]—*School Sisters of Notre Dame.* (Baltimore Prov., St. Louis Prov., Northeastern Prov. and Wilton, CT Prov.).—S.S.N.D.
[0590]—*Sisters of Charity of St. Elizabeth, Convent Station.*—S.C.
[0430]—*Sisters of Charity of the Blessed Virgin Mary.*—B.V.M.
[2575]—*Sisters of Mercy of the Americas.* (Cincinnati and New Jersey Prov.).—R.S.M.
[2549]—*Sisters of Mercy, Co. Sligo, Ireland.*—R.S.M.
[2990]—*Sisters of Notre Dame.* (Chardon, OH).—S.N.D.
[3360]—*Sisters of Providence of St. Mary-of-the-Woods, IN.*—S.P.
[3720]—*Sisters of St. Ann.* (Marlboro, MA).—S.S.A.
[1630]—*Sisters of St. Francis of Penance and Christian Charity.*—O.S.F.
[1650]—*Sisters of St. Francis of Philadelphia.*—O.S.F.
[3830-01]—*Sisters of St. Joseph of Boston.*—C.S.J.
[3840]—*Sisters of St. Joseph of Carondelet.*—C.S.J.
[3830-08]—*Sisters of St. Joseph of Cleveland.*—C.S.J.
[3830-14]—*Sisters of St. Joseph of Rochester.*—S.S.J.
[1990]—*Sisters of the Holy Name of Jesus and Mary.*—S.N.J.M.
[3730]—*Sisters of the Order of St. Basil the Great.*—O.S.B.M.
[1490]—*Sisters of the Third Franciscan Order.* (Syracuse, NY).—O.S.F.
[1710]—*Sisters of the Third Order of St. Francis.*—O.S.F.
[1760]—*Sisters of the Third Order of St. Francis of Penance and of Charity.* (Tiffin, OH).—O.S.F.
[2160]—*Sisters, Servants of the Immaculate Heart of Mary.* (Scranton, PA).—I.H.M.
[4060]—*Society of the Holy Child Jesus.*—S.H.C.J.
[4070]—*Society of the Sacred Heart.*—R.S.C.J.
[4160]—*Vincentian Sisters of Charity.*—V.S.C.

NECROLOGY

† Cronin, David, Punta Gorda, FL Sacred Heart Parish. —Died Feb. 13, 2000.
† Culliton, Leo, Lake Placid, FL St. James Parish. —Died Jan. 18, 2000.

Diocese of Victoria in Texas

(Dioecesis Victoriensis in Texia)

Most Reverend

DAVID E. FELLHAUER, PH.D., J.C.D.

Bishop of Victoria; ordained May 29, 1965; appointed Second Bishop of Victoria in Texas April 7, 1990; consecrated and installed May 28, 1990. *Res., 302 East Red River, Victoria, TX, 77901. Direct all official correspondence to: P.O. Box 4070, Victoria, TX, 77903.*

Legal Title: Diocese of Victoria in Texas.

ESTABLISHED AND CREATED A DIOCESE, MAY 29, 1982.

Square Miles Approximately 9,609.

Comprises the Counties of Calhoun, DeWitt, Goliad, Jackson, Lavaca, Matagorda, Victoria, Wharton and Colorado; also Fayette County west of the Colorado River in the State of Texas.

For legal titles of parishes and diocesan institutions, consult the Chancery Office.

Chancery Office: P.O. Box 4070, Victoria, TX, 77903. Tel.: 361-573-0828; Fax: 361-573-5725.

STATISTICAL OVERVIEW

Personnel	
Bishop	1
Priests: Diocesan Active in Diocese	45
Priests: Active Outside Diocese	2
Priests: Retired, Sick or Absent	9
Number of Diocesan Priests	56
Religious Priests in Diocese	8
Extern Priests in Diocese	7
Ordinations:	
Diocesan Priests	2
Transitional Deacons	1
Permanent Deacons in Diocese	19
Total Sisters	135
Parishes	
Parishes	50
With Resident Pastor:	
Resident Diocesan Priests	37
Resident Religious Priests	5
Without Resident Pastor:	
Administered by Priests	7
Missions	19
Professional Ministry Personnel:	
Sisters	19
Lay Ministers	20
Welfare	
Homes for the Aged	1
Total Assisted	59
Educational	
Diocesan Students in Other Seminaries	7
Total Seminarians	7
High Schools, Diocesan and Parish	2
Total Students	149
High Schools, Private	1
Total Students	393
Elementary Schools, Diocesan and Parish	11
Total Students	2,058
Elementary Schools, Private	1
Total Students	382
Catechesis/Religious Education:	
High School Students	3,006
Elementary Students	6,932
Total Students Under Catholic Instruction	12,927
Teachers in the Diocese:	
Sisters	22
Lay Teachers	234
Vital Statistics	
Receptions into the Church:	
Infant Baptism Totals	1,606
Adult Baptism Totals	92
Received into Full Communion	111
First Communions	1,447
Confirmations	1,212
Marriages:	
Catholic	354
Interfaith	148
Total Marriages	502
Deaths	1,031
Total Catholic Population	107,804
Total Population	210,831

Former Bishops—Most Rev. CHARLES V. GRAHMANN, D.D., ord. March 17, 1956; appt. Titular Bishop of Equilio and Auxiliary of San Antonio, June 30, 1981; cons. Aug. 29, 1981; appt. First Bishop of Victoria, April 14, 1982; installed May 29, 1982; appt. Coadjutor of Dallas, Dec. 18, 1989; succeeded to See, July 14, 1990.

Chancery Office—1505 E. Mesquite Ln., Victoria, 77901., Mailing Address: P.O. Box 4070, Victoria, 77903. Tel: 361-573-0828; Fax: 361-573-5725. Office Hours: Mon.-Fri. 8:30-4:30.

Vicars General—Rev. Msgr. THOMAS C. MCLAUGHLIN, *P.O. Box 4070, Victoria, 77903.* Rev. Msgr. JAMES C. BRUNNER, *P.O. Box 2448, Victoria, 77902.*

Chancellor—Rev. Msgr. THOMAS C. MCLAUGHLIN, V.G., *P.O. Box 4070, Victoria, 77903.* Vice-Chancellor, Rev. GARY W. JANAK, J.C.L., *St. Joseph Church, P.O. Box 734, Yoakum, 77995.* Tel: 361-293-3518.

Diocesan Consultors—Rev. Msgr. THOMAS C. MCLAUGHLIN, V.G.; Rev. Msgr. JAMES C. BRUNNER, V.G.; Revs. JOHN C. BILY; GARY W. JANAK; CASIMIR JARZOMBEK, V.F.; TIMOTHY KOSLER, V.F.; LAWRENCE MATULA; JOHN C. PETERS, V.F.; DONALD R. RUPPERT, V.F.

Vicars Forane—Victoria Deanery: Rev. MICHAEL HARROLD, V.F., *Our Lady of Victory Cathedral, 1309 E. Mesquite Ln., Victoria, 77901.* Tel: 361-575-4741. Cuero Deanery: Rev. FRANK LENZ, V.F., *Holy Cross Church, 1214 Zorn Rd., Yorktown, 78164.* Tel: 361-564-2893. Edna Deanery: Rev. CASIMIR JARZOMBEK, V.F., *Holy Cross Church, 2001 Katy St., Bay City, 77414.* Tel: 979-245-6379. El Campo Deanery: Rev. DONALD RUPPERT, V.F., *Holy Cross Church, P.O. Box 280, East Bernard, 77435.* Tel: 979-335-7551. Hallettsville Deanery: Rev. JOHN C. PETERS, V.F., *Sacred Heart Church, P.O. Box H, Hallettsville, 77964.* Tel: 361-798-5888. Schulenburg Deanery: Rev. TIMOTHY KOSLER, V.F., *St. Rose of Lima Church, 1010 Lyons Ave., Schulenburg, 78956.* Tel: 979-743-3117.

Presbyteral Council—Rev. Msgr. THOMAS C. MCLAUGHLIN, V.G.; Rev. Msgr. JAMES C. BRUNNER, V.G.; Revs. JOHN C. PETERS, V.F.; CASIMIR JARZOMBEK, V.F.; FRANK LENZ, V.F.; DANIEL GIORGI, O.SS.T.; JOHN BILY; MICHAEL HARROLD, V.F.; TIMOTHY KOSLER, V.F.; GARY W. JANAK; CHARLES SONNIER; JOSEPH VRANA; VICTOR SCOCCO, O.SS.T.; EDWARD BOREN; GERARD CERNOCH; DONALD RUPPERT, V.F.; LAWRENCE MATULA.

Diocesan Tribunal—1505 E. Mesquite Ln., Victoria, 77901. Tel: 361-573-0760.

Judicial Vicar—Rev. Msgr. THOMAS C. MCLAUGHLIN, V.G.

Judges—Revs. JOHN C. BILY; MICHAEL HARROLD, V.F.; GARY JANAK, J.C.L.; GABRIEL MAISON, J.C.D.; CELESTINO SAY.

Promoter of Justice—Appointed as needed.

Procurator Advocate—Revs. BENTON THURMOND; MICHAEL LYONS; CHARLES DWOMOH; MATTHEW HUEHLEFELD; SAMUEL APPIASI.

Defenders of the Bond—Revs. EUSTACE HERMES; DAN MORALES; TIMOTHY KOSLER, V.F.; DANIEL P. KAHLICH; THU VAN NGUYEN; FRANK LENZ; GREG KORENEK.

Notaries—Mrs. MINNIE BOCHAT; Mrs. MARY HAAS.

Priests' Personnel Board—Rev. Msgr. THOMAS C. MCLAUGHLIN, V.G., Chancellor; Rev. Msgr. JAMES C. BRUNNER, V.G.; Revs. JOHN C. PETERS, V.F.; MICHAEL HARROLD, V.F.; DONALD RUPPERT, V.F.; TIMOTHY KOSLER, V.F.; FRANK LENZ, V.F.; CASIMIR JARZOMBEK, V.F.

Building Board—Deacon A. R. WEARDEN; Mr. AL HESSLER; Mr. HENRY SCHROEDER; Mr. CHARLES BLUNTZER; Mr. JAMES MIORI; Mr. ED MARTINKA.

Business Administration Office—Deacon A. R. WEARDEN, Mgr.; Mrs. JUNE OHRT; Mrs. SHARON JONES; Mrs. JERI JOSEPH, *P.O. Box 4070, Victoria, 77903.* Tel: 361-573-0828.

Campaign For Human Development and Catholic Relief Services—Rev. GERARD CERNOCH, Dir., *SS. Cyril and Methodius Church, P.O. Box 66, Shiner, 77984.* Tel: 361-594-3836.

Catholic Youth Ministry—Mrs. DEBBIE VANELLI, Dir., *1505 E. Mesquite Ln., P.O. Box 4070, Victoria, 77901.* Tel: 361-573-0828.

Catholic Outreach Prison Ministry—Rev. GARY JANAK, *P.O. Box 697, Cuero, 77954.*

Charismatic Renewal Movement—Sr. PERPETUA HAWES, I.W.B.S., *808 E. Nueces, Victoria, 77902.* Tel: 361-578-8456.

Council of Catholic Women (DCCW)—Rev. MICHAEL O'SHAUGHNESSEY, V.F., Moderator, *506 N. Allen, Edna, 77957.* Tel: 361-782-3588. Mrs. DORIS DOERHMAN, Chm., *670 Doerhman Ln., Meyersville, 77974.* Tel: 361-277-5515.

Diocesan Cemeteries—Rev. EUSTACE HERMES, Dir., *2303 E. Locust, P.O. Box 3098, Victoria, 77903.* Tel: 361-575-7337.

Diocesan Finance Board—Deacon A. R. WEARDEN; Mrs. BEATRICE GONZALEZ; Mr. OTTO KALISHKO; Mr. ROMAN SHIMEK; Mr. GLEN VILLAFRANCA; Mr. JOHN STEVENSON; Rev. DONALD RUPPERT; Rev. Msgr. THOMAS C. MCLAUGHLIN, V.G.; Rev. Msgr. JAMES C. BRUNNER, V.G.

Diocesan Services Appeal—Mrs. JERI JOSEPH, Dir., *1505 E. Mesquite Ln., P.O. Box 4070, Victoria, 77901.* Tel: 361-573-0828.

Diocesan Office of Spiritual Renewal Center—AMADOR AMADOR; CONNIE AMADOR. Tel: 361-572-0836.

Ecumenical Commission—Rev. WAYNE FLAGG, *SS. Peter & Paul Church, Rte. 2, Box 26, New Ulm, 78950.* Tel: 979-732-3430.

Presidio of La Bahia—Mr. NEWTON WARZECHA, *P.O. Box 57, Goliad, 77963*. Tel: 361-645-3752.

Liturgical Commission—Rev. EDWARD J. WINKLER, *P.O. Box 307, Eagle Lake, 77434*. Tel: 979-234-2842.

Office of Catholic Schools—Sr. GLORIA CAIN, S.N.N.D., Supt., *P.O. Box 4070, Victoria, 77903*.

Permanent Diaconate Program—Rev. GABRIEL MAISON, J.C.D., Dir., *1505 E. Mesquite Ln., P.O. Box 4070, Victoria, 77903., P.O. Box 399, Moulton, 77975*.

Propagation of the Faith, Holy Childhood Association—Rev. Msgr. THOMAS C. MCLAUGHLIN, V.G., Dir.

Mission Cooperative Plan—Rev. Msgr. THOMAS C. MCLAUGHLIN, V.G., Dir., *Chancery Office, P.O. Box 4070, Victoria, 77903*.

Religious Education—Sr. DIGNA VELA, I.W.B.S., Dir., *1505 E. Mesquite Ln., P.O. Box 4070, Victoria, 77903*. Tel: 361-573-0828.

Respect Life-Pro Life—Rev. Msgr. JAMES C. BRUNNER, V.G., *P.O. Box 2448, Victoria, 77902*. Tel: 361-573-4328.

Rural Life Conference—Vacant.

Scouting—Vacant.

"The Catholic Lighthouse", Diocesan Newspaper—Mrs. CINDY BREWER, *P.O. Box 4070, Victoria, 77903*. Tel: 361-573-0828.

Vietnamese American Apostolic Center—Rev. JOSEPH PHAM DUC TRIN, *St. Anthony Church, P.O. Box 900, Palacios, 77465*. Tel: 361-972-2685.

Vocations Committee—Revs. MATTHEW HUEHLEFELD, Chm. JOSEPH HYBNER; KIRBY HLAVATY; Sr. MILDRED TRUCHARD, I.W.B.S.; Sr. JACINTA BENAVIDEZ, I.W.B.S.; R. A. STEVENSON, M.D., *P.O. Box 4070, Victoria, 77903*. Tel: 361-573-0828.

Director of Seminarians—Rev. MATTHEW HUEHLEFELD, *St. Joseph Church, P.O. Box 734, Yoakum, 77995*. Tel: 361-741-5302.

CLERGY, PARISHES, MISSIONS AND PAROCHIAL SCHOOLS

CITY OF VICTORIA
(Victoria County)

1—OUR LADY OF VICTORY CATHEDRAL, Revs. Michael Harrold; Kirby Hlavaty.
Res., 1309 E. Mesquite Ln., 77901. Tel: 361-575-4741; Fax: 361-575-3473.
School—Tel: 361-575-5391; 578-5454. Sr. M. Leonita Barron, I.W.B.S., Prin.
Sisters 2; Lay Teachers 29; Students 492.
Catechesis/Religious Programs—Tel: 361-575-8132. Betty Mitchell, D.R.E.
Students 623.

2—HOLY FAMILY OF JOSEPH, MARY & JESUS, Rev. Gregory E. Korenek; Deacon Steve Borowicz. In res., Rev. Gary G. Williams.
Office: 704 Mallette Dr., 77904. Tel: 361-573-5304; Fax: 361-573-6053. [JC]

3—OUR LADY OF LOURDES, Rev. Celestino Say, Admin.
Res., 105 N. William, 77901. Tel: 361-575-3813.

4—OUR LADY OF SORROWS, Revs. Victor Scocco, O.SS.T.; Alberto Rodriguez, O.SS.T.; Wolfgang Mimms, O.SS.T.; Deacons Edward Molina; Jesus Perez.
Res., 208 W. River St., P.O. Box 2548, 77901. Tel: 361-575-2293; Fax: 361-582-0405. [JC]
Catechesis/Religious Programs—Tel: 361-573-2681. Sr. Sylvia Gomez, M.C., D.R.E.
Students 1,015.
Convent—209 W. Murray St., 77901. Tel: 361-575-7654. Missionary Catechists of the Sacred Hearts of Jesus and Mary (Violetas)
Sisters 4.
Mission—Victoria, Victoria Co., Holy Trinity, 2511 Ozark, 77901.

5—ST. MARY'S, Rev. Msgr. James C. Brunner; Deacons Richard Wearden; Dudley Pagel; Jim Koenig.
Res., 402 S. Main, P.O. Box 2448, 77902. Tel: 361-573-4328; Fax: 361-573-4308. [JC]

OUTSIDE THE CITY OF VICTORIA

Ammannsville, Fayette Co., St. John The Baptist, Rev. Timothy Kosler, Admin.
Mailing Address: 7745 Mensik Rd., Schulenburg, 78956. [CEM]
Mission—Holman, St. Wenceslaus. [CEM]

Bay City, Matagorda Co., Holy Cross, Rev. Casimir Jarzombek.
Res., 2001 Katy St., 77414. Tel: 979-245-6379; Fax: 979-244-5481. [CEM 2][JC]
School—Tel: 979-245-5632; Fax: 979-245-6120. Sr. M. Geraldine Pavlik, I.W.B.S., Prin.
Lay Teachers 17; Students 164.
Convent—Tel: 979-245-3173.
Mission—Wadsworth, Sacred Heart.
Our Lady of Guadalupe, Rev. Edward Daniel Boren, O.F.M.
Res., 1412 12th St., 77414. Tel: 979-245-2010.

Blessing, Matagorda Co., St. Peter's, Rev. Samuel Appiasi.
Res., Box 395, 77419. Tel: 361-588-6241; Fax: 361-588-1421. [CEM][JC]
Mission—Markham, St. Robert.

Bloomington, Victoria Co., St. Patrick, Rev. Jacinto Olguin; Deacon Fred Soto.
Res., P.O. Box 217, 77951. Tel: 361-897-1155; Fax: 361-897-1064.

Cistern, Fayette Co., SS. Cyril and Methodius, Rev. Charles B. Carolan.
P.O. Box 186, Flatonia, 78941. Tel: 361-865-3568.
Church—113 Manchester St., Flatonia, 78941. Tel: 361-865-2222. [CEM 2]

Columbus, Colorado Co., St. Anthony's, Rev. Daniel P. Kahlich.
Res., P.O. Box 669, 78934. Tel: 979-732-2562; Fax: 979-732-8636. [CEM]
School—635 Bonham, 78934. Tel: 979-732-5505; Fax: 979-732-9758. Mrs. Charlyne Spanihel, Prin.
Lay Teachers 10; Students 157.

Cuero, Dewitt Co., Our Lady of Guadalupe, Rev. Daniel Giorgi, O.SS.T., Admin.
Res., 705 W. Broadway, P.O. Box 547, 77954. Tel: 361-275-3135.
St. Michael, Rev. Johnson Owusu-Boateng.
Res., 302 E. Church St., 77954. Tel: 361-275-3554; Fax: 361-277-3924.
School—208 N. McLeod, 77954. Tel: 361-277-3854; Fax: 361-275-3618.
Lay Teachers 8; Students 58.

Eagle Lake, Parish of the Nativity (1995), Rev. Edward J. Winkler.
Res., P.O. Box 307, 77434. Tel: 979-234-2842; Fax: 979-234-5828.
Catechesis/Religious Programs—Students 50.

East Bernard, Wharton Co., Holy Cross, Rev. Donald R. Ruppert.
Res., 839 Church St., P.O. Box 280, 77435. Tel: 979-335-7551; Fax: 979-335-7038. [CEM]
Convent—Tel: 979-335-4071.

Edna, Jackson Co., St. Agnes, Rev. Michael A. O'Shaughnessy.
Res., 506 N. Allen, 77957. Tel: 361-782-3588.

El Campo, Wharton Co., St. Philip the Apostle, Revs. Thu Van Nguyen; Michael Petering; Deacon Jarrel Nohavitza.
Res., 304 W. Church St., 77437. Tel: 979-543-3770; Fax: 979-578-8831. [CEM]
School—Tel: 979-543-2901; Fax: 979-578-8835.
Lay Teachers 19; Students 213.
Catechesis/Religious Programs—Students 190.
St. Robert Bellarmine, Rev. Lawrence Matula; Deacon Margarito Cervantez, Jr.
Res., 512 Tegner St., 77437. Tel: 979-543-4298; Fax: 979-541-5399.

Flatonia, Fayette Co., Sacred Heart, Rev. Charles B. Carolan.
Res., P.O. Box 186, 78941. Tel: 361-865-3568; Fax: 361-865-2518. [CEM]

Frelsburg, Colorado Co., SS. Peter and Paul (1836), Rev. Wayne N. Flagg.
Res., 1031 Church Lane, New Ulm, 78950. Tel: 979-732-3430; Fax: 979-732-9204. [CEM]

Ganado, Jackson Co., Assumption of the B.V.M., Rev. Joseph Hybner.
Mailing Address: P.O. Box 369, 77962. Tel: 361-771-3425; Fax: 361-771-3526.
Res., 108 S. Sixth St., 77962. [CEM]

Goliad, Goliad Co., Immaculate Conception, Rev. Raphael Baidoo, O.SS.T.
Res., P.O. Box 49, 77963. Tel: 361-645-3095. [CEM 2]
Missions—Charco, Our Lady of Guadalupe; Fannin, Our Lady of Assumption.
Shrine—Our Lady of Loreto (Old Franciscan Mission).

Hallettsville, Lavaca Co., Sacred Heart, Revs. John C. Peters, V.F.; Robert Knippenberg; Deacons Joey Targac; W.S. (Sonny) Rogers.
Res., P.O. Box H, 77964. Tel: 361-798-5888; Fax: 361-798-4970. [CEM]
School—Tel: 361-798-4251. Mr. David Smolik, Prin. (Elementary & High School).
Sisters 2; Lay Teachers 15; Students 175.
High School—313 S. Texana, 77964.
Sisters 1; Lay Teachers 10; Students 85.
St. Mary, Rev. John C. Peters, Admin.
Church—Rte. 4, Box 369, 77964. Tel: 361-789-2128. [CEM 4]

High Hill, Fayette Co., Nativity of the Blessed Virgin Mary, Rev. Timothy Kosler, Admin.
Mailing Address: 2833 FM 2672, Schulenburg, 78956-5603. Tel: 979-561-8455. [CEM]
Res., 1010 Lyons Ave., Box 310, Schulenberg, 78956. Tel: 979-743-3117.

Hillje, Wharton Co., St. Andrew, Rev. Clement Quainoo; Deacon Edward Wendel.
Mailing Address: Rte. 3, Box 39, El Campo, 77437. Tel: 979-648-2864; Fax: 979-648-2024. [CEM]
Mission—Louise, St. Procopius. [CEM]

Hostyn, Fayette Co., Holy Rosary, Rev. Msgr. Stanley J. Petru.
Res., 936 FM 2436, La Grange, 78945. Tel: 979-247-4441; Fax: 979-247-5008. [CEM]

Hungerford, Wharton Co., St. John the Baptist, Rev. Henry C. Rachunek.
Res., P.O. Box 121, 77448. Tel: 979-532-4747. [CEM]

Inez, Victoria Co., St. Joseph's, Rev. Benton A. Thurmond.
Res., P.O. Box 337, 77968. Tel: 361-782-3181; Fax: 361-782-3181. [CEM]

Koerth, Lavaca Co., St. John the Baptist, Rev. Charles Sonnier.
Res., P.O. Box 201, Sweet Home, 77987. Tel: 361-741-3206; Fax: 361-741-3206. [CEM][JC]

Mentz, Colorado Co., St. Roch (1850), Rev. Wayne N. Flagg.
Mailing Address: Rte. 2, Box 191, Alleyton, 78935. Tel: 979-732-3460; Fax: 979-733-0908. [CEM]

Meyersville, DeWitt Co., SS. Peter & Paul, Rev. Dominic Antwi-Boasiako, Admin.
Res., 11220 FM 237, 77974. Tel: 361-275-3868.
Mission—Westhoff, St. Aloysius.

Moulton, Lavaca Co., St. Joseph's, Rev. Gabriel Maison, J.C.D.
Res., P.O. Box 399, 77975. Tel: 361-596-4674; Fax: 361-596-4826. [CEM]

Nada, Colorado Co., Nativity of the Blessed Virgin Mary, Rev. Joseph A. Koebel.
Res., P.O. Box 97, 77460. Tel: 979-758-3218. [CEM]

New Taiton, Wharton Co., St. John Nepomucene, Rev. Msgr. Julius A. Petru.
Res., Rte. 1, Box 250, El Campo, 77437. Tel: 979-543-6985. [CEM]

Palacios, Matagorda Co., St. Anthony's, Rev. Charles Dwomoh; Deacon Michael Vieira.
Res., 1004 Magnusson, Box 900, 77465. Tel: 361-972-2446; Fax: 361-972-2606.
Vietnamese Apostolate—100 Vietnam, 77465. Tel: 361-972-2685. Rev. Joseph Pham duc Trin.

Plum, Fayette Co., SS. Peter and Paul, Rev. Msgr. Stanley J. Petru.
Res., 936 FM 2436, La Grange, 78945. Tel: 979-247-4441; Fax: 979-247-5008. [CEM 2]

Port Lavaca, Calhoun Co., Our Lady of the Gulf, Revs. Dan Morales; Robert Guerra; Deacon Alonzo F. Calzada.
Res., 319 S. Nueces St., P.O. Box 87, 77979. Tel: 361-552-6140; Fax: 361-552-4300.
Preschool/Daycare—412 W. Austin St., 77979. Tel: 361-553-6358. Kim Windham, Dir.
Lay Teachers 6; Students 49.
School—Tel: 361-552-2774. Sr. Mary Clare Jones, O.S.F., Prin.
Sisters 3; Lay Teachers 12; Students 121.
Catechesis/Religious Programs—Sr. M. Perpetua, I.W.B.S., D.R.E.
Students 654.
Missions—Point Comfort, St. Ann; Port O'Connor, St. Joseph; Seadrift, St. Patrick.

Praha, Fayette Co., St. Mary's, Rev. Edward C. Bartsch.
Res., 821 FM 1295, Flatonia, 78941. Tel: 361-865-3560. [CEM]

St. John, Fayette Co., St. John the Baptist, Rev. Brian Crookes.
Res., Rte. 4, Box 135, Schulenburg, 78956. Tel: 979-562-2222. [CEM]
Mission—Moravia, Lavaca Co., Ascension of Our Lord. [CEM]

Schulenburg, Fayette Co., St. Rose of Lima, Revs. Timothy Kosler, V.F.; Peter Kaplinski.
Res., 1010 Lyons Ave., Box 310, 78956. Tel: 979-743-3117; Fax: 979-743-4712. [CEM]
School—400 Black, 78956. Tel: 979-743-3080. Ms. Judy Roeder, Prin.
Sisters 1; Lay Teachers 10; Students 165.

Shiner, Lavaca Co., SS. Cyril and Methodius, Rev. Gerard Cernoch; Deacon Paul Patek.
Res., 306 S. Ave. F, P.O. Box 66, 77984. Tel: 361-594-3836; Fax: 361-594-2850. [CEM]
School—Tel: 361-594-3843; Fax: 361-594-8599. Mrs. Patricia Pesek, Prin., Tel: 361-594-3843.
Sisters 1; Lay Teachers 15; Students 202.

High School—Tel: 361-594-2313. Mrs. Patricia Pesek, Prin.
Sisters of the Incarnate Word and Blessed Sacrament 1; Lay Teachers 9; Students 64.

Sweet Home, Lavaca Co., Queen of Peace, Rev. Charles Sonnier.
Res., P.O. Box 201, 77987. Tel: 361-741-3206; Fax: 361-741-3206. [CEM][JC]

Vanderbilt, Jackson Co., St. John Bosco, Rev. Michael Lyons.
Office: 232 Main St., P.O. Box 337, 77991-0337. Tel: 361-284-3361; Fax: 361-284-3391.
Res., P.O. Box 163, 121 Garcitas St., 77991. Tel: 361-284-3026.
Mission—LaSalle, St. Theresa. [CEM]

Weimar, Colorado Co., St. Michael, Rev. John C. Bily.
Res., Box 36, 78962. Tel: 979-725-6714. [CEM]
School—Tel: 979-725-8461; Fax: 979-725-8344. Sr. M. Laura Toman, I.W.B.S., Prin.
Sisters of the Incarnate Word and Blessed Sacrament 2; Lay Teachers 7; Students 132.
Mission—Dubina, Fayette Co., SS. Cyril and Methodius.

Wharton, Wharton Co., Holy Family, Rev. Joseph L. Vrana; Deacon Alvin Matthys.
Res., 2011 Briar Ln., 77488. Tel: 979-532-3593.
Mission—Boling, St. Joseph.

Our Lady of Mt. Carmel, Rev. Raymond A. Jackson, C.S.B.
Res., 506 S. East Ave., 77488. Tel: 979-532-3492; Fax: 979-532-2321. [JC]

Yoakum, Lavaca Co., St. Joseph, Revs. Gary W. Janak, J.C.L.; Matthew Huehlefeld.
Res., 210 Schrimscher St., Box 734, 77995. Tel: 361-293-3518; Fax: 361-293-3004. [CEM]
School—Tel: 361-741-5362; Fax: 361-293-2004. Sr. Isabel Estrada, I.W.B.S., Prin.
Sisters of the Incarnate & Blessed Sacrament 2; Lay Teachers 18; Students 179.
Mission—Hochheim, St. Ann. [CEM]

Yorktown, Dewitt Co., Holy Cross, Rev. Frank B. Lenz.
Res., 1214 Zorn Rd., 78164-1907. Tel: 361-564-2893; Fax: 361-564-9315. [CEM 2]
Missions—Yorktown, San Luis; Nordheim, St. Ann's.

On Special or Other Diocesan Assignment:
Reverend Monsignors—
McLaughlin, Thomas C., V.G. Chancellor. Tel: 361-573-0828
Reverend Fathers—
Franks, Gabriel, Hospital Chap., 103 D Sherwood Dr., Victoria, TX 77901. Tel: 361-579-6895

On Duty Outside the Diocese:
Reverend Fathers—
Henninger, George, Indianapolis, IN
Mensah, Gabriel, Military Chap., U.S. Navy

Absent on Sick Leave:
Reverend Fathers—
Anders, Arnold

Retired:
Reverend Monsignors—
Schmidtzinsky, Victor
Reverend Fathers—
Bernasconi, Gino
Caponi, Jerome
Hermes, Eustace A.
Higgins, Peter
Janson, Eugene
O'Brien, Daniel
Quiroz, Guido M.

Permanent Deacons:
Borowicz, Stephen James Michael
Calzada, Alonzo Farias
Cervantez, Margarito Candelario, Jr.
Harper, Linard
Koenig, James Nicholas
Matthys, Alvin
Molina, Edwardo Pina
Nohavitza, Jarrel Joseph
Pagel, Dudley Meryl
Patek, Paul, Sr.
Perez, Jesus Castillo
Rogers, Walter Smith, Jr.
Soto, Fred
Targac, Joseph
Tran, Luan Van
Vieira, Michael
Wearden, Arthur R.
Wendel, Edward

INSTITUTIONS LOCATED IN THE DIOCESE

[A] HIGH SCHOOLS, PRIVATE

VICTORIA. *St. Joseph High School*, 110 E. Red River, 77901. Tel: 361-573-2446; Fax: 361-573-4221.
E-mail: eeilers@stjvic.org
Web site: www.stjvic.org
Mr. William H. McArdle, Jr., Pres.; Sr. M. Emilie Eilers, I.W.B.S., Prin. Sisters 1; Lay Teachers 31; Students 393.

[B] ELEMENTARY SCHOOLS, PRIVATE

VICTORIA. *Nazareth Academy*, 206 W. Convent, 77901. Tel: 361-573-6651; Fax: 361-573-1829.
E-mail: nazareth@icsi.net
Web site: www.nazareth.academy.org
Sr. Kathleen Goike, I.W.B.S., Prin. Sisters of the Incarnate Word and Blessed Sacrament 6; Lay Teachers 24; Students 382. Attended from St. Mary's, Our Lady of Lourdes, Our Lady of Victory, Holy Family and Our Lady of Sorrows' Churches.

[C] HOMES FOR AGED

HILLJE. *Czech Catholic Home For The Aged* Rte. 3, Box 4 El Campo, 77437. Tel: 979-648-2628; Fax: 979-648-2884.
For a complete listing, refer to the Special Care Facilities section.

[D] PERSONAL PRELATURES

SCHULENBURG. *Opus Dei*. Featherock Conference Center, 934 Holub Rd., 78956-5324. Tel: 979-743-4642.

[E] CONVENTS AND RESIDENCES FOR SISTERS

VICTORIA. *Franciscan Monastery of St. Clare*, 107 N. Depot St., 77901. Tel: 361-576-6347.
E-mail: monvctx@attglobal.net
Sr. Antoinette Madden, O.S.C., Supr.

Incarnate Word Convent, 1101 N.E. Water St., 77901-9298. Tel: 361-575-2266; Fax: 361-575-2165.
E-mail: iwbsvic@yahoo.com
Sr. Evelyn Korenek, I.W.B.S., Supr. Gen.; Sr. M. Mildred Truchard, Local Supr. Sisters 58; Annually Professed 2; Postulants 1.

Missionary Catechists of the Sacred Hearts of Jesus and Mary, 209 W. Murray St., 77901. Sr. Antonieta Salazar, M.C.SS.CC.J.M., Supr. Sisters 3.

[F] MONASTERIES & RESIDENCES OF PRIESTS & BROTHERS

VICTORIA. *Trinity House*. Novitiate Holy Trinity Fathers. 1511 E. Commercial St., 77901. Tel: 361-573-7059.
E-mail: damonosst@aol.com
Rev. Damon Geiger, O.SS.T.

[G] CAMPUS MINISTRY

VICTORIA. *Campus Ministry Center*, 2803 N. Ben Jordan, 77901. Tel: 361-578-1428.
E-mail: dtater@vc.cc.tx.us

[H] MISCELLANEOUS

VICTORIA. *Endowment Fund for the Catholic Diocese of Victoria in Texas*, P.O. Box 4070, 77903-4070. Mr. Arthur R. Wearden, Mailing Contact.

Jeanne Chezard De Matel Fund, 1101 N.E. Water St., 77901-9298. Tel: 361-575-2266; Fax: 361-575-2165.

Sisters of the Incarnate Word and Blessed Sacrament, Victoria, Texas, Inc., 1101 N.E. Water St., 77901-9298. Tel: 361-575-2266; Fax: 361-575-2165. Sr. Evelyn Korenek, I.W.B.S., Supr. Gen. & Mailing Contact.

Sisters of the Incarnate Word and Blessed Sacrament of Victoria, Texas, Medical and Retirement Trust, 1011 N.E. Water St., 77901-9298. Tel: 361-572-9321; Fax: 361-575-2165.

RELIGIOUS INSTITUTES OF WOMEN REPRESENTED IN THE DIOCESE

For further details refer to the corresponding bracketed number in the Religious Institutes of Women section.

[2200]—*Congregation of the Incarnate Word and Blessed Sacrament.*—I.W.B.S.

[2700]—*Missionary Catechists of the Sacred Hearts of Jesus and Mary.*—M.C.SS.CC.J.M.

[3760]—*Order of St. Clare.*—O.S.C.

[]—*School Sisters of Notre Dame.*

[]—*School Sisters of St. Francis.*—S.S.S.F.

[0460]—*Sisters of Charity of Incarnate Word.*—C.C.V.I.

[1010]—*Sisters of the Divine Providence of San Antonio, Texas.*—C.D.P.

[]—*Sisters of the Sacred Heart of Jesus.*—S.S.H.J.

[]—*Vietnamese Dominican Sisters.*—O.P.

NECROLOGY

† Doran, William, Meyersville, TX Ss. Peter & Paul. —Died May 25, 2000.

† Halata, William, La Grange, TX Holy Rosary. —Died June 11, 2000.

† Kram, Charles, Chap., Yoakum, TX Yoakum Community Hospital. —Died Aug. 13, 2000.

Archdiocese of Washington

(Archidioecesis Washingtonensis)

His Eminence

JAMES CARDINAL HICKEY, S.T.D., J.C.D.

Archbishop Emeritus of Washington; ordained June 15, 1946; appointed Titular Bishop of Taraqua and Auxiliary Bishop of Saginaw, February 18, 1967; Episcopal ordination April 14, 1967; appointed Bishop of Cleveland May 31, 1974; installed July 16, 1974; appointed Archbishop of Washington June 17, 1980; installed August 5, 1980; created Cardinal June 28, 1988. *Office: Archdiocesan Pastoral Center, 5001 Eastern Ave., Hyattsville, MD, 20782-3447. Mailing Address: P.O. Box 29260, Washington, DC, 20017-0260.* Tel.: 301-853-4500; Fax: 301-853-5346.

Most Reverend

LEONARD J. OLIVIER, S.V.D., D.D., V.G.

Auxiliary Bishop of Washington; ordained June 29, 1951; appointed Titular Bishop of Legia November 10, 1988; consecrated and Episcopal ordination December 20, 1988. *Res., 3340 St. Peter's Church Rd., Waldorf, MD, 20601.* Tel.: 301-843-1388; Fax: 301-843-1041.

His Eminence

THEODORE CARDINAL MCCARRICK, PH.D., D.D.

Cardinal of Washington; ordained May 31, 1958; ordained Auxiliary Bishop of New York and Titular Bishop of Rusibisir May 24, 1977; Episcopal ordination June 29, 1977; appointed First Bishop of Metuchen; appointed November 19, 1981; installed January 31, 1982; appointed Archbishop of Newark May 30, 1986; installed July 25, 1986; appointed Cardinal of Washington November 21, 2000; installed January 3, 2001. *Office: Archdiocesan Pastoral Center, 5001 Eastern Ave., Hyattsville, MD, 20782-3447. Mailing Address: P.O. Box 29260, Washington, DC, 20017-0260.* Tel.: 301-853-4540; Fax: 301-853-5359.

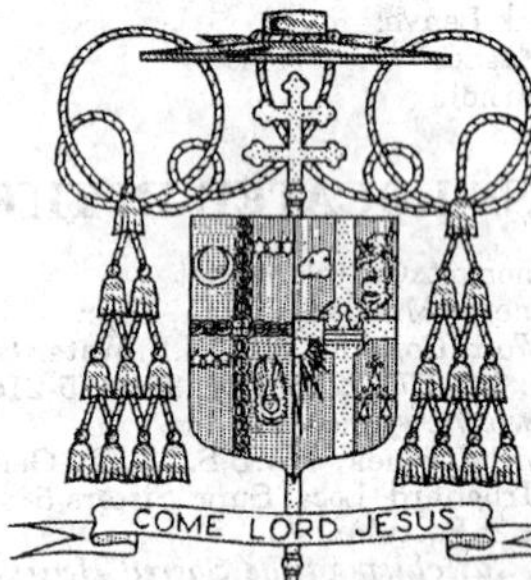

Archdiocesan Pastoral Center: 5001 Eastern Ave., P.O. Box 29260, Washington, DC, 20017. Tel.: 301-853-4500; Fax: 301-853-5346.

E-mail address: chancery@adw.org

Most Reverend

WILLIAM E. LORI, S.T.D., V.G.

Auxiliary Bishop of Washington, Vicar General and Moderator of the Curia; appointed Titular Bishop of Bulla and Auxiliary of Washington February 28, 1995; Episcopal ordination April 20, 1995. *Office: 5001 Eastern Ave., P.O. Box 29260, Washington, DC, 20017. Mailing Address: 5001 Eastern Ave., Hyattsville, MD, 20782-3447.* Tel.: 301-853-4520; Fax: 301-853-5346.

ESTABLISHED ARCHDIOCESE JULY 22, 1939; SEPARATED FROM BALTIMORE.NOVEMBER 15, 1947; BECAME A METROPOLITAN SEE OCTOBER 12, 1965

Square Miles 2,104.

Comprises the District of Columbia and Montgomery, Prince George's, St. Mary's, Calvert and Charles Counties in Maryland.

The Province of Washington has as a Suffragan, the Diocese of St. Thomas in the Virgin Islands.

For legal titles of parishes and archdiocesan institutions, consult the Chancery Office.

STATISTICAL OVERVIEW

Personnel	
Cardinal	1
Retired Cardinal	1
Auxiliary Bishops	2
Abbots	1
Retired Abbots	2
Priests: Diocesan Active in Diocese	211
Priests: Active Outside Diocese	31
Priests: Diocesan in Foreign Missions	2
Priests: Retired, Sick or Absent	74
Number of Diocesan Priests	318
Religious Priests in Diocese	647
Extern Priests in Diocese	189
Ordinations:	
Diocesan Priests	4
Religious Priests	2
Transitional Deacons	4
Permanent Deacons	20
Permanent Deacons in Diocese	226
Total Brothers	137
Total Sisters	748
Parishes	
Parishes	140
With Resident Pastor:	
Resident Diocesan Priests	123
Resident Religious Priests	17
Without Resident Pastor:	
Missions	9
Pastoral Centers	1
Professional Ministry Personnel:	
Brothers	2
Sisters	36
Lay Ministers	396
Welfare	
Catholic Hospitals	3
Total Assisted	427,376
Health Care Centers	5
Total Assisted	99,181
Homes for the Aged	12
Total Assisted	1,247
Residential Care of Children	1
Total Assisted	203
Day Care and Extended Day Care Centers	5
Total Assisted	647
Specialized Homes	9
Total Assisted	419
Special Centers for Social Services	65
Total Assisted	91,767
Residential Care of Disabled	34
Total Assisted	152
Other Institutions	15
Total Assisted	11,725
Educational	
Seminaries, Diocesan	1
Students from This Diocese	10
Students from Other Diocese	86
Diocesan Students in Other Seminaries	27
Seminaries, Religious	30
Students Religious	137
Total Seminarians	174
Colleges and Universities	3
Total Students	20,277
High Schools, Diocesan and Parish	1
Total Students	612
High Schools, Private	16
Total Students	8,388
Elementary Schools, Diocesan and Parish	79
Total Students	23,576
Elementary Schools, Private	9
Total Students	1,481
Non-residential Schools for the Disabled	1
Total Students	175
Catechesis/Religious Education:	
High School Students	2,264
Elementary Students	21,435
Total Students Under Catholic Instruction	78,382
Teachers in the Diocese:	
Priests	23
Scholastics	12
Brothers	13
Sisters	78
Lay Teachers	2,071
Vital Statistics	
Receptions into the Church:	
Infant Baptism Totals	7,084
Adult Baptism Totals	890
Received into Full Communion	734
First Communions	6,472
Confirmations	6,330
Marriages:	
Catholic	1,613
Interfaith	648
Total Marriages	2,261
Deaths	2,930
Total Catholic Population	510,000
Total Population	2,436,407

Former Bishops—Most Rev. MICHAEL J. CURLEY, D.D., cons. Bishop of St. Augustine, June 30, 1914; promoted to the See of Baltimore, Aug. 10, 1921; named Archbishop of Baltimore and Washington, July 22, 1939; died May 16, 1947.—His Eminence PATRICK CARDINAL O'BOYLE, cons. Jan. 14, 1948; retired March 3, 1973; died Aug. 10, 1987.—His Eminence WILLIAM CARDINAL BAUM, installed May 8, 1973; appt. Prefect, Congregation for Catholic Education in the Vatican, Jan. 15, 1980; Major Penitentiary; appt. April 6, 1990.

Auxiliary Bishops—Most Rev. LEONARD J. OLIVIER, S.V.D., D.D., V.G., Auxiliary Bishop of Washington, Office: *3340 St. Peter's Church Rd., Waldorf, MD, 20601.* Tel: 301-843-1388; Fax: 301-843-1041. Most Rev. WILLIAM E. LORI, S.T.D., V.G., Auxiliary Bishop of Washington; Vicar General in Curia, Office: *5001 Eastern Ave., P.O. Box 29260, Washington, 20017.* Tel: 301-853-4520; Fax: 301-853-5346.

Unless otherwise indicated, all Archdiocesan Offices, including the Chancery and the Tribunal, are located in the Archdiocesan Pastoral Center, *5001 Eastern Ave., P.O. Box 29260, Washington, 20017.*

Tel: 301-853-4500; Fax: 301-853-5346. Office Hours: Mon.-Fri. 8:30-5.

Vicars General—Most Rev. WILLIAM E. LORI, S.T.D.; Most Rev. LEONARD J. OLIVIER, S.V.D., D.D.

Episcopal Vicar for Hispanic Catholics—Rev. FRANCISCO GONZALEZ, S.F., *826 Wayne Ave., Silver Spring, MD, 20910.* Tel: 301-589-3261; Fax: 301-589-2550.

Moderator of the Curia—Most Rev. WILLIAM E. LORI, V.G., S.T.D. Tel: 301-853-4520; Fax: 301-853-5346.

Chancellor—Rev. Msgr. BERNARD C. GERHARDT, S.T.L., J.C.D. Tel: 301-853-4520; Fax: 301-853-5346.

Vice Chancellor—Rev. CHARLES ANTONICELLI, J.D., J.C.L. Tel: 301-853-4520; Fax: 301-853-5346.

Canonical Consultant to the Cardinal—Sr. ELIZABETH McDONOUGH, O.P., J.C.D.

Archivist—Deacon BERNARD A. BERNIER. Tel: 301-853-5316.

Secretary To The Archbishop—Rev. BARRY KNESTOUT. Tel: 301-853-4539; 4540; Fax: 301-853-5359.

Secretariats—Sr. BERNADETTE GLODEK, S.N.D., Catholic Education; Rev. WALTER J. TAPPE, Parish Life & Worship; Rev. ROBERT CARY HILL, Clergy; Sr. DANIELLE JOHNSON, R.S.M., Women Religious; Rev. Msgr. KEVIN FARRELL, Finance & Mgmt.; Rev. Msgr. RALPH KUEHNER, Social Concerns. Communications: (See separate sections below).

Executive Directors—Mrs. JACQUELINE E. WILSON, Office of Black Catholics; Sr. ONELLYS VILLEGAS, M.H.S.H., Office of Hispanic Pastoral Affairs; (See separate sections below).

The Tribunal

Tribunal—Tel: 301-853-4543; Fax: 301-853-7674.

Judicial Vicar—Rev. Msgr. JOSEPH F. SADUSKY, M.Div., M.Ch.A., J.C.D. Tel: 301-853-4544.

Assistant Judicial Vicars—Rev. GODFREY T. MOSLEY, J.C.D. Tel: 301-853-4543. Rev. W. BECKET SOULE, O.P., Ph.D., J.C.D. Tel: 301-853-5321.

Judges—Rev. Msgr. BERNARD C. GERHARDT, S.T.L., J.C.D. Tel: 301-853-5324. Revs. G. PAUL HERBERT, J.C.L. Tel: 301-853-5326. FRANCIS G. HORN, O.S.A., J.C.D. Tel: 301-853-4543. VINCENT RIGDON, M.A., J.C.L. Tel: 301-853-4528; Fax: 301-681-3527. GEORGE E. STUART, J.C.L. Tel: 301-853-5327. MARK E. TUCKER, C.SS.R., J.C.L. Tel: 301-853-5322. Deacon JOSEPH B. McGRATH, LL.B., J.C.L. Tel: 301-853-5303. Sr. ELIZABETH McDONOUGH, O.P., J.C.D. Tel: 301-853-4543.

Promoter of Justice—Rev. DAVID F. O'CONNOR, S.T., J.C.D. Tel: 301-853-5319.

Defenders of the Bond—Revs. DAVID F. O'CONNOR, S.T., J.C.D. Tel: 301-853-5319. JOSEPH BUI TRANGH-NGHIEM, M.S., S.T.L., J.U.D. Tel: 301-853-5320. KEVIN T. HART, J.C.D. Tel: 301-853-4543. MICHAEL J. KING, J.C.D. Tel: 301-853-4543.

Advocates—Rev. Msgr. PETER VAGHI, J.D. Tel: 301-853-4543. Revs. ROBERT G. AMEY. Tel: 301-853-4543. MARK E. BRENNAN. Tel: 301-853-4543. DONALD BRICE. Tel: 301-853-4536. JOHN T. DAKES, S.T.L. Tel: 301-853-4543. GEORGE E. GOLDEN, M.Div. Tel: 301-853-5343. PAUL D. LEE, S.T.D. Tel: 301-853-5343.

Notaries—Mrs. PATRICIA A. PERKINSON. Tel: 301-853-4544. Mrs. DENISE SMITH. Tel: 301-853-5324. Sr. MARY PAUL, O.P. Tel: 301-853-4543. Mrs. ANNE McGRATH. Tel: 301-853-4543.

Consultative Groups

Archdiocesan College of Consultors—Most Rev. LEONARD J. OLIVIER, S.V.D., D.D.; Most Rev. WILLIAM E. LORI, S.T.D.; Rev. Msgr. THOMAS M. DUFFY; Rev. Msgr. RAYMOND G. EAST; Rev. Msgr. JOHN J. ENZLER; Rev. Msgr. DONALD S. ESSEX; Rev. Msgr. BERNARD C. GERHARDT; Rev. Msgr. W. RONALD JAMESON; Rev. Msgr. WILLIAM J. KANE; Rev. Msgr. THOMAS A. KANE; Rev. GODFREY T. MOSLEY.

Archdiocesan Pastoral Council—His Eminence THEODORE CARDINAL McCARRICK, Vacant, Sec.; Most Rev. WILLIAM E. LORI; Rev. WALTER J. TAPPE; Ms. DELPHIN CASTRO; Ms. MARY CHAHALIS; Mr. JAMES CURTIS; GEORGE DAMERON; PHILLIP HOULE; Mrs. JANICE HUNTER; RAYMOND D. KANE; EUGENE KAROL; JOSEPH MAUREEN; MICHAEL MORA; NEAL OSTEN; ANN O'NEILL; GLORIA PURVIS; DOLORES STEINHILBER; ARLYN SWEENEY; Ms. ANN VERCAMP; JON WINBORNE.

Archdiocesan Finance Council—His Eminence THEODORE CARDINAL McCARRICK; Most Rev. WILLIAM E. LORI; Rev. Msgr. DONALD ESSEX; Rev. Msgr. KEVIN FARRELL; W. SHEPHERDSON ABELL; FRED J. BRINKMAN; DANIEL CALLAHAN; JEREMIAH C. COLLINS; RICHARD GRAVES; PAUL INTERDONATO; EUGENE I. KANE; Sr. CAROL KEEHAN; ROBERT LIGHTHIZER; ROBERT B. McCAIN; MICHAEL McGARRY; THOMAS P. RODDY; B. FRANCIS SAUL, II.

Deans—Vacant, Northern Prince George's County; Rev. Msgr. JOHN SCANLAN, Middle Prince George's County; Rev. CHARLES McCANN, Southern Prince George's County; Rev. THOMAS KALITA, Upper Montgomery County; Rev. Msgr. WILLIAM KANE, Middle Montgomery County; Rev. FRANCIS KAZISTA, Lower Montgomery County; Rev. PAUL E. LAVIN, Northeast, D.C.; Rev. Msgr. PETER VAGHI, Northwest East, D.C.; Rev. KENNETH W. ROELTGEN, Northwest West, D.C.; Rev. MICHAEL SALAH, Southeast, D.C.; Rev. PETER DALY, Calvert County; Rev. MATTHEW SIEKIERSKI, Charles County; Rev. FRANCIS J. EARLY, St. Mary's County.

Council of Priests—His Eminence THEODORE CARDINAL McCARRICK, Pres.; Rev. KEVIN HART, Moderator; Rev. Msgr. GODFREY MOSLEY, Vice Moderator; Rev. WALTER TAPPE, Sec.; Rev. MICHAEL MELLONE, Treas.

Sisters' Senate—Sr. PATRICE WALES, S.A.C., Pres.; Sr. MARIA LUZ, M.H.S.H., Vice Pres.; Sr. MARY CATHERINE WAREHIME, D.C., Sec.

Secretariat For Education

Secretary for Catholic Education—Sr. BERNADETTE GLODEK, S.N.D. Tel: 301-853-4519; Fax: 301-853-7691.

Assistant Secretary for Education—Rev. CHARLES J. PARRY. Tel: 301-853-5358.

Superintendent of Schools—Mr. LAWRENCE CALLAHAN. Tel: 301-853-4518; Fax: 301-853-7670.

Assistant Superintendent for Secondary Schools—Bro. WILLIAM GRIFFIN, C.F.X. Tel: 301-853-4597.

Assistant Superintendent for Elementary Schools—Mrs. TRUDY SAMPUGNARO. Tel: 301-853-4553.

Director of Curriculum Services—Sr. EILEEN CLINTON, I.H.M. Tel: 301-853-5353.

Director of School Personnel—Ms. DOROTHY THAYER. Tel: 301-853-4549.

Director of Instructional Services—Mrs. NOEL GESSNER. Tel: 301-853-4590.

Director of Professional Development—Sr. PATRICIA GARRAHAN, S.N.D. Tel: 301-853-4552.

Coordinator of Inclusive Education—Ms. PAMELA ALLEN. Tel: 301-853-4569.

Director of Latino and Multicultural Student Initiatives—Ms. BETTY RIVERA. Tel: 301-853-4598.

Financial Officer—Ms. LILLIAN RODRIGUEZ. Tel: 301-853-5356.

Executive Director Center City Consortium—Mrs. MARY ANNE STANTON, *1317 Eighth St., N.W., Washington, D.C., 20001.* Tel: 202-234-4611; Fax: 202-234-4740.

Board of Education—Mr. LAWRENCE JOHNSTON, Pres.

Office of Youth Ministry/CYO—Rev. LeROY FANGMEYER, Exec. Dir. Tel: 202-281-2461; Fax: 202-281-2470.

Our Lady of Mattaponi Retreat Center—Rev. ROBERT MORDINO, Dir., *301-952-9074.* Fax: 301-952-0609.

CYO Programs—THOMAS J. MANCO, Dir. Tel: 202-281-2463.

Coordinator for Youth Adult Ministry—PETER NEWBURN. Tel: 301-853-4559.

Ministry Development Coordinator Adult Training—JAMES PAULEY. Tel: 202-281-2466.

Ministry Development Facilitator—Rev. FRANCO LIPORACE, (Hispanic). Tel: 202-281-2476.

Ministry Development Facilitator—DARREN FOSTER, (African American). Tel: 202-281-2469.

Scouting—Rev. Msgr. JOHN BRADY, Chap. Coord. Tel: 301-769-3332. FRANK ROSSOMONDO, Arch. Lay Coord., Catholic Comm. Boy Scouts & Camp Fire. Tel: 301-770-7450. ROBERT KAMMER, Arch. Lay Chm., Catholic Comm. Boy Scouting. Tel: 301-942-0882. Arch. Co-Chm., Girl Scouts: BARBARA ANN FOSTER. Tel: 301-972-2067. JOAN TREACY. Tel: 301-924-0394.

Our Lady of Mattaponi Youth Retreat and Conference Center—Tel: 301-952-9074; Fax: 301-952-0609.

Office for Religious Education—Mr. LAWRENCE RILLA, S.T.L., Dir. Tel: 301-853-4506; Fax: 301-853-7687.

Hearts Aflame Program—Rev. R. SCOTT HURD, Dir. Tel: 301-853-5386.

Catechist Formation Coordinator—MARY THERESE TUSKEY. Tel: 301-853-4531.

At-Large Field Representative—GREGORY KOLODZIEJCZAK. Tel: 301-853-5385.

Hispanic Catholics Religious Education—Sr. MARIA LUZ ORTIZ, M.H.S.H. Tel: 301-853-5384.

Special Religious Education—DOLORES WILSON, Coord. Tel: 301-853-4560.

Propagation of the Faith—Rev. VINCENT J. RIGDON, Archdiocesan Dir. Tel: 301-853-4527; Fax: 301-853-7684.

Mission Education Coordinator—Sr. MARY OF CHARITY ASENSIO, S.S.V.M. Tel: 301-853-4534.

Holy Childhood Association—Rev. VINCENT J. RIGDON, Dir. Tel: 301-853-4527.

Sacred Heart Basic Adult Education Center—Sr. MARIE LUCEK, O.P., Dir. JOSEPH SHERMAN, Asst. Dir. Tel: 202-462-6499.

Secretariat For Parish Life and Worship

Secretary for Parish Life and Worship—Rev. WALTER J. TAPPE, Acting Sec. Tel: 301-853-4557; Fax: 301-853-7670. Mr. EAMON M. MAGEE, Admin. Asst. Tel: 301-853-4558.

Office for Adult Religious Formation—Mr. THOMAS BURNFORD, Dir. Tel: 301-853-5331.

Office for Ecumenical and Interreligious Affairs—Rev. PAUL LEE, Dir. Tel: 301-853-5378.

Office for Evangelization—Ms. MARTHA FERNANDEZ-SARDINA, Dir. Tel: 301-853-4596.

Hispanic Liturgical Ministry and Hispanic Family Life Ministry - RCIA—MAGDALENA GUTTIEREZ. Tel: 301-853-5334.

Office for Family Life Ministry—Mr. NICK BAGILEO, Dir. Tel: 301-853-4546. Mr. WILLIAM COFFIN, Marriage Prep Coord. Tel: 301-853-4551.

Natural Family Planning—Ms. HEATHER KEIMIG, Dir. Tel: 301-853-4561.

Office for Persons with Disabilities—Ms. DOLORES WILSON, Dir. Tel: 301-853-4560.

Office of Worship—Rev. WALTER J. TAPPE, Dir. Tel: 301-853-4595. JEFFREY McGARRITY, Coord., RCIA Program. Tel: 301-853-5335. Sr. CONSTANCE WARD, S.S.J., Admin. Asst. Tel: 301-853-4594; Fax: 301-853-7684.

Charismatic Renewal Regional Service Committee—Deacon DONALD DeROZE; Mrs. DONALD DeROZE, *13103 Tamarack Rd., Silver Spring, MD, 20994.* Tel: 301-384-5568.

Cursillo Movement—Rev. Msgr. RAYMOND EAST, Spiritual Dir., *Nativity Parish, 600 Georgia Ave., N.W., Washington, 20011.* Tel: 202-726-6262. Directors: MARLO JO BONUCCELLI. Tel: 703-588-1767. SANDRA BARNES. Tel: 301-261-3573.

St. Francis of Assisi Catholic Church and Center for the Deaf—Rev. GERARD A. TRANCONE, Dir., *7202 Buchanan St., Landover Hills, MD, 20784.* Tel: 301-459-7464; Fax: 301-459-8186.

Ministry for the Deaf—Rev. GERARD A. TRANCONE, *Gallaudet University, 800 Florida Ave., N.E., Washington, 20002.* Tel: 301-577-3527 (Voice & TDD).

Holy Name Society—Rev. Msgr. THOMAS A. KANE, *4101 Norbeck Rd., Rockville, MD, 20853.* Tel: 301-924-2284; Fax: 301-929-3017.

Ancient Order of Hibernians—Mr. JAMES CLARKE, *7108 Plantation Ln., Rockville, MD, 20852.* Tel: 301-881-4512.

Archdiocesan Council of Catholic Women—Rev. ROBERT G. AMEY, Spiritual Dir., *11801 Claridge Rd., Wheaton, MD, 20705.* Tel: 301-946-3636; Fax: 301-946-5061. LILLIAN QUEEN, Pres., *463 Madison St., N.E., Washington, 20011.* Tel: 202-832-5453.

Blue Army of our Lady of Fatima—Rev. CHARLES E. POPE, Spiritual Dir., *St. Mary's Parish, 114 St. Mary's Place, Laurel, MD, 20707.* Tel: 301-725-3080. Mrs. ANNA ZACYNSKI, *14518 Perrywood Dr., Burtonsville, MD, 20866.* Tel: 301-236-4012.

Catholic Daughters of the Americas Court District of Columbia No. 212—Ms. GRACE BITONDI, Regent, *4801 Connecticut Ave., N.W., Washington, 20008.* Tel: 202-363-0395.

Catholic Hospital Chaplains—Vacant, *Cardinal O'Boyle Residence, 1150 Varnum St. N.E., Washington, 20017.* Tel: 202-219-7100.

Health Care Concerns Coordinator—Rev. J. WILFRED PARENT, *Archdiocesan Pastoral Center, P.O. Box 29260, Washington, 20017.* Tel: 301-853-4580. *St. Mary, Mother of God, 727 Fifth St., N.W., Washington, 20001.* Tel: 202-289-7771.

Catholic Interracial Council of Washington, DC—Mrs. MADELINE FURTH, Pres., *3224 Northampton St. N.W., Washington, 20015.* Tel: 202-966-6794.

Catholic War Veterans of the United States—Mr. ROBERT A. WAMESTER, Natl. Commander, *441 N. Lee St., Alexandria, VA, 23314-2344.* Tel: 956-580-2298; Fax: 703-684-5196. LORRAINE SATTERSFIELD, Pres., National War Veterans, *441 N. Lee St., Alexandria, VA, 22314.* Tel: 703-549-3622; Fax: 703-684-5196.

Association of St. Francis de Sales—Rev. LEWIS FIORELLI, O.S.F.S., Supr. Gen., *1621 Otis St., N.E., Washington, 20018.* Tel: 202-269-5677. Mrs. JOAN McDERMOTT, Eastern U.S.A. Regl. Dir., *17 Lakeview Trail, Fairfield, PA, 17320.* Tel: 717-642-6647.

First Friday Club—Rev. EVERETT PEARSON, Spiritual Dir., *4000 Harewood Rd. N.E., Washington, 20017.* Tel: 202-397-2525; Fax: 202-397-6639.

International Federation of Catholic Alumnae—The Catholic University of America, 416 Administration Bldg., Washington, 20017. Tel: 202-526-5916.

John Carroll Society—Tel: 703-573-3043. Rev. Msgr. PETER VAGHI, Chap., *619 10th St. N.W., Washington, 20001.* Tel: 202-347-2713. Mr. JAMES MARTIN, *6917 Bradley Blvd., Bethesda, MD, 20817.* Tel: 301-365-9410.

Knights of Columbus—Most Rev. WILLIAM E. LORI, S.T.D., Chap., *P.O. Box 29260, Washington, 20017.* Tel: 202-526-8300.

Knights of St. Jerome—Mr. VINCENT BISBOE, *St. Peter Claver, St. Inigoes, MD, 20684.* Tel: 301-872-5377.

Knights of St. John—Most Rev. LEONARD OLIVIER, *St. Peter's, 3340 St. Peter's Dr., Waldorf, MD, 20601.* Tel: 301-843-1388; Fax: 301-843-1041.

Womens Retreat League—Sr. MARGARET MULLIN, S.A., Dir., *4000 Harewood Rd. N.E., Washington, 20017.* Tel: 202-529-1111; Fax: 202-529-2102.

Engaged Encounter—Contact the Office of Family Life. Tel: 301-853-4561.

Marriage Encounter-Worldwide—Contact the Office of Family Life. Tel: 301-853-4561.

Sodality Union—Rev. GREGORY C. BUTTA, *St. Ann's, 4001 Yuma St., N.W., Washington, 20016.* Tel: 202-966-6288; Fax: 202-916-7722. Mrs. BARBARA B. BECHET, Pres., *11007 Belton St., Largo, MD, 20774.* Tel: 301-336-6835.

Secretariat For Social Concerns

Secretary—Rev. Msgr. RALPH KUEHNER. Tel: 301-853-4556; Fax: 301-853-7671.

Associated Catholic Charities—EDWARD J. ORZECHOWSKI, M.S.W., Pres., *924 G St., N.W., Washington, 20001-4532.* Tel: 202-526-4100.

A.C.C. Housing & Initiative Corp.—924 G St., N.W., Washington, 20001-4532. Tel: 202-526-4100.

A.C.C. Model Cities Corp.—1125 Neal St. N.E., Washington, 20002. Tel: 202-396-8100.

A.C.C. Otis Street Corp.—924 G St., N.W., Washington, 20001-4532. Tel: 202-526-4100.

SHARE, DC, Inc.—5170 Lawrence Pl., P.O. Box 768, Bladensburg, MD, 20710. Tel: 301-864-3115.

Anchor Mental Health Association, Inc.—KERRY SMITH, Dir.; Rev. Msgr. JOHN G. KUHN, Dir. Emeritus, *1001 Lawrence St. N.E., P.O. Box 29058, Washington, 20017-0058.* Tel: 202-635-5900.

Pro-Life Office—Mr. THOMAS GRENCHIK, Dir. Tel: 301-853-4555; Fax: 301-853-7671.

Birthing & Care Center—Ms. MICHELLE WILLIAMS, *817 Varnum St., N.E., Washington, 20017.* Tel: 202-526-2229; Fax: 202-526-1226.

Campaign for Human Development—Mr. CHRISTOPHER WAINWRIGHT. Tel: 301-853-5341.

Office of Social Development—Rev. Msgr. RALPH KUEHNER. Tel: 301-853-4556; Fax: 301-853-7671.

St. Vincent de Paul Society—STANLIE BARTON, Pres. Tel: 202-723-3035.

Project Rachel—Mrs. MAUREEN BREITENBACH, *817 Varnum St., N.E., Washington, 20017.* Tel: 202-269-4673; Fax: 202-526-1226.

Ladies of Charity—ANNA JONES, Pres., *4901 Eastern Ave., Hyattsville, MD, 20782.* Tel: 301-559-5500. Rev. CARL F. DIANDA, Spiritual Dir., *St. Francis de Sales Parish, 2021 Rhode Island Ave., N.E., Washington, 20018., Providence Hospital, 1150 Varnum St., N.E., Washington, 20017.* Tel: 202-269-7000.

Lt. Joseph P. Kennedy Institute—Dr. RICHARD BIRKEL, Pres. & CEO, *801 Buchanan St. N.E., Washington, 20017.* Tel: 202-529-7600.

St. Ann's Infant & Maternity Home—Sr. JOSEPHINE MURPHY, D.C., Admin., *4901 Eastern Ave., Hyattsville, MD, 20782.* Tel: 301-559-5500.

Christ Child Society—MARGARET M. MISSAR, Pres.; Rev. Msgr. W. LOUIS QUINN, Spiritual Dir., *5101 Wisconsin Ave. N.W., Washington, 20016.* Tel: 202-966-9250.

Community Center of the Missionaries of Charity—Sr. LUCIANA, M.C., Supr., *3310 Wheeler Rd. S.E., Washington, 20032.* Tel: 202-562-6890.

Missionaries of Charity—Sr. M. PIETRA, M.C., Supr., *Gift of Peace Home, 2800 Otis St. N.E., Washington, 20017.* Tel: 202-269-3313. Sr. M. FREDINA, Supr., *Mother Teresa's Infant Home, Gift of Love, 5649 Western Ave. N.W., Washington, 20015.* Tel: 202-237-6633.

Cambridge Apartments, Inc., c/o Victory Housing, Inc.—BONNIE THOMSON, Project Developer, *5430 Grosvenor Lane, Ste. 210, Bethesda, MD, 20814.* Tel: 301-493-5508; Fax: 301-493-9788.

Andrew Kim House, Inc., c/o Victory Housing, Inc.—BONNIE THOMSON, Project Developer, *5430 Grosvenor Lane, Ste. 210, Bethesda, MD, 20814.* Tel: 301-493-6000.

Marian Assisted Living—BONNIE THOMSON.

Byron House, Inc.—TAMMY FURNARY, Dir.

Raphael House, Inc.—MICHELINE BUCHANAN, Dir.

Malta House, Inc.—DEBORAH PRESTON, Dir.

Faith House—Sr. JOSEPHINE MURPHY, D.C., Admin., *4903 Eastern Ave., Hyattsville, MD, 20782.* Tel: 301-559-5500.

Bartholomew House, Inc.—LUANNA BARCHIE, Dir.

Avondale Park Apartments, Inc.—Site Supervisors: DAVID DAVIS; JANET HAMMONDS.

Manor Apartments, Inc.—Site Supervisors: DAVID DAVIS; JANET HAMMONDS.

District of Columbia Catholic Conference—Mr. RONALD JACKSON. Tel: 301-853-5342; Fax: 301-853-7671.

Secretariat For The Clergy

Secretary for Services for Clergy, Religious Men and Secular Institutes—Rev. ROBERT CARY HILL. Tel: 301-853-4550; Fax: 301-853-7668.

Director of Priests Personnel—Rev. ROBERT CARY HILL. Tel: 301-853-4550.

Coordinator, Pastoral Care of Priests—Rev. Msgr. JOSEPH RANIERI. Tel: 301-853-5361.

Director, Vocations for Men—Rev. J. WILFRED PARENT. Tel: 301-853-4580.

Continuing Education for Clergy—Rev. PAUL D. LEE. Tel: 301-853-5378.

St. John Vianney House—Rev. MICHAEL J. MURRAY, Dir., *4214 Saul Rd., Kensington, MD, 20895.* Tel: 301-942-1191.

Executive Director, Permanent Diaconate—Rev. MICHAEL J. MURRAY. Tel: 301-853-4582.

Director of Deacon Personnel—Deacon LEON J. BECHET. Tel: 301-853-4591.

Director of Formation—Deacon ALFREDO SOTO. Tel: 301-853-4583.

Priests Retirement Board—Rev. KEVIN HART, Chm. Tel: 301-292-0527.

Cardinal O'Boyle Residence for Priests—Rev. Msgr. LEONARD J. HURLEY, *P.O. Box 29206, Washington, 20017.* Tel: 202-269-7818.

Serra Club of Washington—JOSEPH SPANIOL, JR., *5602 Ontario Circle, Bethesda, MD, 20816.* Tel: 301-229-2176.

Serra Club of Downtown Washington—The Honorable JOHN H. BAYLY, JR., *3512 Runnymede Pl., N.W., Washington, 20015.* Tel: 202-363-6703.

Serra Club of Prince George's Co.—Mr. DAVID GALE, *3804 38th Ave., #2, Cottage City, MD, 20722.*

Serra Club of Southern Maryland—Dr. ROBERT GOLDSMITH, *St. Rt. Box 73, Leonardtown, MD, 20650.* Tel: 301-994-2893.

Liaison with Council of Priests—(see Consultative Bodies) Religious priests and brothers, Secular Institutes, Consultant on Alcoholism.

Secretary For Women Religious

Secretary for Services to Women Religious and Secular Institutes—Sr. DANIELLE JOHNSON, R.S.M. Tel: 301-853-4576; Fax: 301-853-7669.

Liaison with Sisters' Senate—(see Consultative Bodies).

Secretariat For Finance and Management

Secretary For Finance and Management—Rev. Msgr. KEVIN FARRELL. Tel: 301-853-4523; Fax: 301-853-2787.

Accounting and Financial Management—Mr. RICHARD B. GRAVES, Controller. Tel: 301-853-4525.

Parish Accounting—Mr. TERRENCE FARRELL, C.P.A. Tel: 301-853-4511; Fax: 301-853-7664.

Parish Audit Department—Ms. HEATHER HOLLAND, C.P.A. Tel: 301-853-5313.

Office of Investments & Real Estate—ROBERT B. MCCAIN, Dir. Tel: 301-853-5350; Fax: 301-853-7690.

Facilities Management—Mr. RICHARD DE STWOLINSKI. Tel: 301-853-4572; Fax: 301-853-7679.

Materials and Pastoral Center Management—Ms. ALESSANDRA STYLES. Tel: 301-853-4532; Fax: 301-853-7673.

Personnel and Benefits—DOROTHY MOORE, Dir. Tel: 301-853-4513; Fax: 301-853-7680.

Office of Development—Mr. GREGORY F. GANNON, Dir. Tel: 301-853-4574; Fax: 301-853-7678.

Archdiocesan Building Commission—Rev. Msgr. JOSEPH A. RANIERI, Chm.

Cardinal's Stewardship Appeal—Mr. GREGORY F. GANNON, Dir. Tel: 301-853-4575; Fax: 301-853-7678.

Paul VI Institute for the Arts—Rev. Msgr. MICHAEL DI TECCIA FARINA, Dir., *924 G St. N.W., Washington, 20017.* Tel: 202-347-1450.

Offie of Planned Giving—Ms. GRETCHEN KOCH. Tel: 301-853-4573.

Archdiocesan Finance Council—(see Consultative Bodies).

Carroll Publishing Company—(see Secretariat for Communications).

Archdiocesan Sacred Arts Committee—Rev. Msgr. W. RONALD JAMESON, *1725 Rhode Island Ave. N.W., Washington, 20036.* Tel: 202-347-3215; Fax: 202-347-7184.

Cornerstone for Tomorrow, Inc.—Rev. Msgr. KEVIN FARRELL, *P.O. Box 29260, Washington, 20017.* Tel: 301-853-4523.

Priest Retirement Fund of the Archdiocese of Washington, Inc.—Rev. Msgr. KEVIN FARRELL, *P.O. Box 29260, Washington, 20017.* Tel: 301-853-4523.

Development Office

Cardinal's Stewardship Appeal—Tel: 301-853-4575.

Office of Communications

Director—Ms. SUSAN GIBBS. Tel: 301-853-4516; Fax: 301-853-7672.

TV Mass Producer—Mr. JOHN CAPOBIANCO. Tel: 301-853-4515.

Carroll Publishing Company—His Eminence THEODORE CARDINAL MCCARRICK, Publisher; Mr. THOMAS SCHMIDT, Pres. Tel: 202-281-2405; Fax: 202-281-2408.

Newspaper—*"The Catholic Standard";* Mr. MARK ZIMMERMAN, Editor. Tel: 202-281-2412; Fax: 202-281-2418., *"El Pregonero";* Mr. OSCAR REYES, Editor. Tel: 202-281-2441; Fax: 202-281-2448.

Office Of Black Catholics

Executive Director—Mrs. JACQUELINE E. WILSON. Tel: 301-853-4579; Fax: 301-853-7671. Coordinating Office for Black Catholic History; Combating Racism; Black Catholic Congress; REJOICE! Conference on Black Catholic Liturgy; Archdiocesan Mass Choir; Other Programs & Resources for Leadership and Evangelization in the Black Community.

Council of Black Catholics—Dr. JAMES MAYO, Chm.

Office Of Hispanic Pastoral Affairs

Executive Director—Sr. ONELLYS VILLEGAS, M.H.S.H. Tel: 301-853-4566; Fax: 301-853-7671.

Spanish Catholic Center—Rev. BRENDAN BUCKLEY, O.F.M.Cap, Dir., *1618 Monroe St. N.W., Washington, 20010.* Tel: 202-483-5665; Fax: 202-234-7323.

CLERGY, PARISHES, MISSIONS AND PAROCHIAL SCHOOLS

DISTRICT OF COLUMBIA

1—ST. MATTHEW CATHEDRAL (1840), Rev. Msgr. W. Ronald Jameson; Revs. James D. Watkins; G. Paul Herbert; Augustin Mateo Ayala (Spain); Deacons Ulysses Rice; Lawrence C. Gordon; Matthew B. Reilly; Boyd Work; Pamela Erwin, Business Mgr. In res., Rev. Msgr. Bernard C. Gerhardt.

Res., 1725 Rhode Island Ave., N.W., 20036. Tel: 202-347-3215; Fax: 202-347-7184.

Catechesis/Religious Programs—Students 57.

2—ST. ALOYSIUS, Washington, (1859), Revs. R. Bruce Bavinger; John A. Conlin, S.J.; Deacon Willis Daniels.

Res., 19 Eye St., N.W., 20001. Tel: 202-336-7200; Fax: 202-898-1449.

Father McKenna Center—Tel: 202-842-1112. Paul J. Magno, Dir.

3—ST. ANN, Washington, (1869), Revs. Kevin T. Hart; Joseph B. Pierce; Deacon Robert W. Whitaker.

Res., 4001 Yuma St., 20016. Tel: 202-966-6288; Fax: 202-966-7722.

School—(Grades PreK-8). Tel: 202-363-4460; Fax: 202-362-6560. Mrs. Barbara Kelly, Prin.

Catechesis/Religious Programs—Students 269.

4—ANNUNCIATION, Washington, (1948), Rev. Msgr. Kevin J. Farrell; Revs. Patrick E. Dempsey; Donald Brice. In res., Rev. Brien R. McCarthy.

Res., 3125 39th St., N.W., 20016-5409. Tel: 202-362-3323; Fax: 202-237-0652.

School—3825 Klingle Pl., 20016-5434. Tel: 202-362-1408; Fax: 202-363-4057. Mrs. K. Marguerite Conley, Prin.

Sisters of Holy Child Jesus 3; Lay Teachers 15; Students 196.

Catechesis/Religious Programs—Sr. Kathleen O'Neill, S.H.C.J., D.R.E.

Students 73.

Convent—3200 39th St., N.W., 20016. Tel: 202-362-1464.

5—ST. ANTHONY, Washington, (1892), Rev. Msgr. Richard Burton; Rev. Berard L. Marthaler, O.F.M.Conv.; Deacon John Kelly. In res., Revs. Victor Wong (Nanking); John Rodney, S.V.D.; Richard A. Aboumoussa (Lebanon).

Res., 1029 Monroe St., N.E., 20017. Tel: 202-526-8822; Fax: 202-526-1543.

School—Tel: 202-526-4657; Fax: 202-832-5567.

Lay Teachers 24; Students 284.

Catechesis/Religious Programs—Students 20.

6—ASSUMPTION, Washington, (1916), Rev. Msgr. T. Ansgar Laczko.

Res., 3401 Martin Luther King Jr. Ave., S.E., 20032-1597. Tel: 202-561-4178; Fax: 202-561-0336.

School—Tel: 202-562-7070; Fax: 202-574-5829. Mr. Christopher Kelly, Prin.

Lay Teachers 10; Students 165.

Catechesis/Religious Programs—Students 47.

7—St. Augustine, Washington, (1858) (African American), Rev. Msgr. Russell L. Dillard; Rev. Charles C. Green.
Parish Office—1419 V St., N.W., 20009. Fax: 202-234-1787.
Res., 1425 V St., N.W., 20009. Tel: 202-265-1470.
School—1421 V St., N.W., 20009. Tel: 202-667-2608. Shelore C. Williams, Prin.
Lay Teachers 18; Students 190.
Catechesis/Religious Programs—Students 175.

8—St. Benedict the Moor, Washington, (1946) (African American), Revs. Francis M. Hull, S.S.J.; Darren S. Hazeur, S.S.J.
Res., 320 21st St., N.E., 20002. Tel: 202-397-3895; Fax: 202-398-3415.
School—Tel: 202-397-3897; Fax: 202-388-7874. Sr. Brenda Cherry, O.S.P., Prin.
Lay Teachers 15; Students 226.
Catechesis/Religious Programs—Students 17.
Convent—Tel: 202-398-7696.

9—St. Blaise (1984) (Croatian). (Croation Pastoral Mission). Rev. Zdenko Spajic (Bosnia).
Res., St. Jerome House of Study, 1359 Monroe St., N.E., 20017. Tel: 202-832-6364.

10—Blessed Sacrament, Shrine of the Most, Washington, (1911), Rev. Msgr. Thomas M. Duffy; Revs. Percival L. D'Silva; Raymond F. Schmidt; Deacons Joseph B. McGrath; Daniel Thompson.
Res., 6001 Western Ave., N.W., 20015. Tel: 202-966-6575; Fax: 202-966-9255.
School—5841 Chevy Chase Pkwy., N.W., 20015. Tel: 202-966-6682; Fax: 202-966-4938. Mrs. Frances Scango, Prin.
Lay Teachers 32; Students 488.
Catechesis/Religious Programs—Tel: 202-363-8938. D.R.E.: Sr. M. Antoinette Krejsa, S.N.D.; Mrs. Patricia Armelin, (Grades K-6); Joseph Davis, (Grades 7-12).
Students 427.

11—St. Dominic Church & Priory, Washington, (1852), Very Revs. Edward M. Gaffney, O.P., Prior; Donald P. Thibault, O.P., Subprior; Revs. John A. McMahon, O.P.; Robert D. Riley, O.P.; Robert L. Walker, O.P.; Edmund J. Way, O.P.; Fico Barahona Vertiz, O.P.; Kenneth A. France-Kelly, O.P.; Cornelius T. Kane, O.P.; Guy B. Dupont, O.P; William Cenkner, O.P.; Joseph J. Jurasko, O.P.; Joseph A. Cote, O.P.; William Newman, O.P.; Jerome Kennedy, O.P.; Thomas Collins, O.P.; Patrick Walsh, O.P.; Francis Dominic Nealy, O.P.; Peter Batts, O.P.; Mark Heath, O.P.; Becket Soule, O.P.; Bros. Fabian Butler, O.P.; Leon Mancinelli, O.P.
Res., 630 E St., S.W., 20024. Tel: 202-554-7863; Fax: 202-554-0231.

12—Epiphany, Washington, (1923), Rev. Winthrop Brainerd.
Res., 2712 Dumbarton St., N.W., 20007. Tel: 202-965-1610; Fax: 202-337-8377.

13—St. Francis de Sales, Washington, (1722) (African-American), Rev. Carl F. Dianda; Deacons Floyd H. Agostinelli; Harold Jackson. In res., Revs. John S. Wintermyer; Henry Slevin; Romanus Kyomya (Africa); Alphonsus Oha (Africa).
Res., 2021 Rhode Island Ave., N.E., 20018. Tel: 202-529-7451; Fax: 202-529-0050.
School—Tel: 202-529-5394; Fax: 202-529-1620.
Sisters 1; Lay Teachers 9; Students 212.

14—St. Francis Xavier (1924), Rev. Michael A. Salah. In res., Rev. Msgr. John L. Bailey, Pastor Emeritus.
Res., 2800 Pennsylvania Ave., S.E., 20020. Tel: 202-582-5021; Fax: 202-581-7224.
School—Tel: 202-581-2010; 202-234-4611; Fax: 202-582-5244. Mrs. Kathleen Pardue, Prin.
Lay Teachers 10; Students 180.
Catechesis/Religious Programs—Mr. Robert Fuller, D.R.E.
Students 57.
Convent—2812 Pennsylvania Ave., S.E., 20020. Tel: 202-584-5621. Sisters of St. Joseph Sr. M. Brigid S.S.J., Supr.

15—St. Gabriel, Washington, (1919), Revs. Mark Hughes; Vidal Rivas, Spanish Min.; Sr. Maria Faina, S.N.J.M., Pastoral Assoc.; Deacons Robert L. Berry; Morris Williams. In res., Revs. Tesfamariam Baraki; Jonathan Lao.
Res., 26 Grant Cir., N.W., 20011. Tel: 202-726-9092; Fax: 202-291-0334.
School—Tel: 202-726-9212; Fax: 202-726-1881. Mrs. June Felix, Prin.
Lay Teachers 9; Students 250.

16—Holy Comforter—St. Cyprian, Washington, (1893) (African American), Rev. Eddie Tolentino, III; Deacons Charles Edelin; Kevin Butler. In res., Revs. F. Michael Bryant; Reginald Brady.
Res., 1357 E. Capitol St., S.E., 20003. Tel: 202-546-1885; Fax: 202-544-1385.
School—Tel: 202-547-7556; Fax: 202-547-5686. Mrs. Deborah Jackson-Nesmith, Prin.
; Lay Teachers 14; Students 225.
Catechesis/Religious Programs—Tel: 202-547-2510. Mrs. Dolores Gorham, D.R.E.
Students 55.

17—Holy Name, Washington, (1892) (African American), Rev. Everett Pearson; Deacon William Thomas.
Res., 920 11th St., N.E., 20002. Tel: 202-397-2525; Fax: 202-397-6639.
School—Tel: 202-397-1614; Fax: 202-398-4832. Sr. Owen Patricia Bonner, S.S.J., Prin.
Sisters of St. Joseph 2; Lay Teachers 15; Students 230.
Catechesis/Religious Programs—Students 221.

18—Holy Redeemer, Washington, (1922) (African American), Rev. David Bava.
Res., 206 New York Ave., N.W., 20001. Tel: 202-347-7510; Fax: 202-628-0401.
School—Holy Redeemer School, (Grades PreK-8) 1135 New Jersey Ave., N.W., 20001. Tel: 202-638-5789. Mrs. Mildred Tyler, Prin.
Priests 1; Sisters 2; Deacons 1; Lay Teachers 13; Students 230.
Catechesis/Religious Programs—Students 230.

19—Holy Rosary, Washington, (1913) (Italian), Rev. Charles Zanoni, C.S.
Res., 595 Third St., N.W., 20001-2703. Tel: 202-638-0165; Fax: 202-638-0793.

20—Holy Trinity, Washington, (1787), Revs. William J. Byron, S.J.; Bert Akers, S.J.; Vincent Curtin, S.J.; Mark P. Scales, S.J.; Gerard J. Campbell, S.J.; Robert Poirier, S.J.
Church—36th St., N.W., between N and O Sts., 20007.
Parish Center Offices—3513 N St., N.W., 20007.
Res., 3514 O St., N.W., 20007. Tel: 202-337-2840; Fax: 202-337-9048.
School—Tel: 202-337-2339; Fax: 202-337-0368.
Sisters of St. Joseph (Chestnut Hill, PA) 2; Lay Teachers 33; Students 339.
Catechesis/Religious Programs—Students 560.

21—National Shrine Of The Immaculate Conception, Washington,

22—Immaculate Conception, Washington, (1864) (African American), Rev. Msgr. J. Joshua Mundell.
Res., 1315 8th St., N.W., 20001. Tel: 202-332-8888; Fax: 202-332-0173.
School—(Grades PreK-4) 711 N St., N.W., 20001. Tel: 202-234-1093. Sr. Carol Ann Knight, S.H.C.J., Prin.
Sisters 1; Lay Teachers 5; Students 112.
Catechesis/Religious Programs—Students 35.

23—Incarnation, Washington, (1934) (African American), Rev. John A. Carroll, S.S.J.; Deacons Harry Draper; Joseph E. Bell.
Res., 880 Eastern Ave., N.E., 20019. Tel: 202-396-0942; Fax: 202-396-6064.
Catechesis/Religious Programs—Students 60.

24—St. Joseph on Capitol Hill, Washington, (1869), Revs. Paul E. Lavin; Christopher T. Begg. In res., Rev. Eugene Hemrick (JOL).
Res., 313 Second St., N.E., 20002. Tel: 202-547-1223; Fax: 202-547-4189.

25—Kidane-Mehret Ge'ez Rite Catholic Church, Washington, (1984) (Ethiopian-Eritrean), Rev. Tesfamariam Baraki.
Mailing Address: 1001 Lawrence St., N.E., P.O. Box 29616, 20017. Tel: 202-529-8420.
Res., 26 Grant Cir., N.W., 20011. Tel: 202-726-9092; Fax: 202-529-8523.
Catechesis/Religious Programs—Students 127.

26—Church of St. Louis, Washington, (1972) (French). (Paroisse St. Louis de France-French-speaking Parish of Washington). Rev. Andre Millot.
Res., 4125 Garrison St., N.W., 20016. Tel: 202-537-0709; Fax: 202-244-9649.
Catechesis/Religious Programs—Students 240.

27—St. Luke, Washington, (1957) (African American), Revs. James E. McLinden, S.S.J.; Joseph N. Begay, S.S.J.; Deacons Earle W. Coleman; Joseph M. Conrad.
Res., 4925 E. Capitol St., 20019-5202. Tel: 202-584-8322; Fax: 202-584-3421.
Catechesis/Religious Programs—Students 138.

28—St. Martin of Tours, Washington, (1901) (African-American), Rev. Michael J. Kelley.
Res., 1908 N. Capitol St., 20002. Tel: 202-232-1144; Fax: 202-832-6772.
Catechesis/Religious Programs—Students 92.

29—St. Mary, Mother of God, Washington, (1845), Rev. David Conway; Deacon Bernard Johnson. In res., Rev. J. Wilfrid Parent.
Res., 727 Fifth St., N.W., 20001. Tel: 202-289-7771; Fax: 202-408-1989.

30—Nativity, Washington, (1901) (African American), Rev. Msgr. Raymond G. East.
Res., 6000 Georgia Ave., N.W., 20011. Tel: 202-726-6262.
School—Tel: 202-723-3322; Fax: 202-291-0219. Ceasar R. Camarillo, Prin.
Sisters 3; Lay Teachers 15; Students 220.
Catechesis/Religious Programs—Tel: 202-829-4051. Sr. Sally Daniel, S.P.C., D.R.E.
Students 130.

31—Nigerian Catholic Community (1994) (Nigerian), Rev. Pius T. Ajiki.
Res., Nativity Parish, 6000 Georgia Ave., N.W., 20011. Tel: 202-726-8363; 202-726-1513; Fax: 202-882-2854.

32—Our Lady of Perpetual Help, Washington, (1920) (African-American), Revs. Lowell D. Case, S.S.J.; John Hardman, S.S.J.; Deacon Thomas Jones.
Res., 1600 Morris Rd., S.E., 20020. Tel: 202-678-4999; Fax: 202-610-3189.
School—Tel: 202-889-1662 (Grades PreK-4); 678-0211 (Grades 5-8); Fax: 202-610-1519. Principals: Sr. Mary Elizabeth Semmelmayer, S.S.N.D.; Mrs. Charlene Hursey.
School Sisters of Notre Dame 1; Lay Teachers 11; Students 199.
Catechesis/Religious Programs—Students 112.

33—Our Lady Queen of the Americas, Washington, (1986) (Hispanic-Portuguese), Rev. Jose I. Somoza, O.F.M.; Deacon Jorge Vargas. In res., Rev. Demetrio J. Gomez, O.F.M.
Church, Office and Residence—2200 California St., N.W., 20008. Tel: 202-332-8838; Fax: 202-332-2967.
Catechesis/Religious Programs—Sr. Ana C. Hidalgo, D.R.E.
Students 236.

34—Our Lady Queen of Peace, Washington, (1948) (African American), Rev. Alfred J Harris; Deacon Alfred Miller; Mr. Ernest Adams, Pastoral Assoc.
Res., 3800 Ely Pl., S.E., 20019. Tel: 202-582-8600; Fax: 202-575-3317.
School—Tel: 202-584-4278; Fax: 202-584-1922. Deacon Terrell Stackpole, Prin.
Daughters of Charity of St. Vincent de Paul 5; Lay Teachers 13; Students 170.
Catechesis/Religious Programs—Tel: 202-581-4986.
Students 70.
Convent—3740 Ely Pl., S.E., 20019. Tel: 202-581-4963; Fax: 202-584-1922.

35—Our Lady of Victory, Washington, (1906), Rev. William E. Foley; Deacon Edward Redding; Jane Zilles-Sobrano, Pastoral Assoc. In res., Rev. Msgr. Harry A. Echle; Rev. Emanuel Magro (Malta).
Res., 4835 MacArthur Blvd., N.W., 20007. Tel: 202-337-4835; Fax: 202-338-4759.
School—4755 Whitehaven Pkwy., N.W., 20007. Tel: 202-337-1421; Fax: 202-338-4759. Susan Milloy, Prin.
Lay Teachers 19; Students 169.

36—St. Patrick, Washington, (1794), Rev. Msgr. Peter J. Vaghi; Revs. George Madathiparampil; Paul F. Liston; Deacon John J. McGinness. In res., Rev. Msgr. Michael diTeccia Farina; Rev. David Nuss (TOL).
Res., 619 Tenth St., N.W., 20001-4587. Tel: 202-347-2713; Fax: 202-347-1401.

37—St. Peter, Washington, (1821), Rev. Michael J. O'Sullivan. In res., Rev. Msgr. Joseph F. Sadusky; Revs. Thomas J. Sheehan; Joseph R. Sileo.
Res., 313 Second St., S.E., 20003. Tel: 202-547-1430; Fax: 202-547-5732.
School—422 Third St., S.E., 20003. Tel: 202-544-1618; Fax: 202-547-5101. Pamela J. Klobukowski, Prin.
Lay Teachers 23; Students 230.
Catechesis/Religious Programs—Tel: 202-544-1618.
Students 63.

38—Our Lady of Fatima Parish (1999). (Portuguese-speaking Community). Rev. Ademir Guerini, C.S.
Mailing Address: 70 University Blvd. E., Silver Spring, MD 20901. Tel: 301-593-9212; Fax: 301-593-3088.
Catechesis/Religious Programs—10830 Eastwood Ave., Silver Spring, MD 20901.
Students 80.

39—Shrine of the Sacred Heart, Washington, (1899), Revs. Francis X. Russo, O.F.M.Cap.; Stephen Carter, O.F.M.Cap.; Paul Zaborowski, O.F.M.Cap.; Deacons Sylvester Brown, (Retired); James Quander, (Retired). In res., Revs. Joseph Mindling, O.F.M.Cap.; Andre Pierre, O.F.M.Cap. (Haiti).
Res., 3211 Pine St., 20010. Tel: 202-234-8000 (Day); 234-8002 (Night); Fax: 202-234-9159.
School—1625 Park Rd., N.W., 20010. Tel: 202-265-4828; Fax: 202-265-0595. Juana Brown, Prin.
Lay Teachers 17; Students 217.
Catechesis/Religious Programs—Tel: 202-667-2446.
Students 370.

40—St. Stephen Martyr, Washington, (1867), Rev. Msgr. Kenneth W. Roeltgen; Deacon John W. Bobbitt. In res., Revs. Raymond B. Kemp; Robert J. Panke.

Res., 2436 Pennsylvania Ave., N.W., 20037. Tel: 202-785-0982; Fax: 202-785-1574.

41—St. Teresa of Avila, Washington, (1879), Rev. Patrick A. Smith; Deacons Ralph Cyrus; Lawrence Miles.
Res., 1430 Minnesota Ave., S.E., 20020. Tel: 202-678-3709; Fax: 202-678-3325.
Church—1244 V. St. SE, 20020.
Catechesis/Religious Programs—Students 76.

42—St. Thomas Apostle, Washington, (1909), Rev. Mark E. Brennan; Deacon William C. Boesman. In res., Rev. Msgr. William F. O'Donnell; Rev. John K. Sterling (DAV).
Res., 2665 Woodley Rd., N.W., 20008. Tel: 202-234-1488; Fax: 202-234-1480.
Catechesis/Religious Programs—Students 30.

43—St. Thomas More, Washington, Revs. Charles E. Pope; John P. Kinter; Deacon Nerus O. Martin, Jr.
Res., 4275 4th St., S.E., 20032. Tel: 202-562-0431.
School—Mr. Wilford Graham, Prin. Lay Teachers 11; Students 175.

44—St. Vincent De Paul, Washington, (1903) (African American), Revs. Francis M. Hull, S.S.J.; Darren S. Hazeur, S.S.J.; Deacon Francis Kraemer. In res., Bro. Marx Tyree, S.S.J.
Res., 14 M St., S.E., 20003-3511. Tel: 202-488-1354; Fax: 202-488-7899.
Catechesis/Religious Programs—Students 75.

CHURCHES IN MARYLAND

Avenue, St. Mary's Co., Holy Angels (1906), Rev. Msgr. John B. Brady; Rev. Msgr. Aloysius E. O'Connor, Pastor Emeritus.
Res., 21340 Colton Point Rd., 20609-2422. Tel: 301-769-3332; Fax: 301-769-2541. [CEM][JC]
School—Holy Angels-Sacred Heart, Tel: 301-769-3389; Fax: 301-769-4948.
Priests 2; Lay Teachers 11; Students 124.
Catechesis/Religious Programs—Students 51.

Baden, Prince Georges Co., St. Michael (1957), Rev. Louis J. Faust; Deacon Harvey Ballard.
Res. and Mailing Address—17510 Horsehead Rd., Brandywine, 20613. Tel: 301-888-1498; Fax: 301-579-0019.
Catechesis/Religious Programs—Tel: 301-579-6409; Fax: 301-579-0019.
Students 90.
Mission—Aquasco, Prince Georges Co., St. Dominic's, 22300 Aquasco Rd., Aquasco, 20608. [CEM]

Barnesville, Montgomery Co., St. Mary Church and Shrine of Our Lady of Fatima (1807), Revs. Joseph J. Kleinstuber; George B. Reid, Pastor Emeritus; Deacon David Cahoon.
Res., 18230 Barnsville Rd., P.O. Box 67, 20838. Tel: 301-972-8660; Fax: 301-428-8464. [CEM]
Catechesis/Religious Programs—Students 228.

Beltsville, Prince Georges Co., St. Joseph (1963), Rev. Roderick D. McKee; Deacon Andrew J. Betz. In res., Rev. R. Cary Hill.
Res., 11007 Montgomery Rd., 20705. Tel: 301-937-7183; Fax: 301-937-7780.
School—Tel: 301-937-7154; Fax: 301-937-1467.
Lay Teachers 15; Students 277.
Catechesis/Religious Programs—Tel: 301-937-7419.
Students 161.

Benedict, Charles Co., St. Francis de Sales (1903), Rev. Saverio T. Vitturino.
Res., 7185 Benedict Ave., P.O. Box 306, 20612-0306. Tel: 301-274-3416; 870-4991; Fax: 301-274-0689.
Catechesis/Religious Programs—7209 Benedict Ave., 20612.
Students 62.

Bethesda, Montgomery Co.,

1—St. Bartholomew, (1960), Rev. Msgr. James T. Beattie; Revs. Mark Ervin; Luis G. Salcedo.
Res., 7212 Blacklock Rd., 20817. Tel: 301-229-7933; Fax: 301-229-7998.
School—6900 River Rd., 20817. Tel: 301-229-5586. Mrs. Kathleen Miller, Prin.
Sisters 2; Lay Teachers 18; Students 209.
Catechesis/Religious Programs—Tel: 301-229-3431; Fax: 301-229-7998.
Students 353.

2—St. Jane Frances de Chantal, (1950), Rev. Msgr. Donald S. Essex; Revs. Alan R. Helwig; William Joensen (DUB); Deacon Neil Tift.
Res., 9701 Old Georgetown Rd., 20814. Tel: 301-530-1550; Fax: 301-493-8953.
School—9525 Old Georgetown Rd., 20814. Tel: 301-530-1221; Fax: 301-530-1688. Mrs. Betsy Hamilton, Prin.
Lay Teachers 27; Students 544.
Catechesis/Religious Programs—Tel: 301-530-1640; Fax: 301-530-5881.
Students 174.

3—Little Flower, Rev. Msgr. William J. Kane; Revs. David H. Werning; George Stuart; Deacons Gary Davies; Richard Schopfer.
Res., 5607 Massachusetts Ave., 20816. Tel: 301-320-4538; Fax: 301-320-4541.
School—Tel: 301-320-3273; Fax: 301-320-2867.
Sisters of the Immaculate Heart of Mary 5; Lay Teachers 19; Students 267.
Catechesis/Religious Programs—Tel: 301-320-5233.
Students 200.

4—Nativity of the Blessed Virgin (German Mission), (1992), Rev. Msgr. Bernd Kaut.
Liturgy at Our Lady of Bethesda Retreat Center: 7007 Bradley Blvd.; Rectory: 6330 Linway Ter., McLean, VA 22101-4150. Tel: 703-356-4473; Fax: 703-356-4558.

5—Our Lady of Lourdes, (1926) (Spanish), Revs. James P. Meyers; William J. Silk, Senior Priest; Mario E. Dorsonville; Deacon John Shewmaker. In res., Rev. Msgr. W. Louis Quinn.
Res., 7500 Pearl St., 20814. Tel: 301-654-1287; Fax: 301-986-8716.
School—Tel: 301-654-5376; Fax: 301-654-2568. Patrick Serra, Prin.
Sisters 1; Lay Teachers 17; Students 249.
Catechesis/Religious Programs—Tel: 301-654-5954.
Students 131.

6—Our Lady of Vietnam, (1990) (Vietnamese), Revs. Peter Nguyen-Thanh-Long; Hilary Tran-Khac Hy, (Retired); Deacon John Huong Nguyen.
Res., 11812 New Hampshire Ave., Silver Spring, 20904. Tel: 301-622-4895; Fax: 301-625-9384.

Bowie, Prince Georges Co.,

1—Ascension, (1893), Revs. James S. Betz; Samuel L. Craig; Deacons Finis E. Thompson; Ted R. Pillman.
Mailing Address: P.O. Box 96, 20719. Tel: 301-262-2227; Fax: 301-805-5053. [CEM]
Catechesis/Religious Programs—Tel: 301-262-8604. Mrs. Hope A. Benson, D.R.E.
Students 280.

2—Sacred Heart, (1892), Rev. Charles J. Parry; Rev. Msgr. John F. Hogan, Pastor Emeritus; Rev. Stephen F. Nash; Deacons H. Jeffrey Raffensperger; Edward J. Danko, Sr.
Res., 16501 Annapolis Rd., 20715. Tel: 301-262-0704; Fax: 301-805-4686. [CEM]
Catechesis/Religious Programs—Tel: 301-262-1221. Mrs. Mimi Shea, D.R.E.
Students 206.

3—St. Edward, (1972), Rev. Thomas F. Kehoe; Deacons Kevin Barry; David Barnes.
Res., 16304 Pond Meadow Ln., 20716. Tel: 301-249-9199.
Catechesis/Religious Programs—Tel: 301-249-9599; Fax: 301-249-1303.
Students 300.

4—St. Pius X, (1962), Rev. W. Paul Hill; Deacons Andrew Nosacek; Donald Sparling. In res., Revs. Paul Lyttle (Ireland); Thomas McGrath (Ireland).
Res., 3300 Moreland Pl., 20715. Tel: 301-262-2141; Fax: 301-262-2632.
Church—14720 Annapolis Rd., 20715.
School—Tel: 301-262-0203; Fax: 301-805-8875.
Lay Teachers 29; Students 734.
Catechesis/Religious Programs—Tel: 301-262-3644. Debbie Langdon, D.R.E.
Students 289.

Bryantown, Charles Co., St. Mary (1793), Rev. Ralph C. Torsiello; Deacons Eugene Burroughs; Henry Middleton.
Res., 13715 Notre Dame Pl., 20617-2224. Tel: 301-870-2220; 274-3187; Fax: 301-274-0253. [CEM]
School—Tel: 301-932-6883; Fax: 301-274-0626.
School Sisters of Notre Dame 1; Lay Teachers 9; Students 204.
Catechesis/Religious Programs—Tel: 301-274-3800.
Students 215.

Burtonsville, Montgomery Co., Resurrection Parish (1981), Revs. Robert F. Keffer; Charles E. Brown; Sr. Eileen Fitzgerald, S.N.J.M., Pastoral Assoc.; Deacon Donald DeRoze.
Res., 3315 Greencastle Rd., 20866. Tel: 301-236-5200; Fax: 301-236-5204.
Catechesis/Religious Programs—Tel: 301-236-5200.
Students 463.

Bushwood, St. Mary's Co., Sacred Heart (1755), Rev. Francis J. Early.
Res., 20618. Tel: 301-769-3100. [JC]
Catechesis/Religious Programs—See Holy Angels-Sacred Heart School, Avenue, MD, for details.
Students 57.

Camp Springs, Prince Georges Co., St. Philip the Apostle, Revs. Charles McCann; Bernard R. Ihrie, Jr., Senior Priest (Retired). In res., Rev. Jeffrey F. Samaha.
Res., 5416 Henderson Way, 20746. Tel: 301-423-4244; Fax: 301-423-1226.
School—Tel: 301-423-4740; Fax: 301-423-4716.
Lay Teachers 13; Students 285.
Catechesis/Religious Programs—Tel: 301-423-0166.
Students 345.

Chapel Point, Charles Co., St. Ignatius (1641), Rev. Salvador Jordan, S.J.
Res., St. Thomas Manor, 8855 Chapel Point Rd., Port Tobacco, 20677. Tel: 301-934-8245; Fax: 301-934-0944. [CEM]
Catechesis/Religious Programs—Angela Hume, D.R.E.
Students 194.

Chaptico, St. Mary's Co., Our Lady of the Wayside (1938), Rev. John P. Stack.
Mailing Address: Rte. 238, Helen, 20638. Tel: 301-884-3165; Fax: 301-884-3165.
Res., Rte. 238, P.O. Box 97, 20621. Tel: 301-884-2502; Fax: 301-884-0381.
School—Mother Catherine Spalding Tri Parish School, Tel: 301-884-3165.
Lay Teachers 17; Students 213.
Catechesis/Religious Programs—Students 110.

Cheverly, Prince Georges Co., St. Ambrose (1886), Revs. G. William Finch; Timothy K. Baer; Deacon Edwin Beller.
Res., 3107 63rd Ave., 20785. Tel: 301-773-9300; Fax: 301-773-2611.
School—Tel: 301-773-0223; Fax: 301-773-9218. Mr. Vincent Spadoni, Prin.
Lay Teachers 15; Students 265.
Catechesis/Religious Programs—Tel: 301-341-3284.
Students 60.

Chillum, Prince Georges Co., St. John Baptist de la Salle (1951), Rev. Robert C. Richardson.
Res., 5706 Sargent Rd., 20782. Tel: 301-559-3636; Fax: 301-559-3062.
Catechesis/Religious Programs—Students 73.

Clinton, Prince Georges Co., Church of St. John the Evangelist (1875), Revs. Thomas W. Pollard; Richard A. Scott; Deacon Anthony Moll.
Res., 8908 Old Branch Ave., 20735. Tel: 301-868-1070; Fax: 301-868-7915. [CEM]
School—Tel: 301-868-2010; Fax: 301-856-8941. Sr. Jean Louise Bachetti, I.H.M., Prin.
Sisters of the Immaculate Heart of Mary 2; Lay Teachers 21; Students 261.
Catechesis/Religious Programs—Tel: 301-868-3026.
Students 122.

College Park, Prince Georges Co., Holy Redeemer (1912), Rev. William F. Berry.
Res., 4902 Berwyn Rd., 20740. Tel: 301-474-3920; Fax: 301-441-4954.
School—Tel: 301-474-3993; Fax: 301-441-8137. Gregory E. Jones, Prin.
Religious 2; Lay Teachers 18; Students 277.
Catechesis/Religious Programs—Tel: 301-474-4299. Mrs. Sandra Tucker, D.R.E.
Students 123.

St. Andrew Kim (1974) (Korean), Rev. Seung-Chul (Thomas Aquinas) Im (Korea).
Res., 8108 54th Ave., 20740. Tel: 301-474-0681; Fax: 301-474-6785. [CEM][JC]
Catechesis/Religious Programs—Students 282.

Damascus, Montgomery Co., St. Paul (1957), Revs. Peter J. Sweeney; Walter J. Norris, Pastor Emeritus; Deacons John Finerty; David Terrar; Charles Weschler.
Res., 9240 Damascus Rd., 20872. Tel: 301-253-2027; Fax: 301-391-6755.
Catechesis/Religious Programs—Tel: 301-253-5941.
Students 1404.

Darnestown, Montgomery Co., Our Lady of the Visitation (1991), Rev. Raymond L. Fecteau; Deacon Paul DiDuca.
Res., 14200 Darnestown Rd., 20874-3008. Tel: 301-948-5536; Fax: 301-948-7452.
Catechesis/Religious Programs—Students 260.

Mary of Nazareth Roman Catholic Elementary School (1994), Sr. Frances Stavalo, Prin.
Res., 14131 Seneca Rd., 20874. Tel: 301-869-0940; Fax: 301-869-0942.
Catechesis/Religious Programs—Students 230.

Derwood, Montgomery Co., St. Francis of Assisi (1972), Revs. Donald P. Worch; Michael F. Dolan; Deacons Wilbur Pinder; Robert Whitfield. In res., Rev. Msgr. Ralph J. Kuehner.
Res., 6701 Muncaster Mill Rd., 20855. Tel: 301-840-1407; Fax: 301-258-5080.
Catechesis/Religious Programs—Tel: 301-258-9193.
Students 705.

Dunkirk, Calvert Co., Jesus the Good Shepherd (1985), Rev. Paul M. Dudziak; Deacon Emmett "Chad" Martin.
Res., 1555 Mount Harmony Rd. W., Owings, 20736. Tel: 301-855-4400; Fax: 410-257-6334.
School—Cardinal Hickey Academy, 1601 W. Mt. Harmony Rd., Owings, 20736. Tel: 410-286-0404; Fax: 410-286-6334. Ms. Lynn Leaf, Prin.
Catechesis/Religious Programs—Tel: 301-855-5694.
Students 639.

Forestville, Prince George Co., Church of the Holy Spirit (1966), Rev. Joseph A. Jenkins.
Res., 1717 Ritchie Rd., 20747. Tel: 301-336-3707; Fax: 301-324-1649.
Catechesis/Religious Programs—Students 31.

Mt. Calvary (1942), Revs. George E. Golden; David Thompson; Deacon Lawrence Miles; Mr. Mark Cosenza, Pastoral Assoc.
Res., 6700 Marlboro Pike, 20747. Tel: 301-735-5532; Fax: 301-735-2005. [CEM]
School—Tel: 301-735-5262; Fax: 301-736-5044.
Lay Teachers 21; Students 302.
Catechesis/Religious Programs—6704 Marlboro Pike, 20747. Tel: 301-420-4499.
Students 150.

Fort Washington, Prince Georges Co., St. Ignatius (1849), Revs. Robert A. Finamore; Robert P. Wummer. In res., Rev. Salvatore A. Criscuolo.
Res., 2315 Brinkley Rd., Oxon Hill, 20744. Tel: 301-567-4740; Fax: 301-567-0156. [CEM]
School—2317 Brinkley Rd., Oxon Hill, 20744. Tel: 301-567-4090. Ms. Linda Bourne, Prin.
Lay Teachers 12; Students 220.
Catechesis/Religious Programs—Students 70.

Gaithersburg, Montgomery Co., St. John Neumann (1978), Revs. Michael W. Fisher; Paul Tam X. Tran; Deacon Robert Allen.
Church—9000 Warfield Rd., 20882. Tel: 301-977-5492; Fax: 301-977-3559.
Mailing Address: 8900 Lochaven Dr., 20882-4460.
Catechesis/Religious Programs—Tel: 301-977-7990; Fax: 301-330-3235.
Students 725.

St. Martin (1920) (Spanish), Revs. Michael J. Mellone; Kevin C. Kennedy; William A. Ryan; Deacons Lawrence Bell; Eugene J. Cummins, Jr.; Ronald J. Meyer; Kenneth Barrett.
Res., 201 S. Frederick Ave., 20877. Tel: 301-840-1830; Fax: 301-990-7538.
School—Tel: 301-840-1748; Fax: 301-840-1733. Mrs. Shirley Wise, Prin.
Lay Teachers 17; Students 289.
Catechesis/Religious Programs—Tel: 301-840-1838; Fax: 301-840-2008. M. Patricia Dorney, D.R.E.
Students 1,364.

St. Rose of Lima (1972), Rev. Robert D. Duggan; Deacon James McCann.
Mailing Address: 11701 Clopper Rd., 20878-1024. Tel: 301-948-7545; Fax: 301-869-2170. [CEM]
Catechesis/Religious Programs—Tel: 301-948-7545, Ext. 228. Patricia Lawlor, D.R.E.
Students 513.

Garrett Park, Montgomery Co., Holy Cross (1960), Rev. Msgr. Vincent S. Gatto; Rev. Leroy J. Fangmeyer.
Res., 4900 Strathmore Ave., P.O. Box 249, 20896. Tel: 301-942-1020; Fax: 301-949-3543.
School—Tel: 301-949-0053; Fax: 301-949-5074. Sr. Sharon Mihm, Prin.
Lay Teachers 24; Students 249.
Catechesis/Religious Programs—Tel: 301-942-8790.
Students 137.

Germantown, Montgomery Co., Mother Seton Parish (1974), Revs. Ronald A. Potts; Aaron Joseph Coty, O.P.; Deacons William Vita; Timothy Enright; Philip Cooper.
Res., 19951 Father Hurley Blvd., 20874. Tel: 301-924-3838; Fax: 301-428-4951.
Catechesis/Religious Programs—Students 625.

Great Mills, St. Mary's Co., Holy Face (1879), Rev. Kevin O'Reilly.
Res., 20476 Point Lookout Rd., 20634. Tel: 301-994-0525; Fax: 301-994-1547. [CEM]
Mailing Address: P.O. Box 106, 20634.
School—Little Flower, Tel: 301-994-0404.
Lay Teachers 21; Students 325.
Catechesis/Religious Programs—Students 181.

Greenbelt, Prince Georges Co., St. Hugh (1947), Rev. Thomas F. Crowley.
Res., 135 Crescent Rd., 20770. Tel: 301-474-4322; Fax: 301-474-9263.
School—145 Crescent Rd., 20770. Tel: 301-474-4071; Fax: 301-474-3950. Mrs. Mary Elizabeth Whelan, Prin.
Lay Teachers 16; Students 241.
Catechesis/Religious Programs—Tel: 301-474-0239.
Students 59.

Hillcrest Heights, Prince Georges Co., Holy Family (1952) (African-American), Rev. Raymond J. Wadas.
Res., 2210 Callaway St., 20748. Tel: 301-894-2222; Fax: 301-894-2938.
School—2200 Callaway St., 20748. Tel: 301-894-2323.
Catechesis/Religious Programs—Students 235.

Hilltop, Charles Co., St. Ignatius Loyola (1851), Rev. Matthew E. Thompson; Deacon Frank L. Hopson.
Mailing Address: P.O. Box 278, Port Tobacco, 20677. Tel: 301-934-9630. [CEM]

Hollywood, St. Mary's Co., St. John (1690), Rev. Msgr. Martin P. Harris; Rev. John J. Dillon, S.T.B., Ph.D.
Res., P.O. Box 69, 20636. Tel: 301-373-2281; Fax: 301-373-8984. [CEM]
School—Tel: 301-373-2142. Patricia T. Suit, Prin.
Students 254.
Catechesis/Religious Programs—Rev. John J. Dillon, D.R.E.
Students 291.

Huntingtown, Calvert Co., Jesus the Divine Word Parish (1994), Rev. Roger A. Soley.
Res., 710 Joy Lee Ct., 20639-9239. Tel: 301-855-1825; Fax: 410-535-9057.
Catechesis/Religious Programs—Students 198.

Hyattsville, Prince Georges Co., St. Jerome (1886), Rev. James M. Stack; Rev. Msgr. Joseph L. Teletchea, Pastor Emeritus; Deacons Jerome Tintle; David Duggin. In res., Rev. Mark E. Tucker, C.SS.R.
Res., 5205 43rd Ave., 20781. Tel: 301-927-6684; Fax: 301-927-9167.
School—Tel: 301-277-4568; Fax: 301-779-2428. Dr. Joyce Volpini, S.N.D., Prin.
Sisters of Notre Dame de Namur 4; Lay Teachers 26; Students 520.
Convent—5300 43rd Ave., 20781. Tel: 301-864-2016.
Child Center—Tel: 301-699-1314.
Catechesis/Religious Programs—Students 50.

St. Mark (1958), Revs. John T. Dakes; Jeffrey M. Defayette; Deacons Antonio Chaves; Philip Ricker; Mark Gallagher. In res., Rev. Victor Wanjura.
Res., 7501 Adelphi Rd., 20783. Tel: 301-422-8300; Fax: 301-422-2313.
School—Tel: 301-422-7440; Fax: 301-422-7710.
Lay Teachers 30; Students 600.
Catechesis/Religious Programs—Tel: 301-422-7822.
Students 562.

Indian Head, Charles Co., St. Mary Star of the Sea (1918), Rev. William F. Goode; Deacon Thomas O. Hill.
Res., 30 Mattingly Ave., 20640. Tel: 301-753-9177; Fax: 301-753-6995. [CEM]
School—Tel: 301-283-6151.
Lay Teachers 14; Students 213.
Catechesis/Religious Programs—Tel: 301-375-9466.
Students 124.

Issue, Charles Co., Holy Ghost (1880), Rev. Karl A. Chimiak; Deacon Walter Rourke.
Res., 15848 Rock Point Rd., Newburg, 20664. Tel: 301-259-2515; Fax: 301-259-2289. [CEM]
Catechesis/Religious Programs—Tel: 301-259-0237.
Students 55.
Mission—Rock Point, Charles Co., St. Francis de Sales, 13675 Furbush Rd., Newburg, 20664. Tel: 301-259-0254.

Kensington, Montgomery Co., Holy Redeemer (1948), Revs. Walter L. Lawrence; Edward J. Filardi; Deacon Vincent Moskaitis. In res., Rev. Walter J. Tappe.
Res., 9705 Summit Ave., 20895. Tel: 301-942-2333; Fax: 301-942-1041.
School—9715 Summit Ave., 20895. Tel: 301-942-3701; Fax: 301-942-4981. Mrs. Harriann Walker, Prin.
Lay Teachers 34; Students 493.
Catechesis/Religious Programs—Tel: 301-942-3430. Miss Suzanne Shaffer, D.R.E.
Students 112.

Largo, Prince Georges Co., St. Joseph (1922) (African American), Rev. Michael J. King, J.C.D.; Deacon Leon Bechet.
Res., 2020 St. Joseph Dr., 20774. Tel: 301-773-4838; Fax: 301-773-6832.
Catechesis/Religious Programs—Tel: 301-773-2480.
Students 140.

Landover Hills, Prince Georges Co., St. Mary's Catholic Church (1948), Revs. J. William Hines; Michael J. Blackwell, Senior Priest; Deacons B. Paul Blaine, (Retired); Michael J. Taylor; Stephen M. Robinson. In res., Rev. Thomas Poovannal.
Res., 7401 Buchanan St., 20784-2323. Tel: 301-577-8844; Fax: 301-306-5543.
School—7207 Annapolis Rd., 20784. Tel: 301-577-0031; Fax: 301-577-5264. Mr. John E. McCaul, Prin.
Lay Teachers 15; Students 291.
Catechesis/Religious Programs—Tel: 301-577-2478; Fax: 301-459-1355.
Students 87.

Syro-Malankara Mission, Rev. Thomas Poovannal.
Res., 7401 Buchanan St., 20784-9998. Tel: 301-577-8844; Fax: 301-306-5543.
Catechesis/Religious Programs—Students 13.

Lanham, Prince Georges Co., St. Matthias Apostle (1960), Rev. Msgr. John J. Scanlan; Deacons John E. Connor; Ronald W. Schneider; Lawrence W. Murphy.
Res., 9475 Annapolis Rd., 20706. Tel: 301-459-4814; Fax: 301-306-4582. [CEM]
School—Tel: 301-577-9412; Fax: 301-577-8332. Ms. Mary F. Frey, Prin.
Lay Teachers 14; Students 280.
Catechesis/Religious Programs—Tel: 301-577-6567; Fax: 301-306-4582.
Students 144.

La Plata, Charles Co., Sacred Heart (1901), Revs. Matthew J. Siekierski; Joseph Anton Calis; Bernard C. O'Leary, S.J.; Deacons Anthony Barrasso; George V. Foster.
Res., 201 St. Mary's Ave., P.O. Box 1390, 20646. Tel: 301-934-2261; Fax: 301-934-5435. [CEM]
School—Archbishop Neale School, Tel: 301-934-9595; Fax: 301-753-1717. Sr. Helene Fee, Prin.
Sisters of the Immaculate Heart of Mary 2; Lay Teachers 36; Students 525.
Catechesis/Religious Programs—Tel: 301-934-3386. Barbara L. Perricone, D.R.E.
Students 250.

Laurel, Prince Georges Co., St. Mary (1843), Revs. V. James Lockman; William H. Gurnee; Robert L. Keesler, Pastor Emeritus; John Ming Ruan; Deacons Donald Parker; Perfecto Santiago; Douglas Sinchak; Jack Ponzette.
Res., 114 St. Mary's Pl., 20707. Tel: 301-725-3080; 953-3255; Fax: 301-725-2409. [CEM]
School—Tel: 301-498-1433; Fax: 301-498-1170. Darcy Tomko, Prin.
Lay Teachers 27; Students 448.
Catechesis/Religious Programs—Tel: 301-490-8770. Sr. Loretta Primus, S.F.C.C., D.R.E.
Students 730.

St. Nicholas (1967), Rev. Robert P. Buchmeier; Deacon Francis Hannagan.
Res., 8603 Contee Rd., 20708. Tel: 301-490-5116; 5117; Fax: 301-490-1527.
Catechesis/Religious Programs—Tel: 301-776-8303.
Students 218.

Leonardtown, St. Mary's Co., St. Aloysius (1710), Revs. Rory T. Conley; Damian E. Shadwell.
Res., 22800 Washington St., P.O. Box 310, 20650. Tel: 301-475-8064; Fax: 301-475-8762. [CEM]
School—The Father Andrew White, S.J., Tel: 301-475-9795; Fax: 301-475-3537.
Lay Teachers 16; Students 266.
Catechesis/Religious Programs—Students 155.

Lexington Park, St. Mary's Co., Immaculate Heart of Mary (1947), Rev. Thomas A. Gude.
Mailing Address: P.O. Box 6, 20653. Tel: 301-863-8144; Fax: 301-863-8180. [CEM]
Catechesis/Religious Programs—Tel: 301-863-8793. Janet Harmon, D.R.E.
Students 244.

McConchie, Charles Co., St. Catherine of Alexandria (1911), Rev. Matthew E. Thompson; Deacon Frank L. Hopson.
Mailing Address: P.O. Box 278, Port Tobacco, 20677. Tel: 301-934-9630. [CEM]

Mechanicsville, St. Mary's Co., Immaculate Conception (1876), Rev. Msgr. Paul J. Gozaloff; Deacon James E. Conner.
Mailing Address: 28297 Old Village Rd., P.O. Box 166, 20659. Tel: 301-884-3123; Fax: 301-884-7437.
Catechesis/Religious Programs—Tel: 301-884-3016.
Students 172.

Medley's Neck, St. Mary's Co., Our Lady's (1776), Rev. Robert J. Kosty; Deacon Thomas C. Spalding, Sr.
Mailing Address: P.O. Box 111, Leonardtown, 20650. Tel: 301-475-8403; Fax: 301-475-6632. [CEM]
Catechesis/Religious Programs—Students 80.

Mitchellville, Prince Georges Co., Holy Family (1938), Rev. Michael C. Kidd.
Mailing Address: P.O. Box 1599, 20717. Tel: 301-249-2266; Fax: 301-249-2524. [CEM]
Catechesis/Religious Programs—Tel: 301-249-1167.
Students 111.

Morganza, St. Mary's Co., St. Joseph (1700), Rev. Neal A. Ward; Deacons James A. Somerville; Robert Fortney.
Res., P.O. Box 175, 20660. Tel: 301-884-4229; Fax: 301-884-7248. [CEM 2][JC]
Catechesis/Religious Programs—Students 100.

Mount Rainier, Prince Georges Co., St. James (1905) (Hispanic), Revs. Peter R. Alliata; Juan Francisco Molina Monterosa; Deacons Rodney R. Forbes; John H. Turner.
Res., 3628 Rhode Island Ave., 20712. Tel: 301-927-0567; Fax: 301-927-5289.
Catechesis/Religious Programs—Tel: 301-927-0567.
Students 413.

Newport, Charles Co., St. Mary (1674), Rev. Frederick H. MacIntyre.
Res., 11555 St. Mary's Church Rd., Charlotte Hall, 20622. Tel: 301-934-8825; Fax: 301-934-0245. [CEM]
Catechesis/Religious Programs—Students 87.

Newtowne, St. Mary's Co., St. Francis Xavier (1640), Rev. John S. Mattingly.
Res., 21370 Newtowne Neck Rd., Leonardtown, 20650. Tel: 301-475-9885; Fax: 301-475-5662. [CEM]
Catechesis/Religious Programs—Students 127.

Norbeck, Montgomery Co., St. Patrick (1966), Rev. Msgr. Thomas A. Kane; Rev. Auxentius V. Panares; Deacon Ronald Crowley.
Res., 4101 Norbeck Rd., Rockville, 20853. Tel: 301-924-2284; 2285; Fax: 301-929-3017.
Catechesis/Religious Programs—Tel: 301-929-9314.
Students 426.

North Beach, Calvert Co., St. Anthony (1905), Rev. David P. Russell; Deacons John F. Lynch; Michael L. Hoffman.
Res., 8960 Bay Ave., 20714. Tel: 410-257-2368; 301-855-7756 (Washington); Fax: 301-855-6839.
Catechesis/Religious Programs—Tel: 202-855-0897. Sr. Anne Parker, D.R.E.
Students 354.

Olney, Montgomery Co., St. Peter (1898), Revs. Thomas M. Kalita; Keith Woods; Thomas G. LaHood; Deacon John G. Lemon; Ms. Elizabeth Harper, Business Mgr. In res., Rev. Canice Treacy.
Res., 2900 Sandy Spring Rd., 20832. Tel: 301-924-3774; Fax: 301-774-5259.
School—Tel: 301-774-9112; Fax: 301-924-6698. Mrs. Carol Mikoni, Prin.
Lay Teachers 19; Students 401.
Catechesis/Religious Programs—Tel: 301-570-4952. D.R.E.: Mrs. Gloria Zapiain, (Grades PreK-4); Mr. Robert Bellows, (Grades 5-8).
Students 990.

Oxon Hill, Prince Georges Co., St. Columba (1960), Rev. Msgr. Godfrey Mosley; Deacon Richard Fisher.
Res., 7804 Livingston Rd., 20745. Tel: 301-567-5506; Fax: 301-567-6546.
School—7800 Livingston Rd., 20745. Tel: 301-567-6212; Fax: 301-567-6907.
Lay Teachers 14; Students 280.
Catechesis/Religious Programs—Tel: 301-567-6113.
Students 133.

Piscataway, Prince Georges Co., St. Mary (1830), Revs. Julio Alvarez-Garcia; Daniel Paul Leary; Deacon Richard Birkel.
Res., 13401 Piscataway Rd., Clinton, 20735. Tel: 301-292-0527; Fax: 301-292-8786. [CEM]
School—Tel: 301-292-2522.
Lay Teachers 14; Students 247.
Catechesis/Religious Programs—Tel: 301-292-2486.
Students 97.

Pomfret, Charles Co., St. Joseph (1763), Rev. J. Michael Quill.
Mailing Address: 4590 St. Joseph Way, 20675. Tel: 301-870-3041; 609-4670; Fax: 301-609-7564. [CEM]
Catechesis/Religious Programs—Students 272.

Poolesville, Montgomery Co., Our Lady of the Presentation (1992), Rev. Y. David Brault.
Mailing Address: P.O. Box 428, 20837. Tel: 301-349-2045; 972-7504; Fax: 301-349-5423.
Catechesis/Religious Programs—Students 255.

Potomac, Montgomery Co., Our Lady of Mercy (1959) (Korean - Chinese), Rev. Msgr. John J. Enzler; Rev. Mark David Knestout; Deacons F. Ian Ravenscroft; James Yun. In res., Rev. Msgr. William J. Awalt.
Res., 9200 Kentsdale Dr., 20854. Tel: 301-365-1415; Fax: 301-365-3104. [CEM]
School—9222 Kentsdale Dr., 20854. Tel: 301-365-4477; Fax: 301-365-3423. Mrs. Joan C. Hosmer, Prin.
Sisters 1; Lay Teachers 25; Students 280.
Catechesis/Religious Programs—Tel: 301-365-1318.
Students 481.

Prince Frederick, Calvert Co., St. John Vianney (1965), Rev. Peter J. Daly.
Res., 105 Vianney Ln., 20678-4123. Tel: 410-535-0223; 301-855-1928; Fax: 410-535-4422. [CEM]
Catechesis/Religious Programs—Tel: 410-535-4395. Jeanette M. Pedone, D.R.E.
Students 378.

Ridge, St. Mary's Co., St. Michael (1824), Rev. Maurice V. O'Connell.
Res., 20680. Tel: 301-872-4321. [CEM]
School—P.O. Box 429, 20680. Tel: 301-872-5454.
Sisters of St. Joseph of Chambery (Hartford, CT) 3; Lay Teachers 8; Students 220.
Catechesis/Religious Programs—Students 98.

Riverdale, Prince Georges Co., St. Bernard (1950), Revs. John F. McKay; James P. Holloway; Deacon Alfredo Hidalgo.
Res., 5700 St. Bernard Dr., 20737-2185. Tel: 301-277-1000; Fax: 301-277-3464.
School—Tel: 301-864-3801; Fax: 301-864-2912. Mrs. Janet Cantwell, Prin.
Lay Teachers 14; Students 239.
Catechesis/Religious Programs—Tel: 301-277-4220; Fax: 301-277-3464. Mrs. Lucille Kolodrubetz, D.R.E.
Students 392.

Rockville, Montgomery Co.,

1—St. Elizabeth, (1964), Rev. John F. MacFarlane. In res., Revs. Anthony DeConciliis, C.S.C.; Andrew Sroba.
Res., 917 Montrose Rd., 20852. Tel: 301-881-1380; Fax: 301-881-3068.
School—Tel: 301-881-1824; Fax: 301-881-6035.
Lay Teachers 26; Students 480.
Catechesis/Religious Programs—Students 200.

2—Shrine of St. Jude, (1956), Revs. Oliver McGready; G. Ralph Duffy, (Retired); Timothy S. Galban; Alphonso Carew (Sierra Leone); Deacons Nicholas E. Scholz; Donald Mays. In res., Rev. Timothy J. O'Sullivan (Ireland).
Res., 12701 Veirs Mill Rd., 20853. Tel: 301-946-8200; Fax: 301-946-4527.
School—Tel: 301-946-7888; Fax: 301-929-8927.
Lay Teachers 27; Students 527.
Catechesis/Religious Programs—Tel: 301-949-2336.
Students 313.

3—St. Mary, (1813), Revs. John F. Myslinski; L. James Downs; Deacon Daniel Kostka.
Res., 520 Veirs Mill Rd., 20852. Tel: 301-424-5550; Fax: 301-424-5579. [CEM]
School—Tel: 301-762-4179; Fax: 301-762-8507.
Lay Teachers 28; Students 298.
Catechesis/Religious Programs—Tel: 301-762-8750.
Students 400.
Mission—Rockville, Montgomery Co., Our Lady of China, 1001 Grandin Ave., 20851. Tel: 301-294-3574; Fax: 202-635-7563. Rev. Paul Tsau.

4—St. Raphael, (1966), Revs. Michael Wilson; John Dakes; Peter Reymerse; Deacons Lawrence Gordon; Richard Mattocks; Frank Salatto.
Mailing Address: 1592 Kimblewick Rd., 20854.
Res., 1590 Kimblewick Rd., 20854. Tel: 301-762-2143; Fax: 301-762-0719.
Catechesis/Religious Programs—Students 974.

Rosaryville, Prince George's Co., Church of the Most Holy Rosary (1966), Rev. J. Isidore Dixon.
Res., 11704 Duley Station Rd., Upper Marlboro, 20772. Tel: 301-856-3880; 3881; Fax: 301-856-3944. [CEM]
Catechesis/Religious Programs—Tel: 301-868-5475. Mary Farrimond, D.R.E.
Students 98.

St. Inigoes, St. Mary's Co., St. Peter Claver (1903) (African-American), Rev. Raymond H. Moore.
Res., P.O. Box 240, 20684. Tel: 301-872-5460; Fax: 301-872-5672. [CEM]
Catechesis/Religious Programs—Students 74.

St. Mary's City, St. Mary's Co., St. Cecilia (1974), Rev. Francis W. Krastel.
Res., 47950 Mattapany Rd., P.O. Box 67, 20686-0067. Tel: 301-862-4600; Fax: 301-863-7780. [JC]
Catechesis/Religious Programs—Clustered with St. Michael's, Ridge.

Seat Pleasant, Prince Georges Co., St. Margaret (1908) (African American), Revs. Fintan Sheeran, SS.CC.; Benedict Folger, SS.CC.; Deacons Sam Minor; Robert Price; John Somerville.
Res., 408 Addison Rd. S., 20743. Tel: 301-336-3344; Fax: 301-336-5501.
School—410 Addison Rd. S., 20743. Tel: 301-336-3113; Fax: 301-350-1322.
Catechesis/Religious Programs—Tel: 301-336-5976.
Students 225.
Mission—St. Matthias.

Silver Spring, Montgomery Co.,

1—St. Andrew Apostle, (1959), Revs. Joseph P. Kennedy; David W. Beaubien; Deacon Kevin M Mukri. In res., Rev. Michael T. Jones.
Res., 11600 Kemp Mill Rd., 20902. Tel: 301-649-3700; Fax: 301-681-3527.
School—Tel: 301-649-3555; Fax: 301-649-2352. Mrs. Catherine Medlock, Prin.
Lay Teachers 27; Students 536.
Catechesis/Religious Programs—Tel: 301-649-4200.
Students 144.

2—St. Bernadette, (Four Corners) (1948), Revs. William J. Thompson; Karl Bartholomew Smith; Deacon Thomas E. Roszkowski. In res., Rev. Ademir Guerini, C.S., (Portuguese Min.).
Res., 70 University Blvd., E., 20901. Tel: 301-593-0357; Fax: 301-593-3088.
School—Tel: 301-593-5611; Fax: 301-593-9042.
Lay Teachers 21; Students 492.
Catechesis/Religious Programs—Tel: 301-593-5104. Mrs. Jane Bailey, D.R.E.
Students 166.

3—St. Camillus, (1951), Revs. Michael Tyson, O.F.M.; Jose Laboton, O.F.M.; Jacques La Pointe, O.F.M.; Bro. Henry Fulmer, O.F.M.; Deacon Peter Barbernitz.
Res., 1600 St. Camillus Dr., 20903. Tel: 301-434-8400; Fax: 301-434-8041.
School—1500 St. Camillus Dr., 20903. Tel: 301-434-2344; Fax: 301-434-7726.
Sisters 2; Lay Teachers 24; Students 375.
Catechesis/Religious Programs—Tel: 301-434-2111. Mr. Tony Bonanno, D.R.E.
Students 568.
Child Care—(Four Corners), Tel: 301-439-1640; Fax: 301-439-7078. Letitia Thomas, Dir.
Certified Child Care Workers 17.

4—St. Catherine Laboure, (Wheaton) (1951), Revs. Robert G. Amey; Thomas G. Morrow; Deacons Carlos Contreras; Raymond L. Chaput. In res., Rev. Mauricio Henriquez (El Salvador).
Res., 11801 Claridge Rd., 20902. Tel: 301-946-3636; Fax: 301-946-5064.
School—Tel: 301-946-1717; Fax: 301-946-9572.
Daughters of Charity 4; Lay Teachers 30; Students 512.
Catechesis/Religious Programs—Tel: 301-946-3010.
Students 987.

5—Christ the King, (Wheaton) (1961), Revs. Robert J. Bozek; Luis Antonio Marroquin.
Res., 2300 East-West Hwy., 2301 Colston Dr., 20910. Tel: 301-589-8616; Fax: 301-587-1929.
Catechesis/Religious Programs—Tel: 301-589-8620. Sr. Fatima Bonilla, R.S.C.J., D.R.E.
Students 244.

6—St. John the Baptist, (Spring Brook) (1960), Revs. Francis G. Kazista; John M. Barry; Deacons Norman Keller; Bernard Bernier.
Res., 12319 New Hampshire Ave., 20904. Tel: 301-622-1122; Fax: 301-625-9266.
School—Tel: 301-622-3076. Marianne Moore, Prin.
Lay Teachers 22; Students 264.
Catechesis/Religious Programs—Tel: 301-622-3933. Patricia Roberts, D.R.E.
Students 301.

7—St. John the Evangelist, (Wheaton) (1774), Rev. Msgr. William J. English; Revs. Thomas A. Meighan; Joseph F. Perkins; Sr. Theresa McElroy, I.H.M., Pastoral Min.; Deacon Dan P. Stallings.
Res., 10103 Georgia Ave., 20902. Tel: 301-681-7663; Fax: 301-681-8793. [CEM]
School—Tel: 301-681-7656; Fax: 301-681-0754. Sr. Kathleen Lannak, I.H.M., Prin.
Lay Teachers 21; Students 359.
Catechesis/Religious Programs—Tel: 301-681-7634. Sr. Roberta Harding, I.H.M., D.R.E.
Students 212.

8—St. Michael, (Wheaton) (1930), Revs. Vincent J. Rigdon; John R. Clark; Fidel A. de Ramos; Deacons Tom C. Newman; John A. Marinari; Roberto Salgado. In res., Rev. Ramon Masculino (Phillipines) (JARO).
Res., 824 Pershing Dr., 20910-4471. Tel: 301-589-1155; Fax: 301-589-3470.
School—824 Wayne Ave., 20910. Tel: 301-585-6873; Fax: 301-587-1142. Sr. Mary Raymond, S.S.N.D., Prin.
Lay Teachers 13; Students 314.
Catechesis/Religious Programs—Students 279.

9—Our Lady of Grace, (Leisure World) (1983), Rev. Msgr. John J. Madigan.
Mailing Address: 15661 Norbeck Blvd., 20906. Tel: 301-924-0067; Fax: 301-924-6809.
Res., 15665 Norbeck Blvd., 20906. Tel: 301-924-4928.

10—Our Lady Queen of Poland and Saint Maximilian Kolbe, (Leisure World) (1983) (Polish), Rev. Stanislaw Hajkowski, S.Ch. (Poland).
Res., 9700 Rosensteel Ave., 20910. Tel: 301-589-1857; Fax: 301-589-4401.
Catechesis/Religious Programs—Tel: 301-589-7835.
Students 50.

Solomons, Calvert Co., Our Lady Star of the Sea (1888), Rev. Richard E. Gardiner; Deacons John G. Etzel; Robert L. Connelly.
Mailing Address: Box 560, 20688. Tel: 410-326-3535; Fax: 410-326-3679. [CEM]
School—Tel: 410-326-3171; Fax: 410-326-9478. Sr. Rosella Summe, C.D.P., Prin.
Sisters 3; Lay Teachers 11; Students 199.
Catechesis/Religious Programs—Beth Oster, D.R.E. Students 285.

Suitland, Prince George's Co., St. Bernardine (1966), Rev. Arnold W. DePorter.
Res., 2400 Brooks Dr., 20746-1144. Tel: 301-736-0707; Fax: 301-736-2984.
Catechesis/Religious Programs—Fax: 301-736-2884.
Students 48.

Takoma Park, Prince Georges Co., Our Lady of Sorrows (1932), Revs. James J. Suntum, S.F.; Jose Maria Conde, S.F.; Deacons James Wilson, Jr.; Terry Stackpole; Nathanial Cordova-Ferrer.
Res., 1006 Larch Ave., 20912. Tel: 301-891-3500; Fax: 301-891-1523.
School—1010 Larch Ave., 20912. Tel: 301-891-2555; Fax: 301-270-6919. Mrs. Gail Ruffin, Prin.
Lay Teachers 12students236.
Catechesis/Religious Programs—Tel: 301-891-2033.
Students 173.

Upper Marlboro, Prince Georges Co., Saint Mary of the Assumption (1848), Rev. Msgr. Richard A. Hughes; Rev. An Vu; Deacon Frank Klco.
Res., 14908 Main St., 20772. Tel: 301-627-3255; Fax: 301-627-5533. [CEM]
School—Tel: 301-627-4170; Fax: 301-627-6383. Mrs. Patricia Petruzzelli, Prin.
Sisters - Servants of the Immaculate Heart of Mary 3; Students 304.
Catechesis/Religious Programs—Tel: 301-627-4542. Mr. Charles Long, D.R.E.
Students 153.

Valley Lee, St. Mary's Co., St. George (1851), Rev. Robert B. Riedel; Deacons David R. Powell; George A. L'Heureux.
Mailing Address: P.O. Box 9, 20692. Tel: 301-994-0607; Fax: 301-994-1793. [CEM]
Chapel—St. George's Island, St. Francis Xavier.
Catechesis/Religious Programs—Tel: 301-994-0737.
Students 90.

Waldorf, Charles Co., St. Peter (1700), Rev. Msgr. Andrew J. Cassin, Pastor Emeritus; Rev. John R. Pennington; Rev. Msgr. Henry Otero; Deacons Charles J. Wilson; Robert Lyons.
Res., 3320 St. Peter's Dr., 20601. Tel: 301-843-8916; Fax: 301-843-3163. [CEM]
School—Tel: 301-843-1955; Fax: 301-843-6371. Judith DeLucco, Prin.
Lay Teachers 25; Students 514.
Catechesis/Religious Programs—Tel: 301-843-9583; Fax: 301-843-8548. Barbara Perricone, D.R.E.
Students 272.

Our Lady Help of Christians (1980), Rev. Eamon Dignan.
Mailing Address: 100 Village St., 20602-2183. Tel: 301-645-7112.
Res., 930 Barrington Dr., 20602-2838. Tel: 301-843-8823; Fax: 301-645-3635.
Catechesis/Religious Programs—Sr. Margery Rose, M.H.S.H., D.R.E.
Students 525.

Chaplains of Public Institutions

WASHINGTON. *Children's Medical Center* 111 Michigan Ave. N.W., 20010. Tel: 202-884-5050. Rev. Benedict Faneye, O.P., Chap.
General Hospital 1900 Massachusetts Ave. S.E., 20003. Tel: 202-675-5000. Rev. Thomas Poovannal, Chap.
National Rehabilitation Hospital 102 Irving St. N.W., 20010. Tel: 202-877-1000. Rev. James F. Moran, Chap.
Providence Hospital 1150 Varnum St., N.E., 20017-2180. Tel: 202-269-7000. Revs. Carlo Napoli, T.O.R., Chap.; Phelim Jordan, S.V.D., (Ireland) Chap.
St. Elizabeth's Hospital (Government Operated) 2700 Martin Luther King Jr. Ave. S.E., 20032. Tel: 202-373-7018. Rev. Maximo J. Ortiz, O.S.A., Chap.; Sr. Mary Bowman, S.F.C.C., Chap.; Sr. Helen Waugh, S.F.C.C., Chap.
Washington Hospital Center 110 Irving St. N.W., 20010. Tel: 202-877-6691. Revs. John S. Wintermyer, Chap.; Benedict Faneye, O.P., Chap.; Sr. Mary Leo Bryan, S.H.C.J., Chap.; Deacon John A. Connors, Chap.

BETHESDA, MD. *National Institutes of Health, Clinical Center* Tel: 301-496-3407. Rev. Vincent J. O'Brien, O.P., Chap.

LANHAM, MD. *Doctor's Hospital of Prince Georges County*. Served by the priests of St. Matthias Parish. 20706.

Special Ministries:
Reverend Monsignors—
Criscuolo, Salvatore A., Chap., Police and Fire Dept.
Hurley, Leonard F., Rector, Cardinal Boyle Residence
O'Donnell, William F., Priest Dir., Catholic Cemeteries
Reverend Fathers—
Adams, John E., Dir., S.O.M.E.
Begg, Christopher T., Catholic University of America
Bryant, Michael, Chap., District of Columbia Jail
Byrne, William D., Chap., Newman Center, University of Maryland
Conley, Rory T., Archdiocesan Historian
Fangmeyer, Lee J., Exec. Dir., Office of Youth Ministry
Hurd, R. Scott, Hearts Aflame Program
Jones, Michael T., Chap., Good Counsel High School
Kemp, Raymond B., Fellow, Woodstock Theological Center, Georgetown University
Kuhn, John G., Dir. Emeritus, Anchor Mental Health Assoc.
Martin, Francis, Chap., Mother of God Community; Instructor, John Paul II Institute
McCarthy, Brien R., Chap., American University
Montgomery, William L., Teacher, Carroll High School
Mordino, Robert F., Dir. CYO Retreats
Mudd, John, Dir., of Development, Carroll High School
O'Brien, Raymond C., Asst. Dean, Catholic University
Panke, Robert J., Chap., George Washington University Newman Medical Center
Sileo, Joseph R., Coord. of Outreach Svc., Kennedy Institute
Trancone, Gerard A., Center for the Deaf

Pastoral Center Special Ministries:
Most Rev.—
Lori, William E., Vicar Gen. & Mod. of Curia
Reverend Monsignors—
Farrell, Kevin J., Sec., Finance & Mgmt.
Gerhardt, Bernard C., Chancellor
Huebner, Ralph J., Sec. for Social Concerns
Knestout, Barry, Sec., Archbishop
Ranieri, Joseph A., Coord. of Pastoral Care of Priests
Sadusky, Joseph F., Judicial Vicar Tribunal
Reverend Fathers—
Antonicelli, Charles V., Vice Chancellor, 4141 Guildford Dr., College Park, MD 20740
Bui, Joseph, Tribunal
Fangmeyer, Leroy J., Exec. Dir., Office of Youth Ministry
Herbert, G. Paul, Tribunal
Hill, R. Cary, Sec. for Clergy
Hurd, R. Scott, Hearts Aflame Program
Lee, Paul D., Dir., Continuing Educ. of Clergy & Dir., Office for Interreligious & Ecumenical Affairs.
Murray, Michael J., Exec. Dir., Office of the Permanent Diaconate
Parent, J. Wilfrid, Dir. of Priestly Vocations
Parry, Charles J., Asst. Sec. Catholic Educ.
Rigdon, Vincent J., Dir., Propagation of the Faith
Stuart, George E., Tribunal
Tappe, Walter J., Dir., Office of Worship

Hospital & Nursing Home Ministries:
Reverend Monsignors—
Hurley, Leonard F.
Reverend Fathers—
Kinter, John P.
Samaha, Jeffrey F.
Valentine, Keveny M.
Wintermyer, John S.

On Duty Outside the Archdiocese:
Reverend Monsignors—
Albacete, Lorenzo, New York
Bazan, Joaquin, Albuquerque, NM
Langsfeld, Paul J., Mount St. Mary Seminary, Emmitsburg, MD
Roensch, Roger, Vatican City State
Reverend Fathers—
Burke, Herbert, Charlotte, NC
Culkin, Michael, Lancaster, PA
Gancayco, Richard K., Honduras
Giese, Samuel C., West Virginia
Holt, Paul-Stephen, Iowa
Hurley, John J., New Hampshire
Izac, Andre C., North Carolina
Jordan, Milton, Philadelphia
Kuebler, A.M. Seamus, Maine
Metzdorf, William C., California
Murphy, Francis J., Pastoral Center, Reno, NV
Murray, Paul, New York
Nelson, Thomas J., Raleigh, NC
Oberle, James P., S.S., California
Sanz, Jose, D.L.P., California
Slevin, Henry, Vietnam
Twohig, Christopher T., Ireland
Ulshafer, Thomas, S.S., Baltimore, MD
Walsh, Francis M.

Military Chaplains:
Reverend Fathers—
Cunningham, Gerard M.
Cusick, Kevin M.
Fitz-Patrick, David M.
Lee, Matthew (J.T.)
Mudd, David A.
Passamonti, Paul G.
Saltysiak, Paul M.
Siriani, Klaus-Werner J.
Studniewski, Gary R.

Absent On Leave:
Reverend Fathers—
Cocca, Stephen M.
Stankavage, Joseph G.
Umana, Miguel

Retired:
Reverend Monsignors—
Albert, Louis W., 1514 Perrel Ln., Bowie, MD 20716
Arthur, E. Robert, Jeanne Jugan Residence, 4200 Harewood Rd., N.E., Washington, DC 20017
Awalt, William J.
Bailey, John L., St. Francis Xavier, Washington, DC
Benson, John D., Washington, DC
Cassin, Andrew J.
DiNardo, Ramon A., The Westchester, 4000 Cathedral Ave., Apt. 854-B, Washington, DC 20016
Dooley, R. Joseph, Carroll Manor, WDC
Echle, Harry A., Our Lady of Victory, Washington, DC 20007
Farina, Michael F., St. Patrick, Washington, DC
Gillen, James G., Bethesda, MD
Grodavent, Thomas J., P.O. Box 38849, Colorado Springs, CO 80937
Hartman, Joseph W., Carroll Manor, 1150 Varnum St. N.E., Washington, DC 20017
Hogan, John F., Sacred Heart, Bowie, MD
Jimenez, Armando, Cardinal O'Boyle Residence, P.O. Box 29206, Hyattsville, MD 20017
Joy, James B.
McMain, Robert O., St. Ann, Washington, DC
Mohan, Robert Paul
O'Connor, Aloysius E., Holy Angels, Avenue, MD
Quinn, W. Louis, Our Lady of Lourdes, Bethesda, MD
Russell, W. Joyce, Carroll Manor, 1150 Varnum St., N.E., Washington, DC 20017
Teletchea, Joseph L., Cardinal O'Boyle Residence, DC
Reverend Fathers—
Barry, Paul, 5404 Bye St., Capitol Heights, MD 20743
Bender, Lawrence A., S.S., Ft. Washington, MD
Bober, Francis J., 2475 Virginia Ave., N.W., #407, Washington, DC 20037
Branch, Leslie, Carroll Manor, 1150 Varnum St., N.E., Washington, DC 20017
Brogan, Hugh T., 678 Main St., Sugar Notch, PA 18706
Caimi, Luke A., 9840 Sodus Manor Pl., P.O. Box 208, Faulkner, MD 20632
Connor, John V., Holy Cross Rehabilitation, Burtonsville, MD
Duffy, G. Ralph, Shrine of St. Jude, Rockville, MD
Evans, Edward, Mt. Calvary, Forestville, MD
Finan, James
Flaherty, Francis T., The Townhouse, 860 Arnold Ave., Pt. Pleasant, NJ 08742
Gallagher, Roger P., Cardinal O'Boyle Residence, P.O. Box 29206, Washington, DC 20017
Grace, Robert S., 4842 Willows Rd., Chesapeake Beach, MD 20732
Hargrove, Jerry E.
Hartel, Edward T., Washington, DC
Higgins, John J., 300 Ocean Ave., Seabright, NJ 07760
Holden, Paul, DE
Ihrie, Bernard R., Jr., 3637 Bay Dr., Edgewater, MD 21037
Jacobs, Harry W., 3134 Adderley Ct., Silver Spring, MD 20906
Januszkiewicz, Henry, 4281 Inca Dove Ct., Naples, FL 34119
Joyce, George V., 577 Carew St., Springfield, MA 01104
Keesler, Robert L., St. Mary, Laurel, MD
Kemp, Patrick W., 2900 Shipmaster Way, #301, Annapolis, MD 21401
McCormack, Brendan, Raphael House, 1515 Dunster Rd., Rockville, MD 20854

McGuigan, Robert, Jeanne Jugan Residence, 4200 Harewood Rd., N.E., Washington, DC 20017
McManus, Eamon, 215 E. Church St., Frederick, MD 21701
Morel, Paul A.
Newman, Aloysius T., 6260 Crain Hwy., P.O. Box 2225, LaPlata, MD 20646
Norris, Walter J., Marian Assisted Living, Bookeville, MD
Norton, Joseph E., Jeanne Jugan Residence, 4200 Harewood Rd., N.E., Washington, DC 20017
O'Shea, Philip A., Blessed Sacrament, Washington, DC
Petrella, Robert
Powderly, James J., Cardinal O'Boyle Residence, P.O. Box 29206, Washington, DC 20017
Pritchard, Edward
Quinones, Miguel P., Apartado, P.O. Box 40579, Bucaramanga-Santander, Colombia South America
Reid, George B., St. Mary, 18230 Barnesville Rd., Barnesville, MD 20838
Roy, J. Jean, 15 Talmuth Ave., Haverhill, MA 01830
Salcedo, Luis G., St. Bartholomew, Bethesda, MD
Schaefer, Thomas
Schellenberg, Milton A., 5914 Welborn Dr., Bethesda, MD 20816
Sheehan, Thomas J., St. Peter, Washington, DC
Smith, Alphonsus M.
Tou, Louis A., 510 Edmonston Dr., Rockville, MD 20851
Tran-Khac-Hy, Hilarius, Gaithersburg, MD
Treacy, Canice, St. Peter, Olney, MD
Twiddy, Paul, Charlotte Hall Veteran's Home, Rte. 5, Charlotte Hall, MD 20622
Wilson, George W., Hyattsville, MD
Winnenberg, John O., 1536 Todos Santos Pl., Fallbrook, CA 92028
Znotinas, John, 2712 Fairlawn St., Temple Hills, MD 20748

Permanent Deacons:
Abbate, Paul J., (Retired), Archdiocese of Agana
Agostinelli, Floyd D., (Leave of Absence)
Allen, David A., (Retired)
Allen, Robert F., St. John Neumann, Gaithersburg, MD
Bailey, Aston A., Santa Fe, NM
Ballard, Harvey W., (Retired)
Barbernitz, Peter M., St. Camillus, Silver Spring, MD
Barnes, David J., St. Edward the Confessor, Bowie, MD
Barnes, John R., St. Joseph, Pomfret, MD
Barrasso, Anthony T., Sacred Heart, La Plata, MD
Barrett, Kenneth, St. Martin, Gaithersburg, MD
Barrett, Raymond J., (Unassigned)
Barry, T. Kevin, St. Edward, Bowie, MD
Battaglia, Thomas D., (Retired)
Bechet, Leon J., St. Joseph, Largo, MD
Begg, George B., Jr., (Retired)
Bell, Joseph, Incarnation, DC
Bell, Lawrence G., St. Martin, Gaithersburg, MD
Beller, Edwin J., (Retired)
Bernier, Bernard A., Jr., St. John the Baptist, Silver Spring, MD
Berry, Robert L., St. Gabriel, Washington, DC
Betz, Andrew J., St. Joseph, Beltsville, MD
Birkel, Richard, St. Mary's, Piscataway, MD
Black, Joseph L., Santa Fe, NM
Blaine, B. Paul, Jr., (Retired)
Bobbitt, John W., (Retired)
Boesman, William C., St. Thomas the Apostle, Washington, DC
Brink, Edward J., Wilmington, DE
Briscoe, John A., (Retired)
Brokenborough, Alfred T., (Retired)
Brown, James E., Holy Redeemer, Washington, DC
Brown, Sylvester, (Retired)
Burroughs, Eugene, St. Mary, Bryantown, MD
Butler, Kevin A., Sr., Holy Comforter/St. Cyprian, Washington, DC
Cadigan, James, St. Peter, Olney, MD
Cahoon, David L., Jr., St. Mary, Barnesville, MD
Cain, Leonard F., Harrisburg, PA
Carroll, Donald T., Wilmington, DE
Chaput, Raymond L., St. Catherine Laboure, Silver Spring, MD
Chase, Ira E., Basilica of the Immaculate Conception, DC
Chaves, Antonio, (Retired)
Cioffi, Thomas, St. Peter, Olney, MD
Coates, Vincent J., Fall River
Coleman, Earle W., (Retired)
Collins, Gerald A., Holy Family, Hillcrest Hts., MD
Connelly, Robert L., Our Lady Star of the Sea, Solomons, MD
Connor, James E., (Retired)
Connor, John E., St. Matthias, Lanham, MD
Connors, John A., (Retired)
Conrad, Joseph M., St. Luke, Washington, DC
Contreras, Carlos E., St. Catherine La Boure, Silver Spring, MD
Cooper, Philip J., Mother Seton, Germantown, MD
Cordova-Ferrer, Nathaniel, St. Mark, Hyattsville, MD
Crowley, Ronald C., St. Patrick, Rockville, MD
Cummins, Don E., Seattle, WA
Cummins, Eugene J., Jr., St. Martin, Gaithersburg, MD
Cyrus, Ralph W., St. Teresa of Avila, Washington, DC
Daniels, Willis, St. Aloysius, Washington, DC
Danko, Edward, Sacred Heart, Bowie, MD
Dardy, Henry, Holy Family, Mitchellville, MD
Davies, Gary, Little Flower, Bethesda, MD
Davis, Alton, Jr., St. Joseph, Largo, MD
Davis, William E., Las Vegas
DeRoze, Donald G., Resurrection, Burtonsville, MD
DiDuca, Paul, Our Lady of the Visitation, Darnestown, MD
Ditewig, William, Davenport, IA
Donlon, Jerome A., (Unassigned)
Draper, Harry R., (Retired)
Duggin, David, St. Jerome, Hyattsville
Dunne, Joseph E., Pueblo
Ealey, Ronald R., Wichita, KS
Edelin, Charles E., Jr., Holy Comforter-St. Cyprian, Washington, DC
Elliott, Thomas B., Charleston, SC
Emley, William P., Jr., National Institutes of Health, Bethesda, MD
Enderle, Francis X., Harrisburg
Enright, Timothy D., Mother Seton, Germantown, MD
Etzel, John G., Our Lady Star of the Sea, Solomons, MD
Feneis, Albert G., Raleigh, NC
Finerty, John F., St. Paul, Damascus, MD
Fisher, Richard A., St. Columba, Oxon Hill, MD
Flynn, Leo, Erie, PA
Forbes, Rodney R., St. James, Mt. Rainier, MD
Fortney, Charles R., St. Joseph, Morganza, MD
Foster, George, (Retired)
Gallagher, Mark J., St. Mark, Hyattsville, MD
Garcia, David F., Santa Fe, NM
Genis, Thomas P., Immaculate Conception, Washington, DC
Gignilliat, Robert L., St. Joseph, Pomfret, MD
Gordon, Lawrence C., Cathedral of St. Matthew, DC
Hamilton, John G., Palm Beach, FL
Hannagan, Francis L., St. Nicholas, Laurel, MD
Haywood, Hiram H., Jr., (Retired)
Hidalgo, Alfredo, St. Bernard, Riverdale, MD
Hill, Charles, (Retired)
Hill, Thomas O., Sr., (Retired)
Hoffman, Michael R., St. Anthony, North Beach, MD
Holson, Edward, Wilimington, DE
Hong, Pascal, Leave of Absence
Hopson, Frank, St. Ignatius, Hilltop, MD
Hume, W. Michael, Nashville, TN
Interlandi, Joseph S., Orlando, FL
Jackson, Harold I., St. Francis de Sales, Washington, DC
Johnson, Bernard C., (Retired)
Johnson, Samuel A., (Retired)
Jones, Thomas R., Our Lady of Perpetual Help, Washington, DC
Keller, Grafton T., St. Augustine
Keller, Norman B., (Retired)
Kelly, John D., St. Anthony, Washington, DC
Kemp, William, Holy Angels, Avenue, MD
Klco, Frank, St. Mary, Upper Marlboro, MD
Kostka, Daniel S., St. Mary, Rockville, MD
Kraemer, Francis W., Sr., St. Vincent de Paul, Washington, DC
Kronschnabel, Michael C., Phoenix, AZ
Kube, Carl B., Sacramento, CA
Kunsemiller, John H., Colorado Springs, CO
L'Heureux, George G., St. George, Valley Lee, MD
Lacovaro, James G., Archbishop Carroll High School, Washington, DC
Lemon, John, St. Peter, Olney, MD
Lennon, Joseph M., (Retired)
Leonard, John M., (Retired)
Levy, Richard A., Jr., San Francisco, CA
Locke, John W., (Retired)
Luetjen, Palmer, (Unassigned)
Lynch, John F., St. Anthony, North Beach, MD
Lyons, Robert A., St. Peter, Waldorf, MD
Lyons, Robert R., St. Bartholomew, Bethesda, MD
Mallari, Arturo O., Christ the King, Silver Spring, MD
Mallon, Charles A., (Inactive)
Mangold, Charles C., (Retired)
Marinari, A. John, St. Michael, Silver Spring, MD
Martin, E. Chad, Jesus the Good Shephard, Dunkirk, MD
Martin, J. Murry, (Retired)
Martin, Nerus O., Jr., St. Thomas More, Washington, DC
Mastrangelo, Eugene K., St. John Vianney, Prince Frederick, MD
Mattocks, Richard E., St. Raphael, Rockville, MD
Mays, Donald, Shrine of St. Jude, Rockville, MD
McAskill, Donald K., Arlington, VA
McCann, James C., St. Rose of Lima, Gaithersburg, MD
McGinness, John J., St. Patrick, Washington, DC
McGlade, H. Donald, (Retired)
McGrath, Joseph B., (Retired)
Merella, Bartholomew J., St. Joseph, Washington, DC
Meyer, Ferdinand, (Retired)
Meyer, Ronald J., St. Martin, Gaithersburg, MD
Middleton, Henry D., III, (Leave of Absence)
Migliorini, Louis, Sr., (Retired), Crofton, MD
Miles, Lawrence A., Mount Calvary, Forestville, MD
Miller, Alfred A., Jr., Our Lady Queen of Peace, Washington, DC
Miller, Lawrence L., Archdiocese for Military Services, U.S.A.
Minor, Samuel L., Jr., St. Margaret, Seat Pleasant, MD
Moll, Anthony W., St. John, Clinton, MD
Moskaitis, J. Vincent, Holy Redeemer, Kensington, MD
Mukri, Kevin, St. Andrew the Apostle, Silver Spring, MD
Murati, George, Archdiocese for Military Services
Newman, C. Thomas, St. Michael, Silver Spring, MD
Nguyen, John H., Our Lady of Vietnam, Silver Spring, MD
Nosacek, Andrew J., St. Pius X, Bowie, MD
Oettinger, Frank F., Diocese of Orlando
Om, Michael W., Our Lady of Mercy, Potomac, MD
Paolucci, Robert J., (Inactive)
Parker, Charles J., Leave of Absence
Parker, Donald A., St. Mary of the Mills, Laurel, MD
Picard, Adrien D., Springfield
Pillman, Theodore, Ascension, Bowie, MD
Pinder, Wilbur L., Jr., St. Francis of Assisi, Derwood, MD
Ponzette, John, St. Mary of the Mills, Laurel, MD
Powell, David R., St. George, Valley Lee, MD
Price, Robert, St. Margaret of Scotland, Seat Pleasant, MD
Pyle, Jay Allen, Harrisburg, PA
Quander, James W., (Retired)
Raffensperger, Jeffrey, Sacred Heart, Bowie, MD
Ravenscroft, F. Ian, Our Lady of Mercy, Potomac, MD
Redding, Edward R., (Retired)
Reilly, Matthew B., Jr., Cathedral of St. Matthew, DC
Rice, Ulysses, (Retired)
Richards, David C., Leave of Absence
Ricker, Philip W., St. Mark, Hyattsville, MD
Ricker, Thomas B., Jr., St. John Vianney, Prince Frederick, MD
Robinson, John R., Holy Rosary, Upper Marlboro, MD
Robinson, Stephen M., St. Mary, Landover Hills, MD
Roszkowski, Thomas E., St. Bernadette, Silver Spring, MD
Rourke, Walter G., Holy Ghost, Issue, MD
Ruffo, Paul, Our Lady of the Visitation, Darnestown, MD
Salatto, Frank J., Jr., St. Raphael, Rockville, MD
Salgado, Roberto, St. Michael, Silver Spring, MD
Santiago, Perfecto, St. Mary of the Mills, Laurel, MD
Schneider, Ronald W., St. Matthias, Lanham, MD
Scholz, Nicholas E., Shrine of St. Jude, Rockville, MD
Schopfer, Richard J., Little Flower, Bethesda, MD
Serafini, Bartolo, Hispanic Center, Washington, DC
Sferrella, Joseph J., Harrisburg, PA
Shewmaker, John B., Our Lady of Lourdes, Bethesda, MD
Sinchak, J. Douglas, St. Mary of the Mills, Laurel, MD
Smith, Anthony S., Holy Family, Hillcrest Heights, MD
Somerville, James, St. Joseph, Morganza, MD
Somerville, John W., Basilica of the Immaculate Conception, DC
Soto, Alfredo, St. Bartholomew, Bethesda, MD
Spalding, Thomas C., Our Lady's Church, Medley's Neck, MD
Sparling, Donald, St. Pius X, Bowie, MD
Springer, James R., Phoenix, AZ
Stackpole, Terrell U., Our Lady of Sorrows, Takoma Park, MD
Stallings, Dan P., Sr., St. John Evangelist, Silver Spring, MD

Sweeney, Anthony J., III, Immaculate Heart of Mary, Lexington Park, MD
Taylor, Michael J., St. Mary, Landover Hills, MD
Terrar, David B., St. Paul, Damascus, MD
Testudine, Joseph, Airmen's & Soldier's Home, Washington, DC
Thomas, Reginald A., (Unassigned)
Thomas, William, (Retired)
Thompson, Daniel R., Shrine of the Most Blessed Sacrament
Thompson, Finis E., Ascension, Bowie, MD
Thorp, George, St. John the Evangelist, Silver Spring, MD
Tift, Neil J., St. Jane Frances de Chantal, Bethesda, MD
Tintle, Jerome A., St. Jerome, Hyattsville, MD
Tracy, Robert J., Diocese of Wilmington
Trichel, Allen J., Our Lady of Help of Christians, Waldorf, MD
Turner, Al Douglas, Nativity, DC
Turner, John H., St. James, Mt. Rainier, MD
Vargas, Jorge W., Our Lady Queen of the Americas, Washington, DC
Verdon, John, Jesus the Good Shepherd, Dunkirk, MD
Vita, William A., Jr., Mother Seton, Germantown, MD
Wakefield, Walter W., III, Lexington, KY
Walker, George W., Holy Rosary, Rosaryville, MD
Waltz, John F., Leave of Absence
Weightman, Stanley, St. Martin, Gaithersburg, MD
Welch, Joseph, Holy Spirit, Forestville, MD
Weschler, Charles A., St. Paul, Damascus, MD
Whitaker, Robert W., St. Ann, Washington, DC
White, Robert C., Sr., St. Augustine, Washington, DC
Whitfield, Robert J., St. Francis of Assisi, Derwood, MD
Wilbur, Carl, N.I.H., Bethesda, MD
Wilkinson, Lawrence A., St. Anthony, Washington, DC
Williams, Morris, St. Gabriel, Washington, DC
Wilson, Charles J., St. Peter, Waldorf, MD
Wilson, Gerard J., Sec. for the Diaconte, NCCB
Wilson, James, Our Lady of Sorrows, Takoma Park, MD
Work, Boyd, Jr., Cathedral of St. Matthew, DC
Yates, Paul F., Baltimore
Yun, James, Our Lady of Mercy, Potomac, MD
Ziemianski, Lawrence L., Arlington, VA
Zusi, J. Michael, (Retired)

INSTITUTIONS LOCATED IN THE ARCHDIOCESE

[A] SEMINARIES, ARCHDIOCESAN

WASHINGTON. *Theological College of the Catholic University of America*, 401 Michigan Ave., N.E., 20017. Tel: 202-756-4900; Fax: 202-756-4909.
E-mail: decker@theologicalcollege.org
Web site: www.theologicalcollege.org
Sulpician Fathers. Legal Title: *Theological College, Inc.*
Faculty: Revs. Howard P. Bleichner, S.S., Ph.D., Rector; Edward J. Frazer, S.S., M.A., S.T.L.; Albert C. Giaquinto, S.S., M.A., S.T.L.; Gerald D. McBrearity, S.S., M.A., S.T.B., D.Min., Vice Rector; William J. Moorman, O.SS.T.; David D. Thayer, S.S., S.T.L., Ph.D.; Chorbishop Seely Beggiani, S.T.D.; Revs. Hy K. Nguyen, S.T.B., M.Div., M.A.; Jon J. O'Brien, S.J. Priests 8; Religious 3; Students 90.

[B] SEMINARIES, RELIGIOUS OR SCHOLASTICATES

WASHINGTON. *Atonement Seminary-Franciscan Friars of the Atonement*, 5207 Colorado Ave. N.W., 20011. Tel: 202-722-1893; Fax: 202-722-1716. Rev. Patrick Cogan, S.A., Guardian. In res. Rev. Clement St. Jacques, S.A., (Retired). Priests 2; Brothers 1; Students 3.

Augustinian College, Order of St. Augustine, 3700 Oakview Ter., N.E., 20017-2521. Tel: 202-635-5299; Fax: 202-635-5296.
Web site: www.augustinian.org
Revs. Francis J. Caponi, O.S.A., Prior; Francis J. Horn, O.S.A., Treas.; Robert J. Guessetto, O.S.A., Dir., Professed Prog. & Prenovices. In res. Rev. John F. Payne, O.S.A. Solemnly Professed Friars 6; Simply Professed Friars 5; Prenovices 2.

Deshairs Community-Oblates of St. Francis de Sales Residence, 1621 Otis St., N.E., 20018-2321. Tel: 202-526-7403. Revs. Lewis S. Fiorelli, O.S.F.S.; Donald J. Heet, O.S.F.S.; Bro. John M. Carroll, O.S.F.S.; Rev. Michael S. Murray, O.S.F.S. Priests 3; Brothers 1.

Diocesan Laborer Priests, House of Studies (1966), 3706 15th St., N.E., 20017. Tel: 202-832-4217; Fax: 202-526-5692.
E-mail: fcojavier@prodigy.net
Revs. Juan L. Garcia, Dir.; Rutilio J. del Riego, Delegate; Gabriel Calvo; Francisco J. Molina; Thomas E. Murphy. Priests 5; Total Enrollment 2.

Discalced Carmelite Friars, 2131 Lincoln Rd., N.E., 20002-1199. Tel: 202-832-6622; Fax: 2020-832-5711. Legal Title: *Discalced Carmelite Friars, Inc.* Revs. Gregory Burke, O.C.D.; Kieran Kavanaugh, O.C.D., Prior; Theodore Centala, O.C.D.; Francis Miller, O.C.D.; John Sullivan, O.C.D.; Bros. Antonine DiSabella, O.C.D.; Edward O'Donnell, O.C.D.; Bernard Olk, O.C.D.; Bryan Paquette, O.C.D.; Sebastian Reale, O.C.D.; Michael Stoegbauer, O.C.D.; Joseph Girouard, O.C.D. Priests 5; Brothers 7.

Dominican House of Studies, 487 Michigan Ave., N.E., 20017. Tel: 202-529-5300; Fax: 202-636-4460. Very Rev. John C. Vidmar, O.P., Prior; Revs. Brian J. Shanley, O.P., Subprior; Vincent Wiseman, O.P., Student Master; Very Rev. Thomas P. McCreesh, O.P., Pres., Pontifical Faculty; Bro. Martin Downey, O.P., Economic Admin.; Revs. John W. Burke, O.P., Dir. Word of God Institute; Joseph Augustine Di-Noia, O.P., Exec. Dir. Secretariate - Doctrine/Pastoral Practices NCCB; Joseph Tortorici, O.P., Vocation Dir.; Basil Burr Cole, O.P.; Pierre H. Conway, O.P.; John Dominic Corbett, O.P.; Giles Richard Dimock, O.P.; Henry Thomas Donoghue, O.P.; Lawrence J. Donohoo, O.P.; John Martin Egan, O.P.; Norman H. Fenton, O.P.; Peter Michael Girard, O.P.; Kenneth Harkins, O.P.; William J. Hill, O.P.; John Frederick Hinnebusch, O.P.; John Patrick McGovern, O.P.; Albert Paretsky, O.P.; Kurt Pritzl, O.P.; Stephen Desmond Ryan; Matthew Rzeczkowski, O.P.; Malcolm Sylvester Willoughby, O.P. In res. Rev. Vincent Li, O.P. Priests 26; Brothers 1; Clerical Students 22; Seminarians 22.

Franciscan Fathers, T.O.R., Tau Fraternity, 1359 Monroe St., N.W., 20017. Tel: 202-526-6324. Candidates 6.

Franciscan Mission Service of North America, 1323 Quincy St., N.E., P.O. Box 29034, 20017. Tel: 202-832-1762; Fax: 202-832-1778.
E-mail: fms5@juno.com
Co-Directors: Rev. Joseph J. Nangle, O.F.M.; Joanne Blaney. Priests 1; Lay Staff 2.

Josephite Pastoral Center, 1200 Varnum St., N.E., 20017. Tel: 202-526-9270; 9271.
E-mail: ssjpastrcntr@aol.com
Rev. James E. McLinden, S.S.J., Dir.; Maria M. Lannon, Admin. Priests 1; Brothers 1; Deacons 1; Lay Women 3.

Marian Fathers Scholasticate, 3885 Harewood Rd., N.E., 20017. Tel: 202-526-8884; Fax: 202-832-6551.
E-mail: fjoe@jujno.com
Web site: www.marian.org
Revs. Joseph Roesch, M.I.C., Supr. & Formation Dir.; Shaun O'Connor, M.I.C.; Joseph Sielski, M.I.C.; Bro. Leonard Konopka, M.I.C., Asst. Supr. Priests 3; Brothers 2; Novices 3; Seminarians 7.

Marist College, The Scholasticate, 815 Varnum St., N.E., 20017-2199. Tel: 202-529-2821; Fax: 202-635-4627.
E-mail: marist@erols.com
Revs. Mark G. Kenney, S.M., Rector & Supr.; Joseph C. Hurtuk, S.M., Formation Team. Priests 2; Scholastics 8.

Maryknoll Fathers and Brothers, 4834 16th St., N.W., 20011. Tel: 202-726-4252; Fax: 202-726-0466.
E-mail: mkldc@aol.com
Web site: www.maryknoll.org
Revs. Francis Higdon, M.M., Dir.; Daniel Dolan, M.M.; Bro. Peter Brien, M.M.

Office of Justice and Peace, P.O. Box 29132, 20017. Tel: 202-832-1780; Fax: 202-832-5159.
E-mail: mknolldc@igc.org
Marie Dennis, Dir.; Rev. Peter Ruggere, M.M.; Sr. Mary Duffy, M.M., Assoc.; Sr. Mercedes Roman, M.M., Assoc.; Judy Coode, Communications Dir.; Deidre E. Point, Admin. Asst.

Oblates of St. Francis de Sales, 721 Lawrence St., N.E., 20017. Tel: 202-269-9410; Fax: 202-526-4323.
Web site: www.oblates.org
DeSales Hall Residence: Revs. James R. Yeakel, O.S.F.S., Supr. & Dir. Formation Office; James J. Greenfield, O.S.F.S.; John A. Hanley, O.S.F.S., Vocation Dir.; William F. Davis, O.S.F.S.; William N. Dougherty, O.S.F.S., Novice Master; Robert M. Rutledge, O.S.F.S.; Bros. Michael O'Neill McGrath, O.S.F.S., Artist, Bee Still Studio; Robert M. Carter, O.S.F.S.; Daniel P. Wisniewski, O.S.F.S. Priests 6; Brothers 3; Novices 4.

Vocation Office. Tel: 202-526-5651; Fax: 202-526-5653.
E-mail: jhanley@osfs.org

Bee Still Studio. Tel: 202-526-7074; Fax: 202-526-3969.

DeSales Spirituality Center. Tel: 202-526-5651; Fax: 202-526-5653.
E-mail: desales@osfs.org
Rev. Michael Murray, O.S.F.S., Exec. Dir.

Formation Office. Tel: 202-269-9410; Fax: 202-526-4323.

Queen of Pious Schools House of Studies-Piarist Fathers, 1339 Monroe St., N.E., 20017-2510. Tel: 202-529-7734; Fax: 202-526-4014.
Web site: www.piarist.com
Revs. Andrew C. Buechele, Sch.P., Ph.D., Rector & Master of Clerics; Theodore E. Podson, Sch.P., M.E., San Antonio/Amarillo, TX; Mario B. Vizcaino, Sch.P., M.A., S.T.L., Miami, FL; Washington, DC; David B. Powers, Sch.P., Prov.; Leonard Gendernalik, Sch.P. Priests 5.

St. Bonaventure Friary, 3514 15th St., N.E., 20017. Tel: 202-529-5324; 832-0953; Fax: 202-635-4871. Revs. Adam E. Bunnell, O.F.M.Conv., Ph.D.; Berard L. Marthaler, O.F.M.Conv., S.T.D., Ph.D.; Mark Richard Steel, O.F.M.Conv., Ph.D. Priests 3; Brothers 11.

St. Francis Friary-Capuchin College, 4121 Harewood Rd., N.E., 20017-1593. Tel: 202-529-2188; Fax: 202-526-6664.
Web site: www.capcollege.net
Revs. Francis Yacobi, O.F.M.Cap., Vicar; William Graham, O.F.M.Cap., Treas.; Thomas Russman, Supr., Formation Dir.; Adelwald Itatiro, O.F.M.Cap (Tanzania); Robert Malloy, O.F.M.Cap. (DET); Sebastian F. Miklas, O.F.M.Cap.; J. Daniel Mindling, O.F.M.Cap.; Mark Poletunow, O.F.M.Cap.; Christopher Rengers, O.F.M.Cap.; Bros. Michael Letosak, O.F.M.Cap.; Alfred Vincent, O.F.M.Cap. Priests 9; Scholastics 6; Brothers 2; Total Enrollment 6.

St. Joseph's Seminary, 1200 Varnum St., N.E., 20017. Tel: 202-526-4231; 526-4229 (Student); Fax: 202-526-7811.
E-mail: filippellissj@aol.com
St. Joseph's Society of the Sacred Heart-Josephite Fathers & Brothers. Very Rev. John L.M. Filippelli, S.S.J., Rector; Revs. James A. Hayes, S.S.J., Dir. of Maintenance; Stephen Achi, M.S.P. (Nigeria); John Raphael, S.S.J.; James McLinden, S.S.J., Dir. Josephite Pastoral Center; Stephen Brett, S.S.J., Academic Dean; Joseph L. Waters, S.S.J.; Joseph Begay, S.S.J.; Robert DeGrandis, S.S.J.; Bros. Earl Kent, S.S.J.; Thomas Vincent, S.S.J. In res. Revs. Philip Gaiya (Nigeria); Donald Conroy (GBG); Howard Johnson (JKS); Joseph Kamanda (Sierra Leone); Joseph Onuoha (Nigeria); Anthony Oyeyipo (Nigeria); Michael Apochi (Nigeria). Priests 8; Franciscan Sisters of St. Joseph 5; Seminarians 3.

St. Paul's College, 3015 Fourth St., N.E., 20017-1199. Tel: 202-832-6262; Fax: 202-269-2507. Paulist Fathers. Revs. John F. Duffy, C.S.P., Supr. & Dir. Ministerial Formation; Michael J. Martin, C.S.P., Assoc. Dir. of Formation; Kenneth G. Boyack, C.S.P., D.Min.; John J. Geaney, C.S.P.; John E. Hurley, C.S.P., D.Min.; John E. Lynch, C.S.P., Ph.D.; James R. McCauley, C.S.P., Dir. of Novices; Neil J. McEleney, C.S.P., S.S.L.; Lawrence A. Rice, C.S.P.; Robert S. Rivers, C.S.P.; Ronald G. Roberson, C.S.P., S.E.O.D. Priests 11; Sisters 5; Laity 7; Students 15.

Washington Theological Union, 6896 Laurel St., N.W., 20012. Tel: 202-726-8800; Fax: 202-726-1716.
Web site: www.wtu.edu
Legal Title: *Washington Theological Union, Inc.* Established in 1968 as the Coalition of Religious Seminaries. The Union is a school of theology owned by six religious communities: Carmelite Order, Provinces of the Most Pure Heart of Mary and St. Elias; Congregation of the Sacred Hearts of Jesus and Mary; Order of Friars Minor, Province of the Most Holy Name of Jesus; Order of St. Augustine, Province of St. Thomas; Redemptorist Fathers and Brothers. Revs. Daniel McLellan, O.F.M., Pres.; James P. Scullion, O.F.M., Academic Dean. Priests 21; Sisters 5; Lay Teachers 1; Students 275.

Whitefriars Hall, 1600 Webster St., N.E., 20017. Tel: 202-526-1221; Fax: 202-526-9217.
E-mail: egavin@carmelnet.org
Revs. Emmett Gavin, O.Carm., Prior & Formation Dir.; Frank Dixon, O.Carm., Assoc. Dir. of Formation; David Blanchard, O.Carm.; Donald W. Buggert, O.Carm.; Quinn Conners, O.Carm.; Paul Horan, O.Carm.; Patrick McMahon, O.Carm.; Craig Morrison, O.Carm.; Roland Murphy, O.Carm.; Bruce Taggart, O.Carm.; John Welch, O.Carm.; Lambert Yore, O.Carm.; Casimir Zielinski, O.Carm.; Bros. Eric Bell, O.Carm.; Raphael Sutherland, O.Carm. Friars in Solemn Profession 23; Sisters in Final Profession 1; Brothers in First Profession 2.

The Carmelitana Library. Tel: 202-526-1221, Ext. 121; Fax: 202-526-9217. Rev. Patrick McMahon, O.Carm., Ph.D.

BELTSVILLE, MD. *The Saint LaSalle Auxiliary*, P.O. Box 1610-C, 20704-1610. Tel: 301-210-7444; Fax: 301-210-0614. Bro. Thomas Chadwick, F.S.C., Dir.
The Auxiliary is the Development Office for the Christian Brothers of the Baltimore Province. Brothers 2; Lay Staff 3.

CHEVERLY, MD. *Damien House*, 6013 Inwood St., 20785. Tel: 301-386-4840.
E-mail: ssccdc@aol.com
Congregation of the Sacred Hearts. Revs. Marisi Palpale, SS.CC.; Ambrose Forgit, SS.CC.; Bro. Johnathan Hurrell, SS.CC. Priests 2; Brothers 1.

SILVER SPRING, MD. *Austin Friars Hall, Order of St. Augustine*, 2123 Edgewater Pkwy., 20903-1210. Tel: 301-445-2583; Fax: 301-445-0565.
E-mail: wimmer@erols.com
Revs. Joseph F. Wimmer, O.S.A., Prior & Treas.; William M. Cleary, O.S.A.; Maximo J. Ortiz, O.S.A.; Cedric M. Wilson, O.S.A. In res. Rev. John Burkhard, O.F.M.Conv. Priests 5.

Holy Family Seminary, 401 Randolph Rd., P.O. Box 4138, 20904. Tel: 301-622-3582; Fax: 301-622-2959.
E-mail: HolyFamSem@aol.com
Web site: members.aol.com/holyfamsem or www-.manyanet.org
Very Rev. Francisco Gonzalez, S.F., Vice Prov. Supr.; Revs. Miguel Mateo, S.F.; John A. Sierra, S.F.; Palmo Valente, S.F.; Sebastian Lee, S.F. Priests 5; Students 2.

Holy Name College, 1650 St. Camillus Dr., 20903. Tel: 301-434-3400; Fax: 301-434-4624. House of Studies for Holy Name Province of the Order of Friars Minor. Friar Joseph G. Rozansky, O.F.M., Supr. & Dir. Formation; Bro. Kevin Kriso, O.F.M., Vicar & Asst. Dir. Formation; Friars James P. Scullion, O.F.M., Ph.D.; Daniel P. Grigassy, O.F.M., Ph.D.; Nguyen Khoa, O.F.M.; Peter C. Sheridan, O.F.M.; Joseph Sullivan, O.F.M.; Rev. Mathias F. Doyle, O.F.M.; Bro. Juniper Capece, O.F.M. Solemnly Professed Friars 9; Simply Professed Friars 12.

Salvatorian Community, 104 Bishop Dr., 20905. Tel: 301-598-1883.
E-mail: sdsrieden@cs.com
Society of the Divine Savior/Salvatorians. Bro. James Rieden, S.D.S., Area Coord.; Revs. Glen Willis, S.D.S.; Richard Maloney, S.D.S.; Eliot Nitz, S.D.S.; Roman Stadtmueller, S.D.S.; Robert Ross, S.D.S.; F. Philip Vogel, S.D.S.; William J. Remmel, S.D.S., Vicar Coord.; David Bergner, S.D.S.; Robert Nugent, S.D.S.; Donald Skwor, S.D.S.; Joseph Turner, S.D.S.; Julian Guzman, S.D.S.; Bogdan Palka, S.D.S.; Bro. Roger Nelson, S.D.S., First Consultor. Priests 13; Brothers 5; Lay Members 25.

WEST HYATTSVILLE, MD. *Pallottine Seminary at Green Hill*, 2009 Van Buren St., 20782-1761. Tel: 301-422-3777; Fax: 301-422-4070. Society of the Catholic Apostolate. Rev. Bernard P. Carman, S.A.C., Rector, Formation Dir. Priests 1; Brothers 1.

[C] COLLEGES AND UNIVERSITIES

WASHINGTON. *Catholic University of America, The*, (1887) Nugent Hall/Executive Offices, 20064. Tel: 202-319-5000; Fax: 202-319-4441.
E-mail: webmaster@cua.edu
Web site: www.cua.edu
For a complete listing, refer to the Colleges and Universities section.

Georgetown University, (1789) 37th and O Sts., N.W., 20057. Tel: 202-687-0100.
E-mail: umhoferm@gunet.georgetown.edu
Web site: www.georgetown.edu
For a complete listing, refer to the Colleges and Universities section.

Trinity College, Michigan Ave. and Franklin St., N.E., 20017. Tel: 202-939-5000
For a complete listing, refer to the Colleges and Universities section.

[D] HIGH SCHOOLS, ARCHDIOCESAN

WASHINGTON. *Archbishop Carroll High School*. (Coed), 4300 Harewood Rd., N.E., 20017. Tel: 202-529-0900; Fax: 202-529-5989. Mr. John T. Butler, Pres.; Mr. James Mumford, Prin.; Revs. Leslie Branch; William L. Montgomery; John Mudd. Priests 3; Sisters 2; Lay Teachers 50; Students 612.

[E] HIGH SCHOOLS, PRIVATE

WASHINGTON. *Georgetown Visitation Preparatory School*, 1524 35th St., N.W., 20007. Tel: 202-337-3350; Fax: 202-342-5733.
E-mail: name@visi.org
Web site: www.ee.cua.edu/~georgvis
Sr. Mary Berchmans Hannan, V.H.M., Pres.; Mr. Dan Kerns, Headmaster. Sisters 4; Lay Teachers 45; Students 457.

Gonzaga College High School, 19 Eye St., N.W., 20001. Tel: 202-336-7100; Fax: 202-336-7217.
E-mail: www.gonzaga.org
Web site: achilles.gonzaga.pvt.k12.dc.us
Society of Jesus. Rev. Allen P. Novotny, S.J., Pres.; Michael Pakenham, Headmaster; Revs. Daniel K. Lahart, S.J., Vice Pres., Finance & Admin.; Robert J. Rokusek (DET), Chap.; James R. Conroy, S.J., Rector. Jesuit Community. Revs. Lucien F. Longtin, S.J.; Eugene A. Nolan, S.J.; Kenneth E. Meehan, S.J.; Ryan J. Maher, S.J.; Gerald V. O'Connor, S.J.; Bruce A. Steggert, S.J.; John B. Woodward, S.J. In res. Revs. Walter J. Burghardt, S.J.; David R. Brooks, S.J.; John A. Conlin, S.J.; Henry G. Heffernan, S.J.; Raymond M. Lelii, S.J.; Joseph M. McCloskey, S.J.; Anthony I. McHale, S.J.; Bro. Donald Dixon, S.J.; Mr. James Morgan, S.J. Priests 18; Brothers 1; Lay Teachers 66; Scholastics 2; Students 880.

St. Anselm's Abbey School. (Grades 6-12), 4501 South Dakota Ave., N.E., 20017. Tel: 202-269-2350; Fax: 202-269-2373.
E-mail: mainoffice@st-anselms.pvt.k12.dc.us
Web site: www.stanselms.org
Operated by the Benedictine Monks of St. Anselm's Abbey. Seven year college preparatory courses. Rev. Dom Peter Weigand, O.S.B., Headmaster. Priests 5; Brothers 1; Lay Teachers 41; Students 254.

St. John's College High School (1851). (Boys Grade 8, Coed Grades 9-12), 2607 Military Rd., N.W., 20015. Tel: 202-363-2316; Fax: 202-686-5162.
E-mail: stjohnschs@stjohns-chs.org
Web site: stjohns-chs.org
Brothers of the Christian Schools. Legal Title: *St. John's College*. College Preparatory, Elective Army Junior ROTC. Bros. Thomas Gerrow, F.S.C., Pres.; Hal DeLuca, F.S.C., Prin. Brothers 8; Sisters 1; Lay Teachers 65; Students 869.

BETHESDA, MD. *Mater Dei School, Inc.*, 9600 Seven Locks Rd., 20817. Tel: 301-365-2700; 301-365-2701; Fax: 301-365-2710. Mr. Edward N. Williams, Headmaster; Mr. Christopher S. Abell, Pres. Students 225.

Stone Ridge School of the Sacred Heart, 9101 Rockville Pike, 20814. Tel: 301-657-4322; Fax: 301-657-2381.
E-mail: adyer@stoneridge.org
Web site: www.stoneridge.org
Religious of the Sacred Heart. Sr. Anne Dyer, Headmistress. Sisters 7; Lay Teachers 99; Students 809.

BLADENSBURG, MD. *Elizabeth Seton High School*, 5715 Emerson St., 20710-1844. Tel: 301-864-4532; Fax: 301-864-8946.
E-mail: setonhs.org
Web site: www.setonhs.org
Sr. Virginia Ann Brooks, D.C., Pres.; Mrs. Sharon Pasterick, Prin. Daughters of Charity of St. Vincent de Paul 6; Lay Staff 69; Girls 480.

FORESTVILLE, MD. *Bishop McNamara High School*. (Coed), 6800 Marlboro Pike, 20747. Tel: 301-735-8401; Fax: 301-735-0934.
E-mail: clarkm@bmhs.org
Web site: www.bmhs.org
Holy Cross Brothers. Ms. Heather Gossart, Pres.; Mr. Marco Clark, Prin. Brothers 8; Lay Teachers 70; Students 765.

GAITHERSBURG, MD. *Mother of God School*, P.O. Box 2418, 20886. Tel: 301-990-2088; Fax: 301-947-0574.
E-mail: mogsadmn@erols.com
Web site: www.mogschool.com
Students 214.

HYATTSVILLE, MD. *(De Matha) Catholic High School*, 4313 Madison St., 20781. Tel: 301-864-3666; Fax: 301-864-0248.
E-mail: dmmail@dematha.org
Web site: www.dematha.org
Conducted by the Trinitarian Fathers of the Province of the Immaculate Heart of Mary. Rev. William J. Sullivan, O.SS.T., Rector; Dr. Daniel J. McMahon, Prin. Priests 4; Brothers 1; Lay Teachers 68; Students 937.

KENSINGTON, MD. *The Academy of the Holy Cross, Inc.*, 4920 Strathmore Ave., 20895. Tel: 301-942-2100; Fax: 301-929-6440.
E-mail: ahcadmin@erols.com
Web site: academyoftheholycross.org
Legal Title: *The Academy of the Holy Cross, Inc.* Sr. Katherine Kase, C.S.C., Prin. Sisters 10; Lay Teachers 38; Students 480.

LAUREL, MD. *St. Vincent Pallotti High School*, 20707. Tel: 301-725-3228; Fax: 301-776-4343.
E-mail: admissions@pallotti.pvt.k12.md.us
Web site: www.pallotti.pvt.k12.md.us
Missionary Sisters of the Catholic Apostolate. Stephen J. Edmonds, Prin. Priests 1; Sisters 4; Lay Teachers 30; Students 453.

LEONARDTOWN, MD. *St. Mary's Ryken High School*, 22600 Camp Calvert Rd., 20650. Tel: 301-475-2814; 932-4422; Fax: 301-475-7972. Sponsored by the Xaverian Brothers. Mr. Harry L. Swaney, Pres.; Mrs. Mary Joy Hurlburt, Prin. Brothers 1; Lay Teachers 44; Students 622.

MCLEAN, VA. *Oakcrest School*. (Grades 7-12), 850 Balls Hill Rd., 22066. Tel: 703-790-5450; Fax: 703-790-5380.
E-mail: admissions@oakcrest.org
College Preparatory for Girls. Ms. Barbara Falk, Dir. Priests 1; Lay Teachers 25; Students 130.

NORTH BETHESDA, MD. *Georgetown Preparatory School*, 20852. Tel: 301-493-5000; Fax: 301-530-9531.
E-mail: jesuit@gprep.org
Web site: www.gprep.org
Jesuit Community. Society of Jesus. Dr. James P. Power, Headmaster; Revs. Garrett D. Orr, S.J., Supr.; William L. George, Pres.; Gregory J. Quinn; James A.P. Byrne, S.J.; Gregory J. Eck, S.J.; William J. Elliott, S.J.; Aloysius C. Galvin, S.J.; Eugene J. Linehan, S.J.; Vincent M. O'Brien, S.J. Priests 9; Lay Teachers 48; Students 445.

POTOMAC, MD. *Connelly School of the Holy Child*. (Grades 6-12), 9029 Bradley Blvd., 20854. Tel: 301-365-0955; Fax: 301-365-0981.
Web site: www.holychild.org
Sisters of the Holy Child Jesus. College Preparatory for Girls. Maureen K. Appel, Headmistress. Sisters 1; Lay Teachers 53; Students 441.

The Heights School. (Grades 3-12), 10400 Seven Locks Rd., 20854. Tel: 301-365-4300. College Preparatory for Boys. Mr. Richard McPherson, Headmaster. Priests 2; Lay Teachers 38; Students 368.

WHEATON, MD. *Good Counsel High School*, 11601 Georgia Ave., 20902. Tel: 301-942-1155; Fax: 301-942-3656.
E-mail: raimo@olgchs.org
Web site: olgchs.org
Xaverian Brothers. Mr. Arthur Raimo, Pres.; Mr. Patrick Bates, Prin.; Revs. Michael T. Jones, Chap.; Barry R. Gross (LFT). Priests 2; Brothers 2; Lay Teachers 80; Students 1,061.

[F] ELEMENTARY SCHOOLS, PRIVATE

BETHESDA, MD. *The Woods Academy*, 6801 Greentree Rd., 20817. Tel: 301-365-3080. Mary Worch, Head of School. Students 216; Lay Teachers 25.

[G] SPECIAL SCHOOLS

WASHINGTON. *Lt. Joseph P. Kennedy, Jr., Institute*, 801 Buchanan St., N.E., 20017. Tel: 202-529-7600. Deacon Richard C. Birkel, Ph.D., Pres. & CEO.
Nonprofit Organization Serving Children and Adults With Developmental Disabilities: Adult Learning & Employment Services. Staff 40; Participants 315. Family & Personal Support Services. Staff 25; Participants 200. Early Intervention & Preventive Services. Staff 45; Participants 232. Kennedy Education. (Includes Kennedy School, Outreach Program to Catholic Schools and Inclusion 2000). Staff 52; Students 125. Residential Division. Staff 81; Residents 63. Administration Division. Staff 24. Community Living Partnership. Staff 3; Families 50. The Lt. Joseph P. Kennedy, Jr., Institute of the Archdiocese of Washington is a private, nonprofit organization providing education, training and employment, therapeutic and residential services to children and adults with developmental disabilities.

ROCKVILLE, MD. *The Frost Center, Society of the Divine Savior*, 4915 Aspen Hill Rd., 20853. Tel: 301-933-3451; Fax: 301-933-3330.
E-mail: seanmcl@frostcenter.com
Bro. Sean McLaughlin, S.D.S., Dir.; Rev. Glen Willis, S.D.S., Business Mgr.; Bros. Roger Nelson, S.D.S.; Peter Farnesi, S.D.S., Plant Mgr. A School and Therapy Program for Emotionally Disturbed Students and Families. Grades 1-12. Priests 1; Brothers 3; Staff 36; Students 60.

[H] CATHOLIC CHARITIES OF THE ARCHDIOCESE

WASHINGTON. *Catholic Charities of the Archdiocese of Washington, Inc.*, 1438 Rhode Island Ave., N.E., 20018. Tel: 202-526-4100; Fax: 202-526-1829.
Web site: catholiccharitiesdc.org
Mr. Edward Orzechowski, M.S.W., Pres.

Montgomery County Family Center, 11160 Veirs Mill Rd., Ste. 700, Wheaton, MD, 20902. Tel: 301-942-1856; Fax: 301-942-3793.

Prince George's County Family Center, 6706 Marlboro Pike, Forestville, MD, 20747. Tel: 301-568-9529; Fax: 301-568-9567.

Calvert County Family Center, P.O. Box 779, Prince Frederick, MD, 20678. Tel: 410-535-0309; Fax: 410-257-1002.

Charles County Family Center, The Charles Bldg., 513 E. Charles St., La Plata, MD, 20646. Tel: 301-934-2582; Fax: 301-934-3439.

St. Clement's Family Center, P.O. Box 113, Avenue, MD, 20609. Tel: 301-769-2788; Fax: 301-769-2789.

Southeast Family Center, 220 Highview Place, S.E., 20032. Tel: 202-574-3442; Fax: 202-574-3474. Total Assisted 66,187; Total Staff 270.

[I] ARCHDIOCESAN VOLUNTEER ORGANIZATIONS

WASHINGTON. *Archdiocesan Association of Ladies of Charity*, P.O. Box 10038, 20018. Mrs. Patricia Y. Camp, Pres. Purpose: Individual charity work, usually of emergency nature and support various other agencies, foodbanks, child care centers and pregnancy aid centers.

Society of St. Vincent de Paul, Archdiocese of Washington, P.O. Box 92881, 20090-2881.

Office of Archdiocesan Council. Tel: 301-699-3410.

[J] ORPHANAGES AND INFANT HOMES

HYATTSVILLE, MD. *St. Ann's Infant and Maternity Home*, 4901 Eastern Ave., 20782. Tel: 301-559-5500; Fax: 301-853-6985.
E-mail: questions@saint-anns.com
Web site: www.saint-anns.com
For a complete listing, refer to the Special Care Facilities section.

[K] GENERAL HOSPITALS

WASHINGTON. *Center for Life of Providence Hospital*, 1150 Varnum St., N.E., 20017
For a complete listing, refer to the Hospitals section.

De Paul Foundation, Inc., 1150 Varnum St., N.E., 20017
For a complete listing, refer to the Hospitals section.

Georgetown University Hospital, 3800 Reservoir Rd., N.W., 20007. Tel: 202-784-3000; Fax: 202-784-3095.
E-mail: sheamj@gunet.georgetown.edu
Web site: www.georgetown.edu
For a complete listing, refer to the Hospitals section.

Providence Health Services, Inc., 1150 Varnum St., N.E., 20017
For a complete listing, refer to the Hospitals section.

Providence Hospital, 1150 Varnum St., N.E., 20017. Tel: 202-269-7000; Fax: 202-269-7160.
E-mail: srcarol@provhosp.org
Web site: www.provhosp.org
For a complete listing, refer to the Hospitals section.

SILVER SPRING, MD. *Holy Cross Hospital of Silver Spring, Inc.*, 1500 Forest Glen Rd., 20910. Tel: 301-754-7000; Fax: 301-754-7413.
E-mail: holycrosshealth.org
Web site: www/holycrosshealth.org
For a complete listing, refer to the Hospitals section.

[L] HOMES FOR AGED

WASHINGTON. *Cardinal O'Boyle Residence for Priests*, 1150 Varnum St., N.E., 20017. Tel: 202-269-7100; Fax: 202-269-7820
For a complete listing, refer to the Special Care Facilities section.

Jeanne Jugan Residence-St. Joseph's Villa, 4200 Harewood Rd., N.E., 20017-1554. Tel: 202-269-1831; Fax: 202-269-1134
For a complete listing, refer to the Special Care Facilities section.

BELTSVILLE, MD. *Ammendale Normal Institute of Prince George's County-La Salle Hall*, (1880) 6001 Ammendale Rd., 20705. Tel: 301-210-7443; Fax: 301-210-0614
For a complete listing, refer to the Special Care Facilities section.

HYATTSVILLE, MD. *Sacred Heart Home Inc.*, 5805 Queens Chapel Rd., 20782. Tel: 301-277-6500; Fax: 301-277-3181.
E-mail: sacredhearthome@erols.com
For a complete listing, refer to the Special Care Facilities section.

MITCHELLVILLE, MD. *Villa Rosa Nursing Home, Inc.*, 3800 Lottsford Vista Rd., 20721-4026. Tel: 301-459-4700; Fax: 301-459-0754
For a complete listing, refer to the Special Care Facilities section.

[M] MONASTERIES AND RESIDENCES OF PRIESTS AND BROTHERS

WASHINGTON. *Center for Assisted Living.* Dominican Fathers and Brothers. 630 E St., S.W., 20024. Tel: 202-484-0149; Fax: 202-554-5735.
E-mail: JMCMOP@aol.com
Rev. John A. McMahon, O.P., Dir.

Commissariat of the Holy Land, Franciscan Monastery - Mount St. Sepulchre, 1400 Quincy St., N.E., 20017. Tel: 202-526-6800; Fax: 202-529-9889.
E-mail: sebastian@pressroom.com
Web site: www.pressroom.com/franciscan/
Bro. Fabian Adkins, O.F.M., Guardian; Revs. James Brabandt, O.F.M., Dir. of Candidates, Mod. Knights; Kevin Treston, O.F.M., Almanac Editor, Spiritual Asst. to Sec. Franciscan Order; Bro. Callistus Welch, O.F.M., Commissary of the Holy Land & Procurator; Revs. Manuel Ybarra, O.F.M., Asst. Procurator; Patrick Flannigan, O.F.M.; Brian McTommoney, O.F.M.; Sabin Plechta, O.F.M.; Stephen F. Sabbagh, O.F.M.; Francis X. Sihuay, O.F.M. (Peru). Priests 9; Brothers 14; Solemnly Professed 25; Simple Professed 4; Postulants 5; Novices 2; Missionaries in the Holy Land 20.

Divine Word College, 1025 Michigan Ave., N.E., 20017. Tel: 202-526-5047; Fax: 202-529-4489. Rev. Eric P. Vargas, S.V.D., Rector; Bros. G. Raker, S.V.D., Treas.; Daniel Holman, S.V.D., Formation Dir.; Revs. Mariano DaSilva, S.V.D. (Indonesia); Diosnel Centurion, S.V.D. (Paraguay); Henry Gaska, S.V.D. (Poland); Antionius Eko Yuliantoro, S.V.D. (Indonesia); Phelim Jordan, S.V.D. (Ireland); Robert Mertes, S.V.D.; Darius Piwowarczyk, S.V.D. (Poland); German Rodriguez, S.V.D. (Mexico); John Rodney, S.V.D.; Raymond Sanders, S.V.D.; Bros. Brian McLauchlin, S.V.D. (Oakland); Tam Nguyen, S.V.D. (Vietnam). Divine Word College has 32 Priests and Brothers in Residence. 40 of these are members of the S.V.D.; the other 17 are from other religious communities or dioceses in the U.S.A., and are studying at the Catholic University or the John Paul II Institute. We offer them our House for the duration of their studies. Residents 40.

Glenmary House of Studies, 1323 Quincy St., N.E., 20017. Tel: 202-635-0163; 526-1339; Fax: 202-635-0164. Rev. Mike Kerin, Dir. Students in Residence 2; Total in Residence 3; Total Staff 1.

Holy Redeemer College (1930), 3112 Seventh St., N.E., 20017. Tel: 202-529-4410; 529-4484; Fax: 202-832-1321. Opened in 1930. Redemptorist Theology Residence Since 1985. Legal Title: *Holy Redeemer College*. Very Rev. James P. Brennan, C.SS.R., Rector & Dir. Formation; Revs. Kevin O'Neil, C.SS.R., Asst. Dir. Formation; James Wallace, C.SS.R., Vicar; James Dowds, C.SS.R., Vocation Dir.; Thomas Forrest, C.SS.R. Owned and Operated by the Redemptorists of the Baltimore Province for their Own Religious Candidates. Students Attend Washington Theological Union. Priests 5; Religious Students 7.

The Jesuit Community at Georgetown University, 37th and O Sts., N.W., 20057-1200. Tel: 202-687-1700; Fax: 202-687-7679.
E-mail: jbhgu@aol.com
Rev. Brian O. McDermott, S.J., Rector; Bro. John B. Hollywood, S.J., Admin. & Treas.; Rev. Francis Alves, S.J. (Goa); Bro. Steven Alvey, S.J.; Revs. Edward W. Bodnar, S.J.; Thomas J. Buckley, S.J.; Martin J. Casey, S.J.; Paul L. Cioffi, S.J.; T. Byron Collins, S.J.; Patrick J. Conroy, S.J. (Oregon); Robert F. Drinan, S.J. (New England); Joseph T. Durkin, S.J.; Stephen M. Fields, S.J.; Thomas R. Fitzgerald, S.J.; Joseph A. Fitzmyer, S.J.; Gerald P. Fogarty, S.J.; Michael J. Garanzini, S.J. (Missouri); Francis T. Gignac, S.J. (DET); Julio Giulietti, S.J. (New England); Joseph A. Haller, S.J.; Patrick A. Heelan, S.J. (Ireland); Otto H. Hentz, S.J.; David W. Johnson, S.J. (California); Josef Kadlec, S.J.; William J. Kaifer, S.J.; Gustaaf M. Keppens, S.J.; Thomas M. King, S.J.; Josef Kure, S.J. (Czech); John P. Langan, S.J. (DET); Lawrence J. Madden, S.J.; Cesar Maldonado, S.J. (Bolivia); James A. Martin, S.J.; John F. Martin, S.J.; William C. McFadden, S.J.; Dennis L. McNamara, S.J. (Wisconsin); Paul D. McNelis, S.J.; Richard T. McSorley, S.J.; Ralph E. Metts, S.J.; William H. Millerd, S.J.; Joseph M. Moffitt, S.J.; Keith F. Muccino, S.J.; G. Ronald Murphy, S.J.; Jon J. O'Brien, S.J.; Joseph F. O'Connell, S.J.; Leo J. O'Donovan, S.J.; Ladislas Orsy, S.J. (Hungary); Victor Pacharoni, S.J. (Argentina); Janez Percic, S.J. (Slovenia); Scott R. Pilarz, S.J.; Kevin P. Quinn, S.J. (New York); Bro. George F. Reilly, S.J.; Revs. Alvaro Ribeiro, S.J. (China); Solomon I. Sara, S.J. (New England); James V. Schall, S.J. (California); Francis Schemel, S.J.; James M. Shea, S.J.; Christopher W. Steck, S.J. (NO); Daniel R. Sweeney, S.J.; Joseph F. Sweeney, S.J.; John W. Swope, S.J.; Timothy E. Toohig, S.J. (New England); Revs. Joseph N. Tylenda, S.J.; James P.M. Walsh, S.J.; Kevin W. Wildes, S.J.; John W. Witek, S.J. (CHI); Deacons Piotr Aszyk, S.J. (Poland); Brian J. Conley, S.J. (New England); Ivan Rodriguez, S.J. (Spain). Priests 63; Brothers 3; Scholastic 3.

K Street Jesuit Community, 320 K St., N.E., 20002. Tel: 202-546-1958. Revs. James E. Hug, S.J., Supr.; Fred Kammer, S.J.; Joseph R. Hacala, S.J.; Vincent P. DeCola, S.J. Residents 4.

La Salette Community, 1243 Monroe St., N.E., 20017. Tel: 202-526-8070; Fax: 202-529-6577.
E-mail: welch1993@aol.com
Web site: www.lasalette.org
Legal Title: *Missionaries of La Salette Corporation.*

Leonard Neale House, 1726 New Hampshire Ave., N.W., 20009. Tel: 202-387-5375; 387-5376; Fax: 202-387-8220. Revs. John F. Armstrong, S.J.; James A. Casciotti, S.J.; Charles L. Currie, S.J.; George T. Dennis, S.J.; Walter C. Deye, S.J.; Paul C. Kenney, S.J.; James F. Lafontaine, S.J.; John T. Quinn, S.J.; Richard J. Ryscavage, S.J.; Bradley M. Schaeffer, S.J.; Thomas C. Widner, S.J.; Theodore F. Zuern, S.J. Priests 14; Total Staff 14.

Marist Center, 4408 8th St. N.E., 20017-2298. Tel: 202-529-4800; Fax: 202-526-2295.
E-mail: maristprov@aol.com
The Marist Finance Center of the Atlanta Province of the Society of Mary, Fathers and Brothers. Revs. Charles F. Braun, S.M.; Thomas E. Dubay, S.M.; Philip S. Gage, S.M.; John H. Harhager, S.M.; George M. Lepping, S.M.; Howard C. Smith, S.M.; Timothy F. Sugrue, S.M., Business Mgr. & Admin.; Charles J. Barrett, S.M., (Retired), 10300 4th St., N., St. Petersburg, FL, 33716-3813. Tel: 727-576-1025. Rev. Charles F. Brogley, S.M., (Retired), Sacred Heart Manor, 6445 Germantown Ave., Philadelphia, PA, 19119. Tel: 215-438-5268. Rev. Edward C. Corrigan, S.M., (Retired), Sts. Mary & Joseph Home, 4291 Richmond Rd., Cleveland, OH, 44122-6199. Tel: 216-464-1222. Rev. Joseph D. Fenton, S.M., St. Columban Church, 10801 Stanford Ave., Garden Grove, CA, 92640. Tel: 714-534-1174; Fax: 714-534-1937. Rev. Leo A. Foley, S.M., (Retired), Carroll Manor, 1150 Varnum St. N.E., 20017. Tel: 202-269-7100. Rev. Stanley W. Hosie, S.M., 2440 Virginia Ave., N.W., D-1301, 20037-2601. Tel: 202-296-9676. Rev. Eugene E. Hughes, S.M., (Retired), 1497 Ashford Pl. N.E., Atlant, GA, 30319-5105. Tel: 770-454-9594. Rev. John L. Jazwiecki, S.M., (Retired), Our Lady of Perpetual Help Church, 1711 E. 11th Ave., Tampa, FL, 33605-3803. Tel: 813-248-5701; Fax: 813-241-4128. Rev. Timothy G. Keating, S.M., 6200 Westchester Park Dr., Apt. 1113, College Park, MD, 20740-2840. Tel: 301-588-4030. Rev. Leonard P. Kellermann, S.M., (Retired), Mary Joseph Residence, 4201 Woodland Dr., New Orleans, LA, 70131-7398. Tel: 504-394-2200. Rev. Andrew G. McCormack, S.M., Vocation Dir., 1497 Ashford Pl. N.E., Atlanta, GA, 30319-5105. Tel: 770-454-9594. Rev. George J. Meiluta, S.M., (Retired), St. Joseph Home for the Aged, 1182 Holland Rd., Holland, PA, 18966. Tel: 215-357-5511. Rev. Leonard J. Moran, S.M., (Retired), 227 Courtyard Blvd., #206, Sun City Center, FL, 33573-5766. Tel: 813-633-2753; Fax: 813-633-2753. Rev. Patrick D. Primeaux, S.M., 150 Burns St, #6-C, Forest Hills, NY, 11375-6111. Tel: 718-544-8054; Fax: 718-544-6687. Rev. John A. Richmond, S.M., (Retired), Jeanne Jugan Residence, 4200 Harewood Rd., N.E., 20017-1554. Tel: 202-269-1831. Rev. Edward J. Templeton, S.M., (Retired), Our Lady of Wisdom, 5600 General DeGaulle Dr., New Orleans, LA, 70131. Tel: 504-304-5222.

Missionaries of Africa, 1624 21st St., N.W., 20009-1003. Tel: 202-232-5154; Fax: 202-332-8640.
E-mail: r.roy-lapia@juno.com
Province of North America. Revs. Richard P. Roy, Asst. Prov.; Austin MacAdam, M.Afr., Community Coord.; John Philip Reed, M.Afr., Coord. Justice & Peace Office; Roger Bisson, M.Afr.; Sjef Donders, M.Afr. (Holland); John Lynch, M.Afr., Treas.; George Markwell, M.Afr.; Bro. Raphael L. Marin, Dev. Office. Priests 8; Total Staff 8.

Missionary Oblates of Mary Immaculate. Tel: 202-529-4505; Fax: 202-529-4572.
E-mail: province@omiusa.org
Web site: www.omiusa.org
Provincial Offices of the United States Province of the Missionary Oblates of Mary Immaculate, 391 Michigan Ave., N.E., 20017-1516. Tel: 202-529-4505; Fax: 202-529-4572.
E-mail: province@omiusa.org
Web site: www.omiusa.org
Very Revs. David A. Kalert, O.M.I., Prov.; Charles D. Banks, O.M.I., Vicar Prov.; Revs. David Ullrich, O.M.I., Councilor; Thomas Singer, O.M.I., Gen. Councilor; Robert Moosbrugger, O.M.I., Treas.; Charles Hurkes, O.M.I., Dir. Communications; Seamus P. Finn, O.M.I., Dir. Justice & Peace; Armand Mathew, O.M.I., Assoc. Dir. Justice & Peace; Jose Arong, O.M.I., Councilor; Marc Boisvert, O.M.I.; Normand Bonneau, O.M.I.; Richard Cote, O.M.I.; Salvatore DeGeorge, O.M.I., Councilor; Joseph H. Hitpas, O.M.I., Councilor; Thomas M. Killeen, O.M.I.; Etienne LaRose, O.M.I.; Allen Maes, O.M.I., Councilor; Arthur T. Obin, O.M.I.; Dale Schlitt, O.M.I.; Richard Sudlik, O.M.I., Councilor.
Legal Titles and Holdings:

The United States Province of the Missionary Oblates of Mary Immaculate, Inc. Tel: 202-529-4505; Fax: 202-529-4572.

Oblate Service Corporation. Tel: 202-529-4505; Fax: 202-529-4572.

Oblate Shrines and Renewal Centers, Inc. Tel: 202-529-4505; Fax: 202-529-4572.

Oblate Title Holding Corporation. Tel: 202-529-4505; Fax: 202-529-4572.

Oblate Continuing Care Trust. Tel: 202-529-4505; Fax: 202-529-4572.

Oblate Education and Formation Trust. Tel: 202-529-4505; Fax: 202-529-4572.

Oblate Annuity Trust. Tel: 202-529-4505; Fax: 202-529-4572.

Oblate Endowment Trust. Tel: 202-529-4505; Fax: 202-529-4572.

Oblate Patrimony Trust. Tel: 202-529-4505; Fax: 202-529-4572.

Oblate Service Trust. Tel: 202-529-4505; Fax: 202-529-4572.

Oblate Real Estate Trust. Tel: 202-529-4505; Fax: 202-529-4572.

Oblate College/Center for Mission Studies Community, 391 Michigan Ave., N.E., 20017-1586. Tel: 202-529-5244. Revs. William Antonio; Charles D. Banks, O.M.I.; Matthew Casey, O.M.I.; Paul Costello, O.M.I.; Seamus P. Finn, O.M.I., Ph.D.; Charles W. Gilles, O.M.I.; Jef Johnson, O.M.I.; David A. Kalert, O.M.I.; John J. Leddy, O.M.I.; Armand Mathew, O.M.I; Richard McAlear, O.M.I.; George F.

McLean, O.M.I., Ph.D.; Robert Moosbrugger, O.M.I.; Jerry Orsino, O.M.I.; David N. Power, O.M.I., S.T.D.; Ray Prybis, O.M.I., Ph.D. Ed.; Edmund Reginald, O.M.I.; J. William Sheehan, O.M.I.; David Ullrich, O.M.I.; Rufus J. Whitley, O.M.I.; Giovanni Zevola, O.M.I.; Bros. Tim Higgins, O.M.I.; Michael Holly, O.M.I.; Bill Lundberg, O.M.I.; Andrew Small, O.M.I. Priests 21; Brothers 4; Priests Foreign Countries 4.

St. Anselm's Abbey, 4501 South Dakota Ave., N.E., 20017. Tel: 202-269-2300; Fax: 202-269-2312. Benedictine Foundation at Washington, DC, Order of St. Benedict. Rt. Revs. Aidan Shea, O.S.B., Abbot; Alban Boultwood, O.S.B.; Revs. James A. Wiseman, O.S.B., Prior; Bede Bidlack, O.S.B.; Thomas Fahy, O.S.B.; John Farrelly, O.S.B.; David Granfield, O.S.B.; Patrick Granfield, O.S.B.; Michael Hall, O.S.B.; Hilary Hayden, O.S.B.; Edmund Henkels, O.S.B.; Benet Hill, O.S.B.; Joseph Jensen, O.S.B.; Daniel Kirk, O.S.B.; Giles LeVasseur, O.S.B.; Paul McKane, O.S.B.; Gabriel Myers, O.S.B.; Dunstan Robidoux, O.S.B.; Matthew Nylund, O.S.B.; George Porto, O.S.B.; Urban Schnaus, O.S.B.; Mark Sheridan, O.S.B.; Philip Simo, O.S.B.; Boniface von Nell, O.S.B.; Peter Weigand, O.S.B.; Christopher Wyvill, O.S.B. Priests 22; Brothers 4.

St. Louis Friary, 831 Varnum St., N.E., 20017-2144. Tel: 202-529-0171; Fax: 202-832-8513. House of Post-Novitiate Formation for Franciscan Friars, T.O.R., Province of the Most Sacred Heart of Jesus. Revs. Thomas Bourque, T.O.R.; James Morman, T.O.R.; Carlo Napoli, T.O.R. Friars in Post-Novitiate Formation 8; Total in Residence 11.

Woodstock Jesuit Community, 1419 35 St., N.W., 20007. Tel: 202-337-7750.
E-mail: tskretz@erols.com
Revs. Gasper F. LoBiondo, S.J., Supr.; Andrew J. Christiansen, S.J.; James Connor, S.J.; Adrian Lyons, S.J. (Australia); M. Maria Louis, S.J.; Mark P. Scalese, S.J.; James D. Redington, S.J. Priests 7.

ADELPHI, MD. *Missionary Servants of the Most Holy Trinity*, 1733 Metzerott Rd., 20783. Tel: 301-439-3171; Fax: 301-434-0848.
E-mail: fjmcmd@aol.com
Senior Ministry Residence. Revs. Gabriel Hannan, S.T.; Gerald Swift, S.T.; Charles Tague, S.T.; Paul Keenan, S.T.; Shaun McCarty, S.T.; Edwin Dill, S.T.; Martin VanTrieste, S.T.; Hugh Marshall, S.T.; Bros. Malachy Sofield, S.T.; Robert Conway, S.T.; Jonathan Daneski, S.T.; Howard Piller, S.T., Dir.; William Coombs, S.T., Asst. Dir.; Loughlan Sofield, S.T.

Our Lady Missionary Cenacle, 2717 Curry Dr., 20783-1725. Tel: 301-422-8039; Fax: 301-422-6199. Bro. Hilary Mettes, S.T., Supr.; Rev. Domingo Rodriguez, S.T.

BROOKEVILLE, MD. *Marian Monastery-Brookeville*. Marian Residence & Marian Assisted Living, 19101 Georgia Ave., Box 220, 20833. Tel: 301-774-4478; Fax: 301-570-8645.
Web site: www.marian.org
Revs. Bernard Backiel, M.I.C., Rector; Martin Rzeszutek, M.I.C.; John Kobza, M.I.C.; Jaroslaw Gamrot, M.I.C. (Poland). Priests 4.

HYATTSVILLE, MD. *St. John de Matha Monastery, Order of Most Holy Trinity*, 4310 Madison St., 20781. Tel: 301-927-6418; Fax: 301-927-0807. Revs. Damian Anuszewski, O.SS.T., Supr.; Albert M. Anuszewski, O.SS.T., Vicar; Charles Flood, O.SS.T.; Bro. Patrick Wildgen, O.SS.T.; Rev. Iraneusz Ekiert, O.SS.T. Priests 4; Brothers 1; Scholastics 4; Affiliates 4; Total Staff 4.

POTOMAC, MD. *Legionaries of Christ*, 10211 Norton Rd., 20854. Tel: 301-299-0806; Fax: 301-299-0809.
E-mail: rgill@legionaries.org
Revs. William Izquierdo, L.C., Supr.; Richard Gill, L.C.; Robert Presutti, L.C.; Michael Sliney, L.C.; James Swanson, L.C.; Jon Budke, L.C.; John Connor, L.C.; Bros. Albert Assad, L.C.; Michael Brisson, L.C.; Kyle Dardis, L.C.; John Donohue, L.C.

RIVERDALE, MD. *Holy Spirit Missionary Cenacle* 1996, 5809 Riverdale Rd., 20737. Tel: 301-277-7442; Fax: 301-209-0355. Rev. Seraphim Molina, S.T. In res. Rev. Sidney H. Griffith, S.T., Semantics/Early Christian Studies, Faculty, Catholic University of America. Tel: 301-927-4919; Bros. Richard McCann, S.T., Asst. Mission Procurator, Trinity Missions, Silver Spring, MD. Tel: 301-209-9638; Gerardo Oliva, S.T., AIDS Ministry.

SILVER SPRING, MD. *Gemelli House*. Franciscan Friars-Holy Name Province, 10400 Lorain Ave., 20901. Tel: 301-681-9478; Fax: 301-681-7170. Revs. Kenneth R. Himes, O.F.M., Guardian; Vincent de Paul Cushing, O.F.M.; Romuald Green, O.F.M.; Daniel McLellan, O.F.M.; Dominic V. Monti, O.F.M.; Bros. Michael P. Jones, O.F.M.; Stephen Kluge, O.F.M.; Joseph LaGressa, O.F.M.; Steven R. Patti, O.F.M.

TAKOMA PARK, MD. *Society of African Missions (S.M.A.)*, 256 N. Manor Cir., 20912-4551. Tel: 301-270-2008; Fax: 301-270-6370.
E-mail: smausa-v@smafathers.org
Web site: www.smafathers.org
Revs. Eugene Riordan, S.M.A., Supr.; Austin Charles Ochu, S.M.A., Dir. of Formation.

Lay Mission Program, 207 S. Manor Cir., 20912-4555. Tel: 301-891-2014 (Home); 301-891-2037 (Office); Fax: 301-270-8435. Theresa Hicks, Dir.

Vocations Office, 209 Lincoln Ave., 20912-5738. Tel: 301-270-8435; Fax: 301-270-8435. Rev. Thomas Wright, S.M.A., Vocation Dir.

Justice, Peace & Environmental Care Office, 209 Lincoln Ave., 20912-5738. Tel: 301-270-4756; Fax: 301-270-6370. Dr. Stephen Price, Ph.D., Dir. In res. Rev. Daniel Lynch, S.M.A. Priests 3; Lay S.M.A. 1; Lay Candidates 8.

UNIVERSITY PARK, MD. *Holy Trinity Missionary Cenacle* (1995), 4001 Van Buren St., 20782. Tel: 301-779-0939; Fax: 301-699-1745. Bro. Jordan Baxter, S.T., Custodian; Revs. Ralph Frisch, S.T. Tel: 301-864-3470; David O'Connor, S.T. Tel: 301-699-3508; Conrad Schmitt, S.T. Tel: 301-779-0939; Bro. Alexis Norton, S.T. Tel: 301-699-1729.

[N] MINISTRY TO PRIESTS

KENSINGTON, MD. *St. John Vianney House*, 4214 Saul Rd., 20895. Tel: 301-942-1191. Rev. Michael J. Murray.

[O] CONVENTS AND RESIDENCES FOR SISTERS

WASHINGTON. *Archivists for Congregations of Women Religious*, ACWR National Office, Trinity College, 125 Michigan Ave, N.E., 20017. Tel: 202-884-9441; Fax: 202-884-9229.
E-mail: acwr@juno.com
Web site: www.homestead.com/acwr
Purpose: Preservation of the archives of Roman Catholic women religious congregations and collaboration with historians in making known the lives and works of women religious.

Carmelite Sisters of Charity, 1222 Monroe St. N.E., 20017. Tel: 202-265-1349. U.S. Delegation Regional House. Sr. Maria Pilar Chamorro, C.C.V., Regl. Supr.; Sr. Miren A. Lapazaran, First Councilor; Sr. Claudia Paredes, C.C.V., Second Councilor; Sr. Carmen Banegas, C.C.V., Sec.; Sr. M. Carmen de Juan, C.C.V., Treas.; Sr. Amaya Duralde, C.C.V., Formation Dir.

Daughters of Wisdom, 914 Perry Pl., N.E., 20017. Tel: 202-529-3343. Sisters 2.

Franciscan Sisters of Atonement, 4000 Harewood Rd., N.E., 20017. Tel: 202-529-1111. Sr. Margaret Mullin, S.A., Dir. Sisters 7; Total Staff 9.

Georgetown Visitation Convent, 1500 35th St., N.W., 20007. Tel: 202-337-0350; Fax: 202-965-3845.
E-mail: geoviscon@aol.com
Web site: www.ee.cua.edu/~georgvis
Mother Mary deSales McNabb, Supr. Professed Sisters 20.

Institute of Our Lady of Mount Carmel, 4415 Eighth St., N.E., 20017. Tel: 202-526-9180. Total Assisted 48; Total Staff 9.

Little Sisters of Jesus, 1740 Euclid St., N.W., Apt. 1, 20009. Tel: 202-265-6177. Sisters 2.

Little Sisters of the Poor, 4200 Harewood Rd., N.E., 20017. Tel: 202-269-1831; Fax: 202-269-1134. Sisters 16.

Missionaries of Charity, 3310 Wheeler Rd., S.E., 20032. Tel: 202-562-6890. Sisters 6; Total Assisted 16,181.

Missionaries of Charity, Gift of Peace Convent, 2800 Otis St., N.E., 20018. Tel: 202-269-3313. Sr. M. Pietra, M.C., Supr. Total Assisted 69; Total in Residence 53; Total Staff 25.

Oblates Sisters of the Most Holy Eucharist, 2907 Ellicott Ter., N.W., 20008. Tel: 202-244-7714.
E-mail: oblatesl@juno.com
Sr. M. Luz Castro, O.S.S.E., Supr. Sisters 7.

Poor Clares of Perpetual Adoration, 3900 13th St., N.E., 20017-2699. Tel: 202-526-6808; Fax: 202-526-0678. Cloistered Monastery of Perpetual Adoration. Cloistered Nuns 10.

Religious of the Sacred Heart, 1235 Otis St. N.E., 20017. Tel: 202-526-6258;202-832-1598.
E-mail: ckondolf@rscj.org
Sr. Catherine Collins, R.S.C.J., Dir. Center for Educational Design & Communication. Sisters 3.

Religious of the Sacred Heart. Perry Street Community, 1201 Perry St., N.E., 20017. Tel: 202-526-9398. Sr. Marion Duffy, Contact Person.

Religious of the Sacred Heart. Oakview Community. 1215 Perry St., N.E., 20017. Tel: 202-832-0071. Sr. Fleisa Garcia, Contact Person.

Rosary House of Studies-Dominican Sisters of The Presentation, 1201 Monroe St., N.E., 20017. Tel: 202-529-1768; Fax: 202-526-7526.
E-mail: lapointe2@juno.com
Sisters 4.

St. Dominic's Monastery, 4901 16th St., N.W., 20011. Tel: 202-726-2107. Dominican Nuns, a Contemplative Community with Solemn Vows and Papal Enclosure. Sr. Mary Paul, O.P., Prioress. Sisters 11.

Sisters of Notre Dame de Namur, 145 Taylor St. N.E., 20017. Tel: 202-832-6240; Fax: 202-832-6270.
E-mail: jbilliartr@aol.com
Residence for Sisters. Sr. Elizabeth Ann McFadden, S.N.D., Contact Person. Sisters 8.

Sisters of the Holy Child Jesus, 1033 Newton St., N.E., 20017. Tel: 202-526-6832.
Web site: www.shcj.org
Novitiate Community. Sisters 6.
Other Convents: 1244 Monroe St., N.E., 20017. Tel: 202-832-3237. Sisters 4.
Immaculate Conception School (1 Sister); St. Anthony's School (1 Sister).

Sisters of the Third Franciscan Order-Syracuse, NY. Emmaus Convent, 1334 Perry St., N.E., 20017-2531. Tel: 202-526-8017.
E-mail: mlsalerno@aol.com or smcosf@aol.com
Sisters 2.

ANACOSTIA, WASHINGTON. *Missionaries of Charity (Contemplatives)*, 1244 V St., S.E., 20020-7016. Tel: 202-889-6100. Sr. M. Andrea, M.C., Supr.

CHEVY CHASE, MD. *Missionary Sisters of Our Lady of Africa*, 3715 Williams Ln., 20815. Tel: 301-654-2047.
E-mail: msolabev@aol.com

CLINTON, MD. *Religious Sisters of Mercy of Alma, MI*. St. Andrew Home of Mercy, 6100 Wolverton Lane, 20735. Tel: 301-297-5617. Sr. Dolora Keating, Contact Person. Sisters 5.

FORT WASHINGTON, MD. *The Missionary Catechists of St. Therese of the Infant Jesus, Inc.*, 2400 Brinkley Rd., 20744. Tel: 301-839-7751; Fax: 301-839-7751.
E-mail: mcstusa@erols.com
Sr. Marilou P. Paulo, M.C.S.T., Pres. Sisters 4.

HYATTSVILLE, MD. *DeMatha Convent*, 4318 Madison St., 20781. Tel: 301-927-8458; Fax: 301-927-0807. Oblates of St. Martha, Saltillo, Mexico. Sisters 3; Total Staff 3.

KENSINGTON, MD. *Sisters of the Holy Cross*, Saint Angela Hall, 5000 Strathmore Ave., 20895. Tel: 301-949-2244. Legal Title: *Sisters of the Holy Cross, Inc.* Retirement House for the Sisters of the Holy Cross. Sr. Marian Daniel, C.S.C., Supr. Sisters 18.

Academy of the Holy Cross Convent, 4920 Strathmore Ave., 20895. Tel: 301-942-2102. Sisters 14. Legal Title: *The Academy of the Holy Cross, Inc.*

Holy Cross Hospital Convent, 1523 Forest Glen Rd., Silver Spring, 20910. Tel: 301-681-5596. Sisters 6.

Our Lady of the Woods, 9820 Dameron Dr., Silver Spring, 20902. Tel: 301-681-5732.

Sisters of the Holy Cross, 4523 32nd St., Mount Rainier, 20712. Tel: 301-927-0712. Sisters 3. 12623 Laurie Dr., Silver Spring, 20904. Tel: 301-879-9648. Sisters 2. Holy Cross Convent, 4900 Strathmore Ave., Garrett Park, 20896. Tel: 301-933-2213. Sisters 3.

Our Lady of Lourdes Convent, 4511 East-West Hwy., Bethesda, 20814. Tel: 301-986-5741. Sisters 3.

LANHAM-SEABROOK, MD. *Mission Helpers of the Sacred Heart*, 9471 Annapolis Rd., 20706. Tel: 301-459-8078.
E-mail: srsusanne@stmatthias.org
Sisters 9.

LAUREL, MD. *Pallotti Convent*, 404 Eighth St., 20707. Tel: 301-725-1717. Sr. M. Karen Lester, S.A.C., Local Supr. Professed Sisters 8; Total Staff 1.

MOUNT RAINIER, MD. *Congregation of Jesus and Mary, Provincialate*, 3706 Rhode Island Ave., 20712-2009. Tel: 301-277-3594; Fax: 301-277-8656. Sr. Rosemary Mangan, R.J.M., Prov. Administrative Team 3; Staff 2.
Other Residences: Religious of Jesus and Mary, 6709 41st Ave., University Park, 20782. Tel: 301-779-0662; Fax: 301-779-3843. Sisters 3. 4602 Clemson Rd., College Park, 20740. Tel: 301-699-3931; Fax: 301-927-4157. Sisters 3. 3521 13th St., N.W., Washington, DC, 20010. Tel: 202-265-8812; Fax: 202-265-1842. Sisters 3. Jesus Mary Provincialate, St. James Convent, 3706 Rhode Island Ave., 20712-2009. Tel: 301-277-3334; Fax: 301-277-8656. Sisters 7.

NORTH BEACH, MD. *Sisters of St. Dominic of St. Cecilia of Nashville, TN*, St. Anthony Convent, 4104 First St., P.O. Box 600, 20714. Tel: 410-286-3393. Sr. Christine Born, Convent Supr. Sisters 5.

PORT TOBACCO, MD. *Carmel of Port Tobacco* (1790), 5678 Mount Carmel Rd., 20646-9611. Tel: 301-934-1654; Fax: 301-934-0958.
E-mail: steresa@erols.com
Web site: www.erols.com/carmel-of-port-tobacco
Professed 13; Professed Novice 1; Novices 1; Postulants 1.

SILVER SPRING, MD. *Religious of the Sacred Heart*. St. Michael Community. 2524 Locustwood Pl., 20905. Tel: 301-879-2441. Sr. Victoria Rajca, Contact Person.

Sister of Charity of St. Charles Borromeo, Inc., 11320 Classical Ln., 20901. Tel: 301-681-9665.
E-mail: sistersofcb@aol.com
Sr. Caecilia H. Hadiwijana, Pres.

Sisters of Mercy of the Americas Administrative Center, 8300 Colesville Rd., Ste. 300, 20910. Tel: 301-587-0423; Fax: 301-587-0533.
E-mail: srsofmercy@aol.com
Web site: www.sistersofmercy.org
Legal Holdings; Mercy Action, Inc.; McAuley Institute, Inc.; Mercy Corps., Inc. Sr. Marie Chin, R.S.M., Pres. Administrative Team 5.

Sisters of the Good Shepherd, 504 Hexton Hill Rd., 20904-3300. Tel: 301-384-1169; Fax: 301-384-8889. Legal Title: *Sisters of the Good Shepherd of the City of Washington, DC.* Sisters 6.

Good Shepherd Corporation dba Shepherd's Dwelling. (Residence for women with AIDS), Washington, DC. Tel: 301-680-3717; Fax: 301-384-8889.
E-mail: cmdoylergs@aol.com
Total Assisted 4; Total Staff 2.

Proyecto Nino. (Day Care program for children & parents). Tel: 202-588-9892; Fax: 202-588-9808. Total Staff 15.

Sisters of the Holy Names (S.N.J.M.), 715 Pershing Dr., 20910. Tel: 301-587-1717; Fax: 301-587-1717.
E-mail: snjm715@aol.com
Sr. Ann Marean, Supr.
Other Convents: 519 Varnum St., N.W., 20011. Tel: 202-829-8671. Sisters 3. 9212 Glenville Rd., 20901. Tel: 301-593-3385. 10705 Torrance Dr., 20902. Sisters 2.

[P] RETREAT HOUSES

WASHINGTON. *Washington Retreat House, Inc.* (1930), 4000 Harewood Rd., N.E., 20017. Tel: 202-529-1111; Fax: 202-259-2102.
E-mail: washretreat@juno.com
Franciscan Sisters of the Atonement. Sr. Margaret Mullin, S.A., Dir. Sisters 7; Total in Residence 7; Total Staff 10.

FAULKNER, MD. *Loyola on the Potomac Retreat House*, P.O. Box 9, 20632. Tel: 301-934-8862; 870-3515; Fax: 301-392-0808.
E-mail: loyolaretreathouse@erols.com
Web site: www.loyolaretreat.org
Rev. Stephen M. Garrity, S.J., Supr. & Dir. Associate Directors: Revs. Thomas F. Gleeson, S.J.; Frank T. Kaminski, S.J.; Joseph A. Kemme, S.J.; Francis J. Miles, S.J.; Richard C. Schmidt, S.J.; Timothy J. Stephens, S.J.; Sr. Patricia McDermott, I.H.M. Total in Residence 6; Total Staff 8.

UPPER MARLBORO, MD. *Our Lady of Mattaponi Youth Retreat and Conference Center*, 11000 Mattaponi Rd., 20772. Tel: 301-952-9074; Fax: 301-952-0609. Rev. Robert F. Mordino. Total in Residence 1; Total Staff 3.

[Q] NATIONAL SHRINE

WASHINGTON. *Basilica of the National Shrine of the Immaculate Conception*, 400 Michigan Ave., N.E., 20017-1566. Tel: 202-526-8300; Fax: 202-526-8313.
E-mail: info@nationalshrine.com
Web site: http://www.nationalshrine.com
Rev. Paul M. Eversole (ARL), Dir. Liturgy; Rev. Msgr. Michael J. Bransfield (PH), Rector; Revs. Walter R. Rossi (SCR), Dir. Pilgrimages; John J. Leddy, O.M.I., Spiritual Counselor; Leo J. Ovian, M.S.A., Spiritual Counselor.

[R] HOUSES OF PRAYER

WASHINGTON. *Madonna House*, 220 C St., N.E., 20002. Tel: 202-547-0177; Fax: 202-547-8117.
Web site: www.madonnahouse.org
Catherine A. Mitchell, Dir. Total in Residence 4; Total Staff 4.

[S] OFFICES OF CAMPUS MINISTRY

WASHINGTON. *Archdiocesan Campus Ministry.*

American University Catholic Community, Kay Spiritual Life Center, 4400 Massachusetts Ave., N.W., 20016-8010; Fax: 202-885-3317.
E-mail: frbrien@globalatt.net
Rev. Brien R. McCarthy. Tel: 202-885-3327; Dr. Karin Thornton, Assoc. Chap. Tel: 202-885-3326.

Gallaudet University Catholic Community, 20002. Tel: 202-651-5102. Rev. Gerard A. Trancone, 7202 Buchanan St., Landover Hills, MD, 20784. Tel: 301-459-7467; Fax: 301-459-8186.

George Washington Univ. Newman Center, 2210 F St., N.W., 20037. Tel: 202-676-6855; Fax: 202-676-6859. Rev. James J. Greenfield, O.S.F.S., Chap.

Howard Univ. Newman Center, 818 Newman Center, 20059. Tel: 202-238-2687; Fax: 202-806-4641. Rev. John Raphael, S.S.J., Chap.

University of Maryland Catholic Student Center, 4141 Guilford Dr., College Park, MD, 20740. Tel: 301-864-6223; 6224; Fax: 301-864-8411. Rev. William D. Byrne, Chap.; Sr. Rita Ricker, R.J.M., Assoc.

St. Mary's College Campus Ministry, P.O. Box 67, St. Mary's City, MD, 20686. Tel: 301-862-4600. Rev. Francis W. Krastel.

[T] PERSONAL PRELATURES

WASHINGTON. *Prelature of the Holy Cross and Opus Dei*, 2301 Wyoming Ave., N.W., 20008. Tel: 202-234-1567; Fax: 202-238-0621.
Web site: www.opusdei.org
Revs. William H. Stetson; Lawrence A. Kutz; C. John McCloskey.
Other Centers: Tenley Study Center, 4300 Garrison St., N.W., 20016. Tel: 202-362-2419. Revs. Timothy J. Uhen; Ronald Gillis; Orestes Gonzales, 4955 Linnean Ave., N.W., 20008. Tel: 202-237-6894. Rev. Deo G. Rosales.

[U] SECULAR INSTITUTES

WASHINGTON. *Caritas Christi*, Bladensburg Rd., N.E., P.O. Box 41372, 20018. Tel: 301-459-6754; Fax: 202-319-6485.
E-mail: stdenis@cua.edu
A Secular Institute of Pontifical Right. Dr. Helen St. Denis, C.C., Past Pres. US-CSI.

Community of Christ, 1003 Kearney St., N.E., 20017. Tel: 202-832-9710; 797-8806. Rev. John Adams (RIC), Moderator. A Private Association Community of Archdiocesan Right for Priests, Lay Men and Lay Women. The Community of Christ Purpose is Simple Lifestyle, Poverty Ministry, Spiritual Growth and Prayer of Community Members.

WEST BETHESDA, MD. *Missionaries of the Kingship of Christ*, P.O. Box 34513, 20827-0513. Tel: 301-251-5669; Fax: 481-150-8481.
E-mail: cdahlin@aol.com
Web site: www.simkc.org
A Francisan Secular Institute of Pontifical Right. Tel: 301-251-5669; Fax: 481-150-8481. Rev. Dominic V. Monti, O.F.M. Tel: 301-593-4479.

[V] MISCELLANEOUS

WASHINGTON. *"The Americas"*, Catholic University of America, Gibbons Hall, Room B 17, 20064. Tel: 202-319-5890; Fax: 202-319-5569.

Africa Faith & Justice Network, 3035 Fourth St. N.E., 20017. Tel: 202-832-3412; Fax: 202-832-9051.
E-mail: afjn@afjn.org
Web site: www.afjn.cua.edu
Larry Goodwin, Exec. Dir.

Archbishop Carroll High School, 4300 Harewood Rd., N.E., 20017. Tel: 202-529-0900; Fax: 202-529-5989. Records Center for the Archdiocese of Washington.
Alumni Office. John Badaczewski, Dir. Tel: 202-529-0900 Ext. 32.

Archdiocese of Cotabato, 391 Michigan Ave., N.E., 20017. Tel: 202-529-5244. Most Rev. Orlando Quevedo, O.M.I., D.D.; Rev. Robert Moosbrugger, O.M.I.
Mailing Address: *Archdiocese of Washington*, P.O. Box 29260, 20017. Tel: 301-853-4520; Fax: 301-853-5346. Physical Location, 6330 Linway Ter., McLean, VA, 22101. Tel: 703-356-4473. Rev. Msgr. Bernd Kaut.

Association of Catholic Colleges & Universities, One Dupont Cir., Ste. 650, 20036. Tel: 202-457-0605.
E-mail: accu@accunet.org
Dr. Monika K. Hellwig, Exec. Dir.

Black Leadership and Christ's Kingdom Society, P.O. Box 4579, 20017. Tel: 202-529-4860; 301-888-2566; Fax: 202-529-7214. Rev. Robert S. Pittman, S.S.S., Dir. Total in Residence 8; Total Staff 14.

CARA, Center for Applied Research in the Apostolate, Georgetown University, 20057-1203. Tel: 202-687-8080; Fax: 202-687-8083.
E-mail: froehle@gunet.georgetown.edu
Web site: www.georgetown.edu/research/CARA
Dr. Bryan T. Froehle, Exec. Dir.

Carmelite Institute, 1600 Webster St., N.E., 20017. Tel: 202-635-3534; Fax: 202-635-3538.
E-mail: mail@carmeliteinstitute.org
Web site: www.carmeliteinstitute.org
Rev. John Welch, O.Carm., Pres. Tel: 202-526-1221 Ext. 118.

Carroll Manor Nursing & Rehabilitation Center, 1150 Varnum St., N.E., 20017-2180. Tel: 202-269-7100; Fax: 202-269-7816. Rev. Msgr. Leonard F. Hurley, Chap.

Catholic Biblical Association, Catholic University of America, 296 Leahy Hall, 20064. Tel: 202-319-5519; Fax: 202-319-4799.
E-mail: cua-cathbib@cua.edu
Web site: studentlife.cua.edu/students/org/cbib
Rev. Joseph Jensen, O.S.B., Exec. Sec.

Catholic Historical Society of Washington, 619 10th St. N.W., 20001. Mr. Thomas Lalley, Dir.

Catholic Information Center, 815 15th St., N.W., Ste. 102, 20005. Tel: 202-783-2062; Fax: 202-783-6667.
E-mail: frcjm@aol.com
Web site: www.cicdc.org
Rev. C. John McCloskey, III, S.T.D. Total Staff 3.

Center of Concern, 1225 Otis St. N.E., 20017. Tel: 202-635-2757; Fax: 202-832-9494.
E-mail: coc@coc.org
Web site: www.coc.org
Rev. James E. Hug, S.J., Pres.

Centro Maria, 650 Jackson St., N.E., 20017. Tel: 202-635-1697; Fax: 202-635-7246.
E-mail: centroma@erols.com
Web site: www.ymi-world.org
Sr. Ma. Cristina Lopez, R.M.I., Dir.

Christ Child Society of Washington, DC, Inc., 5101 Wisconsin Ave., N.W., 20016. Tel: 202-966-9250; Fax: 202-966-2880.
E-mail: mvmccs@aol.com
Margaret Mary Missar, Pres. A non-profit, volunteer organization of approximately 600 persons serving needing children, regardless of race or creed, through layette distribution, school counseling, camp and camperships and uniform and shoe programs. Volunteer-run except for clinical social workers and camp counselors. Total Assisted 16,000; Total staff 21.

The Christian Institute for the Study of Human Sexuality. 8901 New Hampshire Ave., Silver Spring, MD, 20903-3611. Tel: 301-422-5500; Fax: 301-422-5519.
E-mail: jesedcntr@aol.com
Rev. James J. Gill, S.J., M.D., Dir.

Christian Life Communities, Washington Area Promoters: 5040 Nebraska Ave., N.W., 20008-2938. Tel: 202-363-4593. Ms. Margaret Fox, 201 E. Wayne Ave., Silver Spring, MD, 20901-3808. Tel: 301-495-2969; Fax: 301-495-7318. Fred and Betty Leone.

Communio: International Catholic Review, 487 Michigan Ave., N.E., 20017. Tel: 202-526-0251; Fax: 202-526-1934.
E-mail: communio@aol.com
David L. Schindler, Contact Person.

The Community of St. John, 1215 Quincy St., N.E., 20017; Fax: 202-529-4253.
E-mail: dschundle@aol.com
David L. Schindler, Contact Person. Total in Residence 3.

Consolata Missionaries House of Studies, 1321 Otis St., N.E., 20017. Tel: 202-832-3582; Fax: 202-832-3583.
E-mail: imcwash@aol.com
Web site: www.geocities.com/imcwash
Revs. Mario Barbero, I.M.C., Rector; David K. Gikonyo, I.M.C.; Cyrus Karuthi, I.M.C.; Erasto C. Mgalama, I.M.C.; Ugo Pozzoli, I.M.C.; Deacon Javier Castro, I.M.C.; Bros. Benedict Ngala, I.M.C.; Felix O. Wao, I.M.C.

Council for Research in Values and Philosophy, The Catholic University of America, 20064; Fax: 202-319-6089; 800-659-9962.
E-mail: mclean@cua.edu
Web site: www.crvp.org
Rev. George F. McLean, O.M.I., Sec.

District of Columbia Detention Facility, Office of Chaplain, 1901 D St., S.E., 20003. Tel: 202-547-1715; 673-8400 (Office); Fax: 202-673-8480. Rev. F. Michael Bryant, Ph.D., Chap. Total in Residence 2,000; Total Staff 15.

Dorothy Day Catholic Worker, 503 Rock Creek Church Rd., N.W., 20010. Tel: 202-882-9649. Total Assisted 300; Total Staff 5.

Education for Parish Service Programs, Trinity College, 125 Michigan Ave., N.E., 20017-1094. Tel: 202-884-9020; Fax: 202-483-0253.
E-mail: WaltzB@TrinityDC.edu
Web site: eps.trinitydc.edu
Sr. Mary Ann Cook, S.N.D.deN., Pres.

Equestrian Order of the Holy Sepulchre of Jerusalem - Middle Atlantic Lieutenancy of the U.S., P.O. Box 29260, 20016-0260. Tel: 301-853-5309; Fax: 301-853-7681. His Eminence James Cardinal Hickey, Grand Prior; Edmund Pellegrino, Lieutenant; John C. Piunno, Chancellor.

Ethiopian and Eritrean Catholic Mission, USA, 1001 Lawrence St., N.E., 20017. Tel: 202-829-3934; Fax: 202-529-8523. Rev. Tesfamariam Baraki (Ethiopia), Dir.

Fellowship of Catholic Scholars, John Paul II Institute, 487 Michigan Ave., N.E., 20017. Tel: 219-631-8385; Fax: 219-631-6371. Gerard V. Bradley, Pres.

The Franciscan Federation, Third Order Regular of the Sisters and Brothers of the United States, 817 Varnum St., N.E., P.O. Box 29080, 20017. Tel: 202-529-2334; Fax: 202-529-7016.
E-mail: franfed@aol.com
Web site: www.franfed.org

Holy Childhood Association, 1720 Massachusetts Ave., N.W., 20036. Tel: 202-775-8637; Fax: 202-429-2987.
E-mail: holychildhood.usa@erols.com
Web site: www.holychildhoodusa.org
Rev. Francis W. Wright, C.S.Sp., National Dir.

Institute for Pastoral Renewal, Inc., c/o Jesuit Community, Georgetown University, 20057. Tel: 202-687-4164; Fax: 202-687-2045.
E-mail: 103102.1417@compuserve.com
Web site: paulcioffi@cs.com
Rev. Paul L. Cioffi, S.J., Dir. 900 Priests attend retreats, workshops, and seminars on liturgical renewal. None in residence. Two part-time staff members.

Institute of Carmelite Studies and ICS Publications, 2131 Lincoln Rd., N.E., 20002-1199. Tel: 800-832-8489; Fax: 202-832-8967.
E-mail: brpaquette@aol.com
Web site: www.icspublications
Revs. John Sullivan, O.C.D., Publisher; Kieran Kavanaugh, O.C.D., Editorial Asst.; Bros. Joseph Girouard, O.C.D., Journeyman Editor; Bryan Paquette, O.C.D., Business Mgr. & Promotion Dir.

Jesuit Conference, Inc., 1616 P St., N.W., Ste. 400, 20036-1405. Tel: 202-462-0400; Fax: 202-328-9212.
E-mail: usjc@jesuit.org
Web site: www.jesuit.org
Revs. Bradley M. Schaeffer, S.J., Pres.; James A. Casciotti, S.J., Exec. Sec.

The Jesuit Educational Center for Human Development. 8901 New Hampshire Ave., Silver Spring, MD, 20903-3611. Tel: 301-422-5500; Fax: 301-422-5519.
E-mail: jesedcntr@aol.com
Rev. James J. Gill, S.J., M.D., Dir. Total in Residence 80; Total Staff 16.

Jesuit Missions, Inc., 1616 P St., N.W., #400, 20036. Tel: 202-462-0400; Fax: 202-328-9212.
E-mail: Rryscavage@jesuit.org
Rev. Richard J. Ryscavage, S.J., Exec. Dir.

Jesuit Refugee Service, 1616 P St., N.W., #400, 20036-2286. Tel: 202-462-0400; Fax: 202-328-9212.
E-mail: LOBryon@jesuit.org
Web site: www.jesref.org
Rev. Richard J. Ryscavage, S.J., Natl. Dir.

Jesuit Secondary Education Association, 1616 P St., N.W., Ste. 400, 20036-1405. Tel: 202-667-3888; Fax: 202-387-6305.
E-mail: jsea@jsea.org
Web site: www.jsea.org
Revs. Joseph F. O'Connell, S.J., Pres.; Ralph E. Metts, S.J., Vice Pres.; Bernard L. Bogillette, Ph.D., Vice Pres.; Carolyn E. Lausch, Dir. of Research in Ignatian Pedagogy; La Chan M. Richardson, Admin. Asst.; Lorca Beede-Diaz, Exec. Sec. Total Staff 6.

Jesuit Social and International Ministries-National Office, 1616 P St., N.W., Ste. 400, 20036-1405. Tel: 202-462-0400; Fax: 202-328-9212.
E-mail: brobinson@jesuit.org
Web site: www.jesuit.org
Ms. British Robinson, National Dir.

Jesuit Volunteers International, P.O. Box 3756, 20007-0256. Tel: 202-687-1132; Fax: 202-687-5082.
E-mail: jvi@JesuitVolunteers.org
Web site: www.JesuitVolunteers.org
John Sealey, Acting Dir. Staff 8; Lay Volunteers 75; Foreign Missions 9.

The John Carroll Society, P.O. Box 50188, 20091. Tel: 709-573-3043; Fax: 703-573-3043. James W. Martin, Pres.; Rev. Msgr. Peter J. Vaghi.

McKenna House, 1501 Park Rd., N.W., 20010. Tel: 202-332-7333. Hagos Weldegiorgis, Prog. Mgr.

Missionary Vehicle Association, Inc. MIVA America. 1400 Michigan Ave., N.E., 20017. Tel: 202-635-3444; Fax: 202-526-0830.
E-mail: mivamerica@aol.com
Rev. Philip DeRea, M.S.C., National Dir.

The Morley Institute - CRISIS Magazine, 1814 1/2 N St., N.W., 20036. Tel: 202-861-7790; Fax: 202-861-7788.
E-mail: hudson@crisismagazine.com

Mount Carmel House, 471 G Pl., N.W., 20001. Tel: 202-289-6315; Fax: 202-289-1710.
Web site: www.mtcarmelhouse.org
Sr. Ann Forrest, O.S.F., Dir. Transitional Rehabilitative Housing for Women with 21 beds.

National Black Sisters' Conference, 3027 Fourth St., N.E., 20017. Tel: 202-529-9250; Fax: 202-529-9370.
E-mail: nbsc@igc.org
Sr. Patricia J. Chappell, S.N.D.deN., Pres. Total Staff 2.

National Catholic Conference for Interracial Justice, 1200 Varnum St., N.E., 20017-2796. Tel: 202-529-6480; Fax: 202-526-1262. Deacon Joseph M. Conrad, Jr., Exec. Dir.

National Christ Child Society, Inc., 5101 Wisconsin Ave., N.W., Ste. 304, 20016. Tel: 202-363-9516; 800-814-2149; Fax: 202-966-2880.
E-mail: nccs@nationalchristchildsoc.org
Web site: www.nationalchristchildsoc.org
Mrs. Victoria Riel, Pres., National Christ Child Society, Inc.; Mrs. Margaret Saffell, Exec. Dir. A national non-profit organization with 40 affiliate chapters consisting of over 7,000 member volunteers serving needy children since 1887.

National Institute for the Family, Inc., 3019 Fourth St., N.E., 20017. Tel: 202-462-2591; Fax: 202-462-6534.
E-mail: nacre@earthlink.net
Rev. Donald B. Conroy, S.T.L., Ph.D. (GBG), Exec. Dir.; Dr. Carolyn Gutowski, M.A.T., Ph.D., Assoc.Dir.; Dr. David M. Thomas, Ph.D., Research Dir. Research Program: Intergenerational Parish Ministry. Seminary and Lay Leadership Training in association with the Washington Theological Union.

Notre Dame Education Center, 101 Q St., N.E., 20002. Tel: 202-526-6420; Fax: 202-526-6423. Non-profit, tax exempt adult education program for low income people. The center enables adults to earn a high school diploma and trains them in computers.

Paul VI Institute for the Arts, 619 10th St. N.W., 20001-4587. Tel: 202-347-1450; Fax: 202-347-1401. Rev. Msgr. Michael diTeccia Farina.

Paulist Media Works, 3055 4th St., N.E., 20017-1102. Tel: 202-269-6064; Fax: 202-269-4304.
E-mail: sdonovan@paulist.org
Web site: www.paulist.org/pmw
Sue Donovan, Pres. & Exec. Producer; Jeanean Merkel, Dir. of Opers.; Rev. Lawrence A. Rice, C.S.P., Webmaster.

Paulist National Catholic Evangelization Assoc., 3031 Fourth St., N.E., 20017-1102. Tel: 202-832-5022; Fax: 202-269-0209.
Web site: www.paulist.org/pncea
Rev. Kenneth G. Boyack, C.S.P., Dir.; Sr. Susan Wolf, S.N.D., Exec. Dir.; Rev. Robert S. Rivers, C.S.P., Dir. of Parish & Diocesan Svcs.; Mr. Anthony Bosnick, Dir. Publications; Mr. Joseph Feakes, Dir. Devel.; Ms. Suzanne Nelson, Dir. Parish Based Evangelization; Mr. Mary Weaver, Dir. Finance & HR; Mr. Denny Marcotte, Gen. Business Mgr.; Mr. Michael Scarpato, Dir. Training; Sr. Marie A. Stelmach, Dir. of Prison Ministry.

Rosary Shrine of St. Jude. Dominican Fathers and Brothers. St. Dominic's Church, 501 Sixth St., S.W., 20024. Tel: 202-554-7863; Fax: 202-554-3492. Rev. Kenneth A. France-Kelly, O.P., Dir.

S.M.A. Social Concerns Department, 1242 Newton St., N.E., 20017. Rev. Edward Galvin, S.M.A., Dir.

S.N.D.B.C. Charitable Trust, 3037 Fourth St., N.E., 20017. Tel: 202-832-8770; Fax: 202-635-4912.
E-mail: sndbcunit@aol.com
Web site: www.SNDdeN.org
Sr. Ann Gormly, S.N.D., Trustee; Sr. Ann Theresa Sciannella, S.N.D., Trustee; Sr. Marie-Louise Rossi, S.N.D., Trustee.

St. Vincent Pallotti Center for Apostolic Development, Inc., 415 Michigan Ave., N.E., 20017-1518. Tel: 202-529-3330; 877-VOL-LINK (Toll free); Fax: 202-529-0911.
E-mail: pallotti01@aol.com
Web site: pallotti.cua.edu
Dr. Andrew D. Thompson, Natl. Dir. Total Assisted 15,000; Total Staff 4.

Sisters of Notre Dame de Namur Base Communities, Inc., 3037 Fourth St., N.E., 20017-1102. Tel: 202-832-8770; Fax: 202-635-4912.
E-mail: sndbcunit@aol.com
Web site: www.SNDdeN.org
Sisters 17.

Sovereign Military Order of Malta-Federal Association of the U.S.A., 1730 M St., N.W., Ste. 403, 20036. Tel: 202-331-2494; Fax: 202-331-1149.
E-mail: smomfausa@aol.com
Web site: www.smom.org
William J. Page, Pres.; Joseph J. Dempsey, Jr., Exec. Dir.

Spanish Catholic Center, Administrative Office, P.O. Box 11450, 20008-0650. Tel: 202-939-2437; Fax: 202-234-7323.
E-mail: sccdc@erols.com
Web site: www.centrocatolicohispano.org
Rev. Mark Poletunow, O.F.M.Cap., Dir.

Mt. Pleasant Branch, 1618 Monroe St., N.W., 20010. Tel: 202-939-2437; Fax: 202-234-7323. Medical Clinic. Tel: 202-939-2400; Fax: 202-232-1970. Dental Clinic. Tel: 202-939-2423; Fax: 202-234-7349. Social Services. Tel: 202-939-2414; Fax: 202-232-1970. Immigration Services. Tel: 202-939-2420; Fax: 202-234-7349.
Maryland Locations.

Langley Park Office, 1015 University Blvd. E., Silver Spring, MD, 20903. Tel: 301-431-3773; Fax: 301-431-0886. Medical Clinic. Tel: 301-434-3999; Fax: 301-434-5160. Social, Employment & Immigration Services. Tel: 301-431-3773; Fax: 301-431-0886.

Wheaton Branch, 2424 Reedie Dr., Wheaton, MD, 20903. Tel: 301-929-0207; Fax: 301-929-0594. Medical Clinic. Tel: 301-929-0207; Fax: 301-929-0594.

Gaithersburg Branch, 117 N. Frederick Ave., Gaithersburg, MD, 20877. Tel: 301-417-9113; Fax: 301-417-9895. Social, Employment & Immigration Services. Tel: 301-417-9113; Fax: 301-417-9895. Computer Courses. Tel: 301-330-3339; Fax: 301-417-9895.

Spiritual Life, 2131 Lincoln Rd., N.E., 20002-1199. Tel: 202-832-8489; Fax: 202-832-8967.
E-mail: editor@spiritual-life.org
Web site: www.spiritual-life.org
A Quarterly of Contemporary Spirituality. Bros. Edward O'Donnell, O.C.D., Editor; Bryan Paquette, O.C.D., Business Mgr.; Michael Stoegbauer, O.C.D., Promotion Mgr.; Joseph Girohard, O.C.D., Book Review Editor.

Woodstock Theological Center, Georgetown University, Box 571137, 20057-1137. Tel: 202-687-3532; Fax: 202-687-5837.
E-mail: wtc@gusun.georgetown.edu
Web site: www.georgetown.edu/centers/woodstock
Revs. James L. Connor, S.J., Dir.; Walter J. Burghardt, S.J.; Andrew J. Christiansen, S.J.; J. Leon Hooper, S.J.; Raymond B. Kemp; Gasper F. LoBiondo, S.J.; Joseph N. Tylenda, S.J.; James D. Redington, S.J.

BETHESDA, MD. *Alpha Omega, Inc. The Legion of Christ Inc.*, Our Lady of Bethesda Retreat Center, 7007 Bradley Blvd., 20817. Tel: 301-365-0612; Fax: 301-469-7522. Rev. Richard Gill, L.C.

Avondale Park Apartments, Inc., c/o Victory Housing, 5430 Grosvenor Ln., Ste. 210, 20814-2142. Tel: 301-493-6000; Fax: 301-493-9788.
E-mail: jspencer@victoryhousing.org
Web site: www.victoryhousing.org

Catholic Institute for the Psychological Science, Inc., 7007 Bradley Blvd., 20817. Tel: 203-281-4798. Bro. Juan Sabadell, L.C., Sec. & Treas.

Holy Family Hospital of Bethlehem Foundation, c/o James E. Murray, 4706 Fort Sumner Dr., 20816. Tel: 301-229-1394; Fax: 202-463-7315.

Institute for Evangelization, Inc., 7007 Bradley Blvd., Ste. 300, 20817. Tel: 301-767-6920; Fax: 301-767-6905.
E-mail: ife@familink.com
Web site: www.catechists.org
Steve Grundman, Exec. Dir.

Lay Women's Association, Villa Cortona, P.O. Box 34513, 20827. Tel: 301-251-5669; Fax: 481-150-8481.
E-mail: cdahlin@aol.com
Web site: www.sinkc.org
National Headquarters of the LWA.

Leadership Training Corp., 7007 Bradley Blvd., 20817. Tel: 301-365-7614. Rev. Juan Sabadell, Sec. & Treas.

National Consultants for Education, Inc., 7007A Bradley Blvd., Ste. 200, 20817. Tel: 301-767-6940; Fax: 301-767-6970.
E-mail: consult4ed@erols.com
Gretchen Brey, Bus. Mgr.

Natural Family Planning Center of Washington, DC, Inc., 8514 Bradmoor Dr., 20817-3810. Tel: 301-897-9323; Fax: 301-571-5267.
E-mail: hklaus@dgsys.com
Web site: www2.dgsys.com~hklaus
Sr. Hanna Klaus, M.D., Exec. Dir. Teen STAR & Holistic Sexuality Programs. Total in Residence 3; Total Staff 4.

GAITHERSBURG, MD. *Emmanuel, Inc.* Mailing Address: P.O. Box 2418, 20886-2418. Mother of God School, 20501 Goshen Rd., 20879. Tel: 301-990-2088; Fax: 301-947-0574.
E-mail: mogsadmn@erols.com
Web site: www.mogschool.com
Total Staff 25; Students 204.

GAMBRILLS, MD. *Center for International Resources, Inc. (CIRIMEX)*, 2344 Patuxent River Rd., 21054. Tel: 301-261-0417; 011-52-31-214878 (Mexico); Fax: 703-299-0903; 011-52-31-217738 (Mexico).
E-mail: 103110.1320@compuserve.com
Spanish language and Latin cultural training center. Sr. Kathryn A. Bissell, Chm., Exec. Dir., U.S.A.; Sr. Caridad Inda, Chm., Exec. Dir., Mexico.

HYATTSVILLE, MD. *Faith House, Inc.*, 4901 Eastern Ave., 20782. Tel: 301-559-5500; Fax: 301-853-6985.
E-mail: questions@saint-anns.com
Web site: www.saint-anns.com
Sr. Josephine Murphy, D.C., CEO. Total Assisted 8.

Prison Outreach Ministry, P.O. Box 2173, 20784. Tel: 310-773-1926. Rev. Michael Bryant, Chap. Total in Residence 1,800.

KENSINGTON, MD. *Inter Mirifica*, P.O. Box 241, 20895. Tel: 301-942-9577; Fax: 301-942-9572.
Web site: www.intermirifica.org
Rev. John Hardon, S.J.; Dolores A. O'Connell, Contact Person. Religious publications.

LANDOVER HILLS, MD. *Catholic Deaf Center*, 7202 Buchanan, 20784. Tel: 301-459-7464 (TTY/Voice); Fax: 301-459-8186.
E-mail: deafmindc@aol.com
Web site: www.hometown.aol.com/deafmindc
Rev. Gerard A. Trancone, Dir. Total in Residence 1; Total Staff 3.

POMFRET, MD. *Ministr-O-Media, Inc.*, St. Joseph Church, 20675. Tel: 301-870-3990. Rev. Msgr. John B. Brady, Pres.

POTOMAC, MD. *Youth for the Third Millennium*, P.O. Box 60001, 20859. Tel: 301-365-3205; Fax: 301-365-4241. Mr. Paul Bernetsky, Exec. Dir.

ROCKVILLE, MD. *Irish Apostolate USA, Inc.*, Shrine of St. Jude, 12701 Veirs Mill Rd., 20853. Tel: 301-933-3331; Fax: 301-933-6626.
E-mail: irishlink@erols.com
Web site: www.usairish.org
Rev. Timothy J. O'Sullivan, Dir.

SILVER SPRING, MD. *All Hallows Mission Fund, Inc.*, P.O. Box 3691, 20918.

Apostleship of Prayer, League of the Sacred Heart, 15107 Interlachen Dr. #722, 20906-5632. Tel: 301-438-3753; Fax: 301-924-6809. Rev. Gerard P. Bell, S.J., Archdiocesan Dir.

Archdiocese of Washington Division, The Blue Army. World Apostolate of Fatima, P.O. Box 4934, 20914. Tel: 301-949-4951; Fax: 301-933-3829. Harriet Noye, Pres.; Rev. Charles E. Pope, Spiritual Dir.

Camp St. Charles, Inc., 104 Bishop Dr., 20905. Tel: 301-384-5432; Fax: 301-384-5432.
E-mail: gwillis@frostcenter.com
Web site: www.np.eint.com/csc
Rev. Glen Willis, S.D.S. Total Assisted 600; Total Staff 35.

Catholics Committed to Support the Pope, 9402 Stateside Ct., 20903. Tel: 301-434-3245; 434-7763; Fax: 301-277-4047. George P. Morse, K.G.C.S.G., Pres. & Publisher. Councilors: His Eminence James Cardinal Hickey; His Eminence John Cardinal O'Connor; His Eminence Mario Luigi Cardinal Ciappi; His Eminence Edouard Cardinal Gagnon; His Eminence Alfonso Cardinal Lopez Trujillo; Dr. William E. May. Theological Advisors: Most Rev. William E. Lori; Rev. Msgr. Peter J. Elliott. Prepares and Distributes World-Wide Eleven-Volume Series Precis of Official Catholic Teaching for Rectors, Seminarians, Nuncios, Bishops and Others with Particular Application to Seminaries and Teaching.

Friends of John Paul II Foundation, 9700 Rosensteel Ave., 20910. Tel: 301-589-1857.
Web site: friendsofjohnpaul2foundation.org
Rev. Stanislaw Hajkowski, S.Ch.

Holy Cross Health Corp., 1500 Forest Glen Rd., 20910-1484. Tel: 301-754-7000; Fax: 301-754-7413.
E-mail: @holycrosshealth.org
Web site: www.holycrosshealth.org
Kevin Sexton, Pres. & CEO. Includes Holy Cross Hospital, Home Health Agency, and other services.

Leadership Conference of Women Religious in the U.S.A., 8808 Cameron St., 20910. Tel: 301-588-4955; Fax: 301-587-4575.
E-mail: director@lcwr.org
Web site: www.lcwr.org
Sr. Mary Mollison, C.S.A., Pres.; Sr. Kathleen Pruitt, C.S.J.P., Vice Pres.; Sr. Mary Christine Fellerhoff, C.S.A., Exec. Dir.; Sr. Bernadette McNulty, C.S.J., Treas.; Sr. Carole Shinnick, S.S.N.D., Sec.

Lumen Catechetical Consultants, Inc., P.O. Box 1761, 20915. Tel: 301-593-1066; Fax: 301-593-1689.
E-mail: lumen@lifeaftersunday.com
Web site: lifeaftersunday.com
Mr. John M. Capobianco, Pres. Provides Consulting & Production Services to Catholic Organizations; Assist in Development and Production of Catechetical Materials in Various Media. Publishes "Life After Sunday" Newsletter.

National Association for Treasurers of Religious Institutes, 8824 Cameron St., 20910-4152. Tel: 301-587-7776; Fax: 301-589-2897.
E-mail: natri@natri.org
Web site: www.natri.org
Sr. Lynn Marie Fangman, P.B.V.M., Pres.; Sr. Laura Reicks, R.S.M., Exec. Dir.

Saint Luke Institute, Inc., 8901 New Hampshire Ave., 20903. Tel: 301-445-7970; Fax: 301-422-5400.
E-mail: stever@sli.org
Rev. Stephen J. Rossetti, Ph.D., D. Min., Pres. The Institute is a licensed and accredited treatment center for priests and religious, and a center for education and research. Total Assisted 650; Total Staff 65.

SOAR, 1400 Spring St., Ste. 320, 20910-2735. Tel: 301-589-9811; Fax: 301-589-2482.
E-mail: info@soar-usa.org
Web site: soar-usa.org
Rita A. Hofbauer, Pres.

Washington Catholic Charismatic Service Committee, 13103 Tamarack Rd., 20904. Tel: 301-384-5568; Fax: 301-236-5204.
E-mail: lderoze@cs.com
Deacon Donald DeRoze, Dir.

WALDORF, MD. *Body of Christ Farm Community, Inc.*, 3325 Martha Pl., 20601. Tel: 301-888-2566; Fax: 301-888-2566.
E-mail: r.pittman@erols.com
Rev. Robert S. Pittman, S.S.S., Dir.

WEST HYATTSVILLE, MD. *Dominican Province of Nigeria*, Development and Mission Office, P.O. Box 5087, 20782. Tel: 202-526-4018; Fax: 202-526-4028.
E-mail: bfaneye@aol.com
Web site: dominicanprovineofnigeria
Rev. Benedict Faneye, O.P., Dir.

WHEATON, MD. *U.S. Foundation for the Congregation of the Holy Ghost and the Immaculate Heart of Mary, Inc. (The Spirit*, 11411 Amherst Ave., 20902. Tel: 301-933-6130; Fax: 301-942-5993. Rev. Leonard J. Tuozzolo, C.S.Sp., Exec. Dir.

RELIGIOUS INSTITUTES OF MEN REPRESENTED IN THE ARCHDIOCESE

For further details refer to the corresponding bracketed number in the Religious Institutes for Men or Women section.

[0140]—*The Augustinians.*—O.S.A.
[0200]—*Benedictine Monks.*—O.S.B.
[1350]—*Brothers of St. Francis Xavier.*—C.F.X.
[0330]—*Brothers of the Christian Schools.* (Baltimore Prov.).—F.S.C.
[0600]—*Brothers of the Congregation of Holy Cross.*—C.S.C.
[0400]—*Canons Regular of the Order of the Holy Cross.*—O.S.C.
[0470]—*The Capuchin Friars.* (Prov. of St. Augustine).—O.F.M.Cap.
[0270]—*Carmelite Fathers & Brothers.*—O.Carm.
[1140]—*Congregation of the Sacred Hearts of Jesus and Mary.*—SS.CC.
[0480]—*Conventual Franciscans.*—O.F.M.Conv.
[0260]—*Discalced Carmelite Fathers (Prov. of the Most Pure Heart of Mary).*—O.C.D.
[0520]—*Franciscan Friars (Commissariat of the Holy Land).*—O.F.M.
[0530]—*Franciscan Friars of the Atonement.*—S.A.
[0650]—*Holy Ghost Fathers (Eastern Prov.).*—C.S.Sp.
[0690]—*Jesuit Fathers and Brothers (Prov. of Maryland).*—S.J.
[0730]—*Legionaries of Christ.*—L.C.
[0740]—*Marian Fathers.*—M.I.C.
[0770]—*The Marist Brothers.*—F.M.S.
[0780]—*Marist Fathers.*—S.M.
[0800]—*Maryknoll.*—M.M.
[0850]—*Missionaries of Africa.*—M.Afr.
[0720]—*The Missionaries of Our Lady of La Salette.*—M.S.
[1210]—*Missionaries of St. Charles (Scalabrinians).*—C.S.
[0590]—*Missionaries of the Holy Apostle.*—M.Ss.A.
[0840]—*Missionary Servants of the Most Holy Trinity.*—S.T.
[0870]—*Montfort Missionaries.*—S.M.M.
[0910]—*Oblates of Mary Immaculate (Eastern Prov.).*—O.M.I.
[0920]—*Oblates of St. Francis de Sales.*—O.S.F.S.
[0430]—*Order of Preachers (Dominican) (Prov. of St. Joseph).*—O.P.
[1310]—*Order of the Holy Trinity (American Prov.).*—O.SS.T.
[1030]—*Paulist Fathers.*—C.S.P.
[1040]—*Piarist Fathers.*—Sch.P.
[0610]—*Priests of the Congregation of Holy Cross.* (Indiana Prov.).—C.S.C.
[1070]—*Redemptorist Fathers.* (Baltimore Prov.).—C.Ss.R.
[0700]—*St. Joseph Society of the Sacred Heart.*—S.S.J.
[0110]—*Society of African Missions.*—S.M.A.
[1260]—*Society of Christ.*—S.Ch.
[0990]—*Society of the Catholic Apostolate (Immaculate Conception Prov.).*—S.A.C.
[1200]—*Society of the Divine Savior.* (Milwaukee, WI).—S.D.S.
[0420]—*Society of the Divine Word.*—S.V.D.
[1290]—*Society of the Priests of Saint Sulpice.*—S.S.
[0640]—*Sons of the Holy Family.*—S.F.
[0560]—*Third Order Regular of Saint Francis (Prov. of the Immaculate Conception).*—T.O.R.

RELIGIOUS INSTITUTES OF WOMEN REPRESENTED IN THE ARCHDIOCESE

[1810]—*Bernardine Franciscan Sisters.*—O.S.F.
[0340]—*Carmelite Sisters of Charity.*—C.Ch.
[3803-05]—*Congregation of the Sisters of St. Joseph.* (Rockville Center, Brentwood, NY).—C.S.J.
[1920]—*Congregation of the Sisters of the Holy Cross.*—C.S.C.
[0760]—*Daughters of Charity of St. Vincent de Paul.*—D.C.
[0960]—*Daughters of Wisdom.*—D.W.
[0420]—*Discalced Carmelite Nuns.*—O.C.D.
[1070-13]—*Dominican Congregation of the Most Holy Rosary.* (Adrian, MI).—O.P.
[1050]—*Dominican Contemplative Nuns.*—O.P.
[1070-03]—*Dominican Sisters.* (Sinsinawa, WI).—O.P.
[1100]—*Dominican Sisters of Charity of the Presentation of the Blessed Virgin.*—O.P.
[1470]—*Franciscan Sisters of St. Joseph.*—H.F.S.J.
[1190]—*Franciscan Sisters of the Atonement.*—S.A.
[1250]—*The Institute of the Franciscan Sisters of the Eucharist.*—F.S.E.
[0410]—*Institute of the Sisters of Our Lady of Mt. Carmel.*—O.Carm.
[2330]—*Little Sisters of Jesus.*—L.S.J.
[2340]—*Little Sisters of the Poor.*—L.S.P.
[2345]—*Little Workers of the Sacred Hearts of Jesus and Mary.*—P.O.S.C.
[2490]—*Medical Mission Sisters.*—M.M.S.
[2720]—*Mission Helpers of the Sacred Heart.*—M.H.S.H.
[2710]—*Missionaries of Charity.*—M.C.
[2820]—*Missionary Sisters of Our Lady of Africa.*—M.S.O.L.A.
[2900]—*Missionary Sisters of St. Charles Borromeo.*—M.S.C.S.
[2760]—*Missionary Sisters of the Immaculate Conception of the Mother of God.*—S.M.I.C.
[2865]—*Missionary Sisters of the Sacred Heart of Our Lady of Guadalupe.*—M.S.C.Gpe.
[3530]—*Missionary Sisters, Servants of the Holy Spirit.*—S.Sp.S.
[3040]—*Oblate Sisters of Providence.*—O.S.P.
[]—*Oblate Sisters of the Most Holy Eucharist.*—O.S.S.E.
[3210]—*Poor Clares of Perpetual Adoration.*—P.C.P.A.
[3450]—*Religious of Jesus and Mary.*—R.J.M.
[3460]—*Religious of Mary Immaculate.*—R.M.I.
[2519]—*Religious Sisters of Mercy.* (Alma, MI).—R.S.M.
[3430]—*Religious Teachers Filippini.*—M.P.F.
[2970]—*School Sisters of Notre Dame.*—S.S.N.D.
[3520]—*Servants of the Holy Heart of Mary.*—S.S.C.M.
[3620]—*Sister Servants of Mary Immaculate.*—S.S.M.I.
[0500]—*Sisters of Charity of Nazareth.*—S.C.N.
[0570]—*Sisters of Charity of Seton Hill, Greensburg, Pennsylvania.*—S.C.
[1000]—*Sisters of Divine Providence.* (Melbourne,KY).—C.D.P.
[2575]—*Sisters of Mercy of the Americas.*—R.S.M.
[2990]—*Sisters of Notre Dame.*—S.N.D.
[3000]—*Sisters of Notre Dame de Namur.* (Maryland, Chesapeake & Base Communities Prov.).—S.N.D.deN.
[3360]—*Sisters of Providence of St. Mary-of-the-Woods, IN.*—S.P.
[3893]—*Sisters of Saint Joseph of Chestnut Hill, Philadelphia.*—S.S.J.
[4090]—*Sisters of Social Service.*—S.S.S.
[3718]—*Sisters of St. Ann.*—S.S.A.
[3740]—*Sisters of St. Casimir.*—S.S.C.
[1070-07]—*Sisters of St. Dominic of St. Cecilia.* (Nashville, TN).—O.P.
[1650]—*Sisters of St. Francis of Philadelphia.*—O.S.F.
[1600]—*Sisters of St. Francis of the Martyr St. George.*—O.S.F.
[3830-13]—*Sisters of St. Joseph.*—C.S.J.
[3850]—*Sisters of St. Joseph of Chambery.*—C.S.J.
[3890]—*Sisters of St. Joseph of Peace.*—C.S.J.P.
[3980]—*Sisters of St. Paul de Chartres.*—S.P.C.
[3150]—*Sisters of the Catholic Apostolate (Pallotine).*—S.A.C.
[1830]—*Sisters of the Good Shepherd.*—R.G.S.
[1950]—*Sisters of the Holy Family.*—S.S.F.
[1990]—*Sisters of the Holy Names of Jesus and Mary.*—S.N.J.M.
[2110]—*Sisters of the Humility of Mary.*—H.M.
[3320]—*Sisters of the Presentation of the Blessed Virgin Mary.*—P.B.V.M.
[1490]—*Sisters of the Third Franciscan Order.* (Syracuse, NY).—O.S.F.
[1720]—*Sisters of the Third Order Regular of St. Francis of the Congregation of Our Lady of Lourdes.*—O.S.F.
[2160]—*Sisters, Servants of the Immaculate Heart of Mary.*—I.H.M.
[4060]—*Society of the Holy Child Jesus.*—S.H.C.J.
[4070]—*Society of the Sacred Heart.*—R.S.C.J.
[4120-06]—*Ursuline Nuns of the Congregation of Paris.* (Toledo, OH).—O.S.U.
[4190]—*Visitation Nuns.*—V.H.M.

ARCHDIOCESAN CEMETERIES

WASHINGTON. *The Catholic Cemeteries of the Archdiocese of Washington, Inc.* 13801 Georgia Ave., Silver Spring, MD, 20906. Tel: 301-871-1300. All offices 9-4:30 P.M. Directors: Rev. Msgr. William F. O'Donnell; Mr. Frank Markowski.

Mount Olivet, 1300 Bladensburg Rd., N.E., 20002. Tel: 202-399-3000. Warren A. Meny.

St. Mary's, 2121 Lincoln Rd., N.E., 20002. Tel: 202-635-7444. Warren A. Meny.

CLINTON, MD, 8000 Woodyard Rd., 20735. Tel: 301-868-5141. Harry S. Lancaster, Jr.

LEONARDTOWN, MD, Box 379, 20650. Tel: 301-475-5005. Mr. John A. Spalding.

SILVER SPRING, MD. *Gate of Heaven*, 13801 Georgia Ave., 20906. Tel: 301-871-6500. Samuel E. French, Jr., Mgr.

St. John's Forest Glen, Rosensteel Ave., 20910. Tel: 301-871-6500. Samuel E. French, Jr.

NECROLOGY

† Bloom, R. Frederick, (Retired). —Died Sept. 4, 2000.

† Krastel, Francis W., St. Mary's City, MD St. Cecilia. —Died July 3, 2000.

† McMahon, John B., (Retired). —Died April 9, 2000.

† Montgomery, Rev. Msgr. James F., Washington, DC Church of the Annunciation. —Died Sept. 10, 2000.

† O'Brien, Joseph A., Rector, Washington, DC Cardinal O'Boyle Residence for Priests. —Died Sept. 19, 2000.

† Pagone, Joseph J., (Retired). —Died July 11, 2000.

† Studney, J. Edward, (Retired). —Died Oct. 12, 2000.

† Vail, John D., Newburg, MD Holy Ghost. —Died Jan. 7, 2000.

† Wells, Rev. Msgr. Thomas M., Germantown, MD Mother Seton. —Died June 8, 2000.

Diocese of Wheeling-Charleston

(Dioecesis Vhelingensis carolopolitanus)

Most Reverend

BERNARD W. SCHMITT, D.D.

Bishop of Wheeling-Charleston; ordained May 28, 1955; appointed Titular Bishop of Walla Walla and Auxiliary Bishop of Wheeling-Charleston May 31, 1988; ordained to the Episcopacy August 1, 1988; appointed Seventh Bishop of Wheeling-Charleston March 30, 1989; installed May 17, 1989. *Address all correspondence to: 1300 Byron St., P.O. Box 230, Wheeling, WV, 26003.*

Chancery Office: 1300 Byron St., P.O. Box 230, Wheeling, WV, 26003. Tel.: 304-233-0880; Fax: 304-233-0890.

Web site address: www.dwc.org

E-mail address: Jgallagher@dwc.org

ESTABLISHED AS DIOCESE OF WHEELING JULY 19, 1850.; REDESIGNATED DIOCESE OF WHEELING-CHARLESTON OCTOBER 4, 1974.

Square Miles 24,282.

Comprises the entire State of West Virginia.

For legal titles of parishes and diocesan institutions, consult the Chancery Office.

STATISTICAL OVERVIEW

Personnel	
Bishop	1
Retired Bishops	1
Priests: Diocesan Active in Diocese	113
Priests: Active Outside Diocese	2
Priests: Retired, Sick or Absent	42
Number of Diocesan Priests	157
Religious Priests in Diocese	57
Extern Priests in Diocese	6
Permanent Deacons in Diocese	28
Total Brothers	13
Total Sisters	260
Parishes	
Parishes	112
With Resident Pastor:	
Resident Diocesan Priests	73
Resident Religious Priests	20
Without Resident Pastor:	
Administered by Priests	20
Administered by Women Religious	10
Missions	25
Pastoral Centers	4
Professional Ministry Personnel:	
Brothers	8
Sisters	38
Lay Ministers	24
Welfare	
Catholic Hospitals	3
Total Assisted	407,954
Health Care Centers	2
Total Assisted	10,215
Homes for the Aged	4
Total Assisted	649
Residential Care of Children	1
Total Assisted	25
Day Care and Extended Day Care Centers	4
Total Assisted	440
Specialized Homes	1
Total Assisted	21
Special Centers for Social Services	8
Total Assisted	9,627
Educational	
Diocesan Students in Other Seminaries	9
Seminaries, Religious	9
Total Seminarians	9
Colleges and Universities	1
Total Students	1,497
High Schools, Diocesan and Parish	7
Total Students	1,668
High Schools, Private	1
Total Students	184
Elementary Schools, Diocesan and Parish	26
Total Students	5,186
Elementary Schools, Private	1
Total Students	184
Catechesis/Religious Education:	
High School Students	1,182
Elementary Students	4,334
Total Students Under Catholic Instruction	14,244
Teachers in the Diocese:	
Priests	2
Brothers	2
Sisters	12
Lay Teachers	185
Vital Statistics	
Receptions into the Church:	
Infant Baptism Totals	969
Adult Baptism Totals	257
Received into Full Communion	352
First Communions	1,440
Confirmations	1,522
Marriages:	
Catholic	223
Interfaith	312
Total Marriages	535
Deaths	1,133
Total Catholic Population	97,232
Total Population	1,815,787

Former Bishops—Rt. Rev. RICHARD VINCENT WHELAN, D.D., cons. March 21, 1841; Bishop of Richmond; transferred to Wheeling in 1850; died July 7, 1874.—Rt. Rev. JOHN JOSEPH KAIN, D.D., cons. May 23, 1875; transferred June 15, 1893, to the Titular Archiepiscopal See of Oxyrynchia; appt. July 6, 1893; Coadjutor "cum jure successionis" to the Most Rev. Archbishop of St. Louis, MO; created Archbishop of St. Louis, May 21, 1895; died Oct. 13, 1903.—Rt. Rev. PATRICK JAMES DONAHUE, D.D., cons. April 8, 1894; died Oct. 4, 1922.—Most Rev. THOMAS J. MCDONNELL, D.D., LL.D., cons. Sept. 15, 1947; appt. Auxiliary Bishop of New York, June 21, 1947; appt. Coadjutor of Wheeling, March 7, 1951; died Feb. 25, 1961.—Most Rev. JOHN J. SWINT, D.D., LL.D., appt. Auxiliary Bishop of Wheeling Feb. 22, 1922; cons. May 11, 1922; appt. Bishop of Wheeling Dec. 11, 1922; promoted to rank of Archbishop "ad personam," March 12, 1954; died Nov. 23, 1962.—Most Rev. JOSEPH H. HODGES, D.D., ord. Dec. 8, 1935; appt. Titular Bishop of Rusadus and Auxiliary of Richmond Aug. 8, 1952; cons. Oct. 15, 1952; transferred to Wheeling See as Coadjutor, "cum jure successionis", May 24, 1961; succeeded to the See Nov. 23, 1962; died Jan. 27, 1985.—Most Rev. FRANCIS B. SCHULTE, D.D., ord. May 10, 1952; appt. Titular Bishop of Afufenia and Auxiliary Bishop of Philadelphia; cons. Bishop Aug. 12, 1981; transferred to Wheeling July 31, 1985; transferred to Archdiocese of New Orleans Feb. 14, 1989.

Vicar General—Very Rev. JOHN R. GALLAGHER, V.G., *1300 Byron St., P.O. Box 230, Wheeling, 26003.* Tel: 304-233-0880.

Chancery Office—1300 Byron St., P.O. Box 230, Wheeling, 26003. Office Hours: Mon.-Fri. 8:30-4:30. Tel: 304-233-0880; Fax: 304-233-0890.

Chancellor—Very Rev. JOHN R. GALLAGHER, V.G.

Assistant to the Bishop—Very Rev. KEVIN M. QUIRK, J.C.D.

Diocesan Tribunal—All Rogatory Commissions should be addressed to the office of the Diocesan Tribunal., *P.O. Box 230, Wheeling, 26003.* Tel: 304-233-0880.

Judicial Vicar—Very Rev. KEVIN M. QUIRK, J.C.D.

Promoter Justitiae—Rev. PATRICK A. CONDRON, J.C.L.

Defensores Vinculi—Rt. Rev. JOHN M. LOGAN, O.Praen., J.C.L.

Diocesan Consultors—Very Rev. F. LEON ALEXANDER, V.F.; Rev. JOSEPH L. PETERSON; Very Revs. FREDERICK P. ANNIE; EDWARD M. BELL, V.F.; JOHN R. GALLAGHER, V.G.; Rev. P. EDWARD SADIE.

Vicar for Religious—Sr. MARIAN MADDEN, S.C., *1300 Byron St., P.O. Box 230, Wheeling, 26003.* Tel: 304-233-0880.

Delegate for Clergy—Rev. ROBERT G. PARK, *7 13th St., P.O. Box 230, Wheeling, 26003.* Tel: 304-233-0880.

Vicar for Clergy—Very Rev. FREDERICK P. ANNIE, Dir., *P.O. Box 230, Wheeling, 26003.* Tel: 304-233-0880; Fax: 304-233-0890.

Vicars Forane—Very Rev. STEPHEN D. DUBE, V.F., Wheeling Vicariate; Very Rev. PATSY J. IAQUINTA, V.F., Beckley Vicariate; Very Rev. F. LEON ALEXANDER, V.F., Charleston Vicariate; Very Rev. CARL E. BAUER, V.F., Clarksburg Vicariate; Very Rev. JOHN V. DIBACCO, JR., V.F., Martinsburg Vicariate; Very Rev. EDWARD M. BELL, V.F., Parkersburg Vicariate; Very Rev. WILLIAM A. ANDERSON, V.F., Weston Vicariate.

Finance Council—P.O. Box 230, Wheeling, 26003.

Finance Officer—Very Rev. JOHN R. GALLAGHER, V.G., *P.O. Box 230, Wheeling, 26003.* Tel: 304-233-0880.

Diocesan Offices and Directors

Apostleship of Prayer—Very Rev. KEVIN M. QUIRK, J.C.D., *P.O. Box 230, Wheeling, 26003.*

Archivist—Dr. TRICIA PYNE, Ph.D., *P.O. Box 230, Wheeling, 26003.*

Behavioral Counseling and Ministry—Rev. ROBERT G. PARK, *7 13th St., P.O. Box 230, Wheeling, 26003.* Tel: 304-233-0880.

Board of Education—Mr. JOHN ELCESSER, Pres., *P.O. Box 230, Wheeling, 26003.* Tel: 304-233-0880.

Building Committee—Mr. DONALD P. MORRIS, Building & Property Supvr., *P.O. Box 230, Wheeling, 26003.* Tel: 304-233-0880.

Catholic Community Services, Inc.—Mr. GEORGE E. SMOULDER, Exec. Dir., *7 13th St., P.O. Box 230, Wheeling, 26003-0030.* Tel: 304-233-0880. Northern Regional Office: *7 13th St., P.O. Box 230, Wheeling, 26003-0030.* Tel: 304-233-0880., *3101 Main St., Weirton, 26062-4711.* Tel: 304-748-1081. Western Regional Office: *8024 Court Ave., Hamlin, 25523.* Tel: 304-824-5069. Central Regional Office: *235 High St., Ste. 210, Morgantown, 26505.* Tel: 304-292-6597. Southern Regional Office: *P.O. Box 386, 865 Mercer St., Princeton, 24740-2909.* Tel: 304-425-4306. Eastern Regional Office: *20 S. Marsham St., Romney, 26757.* Tel: 304-822-5414.

Catholic University, Friends of—Very Rev. JOHN R. GALLAGHER, V.G., Dir., *P.O. Box 230, Wheeling, 26003.* Tel: 304-233-0880.

Cemeteries—Very Rev. JOHN R. GALLAGHER, V.G., *1300 Byron St., P.O. Box 230, Wheeling, 26003.* Tel: 304-233-0880.

Censor Librorum—Vacant.

West Virginia Council of Catholic Women—Sr. MARIAN MADDEN, S.C., Diocesan Moderator; BETTY CHARLES, *203 East Dr., Princeton, 24720.* Tel: 304-425-8665.

Stewardship and Development, Office of—Mr. BRYAN MINOR, Dir., *P.O. Box 230, Wheeling, 26003.* Tel: 233-0880.

Diaconal Council—Mr. TRUMAN A. LIPSCOMB, Chm., *P.O. Box 1, Masontown, 26542.* Tel: 304-864-5512 (H); 329-1063 (W).

Finance Office—Very Rev. JOHN R. GALLAGHER, V.G.; Mr. WILLIAM G. FISHER, Finance Dir.; Mr. JOHN L. HOFFMAN, Parish Finance Mgr., *1300 Byron St., P.O. Box 230, Wheeling, 26003.* Tel: 304-233-0880.

Hispanic Affairs—Rev. EUGENE J. WEBER, Dir., *299 School St., P.O. Box 871, Romney, 26757-0871.* Tel: 304-822-5561.

Holy Childhood Association—Sr. MARY DENISE DIETHRIECH, S.C., Dir., *11 13th St., P.O. Box 230, Wheeling, 26003.* Tel: 304-233-0880.

Home and Foreign Missions, Society for the Propagation of the Faith and Catholic Students' Mission Crusade—Very Rev. JOHN R. GALLAGHER, V.G., Diocesan Dir., *P.O. Box 230, Wheeling, 26003.*

Hospitals, Representative for Catholic—Sr. DIANE BUSHEE, S.A.C., *St. Mary's Hospital, 2900 First Ave., Huntington, 25702.* Tel: 304-526-1234.

Human Resources, Office of—Mr. MICHAEL NAU, Dir., *P.O. Box 230, Wheeling, 26003.* Tel: 304-233-0880.

Infirm Priests Association—Most Rev. BERNARD W. SCHMITT, D.D., Pres.; Very Rev. JOHN R. GALLAGHER, V.G., Sec. & Treas., *P.O. Box 230, Wheeling, 26003.* Tel: 304-233-0880.

Justice and Life, Office of—Ms. CAROL WARREN, Dir., *601 Delaware Ave., Charleston, 25301.* Tel: 304-343-3360.

Legion of Mary—Rev. WILLIAM J. STENGER, Spiritual Dir., *St. Jude Parish, 710 Jefferson Ave., P.O. Box 147, Glen Dale, 26038-0147.* Tel: 304-845-8165.

Migration and Refugee Services, Office of—Mrs. KIM KEENE, Dir., *1033 Quarrier St., Ste. 105, Charleston, 25301.* Tel: 304-343-1036.

Natural Family Planning—Ms. NANCY J. BOTKIN, R.N. Tel: 304-343-1036.

Office of Diocesan Planning and Pastoral Services—Rev. JEROME MCKENNA, C.P., *1300 Byron St., P.O. Box 230, Wheeling, 26003.* Tel: 304-233-0880.

Presbyteral Council—Very Rev. JOHN V. DIBACCO, V.F., Chm., *219 S. Queen St., Martinsburg, 25401.* Tel: 304-267-4893.

Priests Eucharistic League—Vacant.

Public Affairs Representative—G. NICHOLAS CASEY, JR., ESQ., *Ste. 700, One Valley Square, P.O. Box 1746, Charleston, 25326.* Tel: 304-345-2000.

Purchasing Agency, Diocesan—*1300 Byron St., P.O. Box 230, Wheeling, 26003.* Tel: 304-233-0880.

Religious Unity, Diocesan Commission for—Rev. JOHN H. MCDONNELL, Chm., *4807 Staunton Ave. S.E., Charleston, 25304-1951.* Tel: 304-925-2864.

Resettlement of Displaced Persons—Mr. GEORGE SMOULDER, Dir., *P.O. Box 230, Wheeling, 26003.* Tel: 304-233-0880.

Respect Life Office—Rev. D. BRIAN SHODA, *St. Leo Parish, Sulphur Spring Rd., P.O. Box 93, Inwood, 25428-0093.* Tel: 304-229-8945.

Scholarship Association—Mr. JOHN ELCESSER, Sec. & Treas., *P.O. Box 230, Wheeling, 26003.* Tel: 304-233-0880.

Scouting—Very Rev. STEPHEN D. DUBE, V.F., *229 California Ave., Weirton, 26062-3729.* Tel: 304-723-2054.

Catholic Charities, Department of—Mr. GEORGE SMOULDER, Exec. Dir., *7 13th St., P.O. Box 230, Wheeling, 26003.* Tel: 304-233-0880.

Vocations, Office of—Very Rev. JOHN R. GALLAGHER, V.G., Dir., *1300 Byron St., P.O. Box 230, Wheeling, 26003.* Tel: 304-233-0880. Rev. CASEY B. MAHONE, Assoc. Dir., *Immaculate Conception Parish, 329 Maryland Ave., P.O. Box 1726 - E, Fairmont, 26555.* Tel: 304-363-1840.

West Virginia State Catholic Conference—Very Rev. JOHN R. GALLAGHER, V.G., Dir., *1300 Byron St., P.O. Box 230, Wheeling, 26003.* Tel: 304-233-0880.

Women, Office of—Sr. MARIAN MADDEN, S.C., *1310 Byron St., P.O. Box 230, Wheeling, 26003-0010.* Tel: 304-233-0880.

Catholic Education and Parish Life

Catholic Education and Parish Life, Dept. of—Vacant, Exec. Dir., *11 13th St., P.O. Box 230, Wheeling, 26003-0030.* Tel: 304-233-0880.

Parish Care & Empowerment—Ms. BARBARA SUTTON, Diocesan Dir., *11 13th St., P.O. Box 230, Wheeling, 26003-0030.* Tel: 304-233-0880.

Catholic Charismatic Renewal—Very Rev. PATSY J. IAQUINTA, V.F., Liaison, *P.O. Box 608, Bluefield, 24701.* Tel: 304-327-5623.

Cursillo—Mr. EDWARD A. MARN, Lay Dir., *200 Church St., Paden City, 26159.* Tel: 304-337-8005.

Communications—Vacant, *1213 Byron St., P.O. Box 230, Wheeling, 26003-0030.* Tel: 304-233-0880.

Audio-Visuals—Mrs. CONNIE GORDER, *1213 Byron St., P.O. Box 230, Wheeling, 26003-0030.* Tel: 304-233-0880.

"Catholic Spirit, The"—Mr. THOMAS PAPEIKA, Editor, *1213 Byron St., P.O. Box 230, Wheeling, 26003-0030.* Tel: 304-233-0880.

Catechetical Ministries—CHERYL J. FOURNIER, Dir., *11 13th St., P.O. Box 230, Wheeling, 26003-0030.* Tel: 304-233-0880.

Evangelization—Mr. BRYAN S. REISING, Diocesan Dir., *1213 Byron St., P.O. Box 230, Wheeling, 26003-0030.* Tel: 304-233-0880.

Family Life—Vacant, Diocesan Dir., *11 13th St., P.O. Box 230, Wheeling, 26003-0030.* Tel: 304-233-0880.

Christian Family Movement—

Marriage Preparation—

Phoenix Group—

Liturgical Practices—Ms. MARIANNE ENGELMANN, Diocesan Dir., *11 13th St., P.O. Box 230, Wheeling, 26003-0030.* Tel: 304-233-0880.

Liturgical Art and Architecture Commission—Very Rev. WILLIAM A. ANDERSON, V.F., Chm.

Schools, Superintendent of—Mr. JOHN F. ELCESSER, Supt.; Mr. VICTOR A. BOERIO, Asst. Supr., Admin. & Finance, *11 13th St., P.O. Box 230, Wheeling, 26003-0030.* Tel: 304-233-0880.

Curriculum—Sr. MARY LOU PALAS, S.C., Diocesan Dir.

Religious Education in Catholic Schools—Sr. MARY DENISE DIETHRIECH, Diocesan Dir., *11 13th St., P.O. Box 230, Wheeling, 26003-0030.* Tel: 304-233-0880.

Ministry with Persons who are Disabled—Ms. ROSE WILKINS, Dir., *1213 Byron St., P.O. Box 230, Wheeling, 26003-0030.* Tel: 304-233-0880.

Youth and Young Adult Ministry—Mr. MICHAEL R. HALL, Diocesan Dir., *7 13th St., P.O. Box 230, Wheeling, 26003-0030.* Tel: 304-233-0880.

Campus Ministry—Mr. MICHAEL R. HALL, Diocesan Dir., *7 13th St., P.O. Box 230, Wheeling, 26003-0030.* Tel: 304-233-0880.

Teens Encounter Christ (TEC)—Mr. MICHAEL R. HALL.

Pastoral Services Liaisons for Catholic Education and Parish Life—

Wheeling Vicariate—Mr. JULIUS DEMASI, *Paul VI Pastoral Center, 667 Stone and Shannon Rd., Wheeling, 26003.* Tel: 304-277-1897.

Charleston Vicariate—Deacon JOHN HANNA, *John XXIII Pastoral Center, 100 Hodges Rd., Charleston, 25314-2281.* Tel: 304-342-5051; Fax: 304-347-9298.

Beckley Vicariate—Ms. ARLENE SMITH, *P.O. Box 653, Princeton, 24740.* Tel: 304-487-1838.

Clarksburg Vicariate—Ms. MARYANN TYRER, *510 E. Pike St., Clarksburg, 26301.* Tel: 304-624-5701.

Parkersburg Vicariate—Mr. ROBERT CHOINIERE, *521 Market St., #12, Parkersburg, 26101.* Tel: 304-424-3457, Ext. 207.

Weston Vicariate—Mrs. CAROLYN SANTILLI, *P.O. Box 278, Buckhannon, 26201.* Tel: 304-472-5698; Fax: 304-472-8170.

Martinsburg Vicariate—Ms. MARY POFFENBERGER, *P.O. Box 808, Charlestown, 25414.* Tel: 304-724-7074; Fax: 304-724-7175.

CLERGY, PARISHES, MISSIONS AND PAROCHIAL SCHOOLS

CITY OF WHEELING
(Ohio County)

1—ST. JOSEPH'S CATHEDRAL (1828). Including former parishes: Blessed Trinity, St. Joan of Arc, and Sacred Heart. Rev. Larry W. Dorsch, Rector. In res., Revs. John R. Gallagher; Robert G. Park; Frederick P. Annie.

Res., 14 13th St., 26003-0051. Tel: 304-233-4121; Fax: 304-233-4129.

School—Wheeling Catholic Elementary School, 26003. Tel: 304-233-1515.

2—BLESSED TRINITY (1931). Closed. Merged with St. Joseph's Cathedral.

3—CORPUS CHRISTI (1916), Rev. Eugene S. Ostrowski.

Res., 1516 Warwood Ave., 26003-7197. Tel: 304-277-2911; Fax: 304-277-2823.

School—Tel: 304-277-1220. Mrs. Erin Olexo, Prin.

Sisters of St. Joseph 2; Lay Teachers 10; Students 208.

Catechesis/Religious Programs—Students 123.

4—IMMACULATE CONCEPTION (ST. MARY) (1873). Closed. Merged with St. Alphonsus.

5—OUR LADY OF PEACE (Mt. Olivet) (1962), Rev. Raymond D. Jablinske.

Res., 2 Allendale Rd., Mt. Olivet, 26003-4601. Tel: 304-242-6575.

School—Tel: 304-242-1383. Mrs. C'Ann Reilly, Prin.

Lay Teachers 12; Students 244.

6—SACRED HEART (1903). Closed. Merged with St. Joseph's Cathedral.

7—ST. ALPHONSUS (1856). Including former parishes St. Mary and St. Ladislaus. Rev. Patrick A. Condron; Pastoral Assocs.: Bro. David Cooney, F.M.S. ; Douglas Breiding.

Church & Res. Address: 2111 Market St., 26003-3827. Tel: 304-232-4353.

School—Wheeling Catholic Elementary School, 26003. Tel: 304-233-1515.

Catechesis/Religious Programs—Students 133.

8—ST. JOAN OF ARC (1923). Closed. Merged with St. Joseph's Cathedral.

9—ST. LADISLAUS (1902). Closed. Merged with St. Alphonsus.

10—ST. MICHAEL'S (1897), Revs. James M. Sobus; Paul D. Yuenger; Deacon Paul J. Smith.

Res., 1225 National Rd., 26003-5791. Tel: 304-242-1560; Fax: 304-243-5710.

School—1221 National Rd., 26003. Tel: 304-242-3966.

Lay Teachers 24; Students 489.

Catechesis/Religious Programs—Tel: 304-242-5897.

Students 105.

11—ST. VINCENT DE PAUL'S (1895), Revs. James LaCrosse, S.M.; H. Joseph Wilhelm, S.M.; Deacons Paul H. Bischof, Jr.; Ronald J. Wojcicki.

Res., 2244 Marshall Ave., 26003-7440. Tel: 304-242-0406; Fax: 304-243-0837.

School—Tel: 304-242-5844.

Sisters 3; Lay Teachers 17; Students 259.

Catechesis/Religious Programs—Students 171.

Mission—Triadelphia, Ohio Co., Our Lady of Seven Dolors, Chapel Hill Rd., Triadelphia, 26059. Tel: 304-547-5342. [CEM]

CITY OF CHARLESTON
(Kanawha County)

1—SACRED HEART CO-CATHEDRAL (1866), Revs. P. Edward Sadie, Rector; Paul Hudock; Deacon John J. Lynch.

Res., 1032 Virginia St. E., 25301-2879. Tel: 304-342-8175; Fax: 304-344-3907. [CEM]

School—Tel: 304-346-5491. Mrs. Jean M. Cavalier, Prin.

Lay Teachers 24; Students 472.

Catechesis/Religious Programs—Students 133.

2—ST. ANTHONY (1905), Rev. Richard J. Zelik, O.F.M.Cap.; Deacon David Wuletich. In res., Rev. Kieran Quinn, O.F.M.Cap.

Res., 1000 Sixth St., 25302. Tel: 304-342-2716; Fax: 304-344-1678.

School—Tel: 304-346-8441. Ms. Myrtolyn English.

Lay Teachers 15; Students 126.

Catechesis/Religious Programs—Students 45.

3—ST. AGNES (1923), Rev. John H. McDonnell.

Res., 4807 Staunton Ave., S.E., 25304. Tel: 304-925-2836; Fax: 304-925-2854.

School—4801 Staunton Ave., S.E., 25304. Tel: 304-925-4341; Fax: 304-925-4423. Sr. Judith Ann Teufel, S.S.J., Prin.

Sisters of St. Joseph 1; Lay Teachers 15; Students 154.

Catechesis/Religious Programs—Students 47.

Convent—300 49th St., S.E., 25304. Tel: 304-925-2480.

OUTSIDE THE CITIES OF WHEELING AND CHARLESTON

Beckley, Raleigh Co., St. Francis De Sales (1907), Revs. Samuel S. Sacus; Pericles P. Malacaman; Deacons W. Donald Wise; John F. Ziolkowski.
Res., 614 S. Oakwood Ave., 25801. Tel: 304-253-3695 (Parish Office); 256-3594 (Rectory); Fax: 304-253-3694. [CEM]
School—Tel: 304-252-4087; Fax: 304-252-4087.
Lay Teachers 9; Students 124.
Catechesis/Religious Programs—626 South Oakwood Ave., 25801. Tel: 304-255-4694.
Students 190.

Beech Bottom, Brooke Co., Holy Family. Closed. See St. John, Wellsburg.

Belington, Barbour Co., Resurrection Mission (1978), Sr. Teresa Reddington, S.S.J., Dir.
Res., 701 Brown Ave., 26250. Tel: 304-823-1576. [CEM]
Catechesis/Religious Programs—Students 3.

Belle, Kanawha Co., St. John (1951), Rev. Albert Alexandrunas, O.F.M.Cap.
Res., 321 E. Tenth St., 25015. Tel: 304-949-3063.
Catechesis/Religious Programs—Students 26.
Mission—Coalburg, Kanawha Co., Good Shepherd, Box 16, East Bank, 25067. Tel: 304-595-6002. Sr. Clara Lill, R.C., Parochial Coord.

Benwood, Marshall Co., St. John's (1875), Rev. Gervase Cain, T.O.R.
Res., 622 Main St., 26031. Tel: 304-232-6455.
School—Sts. James and John Consolidated School, Tel: 304-232-1587. Mrs. Nanette Kennedy, Prin.
Lay Teachers 7; Students 50.

Berkeley Springs, Morgan Co., St. Vincent de Paul (1931), Rev. John S. Ledford; Deacon John W. Locke.
Res., 116 S. Washington St., 25411-1577. Tel: 304-258-1311; Fax: 304-258-7559. [CEM]
Catechesis/Religious Programs—Students 60.

Bluefield, Mercer Co., Sacred Heart (1895), Very Rev. Patsy Iaquinta, V.F.
Res., 1003 Wyoming St., P.O. Box 608, 24701-0608. Tel: 304-327-5623; Fax: 304-327-7769.

Bridgeport, Harrison Co., All Saints (1946), Rev. Harry N. Cramer.
Res., 317 E. Main St., 26330-1750. Tel: 304-842-2283; Fax: 304-842-2283.
School—Harrison Co. Catholic School System, Tel: 304-624-5129.
Catechesis/Religious Programs—Students 288.

Buckhannon, Upshur Co., Holy Rosary (1921), Rev. James B. McCafferty, S.M.
Church—35 Franklin St., P.O. Box 848, 26201-0848. Tel: 304-472-3414; Fax: 304-472-6502.
Rectory: 9 Lincoln Heights, 26021.
Catechesis/Religious Programs—Students 76.
Mission—Pickens, Randolph Co., Sacred Heart, (1902) Pickens, 26230. [CEM]

Camden, Lewis Co., St. Boniface (Leading Creek) (1875), Rev. John H. Finnell.
Res., Rte. 2, Box 25, 26338-9737. Tel: 304-269-1767. [CEM]
Chapel—St. Clara, St. Clare. [CEM]

Cameron, Marshall Co., St. Martin (1871), Rev. Walter M. Jagela.
Church—5 Fitzgerald Ave., 26033. Tel: 304-686-3551. [CEM]

Charles Town, Jefferson Co., St. James (1889). Includes St. Peter, Harper's Ferry. Rev. S. Brian Owens.
Res., 311 S. George St., P.O. Box 370, 25414-0370. Tel: 304-725-5558; Fax: 304-725-1685. [CEM]
Catechesis/Religious Programs—Students 325.

Cheat Lake, Monongalia Co., St. Luke (1980), Rev. Jeremiah F. McSweeney.
Res., 19 Jo Glen Dr., Morgantown, 26508-4434. Tel: 304-594-2353; Fax: 304-594-2359.
School—St. Francis Central Catholic School, 375 Birch St., Morgantown, 26505. Tel: 304-598-0133; Fax: 304-598-2690.
Catechesis/Religious Programs—Students 220.
Mission—Bruceton Mills, Preston Co., Mary Help of Christians, (1983) Bruceton Mills, 26525. Tel: 304-379-4220.

Chester, Hancock Co., Sacred Heart (1902), Rev. F. Rodger Hughes.
Res., 424 Fourth St., Box 313, 26034-0313. Tel: 304-387-0198.

Clarksburg, Harrison Co., Immaculate Conception (1864), Revs. Cesidio J. Federico; Timothy J. Grassi.
Res., 126 E. Pike St., 26301-2155. Tel: 304-622-8280. [CEM]
Parish Office: Tel: 304-622-8243.
Catechesis/Religious Programs—Tel: 304-622-8257.
Students 147.

St. James (1924), Rev. Robert A. Perriello; Deacons Anthony P. Santilli; Donald F. Molinari.
Res., 2107 Pride Ave., 26301-1819. Tel: 304-622-1668; Fax: 304-622-4618.
School—Harrison County Catholic School System, Tel: 304-623-1026; 622-9831.
Catechesis/Religious Programs—Tel: 304-624-5811.
Students 66.

Coalton, Randolph Co., St. Patrick Church (1918), Rev. Roy R. Schuster, O.F.M.Cap.
Res., 200 Church St., P.O. Box 99, 26257-0099. Tel: 304-636-5754. [CEM 4]
Catechesis/Religious Programs—Students 19.

Dunbar, Kanawha Co., Christ the King (1942), Rev. Dean G. Borgmeyer.
Mailing Address: 1508 Grosscup Ave., 25064-2925. Tel: 304-768-2527; Fax: 304-768-8547.
Res., 2219-22nd St., P.O. Box 339, Nitro, 25143. Tel: 304-755-0791.
Church—1504 Grosscup Ave., 25064-2925.
Catechesis/Religious Programs—Students 40.

Elkins, Randolph Co., St. Brendan (1897), Very Rev. William A. Anderson, V.F.
Res., P.O. Box 2205, 26241-2205. Tel: 304-636-0467; 636-0546. [CEM]
Catechesis/Religious Programs—Students 133.

Elkview, Kanawha Co., Our Lady of the Hills (1977), Rev. John P. McDonough.
Res., 4084 Indian Creek Rd., 25071-9366. Tel: 304-965-7670; Fax: 304-965-7670.
Mission—Clendenin, Kanawha Co., St. Anne, 63 Elk River Rd. S., Clendenin, 25045-9710. Tel: 304-548-7147. Co-Directors: Sr. Jacqueline Le Boeuf, S.S.A.; Sr. Marguerite St. Amand, S.S.A.

Fairmont, Marion Co.,

1—St. Peter the Fisherman, (1873). (Formerly St. Peter's, Fairmont. Merged with St. Joseph, Fairmont to form The New St. Peter the Fisherman, Fairmont.). Rev. Stanley T. Tuchalski.
Res., 407 Jackson St., 26554-2941. Tel: 304-363-7434; Fax: 304-363-7516. [CEM 2]
School—Fairmont Catholic Grade School, Tel: 304-363-5313.

2—Immaculate Conception, (1960), Rev. Casey B. Mahone; Sr. Stella Cronauer, C.S.J., Pastoral Assoc.
Church—329 Maryland Ave., P.O. Box 1726-E, 26555-1726. Tel: 304-363-5796; Fax: 304-366-4937.
School—Fairmont Catholic Grade School, Tel: 304-363-5313.
Catechesis/Religious Programs—Students 130.

3—St. Anthony, (1964), Rev. Gary P. Naegele. Pastoral Assocs: Sr. Miriam Sitarz, O.S.F.; Sr. Grace Koszela, O.S.F.
Res., 1660 Mary Lou Retton Dr., 26554-2099. Tel: 304-363-1328.
School—Fairmont Catholic Grade School, Tel: 304-363-5313.
Catechesis/Religious Programs—Students 23.

4—St. Joseph's, (1909). Merged with St. Peter's, Fairmont, to form The New St. Peter the Fisherman, Fairmont.

Farmington, Marion Co., St. Peter's (1921), Rev. Franklin A. Neville. Pastoral Assocs: Sr. Miriam Sitarz, O.S.F.; Sr. Grace Koszela, O.S.F.
Mailing Address: 204 Furbee Ave., Mannington, 26582-1399. Tel: 304-986-2321; Fax: 304-986-1419.
Catechesis/Religious Programs—Students 23.

Follansbee, Brooke Co., St. Anthony (1906), Rev. Anthony Cincinnati.
Res., 1017 Jefferson St., 26037-1334. Tel: 304-527-2286; Fax: 304-527-2548.
Catechesis/Religious Programs—Tel: 304-527-3966.
Students 175.

Fort Ashby, Mineral Co., Annunciation of the Lord (1981), Rev. James J. Chetock.
Res., P.O. Box 553, 26719-0553. Tel: 304-298-3392.
Catechesis/Religious Programs—Students 95.

Franklin, Pendleton Co., St. Elizabeth Ann Seton (1975), Rev. Mario R. Claro; Bros. William Lavigne, F.M.S.; Philip Oullette, F.M.S.; Luke Reddington, F.M.S.
Church & Res.—P.O. Box 890, 26807. Tel: 304-358-7012.

Gary, McDowell Co., Our Lady of Victory (1904), Revs. Thomas Hung Quac Tran, S.V.D.; Marek Pardon, S.V.D.; Sr. Mary Denise Thomas, I.H.M., Parochial Coord.
Church—Church St., P.O. Box 130, 24836-0130. Tel: 304-448-2749.
Res., HC 76, P.O. Box 402, Powhatan, 24877-0167. Tel: 304-862-3494. [CEM]

Gassaway, Braxton Co., St. Thomas (1973), Rev. Elmer Nadicksbernd, S.V.D.; Sr. Ruth Flynn, C.D.P., Pastoral Assoc.
Res., 624 Kanawha St., 26624-1208. Tel: 304-364-5895; Fax: 304-364-8099.

Glen Dale, Marshall Co., St. Jude (1968), Rev. William J. Stenger, Sr.
Res., 710 Jefferson Ave., P.O. Box 147, 26038-0147. Tel: 304-845-8165 (Rectory); 845-2646 (Office).
Catechesis/Religious Programs—Students 90.

Glenville, Gilmer Co., Good Shepherd (1958), Rev. Edwin G. Daschbach, S.V.D.
Res., 701 Mineral Rd., 26351-1310. Tel: 304-462-7130; Fax: 304-462-7130.
Catechesis/Religious Programs—Students 15.

Grafton, Taylor Co., St. Augustine (1852), Rev. Ronald G. Prechtl.
Res., 17 W. Washington St., 26354-1398. Tel: 304-265-1848; 265-3861 (Office); Fax: 304-265-2810. [CEM 2]
Catechesis/Religious Programs—Students 60.

Grant Town, Marion Co., St. Anthony's (1907). Closed. For inquiries for parish records contact the Chancery.

Harpers Ferry, Jefferson Co., St. Peter (1830). Closed. Merged with St. James, Charles Town.

Harrisville, Ritchie Co., Christ Our Hope (1980), Rev. Thomas Karachira; Sr. Kathryn Holohan, O.S.F., Pastoral Assoc.
Res., Rte. 1, Box 44A, 26362-9707. Tel: 304-643-4261.
Church—Pullman Rd. & E. Main, 26362-9707.
Chapel—Pennsboro, St. Joseph, (1870). [CEM]

Hinton, Summers Co., St. Patrick (1874), Rev. Harold F. Dunn, M.S.A.
Res., 309 Second Ave., 25951-0008. Tel: 304-466-3966. [CEM][JC 2]
Mission—Alderson, Greenbrier Co., St. Mary of the Greenbrier, David St., P.O. Box 441, Alderson, 24910. Tel: 304-445-7967.

Holden, Logan Co., St. Mary's (1961). Consolidated with Our Lady of Mount Carmel, Logan, to form St. Francis of Assisi, Logan.

Huntington, Cabell Co.,

1—St. Joseph's, (1872), Rev. Msgr. Lawrence J. Luciana; Rev. M. Julian Marneni.
Res., 1304 Sixth Ave., P.O. Box 369, 25708. Tel: 304-525-5202; Fax: 304-525-0951. [CEM]
School—520 Thirteenth St., 25701. Tel: 304-522-2644; Fax: 304-522-2512. Mr. Todd Faller, Prin.
Lay Teachers 7; Students 158.

2—Our Lady of Fatima, (1952), Rev. Joseph L. Peterson; Sr. Mary Michael, S.A.C., Pastoral Assoc.
Res., 545 Norway Ave., 25705. Tel: 304-525-0866; Fax: 304-525-0390.
School—535 Norway Ave., 25705. Tel: 304-523-2861; 523-2863. Mrs. Marcia McDonald, Prin.
Lay Teachers 13; Students 181.

3—Sacred Heart, (1934), Rev. Andrew G. Kranyc; Sr. Mary Terence Wall, S.A.C., Pastoral Assoc.
Res., 2015 Adams Ave., 25704-1419. Tel: 304-429-5234; 429-4318 (Rectory); Fax: 304-429-4319.

4—St. Peter Claver, (1937) (African American), Rev. Andrew G. Kranyc; Sr. Katherine Shreve, S.S.J., Pastoral Assoc.
Res., 828 Fifteenth St., 25701. Tel: 304-523-7311.
Catechesis/Religious Programs—Students 14.

Hurricane, Putnam Co., Catholic Church of the Ascension (1980), Rev. J. Stephen Vallelonga.
Res., 905 Hickory Mill Rd., 25526. Tel: 304-562-5816; Fax: 304-562-3589.
Catechesis/Religious Programs—Students 220.

Huttonsville, Randolph Co., St. John Bosco (1948), Rev. Roy R. Schuster, O.F.M.Cap., Admin.; Deacon Louis J. Belldina.
Res., Rte. 1, Box 9D, 26273-9737. Tel: 304-335-2165; Fax: 304-335-2165.
Station—Huttonsville Correctional Center, Tel: 304-338-6323.

Inwood, Berkeley Co., St. Leo (1982), Rev. D. Brian Shoda.
Res., Sulphur Springs Rd., P.O. Box 93, 25428-0093. Tel: 304-229-8945; Fax: 304-229-9755.
Catechesis/Religious Programs—Students 360.

Keyser, Mineral Co., Assumption (1874), Rev. Ivan M. Lebar, T.O.R.; Bro. Luke D. Stone, T.O.R., Pastoral Assoc. In res., Bro. Stan J. Prenatt, T.O.R.
Res., 34 James St., 26726-2721. Tel: 304-788-2488; Fax: 304-788-0647. [CEM]
Catechesis/Religious Programs—Students 84.

Kingwood, Preston Co., St. Sebastian's (1914), Revs. Mark Ward, C.P.; Vincent Segotta, C.P.; Deacon Truman A. Lipscomb.
Res., P.O. Box 519, 26537. Tel: 304-329-1519; Fax: 304-329-2546. [CEM 3]
Church—322 E. Main St.

Catechesis/Religious Programs—Students 122.
Mission—Terra Alta, Preston Co., St. Edward.

Logan, Logan Co., St. Francis of Assisi (1996), Rev. David J. Schmitt; Mrs. Connie Bazzilla, Pastoral Assoc.
Res., 561 Main St., 25601-3899. Tel: 304-752-3017.
Church—Stratton St., 25601.
Catechesis/Religious Programs—Students 40.

Lubeck, Wood Co., St. Monica's (1976), Rev. John H. Fahey.
Res., R.R. 1, Box 362, Washington, 26181-9615. Tel: 304-863-5580. [CEM]
Church—State Rte. 68, Lubeck Washington.
Catechesis/Religious Programs—Students 70.

Madison, Boone Co., St. Mary, Queen of Heaven (1957), Rev. James E. O'Connor.
Res., P.O. Box 467, 25130-0467. Tel: 304-369-4538; Fax: 304-369-6268.
Church—51 Madison Ave., 25130.
Catechesis/Religious Programs—Students 35.
Missions—Chapmanville, Logan Co., St. Barbara, (1979) H.C. 74, Box 3018, Chapmanville, 25508-9522. Tel: 304-855-7962. Sr. Carol Symon, S.N.D., Parochial Coord.; Whitesville, Boone Co., St. Joseph the Worker, (1958) P.O. Box 444, Whitesville, 25209-0444. Tel: 304-854-2997; Fax: 304-854-1258. Sr. Ann Marie Liston, S.J.C., Pastoral Coord.

Man, Logan Co., St. Edmund (1961), Rev. David J. Schmitt; Mrs. Connie Bazzilla, Pastoral Assoc.
Mailing Address: 110 Bridge St., 25635.
Res., 561 Main St., Logan, 25601-3899. Tel: 304-752-3017.
Church—110 S. Bridge St., 25635. Tel: 304-583-2476; Fax: 304-239-3131.
Catechesis/Religious Programs—Students 5.

Mannington, Marion Co., St. Patrick's (1897), Rev. Franklin A. Neville. Pastoral Assocs: Sr. Miriam Sitarz, O.S.F.; Sr. Grace Koszela.
Res., 204 Furbee Ave., 26582-1399. Tel: 304-986-2321; Fax: 304-986-1419.
Catechesis/Religious Programs—Students 43.
Mission—Littleton, Wetzel Co., Assumption of the Blessed Virgin Mary, (1859) Long Drain Rd., Littleton, 26581. [CEM 2]

Marlinton, Pocahontas Co., St. John Neumann (1977), Rev. William J. Kuchinsky.
Res., 714 10th Ave., 24954-1314. Tel: 304-799-6778; Fax: 304-799-6778. [CEM]
Mission—Bartow, Pocahontas Co., St. Mark the Evangelist, (1977) Rt. 92-250, Bartow, 24920.

Martinsburg, Berkeley Co., St. Joseph's (1803), Very Rev. John V. DiBacco, Jr., V.F.
Res., 233 S. Queen St., 25401-3213. Tel: 304-264-8947; Fax: 304-263-7357. [CEM]
School—Tel: 304-267-6447; Fax: 304-267-7394.
Daughters of Charity of Vincent de Paul 2; Lay Teachers 24; Students 388.
Catechesis/Religious Programs—Students 205.
Mission—Hedgesville, Berkeley Co., St. Bernadette, 205 W. Main St., P.O. Box 11, Hedgesville, 25427. Tel: 304-754-7830; Fax: 304-754-7830.

Masontown, Preston Co., St. Zita's (1962), Revs. Mark Ward, C.P.; Vincent Segotta, C.P.; Deacon Truman A. Lipscomb.
Res., P.O. Box 519, Kingwood, 26537-0519. Tel: 304-329-1519; Fax: 304-329-2546.
Church—Tel: 304-864-5512.
Catechesis/Religious Programs—Students 24.

Maysel, Clay Co., Risen Lord (1972), Rev. Elmer Nadicksbernd, S.V.D.
Mailing Address: HC 60, Box 7, 25133. Tel: 304-587-4740.
Res., 624 Kanawha St., Gassaway, 26624.

McMechen, Marshall Co., St. James (1900), Rev. Gervase Cain, T.O.R.
Church—326 Logan St., 26040-1096. Tel: 304-232-1227.
School—Sts. James and John Consolidated Schools, Tel: 304-232-1587. Mrs. Nanette Kennedy, Prin.
Lay Teachers 7; Students 60.

Monongah, Marion Co., Holy Spirit (1975), Rev. James J. Neville, S.J.
Res., 687 Maple Ter., 26554-1116. Tel: 304-534-3020; Fax: 304-534-5910. [CEM]

Montgomery, Fayette Co., Immaculate Conception (1888), Rev. Paul J. Wharton.
Res., P.O. Box 65, 25136. Tel: 304-442-2101; Fax: 304-442-4578.
Mission—Boomer, Fayette Co., St. Anthony Shrine, (1928). Tel: 304-779-2561.

Moorefield, Hardy Co., Epiphany of the Lord (1980), Rev. Mario R. Claro.
Church, HC65, Box 400, 26836. Tel: 304-434-2547. [CEM]

Morgantown, Monongalia Co., The New St. Theresa & St. Elizabeth Ann Seton (1901). (Formerly St. Theresa's, Morgantown. Merged with St. Elizabeth Ann Seton, Westover to form The New St. Theresa & St. Elizabeth Ann Seton, Morgantown.). Rev. Colombo F. Bandiera; Sr. Nancy White, S.S.J., Pastoral Assoc.
Res., 44 Beechurst Ave., 26505-4912. Tel: 304-296-5353; Fax: 304-296-8200.
School—St. Francis Central Catholic School, 375 Birch St., 26505. Tel: 304-598-0133.
Catechesis/Religious Programs—Students 90.

St. John University Parish, Newman Hall (1966), Revs. Donald X. Higgs; William K. Matheny, Jr.; Deacon Joseph Prentiss.
Res., 1481 University Ave., 26505-5598. Tel: 304-296-8231; Fax: 304-296-4650.
School—St. Francis Central Catholic School, 375 Birch St., 26505. Tel: 304-598-0133; Fax: 304-598-2690.
Catechesis/Religious Programs—Students 160.

Moundsville, Marshall Co., St. Francis Xavier's (1857), Revs. Ronan J. Deegan, T.O.R.; Albert Driesch, T.O.R.
Res., 912 Seventh St., 26041. Tel: 304-845-1593.
School—(Grades K-8). Tel: 304-845-2562; Fax: 304-845-0016. Mrs. Catherine Frame.
Lay Teachers 11; Students 127; Preschool 19.
Catechesis/Religious Programs—Students 66.
Station—Northern Regional Jail and Correctional Facility, Tel: 304-843-4067.

Mullens, Wyoming Co., St. John the Evangelist (1923), Rev. John C. Reich; Sr. Katherine O'Neil, I.H.M., Pastoral Assoc.
Res., 13 Terry St., 25882-1624. Tel: 304-294-8128.
Catechesis/Religious Programs—Students 13.
Mission—Pineville, Wyoming Co., Holy Cross, Rte. 10, P.O. Box 927, Pineville, 24874. Tel: 304-732-6199; 732-8302 (Rectory).

New Cumberland, Hancock Co., Immaculate Conception (1904), Rev. Ronald A. Getsinger.
Res., 1016 Ridge Ave., P.O. Box 666, 26047-0666. Tel: 304-564-5068.
Catechesis/Religious Programs—Students 36.

New Martinsville, Wetzel Co., St. Vincent de Paul (1901), Rev. Charles J. Schneider, V.F.; Sr. Rose Anne Krantz, S.D.P., Pastoral Assoc.
Res., 21 Rosary Rd., 26155-1602. Tel: 304-455-4615; Fax: 304-455-4617.
Catechesis/Religious Programs—Students 169.

Nitro, Kanawha Co., Holy Trinity (1962), Rev. Dean G. Borgmeyer.
Mailing Address: P.O. Box 339, 25143-0339. Tel: 304-755-0792.
Res., 2219-22nd St., 25143-0339. Tel: 304-755-0791; Fax: 304-755-3473.
Catechesis/Religious Programs—Students 84.
Mission—Bancroft, Putnam Co., St. Patrick, 207 Jefferson St., P.O. Box 238, Bancroft, 25011. Tel: 304-586-3485; Fax: 304-586-3485.

Oak Hill, Fayette Co., SS. Peter and Paul (1906), Revs. Harold W. Moore; Nguyen That Son.
Res., 129 Elmore St., 25901-2628. Tel: 304-465-5445; Fax: 304-465-5445. [CEM]
School—Tel: 304-465-5045; Fax: 304-465-5045. Miss Karen Modzik, Prin.
Lay Teachers 8; Students 121.
Catechesis/Religious Programs—Students 114.

Ona, Cabell Co., St. Stephen (1980), Rev. Bert W. Valdes.
Res., 2491 James River Tpke., 25545-9722. Tel: 304-743-3234.

Paden City, Tyler and Wetzel Cos., Mater Dolorosa (1921), Rev. Joseph Ezharath (India).
Res., 302 E. Main St., 26159-1736. Tel: 304-337-9837.
Mission—Middlebourne, Tyler Co., St. Lawrence, P.O. Box 267, Middlebourne, 26149. Tel: 304-758-4649.

Parkersburg, Wood Co., St. Francis Xavier's (1853), Rev. Michael P. O'Reilly.
Res., 532 Market St., 26101-5144. Tel: 304-422-3145; Fax: 304-422-3142. [CEM 3]

St. Margaret Mary (1923), Very Rev. Edward M. Bell, V.F.; Rev. Neil Buchlein; Deacons Gerald B. Goetemann; George B. Showalter.
Res., 2500 Dudley Ave., 26101-2695. Tel: 304-428-1262; Fax: 304-422-4905.
Catechesis/Religious Programs—Tel: 304-422-4905.
Students 188.

Petersburg, Grant Co., St. Mary's, Rev. Mario R. Claro. Parochial Coordinators: Bros. William Lavigne, F.M.S.; Philip Oullette, F.M.S.; Luke Reddington, F.M.S.
Rectory: 5 Pierpont St., 26847-1633. Tel: 304-257-1057; Fax: 304-257-9442.
Church—4 Grant St., 26847. [JC]
Catechesis/Religious Programs—Students 23.

Philippi, Barbour Co., St. Elizabeth Parish and Newman Center (1953), Rev. Damian P. Drass, T.O.R.
Res., College Hill, Rte. 3, Box 257, 26416-9581. Tel: 304-457-2641. Deacon A. Ray Shaw, III; Res., Rte. 3, Box 38-I, 26416-9581. Tel: 304-457-1408.
Catechesis/Religious Programs—Students 35.

Point Pleasant, Mason Co., Sacred Heart (1948), Rev. Regis Schlick, O.F.M.Cap.
Res., 2222 Jackson Ave., 25550-2004. Tel: 304-675-4602.
Catechesis/Religious Programs—Students 30.
Mission—Mason, Mason Co., St. Joseph, (1856) 3rd St. & Pomeroy St., Mason, 25260. [CEM]

Powhatan, McDowell Co., Sacred Heart (1895), Revs. Thomas Tran, S.V.D.; Marek Pardon, S.V.D.
Res., HC 76, Box 402, 24877. Tel: 304-862-3494.
Catechesis/Religious Programs—Students 10.

Princeton, Mercer Co., Sacred Heart (1915), Rev. Francis A. O'Kruta.
Res., 507 Harrison St., 24740-3198. Tel: 304-425-3664; Fax: 304-425-3676.
Catechesis/Religious Programs—Students 152.
Campus Ministry, Concord College—Athens, 24712. Tel: 304-384-9502.

Rainelle, Greenbrier Co., Sacred Heart, Rev. Harold F. Dunn, M.S.A.
Res., 309-2nd Ave., Hinton, 25951. Tel: 304-438-8687.
Chapel—Springdale, Sacred Heart. (1876). [CEM]
Station—Rainelle.

Ravenswood, Jackson Co., St. Matthew (1957), Rev. John H. Fahey; Sr. Rosanne Fogarty, O.S.M., Parochial Coord.
Res., 600 Crooks Ave., 26164-1312. Tel: 304-273-2175; Fax: 304-273-2175.

Richwood, Nicholas Co., Holy Family (1904), Revs. William F. Seli, S.M.; Jerome D. Rawa, S.M.; Bro. Richard McKenna, S.M.
Res., 4 Maple St., 26261-1318. Tel: 304-846-2873; Fax: 304-846-2873. [CEM]

Ridgeley, Mineral Co., St. Anthony (1916), Rev. James J. Chetock.
Res., Box 553, Fort Ashby, 26719-0553. Tel: 304-298-3392.
Catechesis/Religious Programs—Students 17.

Romney, Hampshire Co., Our Lady of Grace (1951), Rev. Eugene J. Weber.
Res., 299 School St., P.O. Box 871, 26757-0871. Tel: 304-822-5561; Fax: 304-822-5561.
Catechesis/Religious Programs—Students 47.

Ronceverte, Greenbrier Co., St. Catherine of Siena (1892), Rev. Richard W. Shoda, J.C.L.
Res., 407 Walnut St., 24970-1233. Tel: 304-647-4515.
Missions—Lewisburg, Greenbriar Co., St. Louis, King of France, (1977); Union, Monroe Co., St. Andrew the Apostle, (1977) P.O. Box 347, Union, 24983-0347. Tel: 304-772-5849. Sr. Molly Bauer, S.S.J., Parochial Coord.
Station—Williamsburg, Mary Immaculate, (1879). [CEM]
Chaplaincy—WV School of Osteopathic Medicine, Lewisburg.

St. Albans, Kanawha Co., St. Francis of Assisi (1947), Rev. Patrick M. McDonough.
Res., 1023 Sixth Ave., 25177. Tel: 304-727-3033; Fax: 304-727-6640. [CEM]
School—Tel: 304-727-5690; Fax: 304-727-5690.
Priests 1; Lay Teachers 8; Students 131.
Catechesis/Religious Programs—Students 43.

St. Joseph Settlement, Marshall Co., St. Joseph's (1853), Rev. P.J. (Steve) Saju.
Res., R.D. 1, Box 203, Proctor, 26055. Tel: 304-455-4303; Fax: 304-455-4303. [CEM]

St. Marys, Pleasants Co., St. John (1913), Rev. Thomas Karachira (India).
Mailing Address: P.O. Box 338, 26170-0338.
Res., 310 Washington St., 26170-1313. Tel: 304-684-7669. [JC]
Catechesis/Religious Programs—Students 35.

Salem, Harrison Co., Sacred Heart (1915), Rev. Peter A. Giannamore.
Res., Rte. 23 S. & Rte. 50, P.O. Box 248, 26426-0248. Tel: 304-782-2277. [CEM]

Shepherdstown, Jefferson Co., St. Agnes (1794), Rev. T. Matthew Rowgh.
Res., 108 S. Duke, P.O. Box 1603, 25443-1603. Tel: 304-876-6436.
Catechesis/Religious Programs—Students 100.

Shinnston, Harrison Co., St. Ann's (1923), Rev. Karl R. Wohinc.
Res., 610 Pike St., 26431-1451. Tel: 304-592-2733.
Mission—Spelter, Harrison Co., Holy Family, (1925) Spelter, 26438.

Sistersville, Tyler Co., Holy Rosary (1898), Rev. Joseph Ezharath (India).
Church—519 Main St., 26175-1405. Tel: 304-652-6381; 337-9837 (Rectory).

South Charleston, Kanawha Co., Blessed Sacrament (1941), Very Rev. F. Leon Alexander, V.F.; Deacon John J. Hanna.
Res., 305 E St., 25303-1597. Tel: 304-744-5523; Fax: 304-744-5669.
Catechesis/Religious Programs—Students 182.

Spencer, Roane Co., Holy Redeemer (1957), Rev. David Glockner; Bro. Michael Springer, Glmy.
Res., 424 Parkersburg Rd., 25276-1024. Tel: 304-927-2013; Fax: 304-927-3008.
Catechesis/Religious Programs—Students 45.
Missions—Elizabeth, Wirt Co., St. Elizabeth of Hungary, (1977) Hwy. 14, P.O. Box 191, Elizabeth, 26143. Tel: 304-275-4226. Sr. Nancy Fortkort, O.S.F., Pastoral Assoc.; Grantsville, Calhoun Co., Jesus Christ, Prince of Peace, (1977) Hwy. 16, P.O. Box 416, Grantsville, 26147. Tel: 304-354-7937. Trish Russell, Pastoral Assoc.

Star City, Monongalia Co., St. Mary's (1952), Rev. Carl E. Bauer; Jeanne Howell, Pastoral Assoc.; Deacon John Shultz.
Res., 3344 University Ave., P.O. Box 4204, 26504-4204. Tel: 304-599-3747; Fax: 304-599-3769. [CEM]
School—St. Francis Central Catholic School, 375 Birch St., Morgantown, 26505. Tel: 304-598-0133; Fax: 304-598-2690.
Catechesis/Religious Programs—Tel: 304-598-0702.
Students 179.

Stonewood, Harrison Co., Our Lady of Perpetual Help (1955), Revs. Edward Sabo, T.O.R.; Terrence T. Smith, T.O.R.
Res., 707 Third St., 26301-4854. Tel: 304-623-2334; Fax: 304-623-9988.

Summersville, Nicholas Co., St. John The Evangelist (1849), Revs. William F. Seli, S.M.; Jerome D. Rawa, S.M.
Res., 1704 Webster Rd., 26651-1096. Tel: 304-872-2554. [CEM]

Thomas, Tucker Co., St. Thomas Aquinas (1897), Rev. Lino P. Ebejer.
Res., P.O. Box 300, 26292-0300. Tel: 304-463-4488; Fax: 304-463-4488. [CEM]
Church—Brown St. & Third St., 26292.
Catechesis/Religious Programs—Students 38.
Mission—Parsons, Tucker Co., Our Lady of Mercy, (1960) 221 Water St., P.O. Box 97, Parsons, 26287-0097. Tel: 304-478-4575. Sr. Electa Schmidt, I.H.M., Parochial Coord.

Vienna, Wood Co., St. Michael's (1956), Rev. Anthony J. Conlon; Deacon James R. Kelly.
Res., 5501 Fourth Ave., 26105-2007. Tel: 304-295-6109. [JC]
Catechesis/Religious Programs—Students 151.

War, McDowell Co., Christ the King (1942), Revs. Xavier Cooney, S.V.D.; Alex Jebadu, S.V.D.
Church—P.O. Box 728, 24892-0728. Tel: 304-875-3827.

Wayne, Wayne Co., Nativity of Our Lord (1980), Rev. M. Julian Marneni.
Church—Rte. 2, Box 2502, 25570-9738. Tel: 304-272-5832; 525-5202; Fax: 304-272-6176.
Catechesis/Religious Programs—Students 11.
Station—Genoa Christian Center, P.O. Box 67, Genoa, 25517. Tel: 304-385-4583; Fax: 304-385-4583. Sr. Monica Schieber, C.PP.S., Dir.

Webster Springs, Webster Co., St. Anne's (1920), Rev. Dave Cornet, S.V.D.
Res., 160 McGraw, 26288-1134. Tel: 304-847-5512.

Weirton, Brooke Co., St. Paul's (1910), Revs. Thomas E. Schiffer; Anthony Thurston; Deacon Edwin T. Mullavey.
Res., 140 Walnut St., 26062-4521. Tel: 304-748-6710 (Rectory); 748-4118. [CEM]
School—Tel: 304-748-5225; Fax: 304-748-4163. Mr. Frank Carey, Prin.
Lay Teachers 11; Students 210.

Sacred Heart of Mary, Hancock Co., (1916) (Polish), Rev. D. Kent Durig; Deacon Richard W. Mankowski.
Office: 200 Preston Ave., 26062-3994. Tel: 304-723-7175; Fax: 304-723-7176.
School—Tel: 304-723-1560; Fax: 304-723-7176.
Lay Teachers 7; Students 57.
Catechesis/Religious Programs—Students 75.

St. Joseph the Worker, Hancock Co., (1957), Very Rev. Stephen D. Dube, V.F.; Rev. Benedict E. Kapa.
Res., 229 California Ave., 26062-3790. Tel: 304-723-2054; 723-2057; Fax: 304-723-3961.
School—Tel: 304-723-1970; Fax: 304-723-5122. Mr. Alfred Boniti, Prin.
Lay Teachers 12; Students 226.
Catechesis/Religious Programs—Students 147.

Welch, McDowell Co., St. Peter, Revs. Xavier Cooney, S.V.D.; Alex Jebadu, S.V.D.
Res., 111 Virginia Ave., 24801-2424. Tel: 304-436-2014.
Chapel—Kimball, Our Lady Queen of the Apostles. (1959).

Wellsburg, Brooke Co., St. John The Evangelist (1857), Rev. Walter M. Jagela.
Res., 1300 Charles St., 26070-1408. Tel: 304-737-0429. [CEM]
School—Tel: 304-737-0511; Fax: 304-737-0511. Mrs. Tonette Alward, Prin.
Lay Teachers 9; Students 103.
Catechesis/Religious Programs—Students 65.
Mission—Beech Bottom, Brooke Co., Holy Family, (1980). (Formerly Power) Box 7, Beech Bottom, 26030-0007. Tel: 304-394-5929; Fax: 304-394-1256. Sr. Ellen Dunn, O.P., Parochial Coord.

Weston, Lewis Co., St. Patrick's (1845), Rev. James J. Murphy.
Res., 222 Center Ave., 26452-2029. Tel: 304-269-3048; Fax: 304-269-5547.
School—Tel: 304-269-5547. Sr. Eileen Marie Sinnott, S.S.J., Prin.
Lay Teachers 6; Students 106.
Catechesis/Religious Programs—Students 91.
Chapels—Sandfork, St. Bernard. [CEM]
Roanoke, St. Bridget. [CEM]
Chaplaincy—Weston State Hospital, Tel: 304-269-3048.

Westover, Monogalia Co., St. Elizabeth Ann Seton (1977). Merged with St. Theresa, Morgantown, to form The New St. Theresa & St. Elizabeth Ann Seton, Morgantown.

West Union, Doddridge Co., St. Patrick's (1856), Rev. Peter A. Giannamore.
Res., 503 W. Main St., 26456-1129. Tel: 304-873-2547.
Catechesis/Religious Programs—Students 16.

White Sulphur Springs, Greenbrier Co., St. Charles Borromeo (1903), Rev. Joseph F. O'Reilly; Deacon William B. Strange Tel: 304-536-2333.
Res., P.O. Box 598, 24986. Tel: 304-536-1813. [CEM]
Chapel—Sweet Springs, St. John The Evangelist. (1859). [CEM 2]

Whitesville, Boone Co., St. Joseph the Worker (1958). Closed. See St. Mary Queen of Heaven, Madison.

Williamson, Mingo Co., Sacred Heart (1911), Rev. Vincent E. Joseph.
Res., 110 W. Fourth Ave., 25661-3112. Tel: 304-235-2982; Fax: 304-235-3027.
School—126 W. Fourth Ave., 25661. Tel: 304-235-3027.
Sisters 1; Lay Teachers 4; Students 50.
Catechesis/Religious Programs—Students 50.

On Duty Outside the Diocese:
Reverend Fathers—
Cullinane, Jeremiah J., Neuhoff Catholic Center, Southern Methodist University, 3057 University Blvd., Dallas, TX 75205. Tel: 214-987-0044
Fryer, Patrick L., Chief of Chaplains, (PERS 04), 2 Navy Annex, Washington, DC 20370-5000. Tel: 703-614-4326 (Office); 924-1068 (Residence)
Tuchalski, Stanley, Catholic University of America, Washington, D.C. 20017

Absent on Sick Leave:
Reverend Fathers—
Cupp, Edwin
Lee, Michael G.
McCormick, Michael

Absent on Leave:
Reverend Fathers—
Meuret, Donald
Romage, George

Retired:
Reverend Monsignors—
Staud, Sylvester W., Welty Apartments #411, 1276 National Rd., Wheeling, WV 26003-5743

Reverend Fathers—
Arnold, Andrew L., Welty Apartments #402, 1276 National Rd., Wheeling, WV 26003
Bandiera, Colombo F., 442 Ash St., Morgantown, WV 26505-6668
Beyer, Leroy O., 889 Wess Rd., Mineral Point, PA 15942
Briggs, Everett F., Maple Terrace, P.O. Box 9066, Monongah, WV 26555-9066
Brunner, Frank J., Welty Apartments #404, 1276 National Rd., Wheeling, WV 26003
Campi, Vincent L., P.O. Box 856, Frederick, MD 21701
Cann, Hilarion V., 103 Allison Ave., Bridgeport, WV 26330
Chalany, Robert, 17 Cedar Lake Rd., Chester, CT 06412
DeMeester, Peter, 1100 Willard Dr., Blacksburg, VA 24060
Dene, Joseph, 6 Cool View Ln., Bridgeport, WV 26330
Dobosz, Emil J., Good Shepherd Nursing Home, 159 Edgington Ln., Wheeling, WV 26003
Duhaime, John N., 327-13th Ave., P.O. Box 116, Rainelle, WV 25962
Gillooly, Patrick J., 517 S. Green St., Berkeley Springs, WV 25411
Jacobs, Eugene S., Box 54, Loretto, PA 15940
Lombard, Roy A., Welty Apartments, #405, 1276 National Rd., Wheeling, WV 26003-5743
Lukas, Andrew F., P.O. Box 201, Fairmont, WV 26555-0201
Lydon, Leo B., 236 Parkway Dr., Clarksburg, WV 26301
Maguire, Seamus J., Church of Our Lady of Perpetual Help, Harris Promenade, San Fernando, Trinidad, W.I.
Mascioli, Joseph M., P.O. Box 11, Morgantown, WV 26505
McCallister, Charles, P.O. Box 1309, Elkins, WV 26241
McGinnity, John C., 604 Geddings Dr., Myrtle Beach, SC 29577-6029
Nash, Robert C., P.O. Box 793, Deltaville, VA 23043
Nolte, William J., Jr., P.O. Box 1302, Chester, WV 23831
O'Donovan, Donal, Westwood, Chapel St., Dummanway, Co. Cork, Ireland
O'Loughlin, Eugene P., 362 Redford Ct., Greystone, Co. Wicklow, Ireland
Ralph, John, 1757 State St., Biloxi, MS 39531
Schmitt, Eugene A., c/o Ray Schmitt, 43 Williamsburg Cir., Wheeling, WV 26003
Snincak, Stephen A., 2104 Hyde Park St., Sarasota, FL 33579
Werner, Leo E., 324 Kenna Dr., South Charleston, WV 25309
Wojtus, Anthony, P.O. Box 3803, Charleston, WV 24338-3803

Permanent Deacons:
Belldina, Louis J., St. John Bosco, Huttonsville
Bischof, Paul H., Jr., St. Vincent de Paul, Wheeling
Goetemann, Gerald B., St. Margaret Mary, Parkersburg
Grant, Russell J., St. William, Naples, FL
Hanna, John J., Blessed Sacrament, South Charleston
Higgs, Henry F., On Leave
Iafrate, Albert L., Catholic Charities Neighborhood Center, Wheeling
Kelly, James R., St. Michael, Vienna
Lilly, Robert B.
Lipscomb, Truman A., St. Sebastian, Kingwood
Locke, John W., St. Vincent de Paul, Berkeley Springs
Lynch, John J., Sacred Heart, Charleston
Maher, John F., Christ Our Hope, Harrisville; St. John, St. Marys
Mankowski, Richard W., Sacred Heart of Mary, Weirton
Molinari, Donald F., St. James, Clarksburg
Moses, John T., St. Joseph Cathedral, Wheeling
Nedeff, George A., St. Francis Xavier, Parkersburg
Prentiss, Joseph J., St. John University, Morgantown
Santilli, Anthony P., St. James, Clarksburg
Shaw, A. Ray, St. Elizabeth, Phillipi
Showalter, George B., St. Margaret Mary, Parkersburg
Shultz, John A., St. Mary, Star City
Smith, Paul J., St. Michael, Wheeling
Strange, William B., Jr., St. Charles Borromeo, White Sulphur Springs
Wise, W. Donald, St. Francis De Sales, Beckley
Wojcicki, Ronald J., St. Vincent de Paul, Wheeling
Wuletich, David E., St. Anthony, Charleston
Ziolkowski, John F., St. Francis De Sales, Beckley

INSTITUTIONS LOCATED IN THE DIOCESE

[A] COLLEGES AND UNIVERSITIES

WHEELING. *Wheeling Jesuit University*, 316 Washington Ave., 26003-6243. Tel: 304-243-2000; Fax: 304-243-4349.
E-mail: gflundy@wju.edu
Web site: www.wju.edu
For a complete listing, refer to the Colleges and Universities section.

[B] HIGH SCHOOLS, CENTRAL

WHEELING. *Central Catholic High School*, 75-14th St., 26003. Tel: 304-233-1660; Fax: 304-233-3187. Dr. Joseph F. Viglietta, Ph.D., Prin. Sisters of St. Joseph 1; Lay Teachers 33; Students 485.

CHARLESTON. *Charleston Catholic High School*, 1033 Virginia St. E., 25301. Tel: 304-342-8415; Fax: 304-342-1259. Mrs. Debra K. Sullivan, Prin. Lay Teachers 34; Students 480.

CLARKSBURG. *Harrison Co. Catholic School System. Notre Dame High School.* (Grades 7-12), 127 E. Pike St., 26301. Tel: 304-623-1026; Fax: 304-623-1026.
E-mail: ndhs@aol.com
Dr. Carroll Kelly Morrison, Prin. Lay Teachers 10; Students 149.

HUNTINGTON. *St. Joseph Central Catholic High School*, 600 13th St., 25701. Tel: 304-525-5096; Fax: 304-525-5083.
E-mail: tfaller@st.joseph.org
Mr. Tod Faller, Prin.; Rev. Msgr. Lawrence Luciana, Pastor. Lay Teachers 16; Students 185.

MCMECHEN. *Bishop Donahue Memorial High School.* (For Marshall Co.), 325 Logan St., 26040. Tel: 304-233-3850; Fax: 304-233-8677. Bro. Thomas Kelly, Prin. Lay Teachers 15; Students 100.

PARKERSBURG. *Parkersburg Catholic Junior-Senior High School*, 3201 Fairview Ave., 26101. Tel: 304-485-6341; Fax: 304-485-4697.
E-mail: pchs@pchs1.com
Mr. Michael R. Hattman, Prin. Lay Teachers 22; Students 250.

WEIRTON. *Madonna High School*, 150 Michael Way, 26062. Tel: 304-723-0545; Fax: 304-723-0564.
E-mail: csistilli@weirtonmadonna.org
Web site: www.weirtonmadonna.org
Cathy Sistilli, Prin. Lay Teachers 11; Students 169.

[C] HIGH SCHOOLS, PRIVATE

WHEELING. *Mount de Chantal Visitation Academy, Inc.*, 410 Washington Ave., 26003. Tel: 304-233-3771; Fax: 304-233-8598.
E-mail: Mountdec@ovnet.com
Web site: www.mountdechantal.org
Day School. (Girls Grades PreK-12, Boys Grades PreK-6). Visitation Nuns. Sisters 6; Lay Teachers 23; Students 173.

[D] ELEMENTARY SCHOOLS, CENTRAL

WHEELING. *Wheeling Catholic Elementary School*, 77-14th St., 26003. Tel: 304-233-1515; Fax: 304-233-1516.
E-mail: jstechly@acess.k12.wv.us
Consolidation of the following parishes: St. Alphonsus; St. Ladislaus; St. Mary; St. Joseph; Sacred Heart. Sr. Mary Palmer, S.S.J., Pres. Sisters 1; Lay Teachers 8; Students 85.

BENWOOD. *SS. James and John Elementary School*, 52 Seventh St., 26031. Tel: 304-232-1587; Fax: 304-232-4707.
E-mail: saintjj@stratuswave.net
Mrs. Nannette Kennedy, Prin. Consolidation of the following parishes: St. John, Benwood; St. James, McMechen. Lay Teachers 6; Students 75.

CLARKSBURG. *Harrison County Catholic School System. St. Mary's Central Grade School.* (Grades K-6), 107 E. Pike St., 26301. Tel: 304-622-9831; Fax: 304-623-1026. Consolidation of the following parishes: All Saints, Bridgeport; Immaculate Conception, Clarksburg; St. James, Clarksburg; Our Lady of Perpetual Help, Stonewood; St. Ann, Shinnston; Sacred Heart, Salem. Lay Teachers 11; Students 135.

FAIRMONT. *Fairmont Catholic Grade School.* (Grades K-8), 416-A Madison St., 26554. Tel: 304-363-5313; Fax: 304-363-7701.
E-mail: FCSSSchool@mteer.com
Web site: www.fairmontcatholicschool.com
Consolidation of the following parishes: St. Peter; Immaculate Conception; St. Anthony. Sr. Mary DiDomenico, S.S.J., Prin. Sisters 1; Lay Teachers 15; Students 248.

MORGANTOWN. *St. Francis de Sales Central Elementary School*, 375 Birch St., 26505. Tel: 304-598-0133; Fax: 304-598-2690.
E-mail: pfoley@access.k12.wv.us
Web site: www.falcon.sfcc.pvt.k12.wv.us
Sr. Patricia Ann Foley, C.S.J., Prin. Sisters 2; Lay Teachers 27; Students 397.

PARKERSBURG. *Parkersburg Catholic Elementary School*, 810 Juliana St., 26101. Tel: 304-422-6694; Fax: 304-422-2469.
E-mail: pces@pchs1.com
Mr. Kevin Simonton, Prin. Lay Teachers 9; Students 178.

[E] PASTORAL CENTERS

WHEELING. *Paul VI Pastoral Center*, 667 Stone & Shannon Rd., 26003. Tel: 304-277-3300; Fax: 304-277-4320.
E-mail: paulvi@hgo.net
Capacity 72.

CHARLESTON. *John XXIII Pastoral Center*, 100 Hodges Rd., 25314. Tel: 304-342-0507; Fax: 304-342-4786.
E-mail: johnxxiii@newwave.net
Deacon John J. Lynch, Dir. Capacity 166.

HUTTONSVILLE. *Bishop Hodges Pastoral Center*, Rte. 1, Box 9D, 26273. Tel: 304-335-2165; Fax: 304-335-2165.
E-mail: bhpc@neumedia.net
Web site: www.neumedia.net~bhpc
Deacon Louis J. Belldina, Dir. Capacity 72.

KEARNEYSVILLE. *Priest Field Pastoral Center*, State Rte. 51, Box 133, 25430. Tel: 304-725-1435. Rev. Theodore Midile, T.O.R., Dir. Capacity 110.

[F] ASSOCIATED SPIRITUAL AND PASTORAL LIFE CENTERS

WHEELING. *Maryhill Hermitage*, 2264 Marshall Ave., 26003.

St. Joseph Center-Mount St. Joseph, Pogue Run Rd., 26003. Tel: 304-232-8160; Fax: 304-232-1404.
E-mail: SSJWHG@aol.com
Sr. Teresa Fleckenstein, S.S.J., Dir. Overnight Capacity 8; Daytime Capacity 25.

St. Thomas More Center, 26003. Mailing Address: P.O. Box 230, 26003. 2264 Marshall Ave., 26003. Tel: 304-233-0880; Fax: 304-233-0890.
E-mail: jelerick@dwc.org
Accommodations for youth retreats, cursillo and area retreats.

Sisters of the Visitation, 410 Washington Ave., 26003. Tel: 304-232-3771. Legal Title: *Sisters of the Visitation of Holy Mary of Mount de Chantal, Inc.*

MORGANTOWN. *Our Lady of Good Counsel Franciscan Friary*, 493 Tyrone Rd., 26508-2960. Tel: 304-594-1714; Fax: 304-594-9247. Rev. Jude J. Mili, O.F.M., S.T.D., Dir. In res. Rev. John Agapito, C.P.M.; Deacon George J. Doerr.

OLD FIELDS. *Holy Spirit Hermitage*, H.C. 66, Box 20, 26845-9201. In res. Rev. Richard B. Hite, M.S.A.; Sr. Joan Sutherland, Diocesan Hermit.

[G] GENERAL HOSPITALS

WHEELING. *Bishop Joseph H. Hodges Continuous Care Center*, Medical Park, 26003. Tel: 304-243-3800; Fax: 304-243-3398
For a complete listing, refer to the Hospitals section.

Wheeling Hospital, Medical Park, 26003. Tel: 304-243-3000
For a complete listing, refer to the Hospitals section.

BUCKHANNON. *St. Joseph's Hospital of Buckhannon, Inc.*, 1 Amalia Dr., 26201. Tel: 304-473-2000; Fax: 304-472-6620.
Web site: www.stj.net
For a complete listing, refer to the Hospitals section.

HUNTINGTON. *St. Mary's Hospital of Huntington, Inc.*, 2900 First Ave., 25702. Tel: 304-526-1234; Fax: 304-526-1538.
Web site: www.st-marys.org
For a complete listing, refer to the Hospitals section.

[H] NURSING HOMES

WHEELING. *Good Shepherd Nursing Home*, 159 Edgington Ln., 26003. Tel: 304-242-1093; Fax: 304-242-1121
For a complete listing, refer to the Special Care Facilities section.

[I] HOMES FOR AGED

WHEELING. *Welty Home for the Aged, Inc.*, 21 Washington Ave., 26003-6261. Tel: 304-242-5233; Fax: 304-242-1312
For a complete listing, refer to the Special Care Facilities section.

[J] HEALTH SERVICES

HUNTINGTON. *Pallottine Health Services, Inc.*, 2900 First Ave., 25702. Tel: 304-526-8915; Fax: 304-526-8918.
E-mail: srcelest@st-marys.org
Web site: www.st-marys.org
For a complete listing, refer to the Hospitals section.

PINEVILLE. *Children's Health Care, Inc.*, Pineville Children's Clinic, Box 430, 24874. Tel: 304-732-7069; Fax: 304-732-7098.
E-mail: ecatters@marshall.edu
For a complete listing, refer to the Hospitals section.

RHODELL. *Rhodell Health Clinic*, P.O. Box 158, 25915. Tel: 304-683-4318
For a complete listing, refer to the Hospitals section.

[K] SOCIAL SERVICE INSTITUTIONS

WHEELING. *Catholic Charities Neighborhood Center*, 125-18th St., P.O. Box 6176, 26003-0713. Tel: 304-232-7157; Fax: 304-232-4323.
E-mail: doddc2@juno.com
Sr. Constance Dodd, S.M., Dir.

Sisters of St. Joseph House of Hospitality, Inc., 110-15th St., 26003. Tel: 304-232-3129; Fax: 304-232-1404.
E-mail: ssjwhg@aol.com

Society of St. Vincent de Paul, Society of St. Vincent de Paul Store, 348 National Rd., 26003. Tel: 304-232-4230.

HUTTONSVILLE. *Camp Tygart*, Rte. 1, Box 9D, 26273. Tel: 304-335-2130 (In Season); 233-0880 Ext. 335 (Out of Season); Fax: 304-233-9293.
E-mail: mhall@dwc.org
Diocesan Children's Camp. Mr. Michael Hall, Admin.

KERMIT. *A.B.L.E. Families, Inc.*, P.O. Box 1249, 25674. Tel: 304-393-4987.
E-mail: jpeterworth@wizardsinc.net

SALEM. *Nazareth Farm*, Rte. 2, Box 194-3, 26426. Tel: 304-782-2742; Fax: 304-782-4358.
E-mail: nazarethfarm@citynet.net

[L] HOMES FOR DEPENDENT CHILDREN

WHEELING. *St. John's Home for Children*, 141 Key Ave., 26003-7412. Tel: 304-242-5633; Fax: 304-243-4911.
E-mail: stjohns@hgo.net
For a complete listing, refer to the Special Care Facilities section.

[M] MONASTERIES AND RESIDENCES OF PRIESTS AND BROTHERS

WHEELING. *Webb Farm Residence*, 665 Stone & Shannon Rd., 26003. Tel: 304-277-2971; Fax: 304-277-2972. Friar Mark Carter, O.F.M.Cap; Bro. James Townsend, O.F.M.Cap.

CHARLESTON. *Capuchins-St. Anthony Friary*, 1000 Sixth St., 25302. Tel: 304-342-2716.
E-mail: tonycap@citynet.net
Web site: http://home.att.net/~stanthony/capuchinfranciscan.html
Revs. Richard J. Zelik, O.F.M.Cap., Guardian; Kieran Quinn, O.F.M.Cap., Chap.; Albert Alexandrunas, O.F.M.Cap., Vicar; Regis Schlick, O.F.M.Cap.

HINTON. *Monastery of Christ on the Mountain*, P.O. Box 429, 25951-0429. Tel: 304-466-4782; Fax: 304-466-1176.
E-mail: Regisocd@citynet.Net
Discalced Carmelite Hermits. Revs. Bonaventure Lussier, O.C.D.; Regis Jordan, O.C.D.; Bro. Gilbert Tovares, O.C.D.

[N] CONVENTS AND RESIDENCES FOR SISTERS

WHEELING. *Mt. St. Joseph*, Pogue Run Rd., 26003. Tel: 304-232-8160; Fax: 304-232-1404.
E-mail: SSJWHG@aol.com
Motherhouse of the Sisters of St. Joseph. Sr. Marguerite O'Brien, S.S.J., Pres. Professed Sisters 101. Attended by Wheeling Jesuit University.

North America Union Sisters of Our Lady of Charity, Inc., 141 Edgington Ln., 26003. Tel: 304-242-7070; Fax: 304-242-8221. Legal Title: *North American Union Sisters of Our Lady of Charity, Inc.* Sr. Cruz Celia Gomez, Supr.; Sr. Deana Kohlman, Business Mgr.

Sisters of the Visitation, Mount de Chantal, 410 Washington Ave., 26003. Tel: 304-232-1283; Fax: 304-233-8598.
E-mail: Mountdec@ovnet.com
Web site: www.mountdechantal.org
Legal Title: *Sisters of the Visitation of Holy Mary of Mount de Chantal, Inc.* Sr. Catherine Marie Paumier, V.H.M., Supr. Professed Sisters 22. Attended by Wheeling Jesuit University.

[O] FOUNDATIONS

WHEELING. *Central Catholic High School Educational Foundation, Inc.*, 75-14th St., 26003. Tel: 304-233-1660; Fax: 304-233-3187.

Common Fund for Schools, P.O. Box 230, 26003.

John S. Thoner Family Charitable Trust, 1300 Byron St., P.O. Box 230, 26003. Tel: 304-233-0880; Fax: 304-233-0890.
E-mail: jgallagher@dwc.org
Very Rev. John R. Gallagher, V.G., Chancellor & Trustee.

Medical Park Foundation, One Medical Park, 26003. Tel: 304-243-4438; Fax: 304-234-2070.

Sisters of St. Joseph of Wheeling Foundation, Inc., Mount St. Joseph, Pogue Run Rd., 26003. Tel: 304-232-8160; Fax: 304-232-1404.
E-mail: SSJWHG@aol.com

West Virginia Catholic Foundation, P.O. Box 230, 26003. Tel: 304-233-0880; Fax: 304-233-0890.
E-mail: bminor@dwc.org
Web site: www.wvcf.dwc.org
Mr. Bryan E. Minor, Exec. Dir.

CLARKSBURG. *Harrison County Catholic Education Foundation, Inc.*, 126 E. Pike St., 26301-2720.

PARKERSBURG. *Parkersburg Catholic Schools Foundation, Inc.*, 3201 Fairview Ave., 26104-2111. Tel: 304-428-7528; Fax: 304-485-4697.
E-mail: pchsalum@juno.com
Web site: pchsi.com

Sisters of St. Joseph Charitable Fund, Inc., 4420 Rosemar Rd., Ste. 204, P.O. Box 4440, 26104-4440. Tel: 304-424-6080; Fax: 304-424-6081.
E-mail: ssjcf@wirefire.com
Web site: http://home.wirefire.com/ssjcf
Sr. Jane Harrington, S.S.J., Exec. Dir.

WEIRTON. *Society of Friends of Madonna High School, Inc.*, Park Ave., 26062.

[P] NEWMAN CENTERS

CHARLESTON. *University of Charleston Newman Center*, 25364.

ATHENS. *Concord College Newman Center*, 301 Vermillion, P.O. Box 447, 24712. Tel: 304-425-3664. Rev. Francis A. O'Kruta.

BETHANY. *St. John Fisher Catholic Chapel*, 201 Richardson St., Box W, 26032. Tel: 304-829-4622. Very Rev. Kevin M. Quirk, J.C.D.

BUCKHANNON. *West Virginia Wesleyan College Newman Center*, 35 Franklin St., Box 848, 26201-0848. Tel: 304-473-8000.
E-mail: hrchurch@msys.net
Rev. James B. McCafferty, S.M.

FAIRMONT. *Fairmont State College Newman Center*, 1101 Locust Ave., 26554. Tel: 304-363-2300.
E-mail: fatherjz@juno.com
Rev. Jude Molnar, T.O.R.

HUNTINGTON. *Marshall Newman Center*, 1609 Fifth Ave., 25703. Tel: 304-525-4618.
E-mail: Petro@MARShall.edu
Web site: http://webpages.MARShall.Edu/~Petro
Rev. William J. Petro.

PHILIPPI. *Alderson-Broaddus College Newman Center*, College Hill, Rte. 3, Box 257, 26416. Tel: 304-457-2641. Rev. Damian P. Drass, T.O.R.

WEST LIBERTY. *West Liberty State College, St. Thomas Aquinas Campus Ministry*, 134 Chatham St., 26074. Tel: 304-336-7751; 829-4622 (Bethany). Mailing Address: Box W, Bethany, 26032. Very Rev. Kevin M. Quirk, J.C.D.

[Q] CHILD CARE CENTERS

WHEELING. *Holy Family Child Care Center, Inc.*, 161 Edgington Ln., 26003. Tel: 304-242-5222.
E-mail: drp6713@aol.com
For a complete listing, refer to the Special Care Facilities section.

CLARKSBURG. *Madonna Day Care Center*, 444 E. Pike St., 26031. Tel: 304-622-4453
For a complete listing, refer to the Special Care Facilities section.

[R] MISCELLANEOUS

WHEELING. *Retirement Trust Agreement of the Infirm Priests' Association of the Diocese of Wheeling-Charleston*, 1300 Bryon St., 26003. Tel: 304-233-0880; Fax: 304-233-0890.
E-mail: jgallagher@dwv.org
Very Rev. John R. Gallagher, Trustee.

Saint Francis Health System, Inc., Mount Saint Joseph, Poque Run Rd., 26003. Tel: 304-232-8160; Fax: 304-232-1404.
E-mail: SSJWHG@aol.com
Sr. Marguerite O'Brien, S.S.J., Pres.

Saint Francis Hospital, Inc., Mount Saint Joseph, Poque Run Rd., 26003. Tel: 304-232-8160; Fax: 304-232-1404.
E-mail: SSJWHG@aol.com
Sr. Marguerite O'Brien, Pres.

St. Joseph's Hospital of Parkersburg, Inc., Mount St. Joseph, Pogue Run Rd., 26003. Tel: 304-232-8160; Fax: 304-232-1404.
E-mail: SSJWHG@aol.com
Sr. Marguerite O'Brien, S.S.J., Pres.

Sisters of St. Joseph Health System, Inc, Mount St. Joseph, Pogue Run Rd., 26003. Tel: 304-232-8160; Fax: 304-232-1404.
E-mail: SSJWHG@aol.com
Sr. Marguerite O'Brien, S.S.J., Pres.

Sisters of St. Joseph Ministries Support Fund, Inc., Mount St. Joseph, Pogue Run Rd., 26003. Tel: 304-232-8160; Fax: 304-232-1404.
E-mail: SSJWHG@aol.com
Sr. Marguerite O'Brien, S.S.J., Pres.

PRINCETON. *West Virginia Council of Catholic Women*, 203 East Dr., 24720. Tel: 304-425-8665. Sr. Marian Madden, S.C., Diocesan Mod.; Mrs. Betty Charles, Pres.

WEBSTER SPRINGS. *The Catholic Committee of Appalachia*, P.O. Box 662, 26288. Tel: 304-847-7215.
E-mail: appalachia@earthlink.net
Web site: www.cathcomappalachia.org

RELIGIOUS INSTITUTES OF MEN REPRESENTED IN THE DIOCESE

For further details refer to the corresponding bracketed number in the Religious Institutes of Men or Women section.

[0470]—*The Capuchin Friars.*—O.F.M.Cap.
[1330]—*Congregation of the Mission.*—C.M.
[1000]—*Congregation of the Passion.*—C.P.
[0260]—*Discalced Carmelite Fathers.*—O.C.D.
[0820]—*Fathers of Mercy.*—C.P.M.
[0520]—*Franciscan Friars.*—O.F.M.
[0570]—*Glenmary Home Missioners.*—Glmy.
[]—*Heralds of Good News Missionary Society.* (Eluru, India).—H.G.N.
[0690]—*Jesuit Fathers and Brothers.*—S.J.
[0770]—*Marist Brothers.*—F.M.S.
[0780]—*Marist Fathers.*—S.M.
[0590]—*Missionaries of the Holy Apostles.*—M.Ss.A.
[0420]—*Society of the Divine Word.*—S.V.D.
[0560]—*Third Order Regular of St. Francis.*—T.O.R.

RELIGIOUS INSTITUTES OF WOMEN REPRESENTED IN THE DIOCESE

[3110]—*Congregation of Our Lady of the Retreat in the Cenacle.* (Eastern Prov.).—R.C.
[2100]—*Congregation of the Humility of Mary.*—C.H.M.
[1920]—*Congregation of the Sisters of the Holy Cross*.—C.S.C.
[1730]—*Congregation of the Sisters of the Third Order of St. Francis.* (Oldenburg, IN).—O.S.F.
[0760]—*Daughters of Charity of St. Vincent De Paul.* (Emmitsburg Prov.).—D.C.
[0960]—*Daughters of Wisdom.*—D.W.
[1070-14]—*Dominican Sisters.* (Grand Rapids, MI).—O.P.
[1105]—*Dominican Sisters of Hope.* (Ossining, NY).—O.P.
[1070-02]—*Dominican Sisters of St. Mary of the Springs*(Columbus, OH).—O.P.
[1430]—*Franciscan Sisters of Our Lady of Perpetual Help.*—O.S.F.
[2420]—*Marist Missionary Sisters.*—S.M.S.M.
[2430]—*Marist Sisters.*—S.M.
[2490]—*Medical Mission Sisters.*—M.M.S.
[2800]—*Missionary Sisters of the Most Sacred Heart Of Jesus.*—M.S.C.
[3070]—*North American Union Sisters of Our Lady of Charity.*—N.A.U.-O.L.C.
[3150]—*Pallottine Missionary Sisters.*—S.A.C.
[2970]—*School Sisters of Notre Dame.*—S.S.N.D.
[1680]—*School Sisters of St. Francis.*—O.S.F.
[3590]—*Servants of Mary (Servite Sisters).*—O.S.M.
[0570]—*Sisters of Charity of Seton Hill, Greensburg, PA.*—S.C.
[0590]—*Sisters of Charity of St. Elizabeth, Convent Station.* (Southern Province).—S.C.
[0590]—*Sisters of Charity of St. Elizabeth, Convent Station.* (Western Province).—S.C.
[0990]—*Sisters of Divine Providence (St. Peter Prov.).*—C.D.P.
[1000]—*Sisters of Divine Providence, Melbourne, Kentucky.*—C.D.P.
[2360]—*Sisters of Loretto at the Foot of the Cross.*—S.L.
[2575]—*Sisters of Mercy of the Americas.*—R.S.M.
[3000]—*Sisters of Notre Dame de Namur (California Prov.).*—S.N.D.deN.
[3000]—*Sisters of Notre Dame de Namur (Chesapeake Prov.).*—S.N.D.deN.
[3360]—*Sisters of Providence of St. Mary of the Woods, Indiana.*—S.P.
[3720]—*Sisters of St. Anne.*—S.S.A.
[1630]—*Sisters of St. Francis of Penance and Christian Charity.*—O.S.F.
[1650]—*Sisters of St. Francis of Philadelphia.*—O.S.F.
[1530]—*Sisters of St. Francis of the Congregation of Our Lady of Lourdes.*—O.S.F.
[3830-08]—*Sisters of St. Joseph of Cleveland.*—C.S.J.
[3860]—*Sisters of St. Joseph of Cluny.*—S.J.C.
[3830-13]—*Sisters of St. Joseph of Pittsburgh.*—C.S.J.
[3830-05]—*Sisters of St. Joseph of Rockville Centre.*—C.S.J.
[3830-17]—*Sisters of St. Joseph of Wheeling.*—S.S.J.
[2110]—*Sisters of the Humility of Mary.*—H.M.
[3270]—*Sisters of the Most Precious Blood, O'Fallon, MO.*—C.P.P.S.
[3220]—*Sisters of the Poor Child Jesus.*—P.C.J.
[1760]—*Sisters of the Third Order of St. Francis of Penance and Charity.*—O.S.F.
[2160]—*Sisters, Servants of the Immaculate Heart of Mary.* (Scranton).—I.H.M.
[4060]—*Society of the Holy Child Jesus.*—S.H.C.J.
[4120-03]—*Ursuline Nuns of the Congregation of Paris.*—O.S.U.
[4190]—*Visitation Nuns.* (Wheeling, WV).—V.H.M.

DIOCESAN CEMETERIES

WHEELING. *Mount Calvary* (1872), 1685 National Rd., 26003-5599. Tel: 304-242-0460. Very Rev. John R. Gallagher, V.G.

NECROLOGY

† Grondalski, Thaddeus J., (Retired). —Died Dec. 3, 1999.
† Martis, Albin A., (Retired). —Died Feb. 23, 1999.
† O'Reilly, Rev. Msgr. John Lawrence, (Retired). —Died Oct. 1, 1999.
† Rafferty, Thomas A., (Retired). —Died June 17, 1999.
† Savage, Charles H., (Retired). —Died July 14, 2000.
† Wanstreet, Rev. Msgr. Jospeh W., (Retired). —Died Aug. 27, 1999.

Diocese of Wichita

(Dioecesis Wichitensis)

Most Reverend

EUGENE J. GERBER, D.D.

Bishop of Wichita; ordained May 19, 1959; appointed Bishop of Dodge City October 16, 1976; ordained December 14, 1976; installed December 15, 1976; appointed Bishop of Wichita November 23, 1982; installed February 9, 1983. *Res., 307 E. Central, Wichita, KS, 67202.*

The Chancery: 424 N. Broadway, Wichita, KS, 67202. Tel.: 316-269-3900; Fax: 316-269-3936.

ESTABLISHED AUGUST 2, 1887.

Square Miles 20,021.

New boundaries established by Apostolic Letters dated May 19, 1951. Bounded on the west by the west lines of Rice, Reno, Kingman and Harper counties, south by Oklahoma, east by Missouri, and north by the north lines of Bourbon, Allen, Woodson, Greenwood, Morris, Marion, McPherson and Rice Counties in Kansas.

For legal titles of parishes and diocesan institutions, consult the Chancery Office.

STATISTICAL OVERVIEW

Personnel	
Bishop	1
Priests: Diocesan Active in Diocese	80
Priests: Active Outside Diocese	6
Priests: Retired, Sick or Absent	42
Number of Diocesan Priests	128
Religious Priests in Diocese	8
Ordinations:	
Diocesan Priests	4
Transitional Deacons	3
Permanent Deacons in Diocese	2
Total Sisters	332
Parishes	
Parishes	92
With Resident Pastor:	
Resident Diocesan Priests	67
Resident Religious Priests	1
Without Resident Pastor:	
Administered by Priests	24
Professional Ministry Personnel:	
Sisters	18
Lay Ministers	32
Welfare	
Catholic Hospitals	6
Total Assisted	421,013
Health Care Centers	2
Total Assisted	32,011
Homes for the Aged	2
Total Assisted	351
Day Care and Extended Day Care Centers	1
Total Assisted	183
Specialized Homes	1
Total Assisted	96
Special Centers for Social Services	1
Total Assisted	19,851
Other Institutions	1
Total Assisted	3,921
Educational	
Diocesan Students in Other Seminaries	31
Total Seminarians	31
Colleges and Universities	1
Total Students	1,967
High Schools, Diocesan and Parish	4
Total Students	2,143
Elementary Schools, Diocesan and Parish	32
Total Students	8,150
Catechesis/Religious Education:	
High School Students	3,141
Elementary Students	7,095
Total Students Under Catholic Instruction	22,527
Teachers in the Diocese:	
Priests	3
Sisters	21
Lay Teachers	514
Vital Statistics	
Receptions into the Church:	
Infant Baptism Totals	2,533
Adult Baptism Totals	348
Received into Full Communion	486
First Communions	2,513
Confirmations	1,840
Marriages:	
Catholic	452
Interfaith	397
Total Marriages	849
Deaths	902
Total Catholic Population	114,539
Total Population	947,499

Former Bishops—Most Rev. JAMES O'REILLY, D.D., Bishop-Elect; died July 26, 1887.—Most Rev. JOHN JOSEPH HENNESSY, D.D., cons. Nov. 30, 1888; died July 13, 1920.—Most Rev. AUGUSTUS JOHN SCHWERTNER, D.D., ord. June 12, 1897; cons. June 8, 1921; installed June 22, 1921; died Oct. 2, 1939.—Most Rev. CHRISTIAN HERMAN WINKELMANN, S.T.D., ord. June 11, 1907; cons. Auxiliary Bishop of St. Louis, Nov. 30, 1933; installed March 5, 1940; died Nov. 18, 1946.—Most Rev. MARK K. CARROLL, S.T.D., ord. June 10, 1922; appt. Feb. 15, 1947; cons. April 23, 1947; installed May 6, 1947; resigned Sept. 27, 1967; died Jan. 12, 1985.—Most Rev. LEO C. BYRNE, D.D., ord. June 10, 1933; appt. Titular Bishop of Sabidia and Auxiliary of St. Louis, May 21, 1954; cons. June 29, 1954; transferred to Wichita, "cum jure successionis" 1961; appt. Apostolic Administrator, Feb. 25, 1963; transferred to St. Paul and Minneapolis, Sept. 27, 1967; died Oct. 21, 1974.—Most Rev. DAVID M. MALONEY, S.S., S.T.L., J.C.D., former Bishop of Wichita; ord. Dec. 8, 1936; appt. Titular Bishop of Ruspae Auxiliary of Denver, Nov. 9, 1960; cons. Jan. 4, 1961; transferred to Wichita, Dec. 6, 1967; resigned July 16, 1982; died Feb. 15, 1995.

Vicars General—Rev. Msgr. JOHN P. GILSENAN, V.G., J.C.L., *424 N. Broadway, Wichita, 67202.*

Chancery Office—424 N. Broadway, Wichita, 67202. Tel: 316-269-3900; Fax: 316-269-3902.

Vicar for Priests—Rev. JOHN P. GILSENAN, V.G., J.C.L.

Director of Diocesan Planning—Rev. ROBERT E. HEMBERGER, J.C.L.

Director of Diocesan Services—Rev. JOHN P. LANZRATH, S.T.L.

Chancellor—Rev. ROBERT E. HEMBERGER, J.C.L.

Vice Chancellor—Rev. JOHN P. LANZRATH, S.T.L.; Sr. JACINTA LANGLOIS, A.S.C.

Presbyteral Council/Diocesan Consultors—Most Rev. EUGENE J. GERBER; Most Rev. THOMAS J. OLMSTED; Rev. Msgr. JOHN P. GILSENAN, V.G., J.C.L.; Revs. ROBERT E. HEMBERGER, J.C.L., Chm. WILLIAM M. CARR; JOSEPH M. GILE; JOHN V. HOTZE; ANDREW KUYKENDALL; JOHN P. LANZRATH, S.T.L.; H. PATRICK MALONE; SHAWN MCKNIGHT; WAYNE SCHMID; JOHN P. SHERLOCK; THOMAS A. WELK, C.PP.S.

Parish Priest Consultors—Rev. Msgr. CHARLES F. WALSH; Rev. Msgr. JOHN P. GILSENAN, V.G., J.C.L.; Rev. Msgr. CHARLES W. REGAN.

Tribunal—424 N. Broadway, Wichita, 67202. Tel: 316-269-3960.

Judicial Vicar—Rev. ROBERT E. HEMBERGER, J.C.L.

Adjutant Judicial Vicar—Rev. JOHN V. HOTZE, J.C.L.

Judges—Revs. STEPHEN R. BAXTER, J.C.L.; DOUGLAS CAMPBELL, J.C.L.; ROBERT E. HEMBERGER, J.C.L.; JOHN V. HOTZE, J.C.L.; MICHAEL E. NOLAN, J.C.L.

Defenders of the Bond—Rev. Msgr. JOHN P. GILSENAN, V.G., J.C.L.; Rev. J. PATRICK MANNION, J.C.L.

Procurator-Advocates—Sr. JACINTA LANGLOIS, A.S.C.

Notaries—Mrs. ROBERTA RAU; Mrs. CLAUDINE WALD; Mrs. ROSE JONES.

Deans—Revs. WILLIAM M. CARR, North Wichita; DWIGHT J. BIRKET, South Wichita; Rev. Msgr. JOHN P. GILSENAN, V.G., J.C.L., East Wichita; Revs. JAMES BILLINGER, West Wichita; IVAN C. ECK, Hutchinson; PAUL J. OBORNY, Newton; DAVID LINNEBUR, Wellington; THOMAS J. STROOT, Pittsburg; THOMAS F. SCALETTY, Chanute.

Continuing Education of Clergy Committee—Revs. JOSEPH M. GILE; KENT HEMBERGER; ROBERT E. HEMBERGER, J.C.L., Prog. Consultant; DAVID J. LIES; LAWRENCE SANDERS, C.SS.R.; WAYNE L. SCHMID; KENNETH J. SCHUCKMAN; KENNETH S. VAN HAVERBEKE, Prog. Dir.

Diocesan Offices and Directors

Catholic Diocese of Wichita—Most. Rev. EUGENE J. GERBER, D.D., Pres.; Most. Rev. THOMAS J. OLMSTED, Coadjutor Bishop.

Apostleship of Prayer—6900 E. 45th St., N., Wichita, 67226.

Catholic Charities—Ms. JANET PAPE, Dir., *437 N. Topeka, Wichita, 67202.* Tel: 316-264-8344.

Catholic Life Center—424 N. Broadway, Wichita, 67202. Tel: 316-269-3900.

Cemeteries—Mr. JEROME GERBER, *424 N. Broadway, Wichita, 67202.* Tel: 316-269-3900.

Commission for Communications—Rev. JOHN P. LANZRATH, *424 N. Broadway, Wichita, 67202.* Tel: 316-269-3900; Fax: 316-269-3902.

Cursillo—Rev. JEROME A. BEAT, *2007 Arkansas, Wichita, 67203.* Tel: 316-262-4683.

Diocesan Apostolate for Previously Married Catholics—Rev. GERARD PECHT, C.SS.R., *Spiritual Life Center, 7100 E. 45th St., N., Wichita, 67226.* Tel: 316-744-0167.

Diocesan Synod Office—Rev. JOHN P. SHERLOCK, Gen. Sec.; Ms. RHONDA LOHKAMP, Assoc. Gen. Sec., *424 N. Broadway, Wichita, 67202.* Tel: 316-269-3900; Fax: 316-269-3902.

Wichita Diocesan Charismatic Services—Rev. JAMES WELDON, Moderator, *St. Francis of Assisi, 861 N. Socora, Wichita, 67212.* Rev. JAMES S. MAINZER, Assoc. Moderator, *St. James Church, 813 State St., Augusta, 67010.* Tel: 316-775-2155.

Diocesan Apostolate to Engaged Encounter—Rev. DANIEL VACCA, *St. Joseph Hospital, 3600 E. Harry, Wichita, 67218.* Tel: 316-689-5323.

Catholic Marriage Preparation-Evenings for Engaged—Rev. H. PATRICK MALONE, *1425 N. Chautauqua, Wichita, 67214.* Tel: 316-682-8712.

Diocesan Apostolate to Marriage Encounter—Rev. DANIEL J. SPEXARTH, *St. Thomas Aquinas Church, 1321 Stratford Lane, Wichita, 67206.* Tel: 316-683-6569.

Diocesan Apostolate to Widowed Catholics—Rev. GERALD PECHT, C.SS.R., *Spiritual Life Center, 7100 E. 45th St. N., Wichita, 67226.* Tel: 316-744-0167.

Diocesan Building Commission—Rev. JAMES J. BILLINGER; Mr. WILMER FREUND; Revs. KENT A. HEMBERGER; ROBERT E. HEMBERGER, J.C.L., Exec. Sec.; Mr. FRED HERMES; Ms. BRONWEN LEWIS; Mr. DANIEL L. LOUGHMAN; Revs. W. SHAWN MCKNIGHT; THOMAS F. SCALETTY; Mrs. LINDA SNOOK; Mrs. THERESA WHITE.

Diocesan Director of Stewardship and Finance—Mr. DANIEL L. LOUGHMAN, *424 N. Broadway, Wichita, 67202.* Tel: 316-269-3900.

Diocesan Finance Committee—Most. Rev. EUGENE J. GERBER, D.D.; Most. Rev. THOMAS J. OLMSTED; Mr. DANIEL CARNEY; Mr. JOE DELLASEGA; Rev. ROBERT E. HEMBERGER, J.C.L.; Mr. RICHARD KERSCHEN; Rev. JOHN P. LANZRATH, S.T.L.; Mr. DANIEL L. LOUGHMAN; Mr. PATRICK E. O'SHAUGHNESSY; Ms. MARILYN PAULY; Mr. DALE WIGGINS; Mr. PERRY WINTER.

Diocesan Liaison for Health Affairs—Rev. ROBERT E. HEMBERGER, J.C.L., *424 N. Broadway, Wichita, 67202.* Tel: 316-269-3962.

Diocesan Office for Ministry with Persons with Disabilities—Sr. M. VERONICE BORN, C.S.J., Dir., *Holy Family Center, 619 S. Maize Rd., Wichita, 67209.* Tel: 316-722-8159.

Education—Mr. ROBERT VOBORIL, Supt., *424 N. Broadway, Wichita, 67202.* Tel: 316-269-3950.

Office of Religious Education, C.C.D.—Ms. PATRICIA A. YATES, Dir., *424 N. Broadway, Wichita, 67202.* Tel: 316-269-3940.

Special C.C.D. Services—Vacant. Tel: 316-686-7171.

Latin America Mission and Volunteer Services—Sr. URSULA FOTOVICH, C.S.J., Dir., *424 N. Broadway, Wichita, 67202.* Tel: 316-269-3946.

Legion of Mary—Rev. JOHN C. REINKEMEYER, *638 Ave. D. W., Kingman, 67068.* Tel: 316-532-5440.

Marriage and Family Life Services—Coordinated by Spiritual Life Center.

Natural Family Planning Office—Ms. JUDITH LEONARD, Dir., *1515 S. Clifton, Ste. 400, Wichita, 67218.* Tel: 316-685-6776; Fax: 316-685-7540.

Newspaper: "The Catholic Advance" Diocesan Weekly—Mr. CHRISTOPHER M. RIGGS, Editor; Mr. DANIEL L. LOUGHMAN, Business Mgr., *424 N. Broadway, Wichita, 67202.* Tel: 316-269-3965.

Office of Development and Planned Giving—Ms. BRONWEN LEWIS, *424 N. Broadway, Wichita, 67202.*

Office of Pastoral Life and Ministry—*424 N. Broadway, Wichita, 67202.* Tel: 316-269-3947.

Office of Worship—Rev. W. SHAWN MCKNIGHT, Dir., *424 N. Broadway, Wichita, 67202.* Tel: 316-269-3945.

Presbyteral Council—Most Rev. EUGENE J. GERBER; Most Rev. THOMAS J. OLMSTED; Rev. Msgr. JOHN P. GILSENAN, V.G., J.C.L.; Revs. ROBERT E. HEMBERGER, J.C.L., Chm. WILLIAM M. CARR; JOSEPH M. GILE; JOHN V. HOTZE; ANDREW KUYKENDALL; JOHN P. LANZRATH, S.T.L.; H. PATRICK MALONE; SHAWN MCKNIGHT; WAYNE SCHMID; JOHN P. SHERLOCK; THOMAS WELK, C.PP.S.

Propagation of the Faith and Holy Childhood Assn.—Sr. URSULA FOTOVICH, C.S.J., Dir., *424 N. Broadway, Wichita, 67202.* Tel: 316-269-3946.

Respect Life and Social Justice Office—Rev. JOHN B. BRUNGARDT, Dir.; Mr. DION C. SCOTT, Assoc. Dir., *424 N. Broadway, Wichita, 67202.* Tel: 316-269-3935.

Retreats—Rev. JOSEPH M. GILE, Dir., *Spiritual Life Center, 7100 E. 45th St. N., Wichita, 67226.* Tel: 316-744-0167.

Rural Life Ministry—Rev. DARYL BEFORT, *St. Patrick Church, 638 Avenue D, W., Kingman, 67068.* Tel: 316-532-5440.

Social Service—Ms. JANET PAPE, *437 N. Topeka, Wichita, 67202.* Tel: 316-264-8344.

Society of St. Vincent de Paul—Rev. SCOTT NGUYEN, Chap., *Church of the Magdalen, 457 S. Woodlawn, Wichita, 67218.* Tel: 316-683-6516.

Technology Coordinator—Sr. PATRICIA STANLEY, C.S.J., *424 N. Broadway, Wichita, 67202.* Tel: 316-269-3900.

Vocations—Rev. MATTHEW C. MCGINNESS, Dir., *424 N. Broadway, Wichita, 67202.* Tel: 316-269-3900.

Wichita Diocesan Hispanic Council—Rev. JOSE MACHADO, Dir., *424 N. Broadway, Wichita, 67202.* Tel: 316-269-3900.

Youth and Young Adult Ministry—Ms. CHRISTINE EDMONDS, Dir., *424 N. Broadway, Wichita, 67202.* Tel: 316-269-3930.

CLERGY, PARISHES, MISSIONS AND PAROCHIAL SCHOOLS

CITY OF WICHITA
(Sedgwick County)

1—CATHEDRAL OF THE IMMACULATE CONCEPTION (1887), Revs. William M. Carr, Rector; Charles F. Seiwert; Sr. Renee Kirmer, A.S.C., Pastoral Assoc.
Res., 307 E. Central Ave., 67202. Tel: 316-263-6574.
Catechesis/Religious Programs—Students 279.

2—ALL SAINTS (1946), Rev. Dwight J. Birket.
Res., 3205 Grand St., 67218. Tel: 316-682-1415. [JC 3]
School—Tel: 316-682-6021; Fax: 316-682-8734. Dr. John Gahagan, Prin.
Lay Teachers 17; Students 283.
Catechesis/Religious Programs—Tel: 316-687-9981. Terrisa Compton, D.R.E.
Students 65.

3—BLESSED SACRAMENT (1927), Rev. Msgr. John P. Gilsenan; Revs. Joseph C. Tatro; Richard Cleary, O.S.B.
Res., 124 N. Roosevelt Ave., 67208. Tel: 316-682-4557. [JC]
School—Tel: 316-684-3752; Fax: 316-687-1082. Jim Grogan, Prin.
Sisters of St. Joseph 1; Lay Teachers 28; Students 405.
Catechesis/Religious Programs—Cindy Honton, D.R.E.
Students 65.
Convent—138 N. Roosevelt, 67208. Tel: 316-684-3977.

4—CHRIST THE KING (1950), Rev. Robert B. Wachter. In res., Revs. John B. Brungandt; John P. Lanzrath.
Res., 4411 Maple Ave., 67209. Tel: 316-943-4353; Fax: 316-943-8196. [JC]
School—4501 Maple Ave., 67209. Tel: 316-943-4353; Fax: 361-943-7361. Richard Sleefe, Prin.
Sisters, Adorers of the Blood of Christ 1; Lay Teachers 14; Students 270.
Catechesis/Religious Programs—Students 28.

5—CHURCH OF THE MAGDALEN (1950), Revs. Kenneth S. VanHaverbeke; Hien Paul Nguyen; Sr. Connie Beiriger, C.S.J., Pastoral Assoc.
Res., 457 S. Woodlawn St., 67218. Tel: 316-683-6516; Fax: 316-683-8407.
School—Tel: 316-683-5181; Fax: 316-683-9245. Eva Williams, Prin.
Lay Teachers 22; Students 458.
Catechesis/Religious Programs—Students 120.

6—CHURCH OF THE RESURRECTION (1965), Rev. Sherman Orr. In res., Rev. Joseph M. Gile.
Res., 4910 N. Woodlawn, 67220. Tel: 316-744-2776; Fax: 316-744-3027.
School—(Grades Prek-8). Tel: 316-744-3576; Fax: 316-744-3027. Sr. Marietta Conrardy, C.S.J., Prin.
Lay Teachers 14; Students 275.
Catechesis/Religious Programs—Debra Helberg, D.R.E.
Students 100.

7—HOLY SAVIOR (1948) (African American), Rev. H. Patrick Malone; Deacon Ronald Ealey, Pastoral Admin.
Res., 1425 N. Chautauqua, 67214. Tel: 316-682-8712; Fax: 316-682-4797.
School—Tel: 316-684-2141; Fax: 316-682-4797. Mr. James Jerome, Prin.; Mrs. Delia Baenett, Program Admin.
Lay Teachers 12; Students 148.
Catechesis/Religious Programs—Students 72.

8—OUR LADY OF GUADALUPE. Closed. For sacramental records contact St. Margaret Mary, Wichita.

9—OUR LADY OF PERPETUAL HELP (1927), Rev. Jose Machado; Sr. Virginia Alfaro, Pastoral Assoc.
Res., 2351 N. Market St., 67219. Tel: 316-838-8373; Fax: 316-838-8373. [JC]
Catechesis/Religious Programs—Students 230.
Convent—2354 N. Market St., 67219. Tel: 316-838-3190.
Congregation of the Daughters of the Passion of Our Lord Jesus Christ and the Sorrows of Mary 3.
Parish Center—2409 N. Market St., 67219. Tel: 316-838-5750.

10—ST. ANNE (1955), Rev. Kent A. Hemberger; Mary Beth Steiner, Pastoral Assoc.
Office: 2801 S. Seneca, 67217-2399. Tel: 316-522-2809; Fax: 316-524-2370.
School—(Grades K-8). Tel: 316-522-6131. Sr. Margaret Nugent, C.S.J.
Sisters 2; Lay Teachers 13; Students 226.

11—ST. ANTHONY (1887) (German), Rev. Hung Q. Pham.
Res. & Mailing Address: 325 Ohio, 67214. Tel: 316-269-4641.

12—ST. ELIZABETH ANN SETON (1982), Revs. James J. Billinger; Joseph A. Eckberg.
Res., 645 N. 119th St. W., 67235. Tel: 316-721-1686; Fax: 316-721-1723.
School—Tel: 316-721-5693. Mr. David Charles, Prin.; Mrs. Kitty Garcia, Asst. Vice Prin.
Lay Teachers 31; Students 690.
Catechesis/Religious Programs—Tel: 316-721-1686.
Students 364.

13—ST. FRANCIS OF ASSISI (1959), Revs. John V. Hotze; Darrin M. May; James F. Weldon.
Res., 861 N. Socora, 67212. Tel: 316-722-4404; Fax: 316-722-4738.
School—Tel: 316-722-5171; Fax: 316-722-0492. Ms. Candace Buser, Prin.
Adorers of the Blood of Christ 3; Lay Teachers 42; Students 781.
Catechesis/Religious Programs—Richard George, D.R.E.
Students 510.

14—ST. JOSEPH (1886), Revs. Daniel H. Andree, C.SS.R.; Andrew Meiners, C.SS.R.; Walter C. Karrer, C.SS.R.
Res., 145 S. Millwood Ave., 67213. Tel: 316-262-1877; Fax: 316-262-5250. [JC]
School—Tel: 316-265-7962; Fax: 316-265-7963. Ms. Ann Hughes, Prin.
Sisters 1; Lay Teachers 13; Students 200.
Catechesis/Religious Programs—Mrs. Denise Northup, D.R.E.
Students 120.
Convent—St. Joseph's, 128 S. Vine Ave., 67213. Tel: 316-262-4419. Sister Adorers (ASC)

15—ST. JUDE (1958), Rev. Douglas Campbell.
Res., 3130 Amidon Ave., 67204. Tel: 316-838-1963; Fax: 316-838-8513.
School—Tel: 316-838-0800; Fax: 316-838-0866. Mrs. Candace Buser, Prin.
Lay Teachers 13; Students 226.
Catechesis/Religious Programs—Debby Dean, D.R.E.
Students 144.

16—ST. MARGARET MARY (1954), Rev. Scott C. Nguyen.
Res., 2701 Pattie, 67216. Tel: 316-262-1821; Fax: 316-262-4057.
School—(Grades Pre K-8). Tel: 316-267-4911; Fax: 316-267-1707. Mary Samms, Prin.
Lay Teachers 12; Students 206.
Catechesis/Religious Programs—Tel: 316-262-5344. Anne Schock, D.R.E.
Students 75.

17—ST. PATRICK (1895), Rev. Jerome A. Beat.
Res., 2007 Arkansas Ave., 67203. Tel: 316-262-4683; Fax: 316-262-6217. [JC]
School—2023 Arkansas Ave., 67203. Tel: 316-262-4071. Mr. Donald C. Wilson, Prin.
Dominican Sisters 1; Lay Teachers 13; Students 251.
Catechesis/Religious Programs—Linda F. Gosche, D.R.E.
Students 73.
Convent—2045 Arkansas Ave., 67203. Tel: 316-267-0021.

18—ST. PAUL PARISH (1970), Rev. Matthew C. McGinness.
Res., 1810 N. Roosevelt, 67208. Tel: 316-684-6896; Fax: 316-684-2679.

19—ST. THOMAS AQUINAS (1957), Revs. Daniel J. Spexarth; Thomas H. Leland; Sr. Donna Schauf, B.V.M., Pastoral Assoc. & D.R.E.
Res., 1321 Stratford Ln., 67206. Tel: 316-683-6569; Fax: 316-683-6569.
School—Tel: 316-684-9201; Fax: 316-684-7421. Miss Mary Sweet, Prin.
Lay Teachers 37; Students 711.
Catechesis/Religious Programs—Students 152.

20—ST. VINCENT DE PAUL (1955), Rev. Michael E. Baldwin.
Res., 123 N. Andover Rd., Andover, 67002. Tel: 316-733-1423; Fax: 316-733-1687.
Catechesis/Religious Programs—Gayle Beuke, D.R.E.
Students 620.

OUTSIDE THE CITY OF WICHITA

Aleppo, Sedgwick Co., Immaculate Conception (1900) (German), Rev. Philip J. Allen.
Church—25741 W. 13th St. N., Garden Plain, 67050. Tel: 316-531-2662. [CEM]
Catechesis/Religious Programs—Students 12.

Andale, Sedgwick Co., St. Joseph (1890) (German), Rev. Reinhard C. Eck.
Res., 318 Rush Ave., Box 8, 67001. Tel: 316-444-2196. [CEM]
Catechesis/Religious Programs—Mary Jo Hieger, D.R.E.
Students 290.

Anthony, Harper Co., Sacred Heart (1934). Closed. For inquiries for parish records contact St. Joan of Arc, 1023 W. Main St., Box 218, Harper, KS 67058.

Arkansas City, Cowley Co., Sacred Heart (1886), Rev. Ser Khu Wilson (Burma).
Res., 325 S. C St., 67005. Tel: 316-442-0566; Fax: 316-441-0935. [JC]
School—308 S. B St., Tel: 316-442-6550; Fax: 316-441-0935. Sr. Jacklyn Duncan, Prin.
Sisters of St. Joseph 1; Dominican Sisters 1; Lay Teachers 4; Students 53.
Catechesis/Religious Programs—Tel: 316-442-5108. Melanie Biltz, D.R.E.
Students 45.

Arma, Crawford Co., St. Joseph (1934), Rev. Donald R. Thissen.
Res., 310 W. South St., P.O. Box 948, 66712. Tel: 316-347-4525.
Catechesis/Religious Programs—Students 3.

Augusta, Butler Co., St. James (1879), Rev. Samuel J. Pinkerton.
Res., 813 State St., 67010. Tel: 316-775-2155; Fax: 316-775-2131. [CEM]
School—Tel: 316-775-5721; Fax: 316-775-2131. Kathleen Patterson, Prin.
Lay Teachers 9; Students 101.
Catechesis/Religious Programs—Tel: 316-733-5247. D.R.E.: Bonnie Toombs; Lizzie Payne.
Students 210.

Baxter Springs, Cherokee Co., St. Joseph (1868), Rev. Charles Middleton.
Res., 307 Galena, P.O. Box 296, Galena, 66739. Tel: 316-783-1693.
Catechesis/Religious Programs—Students 9.

Burns, Marion Co., Immaculate Conception. Closed. For sacramental records contact Holy Family, Marion.

Bushton, Rice Co., Holy Name of Jesus (1878), Rev. Steven Scheier.
Res., 67427. Tel: 316-562-3427. [CEM]
Catechesis/Religious Programs—Students 55.
Mission—Little River, Rice Co., Holy Trinity.

Caldwell, Sumner Co., St. Martin of Tours (1888), Rev. David W. Linnebur.
Res., 428 N. Main, 67022. Tel: 316-845-6763; Fax: 316-845-6733. [JC]
Catechesis/Religious Programs—Students 45.

Caney, Montgomery Co., Sacred Heart (1914), Rev. Edward J. Steinberger.
Res., P.O. Box 276, Moline, 67353-0276. Tel: 316-647-3577.
Catechesis/Religious Programs—Students 24.

Capaldo, Crawford Co., St. Alice. Closed. For sacramental records contact Sacred Heart, Frontenac.

Castleton, Reno Co., St. Agnes (1872). Closed. For inquiries for sacramental records contact St. Teresa, Hutchinson.

Cedar Vale, Chautauqua Co., St. Joseph. Closed. For inquiries for parish records contact the Chancery.

Chanute, Neosho Co., St. Patrick (1873), Rev. Thomas F. Scaletty.
Res., 424 S. Central, 66720. Tel: 316-431-3165; Fax: 316-431-6587. [CEM 2]
School—(Grades PreK-5). Tel: 316-431-4020. Sr. Sylvana Schulte, Prin.
Sisters 1; Lay Teachers 6; Students 116.
Catechesis/Religious Programs—Tel: 316-431-3165.
Students 160.

Chase, Rice Co., St. Mary (1888) (German), Rev. Joseph P. Slomski, Admin.
Res., P.O. Box 306, 67524. Tel: 316-938-2382. [CEM][JC]
Catechesis/Religious Programs—Students 15.

Cherokee, Crawford Co., St. Anastasia. Closed. For sacramental records contact Our Lady of Lourdes, Pittsburg.

Cherryvale, Montgomery Co., St. Francis Xavier's (1871), Revs. Stephen M. Thapwa (Burma); Kevin Trayers, (Retired).
Res., 202 S. Liberty St., 67335. Tel: 316-336-2941. [CEM]
Catechesis/Religious Programs—Students 30.

Chetopa, Labette Co., Sacred Heart (1873), Rev. Larry Parker.
Res., 1112 W. Third., Oswego, 67356. Tel: 316-795-2262. [CEM]
Catechesis/Religious Programs—Students 11.

Chicopee, Crawford Co., St. Barbara. Closed. For sacramental records contact Our Lady of Lourdes, Pittsburg.

Clonmel, Sedgwick Co., St. John (1879), Rev. Leroy Linnebur.
Res., 18630 W. 71st St., Viola, 67149. Tel: 316-545-7171; 794-2784; Fax: 316-794-2784. [CEM]
Parish Hall: Tel: 316-545-7211.
Catechesis/Religious Programs—D.R.E.: Sylvia Kerschen; Art Gentry.
Students 82.

Coffeyville, Montgomery Co., Holy Name (1869), Rev. Robert J. Hartmann.
Res., 408 Willow St., 67337. Tel: 316-251-0475; Fax: 316-251-6485. [CEM 2]
School—409 Willow St., 67337. Tel: 316-251-0480; Fax: 316-251-1651. Sr. Janice Roberts, Prin.
Sisters of St. Joseph 2; Lay Teachers 10; Students 151.
Catechesis/Religious Programs—Students 60.

Columbus, Cherokee Co., St. Rose (1887), Rev. Eugene W. Grabner.
Res., 115 W. Walnut St., 66725. Tel: 316-429-2639. [JC]
Catechesis/Religious Programs—Clustered with St. Bridget, Columbus.
Students 41.

Colwich, Sedgwick Co., Sacred Heart (1901), Rev. John P. Sherlock.
Res., 231 S. Fifth St., P.O. Box 578, 67030. Tel: 316-796-1224; Fax: 316-796-0735. [CEM]
Catechesis/Religious Programs—Students 356.

Conway Springs, Sumner Co., St. Joseph (1886) (German), Rev. David W. Linnebur.
Res., 217 N. Sixth St., Box 157, 67031. Tel: 316-456-2276; Fax: 316-456-3317. [CEM]
School—Tel: 316-456-2270; Fax: 316-456-2272. Ms. Michaelita J. Wasinger, Prin.
Lay Teachers 9; Students 183.
Catechesis/Religious Programs—D.R.E.: Fax: 316-456-3276. Renee Means; Lillian Palsmeier.
Students 250.

Council Grove, Morris Co., St. Rose (1883), Rev. Chrysostom Ah Maung.
Res., 316 Spencer St., 66846. Tel: 316-767-6412; Fax: 316-767-5370. [CEM][JC 2]
Catechesis/Religious Programs—Joe Glotzbach, Chm. D.R.E. team.
Students 119.

Cunningham, Kingman Co., Sacred Heart (1908) (German), Rev. John Miller.
Res., P.O. Box 216, 67035. Tel: 316-298-2601; Fax: 316-298-2926. [CEM]
Catechesis/Religious Programs—Tel: 316-298-4038. Linda Kerschen, D.R.E.
Students 91.

Danville, Harper Co., Immaculate Conception (1883). Merged For inquiries for parish records contact St. Joan of Arc, 1023 W. Main St., Box 218, Harper, KS 67058.

Derby, Sedgwick Co., St. Mary's (1954), Rev. Wayne Schmid; Kathleen Parisio, Business Mgr.; Sr. Marie Zoglmon, A.S.C., Pastoral Assoc.
Res., P.O. Box 325, 722 N. Derby, 67037. Tel: 316-788-5525; Fax: 316-788-1577.
School—700 N. Derby, 67037. Tel: 316-788-3151; Fax: 316-788-6895. Mr. Richard Montgomery, Prin.
Sisters of St. Joseph 2; Lay Teachers 10; Students 210.
Catechesis/Religious Programs—Tel: 316-788-1253. Janet Clark, D.R.E.
Students 279.

El Dorado, Butler Co., St. John (1915), Rev. Michael E. Nolan.
Res., 302 N. Denver Ave., 67042. Tel: 316-320-4796; Fax: 316-321-1709.
Catechesis/Religious Programs—Tel: 316-321-4933. Annette Hammeke, D.R.E.
Students 220.

Erie, Neosho Co., St. Ambrose (1915), Rev. Larry Parker.
Res., 519 N. Main, 66733. Tel: 316-244-3216.
Catechesis/Religious Programs—Students 57.

Eureka, Greenwood Co., Sacred Heart (1881) (German), Rev. Leo A. Kerschen.
Res., 514 N. Elm St., 67045. Tel: 316-583-7100. [JC]
Catechesis/Religious Programs—Students 63.
Missions—Hamilton, Greenwood Co., St. John, Hamilton, 66853.; Madison, Greenwood Co., St. Teresa Of Avila, Madison, 66860. Tel: 316-437-2504.

Florence, Marion Co., St. Patrick. Closed. Merged with St. Mark, Marion; St. John Nepomucene, Pilsen; and Holy Redeemer, Tampa to form Holy Family, Marion.

Fort Scott, Bourbon Co., Mary Queen of Angels (1860), Rev. Brian Bebak.
Res., 716 S. Eddy St., P.O. Box 271, 66701. Tel: 316-223-4340. [CEM]
School—(Grades K-5). Tel: 316-223-6060; Fax: 316-223-6060. Thomas M. Gorman, Prin.
Lay Teachers 6; Students 54.
Catechesis/Religious Programs—Tel: 316-223-6678. Ken Klassen, D.R.E.
Students 85.

Fredonia, Wilson Co., Sacred Heart (1906), Rev. Stephen R. Baxter.
Res., 428 N. 12th St., 66736. Tel: 316-378-2694; Fax: 316-378-2694. [CEM]
Catechesis/Religious Programs—Tel: 316-378-3565. Judy Puckett, D.R.E.
Students 75.

Frontenac, Crawford Co., Sacred Heart (1891) (Italian), Rev. Robert W. McElwee.
Res., 100 S. Cherokee St., 66763. Tel: 316-231-7747; Fax: 316-231-2550.
Parish Hall: 102 S. Cherokee St., 66763. [CEM]
Catechesis/Religious Programs—Students 115.

Fulton, Bourbon Co., St. Patrick. Closed. For sacramental records contact Mary Queen of Angels, Fort Scott.

Galena, Cherokee Co., St. Patrick (1879), Rev. Charles Middleton.
Res., 307 Galena, P.O. Box 296, 66739. Tel: 316-783-1693.
Catechesis/Religious Programs—Students 16.

Garden Plain, Sedgwick Co., St. Anthony (1901) (German), Rev. Philip J. Allen.
Res., 615 N. Main, 67050. Tel: 316-531-2252; Fax: 316-531-2252. [CEM]
Catechesis/Religious Programs—Tel: 316-535-2593.
Students 332.

Girard, Crawford Co., St. Michael (1925), Rev. Donald R. Thissen.
Res., 106 N. Western, 66743. Tel: 316-724-8717.
Catechesis/Religious Programs—Joan Davied, D.R.E.
Students 158.

Goddard, Sedgwick Co., Holy Spirit (1998), Rev. H. Setter.
Res., 18218 W. Hwy. 54, P.O. Box 787, 67052. Tel: 316-794-3496; Fax: 316-794-3795.
Catechesis/Religious Programs—Students 77.

Greenbush, Crawford Co., St. Aloysius. Closed. For sacramental records contact St. Michael, Girard.

Halstead, Harvey Co., Sacred Heart of Jesus (1874), Rev. James R. O'Shea.
Res., 419 Poplar, 67056. Tel: 316-835-2173. [JC]
Catechesis/Religious Programs—Box 307, Sedgwick, 67135. Tel: 316-772-5841. Tom McVicar, D.R.E.
Students 138.

Hamilton, Greenwood Co., St. John (1888) (German), Rev. Leo A. Kerschen.
Res., 514 N. Elm St., Eureka, 67045. Tel: 316-583-7100.
Catechesis/Religious Programs—Students 2.

Harper, Harper Co., Immaculate Conception. Closed. For inquiries for parish records contact the Chancery.

St. Joan of Arc (1997) (German-Irish), Rev. Michael Peltzer.
Res., 1023 W. Main, P.O. Box 218, 67058. Tel: 316-896-7886; Fax: 316-896-1886; 888-896-1886.
Catechesis/Religious Programs—Tel: 316-896-2251. Tonya Kiley, D.R.E.
Students 87.
Missions—Danville, Harper Co., Danville, 67036. Tel: 316-962-5466; Anthony, Harper Co., 121 S. Madison, Anthony, 67003. Tel: 316-842-5537.

St. Patrick (1882). Closed. For inquiries for parish records contact St. Joan of Arc, 1023 W. Main St., Box 218, Harper, KS 67058.

Haysville, Sedgwick Co., St. Cecilia (1959), Rev. Andy Kuykendall.
Res., 1802 W. Grand, 67060. Tel: 316-524-7801; Fax: 316-524-6183.
School—(Grades K-6) 1912 W. Grand, 67060. Tel: 316-522-0461; Fax: 316-524-6183. Jim Aylward, Prin.
Lay Teachers 8; Students 140.
Catechesis/Religious Programs—JoAnne Audley, D.R.E.
Students 140.

Humboldt, Allen Co., St. Joseph (1867), Rev. Thomas F. Scaletty.
Church—514 Central St., 66748. Tel: 316-473-2129. [CEM]
Res., 424 S. Central Ave., Chanute, 66720. Tel: 316-431-3165.
Catechesis/Religious Programs—Tel: 316-431-4287.
Students 38.

Hutchinson, Reno Co., Holy Cross (1957), Rev. Brian J. Egan.
Res., 2631 Independence Rd., 67502. Tel: 316-665-5163; Fax: 316-662-5085. [JC]
School—2633 Independence Rd., 67502. Tel: 316-665-6168; Fax: 316-665-6168. Mr. Larry Giest, Prin.
Lay Teachers 10; Students 254.
Catechesis/Religious Programs—Students 506.

Our Lady of Guadalupe (1927), Rev. Ned J. Blick.
Res., 612 S. Maple, South Hutchinson, 67505-2099. Tel: 316-662-6443.

Catechesis/Religious Programs—1300 E. 21st, 67502. Tel: 316-663-7968. Mr. Martin Vieyra, D.R.E. Students 101.

St. Teresa (1897), Rev. Richard Stuchlik, S.T.L.
Res., 211 E. Fifth St., 67501. Tel: 316-662-7812; Fax: 316-662-7812. [CEM]
School—215 E. Fifth St., 67501. Tel: 316-662-5601; Fax: 316-662-5601. Ms. Ellen Albert, Prin.
Lay Teachers 8; Students 201.
Catechesis/Religious Programs—Students 180.

Independence, Montgomery Co., St. Andrew (1869), Rev. Stephen M. Thapwa (Burma).
Res., 210 N. Fourth St., 67301. Tel: 316-331-1789; Fax: 316-331-6496. [CEM]
School—Tel: 316-331-2870. Rebecca Brown, Admin.
Lay Teachers 9; Students 120.
Catechesis/Religious Programs—Students 70.

Iola, Allen Co., St. John (1897), Rev. Leon J. Kerschen.
Res., 310 S. Jefferson Ave., 66749. Tel: 316-365-3454. [CEM][JC]
Catechesis/Religious Programs—Tel: 316-365-8278. Mrs. Annette Rexwinkle, D.R.E.
Students 176.

Kingman, Kingman Co., St. Patrick (1885) (Irish), Rev. Daryl Befort.
Res., 638 Ave. D W., 67068. Tel: 316-532-5440; Fax: 316-532-5549. [JC]
School—Tel: 316-532-5338; Fax: 316-532-2966. Mrs. Kristin Schmitz, Prin.
Lay Teachers 9; Students 185.
Catechesis/Religious Programs—Tel: 316-532-5440.
Students 240.

Liberty, Montgomery Co., All Saints. Closed. For inquiries for parish records contact the Chancery.

Lindsborg, McPherson Co., St. Bridget of Sweden (1985), Rev. Paul J. Oborny.
Church—206 W. Swensson, P.O. Box 268, 67456. Tel: 785-227-3588.
Res., 520 E. Northview, McPherson, 67460. Tel: 316-241-0821; Fax: 316-241-8497.
Catechesis/Religious Programs—Mary Patrick, D.R.E.
Students 55.

Little River, Rice Co., Holy Trinity (1885), Rev. Steven Scheier.
296 3rd Rd., Bushton, 67427.
Res., 415 St. Francis St., Lyons, 67554. Tel: 316-562-3427.
Catechesis/Religious Programs—Tel: 316-489-6436. Mary Konen, D.R.E.
Students 44.

Lyons, Rice Co., St. Paul (1927), Rev. James N. Hoagland.
Res., 415 St. Francis St., 67554. Tel: 316-257-3503. [JC]
Catechesis/Religious Programs—Tel: 316-257-3809; Fax: 316-257-2047. Donetta Birzer, D.R.E.
Students 135.

Madison, Greenwood Co., St. Teresa of Avila (1954) (German), Rev. Leo A. Kerschen.
Res., 514 N. Elm St., Eureka, 67045. Tel: 316-583-7100; 437-2504 (Church). [JC]
Catechesis/Religious Programs—Students 5.

Marion, Marion Co., Holy Family 1992. Parish formed from merger of St. Mark, Marion; St. John Nepomucene, Pilsen; St. Patrick, Florence; Holy Redeemer, Tampa; and Immaculate Conception, Burns. Rev. Stephen F. Gronert.
Residence and Mailing: 415 N. Cedar St., 66861. Tel: 316-382-3422. [CEM 5][JC 2]
Catechesis/Religious Programs—Tel: 316-382-3369. Cathy Whitaker, D.R.E.
Students 206.
Mission—Tampa, Marion Co., Holy Redeemer, 66861.

McPherson, McPherson Co., St. Joseph (1880), Rev. Paul J. Oborny.
Res., 520 E. Northview, 67460. Tel: 316-241-0821; Fax: 316-245-9677.
School—Tel: 316-241-3913; Fax: 316-241-3913. Dr. Tamara Arnott, Prin.
Lay Teachers 7; Students 80.
Catechesis/Religious Programs—Anna Ruxlow, D.R.E.
Students 210.
Mission—Lindsborg, McPherson, St. Bridget of Sweden, Box 268, Lindsborg, 67456.

Moline, Elk Co., St. Mary's (1899), Rev. Edward J. Steinberger.
Res., Box 276, 67353-0276. Tel: 316-647-3577. [CEM]

Mount Vernon, Kingman Co., St. Rose (1911) (German-Irish), Rev. Ivan C. Eck.
Res., 13015 E. Maple Grove Rd., Mount Hope, 67108. Tel: 316-444-2210. [CEM]
Catechesis/Religious Programs—Tel: 316-542-3990.
Students 121.

Mulberry, Crawford Co., St. Gabriel. Closed. For sacramental records contact Sacred Heart, Frontenac.

Mulvane, Sumner Co., St. Michael the Archangel (1948), Rev. James S. Mainzer.
Res., 545 E. Main, 67110. Tel: 316-777-4221; Fax: 316-777-1454.
Catechesis/Religious Programs—Tel: 316-777-0444. Karen Oblinger, D.R.E.
Students 250.

Neodesha, Wilson Co., St. Ignatius (1873), Rev. Stephen R. Baxter.
Res., P.O. Box 186, 66757. Tel: 316-378-2694; Fax: 316-378-2694. [CEM]
Catechesis/Religious Programs—Tel: 316-325-3709.
Students 54.

Newton, Harvey Co., St. Mary (1872), Rev. Kenneth J. Schuckman.
Res., 106 E. Eighth St., 67114. Tel: 316-282-0459; Fax: 316-283-0036. [CEM]
School—Tel: 316-282-1974; Fax: 316-283-3642. Mr. Richard Guy, Prin.
Sisters of St. Joseph 1; Lay Teachers 13; Students 230.
Catechesis/Religious Programs—D.R.E.: Sr. Connie Haug, O.P.; Mrs. Marie Morford.
Students 105.

Our Lady of Guadalupe (1919) (Hispanic), Rev. Floyd E. McKinney.
Res., 415 S. Ash St., 67114. Tel: 316-283-3499. [JC]
Catechesis/Religious Programs—Students 134.

Ost, Reno Co., St. Joseph (1880) (German), Rev. Ivan C. Eck.
Res., 13015 E. Maple Grove Rd., Mount Hope, 67108. Tel: 316-444-2210. [CEM]
Catechesis/Religious Programs—Tel: 316-444-2637.
Students 83.

Oswego, Labette Co., Mother of God (1878), Rev. Larry Parker.
Res., 1112 W. Third, 67356. Tel: 316-795-2262. [JC]
Catechesis/Religious Programs—Students 43.

Oxford, Sumner Co., St. Mary (1872), Rev. Bernard X. Gorges.
Res., 412 E. Eighth St., Winfield, 67156. Tel: 316-221-3610. [JC]
Catechesis/Religious Programs—Myra Jacobs, D.R.E.
Students 35.

Parsons, Labette Co., Mary Queen of Peace (1909). Closed. For inquiries for parish records contact St. Patrick, Parsons.

St. Patrick (1872), Rev. Michael J. Schemm.
Res., 1807 Stevens Ave., 67357. Tel: 316-421-6762; Fax: 316-421-4032. [CEM 2][JC]
School—1831 Stevens Ave., 67357. Tel: 316-421-0710; Fax: 316-421-2429. Mr. Harry Heppler, Prin.
Sisters of St. Joseph 1; Lay Teachers 11; Students 147.
Catechesis/Religious Programs—Tel: 316-421-4562.
Students 225.

Pilsen, Marion Co., St. John Nepomucene. Closed. Merged with St. Mark, Marion; St. Patrick, Florence; and Holy Redeemer, Tampa to form Holy Family, Marion.

Piqua, Woodson Co., St. Martin (1884) (German). Closed. For inquiries for sacramental records contact St. John, Iola.

Pittsburg, Crawford Co., Our Lady of Lourdes (1881), Revs. Thomas J. Stroot; Jeffrey A. Fasching; Eric M. Weldon.
Res., 916 N. Locust St., P.O. Box 214, 66762. Tel: 316-231-2135; Fax: 316-231-4804. [CEM]
School—St. Mary's Elementary, (Grades K-6) 213 E. Ninth, 66762. Tel: 316-231-6941. Mr. Francis Smith, Prin.
Sisters of St. Joseph 2; Lay Teachers 18; Students 307.
St. Mary Junior High School—(Grades 7-8) 212 E. 9th, P.O. Box 266, 66762. Tel: 316-231-4690.
Lay Teachers 4; Students 85.
High School—St. Mary-Colgan High School, 212 E. 9th, P.O. Box 266, Pittsburgh, 66762. Tel: 316-231-4690; Fax: 316-231-0690; 231-4804.
Sisters of St. Joseph 1; Priests 1; Lay Teachers 16; Students 159.
Catechesis/Religious Programs—Tama Dutton, D.R.E., Tel: 316-347-8403.
Students 89.
Convent—821 N. Locust St., 66762. Tel: 316-231-6014.

St. Leo, Kingman Co., St. Leo the Great (1902) (German), Rev. John Miller.
Res., 8035 S.W. 160 Ave., Nashville, 67112. Tel: 316-246-5370. [CEM]
Catechesis/Religious Programs—P.O. Box 216, Cunningham, 67035. Tel: 316-298-2601.
Students 40.

St. Mark's, Sedgwick Co., St. Mark (1876) (German), Rev. W. Shawn McKnight.
Res., R.F.D. 1, Colwich, 67030. Tel: 316-796-1604; Fax: 316-769-0511. [CEM][JC]
Catechesis/Religious Programs—Tel: 316-796-1002. Sr. Assumpta, D.R.E.
Students 168.

St. Paul, Neosho Co., St. Francis (1847), Rev. Larry Parker.
Res., 208 Washington St., P.O. Box 216, 66771-0216. Tel: 316-449-2224; Fax: 316-449-8986. [CEM 2]
Catechesis/Religious Programs—Tel: 316-449-2672. Suzan Diskin, D.R.E.
Students 167.

Scammon, Cherokee Co., St. Bridget's (1868), Rev. Eugene W. Grabner.
Res., 115 W. Walnut, Columbus, 66725. Tel: 316-429-2639. [CEM]
Catechesis/Religious Programs—Clustered with St. Rose, Columbus. Tel: 316-479-2236.
Students 66.

Schulte, Sedgwick Co., St. Peter's (1905), Rev. Patrick York.
Parish Offices: 134 W. Peter St., R.R. 24, Wichita, 67215. Tel: 316-524-4259; Fax: 316-524-0932.
Res., 335 N. Annie St., R.R. 24, Wichita, 67215. Tel: 316-522-4728. [CEM]
School—Tel: 316-524-6585; Fax: 316-524-1656. Betty Hunt, Prin.
Lay Teachers 19; Students 328.
Catechesis/Religious Programs—Tel: 316-943-4074. Kathleen Goebel, D.R.E.
Students 217.

Sedan, Chautauqua Co., St. Robert Bellarmine (1962), Rev. Edward J. Steinberger.
Res., P.O. Box 276, Moline, 67353-0276. Tel: 316-647-3577.
Catechesis/Religious Programs—Students 13.

Strong City, Chase Co., St. Anthony of Padua (1880), Rev. Chrysostom Ah Maung.
Res., 316 Spencer, Council Grove, 66846. Tel: 316-767-6412; Fax: 316-767-5370. [CEM]
Catechesis/Religious Programs—Tel: 316-273-8617. Jeanette Black, D.R.E.
Students 53.

Tampa, Marion Co., Holy Redeemer. Now an oratory of Holy Family, Marion.

Walnut, Crawford Co., St. Patrick. Closed. For sacramental records contact St. Francis Church, St. Paul.

Waterloo, Kingman Co., St. Louis (1881) (German-Irish), Rev. Ivan C. Eck.
Res., 13015 E. Maple Grove Rd., Mt. Hope, 67108. Tel: 316-444-2210. [CEM]
Catechesis/Religious Programs—Students 11.

Weir, Cherokee Co., Sacred Heart. Closed. For sacramental records contact St. Rose of Lima, Columbus.

Wellington, Sumner Co., St. Anthony (1884). All information is for both St. Anthony and St. Rose. Rev. Andrew J. Seiler.
Mailing Address: 210 N. B St., 67152. Tel: 316-326-2522; Fax: 316-326-2527.
Catechesis/Religious Programs—Tel: 316-326-3480. Pam Montenegro, D.R.E.
Students 320.

St. Rose of Lima (1949) (Hispanic), Rev. Andrew J. Seiler.
Mailing Address: 210 N. B St., Wellingon, 67152. Tel: 316-326-2522.
Church—1205 E. Harvey, 67152. Tel: 316-326-3572.
Catechesis/Religious Programs—Tel: 316-326-3480.
Students 341.

West Mineral, Cherokee Co., Immaculate Conception. Closed. For sacramental records contact St. Rose of Lima, Columbus.

Willowdale, Kingman Co., St. Peter's (1884) (German), Rev. John P. Miller.
Res., P.O. Box 86, Zenda, 67159. Tel: 316-243-5451. [CEM]

Winfield, Cowley Co., Holy Name (1878), Rev. Bernard X. Gorges.
Res., 412 E. Eighth St., 67156. Tel: 316-221-3610; Fax: 316-221-3528. [JC]
School—Tel: 316-221-0230. Sr. Jacklyn Duncan, Prin.
Lay Teachers 3; Students 44.
Catechesis/Religious Programs—Students 142.

Yates Center, Woodson Co., St. Joseph (1957), Rev. Leon J. Kerschen.
Res., 107 E. Bell St., 66783. [JC]
Catechesis/Religious Programs—Tel: 316-625-2672.
Students 55.

Zenda, Kingman Co., St. John (1908) (German), Rev. John P. Miller.
Res., P.O. Box 86, 67159. Tel: 316-243-5451. [CEM]
Catechesis/Religious Programs—Linda Kerschen, D.R.E.
Students 54.

Chaplains of Public Institutions

WICHITA. *El Dorado Correctional Facility*. Rev. Michael E. Nolan.
Sedgwick County Adult Local Detention Facility. Rev. Dwight J. Birket.
Veterans Administration Hospital. Vacant. Rev. Richard Stuchlik.

HUTCHINSON. *Kansas State Industrial Reformatory*. Rev. Floyd E. McKinney.

On Duty Outside the Diocese:
Reverend Fathers—
Conley, James, Ministry in Rome, Italy
Hoisington, Thomas, Studies in Rome, Italy
McKnight, W. Shawn, Studies in Rome, Italy
Nolan, Joseph T

Retired:
Reverend Monsignors—
Hertel, Herbert N., 3214 Zimmerly, Wichita, KS 67218
Hogan, Vincent, 424 S. Central, Chanute, KS 66720
Lampe, Irvin F., 13014 La Terraza Dr., Sun City West, AZ 85375
Malone, Quintin J., 6900 E. 45th St. N., Wichita, KS 67226
Schmidt, George N., 6900 E. 45th St. N., Wichita, KS 67226
Smith, Charles A., 914 Torrey Pines Dr., Pasa Robles, CA 93446
Tonne, Arthur, 520 N. Freeborn, Marion, KS 66861. Tel: 316-382-3166
Walsh, Charles, 6900 E. 45th St., Wichita, KS 67226

Reverend Fathers—
Bieberle, Victor, 29 Tiburon Way, Hot Springs, AR 71909
Cox, Francis
Curran, John, 6900 E. 45th St., Wichita, KS 67226
Dinan, John, 1915 N. Porter, Apt. A-78, Wichita, KS 67203
Finnegan, Peter J., 6900 E. 45th St. N., Wichita, KS 67226
Freed, Robert, 3330 E. Bellaire St., Wichita, KS 67218
Garrahy, Michael, 6900 E. 45th St. N., Wichita, KS 67226
Harvey, Charles K., 6900 E. 45th St. N., Wichita, KS 67226
Hay, Francis J., 6900 E. 45th St. N., Wichita, KS 67226
Kocour, Robert F., Apartado 407, Barquisimeto Lara, 3001-A Venezuela
Larkin, Patrick, 738 W. Sherman, Kingman, KS 67068
Metcko, Leo E., 6900 E. 45th St. N., Wichita, KS 67226
Mullen, John, P.O. Box 246, Halstead, KS 67056
Mulvihill, Daniel R., RR 10, Box 14, Apt. 4, Joplin, MO 64804
O'Hare, Donald J. q, 950 82nd Ave., Vero Beach, FL 32996
O'Leary, David A., 6900 E. 45th St. N., Wichita, KS 67226
O'Malley, Michael W.
Pepe, Robert F., 4 Circle Dr., Port Duncan, Afton, OK 74331
Regan, Charles, 6900 E. 45th St. N., Apt. E2, Wichita, KS 67226
Reinkemeyer, John, St. Mary, 25741 W. 13th St. N., Garden Plains, KS 67050
Rusteika, John B., 5 Carballo Pl., Hot Springs Village, AR 71909
Spexarth, James, R.R. 1, P.O. Box 30, Marion, KS 66861
Stremel, Adolph, c/o P.A. Sullivan, 801 Main St., Victoria, KS 67671
Trayers, Kevin, 202 S. Liberty, Cherryvale, KS 67335
Walsh, Ulich
Wilkinson, James, 6900 E. 45th St., Wichita, KS 67226
York, Edward, 46 Leicester Dr., Bella Vista, AR 72714

INSTITUTIONS LOCATED IN THE DIOCESE

[A] COLLEGES AND UNIVERSITIES

WICHITA. *Newman University*, 3100 McCormick Ave., 67213-2097. Tel: 316-942-4291; Fax: 316-942-4483.
Web site: www.newmanu.edu
For a complete listing, refer to the Colleges and Universities section.

[B] HIGH SCHOOLS, DIOCESAN

WICHITA. *Bishop Mark K. Carroll Catholic High School*, 8101 W. Central, 67212. Tel: 316-722-2390; Fax: 316-722-6670.
E-mail: BCAROL1@feist.com
Web site: www.feist.com/~bcaroll;
Leticia C. Nielsen, Prin.; Rev. John B. Brungardt, Chap. & Instructor. Tel: 316-943-4353. Priests 1; Sisters 3; Lay Teachers 50; Students 921.
Kapaun Mt. Carmel Catholic High School, 8506 E. Central, 67206. Tel: 316-634-0315; Fax: 316-636-2437.
E-mail: kapaunmountcarmel@yahoo.com
Web site: kapaun.org
Revs. John Sherlock, Chap.; Peter Leigh; Tom Leland, Chap.; Fred N. Spexarth. Sisters 2; Priests 2; Lay Teachers 52; Students 810.

HUTCHINSON. *Trinity High School*, 1400 E. 17th, 67501. Tel: 316-662-5800; Fax: 316-662-1233.
E-mail: bcordel@trinity-hutch.com
Mr. Brian Cordel, Prin.; Rev. Ned J. Blick, Chap. Priests 1; Sisters 3; Lay Teachers 14; Students 253.
The Trinity High School Education Endowment Fund, 1400 E. 17th, 67501. Tel: 316-665-5163; Fax: 316-662-1233. c/o Eugene J. Gerber, 424 N. Broadway, Wichita, 67202. Tel: 316-269-3950. Priests 1; Sisters 3; Lay Teachers 14; Total Enrollment 231.

PITTSBURG. *St. Mary-Colgan High School*, 212 E. 9th St., 66762. Tel: 316-231-4690; Fax: 316-231-0690.
E-mail: smcother@apexcorp.com
Rev. Thomas J. Stroot, Admin.; Mr. Patrick Forbes, Prin. Priests 1; Sisters of St. Joseph 1; Lay Teachers 18; Students 159.

[C] SPECIAL EDUCATION

WICHITA. *Art of Learning Center*, 201 S. Millwood, 67213. Tel: 316-265-6853. Sr. Sibyllina Mueller, O.P., Dir. Speech, Language, Reading Therapy. Total Assisted 1,688; Total Staff 2.

[D] GENERAL HOSPITALS

WICHITA. *Via Christi Regional Medical Center, Inc.*
Web site: www.Via-Christi.org
For a complete listing, refer to the Hospitals section.
Via Christi Rehabilitation Center, Inc., Our Lady of Lourdes Campus, 1151 N. Rock Rd., 67206. Tel: 316-634-3400; Fax: 316-634-1141.
Web site: www.via-christi.org
For a complete listing, refer to the Hospitals section.

COLUMBUS. *Maude Norton Memorial Hospital (MN-MCH, Inc.)*, 220 N. Pennsylvania St., 66725. Tel: 316-429-2545; Fax: 316-429-1984.
E-mail: cneely@stj.com
For a complete listing, refer to the Hospitals section.

FORT SCOTT. *Mercy Health System of Kansas, Inc.*, 821 Burke St., 66701. Tel: 316-223-7057; Fax: 316-223-5327
For a complete listing, refer to the Hospitals section.

INDEPENDENCE. *Mercy Health Systems of Kansas, Inc.-Independence*, 800 W. Myrtle St., P.O. Box 388, 67301. Tel: 316-331-2200; Fax: 316-332-3270.
E-mail: abrau@mhsk.smhs.com
Web site: terraworld.net/mercy/
For a complete listing, refer to the Hospitals section.

OSWEGO. *Oswego Health Center, Inc.*, 800 Barker Dr., 67356-9461. Tel: 316-795-2921; Fax: 316-795-4903.
E-mail: kathym@oswego.net
For a complete listing, refer to the Hospitals section.

PITTSBURG. *Mount Carmel Medical Center; Mount Carmel Foundation*, 1102 E. Centennial, 66762. Tel: 316-231-6100; Fax: 316-232-0493
For a complete listing, refer to the Hospitals section.

[E] HOMES FOR AGED

WICHITA. *Catholic Care Center, Inc.*, 6700 E. 45th St. N., 67226. Tel: 316-744-2020; Fax: 316-744-2182
For a complete listing, refer to the Special Care Facilities section.
Georgetown Village, Inc., 1655 Georgetown St., 67218. Tel: 316-685-0400; Fax: 316-685-0174
For a complete listing, refer to the Special Care Facilities section.

MULVANE. *Villa Maria*, 116 S. Central, 67110. Tel: 316-777-1129; Fax: 316-777-4406.
E-mail: chmathis@hotmail.com
For a complete listing, refer to the Special Care Facilities section.

[F] MONASTERIES AND RESIDENCES FOR PRIESTS AND BROTHERS

WICHITA. *Priests Retirement Center*, 6900 E. 45th St. N., 67226. Tel: 316-744-2020; Fax: 316-744-2182. Thomas M. Church, Admin. Residents 24.
Redemptorist Community, 7100 E. 45th St. N., 67226. Tel: 316-744-0167; Fax: 316-744-8072.
E-mail: spiritlife@feist.com
Web site: www.feist.com/~spiritlife/index.html
Revs. Lawrence E. Sanders, C.SS.R., Supr.; Gerard J. Pecht, C.SS.R.; Edward Thomas Morgan, C.SS.R. Residents 3; Staff 3.
Redemptorist Mission House, 145 S. Millwood Ave., 67213. Tel: 316-262-1877; Fax: 316-262-5250.
E-mail: DANHA@aol.com
Revs. Daniel H. Andree, C.SS.R., Supr.; Walter C. Karrer, C.SS.R.; Andrew Meiners, C.SS.R. Residents 3; Staff 3.

[G] CONVENTS AND RESIDENCES FOR SISTERS

WICHITA. *Adorers of the Blood of Christ*, 1165 Southwest Blvd., 67213. Tel: 316-942-2201; Fax: 1-877-942-0859.
E-mail: stewartj@newmanu.edu
Web site: adorers.org
Rev. Thomas Welk, C.PP.S., Chap. Professed Sisters 209; Novices 1.
Blessed Sacrament Sisters of Charity, 6547 St. James Pl., 67226. Tel: 316-744-8768; Fax: 316-744-3447. Sr. Serena Kim. Sisters 3.
Dominican House of Studies, 201 S. Millwood, 67213. Tel: 316-267-4551. Sisters of the Third Order of St. Dominic (Congregation of the Immaculate Conception, Great Bend, KS). Residents 8.
Medical Sisters of St. Joseph-United States Foundation, 3435 E. Funston, 67218. Tel: 316-686-4746.
E-mail: audrey@qwestinternet.net
Sr. Audrey, Supr. Professed Sisters 5.
Mt. St. Mary Convent, Motherhouse and Novitiate of the Sisters of St. Joseph, 3700 E. Lincoln, 67218-2099. Tel: 316-686-7171; Fax: 316-689-4056.
E-mail: wichitacsj@feist.com
Web site: www.feist.com/~wichitacsj/
Sr. Helene Lentz, C.S.J., Pres.; Rev. Robert E. Hemberger, Chap. Professed Sisters 176.
Sisters of the Immaculate Heart of Mary of Wichita, Inc. (I.H.M.), 605 N. Woodchuck, 67212. Tel: 316-722-9316; Fax: 316-722-4568. Mother Marie Bernadette Mertens, I.H.M., Supr. Professed Sisters 11; Novices 1; Postulants 3.

[H] RETREAT HOUSES

WICHITA. *Spiritual Life Center*, 7100 E. 45th N., 67226. Tel: 316-744-0167; Fax: 314-744-8072.
E-mail: spiritlife@feist.com
Web site: www.feist.com/~spiritlife/index.html
Revs. Joseph M. Gile, Dir.; Lawrence E. Sanders, C.SS.R. Ministry Staff: Revs. Gerard J. Pecht, C.SS.R.; Lawrence E. Sanders, C.SS.R., Spiritual Formation Dir.; Edward Thomas Morgan, C.SS.R.; Chuck Weber, Prog. and Publicity Dir.; Jerrilyn Szelle Holladay, Dir. for Adult Educ. Residents 3; Staff 23.

[I] COMMUNITY CENTERS

WICHITA.
Center of Hope, Inc., 400 N. Emporia, 67202-2514. Tel: 316-267-3999; Fax: 316-267-7778.
E-mail: stellarosenhamer@yahoo.com
Sponsored by Adorers of the Blood of Christ. Sr. Stella Rosenhamer, A.S.C., Dir. Tel: 316-267-0222; Fax: 316-267-7778. Staff 2; Total Assisted 3,921.
Guadalupe Clinic, 940 S. St. Francis, 67211. Tel: 316-264-8974; Fax: 316-262-4938. Ms. Marlene Dreiling, M.N., R.N., Dir. Staff 8; Total Assisted 23,500.

[J] NEWMAN CENTERS

WICHITA. *Wichita State University*. Newman Center, 1810 N. Roosevelt, 67208. Tel: 316-684-6896; Fax: 316-684-2679.
E-mail: nml@veracom.net
Rev. Matthew C. McGinness, Chap.

PITTSBURG. *St. Pius X Center (Pittsburg State University)*, 301A E. Cleveland, 66762. Tel: 316-235-1138.
E-mail: mcelwee@mobile1.net
Web site: www.pittstate.edu/union/organization/newman
Rev. Robert W. McElwee, Chap.

[K] CATHOLIC CHARITIES

WICHITA. *Catholic Charities, Inc.*, 437 N. Topeka, 67202. Tel: 316-264-8344; Fax: 316-264-4442.
E-mail: jvpape@wkscatholiccharities.org
Ms. Janet Valente Pape, Exec. Dir.

Foster Grandparent Program. Provides 84,473 hours of service, 437 N. Topeka, 67202. Tel: 316-264-8344; Fax: 316-264-4442. Staff 3; Total Children Assisted 875; Total Foster Grandparents 124.

Harvest House Program, 437 N. Topeka, 67202. Tel: 316-264-8344; Fax: 316-264-4442. Staff 2; Centers 28; Members Assisted 1,700.

Emergency Services, 437 N. Topeka, 67202. Tel: 316-264-8344; Fax: 316-264-4442. Total Assisted 7,344.

Immigration & Refugee Services, 437 N. Topeka, 67202. Tel: 316-264-0197; Fax: 316-264-4442. Staff 4; Total Assisted 3,969.

Adoption Services, 425 N. Topeka, 67202. Tel: 316-263-0507; Fax: 316-263-5259. Total Assisted 595.

Counseling Services, 425 N. Topeka, 67202. Tel: 316-263-6941; Fax: 316-263-5259. Individuals Served 2,853; Adoptions Completed 31.

Southeast Kansas Counseling, 301 E. Cleveland, Ste. B, Pittsburg, 66762. Tel: 316-231-3638; Fax: 316-230-0477. Staff 2; Clients Assisted 308.

Adult Day Services, 5920 W. Central, 67212. Tel: 316-942-2008; Fax: 316-942-2260. Staff 22; Total Assisted 183.

Anthony Family Shelter, 256 N. Ohio, 67214. Tel: 316-264-7233; Fax: 316-264-6882. Staff 13; Individuals Assisted 438.

Harbor House Shelter, P.O. Box 3759, 67201. Tel: 316-263-6000; Fax: 316-263-8347. Staff 16; Women & Children Assisted 566; Victim's Advocate Program 839.

Mount St. Mary's Learning Lab, 3700 E. Lincoln, 67218. Tel: 316-689-4061; Fax: 316-681-2871. Total Assisted 364.

St. Dismas Missioners, 437 N. Topeka, 67202. Tel: 316-264-8344; Fax: 316-264-4442.

Midtown Learning Center, 1150 N. Broadway, 67214. Tel: 316-303-9001; Fax: 316-303-9002.

Hispanic Social Services, 437 N. Topeka, 67202. Tel: 316-269-5851; Fax: 316-264-4442. Total Agency Staff 103; Total Individuals Assisted 19,969.

[L] MISCELLANEOUS

WICHITA. *De Mattias Jubilee Corporation*, 1400 S. Sheridan, 67213. Tel: 316-943-1203; Fax: 316-943-1427.
E-mail: rosenhamers@newmanu.edu
Sr. Stella Rosenhamer, A.S.C., Pres.

Diocesan Office, Ministry with Persons with Disabilities, 619 S. Maize Rd., 67209. Tel: 316-722-5381; Fax: 316-722-5382.

Gerard House, Inc., 3144 N. Hood, 67204. Tel: 316-832-0777; Fax: 316-832-1327. Deneen Dryden, Dir. Shelter for Needy Pregnant Women. Education Program 51; Total Assisted 45.

Leaven International Corporation, 1400 S. Sheridan, 67213. Tel: 316-943-1203; Fax: 316-943-1427.
E-mail: peterg@newmanu.edu
Greg Peter, Fin. Officer; Sr. Charlotte Rohrbach, Pres. A charitable organization of the Adorers of the Blood of Christ.

The Mary Magdalen Foundation, 457 S. Woodlawn, 67218. Tel: 316-683-6516; Fax: 316-683-8407.

Serra Club of Reno County, 424 N. Broadway, 67202. Rev. Brian J. Egan, Chap.

Serra Club of Wichita - Downtown, 424 N. Broadway, 67202. Tel: 316-269-3900. Rev. Kenneth J. Schuckman, Chap.

Serra Club of Wichita - Metro, 424 N. Broadway, 67202. Tel: 316-269-3900. Rev. Msgr. Thomas McGread, Chap.

Totus Tuus, Inc., 424 N. Broadway, 67202. Tel: 316-685-1337. Sr. Jacinta Langlois.

Via Christi Foundation, Inc., 959 N. Emporia, Ste. 402, 67214. Tel: 316-268-5100; Fax: 316-291-7859. Mr. James N. Barber, Pres. A subsidiary of Via Christi Regional Medical Center. Staff 9.

Via Christi Health Partners, Inc., 959 N. Emporia, Ste. 302, 67214. Tel: 316-268-6944; Fax: 316-291-7966.
Web site: www.Via-Christi.org

Via Christi Health System, Inc., 818 N. Emporia, Ste. 100, 67214. Tel: 316-268-5000; Fax: 316-291-4673.
Web site: www.Via-Christi.org
Mr. LeRoy Rheault, Pres. & CEO; Sr. Sherri Marie Kuhn, S.S.M., Vice Pres. Mission Svcs.; Sr. Marie Veronica Janousek, Vice Pres. Mission Svcs. Owned and operated by the Marian Health System which consists of two sponsoring congregations: The Sisters of St. Joseph of Wichita, Kansas and the Sisters of the Sorrowful Mother of Broken Arrow, Oklahoma. Participating organizations include four acute care facilities, five senior care facilities, and one managed acute care facility, located in three states.

Via Christi Healthcare Outreach Program for Elders, Inc. (HOPE), 3720 E. Bayley, 67218. Tel: 316-689-4000; Fax: 316-689-8928.

Via Christi Home Health Inc., 1122 N. Topeka, 2nd Floor, 67214. Tel: 316-269-1556.

Via Christi Property Services, Inc., 959 N. Emporia, Ste. 302, 67214. Tel: 316-268-6810; Fax: 316-291-7966.
Web site: www.Via-Christi.org

Via Christi Senior Services, Inc., 3720 E. Bayley, 67218. Tel: 316-689-4000; Fax: 316-689-8928.

RELIGIOUS INSTITUTES OF MEN REPRESENTED IN THE DIOCESE

For further details refer to the corresponding bracketed number in the Religious Institutes of Men or Women section.

[1070]—*Redemptorist Fathers*. (Province of St. Louis).—C.SS.R.

[1060]—*Society of the Precious Blood*. (Kansas City Prov.).—C.PP.S.

RELIGIOUS INSTITUTES OF WOMEN REPRESENTED IN THE DIOCESE

[0100]—*Adorers of the Blood of Christ*.—A.S.C.

[]—*Carmelite Sisters of St. Teresa*.—C.S.S.T.

[]—*Charity Sisters of the Blessed Sacrament*. (Korean Foundation).

[]—*Congregation of the Daughters of the Passion of Our Lord Jesus Christ and the Sorrows of Mary*.—C.F.P.

[1070-24]—*Dominican Sisters*.—O.P.

[1430]—*Franciscan Sisters of Our Lady of Perpetual Help*.—O.S.F.

[2575]—*Institute of the Sisters of Mercy of the Americas*.—R.S.M.

[2500]—*Medical Sisters of St. Joseph*.—M.S.J.

[0440]—*Sisters of Charity of Cincinnati, Ohio*.—S.C.

[0430]—*Sisters of Charity of the Blessed Virgin Mary*.—B.V.M.

[3830-18]—*Sisters of St. Joseph*.—C.S.J.

[2185]—*Sisters of the Immaculate Heart of Mary of Wichita*.—I.H.M.

[4100]—*Sisters of the Sorrowful Mother (Third Order of St. Francis)*.—S.S.M.

[2150]—*Sisters, Servants of the Immaculate Heart of Mary*.—I.H.M.

NECROLOGY

† Finnegan, Peter J., (Retired). —Died June 26, 2000.

† Dougherty, Rev. Msgr. Denis R, Colwich, KS Sacred Heart Church. —Died Jan. 9, 2000.

Diocese of Wilmington

(Dioecesis Wilmingtoniensis)

Most Reverend

MICHAEL A. SALTARELLI, D.D.

Bishop of Wilmington; ordained May 28, 1960; appointed Titular Bishop of Mesarfelta and Auxiliary Bishop of Newark, June 12, 1990; Episcopal ordination July 30, 1990; appointed Eighth Bishop of Wilmington November 21, 1995; installed January 23, 1996.

ESTABLISHED MARCH 3, 1868.

Square Miles Delaware 1,932; Maryland 3,375; Total 5,307.

Comprises the State of Delaware and the Counties of Caroline, Cecil, Dorchester, Kent, Queen Anne's, Somerset, Talbot, Wicomico and Worcester in Maryland.

For legal titles of parishes and diocesan institutions, consult the Chancery Office.

Chancery Office: P.O. Box 2030, Wilmington, DE, 19899-2030. Tel.: 302-573-3100; Fax: 302-573-3128.

Web site address: www.cdow.org

E-mail address: ccurtis@cdow.org

STATISTICAL OVERVIEW

Personnel	
Bishop	1
Retired Bishops	1
Priests: Diocesan Active in Diocese	94
Priests: Active Outside Diocese	8
Priests: Retired, Sick or Absent	24
Number of Diocesan Priests	126
Religious Priests in Diocese	85
Extern Priests in Diocese	15
Ordinations:	
Diocesan Priests	3
Permanent Deacons in Diocese	45
Total Brothers	25
Total Sisters	270
Parishes	
Parishes	56
With Resident Pastor:	
Resident Diocesan Priests	51
Resident Religious Priests	4
Without Resident Pastor:	
Administered by Priests	1
Missions	21
Pastoral Centers	8
Professional Ministry Personnel:	
Sisters	32
Lay Ministers	69
Welfare	
Catholic Hospitals	1
Total Assisted	217,707
Health Care Centers	2
Total Assisted	1,050
Homes for the Aged	5
Total Assisted	366
Residential Care of Children	4
Total Assisted	99
Day Care and Extended Day Care Centers	2
Total Assisted	252
Specialized Homes	2
Total Assisted	413
Special Centers for Social Services	18
Total Assisted	338,951
Residential Care of Disabled	1
Total Assisted	62
Educational	
Diocesan Students in Other Seminaries	14
Total Seminarians	14
High Schools, Diocesan and Parish	5
Total Students	2,942
High Schools, Private	3
Total Students	1,712
Elementary Schools, Diocesan and Parish	25
Total Students	9,825
Elementary Schools, Private	4
Total Students	1,050
Non-residential Schools for the Disabled	1
Total Students	100
Catechesis/Religious Education:	
High School Students	1,117
Elementary Students	10,313
Total Students Under Catholic Instruction	27,073
Teachers in the Diocese:	
Priests	18
Brothers	5
Sisters	48
Lay Teachers	910
Vital Statistics	
Receptions into the Church:	
Infant Baptism Totals	3,028
Adult Baptism Totals	353
Received into Full Communion	315
First Communions	2,953
Confirmations	1,893
Marriages:	
Catholic	493
Interfaith	388
Total Marriages	881
Deaths	1,527
Total Catholic Population	205,000
Total Population	1,137,988

Former Bishops—Rt. Rev. THOMAS A. BECKER, D.D., cons. Aug. 16, 1868; transferred to Savannah, 1886; died July 29, 1899.—Rt. Rev. ALFRED A. CURTIS, D.D., cons. Nov. 14, 1886; resigned 1896; named Titular Bishop of Echinus; died July 11, 1908.—Most Rev. JOHN J. MONAGHAN, D.D., cons. May 9, 1897; resigned and named Titular Bishop of Lydda, July 10, 1925; died Jan. 7, 1935.—Most Rev. EDMOND JOHN FITZMAURICE, D.D., cons. Nov. 30, 1925; resigned March 2, 1960 and named Titular Archbishop of Tomi; died July 25, 1962.—Most Rev. HUBERT J. CARTWRIGHT, D.D., cons. Coadjutor "with right of succession," Oct. 24, 1956; Titular Bishop of Neve; died March 6, 1958.—Most Rev. MICHAEL W. HYLE, D.D., cons. Sept. 24, 1958 as Titular Bishop of Christopolis and Coadjutor with right of succession; succeeded to See, March 2, 1960; died Dec. 26, 1967.—Most Rev. THOMAS J. MARDAGA, D.D., cons. Jan. 25, 1967; named Titular Bishop of Mutugenna; appt. Bishop of Wilmington, March 13, 1968; installed April 6, 1968; died May 28, 1984.—Most Rev. JAMES C. BURKE, O.P., cons. May 25, 1967; named Titular Bishop of Lamiggiga; Vicar Apostolic of Chimbote, Peru, 1962-1978 Served in Diocese of Wilmington, 1978-1994; died May 28, 1994.—Most Rev. ROBERT E. MULVEE, D.D., J.C.D., ord. June 30, 1957; Auxiliary Bishop of Manchester and Titular Bishop of Summa, Feb. 15, 1977; cons. April 14, 1977; appt. Bishop of Wilmington, Feb. 19, 1985; installed April 11, 1985; appt. to Diocese of Providence as Coadjutor Bishop of Providence, Feb. 7, 1995; installed March 27, 1995; succeeded to See, June 11, 1997.

Office of the Bishop—P.O. Box 2030, Wilmington, 19899. PATRICIA SLEPESKY-BOSSI, Sec. to Bishop & Notary for the Curia. Tel: 302-573-3100; Fax: 302-573-2391.

Vicar General for Administration and Moderator of the Curia—Rev. Msgr. J. THOMAS CINI, V.G., *1925 Delaware Ave., P.O. Box 2030, Wilmington, 19899.* Tel: 302-573-3118; Fax: 302-573-3128.

Vicar General for Pastoral Services—Rev. Msgr. JOSEPH F. REBMAN, V.G., S.T.L., J.C.L., *1925 Delaware Ave., P.O. Box 2030, Wilmington, 19899.* Tel: 302-573-3100; Fax: 302-254-4044.

Vicar for Priests—Rev. Msgr. CLEMENT P. LEMON, V.P., *1925 Delaware Ave., P.O. Box 2030, Wilmington, 19899.* Tel: 302-573-3144; Fax: 302-573-3128.

Pastoral Services Department

Secretary, Pastoral Services Department—Rev. Msgr. JOSEPH F. REBMAN, V.G., S.T.L., J.C.L.

Chancery Office—Rev. Msgr. JOHN O. BARRES, S.T.D., J.C.L., Chancellor, *Mailing Address: P.O. Box 2030, Wilmington, 19899.* Office: *1925 Delaware Ave., Wilmington, 19806.* Office Hours: Mon.-Fri. 8:30-4:30. Tel: 302-573-3100; Fax: 302-254-4044. Send all marriage dispensation requests to Chancery Office.

Archives—Mr. DONN DEVINE, Archivist, *P.O. Box 4019, Greenville, 19807.* Tel: 302-655-0597.

Diocesan Tribunal—Mailing Address: P.O. Box 2030, Wilmington, 19899. 1925 Delaware Ave., Wilmington, 19806. Tel: 302-573-3107; Fax: 302-573-3128.

Judicial Vicar—Very Rev. THEODORE E. OLSON, J.C.L.

Office Supervisor—Mrs. JOANN KUBASKO.

Court of First Instance Judges—Revs. STANLEY R. DRUPIESKI, O.S.F.S.; GEORGE J. BRUBAKER, J.C.L.; Sr. JEANNE HAMILTON, O.S.U., J.C.L.; Ms. JACQUELINE E. HANNEM, J.C.L.

Auditor—Deacon FRANCIS STAAB.

Defenders of the Bond—Mr. JACK D. ANDERSON, J.C.D.; Rev. CYPRIAN ROSEN, O.F.M.Cap., J.C.L.

Secretaries/Notaries—Mrs. MARIE BRADLEY; Mrs. GAIL ESPOSITO; Mrs. PATRICIA KILLEN.

Catholic Cemeteries—Rev. Msgr. JOSEPH F. REBMAN, V.G., C.C.C.E., Dir.; Mr. MARK A. CHRISTIAN, C.C.C.E., Exec. Dir., *Mailing Address: P.O. Box 2506, Wilmington, 19805.* Tel: 302-656-3323; Fax: 302-656-1069.

Coordinator of Institutional Chaplains—Rev. Msgr. JOHN O. BARRES, *1925 Delaware Ave., P.O. Box 2030, Wilmington, 19899.* Tel: 302-573-3100; Fax: 302-254-4044.

Vocation Office—Rev. JAMES NASH, Dir., *1925 Delaware Ave., P.O. Box 2030, Wilmington, 19899.* Tel: 302-573-3113; Fax: 302-573-3128.

Office for Deacons—Deacon HAROLD D. JOPP, JR., Dir., *1925 Delaware Ave., P.O. Box 2030, Wilmington, 19899.* Tel: 302-573-2390; Fax: 302-573-3128.

Office of Worship—Vacant, Dir., *1626 N. Union St., Wilmington, 19899.* Tel: 302-573-3137; Fax: 302-573-2393.

Delegate for Religious—Sr. CELESTE CRINE, O.S.F., *1925 Delaware Ave., P.O. Box 2030, Wilmington, 19899.* Tel: 302-573-3124; Fax: 302-573-3128.

Mission Office—Propagation of the Faith and Holy Childhood Association, Rev. JOHN P. KLEVENCE, Dir., *1626 N. Union St., P.O. Box 2030, Wilmington, 19899.* Tel: 302-573-3104; Fax: 302-573-2393.

Apostolate for Ethnic Ministries—P.O. Box 2030, Wilmington, 19899. Tel: 302-573-3100.

Ministry of Black Catholics—Mr. ALVIN RULEY, Co-ord., *Mailing Address: P.O. Box 617, Cecilton, MD, 21913.* Tel: 410-275-2410.

Hispanic Community—

Wilmington Office—Rev. CHRIS POSCH, O.F.M., Dir., *1010 W. Fourth St., Wilmington, 19805.* Tel: 302-655-0518; Fax: 302-655-7684.

Georgetown Office—Sr. FRANCISCA MOTA, C.C.V., Assoc. Dir., *302 W. Laurel St., Georgetown, 19947.* Tel: 302-855-1253.

Korean Catholics—Rev. STEPHEN DO, Pastoral Min.; Mr. JOHN KO, Lay Leader, *2710 Duncan Rd., Wilmington, 19808.* Tel: 302-998-7609; Fax: 302-798-4785.

Native American Community—Ms. GAIL RANDO, Contact, *1200 Windon Dr., Wilmington, 19803.* Tel: 302-478-5412.

Catholic Education Department

Secretary—Mr. EDMUND F. GORDON.

Catholic Schools—Bro. JAMES MALONE, C.F.X., Supt.; Sr. KATHLEEN CALLAGHAN, S.S.J., Assoc. Supt.; Sr. KATHLEEN FINERTY, O.S.U., Asst. Supt., *1626 N. Union St., Wilmington, 19806.* Tel: 302-573-3133; Fax: 302-573-3143.

Religious Education—Mr. EDMUND F. GORDON, Diocesan Dir. GLORIA REINHARDT, Assoc. Dir., *1626 N. Union St., Wilmington, 19806.* Tel: 302-573-3130; Fax: 302-573-2393.

Education Ministry for Persons With Special Needs—Mrs. JO-ANN DORA, Coord. Spec. Rel. Educ. Tel: 302-573-3130. Mrs. MARGARET WYNN, Coord. Hearing Impaired, *1626 N. Union St., Wilmington, 19806.* Tel: 302-573-3130.

Educational Resource Center—Ms. SUZANNE GIERKE, Admin., *1626 N. Union St., Wilmington, 19806.* Tel: 302-573-3136.

Catholic Youth Ministry—Mr. PATRICK DONOVAN, Dir. AMY HAEGEN, Coord. Leadership Devel. JOE MCNESBY, Coord. Athletics; MARTINA SOBOLESKI, Coord. Youth at Risk, *803 N. Broom St., Wilmington, 19806.* Tel: 302-658-3800; Fax: 302-658-7617.

Catholic Campus Ministry—Very Rev. MICHAEL F. SZUPPER, Ph.D., V.F., Dir., *University of Delaware, 45 Lovett Ave., Newark, 19711.* Tel: 302-368-4728; Fax: 302-368-2548.

Communications Department

Secretary—Mr. ROBERT KREBS.

Office of Public Relations, Radio and T.V.—Mr. ROBERT KREBS, Dir., *1626 N. Union St., Wilmington, 19899.* Tel: 302-573-3116; Fax: 302-573-2393.

Finance Department

Chief Financial Officer and Secretary—Mr. JOSEPH P. CORSINI, *Mailing Address: P.O. Box 2030, Wilmington, 19899. 1925 Delaware Ave., Wilmington, 19806.* Tel: 302-573-3105; Fax: 302-573-3129.

Development Department

Secretary and Diocesan Development Director—Mrs. DEBORAH A. FOLS; Mrs. GRACE BEEBE, Assoc. Devel. Dir., *P.O. Box 2030, Wilmington, 19899.* Tel: 302-573-3121; Fax: 302-573-3128.

Annual Catholic Appeal—Mrs. DEBORAH A. FOLS, Dir., *P.O. Box 2030, Wilmington, 19899.* Tel: 302-573-3100; Fax: 302-573-3128.

Catholic Charities Department

Catholic Charities—Mr. ALLAN J. DAUL, A.C.S.W., Exec. Dir.; Mrs. BARBARA GRIECO, M.C., M.B.A., Deputy Dir., *Fourth St. & Greenhill Ave., P.O. Box 2610, Wilmington, 19805.* Tel: 302-655-9624; Fax: 302-655-9753. (Refer to separate listings in the Institutions for detailed information on Catholic Charities and related organizations.).

Parish Social Ministry—Mr. ANDREW ZAMPINI, Dir., *Fourth St. & Greenhill Ave., P.O. Box 2610, Wilmington, 19805.* Tel: 302-655-9624; Fax: 302-655-9753.

Offices Reporting to Vicar General for Adminstration/Moderator of the Curia

Catholic Press Inc., "The Dialog"—Most Rev. MICHAEL A. SALTARELLI, Publisher; Mr. JIM GRANT, Editor & Gen. Mgr., *P.O. Box 2208, Wilmington, 19899. 1925 Delaware Ave., Wilmington, 19806.* Tel: 302-573-3109 (Newsroom); 302-573-3112 (Advertising); Fax: 302-573-2397.

Human Resources Office—Sr. SUZANNE DONOVAN, S.C., Dir., *P.O. Box 2030, Wilmington, 19899.* Tel: 302-573-3126.

Management Information System (MIS)—Mrs. NANCY MOORE, Dir., *P.O. Box 2030, Wilmington, 19899. 1925 Delaware Ave., Wilmington, 19806.* Tel: 302-573-3122.

Legal Services—JAMES P. COLLINS, SR., Esq., Diocesan Attorney, *P.O. Box 2030, Wilmington, 19899. 1626 N. Union St., Wilmington, 19806.* Tel: 302-573-3138; Fax: 302-573-2351.

Diocesan Planning—Rev. Msgr. J. THOMAS CINI, V.G., *P.O. Box 2030, Wilmington, 19899.* Tel: 302-573-3118.

Diocesan Real Estate Committee—Rev. Msgr. J. THOMAS CINI, V.G., Sec., *P.O. Box 2030, Wilmington, 19899.* Tel: 302-573-3118.

Catholic Ministry to the Elderly—Rev. Msgr. J. THOMAS CINI, V.G., Sec., *P.O. Box 2030, Wilmington, 19806.* Tel: 302-573-3118.

Other Ministries

Catholic Scouting Program—Rev. MICHAEL J. CARRIER, Chap. for Girl Scouts, *P.O. Box 8093, Newark, 19714.* Tel: 302-368-4665. Revs. JAMES D. HREHA, Chap. for Boy Scouts; MICHAEL DARCY, Assoc. Chap., *P.O. Box 646, Rehoboth Beach, 19971.* Tel: 302-227-4550.

Censor of Books—Rev. Msgr. JOHN H. DEWSON, S.T.L., *St. Thomas Parish, 301 N. Bancroft Pkwy., Wilmington, 19805.* Tel: 302-658-5131.

Liaison for Non-Christian Religions—Rev. LEONARD J. KEMPSKI, Liaison, *Church of the Good Shepherd, 828 Aiken Ave., Perryville, MD, 21903.* Tel: 410-642-6534.

Liaison for Evangelization—Rev. WILLIAM J. LAWLER, Liaison, *Mailing Address: 303 Chesterfield Ave., Centreville, MD, 21617.* Tel: 410-758-0140.

Ecumenical Liaison—Rev. Msgr. JOSEPH F. REBMAN, V.G., Dir., *Mailing Address: P.O. Box 2030, Wilmington, 19899.* Tel: 302-573-3100.

Marian Devotions—Rev. Msgr. JOHN O. BARRES, Dir.; Rev. JOSEPH J. PIEKARSKI, Assoc. Dir., *Mailing Address: P.O. Box 2030, Wilmington, 19899.* Tel: 302-573-3100.

Volunteer Liaison for the Physically Disabled—Mr. BOB CICHOCKI, M.H.S., *260 Christiana Rd., #B-3, New Castle, 19720;* Fax: 302-325-2131.

Principal Advisory Groups to the Bishop

College of Consultors—Rev. Msgr. JOSEPH F. REBMAN, V.G.; Rev. Msgr. J. THOMAS CINI, V.G.; Rev. Msgr. PAUL J. TAGGART; Rev. Msgr. CLEMENT P. LEMON; Rev. Msgr. JOHN O. BARRES; Revs. MICHAEL A. ANGELONI; JOHN P. HOPKINS; WILLIAM F. GRANEY, *P.O. Box 2030, Wilmington, 19899.*

Priests' Council—Rev. JOHN P. HOPKINS, Exec. Officer; Rev. Msgr. JOHN O. BARRES, Sec., *P.O. Box 2030, Wilmington, 19899.* Tel: 302-573-3100.

Deans—Very Rev. JOHN F. O'BRIEN, Coord. of Deans; Very Rev. DANIEL W. GERRES, V.F.; Very Rev. MICHAEL F. SZUPPER, V.F.; Very Rev. ARTHUR B. FIORE, V.F.; Very Rev. GEORGE J. BRUBAKER, V.F.; Very Rev. STEPHEN J. CONNELL, V.F.; Very Rev. THOMAS J. PETERMAN, V.F.; Very Rev. RAYMOND F. WEISMAN, V.F.; Very Rev. JOHN J. KAVANAUGH, V.F.

Finance Council—Mr. JOSEPH P. CORSINI, Sec., *P.O. Box 2030, Wilmington, 19899.* Tel: 302-573-3105.

Parish Priest Consultors—Revs. CHARLES L. BROWN; CHARLES C. DILLINGHAM; THOMAS E. HANLEY; JOHN J. KAVANAUGH; CHRIS LABARGE; STANLEY J. RUSSELL.

Priests' Personnel Committee—Rev. JOHN J. MINK, Dir., *P.O. Box 2030, Wilmington, 19899.* Tel: 302-328-1790.

Women's Commission—Co-Chairs: Sr. DORIS MICAL, C.S.J.P., *5700 Kirkwood Hwy., Ste. 104, Wilmington, 19808.* KIM ZITZNER, *45 Lovett Ave., Newark, 19711.*

Other Advisory Groups

Priests' Continuing Formation Committee—Rev. JOHN P. HOPKINS, Chm., *St. Margaret of Scotland, 230 Executive Dr., Ste. 8, Newark, 19702.* Tel: 302-369-8100; Fax: 302-369-6200.

Council of Religious—Sr. CELESTE CRINE, Contact, *Mailing Address: P.O. Box 2030, Wilmington, 19899.* Tel: 302-573-3124; Fax: 302-573-3128.

Diocesan School Board—Bro. JAMES MALONE, C.F.X., Sec., *Mailing Address: P.O. Box 2030, Wilmington, 19899.* Tel: 302-573-3133.

Diocesan Religious Education Board—Mr. EDMUND F. GORDON, Sec., *Mailing Address: 1626 N. Union St., Wilmington, 19806.* Tel: 302-573-3130; Fax: 302-573-2393.

Diocesan Building Committee—Mr. PAUL S. ADAMS, JR., Chm.; Rev. Msgr. J. THOMAS CINI, V.G., Episcopal Liaison, *P.O. Box 2030, Wilmington, 19899.* Tel: 302-573-3118; Fax: 302-573-3128.

Office for Pro Life Activities—Mr. THOMAS JEWETT, Chm., *P.O. Box 2610, Wilmington, 19805.* Tel: 302-655-9624; Fax: 302-655-9753.

Pastoral Council—Mr. LAWRENCE BUCCI, Exec. Officer; Rev. Msgr. JOHN O. BARRES, Sec., *Mailing Address: P.O. Box 2030, Wilmington, 19899.* Tel: 302-573-3100; Fax: 302-254-4044.

Public Affairs Advisory Committee—Rev. Msgr. J. THOMAS CINI, V.G., Chm., *P.O. Box 2030, Wilmington, 19899.* Tel: 302-573-3118; Fax: 302-573-3128.

Respect Life Committee—Mr. THOMAS JEWETT, Chm., *Fourth St. & Greenhill Ave., Wilmington, 19805.* Tel: 302-655-9624; Fax: 302-655-9753.

Due Process Commission—Contact: Very Rev. THEODORE E. OLSON, Clerk, *P.O. Box 2030, Wilmington, 19899.* Tel: 302-573-3107; Fax: 302-573-3128.

Diocesan Corporations

Catholic Cemeteries, Inc.—Rev. Msgr. JOSEPH F. REBMAN, V.G., Vice Pres.; Mr. MARK A. CHRISTIAN, Sec., *P.O. Box 2506, Wilmington, 19805.* Tel: 302-656-3323.

Catholic Diocese of Wilmington, Inc.—A corporation sole under the laws of the State of Delaware. Rev. Msgr. JOSEPH F. REBMAN, V.G., Vice Pres.; Rev. Msgr. J. THOMAS CINI, V.G., Sec., *Mailing Address: P.O. Box 2030, Wilmington, 19899.* Tel: 302-573-3118. Office: *1925 Delaware Ave., Wilmington, 19899.*

Catholic Diocese Foundation—Mr. JOSEPH P. CORSINI, Exec. Dir., *P.O. Box 2030, Wilmington, 19899.* Tel: 302-573-3105.

Catholic Ministry to the Elderly, Inc.—Rev. Msgr. J. THOMAS CINI, V.G., Vice Pres., *P.O. Box 2030, Wilmington, 19899.* Tel: 302-573-3118.

Catholic Press of Wilmington, Inc.—Rev. Msgr. J. THOMAS CINI, V.G., Vice Pres., *P.O. Box 2208, Wilmington, 19899.* Tel: 302-573-3118.

Catholic Charities, Inc.—Mr. ALLAN J. DAUL, A.C.S.W., Sec., *Fourth St. & Greenhill Ave., P.O. Box 2610, Wilmington, 19806.* Tel: 302-655-9624.

Catholic Youth Organization, Inc.—Rev. Msgr. J. THOMAS CINI, V.G., Vice Pres., *Mailing Address: P.O. Box 2030, Wilmington, 19899.* Tel: 302-573-3118.

Children's Home, Inc.—Mr. ALLAN J. DAUL, A.C.S.W., Sec., *Fourth St. & Greenhill Ave., P.O. Box 2610, Wilmington, 19806.* Tel: 302-655-9624.

Diocese of Wilmington Schools, Inc.—Bro. JAMES MALONE, C.F.X., Sec., *1626 N. Union St., Wilmington, 19806.* Tel: 302-573-3133.

Seton Villa, Inc.—Mr. ALLAN J. DAUL, A.C.S.W., Sec., *Fourth St. & Greenhill Ave., P.O. Box 2610, Wilmington, 19806.* Tel: 302-655-9624.

Siena Hall, Inc.—Mr. ALLAN J. DAUL, A.C.S.W., Sec., *Fourth St. & Greenhill Ave., P.O. Box 2610, Wilmington, 19806.* Tel: 302-655-9624.

Activities

Apostleship of Prayer—Rev. JOSEPH R. MCMAHON, *2013 Gilpin Ave., Wilmington, 19806.* Tel: 302-654-5519.

Campaign for Human Development—Mr. ALLAN J. DAUL, A.C.S.W., Diocesan Dir., *Fourth St. & Greenhill Ave., P.O. Box 2610, Wilmington, 19806.* Tel: 302-655-9624.

Catholic Charismatic Renewal—Rev. STANLEY A. IANIERI, Chap., *St. John the Beloved, 907 Milltown Rd., Wilmington, 19808.* Tel: 302-999-0211.

Catholic Relief Services Inc.—Very Rev. GEORGE J. BRUBAKER, V.F., Diocesan Dir., *506 Seabury Ave., Milford, 19963.* Tel: 302-422-5123.

Commission for the Catholic Missions Among the Colored People and the Indians—Rev. Msgr. JOSEPH F. REBMAN, V.G., Diocesan Dir., *P.O. Box 2030, Wilmington, 19899.* Tel: 302-573-3100; Fax: 302-573-3128.

Cursillo Movement—Rev. THOMAS E. HANLEY, Spiritual Dir., *631 S. State St., Dover, 19901.* Tel: 302-674-5787. JEAN REYNOLDS, Lay Dir., *528 Troon Rd., Dover, 19904.* Tel: 302-736-6636.

Delmarva Catholic Network, Inc.—Mr. ROBERT KREBS, Contact Person, *P.O. Box 2030, Wilmington, 19899.* Tel: 302-573-3116.

Diocesan Healing Ministry—JEANNE CASEY, Lay Dir., *533 Waterford Dr., Hockessin, 19707.* Tel: 302-239-5982.

KAIROS Ministries, Inc.—Rev. GREGORY CORRIGAN, Contact Person, *P.O. Box 269, Claymont, 19703.* Tel: 302-798-2904.

Korean Catholic Community, Inc.—Rev. STEPHEN CHANG-HOWN DO, Chap.; Mr. JOHN KO, Lay Leader, *2712 Duncan Rd., Wilmington, 19808.* Tel: 302-998-7730.

St. Thomas More Society—Rev. Msgr. PAUL J. TAGGART, Chap.; Very Rev. THEODORE E. OLSON, Assoc. Chap., *Mailing Address: P.O. Box 2030, Wilmington, 19899.* Tel: 302-573-3100.

St. Vincent dePaul Society—Mr. PAUL COLLINS, *312 Hazlett Rd., New Castle, 19720.* Tel: 302-328-5166.

Organizations With Which Diocese Has Liaison

[*]Birthright of Delaware, Inc.—Mrs. MARY JO FROHLICH, Dir., *1311 N. Scott St., Wilmington, 19806.* Tel: 302-656-7080.

The Christian Council of DE & MD's Eastern Shore—Rt. Rev. WAYNE P. WRIGHT, Chm., *2020 N. Tatnall St., Wilmington, 19802.* Tel: 302-656-5441.

[*]Delaware Citizens for Life—Mr. THOMAS JEWETT, Chm., *4019 Greenmount Rd., Wilmington, 19810.*

Delawareans United for Education—Rev. Msgr. J. THOMAS CINI, V.G., *P.O. Box 2030, Wilmington, 19899.* Tel: 302-573-3118.

[*]Jesus House—Mr. CHRISTIAN MALMGREN, Dir. ANGELA MALMGREN, Assoc. Dir.; Deacon JOSEPH CONTE, Chap., *2501 Milltown Rd., Wilmington, 19808.* Tel: 302-995-6859; Fax: 302-995-6833.

Maryland Catholic Conference—(An agency of the Archdiocese of Baltimore, Washington and the Diocese of Wilmington); Mr. RICHARD J. DOWLING, Exec. Dir., *309 Cathedral St., Baltimore, MD, 21201.* Tel: 301-322-0901. Rev. Msgr. J. THOMAS CINI, V.G., Diocesan Liaison, *P.O. Box 2030, Wilmington, 19899.* Tel: 302-655-3130.

National Catholic Ministry to the Bereaved—Mr. THOMAS R. JEWETT, Contact, *P.O. Box 2610, Wilmington, 19805.* Tel: 302-655-9624; Fax: 302-655-9753.

National Conference for Community and Justice—Rev. CLEMENS D. MANISTA, *3200 Philadelphia Pike, Claymont, 19703.* Tel: 302-798-2904.

Operation Help, Inc.—Rev. PATRICK SHAULES, S.J., Pres. MARCINDA HAEDGE, Sec. & Treas., *P.O. Box 134, Hartly, 19953.* Tel: 302-492-8985; Fax: 302-492-8360.

Regina Coeli Society—Rev. JOHN F. HECKEL, O.S.F.S., Chap., *1801 N. Broom St., Wilmington, 19802.* Tel: 302-655-1592.

World Wide Marriage Encounter—Contact Persons: JOE HUNTER; ANN HUNTER. Tel: 302-734-4089; Fax: 302-734-7898.

CLERGY, PARISHES, MISSIONS AND PAROCHIAL SCHOOLS

DELAWARE, CITY OF WILMINGTON
(New Castle County)

1—CATHEDRAL OF ST. PETER (1796), Rev. William B. Kauffman, Rector; Deacon George M. Taylor, Jr. In res., Revs. William P. Mathesius; Carlos R. Vazquez.
Res., 500 West St., 19801. Tel: 302-654-5920; Fax: 302-654-3197.
School—310 W. 6th St., 19801. Tel: 302-656-5234; Fax: 302-658-6489.
Daughters of Charity of St. Vincent de Paul 3; Lay Teachers 13; Students 216.
Catechesis/Religious Programs—Students 210.

2—ST. ANN (1887), Revs. Joseph R. McMahon; Roger F. Dibuo. Pastoral Assocs.: Sr. John Regina Lang, M.S.B.T.; Sr. Marie Bernadette Lang, M.S.B.T. In res., Rev. Msgr. John O. Barres.
Res., 2013 Gilpin Ave., 19806. Tel: 302-654-5519; 652-0152; Fax: 302-654-5527.
School—Tel: 302-652-6567; Fax: 302-652-4156. Mr. Ronald Bogia, Prin.
Lay Teachers 17; Students 266.
Catechesis/Religious Programs—Tel: 302-654-8504. Anita Wood, D.R.E.
Students 266.

3—ST. ANTHONY OF PADUA (1924) (Italian), Revs. Mark A. Hushen, O.S.F.S.; Charles C. Garst, O.S.F.S.; Bro. Michael J. Rosenello, O.S.F.S. In res., Revs. Roberto Balducelli, O.S.F.S.; Mario Bugliosi, O.S.F.S.
Res., 901 N. DuPont St., 19805. Tel: 302-421-3700; Fax: 302-421-3709.
School—9th & Scott Sts., 19805. Tel: 302-421-3743; Fax: 302-421-3796. Mr. Bernard J. Fisher, Prin.
Sisters of St. Francis of Philadelphia 2; Lay Teachers 21; Students 510.
High School—Padua Academy, 905 N. Broom St., 19805. Tel: 302-421-3739; Fax: 302-421-3748. Sr. Ann Michele Zwosta, O.S.F., Prin.
Sisters 2; Lay Teachers 55; Brothers 1; Students 605.
Catechesis/Religious Programs—Tel: 302-421-3706.
Students 45.
Convents—1710 W. 9th St., 19805. Tel: 302-421-3754.
Sisters 2; 1401 W. 10th St., 19806. Tel: 302-421-3739.
Sisters 5.
St. Anthony's Education Fund, Inc.—901 N. DuPont St., 19805. Tel: 302-421-3700; Fax: 302-421-3709.

4—CHRIST OUR KING (1926), Rev. Leonard J. Kempski; Deacon William J. Maloney, Jr.
Res., 2810 N. Monroe St., 19802. Tel: 302-762-4140; Fax: 302-762-8414.
School—28th & Madison Streets, 19802. Tel: 302-762-4031.
Sisters of St. Francis 5; Lay Teachers 9; Students 150.

5—ST. ELIZABETH (1908), Revs. Charles C. Dillingham; Warren R. Hall; James D. Bagnato, O.Praem.
Res., 809 S. Broom St., 19805-4296. Tel: 302-652-3626; Fax: 302-658-5957.
School—1500 Cedar St., 19805-4249. Tel: 302-655-8208; Fax: 302-655-5457. Sr. M. Gerard, O.S.B., Prin.
Sisters of St. Benedict 2; Lay Teachers 24; Aides 8; Students 557.
High School—Tel: 302-656-3369; Fax: 302-656-7513. Sr. Mary Ellen, O.S.B., Prin.
Sisters 5; Lay Teachers 31; Students 439.
Catechesis/Religious Programs—St. Hedwig, 408 S. Harrison St., 19805. Tel: 302-594-1400, Ext. 3; Fax: 302-594-1407.
Students 31.

6—ST. HEDWIG (1890) (Polish), Revs. Andrew Molewski; Joseph E. Wharton.
Res., 408 S. Harrison St., 19805. Tel: 302-594-1400; Fax: 302-594-1415.
School—Linden & Harrison Sts., 19805. Tel: 302-594-1402; Fax: 302-594-1407.
Felician Sisters 1; Lay Teachers 14; Students 290.
Catechesis/Religious Programs—Students 80.

7—ST. JOSEPH'S R.C. CHURCH OF WILMINGTON, INC. (1889), Franciscan Pastoral Team: Rev. Barry J. Langley, O.F.M., Pastoral Mod.; Bro. David W. Schlatter, O.F.M., Admin.
Church—1012 French St., 19801. Tel: 302-658-4535; Fax: 302-656-2167.
Res., 1010 W. 4th St., 19805.

8—ST. MARY OF THE IMMACULATE CONCEPTION (1858), Revs. James F. Trainor; Philip P. Sheekey.
Res., 1414 King St., 19801. Tel: 302-652-0743.
Church—6th & Pine Sts., 19801.

9—ST. PATRICK (1880), Revs. James F. Trainor; Philip P. Sheekey.
Res., 1414 King St., 19801. Tel: 302-652-0743.

10—ST. PAUL'S (1869), Franciscan Pastoral Team: Rev. Lawrence J. Hayes, O.F.M., Pastoral Mod. In res., Revs. Barry J. Langley, O.F.M.; Christopher J. Posch, O.F.M.; Bro. David Schlatter, O.F.M.; Revs. Flavian A. Walsh, O.F.M.; Thomas M. Gallagher, O.F.M.
Res., 1010 W. 4th St., 19805. Tel: 302-655-6596; Fax: 302-655-7684.
School—3rd & Van Buren Sts., 19805. Tel: 302-656-1372; Fax: 302-656-5238. Mrs. Cindy Mann, Prin.
Lay Teachers 16; Students 240.

11—SACRED HEART (1874). Closed. For inquiries for sacramental records contact Cathedral of St. Peter. Tel: 302-654-3197; Fax: 302-654-6850.

12—ST. STANISLAUS KOSTKA (1912) (Polish), Rev. Edward J. Kaczorowski.
Mailing Address: P.O. Box 30110, 19805-7110.
Res., 901 E. 7th St., 19801. Tel: 302-571-0622; Fax: 302-571-1508.

13—ST. THOMAS (1903), Rev. Daniel W. Gerres. In res., Rev. Msgr. John H. Dewson.
Res., 301 N. Bancroft Pkwy., 19805. Tel: 302-658-5131; Fax: 302-652-6222.
School—201 Bayard Ave., 19805. Tel: 302-654-0746; Fax: 302-426-1738.
Lay Teachers 17; Students 253.

DELAWARE
OUTSIDE THE CITY OF WILMINGTON

Bear, New Castle Co., St. Elizabeth Ann Seton (1978), Revs. Charles L. Brown, III; Joseph V. Bozzelli.
Res., 345 Bear-Christiana Rd., 19701-1048. Tel: 302-322-6430; Fax: 302-322-6297.
Catechesis/Religious Programs—Tel: 302-322-8194. Mrs. Sylvia Deputy, D.R.E.
Students 474.

Bellefonte, New Castle Co., St. Helena (Wilmington P.O.) (1936), Revs. Stanley J. Russell; Joseph M. LaForge (TR); Deacon Edward A. Dunning.
Res., 602 Philadelphia Pike, Wilmington, 19809. Tel: 302-764-0325; Fax: 302-764-1068.
School—210 Bellefonte Ave., Willmington, 19809. Tel: 302-762-5595; Fax: 302-762-6329.
Lay Teachers 11; Assistants 4; Students 225.
Catechesis/Religious Programs—Tel: 302-762-4280. Hummy Pennell, D.R.E.
Students 103.
Convent—610 Philadelphia Pike, Willmington, 19809. Tel: 302-764-3427.

Bethany Beach, Sussex Co., St. Ann (1955), Rev. David F. Kelley; Deacons Edward Brink; Robert Tracy; Donald Lydick.
Res., 691 Garfield Ave., P.O. Box 149, 19930. Tel: 302-539-6449; Fax: 302-539-0657.
Catechesis/Religious Programs—Tel: 302-539-5443; Fax: 302-539-5509.
Students 313.

Brandywood, New Castle Co., Church of the Holy Child (Wilmington P.O.) (1969), Revs. James T. Kirk, Jr.; Francis P. Kenney; Deacon Samuel Torres.
Res., 2500 Naamans Rd., Wilmington, 19810. Tel: 302-475-6486; Fax: 302-475-3458.
Catechesis/Religious Programs—Tel: 302-475-5477. Sr. Margaret Cunniffe, O.S.F., D.R.E.
Students 236.

Claymont, New Castle Co., Holy Rosary (1921), Revs. Clemens D. Manista; David F. Murphy; Deacons Richard J. Maichle; Allen Wolf. In res., Rev. Gregory M. Corrigan.
Res., 3200 Philadelphia Pike, 19703. Tel: 302-798-2904; 798-2987; Fax: 302-798-3609.
School—3110 Philadelphia Pike, 19703. Tel: 302-798-5584.
Sisters of St. Joseph 3; Lay Teachers 25; Students 433.
Catechesis/Religious Programs—Tel: 302-798-0123. Sr. Maryanne Bemiller, S.S.J., D.R.E.
Students 174.

Delaware City, New Castle Co., St. Paul (1852), Rev. Philip L. Siry.
Res., 209 Washington St., P.O. Box 544, 19706. Tel: 302-834-4321; Fax: 302-834-1757.

Glasgow, New Castle Co., St. Margaret of Scotland (1999), Rev. John P. Hopkins.
Res., 230 Executive Dr., Ste. #8, Newark, 19702. Tel: 302-369-8100; Fax: 302-369-6200.
Catechesis/Religious Programs—Students 320.

Dover, Kent Co., Holy Cross (1870), Revs. Thomas E. Hanley; James B. Smith; Michael P. Darcy; Deacon Anthony Vinciguerra.
Res., 631 S. State St., 19901. Tel: 302-674-5780; Fax: 302-674-5783. [CEM]
School—Tel: 302-674-5784. Ms. Marcia Bertino, Prin.
Lay Teachers 33; Students 694.
Catechesis/Religious Programs—Tel: 302-674-5786. Carmella Jones, D.R.E.
Students 750.

Elsmere, New Castle Co., Corpus Christi (Wilmington P.O.) (1948), Rev. Francis J. Rogers; Deacon John G. Parisi. In res., Very Rev. Theodore E. Olson, J.V.
Res., 901 New Rd., Elsmere, Wilmington, 19805. Tel: 302-994-2922; Fax: 302-892-3315.
School—907 New Rd., Elsmere, Wilmington, 19805. Tel: 302-995-2231; Fax: 302-993-0767. Sr. Donna Desien, O.S.F., Prin.
Sisters 4; Lay Teachers 28; Students 567.
Catechesis/Religious Programs—Tel: 302-998-2864. Joanne Huhn, D.R.E.
Students 73.
Convent—912 New Rd., Elsmere, Wilmington, 19805. Tel: 302-994-5641.

Fairfax, New Castle Co., St. Mary Magdalen (Wilmington P.O.) (1951), Very Rev. John F. O'Brien; Revs. Stephen C. Lonek; Joseph M.P.R. Cocucci; Deacon Tony Catka.
Res., 7 Sharpley Rd., Wilmington, 19803. Tel: 302-652-6800; Fax: 302-652-4771.
School—9 Sharpley Rd., Wilmington, 19803. Tel: 302-656-2745; Fax: 302-656-7889. Barbara Wanner, Prin.
Lay Teachers 43; Students 540.
Catechesis/Religious Programs—Tel: 302-652-7141. Sheila Meara, D.R.E.
Students 211.

Garfield Park, New Castle Co., Holy Spirit (New Castle P.O.) (1954), Rev. Charles W. Wiggins.
Res., 12 Winder Rd., Garfield Park, New Castle, 19720. Tel: 302-658-1069; Fax: 302-658-6890.
School—Church Dr., New Castle, 19720. Tel: 302-658-5345.
Sisters 2; Lay Teachers 15; Students 296.
Catechesis/Religious Programs—Students 50.

Georgetown, Sussex Co., St. Michael the Archangel (1956), Rev. Daniel J. McCloskey; Deacons Joseph Baker; Donald Carroll.
Res., 202 Edward St., 19947. Tel: 302-856-6451; Fax: 302-856-3790.
Catechesis/Religious Programs—Students 141.

Mission—Millsboro, Sussex Co., Mary Mother of Peace, Rte. 24, 19966. Tel: 302-945-4044.

Greenville, New Castle Co., St. Joseph on the Brandywine (1841), Rev. Msgr. Joseph F. Rebman, V.G.; Deacon F. Edmund Lynch. In res., Very Rev. Stephen J. Connell.
Res., 10 Old Church Rd., Wilmington, 19807. Tel: 302-658-7017; Fax: 302-428-0639. [CEM 2]
Catechesis/Religious Programs—Tel: 302-656-7185. Sr. Imelda P. Dooley, O.S.F., D.R.E.
Students 203.

Hockessin, New Castle Co., St. Mary of the Assumption (1882), Revs. Roy F. Pollard; Steven Giuliano; Michael McDermott; Deacon John W. Freebery, Jr. In res., Rev. Paul G. Mast.
Res., 7200 Lancaster Pike, P.O. Box 1240, 19707. Tel: 302-239-7100; Fax: 302-239-8219. [CEM]
Catechesis/Religious Programs—Tel: 302-239-7100, Ext. 17.
Students 735.

Liftwood, New Castle Co., Immaculate Heart of Mary (Wilmington P.O.) (1955), Rev. Msgr. Clement P. Lemon; Rev. William D. Melnick; Deacon Austin M. Snow, Jr.; Theresa H. Gerlach, Pastoral Assoc. In res., Rev. Msgr. J. Thomas Cini.
Res., 4701 Weldin Rd., Liftwood, Wilmington, 19803. Tel: 302-764-0357; Fax: 302-764-4381.
School—1000 Shipley Rd., Liftwood, Wilmington, 19803. Tel: 302-764-0977; Fax: 302-764-0375. Catherine Weaver, Prin.
Lay Teachers 29; Students 523.
Catechesis/Religious Programs—Tel: 302-762-5550. Sharon B. Hayes, D.R.E.
Students 206.

Middletown, New Castle Co., St. Joseph (1883), Rev. Thomas A. Flowers.
Res., 115 Cleaver Farm Rd., P.O. Box 196, 19709. Tel: 302-378-5800; Fax: 302-378-5808. [CEM]
Catechesis/Religious Programs—Tel: 302-378-5802. Paulette R. Cotnoir, D.R.E.
Students 700.
Mission—Chesapeake City, Cecil Co., St. Rose of Lima, Lock St., 21915. Tel: 410-885-5533.
Shrine—Warwick, St. Francis Xavier-Old Bohemia.

Milford, Kent and Sussex Cos., St. John the Apostle (1910), Revs. George J. Brubaker; John L. Taggart; Deacons James D. Malloy; Anthony Bianco.
Res., 506 Seabury Ave., 19963-2217. Tel: 302-422-5123; Fax: 302-422-5720.
Catechesis/Religious Programs—Tel: 302-422-5319; Fax: 302-422-5729.
Students 318.
Mission—Harrington, Kent Co., St. Bernadette, 109 Dixon, Harrington, 19952. Tel: 302-398-8269.

New Castle, New Castle Co., St. Peter (1845), Very Rev. Arthur B. Fiore, V.F. In res., Rev. Paul D. Calamari.
Church & Mailing:, 521 Harmony St., 19720.
Res., 35 E. 5th St., 19720. Tel: 302-328-2335; Fax: 302-328-0519. [CEM]
School—6th & Harmony Sts., 19720. Tel: 302-328-1191; Fax: 302-328-8049.
Lay Teachers 10; Students 292.
Catechesis/Religious Programs—Tel: 302-322-5177. Sr. Joan Lewis, S.S.J., D.R.E.
Students 105.

Newark, Newcastle Co., Parish of the Resurrection (1969), Rev. Joseph J. Drobinski; Deacons Joseph J. Conte; Francis J. Huhn; Al Rose, Sr.
Office: 3000 Videre Dr., Skyline Ridge, Wilmington, 19808. Tel: 302-368-0146; Fax: 302-368-3536.
Res., 119 Larkspur Rd., 19711. Tel: 302-737-3066; Fax: 302-368-3536.
Catechesis/Religious Programs—Tel: 302-366-1596. Jo Singer, D.R.E.
Students 312.

St. John the Baptist-Holy Angels, New Castle Co., (1891), Revs. Richard A. Reissmann; David A. Baumgartel; Mark A. Kelleher; Deacon Hugh J. McCann.
Res., 82 Possum Park Rd., 19711. Tel: 302-731-2200; Fax: 302-731-2434. [CEM]
School—Tel: 302-731-2210; Fax: 302-731-2211.
Lay Teachers 25; Students 544.
Catechesis/Religious Programs—Tel: 302-731-2209.
Students 521.

St. Thomas More Oratory, New Castle Co., (1975). (Personal Parish for Students & Faculty of University of Delaware). Very Rev. Michael F. Szupper, V.F.; Rev. Mark Kopacz; Kim Zitzner, Pastoral Assoc.
Res., 155 Haines St., 19711. Tel: 302-368-4728; Fax: 302-368-2548.
Church & Mailing:, 45 Lovett Ave., 19711. Tel: 302-368-4728.
Catechesis/Religious Programs—Students 30.

Ogletown, New Castle Co., Holy Family (Newark P.O.) (1979), Revs. Michael Angeloni; Michael J. Carrier; John Grasing; Deacon William Murrian.
Res., 15 Gender Rd., P.O. Box 8093, Newark, 19714. Tel: 302-368-4665; Fax: 302-368-4667.
Catechesis/Religious Programs—Tel: 302-368-8976; Fax: 302-368-5184. D.R.E.: Melody Duffy; Geralyn Ryerson.
Students 607.

Wilmington, New Castle Co., St. Catherine of Siena (Wilmington P.O.) (1960), Revs. John M. Hynes; Ralph Castelow; Deacons John J. Falkowski, Jr.; Francis J. Staab.
Res., 2503 Centerville Rd., 19808. Tel: 302-633-4900; Fax: 302-633-4960.
School—Tel: 302-633-4901; Fax: 302-633-4902.
Lay Teachers 17; Students 303.
Catechesis/Religious Programs—2503 Centerville Rd., Tel: 302-633-4903. Sr. Theresa Cappelli, D.R.E.
Students 355.

Rehoboth, Sussex Co., St. Edmond (1952), Revs. Raymond L. Forester; James D. Hreha; Deacon John A. Smith.
Office: 409 King Charles St., P.O. Box 646, Rehoboth Beach, 19971. Tel: 302-227-4550; Fax: 302-227-4557.
Res., 402 King Charles St., P.O. Box 646, Rehoboth Beach, 19771.
Catechesis/Religious Programs—Tel: 302-227-4553. Mrs. Geraldine Buckley, D.R.E.
Students 296.
Mission—Lewes, Sussex Co., Shrine of St. Jude, Rt. 1, Lewes, 19958. Tel: 302-227-4550.

Seaford, Sussex Co., Our Lady of Lourdes (1945), Revs. John Harrison, C.SS.R.; Pasquale Tremonte, C.SS.R.; Deacon Arcy Passwaters.
Res., 528 Stein Hwy., P.O. Box 719, 19973-0719. Tel: 302-629-3591; Fax: 302-629-6758. [CEM]
Catechesis/Religious Programs—Tel: 302-629-7999. Mrs. Debra Depta, D.R.E.
Students 275.

Sherwood Park, New Castle Co., St. John the Beloved (1955), Very Rev. John J. Kavanaugh, V.F.; Revs. Stanley A. Ianieri; Richard Smith; Deacon James Haley.
Res., 907 Milltown Rd., Wilmington, 19808. Tel: 302-999-0211; Fax: 302-999-9184.
School—903 Milltown Rd., Wilmington, 19808. Tel: 302-998-5525.
Sisters of St. Francis of Philadelphia 2; Lay Teachers 29; Students 612.
Catechesis/Religious Programs—Tel: 302-994-7757. Pauline Berlingieri, D.R.E.
Students 614.

Smyrna, Kent Co., St. Polycarp (1883), Rev. Ralph L. Martin.
Res., 135 Ransom Ln., 19977. Tel: 302-653-8279; Fax: 302-653-3509.
Catechesis/Religious Programs—Tel: 302-653-4101. Sr. Ellen Gerlach, D.R.E.
Students 200.

Wilmington Manor, New Castle Co., Our Lady of Fatima (New Castle P.O.) (1948), Revs. John J. Mink; Thomas J. Protack, S.T.L.; Joseph J. Narimattam; Deacon Joseph C. Romans.
Res., 801 Dupont Blvd., New Castle, 19720. Tel: 302-328-3431; 328-5773; Fax: 302-328-6318.
School—Tel: 302-328-2803; Fax: 302-328-5427.
Lay Teachers 28; Students 596.
Catechesis/Religious Programs—Tel: 302-328-0307. D.R.E.: Patricia Walker; Debra Menard.
Teachers 25; Students 255.

Woodcrest, New Castle Co., St. Matthew (1941), Revs. Michael J. Cook; William M. Hazzard; William J. Klapps, (Retired U.S.N.); Deacon Harold Chalfant.
Res., 3 Curtis Ave., Wilmington, 19804. Tel: 302-633-5850; Fax: 302-633-6022.
School—One Fallon Ave., 19804. Tel: 302-633-5860; Fax: 302-633-3787.
Lay Teachers 28; Students 520.
Catechesis/Religious Programs—811 Newport Pk, Wilmington, 19804. Tel: 302-633-5858.
Students 148.

MARYLAND

Cambridge, Dorchester Co., St. Mary Refuge of Sinners (1885), Rev. Bruce Byrolly.
Res., 1515 Glasgow St., Box 218, 21613. Tel: 410-228-4770; Fax: 410-228-0969. [CEM]
Catechesis/Religious Programs—Tel: 410-228-2701. Sr. Kathleen Winkleman, O.S.F., D.R.E.
Students 70.
Mission—Meekin's Neck, Dorchester Co., St. Mary, Star of the Sea. [CEM]

Centreville, Queen Anne Co., Our Mother of Sorrows (1890), Rev. William J. Lawler.
Res., 303 Chesterfield Ave., 21617. Tel: 410-758-0140. [CEM]
Catechesis/Religious Programs—Tel: 410-758-0143; Fax: 410-758-5463. Sr. Elaine McCarron, S.C.N., D.R.E.
Students 209.
Mission—Queenstown, Queen Anne Co., St. Peter, 5319 Ocean, Gateway, 21658. Tel: 410-827-8084.

Chester, Kent Island, Queen Anne Co., St. Christopher (1954), Revs. Paul F. Jennings, Jr.; Rene Mangahas.
Res., Box 660, 1861 Harbor Dr., Chester, 21619. Tel: 410-643-6220; Fax: 410-643-4055.
Catechesis/Religious Programs—Tel: 410-643-8489.
Students 445.

Chestertown, Kent Co., Sacred Heart (1876), Rev. Leonard J. Blakely.
Res., 508 High St., 21620. Tel: 410-778-3160; Fax: 410-810-0427. [CEM]
Catechesis/Religious Programs—Tel: 410-778-4650. Sr. Elaine McCarron, S.C.N., D.R.E.
Students 159.
Missions—Rock Hall, Kent Co., St. John, W. Main St., Rock Hall, 21661. Tel: 410-778-3160; Betterton, Kent Co., Most Precious Blood, 1910 Main St., Betterton, 21610.

Easton, Talbot Co., SS. Peter and Paul (1868), Revs. Robert E. Coine; Edmund T. Coppinger; Cornelius J. Breslin.
Res., 215 Goldsborough St., 21601. Tel: 410-822-2344; Fax: 410-770-5080. [CEM]
School—900 High St., 21601. Tel: 410-822-2275; Fax: 410-820-0136.
Lay Teachers 28; Students 513.
High School—Fax: 410-822-1767.
Lay Teachers 24; Students 231.
Catechesis/Religious Programs—Tel: 410-822-6581. Sr. Marianne Wegener, D.R.E.
Students 744.
Missions—Cordova, Talbot Co., St. Joseph, 21625. Tel: 410-364-5543; St. Michaels, Talbot Co., St. Michael, Lincoln Ave., 21663. Tel: 410-745-2822.

Elkton, Cecil Co., Immaculate Conception (1849), Revs. Daniel J. McGlynn; John J. Gayton, M.I.C.
Res., 300 Maryland Ave., P.O. Box 345, 21922. Tel: 410-398-1100; Fax: 410-398-1175. [CEM 2]
School—452 Bow St., 21921. Tel: 410-398-2636; 398-4161; Fax: 410-398-1190.
Sisters of St. Francis of Philadelphia 2; Lay Teachers 19; Students 270.
Catechesis/Religious Programs—Tel: 410-392-3551; Fax: 410-392-9917. Sr. Grace Andrew, D.R.E.
Students 578.
Mission—North East, Cecil Co., St. Jude, 928 Turkey Point, 21901.

Galena, Kent Co., St. Dennis, Very Rev. Thomas J. Peterman, V.F.
Mailing Address: P.O. Box 249, 21635. Tel: 410-648-5145; Fax: 410-648-5767. [CEM]
Catechesis/Religious Programs—Tel: 410-648-5287.
Students 86.

Marydel, Caroline Co., Immaculate Conception (1916), Rev. Christopher LaBarge.
Res., 522 Main St., Box 399, 21649. Tel: 410-482-7687; Fax: 410-482-7253.
Catechesis/Religious Programs—Tel: 410-482-8939.
Students 128.

Ocean City, Worcester Co., St. Mary, Star of the Sea (1877), Rev. John P. Klevence; Deacon Richard McCarthy.
Res., 208 S. Baltimore Ave., 21842-4106. Tel: 410-289-9419.
Catechesis/Religious Programs—Tel: 410-289-7038; Fax: 410-289-4385. Elizabeth A. Sacca, D.R.E.
Students 191.
Mission—Ocean City, Worcester Co., Holy Saviour, Philadelphia Ave. & 17th St., Ocean City, 21842. Tel: 410-289-3463.

St. Luke and St. Andrew (1985), Revs. William J. Porter; Joseph J. Piekarski; Edward J. Fahey; Deacons Jack H. Campbell; Edward Holson.
Office: 144th St. & Lighthouse Ave., P.O. Box 3400, 21843. Tel: 410-250-0300; 0301; Fax: 410-250-0417.
Res., 403 141st St., 21843. Tel: 410-250-0399; Fax: 410-250-0417.
Catechesis/Religious Programs—Tel: 410-250-0342. Mrs. Mary Anne Blatzheim, D.R.E.
Students 363.
Mission—Ocean Pines, Worcester Co., St. John Neumann, Rt. 589 & Beauchamp Rd., 21811. Tel: 410-208-2956.

Perryville, Cecil Co., Church of the Good Shepherd (1949), Rev. Leonard J. Kempski. In res., Rev. Donald Grecco.
Res., 828 Aiken Ave., 21903. Tel: 410-642-6534; Fax: 410-642-2234.
School—810 Aiken Ave., 21903. Tel: 410-642-6265; Fax: 410-642-6522.
Lay Teachers 12; Students 200.
Catechesis/Religious Programs—Tel: 410-642-2439.
Students 148.
Missions—Port Deposit, Cecil Co., St. Teresa, 162 N. Main St., Port Deposit, 21904.; Pilottown, Cecil

Co., St. Patrick Bald Friar Rd.; Rising Sun, Cecil Co., St. Agnes, 150 S. Queen St., Rising Sun, 21911. Tel: 410-658-9422.

Pocomoke City, Worcester Co., Holy Name of Jesus (1943), Very Rev. Raymond F. Weisman, V.F.
Res., 1913 Old Virginia Rd., P.O. Box 179, 21851. Tel: 410-957-1215; Fax: 410-957-1214.
Catechesis/Religious Programs—Fax: 410-957-1215. Patrick Russo, D.R.E.
Students 105.
Mission—Westover, Somerset Co., St. Elizabeth, 8734 Old Westover Rd., Westover, 21871. Tel: 410-651-9117.

Ridgely, Caroline Co., St. Benedict (1896), Rev. Norman P. Carroll; Deacon Harold D. Jopp, Jr.
Res., 408 Central Ave., P.O. Box 459, 21660. Tel: 410-634-2253; Fax: 410-634-1997. [CEM 2]
Catechesis/Religious Programs—Tel: 410-634-1921.
Students 200.
Mission—Denton, Caroline Co., St. Elizabeth, First St. & Franklin St., Denton, 21629. [CEM]

Salisbury, Wicomico Co., St. Francis De Sales (1910), Revs. Edward M. Aigner; Paul J. Campbell, O.S.F.S.; Joseph Kandathiparampil; Michael B. Roark; Deacons Carl R. Beers; Ron R. Siers.
Res., 514 Camden Ave., 21801. Tel: 410-742-6443; Fax: 410-742-9410.
School—500 Camden Ave., 21801. Tel: 410-749-9907; Fax: 410-749-9507. Mr. Richard Adamo, Prin. Lay Teachers 20; Students 298.
Catechesis/Religious Programs—Tel: 410-546-2908. Mrs. Michele Harris, D.R.E.
Students 622.
Convent—417 Wicomico St., 21801. Tel: 410-742-9343.
Mission—Delmar, Wicomico Co., Holy Redeemer, Bi-State Blvd. & Chestnut St., Delmar, 21875.

Secretary, Dorchester Co., Our Lady of Good Counsel (1891), Rev. Anthony F. Greco.
Res., 109 Willow Street, P.O. Box 278, 21664. Tel: 410-943-4300; Fax: 410-943-1357. [CEM]
Catechesis/Religious Programs—Students 87.
Mission—Bethlehem, Caroline Co., Holy Child, P.O. Box 278, Bethlehem, 21664.

Chaplains of Public Institutions

National Guard

WILMINGTON. *Delaware Air National Guard.* 901 New Rd., 19805. Tel: 302-994-2922. Rev. Francis J. Rogers, Chap., 506 Seabury Ave., Milford, 19963. Tel: 302-422-5123. Very Rev. George J. Brubaker.
Delaware Army National Guard 301 N. Bancroft Pkwy., 19805. Chaplains: Revs. John J. Mink; David F. Murphy.

Health Care

WILMINGTON. *A.I. du Pont Institute.* Rev. David A. Baumgartel, Chap., Tel: 302-764-0357.
St. Francis Hospital 7th St. & Clayton St., 19805. Tel: 302-421-4577. Revs. John Finn; Joseph J. McKenna, O.S.F.S.

DELAWARE CITY. *Governor Bacon Health Center.* Rev. Philip L. Siry, Chap., Tel: 302-834-4321.

ELSMERE. *Veteran's Hospital* 1601 Kirkwood Hwy., Tel: 302-994-2511. Chaplains: Revs. John P. Connery, O.S.F.S.; William J. Dougherty, O.S.F.S., Asst. Chap.

NEW CASTLE. *Delaware Psychiatric Hospital.* Rev. Carlos R. Vazquez, Chap., Tel: 302-577-4360.

NEWARK. *Christiana Care Health Services, Inc* 4755 Ogletown-Stanton Rds., Tel: 302-733-1900; 733-1280. Wilmington Hospital, 14th & Washington Sts., Wilmington, 19805. Tel: 302-428-2233. Chaplains: Revs. William F. Graney; Paul Calamari.

PERRY POINT, MD. *Veterans Admin.* Rev. Jeffrey Reynolds.

SMYRNA, MD. *Delaware Home & Hospital for the Chronically Ill.* Rev. Ralph L. Martin, Chap., Tel: 302-653-8279.

Correctional Facilities

WILMINGTON. *Ferris School and Bridge House.* Deacon George M. Taylor, Jr., Chap., Tel: 302-995-2350.
Gander Hill Correctional Center. Rev. Daniel W. Gerres, Chap., Tel: 302-764-0357.

SMYRNA, MD. *Delaware State Correctional Center.* Rev. William P. Mathesius, Chap., Tel: 302-653-9261 Ext. 487.

WESTOVER, MD. *Eastern Correctional Institution.* Rev. Edward M. Aigner, Jr., Chap., Tel: 410-742-6443.

Campus Ministry

CHESTERTOWN, MD. *Washington College* Sacred Heart, 508 High St., 21620. Tel: 410-778-3160. Rev. Leonard J. Blakely, Chap.

DOVER. *Wesley College.* Very Rev. Michael F. Szupper, Chap., Tel: 302-368-4728.

NEWARK. *University of Delaware* St. Thomas More Oratory, 45 Lovett Ave., 19711. Tel: 302-368-4728. Very Rev. Michael F. Szupper, Ph.D., Chap. & Dir. Campus Ministry.

SALISBURY, MD. *Salisbury State College* 211 W. College Ave., 21801. Tel: 410-219-3376. Laura St. Marie, Campus Min.
University of Maryland, Eastern Shore 211 W. College Ave., 21801. Tel: 410-219-3376. Laura St. Marie, Campus Min.

Apostleship of the Sea:
Reverend Fathers—
Kauffman, William B., Chap., Cathedral of St. Peter, 500 West St., Wilmington, DE 19801. Tel: 302-654-5920

Nursing Homes:
Reverend Fathers—
Eckrich, James P., Asst. Chap. to Health Care Facilities, 773 Paper Mill Rd., Newark, DE 19711. Tel: 302-737-7142
Storck, Edward J., Chap., 1504-2 N. Broom St., #17, Wilmington, DE 19806-3048. Tel: 302-428-1415

Special or Other Diocesan Assignment:
Reverend Fathers—
Glapiak, Edward, 3 Towne Estates, Apt. G3, Wilmington, DE 19805
Richardson, James E., 2504 Blackwood Rd., Wilmington, DE 19810. Tel: 302-475-6252

On Duty Outside the Diocese:
Reverend Monsignors—
Koper, Francis B., SS. Cyril and Methodius Seminary, Orchard Lake, MI 48033
Reverend Fathers—
Gallagher, Michael J., Trinity College, Theology Dept., 125 Michigan Ave., Washington, DC 20017
Gomolski, Joseph T., 241 Balboa Dr., Poinciana, FL 34758
Martin, Kenneth J., 4001 14th St., N.E., Washington, DC 20017
McMahon, Kevin T., St. Charles Borromeo Seminary, 1000 E. Wynnewood Rd. Overbrook, Philadelphia, PA 19096
Pagano, Bernard T., St. Mary of Mt. Virgin, 190 Sanford St., New Brunswick, NJ 08901
Turley, Sean F., SS. Michael and James, Haunton near Tamworth, Staffordshire, B799HL (1848), Great Britain

Military Chaplains:
Reverend Fathers—
Mullen, Owen J., 91-1009 Kaiopua St., Ewa Beach, HI 96706
Volmi, Dennis G., 4WGHC, 1505 Vermont Garrison St., Seymour Johnson AFB, NC 27531-2449

Absent on Sick Leave:
Reverend Fathers—
Casari, Michael T., P.O. Box 2030, Wilmington, DE 19899
Jackson, James M., P.O. Box 2030, Wilmington, DE 19899
O'Neill, Patrick J., P.O. Box 2030, Wilmington, DE 19899

Retired:
Reverend Monsignors—
Brady, Patrick A., Vianney House, 905 Milltown Rd., Wilmington, DE 19808
Dewson, John H., St. Thomas the Apostle, 301 N. Bancroft Pkwy., Wilmington, DE 19805
Taggart, Paul J., 1401 Pennsylvania Ave., #1411, Wilmington, DE 19806
Reverend Fathers—
Breen, Stephen B., Vianney House, 905 Milltown Rd., Wilmington, DE 19808
Clark, Howard T., P.O. Box 147, Essington, PA 19029
DeLuca, Francis G., Fahey Court, 100 Pastime Dr., Apt. 307, Syracuse, NY 13208
Dempster, Douglas W., P.O. Box 370, Marydel, MD 21649
Frundt, Oscar H., 417 Delaware Ave. W., Wilmington, DE 19803
Gardocki, Thomas F., 4620 Sylvanus Dr., Wilmington, DE 19803
Gorski, Alex F., 1401 Pennsylvania Ave., Apt. 1205, Wilmington, DE 19806
Jennings, William E., 2303 Inglewood Dr., Wilmington, DE 19803
Klapps, William J., Caravel Farms, 260 Benjamin Blvd., Bear, DE 19701
McGann, L. Philip, 5541 Bay Ave., Ocean City, NJ 08226
Paris, Charles W., Box 752, Toms River, NJ 08754
Perkins, Russell H., P.O. Box 2437, Manteo, NC 27954
Plokhooy, Christopher H., Vianney House, 905 Milltown Rd., Wilmington, DE 19808
Rhodes, George V., Vianney House, 905 Milltown Rd., Wilmington, DE 19808
Sarro, John A., 1003 Melrose Ave., Wilmington, DE 19809

Permanent Deacons:
Bailey, Thomas A., Resurrection Parish, Newark, DE
Baker, Joseph G., (Retired)
Beers, Carl (NYC), St. Francis de Sales, Salisbury, MD
Bianco, Anthony A., St. Bernadette, Milford, DE
Brink, Edward J., St. Ann, Bethany Beach, DE
Campbell, Jack H., (Retired)
Carroll, Donald T., St. Michael the Archangel, Georgetown, DE
Catka, Tony E., St. Mary Magdalen and Family Life Bureau, Wilmington, DE
Chalfant, Harold F., St. Matthew, Wilmington, DE
Cimino, Thomas S., Eastern Correctional Institute, Westover, MD
Conte, Joseph J., Parish of the Resurrection, Newark, DE
Costello, John L., Holy Name of Jesus, Pocomoke City, MD
Dunning, Edward A., (Retired)
Falkowski, John J., Jr., St. Catherine of Siena, Wilmington, DE
Freebery, John W., Jr., St. Mary of the Assumption, Hockessin, DE
Giacci, John, St. Mary of the Assumption, Hockessin, DE
Haley, James J., St. John the Beloved, Wilmington, DE
Hanbury, Kenneth M., Our Mother of Sorrows, Centreville, MD
Handlir, James, St. Peter, New Castle, DE
Hardy, Robert W., St. Anthony of Padua, Wilmington, DE
Holson, Edward G., St. Luke/St. Andrew, Ocean City, MD
Huhn, Francis J., Parish of the Resurrection, Newark, DE
Johnston, Patrick K., Holy Spirit Parish, New Castle, DE
Johnston, William J., Corpus Christi Parish, Elsmere, DE
Jopp, Harold D., Jr., St. Benedict's, Ridgely, MD
Lafferty, James J., Jr., St. Ann's, Wilmington, DE
Lydick, Donald E., St. Ann, Bethany Beach, DE
Lynch, Edmund F., St. Joseph on the Brandywine, Greenville, DE
Maichle, Richard J., Sr., Holy Rosary, Claymont, DE
Malloy, James D., St. John the Apostle, Milford, DE
Maloney, William, Jr., (Retired)
McCann, Hugh J., (Retired)
McCarthy, Richard, St. Mary Star of the Sea, Ocean City, MD
Miller, Thomas H., Campus Ministry, University of Delaware, Newark, DE
Murrian, William J., Holy Family, Ogletown, DE
Normoyle, Robert H., (Retired)
O'Connor, Howard J., (Retired)
Parisi, John G., Corpus Christi, Wilmington, DE
Passwaters, Arcy A., Our Lady of Lourdes, Seaford, DE
Recce, Richard L., (Retired)
Robinson, Charles, St. Polycarp Parish, Smyrna, DE and De State Correctional Center, Smyrna, DE
Romans, Joseph C., Our Lady of Fatima, New Castle and Christiana Div., Christiana Care Health System, Newark, DE
Rose, Albert F., (Retired)
Siers, Ronald (L), St. Francis de Sales, Salisbury, MD
Smith, John A., St. Edmond, Rehoboth Beach, DE
Snow, Austin M., Jr., Immaculate Heart of Mary, Wilmington, DE; Chap., Seton Villa & Siena Hall, Wilmington, DE
Staab, Francis J., St. Catherine of Siena, Wilmington, DE
Taylor, George M., Jr., Cathedral of St. Peter & Ferris School, Wilmington, DE
Torres, Samuel, Church of the Holy Child, Wilmington, DE
Tracy, Robert, St. Ann, Bethany Beach, DE
VanBourgondien, Cornelius J., (Retired)
Vinciguerra, Anthony P., Holy Cross, Dover, DE
Wolf, Allen S., Claymont, DE, Holy Rosary; Christiana Div., Christiana Care Health System, Newark, DE

INSTITUTIONS LOCATED IN THE DIOCESE

[A] HIGH SCHOOLS, DIOCESAN

WILMINGTON. *St. Mark's High School*, 2501 Pike Creek Rd., 19808. Tel: 302-738-3300; Fax: 302-738-5132.
E-mail: mfreund@stmarks.pvt.k12.de.us
Mr. Mark John Freund, Prin.; Rev. Gregory M. Corrigan. Priests 1; Sisters 5; Lay Teachers 108; Students 1,560.

MAGNOLIA. *St. Thomas More Academy*, 133 Thomas More Dr., 19962. Tel: 302-697-8100; Fax: 302-697-8122.
E-mail: msoltys@saintmore.com
Mary L. Soltys, Ed.D., Prin.; Rev. Michael Darcy, Chap. Priests 1; Lay Teachers 12; Part-time Lay Teachers 4; Students 130.

[B] HIGH SCHOOLS, PRIVATE

WILMINGTON. *Salesianum School*, 1801 N. Broom St., 19802. Tel: 302-654-2495; Fax: 302-654-7767.
E-mail: saloblates@aol.com
Web site: www.salesianum.org
Revs. John J. Fisher, O.S.F.S., Prin.; Robert D. Kenney, O.S.F.S.; Thomas B. Curran, Pres.; James Dalton, O.S.F.S., Asst. Prin.; Stephen E. Shott, O.S.F.S., Asst. Prin.; Thomas J. Tucker, O.S.F.S., Supr.; John P. Connery, O.S.F.S.; John A. Kolodziej, O.S.F.S.; John A. Kowalewski, O.S.F.S.; Stanley R. Drupieski, O.S.F.S.; Joseph J. McKenna, O.S.F.S.; John P. Spellman, O.S.F.S.; John M. Mokluk, O.S.F.S.; Bros. Joseph G. Schodowski, O.S.F.S.; Edward F. Ogden, O.S.F.S. Priests 13; Brothers 2; Seminarians 1; Lay Teachers 61; Boys 1027.

Ursuline Academy of Wilmington, DE, Inc., 1106 Pennsylvania Ave., 19806. Tel: 302-658-7158; Fax: 302-658-4297.
E-mail: bgriffin@ursuline.org
Web site: www.ursuline.org
(Coed Grades Early Childhood-3, All Girls Grades 4-12). Barbara C. Griffin, Pres. Lay Faculty 85; Ursuline Nuns 1; Students 713.

CLAYMONT. *Archmere Academy*, 3600 Philadelphia Pike, 19703. Tel: 302-798-6632; Fax: 302-798-7290.
E-mail: generale-mailbox@archmereacademy.com
Web site: www.archmereacademy.com
Coed College Prepatory High School. Rt. Rev. Robert F. Kelly, O.Praem., Prior; Revs. Timothy F. Mullen, O.Praem., Headmaster; Jeffrey T. Cesarone, O.Praem.; Michael T. Collins, O.Praem.; William R. Craig; Paul J. DeAntoniis, O.Praem.; Blaise P. Krautsack, O.Praem. Priests 6; Lay Teachers 55; Students 484.

RIDGELY, MD. *The Benedictine School Habilitation Center*, 21660. Tel: 410-634-2115. Carlene Zierfuss, Co-ord. Sisters 2; Lay Personnel 32; Students 32. Open Community Program MD/DE. Ages 21 and older. Tel: 410-634-1990. Dixie Hughlett, Coord. Students 62; Lay Teachers 17.

[C] ELEMENTARY SCHOOLS, PRIVATE

WILMINGTON. *Saint Edmond's Academy*. (Grades 4-8), 2120 Veale Rd., 19810. Tel: 302-475-5370; Fax: 302-475-2256. Bros. Michael A. Smith, C.S.C., Headmaster; Joseph Ash, C.S.C.; James DeTemple, C.S.C.; Thomas Durney, C.S.C.; Thomas Meany, C.S.C.; David Parrish, C.S.C.; Edward Quintal, C.S.C. Brothers of Holy Cross 7; Lay Teachers 20; Boys 257.

CHILDS, MD. *Mount Aviat Academy*. (Grades PreK-8), 399 Childs Rd., 21916. Tel: 410-398-2206; Fax: 410-398-8063.
E-mail: monavi01@dpnet.net
Oblate Sisters of St. Francis de Sales. Sr. John Elizabeth, O.S.F.S., Prin. Sisters 7; Lay Teachers 12; Students 262.

RIDGELY, MD. *The Benedictine School for Exceptional Children*, 14299 Benedictine Ln., 21660. Tel: 410-634-2112; Fax: 410-634-2640.
E-mail: benefound@aol.com
Web site: www.benschool.com
Sisters of St. Benedict. Sr. Jeanette Murray, O.S.B., Dir.; Rev. Francis J. Rinaldi, O.S.F.S., Chap. Sisters 7; Students 100.

Benedictine School for Exceptional Children Foundation, Inc., 14299 Benedictine Ln., 21660. Tel: 410-634-2292; Fax: 410-634-1855.
E-mail: benefound@aol.com
Web site: benschool.com
Sr. Jeannette Murray, O.S.B., Dir. Sisters 1; Lay Staff 3.

[D] DIOCESAN CATHOLIC CHARITIES PROGRAM

WILMINGTON. *Catholic Charities, Inc.*, 2601 W. 4th St., P.O. Box 2610, 19805-0610. Tel: 302-655-9624; Fax: 302-655-9753. Mr. Allan J. Daul, A.C.S.W., Diocesan Sec., Exec. Dir.; Ms. Barbara Grieco, M.C., M.B.A., Deputy Dir.; Katrina Furlong, B.A., Dir. Community & Family Support Svcs.; Mr. Frederick Jones, M.S., Dir. of Children's Services; Ms. Donna Connor, B.A., C.F.R.E., Dir. Devel. & Community Rels. Staff 180; Individuals Served 54,506; Fuel Program 28,400.

Energy Assistance Program. New Castle Office. Tel: 302-654-9295. Sussex Office. Tel: 302-856-6310. Kent Office. Tel: 302-674-1782.

Social Service Counseling Centers. 4th St. & Greenhill Ave., P.O. Box 2610, 19805-0610. Tel: 302-655-9624.

Dover Office, 1155 W. Walker Rd., Dover, 19904. Tel: 302-674-1600.

Georgetown Office, 406 S. Bedford St., Ste. 9, Georgetown, 19947. Tel: 302-856-9578.

Sailsbury Office, 1405 Wesley Dr., Salisbury, MD, 21801. Tel: 410-749-1121.

Children's Services (Adoption & Foster Care). 4th St. & Greenhill Ave., P.O. Box 2610, 19805-0610. Tel: 302-655-9624. Ms. Neomi Litonjua, L.C.S.W., Supvr.

Family & Individual Services (including Family Life Bureau). 4th St. & Greenhill Ave., P.O. Box 2610, 19805-0610. Tel: 302-655-9624. Mr. Thomas R. Jewett, M.C., Prog. Dir.

HIV Family Resource Center (AIDS Ministry), 2825 Madison St., 19802. Tel: 302-762-9244. Sr. Jeanne Barnard, S.S.J., Contact Person.

Community and Family Support Services.

Crisis Alleviation. 4th St. & Greenhill Ave., P.O. Box 2610, 19805-0610. Tel: 302-654-6473. Sharon Truitt, Contact Person, 1155 W. Walker Rd., Dover, 19904. Tel: 302-674-4016; Fax: 302-674-4018. Sheena Naber, Contact Person; Katrina Furlong, B.A., Dir. Community & Family Support Svcs., New Castle Co. Tel: 302-654-6473. Kent Co. Tel: 302-674-4016. Sussex Co. Tel: 302-856-6310.

Energy Assistance. New Castle Co. Tel: 302-654-9295. Kent Co. Tel: 302-674-1782. Sussex Co. Tel: 302-856-6310.

Immigration & Refugee Services. 4th St. and Greenhill Ave., P.O. Box 2610, 19805-0610. Tel: 302-654-6460. Maria Rodriguez, Contact Person, 406 S. Bedford St., Ste. 9, Georgetown, 19947. Tel: 302-856-9578. Leila Krouse, Contact Person.

Catholic Charities Thrift Shop. 1320 E. 23rd St., 19802. Tel: 302-764-2717. Diane Kelly, Mgr.

Catholic Charities Thrift Shop. 2000 W. Union St. (4th St. & Union Sts.), 19805. Tel: 302-655-9300. Lorraine Shannon, Mgr.

Child & Adult Care Food Program. 1155 W. Walker Rd., Dover, 19904. Tel: 302-674-1600; 1-800-239-2839. Donna Costilow, Contact Person, New Castle Co. Tel: 302-655-9624. Hanne Dawson-Holt, Contact Person, Sussex Co. Tel: 302-856-3414. Pat Miller, Contact Person; Karen Adams.

Counseling and Substance Abuse Services. Fifth St. & Greenhill Ave., P.O. Box 2610, 19805-0610. Tel: 302-656-0651. Laura Hummel, M.S.N., R.N.C.S., C.A.D.C, Program Mgr.

Residential Services. 2307 Kentmere Pkwy., 19806. Tel: 302-656-2183. Frederick Jones, M.S., Dir. Children's Svcs.

Siena Hall, Inc. 2307 Kentmere Pkwy., 19806. Tel: 302-656-2183. Frederick Jones, M.S., Dir. Children's Svcs.

Seton Villa, Inc. 800 Bellevue Rd., 19809. Tel: 302-762-2982. Frederick Jones, M.S., Dir. Children's Svcs.

Children's Home. 2901 Green St., Claymont, 19703. Tel: 302-798-0601. Frederick Jones, M.S., Dir. Children's Svcs.

Casa San Francisco. 127 Broad St., P.O. Box 38, Milton, 19968. Tel: 302-684-8694; Fax: 302-684-2808. Ms. Marion Bau, M.A., Program Dir.; Pat Saez, Contact Person.

Seton Center. 30632 Hampden Ave., P.O. Box 401, Princess Anne, MD, 21853. Tel: 410-651-9608.

Office for Parish Social Ministry. 4th St. & Greenhill Ave., P.O. Box 2610, 19805-0610. Tel: 302-655-9624. Andrew Zampini, S.F.O., Dir.

[E] RESIDENCES FOR CHILDREN

WILMINGTON. *Seton Villa, Inc.*, 800 Bellevue Rd., 19809. Tel: 302-762-2982; Fax: 302-762-3187
For a complete listing, refer to the Special Care Facilities section.

Siena Hall, Inc., 2307 Kentmere Pkwy., 19806. Tel: 302-656-2183; Fax: 302-658-2189
For a complete listing, refer to the Special Care Facilities section.

CLAYMONT. *Children's Home, Inc.*, 2901 Green St., 19703. Tel: 302-798-0601; Fax: 302-798-0604
For a complete listing, refer to the Special Care Facilities section.

[F] OTHER WELFARE AGENCIES

(Not under jurisdiction of Department of Social Concerns)

WILMINGTON. *Home of Divine Providence, Inc.-Bayard House*, 300 Bayard Ave., 19805. Tel: 302-654-1184; Fax: 302-654-8570
For a complete listing, refer to the Special Care Facilities section.

Ministry of Caring, Inc., 506 N. Church St., 19801-4812. Tel: 302-652-5523; Fax: 302-652-1919.
E-mail: mail@ministryofcaring.org
For a complete listing, refer to the Special Care Facilities section.

NEWARK. *Our Lady of Grace Home for Children, Inc.*, 487 E. Chestnut Hill Rd., 19713. Tel: 302-738-4658; 737-6650; Fax: 302-369-1395
For a complete listing, refer to the Special Care Facilities section.

RIDGELY, MD. *St. Martin's Ministries*, 14259 Benedictine Ln., 21660. Tel: 410-634-2497; Fax: 410-634-1410.
E-mail: corta@juno.com
For a complete listing, refer to the Special Care Facilities section.

[G] HOMES FOR AGED

WILMINGTON. *The Antonian*, 1701 W. 10th St., 19805. Tel: 302-421-3758
For a complete listing, refer to the Special Care Facilities section.

Franciscan Health System / Care at Wilmington, 801 N. Broom St., 19806. Tel: 302-652-3861
For a complete listing, refer to the Special Care Facilities section.

St. Patrick's House, Inc., 115 E. 14th St., 19801. Tel: 302-654-6908
For a complete listing, refer to the Special Care Facilities section.

Vianney House, 905 Milltown Rd., 19808. Tel: 302-636-0200
For a complete listing, refer to the Special Care Facilities section.

HOCKESSIN. *Franciscan Health System / Care at Brackenville*, 100 St. Clare Dr., 19707. Tel: 302-234-5420; Fax: 302-234-5424
For a complete listing, refer to the Special Care Facilities section.

NEWARK. *Jeanne Jugan Residence*, 185 Salem Church Rd., 19713. Tel: 302-368-5886; Fax: 302-738-5610
For a complete listing, refer to the Special Care Facilities section.

Marydale Retirement Village, 135 Jeandell Dr., 19713. Tel: 302-368-2784; Fax: 302-731-0584.
E-mail: rpierce384@aol.com
For a complete listing, refer to the Special Care Facilities section.

[H] GENERAL HOSPITALS

WILMINGTON. *St. Francis Hospital, Inc.*, 7th and Clayton Sts., P.O. Box 2500, 19805-0500. Tel: 302-575-8301; Fax: 302-575-8320.
E-mail: juliekeegan@chi-east.org
Web site: www.stfrancishealthcare.org
For a complete listing, refer to the Hospitals section.

[I] MONASTERIES AND RESIDENCES OF PRIESTS AND BROTHERS

WILMINGTON. *Brothers of Holy Cross, St. Edmond's Academy*, 2120 Veale Rd., 19810. Tel: 302-475-5321.
E-mail: veal2120@aol.com
Bro. Joseph W. Ash, C.S.C., Dir. Religious. Brothers 7.

Capuchin Franciscan Friars, St. Francis Renewal Center, 1901 Prior Rd., 19809. Tel: 302-798-1454; Fax: 302-798-3360. Revs. Cyprian Rosen, O.F.M.Cap., Guardian, Dir.; Thomas Pietrantonio, O.F.M.Cap., Vicar; Edward Henning, O.F.M.Cap.; Bro. Nicholas Mormando, O.F.M.Cap.; Rev. Edmund Walker, O.F.M.Cap.

DeSales House, 1600 Brinckle Ave., 19806. Tel: 302-656-4342; Fax: 302-656-6108. Revs. Joseph J. McKenna, O.S.F.S.; John P. Connolly, O.S.F.S.; William J. Dougherty, O.S.F.S.; John A. Finn, O.S.F.S.; John J. Hurley, O.S.F.S.; William H. Juergens, O.S.F.S.; William J. Keech, O.S.F.S.; Richard D. Leone, O.S.F.S. Priests 8.

Oblates of St. Francis De Sales. Tel: 302-656-8529; Fax: 302-658-8052.
Web site: www.oblates.org
Residence of the Provincial, 2200 Kentmere Pkwy., 19806. Tel: 302-656-8529; Fax: 302-658-8052. Very Rev. Joseph G. Morrissey, O.S.F.S., Prov.; Revs. Edward T. Fitzpatrick, O.S.F.S., Asst. Prov. & Dir. Personnel; Michael T. Cavanaugh, O.S.F.S., Rel.-In-Charge; Richard R. De Lillio, O.S.F.S., Dir. Devel.; Francis J. Hanlon, O.S.F.S., Dir. Senior Oblates;

Robert A. Mancini, O.S.F.S., Treas.; John P. Spellman, O.S.F.S.
Rev. Oblates Attached to the Provincial Residence: Revs. Walter R. Dean, O.S.F.S.; William J. Hultberg, O.S.F.S.; George S. Salzmann, O.S.F.S.; James J. MacNew, O.S.F.S., Military Chap.; John W. Lyle, O.S.F.S., Military Chap.; Paul T. Frey, O.S.F.S., Missions; William R. Gore, O.S.F.S., Missions; Anthony J. Pinizzotto, O.S.F.S., Educ.; John A. Gilvey, O.S.F.S. Priests 16.

St. Felix Friary, 119 N. Jackson St., 19805-3670. Tel: 302-652-7010; Fax: 302-652-8943.
E-mail: stfelix@ministryofcaring.org
Rev. Ronald Giannone, O.F.M.Cap., Guardian; Bro. Kevin O'Loughlin, O.F.M.Cap., Vicar. Brothers 5.

CHILDS, MD. *Oblates of St. Francis De Sales.* Tel: 410-398-3040; Fax: 410-620-6131.
E-mail: jjocco@dol.net
Web site: www.oblates.org
Retirement and Retreat Center, 1120 Blue Ball Rd., 21916-0043. Tel: 410-398-3040; Fax: 410-620-6131.
Rev. Joseph P. Jocco, O.S.F.S., Supr. in residence. In res. Revs. Joseph A. Baird, O.S.F.S.; John J. Bradunas, O.S.F.S.; George J. Brownholtz, O.S.F.S.; Francis T. Christof, O.S.F.S.; George W. Martyn, O.S.F.S.; John J. Conmy, O.S.F.S.; Hugh E. Duffy, O.S.F.S.; Paul E. Burke, O.S.F.S.; James P. Harvey, O.S.F.S.; Manning C. Moore, O.S.F.S.; Thomas F. Malloy, O.S.F.S.; Louis R. McCartney, O.S.F.S.; James J. McGuire, O.S.F.S.; Michael B. Donovan, O.S.F.S.; Anthony T. Schelich, O.S.F.S.; Vincent Burke, O.S.F.S.; Gerard R. Clarke, O.S.F.S.; James O. Keenan, O.S.F.S.; Francis Greene, O.S.F.S.; Robert Hanlon, O.S.F.S.; John Heckel, O.S.F.S.; Bros. John J. Dochkus, O.S.F.S.; Joe H. Hayden, O.S.F.S.; Frank J. Konstanty, O.S.F.S.; Anthony F. Rifkin, O.S.F.S.; Paul A. Schuler, O.S.F.S.; Gerald M. Sweeney, O.S.F.S.; Thomas J. Nee, O.S.F.S.; Henry J. Fiegl, O.S.F.S. Brothers 8.

CLAYMONT. *Immaculate Conception Priory of the Canons Regular of Premontre*, 3600 Philadelphia Pike, 19703-0103. Tel: 302-792-2791; Fax: 302-792-2998.
E-mail: jdant1947@aol.com
Rt. Revs. Robert F. Kelly, O.Praem., Prior; John M. Logan, O.Praem.; Revs. Timothy F. Mullen, O.Praem, Headmaster; Walter J. Burke, O.Praem.; Jeffrey T. Cesarone, O.Praem.; Francis J. Ciliberti, O.Praem.; John V. Cimino, O.Praem.; Michael T. Collins, O.Praem.; Paul J. DeAntoniis, O.Praem., Sub Prior; Martin A. Frigo, O.Praem.; Blaise P. Krautsack, O.Praem.; Edward J. Smith, O.Praem., Treas.; Bro. Joseph Mulholland, O. Praem. Priests 20; Brothers 1.

Norbertine Fathers of Delaware, Inc., 3600 Philadelphia Pike, 19703-0130. Tel: 302-792-2791; Fax: 302-792-2998.
E-mail: jdant1947@aol.com
Rt. Rev. Robert F. Kelly, O.Praem., Prior; Revs. James D. Bagnato, O.Praem., Sub-Prior; Jeffrey T. Cesarone, O.Praem., Vocation Dir.; Edward J. Smith, O.Praem, Treas.

[J] CONVENTS AND RESIDENCES FOR SISTERS

WILMINGTON. *Monastery of St. Veronica Giuliani.* (Strict Enclosure), 816 Jefferson St., 19801. Tel: 302-654-8727; Fax: 302-652-3929. Capuchin Poor Clare Nuns of Delaware. Mother Maria Imelda Valencia, O.S-.C.Cap., Abbess; Rev. Ronald Giannone, O.F.M.Cap., Chap. Sisters 14.

Our Lady of Peace Convent, 1801 W. 8th St., 19805. Tel: 302-426-1809.
Web site: osfphila.org
The Sisters of St. Francis of Philadelphia 2.

St. Benedict, 113 Canterbury Dr., 19803. Tel: 302-478-3754; Fax: 302-478-9305.
E-mail: margosb@aol.com
Sisters of St. Benedict 3.

St. Francis Convent, 701 N. Rodney St., 19805. Tel: 302-652-8489. The Sisters of St. Francis of Philadelphia 9.

St. Mark's Faculty Residence, 2503 Pike Creek Rd., 19808-3615. Intercommunity Sisters 15.

Ursuline Academy Inc., The, 1104 Pennsylvania Ave., 19806. Tel: 302-656-5890; Fax: 302-656-2315. Sr. Frances Lyle, O.S.U., Supr. Sisters 19.

CHILDS, MD. *Villa Aviat Convent*, 399 Childs Rd., 21916. Tel: 410-398-3699; Fax: 410-398-5801.
E-mail: oblatesisters@mountaviat.org
Oblate Sisters of St. Francis de Sales. Sr. Anne Elizabeth, O.S.F.S., Supr. Sisters 9.

EASTON, MD. *Eastern Shore Co-op*, 304 Prospect Ave., 21601. Tel: 410-820-7437. Sisters 2.

PRINCESS ANNE, MD. *Seton Center, Sisters of Charity.* (Convent Station), P.O. Box 401, 21853. Tel: 410-651-9608; Fax: 410-651-1437.
E-mail: seton-center@juno.com
Sisters 4; Assisted 15,277.

RIDGELY, MD. *St. Gertrude's Monastery, Motherhouse and Novitiate of the Sisters of St. Benedict*, 14259 Benedictine Ln., 21660. Tel: 410-634-2497; Fax: 410-634-1410.
E-mail: smp52@juno.com
Web site: www.ridgelybenedictines.org
Sr. Mary Paul McLaughlin, O.S.B., Prioress. In res. Rev. Francis J. Rinaldi, O.S.F.S., Chap. Sisters 39.

SALISBURY, MD. *Joseph House, Little Sisters of Jesus & Mary.*, P.O. Box 1755, 21802. Tel: 410-543-1645; Fax: 410-742-3390.
E-mail: convent@thejosephhouse.org
Web site: www.thejosephhouse.org
Sr. Mary Elizabeth Gintling, Dir. Sisters 7.

[K] SECULAR INSTITUTES

WILMINGTON. *Secular Franciscan Order.* (St. Patrick's Fraternity), 1901 Prior Rd., 19809. Tel: 302-571-8503. Loretta Juras, S.F.O., Min.; Bro. Nicholas Mormando, O.F.M.Cap., Spiritual Asst.

CHESTERTOWN, MD. *Secular Order of Discalced Carmelites.* (Annunciation Community), 201 N. Queen St., 21620. Tel: 410-778-0557. Mrs. Bernadette M. Stenger, Pres.; Bro. Bryan Paquette, O.C.D., Spiritual Asst.

DOVER. *Secular Institute of the Two Hearts*, P.O. Box 1719, 19903. Tel: 302-678-1358; Fax: 302-678-3246.
E-mail: sith_usa@aol.com
Agnes Frias, Intl. Supr.; Marilyn Parra, Natl. Supr.; Revs. Edgardo M. Arellano, Spiritual Dir.; John R. Santos, Asst. Spiritual Dir.

KENNETT SQUARE, PA. *Secular Franciscan Order.* (San Damiano Fraternity), 412 Narrum Dr., 19348. Tel: 610-388-6423. Sr. Elixe Betz, O.S.F.

MIDDLETOWN. *St. Francis De Sales Secular Institute*, 108 W. Cochran St., 19709. Tel: 302-378-2423; Fax: 302-378-9127.
E-mail: jackied@gateway.net
Jacquelyn Delaporte, Contact; Therese Keyes, Dir. U.S.A. Tel: 203-469-3277.

SALISBURY, MD. *Secular Order of Discalced Carmelites.* (Mary, Mother of Life Community), 631 Ridge Rd., 21811. Tel: 410-742-1777. Mrs. Marianne Chapin; Bro. Bryan Paquette, O.C.D., Spiritual Asst.

[L] RETREAT HOUSES, GENERAL

WILMINGTON. *St. Francis Renewal Center*, 1901 Prior Rd., 19809. Tel: 302-798-1454; Fax: 302-798-3360. Revs. Cyprian Rosen, O.F.M.Cap., Guardian, Dir.; Thomas Pietrantonio, O.F.M.Cap., Vicar; Edward Henning, O.F.M.Cap.; Edmund Walker, O.F.M.Cap.; Bro. Nicholas Mormando, O.F.M.Cap. Priests 4; Brothers 1.

CHILDS, MD. *De Sales Centre*, 1120 Blue Ball Rd., 21916-0043. Tel: 410-398-3383; Fax: 410-398-0116.
E-mail: retreathouse@osfs.org
Web site: www.oblates.org/retreat
Rev. Michael B. Donovan, O.S.F.S., Dir. Oblate Retreat House.

CLAYTON. *St. Joseph's Center for Prayer*, 355 W. Duck Creek Rd., 19938. Tel: 302-653-8814. Rev. Nelson Moreira, S.S.J., Admin.

[M] RETREAT HOUSES, WOMEN

CHILDS, MD. *Oblate Sisters of St. Francis de Sales*, Villa Aviat, 399 Childs Rd., 21916. Tel: 410-398-3699; Fax: 410-398-5801.
E-mail: oblatesisters@mountaviat.org

RIDGELY, MD. *Berg Retreat Center*, St. Gertrude's Monastery, 14259 Benedictine Ln., 21660. Tel: 410-634-2497; Fax: 410-634-1410.
E-mail: smp52@juno.com
Web site: www.ridgelybenedictines.org
Benedictine Sisters.

[N] INFORMATION CENTERS

WILMINGTON. *The Franciscan Center*, 833 N. Market St., 19801-3078. Tel: 302-656-0711; Fax: 302-656-2167. Bro. David W. Schlatter, O.F.M., Dir.; Revs. Barry J. Langley, O.F.M., Asst. Dir.; James Richardson, C.A.D.C.

[O] NEWMAN CENTERS

CHESTERTOWN, MD. *Washington College Catholic Campus Ministry*, Sacred Heart, 508 High St., 21620. Tel: 410-778-3160. Rev. Leonard J. Blakely, Chap.

NEWARK. *Univ. of Delaware Newman Center*, St. Thomas More Oratory, 45 Lovett Ave., 19711. Tel: 302-368-4728; Fax: 302-368-2548.
E-mail: szuptmo@udel.edu
Very Rev. Michael F. Szupper, Ph.D., Chap. & Diocesan Dir. Campus Ministry.

Delmar Organization of Catholic Students - DOCS. Tel: 302-368-4728; Fax: 302-368-2548. Kimberly S. Zitzner, B.A., Dir., Salisbury State College, 211 W. College Ave., Salisbury, MD, 21801. Tel: 410-219-3376; Fax: 410-219-3376. Laura St. Marie, Campus Min., University of Maryland Eastern Shore, 211 W. College Ave., Salisbury, MD, 21801. Tel: 410-219-3376; Fax: 410-219-3376. Laura St. Marie, Campus Min.

Wesley College Newman Center. Tel: 302-368-4728; Fax: 302-368-2548.
E-mail: szuptmo@udel.edu
Very Rev. Michael F. Szupper, Chap.

Washington College, 508 High St., Chestertown, MD, 21260. Tel: 410-778-3160; Fax: 410-810-0427. Rev. Leonard J. Blakely, Chap.

Wesley College Catholic Campus Ministry, St. Thomas More Oratory, 45 Lovett Ave., 19711. Tel: 302-368-4728.
E-mail: szuptmo@udel.edu

RELIGIOUS INSTITUTES OF MEN REPRESENTED IN THE DIOCESE

For further details refer to the corresponding bracketed number in the Religious Institutes of Men or Women section.

[1350]—*Brothers of St. Francis Xavier.*—C.F.X.
[0600]—*Brothers of the Congregation of Holy Cross.* (Eastern Province).—C.S.C.
[0900]—*Canons Regular of Premontre.*—O.Praem.
[0470]—*The Capuchin Friars.* (Prov. of the Stigmata).—O.F.M.Cap.
[0740]—*Congregation of Marian of the Immaculate Conception.*—M.I.C.
[0520]—*Franciscan Friars.* (Holy Name Province).—O.F.M.
[0690]—*Jesuit Fathers and Brothers.*—S.J.
[0855]—*Missionary Fraternity of Mary.*—F.M.M.
[]—*Oblate Apostles of the Two Hearts.*—O.A.T.H.
[0920]—*Oblates of St. Francis de Sales.*—O.S.F.S.
[1070]—*Redemptorist Fathers.* (Baltimore, MD).—C.SS.R.

RELIGIOUS INSTITUTES OF WOMEN REPRESENTED IN THE DIOCESE

[0100]—*Adorers of the Blood of Christ.*—A.S.C.
[0230]—*Benedictine Sisters of Pontifical Jurisdiction.*—O.S.B.
[3765]—*Capuchin Poor Clare Sisters.*—O.S.C.Cap.
[]—*Carmelites of Charity of Verduna.*—C.C.V.
[0760]—*Daughters of the Charity of St. Vincent de Paul.*—D.C.
[1070-11]—*Dominican Sisters.*—O.P.
[1170]—*Felician Sisters.*—C.S.S.F.
[1180]—*Franciscan Sisters of Allegheny, New York.*—O.S.F.
[2331]—*Little Sisters of Jesus and Mary.*—L.S.J.M.
[2340]—*Little Sisters of the Poor.*—L.S.P.
[2720]—*Mission Helpers of the Sacred Heart.* (Prov. of Baltimore).—M.H.S.H.
[2790]—*Missionary Servants of the Most Blessed Trinity.*—M.S.B.T.
[3060]—*Oblates Sisters of St. Francis de Sales.*—O.S.F.S.
[2575]—*Religious Sisters of Mercy of the Americas.* (Baltimore, MD; Merion, PA).—R.S.M.
[2970]—*School Sisters of Notre Dame.*—S.S.N.D.
[0440]—*Sisters of Charity of Cincinnati.*—S.C.
[0500]—*Sisters of Charity of Nazareth.*—S.C.N.
[0590]—*Sisters of Charity of Saint Elizabeth, Convent Station.* (Southern, Western Provs.).—S.C.
[3000]—*Sisters of Notre Dame.*—S.N.D.deN.
[3780]—*Sisters of Saints Cyril and Methodius.*—SS.C.M.
[1650]—*Sisters of St. Francis of Philadelphia.*—O.S.F.
[3893]—*Sisters of St. Joseph of Chestnut Hill, Philadelphia.*—S.S.J.
[3890]—*Sisters of St. Joseph of Peace.*—C.S.J.P.
[0970]—*Sisters of the Divine Compassion.*—R.D.C.
[3730]—*Sisters of the Order of St. Basil the Great.*—O.S.B.M.
[2160]—*Sisters, Servants of Immaculate Heart of Mary.*—I.H.M.
[4110]—*Ursuline Nuns (Roman Union).* (Eastern Prov.).—O.S.U.

DIOCESAN CEMETERIES

WILMINGTON. *All Saints*, Box 2506, 19805. Tel: 302-737-2524; Fax: 302-737-4091. Office, Kirkwood Hwy., 19805. Mark A. Christian, Exec. Dir.; Thomas J. Kane, Supt.

Cathedral, Box 2506, 19805. Tel: 302-656-3323; Fax: 302-656-1069. Office, 2400 Lancaster Ave., 19805. Mark A. Christian, Exec. Dir. & Supt.

NECROLOGY

† Harney, Peter P., Greenville, DE St. Joseph on the Brandywine. —Died April 16, 2000.
† Masterson, John J., Bethany Beach, DE St. Ann. —Died June 19, 2000.

Diocese of Winona

(Dioecesis Vinonaensis)

Most Reverend

BERNARD J. HARRINGTON, D.D.

Bishop of Winona; ordained June 6, 1959; appointed Auxiliary Bishop of the Archdiocese of Detroit and Titular Bishop of Uzali November 23, 1993; transferred to Winona November 6, 1998; installed January 6, 1999.

Most Reverend

LORAS J. WATTERS, D.D.

Retired Bishop of Winona; ordained June 7, 1941; appointed Titular Bishop of Fidoloma and Auxiliary Bishop of Dubuque June 23, 1965; consecrated August 26, 1965; transferred to Winona January 8, 1969; retired October 14, 1986; appointed Apostolic Administrator October 14, 1986. *Res., 618 Forest, Apt. D., Pacific Grove, CA, 93950.* Tel.: 408-373-3715.

Pastoral Center: 55 W. Sanborn St., P.O. Box 588, Winona., MN, 55987. Tel.: 507-454-4643; Fax: 507-454-8106.

Web site address: www.dow.org

E-mail address: diocese@dow.org

ESTABLISHED NOVEMBER 26, 1889.

Square Miles 12,282.

Comprises the Counties of Winona, Wabasha, Olmsted, Dodge, Steele, Waseca, Blue Earth, Watonwan, Cottonwood, Murray, Pipestone, Rock, Nobles, Jackson, Faribault, Martin, Freeborn, Mower, Fillmore and Houston in the State of Minnesota.

For legal titles of parishes and diocesan institutions, consult the Pastoral Center.

STATISTICAL OVERVIEW

Personnel	
Bishop	1
Retired Bishops	1
Priests: Diocesan Active in Diocese	73
Priests: Active Outside Diocese	5
Priests: Retired, Sick or Absent	50
Number of Diocesan Priests	128
Religious Priests in Diocese	8
Extern Priests in Diocese	3
Ordinations:	
Diocesan Priests	3
Transitional Deacons	1
Permanent Deacons in Diocese	5
Total Brothers	22
Total Sisters	449
Parishes	
Parishes	118
With Resident Pastor:	
Resident Diocesan Priests	58
Resident Religious Priests	4
Without Resident Pastor:	
Administered by Priests	51
Administered by Women Religious	3
Administered by Lay People	2
Missions	1
Pastoral Centers	2
Professional Ministry Personnel:	
Brothers	1
Sisters	15
Lay Ministers	64
Welfare	
Catholic Hospitals	2
Total Assisted	71,207
Health Care Centers	1
Total Assisted	4,100
Homes for the Aged	8
Total Assisted	874
Day Care and Extended Day Care Centers	3
Total Assisted	9,500
Specialized Homes	2
Total Assisted	83
Special Centers for Social Services	7
Total Assisted	13,001
Residential Care of Disabled	1
Total Assisted	16
Other Institutions	1
Total Assisted	108
Educational	
Seminaries, Diocesan	1
Students from This Diocese	3
Students from Other Diocese	54
Diocesan Students in Other Seminaries	3
Total Seminarians	6
Colleges and Universities	1
Total Students	1,364
High Schools, Diocesan and Parish	4
Total Students	1,396
Elementary Schools, Diocesan and Parish	28
Total Students	5,020
Catechesis/Religious Education:	
High School Students	4,838
Elementary Students	12,114
Total Students Under Catholic Instruction	24,738
Teachers in the Diocese:	
Priests	7
Brothers	1
Sisters	17
Lay Teachers	362
Vital Statistics	
Receptions into the Church:	
Infant Baptism Totals	1,881
Adult Baptism Totals	77
Received into Full Communion	232
First Communions	1,948
Confirmations	2,166
Marriages:	
Catholic	395
Interfaith	357
Total Marriages	752
Deaths	1,122
Total Catholic Population	150,370
Total Population	528,303

Former Bishops—Rt. Rev. JOSEPH B. COTTER, D.D., cons. Dec. 27, 1889; died June 28, 1909.—Rt. Rev. PATRICK R. HEFFRON, D.D., cons. May 19, 1910; died Nov. 23, 1927.—Most Rev. FRANCIS M. KELLY, D.D., cons. June 9, 1926; transferred to Diocese of Winona, Feb. 10, 1928; transferred to Titular See of Nasal, Oct. 17, 1949; died June 24, 1950.—Most Rev. EDWARD A. FITZGERALD, D.D., cons. Sept. 12, 1946; Auxiliary Bishop of Dubuque; transferred to Winona, Oct. 20, 1949; retired and transferred to the Titular See of Zerta, Jan. 8, 1969; died March 30, 1972.—Most Rev. LORAS J. WATTERS, D.D., ord. June 7, 1941; appt. Titular Bishop of Fidoloma and Auxiliary Bishop of Dubuque, June 23, 1965; cons. Aug. 26, 1965; transferred to Winona, Jan. 8, 1969; retired Oct. 14, 1986; appt. Apostolic Administrator, Oct. 14, 1986.—Most Rev. JOHN G. VLAZNY, D.D., ord. Dec. 20, 1961; appt. Auxiliary Bishop of Chicago and Titular Bishop of Stagno, Oct. 31, 1983; cons. Dec. 13, 1983; appt. Bishop of Winona, May 19, 1987; installed July 29, 1987; appt. Archbishop of Portland, Oct. 28, 1997.

Vicar General and Moderator of the Curia—Rev. MICHAEL J. HOEPPNER, V.G.

Chancellor—Rev. EDWARD F. MCGRATH, *55 W. Sanborn St., P.O. Box 588, Winona, 55987.* Tel: 507-454-4643; Fax: 507-454-8106.

Deans—Rev. EDWARD F. MCGRATH, Winona; Rev. DALE E. TUPPER, Rochester; Rev. GREGORY P. LEIF, Austin-Albert Lea; Rev. JOHN M. KUNZ, Mankato; Rev. GERALD C. KOSSE, Worthington.

Diocesan Consultors—Rev. Msgr. ROY E. LITERSKI; Rev. Msgr. DONALD P. SCHMITZ; Revs. THOMAS J. JENNINGS; JOSEPH L. KEEFE; ROBERT G. MEYER; JAMES D. RUSSELL.

Finance Council—Revs. MICHAEL J. HOEPPNER, V.G.; ROBERT G. MEYER; Sr. JOAN BLANK, O.S.F.; Mr. ROBERT HOODECHECK; Mrs. SHARON WAGNER; Mr. ROCKY SIELER; Mr. JAMES WIEKAMP; Mr. LAWRENCE J. DOSE, Dir.

Diocesan Board of Administration—(Civil Corporation): Most Rev. BERNARD J. HARRINGTON, Pres.; Revs. MICHAEL J. HOEPPNER, V.G., Vice Pres. EDWARD F. MCGRATH, Sec.; Mr. ROBERT HOODECHEK; Mrs. SHARON WAGNER.

Tribunal—55 W. Sanborn St., P.O. Box 588, Winona, 55987. Tel: 507-454-4643.

Judicial Officers—Rev. EDWARD F. MCGRATH, J.C.L., Vicar Judicial; Mr. LAWRENCE G. PRICE, J.D., J.C.L., Dir.

Censors of Books and Periodicals—Revs. WILLIAM M. BECKER, S.T.D.; JACK L. KROUGH, M.A.; JOHN M. SAUER, S.T.L.; TIMOTHY T. REKER, S.T.L.; ANDREW J. BEERMAN, S.T.L.

Associate Judges—Revs. WILLIAM KULAS, J.C.L.; ROBERT G. MEYER; DAVID WECHTER, O.Cist., J.C.L.; Mr. LAWRENCE G. PRICE, J.D., J.C.L.
Regional Tribunal Judge—Rev. WILLIAM J. KULAS, J.C.L.
Regional Tribunal Defender of the Bond—Rev. DONALD J. SCHMITZ, M.A.
Defenders of the Bond—Rev. Msgr. DONALD P. SCHMITZ, M.Ch.A.; JACK L. KROUGH.
Advocates—Revs. GERALD C. KOSSE; PAUL HEITING; MICHAEL J. CRONIN; Mr. THOMAS HEALY, J.D.
Promoter of Justice—Rev. Msgr. DONALD P. SCHMITZ.
Notaries—Mrs. CAROL NEPPL; Ms. PAULA WATEMBACH; Mrs. JULIE WRIGHT.

Diocesan Offices and Directors

All Diocesan Offices and Directors are located at the Pastoral Center (unless otherwise indicated), 55 W. Sanborn St., P.O. Box 588, Winona, 55987. Tel: 507-454-4643; Fax: 507-454-8106. Please send all matrimonial dispensations and permissions to the Tribunal office

Curia—
Chancellor—Rev. EDWARD F. MCGRATH, J.C.L.
Pastoral Planning—Rev. MICHAEL J. HOEPPNER, V.G.
Finances—Mr. LAWRENCE J. DOSE, Dir.
Catholic Charities—Mr. ROBERT TEREBA, *111 Market St., P.O. Box 379, Winona, 55987.* Tel: 507-454-2270; Fax: 507-457-3027.
Communications - "The Courier"—Mr. IVAN KUBISTA.
Office of RCIA, Liturgy and Evangelization—Ms. PEGGY LOVRIEN.
Education, Human Resources and Schools—Mrs. P. J. THOMPSON.
Faith Formation—Mr. MARK NUEHRING.
Youth and Family Life—Mrs. ALMA RICHARD.
Diaconate Formation—Rev. TIMOTHY T. REKER, *St. Francis of Assisi Church, 1114 3rd St., S.E., Rochester, 55904.* Tel: 507-288-7313. Mr. TODD GRAFF, Contact Person.
Vocations—Rev. JAMES P. STEFFES, Dir.
Lay Ministry Formation—Mr. TODD GRAFF.
Stewardship and Development—Deacon LEONARD FULLER.
Additional Ministries—
Annual Diocesan Appeal—Mrs. DIANE M. ZITTEL, Dir.
Director of Clergy Education—Rev. MICHAEL J. HOEPPNER, V.G.
Ecumenism—Rev. WILLIAM M. BECKER, *Saint Mary's University, 700 Terrace Heights, Winona, 55987.* Tel: 507-457-7373.
Propagation of the Faith—Rev. CHARLIE I. COLLINS, *Christ the King Church, 202 4th St., N.W., P.O. Box 1000, Byron, 55920-1000.* Tel: 507-775-6455.
Hispanic Ministry—Rev. HILARY R. BRIXIUS, *Church of St. Mary, 1215 7th Ave., Worthington, 56187-2297.* Tel: 507-376-6005.
Coordinator of Diocesan Health Ministry—Rev. JAMES F. BURYSKA, Diocesan Dir. of Hospitals, *Rochester Methodist Hospital Chaplain Services, 201 W. Center St., Rochester, 55902.* Tel: 507-255-5551; Fax: 507-255-3125.

Advisory Bodies—
Presbyteral Council—
Ex Officio—Rev. MICHAEL J. HOEPPNER, V.G.
Elected Senior Member—Rev. GERALD W. CONWAY.
Appointed Members—Rev. Msgr. ROY E. LITERSKI; Rev. Msgr. DONALD P. SCHMITZ; Revs. THOMAS J. JENNINGS, Pres. JOSEPH L. KEEFE; THOMAS A. LOOMIS; THOMAS E. COOK, Sec.
Elected At-Large Representatives—Revs. JAMES D. RUSSELL; PAUL E. NELSON.
Elected Deanery Representatives—Revs. GERALD C. KOSSE; ROBERT J. SCHNEIDER; JOHN OZBUN, Vice Pres. GREGORY G. HAVEL; PETER L. SCHUSTER.
Priestly Assignments Committee—Rev. MICHAEL J. HOEPPNER, V.G.; Rev. Msgr. DONALD P. SCHMITZ; Rev. RICHARD M. COLLETTI.
Diocesan Pastoral Council—Revs. MICHAEL J. HOEPPNER, V.G.; JOSEPH P. PETE; Bro. PATRICK CONWAY; Sr. JOAN LEWISON, O.S.F.; Sr. BRENDA PENNING, S.S.N.D.; Mrs. PAT MCCORMICK; Mrs. JOYCE ARNDORFER; Mrs. ROSEMARY MURPHY; Mr. DANIEL BRODERICK.
Bishop's Council—Revs. MICHAEL J. HOEPPNER, V.G.; GERALD C. KOSSE; JOHN M. KUNZ; GREGORY P. LEIF; EDWARD F. MCGRATH; DALE E. TUPPER; Sr. IRENE DOHMEN, S.S.N.D.; Sr. MONIQUE SCHWIRTZ, O.S.F.
Priests' Pension Board—Revs. GERALD W. CONWAY; PAUL E. NELSON; JAMES A. MCCAULEY; Bro. LOUIS DETHOMASIS; Mr. TIMOTHY GEISLER; Mr. LAWRENCE J. DOSE, Treas.; Mr. THOMAS CROWLEY.
Commission on Sacred Liturgy—Ms. PEGGY LOVRIEN, Ex Officio; Rev. JOHN M. SAUER, Exec. Chm.; Rev. GERALD C. KOSSE; Sr. BRENDA PENNING, S.S.N.D.; Mr. ROBERT HACKMEISTER; Mrs. SUSAN SHEPHARD; THERESA HOFFMAN; Mr. JAMES STOLPA; Ms. BETSY DIERCKS; Ms. JACKIE PETERSON.
Vocations Advisory Council—Revs. JAMES P. STEFFES, Dir. THOMAS A. LOOMIS; ANDREW J. BEERMAN; TIMOTHY E. BIREN; Sr. JOYCE KOLBET, S.S.N.D.; Sr. MARY BETH SCHRAML, S.S.N.D.; Mrs. PAMELA J. THOMPSON; DICK BREITER; THERESE BREITER.

Winona Diocesan Organizations-Agencies-Programs

Archives—Rev. EDWARD F. MCGRATH, *Pastoral Center, 55 W. Sanborn St., P.O. Box 588, Winona, 55987.* Tel: 507-454-4643; Fax: 507-454-8106.
Boy Scouts—Mrs. ALMA RICHARD, Coord.
Chaplain—Rev. JAMES C. BERNING. Tel: 507-642-8305.
Catholic Charities—Mr. ROBERT TEREBA, Exec. Dir., *111 Market St., P.O. Box 379, Winona, 55987.* Tel: 507-454-2270; Fax: 507-457-3027.
Catholic Charities Board—JOE STILES, Chm.
Albert Lea—308 E. Fountain, Albert Lea, 56007. Tel: 507-377-3664.
Austin—2001 2nd Ave., N.W., Austin, 55912. Tel: 507-433-3062.
Mankato—423 W. 7th St., Mankato, 56001. Tel: 507-387-5586.
Owatonna—140 1/2 E. Rose St., Owatonna, 55060. Tel: 507-455-2008.
Pipestone—106 4th St., S.E., Pipestone, 56164. Tel: 507-825-2146.
Rochester—117 E. Center St., Ste. B, Rochester, 55904. Tel: 507-287-2047; Fax: 507-287-2050.
Winona—111 Market St., P.O. Box 379, Winona, 55987. Tel: 507-454-2270; Fax: 507-457-3027.
Worthington—1118 Oxford St., Worthington, 56187. Tel: 507-376-9757.
Hispanic Ministry—KELLY MOMSEN, Coord., *111 Market St., P.O. Box 379, Winona, 55987.* Tel: 507-454-2270; Fax: 507-457-3027.
Parish and Community Social Action Office—SUZANNE BELONGIA, Supvr., *111 Market St., P.O. Box 379, Winona, 55987.* Tel: 507-454-2270; Fax: 507-457-3027. Coordination of:
Parish Social Ministry—
Rural Life Ministry—
Campaign for Human Development—
Catholic Relief Services—
Developmentally Challenged—
HIV-AIDS Ministry—
Disaster Relief Services—
Refugee Resettlement—Sr. MARILYN ORCHARD, S.S.N.D., Supvr., *117 E. Center St., Ste. B, Rochester, 55904.* Tel: 507-287-2047; Fax: 507-287-2050.
Cemeteries—Rev. EDWARD F. MCGRATH.
Charismatic Renewal—Sr. MARY ANN SCHAENZER, S.S.N.D., *R.R. 1 Box 339, Mankato, 56001-9752.* Tel: 507-345-2989 (Office); 507-345-5880 (Res.).
Council of Catholic Women—Mrs. MARY CONLEY, Pres., *1026 Rolling Green Dr., Owatonna, 55060.* Tel: 507-451-1742. Rev. THOMAS J. HARGESHEIMER, Diocesan Moderator. Tel: 507-451-4845.
Diocesan Self-Insurance Plan—Gallagher-Bassett Insurance Service, 111 Riverfront, P.O. Box 30127, Winona, 55987. Tel: 507-454-6452.
Hospitals—Rev. JAMES F. BURYSKA, *Rochester Methodist Hospital, 201 W. Center St., Rochester, 55902.* Tel: 507-255-5551.
Girl Scouts—Mrs. ALMA RICHARD, Coord., *55 W. Sanborn St., P.O. Box 588, Winona, 55987.* Tel: 507-454-4643; Fax: 507-454-8106.
Marriage Preparation/Enrichment—Mrs. ALMA RICHARD, *55 W. Sanborn St., P.O. Box 588, Winona, 55987.* Tel: 507-454-4643; Fax: 507-454-8106.
Pathways TEC (Teens Encounter Christ)—Mrs. ALMA RICHARD, Diocesan Liaison, *55 W. Sanborn St., P.O. Box 588, Winona, 55987.* Tel: 507-454-4643; Fax: 507-454-8106. Rev. JAMES C. BERNING, Spiritual Dir., *Church of St. Mary, 212 1st St., N.E., Madelia, 56062-1702.* Tel: 507-642-8305.
Respect Life—Mrs. ALMA RICHARD, *55 W. Sanborn St., P.O. Box 588, Winona, 55987.* Tel: 507-454-4643; Fax: 507-454-8106.
Misconduct Issues—Rev. EDWARD F. MCGRATH; Mrs. PAMELA J. THOMPSON, *55 W. Sanborn St., P.O. Box 588, Winona, 55987.* Tel: 507-454-4643; Fax: 507-454-8106.
Southern Minnesota Retrouvaille—Rev. THEODORE J. HOTTINGER, S.J., Dir., *Ss. Peter & Paul Church, 105 N. 5th St., Mankato, 56001-4442.* Tel: 507-388-2995; 386-1369 (Couple Contact).

CLERGY, PARISHES, MISSIONS AND PAROCHIAL SCHOOLS

CITY OF WINONA
(Winona County)

1—CATHEDRAL OF THE SACRED HEART (1950), Revs. John M. Sauer, Rector; Shawn T. Haremza. In res., Revs. Cyril Fabian, O.P. Tel: 507-452-5428 (Res); 457-1539; Michael J. Hoeppner Tel: 507-454-4643.
Res., 360 Main St., 55987-3299. Tel: 507-452-4770; Fax: 507-454-1974. [JC]
School—See listings under Centralized Catholic Schools.
Catechesis/Religious Programs—Students 199.

2—ST. CASIMIR'S (1906), Rev. James W. Hennessy.
Res., 624 W. Broadway, 55987-2721. Tel: 507-452-3434; Fax: 507-452-5535. [JC]
Catechesis/Religious Programs—Tel: 507-454-7311.
Students 50.

3—ST. JOHN NEPOMUCENE (1888). Attended by St. Stanislaus, Winona.
625 E. Fourth St., 55987-4297. Tel: 507-452-5430; Fax: 507-452-3355.
Catechesis/Religious Programs—602 E. Fifth St., 55987.
Students 42.

4—ST. MARY'S (1911), Rev. Joseph L. Keefe; Deacon Gordon D. Richard.
Res., 1303 W. Broadway, 55987-2395. Tel: 507-452-5656; Fax: 507-452-5477. [JC]
School—See listings under Centralized Catholic Schools.
Catechesis/Religious Programs—Tel: 507-452-5656; Fax: 507-452-5477.
Students 267.

5—ST. STANISLAUS (1871), Rev. Daniel R. Dernek.
Res., 625 E. Fourth St., 55987-4297. Tel: 507-452-5430; Fax: 507-452-3355.
School—See listings under Centralized Catholic Schools. Tel: 507-452-3766.
Catechesis/Religious Programs—602 E. Fifth St., 55987.
Students 150.

OUTSIDE THE CITY OF WINONA

Adams, Mower Co., Sacred Heart (1886), Rev. Gregory P. Leif.
Res., 412 Main St., P.O. Box 352, 55909-9998. Tel: 507-582-3321; Fax: 507-582-1033. [CEM]
School—(Grades 1-8). Tel: 507-582-3120. Mrs. Joanne Croker, Prin.
Sisters 1; Lay Teachers 7; Students 130.
Catechesis/Religious Programs—Tel: 507-582-3321.
Students 78.
Convent—Tel: 507-582-3304.

Adrian, Nobles Co., St. Adrian (1877), Rev. Gerald C. Kosse.
Res., 512 Maine Ave., P.O. Box 475, 56110-0475. Tel: 507-483-2317; Fax: 507-483-2460. [CEM]
Catechesis/Religious Programs—108 E. Sixth St., 56110. Tel: 507-483-2480.
Students 244.

Albert Lea, Freeborn Co., St. Theodore's (1882), Rev. Robert J. Schneider.
Res., 308 E. Fountain, 56007-2456. Tel: 507-373-0603; Fax: 507-373-9657. [CEM]
Parish Center & School—See listings under Centralized Catholic Schools. 323 E. Clark St., 56007. Tel: 507-373-9657.
Catechesis/Religious Programs—Tel: 507-373-2987; Fax: 507-373-9657.
Students 438.

Altura, Winona Co., St. Anthony's (1919). Attended by St. Rose of Lima.
180 S. Fremont, P.O. Box 727, Lewiston, 55952-0727. Tel: 507-796-6271; 507-523-2428 (Rectory). [JC]
Catechesis/Religious Programs—Students 85.

Austin, Mower Co., St. Augustine's (1857), Rev. Paul E. Nelson.
Res., 405 Fourth St., N.W., 55912-3091. Tel: 507-437-4537. [JC]
School—See listings under Centralized Catholic Schools.
Catechesis/Religious Programs—Students 194.

St. Edward's (1960), Revs. Hubert Boschert, S.J.; Timothy E. Biren.
Res., 2000 Oakland Ave., W., 55912-1599. Tel: 507-433-1841; Fax: 507-433-9680. [JC]
School—See listings under Centralized Catholic Schools.
Catechesis/Religious Programs—Students 92.

Queen of Angels (1936), Rev. Virgil S. Duellman.
Res., 1001 Oakland Ave. E., 55912-3896. Tel: 507-433-1888; Fax: 507-433-1889. [JC]
School—See listings under Centralized Catholic Schools. Tel: 507-433-8745.
Catechesis/Religious Programs—912 First Ave., N.E., 55912. Tel: 507-433-8474.
Students 152.

Convent/Retreat House—1009 E. Oakland Ave., 55912. Tel: 507-437-4015.

Blooming Prairie, Steele Co., St. Columbanus (1878), Rev. Richard J. Dernek.
Res., 114 E. Main, 55917-1427. Tel: 507-583-2529; 583-2784. [CEM]
Catechesis/Religious Programs—Tel: 507-583-2784.
Students 148.

Blue Earth, Faribault Co., SS. Peter and Paul's (1866), Rev. John W. Ozbun.
Res., 214 S. Holland, 56013-1331. Tel: 507-526-5626. [CEM]
Catechesis/Religious Programs—Tel: 507-526-2816.
Students 171.

Brewster, Nobles Co., Sacred Heart (1901). Attended by St. Francis Xaiver, Windom.
548 17th St., Windom, 56101-1217. Tel: 507-831-3300. [CEM]
Catechesis/Religious Programs—P.O. Box 187, 56119. Tel: 507-842-5584. Loretta Smith, D.R.E.
Students 78.

Brownsdale, Mower Co., Our Lady of Loretto (1946). Attended by St. Edward, Austin. Rev. Hubert Boschert, S.J.
2000 Oakland Ave., W., Austin, 55912-1599. Tel: 507-433-1841; Fax: 507-433-9680.
Catechesis/Religious Programs—Tel: 507-584-6476.
Students 36.

Brownsville, Houston Co., St. Patrick's (1871). Attended by St. Peter.
P.O. Box 355, Hokah, 55941-0355. Tel: 507-894-4242. [CEM][JC 2]
Catechesis/Religious Programs—P.O. Box 155, 55919. Tel: 507-482-6769.
Students 55.
Mission—Freeburg, St. Nicholas.

Byron, Olmsted Co., Christ the King (1965), Rev. Charlie I. Collins.
Res., 202 Fourth St., N.W., P.O. Box 1000, 55920-1000. Tel: 507-775-6455; Fax: 507-775-0501.
Catechesis/Religious Programs—Tel: 507-775-0501.
Students 230.

Caledonia, Houston Co., St. Mary (1975), Rev. Donald J. Schmitz.
Res., 513 S. Pine St., P.O. Box 406, 55921-0406. Tel: 507-725-3804; Fax: 507-725-2001. [CEM]
School—(Grades K-8). Tel: 507-725-3355. Mrs. Gail Trocinski, Prin.
Priests 1; Lay Teachers 14; Students 180.
Catechesis/Religious Programs—Students 196.
Convent—308 E. South, 55921.

Canton, Fillmore Co., The Assumption (1891). Attended by Nativity of B.V.M.
640 First Ave., S.W., Harmony, 55939-0596. Tel: 507-886-2393; Fax: 507-886-2393. [CEM][JC]

Chatfield, Fillmore Co., St. Mary's (1866). Attended by St. Columban, Preston. Rev. Thomas A. Loomis Tel: 507-765-3886.
408 N.W. Preston St., Preston, 55965.; Office: 405 S.W. Bench St., 55923. Tel: 507-867-3922; Fax: 507-867-3922. [CEM 2][JC]
Catechesis/Religious Programs—405 Bench St., S.W., 55923. Tel: 507-867-3138.
Students 179.

Claremont, Dodge Co., St. Francis de Sales (1869). Attended by St. John Baptist de La Salle, Dodge Center.
20 Second St., N.E., P.O. Box 310, Dodge Center, 55927-0310. Tel: 507-374-6830. [CEM][JC]
Catechesis/Religious Programs—Tel: 507-528-2200.
Students 40.

Currie, Murray Co., Immaculate Heart of Mary (1883), Rev. Msgr. Paul C. Evers.
Res., 510 Mill St., P.O. Box 174, 56123-0174. Tel: 507-763-3145.
Catechesis/Religious Programs—Students 107.

Dakota, Winona Co., Holy Cross (1890), Rev. Joseph C. Frisch.
Res., P.O. Box 387, 55925-0387. Tel: 507-643-6163.
Catechesis/Religious Programs—Students 34.

Deerfield, Steele Co., Corpus Christi (1869). Attended by Christ the King, Medford.
205 N.W. Second Ave., P.O. Box 120, Medford, 55049-0120. Tel: 507-451-6353.

Delavan, Faribault Co., Mater Dolorosa (1889). Attended by St. Mary, Winnebago.
P.O. Box 308, Winnebago, 56098-0308. Tel: 507-893-4242. [CEM]
Catechesis/Religious Programs—Tel: 507-893-4242.
Students 34.

Dodge Center, Dodge Co., St. John Baptist de La Salle (1945), Rev. James J. Seitz.
Res., 20 Second St. N.E., P.O. Box 310, 55927-0310. Tel: 507-374-6830.
Catechesis/Religious Programs—Tel: 507-374-6765.
Students 78.

Dundee, Nobles Co., St. Mary. Closed. For inquiries for parish records contact the Chancery.

East Chain, Martin Co., Holy Family (1925). Attended by St. John Vianney, Fairmont.
Res., 901 S. Prairie Ave., Fairmont, 56031-3098. Tel: 507-235-5535; Fax: 507-235-5639. [CEM][JC]
Catechesis/Religious Programs—Students 43.

Easton, Faribault Co., Our Lady of Mount Carmel (1866), Rev. John P. Wilmot.
Res., 27 Main St., P.O. Box 8, 56025-0008. Tel: 507-787-2303; Fax: 507-787-2221. [CEM]
School—(Grades K-8). Tel: 507-787-2233. Darlene Yonkey, Prin.
Priests 1; Lay Teachers 7; Students 40.
Catechesis/Religious Programs—Students 60.

Elba, Winona Co., St. Aloysius (1877). Attended by St. Charles Borromeo, St. Charles.
736 Church Ave., St. Charles, 55972-1426. Tel: 507-932-3294; Fax: 507-932-3393. [CEM]
Catechesis/Religious Programs—Attend St. Charles Borromeo program, Tel. No. 507-932-3303.

Ellendale, Freeborn Co., St. Aidan (1857). Attended by St. Edward, Austin.
c/o St. Edward Church: 2000 Oakland Ave. W., Austin, 55912-1599. Tel: 507-433-1841; Fax: 507-433-9680. [CEM]
Catechesis/Religious Programs—Tel: 507-684-2245.
Students 82.

Ellsworth, Nobles Co., St. Mary's (1885). Attended by St. Catherine, Luverne.
203 E. Brown St., Luverne, 56156-1599. Tel: 507-283-8502; Fax: 507-283-3638. [CEM]
Catechesis/Religious Programs—Tel: 712-479-2444.
Students 39.

Eyota, Olmsted Co., Holy Redeemer (1891). Attended by St. Charles Borromeo, St. Charles.
Mailing Address: 736 Church Ave., St. Charles, 55972-1426.
761 Whitewater Ave., St. Charles, 55972-1426. Tel: 507-932-3294; Fax: 507-932-3393.
Catechesis/Religious Programs—Tel: 507-545-2161; Fax: 507-545-2161.
Students 167.

Fairmont, Martin Co., St. John Vianney (1952), Revs. Joseph B. Fogal; Richard P. Loomis.
Parish Office: 901 S. Prairie Ave., 56031-3098. Tel: 507-235-5535; Fax: 507-235-5639. [CEM]
School—(Grades PreK-7) 911 S. Prairie Ave., 56031. Tel: 507-235-5304; Fax: 507-235-9099. Bruce Tepfer, Prin.
Priests 2; Lay Teachers 11; Students 180.
Catechesis/Religious Programs—Tel: 507-235-5903; Fax: 570-235-5659.
Students 367.

Fountain, Fillmore Co., St. Lawrence O'Toole (1872). Attended by St. Columban, Preston.
408 N.W. Preston St., Preston, 55965. Tel: 507-765-3886. [JC]
Catechesis/Religious Programs—Students 3.

Fulda, Murray Co., St. Gabriel's (1882). Attended by Immaculate Heart of Mary, Currie.
501 Mill St., P.O. Box 174, Currie, 56123-0174. Tel: 507-763-3145.
Res., 307 W. Lake Ave., 56131-9402. Tel: 507-425-2595. [CEM]
Catechesis/Religious Programs—Tel: 507-425-2369.
Students 158.

Geneva, St. Mary (1867). Attended by All Saints, New Richland. Rev. Thien Nguyen.
307 1st St., S.W., P.O. Box 185, New Richland, 56072-0185. Tel: 507-465-8217; 465-8381. [CEM]
Catechesis/Religious Programs—Tel: 507-583-7530.
Students 43.

Good Thunder, Blue Earth Co., St. Joseph (1879). Attended by St. Teresa, Mapleton.
104 Silver St. W., P.O. Box 305, Mapleton, 56065. Tel: 507-524-3127; Fax: 507-524-4423. [CEM]
Catechesis/Religious Programs—Tel: 507-278-3444.
Students 63.

Grand Meadow, Mower Co., St. Finbarr's (1878). Attended by St. Ignatius, Spring Valley.
213 W. Franklin St., Spring Valley, 55975-1312. Tel: 507-346-7565. [CEM]
Church—504 1st St. S.W., P.O. Box 326, 55951. Tel: 507-754-5190.
Catechesis/Religious Programs—Students 107.

Guckeen, Faribault Co., Our Lady of Mercy (1902). Attended by Sts. Peter and Paul, Blue Earth. Rev. John W. Ozbun.
214 S. Holland, Blue Earth, 56013-1331. Tel: 507-526-5626.
Catechesis/Religious Programs—Students 11.

Hammond, Wabasha Co., St. Clement's. Closed. For inquires for parish records contact SS. Peter and Paul, Mazeppa.

Harmony, Fillmore Co., The Nativity of the Blessed Virgin (1906), Rev. Stephen J. Peterson.
Res., 640 First Ave., S.W., 55939-0596. Tel: 507-886-2393; Fax: 507-886-2393.
Catechesis/Religious Programs—Students 82.

Hayfield, Dodge Co., Sacred Heart (1935). Attended by St. Columbanus, Blooming Prairie. Rev. Richard J. Dernek.
114 E. Main St., Blooming Prairie, 55917-1427. Tel: 507-583-2529.
Catechesis/Religious Programs—Tel: 507-477-2297.
Students 96.

Heron Lake, Jackson Co., Sacred Heart (1884). Attended by St. Francis Xavier, Windom.
548 17th St., Windom, 56101-1217. Tel: 507-831-3300; Fax: 507-831-3300. [CEM]
Catechesis/Religious Programs—Tel: 507-793-2773.
Students 124.

Hokah, Houston Co., St. Peter's (1876), Rev. Paul J. Breza.
Res., P.O. Box 355, 55941-0355. Tel: 507-894-4242. [CEM][JC 2]
School—(Grades K-8). Tel: 507-894-4375; 894-4944. Norman Valiska, Prin.
Lay Teachers 7; Students 80.
Catechesis/Religious Programs—Students 23.

Houston, Houston Co., St. Mary's (1873). Attended by St. Joseph, Rushford.
101 Rushford Ave. W., P.O. Box 577, Rushford, 55971-0557. Tel: 507-864-2257; Fax: 507-864-2257. [CEM]

Iona, Murray Co., St. Columba's (1891). Attended by St. Ann, Slayton.
2747 29th St., Slayton, 56172-1485. Tel: 507-836-8030. [CEM]
Catechesis/Religious Programs—Students 93.

Jackson, Jackson Co., Good Shepherd (1891), Rev. Charles J. Quinn.
Res., 311 N. Sverdrup Ave., P.O. Box 65, 56143-1329. Tel: 507-847-2504; Fax: 507-847-5322. [CEM]
Catechesis/Religious Programs—Tel: 507-847-2719. Susanne Foster, D.R.E.
Students 150.

Janesville, Waseca Co., St. Ann's (1876), Rev. Sylvester F. Brown.
307 W. Second St., P.O. Box 218, 56048-0218. Tel: 507-234-6244; Fax: 507-234-6237. [CEM]
Catechesis/Religious Programs—Tel: 507-234-5753.
Students 178.

Jasper, Pipestone Co., St. Joseph's (1890). Attended by St. Leo's, Pipestone.
106 4th St., S.E., P.O. Box 36, Pipestone, 56154-0036. Tel: 507-825-3152; Fax: 507-825-4492. [CEM]
Catechesis/Religious Programs—Students 45.

Jeffers, Cottonwood Co., St. Augustine's (1912). Closed. For inquiries for parish records contact the Chancery.

Johnsburg, Mower Co., St. John's (1859). Attended by Sacred Heart, Adams.
412 Main St., P.O. Box 352, Adams, 55909-9998. Tel: 507-582-3321; Fax: 507-582-1033. [CEM]

Kasson, Dodge Co., Holy Family (1976). Attended by Christ the King, Byron. Rev. Charlie I. Collins.
202 Fourth St., N.W., P.O. Box 1000, Byron, 55920-1000. Tel: 507-775-6455; Fax: 507-775-0501. [CEM]
Catechesis/Religious Programs—Tel: 507-634-7599.
Students 280.

Kellogg, Wabasha Co., St. Agnes (1900). Attended by St. Felix, Wabasha.
117 3rd St. W., Wabasha, 55981-1201. Tel: 651-565-3931; Fax: 651-565-4363.
Catechesis/Religious Programs—Tel: 507-767-4780.
Students 68.

Immaculate Conception (1881). Attended by St. Felix, Wabasha.
117 3rd St. W., Wabasha, 55981-1201. Tel: 651-565-3931; Fax: 651-565-4363.
Catechesis/Religious Programs—Tel: 507-534-3588.
Students 68.

La Crescent, Houston Co., The Crucifixion (1856), Rev. Msgr. Donald W. Grubisch.
Res., 407 S. Second St., 55947-1326. Tel: 507-895-4720; Fax: 507-895-4720. [CEM 2]

School—(Grades K-6) 420 S. Second St., 55947. Tel: 507-895-4402; Fax: 507-895-4403. Robert Adams, Prin.
Lay Teachers 10; Students 124.
Catechesis/Religious Programs—1380 Lancer Blvd., 55947. Tel: 507-895-2700.
Students 310.
Convent—423 S. Second St., 55947. Tel: 507-895-6867.

Lake City, Wabasha Co., St. Mary's of the Lake (1877), Rev. James D. Russell.
Res., 419 Lyon Ave., 55041-1649. Tel: 651-345-4134; Fax: 651-345-6134.
Catechesis/Religious Programs—Tel: 651-345-3535.
Students 270.

Lake Crystal, Blue Earth Co., Holy Family (1900). Attended by St. Joseph the Worker, Mankato. Revs. Joseph P. Pete; Kurt Farrell, Admin.
Res., 816 Hubbell Ave., Mankato, 56001-2197. Tel: 507-388-3766; Fax: 507-388-3766. [CEM]
Catechesis/Religious Programs—Tel: 507-726-2725.
Students 121.

Lakefield, Jackson Co., St. Joseph (1897). Attended by Good Shepherd, Jackson.
311 N. Sverdrup Ave., P.O. Box 65, Jackson, 56143-1329. Tel: 507-847-2504. [CEM]
Catechesis/Religious Programs—410 Broadway Ave., Box 517, 56150. Tel: 507-662-5819.
Students 112.

Lake Wilson, Murray Co., St. Mary (1916). Attended by St. Ann, Slayton.
2747 29th St., Slayton, 56172-1485. Tel: 507-836-8030. [JC]
Catechesis/Religious Programs—Students 55.

Lamoille, Winona Co., Precious Blood (1900). Closed. For inquiries for parish records contact the Chancery.

Lanesboro, Fillmore Co., St. Patrick (1871). Attended by St. Columban, Preston.
408 N.W. Preston St., Preston, 55965. Tel: 507-765-3886. [JC]
Catechesis/Religious Programs—Students 24.

Le Roy, Mower Co., St. Patrick's (1878). Attended by St. Ignatius, Spring Valley. Rev. Russell G. Scepaniak.
213 W. Franklin St., Spring Valley, 55975-1312. Tel: 507-324-5203. [CEM]
Catechesis/Religious Programs—Students 125.

Lewiston, Winona Co., St. Rose of Lima (1876), Rev. Peter Schuster.
Res., 180 S. Fremont, P.O. Box 727, 55952-0727. Tel: 507-523-2428. [CEM]
Catechesis/Religious Programs—Tel: 507-523-3548.
Students 180.

Lismore, Nobles Co., St. Anthony's (1887), Rev. Gerald C. Kosse, Priest Mod.; Ms. Roxanne Lisnak, Parish Dir.
Mailing Address: 310 Third Ave. S., P.O. Box 158, 56155-0158. Tel: 507-472-8262; Fax: 507-472-8454. [CEM]
Catechesis/Religious Programs—Tel: 507-472-8262.
Students 53.

Litomysl, Holy Trinity (1877). Attended by St. Edward, Austin.
2000 Oakland Ave. W., Austin, 55912-1599. Tel: 507-433-1841.
School—St. Isidore, (Grades K-8). Tel: 507-451-5876; Fax: 507-433-9680. Ann Nylund, Prin.
Priests 2; Lay Teachers 4; Students 46.
Catechesis/Religious Programs—Students 13.

Luverne, Rock Co., St. Catherine's (1881), Rev. Andrew J. Beerman.
203 E. Brown, 56156-1599. Tel: 507-283-8502; Fax: 507-283-3638. [CEM]
Catechesis/Religious Programs—Tel: 507-283-8071.
Students 201.

Lyle, Mower Co., Queen of Peace (1946) (German). Attended by St. Peter, Rose Creek.
302 Maple St. S.W., Rose Creek, 55970-9701. Tel: 507-433-1532.
Catechesis/Religious Programs—Tel: 507-325-4677.
Students 54.

Mabel, Fillmore Co., St. Olaf (1954). Attended by Nativity of B.V.M., Harmony.
640 First Ave. S.W., Harmony, 55939-0596. Tel: 507-886-2393. [JC]
Catechesis/Religious Programs—Students 85.

Madelia, Watonwan Co., St. Mary (1872), Rev. James C. Berning.
Res., 212 First St., N.E., 56062-1702. Tel: 507-642-8305.
School—(Grades PreK-6). Tel: 507-642-3324. Mrs. Janel Sasser, Prin.
Priests 1; Lay Teachers 8; Students 84.
Convent—13 Crosby Ave., N.E., 56062. Tel: 507-642-3323.
Catechesis/Religious Programs—Students 123.

Madison Lake, Blue Earth Co., All Saints (1894), Rev. Kevin Connolly.
Parish Endowment Fund, Inc. of All Saints Church: 600 3rd St., P.O. Box 217, 56063-0217. Tel: 507-243-3319; Fax: 507-243-3319. [CEM]
School—(Grades PreK-6) P.O. Box 158, 56053-0158. Tel: 507-243-3819; Fax: 507-243-3319. Sr. Mary Beth Schraml, S.S.N.D., Prin.
Priests 1; Sisters 2; Lay Teachers 3; Students 68; Preschool 19.
Catechesis/Religious Programs—Students 181.
Convent—Tel: 507-243-3010.

Mankato, Blue Earth Co.,

1—SS. Peter and Paul's, (1854), Revs. Karl Voelker, S.J.; Theodore Hottinger, S.J.; Charles L. Kerr, S.J.; Bro. James Becwar, S.J.
Res., 105 N. Fifth St., 56001-4442. Tel: 507-388-2995; Fax: 507-388-7628.
School—See listings under Centralized Catholic Schools. Tel: 507-387-3316.
Pastoral Center—512 Mulberry St., 56001-4442. Tel: 507-388-1664.
Catechesis/Religious Programs—Tel: 507-387-6228; Fax: 507-388-7628.
Students 263.
Mission—Mankato, Blue Earth Co., St. Francis Xavier, Harper & 3rd Ave., 56001.

2—St. Francis Xavier Mission Chapel. Attended by SS. Peter and Paul, Mankato, 105 N. Fifth St., 56001. Tel: 507-388-2995.
Church—Harper & 3rd Ave., 56001.
Catechesis/Religious Programs—Students 144.

3—St. John the Baptist's, (1884), Rev. Richard M. Colletti.
Res., 632 S. Broad St., 56001-3890. Tel: 507-625-3131; Fax: 507-625-3270. [JC]
School—See listings under Centralized Catholic Schools.
Catechesis/Religious Programs—Tel: 507-625-3389.
Students 383.

4—St. Joseph the Worker, (1957), Rev. Joseph P. Pete.
Res., 816 Hubbell Ave., 56001-2197. Tel: 507-388-3766; Fax: 507-388-3766. [JC]
School—See listings under Centralized Catholic Schools.
Catechesis/Religious Programs—423 W. 7th St., 56001. Tel: 507-625-3450.
Students 170.
Convent—Tel: 507-388-2515.

Mapleton, Blue Earth Co., St. Teresa's (1876), Rev. Joseph W. Mountain, Priest Mod.; Sr. Lalande Hennen, S.S.N.D., Parish Dir.
Res., 104 Silver St., P.O. Box 305, 56065. Tel: 507-524-3127; Fax: 507-524-4423. [CEM]
Catechesis/Religious Programs—Tel: 507-524-4606.
Students 164.

Mazeppa, Wabasha Co., SS. Peter and Paul (1860), Rev. Robert G. Meyer.
Res., 1st St. S., P.O. Box 224, 55956-0224. Tel: 507-843-3885.
Catechesis/Religious Programs—Tel: 507-843-4600.
Students 78.

Medford, Steele Co., Christ the King (1943), Rev. Robert D. Herman.
Res., 205 N.W. Second Ave., P.O. Box 120, 55049-0120. Tel: 507-451-6353.
Catechesis/Religious Programs—Tel: 507-451-8898.
Students 132.

Minneiska, Wabasha Co., St. Mary's (1867). Attended by Holy Trinity, Rollingstone.
83 Main St., Rollingstone, 55969-9759. Tel: 507-689-2351.

Minnesota City, Winona Co., St. Paul's (1924), Rev. Edward Cunningham, O.M.I.
Res., P.O. Box 26, 55959-0026. Tel: 507-689-2485; Fax: 507-689-4559. [CEM]
Catechesis/Religious Programs—Students 24.

Minnesota Lake, Faribault Co., St. John the Baptist (1865). Attended by Our Lady of Mount Carmel, Easton. Rev. John P. Wilmot.
Mailing Address: P.O. Box 8, Easton, 56025-0008. Tel: 507-787-2303; Fax: 507-787-2221.
Church—P.O. Box 158, 56068. Tel: 507-462-3636; Fax: 507-462-3212. [CEM]
Catechesis/Religious Programs—Tel: 507-462-3791.
Students 91.

New Richland, Waseca Co., All Saints (1879), Rev. Thien Van Nguyen.
Res., 307 1st St. SW, P.O. Box 185, 56072-0185. Tel: 507-465-8217. [CEM]
Catechesis/Religious Programs—Students 104.

Oak Ridge, Winona Co., Immaculate Conception (1875). Closed. For inquiries about sacramental records contact Holy Trinity, Rollingstone.

Owatonna, Steele Co., St. Joseph's (1891), Rev. Thomas J. Hargesheimer; Deacon Paul Hillyer.
Res., 512 S. Elm St., 55060-3399. Tel: 507-451-4845; Fax: 507-451-4651.
School—See listings under Centralized Catholic Schools.
Catechesis/Religious Programs—Students 411.

Sacred Heart (1866), Rev. Peter J. Klein; Deacon George Anderberg.
Res., 810 S. Cedar Ave., 55060-3297. Tel: 507-451-1588; Fax: 507-446-9979. [JC]
School—See listings under Centralized Catholic Schools. Tel: 507-451-2694; Fax: 507-451-9554.
Catechesis/Religious Programs—Marian Dr., 55060. Tel: 507-451-2699.
Students 400.

Pipestone, Pipestone Co., St. Leo's (1887), Rev. Martin T. Schaefer.
Res., 106 Fourth St. S.E., P.O. Box 36, 56164-0036. Tel: 507-825-3152; Fax: 507-825-4492. [CEM]
Catechesis/Religious Programs—Students 285.

Plainview, Wabasha Co., St. Joachim's (1858), Rev. Donald F. Connelly.
Res., 900 W. Broadway, 55964-1039. Tel: 507-534-3321. [CEM]
Catechesis/Religious Programs—Tel: 507-534-2887.
Students 446.

Preston, Fillmore Co., St. Columban (1869), Rev. Thomas A. Loomis.
Res., 408 N.W. Preston St., 55965. Tel: 507-765-3886. [CEM 2][JC]
Catechesis/Religious Programs—Students 63.

Rochester, Olmsted Co.,

1—Holy Spirit, (1990), Rev. Dale E. Tupper.
Office: 5455 50th Ave., N.W., 55901. Tel: 507-280-0638; Fax: 507-292-9547.
Res., Tel: 507-281-8323. [JC]
School—See listings under Centralized Catholic Schools.
Catechesis/Religious Programs—Students 179.

2—Pax Christi, (1973), Revs. LaVern E. Trocinski; Patrick O. Arens.
Res., 4135 18th Ave., N.W., 55901-0460. Tel: 507-282-8542; Fax: 507-289-8741. [JC]
School—See listings under Centralized Catholic Schools. Tel: 507-280-0349; Fax: 507-289-4008.
Catechesis/Religious Programs—Fax: 507-289-8741.
Students 592.

3—Resurrection, (1967), Rev. Msgr. Donald P. Schmitz. In res., Rev. David Byrne.
Res., 1600-11th Ave., S.E., 55904-5499. Tel: 507-288-5528; Fax: 507-252-0763. [JC]
School—See listings under Centralized Catholic Schools.
Catechesis/Religious Programs—Students 500.

4—St. Bridget's, (1857). Attended by St. Bernard, Stewartville. Rev. Gregory G. Havel.
116 4th Ave., S.E., Stewartville, 55976. Tel: 507-533-8257. [CEM]
Catechesis/Religious Programs—Tel: 507-533-8757.
Students 80.

5—St. Francis of Assisi, (1937), Revs. Timothy T. Reker; Glenn K. Frerichs.
Res., 1114 3rd St., S.E., 55904-7293. Tel: 507-288-7313; Fax: 507-281-5997. [JC]
School—See listings under Centralized Catholic Schools. Tel: 507-288-4816; Fax: 507-288-4815.
Catechesis/Religious Programs—Tel: 507-289-2427.
Students 142.

6—St. John's, (1863), Rev. Msgr. Gerald A. Mahon; Deacon Gumisindo Gonzales.
Res., 11 4th Ave., S.W., 55902-3098. Tel: 507-288-7372; Fax: 507-288-7373. [JC]
School—See listings under Centralized Catholic Schools. Tel: 507-282-5248.
Catechesis/Religious Programs—Students 200.

7—St. Pius X, (1954), Revs. Paul W. Surprenant; Thomas E. Cook; Jack L. Krough Tel: 507-282-7441.
Res., 1315 12th Ave., N.W., 55901-1744. Tel: 507-288-8238; Fax: 507-286-8769. [JC]
School—See listings under Centralized Catholic Schools. Tel: 507-282-5161; Fax: 507-282-5107.
Catechesis/Religious Programs—Tel: 507-289-6317; Fax: 507-286-8769.
Students 282.

Rollingstone, Winona Co., Holy Trinity (1862), Rev. Edward F. McGrath.
Res., 83 Main St., 55969-9759. Tel: 507-689-2351. [CEM]
Catechesis/Religious Programs—Students 54.
Oratory—Oak Ridge, Immaculate Conception Chapel.

Rose Creek, Mower Co., St. Peter's (1885), Rev. Ruben C. Spinler.
Res., 302 Maple St. S.W., 55970-9701. Tel: 507-433-1532. [CEM]
Catechesis/Religious Programs—Tel: 507-433-6472.
Students 87.

Rushford, Fillmore Co., St. Joseph's (1868), Rev. William J. Kulas.
Res., 101 Rushford Ave. W., P.O. Box 577, 55971-0577. Tel: 507-864-2257; Fax: 507-864-2257. [CEM]
Catechesis/Religious Programs—Students 95.

St. Charles, Winona Co., St. Charles Borromeo (1867), Rev. James F. Callahan, S.M.A.
Mailing Address: 736 Church Ave., 55972-1426. Tel: 507-932-3294; Fax: 507-932-3393. [CEM]
Church—761 Whitewater Ave., 55972-1426.
Catechesis/Religious Programs—Tel: 507-932-3303.
Students 227.

St. Clair, Blue Earth Co., Immaculate Conception (1874). Attended by All Saints Church, 600 3rd St., P.O. Box 217, Madison Lake 56063-0217. Rev. Kevin Connolly.
Tel: 507-243-3319. [CEM]
Catechesis/Religious Programs—Students 196.

St. James, Watonwan Co., St. James (1873). Attended by St. Mary Church, Madelia. Rev. James C. Berning Tel: 507-642-8305; Sr. Lucille Hass, O.S.F., Pastoral Assoc.
Church—707 4th St.S., 56081-1824. Tel: 507-375-3542. [CEM]
Catechesis/Religious Programs—Tel: 507-375-4432. D.R.E.: Nonnie Hanson; Cleo Erickson.
Students 200.

St. Kilian, Nobles Co., St. Kilian (1903). Attended by St. Anthony, Lismore.
Mailing Address: 310 Third Ave. S., P.O. Box 158, Lismore, 56155-0158. Tel: 507-472-8262; Fax: 507-472-8454. [CEM]
Catechesis/Religious Programs—Tel: 507-472-8206.
Students 10.

Sherburn, Martin Co., St. Luke's (1888). Attended by Good Shepherd, Jackson.
Res., 311 N. Sverdrup Ave., P.O. Box 65, Jackson, 56143-1329. Tel: 507-847-2504; Fax: 507-847-5322. [CEM]
Catechesis/Religious Programs—Tel: 507-764-5091.
Students 110.

Slayton, Murray Co., St. Ann's (1897), Rev. Mark C. McNea.
Res., 2747 29th St., 56172-1485. Tel: 507-836-8030; Fax: 507-836-6261. [CEM]
Catechesis/Religious Programs—Tel: 507-836-6261.
Students 158.

Spring Valley, Fillmore Co., St. Ignatius (1878), Rev. Russell G. Scepaniak.
Res., 213 Franklin St., 55975-1312. Tel: 507-346-7565. [CEM]
Catechesis/Religious Programs—Students 135.
Oratory—Wykoff, St. Kilian.

Stewartville, Olmsted Co., St. Bernard's (1894), Rev. Gregory G. Havel.
Res., 116 Fourth Ave. S.E., 55976. Tel: 507-533-8257. [CEM]
Catechesis/Religious Programs—Tel: 507-533-8192.
Students 270.

Theilman, Wabasha Co., St. Joseph's (1903). Attended by St. Mary of the Lake, Lake City.
419 Lyon Ave., Lake City, 55041-1649. Tel: 651-345-4134. [CEM]

Trimont, Martin Co., St. Joseph. Closed. For inquiries for parish records contact the Chancery.

Truman, Martin Co., St. Katherine (1954). Attended by St. Mary, Madelia.
212 First St., N.E., Madelia, 56062-1702. Tel: 507-642-8305.
Catechesis/Religious Programs—Students 67.

Twin Lakes, Freeborn Co., St. James (1876), Rev. Donald W. Zenk, Admin.
Res., 602 31st St., N.W., Austin, 55912. Tel: 507-437-3579.

Vernon Center, Blue Earth Co., St. Matthew (1911). Attended by St. Teresa, Mapleton.
Mailing Address: 104 Silver St. W., P.O. Box 305, Mapleton, 56065. Tel: 507-524-3127; Fax: 507-524-4423. [CEM]
Catechesis/Religious Programs—Tel: 507-549-3358.
Students 69.

Wabasha, Wabasha Co., St. Felix (1858), Rev. Donald J. Lovas.
Res., 117 W. Third St., 55981-1201. Tel: 651-565-3931; Fax: 651-565-4363. [CEM]
School—(Grades PreK-6) 130 Third St. E., 55981. Tel: 651-564-4446; Fax: 651-565-0244. Sr. M. Joann McMahon, S.S.N.D., Prin.
Priests 1; Sisters 2; Lay Teachers 7; Students 185.
Catechesis/Religious Programs—Tel: 651-565-3718; Fax: 651-565-4363.
Students 171.
Convent—36 Bailey Ave., 55981. Tel: 651-565-4578.

Waldorf, Waseca Co., St. Joseph's (1878). Attended by All Saints, New Richland, 307 1st. St. S.W., P.O. Box 185, New Richland, MN 56072-0185.
Tel: 507-465-8217. [CEM]
Catechesis/Religious Programs—Students 64.

Waseca, Waseca Co., Sacred Heart (1869), Rev. John M. Kunz.
Res., 111 Fourth St., N.W., 56093-2413. Tel: 507-835-1222; Fax: 507-835-4149. [CEM][JC 2]
School—(Grades PreK-4) 308 W. Elm Ave., 56093. Tel: 507-835-2780. Patricia Dunder, Prin.
Priests 1; Lay Teachers 11; Students 232.
Catechesis/Religious Programs—Tel: 507-835-1500.
Students 471.
Convent—400 Second Ave., N.W., 56093. Tel: 507-835-4867.

Wells, Faribault Co., St. Casimir's (1880), Rev. Eugene F. Stenzel.
Res., 320 Second Ave. S.W., 56097-1399. Tel: 507-553-5391. [CEM]
School—(Grades K-8) 330 Second Ave., S.W., 56097. Tel: 507-553-5822. Katy Schmitz, Prin.
Lay Teachers 12; Students 102.
Catechesis/Religious Programs—Students 175.

West Albany, Wabasha Co., St. Patrick's of West Albany (1865). Attended by SS. Peter and Paul.
1st St. S., P.O. Box 224, Mazeppa, 55956-0224. Tel: 507-843-3885. [CEM]
Catechesis/Religious Programs—Tel: 507-753-2424.
Students 56.

Westbrook, Cottonwood Co., St. Anthony's (1909). Attended by Immaculate Heart of Mary, Currie.
501 Mill St., P.O. Box 174, Currie, 56123-0174. Tel: 507-763-3145. [CEM]

West Concord, Dodge Co., St. Vincent de Paul (1945). Attended by St. John Baptist de La Salle, Dodge Center.
20 Second St., N.E., P.O. Box 310, Dodge Center, 55927-0310. Tel: 507-374-6830. [CEM]
Catechesis/Religious Programs—P.O. Box 117, 55985. Tel: 507-527-2384.
Students 79.

Wilmont, Nobles Co., Our Lady of Good Counsel (1903). Attended by St. Adrian, Adrian.
512 Main Ave., P.O. Box 475, Adrian, 56110-0475. Tel: 507-483-2317; Fax: 507-483-2460. [CEM]
Catechesis/Religious Programs—Tel: 507-926-5305.
Students 77.

Wilson, Winona Co., Immaculate Conception (1874). Attended by Cathedral of the Sacred Heart.
360 Main St., Winona, 55987-3299. Tel: 507-452-4770.

Windom, Cottonwood Co., St. Francis Xavier's (1898), Rev. Andrew D. Olsem.
Res., 548 17th St., 56101-1217. Tel: 507-831-3300.
Catechesis/Religious Programs—532 17th St., 56101. Tel: 507-831-1985.
Students 220.

Winnebago, Faribault Co., St. Mary's (1893), Rev. John F. Traufler.
Res., 32 1st St. N.E., P.O. Box 308, 56098-0308. Tel: 507-893-4242. [CEM]
Catechesis/Religious Programs—Students 70.

Woodstock, Pipestone Co., St. Martin's (1882). Attended by St. Leo, Pipestone.
Mailing Address: 106 Fourth St., S.E., P.O. Box 36, Pipestone, 56164-0036. Tel: 507-825-3152; Fax: 507-825-4492. [CEM]

Worthington, Nobles Co., St. Mary's (1886), Rev. Hilary R. Brixius.
Res., 1215 Seventh Ave., 56187-2297. Tel: 507-376-6005; Fax: 507-376-9167. [CEM]
School—(Grades K-6) Twelfth St. & Eighth Ave., 56187. Tel: 507-376-5236; Fax: 507-376-6159. Laura Pass, Prin.
Sisters 1; Lay Teachers 8; Students 138.
Catechesis/Religious Programs—1206 Eighth Ave., 56187. Tel: 507-372-2090.
Students 256.
Convent—1221 Seventh Ave., 56187. Tel: 507-376-4035.

Wykoff, Fillmore Co., St. Kilian's (1887). Closed. For inquiries for parish records contact the Chancery.

Chaplains of Public Institutions

ROCHESTER. *Federal Medical Center* Bureau of Prisons, 2110 Center St. E., 55904. Sr. Emile Bormann, P.B.V.M., Chap.

WASECA. *Federal Correctional Institution*. Vacant. 920 St. Andrews Pl., Owatonna, 55060.

On Special or Other Diocesan Assignment:
Reverend Fathers—
Buryska, James F., Rochester Methodist Hospital, 201 W. Center St., Rochester, MN 55902. Tel: 507-255-5551
Kunz, James H., Mayo Medical Center, 1216 2nd St., SW, Rochester, MN 55902. Tel: 507-285-5123
Marek, Dean V., Mayo Medical Center, 1216 2nd St., SW, Rochester, MN 55902. Tel: 507-255-5780

On Duty Outside the Diocese:
Reverend Fathers—
Brandenhoff, Peter B., 8859 Spring Lane, Woodbury, MN 55125. Tel: 612-578-0957
Heiting, Paul, Casa Santa Maria, Uia dell' Umilta 30, Rome, 00187 Italy
Moore, Jon H., 600 Laurel Ave., Hudson, WI 54016-1903
Murtagh, Lawrence, Box 66, Stockholm, SD 57264. Tel: 605-676-2550

Military Chaplains:
Reverend Fathers—
Arnoldt, David M., CMR 430 Box 227, APO AE, 09096. Tel: Work: 49-611-705-1570/6248/6247

Absent on Leave:
Reverend Fathers—
Cashman, Joseph C.
Hodapp, Timothy L., 224 Lexington Pkwy. S., St. Paul, MN 55105. Tel: 651-848-0805
Taylor, Robert H., Diocese of Winona, P.O. Box 588, Winona, MN 55987

Retired:
Reverend Monsignors—
Egan, Eugene E., 401 N. Maple St., Ellsworth, MN 56129. Tel: 507-967-2382
Enright, Frank E., Sacred Heart Care Center, Inc., 1200 12th St., S.W., Austin, MN 55912-2699. Tel: 507-437-8309
Galles, Francis A., 500 Preston St. N.W., Preston, MN 55965. Tel: 507-765-2756
Habiger, James D., Univ. of St. Thomas, 2115 Summit Ave., Box 4174, St. Paul, MN 55105. Tel: 612-962-8065(Res); 612-227-8777
Klein, Edward, St. Elizabeth Hospital, 1200 W. 5th Grant Blvd., Wabasha, MN 55981-1098. Tel: 651-565-2104
Klein, Frank W., Callista Court, 1455 W. Broadway, Apt. 215, Winona, MN 55987
Literski, Roy E., 1328 D. McNally Dr., Winona, MN 55987. Tel: 507-452-7685
McGinnis, Joseph R., St. Elizabeth Hospital, 1200 W. 5th Grant Blvd., Wabasha, MN 55981-1098. Tel: 651-565-5513
Mountain, Joseph W., 5371 Elkton Tr., Faribault, MN 55021-8453
Ploof, Thomas M., 220 S. Broadway, 1122 Center Plaza, Rochester, MN 55904-6514. Tel: 507-282-0445
Tighe, Emmett F., Madonna Towers #800/802, 4001 19th Ave. N.W., Rochester, MN 55901. Tel: 507-288-3911
Reverend Fathers—
Conway, Gerald W., 728 First Ave. S.W., #404, Rochester, MN 55902-3307. Tel: 507-285-1279
Cook, Louis G., 495 8th St. SW, Plainview, MN 55964
Curtis, William D., St. Elizabeth Hospital, 1200 W. 5th Grant Blvd., Wabasha, MN 55981-1098. Tel: 612-565-4531
Dandelet, James D., P.O. Box 46, Easton, MN 56025-0046. Tel: 507-787-2520
Eikens, Leroy F., 728 First Ave., S.W. #403, Rochester, MN 55902-3307. Tel: 507-280-7692
Engels, Richard J., 205 Dugan St., Wabasha, MN 55981
Ernster, Milo, 163 Pioneer Dr., Wabasha, MN 55981. Tel: 612-565-2191
Ginther, Lawrence P., 5125 W. Seventh St., Apt. 8, Winona, MN 55987-5616. Tel: 507-454-4789
Gits, Douglas J., 1420 4th St. S.E., Rochester, MN 55904-4716. Tel: 507-286-7874
Glynn, Francis M., St. Elizabeth Hospital, 1200 W. 5th Grant Blvd., Wabasha, MN 55981-1098. Tel: 507-332-5150
Haberman, Clayton J., 5371 Elkton Tr., Faribault, MN 55021-8453. Tel: 507-334-0610
Halloran, Jerome D., 5653 B Lake Murray Blvd., La Mesa, CA 92041. Tel: 619-463-9685

Halloran, Paul F., 7646 Sixth Lake Rd., N.W., Akeley, MN 56433-9507
Jewison, Harry P., 1024 Ninth St., N.E., Rochester, MN 55906. Tel: 507-285-5515
Kellen, Elmer W., 104 Park St., P.O. Box 171, Minnesota Lake, MN 56068. Tel: 507-462-3565
Kerrigan, Bernard A., 626 Shields Ave., Wabasha, MN 55981
Kulas, Robert A., 7510 Cahill Rd., #201B, Edina, MN 55439. Tel: 612-946-8972
Kunz, Francis P., 240 Hudson Ave. E., Mankato, MN 56001. Tel: 507-625-6217
LaPlante, Joseph A., 31 Robinson Dr., Wabasha, MN 55981-3016. Tel: 651-565-2441
Leary, Donald G., #1504, 220 S. Broadway, Rochester, MN 55902. Tel: 507-288-5813
Loosbrock, Donald L., 149 Pioneer Dr., Wabasha, MN 55981-3214. Tel: 651-565-6531
Maher, Robert G., 9505 Salem Hills Court, Las Vegas, NV 89134-4600. Tel: 702-804-2718
Mountain, Edward C., 420 11th St., S.E., Owatonna, MN 55060-4008. Tel: 507-451-6752
Mountain, Harold B., 50 Teton Ln., #124, Mankato, MN 56001-4813. Tel: 507-345-8933
Peterson, Cyril P., c/o Jack Peterson, Box 238, Missouri Valley, IA 51555-0238. Tel: 712-322-4381
Quesnel, Raymond, O.M.I., Madonna Towers, 4001 19th Ave., N.W., Rochester, MN 55901-0553. Tel: 507-288-3911
Schaefer, Edgar J., 9659 111th Ave., N, Sun City, AZ 85351. Tel: 602-875-9749
Schiltz, Roger J., 1532 Glenrosa Dr., N. Las Vegas, NV 89031-5548
Smith, Leland J., 468 Center St., Winona, MN 55987. Tel: 507-454-8464
Speck, James A., 528 Maceman St., Apt. 108, Winona, MN 55987-2479. Tel: 507-454-2129
Stamschror, Robert P., 2480 Goodview Rd., Winona, MN 55987. Tel: 507-452-4202
Verdick, Jerome F., 210 E. Paddock, P.O. Box 87, Alpha, Mn 56111-0087. Tel: 507-847-2939
Vincent, John F., 513 S. Seventh St., Apt. C, LaCrescent, MN 55947-1275. Tel: 507-895-6736
Zenk, Donald W., St. James Church, c/o 602 31st St., N.W., Austin, MN 55912

INSTITUTIONS LOCATED IN THE DIOCESE

[A] SEMINARIES, DIOCESAN

WINONA. *Immaculate Heart of Mary Seminary*, 700 Terrace Hts. #43, 55987-1399. Tel: 507-457-7373; Fax: 507-457-8601.
E-mail: ihms@smumn.edu
Affiliated with Saint Mary's University of MN. Revs. David C. Kunz, Rector; James P. Steffes, Dir. Spiritual Formation & Spiritual Dir. Tel: 507-454-4643; Thomas J. Jennings, Vice Rector & Dean of Students. Extern Spiritual Directors: Rev. Msgr. Donald P. Schmitz; Revs. Joseph A. LaPlante; Edward F. McGrath; Joseph L. Keefe; Gregory P. Leif; Mark Pierce (LC); Edward Thome (LC); Mr. Lawrence G. Price, Coord., Liturgy & Music. Priests 3; Lay Staff 4; Students 57.

[B] COLLEGES AND UNIVERSITIES

WINONA. *Saint Mary's University of Minnesota*, 700 Terrace Hts., 55987-1399. Tel: 507-452-4430; 800-635-5987; Fax: 507-457-1633.
E-mail: admissions@smumn.edu
Web site: www.smumn.edu
For a complete listing, refer to the Colleges and Universities section.

[C] CENTRALIZED CATHOLIC SCHOOLS

WINONA. *Cotter High School & Junior High School*. (Grades 7-12), 1115 W. Broadway, 55987. Tel: 507-453-5002; Fax: 507-453-5006.
E-mail: sblank@mps.org
Web site: www.mps.org
Bro. Louis DeThomasis, F.S.C., CEO; Sandra Blank, Prin. Cotter High School; Scott Walker, Prin. Cotter Junior High School; Craig Junker, Pres.; Deacon Gordon D. Richard, Campus Min. Priests 1; Sisters 1; Lay Teachers 48; Students 525.

Winona Area Catholic Schools, 352 Center St., 55987. Tel: 507-452-4936.
E-mail: cwilant@tvsw.org
Mrs. Carol Wilant, Prin. Religious 1; Lay Teachers 34.

St. Mary's Primary School. (Grades PreK-K), 1315 W. Broadway, 55987. Tel: 507-452-2890; Fax: 507-452-2898.
E-mail: cwilant@tvsw.org
Mrs. Carol Wilant, Prin. Students 175.

Cathedral Elementary School. (Grades 1-3), 352 Center St., 55987. Tel: 507-452-4936; Fax: 507-454-1473.
E-mail: cwilant@tvsw.org
Mrs. Carol Wilant, Prin. Students 176.

St. Stanislaus Middle School. (Grades 4-6), 602 E. Fifth St., 55987. Tel: 507-452-3766; Fax: 507-452-5497.
E-mail: cwilant@tvsw.org
Mrs. Carol Wilant, Prin. Students 190.

Winona Area Catholic Schools Foundation, 360 Main St., 55987. Tel: 507-454-7449.

ALBERT LEA. *St. Theodore School*. (Grades K-7), 323 E. Clark St., 56007. Tel: 507-373-9657; Fax: 507-373-9657.
E-mail: jfc@sttheo.org
Web site: www.sttheo.org
Rev. Robert J. Schneider, Acting Prin. Lay Teachers 7; Students 102.

AUSTIN. *Austin Area Catholic Schools*, 511 N.W. Fourth Ave., 55912. Tel: 507-433-6630; Fax: 507-433-6630.

St. Augustine's - St. Edward. (Grades PreK-4), 511 N.W. Fourth Ave., 55912. Tel: 507-433-8859; Fax: 507-433-6630.
E-mail: winqoa@impresso.com
Richard J. Cook, Prin. Lay Teachers 14; Students 197.

Queen of Angels. (Grades 5-8), 912 First Ave., N.E., 55912. Tel: 507-433-8745; Fax: 507-433-6630.
E-mail: winqoa@impresso.com
Richard J. Cook, Prin. Lay Teachers 9; Students 112.

Pacelli Senior High School. (Grades 9-12), 311 Fourth St., N.W., 55912. Tel: 507-437-3278; Fax: 507-433-5693. Norman Blazer, Dean of Students; Alice Duffy-Meyer, Campus Min. Lay Teachers 12; Students 73.

United Catholic Schools Foundation of Austin, MN, Inc., 511 N.W. Fourth Ave., 55912. Tel: 507-433-6630; Fax: 507-433-6630. Mrs. Alice Snater, Financial Sec.

MANKATO. *Mankato Area Catholic Schools*, 145 Good Counsel Dr., 56001-3146. Tel: 507-388-3997; Fax: 507-388-3081.
E-mail: ttacheny@mail.macs.mankato.mn.us
Thomas Tacheny, D.Ed., Supt. Total Enrollment 716.

St. Joseph - St. John School. (Grades K-3), 820 Hubbell, 56001-2100. Tel: 507-388-2536; Fax: 507-388-2536.
E-mail: nhackenmiller@yahoo.com
Ms. Nancy Hackenmiller, Prin. Sisters 1; Lay Teachers 4; Students 58.

SS. Peter and Paul School. (Grades K-3), 110 N. Sixth St., 56001. Tel: 507-387-3316; Fax: 507-388-2750.
E-mail: nhackenmiller@yahoo.com
Ms. Nancy Hackenmiller, Prin. Sisters 1; Lay Teachers 10; Students 156.

Fitzgerald Middle School. (Grades 6-8), 110 N. Fifth St., 56001-4499. Tel: 507-388-9344; Fax: 507-388-2750.
E-mail: marydonaldssnd@yahoo.com
Sr. Mary Donald Miller, S.S.N.D., Prin. Sisters 2; Lay Teachers 10; Students 190.

Loyola High School. (Grades 9-12), 145 Good Counsel Dr., 56001-3146. Tel: 507-388-2997; Fax: 507-388-3081.
E-mail: schultz@mail.macs.mankato.mn.us
Shelley Schultz, Prin.; Sid McGee, Campus Min. Lay Teachers 15; Students 210.

Holy Rosary School. (Grades 4-5), 546 Grant Ave., North Mankato, 56003. Tel: 507-345-6765; Fax: 507-388-2017.
E-mail: marydonaldssnd@yahoo.com
Sr. Mary Donald Miller, S.S.N.D., Prin. Lay Teachers 5; Students 104.

OWATONNA. *St. Mary's School*. (Grades PreK-8), 730 South Cedar St., 55060. Tel: 507-451-2694; Fax: 507-451-9554.
E-mail: smsowat@mnic.net
Mr. Gerald Kent, Prin. Sisters 1; Lay Teachers 28; Students 405.

ROCHESTER. *Rochester Catholic Schools*, 621 W. Center St., 55902. Tel: 507-280-0349; Fax: 507-289-4008.
E-mail: dschwinghammer@rochestercatholic.k12.mn.us
Mrs. Diane Schwinghammer, Supt.

St. Francis School. (Grades PreK-8), 318 11th Ave., S.E., 55904. Tel: 507-288-4816; Fax: 507-288-4815.
E-mail: bplenge@rochestercatholic.k12.mn.us
Mrs. Barb Plenge, Prin. Priests 2; Lay Teachers 28; Students 510.

St. John School. (Grades K-8), 424 W. Center St., 55902. Tel: 507-282-5248; Fax: 507-282-1343.
E-mail: dkutzke@rochestercatholic.k12.mn.us
Mrs. Denise Kutzke, Prin. Priests 1; Lay Teachers 17; Students 308.

St. Pius X School. (Grades K-8), 1205 12th Ave., 55901. Tel: 507-282-5161; Fax: 507-282-5107.
E-mail: mklebe@rochestercatholic.k12.mn.us
Mr. Matthew Klebe, Prin. Priests 5; Lay Teachers 23; Students 464.

Lourdes High School of Rochester, Inc. (Grades 9-12), 621 W. Center St., 55902. Tel: 507-289-3991; Fax: 507-289-4008.
E-mail: dnigon@rochestercatholic.k12.mn.us
Mr. Dennis Nigon, Prin.; Anita Loechler, Campus Min. Priests 1; Sisters 1; Lay Teachers 40; Students 552.

Holy Spirit School. (Grades K-8), 5455 50th Ave., N.W., 55901. Tel: 507-288-8818; Fax: 507-288-5155.
E-mail: rgaines@rochestercatholic.k12.mn.us
Ronald Gaines, Prin. Lay Teachers 22; Students 400.

[D] GENERAL HOSPITALS

ROCHESTER. *Saint Marys Hospital*, 55902-1970. Tel: 507-255-5123; Fax: 507-255-3125
For a complete listing, refer to the Hospitals section.

WABASHA. *St. Elizabeth's Hospital of Wabasha, Inc.*, 1200 Fifth Grant Blvd., W., 55981. Tel: 651-565-4531; Fax: 651-565-2482.
Web site: www.ministryhealth.com
For a complete listing, refer to the Hospitals section.

[E] SPECIAL HOSPITALS AND REHABILITATION FACILITIES

WINONA. *Franciscan Skemp Behavioral Health*, 725 W. Broadway, 55987. Tel: 507-454-7711; Fax: 507-452-0325
For a complete listing, refer to the Special Care Facilities section.

ROCHESTER. *Guest House*, 4800 48th St., N.E., P.O. Box 954, 55903. Tel: 800-634-4155; 507-288-4693.
E-mail: ghousemn@infonet.isl.net
Web site: www.ic.net/fighouse/ghouse.html
For a complete listing, refer to the Special Care Facilities section.

[F] HOMES FOR AGED

WINONA. *St. Anne Retirement Community, Inc.*, 1347 W. Broadway, 55987. Tel: 507-454-3621; Fax: 507-452-2556
For a complete listing, refer to the Special Care Facilities section.

AUSTIN. *Burr Oak Care Center*, 400 10th Ave., NW, P.O. Box 429, 55912. Tel: 507-433-7391
For a complete listing, refer to the Special Care Facilities section.

Sacred Heart Care Center, Inc., 1200 Twelfth St., S.W., 55912. Tel: 507-433-1808
For a complete listing, refer to the Special Care Facilities section.

ROCHESTER. *Madonna Towers of Rochester, Inc.*, 4001 19th Ave., N.W., 55901. Tel: 507-288-3911; Fax: 507-288-0393.
E-mail: mccairns@BHShealth.org
For a complete listing, refer to the Special Care Facilities section.

WABASHA. *St. Elizabeth's Health Care Center*, 626 Shields Ave., 55981. Tel: 651-565-4581.
Web site: www.ministryhealth.org
For a complete listing, refer to the Special Care Facilities section.

[G] CONVENTS AND RESIDENCES FOR SISTERS

WINONA. *Third Order Regular Common Franciscan Novitiate, Inc.*, Tau Center, 511 Hilbert St., 55987. Tel: 507-454-0184; Fax: 507-453-0910.
E-mail: cfn@luminet.net
Sr. Diane Jamison, O.S.F., Novice Min.; Sr. JoAnn Haney, O.S.F., Co-Min. Total in Residence 7; Total Staff 2.

HOUSTON. *Hermits of St. Mary of Carmel, H.S.M.C.* Carmelite eremitical community of Diocesan Right, R.R. 1, Box 143, 55943-9737. Tel: 507-896-2125; Fax: 507-896-4349. Mother Rosemary Therese Quinn, H.S.M.C., Prioress; Rev. David Wechter, O.C.S.O. (DUB). Tel: 507-896-2125. Sisters 5.

JACKSON. *Convent of Religious Sisters of Mercy*, R.R. 3, Box 79, 56143. Tel: 507-847-5498; Fax: 507-847-5689. Sr. Marie Paul Lockerd, R.S.M., Local Supr. Sisters 2.

MANKATO. *Provincial House of the School Sisters of Notre Dame*, Convent of Our Lady of Good Counsel, 170 Good Counsel Dr., 56001-3138. Tel: 507-389-4200; Fax: 507-345-6679.
E-mail: kduvalssnd@juno.com
Web site: www.ssndmankato.org
Religious in Province 438; Sisters in Motherhouse 151; Lay Staff 175.

School Sisters of Notre Dame at Mankato, MN, Inc. Tel: 507-389-4200; Fax: 507-345-6679.

School Sisters of Notre Dame at Mankato, MN, Inc. Charitable Trust. Tel: 507-389-4200; Fax: 507-345-6679.

School Sisters of Notre Dame Cooperative Investment Fund. Tel: 507-389-4200; Fax: 507-345-6679.

ROCHESTER. *Congregational Center of the Third Order Regular of St. Francis of the Congregation of Our Lady of Lourde,* Assisi Heights, 1001 14th St., N.W., Ste. 100, 55901-2511. Tel: 507-282-7441; Fax: 507-282-7762.
Web site: www.Rochesterfranciscan.org
Sr. Dolore M. Rockers, O.S.F., Pres. & Community Min.; Rev. Jack L. Krough. Legal Title: *Academy of Our Lady of Lourdes.* Religious in Prov. 367; Sisters in Motherhouse 161; Novices 1; Lay Staff 154.

[H] RETREAT HOUSES AND CENTERS OF SPIRITUALITY

WINONA. *Tau Center,* 511 Hilbert St., 55987. Tel: 507-454-2993.
E-mail: taucentr@luminet.net
Web site: www.winonanet.com/orgs/taucenter
L. Susan Althoff, Conference & Retreat Dir. Total in Residence 9; Total Staff 17.

AUSTIN. *Queen of Angels Center,* 1009 Oakland Ave. E., 55912. Tel: 507-437-4015. Kathleen Finnegan, Dir. Volunteers 25.

JANESVILLE. *Holy Spirit Retreat Center,* 3864 420th Ave., 56048. Tel: 507-234-5712.
E-mail: retreat@frontiernet.net
Directors: Sr. Elaine Frank, O.S.F.; Sr. Colleen Bryon, O.S.F.

MANKATO. *Good Counsel Education Center,* 151 Good Counsel Dr., 56002. Tel: 507-389-4287; Fax: 507-389-4119. Sr. Lois Wickenhauser, S.S.N.D., Dir.

ROCHESTER. *Assisi Community Center,* Assisi Heights., 1001 14th St., N.W., Ste. 100, 55901-2511. Tel: 507-280-2180; Fax: 507-282-7762.
E-mail: acomc@aol.com
Sr. Joy Barth, O.S.F., Contact Person. Total Staff 6.

[I] NEWMAN CENTERS

WINONA. *St. Thomas Aquinas Newman Center,* 475 Huff St., 55987. Tel: 507-452-2781; Fax: 507-454-0660.
E-mail: newmancenter@vax2.winona.msus.edu
Mr. Thomas Parlin, Dir.; Rev. Shawn T. Haremza, Chap.

MANKATO. *St. Thomas More Newman Center, Minnesota State University,* 1331 Warren St., 56001. Tel: 507-387-4154.
E-mail: mccabs@mail.mankato.msus.edu
Ms. Sydelle McCabe, Dir.; Rev. Kurt Farrell, Chap.

[J] MISCELLANEOUS LISTINGS

WINONA.
Diocese of Winona Deposit & Loan, 55 W. Sanborn St., P.O. Box 588, 55987. Tel: 507-454-4643; Fax: 507-454-8106.

Diocese of Winona Foundation, 55 W. Sanborn St., P.O. Box 588, 55987. Tel: 507-454-4643; Fax: 507-454-8106.
E-mail: 1fuller@dow.org
Web site: www.dow.org

St. Mary's Parish of Winona Endowment Fund, Inc., 1303 W. Broadway, 55987. Tel: 507-452-5656; Fax: 507-452-5477. Rev. Joseph L. Keefe, Contact.

Saint Mary's Press, Christian Brothers Publications, 702 Terrace Hts., 55987. Tel: 507-457-7900; Fax: 507-457-7990.
E-mail: smpress@smp.org
Web site: www.smp.org
Bro. Damian Steger, F.S.C., Pres.; John M. Vitek, Vice Pres.

ALBERT LEA. *St. Theodore Catholic School Endowment,* 308 E. Fountain St., 56007-2456. Tel: 507-373-0603; Fax: 507-373-9657.
E-mail: sttheo@sttheo.org
Web site: www.sttheo.org
Rev. Robert J. Schneider, Contact.

JACKSON. *Sacred Heart Mercy Health Care Center,* 803 Fourth St., 56143. Tel: 507-847-3571; Fax: 507-847-5664. Sr. Margaret Mary Turner, R.S.M., Admin. Patients assisted annually 4,600; Total Staff 9.

ROCHESTER. *Poverello Foundation,* St. Mary's Hospital, 1216 S.W. Second St., 55902. Tel: 507-255-5158; Fax: 507-255-3125. Sr. Generose Gervais, O.S.F., Pres.

The Roman Catholic Pontifical Lay Association Memores Domini, 6006 Woodridge Ct., 55906. Tel: 507-292-0551; Fax: 507-288-7373.

RELIGIOUS INSTITUTES OF MEN REPRESENTED IN THE DIOCESE

For further details refer to the corresponding bracketed number in the Religious Institutes of Men or Women section.

[0330]—*Brothers of the Christian Schools.*—F.S.C.

[0340]—*Cistercian Fathers.* (Abbey of Our Lady of New Malleray).—O.Cist.

[0690]—*Jesuit Fathers and Brothers.* (Wisconsin Province).—S.J.

[0910]—*Oblates of Mary Immaculate.* (Central Province).—O.M.I.

[0430]—*Order of Preachers (Dominicans).* (Chicago Province).—O.P.

[0110]—*Society of African Missions.*—S.M.A.

RELIGIOUS INSTITUTES OF WOMEN REPRESENTED IN THE DIOCESE

[0230]—*Benedictine Sisters of Pontifical Jurisdiction.*—O.S.B.

[1780]—*Congregation of the Sisters of the Third Order of St. Francis of Perpetual Adoration.* (Eastern, Central Regions).—F.S.P.A.

[1310]—*Franciscan Sisters of Little Falls.*—O.S.F.

[]—*Hermits of St. Mary of Carmel (Contemplative Community).*—H.S.M.C.

[2470]—*Maryknoll Sisters of St. Dominic.*—M.M.

[2519]—*Religious Sisters of Mercy of Alma, Michigan.*—R.S.M.

[2970]—*School Sisters of Notre Dame.*—S.S.N.D.

[1680]—*School Sisters of St. Francis.*—O.S.F.

[0430]—*Sisters of Charity of the Blessed Virgin Mary.*—B.V.M.

[1705]—*The Sisters of St. Francis of Assisi.*—O.S.F.

[1570]—*Sisters of St. Francis of the Holy Family.*—O.S.F.

[3320]—*Sisters of the Presentation of the B.V.M.*—P.B.V.M.

[4100]—*Sisters of the Sorrowful Mother (Third Order of St. Francis).*—S.S.M.

[1720]—*Sisters of the Third Order Regular of St. Francis of the Congregation of Our Lady of Lourdes.*—O.S.F.

[]—*Third Order Regular Common Franciscan.*—S.S.S.F.

DIOCESAN CEMETERIES

WINONA. *Catholic Cemeteries of Winona,* 55 W. Sanborn St., P.O. Box 588, 55987. Rev. Edward F. McGrath.

NECROLOGY

† Clinton, Kenneth J., (Retired). —Died Dec. 19, 1999.

† Dittman, Rev. Msgr. Harold J., (Retired). —Died Dec. 25, 1999.

† Schaefer, Vernon J., (Retired). —Died Nov. 16, 2000.

Diocese of Worcester

(Dioecesis Wigorniensis)

Most Reverend

DANIEL P. REILLY, D.D.

Bishop of Worcester; ordained May 30, 1953; appointed Bishop of Norwich June 17, 1975; consecrated August 6, 1975; appointed Bishop of Worcester October 27, 1994; installed December 8, 1994. *Res., 2 High Ridge Rd., Worcester, MA, 01602.*

Most Reverend

GEORGE E. RUEGER, D.D., V.G.

Auxiliary Bishop of Worcester; ordained January 6, 1958; appointed Auxiliary Bishop of Worcester and Titular Bishop of Maronana January 19, 1987; consecrated February 25, 1987 St. Stephen's Rectory, 16 Hamilton St., Worcester, MA, 01604.

ESTABLISHED JANUARY 14, 1950.

Square Miles 1,532.

Comprises the County of Worcester in the State of Massachusetts.

For legal titles of parishes and diocesan institutions, consult the Chancery Office.

Chancery Office: 49 Elm St., Worcester, MA, 01609. Tel.: 508-791-7171; Fax: 508-753-7180.

Web site address: www.worcesterdiocese.org

STATISTICAL OVERVIEW

Personnel	
Bishop	1
Auxiliary Bishops	1
Abbots	3
Priests: Diocesan Active in Diocese	176
Priests: Active Outside Diocese	18
Priests: Retired, Sick or Absent	47
Number of Diocesan Priests	241
Religious Priests in Diocese	111
Permanent Deacons in Diocese	76
Total Brothers	85
Total Sisters	446
Parishes	
Parishes	126
With Resident Pastor:	
Resident Diocesan Priests	122
Resident Religious Priests	4
Welfare	
Catholic Hospitals	1
Total Assisted	185,000
Homes for the Aged	7
Total Assisted	25,000
Residential Care of Children	1
Total Assisted	20
Day Care and Extended Day Care Centers	6
Total Assisted	1,750
Specialized Homes	2
Total Assisted	285
Special Centers for Social Services	10
Total Assisted	32,000
Other Institutions	1
Total Assisted	180
Educational	
Seminaries, Diocesan	1
Students from This Diocese	6
Diocesan Students in Other Seminaries	11
Students Religious	4
Total Seminarians	21
Colleges and Universities	3
Total Students	6,501
High Schools, Diocesan and Parish	4
Total Students	2,726
High Schools, Private	4
Total Students	1,557
Elementary Schools, Diocesan and Parish	22
Total Students	5,494
Elementary Schools, Private	2
Total Students	638
Non-residential Schools for the Disabled	1
Total Students	80
Catechesis/Religious Education:	
High School Students	7,581
Elementary Students	26,135
Total Students Under Catholic Instruction	50,733
Teachers in the Diocese:	
Priests	1
Brothers	8
Sisters	32
Lay Teachers	649
Vital Statistics	
Receptions into the Church:	
Infant Baptism Totals	4,416
Adult Baptism Totals	145
Received into Full Communion	242
First Communions	4,622
Confirmations	2,936
Marriages:	
Catholic	978
Interfaith	253
Total Marriages	1,231
Deaths	3,722
Total Catholic Population	306,213
Total Population	790,705

Former Bishops—His Eminence JOHN CARDINAL WRIGHT, D.D., ord. Dec. 8, 1935; appt. Titular Bishop of Aegea and Auxiliary Bishop of Boston, May 10, 1947; cons. June 30, 1947; transferred to new See of Worcester, Jan. 28, 1950; enthroned March 7, 1950; appt. Bishop of Pittsburgh, Jan. 28, 1959; created Cardinal, April 28, 1969; transferred to the Roman Curia Prefect, Sacred Congregation for the Clergy; died Aug. 10, 1979.—Most Rev. BERNARD J. FLANAGAN, D.D., J.C.D., resigned March 31, 1983; died Jan. 28, 1998.—Most Rev. TIMOTHY J. HARRINGTON, D.D., retired Oct. 27, 1994; died March 23, 1997.

Vicars General—Most Rev. GEORGE E. RUEGER, D.D., V.G., Moderator of the Curia, *St. Stephen's Rectory, 16 Hamilton St., Worcester, 01604.* Tel: 508-791-7171.

Chancery Office—Rev. THOMAS SULLIVAN, Chancellor, *49 Elm St., Worcester, 01609.* Tel: 508-791-7171; Fax: 508-753-7180.

Diocesan Director of Educational Services—Most Rev. GEORGE E. RUEGER, D.D., V.G., *49 Elm St., Worcester, 01609.* Tel: 508-791-7171.

Diocesan Director of Fiscal Affairs—Rev. Msgr. EDMOND T. TINSLEY, V.G., *49 Elm St., Worcester, 01609.* Tel: 508-791-7171.

Diocesan Director for Human Services (and Catholic Relief Services)—Rev. Msgr. EDMOND T. TINSLEY, V.G., *Res., 77 Mulberry St., Leicester, 01524.* Tel: 508-892-4886.

Diocesan Expansion Fund—Most Rev. GEORGE E. RUEGER, D.D.; Mrs. PATRICIA JONES, Chm., *49 Elm St., Worcester, 01609.* Tel: 508-791-7171.

Diocesan Finance Committee—JOSEPH GIOVINO, Chm., *49 Elm St., Worcester, 01609.*

Diocesan Tribunal—Address all communications to: *49 Elm St., Worcester, 01609.* Tel: 508-791-7171.

Vicar for Canonical Affairs and Judicial Vicar—Rev. F. STEPHEN PEDONE, J.C.L., *49 Elm St., Worcester, 01609.*

Associate Judicial Vicars—Rev. PAUL T. O'CONNELL, J.C.D., Assoc. Judicial Vicar.

Judges—Rev. HENRY G. BOWEN, J.C.D.; Rev. Msgr. JOHN J. KELLIHER; Revs. ROBERT J. KASLYN, S.J., J.C.D.; PAUL T. O'CONNELL, J.C.D.; F. STEPHEN PEDONE, J.C.L.

Promoter of Justice—Rev. HENRY G. BOWEN, J.C.D.

Psychologist—Sr. MARY DANIEL MALLOY, R.S.M.

Secretary to the Tribunal—Deacon GEORGE L. O'TOOLE.

Defenders of the Bond—Rev. Msgr. ANTHONY S. CZARNECKI, J.C.L.; Rev. JOHN J. ROY, J.C.L.; Deacon GEORGE L. O'TOOLE.

Advocates—Revs. ROLAND L. GAMACHE; THOMAS E. MAHONEY; LEO BARRY; JAMES P. KERRIGAN; WILLIAM F. SANDERS; MICHAEL A. DIGERONIMO.

Notary—JUDITH M. GAUTHIER,Address all requests for dispensations to: *Diocesan Tribunal, 49 Elm St., Worcester, 01609.*

Diocesan Consultors—Most Rev. GEORGE E. RUEGER, D.D., V.G.; Rev. Msgr. RICHARD J. CARELLI; Revs. CHARLES DUMPHY; ROLAND GAMACHE; JOSEPH NALLY; ARTHUR OUILLETTE; F. STEPHEN PEDONE; ROCCO M. PICCOLOMINI; Rev. Msgr. FRANCIS J. SCOLLEN; Rev. JOSEPH SZWACH; Rev. Msgr. EDMOND T. TINSLEY.

Deans—Rev. MICHAEL A. DIGERONIMO, Area I; Rev. MICHAEL BAFARO, Area II; Rev. JAMES B. O'SHEA,

Area III; Rev. MARTIN P. DONAHUE, Area IV; Rev. BRIAN P. O'TOOLE, Area V; Rev. PAUL J. TOUGAS, Area VI; Rev. JAMES M. STEUTERMAN, Area VII; Rev. JEAN-PAUL GAGNON, Area VIII; Rev. ROLAND L. LAJOIE, Area IX; Rev. FRANCIS T. GOGUEN, Area X; Rev. H. EDWARD CHALMERS, Area XI; Rev. ROLAND J. GAMACHE, Area XII; Rev. ARTHUR C. OUELLETTE, (Retired Priests); Area XIII.

Vicar for Clergy—Rev. ROCCO M. PICCOLOMINI, *Res., Our Lady of Mt. Carmel-St. Ann, 53 E. Central St., Worcester, 01605.*

Vicar for Religious—Sr. PAULA KELLEHER, S.S.J., *49 Elm St., Worcester, 01609.* Tel: 508-791-7171.

Diocesan Offices and Directors

The Adopt-a-Student Endowment Trust—MICHAEL J. COOGAN, Dir., *49 Elm St., Worcester, 01609.* Tel: 508-791-7171.

Apostleship of Prayer and Eucharistic Crusade—Rev. THADDEUS X. STACHURA, *Our Lady of Czestochowa, 34 Ward St., Worcester, 01610.* Tel: 508-755-5959.

Apostolate Office of Divine Mercy and Healing—Rev. RALPH A. DIORIO, Dir., *P.O. Box 668, Worcester, 01613-0668.* Tel: 508-791-0427.

Archivist—Most Rev. GEORGE E. RUEGER, *49 Elm St., Worcester, 01609.* Tel: 508-791-7171.

Brazilian Pastoral Ministry—Sr. BARBARA CICCOLINI, *49 Elm St., Worcester, 01609.* Tel: 508-791-7171, Ext. 153; Fax: 508-753-7180.

Bishop's Fund—OWEN C. COOGAN, Dir., *49 Elm St., Worcester, 01609.* Tel: 508-791-7171.

Building Commission Members—Rev. Msgr. GEORGE E. DENOMME; Most Rev. GEORGE E. RUEGER, D.D., V.G.; Rev. Msgr. EDMUND G. HADDAD; Rev. Msgr. EDMOND T. TINSLEY; Revs. LEE BARTLETT, Chm. JOHN FOLEY; ROBERT JOHNSON; THADDEUS STACHURA; JOHN THOMAS; Mr. HENRY MILLER; Mrs. MARY SLOCUM, *49 Elm St., Worcester, 01609.* Tel: 508-791-7171.

Campus Ministry—Rev. PETER J. SCANLON, Vicar for College Communities, *Diocesan Office, P.O. Box 903, Worcester, 01613., Res., The Center, 19 Schussler Rd., Worcester, 01609.* Tel: 508-757-6097., Newman Center: *281 Highland Ave., Fitchburg, 01420.* Tel: 508-345-2688.

Catholic Charities—CATHERINE LOEFFLER, Dir., *10 Hammond St., Worcester, 01610-1513.* Tel: 508-798-0191. (Refer to separate listings for detailed information on Catholic Charities and related organizations).

Cemeteries—Mr. FRANCIS F. ELLIOTT, Dir.; Rev. JOHN CAHILL, Priest liaison, *260 Cambridge St., Worcester, 01610.* Tel: 508-757-7415.

Charismatic Renewal, Office of—Mr. MICHAEL FREEL, Liaison, *St. Joseph, West St., P.O. Box 284, Berlin, 01503.* Tel: 508-365-6492.

Clergy Benefit Plan—Rev. JOHN J. FOLEY, *1052 Pleasant St., Worcester, 01602.*

Collaborative for Education and Ministry: Institute for Academic and Pastoral Development—Most Rev. GEORGE E. RUEGER, Chm.

Communication Office—RAYMOND L. DELISLE, Dir., *49 Elm St., Worcester, 01609.* Tel: 508-791-5357.

Continuing Education of the Clergy—Rev. MICHAEL ROSE, Dir., *89 Main St., S. Grafton, 01560.* Tel: 508-839-5354.

Cursillo—Rev. ROBERT A. GRATTAROTI, Dir., *37 Worcester Rd., Charlton City, 01508.* Tel: 508-248-7862.

Development Office—Bishop's Fund, Good Shepherd Endowment Fund, Adopt-A-Student, Annual Catholic School Appeal, Project Share for Christ, The Adopt-A-Student Endowment Trust. Mr. OWEN C. COOGAN, Dir., *49 Elm St., Worcester, 01609.* Tel: 508-754-0574; Fax: 508-754-2768.

Diocesan Expansion Fund—Members: JANET S. SIMONDS; Revs. RICHARD REIDY; PAUL LEMIRE; Most Rev. GEORGE E. RUEGER; Rev. Msgr. EDMOND T. TINSLEY; Mrs. HELEN G. SHAUGHNESSY; DENNIS F. GORMAN, Chm.; Mr. ANDREW STANHOPE.

Diocesan Scouts—Boy Scout Office: *120 Hill St., Whitinsville, 01588.* Tel: 508-234-0346., Girl Scout Office:*120 Hill St., Whitinsville, 01588.* Tel: 508-234-0346. Rev. RICHARD REIDY, *19 Chatham St., Worchester, 01609.*

Ecumenical and Interreligious Affairs, Diocesan Office for—Sr. THERESE DION, S.S.A., *49 Elm St., Worchester, 01609.*

Office for Ethnic Ministries—Sr. MARIE PREFONTAINE, S.N.D., Dir., *49 Elm St., Worcester, 01609.* Tel: 508-791-7171; Fax: 508-753-7180.

Evangelization, Office of—Rev. LAWRENCE J. ESPOSITO, Chm., *49 Elm St., Worcester, 01609.*

Family Life Ministry—Co-Directors: Mr. RONALD V. ARCIERI; Mrs. JANET M. ARCIERI, *49 Elm St., Worcester, 01609.* Tel: 508-791-7171.

Finance Office—Rev. Msgr. EDMOND T. TINSLEY, V.G., Fiscal Affairs; JEROME D. JUSSAUME, Mgr. Finance, *49 Elm St., Worcester, 01609.* Tel: 508-791-7171.

Rev. James Fitton House of Priestly Formation—Rev. THOMAS SULLIVAN, Dir., *761 Main St., Leicester, 01524.* Tel: 508-892-8439; Fax: 508-892-4539.

Haitian Ministries Coalition of the Diocese of Worcester—Deacon PETER R. FAFORD, Co-Chm. LINDA M. FAFORD, Co-Chm. & Treas.; Mrs. CONNIE BARNA, Sec.; Rev. WILLIAM KONICKI, Project Coord.; Dr. SITA RAM UPADHYAY; Rev. BRIAN O'TOOLE; Mrs. LOIS KOLOSKY, Adopt-A-Student; Rev. OLIVER BLANCHETTE, Advisory Board; Sr. ALICE RICHARDS, Advisory Board; ROBERT LANGLOIS, Micro Loan Project, *Office for Youth Ministry, 120 Hill St., Whitinsville, 01588.* Tel: 508-234-0346; Fax: 508-234-0348.

Haitian Apostolate—CONNIE BARNS, Dir.; Sr. THERESITA DONACH, C.S.F.N. Assoc. Dir. SUSAN JIMERSON, Project Coord., *120 Hill St., Whitinsville, 01588.* Tel: 508-234-9115.

Holy Childhood Association—Rev. Msgr. THOMAS J. NEEDHAM, Dir., *353 Grove St., Worcester, 01605.* Tel: 508-754-8419.

Meet-the-Father Ministry, Inc.—Mrs. EILEEN GEORGE, Contact Person, *363 Greenwood St., Millbury, 01527.*

Newspaper—"The Catholic Free Press"; Mrs. MARGARET M. RUSSELL, Exec. Editor, *51 Elm St., Worcester, 01609.* Tel: 508-757-6387.

Office for Worship—Rev. ROBERT JOHNSON, Dir., *19 Chatham St., Worcester, 01609.* Tel: 508-798-0417.

Pastoral Associate Ministry Consultative Board—Sr. PAULA KELLEHER, S.S.J., Chm., *49 Elm St., Worcester, 01609.* Tel: 508-791-7171.

Permanent Diaconate—Co-Directors: Revs. ROCCO M. PICCOLOMINI; JAMES AQUINO, *49 Elm St., Worcester, 01609.*

Presbyteral Council—Most Rev. DANIEL P. REILLY, Pres.; Most Rev. GEORGE E. RUEGER; Revs. F. STEPHEN PEDONE; JAMES J. AQUINO; Rev. Msgr. RICHARD J. CARELLI; Revs. JOSEPH M. NALLY, Chm. ROCCO M. PICCOLOMINI; JOSEPH F. SZWACH; Rev. Msgr. EDMOND T. TINSLEY, Sec.; Revs. PAUL J. TOUGAS, Treas. CHARLES F. MONROE, Vice Chm., *Chancery Bldg., 49 Elm St., Worcester, 01609.* Tel: 508-791-7171.

Priests' Personnel Board—Rev. ROCCO M. PICCOLOMINI, *Our Lady of Mt. Carmel-St. Ann, 53 E. Central St., Worcester, 01605.* Tel: 508-792-4574.

Priests' Retirement Residence—Rev. JOHN F. CAHILL, Admin., *222 June St., Worcester, 01602.* Tel: 508-791-0311.

Pro-Life—Rev. CHESTER J. DEVLIN, Dir. & Educational Coord., *49 Elm St., Worcester, 01609.*

Propagation of the Faith—Rev. Msgr. THOMAS J. NEEDHAM, Dir., *353 Grove St., Worcester, 01605.* Tel: 508-754-8419.

Religious Education Office—Rev. Msgr. LOUIS R. PIERMARINI, Dir., *49 Elm St., Worcester, 01609.* Tel: 508-791-7171., *Res., St. Roch, 334 Main St., Oxford, 01540.*

North County Office Fitchburg—Mrs. MARY G. HOVENESIAN, Assoc. Dir. & North Country Coord., *89 Sheridan St., Fitchburg, 01420.* Tel: 508-345-6636.

School Department—Mr. CHARLES E. MCMANUS, Supt. PATRICIA M. HALPIN; Sr. RANAH PHELAN, *49 Elm St., Worcester, 01609.* Tel: 508-791-7171.

Social Justice, Peace and Integrity of Creation, Office of—*49 Elm St., Worcester, 01609.* Tel: 508-791-7171.

Spanish Apostolate—Rev. JOSE A. RODRIGUEZ, Bishop's Liaison, *429 Main St., Worcester, 01610., 49 Elm St., Worchester, 01609.* Tel: 508-791-7171.

St. Vincent dePaul Society—Central and Greater Worcester District Council—FRANCES PIKE, Pres.; Rev. Msgr. EDMOND T. TINSLEY, Spiritual Dir., *Res., 77 Mulberry St., Leicester, 01524.* Tel: 508-892-4886.

Northern Worcester County District Council—JOHN YOVINO, Pres.; Rev. Msgr. LEO J. BATTISTA, Chap.

Southern Worcester County District Council—ALFRED E. BALLARD, Pres.; Rev. J. NORMAND TREMBLAY, Chap.

Tri-Conference Retirement Fund for Religious—Sr. PAULA KELLEHER, S.S.J., Diocesan Coord., *49 Elm St., Worcester, 01609.* Tel: 508-791-7171.

Vicar for Priests—Rev. ROCCO M. PICCOLOMINI, *53 E. Central St., Worcester, 01605.*

Vicar for Religious—Sr. PAULA KELLEHER, S.S.J., *49 Elm St., Worcester, 01609.* Tel: 508-791-7171.

Vietnamese Apostolate—Rev. PHUONG VAN NGUYEN, *1052 Pleasant St., Worcester, 01602., 44 Temple St., Worcester, 01605.* Tel: 508-756-7165.

Vocation Office—Rev. THOMAS SULLIVAN, Dir., *49 Elm St., Worcester, 01609.* Tel: 508-791-7171.

Worcester Diocesan Commission for Women—Mrs. MARY DONOVAN, Chm., *49 Elm St., Worcester, 01609.* Tel: 508-791-7171.

Youth Ministry—Sr. BETTY PAUL, S.P., Dir. Youth Ministry, Office: *Oakhurst, 120 Hill St., Whitinsville, 01588.* Tel: 508-234-0346.

CLERGY, PARISHES, MISSIONS AND PAROCHIAL SCHOOLS

CITY OF WORCESTER
(Worcester County)

1—ST. PAUL'S CATHEDRAL (1866), Revs. Richard F. Reidy, Rector; Joseph P. Mahoney; Deacons James P. Quinlivan, Sr.; Francisco Escobar. In res., Revs. David E. Doiron; Robert K. Johnson.
Res., 38 High St., 01609. Tel: 508-799-4193; Fax: 508-752-6308.
Catechesis/Religious Programs—Tel: 508-755-1414; Fax: 508-755-1414.
Students 210.

2—ASCENSION (1911), Rev. Joseph A. Adamo.
Res., 48 Vernon St., 01610. Tel: 508-752-4459; Fax: 508-752-8821.

3—BLESSED SACRAMENT (1912), Revs. Charles J. Dumphy; Thomas J. Markey. In res., Rev. Thomas Landry.
Res., 551 Pleasant St., 01602. Tel: 508-755-5291; Fax: 508-755-6891.
Catechesis/Religious Programs—Epiphany House, Tel: 508-752-4368.
Students 193.

4—CHRIST THE KING (1936), Revs. John J. Foley; Phuong Van Nguyen; James S. Mazzone; Sr. Bernadette Lavoie, S.S.A., Pastoral Assoc.; Deacon Joseph M. Banieukiewicz.
Res., 1052 Pleasant St., 01602. Tel: 508-754-5361; Fax: 508-753-0448.
Catechesis/Religious Programs—Tel: 508-752-5514. Susan J. Wenc, D.R.E.
Students 578.

5—HOLY NAME OF JESUS (1893) (French), Rev. Msgr. Joseph V. Sirois.
Res., 51 Illinois St., 01610. Tel: 508-799-2792; Fax: 508-799-2368.
Catechesis/Religious Programs—Tel: 508-754-6722; Fax: 508-797-1191.
Students 62.

6—IMMACULATE CONCEPTION (1873), Rev. Msgr. Thomas J. Needham.
Res., 353 Grove St., 01605. Tel: 508-754-8419; Fax: 508-756-2192.
Catechesis/Religious Programs—Father Connor Center, Tel: 508-791-5887; Fax: 508-754-8508.
Students 115.

7—NOTRE DAME DES CANADIENS - ST. JOSEPH (1869) (French), Revs. Richard G. Roger; Thomas B. Fleming; Mary G. Guerin, Pastoral Assoc.
Res., 5 Whitman Rd., 01609. Tel: 508-754-6722; Fax: 508-797-1191. [CEM]
Catechesis/Religious Programs—Students 78.

8—OUR LADY OF THE ANGELS (1916), Revs. Charles F. Monroe; William E. Champlin. Pastoral Assocs.: Sr. Barbara Collins, S.N.D.; Deacon Alphonse Desautels.
Res., 1222 Main St., 01603. Tel: 508-791-0951; Fax: 508-753-9531.
School—1220 Main St., Rear, 01603. Tel: 508-752-5609; Fax: 508-798-9634. John F. Hanson, Prin.
Lay Teachers 18; Students 303.
Catechesis/Religious Programs—Tel: 508-754-4165.
Students 451.

9—OUR LADY OF CZESTOCHOWA (1903) (Polish), Revs. Thaddeus X. Stachura; Anthony S. Kazarnowicz.
Res., 34 Ward St., 01610. Tel: 508-755-5959; Fax: 508-767-1644.
School—St. Mary's, (Grades K-6) 50 Richland St., Tel: 508-753-0484; Fax: 508-795-0506. Sr. Roberta Garczynska, Prin. & D.R.E.
Sisters of the Holy Family of Nazareth 3; Lay Teachers 8; Students 154.
St. Mary's Jr. & Sr. High School—Tel: 508-753-1170; Fax: 508-795-0560. Paul DiDomenico, Prin.
Sisters 1; Lay Teachers 14; Students 177.
Catechesis/Religious Programs—Students 120.

10—OUR LADY OF FATIMA (1952) (Spanish), Rev. Edward M. Ryan; Sr. Mariapia Gonza, X.M.M., Spanish Apostolate; Deacon Vincent Librandi. In res., Rev. Conrad S. Pecevich.
Res., 7 Auburn St., 01605. Tel: 508-755-3820; Fax: 508-755-7196.
Catechesis/Religious Programs—Tel: 508-755-3830.
Students 145.

11—OUR LADY OF LORETO (1966) (Italian), Rev. James J. Aquino; Deacon Pasquale Mussulli.
Res., 33 Massasoit Rd., 01604. Tel: 508-753-5001; Fax: 508-754-1537.
Catechesis/Religious Programs—37 Massasoit Rd., 01604. Tel: 508-799-2445. Sr. Mary Rose Zaccari, M.P.V., D.R.E.
Students 169.

12—OUR LADY OF LOURDES (1949), Rev. James B. O'Shea. In res., Revs. Bernard J. Conlin, (Retired); Francis J. Roach.
Res., 1290 Grafton St., 01604. Tel: 508-757-0789; Fax: 508-757-0048.
Catechesis/Religious Programs—Tel: 508-753-5773. Jo-Ann Bafaro, D.R.E.
Students 215.

13—OUR LADY OF MT. CARMEL AND ST. ANN (1872), Rev. Michael P. Bafaro. In res., Rev. Rocco Piccolomini.
Res., 53 E. Central St., 01605. Tel: 508-752-2964; Fax: 508-755-3506.
Catechesis/Religious Programs—Tel: 508-791-6139. Joan D'Argenis, D.R.E.
Students 215.

14—OUR LADY OF THE ROSARY (1911), Rev. Msgr. John J. Kelliher; Rev. James M. Shea.
Res., 23 Fales St., 01606. Tel: 508-853-1640; Fax: 508-853-2426.
Catechesis/Religious Programs—Father Riley Center, 9 Emerson Rd., 01604. Tel: 508-852-5474. Sr. Irene Moran, M.P.V., D.R.E.
Students 485.

15—OUR LADY OF VILNA (1925) (Lithuanian), Rev. Alphonse A. Volungis.
Res., 153 Sterling St., 01610. Tel: 508-752-1825; Fax: 508-756-1267.

16—SACRED HEART (1880), Rev. Lee F. Bartlett. In res., Rev. Peter J. Scanlon.
Res., 596 Cambridge St., 01610. Tel: 508-752-1608; 753-2555; Fax: 508-757-2462.
Catechesis/Religious Programs—Students 145.

17—ST. ANDREW THE APOSTLE (1954), Rev. James F. Carmody; Sr. Therese Gosselin, S.S.A., Pastoral Assoc.
Res., 16 Vineyard St., 01603. Tel: 508-754-6057; Fax: 508-754-0830.
Catechesis/Religious Programs—Tel: 508-752-4701.
Students 116.

18—ST. BERNARD (1916), Rev. Richard F. Trainor.
Res., 236 Lincoln St., 01605. Tel: 508-791-3104; Fax: 508-791-7124.
Catechesis/Religious Programs—One Harlow St., 01605.
Students 36.

19—ST. CASIMIR'S (1894) (Lithuanian), Rev. Anthony N. Nockunas, M.I.C., Temp. Admin. In res., Rev. John C. Petrauskas, M.I.C.
Res., 41 Providence St., 01604. Tel: 508-754-5142; Fax: 508-770-8060.

20—ST. CATHERINE OF SWEDEN (1952), Rev. George J. Ridick; Sr. Kathleen McGurk, Pastoral Assoc.; Deacon Thomas Wagner.
Res., 3 Wiser Ave., 01607. Tel: 508-752-1624; Fax: 508-797-1196.
Catechesis/Religious Programs—Tel: 508-793-2187.
Students 86.

21—ST. CHARLES BORROMEO (1954), Revs. Henry G. Bowen; Leo J. O'Neil; Deacon Peter R. Faford.
Res., 341 June St., 01602. Tel: 508-799-4031; Fax: 508-792-6675.
Catechesis/Religious Programs—Sr. Elaine Potvin, S.S.A., D.R.E.
Students 180.

22—ST. CHRISTOPHER (1956), Rev. Martin P. Donahue; Deacon Henry Morrissey.
Res., 950 W. Boylston St., 01606. Tel: 508-853-1492; Fax: 508-853-4338.
Catechesis/Religious Programs—Tel: 508-853-3302.
Students 128.

23—ST. GEORGE (1951), Revs. Henry A. Donoghue; Stephen G. Copper. In res., Rev. F. Stephen Pedone.
Res., 40 Brattle St., 01606. Tel: 508-853-0183; Fax: 508-854-0864.
Catechesis/Religious Programs—Tel: 508-852-1784. Miss Diane Fitch, Admin.
Students 718.

24—ST. JOAN OF ARC (1950), Revs. Joseph M. Nally; Emerito Ortiz. Pastoral Assocs.: Sr. Soledad Chacon, R.O.D.A.; Sr. Mary Christopher Power, S.S.J.
Res., 570 Lincoln St., 01605. Tel: 508-852-3232; Fax: 508-852-3223.
Catechesis/Religious Programs—Students 248.

25—ST. JOHN'S (1834), Rev. Joseph A. Coonan. In res., Rev. Joseph P. Mahoney.
Res., 44 Temple St., 01604. Tel: 508-756-7165; Fax: 508-754-5153.
Catechesis/Religious Programs—Mrs. Donna Mastrovito, D.R.E.
Students 177.

26—ST. MARGARET MARY (1922), Rev. Patrick J. Hawthorne; Deacon Bruce Vidito.
Res., 77 Alvarado Ave., 01604. Tel: 508-753-5788; Fax: 508-797-1644.
Catechesis/Religious Programs—Students 90.

27—ST. PETER (1884), Rev. Msgr. Francis J. Scollen; Rev. Jose Andres Rodriguez.
Res., 929 Main St., 01610. Tel: 508-752-4674; Fax: 508-767-1511.
Catechesis/Religious Programs—Tel: 508-752-0797; Fax: 508-767-1511.
Students 275.

28—ST. STEPHEN'S (1887), Revs. William F. Sanders; Daniel J. Becker; Deacon James F. DiPadua, Jr. In res., Most Rev. George E. Rueger.
Res., 16 Hamilton St., 01604. Tel: 508-755-3165; Fax: 508-755-0937.
School—(Grades PreK-8) 355 Grafton St., Tel: 508-755-3209; Fax: 508-770-1052. Ruth O. McGinn, Prin.
Sisters 2; Lay Teachers 13; Students 238.
Catechesis/Religious Programs—Ramona Kneeland, D.R.E.
Students 227.

OUTSIDE THE CITY OF WORCESTER
(In the County of Worcester)

Ashburnham, St. Denis (1951), Rev. Joseph J. Jurgelonis; Deacons Michael P. Connor; Richard DesJardins.
Res., 85 Main St., P.O. Box 418, 01430. Tel: 978-827-5806; Fax: 978-827-1191. [CEM]
Catechesis/Religious Programs—Tel: 978-827-4892.
Students 310.

Athol, Our Lady Immaculate (1882), Revs. Stephen D. Johnson; James B. Callahan; Deacons James L. Linderman; Robert Dio.
Res., 192 School St., 01331-2399. Tel: 978-249-2738; Fax: 978-249-0447.
Catechesis/Religious Programs—Tel: 978-249-7690. Sharon Maher, D.R.E.
Students 297.
Mission—South Royalston, Worcester Co., Our Lady Queen of Heaven, Rte. 68, South Royalston, 01368. Tel: 978-249-4103.

St. Francis (1912), Rev. Raymond P. Messier.
Res., 105 Main St., 01331. Tel: 978-249-3361; Fax: 978-249-8924.

Auburn, St. Joseph's (1907), Revs. Lawrence J. Esposito; Dennis O. O'Malley; Deacon Peter Ryan.
Res., 194 Oxford St., 01501. Tel: 508-832-2074; Fax: 508-832-8894.
Catechesis/Religious Programs—Tel: 508-832-5975; Fax: 508-721-7607. Ms. Susan Landry, D.R.E.
Students 699.

North American Martyrs (1952), Rev. John F. Gee.
Res., 8 Wyoma Dr., 01501. Tel: 508-798-8779; Fax: 508-791-6614.
Catechesis/Religious Programs—Tel: 508-798-0612. Joan Sundstrom, D.R.E.
Students 195.

Baldwinville, St. Vincent De Paul (1955), Rev. John E. Kelley.
Res., 18 Pleasant St., 01436. Tel: 978-939-8851; Fax: 978-939-2120.
Catechesis/Religious Programs—Tel: 978-939-8290.
Students 161.

Barre, St. Joseph's (1896), Rev. Thomas H. Hultquist.
Res., 90 Common St., 01005. Tel: 978-355-4463; Fax: 978-355-0136. [CEM]
Catechesis/Religious Programs—Tel: 978-355-6402.
Students 188.
Mission—Wheelwright, Hardwick Co., St. Augustine, 98 Church Ln., Wheelwright, 01094. Tel: 978-355-4463.

Berlin, St. Joseph the Good Provider (1973), Rev. Robert M. Spellman.
Res., 52 West St., Box 284, 01503-0284. Tel: 978-365-6492; 838-2915; Fax: 978-365-9133.
Catechesis/Religious Programs—Students 190.

Blackstone, St. Paul's (1850), Rev. James D. Champion.
Res., 48 St. Paul St., 01504. Tel: 508-883-6726; Fax: 508-883-2079. [CEM]
Catechesis/Religious Programs—Tel: 508-883-2590; Fax: 508-883-2079.
Students 387.

St. Theresa (1929) (French), Rev. Richard H. Labonte.
Res., 630 Rathbun St., 01504. Tel: 508-883-7206; Fax: 508-883-5250.
Catechesis/Religious Programs—Tel: 508-883-7527.
Students 179.

Bolton, St. Francis Xavier (1953), Rev. Robert L. Killion.
Res., 808 Main St., 01740. Tel: 508-779-2750; Fax: 508-779-0337.
Catechesis/Religious Programs—Students 135.

Boylston, St. Mary of the Hills (1952), Rev. Paul J. Tougas; Deacon Raymond H. Bolduc, (Retired).
Res., 620 Cross St., 01505. Tel: 508-869-6771; Fax: 508-869-3465.
Catechesis/Religious Programs—Tel: 508-869-6776; Fax: 508-869-0418. Marcella Wilson, D.R.E.
Students 250.

Brookfield, St. Mary's (1885), Rev. John G. Hillier.
Res., 4 Howard St., 01506. Tel: 508-867-3188; Fax: 508-867-4313.
Catechesis/Religious Programs—Students 76.

Charlton City, St. Joseph's (1900), Revs. Robert A. Grattaroti; J. Normand Tremblay; Deacons Lawrence F. Miskell; William S. Miller.
Res., Box 338, 01508. Tel: 508-248-7862; Fax: 508-248-5832.
Catechesis/Religious Programs—Tel: 508-248-7986. D.R.E.: Michael Gillespie, (High School); Cheryl Kingston, (Elementary).
Students 885.

Clinton, St. John the Evangelist (1849), Revs. Thomas V. Walsh; Dennis J. Rocheford. Pastoral Assocs.: Sr. Theresa Sullivan, P.B.V.M.; Sr. Sheila Finnegan, S.N.D.
Res., 149 Chestnut St., 01510. Tel: 978-368-0366; Fax: 978-368-4359. [CEM]
Catechesis/Religious Programs—Tel: 508-368-0052.
Students 625.

Our Lady of Jasna Gora (1913) (Polish), Rev. John F. Madden.
Res., 128 Franklin St., 01510. Tel: 978-365-2724; Fax: 978-365-5705.
School—St. Mary's, R128 Franklin St., 01510. Tel: 978-365-3137; Fax: 978-365-3380. Marilyn Blanchard, Prin.
Lay Teachers 10; Students 178.
Catechesis/Religious Programs—Students 55.

Our Lady of the Rosary (1909), Rev. J. Brendan Nally.
Res., One Cross St., 01510. Tel: 508-365-3621; Fax: 508-368-3082.
Catechesis/Religious Programs—Students 79.

Dudley, St. Andrew Bobola (1963) (Polish), Revs. Joseph F. Szwach; Joseph Bielonko.
Res., 54 W. Main St., P.O. Box 98, 01571. Tel: 508-943-5633; Fax: 508-949-6701. [JC]
Catechesis/Religious Programs—Students 83.

St. Anthony's (1969), Rev. Paul F. Campbell.
Res., 22 Dudley Hill Rd., Box 277, 01571-0277. Tel: 508-943-0470; Fax: 508-943-5663. [CEM]
Catechesis/Religious Programs—Tel: 508-949-0335; Fax: 508-943-5663.
Students 320.

East Brookfield, St. John the Baptist (1952), Rev. George A. Charland.
Res., 121 Blaine Ave., 01515. Tel: 508-867-3738; Fax: 508-867-3301.
Catechesis/Religious Programs—Tel: 508-885-4506.
Students 85.

East Douglas, St. Denis (1870), Rev. William N. Cormier.
Res., 23 Manchaug St., 01516. Tel: 508-476-2002; Fax: 508-476-2022. [CEM]
Catechesis/Religious Programs—Students 493.

East Templeton, Holy Cross (1952), Rev. George L. O'Brien.
Res., 25 Lake Ave., P.O. Box 418, 01438. Tel: 978-632-2121; Fax: 978-630-3890.
Catechesis/Religious Programs—Tel: 978-632-2194.
Students 230.

Fiskdale, St. Anne's and St. Patrick's (1886), Revs. Donald B. Espinosa, A.A.; Paul Vaudreuil, A.A.; Aidan M. Furlong, A.A.; Deacon Clarence H. Martel.
Res., 16 Church St., 01518. Tel: 508-347-7338; Fax: 508-347-2982. [CEM]
Catechesis/Religious Programs—Tel: 508-347-9353; Fax: 508-347-9353.
Students 347.

Fitchburg

1—ST. ANTHONY OF PADUA (1908) (Italian), Rev. Robert D. Bruso; Deacon John B. LeBlanc. In res., Rev. Jerry Orsino, O.M.I.
Res., 2 Beekman St., 01420. Tel: 978-342-4706; Fax: 978-342-8160.
School—(Grades PreK-8). Tel: 978-345-7785; Fax: 978-342-5110. Rosemary Thibodeau, Prin.
Sisters 1; Lay Teachers 11; Students 254.
Catechesis/Religious Programs—Tel: 978-342-2491. Ellen DePatie, D.R.E.
Students 138.

2—ST. BERNARD'S (1847) (Irish), Revs. H. Edward Chalmers; Paul J. Theisen. In res., Revs. Thomas M. Tierney; Theodore R. Laperle.
Res., 240 Water St., 01420. Tel: 978-343-7459; Fax: 978-343-0193. [CEM]
School—254 Summer St., 01420. Tel: 978-342-1948; Fax: 978-342-1153.
Sisters of the Presentation of the Blessed Virgin Mary 2; Lay Teachers 10; Students 250.
Catechesis/Religious Programs—Students 190.

3—ST. CAMILLUS DE LELLIS (1953), Rev. Richard P. Lewandowski; Deacon Benjamin A. Nogueira.
Res., 333 Mechanic St., 01420. Tel: 978-342-7921; Fax: 978-345-2688.
Catechesis/Religious Programs—Students 81.

4—ST. FRANCIS OF ASSISI (1903) (French), Rev. Gerald A. Dorais; Deacon William Colon, Spanish Ministry. In res., Rev. Angel Matos, Spanish Ministry.
Res., 63 Sheridan, 01420. Tel: 978-342-9651; Fax: 978-342-7936.
Catechesis/Religious Programs—Tel: 508-342-3521. Robert Jones, D.R.E.
Students 98.

5—IMMACULATE CONCEPTION (1886) (French), Rev. Msgr. Richard E. Collette.
Res., 59 Walnut St., 01420. Tel: 978-342-5851; Fax: 978-345-2491.
Catechesis/Religious Programs—Tel: 978-345-2491.
Students 42.

6—ST. JOSEPH'S (1890), Rev. John R. Dolan, M.S.; Deacon Andre W. Croteau. In res., Revs. John J. Nally, M.S.; John Hughes, M.S.; Maurice Linehan, M.S.; James B. Quilty, M.S.; Edmund Normantowicz, M.S.
Res., 49 Woodland St., 01420. Tel: 978-345-7997; Fax: 978-345-7678. [CEM]
School—35 Columbus St., 01420. Tel: 978-343-3630; Fax: 978-343-2671. Cheryl Slattery, Prin.
Lay Teachers 10; Students 172.
Catechesis/Religious Programs—Tel: 978-345-7997. Bette Brunell, D.R.E.
Students 145.

7—MADONNA OF THE HOLY ROSARY (1955), Rev. Frank J. Liistro.
Res., 118 Theresa St., 01420. Tel: 978-342-1290; Fax: 978-345-3032.
Catechesis/Religious Programs—Tel: 978-345-4906. Judy A. Alario, D.R.E.
Students 190.

8—SACRED HEART OF JESUS (1867) (Irish), Rev. John A. Dwyer; Deacon Edgar B. Blackwelder.
Res., 22 Cottage St., 01420. Tel: 978-342-9606; Fax: 978-342-7131.
Catechesis/Religious Programs—Students 54.

Gardner

1—HOLY SPIRIT (1955), Revs. Andre M. Gariepy; Angel Matos, Spanish Ministry.
Res., 45 Metcalf St., 01440. Tel: 978-632-3333; Fax: 978-632-3630.
Catechesis/Religious Programs—Students 131.

2—ST. JOSEPH'S (1908) (Polish), Rev. Thomas M. Tokarz.
Res., 358 Pleasant St., 01440. Tel: 978-632-0375; Fax: 978-632-1282. [CEM]
Catechesis/Religious Programs—Students 24.

3—OUR LADY OF THE HOLY ROSARY (1884) (French), Revs. J. Andre Guenette; Laurie Leger, M.S.; Deacon Arthur Giard.
Res., 135 Nichols St., 01440. Tel: 508-632-0253; Fax: 508-630-1773. [CEM]
School—99 Nichols St., 01440. Tel: 508-632-8656; Fax: 508-630-1433.
Sisters of the Presentation of Mary 1; Lay Teachers 21; Students 410.
Catechesis/Religious Programs—Students 64.

4—SACRED HEART OF JESUS (1874), Rev. Donald H. Baker; Deacon Paul J. Carrier.
Res., 166 Cross St., 01440. Tel: 978-632-0237; Fax: 978-630-2459. [CEM]
Parish Center: 100 Central St., 01440. Tel: 978-632-0217 (Deacon's Office).
School—Sacred Heart, (Grades K-8) Lynde St., 01440. Tel: 978-632-0950; Fax: 978-630-2448. Linda Rice, Prin.
Lay Teachers 9; Students 190.
Catechesis/Religious Programs—Tel: 978-632-0218.
Students 350.
Day Care—Tel: 978-632-5745. Mrs. Jane Pineo, Dir.

Gilbertville, St. Aloysius (1894), Rev. Chester J. Misiewicz.
Res., 58 Church St., P.O. Box 542, 01031-0542. Tel: 413-477-6493; Fax: 413-477-0140. [CEM]
Catechesis/Religious Programs—Students 52.

Grafton, St. Philip's (1869), Rev. Anthony T. Marteka.
Res., 12 West St., 01519. Tel: 508-839-3325; Fax: 508-839-1310. [CEM]
Catechesis/Religious Programs—Tel: 508-839-9130.
Students 204.

Harvard, St. Theresa's (1950), Rev. Normand R. Gaumond.
Res., 15 Still River Rd., P.O. Box 746, 01451. Tel: 978-456-3563; Fax: 978-456-8352.
Catechesis/Religious Programs—Tel: 978-456-8807. Lorretta DiPietro, D.R.E.
Students 270.

Hopedale, Sacred Heart of Jesus (1935), Rev. Raymond M. Goodwin, Jr.; Deacon Joseph Manella.
Res., 187 Hopedale St., Box 16, 01747. Tel: 508-473-1900; Fax: 508-473-1745.
Catechesis/Religious Programs—Tel: 508-473-1701. Carol Pellegrino, D.R.E.
Students 519.

Jefferson, St. Mary's (1884), Rev. Andre N. Remillard; Maureen Smith, Pastoral Assoc.
Res., 114 Princeton St., 01522. Tel: 508-829-4508; Fax: 508-829-0429. [CEM]
Catechesis/Religious Programs—Tel: 508-829-6758.
Students 494.

Lancaster, Immaculate Conception (1915), Rev. Edward P. Lettic.
Res., 28 Packard St., P.O. Box 95, 01523. Tel: 508-365-6582; Fax: 508-365-3097.
Catechesis/Religious Programs—Students 179.

Leicester, St. Joseph's (1851), Revs. Michael A. DiGeronimo; Paul W. Lemire; Carol Cornacchioli, Pastoral Assoc.
Res., 759 Main St., 01524. Tel: 508-892-7407; Fax: 508-892-4753. [CEM]
Catechesis/Religious Programs—Combined with St. Pius X. Kathleen A. Cherry, C.R.E.
Students 377.
Day Care, Caring Place—Tel: 508-892-3168.
Students 68.

St. Pius X (1956), Revs. Michael A. DiGeronimo; Paul W. Lemire; Carol A. Cornacchioli, Pastoral Assoc.
Mailing Address: 759 Main St., 01524. Tel: 508-892-7407; Fax: 508-892-4753.
Church—1161 Main St., 01524.
Catechesis/Religious Programs—Clustered with St. Joseph's, Leicester.
Students 377.

Leominster

1—ST. ANNA'S (1937) (Italian), Rev. Ronald G. Falco; Deacon Robert Leger.
Res., 199 Lancaster St., 01453. Tel: 978-537-5293; Fax: 978-537-2950.
School—Tel: 978-534-4770; Fax: 978-466-1167. Rita Bernard, Prin.
Priests 1; Lay Teachers 12; Students 229.
Catechesis/Religious Programs—Tel: 978-537-2945.
Students 350.

2—HOLY FAMILY OF NAZARETH (1963), Rev. Thomas F. Egan.
Res., 800 Union St., 01453. Tel: 978-537-3016; Fax: 978-534-1119.
Catechesis/Religious Programs—Tel: 978-537-5660. Anne Booth, D.R.E.
Students 220.

3—ST. CECILIA'S (1900) (French), Rev. Francis T. Goguen; Rev. Msgr. George E. Denomme; Rev. Richard A. Jakubauskas; Deacon Ronald J. Aubuchon.
Res., 170 Mechanic St., 01453. Tel: 978-537-6541; Fax: 978-840-1965. [CEM]
Catechesis/Religious Programs—Tel: 978-537-4673. Patricia Secino, D.R.E.
Students 321.
Convent—190 Mechanic St., 01453. Tel: 978-534-6907.

4—ST. LEO'S (1872), Revs. John E. Doran; Joseph M. Dolan.
Res., 108 Main St., 01453. Tel: 978-537-7257; Fax: 978-840-6182. [CEM]
School—120 Main St., 01453. Tel: 978-537-1007. Mrs. Carolyn Polselli, Prin.
Sisters of the Presentation of the Blessed Virgin Mary 2; Lay Teachers 24; Students 316.
Catechesis/Religious Programs—Tel: 978-537-1194.
Students 340.

5—OUR LADY OF THE LAKE (1952), Rev. Timothy M. Brewer; Sr. Paulette Gariepy, D.H.S., Pastoral Assoc.; Deacon Fred A. Harkins.
Res., 1400 Main St., 01453. Tel: 978-342-2978; Fax: 978-342-8738.
Catechesis/Religious Programs—Tel: 978-345-7469. Lisa Sciacca, D.R.E.
Students 516.

Linwood, Good Shepherd (1904), Rev. Daniel R. Mulcahy, Jr.
Res., 121 Linwood St., P.O. Box 517, 01525. Tel: 508-234-7726; Fax: 508-234-0964.
Catechesis/Religious Programs—Tel: 508-234-5340. Deborah R. Blicharz, Pastoral Assoc. & D.R.E.
Students 295.

Lunenburg, St. Boniface (1950), Rev. Edward D. Niccolls; Sr. Mary E. LeBlanc, P.B.V.M., Pastoral Assoc.; Deacon Joseph M. Cieri. In res., Rev. Donald C. Ouellette.
Res., 817 Massachusetts Ave., 01462. Tel: 978-582-4008; Fax: 978-582-9355.
Catechesis/Religious Programs—Tel: 978-582-6650; Fax: 978-582-9355. Mr. Thomas J. Griffin, D.R.E.
Students 491.

Manchaug, St. Anne's (1900), Rev. Stanley F. Krutcik.
Res., 31 Main St., P.O. Box 311, 01526. Tel: 508-476-2405; Fax: 508-476-4443.
Catechesis/Religious Programs—Students 34.

Mendon, St. Michael's (1952), Rev. Thomas E. Mahoney; Deacon Ernest E. Desmarais.
Res., 29 North Ave., P.O. Box 33, 01756. Tel: 508-478-4456; Fax: 508-634-2664.
Catechesis/Religious Programs—Students 347.

Milford, St. Mary of the Assumption (1848), Revs. Michael G. Foley; David B. Galonek; Eusiquio Munoz; Sr. Theresa Lucier, S.P., Pastoral Assoc.
Res., 27 Pearl St., 01757. Tel: 508-473-2000; Fax: 508-473-6907. [CEM]
Catechesis/Religious Programs—St. Mary's Parish Center, 17 Winter St., 01757. Tel: 508-478-7440. Martha LaFreniere Harris, D.R.E.
Students 860.

Sacred Heart (1905), Revs. Paul D. Burns, C.S.S.; Edward J. Hanlon. Pastoral Ministers: Sr. Claire Belforti, S.S.J.; Sr. Estelle Santarpia, S.S.J.
Res., 5 E. Main St., 01757. Tel: 508-473-0331; Fax: 508-478-4993. [CEM]
Catechesis/Religious Programs—Tel: 508-473-1036. Sr. Catherine Walsh, R.S.M., D.R.E.
Students 591.

Millbury, Assumption (1884) (French), Rev. Richard A. Fortin.
Res., 12 Waters St., 01527. Tel: 508-865-2657; Fax: 508-865-4866.
School—17 Grove St., 01527. Tel: 508-865-5404; Fax: 508-581-8974. Sr. Gertrude Lanouette, D.H.S., Prin.
Lay Teachers 14; Students 215.
Assumption Preschool—Tel: 508-865-5404.
Catechesis/Religious Programs—Students 80.

St. Brigid (1849), Revs. John E. Horgan; Robert E. Kelley.
Res., 59 Main St., 01527. Tel: 508-865-6624; Fax: 508-865-3101.
Catechesis/Religious Programs—Tel: 508-865-2752. Mrs. Gloria Schimke, D.R.E.
Students 555.

Millville, St. Augustine's (1884), Rev. Jean Paul Gagnon; Deacon William Lucier.
Res., 17 Lincoln St., 01529. Tel: 508-883-6678; Fax: 508-883-5878.
Catechesis/Religious Programs—15 Lincoln St., 01529. Tel: 508-883-8794.
Students 158.

Northboro, St. Bernadette (1959), Rev. Chester J. Devlin.
Res., 266 Main St., P.O. Box 743, 01532. Tel: 508-393-2838; Fax: 508-393-2718.
School—(Grades PreK-8) 266 Main St., 01532. Tel: 508-351-9905. Mrs. Josephine R. Dansereau, Prin.; Sr. Roberta Salah, S.S.J., Asst. Prin.
Sisters 3; Lay Teachers 30; Students 430.
Catechesis/Religious Programs—Tel: 508-393-7445.
Students 105.

St. Rose of Lima (1883), Rev. James A. Houston; Sr. M. Cathleen Toomey, R.S.M., Pastoral Assoc.
Res., 244 W. Main St., P.O. Box 685, 01532. Tel: 508-393-2413; Fax: 508-393-4922.
Catechesis/Religious Programs—P.O. Box 387, Tel: 508-393-6444. Mrs. Patricia Morin, D.R.E.
Students 752.

Northbridge, St. Peter (1904), Rev. John F. Connell.
Res., 39 Church Ave., 01534. Tel: 508-234-2156; Fax: 508-234-5123.
Catechesis/Religious Programs—Tel: 508-234-6355. Barbara Ramian, D.R.E.
Students 146.

North Brookfield, St. Joseph's (1867), Rev. Richard T. Carey.
Res., 28 Mt. Pleasant St., 01535. Tel: 508-867-6811; Fax: 508-867-7756. [CEM]
Catechesis/Religious Programs—27 Mt. Pleasant St., 01535. Tel: 508-867-9302.
Students 343.

North Grafton, St. Mary's (1952), Rev. John J. Bagley; Deacon Nicholas M. CaraDonna, Jr.
Res., 17 Waterville St., 01536. Tel: 508-839-3993; Fax: 508-839-1330.

Catechesis/Religious Programs—Tel: 508-839-3993, Ext. 12. Patricia Verderese, D.R.E.
Students 261.

North Oxford, St. Ann's (1906), Rev. James M. Steuterman; Sr. Jeanne Rouillard, S.A.S.V., Pastoral Assoc.; Deacon James Denning.
Res., 652 Main St., P.O. Box 488, 01537. Tel: 508-987-8892; Fax: 508-987-1598.
Catechesis/Religious Programs—P.O. Box 488, N. Oxford, 01537. Tel: 508-987-1869.
Students 226.

Otter River, St. Martin's (1864), Rev. Cornelius F. O'Leary.
Res., 248 State Rd., 01436. Tel: 508-939-5588; Fax: 508-939-2305.
Church—247 State Rd., 01436.
Catechesis/Religious Programs—Students 61.

Oxford, St. Roch's (1886), Rev. Gerard P. Walsh. In res., Rev. Msgr. Louis R. Piermarini.
Res., 334 Main St., 01540. Tel: 508-987-8987; Fax: 508-987-8938. [CEM]
Catechesis/Religious Programs—Tel: 508-987-2382.
Students 380.

Paxton, St. Columba's (1951), Rev. John D. Thomas.
Res., 10 Richards Ave., 01612. Tel: 508-755-0408; Fax: 508-767-0759.
Catechesis/Religious Programs—Tel: 508-755-0601.
Students 322.

Petersham, St. Peter (1968), Rev. Raymond P. Messier.
Mailing Address: Main St., 01366. Tel: 978-249-3361; Fax: 978-249-8924.
Res., St. Francis, 105 Main St., Athol, 01331.
Catechesis/Religious Programs—Students 30.

Princeton, Prince of Peace (1967), Rev. James J. Caldarella; Sr. Teresa Rose Carchidi, Pastoral Assoc.
Res., 5 Worcester Rd., P.O. Box 305, 01541. Tel: 508-464-2871; Fax: 508-464-0449.
Catechesis/Religious Programs—Students 230.

Rochdale, St. Aloysius-St. Jude (1904), Rev. Peter H. White.
Res., 2 Church Pl., P.O. Box 296, 01542-0296. Tel: 508-892-8296; Fax: 508-892-8296.
Catechesis/Religious Programs—Mrs. Ann Listenic, D.R.E.
Students 190.

Rutland, St. Patrick's (1938), Rev. James P. Kerrigan; Deacon William J. Vigliotti.
Res., 290 Main St., Box 939, 01543. Tel: 508-886-4309; Fax: 508-886-2897.
Church—258 Main St., 01543. Tel: 508-886-6131.
Catechesis/Religious Programs—Tel: 508-886-4984. Michele Curtis, D.R.E.
Students 465.

Shrewsbury, St. Anne's (1950), Revs. Edward J. Moran; Robert A. Loftus; Sr. Charlene O'Leary, P.B.V.M., Pastoral Assoc.
Res., 130 Boston Tpke., 01545. Tel: 508-757-5154; Fax: 508-797-9520. [CEM]
Catechesis/Religious Programs—Tel: 508-752-5040. Karen Weigold, D.R.E.
Students 805.

St. Mary's (1922), Revs. Paul T. O'Connell; Dennis J. O'Brien; Leo Lancaster.
Res., 18 Summer St., 01545. Tel: 508-845-0161; Fax: 508-842-9132.
School—Tel: 508-842-1601; Fax: 508-845-1535. Joanne Gannon, Prin.
Sisters 1; Lay Teachers 20; Students 243.
Catechesis/Religious Programs—Tel: 508-845-1154.
Students 1062.

South Ashburnham, St. Anne (1895), Rev. Joseph J. Jurgelonis; Deacons Michael P. Connor; Richard DesJardins.
Pastoral Office: 85 Main St., P.O. Box 418, Ashburnham, 01430-0418. Tel: 978-827-5806; Fax: 978-827-1191.
Catechesis/Religious Programs—Combined with St. Denis.

South Barre, St. Thomas-A-Becket (1923), Rev. Ernest Allega.
Res., P.O. Box 186, Vernon Ave., 01074. Tel: 978-355-2228; Fax: 978-355-0042.
Catechesis/Religious Programs—Fax: 978-355-2228.
Students 144.

Southborough, St. Anne (1886), Rev. Thirburse F. Millott.
Res., 20 Boston Rd., P.O. Box 403, 01772. Tel: 508-485-0141; Fax: 508-481-9374.
Catechesis/Religious Programs—Tel: 508-481-3159. Teresa F. Katuska, C.R.E.
Students 488.

St. Matthew (1956), Rev. James B. Flynn.
Res., 105 Southville Rd., 01772. Tel: 508-485-2285; Fax: 508-485-4437. [JC]
Catechesis/Religious Programs—Tel: 508-229-2429; Fax: 508-229-0837.
Students 443.

Southbridge

1—St. Hedwig's (1916) (Polish), Rev. Charles E.J. Borowski.
Res., 29 Summer St., 01550. Tel: 508-764-6947; Fax: 508-764-7707. [CEM]
Catechesis/Religious Programs—Students 29.

2—Notre Dame (1869) (French-Canadian), Revs. Maurice L. Gilbert; Leo-Paul J. LeBlanc; Deacon Michael J. Corby.
Res., 61 Marcy St., 01550. Tel: 508-765-0601; Fax: 508-764-4148.
Catechesis/Religious Programs—Religious Education Center, 20 Marcy St., 01550. Tel: 508-764-8018.
Students 242.

3—Sacred Heart (1908) (French), Rev. Charles R. Armey; Deacon Thomas Skonieczny.
Res., 40 Charlton St., 01550. Tel: 508-764-6964; Fax: 508-764-3320.
Catechesis/Religious Programs—Tel: 508-765-5597.
Students 102.

4—St. Mary's (1861), Revs. Peter Joyce; Kenneth R. Cardinale; Deacon Richard Olson.
Res., 263 Hamilton St., 01550. Tel: 508-764-3226; Fax: 508-764-3209. [CEM]
Catechesis/Religious Programs—Tel: 508-765-0245; 765-0394 (Spanish). Sr. Estelia Viquez, R.O.D.A.
Students 407.

South Grafton, St. James (1887), Rev. Michael F. Rose; Deacon Edward Richards.
Res., 89 Main St., 01560. Tel: 508-839-5354; Fax: 508-839-5430.
Catechesis/Religious Programs—Tel: 508-839-6800.
Students 417.

Spencer, Mary, Queen of the Rosary (1994). Merger of St. Mary and Our Lady of the Rosary. Revs. James F. Hoey; Thomas M. Barry; Deacon Harry M. Sweet.
Office: 60 Maple St., 01562. Tel: 508-885-3111; Fax: 508-885-4905.
Res., 46 Maple St., 01562. Tel: 508-885-3806. [CEM]
Catechesis/Religious Programs—Tel: 508-885-3332. Mrs. Carol St. John, D.R.E.
Students 512.

Our Lady of the Rosary (1854). Merged with St. Mary's to form Mary, Queen of the Rosary.

Sterling, St. Richard of Chichester (1953), Rev. Thomas B. Garlick; Sr. Anne Marie Wildenhain, S.S.J., Pastoral Assoc.; Jeanne A. Whitford, Business Mgr.
Res., 4 Bridge St., P.O. Box 657, 01564. Tel: 508-422-8881; Fax: 508-422-0291.
Catechesis/Religious Programs—Tel: 508-422-8921. Patricia Cole, D.R.E.
Students 416.

Sutton, St. Mark (1966), Revs. Brian P. O'Toole; Joseph W. McKiernan; Deacon Walter Doyle.
Res., 356 Boston Rd., 01590. Tel: 508-865-3860; Fax: 508-865-5095.
Catechesis/Religious Programs—D.R.E.: Marianne Raeke; Kathleen Mahoney; Robin Boria.
Students 800.

Upton, Holy Angels (1900), Rev. Laurence V. Brault.
Res., 2 Nelson St., 01568. Tel: 508-529-6981; Fax: 508-529-6317.
Catechesis/Religious Programs—Tel: 508-529-3109. Simone Caron, D.R.E.
Students 480.

Uxbridge, St. Mary's (1853), Rev. Paul J. Doherty; Deacon Paul Brown; Mrs. Rosemary Seibold, Pastoral Assoc.
Res., 77 Mendon St., 01569. Tel: 508-278-2226; Fax: 508-278-7949. [CEM]
Catechesis/Religious Programs—Tel: 508-278-3777.
Students 444.

Warren, St. Paul's (1872), Rev. Roland L. Lajoie.
Res., 1082 Main St., P.O. Box 1027, 01083-1027. Tel: 413-436-7327; Fax: 413-436-9677. [CEM]
Catechesis/Religious Programs—Clustered with St. Thomas Aquinas, Warren.
Students 120.

Webster, St. Joseph's Basilica (1887) (Polish), Rev. Msgr. Anthony Czarnecki; Rev. Paul M. LaPalme.
Res., 53 Whitcomb St., 01570. Tel: 508-943-0467; Fax: 508-943-0808. [CEM]
School—Tel: 508-943-0378; Fax: 508-949-0581. Sr. Marie JoAnn Lewko, Prin.
Felician Sisters 3; Lay Teachers 14; Students 300.
Catechesis/Religious Programs—Tel: 508-943-2738.
Students 65.

Sacred Heart of Jesus (1870), Rev. Michael J. Roy; Deacons Roland R. Michaud; Laurent Mongeau.
Res., 18 E. Main St., 01570. Tel: 508-943-3140; Fax: 508-943-2213. [CEM]
School—Tel: 508-943-2735; Fax: 508-943-6215. Sr. Constance Bayeur, S.S.A., Prin.
Sisters of St. Anne 2; Lay Teachers 11; Students 237.
Catechesis/Religious Programs—Tel: 508-943-0113.
Students 165.

St. Louis (1853), Revs. Joseph A. Marcotte; Bernard Davenport.
Res., 15 Lake St., 01570. Tel: 508-943-0240; Fax: 508-943-0801. [CEM]
School—Tel: 508-943-0257; Fax: 508-943-0257.
Lay Teachers 12; Students 217.
Catechesis/Religious Programs—Tel: 508-943-0817.
Students 500.

Westborough, St. Luke the Evangelist (1870), Revs. George O. Lange; Steven M. LaBaire.
Res., 70 W. Main St., 01581. Tel: 508-366-5502; Fax: 508-366-6049. [CEM]
Catechesis/Religious Programs—One Ruggles St., 01581. Tel: 508-366-8509. Margaret Bissonnette, D.R.E.
Students 1,083.

West Boylston, Our Lady of Good Counsel (1869), Rev. John F. Burke. In res., Rev. Francis A. Roberge.
Res., 111 Worcester St., 01583. Tel: 508-835-3606; Fax: 508-835-5456. [CEM]
Catechesis/Religious Programs—Tel: 508-835-6336. Thomas Faucher, D.R.E.
Students 492.

West Brookfield, Sacred Heart of Jesus (1950), Rev. Peter D. Shea.
Res., 10 Milk St., 01585-0563. Tel: 508-867-6469; Fax: 508-867-3670. [CEM]
Parish Center: Tel: 508-867-4460.
Catechesis/Religious Programs—Tel: 508-867-4460.
Students 170.

Westminster, St. Edward the Confessor (1951), Rev. Terence T. Kilcoyne, D.Min.; Deacon Roderick F. Cashes.
Res., 10 Church St., 01473. Tel: 978-874-2362; Fax: 978-840-1024.
Catechesis/Religious Programs—Tel: 978-874-1559.
Students 250.

West Warren, St. Stanislaus (1913) (Polish), Rev. Peter P. Hamernik, Admin.
Res., 2270 Main St., P.O. Box 723, 01092-0503. Tel: 413-436-5110; Fax: 413-436-0556.
Catechesis/Religious Programs—Students 23.

St. Thomas Aquinas (1893), Rev. Roland L. Lajoie.
Res., St. Paul's Rectory, 1082 Main St., P.O. Box 323, 01092. Tel: 413-436-7327; Fax: 413-436-7324.
Catechesis/Religious Programs—Clustered with St. Paul, Warren. Fax: 413-436-9677.
Students 120.

Whitinsville, St. Patrick's (1889), Rev. Michael Broderick; Deacon Anthony R. Surozenski.
Res., 7 East St., P.O. Box 60, 01588. Tel: 508-234-5656; Fax: 508-234-6845. [CEM]
Catechesis/Religious Programs—Tel: 508-234-3511. MaryAnn DiGregorio, D.R.E.
Students 561.

Winchendon, Immaculate Heart of Mary (1870), Rev. Roland L. Gamache. Pastoral Assistants: Sr. Anne O'Shea, P.M.; Mr. Mark J. Carrier.
Res., 52 Spruce St., 01475. Tel: 508-297-0280; Fax: 508-297-3577. [CEM]
Catechesis/Religious Programs—Tel: 508-297-2699. Sr. Pauline Grenier, P.M., D.R.E.
Students 204.
Convent—Our Lady of Sorrows, Tel: 508-297-0275. Sisters of the Presentation of Mary 2.

Chaplains of Public Institutions

Worcester. *ADCARE Hospital of Worcester*. Vacant.
Air National Guard. Serviced by Catholic Charities priests.
Hahnemann Hospital. Serviced by Priests of St. Bernard, St. Joan of Arc, Immaculate Conception, Our Lady of the Rosary Churches.
Memorial Hospital. Catholic Pastoral Ministry: Rev. Thomas Landry.
University of Mass Medical Center. Rev. Francis Roach.
Worcester Belmont House. Serviced by St. Margaret Mary Church.
Worcester Detention Center. Serviced by Urban Ministry.
Worcester State Hospital. Vacant.

Boylston. *Worcester County Jail and House of Correction*. Deacon Gary Miller.

Worcester County Sanitarium. Rev. Leo J. O'Neil, Chap.

GARDNER. *Massachusetts Correctional Institution*. Rev. Thomas M. Tierney, Chap.

LANCASTER. *Massachusetts Correctional Institution*. Vacant.

OTTER RIVER. *Walter E. Fernald State School*. Rev. John E. Kelley.

On Special or Other Diocesan Assignment:
Reverend Fathers—
Banach, Michael, Vatican Diplomatic Corp.
Ciambelli, Blase A., Westboro State Hospital
DiOrio, Ralph A., Apostolate of Healing
Doiron, David E., Pastoral Counseling
Gothing, Donald B., Admin., Capilia de la Santisima Trinidad, 69 Lincoln Ter. P.O. Box 667, Leominster, MA 01453. Tel: 978-534-5258

On Duty Outside the Diocese:
Reverend Monsignors—
Banach, Michael, Nunciatura Apostolica, Avenida Arce 2990, Casilla Postal 136, La Paz, Bolivia
Kelly, Francis D., Rector, Pope John XXIII Seminary
Mongelluzzo, James A., P.O. Box 2545, Worcester, MA 01613
Reverend Fathers—
Carr, David W., 740 Palm Trail, Delray Beach, FL 33447
Damian, Ronald
Dunkley, George
Hill, George H., Abbey of the Genesee, Piffard, NY 14533
Inzerillo, Peter, Pastoral Studies
Kelly, David F., Duquesne Univ., Theology Dept., Pittsburgh, PA 15219
Mattimore, William F., St. George, 41-1323 Kalanianole Hwy., Waimanalo, HI 96795. Tel: 808-259-7188; Fax: 808-259-0169
Moroney, James P., Exec. Dir., National Conference of Catholic Bishops, Secretariat for the Liturgy, 3211 4th St., N.E., Washington, DC 20017-1194. Tel: 202-541-3060; Fax: 202-541-3088
Roy, F. Gilles, Apartado 46, Sicuani (Via Cuzco), Peru

Military Chaplains:
Reverend Fathers—
Bomba, Paul M.
Boucher, Roger R.
Grochowski, Bernard J.

Absent on Leave:
Reverend Fathers—
Branconnier, Gerard
Gelineau, H. Raymond
Kane, Thomas
Kardas, Thaddeus
Kelly, Robert
Nicewicz, Edward
Ritacco, Richard
Siciliano, John
Szantyr, John
Teczar, Thomas

Retired:
Reverend Monsignors—
Battista, Leo, 30 Julio Dr., Shrewsbury, MA 01545
Carelli, Richard J., 30 Julio Dr., Shrewsbury, MA 01545
Daley, Thomas J., Vianney House, 222 June St., Worcester, MA 01602
Haddad, Edmond G., Vianney House, 222 June St., Worcester, MA 01602
Lenk, Charles, Southgate, 30 Julia Dr., Shrewsbury, MA 01545
Reverend Fathers—
Anger, Raymond G., 30 Julio Dr., Apt. 317, Shrewsbury, MA 01545
Archey, Eugene C., P.O. Box 2025, Central Berkshire Blvd., Pittsfield, MA 01202
Ash, Joseph H., 222 June St., Worcester, MA 01602
Banach, Henry S., 64 Oakwood Ln., Worcester, MA 01604
Barrett, John W., 49 Elm St., Worcester, MA 01609
Barry, Leo, 15 Sandro Cir., Warwick, RI 02886
Bedard, J. Raymond, Hilltop Condo #23, Shawne Rd., Sandwich, MA
Berthiaume, Eugene F., P.O. Box 415, West Warren, MA 01092
Clifford, James J., 222 June St., Shrewsbury, MA 01602
Conlin, Bernard J., Our Lady of Lourdes Rectory, 1290 Grafton St., Worcester, MA 01604
Debitetto, Ronald E., 66 Stetson St., Hyannis, MA 02601
Devaney, Roy J., 532 Grove St., Worcester, MA 01605
Dutram, Charles J., 880 School St., Webster, MA 01570
Dyer, Edward J., 30 Apricot St., Worcester, MA 01603
Falvey, Edmund F., 13 Blaine St., Worcester, MA 01603
Foley, Paul T., Shrewsbury Nursing Home, 66 S. Shrewsbury, Shrewsbury, MA 01545
Fontaine, John-Paul, 68 Natal Ave., East Falmouth, MA 02536
Gallagher, William J., 49 Elm, Worcester, 01609
Gariepy, Robert E., 320 Sprice Dr., Ashburnham, MA 01453
Gilgun, Bernard E., St. Anne's, Shewsbury, MA
Gionet, Urbain J., Southgate of Shrewsbury, 30 Julio Dr., Apt. 112, Shrewsbury, MA 01545
Harrity, Francis P., 115 Prescott St., Clinton, MA 01510
Hebert, Roland G., Southgate of Shrewsbury, 30 Julio Dr., Apt. 109, Shrewsbury, MA 01545
Holland, George G., Box 488, North Oxford, MA 01537
Kurzawski, Casimir J., 220 Lakeview Ave., Syracuse, NY 13204
Lamothe, C. Romero, 51 Chapel St., Chicopee, MA 01020
Lange, Raymond L., Southgate of Shrewsbury, 30 Julio Dr., Apt. 219, Shrewsbury, MA 01545
Laperle, Theodore R., St. Bernard Rectory, 240 Water St., Fitchburg, MA 01420
LeBeau, Cyril A., Vianney House, 222 June St., Worcester, MA 01602
Loiselle, Joseph G., 48 West Main St., Millbury, MA 01527
Manahan, Martin J., 865 Grove St., Worcester, MA 01605
McGovern, William W., Vianney House, 222 June St., Worcester, MA 01602
McKenna, John J., 88 Melba Ave., Springfield, MA 01104
McNamara, Philip D., 30 Julio Dr., Shrewsbury, MA 01545
O'Brien, Thomas F., 7 Woodland Dr., Paxton, MA 01612
O'Brien, William G., P.O. Box 307, Dennis, MA 02638
O'Donoghue, Brendon W., 30 Julio Dr., Apt. 246, Shrewsbury, MA 01545
Ouillette, Arthur A., 165 Sunset Dr., P.O. Box 1285, Charlton City, MA 01508
Pelletier, Edgar A., 9504 Via Segovia, New Port Richey, FL 33552
Prunier, Arthur J., 22 Thorne St., Worcester, MA 01604
Raftery, William J., Tara Knoll, Box 307, Manomet, MA 02345
Sullivan, Andrew J., 20 Birmingham Rd., Worcester, MA 01606
Yankauskas, Albin J., Shrewsbury Nursing Home, 66 South St., Shrewsbury, MA 01545

Permanent Deacons:
Aiken, Raymond E., (Retired)
Aliskevicz, John J., St. Vincent Hospital, Worcester
Arsenault, Roger D., Holy Rosary, Gardner
Aubuchon, Ronald J., St. Cecilia, Leominster
Baniukiewicz, Joseph M., Christ the King, Worcester
Benvenuti, Clement E., (Retired)
Blackwelder, Edgar B., (Retired)
Bolduc, Raymond H., (Retired)
Bosse, Raymond J., (Retired)
Brown, Paul E., Deaf Ministry Catholic Charities, Worcester; St. Mary, Uxbridge
CaraDonna, Nicholas M., Jr., St. Mary's, North Grafton
Carbone, Francis A., (Retired)
Carrier, Paul J., Sacred Heart of Jesus, Gardner
Cashes, Roderick F., St. Edward the Confessor, Wesminster
Cieri, Joseph M., St. Boniface, Lunenburg
Colon, William B., Hispanic Community, St. Francis, Fitchburg
Connor, Michael P., St. Dennis, Ashburnham; St. Ann, South Ashburnham
Corby, Michael P., Notre Dame, Southbridge
Croteau, Andre W., St. Joseph, Fitchburg
Daluga, Richard B., St. Mary, Milford
Denning, James, St. Anne, North Oxford
Desautels, Alphonse T., Our Lady of the Angels, Worcester
Desjardin, Richard C., St. Dennis/St. Ann, Ashburnham
Desmarais, Ernest E., St. Michael the Archangel, Mendon
Devine, Philip E., St. Mary, Shrewsbury
DeVito, Frederick A., (Retired)
Dio, Robert F., Our Lady Queen of the Rosary, South Royalston
DiPadua, James F., Jr., St. Stephen, Worcester
Doyle, Walter F., Refugee Apostolate, Worcester; St. Mark's, Sutton
Dunphy, Melvin A., On Duty Outside the Diocese
DuVarney, Joseph T., 49 Elm St., Worcester
Escobar, Francisco, St. Paul Cathedral, Worcester
Faford, Peter R., St. Charles Borromeo
Fenner, Harry, (Retired)
Foster, Deane C., (Retired)
Giard, Arthur J., Jr., Our Lady of the Holy Rosary, Gardner
Green, Amos H., Sr., (Retired)
Harkins, Frederick A., Our Lady of the Lake, Leominster
Isabel, David R., Souza-Baranouski Correction Center, Lancaster
King, Loren M., Our Lady of Jasna Gora, Clinton
Ladroga, William J., On Duty Outside the Diocese
LeBlanc, John B., St. Anthony of Padua, Fitchburg
Leger, Robert, St. Anna, Leominster
Librandi, Vincent A., Our Lady of Fatima, Worcester
Linderman, James L., Our Lady Immaculate, Athol
Lucier, William J., St. Augustine, Millville
Manella, Joseph R., Sacred Heart, Hopedale
Martel, Clarence H., St. Anne's/St. Patrick, Sturbridge
McCaffrey, Joseph A., St. Anne, Southboro
Michaud, Roland R., Sacred Heart, Webster
Miller, Gary, Worchester County Jail and House of Corrections
Miller, William S., St. Joseph, Charlton
Miskell, Lawrence F., St. Joseph, Charlton
Mongeau, Laurent M., Sacred Heart, Webster
Montiverdi, Gerald M., University of Massachusetts Medical Center, Worcester
Morrissey, Henry F., Medical Leave of Absence
Mussulli, Pasquale, Our Lady of Loreto, Worcester
Neal, Edmond
Nogueira, Benjamin A., Campus Ministry, Fitchburg State College, Fitchburg
O'Connor, Richard J., (Retired)
O'Toole, George L., Diocesan Tribunal, Diocese of Worcester
Olson, Richard V., St. Mary, Southbridge
Prince, Norman A., Immaculate Conception, Fitchburg
Quinlivan, James P., Sr., St. Paul, Worcester
Richards, Edward J., St. James, South Grafton
Ryan, Peter, St. Joseph, Auburn
Showalter, John A.
Skonieczny, Thomas A., Sacred Heart, Southbridge
Starr, Peter J., Medical Leave of Absence
Surozenski, Anthony R., St. Patrick, Whitinsville
Sweet, Harry M., Mary Queen of the Rosary, Spencer
Tatro, Leo J., (Retired)
Vidito, Bruce R., St. Margaret Mary, Worcester
Vigliotti, William J., St. Patrick, Rutland
Wagner, Thomas A., St. Catherine of Sweden, Worcester

INSTITUTIONS LOCATED IN THE DIOCESE

[A] SEMINARIES, RELIGIOUS, OR SCHOLASTICATES

SPENCER. *St. Joseph's Abbey School of Theology and Institute of Monastic Studies*, 01562. Tel: 508-885-8700; Fax: 508-885-8701.
E-mail: sjasecrt@mindspring.com
Web site: www.spencerabbey.com
Rt. Rev. Damian Carr, Abbot & Rector; Revs. Isaac Keeley, Prior; Dominic Whedbee, O.C.S.O., Novice Master; Edward John Mullaney, O.C.S.O., Vocation Dir.; Luke Truhan, O.C.S.O., Dean of Studies; Bros. Robert Robinson O.C.S.O., Subprior; James Palmigiano, Dean of Juniors. Professors 6; Students 4.

[B] COLLEGES AND UNIVERSITIES

WORCESTER. *Assumption College*, 500 Salisbury St., 01615-0005. Tel: 508-767-7000; Fax: 508-756-1780.
E-mail: info@ave.assumption.edu
Web site: www.assumption.edu
For a complete listing, refer to the Colleges and Universities section.

College of the Holy Cross, Inc., 01610. Tel: 508-793-2011; Fax: 508-793-3030.
Web site: www.holycross.edu
For a complete listing, refer to the Colleges and Universities section.

PAXTON. *Anna Maria College*, Sunset Lane, 01612. Tel: 508-849-3300; Fax: 508-849-3334.
E-mail: jprice@annamaria.edu
Web site: www.annamaria.edu
For a complete listing, refer to the Colleges and Universities section.

[C] HIGH SCHOOLS, CENTRAL

WORCESTER. *Holy Name Central Catholic Junior/Senior High School*, 144 Granite St., 01604. Tel: 508-753-6371; Fax: 508-831-1287. Mr. Timothy M. Rioux, Headmaster; Mrs. Mary E. Riordan, Prin.; Mr. George Olson, Admin.; Mrs. Arlene Maurello, Vice Prin.; Rev. James B. Flynn, Senior Counselor. Priests 1; Sisters 2; Lay Teachers 55; Students 860.

St. Peter-Marian Central Catholic Junior/Senior High School, 781 Grove St., 01605-3196. Tel: 508-852-5555; Fax: 508-852-7238.
E-mail: spmoffice@netscape.net
Mr. Matthew R. Sturgis, Headmaster; Miss Patricia Aubertine, Prin.; Mrs. Joanne Ethier, Asst. Prin.; Mr. John Pace, Asst. Prin.; Rev. Daniel J. Becker. Priests 1; Sisters 3; Lay Teachers 66; Students 1,181.

FITCHBURG. *St. Bernard's Central Catholic High School*, 45 Harvard St., 01420. Tel: 978-342-3212; Fax: 978-345-8067.
E-mail: stbernhs@net/plus.com
Web site: www.netplus
Mr. John A. Bierden, Headmaster; Daniel Costello, Prin. In res. Rev. Donald C. Ouellette. Priests 1; Sisters 3; Lay Teachers 30; Students 555.

SOUTHBRIDGE. *Trinity Catholic Academy*. Elementary School, 11 Pine St., 01550. Tel: 508-765-5991; Fax: 508-765-0017.
E-mail: mbrouillar@aol.com
Mrs. Madeleine Brouillard, Prin. Lay Teachers 11; Students 249; Total Staff 18.

[D] HIGH SCHOOLS, PAROCHIAL

WORCESTER. *St. Mary's Junior/Senior High School*, 50 Richland St., 01610. Tel: 508-753-1170; Fax: 508-795-0560. Congregation of the Sisters of the Holy Family of Nazareth. Sisters 1; Lay Teachers 15; Students 130.

[E] HIGH SCHOOLS, PRIVATE

WORCESTER. *Notre Dame Academy*, 425 Salisbury St., 01609. Tel: 508-757-6200; Fax: 508-757-7200.
E-mail: morrisoa@nda.mec.edu
A Private Day School for Girls. Sr. Ann Morrison, S.N.D., Prin. Sisters of Notre Dame de Namur 4; Other Religious Orders 2; Lay Teachers 31; Girls 312.

FITCHBURG. *Notre Dame Preparatory School*. (Grades 7-12), 171 South St., 01420. Tel: 978-343-7635; Fax: 978-343-6579. Mr. Jeff Hammond, Headmaster. Lay Teachers 13; Students 64.

LANCASTER. *Trivium School*, 471 Langen Rd., 01523. Tel: 978-365-4795; Fax: 978-365-4795.
E-mail: trivium@altavista.com
Web site: triviumschool.com
Mailing Address: P.O. Box 597, South Lancaster, 01561. Dr. William M. Schmitt, Headmaster. Lay Teachers 9; Students 63.

SHREWSBURY. *St. John's High School*, 378 Main St., 01545. Tel: 508-842-8934; Fax: 508-842-3670.
Web site: www.stjohns.shrewsbury.ma.us
Xaverian Brothers. Bro. J. Conal Owens, C.F.X., Headmaster. Brothers 12; Lay Teachers 72; Boys 1,118.

STILL RIVER. *Immaculate Heart of Mary School*, 254 Still River Rd., P.O. Box 22, 01467. Tel: 978-456-8017. Sr. Ann Mary, M.I.C.M., Prin. Sisters 1; Students 2.

[F] ELEMENTARY SCHOOLS, CENTRAL

WORCESTER. *St. Peter's Central Catholic Elementary School*, 865 Main St., 01610. Tel: 508-791-6496; Fax: 508-770-0818. Sisters of St. Joseph. Mrs. Meg Kursonis, Head of School. Lay Teachers 20; Students 354; Preschool Students 31; Total Enrollment 385.

MILFORD. *Milford Catholic Elementary School*, 11 E. Main St., 01757. Tel: 508-473-7303; Fax: 508-478-4902.
E-mail: milfordcatholic@mediaone.net
Sr. Patricia Murphy, S.S.J., Prin. Sisters of St. Joseph 1; Lay Teachers 14; Students 275; Aids 2.

UXBRIDGE. *Our Lady of Valley Regional Elementary School*, 75 Mendon St., 01569. Tel: 508-278-5851; Fax: 508-278-0391. Sr. Kathleen Duffy, S.S.J., Prin. Sisters 1; Lay Teachers 9; Students 226; Part-Time Teachers 3.

[G] ELEMENTARY SCHOOLS, PRIVATE

WORCESTER. *Venerini Academy*, 27 Edward St., 01605. Tel: 508-753-3210; Fax: 508-754-6050.
E-mail: pmarmen@venerini.org
Mrs. Patricia Marmen, Prin. Sisters 5; Lay Teachers 21; Students 357.

LEOMINSTER. *Julie Country Day School*, 365 Lindell Ave., 01453. Tel: 978-537-4939; Fax: 978-534-0347.
E-mail: jcdcoed@aol.com
Sr. Marguerite Timothy, S.N.D., Prin. Sisters 8; Lay Teachers 23; Students 281.

[H] CATHOLIC CHARITIES

WORCESTER. *Catholic Charities*, 10 Hammond St., 01610-1513. Tel: 508-798-0191; Fax: 508-797-5659.
E-mail: billk@ccworc.cnchost.com
Catherine Loeffler, Diocesan Dir.

Northern Worcester Co., 53 Highland Ave., Fitchburg, 01420-7896. Tel: 978-343-4879; Fax: 978-345-4161.

Athol Office, 12 Riverbend St., Athol, 01331-2520. Tel: 978-249-4563; Fax: 978-249-2545. Jacqueline Hager, Area Admin.

Southbridge Office, 79 Elm St., Southbridge, 01550-2601. Tel: 508-765-5936; Fax: 508-764-4153. Edelmira A. Spence, Area Admin.

Blackstone Valley/Greater Milford Area Office, 9 Spring St., Whitinsville, 01588-1409. Tel: 508-234-3800; Fax: 508-234-2321. 126 Main St., Room 6, Milford, 01757. Tel: 508-478-9632; Fax: 508-478-9632. Noreen Landry, Area Admin.

Senior Employment Service, 10 Hammond St., 01610-1513. Tel: 508-798-0191; Fax: 508-797-5659. Edward P. Binnall, Admin.

Refugee Resettlement, 10 Hammond St., 01610-1513. Tel: 508-798-0191; Fax: 508-797-5659. Sr. Theresa Khen Doan, Admin.

Family & Community Services, 10 Hammond St., 01610-1513. Tel: 508-798-0191; Fax: 508-797-5659. Sara Glenn, Admin.

Home Care Services, 10 Hammond St., 01610-1513. Tel: 508-798-0191; Fax: 508-797-5659. Rachel T. Renaud, Admin.

Literacy Volunteers, 10 Hammond St., 01610-1513. Tel: 508-798-0191; Fax: 508-797-5659. Madelyn Morales, Admin.

Crozier House, 10 Hammond St., 01610-1513. Tel: 508-798-0191; Fax: 508-797-5659. A Half-Way House for Substance Abusing Men. J. David Mulrooney, Admin.

Mercy Centre (Developmental Disabilities). Special Education Day Program and Sheltered Workshop for Developmentally Disabled Youngsters and Adults, 25 W. Chester St., 01605-1136. Tel: 508-852-7165; Fax: 508-856-9755. Heather McDonald, Admin.

Youville House Shelter for Homeless Families, 133 Granite St., 01604-4500. Tel: 508-753-3084; Fax: 508-754-0139. Sara Glenn, Admin. Total Assisted 47,000; Total Staff 375.

Office of AIDS Ministry, 10 Hammond St., 01610-1513. Tel: 508-792-5752; Fax: 508-797-5659. Rev. Thomas B. Fleming, Dir.

[I] CHILD CARE AGENCIES

WORCESTER. *Guild of St. Agnes*, 133 Granite St., 01604. Tel: 508-755-2238; Fax: 508-754-2026.
Web site: www.guildofstagnes.org
Mr. Edward Madaus, Dir. Day Care Centers for Infants, Toddlers, Preschoolers & School-age Children. Children aged 8 weeks-12 years. Children 1,250. Family Day Care Program ages 2 months-5 years. Children 320. For all: Total Staff 295.

FITCHBURG. *Guild of St. Agnes*, 62 Dover St., 01420. Tel: 978-343-3042; Fax: 978-343-2610. Total Assisted 145; Total Staff 12.

LEICESTER. *McAuley Nazareth Home for Boys*, 01524. Tel: 508-892-4886; Fax: 508-892-9736.
E-mail: naz1901@aol.com
Sisters of Mercy. Sr. Mary T. Barry, R.S.M., Exec. Dir.; Rev. Msgr. Edmond T. Tinsley, Chap. Sisters 5; Boys 18; (Residents); Special Education School: Boys 20; Lay Teachers 4.

[J] GENERAL HOSPITALS

WORCESTER. *Saint Vincent Hospital, Inc.*, 25 Winthrop St., 01604. Tel: 508-798-1234; Fax: 508-798-1240.
E-mail: beap01@svh-worc.com
For a complete listing, refer to the Hospitals section.

[K] SPECIAL HOSPITALS AND SANATORIA

WORCESTER. *Providence Extended Care Center*, 119 Providence St., 01604. Tel: 508-860-5000; Fax: 508-860-5109
For a complete listing, refer to the Special Care Facilities section.

Saint Francis Home, 101 Plantation St., 01604. Tel: 508-755-8605; Fax: 508-798-0625.
E-mail: admin@saintfrancishome.org
For a complete listing, refer to the Special Care Facilities section.

MILLBURY. *Providence House Nursing Home of Millbury*, 29 Main St., 01527. Tel: 508-865-6106
For a complete listing, refer to the Special Care Facilities section.

WHITINSVILLE. *St. Camillus Hospice, Inc.*, 447 Hill St., 01588. Tel: 508-234-7306; Fax: 508-234-7597
For a complete listing, refer to the Special Care Facilities section.

St. Camillus Nursing Home Inc., 447 Hill St., 01588. Tel: 508-234-7306
For a complete listing, refer to the Special Care Facilities section.

[L] HEALTH SERVICES

WORCESTER. *Compassion House*, 36 King St., 01610. Tel: 508-756-2713
For a complete listing, refer to the Hospitals section.

Our Lady of Mercy Health Care Center, Inc., 101 Barry Rd., 01609. Tel: 508-798-3727; Fax: 508-757-9415.
E-mail: olmhcc@aol.com
For a complete listing, refer to the Hospitals section.

Pernet Family Health Service, 237 Millbury St., 01610. Tel: 508-755-1228; Fax: 508-797-3477
For a complete listing, refer to the Hospitals section.

[M] HOMES FOR AGED

WORCESTER. *Vianney House*, 222 June St., 01602. Tel: 508-791-0311
For a complete listing, refer to the Special Care Facilities section.

LEOMINSTER. *Presentation Health Care Center*, 99 Church St., 01453-3147. Tel: 978-537-7856; Fax: 978-840-1564
For a complete listing, refer to the Special Care Facilities section.

[N] MONASTERIES AND RESIDENCES OF PRIESTS AND BROTHERS

WORCESTER. *Assumptionists (Augustinians of the Assumption)*, 50 Old English Rd., 01609. Tel: 508-754-6276; Fax: 508-797-1789. Revs. Alexis A. Babineau, A.A.; Albert E. Brochu, A.A.; Andre E. Dargis, A.A.; Louis F. Dion, A.A.; Bernard Guillet, A.A.; Roland O. Guilmain, A.A.; Leonard LaRocque, A.A.; Joseph Richard, A.A.; Wilfred J. Dufault, A.A.; Bros. Paul Maurice Gosselin, A.A., Treas.; Omer Gemme, A.A.; Armand Lemaire, A.A.; John-Thomas McHugh, A.A. Priests 9; Brothers 4; Total Staff 13.

Assumptionists of Assumption College, Emmanuel House, 512 Salisbury St., 01609-1326. Tel: 508-767-7523; Fax: 508-793-9701.
E-mail: rcorrive@assumption.edu
Web site: www.assumption.edu
Revs. Roger R. Corriveau, A.A., Supr.; Donat R. Lamothe, A.A., Treas.; Barry Bercier, A.A.; David M. Gallo, A.A.; Dennis Gallagher, A.A.; Eugene V. Laplante, A.A.; Bros. Robert Francis Beaulac, A.A.; Jerome Lively, A.A. Total in Residence 7; Total Staff 1.

Jesuits of Holy Cross College, Inc., 01610. Tel: 508-793-2011; Fax: 508-793-2624.
E-mail: akuzniew@Holycross.edu
Web site: Holy Cross
Revs. John E. Brooks, S.J.; Terrence W. Curry, S.J.; Alfred R. Desautels, S.J.; James J. Drohan, S.J.; Charles J. Dunn, S.J.; Michael F. Ford, S.J.; Lionel P. Honore, S.J.; Robert J. Kaslyn; Anthony J. Kuzniewski, S.J., Rector; Joseph J. LaBran, S.J.; Vincent A. Lapomarda, S.J.; Brian F. Linnane, S.J.; John J. MacDonnell, S.J.; Gerard R. McKeon, S.J.; Earle L. Markey, S.J.; Charles R. McKenney, S.J.; Francis X. Miller, S.J.; James J. Miracky, S.J.; Paul J. Nelligan, S.J.; William J. O'Halloran, S.J.; Joseph B. Pomeroy, S.J.; John P. Reboli, S.J.; William E. Reiser, S.J.; Philip C. Rule, S.J.; William E. Stempsey, S.J.; Edward J. Vodoklys, S.J.; Thomas W. Worcester, S.J. Priests 26. Casa Santa Maria del Camino, Inc., 6 Claremont St., 01610. Tel: 508-798-0104. Rev. William E. Reiser, S.J., Pres.

FITCHBURG. *Missionaries of Our Lady of LaSalette Corp.*, St. Joseph, 46 Woodland St., 01420. Tel: 978-342-7907; Fax: 978-345-7678. Bro. G. Peter Collins, M.S., Treas. & Contact Person. Total in Residence 6.

LEICESTER. *Father James Fitton House of Priestly Formation*, 761 Main St., 01524. Tel: 508-892-8439; Fax: 508-892-4539.
E-mail: vocdir@aol.com
Rev. Thomas J. Sullivan, Dir.

PETERSHAM. *St. Mary's Monastery*, N. Main St., P.O. Box 345, 01366. Tel: 978-724-3350.
E-mail: franselm@one800.net
Revs. Anselm Atkinson, O.S.B., Supr.; Bede Kierney, O.S.B. Priests-Monks 2; Monks 4.

SHREWSBURY. *Calvery Retreat Center, Passionist Fathers of Shrewsbury, Inc.*, 59 South St., P.O. Box 219, 01545-0219. Tel: 508-842-8821; Fax: 508-842-5356.
E-mail: jpowers@cpprov.org
Web site: calvaryretreat.org
Very Rev. John Powers, C.P., Retreat-Community Dir.; Revs. Brice Edwards, C.P., Vicar; Joseph Sedley, C.P.; Fidelis Connolly, C.P.; Edward Wolanski, C.P.; Bonaventure Moccia, C.P.; Bro. August Parlavechio, C.P. Priests 6; Brothers 1.

Xaverian Brothers, 378 Main St., 01545. Tel: 508-845-1878; Fax: 508-842-3670. Bro. Stephen Comeau, C.F.X., Dir. Brothers 10.

SPENCER. *St. Joseph's Abbey*, 01562-1233. Tel: 508-885-8700; Fax: 508-885-8701.
E-mail: sjaspencer@aol.com
Web site: www.SpencerAbbey.org

The Cistercian Order of the Strict Observance (Trappists). Legal Title: *The Cistercian Abbey of Spencer, Inc.* Rt. Rev. Damian Carr, O.C.S.O.; Very Rev. Joseph Chu Cong, O.C.S.O., Prior; Revs. Laurence Bourget, O.C.S.O.; Peter Zemanick, O.C.S.O., (On Leave); Adrian Proback, O.C.S.O.; Raphael Simon, O.C.S.O.; Pius Rivera-Martinez, O.S.C.O.; Basil Byrne, O.C.S.O.; Eugene Lacasse, O.C.S.O.; Robert Kevin Anderson, O.C.S.O., (In Service Outside the Community); Simon Sansone, O.C.S.O.; Edward Steriti, O.C.S.O.; Matthew Flynn, O.C.S.O.; Gabriel Bertoniere, O.C.S.O.; Patrick Brown, O.C.S.O.; Kevin Hunt, O.C.S.O.; Robert Morhous, O.C.S.O.; Vincent Dwyer, O.C.S.O., (In Service Outside the Community); Henry Scarborough, O.C.S.O.; Peter Schmidt, O.C.S.O.; Gerald Sears, O.C.S.O.; Edward John Mullaney, O.C.S.O.; Kizito Thompson, O.C.S.O., (On Leave); Marius Granato, O.C.S.O.; Aquinas Keane, O.C.S.O., (In Service Outside the Community); Luke Truhan, O.C.S.O.; Aidan Logan, O.C.S.O., (On Leave to Military Ordinariate); Francis Rodriguez, O.C.S.O.; Andrew Johnson, O.C.S.O., (On Leave); Isaac Keeley, O.C.S.O.; Dominic Whedbee, O.C.S.O.; David Lavich, O.C.S.O., (In Service Outside the Community); James Palmigiano, O.C.S.O. Solemnly Professed 76; Simply Professed 4; Novices 3; Total Priests in Community 35; Total in Community 84.

STILL RIVER. *Benedictine Monks, St. Benedict Abbey* (Harvard), 252 Still River Rd., P.O. Box 67, 01467. Tel: 978-456-3221. Rt. Rev. Gabriel Gibbs, O.S.B., Abbot; Very Rev. Xavier Connelly, O.S.B., Prior; Revs. Basil Rechenburg, O.S.B.; Peter Connelly, O.S.B.; Anthony Kloss, O.S.B.; Marc Crilly, O.S.B.; Andrew Koch, O.S.B.; James Doran, O.S.B. In res. Rev. Francis Xavier (Sri Lanka). Priests 8; Brothers 10; Oblates 1.

WHITINSVILLE. *St. Camillus Community*, 497 Hill St., 01588. Tel: 617-234-3648; Fax: 508-234-7597. Bros. Thomas Farrell, O.S.Cam., Supr.; John Wiejkus, O.S.Cam.; Rev. John Gallagher, O.S.Cam. Priests 1; Brothers 2.

[O] CONVENTS AND RESIDENCES FOR SISTERS

WORCESTER. *Carmelite Sisters of the Eucharist of Worcester, MA*, 8 Berwick St., 01602. Tel: 508-799-2092; Fax: 508-799-2137. Sisters 5.

Harper Residence, Res., 11 Beechmont St., 01609. Tel: 508-792-1619; Fax: 508-792-2067.
E-mail: lcsasv@yahoo.com
Sisters 5.

Little Franciscans of Mary, 55 Moore Ave., 01602-1819. Tel: 508-755-0878; Fax: 508-799-4337.
E-mail: rmgpfm@yahoo.com
Sr. Rena Mae Gagnon, P.F.M., Regl. Supr. Tel: 508-755-0878. Sisters 20.

Little Franciscans of Mary, 101 Plantation St., 01604. Tel: 508-755-8605; Fax: 508-799-4337. Sr. Gertrude Emond, P.F.M. Sisters 16.

Little Sisters of the Assumption, Pernet Family Health Service, Inc., 237 Millbury St., 01610. Tel: 508-755-1228; Fax: 508-797-3477. Family Health Agency. Nursing and Family Development Services-Home Based.

Religious Venerini Sisters Provincial Office, 23 Edward St., 01605. Tel: 508-745-1020; Fax: 508-852-1677.
E-mail: ponte@venerini.org
Web site: www.venerinisisters.org
Sr. Hilda Ponte, M.P.V., Prov. Coord. Sisters 32; Total in Residence 23.

St. Joseph Residence for Women, 52 High St., 01609. Tel: 508-755-7707; Fax: 508-756-6842. Sr. Ellen Kurtz, R.S.M., Admin.; Yvette Boire, Asst. Admin. Sisters of Mercy 1; Women 65; Total Staff 9.

Sisters of Mercy, 101 Barry Rd., 01609. Tel: 508-798-3727; Fax: 508-757-9415.
E-mail: mercyma@aol.com
Sisters 17.

Sisters of St. Anne, Esther House, 1015 Pleasant St., 01602. Tel: 508-757-6053.
E-mail: smdugas@hotmail.com
Web site: www.annamaria.edu/ssa
Sisters 5; Total in Residence 4; Total Staff 4.

Sisters of St. Joseph, S.S.J., 783 Grove St., 01605. Tel: 508-852-1659. Sisters 3.

Sisters of the Assumption of the Blessed Virgin, 316 Lincoln St., 01605. Tel: 508-856-9383; Fax: 508-853-0881.
E-mail: lono9595@aol.com
Sr. Estelle Dube, S.A.S.V. Tel: 978-724-3468; Sr. Lorraine Normand, S.A.S.V., Treas. Tel: 508-856-9450.

Sisters of the Holy Family of Nazareth, 119 Endicott St., 01610. Tel: 508-753-3835. Sr. M. Roberta, C.S.F.N., Supr. Sisters 3.

Xaverian Missionary Society of Mary, Headquarters: 242 Salisbury St., 01609-1639. Tel: 508-757-0514; Fax: 508-757-0514. Sr. Stefanina Loi, X.M.M., Supr. Sisters 6.

LEOMINSTER. *St. Cecilia's Convent*, 196 Mechanic St., 01453. Tel: 978-534-6907. Daughters of the Holy Spirit 3.

St. Julie Convent, 342 Lindell Ave., 01453. Tel: 978-537-5822; Fax: 978-534-0347. Sr. Marguerite Timothy, S.N.D., Prin. Sisters of Notre Dame de Namur 4.

The Sisters of the Presentation of the Blessed Virgin Mary, New Windsor, NY, 9 Church St., 01453. Tel: 978-537-7108; Fax: 978-840-1564. Mt. St. Joseph, 880 Jackson Ave., New Windsor, NY, 12553. Tel: 914-564-6620; 564-0513 (Admin. Office); Fax: 914-567-0219 (Admin. Office). Ministries are in the areas of education in parochial elementary and high schools; pastoral services; health care; social services. Sr. Catherine Cleary, Pres.; Sr. Brian Elizabeth Barnicle, House Coord. Professed Sisters 182.

PETERSHAM. *Assumption Residence of the Sisters of the Assumption of the Blessed Virgin*, 211 N. Main St., Box 128, 01366. Tel: 978-724-3468; Fax: 978-724-0200. Co-Administrators: Sr. Estelle Dube, S.A.S.V.; Sr. Alice Parent, S.A.S.V.; Sr. Aline Prince, S.A.S.V. Professed Sisters 56.

St. Scholastica Priory, 271 N. Main St., Box 606, 01366. Tel: 978-724-3213; Fax: 978-724-3216. Benedictine Nuns (Cloistered). Very Rev. Mary Clare Vincent, O.S.B., Prioress; Sr. Mary Frances Wynn, O.S.B., Sub Prioress. Nuns in Solemn Vows 7; in Simple Vows 2; Claustral Oblates 1; Novices 1.

STILL RIVER. *Sisters of Saint Benedict Center, Slaves of the Immaculate Heart of Mary Inc.*, St. Ann House, 254 Still River Rd., P.O. Box 22, 01467. Tel: 978-456-8017; Fax: 978-456-8508.
E-mail: micm@bicnet.net
Mother Teresa Beneway, M.I.C.M. Professed Sisters 16; Postulants 1; Live-In Oblates 2.

WEBSTER. *St. Joseph Convent*, 5 Maynard St., 01570. Tel: 508-943-2228.
E-mail: cssfwebster@yahoo.com
Sr. Marie JoAnn Lewko, C.S.S.F., Supr. Felician Sisters 3.

[P] RETREAT HOUSES AND HOUSE OF PRAYER

SPENCER. *Mary House, Inc.*, 186 N. Spencer Rd. (Rte. 31), P.O. Box 20, 01562. Tel: 508-885-5450. House of Prayer and Contemplation. Ms. Joyce Thomasmeyer, Pres.

St. Joseph Abbey, 167 N. Spencer Rd., 01562-1233. Tel: 508-885-8710; Fax: 508-885-8701.
E-mail: spenabby@spencerabbey.org
Web site: www.spencerabbey.org
Guest house and Retreat house. Rev. Matthew Flynn, O.C.S.O., Guestmaster.

STILL RIVER. *Benedictine Monks, St. Benedict Abbey* (Harvard). (See separate listing under Monasteries and Residences for Men.), 252 Still River Rd., P.O. Box 67, 01467. Tel: 978-456-3221. Rt. Rev. Gabriel Gibbs, O.S.B., Abbot.

[Q] NEWMAN CHAPLAINS AND CENTERS

WORCESTER. *Campus Ministry*, P.O. Box 903, 01613. Tel: 508-757-6097.
E-mail: priest@WPI.edu
Web site: www.wpi.edu/~newman
Rev. Peter J. Scanlon, S.T.L., Vicar. Total Staff 23.

Assumption College, 500 Salisbury St., 01609. Tel: 508-767-7419.
E-mail: godonline@assumption.edu
Rev. Roland O. Guilmain, A.A.; Mr. Peter Hart; Mr. John Fleming; Sr. Cecilia Hervas, R.A.; Frank Corbin, Ph.D.

Becker College, 19 Schussler Rd., 01609. Tel: 508-757-6097.
E-mail: priest@wpi.edu
Rev. Peter J. Scanlon, S.T.L., Chap., Religious Center at W.P.I.

Clark University, Box A-62, 01610. Tel: 508-793-7737.
E-mail: eschaper@clark.edu
Beth Duffy Schaper, M.Ed.

Holy Cross College, The Office of the College Chaplain. Tel: 508-793-2448.
E-mail: kmcelane@holycross.edu
Ms. Katherine McElaney, Dir.; Revs. Joseph J. LaBran, S.J.; Gerard R. McKeon; Michael F. Ford, S.J.; Paul Covino; Marybeth Cearns-Barrett; Sr. Lucille Cormier, S.A.S.V.

Becker College at Leicester. Refer to Diocesan Office. Tel: 508-757-6097.
E-mail: priest@wpi.edu

Quinsigamond Community College, 670 W. Boylston St., 01606. Tel: 508-853-2300, Ext. 300.
E-mail: helene@qcc.mass.edu
Sr. Helen Egan, S.S.J., M.A.

University of Massachusetts Medical School. Refer to Diocesan Office. Tel: 508-757-6097.
E-mail: priest@wpi.edu

Worcester State College, Campus Ministry Center, 486 Chandler St., 01602. Tel: 508-793-8017.
E-mail: froberge@juno.com
Rev. Francis A. Roberge, M.A., M.Div.

Worcester Polytechnic Institute, Religious Center at WPI, 19 Schussler Rd., 01609. Tel: 508-757-6097.
E-mail: priest@wpi.edu
Rev. Peter J. Scanlon, S.T.L.

Nichols College (Dudley), 01570. Tel: 508-943-1560.
E-mail: pecevics@nichols.edu
Rev. Conrad S. Pecevich, D.Min.

Fitchburg State College (Fitchburg), Newman Center, 281 Highland Ave., 01420. Tel: 508-345-2688.
E-mail: loisnc@fsc.edu
Rev. Richard P. Lewandowski, M.A., M.Div.; Deacon Benjamin A. Nogueira; Lois I. Nogueira, Chap.

Mt. Wachusett Community College (Gardner), Campus Ministry at MW CC, 419 Green St., Gardner, 01440. Tel: 508-632-6600, Ext. 193.
E-mail: watkin@juno.com
Ms. Corrine Watkins.

Anna Maria College, Box 35, Paxton, 01612. Tel: 508-849-3399.

PAXTON. *Anna Maria College*, Office of Campus Ministry, 01612-1198. Tel: 508-849-3399; Fax: 508-849-3319.
E-mail: @annamaria.edu
Web site: www.annamaria.edu
Sr. Sarah Landis, I.H.M. Total Staff 1.

[R] MISCELLANEOUS

WORCESTER. *Casa Santa Maria del Camino, Inc.*, 6 Claremont Sq., 01610. Tel: 508-798-0104. Rev. William E. Reiser, S.J., Pres. Total in Residence 2; Total Staff 1. Pastoral Outreach Center for the Hispanic Community.

The Charlton Charitable Corporation, Inc. Diocese of Worcester. 49 Elm St., 01609. Tel: 508-791-7171; Fax: 508-754-2768.

The Guild of Our Lady of Providence. Tel: 508-791-7171. Mailing Address: Chancery Office of the Diocese of Worcester, 49 Elm St., 01609. Tel: 508-791-7171; Fax: 508-753-7180.

Mendon Charitable Corporation, Inc., 49 Elm St., 01609. Tel: 508-791-7171; Fax: 508-754-2768. Most Rev. George E. Rueger, Contact Person.

Monsignor Thomas Griffin Foundation, 49 Elm St., 01609. Tel: 508-791-7171; Fax: 508-753-7180. Rev. Msgr. Edmond T. Tinsley, Contact Person.

Office for Ethnic Ministries, 49 Elm St., 01609. Tel: 508-791-7171; Fax: 508-753-7180.
E-mail: sprefontaire@worcesterdiocese.org
Web site: www.worcesterdiocese.org
Sr. Marie Prefontaine, S.N.D., Dir.

St. Peter-Marian Endowment Trust, c/o St. Peter-Marian Central Catholic Junior/Senior High School, 781 Grove St., 01605. Tel: 508-852-5555; Fax: 508-852-7238.
E-mail: alumspm@aol.com

FITCHBURG. *PACE - Parents Alliance for Catholic Education*, 124 Summer St., 01420. Tel: 978-665-9890; Fax: 978-665-9885.
E-mail: PACE@tiac.net
Web site: www.pacesite.org
Stephen A. Perla, Exec. Dir.

GARDNER. *House of Peace & Education, Inc.*, 20 Barthel Ave., 01440. Tel: 978-630-4752; Fax: 978-630-4752.
E-mail: hope@net1plus.com
Maxyne D. Schneider, S.S.J., Exec. Dir. Purpose: Neighborhood educational center for disadvantaged women and children.

PETERSHAM. *St. Bede's Publications*, 271 N. Main St., P.O. Box 545, 01366-0545. Tel: 978-724-3407; Fax: 978-724-3574. Mother Mary Clare Vincent, O.S.B.

St. Mary and St. Scholastica Church, Inc., 271 N. Main St., 01366-9503.

SPENCER. *Cistercian Publications, Inc.*, St. Joseph's Abbey, 01562. Tel: 508-885-8730; Fax: 508-885-4687.
E-mail: trappist@ultranet.com
Web site: www.spencerabbey.org/cistpub
Dr. Ernst Breisach, Pres.; Dr. E. Rozanne Elder, Exec. Vice Pres. & Mng. Editor; Rev. M. Basil Pennington, O.C.S.O., Sec.

WHITINSVILLE. *St. Camillus Institute, Inc.*, 447 Hill St., 01588. Tel: 617-234-7306. Very Rev. William F. Cronin, O.S.Cam., Pres. Order of the Servants of the Sick (St. Camillus).

RELIGIOUS INSTITUTES OF MEN REPRESENTED IN THE DIOCESE

For further details refer to the corresponding bracketed number in the Religious Institutes of Men or Women section.

[0130]—*Assumptionists.*—A.A.

[0200]—*Benedictine Monks.* (Petersham; Still River).—O.S.B.

[1350]—*Brothers of St. Francis Xavier.*—C.F.X.

[0350]—*Cistercians Order of the Strict Observance (Trappists).*—O.C.S.O.

[0790]—*Congregation of Maronite Monks.*—O.Mar.

[1000]—*Congregation of the Passion.*—C.P.
[0690]—*Jesuit Fathers and Brothers.*—S.J.
[0740]—*Marian Fathers.*—M.I.C.
[0720]—*Missionaries of Our Lady of LaSalette.* (Seven Dolors Prov.).—M.S.
[0240]—*Order of St. Camilus - Camillian Fathers and Brothers.*—O.S.Cam.
[1280]—*Stigmatine Fathers and Brothers.*—C.S.S.

RELIGIOUS INSTITUTES OF WOMEN REPRESENTED IN THE DIOCESE

[0230]—*Benedictine Sisters of Pontifical Jurisdiction.* (Petersham; Rutland; Eau Clare, WI).—O.S.B.
[0192]—*Carmelite Sisters of the Eucharist, Inc.*—C.S.E.
[0820]—*Daughters of the Holy Spirit.*—D.H.S.
[1070-06]—*Dominican Sisters.* (Newburgh, NY).—O.P.
[1170]—*Felician Sisters.*—C.S.S.F.
[2575]—*Institute of the Sisters of Mercy of the Americas.* (New York, NY).—R.S.M.
[2280]—*Little Franciscans of Mary.*—P.F.M.
[2310]—*Little Sisters of the Assumption.*—L.S.A.
[2790]—*Missionary Servants of the Most Blessed Trinity.*—M.S.B.T.
[2420]—*Missionary Sisters of the Society of Mary (Marist).*—S.M.S.M.
[3390]—*Religious of the Assumption.*—R.A.
[2070]—*Religious of the Holy Union of the Sacred Hearts.*—S.U.S.C.
[4180]—*Religious Venerini Sisters.*—M.P.V.
[]—*Sisters Oblates to Divine Love.*—R.O.D.A.
[3000]—*Sisters of Notre Dame de Namur.* (Boston, Ipswich, Japan and Connecticut Provs.).—S.N.D.deN.
[3340]—*Sisters of Providence.*—S.P.
[3720]—*Sisters of Saint Anne.*—S.S.A.
[1650]—*The Sisters of St. Francis of Philadelphia.*—O.S.F.
[3830-01]—*Sisters of St. Joseph.* (Boston, Brighton).—C.S.J.
[3830-16]—*Sisters of St. Joseph.*—S.S.J.
[3815]—*Sisters of Ste. Jeanne D'Arc.*—S.J.A.
[0150]—*Sisters of the Assumption.*—S.A.S.V.
[1970]—*Sisters of the Holy Family of Nazareth.*—C.S.F.N.
[3310]—*Sisters of the Presentation of Mary.*—P.M.
[3320]—*Sisters of the Presentation of the B.V.M.*—P.B.V.M.
[4230]—*Xaverian Missionary Society of Mary, Inc..*—X.M.M.

DIOCESAN CEMETERIES

WORCESTER. *St. John's.*

NECROLOGY

† Moynahan, Joseph A., Worcester, St. Christopher Parish. —Died Mar. 13, 2000.
† Poulin, Robert P., Southbridge, Notre Dame Parish. —Died Sept. 23, 2000.

Diocese of Yakima

(Dioecesis Yakimensis)

Most Reverend

CARLOS A. SEVILLA, S.J., D.D.

Bishop of Yakima; ordained June 3, 1966; appointed Auxiliary Bishop of San Francisco December 6, 1988; Episcopal ordination January 25, 1989; appointed Bishop of Yakima December 31, 1996; installed February 17, 1997. *Address all correspondence to: 5301-A Tieton Dr., Yakima, WA, 98908.*

Pastoral Office (Chancery): 5301-A Tieton Dr., Yakima, WA, 98908. Tel.: 509-965-7117; Fax: 509-966-8334.

E-mail address: dioyak@televar.com

ESTABLISHED JUNE 23, 1951.

Square Miles 17,787.

Legal Title: Corporation of the Catholic Bishop of Yakima.

Comprises the following Counties in the State of Washington: Benton, Chelan, Douglas, Grant, Kittitas, Klickitat and Yakima.

For legal titles of parishes and diocesan institutions, consult the Pastoral Office.

STATISTICAL OVERVIEW

Personnel	
Bishop	1
Priests: Diocesan Active in Diocese	42
Priests: Active Outside Diocese	9
Priests: Retired, Sick or Absent	14
Number of Diocesan Priests	65
Religious Priests in Diocese	11
Extern Priests in Diocese	6
Ordinations:	
Diocesan Priests	3
Permanent Deacons in Diocese	25
Total Brothers	8
Total Sisters	55
Parishes	
Parishes	41
With Resident Pastor:	
Resident Diocesan Priests	37
Resident Religious Priests	4
Missions	4
Pastoral Centers	2
Professional Ministry Personnel:	
Sisters	12
Lay Ministers	14
Welfare	
Catholic Hospitals	3
Total Assisted	305,306
Day Care and Extended Day Care Centers	2
Total Assisted	391
Special Centers for Social Services	5
Total Assisted	36,570
Educational	
Diocesan Students in Other Seminaries	23
Total Seminarians	23
High Schools, Private	1
Total Students	140
Elementary Schools, Diocesan and Parish	6
Total Students	1,888
Elementary Schools, Private	1
Total Students	135
Catechesis/Religious Education:	
High School Students	2,031
Elementary Students	5,815
Total Students Under Catholic Instruction	10,032
Teachers in the Diocese:	
Brothers	8
Sisters	5
Lay Teachers	117
Vital Statistics	
Receptions into the Church:	
Infant Baptism Totals	3,312
Adult Baptism Totals	135
Received into Full Communion	122
First Communions	2,161
Confirmations	933
Marriages:	
Catholic	417
Interfaith	176
Total Marriages	593
Deaths	443
Total Catholic Population	62,587
Total Population	461,600

Former Bishops—Most Rev. JOSEPH P. DOUGHERTY, D.D., First Bishop of Yakima; ord. June 14, 1930; appt. July 9, 1951; cons. Sept. 26, 1951; resigned Feb. 5, 1969; died July 10, 1970.—Most Rev. CORNELIUS M. POWER, D.D., Second Bishop of Yakima; ord. June 3, 1939; appt. Feb. 5, 1969; cons. May 1, 1969; elevated to Metropolitan See of Portland in Oregon, Jan. 24, 1974; died May 22, 1997.—Most Rev. NICOLAS E. WALSH, D.D., Third Bishop of Yakima; ord. June 6, 1942; appt. Sept. 5, 1974; cons. Oct. 28, 1974; installed Oct. 30, 1974; transferred to Archdiocese of Seattle as Auxiliary Bishop, Aug. 10, 1976; resigned Sept. 6, 1983; died April 22, 1997.—Most Rev. WILLIAM S. SKYLSTAD, D.D., Fourth Bishop of Yakima; ord. May 21, 1960; appt. Feb. 22, 1977; cons. May 12, 1977; transferred to Spokane as Bishop of Spokane, April 17, 1990.—Most Rev. FRANCIS E. GEORGE, O.M.I., Ph.D., S.T.D., Fifth Bishop of Yakima; ord. Dec. 21, 1963; appt. July 10, 1990; cons. Sept. 21, 1990; appt. Metropolitan See of Portland in Oregon, April 30, 1996; appt. Metropolitan See of Chicago, April 8, 1997; created Cardinal Priest, Feb. 21, 1998.

Pastoral Office (Chancery)—5301-A Tieton Dr., Yakima, 98908. Tel: 509-965-7117; Fax: 509-966-8334.

Vicar General—Rev. Msgr. PERRON J. AUVE, *5301-A Tieton Dr., Yakima, 98908-3493.*

Vicar for Priests—Rev. Msgr. JOHN J. MCDONNELL; Rev. MARIO A. SALAZAR.

Chancellor and Moderator of the Curia—Very Rev. RONALD W. METHA.

Vice-Chancellor—Mrs. GAYLE A. MILLER.

Diocesan Tribunal—5301-D Tieton Dr., Yakima, 98908. Tel: 509-965-7123.

Judicial Vicar—Very Rev. MICHAEL J. IBACH, J.C.L.

Adjutant Judicial Vicar—Very Rev. Sir JOHN F. HENEGHAN, J.C.L.

Bilingual Administrator—Mrs. ANGELITA T. SALDIVAR.

Judges—Very Rev. MICHAEL J. IBACH, J.C.L.; Very Rev. Sir JOHN F. HENEGHAN, J.C.L.; Rev. JOSE JOAQUIN ESTRADA, J.C.L.

Defenders of the Bond—Rev. Msgr. PERRON J. AUVE; Rev. Msgr. JOHN A. ECKER; Revs. THOMAS C. CHAMPOUX; RICHARD A. WUERTZ; SALOMON COVARRUBIAS-PINA; Mrs. MATILDA M. SMITH.

Advocates—Clergy and pastoral ministers by appointment.

Notaries—Rev. ANTONIO CASTANEDA; Miss ELIZABETH CASTRO; Mrs. EILEEN WALKER.

Diocesan Consultors—Rev. OSMAR AGUIRRE; Rev. Msgr. PERRON J. AUVE; Rev. THOMAS C. CHAMPOUX; Rev. Msgr. JOHN A. ECKER; Very Rev. RONALD W. METHA; Revs. JOSE DE JESUS RAMIREZ; RICHARD D. SEDLACEK; RICHARD A. WUERTZ.

Diocesan Offices, Commissions, Committees

Campaign for Human Development—Mr. JOHN L. YOUNG, *5301-C Tieton Dr., Yakima, 98908.*

Catholic Charities—Mr. JOHN L. YOUNG, Exec. Dir., Office: *5301-C Tieton Dr., Yakima, 98908.* Tel: 509-965-7100.

Catholic Women, Council of—Rev. SEAMUS KERR, *323 "D" St., Ephrata, 98823.* Tel: 509-754-3640.

Charismatic Renewal, English—Rev. Msgr. PERRON J. AUVE, Liaison, *5301-A Tieton Dr., Yakima, 98908.* Tel: 509-965-7117.

Charismatic Renewal, Spanish—Rev. MANUEL MENDEZ, *520 S. Garfield, Kennewick, 99336.* Tel: 509-586-3820.

Conciliation Board—Rev. THOMAS C. CHAMPOUX; Mr. PAT COCKRILL; Mrs. MARY KOWALSKI; Mrs. TRUDY LEDWICH; Mrs. SANDY SEWARD, *5301-C Tieton Dr., Yakima, 98908.* Tel: 509-965-7100.

Cursillo, English—Rev. JOHN G. O'SHEA, *7409 W. Clearwater, Kennewick, 99336.* Tel: 509-735-8558.

Spanish—Deacon FRANK MARTINEZ, *3790 Rd. 10.4 S.W., Royal City, 99357.* Tel: 509-346-9536. VIOLA MATA, *1706 Vancouver, Kennewick, 99337.* Tel: 509-586-9995.

Development Office / Stewardship—Mr. DONALD M. KLIPPSTEIN, Dir., *5301-A Tieton Dr., Yakima, 98908.* Tel: 509-965-7117.

Diocesan Coordinator for Health Affairs—Rev. THOMAS C. CHAMPOUX, *5301-C Tieton Dr., Yakima, 98908.* Tel: 509-965-7100.

Diocesan Commission for the Catechumenate—Mr. PETE BRAUN, Chm.; Mrs. LUCY GARCIA; Mrs. MARY HAMELIN; KAY SHEPARD; Mrs. JACQUE LOYND; Deacon ROBERT SCHROM; Mrs. AUROLYN WATLAMET.

Diocesan Commission on Public Worship—Revs. JUAN FLORES; THOMAS S. KUYKENDALL, Chm.; Mrs. PAT MANDELAS; Deacon RAY MILLER; DAVID SIEVERS; Sr. MARIA DE JESUS YBARRA, O.P.

Diocesan Pastoral Council—Deacon BERNEY ALVARADO; Rev. Msgr. DESMOND P. DILLON; EVANGELINA AGUILAR; ANDRES ESCAMILLA; PAMELA FABELLA; FRED DEL POZO; RANULFO PEREZ; TOM MURPHY; Most Rev. CARLOS A. SEVILLA, S.J.; SANDY SEWARD; MARY KAY RAZEY; DOUG STETNER; KAY SHEPARD; Sr. PATRICIA WINDER, M.S.B.T.; BARBARA ROOS; Sr. MARIA ELENA CASILLAS, M.D.P.V.M.

Ecumenical Liaison—Rev. Msgr. JOHN A. ECKER, *15 S. 12th Ave., Yakima, 98902.* Tel: 509-575-3713.

Engaged Encounter—Mrs. DeNeen Koch; Mr. Michael Koch, *2650 Eastwood, Richland, 99352.* Tel: 509-627-0783.

Engaged Encounter, Spanish—Sr. Maria de Jesus Ybarra, O.P., *5301-B Tieton Dr., Yakima, 98908.* Tel: 509-965-7110.

Diocesan Finance Council—Most Rev. Carlos A. Sevilla, S.J.; Rev. Msgr. Perron J. Auve, *Pastoral Center, 5301-A Tieton Dr., Yakima, 98908.* Very Rev. Ronald W. Metha, *5301-A Tieton Dr., Yakima, 98908.* Mr. Robert Cash; Mr. Nicanor DeLeon; Ms. Ann Drader; Mr. Richard Gasseling; Mrs. Colleen Kelleher; Mr. Donald M. Klippstein; Mrs. Pat Myers; Mr. Alex Santillanes; Rev. Dan Dufner; Jeff Peterson, Consultant; Mrs. Peggy Roy; Mr. Larry Wright.

Marriage Encounter, English—Mrs. Erin Gaston; Mr. Jim Gaston, *2657 Quaterhorse Way, Richland, 99352.* Tel: 509-627-6386.

Spanish—Rev. Jose de Jesus Ramirez, *P.O. Box 340, Royal City, 99357-0340.* Tel: 509-346-2730.

Ministry & Education Center—Mrs. Cathy Colver, Admin. & Supt. of Schools, *5301-B Tieton Dr., Yakima, 98908.* Tel: 509-965-7110.

Hispanic Religious Education and Ministry Formation—Sr. Maria de Jesus Ybarra, O.P., Dir.

Evangelization and Lay Formation, Deacon Formation, Pastoral Council, Small Church Communities—Mr. Robert Fontana, Dir.

Family Ministries—Sr. Susanne Thibault, M.S.B.T., *5301-C Tieton Dr., Yakima, 98908-3493.* Tel: 509-965-7100.

Religious Education—Ms. Ree Kearns, Dir.

Youth / Young Adult Director—Mr. Chris Berghout.

Youth / Young Adult Hispanic Ministry—Mr. Carlos Carrillo.

Deacon Director—Deacon Frank Martinez, *3790 Rd. 10.4 S.W., Royal City, 99357.* Tel: 509-346-9536.

Personnel Board—Most Rev. Carlos A. Sevilla, S.J.; Rev. Msgr. Perron J. Auve; Rev. Msgr. John J. McDonnell; Rev. Msgr. John A. Ecker; Very Rev. Ronald W. Metha; Revs. Thomas C. Champoux; Argemiro Orozco; Lawrence T. Reilly; Mario A. Salazar.

Press (Central Washington Catholic)—Very Rev. Ronald W. Metha, Exec. Editor; Mrs. Jonella Leadon, Mng. Editor, *5301-A Tieton Dr., Yakima, 98908.* Tel: 509-965-7117.

Presbyteral Council Executive Committee—Most Rev. Carlos A. Sevilla, S.J.; Rev. Osmar Aguirre; Rev. Msgr. Perron J. Auve; Revs. Salomon Covarrubias-Pina; Ricardo Villarreal; Thomas Kuykendall; Very Rev. Ronald W. Metha; Revs. John Morse, S.J.; John Murtagh; Argemiro Orozco; Ronald J. Patnode; Richard Sedlacek; John Shaw.

Native American Ministries—Sr. Margaret Ball, S.N.J.M., *109 N. E St., Toppenish, 98948.* Tel: 509-877-2751.

Natural Family Planning—Mrs. Jane Villanueva, *5301-B Tieton Dr., Yakima, 98908.* Tel: 509-965-7110.

Jail Ministry—Rev. George Purdy, S.J., *P.O. Box 128, Naches, 98937.* Tel: 509-653-2534. Deacon Nestor Chavez, *710 E. Race St., Yakima, 98901.*

Retreat Center—

St. Peter Retreat Center—Mr. Bill Hudson, Dir., *15880 Summitview Rd., Cowiche, 98923.* Tel: 509-678-4935.

Respect Life Committee—Mr. Ruben Beedle; Rev. Thomas C. Champoux; Mrs. Barb Cruz; Mr. Bill Fromherz; Mr. Chuck Gonsalez; Mrs. Dee Gonsalez; Dr. Anne Nealen; Mrs. Susan Schwaegler; Mrs. Dee Schwab; Mrs. Cheri Vause; Mrs. Jane Villanueva; Sr. Maria de Jesus Ybarra, O.P., *5301-B Tieton Dr., Yakima, 98908.* Tel: 509-965-7110.

Scouting—Rev. William E. Shaw, Chap., *P.O. Box 567, Zillah, 98953.* Tel: 509-829-5433. Deacon Bill Dronen, Chm.; Mr. Carlos Carrillo; Mr. Marc Desgroseillier; Mrs. Cindy Desgroseillier; Mrs. Charlene Dronen; Mrs. Iliana Garza; Mr. John Warren.

Social Justice Commission—Rev. Osmar Aguirre; Sr. Maria De Jesus Ybarra, O.P.; Mrs. Jane Villanueva; Mr. John Young; Mr. Chris Cassidy; Mrs. Terri Aguilera-Flemming; Mr. Frank McGree; Mr. Vic Rohret; Sr. Graciela Rosas, M.D.P.V.M.; Mrs. Yvonne Smith, *5301-B Tieton Dr., Yakima, 98908.* Tel: 509-965-7110.

Hispanic Ministries—Rev. Argemiro Orozco, Dir., *210 N. Beech, Toppenish, 98948.* Tel: 509-865-4040.

St. Vincent de Paul Society—Rev. Thomas C. Champoux, Spirtual Dir., *1126 Long Ave., Richland, 99352.* Tel: 509-946-1675. Amey Betancourt, Exec. Dir., *305 North Ave., Sunnyside, 98944.* Tel: 509-837-7968.

Vocations—Rev. Msgr. John A. Ecker, Dir., *15 S. 12th Ave., Yakima, 98902.* Tel: 509-575-3713.

CLERGY, PARISHES, MISSIONS AND PAROCHIAL SCHOOLS

CITY OF YAKIMA
(Yakima County)

1—St. Paul Cathedral (1914), Rev. Msgr. John A. Ecker; Revs. Michael Brzezowski; Isaias Hernandez; Deacon Ray Miller; Alma Ahlbrecht, Pastoral Assoc.
Res., 15 S. 12th Ave., 98902. Tel: 509-575-3713; Fax: 509-453-7497. [CEM]
School—(Grades K-8) 1214 W. Chestnut Ave., 98902. Tel: 509-575-5604; Fax: 509-577-8817.
Lay Teachers 20; Students 337.
Catholic Student Center—810 S. 16th Ave., 98902. Tel: 509-249-6238.
Catechesis / Religious Programs—Students 500.

2—Holy Family (1959), Rev. John J. Murtagh; Rev. Msgr. John J. McDonnell; Rev. Gary Desharnais; Deacons John Cornell; Jim Kramper.
Res., 5315 Tieton Dr., 98908. Tel: 509-966-0830; Fax: 509-965-1742.
Catechesis / Religious Programs—Tel: 509-966-0788; Fax: 509-965-0288.
Students 518.
Mission—Yakima, Yakima Co., Ahtanum, 17740 Ahtanum Rd., 98908. Tel: 509-966-0865.

3—Holy Redeemer (1962), Revs. Donal P. Kennedy; Roberto B. Saenz, S.J., Admin.; Deacon Duane Berger.
Res., 1609 Landon Ave., 98902. Tel: 509-248-2241; Fax: 509-457-3312. [JC]
Catechesis / Religious Programs—Tel: 509-457-3435.
Students 160.

4—St. Joseph's, Revs. Patrick C. Carroll, S.J.; Thomas R. Royce, S.J.; William Vogel, S.J.; Mary E. Bischoff, Admin. In res., Revs. Neill R. Meany, S.J.; Charles E. Schmitz, S.J.
212 N. 4th St., 98901-2499. Tel: 509-248-1911; Fax: 509-248-2604.
School—St. Joseph/Marquette, Tel: 509-575-5555; Fax: 509-457-5621.
Sisters of Providence 2; Lay Teachers 26; Students 400.
Catechesis / Religious Programs—Students 321.

OUTSIDE THE CITY OF YAKIMA

Benton City, Benton Co., St. Frances Xavier Cabrini (1963), Rev. James Spezzano.
Mailing Address: P.O. Box 179, 99320-0179. Fax: 509-588-3636.
Church—Horn Rd., 99320. Tel: 509-588-3636.
Catechesis / Religious Programs—Tel: 509-588-4235.
Students 125.

Bridgeport, Douglas Co., St. Anne's (1964) (Hispanic-Mexican), Rev. Daniel G. Dufner.
P.O. Box 1089, Chelan, 98816-1089. Tel: 509-682-5730.
Catechesis / Religious Programs—Students 26.
Mission—Mansfield, Douglas Co., St. Mary, (1909).

Cashmere, Chelan Co., St. Francis Xavier (1915), Rev. Juan Flores; Deacon Bill Dronen.
Res., 307 Angier, 98815. Tel: 509-782-2643; Fax: 509-782-2686.
Catechesis / Religious Programs—Tel: 509-782-1277.
Students 84.

Chelan, Chelan Co., St. Francis de Sales (1904), Revs. Richard A. Wuertz Tel: 509-682-2433; Daniel G. Dufner, Hispanic Ministry, Tel: 509-682-5730.
215 W. Allen Ave., P.O. Box 1089, 98816-1089. Tel: 509-682-2433; Fax: 509-682-9147.; 621 Cedar St., P.O. Box 1089, 98816-1089.
Catechesis / Religious Programs—Students 180.

Cle Elum, Upper Kittitas Co., St. John the Baptist (1913), Rev. Ronald J. Patnode.
Office: 303 W. 2nd St., 98922. Tel: 509-674-2531; Fax: 509-674-1894.
Catechesis / Religious Programs—D.R.E. Larry Cates; Helen Wanachek.
Students 51.

Cowiche, Yakima Co., St. Peter's (1959) (Spanish), Rev. David J. Jimenez; Deacon Walter A. Burnham.
Res., 15880 Summitview Rd., 98923. Tel: 509-678-4164.
Catechesis / Religious Programs—Fax: 509-678-4164.
Students 62.

East Wenatchee, Douglas Co., Holy Apostles (1962), Revs. Maurice F. Peterson; Alvaro Diez; Deacon Bill Loranger.
Res., P.O. Box 7279, 98802. Tel: 509-884-5444; Fax: 509-886-3424.
Catechesis / Religious Programs—1315 N.E. 8th St., 98801. Tel: 509-884-5444. D.R.E.: Debbie Patterson; Kristie Tuttle.
Students 95.

Ellensburg, Kittitas Co., St. Andrew's (1884), Rev. Msgr. Perron Joseph Auve; Deacon Jack Spence.
Res., 401 S. Willow St., 98926. Tel: 509-962-9819; Fax: 509-962-9846. [CEM]
Catechesis / Religious Programs—Students 182.

Ephrata, Grant Co., St. Rose of Lima (1941), Rev. Richard Mel House.
Parish Office: 323 D St., S.W., 98823. Tel: 509-754-3640; Fax: 509-754-4064. [CEM]
School—(Grades PreK-6) 520 S.E. Blvd., 98823. Tel: 509-754-4901; Fax: 509-754-9274.
Lay Teachers 6; Students 85.
Catechesis / Religious Programs—Students 130.

Goldendale, Klickitat Co., Holy Trinity (1884), Rev. William Byron.
Res., 210 S. Schuster St., 98620. Tel: 509-773-4516; Fax: 509-773-6983. [CEM]
Catechesis / Religious Programs—Lynette Anderson, D.R.E.
Students 30.

Grand Coulee, Grant Co., St. Henry's (1955), Rev. Robert P. Himes; Deacon Dan Farrell.
Res., 590 Grand Coulee Ave. W., P.O. Box P, 99133. Tel: 509-633-1180; Fax: 509-633-6859. [JC]
Catechesis / Religious Programs—Students 50.

Grandview, Yakima Co., Blessed Sacrament (1954), Revs. Salomon Covarrubras-Pina; John C. Vogl.
Res., 1201 Missouri, 98930. Tel: 509-882-1657; Fax: 509-882-1107.
Catechesis / Religious Programs—Students 219.

Granger, Yakima Co., Our Lady of Guadalupe (1966) (Hispanic), Rev. Mario P. Salazar; Deacon John Kassinger.
Res., 608 Ave. E., P.O. Box 308, 98932. Tel: 509-854-1558; Fax: 509-854-7326. [JC]
Catechesis / Religious Programs—Tel: 509-854-1964.
Students 120.

Hartline, Grant Co., St. Patrick's (1955). Served from St. Henry's, P.O. Box P, Grand Coulee 99133. Revs. Robert P. Himes; Daniel J. Farrell.
P.O. Box 925, Coulee City, 99115. Tel: 509-633-1180; Fax: 509-633-6859. [CEM]
Catechesis / Religious Programs—Students 24.
Mission—Coulee City, Grant Co., Holy Angels, Grand Coulee, 99133.

Kennewick, Benton Co., Holy Spirit (1980), Rev. John G. O'Shea; Deacon John E. Powers.
Office: 7409 W. Clearwater, 99336. Tel: 509-735-8558; Fax: 509-735-8559.
Catechesis / Religious Programs—D.R.E.: Lori Casey; Isabelle Ryan.
Students 258.

St. Joseph's (1911), Revs. Richard D. Sedlacek; Manuel Mendez; Sr. Robert Joseph, C.S.J., Pastoral Assoc.; Deacons William Mich; Gilberto Garcia. In res., Rev. Msgr. Desmond P. Dillon.
Res., 520 S. Garfield, 99336. Tel: 509-586-3820; Fax: 509-586-3558.
School—901 W. 4th Ave., 99336. Tel: 509-586-0481; Fax: 509-585-9781.
Sisters of St. Joseph of Carondelet 3; Lay Teachers 15; Students 458.
Catechesis / Religious Programs—Tel: 509-582-8460.
Students 340.

Leavenworth, Chelan Co., Our Lady of the Snows (1912), Rev. Juan Flores; Deacon Don Griek.
Res., 145 Wheeler St., 98826. Tel: 509-548-5119; Fax: 509-548-5051.
Catechesis / Religious Programs—Tel: 509-548-8314.
Students 42.

Mabton, Yakima Co., Immaculate Conception (1910), Mailing Address: P.O. Box 275, 98935. Tel: 509-882-1657; Fax: 509-882-1107.
Res., 1201 Missouri, Grandview, 98930. Tel: 509-882-1657; Fax: 509-882-1107.
Catechesis / Religious Programs—Students 70.

Mattawa, Grant Co., Our Lady of the Desert (1987), Rev. Jose de Loza.
Mailing Address: P.O. Box 2268, 99349. Tel: 509-932-5424; Fax: 509-932-5424. [JC]
Catechesis / Religious Programs—Students 90.

Moses Lake, Grant Co., Our Lady of Fatima (1955), Revs. John Morse, S.J.; Antonio Castaneda, Pastoral Assoc.; Deacon Robert Schrom. In res., Rev. Msgr. Martin O. Skehan, (Retired).
Res., 318 W. Northshore Dr., 98837. Tel: 509-765-6729; Fax: 509-765-0114.

Parish Center—200 Dale Rd., 98837. Tel: 509-766-5912.
Catechesis/Religious Programs—Elsa Meservy, D.R.E.
Students 241.

Moxee City, Yakima Co., Holy Rosary (1900) (French-Canadian), Rev. Thomas V. Lane. In res., Rev. Msgr. Edmund G. McGrath, (Retired).
Res., 201 N. Iler., P.O. Box 279, Moxee, 98936. Tel: 509-453-4061; Fax: 509-576-6290. [CEM]
Catechesis/Religious Programs—Tel: 509-453-6754. Patricia Verhey, D.R.E.
Students 247.

Naches, Yakima Co., St. John's (1959), Rev. George Purdy, S.J.
Res., 204 Moxee Ave., P.O. Box 128, 98937. Tel: 509-653-2534; Fax: 509-653-2534.
Catechesis/Religious Programs—Students 22.

Prosser, Benton Co., Sacred Heart (1899), Rev. Francisco J. Hernandez.
Res., 1905 Highland Dr., 99350. Tel: 509-786-1783; Fax: 509-786-1747.
Catechesis/Religious Programs—Tel: 509-973-2265. D.R.E. Cynthia O'Brien, (English Program); Juanita Lopez, (Spanish Program), Tel: (509) 882-5460.
Students 350.

Quincy, Grant Co., St. Pius X (1955), Rev. Mario A. Salazar.
Res., 805 N. Central Ave., P.O. Box 308, 98848. Tel: 509-787-2622; 787-3116; Fax: 509-787-6068.
Catechesis/Religious Programs—D.R.E.: Kathleen Horning; Esperanza Hernandez, (Spanish).
Students 404.

Richland, Benton Co., Christ the King (1946), Revs. Thomas C. Champoux; Darell J. Mitchell; Deacons Robert DaValle; LeRoi Rice; Alfred Rizzo.
Office: 1126 Long Ave., 99352. Tel: 509-946-1675; Fax: 509-946-9940.
School—1122 Long Ave., 99352. Tel: 509-946-6158.
Lay Teachers 29; Students 449.
Catechesis/Religious Programs—Tel: 509-946-1154. Deacon LeRoi Rice, D.R.E.
Students 513.

Roslyn, Upper Kittitas Co., Immaculate Conception (1887), Rev. Ronald J. Patnode.
Mailing Address: 303 W. 2nd St., Cle Elum, 98922. Tel: 509-674-2531; Fax: 509-674-1894.
Res., 211 N. 8th St.
Catechesis/Religious Programs—Twinned with St. John the Baptist, Cle Elum.

Royal City, Grant Co., St. Michael the Archangel (1966), Rev. J. Jesus Ramirez; Deacon Francisco Martinez.
Res., 145 Daisy St., N.W., P.O. Box 340, 99357. Tel: 509-346-2730; Fax: 509-346-2901.
Catechesis/Religious Programs—Tel: 509-246-2730.
Students 61.

Selah, Yakima Co., Our Lady of Lourdes (1975), Very Rev. Michael J. Ibach.
Res., 1112 W. Fremont, 98942. Tel: 509-697-4633; Fax: 509-697-3134.
Catechesis/Religious Programs—Mary Payment, D.R.E.
Students 168.

Sunnyside, Yakima Co., St. Joseph's (1936), Revs. Osmar Aguirre; Felix Rodriquez.
Res., 920 S. 6th St., 98944. Tel: 509-837-2243; Fax: 509-837-7063.
Catechesis/Religious Programs—Tel: 509-839-4758.
Students 350.
Convent—Tel: 509-837-2242.
Missionary Daughters of the Most Pure Virgin Mary 4.

Toppenish, Yakima Co., St. Aloysius (1908), Revs. Argemiro Orozco, Hispanic Ministry; L. Michael Pope, S.J.; Deacon Berny Alvarado.
Mailing Address: 213 N. Beech St., 98948. Tel: 508-865-4725; Fax: 508-865-7882. [JC]
Religious Education Center—214 N. Beech St., 98948. Tel: 509-865-2565; 865-4725; 865-2380; Fax: 509-865-3462.
St. Vincent De Paul Center—11 S. B, 98948. Tel: 509-865-5311.
Catechesis/Religious Programs—Darlene Riojas, D.R.E.
Students 527.

Wapato, Yakima Co., St. Peter Claver (1908), Revs. William E. Shaw; Jose Joaquin Estrada (Columbia); Deacons John Kassinger; Antonio Osorio.
Res., 509 S. Satus Ave., 98951. Tel: 509-877-2813; Fax: 509-877-6207.
Catechesis/Religious Programs—Tel: 509-877-4881.
Students 450.

Warden, Grant Co., Queen of All Saints (1966), Revs. John Morse, S.J.; Antonio Castaneda, Pastoral Assoc.
318 W. Northshore Dr., Moses Lake, 98837. Tel: 509-765-6729; Fax: 509-765-0114.
Catechesis/Religious Programs—Tel: 509-349-2757.
Students 165.

Waterville, Douglas Co., St. Joseph's (1892), Rev. Bonifacio Salvana.
Res., Poplar St., P.O. Box 519, 98858. Tel: 509-745-8205. [CEM]
Catechesis/Religious Programs—Noreen Daling, D.R.E.
Students 62.

Wenatchee, Chelan Co., St. Joseph's (1903), Revs. Thomas Kuykendall; Ricardo A. Villarreal; Deacon Bill Osborn.
Res., 504 S. Chelan, P.O. Box 2138, 98807. Tel: 509-662-4569; Fax: 509-663-8437.
School—(Grades PreK-5). Tel: 509-663-2644; Fax: 509-663-8474.
Lay Teachers 9; Students 159.
Catechesis/Religious Programs—600 St. Joseph Pl., 98801.
Students 333.

White Salmon, Klickitat Co., St. Joseph (1912) (Spanish), Rev. Thomas S. Dahlquist.
Res., 240 N.W. Washington., P.O. Box 2049, 98672. Tel: 509-493-2828; Fax: 509-493-2828.
Catechesis/Religious Programs—Tel: 509-493-2961.
Students 66.

White Swan, Yakima Co., St. Mary's (1847) (Native American-Hispanic), Rev. John Shaw.
Res., P.O. Box 417, 98952. Tel: 509-874-2436; Fax: 509-874-2436. [CEM]
Catechesis/Religious Programs—Lola Sarsfield, D.R.E., Tel: 509-848-2371.
Students 105.

Zillah, Yakima Co., Resurrection (1963), Rev. Emmett Sarsfield. In res., Rev. Jorge Granados Lopez, Spanish Min., Tel: 509-829-5312.
Mailing Address: P.O. Box 567, 98953-0567. Tel: 509-829-5433.
Catechesis/Religious Programs—Tel: 509-829-6244. Betty Collins, D.R.E.
Students 125.

Special Assignment:
Reverend Fathers—
Bunnell, Thomas J., S.J., P.O. Box 4744, Tri Cities, WA 99302-4744
Minder, Kevin, Casa Santa Maria, Via dell'Umilta.30, Rome, 00187 Italy
Reilly, Lawrence T., c/o 5301-A Tieton Dr., Yakima, WA 98908

On Duty Outside the Diocese:
Reverend Fathers—
Cerezo, Alberto F., 11637 100th Ave., N.E., #C2W, Kirkland, WA 98034
Gallagher, Brian T., 55743 Navajo Tr., Yucca Valley, CA 92284
Kenna, Joseph J., 929 Lakefront Dr., Bowie, MD 20721
Keolker, Richard F., Mount Angel Seminary, 119 Anselm, St. Benedict, OR 97373
Norman, Gary, c/o St. Philip Bonitus, P.O.Box 827, Scobey, MT 59263
Sewvello, Robert, 2003 Woody Dr., #3, Billings, MT 59102

Military Chaplains:
Reverend Fathers—
Greene, Daniel P., V.A. Admin. Med. Ctr., Chaplain Serv., Bay Pines, FL 33744
House, Richard M., c/o St. Rose of Lima, 323 D St., Ephrata, WA 98823

Retired:
Reverend Monsignors—
Dillon, Desmond P., St. Joseph Parish, 520 S. Garfield, Kennewick, WA 99336
Marasciulo, John
McGrath, Edmund G., P.O. Box 279, Moxee City, WA 98936-0279
Skehan, Martin O., W. 318 Northshore Dr., Moses Lake, WA 98837
Reverend Fathers—
Byron, Patrick J., The Grotto, Pallashill, Pallasgreane, Limerick, Ireland
Camacho, Enrique, Apartado Postal 7 Cocula, Jalisco, CP 48500 Mexico
Dorian, Brendan, Duffy's Cross, Readpenny, Co. Louth, Ireland
Hannick, Anthony S., 1600 Roosmoor Pkwy., Walnut Creek, CA 94553
Heneghan, John F., Waverly Collacoon, Co. Mayo, Ireland
King, Anthony S., 5602 W. Chestnut Ave., Yakima, WA 98908
Shields, Robert J., 4602 Tieton Dr., Apt. P-74, Yakima, WA 98908
Tholen, John, 5301-A Tieton Dr., Yakima, WA 98908
Wawrzynski, Edward A., U.S.A.F.R., 5856 106th Ter. N., Pinellas Park, FL 34666

Permanent Deacons:
Alvarado, Berney, 15 S. Date St., Toppenish, WA 98948
Berger, Duane, 1706 Lower Ahtanum, Yakima, WA 98903
Burnham, Walter, 300 S. 76th Ave., #67, Yakima, WA 98908
Chavez, Nestor, 710 E. Race St., Yakima, WA 98901
Cornell, John, 2504 W. Chestnut, Yakima, WA 98902
DaValle, Robert, 1837 Marshall Ave., Richland, WA 99352
Dronen, Bill, 306 Railroad Ave., Cashmere, 98815
Garcia, Gilberto, 18 N. Mayfield, Kennewick, WA 99336
Griek, Don, P.O. Box 1023, Leavenworth, WA 98826
Henn, Thomas W., 22402 N. Vega Dr., Sun City, AZ 85375-2046
Kassinger, John, 1314 N. Ave., #4, Sunnyside, WA 98944
Kramper, James, 7304 Spokane St., Yakima, WA 98908
Loranger, Bill, 613 Briarwood Dr., East Wenatchee, WA 98802
Martinez, Frank, 3790 Rd. 10.4 S.W., Royal City, WA 99357
Mich, William, 601 N. Reed, Kennewick, WA 99336
Miller, Ray, 2412 W. Chestnut, Yakima, WA 98902
Osborn, Bill, 410 Cottage Ave., Cashmere, WA 98815
Osorio, Antonio, 14 S. I St., Toppenish, WA 98948
Powers, John, 3614 S. Green St., Kennewick, WA 99337
Reyna, Lupe, 1130 S. Grand, Moses Lake, WA 98837
Rice, LeRoi, 1845 Mahan Ave., Richland, WA 99352
Rizzo, Al, 135 MacArthur St., Richland, WA 99352
Schrom, Robert, 7240 Rd. 17, S.W., Royal City, WA 99357
Spence, Jack, 351 Hanson Rd., Ellensburg, WA 98926

INSTITUTIONS LOCATED IN THE DIOCESE

[A] COLLEGES AND UNIVERSITIES

TOPPENISH. *Heritage College*, 3240 Fort Rd., 98948. Tel: 509-865-2244; Fax: 509-865-4469.
Web site: www.heritage.edu
For a complete listing, refer to the Colleges and Universities section.

[B] HIGH SCHOOLS

UNION GAP. *La Salle High School*, 3000 Lightning Way, 98903. Tel: 509-225-2900; Fax: 509-225-2950.
E-mail: lasallehs@aol.com
Web site: www.lasallehs.net
Timothy McGree, Pres.; Bro. Daniel Morgan, F.S.C., Prin. Brothers 5; Sisters 1; Lay Teachers 5; Total Staff 14; Students 140.

[C] ELEMENTARY SCHOOLS

SUNNYSIDE. *St. Joseph School*. (Grades K-8), 920 S. 6th St., 98944. Tel: 509-839-2241; Fax: 509-839-7171.
E-mail: st_joseph@Futurelink.net
Brothers of the Christian Schools. Bro. Robb Wallace, Prin. Lay Teachers 7; Religious Brothers 3; Students 125.

[D] HOSPITALS

YAKIMA. *Providence Yakima Medical Center*, 110 S. 9th Ave., 98902. Tel: 509-575-5000; Fax: 509-454-6193
For a complete listing, refer to the Hospitals section.

RICHLAND. *Lourdes Counseling Center*, 1175 Carondelet Dr., 99352. Tel: 509-943-9104; Fax: 509-943-7206.
E-mail: bmead@lourdesonline.org
Web site: lourdesonline.org
For a complete listing, refer to the Hospitals section.

TOPPENISH. *Providence Hospital*, 504 W. 4th Ave., P.O. Box 672, 98948. Tel: 509-865-3105; Fax: 509-865-1519.
Web site: www.providence.org
For a complete listing, refer to the Hospitals section.

[E] CATHOLIC SOCIAL SERVICE CATHOLIC CHARITIES

YAKIMA. *Carroll Children's Center*, 5301 Tieton Dr., Ste. C, 98908. Tel: 509-965-7104; Fax: 509-966-9750. Maureen Mould, Dir. Capacity 140; Total Assisted 320; Total Staff 25.

Catholic Charities of the Diocese of Yakima, 5301-C Tieton Dr., 98908. Tel: 509-965-7100; Fax: 509-966-9750. Mr. John L. Young, Exec. Dir.

Catholic Family and Child Service, 5301 Tieton Dr., Ste. C, 98908. Tel: 509-965-7100; Fax: 509-966-9750. Mrs. Darlene Darnell, M.S.W., Agency Dir. Total Assisted 26,700; Total Staff 100.

Child Care Nutrition, P.O. Box 2399, 98908. Tel: 509-965-7107; Fax: 509-965-7108.

St. Vincent de Paul Store, 2629 S. First St., 98903. Tel: 509-457-5111. Mr. Frank McGree, Mgr. (Of All Stores in Diocese). Total Staff 14.

CHELAN. *St. Vincent de Paul Store*, 404 E. Woodin, P.O. Box 2387, 98816. Tel: 509-682-3655.

ELLENSBURG. *St. Vincent de Paul Store*, 1200 Canyon St., 98926. Tel: 509-925-2167. Total Staff 9.

GRANDVIEW. *Catholic Family and Child Service*, 322 Division, P.O. Box 22, 98930. Tel: 509-882-3050. Total Assisted 1,200; Total Staff 6.

KENNEWICK. *St. Vincent de Paul Store*, 1401 W. Kennewick Ave., 99336. Tel: 509-586-1053; Fax: 509-586-6910.

MOSES LAKE. *Catholic Family and Child Service of Moses Lake-Ephrata*, 414 Burress St., 98837. Tel: 509-765-1875; Fax: 509-766-1836. Total Assisted 500; Total Staff 5.

RICHLAND. *Catholic Family and Child Service*, 2139 Van Giesen, P.O. Box 1504, 99352. Tel: 509-946-4645; Fax: 509-943-2068.
E-mail: jkdcf@owt.com
Judith Dirks, Branch Dir. Total Assisted 2,250; Total Staff 35.

SUNNYSIDE. *St. Vincent de Paul Store*, 305 North Ave., 98944. Tel: 509-837-2055; Fax: 509-837-2033.
E-mail: svdp@televar.com
Total Staff 13.

WENATCHEE. *Catholic Family and Child Service*, Morris Bldg., No. 320, 23 S. Wenatchee Ave., # 320, 98801. Tel: 509-662-6761; Fax: 509-663-3182.
E-mail: stryon@cfcs.net
Total Assisted 5,920; Total Staff 28.

St. Vincent de Paul Store, 330 S. Wenatchee Ave., 98801. Tel: 509-662-6010; Fax: 509-662-2810. Total Staff 8.

[F] RETIREMENT HOMES

YAKIMA.
The Gamelin Association-Providence House, 314 N. 4th St., 98901-2459. Tel: 509-452-5017; Fax: 509-452-1947.
E-mail: drrodrigues@providence.org
Web site: www.seniorhousing.net/ad/providence house
Sr. Dawn Rodrigues, Dir. Low income housing for elderly.

[G] VOLUNTEER SERVICES

YAKIMA. *Holy Family Parish Conference*, 5315 Tieton Dr., 98908. Tel: 509-966-0830; Fax: 509-965-1742.

Holy Redeemer Parish Conference, 1609 Landon Ave., 98902. Tel: 509-248-2241; Fax: 509-457-3312. Raymond Faith, Pres.

St. Joseph's Parish Conference, 212 N. 4th St., 98901. Tel: 509-248-1911; Fax: 509-248-2604. Mrs. O. Gress, Pres.

St. Paul's Parish Conference, 15 S. 12th Ave., 98902. Tel: 509-575-3713; Fax: 509-453-7497.
E-mail: stpaul@wolfenet.com
Dave Uhlman, Pres.; Fred Schilling, Treas.

Society of St. Vincent de Paul, Particular Council of Yakima, 2629 S. First St., 98903. Tom Gehlen, Pres. Total Staff 13.

EAST WENATCHEE. *Holy Apostles Parish Conference*, P.O. Box 7279, 98801. Tel: 509-884-5444; Fax: 509-886-3424. Chris McCarthy, Pres.

KENNEWICK. *St. Joseph Parish Conference*, 520 S. Garfield, 99336. Tel: 509-586-3820; Fax: 509-586-3558.
E-mail: cp1353@3-cities.com
Web site: cbvcp.com/stjocath/default.htm
Dick McAloon, Pres.

MOSES LAKE. *Our Lady of Fatima Parish Conference*, W. 318 Northshore Dr., 98837. Tel: 509-765-6729; Fax: 509-765-0114.
E-mail: jmorse@nwi.net
Wayne Vadnais, Pres.

RICHLAND. *Christ the King Parish Conference*, 1126 Long Ave., 99352. Tel: 509-946-1675; Fax: 509-946-9940.
E-mail: ckparish@gte.net
Web site: home1.gte.net/ckparish
Bob Morford, Pres.

TOPPENISH. *St. Aloysius Parish Conference*, 213 N. Beech St., 98948. Tel: 509-865-4725; Fax: 509-865-7882. Adrianna Hede, Pres.

St. Vincent de Paul Center, 213 N. Beech St., 98948. Tel: 509-865-5311; Fax: 509-865-7882. 11 S. B St., 98948. Tel: 509-865-5311. Adriana Hede, Dir. Total Assisted 5,771; Total Staff 1.

WENATCHEE. *St. Joseph Parish Conference, St Vincent de Paul*, 504 S. Chelan, 98801. Tel: 509-662-4569. V. E. Houck, Pres.

[H] RETREAT HOUSES

COWICHE. *St. Peter the Apostle Retreat Center*, 15880 Summitview Rd., 98923. Tel: 509-678-4935; Fax: 509-678-8758.
E-mail: stpetersretreat@juno.com
William D. Hudson, Admin. Dir. Total in Residence 3; Total Staff 4.

[I] CAMPUS MINISTRY

ELLENSBURG. *Catholic Campus Ministry at Central Washington University*, 706 N. Sprague, 98926. Tel: 509-925-3043.
E-mail: ccm-cwu@televar.com
Mr. Joseph Kiesel-Nield, Dir. & Campus Min. Total in Residence 3; Total Staff 1.

[J] MISCELLANEOUS LISTINGS

YAKIMA. *Diocese of Yakima Housing Services*, 5301 Tieton Dr., Ste. C, 98908-3478. Tel: 509-965-7100; Fax: 509-966-9750.
E-mail: mariov@dioceseofyakima.org
Mr. John L. Young, Pres.

COWICHE. *REACH Youth Ministry*, P.O. Box 130, 98923-0130. Tel: 509-678-8754; Fax: 509-678-8758.
E-mail: reachym@prodigy.net
Web site: pages.prodigy.net/reachym
Gina Morrissey, Dir. Total Assisted 8,000; Total Staff 4.

SUNNYSIDE. *Ministerio Nueva Vida*, 710 S. 6th St., 98944. Tel: 509-839-0553; Fax: 509-839-4101.

TOPPENISH. *Association of Catholic Sisters for Educational Opportunities for the Poor*, 3240 Fort Rd., 98948. Sr. Kathleen Ross, S.N.J.M., Pres.

UNION GAP. *La Salle Foundation of Yakima*, 3000 Lightning Way, 98903. Tel: 509-225-2900; Fax: 509-225-2950.
E-mail: lasallehs@aol.com
Web site: www.lasallehs.net
Bro. Daniel Morgan, F.S.C., Prin.; Timothy McGree, Pres.; Tom Savre, Chairperson.

RELIGIOUS INSTITUTES OF MEN REPRESENTED IN THE DIOCESE

For further details refer to the corresponding bracketed number in the Religious Institutes of Men or Women section.

[0200]—*Benedictine Monks (American Cassinese Congregation).*—O.S.B.

[0330]—*Brothers of the Christian Schools.* (Prov. of San Francisco).—F.S.C.

[0690]—*Jesuit Fathers and Brothers (Oregon Providence).*—S.J.

RELIGIOUS INSTITUTES OF WOMEN REPRESENTED IN THE DIOCESE

[0230]—*Benedictine Sisters of Pontifical Jurisdiction.*—O.S.B.

[1070-20]—*Dominican Sisters.*—O.P.

[]—*Missionary Daughters of the Most Pure Virgin Mary.*

[2790]—*Missionary Servants of the Most Blessed Trinity.*—M.S.B.T.

[3350]—*Sisters of Providence (Prov. of Sacred Heart).*—S.P.

[3840]—*Sisters of St. Joseph of Carondelet.*—C.S.J.

[1990]—*Sisters of the Holy Names of Jesus and Mary.*—S.N.J.M.

[2160]—*Sisters, Servants of the Immaculate Heart of Mary.*—I.H.M.

NECROLOGY

† Moore, Michael, (Retired). —Died Jan. 12, 2000.

† Schindler, John, (Retired). —Died April 13, 2000.

Diocese of Youngstown

(Dioecesis Youngstoniensis)

Most Reverend

THOMAS J. TOBIN, D.D.

Bishop of Youngstown; ordained July 21, 1973; appointed Titular Bishop of Novica and Auxiliary Bishop of Pittsburgh, November 3, 1992; appointed Fourth Bishop of Youngstown; installed February 2, 1996.

Most Reverend

BENEDICT C. FRANZETTA, D.D.

Retired Auxiliary Bishop of Youngstown; ordained April 29, 1950; appointed Titular Bishop of Oderzo and Auxiliary July 29, 1980; consecrated September 4, 1980; retired September 4, 1996. *Res., St. Columba Rectory, 159 W. Rayen Ave., Youngstown, OH, 44503.*

ESTABLISHED MAY 15, 1943.

CANONICALLY ERECTED JULY 22, 1943.

Square Miles 3,404.

Comprises six Counties in the northeastern part of the State of Ohio, namely, Ashtabula, Columbiana, Mahoning, Portage, Stark and Trumbull Counties.

For legal titles of parishes and diocesan institutions, consult the Chancery Office.

Chancery Office: 144 W. Wood St., Youngstown, OH, 44503. Tel.: 330-744-8451; Fax: 330-742-6448; 744-2848.

Web site address: www.doy.org

E-mail address: doychancery@impresso.com

STATISTICAL OVERVIEW

Personnel	
Bishop	1
Retired Bishops	1
Priests: Diocesan Active in Diocese	116
Priests: Active Outside Diocese	5
Priests: Diocesan in Foreign Missions	1
Priests: Retired, Sick or Absent	62
Number of Diocesan Priests	184
Religious Priests in Diocese	24
Extern Priests in Diocese	1
Ordinations:	
Diocesan Priests	3
Transitional Deacons	2
Permanent Deacons	7
Permanent Deacons in Diocese	71
Total Brothers	20
Total Sisters	236
Parishes	
Parishes	116
With Resident Pastor:	
Resident Diocesan Priests	104
Resident Religious Priests	6
Without Resident Pastor:	
Administered by Priests	5
Administered by Women Religious	1
Missions	2
Professional Ministry Personnel:	
Sisters	29
Lay Ministers	100
Welfare	
Catholic Hospitals	3
Total Assisted	955,152
Health Care Centers	5
Total Assisted	159,638
Homes for the Aged	9
Total Assisted	536
Day Care and Extended Day Care Centers	3
Total Assisted	395
Specialized Homes	3
Total Assisted	405
Special Centers for Social Services	7
Total Assisted	312,976
Other Institutions	2
Total Assisted	55
Educational	
Diocesan Students in Other Seminaries	13
Total Seminarians	13
Colleges and Universities	1
Total Students	1,580
High Schools, Diocesan and Parish	6
Total Students	2,686
Elementary Schools, Diocesan and Parish	44
Total Students	11,418
Catechesis/Religious Education:	
High School Students	3,190
Elementary Students	15,398
Total Students Under Catholic Instruction	34,285
Teachers in the Diocese:	
Priests	3
Sisters	29
Lay Teachers	761
Vital Statistics	
Receptions into the Church:	
Infant Baptism Totals	3,061
Adult Baptism Totals	322
Received into Full Communion	548
First Communions	3,457
Confirmations	2,904
Marriages:	
Catholic	723
Interfaith	593
Total Marriages	1,316
Deaths	3,057
Total Catholic Population	262,020
Total Population	1,217,333

Former Bishops—Most Rev. JAMES A. MCFADDEN, S.T.D., LL.D., appt. Titular Bishop of Bida and Auxiliary of Cleveland, May 13, 1932; cons. Sept. 8, 1932; appt. Bishop of Youngstown, June 2, 1943; died Nov. 16, 1952.—Most Rev. EMMET M. WALSH, D.D., ord. Jan. 15, 1916; appt. Bishop of Charleston, June 20, 1927; appt. Titular Bishop of Rhaedestus and Coadjutor, Sept. 8, 1949; succeeded to See, Nov. 16, 1952; died March 16, 1968.—Most Rev. JAMES W. MALONE, D.D., ord. May 26, 1945; appt. Titular Bishop of Alabanda and Auxiliary, Jan. 2, 1960; appt. Apostolic Administrator, Jan. 22, 1966; succeeded to See, May 2, 1968; retired Dec. 4, 1995; died April 9, 2000.—

All Diocesan offices and personnel can be reached at 144 W. Wood St., Youngstown, OH, 44503, Tel: 330-744-8451, Fax: 330-742-6448; 744-2848 unless otherwise indicated.

Chancery Office

Vicar General and Moderator of the Curia—Rev. Msgr. ROBERT J. SIFFRIN.

Chancellor—Mrs. NANCY YUHASZ.

"The Catholic Exponent", Diocesan Newspaper—Most Rev. THOMAS J. TOBIN, Publisher; Mr. LOUIS JACQUET, Editor & Gen. Mgr. Tel: 330-744-5251.

College of Consultors—Rev. Msgr. MICHAEL CARIGLIO; Rev. GERALD DELUCIA; Rev. Msgr. JOHN DEMARINIS; Rev. Msgr. JOHN FINNIGAN; Revs. TERRENCE HAZEL; JOHN MULQUEEN; Rev. Msgr. ROBERT SIFFRIN; Rev. DANIEL VENGLARIK.

Communications—

Catholic Television Network of Youngstown (CTNY)—Rev. JEFFREY MICKLER, S.S.P., Pastoral Dir., *P.O. Box 430, Canfield, 44406-0430.* Tel: 330-533-2243.

Public-Media Relations—NANCY YUHASZ.

Development/Stewardship—Mr. PAT PALOMBO, Dir., The Foundation of the Roman Catholic Diocese of Youngstown.

Ecumenism—Rev. JOSEPH WITMER, Dir., Ecumenical Commission, *342 S. Chillicothe, Aurora, 44202.* Tel: 330-562-8519.

Office of Missions/Evangelization—Rev. PAUL HILL, M.S.C., Dir.

Office of Pro-Life Activities—MARIE MILBURN, Dir.

Scouting, Diocesan Office—Rev. LEO WEHRLIN, Dir., *3430 St. Michael Dr., N.W., Canton, 44718.* Tel: 330-492-3119.

Department of Canonical Services

Department of Canonical Services—Rev. Msgr. WILLIAM J. CONNELL, J.C.L., Exec. Dir., *141 W. Rayen Ave., Youngstown, 44503.* Tel: 330-744-8451.

Office of Conciliation—

Matrimonial Dispensations—

Tribunal—

Judicial Vicar—Rev. Msgr. WILLIAM J. CONNELL, J.C.L.
Adjutant Judicial Vicar—Rev. Msgr. MICHAEL J. CARIGLIO, J.C.L.
Judges—Rev. Msgr. FRANK A. CARFAGNA; Rev. Msgr. JOHN H. DEMARINIS; Rev. Msgr. PETER M. POLANDO, J.C.L.; Rev. Msgr. DAVID W. RHODES; Rev. Msgr. FREDERICK SLAVEN; Rev. Msgr. MARTIN S. SUSKO, J.C.L.; Rev. Msgr. LAWRENCE C. FYE; Revs. ROBERT G. GIBAS; JOHN E. KEEHNER, J.C.L.; DANIEL J. KULESA; THOMAS J. MCCARTHY; JOHN A. MURRAY; JOHN NAGELE, C.PP.S.; JOHN R. OLSAVSKY, J.C.L.; ROBERT F. PFEIFFER, J.C.L.; ROBERT A. SABATINO, Ph.D.; GARY D. YANUS, J.C.D.
Defenders of the Bond—Rev. Msgr. JOHN ZURAW, J.C.L.; Revs. TERRENCE HAZEL; FREDERICK LUKEHART; DONALD J. OSER; RAYMOND PAUL; JOHN F. WARNER.
Advocates—Revs. BERNARD N. GAETA; J. PATRICK MANNING, Ph.D.; BRIAN MULCAHY, O.P.; Mrs. BARBARA ROGICH.
Promoter of Justice—Rev. Msgr. JOHN A. ZURAW, J.C.L.
Notaries—COLLEEN HARRIS; PHYLLIS KULICS; BARBARA ROGICH; JULIE TABAKA.

Department of Catholic Charities Services

Department of Catholic Charities Services—Sr. CONSOLATA KLINE, H.M., Exec. Dir. Health & Human Services Commission; Antonine Sisters Adult Day Care Center; Liaison to St. Vincent DePaul Society.
Office of Social Action—Mr. BRIAN CORBIN, Dir., Environment, Hunger & Rural Life Committee; Housing & Community Devel. Committee; Minorities Commission; Respect Life Committee; Parish Social Ministry; Criminal Justice Ministry.
Office of Social Services—Mrs. MARY ELLEN ANDERSEN, Dir., Aging Services; Pres., Diocese of Youngstown Catholic Charities Corporation; Diocesan Commission on the Role of Women in the Church and in Society.
St. Vincent DePaul Society—Mr. THOMAS MARTINKO, Pres., Particular Council of Youngstown, *235 Wick Ave., Youngstown, 44503*. Tel: 330-746-5222. Mr. VINCENT SCHUYLER, Pres., Particular Council of Trumbull Deanery, *2415 Niles Rd., S.E., Warren, 44484*. Tel: 330-369-4198.

Department of Clergy and Religious Services

Department of Clergy and Religious Services—Rev. Msgr. JOHN ZURAW, Exec. Dir.
Office of Vocations—Rev. Msgr. JOHN ZURAW, Dir.
Serra International, Serra Club of Youngstown—Rev. FREDERICK LUKEHART, Chap., *1000 Tod Ave., Warren, 44485*. Tel: 330-395-3747.
Office for Clergy Services—Rev. Msgr. JOHN ZURAW, Dir.
Priests' Council—Rev. J. JAMES KORDA, Exec. Sec., *4545 New Rd., Youngstown, 44515*. Tel: 330-792-1919.
Office of Continuing Education and Formation of Priests—Rev. STEPHEN POPOVICH, Dir., *4490 Norquest Blvd., Youngstown, 44515*. Tel: 330-793-9988.
Office of Priests' Personnel Advisor—Vacant.
Office of Permanent Diaconate—Rev. Msgr. JOHN ZURAW, Dir.
Office of Religious—Sr. ROSEMARY MURRAY, H.M., Dir.
Diocesan Conference of Religious—Sr. ROSEMARY MURRAY, H.M., Dir.

Department of Financial Services

Department of Financial Services—Rev. Msgr. JOHN H. DEMARINIS, Treas. & Econome; Mr. ROBERT A. HOFFMAN, Exec. Dir. Finance & Oper.
Office of Finance—Mr. JOHN DIDEK, JR., Dir. Finance; Mrs. MARGARET FISHER, Dir. Finance; Mr. LEONARD W. DERSHAW, Dir. Auditing; Mr. KEVIN C. O'DONNELL, Financial Accountant; Sr. M. GERTRUDE PARIS, O.S.U, Dir. Admin. Svcs.
Office of Data Processing—Mr. LOUIS ORBIN, Dir.

Department of Pastoral and Educational Services

Pastoral and Educational Services—Sr. M. BRENDON ZAJACK, S.N.D., Exec. Dir.
Office of Catholic Schools—Dr. NICHOLAS WOLSONOVICH, Supt.; Dr. ALAN DIGIANANTONIO, Dir. Curriculum Instruction & Technology; Mr. THOMAS WELCSH, Dir. Certificated Personnel; Mr. WALLACE DUNNE, Dir. Gov't Programs & Resource Devel.
Superintendent's School Advisory Council—Revs. DANIEL VENGLARIK, Pres. TERRENCE HAZEL, Vice Pres.
The Catholic Diocese of Youngstown Educational Fund, Inc.
Office of Religious Education—BARBARA WALKO, Diocesan Dir., *225 Elm St., Youngstown, 44503*. Tel: 330-744-8451. THOMAS SAULINE, Consultant; CARLETTE CHORDAS, Media Resources.
Diocesan Council for Catechesis—MARGARET HARVAN, Chm. ROSEANNE SCHAEFFER, Vice Chm.
Office of Youth Ministry—AMY ZEAFLA, Dir. FAYE ABBONDANZA, Assoc. Dir.
Office of Campus Ministry—Rev. JOHN JEREK, Diocesan Dir., *1424 Horning Rd., Kent, 44240*. Tel: 330-678-0240.
Hiram College—Rev. RICHARD J. PENTELLO, *St. Ambrose Parish, 10692 Freedom St., Garrettsville, 44231*. Tel: 330-527-4105.
Immaculate Heart of Mary University Parish (Kent State Newman Center)—Rev. JOHN JEREK, Pastor; Mrs. CARMEN ROEBKE, Campus Min., *1424 Horning Rd., Kent, 44240*. Tel: 330-678-0240.
Stark State College of Technology-Kent State Stark—MARCIE BIRCHER; THOMAS DOUCE, *Interfaith Campus Ministry, 6200 Frank Ave., N.W., Canton, 44720*. Tel: 330-494-6170, Ext. 4264.
Walsh University—Rev. DON MILLER, O.F.M.; Sr. CAROL HEBERT, S.S.J., *2020 Easton St., N.W., North Canton, 44720*. Tel: 330-490-7341; 7342.
Youngstown State University—Rev. BRIAN MULCAHY, O.P., *254 Madison Ave., Youngstown, 44504*. Tel: 330-747-9202.
Office of Worship—FRAN AMER, Dir.
Office of Lay Ministry Formation—EILEEN NOVOTNY, Dir.
Office of Marriage & Family Life—Mr. JOHN DAMICO, Dir.

Other Ministries

Catholic Alumni Club of Youngstown, Inc.—Rev. VINCENT FREEH, M.S.C., Chap., *3128 Logan Ave., Youngstown, 44505*. Tel: 330-759-9539.
Catholic Women, Diocesan Council of—Rev. Msgr. JAMES A. CLARKE, Moderator, *241 S. Main St., North Canton, 44720*. Tel: 330-499-2201.
Charismatic Prayer Group—Rev. ROBERT EDWARDS, Dir., *271 Chestnut St., Lisbon, 44432*. Tel: 330-424-7648.
Disabled Services—
Physically and Developmentally—Rev. TERRENCE HAZEL, Chap., *281 Glenview Dr., Canfield, 44406*. Tel: 330-533-6839.
Deaf and Hearing Impaired—Rev. TERRENCE HAZEL, Chap., *281 Glenview Dr., Canfield, 44406*. Tel: 330-533-6839.
Spanish Speaking—Rev. THOMAS CARNEY, M.S.C., *50 Struthers-Coitsville Rd., Youngstown, 44505*. Tel: 330-755-3633.

CLERGY, PARISHES, MISSIONS AND PAROCHIAL SCHOOLS

CITY OF YOUNGSTOWN
(Mahoning County)

1—CATHEDRAL OF ST. COLUMBA (1847), Rev. Msgr. Lawrence C. Fye, M.Ed., V.F.; Rev. John Keehner, J.C.L., Vice Rector. In res., Most Rev. Benedict C. Franzetta, D.D., V.G., (Retired).
Res., 159 W. Rayen Ave., 44503. Tel: 330-744-5233; Fax: 330-744-2282. [JC]
Catechesis/Religious Programs—Students 49.

2—HOLY NAME (1916) (Slovak), Rev. Msgr. Michael E. Ronik.
Res., 613 N. Lakeview Ave., 44509. Tel: 330-799-8873.
Catechesis/Religious Programs—Students 40.

3—IMMACULATE CONCEPTION (1882), Rev. Msgr. John A. Zuraw, Admin.; Sr. Mary Lee Nalley, O.S.U., Pastoral Min.
Res., 811 Oak St., 44506. Tel: 330-747-3533; Fax: 330-747-3533.
School—810 Oak St., 44506. Tel: 330-747-9471; Fax: 330-747-5022. Mr. Robert Sferra, Prin.
Lay Teachers 9; Students 168.
Catechesis/Religious Programs—Sr. Kathleen McCarragher, O.S.U., D.R.E.
Students 35.

4—IMMACULATE HEART OF MARY, Mahoning Co., (1954), Rev. Stephen Popovich.
Res., 4490 Norquest Blvd., 44515. Tel: 330-793-9988.
School—Tel: 330-799-1944; Fax: 330-799-0151.
Sisters 2; Lay Teachers 10; Students 193.
Catechesis/Religious Programs—Tel: 330-799-4202.
Students 275.

5—OUR LADY OF HUNGARY (1929) (Hungarian), Rev. John E. Reiss, O.F.M.
Office: 545 N. Belle Vista Ave., 44509. Tel: 330-799-6829.
Res., Mt. Alverna Friary, 517 S. Belle Vista Ave., 44509. Tel: 330-799-1880.
Catechesis/Religious Programs—Students 25.

6—OUR LADY OF MT. CARMEL (1908) (Italian), Rev. Msgr. Michael J. Cariglio, J.C.L.; Deacon Joseph Nohra.
Res., 343 Via Mt. Carmel, 44505. Tel: 330-743-4144; Fax: 330-743-1035.
Catechesis/Religious Programs—Tel: 330-743-3508.
Students 181.

7—SACRED HEART OF JESUS (1888), Revs. Joseph P. Martin; Thomas Eisweirth.
Res., 400 Lincoln Park Dr., 44506. Tel: 330-747-6080; Fax: 330-747-7003.
School—Combined with Immaculate Conception. Tel: 330-747-9471; Fax: 330-747-3533.
Catechesis/Religious Programs—Sr. Kathleen McCarragher, O.S.U., D.R.E.
Students 87.

8—ST. ANTHONY'S (1898) (Italian), Rev. Msgr. John H. DeMarinis.
Res., 1125 Turin Ave., 44510. Tel: 330-744-5091; Fax: 330-744-1407.
Catechesis/Religious Programs—Students 35.

9—ST. BRENDAN'S (1923), Rev. James M. Daprile. In res., Rev. Msgr. Robert Siffrin.
Res., 2800 Oakwood Ave., 44509. Tel: 330-792-3875; Fax: 330-792-9080.
School—144 N. Schenley Ave., 44509. Tel: 330-799-9741; Fax: 330-799-1113.
Catechesis/Religious Programs—Students 247.

10—ST. CASIMIR'S (1906, Rev. Sy Kaminski.
Church & Mailing: 149 Jefferson St., 44510. Tel: 330-743-3951.
Res., 1115 Eveningstar Dr., Rome, 44085-9763. Tel: 440-563-5316.

11—ST. CHRISTINE'S (1953), Rev. Msgr. David W. Rhodes; Rev. Dennis Bliss; Sr. Ann McManamon, Pastoral Assoc.; Deacons David Beil; Ronald Layko; Robert Cuttica, M.D.; Jim Brown.
Res., 3165 S. Schenley Ave., 44511. Tel: 330-792-3829; Fax: 330-792-6587. [CEM]
School—3125 S. Schenley Ave., 44511. Tel: 330-792-4545; Fax: 330-792-6888.
Lay Teachers 22; Students 504.
Catechesis/Religious Programs—Tel: 216-793-0544; Fax: 216-792-3820. Colleen Boyle, D.R.E.
Students 550.

12—SS. CYRIL AND METHODIUS, Mahoning Co., (1896) (Slovak). Unassigned.
Res., 252 E. Wood St., 44503. Tel: 330-743-5291; Fax: 330-746-1207.
Catechesis/Religious Programs—Students 26.

13—ST. DOMINIC'S (1923), Revs. Joseph P. Allen, O.P.; William J. Rock, O.P.; Ernest Kelly, O.P., Chap. South Side; Brian Mulcahy, O.P.; Robert R. Heuschkel.
Res., 77 E. Lucius Ave., 44507. Tel: 330-783-1900; Fax: 330-783-2396.
Parish Center:—3403 Southern Blvd., 44507. Tel: 330-782-1123; Fax: 330-782-4616.
Catechesis/Religious Programs—Students 147.

14—ST. EDWARD'S (1917), Rev. Frank M. Lehnerd.
Res., 240 Tod Ln., 44504. Tel: 330-743-2308; Fax: 330-743-8321.
School—(Grades K-8). Tel: 330-746-0576; Fax: 330-744-7042.
Lay Teachers 15; Students 217.
Catechesis/Religious Programs—Students 27.

15—ST. ELIZABETH'S (1922) (Slovak), Rev. George M. Duritsa, Admin.
Res., 124 Keystone St., Campbell, 44405. Tel: 330-747-4085; Fax: 330-747-8647.
Catechesis/Religious Programs—Students 32.

16—ST. JOSEPH (1966), Rev. J. James Korda; Deacon Michael Roberts.
Res., 4545 New Rd., Austintown, 44515. Tel: 330-792-1919; Fax: 330-792-5233.
School—Tel: 330-793-1250; Fax: 330-793-2377.
Lay Teachers 13; Students 227.
Catechesis/Religious Programs—Tel: 330-792-1934. Mrs. Lori Pugh, D.R.E.
Students 466.

17—ST. MATTHIAS (1914) (Slovak), Rev. Msgr. Peter M. Polando, J.C.L.; Deacon Salvatore DiFrancesco.
Res., 915 Cornell St., 44502-2765. Tel: 330-788-5082; Fax: 330-788-2383.
School—2800 Shady Run Rd., 44502-2700. Tel: 330-788-0241.
Vincentian Sisters of Charity 2; Lay Teachers 13; Students 163.
Catechesis/Religious Programs—Tel: 330-788-5732.
Students 83.

Convent—937 Cornell St., 44502-2765. Tel: 330-788-5732.

18—ST. PATRICK'S (1911), Rev. Edward P. Noga.
Res., 1420 Oak Hill Ave., 44507. Tel: 330-743-1109; Fax: 330-743-8810.
Catechesis/Religious Programs—Students 87.

19—SS. PETER AND PAUL'S, Mahoning Co., (1911) (Croatian), Rev. John Warner.
Res., 421 Covington St., 44510. Tel: 330-747-6762.
Catechesis/Religious Programs—Students 62.

20—ST. ROSE OF LIMA (1961) (Hispanic), Rev. Thomas A. Carney, M.S.C.; Deacons Felipe Colon; Enrique Santiago; John Rentas.
Res., 50 Struthers-Coitsville Rd., 44505. Tel: 330-755-3633; Fax: 330-755-3683.
Catechesis/Religious Programs—Students 125.

21—ST. STANISLAUS KOSTKA'S (1902) (Polish), Rev. Edward J. Neroda; Deacon Michael Schlais.
Res., 430 Williamson Ave., 44507. Tel: 330-747-8503; Fax: 330-747-6334.
Catechesis/Religious Programs—Tel: 330-747-3015.
Students 22.

22—ST. STEPHEN OF HUNGARY (1905) (Hungarian), Rev. Melvin E. Rusnak; Sr. Annette Amendolia, S.N.D., Pastoral Assoc.; Deacon Al Medvez.
Church—854 Wilson Ave., 44506. Tel: 330-743-1905; Fax: 330-743-1905.
Catechesis/Religious Programs—Twinned with SS. Cyril and Methodius, 252 E. Wood St., Youngstown Tel: 330-743-5291; Fax: 330-746-1207.

OUTSIDE THE CITY OF YOUNGSTOWN

Alliance, Stark Co., St. Joseph's (1859), Rev. Donald L. Feicht.
Res., 427 E. Broadway, 44601. Tel: 330-821-5760; Fax: 330-821-5783. [CEM]
Catechesis/Religious Programs—Students 164.

Regina Coeli (1958), Rev. J. Patrick Manning; Sr. Yvonne Horning, O.P., Pastoral Assoc.
Res., 663 Fernwood Blvd., 44601-2796. Tel: 330-821-5880; Fax: 330-821-8837. [JC]
School—733 Fernwood Blvd., 44601-2796. Tel: 330-829-9239; Fax: 330-823-1877.
Religious 1; Lay Teachers 11; Students 238.
Catechesis/Religious Programs—D.R.E.: Yvonne Welch; Amy Benodetti.
Students 65.

Andover, Ashtabula Co., Our Lady of Victory (1949), Rev. Lawrence Frient.
Res., 481 S. Main St., P.O. Box 669, 44003-9778. Tel: 440-293-6218; Fax: 440-293-7778.
Catechesis/Religious Programs—Students 38.

Ashtabula, Ashtabula Co., Mother of Sorrows (1890) (Irish-Finnish), Rev. Kevin Peters.
Res., 1514 W. 6th St., 44004. Tel: 440-964-3277 (Office); Fax: 440-964-6780.
Catechesis/Religious Programs—Students 87.

Our Lady of Mt. Carmel (1902) (Italian), Rev. Michael D. Balash; Sr. Laurie Divoky, S.N.D., Pastoral Min.
Res., 1200 E. 21st St., 44004. Tel: 440-998-4111; Fax: 440-998-7829.
Catechesis/Religious Programs—Students 172.

St. Joseph's (1862), Rev. Philip Miller; Deacons Richard Johnson; Alan Prasek; Donald Johnson; Peter Olsen, Business Mgr.
Res., 3330 Lake Ave., 44004. Tel: 440-992-0330; Fax: 440-993-3579. [CEM]
Mission—Ashtabula, Ashtabula Co., Our Lady of Miracles (St. Joseph Mission), 4317 West Ave., 44004. Tel: 440-997-7121.
Catechesis/Religious Programs—Students 145.

Aurora, Portage Co., Our Lady of Perpetual Help (1955), Rev. Joseph W. Witmer; Sr. Lu Haidnick, C.D.P., Pastoral Assoc.
Res., 342 S. Chillicothe Rd., 44202-7814. Tel: 330-562-8519; Fax: 330-562-2529.
Catechesis/Religious Programs—Dr. Thomas Brozich, D.R.E.
Students 575.

Boardman, Mahoning Co., St. Charles Borromeo's (1926), Revs. Daniel M. Venglarik; James Zanni; Deacon Michael A. Kocjancic; Peter Gross, Business Mgr. Pastoral Assocs.: Sue Heher; Linda O'Brien.
Res., 7345 Westview Dr., Youngstown, 44512. Tel: 330-758-2325; Fax: 330-758-2004.
School—7325 Westview Dr., Youngstown, 44512. Tel: 330-758-6689; Fax: 330-758-7404.
Sisters 1; Lay Teachers 30; Students 703.
Catechesis/Religious Programs—Tel: 216-758-8063. Mrs. Judy Magielski, D.R.E.
Students 1110.
Convent—7515 Oregon Tr., Youngstown, 44512. Tel: 330-758-2396.

St. Luke (1962), Revs. Joseph A. Fata; Richard A. Brobst; Deacon Richard Milanek.
Res., 5235 South Ave., 44512. Tel: 330-782-9783; Fax: 330-782-1574.
School—Tel: 330-782-4060; Fax: 330-782-4842.
Lay Teachers 12; Students 205.
Catechesis/Religious Programs—Students 275.

Brewster, Stark Co., St. Therese (1928), Rev. Robert W. Kaylor, Admin.
Res., 456 Wabash Ave. S., 44613. Tel: 330-767-3622. [JC]
Catechesis/Religious Programs—Students 50.

Campbell, Mahoning Co., St. John the Baptist (1919) (Slovak), Rev. John S. Trimbur; Deacon Ronald J. Bunofsky.
Res., 159 Reed Ave., 44405. Tel: 330-755-4141; Fax: 330-755-1022. [CEM]
Catechesis/Religious Programs—Students 51.

St. Joseph the Provider (1919) (Polish), Rev. Michael Swierz.
Res., 633 Porter Ave., 44405. Tel: 330-755-0266; Fax: 330-755-1988.
School—Tel: 330-755-4747; Fax: 330-755-4749.
Lay Teachers 9; Students 131.
Catechesis/Religious Programs—Students 15.

St. Lucy's (1937) (Italian), Rev. Msgr. John P. Ashton, Ph.D.
Res., 394 Tenney Ave., 44405-1695. Tel: 330-755-4132; Fax: 330-755-1988.
Catechesis/Religious Programs—Tel: 330-755-1367.
Students 98.

Canal Fulton, Stark Co., SS. Philip and James (1845), Rev. John R. Lody.
Res., 412 High St., 44614. Tel: 330-854-2332. [CEM]
School—Tel: 330-854-2823; Fax: 330-854-1109. Mrs. Donna Mertes, Prin.
Lay Teachers 12; Students 264.
Catechesis/Religious Programs—Students 169.

Canfield, Mahoning Co., St. Michael's (1963), Rev. Terrence J. Hazel; Deacon Tom Soich; Sr. Brendan Sherlock, O.S.U., Pastoral Min.; Mrs. Barbara Spencer, Pastoral Min.; Ms. Maureen Hall, Pastoral Min.
Res., 281 Glenview Dr., 44406. Tel: 330-533-6839; Fax: 330-533-6839.
Catechesis/Religious Programs—Tel: 330-533-5275. Jim Merhaut, D.R.E.
Students 737.

Canton, Stark Co.,

1—ALL SAINTS, (1920) (Polish), Rev. Thomas G. Bishop, Admin.
Res., 1386 Henry Ave., S.W., 44706. Tel: 330-453-6429; Fax: 330-452-4870.
Catechesis/Religious Programs—Students 30.

2—OUR LADY OF PEACE, (1952), Rev. John Nentwick.
Res., 833 39th St., N.W., 44709. Tel: 330-492-0757; Fax: 330-492-1214.
School—1001 39th St., N.W., 44709. Tel: 330-492-0622; Fax: 330-492-0959.
Sisters 1; Lay Teachers 22; Students 429.
Catechesis/Religious Programs—Tel: 330-492-0929.
Students 193.

3—SACRED HEART, (1922) (Slovak), Rev. William Shipe; Deacon Edward Briestensky.
Res., 1620 Clark Ave., S.W., 44706. Tel: 330-453-1028.

4—ST. ANTHONY'S, (1908) (Italian), Rev. Thomas G. Bishop.
Res., 1530 11th St., S.E., 44707. Tel: 330-452-9539; Fax: 330-452-4870.
Catechesis/Religious Programs—Students 126.

5—ST. BENEDICT, (1923), Rev. John Zuzik.
Res., 2207 Third St., S.E., 44707. Tel: 330-452-0751.
Benedict Center: Tel: 330-453-3642.
Church—E. Tuscarawas St. & Girard Ave., S.E., 44707.
Catechesis/Religious Programs—Students 70.

6—ST. JOAN OF ARC, (1944), Revs. Thomas P. Dyer; Joseph Ruggieri; Deacon David Conversino. In res., Rev. Msgr. John J. Daum.
Res., 4940 Tuscarawas St. W., 44708-5012. Tel: 330-477-6796; 6797; Fax: 330-477-0594.
School—120 Bordner Ave., S.W., 44710. Tel: 330-477-2972; Fax: 330-478-2606.
Lay Teachers 19; Students 475.
Catechesis/Religious Programs—166 Bordner Ave., S.W., 44710. Tel: 330-477-6790.
Students 347.

7—ST. JOHN THE BAPTIST, (1823), Rev. Ronald M. Klingler; Deacon Carl Burkhardt.
Res., 627 McKinley Ave., N.W., 44703. Tel: 330-454-8044; Fax: 330-454-1397. [CEM]
Catechesis/Religious Programs—Tel: 330-453-5418.
Students 90.

8—ST. JOSEPH'S, (1902), Rev. Msgr. Frank A. Carfagna; Rev. Timothy J. Huffman (STU); Deacon Wilbur J. Bagley.
Res., 2427 W. Tuscarawas St., 44708. Tel: 330-453-2526.
School—126 Columbus Ave., N.W., 44708. Tel: 330-454-9787; Fax: 330-454-9866.
Lay Teachers 17; Students 259.
Catechesis/Religious Programs—Tel: 330-454-2144.
Students 212.

9—ST. MARY, (1899), Rev. Gerald J. Sommer, M.S.C.
Res., 1602 Market Ave. S., 44707. Tel: 330-453-2110; Fax: 330-453-4008.
Catechesis/Religious Programs—Students 98.

10—ST. MICHAEL THE ARCHANGEL, (1952), Revs. Bradford N. Helman; Leo J. Wehrlin. Pastoral Assocs.: Sr. Carol McHenry, S.N.D.; Mrs. Faith Wackerly.
Res., 3430 St. Michael Blvd., N.W., 44718. Tel: 330-492-3119; Fax: 330-492-0339.
School—3431 St. Michael's Blvd., N.W., 44718. Tel: 330-492-2657; Fax: 330-492-9618. Mrs. Patricia Lamielle, Prin.
Sisters 2; Lay Teachers 22; Students 553.
Catechesis/Religious Programs—Mr. Michael Ress, D.R.E.
Students 950.

11—ST. PAUL'S, (1907), Rev. John E. Zuzik, Admin.; Mrs. Sally Dick, Pastoral Min. In res., Rev. Nicholas J. Mancini.
Res., 1459 Superior Ave., N.E., 44705. Tel: 330-456-7555; Fax: 330-452-7716. [JC]
Catechesis/Religious Programs—Students 90.

12—ST. PETER'S, (1845), Rev. Msgr. John C. Finnigan; Deacon Robert Klein.
Res., 726 Cleveland Ave., N.W., 44702. Tel: 330-453-8493; Fax: 330-453-8083. [CEM]
School—702 Cleveland Ave., N.W., 44702. Tel: 330-452-0125.
Sisters of Notre Dame 2; Lay Teachers 11; Students 200.
Catechesis/Religious Programs—Students 145.

Champion, Trumbull Co., St. William (1963), Rev. Michael J. Smar; Sr. Mary Cora Skrivan, S.N.D., D.R.E.
Res., 5411 Mahoning Ave., N.W., Warren, 44483. Tel: 330-847-8677.
Catechesis/Religious Programs—Tel: 330-847-8627.
Students 181.

Columbiana, Columbiana Co., St. Jude (1966), Rev. Thomas G. Ziegler.
Res., 180 7th St., 44408. Tel: 330-482-2351.
Catechesis/Religious Programs—Tel: 330-482-2888. Ms. Mary Glasser, D.R.E.
Students 203.

Conneaut, Ashtabula Co., St. Mary's (1888), Rev. Raymond J. Thomas.
Res., 480 State St., P.O. Box 619, 44030. Tel: 440-599-8855; Fax: 440-593-6772. [CEM][JC]
Catechesis/Religious Programs—Tel: 440-599-8570.
Students 95.

St. Frances Cabrini (1954), Rev. Raymond J. Thomas.
Res., 744 Mill St., P.O. Box 619, 44030. Tel: 440-599-8570; Fax: 440-593-6772.
School—Tel: 440-593-1677; Fax: 440-599-9576.
Oblate Sisters of the Sacred Heart 1; Lay Teachers 10; Students 115.
Catechesis/Religious Programs—Students 58.

Cortland, Trumbull Co., St. Robert Bellarmine Parish (1952), Rev. Carl Kish.
Res., 4659 Niles-Cortland Rd., N.E., 44410. Tel: 330-637-4886; Fax: 330-637-0608. [CEM]
Catechesis/Religious Programs—Students 420.

Dungannon, Columbiana Co., St. Philip Neri (1817), Rev. John P. Tully.
Mailing Address: P.O. Box 309, Hanoverton, 44423-0309.
Office & Res.: 16017 Smith Rd., Summitville, 43962. Tel: 330-223-1871. [CEM]
Church—11328 Gavers Rd., 44423. Tel: 330-223-1973.
Catechesis/Religious Programs—Students 9.

East Liverpool, Columbiana Co., St. Aloysius (1838) (Irish), Rev. Bernard N. Gaeta.
Res., 235 W. 5th St., 43920. Tel: 330-385-7131; Fax: 330-385-3025. [CEM]
School—335 W. 5th St., 43920. Tel: 330-385-5963; Fax: 330-385-6455.
Lay Teachers 11; Students 163.
Catechesis/Religious Programs—Tel: 330-385-6472.
Students 69.

St. Ann's (1915), Rev. George J. Balasko.
Res., 1506 Pennsylvania Ave., 43920. Tel: 330-385-5582; Fax: 330-386-5246.
Catechesis/Religious Programs—Students 32.

East Palestine, Columbiana Co., Our Lady of Lourdes (1880), Rev. Daniel Cipar, M.S.C.; Rev. Msgr. Dezso Torok, Pastor Emeritus.
Res., 200 E. Main St., 44413. Tel: 330-426-9346; Fax: 330-426-9846. [CEM]

Catechesis/Religious Programs—20 N. James St., 44413. Tel: 330-426-2254.
Students 128.

Garrettsville, Portage Co., St. Ambrose (1944), Rev. Richard J. Pentello; Deacon Robert Rapp.
Res., 10692 Freedom St., 44231. Tel: 330-527-4105; Fax: 330-527-2500.
Catechesis/Religious Programs—Students 166.

Geneva, Ashtabula Co., Assumption B.V.M. (1915), Rev. Paul R. Tobin.
Res., 594 W. Main St., 44041. Tel: 440-466-3427; Fax: 440-466-4670.
School—Tel: 440-466-2104. Sr. Mary Gloria Auer, R.S.M., Prin.
Lay Teachers 12; Students 130.
Catechesis/Religious Programs—Students 200.

Girard, Trumbull Co., St. Rose (1892), Rev. Msgr. Martin S. Susko; Rev. Charles Poore; Deacons Kevin Lamar; Paul Milligan.
Res., 48 E. Main St., 44420. Tel: 330-545-4351; Fax: 330-545-0119.
School—65 E. Main St., 44420. Tel: 330-545-1163. Sr. Carole Suhar, O.S.U., Prin.
Sisters 2; Lay Teachers 17; Students 313.
Catechesis/Religious Programs—Tel: 216-545-1216. Marjorie O'Malley, D.R.E.
Students 426.

Hubbard, Trumbull Co., St. Patrick's (1869), Revs. Timothy H. O'Neill; James R. Johnson, S.P.; John A. Murray, (Retired); Deacon Robert Friedman.
Res., 315 N. Main St., 44425. Tel: 330-534-1928; Fax: 330-534-0820. [CEM]
School—38 E. Water St., 44425. Tel: 330-534-2509; Fax: 330-534-0305.
Lay Teachers 14; Students 232.
Catechesis/Religious Programs—225 N. Main St., 44425. Tel: 330-534-8304; 534-4111. Karen Bartos, D.R.E.
Students 472.

Jefferson, Ashtabula Co., St. Joseph Calasanctius (1858), Rev. Stephen M. Wassie.
Res., 32 E. Jefferson St., 44047. Tel: 440-576-3651.
Catechesis/Religious Programs—Tel: 440-576-3339.
Students 136.

Kent, Portage Co., St. Patrick's (1864), Rev. Msgr. Timothy Kenney; Rev. Thomas J. Kraszewski; Deacon Timothy DeFrange.
Res., 313 N. Depeyster St., 44240. Tel: 330-673-5849; Fax: 330-673-5849. [JC]
School—127 Portage St., 44240. Tel: 330-673-7232; Fax: 330-678-6612.
Lay Teachers 20; Students 376.
Catechesis/Religious Programs—Tel: 330-677-4433.
Students 348.

Immaculate Heart of Mary (1953), Rev. John M. Jerek.
Res., 1424 Horning Rd., 44240. Tel: 330-678-0240; Fax: 330-678-7780.
Catechesis/Religious Programs—Students 125.

Kingsville, Ashtabula Co., St. Andrew (1936), Rev. Nathan S. Willis.
Res., 3700 Rte. 193, 44048. Tel: 440-224-0987 (Church). [CEM]
Catechesis/Religious Programs—Students 39.

Kinsman, Trumbull Co., St. Patrick (1957). Attended by Our Lady of Victory, Andover.
481 S. Main St., P.O. Box 669, Andover, 44003-9778. Tel: 440-293-6218; Fax: 440-293-7778.
Catechesis/Religious Programs—6397 State Rte. 87, N.E.
Students 52.

Lake Milton, Mahoning Co., St. Catherine (1956), Rev. David W. Merzweiler; Deacon Ralph T. Chase.
Res., 1254 Grandview Rd., 44429-9542. Tel: 330-654-4001.
Catechesis/Religious Programs—Sr. Janice Kusick, O.S.U., D.R.E.
Students 29.

Leetonia, Columbiana Co., St. Patrick's (1861), Rev. Thomas J. Ungashick.
Res., 167 Main St., P.O. Box 67, 44431. Tel: 330-427-6577. [CEM]
Catechesis/Religious Programs—Students 51.

Lisbon, Columbiana Co., St. George (1820), Rev. Robert Edwards; Deacon David H. Arend.
Res., 271 W. Chestnut St., 44432. Tel: 330-424-7648; Fax: 330-424-7648.
Catechesis/Religious Programs—Tel: 330-424-0109.
Students 80.
Mission—West Point, Columbiana Co., St. Agatha, P.O. Box 462, West Point, 44492. Tel: 330-424-0155.

Louisville, Stark Co., St. Louis (1838) (French-German), Revs. Kenneth E. Miller; Homer G. Oliver.
Res., 300 N. Chapel St., 44641. Tel: 330-875-1658; Fax: 330-875-1657. [CEM]
School—Tel: 330-875-1467; Fax: 330-875-2511.
Lay Teachers 12; Students 216.
Catechesis/Religious Programs—Students 229.

Sacred Heart of Mary (1833), Rev. William B. Kraynak.
Res., 8277 Nickelplate Ave., N.E., 44641. Tel: 330-875-2827; Fax: 330-875-2410. [CEM]
School—8267 Nickelplate Ave., N.E., 44641. Tel: 330-875-5167. Jane Burgess, Prin.
Lay Teachers 11; Students 91.
Catechesis/Religious Programs—Tel: 330-875-7705.
Students 93.

Lowellville, Mahoning Co., Our Lady of the Holy Rosary (1867), Rev. Gerald M. DeLucia.
Res., 131 E. Wood St., 44436. Tel: 330-536-6436; Fax: 330-536-9188. [CEM]
Catechesis/Religious Programs—Students 230.

McDonald, Trumbull Co., Our Lady of Perpetual Help (1943), Rev. Daniel J. Kulesa.
Res., 618 Ohio Ave., 44437. Tel: 330-530-6929; Fax: 330-530-2488.
Catechesis/Religious Programs—601 Indiana Ave., 44437. Tel: 330-530-1111.
Students 209.

Mantua, Portage Co., St. Joseph's (1923), Rev. Thomas J. McCarthy.
Res., 11045 St. Joseph Blvd., 44255. Tel: 330-274-2114; Fax: 330-274-2254.
Parish Center—Tel: 330-274-2253.
School—Tel: 330-274-2268; Fax: 330-274-2412.
Lay Teachers 14; Students 201.
Catechesis/Religious Programs—Students 245.

Massillon, Stark Co., St. Barbara's (1867) (German), Rev. Thomas Cebula; Mrs. Marcia Popovich, Pastoral Assoc.
Res., 2813 Lincoln Way, N.W., 44647. Tel: 330-833-6898; Fax: 330-833-5164. [CEM]
School—2825 Lincoln Way, N.W., 44647. Tel: 330-833-9510; Fax: 330-833-3297.
Sisters 1; Lay Teachers 11; Students 249; Preschool Children 29.
Catechesis/Religious Programs—Students 104.

St. Joseph's (1863), Rev. Raymond L. Paul; Deacon Steven A. Wyles.
Res., 322 Third St., S.E., 44646. Tel: 330-833-2607. [CEM]
Parish Center and Office—330 Fourth St., S.E., 44646. Tel: 330-833-4907; 833-6088; Fax: 330-833-3907.
Catechesis/Religious Programs—Students 148.

St. Mary's (1839), Revs. A. Edward Gretchko; John-Michael Lavelle; James R. Kolp, (Retired); Deacons Edwards Kurkas; Joseph Fries.
Res., 206 Cherry Rd., N.E., 44646. Tel: 330-833-8501; Fax: 330-833-3359. [CEM]
School—640 First St., N.E., 44646. Tel: 330-832-9355; Fax: 330-832-9030.
Sisters 2; Lay Teachers 19; Students 414.
Catechesis/Religious Programs—Tel: 216-832-5719.
Students 170.

Masury, Trumbull Co., St. Bernadette (1940), Rev. Robert J. Hannon.
Res., 7800 Locust St., 44438. Tel: 330-448-8015; Fax: 330-448-0432.
Catechesis/Religious Programs—Brookfield Junior High, Brookfield, Tel: 330-448-3003.
Students 117.

Maximo, Stark Co., St. Joseph (1850), Rev. William E. Bantz.
Res., 12055 Easton St., N.E., P.O. Box 219, 44650. Tel: 330-823-7809. [CEM]
Catechesis/Religious Programs—Tel: 330-823-5233.
Students 124.

Middlebranch, Stark Co., St. Therese Little Flower (1929), Revs. Kevin L. Fete; Edward F. Varble, Pastor Emeritus; Mr. David R. Schmidt, Pastoral Assoc.; Deacon Harold Krause.
Res., 2040 Diamond St., N.E., North Canton, 44720. Tel: 330-494-2759; Fax: 330-494-2536.
Catechesis/Religious Programs—Students 328.

Mineral Ridge, Trumbull Co., St. Mary's (1870), Rev. Richard Murphy.
Res., 3504 Main St., 44440. Tel: 330-652-7761; Fax: 330-652-7765.
Catechesis/Religious Programs—Students 95.

Navarre, Stark Co., St. Clement's (1830), Rev. Robert G. Gibas.
Res., 216 Wooster St. E., 44662. Tel: 330-879-5900; Fax: 330-879-5138. [CEM]
School—Tel: 330-879-2645; Fax: 330-879-3242.
Lay Teachers 9; Students 155.
Catechesis/Religious Programs—Students 63.

New Middletown, Mahoning Co., St. Paul the Apostle (1952), Rev. Nicholas R. Shori.
Res., 10143 Main St., P.O. Box 515, 44442. Tel: 330-542-3466. [JC]
Catechesis/Religious Programs—Tel: 330-542-3824.
Students 355.

Newton Falls, Trumbull Co., St. Joseph (1846) (Slovak), Rev. John P. Madden.
Res., 131 W. Quarry St., 44444-1560. Tel: 330-872-5742; Fax: 330-872-5744. [CEM]
School—Tel: 330-872-7676; Fax: 330-872-1013.
Students 206.
Catechesis/Religious Programs—Tel: 330-872-9947.
Students 121.

St. Mary (1928) (Polish), Rev. John P. Madden.
Res., 131 West Quarry St., 44444. Tel: 330-872-5742; Fax: 330-872-5744. [JC]
Catechesis/Religious Programs—Tel: 330-872-9947.
Students 6.

Niles, Trumbull Co., Our Lady of Mt. Carmel (1907) (Italian), Rev. Msgr. Robert Reidy; Rev. John D. Mulqueen.
Res., 381 Robbins Ave., 44446. Tel: 330-652-5825; Fax: 330-544-1872.
School—Tel: 330-652-5547; Fax: 330-652-1921.
Sisters 1; Lay Teachers 15; Students 242.
Catechesis/Religious Programs—Students 240.

St. Stephen's (1853), Rev. John H. Gubser.
Res., 129 W. Park Ave., 44446. Tel: 330-652-4396; Fax: 330-652-9317. [CEM]
School—(Grades PreK-8) 45 S. Chestnut, 44446. Tel: 330-652-5511; Fax: 330-652-4264.
Lay Teachers 14; Students 188; Preschool 58.
Catechesis/Religious Programs—Students 160.

North Canton, Stark Co., St. Paul's (1845), Rev. Msgr. James A. Clarke; Revs. Joseph Rudjak; James E. McKarns, (Retired); Donald J. Oser, (Retired); Judy Piero, Pastoral Min.; Deacons William Lambert; Ron Reolfi; Carol Rondini, Business Mgr.
Res., 241 S. Main St., 44720. Tel: 330-499-2201; Fax: 330-499-8106. [CEM]
School—303 S. Main St., 44720. Tel: 330-494-0223; Fax: 330-494-3226. Jackie Zufall, Prin.
Lay Teachers 22; Students 438.
Catechesis/Religious Programs—Tel: 330-494-4036. Kathy Weber, D.R.E.
Students 491.

North Jackson, Mahoning Co., St. James Parish Family (1943), Rev. David W. Merzweiler.
Mailing & Office Address: 50 Rosemont Rd., 44451. Tel: 330-538-2602.
Res., 1254 Grandview Rd., Lake Milton, 44429. Tel: 330-654-4001.
Catechesis/Religious Programs—Sr. Janice Kuscik, O.S.U.
Students 105.

Orwell, Ashtabula Co., St. Mary (1922), Rev. Gregory F. Fedor.
Res., 103 N. Maple, Box 217, 44076. Tel: 440-437-6262; Fax: 440-437-8216. [CEM]
Catechesis/Religious Programs—Tel: 440-437-8216.
Students 116.

Poland, Mahoning Co., Holy Family (1956), Rev. Msgr. William J. Connell; Rev. Pat Ferraro; Deacon Ray Hatala.
Res., 2729 Center Rd., 44514. Tel: 330-757-1545; Fax: 330-757-4443.
School—Tel: 330-757-3713; Fax: 330-757-7648.
Sisters 2; Lay Teachers 27; Students 398.
Catechesis/Religious Programs—Students 575.

Randolph Township, Portage Co., St. Joseph (1831), Rev. Edward R. Wieczorek; Deacon James White.
Res., 2643 Waterloo Rd., Mogadore, 44260. Tel: 330-628-9941; Fax: 330-628-9942. [CEM]
School—Tel: 330-628-9555.
Lay Teachers 11; Students 209.
Catechesis/Religious Programs—Tel: 330-628-4844. Linda Shaw, D.R.E.
Students 275.

Ravenna, Portage Co., Immaculate Conception (1854), Rev. Msgr. Robert A. Sabatino; Rev. David M. Misbrener; Deacons Russell J. Brode; Steven Gies.
Res., 409 W. Main St., 44266. Tel: 330-296-6434; Fax: 330-296-9193. [CEM]
School—225 S. Sycamore St., 44266. Tel: 330-296-4817; Fax: 330-296-2925.
Lay Teachers 9; Students 159.
Catechesis/Religious Programs—Tel: 330-296-4549.
Students 433.

Rock Creek, Ashtabula Co., Sacred Heart (1956), Rev. Msgr. Edward Kowaleski; Deacon John D. Pallo.
Res., 3409 N. Main St., P.O. Box 305, 44084. Tel: 440-563-3010. [JC]
Catechesis/Religious Programs—Students 81.

Rootstown, Portage Co., St. Peter of the Fields (1868), Rev. Thomas J. Crum; Sr. Regina Zeleznik, S.N.D., Pastoral Min.; Deacon Thomas Shay.

Res., 3487 Old Forge Rd., 44272. Tel: 330-325-7543. [CEM]
Catechesis/Religious Programs—Students 132.

Salem, Columbiana Co., St. Paul's (1881), Rev. Thomas Eisweirth. Pastoral Assocs.: Donna Lynn; Amanda Raymond.
Res., 157 Ohio Ave., 44460. Tel: 330-332-0336; Fax: 330-332-7982.
School—925 E. State St., 44460. Tel: 330-337-3451; Fax: 330-337-3452.
Lay Teachers 13; Students 152.
Catechesis/Religious Programs—Tel: 330-332-4373; Fax: 330-332-4373. D.R.E.: Joan Reedy; Donna Dermotta.
Students 308.

Salineville, Columbiana Co., St. Patrick's (1873), Rev. John P. Tully.
Mailing Address: P.O. Box 309, Hanoverton, 44423-0309.
Office & Res.: 16017 Smith St., Summitville, 43962. Tel: 330-223-1871.
Church—611 Jefferson St., 43945. Tel: 216-223-1871. [CEM]
Catechesis/Religious Programs—Students 28.

Sebring, Mahoning Co., St. Ann (1908), Sr. Maureen Smith, H.M.
Res., 323 S. 15th St., 44672. Tel: 330-938-2033; Fax: 330-938-2033.
Catechesis/Religious Programs—Students 92.

Streetsboro, Portage Co., St. Joan of Arc (1965), Rev. Msgr. Frederick Slaven; Rev. Robert V. Flynn, Pastor Emeritus.
Res., 8894 State Rte. 14, 44241. Tel: 330-626-3424; Fax: 330-626-3422.
Catechesis/Religious Programs—Tel: 330-626-2050.
Students 289.

Struthers, Mahoning Co., Holy Trinity (1907) (Slovak), Rev. Stephen C. Karas.
Res., 250 N. Bridge St., 44471. Tel: 330-755-2115; Fax: 330-750-9431.
Catechesis/Religious Programs—Tel: 330-755-4133.
Students 28.

St. Nicholas (1865), Revs. Philip E. Rogers; August Coccarelli; Deacons John Terranova; Paul Lisko; Mrs. Rita DeFrance, Pastoral Min.
Res., 775 5th St., 44471-1795. Tel: 330-750-2555.
Parish Office—764 5th St., 44471-1704. Tel: 330-755-9819; Fax: 330-755-9949.
School—762 5th St., 44471-1704. Tel: 330-755-2128.
Lay Teachers 17; Students 226.
Catechesis/Religious Programs—Tel: 330-755-6245. Miss Stephanie Tarajack, D.R.E.
Students 462.

Summitville, Columbiana Co., St. John's (1846), Rev. John P. Tully.
Mailing Address: P.O. Box 309, Hanoverton, 44423-0309.
Office & Res.: 16017 Smith Rd., 43962. Tel: 216-223-1871. [CEM]
Catechesis/Religious Programs—Students 49.

Uniontown, Stark Co., Holy Spirit (1979), Rev. John Zapp.
Res., 2952 Edison St., N.W., 44685. Tel: 330-699-4500.
Catechesis/Religious Programs—Students 282.

Vienna, Trumbull Co., Queen of the Holy Rosary (1997), Revs. Gary Dilley, F.S.S.P.; Howard Remski, F.S.S.P.
Res., 291 Scoville Dr., 44473. Tel: 330-856-4204; Fax: 330-856-9587.
Catechesis/Religious Programs—Students 60.

St. Vincent de Paul (1879), Rev. Frank L. Zanni.
Res., 4453 Warren-Sharon Rd., 44473. Tel: 330-394-2461; Fax: 330-609-0320.
Catechesis/Religious Programs—Tel: 330-394-2361.
Students 162.

Warren, Trumbull Co.,

1—Blessed Sacrament, (1959), Rev. Donald E. King.
Res., 3020 Reeves Rd., N.E., 44483. Tel: 330-372-2215; Fax: 330-372-6380.
School—Notre Dame, (Grades PreK-3). Queen of All Saints Building 3000 Reeves Rd., N.E., 44483. Tel: 330-372-2375; Fax: 330-372-2465. Mrs. Theresa A. Dolan-Dixon, Prin.
Lay Teachers 14; Students 205.
Catechesis/Religious Programs—Tel: 330-372-6930.
Students 476.

2—Christ Our King, (1951), Rev. Frederick Lukehart.
Res., 1000 Tod Ave., S.W., 44485. Tel: 330-395-3747; Fax: 330-395-3747.
Catechesis/Religious Programs—Students 44.

3—SS. Cyril and Methodius, (1928) (Slovak), Rev. James P. Walker.
Res., 185 Laird Ave., N.E., 44483. Tel: 330-393-9766; Fax: 330-393-0555.
Catechesis/Religious Programs—Tel: 330-393-0781.
Students 47.

4—St. James, (1947), Rev. Charles W. Crumbley Tel: 330-369-3518.
Res., 2533 Burton St., S.E., 44484. Tel: 330-369-3888; Fax: 330-369-2761.
Schools—Queen of Angels Building, (Grades 2-5) 44484. Tel: 330-369-4218; Fax: 330-369-2541.
Lay Teachers 19; Students 178; Notre Dame Queen of Peace, (Grades 5-8) 261 Elm Rd., 44483. Tel: 330-399-5154. Sr. Mary Judith Anne Sabau, S.N.D., Prin.
Catechesis/Religious Programs—2106 Arbor St., S.E., 44484. Tel: 330-369-3518. Mary Theisler, D.R.E.
Students 89.

5—St. Joseph, (1928) (Polish), Rev. Fred Trucksis. In res., Rev. George Popovich.
Res., 1346 Vernon St., N.W., 44483. Tel: 330-393-0226; Fax: 330-393-4764. [CEM]
Catechesis/Religious Programs—Students 25.

6—St. Mary's, (1835), Rev. Bernard R. Schmalzried. In res., Rev. Thomas M. Spisak.
Res., 232 Seneca St., N.E., 44481. Tel: 330-393-8721; 394-3426. [CEM]
Catechesis/Religious Programs—Tel: 330-393-8721.
Students 67.

7—St. Pius X, (1959), Rev. William J. Loveless.
Res., 1401 Moncrest Ave., N.W., 44485. Tel: 330-399-8881; 399-8882; Fax: 330-399-1361.
Schools—Queen of Apostles Building, (Grades K-4). Tel: 330-399-5411; Fax: 330-399-7364.; Notre Dame, (Grades 5-8). Tel: 330-399-5411; Fax: 330-399-2499. Mary Jo Dugan, Prin.
Lay Teachers 9; Students 87.
Catechesis/Religious Programs—Tel: 330-394-4343.
Students 56.

Waynesburg, Stark Co., St. James (1928), Rev. Michael D. Seifert.
Res., 400 W. Lisbon St., 44688. Tel: 330-866-9449.
School—Tel: 330-866-9556; Fax: 330-866-4075.
Lay Teachers 8; Students 108.
Catechesis/Religious Programs—Tel: 330-866-9449.
Students 118.

Wellsville, Columbiana Co., Immaculate Conception (1842), Rev. Bernard N. Gaeta; Mary E. Frost, Business Mgr.
Res., 1021 Riverside Ave., 43968. Tel: 330-532-3445; Fax: 330-532-3445. [CEM]
Catechesis/Religious Programs—Tel: 330-532-2382. Mr. Robert Barto, D.R.E.
Students 93.

Windham, Portage Co., St. Michael's (1943), Rev. James Paul Lang.
Res., 9736 E. Center St., 44288. Tel: 330-326-3531.
Catechesis/Religious Programs—Students 36.

On Duty Outside the Diocese:
Reverend Fathers—
Bonnot, Bernard R., Studio City, CA
Dailey, John, El Salvador, Central America
Deffenbaugh, Joseph T., Pensacola, FL
Nuzzi, Ronald, St. Louis, MO

Military Chaplains:
Reverend Fathers—
Garvey, Michael, U.S. Navy
Mikstay, Michael, U.S. Marines

Absent on Leave:
Reverend Fathers—
Brienz, Edward
Grabowski, Dennis
Santucci, Louis
Vazquez, Jose
Ziemba, Howard

Retired:
Reverend Monsignors—
Adamko, Cyril A.
Daum, John J.
Kelly, Thomas F.
Kolp, James
Oliver, Homer G.
Radetic, Branimir
Reagan, Donald
Torok, Dezso
Winca, George F.
Reverend Fathers—
Bakos, Stephen
Barrett, Robert P.
Bruce, Robert J.
Cavanaugh, James K.
Chonko, Michael J.
Curran, Gerald X.
Czaja, Joseph S.
Dobosiewciz, Leon W.
Duritsa, George M.
Esposito, Anthony
Fasline, Anthony
Flynn, Robert V.
Forgach, Carl J.
Franko, George M.
Friedrich, Ralph
Gubser, Paul
Herttna, Matthew M.
Hill, Robert
Horvath, Stephen
Klein, Albert J.
Lettau, David
Lyons, John F.
Marrokal, Donald, C.R.
McKarns, James
Mintjal, Frank
Murphy, Thomas
Murray, John
Nachtigal, Fred
Nist, Arthur
O'Brien, James E.
O'Leary, Patrick D.
Oser, Donald
Pierce, Blaine F.
Platt, Stewart
Pleban, Leo
Rath, John G.
Rich, Orlando S.
Sargent, John
Schmidt, John W.
Slipski, William P.
Snock, Francis
Spitale, John
Summers, John
Tamburrini, Joseph
Vacca, Bernard
Varble, Edward F.
Welsch, John
Witt, William
Yablonsky, Gabriel

Permanent Deacons:
Arend, David H., St. George, Lisbon
Bagley, Wilbur J., St. Joseph, Canton
Beil, David C., St. Christine, Youngstown
Boccieri, Nicholas J., St. Anthony, Youngstown
Brechbill, Kenneth W., (Retired)
Briestensky, Edward L., Sacred Heart, Canton
Brode, Russell J., Immaculate Conception, Ravenna
Brown, James, St. Christine, Youngstown
Bunofsky, Ronald J., St. John, Campbell
Burkhardt, Carl R., St. John the Baptist, Canton
Carney, John F., St. Joan of Arc, Streetsboro
Centric, Louis
Chase, Ralph, St. Catherine, Lake Milton
Cobett, Edgar, Little Flower, Middlebranch
Colon, Felipe, St. Rose of Lima, Youngstown
Conversino, David, St. Joan of Arc, Canton
Cosentino, Louis A., St. Jude, Columbia
Coulter, Terry L., St. Jude, Columbiana
Cuttica, Robert J., St. Christine, Youngstown
Davies, Martin H., On Duty Outside the Diocese.
DeFrange, Tim, St. Patrick, Kent
DiFrancesco, Salvatore, St. Matthias, Youngstown
Dubois, Bartley, St. William, Warren
Friedman, Robert J., St. Patrick, Hubbard
Fries, Joseph K., St. Mary, Massillon
Gies, Steven R., Immaculate Conception, Ravenna
Harvey, James G., St. William, Warren
Hatala, Ray H., Office of Permanent Diaconate
Hawkins, Edward, (Leave of Absence)
Heinz, Edward, St. Mary, Orwell
Ivan, Ellis C., Holy Spirit, Uniontown
Jaskiewicz, Albert F., St. Pius X, Warren
Johnson, Don, St. Joseph, Ashtabula
Johnson, Richard M., St. Joseph, Ashtabula
Klein, Robert E., St. Peter, Canton
Kocjancic, Michael A., St. Charles, Boardman
Krause, Harold R., Little Flower, North Canton
Kurkas, Edward G., St. Mary, Massillon
Lamar, Kevin T., St. Vincent de Paul, Vienna
Lambert, William H., St. Paul, North Canton
Layko, Ronald J., St. Christine, Youngstown
Lewis, David, St. James, Warren
Lisko, Paul, St. Nicholas, Struthers
Mastrovich, George, St. Ann, East Liverpool & Immaculate Conception, Wellsville
Medvez, Alvin A., St. Stephen, Youngstown; C.T.N.Y.
Milanek, Richard, St. Luke, Boardman
Milligan, Paul, St. Rose, Girard
Nohra, Joseph S., St. Maron & Mt. Carmel, Youngstown
O'Neill, Russell, Holy Spirit, Uniontown
Pallo, John D., Sacred Heart, Rock Creek

Pasko, Lawrence, St. Patrick, Leetonia
Pepoy, Joseph E., Our Lady of Perpetual Help, Aurora
Pohl, Peter P., SS. Philip & James, Canal Fulton
Prasek, Alan, St. Joseph, Ashtabula
Rapp, Robert, St. Ambrose, Garrettsville
Rentas, John, St. Rose of Lima, Youngstown
Reolfi, Ron, St. Paul, North Canton
Roberts, Michael R., Jr., St. Joseph, Austintown
Rohr, Thomas J., SS. Philip & James, Canal Fulton
Santiago, Enrique, St. Rose of Lima, Youngstown
Scarletto, Frederick C., Our Lady of Peace, Canton
Schlais, Michael, St. Stanislaus, Youngstown
Shay, Thomas R., Sr., St. Peter of the Fields, Rootstown
Sherwood, Ronald D., St. Benedict, Canton
Smith, James, St. Edward, Youngstown
Soich, Thomas G., St. Michael, Canfield
Terranova, John, St. Nicholas, Struthers
Toth, Joseph P., Blessed Sacrament, Warren
White, James A., St. Joseph, Randolph
Williams, Don, Our Lady of Peace, Canton
Wyles, Steve, St. Joseph, Massillon

INSTITUTIONS LOCATED IN THE DIOCESE

[A] SEMINARIES, RELIGIOUS, OR SCHOLASTICATES

YOUNGSTOWN. *Sacred Heart Retreat House & Renewal Center*, 3128 Logan Ave., P.O. Box 6074, 44501. Tel: 330-759-9539; Fax: 330-759-8235.
E-mail: mscyng@aol.com
Very Rev. Vincent T. Freeh, M.S.C., Supr.; Revs. Paul J. Hill, M.S.C., Dir. Novices; Thomas Carney, M.S.C., St. Rose of Lima, 50 Struthers-Coitsville Rd., Youngstown, OH 44505. Tel: 330-755-3633; Daniel Cipar, M.S.C., Our Lady of Lourdes, 200 E. Main St., East Palestine, OH 44413. Tel: 330-426-9346; Gerald J. Sommer, M.S.C., St. Mary, 1602 Market Ave. S., Canton, OH. Tel: 330-453-2110; Stephen Boland, M.S.C. Applications for missions, retreats, recollection days, novenas and Forty Hours to be made to the Rev. Father Superior. Priests 3; Brothers 4; Total Staff 11.

CANFIELD. *Society of St. Paul*, P.O. Box 595, 44406. Tel: 330-533-5503; 533-1076; Fax: 330-533-1076.
E-mail: paultheapostle@msn.com
Web site: www.albahouse.org
Revs. Matthew Roehrig, S.S.P., Supr.; Thomas Fogarty, S.S.P.; Jeffrey Mickler, S.S.P.; Francis J. Parella, S.S.P.; Angelo Y. Sye, S.S.P.; Bros. Luke Bedard, S.S.P.; Dismas Beique, S.S.P.; Richard Brunner, S.S.P.; Arthur McClelland, S.S.P.; Aloysius Milella, S.S.P.; John Joachim Naranjo, S.S.P.; Peter Scalise, S.S.P.; Joshua Seidl, S.S.P..Priests 5; Brothers 8.

[B] COLLEGES AND UNIVERSITIES

NORTH CANTON. *Walsh University*, 2020 Easton St., N.W., 44720-3396. Tel: 330-490-7090; Fax: 330-490-7165.
E-mail: admissions@walsh.edu
Web site: www.walsh.edu
For a complete listing, refer to the Colleges and Universities section.

[C] HIGH SCHOOLS, DIOCESAN

YOUNGSTOWN. *Cardinal Mooney High School*, 2545 Erie St., 44507. Tel: 330-788-5007; Fax: 330-788-4511.
E-mail: jmkudlacz@aol.com
Web site: www.cardinalmooney.com
Sr. Jane Marie Kudlacz, H.M., Prin..Sisters 1; Lay Teachers 49; Students 613.
Ursuline High School, 750 Wick Ave., 44505. Tel: 330-744-4563; Fax: 330-744-3358.
E-mail: ygnursuline@impresso.com
Web site: www.ursuline.com
Patricia Fleming, Prin..Priests 1; Sisters 3; Lay Teachers 36; Students 560.

ASHTABULA. *SS. John & Paul School*. (Grades 7-12). St. John High School Building, 541 W. 34th St., 44004. Tel: 440-997-5531; Fax: 440-998-1661.
E-mail: ssjp@knownet.net
Web site: www.knownet.net/users/ssjp
Miss Albina Larson, Prin..Lay Teachers 15; Students 185.

CANTON. *Central Catholic High*, 4824 Tuscarawas St. W., 44708-5198. Tel: 330-478-2131; Fax: 330-478-6086.
Web site: centcath.neo.rr.com
Rev. Robert W. Kaylor, Prin.; Mr. John Korecki, Asst. Prin.; Mr. Leo DeMatteis, Dean of Students; Mr. James Naegeli, Campus Ministry Dir..Priests 1; Lay Teachers 48; Total Staff 48; Students 665.

LOUISVILLE. *St. Thomas Aquinas High School*, 2121 Reno Dr., N.E., 44641. Tel: 330-875-1631; Fax: 330-875-8469. Mr. Joseph Meranto, Prin.; Mrs. Mary Ann McClellan, Asst. Prin.; Miss Cindi Eby, Dir. of Student Svcs. Lay Teachers 33; Religious 1; Total Staff 50; Students 488.

WARREN. *John F. Kennedy High School*, 2550 Central Pkwy., S.E., 44484. Tel: 330-369-1804; Fax: 330-369-1125.
E-mail: ygnkennedy@firststep
Girard-Niles-Youngtown. Rev. William Petrunak, Chap.; Mrs. June Drennen, Prin.; Mr. James Boyle, Asst. Prin. Priests 1; Lay Teachers 26; Students 371.

[D] ELEMETARY SCHOOLS, DIOCESAN

ASHTABULA. *SS. John & Paul School*. (Grades K-6). Our Lady of Mt. Carmel Building, 2150 Columbus Ave., 44004. Tel: 440-997-5821; Fax: 440-998-0514.
E-mail: ssjpmtc@knownet.net
Web site: www.knownet.net/users/ssjp
Consolidated school for Mother of Sorrows, St. Joseph & Our Lady of Mt. Carmel. Mrs. Donna Timonere, Prin. Lay Teachers 9; Students 200.

[E] MIDDLE SCHOOLS, DIOCESAN

WARREN. *Notre Dame School*. Queen of Peace Building, 261 Elm Rd., N.E., 44483. Tel: 330-399-5154; Fax: 330-399-2499.
E-mail: ygnpeace@impresso.com
Mr. Howard Mancini, Prin..Lay Teachers 18; Students 270.

[F] PRIVATE SCHOOLS

CANFIELD. *Ursuline Preschool & Kindergarten*, 4300 Shields Rd., 44406. Tel: 330-792-4150; Fax: 330-792-9553. Sr. Jacquelyn Herpy, O.S.U., Dir. & Prin. Ursuline Sisters 2; Lay Teachers 17; Students 300.

[G] GENERAL HOSPITALS

YOUNGSTOWN. *Humility of Mary Health Partners*, 5211 Mahoning Ave., 44515. Tel: 330-480-3776; Fax: 330-480-4548
For a complete listing, refer to the Hospitals section.
Humility of Mary Health Partners, St. Elizabeth Health Center, 1044 Belmont Ave., Box 1790, 44501. Tel: 330-746-7211; Fax: 330-480-7974
For a complete listing, refer to the Hospitals section.

CANTON. *CSAHS/UHHS - Canton, Inc.*, Mercy Medical Center, 1320 Mercy Dr., N.W., 44708. Tel: 330-489-1000; Fax: 330-489-1312.
E-mail: mail@cantonmercy.com
Web site: www.thequalityhospital.com
For a complete listing, refer to the Hospitals section.

WARREN. *St. Joseph Health Center*, 667 Eastland Ave., S.E., 44484. Tel: 330-841-4000; Fax: 330-841-4019
For a complete listing, refer to the Hospitals section.

[H] SPECIAL CARE FACILITIES

NORTH LIMA. *The Assumption Village*, 9800 Market St., 44452. Tel: 330-549-0740; Fax: 330-549-0701
For a complete listing, refer to the Special Care Facilities section.

[I] HOMES FOR AGED

AUSTINTOWN. *Humility House*, 755 Ohltown Rd., 44515. Tel: 330-505-0411; Fax: 330-544-5694
For a complete listing, refer to the Special Care Facilities section.

CANTON. *House of Loreto*, 2812 Harvard Ave., N.W., 44709. Tel: 330-453-8137; Fax: 330-453-8140
For a complete listing, refer to the Special Care Facilities section.

HUBBARD. *Villa Maria Teresa*, 50 Warner Rd., 44425. Tel: 330-759-9329 (Villa); 875-4635 (Emmaus House); Fax: 330-759-7290.
E-mail: jcoblate@aol.com
Web site: www.oblatesistersofshj.com
For a complete listing, refer to the Special Care Facilities section.

LOUISVILLE. *Emmaus House*, 1515 California Ave., 44641. Tel: 330-875-4635.
E-mail: rsacred@neo.rr.com
For a complete listing, refer to the Special Care Facilities section.
St. Joseph Care Center, 2308 Reno Dr., 44641. Tel: 330-875-5562; Fax: 330-875-8947.
E-mail: sjcc@neo.rr.com
For a complete listing, refer to the Special Care Facilities section.

NORTH LIMA. *The Assumption Village*, 9800 Market St., 44452. Tel: 330-549-0740; Fax: 330-549-0701
For a complete listing, refer to the Special Care Facilities section.

[J] MONASTERIES AND RESIDENCES OF PRIESTS AND BROTHERS

YOUNGSTOWN. *Mt. Alverna Friary*, 517. S. Belle Vista Ave., 44509. Tel: 330-799-1888; Fax: 330-799-0723.
E-mail: bruit@hotmail.com
Franciscan Friars. Revs. John E. Reiss, O.F.M., Pastor of Our Lady of Hungary; Vit Fiala, O.F.M., Dir.; Sandor Krupa, O.F.M.; Bro. Reginald Antal, O.F.M. Total in Residence 4; Total Staff 4.

[K] CONVENTS AND RESIDENCES FOR SISTERS

CANFIELD. *Motherhouse and Educational Center of the Ursuline Sisters*, 4250 Shields Rd., 44406. Tel: 330-792-7636; Fax: 330-792-9553. Sr. Nancy Dawson, O.S.U., Gen. Supr. Total in Community 71; Total in Residence 72; Total Staff 5.
Ursuline Center, 4280 Shields Rd., 44406. Tel: 330-799-4941; Fax: 330-792-9553.

CANTON. *Sancta Clara Monastery*, 4200 N. Market Ave., 44714. Tel: 330-492-1171; Fax: 330-492-2227.
E-mail: clares@ezo.net
Rev. Nickolas Lohkamp, O.F.M., Chap. Poor Clares of Perpetual Adoration. Cloistered Professed Nuns 12.

HUBBARD. *Villa Maria Teresa*, 50 Warner Rd., 44425. Tel: 330-759-9329; Fax: 330-759-7290.
E-mail: jcoblate@aol.com
Web site: www.oblatesistersofshj.com
Sr. Teresina Rosa, O.S.H.J., Regl. Supr. & Convent Supr. Novitiate and American Headquarters of Oblate Sisters of the Sacred Heart of Jesus..Sisters 20; Total Staff 7.

[L] CATHOLIC CHARITIES SOCIAL SERVICE AGENCIES

YOUNGSTOWN. *Diocese of Youngstown Catholic Charities Corporation*, 144 W. Wood. St., 44503. Tel: 330-744-8451; Fax: 330-742-6447.
E-mail: ccadmin@cboss.com
Web site: www.doy.org

ASHTABULA. *Catholic Charities of Ashtabula County*, 4200 Park Ave., 3rd Floor, 44004. Tel: 440-992-2121; Fax: 440-992-5974.
E-mail: csl@ncweb.com
Danita M. Eartly, Exec. Dir..Total Assisted 5,000; Total Staff 18.

CANTON. *Catholic Charities of Stark County*, 1500 Market Ave. N., Ste. 3, 44714. Tel: 330-454-2220; Fax: 330-454-2255. Mr. Ed Baur, Exec. Dir. Total Assisted 350.

RAVENNA. *Catholic Charities of Portage County*, 206 W. Main St., P.O.Box 471, 44266. Tel: 330-297-7745; Fax: 330-297-7763.

WARREN. *Catholic Community Services*, P.O. Box 1740, 44482. Tel: 330-393-4254; Fax: 330-393-4050.
E-mail: nancy-ccs@cboss.com
Nancy Voitus, Interim Dir. Family and Child Welfare Work in Mahoning, Trumbull and Columbiana Counties. Total Staff 60.

[M] HOMES FOR WOMEN

YOUNGSTOWN. *Beatitude House*, 1515 Fifth Ave., 44504. Tel: 330-744-3147; Fax: 330-744-3991.
E-mail: sispeg@netzero.net
Transitional Housing, Job Preparation, Job Training, Counseling, and Case Management for Economically Disadvantaged Women. Sr. Margaret Scheetz, O.S.U., Exec.Dir. Total Assisted 113; Total Staff 16.

[N] RETREAT HOUSES

YOUNGSTOWN. *Sacred Heart Retreat and Renewal Center*, 3128 Logan Way, P.O. Box 6074, 44501. Tel: 330-759-9539; Fax: 330-759-8235.
E-mail: MSCYNG@aol.com
Society of the Missionaries of the Sacred Heart. Revs. Vincent T. Freeh, M.S.C., Dir.; Steve Boland, M.S.C., Coord.; Bro. Eugene Thomas, M.S.C., House Mgr. Residents 3; Total Staff 3.

[O] NEWMAN CENTERS

YOUNGSTOWN. *Newman Center at Youngstown State University*, 254 Madison Ave., 44504-1627. Tel: 330-747-9202; Fax: 330-747-1667.
E-mail: Newman@ysunewmancenter.com
Web site: www.ysunewmancenter.com
Total Staff 3.

KENT. *Kent State University Newman Center*, 1424 Horning Rd., 44240. Tel: 330-678-0240; Fax: 330-678-7780.
E-mail: jjerek@kent.edu
Rev. John M. Jerek; Sr. Nancy DiCola, O.S.U., Pastoral Min.; Mrs. Carmen Roebke, Pastoral & Campus Min.; Mrs. Barbara DeGrand, Office Mgr. Total in Residence 1; Total Staff 5.

[P] MISCELLANEOUS LISTINGS

YOUNGSTOWN. *"The Catholic Exponent"*, 144 W. Wood St., P.O. Box 6787, 44503. Tel: 330-744-5251; Fax: 330-742-5252.
E-mail: exponent@cboss.com
Web site: www.doy.org

Caritas Communities, 225 Elm St., 44503. Tel: 330-744-8451; 384-1555; Fax: 330-742-6447.
E-mail: bcorbin@cboss.com
Web site: www.rc.net/youngstown/catholic_charities
Sr. Denise Maher, H.M., Pres. & CEO; Brian Corbin, Chm.
As a member of Corporation of Catholic Charities Housing Opportunities and the Humility of Mary Housing Program, Caritas Communities will serve as Property Management Corporation for low income and special needs housing. Families Assisted 154; Total Staff 5.

Catholic Charities Housing Opportunities Corporation, 225 Elm St., 44503. Tel: 330-744-8451, Ext. 275; Fax: 330-742-6447.
E-mail: ccho@cboss.com
Web site: www.rc.net/youngstown/catholic_charities
Mr. Brian Corbin, Pres.; George Garchar, Ex. Dir.
Purpose: Provides coordination, integration and leadership in the provision of housing services which promote affordable housing in the community. Total Families Assisted 490; Total Staff 2.

Declaration of Trust of Trumbull, Department of Education,144 W. Wood St., 44503. Tel: 330-744-8451; Fax: 330-742-6448.
E-mail: ygnsupt@connect.com
County Catholic School Endowment Fund.

Humility of Mary Information Systems, Inc., 1343 Belmont Ave., 44504. Tel: 330-746-1010; Fax: 330-746-6824.
E-mail: chuck_folkwein@hmis.org
Chuck Folkwein, Senior Vice Pres. & CIO.

St. Elizabeth Development Foundation, 1044 Belmont Ave., P.O. Box 1790, 44501-1790. Tel: 330-480-3349; Fax: 330-480-2957.
E-mail: edward_toth@hmis.org
Edward R. Toth, Jr., Pres. & CEO..Total Staff 2.

CANFIELD. *The Ursuline Center*, 4280 Shields Rd., 44406. Tel: 330-799-4941; Fax: 330-792-9553.
E-mail: treerich@aol.com
Web site: www.theursulines.org
Resource and outreach services for the poor, including prison ministry, AIDS ministry, retreats, and adult formation. Total Assisted 21,000; Sisters 8; Total Staff 10.

CANTON. *Sisters of Charity Foundation of Canton*, The United Band Bldg., Ste. 500, 220 Market Ave. S., 44702. Tel: 330-454-5800; Fax: 330-454-5909.
E-mail: vconley@scfcanton.org
Victoria Conley, Exec. Dir.

LOUISVILLE. *St. Thomas Aquinas High School Endowment Fund*, 2121 Reno Drive, N.E., 44641. Tel: 330-875-1631; Fax: 330-875-8469. Joseph Meranto, Pres.; Vickie Frustaci, Business Mgr.

MASSILLON. *National Shrine of St. Dymphna* (1938), 3000 Erie St. S., P.O. Box 4, 44648-0004. Tel: 330-833-8478. Located on the grounds of Heartland Behavioral Healthcare. Rev. Matthew M. Herttna, Chap. & Dir.

WARREN. *St. Joseph Development Foundation*, 667 Eastland Ave., S.E., 44484. Tel: 330-841-4198; Fax: 330-841-4019.
E-mail: edward_toth@hmis.org
Edward R. Toth, Jr., Pres. & CEO..Total Staff 2.

[Q] DIOCESAN CEMETERIES

YOUNGSTOWN. *Calvary*, 248 S. Belle Vista Ave., 44509.
Catholic Cemeteries of the Diocese of Youngstown, 144 W. Wood St., 44503. Tel: 330-744-8451; Fax: 330-742-6448. Rev. Msgr. Frank A. Carfagna, Dir.
Resurrection, 300 N. Racoon Rd., 44515. Tel: 216-799-1900.

MASSILLON. *Calvary*, 3469 Lincoln Way E., 44647.

WARREN. *All Souls*, Rte. 3, Box 500, 44483.

RELIGIOUS INSTITUTES OF MEN REPRESENTED IN THE DIOCESE

For further details refer to the corresponding bracketed number in the Religious Institutes of Men or Women section.

[0320]—*Brothers of Christian Instruction*.—F.I.C.
[]—*Congregation of the Apostles of Jesus*.—A.J.
[0520]—*Franciscan Friars*. (Immaculate Conception Prov. of New York).—O.F.M.
[]—*Franciscans-Province of St. John the Baptist*.—O.F.M.
[1110]—*Missionaries of the Sacred Heart*.—M.S.C.
[0430]—*Order of Preachers (Dominicans)*. (Prov. of St. Joseph).—O.P.
[1020]—*Pauline Fathers and Brothers*.—S.S.P.
[]—*Priestly Fraternity of St. Peter*.—F.S.S.P.
[1230]—*Servants of the Paraclete*.—s.P.

RELIGIOUS INSTITUTES OF WOMEN REPRESENTED IN THE DIOCESE

[0100]—*Adorers of the Blood of Christ*.—A.S.C.
[]—*Antonine Sisters*.—A.S.
[]—*Benediction Sisters (Byzantine Sisters)*.—O.S.B.
[1040]—*Congregation of the Divine Spirit*.—C.D.S.
[1710]—*Congregation of the Third Order of St. Francis of Mary Immaculate, Joliet, IL*.—O.S.F.
[1070-28]—*Dominican Sisters*.—O.P.
[]—*Mission Helpers of the Sacred Heart*.—M.H.S.H.
[3050]—*Oblate Sisters of the Sacred Heart of Jesus*.—O.S.H.J.
[3210]—*Poor Clares of Perpetual Adoration*.—P.C.P.A.
[0580]—*Sisters of Charity of St. Augustine*.—C.S.A.
[0990]—*Sisters of Divine Providence*.—C.D.P.
[2575]—*Sisters of Mercy of the Americas*.—R.S.M.
[2990]—*Sisters of Notre Dame*.—S.N.D.
[]—*Sisters of Our Lady of Kilimanjaro*.—C.D.N.K.
[3830-08]—*Sisters of St. Joseph*.—C.S.J.
[]—*Sisters of St. Joseph of Springfield*.—S.S.J.
[3910]—*Sisters of St. Joseph of St. Mark*.—S.J.S.M.
[2110]—*Sisters of the Humility of Mary*.—H.M.
[3730]—*Sisters of the Order of St. Basil the Great*.—O.S.B.M.
[4120-07]—*Ursuline Nuns of the Congregation of Paris*.—O.S.U.
[4160]—*Vincentian Sisters of Charity*.—V.S.C.

NECROLOGY

✠ Malone, Most Rev. James W., (Retired). —Died April 9, 2000.
† Conley, Philip P, Poland, OH Holy Family. —Died May 9, 2000.
† Fannon, Rev. Msgr. Robert C., (Retired). —Died April 5, 2000.
† Turk, John P., Warren, OH St. Joseph. —Died March 9, 2000.

Apostolate to Hungarians

Most Reverend

ATTILA MIKLOSHAZY, S.J., S.T.D.

Titular Bishop of Castel Minore and Bishop for the spiritual assistance to the Hungarian emigrant people; ordained June 18, 1961; appointed August 12, 1989; consecrated November 4, 1989. *Res., St. Augustine's Seminary, 2661 Kingston Rd., Scarborough, Ontario, Canada, M1M 1M3.* Tel.: 416-261-7207; Fax: 416-261-2529.

ESTABLISHED MAY 20, 1983.

The Apostolate of the Bishop of Hungarians living outside of Hungary extends territorially to all the Hungarian communities existing outside of Hungary. The main purpose of the Apostolate is to give spiritual assistance to them through and in cooperation with the local ordinary and pastors.

Former Bishop—Most Rev. LADISLAUS A. IRANYI, Sch.P., ord. March 13, 1938; appt. May 20, 1983; cons. July 27, 1983; died March 6, 1987.

Bishop's Office—2661 Kingston Rd., Scarborough, Ontario, Canada, M1M 1M3. Tel: 416-261-7202; Fax: 416-261-2529.

Delegate of the Bishop in Europe—Rev. Dr. FERENC CSERHATI, *Ung.Kath.Mission, Oberfohringerstr.40, D-81925, Munchen, Germany.* Tel: 49-89-982-637; Fax: 49-89-985-419.

Delegate of the Bishop in the U.S.A.—Rev. STEPHEN N. MUSTOS, Sch.P., *223 Third St., Passaic, NJ, 07055.* Tel: 973-779-0332; Fax: 973-778-4263.

American Hungarian Catholic Priests' Association—East Coast Division: Rev. STEPHEN MUSTOS, Sch.P., *223 Third St., Passaic, NJ, 07055.* Tel: 973-779-0332; Fax: 973-778-4263. Middle East Division: Rev. BARNABAS G. KISS, O.F.M., *8423 South St., Detroit, MI, 48209.* Tel: 313-842-1133; Fax: 313-842-2773.

Hungarian Catholic League of America, Inc.—Rev. Msgr. WILLIAM I. VARSANYI, P.A., Chm., *One Cathedral Sq., Providence, RI, 02903.* Tel: 401-278-4520; Fax: 401-278-4548.

Hungarian Priests' Association in Canada—Rev. ALEXANDER EROS, *337 Hellems Ave., Welland, Ontario, Canada, L3B 3C2.* Tel: 905-734-3772.

Newspapers & Magazines—"Eletunk", (Our Life); Rev. OTTO FEJOS, Editor, *Landwehrstrasse 66, D-80336, Munchen 2, Germany.* Tel: 49-89-532-8288; Fax: 49-89-532-8245.

"HIS- Press Service"—published by the Hungarian Institute for Sociology of Religion. Rev. EMERIC ANDRAS, S.J., Editor, *Gerlgasse 10/3, A-1030, Wien, Austria.* Tel: 43-1-798-0233; Fax: 43-1-798-4181.

"Tavlatok"—(Perspectives), Quarterly on Worldview, Spirituality and Culture, ed. by the Unio Cleri Hungarici. Revs. FERENC SZABO, S.J.; FERENC NAGY, S.J., *Sodras u. 13, H-1026, Budapest, Hungary.* Tel: 36-1-176-7062; Fax: 36-1-275-0269.

"A Sziv"—(Sacred Heart Messenger), monthly, published by the Hungarian Jesuit Fathers. Rev. NEMESHEGYI PETER, S.J., Editor, *Pf. 586, H-1398, Budapest, Hungary.* Tel: 36-1-176-7062; Fax: 36-1-275-0269., Address in Canada: *432 Sheppard Ave. E., Willowdale, Ontario, Canada, M2N 3B7.*

STATISTICS

Most personnel and institutions are under the jurisdiction of their local ordinaries.

NECROLOGY

Incorporated in diocesan and archdiocesan listings.

Apostolate For Lithuanian Catholics

Living Outside Lithuania

Most Reverend

PAUL A. BALTAKIS, O.F.M.

Titular Bishop of Egara and Bishop for Spiritual Assistance of Lithuanian Catholic; Living Outside Lithuania; ordained August 24, 1952; appointed June 1, 1984; consecrated September 14, 1984. *Res., 361 Highland Blvd., Brooklyn, NY, 11207.* Tel.: 718-827-7932; Fax: 718-827-6696.

IN CARITATE SERVIAMUS DEO

ESTABLISHED JUNE 1, 1984.

The Apostolate of the Bishop for Lithuanian Catholics extends worldwide to all Lithuanian communities existing outside Lithuania, 75 percent of them in the U.S.A. The purpose of the apostolate is to give spiritual assistance to them, in cooperation with the local ordinaries and pastors. Specific faculties enabling the implementation of the Bishop's responsibilities were granted by the Holy See on July 21, 1986.

E-mail address: lcra@earthlink.net:

Former Lithuanian Bishops—Most Rev. VINCENTAS BRIZGYS, Ph.D., J.C.D., cons. May 19, 1940; Titular Bishop of Bosana; Auxiliary Bishop of Kaunas, Lithuania (Impeditus); died April 23, 1992.—Most Rev. ANTANAS DEKSNYS, Ph.D., cons. Jan. 15, 1969; Titular Bishop of Lavello, *Res., Villa Lithuania, Piazza Asti, Rome, Italy, 00182.* died May 5, 1999.

Bishop's Office—361 Highland Blvd., Brooklyn, NY, 11207. Tel: 718-827-7932; Fax: 718-827-6696.

Secretary to the Bishop—Rev. EDMUNDAS PUTRIMAS.

"Bishop's Brief"—Quarterly information bulletin.

Bishop's Pastoral Council—Rev. ANTANAS SAULAITIS, S.J., Vice Pres.; Sr. IGNE MARIJOSIUS, Prog. Dir.; Mr. ALGIS SILBAJORIS, Information; SAULIUS V. KUPRYS, Gen. Counsel.

[*]Lithuanian R. Catholic Religious Aid—Mrs. VIDA JANKAUSKAS, Exec. Dir., *351 Highland Blvd., Brooklyn, NY, 11207.* Tel: 718-647-2434; Fax: 718-827-6696.

Pontifical Lithuanian College of St. Casimir—Rev. Msgr. ALGIMANTAS BARTKUS, J.C.L., Rector, *via Casalmonferrato 20, Rome, Italy, 00182.* Tel: 06-70-24-908; Fax: 06-70-11-659.

Vocations and Public Relations Director—Rev. EDMUNDAS PUTRIMAS, *1011 College St., Toronto, Ontario, Canada, M6H-1A8.* Tel: 416-533-0621.

Publications—The Observer, Darbininkas, Draugas, Journeys, Laiskai Lietuviams, Vytis, Musu Zinios, I Laisve, Garsas, Laivas.

World Lithuanian R. Catholic Priests' League—Rev. AGUSTINAS SIMANAVICIUS, O.F.M., Pres., *1011 College St., Toronto, Ontario, Canada, MGH 1A8.* Tel: 416-533-0621; Fax: 416-532-4816.

Lithuanian R. Catholic Priests' League of America—Rev. Msgr. ALBERT CONTONS, Pres., *P.O. Box 1025, Hamerock, MA, 02047.* Tel: 781-834-4079.

Lithuanian Franciscan Province of St. Casimir—Very Rev. PLACIDAS BARIUS, O.F.M., Prov., *Kennebunkport, ME, 04046.* Tel: 207-967-2031; Fax: 207-967-5721.

Lithuanian Jesuit Province—Very Rev. ANTANAS SAULAITIS, S.J., Prov., *2345 W. 56th St., Chicago, IL, 60636.* Tel: 312-737-8400.

Lithuanian Marian Province of St. Casimir—Very Rev. DONALD PETRAITIS, M.I.C., Prov., *6336 Kilbourn Ave., Chicago, IL, 60636.* Tel: 312-582-1666.

Sisters of the Immaculate Conception of the Blessed Virgin Mary—Sr. PAULE SAVICKAITE, Prov., *Rte. 21, R.D. 2, Putnam, CT, 06260.* Tel: 203-928-7955; Fax: 203-928-1930.

Poor Sisters of Jesus Crucified and the Sorrowful Mother—Sr. MARY J. VALLERE, Supr. Gen., *261 Thatcher St., Brockton, MA, 02402.* Tel: 617-588-5070.

Sisters of St. Casimir—Sr. IMMACULATA WENDT, Gen. Supr., *2601 W. Marquette Rd., Chicago, IL, 60609.* Tel: 312-776-1324.

Sisters of St. Francis—Sr. JOAN BRAZINSKI, Dir., *3603 McRoberts Rd., Pittsburgh, PA, 15234.* Tel: 412-882-9911.

INSTITUTIONS LOCATED IN THE DIOCESE

[A] SCHOOLS

CHICAGO, IL. *Maria High School.*

THOMPSON, CT. *Marionapolis Prep School.*

[B] HOSPITALS

CHICAGO, IL. *Holy Cross Hospital.*

[C] NURSING HOMES AND HOMES FOR THE AGED

BROCKTON, MA. *St. Joseph Manor Nursing Home.*

ELMHURST, PA. *St. Mary's Villa.*

HOLLAND, PA. *St. Joseph Nursing Home.*

LEMONT, IL. *Holy Family Villa.*

PUTNAM, CT. *Maulaitis Nursing Home.*

[D] MISCELLANEOUS

BROOKLYN, NY. *Franciscan Cultural Center.*

CHICAGO, IL. *Catholic Action Fund.*

Jesuit Lithuanian Center.

Lithuanian Roman Catholic Charities, 4545 W. 63rd St., 60629.

Matulaitis Institute.

MANCHESTER, MI. *Lithuanian American R. Catholic Federation Youth Camp,* 15100 Austin Rd., 48158.

PUTNAM, IL. *American Lithuanian Catholic Archives.*

WEST BRATTLEBORO, VT. *Camp Neringa.*

[E] CEMETERIES

CHICAGO, IL. *St. Casimir Lithuanian.*

RELIGIOUS INSTITUTES OF MEN REPRESENTED IN THE DIOCESE

For further details refer to the corresponding bracketed number in the Religious Institutes of Men or Women section.

[]—*Congregation of the Marians Province of St. Casimir.* (Chicago, IL).

[]—*Franciscan Fathers of the Lithuanian Province of St. Casimir.* (Kennebunkport, ME).

[]—*Jesuit Fathers of Della Strada.* (Chicago, IL).

RELIGIOUS INSTITUTES OF WOMEN REPRESENTED IN THE DIOCESE

[3240]—*Poor Sisters of Jesus Crucified and the Sorrowful Mother.* (Brockton, MA).—C.J.C.

[2140]—*Sisters of Immaculate Conception of the Blessed Virgin Mary.* (Putnam, CT).

[3740]—*Sisters of St. Casimir.* (Chicago, IL).—S.S.C.

[1690]—*Sisters of St. Francis.* (Pittsburgh, PA).—O.S.F.

STATISTICS

Most personnel and institutions are under the jurisdiction of their local ordinaries.

NECROLOGY

(No Deaths)

Personal Prelatures

Personal Prelatures

Personal prelatures are jurisdictional structures of a secular type which are established by the Holy See as an instrument within the hierarchical pastoral work of the Church to carry out special pastoral or missionary tasks. Personal prelatures are based on the principle of insertion into the local Church. In this they differ essentially from the personal dioceses, such as those constituted for the faithful of a particular rite, which are based on the principle of independence or autonomy in regard to local Churches.

Vatican II provided for setting up personal prelatures (see Decree, Presbyterorum ordinis, no. 10). Additional norms were established in subsequent pontifical legislation (see Motu proprio Ecclesiae Sanctae no. 1, no. 4, August 6, 1966 and the Apostolic Constitution Regimini Ecclesiae Universae, no. 49, no. 1, Aug. 15, 1967). General legislation concerning personal prelatures is contained in canons 294 to 297 of the 1983 Code of Canon Law.

Personal prelatures are to be established by the Holy See after hearing the views of the respective Episcopal Conferences (can. 294). They are governed by a Prelate according to statutes given by the Holy See. The Prelate is their proper Ordinary, who may incardinate priests and must look after their spiritual and temporal welfare (can. 295). Lay people can dedicate themselves by means of a contractural agreement, to the apostolic activities of the prelature (can. 296). And the statutes are to determine the relations of the prelature with the Ordinaries of the places in which the prelature works, with the prior consent of the Ordinaries (can. 297).

PRELATURE OF OPUS DEI

(Praelatura Sanctae Crucis et Operis Dei)

Most Reverend

JAVIER ECHEVARRIA, J.D., J.C.D.

Prelate of the Prelature of the Holy Cross and Opus Dei; ordained August 7, 1955; appointed April 20, 1994; episcopal ordination January 6, 1995. *Curia of the Prelature, Viale Bruno Buozzi 73, 00197, Rome, Italy. Tel: 39-06-808-961.*

Erected by the Apostolic Constitution, "Ut sit," on November 28, 1982 by Pope John Paul II.

Opus Dei was founded on October 2, 1928 by Blessed Josemaria Escriva, to spread in all sectors of society a profound awareness of the universal call to sanctity in ordinary life and, more specifically, in the exercise of one's work.

Curia of the Prelature—Viale Bruno Buozzi, 73, 00197. Rome, Italy. Tel: 39-06-808-961.

Vicar General—Rev. Msgr. Fernando Ocariz, Ph.D., S.T.D., *Viale Bruno Buozzi 73, 00197. Rome, Italy.* Rev. Thomas Bohlin, residing at the Curia of the Prelature.

Regional Vicar for the United States—Very Rev. Arne A. Panula, Ph.D., S.T.D., *139 East 34th St., New York, NY 10016.* Tel: 646-742-2700.

Vicar for the Midwest—Very Rev. Peter V. Armenio, B.S., Ph.D., *5800 N. Keating Ave., Chicago, IL 60646.* Tel: 312-283-5800. Embracing the states of Illinois, Indiana, Missouri and Wisconsin.

Vicar for California—Very Rev. George M. Rossman, Ph.D., *765 14th Ave., San Francisco, CA 94118.* Tel: 415-386-0431.

Acting Vicar for Texas—Very Rev. Gerald Kolf, B.S., M.B.A., S.T.D., *5505 Chaucer Dr., Houston, TX 77005.* Tel: 715-523-4351.

Represented in the Archdioceses of Boston, Chicago, Los Angeles, Milwaukee, Newark, New York, St. Louis, San Antonio, San Francisco, Washington and in the Dioceses of Burlington, Dallas, Fort Wayne-South Bend, Galveston-Houston, Gary, Oakland, Palm Beach, Peoria, Pittsburgh, Providence, Trenton and Victoria.

CHAPLAINS FOR THE UNITED STATES

State of New York

New Rochelle—Revs. Bradley K. Arturi; Martin Heneghan. *99 Overlook Circle, New Rochelle, NY 10804.* Tel: 914-235-6128.

New York—Very Rev. Arne A. Panula, Ph.D., S.T.D., Reg. Vicar; Rev. Msgr. Javier Garcia de Cardenas; Rev. Msgr. James A Kelly; Revs. James Albrecht; Robert Brisson. *139 East 34th St., New York, NY 10016.* Tel: 646-742-2700; Rev. Malcolm M. Kennedy. *330 Riverside Dr., New York, NY 10025.* Tel: 212-222-3285.

District of Columbia

Washington—Revs. William H. Stetson; Lawrence A. Kutz; C. John McCloskey, III. *2301 Wyoming Ave. N.W., Washington, DC 20008.* Tel: 202-234-1566; Revs. Ronald S. Gillis; Timothy J. Uhen. *4300 Garrison St. N.W., Washington, DC 20016.* Tel: 202-362-2419; Rev. Deo G. Rosales, *4955 Linnean Ave., N.W., Washington, DC 20008.* Tel: 202-237-6894.

State of Massachusetts

Cambridge—Revs. Robert P. Bucciarelli; Juan Velez. *25 Follen St., Cambridge, MA 02138.* Tel: 617-354-3204.

Chestnut Hill—Revs. Raphael F. Caamano; Richard W. Rieman; Michael Giesler; Alvaro Silva (in res., St. Ann, Quincy, MA). *481 Hammond St., Chestnut Hill, MA 02167.* Tel: 617-738-7348.

State of New Jersey

Princeton—Rev. William G. Shaughnessy. *34 Mercer St., Princeton, NJ 08540.* Tel: 609-497-9448.

South Orange—Rev. Robert A. Connor. *170 Montrose Ave., South Orange, NJ 07079.* Tel: 201-763-8397.

State of Pennsylvania

Pittsburgh—Revs. Joseph P. Landauer; Martin J. Miller. *5090 Warwick Ter., Pittsburgh, PA 15213.* Tel: 412-683-8448.

State of Florida

Delray Beach—Rev. Christopher Schmitt., *4409 Frances Dr., Delray Beach, FL 33445.* Tel: 305-498-1249.

Miami—Revs. Salvador S. Vahi; Orestes Gonzalez., *4415 S.W. 88th Ave., Miami, FL 33165.* Tel: 305-551-7965.

State of Rhode Island

Providence—Rev. Thomas J. Lamb., *224 Bowen St., Providence, RI 02906.* Tel: 401-272-7834.

State of Illinois

Chicago—Very Rev. Peter V. Armenio, Ph.D., Vicar for the Midwest; Revs. John C. Agnew; Edward G. Maristany; Frank Hoffman. *5800 N. Keating Ave., Chicago, IL 60646.* Tel: 312-283-5800; Rev. James Socias. *7225 N. Greenview Ave., Chicago, IL 60646.* Tel: 312-465-3486; Revs. John Debicki; Hilary Mahaney; Charles Ferrer; Fred Piegl. *1825 N. Wood St., Chicago, IL 60622.* Tel: 312-278-2644.

Oak Park—Revs. Richard Schendt; Barry Cole. *829 S. Euclid, Oak Park, IL 60304.* Tel: 708-383-0928.

Urbana—Rev. Jerome L. Jung. *715 W. Michigan, Urbana, IL 61801.* Tel: 217-367-6650.

State of Indiana

South Bend—Rev. David J. Cavanagh, *1121 N. Notre Dame Ave., South Bend, IN 46617.* Tel: 219-232-0550.

State of Missouri

Kirkwood—Revs. Mark Mannion; John J. Alvarez. *100 E. Essex Ave., Kirkwood, MO 63122.* Tel: 314-821-1608.

State of Wisconsin

Brookfield—Revs. Gregory Coyne; John Kubeck. *12900 W. North Ave., Brookfield, WI 53005.* Tel: 414-784-1523.

State of California

San Francisco—Very Rev. George M. Rossman, Ph.D., Vicar for California; Revs. Torlach C. Delargy; John Meyer. *765 14th Ave., San Francisco, CA 94118.* Tel: 415-386-0431.

Menlo Park—Rev. Matthew Bloomer. *1160 Santa Cruz Ave., Menlo Park, CA 94025.* Tel: 415-327-1675.

Mill Valley—Rev. Jose P. Ruisanchez. *108 Kipling Dr., Mill Valley, CA 94941.* Tel: 415-388-4531.

Los Angeles—Revs. Rene J. Schatteman; John R. Waiss. *655 Levering Ave., Los Angeles, CA 90024.* Tel: 213-208-0941.

Berkeley—Rev. Paul A. Donlan. *2710 College Ave., Berkeley, CA 94705.* Tel: 510-548-2819.

State of Texas

Houston—Very Rev. Gerald Kolf, B.S., M.B.A, S.T.D., Acting Vicar for Texas; Revs. Michael Barrett; Michael J. Manz. *5505 Chaucer Dr., Houston, TX 77005.* Tel: 713-523-4351.

Irving—Rev. John E. Solarski. *3610 Wingren, Irving, TX 75062.* Tel: 214-650-0064.

San Antonio—Rev. George W. Crafts. *345 E. Summit Ave., San Antonio, TX 78212.* Tel: 210-732-3065.

Eastern Church

Eastern Catholic Association (ECA)
The Eastern Catholic Associates is the association of all Eastern Catholic Bishops in the United States. All Eastern Catholic Bishops, diocesan bishops (and their equivalent in law) and auxiliaries are members. The Association represents the Armenian, Chaldean, Maronite Melkite, Romanian, Ruthenian and Ukrainian Churches. The Syriac, Syro-Malabar and Russian churches are also represented but without a bishop member since they presently have no established hierarchy in the United States. Officers of the Association are—President: Most Rev. Nicholas J. Samra, D.D., V.G., Auxiliary Bishop of Newton, 8525 Cole, Warren MI 48093-5239. Tel: 810-558-0143; Fax: 810-558-0144. Vice President: Most Rev. Robert M. Moskal, D.D., Bishop of the Ukrainian Diocese of St. Josaphat in Parma, 5720 State Rd., Parma, OH 44134-7180. Tel: 216-888-1522; Fax: 216-888-3477. Secretary: Most Rev. John Botean, Bishop of Romanian Catholic Diocese of St. George, Canton, 1121 44th St., N.E., Canton, OH 44714-1297. Tel: 330-492-4086; Fax: 330-493-1416.

Religious Education Department
The ECA has established the ECDD - The Eastern Catholic Conference of Diocesan Directors of Religious Education which oversees, through God With Us Publications, all publications of catechetical materials published by it and used in Eastern Catholic Churches, mainly of Byzantine tradition. Rev. John S. Kachuba, M.A., Chm.-ECDD & Dir.-Religious Education, Eparchy of Parma, 532 Lloyd R., Euclid, OH 44132. Tel: 216-732-7292; Fax: 216-732-9434. Rev. Fred Saato, Asst. Chm./Dir.-Publications & Dir.-Education Services, Eparchy of Newton, 27 Lake Ave., Yonkers, NY 10703. Tel: 914-968-2428; Fax: 914-423-9239. Sr. Ann Laszok, O.S.B.M., Treas. & Bus. Mgr.-ECDD, 204 Olivia St., McKeesrocks, PA 15136. Tel: 412-481-9778; Fax: 412-331-8140. God With Us Publications, P.O. Box 99203, Pittsburgh, PA 15233. Tel: 412-771-9119; Fax: 412-766-8244.

In addition to the Eastern Churches listed below there are other Eastern Churches in communion with Rome which do not have Ordinaries of their own in the United States. Consequently they are under the jurisdiction of the local Ordinary and the various parishes and institutions are incorporated in the Archdiocesan and Diocesan listings. Please consult these pages for full information regarding churches, personnel and statistics. For convenience, however, listed below are the Russian Eastern Churches and the cities in which they are located.

RUSSIAN

California
El Segundo (LA), St. Andrew
San Francisco (SFR), Our Lady of Fatima Center

New York
New York (NY), St. Michael Chapel (St. Patrick's Old Cathedral)

Armenian Catholic Exarchate of U.S.A. and Canada.

Most Reverend

NERSES MIKAEL SETIAN, D.D., J.C.D.

Former Apostolic Exarch for the Armenian Catholics in the U.S.A. and Canada; born October 18, 1918; appointed Titular Bishop of Ancera and Apostolic Exarch for the Armenian Catholics in the U.S.A. and Canada July 3, 1981; ordained December 5, 1981; installed December 27, 1981; retired. *Res., c/o Our Lady Queen of Martyrs Church, 1327 Pleasant Ave., Los Angeles, CA, 90033-2328.*

Legal Title: Apostolic Exarchate for Armenian Catholics In the United States of America.

(Vacant See)

Chancery & Vicar General Office: 110 E. 12th St., New York, NY, 10003-5395. Tel.: 212-477-2030; Fax: 212-477-2185.

STATISTICAL OVERVIEW

Personnel	
Retired Bishops	2
Priests: Diocesan Active in Diocese	6
Number of Diocesan Priests	6
Religious Priests in Diocese	7
Permanent Deacons in Diocese	1
Total Sisters	15
Parishes	
Parishes	7
With Resident Pastor:	
Resident Diocesan Priests	5
Resident Religious Priests	2
Educational	
Elementary Schools, Diocesan and Parish	4
Total Students	1,005
Catechesis/Religious Education:	
Total Students Under Catholic Instruction	1,005
Teachers in the Diocese:	
Priests	2
Sisters	15
Lay Teachers	85
Vital Statistics	
Receptions into the Church:	
Infant Baptism Totals	68
Adult Baptism Totals	1
Received into Full Communion	69
First Communions	55
Confirmations	69
Marriages:	
Catholic	13
Interfaith	10
Total Marriages	23
Deaths	35
Total Catholic Population	25,000

Chancery & Vicar General Office—*110 E. 12th St., New York, NY, 10003-5395.* Tel: 212-477-2030; Fax: 212-477-2185.

Vicar General—Rev. GEORGES ZABARIAN. Tel: 212-477-2030.

Chancellor—Rev. RAPHAEL ANDONIAN, O.Mech. Tel: 212-477-2030.

Newspaper Diocesan Bulletin—"The Eternal Flame", Office: *110 E. 12th St., New York, NY, 10003-5395.* Tel: 212-477-2030.

Newspaper Diocesan Bulletin "VERELK"—Office: *1327 Pleasant Ave., Los Angeles, CA, 90033-2328.* Tel: 323-267-1740.

CLERGY, PARISHES, MISSIONS AND PAROCHIAL SCHOOLS

STATE OF NEW YORK

Brooklyn, Kings Co., Visitation. Closed. For inquiries for parish records contact the Chancery.

New York, New York Co., St. Ann's Cathedral (1983), Most Rev. Hovhannes Tertzakian, O. Mech.
Res., 110 E. 12th St., 10003-5395. Tel: 212-477-2030; Fax: 212-477-2185.

STATE OF CALIFORNIA

Los Angeles, Los Angeles Co., Our Lady Queen of Martyrs (1951), Revs. Raphael Minassian; Antoine Panossian.
Res., 1327 Pleasant Ave., 90033-2328. Tel: 323-261-9898; Fax: 323-261-0522.

Glendale, Los Angeles Co., St. Gregory (1998), Rev. Raphael Minassian.
Res., 1504-10 E. Mountain St., 91207-1226. Tel: 818-243-8400; Fax: 818-243-0095.

STATE OF MASSACHUSETTS

Boston, Middlesex Co., Holy Cross (1940), Revs. Raphael Andonian, O.Mech.; Paul A. O'Connor, A.A.; Archdeacon M.J. Connolly.
Res., 200 Lexington St., Belmont, 02478-1241. Tel: 617-489-2280; Fax: 617-489-0218.

STATE OF MICHIGAN

Detroit, Wayne Co., St. Vartan's (1948), Rev. Antoine Saroyan.
Res., 8541 Greenfield Rd., 48228-2224. Tel: 313-584-3345; Fax: 313-582-7012.

STATE OF NEW JERSEY

Paterson, Passaic Co., Sacred Heart (1927), Rev. George Kalousieh.
Res., 155 Long Hill Rd., Little Falls, 07424-2374. Tel: 973-890-0447; Fax: 973-890-0292.

STATE OF PENNSYLVANIA

Philadelphia, Philadelphia Co., St. Mark's Armenian Catholic (1924), Rev. Antranik Atamian.
Res., 400 Haverford Rd., Wynnewood, 19096-2699. Tel: 610-896-7789; Fax: 610-896-0915.

INSTITUTIONS LOCATED IN THE DIOCESE

[A] SCHOOLS

STATE OF CALIFORNIA

LA CRESCENTA. *Mekhitarist School.* Mailing Address: P.O. Box 8407, 91224-0407. 6470 Foothill Blvd., Tujunga, 91042-2729. Tel: 818-353-3003; 352-3048 (Convent); Fax: 818-353-0815; 352-2647.
E-mail: school@mekhitarist.org
Revs. Augustin Szekula, O.Mech., Prin.; Nerses Sakayan, O.Mech.

MONTROSE. *Armenian Sisters of the Immaculate Conception*, 2361 Florencita Dr., 91020-1817. Tel: 626-249-8783; Fax: 626-249-7288. Sr. Eutoxia Keshishian, Supr. & Prin.

STATE OF MASSACHUSETTS

LEXINGTON. *Armenian Sisters Academy*, 20 Pelham Rd., 02421-5702. Tel: 781-861-8303; Fax: 781-862-8479. Sr. Veronique Achikian, Supr. & Prin.

STATE OF PENNSYLVANIA

RADNOR. *Armenian Sisters Academy*, 440 Upper Gulph Rd., 19087-4699. Tel: 610-687-4100; Fax: 610-687-2430.
E-mail: armeniansrsacademy.org
Sr. Louisa Kassarjian, Prin.

[B] RELIGIOUS INSTITUTES AND CONVENTS FOR WOMEN

STATE OF CALIFORNIA

MONTROSE. *Armenian Sisters of the Immaculate Conception*, 2361 Florencita Dr., 91020-1817. Tel: 626-249-8783; 818-249-7493 (convent); Fax: 626-249-7288; 818-242-4610 (convent). Sr. Eutoxia Keshishian, Supr. & Prin.

STATE OF MASSACHUSETTS

LEXINGTON. *Armenian Sisters of the Immaculate Conception*, 6 Eliot Rd., 02173. Tel: 781-863-5962; Fax: 781-674-0410. Sr. Veronique Achikian, Supr. & Prin.

STATE OF PENNSYLVANIA

RADNOR. *Armenian Sisters of the Immaculate Conception*, 440 Upper Gulph Rd., 19087-4699. Tel: 610-687-4100; 610-688-9360 (convent); Fax: 610-687-2430. Sr. Louisa Kassarjian, Prin.

[C] EDUCATIONAL FOUNDATIONS

STATE OF CALIFORNIA

GLENDALE.
Mekhitarian Educational Foundation, 702 E. Glenoaks Blvd., 91207-1714. Tel: 818-546-1967; Fax: 818-548-1166. Revs. Dadjad Yardemian, O.Mech., Exec. Dir.; Mesrop Sulahian.

NECROLOGY

† Kalayjian, Rev. Msgr. Joseph, Detroit, MI St. Vartan Church. —Died Nov. 20, 1999.

Diocese of Newton (Melkite-Greek Catholic)

Most Reverend

JOHN A. ELYA, B.S.O., D.D.

Eparch of Newton; ordained February 17, 1952; appointed Auxiliary Bishop of Newton April 2, 1986; appointed Eparch of Newton November 25, 1993; installed January 25, 1994. *Res., 158 Pleasant St., Brookline, MA, 02446.* Tel.: 617-566-4511; Fax: 617-566-4115.

Most Reverend

NICHOLAS J. SAMRA, D.D.

Auxiliary Bishop of Newton and Protosyncellus; ordained May 10, 1970; appointed Auxiliary Bishop of Newton June 29, 1989. *Res., 8525 Cole St., Warren, MI, 48093.* Tel.: 810-558-0143; Fax: 810-558-0144.

The Chancery: 158 Pleasant St., Brookline, MA, 02446. Tel.: 617-566-4511; Fax: 617-566-4115.

Web site address: melkite.org

E-mail address: dioceseofnewton@aol.com

ESTABLISHED AS AN APOSTOLIC EXARCHATE JANUARY 10, 1966.

ELEVATED TO EPARCHY, JUNE 28, 1976; EMBRACES ALL MEMBERS OF THE MELKITE GREEK CATHOLIC CHURCH IN THE UNITED STATES.

For legal titles of parishes and institutions, consult the Chancery Office.

STATISTICAL OVERVIEW

Personnel	
Bishop	1
Auxiliary Bishops	1
Priests: Diocesan Active in Diocese	34
Priests: Active Outside Diocese	2
Priests: Retired, Sick or Absent	8
Number of Diocesan Priests	44
Religious Priests in Diocese	17
Extern Priests in Diocese	3
Ordinations:	
Diocesan Priests	1
Permanent Deacons	2
Total Sisters	3
Parishes	
Parishes	35
With Resident Pastor:	
Resident Diocesan Priests	28
Resident Religious Priests	7
Missions	7
Educational	
Seminaries, Diocesan	1
Seminaries, Religious	1
Catechesis/Religious Education:	
High School Students	362
Elementary Students	1,260
Total Students Under Catholic Instruction	1,622
Vital Statistics	
Receptions into the Church:	
Infant Baptism Totals	394
Adult Baptism Totals	18
Received into Full Communion	4
First Communions	407
Confirmations	431
Marriages:	
Catholic	139
Interfaith	22
Total Marriages	161
Deaths	183
Total Catholic Population	27,394

Former Bishops—Most Rev. JUSTIN A. NAJMY, B.A.O., D.D.,born April 23, 1898; ord. Dec. 25, 1926; cons. May 29, 1966; installed June 4, 1966; died June 11, 1968.—Most Rev. JOSEPH E. TAWIL, D.D., LL.D., ord. July 20, 1936; cons. Jan. 1, 1960; appt. Apostolic Exarch, Oct. 30, 1969; appt. Eparch, June 28, 1976 became emeritus Dec. 2, 1989. died Feb. 17, 1999.—Most Rev. IGNATIUS GHATTAS, B.S.O., D.D.,born Dec. 25, 1920; ord. July 7, 1946; appt. Dec. 2, 1989; cons. Feb. 23, 1990; died Oct. 11, 1992.

Diocesan Administration

Chancery Office—158 Pleasant St., Brookline, MA, 02446. Tel: 617-566-4511; Fax: 617-731-3790. Office Hours: Mon.-Fri. 9-5.

Protosyncellus—Most Rev. NICHOLAS J. SAMRA, D.D.

Chancellor—Protodeacon PAUL F. LAWLER.

Diocesan Tribunal—18 New Dunstable Rd., Nashua, NH, 03060. Tel: 603-595-9815; Fax: 603-595-2389.

Judicial Vicar—Rt. Rev. GERASIMOS MURPHY, B.S.O., D.Min., J.C.D., *18 New Dunstable Rd., Nashua, NH, 03060.* Tel: 603-595-9815; Fax: 603-595-2389.

Defender of the Bond and Promoter of Justice—Rt. Rev. JOSEPH S. HAGGAR, M.A., J.C.L.; Sr. LOUISE TESSIER, J.C.L.

Judges—Revs. JOSEPH KOURY, J.C.D.; JOHN FARAJ, J.C.D.; HERBERT MAY, J.C.L.

Notaries—Deacons GEORGE YANY; PAUL LAWLER; Ms. LUCILLE LAROCHE.

Economos—Rev. ANDRE ST. GERMAIN.

Protopresbyters—Rt. Rev. JOSEPH S. HAGGAR, New England; Rev. JOHN FARAJ, B.S.O., Mid-Atlantic; Rt. Rev. FRANK MILIENEWICZ, Southeast; Revs. IBRAHIM IBRAHIM, B.S.O., Great Lakes; ALEXEI SMITH, West.

Consultative Bodies

College of Eparchial Consultors—Most Rev. NICHOLAS J. SAMRA; Rt. Rev. JOSEPH S. HAGGAR, J.C.L.; Rt. Rev. GERASIMOS MURPHY, B.S.O., D.Min., J.C.D.; Rt. Rev. ROMANOS V. RUSSO; Rt. Rev. FRANK J. MILIENEWICZ; Revs. IBRAHIM IBRAHIM, B.S.O.; ANDRE ST. GERMAIN; EUGENE MITCHELL, B.S.O.

Presbyteral Council—Most Rev. JOHN A. ELYA, Pres.; Most Rev. NICHOLAS J. SAMRA; Rt. Rev. JOSEPH S. HAGGAR; Rt. Rev. EDWARD KAKATY; Rt. Rev. FRANK MILIENEWICZ; Rt. Rev. GERASIMOS MURPHY, B.S.O.; Rt. Rev. PHILIP RACZKA; Revs. ALAM ALAM; PHILIP AZOON; GREGORY EL-THOM; JOHN FARAJ, B.S.O.; IGNATIUS HARRINGTON; IBRAHIM IBRAHIM, B.S.O.; EMMANUEL CHARLES MCCARTHY; MICHAEL SKROCKI; ALEXEI SMITH; ALBERT WEHBY, B.A.O.

Diocese of Newton for the Melkites in the USA, Inc., a Massachusetts Corporation—Most Rev. JOHN A. ELYA; Most Rev. NICHOLAS J. SAMRA; Rt. Revs. JOSEPH S. HAGGAR; GERASIMOS MURPHY, B.S.O.; PHILIP RACZKA; ROMANOS RUSSO; Rev. ANDRE ST. GERMAIN; Protodeacon PAUL F. LAWLER.

Finance Council—Most Rev. NICHOLAS J. SAMRA; Rev. ANDRE ST. GERMAIN, Economos; Mr. JOSEPH GHOLL; Mr. STANLEY SABA; Dr. JOHN NAZARIAN; Deacon ROBERT SHALHOUB; GILBERT SHASHA; RAYMOND KAYAL; EDMUND NAHOM; BASIL ZALOOM.

Priest's Sickness & Disability, and Retirement Plans—Most Rev. NICHOLAS J. SAMRA; Rt. Rev. JOSEPH FRANCAVILLA; Rt. Rev. JOSEPH S. HAGGAR; Rt. Rev. FRANK MILIENEWICZ; Rt. Rev. PHILIP RACZKA; Revs. JOHN FARAJ; ALEXEI SMITH; ANDRE ST. GERMAIN.

Canonical Consultants—Rt. Rev. Archimandrite VICTOR J. POSPISHIL, J.C.D.; Rev. JOHN FARAJ, B.S.O., J.C.D; Rt. Rev. JOHN D. FARIS, J.C.O.D.; Rev. GEORGE D. GALLARO, J.C.O.D.

Legal Consultant—CAMILLE F. SARROUF, JR., Esq., *95 Commercial Wharf, Boston, MA, 02110.* Tel: 617-227-5800.

Liturgical Consultants—Rev. ROBERT TAFT, S.J.; Archimandrite EUTHIMIOS SKAFF, B.S.O.

Pastoral Offices and Commissions

Continuing Education of Clergy Office—Rev. PAUL FRECHETTE; Rt. Rev. GABRIEL GHANOUM; Revs. IGNATIUS HARRINGTON; FRED SAATO; ALEXEI SMITH.

National Association of Melkite Youth—Archdeacon GEORGE YANY, *1 Valley St., Central Falls, RI, 02863.* Tel: 401-722-0017.

MAYA (Melkite Assoc. of Young Adults)—Rev. JUSTIN ROSE, *923 W. Congress St., San Bernardino, CA, 92410.* Tel: 909-889-3579.

Ambassadors—Rt. Rev. GABRIEL GHANOUM, B.S.O., *126 S.E. 15 Rd., Miami, FL, 33129.* Tel: 305-856-8666.

National Association of Melkite Women—Rev. EDWARD

KAKATY, *7 V.F.W. Pkwy., Boston, MA, 02131.* Tel: 617-323-5242.

Liturgical Commission—Most Rev. NICHOLAS SAMRA, Chm.; Rt. Rev. JOSEPH HAGGAR; Rt. Rev. VICTOR SAMAHA; Rt. Rev. EDWARD KAKATY; Rt. Rev. ROMANOS RUSSO; Rev. MARK MELONE.

Educational Services—Rev. FRED SAATO, M.A.; Dr. FRANCES COLIE, Assoc. Dir., *491 Palisade Ave., Yonkers, NY, 10703.* Tel: 914-963-6680.

Vocations Office—Rt. Rev. PHILIP RACZKA, Coord., *600 W. Exchange St., Akron, OH, 44302.* Tel: 330-535-7364; Fax: 330-535-8037. Rt. Rev. EDWARD KAKATY; Rt. Rev. FRANK MILIENEWICZ; Revs. SAMI BAROODY; IGNATIUS HARRINGTON; ALEXEI SMITH.

"Sophia" (A Journal)—Rev. ROBERT RABBAT, Editor-in-Chief. Associates: Rev. JAMES GRAHAM; Deacon ELIAS SAHYOUNI; Rev. JOSEPH A. BOU-SLIMAN, *200 E. North Ave., Northlake, IL, 60164.* Tel: 708-865-7050; Fax: 708-865-7050.

Ecumenical & Interreligious Commission—Rev. IBRAHIM IBRAHIM, B.S.O., *8023 Memphis Ave., Brooklyn, OH, 44114.* Rt. Rev. EDWARD G. KAKATY.

Order of St. Nicholas—Most Rev. NICHOLAS J. SAMRA, Grand Advisor; RAYMOND KAYAL, National Chm.; Rev. ANDRE ST. GERMAIN, Treas. Chaplains: Revs. GABRIEL GHANOUM, B.S.O.; IBRAHIM IBRAHIM, B.S.O., Mailing Address: *158 Pleasant St., Brookline, MA, 02446.* Tel: 617-566-4511; Fax: 617-731-3790.

Associated Melkite Charities—Rev. PHILARET LITTLEFIELD, *1617 W. State St., Milwaukee, WI, 53233.* Tel: 414-342-1543.

Sophia Press—158 Pleasant St., Brookline, MA, 02446. Tel: 617-566-4511; Fax: 617-731-3790.

CLERGY, PARISHES, MISSIONS AND PAROCHIAL SCHOOLS

STATE OF MASSACHUSETTS

Boston, Suffolk Co., Annunciation Cathedral, Rt. Rev. Edward G. Kakaty; Rev. Alam Alam; Deacons Paul Lawler; John Moses.
Res., 7 V.F.W. Pkwy., 02131. Tel: 617-323-5242; Fax: 617-325-2662.

Lawrence, Essex Co., St. Joseph, Rev. Youssef A. Youssef, B.S.O.; Deacons Bryan McNeil; John MacMillan.
Res., 241 Hampshire St., 01841. Tel: 978-682-8152; Fax: 978-682-6114.

Worcester, Worcester Co., Our Lady of Perpetual Help, Rev. Paul G. Frechette.
Res., 256 Hamilton St., 01604. Tel: 508-752-4174; Fax: 508-752-8351.

STATE OF ALABAMA

Birmingham, Jefferson Co., St. George, Rev. Frank J. Milienewicz; Deacon Seraphim Ritchey.
Res., 425-Sixteenth Ave. S., 35205. Tel: 205-252-5788; Fax: 205-252-1085.

STATE OF ARIZONA

Phoenix, Maricopa Co., St. John of the Desert, Rt. Rev. Robert Skager, Admin.; Rev. Samir Abu Leil.
Res., 2525 E. Osborn, 85016. Tel: 602-954-7258.

STATE OF CALIFORNIA

El Cajon, San Diego Co., St. Jacob Mission, Rev. George Said Bisharat; Deacon Edward Bagdasar.
Mailing Address: 722 Medford St., 92020. Tel: 619-460-0444; Fax: 619-462-0219.
Our Lady of Grace Church: 2766 Navajo Rd., 92020.

El Segundo, Los Angeles Co., St. Paul, Rev. Alexei R. Smith, Admin.; Deacon Irenaeus Dionne.
Res., 538 Concord St., 90245. Tel: 310-322-1892; Fax: 310-322-1919.

North Hollywood, Los Angeles Co., St. Anne, Revs. Albert Wehby, B.A.O.; Alam Alam; Deacons George Sayegh; Marion Rimmer; George Karout.
Res., 11245 Rye St., 91602. Tel: 818-761-2034; Fax: 818-761-2922.

Oakland, Alameda Co., St. John The Theologian, Revs. Owen Carroll (OAK); Eugene M. Ludwig, O.F.M.Cap (OAK).
Res., 5 Gleneden Ave., 94611. Tel: 510-428-2234.

Placentia, Orange Co., Holy Cross, Rev. James K. Babcock.
Church & Res.: 451 W. Madison Ave., 92870. Tel: 714-985-1710; Fax: 714-985-1765.

Sacramento, Sacramento Co., St. George, Rev. Mark E. Melone.
Church—1620 Bell St., 95825. Tel: 916-920-2900; Fax: 916-920-2900.

San Bernardino, San Bernardino Co., St. Philip, Rev. Justin Rose.
Mailing Address: 923 W. Congress St., 92410. Tel: 909-889-3579; Fax: 909-889-5461.

San Jose, Santa Clara Co., St. Elias, Rev. James K. Graham.
Res., 3088 Kentridge Dr., 95133. Tel: 408-259-0259; Fax: 408-259-0239.
Church—4411 Hyland Ave., 95127.

Temecula, Riverside Co., Virgin Mary Mission, Rt. Rev. Nassir Matta, Admin.
Mailing Address: 2700 Iowa Ave., Apt. 59, Riverside, 92507. Tel: 909-308-1060.
St. Mark Church: Twin Oaks & Silver St., San Marcos.

STATE OF CONNECTICUT

Danbury, Fairfield Co., St. Ann, Rev. Basil R. Parent.
Mailing Address: 181 Clapboard Ridge Rd., 06811. Tel: 203-743-5119.

Waterford, New London Co., St. Ann, Rev. Michael Skrocki.
Res., 41 Cross Rd., 06385. Tel: 860-442-2211; Fax: 860-442-2211.

STATE OF FLORIDA

Miami, Dade Co., St. Jude, Rt. Rev. Gabriel Ghanoum, B.S.O.; Deacon Magdi Negm.
Res., 126 S.E. 15 Rd., 33129. Tel: 305-856-8666; Fax: 305-859-7982.

Delray Beach, Palm Beach Co., St. Nicholas. Served by Miami. Rt. Rev. Gabriel Ghanoum, B.S.O.; Deacon Magdi Negm.
Res., 126 S.E. 15 Rd., Miami, 33129. Tel: 305-856-8666.

STATE OF GEORGIA

Atlanta, Fulton Co., St. John, Rev. John Azar.
Res., 1428 Ponce de Leon Ave., N.E., 30307. Tel: 404-373-9522; Fax: 404-373-9522.

Augusta, Richmond Co., St. Ignatios of Antioch, Revs. Daniel Munn; Miguel Grave de Peralta; Deacon Kent Plowman.
Church—1003 Merry St., 30904. Tel: 706-738-9388.
Mailing Address: P.O. Box 3351, 30914-3351.
Res., 967 Meigs St., 30904. Tel: 706-738-5623.

STATE OF ILLINOIS

Northlake, Cook Co., St. John the Baptist, Rev. Robert Rabbat; Deacon Elias Sahyouni.
Res., 200 E. North Ave., 60164. Tel: 708-865-7050; Fax: 708-865-7050.

STATE OF INDIANA

Hammond, Lake Co., St. Michael the Archangel, Rev. Robert Rabbat, Admin.
Mailing Address: 7113 Columbia Ave., 46324. Tel: 219-844-9027; Fax: 219-844-6986.
Church—619 E. Sibley Ave., 46320.

South Bend, St. Joseph Co., St. John of Damascus, Rev. Robert L. Kerby; Deacon Lawrence Farhat.
Church—839 Woodcliff Dr., 46615.
Res., 918 Simon Ct., 46615. Tel: 219-233-5338.

STATE OF MICHIGAN

Lansing, Ingham Co., St. Joseph, Rt. Rev. Victor M. Samaha, B.C.O.
Res., 912 Westover Circle, 48917. Tel: 517-327-6394.

Plymouth, Wayne Co., St. Michael, Rev. Edmond J. Ghazal, B.C.O., Admin.
Church—585 N. Mill St., 48170. Tel: 734-414-6110.

Warren, Macomb Co., Our Lady of Redemption, Most Rev. Nicholas J. Samra; Revs. George D. Gallaro; Gregory El-Thom, B.C.O.; Deacons Joseph Daratony; James Soloman.
Res., 8525 Cole St., 48093. Tel: 810-751-6017; Fax: 810-588-0144.

STATE OF NEW HAMPSHIRE

Manchester, Hillsborough Co., Our Lady of the Cedars, Rev. Eugene Mitchell, B.S.O.; Deacon Thomas P. Steinmetz.
Res., 161 S. Beech St., 03103. Tel: 603-623-8944; Fax: 603-645-6017.

STATE OF NEW JERSEY

Cliffside Park, Bergen Co., St. Demetrius, Rt. Rev. Romanos Russo, Admin.
Res., 228 91st St., Brooklyn, NY 11209. Tel: 718-836-7311; Fax: 718-921-5290.
Church—184 Cliff St., 07010. Tel: 201-840-8554.

West Paterson, Passaic Co., St. Ann, Revs. Sami W. Baroody; Jean Ghaby; Deacons Michael Jolly; Edward Bsarany; Roland Basinski; Robert Shalhoub.
Res., 802 Rifle Camp Rd., 07424. Tel: 973-785-4144; Fax: 973-890-9599.

STATE OF NEW YORK

Brooklyn, Kings Co., Church of the Virgin Mary, Rev. John Faraj, B.S.O.
Res., 216 Eighth Ave., 11215. Tel: 718-788-5454; Fax: 718-499-7702.

Rochester, Monroe Co., St. Nicholas, Rev. Kenneth Sherman; Deacon Edmond Elhilow.
Res., 1492 Spencerport Rd., 14606. Tel: 716-426-4218.

Utica, Oneida Co., St. Basil, Rt. Rev. Julien A. Eliane; Deacon Daniel Klockowski.
Res., 901 Sherman Dr., 13501. Tel: 315-732-4662; Fax: 315-797-4895.

Yonkers, Westchester Co., Christ the Savior Church, Rev. Fred Saato.
Res., 491 Palisade Ave., 10703. Tel: 914-963-6680; Fax: 914-963-1058.

STATE OF OHIO

Akron, Summit Co., St. Joseph, Rt. Rev. Philip Raczka.
Res., 600 W. Exchange St., 44302. Tel: 330-535-7364; Fax: 330-535-8037.

Brooklyn, Cuyahoga Co., St. Elias, Rev. Ibrahim Ibrahim, B.S.O.
Res., 8023 Memphis Ave., 44144. Tel: 216-661-1155; Fax: 216-661-3838.

Columbus, Franklin Co., Holy Resurrection, Rev. Ignatius Harrington.
Res., 7752 Deercrest Ct., Dublin, 43016. Tel: 614-761-7975; Fax: 614-761-7975.

Zanesville, Muskingum Co., Holy Trinity, Rev. Ignatius Harrington.
Res., 7752 Deercrest Ct., Dublin, 43016. Tel: 614-761-7975; Fax: 614-761-7975.
Church—317 Wayne Ave., 43701.

STATE OF PENNSYLVANIA

Scranton, Lackawanna Co., St. Joseph, Rev. Philip Azoon.
Res., 130 N. Cabrini Ave., 18504. Tel: 570-343-6092; Fax: 570-969-0862.

STATE OF RHODE ISLAND

Lincoln, Providence Co., St. Basil the Great, Rt. Rev. Joseph S. Haggar; Archdeacon George M. Yany; Deacon Edmond Raheb.
Church—15 Skyview Dr., 02865.
Res., 111 Cross St., Central Falls, 02863. Tel: 401-722-1345; Fax: 401-722-2436.

Woonsocket, Providence Co., St. Elias, Rt. Rev. Joseph S. Haggar.
Church—80 Hamilton St., 02895.
Res., 111 Cross St., Central Falls, 02863. Tel: 401-722-1345.

STATE OF VIRGINIA

McLean, Fairfax Co., Holy Transfiguration, Rt. Rev. Joseph F. Francavilla; Deacons Paul Weyrich; Ephrem Handal.
Res., 8501 Lewinsville Rd., 22102. Tel: 703-734-9198; Fax: 703-734-5148.

STATE OF WISCONSIN

Milwaukee, Milwaukee Co., St. George, Rev. Philaret Littlefield.
Res., 1617 W. State St., 53233. Tel: 414-342-1543; Fax: 414-933-3755.

On Special Projects:
Reverend Fathers—
Boutros, Peter, 6539 Steeplechase Dr., Tampa, FL 33625-1631. Tel: 813-926-2241
Grave de Peralta, Miguel, 1000 Merry St., Augusta, GA 30914. Tel: 706-228-4938 Fax: 706-738-6559
St. Germain, Andre, Economos

Military Chaplains:
Reverend Fathers—
Brown, Shaun
Gosselin, Lawrence

Leave of Absence:
Reverend Fathers—
Golini, Ronald
Kirk, David
Koury, James
Moloney, Patrick W.
Samra, Basil

Retired:
Reverend Fathers—
Hassey, Athanase
King, James E.

Rt. Rev. Archimandri—
Aboody, Charles
Badaoui, Adib, B.S.O.
Chalhoub, Maximos
Dagher, George, B.S.O.
Haddad, William, B.S.O.
Hage, Simon
Jadaa, John
Skaff, Elias B.

Deacons:
Bagdasar, Edward, San Diego, CA
Basinski, Roland, West Paterson, NJ
Bsarany, Edward, West Paterson, NJ
Daratony, Joseph, Warren, MI
Dionne, Irenaeus, El Segundo, CA
Elhilow, Edmond, Rochester, NY
Farhat, Lawrence, Southbend, IN
Handal, Ephrem, McLean, VA
Heinemeyer, Carl, (Retired)
Jolly, Michael, Paterson, NJ
Karout, George, North Hollywood, CA
Klockowski, Daniel, Utica, NY
Lawler, Paul, Boston, MA
MacMillan, John, Lawrence, MA
McNeil, Bryan, Lawrence, MA
Moses, John, Boston, MA
Negm, Magdi, Miami, FL
Plowman, Kent, Augusta, GA
Raheb, Edmond, Lincoln, RI
Rimmer, Marion, North Hollywood, CA
Ritchey, Seraphim, Birmingham, AL
Sahyouni, Elias, Northlake, IL
Sayegh, George, North Hollywood, CA
Shalhoub, Robert, West Paterson, NJ
Soloman, James, Warren, MI
Steinmetz, Thomas, Manchester, NH
Weyrich, Paul, McLean, VA
Yany, George, Central Falls, RI

Deacons Serving Outside the Eparchy:
Haddad, Gregory
Nasser, Andre P.
Richardson, David W.
Versage, Joseph V.

INSTITUTIONS LOCATED IN THE DIOCESE

[A] SEMINARIES

STATE OF MASSACHUSETTS

BROOKLINE. *Seminary of St. Gregory the Theologian*, 158 Pleasant St., 02446. Rev. Emmanuel Charles McCarthy. Priests 1.

METHUEN. *Seminary of St. Basil the Great*, 30 East St., 01844. Tel: 978-683-2471. Rt. Rev. Gerasimos Murphy, B.S.O., J.C.D., Dean. Priests 3.

[B] MONASTERIES AND RESIDENCES FOR PRIESTS AND BROTHERS

STATE OF MASSACHUSETTS

METHUEN. *Basilian Salvatorian Order*, 30 East St., 01844. Tel: 978-683-2471; Fax: 978-794-3452. Rt. Rev. Gerasimos Murphy, B.S.O., J.C.D., Reg. Supr.; Revs. Eugene Mitchell, B.S.O., General Economos; J.P. Martin A. Hyatt, B.S.O., Local Supr.; Lawrence Tumminelli, B.S.O.; Naim Khalil, B.S.O.; Rt. Revs. George Dagher, B.S.O., (Retired); Simon Hage, B.S.O., (Retired).

[C] CONVENTS AND RESIDENCES FOR SISTERS

STATE OF CONNECTICUT

DANBURY. *Community of The Mother of God of Tenderness*, 79 Golden Hill Rd., 06811-4631. Tel: 203-794-1486. Sr. Mary Ann Socha, C.M.G.T., Pres. Sisters 3.

[D] MISCELLANEOUS

STATE OF ALABAMA

BIRMINGHAM. *National Shrine of St. George*, 425 16th Ave. S., 35205. Tel: 205-252-5788. Rt. Rev. Frank J. Milienewicz.

STATE OF MASSACHUSETTS

LAWRENCE. *St. Joseph's Plains Community Center*, 245 Hampshire St., 01841. Tel: 978-685-6001. Rev. Youssef A. Youssef, B.S.O.

METHUEN. *St. Basil's Salvatorian Center*, 30 East St., 01844. Tel: 978-683-2959; Fax: 978-794-3379. Richard Daggett, Dir.

STATE OF NEW YORK

WHITE PLAINS. *The Friends of the Holy Land, Inc.*, 15 Baylor Cir., 10605. Tel: 914-969-0887; 949-2106. Ernest F. Russo, Governor Gen., Patriarchal Order of the Holy Cross of Jerusalem.

RELIGIOUS INSTITUTES OF MEN REPRESENTED IN THE EPARCHY

For further details refer to the corresponding bracketed number in the Religious Institutes of Men or Women section.

[]—*Basilian Aleppian Order*. (Deir-es-Chir, Lebanon).—B.A.O.

[]—*Basilian Chouerite Order*. (St. John Monastery, Khonchara, Lebanon).—B.C.O.

[0190]—*Basilian Salvatorian Order*. (Holy Saviour Monastery, Sidon, Lebanon).—B.S.O.

NECROLOGY

Mardelli, Maximos, (Retired). —Died Oct. 2000.

Diocese of Our Lady of Deliverance

For Syriac Catholics in the United States and Canada

Most Reverend

JOSEPH YOUNAN, D.D.

Bishop of Our Lady of Deliverance; ordained September 12, 1971; ordained Bishop January 7, 1996; installed February 10, 1996. *Chancery Office: 502 Palisade Ave., Union City, NJ, 07087-5213.*

DIOCESE ESTABLISHED NOVEMBER 18, 1996.

Chancery Office: 502 Palisade Ave., Union City, NJ, 07087-5213. Mailing Address: P.O. Box 8366, Union City, NJ, 07087-8262.

Web site address: www.syriac-catholic.org

E-mail address: frsyriac@aol.com

STATISTICAL OVERVIEW

Personnel	
Bishop	1
Priests: Diocesan Active in Diocese	8
Priests: Active Outside Diocese	1
Number of Diocesan Priests	9
Parishes	
Parishes	8
With Resident Pastor:	
Resident Diocesan Priests	6
Without Resident Pastor:	
Administered by Priests	1
Administered by Deacons	1
Administered by Lay People	1
Missions	2
New Parishes Created	2
Educational	
Diocesan Students in Other Seminaries	1
Total Seminarians	1
Catechesis/Religious Education:	
High School Students	130
Elementary Students	260
Total Students Under Catholic Instruction	391
Vital Statistics	
Receptions into the Church:	
Infant Baptism Totals	66
Adult Baptism Totals	2
Received into Full Communion	18
First Communions	72
Confirmations	68
Marriages:	
Catholic	14
Interfaith	4
Total Marriages	18
Deaths	22
Total Catholic Population	12,100

Chancery—502 Palisade Ave., Union City, NJ, 07087-5213. Tel: 201-583-1067; Fax: 201-583-0212., *P.O. Box 8366, Union City, NJ, 07087-8262.*

Vicar General—Chorbishop PIERRE MELKI.

Chancellor—Rev. ST SUTTON. Tel: 201-583-1067.

Secretary—Rev. ST SUTTON. Tel: 201-583-1067.

CLERGY, PARISHES, MISSIONS AND PAROCHIAL SCHOOLS

STATE OF NEW JERSEY

1—OUR LADY OF DELIVERANCE (1986), Rev. Yousif Abdulmasih Tel: 201-583-1093.
Res., 502 Palisade Ave., Union City, 07087-5213. Tel: 201-583-9590; Fax: 201-583-9639.

STATE OF CALIFORNIA

North Hollywood, Los Angeles Co., Sacred Heart Syriac. Served by Chancery personnel. Rev. Huytham Bashir Zallo, Admin.; Deacons Elia Azouz; George Qatto; Faisal Karesh.
Res., 10837 Collins St., 91601-2009. Tel: 818-766-7001; Fax: 818-766-7254.

San Diego, San Diego Co., Our Mother of Perpetual Help Mission, Deacon Emad Hanna Al-Shaikh, Pastoral Assoc.
Mailing Address: P.O. Box 152229, 92295. Tel: 619-660-1492.

STATE OF FLORIDA

Jacksonville, Duval Co., St. Ephrem. Served by Chancery personnel. Rev. Selwan A. Sulaiman, Admin.
Res., 14608 Stacey Rd., 32250. Tel: 904-992-0025.

STATE OF ILLINOIS

Northbrook, Saint Mary Virgin Immaculate Syriac Catholic Mission. Administered by the Chancery Office.
Res., 425 N. Hillside, Hillside, IL 60162. Tel: 708-449-7947; Fax: 708-449-9813.

STATE OF MICHIGAN

Farmington Hills, Oakland Co., St. Toma, Rev. Toma B. Azizo.
Res., 30465 Farmington Rd., 48334-1940. Tel: 248-788-3437; Fax: 248-642-0645.

CANADA

Toronto, St. Joseph, Rev. Yousif Mansour Abba, Admin.
Res., 222 Ridley Blvd., ON M5M 3M6. Tel: 416-485-7781; Fax: 416-489-4183.

Laval, St. Ephrem, Chorbishop Pierre Melki, Vicar Gen.
Res., 3000 Edouard Monpetit, PQ H7T 2T5. Tel: 450-682-7546; Fax: 450-682-7603.

Special Assignment:
Reverend Fathers—
Sutton, ST, Chancellor & Sec. to the Bishop

NECROLOGY

(No Deaths)

Eparchy of Our Lady of Lebanon of Los Angeles

Most Reverend

ROBERT J. SHAHEEN

Bishop of Our Lady of Lebanon of Los Angeles; ordained May 2, 1964; appointed December 5, 2000.

Comprises the States of Ohio, West Virginia, Illinois, Alabama, Michigan, Minnesota, Missouri, Texas, Utah, Arizona, Nevada, Oregon, California, Alaska, Hawaii, Indiana, Kentucky, Tennessee, Mississippi, Wisconsin, Iowa, Arkansas, Louisiana, North Dakota, South Dakota, Kansas, Oklahoma, Nebraska, Montana, Wyoming, Colorado, New Mexico, Idaho and Washington.

Chancery Office: P.O. Box 16397, Beverly Hills, CA, 90209. Mailing Address: 331 S. San Vicente Blvd., Los Angeles, CA, 90048. Tel.: 310-247-8322; Fax: 310-247-9297.

Web site address: www.eparchyla.org

E-mail address: eparchy@aol.com

STATISTICAL OVERVIEW

Personnel	
Bishop	1
Priests: Diocesan Active in Diocese	28
Priests: Active Outside Diocese	1
Priests: Retired, Sick or Absent	2
Number of Diocesan Priests	31
Religious Priests in Diocese	9
Permanent Deacons in Diocese	8
Total Sisters	8
Parishes	
Parishes	29
With Resident Pastor:	
Resident Diocesan Priests	22
Resident Religious Priests	6
Without Resident Pastor:	
Administered by Priests	3
Missions	10
New Parishes Created	2
Welfare	
Homes for the Aged	1
Total Assisted	55
Educational	
Diocesan Students in Other Seminaries	7
Total Seminarians	7
Catechesis/Religious Education:	
Total Students Under Catholic Instruction	7
Vital Statistics	
Receptions into the Church:	
Infant Baptism Totals	457
Adult Baptism Totals	23
First Communions	339
Confirmations	480
Marriages:	
Catholic	99
Interfaith	34
Total Marriages	133
Deaths	181
Total Catholic Population	24,411

Former Bishop—MOST REV. JOHN GEORGE CHEDID, D.D.; ordained Dec. 21, 1951; appointed Titular Bishop of Callinicum and Auxiliary Bishop of St. Maron of Brooklyn, Oct. 28, 1980; consecrated Jan. 25, 1981; appointed Bishop of Our Lady of Lebanon of Los Angeles, Feb. 19, 1994; retired Dec. 5, 2000.

Chancery—Chorbishop GREGORY J. MANSOUR, S.T.L., Protosyncellus and Chancellor *331 S. San Vicente Blvd., Los Angeles, CA, 90048.* Tel: 310-247-8322; Fax: 310-247-9297., *P.O. Box 16397, Beverly Hills, CA, 90209.*

Advisor for Priests—Chorbishop ROBERT SHAHEEN.

College of Consultors—Chorbishop ROBERT SHAHEEN; Chorbishop MICHAEL KAIL; Revs. ABDALLAH ZAIDAN, M.L.M.; DONALD SAWYER; FAOUZI ELIA; Chorbishop BERNARD KHACHAN; Chorbishop GREGORY J. MANSOUR.

Commission for Lebanon—Rev. ABDALLAH ZAIDAN, M.L.M.

Tribunal—

Defender of the Bond—Rev. ROBERT BISHOP, C.F.M.

Judicial Vicar—Chorbishop WILLIAM LESER, S.T.B.

Moderator of the Tribunal—Bishop JOHN CHEDID, J.C.D., S.T.L.

Procurator/Advocate—Rev. ABDALLAH E. ZAIDAN, M.L.M.; Chorbishop GREGORY J. MANSOUR, S.T.L.

Promoter of Justice—Rev. ROBERT BISHOP, C.F.M.

Notary—Miss SIUIN MORRISSY.

Eparchial Newsletter—"Maronites Today"; Rev. DONALD J. SAWYER, Editor, *P.O. Box 1891, Austin, TX, 78767.*

Office for Immigration—Rev. FAOUZI ELIA.

Office for Missions—Revs. DONALD J. SAWYER; ANTHONY SPINOSA.

Office for Pastoral Leadership and Stewardship—Chorbishop MICHAEL KAIL.

Office of Communications—Rev. Msgr. RICHARD SAAD.

Office of Inter-faith/Ecumenical Affairs—Rev. ANTHONY SPINOSA.

Office of Liturgy—Chorbishop MICHAEL KAIL.

Office of Ministries—Rev. Msgr. RICHARD SAAD.

Office of Priestly Vocations—Rev. SHARBEL MAROUN.

Office of Religious Education—Rev. ANTHONY SALIM.

Office of Youth Ministries—Rev. SHARBEL MAROUN.

Presbyteral Council—Chorbishop MICHAEL KAIL, Exec. Dir.; Rev. Msgr. RICHARD SAAD, Sec.; Chorbishop ROBERT SHAHEEN; Revs. ABDALLAH ZAIDAN, M.L.M.; DONALD SAWYER; Rev. Msgr. WILLIAM BONCZWESKI; Revs. FAOUZI ELIA; GHATTAS KHOURY; Chorbishop BERNARD KHACHAN; Chorbishop GREGORY J. MANSOUR, Ex Officio.

Pro-Life Office—Rev. ANTOINE BAKH, Dir.; Mrs. MARILUE SIMON, Assoc. Dir.

Family Life Office—Chorbishop ROBERT SHAHEEN, Dir.; Mrs. MARILUE SIMON, Assoc. Dir.

Office for the Third Millenium—Rev. ANTHONY SPINOSA.

Eparchial Webmaster—Rev. JEAN AL NAHAL, M.L.M.

Properties Owned—

St. Maron Office Building—Detroit, MI.

Father Toubia Retirement Home—North Jackson, OH.

Bishop's Residence—Bel Air, CA.

Protopresbyters—Chorbishop ROBERT SHAHEEN, Mid-America Region; Chorbishop MICHAEL KAIL, Midwest Region; Revs. ABDALLAH ZAIDAN, M.L.M., Southwest Region; DONALD SAWYER, Southern Region.

Spiritual Director for the National Apostolate of Maronites—Chorbishop MICHAEL KAIL.

Order of St. Sharbel—PHILLIP BAROUD, Pres. NINA BEJANY, Vice Pres., *Eparchy of Our Lady of Lebanon of Los Angeles, P.O. Box 16397, Beverly Hills, CA, 90209.* Chorbishop ROBERT SHAHEEN, Spiritual Dir.

CLERGY, PARISHES, MISSIONS AND PAROCHIAL SCHOOLS

STATE OF CALIFORNIA

Los Angeles, Los Angeles Co., Our Lady of Mt. Lebanon-St. Peter Cathedral (1923) (Lebanese), Most Rev. John Chedid, J.C.D., S.T.L.; Rev. Abdallah E. Zaidan, M.L.M., Rector; Deacon Edward Corey. In res., Chorbishop Gregory J. Mansour, S.T.L., Chancellor.

Res., 333 S. San Vicente Blvd., 90048. Tel: 310-275-6634; Fax: 310-858-0856.

Catechesis/Religious Programs—Students 64.

St. Jude Mission (1999) (Lebanese), Rev. Abdallah E. Zaidan, M.L.M., Contact Person.

Res., 333 S. San Vincent Blvd., 90048. Tel: 310-275-6634; Fax: 310-858-0854.

Catechesis/Religious Programs—P.O. Box 885, San Dimas, 91773.

Students 35.

Anaheim, Orange Co., St. John Maron Mission (1988), Rev. Antoine Bakh; Subdeacon Alfred Harb.

Mailing & Church Address: 1546 E. La Palma Ave., 92805. Tel: 714-520-5303; Fax: 714-520-4273.

Res., 601 N. Woods Ave., Fullerton, 92832. Tel: 714-525-4216.

Catechesis/Religious Programs—Students 55.

Mission—Anaheim, Orange Co., Maronite Catholic Community of Riverside.

Millbrae, San Mateo Co., Our Lady of Lebanon (1979) (Lebanese), Rev. Georges Channine.

Res., 600 El Camino Real N.W., P.O. Box 896, 94030. Tel: 650-589-9653; Fax: 650-866-3091. [JC]

Mission—Stockton, San Joaquin Co., Maronite Catholic Community of Stockton.

San Diego, San Diego Co., Saint Ephrem Mission (1989), Rev. Nabil Mouannes, Admin.

Mailing Address: 750 Medford St., Elcajon, 92020. Tel: 619-337-1350; Fax: 619-337-1350. [CEM]

Res., 766 Medford St., Elcajon, 92020. Tel: 619-697-3040; Fax: 619-697-3040.

STATE OF ALABAMA

Birmingham, Jefferson Co., St. Elias (1910) (Lebanese), Rev. Msgr. Richard D. Saad; Deacon Joseph Stephens; Subdeacon Samuel Wehby.

Res., 836 Eighth St. S., 35205-4567. Tel: 205-251-5057; 252-3867; Fax: 205-251-5028.
Catechesis / Religious Programs—Students 100.

Maronite Catholic Community of Mobile (1910) (Lebanese), Rev. Msgr. Richard D. Saad, Contact Person.
Mailing Address: St. Elias Church, 836 8th St. S., 35205. Tel: 205-251-5057; Fax: 205-251-5028.

STATE OF ARIZONA

Phoenix, Maricopa Co., St. Joseph Mission (1992), Rev. Ghassan Matar, M.L.M.
Res., 5406 E. Virginia Ave., 85008. Tel: 602-667-3280; Fax: 602-468-0174.
Catechesis / Religious Programs—Students 35.

STATE OF COLORADO

Denver, Denver Co., Maronite Catholic Community of Denver, Rev. Abdallah E. Zaidan, M.L.M., Protopresbyter & Admin., Tel: 310-275-6634.

STATE OF ILLINOIS

Hillside, Cook Co., Our Lady of Lebanon Church (1952) (Lebanese), Rev. Victor Kayrouz.
Res., 425 N. Hillside Ave., 60162. Tel: 708-449-5558; Fax: 708-449-9813.
Catechesis / Religious Programs—Students 85.
Mission—Michigan City, La Porte Co., Maronite Catholic Community, Sacred Heart Church, Eighth St., Michigan City, IN 46360. Tel: 219-874-3491. Rev. Victor Kayrouz.

Peoria, Peoria Co., St. Sharbel (1973), Rev. Faouzi Y. Elia; Deacon James Siedlecki; Subdeacon Bechara Awada.
Res., 2914 W. Scenic Dr., 61615. Tel: 309-688-5555; Fax: 309-688-0431.
Catechesis / Religious Programs—Students 40.

STATE OF KENTUCKY

Louisville, Jefferson Co., Maronite Catholic Community of Louisville (1910) (Lebanese), Rev. Ghattas Khoury.
Mailing Address: 2530 Victory Pkwy., Cincinnati, OH 45206. Tel: 513-961-0120; Fax: 513-861-5075.

STATE OF LOUISIANA

Baton Rouge, Maronite Catholic Community, Rev. Donald Sawyer, Admin.
Tel: 512-458-3693; Fax: 512-451-9554.

Lafayette, Maronite Catholic Community, Rev. Kenneth Morvant, Admin.

Lake Charles, Maronite Catholic Community, Rev. Donald Sawyer, Admin.
Tel: 512-458-3693; Fax: 512-451-9554.

New Orleans, Maronite Catholic Community, Rev. Msgr. Richard D. Saad, Admin.
Tel: 205-251-5057; Fax: 305-251-5028.

STATE OF MICHIGAN

Detroit, Wayne Co., St. Maron (1909) (Lebanese), Rev. Msgr. Louis Baz.
Res., 11466 Kercheval, 48215. Tel: 313-824-0196; Fax: 313-824-6418. [CEM]
Catechesis / Religious Programs—Students 162.

Warren, Macomb Co., St. Sharbel (1987), Rev. Msgr. Kenneth A. Michael; Rev. Pierre Bassil.
Res., 31601 Schoenherr Rd., 48093-1977. Tel: 810-826-9688; Fax: 810-826-3521.
Catechesis / Religious Programs—Students 121.

Flint, Genesee Co., Our Lady of Lebanon (1973), Rev. Anthony S. Spinosa; Deacon Martin J. Rachid; Subdeacons Earl Matte; Charles Rossie.
Res., 4133 Calkins Rd., 48532. Tel: 810-733-1259; Fax: 810-732-2760.
Catechesis / Religious Programs—Students 65.

STATE OF MINNESOTA

Minneapolis, Hennepin Co., St. Maron (1948) (Lebanese), Rev. Sharbel G. Maroun.
Res., 219 Sixth Ave., N.E., 55413. Tel: 612-379-2758; Fax: 612-379-7647. [CEM][JC]
Catechesis / Religious Programs—Tel: 612-631-2182.
Students 56.

St. Paul, Ramsey Co., Holy Family Church (1918) (Lebanese), Rev. Bakhos Chidiac.
Res., 203 E. Robie St., 55107. Tel: 651-291-1116; Fax: 651-291-7009.

STATE OF MISSOURI

Columbia, Boone Co., Maronite Catholic Community (1998), Chorbishop Robert J. Shaheen, Admin.
Tel: 314-621-0056; Fax: 314-231-9057.

St. Louis, St. Louis City Co., St. Raymond (1913) (Lebanese), Chorbishop Robert J. Shaheen; Subdeacons Louis Peters; George Simon.
Res., 931 Lebanon Dr., 63104. Tel: 314-621-0056; Fax: 314-231-9057.
Catechesis / Religious Programs—Students 105.

STATE OF NEVADA

Las Vegas, Clark Co., St. Sharbel Mission, Rev. Toufic Nasr, Admin., Tel: 650-375-1536; Fax: 650-866-3091.
766 Medford St., El Cajon, CA 92020. Tel: 619-697-3040.

STATE OF OKLAHOMA

Tulsa, Tulsa Co., Maronite Catholic Community (1998), Rev. Stephen Bonian, S.J., Admin.
Res., 6812 S. Toledo Ave., No. 312, OK 74136. Tel: 918-492-4534.

STATE OF OHIO

Cincinnati, Hamilton Co., St. Anthony of Padua (1910) (Lebanese), Rev. Ghattas Khoury; Subdeacons Joseph Mousie; Arthur Evans.
Res., 2530 Victory Pkwy., 45206. Tel: 513-961-0120; Fax: 513-961-6058. [CEM]

Cleveland, Cuyahoga Co., St. Maron (1915), Chorbishop Bernard C. Khachan; Deacon George M. Khoury; Subdeacon James Peters.
Res., 1245 Carnegie Ave., 44115. Tel: 216-781-6161; Fax: 216-781-6162. [JC]
Catechesis / Religious Programs—Students 109.

Columbus, Franklin Co., Maronite Catholic Community, Chorbishop Michael J. Kail, Protopresbyter & Admin., Tel: 330-666-3598.

Dayton, Montgomery Co., Saint Ignatius Mission (1993), Rev. Alfred Al-Badwi.
Mailing Address: 727 Beckman St., 45410. Tel: 937-256-3134; Fax: 937-256-3134. [JC]

Fairlawn, Summit Co., Our Lady of the Cedars of Mt. Lebanon (1937), Chorbishop Michael J. Kail; Deacons Robert Foster; Fred Browne.
Res., 507 S. Cleveland-Massillon Rd., 44333-3019. Tel: 330-666-3598; Fax: 330-666-3897.
Catechesis / Religious Programs—Students 58.

Toledo, Lucas Co., Maronite Catholic Community (1999), Rev. Anthony Spinosa.
Mailing Address: 4133 Calkins Rd., Flint, MI 48523. Tel: 810-733-1259.

Youngstown, Mahoning Co., St. Maron (1902), Revs. Anthony J. Salim; Gary George, C.SS.R.; Deacon Joseph Nohra; Subdeacon Thomas Craven.
Res., 1555 S. Meridian Rd., 44511-1199. Tel: 330-792-2371; 792-7671 (Center); Fax: 330-792-3026.
Catechesis / Religious Programs—Tel: 330-538-2567; Fax: 330-538-9820.
Students 149.

STATE OF OREGON

Portland, Multnomah Co., Saint Sharbel (1970), Rev. William Jonathan Decker.
Res., 1804 S.E. 16th Ave., 97214. Tel: 503-231-3853.
Catechesis / Religious Programs—Students 24.
Mission—Seattle, Maronite Catholic Community, 97214. Rev. William Jonathan Decker, Admin.

STATE OF TEXAS

Austin, Travis Co., Our Lady's Maronite Parish (1982), Rev. Donald Sawyer, D.Min.; Deacon Joseph Crowley.
Mailing Address: (Church) 1320 E. 51st St., 78723. Tel: 512-458-3693; Fax: 512-451-9554.
Res., 5010 Caswell Ave., 78751. Tel: 512-454-6342.
Catechesis / Religious Programs—Students 26.

El Paso, El Paso Co., St. Anthony of the Desert Mission (1997) (Lebanese), Rev. Georges Bou-Msallem, Admin.
Res., 3617 Breckenridge St., 79936. Tel: 915-593-3121; Fax: 915-594-8515.
Catechesis / Religious Programs—Students 5.

Houston, Harris Co., Our Lady of the Cedars Maronite Mission (1990), Revs. Milad T. Yaghi, M.L.M.; Andre Estephan.
Res., 11935 Belfort Village, 77031. Tel: 713-568-6800; Fax: 713-564-6961. [JC]
Catechesis / Religious Programs—Students 80.

Lewisville, Denton Co., Our Lady of Lebanon Mission (1990) (Lebanese), Rev. Assaad El-Bacha, M.L.M.
Res., 719 University Pl., 75067. Tel: 972-436-7617; Fax: 972-221-3430.
Catechesis / Religious Programs—Students 70.

San Antonio, Bexar Co., St. George Maronite (1925) (Maronite), Rev. Jean Al-Nahal, M.L.M.; Subdeacon Raymond E. Casillas.
Res., 6070 Babcock Rd., 78240. Tel: 210-690-9569; Fax: 210-690-5093. [JC]
Catechesis / Religious Programs—Students 90.

STATE OF UTAH

Murray, Salt Lake Co., Saint Jude Church (1975) (Lebanese), Rev. Gebran Bou-Merhi.
Res., 4893 Wasatch St., 84107. Tel: 801-268-2820.
Church—4900 Wasatch St., 84107. Tel: 801-265-2195; Fax: 801-268-2820.
Catechesis / Religious Programs—Students 10.

STATE OF WEST VIRGINIA

Wheeling, Ohio Co., Our Lady of Lebanon (1906) (Lebanese), Rev. Georges Chaanine.
Res., 2216 Eoff St., 26003. Tel: 304-233-1688; Fax: 304-233-4714. [JC]
Catechesis / Religious Programs—Students 3.

Special Assignment:
Reverend Fathers—
Fisher, David, Adjunct Prof. of Theology, Marianist University of Dayton
Karem, Peter, Doctoral Studies
Krimes, John Paul, North American College, Rome, Italy

Retired:
Chorbishop—
Trad, John
Reverend Fathers—
Hitti, Michael

INSTITUTIONS LOCATED IN THE DIOCESE

[A] MONASTERIES AND RESIDENCES OF PRIESTS AND BROTHERS

ANN ARBOR, MI. *Maronite Order of Blessed Virgin Mary*, 4405 Earhart Rd., 48105. Tel: 313-662-4822; Fax: 313-662-4822. Revs. Roger Chikri, O.M.M.; Paul Asaf; Nahed Tarabay. Total in Residence 3.

HOUSTON, TX. *The Congregation of Maronite Lebanese Missionaries*, Our Lady of the Cedars, 11935 Bellfort Village, 77031. Tel: 281-568-6800; Fax: 281-564-6961.
E-mail: st.georgesa@stgeorgesa.org
Web site: www.stgeorgesa.org
Revs. Abdallah E. Zaidan, M.L.M., Supr.; Milad T. Yaghi, M.L.M.; Andre S. Estephan, M.L.M.; John Al-Nahal, M.L.M.; Assaad El-Bacha, M.L.M.; Ghassan Matar, M.L.M.; George Bou Sallem, M.L.M.

[B] CONVENTS AND RESIDENCES FOR SISTERS

NORTH JACKSON, OH. *Antonine Maronite Sisters of Youngstown, Inc.*, 2691 N. Lipkey Rd., 44451. Tel: 330-538-2567; Fax: 330-538-9820.
E-mail: anto9srs@aol.com
Sisters 7. Antonine Sisters Adult Day Care, Inc., 2675 N. Lipkey Rd., 44451. Tel: 330-538-9822; Fax: 330-538-9820. Total Staff 15; Total Assisted 55.

[C] NATIONAL SHRINES

NORTH JACKSON, OH. *National Shrine of Our Lady of Lebanon*, 2759 N. Lipkey Rd., 44451. Tel: 330-538-3351; Fax: 330-538-0455.
Web site: www.nationalshrine.org
Rev. Msgr. William D. Bonczewski.

[D] RELIGIOUS COMMUNITIES OF MEN

PHILIPPI, WV. *Our Lady of Solitude, Inc.*, 334 S. Main St., 26416. Tel: 304-457-3330. Rev. Bernard Grunewald, Er.O.L.S, Supr. Total in Residence 1; Total Staff 2.

[E] RESIDENCES FOR CLERGY

NORTH JACKSON, OH. *Father Toubia Retirement Home*, 2759 N. Lipkey Rd., 44451. Tel: 330-538-3351; Fax: 330-538-0455.
Web site: www.nationalshrine.org

[F] MISCELLANEOUS

LOS ANGELES. *Bishop's Retirement Home*, 850 Stone Canyon Rd., 90077. Tel: 310-247-8322; Fax: 310-247-9297.

Bishop's Retirement Trust Fund, c/o Eparchy of Our Lady of Lebanon of Los Angeles, 331 S. San Vicente Blvd., 90048. Tel: 310-247-8322; Fax: 310-247-9297. Chorbishop Gregory J. Mansour, S.T.L.

Eparchial Endowments, c/o Eparchy of Our Lady of Lebanon of Los Angeles, 331 S. San Vincente Blvd., 90048. Tel: 310-247-8322; Fax: 310-247-9297. Chorbishop Gregory J. Mansour, S.T.L.

Priest's Retirement Fund, 333 S. San Vicente Blvd., 90048. Tel: 310-247-8322; Fax: 310-247-9297.

RELIGIOUS INSTITUTES OF MEN REPRESENTED IN THE DIOCESE

For further details refer to the corresponding bracketed number in the Religious Institutes of Men section.

[0785]—*The Congregation of Maronite Lebanese Missionaries.* (San Antonio, TX).—M.L.M.

[0782]—*Maronite Order of Blessed Virgin Mary.* Ann Arbor, MI.—O.M.M.

NECROLOGY

† Abi-Nader, Maron, (Retired). —Died Dec. 19, 1996.

† Feghali, Chorbishop Joseph, (Retired). —Died Dec. 29, 1998.

† Naffah, Rev. Msgr. John, (Retired). —Died Sept. 9, 1999.

Byzantine Eparchy of Parma

Most Reverend

BASIL M. SCHOTT, O.F.M., D.D.

Bishop of Parma; ordained August 29, 1965; consecrated and installed July 11, 1996.

ESTABLISHED FEBRUARY 21, 1969.

Embraces all Byzantine Ruthenian Rite Catholics in the States of Illinois, Indiana, Iowa, Kansas, Michigan, Minnesota, Missouri, Nebraska, North Dakota, South Dakota and Wisconsin. Also the entire State of Ohio excluding the Counties of Ashtabula, Trumbull, Mahoning, Columbiana, Carroll, Harrison, Guernsey, Noble, Morgan, Athens, Meigs, Gallia and Lawrence.

For legal titles of parishes and diocesan institutions, consult the Chancery Office.

Chancery Office: 1900 Carlton Rd., Parma, OH, 44134. Tel.: 216-741-8773; Fax: 216-741-9356.

Web site address: www.parma.org

STATISTICAL OVERVIEW

Personnel	
Bishop	1
Priests: Diocesan Active in Diocese	28
Priests: Active Outside Diocese	1
Priests: Retired, Sick or Absent	9
Number of Diocesan Priests	38
Religious Priests in Diocese	3
Extern Priests in Diocese	9
Ordinations:	
Diocesan Priests	1
Permanent Deacons in Diocese	4
Total Sisters	14
Parishes	
Parishes	37
With Resident Pastor:	
Resident Diocesan Priests	30
Resident Religious Priests	1
Without Resident Pastor:	
Administered by Priests	8
Missions	1
Pastoral Centers	1
Professional Ministry Personnel:	
Sisters	2
Lay Ministers	1
Welfare	
Day Care and Extended Day Care Centers	2
Total Assisted	93
Special Centers for Social Services	2
Total Assisted	8,500
Educational	
Diocesan Students in Other Seminaries	1
Total Seminarians	1
Elementary Schools, Diocesan and Parish	2
Total Students	339
Catechesis/Religious Education:	
High School Students	193
Elementary Students	693
Total Students Under Catholic Instruction	1,226
Teachers in the Diocese:	
Sisters	4
Lay Teachers	23
Vital Statistics	
Receptions into the Church:	
Infant Baptism Totals	120
Adult Baptism Totals	13
Received into Full Communion	29
First Communions	85
Confirmations	96
Marriages:	
Catholic	44
Interfaith	15
Total Marriages	59
Deaths	224
Total Catholic Population	12,572

Former Bishops—Most Rev. EMIL J. MIHALIK, D.D., ord. Sept. 21, 1945; appt. first Bishop of the Ruthenian Eparchy of Parma, March 22, 1969; installed June 12, 1969; died Jan. 27, 1984.—Most Rev. ANDREW PATAKI, D.D., appt. Titular Bishop of Tellmisus and Auxiliary of Passaic, NJ, May 30, 1983; installed Aug. 23, 1983; succeeded to See, June 19, 1984; transferred Parma See, Aug 16, 1984; transferred Byzantine Eparchy of Passaic, Nov. 21, 1995.

Chancery Office—1900 Carlton Rd., Parma, OH, 44134. Tel: 216-741-8773; Fax: 216-741-9356.

Chancellor—Rev. MICHAEL J. HUSZTI, J.C.L.

Presbyteral Council—Rev. Msgr. ROBERT YARNOVITZ; Very Revs. MICHAEL EVANICK; DAVID HANNES, J.C.L.; Revs. EDWARD ZAVELL; JOHN KACHUBA; BRYAN EYMAN; BASIL HUTSKO; DENNIS HRUBIAK; JOHN KAPITAN, O.F.M.; DAVID PETRAS, S.E.O.D.; JOHN KEBLESH; JOSEPH REPKO.

Eparchial Finance Officer—Rev. EDWARD ZAVELL; Sr. HELEN MILLOW, Sec. Eparchial Finance: JEROME J. LUCAS; EDWARD MAHER; THOMAS PERCIAK; HELEN IRION, Sec.

Eparchial Consultors—Rev. Msgr. ROBERT V. YARNOVITZ; Revs. EDWARD ZAVELL; MICHAEL EVANICK; DAVID PETRAS, S.E.O.D.; DAVID HANNES, J.C.L.; JOHN KACHUBA.

Protopresbyters—Ohio: Rev. EDWARD ZAVELL,Midwest: Rev. Msgr. FRANK KORBA,Great Lakes: Rev. JAMES KUBAJAK, M.Div.

Vicar Judicialis—Rev. DAVID HANNES, J.C.L.

Vicar Adjutant—Rev. MICHAEL J. HUSZTI, J.C.L.

Judge—Rev. NICHOLAS R.A. RACHFORD, J.C.L.

Secretary—Rev. NICHOLAS R.A. RACHFORD, J.C.L.

Defender of the Bond—Rev. JAMES KUBAJAK, M.Div.

Promoter of Justice—Rev. JAMES KUBAJAK, M.Div.

Notaries—Rev. JAMES BATCHA; HELEN IRION.

Eparchial Censors—Revs. DAVID PETRAS, S.E.O.D.; JOHN KACHUBA, M.A.

Eparchial Commissions

Sacred Liturgy—Rev. DAVID PETRAS, S.E.O.D., Chm.; Rev. Msgr. ROBERT V. YARNOVITZ; Revs. ROBERT BARTER; MICHAEL HAYDUK; VLADIMIR VANCIK, S.T.D.; STEVEN KOPLINKA; STEVEN HAWKES-TEEPLES.

Apostolate of St. Nicholas—Eparchial Director Cleveland West, Ohio: LORETTA NEMETH, Spiritual Dir.; Rev. JAMES BATCHA, Dir. Cleveland East: Rev. BRYAN R. EYMAN, (Chap.) Spiritual Dir. BRUCE ROYKO, Dir. Midwest: Chapter Directors: PAUL HOHRAN, St. Michael, Merrillville, IN; ANN MARIE ZIMA, St. Nicholas, Munster, IN; DON GRISHAM, Annunciation, Lockport, IL; HELEN TIMURA, St. Nicholas, Barberton, OH Great Lakes: Vacant.

Building Commission—Rev. Msgr. ROBERT V. YARNOVITZ, V.G., Chm.; Revs. DAVID PETRAS, S.E.O.D.; BRYAN EYMAN; CHARLES LIZANICH.

Cantors' Institute—NICOLETTE BOROS, Dir. Cantors' Institute Faculty: Revs. DAVID PETRAS, S.E.O.D.; DENNIS HRUBIAK; MICHAEL HAYDUK; MICHAEL J. HUSZTI, J.C.L.; JAMES BATCHA; NICHOLAS RACHFORD, J.C.L., Cantors' Institute Advisory Board: EDWARD MAHER; VICTORIA BOROS; JEROME J. LUCAS; Revs. EDWARD ZAVELL; NICHOLAS RACHFORD.

Office of Religious Education—JOHN KACHUBA, M.A., Dir. Tel: 216-741-4102. Rev. BASIL HUTSKO, Great Lakes; Rev. Msgr. FRANK KORBA, Midwest.

Catechetical Board—Rev. Msgr. FRANK KORBA; Rev. JOHN KEBLESH; Sr. ELIZABETH JANE TEPLEY, O.S.B.M.; BETTY BARANKO; MELVIN CANNON; RENA FULKA; Deacon RICHARD GUIDEN; LISA STANICH.

Associate Religious Education Directors—Midwest: Rev. Msgr. FRANK KORBA, Great Lakes: Rev. BASIL HUTSKO.

Office of Youth Ministry—Revs. BRUCE RIEBE, Dir. BASIL HUTSKO, Great Lakes; JOHN KEBLESH, Ohio; THOMAS LOYA, Midwest.

Young Singles—Rev. MICHAEL J. HUSZTI.

Office of Family Life—VIRGIL DANIELS, Dir.

Office of Lay Apostolate—ROBERT SHIRILLA, Dir.

Office of Evangelization and Missionary Activity—Rev. JAMES BATCHA, Dir.

Office of the Diaconate—Rev. DENNIS HRUBIAK, Dir.

Office of Vocations—Rev. DENNIS HRUBIAK, Dir.

Seminary Education and Priestly Formation Board—Rev. DAVID PETRAS, S.E.O.D., Chm.; Rev. Msgr. ROBERT V. YARNOVITZ; Revs. MICHAEL HAYDUK; DENNIS HRUBIAK; JOHN KACHUBA, M.A.; NICHOLAS RACHFORD, J.C.L.; EDWARD ZAVELL.

Clergy Life Commission—Rev. DENNIS HRUBIAK, Chm.; Rev. Msgr. BASIL SMOCHKO; Rev. Msgr. ROBERT V. YARNOVITZ; Revs. MICHAEL EVANICK; DAVID HANNES, J.C.L.; MICHAEL J. HUSZTI, J.C.L.; JAMES KUBAJAK, M.Div.; DAVID PETRAS, S.E.O.D.; NICHOLAS RACHFORD, J.C.L.; EDWARD ZAVELL.

Office of Communication—Rev. NICHOLAS RACHFORD, J.C.L., Dir. Eparchial Newspaper, "Horizons". Tel: 216-741-3312; Fax: 216-741-9356.

Vicar for Religious—Rev. MICHAEL J. HUSZTI.

Delegates for Priests—Rev. Msgr. ROBERT V. YARNOVITZ, Chm.; Rev. MICHAEL EVANICK; Rev. DENNIS HRUBIAK.

Priest's Pension Board—Rev. Msgr. ROBERT V. YARNOVITZ, Chm.; Rev. Msgr. FRANK KORBA; Revs. ROBERT BARTER; JAMES BATCHA; BASIL HUTSKO; JOSEPH POHORLAK; JOSEPH RADVANSKY; EDWARD ZAVELL.

Office of Ecumenical Activity—Rev. DAVID PETRAS, S.E.O.D., Dir.

History and Research—Rev. MICHAEL J. HUSZTI, J.C.L., Dir.

Stewardship Office—MARY S. LIZANICH.
Scouting Office—Rev. NICHOLAS RACHFORD, J.C.L., Dir. & Chap., Boy Scouts.
Eparchial Shrine of the Weeping Madonna of Mariapoch—(Burton, OH): President, The Most Rev. Ordinary of the Parma Eparchy. Revs. MICHAEL J. HUSZTI, J.C.L., Dir. & Admin. JOHN KOVACH, Parochial Vicar. Tel: 440-834-8807. Assisted by the Social Mission Sisters. Sr. M. FLORA, S.M.S., Supr. Tel: 440-834-4078.
Respect Life Office—PATRICK PEROTTI.
Pre-Cana Office—Rev. MICHAEL HAYDUK.

CLERGY, PARISHES, MISSIONS AND PAROCHIAL SCHOOLS

STATE OF OHIO

Parma, Cuyahoga Co., Saint John the Baptist, Cathedral, Rev. Msgr. Robert Yarnovitz.
Church—1900 Carlton Rd., 44134-3129. Tel: 216-661-8658; Fax: 216-741-9356.
Res., 1703 Carlton Rd., 44134.
Holy Spirit, Rev. Dennis M. Hrubiak.
Res., 5500 W. 54th St., 44129-2274. Tel: 440-884-8452; Fax: 440-884-8453.

Akron, Summit Co., St. Michael the Archangel, Rev. James Atkins, Admin.
Res., 847 Crouse St., 44306-1125. Tel: 330-376-6633; Fax: 330-376-4149.

Barberton, Summit Co., St. Nicholas, Rev. Stephen Muth, Admin.
Res., 1051 E. Robinson St., 44203-3852. Tel: 330-753-2031.

Bedford, Cuyahoga Co., St. Eugene, Rev. Joseph Repko.
Res., 264 Warrensville-Center Rd., 44146-2741. Tel: 440-232-7302; Fax: 440-439-9537.

Brecksville, Cuyahoga Co., St. Joseph, Rev. Bruce Riebe.
Res., 8111 Brecksville, 44141-1204. Tel: 440-526-1818; Fax: 440-526-0016.

Brunswick, Medina Co., St. Emilian, Rev. John W. Keblesh.
Res., 1231 Substation Rd., 44212-0843. Tel: 330-225-9857; Fax: 330-220-5963.

Burton, Geauga Co., Church of Mariapoch, Revs. Michael J. Huszti, Shrine Dir.; John Kovach.
Res., 17486 Mumford Rd., 44021-9640. Tel: 440-834-8807.
Shrine—Shrine of Mariapoch, Tel: 440-834-4078.
Social Mission Sisters of Hungary 2.

Cleveland, Cuyahoga Co., Holy Ghost, Rev. Joseph Repko, Admin.
Res., 2420 W. 14th St., 44113-4406. Tel: 216-861-2177; Fax: 216-623-0167.
St. Mary, Rev. Steven Koplinka. In res., Rev. Robert St. Martin.
Res., 4600 State Rd., 44109-5243. Tel: 216-741-7979; Fax: 216-741-6622.
School—Tel: 216-749-7980; Fax: 216-749-7981. Sr. Joanne Lickvar, Prin.
Sisters of St. Basil the Great 4; Lay Teachers 10; Students 351.
St. Nicholas (Croatian), Rev. Michael Hayduk.
Res., 3431 Superior Ave., 44114-4160. Tel: 216-361-5069; Fax: 216-361-2455.

Columbus, Franklin Co., St. John Chrysostom, Rev. Eugene R. Linowski.
Res., 5858 Cleveland Ave., 43231-2862. Tel: 614-882-7578; Fax: 614-890-6048.

Dayton, Montgomery Co., St. Barbara, Revs. Eugene R. Linowski, Admin.; Waldemar J. Kuchta.
Res., 5915 Springboro Pk., 45449-3249. Tel: 937-434-9205; Fax: 937-435-2454.

Euclid, Cuyahoga Co., St. Stephen, Revs. John S. Kachuba; Robert D. Kelly.
Res., 532 Lloyd Rd., 44132-1721. Tel: 216-732-7292; Fax: 216-732-9434.

Fairport Harbor, Lake Co., St. Michael, Rev. Bryan R. Eyman.
Mailing Address: St. Andrew, c/o 5768 Andrews Rd., Mentor-on-the-Lake, 44060-2608.
Res., 630 Plum St., 44077-5660. Tel: 440-257-3620; Fax: 440-257-6524.

Fairview Park, Cuyahoga Co., St. Mary Magdalene, Rev. Edward Zavell, V.F.
Res., 5390 W. 220th St., 44126-2968. Tel: 440-734-4644; Fax: 440-734-4645.

Lakewood, Cuyahoga Co., St. Gregory the Theologian, Rev. Gerald P. Schmitz.
Res., 2035 Quail Ave., 44107-5217. Tel: 216-521-1081; Fax: 216-521-1020.

Lorain, Lorain Co., St. Michael, Rev. James Batcha.
Res., 3056 Reeves Ave., 44052-4274. Tel: 440-282-3808.
St. Nicholas, Rev. James Batcha.
Res., 2711 W. 40th St., 44053-2252. Tel: 440-282-7525; Fax: 440-282-9185.
School—2707 W. 40th St., 44053-2252. Tel: 440-282-3289. Mr. Russell Tabak, Prin.
Lay Teachers 7; Students 91.

Marblehead, Ottawa Co., St. Mary, Rev. Joseph R. Radvansky.
Res., 506 E. Main St., 43440-2232. Tel: 419-798-4283.

Mentor-on-the-Lake, Lake Co., St. Andrew the Apostle, Rev. Bryan R. Eyman.
Res., 5768 Andrews Rd., 44060-2608. Tel: 440-257-3620; Fax: 440-257-6524.

Northwood, Lucas Co., St. Michael the Archangel, Rev. James Kubajak.
Res., 2526 Skagway Dr., 43619. Tel: 419-691-5656; Fax: 419-691-7669.
Church—4001 Navarre Ave., Oregon, 43616.

Solon, Cuyahoga Co., St. John the Baptist, Rev. Michael J. Huszti.
Res., 36125 Aurora Rd., 44139-3841. Tel: 440-248-0417; Fax: 440-248-8044.

STATE OF ILLINOIS

Chicago, Cook Co., St. Mary. Closed. For inquiries for parish records contact the Chancery.

Joliet, Will Co., St. Mary Assumption. Closed. For inquiries for parish records contact the Chancery.

Lockport, Will Co., Annunciation Byzantine Catholic Church, Rev. Thomas J. Loya.
Res., 14610 S. Will-Cook Rd., 60441-9212. Tel: 708-645-0241; Fax: 708-645-0243.

STATE OF INDIANA

East Chicago, Lake Co., St. Basil's. Closed. For inquiries for parish records contact the Chancery.

Indiana Harbor Co., Holy Ghost. Closed. For inquiries for parish records contact the Chancery.

Indianapolis, Marion Co., St. Athanasius Church, Rev. John Kapitan, O.F.M., Admin.
Res., 1117 S. Blaine Ave., 46221-1110. Tel: 317-632-4157; Fax: 317-632-2988.

Merrillville, Lake Co., St. Michael, Very Rev. Michael Evanick.
Res., 557 W. 57th Ave., 46410-2540. Tel: 219-980-0600.

Munster, Lake Co., Saint Nicholas, Rev. Msgr. Frank Korba, V.F.
Res., 8103 Columbia Ave., 46321-1802. Tel: 219-838-9380; Fax: 219-838-1265.

Whiting, Lake Co., Assumption of the Blessed Virgin, Rev. Joseph Pohorlak.
Res., 2011 Clark St., 46394-2023. Tel: 219-659-0277.

STATE OF MICHIGAN

Allen Park, Wayne Co., St. Stephen, Rev. Cyril Attak. In res., Rev. Msgr. John Kurty.
Res., 4141 Laurence Ave., 48101-3049. Tel: 313-382-5901.

Bay City, Bay Co., Saint George, Rev. Robert Stash.
Res., 204 N. Van Buren St., 48706-6519. Tel: 517-892-0763.

Detroit, Wayne Co., St. Nicholas, Rev. Robert J. Barter.
Church—19130 Beaconsfield St., 48224-1177. Tel: 313-521-6827.
St. John the Baptist. Closed. For inquiries for parish records contact the Chancery.

Flushing, Genesee Co., St. Michael, Very Rev. David A. Hannes, J.C.L.
Res., 2333 N. Elms Rd., 48433-9426. Tel: 810-659-4887; Fax: 810-659-8363.

Livonia, Wayne Co., Sacred Heart, Rev. Nicholas Ivan.
Res., 29125 W. Six-Mile Rd., 48152-3661. Tel: 734-522-3166.

Omer, Arenac Co., St. John, Rev. Robert Stash.
Mailing Address: P.O. Box 236, 48749-0236. Tel: 517-892-0763.
Res., 204 N. Van Buren St., Bay City, 48706-6519.

Sterling Heights, Macomb Co., St. Basil, Rev. Basil J. Hutsko.
Res., 4700 Metropolitan Pkwy., 48310-3905. Tel: 810-268-1082.

Taylor, Wayne Co., Christ the King. Closed. For inquiries for parish records contact the Chancery.

STATE OF MINNESOTA

Minneapolis, Hennepin Co., St. John the Baptist, Rev. Edward C. Wojciechowski.
Res., 2215 Third St., N.E., 55418-3422. Tel: 612-789-6252.

STATE OF MISSOURI

St. Louis, St. Louis Co., St. Louis Mission, Revs. Eugene P. Selzer; Paul Niemann; Joseph A. Weber.
Res., 9311 Stansberry Ave., 63134-3635. Tel: 314-428-7371; Fax: 314-428-1158.

Sugar Creek, Jackson Co., St. Luke, Byzantine Catholic Parish, Rev. Francis McGlynn.
Mailing Address: 700 E. 8th St., #910, Kansas City, 64106-1635.
Church—11411 Chicago, 64054. Tel: 816-842-3454.

STATE OF WISCONSIN

Bristol, Kenosha Co., St. Irene. Closed. For information regarding the Byzantine Catholic Community contact the Chancery.

On Special or Other Diocesan Assignment:
Reverend Fathers—
Rachford, Nicholas, 1703 Carlton Rd., Apt. A, Parma, OH 44134-3126. Tel: 216-661-9264

On Duty Outside the Diocese:
Reverend Fathers—
Petras, David M., Byzantine Catholic Seminary, 3605 Perrysville Ave., Pittsburgh, PA 05214. Tel: 412-321-5133

Absent on Leave:
Reverend Fathers—
Chelena, Thomas
Francisko, Gary
Rebovich, John
Ruglovsky, Robert
St. Germain, Brian

Retired:
Reverend Monsignors—
Kurty, John, 4141 Laurence Ave., Allen Park, MI 48101-3049. Tel: 313-382-5901
Reverend Fathers—
Jadwisiak, Edmund, 3964 E. State Rd., Port Clinton, OH 43452. Tel: 419-734-9923
Smochko, Basil, 66399 Estrella Ave., Desert Hot Springs, CA 82240-4525. Tel: 760-251-0802
Vancik, Vladimir, Mt. Macrina Manor, 520 W. Main St., Uniontown, PA 15401

Permanent Deacons:
Guiden, Richard
Hendricks, Lawrence
Kenes, Michael
Marquis, Joseph

INSTITUTIONS LOCATED IN THE DIOCESE

[A] CONVENTS AND RESIDENCES FOR SISTERS

NORTH ROYALTON. *Motherhouse and Novitiate*, 6688 Cady Rd., 44133. Tel: 440-237-6800. Byzantine Nuns of St. Clare. Sisters, Parma Eparchy, Byzantine Ruthenian Province, Monastery of the Holy Protection of the Mother of God. Sr. Mary Philomena Horkavi, B.N.S.C., Supr.

[B] RELIGIOUS SHRINES

BURTON. *Shrine of Mariapoch*, 17486 Mumford Rd., 44021. Tel: 440-834-8807. Revs. Michael J. Huszti, Shrine Dir.; John Kovach, Parochial Vicar; Sr. Flora, Supr. Tel: Convent Tel.: 440-834-4078.

[C] MISCELLANEOUS

CLEVELAND. *St. Mary Hospitality House*, 4600 State Rd., 44109. Tel: 216-749-7288. Dorothy Papke, Dir.

KENOSHA, WI. *Byzantine Catholic Center*, 7617 Sheridan Rd. # 6, 53143. Tel: 262-605-4829. Rev. Stephen Wiese, S.C.J.

RELIGIOUS INSTITUTES OF WOMEN REPRESENTED IN THE DIOCESE

For further details refer to the corresponding bracketed number in the Religious Institutes of Women section.

[]—*Byzantine Nuns of St. Clare.* (Parma Eparchy).—B.N.S.C.

[3730]—*Sisters of the Order of St. Basil the Great.*—O.S.B.M.

[]—*Social Mission Sisters of Mariapoch.*—S.M.S.

NECROLOGY

(No Deaths)

Byzantine Catholic Eparchy of Passaic

Most Reverend

ANDREW PATAKI, J.C.L., D.D.

Bishop of Passaic; appointed Titular Bishop of Tellmisus and Auxiliary Bishop of Passaic, May 30, 1983; consecrated August 23, 1983; appointed Bishop June 19, 1984; transferred to Parma See August 16, 1984; transferred to Passaic November 21, 1995.

Most Reverend

MICHAEL J. DUDICK, D.D.

Retired Bishop of Passaic; ordained November 13, 1945; appointed Bishop August 21, 1968; consecrated and installed October 24, 1968; retired November 21, 1995. *Res., 445 Lackawanna Ave., West Paterson, NJ, 07424.*

ESTABLISHED JULY 31, 1963.

Embraces all Catholics of the Byzantine-Ruthenian Rite in the States of New Jersey, Connecticut, Delaware, District of Columbia, Florida, Georgia, Maine, Maryland, Massachusetts, New Hampshire, New York, North Carolina, Rhode Island, South Carolina, Vermont, Virginia and all Eastern Pennsylvania within the western boundaries of the Counties of Franklin, Juniata, Lycoming, Mifflin, Union and Tioga.

For legal titles of parishes and diocesan institutions, consult the Chancery Office.

Chancery Office: 445 Lackawanna Ave., West Paterson, NJ, 07424. Tel.: 973-890-7777; Fax: 973-890-7175.

Web site address: members.aol.com/byzruth/index/htm

E-mail address: ECLnews@aol.com

STATISTICAL OVERVIEW

Personnel	
Bishop	1
Retired Bishops	1
Priests: Diocesan Active in Diocese	67
Priests: Active Outside Diocese	7
Priests: Retired, Sick or Absent	14
Number of Diocesan Priests	88
Religious Priests in Diocese	11
Extern Priests in Diocese	4
Permanent Deacons in Diocese	15
Total Brothers	2
Total Sisters	19
Parishes	
Parishes	93
With Resident Pastor:	
Resident Diocesan Priests	63
Resident Religious Priests	3
Without Resident Pastor:	
Administered by Priests	27
Missions	6
Closed Parishes	3
Educational	
Diocesan Students in Other Seminaries	3
Total Seminarians	3
Elementary Schools, Diocesan and Parish	2
Total Students	245
Catechesis/Religious Education:	
High School Students	384
Elementary Students	1,863
Total Students Under Catholic Instruction	2,495
Teachers in the Diocese:	
Sisters	5
Lay Teachers	15
Vital Statistics	
Receptions into the Church:	
Infant Baptism Totals	287
Adult Baptism Totals	15
Received into Full Communion	39
First Communions	304
Confirmations	266
Marriages:	
Catholic	97
Interfaith	26
Total Marriages	123
Deaths	606
Total Catholic Population	32,860

Former Bishops—Most Rev. STEPHEN J. KOCISKO, D.D., ord. March 30, 1941; appt. Titular Bishop of Theveste and Auxiliary of Exarchate of Pittsburgh, July 20, 1956; appt. First Eparch of Passaic, July 31, 1963; appt. Eparch of Pittsburgh, Dec. 21, 1967; installed March 5, 1968; elevated to Metropolitan Archbishop of Pittsburgh, Feb. 21, 1969; retired June 12, 1991; died March 7, 1995.—Most Rev. MICHAEL J. DUDICK, D.D., ord. Nov. 13, 1945; appt. Bishop of Passaic, Aug. 21, 1968; installed Oct. 24, 1968; retired Nov. 21, 1995.

Protosyncellus-Vicar General—Very Rev. GERALD N. DINO, O.E.S.L.

Syncellates and Protopresbyterates—

Susquehanna Valley Syncellate—

Syncellus—Vacant.

Northern Pennsylvania/Northern New York Protopresbyterate—Rev. Msgr. JOHN T. SEKELLICK, J.C.L., Protopresbyter, *Holy Ghost Church, 313 First St., Jessup, PA, 18434.* Tel: 570-489-2353.

Wyoming Valley Protopresbyterate—Vacant.

Central Pennsylvania Syncellate—

Syncellus—Very Rev. LEONARD M. HOLLICK, *St. Michael Church, 17 E. Blaine St., McAdoo, PA, 18237.* Tel: 570-929-1062.

Mid-Pennsylvania Protopresbyterate—Very Rev. MICHAEL MONDIK, Protopresbyter, *SS. Peter & Paul Church, 107 S. Fourth St., Minersville, PA, 17954.* Tel: 570-544-2074.

South Pennsylvania Protopresbyterate—Very Rev. GREGORY J. NOGA, M.A., Protopresbyter, *SS. Peter & Paul Church, 1140 Johnston Dr., Bethlehem, PA, 18017-1934.* Tel: 610-867-2322.

New Jersey Syncellate—

Syncellus—Very Rev. BASIL RAKACZKY, O.S.B.M., S.T.L., *St. Michael Church, 401 Hall Ave., Perth Amboy, NJ, 08861.* Tel: 732-826-0792.

Northern New Jersey Protopresbyterate—Rev. Msgr. ROBERT G. MONETA, Protopresbyter, *St. George Church, 214 Warwick St., Newark, NJ, 07105.* Tel: 973-589-7202.

Central New Jersey Protopresbyterate—Very Rev. ROBERT RADVANSKY, Protopresbyter, *St. Nicholas Church, 320 Washington St., Perth Amboy, NJ, 732-442-0418.*

New York-New England Syncellate—

Syncellus—Vacant.

New York/New England Protopresbyterate—Very Rev. ROBERT J. HOSPODAR, J.C.L., Protopresbyter, *St. Mary Church, 246 E. 15th St., New York, NY, 10003.* Tel: 212-677-0516.

Middle States Syncellate—

Syncellus—Very Rev. JOHN G. BASARAB, M.A., *Epiphany of Our Lord Church, 3410 Woodburn Rd., Annandale, VA, 22003.* Tel: 703-573-3986. Very Rev. CONAN TIMONEY, Ph.D., Protopresbyter, *Patronage of Mother of God Church, 1260 Stevens Ave., Baltimore, MD, 21227.* Tel: 410-247-4936.

Southern States Syncellate—

Syncellus—Very Rev. PETER LICKMAN, *St. Basil Church, 1475 N.E. 199th Street, Miami, FL, 33179.* Tel: 305-651-0991. Very Rev. ROBERT EVANCHO, Protopresbyter, *St. Therese Church, 4265 13th Ave. N., St. Petersburg, FL, 33713.* Tel: 727-323-4022.

Chancery Office—*Eparchial Center, 445 Lackawanna Ave., West Paterson, NJ, 07424.* Tel: 973-890-7777; Fax: 973-890-7175. Office Hours: Mon.-Fri. 9-12 & 1-4.

Chancellor—Very Rev. ROBERT J. HOSPODAR, J.C.L.

Eparchial Finance Officer—Mr. NICHOLAS LUCARELLA, C.P.A.

Eparchial Finance Council—Very Rev. GERALD N. DINO, O.E.S.L.; Mr. NICHOLAS LUCARELLA, C.P.A.; Mr. FRANK FERRANTE, Attorney; Mr. BERT REIMAN; Mr. JERRY LUCAS, C.P.A.; Ms. VICKI WINDSOR.

Canonical Consultant to the Bishop—Rev. BENEDICT A. DESOCIO, J.C.L.

Eparchial College of Consultors—Very Revs. GERALD N. DINO, O.E.S.L.; LEONARD M. HOLLICK; BASIL RAKACZKY, O.S.B.M., S.T.L.; JOHN G. BASARAB, M.A.; PETER LICKMAN; ROBERT J. HOSPODAR, J.C.L., Sec.

Presbyteral Council—Ex Officio Members: Very Revs. GERALD N. DINO, O.E.S.L.; LEONARD M. HOLLICK; BASIL RAKACZKY, O.S.B.M., S.T.L.; JOHN G. BASARAB, M.A.; PETER LICKMAN; Rev. Msgr. JOHN T. SEKELLICK, J.C.L. Elected Members: Very Revs. EDWARD G. CIMBALA, D.Min.; GREGORY J. NOGA, M.A.; ROBERT RADVANSKY; CONAN TIMONEY, Ph.D.; Revs. EDWARD J. HIGGINS; MICHAEL KANE, Ph.D.; THEODORE KREPP; MICHAEL POPSON. Appointed Members: Rev. Msgr. ALAN BORSUK; Very Rev. ROBERT J. HOSPODAR, J.C.L., Sec.

Eparchial Tribunal—445 Lackawanna Ave., West Paterson, NJ, 07424. Tel: 973-890-7777.
Judicial Vicar—Rev. Msgr. JOHN T. SEKELLICK, J.C.L.
Moderator of the Tribunal/Adjutant Judicial Vicar—Rev. BENEDICT A. DESOCIO, J.C.L.
Defender of the Bond—Very Rev. ROBERT J. HOSPODAR, J.C.L.
Advocates—Rev. ANDOR RAKACZKI, S.T.D.; Very Rev. BASIL RAKACZKY, O.S.B.M., S.T.L.
Promoter of Justice—Very Rev. ROBERT J. HOSPODAR, J.C.L.
Notaries—Rev. VLADIMIR ZABLOTSKI; Mrs. MARY ELLEN GAFFNEY.

Commissions, Departments and Institutions

Boy Scouts—Vacant.

Building and Properties Commission—Rev. Msgr. ALAN BORSUK, Chm.

Cemeteries Commission—Very Rev. LEONARD M. HOLLICK, Chm.

Clergy Continued Education—Rev. JOHN ZEYACK, S.T.L., Dir.

Commission for Ecumenism—Rev. Msgr. ALAN BORSUK, Chm.

Communications and Telecommunications—Rev. JAMES HAYER.

Evangelization—Rev. JOSEPH BERTHA, Chm.

Respect Life—Very Rev. ROBERT J. HOSPODAR, J.C.L., Dir.

Family Life—Rev. Msgr. JOHN T. SEKELLICK, J.C.L., Dir.

Eparchial Historian—Very Rev. ROBERT J. HOSPODAR, J.C.L.

Holy Name Society—Rev. Msgr. ROBERT G. MONETA, Chm.

Eparchial Liturgy and Art Commission—Rev. Msgr. ALAN BORSUK, Chm.

Eparchial Music Commission—Rev. ROBERT G. MONETA, Chm.

Eparchial Newspaper—The Eastern Catholic Life; Rev. EUGENE M. HUTTER, Editor; Rev. GEORGE M. MALITZ, Business Mgr. Associate Editors: Revs. GLENN DAVIDOWICH; JAMES HAYER. Tel: 973-890-7794.

Office for Eastern Christian Formation (formerly: Office of Religious Education)—Very Rev. GREGORY J. NOGA, M.A., Dir.

Secretariat for Youth—Rev. GEORGE M. MALITZ, Moderator.

Retirement Plan Board—Very Revs. GERALD N. DINO, O.E.S.L.; ROBERT J. HOSPODAR, J.C.L., Sec. ROBERT RADVANSKY; Rev. Msgr. ROBERT G. MONETA; Revs. MYRON BADNEROSKY; RONALD HATTON; GEORGE M. MALITZ; MICHAEL SALNICKY.

Saint Nicholas Shrine - Carpathian Village—Rev. MICHAEL SALNICKY, Dir., *P.O. Box 616, Canadensis, PA, 18325.* Tel: 717-595-3265.

Vocations—Rev. EDWARD G. CIMBALA, D.Min., Dir.

Priesthood & Diaconate Formation Programs—Rev. EDWARD G. CIMBALA, D.Min., Dir.

Vicar for Clergy—Vacant.

Vicar for Religious—Vacant.

Eastern Catholic Associates—Publication: God With Us; *445 Lackawanna Ave., West Paterson, NJ, 07424.*

CLERGY, PARISHES, MISSIONS AND PAROCHIAL SCHOOLS

STATE OF NEW JERSEY

Passaic, Passaic Co., St. Michael Cathedral, Rev. Marcel Szabo.
Res., 96 First St., 07055. Tel: 973-777-2553; Fax: 973-777-9474. [CEM]
Chapel—415 Lackawanna Ave., West Paterson, 07424. Tel: 973-256-0134; Fax: 973-777-9474.

Bayonne, Hudson Co., St. John the Baptist, Rev. Michael Yurista.
Res., 15 E. 26th St., 07002. Tel: 201-339-1840; Fax: 201-339-6255.

Carteret, Middlesex Co., St. Elias, Rev. Edward Semko.
Res., 42 Cooke Ave., 07008. Tel: 732-541-5213; Fax: 732-541-9637.

Dunellen, Middlesex Co., St. Nicholas, Rev. J. Michael Venditti, Admin.
Res., 121 Madison Ave., 08812. Tel: 732-968-3337.

East Brunswick, Middlesex Co., Nativity of Our Lord, Rev. J. Michael Venditti.
Res., 700 Old Bridge Tpke., 08816. Tel: 732-238-0865; Fax: 732-238-2950.

Edison, Middlesex Co., St. Nicholas, Very Rev. Robert J. Radvansky, Admin.
Res., 215 May St., 08837. Tel: 732-661-1160.

Elizabeth, Union Co., SS. Peter and Paul. Administered from St. George's, Linden, NJ. In res., Rev. Michael Chubirko, S.D.B.
Res., 316 First Ave., 07206. Tel: 908-353-7246.

Flanders, Morris Co., Holy Wisdom, Rev. Daniel Staniskis.
Res., 197 Emmans Rd., 07836. Tel: 973-584-0414.

Hillsborough Township, Somerset Co., St. Mary's, Rev. Msgr. Alan J. Borsuk; Rev. Vladimir Zablotski.
Res., 1900 Brook Blvd., 08876. Tel: 908-725-0615; Fax: 908-725-9615.

Jersey City, Hudson Co., St. Mary's, Rev. Robert J. Skurla.
Res., 231 Pacific Ave., 07304. Tel: 201-333-2975.

Linden, Union Co., St. George's, Very Rev. Gerald N. Dino, O.E.S.L.; Deacon William Tizio.
Res., 417 McCandless St., 07036. Tel: 908-486-6500; Fax: 908-486-6523.

Mahwah, Bergen Co., Holy Spirit. Unassigned. Administered from St. Michael Cathedral, Passaic, NJ.
Mailing Address: c/o, 96 First St., Passaic, 07055.

Newark, Essex Co., St. George, Rev. Msgr. Robert G. Moneta.
Res., 214 Warwick St., 07105. Tel: 973-589-7202.

New Brunswick, Middlesex Co., St. Joseph, Rev. Stephen J. Skinta, O.S.B.M., Admin.
Res., 30 High St., 08901. Tel: 732-545-1686.

Perth Amboy, Middlesex Co., St. Nicholas, Very Rev. Robert J. Radvansky.
Res., 320 Washington St., 08861. Tel: 732-442-0418; Fax: 732-442-9120. [CEM]
St. Michael, Very Rev. Basil M. Rakaczky, O.S.B.M.
Res., 401 Hall Ave., 08861. Tel: 732-826-0792; Fax: 732-826-7993.

Phillipsburg, Warren Co., SS. Peter and Paul, Rev. Steven Safko, Admin.
Res., 723 S. Main St., 08865. Tel: 908-454-5482.

Rahway, Union Co., St. Thomas the Apostle, Rev. John Zeyack, S.T.L.
Res., 1410 Church St., 07065. Tel: 732-382-5300.

Roebling, Burlington Co., St. Nicholas, Rev. Lawrence Robert Wolf, O.S.B.M., Admin.
Res., 191 Norman Ave., 08554. Tel: 609-499-0058. [CEM]
Mission—South Hampton Twp., Vincentown Co., St. Jude, 50 Burrs Mill Rd., South Hampton Twp., 08088.

Somerset, Somerset Co., SS. Peter and Paul, Rev. Christopher Petruska.
Res., 285 Hamilton St., 08873. Tel: 732-545-5500; Fax: 732-545-3466.

Toms River, Ocean Co., Our Lady of Perpetual Help, Rev. Charles Yastishock.
Res., 1937 Church Rd., 08753. Tel: 732-255-6272; Fax: 732-279-0206.

Trenton, Mercer Co., St. Mary of the Assumption, Rev. Edward G. Cimbala, D.Min.; Deacon Thomas L. Vanisko.
Res., 411 Adeline St., 08611. Tel: 609-394-5004. [CEM]
Chapel—Hamilton Township, St. Mary Chapel.
St. Nicholas. Closed. For parish records, contact St. Mary of the Assumption, Trenton, NJ.
Mailing Address: c/o, 411 Adeline St., 08611.

STATE OF CONNECTICUT

Bridgeport, Fairfield Co., Holy Trinity. Administered from St. John the Baptist, Trumball, CT.
Mailing Address: c/o 100 St. John's Dr., Trumball, 06611.
Church—155 Scofield Ave., 06605.

Danbury, Fairfield Co., St. Nicholas, Rev. Michael George Popson.
Res., 13 Pembroke Rd., 06811. Tel: 203-743-1106; Fax: 203-743-5326.

Meriden, New Haven Co., St. Nicholas of Myra. Administered from St. Nicholas, Danbury, CT.
Mailing Address: c/o 13 Pembroke Rd., Danbury, 06810.

New Britain, Hartford Co., Holy Trinity, Rev. Robert Woytek.
Res., 121 Beaver St., 06051. Tel: 860-229-2531; Fax: 860-827-0564. [CEM]

Trumbull, Fairfield Co., St. John the Baptist, Rev. George M. Malitz.
Res., 100 St. John's Dr., 06611. Tel: 203-377-5967; Fax: 203-377-5968.

STATE OF FLORIDA

Coconut Creek, Broward Co., Our Lady of the Sign, Rev. Michael N. Kane, Ph.D.
Res., 7311 Lyons Rd., 33073. Tel: 954-429-0056.

Fort Pierce, Port St. Lucie Co., SS. Cyril and Methodius, Rev. Michael Sopoliga, Admin.
Church—1002 Bahama Ave., 34982. Tel: 561-595-1021; 561-595-8862 (Res.); Fax: 561-461-1436.

Jacksonville, Duval Co., Protection of the Mother of God. Closed. For parish records, contact Holy Dormition, Ormond Beach, FL.

Lake Worth, Duval Co., Holy Apostles, Rev. Nicholas C. Kusevich.
Res., 4788 Clock Rd., 33463. Tel: 561-968-8500; Fax: 561-968-2021.

Miami, Dade Co., St. Basil's, Very Rev. Peter Lickman.
Res., 1475 N.E. 199 St., 33179. Tel: 305-651-0991; Fax: 305-651-4902.

New Port Richey, Pasco Co., St. Anne's, Rev. Basil William Kraynyak.
Church and Res.: 7120 Massachusetts Ave., 34653. Tel: 727-849-1190.

North Fort Myers, Lee Co., All Saints Byzantine Catholic, Rev. James Mitchko.
Res., 10291 Bayshore Rd., 33917. Tel: 941-543-6363; Fax: 941-543-6363.
Mission—Naples.

Orlando, Orange Co., St. Nicholas of Myra, Rev. Salvatore A. Pignato; Deacon Robert Thanski.
Res., 5135 Sand Lake Rd., 32819. Tel: 407-351-0133; Fax: 407-351-0133[*]51.
Mission—Melbourne.

Ormond Beach, Volusia Co., Holy Dormition, Rev. Francis Gera.
Res., 17 Buckskin Ln., 32174. Tel: 904-677-8704; Fax: 904-677-8704.

St. Petersburg, Pinellas Co., St. Therese, Very Rev. Robert Evancho; Deacon Joseph Ciarciaglino.
Res., 4226 33rd Ave. N., 33713. Tel: 727-323-4022; Fax: 727-323-8351.
Convent—1200 37th St. N., 33713. Tel: 727-322-0003.

STATE OF GEORGIA

Roswell, Fulton Co., Epiphany Byzantine Church, Rev. Philip P. Scott, Ph.D.
Res., 2030 Old Alabama Rd., 30076. Tel: 770-993-0973; Fax: 770-993-2419.

STATE OF MARYLAND

Baltimore, Baltimore Co., Patronage of the Mother of God, Very Rev. Conan H. Timoney, Ph.D.
Church—1260 Stevens Ave., 21227. Tel: 410-247-4936.
Missions—Abingdon, St. Francis; Hagerstown, St. Ann's.

Beltsville, Prince George's Co., St. Gregory of Nyssa, Rev. Michael Kerestes.
Res., 12420 Old Gunpowder Rd., 20705. Tel: 301-953-9323; Fax: 301-953-1529.

STATE OF MASSACHUSETTS

South Hadley, Hampshire Co., St. Michael's. Closed. For parish records, contact Holy Trinity, New Britain, CT.
Mailing Address: c/o, 121 Beaver St., New Britain, CT 06051.

STATE OF NEW YORK

Amherst, Erie Co., St. Stephen's, Rev. Joseph Bertha; Deacon Chester Fortuna, M.D.
Res., 620 Ayer Rd., Williamsville, 14221. Tel: 716-688-9290.

Binghamton, Broome Co., Holy Spirit, Very Rev. John J. Cigan, J.C.B.
Res., 360 Clinton St., 13905. Tel: 607-797-2122; Fax: 607-797-2167. [CEM]

Brooklyn, Kings Co., St. Elias. Administered from St. Mary's, New York.
Mailing Address: c/o, 246 E. 15th St., New York, 10003.
Saint Mary's Chapel. Closed.

Endicott, Broome Co., SS. Peter and Paul's, Rev. Vincent M. Brady, Admin.
Res., 106 N. Rogers Ave., 13760. Tel: 607-785-3132; Fax: 607-748-1138. [CEM]

Granville, Washington Co., SS. Peter and Paul. Administered from SS. Peter and Paul, Peekskill, NY. In res., Rev. Harold Stockert.
Res., 2 Park Ave., 12832. Tel: 518-642-2884; Fax: 518-642-1556. [CEM]

New York, New York Co., Exaltation of Holy Cross. Administered from St. Nicholas of Myra, White Plains, NY. Tel: 914-681-0659.
Mailing Address: c/o, 768 North St., White Plains, 10605.
St. Mary's, Very Rev. Robert J. Hospodar, J.C.L., Admin.
Res., 246 E. 15th St., 10003. Tel: 212-677-0516; Fax: 212-260-6071.

Olean, Cattaragus Co., St. Mary's. Administered from St. Stephen Church, Amherst, NY.
Mailing Address: c/o, 620 Ayer Rd., Williamsville, 14221.

Peekskill, Westchester Co., SS. Peter and Paul, Rev. Msgr. Robert Senetsky, J.C.D.
Res., 705 Shenandoah Ave., 10566. Tel: 914-737-8249; Fax: 914-737-8438.

Smithtown, Suffolk Co., Resurrection, Rev. Daniel J. Bitsko.
Res., 37 Juniper Ave., 11787. Tel: 516-724-4979.

Westbury, Nassau Co., St. Andrew the Apostle, Rev. Daniel J. Bitsko, Admin.; Deacon Nicholas Daddona.
Church—275 Ellison Ave., 11590. Tel: 516-333-3266; 724-4979 (Office).

White Plains, Westchester Co., St. Nicholas of Myra, Rev. Andor Rakaczki, S.T.D.
Res., 768 North St., 10605. Tel: 914-681-0659; Fax: 914-681-0238.

Yonkers, Westchester Co., St. Nicholas of Myra. Administered from St. Nicholas of Myra, White Plains.
Mailing Address: c/o St. Nicholas of Myra, 768 North St., White Plains, 10605. Tel: 914-681-0659.

STATE OF NORTH CAROLINA

Cary, Wake Co., SS. Cyril & Methodius Byzantine Catholic, Rev. Richard Rohrer.
Res., 2510 Piney Plains Rd., 27511. Tel: 919-851-9266; Fax: 919-233-3997.

STATE OF PENNSYLVANIA

Allentown, Lehigh Co., St. Andrew the Apostle. Closed. For parish records, contact St. Michael, Allentown.
St. Michael, Rev. Peter J. Hosak, M.S.
Res., 156 Green St., 18102. Tel: 610-432-6773; Fax: 610-432-6773.

Beaver Meadows, Carbon Co., SS. Peter and Paul, Rev. James J. Demko; Deacon Michael Pataki.
Res., P.O. Box 206, 18216. Tel: 570-455-1442; Fax: 570-455-7144. [CEM]

Bethlehem, Northampton Co., SS. Peter and Paul, Very Rev. Gregory J. Noga, M.A.
Res., 1140 Johnston Dr., 18017. Tel: 610-867-2322; Fax: 610-867-7274.

Brockton, Schuylkill Co., St. Mary's. Administered from St. Mary's, Mahanoy City, PA.
Mailing Address: c/o, 621 Mahanoy Ave., Mahanoy City, 17948.

Clarks Summit, Lackawanna Co., Transfiguration. Administered from St. Mary, Scranton, PA.
Mailing Address: c/o, 310 Mifflin Ave., Scranton, 18503.

Coatesville, Chester Co., St. Mary's. Administered from St. Michael's, Mont Clare, PA.
Mailing Address: c/o St. Michael's, 203 Jacob St., Mont Clare, 19453. Tel: 610-933-2819; Fax: 610-935-9460.

Dunmore, Lackawanna Co., St. Michael, Rev. Theodore Rudy.
Res., 511 E. Drinker St., 18512. Tel: 570-344-2521; Fax: 570-344-4535. [CEM]

Forest City, Susquehanna Co., St. John the Baptist. Administered from St. John the Baptist, Scranton, PA.
Mailing Address: c/o, 310 Broadway, Scranton, 18505.

Freeland, Luzerne Co., St. Mary's, Rev. Msgr. Nicholas I. Pohak.
Res., 643 Fern St., 18224. Tel: 570-636-0700. [CEM]

Glen Lyon, Luzerne Co., St. Michael. Administered from St. Mary's, Kingston, PA.
Mailing Address: c/o, 321 Chestnut Ave., Kingston, 18704.

Harrisburg, Dauphin Co., St. Ann, Rev. Michael P. Shear.
Res., 5408 Locust Ln., 17109. Tel: 717-652-1415; Fax: 717-652-5471.

Hazleton, Luzerne Co., St. John the Baptist Church, Rev. Eugene Hutter.
Res., 5 E. 20th St., 18201. Tel: 570-454-1142; Fax: 570-454-6120. [CEM 2]
School—201 N. Wyoming St., 18201. Tel: 570-454-5812; Fax: 570-454-8757. Mr. Lawrence Foran, Prin.
Sisters of St. Basil the Great 3; Lay Teachers 6; Students 97.
St. Mary's, Rev. Michael Krulak.
Res., 227 E. Beech St., 18201. Tel: 570-455-3232; Fax: 570-454-8447. [CEM]

Hilltown, Bucks Co., Byzantine Catholic Mission of Bucks County, PA. Closed. For mission records, contact Holy Ghost, Philadelphia, PA.
Mailing Address: c/o, 2310 S. 24th St., Philadelphia, 19145.

Jessup, Lackawanna Co., Holy Ghost, Rev. Msgr. John T. Sekellick, J.C.L.
Res., 313 First Ave., 18434. Tel: 570-489-2353; Fax: 570-489-7049. [CEM]
School—LaSalle Academy, Tel: 570-489-2010; Fax: 570-489-3887. Dr. James Tarity, Jr., Prin.
Sisters 2; Lay Teachers 26; Students 468.

Kingston, Luzerne Co., St. Mary's, Rev. Theodore Krepp.
Res., 321 Chestnut Ave., 18704. Tel: 570-287-0282; Fax: 570-283-0464. [CEM]

Lansford, Carbon Co., St. John the Baptist, Rev. Ronald Barusefski.
Res., 116 E. Bertsch St., 18232. Tel: 570-645-2640. [CEM]

Levittown, Bucks Co., Our Lady of Perpetual Help, Rev. Myron M. Badnerosky.
Res., 1787 Woodbourne Rd., 19056. Tel: 215-945-5122.

Lopez, Sullivan Co., SS. Peter and Paul. Administered from St. Nicholas Church, Old Forge, PA.
Mailing Address: c/o, 140 Church St., Old Forge, 18518.

McAdoo, Schuylkill Co., St. Michael, Very Rev. Leonard Hollick.
Res., 17 E. Blaine St., 18237. Tel: 570-929-1062; Fax: 570-929-3239. [CEM]

Mahanoy City, Schuylkill Co., St. Mary's, Rev. Gary Mensinger, Admin.
Res., 621 W. Mahanoy Ave., 17948. Tel: 570-773-2631. [CEM]

Minersville, Schuylkill Co., SS. Peter and Paul, Very Rev. Michael Mondik.
Res., 107 S. Fourth St., 17954. Tel: 570-544-2074; Fax: 570-544-2074. [CEM]

Mont Clare, Montgomery Co., St. Michael, Rev. Glenn M. Davidowich.
Res., 203 Jacob St., 19453. Tel: 610-933-2819; Fax: 610-935-9460.

Nanticoke, Luzerne Co., St. Mary's (Hanover). Administered from St. John's, Wilkes Barre, PA.
Mailing Address: c/o, 526 Church St., Wilkes-Barre, 18702.

Nesquehoning, Carbon Co., St. Mary's. Administered from St. John the Baptist, Lansford, PA.
Mailing Address: c/o, 116 E. Bertsch St., Lansford, 18232. [CEM]

Old Forge, Lackawanna Co., St. Nicholas, Revs. Peter M. Donish; Nicholas Kraynak.
Res., 140 Church St., 18518. Tel: 570-457-3042; Fax: 570-457-1906. [CEM]
Mission—Mount Pocono, Monroe Co., St. Nicholas, (1973) Rte. 940, Mt. Pocono, 18344. Tel: 570-839-8090; Fax: 570-595-6177. Rev. Michael J. Salnicky, Admin., Tel: 570-839-8090; Fax:570-595-6177.

Palmerton, Carbon Co., SS. Peter and Paul. Administered from St. Michael's, Allentown, PA.
Mailing Address: c/o, 156 Green St., Allentown, 18102. Tel: 610-432-6773.

Philadelphia, Philadelphia Co., Holy Ghost, Rev. Edward J. Higgins.
Res., 2310 S. 24th St., 19145. Tel: 215-334-5129; Fax: 215-334-1797.
Holy Trinity. Administered from Holy Ghost, Philadelphia, PA. In res., Rev. Austin Mohrbacher.
Res., 6801 N. 10th St., 19126. Tel: 215-548-2837.

Pittston, Luzerne Co., St. Michael, Rev. Robert Kemeter.
Res., 205 N. Main St., 18640. Tel: 570-654-4564; Fax: 570-654-5349. [CEM]

Pottstown, Montgomery Co., St. John the Baptist, Rev. Nicholas DeProspero; Deacon Michael Erdek.
Res., 301 Cherry St., 19464. Tel: 610-326-1877; Fax: 610-326-1890. [CEM]

St. Clair, Schuylkill Co., St. Mary's. Administered from SS. Peter and Paul, Minersville, PA.
Mailing Address: 107 S. 4th St., Minersville, 17954. [CEM]

Scranton, Lackawanna Co., St. John the Baptist, Rev. Robert W. Lozinski, C.S.C., Admin.
Res., 310 Broadway, 18505. Tel: 570-342-8930; Fax: 570-342-8930. [CEM]
St. Mary's, Rev. Francis M. Twardzik, S.D.B.
Res., 310 Mifflin Ave., 18503. Tel: 570-342-8429; Fax: 570-342-6773. [CEM]

Sheppton, Schuylkill Co., St. Mary's. Administered from SS. Peter and Paul, Beaver Meadows.
Mailing Address: c/o, P.O. Box 206, Beaver Meadows, 18216. [CEM]

Swoyersville, Luzerne Co., St. Nicholas. Administered from St. Mary's, Kingston, PA. In res., Rev. Jody Baran.
Res., 271 Tripp St., 18704. Tel: 570-287-4418. [CEM]

Taylor, Lackawanna Co., St. Mary's. Administered from St. Nicholas, Old Forge.
Mailing Address: c/o, 140 Church St., Old Forge, 18518. Tel: 570-457-3042. [CEM]

Wilkes-Barre, Luzerne Co., St. Mary's, Rev. James Hayer.
Res., 695 N. Main St., 18705. Tel: 570-822-6028; Fax: 570-823-5423. [CEM]
School—522 Madison St., 18705. Tel: 570-823-8003; Fax: 570-823-8003. Sr. Janet Decker, O.S.B.M., Prin.
Sisters of St. Basil the Great 2; Lay Teachers 9; Students 148.
St. John's, Rev. James Badeaux.
Res., 526 Church St., 18702. Tel: 570-825-4338; Fax: 570-825-0786.

Williamstown, Dauphin Co., Holy Spirit. Administered from SS. Peter and Paul, Minersville, PA.
Mailing Address: c/o, 107 S. Fourth St., Minersville, 17954. Tel: 570-544-2074. [CEM]

STATE OF VIRGINIA

Annandale, Fairfax Co., Epiphany of Our Lord, Very Rev. John G. Basarab, M.A.; Deacon Gerald McDonnell.
Res., 3410 Woodburn Rd., 22003. Tel: 703-573-3986; Fax: 703-573-0344.

Williamsburg, York Co., Ascension of Our Lord, Rev. Ronald Hatton.
Res., 4528 Wimbledon Way, 23188. Tel: 757-253-5641; Fax: 757-253-9423.
Church—114 Palace Ln., 23185. Tel: 757-220-8098.
Mission—Virginia Beach, Virginia Beach Co., Our Lady of Perpetual Help, 216 S. Parliament Dr., Virginia Beach, 23462. Tel: 757-456-0809.

Special or Other Diocesan Assignment:
Reverend Fathers—
DeSocio, Benedict, J.C.L., Chancery Office, 445 Lackawanna Ave., West Paterson, NJ 07424
Paulshock, Emil

On Duty Outside Diocese:
Reverend Fathers—
Custer, John S., SS. Cyril & Methodius Seminary, 3605 Perrysville Ave., Pittsburgh, PA 15214. Tel: 412-321-8383; Fax:412-321-9936
DeFronzo, Anthony R., 767 Elm St., Rocky Hill, CT 06064
Drucker, James
Fulton, Eugene, Larchmont Trinity Retreat, One Pryer Manor Rd., Larchmont, NY 10538. Tel: 914-632-3743
Hamperzonian, Jerry, Chap., VA Medical Center, 3350 La Jolla Village Dr., San Diego, CA 92161
Kapron, Alan, 3600 Biddulph Rd., Cleveland, OH 44109. Tel: 216-398-4866
Slesinski, Robert, Ph.D., Vysshaia Dukhovnaia Seminaria "Maria Tsaritsa Apostolov", la Krasnoarmeiskaia vl., 11, Sankt-Peterburg, Russia 198005. Tel: 011-7-812-316-15-95

Leave of Absence:
Reverend Fathers—
Siroki, David

Absent on Sick Leave:
Reverend Fathers—
Bujnak, George A.
Czachor, Christopher
Kanar, Richard

Retired:
Reverend Monsignors—
Jackanich, Joseph, 4036 Lockwood Blvd., Youngstown, OH 44511
Misolich, Raymond M., J.C.L., 4 Springbrook Ter., Lake Hopatcong, NJ 07849. Tel: 973-663-3093
Reverend Fathers—
Billy, George
Brown, Charles, M.D., Santa Teresita del Nino Jesus, 2 Poniente, Puebla, Pue CP 72140 Mexico. Tel: 011-22-48-38-78
Danilak, John, 2711 Veser Ln., Willow Grove, PA 19090. Tel: 610-495-0909
Eles, Joseph, 150 Horizons E., Apt. 305, Boynton Beach, FL 33435. Tel: 407-731-2682
Homa, Joseph, 25 Runnymede Rd., Colonia, NJ 07067
Luzetsky, Stephen, Juniper Manor, 70 W. Juniper St., Hazleton, PA 18201
Musko, Andrew, Holy Family Manor, 1200 Spring St., Bethlehem, PA 18018. Tel: 610-865-5595
Tigyer, Paul, P.O. Box 658, Hamlin, PA 18427. Tel: 717-689-2153

Permanent Deacons:
Behrens, Robert
Ciarciaglino, Joseph M.
Daddona, Nicholas

Erdek, Michael A.
Fortuna, Chester
Guze, John G.
Kashi, George
McDonnell, Gerald E.
Obsitnik, Vincent
Pataki, Michael
Sotak, Nicholas
Szewczyk, William
Thanski, Robert
Tizio, William
Vanisko, Thomas L.

INSTITUTIONS LOCATED IN THE DIOCESE

[A] MONASTERIES

MATAWAN. *Basilian Fathers of Mariapoch*, 360 Monastery Ln., 07747-9703. Tel: 732-566-8445. Very Rev. Joseph J. Erdei, O.S.B.M., Supr.; Revs. Basil M. Rakaczky, O.S.B.M.; Stephen J. Skinta, O.S.B.M.; Lawrence Robert Wolf, O.S.B.M.

SYBERTSVILLE, PA. *Holy Dormition Friary*, P.O. Box 270, 18251. Tel: 570-788-1212; Fax: 570-788-1212. Revs. Carmen Scuderi, O.F.M., Guardian; Anthony Skurla, O.F.M.; James Carroll, O.F.M.; Bros. Augustine Paulik, O.F.M.; Andrew Martino, O.F.M.

[B] CONVENTS AND RESIDENCES FOR SISTERS

SUGARLOAF, PA. *Holy Annunciation Monastery*, R.R. 1, Box 1336, 18249. Tel: 570-788-1205; Fax: 570-788-3329. Discalced Byzantine Carmelite Nuns. Mother Marija of the Holy Spirit, O.C.D., Prioress. Nuns with Solemn Vows 10; Nuns with Temporary Vows 1; Novices 1.

[C] MISCELLANEOUS

PASSAIC. *Eastern Catholic Associates*, 96 First St., 07055. God with Us Publications, 445 Lackawanna Ave., West Paterson, 07424. Most Revs. Nicholas Samra, Pres.; Robert Moskal, Vice Pres.; Rt. Rev. John M. Boean, Sec.; Most Rev. Andrew Pataki, J.C.L., Registered Agent.

MIAMI, FL.

Holy Cross Community, 1245 Sunset Dr., 33183. Tel: 305-598-0009; Fax: 305-598-8455. Rev. Archimandrite Frank Wendt; Rev. Damian Gibault.

RELIGIOUS INSTITUTES OF MEN REPRESENTED IN THE DIOCESE

For further details refer to the corresponding bracketed number in the Religious Institutes of Men or Women section.

[0520]—*Franciscan Friars*.—O.F.M.

[0180]—*Order of St. Basil the Great*.—O.S.B.M.

RELIGIOUS INSTITUTES OF WOMEN REPRESENTED IN THE DIOCESE

[0420]—*Discalced Carmelite Nuns (Byzantine Rite)*.—O.C.D.

[3730]—*Sisters of the Order of St. Basil the Great*.—O.S.B.M.

NECROLOGY

† Balog, John, Wilkes-Barre, PA St. John the Baptist Church. —Died June 11, 2000.

† Kuberski, Leonard, M.A, Dunellen, NJ St. Nicholas of Myra Church. —Died Aug. 18, 2000.

† Opalenick, Rev. Msgr. John, O.E.S.L, Old Forge, PA St. Nicholas of Myra Church. —Died June 19, 2000.

Metropolitan Archdiocese of Philadelphia Ukrainian

Most Reverend

STEPHEN SOROKA

Archbishop of Philadelphia Ukrainian; ordained June 13, 1982; appointed Auxiliary Bishop of Winnipeg (Ukrainian) March 29, 1996; ordained Auxiliary Bishop of Winnipeg (Ukrainian) June 13, 1996; appointed Archbishop of Philadelphia Ukrainian November 29, 2000; installed Archbishop of Philadelphia Ukrainian February 27, 2001.

Most Reverend

WALTER PASKA

Auxiliary Bishop of Philadelphia Ukrainian; appointed February 4, 1992; retired November 29, 2000.

ESTABLISHED MAY 28, 1913.

The jurisdiction of the Metropolitan Archdiocese of Philadelphia includes the District of Columbia, the States of Virginia, Maryland, Delaware, New Jersey and eastern Pennsylvania to the eastern boundaries of the following Counties: Potter, Clinton, Center, Mifflin, Huntington and Fulton. With regard to persons, his subjects are all Catholics of the Byzantine Rite: 1. Who immigrated to this country from Galicia, Bucovina and other Ukrainian provinces; 2. Who descend from such persons (can. 755); 3. Women married to men referable to 1. and 2. if they comply with can. 98, n. 4; 4. Who in accordance with can. 98, n. 3 changed their Rite; 5. Converts to the Catholic Church of the Byzantine Rite; 6. And in fact all other Catholics of the Byzantine Rite who are attached to parishes subject to the jurisdiction of the Archbishop.

For legal titles of parishes and archdiocesan institutions, consult the Chancery Office.

Chancery Office: 827 N. Franklin St., Philadelphia, PA, 19123. Tel.: 215-627-0143; Fax: 215-627-0377.

E-mail address: srtom@catholic.org

STATISTICAL OVERVIEW

Personnel	
Archbishop	1
Auxiliary Bishops	1
Priests: Diocesan Active in Diocese	47
Priests: Retired, Sick or Absent	12
Number of Diocesan Priests	59
Religious Priests in Diocese	6
Extern Priests in Diocese	12
Ordinations:	
Diocesan Priests	1
Permanent Deacons in Diocese	6
Total Sisters	81
Parishes	
Parishes	74
With Resident Pastor:	
Resident Diocesan Priests	45
Resident Religious Priests	4
Without Resident Pastor:	
Administered by Priests	25
Professional Ministry Personnel:	
Sisters	4
Lay Ministers	4
Welfare	
Day Care and Extended Day Care Centers	2
Total Assisted	120
Educational	
Seminaries, Diocesan	1
Students from This Diocese	9
Diocesan Students in Other Seminaries	6
Total Seminarians	15
High Schools, Private	1
Total Students	352
Elementary Schools, Diocesan and Parish	7
Total Students	1,020
Catechesis/Religious Education:	
High School Students	215
Elementary Students	1,120
Total Students Under Catholic Instruction	2,722
Teachers in the Diocese:	
Priests	2
Sisters	15
Lay Teachers	325
Vital Statistics	
Receptions into the Church:	
Infant Baptism Totals	210
Adult Baptism Totals	19
Received into Full Communion	35
First Communions	214
Confirmations	202
Marriages:	
Catholic	66
Interfaith	32
Total Marriages	98
Deaths	413
Total Catholic Population	67,800

Former Bishops—Most Rev. STEPHEN SOTER ORTYNSKY, O.S.B.M., D.D.,First Ukrainian Catholic Bishop of the United States; ord. July 18, 1891; cons. May 12, 1907; died March 24, 1916.—Most Rev. CONSTANTINE BOHACHEVSKY, D.D., S.T.D., appt. Bishop in the United States, May 20, 1924; appt. Metropolitan Archbishop of the Philadelphia Archeparchy, Byzantine Rite, Aug. 6, 1958; cons. June 15, 1924; died Jan. 6, 1961.—Most Rev. JOSEPH M. SCHMONDIUK, D.D., appt. Titular Bishop of Zeugma and Auxiliary of the Archeparchy of Philadelphia, July 20, 1956; transferred to the Diocese of Stamford See, Nov. 9, 1961; appt. Metropolitan Archbishop of Philadelphia, Oct. 1, 1977.—Most Rev. JOHN STOCK, D.D., appt. Titular Bishop of Pergamum and Auxiliary Bishop to the Archeparchy, Feb. 22, 1971; cons. May 25, 1971; died June 29, 1972.—Most Rev. AMBROSE SENYSHYN, O.S.B.M., D.D., appt. Auxiliary Bishop to the Philadelphia Bishop, July 6, 1942; appt. Exarch of Stamford, July 20, 1956; appt. Eparch of Stamford, Nov. 1, 1958; appt. Metropolitan Archbishop of Philadelphia, Aug. 14, 1961; died Sept. 11, 1976.—Most Rev. JOSEPH M. SCHMONDIUK, D.D., cons. Nov. 8, 1956; Archbishop of Archeparchy, Oct. 1, 1977; died Dec. 25, 1978.—His Eminence MYROSLAV CARDINAL LUBACHIVSKY, D.D., appt. Metropolitan Archbishop of Philadelphia, Sept. 21, 1979; appt. Apostolic Administrator of Philadelphia, Oct. 3, 1979; cons. in Rome, Nov. 12, 1979; named Coadjutor Major Archbishop of Lviw, March 24, 1980; transferred to Rome Assumed position of Major Archbishop of Lviw, Sept. 7, 1984. Created Cardinal, May 25, 1985.

Protosycellus—Most Rev. WALTER PASKA, J.C.D.

Chancellor—Sr. THOMAS HRYNEWICH, S.S.M.I. Tel: 215-627-0143.

Chancery Office—827 N. Franklin St., Philadelphia, PA, 19123-2097. Tel: 215-627-0143; Fax: 215-627-0377.

College of Archeparchial Counsultors—Most Rev. STEPHEN SULYK, D.D.; Most Rev. WALTER PASKA, J.C.D.; Rev. Msgr. JOHN BURA; Rev. Archpriest DAVID CLOONEY; Rev. Archpriest DANIEL GUROVICH; Rev. Archpriest JOHN FIELDS; Rev. ROMAN DUBITSKY; Rev. Msgr. JAMES MELNIC.

Presbyteral Council—Most Rev. STEPHEN SULYK, D.D.; Most Rev. WALTER PASKA, J.C.D.; Rev. Msgr. JOHN BURA; Rev. ROMAN DUBITSKY; Rev. Msgr. MICHAEL FEDOROWICH; Rev. Archpriest MICHAEL HUTSKO; Rev. Archpriest DAVID CLOONEY; Rev. Archpriest DANIEL GUROVICH; Rev. Archpriest JOHN FIELDS; Rev. PAUL LABINSKY; Rev. Msgr. JAMES MELNIC.

Archeparchial Corporation—Most Rev. STEPHEN SULYK, D.D., Pres.; Rev. Msgr. JAMES MELNIC; Rev. ROMAN DUBITSKY; Rev. Archpriest DANIEL GUROVICH, Sec.; Rev. Archpriest JOHN FIELDS.

Archdiocesan Tribunal—827 N. Franklin St., Philadelphia, PA, 19123. Tel: 215-627-0143.

Judicial Vicar—Most Rev. WALTER PASKA, J.C.D.

Adjunct Judicial Vicar—Rev. Archpriest DANIEL GUROVICH.

Synodal Judges—Rev. Msgr. STEPHEN HRYNUCK, Ph.D.; Rev. Msgr. JOHN BILANYCH, J.U.D.

Defender of the Bond—Rev. JAMES GRANT.

Promoter of Justice—Rev. Msgr. RONALD POPIVCHAK, Ph.D.

Notary—Sr. THOMAS HYRNEWICH, S.S.M.I.

Archeparchial Council for Economic Affairs—Most Rev. STEPHEN SULYK, D.D.; Rev. Msgr. JAMES MELNIC; Rev. Archpriest JOHN FIELDS; ANDREW FYLYPOWYCH; RICHARD HANUSEY; JOSEPH REH; IHOR SHUST.

Archeparchial Econom—Rev. Msgr. JAMES MELNIC; JOSEPH REH, Fin. Dir.

Protopresbyters (Deans)—Rev. Msgr. RONALD POPIVCHAK, Reading; Rev. Msgr. JAMES MELNIC, Philadelphia; Rev. Mitred Msgr. STEPHEN CHOMKO, Scranton; Rev. Msgr. JOSEPH FEDOREK, New Jersey; Rev. Archpriest MICHAEL HUTSKO, Shamokin.

Diocesan Offices and Directors

Acolyte Confraternity—Rev. Archpriest MICHAEL HUTSKO.

Apostleship of Prayer—Rev. Msgr. MYRON GRABOWSKY.

Apostolate—Most Rev. STEPHEN SULYK, D.D.; Most. Rev. WALTER PASKA, J.C.D.; Rev. Archpriest JOHN FIELDS.

Cemeteries—Sr. THOMAS HRYNEWICH, S.S.M.I.

Censors—Rev. Msgr. Dr. RONALD POPIVCHAK; Rev. Msgr. JOHN BURA.

Holy Name Society—Rev. JOHN CIURPITA.

Insurance Commission—Rev. Msgr. JAMES MELNIC; JOSEPH REH.

League of Ukrainian Catholics—Sr. THOMAS HRYNEWICH, Archdiocesan Dir.

Press, The Way—Rev. ROBERT HITCHENS, English Editor; Rev. NESTOR IWASIW, English Co-Editor; IVAN SKOCZYLAS, Ukrainian Editor; Rev. LYUDMILIA VNUKOVA, Business Mgr.

Archdiocesan Bulletin—Office: *827 N. Franklin St., Philaldephia, PA, 19123.*

Priests Beneficial Fund—Most Rev. STEPHEN SULYK, D.D., Pres.; Rev. DANIEL GUROVICH, Sec. & Treas. Board Members: Rev. Msgr. JAMES MELNIC; Rev. ROMAN DUBITSKY; Rev. Msgr. JOHN BURA; Rev. Msgr. JAMES MELNIC; Rev. JOSEPH SZUPA.

Office of Vocations—Rev. ROBERT HITCHENS.

Archdiocesan Radio Programs—"Christ Among Us", aired Sundays 9-9:30 am WTEL, 860 AM (Phila.); Rev. Msgr. JAMES MELNIC; Rev. VASYL SIVINSKIJ.

Archieparchial Seminary Advisory and Admissions Board—Most Rev. STEPHEN SULYK, D.D.; Most Rev. WALTER PASKA, J.C.D.; Rev. Archpriest DAVID CLOONEY, Rector; Rev. Archimandrite JOSEPH LEE, Academic Dean; Rev. Msgr. JAMES MELNIC; Rev. Archpriest MICHAEL HUTSKO; Rev. Archpriest JOHN FIELDS; Rev. ROMAN DUBITSKY.

CLERGY, PARISHES, MISSIONS AND PAROCHIAL SCHOOLS

CITY OF PHILADELPHIA
(Philadelphia County)

1—IMMACULATE CONCEPTION OF BLESSED VIRGIN MARY, CATHEDRAL, Most Rev. Walter Paska, J.C.D.
Res., 833 N. Franklin St., 19123. Tel: 215-922-2845. [CEM]
Chapels—Immaculate Conception Cathedral Convent.; Missionary Sisters of Mother God Convent.; Chapel of St. Joseph of Arimathea and the Holy Myrrh-Bearing Women.

2—PROTECTION OF BLESSED VIRGIN MARY, Rev. T. Frank Patrylak.
Res., 100 S. Penn St., Clifton Heights, 19018. Tel: 610-626-9495.

3—ST. ANDREW. Attended by Cathedral of the Immaculate Conception, Philadelphia.
Mailing Address: 833 N. Franklin St., 19123-2097. 427 Pine St., 19106. Tel: 215-925-7024.

4—ANNUNCIATION OF THE B.V.M., Rev. Msgr. James Melnic.
Res., 1204 Valley Rd., Melrose Park, 19027-3035. Tel: 215-635-1627; Fax: 215-635-9203.
Church—1206 Valley Rd., Melrose Park, 19127-3035. Tel: 215-782-9865.

5—ST. NICHOLAS, Rev. Evhen Moniuk (Ukraine).
Res., 871 N. 24th St., 19130-1988. Tel: 215-769-3863.
Church—24th & Poplar Sts., 19130-1988.

6—ST. JOSAPHAT'S, Rev. Wasyl Sivinsky (Ukraine).
Res., 2236 Orthodox St., 19137. Tel: 215-533-7968.
School—4521 Longshore Ave., 19135. Tel: 215-332-8008. Sr. Theodosia O.S.B.M., Prin.
Sisters 3; Lay Teachers 12; Students 360.
Convent—6932 Ditman St., 19135. Tel: 215-332-8488. Sisters of St. Basil the Great

7—SACRED HEART. Closed. For inquiries for parish records contact the Chancery.

8—CHRIST THE KING, Rev. Yaroslav Kurpel (Ukraine).
Res., 1629 W. Cayuga St., 19140. Tel: 215-455-2416.

STATE OF DELAWARE

Wilmington, New Castle Co., St. Nicholas. Unassigned.
Res., 801 Lea Blvd., 19802. Tel: 302-762-5511; Fax: 302-656-6108.

STATE OF MARYLAND

Baltimore, Baltimore Co., St. Michael's, Rev. Michael Michlik.
Res., 2401 Eastern Ave., 21224. Tel: 410-675-7557; Fax: 410-675-7557. [CEM]

Curtis Bay, Baltimore Co., SS. Peter and Paul. Attended by St. Michael's, Baltimore.
Mailing Address: 2401 Eastern Ave., Baltimore, 21224.
Church—1506 Church St., 21226-1440.

Chesapeake City, Cecil Co., St. Basil the Great. Attended by St. Nicholas, Wilmington.
Mailing Address: 801 Lea Blvd., Wilmington, DE 19802.
Chapel—Chesapeake City, Sisters of St. Basil the Great.

Silver Spring, Montgomery Co., Holy Trinity, Rev. Taras R. Lonchyna, Admin.
Res., 16631 New Hampshire Ave., 20905-3919. Tel: 301-989-3318; Fax: 301-989-1494.

STATE OF NEW JERSEY

Bayonne, Hudson Co., Assumption B.V.M. Attended by SS. Peter and Paul, Jersey City.
Mailing Address: c/o SS. Peter and Paul, 30 Bentley Ave., Jersey City, 07304. Tel: 201-432-3122.
Church—30 E. 25th St., Box 260, 07002.

Carteret, Middlesex Co., St. Mary's, Rev. Viktor Bek (Ukraine).
Res., 719 Roosevelt Ave., 07008. Tel: 732-541-7678.

Cherry Hill, Camden Co., St. Michael's, Rev. John Ciurpita.
Res., 675 Cooperlanding Rd., 08002. Tel: 856-482-0938; Fax: 609-482-9092.

Elizabeth, Union Co., St. Vladimir's, Rev. Msgr. Joseph J. Fedorek; Rev. Petro Zvarych (Ukraine).
Res., 309 Grier Ave., 07202-3310. Tel: 908-352-8823; Fax: 908-352-7648. [CEM]
Catechesis/Religious Programs—Students 75.

Great Meadows, Warren Co., St. Nicholas. Attended by Holy Ghost, West Easton, PA. Rev. Petro Semanych (Ukraine).
Mailing Address: c/o 315 Fourth St., West Easton, PA 18042. Tel: 610-252-4266; Fax: 610-252-8533.
Church—Rte. 46, P.O. Box 162, 07838.

Hillside, Union Co., Immaculate Conception. Attended by St. John the Baptist, Newark.
Mailing Address: 719 Sandford Ave., Newark, 07106. Tel: 973-371-1356; Fax: 973-416-0085.
Church—Bloy St. and Liberty Ave., 07205. Tel: 973-354-0472.

Jersey City, Hudson Co., SS. Peter and Paul, Rev. Marian Struc.
Res., 30 Bentley Ave., 07304. Tel: 201-432-3122; Fax: 201-432-3122.

Manville, Somerset Co., St. Michael's. Attended by Nativity of the B.V.M., New Brunswick. Rev. Paul Labinsky.
Mailing Address: 86 Livingston Ave., New Brunswick, 08901-2519.
Church—1700 Brooks Blvd., 08835. Tel: 732-526-9195.

Marlboro, Monmouth Co., St. Volodymyr's. Attended by St. Mary's, Carteret. Rev. Viktor Bek (Ukraine); Deacon Michael Waak.
Mailing Address: 719 Roosevelt Ave., Carteret, 07008. Tel: 732-541-7678.
Church—Rte. 520, 07746.
Catechesis/Religious Programs—Students 65.

Millville, Cumberland Co., St. Nicholas. Attended by Holy Ghost, Chester, PA. Rev. Msgr. John Bura.
Mailing Address: 3015 W. Third St., Chester, PA 19013.
Church—373 Carmel Rd., 08332. Tel: 609-825-4826. [CEM]

Newark, Essex Co., St. John the Baptist, Revs. Bohdan Lukie, C.SS.R.; Leonid Malkov, C.SS.R.; Andriy Manko, C.SS.R.
Res., 719 Sandford Ave., 07106. Tel: 973-371-1356; Fax: 973-416-0085.
School—Tel: 973-373-9359. Sr. Evelyn Stock, S.S.M.I., Prin.
Sisters Servants of Mary Immaculate 2; Lay Teachers 15; Students 118.
Catechesis/Religious Programs—Students 26.

New Brunswick, Middlesex Co., Nativity of B.V.M., Rev. Paul Labinsky.
Res., 86 Livingston Ave., 08901. Tel: 732-246-8385.

Passaic, Passaic Co., St. Nicholas, Revs. Joseph Szupa; Vasyl Bunyk (Ukraine).
Res., 216 President St., 07055. Tel: 973-777-0230; Fax: 973-471-4714.
School—Tel: 973-779-0249. Sr. Kathleen S.S.M.I., Prin.
Sisters 3; Lay Teachers 7; Students 122.

Perth Amboy, Middlesex Co., Assumption of B.V.M., Revs. Roman Dubitsky; Augustine Molodowitz; Deacon Paul Makar.
Res., 684 Alta Vista Pl., 08861. Tel: 732-826-0767; Fax: 732-826-6744.
School—Tel: 732-826-8721. Sr. Vladymira M.S.M.G., Prin.
Missionary Sisters of Mother of God 2; Lay Teachers 11; Students 240.

Ramsey, Bergen Co., St. Paul. Attended by St. John the Baptist, Whippany.
Mailing Address: 7 S. Jefferson Rd., Whippany, 07981. Tel: 973-887-3616.

Rutherford, Bergen Co., Annunciation B.V.M. Attended by St. Nicholas, Passaic.
Mailing Address: St. Nicholas, 216 President St., Passaic, 07055. Tel: 973-777-0230; Fax: 973-471-4714.
Church—70 Home Ave., 07070.

Toms River, Ocean Co., St. Stephen's. Attended by Assumption of B.V.M., Perth Amboy. Rev. Roman Dubitsky; Deacon Paul Makar.
Mailing Address: Assumption of B.V.M., 684 Alta Vista Pl., Perth Amboy, 08861. Tel: 732-826-0767; Fax: 732-826-6744.
Church—1344 White Oak Bottom Rd., 08755. Tel: 732-505-6293; Fax: 732-826-6744.

Trenton, Mercer Co., St. Josaphat's, Rev. Vasyl Repela (Ukraine).
Res., 1195 Deutz Ave., 08611. Tel: 609-695-3771.

Whippany, Morris Co., St. John the Baptist, Rev. Archpriest Uriy Markewuch.
Res., 7 S. Jefferson Rd., 07981. Tel: 973-887-3616.
Church—Rte. 10, 07981.

Williamstown, Gloucester Co., SS. Peter and Paul. Attended by St. Michael's, Cherry Hill.
Mailing Address: 675 Cooperlanding Rd., Cherry Hill, 08002. Tel: 856-482-0938. [CEM]

Woodbine, Cape May Co., St. Nicholas. Closed. For inquiries for parish records contact St. Nicholas, Millville, NJ.

STATE OF PENNSYLVANIA

Alden Station, Luzerne Co., St. Vladimir. Closed. For inquiries for parish records contact St. Nicholas, Glen Lyon, PA.

Allentown, Lehigh Co., Immaculate Conception of B.V.M. Closed. For inquiries for parish records contact St. Josaphat, Bethlehem, PA.

Berwick, Columbia Co., SS. Cyril and Methodius, Rt. Rev. Mitred Msgr Stephen Chomko.
Res., 706 Warren St., 18603. Tel: 570-752-3172. [CEM]
Catechesis/Religious Programs—Students 66.

Bethlehem, Lehigh Co., St. Josaphat's, Rev. Archpriest Daniel Gurovich.
Res., 1826 Kenmore Ave., 18018-3305. Tel: 610-865-2521. [CEM]
Catechesis/Religious Programs—Students 169.

Bridgeport, Montgomery Co., SS. Peter and Paul, Rev. Msgr. Ronald P. Popivchak.
Res., 519 Union Ave., P.O. Box 126, 19405. Tel: 610-272-7035. [CEM]
Catechesis/Religious Programs—George Maxim, D.R.E.
Students 145.

Bristol, Bucks Co., St. Mary's, Rev. Msgr. Myron Grabowsky.
Res., 2026 Bath Rd., 19007. Tel: 215-788-7117; Fax: 215-788-7175.

Centralia, Columbia Co., Assumption of B.V.M. Attended by Mount Carmel. Rev. Bohdan Kudleychuk (Ukraine).
Mailing Address: 131 N. Beech St., Mount Carmel, 17851. Tel: 570-339-0650; Fax: 570-339-2715. [CEM]

Chester, Delaware Co., Holy Ghost, Rev. Msgr. John Bura.
Res., 3015 W. Third St., 19013. Tel: 610-494-7899; Fax: 610-494-2350.

Clifton Heights, Delaware Co., SS. Peter and Paul, Rev. T. Frank Patrylak.
Res., 104 S. Penn St., 19108.
Church—100 S. Penn St., 19018. Tel: 610-626-9495.

Edwardsville, Luzerne Co., St. Vladimir's, Revs. Alex Burak; Vasyl Putera (Ukraine).
Res., 87 Zerbey Ave., 18704. Tel: 570-287-8471. [CEM]
Catechesis/Religious Programs—Tel: 717-822-1589. Mary Ann Mudrak, D.R.E.
Students 144.

Frackville, Schuylkill Co., St. Michael's, Rev. Nestor Iwasiw.
Res., 45 S. Second St., 17931. Tel: 570-874-1101; Fax: 570-874-0448.
Catechesis/Religious Programs—Tel: 717-874-1101.
Students 50.

Glen Lyon, Luzerne Co., St. Nicholas. Attended by St. Nicholas, Nanticoke, PA.
Mailing Address: 430 N. Seventh St., Scranton, 18503.
Church—153 Main St., 18617.

Hazleton, Luzerne Co., St. Michael's. Attended by St. Mary's, McAdoo. Rev. Gregory Maslak.
Mailing Address: 210 W. Blaine St., McAdoo, 18237.

Jenkintown, Montgomery Co., St. Michael the Archangel, Rev. Orest Mykhayliuk.
Res., 1013 Fox Chase Rd., 19046. Tel: 215-576-5827.

Lansdale, Montgomery Co., Presentation of Our Lord. Attended by St. Anne's, Warrington. Rev. Archpriest John Fields.
Mailing Address: 1545 Easton Rd., P.O. Box 417, Warrington, 18976.
Church—1564 Allentown Rd., 19446. Tel: 215-368-3993; Fax: 215-343-8060.

McAdoo, Schuylkill Co., St. Mary's, Rev. Gregory Maslak.
Church—210 W. Blaine St., 18237. Tel: 570-929-2804; Fax: 570-462-0517.

Mahanoy City, Schuylkill Co., St. Nicholas. Attended by St. Michael, Shenandoah.
Mailing Address: 114 Chestnut St., Shenandoah, 17976. Tel: 570-773-0115. [CEM]

Maizeville, Schuylkill Co., St. John the Baptist. Attended by St. Michael, Frackville.
Mailing Address: 45 S. Second St., Frackville, 17931. Tel: 570-874-1821. [CEM]
Church—Main St., 17934.

Marion Heights, Northumberland Co., Patronage of the Mother of God. Attended by SS. Peter & Paul, Mount Carmel.
Mailing Address: 131 N. Beech St., Mount Carmel, 17851.

Middleport, Schuylkill Co., Nativity of B.V.M., Rev. Archpriest Michael Hutsko.
Mailing Address: 415 N. Front St., Minersville, 17954. Tel: 570-544-4581; Fax: 570-544-9653. [CEM]
Church—Kaska St., 17953.

Minersville, Schuylkill Co., St. Nicholas, Rev. Archpriest Michael Hutsko.
Res., 415 Front St., 17954. Tel: 570-544-4581; Fax: 570-544-9653. [CEM]
School—Tel: 570-544-2800; Fax: 570-544-6471. Sr. Stephanie S.S.M.I., Prin.
Sisters 3; Lay Teachers 13; Students 175.
Catechesis/Religious Programs—Students 105.

Moscow, Lackawanna Co., Holy Ghost. Closed. For inquiries for parish records contact St. Vladimir, Scranton, PA.

Mount Carmel, Northumberland Co., SS. Peter and Paul, Rev. Bohdan Kudleychuk (Ukraine); Deacon Theodore Spotts.
Res., 131 N. Beech St., 17851. Tel: 570-339-0650; Fax: 570-339-2715. [CEM]

Nanticoke, Luzerne Co., St. Nicholas, Rev. Michael Mokris (PSC).
Res., 472 Church St., Swoyersville, 18704. Tel: 570-287-2306.
Church—111 Green St., 18634.
Transfiguration of Our Lord. Attended by Sts. Peter and Paul, Plymouth, PA. Rev. Wasyl Kharuk (Ukraine).
Mailing Address: 20 Turner St., Plymouth, 18651. Tel: 570-779-4411.

Northampton, Northampton Co., St. John the Baptist, Rev. George Kuzara, C.PP.S.
Res., 1343 Newport Ave., 18067. Tel: 610-262-4104. [CEM]
School—Tel: 610-262-2231. Michael Duda, Prin.
Lay Teachers 9; Students 130.

Olyphant, Lackawanna Co., SS. Cyril and Methodius, Very Rev. Msgr. Stephen Hrynuck.
Res., 135 River St., 18447. Tel: 570-489-2271. [CEM]
Catechesis/Religious Programs—Students 119.

Palmerton, Carbon Co., St. Vladimir's, Rev. Edward Levandusky.
Res., 101 Lehigh Ave., 18071. Tel: 610-826-2359.

Phoenixville, Chester Co., SS. Peter and Paul. Attended by SS. Peter and Paul, Bridgeport. Rev. Msgr. Ronald P. Popivchak.
Mailing Address: 519 Union Ave., P.O. Box 126, Bridgeport, 19405. Tel: 610-272-7035.

Plymouth, Luzerne Co., SS. Peter and Paul, Rev. Wasyl Kharuk (Ukraine) Admin.
Res., 20 Turner St., 186514. Tel: 570-779-4411; Fax: 570-779-4411.

Pottstown, Montgomery Co., St. Michael's. Attended by Nativity B.V.M., Reading. Rev. Leonard Sinatra.
Mailing Address: 1814 Philadelphia Ave., Reading, 19607. Tel: 610-376-0586. [CEM]

Reading, Berks Co., Nativity of Blessed Virgin Mary, Rev. Leonard Sinatra.
Res., 1814 Philadelphia Ave., 19607. Tel: 610-376-0586. [CEM]

St. Clair, Schuylkill Co., St. Nicholas. Attended by Holy Trinity, St. Clair. Rev. John Wysochansky; Deacon James Bremer.
Mailing Address: Holy Trinity, 254 N. Mill St., 17970. Tel: 570-429-2212. [CEM]
Church—N. Morris St., 17970.
Holy Trinity, Rev. John Wysochansky; Deacon James Bremer.
Res., 254 N. Mill St., 17970. Tel: 570-429-2212. [CEM]

Sayre, Bradford Co., Ascension of Our Lord. Attended by Elmira Heights, NY.
Res., 110 N. Higgins Ave., 18840. Tel: 570-888-2207. [CEM]

Scranton, Lackawanna Co., St. Vladimir's, Rev. Paul Guthrie, O.F.M.
Res., 430 N. Seventh St., 18503. Tel: 570-342-7023. [CEM]

Shamokin, Northumberland Co., Transfiguration of Our Lord, Rev. Msgr. Michael Fedorowich.
Res., 303 N. Shamokin St., 17872-5460. Tel: 570-648-5932. [CEM]
School—Tel: 570-648-6435. Sr. Anne Roman, S.S.M.I., Prin.
Sisters Servants of Mary Immaculate 2; Lay Teachers 9; Students 130.

Shenandoah, Schuylkill Co., St. Michael's, Rev. Robert Hitchens.
Res., 114 S. Chestnut St., 17976. Tel: 570-462-0809; Fax: 570-462-0517. [CEM]

Simpson, Lackawanna Co., SS. Peter and Paul, Rev. Theodore Boholnick.
Res., 43 Rittenhouse St., 18407. Tel: 570-282-0331. [CEM]

Warrington, Bucks Co., St. Anne's, Rev. Archpriest John Fields.
Res., 1545 Easton Rd., Box 417, 18976. Tel: 215-343-0779; Fax: 215-343-8060.
Catechesis/Religious Programs—Students 58.

West Easton, Northampton Co., Holy Ghost, Rev. Petro Semenych (Ukraine).
Res., 315 Fourth St., 18042. Tel: 610-252-4266; Fax: 610-252-8533. [CEM]

Wilkes-Barre, Luzerne Co., SS. Peter and Paul. Attended by St. Vladimir's, Edwardsville. Revs. Alex Burak, Admin.; Vasyl Putera (Ukraine).
Mailing Address: 87 Zerby Ave, Edwardsville, 18704.
Church—635 N. River St., 18701. Tel: 570-823-1821. [CEM]
Catechesis/Religious Programs—Mary Ann Mudrak, D.R.E.
Students 49.

STATE OF VIRGINIA

Manassas, Prince William Co., Annunciation of the Blessed Virgin Mary. Attended by Holy Trinity, Silver Spring, MD. Rev. Taras R. Lonchyna, Admin.
Mailing Address: 16631 New Hampshire Ave., Silver Spring, MD 20905-3919. [CEM]
Church—6719 Hoadly Rd., 20108-0878. Tel: 301-421-1739.

Richmond, Henrico Co., St. John the Baptist. Attended by Holy Trinity, Silver Spring, MD. Rev. Taras R. Lonchyna, Admin.
Mailing Address: 16631 New Hampshire Ave., Silver Spring, MD 20905-3919. Tel: 301-421-1739.
Chapel—Sisters of Verona Chapel, Tel: 804-359-4934.

DISTRICT OF COLUMBIA

Washington, District of Columbia, Ukrainian Catholic National Shrine of the Holy Family, Rev. Thaddeus Krawchuk, C.Ss.R.; Deacons Theophil Staruch; Donald Latrick.
Res., 4250 Harewood Rd., N.E., 20017. Tel: 202-526-3737; Fax: 202-526-1327.
Catechesis/Religious Programs—Students 152.

Absent on Leave:
Reverend Monsignors—
Canavan, Martin
Reverend Fathers—
Batcho, Michael
Kin, Bohdan
Korinchock, Joseph
Seniw, John
Worschak, George D.

Retired:
Reverend Monsignors—
Bilanych, John, 1627 W. Cayuga St., Philadelphia, PA 19140
Pospishil, Victor J., 6 Michigan Dr., Matawan, NJ 07747
Reverend Fathers—
Dawydowych, Ivan
Horoshko, Michael
Kostiuk, Nick
Radchuk, Anthony, 14 Monastery Rd., Elysburg, PA 17824

Permanent Deacons:
Bremer, James, Holy Trinity & St. Nicholas, St. Clair, PA
Latrick, Donald, Holy Family Ukrainian Catholic National Shrine, Washington, DC
Makar, Paul, Perth Amboy, NJ
Spotts, Theodore, SS. Peter & Paul, Mt. Carmel, PA; Protection BVM, Marion Heights, PA; Assumption BVM, Centralia, PA
Staruch, Theophil, Holy Family Ukrainian Catholic National Shrine, Washington, DC
Waak, Michael P., Perth Amboy, NJ

INSTITUTIONS LOCATED IN THE ARCHDIOCESE

[A] SEMINARIES, ARCHEPARCHY

WASHINGTON, DC. *St. Josaphat Seminary*, 201 Taylor St., N.E., 20017. Tel: 202-529-1177. Rev. Archpriest David Clooney, Rector; Rt. Revs. Archimandrite Joseph Lee, Academic Dean; Hieromonk David Siebert, Spiritual Dir.

[B] COLLEGES AND UNIVERSITIES

JENKINTOWN. *Manor College*, 700 Fox Chase Rd., 19046. Tel: 215-885-2360; Fax: 215-576-6564.
E-mail: scecilia@mail.manor.edu
Web site: www.manor.edu
For a complete listing, refer to the Colleges and Universities section.

[C] HIGH SCHOOLS, PRIVATE

FOX CHASE MANOR. *St. Basil Academy*, 711 Fox Chase Rd., 19046. Tel: 215-745-5550; Fax: 215-885-4025.
E-mail: admissions@stbasilacademy.org
Web site: www.stbasilacademy.org
Sr. Carla Hernandez, O.S.B.M., Prin. Sisters 7; Lay Teachers 32; Students 350.

[D] HOMES FOR SENIOR CITIZENS

PHILADELPHIA. *Ascension Manor, Inc.*, 911 N. Franklin St., 19123. Tel: 215-922-1116
For a complete listing, refer to the Special Care Facilities section.

[E] MONASTERIES AND RESIDENCES OF PRIESTS AND BROTHERS

WASHINGTON, DC. *Monastery of the Holy Cross*, 1302 Quincy St., N.E., 20017-2614. Tel: 202-832-8519. Rev. Archimandrite Joseph (Richard) Lee; Rev. David (Thomas) Siebert.

[F] CONVENTS AND RESIDENCES FOR SISTERS

PHILADELPHIA. *Motherhouse of the Missionary Sisters of Mother of God*, 711 N. Franklin St., 19123. Sr. Josepha Kruchinsky, M.S.M.G., Supr. Gen.
Nursery School. Students 35. Professed Nuns 12.
Sacred Heart Convent, 160 W. Carpenter Ln., 19119. Tel: 215-843-2266. Sr. Daniella, P.O.S.C., Supr. Nursery School; Students 20.

CHESAPEAKE CITY, MD. *St. Basil's Convent*, 415 Lock St., 21915. Sisters O.S.B.M. Sr. M. Augustine, Supr.

FOX CHASE MANOR. *Provincial Motherhouse of the Sisters of St. Basil the Great*, 710 Fox Chase Rd., 19046. Tel: 215-663-9153; Fax: 215-728-6129. Sr. Dorothy Ann Busowski, O.S.B.M., Prov. Supr.; Sr. Laura Palka, O.S.B.M., Asst. Prov.; Rev. Michael Rozmarynowcz (SJP). Councilors: Sr. Mary Cecilia Jurasinski, O.S.B.M.; Sr. Miriam Clair Kowal, O.S.B.M.; Sr. Paula Jacynyk, O.S.B.M. Professed Sisters 67.

[G] MISCELLANEOUS

FOX CHASE MANOR. *Basilian Spirituality Center*, 710 Fox Chase Rd., 19046. Tel: 215-342-8381. Sr. Marina Bochnewich, O.S.B.M., Dir.

JENKINTOWN. *The Basileiad Library*, 700 Fox Chase Rd., 19046. Sisters of St. Basil the Great. Brian T. Johnstone, Librarian.

RELIGIOUS INSTITUTES OF MEN REPRESENTED IN THE ARCHEPARCHY

For further details refer to the corresponding bracketed number in the Religious Institutes of Men or Women section.

[1070]—*Redemptorist Fathers*.—C.SS.R.

RELIGIOUS INSTITUTES OF WOMEN REPRESENTED IN THE ARCHEPARCHY

[2345]—*Little Workers of the Sacred Heart of Jesus and Mary*.—P.O.S.C.

[2810]—*Missionary Sisters of Mother of God*.—M.S.M.G.

[3730]—*Sisters of the Order of St. Basil the Great*.—O.S.B.M.

[3610]—*Sisters Servants of Mary Immaculate*.—S.S.M.I.

ARCHDIOCESAN CEMETERIES

LANGHORNE. *Mother of Sorrows*, Langhorne & Yardley Rd., 19047. Tel: 215-627-0143.

NECROLOGY

† Oryshkewych, Ostap, Ph.D, Philadelphia, PA St. Andrew. —Died Jan. 13, 2000.

Metropolitan Archeparchy of Pittsburgh, Byzantine

Most Reverend

JUDSON M. PROCYK, D.D.

Metropolitan Archbishop of Pittsburgh Byzantine; ordained May 19, 1957; appointed Archbishop of Pittsburgh Byzantine November 15, 1994; installed February 7, 1995. *Office: 66 Riverview Ave., Pittsburgh, PA, 15214. Res., 50 Riverview Ave., Pittsburgh, PA, 15214.*

ESTABLISHED FEBRUARY 25, 1924.

RAISED TO ARCHEPARCHY FEBRUARY 21, 1969.

Embraces all Byzantine Ruthenian Rite Catholics in that part of the State of Pennsylvania west of the western boundaries of the Counties of Tioga, Lycoming, Union, Mifflin, Juniata and Franklin. In the State of Ohio, the Counties of Ashtabula, Athens, Belmont, Carroll, Columbiana, Gallia, Guernsey, Harrison, Jefferson, Lawrence, Mahoning, Meigs, Morrow, Morgan, Noble, Trumbull and Washington and also the States of Alabama, Arkansas, Kentucky, Louisiana, Mississippi, Oklahoma, Tennessee, Texas and West Virginia.

For legal titles of parishes and diocesan institutions, consult the Chancery Office.

Chancery Office: 66 Riverview Ave., Pittsburgh, PA, 15214. Tel.: 412-231-4000; Fax: 412-231-1697.

STATISTICAL OVERVIEW

Personnel	
Archbishop	1
Abbots	1
Priests: Diocesan Active in Diocese	60
Priests: Retired, Sick or Absent	4
Number of Diocesan Priests	64
Religious Priests in Diocese	8
Ordinations:	
Diocesan Priests	2
Transitional Deacons	1
Total Brothers	4
Total Sisters	104
Parishes	
Parishes	86
With Resident Pastor:	
Resident Diocesan Priests	55
Resident Religious Priests	3
Without Resident Pastor:	
Administered by Priests	28
Professional Ministry Personnel:	
Brothers	1
Sisters	6
Welfare	
Homes for the Aged	2
Total Assisted	488
Educational	
Seminaries, Diocesan	1
Students from This Diocese	3
Students from Other Diocese	4
Total Seminarians	3
Elementary Schools, Diocesan and Parish	2
Total Students	374
Catechesis/Religious Education:	
High School Students	517
Elementary Students	1,823
Total Students Under Catholic Instruction	2,717
Teachers in the Diocese:	
Sisters	5
Lay Teachers	20
Vital Statistics	
Receptions into the Church:	
Infant Baptism Totals	308
Adult Baptism Totals	26
Received into Full Communion	60
First Communions	530
Confirmations	401
Marriages:	
Catholic	88
Interfaith	49
Total Marriages	137
Deaths	584
Total Catholic Population	64,986

Former Bishops—Most Rev. BASIL TAKACH, ord. Dec. 12, 1902; appt. May 20, 1924; cons. June 15, 1924; died May 13, 1948.—Most Rev. DANIEL IVANCHO, D.D., Titular Bishop of Europus; ord. Sept. 30, 1934; appt. Coadjutor Bishop, Aug. 29, 1946; cons. Nov. 5, 1946; succeeded to May 13, 1948; retired Dec. 2, 1954; died Aug. 2, 1972.—Most Rev. NICHOLAS T. ELKO, D.D., cons. March 6, 1955; transferred to Rome, Dec. 22, 1967; died May 18, 1991.—Most Rev. STEPHEN J. KOCISCKO, D.D., cons. Oct. 23, 1956; retired June 12, 1991; died March 7, 1995.—Most Rev. THOMAS V. DOLINAY, ord. May 16, 1948; appt. Titular Bishop of Thyatira and Auxiliary of Passaic, Sept. 23, 1976; cons. Nov. 23, 1976; appt. First Ordinary of the Byzantine Catholic Diocese of Van Nuys; installed March 1982; appt. Coadjutor Archbishop of Pittsburgh, March 13, 1990; installed May 29, 1990; succeeded to June 12, 1991; died April 13, 1993.—Most Rev. JOHN M. BILOCK, ord. Feb. 3, 1946; appt. Titular Bishop of Pergamo and Auxiliary Bishop to the Metropolitan Archbishop of Pittsburgh; installed March 1, 1973; cons. May 15, 1973; appt. Archieparchial Administrator, April 20, 1993; died Sept. 8, 1994.

Chancery Office—66 Riverview Ave., Pittsburgh, 15214. Office Hours: Mon.-Fri. 9:30-12 and 12:30-4. Tel: 412-231-4000; Fax: 412-231-1697.

Protosyncellus—Rev. Msgr. RUSSELL A. DUKER, S.E.O.D.

Chancellor—Rev. Msgr. RUSSELL A. DUKER, S.E.O.D.

Vice Chancellor—Very Rev. Archpriest JOHN M. KUDRICK.

Vicar for Canonical Services—Very Rev. RICHARD J. WHETSTONE, J.C.O.L.

Syncellus for Clergy—Very Rev. Archpriest JOHN G. PETRO.

Syncellus for Religious—Very Rev. JAMES A. SPONTAK.

Secretary to the Metropolitan—Sr. ELAINE KISINKO, O.S.B.M.

Treasurer—GREGORY S. POPIVCHAK.

Consultors—Revs. DENNIS M. BOGDA; JOSEPH J. BORODACH; Rev. Msgr. RUSSELL A. DUKER, S.E.O.D.; Rev. RICHARD I. LAMBERT; Very Revs. SIMEON B. SIBENIK; JAMES A. SPONTAK; RICHARD J. WHETSTONE.

Presbyteral Council—Most Rev. JUDSON M. PROCYK, D.D., Pres.; Revs. DENNIS M. BOGDA; JOSEPH J. BORODACH; GEORGE EVANCHO; Rev. Msgr. RUSSELL A. DUKER, S.E.O.D.; Very Rev. Archpriest JOHN M. KUDRICK; Revs. RICHARD I. LAMBERT; RONALD P. LARKO; Very Rev. Archpriest JOHN G. PETRO; Very Revs. LEO SCHLOSSER, O.S.B.; SIMEON B. SIBENIK; JAMES A. SPONTAK; RICHARD J. WHETSTONE, J.C.O.L; Rev. MICHAEL JUDE WYTISH, J.C.B.

Protopresbyters—Most Rev. JUDSON M. PROCYK, D.D.; Rev. Msgr. RUSSELL A. DUKER; Rev. Msgr. WILLIAM G. LEVKULIC, Clairton; Rev. Msgr. RAYMOND A. BALTA, Johnstown; Very Rev. Archpriest JOHN M. KUDRICK; Very Rev. Archpriest JOHN G. PETRO; Rev. ROBERT J. KARL; Very Rev. Archpriest JOHN J. BORODACH; Rev. JOSEPH KAPUSNAK; Very Rev. JOHN H. SALKO, Mon-Valley; Very Rev. SIMEON B. SIBENIK, North-Central; Rev. Msgr. NICHOLAS X. SMICIKLAS, Pittsburgh; Very Rev. JOHN J. MIHALCO, Southwest; Very Rev. JOSEPH J. JUGAN, Tri-State; Rev. Msgr. SYLVESTER HLADKY, Youngstown.

Finance Council—Most Rev. JUDSON M. PROCYK; GREGORY S. POPIVCHAK; Rev. JOHN J. BORODACH; MICHAEL I. ROMAN.

Tribunal—

Judicial Vicar—Very Rev. RICHARD J. WHETSTONE, J.C.O.L.

Pro-Synodal Judges—Revs. MICHAEL JUDE WYTISH, J.C.B.; ANSELM ORLOSKY, O.S.B.

Defender of the Bond—Very Rev. JOHN J. MIHALCO, S.E.O.L.

Promoter of Justice—Rev. Msgr. ALEXIS E. MIHALIK.

Secretary—Sr. ELAINE KISINKO, O.S.B.M.

Notaries—Rev. GREGORY J. MICHALISIN; DONNA OBSINCS.

Archieparchial Choir—DARLENE FEJKA, Dir.

Archives—Rev. JOHN L. MINA, Archivist; Rev. ROBERT F. ORAVETZ, Asst.; Sr. ELAINE KISINKO, O.S.B.M., Asst.

Clergy Continuing Formation—

Presbyteral Council—Very Rev. JAMES A. SPONTAK, Dir.

Communications—Rev. MICHAEL JUDE WYTISH, Dir.

Diaconate Program—Rev. STEPHEN HAWKES-TEEPLES, S.J., Dir.

Evangelization, Mission Activity and Ecumenism—Rev. ROBERT F. ORAVETZ, Dir.

Vocations—Rev. DENNIS M. BOGDA, Dir.; Sr. JEAN MARIE CIHOTA, O.S.B.M., Asst.

Priests' Pension Board—Ex Officio Members: Most Rev. JUDSON M. PROCYK, Chm.; Rev. Msgr. RUSSELL A. DUKER, Vicar General; GREGORY S. POPIVCHAK, Archieparchial Treas.

Elected Deanery Representatives—Rev. Msgr. WILLIAM G. LEVKULIC, Sec., Clairton; Rev. RONALD P. LARKO, Greater Pittsburgh; Rev. DANIEL J. LOYA, Johnstown; Rev. JEROME G. BOTSKO, Mon Valley; Rev. DONALD R. VALASEK, North Central; Rev. SERAPHIM J. CHEWNING, Tri State; Rev. FRANK A. FIRKO, Youngstown.

Office of Religious Education—Rev. ELIAS L. RAFAJ, Asst. Dir.; Sr. MARION DOBOS, O.S.B., Dir., *Archieparchial Catechetical Center, 3605 Perrysville Ave., Pittsburgh, 15214.* Tel: 412-322-8773; Fax: 412-322-8737.

Building Commission—Very Rev. Archpriest JOHN M. KUDRICK; PAUL CHEKAN; GEORGE KURTANICH; ALEX WOZNIAK.

Liturgy Commission—Rev. Msgr. WILLIAM G. LEVKULIC; Rev. Msgr. ALEXIS E. MIHALIK.

Music Commission—J. MICHAEL THOMPSON; Very Rev. Archpriest JOHN G. PETRO; COREEN POKLEMBO; Rev. RICHARD I. LAMBERT; Rev. Msgr. ALEXIS E. MIHALIK; Revs. ELIAS O'BRIEN, O.Carm.; JOSEPH R. RAPTOSH; DONALD R. VALASEK.

Revitalization and Renewal Commission—Presbyteral Council.

Archieparchial Newspaper—Byzantine Catholic World; Rev. MICHAEL JUDE WYTISH, Editor; Sr. ELAINE KISINKO, Copy Editor, *66 Riverview Ave., Pittsburgh, 15214.* Tel: 412-231-4000; Fax: 412-231-1697.

Byzantine Catholic Seminary Press—Sr. SERAPHIM OLSAFSKY, O.S.B.M., Mgr., *3605 Perrysville Ave., P.O. Box 7626, Pittsburgh, 15214.* Tel: 412-322-8307; Fax: 412-322-9530.

CLERGY, PARISHES, MISSIONS AND PAROCHIAL SCHOOLS

STATE OF LOUISIANA

New Orleans, Orleans Parish, St. Nicholas of Myra Mission (1984), Rev. Ellis De Priest, S.M., Admin.
2435 S. Carrollton Ave., 70118. Tel: 504-524-5192; Fax: 504-524-9796.
Res., 1706 Jackson Ave., 70113-1510.

STATE OF PENNSYLVANIA

Munhall, Allegheny Co., St. John the Baptist Cathedral, Very Rev. Archpriest John M. Kudrick, Rector.
Res., 210 Greentree Rd., 15120. Tel: 412-461-0944; Fax: 412-462-3495. [CEM]
St. Elias, Rev. Eugene P. Yackanich.
Res., 4200 Homestead, Duquesne Rd., 15120. Tel: 412-461-1712; Fax: 412-461-1712. [CEM]

Aliquippa, Beaver Co., St. George the Great Martyr, Rev. Elias O'Brien, O.Carm.
Res., 1001 Clinton St., 15001. Tel: 724-375-2742; Fax: 724-375-8776.

Ambridge, Beaver Co., St. Mary's, Rev. Msgr. Edward V. Rosack.
Res., 624 Park Rd., 15003. Tel: 724-266-2030; Fax: 724-266-0799.

Arcadia, Indiana Co., Ascension. Attended by Northern Cambria.
719 Chestnut Ave., Northern Cambria, 15714-1459. Tel: 814-948-8242; Fax: 814-948-8252. [CEM]

Avella, Washington Co., St. John the Baptist. Attended by St. Mary's, Weirton, WV.
Res., P.O. Box 565, 15312. Tel: 724-587-5819. [CEM]

Beaver, Beaver Co., Saint Nicholas Chapel, Very Rev. Archpriest John G. Petro, Admin.
Res., 5400 Tuscarawas Rd., 15009-9513. Tel: 724-495-3400.

Beaverdale, Cambria Co., St. Mary's, Rev. Stephen Kolcun.
Res., P.O. Box 610, 15921. Tel: 814-487-7458; Fax: 814-487-4830. [CEM]

Braddock, Allegheny Co., SS. Peter and Paul, Rev. Blaise Kovach.
Res., 431 George St., 15104. Tel: 412-271-1297; Fax: 412-351-4015.

Bradenville, Westmoreland Co., St. Mary's, Rev. Joseph Borodach.
Res., R.R. #1, Box 75, 15620-9711. Tel: 724-537-5839; Fax: 724-532-1499. [CEM]

Brownsville, Fayette Co., St. Nicholas, Rev. Jerome G. Botsko.
Res., 302 Third Ave., 15417. Tel: 724-785-7573; Fax: 724-785-4649. [CEM]

Canonsburg, Washington Co., St. Michael, Very Rev. Joseph Jugan.
Res., 166 E. College St., 15317. Tel: 724-745-7117; Fax: 724-745-3097.

Charleroi, Washington Co., Holy Ghost, Very Rev. James A. Spontak.
Res., 828 Meadow Ave., 15022. Tel: 724-483-8622; Fax: 724-483-0696.

Clairton, Allegheny Co., Ascension of Our Lord, Rev. John L. Mina, Ph.D.
Res., 318 Park Ave., 15025. Tel: 412-233-7422; Fax: 412-233-0529. [CEM]

Clarence, Centre Co., St. Mary's. Attended by St. John the Baptist Church, Hawk Run. Rev. Donald J. Voss.
c/o St. John the Baptist Church, Hawk Run, 16840. Tel: 814-342-4315. [CEM]

Clymer, Indiana Co., St. Anne. Attended by St. Jude Thaddeus, Ernest.
P.O. Box 130, Ernest, 15739. Tel: 724-463-3397; Fax: 724-465-5773.

Coal Run, Indiana Co., Holy Cross. Attended by Holy Protection of Mary, Homer City.
279 Yellow Creek St., Homer City, 15748. Tel: 724-479-2206.

Conemaugh, Cambria Co., Holy Trinity, Rev. Ronald W. Borsuk.
Res., 217 Fourth St., 15909. Tel: 814-535-5231; Fax: 814-535-2417.

Donora, Washington Co., St. Michael, Very Rev. Archpriest John J. Borodach.
Res., 511 Murray Ave., 15033. Tel: 724-379-9751; Fax: 724-379-9752. [CEM]

Du Bois, Clearfield Co., Nativity of the Mother of God. Attended by Holy Trinity, Sykesville. Very Rev. Simeon B. Sibenik.
Res., 200 McCullough St., 15801. Tel: 814-894-5440; Fax: 814-894-2412.

Dunlo, Cambria Co., SS. Peter and Paul. Attended by St. Mary's, Beaverdale.
P.O. Box 610, Beaverdale, 15921. Tel: 814-487-7458. [CEM]

Duquesne, Allegheny Co., SS. Peter and Paul, Rev. Msgr. William Levkulic.
Res., 701 Foster Ave., 15110. Tel: 412-466-3578; Fax: 412-466-3578. [CEM]
St. Mary's. Attended by St. Elias, Munhall.
Res., 1209 Kennedy Ave., 15110. Tel: 412-461-1712; Fax: 412-461-1712.

East Pittsburgh, Allegheny Co., St. Mary's, Rev. George Evancho.
Res., 317 Howard St., 15112. Tel: 412-824-1622.

Erie, Erie Co., SS. Peter and Paul, Rev. Julius Kubinyi.
Res., 3415 Wallace St., 16504. Tel: 814-825-8140.

Ernest, Indiana Co., St. Jude Thaddeus, Rev. James A. Ragan.
Res., Box 130, 15739. Tel: 724-463-3397; Fax: 724-465-5773.

Girard, Erie Co., SS. Cyril and Methodius, Rev. Dennis Logue, S.V.D.
Res., 1022 Tilden Ave., 16417. Tel: 814-774-3281; Fax: 814-774-5405.

Gibsonia, Allegheny Co., St. Andrew the Apostle, Rev. Andrew J. Deskevich.
Res., 235 Logan Rd., 15044. Tel: 724-625-1160; Fax: 724-625-1085.

Greensburg, Westmoreland Co., St. Nicholas of Myra, Rev. Regis Dusecina.
Res., 622 E. Pittsburgh St., 15601. Tel: 724-837-0295; Fax: 724-837-9042.

Hannastown, Westmoreland Co., St. Mary's. Attended by St. Nicholas of Myra, Greensburg.
622 E. Pittsburgh St., Greensburg, 15601. Tel: 724-837-0295.

Hawk Run, Clearfield Co., St. John the Baptist, Rev. Donald J. Voss.
Mailing Address: P.O. Box 2, 16840. Tel: 814-342-4315.

Herminie, Westmoreland Co., St. Mary's. Attended by St. Stephen's, North Huntington.
7 Second St., 15637. Tel: 724-446-5570.

Hermitage, Mercer Co., St. Michael, Rev. Frank A. Firko, S.T.L.
Res., 2230 Highland Rd., 16148. Tel: 724-981-6680; Fax: 724-981-7422. [CEM]

Homer City, Indiana Co., Holy Protection of Mary, The Mother of God, Rev. Edward J. Pyo.
Res., 279 Yellow Creek St., 15748. Tel: 724-479-2206; Fax: 724-479-9506.

Jerome, Somerset Co., SS. Peter and Paul. Attended by St. Mary, Windber.
803 Somerset Ave., Windber, 15963. Tel: 814-467-8044; Fax: 814-467-8044. [CEM]

Johnstown, Cambria Co., St. Mary's, Rev. Msgr. Raymond A. Balta.
Res., 411 Power St., 15906. Tel: 814-535-4132; Fax: 814-536-9017. [CEM]

Leisenring, Fayette Co., St. Stephen, Rev. Joseph Kapusnak.
Res., P.O. Box 128, 15455. Tel: 724-628-6611; Fax: 724-628-5009. [CEM]

Lyndora, Butler Co., St. John the Baptist, Rev. Dennis M. Bogda.
Res., 105 Kohler Ave., 16045. Tel: 724-287-5000; Fax: 724-287-6769. [CEM]

McKeesport, Allegheny Co., St. Nicholas, Rev. John J. Cuccaro.
Res., 410 Sixth Ave., 15132. Tel: 412-664-9131; Fax: 412-664-0854. [CEM]
Transfiguration of Our Lord. Attended by St. Nicholas, McKeesport.
Res., 121 Sixth Ave., 15132. Tel: 412-672-0728.

McKees Rocks, Allegheny Co., Holy Ghost, Rev. Ronald P. Larko.
Res., 225 Olivia St., 15136. Tel: 412-771-3324; Fax: 412-331-1870.

Monessen, Westmoreland Co., Assumption of the Blessed Virgin, Rev. Msgr. Andrew D. Parvensky.
Res., 125 McKee Ave., 15062. Tel: 724-684-5662; Fax: 724-684-3301. [CEM]

Monongahela, Washington Co., St. Macrina. Attended by Holy Ghost, Charleroi.
Church—c/o 828 Meadow Ave., Charleroi, 15022.

Monroeville, Allegheny Co., Church of the Resurrection, Rev. Richard Joseph Raptosh, Admin.
Res., 455 Center Rd., 15146. Tel: 412-372-8650; Fax: 412-372-1442.

Nanty-Glo, Cambria Co., St. Nicholas. Attended by Holy Trinity, Conemaugh.
Res., 1191 Second St., 15943. Tel: 814-749-0421.

New Salem, Fayette Co., St. Mary's. Attended by St. Nicholas, Brownsville.
P.O. Box 487, 15468. Tel: 724-245-7188. [CEM]

Northern Cambria, Cambria Co., St. John the Baptist, Rev. Donald Valasek.
Res., 719 Chestnut Ave., 15714-1459. Tel: 814-948-8242; Fax: 814-948-8252. [CEM]

North Huntingdon, Westmoreland Co., St. Stephen's, Rev. Gregory Michalisin.
Res., 90 Bethel Rd., 15642. Tel: 724-863-6776; Fax: 724-864-9685.

Patton, Cambria Co., SS. Peter and Paul. Attended by St. John, Northern Cambria.
Church—516 Palmer Ave., 16668. Tel: 814-674-5552. [CEM]

Perryopolis, Fayette Co., St. Nicholas, Rev. Robert E. Halus.
Res., 102 Railroad St., 15473. Tel: 724-736-4344; Fax: 724-736-4642. [CEM]

Pittsburgh, Allegheny Co.,

1—Holy Spirit, Rev. Msgr. Russell A. Duker, S.E.O.D.
Res., 4815 Fifth Ave., 15213. Tel: 412-687-1220; Fax: 412-687-1520.

2—Holy Ghost, Rev. Msgr. Peter Tay.
Res., 1437 Superior Ave., 15212. Tel: 412-321-5072; Fax: 412-321-0260.

3—St. John the Baptist, Rev. Elias L. Rafaj.
Res., 1720 Jane St., 15203. Tel: 412-431-1090; Fax: 412-431-2059. [CEM]

4—St. John Chrysostom, Rev. Richard Lambert.
Res., 506 Saline St., 15207. Tel: 412-421-0243; Fax: 412-422-3624.

5—Nativity of B.V.M . Attended by St. John Chrysostom, Pittsburgh.
Res., 4027 Beechwood Blvd., 15217. Tel: 412-421-5231.

6—St. Pius X, Rev. Msgr. Nicholas X. Smiciklas.
Res., 2336 Brownsville Rd., 15210. Tel: 412-881-8344; Fax: 412-884-7504.

Portage, Cambria Co., SS. Peter and Paul, Rev. Robert J. Karl.
Res., 143 Church Rd., 15946. Tel: 814-736-9780; Fax: 814-736-8701. [CEM]

Punxsutawney, Jefferson Co., SS. Peter and Paul, Rev. Robert K. Yetsko, T.O.R.
Res., 714 Second Ave., 15767. Tel: 814-938-6564; Fax: 814-938-6551. [CEM 2]

Rankin, Allegheny Co., St. John's. Attended by St. Mary's, East Pittsburgh. Rev. George Evancho.
317 Howard St., East Pittsburgh, 15112. Tel: 412-824-1622.
Church—44 Miller Ave., 15104.

Sagamore, Armstrong Co., St. Mary's. Attended by St. Jude Thaddeus, Ernest.
Box 130, Ernest, 15739. Tel: 724-463-3397. [CEM]

Scottdale, Westmoreland Co., St. John the Baptist, Very Rev. John H. Salko.
Res., 525 Porter Ave., 15683. Tel: 724-887-5072; Fax: 724-887-3365. [CEM]

Sheffield, Warren Co., St. Michael, Very Rev. Leo R. Schlosser, O.S.B.
Res., 407 School St., 16347. Tel: 814-968-5478; Fax: 814-968-4445. [CEM]

South Fork, Cambria Co., St. Michael's. Attended by SS. Peter and Paul Church, Portage. Rev. Robert J. Karl, Admin.
143 Church Rd., Portage, 15946. Tel: 814-736-9780; Fax: 814-736-8701. [CEM]

Sykesville, Jefferson Co., Holy Trinity, Very Rev. Simeon B. Sibenik.
Res., 104 Shaffer St., 15865. Tel: 814-894-5440; Fax: 814-894-2412. [CEM]

Tarentum, Allegheny Co., Sts. Peter and Paul, Rev. Robert F. Oravetz.
Res., 339 E. 10th Ave., 15084-1003. Tel: 724-224-3026; Fax: 724-224-5242.

Trauger, Westmoreland Co., St. Mary's, Rev. Christopher R. Burke.
Res., R.D. 3, Box 373-C, Latrobe, 15650. Tel: 724-423-3673; Fax: 724-423-1808. [CEM]

Uniontown, Fayette Co., St. John the Baptist, Very Rev. Richard J. Whetstone, J.C.O.L.
Res., 185 E. Main St., 15401. Tel: 724-438-6027; Fax: 724-438-1382. [CEM]

Upper St. Clair, Allegheny Co., St. Gregory Nazianzus, Rev. Bruno Asturi.
Res., 2005 Mohawk Rd., 15241. Tel: 412-835-7800; Fax: 412-835-7890.

Wall, Allegheny Co., Holy Trinity, Rev. Anselm Orlosky, O.S.B.
Res., 470 Wall Ave., 15148. Tel: 412-824-9803; Fax: 412-824-9803.

Windber, Somerset Co., St. Mary (Dormition) Church, Rev. Daniel Loya.
Res., 803 Somerset St., 15963. Tel: 814-467-8044; Fax: 814-467-8044. [CEM]

STATE OF OKLAHOMA

Oklahoma City, Oklahoma Co., Byzantine Catholic Community of Oklahoma City, Rev. Philip M. Seeton, Admin.
Res., 1010 N.W. 82nd St., Lawton, 73506. Tel: 580-531-2607; Fax: 580-531-2608.

STATE OF OHIO

Ashtabula, Ashtabula Co., St. Nicholas, Rev. A. Edward Gretchko.
Res., 206 Cherry Rd. NE, Massilon, 44646.
Church—1104 E. Fifteenth St., 44004. Tel: 330-833-8501; Fax: 330-833-3359.

Boardman, Mahoning Co., Infant Jesus of Prague, Rev. Msgr. Alexis E. Mihalik.
Res., 7754 S. Ave. Extension, P.O. Box 7006, 44512. Tel: 330-758-6019; Fax: 330-758-6776.

Campbell, Mahoning Co., St. Michael, Rev. Msgr. Victor G. Romza.
Res., 463 Robinson Rd., Box 426, 44405. Tel: 330-755-4831; Fax: 330-755-1818. [CEM]

Mingo Junction, Jefferson Co., St. John the Baptist. Attended by St. Joseph, Toronto.
Church—207 Standard St., 43938. Tel: 740-535-0271; Fax: 740-537-9802.

Newton Falls, Trumbull Co., St. Michael, Rev. John Kasarda.
Res., 737 Ridge Rd., 44444. Tel: 330-872-5216; Fax: 330-872-0200. [CEM]

Pleasant City, Guernsey Co., St. Michael, Rev. Seraphim John Chewning.
Res., 408 Walnut St., 43772. Tel: 740-685-3292; Fax: 740-685-1015. [CEM]

Toronto, Jefferson Co., St. Joseph, Rev. Andrew Chura.
Res., 814 N. Fifth St., 43964. Tel: 740-537-1026; Fax: 740-537-9802.

Warren, Trumbull Co., SS. Peter and Paul's, Rt. Rev. Msgr. Sylvester Hladky; Rev. John J. Koza, III.
Res., 180 Belvedere Ave., N.E., 44483. Tel: 330-372-1875; Fax: 330-372-5965. [CEM]
School—195 Belvedere Ave., N.E., 44483. Tel: 330-372-1312; Fax: 330-372-5965. Sr. Margaret Mary, O.S.B., Ph.D., Prin.
Sisters of the Order of St. Benedict 3; Lay Teachers 13; Students 174.

Youngstown, Mahoning Co.,

1—Assumption of the Blessed Virgin, Revs. John D. Ycoback; Thomas J. Wesdock.
Res., 356 S. Belle Vista, 44509. Tel: 330-799-8163; Fax: 330-793-5360. [CEM]

2—St. Nicholas, Rev. David J. Shortt.
Res., 1898 Wilson Ave., 44506. Tel: 330-743-0419; Fax: 330-743-6888. [CEM]
School—Byzantine Catholic Central, 5512 Youngstown-Poland Rd., 44514. Tel: 330-757-9185; Fax: 330-757-8150.
Sisters 2; Lay Teachers 7; Students 200.

3—St. George. Attended by St. Nicholas, Youngstown. 1726 Canfield Rd., 44511. Tel: 330-782-2865.

4—St. John the Baptist. Closed. For inquiries for parish records contact St. Nicholas, 1898 Wilson Ave., Youngstown, OH 44506. Tel.: 330-743-0419.

STATE OF TEXAS

Houston, Harris Co., St. John Chrysostom, Very Rev. John J. Mihalco.
Res., 5402 Acorn St., 77092-4255. Tel: 713-681-3580; Fax: 713-681-3466.
Mission—San Antonio, Bexar Co., Byzantine Catholic Mission.

Irving, Dallas Co., St. Basil the Great, Rev. David A. Bosnich.
Res., 1118 E. Union Bower Rd., 75061. Tel: 972-438-5644; Fax: 972-721-0696.

STATE OF WEST VIRGINIA

Morgantown, Monongalia Co., St. Mary Holy Protection, Rev. Michael Jude Wytish.
2115 Listravia Ave., 26505. Tel: 724-438-8060; Fax: 724-438-3463.
Church—Tel: 304-296-2455.

Weirton, Hancock Co., St. Mary's, Rev. Edward Lucas.
Res., 3116 Elm St., 26062. Tel: 304-748-2087; Fax: 304-748-7550.

Retired:
Reverend Monsignors—
Macko, John, 101 Whitestown Rd., Lyndora, PA 16045
Reverend Fathers—
Chornyak, Joseph I., P.O. Box 338, Perryopolis, PA 14573-0338
Gnall, Julian M., O.S.B., Chap., U.S. Navy, San Diego, CA
Gran, Thomas, 401 Cambria Ave., Windber, PA 15963
Mokris, Michael, 472 Church St., Swoyersville, PA 18704

INSTITUTIONS LOCATED IN THE ARCHDIOCESE

[A] SEMINARIES, ARCHDIOCESAN

Pittsburgh. *Byzantine Catholic Seminary of SS. Cyril and Methodius*, 3605 Perrysville Ave., 15214-2297. Tel: 412-321-8383; Fax: 412-321-9936.
E-mail: byzcathsem@att.net
Very Rev. John G. Petro, Rector. Tel: 412-321-7550; Revs. David M. Petras, Spiritual Dir. Tel: 412-321-5133; John S. Custer, Dean. Tel: 412-321-5993. Students for Priesthood 7.

[B] HOMES FOR AGED

Uniontown. *Mt. Macrina Manor*, 520 W. Main St., 15401-2602. Tel: 724-437-1400; Fax: 724-430-1095
For a complete listing, refer to the Special Care Facilities section.

Warren, OH. *Infant of Prague Manor*, 169 Kenmore, N.E., 44483. Tel: 330-372-4700; Fax: 330-372-5965.
E-mail: smm@netdotcom.com
Web site: www.stspeterandpaulbyz.org
For a complete listing, refer to the Special Care Facilities section.

[C] MONASTERIES AND RESIDENCES OF PRIESTS AND BROTHERS

Butler. *Holy Trinity Monastery*, P.O. Box 990, 16003. Tel: 724-287-4461; Fax: 724-287-6160. Rt. Rev. Leo R. Schlosser, O.S.B., Abbot/Hegumen; Very Rev. Anselm Orlosky, O.S.B., Prior; Bro. Michael Zetzer, O.S.B., Procurator. Priests 5; Brothers 3.

[D] CONVENTS AND RESIDENCES FOR SISTERS

Uniontown. *Motherhouse and Novitiate of the Sisters of St. Basil the Great.* Mailing Address: 500 W. Main St., P.O. Box 878, 15401. Tel: 724-438-8644; Fax: 724-438-8660.
E-mail: osbmolph@stargate.net
Sr. Ruth Plante, O.S.B.M., Prov. Supr.; Rev. Michael Jude Wytish, Chap. Professed Sisters 92.

Warren, OH. *Queen of Heaven Monastery*, 8640 Squires Ln., N.E., 44484. Tel: 330-856-1813; Fax: 330-856-9528.
E-mail: gohm@netdotcom.com
Web site: benedictinebyzantine.org
Sr. Margaret Mary Schima, O.S.B., Prioress. Benedictine Sisters of the Byzantine Rite 10.

Youngstown, OH. *Byzantine Convent*, 5512 Youngstown-Poland Rd., 44514. Tel: 330-757-9186; Fax: 330-757-1950. Sisters of St. Basil the Great 3.

[E] MISCELLANEOUS

Uniontown. *Mt. St. Marcina Retreat Center*, 510 W. Main St., P.O. Box 878, 15401-0878. Tel: 724-438-7149; Fax: 724-438-8660. Sr. Carol Petrasovich, O.S.B.M., Dir.

RELIGIOUS INSTITUTES OF MEN REPRESENTED IN THE ARCHDIOCESE

For further details refer to the corresponding bracketed number in the Religious Institutes of Men or Women section.

[0200]—*Benedictine Monks.*—O.S.B.

RELIGIOUS INSTITUTES OF WOMEN REPRESENTED IN THE ARCHDIOCESE

[0230]—*Benedictine Sisters of the Byzantine Rite.*—O.S.B.

[3730]—*Sisters of the Order of St. Basil the Great.*—O.S.B.M.

NECROLOGY

(No Deaths)

Romanian Catholic Diocese of Saint George's in Canton

Most Reverend

JOHN MICHAEL BOTEAN, D.D.

Bishop for the Romanian Byzantine Faithful of the United States; ordained May 18, 1986; appointed July 15, 1993; Episcopal Ordination August 24, 1996. *Res., 1121 44th St., N.E., Canton, OH, 44714-1297.* Tel.: 330-492-4086 (Office); Fax: 330-493-1416.

Most Reverend

LOUIS PUSCAS, D.D.

Bishop Emeritus for the Romanian Byzantine Faithful of the United States; ordained May 14, 1942; appointed Exarch December 4, 1982; Episcopal ordination June 26, 1983; installed August 28, 1983; promoted first Eparch April 16, 1987; retired July 15, 1993. *Mailing Address: 609 N. Lincoln Ave., Aurora, IL, 60505-2112.* Tel.: 630-859-3961.

ESTABLISHED DECEMBER 4, 1982.

ELEVATED FROM APOSTOLIC EXARCHATE FOR ROMANIAN BYZANTINE TO THE RANK OF AN EPARCHY (DIOCESE) MARCH 26, 1987.

Legal Title: The Romanian Catholic Diocese of Canton.

The Jurisdiction of the Romanian Catholic Diocese of Canton extends territorially to all of the United States.

Diocesan Offices: 1121 44th St., N.E., Canton, OH, 44714-1297. Tel.: 330-492-4086; Fax: 330-493-1416.

Web site address: www.RomanianCatholic.org

E-mail address: Romanian_Catholic@compuserve.com

STATISTICAL OVERVIEW

Personnel	
Bishop	1
Retired Bishops	1
Priests: Diocesan Active in Diocese	9
Priests: Active Outside Diocese	2
Priests: Retired, Sick or Absent	4
Number of Diocesan Priests	15
Religious Priests in Diocese	2
Ordinations:	
Diocesan Priests	1
Parishes	
Parishes	15
With Resident Pastor:	
Resident Diocesan Priests	10
Resident Religious Priests	2
Without Resident Pastor:	
Administered by Priests	4
Missions	4
Educational	
Diocesan Students in Other Seminaries	3
Total Seminarians	3
Catechesis/Religious Education:	
High School Students	6
Elementary Students	10
Total Students Under Catholic Instruction	19
Vital Statistics	
Receptions into the Church:	
Infant Baptism Totals	19
Received into Full Communion	16
Marriages:	
Catholic	14
Interfaith	3
Total Marriages	17
Deaths	12
Total Catholic Population	5,000

Former Bishop—Most Rev. LOUIS PUSCAS, ord. May 14, 1942; appt. Exarch, Dec. 4, 1982 Episcopal ordination, June 26, 1983; installed Aug. 28, 1983; promoted to first Eparch, April 16, 1987; retired July 15, 1993.

Chancellor—Rev. JOHN J. SKALA.

Vice Chancellor—Very Rev. Archpriest CHARLES A. MEZZOMO.

Economos—Mr. JAMES P. DERSHAW, C.P.A.

Board of Consultors—Very Rev. GEORGE DAVID, V.G.; Very Rev. AUREL PATER; Revs. MICHAEL MOISIN; MICHAEL KIRILA; GEORGE GAGE; ANDRE MATTHEWS.

Protosyncellus—Very Rev. GEORGE DAVID, V.G.

Vicar for Theological Affairs—Sr. THERESA KOERNKE, I.H.M., Ph.D.

Director of Religious Education—Rev. EMMANUEL G. SAMAYOA.

Pro-Life Commission—Mrs. ELIZABETH KIRILA, Chm.

Director of Scouting Svcs.—Rev. Deacon GARY A. BOYCE, Dir.

Formation Council—Rev. RICHARD J. MUCOWSKI, O.F.M., Ph.D.; Sr. THERESA KOERNKE, I.H.M., Ph.D.; Rev. AUGUST J. DEASIO, M.A.; Very Rev. Archpriest CHARLES A. MEZZOMO.

Director of Vocations—Very Rev. Archpriest CHARLES A. MEZZOMO.

Office to Aid the Church in Romania—Rev. MICHAEL MOISIN, Coord.

Moderator of the Curia—Very Rev. Archpriest CHARLES A. MEZZOMO.

CLERGY, PARISHES, MISSIONS AND PAROCHIAL SCHOOLS

STATE OF CALIFORNIA

Los Angeles, Los Angeles Co., St. Mary Romanian Catholic Mission,

STATE OF ILLINOIS

Aurora, Kane Co., St. George, Rev. Frederick Peterson, O.S.B.
Res., 850 Butterfield Rd., 60504-8609. Tel: 630-897-7215, Ext. 346; Fax: 630-897-0393.
Church—720 Rural St., 60505-2551. Tel: 630-851-4002; Fax: 630-851-4002.

St. Michael, Du Page Co., Very Rev. Aurel Pater.
Res. & Church—609 N. Lincoln Ave., 60505-2112. Tel: 630-897-8115; Fax: 630-897-5923.

Chicago, Cook Co., Ss. Peter and Paul Mission, Rev. Sergio Cornea, Admin.
Res., 208 Lilac Ln., North Aurora, 60542-1310. Tel: 630-896-4807.
Mission—Chicago, Cook Co., Holy Redeemer Church, 3107 Fullerton Ave., 60647.

STATE OF INDIANA

East Chicago, Lake Co., St. Nicholas, Rev. Gheorghe Opris, Admin.
Church & Res.: 4309 Olcott Ave., 46312-2649. Tel: 219-398-3760; Fax: 219-398-3760.

STATE OF MASSACHUSETTS

Boston, Middlesex Co., Romanian Catholic Mission of Boston, Rev. Michael Moisin, Admin.
Res. & Mailing Address: 8 Druce St., Brookline, MA 02146-4213. Tel: 617-566-4345; Fax: 617-566-3073.

STATE OF MICHIGAN

Dearborn, Wayne Co., St. Mary, Rev. Emmanuel G. Samayoa.
Church & Res.: 823 S. Military, 48124-2109. Tel: 313-274-2347.

Detroit, Wayne Co., St. John the Baptist, Rev. Michael Kirila.
Res., 2371 Woodstock Dr., 48203-1060. Tel: 313-386-1046; Fax: 313-368-5358.

STATE OF NEW JERSEY

Roebling, Burlington Co., St. Mary. Attended by St. Basil, Trenton. Very Rev. George David, V.G.
Church—181 Norman Ave., 08554-1125. Tel: 609-695-6093.

Trenton, Mercer Co., St. Basil, Very Rev. George David, V.G.
Church & Res.: 238 Adeline St., 08611-2420. Tel: 609-695-6093.

STATE OF NEW YORK

Astoria, Queens Co., St. Mary Romanian Catholic Mission,
Church—Holy Cross Church, 31-12 30th St., Long Island City, 11106-2802.

STATE OF OHIO

Alliance, Stark Co., St. Theodore. Attended by St. George, Canton. Very Rev. Archpriest Charles A. Mezzono.

Mailing Address: 1123 44th St., N.E., Canton, 44714-1297. Tel: 330-492-8413; Fax: 330-493-1416. *Church*—820 S. Linden St., 44601.

Canton, Stark Co., St. George Cathedral, Very Rev. Archpriest Charles A. Mezzono, Rector; Rev. John J. Skala.
Church & Res.: 1123 44th St., N.E., 44714-1297. Tel: 330-492-8413; Fax: 330-493-8413. Most Rev. John Michael Botean, D.D.; Bishop's Residence: 1121 44th St., N.E., 44714-1297. Tel: 330-492-4086 (Chancery Office); Fax: 390-493-1416.

Chesterland, Geauga Co., Most Holy Trinity, Rev. Albert Marflak, O.S.B., Admin.
Res., 10510 Buckeye Rd., Cleveland, 44104-3725. Tel: 216-721-5300; Fax: 216-791-8268.
Church—8549 Mayfield Rd., 44026-2625. Tel: 216-729-7636.

Cleveland, Cuyahoga Co., St. Helena, Rev. Andre Matthews.
Church & Res.: 1367 W. 65th St., 44102-2109. Tel: 216-651-0965; Fax: 216-631-3853.

Lorain, Lorain Co., St. Basil. Served from St. Helena, Cleveland. Rev. Andre Matthews.
Res., St. Helena, 1367 W. 65th St., Cleveland, 44102-2109. Tel: 216-651-0965; Fax: 216-631-3853. *Church*—2305 E. 31st St., 44052-2015. Tel: 216-277-5646.

Youngstown, Mahoning Co., St. Mary, Rev. George D. Gage.
Church & Res.: 7782 Glenwood Ave., Boardman, 44512-5823. Tel: 330-726-8573; Fax: 330-726-4102.

STATE OF PENNSYLVANIA

McKeesport, Allegheny Co., St. Mary, Revs. John M. Elanjileth; James Reiter (Canada).
Church & Res.: 318 26th St., 15132-7014. Tel: 412-673-5552. Rev. James E. Reiter.
Res., 1105 10th Ave., Irwin, 15642-3827. Tel: 412-863-6837; Fax: 412-863-6997.

Sharon, Mercer Co., St. John the Baptist. Attended by by St. Mary, Youngstown. Rev. George D. Gage.
Res., 7782 Glenwood Ave., Boardman, OH 44512-5823. Tel: 330-726-8573; Fax: 330-726-4102.
Church—3056 Morefield Rd., Hermitage, 16148.

Special Assignment or On Duty Outside the Diocese:
Reverend Fathers—
Brown, Konstantin K.
Kusevich, Nicholas C.
Yossa, Kenneth F.

Unassigned:
Reverend Fathers—
Buga, John

Retired:
Most Rev.—
Puscas, Louis, D.D., 609 N. Lincoln Ave., Aurora, IL 60505-2112. Tel: 630-859-3961
Reverend Fathers—
Ciungu, John
Filip, John T.
Streza, Charles V.

NECROLOGY

(No Deaths)

Ukrainian Catholic Diocese of St. Josaphat in Parma

Most Reverend

ROBERT M. MOSKAL, D.D.

Bishop of St. Josaphat in Parma; ordained March 25, 1963; appointed Titular Bishop of Agathopolis and Auxiliary Bishop of the Archeparchy of Philadelphia August 3, 1981; consecrated October 13, 1981; appointed First Bishop of St. Josaphat in Parma December 5, 1983. *Res., 5720 State Rd., P.O. Box 347180, Parma, OH, 44134.*

Chancery: 5720 State Rd., P.O. Box 347180, Parma, OH, 44134-7180. Tel.: 440-888-1522; Fax: 440-888-3477.

E-mail address: 110330.137@compuserve.com

ESTABLISHED DECEMBER 3, 1983.

The jurisdiction of the Bishop of St. Josaphat in Parma extends territorially through all the States of Ohio, Mississippi, West Virginia, Kentucky, Tennessee, Alabama, Georgia, North Carolina, South Carolina, Florida and western Pennsylvania. With regards to persons, his subjects are Catholics of the Byzantine Ukrainian Rite: 1. Who immigrated to this country from Galicia, Bucovina and other Ukrainian provinces; 2. Who descend from such persons (Can. 755); 3. Women married to men referable to 1 and 2, if they comply with (Can. 98, n.4); 4. Who in accordance with (Can. 98, n.3) changed their Rite; 5. Converts to the Catholic Church of the Byzantine Ukrainian Rite; 6. And in fact, all other Catholics of the Byzantine Ukrainian Rite who are attached to parishes subject to the jurisdiction of the Bishop of St. Josaphat in Parma.

For legal titles of parishes and diocesan institutions, consult the Chancery.

STATISTICAL OVERVIEW

Personnel	
Bishop	1
Priests: Diocesan Active in Diocese	31
Priests: Active Outside Diocese	1
Priests: Retired, Sick or Absent	8
Number of Diocesan Priests	40
Religious Priests in Diocese	1
Extern Priests in Diocese	8
Ordinations:	
Permanent Deacons	1
Permanent Deacons in Diocese	7
Total Brothers	10
Total Sisters	10
Parishes	
Parishes	38
With Resident Pastor:	
Resident Diocesan Priests	31
Resident Religious Priests	1
Without Resident Pastor:	
Administered by Priests	6
Missions	3
Professional Ministry Personnel:	
Sisters	2
Welfare	
Homes for the Aged	2
Total Assisted	146
Educational	
Diocesan Students in Other Seminaries	4
Total Seminarians	4
Elementary Schools, Diocesan and Parish	2
Total Students	307
Catechesis/Religious Education:	
High School Students	65
Elementary Students	575
Total Students Under Catholic Instruction	951
Teachers in the Diocese:	
Sisters	2
Lay Teachers	29
Vital Statistics	
Receptions into the Church:	
Infant Baptism Totals	112
Adult Baptism Totals	6
Received into Full Communion	4
First Communions	99
Confirmations	121
Marriages:	
Catholic	57
Interfaith	5
Total Marriages	62
Deaths	240
Total Catholic Population	11,299

Vicar General—Rev. Msgr. Mitrat LEO ADAMIAK.

Vicar General in Curia—Rev. Msgr. Mitrat THOMAS A. SAYUK.

Chancellor—Rev. Msgr. Mitrat THOMAS A. SAYUK.

Vice Chancellor—Rev. Msgr. PETER WASLO.

Diocesan Treasurer—Rev. Msgr. Mitrat THOMAS A. SAYUK.

Chancery—5720 State Rd., P.O. Box 347180, Parma, OH, 44134-7180. Tel: 440-888-1522; Fax: 440-888-3477. Office Hours: Mon.-Fri. 10-12 & 2-4.

Secretary—Sr. LAURENCE M. LALIK, O.S.B.M.

Diocesan Consultors—Rev. Msgr. Mitrat LEO ADAMIAK; Rev. Msgr. Mitrat MICHAEL POLOWAY; Rev. Msgr. Mitrat MICHAEL REWTIUK; Rev. Msgr. GEORGE APPLEYARD; Rev. Msgr. RICHARD SEMINACK; Rev. Msgr. Mitrat THOMAS A. SAYUK; Very Rev. Canon JAROSLAW MYCHAJLENKO; Very Rev. Canon ROBERT HNATYSHYN.

Diocesan Corporation—Most Rev. ROBERT M. MOSKAL, Pres.; Rev. Msgr. PETER WASLO, Vice Pres.; Rev. Msgr. Mitrat THOMAS A. SAYUK, Sec. & Treas.

Diocesan Administrative Council—Most Rev. ROBERT M. MOSKAL; Rev. Msgr. Mitrat LEO ADAMIAK; Rev. Msgr. PETER WASLO; Rev. Msgr. Mitrat THOMAS SAYUK; Rev. MARK MOROZOWICH.

Protopresbyters-Deans—Western Deanery: Very Rev. Canon JAROSLAW MYCHAJLENKO, Dean; Central Deanery: Rev. Msgr. Mitrat MICHAEL POLOWAY, Dean; Eastern Deanery: Very Rev. Canon JAMES POORMAN, Dean; Southern Deanery: Very Rev. Archpriest Mitrat MATTHEW BERKO, Dean; Rev. Msgr. JOHN STEVENSKY, Vice Dean.

Vicar for Clergy—Rev. Msgr. PETER WASLO.

Vicar for Religious—Rev. Msgr. GEORGE APPLEYARD.

Liturgical Commission—Most Rev. ROBERT MOSKAL; Rev. Msgr. THOMAS SAYUK; Rev. Msgr. GEORGE APPLEYARD; Rev. MARK MOROZOWICH.

Diocesan Offices and Directors

Acolyte Confraternity—Deacon MICHAEL LEVY.

Catechetical Planning Committee—Sr. ANN LASZOK, O.S.B.M., Chm.; Rev. Msgr. RICHARD SEMINACK, D.R.E.; Rev. Msgr. GEORGE APPLEYARD; Sr. OLGA MARIE FARYNA, O.S.B.M.; Very Rev. Canon JAROSLAW MYCHAJLENKO; Revs. XAVIER ELAMBASSERY; ANTHONY BALISTRERI; Rev. Msgr. PETER WASLO.

Clergy Examiners—Rev. Msgr. Mitrat LEO ADAMIAK; Rev. Msgr. RICHARD SEMINACK; Rev. MARK MOROZOWICH; Rev. Msgr. PETER WASLO; Rev. Msgr. Mitrat THOMAS A. SAYUK.

Department of Religious Education—Rev. Msgr. RICHARD SEMINACK, Dir.; Sr. ANN LASZOK, O.S.B.M., Asst. Dir., *726 Washington Ave., Carnegie, PA, 15106.* Tel: 412-279-4652.

Diocesan Ecumenical Office—Rev. Msgr. GEORGE APPLEYARD, Dir.

Diocesan Promoter for the Cause of Metropolitan Andrew Sheptytsky—Rev. Msgr. Mitrat THOMAS A. SAYUK.

Diocesan Resource Committee—Rev. Msgr. GEORGE APPLEYARD, Spiritual Dir. NICKOLAUS KOTOW, Chm. DAVID HODOWANEC, Vice Chm. LILLIAN MISKO COURY, Sec. PETER HLUTKOWSKY, Treas.

Director of Liturgical Chant—STEPHEN ZINSKI; LILLIAN MISKO COURY; BRUCE SCILENY.

Director of Youth Ministries—Rev. ANTHONY BALISTRERI.

Lay Ministries—Sr. ANN LASZOK, O.S.B.M.; Sr. OLGA MARIE FARYNA, O.S.B.M.

League of Ukrainian Catholics (LUC)—Rev. MICHAEL POLOSKY, Spiritual Dir. of Western PA Council; Rev. Msgr. JOHN STEVENSKY, Organizer of Southern Deanery LUC.

League of Ukrainian Catholic Youth (LUCY)—Rev. ANTHONY BALISTRERI, Spiritual Dir.

Lector Training Team—Sr. ANN LASZOK, O.S.B.M., Dir.

Marian Sodalities—Sr. LAURENCE M. LALIK, O.S.B.M.

Obnova—Rev. Mitrat WOLODYMYR WOLOSZCZUK, Dir.

Office for Evangelization—Rev. MICHAEL POLOSKY, Liaison.

Pastoral Ministry Office—Sr. ANN LASZOK, O.S.B.M., Coord. Adult Religious Education: Dr. VERA KROKONKO; Deacon JEFFREY SMOLILO, *727 E. Carson St., Pittsburgh, PA, 15203.* Tel: 412-481-9778.

Permanent Diaconate Program—Rev. Msgr. GEORGE APPLEYARD, Dir.; Rev. Msgr. Mitrat MICHAEL POLOWAY; Rev. Msgr. RICHARD SEMINACK; Rev. Msgr. PETER WASLO; Rev. Canon JOHN ROPKE.

Prayer League for Canonization of Metropolitan Andrew Sheptytsky—Rev. Msgr. Mitrat THOMAS SAYUK.

Presbyteral Council—Rev. Msgr. Mitrat LEO ADAMIAK; Rev. Msgr. Mitrat THOMAS A. SAYUK; Rev. Msgr. Mitrat MICHAEL POLOWAY; Rev. Msgr. Mitrat MICHAEL REWTIUK; Rev. Msgr. RICHARD SEMINACK; Very Rev. Canon JAMES POORMAN; Very Rev. Canon WALTER WYSOCHANSKY; Rev. XAVIER ELAMBASSERY; Rev. Msgr. PETER WASLO; Revs. STEVEN PALIWODA; ANTHONY BALISTRERI; MICHAEL POLOSKY; MICHAEL KRUPKA; Rev. Canon JOHN ROPKE; Rev. Msgr. JOHN STEVENSKY; Rev. Msgr. GEORGE APPLEYARD.

Priests' Continuing Education—Rev. Canon Dr. JOHN ROPKE.

Vocation Director—Revs. STEVEN PALIWODA; MICHAEL POLOSKY.

Diocesan Personnel Board—Rev. Msgr. RICHARD SEMINACK, Chm.; Rev. Canon Dr. JOHN ROPKE, Sec.; Rev. Msgr. Mitrat MICHAEL POLOWAY; Revs. XAVIER ELAMBASSERY; GEORGE MULLONKAL.

Tribunal—

Judicial Vicar—Rev. Msgr. PETER WASLO.

Judge—Rev. W. BECKETT SOULE, O.P.

Defender of the Bond—Rev. MARK Q. FEDOR.

Notary—Very Rev. Canon JAROSLAW MYCHAJLENKO; Sr. LAURENCE LALIK, O.S.B.M.

CLERGY, PARISHES, MISSIONS AND PAROCHIAL SCHOOLS

STATE OF OHIO

Parma, St. Josaphat Cathedral, Rev. Msgr. Mitred Michael Rewtiuk, Archpriest; Rev. Canon Andrew Hanowsky; Rev. Valerian Michlik.
Res., 5720 State Rd., 44134-2536. Tel: 440-886-2108.
School—Tel: 440-884-1812; Fax: 440-884-3435.
Sisters of St. Basil the Great 2; Lay Teachers 15; Students 177.

St. Andrew, Rev. Msgr. Peter Waslo; Rev. Michael Bliszcz.
Res., 7700 Hoertz Rd., 44134-6404. Tel: 440-843-9149.

Pokrova Ukrainian Catholic Parish, Rev. Vasil Petriv.
Office: 6812 Broadview Rd., 44134. Tel: 216-524-0918; Fax: 216-524-0919. [CEM]
Res., 6790 Broadview Rd., 44134-4804. Tel: 440-524-2505.

Akron, Summit Co., Holy Ghost, Rev. Michael Krupka.
Res., 1859 Carter Ave., 44301. Tel: 330-724-8277.

Austintown, Mahoning Co., St. Anne, Rev. Msgr. George Appleyard; Rev. Andrew Marko.
Res., 3055 S. Raccoon Rd., 44515-5351. Tel: 330-793-5436; 792-8555; Fax: 330-793-5436.
Church—4310 Kirk Rd., 44511-1899.
School—Tel: 330-792-9806; Fax: 330-792-3995.
Lay Teachers 14; Students 130.

Canton, Stark Co., St. Nicholas. Attended by Akron.
Church—1020 Lippert Rd., 44704.

Cleveland, Cuyahoga Co., Ss. Peter and Paul, Rev. Steven Zarichny.
Res., 2280 W. 7th St., 44113. Tel: 216-861-2176. [CEM]

Lorain, Lorain Co., St. John the Baptist, Rev. Peter Tomas.
Res., 3038 Charleston Ave., 44055-2164. Tel: 440-277-7114.
Church—2445 E. 31st St., 44055.
Mission—Brunswick, Medina Co.

Rossford, Wood Co., St. Michael. Unassigned.
Res., 133 Walnut St., 43460-1248. Tel: 419-666-5627.

Solon, Cuyahoga Co., Protection B.V.M., Very Rev. Canon Jaroslaw Mychajlenko.
Res., 27275 Aurora Rd., 44139-1804. Tel: 440-248-4549.

Youngstown, Mahoning Co., Holy Trinity, Rev. Msgr. Mitred Leo Adamiak, V.G.
Res., 526 W. Rayen Ave., 44502-1124. Tel: 330-744-5820.

STATE OF FLORIDA

Apopka, Orange Co., St. Mary's, Mitred Archpriest Matthew Berko.
Res., 20 E. Nightingale St., 32712. Tel: 407-880-1640.
Mission—Daytona Beach.

Miami, Dade Co., Assumption of B.V.M., Rev. John Chirovsky.
Res., 11000 SW 128th St., 33126. Tel: 305-262-4192; Fax: 305-261-9759.
Mission—Lantana.

North Port, Sarasota Co., Entrance of B.V.M. into the Temple, Mitred Archpriests Wolodymyr Woloszczuk; Mitrat Iwan Tylawskyj, Pastor Emeritus.
Res., 1078 N. Biscayne Dr., 34286. Tel: 941-426-7931.

St. Petersburg, Pinellas Co., Epiphany of Our Lord, Mitred Archpriest Matthew Berko; Rev. Andrew Krasulski.
Res., 434 90th Ave. N., 33702. Tel: 727-576-1001 (Office); 727-577-0385 (Res.).

Spring Hill, Hernando Co., St. Andrew, Rev. Boris Dukeley.
Mailing Address: P.O. Box 5902, 3611-5902. Tel: 813-577-0385.
Res., 415 Montpellier Ct., 34608. Tel: 352-684-4876.

STATE OF GEORGIA

Conyers, Rockdale Co., Mother of God, Rev. Msgr. John Stevensky, Pastor.
Res., 2880 Highway 138 N.E., 30013. Tel: 770-760-1111.

STATE OF PENNSYLVANIA

Aliquippa, Beaver Co., Ss. Peter and Paul, Rev. Michael Derbish, O.F.M.
Res., 2001 Main St., 15001. Tel: 412-375-7016.

Altoona, Blair Co., Immaculate Conception. Served by Northern Cambria.
Res., 2020 20th St., 16601. [CEM]

Ambridge, Beaver Co., Ss. Peter and Paul, Rev. Michael Polosky; Rev. Canon Walter Wysochansky.
Res., 404 6th St., 15003. Tel: 412-266-2262; Fax: 412-266-2262.

Northern Cambria, Cambria Co., Immaculate Conception, Rev. Emanuel Rathapilly.
Res., 300 Campbell Ave., P.O. Box 1066, 15714. Tel: 814-948-9193.

Carnegie, Allegheny Co., Holy Trinity, Rev. Msgr. Richard Seminack.
Res., 730 Washington Ave., 15106. Tel: 412-279-4652. [CEM]

Ford City, Armstrong Co., St. Mary, Rev. Michael Sopp, Admin.
Res., 514 Ninth St., 16226. Tel: 724-763-1203. [CEM]

Jeannette, Westmoreland Co., St. Demetrius, Rev. John Gribik.
Res., 1013 Gaskill Ave., 15644-3307. Tel: 724-523-9389.

Johnstown, Cambria Co., St. John the Baptist, Rev. Anthony Balistreri.
Res., 606 Maple Ave., 15901. Tel: 814-535-2634. [CEM]

Latrobe, Westmoreland Co., Assumption of B.V.M., Rev. Xavier Elambassery.
Res., 526 Hillview Ave., 15650. Tel: 412-537-6450.

Lyndora, Butler Co., St. Michael, Rev. Douglas Lorance.
Res., 610 Hansen Ave., 16045-1325. Tel: 724-283-6230; Fax: 724-283-0363.

McKeesport, Allegheny Co., St. John the Baptist, Very Rev. Canon Robert Hnatyshyn.
Res., 1907 Eden Park Blvd., 15132. Tel: 412-672-0923.

McKees Rocks, Allegheny Co., St. John the Baptist, Rev. Roman Harwas.
Res., 204 Olivia St., 15136. Tel: 412-331-5605.

New Alexandria, Westmoreland Co., Nativity B.V.M. Attended by Latrobe.
526 Hillview Ave., Latrobe, 15650. Tel: 412-537-6450.
Church—Shersburg Rd., 15670. [CEM]

New Kensington, Westmoreland Co., St. Vladimir, Rev. Dr. Canon John Ropke.
Res., 1601 Kenneth Ave., Arnold, 15068. Tel: 724-339-9622; Fax: 724-339-9622.

Pittsburgh, Allegheny Co., St. George, Rev. Steven Paliwoda.
Res., 3455 California Ave., 15212. Tel: 412-766-8801; Fax: 412-766-8244.

St. John the Baptist, Rev. Msgr. Mitred Michael Poloway; Rev. Joseph Tamburro.
Res., 109 S. Seventh St., 15203. Tel: 412-431-2531; Fax: 412-431-0727. [CEM]

Ramey, Clearfield Co., Annunciation B.V.M., Very Rev. Canon James E. Poorman.
Res., P.O. Box 205, 16671. Tel: 814-378-7688. [CEM]

Revloc, Cambria Co., Protection Blessed Virgin Mary. Attended by Johnstown.
606 Maple Ave., Johnstown, 15901. Tel: 814-535-2634.
Church—560 Cambria Ave., P.O. Box 194, 15948-0914.

West Leechburg, Armstrong Co., St. Michael. Attended by Ford City, PA.
Mailing Address: 514 Ninth St., Ford City, 16226. Tel: 724-763-1203.
Church—Main St., 15656.

Wilmerding, Allegheny Co., Ss. Peter and Paul. Attended by Jeannette, PA.
Mailing Address: 1013 Gaskill Ave., Jeannette, 15644-3307. Tel: 724-523-9389.
Church—163 State St., 15148-1323. Tel: 724-829-1833.

STATE OF WEST VIRGINIA

Wheeling, Ohio Co., Our Lady of Perpetual Help, Very Rev. Archpriest Philip Bumbar.
Res., 4136 Jacob St., 26003. Tel: 304-232-2168.

On Sick Leave:
Reverend Fathers—
Ganzy, Alexander

Retired:
Reverend Monsignors—
Fedyk, Jaroslaw, Hollywood Trailer Park, 7230 4th St. N., Lot 1102, St. Petersburg, FL 33702
Kachmar, Walter, R.D. No. 5, Box 54, Blairsville, PA 15717-9139. Tel: 724-459-8614
Nestor, Michael, 867 N. Concord St., Gilbert, AZ 85234. Tel: 602-507-5015
Reverend Fathers—
Adamiak, Stephen, 6000 21st St. N., St. Petersburg, FL 33714
Balaban, Oryst, 1532 Fourth Ave., Arnold, PA 15068-4402
Griffiths, James, 111 S. Cliff St., Apt. 6B6, Butler, PA 16001-6045
Tylawskyj, Mitrat Iwan, 7919 Hyde Park Ave., North Port, FL 34286. Tel: 941-429-0085

Permanent Deacons:
Billy, Donald, 2515 McCollum Rd., Youngstown, OH 44509. Tel: 330-792-3166
Boyce, Gary, 6976 S. Evening Glow Pl., Gold Canyon, AZ 85219-2946. Tel: 480-288-6854
Dobosh, Michael, 7935 Carlyle Ave., Apt. 10, Miami Beach, FL 33141. Tel: 305-864-7991
Kulick, Michael, 8455 Sunnydale Dr., Brecksville, OH 44141. Tel: 440-526-4517
Levy, Joseph M., 5216 Kerrington Dr., Gibsonia, PA 15044. Tel: 724-443-8764
Poklemba, Joseph, 904 W. Grant St., Blakely, PA 18447. Tel: 507-489-0005
Smolilo, Jeffery, 4546 Shelly Dr., Seven Hills, OH 44131. Tel: 216-328-0743

INSTITUTIONS LOCATED IN THE DIOCESE

[A] CONVENTS

PARMA. *St. Josaphat Convent*, 5720 State Rd., 44134-2536. Tel: 440-885-1245. Sisters of St. Basil the Great.

[B] HOMES FOR THE AGED

PARMA. *Shevchenko Manor*, 5620 W. 24th St., 44134-2751. Tel: 216-459-1440; Fax: 216-459-1442. Jennie Bochar, Mgr.

PITTSBURGH, PA. *Sheptytsky Arms*, 3505 Mexico St., 15212. Tel: 412-766-8802; Fax: 412-766-0938. Sr. Bernardine Symionow, S.S.M.I., Mgr.; Sr. Consolata Trudick, S.S.M.I., Sec.

NECROLOGY

† Kubacki, Anthony, Johnstown, PA St. John the Baptist Church. —Died Dec. 9, 1999.

Eparchy of St. Maron of Brooklyn

Most Reverend

STEPHEN HECTOR DOUEIHI, S.T.D.

Bishop, Eparchy of Saint Maron of Brooklyn; born June 25, 1927; ordained August 14, 1955; appointed Second Eparchial Bishop of the Eparchy of Saint Maron of Brooklyn November 23, 1996; consecrated January 11, 1997; enthroned February 5, 1997. *Res., 8070 Harbor View Terrace, Brooklyn, New York, 11209.*

Most Reverend

FRANCIS M. ZAYEK, D.D., S.T.D., J.C.D.

Retired Bishop, Eparchy of St. Maron of Brooklyn; born October 18, 1920; ordained March 17, 1946; appointed Titular Bishop of Callinicum May 30, 1962; consecrated August 5, 1962; appointed Eparch of the Diocese of Saint Maron November 11, 1971; installed June 4, 1972; elevated to Archbishop December 22, 1982. *Res., 4010 - Galt Ocean Dr., Apt. 1203, Fort Lauderdale, FL, 33308.*

ESTABLISHED AS AN APOSTOLIC EXARCHATE JANUARY 10, 1966; ELEVATED TO A DIOCESE NOVEMBER 11, 1971.

The jurisdiction of the Diocese extends to all the Maronite Catholics in New York, New Jersey, Pennsylvania, Florida, Georgia, North Carolina, South Carolina, Delaware, Virginia, District of Columbia, Maine, New Hampshire, Vermont, Massachusetts, Rhode Island, Connecticut and Maryland.

For legal titles of parishes and diocesan institutions, consult the Chancery Office.

Chancery Office: 109 Remsen St., Brooklyn, NY, 11201. Tel.: 718-237-9913; Fax: 718-243-0444.

STATISTICAL OVERVIEW

Personnel	
Retired Archbishops	1
Bishop	1
Priests: Diocesan Active in Diocese	45
Priests: Active Outside Diocese	6
Priests: Retired, Sick or Absent	14
Number of Diocesan Priests	65
Religious Priests in Diocese	12
Ordinations:	
Transitional Deacons	1
Permanent Deacons	1
Permanent Deacons in Diocese	13
Total Brothers	7
Total Sisters	2
Parishes	
Parishes	33
With Resident Pastor:	
Resident Diocesan Priests	31
Resident Religious Priests	1
Without Resident Pastor:	
Administered by Priests	1
Missions	4
Educational	
Seminaries, Diocesan	1
Students from This Diocese	1
Diocesan Students in Other Seminaries	2
Total Seminarians	3
Catechesis/Religious Education:	
High School Students	299
Elementary Students	1,503
Total Students Under Catholic Instruction	1,805
Vital Statistics	
Receptions into the Church:	
Infant Baptism Totals	447
Adult Baptism Totals	20
Received into Full Communion	13
First Communions	286
Confirmations	280
Marriages:	
Catholic	107
Interfaith	33
Total Marriages	140
Deaths	216
Total Catholic Population	30,000

Protosyncellus (Vicar General)—Chorbishop JOSEPH F. KADDO.

Chancellor—Rev. FRANCIS J. MARINI, J.D., J.C.O.D.

Vicar for Canonical Services/Administration—Rev. FRANCIS J. MARINI, J.D., J.C.O.D.

The Chancery—109 Remsen St., Brooklyn, NY, 11201. Tel: 718-237-9913; Fax: 718-243-0444. Office Hours: Mon.-Fri. 9-12 & 1-4. Closed on Maronite holy days and national holidays.

Tribunal of the Eparchy of Saint Maron of Brooklyn—

Judicial Vicar—Rev. MICHAEL G. THOMAS, J.C.D., *2055 Coral Way, Miami, FL, 33145.* Tel: 305-762-1269; Fax: 305-856-5740.

Defender of the Bond—Rev. CARL MORRISON, J.C.L.

Promoter of Justice—Very Rev. THOMAS M. MARIN, J.C.L.

Advocates—Rev. Msgr. NEVIN KLINGER, J.C.L.; Rev. MICHAEL SOUCKAR, J.C.D.

Presbyteral Council-Ex Officio Members—Most Rev. STEPHEN HECTOR DOUEIHI; Chorbishop SEELY BEGGIANI; Chorbishop JOSEPH LAHOUD, Northern District; Chorbishop JOSEPH F. KADDO; Rev. Msgr. IGNACE SADEK; Rev. FAHED AZAR, Central District; Rev. GEORGE SEBAALI, Southern District.

Elected Members—Chorbishop JOSEPH LAHOUD; Rev. FRANCIS J. MARINI; Rev. Msgr. DAVID M. GEORGE.

Appointed Members—Rev. Msgr. NORMAN FERRIS; Rev. EDWARD T. NEDDER.

Protopresbyters—(I); Chorbishop JOSEPH LAHOUD,(Northern); Rev. FAHED AZAR,(Central); Rev. GEORGE SEBAALI,(Southern).

Lebanon Commission—Chorbishop SEELY BEGGIANI, Chm., *7164 Alaska Ave., N.W., Washington, DC, 20012.* Tel: 202-723-8831.

National Apostolate of Maronites National Office—Mr. ANTHONY T. BUDWAY, Pres. ED SHINER, Exec. Sec., *P.O. 126, Dyker Heights Stn., Brooklyn, NY, 11228.* Tel: 718-232-7292.

Diocesan Offices and Directors

Communications—Rev. GEORGE SEBAALI, *4611 Sadler Rd., Glen Allen, VA, 23060.* Tel: 804-270-7234; Fax: 804-273-9914.

(Diocesan Newspaper) "The Maronite Voice"—Rev. GEORGE SEBAALI, Editor, *4611 Sadler Rd., Glen Allen, VA, 23060.* Tel: 804-762-4301; Fax: 804-273-9914.

Finance Council—Most Rev. STEPHEN HECTOR DOUEIHI, Chm.

Office of Jubilee 2000—Rev. Msgr. RONALD BESHARA, Dir., *55 N. Lakeshore Dr., Hypoluxo, FL, 33462-6077.* Tel: 561-840-6196; Fax: 561-882-1025.

Liturgy—Most Rev. STEPHEN HECTOR DOUEIHI, Chm.; Rev. CLAUDE W. FRANKLIN, JR., Asst., *109 Remsen St., Brooklyn, NY, 11201.* Tel: 718-237-9913; Fax: 718-243-0444.

Ministries (Permanent Deacons and Subdeacons)—Rev. EDWARD T. NEDDER, *375 Island Pond Rd., Springfield, MA, 01118.* Tel: 413-732-0589.

Order of Saint Sharbel—Mr. PHILLIP BARROOD, *National Office, 109 Remsen St., Brooklyn, NY, 11201.*

Office of Outreach—Rev. Msgr. RONALD BESHARA, Dir., *55 N. Lakeshore Dr., Hypoluxo, FL, 33462-6077.* Tel: 561-840-6196; Fax: 561-882-1025.

Pro-Life Director—Rev. KEVIN BEATON, *2 W. Reynolds St., New Castle, PA, 16101.* Tel: 724-658-0787.

Religious Education—Chorbishop DOMINIC ASHKAR, *7164 Alaska Ave., N.W., Washington, DC, 20012.* Tel: 202-826-5554.

Vocations—Rev. JAMES ROOT, *1000 Lindsay Rd., Carnegie, PA, 15106.* Tel: 412-278-0841; Fax: 412-278-0846.

Youth Ministry Office—Rev. JOHN MORRISON, *806 Arsenal Ave., Fayetteville, NC, 28305.* Tel: 910-484-1531.

CLERGY, PARISHES, MISSIONS AND PAROCHIAL SCHOOLS

STATE OF NEW YORK

Brooklyn, Kings Co., Cathedral of Our Lady of Lebanon, Rev. Msgr. Ignace Sadek, Rector. In res., Rev. Francis J. Marini, J.D., J.C.O.D.
Res., 113 Remsen St., 11201. Tel: 718-624-7228; Fax: 718-624-8034.

Olean, Cattaraugus Co., St. Joseph, Rev. Joseph G. Akiki.
Res., 331 N. Fourth St., 14760. Tel: 716-372-4311.

Troy, Rensselaer Co., St. Ann, Rev. David William Mickiewicz.
Church—182 Fourth St., 12180. Tel: 518-272-6073.

Utica, Oneida Co., St. Louis Gonzaga, Rev. Bassam Saade.
Res., 520 Rutger St., 13501. Tel: 315-732-6019; Fax: 315-732-3047.

Williamsville, Erie Co., St. John Maron, Rev. Georges El-Khalli.

Res., 2040 Wehrle Dr., 14221-7041. Tel: 716-634-0669; Fax: 716-634-0674.

STATE OF CONNECTICUT

Danbury, Fairfield Co., St. Anthony, Rev. Larry Jensen.
Res., 17 Granville Ave., 06810. Tel: 203-744-3372; Fax: 203-794-0949.

Torrington, Litchfield Co., St. Maron, Rev. Lawrence P. Michael.
Res., 613 Main St., 06790. Tel: 860-489-9015; Fax: 860-482-1614.

Waterbury, New Haven Co., Our Lady of Lebanon, Rev. Msgr. David M. George.
Res., 8 E. Mountain Rd., 06706. Tel: 203-753-6633; 753-9428; Fax: 203-573-8384.

STATE OF FLORIDA

Miami, Dade Co., Our Lady of Lebanon (1973), Revs. Michael G. Thomas; Michel Freifer.
Mailing Address: 2055 Coral Way, 33145. Tel: 305-856-7449; Fax: 305-856-5740.
Res., 420 Como Ave., Coral Gables, 33146.

Orlando, Orange Co., St. Jude Mission, Rev. George Zina.
Res., 6282 Sandcrest Cir., 32819. Tel: 407-363-7405; Fax: 407-363-7793.

West Palm Beach, Palm Beach Co., Mary Mother of Light Maronite Mission, Rev. Leonard Basinow.
Res., 3138 Via Poinciana Dr., Lake Worth, 33467. Tel: 561-433-8831.

Jacksonville, Duval Co., St. Maron Maronite, Rev. Elie Abichedid.
Res., P.O. Box 350148, 32235-0148. Tel: 904-721-3334.

STATE OF GEORGIA

Atlanta, Fulton Co., St. Joseph's Maronite Church, Rev. Peter Boulos.
Res., 502 Seminole Ave., N.E., 30307. Tel: 404-525-2504; Fax: 404-589-1744.

STATE OF MAINE

Waterville, Kennebec Co., St. Joseph, Rev. Samuel A. Najjar.
Res., 3 Appleton St., 04901. Tel: 207-872-8515.

STATE OF MASSACHUSETTS

Brockton, Plymouth Co., St. Theresa, Rev. Christopher J. Henderson.
Mailing Address: P.O. Box 2567, 02305-2567. Fax: 508-587-8139.
Res., 10 Lebanon St., 02301. Tel: 508-586-1428.

Fall River, Bristol Co., St. Anthony of the Desert, Rev. Msgr. Norman J. Ferris; Rev. Boutros Sleiman Kass-Hanna Saissa.
Res., 300 N. Eastern Ave., 02723. Tel: 508-672-7653; Fax: 508-678-1474.

Jamaica Plain, Suffolk Co., Our Lady of the Cedars of Lebanon, Rev. Msgr. Joseph F. Lahoud.
Res., 61 Rockwood St., 02130. Tel: 617-522-0225; Fax: 617-522-0194.

Lawrence, Essex Co., St. Anthony, Rev. Msgr. James T. Khoury; Rev. Elie Hares Mikhael.
Res., 145 Amesbury St., 01841. Tel: 617-685-7233; Fax: 978-688-4475. [CEM]

New Bedford, Bristol Co., Our Lady of Purgatory, Rev. Charbel T. Semaan.
Res., 11 Franklin St., 02740. Tel: 508-996-8934; Fax: 508-996-2744.

Springfield, Hampden Co., St. Anthony, Rev. Edward T. Nedder; Deacon Terrence O'Connell.
Mailing Address: 375 Island Pond Rd., 01118-1002.
Res., 419 Island Pond Rd., 01118-1002. Tel: 413-732-0589.

Worcester, Worcester Co., Our Lady of Mercy, Rev. Msgr. Assad Awad.
Res., 74 Mulberry St., 01605. Tel: 508-752-4287.

STATE OF NEW HAMPSHIRE

Dover, Strafford Co., St. George, Rev. Bartholomew Leon, O.S.B.
Res., 66 Portland Ave., 03820. Tel: 603-742-1149.
Church—Tel: 603-742-1149 (Rectory); 603-740-4287 (Church).

STATE OF NEW JERSEY

Somerset, Somerset Co., St. Sharbel, Rev. Maroun Asmar.
Res., 12 Reeve St., 08873. Tel: 908-828-2055; Fax: 908-828-5488.

STATE OF NORTH CAROLINA

Fayetteville, Cumberland Co., St. Michael the Archangel, Rev. John Morrison.
Res., 806 Arsenal Ave., 28305. Tel: 910-484-1531; Fax: 910-484-5387.

STATE OF PENNSYLVANIA

Carnegie, Allegheny Co., Our Lady of Victory, Revs. James A. Root; David F. Michael.
Res., 1000 Lindsay Rd., 15106. Tel: 412-278-0841; Fax: 412-278-0846.

Easton, Northampton Co., Our Lady of Lebanon, Rev. Msgr. Sami Hayek; Rev. Joseph Khoueiry.
Res., 54 S. Fourth St., 18042. Tel: 610-252-5275; Fax: 610-252-1737.

New Castle, Lawrence Co., St. John the Baptist, Rev. Kevin J. Beaton.
Res., 2 W. Reynolds St., 16101. Tel: 724-658-0787.

Newtown Square, Delaware Co., St. Sharbel, Rev. Paul Mooradd.
Res., 3679 Providence Rd., Newton Square, 19073-3006. Tel: 610-353-5952.

Philadelphia, Philadelphia Co., St. Maron, Rev. Msgr. Sharbel Lischaa; Deacon Joseph Regan.
Res., 1010 Ellsworth St., 19147. Tel: 215-389-2000.

Scranton, Lackawanna Co., St. Ann, Rev. Claude W. Franklin, Jr.
Res., 1320 Price St., 18504-3336. Tel: 570-344-2129; Fax: 570-344-3920.

Uniontown, Fayette Co., St. George, Rev. Joseph David.
Res., Lebanon Ter., 15401. Tel: 724-437-5589; Fax: 724-437-3819.

, St. Anthony. Merged with St. George, Wilkes-Barre to form St. Anthony/St. George, Wilkes-Barre.

Wilkes-Barre, Luzerne Co., St. George. Merged with St. Anthony, Wilkes-Barre to form St. Anthony/St. George, Wilkes-Barre.
St. Anthony/St. George, Rev. Fahed Azar.
Res., 79 Loomis St., 18702. Tel: 570-824-3599; Fax: 570-824-1747.

STATE OF RHODE ISLAND

Pawtucket, Providence Co., Holy Trinity-St. George, Rev. Paul Mouawad.
Res., 50 Summit St., 02860. Tel: 401-723-8444.

STATE OF VIRGINIA

Glen Allen, Henrico Co., St. Anthony, Rev. George M. Sebaali.
Res., 4611 Sadler Rd., 23060. Tel: 804-270-7234; Fax: 804-273-9914.

Roanoke, Roanoke City Co., St. Elias, Rev. Rodolph Wakim.
Res., 4730 Cove Rd., N.W., 24017. Tel: 540-562-0012; Fax: 540-562-1300.

DISTRICT OF COLUMBIA

Washington, District of Columbia, Our Lady of Lebanon Church, Chorbishop Dominic F. Ashkar.
Res., 7164 Alaska Ave., N.W., 20012. Tel: 202-829-5554.

On Duty Outside the Diocese:
Chorbishop—
Faris, John D.
Reverend Monsignors—
Beshara, Ronald N.
Reverend Fathers—
Amar, Joseph P.
Bartoul, William
Coover, Thomas
Joseph, Moussa

Unassigned:
Reverend Fathers—
Abi-Sarkis, Elias
Shaheen, Joseph

Retired:
Chorbishop—
Abi-Nader, Joseph
Saidi, Joseph
Trad, John
Most Rev.—
Tayah, Wadih B.
Zayek, Francis M.
Reverend Monsignors—
Antoun, Elie
Bistany, Joseph
Joseph, Joseph D.
Reverend Fathers—
Andary, John S.
Boackle, Paul H.
El-Hayek, Nehmatallah
Hitti, Michael
Hoyek, Elias
Mahfoud, Peter
Saad, Antoun
Thomas, Donald N.
Zogheib, Hares

Permanent Deacons:
Calabrese, Robert, Danbury, CT
Caporiccio, Richard, Springfield, MA
Joseph, Peter, Waterville, ME
Koury, Anthony, Easton, PA
Massoud, Donald, Fall River, MA
Mattar, Jean E., New Bedford, MA
Nashawaty, Nicholas, MA
Nasser, Andre, Fall River, MA
O'Connell, Terrence J., Springfield, MA
Ramey, Al, Lawrence, MA
Regan, Joseph W., Sewell, NJ
Salamy, Paul A., Utica, NY
Stone, Richard, New Castle, PA

INSTITUTIONS LOCATED IN THE DIOCESE

[A] SEMINARIES, DIOCESAN

WASHINGTON, DC. *Our Lady of Lebanon Maronite Seminary*, 7164 Alaska Ave., N.W., 20012. Tel: 202-723-8831; Fax: 202-829-6053. Chorbishop Seely Beggiani, S.T.D., Rector.

[B] CONVENTS AND RESIDENCES FOR SISTERS

NORTH BROOKFIELD, MA. *Hermits of Jesus The Eternal Priest*, P.O. Box 216, 01535. Tel: 508-867-0134.
E-mail: hjep@juno.com
Mother Elias, Supr.

[C] RELIGIOUS COMMUNITIES OF MEN

PETERSHAM, MA. *Most Holy Trinity Monastery*, 67 Dugway Rd., 01366. Tel: 978-724-3347. Revs. William J. Driscoll, O.Mar., Abbot; Giles R. Goyette, O.Mar., Vicar; Michael Cernak, O.Mar.; John Marie Choiniere, O.Mar.; Louis Marie Dauphinais, O.Mar.; Elias Havel, O.Mar.; Francis DeGuzman, O.Mar.; Maron Morgan, O.Mar.; Martin Ferland, O.Mar.; Anthony Kramer, O.Mar.; David Fitzhugh. Priests 11; Brothers 7.

[D] RESIDENCES FOR CLERGY

BROOKLYN. *Bishop's Residence*, 8070 Harbor View Ter., 11209. Chorbishop Joseph F. Kaddo.

[E] MISCELLANEOUS

BROOKLYN. *Bishops Retirement Trust Fund*, 109 Remsen St., 11201.
Order of St. Sharbel Trust Fund, 109 Remsen St., 11201.
Priest Retirement Trust Fund, 109 Remsen St., 11201.

NEW BEDFORD, MA. *Cedar Holdings, Inc.*, P.O. Box 51021, 02745-0035. Tel: 508-996-8934; Fax: 508-996-2744.

SHELBOURNE, VT. *Blessed Rafka Retreat Center*, 6420 Rte. 116, 05482-7191. Tel: 802-660-2528; Fax: 802-863-8456. Rev. Anthony Weiler.

NECROLOGY
(No Deaths)

Diocese of St. Nicholas in Chicago for Ukrainians

Most Reverend

MICHAEL WIWCHAR, C.SS.R., D.D.

Diocesan Administrator; ordained June 28, 1959; appointed Third Bishop of the St. Nicholas Diocese; installed September 28, 1993. *Mailing Address: 2245 W. Rice St., Chicago, IL, 60622.*

(Vacant See)

Chancery Office: 2245 W. Rice St., Chicago, IL, 60622. Tel.: 312-276-5080; 276-4537; Fax: 312-276-6799.

E-mail address: sneparchy@iols.com

Most Reverend

INNOCENT LOTOCKY, O.S.B.M., D.D., PH.D.

Retired Bishop of Chicago; ordained November 24, 1940; appointed Second Bishop of Chicago January 29, 1981; consecrated March 1, 1981; installed April 2, 1981; retired September 28, 1993. *Mailing Address: 2245 W. Rice St., Chicago, IL, 60622.* Tel.: 773-276-8981.

Comprises all of the United States west of the western borders of Ohio, Kentucky, Tennessee and Mississippi.

For legal titles of parishes and diocesan institutions, consult the Chancery Office.

STATISTICAL OVERVIEW

Personnel	
Bishop	1
Retired Bishops	1
Abbots	1
Retired Abbots	1
Priests: Diocesan Active in Diocese	16
Priests: Active Outside Diocese	3
Priests: Retired, Sick or Absent	7
Number of Diocesan Priests	26
Religious Priests in Diocese	13
Extern Priests in Diocese	19
Ordinations:	
Transitional Deacons	1
Permanent Deacons	2
Permanent Deacons in Diocese	12
Total Brothers	2
Total Sisters	4
Parishes	
Parishes	37
With Resident Pastor:	
Resident Diocesan Priests	23
Resident Religious Priests	3
Without Resident Pastor:	
Administered by Priests	9
Administered by Deacons	2
Missions	7
New Parishes Created	1
Educational	
Diocesan Students in Other Seminaries	3
Total Seminarians	3
High Schools, Diocesan and Parish	1
Total Students	82
Elementary Schools, Diocesan and Parish	2
Total Students	380
Catechesis/Religious Education:	
High School Students	150
Elementary Students	310
Total Students Under Catholic Instruction	925
Teachers in the Diocese:	
Sisters	4
Lay Teachers	52
Vital Statistics	
Receptions into the Church:	
Infant Baptism Totals	244
Adult Baptism Totals	10
Received into Full Communion	4
First Communions	230
Confirmations	260
Marriages:	
Catholic	56
Interfaith	18
Total Marriages	74
Deaths	240
Total Catholic Population	10,000

Former Bishops—Most Rev. JAROSLAV GABRO, D.D., appt. First Bishop of Chicago, July 12, 1961; cons. Oct. 26, 1961; died March 28, 1980.—Most Rev. INNOCENT LOTOCKY, O.S.B.M., D.D., Ph.D., ord. Nov. 24, 1940; appt. Second Bishop of Chicago, Jan. 29, 1981; cons. March 1, 1981; installed April 2, 1981; retired Sept. 28, 1993.

Protosyncellus—Very Rev. Canon WAYNE RUCHGY.

Chancellor—Rev. MYKHAILO KUZMA.

Econome—Rev. ABRAHAM MILLER.

Chancery Office—2245 W. Rice St., Chicago, IL, 60622. Tel: 773-276-5080; Fax: 773-276-6799. Office Hours: Mon.-Fri. 9-4.

Diocesan Consultors—Very Rev. Canon WAYNE RUCHGY; Very Rev. BASIL SALKOVSKI, O.S.B.M.; Revs. MYRON PANCHUK; RICHARD JANOWICZ; Very Rev. Canon MICHAEL STELMACH; Rev. MYKHAILO KUZMA.

Presbyteral Council—Most Rev. MICHAEL WIWCHAR, C.SS.R., Ex Officio; Very Rev. Canon WAYNE RUCHGY, Chm.; Revs. ABRAHAM MILLER; MYRON PANCHUK; MYKHAILO KUZMA; PAVLO HAYDA, Vice Chm. RICHARD JANOWICZ, Sec. & Treas.; Very Rev. BASIL SALKOVSKI, O.S.B.M.; Very Rev. Canon MICHAEL STELMACH; Revs. WALTER RYBICKY, O.S.B.M.; BOHDAN NALYSNYK.

Personnel Board—Most Rev. MICHAEL WIWCHAR, C.SS.R.; Very Rev. Canon WAYNE RUCHGY, Chm.; Revs. MYKHAILO KUZMA; ABRAHAM MILLER; RICHARD JANOWICZ; MYRON PANCHUK.

Tribunal—Through Special Permission of the Holy See, Local Latin Rite Tribunals Handle the Cases Within the Diocese.

Protopresbyters (Deans)—Detroit: Very Rev. BASIL SALKOVSKY, O.S.B.M., Protopresbytery; Rev. ROBERTO LUCAVEI, O.S.B.M., Vice Protopresbytery; Chicago: Rt. Rev. Mitred Archpriest IVAN KROTEC, Protopresbytery; Rev. MYKHAILO KUZMA, Vice Protopresbytery; Minneapolis: Very Rev. Canon MICHAEL STELMACH, Protopresbytery; Rev. PETER LEIGH, Vice Protopresbytery; South-West: Very Rev. RICHARD JANOWICZ, Protopresbytery; Very Rev. Canon THOMAS GLYNN, Vice Protopresbytery.

Eparchial Censor—Rev. DEMETRIUS WYSOCHANSKY, O.S.B.M.

Eparchial Catechetical Office—Rev. RICHARD L. KIROUAC, Dir., *2208 W. Chicago Ave., Chicago, IL, 60622.* Tel: 773-227-3970; Fax: 773-227-3971.

Office of Communication and Development—Rev. THEODORE WROBLICKY, Dir., *2208 W. Chicago Ave., Chicago, IL, 60622.*

Office of Stewardship—BARBARA WROBLICKY, Dir., *2208 W. Chicago Ave., Chicago, IL, 60622.*

Finance Officer—Rev. WILLIAM H. MACKINNON, S.O.L.T., *2208 W. Chicago Ave., Chicago, IL, 60622.*

CLERGY, PARISHES, MISSIONS AND PAROCHIAL SCHOOLS

STATE OF ILLINOIS

Chicago

1—ST. NICHOLAS UKRAINIAN CATHOLIC CATHEDRAL (1906) (Ukrainian), Most Rev. Michael Wiwchar, C.SS.R., Bishop; Rev. Msgr. Jaroslaw Swyschuk, Rector; Rev. Bogdan Nalysnyk, Vice Rector; Deacon Mychajlo Horodysky. In res., Revs. Richard Kirouac; Taras Miles.
Res., 2238 W. Rice St., 60622. Tel: 773-276-4537; Fax: 773-276-5558. [CEM]
School—2200 W. Rice St., 60622. Tel: 773-384-7243; Fax: 773-384-7283. Sr. Irenea Hankewych, O.S.B.M., Supr. & Prin.
Sisters 2; Lay Teachers 14; Students 176.
Convent—2230 W. Rice St., 60622. Tel: 773-486-6820. Sisters of St. Basil the Great

2—ST. JOSEPH (N.W. Chicago) (1956) (Ukrainian), Rev. Pavlo Hayda.
Res., 5000 N. Cumberland Ave., 60656. Tel: 773-625-4833; 625-4805 (Office); Fax: 773-625-4148.
Catechesis/Religious Programs—Students 60.

3—SS. VOLODYMYR AND OLHA (1968) (Ukrainian), Rt. Rev. Mitred Arch Ivan Krotec Tel: 312-455-0178; Revs. Myron Panchuk Tel: 312-666-6051; Yaroslav Mendyuk Tel: 773-384-0247; Oleh Kryvokulsky Tel: 312-455-0441; Deacon Michael Szyjan Tel: 773-252-1711.

Parish Office: 2245 W. Superior St., 60612. Tel: 312-829-5209; Fax: 312-829-4113. [JC]

4—ST. MICHAEL'S (1917) (Ukrainian), Rev. Abraham Miller, Admin.

Mailing Address: 12211 S. Parnell, 60628. Tel: 773-334-4512.

Church—2238 W. Rice St., 60622. Tel: 773-276-4537; Fax: 773-276-5558. [JC]

Madison, Madison Co., St. Mary's, Rev. Robert Piorkowski.

Res., 1312 Iowa St., 62060. Tel: 616-452-9118. [JC]

Palatine, Immaculate Conception (1963) (Ukrainian), Very Rev. Mykhailo Kuzma; Deacon Andrew Plishka.

Res., 745 S. Benton, 60067. Tel: 847-991-0820; Fax: 847-991-7873.

Catechesis/Religious Programs—Students 9.

Palos Park, Cook Co., Nativity of B. V. M. (1911) (Ukrainian), Revs. Walter Rybicky, O.S.B.M.; Demetrius Wysochansky, O.S.B.M.

Res., 8530 W. 131 St., 60464. Tel: 708-361-8876; 361-8820; Fax: 1-708-361-8820.

STATE OF ARIZONA

Phoenix, Maricopa Co., Assumption of B.V.M. (1959), Rev. Hugo Soutus.

Res., 3730 W. Maryland Ave., 85019. Tel: 602-973-3667; Fax: 602-973-3667.

Church—3720 W. Maryland Ave., 85019.

Tucson, Pima Co., St. Michael (1978) (Ukrainian), Rev. Basil Buchek.

Res., 1557 N. Brown Way, 85715-5578. Tel: 520-298-4967. [JC]

STATE OF CALIFORNIA

Los Angeles, Los Angeles Co., Nativity of B.V.M. (1947) (Ukrainian), Rev. Oleh Romanenko.

Res., 5154 De Longpre Ave., Hollywood, 90027. Tel: 323-663-6307; Fax: 323-663-0369.

Sacramento, St. Andrew the Apostle, Revs. Alex Avramenko; Theodore Wroblicky, Admin.; Volodymyr Petriv.

Res., c/o 215 Silliman, San Francisco, 94134. Tel: 415-468-2601; Fax: 415-715-0291.

San Diego, San Diego Co., Our Lady of Perpetual Help (1960) (Ukrainian), Rev. Myron Mykyta; Very Rev. Canon Michael Kurylo, Pastor Emeritus.

Res., 4061 Winona Ave., 92105. Tel: 619-282-9538; Fax: 619-282-9538.

San Francisco, San Francisco Co., Immaculate Conception (1957) (Ukrainian), Rev. Alexander Avramenko, Admin.

Res., 215 Silliman, 94134. Tel: 415-468-2601; Fax: 415-715-0291.

Santa Clara, Santa Clara Co., St. Vladimir. Attended by San Francisco. Rev. Alexander Avramenko.

Ukiah, Ukiah Co., Ukrainian Catholic Mission (1999) (Ukrainian), Rev. David Anderson.

Res., 2975 Mill Creek Rd., 95482. Tel: 707-468-4348; Fax: 707-467-0505.

STATE OF COLORADO

Denver, Denver Co., Transfiguration of Our Lord (1954) (Ukrainian), Rev. Peter Bohdanowycz; Deacon Michael Bozio, Admin.

Res., 4118 Shoshone St., 80211. Tel: 303-433-2347. [JC]

STATE OF HAWAII

Honolulu, Byzantine Missions, Rev. Thomas D. Marick.

Res., 1121 Ala Napunani, 704, HI 96818. Tel: 808-833-2472.

Waianae, St. Sophia Byzantine Missions, Rev. Philip Gregory Harmon, Admin.

Res., 86-660 Lua Lualei Homestead Rd., HI 96792. Tel: 808-696-2655; Fax: 808-696-2030.

STATE OF INDIANA

Mishawaka, St. Joseph Co., St. Michael (1962), Rev. Thomas Dobrowolski.

Res., 712 E. Lawrence St., 46544. Tel: 219-259-7173.

Munster, Lake Co., St. Josaphat (1958) (Ukrainian), Rev. John Hritzko.

Res., 8624 White Oak Ave., 46321. Tel: 219-923-0984; Fax: 219-923-0984.

STATE OF MICHIGAN

Dearborn, Wayne Co., St. Michael's (1962), Very Rev. Canon Wayne J. Ruchgy.

Res., 6340 Chase Rd., 48126. Tel: 313-582-1424; Fax: 313-582-8157.

Dearborn Heights, Wayne Co., Our Lady of Perpetual Help (1963) (Ukrainian), Very Rev. Archpriest John Lazar.

Res., 26606 Ann Arbor Trail, 48127. Tel: 313-278-0470.

Catechesis/Religious Programs—Students 20.

Detroit, Wayne Co., St. John the Baptist (1918) (Ukrainian), Rev. Volodymyr Petriv.

Res., 3877 Clippert Ave., 48210. Tel: 313-897-7300; Fax: 313-897-7304.

Hamtramck, Wayne Co., Immaculate Conception of B.V.M. (1914) (Ukrainian), Very Rev. Tarcisio Lucavei, O.S.B.M., Pastor & Supr.; Revs. Constantine Wysochansky, O.S.B.M.; Lauro Schaicoski, O.S.B.M.

Res., 11700 McDougall St., 48212. Tel: 313-893-1710; Fax: 313-893-0770.

School—29500 Westbrook, Warren, 48093. Tel: 810-574-2480; Fax: 810-574-0867. Rosemary Sobol, Prin.

Sisters 2; Lay Teachers 17; Students 238.

High School—29400 Westbrook, Warren, 48092. Tel: 810-574-0510; Fax: 810-574-2723. Michalene Weigle, Prin.

Priests 1; Lay Teachers 14; Students 81.

Catechesis/Religious Programs—Students 319.

Convent—11745 Gallagher, 48212. Tel: 313-366-2061. Sisters of St. Basil the Great Sr. Frances O.S.B.M., Supr.

Sisters 2.

Flint, Genesee Co., St. Vladimir's (1950), Rev. Volodymyr Petriv, Admin., Hamtramck, MI.

Res., c/o 3877 Clippert Ave., Detroit, 48210. Tel: 313-897-7300.

Grand Rapids, Kent Co., St. Michael's (1949) (Ukrainian), Rev. Stepan Vasyliv, Admin.; Deacons Jaroslaw Bohatch, Admin. Asst.; Russell Anthony.

Mailing Address: 4390 Woodside Oaks Dr., S.E., 49546-6216. Tel: 616-949-9597; Fax: 616-949-1151. [JC]

Warren, Macomb Co., St. Josaphat (1961) (Ukrainian), Revs. Basil Salkovski, O.S.B.M.; Sebastian Sabol, O.S.B.M.; Roman Hykavy, O.S.B.M.

Res., 26401 St. Josaphat Dr., 48091. Tel: 810-755-1740; Fax: 810-755-1399. [CEM]

STATE OF MINNESOTA

Minneapolis, Hennepin Co., St. Constantine (1913) (Ukrainian), Rev. Michael Stelmach.

Res., 515 University Ave., N.E., 55413-1944. Tel: 612-379-2394; Fax: 612-379-2470.

St. Paul, Ramsey Co., St. Stephen (1951) (Ukrainian). Attended by St. Constantine Church, Minneapolis.

Church—1260 Greenbrier St., 55106. Tel: 612-379-2394; Fax: 612-379-2470.

STATE OF MISSOURI

St. Joseph, Buchanan Co., St. Joseph's (1918) (Ukrainian). Attended by Omaha, NE. Rev. William H. MacKinnon, III, S.O.L.T., Admin.

Church—526 Virginia, 64504. Tel: 816-238-1187.

St. Louis, St. Louis Co., Assumption B.V.M. (1894) (Ukrainian), Rev. Robert Piorkowski, Admin.

Church—11363 Oak Branch Dr., 63129.

STATE OF NEBRASKA

Lincoln, Lancaster Co., St. George's (1950) (Ukrainian), Rev. William H. MacKinnon, III, S.O.L.T., Admin.

Res., 1513 Martha St., Omaha, 68108.

Church—3330 N. 13th St., 68521. Tel: 402-435-5882; 345-1552.

Omaha, Douglas Co., Assumption of B.V.M. (1950) (Ukrainian), Rev. William H. MacKinnon, III, S.O.L.T., Admin.

Res., 1513 Martha St., 68108. Tel: 402-345-1552.

STATE OF NORTH DAKOTA

Belfield, Stark Co., St. John the Baptist (1946) (Ukrainian), Rev. Yaroslaw Dowbush, Admin.
Res., P.O. Box 428, 58622-0428. Tel: 701-575-4281. [CEM]

Fairfield, Billings Co., St. Demetrius (1905) (Ukrainian), Rev. Yaroslaw Dowbush, Admin.
Res., P.O. Box 428, Belfield, 58622-0428. Tel: 701-575-4281. [CEM]

Wilton, McLean Co., SS. Peter and Paul (1890) (Ukrainian), Rev. George L. Pruys, Admin.
Res., 106 N. 7th St., P.O. Box 275, 58579. Tel: 701-734-6464. [CEM]
Catechesis/Religious Programs—Students 18.
Missions—Minot, Ward Co., St. Michael, 812 N. Main St., Minot, ND 58703. Tel: 701-839-4756; Mobridge.

STATE OF OREGON

Springfield, Lane Co., Nativity of the Mother of God (1981) (Ukrainian), Very Rev. Richard Janowicz.
Res., 704 Aspen St., 97477. Tel: 541-726-7309; Fax: 541-726-7309.

STATE OF TEXAS

Houston, Harris Co., Protection of the Mother of God (1957) (Ukrainian), Rev. Andrij Taras Dwulit, Admin.
Res., 9102 Meadowshire St., 77037. Tel: 713-447-2749; Fax: 713-447-2749. [JC]
Catechesis/Religious Programs—Students 74.

The Colony, St. Sophia Ukrainian Catholic Church (1999), Rev. Vasyl Savchyn.
Church—5600 N. Colony Blvd., 75075. Tel: 972-379-4700.
Res., St. Mark, 1201 Alma Dr., Plano, 75075. Tel: 972-509-0237.

STATE OF WISCONSIN

Milwaukee, Milwaukee Co., St. Michaels (1950) (Ukrainian), Rev. Volodymyr Zaiats.
Res., 1025 S. 11th St., P.O. Box 64012, 53204. Tel: 414-672-5616. [JC]

Chaplains of Public Institutions

Hospitals

CHICAGO, IL. *Resurrection and Our Lady of Resurrection.* 4000 Forest Dr., Delavan, WI 53115. Tel: 262-728-9930; Fax: 262-728-1020. Rev. Msgr. Canon William M. Bilinsky, Chap., Dir. of Clinical Ethics.
St. Mary of Nazareth Hospital Center. Rev. Abraham Miller, Chap.

On Duty Outside the Diocese:
Reverend Fathers—
Kassian, Jeffrey, 209 S. Brown St., Paw Paw, MI 49079. Tel: 616-657-4459
Leigh, Peter, 4032 West 10th St., Wichita, KS 67212
Very Rev.—
Klimchuk, Walter, Winnipeg, Canada

Absent on Sick Leave:
Reverend Fathers—
Prodywus, Alexander

Retired:
Reverend Fathers—
Kmech, John, Rest Haven, 16300 Wausau Ave., South Holland, IL 60473
Pedelesky, Nestor, Lakefront Health Care Center, 7618 N. Sheridan Rd., Chicago, IL. Tel: 773-743-7711
Skaskiw, Bohdan, 3805 Dora Dr., Warren, MI 48091
Rt. Rev. Mitred Arch—
Mykyta, Andrew, 2308 W.Rice St., Chicago, IL 60616
Very Rev. Canon—
Bobersky, Michael, 6209 E. McKellips, Mesa, AZ 85205. Tel: 602-985-7620
Kurylo, Michael, 3821-49th St., San Diego, CA 92105. Tel: 619-282-7958

Permanent Deacons:
Bohatch, Jaroslav, St. Michael, Grand Rapids, MI
Bozio, Michael, Transfiguration of Our Lord, Denver, CO
Chabin, Nicholas, Milwaukee, WI
Horodysky, Mychajlo, St. Nicholas Cathedral, Chicago, IL
Huskey, Michael, Christ the Redeemer, Chicago, IL
Kordonowy, Leonard, St. John the Baptist, Belfield, ND; St. Demetrius, Fairfield, ND
May, Andrew, Downers Grove, IL
Plishka, Andrew, St. Joseph, Chicago, IL
Russell, Anthony, St. Michael, Grand Rapids, MI
Szyjan, Michael, Ss. Volodymyr & Olha, Chicago, IL
Wasylyna, E., (Retired), Denver, CO

INSTITUTIONS LOCATED IN THE DIOCESE

[A] MONASTERIES

EAGLE HARBOR, MI. *Skete of Holy Transfiguration Monastery.* Society of St. John, Star Rte. 1, P.O. Box 226, 49950. Tel: 906-289-4384; Fax: 906-289-4388. Very Rev. Nicholas Glenn, Hegumen; Subdeacon Ambrose; Rev. Basil Paris. Priests 2; Professed Monks 4.

REDWOOD VALLEY, CA. *Holy Transfiguration Monastery,* 17001 Tomki Rd., 95470. Tel: 707-485-8959; Fax: 707-485-1122. Mailing Address: P.O. Box 217, 95470. Monks of Mount Tabor. Very Rev. Joseph Homick, Abbot; Rev. Theodore Zientek. Priests 4; Deacons 1; Novices 2; Professed Monks 12; Aggregates 12; Postulants 2.

RELIGIOUS INSTITUTES OF MEN REPRESENTED IN THE DIOCESE

For further details refer to the corresponding bracketed number in the Religious Institutes of Men or Women section.

[]—*Monks of Mt. Tabor.*

[0180]—*Order of St. Basil the Great.*—O.S.B.M.

[]—*Skete of Mt. Tabor.*

RELIGIOUS INSTITUTES OF WOMEN REPRESENTED IN THE DIOCESE

[3730]—*Sisters of the Order of St. Basil the Great.*—O.S.B.M.

NECROLOGY

† Leskiw, Rt. Rev. Mitred Msgr Peter, (Retired). —Died Feb. 12, 2000.

† Riotte, Rt. Rev. Mitred Msgr Jules, (Retired). —Died May 10, 2000.

Eparchy of Saint Thomas the Apostle

Most Reverend

IBRAHIM N. IBRAHIM, D.D.

First Bishop-Eparch of the Eparchy of Saint Thomas the Apostle-Chaldean Catholic Diocese of America; ordained December 30, 1962; appointed Chaldean Apostolic Exarch and Titular Bishop of Anbar January 26, 1982; consecrated Bishop March 7, 1982 in Baghdad, Iraq; installed April 18, 1982 in Detroit; appointed First Bishop Eparch to the Eparchy of Saint Thomas the Apostle-Chaldean Catholic Diocese of America September 14, 1985. *Res., Chaldean Catholic Diocese of U.S.A., 25603 Berg Rd., Southfield, MI, 48034.*

Chancery Office: 25603 Berg Rd., Southfield, MI, 48034. Tel.: 248-351-0440; Fax: 248-351-0443.

E-mail address: Cryst96@aol.com

EXARCHATE ERECTED JANUARY 26, 1982. ELEVATED TO THE RANK OF EPARCHY SEPTEMBER 14, 1985.

The Jurisdiction of the Eparchy extends territorially to all of the United States of America inclusive. With regard to persons, its subjects are all Catholics of the Chaldean or Assyrian-Chaldean Church: (1) Who immigrated to this country from the Middle East, especially from Iraq and Iran; (2) Who descends from such persons (can. 755); (3) Women married to men referable to (1) & (2) if they comply with can. 98, n. 4; (4) Who in accordance with can. 98, n. 3., changed their Rite; (5) Converts to the Catholic Church of the Chaldean Rite; (6) And in fact, all other Catholics of the Chaldean Rite who are attached to the parishes subject to the jurisdiction of the Eparch.

For legal titles of parishes and diocesan institutions, consult the Chancery Office.

STATISTICAL OVERVIEW

Personnel	
Bishop	1
Priests: Diocesan Active in Diocese	17
Priests: Active Outside Diocese	2
Priests: Diocesan in Foreign Missions	2
Priests: Retired, Sick or Absent	1
Number of Diocesan Priests	22
Parishes	
Parishes	13
With Resident Pastor:	
Resident Diocesan Priests	12
Without Resident Pastor:	
Administered by Priests	1
Welfare	
Homes for the Aged	3
Educational	
Diocesan Students in Other Seminaries	1
Total Seminarians	1
Catechesis/Religious Education:	
Total Students Under Catholic Instruction	1
Vital Statistics	
Receptions into the Church:	
Infant Baptism Totals	1,078
Adult Baptism Totals	3
First Communions	1,029
Marriages:	
Catholic	381
Interfaith	24
Total Marriages	405
Deaths	191
Total Catholic Population	85,800

Chancery Office—25603 Berg Rd., Southfield, MI, 48034. Tel: 248-351-0440; Fax: 248-351-0443.

Vicar General—Rt. Rev. SARHAD Y. JAMMO, *2442 E. Big Beaver Rd., Troy, MI, 48083.* Tel: 248-528-3676; Fax: 248-524-1957.

Eparchial College of Consultors—Rt. Rev. SARHAD Y. JAMMO, Vicar Gen.; Revs. MANUEL BOJI; STEPHEN KALLABAT; HANNA CHEIKHO; JACOB YASSO; MICHAEL BAZZI; KAMAL BIDAWID; YOSHIA SANA; EMANUEL ISHO; NOEL GORGIS; EMANUEL RAYES; FRANK KALABAT.

Diocesan Corporation-The Chaldean Catholic Church of U.S.A.—Most Rev. IBRAHIM N. IBRAHIM, D.D., Pres.; Revs. MANUEL Y. BOJI, Sec. SARHAD Y. JAMMO, Treas.

Diocesan Bulletin—"The Star of Chaldeans", 25603 Berg Rd., Southfield, MI, 48034. Tel: 248-351-0440.

Eparchial Tribunal—Rev. STEPHEN H. KALLABAT, *Court of the First Instance, Chancery Office, 25603 Berg Rd., Southfield, MI, 48034.*

CLERGY, PARISHES, MISSIONS AND PAROCHIAL SCHOOLS

STATE OF MICHIGAN

Detroit, Wayne Co., Sacred Heart Chaldean Parish (1973), Rev. Jacob O. Yasso.
Res., 310 W. Seven Mile Rd., 48203. Tel: 313-368-6214 (Church); Fax: 313-891-0132.
Catechesis/Religious Programs—Tel: 248-548-0066.
Students 140.
Convent—19138 Danbury, 48203. Tel: 313-368-7999. Chaldean Sisters

Oak Park, Oakland Co., Mar Addai Chaldean Parish (1979) (Chaldean), Revs. Stephen Kallabat; Suleiman Denha.
Res., 24010 Coolidge Hwy., 48237. Tel: 248-547-4648; Fax: 248-399-9089.
Catechesis/Religious Programs—Students 215.

Southfield, Oakland Co., Our Lady of Chaldeans Cathedral, Mother of God Chaldean Parish (1948), Most Rev. Ibrahim Ibrahim; Revs. Manuel Y. Boji, Rector; Frank Y. Kalabat.
Res., 25585 Berg Rd., 48034. Tel: 248-356-0565; 356-0569; 356-9809 (Hall); Fax: 248-356-5235.
Catechesis/Religious Programs—Tel: 248-356-2448. Joyce Appelt, D.R.E.
Students 170.
Convent—23754 Clarkson, 48034. Tel: 248-355-1318. Chaldean Sisters
Chaldean Manor Housing for Elders—(Middle Age & up) 25775 Berg Rd., 48034. Tel: 248-355-9491.

Troy, Oakland Co., St. Joseph Chaldean Parish (1981), Rt. Rev. Sarhad Jammo; Revs. Emanuel Rayes; Jirjis Abrahim.
Res., 2442 E. Big Beaver Rd., 48083. Tel: 248-528-3676; 524-1144 (Church); Fax: 248-524-1957.
Catechesis/Religious Programs—Students 240.
Convent—2554 Parasol, 48083. Tel: 248-740-2741. Chaldean Sisters
Mission—Flint, Genesee Co., (1993).

West Bloomfield, Oakland Co., St. Thomas Chaldean Catholic Parish (1992) (Chaldean), Rev. John Hanna Cheikho.
Mailing Address: 6900 Maple Rd., 48322. Tel: 248-788-2460; Fax: 248-788-2153.
Res., 6900 Maple Rd., 48322. Tel: 248-788-2460.
Catechesis/Religious Programs—Students 120.

STATE OF ILLINOIS

Chicago, Cook Co., St. Ephrem's Church (1904) (Chaldean-Assyrian), Rev. Msgr. Edward J. Bikoma.
Res., 2537 W. Bryn Mawr Ave., 60659-4996. Tel: 773-271-8899; Fax: 773-271-8866. [JC]
Catechesis/Religious Programs—Students 60.

Mart Mariam Parish (1986) (Chaldean-Assyrian), Rev. Msgr. Edward J. Bikoma.
Mailing Address: 2537 W. Bryn Mawr, 60659. Tel: 773-271-8899; Fax: 773-271-8866.
Res., 2847 W. Chase Ave., 60645. Tel: 773-761-9401; Fax: 773-271-8866. [JC]
Catechesis/Religious Programs—Students 160.

STATE OF CALIFORNIA

El Cajon, St. Michael Chaldean Catholic Church,
Church—799 E. Washington Ave., 92020. Tel: 619-444-9911; Fax: 619-444-7989. Rev. Sabri A. Iskander.

St. Peter Chaldean Parish, San Diego Co., (1973) (Chaldean), Rev. Michael J. Bazzi; Najib Konja, Parish Council Pres.
Res., 1627 Jamacha Way, 92019. Tel: 619-579-7913; 588-9921; Fax: 619-588-8281.
Catechesis/Religious Programs—Tel: 619-579-7913. Khelood Allos, D.R.E.
Students 710.
Convent—1591 Jamacha Way, 92019. Tel: 619-447-4842. Chaldean Sisters

North Hollywood, Los Angeles Co., St. Paul Assyrian-Chaldean Catholic Parish (1980), Revs. Noel Gorgis; Poulos Ghozairan.
Res., 13050 Vanowen St., 91605. Tel: 818-765-3665; Fax: 818-765-0493.
Mission—Placentia, Orange Co., St. George, 451 W. Madison, Placentia, 92632.

San Jose, Santa Clara Co., St. Mary Assyrian-Chaldean Parish (1987), Rev. Yoshia Sana.
Church & Rectory: 109 N. First St., Campbell, 95008. Tel: 408-378-6212. [JC]
Catechesis/Religious Programs—Students 50.

Turlock, Stanislaus Co., St. Thomas Assyrian-Chaldean Parish, Rev. Kamal Warda Bidawid.
Res., 2901 N. Berkeley Ave., 95380. Tel: 209-668-4500; Fax: 209-668-2762.
Convent—2937 N. Berkeley Ave., 95380. Tel: 209-634-2043. Chaldean Sisters
St. Thomas Retirement Center—Tel: 209-634-7252.

STATE OF ARIZONA

Scottsdale, Maricopa Co., Mar Auraha Chaldean Catholic Parish (1992), Rev. Noel Gorgis, Admin.
Res., 6816 E. Cactus Rd., 85254. Tel: 480-596-6798; Fax: 480-596-9067.
Catechesis/Religious Programs—Students 60.

On Assignment Outside the Diocese:
Reverend Fathers—
Buffington, Jon
Yadegar, Benn Beth

Retired:
Reverend Fathers—
Ablahad, Najor, 28454 Red Leaf, Southfield, MI 48076. Tel: 248-569-5736

INSTITUTIONS LOCATED IN THE DIOCESE

RELIGIOUS INSTITUTE OF WOMEN IN THE EPARCHY

Institute of Sisters: Daughters of Mary Immaculate, founded in 1922 in Baghdad, Iraq. Convents in Detroit, Troy and Southfield, MI; Turlock, and San Diego, CA.

NECROLOGY

(No Deaths)

Ukrainian Catholic Diocese of Stamford

Most Reverend

BASIL H. LOSTEN, D.D., S.T.L., LL.D. (HON.)

Bishop of Stamford; ordained June 10, 1957; appointed Titular Bishop of Arcadiopolis and Auxiliary of Ukrainian Catholic Archeparchy of Philadelphia March 15, 1971; consecrated May 25, 1971; appointed Apostolic Administrator of Archeparchy of Philadelphia June 8, 1976; transferred to the Stamford See September 20, 1977. *Res., 161 Glenbrook Rd., Stamford, CT, 06902.*

ESTABLISHED AUGUST 8, 1956.

The jurisdiction of the Bishop of Stamford extends territorially throughout all of New York State and the New England States. With regard to persons, his subjects are all members of the Ukrainian Catholic Church (Byzantine Rite), irrespective of where they received Baptism.

For legal titles of parishes and diocesan institutions, consult the Chancery Office.

Chancery Office: 14 Peveril Rd., Stamford, CT, 06902-3019. Tel.: 203-324-7698; Fax: 203-967-9948.

E-mail address: BASILEOS@aol.com

STATISTICAL OVERVIEW

Personnel	
Bishop	1
Priests: Diocesan Active in Diocese	20
Priests: Retired, Sick or Absent	10
Number of Diocesan Priests	30
Religious Priests in Diocese	12
Extern Priests in Diocese	30
Ordinations:	
Transitional Deacons	2
Permanent Deacons in Diocese	5
Total Brothers	5
Total Sisters	38
Parishes	
Parishes	51
With Resident Pastor:	
Resident Diocesan Priests	40
Resident Religious Priests	5
Without Resident Pastor:	
Administered by Priests	6
Missions	4
Pastoral Centers	1
Welfare	
Homes for the Aged	1
Total Assisted	28
Day Care and Extended Day Care Centers	1
Total Assisted	44
Special Centers for Social Services	2
Total Assisted	250
Educational	
Seminaries, Diocesan	1
Students from Other Diocese	28
Diocesan Students in Other Seminaries	1
Total Seminarians	1
High Schools, Diocesan and Parish	1
Total Students	165
Elementary Schools, Diocesan and Parish	3
Total Students	331
Catechesis/Religious Education:	
High School Students	359
Elementary Students	795
Total Students Under Catholic Instruction	1,651
Teachers in the Diocese:	
Priests	6
Sisters	4
Lay Teachers	29
Vital Statistics	
Receptions into the Church:	
Infant Baptism Totals	213
Adult Baptism Totals	3
Received into Full Communion	5
First Communions	168
Confirmations	219
Marriages:	
Catholic	50
Interfaith	10
Total Marriages	60
Deaths	350
Total Catholic Population	15,501

Former Bishops—Most Rev. AMBROSE SENYSHYN, O.S.B.M., D.D., installed as first Bishop of Stamford, Dec. 15, 1956; transferred to the Archeparchy of Philadelphia, Oct. 26, 1961; died Sept. 11, 1976.—Most Rev. JOSEPH M. SCHMONDIUK, D.D., Bishop of Stamford, Nov. 9, 1961; transferred to the Archeparchy of Philadelphia, Sept. 20, 1977; died Dec. 25, 1978.

Chancery Office—14 Peveril Rd., Stamford, CT, 06902-3019. Tel: 203-324-7698; Fax: 203-967-9948. Office Hours: 9-5.

Vicar General—Very Rev. PATRICK PASCHAK, O.S.B.M., V.G.

Econome—Rt. Rev. Mitred Msgr. JOHN TERLECKY.

Chancellor & Archivist—Rev. Msgr. LEON A. MOSKO.

Vice Chancellor—Rev. IHOR MIDZAK.

Secretary—OKSANA DRAGAN.

Notary Public—OLGA KROHLEY.

Diocesan Consultors—Very Rev. PATRICK PASCHAK, O.S.B.M., V.G.; Rt. Rev. Mitred Msgr. JOHN TERLECKY; Rev. Msgr. LEON MOSKO; Rev. JAROSLAW NALYSNYK; Rev. VLADIMIR MARUSCEAC; Rev. IHOR MIDZAK.

Diocesan Tribunal—14 Peveril Rd., Stamford, CT, 06902-3019. Tel: 203-324-7698.

Vicar Judicial—Rt. Rev. Archimandrite Msgr. VICTOR POSPISHIL, J.C.D., S.E.O.D.

Judges—Rev. Msgr. GEORGE BINKOWSKI, B.S., M.S., B.D.; Rev. PAUL LUNIW.

Defender of the Bond—"Ad Hoc" Appointment.

Notaries—Rev. MARK HIRNIAK.

Diocesan Protopresbyters (Deans)—Albany: Rev. VLADIMIR MARUSCEAC, Acting Dean; Boston: Rev. JAROSLAW NALYSNYK, Acting Dean; Brooklyn: Rev. Msgr. GEORGE BINKOWSKI, B.S., M.S., B.D., Buffalo: Very Rev. MARIJAN PROCYK, Hartford: Rev. PAUL LUNIW, Dean; New York: Rev. PHILIP WEINER, Acting Dean; Syracuse: Very Rev. JEFFREY A.G. RODEGHERO, Dean.

Presbyteral Council—Most Rev. BASIL LOSTEN; Very Rev. PATRICK PASCHAK, O.S.B.M., V.G.; Rev. Msgr. LEON MOSKO; Very Rev. MARIJAN PROCYK; Rev. MICHAEL BUNDZ; Rev. IVAN KASZCZAK; Very Rev. EDWARD YOUNG, B.A., S.T.B.; Rev. IVAN MAZURYK; Rev. Canon LUBOMYR MUDRY; Rt. Rev. Mitred Msgr. JOHN TERLECKY, B.A., M.A., M.L.S.

Diocesan Offices and Directors

All offices are located at the following address unless otherwise noted., 14 Peveril Rd., Stamford, CT, 06902-3019. Tel: 203-325-2116; Fax: 203-967-9948

Administrative Council—Most Rev. BASIL H. LOSTEN; Very Rev. PATRICK PASCHAK, O.S.B.M., V.G.; Rev. Msgr. LEON MOSKO; Rt. Rev. Mitred Msgr. JOHN TERLECKY; Revs. IVAN KASZCZAK; ZBIGNIEW BRZEZIKI; IHOR MIDZAK.

Apostolate—Vacant.

Apostleship of Prayer—Rev. MARIJAN PROCYK.

Catechetics (Heritage Schools)—Rev. IHOR MIDZAK, S.T.B.

Cemeteries—Directors: Most Rev. BASIL H. LOSTEN, Pres. & Chm.; Rev. ZBIGNIEW BRZEZICKI, Exec. Dir.; Rev. Msgr. LEON MOSKO, Sec.; Very Rev. PATRICK PASCHAK, O.S.B.M., V.G.; Rt. Rev. Mitred Msgr. JOHN TERLECKY; Mr. LOUIS NIGRO; Mr. JOHN SENKO; Mr. ROMAN KOZICKY, ESQ., *Holy Spirit Ukrainian Catholic Cemetery, 141 Sarah Wells Trail, Campbell Hall, NY, 10916.* Tel: 914-496-5506.

Censors—Very Rev. Archpriest EDWARD YOUNG; Rev. JONATHAN MORSE, Ph.D.

Communications—Rev. Msgr. LEON MOSKO.

Development Office—Ms. ALEXANDRA LENCYK.

Diaconate, Permanent—Deacon WILLIS HOMICK.

Diocesan Charities and Missions—Most Rev. BASIL H. LOSTEN.

Ecumenical Commission—Most Rev. BASIL H. LOSTEN; Revs. MIHAI DUBOVICI; THEODOSIUS ILNICKI, O.S.B.M., J.C.L.; Very Rev. EDWARD YOUNG.

Educational Institutions—Most Rev. BASIL H. LOSTEN; Revs. JAMES MORRIS; JEFFREY A.G. RODEGHERO; Sr. MICHELE YAKYMOVITCH, S.S.M.I.; Rev. Msgr. GEORGE BINKOWSKI, B.S., B.D., M.S., Supt. of Diocesan Schools.

Family Life—Rev. JONATHAN MORSE.

Holy Name Societies—Rev. PHILIP WEINER.

League of Ukrainian Catholics—Rev. MIROSLAW JATSIV, Spiritual Dir. (New England); Very Rev. MARIJAN PROCYK, Spiritual Dir. (New York).

Liturgical Commission—Rev. Msgr. LEON MOSKO; Rev. Msgr. PETER SKRINCOSKY; Rev. PHILIP WEINER.

Missionaries, Diocesan—Revs. PHILIP SANDRICK, O.S.B.M.; BERNARD PANCZUK, O.S.B.M.

Ukrainian Diocesan Museum—WASYL LENCYK, Ph.D., Dir. LUBOW WOLYNETZ, Curator.

Ukrinian Diocesan Library and Research Center—Rt. Rev. Mitred Msgr. JOHN TERLECKY, Dir.; Mrs. LUBOW WOLYNETZ, Librarian Archivist.

Press, Diocesan: "The Sower"—Rev. Msgr. LEON MOSKO, English Editor; Rev. MYROSLAVA ROZDOLSKA, Ukrainian Editor; WASYL LENCYK, Ph.D., Contributing Editor.

Priests' Benevolent Association—Rt. Rev. Mitred Msgr. JOHN TERLECKY.

Religious Communities, Vicar—Very Rev. PATRICK PASCHAK, O.S.B.M., V.G.

Religious Education—Rev. JONATHAN MORSE.

Sodalities, B.V.M.—Rev. STEPHEN YANOWSKI.

Ukrainian Catholic Relief, Inc.—Rev. JONATHAN MORSE.

Ukrainian Library & Research Center—Mrs. LUBOW WOLYNETZ, Dir., *39 Clovelly Rd., Stamford, CT, 06902.* Tel: 203-324-7698; Fax: 203-967-9948.

Vocations—Rev. IVAN KASZCZAK.

Youth Apostolate—Rev. JONATHAN MORSE.

Youth-For-Christ Association—Sr. NATALYA STOCZANYN, S.S.M.I.

CLERGY, PARISHES, MISSIONS AND PAROCHIAL SCHOOLS

STATE OF CONNECTICUT

Stamford, Fairfield Co., St. Vladimir Cathedral (1916) (Ukrainian), Rt. Rev. Mitred Msgr John Terlecky.
Res., 24 Wenzel Ter., 06902. Tel: 203-324-0242; Fax: 203-316-8284.
Catechesis/Religious Programs—Priests 1; Lay Teachers 2; Students 27.

Ansonia, New Haven Co., SS. Peter and Paul (1897) (Ukrainian), Rev. Miroslaw Jatsiv.
Res., 105 Clifton Ave., 06401. Tel: 203-734-3895; Fax: 203-732-3191. [CEM]

Bridgeport, Fairfield Co., Protection of B.V.M. (1950) (Ukrainian), Rev. Stepan Yanovski.
Church—Holy Protection of B.V.M. Ukrainian Catholic Church, 457 Noble Ave., 06608. Tel: 203-367-5054.
Res., 255 Barnum Ave., 06608. Tel: 203-367-5054.

Colchester, New London Co., St. Mary Dormition (1948) (Ukrainian), Rev. Ihor Papka.
Res., 178 Linwood Ave., 06415. Tel: 860-537-2069. [CEM]

Glastonbury, Hartford Co., St. John The Baptist (1925) (Ukrainian). Attended by St. Michael's, Hartford. Rev. Paul Luniw.
Church—26 New London Tpke., 06033.
Res., 135 Wethersfield Ave., Hartford, 06114. Tel: 860-525-7823; Fax: 860-548-1049.

Hartford, Hartford Co., St. Michael (1907) (Ukrainian), Rev. Paul Luniw.
Church—125 Wethersfield Ave., 06114.
Res., 135 Wethersfield Ave., 06114. Tel: 860-525-7823; Fax: 860-548-1049. [CEM]
Saturday Ukrainian School—Tel: 860-728-8792.
Priests 1; Lay Teachers 11; Students 89.

New Britain, Hartford Co., St. Josaphat (1951) (Ukrainian), Rev. Stepan Bereza.
Res., 303 Eddy Glover Blvd., 06053. Tel: 860-225-7340; Fax: 860-229-5490.
Catechesis/Religious Programs—Priests 1; Lay Teachers 2; Students 25.

New Haven, St. Michael (1909) (Ukrainian), Rev. Ihor Midzak.
Res., 569 George St., 06511. Tel: 203-865-0388; Fax: 203-752-0327.
St. Michaels Ukrainian Heritage School—(Saturdays).
Saturday Nursery School—Myron Melnyk, Prin.
Priests 1; Lay Teachers 5; Students 25.

Terryville, Litchfield Co., St. Michael (1910) (Ukrainian), Rev. Robert J. Smolley.
Res., 35 Allen St., 06786. Tel: 860-583-7588; Fax: 860-582-8064. [CEM]
Catechesis/Religious Programs—Tel: 860-582-1850. Frank Dziubek, D.R.E.
Priests 1; Lay Teachers 4; Students 10.

Willimantic, Windham Co., Protection of B.V.M. (1950) (Ukrainian), Rev. Pawlo Martyniuk, Admin.
Res., 69 Oak St., 06226. Tel: 860-423-5031; Fax: 860-423-5031.

STATE OF MASSACHUSETTS

Boston, Suffolk Co., Christ the King (1968), Rev. Jaroslaw Nalysnyk, Admin.
Res., 146 Forest Hills St., Jamaica Plain, 02130. Tel: 617-522-9720; Fax: 617-983-0309. [CEM]
Saturday Ukrainian School—.
Priests 1; Lay Teachers 3; Students 40.
Catechesis/Religious Programs—Priests 1; Lay Teachers 2; Students 25.

Fall River, Bristol Co., St. John-the-Baptist (1914). Attended by Woonsocket, RI. Rev. Msgr. Roman Golemba.
Church—339 Center St., 02724. Tel: 508-673-2353; Fax: 401-762-2733.
Res., 394 Blackstone St., Woonsocket, RI 02895. Tel: 401-762-2733. [JC]

Ludlow, Hampden Co., SS. Peter and Paul (1912)(1924) (Ukrainian), Rev. Kiril Angelov.
Res., 45 Newbury St., 01056. Tel: 413-583-2140.
Catechesis/Religious Programs—Priests 1; Students 14.

Pittsfield, Berkshire Co., St. John the Baptist (1921) (Ukrainian), Rev. Jaroslaw Kostyk.
Res., Tel: 518-828-5226; Fax: 518-828-6749.

Salem, Essex Co., St. John the Baptist (1918) (Ukrainian), Rev. James Morris, Admin.
Mailing Address: P.O. Box 206, 01970-0206. Tel: 978-745-3151.
Church—124 Bridge St., 01970.
Catechesis/Religious Programs—Tel: 617-599-8138.
Students 7.

South Deerfield, Franklin Co., Holy Ghost (1920) (Ukrainian), Rev. Kiril Angelov.
Res., 44 Sugarloaf St., 01373. Tel: 413-665-3880.
Catechesis/Religious Programs—Priests 1; Lay Teachers 2; Students 15.

STATE OF NEW HAMPSHIRE

Manchester, Hillsboro Co., Protection of B.V.M. (1908) (Ukrainian), Rev. Joseph Lazor.
Church—54 Walnut St., 03104. Tel: 603-622-0034; Fax: 603-642-8961.
Res., 2 Partridge Ln., East Kingston, 03827. Tel: 603-642-5865.
Catechesis/Religious Programs—Priests 1; Lay Teachers 6; Students 32.

STATE OF NEW YORK

Amsterdam, Montgomery Co., St. Nicholas (1909) (Ukrainian), Rev. Marian Kostyk.
Res., 24 Pulaski St., 12010. Tel: 518-842-8731; Fax: 518-842-1384. [CEM]

Auburn, Cayuga Co., SS. Peter and Paul (1901) (Ukrainian), Rev. Robert Batcho.
Res., 132 Washington St., 13021. Tel: 315-252-5573; Fax: 315-252-7469.
School—(Grades K-8). Tel: 315-252-5567. Sr. M. Boniface, O.S.B.M., Prin.
Lay Teachers 8; Students 135.
Catechesis/Religious Programs—Lay Teachers 3; Students 30.

Bath, Steuben Co., Christ the King. Closed. For inquiries for parish records contact the Chancery.

Bronx, Bronx Co., St. Mary Protectress (1943) (Ukrainian), Rev. Mauricio Popadiuk, O.S.B.M.
Church—1745 Washington Ave., 10457. Tel: 718-731-9392.
Res., East Beach Dr., Glen Cove, 11542. Tel: 516-671-0545; Fax: 516-676-7465. [JC]

Brooklyn, Kings Co., Holy Ghost (1913) (Ukrainian), Rev. Paul Wolensky.
Church—160 N. 5th St., 11211. Tel: 718-782-9592; Fax: 718-599-2905.
Mailing Address: 161 N. Fifth St., 11211.

St. Nicholas (1916) (Ukrainian), Rev. Wolodymyr Kucaj, Admin.
256 19th St., 11215. Tel: 718-389-8744.

Buffalo, Erie Co., St. Nicholas (1894) (Ukrainian), Very Rev. Marijan Procyk.
Res., 308 Fillmore Ave., 14206. Tel: 716-852-7566; Fax: 716-855-1319.
Catechesis/Religious Programs—Elaine P. Nowadly, D.R.E.
Priests 1.

Cohoes, Albany Co., SS. Peter and Paul (1907) (Ukrainian), Rev. Vladimir Marusceac.
Res., 198 Ontario St., 12047. Tel: 518-237-0535; Fax: 518-237-2397.

Elmira Heights, Chemung Co., St. Nicholas (1895) (Ukrainian), Rev. Janusz Jedrychowski.
Res., 410 E. McCanns Blvd., 14903. Tel: 607-734-1221; Fax: 607-737-7569.
Catechesis/Religious Programs—Irene Moffe, D.R.E.
Priests 1; Lay Teachers 6; Students 24.

Fresh Meadows, Queens Co., Annunciation of the B.V.M. (1957) (Ukrainian), Rev. Msgr. George Binkowski.
Res., 48-26 171st St., 11365. Tel: 718-939-4116; Fax: 718-939-3696.

Glen Spey, Sullivan Co., St. Volodymyr (1961) (Ukrainian), Rev. Oleska Kostyk.
Res., 2105 Rte. 41, 12737-5618. Tel: 914-856-5500. [JC]

Hamptonburgh, Orange Co., St. Andrew's (1983) (Ukrainian), Rev. Zbigniew Brzezicki.
Res., 141 Sarah Wells Tr., Campbell Hall, 10916. Tel: 914-496-5506.
Catechesis/Religious Programs—Priests 1; Lay Teachers 1; Students 4.

Hempstead, Nassau Co., St. Vladimir (1944) (Ukrainian), Very Rev. Maxim Kobasuk, O.S.B.M.
Res., 709 Front St., 11550. Tel: 516-481-7717; Fax: 516-481-3435.
Parish Center: 226 Uniondale Ave., Uniondale, 11553. Tel: 516-485-0775.
Saturday Ukrainian School—.
Priests 1; Lay Teachers 8; Students 36.
Catechesis/Religious Programs—Priests 1; Lay Teachers 7; Students 38.

Hudson, Columbia Co., St. Nicholas (1923) (Ukrainian), Rev. Jaroslaw Kostyk.
Res., 29 S. Second St., 12534. Tel: 518-828-5226; Fax: 518-828-6749.

Hunter, Greene Co., St. John the Baptist (1962) (Ukrainian). Administered from Holy Trinity Parish, R.R. 1, Box 129 Foordmore Rd., Kerhonkson, NY 12446, 914-626-2864.

Johnson City, Broome Co., Sacred Heart Ukrainian Catholic Church (1944) (Ukrainian), Rev. Ivan Mazyryk.
Res., 230 Ukrainian Hill Rd., 13790. Tel: 607-797-6293; Fax: 607-797-6293. [CEM]
Saturday Ukrainian School—Tel: 607-798-9148.
Lay Teachers 3; Students 11.
Catechesis/Religious Programs—Tel: 607-723-7660. Christina Litwak, D.R.E.
Lay Teachers 4; Students 36.

Kenmore, Erie Co., St. John the Baptist (1904) (Ukrainian), Rev. Stepan Kuklich.
Res., 3275 Elmwood Ave., 14217. Tel: 716-873-5011; Fax: 716-871-8804.

Kerhonkson, Ulster Co., Holy Trinity (1965) (Ukrainian), Rev. Iura Godenciuc.
Mailing Address: 211 Foordmore Rd., 12446.
Church—211 Foordmore Rd., 12446. Tel: 914-626-2864.
Saturday Ukrainian School—.
Priests 1; Lay Teachers 2; Students 12.

Lackawanna, Erie Co., Our Lady of Perpetual Help (1925) (Ukrainian), Rev. Wasyl Hrynkiw.
Res., 1182 Ridge Rd., 14218. Tel: 716-823-6182; Fax: 716-823-6550.
Catechesis/Religious Programs—D.R.E.: Annette M. Nayda; Maria Slabyk.
Priests 1; Lay Teachers 2; Students 8.

Lancaster, Erie Co., St. Basil (1921) (Ukrainian), Rev. Robert Moreno.
Res., 12 Embry Pl., 14086. Tel: 716-683-0313; Fax: 716-651-9873.
Church—3657 Walden Ave., 14086.

Little Falls, Herkimer Co., St. Nicholas (1912). Attended by Amsterdam. Rev. Marian Kostyk.
Res., 150 Furnace St., 13365. Tel: 315-823-4474.

Long Island City, Queens Co., Holy Cross (1944) (Ukrainian), Rev. Theodosius Ilnicki, O.S.B.M.; Very Rev. Chistopher Woytyna, O.S.B.M., Prov.
Res., 31-12 30th St., 11106. Tel: 718-932-4060.
Catechesis/Religious Programs—Priests 2; Religious 1; Lay Teachers 3; Students 21.

New York, New York Co., St. George (1905) (Ukrainian), Revs. Mario Daechen, O.S.B.M.; Lawrence Lawryniuk, O.S.B.M.; Patrick Paschak, O.S.B.M.; Taras Prokopiw, O.S.B.M.; Bro. Emil Turko, O.S.B.M.
Res., 30 E. Seventh St., 10003. Tel: 212-674-1615; Fax: 212-475-7017.
School—215 E. Sixth St., 10003. Tel: 212-473-3130; Fax: 917-534-0819. Sr. Gabriel O.S.B.M., Prin.
Sisters of St. Basil the Great 2; Lay Teachers 7; Students 120.
High School—Tel: 212-473-3323.
Sisters 1; Lay Teachers 11; Students 160.

Niagara Falls, Niagara Co., Protection of B.V.M. (1920) (Ukrainian), Rev. Demetrius Laptuta, C.SS.R.
Res., 2713 Ferry Ave., 14301. Tel: 716-284-7066; Fax: 716-282-6902.

Ozone Park, Queens Co., St. Mary Protectress (1954) (Ukrainian), Rev. Vasile Tivadar.
Res., 97-06 87th St., 11416. Tel: 718-845-5366.

Riverhead, Suffolk Co., St. John the Baptist (1924) (Ukrainian), Rev. Ihor Tarasiw.
Res., 820 Pond View Rd., 11901. Tel: 631-727-2766; Fax: 631-727-4141. [CEM]
Church—Franklin St., 11901.

Rochester, Monroe Co., St. Josaphat (1909) (Ukrainian), Very Rev. Archpriest Edward P. Young; Rev. Volodymyr Piso; Deacon Stepan Bilyk.
Res., 940 Ridge Road E., 14621. Tel: 716-467-6457; Fax: 716-467-7296.
School—95 Stanton Ln., 14621. Tel: 716-266-8700; Fax: 716-266-8837. Sr. Bernitta Dub, S.S.M.I., Prin.
Priests 2; Sisters Servants of Mary Immaculate 2; Lay Teachers 14; Students 80.
Catechesis/Religious Programs—Lay Teachers 9; Students 55.
Convent—910 Ridge Rd. E., 14621. Tel: 716-266-1540.

Epiphany of Our Lord (1958) (Ukrainian), Rev. Vasile Godenciuc.
Res., 202 Carter St., 14621. Tel: 716-266-4036; Fax: 716-323-9691. [JC]

Rome, Oneida Co., St. Michael (1914) (Ukrainian). Attended by St. Vladimir, Utica. Rev. Michael Bundz.
Res., 296 Genessee St., Utica, 13502. Tel: 315-735-5138; Fax: 315-735-0443.
Church—133 River St., 13440. [CEM]

Spring Valley, Rockland Co., SS. Peter and Paul (1913) (Ukrainian), Rev. Ivan Tykhovytch.
Res., 41 Collins Ave., 10977. Tel: 914-356-1634; Fax: 914-425-2749.

Catechesis/Religious Programs—Tel: 201-529-4208. Irene Gojdycz, D.R.E.
Lay Teachers 3; Students 14.

Staten Island, Richmond Co., Holy Trinity (1949) (Ukrainian), Rev. Wolodymyr Kucaj.
Res., 288 Vanderbilt Ave., 10304. Tel: 718-442-2555.

Syracuse, Onondaga Co., St. John the Baptist (1900), Very Rev. Jeffery A.G. Roderhero.
Res., 207 Tompkins St., 13204. Tel: 315-478-5109; Fax: 315-471-9867.
Catechesis/Religious Programs—Priests 1; Lay Teachers 9; Students 50.

Troy, Rensselaer Co., Protection of B.V.M. (1952) (Ukrainian). Attended by SS. Peter and Paul, Cohoes. Rev. Vladimir Marusceac.
Res., 198 Ontario St., Cohoes, 12047. Tel: 518-237-0535; Fax: 518-237-2397. [JC]
Church—459 Second St., 12180. Tel: 518-274-5318.

Utica, Oneida Co., St. Volodymyr the Great (1950) (Ukrainian), Rev. Michael Bundz, Admin.
Res., 296 Genessee St., 13502. Tel: 315-735-5138; Fax: 315-735-0443. [CEM]
Saturday Ukrainian School—.
Priests 1; Lay Teachers 1; Students 8.

Watervliet, Albany Co., St. Nicholas (1905) (Ukrainian), Rev. Mikhail Myshchuk.
Res., 2410-4th Ave., 12189. Tel: 518-273-6752; Fax: 518-273-4456. [CEM][JC]

Saturday Ukrainian School & C.C.D.—.
Lay Teachers 8; Students 36.

West Islip, Suffolk Co., Holy Family (1924) (Ukrainian), Rev. Ovian Popovich.
Res., 471 Montauk Hwy., 11795-4475. Tel: 516-661-0031; Fax: 516-321-4368.

Yonkers, Westchester Co., St. Michael (1899) (Ukrainian), Revs. Philip Weiner; Peter Gronski.
Res., 21 Shonnard Pl., 10703. Tel: 914-963-0209; Fax: 914-969-6269.
Catechesis/Religious Programs—Priests 1; Students 163.
Mission—Yonkers, Westchester Co., Holy Protection of the Mother of God, 10703.

STATE OF RHODE ISLAND

Woonsocket, Providence Co., St. Michael (1908), Rev. Msgr. Roman Golemba.
Res., 394 Blackstone St., 02895. Tel: 401-762-2733; Fax: 401-762-2733. [CEM][JC]
Church—396 Blackstone St., 02895.

Special Assignment:
Reverend Monsignors—
Mosko, Leon A., Chancellor
Reverend Fathers—
Hirniak, Mark, Bishop's Chancery, 14 Peveril Rd., Stamford, CT 06902
Morse, Jonathan, Ukrainian Catholic Relief, Inc.
Shubiak, Stephen, U.S. Chap. Corps

Retired:
Mitred Archpriest—
Andrushkiw, Vladimir, 195 Glenbrook Rd., Stamford, CT 06902
Rev. Archpriest—
Pelensky, Ihor, P.O. Box 533, Westmoreland, NY 13490
Reverend Monsignors—
Chrepta, Stephen J., 16134 Veronica St., East Detroit, MI 48021
Reverend Canons—
Sharanevych, Emile, 332 Foordmore Rd., Kerhonkson, NY 12446. Tel: 914-626-4947
Reverend Fathers—
Graskow, Paul, 3415 La Fayette Ave. S., Seattle, WA 98144
Rt. Rev. Mitred Msgr—
Chomko, Stephen, 706 Warren St., Berwick, PA 18603
Very Rev.—
Ohirko, Peter, St. Joseph's Home, 125 Sister's Servants Lane, Box 25, Sloatsburg, NY 10974-0025. Tel: 914-753-2555

Permanent Deacons:
Homick, Willis, SS. Peter & Paul, Auburn, NY
Kotch, Myron, Syracuse, NY
Malachowsky, Yourij, Holy Cross, Long Island City, NY

INSTITUTIONS LOCATED IN THE DIOCESE

[A] SEMINARIES, DIOCESAN

STAMFORD. *St. Basil College*, 195 Glenbrook Rd., 06902-3099. Tel: 203-324-4578; Fax: 203-357-7681. Most Rev. Basil H. Losten, D.D., S.T.L., LL.D., Chm., Board of Directors; Rev. Msgr. John Squiller, B.A., S.T.L., Pres. & Rector; Rev. Ivan Kaszczak, B.A., M.A., M.Ed., Vice Rector; Very Rev. Canon Lubomyr Mudry, Dir. of Spiritual Formation; Rt. Rev. Mitred Msgr John Terlecky, B.A., M.A., M.L.S., Librarian; Revs. Ihor Midzak, Formation Dir.; Bohdan Danylo, B.S., S.T.B., Dean of Men; Mihai Dubovici, B.A., S.T.B., Bursar, Procurator & Dir. of Operations; Patrick J. Holt, B.A., M.Th., A.B.D., Dean and Registrar; Ms. Lubow Wolynetz, B.A., M.L.S., Asst. Librarian. Household Dept. Institute of Catechists of the Heart of Jesus.

[B] SEMINARIES, RELIGIOUS

GLEN COVE, NY. *Basilian Fathers Novitiate of the Order of St. Basil the Great*, E. Beach Dr., 11542. Tel: 516-671-0545; Fax: 516-676-7465. Very Rev. Cyril Izczuk, O.S.B.M., Supr. & Master of Novices; Revs. Januario Lucavei, O.S.B.M., Asst. Master of Novices; Hilarion Benedik, O.S.B.M.; Athanasius B. Pekar, O.S.B.M. Priests 4; Brothers 2; Novices 4; Scholastics 9.

[C] NURSERY SCHOOLS

STAMFORD. *St. Ann's Nursery School*, 111 W. North St., 06902. Tel: 203-323-1237; 348-5675. Missionary Sisters of Mother of God 6; Nursery 44; Staff 3.

[D] ADULT FACILITIES

SLOATSBURG, NY. *St. Joseph's Home*, 125 Sisters Servants Ln., Box 25, 10974-0025. Tel: 845-753-2555; Fax: 845-753-6910
For a complete listing, refer to the Special Care Facilities section.

[E] MONASTERIES AND RESIDENCES OF PRIESTS AND BROTHERS

NEW YORK, NY. *Provincialate of Basilian Fathers.* Res., 29 Peacock Ln., Locust Valley, 11560. Tel: 516-609-3262; Fax: 516-609-3264. Rev. Mauricio Popadiuk, O.S.B.M., Protohegumen. Priests 22; Scholastics 9; Brothers 3.

WEST BURKE, VT. *Mary Theotokos Centre*, P.O. Box 88, 05871-0088. Tel: 802-467-1132.
E-mail: stefan@sover.net
Rev. Stephen C. von Fauer, Supr.

[F] MONASTERIES OF NUNS

STAMFORD. *Missionary Sisters of Mother of God*, 111 W. North St., 06902. Tel: 203-323-1237. Sr. Josepha Kruchinsky, M.S.M.G., Supr.; Rev. Jonathan Morse, Chap.

MIDDLETOWN, NY. *Nuns of St. Basil the Great*, Sacred Heart Monastery, 209 Keasel Rd., 10940-6287. Tel: 845-343-1308. Mother M. Georgianna Snihur, O.S.B.M., Supr. Sisters 5.

SLOATSBURG, NY. *Immaculate Conception Provincialate*, Sisters Servants Ln., 9 Emmanuel Dr., P.O. Box 6, 10974-0006. Tel: 845-753-2840; Fax: 845-753-1956. Sisters Servants of Mary Immaculate Conception Province. Sr. Michele Yakymovitch, S.S.M.I., Prov. Supr. Sisters 19.

[G] MISCELLANEOUS

STAMFORD. *Institute of Catechists of the Heart of Jesus*, 161 Glenbrook Rd., 06902. Tel: 203-327-6374. Cecilia Daciuk, Supr. Total Members 7.

Ukrainian Catholic Relief, Inc., 14 Peveril Rd., 06902.
E-mail: morseucrstamford@worldnet.att.net

SLOATSBURG, NY. *St. Mary's Villa Spiritual, Cultural & Educational Center*, 150 Sisters Servants Ln., P.O. Box 6, 10974-0006. Tel: 914-753-5100; Fax: 914-753-5100. Sr. Jonathan Duchensky, S.S.M.I., Coord.

RELIGIOUS INSTITUTES OF MEN REPRESENTED IN THE DIOCESE

For further details refer to the corresponding bracketed number in the Religious Institutes of Men or Women section.

[0180]—*Order of St. Basil the Great.*—O.S.B.M.
[1070]—*Redemptorists.*—C.Ss.R.

RELIGIOUS INSTITUTES OF WOMEN REPRESENTED IN THE DIOCESE

[]—*Institute of Catechists of the Heart of Jesus.*
[2810]—*Missionary Sisters of Mother of God.*—M.S.M.G.
[3730]—*Sisters of the Order of St. Basil the Great.*—O.S.B.M.
[3610]—*Sisters Servants of Mary Immaculate.*—S.S.M.I.

NECROLOGY

† Figol, Reverend Father Wolodymyr, (Retired). —Died Dec. 27, 1999.
† Humanitzki, Reverend Father Theodore, (Retired). —Died April 7, 2000.

Byzantine Eparchy of Van Nuys

(Vacant See)

Chancery Office: 8131 N. 16 St., Phoenix, AZ, 85020. Tel.: 602-861-9778; Fax: 602-861-9796.

Web site address: eparchy-of-van-nuys.org

E-mail address: EVNizer@aol.com

ESTABLISHED DECEMBER 3, 1981.

Embraces all Catholics of the Byzantine-Ruthenian Church in the States of California, Oregon, Washington, Idaho, Nevada, Arizona, Utah, Wyoming, Montana, Colorado, New Mexico, Alaska and Hawaii.

For legal titles of parishes and diocesan institutions, consult the Chancery Office.

Legal Title: The Byzantine Catholic Bishop of Van Nuys, a Corporation Sole.

Principal Patron-Patronage of the Mother of God (Pokrov).

STATISTICAL OVERVIEW

Personnel	
Priests: Diocesan Active in Diocese	16
Priests: Active Outside Diocese	2
Priests: Retired, Sick or Absent	3
Number of Diocesan Priests	21
Religious Priests in Diocese	5
Extern Priests in Diocese	3
Ordinations:	
Diocesan Priests	1
Transitional Deacons	1
Permanent Deacons	1
Permanent Deacons in Diocese	4
Total Brothers	7
Total Sisters	4
Parishes	
Parishes	18
With Resident Pastor:	
Resident Diocesan Priests	15
Resident Religious Priests	3
Pastoral Centers	1
Professional Ministry Personnel:	
Brothers	7
Sisters	4
Welfare	
Other Institutions	1
Total Assisted	30
Educational	
Diocesan Students in Other Seminaries	1
Total Seminarians	1
Catechesis/Religious Education:	
High School Students	165
Elementary Students	437
Total Students Under Catholic Instruction	603
Vital Statistics	
Receptions into the Church:	
Infant Baptism Totals	102
Adult Baptism Totals	22
Received into Full Communion	20
First Communions	151
Confirmations	171
Marriages:	
Catholic	16
Interfaith	7
Total Marriages	23
Deaths	43
Total Catholic Population	3,121

Former Bishop—Most Rev. THOMAS V. DOLINAY, D.D., ord. May 16, 1948; cons. Nov. 23, 1976; appt. Titular Bishop of Thyatira and Auxiliary of Passiac, Sept. 23, 1976; appt. First Ordinary of the Byzantine Catholic Diocese of Van Nuys, CA; installed March 9, 1982; appt. Coadjutor Archbishop of Pittsburgh Byzantine Rite, March 13, 1990; succeeded to June 12, 1991; died April 13, 1993.

Chancery Office—Byzantine Catholic Eparchy of Van Nuys, Pastoral Center, 8105 N. 16th St., Phoenix, AZ, 85020. Tel: 602-861-9778; Fax: 602-861-9796. Office Hours: Mon.-Thurs. 10-3; Fri. 10-1.

Protosyncellus and Chancellor—Rt. Rev. WESLEY IZER, S.D.B.

Syncelli—Northwest Vicariate: Very Rev. STEPHEN GRESKOWIAK, Italo-Greeks Vicariate: Rt. Rev. FRANCIS M. VIVONA, S.T.M., J.C.L., Southwest Vicariate: Rt. Rev. STEPHEN WASHKO.

Treasurer—Sr. CELESTINE PETRUSKA, O.S.B.M.

Eparchial Consultors - Presbyteral Council—Very Rev. STEPHEN GRESKOWIAK; Rt. Rev. WESLEY IZER, S.D.B.; Very Revs. MICHAEL MORAN; WILLIAM SKURLA; Rt. Rev. STEPHEN WASHKO; Rt. Rev. FRANCIS M. VIVONA, S.T.M., J.C.L.

Diocesan Matrimonial Tribunal—Office of the Tribunal Eparchy of Van Nuys, 2120 Lindell Rd., Las Vegas, NV, 89146. Tel: 702-873-5102; Fax: 702-873-5104.

Judicial Vicar—Rt. Rev. FRANCIS M. VIVONA, S.T.M., J.C.L.

Promoter of Justice—Very Rev. Archpriest MICHAEL MORAN, J.C.D.

Secretary—Mrs. CECILIA CAMMARANO.

Defender—Rev. PHILIP ACQUARO, C.S.B., J.C.D.

Judge—Rt. Rev. FRANCIS VIVONA.

Building Commission—Most Rev. GEORGE M. KUZMA; Rt. Rev. WESLEY IZER, S.D.B.; Mr. JOHN MONTALVO, III; Mr. JOEL WEISHEIT.

Director of Religious Education and Evangelization—Sr. BARBARA SWINDELLS, O.S.B.M.

Eparchial Finance Commission—Most Rev. GEORGE M. KUZMA, Chm.; Rt. Rev. WESLEY IZER, S.D.B.; Sr. CELESTINE PETRUSKA, O.S.B.M.; Mrs. JOSEFINA DANOVICH; Mr. WILLIAM GOMBAR.

Vocation Director—Rev. ROBERT M. PIPTA.

Ecclesiatical Notary—Rev. ROBERT M. PIPTA; Rt. Rev. STEPHEN WASHKO.

Liturgy & Music Commission—Rt. Rev. STEPHEN WASHKO, Chm.; Revs. JOSEPH HUTSKO; ROBERT M. PIPTA; Sr. CHRISTOPHER MALCOVSKY, O.S.B.M.; Mr. BASIL RABAYDA, JR.

"Eparchial Newsletter"—Rt. Rev. WESLEY IZER, S.D.B., Editor. Assoc. Editors: Rev. WILLIAM SKURLA; Sr. MADELINE BOBACK, O.S.B.M.

Director of Development & Stewardship—Sr. CHRISTOPHER MALCOVSKY, O.S.B.M.

Director of Ecumenical Affairs—Rt. Rev. STEPHEN WASHKO.

Censor—Rt. Rev. FRANCIS VIVONA.

Administrative Secretary—Sr. MADELINE BOBACK, O.S.B.M.

Commission for the Implementation of the Particular Law—Rt. Rev. WESLEY IZER, S.D.B., Chm.; Rev. PHILIP ACQUARO, C.S.B.; Very Rev. MICHAEL MORAN; Rt. Rev. FRANCIS VIVONA.

CLERGY, PARISHES, MISSIONS AND PAROCHIAL SCHOOLS

STATE OF ARIZONA

Gilbert, Maricopa Co., St. Thomas the Apostle (1982), Rev. Philip A. Acquaro, C.S.B., Admin.; Deacon Douglas M. LeClair.
Mailing Address: P.O. Box 667, 85299-0667. Tel: 480-497-5799.
19 W. Bruce Ave., 85233. Tel: 480-497-6726.

Phoenix, Maricopa Co., St. Stephen (1968). (Byzantine Catholic Pro-Cathedral). Rt. Rev. Stephen G. Washko, Rector; Sr. Christopher Malcovsky, O.S.B.M., Pastoral Assoc.
Res., 8141 N. 16th St., 85020-3999. Tel: 602-943-5379; Fax: 602-861-9796.
Convent—St. Stephen Convent, 8141 N. 16th St. #27, 85020. Tel: 602-944-5121; Fax: 602-861-9796. Sisters 3.

Tucson, Pima Co., St. Melany (1977), Rev. William Skurla.
Church—1212 N. Sahuara, 85712-5018. Tel: 520-886-4225; Fax: 520-751-4574.

STATE OF ALASKA

Anchorage, Anchorage Co., Saint Nicholas of Myra (1957), Rev. Stephen Greskowiak.
Res., 2200 Arctic Blvd., 99503-1909. Tel: 907-277-6731; Fax: 907-277-6731.

STATE OF CALIFORNIA

Van Nuys, Los Angeles Co., Cathedral of St. Mary (1956), Very Rev. Archpriest Michael Moran, Rector; Sr. Barbara Swindells, O.S.B.M., Pastoral Assoc.; Deacon Michael Hladky, (Retired).
Res., 5329 Sepulveda Blvd., 91411-3441. Tel: 818-907-5511; Fax: 818-981-7107.
Convent—5335 Sepulveda Blvd., 91411-3441. Tel: 818-907-1261.

Anaheim, Orange Co., Annunciation (1969), Rev. Msgr. George N. Vida.
Res., 319 N. Harbor Blvd., 92805-2599. Tel: 714-533-6292; Fax: 714-533-6292.

Fontana, San Bernardino Co., St. Nicholas (1958), Rev. Joseph Hutsko.
Res., 9112 Oleander Ave., 92335-5599. Tel: 909-822-9917; Fax: 909-822-7663.

Fresno, Fresno Co., Byzantine Catholic Community of Fresno, CA. Closed. For inquiries for parish records contact the Chancery.

Los Gatos, Santa Clara Co., St. Basil the Great (1986), Rev. Anthony Hernandez.

Res., 14263 Mulberry Ave., 95032-1208. Tel: 408-871-0919; Fax: 408-871-0911.

Palm Springs, Riverside Co., Byzantine Catholic Community of Palm Springs, CA. Closed. For inquiries for parish records contact the Chancery.

Sacramento, Sacramento Co., St. Philip the Apostle (1971), Rt. Rev. Januarius Izzo, O.F.M., Admin.
Church—3866 65th St., 95820-2033. Tel: 916-383-1552 (Rectory); 916-452-1888 (Office).

San Diego, San Diego Co., Holy Angels (1958), Rev. Melvin Rybarczyk, C.R., Admin.; Deacon David Hess.
Mailing Address: 2235 Galahad Rd., 92123-3931. Tel: 858-277-2511; Fax: 858-277-5792.

San Luis Obispo, San Luis Obispo Co., Saint Anne (1986), Rev. Edmund M. Idranyi, Admin.; Mr. Julius Dicky, Financial Admin.
Mailing Address: 222 Foothill Blvd., 93405-1540. Tel: 805-543-8883 (Voice/Fax).

San Mateo, San Mateo Co., St. Macrina. Closed. All records at the Chancery Office.

Stockton, San Joaquin Co., Byzantine Catholic Community of Stockton. Closed. For inquiries for parish records contact the Chancery.

STATE OF COLORADO

Colorado Springs, El Paso Co., Byzantine Catholic Mission. Closed. For inquiries for parish records contact the Chancery.

Denver, Denver Co., Holy Protection of the Mother of God (1974), Rev. Chrysostom Frank.
Mailing Address: P.O. Box 3490, Littleton, 80161-3490.
Res., 1074 S. Cook St., 80209-4923.
Church—1201 S. Elizabeth St., 80210. Tel: 303-778-8283.

STATE OF NEVADA

Las Vegas, Clark Co., Our Lady of Wisdom Italo-Greek Mission (1993), Rt. Rev. Archimandri Francis Vivona, Syncellus.
Church—2120 Lindell Rd., 89146. Tel: 702-873-5101; Fax: 702-873-5104.
St. Gabriel the Archangel (1977), Rev. Robert M. Pipta, Admin.
Church—2250 E. Maule Ave., 89119-4607. Tel: 702-361-2431; Fax: 702-361-2431.

STATE OF NEW MEXICO

Albuquerque, Bernalillo Co., Our Lady of Perpetual Help (1974), Rev. Christopher L. Zugger.
Church—1837 Alvarado Dr., N.E., 87110. Tel: 505-256-1539; 256-1787 (Res.); Fax: 505-256-1278.

Las Cruces, Dona Ana Co., Byzantine Catholic Mission. Closed. Records are located at Albuquerque Parish.

STATE OF OREGON

Portland, Multnomah Co., St. Irene Byzantine Catholic Church, Rev. Kurt Burnette, Admin.
Mailing Address: 8261 S.E. Clatsop, 97266. Tel: 503-777-1814; Fax: 503-775-9368.
Church—4630 N. Maryland Ave., 97266.

STATE OF UTAH

Salt Lake City, Salt Lake Co., Byzantine Catholic Mission. Closed. For inquiries for parish records contact the Chancery.

STATE OF WASHINGTON

Olympia, Thurston Co., St. George Byzantine (1989), Rev. Michael Durka, Admin.
Res., 9730 Yelm Hwy, 98513. Tel: 360-413-5651.

Seattle, King Co., St. John Chrysostom (1981), Rt. Rev. Joseph Stanichar, Pastor; Rev. William O'Brien.
Res., 1305 S. Lander St., 98144-5038. Tel: 206-329-9219; Fax: 206-322-6930.

Spokane, Spokane Co., SS. Cyril & Methodius (1979), Rev. David Logan, Admin.
Res., N. 4315 Evergreen Rd., 99216-1298. Tel: 509-922-4527.

Walla Walla, Walla Walla Co., Byzantine Catholic Mission. Closed. For inquiries for parish records contact the Spokane parish.

On Special Assignment:
Reverend Fathers—
Kovach, John, Shrine of the Weeping Madonna, 17486 Mumford Rd., Burton, OH 44021-9640
Michalenko, Alexei, Chap., Georgetown Law Center, 600 New Jersey Ave., N.W., Washington, DC 20001

On Leave:
Reverend Fathers—
Barrand, James

Retired:
Reverend Fathers—
Dorich, John M., 8141 N. 16th St., #2, Phoenix, AZ 85020-3999
Ridella, Joseph, 66295 Hacienda Ave., Desert Hot Springs, CA 92240
Rt. Rev.—
Artim, Michael, 13211 Venus Way, Anchorage, AK 99515-3915

Permanent Deacons:
Hess, David, San Diego, CA
Hladky, Michael, (Retired)
LeClair, Douglas (PHX), Gilbert, AZ
Wortman, Richard, On Leave

INSTITUTIONS LOCATED IN THE DIOCESE

[A] RELIGIOUS COMMUNITIES

PHOENIX. *Congregation of Saint Basil*, 8141 N. 16th St., #22, 85020-3901. Tel: 602-395-0457. Rev. Philip A. Acquaro, C.S.B.
St. Stephen Convent, 8141 N. 16th St. #27, 85020. Tel: 602-944-5121; Fax: 602-861-9796. Sr. Christopher Malcovsky, O.S.B.M.; Sr. Celestine Petruska, O.S.B.M.; Sr. Madeline Boback, O.S.B.M.
Salesians of Don Bosco, 8141 N. 16th St., #19, 85020-3999. Tel: 602-861-9443. Rt. Rev. Wesley W. Izer, S.D.B.

NEWBERRY SPRINGS, CA. *Holy Resurrection Monastery*. (Monastic Community of Men est. Aug. 4, 1995), 45704 Valley Center Rd., P.O. Box 130, 92365. Tel: 760-257-4008; Fax: 760-257-3362. Rev. Nicholas Zachariadis, Hegumen; Bros. Maximos Davies, Protos; Basil Doty; Moses Wright.

RAMONA, CA. *Good Shepherd Monastery*. (Monastic Community of Men est. Oct. 1, 1998), P.O. Box 2822, 92065. Tel: 760-788-2852.
E-mail: monasterygs@hotmail.com
Res., 18840 Littlepage Rd., 92065. Rev. Juan Jensen Hegumen, Supr.; Bros. Francisco Gallegos Marin; Jorge Ortega Cordova.

REDLANDS, CA. *Byzantine Brothers of St. Francis*, 9458 Buckeye St., 92374. Tel: 909-793-1127.
E-mail: brmike7@aol.com
Bros. Michael Sullivan, B.B.S.F., Supr.; John Gray, B.B.S.F., Treas.

VAN NUYS, CA. *Saint Mary Convent*, 5335 Sepulveda Blvd., 91411-3441. Tel: 818-907-1261. Order of Sisters of St. Basil the Great. Sr. Barbara Swindells, O.S.B.M.

RELIGIOUS INSTITUTES OF MEN REPRESENTED IN THE DIOCESE

For further details refer to the corresponding bracketed number in the Religious Institutes of Men or Women section.

[0170]—*Basilian Fathers.*—C.S.B.
[]—*Byzantine Brothers of St. Francis.*—B.B.S.F.
[0520]—*Franciscan Friars.*—O.F.M.
[1190]—*Salesians of Don Bosco.*—S.D.B.

RELIGIOUS INSTITUTES OF WOMEN REPRESENTED IN THE DIOCESE

[3730]—*Sisters of the Order of St. Basil the Great.*—O.S.B.M.

NECROLOGY

(No Deaths)

U.S. TERRITORIAL SEES

Archdiocese of Agana

Most Reverend

ANTHONY SABLAN APURON, O.F.M.CAP., D.D.

Archbishop of Agana; ordained August 26, 1972; appointed Auxiliary Bishop December 8, 1983; ordained Titular Bishop of Muzuca February 19, 1984; appointed Apostolic Administrator to the Archdiocese October 27, 1985; succeeded to Metropolitan See May 11, 1986. *Res., Archbishop's Residence, 196-B Cuesta San Ramon, Agana, GU, 96910.* Tel.: 671-472-6116; 472-6573; Fax: 671-477-3519.

ERECTED BY POPE PIUS X, MARCH 1, 1911 AND COMMITTED TO THE ORDER OF FRIARS MINOR CAPUCHIN. EXTENDED TO ALL THE MARIANAS ISLANDS, JULY 4, 1946, WAKE ISLAND, JUNE 14, 1948. ELEVATED TO A DIOCESE, OCTOBER 14, 1965, AS A SUFFRAGAN OF SAN FRANCISCO. ELEVATED TO METROPOLITAN ARCHDIOCESE, MAY 20, 1984 WITH A SUFFRAGAN SEE, DIOCESE OF CAROLINE-MARSHALLS AND DIOCESE OF CHALAN KANOA (SUBSEQUENTLY ADDED JANUARY 13, 1985). MEMBER OF CEPAC CONFERENCE. MEMBER OF FEDERATION OF CATHOLIC BISHOPS CONFERENCE OF OCEANIA. OBSERVER TO NCCB-USCC CONFERENCE.

GUAM IS A TERRITORY OF THE U.S.A. BY ACT OF THE U.S. CONGRESS JULY 21, 1949.

Legal Title: *Archbishop of Agana, a Corporation Sole.*

STATISTICAL OVERVIEW

Personnel	
Archbishop	1
Priests: Diocesan Active in Diocese	29
Priests: Active Outside Diocese	2
Priests: Retired, Sick or Absent	2
Number of Diocesan Priests	33
Religious Priests in Diocese	16
Ordinations:	
Permanent Deacons	7
Permanent Deacons in Diocese	7
Total Brothers	1
Total Sisters	125
Parishes	
Parishes	24
With Resident Pastor:	
Resident Diocesan Priests	16
Resident Religious Priests	8
Welfare	
Homes for the Aged	1
Total Assisted	59
Day Care and Extended Day Care Centers	3
Total Assisted	136
Specialized Homes	11
Total Assisted	599
Special Centers for Social Services	1
Total Assisted	8,496
Educational	
Seminaries, Diocesan	1
Students from This Diocese	14
Diocesan Students in Other Seminaries	4
Seminaries, Religious	1
Students Religious	5
Total Seminarians	23
High Schools, Diocesan and Parish	2
Total Students	788
High Schools, Private	244
Total Students	1,032
Elementary Schools, Diocesan and Parish	7
Total Students	2,114
Catechesis/Religious Education:	
Total Students Under Catholic Instruction	5,398
Teachers in the Diocese:	
Priests	1
Sisters	41
Lay Teachers	220
Vital Statistics	
Receptions into the Church:	
Infant Baptism Totals	2,272
Adult Baptism Totals	14
Received into Full Communion	42
First Communions	1,349
Confirmations	873
Marriages:	
Catholic	254
Interfaith	10
Total Marriages	264
Deaths	462
Total Catholic Population	150,563
Total Population	167,292

Former Vicars-Apostolic—Most Rev. FRANCIS X. VILLA Y MATEU, O.F.M.Cap., D.D., cons. Titular Bishop of Adraha, Oct. 1, 1911; died at Agana, Jan. 1, 1913.—Most Rev. AUGUSTIN BERNAUS Y SERRA, O.F.M.Cap., D.D., cons. Titular Bishop of Milopotamo, May 9, 1913; transferred to Vicariate-Apostolic of Bluefields, Nicaragua, 1914.—Most Rev. JOAQUIN FELIPE OLAIZ Y ZABALZA, O.F.M.Cap., D.D., cons. Titular Bishop of Docimeo, Nov. 30, 1914; died at Pamplona, Spain, Dec. 8, 1945.—Most Rev. MIGUEL ANGEL OLANO Y URTEAGA, O.F.M.Cap., D.D., cons. Titular Bishop of Lagina, May 5, 1935; resigned and made Asst. at Pontifical Throne Aug. 20, 1945; died at Agana, Guam May 21, 1970.—Most Rev. APOLLINARIS W. BAUMGARTNER, O.F.M.Cap., D.D., cons. Sept. 18, 1945; appt. First Bishop of Agana, Oct. 14, 1965; died at Agana, Guam Dec. 18, 1970.—Most Rev. FELIXBERTO CAMACHO FLORES, ord. April 30, 1949; appt. Apostolic Admin., Diocese of Agana, May 2, 1969; appt. Titular Bishop of Stonj, March 19, 1970; cons. May 17, 1970; succeeded to See, May 15, 1971; died Oct. 25, 1985.

Vicar General and Moderator of the Curia—Rev. DAVID C. QUITUGUA, J.C.D.

Chancellor—Rev. ADRIAN CRISTOBAL.

Archdiocesan College of Consultors—Revs. DAVID C. QUITUGUA, J.C.D.; ADRIAN CRISTOBAL; ERIC FORBES, O.F.M.Cap.; JOSE ANTONIO ABAD; JAMES L.G. BENAVENTE; KENNETH HEZEL, S.J.; JOSE VILLAGOMEZ, O.F.M.Cap.

Archdiocesan Finance Council—Rev. JAMES L.G. BENAVENTE. Tel: 671-472-6201. Sr. MARY STEPHEN TORRES, R.S.M. Tel: 671-646-7246. Mr. T. ROY SULLIVAN, Pres. Tel: 617-472-8891. Mr. DOMINIC KIM; Mr. RICHARD UNTALAN; Mr. JOSEPH DUENAS.

Archdiocesan Presbyteral Council—Revs. DAVID C. QUITUGUA, J.C.D., Vicar Gen. ADRIAN CRISTOBAL, Chancellor; ERIC FORBES, O.F.M.Cap., Vice Provincial; JOSE ANTONIO ABAD; DAVID I.A. QUITUGUA; WILFREDO LORILLA; PATRICK CASTRO, O.F.M.Cap.; JOSE VILLAGOMEZ, O.F.M.Cap.; JOSEPH ENGLISH, O.F.M.Cap.; DANIEL CRISTOBAL, O.F.M.Cap.; KENNETH HEZEL, S.J.; BRIGIDO ARROYO; JAMES L.G. BENAVENTE.

Archdiocesan Offices and Directors

Catholic Schools Office—Vacant, Supt. Tel: 671-472-6116; Fax: 671-477-3519.

Division of Pastoral Ministries—Sr. MARIAN ARROYO, R.S.M., Exec. Dir. Tel: 671-472-6116; Fax: 671-472-3519.

Pontifical Holy Childhood Association & Pontifical Society for the Propagation of the Faith—Rev. DAVID C. QUITUGUA, *196-B Cuesta San Ramon, Agana, 96910.* Tel: 671-472-6116; Fax: 671-477-3519.

Office of Faith Formation—CONNIE P. GUERRERO, Dir.

Family and Youth Ministry—CYNTHIA AGBULOS, Dir., *196-B Cuesta San Ramon, Agana, 96910.* Tel: 671-472-6116; Fax: 671-472-4406. Mr. JOHN LIZAMA, *P.O. Box 306, Agana, 96910.* Tel: 671-472-6068.

Evenings for the Engaged—Coordinators: FRANCIS GUERRERO; CONNIE GUERRERO, *c/o Barrigada Church, 229 San Roke St., Barrigada, 96913.*

Marriage Encounter—Coordinators: RAY FERNANDEZ; JOSEPHINE FERNANDEZ.

Natural Family Planning—CYNTHIA AGBULOS, Coord.

Sponsor Couple Program—CYNTHIA AGBULOS, Coord.

Office of Pastoral Planning—LOUIS T. AGBULOS, JR., Dir.

Office of Worship—Sr. MARIAN THERESE ARROYO, R.S.M., Dir., *Cuesta San Ramon, Agana, 96910.* Tel: 671-472-6201.

Resource Center—Vacant.

Chancery Office—

Finance Officer and Business Mgr.—Mr. DOMINIC KIM.

Records Office—Mrs. JUNE UNGACTA.

Computers—Mr. MANNY CRUZ, Chancery Office: *196-B Cuesta San Ramon, Agana, 96910.* Tel: 671-472-6116; 472-8024; 472-6573; Fax: 671-477-3519. Office Hours: Mon.-Fri. 8-12 & 1-4.

Tribunal—

Judicial Vicar—Rev. DAVID C. QUITUGUA, J.C.D.

Promoter of Justice—Rev. JOSE VILLAGOMEZ, O.F.M.Cap.

Defender of the Bond—Rev. ADRIAN CRISTOBAL.

Associate Judges—Rev. Msgr. ZOILO CAMACHO; Rev. RAYMOND CEPEDA, J.C.L.; Sr. MARIA ANA LEE, O.P., J.C.L.

Advocate—Rev. JAMES L.G. BENAVENTE.

Notary—Rev. FELIXBERTO LEON GUERRERO, O.F.M.Cap.

Archdiocesan Cemetery Office—Rev. JAMES L.G. BENAVENTE, Dir. Tel: 671-472-6201.

Chaplains—See separate listing.

Catholic Charities Appeal - Guam—Rev. ADRIAN CRISTOBAL, Dir., *196-B Cuesta San Ramon, Agana, 96910.* Tel: 671-472-6116.

Office of Vocations—Revs. ADRIAN CRISTOBAL, Co-Dir. JAMES L.G. BENAVENTE, Co-Dir., *196-B Cuesta San Ramon, Agana, 96910.* Tel: 671-472-6116; 472-8024; 472-6201; Fax: 671-472-3519; 472-1729.

Catholic Social Services—Mrs. CERILA RAPADAS, Exec. Dir.; Sr. CALLISTA CAMACHO, R.S.M., Deputy Dir., *P.O. Box EJ, Hagatna, 96932.* Tel: 671-635-1410; Fax: 671-635-1444.

Alee Shelter Program for Spousal Abuse—Sr. MARIE MAURER, R.G.S., Dir., *c/o Catholic Social Services, P.O. Box EJ, Hagatna, 96932.* Tel: 671-635-1409.

Kamalen Karidad—Deacon FRANK TENORIO, Gen. Mgr., *Tai Thrift Shop.* Tel: 671-734-2479., *Quality Thrift Shop.* Tel: 671-734-2483., *Kusinan Kamalen Karidad.* Tel: 671-472-6068.

Catholic Pro-Life Committee—

Gentle Refuge Crisis Pregnancy Center—

Project Rachel (Abortion Aftermath Counseling)—Deacon FRANK TENORIO, Dir., *P.O. Box 23006, GMF, 96921.* Tel: 671-477-1742.

Catholic Campus Ministry, Newman Center, University of Guam—Revs. LEO J. DALY, S.J., Dir. KENNETH J. HEZEL, S.J., *P.O. Box 23142, Barrigada, 96921.* Tel: 671-734-3507; Fax: 671-734-2943.

Office of Communications—Rev. BRIGIDO ARROYO, Dir.; Mr. TERRY MORTERA, Gen. Mgr., *P.O. Box 2553, Hagatna, 96932.* Tel: 671-472-6427.

Catholic Educational Radio, KOLG—Mr. JOHN DUNGCA, Program Mgr., *P.O. Box DZ, Hagatna, 96932.* Tel: 671-477-5654; Fax: 671-477-5656.

Pacific Voice—Rev. HERMES LOSBANES, Editor, *P.O. Box 2553, Hagatna, 96932.* Tel: 671-472-6427; Fax: 671-477-5224.

Records—JUNE UNGACTA.

Catholic Daughters of America—Rev. BRIGIDO ARROYO, Chap. Tel: 671-646-7181.

Court of Our Lady of Camarin #2047—Mrs. MAE QUINATA, Regent.

Court of Maria Rainan Y Familia #2450—Mrs. DORA SALAZAR, Regent.

Confraternity of Christian Mothers—Rev. MICHAEL TENORIO, O.F.M.Cap., Spiritual Dir.; Mrs. MAE QUINATA, Island Bd. Pres.

Cursillo in Christianity—Rev. JOEL DE LOS REYES, Spiritual Dir.; Mr. ROLAND BISCOE, Pres. Tel: 671-472-6116.

Legion of Mary—Rev. DAVID C. QUITUGUA, Spiritual Dir.; Mrs. CONSEJO HAUTEA, Pres.

Secular Franciscans (Third Order)—Rev. DANIEL CRISTOBAL, O.F.M.Cap., Spiritual Dir., *135 Gunut Cir., Agana Heights, 96910.* Mrs. CARMEN MANIBUSAN, Pres.

Knights of Columbus—Most Rev. ANTHONY SABLAN APURON, O.F.M.Cap., D.D., Spiritual Dir.; Sir Knight CLYDE SAUGET, Territorial Deputy, *P.O. Box 225404, GMF, 96921.* Tel: 671-477-2703. Sir Knight BERT UNPINGCO, Master of the Fourth Degree. Tel: 671-477-4700.

Knights of Columbus No. 5666—P.O. Box BP, Agana, 96910. Pale San Vitores Council, Mr. CLYDE SAUGET, Grand Knight Archbishop Felixberto Flores Council, Mr. EDWIN CARBONEL, Grand Knight, *P.O. Box 1252, Tamuning, 96911.*

Knights of Saint Sylvester—Sir Knights CRISTOBAL DUENAS; LUCAS SAN NICOLAS; PETE SGRO; FRANK CRUZ; PEDRO M. CAMACHO; RICHARD UNTALAN; FRANK SANTOS. Tel: 671-472-6201.

Knights of Saint Gregory The Great—Sir Knight CRISTOBAL DUENAS.

United Catholic Charismatic Groups of Guam—P.O. Box 9998, Tamuning, 96931.

Couples for Christ—Bro. ARMAND LINCO.

Catholic Charismatic Community—Sr. MARIA LEON GUERRERO.

Catholic Covenant Community—Bro. CARLOS T. SAN AGUSTIN.

Cell Prayer Community—Bro. ROQUE MENDIOLA.

El Shaddai DWXI Prayer Partner International, Guam Chapter—Sr. ALBINA SANTOS.

Our Lady of Lourdes Catholic Charismatic Group—Sr. LINDA ESTRELLA.

Worship and Praise—Sr. FLO SANCHEZ.

CLERGY, PARISHES, MISSIONS AND PAROCHIAL SCHOOLS

CITY OF AGANA
ISLAND OF GUAM

1—DULCE NOMBRE DE MARIA CATHEDRAL - BASILICA (1669), Most Rev. Anthony Sablan Apuron, O.F.M.Cap., D.D.; Revs. James L.G. Benavente; David C. Quitugua, J.C.D.; Thomas B. McGrath, S.J.; Deacon John Dierking.
Res., 207 Archbishop Felixberto C. Flores St., 96910. Tel: 671-472-6201; 477-1842; Fax: 671-472-1729.
Catechesis/Religious Programs—Students 110.

2—ST. ANDREW KIM. Unassigned. (Quasi-parish).
Mailing Address: P.O. Box 155, 96910. Tel: 671-637-4148; Fax: 671-637-4149.

OUTSIDE THE CITY OF AGANA

Agana Heights, Our Lady of the Blessed Sacrament (1948), Rev. Paulo R. Kosaka, O.F.M.Cap.
Res., 135 Gunut Cir., 96919. Tel: 671-472-6246.
Catechesis/Religious Programs—Eleanor Cruz, D.R.E.
Students 252.

Agat, Our Lady of Mount Carmel (1957), Rev. Jose Villagomez, O.F.M.Cap.; Deacon Frank Tenorio.
Res., 135 Gunut Cir., Agana Heights, 96919. Tel: 671-565-2136; Fax: 671-565-9678. [CEM]
Catechesis/Religious Programs—Tel: 671-565-9676.
Students 459.

Asan, Holy Family, Nino Perdido, Rev. Rodolfo Arejola.
Res., P.O. Box 45, Agana, 96910. Tel: 671-477-2211.

Barrigada, San Vicente Ferrer (1947), Revs. Adrian F. Cristobal; Joel de los Reyes.
Res., 229 San Roke St., 96913. Tel: 671-734-4573; Fax: 671-734-5858.
Catechesis/Religious Programs—Sr. Mary Gertrude Quitugua, R.S.M., D.R.E.
Students 432.

Chalan Pago, Nuestra Senora de la Paz y Buen Viaje, Rev. Felixberto C. Leon Guerrero, O.F.M.Cap.
Res., 135 Gunut Cir., Agana Heights, 96919. Tel: 671-734-3723; Fax: 671-472-8431.
Catechesis/Religious Programs—Tel: 671-734-4223.
Students 380.

Dededo, Santa Barbara (1947), Rev. Raymond F. Cepeda; Rev. Msgr. Zoilo L.G. Camacho, Pastor Emeritus; Revs. Tomasito Tibudan; James McDonough; Virgil Paras; Tony Camora; Deacon Ramon Diaz. In res., Rev. Efren Adversario.
Res., 315 W. Sta., Barbara Ave., 96912. Tel: 671-632-5659; 632-9534; Fax: 617-632-1713.
Catechesis/Religious Programs—D.R.E.: Vangie Cepeda; Alvin Alvarez; Virginia Avaricio; Cristeta Deliquina.
Students 1,307.

Inarajan, St. Joseph (1680), Rev. Manuel Ombao.
Res., P.O. Box 170022, 96917. Tel: 671-828-8102; Fax: 671-477-3519. [CEM]
Catechesis/Religious Programs—Students 124.

Maina, Our Lady of the Purification (1949), Rev. Simeon Balmeo.
Res., P.O. Box 4477, Agana, 96910. Tel: 671-477-7256.
Catechesis/Religious Programs—Students 60.

Malojlo, San Isidro (1977), Rev. Manuel Trenchera.
Res., HCR Box 17083, Inarajan, 96917. Tel: 671-828-8454; Fax: 671-828-0001. [JC]
Catechesis/Religious Programs—Students 175.

Mangilao, Santa Teresita (1951), Rev. Joseph English, O.F.M.Cap.
Res., 192 Rte. 10, P.O. Box 306, Agana, 96910. Tel: 671-734-2100; Fax: 671-734-2171.
Catechesis/Religious Programs—Students 386.

Merizo, San Dimas and Our Lady of the Rosary (1680), Rev. Michael Crisostomo.
Res., P.O. Box 6099, 96916. Tel: 671-828-8056; Fax: 671-828-3100. [CEM]
Catechesis/Religious Programs—Students 364.

Mongmong, Nuestra Senora de Las Aquas (1969), Rev. Patrick Kenny Q. Garcia.
Res., P.O. Box 163, Agana, 96910. Tel: 671-477-6754; Fax: 671-477-3766.
Catechesis/Religious Programs—Tel: 671-477-3422. Mrs. Luisa M. Grino, D.R.E.
Students 178.

Ordot, San Juan Bautista (1947) (Chamorro), Rev. David I.A. Quitugua.
Res., P.O. Box 49, Agana, 96910. Tel: 671-472-8341; Fax: 671-472-2324.
Catechesis/Religious Programs—Students 122.

Piti, Assumption of Our Lady (1930) (Chamorro), Rev. Wilfredo Lorilla.
Mailing Address: 314 Assumption Dr., 96925. Tel: 472-2272; Fax: 477-1955.
Res., 96910. Tel: 671-472-2272; Fax: 671-477-1955.
Catechesis/Religious Programs—Students 167.

Santa Rita, Our Lady of Guadalupe (1944), Rev. Agustin Gumataotao, O.F.M.Cap.
Res., P.O. Box 4632, Agana, 96910. Tel: 671-565-2160; Fax: 671-565-7078.
Catechesis/Religious Programs—Mrs. Cecilia Cruz, D.R.E.
Students 405.

Sinajana, Saint Jude Thaddeus (1962), Rev. Michael Tenorio, O.F.M.Cap.; Deacon Anthony C. Leon Guerrero.
Church & St. Jude Rectory—122 Avenida Bien Venida, 96926. Tel: 671-475-6530; 6531; Fax: 671-477-5353.
Catechesis/Religious Programs—Sr. Gloria Aquon, F.S.P.A., D.R.E.
Students 383.

Talofofo, San Miguel (1945), Rev. Daniel Cristobal, O.F.M.Cap.
Res., 71 San Miguel St., 96930. Tel: 671-789-1069; Fax: 671-789-7665.
Catechesis/Religious Programs—Tel: 671-789-0130. Marie E. Meno, D.R.E.
Students 300.

Tamuning, St. Anthony and St. Victor (1946), Revs. Brigido U. Arroyo; James Ch'e; Jose Antonio P. Abad; Deacon Mario L. Celis. In res., Revs. Antonio Bobis; Edwin Musico; Jorge Carao.
Res., P.O. Box 7707, 96931. Tel: 671-646-7181; 646-8044; Fax: 671-646-1039.
Catechesis/Religious Programs—Students 411.

Toto, Immaculate Heart of Mary (1948), Rev. Alfonso Asis; Deacon Jose Santos.
Res., P.O. Box 2552, Agana, 96910. Tel: 671-477-9118.
Catechesis/Religious Programs—Students 130.

Tumon Bay, Blessed Diego Luis de San Vitores Church (1970), Rev. Hermes G. Losbanes.
Res., 884 Pale' San Vitores Rd., Tumon, 96911-4013. Tel: 671-646-5649; Fax: 671-649-6887.
Catechesis/Religious Programs—Students 58.

Umatac, San Dionisio (1680), Rev. Michael Crisostomo.
Res., P.O. Box 6099, Merizo, 96916. Tel: 671-828-8056; Fax: 671-828-3100. [CEM]
Catechesis/Religious Programs—Students 108.

Yigo, Our Lady of Lourdes (1947), Revs. Vito B. San Andres; Jeffrey San Nicolas; Deacon Fred Otte.
Res., P.O. Box 11001, 96929. Tel: 671-653-2584; Fax: 671-653-4746.
Catechesis/Religious Programs—Tel: 671-653-1102. D.R.E.: Femy Castro; Trinie Cruz; Elaine Gogue; Thelma Lumbre.
Students 791.
Mission—Agafa Gumas, Santa Bernadita Mission Chapel.

Yona, San Francisco d'Assisi (1954), Rev. Patrick Castro, O.F.M.Cap.
Res., San Fidelis Friary, 135 Gunut Cir., Agana Heights, 96919. Tel: 671-789-1491; 1492; Fax: 671-789-1400; 1404. [CEM]
Catechesis/Religious Programs—Josephine L.G. Santos, D.R.E.
Students 252.

On Duty Outside the Archdiocese:
Reverend Fathers—
Adversario, Efren, Military Chap., U.S. AF
Perez, Antonio, St. Mary's Seminary, Baltimore, MD

Retired:
Reverend Monsignors—
Camacho, Zoilo L.G., 315 W. Santa Barbara Ave., Dededo, GU 96912. Tel: 671-632-5659
Reverend Fathers—
Brouillard, Louis A., 525 9th St., Pine City, MN 55063
D'Arcy, William

Permanent Deacons:
Barcinas, Joseph
Celis, Mario
Dierking, John
Guerrero, Anthony Leon
Otte, Fred
Santos, Jose
Tenorio, Francisco

INSTITUTIONS LOCATED IN THE ARCHDIOCESE

[A] SEMINARIES

AGANA. *Redemptoris Mater Seminary*, 196-B Cuesta San Ramon, 96910. Tel: 671-734-0680; Fax: 671-734-6520.
E-mail: rmsguam@ite.net
Rev. Raymond LaBranche, Rector. Seminarians 14.

[B] HIGH SCHOOLS

AGANA. *Academy of Our Lady of Guam*, 233 W. Archbishop Felixberto C. Flores St., 96910. Tel: 671-477-8203; Fax: 671-477-8555.
E-mail: acad@aolg.edu.gu
Web site: http://www.aolg.edu.gu
Sisters of Mercy. Sr. Francis Jerome Cruz, R.S.M., Prin. Sisters 2; Lay Teachers 27; Staff 10; Students 394.

The Father Duenas Memorial School, P.O. Box FD, 96932. Tel: 671-734-2261; 734-2263; Fax: 671-734-5738.
E-mail: fdms2@ite.net
Web site: www.fatherduenas.com
Mr. William Roth, Prin. Priests 1; Sisters 1; Lay Teachers 26; Students 394.

TALOFOFO. *Notre Dame High School*, 480 San Miguel St., 96930. Tel: 671-789-1676; 789-1745; Fax: 671-789-4847.
E-mail: ndhs@netpci.com
Dr. Regina Paulino, S.S.N.D., Ed.D., Pres.; Pilar Perez Williams, Prin. Sisters 3; Lay Teachers 14; Students 244.

[C] ELEMENTARY AND JUNIOR HIGH SCHOOLS

AGAT. *Our Lady of Mt. Carmel School*, P.O. Box 7830, 96928. Tel: 671-565-5128; Fax: 671-565-3539. Sr. Lydia Marie Borja, S.S.N.D., Prin. Sisters 3; Lay Teachers 9; Students 90.

DEDEDO. *Santa Barbara School*, 274-A W. Santa Barbara Ave., 96912. Tel: 671-632-4478; 632-2789; Fax: 671-632-1414.
E-mail: info@sbs.edu.gu
Web site: www.sbs.edu.gu
Mailing Address: 274-B W. Santa Barbara Ave., 96912. Sr. Jeanette Marie Pangelinan, R.S.M., Prin. Sisters 3; Lay Teachers 28; Students 358.

GMF. *St. Francis School*, P.O. Box 22199, 96921. Tel: 671-789-1270; 789-1350; Fax: 671-789-3900. Sr.

Lourdes Pangelinan, S.S.N.D., Prin. Sisters 2; Lay Teachers 9; Students 174.

San Vicente School. 196 Bejong St., Barrigada, 96913. Tel: 671-735-4240; Fax: 671-734-8718.
E-mail: ssndbarr@ite.net
Sr. Mary Juan Camacho, S.S.N.D., Prin. Sisters 2; Lay Teachers 27; Students 247.

SINAJANA. *Bishop Baumgartner Memorial School,* 281 Calle Angel Flores St., 96926. Tel: 671-472-6670; 477-2677; 477-4010; Fax: 671-477-4028.
E-mail: mcharles@bbms.edu.gu
Sr. Mary Charles Cameron, R.S.M., Pres.; Sr. M. McAuley, R.S.M., Prin. Cathedral Grade School merged with Bishop Baumgartner Middle School to form Bishop Baumgartner Memorial School. Sisters 7; Lay Teachers 30; Students 565.

TAMUNING. *Saint Anthony School,* 529 Chalan San Antonio, 96911. Tel: 671-647-1140; Fax: 671-649-7130.
E-mail: sasadm@ite.net
Sr. Doris San Agustin, R.S.M., Prin. Sisters 3; Lay Teachers 33; Students 547.

YIGO. *Dominican School,* 114 Chalan Pale Ramon - Lagu, Rte. 1, 96929. Tel: 671-653-3021; Fax: 671-653-3090. Sr. Zenaida Ancheta, O.P., Prin. Sisters 6; Lay Teachers 8; Students 123.

[D] KINDERGARTEN AND NURSERY SCHOOLS

AGANA HEIGHTS. *Maria Artero Nursery,* 161 A Sunset Dr., 96919. Tel: 671-472-8777. Sr. Katherine E. Bromwell, M.M.B., Prin. Sisters 4; Lay Teachers 4; Students 65.

ORDOT. *Dominican Child Development Center.* P.O. Box 5668, Agana, 96932. Tel: 671-477-7228; Fax: 671-472-4282. Sr. Josefina Manago, O.P., Contact Person. Sisters 4; Lay Teachers 4; Aides 3; Students 75.

PEREZVILLE-TAMUNING. *Mercy Heights Nursery and Kindergarten, Inc.,* 211 San Vitores St., 96911. Tel: 671-646-1185; Fax: 671-649-1822. Sr. Mary Roberta Taitano, R.S.M., Admin. Students 185.

TAI. *Infant of Prague Nursery and Kindergarten, Inc.* P.O. Box 22865, GMF, 96921. Tel: 671-734-2785; Fax: 671-734-2785. Sisters of Mercy. Sr. Barbara Ungacta, R.S.M., Admin. Students 187.

[E] CATHOLIC CHARITIES

AGANA. *Catholic Social Services of Guam,* P.O. Box EJ, 96910. Tel: 671-649-5717; 646-1924; 646-4974; Fax: 671-649-9224. Mrs. Cerila Rapadas, Exec. Dir.; Sr. Callista Camacho, R.S.M., Deputy Dir. Total Elderly Assisted 1,658; Total Adults Assisted 5,603; Total Children Assisted 2,008; Total Families Assisted 8,345; Total Staff 246.

Alee Shelter Program for Spouse Abuse, P.O. Box EJ, 96910. Tel: 472-6729; 472-6709. Sr. Eileen Mearns, R.G.S., Dir.

[F] MONASTERIES AND RESIDENCES OF PRIESTS

AGANA HEIGHTS. *St. Fidelis Friary.* Mailing Address: 135 Gunut Cir., 96919. Tel: 671-472-6339; Fax: 671-472-3335. Headquarters of Capuchin Friars (Vice Province, Star of the Sea). Very Revs. Agustin Gumataotao, O.F.M.Cap., Vice Prov.; Eric Forbes, O.F.M.Cap., Vice Prov., Guardian; Revs. Felix Leon Guerrero, O.F.M.Cap., Councilor; Paulo R. Kosaka, O.F.M.Cap., Councilor; George Maddock, O.F.M.Cap., Councilor; Daniel Cristobal, O.F.M.Cap.; Patrick Castro, O.F.M.Cap.; Joseph English, O.F.M.Cap.; Michael Tenorio, O.F.M.Cap.; Bros. Brian Champoux, O.F.M.Cap., Post-Noviate Formation Dir.; Maurice Moreau, O.F.M.Cap.
In Formation: Bros. Bryant Bamba; Robert Wolford; Hamilton Nukuto; Revs. Michael Cruz, O.F.M.Cap., Hawaii; Soke Maluafiti, O.F.M.Cap., Hawaii; Andre Eduvala, O.F.M.Cap.; Douglas Antipas, O.F.M.Cap.
Priests Retired: Revs. Eymard McKinnon, O.F.M.Cap.; Randolph Nowak, O.F.M.Cap., Hawaii. Priests Abroad: Revs. Paul Minchak, O.F.M.Cap., Hawaii; Gordon Combs, O.F.M.Cap., Hawaii; Robert Phelps, O.F.M.Cap., Hawaii; Andrew Mannetta, O.F.M.Cap., Hawaii; Michel W. Dalton, O.F.M.Cap., Hawaii.

AGAT. *Capuchin Fraternity,* P.O. Box 7787, 96928. Tel: 671-565-2136; Fax: 671-565-9678. Revs. Randolph Nowak, O.F.M.Cap., Senior Friar; Jose Villagomez, O.F.M.Cap.; Agustin Gumataotao, O.F.M.Cap.

YIGO. *St. Ignatius of Loyola House of Studies.* P.O. Box 20516, GMF, 96921. Tel: 671-653-5348; Fax: 671-653-5162.
E-mail: dmlhsr@ite.net
Rev. Daniel J. Mulhauser, S.J., Dir. Seminarians 5.

[G] CONVENTS AND RESIDENCES FOR SISTERS

AGANA. *Cathedral Mercy Convent.* Tel: 671-477-9291. P.O. Box 3070, Hagatna, 96932. Sisters of Mercy 8.

AGANA HEIGHTS. *Mercedarian Missionaries of Berriz,* 161 A Sunset Dr., 96919.
E-mail: mmbmicro@ite.net
Mailing Address: P.O. Box 3487, Agana, 96932. Tel: 671-477-8303; Fax: 671-472-2326. Sr. Mary Pilar Latasa, M.M.B., Regl. Vicar; Sr. Isabel Seman, M.M.B., Regl. Coord. Sisters 8.

AGAT. *Mt. Carmel Community,* P.O. Box 7705, 96928. Tel: 671-565-2369. Sr. Carmen Francis Siguenza, S.S.N.D.; Sr. Bernadette Quintanilla, S.S.N.D.; Sr. Clare Marie Quichocho, S.S.N.D.; Sr. Rose Marie Manibusan, S.S.N.D. Sisters 4. Sisters teach at Mt. Carmel Elementary & Jr. High.

BARRIGADA. *San Vicente Community,* 201 Bejong St., 96913. Tel: 671-734-3010. Sisters 4. Sisters teach at San Vicente Elementary & Jr. High, St. Francis School, and work at the Catholic Schools Office - Chancery.

DEDEDO. *Santa Barbara Convent,* 274 B. W. Santa Barbara St., 96912. Tel: 671-632-2384; Fax: 671-632-1414. Institute of the Sisters of Mercy of the Americas, North Carolina Region.

Kamalin House, P.O. Box 4678, Hagatna, 96932. Tel: 671-632-3211. Sisters 4.

INARAJAN. *Convent of Mercy Sisters,* P.O. Box 17211, 96916. Tel: 671-828-8285. Institute of Sisters of Mercy of the Americas, North Carolina Region 3.

St. Joseph Convent, P.O. Box 17211, 96917. Tel: 671-828-8285. Sisters 3.

MALOJLO. *Discalced Order Of Carmelites Monastery.* P.O. Box 17084, Inarajan, 96917. Tel: 671-828-8280; Fax: 671-828-8972. Order of Discalced Carmelites. Mother Bernadette Siew, O.C.D., Prioress. Sisters 14.

ORDOT. *Religious Missionaries of St. Dominic.* Tel: 671-477-7228; 472-1524. P.O. Box 5668, Agana, 96932. Total in Residence 5; Total Staff 5.

Sisters of the Good Shepherd Convent. P.O. Box 3596, Agana, 96932. Tel: 671-472-3393; Fax: 671-472-8486. Sr. Marie Maurer, R.G.S., Coord.; Sr. Helena Cusack, R.G.S., Supr.; Sr. Eileen Mearns, R.G.S.; Sr. Carol McClenon, R.G.S.; Sr. Stella Mangona, R.G.S. Total Assisted 400; Total Staff 16. Sisters work at abuse shelters under Catholic Social Services.

PEREZVILLE-TAMUNING. *Mercy Heights Convent,* 211 San Vitores St., 96911. Tel: 671-646-7246; Fax: 671-649-1822.
E-mail: guamrsm@iftech.net
Sr. Mary Angela Perez, R.S.M., Guam Region Pres. Administrative Residence and Offices of the Institute of the Sisters of Mercy of the Americas, North Carolina Region. Sisters in residence teaching and working in Tamuning and Agana. Sisters 11.

SINAJANA. *St. Jude Thaddeus Convent.* P.O. Box 394, Hagatna, 96932. Tel: 671-472-9687. Franciscan Sisters of Perpetual Adoration.

TAI. *Mercy Convent and Formation House.* P.O. Box 22865, Barrigada, 96921. Tel: 671-734-3312; Fax: 671-734-2260. Institute of the Sisters of Mercy of the Americas, North Carolina Region. Professed Sisters in various Apostolates and Sisters in basic formation. Sisters 13.

TALOFOFO. *Notre Dame Community,* 480 San Miguel St., 96930. Tel: 671-789-1629; Fax: 671-789-3810.

S.S.N.D. Regional House, 480 San Miguel St., 96930. Tel: 671-789-7763; 789-0501; Fax: 671-789-3810.
E-mail: guamregion@kuentos.guam.net

St. Augustine Community. Tel: 671-789-5965.

Mother Theresa. Tel: 671-789-0501.

Notre Dame Community. Tel: 671-789-1629.

Mother Caroline Community. Tel: 671-789-2919.

Mt. Carmel Community. Regional Councilors: Sr. Joseph Ann Quinene, S.S.N.D., Regl. Leader; Sr. Ignatia Sanchez, S.S.N.D.; Sr. Tarcisia Sablan, S.S.N.D. Sisters 28.

[H] MISCELLANEOUS LISTINGS

AGANA. *Our Lady of the Waters House of Prayer.* (Retreat Center), P.O. Box 163, 96932. Tel: 671-477-3122; Fax: 671-477-3766. Rev. Patrick K.Q. Garcia, Dir.

Saint Vincent de Paul Society, c/o Santa Teresita Parish, P.O. Box 306, 96910. Tel: 671-734-2100. Mr. John Lizama, Pres. Tel: 671-472-6068.

Secular Franciscans, P.O. Box CF, 96910. Tel: 671-472-6023; 472-6339. Rev. Daniel Cristobal, O.F.M.Cap., Spiritual Dir.; Mrs. Carmen Manibusan, Pres.

BARRIGADA. *Saint Dominic's Senior Care Home.* 350 N. Sabana Barrigada Dr., Barrigada Heights, 96913. Tel: 671-632-9370; 632-9378; 9379; Fax: 671-637-1679.
E-mail: Stdom@ite.net
Sr. Fe Dural, O.P., Admin. Total in Residence 59; Total Staff 70.

MANGILAO. *Campus Ministry, Newman Center, University of Guam.* Box 23142, Barrigada, 96921. Tel: 671-734-3507; Fax: 671-734-2943.
E-mail: khezel@ite.net
Revs. Kenneth J. Hezel, S.J.; William T. Suchan, S.J. Total in Residence 1; Total Staff 3.

RELIGIOUS INSTITUTES OF MEN REPRESENTED IN THE ARCHDIOCESE

For further details refer to the corresponding bracketed number in the Religious Institutes of Men or Women section.

[0470]—*The Capuchin Friars.* (Vice Prov. of Mary, Star of the Sea).—O.F.M.Cap.

[0690]—*The Society of Jesus- Jesuit Fathers and Brothers.* (N.Y. Prov.).—S.J.

RELIGIOUS INSTITUTES OF WOMEN REPRESENTED IN THE ARCHDIOCESE

[1780]—*Congregation of the Sisters of the Third Order of St. Francis of Perpetual Adoration.* (La Crosse, WI).—F.S.P.A.

[0420]—*Discalced Carmelite Nuns.*—O.C.D.

[2510]—*Mercedarian Missionaries of Berriz.*—M.M.B.

[]—*Order of Saint Benedict.*—O.S.B.

[]—*Religious Missionaries of St. Dominic.*—O.P.

[2970]—*School Sisters of Notre Dame.* (Mequon, WI).—S.S.N.D.

[2575]—*Sisters of Mercy of the Americas.* (Belmont, NC).—R.S.M.

[]—*Sisters of St. Francis.*—O.S.F.

[1830]—*Sisters of the Good Shepherd.*—R.G.S.

NECROLOGY

† Calvo, Rev. Msgr. Oscar L., (Retired). —Died July 28, 2000.

Diocese of Arecibo, Puerto Rico

(Dioecesis Arecibensis)

Most Reverend

INAKI MALLONA TXERTUDI, C.P.

Bishop of Arecibo; ordained March 27, 1956; appointed December 14, 1991; consecrated January 6, 1992; installed January 25, 1992. *Res., 206 Dr. Salas St., P.O. Box 616, Arecibo, PR, 00613-0616.*

Most Reverend

MIGUEL RODRIGUEZ, C.SS.R., D.D.

Retired Bishop of Arecibo; ordained June 22, 1958; appointed January 21, 1974; consecrated March 23, 1974; retired March 1990. *Res., Apartado 238, Aguadilla, PR, 00605-0238.*

ESTABLISHED APRIL 30, 1960.

Square Miles 833.08.

Comprises the mid-northern part of the Island.

The Chancery: 206 Dr. Salas St., P.O. Box 616, Arecibo, PR, 00613. Tel.: 787-878-3180; Fax: 787-880-2661.

E-mail address: obispado@xsn.net

STATISTICAL OVERVIEW

Personnel	
Bishop	1
Retired Bishops	1
Priests: Diocesan Active in Diocese	101
Priests: Active Outside Diocese	7
Priests: Retired, Sick or Absent	11
Number of Diocesan Priests	119
Religious Priests in Diocese	41
Extern Priests in Diocese	8
Ordinations:	
Diocesan Priests	1
Religious Priests	15
Permanent Deacons in Diocese	11
Total Brothers	8
Total Sisters	163
Parishes	
Parishes	59
With Resident Pastor:	
Resident Diocesan Priests	42
Resident Religious Priests	17
Missions	230
Pastoral Centers	1
Welfare	
Homes for the Aged	4
Total Assisted	9,490
Residential Care of Children	3
Total Assisted	69
Specialized Homes	1
Total Assisted	35
Special Centers for Social Services	2
Total Assisted	13,518
Educational	
Seminaries, Diocesan	1
Students from This Diocese	4
Diocesan Students in Other Seminaries	5
Total Seminarians	9
Colleges and Universities	1
Total Students	867
High Schools, Diocesan and Parish	14
Total Students	2,617
Elementary Schools, Diocesan and Parish	14
Total Students	4,286
Catechesis/Religious Education:	
High School Students	3,996
Elementary Students	12,990
Total Students Under Catholic Instruction	24,765
Teachers in the Diocese:	
Priests	7
Brothers	3
Sisters	40
Lay Teachers	478
Vital Statistics	
Receptions into the Church:	
Infant Baptism Totals	3,515
Adult Baptism Totals	258
Received into Full Communion	83
First Communions	3,180
Confirmations	2,196
Marriages:	
Catholic	733
Interfaith	31
Total Marriages	764
Deaths	1,670
Total Catholic Population	386,874
Total Population	609,690

Former Bishops—Most. Rev. ALFRED F. MENDEZ, C.S.C., ord. 1935; cons. Oct. 28, 1960; retired Jan., 1974; died Jan. 28, 1995.—Most. Rev. MIGUEL RODRIQUEZ, C.S.S.R., D.D., ord. June 22, 1958; appt. Jan. 21, 1974; cons. March 23, 1974; retired March, 1990.

Secretary to the Bishop—Sr. SELENIA CASTRO, O.P.

Chancery Office—206 Dr. Salas St., P.O. Box 616, Arecibo, 00613-0616. Tel: 787-878-3180; 878-3110; Fax: 787-880-2661.

Vicar General—Rev. JOSE D. SOBERAL, V.G., *P.O. Box 616, Arecibo, 00613.* Tel: 787-878-3180; 878-3110.

Chancellor—Rev. JOSEPH D. SCHRECK, O.F.M.Cap., *P.O. Box 616, Arecibo, 00613.* Tel: 787-878-3180.

Vice Chancellor & Secretary—Miss SYLVIA VARGAS.

Diocesan Tribunal of Arecibo—Rev. JORGE L. VIRELLA SANCHEZ, J.C.L., Official, *P.O. Box 143964, Arecibo, 00613.* Tel: 787-816-5614; Fax: 787-816-5614.

Judicial Vicar—Rev. EDWIN MERCADO VIERA, J.C.L., Presiding Judge.

Promoter of Justice—Rev. GABRIEL MADURO LOPEZ.

Defenders of the Bond—Revs. ALBERTO DIAZ COLON; GABRIEL MADURO; JOSEPH SCHRECK, O.F.M.Cap.

Advocate—Miss SARAH R. LOPEZ ALBERTI.

Notary—Mrs. JOSEPHINE BURGOS.

Secretary—Mrs. LIVIA E. SERRANO.

Vicar of Diocesan Pastoral Affairs—Rev. JOSE D. SOBERAL.

Diocesan Consultors—Rev. Msgr. BUENAVENTURA BALLESTER, P.H.; Revs. MIGUEL MERCADO; JOSE D. SOBERAL, V.G.; ELIAS FERNANDEZ, O.SS.T.; CARMELO URARTE; FRANCISCO CONCEPCION; VICTOR ROJAS.

Diocesan Pastoral Council—Revs. MIGUEL MERCADO; ELIAS FERNANDEZ; BENJAMIN QUINONES; MELQUIADES ROJAS; Sr. ROSA DE FATIMA, O.P.

Dean of Arecibo Zone—Rev. Msgr. BUENAVENTURA BALLESTER, P.H., *P.O. Box 140637, Arecibo, 00614-0637.* Tel: 787-878-4910.

Dean of El Calvario Zone—Rev. ELIAS FERNANDEZ, O.SS.T., *P.O. Box 525, Isabela, 00662.* Tel: 787-872-2563.

Dean of Vega Baja Zone—Rev. Msgr. FRANCISCO CONCEPCION, *P.O. Box 775, Vega Alta, 00692.* Tel: 787-883-4875.

Diocesan Offices and Directors

Ayuda Social Movimiento Juan XXIII—MARIA S. SANTIAGO, Coord., *P.O. Box 241, Sabana Hoyos, P.R., 00688-0241.* Tel: 787-881-7141; 881-2342; Fax: 787-881-7141.

Confraternity of Christian Doctrine—Sr. ROSA DE FATIMA, O.P., *5 Calle Mariano Abril, Box 1151, Arecibo, 00612.* Tel: 787-878-8401.

Cursillos de Cristiandad—Rev. VICTOR ROJAS, *P.O. Box 1826, Arecibo, 00613.* Tel: 787-872-2563.

Diocesan Council of Catholic Women—Vacant.

Propagation of Faith—Rev. MANUEL P. CARDENAS, M.N.M.

Holy Childhood—Rev. MANUEL P. CARDENAS, M.N.M.

Director of Youth—Rev. CARLOS E. GRANADOS.

Legion of Mary—Vacant.

Movimiento Familiar Cristiano (CFM)—Vacant.

Prison Services—Rev. ELVIN IRIZARRY, *Box 673, Arecibo, 00613.* Tel: 787-878-4910.

Seminario Jesus Maestro College Seminary—Rev. DANIEL FERNANDEZ, Dir., *Box 2164, Arecibo, 00613.* Tel: 787-878-1528.

Seminary Board—Rev. JORGE L. VIRELLA.

Pastoral Vocational Program—Revs. DANIEL FERNANDEZ; CARLOS E. GRANADOS; RAMON OLIVENCIA; VICTOR ROJAS; ROBERTO VEGA.

Superintendent of Schools—Miss LYDIA HERNANDEZ;

Mrs. TRINIDAD GONZALEZ, *P.O. Box 1683, Arecibo, 00613.* Tel: 787-878-1095; Fax: 787-878-1095.

Catholic Charities—Sr. ROBERTA GRZELAK, C.D.P., Promotion of Human Development Office, *P.O. Box 353, Arecibo, 00613.* Tel: 787-817-6951; Fax: 787-817-7597.

Retreat House, Centro Diocesano Mons. Mendez—Rev. DANIEL FERNANDEZ, *Apdo. 2164, Arecibo, 00613.* Tel: 787-878-4796.

Boy Scouts—Vacant.

Hospital Chaplains—

Arecibo Hospital—Dr. COLL Y TOSTE; Rev. DELFIN RODRIGUEZ; Miss ESTHER COSTA.

Buen Hospital Pastor—Rev. P. GABRIEL MADURO, and priests of Cathedral of San Felipe Apostol: Revs. ROBERTO VEGA; JORGE PAREDES.

Susoni Hospital—Rev. P. GABRIEL MADURO.

Vocations—Rev. DANIEL FERNANDEZ, *Apdo. 2164, Arecibo, 00613.* Tel: 787-878-1528.

Police Chaplain—Rev. Msgr. FRANCISCO CONCEPCION.

Sociedad San Vincente de Paul (Vincentinos)—Mr. ANGEL GINES, Pres. Consejo Diocesano. Tel: 787-884-5087; 854-2562.

CLERGY, PARISHES, MISSIONS AND PAROCHIAL SCHOOLS

CITY OF ARECIBO

1—CATHEDRAL OF SAN FELIPE APOSTOL (1616), Revs. Roberto Vega, Rector; Gabriel Maduro; Jorge Paredes.
Res., De Diego St., Box 577, 00613. Tel: 809-878-1149; Fax: 787-878-1149. [JC]
Chapels—Islote II, Sagrada Familia.; Islote III (Sector Vibora), San Juan Evangelista.; Sector Boam, Maria Reina.; Islote I (Vigia), N.S. del Carmen.

2—CHURCH OF SAGRADO CORAZON DE JESUS (1961), Rev. Msgr. Buenaventura Ballester, P.H.; Rev. Cesar Ramirez.
Res., Box 140637, 00614. Tel: 787-878-4910; Fax: 787-879-2124. [JC]
School—Colegio San Felipe, Box 673, 00613. Tel: 809-878-3532.
Lay Teachers 30; Students 337. Principals: Judith Colon; Gregoria Perez.
Catechesis/Religious Programs—Students 87.
Chapel—Bo. Obrero, Inmaculada Concepcion.

3—NUESTRA SENORA DEL CARMEN (1961), Revs. Alberto Diaz; Delfin Rodriguez.
Res., Bo. Cotto No. 985, P.O. Box 9949, Cotto Sta., 00613. Tel: 787-878-1268; Fax: 787-817-5062. [JC]
School—Hogar-Colegio La Milagrosa, Ave., Cotto, 00613. Tel: 809-878-0341.
Sisters of Charity 7; Lay Teachers 25; Students 438.
Catechesis/Religious Programs—Students 218.
Chapels—Abra S. Francisco, San Antonio.; Rodriguez Olmo, San Francisco.

4—SANTA ANA (1961), Revs. Victor Rojas; Elvin Irizarry.
Res., Bo. Santana, Box 318, 00613. Tel: 787-881-6005. [JC]
Catechesis/Religious Programs—Tel: 787-881-6882.
Students 119.
Chapels—Factor II, N.S. del Carmen.; Santuario Cristo de los Milagros.

5—CHURCH OF CHRIST THE KING (1967), Rev. Serapio Fernandez.
Res., Box 1932, 00613. Tel: 809-878-9214.
Catechesis/Religious Programs—Students 155.
Chapel—Bo. Hato Arriba, Maria Auxiliadora.

6—OUR LADY OF HOPE (1986), Rev. Angel M. Pagan.
Res., Box 489, 00613. Tel: 787-880-1943. [JC]
Catechesis/Religious Programs—Students 37.
Chapels—Cantagallo, Sgdo. Corazon de Jesus.; Plan Bonito, San Rafael.

7—NUESTRA SENORA DE FATIMA (1967), Revs. Ignacio Pili, C.M.V.; Gilberto Da Silva, C.M.V.; Jesus Gonzalez, C.M.V.
Res., Box 667, Sabana Hoyos, 00688. Tel: 787-881-8274. [JC]
Catechesis/Religious Programs—Students 145.
Chapels—Garrochales, S. Fco. de Asis.; Ballaja, N.S. del Carmen.; Garrochales, La Milagrosa, San Luis.; Espino, Immaculada Concepcion.

8—INMACULADO CORAZON DE MARIA (1987), Revs. Cornelius T. McQuillan, C.S.Sp.; Christopher Chukwu, C.S.Sp.
Res., Box 1282, Sabana Hoyos, 00688. [JC]
Chapels—Bo. Asomante, San Isidro.; Bo. Carolina, Sagrado Corazon de Jesus.; Bo. Arrozal, San Jose.; Los Muertos, San Francisco.

9—LA MILAGROSA (1973), Rev. Angel M. Santos.
Res., Box 204, Bajadero, 00616. Tel: 787-881-0295. [JC]
Catechesis/Religious Programs—Students 310.
Chapels—Bajadero, Immaculada Concepcion.; Domingo Ruiz, N.S. La Providencia.; Carreras, San Judas.; Biafara, N.S. La Virgen del Carmen.

10—SAN JUAN BOSCO (1971), Rev. Melquiades Rojas.
Res., Urb. Jardines de Arecibo, Calle R-Y-26, 00612. Tel: 787-879-1070; Fax: 787-817-4107.
School—Tel: 809-879-2069.
Lay Teachers 25; Students 413.
Catechesis/Religious Programs—Students 194.
Chapel—Las Canelas, N.S. La Dolorosa, San Daniel.
Sisters of Mercy 3.

11—CHURCH OF SAN MARTIN DE PORRES (1973), Rev. Edwin Mercado.
Res., Calle 6 F-12, Box 14-2142, Urb. Univ. Gardens, 00613. Tel: 787-878-1822.
Catechesis/Religious Programs—Students 225.
Chapel—Victor Rojas II, San Jose Obrero.

12—CHURCH OF SANTA TERESITA (1980), Rev. Luis A. Vazquez.
Res., Road 492, KM 1.9, P.O. Box 9242, Cotto Station, 00613. Tel: 787-878-7015. [JC]
Catechesis/Religious Programs—Students 60.
Chapels—Hato Arriba, N.S. La Providencia.; Barrancas, La Milagrosa.

13—CHURCH OF SANTA CECILIA (1981), Rev. Carlos E. Granados.
Res., HC-02 Box 13674, 00612. Tel: 787-879-3364. [JC]
Catechesis/Religious Programs—Students 120.
Chapels—Calichosa, San Jose.; Los Canos, San Martin de Porres.; La Guinea, La Milagrosa.

14—SANTISIMO SACRAMENTO (1990), Rev. Enrique A. Perez.
Res., Ste. 109, P.O. Box 4015, 00613. Tel: 787-880-6513. [JC]
Catechesis/Religious Programs—Students 65.
Chapels—Del Valle, La Milagrosa.; Jobos, San Pascual.

OUTSIDE OF ARECIBO

Barceloneta, Church of Our Lady of Mt. Carmel (1882), Revs. William Murphy, Pastor; Scott Brockson.
Res., P.O. Box 2062, 00617. Tel: 809-846-5625. [JC]
Catechesis/Religious Programs—Tel: 787-846-7343.
Students 209.
Chapels—Garrochales I, N.S. de Fatima.; Palmas Altas, San Antonio.; Punta Palma, N.S. del Mar.

Our Lady of Victory (1963), Rev. Leon Perez, Admin.
Res., Ste. 125, Call Box 2020, 00617. Tel: 809-846-6120. [JC]
Catechesis/Religious Programs—Students 107.
Chapels—Parcelas Imberry, San Jose Obrero.; Quebrada, Immaculate Heart of Mary.; Tiburones, N.S. de Fatima.; Palenque, San Juan Bautista.

Camuy

1—ST. JOSEPH (1827), Revs. Adrian Jimenez; Eliud Aponte.
Res., P.O. Box 414, 00627. Tel: 787-898-3620; Fax: 787-898-3620. [JC]
Catechesis/Religious Programs—Students 451.
Convent—.San Jose Hermanas Terciarias Capuchinas 4.
Chapels—Membrillo, N.S. La Monserrate.; Puente (Zarzas), Sagrado Corazon.; Puente (Zarza Parcelas), N.S. La Milagrosa.; Puente (Sector Pica), N.S. del Rosario.; Abra Honda, Espiritu Santo.; Zanjas, Immaculada Concepcion.

2—OUR LADY OF THE MIRACULOUS MEDAL (1962). (El Calvario). Revs. Zenaido Martin; Apolonio Duron, M.N.M.; Juan J. Ortiz.
Res., HC-01 Buzon 5240, 00627. Tel: 787-898-5825. [JC]
Catechesis/Religious Programs—Tel: 787-898-4841.
Students 436.
Chapels—Planas II, Santiago Apostol.; Puertos, Sagrado Corazon.; Cienaga, Cristo Rey.; Camuy Arriba, N.S. del Carmen.; Sector Riego, Santa Clara.; Sector Mani, Sagrado Corazon.

3—OUR LADY OF ASUMPTION (1984), Rev. Antonio Caraballo.
Res., HC-02 Box 8047, 00627. Tel: 787-898-8038. [JC]
Catechesis/Religious Programs—Students 372.
Chapels—Cibao Ocasio, N.S. del Perpetuo Socorro.; Callejones, Sagrado Corazon.; Callejones II, San Pablo de la Cruz.; Cibao Lugo, Maria Auxiliadora.

4—OUR LADY OF MONSERRATE (1961), Revs. Manuel M. Flores, M.N.M.; Victor Lugo, M.N.M.
Res., HC-03 Box 16512, Quebradillas, 00678-9820. Tel: 787-898-6784. [JC]
Catechesis/Religious Programs—Students 200.
Convent—Tel: 787-896-6176.
Hermanes Angeles Custodios 2.
Chapels—Piletas (Lares), N.S. del Carmen.; Guajataca (Queb.), N.S. de Fatima.; Aibonito Beltran, San Antonio.; Cibao (S. Sebastian), Santa Ana.; Planas I (Isabela), Santa Cruz.; Planas II, N.S. del Rosario.

Ciales, Holy Rosary (1820), Revs. Antonio Rodriguez, O.Carm.; Elias Pascual; Luis Miranda, O.Carm.; Gabriel M. Torres, Pastor.
Res., P.O. Box 26, 00638. Tel: 787-871-2205; 871-3485. [JC]
School—P.O. Box 1334, 00638. Tel: 787-871-1318. Mrs. Juanita Natal, Prin.
Lay Teachers 28; Students 363.
Catechesis/Religious Programs—Tel: 787-871-1492.
Students 760.
Chapels—Pozas, San Elias.; Cialitos, Buen Pastor.; Hato Viejo, Corazon de Jesus.; Hato Viejo, San Antonio.; Jaguas, Santa Clara.; Pesa, San Ignacio.; Cialitos-Cruces, Corazon de Maria.; Toro Negro, N.S.; Bo. Marias, Maternidad de la Virgen.

N.S. Madre del Redentor (1988), Rev. Wiktor Tarnawski.
Res., P.O. Box 1181, 00638. Tel: 787-871-2404. [JC]
Catechesis/Religious Programs—Students 200.
Chapels—Yunes, San Jose.; Fronton (Sabana), Perpetuo Socorro.; Cordillera 5, N.S. La Providencia.; Limon, Smo. Rosario.; Cordillera 7, Sagrada Familia.

Corozal, Holy Family (1804), Revs. Eugenio Gayarre; Ovidio Perez Perez.
Res., P.O. Box 474, 00783. Tel: 787-859-2595. [JC]
School—Tel: 787-859-2420.
Sisters of St. Joseph 9; Lay Teachers 50; Students 942.
Catechesis/Religious Programs—Students 1,025.
Chapels—Guarico Palmarejo I, San Judas Tadeo.; Palmarejo II, San Vicente.; Palmarejo II, San Francisco de Asis.; Dos Bocas II, Santa Teresita.; Cibuco, N.S. del Carmen.; Abras, San Jose.; Urb. Sylvia, Perpetuo Socorro.

Corozal-Padilla, Our Lady of the Seven Sorrows (1984), Revs. Miguel Rivera; Juan R. Mora.
Res., P.O. Box 740, 00783. Tel: 787-859-1900.
Catechesis/Religious Programs—Students 700.
Chapels—Padilla Hermita, San Rafael.; Padilla Hormiga, San Martin.; Cieneguita (V.A.), N.S. del Perpetuo Socorro.

Corozal-Palmarito, La Milagrosa, Revs. Benjamin Quinones, C.R.L.; Manuel Rabadan, C.R.L.; Rafael J. Gonzalez, C.R.L., Pastor.
Res., HC-03 Box 13976, 00783. Tel: 787-859-5306.
Catechesis/Religious Programs—Students 514.
Convent—HC-03 Box 14048, 00783. Tel: 787-859-8151.
Hnas. de San Francisco (Secular Institute) 3.
Chapels—Maguelles, Cristo Rey.; Mana, N.S. de Fatima.; Radio Oro, Nuestra Senora del Carmen.

Corozal-Palos Blancos, Christ the King (1968), Rev. David Rivas, Pastor.
Res., P.O. Box 1091, Corozal, 00783. Tel: 787-859-7313. [JC]
Catechesis/Religious Programs—Students 725.
Chapels—Cuchillas, N.S. del Perpetuo Socorro.; Negros, N.S. del Rosario.; Palos Blancos, Santa Teresita.; Palos Blancos, San Antonio.

Florida, Our Lady of Mercy (1887), Rev. Casimiro Domeck.
Res., P.O. Box 437, 00650. Tel: 787-822-2670. [JC]
Catechesis/Religious Programs—Tel: 787-822-2045.
Students 100.
Chapels—Monte Bello, N.S. del Carmen.; Pajornal (Bta.), Santa Rosa de Lima.

Hatillo, Our Lady of Mt. Carmel (1830), Revs. Fernando Morell, Pastor; Rafael Mendez.
Res., P.O. Box 2, 00659. Tel: 809-898-5300. [JC]
School—Tel: 787-898-2800.
Sisters de la Caridad del Cardenal Sancha 4; Lay Teachers 55; Students 869.
Catechesis/Religious Programs—Tel: 787-898-3302.
Students 610.
Chapels—Carrizales, Sagrado Corazon.; Corcovados, Immaculada Concepcion.; Capaez, N.S. Perpetuo Socorro.; Carrizales, San Jose.; Santa Rosa, Santa Rosa de Lima.; Lechuga: San Pio X.; Palma Gordo: Sagrada Familia.

Our Lady of Guadalupe (1961), Revs. Victor R. Borrero, S.E.M.V., Prior; Luis Maria de la Cruz, S.E.M.V.; Rene A. Maria del Nino Jesus, S.E.M.V.; Anibal Jesus Hostia de la Purisima, S.E.M.V.; David A. Maria Alabanza de la Trin, S.E.M.V.; Alberto Jesus Gloria de la Inmaculada, S.E.M.V.;

Antonio Ofray, S.E.M.V.; Sr. Teresa Maria V. de la Eucaristia.
Res., Carr. Ins. 129, Arecibo to Lares, P.O. Box 1131, Arecibo, 00613. Tel: 787-898-8035. [JC]
Catechesis/Religious Programs—Students 296.
Chapels—Pajuil, Santa Rosa de Lima.; Buena Vista, Inmaculada Concepcion.; Bda Colon, N.S. La Providencia.; Sector Naranjito, San Jose.

Perpetual Help (1961), Rev. Jose Estensoro.
Res., Ste. 113, P.O. Box 59003, 00659. Tel: 787-898-7771. [JC]
Catechesis/Religious Programs—Tel: 787-820-2819.
Students 140.
Chapels—Aibonito, Cristo Rey.; Berrocal, Sagrado Corazon de Jesus.; Sonadora, La Milagrosa.; Mariposa, N.S. del Carmen.; Cantera, Ntra. Sra. de la Providencia.

Isabela, St. Anthony (1835), Revs. Alejandro Nistal; Wilfredo Echevarria, O.SS.T.; Johnny Cruz; Epifanio Fernandez, O.SS.T.
Res., Box 525, 00662. Tel: 787-872-2563; Fax: 787-872-4393. [JC]
School—Sisters of St. Dominic 4; Lay Teachers 31; Students 500.
Catechesis/Religious Programs—Students 608.
Chapels—Medina, Sma. Trinidad.; Curva, Santa Rosa de Lima.; Cotto, San Martin de Porres.; Arenales Bajo, N.S. La Monserrate.; Vendrel, N.S. La Providencia.; Jobos, Buen Pastor.; Guayabos, Espiritu Santo.; Arenales A., El Salvador.; Arenales Alto, Sagrado Corazon, Tel: 787-872-0015.
Sister of Trinity (Valencia) 4.; Hogar Infantil/Jesus Nazareno, Isabella.

Our Lady of Mount Carmel (1983), Rev. Elias Fernandez, O.SS.T.
Res., Box 1555, 00662. Tel: 787-872-5550. [JC]
Catechesis/Religious Programs—Students 390.
Chapels—Poncito, Santos Inocentes.; Planas, San Juan Bautista.; La Tuna, San Juan de Mata.; Galateo Bajo, La Milagrosa.

Lares, St. Joseph (1827), Revs. Esteban Barruetabena; Ignacio Goiburu, C.P.; Mariano Arrien, C.P.; Luis A. Lopez, C.P.
Res., P.O. Box 103, 00669. Tel: 787-897-2067. [JC]
School—Tel: 809-897-2640.
Hermanas Pasionistas 1; Lay Teachers 17; Students 209.
Catechesis/Religious Programs—Tel: 787-897-2717.
Students 850.
Chapels—Piletas II, San Carlos.; Sebruguillo, La Resurreccion.; Piletas Arece, La Milagrosa.; Piletas, Saint Maria Goretti.; Tabonuco, La Providencia.
Hermanas Josefinas de Mexico 6.

St. Judas Tadeos (1986), Rev. Angel R. Diaz, Admin.
Res., P.O. Box 1109, 00669. Tel: 809-897-3540. [JC]
Catechesis/Religious Programs—Students 240.
Chapels—Palmar Llano, Perpetuo Socorro.; Vega de los Acevedo, La Dolorosa.; Buenos Aires, Sgda. Familia de Nazaret.; Matilde, San Antonio.

Manati

1—La Candelaria (1738), Revs. Emilio Tovar, C.M.; Santiago Arribas, C.M.
Res., Calle Padial #2, 00674. Tel: 787-854-2013. [JC]
School—Sisters of Charity 5; Lay Teachers 45; Students 985.
Catechesis/Religious Programs—Tel: 787-854-4021.
Students 77.
Chapels—Pugnado, N.S. del Perpetuo Socorro.; Villa Amalia, La Milagrosa.; Cortes, Sagrado Corazon.; Polvorin, La Monserrate.; Ceiba, Espiritu Santo.

2—Our Savior, Rev. Victor Sanchez.
Res., P.O. Box 465, 00674. Tel: 787-884-3664.
School—Colegio Marista, P.O. Box 462, 00764. Tel: 787-854-1075.
Marist Brothers 3; Lay Teachers 29; Students 491.
Catechesis/Religious Programs—Students 100.
Chapels—San Jose, San Jose.; Lagunas Tierra Nueva, N.S. de Lourdes.; Guayaney, San Martin de Porres.

3—Sagrada Familia (1972), Revs. Francisco J. Marrodan, C.M.; Manuel Araujo, C.M.
Res., P.O. Box 704, 00674. Tel: 787-854-2858. [JC]
Catechesis/Religious Programs—Students 216.
Chapels—Parcelas Marquez, San Judas Tadeo.; Palo Alto, N.S. La Monserrate.; Polvorin, La Milagrosa.

4—Nuestra Senora del Mar (1978), Rev. Jesus A. Rodriguez.
Res., Apdo. 1183, 00674. Tel: 787-854-5388. [JC]
Catechesis/Religious Programs—Tel: 787-854-9252.
Students 276.
Chapels—Tierras Nuevas, Santa Rosa de Lima.; Sector Cantito, La Milagrosa.; Boquillas, Nuestra Senora de Lourdes.

Morovis, Nuestra Senora del Carmen (1820), Revs. Ramon Gomez, O.Carm.; Enrique Oria, O.Carm.; Jose Oliveras, O.Carm.; Jesus Monreal, O.Carm., Pastor.
Res., Box 428, 00687. Tel: 787-862-2620. [JC]
Catechesis/Religious Programs—Students 2,176.
Chapels—San Lorenzo, N.S. del Rosario.; Perchas, N.S. del Carmen.; Pastos, N.S. del Carmen.; Rio Grande, La Milagrosa.; Morovis Sur, San Jose.; Unibon, San Miguel.; Vaga III, La Milagrosa.; MPatron I, Sagrada Familia.; Cuchillas, Segrado Corazon.; Morovis Sur, Inmaculada Concepcion.

St. Paul Apostle (1985), Rev. Tomas Santos.
Res., P.O. Box 537, 00687. Tel: 787-862-3445. [JC]
Catechesis/Religious Programs—Students 690.
Chapels—Franquez, Nino de Praga.; Franquez Carretera, La Providencia.; Torrecillas, Senor de los Milagros.

Orocovis, San Juan Bautista (1838), Revs. Jose L. Gomez, S.D.B.; Julian San Nicasio, S.D.B.; Francisco Juan, S.D.B.; Abrahan Cepeda, S.D.B.
Res., P.O. Box 2114, 00720. Tel: 787-867-2210; Fax: 787-867-5675. [JC]
School—Tel: 787-867-2295.
Salesians Sisters 4; Lay Teachers 23; Students 251.
Catechesis/Religious Programs—Students 991.
Chapels—Sabana, Angeles Custodios.; Botijas I, Cristo Resucitado.; Botijas II, Santa Clara.; El Puente, San Pablo.; Mata de Cana, Sagrado Corazon.; Damian Arriba, Espiritu Santo.; Montebello, N.S. del Carmen.; Guadalupe, N.S. La Guadalupe.; Gato Bajura, N.S. La Providencia.; Gato, San Judas Tadeo.

Our Lady of Fatima (1975), Revs. Tosello Giangiacomo, C.S.Sp.; Jose Alamo, C.S.Sp.
Res., Box 2118, 00720. Tel: 787-867-3277. [JC]
Catechesis/Religious Programs—Students 475.
Chapels—Bermejales, Cristo de la Salud.; Bauta, N.S. La Dolorosa.; Damian Arriba, N.S. del Perpetuo Socorro.; Pellejas I, Espiritu Santo.; Miraflores, San Martin.

Quebradillas, San Raphael (1828), Revs. Miguel Mercado; Salomon de Jesus Morales. In res., Rev. Msgr. Ernesto Munoz.
Res., Box 57, 00678. Tel: 787-895-2035. [JC]
School—Tel: 809-895-2280.
Sisters 2; Lay Teachers 19; Students 363.
Catechesis/Religious Programs—Students 450.
Chapels—San Jose, San Jose.; Quebrada, N.S. del Carmen.; Chivos, Santa Cruz.; Cacao, La Milagrosa.; Parcelas San Antonio, N.S. La Monserrate.; San Antonio, San Antonio.; Charcas, N.S. del Perpetuo Socorro.; Las Talas, La Guadalupe.
Hermanes Dominicas Presentacion 5.

Sacred Heart (1977), Rev. Carmelo Urarte.
Res., Box 1569, 00678. Tel: 787-895-3033; Fax: 787-895-3033. [JC]
Catechesis/Religious Programs—Students 250.
Chapels—San Antonio, San Miguel.; Yeguada, N.S. del Perpetuo Socorro.; El Verde, Madre Dolorosa.

Utuado

1—San Miquel (1746), Revs. Roy Martinez, O.F.M.Cap., Pastor; Pedro Silva, O.F.M.Cap.; Joseph Schreck, O.F.M.Cap.; Jose McCarthy, O.F.M.Cap. In res., Bros. Bernardo Ayala, O.F.M.Cap.; Jose E. Sanchez, O.F.M.Cap.; Reynaldo Saliva, O.F.M.Cap; Jose A. Villaran, O.F.M.Cap.
Res., 8 Barcelo St., P.O. Box 10, 00641. Tel: 787-894-2696; 3108; Fax: 787-894-3812. [JC]
Schools—Elementary School, Progreso St., Box 10, 00641. Mrs. Nereida Huertas, Prin.
Lay Teachers 22; Students 123; Intermediate and High School, San Miguel Ave., Box 10, 00641. Tel: 809-894-9386. Mrs. Lydia M. Giusti, Prin.
Lay Teachers 26; Students 198.
Catechesis/Religious Programs—Students 536.
Chapels—Puente Blanco, San Fidel.; Arenas, San Martin.; Sabana Grande, N.S. del Perpetuo Socorro.

2—San Pedro y San Pablo (1988), Rev. Rafael Nuno.
Res., Box 679, 00641. Tel: 787-894-0696. [JC]
Catechesis/Religious Programs—Students 146.
Chapels—Las Palmas, San Francisco.; Vivi Arriba, Immalculada Concepcion.; La Pica, La Milagrosa.; Consejo, San Jose.; Vivi Abajo, Nuestra Senora de la Divina Providencia.
Monastery Mother of God Cloistered 33.

3—Our Lady of Angels (1967), Rev. Andres Davila.
Res., Box 98, Angeles, 00611. Tel: 809-894-7722. [JC]
Catechesis/Religious Programs—Students 59.
Chapels—Corcho, San Jose.; Santa Isabela, N.S. La Monserrate.; Las Vegas, Sagrada Familia.

4—Nuestra Senora del Monte Carmelo (1981), Rev. Pedro Hernandez.
Res., P.O. Box 299, Caonillas-Utuado, 00641. Tel: 787-894-7340. [JC]
Catechesis/Religious Programs—Students 8.
Chapels—Mameyes, San Antonio.; Tetuan III, Sagrado Corazon.; Tetuan I, Cristo Salvador.; Don Alonso, La Milagrosa.

5—Our Lady of Sorrows (1983), Rev. Bertulfo Acevedo.
Res., Box 161, Angeles, 00611. Tel: 787-894-7144. [JC]
Catechesis/Religious Programs—Students 54.
Chapels—Roncador, San Martin de Porres.; Cayuco, Cristo Rey.; Jacanas, N.S. la Monserrate.

Vega-Alta, Immaculate Conception of Blessed Virgin Mary (1805), Rev. Msgr. Francisco Concepcion; Rev. Ramon Olivencia.
Res., P.O. Box 775, 00692. Tel: 787-883-4875.
Catechetical Center—Calle Colon 17, 00692.
Sisters of Charity 4; Students 464.
Chapels—Maricao IV, Sagrado Corazon.; Bajura II, San Vicente.; Bajura I, Santa Ana.; Candelaria, Inmaculado Corazon de Maria.; Maricao II, N.S. La Guadalupe.

Santa Ana (1967), Rev. Msgr. Jesus Diaz.
Res., Urb. Santa Ana, Apartado 2105, Calle 3H9, 00692. Tel: 787-883-2502.
Catechesis/Religious Programs—Students 190.
Chapel—Espinosa, N.S. del Carmen.

Perpetuo Socorro (1975), Rev. Francisco Jimenez, Admin.
Res., Box 9018, Sabana Branch, Vega-Baja, 00694. Tel: 787-883-5776; Fax: 787-270-3103. [JC]
Catechesis/Religious Programs—Students 111.
Chapels—Sabana (V.B.), San Vicente.; Cerro Gordo, N.S. del Carmen.

Vega-Baja

1—Holy Rosary (1794), Revs. Jose A. Rodriguez, Admin.; Francisco R. Tejada.
Res., P.O. Box 1388, 00694. Tel: 787-858-2969. [JC]
School—Sisters 3; Lay Teachers 38; Students 545.
Catechesis/Religious Programs—Students 232.
Chapels—Arenales, San Jose.; Almirante, N.S. de Fatima.

2—N.S. de la Providencia (1970), Rev. Angel Diaz.
Res., Guarico Rd. 14 Urb. Box 4056, Jardines de Vega Baja, 00694. Tel: 809-858-2171. [JC]
Catechesis/Religious Programs—Students 356.
Chapels—Brisas de Tortuguero, San Jose.; Vega Baja Lakes, San Pedro.

3—The Blessed Trinity (1971), Rev. Hernando A. Martinez-Gomez, Admin.
Res., P.O. Box 58, Almirante Sur Station, 00694. Tel: 809-858-8743.
Catechesis/Religious Programs—Students 310.
Chapels—Almirante Norte, Sagrada Familia.; Patron II, N.S. La Providencia.

4—Our Lady of Carmen-Playa (1976), Rev. Cesar E. Santos, Admin.
Res., Apdo. 4095, 00694. Tel: 809-858-4275; Fax: 787-855-3345. [JC]
Catechesis/Religious Programs—Students 122.
Chapels—Naranjos, San Judas Tadeo.; San Demetrio, Divino Nino Jesus.

5—Parroquia de San Martin de Porres (1967), Rev. Efrain Montesino.
Res., P.O. Box 254, Vega Baja, 00694. Tel: 787-858-1485; Fax: 787-858-1485. [JC]
Catechesis/Religious Programs—Tel: 787-858-8651.
Students 271.
Chapels—Panaini, Del Carmen.; Pugnado Adentro, San Jose.; Vila Colombo, St. Anthony.

6—Our Lady of Lourdes (1984), Rev. Jose A. Acaba.
Res., P.O. Box 4414, 00694. Tel: 787-855-4942. [JC]
Catechesis/Religious Programs—Students 515.
Convent—Tel: 787-855-0341.
Hermanas Terciarias Capuchinas 3.
Chapels—Rio Abajo, Santa Rosa de Lima.; Quebrada Arenas, San Juan Bautista.; Las Granjas, S. Francisco de Asis.

7—Our Lady of Mt. Carmel (1968), Rev. Luis Velazquez.
Res., P.O. Box 1417, 00694. Tel: 787-855-0159. [JC]
Catechesis/Religious Programs—Students 490.
Chapels—Pueblo Nuevo, La Milagrosa.; Sabana Hoyos, San Judas.; Santa Rosa, La Guadalupe.

Special Assignment:
Reverend Fathers—
Portalatin, Antonio, Vice Rector, Seminario Sta. Maria de los Angeles, San Juan, PR

On Duty Outside the Diocese:
Reverend Fathers—
Gomez, Walter, Archdiocese of San Juan
Guerrero, Jose Ma., Espana
Lopez, Juan J., Lyons, CA
Morales, Angel L., Archdiocese of San Juan
Nunez, Philip, III, Miami, FL

Rios Capiello, Luis B., Mayaguez, Puerto Rico

Retired:
Reverend Monsignors—
Salvador, Antonio, Espana
Reverend Fathers—
Burgos, Jose Casco, Espana
Hernandez, Jimmy, Quebradillas, Puerto Rico
Irizarry, Rafael, Quebradillas, Puerto Rico
Martinez, Francisco, Spain
San Llorente, Faustino, P.O. Box 4196, Vega Baja, PR 00694

INSTITUTIONS LOCATED IN THE DIOCESE

[A] EDUCATIONAL

ARECIBO. *Pontificia Universidad Catholica de Puerto Rico, Recinto de Arecibo*, Mailing Address: P.O. Box 144045, 00614-4045. Tel: 787-881-1212. Rev. Victor Rojas, Chap. Priests 5; Lay Teachers 41; Students 867.

Seminario de Jesus Maestro, Mailing Address: P.O. Box 2164, 00613. Tel: 787-878-1528. Rev. Daniel Fernandez. Total Enrollment 11.

[B] HOMES FOR AGED AND ORPHANS

ARECIBO. *Hogar de Ancianos San Vicente* Mailing Address: P.O. Box 4196 Vega Baja, 00694.
For a complete listing, refer to the Special Care Facilities section.

Hogar Sta. Maria Eufrasia Mailing Address: P.O. Box 1909, 00612 Fax: 787-880-2632.
For a complete listing, refer to the Special Care Facilities section.

La Milagrosa Home for Orphan Girls, Cotto Ave., No. 987, 00612. Tel: 809-878-6231
For a complete listing, refer to the Special Care Facilities section.

San Rafael Home for Aged, 00612
For a complete listing, refer to the Special Care Facilities section.

ISABELA. *Hogar Infantil Jesus Nazareno, Inc.*, P.O. Box 1671, 00662
For a complete listing, refer to the Special Care Facilities section.

LARES. *Fundacion Irma Fe*, Calle Comerio No. 52, 00669. Tel: 787-897-6090
For a complete listing, refer to the Special Care Facilities section.

VEGA ALTA. *Mision Juan XXIII*, 00692
For a complete listing, refer to the Special Care Facilities section.

[C] MISCELLANEOUS

ARECIBO. *Hogar Infantil Santa Teresita del Nino Jesus, Inc.*, P.O. Box 140057, 00614-0057. Tel: 787-817-6651; Fax: 787-817-6651. Hnas. Dominicas de la Presentacion.

UTUADO. *Fondita Santa Marta*, P.O. Box 10, 00631-0010. Tel: 787-894-3108; Fax: 787-894-3812. Bro. Jose Enrique Sanchez, O.F.M. Cap.

RELIGIOUS INSTITUTES OF MEN REPRESENTED IN THE DIOCESE

For further details refer to the corresponding bracketed number in the Religious Institutes of Men or Women section.

[]—*Canonigos Regulares Lateranenses de San Agustin.* (Bronx, NY).—C.R.L.

[0470]—*Capuchin Friars.* (Province of Pittsburgh).—O.F.M.Cap.

[0270]—*Carmelite Fathers and Brothers.* (Province de Aragon, Valencia, Espana).—O.Carm.

[1330]—*Congregation of the Mission.* (Vice-Province of Puerto Rico).—C.M.

[1000]—*Congregation of the Passion.* (Bilbao, Spain).—C.P.

[]—*Esclavos de la Eucaristia y Maria Virgen.*—E.E.M.V.

[0650]—*Holy Ghost Fathers.* (Eastern Province).—C.S.Sp.

[0770]—*Marist Brothers.*—F.M.S.

[]—*Misioneros Natividad de Maria.* (Mexico).—M.N.M.

[]—*Misioneros de Villa Regia - Italia.*—C.M.V.

[1310]—*Order of the Holy Trinity.* (Viscaya, Spain Province).—O.SS.T.

[1190]—*Salesians of Don Bosco.* (Province of Madrid).—S.D.B.

RELIGIOUS INSTITUTES OF WOMEN REPRESENTED IN THE DIOCESE

[]—*Congregation of Sisters of Passion.* (Mexico).

[0760]—*Daughters of Charity of St. Vincent de Paul.*—D.C.

[1070-05]—*Dominican Sisters.*—O.P.

[]—*Dominican Sisters of Amityville, N.Y.*.

[1100]—*Dominican Sisters of Charity of the Presentation of the Blessed Virgin.*—O.P.

[]—*Dominican Sisters of Fatima.* (Yauco PR).

[]—*Hermanas de San Jose de Corozal.* (Corozal).

[]—*Hermanas del Buen Pastor.*

[]—*Hermanas Esclaves del Santisimo y la Inmaculada.*

[]—*Hermanas Josefinas.* (Mexico).

[]—*Hermanas San Francisco.* (Instituto Secular).

[]—*Hnas. Apostolado Corzon de Jesus.* (Madrid).—R.A.

[2460]—*Hnas. Carmelitas Madre Candelaria, Carmelite Nuns.* (Venezuela).

[]—*Hnas. Religiosas Angeles Custodios.* (Madrid, Spain).

[]—*Hnas.Carmelitas.* (Madrid, Spain).

[]—*Instituto Sma. Trinidad.* (Valencia, Spain).

[]—*Misioneras de la Sagrada Familia.* (Instituto Secular).

[]—*Misioneras Sagrado Corazon.* (Santo Domingo).

[]—*Misioneras Villa Regia - Italia.*

[]—*Monasterio Madre de Dios - Cloistered Dominican Nuns.*

[]—*Salesian Sisters.* (Roma).

[]—*Siervas de Maria.*

[]—*Sisters of Charity of Cardinal Sancha.* (Santo Domingo).

[0990]—*Sisters of Divine Providence.* (Pittsburgh).—C.D.P.

[]—*Sisters of Mercy.* (Spain).

[3930]—*Sisters of St. Joseph of the Third Order of St. Francis.* (South Bend, IN).—S.S.J.-T.O.S.F.

NECROLOGY

† Cobeaga, Victoriano, Vega-Baja, PR Our Lady of Lourdes Church. —Died Dec. 16, 1999.

Diocese of Caguas, Puerto Rico

(Dioecesis Caguana)

Most Reverend

RUBEN ANTONIO GONZALEZ MEDINA, C.M.F.

Bishop of Caguas; ordained February 9, 1949; appointed Bishop of Caguas December 12, 2000; consecrated February 4, 2001

Most Reverend

ENRIQUE HERNANDEZ RIVERA, D.D.

Bishop Emeritus of Caguas; ordained June 8, 1968; appointed Titular Bishop of Vanalla, North Africa and Auxiliary Bishop of San Juan June 11, 1979; consecrated August 17, 1979; appointed Bishop of Caguas February 13, 1981; officially installed March 8, 1981; retired July 28, 1998. *Res., Bishop's House, Box 8698, Caguas, PR, 00726.* Tel.: 787-747-5885; 747-5787; Fax: 787-747-5616; 747-5767.

ESTABLISHED NOVEMBER 1964.

Square Miles 737.

Comprises east and southeast portion of Puerto Rico and the Islands of Culebra and Vieques.

Patroness of the Diocese: Maria, Madre de la Iglesia - November 12, 1988.

Web site address: www.home.coqui.net/obicag:

E-mail address: obicag@coqui.net

STATISTICAL OVERVIEW

Personnel	
Bishop	1
Retired Bishops	1
Abbots	1
Retired Abbots	1
Priests: Diocesan Active in Diocese	66
Priests: Active Outside Diocese	6
Priests: Diocesan in Foreign Missions	1
Number of Diocesan Priests	73
Religious Priests in Diocese	51
Extern Priests in Diocese	2
Ordinations:	
Diocesan Priests	3
Religious Priests	1
Permanent Deacons in Diocese	69
Total Brothers	18
Total Sisters	154
Parishes	
Parishes	43
With Resident Pastor:	
Resident Diocesan Priests	34
Resident Religious Priests	9
Welfare	
Specialized Homes	3
Total Assisted	654
Educational	
Seminaries, Diocesan	1
Students from This Diocese	12
Diocesan Students in Other Seminaries	8
Total Seminarians	20
High Schools, Diocesan and Parish	1
Total Students	113
High Schools, Private	6
Total Students	3,896
Elementary Schools, Diocesan and Parish	4
Total Students	670
Elementary Schools, Private	13
Total Students	4,164
Catechesis/Religious Education:	
High School Students	4,102
Elementary Students	5,670
Total Students Under Catholic Instruction	18,635
Teachers in the Diocese:	
Priests	19
Scholastics	4
Brothers	4
Sisters	17
Lay Teachers	370
Vital Statistics	
Receptions into the Church:	
Infant Baptism Totals	6,188
Adult Baptism Totals	500
First Communions	5,670
Confirmations	4,102
Marriages:	
Catholic	1,222
Interfaith	45
Total Marriages	1,267
Deaths	2,248
Total Catholic Population	515,000
Total Population	653,012

Former Bishops—Most Rev. RAFAEL GROVAS, D.D., S.T.D., Ph.D., J.C.L., ord. April 7, 1928; appt. Jan. 19, 1965; cons. March 28, 1965; retired Feb. 13, 1981; died Sept. 9, 1991.—Most Rev. ENRIQUE HERNANDEZ RIVERA, D.D., ord. June 8, 1968; cons. Aug. 17, 1979; appt. Feb. 13, 1981; retired July 28, 1998.

Vicar General—Rev. EDWARD SANTANA.

Sec. Chancellor—Rev. DANIEL P. CRONIN.

Sec. Vice Chancellor—Rev. ANGEL MOLINA; Sr. CARMEN GONZALEZ, C.D.P.

Diocesan Consultors—Rev. Msgr. MIGUEL A. MENDOZA; Revs. HIPOLITO TORRES; AURELIO ADAN; JOSE M. CALVO; EUSEBIO RAMOS; EDWARD SANTANA.

Diocesan Tribunal of Caguas—Rev. EDWARD SANTANA, J.C.D., Judicial Vicar; Sr. CARMEN GONZALEZ, C.D.P., J.C.L., Dir., *P.O. Box 9779, Caguas, 00726.* Tel: 787-286-8595; Fax: 787-286-8620.

Board of Diocesan Government—Rev. FELIX OLIVERAS VILLANUEVA; Deacon JOSE RODRIGUEZ.

Priests Senate—Rev. Msgr. MIGUEL A. MENDOZA; Revs. HIPOLITO TORRES; JOSE M. CALVO; JAVIER HERNANDEZ; AURELIO ADAN; EDWARD SANTANA; ELIAS LORENZANA; FELICIANO RODRIGUEZ; ANGEL MOLINA; DANIEL CRONIN; ROBERTO SOTO; ANGEL LUIS CINTRON; OSCAR RIVERA, O.S.B.; JUAN B. MEDINA.

Diocesan Offices and Directors

Economic Administrator—Rev. FELIX OLIVERAS VILLANUEVA, *P.O. Box 8698, Caguas, 00726.* Tel: 787-747-5885; 747-5787, Ext. 227.

Planning Vicar—Vacant, *P.O. Box 8698, Caguas, 00726.* Tel: 787-747-5885; 747-5787.

Cursillos de Cristiandad—MIGUEL A. CASUL, Pres.

Renovacion Carismatica—MARIA DE LOS A. PINTO, Pres.

Movimiento de Retiro Juan XXIII—MAXIMILIANO RIVERA MILLAN, Pres.

Sociedad del Santo Nombre—EVARISTO RUIZ, Pres.

Caballeros de Colon—DARWIN HERNANDEZ, Gran Caballero.

Talleres de Oracion y Vida—LYDIA E. SALABARRIA, Pres.

Apostolado de la Cruz—ELVIN PENA, Encargado.

Hermanos Cheos—EDUARDO VAZQUEZ, Pres.

Hijas Catolicas de America—IRMA RUIZ DE MERCED, Regente.

Mariano de Shoenstatt—JOSE N. BRACERO, Pres.

Misioneros del Padre Nuestro—RAFAEL TIRADO, Pres.

Catholic Youth—Rev. JOHN ALICEA, *P.O. Box 8698, Caguas, 00726.* Tel: 787-744-6738, Ext. 229.

Catholic Social Action—Vacant, *P.O. Box 8698, Caguas, 00726.* Tel: 787-747-5885; 747-5787.

Catholic School Consultors—DOMICIANO GARCIA, *P.O. Box 8699, Caguas, 00726.* Tel: 787-743-1171.

Catechetical Delegate—Deacon JOSE RODRIGUEZ, *P.O.Box 8698, Caguas, 00726.* Tel: 787-747-5885, Ext. 223.

Building Commission—Vacant, *P.O. Box 8698, Caguas, 00726.* Tel: 787-747-5885; 747-5787.

Liturgical Consultor—Revs. DANIEL CRONIN; LUIS ALICEA, *P.O. Box 8698, Caguas, 00626.* Tel: 787-747-5885, Ext. 222.

Communication Office—Mrs. DAYANI CENTENO, *P.O. Box 8698, Caguas, 00726.* Tel: 809-746-3783.

Guerra Contra el Hambre (War on Hunger)—Rev. ANGEL MOLINA, *P.O. Box 8698, Caguas, 00726.* Tel: 787-747-5767.

Vincentian Society—Mr. EMILIANO VAZQUEZ, *P.O. Box 8698, Caguas, 00726.*

Hospitals—Rev. FREDDY CELANO, *P.O. Box 8698, 00726.*

Legion of Mary—Rev. CLEMENTE CAHILL, C.SS.R., *P.O. Box 967, Caguas, 00726.* Mr. ISABELO HUERTAS, *P.O. Box 8698, Caguas, 00726.*

Master of Ceremonies—Vacant, *P.O. Box 8698, Caguas, 00726.* Tel: 809-747-5885.

Pastoral Vicar—Rev. FELICIANO RODRIGUEZ, *P.O. Box 8698, Caguas, 00726.* Tel: 787-286-0075, Ext. 245.

Schools—*P.O. Box 8699, Caguas, 00726.* Tel: 787-743-1171.

School Superintendent—Mr. DOMICIANO GARCIA.

Vocations—Rev. RAMON SANTANA, *P.O. Box 8698, Caguas, 00726.* Tel: 787-747-5885, Ext. 243; Fax: 787-857-3585.

Catholic Charities—Deacon CLEMENTE GUZMAN, *P.O. Box 8698, Caguas, 00726.* Tel: 787-703-0775; Fax: 787-747-5616.

Commission of Permanent Deacons—Deacon RAFAEL UFRET.

CLERGY, PARISHES, MISSIONS AND PAROCHIAL SCHOOLS

CITY OF CAGUAS

1—CATHEDRAL DULCE NOMBRE DE JESUS (1730). Redemptorist Fathers. Revs. Gerardo Campbell, C.SS.R., Rector; Clemente Cahill, C.SS.R.; William Spillane, C.SS.R.; Ricardo Reillo, C.SS.R.; Andres Spacht, C.SS.R. In res., Rev. Damian Wall.
Res., 3 Corchado St., Box 967, 00726. Tel: 787-743-4311; 2927; Fax: 787-743-7567.
School—Colegio Catolico de Caguas, Acosta St., Box 967, 00726. Tel: 787-743-2385. School Sisters of Notre Dame. Sr. Bernardine Marie, S.S.N.D.
Sisters 2; Lay Teachers 43; Students 1,031; Aids 10.
High School—Notre Dame, Urb. Borinquen, Box 541, 00726. Tel: 787-743-3693; 5501; Fax: 787-258-9648. School Sisters of Notre Dame. Mr. Jose G. Grillo.
Priests 2; Sisters 4; Lay Teachers 68; Students 1,200.
Chapels—Nuestra S. Perpetuo Socorro, (1929), 24 Aguayo St., 00726; San Gerardo, (1940), 221 B St., B-14, Jardines de Caguas, 00726; San Vicente de Paul, 221 B St., Brooklyn; La Sagrada Familia, (1978), 1004 P St., Bda. Morales.

2—SAN JOSE (1960). (Discalced Carmelites from Spain). Revs. Antonio Mata, O.C.D.; Alejandro Moral, O.C.D.; Luis Cestero; Miguel A. Arroyo, O.C.D.
Res., Coral St., Villa Blanca, Box 1101, 00726. Tel: 787-743-5889; Fax: 787-258-0683.
School—(Spanish Discalced Carmelite Sisters) Box 806, 00625. Tel: 787-743-2032; Fax: 787-258-0683. Sr. Soledad Diaz, C.M., Prin.
Priests 1; Sisters 5; Lay Teachers 28; Students 609.
High School—Tel: 787-744-8993; Fax: 787-744-4111. Mrs. Brenda Figueroa de Soler, Prin.
Priests 1; Lay Teachers 21; Students 450.
Chapel—Bairoa, Nuestra Senora del Rosario, (1981), Tel: 787-743-5889.

3—SAGRADO CORAZON DE JESUS (1963), Rev. Felix Oliveras Villanueva.
Res., HC 04, Box 45078, Bo. Beatriz, 00726. Tel: 787-747-5170.
Chapels—Bo. Beatriz, Cristo Rey, (1960); San Martin, (1994).

4—NUESTRA SENORA DE LA PROVIDENCIA (1967), Revs. Juan B. Medina; Pedro Ortiz.
Res., Urb. Villa del Carmen, Box 6318, 00725. Tel: 787-743-8200.
Stations—Urb. Mariolga; Caserio Publico; Los Flamboyanes; Rio Verde.

5—SANTISIMO SACRAMENTO (1967). Blessed Sacrament Fathers. Revs. Jose' Martin Eguiguren; Jesus Maria Maiza, S.S.S.; Adrian Alicea, S.S.S.; Domingo Gayarre, S.S.S.
Res., Calle Caney A-11, Caguax, 00725. Tel: 787-743-8444; Fax: 787-745-5165.
Chapels—Urb. Caguas Norte, San Antonio de Padua; Nuestra S. de Guadalupe, 5th St., Urb. Jose Delgado.

6—NUESTRA SENORA DEL PERPETUO SOCORRO (1968), Revs. Oscar Rivera; Angel Molina.
Res., Calle 2, A-13, Villa Nueva, 00725. Tel: 787-744-1420; Fax: 787-258-4341.
Stations—Bo. Canaboncito, San Patricio, (1926).; Villa Esperanza, San Judas Tadeo, (1960).; Bo. Canaboncito (Las Parcelas), Sagrado Corazon.; Urb. Turabo Gardens, Nuestra S. del Carmen, (1988).

7—EL SALVADOR (1970), Rev. Orlando De Jesus Gomez.
Res., Parcelas Bo. Boringuen, HC 03, Buzon 38888, 00625-9723. Tel: 787-747-0091; Fax: 787-747-0091.
Catechesis/Religious Programs—Students 300.
Chapels—Bo. San Salvador, Cristo Rey, (1922); Sector Anon, San Alfonso, (1929); Bo. San Salvador, Sector Hato, Nuestra S. del Carmen, (1911).

8—INMACULADO CORAZON DE MARIA (1971), Revs. Toribio Nicholas Garcia, C.M.F.; Pedro Lopez Moran, C.M.F.
Mailing Address: HC 05, Box 57564, Caguas, 00725-9233. Tel: 787-747-6336.
Catechesis/Religious Programs—Students 230.
Chapels—Bo. La Barra, Cristo Rey, (1971); San Antonio, (1950); Bo. La Mesa, N.S. Providencia, (1982); Bo. La Mesa, Nuestra S. del Carmen; Bo. Quebrada Arenas, San Felipe; Guasabara, Sta. Teresa del Nino Jesus, (1995).

9—SAN PABLO APOSTOL (1982) (Hispanic), Rev. Gervasio Malave.
Res., Kennedy U-32 Urb. Jose Mercado, Caguas, 00625. Tel: 787-743-3546; Fax: 787-743-3546.
Chapels—Bo. Tomas de Castro I, Nuestra S. de Guadalupe, (1928); Bo. Tomas de Castro II, Santa Rose de Lima; Sector Ramal, San Martin, (1969); Sector Buenos Aires, San Juan Bautista; Sector RM5, Virgen de la Monserrate.
Catechesis/Religious Programs—Students 134.

10—SAN PEDRO APOSTOL (1982), Rev. Antonio Munoz.
Res., Urb. Bonneville, Box 8878, Caguas, 00726. Tel: 787-744-2036.

11—SAN JUAN APOSTOL Y EVANGELISTA (1982), Rev. Antonio Cartagena.
Res., Apartado 459, Avenida Bairoa, Gguas, 00726. Tel: 787-744-6359; Fax: 787-743-8266.
Catechesis/Religious Programs—Students 200.

12—SANTISIMA TRINIDAD (1986), Rev. Efrain Zabala.
Res., Box 9630, Caguas, 00726. Tel: 787-747-6967; Fax: 787-747-6967.

13—MARIA MADRE DE LA IGLESIA, Rev. Hermenegildo Alayon.
Calle Juan M. Morales D-23 Urb Valle Tolima, Caguas, 00725. Tel: 787-258-4481.

14—DIVINO NINO (1995), Rev. Campo Emilio Ariza; Deacons Leonardo Matos; Rolando Rocafort.
Mailing Address: P.O. Box 9416, 00726. Tel: 787-746-1450; Fax: 787-746-1450.
Catechesis/Religious Programs—Students 137.
Chapel—San Francisco Javier.

OUTSIDE THE CITY OF CAGUAS FROM LAS AMERICAS EXPRESS WAY TOWARD THE WEST

Aibonito, Aibonito Co., Church of St. Joseph (1897), Revs. Pedro Oyarbide; Israel Berrios; Deacons Antonio Torres; Modesto Reyes; Ezequiel Collazo; Cristobal Rolon; Otilio Rivera; Angel Luis Berrios; Pablo Ortiz.
Res., Box 2038, 00705. Tel: 787-735-3741; Fax: 787-735-4436.
Catechesis/Religious Programs—Students 1,900.
Chapels—Bo. Asomante (Cuadritos), Nuestra S. del Carmen, (1959); Bo. Asomante (Abejas), Inmaculada Concepcion (1965); Bo. Pasto, Nuestra S. de Guadalupe, (1970); Nuestra S. de la Providencia, (1982), Palestina St; Bo. Rabanal (Parcelas), Nuestra S. de Fatima, (1972); Ext. San Luis, Nuestra S. del Carmen, (1986); La Plata, La Milagrosa, (1986).
Mission—Llanos, Sector El Juicio.
Chapel—La Sierra, San Judas Tadeo.

Aguas Buenas, Aguas Buenas Co., Church of Tres Santos Reyes (1838). Redemptorist Fathers. Revs. Terry Tull, C.Ss.R.; Tomas Gavigan, C.Ss.R.; Carlos Corbett, C.Ss.R.; Roberto McMurrer, C.Ss.R.; Angelo Sanchez, C.Ss.R.; Bro. Jose E. Hernandez.
Res., 4 Munoz Rivera St., Box 1, 00703. Tel: 787-732-2741; Fax: 787-732-2185.
School—Academia San Alfonso, Tel: 787-732-8288; Fax: 787-732-4115. Sr. Myrtha E. Arroyo de Lopez, Prin.
Lay Teachers 15; Students 181.
Chapels—Bo. Sumidero, Nuestra S. del Perpetuo Socorro, (1933); Sector Corujas del Barrio Sumidero, Sta. Juliana, (1984); Bo. Sonadora, Sagrado Corazon, (1937); Bo. Jagueyes Abajo, San Jose, (1939); Bo. Jagueyes Quinta, Divino Redentor, (1947); Bo. Caguitas, Madre del Perpetuo Socorro, (1941); Bo. Caguitas, Sector La Brusca, (1996); Parcelas Santa Clara, Santa Clara, (1974).

Espiritu Santo, Rev. Encarnacion Nieves.
Res., Box 1250, 00703. Tel: 787-732-1270.
Chapels—Carr. 156, Santa Teresita, (1929); Bo. Mulitas Alvelo, De Todos los Santos, (1974); Bo. Mulitas Tiza, San Gerardo Mayela, (1974).

Barranquitas, Barranquitas Co., Church of St. Anthony of Padua (1808; 1988), Rev. Msgr. Miguel A. Mendoza; Revs. Juan Jose Colon; R. Miguel A. Merced Reyes.
Res., Box 1099, 00794. Tel: 787-857-3585.
Catechesis/Religious Programs—Students 1,800.
Chapels—San Francisco de Asis, (1960); Bo. Mana, Virgen del Carmen, (1963); Bo. Canabon, Virgen de la Providencia, (1968); Bo. Helechal, San Jose Obrero, (1968); Bo. Quebrada Grande, Nuestra Sra. de la Monserrate, (1968); Bo. Palo Hincado, Virgen del Perpetuo Socorro, (1975); Bo. Lajitas, Nuestra S. del Pilar, (1970); Sector La Torre, Santa Cruz, (1975); Bo. Helechal, San Martin de Porres, (1950).

San Andres Apostol (1986), Revs. Jose A. de Leon; Jose L. Ortiz; Deacons Joaquin Ortiz; Optaciano Rivera; Angel Mercado.
Res., Bo. Quebradillas, Box 490, 00794. Tel: 787-875-5424; Fax: 787-875-5424.
Catechesis/Religious Programs—Students 241.
Chapels—Bo. Palomas, Comerio, San Jose, (1925); Bo. Quebradillas, Barranquitas, Corazon de Jesus, (1940; 1987); Bo. Cedro Arriba, Naranjito, San Antonio de Padua, (1864); Bo. Quebradillas, Barranquitas, Inmaculada Concepcion y Santa Cruz, (1957); Bo. Cedro Arriba, Naranjito, Santuario Maria Auxiliadora, (1992).

Cayey, Cayey Co., Nuestra Senora de la Asuncion (1787). Mercedarian Fathers. Revs. Fidel Fernandez, O.M., Supr.; Antonio Garcia, O.deM.; Wilfredo Riveros, O.deM.; Pedro Ruiz Valero, O.M.
Res., Casa Parroquial, P.O. Box 37 2887, 00737-2887. Tel: 787-738-2763; Fax: 787-738-2763.
Catechesis/Religious Programs—Students 1,069.
Chapels—Bo. Jajome, Sagrado Corazon de Jesus, (1935); Bo. Pasto Viejo, Nuestra S. del Carmen, (1937; 1988); Bo. Toita, Nuestra S. de la Merced, (1946); Res. Brisas de Cayey, San Ramon Nonato, (1978); Bo. Maton Arriba, Santa Teresita del Nino Jesus, (1987).

Nuestra Senora de la Merced (1968), Revs. Jesus Saez Castrillo, O.de.M.; Elias Lorenzana, O.de.M.; Gregorio Dafonte.
Res., Reparto Montellano, Box 1840, 00737. Tel: 787-738-3872.
Chapels—Bo. Vegas, San Ramon Nonato, (1961); Bo. Culebras, Nuestra S. del Carmen, (1973); Bo. Farallon, San Pedro Nolasco, (1980); San Pedro Armengol (La Plata), (1994).

San Esteban Protomartir (1985), Revs. Jose Antonio Ortiz; Hector Bruno de Jesus; Deacons Anibal Gonzalez; Felix Montanez; Silvestre Rodriguez.
Res., Bo. Guavate, 22601 Sector Nieves, 00736-9522. Tel: 787-747-4555.
Chapels—Bo. Borinquen Pradera, Nuestr Senora del Carmen, (1910); Bo. Guavate, San Jose de la Montana, (1951; 1990).

Cidra, Cidra Co., Nuestra Senora del Carmen (1818), Revs. Raul Morales Berrios; Angel Luis Cintron; Deacons Diego Reyes; Alfonso Delgado; Carlos A. Sola.
Res., Centro Plaza Municipal, Box 359, 00739. Tel: 787-739-2406; Fax: 787-739-4991.
Chapels—Bo. Rio Abajo, Madre del Salvador; Urb. Treasure Valley, La Milagrosa; Bo. Bayamon-Centenejas I, La Inmaculada; Bo. Montellano, Santa Teresa del Nino Jesus; Bo. Bayamon-Certenejas II, Perpetuo Socorro; Bo. Bayamon-Juan del Valle, Nuestra Senora del Rosario; Bo. Arena-Santa Clara, San Joaquin; Bo. Ceiba-Hevia, Nuestra Senora del Rosario; Bo. Arenas, Nuestra Senora de la Providencia; Bo. Ceiba, Cristo Rey; Bo. Bayamon-San Jose, San Jose; Bo. Rincon, San Francisco de Asis; Bo. Sud, La Milagrosa; Bo. Sud, San Pablo.

Nuestra Senora de Fatima (1963), Rev. Isidro Nazabal.
Res., Bo. Rabanal, Box 214, 00739. Tel: 787-739-0633.
Catechesis/Religious Programs—Students 596.
Chapels—Bo. Toita, Sagrado Corazon de Jesus, (1960); Bo. Salto, San Vicente, (1965); Bo. Honduras, Perpetuo Socorro, (1970); Bo. Rabanal, Bo. Salvador, (1970); Bo. Parcelas, La Milagrosa, (1978); Bo. Salto, Nuestra Senora de la Providencia; Bo. Salto, Santa Teresita, (1982); Santo Cristo de Los Milagros, (1987).

Comerio, Comerio Co., Santo Cristo de la Salud (1832), Rev. Roberto Solivan.
Box 1139, 00762. Tel: 787-875-4525.
Res., Calle Santiago R Palmer #12, 00782.
Chapels—Bo. Sabana, Nuestra Senora del Santisimo Rosario, (1966); Bo. Rio Hondo, Nuestra Senora de Fatima, (1953); Bo. Palomas, Santa Ceceilia, (1954); Bo. Cedrito, Virgen de la Providencia, (1958); Bo. Rio Hondo-Sector Las Parcelas, San Pablo, (1965); Bo. Pinas Arriba, Nuestra Senora del Carmen, (1973); Bo. Naranjo-Sector Las Parcelas, San Antonio de Padua, (1977); Bo. Vega Redonda, San Francisco de Asis, (1977); Bo. Cejas, Santa Rose de Lima, (1980); Bo. Dona Elena, San Martin de Porres, (1950); Rio Hondo II, Maria Madre de la Iglesia.

Naranjito, Naranjito Co., San Miguel Arcangel (1831), Revs. Hipolito Torres; Enrique Gomez.
Res., Centro Parroquial, Box 68, 00719. Tel: 787-869-2840; Fax: 787-869-3050.
Chapels—Bo. Nuevo, Santa Rosa de Lima, (1953); Bo. Lomas Centro, Virgen del Carmen, (1954); Bo. Anones, La Milagrosa, (1962); Bo. Lomas Valles, San Judas Tadeo, (1963); Bo. Guadiana, La Monserrate, (1967); Bo. Achiote, Sagrado Corazon, (1978); Bo. Nuevo Parcelas, San Vicente de Paul, (1981); Bo. Cedro Abajo, San Jose, (1981).

OUTSIDE THE CITY OF CAGUAS FROM LAS AMERICAS EXPRESS WAY TOWARD THE EAST COAST

Ceiba, Ceiba Co., San Antonio de Padua (1840), Rev. Hilario Rivera.
Res., Plaza St., Box 77, 00735. Tel: 787-885-2530.
Missions—Ceiba, Sagrado Corazon de Jesus, Bo. Saco, 00735; Ceiba, Ceiba Co., N.S. del Carmen, Parcelas de Aguas Claras, 00735; Bo. Rio Abajo, Ceiba Co., N.S. del Perpetuo Socorro Bo. Rio Abajo, Ceiba, 00735.
Chapel—Bo. Daguao, Nuestra Senora de Fatima, (1968).
Catechesis/Religious Programs—Students 110.

Fajardo, Fajardo Co., Santiago Apostol (1766). Redemptorist Fathers. Revs. Henry Beachamp, C.Ss.R.; Alfonso Amador, C.Ss.R.; Gerardo McSwigan, C.Ss.R. In res., Revs. Manuel Rodriguez, C.Ss.R.; Jose Roberto Gandara, C.Ss.R.
Res., 16 Garrido Morales St., Box 806, 00738. Tel: 787-863-2365; Fax: 787-860-1837.
Chapels—Bo. Florencio, Santa Elena, (1962); Bo. Quebrada Vueltas, Perpetuo Socorro, (1965); La Milagrosa, (1978); Santa Isidra, Santiago Apostol.
Santisimo Redentor (1993), Rev. Javier Hernandez.
Res., Urb. Monte Brisas, Calle C-V-19, 00738. Tel: 787-863-5227; Fax: 787-860-0560.
Catechesis/Religious Programs—Students 140.
Chapels—Puerto Real, Ntra. Sra. de Carmen; Sardinera, San Juan Bautista.; Las Croabas, Maria, Madre del Senor; Fajardo Gardens, Maria, Madre de la Providencia.

Gurabo, Gurabo Co., San Jose (1822), Revs. Roberto Angel Soto; Leonardo Valero.
Res., 7 Santiago Iglesias St., Box 733, 00778. Tel: 787-737-2656.
Chapels—Bo. Jagual, Sagrado Corazon de Jesus, (1951); Bo. Jaguas Llano, Virgen del Carmen, (1967); Bo. Navarro, San Francisco Javier, (1968); Bo. Santa Rita, Santa Rita, (1968); La Milagrosa, (1973), Bo. Hato Nuevo; Bo. Celada, Santa Francisca Javier Cabrini, (1967); Bo. Santa Barbara, Santa Maria del Camino, (1987); Bo. Hato Nuevo, La Milagrosa, (1982); Bo. Jaguas Loma, San Miguel, (1989); Bo. Mamey II, Ntra. Sra. del Carmen.
Catechesis/Religious Programs—Students 315.

Humacao, Humacao Co., Dulce Nombre de Jesus (Pueblo) (1763), Revs. Eusebio Ramos Morales; Jose Antonio Arocho; David Diaz Matos; Jhon Jaime Florez; Deacons Angel Cruz Cruz; Justino Cruz; Frank Colon.
Res., 3 Font Martelo St., Box 9087, 00791. Tel: 787-852-0868; Fax: 787-850-6448. [JC]
Chapels—San Agustin, (1955), Parcela No. 44, Bo. Anton Ruiz; Nuestra Senora de la Candelaria, (1956), Parcela No. 30, Candelero Arriba; San Jose, (1957), Carr. 922 Cotto Mabu; Nuestra Senora de Fatima, (1962), Bo. Juniquito; Santa Teresita, (1965), Bo. Candelero Abajo; San Pedro y San Pablo, (1986), Caserio Roig; Nuestra Senora de la Providencia, (2000), Bo. Catano; Perpetuo Socorro, (1944), Bo. Buena Vista; Inmaculada Concepcion, (1996), Urbanizacion Villa; Maria Auxiliadora, (1999), Bo. Candelero Abajo, Parcelas Martinez.
Maria Reina de la Paz (Pueblo) (1989), Revs. Kharlosg Lopez; Eric R. Buermann, O.S.B.; Mauro Simpson, O.S.B.; Ignacio Aguirre, O.S.B.; Deacons Rafael Ulfret; Clemente Guzman.
Mailing Address: Villa Universitaria, Box 10160, 00792.
Res., Villa Universitaria, Calle 4 A20, 00792. Tel: 787-850-3081; Fax: 787-850-3080.
Catechesis/Religious Programs—Students 120.
Chapels—Sagrado Corazon de Jesus, (1940); San Martin de Porres, (1962); Bo. Mariana IV; Buen Pastor, (1970); Bo. Tejas, Cristo Rey, (1976); Bo. Mariana II, Santa Rosa de Lima, (1978); Comunidad Vista Hermosa.

Humacao Playa, Humacao Co., Nuestra Senora del Carmen (Punta Santiago) (1970), Rev. Jorge D. Cardona.
Res., Box 91, Punta Santiago, 00741. Tel: 787-850-2125; Fax: 787-850-2125.
Catechesis/Religious Programs—Calle 5 #103 Verde Mar, P.O. Box 91, Punta Santiago, 00741. Students 125.
Chapel—Bo. Pasto Viejo, Sector El batey, Nuestra Senora del Perpetuo Socorro, (1937; 1986).

Juncos, Juncos Co., Inmaculada Concepcion (1797), Revs. Jose M. Calvo Muniain; Miguel Arregui Moso.
Res., Almodovar St. #18, Box 1728, 00777. Tel: 787-734-2431; Fax: 787-734-0350.
Catechesis/Religious Programs—Students 81.
Chapels—Bo. Canta Gallo, Cristo Redentor, (1975); Bo. Ceiba Sur, Sagrado Corazon, (1976); Bo. Valenciano Sector Amigo, Espiritu Santo, (1976); Bo. Ceiba Norte, Cristo Rey, (1978); Bo. Valenciano Arriba, San Juan Bautista, (1979); Bo. Ceiba Norte Sector Chinos, Buen Pastor, (1979); Bo. Pinas, Santa Cruz, (1981); Bo. Lirios, San Jose, (1978); Bo. Canta Gallo Secto Reparto Valenciano, Maria Reina De La Paz, (1993).
Mission—Bo. Placita.

Las Piedras, Las Piedras Co., Inmaculada Concepcion (1801), Revs. Boris Espinoza Perez; Carlos R. Soto.
Res., Box 324, 00771. Tel: 787-733-2381; Fax: 787-733-1180.
Catechesis/Religious Programs—Tel: 787-733-8325. D.R.E.: Sor Miriam Nieves; Hnas Fatima. Students 186.
Chapels—Bo. Montones I, Perpetuo Socorro, (1935); Bo. Tejas Asomonte, Nuestra Senora de la Providencia, (1955); Bo. La Fermina, Jesus de Nazaret, (1979); Bo. Montones IV, Santa Teresa del Nino Jesus, (1980); Bo. Montones II, San Juan Bautista, (1982).
Mission—Salon Usos Multiples-Urb. April Gardens, Las Piedras.
San Juan Bautista (Bo. Pueblito del Rio) (1971), Rev. Tomas Galarza.
Res., Bo. Pueblito del Rio, HC 02, Buzon 4467, 00771. Tel: 787-733-6444.
Chapels—Finca Roig, San Juan Bautista, (1911; 1940); Bo. Boqueron, La Sagrada Familia, (1957); Bo. Pena Pobre, Santo Tomas de Aquino, (1964); Bo. Rio Blanco, La Milagrosa, (1972); Bo. Mango, San Francisco Javier; Bo. Pasto Seco, El Buen Pastor.

Maunabo, Maunabo Co., San Isidor Labrador (1799), Revs. Luis Antonio Alicea; Franklin Rodriguez Cotton.
Res., Box 248, 00707. Tel: 787-861-2595; Fax: 787-861-2595.
Chapels—Nuestra Senora del Carmen, (1962); Bo. Calzada, Nuestra Senora de la Providencia, (1971); Bo. Matuyas, Nuestra Senora de la Candelaria, (1974); Bo. Palo Seco, San Judas Tadeo, (1975); Bo. Emajaguas, San Antonio de Padua, (1977).
Missions—Bo. Quebrada Arenas; Bo. Lizas; Bo. Talante; Bo. Paloseco; Bo. Talante (La Pica); Bo. Calzada.

Naguabo, Naguabo Co., Nuestra Senora del Rosario (1794), Revs. P. Jose A. Rivera Maldonado; Luis Ruiz.
Res., Box 665, 00718. Tel: 787-874-2235; Fax: 787-874-0150. [JC]
Chapels—Nuestra Senora del Perpetuo Socorro, (1946); Bo. Maizales, Nuestra Senora de la Altagracia, (1963); Bo. Duque, Nuestra Senora de Fatima, (1965); Bo. Florida, Nuestra Senora del Perpetuo Socorro, (1942); Nuestra Senora del Carmen Playa Hucares, (1920); Bo. Mariana, Nuestra Senora de la Providencia, (1965); Bo. Santiago y Lima (Botija), Santa Rosa de Lima, (1975).
Missions—Barrio Rio, Sector Brazo Seco; Barrio Cecilia, Sector La Fe.

San Lorenzo, San Lorenzo Co., Nuestra Senora de la Mercedes (1810), Revs. Dennis Demko, C.Ss.R.; Juan Ramon Hernandez, C.Ss.R.; Federico J. Consla, C.Ss.R.; Santiago Mallen, C.Ss.R.
Res., Munoz Rivera 55, Apartado 1280, 00754-1280. Tel: 787-736-2571; Fax: 787-736-1213.
Chapels—Bo. Quebrada Honda, Santa Teresita de Jesus, (1948); Bo. Jagual, Nuestra Senora del Carmen, (1952); Bo. Quemados, Nuestra Senora del Perpetuo Socorro, (1957).; Bo. Cerro Gordo Abajo, Cristo Redentor, (1965); Bo. Quebrada, Jesus Maestro.; Bo. Florida, Santa Monica; Bda. Roosevelt, Nuestra Senora del Carmen, (1968); Bo. Hato Km. 6, Nuestra Senora del Perpetuo Socorro, (1968); Bo. Cayaguas, San Pedro Apostol, (1972); Bo. Cerro Gordo Arriba, Nuestra Senora del Perpetuo Socorro, (1977); Bo. Lorenzo del Valle, Inmaculado Corazon de Maria, (1978); Bo. Santa Clara, San Gerardo, (1986); Urb. Los Flamboyanes, Bo. Florida, Nuestra Senora de Lourdes, (1988).
Catechesis/Religious Programs—Students 850.
Sagrado Corazon de Jesus y 12 Apostoles (Bo. Espino) (1986), Rev. Luis Antonio Rivera.
Res., Bo. Espino, HC 30, Box 32716, 00754. Tel: 787-736-9090; Fax: 787-736-9090.
Chapels—San Francisco de Asis, (1988), Carr. 181, 00754; Santa Rosa de Lima, (1989), Carr. 181, 00754; San Jose, (1959), Carr. 181, 00754; Nstra. Sra. del Rosario, (1994), Carr. 181, Ramal 745, 00754; Maria Madre de la Iglesia, (1990), Carr. 181, 00754.

Yabucoa, Yabucoa Co., Santos Angeles Cutodios (1793), Revs. Rafael Rodriguez; P. Rafael Mateo, C.Ss.R.; Alvaro Jimenez; Luis Sierra; Deacons Rafael Medina; Juan Ramon Delgado.
Res., Box 7, 00767. Tel: 787-893-2250 (Res.); 893-3347 (Office); Fax: 787-266-0841.
Catechesis/Religious Programs—Students 335.
Chapels—Bo. Rosa Sanchez, Santa Rosa de Lima; Bo. Jacanas Granjas, San Juan Evangelista; Bo. Jac. Piedra Blanca, Sagrado Corazon, (1976); Bo. Tejas Piedra Azul, Sta. Maria Reina Paz; Bo. Martorell, Santa Teresita del Nino Jesus; Bo. Tejas, Ntra. Sra. de la Divina Providencia; Bo. Playita Cuesta, San Bernardo; Bo. Playita Arriba, S. Antonio de Padua, (1947); Bo. Playita Parcelas, Virgen Milagrosa; Bo. Quebradillas, Ntra. Sra. del Carmen; Bo. Guayabota, La Sagrada Familia, (1948); Bo. Calabazas Arriba, San Jose, (1942); Bo. Quebrada Grande, San Benito; Bo. Playa Guayanes, Ntra. Sra. del Carmen; Bo. Aguacate, Ntra. Sra. del Perpetuo Socorro, (1937); Bo. Jagueyes, Inmaculada Concepcion, (1910); Bo. Ingenio, Santisima Trinidad; Bo. Camino Nuevo, San Jeronimo; Bo. Jacanas Sur, Divino de Jesus y Beato Diego, (1999).

OUTSIDE THE MAIN ISLAND OF PUERTO RICO, THE SMALL ISLANDS

Culebra, Culebra Co., Nuestra Senora del Carmen (1889; 1990), Rev. Renelmo Ramirez.
Mailing Address: P.O. Box 236, 00775. Tel: 787-742-0133.

Vieques, Vieques Co., Inmaculada Concepcion (1840), Revs. Nelson Lopez Aponte; Angel Colon; Deacons Justino Lopez Ortiz; Pedro Ramos.
Res., 442 Lebruon St., 00765. Tel: 787-741-2241.
Chapels—Bo. Puerto Real, Sagrado Corazon de Jesus, (1949); Bo. Esperanza, San Gerardo, (1952); Bo. Monte Santo, Nuestra Senora del Perpetuo Socorro, (1945); Bo. Santa Maria, Virgen del Carmen, (1942); Bo. Destino, Nuestra Senora de Fatima, (1950).

Chaplains of Public Institutions

CAGUAS. *Government Regional Hospital*. Rev. Freddy Celano.
Hospital Hima. Rev. Freddy Celano.

Unassigned:
Reverend Fathers—
Garcia, Hector de Jesus
Hernandez, Felix Nunez

Retired:
Reverend Fathers—
Gutierrez, Julio
Martinez, Alfredo

INSTITUTIONS LOCATED IN THE DIOCESE

[A] PAROCHIAL SCHOOLS

CAGUAS. *Academia Cristo de los Milagros*, Box 7618, 00726-7618. Tel: 787-743-4855; 743-3131; 743-4242; Fax: 787-746-1428.
E-mail: acdlm@caribe.net
Priests 1; Deacons 1; Lay Teachers 58; Students 1,350.
Colegio Catolico Notre Dame Elemental, Box 967, 00726. Tel: 787-743-2385; 743-2524; Fax: 787-743-7567; 744-6464.
E-mail: tecumsa@coguinet.com
Priests 1; Sisters 4; Lay Teachers 49; Aids 10; Students 1,085.
Colegio Catolico Notre Dame Superior, Box 541, 00726. Tel: 787-743-3693; 743-5501; Fax: 787-258-9648.
Web site: www.ccnd.org
Priests 1; Sisters 4; Lay Teachers 81; Students 1,226.
Colegio San Jose Elemental, Box 806, 00726. Tel: 787-743-2032; Fax: 787-258-0683.
E-mail: sjosepk6@cogui.net
Priests 2; Sisters 4; Lay Teachers 26; Students 600.
Colegio San Jose Superior, Box 1101, Y/O 1749, 00726. Tel: 787-744-8993; Fax: 787-744-4111.
Web site: www.san.jose@prw.net
Priests 1; Lay Teachers 21; Students 450.
Colegio San Juan Apostol y Evangelista, P.O. Box 459, 00726-0459; Fax: 787-743-8266. Lay Teachers 23; Students 425.
Escuela Nuestra Sra. de la Providencia, P.O. Box 1723, 00726. Tel: 787-747-8866. Students 55.

AGUAS BUENAS. *Academia San Alfonso*. (Grades PreK-9), Pio Rechani St., Box 1, 00703. Tel: 787-732-8288; Fax: 787-732-2188. Lay Teachers 13; Students 200.

AIBONITO. *Colegio Parroquial San Jose*, Box 812, 00705. Tel: 787-735-7235; Fax: 878-735-7235. Priests 2; Brothers 1; Sisters 1; Lay Teachers 15; Students 200.

BARRANQUITAS. *Colegio San Francisco de Asis Elemental y Superior*, Box 789, 00794. Tel: 787-857-2123. Brothers 2; Sisters 3; Students 280.

CAYEY. *Colegio Nuestra Senora de la Merced*, Lucia Vazquez St., 00736. Tel: 787-738-3438; Fax: 787-263-5837. (Nuestra Senora de la Asuncion Parish). Priests 1; Lay Teachers 23; Students 440.

FAJARDO. *Colegio Santiago Apostol*. (Grades K-12), Box 907, 00738. Tel: 787-863-0524; 863-0445; Fax: 787-860-6655. Students 655; Priests 2; Sisters 1; Lay Teachers 33.

GURABO. *Colegio Ntra. Sra. De Pilar*, P.O. Box 733, 00778. Tel: 787-737-1400. Mrs. Awilda Velazquez Cotto. Students 132.

HUMACAO. *Colegio Nuestra Senora del Perpetuo Socorro de Humacao, Inc.*, P.O. Box 9107, 00792. Tel: 787-852-0845; 850-0025; Fax: 787-852-8706.
E-mail: perpetuo@east-net.net
Lay Teachers 27; Students 402.

Colegio San Antonio Abad. (Benedictines), Box 729, 00792. Tel: 787-852-1616; Fax: 787-852-1920. Carmen Solis, Prin. Students 470; Priests 2; Lay Teachers 29.

Colegio San Benito, Box 728, 00792. Tel: 787-852-1365; 850-7075; Fax: 787-285-8137. Students 796; Sisters 1; Lay Teachers 40.

JUNCOS. *Colegio Corazon de Maria.* (Grades PreK-9), Box 1776, Calle Fraternidad Esq. Escute, 00777-1776. Tel: 787-734-5551; 734-5565; Fax: 787-734-2724. Priests 1; Sisters 2; Lay Teachers 19; Students 197.

NARANJITO. *Academia Santa Teresita*, Box 244, 00719. Tel: 787-869-7968; 869-6731; 869-8357; Fax: 787-869-8357.
E-mail: astnar@prtc.net
Lay Teachers 32; Students 489.

[B] RETREAT HOUSES

AGUAS BUENAS. *Casa Cristo Redentor* (1967), Box 8, 00703-0008. Tel: 787-732-5161; Fax: 787-732-1115. Revs. Marcos Wise, C.SS.R.; Damian Wall, C.SS.R.; Bro. Mateo Perez, C.SS.R.

AIBONITO. *Casa Manresa*, Box 1319, 00705. Tel: 787-735-8016; 8017; Fax: 787-735-2421. Revs. Aurelio Adan, Dir.; Enrique Asencio.

JUNCOS. *Casa Cursillos de Cristiandad of Caguas.* (Lay Corp. of Cursillistas), Salida de Juncos Carretera 919, P.O. Box 1761, 00777. Tel: 787-734-7068.

SAN LORENZO. *Casa Charlie Rodriguez*, P.O. Box 1190, 00754. Tel: 787-736-5750. Rev. Edward Santana, J.C.D.

[C] MONASTERIES AND RESIDENCES OF PRIESTS

CAGUAS. *Misioneros Hijos del Inmaculado Corazon de Maria (Claretianos)*, Bo. Rio Canas HC-05 Box 57564, 00725-9233.

AIBONITO. *Casa Salesiana de Retiros*, P.O. Box 2019, 00705. Tel: 787-735-2486; Fax: 787-735-5501.
E-mail: sdbaibon@cogui.net
Revs. Antonio Robles, Dir.; Luis Dalbon, Vicar; Bros. Santiago Arroyo; Jose Artigas, Admin.

HUMACAO. *San Antonio Abad Abbey of the Order of St. Benedict*, Box 729, 00792. Tel: 787-852-1616; Fax: 787-852-1920.
E-mail: santabad@east-net.com
Rt. Rev. Oscar Rivera, O.S.B., Abbot; Very Rev. Eduardo Torrelas, Prior; Revs. Rafael Perez, O.S.B.; Jaime Reyes, O.S.B.; Bros. Aristedes Pacheco, Sub Prior; Felix Neussendorfer; Tarcisio Medina; Gregorio Valentin; Randolph Perkins; Roberto Rossi; Jaime Trevino; Ricardo Padilla. Brothers 8; Novices 2.

[D] CLOISTER SISTERS

AGUAS BUENAS. *Reina de la Paz Convent*, Box 1183, 00703. Tel: 787-732-5339.

[E] SHRINES

SAN LORENZO. *Diocesan Shrine Our Lady of Mount Carmel*, P.O. Box 1190, 00754. Tel: 787-736-5750. Rev. Edward Santana, J.C.D., Rector.

[F] MISCELLANEOUS

CAGUAS. *Diocesan Tribunal of Caguas*, P.O. Box 9779, 00726. Tel: 787-286-8595; Fax: 787-286-8620. Rev. Edward Santana, J.C.D., Judicial Vicar.

Instituto Secular de Ntra. Sra. de la Altagracia, Calle 13, L23. Urb. Delgado, 00725. Tel: 787-744-3628; Fax: 787-744-3628. Isabel Vazquez Rivera; Maria Melendez Sanchez; Ramonita Lopez Diaz; Zoraida Santos Santos; Judith Colon Cruz; Olga Rodriguez Berrios; Maria Isabel Colon; Prixda Santos Agosto; Doris Roque Julia; Natividad Ramos Ramos; Evelyn Rosado Rivera.

Movimiento Juan XXIII, P.O. Box 7229, 00726. Tel: 787-747-3748. Rev. Orlando de Jesus.

Voluntarios y Acompanantes Comprometidos con el SIDA (VACS), P.O. Box 656, 00726. Tel: 747-286-3333; Fax: 787-286-3612.

NARANJITO. *Seminario Pablo VI - Propedeutico*, P.O. Box 302, 00719. Tel: 787-869-0861; Fax: 787-869-0861.
E-mail: seminario@prtc.net
Revs. Juan Luis Negron, Rector; Baltazar Nunez Hernandez, Vocation Dir.

RELIGIOUS INSTITUTES OF MEN REPRESENTED IN THE DIOCESE

For further details refer to the corresponding bracketed number in the Religious Institutes of Men or Women section.

[0200]—*Benedictine Monks.* (Collegeville, MN).—O.S.B.
[]—*Claretian Fathers.*—C.M.F.
[0220]—*Congregation of the Blessed Sacrament.* (N. Spain Prov.).—S.S.S.
[]—*Mercedarian Fathers.* (Spain).
[]—*Order of Carmelites.*—O.Carm.
[1070]—*Redemptorist Fathers.* (San Juan Prov.).—C.SS.R.
[1190]—*Salesians of Don Bosco.* (Cuba).—S.D.B.

RELIGIOUS INSTITUTES OF WOMEN REPRESENTED IN THE DIOCESE

[0230]—*Benedictine Sisters of Pontifical Jurisdiction.* (St. Joseph, MN).—O.S.B.
[0420]—*Discalced Carmelite Nuns.* (Spain).—O.C.C.
[]—*Franciscan Nuns (Cloistered).*
[2790]—*Missionary Servants of the Most Holy Trinity.* (Spain).—M.S.B.T.
[3760]—*Order of St. Clare.*—P.C.C.
[]—*Sacred Heart Sisters.*
[]—*Salesian Sisters.*
[2970]—*School Sisters of Notre Dame.* (Wilton, CT).—S.S.N.D.
[]—*Siervas de Maria.* (Spain).
[0640]—*Sisters of Charity of St. Vincent de Paul.* (Puerto Rico Prov.).—S.C.
[]—*Sisters of Fatima.* (Diocesan).
[1650]—*The Sisters of St. Francis of Philadelphia.*—O.S.F.
[2150]—*Sisters Servants of the Immaculate Heart of Mary.*—I.H.M.

NECROLOGY

† Cotto Rodriguez, Carlos N, Ceiba, Puerto Rico San Antonio de Padua. —Died March 11, 2000.

Diocese of the Caroline Islands

Most Reverend

AMANDO SAMO, D.D.

Bishop of the Caroline Islands; ordained Priest December 10, 1977; appointed Titular Bishop of Libertina and Auxiliary Bishop of the Caroline and Marshalls May 10, 1987; ordained Bishop August 15, 1987; named Coadjutor February 3, 1994; named Bishop of the Diocese March 25, 1995; installed June 6, 1995. *Res., P.O. Box 939, Chuuk, Caroline Islands, FM, 96942.* Tel.: 691-330-2399; Fax: 691-330-4585.

Most Reverend

MARTIN J. NEYLON, S.J., D.D.

Retired Bishop of the Caroline Islands; ordained June 18, 1950; appointed Titular Bishop of Libertina October 2, 1969, *"cum jure successionis"*; consecrated February 2, 1970; succeeded as Vicar Apostolic September 20, 1971; appointed First Bishop of Carolines-Marshalls May 3, 1979; installed February 3, 1980; retired June 6, 1995. *Res., St. Ignatius Loyola Residence, 53 E. 83rd St., New York, NY, 10028.* Tel.: 212-288-3588; Fax: 212-734-3671.

Square Miles Ocean 1,725,000.

Total Population of 135,831.

Vicariate of the Caroline Islands erected December 10, 1905 and committed to the Order of Friars Minor Capuchin, extended to the Mariana Islands March 1, 1911.

Vicariate of the Marianas and Caroline and Marshall Islands erected May 4, 1923 and committed to the Society of Jesus. Marianas Islands separated July 4, 1946. Diocese of the Caroline-Marshalls created February 3, 1980. The Marshalls made a separate Prefecture Apostolic August 15, 1993, and the Diocese renamed "Diocese of the Caroline Islands."

Civilly it includes the four Federated States of Micronesia (Chuuk, Kosrae, Pohnpei and Yap) and the Republic of Palau.

Web site address: www.diocesecarolines.org

E-mail address: diocese@mail.fm

STATISTICAL OVERVIEW

Personnel	
Bishop	1
Retired Bishops	1
Priests: Diocesan Active in Diocese	12
Number of Diocesan Priests	12
Religious Priests in Diocese	14
Ordinations:	
Permanent Deacons	4
Permanent Deacons in Diocese	40
Total Brothers	3
Total Sisters	31
Parishes	
Parishes	26
With Resident Pastor:	
Resident Diocesan Priests	8
Resident Religious Priests	3
Without Resident Pastor:	
Administered by Priests	6
Administered by Deacons	9
Missions	4
New Parishes Created	5
Professional Ministry Personnel:	
Brothers	3
Sisters	5
Lay Ministers	3
Educational	
Diocesan Students in Other Seminaries	8
Total Seminarians	8
High Schools, Diocesan and Parish	3
Total Students	481
High Schools, Private	2
Total Students	317
Elementary Schools, Diocesan and Parish	4
Total Students	1,537
Elementary Schools, Private	1
Total Students	230
Catechesis/Religious Education:	
High School Students	230
Elementary Students	750
Total Students Under Catholic Instruction	3,553
Teachers in the Diocese:	
Priests	4
Scholastics	3
Brothers	2
Sisters	21
Lay Teachers	160
Vital Statistics	
Receptions into the Church:	
Infant Baptism Totals	1,667
Adult Baptism Totals	295
Received into Full Communion	65
First Communions	1,308
Confirmations	929
Marriages:	
Catholic	480
Interfaith	86
Total Marriages	566
Total Catholic Population	70,185
Total Population	135,831

Former Bishops—Most Rev. SALVADOR WALLAESER, O.F.M.Cap., cons. Vicar Apostolic and Titular Bishop of Tanagra, Aug. 21, 1912; resigned June 23, 1919; died Jan. 1, 1946; Most Rev. SANTIAGO LOPEZ DE REGO, S.J., cons. Vicar Apostolic and Titular Bishop of Dionisiopolis, Aug. 26, 1923; resigned June 2, 1939; died Aug. 5, 1940; Most Rev. THOMAS J. FEENEY, S.J., cons. Vicar Apostolic and Titular Bishop of Agno, Sept. 8, 1951; died Sept. 9, 1955; Most Rev. VINCENT I. KENNALLY, S.J., cons. Vicar Apostolic and Titular Bishop of Sassura, March 25, 1957; resigned Sept. 20, 1971; died April 12, 1977; Most Rev. MARTIN J. NEYLON, S.J., ord. Bishop, Feb. 2, 1970; succeeded to as Vicar Apostolic, Sept. 20, 1970; named to be Bishop of the new diocese, May 3, 1979; installed as first Bishop of the Diocese of the Carolines-Marshalls, Feb. 3, 1980; retired June 6, 1995.

Chancery Office—P.O. Box 939, Chuuk, FM, 96942. Tel: 691-330-2399; Fax: 691-330-4585.

Vicar General—Rev. JOHN F. CURRAN, S.J., J.C.L.

Chancellor—Rev. NICHOLAS RAHOY.

Diocesan Consultors—Revs. JOHN F. CURRAN, S.J., J.C.L.; RUSK SABURO; WILLIAM J. MCGARRY, S.J.; APOLLINARIS THALL, S.J.; ADALBERT UMWECH.

Finance Committee—Rev. JOHN F. CURRAN, S.J., J.C.L.; Mr. SANTI ASANUMA; Mr. ANGKEN XYMOON; Mr. TONY GANNGIYAN; Mr. WILLIAM IRIARTE; Mr. T. ROY SULLIVAN, Consultant.

Episcopal Vicars—

Chuuk—Rev. DAVID ADALBERT, *P.O. Box 337, Chuuk, FM, 96942.* Tel: 691-330-2672; Fax: 691-330-4394.

Palau—Rev. JOHN PAUL ILILAU, *P.O. Box 128, Palau, PW, 96940.* Tel: 680-488-6539; 2226; Fax: 680-488-1819.

Pohnpei-Kosrae—Rev. WILLIAM J. MCGARRY, S.J., *P.O. Box 160, Pohnpei, FM, 96941.* Tel: 691-320-4661; Fax: 691-320-5876.

Yap—Rev. APOLLINARIS THALL, S.J., *P.O. Box "A", Yap, FM, 96943.* Tel: 691-350-2265; Fax: 691-350-2784.

Diocesan Tribunal—

Judical Vicar—Rev. WILLIAM J. RAKOWICZ, S.J., *P.O. Box 128, Palau, PW, 96940.* Tel: 680-488-2226; Fax: 680-488-1819.

Defenders of the Bond—Most Rev. MARTIN J. NEYLON, S.J., D.D.; Revs. FLORENTINUS AKKIN; NEIL POULIN, S.J.; RUSK SABURO.

Notaries—Rev. JOHN F. CURRAN, S.J., J.C.L.; Mrs. MIRIAM CHIN; Ms. FILIPANA PHILLIP.

Vocations—Most Rev. AMANDO SAMO.

CLERGY, PARISHES, MISSIONS AND PAROCHIAL SCHOOLS

CHUUK (TRUK) STATE, CAROLINE ISLANDS

Mailing Address: for the Vicariate of Chuuk: Rev. Adalbert Umwech, P.O. Box 250, Chuuk, Caroline Islands, FM 96942. Tel: 691-330-2672; Fax: 691-330-4394 (unless otherwise noted).

Tunnuk, Immaculate Heart of Mary Cathedral, Rev. Basilio Dilipiy; Deacons Edwin Shuru; Chitaro William; Yostaro Noporu.
School—St. Cecilia's, Tel: 691-330-4525; Fax: 691-330-4394. Mr. Mariano Marcus, Prin.
Mercedarian Missionaries of Berriz 2; Lay Teachers 28; Students 725.

Neepwukos, Holy Family Church, Rev. Julio Angkel; Deacons Eliot Cholymay; Bername Itiraw.

Fefan, Sacred Heart, Rev. Florentinus Akkim.
Missions—Parem; Tsis.

Uman, Holy Cross, Rev. David Lewis; Deacons Audreas Nimas; Carlos Sam; Salvador Mailos; Akiuo Meisa; Joseph Albert; Nori Oneitam.

Udot, St. Francis Assisi, Deacons John Fritz; Eichy Karsom.
Mission—Romanum, St. Joseph.

Tol, Assumption of the Blessed Virgin Mary, Rev. Adalbert Umwech; Deacons Angken Rapun; Roke Rokop; Kintin Rawit; Itoi Ruta; Oiken Victus; Missa Sewell; Francisco Ykuta; Lukas Paulus.
School—St. Julia. Sr. Yolanda Delgadillo, M.M.B., Prin.
Mercedarian Missionaries of Berriz 4; Lay Teachers 6; Students 107.

Tolowas, St. Anthony's, Revs. David Lewis; Florentinus Akkin; Deacon Tobias Soram.

Lukunor, Sacred Heart, Rev. Nickolas Rahoy.
Missions—Satowan; Kuttu; Moch; Ettal; Namoluk; Oneop; Ta; Nama; Piis; Losap.

POHNPEI STATE, CAROLINE ISLANDS

Mailing Address: for the Vicariate of Pohnpei: Rev. William J. McGarry, S.J., P.O. Box 160, Pohnpei, Caroline Islands, FM 96941. Tel: 691-320-4661; Fax: 691-320-5876 (unless otherwise noted).

Kolonia, Our Lady of Mercy, Rev. Rex Edwin; Deacons Edgar Martin; Martiniano Rodriguez; Geronimo Victor.
Tel: 691-320-2557; Fax: 691-320-5876.
School—Pohnpei Catholic School.
Sisters 3; Lay Teachers 12; Students 190.

Awak, St. Joseph, Deacons Adelino Lorens, Admin.; Manuel Amor; Tarsisio Amor.
Tel: 691-320-6025.

Ipwutek, St. Augustine, Deacon Alius Dorres, Admin.
Tel: 691-320-8930.

Palikir, Sts. Paul and Barnabas, Deacon Thomas Santos, Admin.
Tel: 691-320-5822.

Porrassapw, Christ the King, Deacons Koropin Kermen, Admin.; Saulus Olbet.
Tel: 691-320-3744.

Seinwar, Most Pure Heart of Mary, Deacon Luciano Iowanis.
Tel: 691-320-3573.

Sokehs, St. Peter's, Deacon Albert Linny, Admin.
Tel: 691-320-4667; 320-6923.

Tamoroi, Sacred Heart, Deacon Peter Silbanuz, Admin.
Tel: 691-320-5742.
Mission—Metip.

YAP STATE, CAROLINE ISLANDS

Mailing Address: for the Vicariate of Yap: Rev. Apollinaris Thall, S.J., Vicar, P.O. Box A, Yap, FM 96943. Tel: 691-350-2265; Fax: 350-2784.

Nemar, St. Mary, Rev. Apollinaris I. Thall, S.J.
School—St. Mary's. Sr. Walter Marie Ray, S.S.N.D., Prin.
Priests 1; Sisters 2; Lay Teachers 12; Students 284.

Gagil-Tomil, St. Joseph, Rev. Neil C. Poulin, S.J.
Tel: 691-350-2598.

Ulithi and Neighboring Islands, Queen of Heaven, Rev. Cuthbert Yiftheg; Deacon John Rulmal.
Mission—Ngulu.

Woleai and Neighboring Islands, St. Ignatius, Rev. John S. Hagileiram, S.J.

REPUBLIC OF PALAU, CAROLINE ISLANDS

Mailing Address: for the Vicariate of Palau: Rev. John Paul Iliau, Vicar, P.O. Box 128, Koror, Palau PW 96940. Tel: 680-488-1758; Fax: 680-488-1819.

Koror, Sacred Heart, Rev. Rusk R. Saburo.
School—Maris Stella. Mr. Felix Okabe, Prin.
Brothers 1; Mercedarian Missionaries of Berriz 4; Lay Teachers 23; Students 330.
Missions—Ngcheangl; Sonsorol.
Convent— Our Lady of Lourdes
Mercedarian Missionaries of Berriz 7.
Manresa Jesuit Novitiate—Very Rev. Felix K. Yaoch, S.J., Dir.

Ioueldoab, St. John Baptist, Rev. John Paul Ililau, Admin.

Babeldaob, St. Thomas Apostle, Rev. John Paul Ililau, Admin.

Permanent Deacons:
Albert, Joseph, Uman, Chuuk
Amor, Manuel, Awak, Pohnpei
Amor, Tarsisio, Awak, Pohnpei
Cholymay, Eliot, Moen, Chuuk
Dorres, Aluis, Enimwahn, Pohnpei
Edgar, Martin, Kolonia, Pohnpei
Else, Pelsiano, Sapwuahfik, Pohnpei
Elukan, Augustine, (Retired), Gagil-Tomil, Yap
Felichoo, Francisco, Gagil-Tomil, Yap
Fichibman, Donald, Gagil-Tomil, Yap
Fritz, John, Udot, Chuuk
Iowanis, Tuciano, Seinwar, Pohnpei
Itiraw, Bername, Neepwukos, Chuuk
Karsom, Eichy, Udot, Chuuk
Kermen, Koropin, Kiti, Pohnpei
Linny, Albert, Sokehs, Pohnpei
Lorens, Adelino, Uh, Pohnpei
Mailos, Salvador, Uman, Chuuk
Meisa, Akiuo, Uman, Chuuk
Nimas, Andreas, Uman, Chuuk
Noporu, Yostaro, Fono, Chuuk
Olbet, Saulus, Wene, Pohnpei
Oneitam, Nory, Uman, Chuuk
Paulus, Lucas, Fanapanges, Chuuk
Rapun, Angken, Tol, Chuuk
Rawit, Kintin, Wonei, Chuuk
Rodriguez, Martiniano, Kolonia, Pohupei
Rokop, Roke, Tol, Chuuk
Rulmal, John B., Ulithi, Yap
Ruta, Itol, Tol, Chuuk
Sam, Karlos, Uman, Chuuk
Santos, Thomas, Palikir, Pohnpei
Sewell, Meisa, Tol, Chuuk
Shuru, Edwin, Moen, Chuuk
Silbanuz, Peter, Tamworoi, Pohnpei
Soram, Tobias, Tolowas, Chuuk
Sos, Iakim, Hall Islands, Chuuk
Victor, Geronimo, Kolonia, Pohnpei
Victus, Oiken, Pwene, Chuuk
William, Chitaro, Moen, Chuuk
Ykuta, Francisco, Pwene, Chuuk

INSTITUTIONS LOCATED IN THE DIOCESE

[A] PASTORAL RESEARCH INSTITUTE

POHNPEI. *Micronesian Seminar*, P.O. Box 160, 96941. Tel: 691-320-4067; Fax: 691-320-5876. Rev. Francis X. Hezel, S.J., Dir. Lay Assistants 2.

[B] HIGH SCHOOLS

CHUUK. *Saramen Chuuk Academy*, P.O. Box 662, 96942. Tel: 691-330-4442; Fax: 691-330-4452. Mr. John Martin, Prin.; Rev. John Ikataere, M.S.C., Chap.; Deacon Eliot Cholymay. Sisters 3; Lay Teachers 14; Students 247.
Xavier High School, P.O. Box 220, 96942. Tel: 691-330-4266; Fax: 691-330-4753. Rev. James P. Croghan, S.J., Dir.; Mrs. Lynn Polloi, Prin. Lay Teachers 9; Scholastics 3; Students 156.

PALAU, PW. *Mindszenty High School*, P.O. Box 69, 96940. Tel: 680-488-2437. Ms. Justa Polloi, Prin. Priests 1; Mercedarian Sisters 1; Lay Teachers 16; Students 172.

POHNPEI. *Our Lady of Mercy Vocational Training School*, P.O. Box 73, 96941. Tel: 691-320-3168. Sr. Maria Perez-Caballero, M.M.B., Prin. Mercedarian Sisters 2; Lay Teachers 5; Students 61.
PATS (Pohnpei Agriculture and Trade School), P.O. Box 39, 96941. Tel: 691-320-2991; Fax: 691-320-6046. Revs. Gregory F. Muckenhaupt, S.J., Dir.; Paul L. Horgan, S.J., Chap.; Bro. Terence N. Todd, S.J., Asst. Dir. Priests 2; Brother Teaching 1; Lay Teachers 31; Students 160.

[C] RESIDENCES OF PRIESTS AND BROTHERS

KOLONIA, POHNPEI. *Jesuit House*, P.O. Box 160, 96941. Tel: 691-320-2317; Fax: 691-320-5876. In res. Revs. Francis X. Hezel, S.J., Supr.; William J. McGarry, S.J., Vicar; Joseph A. Cavanagh, S.J.

KOROR, PALAU, PW. *Manresa Jesuit House*, P.O. Box 128, 96940. Tel: 680-488-2226; Fax: 680-488-1819; 488-1725. Very Rev. Felix K. Yaoch, S.J., Regl. Supr.; Revs. Richard S. McCouch, S.J.; William J. Rakowiez, S.J.

TUNNUK, CHUUK. *Vicariate Residence*, P.O. Box 250, 96942. Tel: 691-330-2313; Fax: 691-330-4394. In res. Revs. Basilio Dilipiy, Admin.; Julio Angkel; David Lewis. Priests 2.

[D] RESIDENCES OF SISTERS

AWAK, POHNPEI. *Sisters of Marie Auxiliatrice*, P.O. Box 1375, 96942. Tel: 691-320-2626. Sr. Keiko Akaiwa, M.A., Supr. Sisters 6.

COLONIA, YAP. *Maryknoll Sisters*, P.O. Box 26, 96943. Tel: 691-350-2148 (Colonia). Sr. Joanne McMahon, M.M., Contact Person. Sisters 3.
School Sisters of Notre Dame, P.O. Box 111, 96943. Tel: 691-350-2345. Sr. Vincent Marie Balajadia, S.S.N.D., Contact Person. Sisters 2.

KOLONIA, POHNPEI. *Mercedarian Missionaries of Berriz*, P.O. Box 73, 96941. Tel: 691-320-2558. Sr. Maria Perez-Caballero, M.M.B., Coord. Sisters 4.

KOROR, PALAU, PW. *Mercedarian Missionaries of Berriz*, P.O. Box 56, 96940. Tel: 680-488-2272. Sr. Micaela Udui, M.M.B., Coord. Sisters 7.

NEEPWUKOS, CHUUK. *Religious Sisters of Mercy*, 96942. Tel: 691-330-3363. Sr. Grace Joseph, R.S.M., Coord. Sisters 1.

TOL, CHUUK. *Mercedarian Missionaries of Berriz*, P.O. Box 190, 96942. Sr. Yolanda Delgadillo, M.M.B., Coord. Sisters 5.

TUNNUK, CHUUK. *Mercedarian Missionaries of Berriz*, P.O. Box 67, 96942. Tel: 691-330-4587. Sr. Faustina Nedelec, M.M.B., Coord. Sisters 4.

RELIGIOUS INSTITUTES OF MEN REPRESENTED IN THE DIOCESE

For further details refer to the corresponding bracketed number in the Religious Institutes of Men or Women section.

[0690]—*Jesuit Fathers and Brothers.* (New York Prov.).—S.J.

[1110]—*Missionaries of the Sacred Heart.*—M.S.C.

RELIGIOUS INSTITUTES OF WOMEN REPRESENTED IN THE DIOCESE

[2470]—*Maryknoll Sisters of St. Dominic.*—M.M.

[2510]—*Mercedarian Missionaries of Berriz.*—M.M.B.

[2970]—*School Sisters of Notre Dame.*—S.S.N.D.

[2575]—*Sisters of Mercy of the Americas.*—R.S.M.

[]—*Sisters of Marie Auxiliatrice.*—M.A.

NECROLOGY

(No Deaths)

Diocese of Chalan Kanoa

(Dioecesis Vialenbensis)

Most Reverend

TOMAS A. CAMACHO, D.D.

Bishop of Chalan Kanoa; ordained June 14, 1961; appointed Prelate of Honor by Pope Paul VI in 1974; appointed Bishop of Chalan Kanoa November 8, 1984; consecrated and installed January 13, 1985. *Res., Bishop's Residence, P.O. Box 500745 CK, Saipan, MP, 96950.* Tel.: 670-234-3000.

ESTABLISHED NOVEMBER 8, 1984.

Square Miles 183.61.

Corporate Title: "Bishop of Chalan Kanoa, a Corporation Sole."

Comprises the Mariana Island chain except for Guam, known legally as the Commonwealth of the Northern Mariana Islands.

For legal titles of parishes and diocesan institutions, consult the Diocesan Curia.

Web site address: www.mtccnmi.com / community / diocese:

E-mail address: diocese@gtepacifica.net

STATISTICAL OVERVIEW

Personnel	
Bishop	1
Priests: Diocesan Active in Diocese	12
Priests: Active Outside Diocese	1
Number of Diocesan Priests	13
Religious Priests in Diocese	2
Permanent Deacons in Diocese	3
Total Sisters	9
Parishes	
Parishes	11
With Resident Pastor:	
Resident Diocesan Priests	10
Resident Religious Priests	1
Missions	2
Welfare	
Special Centers for Social Services	1
Total Assisted	2,960
Educational	
Diocesan Students in Other Seminaries	4
Total Seminarians	4
High Schools, Diocesan and Parish	1
Total Students	239
Elementary Schools, Diocesan and Parish	4
Total Students	408
Catechesis/Religious Education:	
High School Students	626
Elementary Students	1,650
Total Students Under Catholic Instruction	2,927
Teachers in the Diocese:	
Sisters	7
Lay Teachers	47
Vital Statistics	
Receptions into the Church:	
Infant Baptism Totals	760
Adult Baptism Totals	17
First Communions	680
Confirmations	405
Marriages:	
Catholic	96
Total Marriages	96
Deaths	144
Total Catholic Population	53,066
Total Population	66,559

Diocesan Curia—*P.O. Box 500745, Saipan, MP, 96950.* Tel: 670-234-3000; Fax: 670-235-3002.

Vicar General—Rev. JOSEPH E. BILLOTTI, S.J.

Chancellor—Rev. ROGER P.T. TENORIO, J.C.L.(Cand.).

Vice Chancellor—Vacant.

Finance Officer—Rev. JOSEPH E. BILLOTTI, S.J., Acting Officer.

Personnel Officer—Vacant.

Director of Vocations—Rev. ROGER P.T. TENORIO, J.C.L.(Cand.).

Director of Religious Education—Sr. MARIANA T. SALMO, O.P.

Superintendent of Catholic Schools—Rev. ROGER P.T. TENORIO, J.C.L.(Cand.).

Director of Worship—Rev. ISAAC M. AYUYU.

Director of Youth Ministry—Rev. JOSE RODOLFO COLENDRINO.

Diocesan Curia Staff—Mrs. LOLITA M. BABAUTA, Office Mgr.; Rev. JOSE A. DAVID, JR., Bishop's Sec.; Sr. ASCENSION ZAMBRA, O.P., Archivist & Librarian.

Consultative Bodies

Presbyteral Council—Rev. ROGER P.T. TENORIO, J.C.L.(Cand.); Rev. Msgr. LOUIS ANTONELLI; Revs. MANUEL CORCUERA; SALVADOR DUMAS; ISAAC AYUYU; MATTHEW BLOCKLEY; JOSE DAVID, JR.; JOSE RODOLFO COLENDRINO; ROLANDO C. PETRONIO; MATTHEW PARK; BONIFACIO G. ESPELETA; GIOVANNI D. BILIRAN, S.V.D.; JOSEPH E. BILLOTTI, S.J.

College of Consultors—Revs. MANUEL CORCUERA; SALVADOR DUMAS; ROGER P.T. TENORIO, J.C.L.(Cand.); JOSEPH E. BILLOTTI, S.J.; ISAAC M. AYUYU; MATTHEW BLOCKLEY.

Diocesan Finance Council—Mr. MICHAEL JOHNSON; Mr. KARL REYES; Mr. JESUS Q. GUERRERO; JOAQUIN Q. DELA CRUZ.

Diocesan Pastoral Council—Representatives from every Parish Pastoral Council, Clergy and Religious.

Diocesan Tribunal

Judicial Vicar—Rev. GIOVANNI D. BILIRAN, S.V.D.

Marriage Tribunal Judge—Rev. ROGER P.T. TENORIO, J.C.L.(Cand.).

Defender of the Bond—Mrs. DEBORAH BARTON, J.C.L.

Tribunal Auditor—Vacant.

Diocesan Commissions

Commission on Worship—Rev. ISAAC M. AYUYU, Acting Chm.

Commission on Justice and Development—Mr. JOHN R. GONZALES, Chm.

Commission on Evangelization—Awaiting formal establishment and appointment of members.

Commission on Family Life—Mr. ROSIKY CAMACHO, Chm.

Commission on Vocation Team—Rev. ROGER P.T. TENORIO, J.C.L.(Cand.), Chm.

Apostolic Works of the Diocese

Human Rights Advocacy Office—Vacant.

Diocesan Publications Office—Rev. ISAAC M. AYUYU, Dir.; Mr. RUY V. POLISTICO, Editor of "North Star" (Diocesan Newspaper); Mrs. MARGRET T. CABRERA, Advertising Mgr.

Electronic Media—Rev. ISAAC M. AYUYU.

Hospital Chaplaincy (Saipan)—Rev. BONIFACIO G. ESPELETA.

Mt. Carmel Catholic Cemetery—Consultants: Mr. MARLON CARLOS; Mr. CRIS M. SABLAN.

Prison Chaplaincy—Rev. JOSEPH E. BILLOTTI, S.J.

Police and Fire Departments Chaplaincy—Rev. JOSEPH E. BILLOTTI, S.J.

St. Joseph Catholic School (Tinian)—Sr. DELIA OBENZA, O.P., Admin. & Prin.

Santa Soledad Catholic School—Rev. ROGER P.T. TENORIO, J.C.L.(Cand.), Admin., Dominican Sisters of the Most Holy Rosary of the Philippines.

Civilly Incorporated Activities of the Diocese

Mount Carmel School, Inc. (Saipan)—Mr. JERRY FACEY, Chm.; Mrs. MARGARET C. DELA CRUZ, Pres.; Mr. TYLER BANGERT, High School Prin.; Mr. MICHAEL MILLER, Elem. School Prin.; Rev. JOSE RODOLFO COLENDRINO, School Chap.

Eskuelan San Francisco de Borja School, Inc. (Rota)—Mr. VINCENT M. ATALIG, Chm.; Sr. BRIGID PEREZ, R.S.M., Admin.

Karidat, Inc.—Mr. NED ARRIOLA, Pres. Bd. Directors; Mrs. ANGIE V. GUERRERO, Exec. Dir.

Associations of the Faithful

A.G.A.P.E. (Almighty God and People Encounter)—Adult Leaders: CRIS SABLAN; LUCINDA SABLAN; Rev. JOSE RODOLFO COLENDRINO, Spiritual Dir.

Catholic Daughters of America—Mrs. THOMASA T. ADA, Regent & Spiritual Dir.

Children of God the Father, Inc.—Mrs. ROMA DIAZ-ARANDA, Pres.; Rev. ROGER P.T. TENORIO, J.C.L.(Cand.), Spiritual Dir.

Confraternity of Christian Mothers—Mrs. ROSA S. CABRERA, Island Board Pres.; Rev. ROGER P.T. TENORIO, J.C.L.(Cand.), Spiritual Dir.

Couples for Christ—Mr. RUFO MAFNAS, Household Leader; Rev. ROLANDO C. PETRONIO, Spiritual Dir.

Cursillo Movement—Mr. BENJAMIN SEMAN, Pres.; Rev. MANUEL CORCUERA, Spiritual Dir.

El Shaddai Movement—Mr. EDUARDO I. BALLESTEROS, Leader; Rev. JOSE RODOLFO COLENDRINO, Spiritual Dir.

Eucharistic Adoration Society—Most Rev. TOMAS A. CAMACHO; ELIZABETH CHO; FRANCISCO PALACIOS.

Knights of Columbus—Sir Knight ANTONIO L. TAISACAN, District Deputy; Rev. ISIDRO T. OGUMORO, Spiritual Dir. for Rev. Msgr. Vicente T. Martinez Council; Rev. ROGER P.T. TENORIO, J.C.L.(Cand.), Spiritual Dir. for Pale Luis Medina Council.

Legion of Mary—

San Vicente Parish - Our Lady, Queen of the Family Praesidium—Rev. ROGER P.T. TENORIO, J.C.L.(Cand.), Spiritual Dir. Assistants: Dominican Sisters.

San Roque Parish - Mother of Divine Love Praesidium—Rev. MANUEL CORCUERA, Spiritual Dir.

Light & Salt Catholic Charismatic Community—Mr. ELMER PASCUAL, Head Secretariat; Rev. JOSE DAVID, JR., Spiritual Dir.

Marriage Encounter—Main Contact: Mr. JESUS SONODA; Mrs. ANICIA SONODA; Rev. ISAAC M. AYUYU, Spiritual Dir.

CLERGY, PARISHES, MISSIONS AND PAROCHIAL SCHOOLS

ISLAND OF SAIPAN

Chalan Kanoa Village, Cathedral of Our Lady of Mt. Carmel, Most Rev. Tomas A. Camacho; Revs. Giovanni D. Biliran, S.V.D.; Jose A. David, S.V.D.

Res., Mt. Carmel Rectory, P.O. Box 500745, Saipan, 96950. Tel: 670-234-3000.

Mission—Saipan, Korean Catholic Community, P.O. Box 693, 96950. Tel: 670-235-1449;1450.

Oratory—Mercedarian Missionary Sisters of Berriz. Formation House and Little House.

Garapan Village, District 11, Kristo Rai Parish, Revs. Isaac M. Ayuyu; Bonifacio G. Espeleta.

Oratories—Maturana House of Prayer; Navy Hill, Commonwealth Health Center Chapel.

San Antonio Village, District 6, San Antonio De Padua Parish, Rev. J. Rudolpho Colendrino.

Res., San Antonio Rectory, P.O. Box 500745, Saipan, 96950. Tel: 670-235-4515.

San Jose Village, District 7, San Jose Parish, Rev. Isidor T. Ogumoro.

Res., P.O. Box 500745, Saipan, 96950. Tel: 670-234-3000.

Tanapag Village, District 8, Santa Remedios Parish, Rev. Manuel Corcuera.

Res., Cathedral Rectory, P.O. Box 500745, Saipan, 96950. Tel: 670-234-3000.

San Roque Village, District 9, San Roque Parish, Rev. Manuel Corcuera.

Res., Cathedral Rectory, P.O. Box 500745, Saipan, 96950. Tel: 670-234-3000.

San Vicente Village, District 10, San Vicente Parish, Revs. Roger P.T. Tenorio; Jose A. David, Jr.

Res., San Vicente Rectory, P.O. Box 500745, Saipan, 96950. Tel: 670-235-8208.

School—Tel: 670-256-7767.

Mission—Saipan, Santa Soledad Mission, (1995). Rev. Roger P.T. Tenorio.

Oratory—Dominican Sisters of the Most Holy Rosary Convent.

Saipan, San Jude Parish, Rev. Joseph E. Billotti, S.J. Mailing Address: P.O. Box 500745, 96950. Tel: 670-288-0269; Fax: 670-235-3002.

ISLAND OF ROTA

Rota, San Isidro (1999), Rev. Msgr. Louis Antonelli. Mailing Address: P.O. Box 590, 96951. Tel: 670-532-0720.

Songsong Village, San Francisco de Borja Parish, Rev. Rolando Petronio.

Res., San Francisco de Borja Rectory, Songsong Village, P.O. Box 542, Rota, 96951. Tel: 670-532-3522.

San Isidro Parish (Sinapalo), Rev. Msgr. Louis Antonelli.

Res., Sinapalo Village, P.O. Box 590, Rota, 96951. Tel: 670-532-0720.

ISLAND OF TINIAN

San Jose Village, San Jose, Rev. Salvador Dumas; Deacon Segundo Castro.

Res., Catholic Rectory, San Jose Village, Tinian, 96952. Tel: 670-433-3000.

School—St. Joseph Catholic School, P.O. Box 282, Tinian, 96952. Tel: 670-433-7527; Fax: 670-433-3000. Sr. Delia Obenza, O.P., Admin. & Prin.

DIOCESAN MISSIONS

1—SAN JOSE CHAPEL. (Island of Anatahan).

2—SANTA CRUZ CHAPEL. (Island of Alamagan).

3—SAN IGNACIO CHAPEL. (Island of Pagan).

4—SANTA CRUZ CHAPEL. (Island of Agrihan).

INSTITUTIONS LOCATED IN THE DIOCESE

[A] ELEMENTARY AND HIGH SCHOOLS

SAIPAN. *Santa Soledad Catholic School*, P.O. Box 500745, 96950. Tel: 670-235-8208; 8209; Fax: 670-235-6396. Rev. Roger P.T. Tenorio.

TINIAN. *St. Joseph Catholic School*, P.O. Box 282, 96952. Tel: 670-433-7527; Fax: 670-433-3000. Sr. Delia Obenza, O.P., Admin. & Prin.

[B] RESIDENCES OF SISTERS

SAIPAN. *M.M.B. Formation House*, P.O. Box 136, 96950. Tel: 670-234-6214. Sr. Helena Ngirkelau, M.M.B., Local Coord. Sisters 8; Novices 4.

M.M.B. Little House, P.O. Box 245, 96950. Tel: 670-234-6127. Sr. Concepcion Kinosta, M.M.B., Local Coord. Sisters 8; Aspirant 4.

M.M.B. Maturana Hill Community, P.O. Box 1178-CK, 96950. Tel: 670-322-9713; Fax: 670-323-4673. Sr. Martha Ramarui, M.M.B., Local Coord. Sisters 9.

Mercy Sisters Convent (San Antonio Parish), P.O. Box 745, 96950. Tel: 670-234-1752. Sr. Seville Cabuhat, R.S.M., Local Coord. Sisters 2.

ROTA. *Rota Mercy Convent*, P.O. Box 542, 96951. Tel: 670-532-5000; Fax: 670-532-3151. Local Coordinators: Sr. Mary Brigid Perez, R.S.M.; Sr. Orlean Pereda, R.S.M. Sisters 2.

RELIGIOUS INSTITUTES OF MEN REPRESENTED IN THE DIOCESE

For further details refer to the corresponding bracketed number in the Religious Institutes of Men or Women section.

[0690]—*The Society of Jesus.*—S.J.

RELIGIOUS INSTITUTES OF WOMEN REPRESENTED IN THE DIOCESE

[]—*Dominican Sisters of the Holy Rosary.*—O.P.

[]—*Dominican Sisters of the Philippines-Saipan.*—O.P.

[]—*Dominican Sisters of the Philippines-Tinian.*—O.P.

[2510]—*Mercedarian Missionaries of Berriz.*—M.M.B.

[0420]—*Religious Sisters of Mercy.*—R.S.M.

NECROLOGY

(No Deaths)

Prefecture Apostolic of the Marshall Islands

Very Reverend

JAMES C. GOULD, S.J.

First Prefect Apostolic of the Marshall Islands; appointed First Prefect Apostolic of the Marshall Islands April 23, 1993; installed August 15, 1993. *Res., Cathedral of the Assumption, P.O. Box 8, Majuro, MH, 96960.* Tel.: 011-692-625-6675; Fax: 011-692-625-5520.

Square Miles 500,000.

Total Population (est.) 50,000.

Prefecture Apostolic of the Marshall Islands divided from the Diocese of the Carolines-Marshalls and erected on August 15, 1993 and committed to the Society of Jesus, New York Province. Area is that of the Republic of the Marshall Islands which is civilly under a Compact of Free Association with the United States.

P.O. Box 8, Majuro, MH, 96960. Tel.: 011-692-625-6675; Fax: 011-692-625-5520.

E-mail address: catholic@ntamar.com

STATISTICAL OVERVIEW

Personnel	
Religious Priests in Diocese	6
Ordinations:	
Transitional Deacons	1
Permanent Deacons	2
Permanent Deacons in Diocese	2
Total Sisters	16
Parishes	
Parishes	4
With Resident Pastor:	
Resident Religious Priests	3
Without Resident Pastor:	
Administered by Priests	1
Pastoral Centers	1
Professional Ministry Personnel:	
Sisters	16
Lay Ministers	33
Educational	
Elementary Schools, Diocesan and Parish	6
Total Students	1,325
Catechesis/Religious Education:	
High School Students	24
Elementary Students	250
Total Students Under Catholic Instruction	1,599
Teachers in the Diocese:	
Sisters	6
Lay Teachers	75
Vital Statistics	
Receptions into the Church:	
Infant Baptism Totals	70
Received into Full Communion	52
First Communions	42
Confirmations	12
Marriages:	
Catholic	21
Interfaith	13
Total Marriages	34
Deaths	10
Total Catholic Population	4,427
Total Population	50,894

Prefecture Consultors—Rev. R. RICHARD MCAULIFF, S.J.; Sr. JOAN CREVCOURE, M.M.; Mrs. NEIMAT REIMERS; Mr. OSCAR DE BRUM; Mr. DENNIS MOMOTARO; Mrs. DAISEY MOMOTARO.

Finance Committee—Sr. ROSE LAUREN EARL, M.M.; Mr. ALEX BING; Mr. ALAN FOWLER; Mr. DENNIS MOMOTARO.

Judicial Vicar—Rev. WILLIAM J. RAKOWICZ, S.J., *P.O. Box 250, Chuuk, FM, 96942.*

Defenders of the Bond—Most Rev. MARTIN J. NEYLON, S.J.; Rev. R. RICHARD MCAULIFF, S.J.

Notary—Mrs. VERONICA KILUWE.

Vocations—Rev. Msgr. JAMES C. GOULD, S.J., *P.O. Box 8, Majuro, MH, 96960.*

CLERGY, PARISHES, MISSIONS AND PAROCHIAL SCHOOLS

MARSHALL ISLANDS

Mailing Address: for the Marshalls: P.O. Box 8, Majuro, MH 96960. Tel: (011) 692-625-6675; Fax: (011) 692-625-5520, unless otherwise noted.

Majuro, Cathedral of the Assumption, Rev. Msgr. James C. Gould, S.J.; Revs. R. Richard McAuliff, S.J.; Leonard G. Hacker, S.J.; Deacon Alfred Capelle.
Tel: 692-625-8307; Fax: 692-625-6507.
School—Sisters 2; Lay Teachers 16; Students 343.
High School—Sisters 2; Lay Teachers 10; Students 142.
Mission—Majuro Atoll, Laura.

Ebeye, Queen of Peace, Rev. Edward Soucie, S.J.
Mailing Address: P.O. Box 5065, Marshall Islands, 96960. Tel: 692-329-3826; Fax: 692-625-3689.
School—School Sisters of Notre Dame 2; Lay Teachers 24; Students 510.
High School—Lay Teachers 13; Students 250.
Mission—Kwajalein, Santo.

Kwajalein, Blessed Sacrament, Rev. William Sullivan, S.J.
Mailing Address: P.O. Box 1711, APO AP, 96555. Tel: 805-355-2116; 355-4535; Fax: 805-355-8404.

Outer Island Parish, Rev. Msgr. James C. Gould, S.J.
Schools—Arno.
Lay Teachers 5; Students 101; Jaluit.
Lay Teachers 5; Students 85; Wotje.
Lay Teachers 4; Students 81.
Missions—Arno; Ailinglaplap; Buoj; Jaluit; Likiep; Namorik; Woja; Wotje.

Special Assignment:
Reverend Fathers—
Young, David, Military Chap.

INSTITUTIONS LOCATED IN THE DIOCESE

[A] MISCELLANEOUS

MAJURO. *Catholic Pastoral Center: Ajeltake*, P.O. Box 8, 96960. Tel: 011-692-247-7797; Fax: 011-692-625-5520. Mrs. Adella Hone, Contact Person.

NECROLOGY

(No Deaths)

Diocese of Mayaguez, Puerto Rico

(Dioecesis Maiaguezensis)

Most Reverend

ULISES AURELIO CASIANO VARGAS, D.D.

Bishop of Mayaguez; ordained May 30, 1967; appointed Bishop March 4, 1976; ordained April 30, 1976. *Res., P.O. Box 2272, Mayaguez, PR, 00709.* Tel.: 809-833-2475; 833-5411 (Office).

Erected by the Bull *"Qui arcano Dei"* on March 1, 1976, by Pope Paul VI.

Comprises a portion of the southwest of the Island.

STATISTICAL OVERVIEW

Personnel	
Bishop	1
Priests: Diocesan Active in Diocese	31
Priests: Active Outside Diocese	2
Priests: Retired, Sick or Absent	8
Number of Diocesan Priests	41
Religious Priests in Diocese	31
Extern Priests in Diocese	4
Ordinations:	
Permanent Deacons	4
Permanent Deacons in Diocese	4
Total Brothers	3
Total Sisters	135
Parishes	
Parishes	29
With Resident Pastor:	
Resident Diocesan Priests	21
Resident Religious Priests	8
Pastoral Centers	154
Professional Ministry Personnel:	
Brothers	3
Sisters	14
Lay Ministers	618
Welfare	
Catholic Hospitals	1
Total Assisted	80,000
Homes for the Aged	1
Total Assisted	133
Special Centers for Social Services	1
Total Assisted	1,780
Educational	
Diocesan Students in Other Seminaries	6
Total Seminarians	6
Colleges and Universities	1
Total Students	1,750
High Schools, Diocesan and Parish	3
Total Students	635
High Schools, Private	4
Total Students	1,394
Elementary Schools, Diocesan and Parish	3
Total Students	924
Elementary Schools, Private	7
Total Students	3,043
Catechesis/Religious Education:	
High School Students	12,500
Total Students Under Catholic Instruction	20,252
Teachers in the Diocese:	
Priests	5
Brothers	3
Sisters	6
Lay Teachers	315
Vital Statistics	
Receptions into the Church:	
Infant Baptism Totals	4,547
Adult Baptism Totals	132
First Communions	3,485
Confirmations	3,083
Marriages:	
Catholic	959
Interfaith	34
Total Marriages	993
Deaths	1,683
Total Catholic Population	360,000
Total Population	491,518

Vicar General—Rev. Msgr. GONZALO DIAZ.

Episcopal Vicars—

For Pastoral—Rev. ROGELIO MUR, O.Carm.

For Diocesan Administration—Rev. Msgr. GONZALO DIAZ.

Chancery Office—P.O. Box 2272, Mayaguez, 00681. Tel: 787-833-5411.

Chancellor—Rev. Msgr. GONZALO DIAZ.

Diocesan Consultors—Rev. Msgr. GONZALO DIAZ; Rev. Msgr. ROGELIO MUR, O.Carm; Revs. TORIBIO PASCUAL, O.S.B.; ANGEL MENDEZ; HUMBERTO LOPEZ; JOSE F. BAEZ.

Diocesan Board of Administration—Rev. Msgr. FRANCIS R. LOPEZ; Rev. Msgr. GONZALO DIAZ HERNANDEZ; Revs. ROGELIO MUR, O.Carm.; ALBERTO CASTRO, P.D.

Administrator—Mr. ALBERTO RODRIGUEZ.

Censor Librorum—Rev. JULIO FERNANDEZ.

Parish Priests Consultors—Rev. Msgr. GONZALO DIAZ HERNANDEZ; Revs. ROGELIO MUR, O.Carm.; TORIBIO PASCUAL, O.S.B.

Diocesan Offices and Directors

Youth Apostolate—Rev. RAFAEL MENDEZ.

Communications Media—Rev. NOMAR J. CALERO; Sr. MARIA SOCORRO BONILLA, O.P.

Cursillos de Cristiandad—Rev. Msgr. GONZALO DIAZ.

Holy Childhood—Most Rev. HERMIN NEGRON.

Legion of Mary—Rev. HECTOR RIVERA.

Supt. of Schools—Sr. VIVINA GRACIA, C.S.J.

Religious Consultor—JOSE MORENO.

Catechetics—Sr. CARLETA MUNOZ, C.S.J.

Christian Family Movement—Rev. LEONIDES SOTO.

Religious Coordinator—Rev. JULIO FERNANDEZ.

Development and Planification—Rev. Msgr. FRANCIS R. LOPEZ; Rev. ROGELIO MUR, O.Carm.

Vocations—Rev. NOMAR J. CALERO.

Lay Pastoral Development—Rev. Msgr. FRANCIS R. LOPEZ, Rector, *Instituto de la Fe, Box 2272, Mayaguez, 00709.*

Catholic Social Services—Sr. LOURDES T. TORO, M.S.B.T., Dir., *Ramos Antonini No. 25 Oeste, Box 2272, Mayaguez, 00681.*

CLERGY, PARISHES, MISSIONS AND PAROCHIAL SCHOOLS

CITY OF MAYAGUEZ

1—CATHEDRAL OF OUR LADY OF PURIFICATION (1763), Revs. Hector E. Rivera Ramos; Nomar J. Calero; Rene J. Hernandez.
Res., P.O. Box 220, Mayaguez, 00681-0220. Tel: 787-831-2444.
Schools—Academy of the Immaculate Conception, Tel: 787-834-5400; 787-834-7824 (High School). Mrs. Marlene Rosa, Elementary Prin.; Mr. Rene Torres, High School Prin.
Lay Teachers 42; Students: Elementary 408; High School 404; Colegio La Milagrosa, Tel: 787-834-0350. Sr. Trinidad Irizarry, Prin.
Sisters of Charity 6; Lay Teachers 27; Students: Elementary 281; High School 162.
Missions—Mayaguez, Maria Socorro de los Cristianos Barrio Leguisamo,; Mayaguez, Santa Ana. Quebrada Grande.
Catechesis/Religious Programs—Students 143.

2—OUR LADY OF MT. CARMEL, Revs. Miguel A. Garcia, C.SS.R.; Jose Chechia, C.SS.R.; Jorge Colon, C.SS.R.; Sr. Elisa Doherty, O.P., Pastoral Min.
Res., Box 3166, Mayaguez, 00681. Tel: 787-831-6544; 832-2036 (Office); Fax: 787-834-2777.
Missions—Mani, Infant of Prague; Jardines del Caribe, Perpetuo Socorro.
Catechesis/Religious Programs—Students 207.

3—ASCENSION (1968), Rev. Jose Fco. Baez Camacho.
Res., Box 4361, Salud Sta., Mayaguez, PR 00681-4361. Tel: 787-832-0766; Fax: 787-832-0766.
Missions—Bo. Limon, St. Teresita; Bo. Las Vegas, Our Lady of Perpetual Help; Bo. El Porvenir, Ntra. Sra. de la Providencia (Rep. Masias).
Catechesis/Religious Programs—Students 160.

4—CHURCH DE EL BUEN PASTOR (1986), Rev. Patrick O. Erwin.
Res., Urb. Mayaguez Ter., 5000 Calle San Gerardo, Mayaguez, 00682-6627. Tel: 787-833-8800; Fax: 787-805-3660.
Catechesis/Religious Programs—Students 151.
Missions—Alturas de Mayaguez, El Senor de Los Milagros, Tel: 787-265-5936; Parcelas Soledad, Sta. Teresita.

5—NUESTRA SENORA DE FATIMA (1986), Rev. Edwin Lugo Silva, Admin.
Res., Parcelas Castillo C-2, Mayaguez, 00680. Tel: 787-833-0794. [JC]
Catechesis/Religious Programs—Students 101.
Missions—Mayaguez, Cristo Rey, Andalucia St., Sultana, 00680.; Mayaguez, Espiritu Santo, Sagitario St., Villa del Oeste, Sabalos, 00680.; Mayaguez, Corpus Christi, Urb. Vista Verde, 00680.

6—SACRED HEART (1959), Revs. Toribio Pascual Diez, O.S.B.; Paulino Mazuelas, O.S.B.; Antonio M. Galban, O.S.B.; Gerardo Ibarra Rodriguez, O.S.B.; Frank Perez Martinez, O.S.B.
Res., R.F.D. 348 Buzon 400, Mayaguez, 00680. Tel: 787-832-1464.
School—St. Benedict College, Tel: 787-832-9626. Rev. Paulino Mazuelas, O.S.B., Prin.
Lay Teachers 31; Students: Elementary 322; High School 220.
Catechesis/Religious Programs—Students 320.
Missions—Rosario, San Jose; Rio Hondo, San Carlos y San Antonio; Bo. Malezas, La Milagrosa.

7—Santa Teresita (1970), Rev. Harry Lopez Vazquez, Admin.
Res., Principe St., 203 Bo. Colombia, Mayaguez, 00680. Tel: 787-832-2872.
Catechesis/Religious Programs—Students 88.

8—San Vicente (1965), Revs. Teodoro Calzada, C.M.; Prudencio Sanchez, C.M.; Tomas de la Puebla, C.M.
Res., Ave. Guanajibo, No. 401, Mayaguez, 00680. Tel: 787-832-8874. [JC]
Catechesis/Religious Programs—Students 63.

9—Church of the Resurrection (1988), Rev. Marcelino Arocho, Admin.
Res., Balboa 285, Mayaguez, 00680. Tel: 787-831-6180.
Catechesis/Religious Programs—Students 56.
Chapels—Consumo, Jesus Redentor.; Rio Canas, Nuestra Senora del Perpetuo Socorro.; Barrio Quemado, Nuestra Senor del Carmen.

OUTSIDE THE CITY OF MAYAGUEZ

Aguada, St. Francis of Assisi (1692), Revs. Jose Luis Diez Gabela, O.S.A. (Spain); Lesmes Bernabe Lazaro, O.S.A. (Spain); German Lombo, O.S.A. (Spain); Isaias Revilla, O.S.A. (Spain).
Res., P.O. Box 608, 00602. Tel: 787-868-2630; Fax: 787-868-8561.
Catechesis/Religious Programs—Students 2,124.
Convent—Calle Jose Hernandez, Box 1136, 00602. Tel: 787-868-8257; Fax: 787-868-8257. Hermanas de la Caridad del Cardenal Sancha
Missions—Sabana, San Jose; Laguna, Santa Rita; Cruces, Santa Monica; Galicia-Columbani, Santo Tomas de Villanueva; Jaguey Chiquito, San Augustin; Rio Grande, Perpetuo Socorro; Naranjo Militar, Ntra. Sra. de Monserrate; Atalaya, Ntra. Sra. de Altagracia; Naranjo-Guanabanas, San Pablo; Marias, Asuncion de Maria; Cerro Gordo, Buen Consejo; Mamey, Perpetuo Socorro; Guaniquilla, Ntra. Sra. del Carmen; Carrizales, Ntra. Sra. de las Mercedes; Malpaso-Cesar Ruiz, Immaculada Concepcion; Bajio, Sagrada Familia; Quebrada Larga, Sgdo. Corazon de Jesus; Rio Grande-Playa, Ntra. Sra. del Carmen; Guayabo, El Buen Pastor; Piedras Blancas, Ntra. Sra. Reina de la Paz.

Santuario Protomartires de la Concepcion (1524), Rev. Roberto Soler.
Res., Bo. Espinar, Buzon 1162, 00602. Tel: 787-891-2889.
Chapels—Bo. Palmar, El Buen Pastor.; Bo. Tablonar, El Nino Jesus.
Catechesis/Religious Programs—Students 88.

Aguadilla, St. Charles Borromeo, Revs. Angel Mendez; Urian Perez.
Res., P.O. Box 238, 00605. Tel: 787-891-0575; Fax: 787-891-3622. [CEM]
School—Tel: 787-891-1445; Fax: 787-882-3270. Mrs. Lizzette Ortiz, Prin.
Lay Teachers 41; Students: Elementary 351; High School 301.
Catechesis/Religious Programs—Students 652.
Convents—Tel: 787-882-3629. Sr. Nilsa Gonzalez, Supr.
Salesian Sisters 4; Tel: 787-891-7496. Sr. Violeta Meduvely, M.C., Supr.
Missionaries of Charity 4.
Chapels—Bo. Corrales, Our Lady of Perpetual Help.; Caimital Alto, St. John Baptist.; Victoria-Nuestra, Senora de la Victoria.; Esteves, N. S. del Rosario.; Bda. Caban, Ntra. Sra. de la Sagrada Familia.

La Milagrosa (1920), Rev. Ramon E. Albino.
Res., Urb. Marbella, Calle 1 Num. 379, 00605. Tel: 787-891-7014.
Catechesis/Religious Programs—Students 198.
Missions—Borinquen, Our Lady of Victory; Camaseyes, Our Lady of Fatima; San Judas Tadeo, Playuelas.

San Jose Obrero (1975), Revs. Christian Jose Then Henriquez, S.D.B., Admin.; Hiram Santiago, S.D.B.; Mario Borgonovo, S.D.B.
Res., Poblado San Antonio, P. O. Box 787, San Antonio, 00690-0787. Tel: 787-890-2449; Fax: 787-826-2494.
Catechesis/Religious Programs—Students 225.
Missions—Bo. Guerrero, La Providencia; Ramey-Maleza, Los Santos Reyes.

Anasco, St. Anthony Abbot (1730), Revs. Rogelio Mur Aguilar, O.Carm.; Juan Maria Amoros, O.Carm.; Francisco Ortiz, O.Carm.
Res., Box 392, 00610. Tel: 787-826-2215.
Catechesis/Religious Programs—Students 450.
Missions—Miraflores, Chapel of Our Lady of Perpetual Help; La Playa, Our Lady of Carmel; Bo. Espino, St. Lawrence Martyr; Bo. Pinales, La Immaculade; Bo. Carreras, La Providencia; Bo. Cerro Gordo, Our Lady of Monserrat; Bo. Marias, St. Rita; Bo. Oveja, Cristo Redentor; Bo. Pozo Hondo, Santa Rosa de Lima.
Jesus Maestro Casa de Formaction—.

Cabo Rojo, St. Michael (1783), Revs. Angel Ortiz, Admin.; Jose R. Linares; Edgardo Lopez.
Res., Box 625, 00623. Tel: 787-851-1283; Fax: 787-851-1970.
School—Miss Elba I. Santana Colon, Dir. Sisters 1; Lay Teachers 39; Students: High School 247; Elementary 380.
Catechesis/Religious Programs—Students 627.
Missions—Puerto Real, Our Lady of Mt. Carmel; Joyuda, St. John the Baptist; Boqueron, St. Joseph; Llanos Tunas, Our Lady of Good Counsel; Las Palmas, St. Rita; Monte Grande, St. Jude Thaddeus; El Corozo, Cristo Rey; Betances, Our Lady of Fatima; Conde Avila, St. Martin de Porres; Bo. Miradero, Ntro. Sra. de la Providencia.

Hormigueros, Shrine of Our Lady of Monserrate (1874), Rev. Msgr. Gonzalo Diaz Hernandez; Rev. Angel Roman Ramos.
Res., Box 24, 00660. Tel: 787-849-2260.
Convent—Box 185, 00660. Tel: 787-849-2055. Sr. Socorro Bonilla, O.P., Supr.
Sisters of Fatima for Social Work 4.
Missions—Bo. Lavadero, Sagrado Corazon de Jesus; Bo. Jaquitas, Ntra. Sra. de la Paz; Bo. Carretera Nueva, La Asuncion; Bo. Guanajibo, San Martin de Porres; Bo. El Hoyo, Santa Rosa de Lima.

El Salvador (1969), Rev. Angel Sanchez, Admin.
Res., Box 567, 00660. Tel: 787-834-1993.
Catechesis/Religious Programs—Students 80.
Chapels—Valle Hermoso Arriba, San Judas Tadeo.; Parcelas S. Romualdo, Sta. Teresita.

Lajas, Our Lady of the Purification (1883), Revs. Rafael Mendez, Admin.; P. Floyd McCoy.
Res., Box 425, 00667. Tel: 787-899-1911; Fax: 787-899-2455.
School—St. Louis Academy Sisters of St. Joseph. (Brooklyn). Tel: 787-899-4080. Sr. Luz Ley de Visot, C.S.J., Prin.
Sisters 2; Lay Teachers 23; Students: Elementary 149; High School 145.
Catechesis/Religious Programs—Students 281.
Convent—Tel: 787-899-5180. La Providencia
Missions—Bo. La Plata, Sagrado Corazon de Jesus, Parcelas #201, 00667.; Bo. Lajas Arriba (La Tea), Ntra. Sra. del Perpetuo Socorro, Carretera 118 Km 0, 00667.; Bo. Lajas Arriba (Parcelas), San Pablo, Parcelas #48, 00667.; Bo. Parcelas Santa Rosa, Santa Rosa de Lima, Comunidad Sta. Rosa #35, 00667.; Bo. Parcelas Palmarejo, San Judas Tadeo, Parcelas #172, 00667.; Bo. Palmarejo II, San Juan Bautista, Parcela #80, 00667.

De la Merced Parish (1971), Rev. Edgar Carlo, Admin.; Deacon Ramon Cardona, P.D.
Res., P.O. Box 1023, 00667-1063. Tel: 787-899-1910.
Catechesis/Religious Programs—Students 110.
Missions—Bo. Maguayo, Ntra. Sra. de la Monserrate, Carr. 101 Ramal 303 K.2.4, Bo. Maguayo, 00667.; Bo. Parguera, San Pedro, Carr. 304 Calle Principal, Bo. Parguera, 00667.; Bo. Cuesta Blanca, Ntra. Sra. de Monserrate, Carr. 116 Parcellas Cuesta Blanca #264, Bo. Cuesta Blanca, 00667.; Bo. Salinas, Ntra. Sra. del Carmen, Carr. 324 K. 5.6, Bo. Salinas, 00667.; Bo. Paris, Ntra Sra. del Perpetuo Socorro, Carr. 306, Bo. Paris, 00667.

Las Marias, Immaculate Heart of Mary (1863), Rev. Delroy Thomas Scott.
Res., Box 126, 00670. Tel: 787-827-3300.
Catechesis/Religious Programs—Students 177.
Missions—Anones, San Jose, Carr. 406, Km. 3.9, 00607.; Buena Vista, La Milagrosa, Carr. 124, R. 370, Km. 6.8 Int Buena Vista, 00670.; Palma Escrita, N.S. de Fatima.

Maricao, St. John the Baptist (1864), Rev. Angel L. Rios, M.C.
Res., Box 453, 00606. Tel: 787-838-2014.
Catechesis/Religious Programs—Students 142.
Missions—Bucarabones, Sagrado Corazon; Indiera Fria, Santa Rosa.
Chapel—Montoso, Immaculado Corazon de Maria, Tel: 787-838-2272. Sr. Inocencia Olmeda, O.P., Supr.
Dominican Sisters of Our Lady of Fatima 6.

Moca, Our Lady of Monserrate (1772), Revs. Santiago Rivera Allende; David Perez Mendez; Orlando Rosas Muniz; Juan Bautista Morales; Rev. Msgr. Hector Ortiz.
Res., P.O. Box 435, 00716. Tel: 787-877-2765.
Catechesis/Religious Programs—Lydia Soto, D.R.E. Students 1,738.
Missions—Bo. Cerro Gordo, San Judas; Bo. Voladoras Lomas, Espiritu Santo; Bo. Voladoras Parcelas, Sagrada Familia; Bo. Naranjo, Corazon de Jesus; Bo. Cuchillas La Salle, Santos Guillermo y Mateo; Bo. Chucillas Sabana, Corazon de Jesus; Bo. Limon, Virgen del Rosario; Bo. Cuchillas Loperena, Virgen del Carmen; Bo. Cordero, Virgen Monserrate; Bo. Rocha Magueyes, La Providencia; Bo. Punta Brava, San Pedro; Bo. Capa Barreto, Virgen del Rosario; Bo. Capa Bosque, Cristo Salvador; Bo. Cerro Gordo, La Inmaculada; Bo. Aceituna, San Martin de Porres.

Rincon, St. Rose of Lima (1789), Revs. Angel L. Soto Barreto, Admin.; Luis B. Rios Capiello; Deacon Fausto Duran, P.D.
Res., Box 128, 00677. Tel: 787-823-2650; Fax: 787-823-4400.
Catechesis/Religious Programs—Students 600.
Missions—Bo. Calvache, Santa Rosa; Bo. Atalaya, El Cristo de la Reconciliacion; Bo. Corcega, La Milagrosa; Bo. Cruces, Sagrado Corazon de Jesus; Bo. Puntas, Nuestra Senora del Carmen; Bo. Jaguey, San Jose.

Rosario, Rosary, Rev. Vicente Perez Roig.
Res., Box 692, 00636. Tel: 787-832-3533.
Missions—Rosario, Nuestra Senora del Rosario; Bo. Rosario Penon, La Monserrate, Bo. Rosario Penon, 00680.
Catechesis/Religious Programs—Students 40.

Sabana Grande, Church of San Isidro (1813), Revs. Jorge L. Caro Morales; Edward Acevedo; Edgardo Acosta.
Res., Box 817, 00637. Tel: 787-873-4475.
Catechesis/Religious Programs—Students 889.
Convent—Tel: 787-873-2750. Sr. Barbara Duran, O.P., Supr.
Sisters 4.
Missions—El Papayo, Cristo Rey, Carr.368 R.367 KM.2.0, 00637.; Susua, La Resurreccion, Carr.121 Calle Azucena, 00637. Tel: 809-873-0382; Bo. Maginas, Sagrado Corazon de Jesus, Calle Rable #44-Carr.121 K. 5.0, 00637. Tel: 809-873-1368; Bo. La Pica, San Jose, Carr. 121 Km. 4.1, 00637. Tel: 809-873-4231; Bo. Cerro Gordo, San Francisco de Asis, Carr.369 Km.1.4, 00637. Tel: 809-873-8048; Bo. Molinas, Ntra. Sra. de Monserrate, Carr.2 R.365 Km.2.8 Int., 00637. Tel: 809-873-2656; Bo. Guaras, Ntra. Sra. de Fatima, Carr.328 Km.3.6, 00637. Tel: 809-873-0886; Bo. La Torre, Santa Catalina de Siena, Carr.388 Km.5.9 Int., 00637. Tel: 809-873-7591; Bo. La Maquina, Santa Ana, Carr.114 R.363 Km.2.4, 00637.; Bo. Santana Pichel, Ntra. Sra. del Rosario, Carr.120 Km.6, 00637. Tel: 809-873-3707; Bo. El Hoyo, La Virgen Milagrosa, Carr.364 Km.7 Interior, 00637.; Bo. Rayo Plata, San Judas Tadeo, Carr.117 Km.10.7, 00637.; Bo. Sta. Ana Moreno, Sta Lucia, Carr.120 Km.3.1, 00637. Tel: 809-873-7962.

San German, San German de Auxerre, Revs. Humberto Lopez; Julio Vera; Rev. Msgr. Francis R. Lopez; Rev. Fernando Palacio Salazar.
Res., Box 305, 00683. Tel: 787-892-1027.
School—Tel: 787-892-1009. Sr. Maria Ines Martin, C.S.J., Prin.
Sisters of St. Joseph (Brooklyn) 1; Lay Teachers 37; Students: Elementary 478; High School 165.
Catechesis/Religious Programs—Students 318.
Missions—Duey, Chapel of St. Augustin; Hoconuco, Chapel of St. Joseph; Maresua, Gruta de Lourdes; Cotuy, Our Lady of Fatima; Sabana Eneas, San Judas Tadeo.

St. Rose of Lima (1967), Revs. Urbano Saenz, O.S.A.; Roberto Garcia, O.S.A.; Francisco Larran, O.S.A.
Res., Box 364, 00683. Tel: 787-892-1276.
Catechesis/Religious Programs—Students 542.
Missions—Bo. Guama, N. Sra. de la Consolacion; Bo. Minillas Carretera, Perpetuo Socorro; Bo. Retiro Tea, Santa Rita; Bo. Minillas Valle, Santa Monica; Bo. Cain, St. Martin de Porres.

San Sebastian, San Sebastian Martir (1752), Revs. Jose R. Montanez Lopez, C.P.; Bernardo Onaindia, C.P.; Miguel Angel San Martin, C.P.; Jose Lizarralde, C.P.
Res., P.O. Box 801, 00685. Tel: 787-896-1028.
School—San Sebastian Martir, Tel: 787-896-5728. Jose Joaquin Rivera, Prin.
Lay Teachers 29; Students 425.
Catechesis/Religious Programs—Students 1,181.
Missions—Bo. Perchas 1, Cristo Rey; Bo. Perchas 11, La Pasion; Bo. Calabazas, San Gabriel de la Dolorosa; Bo. La Lechuza, La Asuncion; Bo. Juncal, Santa Teresita; Bo. Aibonito Guerrero, Ntra. Sra. del Carmen; Bo. Saltos, San Judas Tadeo; Bo. Hato Arriba, San Patricio; Bo. Hato Arriba (Parcelas), San Pablo de la Cruz; Bo. Altozano, Ntra. Sra. de Fatima; Bo. Robles, Sagrado Corazon; Bo. Hoyamala, San Jose Obrero; Bo. Parcelas Guacio (Parcelas), Santa Cruz.

On Special Assignment:
Reverend Fathers—
Diaz, Gonzalo, Chancellor, Vicar General, Box 24, Hormingueros, PR

INSTITUTIONS LOCATED IN THE DIOCESE

[A] COLLEGES AND UNIVERSITIES

ANASCO. *De La Salle Catholic College*, Apartado 61, 00610. Tel: 787-826-6071; Fax: 787-826-5185. Rene Hernandez Perez, Contact Person.

AQUADILLA. *Corpus Christi College*, Apartado 4021, 00605-4021. Tel: 787-882-8433; Fax: 787-891-4555. Rev. Ramon E. Albino.

MOCA. *Nuestra Senora de la Monserrate College*, Apartado 435, 00676. Tel: 787-877-2765; Fax: 787-877-7795. Hilda Perez, Prin.

[B] SCHOOLS

RINCON. *Santa Rosa de Lima Academy*, Apartado 128, 00677. Tel: 787-823-0496. Sr. Samuel Collazo, Prin.

[C] HOSPITALS

SAN GERMAN. *Hospital of the Immaculate Conception*, Box 285, 00683

For a complete listing, refer to the Hospitals section.

[D] INSTITUTIONS

MAYAGUEZ. *Asylum for the Poor and Aged*, Calle Post 62, 00680. Sisters of Charity (Spanish). Sr. Cruz M. Fontan, Supr. Sisters 4; Beds 112; Residents 87.

Convent of the Servants of Mary, Hostos Ave. 401, 00708. Tel: 787-832-0391. Sisters care for the sick in their homes and hospital. Sr. Milagros Santos, Supr. Sisters 16.

HORMIGUEROS. *Residence for the Aged, San Jose*, Valle Hermoso, 00660. Tel: 787-832-4243. Sr. Purificacion Rubenaque, Supr. Sisters 13; Residents 150.

[E] PERSONAL PRELATURES

MAYAGUEZ. *Opus Dei (Prelature of the Holy Cross and Opus Dei)*, 69 Orquideas St., Ensanche Martinez, 00680. Tel: 787-833-6461. Rev. Ramon Alvarez Infiesta.

RELIGIOUS INSTITUTES OF MEN REPRESENTED IN THE DIOCESE

For further details refer to the corresponding bracketed number in the Religious Institutes of Men or Women section.

[]—*Acies Christi*. (Spain).
[0140]—*Augustinians*.—O.S.A.
[0200]—*Benedictine Monks*. Spain.—O.S.B.
[0270]—*Carmelite Fathers and Brothers*. (Spain).—O.Carm.
[1330]—*Congregation of the Mission*. (Vice Province of Puerto Rico).—C.M.
[1000]—*Congregation of the Passion*.—C.P.
[1070]—*Redemptorist Fathers*.—C.SS.R.
[]—*Salesian Fathers*.

RELIGIOUS INSTITUTES OF WOMEN REPRESENTED IN THE DIOCESE

[]—*Acies Christi*. (Spain).
[]—*Carmelitas de Clausura*. (Spain).
[1070-13]—*Dominican Sisters*.—O.P.
[]—*Hermanas de la Caridad*.
[]—*Hermanas MM. del Buen Pastor*. (Puerto Rico).
[]—*Hermanas Salesianas*. (Spain).
[]—*Hermanas Teatinas*. (Spain).
[2340]—*Little Sisters of the Poor*.—L.S.P.
[]—*Madames of the Sacred Heart*.
[2790]—*Missionary Servants of the Most Blessed Trinity*.—M.S.B.T.
[]—*Monasterio Santa Maria del Monte Carmelo*.
[3580]—*Servants of Mary*. (Spain).—O.S.M.
[0650]—*Sisters of Charity of St. Vincent de Paul*. (Spanish).—S.C.
[]—*Sisters of Fatima*. (Puerto Rico).
[]—*Sisters of Schoenstatt*. (Germany).
[]—*Sisters of St. Joseph*. (Brooklyn).

NECROLOGY

(No Deaths)

Diocese of Ponce, Puerto Rico

(Dioecesis Poncensis)

Most Reverend

RICARDO SURINACH CARRERAS, D.D.

Bishop of Ponce; ordained April 13, 1957; appointed May 26, 1975; consecrated July 25, 1975; appointed November 10, 2000; installed November 30, 2000. *Res., P.O. Box 32205, Ponce, PR, 00732-2205.* Tel.: 787-848-5265; Fax: 787-841-1778.

Most Reverend

FREMIOT TORRES OLIVER, D.D.

Bishop Emeritus of Ponce; ordained April 10, 1950; appointed Bishop November 4, 1964; consecrated December 21, 1964; retired November 10, 2000. *Res., Bishop's House, P.O. Box 32205, Ponce, PR, 00732-2205.* Tel.: 787-848-5265; Fax: 787-841-1778.

ESTABLISHED NOVEMBER 21, 1924.

Square Miles 830.

Comprises the south portion of the Island of Puerto Rico and is in the Ecclesiastical Province of Puerto Rico.

Web site address: www.pucpr.edu:

E-mail address: obispadoponce@pucpr.edu

STATISTICAL OVERVIEW

Personnel	
Bishops	1
Retired Bishops	1
Priests: Diocesan Active in Diocese	39
Priests: Active Outside Diocese	28
Priests: Retired, Sick or Absent	8
Number of Diocesan Priests	75
Religious Priests in Diocese	53
Extern Priests in Diocese	17
Ordinations:	
Diocesan Priests	2
Permanent Deacons in Diocese	71
Total Brothers	1
Total Sisters	218
Parishes	
Parishes	40
With Resident Pastor:	
Resident Diocesan Priests	27
Resident Religious Priests	13
Missions	2
Pastoral Centers	231
Welfare	
Homes for the Aged	2
Total Assisted	262
Specialized Homes	1
Total Assisted	83
Special Centers for Social Services	3
Total Assisted	4,412
Other Institutions	1
Total Assisted	1,653
Educational	
Seminaries, Diocesan	1
Students from This Diocese	7
Students from Other Diocese	3
Diocesan Students in Other Seminaries	3
Seminaries, Religious	2
Students Religious	8
Total Seminarians	18
Colleges and Universities	1
Total Students	10,365
High Schools, Diocesan and Parish	20
Total Students	1,612
Elementary Schools, Diocesan and Parish	22
Total Students	8,075
Catechesis/Religious Education:	
Total Students Under Catholic Instruction	20,070
Teachers in the Diocese:	
Priests	13
Sisters	3
Lay Teachers	1,030
Vital Statistics	
Receptions into the Church:	
Infant Baptism Totals	4,327
Adult Baptism Totals	2,980
Received into Full Communion	36
First Communions	5,609
Confirmations	5,523
Marriages:	
Catholic	1,183
Interfaith	37
Total Marriages	1,220
Total Catholic Population	484,000
Total Population	604,210

Former Bishops—Most Rev. EDWIN V. BYRNE, D.D., cons. in Philadelphia, Nov. 30, 1925; transferred to San Juan, PR; promoted to Archbishop of Santa Fe, NM, June 15, 1943; died July 25, 1963.—Most Rev. ALOYSIUS J. WILLINGER, C.Ss.R., D.D., ord. July 2, 1911; appt. Bishop of Ponce March 8, 1929; cons. Oct. 28, 1929; appt. Titular Bishop of Bida and Coadjuctor of Monterey-Fresno (cum jure successionis), Dec. 12, 1946; installed Bishop of Monterey-Fresno, Jan. 3, 1953; resigned Oct. 25, 1967; died July 25, 1973.—Most Rev. JAMES E. MCMANUS, C.SS.R., D.D., J.C.D., transferred to the Archdiocese of New York, Nov. 27, 1963.—His Eminence LUIS CARDINAL APONTE, D.D., ord. April 10, 1950; appt. Titular Bishop of Lares and Auxiliary of Ponce, July 23, 1960; cons. Oct. 12, 1960; appt. Coadjuctor Bishop of Ponce, April 16, 1963; appt. Bishop of Ponce, Nov. 18, 1963; installed Feb. 20, 1964; promoted to Archbishop of San Juan, Nov. 4, 1964; installed Jan. 15, 1965; created Cardinal, March 5, 1973; resigned May 8, 1999.

Vicar General—Most Rev. RICARDO SURINACH, D.D.

Pro-Vicar General—Rev. Msgr. PEDRO J. BALLESTER.

Chancellor—Rev. Msgr. HERMINIO DE JESUS.

Vice Chancellor—Rev. Msgr. JUAN ESPONA.

Bishop's Secretary—Rev. Msgr. JUAN ESPONA.

Episcopal Vicar for Diocesan Administration—Rev. Msgr. HERMINIO DE JESUS.

Episcopal Vicar for Pastoral Coordination—Rev. Msgr. ANDRES GUERRERO.

Episcopal Vicar for Clergy Affairs—Rev. Msgr. ROBERTO GARCIA-BLAY.

Tribunal Interdiocesano de Puerto Rico—*P.O. Box 32209, Calle Isabel No. 31, Ponce, 00732-2732.* Tel: 787-843-4630; Fax: 787-841-7483. First instance for the Dioceses of Mayaguez and Ponce. Second Instance for the Archdiocese of San Juan.

Judicial Vicar—Rev. Msgr. ELIAS MORALES, J.C.L.

Associate Judicial Vicars—Rev. MANUEL SANTIAGO, J.C.L.

Moderator—Most Rev. FREMIOT TORRES OLIVER, D.D.

Judge—Mayaguez: Rev. Msgr. GONZALO DIAZ.

Diocesan Consultors—Most Rev. RICARDO SURINACH, D.D.; Rev. Msgr. PEDRO J. BALLESTER; Rev. Msgr. HERMINIO DE JESUS; Rev. Msgr. MARCOS A. PANCORBO; Rev. Msgr. JESUS R. DIEZ ANTONANZAS; Rev. Msgr. JUAN ESPONA; Revs. JOSE LOZANO; JUAN RODRIGUEZ ORENGO.

Diocesan Board of Administration—Most Rev. RICARDO SURINACH, D.D.; Rev. Msgr. MARCOS PANCORBO; Rev. Msgr. PEDRO J. BALLESTER; Mr. FERNANDO ROSADO; Deacon ALBERTO CASTRO; Mr. SANTIAGO RAMOS.

Parish Priests Consultors—Rev. Msgr. MARCOS PANCORBO; Rev. Msgr. ANDRES GUERRERO; Rev. Msgr. HERMINIO DE JESUS; Rev. JOSE LOZANO.

Notaries—Rev. Msgr. JUAN ESPONA; Mrs. LUZ DELIA MEDINA; Mrs. MARIA V. RODRIGUEZ; Mrs. IRIS YOLANDA PAGAN, M.J.

Censores Librorum—Revs. PERFECTO ALVAREZ, O.S.A.; FELIX LAZARO, Sch.P.; BRIAN HARRISON, O.S.

Administrator—Rev. Msgr. JUAN ESPONA.

Diocesan Offices and Directors

Catechesis—Sr. LUISA CARABALLO, O.P., *P.O. Box 331064, Ponce, 00733-1064.* Tel: 787-842-9178; Fax: 787-259-1718.

Catholic Youth Organization—Vacant.

Children of Mary—Rev. Msgr. ANDRES GUERRERO.

Committee for Community Planning—Rev. Msgr. HERMINIO DE JESUS.

Communications—Sr. LOURDES MERCADO, O.P., *P.O. Box 330986, Ponce, 00733-0986.* Tel: 809-843-1548.

Cursillos de Cristiandad—Deacon BENJAMIN PAGAN, *Marvesa, La Rambla, Ponce, 00731.*

Ecumenism—Rev. Msgr. ANDRES GUERRERO, *P.O. Box 32205, Ponce, 00732-2205.*

Legion of Mary—Rev. Msgr. ANDRES GUERRERO, *P.O. Box 32205, Ponce, 00732-2205.*

Liturgical Commission—Most Rev. RICARDO SURINACH, D.D.; Rev. Msgr. JUAN ESPONA, *P.O. Box 32205, Ponce, 00732-2205.*

Sacred Music Commission—Rev. Msgr. ABEL DI MARCO.

St. Vincent de Paul Conferences—Dr. RAFAEL BLASINI, *Cristo Rey Parish, 7W Ext. La Rambla, Ponce, 00731.*

Superintendent of Schools—Sr. MARIA UNA, R.A.D., *P.O. Box 32552, Ponce, 00732-2552.* Tel: 787-848-4020; Fax: 787-844-5987.

Vigilance for the Faith—Most Rev. RICARDO SURINACH, D.D.

Vocations—Rev. Msgr. JESUS R. DIEZ ANTONANZAS; Rev. ALFREDO ALVAREZ LACRUZ, *P.O. Box 32110, Ponce, 00732-2110.* Tel: 787-848-5265; Fax: 787-848-5265.

Institute of Family Orientation—Deacon JESUS M. PAGAN, *P.O. Box 32214, Ponce, 00732-2214.* Tel: 787-840-6018; Fax: 787-848-4523.

CLERGY, PARISHES, MISSIONS AND PAROCHIAL SCHOOLS

CITY OF PONCE

1—CATHEDRAL OF OUR LADY OF GUADALUPE (1692), Rev. Msgr. Marcos A. Pancorbo; Rev. Rafael Alvarado de Jesus; Deacon Jose Mercado.
Res., 28 Cristina St., Box 32210, 00732-2210. Tel: 787-842-0134; Fax: 787-848-9104.

2—CHRIST THE KING (1964), Revs. Juan Rodriguez Orengo; Luis A. Cruz; Deacons Anibal Rosario; Eduardo A. Dosal; Manuel Roman.
Res., 7 W. Ext., La Rambla, 00731. Tel: 787-843-3028; Fax: 787-840-7398.
School—Tel: 787-843-0766; Fax: 787-843-6443. Mrs. Daisy Lopez, Prin.
Missions—Urb. Santa Teresita, Ponce Co., Santa Teresita Calle 33, Parque Central; Rio Chiquito, Ponce Co., Nino Jesus de Praga Bo. Los Claves; Ponce, La Dolorosa. Villa Ponce - Rambla #4st.

3—CHURCH OF THE RESURRECTION (1967), Rev. Msgr. Roberto Garcia Blay; Revs. Esteban Santaella; Jose M. Herrero; Deacon Rafael Castro.
Res., Glenview Gardens, PMB-98, P.O. Box 2000, Mercedita, 00715. Tel: 787-842-7167; Fax: 787-848-5458.
Missions—Bo. La Yuca, Ponce Co., Immaculate Heart of Mary; Bo. Collado, Ponce Co., Our Lady of Monserrate; Bo. Las Vallas, Ponce Co., San Lucas; Ponce, Saint Joseph Bo. La Yuca; Ponce, Our Lady of Carmel. Bo. Carmelita.

4—OUR LADY OF MT. CARMEL (1883), Revs. Miguel Alvarez, Sch.P.; Jose Mateo, Sch.P.; Francisco J. Lopez, Sch.P.; Deacon Jose Rivera.
Res., P.O. Box 30118, Playa de Ponce, 00734-0118. Tel: 787-842-1333; Fax: 787-841-6861.
School—Tel: 787-842-5018. Mrs. Paquita Alvarado, Prin.
Missions—Villa del Carmen, Ponce Co., San Martin de Porres, Constancia Ave., 00734. Tel: 787-848-4355; Bo. Salistral, Ponce Co., Santa Marta.

5—SANTA TERESITA (1930), Revs. Jose A. Carrion, O.F.M.Cap.; Roberto Martinez, O.F.M.Cap.; Mario Mastrangelo, O.F.M.Cap.; Francisco Garcia, O.F.M.Cap.; Deacon Casildo Rodriguez.
Res., Box 7244, 342 Victoria St., 00732. Tel: 787-842-3137; 842-5055 (Friary); Fax: 787-844-7267.
School—342 Victoria St., 00732. Tel: 787-842-4110. Mrs. Mildred Reyes, Prin.

6—SAN CONRADO (1948), Rev. Msgr. Pedro J. Ballester; Deacon Emerito Lopez.
Res., Box 7362, 00732. Tel: 787-843-0560.
School—P.O.Box 7111, 00732. Tel: 787-843-1405; 842-2293; Fax: 787-841-7303. Sr. Nildred Rodriguez, C.S.J., Prin.

7—SANTA MARIA (1952), Revs. Thomas Cahill, M.J.; Daniel Ewald, M.J.; Michael J. Diemer, M.J.
Res., P.O. Box 32101, 00732-2101. Tel: 787-848-5370; Fax: 787-848-3313.
School—Tel: 787-842-1164. Mrs. Lydia Otero, Prin.

8—LA MILAGROSA (1928), Revs. Juan Lamela, C.M.; Manuel Prado, C.M.; Deacons Ramon L. Vazquez; Carlos Burgos.
Res., Guadalupe No. 2, 00731. Tel: 787-842-3188; Fax: 787-284-1100.
School—Tel: 787-842-1164. Mrs. Carmen Pasarell, Prin.

9—LA MERCED (1928), Revs. Ramon Conde Ocampo, O.de.M.; Silvino Gonzalez, O.de.M.; Jose Luis Iturraran, O.de.M.; Deacons Carlos M. Rodriguez-Guilbe; Jose D. Ruiz.
Res., 4632 Luna St., 00717-2000. Tel: 787-842-0069; Fax: 787-842-0603.

10—LA SANTISIMA TRINIDAD (1971), Revs. Jose Luis Fernandez, O.SS.T.; Alfonso Rementeria, O.SS.T.; German Rementeria, O.SS.T.; Deacons Francisco Lugo; Jose Rodriguez.
Res., Las Delicias, Box 8226, 00732. Tel: 787-842-6073; Fax: 787-842-6073.
Missions—Bo. Magueyes, Ponce Co., San Juan de Mata, Box 8226, 00732; Bo. Guaragoa, Ponce Co., San Andres, 00732; Bo. Guaragoa, Arriba, Ponce Co., Santa Ana, 00732; Bo. Marueno, Arriba, Ponce Co., N.S. Fatima, 00732; Parcelas de Marueno, Ponce Co., San Antonio de Padua, 00732; Bo. Madrigal, Ponce Co., N.S. del Rosario, 00732; Bo. Pastillo, Ponce Co., Inmaculada, 00732; Bo. Corral Viejo, Ponce Co., Cristo Rey, 00732; Bo. Santas Pascuas, Ponce Co., Resurreccion, 00732.

11—SAN JOSE OBRERO (1979), Revs. Brian W. Harrison, O.S.; Christopher de Herrera, O.S.; Deacons Nestor Rentas; Angel R. Mendez.
Res., El Tuque, Calle 1 No. 3, Box 8027, 00732. Tel: 787-843-9072; Fax: 787-843-9072.
Mission—Punto Oro, Ponce Co., Ntra. Sra. del Pilar.

12—SAN JOSE (1965), Revs. Santiago Soria, O.C.D.; Mariano Fraile, O.C.D.; Alexio Jose de Armas, O.C.D.; Bro. Fray Jorge Llorentes, O.C.D.; Deacons David Rodriguez; Benjamin Pagan.
Res., Urb. San Jose, Calle 6, Box 8414, 00732. Tel: 787-843-3910; Fax: 787-843-1994.

13—SANTUARIO SAN JUDAS TADEO (1964), Revs. Jose Maria Reyes, O.de. M.; Modesto Vaca, O.de.M.; Javier Errecalde, O.de.M.; Vicente Salas Avello, O.de.M.; Javier Gutierrez, O.de.M.
Res., P.O. Box 7046, 00732. Tel: 787-843-0572; Fax: 787-842-0148.
School—Oblates to the Divine Love, Tel: 787-844-2610. Mrs. Zaida Toro, Prin.
Kindergarten—Urb. Constancia H-467, 00731. Tel: 787-843-5378; Fax: 787-842-5079. Sisters of the Love of God (Spain). Sr. Paz Martinez, R.A.D., Prin.
Mission—Bo. Cuatro Calles, Ponce Co., St. Anthony.

14—SAN VICENTE-CANTERA, Revs. Luis Brioso, C.M.; Bernardo Hernandez, C.M.
Res., Mayor Cantera No. 67, 00731. Tel: 809-843-1976.
Mission—Rio Chiquito, Ponce Co., San Vicente.

15—CHURCH OF THE SACRED HEART (1969), Revs. Jose M. Galan; Perfecto Alvarez, O.S.A.; Deacon Reinaldo Rivera.
Res., P.O. Box 577, Mercedita, 00715-0577. Tel: 787-848-9212; Fax: 787-848-9212.
Mission—Bo. La Cuarta, Ponce Co., San Pedro Nolasco.

16—CHURCH OF THE GOOD SHEPHERD (1968), Rev. Msgr. Elias Morales; Deacons David Ramos; Rafael D. Ruiz; Andres Maldonado; Jose A. Perez; Juan Rodriguez.
Res., Calle 35, H.H. 14, Jardines del Caribe, 00731. Tel: 787-843-6202.
Mission—Bo. Quebrado del Agua, Ponce Co., La Milagrosa, 00731.

17—OUR LADY OF MT. CARMEL (1973), Rev. Jose Antonio Lopez Vega; Deacons Ladislao Laboy; Jose M. Vazquez.
Res., Box 187, Coto Laurel, 00780. Tel: 787-848-2030.
Missions—Bo. Hoyos, Ponce Co., Santa Maria Virgen, 00780; Bo. Las Raices, Ponce Co., Sagrado Corazon de Jesus, Carr. 511 K. 15, 00780; Bo. Real Anon Abajo, Ponce Co., San Mateo, 00780; Bo. Real Anon Arriba, Ponce Co., San Martin de Porres, 00780.

18—CHURCH SANTISIMO SACRAMENTO (1984), Revs. Jesus de Duenas, L.D.; Juan Ramon Andres, L.D.
P.O. Box 32212, 00732-2212.
Res., Urb. Lirios del Sur, Calle 15-I #1, 00731. Tel: 787-843-0245; Fax: 787-284-1032.

Parishes in Formation

1—CHURCH OUR LADY OF MIRACULOUS MEDAL, Rev. Msgr. Marcos A. Pancorbo, Admin.
Res., P.O. Box 210, Sta. 6, 00732. Tel: 787-842-0134.

2—CHURCH SAN PATRICIO, Rev. Esteban Santaella, Admin.
Res., La Pica, Cr. Buzon 234-B, 00730. Tel: 787-828-6350.

OUTSIDE THE CITY OF PONCE

Adjuntas, Adjuntas Co., St. Joachim (1815), Revs. Carlos G. Santiago, O.R.C.; Carlos Alberto Reinoso, O.R.C.; Deacons Samuel Sepulveda; Radames Marcucci; Edwin Figueroa; Wilfredo Torres.
Res., 14 Rius Rivera St., 00601. Tel: 787-829-3145; Fax: 787-829-3145.
School—San Joaquin Elementary and Intermediate, 12 Primo Delgado St., 00601. Tel: 787-829-3040. Mr. Rolando Torres, Prin.
Missions—Garzas, San Francisco; Vegas Arriba, Sta. Ana; Tres de Jayuya, Santa Teresita; Pellejas, Santa Rosa; Yahuecas, Virgen del Carmen; Tanama, Sagrado Corazon; Guilarte, San Antonio; Vegas Abajo, La Milagrosa; Limani, Inm. Corazon de Maria.

Aguirre, Guayama Co., Sacred Heart (1946), Rev. Juan J. Saliva; Deacons Luis Gonzalez; Pedro Rivera.
Res., Box 260, 00704. Tel: 787-853-3620; Fax: 787-853-3620.
School—Perpetuo Socorro, Box 260, 00704. Tel: 787-853-2270. Sr. Isabel Cruz, R.A., Prin.
Students 672.
Missions—Las Mareas, St. Judas; Coqui, Our Lady of Perpetual Help; San Felipe, St. Martin de Porres; Aguirre, La Milagrosa.

Arroyo, Arroyo Co., Our Lady of Mt. Carmel (1855), Revs. Eduardo Garcia; Orlando Rivera; Deacon Luis A. Melendez.
Res., Box 388, 00714. Tel: 787-839-3465; Fax: 787-839-1552.
Missions—Bo. Pitahaya, Ntra Sra. del Carmen; Bda. Marin, La Milagrosa; Bo. Yaurel Palmarejo, San Jose; Bo. Palmas, Ntra Sra. de Fatima; Bo. Yaurel Santa Clara, San Martin.

Castaner, Our Lady of the Miraculous Medal (1969), Rev. Macario P. Serrano, O.R.C.; Deacon William Ramos.
Res., Box 1006, 00631. Tel: 787-897-5843.
Missions—Bartolo, Immaculate Conception; Mirasol, La Virgen; Rio Prieto, Milagrosa.

Coamo, Coamo Co., St. Blase (1616), Rev. Msgr. Andres Guerrero; Revs. Julio Rolon; Victor Bruno Lopez; Jose A. Barrera; Cristobal Reilly, S.T.; Deacon Angel A. Negron.
Res., Box 196, 00769. Tel: 787-825-1122; Fax: 787-825-7006.
School—Ntra. Sra. de Valvanera, Box 1903, 00769. Tel: 787-825-1145. Mrs. Maria Rivera Cansobre, Prin.
Missions—Coamo Arriba, Coamo Co., Sacred Heart, Box 196, 00769; Los Llanos, Coamo Co., St. Anthony, 00769; Palmarejo, Coamo Co., Sacred Heart of Mary, 00769; Pulguillas, Coamo Co., Christ the King, 00769; Hayales, Coamo Co., Our Lady of Mt. Carmel, 00769; Santa Catalina, Coamo Co., Miraculous Virgin, 00769; Santa Catalina, Coama Co., Sacred Heart, Sector Descalabrado, 00769; Coamo, Coamo Co., Saint James, Sector Cilantro, 00769; Pedro Garcia, Coamo Co., Miraculous Virgin, 00769; Santa Ana, Coamo Co., Santa Ana, 00769; Rio Jueyes, Coamo Co., Our Lady of Lourdes, 00769.; San Diego, Coamo Co., San Diego, 00769; Emanueli, Coamo Co., Holy Family, 00769; Las Flores, Coamo Co., San Martin, 00769; Melendez, Coamo Co., Our Lady of Fatima, 00769.

Ensenada, Sacred Heart (1963), Rev. Samuel Santiago; Deacon Wallis S. Sanchez.
Res., Box 179, 00647. Tel: 787-821-2857.
Missions—Salinas-Providencia, Divina Providencia; Bo. Fuig., Monserrate.

Guanica, Guanica Co., St. Anthony Abbot (1888), Rev. Jose Carlos Vargas; Deacon Reinaldo Galarza.
Res., Box 804, 00653. Tel: 787-821-2147.
School—Blessed Imelda, Dr. Veve Str. 26, 00653. Tel: 787-821-2714; Fax: 787-821-2714. Mrs. Nancy Camacho, Prin.
Missions—Bo. Belgica, Guanica Co., Cristo Rey; Bo. Santa Juanita, Guanica Co., N. Sra. Rosario; Bo. Luna, Guanica Co., San Judas; Bo. La Luna, Guanica Co., N. Sra Fatima; Bda. Esperanza, Guanica Co., La Providencia.

Guayama, Guayama Co., St. Anthony of Padua (1736), Revs. Antonio A. Hernandez, C.Ss.R.; Virgilio Caskey, C.Ss.R.; Vincente Dionne, C.Ss.R.; Juan Rosario, C.Ss.R.; Deacons Alberto Montanez; Gerardo Rivera.
Res., Box 2820, 00785. Tel: 787-864-4100; Fax: 787-864-5494.
Schools—St. Anthony, Box 777, 00785. Tel: 787-864-2062; Fax: 787-864-1450. Mrs. Evelyn Adams, Prin.; St. Alphonse Liguori, Box 777, 00785. Mr. Luis C. Ayes, Prin.
Missions—Caimital, Our Lady of Perpetual Help; Bo. Puente Jobos, SS. Peter and Paul; Palmas, St. Gerard; Carmen, Our Lady of Mt. Carmel; Bo. Olimpo, Cristo Rey; Bo. Corazon, La Candelaria; Colonia Villodos, Perpetuo Socorro; Bo. Puerto Jobos, San Francisco de Asis; Bo. Guamani, Sgdo. Corazon; Bo. Carite, San Martin; Bo. Barrancas, La Monserrate.

Guayanilla, Guayanilla Co., Immaculate Conception (1841), Revs. Raymond L. Rivera; Jery Rivera; Deacons Miguel Sepulveda; Jesus Rodriguez.

Res., P.O. Box 560573, 00656-0573. Tel: 787-835-3035.
School—Immaculate Conception, P.O. Box 560573, 00656-0573. Tel: 787-835-2230; Fax: 787-835-3035. Mr. Rafael Ortiz, Prin.
Missions—Barrio Sierra Baja, Our Lady of Mt. Carmel; Magas Arriba, Perpetuo Socorro; Quebradas, San Francisco de Asis; Barrio Indios, San Juan Bosco; Consejo Alto, La Monserrate; Macana Rio, Virgen de Fatima; Quebrada Honda, Nuestra Senora; Macana Parcelas, San Martin de Porres.

Jayuya, Jayuya Co., Our Lady of Monserrate (1883), Revs. Pedro Faustino Echevarria; Jose Florencio Martinez; Jose Luis Larreategui, Sch.P.; Felix Lazaro, Sch.P.; Deacons Luis Rosario; Carlos Orama; Jose A. Perez.
Res., Calle Figueras 13, 00664. Tel: 787-828-6350; Fax: 787-828-5062.
Missions—Collares, Jayuya Co., Cristo Rey, Figueras #13, 00664; Coabbey, Jayuya Co., San Jorge, 00664; Canalizo, Jayuya Co., La Milagrosa, 00664; Gripinas, Jayuya Co., Buen Pastor, 00664; Zama, Jayuya Co., Santa Cecila, 00664; Hoyo Planas, Jayuya Co., Esp. Santo, 00664; Mameyes, Jayuya Co., S. Antonio, 00664; Salto, Jayuya Co., Santos Reyes, 00664; Saliente, Jayuya Co., San Francisco, 00664; Puerto Plata, Jayuya Co., San Juan, 00664; La Pica, San Patricio Co., 00664; Hogares Seguros, San Antonio Co., 00664.

Juana Diaz, Juana Diaz Co., St. Raymond Nonato (1798), Rev. Msgr. Jose Lozano; Rev. Santiago Solla; Deacons Hector L. Santiago; Narciso Ortiz.
Res., Box 1426, 00795. Tel: 787-837-2390; Fax: 787-837-2390.
Missions—Pastillo, Cotopaso Co., Santiago Apostol; Rio Canas, Rio Canas Abajo, San Judas; Jacaquas, Bo. Jacaguas, N.S. de Fatima; Collores, Bo. Jacaguas, La Milagrosa; Las Margaritas, Bo. Collores Arriba, Santiago, Ap.; Corral, P. Socorro; Guayabal, Bo. Guayabal, Our Lady of the Rosary; Callabo, Bo. Callabo, San Ramon; Bo. Rio Cana Arriba, La Merced.

Santa Teresita (Arus) (1984), Rev. Adalin Rivera; Deacons Pedro Garcia-Malavet; Secundino Torres.
Res., P.O. Box 32131, Ponce, 00732-2131. Tel: 787-844-6670.
Missions—San Martin de Porres. (Singapur); Divine Mercy. (Piedra Aguza); Pastillito, Manzanilla, Our Lady of Carmel. (Galicia).

Nuestra Senora de Lourdes (Aguilita) (1984), Rev. Msgr. Herminio de Jesus; Deacons Jose Mendez; Cirilo Carmona; Ruperto Reyes; Jaime Velez; Fernando Perez.
Res., P.O. Box 1824, 00795. Tel: 787-837-1097.

Patillas, Inmaculado Corazon de Maria (1811), Revs. Gerardo Ramirez; Roberto Garcia Echevarria; Deacon Ruben Pabon.
Res., Box 635, 00723. Tel: 787-839-5333.
Missions—Bo. Marin Alto, Pastillas, Pastillas Co., Perpetuo Socorro; Bo. Guarderraya, Pastillas, Pastillas Co., Madre Cabrini; Bo. Recio, Pastillas, Pastillas Co., Sto. Cristo de Los Milagros; Bo. Jacaboa, Pastillas, Pastillas Co., Carmen; Bo. El Bajo, Pastillas, Pastillas Co., Cristo Rey; Bo. Providencia, Pastillas, Pastillas Co., Providencia; Bo. Los Pollos, Pastillas, Pastillas Co., Santa Rosa de Lima; Bo. Los Barros, Pastillas, Pastillas Co., S. Juan Evangelista; Bo. El Real, Pastillas, Pastillas Co., San Guillermo; Bo. Jagual, Pastillas, Pastillas Co., Carmen.

Penuelas, Penuelas Co., St. Joseph (1793), Revs. Francesco Carraro; Gioacchino Basile; Deacons Carmelo Vazquez; Jose E. Gelpi; Glidden R. Perez; Jose A. Rosario; Jose Torres.
Res., Box 25, 00624. Tel: 787-836-1038; Fax: 787-836-0167.
Missions—El Rucio, Penuelas Co., La Milagrosa, Carr. #391, 00624.; El Alto, San Antonio Carr. #132,; Macana, Fatima Carr. #131,; Tallaboa Alta, Santa Ana St. Domingo, Carmen Carr. #124,; Bo Barreal, Cristo de la Salud Carr. #386,; Quebrada Ceiba, Milagrosa Carr. #387,; Corozal, San Antonio. Carr. #387.

Sacred Heart (Tallaboa) (1928), Rev. Agustin Grinena.
Res., HC 01, Box 13063, 00624. Tel: 787-836-1164.
Mission—Bo. Buena Vista, Holy Family.

Salinas, Our Lady of Monserrat (1854), Revs. Angel Sanchez; Edwin Vazquez-Vega; Deacon Pablo F. Miranti.
Res., Box 1172, 00751. Tel: 787-824-2215.
Missions—Plena, San Jose; Coco, Santa Ana; Parcelas Vazquez, Esp. Santo; Bo. Las Palmas, Virg. del Carmen; Naranjo, Santa Marta; Las Ochenta, Inmaculada Concepcion; Bo. Playita, Virgen Milagrosa; Bo. Playa, Carmen; Sabana Llana, Perpetuo Socorro.

Santa Isabel, St. James (1854), Revs. Ismael Larena; Moises Navascues, Sch.P.; Deacon Jaime Martinez.
Res., Box 137, 00757. Tel: 787-845-2450; Fax: 787-845-2485.
Missions—Playita Cortada, San Patricio; Bo. Penuelas, Virgen del Rosario; Bo. Paso Secos, Virgen del Rosario; Bo. Ollas, Monserrate; Jauca, San Ignacio de Loyola.

Villalba, Our Lady of Mt. Carmel (1917), Revs. Jose Diego Rodriguez; Emiliano Alamo; Manuel Santiago; Fausto Ramos; Deacons Javier Gonzalez; Ramon A. Resto; Jose A. Pagan.
Res., Box 432, 00766. Tel: 787-847-0695; Fax: 787-847-8137.
School—Box 1033, 00766. Tel: 787-847-2875. Sr. Ana M. Santamarta, R.A.D., Prin.
Convent—Tel: 787-847-2874; 847-2391. Sisters of the Love of God
Missions—Romero, Sagrado Corazon, HC01 Box 5081, 00766. Tel: 787-847-1591; Bo. Vista Alegre, Jesus Crucificado, 00766; Bo. Mogote, Santisima Tinidad, 00766; Bo. Cerro Gordo, Espiritu Santo, 00766; Bo. Jagueyes Arriba, La Milagrosa, 00766; Bo. Corillo, San Pedro, 00766; Bo. Palmarejo, San Jose, 00766; Bo. Higuero, Santisimo Sacramento, 00766; Bo. Camarones, Jesus Crucificado, 00766; Bo. Canonilla Abajo, Maria Madre de la Iglesia, 00766; Bo. Sierrita Caonillas, Cristo de la Salud, 00766; Barrio Jaguey, Madre Cabrini, 00766; Barrio Semil, Santa Cecilia, 00766; Barrio Apeadero, San Alfonso, 00766; Barrio Hatillo, Sagrada Familia, 00766; Bo. Camarones-Los Robles, San Antonio, 00766; Bo. Hatillo Viejo, La Milagrosa, 00766; Bo. Cuchilla del Limon, La Asuncion, 00766; Bo. Limon, Virgen de la Amargura, 00766; Bo. Dajas, N.S. del Carmen, 00766.

Our Lady Mother of Divine Providence (Mission Noell) (1962), Revs. Raymond D. Middendorf, S.M.; George Onida, S.M.; Vincent A. Plassenthal, S.M.
Res., Box 1556, 00766. Tel: 787-867-2052; Fax: 787-867-7464.
Missions—Bo. Alturita, Cacao Co., Our Lady of Mt. Carmel; Bo. Cacao, Cacao Co., Imm. Concepcion; Bo. El Frio, Ala de La Piedra Co., Nino de Praga; Bo. Guineo, Ala de La Piedra Co., Santa Ana; Bo. Bauta, Bauta Abajo Co., N.S. del Rosario; Bo. Damian Abajo, Damian Abajo Co., N.S. del Pilar; Bo. Pozas, Damian Abajo Co., N.S. Monserrate; La Piedra, Ala de La Piedra Co., O.L. of Perp. Help; Matrullas, Cacao Co., Sacred Heart of Jesus; Ortiga, Bauta Abajo Co., San Mateo.

Yauco, Holy Rossary (1756), Revs. Jose Martin, O.P.; Jose Luis Alonso, O.P.; Alfredo Vallina, O.P.; Fortunato Bodero, O.P.; Jose Fernandez, O.P.; Deacons Victor Sanchez; Jesus Vazquez.
Res., Box 46, 00698. Tel: 787-856-1222; Fax: 787-856-6845.
School—Box 26, 00698. Tel: 787-856-1001; Fax: 787-267-1238. Mrs. Judith Negron, Prin.
Convent—Tel: 787-856-1573. Sisters Of Fatima for Social Work Sr. Luisa Caraballo, O.P., Supr. Sisters 17.
Missions—Collores, Sacred Heart; Duey, Virgin of Mt. Carmel; Barinas, St. James; Las Vegas, Sta. Teresita; Lluberas, St. Joseph; Cambalaches, Our Lady of Perpetual Help; Carrizales, Our Lady of Montserrat; Algarrobos, Our Lady of Fatima; Sierra Alta, St. Lucy; Almacigo Bajo, St. Martin de Porres; Naranjo, St. Anthony; Diego Hdez, St. Anthony; Quebradas, Sacred Heart; Aguas, St. Martin; Almacigo Alto, S. Juan Macias.

St. Martin de Porres (1969), Rev. Segismundo Cintron; Deacon Saba Gonzalez.
Res., Las Palomas, Box 2005, 00698. Tel: 787-856-3617.
Convent—Box 62, Santa Rita, 00698. Tel: 787-856-1476. Sisters of Fatima-Motherhouse Sr. Celeste Ortiz, O.P., Mother Gen.
Sisters 125; Novices 7.
Missions—Bo. Susa, Guanica Co., Santa Rita; Bo. Susa, Guanica Co., N.S. de La Providencia; Bo. Arenas de Guancia, Guancia Co., S. Martin de Porres; Bo. Susa, Yauco Co., S. Francisco de Asis; Bo. Susa, Yauco Co., N.S. de La Monserrate.

Special Assignment:
Reverend Monsignors—
Bellester, Pedro J., Pro-Vicar Gen.
Espona, Juan, Admin. & Vice Chancellor

On Duty Outside the Diocese:
Reverend Fathers—
Alvarez, Pablo D., F.S.S.P., 110 W. 35th St., Apt. 3, Hialeah, FL 33012
Aponte, Eliud, P.O.Box 765, Penuelas, PR 00624
Arguinzoniz, Francisco, Apartado 70, Durango, Vizcaya, Spain
Barrett, Kevin S., Chap., Apostolate of Family Consecration, P.O. Box 151, Bloomingdale, OH 43910-0151
Colon, Jose E., Colinas Montecarlo, Bldg. D-35, San Juan, PR 00927
DuChez, Daniel B., O.S., 810 Pearl St., Chippewa Falls, WI 54729
Duran, Alfonso M., M.J., Via Tespi 176, Rome, 00125 Italy
Fletcher, Patrick, 62 AW/Chapel, 746 Main St., McChord AFB, WA 98438
Floeckler, Christopher M.J., P.O. Box 256528, Chicago, IL 60625
Gelis, Mark, M.J., Via Tespi 176, Rome, 00125 Italy
Gusiora, Alphonsus, P.O. Box 61, Enugwu-Ukwu (Anambra State), Nigeria
Kelty, Edward, O.S., Via Antonio Zanoni 44, Rome, 00134 Italy
MacIssac, Charles S., O.S., c/o J. Joseph MacIsaac, 281 York St., Canton, MA 02021
Malachowski, Christopher, O.S., Instytut Emaus, ul. Deotymy 41, Warszawa, 01-991 Polonia
Margola, Joseph F., 1633 North Arlington Pl., Milwaukee, WI 53202-225
Medina, George, P.O. Box 286, East Boston, MA 02128
Mezquida, Ramon, San Jose 4, Alqueria Condesa 46715, Valencia, Spain
Muniz, Alberto, P.O.Box 790, Arroyo, PR 00714-0790
Munoz, Rafael, P.O. Box 187, Barceloneta, PR 00657
Nicoletti, Robert, M.J., Via Tespi 176, Rome, 00125 Italy
Nischan, James R., 1625 Mayo Ave., Owensboro, KY 42301
Porada, Casey, O.S., St. Mary's Rectory, 580 I St., David City, NE 68632
Quinones, Leoncio, Urb. Apolo, Guaynabo, PR 00657
Roman, Carlos, P.O.Box 3043, Yauco, PR 00698
Sancho Piquer, Enrique, Calvario 49, 2, 4, Pafelbunoli, Valencia, Spain
Serrano, Dionisio, Maestro Ripoll 14, 28006 Madrid, Spain
Sirvent, Francisco, Capitan Cortes 8-2, Valencia
Tyrrell, Anthony, P.O.Box 943, Greentown, PA 18426-0943
Vota, Paul, M.J., P.O. Box 256528, Chicago, IL 60625
Weslin, Norman U., O.S., 151 Harvard St., Colorado Springs, CO 80911
Zayas, Antonio, Naranjito, PR 00767

Retired:
Reverend Monsignors—
Colon, Jose, Box 242, Merceditas, PR 00715
Irizarry, Raul, Marginal 11 Urb. Mercedita, Ponce, PR 00731
Santiago, Rafael, Villa 269-B, Ponce, PR 00731
Reverend Fathers—
Cano, Emilio, Box 21012, Rio Piedras, PR 00928
Ferre, Antonio, Villa del Carmen, Calle 23-Y-11, Ponce, PR 00734
Pacho, Jesus, 2065 Ave. Las Americas, Apt. 207, Ponce, PR 00731-9427
Ramos, Fausto, Box 5081 HC-01, Villalba, PR 00766

INSTITUTIONS LOCATED IN THE DIOCESE

[A] SEMINARIES

PONCE. *Diocesan Seminary.* (Major Interdiocesan), P.O. Box 32110, 00732-2110. Tel: 787-848-4380; Fax: 787-848-4380. Rev. Msgr. Jesus R. Diez Antonanzas, Rector; Rev. Alfredo Alvarez Lacruz, Spiritual Dir. Priests 2; Lay Staff 2; Seminarians 10.

[B] COLLEGES & UNIVERSITIES

PONCE. *The Pontifical Catholic University of Puerto Rico*, 2250 Avenida de las Americas, 00717-0777. Tel: 787-841-2000; Fax: 787-840-4295.
Web site: www.pucpr.edu
For a complete listing, refer to the Colleges and Universities section.

[C] SCHOOLS - INSTITUTES OF EDUCATION

PONCE. *Centro San Francisco.* Mailing Address: Box 10479, 00732. Tel: 787-844-2434; Fax: 787-842-2776. Sisters of St. Joseph. Sr. Anita Moseley, C.S.J., Prin. Sisters 3; Lay Teachers 24; Librarians 2; Social Workers 2; Counselor 1.

Colegio El Ave Maria, Dr. Luis Bartolomei 6, Rep. Valle Alegre, 00731. Tel: 787-284-2453. Operarias del Divino Maestro. Sr. Milagros Pizarro, O.D.M., Prin. Sisters 4; Lay Teachers 9.

Colegio Sagrado Corazon, Calle Obispado Final, 00731. Tel: 787-842-0339; Fax: 787-843-0250. Religious of the Sacred Heart. Mrs. Maria Serrano, Prin. Sisters 2; Lay Teachers 41.

Holy Family School, Avenida Hostos 7, 00731. Tel: 787-842-3208; Fax: 787-844-6773. Sisters of Charity. Sr. Ediltrudis Acevedo, H.C., Prin. Sisters 5; Lay Teachers 20.

COTO LAUREL. *Colegio Ponceno.* (Day School). Mailing Address: Colegio Ponceno, 00780-9508. Tel: 787-848-2525; Fax: 787-259-4282. Piarists Fathers. Revs. Julio Torralba, Sch.P.; Juan L. Cabrerizo, Sch.P.; Jose A. Basols, Sch.P.; Fernado Torres, Sch.P. Priests 4; Lay Teachers 66.

PLAYA PONCE. *Centros Sor Isolina Ferre, Inc.*, P.O. Box 34213, 00734-4213. Tel: 787-843-1910. Missionary Servants of the Most Blessed Trinity. Sr. Rosita M. Bauza, M.S.B.T., Exec. Dir. Center for social services, health and technical education, artistic, cultural, economic, domestic and spiritual formation. Priests 1; Sisters 3; Lay Teachers 38; Councilors 5; Coordinators 26; Community Lay Leaders 27.

[D] HOMES FOR THE AGED

PONCE. *Home for Aged and Infirm*, Barrio Sabenetas, P.O. Box 2127, 00731. Tel: 787-840-7575
For a complete listing, refer to the Special Care Facilities section.

[E] MONASTERIES AND RESIDENCES OF PRIESTS AND BROTHERS

PONCE. *Residencia Asis.* (Postulantado), 342 Victoria St., Box 7244, 00732. Tel: 787-842-5055; Fax: 787-844-7267. Revs. Jose A. Carrion, O.F.M.Cap., Guardian & Postulant Dir.; Roberto Martinez, O.F.M.Cap.; Francisco Garcia, O.F.M.Cap. Postulants 3.

[F] CONVENTS & RESIDENCES OF SISTERS

PONCE. *Convent Apostolate.* Mailing Address: Box 8300, 00732. Tel: 787-842-4340. Mother Teresita Herrera, R.A., Supr. Sisters Apostolate of the Sacred Heart of Jesus 12.

Convent of Servants of Mary, Ext. La Rambla, Calle Siervas de Maria 500, 00731. Tel: 787-842-2336. Mother Maximina Galvez, S.M., Supr. Religious 21; Postulants 3; Novices 14; Administered in the home 1,832.

PLAYA DE PONCE. *Blessed Trinity Missionary Cenacle*, Box 213, 00734. Tel: 787-844-1627. Sr. Rosita Maria Bauza, M.S.B.T., Custodian. Sisters 3.

[G] PERSONAL PRELATURES

ALHAMBRA, PONCE. *Prelature of the Holy Cross and Opus Dei*, 8 Alcazar, 00731. Tel: 787-844-2661. Revs. Pablo J. Concepcion; Jose F. Tejeda.

[H] MISCELLANEOUS

PONCE. *Albergue La Providencia, Inc.*, P.O. Box 10142, 00732. Tel: 787-841-2119. Rev. Francisco Garcia, O.F.M.Cap., Dir. Refuge Center for AIDS patients. Total Assisted 64; Total Staff 30.

Apostolate for Family Consecration. Mailing Address: International Spanish Center, P.O. Box 32205, 00732-2205. Tel: 787-848-5265.

Institucion Magdalena Aulina - Operarias Parroquiales. (Secular Institute), Simon de la Torre 43, 00731. Tel: 787-842-7209.

Memores Domini, P.O. Box 32197, 00732-2197. Tel: 787-844-0464.

Miles Jesu, Ladies House, P.O. Box 32165, 00732-2165. Tel: 787-840-9436. Men's House, Parroquia Santa Maria Reina, P.O. Box 32166, 00732-2166. Tel: 787-848-5370.

Oblates of Wisdom. Mailing Address: Box 8027, 00732. Rev. Brian W. Harrison, O.S., Reg. Dir.

Pastoral Care of the Sick. Mailing Address: P.O. Box 32205, 00732-2205. Tel: 787-844-2080 Ext. 1208, 787-848-7157. Sr. Teresa Jensen, C.S.J., Dir.

Shelter for the Homeless. Mailing Address: Misioneras De La Caridad, P.O. Box 32177, 00732-2177. Tel: 787-841-5443. Sr. Mary Selma Thomas, M.C., Supr. Missionaries of Charity (Mother Theresa of Calcutta). Sisters 6; Residents 46; Total Assisted 50.

PENUELAS. *Training School for the Lay Apostolate (Hermanos Cheos).* Mailing Address: P.O. Box 120, 00624. Rev. Msgr. Marcos A. Pancorbo, Dir.; Bro. William Perez Ramos, Pres. Brothers 97.

RELIGIOUS INSTITUTES OF MEN REPRESENTED IN THE DIOCESE

For further details refer to the corresponding bracketed number in the Religious Institutes of Men or Women section.

[0140]—*The Augustinians.*—O.S.A.
[0470]—*The Capuchin Friars (Vice Province of Puerto Rico).*—O.F.M.Cap.
[0270]—*Carmelite Fathers & Brothers.*—O.Carm.
[1330]—*Congregation of the Mission.*—C.M.
[]—*Esclavos de la Eucaristia y Maria Virgen.*—S.E.M.V.
[0650]—*Holy Ghost Fathers.* (Eastern Prov.).—C.S.Sp.
[]—*Lumen Dei.*—L.D.
[]—*Operarios Del Reino De Cristo.*—O.R.C.
[0430]—*Order of Preachers-Dominicans.* (Holland Prov.).—O.P.
[1310]—*Order of the Holy Trinity.* (Spain).—O.SS.T.
[1040]—*Piarist Fathers.* (Spain).—Sch.P.
[1070]—*Redemptorist Fathers.* (San Juan Prov.).—C.SS.R.

RELIGIOUS INSTITUTES OF WOMEN REPRESENTED IN THE DIOCESE

[0130]—*Apostles of the Sacred Heart of Jesus.*—A.S.C.J.
[0340]—*Carmelite Sisters of Charity.*—C.a.Ch.
[]—*Congregacion Hermanas de N.S. del Perpetuo Socorro.*—N.S.P.S.
[1070-05]—*Dominican Sisters.*—O.P.
[]—*Hermanas Del-Amor De Dios.*
[]—*Hermanas Dominicas de Fatima.*—O.P.
[]—*Hermanas Ntra. Sra. del Perpetuo Socorro.* Tuana Diaz, Ponce.—N.S.P.S.
[]—*Hijas de la Caridad del Card. Sancha.*—H.C.C.S.
[2340]—*Little Sisters of the Poor.*—L.S.P.
[2710]—*Missionaries of Charity.*—M.C.
[2790]—*Missionary Servants of the Most Blessed Trinity.*—M.S.B.T.
[]—*Religious de los Santos Angeles Custodios (Adjuntas, Ponce).*—R.A.C.
[3580]—*Servants of Mary.*—O.S.M.
[]—*Sisters of Charity of St. Vincent de Paul.*—H.C.
[]—*Sisters of St. Joseph.*—S.S.J.
[2150]—*Sisters, Servants of the Immaculate Heart of Mary.*—I.H.M.

NECROLOGY

† Gonzalez, Miguel, Ponce, PR Cathedral of Our Lady of Guadalupe. —Died Nov. 17, 1999.

Diocese of Samoa-Pago Pago

Most Reverend

JOHN QUINN WEITZEL, M.M.

Bishop of Samoa-Pago Pago; ordained June 11, 1955; appointed First Bishop of Samoa-Pago Pago October 29, 1986. *Fatuaiga: P.O. Box 596, Pago Pago, American Samoa, 96799.* Tel.: 684-699-1402; Fax: 684-699-1459.

E-mail address: QUINN@samoatelco.com

CREATED A DIOCESE NOVEMBER, 1982.

The Diocese of Samoa-Pago Pago includes the islands of Tutuila; Swains; Manu'a Is., Ofu, Olosega & Ta'u; Aunu'u and Rose Island.

STATISTICAL OVERVIEW

Personnel	
Bishop	1
Priests: Diocesan Active in Diocese	8
Priests: Diocesan in Foreign Missions	1
Number of Diocesan Priests	9
Religious Priests in Diocese	2
Permanent Deacons in Diocese	17
Total Sisters	11
Parishes	
Parishes	11
With Resident Pastor:	
Resident Diocesan Priests	5
Resident Religious Priests	1
Without Resident Pastor:	
Administered by Deacons	1
Administered by Professed Men Religious	4
Welfare	
Homes for the Aged	1
Total Assisted	26
Day Care and Extended Day Care Centers	1
Total Assisted	95
Special Centers for Social Services	1
Total Assisted	400
Educational	
Diocesan Students in Other Seminaries	14
Total Seminarians	14
High Schools, Diocesan and Parish	1
Total Students	229
Elementary Schools, Diocesan and Parish	2
Total Students	426
Catechesis/Religious Education:	
High School Students	180
Elementary Students	1,700
Total Students Under Catholic Instruction	2,549
Teachers in the Diocese:	
Sisters	5
Lay Teachers	69
Vital Statistics	
Receptions into the Church:	
Infant Baptism Totals	301
Adult Baptism Totals	107
Received into Full Communion	18
First Communions	210
Confirmations	180
Marriages:	
Catholic	28
Interfaith	15
Total Marriages	43
Deaths	28
Total Catholic Population	12,250
Total Population	62,000

Vicar General of Diocese—Very Rev. VAN CAMP TAVAI.

Chancellor—IVONA T. MAUGA.

Diocesan Consultors—Revs. VAN CAMP TAVAI; MASELINO PAULO; PETELO SILIAKO; VIANE ETUALE.

Bishop's Pastoral Council—TE'O FUAVAI, Chm. TOLEAFOA PAUL FELISE, Vice Chm. CECILIA PAPALI'I, Sec. IULI MULIAGA ALEXANDER GODINET.

Fatu-O-Aiga Multipurpose Cultural and Pastoral Center—Pastoral Team: Rev. VAN CAMP TAVAI, Dir.; Mrs. ALOFA LEASIOLAGI, Sec. Faculty Members: Revs. EMANI TEVAGA; VIANE ETUALE.

Sagata Ana Society—Mrs. VERONIKA TAVALE, Pres.; Mrs. NELLIE TOILOLO, Vice Pres.; Mrs. MALIA PEPE, Treas.; Mrs. IVONA T. MAUGA, Sec.

Sacred Heart Society—AGNES GABBARD, Pres. VERA ANNESLEY, Vice Pres. TINA MOANANU, Treas. MUA POTASI, Sec.

Vicar for Youth—Mr. TAVITA LEMISIO, Dir. Youth.

Director of Vocations—Rev. VIANE ETUALE.

Port Chaplain—Deacon NIKOLAO PULA; Rev. EMANI TEVAGA, Asst.

Hospital Chaplain—Deacon LUTIA TIMOTEO, Chap.

Prison Chaplain—Deacon TOETOFI TAVALE, F.K.

Director of Propagation of the Faith—Vacant.

CLERGY, PARISHES, MISSIONS AND PAROCHIAL SCHOOLS

SAMOA-PAGO PAGO

1—CATHEDRAL OF THE HOLY FAMILY (1986), Most Rev. John Quinn Weitzel, M.M.; Revs. Petelo Siliako; Falaniko Atonio; Deacons Anetele'a Puletasi; Lito Roque; Francis Leasiolagi; Toetofi Tavale; Edward Simon.
Mailing Address: Fatuoaiga, P.O. Box 3594, 96799-3594. Tel: 684-699-1446; Fax: 684-699-1459.
Catechesis/Religious Programs—Tel: 684-699-2209; Fax: 684-699-1459. D.R.E.: Deacon Toetofi Tavale; Mrs. Lydia Faleafine-Nomura; Mrs. Palu Vitale; Miss Christina Iosefo.
Students 480.
Mission—Manu'a Island, Mary, Star of the Sea, Tel: 684-677-3103.

2—CO-CATHEDRAL OF ST. JOSEPH THE WORKER (Fagatogo) (1974), Rev. Emani Tevaga, Admin.; Deacons Lutia Timoteo; Nikolao Pula; Tavita Pereira; Lafaele Aunoa.
Mailing Address: Fagatogo, P.O. Box AA, 96799. Tel: 684-633-1548.
Catechesis/Religious Programs—Sauileone Aigofie, D.R.E.
Students 180.
Missions—Utulei,; Fagasa, Tel: 684-633-1352; Pago Pago, Tel: 684-633-4035; Faga'alu, Tel: 684-633-2560.

3—CHRIST THE KING (Amanave), Silivelio Tufele, Admin.
Mailing Address: P.O. Box 5408, 96799. Tel: 684-688-1542.
Catechesis/Religious Programs—Students 42.

4—CHRIST THE KING (Malaeloa) (1997), Paulo Luamanu, Admin.
Mailing Address: P.O. Box 596, 96799. Tel: 684-688-2438; Fax: 684-699-1459.
Catechesis/Religious Programs—Students 88.

5—CHRIST THE KING (Nu'uuli) (1983), Malaki Timu, D.R.E.
Mailing Address: P.O. Box 596, 96799. Fax: 684-699-1459.
Catechesis/Religious Programs—Students 165.

6—ST. PAUL (Ili'ili) (1974), Rev. Viane Etuale; Deacons Sagapolutele Malaeola, Pastoral Assoc.; Felise Toilolo.
Mailing Address: Ili'ili, P.O. Box 2004, 96799. Tel: 684-699-7572; Fax: 684-699-1459.
Office: Fatuoaiga—P.O. Box 596, 96799. Tel: 684-699-5710.
Catechesis/Religious Programs—Felise Toilolo, D.R.E.
Students 420.
Missions—Faleniu,; Futiga,; Pava'ia'i, Tel: 684-699-7613; Aasu/Aoloau, Tel: 684-699-9766.

7—STS. PETER & PAUL (Asili), Meaalofa Lotomau, Admin.
Mailing Address: P.O. Box 7286, 96799. Tel: 684-688-7236.
Catechesis/Religious Programs—Students 50.

8—CHURCH OF ST. PETER AND PAUL (Lauli'i) (1969), Rev. Falaniko Auva'a; Deacons Setefano Lesa; Fred Pele.
Mailing Address: P.O. Box 985, 96799. Tel: 684-644-5581.
Catechesis/Religious Programs—Tel: 684-644-4697. Sefo Tanuvasa, D.R.E.
Students 200.
Missions—Masefau, Tel: 684-622-7131; Faga'itua, Tel: 684-622-7130; Sa'ilele.

9—CHURCH OF THE HOLY CROSS (Leone) (1861), Rev. Van Camp Tavai.
Mailing Address: Leone, P.O. Box 1206, 96799. Tel: 684-688-7663; Fax: 684-699-1459.
Mission—Amaluia.
Catechesis/Religious Programs—Anitele'a Iese, D.R.E.
Students 207.

10—CHURCH OF THE IMMACULATE CONCEPTION (Lepua) (1867), Rev. Paulino Kolio, Admin.
Mailing Address: Lepua, P.O. Box 398, 96799. Tel: 684-644-5512.
Catechesis/Religious Programs—Tel: 684-644-2411. D.R.E.: Asalemo Taulamano; Teofilo Laulu.
Students 225.
Missions—Afono, Tel: 684-644-4797. Deacon Ioane Leota.; Aua, Tel: 684-644-5826.

11—CHURCH OF SACRED HEART (Alao) (1989), Deacon Sogimaletavai Leo.
Mailing Address: Alao, P.O. Box 4175, 96799. Tel: 684-622-7029; Fax: 684-699-1459.
Catechesis/Religious Programs—Students 48.
Missions—Aoa, Tel: 684-622-7416; Amouli, Tel: 684-622-7613.

Permanent Deacons:
- Aunoa, Lafaele
- Folau, Kalini
- Gabriel, August
- Lafaele, Setefano
- Leasiolagi, Francis
- Leo, Herman Sogimaletavai
- Ma'ileoi, Naisina
- Maugaotega, Tagataese, (On leave)
- Pele, Tupuaga Fred
- Pereira, Tavita
- Pula, Taafulisia Nikolao
- Puletasi, Niuatoa Andy
- Sagapolutele, Anthony Malaeola
- Simon, Edward
- Tavale, Toetofi
- Timoteo, Lutia Laupapa
- Toilolo, Felise

INSTITUTIONS LOCATED IN THE DIOCESE

[A] PRESCHOOLS

PAGO PAGO. *Mary The Mother Montessori Early Education Center*, c/o Diocese of Samoa-Pago Pago, Fatuoaiga-P.O. Box 596, 96799. Tel: 684-644-1311; Fax: 684-699-1459. Sr. Marilyn Evans, M.M., Prin. & Supr. Sisters 1; Lay Teachers 7; Students 90.

[B] ELEMENTARY SCHOOLS, PAROCHIAL

LEONE. *St. Theresa*, P.O. Box 883, 96799-0596. Tel: 684-688-1105; Fax: 684-688-1114. Missionary Sisters of the Society of Mary. Sr. Sisi Marama, S.M.S.M., Prin. Sisters 2; Lay Teachers 15; Students 249.

LEPUA. *Marist St. Francis*, Fatuoaiga, P.O. Box 429, 96799-0429; Fax: 684-688-1459. Missionary Sisters of the Society of Mary. Sr. Pesio Iosefo, S.M.S.M., Prin. Sisters 2; Lay Teachers 11; Students 178.

[C] HIGH SCHOOLS, PAROCHIAL

LEPUAPUA. *Faasao Marist College Preparatory School*, P.O. Box 729, 96799; Fax: 684-688-2055. E-mail: courgars@faasao.com Mrs. Veronika Mortenson Mata'utia, Prin.; Catherine Satele, Co-Admin. Sisters 2; Lay Teachers 10; Volunteer Lay Missionaries 5; Students 229.

MALAELOA. *Fassao Marist College Preparatory School*, Fatuoaiga, P.O. Box K, 96799; Fax: 684-688-2336. Mr. Mark McGreevy, Prin.; Lolesio Iosefo, Vice Prin. Lay Teachers 8; Students 120.

[D] HOMES FOR AGED & SPECIAL CARE FOR CHILDREN

PAGO PAGO. *Nazareth House*, P.O. Box 1510, 96799. Tel: 684-699-2101; Fax: 684-699-1459
For a complete listing, refer to the Special Care Facilities section.

[E] MISCELLANEOUS

PAGO PAGO. *Catholic Social Services, Inc.*, P.O. Box 596, 96799. Tel: 684-699-5683; Fax: 684-699-1459. E-mail: ccs1@samoatelco.com Miss Faleupolu Fuatagavi, B.S., Dir. Total Assisted 400; Total Staff 2.

RELIGIOUS INSTITUTES OF MEN REPRESENTED IN THE DIOCESE

For further details refer to the corresponding bracketed number in the Religious Institutes of Men or Women section.

[0800]—*Maryknoll*.—M.M.

RELIGIOUS INSTITUTES OF WOMEN REPRESENTED IN THE DIOCESE

[2420]—*Marist Missionary Sisters, Inc. (Missionary Sisters of the Society of Mary)*.—S.M.S.M.

[2470]—*Maryknoll Sisters of St. Dominic*.—M.M.

[3242]—*Poor Sisters of Nazareth*.—P.S.O.N.

[]—*Religious Sisters of the Virgin Mary*.—R.V.M.

NECROLOGY

† Falaniko, Mikaele, Lauli'i, Ss. Peter & Paul. —Died Oct. 21, 1999.

Archdiocese of San Juan, Puerto Rico

(Sancti Joannis Portoricensis)

His Eminence

LUIS CARDINAL APONTE MARTINEZ, D.D.

Retired Archbishop of San Juan; ordained April 10, 1950; appointed Titular Bishop of Lares and Auxiliary of Ponce July 23, 1960; consecrated October 12, 1960; appointed Coadjutor Bishop of Ponce April 16, 1963; appointed Bishop of Ponce November 18, 1963; installed February 20, 1964; promoted to Archbishop of San Juan November 4, 1964; installed January 15, 1965; Created Cardinal March 5, 1973.

Most Reverend

FRANCOIS BACQUE

Apostolic Delegate for Puerto Rico. *Office: Ponce de Leon Ave. #256, San Juan, PR, 00907. Mailing Address: P.O. Box 191771, San Juan, PR, 00919-1771.* Tel.: 809-723-1280; Fax: 809-723-1280.

Most Reverend

ROBERTO O. GONZALEZ, O.F.M.

Archbishop of San Juan; ordained May 1977; appointed Titular Bishop of Ursona and Auxiliary Bishop of Boston July 19, 1988; consecrated October 3, 1988; appointed Coadjutor Bishop of Corpus Christi May 16, 1995; transferred to Corpus Christi June 26, 1995; succeeded to See April 1, 1997; appointed Bishop of Corpus Christi March 26, 1999.

Chancery Office: P.O. Box S-1967, San Juan, PR, 00902.

Most Reverend

HECTOR M. RIVERA, D.D.

Titular Bishop of Tubune in Numidia and Auxiliary Bishop of San Juan PR; ordained June 12, 1966; appointed June 11, 1979; consecrated August 17, 1979. *Res., Lomas de Carolina, Calle Yunquecito UU #18, Carolina, PR, 00987.* Tel.: 727-7373. *Mailing Address: P.O. Box 1967, San Juan, PR, 00902-1967.*

Most Reverend

HERMIN NEGRON SANTANA, D.D.

Titular Bishop of Gegi, North Africa and Auxiliary Bishop of San Juan, PR; ordained May 30, 1969; appointed June 30, 1981; consecrated September 7, 1981. *Res., Calle 6, D-9 Urb. Royal Town, Bayamon, PR, 00956.* Tel.: 809-730-4310. *Archbishop's Office: San Jorge St., No. 201, Santurce, P.P. Mailing Address: P.O. Box S-1967, San Juan, PR, 00903.* Tel.: 809-727-7373.

ERECTED AUGUST 8, 1511.

ERECTED AN ARCHDIOCESE APRIL 30, 1960.

Square Miles 353.

Comprises the northeast portion of the Island of Puerto Rico, with a Total Population of 1,260,000.

STATISTICAL OVERVIEW

Personnel	
Retired Cardinals	1
Archbishop	1
Auxiliary Bishops	2
Priests: Diocesan Active in Diocese	66
Priests: Active Outside Diocese	11
Priests: Retired, Sick or Absent	14
Number of Diocesan Priests	91
Religious Priests in Diocese	205
Extern Priests in Diocese	69
Ordinations:	
Diocesan Priests	2
Religious Priests	3
Transitional Deacons	2
Permanent Deacons	24
Permanent Deacons in Diocese	273
Total Brothers	23
Total Sisters	506
Parishes	
Parishes	154
With Resident Pastor:	
Resident Diocesan Priests	109
Resident Religious Priests	45
Without Resident Pastor:	
Administered by Priests	1
Missions	178
Professional Ministry Personnel:	
Brothers	47
Sisters	506
Lay Ministers	2,577
Welfare	
Catholic Hospitals	1
Total Assisted	180
Health Care Centers	2
Total Assisted	7,880
Homes for the Aged	22
Residential Care of Children	7
Total Assisted	55
Day Care and Extended Day Care Centers	36
Total Assisted	7,674
Specialized Homes	12
Total Assisted	588
Special Centers for Social Services	4
Total Assisted	41,852
Educational	
Seminaries, Diocesan	1
Students from This Diocese	9
Students from Other Diocese	7
Diocesan Students in Other Seminaries	2
Seminaries, Religious	15
Students Religious	37
Total Seminarians	48
Colleges and Universities	2
Total Students	8,361
High Schools, Diocesan and Parish	20
Total Students	4,397
High Schools, Private	26
Total Students	6,611
Elementary Schools, Diocesan and Parish	28
Total Students	9,683
Elementary Schools, Private	40
Total Students	13,539
Catechesis/Religious Education:	
Total Students Under Catholic Instruction	42,639
Teachers in the Diocese:	
Priests	36
Brothers	23
Sisters	80
Lay Teachers	2,191
Vital Statistics	
Receptions into the Church:	
Infant Baptism Totals	11,397
Adult Baptism Totals	1,353
First Communions	6,925
Confirmations	3,675
Marriages:	
Catholic	2,049
Interfaith	112
Total Marriages	2,161
Total Catholic Population	1,007,197
Total Population	1,393,611

Former Bishops—Most Rev. ALONSO MANSO, D.D., appt. May 1513.—Most Rev. JAMES H. BLENK, S.M.D.D., appt. Bishop of Puerto Rico, June 12, 1899; died April 20, 1917.—Most Rev. WILLIAM A. JONES, O.S.A., cons. Feb. 24, 1907; died Jan. 1921.—Most Rev. GEORGE J. CARUANA, D.D., promoted to the Apostolic Delegation of Mexico, 1925; promoted to Nunciature Apostolic of Cuba, 1927.—Most Rev. EDWIN VINCENT BRYNE, D.D., former Bishop of Ponce, Puerto Rico; cons. Nov. 30, 1925; appt. March 1929; promoted to Archdiocese of Santa Fe, June 15, 1943; died July 25, 1963.—Most Rev. JAMES PETER DAVIS, cons. Oct. 9, 1943; transferred to Archdiocese of Santa Fe, June, 1943; installed Feb. 25, 1964; retired Oct. 1974.—His Eminence LUIS CARDINAL APONTE MARTINEZ, D.D., cons. Oct. 12, 1960; retired March 25, 1999.

Vicars General—Most Rev. HECTOR RIVERA, D.D.; Most Rev. HERMIN NEGRON SANTANA, D.D.; Rev. Msgr. CELESTINO LINERA.

Episcopal Vicars—

for Administration of Temporalities—Rev. Msgr. BAUDILIO MERINO; Rev. CARLOS QUINTANA, Asst.

for Religious Women for Education—Rev. Msgr. BAUDILIO MERINO.

for Pastoral Affairs—Rev. Msgr. EMILIO TORO.

for Geographic-Pastoral Zones—San Juan-Santurce: Rev. JUAN MARTINEZ, S.D.B., Bayamon: Rev. DANIEL TRUJILLO, Carolina: Rev. NESTOR YULFO-HOFFMAN, Rio Piedras: Rev. REINALDO SAGARDIA, Rio Grande: Rev. VICENTE PASQUALETTO, Guaynabo-Puerto Nuevo: Rev. Msgr. MARIO A. GUIJARRO.

Chancery Office—P.O. Box 9021967, San Juan, 00902-1967.

Chancery Affairs—Rev. Msgr. FERNANDO B. FELICES-SANCHEZ, Chancellor; Rev. CARLOS JIMENEZ, Vice Chancellor.

Metropolitan Tribunal—

Moderator—Most Rev. ROBERTO O. GONZALEZ-NIEVES, O.F.M.

Secretary to the Archbishop—Rev. ALFONSO GUZMAN, O.F.M. Tel: 787-725-4975.

Executive Assistant to the Archbishop—Mr. SAMUEL SOTO-ALONSO. Tel: 787-725-4975.

Assistant to the Archbishop and Secretary to the Cardinal—Miss MIRIAM RAMOS.

Adjunt Judicial Vicar—Rev. Msgr. JAIME CAPO-BOSCH; Rev. PEDRO REYES.

Judges—Miss MARIA LUCIA SANCHEZ; Revs. REINALDO SAGARDIA; JOSE A. LANDRAU-ROMAN.

Defenders of the Bond—Rev. FLORENTINO SANZ.

Instructors—Rev. Msgr. JAIME CAPO-BOSCH; Revs. PEDRO REYES; JOSE A. LANDRAU; Miss MARIA LUCIA SANCHEZ; Mr. RIGOBERTO HIRALDO; Mr. JOSE GARCIA; Mr. ROLANDO QUEVEDO; Mr. PLINIO RODRIGUEZ.

Diocesan Consultors—Most Rev. HERMIN NEGRON SANTANA, D.D.; Most Rev. HECTOR RIVERA; Rev. Msgr. CELESTINO LINERA; Rev. Msgr. RAFAEL FONTANEZ; Rev. Msgr. JAMIE CAPO-BOSCH; Rev. Msgr. BAUDILIO MERINO; Rev. Msgr. FERNANDO FELICES-SANCHEZ.

Censor Librorum—Rev. Msgr. JAIME CAPO-BOSCH.
Examinatores Cleri—Vacant.
Pro-Synodal Examiner—Vacant.

Archdiocesan Offices and Directors

Boy Scouts—Rev. LORENZO RUIZ, S.D.B., *Calle Lutz 370, Santurce, 00910.*

Catechetics—Most Rev. HECTOR RIVERA, Archdiocesan Coord., *Calle San Jorge 201, Santurce, 00914.*

Catechetics Center—San Juan-Santurce: Sr. MARIA ELENA PEREZ-CORTEZ, M.G.Sp.S.; Sr. OCTAVIA ORTEGA, M.G.Sp.S., *P.O. Box 9021967, San Juan, 00902-1967.* Bayamon: Sr. IMELDA MORALES, M.SS.S., *P.O. Box 4152, Bayamon, 00958.* Tel: 787-780-1173. Rio Piedras: Sr. AILEEN BARDEN, C.S.J., *1744 Calle Echegaray, Bajo, San Juan, 00926.* Tel: 787-761-4280. Guaynabo-PtoNuevo: Sr. ROSE MORALES, M.S.B.T., *P.O. Box 9021967, San Juan, 00902-1967.* Tel: 787-731-6100. Rio Grande: Sr. ISABEL SOTO, M.SS.S.; Sr. MAYRA FIGUEROA, M.SS.S., *P.O. Box 1793, Rio Grande, 00745.* Tel: 787-888-5317. Carolina: Sr. MARIA EUGENIA MORENO, M.G.Sp.S., *Urb. Valle Arriba Heights, BF-20, Calle Alamo, Carolina, 00983.* Tel: 787-276-1413.

Catholic Charities—Mr. AMERICO P. LOPEZ ORTIZ, *P.O. Box 9021967, San Juan, 00902-1967.* Tel: 787-727-7373; Fax: 787-728-1719.

Daughters of Mary—Vacant.

Pre Cana Conferences—Rev. DAMIAN ARTIAGA, Dir., *Parroquia Santa Rosa Lima, 1765 Calle Lesbos, San Juan, 00926.* Tel: 787-761-6586. Mr. ALVAREZ, *Urb. Country Club, 1102 Calle Maria Cadilla, San Juan, 00924.* Tel: 787-769-1763. Mr. MANUEL SANCHEZ, *Urb. Country Club, 1031 Calle Genoveva De Lugo, San Juan, 00924.* Tel: 787-769-3565.

"El Visitante"—Weekly Catholic Paper for All Dioceses (Interdiocesan). Published By The P.R., Episcopal Conference. Most Rev. ROBERTO GONZALEZ NIEVES, Pres.; Rev. EFRAIN ZABALA, Editor; Dr. JOSE R. ORTIZ-VALLADARES, Dir., *Mailing Address: P.O. Box 41305, Minillas Sta., San Juan, 00940-1305.* Tel: 787-728-3710; Fax: 787-728-3656. Offices: *Pumarada St. 1704, Santurce, 00914.*

Radio Stations—WORO-FM and WKVM-AM 81, Mrs. ANA D. MELENDEZ, Dir., *Urb. Baldrich, 415 Calle Ingenioro Carbonell, San Juan, 00918., c/o P.O. Box 9021967, San Juan, 00902-1967.* Tel: 787-731-1380; 751-1018; Fax: 787-758-9967.

Television Station—WPRV-TV CHANNEL 13, Rev. Msgr. WILFREDO PENA-MORENO, Exec. Dir.; Mr. JUAN M. MUNIZ, Gen. Mgr., *Ave Iturregui Esq. Marginal, Baldorioty De Castro Ave., Carolina, 00982.* Tel: 787-276-1300; Fax: 787-276-1307., *P.O. Box 9021967, San Juan, 00902-1967.*

Commission for Sacred Art—Dr. ARTURO DAVILA, *Urb. Baldrich, Calle Rossy #202, San Juan, 00918.*

Commission for Sacred Liturgy—Rev. LEONARDO RODRIGUEZ-JIMENEZ, *P.O. Box 11714, San Juan, 00922-1714.* Tel: 787-783-0645.

Commission for Sacred Music—Vacant.

Clergy Social Security (Prevision Social del Clero)—Rev. Msgr. EMILIO TORO, Pres.; Revs. CARLOS QUINTANA-PUENTE, Treas. ALBERTO DIAZ, Sec., *CEP, P.O. Box 40682, San Juan, 00940-0682.* Tel: 787-728-1650; Fax: 787-728-1654.

Cursillos De Cristiandad—Rev. Msgr. JAIME CAPO-BOSCH; Rev. VINCENTE FERNANDEZ-MARINO, *P.O. Box 361809, San Juan, 00936-1809.* Tel: 787-789-7596.

Catholic Social Services—Prof. AMERICO LOPEZ-ORTIZ, Exec. Dir.

Emigrant Aid—Miss LAURA FELICIANO, *Catholic Social Services, P.O. Box 9021967, San Juan, 00902-1967.* Tel: 787-727-7373.

Holy Childhood Association—Rev. PRISCILIANO CARDENAS-RUIZ, *106 Ruiz Belvis St., Floral Park, P.O. Box 191882, San Juan, 00919.* Tel: 787-754-0995; Fax: 787-754-0749.

Holy Name Society—Rev. OMAR MARTINEZ, O.P., *Convento Del Sno. Rosario, P.O. Box 1968, Bayamon, 00960-1942.* Mr. MIGUEL A. RODRIGUEZ, Archdiocesan Dir., *P.O. Box 31164, San Juan, 00929.* Tel: 787-276-2212; 764-4813.

Renovacion Conyugal—Rev. JORGE AMBERT, S.J., Dir., *Urb. Ext. Roosevelt, 363 Calle Sargento Medina, San Juan, 00918.* Tel: 787-751-6001; 766-1363.

Istepa—Deacon RAFAEL L. MORALES, *Camino Alejandrino KM 3.4, Antiguo, Guaynabo, 00969., Mailing Address: Instituto Superior de Teologia y Pastoral, Edificio 2021, Carretera #177, Guaynabo, 00969-5140.* Tel: 787-731-6100; Fax: 787-731-0000.

Labor Relations—Vacant.

Legion of Mary—Mrs. ROSITA SANTANA, Pres., *RR 4 Box 833, Carpetera 830, BO. Cerro Gordo, Bayamon, 00956.* Tel: 787-797-8447.

Marriage Encounter—Hon. JUAN PEREZ JIMENEZ, *Urb. Caparra Hills, 67 Calle Nogal, Guaynabo, 00968.* Tel: 787-783-4292.

Spiritual Director—Rev. RICKY ROIC, *San Juan De Dios Parish.* Tel: 787-757-5060.

Master of Ceremonies to the Archbishop—Deacon PEDRO AREVALO.

Movimiento "Por Un Mundo Mejor"—Rev. JUAN J. GENOVARD, M.SS.CC., *Calle Duke 211, University Gardens, Rio Piedras, 00927.* Tel: 787-765-2255; 765-8042.

Nocturnal Adoration—Mr. EDGARD ARROYO, Pres., *423 Calle San Jorge, San Juan, 00912-3313.* Tel: 787-727-6359.

Spiritual Director—Rev. RICARDO HERNANDEZ, *Parro Quia Guadalupe, P.O. Box 364125, San Juan, 00936-4125.* Tel: 787-782-0016.

Head Start-Municipality of Carolina—Rev. SILVERIO RUEDA, Dir., *P.O. Box 9689, Carolina, 00988-9689.* Tel: 787-752-3040; Fax: 787-276-2420.

Head Start-Municipality of San Juan—Mrs. IVETTE SEPULVEDA, Dir., *Urb. Country Club, Calle 900, San Juan, 00924.* Tel: 787-757-1913; 768-0580; Fax: 787-257-6680.

Talleres De Oracion y Vida—Mrs. LEONOR PITA, Dir., *Urb. Baldrich, 168 Calle Presidente Ramirez, San Juan, 00918.* Tel: 787-766-0743; 781-5247.

Grupo Reina De La Paz—Rev. MANUEL GAMARRA, Spiritual Dir.; Mrs. MILLIE REXACH, Pres., *Urb. Villa Verde, 20 Calle A, Guaynabo, 00966.* Tel: 787-781-8777; Fax: 787-792-0813. Mrs. SUSANA FERNANDEZ, Sec. Tel: 787-789-9454.

Focolares—LUIS NOEL SOTO, Dir., *Q2 Calle 21, Ciudad Universitaria, Trujillo Alto, 00976.* Tel: 787-761-5721; 767-2346.

Catholic Charismatic Renewal—Rev. Msgr. BANDILIO MERINO, Dir., *Arzobispado De San Juan.* Tel: 787-765-6240; 727-7373.

Secretariado Sagrado Corazon—Mrs. ANA M. BONET, Pres., *Urb. Prado Alto, C6 Calle 4, Guaynabo, 00966.* Tel: 787-757-1413.

Catholic Daughters of America—Mrs. DAMARIS Y. VARGAS, *236 Dos Palmas Corozo, Moca, 00676.* Tel: 787-877-0295.

Equipo Camino Neocatecumenal—Mr. JULIO ALVAREZ, *Urb. Lago Alto, F81 Calle Loiza, Trujillo Alto, 00976.* Tel: 787-755-4320.

Union Eucaristica Reparadora (UNER)—Rev. PEDRO REYES, Spiritual Dir. Tel: 787-761-0571.

Sociedad San Vicente De Paul—Mrs. PETRIN, Pres., *938 Calle Azabache, San Juan, 00924.* Mrs. LILLIAN RIVERA, Vice Pres., *P.O. Box 29585, 65th Infantry Station, San Juan, 00924.* Tel: 787-762-8632.

Movimiento San Vicente Ferrer—Mrs. GLADYS FUSTER, Dir., *P.O. Box 3902, Bayamon Gardens Station, 00958.* Tel: 787-797-3432.

Hermandad N. Sra. De La Caridad—Rev. NICANOR VALDEZ, Dir., *P.O. Box 10151, San Juan, 00922-0151.* Tel: 787-783-3522.

Knights of Columbus—Mr. EDMUNDO NEVAREZ ORTEGA, *SD 38 Plaza 7, Urb. Mansion Del Sur, Levittown, 00949.* Tel: 787-795-9692; 728-2960.

Movimiento Juan XXIII—Mr. ANGEL L. RIOS, Pres., *Villa Contessa, F35 Calle Aragon, Bayamon, 00976.* Tel: 787-787-5984; Fax: 787-785-1024.

Movimiento De Schoenstatt—MARCOS RODRIGUEZ, Attorney, *Villa Verde, C1 Calle B, Guaynabo, 00966.* Tel: 787-781-3577.

Fatima Blue Army—Mr. AMERICO LOPEZ-ORTIZ, *P.O. Box 19671, Fernandez Juncos Station, San Juan, 00910.* Tel: 787-727-7373.

Our Lady of Providence Association—Mrs. DAPHNE ROJO. Tel: 787-722-0524.

Perpetual Adoration—Mrs. VIRGINIA ALVAREZ, Asst., *Mailing Address: Box S-763, San Juan, 00902.* Tel: 787-725-7734.

Pius Union of the Clergy—Rev. Msgr. CELESTINO LINERA, *Mailing Address: P.O. Box 9021967, San Juan, 00902-1967.* Tel: 787-727-7373.

Propagation of the Faith—Rev. PRISCILIANO CARDENAS-RUIZ, *106 Ruiz Belvis St., Floral Park, P.O. Box 191882, San Juan, 00919.*

San Juan Bautista Regional Seminary—Rev. LEONARDO RODRIGUEZ-JIMENEZ, Rector; Rev. ANTONIO PORTALATIN RODRIGUEZ, Vice Rector; Rev. DANIEL FERNANDEZ, Dean of Studies, *P.O. Box 11714, San Juan, 00922-1714.* Tel: 787-783-0645; 273-8090; Fax: 787-783-0645. *Ave. De Diego 930, Urb. La Riviera, Rio Piedras, 00921.*

San Jose Minor Seminary—Rev. FREDDY ALECIO, Rector, *Demetrio O'Dally St. 1000, Country Club, San Juan, 00924.* Tel: 787-768-3157.

Serra Clubs—Vacant.

Vocations Promoter—Rev. IVAN L. HUERTAS-COLON, *P.O. Box 11714, San Juan, 00922-1714.* Tel: 787-783-0645; 273-8090.

Society For The Protection of Children—Most Rev. ROBERTO GONZALEZ NIEVES, O.F.M., *Mailing Address: P.O. Box 9021967, San Juan, 00902-1967.* Tel: 787-727-7373.

Superintendent of Schools—Mr. RAFAEL MORALES, Supt.; Mrs. BLANCA MARQUEZ, Asst.; Sr. MARY ELLEN GEMMELL, Religion Program Dir., *Mailing Address: Edificio 2021, Carretera 177, Guaynabo, 00969-5140.* Tel: 787-731-6100; Fax: 787-731-0000.

War Against Hunger—Mrs. LAURA BLIZZARD DE APONTE, *San Jorge St., No. 201, Santurce, 00914., Mailing Address: P.O. Box 11547, San Juan, 00910-2647.* Tel: 787-727-7373, Ext. 240; 237; 238; Fax: 787-727-7938.

Young Catholic Action—Vacant.

Young Catholic University Students—Rev. JOSE ANGEL BORGES, S.J., *Mariana Bracetti 10, Rio Piedras, 00925.* Tel: 787-767-3348.

Young Christian Workers—Vacant.

Archdiocesan Historical Archive—Mrs. ELSE ZAYAS LEON, *Calle San Sebastian S-N, San Juan, 00902., P.O. Box 9021967, San Juan, 00902-1967.* Tel: 787-725-4975.

Tourism and Apostleship of the Sea—

Casamar—P. JUAN CRUZ PEREZ VAZQUEZ, *Calle Tejuan 205, Viego, San Juan, 00901.* Tel: 787-725-8730; 9606.

Youth Ministries—Rev. NESTOR YULFO, *Parroquia San Andres, MF15 Calle 482, Ext. Country Club, Carolina, 00982.* Tel: 787-769-7076. Rev. RUBEN GONZALEZ, C.M.F., *Parroquia San Jose Obrero, 470 Calle Belmonte, San Juan, 00923.* Tel: 787-767-1448.

Police Chaplains—Rev. VALERIANO MIGUELEZ. Tel: 787-754-0570. Rev. LUIS ANGEL TORRES. Tel: 787-769-5665. Rev. GREGORIO BRAVO. Tel: 787-765-0600. Rev. FELIX VARAS. Tel: 787-793-1234, Ext. 2196. Rev. Msgr. BAUDILIO MERINO. Tel: 787-767-6552.

San Juan International Airport Chapel—Rev. BRUCE LINCON, Chap. Tel: 787-791-2594. Deacon EDUARDO GONZALEZ. Tel: 787-769-3549.

Carmelite Third Order—Rev. LUIS MIRANDA, O.Carm. Tel: 787-727-0030; 0181.

CLERGY, PARISHES, MISSIONS AND PAROCHIAL SCHOOLS

CITY OF SAN JUAN

1—CATEDRAL DE SAN JUAN BAUTISTA (1522). (Nuestra Sra. de los Remedios). Revs. Raul Saez Munoz, Rector; Ricardo Gerena; Richard Marmol (Venezuela).
Res., 151 Cristo St., Box 9022145, 00902-2145. Tel: 787-722-0861.
Chapels—Santo Cristo; San Jose; Santa Ana.

2—SAN AGUSTIN (1889), Revs. Tomas J. Travers, C.SS.R.; Robert Gaugler, C.SS.R.; Carlos R. Valles, C.SS.R.; Philip Andrews, C.SS.R.; Bro. Mateo Perez, C.SS.R., Pastoral Assoc. In res., Revs. Jose Rached, C.SS.R., Prov. Supr.; Juan A. Gaucci, C.SS.R.; Arthur Donnelly, C.SS.R.
Mailing Address: P.O. Box 9066557, 00906-6557.
Res., 265 Ponce de Leon Ave., Pta. de Tierra, 00906. Tel: 787-722-4289; Fax: 787-725-7737.
School—Colegio San Agustin, 225 Ponce de Leon Ave., Box 9066, 00906. Tel: 787-722-4544; Fax: 787-997-1700. Marie Benitez Alonso, Prin.
Lay Teachers 18; Students 462.

3—NUESTRA SENORA DE LA ALTAGRACIA (1958), Rev. Franco Gutierrez (Spain); Deacons Ildefonso Lugo; Rafael Colon.
Mailing Address: Apartado 29493, 00929-0493. Tel: 787-765-0281.
Res., Calle Felipe Gutierrez 672, Urb. Villa Prades, Rio Piedras, 00924. Tel: 787-765-0281.
Catechesis/Religious Programs—Students 376.

4—SAN ANTONIO (1908), Revs. Jose Antonio Cruz; Edward Maldonado; Luis Francisco Gonzalez.
Res., Calle Arzuaga #218, Esq. Frailes Capuchinos, Apartado 21350, 00928. Tel: 787-765-0606; Fax: 787-765-1180.
School—Tel: 787-764-0090; Fax: 787-763-7592. John Bartemas, Admin.
Priests 2; Sisters 2; Lay Teachers 77; Students 1,400. Principals: Belicis Aponte, Preschool; Fe Villafane, Elementary; Miguel Rosa, Intermediate & High School.
Mission—Nuestra Senora del Buen Consejo.

5—ASUNCION DE LA VIRGEN (1972), Rev. P. Ruben Rodriguez, O.Carm.
Res., Calle Calve No. 1484, Urb. Antonsanti, Rio Piedras, 00928. Tel: 787-250-6771. [CEM]

6—NUESTRA SENORA DE BELEN (1960), Rev. Joaquin Mansilla (Spain).
Mailing Address: P.O. Box 10,845, Caparra Heights, 00922. Tel: 787-793-2485.
Res., Urb. Los Caobos, Calle Jacinto Galib Final Avda San Patricio, Caparra Heights.

7—NTR. SRA. DE LA CARIDAD DEL COBRE (1969), Revs. Victor Torres, O.M.I. (Panama); Neil Macaulay, O.M.I. (Canada).

Mailing Address: Box 4023, 00936-4023.
Res., Urb. Buena Vista, Calle 5, No. 124, Hato Rey, 00917. Tel: 787-753-0108; Fax: 787-751-0108; 751-5976.
Mission—Hato Rey, San Juan, Sma. Trinidad, Calle Buenos Aires, No. 25, Parada 27, Hato Rey 00919.

8—NUESTRA SENORA DEL CARMEN (1923), Rev. P. Demetrio Torres-Tarazona, O.M.I. (Peru).
Mailing Address: P.O. Box 7275, 00916-7275. Tel: 787-727-0737.
Res., Ave., Borinquen, Esq., Calle Tapia, Num. 609, Barrio Obrero, Santurce, 00916.
School—Father Berrios, Tel: 787-726-4851; Fax: 787-728-4860. Sr. Nilsa Cruz Rodriguez, H.C.C.S., Prin.
Sisters 3; Lay Teachers 9; Students 250.
Mission—San Martin de Porres, Calle: Tito Rodriguez #719 Barrio Obrero, 00916.

9—SANTA CATALINA LABOURE (1977), Rev. Carlos D. Cruz Davila; Deacon Jacinto Ortiz.
Mailing Address: Urb. La Cumbre 497 Emiliano Pol, Ste. 507, 00926-5636. Tel: 787-720-0303.
Res., Carretera 842 Km. 4.0 Barrio Caimito, Rio Piedras.
Missions—Medalla Milagrosa Barrio Los Romeros,; San Pablo. Carretera 842.

10—SANTA CECILIA (1969), Rev. Jose Ma. Lopez Mairal (Spain); Deacon Victor Merced de la Paz.
Mailing Address: P.O. Box 415, El Senorial Sta., 00926-0415.
Res., Carr Cupey Km. 3 Hm. 8, Rio Piedras, Tel: 787-755-8670; 761-5461 (Parish House).
Catechesis/Religious Programs—Students 127.
Chapels—Hogar Santa Teresa Jornet, Tel: 787-761-5805; Fax: 787-755-5575; Capilla San Agustin, Carretera 744, Cupey Bajo.

11—CORPUS CHRISTI (1972), Rev. Pablo Valenzuela (Spain); Deacons Francisco Gierbolini; Miguel Mendez; Luis R. Perez; Juan Figueroa; Reinaldo Del Valle; Jose Perez; Casiano Lugo.
Res., Calle Jose Abad, 1224 Urb. Club Manor, Rio Piedras, 00924. Tel: 787-757-5821.
Mission—Sector Santo Domingo, Santo Domingo. Carretera 849 Km. 8.7.

12—CRISTO REDENTOR (1971), Rev. Damian Carvajal (Spain); Deacon Wilfredo Rodriguez.
Res., Calle Ganges 140, Urb. El Paraiso, Rio Piedras, 00926. Tel: 787-764-1583; Fax: 787-761-6617.

13—CRISTO REY (1956), Rev. Msgr. Antonio Gomez (Spain); Deacons Victor Reyes; Miguel Roman Del Valle.
Mailing Address: P.O. Box 29695, 65 Inf., Rio Piedras, 00929-0695.
Res., Calle Jaime Drew, No. 789, Urb. Los Maestros, Rio Piedras, 00923. Tel: 787-767-3289.

14—NUESTRA SENORA DE LA ESPERANZA (1962), Rev. Manuel J. Gamarra (Peru).
Mailing Address: P.O. Box 8532, 00910-8532.
Res., Calle Republica No. 864, Urb. Hipodromo, Parada 20, Santurce, 00910. Tel: 787-723-5998.
Mission—Ntra. Sra. de la Providencia. Barriada Figueroa.
Chapel—Doctors Hospital, Tel: 787-723-2950; Fax: 787-721-3155.

15—ESPIRITU SANTO (1941), Rev. Valeriano Miguelez (Spain).
Mailing Address: P.O. Box 190259, 00919-0259.
Res., 75 Ruiz Belvis St., Floral Park, Hato Rey, 00919. Tel: 787-754-0570.
School—Aptdo. 191715, 00919-1715. Tel: 787-754-0490; 754-0555; Fax: 787-754-7154.
Priests 1; Lay Teachers 46; Students 701.
Calle Pachin Marin, Esq. Suiza, Hato Rey. Sr. Enedina Santos, Prin.

16—NTRA. SRA. DE FATIMA (1967), Revs. Mario Velazquez; Julio Fernandez Dominguez, O.M. (Spain); Martin Garamendi, O.M. (Spain); Jose M. Gallego, O.M. (Spain); William Rabelo Ortiz, O.M.
Mailing Address: P.O. Box 190396, 00919-0396. Tel: 787-753-6334; Fax: 787-764-3571.
Res., 608 Munoz Rivera Ave., Stop 34, Urb. Baldrich, Hato Rey, 00919.
School—La Merced, (1949), P.O. Box 364048, 00936-4048. Tel: 787-765-7342; 754-1162; Fax: 787-765-3970. Mrs. Rosa M. Figueroa, Prin., Tel: 809-766-3181.
Lay Teachers 36; Students 477.
Mission—Egida del Maestro.

17—FRANCISCA JAVIERA CABRINI (1968). (Mother Cabrini). Rev. Angel Ciappi-Azcorra; Deacon Luis Magin Nieves.
Res., 1564 Encarnacion St., 00920. Tel: 787-783-7447; Fax: 787-792-7233.
Catechesis/Religious Programs—Students 125.

18—SAN FRANCISCO DE ASIS (1858), Revs. Ramon Jaime Casellas, O.F.M.Cap.; Ricardo Colon; Alberto Figueroa, Vice Prov.; Bro. Jorge Macias.
Res., 301 San Francisco St., Box 9024231, 00902. Tel: 787-724-1131; Fax: 787-721-4616.
Catechesis/Religious Programs—Students 10.
Mission—San Juan, Capilla San Conrado, Bo. La Perla, 00902.

19—SAN FRANCISCO DE MONTE ALVERNIA (1985), Rev. Perfecto Fondevilla (Spain); Deacon Juan Bantista Perez.
Res., Calle 10 #15 Ext. San Augustin, Rio Piedras, 00926. Tel: 787-765-8824.

20—SAN FRANCISCO JAVIER (1967), Rev. Julio V. Garcia-Padron (Cuba); Deacons Elidio Aldarondo; Abel De Varona; Jose Hernandez.
Res., Calle 19, G46. Urb. Fair View, 00926. Tel: 787-761-2115.
Catechesis/Religious Programs—Students 120.

21—NUESTRA SRA. DE GUADALUPE (1951), Rev. Msgr. Juan Miranda (Spain); Rev. Ricardo Hernandez-Morales. In res., Rev. Msgr. Fernando B. Felices-Sanchez.
Mailing Address: G.P.O. Box 4125, 00936. Tel: 787-782-0016.
Res., 19th St., N.E. No. 1, Puerto Nuevo, 00920.
School—Tel: 787-782-0330; Fax: 787-724-5925. Mrs. Idalia Molina, Prin.
Lay Teachers 35; Students 789.

22—SAN IGNACIO DE LOYOLA (1956), Revs. Lawrence Searles, S.J.; Donald Vega; Jorge Ambert, S.J.
Res., Calle Narciso 1904, Rio Piedras, 00927-6706. Tel: 787-751-7680.
School—Academia San Ignacio De Loyola, 1908 Calle Narcisco, Rio Piedras, Tel: 787-765-8190; Fax: 787-765-3635. Sr. Risario Morales, C.S.J., Prin.
Students 535.
Chapel—Hospital Psiquiatria.

23—INMACULADO CORAZON DE MARIA (1961), Rev. Msgr. Rafael Matienzo; Deacons Benjamin Totti; Jose Rodriguez; Israel Suarez.
Mailing Address: P.O. Box 11929, 00922. Tel: 787-782-4176.
Res., Rodriguez Vera y Ferrer St., Urb. Santiago Iglesias, 00922.
Catechesis/Religious Programs—Students 260.
Mission—Monacillos, San Fernando.
Chapels—Colegio Ntra. Sra. de la Providencia.; N. Sra. Del Camino, Metropolitan Hospital.

24—JESUS MAESTRO (1969), Revs. P. Ricardo Fernandez, C.M. (Spain); Eugenio Villafranca, C.M. (Spain); Deacons Rafael Velazquez; William Gomez Soto.
Res., Segre 1725 Urb. Rio Piedras Heights, Rio Piedras, 00926. Tel: 787-763-8291.
Mission—Jesus Nazareno, Calle Guadiana #1666. [JC]

25—SAN JORGE (1965), Rev. Msgr. Jesus Santoalla; Rev. Msgr. Francisco Arenas; Rev. Carlos Jimenez.
Mailing Address: P.O. Box 6427, Loiza Sta., 00914-6427.
Res., Calle San Jorge 157, Santurce, 00914. Tel: 787-724-7780.

26—SAN JOSE (Villa Caparra), Rev. Msgr. Rafael Fontanez; Rev. Walter Gomez; Deacons Luis Colon; Luis Cordero; Ramon Rodriguez.
Res., 1948 Urb. Villa Caparra, Bloque ZM 215, Guaynabo, 00966. Tel: 787-781-1155; Fax: 787-783-8147.
School—Calle A. 32, (Villa Caparra), Tel: 787-783-1995; Fax: 787-792-7440.
Priests 2; Sisters 5; Lay Teachers 76; Students 1,134. Prins.: Sr. Catherine Ortiz, O.P., (Elementary); Sr. John Christian, (High School).

27—SAN JOSE OBRERO (1956), Revs. Ruben Gonzalez, C.M.F.; Jose Munez, C.M. (Spain); Deacon Eugenio Rivera.
Mailing Address: Calle Belmonte 470, 00923. Tel: 787-767-1448; Fax: 787-753-5392.
Res., Urb. San Jose, Calle Belmonte 470, Rio Piedras, 00923.
Missions—Embalse Sector, San Antonio Ma. Claret; San Martin de Porres, Bitumul.

28—SAN JUAN BOSCO (1945), Revs. Juan Martinez, S.D.B.; Jorge Santiago, S.D.B.; Enrique Mendez, S.D.B.; Lorenzo Ruiz; Francisco Quintero, S.D.B.
Mailing Address: P.O. Box 14125 Barrio Obrero Sta., 00915.
Res., 370 Lutz St., 00915. Tel: 787-726-1420; 726-0232; Fax: 787-726-7317.
Missions—Santurce, La Milagrosa, Villa Palmeras, Lutz Final, 00915; San Juan, Ntra. Sra. del Rosario, Fajardo St., 00915; San Juan, San Martin de Porres, Union St. #58, 00915.

29—SAN JUAN DE LA CRUZ (1990), Rev. Mario Mesa, O.F.M.Cap. (Spain); Deacon Martin Nieves.
Mailing Address: MSC 216, Urb. La Cumbre, Emiliano Pol Sta., 00926.
Res., Urb. La Cumbre, Calle Julio Ruedas #1935, Borinquen Gardens, Rio Piedras, 00926. Tel: 787-731-2016; Fax: 787-731-2016. [JC]

30—SAN JUAN EVANGELISTA (1962), Rev. Nicanor Valdes (Cuba); Deacon Miguel De La Sota.
Mailing Address: P.O. Box 10151, 00922.
Res., Calle Church Hill, J-5, Urb. Torrimar, Guaynabo, 00966. Tel: 787-783-3522; Fax: 787-781-0236.
School—Tel: 787-781-5325. Rev. Nicanor Valdes, Dir.
Priests 1; Sisters 1; Lay Teachers 22; Students 120.
Mission—San Francisco de Asis. Carretera 19, La Marina.

31—NUESTRA SENORA DE LOURDES (1969), Rev. Msgr. Efrain Rodriguez; Deacon Dionilo Torres.
Mailing Address: P.O. Box 14452, Bo. Obrero Sta., 00916.
Res., Gilberto Monroig Ave., Cr. of Colton St., 288, 00916. Tel: 787-726-4643.

32—SAN LUCAS (1972), Rev. Reinaldo Sagardia; Deacons Jose Rodriguez; Miguel Colon; Hector Cruz D'Choudens.
Mailing Address: Urb. El Senorial Calle Pio Baroja 380, 00926.
Res., Pio Baroja St., No. 380, Urb. El Senorial, 00926. Tel: 787-764-5476.

33—SANTA LUISA DE MARILLAC (1962), Rev. Victoriano Ramos (Spain); Deacon Francisco Colon.
Mailing Address: Urb. La Cumbre Ave., Emiliano Pol Sta. 497, Ste. #17, 00926.
Res., Ave. Emiliano Pol, Urb. La Cumbre, Rio Piedras, 00926. Tel: 787-720-3150.

34—SAN LUIS GONZAGA (1965), Rev. Virgilio Martinez (Spain).
Res., Calle Ronda A-17, Urb. Villa Andalucia, 00926. Tel: 787-761-9438; 283-6120.

35—SAN LUIS REY (1968), Rev. Jose Antonio Landrau.
Mailing Address: P.O. Box 71325, Ste. 65, 00936-8425.
Res., Calle 43 S.E. Final, Urb. Reparto Metropolitano, Rio Piedras, Tel: 787-767-6235.
School—Calle 43 S.E. #869, Reparto Metropolitano, Rio Piedras, 00921. Tel: 787-767-4006; Fax: 787-767-6235. Silvia Almenas, Prin.
Sisters 1; Lay Teachers 10; Students 213.

36—MARIA MADRE DE LA IGLESIA (1967), Rev. Gregorio Bravo (Spain); Deacons George Gonzalez; Eugenio Torres.
Res., 1120 Calle 5, Urb. Villa Nevarez, 00927. Tel: 787-765-0600.

37—MARIA AUXILIADORA (1962), Revs. Nicolas Navarro; Wilfredo Calderon; Rogelio Barranco, S.D.B.; Andres Rivera, S.D.B.; Antonio Polo, S.D.B.; Bros. Jose Cabo; Alberto Barrera.
Mailing Address: P.O. Box 14367, 00916.
Res., C. Constitucion Esq. Sta. Elena, Cantera, Tel: 787-726-1995; 727-5346, Ext. 261, 267.
Catechesis/Religious Programs—Students 300.
Missions—Sector Buenavista, Sagrado Corazon; Sector Buenavista, Nra. Sra. del Altagracia; Sector Ultimo Chance-Cerro, Ntra. Sra. de Fatima; Santisima Trinidad. Ave. Borinquen Final.

38—SANTA MARIA DE LOS ANGELES (1954), Revs. Isidro G. Valero (Cuba); Anibal R. Torres-Ortiz; Deacons Jose A. Torres; Rafael Reyes Crespo; Manuel Camacho.
Mailing Address: Box 10716, 00922-0716. Tel: 787-792-2640.
Res., De Diego Ave., No. 930, Urb. La Rivera, Rio Piedras.
Mission—San Juan, Ntra. Senora de la Caridad del Cobre, Urb. La Riviera, Calle 3 S.O. 1027, 00921-2517. Tel: 787-792-6613. Rev. Pedro Zaballa (Spain).

39—SAN MATEO (1773), Rev. Eddie Rivera.
Mailing Address: P.O. Box 6081, 00914-6081.
Res., Calle San Mateo, Esq. San Jorge, Stop 25, Santurce, 00912. Tel: 787-722-4158.

40—NUESTRA SENORA DE LA MERCED (1940), Revs. Jose Benito Osorio, O.de.M. (Spain); Jose Luis Garcia, O.de.M. (Spain); Angel Cuadrado, O.de.M. (Spain); Jose Esteves Iglesias, O.de.M. (Spain).
Mailing Address: P.O. Box 364133, 00936-4133.
Res., C/Pedro Espada 430, Urb. Roosevelt, Hato Rey, Tel: 787-763-3657.
Catechesis/Religious Programs—Students 50.

41—NTRA. SRA. DE LA MEDALLA MILAGROSA (1957), Rev. Ovidio Ortega Lemus.
Mailing Address: Urb. Perez Moris, Calle Mayaguez 209, 00917.
Res., 209 Mayaguez St., 00917. Tel: 787-751-2335.

42—NTRA. SRA. DE LA MONSERRATE (1916), Revs. Felipe Fernandez, O.S.A. (Spain); Isaias Alvarez, O.S.A. (Spain); Felix Moratiel, O.S.A. (Spain).
Mailing Address: P.O. Box 13726, 00908-3726.
Res., 1058 Fernandez Juncos Ave., 00907. Tel: 787-722-3134; Fax: 787-722-3134.
School—Santa Monica, Tel: 787-723-2573; 723-3845; Fax: 787-723-3992. Mr. Jose Ramos, Prin.
Lay Teachers 35; Students 390.

Catechesis/Religious Programs—Fax: 787-723-7838.
Students 60.
Mission—Santa Ana. Trastalleres.

43—SAN PABLO (1965), Rev. Ramon Orlando Tirado; Deacons Tomas Ramirez; Orlando Sanchez.
Res., Duero St., No. 370, Urb. Villa Borinquen, Puerto Nuevo, 00920. Tel: 787-706-0412; Fax: 787-706-0412.
Mission—Puerto Nuevo, Ntra. Sra. de la Caridad. Borinquen Tower.

44—SANTOS PEDRO Y PABLO LOS APOSTOLES (1980), Rev. Vicente Egurrola (Spain).
Mailing Address: Box 29231, 65 de Inf., 00929.
Res., Urb. Jardines De Berwind, Calle Las Casitas, Lote K, 65 Infanteria, Rio Piedras, 00929. Tel: 787-768-7424.

45—NTRA. SRA. DEL PERPETUO SOCORRO (1941), Revs. Armando Alvarez; Reinalo Terrero Vasquez (Cuba).
Res., Calle Marti 704, Miramar, Santurce, 00907-3227. Tel: 787-721-1015; 721-1016.
School—Jose Marti St. 704, 00907. Tel: 787-724-1447; 721-4540; Fax: 787-725-8104 (Elem.); 723-4550 (H.S.). Sr. Armand Marie, S.S.N.D., Prin.
Priests 1; Lay Teachers 102; Students 1,312.

46—NUESTRA SENORA DE LA PIEDAD (1956), Revs. Jesus Echeandia, C.P. (Spain); Juan Bautista Benguria, C.P. (Spain); Jose Ramon Zubizarreta, C.P., (Spain) Supr.; Joseba I. Goiogana, C.P. (Spain); Bro. Juan Landia, C.P.
Mailing Address: Box 6277, Loiza Sta., 00914-6277.
Res., Calle Marginal, AB-1, Ext. Villamar, Isla Verde, 00979. Tel: 787-726-2880; Fax: 787-268-5625.
School—Tel: 787-727-7585; Fax: 787-728-0125.
Priests 1; Lay Teachers 77; Students 756. Principals: Mrs. Nilda Ramos, (High School); Dr. Juan B. Benguria, C.P.

47—NUESTRA SENORA DEL PILAR (1714), Revs. Ignacio Alonso, C.M. (Spain); Higinio Madrazo, C.M. (Spain); Maximiano Santos, C.M. (Spain).
Mailing Address: Box 21134, 00928-1134.
Res., Plaza de Recreo, Rio Piedras, 00928. Tel: 787-764-5088; 763-3161.
Mission—Rio Piedras, Ba. Venezuela Co., Santa Teresita de Nino Jesus, Calle Tanque, 37, Rio Piedras, 00925.
Chapels—Colegio La Milagrosa, De Diego St. 107, Rio Piedras, Tel: 787-765-6114; Hogar Crea, Barriada Venezuela.

48—NUESTRA SENORA DE LA PROVIDENCIA (1959), Rev. Msgr. Baudilio Merino (Spain); Deacons Luis Vazquez; Pedro Rivera; Ricardo Martinez.
Res. & Mailing Address: Santa Agueda St., No. 1730, Urb. San Gerardo, Rio Piedras, 00926. Tel: 787-765-6240; Fax: 787-765-4821.
School—Carretera #176, Km. 2.7-C/Sta. Agueda 1733-Urb. San Gerardo, Rio Piedras, 00926. Tel: 809-767-6552; 767-6755. Melisa Sanabria, Prin.
Lay Teachers 42; Students 460.
Catechesis/Religious Programs—Students 454.

49—NUESTRA SENORA DE LA PROVIDENCIA (1973), Rev. Hermenegildo Vicedo (Spain).
Res. & Mailing Address: 219 Aponte St., 00912. Tel: 787-727-1878.

50—MARIA REINA DEL MUNDO (1971), Rev. Felix Varas (Spain).
Mailing Address: G.P.O. Box 3828, 00936-3828. Tel: 787-767-1372; 781-0303.
Res., Caserio Nemesio Canales, Roosevelt Ave. Puerto Nuevo, Rio Piedras.

51—RESURRECCION DEL SENOR (1968), Revs. Cruz Ajuria, O.F.M. (Spain); Luis Zabala, O.F.M.; Samuel Azcona, O.F.M. (Spain).
Res., Calle 31, S.O. #797, Urb. Las Lomas, 00921-1205. Tel: 787-792-1416; 792-5939.

52—SANTA ROSA DE LIMA (1971), Rev. Jose D'Artiaga (Spain); Deacons Pedro Costa; Vicente Rios.
Res., Calle Lesbos No. 1765, Urb. Venus Gardens, 00926. Tel: 787-761-6586.

53—SAGRADA FAMILIA (1971), Rev. Msgr. Tomas Su (China); Deacon Vicente Colon.
Mailing Address: P.O. Box 29311, 00929.
Res., Ave 65 de Inf., Esquina Calle 7, No. 112, Hills Brothers, Sabana Llana, 00929. Tel: 787-767-1723. [CEM]

54—SAGRADO CORAZON DE JESUS (1971), Revs. Basilio Roldan (Spain); Jaime Vergara, C.M. (Spain); Jose Yanez, C.M. (Spain).
Res. & Mailing Address: Calle Oxford 251, Esq. Howard Urb. University Gardens, 00927. Tel: 787-765-4798.
School—Iteramericana y Palma Real: Urb. University Gardens, Rio Piedras, 00927. Tel: 787-765-9430; Fax: 787-765-5267. Mary Andreen, Prin. Sup.; Sr. Maria Kivick, O.S.F., Prin. Elm.

55—SAGRADO CORAZON DE JESUS (1909), Rev. Rafael Candelas; Deacon Francisco Martinez.
Mailing Address: Box 8312, F. Juncos Sta., 00910-8312.
Res., Ponce de Leon Ave., #1308, Stop 19, Santurce, 00910. Tel: 787-722-0235; Fax: 787-722-4845.

56—SANTISMO SACRAMENTO (1967), Rev. Gabriel A. Jimenez (Columbia).
Mailing Address: P.O. Box 9300315, 00930-0315.
Res., 500 Jerusalem St., Urb. Matienzo Cintron, Rio Piedras, 00923. Tel: 787-764-3448.

57—SANTISIMO SALVADOR (1966), Revs. Leopoldo Laredo, Sch.P. (Spain); Cecilio Lacruz, Sch.P. (Spain); Rafael Capo Iriarte, Sch.P.; Benito Forcano, Sch.P., (Spain) Supr.; Miguel Angel Medina, Sch.P. (Spain); Deacons Julio Alvarez; Luis A. Medina; Luis O. del Rio.
Res., Niza St., 575, Urb. Villa Capri, 00924. Tel: 787-761-3314; Fax: 787-755-1595.
School—Calasanz, (1968), Ave. Montecarlo, P.O. Box 29067, 65 Inf. Sta., Rio Piedras, 00929. Tel: 787-750-2500; Fax: 787-257-0450.
Priests 5; Lay Teachers 34; Students 518. Principals: Celia Santos, High School; Leticia Santiago Orria, Elementary.
Catechesis/Religious Programs—Students 65.
Missions—Rio Piedras, N. Sra. Reina de la Paz, C/1 Esq. C/8 Urb. Berwind States, 00924.; Rio Piedras, San Jose de Calasanz, Calle #23 408, Parc. Hills Brothers, 00924. Rev. Agustin Lopez, Sch.P., (Spain) Dir.

58—SANTA TERESA JORNET (1985), Rev. Francisco J. Quinonez; Deacons Vicente Lasanta; Martin Cuevas.
Mailing Address: Aptdo. 415, El Senorial Mail Sta., 00926-0415.
Res., Carr. 176 Camino el Mundo, Km. 10.0 Cupey Alto, 00926. Tel: 787-748-2978; 760-8376.
Missions—Cupey, San Martin de Porres Camino El Mudo,; Cupey, Virgen de la Salud Camino Guayabos Carr. 176, Km. 9.5,; Ermita N. Sra. Providencia. Camino Los Gonzalez, Km. 5.3.

59—SANTA TERESITA DEL NINO JESUS (1930), Revs. Tomas Ciscar, O.Carm., (Spain) Sup. Regional; Franco Barreneche, O.Carm. (Spain); Francisco Armell, O.Carm.; Enrique Oria, O.Carm. (Spain); Jorge Rivera, O.Carm.; Salvador Rodrigo, O.Carm. (Spain).
Res., 2059 Loiza St., 00911-1799. Tel: 787-727-0181; 727-0030; Fax: 787-728-0056.
School—Tel: 787-727-4260; 727-4317; 727-4358. Brenda Arroyo, Prin.
Priests 1; Sisters 1; Lay Teachers 47; Students 440.
Mission—Sagrada Familia, Tel: 809-726-0570.

60—SAN VICENTE DE PAUL (1940), Revs. P. Gregorio Alegria, C.M., (Spain) Prov. Supr.; Evaristo Oliveras, C.M.; Manuel Aznar, C.M. (Spain); P. Pascual Sota, C.M. (Spain); Javier Inigo, C.M. (Spain); Victor Santos, C.M.; Jeronimo Sola, C.M. (Spain); Bros. Wilfredo Acevedo, C.M.; Jean Ketel Bonhommete, C.M.
Mailing Address: P.O. Box 19118, 00910-0118.
Res., 1651 Los Angeles, Corner to Fernandez Juncos Ave., 19118, Fernandez Juncos Sta., Santurce, 00910. Tel: 787-727-3963; Fax: 787-726-4126. [CEM][JC]
School—709 Bolivar St., Box 8699, Tel: 787-727-4273; Fax: 787-728-2266. Mrs. Isabel Casanas, Prin.
Lay Teachers 31; Students 658.
Catechesis/Religious Programs—Students 80.

61—STELLA MARIS (1965), Rev. Eral Jose Rivas-Campiz; Deacon Wayne Matthews.
Res., 69 Cervantes St., Condado, San Juan, 00907-1947. Tel: 787-723-2240; 723-2359; Fax: 787-722-3200.

OUTSIDE THE CITY OF SAN JUAN

Bayamon

1—SAN AGUSTIN (1964), Revs. Ildefonso Blanco, O.S.A. (Spain); Gonzalo Gonzalez, O.S.A. (Spain); Eliseo Garcia, O.S.A. (Spain); Carlos Cordero, O.S.A.; Deacons Ignacio Perez; Cristobal Rivera; Pedro Miranda.
Mailing Address: P.O. Box 4283, Bayamon Gardens Sta., 00958-4283.
Res., Lomas Verdes, Calle Duende Bloque 2, E #21, 00956. Tel: 787-785-8611; Fax: 787-785-8611.
School—(1964), Tel: 787-786-8055. Mrs. Mary Jo Duran, Prin.
Sisters 3; Lay Teachers 23; Students 503.
Missions—Bayamon, San Martin de Porres, c/1 Barrio Juan Sanchez, 00959.; Bayamon, N. Sra. Del Buen Consejo, Villas de San Agustin.

2—SAN ANTONIO MARIA CLARET (1966), Revs. Marcelino Romero, C.M.F. (Spain); Salvador Salgado, C.M.F.; Deacon Jose Dolores Rivera.
Mailing Address: P.O. Box 3292, 00958-3292.
Res., D-24 Castiglioni Ave., Urb. Bayamon Gardens, 00957. Tel: 787-797-3337.

3—CATALINA DE SIENA (1963), Revs. Alberto Pagan, O.P.; Victor Perez, O.P.; Deacons Francisco Cruz; Victor Lopez; Antonio Santiago; Jose Rios; Agapito Diaz.
Mailing Address: P.O. Box 4188, 00959-4188.
Res., Urb. Hermanas Davila, Calle 10, Q-3, 00959. Tel: 787-785-2381; Fax: 787-269-5065.
Catechesis/Religious Programs—Students 109.

4—CRISTO SALVADOR (1998), Rev. Ivan L. Huertas.
Mailing Address: P.O. Box 362982, San Juan, 00936-2982.
Church—Carr. 177, Los Filtros, 00959. Tel: 787-287-5678.

5—NUESTRA SRA. DE LOS DOLORES (1976), Rev. Raul Quesada Gil (Cuba); Deacon Francisco Hernandez.
Res., Bloque DD-25, 18th St., Urb. Alturas de Flamboyan, 00957. Tel: 787-786-7494.

6—SANTO DOMINGO DE GUZMAN (1976), Rev. Juan Burgos, O.P.; Deacons Hector Negron; William Rodriguez.
Mailing Address: P.O. Box 4188, 00960-4188.
Res., Ext. La Milagrosa Calle 2, 00960. Tel: 787-786-8592; 785-2381; Fax: 787-269-5065.
Catechesis/Religious Programs—Students 64.

7—SANTA ELENA (1978), Revs. Daniel Trujillo (Columbia); Rodrigo Manrique Hernandez (Columbia).
Mailing Address: P.O. Box 366, Garden Sta., 00960-0366.
Res., Calle 6, H-14, Urb. Sta. Elena, 00960. Tel: 787-785-6604; Fax: 787-785-6604.

8—INVENCION DE LA SANTA CRUZ (1772), Revs. Edgardo Sanabria, O.P.; Marcos Espinel (Spain); Ivan Almodovar, O.P. (Spain); Deacon Jose A. Bermudez.
Res., 12 Degetau St., 00619. Tel: 787-785-2134; Fax: 787-778-7867.

9—SAN JOSE (1964), Revs. Jose Nieto, C.M.F. (Spain); Hector F. Cuadrado, C.M.F.; Camilo Riano, C.M.F. (Spain); Romualdo Fernandez, C.M.F. (Spain).
Res., Dakar, F-169, Forest View, 00956. Tel: 787-785-6675; Fax: 787-785-0670.
School—Academia Claret, Tel: 787-787-6685. Yolanda Martinez, Prin.
Priests 2; Lay Teachers 30; Students 467.

10—SAN JUAN BAUTISTA DE LA SALLE (1979), Revs. Jose M. Garcia Bazton, M.SS.CC. (Spain); Jesus M. Ciriza, M.SS.CC. (Spain); Deacons Francisco Ortiz; Jose Vega; Jorge Rivera.
Res., 19 Rio Cialitos St., 1ra. Secc. Estancias Rio Hondo, 00961. Tel: 787-787-9567; Fax: 787-798-5071.

11—SAN MIGUEL ARCANGEL (1962), Rev. Francisco Medina; Deacons Jose Pena; Santiago Latorre.
Mailing Address: P.O. Box 361714, San Juan, 00936-1714. Tel: 787-787-4459; Fax: 787-787-4459. [JC]
Res., Urb. Jardines de Caparra, Calle 12A Bloque AB., No. 32, 00959.

12—NUESTRA SENORA DE LA MILAGROSA (1968), Rev. Hernan Adarve (Columbia).
Mailing Address: P.O. Box 2104, 00960-2104.
Res., Carr. 864, No. 82, Bo. Hato Tejas, 00960. Tel: 787-785-6620.

13—ASCENSION DEL SENOR (1984), Revs. Jose A. Santiago, O.SS.T.; Javier Elorriaga, O.SS.T. (Spain); Deacons Aureliz Garcia; Juan Perez del Valle. In res., Rev. Pedro Gorena, O.SS.T. (Spain).
Mailing Address: P.O. Box 3367, 00958-3367. Tel: 787-799-6120; Fax: 787-799-1977.
Res., Calle 31, Final, Urb. Rexville, 00957.

14—ESPIRITU SANTO. (Parish in Formation). Rev. Pedro Gorena, O.SS.T. (Spain).
Mailing Address: & Res.: Calle 1, E #18, Bella Vista Gardens, 00957. Tel: 787-799-6120; Fax: 787-797-2842.

15—NTRA. SRA. DE LA MONSERRATE (1985), Revs. Carlos R. Morales, O.S.A.; Saturnino Juan, O.S.A. (Spain); Deacons Luis A. Rodriguez; Jesus Lopez.
Mailing Address: P.O. Box 3948, Bayamon Gardens, 00958.
Res., Carr. 829, Km. 6.2, Bo. Santa Olaya, Bayamon Gardens, 00958. Tel: 787-797-0708; 799-7340; Fax: 787-797-9953.
Missions—Sector La Morenita, Cristo Rey Bo. Guaragoao,; Bayamon, Sector Pena, Santa Monica. Bo. Guaragoao.

16—NUESTRA SENORA DEL PERPETUO SOCORRO (1976), Rev. Roberto Arzola, O.P.; Deacons Ramon L. Ramon; Miguel Velez; Rafael Ortiz.
Res., Comerio St. No. 192, 00956. Tel: 787-785-2381; 780-4367.
Convent—Tel: 787-785-6542.

17—LA RESURRECCION DEL SENOR (1987), Rev. Juan Santa; Deacons Angel Luis Oyola; Nicanor Mercado.
Res., Calle 12 F-1, Urb. Royal Town, 00956. Tel: 787-730-4310.

18—SANTA RITA DE CASIA (1967), Revs. Mario Gonzalez, O.S.A., (Spain) Supr.; Heber Nazario, O.S.A.; Benigno Palomo, O.S.A. (Spain); Bro. Agustin Sanchez, O.S.A; Deacons Eliezer Toro; Gregorio Velez (MIA); Ramon Luis Rivera (PCE); Noel Vasquez.

Res., Ave. Hostos NS-8, Urb. Santa Juanita, 00956. Tel: 787-786-3971; Fax: 787-778-3806.
Retired House—Ntra. Sra. del Buen Consejo.
Missions—Bayamon, San Jose Carretera 831, Bo. Minillas,; Bayamon, N. Sra. Del Carmen Calle Reno P-54,; Bayamon, Sagrado Corazon De Jesus. Calle Palestina D, Z-10.

19—SANTA ROSA DE LIMA (1976), Rev. Pedro Campana (Spain); Deacons Ricardo D'Auria; Ricardo Longueira; Juan R. Santos.
Mailing Address: Calle 12, Bloque No. 28 No. 9, Urb. Santa Rosa, 00959. Tel: 787-798-2300; 787-1676; Fax: 787-780-3680.
Res., Urb. Sta. Rosa, Av. Main, Calles 11, 12, 13.
School—Calle Main, Tel: 787-798-2829; Fax: 787-780-3680. Sr. Selenia, Prin.
Sisters 8; Lay Teachers 40; Students 882.

20—NUESTRA SENORA DEL ROSARIO (1971), Rev. Jaime Vazquez Rojas; Deacons Luis Echegaray; Luis A. Navedo.
Res., Calle Zaragoza, Bloque, B No. 35, Esq. Calle Vizcaya, Urb. Villa Espana, 00961. Tel: 809-787-0418.

21—NUESTRA SRA. DEL ROSARIO (1993), Rev. Heriberto Londono (Columbia); Deacon Hector Rivera.
Mailing Address: Box 3917, 00958.
Res., Carr. 816 Km. 5.6, Barrio Nuevo, Tel: 787-730-6000.

22—SAGRADA FAMILIA (1976), Rev. Alvaro Silva (Colombia); Deacons Americo Arroyo; Gumersindo Colon; Ramon L. Ortiz.
Mailing Address: P.O. Box 8478, 00960-8478.
Res., Calle Caracas and Valparaiso, Urb. Ext. Forest Hills, 00960. Tel: 787-798-2010.
Catechesis/Religious Programs—Students 160.

23—SANTA MARIA (1984), Revs. Juan Alexis Diaz, C.M.F.; Vicente Penalba, C.M.F. (Spain); Bro. Zacarias Pichardo; Deacons Jose Ramon Cruz; Rafael Araya.
Mailing Address: Urb. Cana, Calle 24 #II-1, 00957.
Res., Calle 24, II No. 1, Carr 167, Urb. Cana, 00957. Tel: 787-797-7248; 797-8230; Fax: 787-279-5292.
Missions—Bayamon, San Gerardo de Mayela, Bo. Buena Vista, 00957.; Bayamon, Sagrado Corazon, Bo. Cerro Gordo, 00956.

24—SANTA TERESA DE JESUS (1983), Rev. Angel Figueroa, O.M.I.; Deacon Eugenio Torres.
Mailing Address: P.O. Box 9204, 00960-9204.
Res., Calle 12 F #10, Urb. Teresita, 00960. Tel: 787-269-6749.
Missions—San Martin de Porres Rio Plantation Urb.,; Sector Punta Brava, Convento Missioneras De La Caridad.

25—SANTIAGO APOSTOL (1966), Revs. Antonio Picornell, M.SS.CC. (Spain); Jesus Jordan, M.SS.C. (Spain); Deacons Felix Lopez; Juan Melendez; Angel Pabon; Raul Perez.
Res., Urb. Sierra Bayamon, Calle 23, Bloque 23, Num. 17, 00961. Tel: 787-786-9679; 288-1966.
School—Mrs. Zoraida N. de Alonso, Prin. Priests 1; Lay Teachers 11; Students 466.

26—SANTO DOMINGO DE GUZMAN (1984), Rev. Orlando London (Columbia); Deacons Virgilio Andino; Ramon Ramos.
Mailing Address: P.O. Box 3342, 00958-3342.
Res., Parcelas Van Scoy Esq.Principal Calle, 3, 00958. Tel: 787-797-5510; 799-2377.

Canovanas

1—NUESTRA SENORA DEL PILAR (1960), Rev. Fabio Moncada (Columbia); Deacon Jose Rivera.
Mailing Address: P.O. Box 1615, 00729-1615.
Res., Luis Hernaiz St., #3, 00729. Tel: 787-876-2655; 876-3020; Fax: 787-256-5767.
School—3 Luis Hernaiz St., 00729. Tel: 787-876-3020. Mr. Victor Hernandez, Dir.
Lay Teachers 19; Students 810.
Mission—San Francisco Javier.

2—RESURRECCION DEL SENIOR (1978), Rev. Luis E. Villada (Colombia); Deacons Pedro Florez; Miguel Roman.
Mailing Address: P.O. Box 896, 00729.
Res., Las Parcelas de San Isidro, 188 Carret. Bo. Mediania Km. 2.0, 00729. Tel: 787-876-3917; Fax: 787-256-4836.
Mission—Ntra. Sra. de la Providencia. Villas De Loiza.

3—SAGRADO CORAZON DE JESUS (1991), Rev. Guillermo Piedrahita (Columbia); Deacons Julio Ortiz; Anthony Calderon.
Mailing Address: P.O. Box 35000, Ste. 20147, 00729. Tel: 787-876-1355.
Res., Bo. Cubuy, Carretera 186 Km. 77, 00729.

4—SANTA MARIA MADRE DE DIOS (1971), Rev. Vicente Pasqualetto, S.T.; Deacon Jose L. Casaigne.
Mailing Address: E-189 Girasol St., Loiza Valley, 00729. Tel: 787-876-0827; Fax: 787-256-2142.
Res., Bo. La Central, Carretera 8874, Urb. Loiza Valley, Calle Camelia.

Mission—Capilla Cristo Salvador. Sector Pueblo Indio.

5—SAN JOSE (1971), Rev. Jose Francisco Quintero; Deacon Felipe Rivera.
Mailing Address: P.O. Box 807, 00729-0807.
Res., Bo. Campo Rico, Carretera 185, 00729. Tel: 787-876-7167.
Missions—Palma Sola, Ntra. Sra. de la Asuncion Carrt. 957 Km. 6.8,; Alturas de Campo Rico, Ntra. Sra. Del Carmen. Carrt. 185 Km. 5.3.

Carolina

1—SAN ANDRES (1982), Rev. Nestor Yulfo; Deacons Marino Hernandez; Gilberto Mejias.
Mailing Address: MF-15 Calle 482, Urb. Country Club, 00982. Tel: 787-769-7076; Fax: 787-769-7076.

2—SANTA BERNARDITA SOUBIROUS (1982), Rev. Msgr. Wilfredo Pena Moreno; Deacons Ismael Colon; Angel Rivera; Rafael Zanabria; Ramon Santiago.
Mailing Address: P.O. Box 29826, 65 Infanteria Sta., San Juan, 00929-0826. Tel: 787-762-0375; 257-7643; Fax: 787-257-6642.
Res., Calle Espioncela, Esquina Calle Torcaza, Country Club, Rio Piedras, 00924.

3—SANTA CLARA DE ASIS (1966), Revs. Fernando Hortiguela, O.F.M. (Spain); Leandro Abarrategui, O.F.M. (Spain); Luis S. Olmo, O.F.M. (Spain); Deacons Luis Del Rio Pitre; Jose A. Morales; Luis Montes; Juan F. Ubarri.
Mailing Address: Urb. Villa Fontana, JL-456 Via 14, 00983.
Res., Via 14 JL No. 456 Urb. Villa Fontana, 00983. Tel: 787-768-1708; Fax: 787-750-2898.
School—(1968), Tel: 787-768-7110. Mrs. Lillivette Torres, Prin.; Rev. Leanadro Abarrategui, O.F.M., Dir.
Lay Teachers 23; Students 355.
Missions—San Francisco de Asis; Carolina, Parque Boliviano 5-JL, Villa Fontana Park, 00983.

4—SANTO CRISTO DE LA AGONIA (1971), Rev. Jorge J. Castillejo-Llusia (Spain); Deacon Ernesto Rivera.
Mailing Address: P.O. Box 5108, 00984-5108.
Res., Calle Robles C-29, Urb. Eduardo J. Saldana, 00984. Tel: 787-768-0374.
Catechesis/Religious Programs—Students 95.

5—SANTO CRISTO DE LOS MILAGROS (1971), Rev. Celso Martinez (Spain).
Mailing Address: P.O. Box 834, 00986-0834.
Res., Ave. Sanchez Castano, Urb. Villa Carolina, 00985. Tel: 787-768-3810.

6—EPIFANIA DEL SENOR (1982), Rev. Juan Patron Kastner; Deacon Ibrahim Mestre.
Mailing Address: & Res.: Calle Calais 425, Ext. El Comandante, 00982-3601. Tel: 787-752-1149.

7—SAN FELIPE APOSTOL (1971), Rev. Rafael Suazo; Deacons Eugenio Balasquide; Jose Rafael Vazquez.
Mailing Address: P.O. Box 1494, 00984-1494.
Res., Calle 419, Bloque 165, No. 3, 4 ta. Ext. Villa Carolina, 00964. Tel: 787-762-6520. [CEM]

8—SAN FERNANDO (1851), Rev. Miguel Ferrer; Deacons Jose Birriel; Enrique Colon; Santiago Diaz Rosa; Presbitero Rivera; Jose Torres.
Mission—Carolina, P.O. Box 128, 00986-0128.
Res., Calle Munoz Rivera, No. 65, fuenta a Plaza de Recreo, 00986. Tel: 787-769-0170.

9—SANTA GEMA GALGANI (1971), Revs. Manuel Elejalde, C.P. (Spain); Felix Barruetabena, C.P. (Spain).
Mailing Address: P.O. Box 2789, 00984-2789.
Res., Av. Galicia Final, Urb. Bahia Vistamar, 00984. Tel: 787-769-5663.
School—Tel: 787-768-3082; 757-2505; Fax: 787-750-3090. Mrs. Lilia Luna de Anaya, Prin.
Sisters 1; Lay Teachers 26; Students 606.

10—INMACULADA CONCEPCION (1966), Rev. Hernan Berdugo.
Mailing Address: Apartado 3562, 00984-3562.
Res., Urb. Valle Arriba Heights, Calle Alemendro A-15, 00984. Tel: 787-276-1527; Fax: 787-276-1527. [CEM]

11—JESUS MEDIADOR (1988), Rev. Freddy Alecio (Guatemala); Deacons Candido Martinez; Edwin Rivera.
Mailing Address: & Res.: Calle Demetrio O'Dally 1000, Urb.Country Club, San Juan, 00924. Tel: 787-768-3157; Fax: 787-752-2410.

12—SAN JUAN DE DIOS (1971), Rev. Ricardo A. Roig; Deacon Luis R. O'Neill.
Mailing Address: P.O. Box 3179, 00984-3179.
Res., R-19-A Canaria St., Jardines de Borinquen, P.O. Box 3179, 00984. Tel: 787-757-5060; Fax: 787-757-5060.
Mission—La Sagrada Familia. Villa Esperanza, Calle Matadero.

13—NUESTRA SENORA DE LOURDES (1956), Rev. David Arrieta (Spain); Deacons Emilio Caceres; Edwin Perez; Nelson Soto.
Mailing Address: Urb. El Comandante, 1173 Calle Alejo Cruzado, San Juan, 00924.
Res., 1173 Alejo Cruzado, Ext. El Comandante, Tel: 787-750-4787; 752-3716.

14—NTRA. SRA. DEL CARMEN (1984), Rev. Antonio Garcia (Spain); Deacons Ernie Diaz; Cesar Avila.
Mailing Address: P.O. Box 299, 00986-0299.
Res., Urb. Lomas de Carolina, Monte Membrillo Km. 8, 00986-0299. Tel: 787-752-8708; Fax: 787-752-4454.
School—Tel: 787-757-4489. Sr. Yolanda M. Aguiar, R.M., Prin.
Priests 1; Sisters 3; Lay Teachers 20; Students 252.
Catechesis/Religious Programs—Students 112.

15—NTRA. SRA. REINA DE LA PAZ (1969), Rev. Jesus A. Garcia (Venezuela); Deacons Euripides Lugo; Miguel Marrero; Manuel Reyes; Efigenio Rivera.
Mailing Address: P.O. Box 3688, 00984-6388.
Res., Calle 6, Final, Urb. Sabana Gardens, 00983. Tel: 787-752-5607; Fax: 787-762-4277.

16—NTRA. SRA. REINA DE LOS ANGELES (1960), Rev. J. Bruce Lincon (BGP); Deacon Ildefonso Berrios.
Mailing Address: Urb. Los Angeles, Bloque W17A Calle N, 00979-1154.
Res., W17A Calle N, Urb. Los Angeles, Tel: 787-791-2594; Fax: 787-791-2594.
Catechesis/Religious Programs—Students 110.

17—SANTISIMA TRINIDAD (1982), Rev. Luis Angel Torres; Deacons Ibrahim Suarez; Esteban Valle; Bienvenido Domenech; Gaspar Orozco.
Mailing Address: Urb. Country Club, 3 RA Ext., Ave. Campo Rico PA-16, 00982. Tel: 787-769-5665. [JC]
Res., Aveida Campo Rico PA-16, Urb. Country Club.

18—CRISTO REY (1971), Rev. Miguel A. Corrales (Colombia).
Mailing Address: P.O. Box 1215, 00986-1215.
Res., Urb. Parque Ecuestre, Calle Dulce Sueno U-8, 00987. Tel: 787-757-8712.
Missions—Parque Encuestre, S. Francisco de Asis Entre las calles Tinajero y Dulce Sueno; Bo. Canovanillas, Maria Auxiliadora Carrt. 857 Km. 3.6; Bo. Cambute, Divino Nino Ubanizaciones: Ciudad Jardin y Colobos Park; Cristo Rey. Bo. Carruzos.

19—NTRA. SRA. DE FATIMA (1998), Rev. Mario Velazquez (Columbia); Deacons Domingo Ocasio; Orlando Rodriguez.
Mailing Address: HC-3 Box 12076, Barrio Cedros, 00985.
Res., Bo. Cedros, Carr 853, Km. 13.6, Tel: 787-750-8562; Fax: 787-750-8562.

20—SAN VALENTIN (1971), Rev. Francisco Jose Quiceno (Columbia); Deacons Miguel Diaz; Antonio Quintana; Jose A. Pappaterra.
Mailing Address: P.O. Box 9382, 00988-9382.
Res., Calle San Luis 128, Urb. Rolling Hills, 00988. Tel: 787-750-5277; Fax: 787-750-5277.
Missions—Jardines de Carolina, Santa Rosa, Calle E, esq. Calle F, Jardines de Carolina, 00987; Carolina, San Antonio, Urb. San Anton, Calle Tomas Ortiz, esq. Kercado, 00987.

21—SAN FRANCISCO DE ASIS (1988), Rev. Frank de la Rosa Peguero (Dominican Republic); Deacon Justo Montanez.
Mailing Address: & Res.: Calle 22 #0-31 A, Urb. Metropolis, 00987. Tel: 787-768-8860.

Catano, San Francisco de Sales (1969), Revs. Jorge L. Gonzalez, S.D.B.; Adan Marrero, S.D.B.
Mailing Address: P.O. Box 567, 00963-8163.
Res., Ave. Flor del Valle Bloque BB-No. 108, Urb. Las Vegas, 00963. Tel: 787-788-5036; Fax: 787-788-8163.
Missions—Santo Domingo De Guzman, Puente Blanco; Maria Auxiliadora Urb. Vistas Del Morro; San Judas Tadeo (Santuario) Parcelas Bo. Palmas; Sector La Cucharilla, Immaculada Concepcion.

Nuestra Senora del Carmen (1893), Revs. Silvestre Gomez (Bolivia); Felix A.P. Struik, O.P. (Holland); Deacons Angel Oquendo; Enrique Rivera. In res., Revs. Malac Clune, O.P. (Ireland); Oscar Morales, O.P.
Mailing Address: P.O. Box 427, 00963-0427.
Res., Calle Tren Num. 42, 00963. Tel: 787-788-1098; Fax: 787-788-5905.
Missions—San Martin de Porres Bayview Urb.; San Jose Obrero. Rev. Juan A. Matos.

Dorado, San Antonio de Padua (1842), Revs. Angel Luis Morales; Jose Miguel Cardona-Matta; Deacons Jose Marrero; Luis Marcial Rivera; Romulo Rodriguez.
Mailing Address: P.O. Box 602, 00646-0602. Tel: 787-278-1416; 728-1154 (Res.); Fax: 787-278-4759.

Ntra. Sra. de La Salud (1982), Rev. Manuel Garcia (Spain); Deacons Hilario De Leon; Cresencio Rosario.
Mailing Address: Bo. Higuillar, P.O. Box 470, 00646-0470.
Res., Parcela 202, Calle Principal 210, Sector San Antonio, 00646. Tel: 787-796-3418.

Guaynabo
1—Corazon de Jesus (1992), Revs. Esteban Beltran, SS.CC. (Spain); Alberto Ramirez, SS.CC. (Spain); Deacon Andres Figueroa Acevedo.
Mailing Address: P.O. Box 225, 00970-0225. Tel: 787-789-2014.
Res., Carr. 834 Km. 4.0, Bo. Sonadora, 00970.
2—El Buen Pastor (1970), Rev. Francisco Jimenez (Spain).
Mailing Address: & Res.: Avenida Apolo, Urb. Apolo, 00969. Tel: 787-789-2653.
3—Maria Madre de Mi Senor, Rev. P. Mario Velazquez Heredia (Colombia).
Mailing Address: P.O. Box 2150, 00970-2150. Tel: 787-789-1837; 720-1709.
Res., Bo. Tortugos, Carretera 873, #1904.
Mission—Guaynabo, Ntra. Sra. del Carmen. Bo. Frailes Llanos Sector Los Baez.
4—San Juan M. Vianney (1972). (Santo Cura de Ars). Rev. Florentino Sanz (Spain); Deacon Manuel Caban.
Mailing Address: & Res.: Calle-2-F-14, Urb. Hillside, San Juan, 00926. Tel: 787-790-2014.
Missions—La Milagrosa; Cristo del Perdon Parcelas Canejas, Bo. Camito Bajo; Dulce Nombre de Maria Bo. Dulce, Caimito Bajo; Ntra. Sra. del Carmen. Calle Fidalgo, Sector Corea, Bo. Caimito Bajo.
5—Maria Madre de la Misericordia (1995), Revs. Eliades Petit; Vicente Fernandez.
Mailing Address: Ave. Santa Maria #150, 00969. Tel: 787-790-1343.
Res., Carretera 833 Km. 13.2, Bo. Santa Rosa 3, 00969. Tel: 787-789-0090; Fax: 787-790-7596.
6—San Pedro Martir de Verona (1769), Rev. Msgr. Mario A. Guijarro de Corzo (Cuba); Rev. Johnny Cruz; Deacons Carlos Rivera Martinez; Gumersindo Negron Morales; Humberto Reyes Anciano; Angel Loyola Zayas; Gregory A. Guijarro; Jorge Encarnacion.
Mailing Address: P.O. Box 32, 00970-0032.
Res., Calle Tapia No. 5, 00970. Tel: 787-720-2361; 272-6739; 287-1791; Fax: 787-287-2833.
School—Alpierre St., Urb. Colimar, P.O. Box 2560, 00970. Tel: 787-720-2219; Fax: 787-272-8770. Mrs. Ivonne D. Carlo, Prin.; Gregory A. Guijarro, Prof. & Vice Dir.
Priests 2; Sisters 9; Lay Teachers 45; Students 610.
Catechesis/Religious Programs—Students 267.
7—Divino Nino Jesus (1992), Rev. Rodolfo Lamas (Cuba); Deacons Gerardo Comulada; Milton Valladares.
Mailing Address: PBM 143, HC-01, Box 29030, Caguas, 00725-8900. Tel: 787-720-0203; Fax: 787-720-0203. [JC]
Res., Urb. Lomas Del Sol, Calle Principal Y-6.
Missions—Guaynabo, San Rafael Arcangel, Barrio Camarones, Carr. #20, 00970.; Guaynabo, Jesus Nazareno, Bo. Mamey, 00970.; Guaynabo, El Buen Pastor, Carr. #1, 00970. Tel: 787-798-9596.
8—Nuestra Senora de la Paz (1992), Revs. Javier Esparza, SS.CC. (Spain); Jesus Vietes, SS.CC. (Spain).
Mailing Address: P.O. Box 225, 00970-0225. Tel: 787-789-2014.
Res., Bo. Guaraguao, 00970.
9—Sagrados Corazones (1968), Revs. Mateo Mateo, SS.CC.; Esteban Beltran, SS.CC.; Jose Ma. Garcia, SS.CC.; Deacons Ivan E. Dominguez; Ulpiano H. Rivera; Julio Toro.
Mailing Address: P.O. Box 3902, 00970-3902.
Res., Urb. Ponce de Leon, 208 Ave. Esmeralda, 00969. Tel: 787-720-6151; Fax: 787-720-6035.
School—Avenue A., Tel: 787-720-2585; Fax: 787-720-6035. Edith Casiano, Prin.
Sisters 3; Lay Teachers 35; Students 796.
Mission—Guaynabo, Virgen de la Paz. Bo. Cruz Melendez.
10—Santa Rosa de Lima (1973), Rev. Antonio Jose Vazquez-Colon; Deacon Filiberty De Jesus.
Mailing Address: & Res.: 16 Parque St., Barrio Amelia, 00965. Tel: 787-781-5855; 783-9731; Fax: 787-781-5855; 783-9731.
Mission—Barriada Vietnam, La Milagrosa.
Loiza, San Patricio (1719), Rev. Harold Stone, S.T.; Deacons Santiago Acosta; Marcos Penaloza; Pastor Perez; Manuel Pizarro.
Mailing Address: Box 504, 00772-0504.
Res., Calle Espiritu Santo #10, 00772. Tel: 787-876-2229; Fax: 787-876-7828.
Missions—Santa Rosa Bo. Pinones; Ntra. Sra. del Perpetuo Socorro Bo. La Torre; Santisima Trinidad Bo. Mediana Baja; San Antonio Bo. Las Cuevas,; Ntra. Sra. de Fatima Villa Canona; San Rafael. Villa Nevarez.
Santiago Apostol, El Mayor (1971), Revs. Francis J. Conkle, S.T.; Eduardo Sittinger, S.T.
Mailing Address: P.O. Box 118, 00772-0118.
Res., Carretera 187 Km. 6.0, Bo. Mediania Alta, 00772. Tel: 787-876-1879; Fax: 787-876-3060.
Missions—Parcelas Suarez, Ntra. Sra. Perpetuo Socorro; La Milagrosa Bo. El Jobos; La Providencia Bo. Mini Mine; N. Sra. De Fatima. Parcelas Vieques.
Luquillo, Madre del Redentor (1997), Rev. Luis H. Quinonez-Murillo (Colombia).
Mailing Address: P.O. Box 591, 00773—0591. Tel: 787-889-0733; Fax: 787-889-0733.
Res., Barrio Pitaya, Sector Casablanca, Carr. 183, Km. 1.5, 00773.
San Jose (1797), Rev. Msgr. Emilio Toro (Colombia); Deacons Jesus Ramos; Frank Rivera.
Mailing Address: P.O. Box 493, 00773-0493.
Res., Calle Soledad No. 15, fronte a Plaza De Recreo, 00773. Tel: 787-889-2590; Fax: 787-889-6180.
Missions—San Judas Bo. Mata de Platano; Ntra. Sra. del Cobre. Parcelas Fortuna.
Rio Grande, Cristo Rey (1970), Rev. P. Jose Emilio Cummings, C.M.
Mailing Address: P.O. Box 382, Palmer, 00721-0382.
Res., Calle Principal, #50, Palmer, 00721. Tel: 787-887-3552.
Missions—Palmer, Hato Rio Grande, La Milagrosa Bo. Carola, Parcela 69; Palmer, Rio Grande, Ntra. Sra. de la Providencia. Bloque S-1 #7.
Nuestra Senora del Carmen (1840), Revs. James Gil De La Madrid, M.SS.CC.; Jose Miguel Echevarria, M.SS.CC.; Deacons Jose Carrasquillo; Vidal Diaz; Juan Rodriguez.
Mailing Address: P.O. Box 845, 00745-0845.
Res., No. 9 del Carmen St., 00745. Tel: 787-887-2365; Fax: 787-888-3991.
School—Calle 14 Urb. Alturas de Rio Grande, P.O. Box 818, 00745. Tel: 787-887-4099. Mrs. Maria Guzman, Prin.
Missions—Rio Grande, Nuestra Senora de Fatima Bo. El Verde; Jardines de Rio Grande, Ntra. Sra. de Guadalupe; Rio Grande, San Pedro Bo. Bartolo; Alturas de Rio Grande, La Milagrosa. Calle 14.
San Francisco de Asis (1986), Rev. Yesid Ricardo Castellanos Ruiz (Colombia); Deacon Manuel Llanos.
Mailing Address: P.O. Box 1449, Bo. Malpica, 00745.
Res., Barrio Malpica, 00745. Tel: 787-888-5302; Fax: 787-888-5302.
Toa Alta
1—San Esteban, Protomartir (1997), Rev. Jose Antonio Carrion (Cuba); Deacon Jose Ramon Perez-Bracero.
Mailing Address: Letters 118, Box 391, 00954.
Res., Ave. Hato Tejas, Esq. Carretera 861, Km. 4.0, 00953. Tel: 787-799-2925; Fax: 787-279-8439.
Catechesis/Religious Programs—Students 120.
Convent—Santa Cruz Convent, Barrio Pajaros, Sector Los Frailes, 00953. Tel: 787-799-7950. Dominican Sisters of the Holy Cross of Amityville
Mailing Address: RR-5, Box 4103, Bayamon, 00956. Tel: 787-799-7950.
Chapel—Capilla Cristo Rey, Sector La Cuerda, Barrio Bucarabones, 00953.
2—San Fernando Rey (1751), Rev. Natividad Acevedo, O.P.; Deacons Jose Narvaez; Felipe Collazo; Pablo Irene.
Mailing Address: P.O. Box 63, 00954-0063.
Res., Calle Jose de Diego #10, 00953. Tel: 787-870-2585.
Mission—San Antonio. Rio Lajas, Dorado.
3—San Jose (1998), Rev. Calixto Soto (Colombia); Deacons Francisco Villamil; Enrique Laureano; Rafael Morales.
Mailing Address: P.O. Box 777, 00954-0777.
Res., Sector Jazmin, Carretera 823, Rio Lajas, Tel: 787-870-6415.
Missions—Ntra. Sra. del Camino Bo. Espinosa, Carretera #2, Dorado; S. Francisco De Asis Bo. Maguayo, Dorado; Cristo de los Milagros; Toa Alta, Santa Teresita Bo. Rio Lajas; Toa Alta, Sector Marzan, Sagrada Familia Bo. Rio Lajas; Toa Alta, Sector Los Mudos, Sagrado Corazon. Bo. Quebrada Arenas.
4—Nuestra Senora de la Medalla Milagrosa, Rev. Jairo Salazar (Colombia); Deacons German Hernandez; Santos Nieves.
Mailing Address: P.O. Box 335, 00954-0335.
Res., Bo. Quebrada Cruz, Carretera 824, Km. 3.8, 00954. Tel: 787-870-4090; Fax: 787-870-8125.
Missions—Toa Alta, Nuestra Senora del Carmen Sector El Cuco, Bo. Quebrada Cruz; Toa Alta, Sagrado Corazon de Jesus. Carretera 165 Km. 3.1, Quebrada Cruz.
5—N. Sra. de la Providencia (1988), Rev. Carlos Verdia, C.M.F.; Deacons Gregorio Cuevas; Jose C. Pacheco.
Mailing Address: P.O. Box 3836, Bayamon Gardens Sta., Bayamon, 00958-3836. Tel: 787-797-1618; Fax: 787-279-8439.
Res., Bo. Pinas, Carretera 861 Km. 5.6.
Missions—Sector Rincon, N. Sra. de Fatima; La Resurreccion Villa Del Rio, Bo. Pinas; Sector Del 7, N. Sra. Del Carmen; Sagrada Familia. Villa Juventud.
6—San Judas Tadeo, Rev. Juan De La Cruz Perez-Vasquez; Deacons Luis Rivera-Albino; Jose Diaz.
Mailing Address: RP-03, Box 9169, 00954.
Res., Carretera 804 Km. 1.2, Bo. Galateo Centro.
Missions—S. Martin De Porres Bo. Galateo; Toa Alta, Santa Teresa De Jesus. Bo. Quebrada Cruz.
Toa Baja
1—Nuestra Senora de Covadonga (1984), Rev. Francisco Arana (Spain); Deacon Efrain Narvaez.
Mailing Address: P.O. Box 9076, Bayamon, 00960-9076. Tel: 787-251-6466.
Res., Calle 13, 2-C-4, Esq. Calle 14, Urb. Covadonga, 00949.
Missions—Toa Baja, Ntra. Sra. de Lourdes Bo. Candelaria Arenas; Toa Baja, San Martin de Porres Bo. Kennedy; Toa Baja, Divino Nino Jesus. Urb. El Plantio.
2—Ntra. Sra. de la Candelaria (1960), Rev. Jose Dario Martinez Tobon (Colombia); Deacons Anselmo Miranda; Roberto Ortiz; Camildo Ortiz.
Mailing Address: P.O. Box 892, 00951-0892.
Res., Carret. No. 863, Km. 0.6, Bo. Pajaros, 00951. Tel: 787-251-0503.
Missions—Toa Alta, Cristo Rey Calle 10, Bo. Bucarabones; Toa Baja, Santa Maria La Mayor Carretera #2 R063, Bo. Macun; Toa Baja, Santisima Trinidad Urb. Las Colinas; Toa Baja, Buen Pastor. Urb. Sta. Maria.
3—Espiritu Santo (1965), Revs. Luis Gonzalez-Chao (Spain); Miguel Angel Trinidad-Fonseca; Deacons Pablo Maldonado; Jose Miranda.
Mailing Address: P.O. Box 50272, Levittown Sta., 00950.
Res., Paseo Damisela No. 1452, Urb. Levittown, 00950. Tel: 787-784-4805; Fax: 787-784-3051.
School—Paseo Damisela 1453, 00632. Tel: 787-784-0905; Fax: 787-795-5418. Rosa I. Perez, Prin.; Jose A. Ruiz, Dir.
Lay Teachers 16; Students 650.
Mission—Toa Baja, N. Sra. del Carmen, Calle Carmen, Bo. Palo Seco, 00759.
4—San Jose Obrero (1965) (Puerto Rican), Revs. Luis Lizarralde, O.F.M. (Spain); Dario Carrero, O.F.M., Supr.; Alfonso Guzman, O.F.M.; Deacon Ramon L. Colon.
Mailing Address: Box 173, Sabana Seca, 00952-0173.
Res., Carretera 2-R 866, Km. 3 #6, 00952. Tel: 787-784-1400; 795-3141; Fax: 787-261-3469.
Missions—Sector Los Bravos, Ntra. Sra. del Carmen; San Martin de Porres. Villa Marisol.
5—San Pedro Apostol (1745), Rev. Jose Maria Solano-Uribe (Colombia); Deacon Gerardo Trujillo.
Mailing Address: P.O. Box 513, 00951-0513.
Res., 45 Las Flores St., 00951. Tel: 787-794-1327.
Catechesis/Religious Programs—Students 260.
Missions—St. Teresita Calle Quintero; Ntra. Sra. de Guadalupe Calle Crisantemo, Parcela 137-A; San Jose Calle San Jose #303; San Pablo Calle Universo, Parcela #9, Toaville; La Virgen de la Providencia. Bo. Villa Calma.
6—Santisima Trinidad (1978), Rev. Juan M. Beristain (Spain); Deacons Eusebio Jaca; Justo Ortiz; Edwin Negron.
Mailing Address: Apartado 50378, Levittown, 00950-0378. Tel: 787-784-2889; Fax: 787-261-2911.
Res., Ave. Los Dominicos, Esquina Dr. Sanchez Cardona, Levittown, 00950. Tel: 787-261-2716; 784-2889.
Trujillo Alto
1—San Bartolome (1988), Rev. P. Jose Alcocer Corbaton, M.SS.CC. (Spain); Deacon Alberto Gomez.
Mailing Address: & Res.: Ciudad Universitaria, X-1 Calle 16, Urb., 00976. Tel: 787-755-0120.
2—San Pio X (1971), Rev. Alberto Lopez; Deacon Julio Sanchez.
Mailing Address: P.O. Box 631, St. Just, 00978.
Res., Carretera 848, K-1.4, Bo. Sain Just, 00978. Tel: 787-761-5040.
Mission—Rio Piedras, N. Sra. Del Rosario. Calle Lirio, Esq. Orquidea, Urb. Round Hill.
3—Santa Cruz (1801), Rev. Leonardo Rodriguez-Ochoa; Deacons Alfredo Aponte; Domingo Vargas.
Mailing Address: Box 1808, Truijillo Alto, 00977-1808.
Res., J. Diaz St., #515, 00977. Tel: 787-761-0507; Fax: 787-755-3065.
4—San Francisco de Asis (1992), Deacons Hector Rivera; Alfredo Aponte; William Rios.
Mailing Address: P.O. Box 1316, 00977-1316.
Res., Parcela Ramon T. Colon, Calle 2, Parcelas #32, Quebrada Negrito, 00977. Tel: 787-748-5584.
Missions—Espiritu Santo Bo. Kennedy Hills, Carretera 181 Km. 10; San Jose de la Montana Bo.

Sabana, Carretera #181 R-851; La Inmaculada Concepcion. Bo. Talanco, Carretera #181 R-852.

5—BIENVENTURADA VIRGEN MARIA DE LOURDES (1975), Rev. Pedro Luis Reyes Lebron; Deacons Oscar Sanchez; Edwin Hernandez-Ralat; Pablo Torres. Mailing Address: P.O. Box 1081, 00977. Res., Santuario, Gruta de Lourdes, Carretera 876 Km. 1.6, Barrio Cuevas, 00977. Tel: 787-761-0571; Fax: 787-761-0571. [JC]

6—SAN JUDAS TADEO (1980), Rev. Miguel Pons; Deacons Jose Baez; Jose Ramon Oliveras. Mailing Address: Apartado 1535, 00977-1535. Res., Calle 7, Esq. 8 Urbanizacion El Conquistador, 00977-1535. Tel: 787-755-5993.
Catechesis/Religious Programs—Students 75.
Missions—Trujillo Alto, El Divino Pastor Carretera 844 Km. 0.2, Parcelas Carraizo; Trujillo Alto, Ntra. Sra. del Carmen. Carretera 175, Bo. Capraizo Alto.

Chaplains of Public Institutions

SANTURCE. *Ashford Presbyterian Community Hospital* 1451 Ave. Ashford, Condado, Tel: 787-725-8820; 724-8320. Rev. Msgr. Jesus Santoalla Tel: 787-724-7780.
Doctors Community Hospital 1395 Calle San Rafael, Tel: 787-723-2950. Rev. Manuel Gamarra Tel: 787-723-5998.
Hospital Del Nino San Jorge 255 Calle San Jorge, Tel: 787-727-1000. Rev. Eddie Rivera Tel: 787-722-4158.
Hospital Pavia-Santurce 1462 Calle Asia, Tel: 787-727-6060. Rev. Evaristo Olivares, C.M. Tel: 787-727-3963.

Resident Chaplains:
Reverend Monsignors—
Valdes, Angel, Hospital del Maestro, Hato Rey
Reverend Fathers—
Mairal, Jose Ma. Lopez, Hogar de Sta. Teresa Jornet, Bo. Cupey, Rio Piedras, Trujillo Alto, PR
Ortega, Ovidio, Hogar de Ntra. Sra. de la Providencia, Ave. Ponce de Leon, Puerta de Tierra, San Juan, PR

On Duty Outside the Archdiocese:
Reverend Fathers—
Del Valle, Tomas, New York
McCoy, Floyd, Mayagueo Diocese
Parello, Joseph J., St. Patrick Church, Smithtown, NY
Roldan, Juan, Caguas Diocese
Sutil, Florencio, Spain
Torres, Ivan, New York

Graduate Studies:
Reverend Fathers—
Capacetti, Luis O., Rome
Hernandez, Guillermo, Washington
Mejias, Carlos Ortiz, Rome
Toro, Carlos Perez, Rome
Torres, William, Madrid

Military Services:
Reverend Monsignors—
Matienzo, Rafael, (National Guard). Tel: 787-782-4176
Reverend Fathers—
Castille, Jorge Jo, (Army)
Tirado, Orlando, C.M., (Air Force)

Detention Ministries:
Reverend Fathers—
Ferrer, Miguel, San Fernando Parish, Carolina, P.R. Tel: 787-767-9600, Ext. 2331; 2312

Retired:
Reverend Monsignors—
Cruz, Remberto
Ortiz, Tomas Maisonet
Valdes, Angel Valdes
Reverend Fathers—
Coroztieta, Jose Madoz
Cruz, Gilbert J. (Spain)
Diaz, Alvaro
Egurrola, Vicente
Gonzalez, Cruz Gil
Marks, Teodoro Gray
Mena, Francisco De Carlo
Mendez, Jose R. Ferendez
Nuin, Jeronimo Sola
Rivera, Leoncio Quijones
Rivera Ribo, Francisco J.
Rodriquez, Josi Fuentes
Sanz, Florentino, (Spain)

Permanent Deacons:
Acosta Osorio, Santiago
Aldarondo Galvan, Elidio
Alicea Rivera, Angel L.
Alvarez Granada, Enrique
Alvarez Torano, Julio
Amador Melendez, Luis F.
Andino Cintron, Virgilio
Andino Santos, Manuel
Aponte Diaz, Alfredo
Araya Brenes, Rafael F
Araya Fernandez, Antonio
Arevalo, Pedro Nel
Arroyo Acevedo, Americo
Avila Rodriguez, Cesar
Ayala Garay, Gregorio
Baez Cotto, Pedro J.
Baez Navarro, Jose
Balasquide Vargas, Eugenio
Bermudez Martes, Jose A.
Berrios Rodriguez, Ildefonso
Birriel Rodriguez, Jose
Caban Roman, Manuel
Caceres Paredes, Emilio
Calderon Rodriguez, Anthony
Camacho Rivera, Manuel
Carmona, Eduardo
Carrasquillo Rodz, Jose M.
Casaigne Ayala, Jose L.
Casanova Calzada, Jorge
Castillo Lopez, Jose M.
Claudio Flores, Pedro
Collazo Montalvo, Felipe
Colon Andino, Gumersindo
Colon Colon, Rafael
Colon Febres, Ismael
Colon Hernandez, Ramon L.
Colon Mallen, Vicente
Colon Marrero, Miguel
Colon Melendez, Enrique
Colon Ramos, Luis
Colon Rivera, Francisco
Comulada Pabon, Gerardo
Cordero Mercado, Luis
Cosme Varela, Nicomedes
Costa, Pedro Tomas
Cotto Velez, Felix
Cruz De Choudens, Hector M.
Cruz Ortiz, Francisco
Cruz Vazquez, Jose R.
Cuevas Alfonso, Martin
Cuevas Nieves, Gregorio
D'Auria, Ricardo
De Jesus Robles, Filiberty
De La Sota Pumarejo, Miguel
De Leon Sanchez, Hilario
De Varona Juarez, Abel
Del Rio Del Rio, Anastasio
Del Rio Ortiz, Luis O.
Del Rio Pitre, Luis
Del Valle Gonzalez, Reinaldo
Delgado Maldonado, Alfonso
Diaz Diaz, Miguel A.
Diaz Miranda, Ernie P.
Diaz Rivera, Jose
Diaz Rivera, Vidal
Diaz Rosa, Santiago
Diaz Sifonte, Agapito
Domenech, Bienvenido
Dominguez, Ivan
Echegaray Martinez, Luis
Encarnacion Torres, Jorge
Estrada Galarza, Martin
Falcon Matos, Jose E.
Figueroa Acevedo, Andres
Figueroa Carrasquillo, Raul
Figueroa Dominguez, Nelson
Figueroa Sanchez, Juan
Flores Torres, Pedro
Franco Torres, Porfirio
Garcia Cosme, Aureliz
Garcia Diaz, Enemias
Giierbolini Santiago, Fco.
Gomez Maldonado, Alberto
Gomez Soto, William
Gonzalez Quintana, Antonio
Gonzalez Rodz, Eduardo
Gonzalez Rosario, Pablo
Gonzalez Rosario, Pedro
Gonzalez Segarra, George
Guijarro, Gregory A.
Guiven Flores, Cesar H.
Guzman Rosario, Jose A.
Hernandez, German
Hernandez, Marino
Hernandez Adorno, Fco.
Hernandez Jorge, Jose A.
Irene Vargas, Pablo
Jaca Hernandez, Eusebio
LaSanta Arroyo, Vicente
LaTorre, Santiago
Laureano, Enrique
Laureano Rvera, Juan
LLanos Calderon, Enrique
Longueira, Ricardo
Lopez Cepero, Victor
Lopez Collazo, Jesus
Lopez Echevarria, Felix
Loyola Zayas, Angel A.
Lugo Cordero, Casiano
Lugo Lugo, Euripides
Lugo Martinez, Ildefonso
Maldonado Febo, Pablo J.
Maldonado Lopez, Eliecer
Marin Mingaro, Louis
Marrero Nieves, Miguel A.
Marrero Picorneli, Jose M.
Martinez Duran, Ricardo L
Martinez Pacini, Fco.
Martinez Stgo., Candido
Matthews, Wayne
Medina Nunez, Bernardino
Medina Rivera, Luis A.
Mejias Nunez, Gilberto
Melendez Lozano, Juan R.
Mendez Santiago, Miguel
Mendia Colon, Roberto
Mercado Vila, Nicanor
Merced De La Paz, Victor
Merino Raposo, Latino
Mestre Sanchez, Ibrahim
Miranda, Anselmo
Miranda Berrios, Pedro
Miranda Cruz, Jose
Montanez, Justo
Montes Quevedo, Luis J.
Morales, Rafael
Morales Gonzalez, Jose A.
Morales Morales, Angel
Morales Rdz., Carlos R.
Morales Rdz., Rene
Narvaez Hndz., Jose R.
Narvaez Stgo., Efraim
Navedo Rdz., Luis A.
Negron, Gumersindo
Negron Rivera, Edwin
Negron Santana, Hector
Nerys Gonzalez, Jose A.
Nieves Carbona, Luis M.
Nieves Nieves, Martin
Nieves Vazquez, Santos
Nunez, Pedro Arcadio
O'Neill Rosario, Luis R.
Ocasio Glz., Domingo
Oliveras Rivera, Jose
Oquendo Serrano, Angel
Orozco, Gaspar
Ortiz Alvarado, Justo
Ortiz Collazo, FCO
Ortiz Core, Ramon L.
Ortiz Mangual, Julio
Ortiz Rdz., Jacinto
Ortiz Rosado, Camildo
Ortiz Rosado, Roberto
Ortiz Rosario, Rafael
Ortiz Toro, Julio
Oyola Figueroa, Angel L.
Pabon Hernandez, Angel
Pabon Molina, Angel A.
Pacheco Diaz, Jose C.
Padilla Vega, Isaias
Pappeterra Arthur, Jose A.
Pena Gonzalez, Jose
Penaloza Lacen, Marcos
Perez Ayala, Edwin
Perez Bracero, Jose R.
Perez Del Valle, Juan B.
Perez Fuentes, Raul
Perez Gonzales, Ignacio
Perez Gonzalez, Luis R.
Perez Guadalupe, Jose
Perez Pizarro, Pastor
Perez Silva, Juan B.
Pineiro Nazario, Carlos
Pizarro Davila, Angel M.
Quintana Medina, Antonio
Ralat Saiz, Carlos
Ramirez Abreu, Tomas
Ramirez Stgo., Ferdinand
Ramos Rodz., Ramon L.
Ramos Torres, Jesus R.
Reyes Anciano, Humberto
Reyes Crespo, Rafael
Reyes Matos, Manuel
Reyes Torres, Victor
Rios Aponte, William
Rios Arroyo, Jose A.
Rios Torres, Vicente
Rivera, Enrique
Rivera, Luis Marcial
Rivera, Prudencio I.
Rivera, Ramon L.
Rivera, Ulpiano
Rivera Albino, Luis
Rivera Archilla, Pedro
Rivera Baez, Eugenio
Rivera Collazo, Angel

Rivera De Jesus, Efigenio
Rivera Diaz, Hector R.
Rivera Estremera, Felipe
Rivera Fuentes, Jorge I.
Rivera Garcia, Edwin
Rivera Lopez, Hector M.
Rivera Martinez, Carlos
Rivera Matos, Frank
Rivera Mojica, Jose D.
Rivera Negron, Ernesto
Rivera Rios, Cristobal
Rivera Rivera, Jose R.
Rivera Rodz., Presbitero
Rivera Torres, Jose A.
Robiles Morales, Jose L.
Rodriguez, Luis A.
Rodriguez Acevedo, Ramon
Rodriguez Marrero, Romulo
Rodriguez Martinez, Jose
Rodriguez Mldz., Orlando
Rodriguez Perazza, Jose R.
Rodriguez Rdgz., Wilfredo
Rodriguez Rodz., Jose M.
Rodriguez Rodz., Juan
Rodriguez Serrano, William
Roman Del Valle, Miguel
Roman Maldonado, Jose M.
Roman Maldonado, Miguel A.
Rondon Martinez, Angel
Rosario Rodz., Crescencio
Rubio Roman, Silverio
Sanabria Lopez, Rafael
Sanchez, Oscar
Sanchez, Samuel Aldjandro
Sanchez Munoz, Orlando
Sanchez Ortiz, Julio
Santiago, Antonio
Santiago Correa, Ramon
Santos Bello, Juan R.
Santos Negron, Marcos A.
Soto Mirando, Nelson
Suarez, Ibrahim
Suarez, Israel
Toro Toro, Obed E.
Torres Acevedo, Pablo
Torres Burgos, Miguel A.
Torres Diaz, Eugenio
Torres Labauld, Jose A.
Torres Rodriguez, Dionilo
Torres Torres, Jose A.
Totti Lugo, Benjamin
Trujullo Cardona, Gerardo
Ubarri Mestres, Juan
Valazquez Reyes, Rafael
Valladares, Milton
Valle Valle, Esteban
Vargas Ramos, Domingo
Vazquez, Jose R.
Vazquez Garcia, Luis A.
Vazquez Rosario, Noel A.
Vega Vega, Jose P.
Velazquez Gonzalez, Jose L.
Velez, Gregorio
Velez Roman, Miguel
Villamil Marrero, Fco. E.

INSTITUTIONS LOCATED IN THE ARCHDIOCESE

[A] COLLEGES & UNIVERSITIES

SAN JUAN. *Sacred Heart University*. Calle Rosales esq. San Antonio, Parada 26 1/2, Santurce.
E-mail: www.sagrado.edu
Mailing Address: P.O. Box 12383, 00914-0383. Tel: 787-728-1515.
E-mail: www.sagrado.edu
The University has the following Departments and Programs: Departments of Communications, Humanities, Business Administration, Education, Natural Sciences and Social Sciences. The Graduate Programs include: Masters of Business Administration in Management of Systems Information, Masters of Arts & Communications, Masters of Art & Education, Masters of Occupational Nursing, Medical Technology Certificate.
Governing Board: Mr. Alberto Paraccini, Pres. Bd. of Trustees; Dr. Jose Jaime Rivera, Pres.; Dr. Cesar A. Rey, Dean of Academic Affairs; Ms. Lourdes Beltran, Dean of Admin.; Sr. Sororro Julia, Dean of Devel.; Dr. Manuel De Jesus, Assoc. Dean Student Affairs; Dr. Isabel Yamin, Dir. Of Humanities; Maria T. Martinez, Prof. & Dir. of Communications; Dr. Adalexis Rios, Dir. of Educ.; Yezmin Hernandez, Prof. & Dir. of Bus. Admin.; Dr. Maria B. Rodriguez, Dir. of Natural Sciences; Fernando Medina, Dir. of Social Sciences; Hylsa Silva Janer, Lic. & Legal Counsel; Ms. Hilda Mendez, Registrar; Daniel Rodriguez, Prof. & Dir. of Admin.; Mr. Luis A. Quiles, Dir. of Student Fin. Aid; Norma T. Diaz, Dir. of Campus Ministry. Faculty 136; Total Enrollment 5,234.

BAYAMON. *Bayamon Central University*, Avenida Zaya Verde, Bo. Hato Tejas, P.O. Box 1725, 00960-1725. Tel: 787-786-3030. The University has the following Departments and Programs: Humanites; Business Administration; National Sciences; Education; Graduate Studies; Adult Education Program; Student Support Services; Upward Bound.
Governing Board: Rev. Mario Rodriguez-leon, Pres. Council of Founders; Dr. Hermenegildo Ortiz, Pres. Bd. of Trustees.
Administration: Dr. Anibal Colon-Rosado, Pres.; Dr. Blanco Berio, Dean Academic Affairs; Mr. Mario Medina, Dean Admin. & Finances; Mr. Yanius Alvarado, Dean Student Affairs; Dr. Modesto Fernandez, Dir. Humanities; Dr. Robert Turner, Dir. Education; Norma Moctezuma, Prof. & Dir. Natural Sciences; Mr. Angel Berrios, Dir. Institutional Devel.; Mr. Enrique Arias, Esq., Legal Counsel; Antonio Suarez, Dir. of Human Resources; Mr. Victor Colon, Registrar; Mrs. Christine Hernandez, Dir. Admissions; Mr. Henry Miranda, Dir. Student Financial Aid; Mr. Carlos Altamirano, Dir. Academic Resource Ctr.
Faculty: Revs. Felix A.P. Struik, O.P.; Luis Espinel, O.P.; Enrique Oria, O.Carm.; Angel Diaz Caceres; Mario Rodriguez Leon, O.P.; Angel Dario Carrero; Teodoro Veerkamp, O.P.; Marcelino Romero, C.M.F.; Domingo Aller, O.S.A.; Jorge Macias, C.S.S.R.; Jose Diman Soberal; Manuel Soler Pala, M.SS.CC. Lay Teachers 143; Total Enrollment 3,320.

[B] ELEMENTARY & HIGH SCHOOLS

SAN JUAN, P.R. *Colegio Corazon De Maria*. (Archdiocesan School), Ferrer, Ferrer St, Santiago, Igesias, 00922. Tel: 787-783-3275. Priests 1; Lay Teachers 18; Students 349.

Colegio Maria Auxiliadora, 2273 Eduardo Conde, 00915. Tel: 787-726-8288; Fax: 787-727-6497. Sr. Margarita Fontan, F.M.A., Prin. Sisters 7; Lay Teachers 18; Students 364.

Colegio Parvulos Inmaculada Corazon de Maria, 263 San Sebastian St., 00901. Tel: 787-722-1334; Fax: 787-724-2043. Sr. Cecilia Serrano, H.C. Sisters 5; Lay Teachers 8; Students 146.

Cristo Rey. (Archdiocesan School). Tel: 809-767-0922; Fax: 809-764-9164. Sr. Irene Martin, H.T.F. Sisters 2; Lay Teachers 15; Students 250.

Nuestra Senora De Belen. (Archdiocesan School). Tel: 787-792-3115; Fax: 787-781-4920. Eleonor Marrero, Prin.; Maira Mendez Barreto, Dir.; Lay Teachers 73; Students 853.

Nuestra Senora de la Altagracia. (Archdiocesan School). Tel: 809-763-7755; Fax: 809-756-5195. Mrs. Mirta Alicea, Prin.; Mr. Angel Castillo, Dir.

San Jorge. (Archdiocesan School), 1701 Colon St., 00911. Tel: 787-722-3182. Mrs. Maritza Rosario, Prin.; Vanessa Valdez, Dir. Brothers 1; Lay Teachers 70; Students 700.

BAYAMON. *Colegio Ntra. Sra. del Rosario*, Calle 5, AA-7, Repto. Valencia, 00619. Tel: 787-798-5100. Sr. Ma. Ana Jimenez Maldonado, O.P., Dir.; Elba I. Soto, Prin. Students 300.

Colegio Santa Rosa, Calle Marti 15, P.O. Box 6032, 00619. Tel: 787-785-1195; Fax: 787-740-0115. Mrs. Luz Valentin, Prin. Priests 1; Lay Teachers 30; Total Enrollment 607.

Colegio Santa Rosa Elemental, 191 Comerio St., 00619. Tel: 787-785-0381. Mrs. Mana A. Rodriguez Reyes, Prin. Sisters 2; Brothers 1; Lay Teachers 19; Students 265.

Escuela Archdiocesan Superior Catolica de Bayamon, Jazmin Esq. Millones, 2na. Ext. Lomas Verdes, P.O. Box 4225, 00956. Tel: 787-798-5260; 798-2329; 798-2747; Fax: 787-798-2620.
E-mail: escb@crcnet.net
Web site: familyeducation.com/pr
Mrs. Maria C. de Marxuach, Dir. & Prin. Students 621.

Sagrada Familia. (Archdiocesan School). Mailing Address: P.O. Box 4153, Bayamon Garden Sta., 00961. Mendez Bosque, Prin.; Rev. Alvaro Silva, Dir. Lay Teachers 14; Students 301.

Santo Tomas de Aquino. Mailing Address: P.O. Box 1557, 00960-1557. Tel: 787-786-5015 (High School); 785-3838 (Elementary); Fax: 787-786-5015 (H.S.); 798-0180 (Elem.). P.O. Box 4098, 00958-1098. Mrs. Carmen J. Acosta, Elem. Prin.; Miss Micaela Hurtado, H.S. Prin. Lay Teachers 50; Students 1,311.

CANTERA. *Colegio San Juan Bosco*. (Archdiocesan School), Carpenter Rd. Rev. Nicolas Navarro, Dir.; Mrs. Lissette M. Ruiz. Priests 2; Religious 15; Lay Teachers 12; Students 288.

CAROLINA. *Colegio Maria Auxiliadora*, Box 797, 00986. Tel: 787-762-0350. Lelis R. Iglesias, Prin. Sisters 5; Lay Teachers 23; Students 1,592.

GUAYNABO. *Colegio Marista*, Alturas de Torrimar, 00969. Tel: 787-789-2186; 789-2187; Fax: 787-720-7020.
E-mail: marista1@prtc.net
Bro. Ricardo Herrero, Dir. Priests 1; Brothers 5; Lay Teachers 79; Students 1,320.

Colegio Ntra. Sra. De La Caridad, Carretera Estatal #19, X-19, Villa Caparra., 00966. Tel: 787-781-8835. St. Joseph of the Mountain Sisters. Mother Josefina Jimenez, S.J., Prin. Sisters 9; Lay Teachers 14; Students 195.

HATO REY. *Colegio Lourdes*, 87 Mayaguez St., 00917. Tel: 787-767-6106; 756-5436; Fax: 787-767-5282.
E-mail: clourdes@coqui.net
Web site: colegiolourdes.com
Mailing Address: P.O. Box 190847, San Juan, 00919-0847. Sr. Maria Paz Asiain, O.P., Dir. Sisters 5; Lay Teachers 40; Students 690.

RIO PIEDRAS. *Colegio La Milagrosa*, 107 De Diego Ave., 00925. Tel: 787-765-6114. Sr. Maria Flores., H.C., Prin. Sisters 8; Lay Teachers 15; Students 467.

Colegio Nuestra Senora De La Providencia. (Girls), Ave. San Ignacio #1358, Urb. Altamesa, 00921. Tel: 787-781-7506. Spanish Mercedarian Sisters. Sr. Lourdes Martinez, Prin. Sisters 7; Lay Teachers 46; Students 925.

Colegio Nuestra Senora Del Carmen, R.R. 2, Box 15, 00928. Tel: 787-761-8010; Fax: 787-748-2505.
E-mail: melisea@coqui.net
Sr. Arly Medina, Dir. Principals: Lisette Torres; Liliana Santiago. Sisters 7; Lay Teachers 32; Students 516.

Colegio San Jose. Tel: 787-751-8177; Fax: 787-767-1746.
E-mail: sanjose@yungue.net
Web site: www.csj-pr.org
Mailing Address: Box 21300, San Juan, 00928-1300. Bro. Francisco T. Gonzalez, S.M., M.D., Dir. & Prin. Brothers 4; Lay Teachers 46; Students 569.

SANTURCE. *Academia Sagrado Corazon*. Mailing Address: Box 11368, Fernandez Juncos Sta., 00910. Tel: 787-721-3300. Rev. Francisco Quinones, Spiritual Dir.; Mrs. Alma de la Vega, Prin. Lay Teachers 37; Students 410.

Colegio La Inmaculada, Stop 26, Ave. Ponce De Leon #1711, 00909. Tel: 787-727-6673; Fax: 787-727-5330. Sr. Mary Arzuaga, H.C., Dir.; Mr. Jose Acevedo, Prin. Sisters 10; Lay Teachers 25; Students 430.

Colegio Sagrada Familia. (Archdiocesan School), Urb. Llorens Torres. Tel: 787-726-1742; Fax: 787-726-0718. Ines Elias, Prin.; Vanessa Valdez, Dir. Lay Teachers 6; Students 164.

TRUJILLO ALTO. *Santa Cruz*. (Archdiocesan School), Dr. Fernandez St., #203, 00977. Tel: 787-761-1100; Fax: 787-761-1100. Sr. Maria Ramon Santiago, O.S.F., Dir.; Mrs. Ana L. Monzon de Matos, Prin. Sisters 3; Lay Teachers 25; Students 430.

[C] SPECIAL SCHOOLS AND SEMINARIES

SAN JUAN. *Instituto Psicopedagogico De P.R.*, P.O. Box 363744, 00936-3744. Tel: 787-782-4640; 783-5431; Fax: 787-792-3610. Jesus Nazarene Sisters. Mother Isabel Lauado, Supr. Beds 130; Sisters 4; Patients assisted annually 129.

Seminario Carmelita, Calle Loiza 2059, 2059. Tel: 787-726-2655.

Seminario Menor San Jose, Demetrio O'Dally St. 1000 Country Club, 00924. Tel: 787-768-3157; Fax: 787-752-2410. Rev. Freddy Alecio, Rector. Priests 1; Lay Teachers 2.

BAYAMON. *Casa Beato Pedro Donders*, Carretera 864 #127, Hato Tejas, 00959. Tel: 787-785-2867.

Centro Vocational Claretiano, Urb. Cana, Calle 24 esq. Calle 23. Tel: 787-797-8230.

Convento Del Santisimo Rosario, Calle Capitan Correa N-27, Reparto Flamingo, P.O. Box 1968, 00960-1942. Tel: 787-785-6542.

Seminario Agustiniano Sto. Tomas De Villanueva, Carpetera 830 km 5.1, Camino Los Muleros, Barrio Santaolaya. Mailing Address: P.O. Box 3948, 00958. Tel: 787-797-0708; Fax: 787-797-9953.

Seminario Misionero del Espiritu Santo, Calle Zaya Verde #44-A, Hato Tejas, 00959. Tel: 787-786-8231; Fax: 787-787-2398.
E-mail: opgcssp@caribe.net
Rev. Osualdo Perez Gonzalez, C.S.Sp., M.Div., Prin. Supr.

CATANO. *Prenoviciado Salesiano*, Ave. Flor Del Valle, Bloque BB #108, Urb. Las Vegas. Mailing Address: P.O. Box 567, 00963-8163. Rev. Adan Merrero, S.D.B.

DORADO. *Estudiantado Pasionista*, Carpetera 695 km. 3.3, Sector Los Puertos, Barrio Higuillar, P.O. Box 593, 00646-0593. Tel: 787-278-0517.

GUAYNABO. *Casa Padre Damian*, Calle P. Damian Final, Aptdo. 225, 00970-0225. Tel: 787-789-2014.

RIO PIEDRAS. *Fraternidad San Lorenzo de Brindis (Postnovitiate)*, P.O. Box 21350, 00928-1350. Tel: 787-765-8247; Fax: 787-763-9832.

Jesuit Novitiate, 2106 Calle Jose Fidalgo Diaz, Sector Chapero, Bo. Caimito Bajo. Tel: 787-790-3557; Fax: 787-790-3162.
E-mail: otorres@icepr.com
Mailing Address: R.R. 9, Buzon 5348, San Juan, 00926-9675. Revs. P.L. Orlando Torres, S.J., Master of Novices & Supr.; P. Jorge Ferrer, S.J.; John F. Talbot, S.J.; P. Fabian, Rodriguez, S.J. Priests 4.

Seminario Mayor Regional San Juan Bautista, Ave. De Diego No. 930, Urb. La Riviera, 00922-1714. Tel: 787-273-8090; 783-0645; Fax: 787-783-0645.
E-mail: seminary@coqui.net
Mailing Address: P.O. Box 11714, San Juan, P.R., 00922-1714. Revs. Leonardo J. Rodriguez, Rector; Antonio Portalatin, Vice Rector. Priests 9; Brothers 1; Lay Teachers 10; Total Staff 20.

TRUJILLO ALTO. *Fraternidad Santa Maria de Los Angeles*, Expreso Trujillo Alto, Km. 1 Hm. 1. Tel: 787-761-8060; Fax: 787-755-8998. Mailing Address: Aptdo. 1865, 00977-1865.

[D] SPECIAL CENTERS

SAN JUAN. *Renovacion Conyugal*, 576 Calle Eddie Gracia, 00918. Tel: 787-751-6001; Fax: 787-766-1363.
E-mail: jarsi@prtc.net
Rev. Jorge Ambert, S.J., Dir.

Santa Ana Chapel. Perpetual Adoration (Temporarily Closed For Renovations), Calle Tetuan 203, Box 763, 00902. Tel: 787-725-7734. Rev. Raul Saez, Rector.

PUERTO NUEVO. *San Gabriel School For The Deaf*, Prolongacion Calle 19 NE. Tel: 787-783-3455; Fax: 787-781-3770. Mailing Address: P.O. 360347, San Juan, 00936-0347. Sr. Amparo Blasco, Dir.

RIO PIEDRAS. *Centro Capuchino*, Expreso Trujillo Alto, Km. 1 Hm. 1. Tel: 787-761-8410. Mailing Address: Apto. 1865, 00977-1865. Rev. Jaime Perez Munoz, O.F.M.Cap., Dir.

Centro Universitario Catolico, 10 Mariana Bracetti St., 00925-2201. Tel: 787-767-3348.
E-mail: el_cue@hotmail.com
Revs. Jose A. Borges, S.J., Dir.; Fernando Gomez, S.J., Coop.

[E] CLINICS, HEALTH CENTERS

SAN JUAN. *Casa La Providencia, Inc.* Tel: 787-725-5358; Fax: 787-725-0058.
E-mail: info@casalaprovidencia.org
Web site: casalaprovidencia.org
Mailing Address: P.O. Box 9020614, 00902-0614. Tel: 787-725-5358; Fax: 787-725-0058.
For a complete listing, refer to the Hospitals section.

Centro Medico de P.R., Calle 10 #1030, Puerto Nuevo, 00920. Apdo. 347, 00936. Tel: 787-763-7272
For a complete listing, refer to the Hospitals section.

VA Medical Center, One Veterans Plaza, 00927-5800. Tel: 787-641-7582, Ext. 12167
For a complete listing, refer to the Hospitals section.

RIO PIEDRAS. *Hospital del Maestro*, Calle Flamboyanes #218, Hyde Park, 00929. Tel: 787-763-8383
For a complete listing, refer to the Hospitals section.

[F] HOMES AND RESIDENCES

SAN JUAN. *Casa La Providencia*, Blvd. Del Valle 2000. Tel: 787-725-5358 Mailing Address: P.O. Box 614, 00902.
For a complete listing, refer to the Special Care Facilities section.

Hogar Fatima, Floral Park, 20 C. Matienzo Citron, 00919. Tel: 787-250-6323
For a complete listing, refer to the Special Care Facilities section.

BAYAMON. *Hogar Del Nino "Elave Maria"*, Carpetera 861, km 2.0, Bo. Pajaros Americanos. Tel: 787-797-2382; 279-3003 Mailing Address: P.O. Box 3367, 00958-3367.
For a complete listing, refer to the Special Care Facilities section.

Hogar Escuela Sop Maria Rafaela, Carpetera 871, km 1.0, Bo. El Volcan, Hato Tejas. Tel: 787-785-9586; Fax: 787-785-9586 Mailing Address: P.O. Box 3024, 00960.
For a complete listing, refer to the Special Care Facilities section.

Hogar Fatima, Ave. Santa Juanita Final, Camino Esteban Cruz Mailing Address: P.O. Box 4228 Bayamon Garden Sta., 00958-1218.
For a complete listing, refer to the Special Care Facilities section.

CANOVANAS. *Hogar Teresa Toda*, P.O. Box 868, 00729. Tel: 787-886-2060
For a complete listing, refer to the Special Care Facilities section.

DORADO. *Santuario del Espiritu Santo*, Box 187, 00646-0187. Tel: 787-796-2798.
E-mail: orlycssp@coqui.net
For a complete listing, refer to the Special Care Facilities section.

PUERTA DE TIERRA. *Asylum For The Aged and Infirm*, Hogar de la Providencia, Stop 5, 00906. Tel: 787-722-1331
For a complete listing, refer to the Special Care Facilities section.

RIO PIEDRAS. *Asylum For Orphan Girls*, 107 Jose de Diego St. S., 00925. Tel: 787-765-6114
For a complete listing, refer to the Special Care Facilities section.

Centro N. Sra. de la Providencia, R.F.D. #2, Box 16T, 00928. Tel: 787-761-0273
For a complete listing, refer to the Special Care Facilities section.

Centro Santa Luisa, Carpetera 842, Camino Los Romeros km 1.9, Bo. Caimito. Tel: 787-720-2764; Fax: 787-731-7795 Mailing Address: RR6, Box 9492 San Juan, 00926.
For a complete listing, refer to the Special Care Facilities section.

Hogar Carmelitano, Urb. San Martin, 00924. Tel: 787-769-6510; 769-3110; Fax: 787-768-1240
For a complete listing, refer to the Special Care Facilities section.

Hogar Santa Teresa Jornet for the Aged, Cupey Alto, Km. 3, Hm. 8, Box 21012, 00928. Tel: 787-761-5805; Fax: 787-755-5575
For a complete listing, refer to the Special Care Facilities section.

SANTURCE. *Casa Manuel Fernandez Juncos*, Calle Villa Verde Esq. Refugio, PDA 11, Miramar. Tel: 787-724-2904;725-6328; Fax: 787-724-0908 Mailing Address: P.O. Box 9020163 San Juan, 00902-0163.
For a complete listing, refer to the Special Care Facilities section.

TOA ALTA. *Hogar Santisima Trinidad*, Lote A y Loted, km 7.0, Bo Mucarabones. Tel: 787-799-6208 Mailing Address: P.O. Box 3367 Bayamon, 00958-3367.
For a complete listing, refer to the Special Care Facilities section.

[G] PERSONAL PRELATURES

GUAYNABO. *Opus Dei*. (Prelature of the Holy Cross and Opus Dei), Region of Puerto Rico of the Prelature, A-35, Villa Caparra, 00966. Tel: 787-783-6206. Very Rev. Vicente Ariza, Reg. Vicar; Revs. Alfredo Gastalver; Gonzalo Diaz; Martin Llambias; Jaime Guixa; Andres Eiroa Sanchez.

[H] MONASTERIES AND RESIDENCES FOR PRIESTS AND BROTHERS

SAN JUAN. *The Capuchin Formation Trust of Puerto Rico.*

Capuchin Health and Retirement Trust of Puerto Rico. Legal Title: *Asociacion Frailes Capuchinos, Inc.*

HATO REY. *Jesuit Community - Casa Claver*, 398 Francisco Sein, 00917. Tel: 787-759-7654; Fax: 787-790-3162. Mailing Address: Apto. 22634 U.P.R. Sta., San Juan, P.R., 00931-2634. Rev. Fernando Pico, S.J.

RIO PIEDRAS. *Communidad Jesuita C.S.I.*, Calle Sauco 1940, Urb. Santa Maria, 00927-6728. Tel: 787-758-1717; 764-4324, Ext. 1721; Fax: 787-758-4145.

The Viceprovince of Saint John the Baptist, Puerto Rico, of the Order Friars Minor Capuchin, Calle Arzuaga, 218, Apartado Postal 21350, 00928-1350. Tel: 787-764-3090; Fax: 787-764-4070. Rev. Alberto Figueroa, O.F.M. Cap., Vice Prov. Min.

TRUJILLO ALTO. *Carmelite Monastery* (1650). (Monasterio Carmelita De San Jose), 00977-0568. Tel: 787-761-9548; Fax: 787-283-7235. Mailing Address: P.O. Box 568, 00977-0568. Sr. M. Blanca Ocasio, Prioress.

[I] MISCELLANEOUS

SAN JUAN. *Casa San Clemente*. (Spiritual, Personal, Pastoral, and Psychological Counseling), Ave. Ponce De Leon 257, Puerta De Tierra, 00901. Tel: 787-723-6915. Mailing Address: P.O. Box 9066315, 00906-6315. Bro. Mateo Perez, C.SS.R.; Rev. Tomas Travers, C.SS.R., Exec. Dir.

Centro Sor Isolina. (Social Improvement of the Poor), R.R. 6, Box 9541, 00928. Tel: 787-731-5700. Sr. Teresa Geigel, M.S.B.T.

Hogar Buen Pastor. (Homeless Shelter), Ave. Ponce De Leon #250, Pueroa De Tierra, 00901. Tel: 787-721-8579. Mailing Address: P.O. Box 9066547, 00906-6547. Sr. Rose Mary Gonzalez.

MEDIANIA ALTA WARD, LOIZA. *Centro Esperanza, Inc.*, 1st St., Parcelas Vieques Development, 00772. Tel: 787-876-1545; Fax: 787-876-1545. Mailing Address: P.O. Box 482, Loiza, 00772-0482. Tel: 787-876-1545. Sr. Carmen Gloria Alayon, H.C., Dir. & Contact Person. Sponsored by: Sisters of Charity, Saint Vincent de Paul.

SANTURCE. *Beth Yash'ah*. (Spiritual and Psychological Counseling), 1708 Calle Pumarada. Tel: 787-763-6708; 268-2661; 727-4100. Dr. Lucy Lopez-Roig; Dr. Cecilia Arias.

Fondita De Jesus. (Soup Kitchen), Calle Monserrate 704, PDA 16 1/2. Mailing Address: P.O. Box 19384, San Juan, 00910-1384. Mrs. Ivis Carrion, Dir.

RELIGIOUS INSTITUTES OF MEN REPRESENTED IN THE ARCHDIOCESE

For further details refer to the corresponding bracketed number in the Religious Institutes of Men or Women section.

[0140]—*Augustinian Friars*. (Spain).—O.S.A.
[0470]—*The Capuchin Friars*. (Vice Prov. of Puerto Rico).—O.F.M.Cap.
[0270]—*Carmelite Fathers & Brothers*. (Prov. of Aragon, Valentina, Spain).—O.Carm.
[0360]—*Claretian Missionaries*. (Spain).—C.M.F.
[0310]—*Congregation of Christian Brothers*. (Antilles Prov.).—C.F.C.
[0820]—*Congregation of the Fathers of Mercy*. (Madrid, Spain).—C.P.M.
[1330]—*Congregation of the Mission*. (Prov. of Puerto Rico).—C.M.
[1000]—*Congregation of the Passion*. (Bibao).—C.P.
[]—*Congregation of the Sacred Heart*. (Spain).—C.SS.CC.
[]—*Congregation of the Terciarios Capuchinos Ntra. Sra. de los Dolores*. (Spain).—T.C.
[0520]—*Franciscan Friars*. (Spain).—O.F.M.
[0650]—*Holy Ghost Fathers*. (American Prov.).—C.S.Sp.
[0690]—*Jesuit Fathers and Brothers*. (Prov. of Puerto Rico).—S.J.
[0740]—*Marian Fathers*.—M.I.C.
[0770]—*The Marist Brothers*.—F.M.S.
[1120]—*Missionaries of the Sacred Hearts of Jesus and Mary*. (Spain).—M.SS.CC.
[0840]—*Missionary Servants of the Most Holy Trinity*.—S.T.
[0910]—*Oblates of Mary Immaculate*. (Peru Prov.).—O.M.I.
[0430]—*Order of Preachers-Dominicans*. (Gen. Vicariate of P.R.).—O.P.
[1310]—*Order of the Holy Trinity*. (Spain).—O.SS.T.
[1040]—*Piarist Fathers*. (Spain).—Sch.P.
[1070]—*Redemptorist Fathers*. (San Juan Prov.).—C.SS.R.
[1190]—*Salesians of Don Bosco*. (Antilles Prov.).—S.D.B.
[0760]—*Society of Mary*. (New York Prov.).—S.M.

RELIGIOUS INSTITUTES OF WOMEN REPRESENTED IN THE ARCHDIOCESE

[]—*Apostolado del Sagrado Corazon de Jesus*. (Madrid, Spain).
[1810]—*Bernardine Sisters of the Third Order of St. Francis*. (Villanova, PA).—O.S.F.
[0760]—*Compania de las Hijas de la Caridad de San Vicente de Paul*. (Paris, France).—H.C.
[]—*Daughters of St. Paul*.—F.S.P.
[1070-02]—*Dominican Sisters*.—O.P.
[1070-05]—*Dominican Sisters*.—O.P.
[1070-06]—*Dominican Sisters*.—O.P.
[1070-13]—*Dominican Sisters*.—O.P.
[]—*Dominicanas Terciarieas del Santisimo Sacramento*. (Cadiz, Spain).
[]—*Eumen Dei*. (Madrid, Spain).—U.L.D.
[]—*Hermanas Carmelitas de la Caridad*. (Rome, Italy).—C.ach.
[]—*Hermanas Carmelitas de Madre Candelaria (Venezuela)*.
[]—*Hermanas Carmelitas Teresas de San Jose (Barcelona, Spain)*.
[]—*Hermanas de la Amistad Misionera en Cristo Obrero*. (Amico and Madrid, Spain).
[]—*Hermanas de la B.V. Maria del Monte Carmelo*. (Madrid, Spain).—H.Carm.
[]—*Hermanas De La Capidad Del Sagrado Corazon De Jesus*. (Madrid, Spain).
[]—*Hermanas de la Caridad del Cardenal Sancha*. (San Domingo).—HCCS.
[]—*Hermanas de la Compania del Salvador*. (Spain).
[]—*Hermanas de Santos Angeles Custodios*. (Bilbao, Spain).
[]—*Hermanas Dominicas de la Presentacion*. (Tburs, France; Colombia).
[]—*Hermanas Dominicas de Nuestra Senora del Rosario de Fatima*. (Yauco).
[]—*Hermanas Hospitalarias de Jesus Nazareno*. (Cordoba, Spain).
[]—*Hermanas Mercedarias de la Caridad*. (Madrid, Spain).
[]—*Hermanas Misioneras de los Sagrados Corazones*. (Palma de Mallorca, Spain).
[]—*Hermanitas de los Ancianos Desamparados*. (Valencia, Spain).
[]—*Hermans De La Divina Providencia*. (Rome, Italy).—CDP.

[]—*Hijas de Maria Auxiliadora.* (Torino, Italy).
[]—*Hijas Del Corazon Misericordioso De Maria.* (Bogota, Columbia).
[0950]—*Instituto Misionero Hijas de San Pablo.* (Rome, Italy).
[]—*Instituto Santa Mariana de Jesus (Hermanas Marianitas).* (Ecuador).—R.M.
[]—*Madres de Desamparados y San Jose de la Montana.* (Valencia, Spain).
[]—*Madres Escolapis.* (Rome).
[]—*Misioneras de Cristo Salvador.*
[2710]—*Misioneras De La Capidad.* (Calcutta, India).—M.C.
[]—*Misioneras del Buen Pastor.* (Caguas).
[]—*Misioneras del Santisimo Sacramento y Maria Inmaculada.* (Spain).
[]—*Misioneras Dominicas del Santisimo Rosario.* (Madrid, Spain).
[1845]—*Misioneras Guadalupanas del Espiritu Santo.* (Morelia, Mexico).
[2720]—*Mission Helpers of the Sacred Heart.*—M.H.S.H.
[2790]—*Missionary Servants of the Most Blessed Trinity.* (Philadelphia, PA).—M.S.B.T.
[]—*Monjas de la Orden de la Bienventurada Virgen Maria de Monte Carmelo.*—O.Carm.
[]—*Oblates De La Santisima Trinidad.* (Spain).
[]—*Oblates del Santisimo Redenteor.* (Madrid, Spain).
[]—*Operarias Del Divino Maestro.* (Valenzia, Spain).
[]—*Religiosas del Sagrado Corazon.* (Rome, Italy).
[]—*Religiosas Oblates del Divino Amor.*
[]—*Religiosas Teatinas de la Inmaculada Concepcion.* (Rome).—R.T.
[]—*Religiosas Terciarias de San Francisco de Asis y de la Inmaculada Concepcion.* (Valencia, Spain).
[2970]—*School Sisters of Notre Dame.* (Wilton, CT).—S.S.N.D.
[]—*Siervas De La Verdad.* (Bayamon, Puerto Rico).
[3600]—*Siervas de Maria y Ministras de los Enfermos.* (Rome, Italy).—S.M.
[2570]—*Sisters of Mercy.* (Pittsburgh, PA).—R.S.M.
[1620]—*Sisters of Saint Francis of Millvale, Pennsylvania.*—O.S.F.
[1650]—*Sisters of St. Francis of Philadelphia.*—O.S.F.
[1800]—*Sisters of St. Francis of the Third Order Regular.* (Williamsville, New York).—O.S.F.
[3830]—*Sisters of St. Joseph.* (Brentwood).—C.S.J.
[3930]—*Sisters of St. Joseph of the Third Order of St. Francis.*—S.S.J.-T.O.S.F.
[1970]—*Sisters of the Holy Family of Nazareth.*—C.S.F.N.
[1490]—*Sisters of the Third Franciscan Order.*—O.S.F.
[2150]—*Sisters, Servants of the Immaculate Heart of Mary.*—I.H.M.
[]—*Terciarias Franciscanas de la Purisima.* (Murcia, Spain).

NECROLOGY

† Feliz, Felix, (Retired). —Died May 12, 2000.
† Hernandez, Antonio. —Died Jan. 16, 1998.
† Pagan, Joaquin Rivera, Carolina, P.R. San Fernando Parish. —Died July 12, 1999.
† Pereda, Guillermo, (Retired). —Died Oct. 17, 1999.
† Vela, Santiago, (Retired). —Died Aug. 25, 1999.

Diocese of St. Thomas in the Virgin Islands

Most Reverend

GEORGE V. MURRY, S.J.

Bishop of St. Thomas in the Virgin Islands; ordained June 9, 1979; appointed May 5, 1998; installed June 30, 1999.

ESTABLISHED AS PRELATURE OF VI, JULY 23, 1960.

ESTABLISHED AS DIOCESE OF ST. THOMAS IN THE VIRGIN ISLANDS APRIL 20, 1977.

Comprises the Islands of St. Thomas, St. Croix and St. John.

Chancery Office: P.O. Box 301825, Charlotte Amalie, VI, 00803. Tel.: 340-774-3166; 776-1865; Fax: 340-774-5816.

Web site address: www.islands.vi / ~ chancery

E-mail address: chancery@islands.VI

STATISTICAL OVERVIEW

Personnel	
Bishop	1
Retired Bishops	1
Priests: Diocesan Active in Diocese	8
Priests: Active Outside Diocese	4
Number of Diocesan Priests	12
Religious Priests in Diocese	5
Extern Priests in Diocese	1
Ordinations:	
Transitional Deacons	2
Permanent Deacons in Diocese	18
Total Brothers	4
Total Sisters	17
Parishes	
Parishes	8
With Resident Pastor:	
Resident Diocesan Priests	6
Resident Religious Priests	2
Missions	2
Welfare	
Special Centers for Social Services	4
Total Assisted	808
Educational	
Diocesan Students in Other Seminaries	3
Total Seminarians	3
High Schools, Diocesan and Parish	2
Total Students	240
Elementary Schools, Diocesan and Parish	3
Total Students	558
Catechesis/Religious Education:	
High School Students	297
Elementary Students	720
Total Students Under Catholic Instruction	1,818
Teachers in the Diocese:	
Brothers	1
Sisters	3
Lay Teachers	64
Vital Statistics	
Receptions into the Church:	
Infant Baptism Totals	347
Adult Baptism Totals	16
Received into Full Communion	13
First Communions	290
Confirmations	189
Marriages:	
Catholic	75
Interfaith	34
Total Marriages	109
Deaths	158
Total Catholic Population	30,000
Total Population	110,000

Former Bishops—Most Rev. EDWARD J. HARPER, C.SS.R., D.D., ord. June 18, 1939; appt. July 23, 1960; cons. Oct. 6, 1960; named first residential bishop of Diocese of St. Thomas in the Virgin Islands, April 20, 1977; retired Oct. 15, 1985; died Dec. 2, 1990.—Most Rev. SEAN P. O'MALLEY, O.F.M.Cap., ord. Aug. 29, 1970; named coadjutor, May 30, 1984; ord. Bishop, Aug. 2, 1984; installed Oct. 16, 1985; transferred to Fall River Aug. 11, 1992.—Most Rev. ELLIOTT G. THOMAS, D.D., ord. June 6, 1986; cons. and installed as Bishop Dec. 12, 1993; retired June 30, 1999.

Chancery Office—*P.O. Box 301825, Charlotte Amalie, 00803.* Tel: 340-774-3166; 776-1865; Fax: 340-774-5816.

Chancellor—Rev. NEIL SCANTLEBURY. Tel: 340-774-3166.

Fiscal Officer—JOSEPH HOSIE.

Diocesan Consultors—Revs. ALFRED BRADLEY, C.SS.R.; SIMON PETER OPIRA; JEROME FEUDJIO; Very Rev. KENNETH GADDY, C.SS.R., V.G.; Rev. Msgr. MICHAEL KOSAK; Rev. NEIL SCANTLEBURY.

Religious Education Office—Vacant.

Youth Coordinator—Very Rev. KENNETH GADDY, C.SS.R., *P.O. Box 547, Frederiksted, St. Croix, 00841.* Tel: 340-772-0138.

Hispanic Ministry—Vacant.

Catholic Charities of the Virgin Islands, Inc.—Ms. DEBRA BROWN-ROUMO, Exec. Dir., *P.O. Box 10736, Charlotte Amalie, 00801.* Tel: 340-777-8518; Fax: 340-777-4875.

Catholic Schools Office—Mrs. DIANA PARKER, Supt., *P.O. Box 301825, Charlotte Amalie, 00803.* Tel: 340-774-3166; Fax: 340-774-5816.

Vocations—Rev. Msgr. MICHAEL F. KOSAK, *P.O. Box 1160, Kingshill, St. Croix, 00851.* Tel: 340-778-0484.

Charismatic Movement—Deacon HYACINTHE GEORGE, St. Croix; Rev. Msgr. MICHAEL KOSAK, St. Croix.

Diocesan Television Network—Mr. RONALDO BOSCHULTE, Dir. of Operations, *P.O. Box 301825, VDS, Charlotte Amalie, 00803.* Tel: 340-777-4828.

Caribbean Catholic Network—Channel 7, *P.O. Box 1160, Kingshill, St. Croix, 00851.* Tel: 340-779-3000.

Catholic Television Network (CTN)—Channel 16, *P.O. Box 301825, Charlotte Amalie, 00803.* Tel: 340-777-4828.

Diocesan Newspaper—*"The Catholic Islander"*, SANDRA ROSS, Editor, *P.O. Box 301825, Charlotte Amalie, 00803.* Tel: 340-774-3166; Fax: 340-774-5816.

Communications Coordinator—Rev. Msgr. MICHAEL KOSAK.

Prison Ministry—Deacon ARNOLD HELENESE, St. Croix; Rev. JEROME FEUDJIO, St. Thomas.

Natural Family Planning Coordinator—Rev. TROY SCHUSTER, *P.O. Box 304983, St. Thomas, 00803-4983.* Tel: 340-774-0885.

Permanent Diaconate—Bro. PATRICK CLEMENT LEAVY, Dir. Tel: 340-774-3166; Fax: 340-774-5816.

Shelters for the Homeless—Ms. DEBRA BROWN-ROUMO, Exec. Dir., *Bethlehem House, P.O. Box 10736, Charlotte Amalie, 00801.* Tel: 340-774-4663., St. Croix: Tel: 340-778-1227., Administration: Tel: 340-777-8518; Fax: 340-777-4475.

CLERGY, PARISHES, MISSIONS AND PAROCHIAL SCHOOLS

ISLAND OF ST. THOMAS
(Catholic Population, 12,500)

1—CATHEDRAL OF STS. PETER AND PAUL (1773) (West Indian), Rev. Jerome Feudjio; Deacons William Kenny; Jose Vasquez; Austin Medina. In res., Revs. George Franklin; Ben Calip (Philippines); Troy Schuster.

Mailing Address: P.O. Box 301767, Charlotte Amalie, 00803. Tel: 340-774-0201; 776-7384; Fax: 340-776-9586.

Res., 22A Kronprindsens Gade (Main St.), Charlotte Amalie, 00803.

Schools—Sts. Peter and Paul School, (Grades Jr.K-12) P.O. Box 301706, 00803. Tel: 340-774-5662; Fax: 340-777-5355. Mrs. Barbara Kenny, Asst. Prin.

Sisters 1; Lay Teachers 11; Students (Grades Jr.K-6) 114; Tel: 340-774-2199. Bro. Lawrence Lavallee, F.M.S., Prin.

Lay Teachers 14; Students (Grades 7-12) 154.

Catechesis / Religious Programs—Students 36.

Convent—31 A Prindcesse Gade, P.O. Box 303785, Charlotte Amalie, 00803. Tel: 340-774-0248; Fax: 340-776-9586. Sisters of Charity of St. Elizabeth

Mission—Carenage, Chapel of St. Anne, P.O. Box 306810, 00803. Tel: 340-714-1101; Fax: 340-775-1750. Deacon Alberto Olive.

2—OUR LADY OF PERPETUAL HELP (1926), Rev. Troy Schuster; Deacon William Summer.

Mailing Address: P.O. Box 304983, Charlotte Amalie, 00803. Tel: 340-774-0885; Fax: 340-774-5896. [CEM]

Catechesis / Religious Programs—Students 45.

3—HOLY FAMILY PARISH (1969), Rev. Simon Peter Opira (Uganda); Deacon Leonard Monsanto.

Res., Cassi Hill, P.O. Box 502218, St. Thomas,

00805. Tel: 340-775-1650; Fax: 340-775-1750. [JC]
Catechesis/Religious Programs—Tel: 340-775-5466. Gloria Etienne, D.R.E.
Students 133.

ISLAND OF ST. JOHN
(Catholic Population 300)

1—OUR LADY OF MT. CARMEL PARISH (1962), Rev. Neil Scantlebury.
Res., P.O. Box 241, St. John, 00831. Tel: 340-776-6339 (Res. & Office); Fax: 340-693-7685.

ISLAND OF ST. CROIX
(Catholic Population, approx. 17,200)

1—CHURCH ST. ANN (1823), Rev. Msgr. Michael F. Kosak; Rev. Bernard Campbell; Deacons Arnold Helenese; Joseph Mark; Norbert Xavier; Hyacinthe George, Pastoral Assoc.
Mailing Address: 42 Barrenspot Hill, P.O. Box 1160, Kingshill, St. Croix, 00851-1160. Tel: 340-778-0484; Fax: 340-779-3151.
Catechesis/Religious Programs—Deacon Joseph Mark, D.R.E.
Students 243.
School—School of Evangelization. Rev. Msgr. Michael F. Kosak, Coord.; Deacon Joseph Mark, Prin.; Sr. Patricia Alexander, W.I.F., Spiritual Dir.; Deacon Hyacinthe George, Asst. Prin.
Students 80.
Chaplaincy—Herbert Grigg Home for the Aged, Tel: 340-778-0708.
Shrine—Our Lady of Barrenspot Hill.

2—CHURCH OF THE HOLY CROSS (1755), Revs. Alfred Bradley, C.SS.R.; Scott Bailey, C.SS.R.; Michael Houston, C.SS.R.; Bro. Leonard Samuel, C.SS.R.; Deacons Ulric Benjamin; James Matthews; David Capriola; Sr. Claudia Palacios, R.G.S., Pastoral Assoc.
Res., Box 1069, Christiansted, St. Croix, 00821-1069. Tel: 340-773-7564; Fax: 340-713-9149. [JC]
School—St. Mary's, P.O. Box 4090, Christiansted, St. Croix, 00822. Tel: 340-773-0117; Fax: 340-773-1166. Susan Diverio, Prin.; Mrs. Elizabeth Hering, Assistant Prin.
Lay Teachers 19; Students 211.
Catechesis/Religious Programs—Tel: 340-773-7564; Fax: 340-713-9149. D.R.E.: Rev. Scott Bailey, C.SS.R; Mrs. Christina James, Coord.
Students 140.
Mission—LBJ Village, U.S.V.I., Sacred Heart Chapel, P.O. Box 1069, Christiansted, 00821. Tel: 340-773-7564; Fax: 340-713-9149.
Blessed Peter Donder's Formation Residence—P.O. Box 24839-Gallows Bay, Christiansted, St. Croix, 00824-0839. Tel: 340-692-9999; Fax: 340-692-9997. Bro. Leonard Samuel, C.Ss.R., Dir.
Res., 20 Prince St., Christiansted, St. Croix, 00820. Tel: 340-692-9999; Fax: 340-692-9997.
Convents—P.O. Box 3058, Christiansted, St. Croix, 00821. Tel: 340-773-1950. Missionaries of Charity; P.O. Box 2984, Christianhead, St. Croix, 00821. Tel: 340-713-8724. Sisters of the Good Shepherd

3—CHURCH OF ST. PATRICK (1846) (African-Caribbean), Revs. Joseph Bertrand, C.SS.R.; Kenneth Gaddy, C.SS.R.; Deacons Ed Cave; Emith Fludd.
Mailing Address: P.O. Box 547, Frederiksted, St. Croix, 00841. Tel: 340-772-0138; Fax: 340-772-0142.
School—P.O. Box 988, Frederiksted, St. Croix, 00841. Tel: 340-772-5052; Fax: 340-772-4488. Mary McIntosh, Prin.
Lay Teachers 11; Students 233.
Catechesis/Religious Programs—Students 110.
Convent—Caribbean Center, P.O. Box 95, Frederiksted, St. Croix, 00841. Tel: 340-772-0341; Fax: 340-772-4908. Missionary Sisters of the Immaculate Heart of Mary
DeMeester Residence: P.O. Box 52, St. Croix, 00841. Tel: 340-772-0132.
Light of Christ Retreat Center—301 New St., P.O. Box 547, St. Croix, 00841. Tel: 340-772-4782; Fax: 340-772-0142.

4—CHURCH OF ST. JOSEPH (1947), Rev. Cecil Corneille; Deacons James Verhoff; Conrad Williams; Neville Charles. In res., Bro. James A. Petrait, O.S.F.S.
Mailing Address: P.O. Box 2150, Kingshill, St. Croix, 00851-2150. Tel: 340-692-2005; Fax: 340-692-2748. [JC]
Res., Mt. Pleasant, Frederiksted, St. Croix, 00841.
Catechesis/Religious Programs—Students 280.
Convent—P.O. Box 1847, Kingshill, St. Croix, 00851. Tel: 340-778-5773; Fax: 340-778-5773. West Indian Franciscans

Chaplaincies

These chaplaincies only pertain to the Island of St. Thomas.

ST. THOMAS. *Lucinda Millin Home for the Aged.*
Queen Louise Home for the Aged.
St. Thomas Hospital and Community Health Center.
Seaview Nursing and Rehabilitation Center.

On Duty Outside the Diocese:
Reverend Fathers—
Franklin, George, 1927A Senate St., St. Louis, MO 63118. Tel: 314-664-2413
Herrera, Jose
Obeng, Simon
Onyekwere, Michael
Sanchez, Alejandro

Permanent Deacons:
Benjamin, Ulric
Capriola, David
Cave, Edward
Charles, Neville
Fludd, Emith
George, Hyacinthe
Helenese, Arnold
Kenny, William
Mark, Joseph T.
Matthew, James
Medina, Austin
Monsanto, Leonard
Olive, Alberto
Summer, William
Vazquez, Jose
Verhoff, James
Williams, Conrad
Xavier, Norbert

INSTITUTIONS LOCATED IN THE DIOCESE

[A] INTERPAROCHIAL HIGH SCHOOLS

ST. CROIX. *St. Joseph High School*, 3 Mt. Pleasant, Rte. 2, Frederiksted, 00840. Tel: 340-692-2455; Fax: 340-692-2458.
E-mail: sjhs@islands.vi
Web site: www.islands.vi/~sjhs
Sr. Claina Letang, I.C.M., Prin. Brothers 1; Sisters 2; Lay Teachers 9; Students 86.

[B] ORGANIZATIONS IN THE DIOCESE

ST. THOMAS. *Miscellaneous Organizations.* (For further information contact the Chancery Office.). Box 301825, Charlotte Amalie, 00803. Tel: 340-774-3166; Fax: 340-774-5816.
E-mail: chancery@islands.vi
Catholic Charismatic Renewal. Tel: 340-778-0484. Rev. Msgr. Michael F. Kosak, Dir.; Sr. Patricia Alexander, Asst. Dir.
Catholic Daughters of the Americas; Fax: 340-776-9586. Mrs. Carmen Grant, Regent. Tel: 340-775-5369.
Children of Mary; Fax: 340-775-1750. Wende Rouse. Tel: 340-775-1351; 340-775-1750 (Fax).
COR (Christ in Others Retreat); Fax: 340-772-0142. Rev. Kenneth Gaddy, C.SS.R. Tel: 340-772-0138.
Spanish Ministry, St. Croix. Tel: 340-773-7564; Fax: 340-713-9149. Rev. Michael Houston, C.SS.R.; Sr. Claudia Palacios, R.G.S. Tel: 340-773-7564; 340-713-9149 (Fax).
Knights of Columbus, St. Croix. Bertil MacGregor, Deputy. Tel: 340-773-7135.
Legion of Mary, St. Croix. Rev. Michael Houston, C.SS.R. Tel: 340-773-7564.
Legion of Mary, St. Thomas. Tel: 340-775-3503; Fax: 340-775-1750. Eubald Rene. Tel: 340-775-3503.
Lumen 2000/Caribbean Region. Rev. Msgr. Michael F. Kosak. Tel: 340-778-0484.
Propagation of the Faith; Fax: 340-775-1750. Rev. Simon Peter Opira, Dir. Tel: 340-775-1650.
Secular Franciscans. Sr. Patricia Alexander, W.I.F., Spiritual Asst. Tel: 340-778-5773.
Fraternity Our Lady of the Angels. Deacon Conrad Williams, Min. Tel: 340-778-1733; Mrs. Cleo Hobson, Min. Tel: 340-775-0666.
St. Vincent de Paul Society, St.Thomas; Fax: 340-775-1750. Alma Wells. Tel: 340-775-0839.
Catholic Charities of the Virgin Islands. Tel: 340-777-8518; Fax: 340-777-4475. Debra Brown-Roumo, Exec. Dir.
Disciples of the Holy Spirit, Inc., P.O. Box 1160, Kingshill, St. Croix, 00851. Tel: 340-778-0484; Fax: 340-779-3151. Rev. Msgr. Michael F. Kosak, Dir.
St. Joseph Workers; Fax: 340-775-1750. Orville Rouse. Tel: 340-775-1351.
Secular Order Discalced Carmelites, St. Croix. Barbara O'Dea, Dir. Tel: 340-778-0933.
Men's Fellowship, St. Croix. Cecil George. Tel: 340-772-2573.
Cursillo Movement, St. Croix. Tel: 340-692-2005; Fax: 340-692-2748. Victoria Soto. Tel: 340-772-1118.

RELIGIOUS INSTITUTES OF MEN REPRESENTED IN THE DIOCESE

For further details refer to the corresponding bracketed number in the Religious Institutes of Men or Women section.

[0310]—*Congregation of Christian Brothers.*—C.F.C.
[0770]—*Marist Brothers.*—F.M.S.
[0920]—*Oblates of St. Francis De Sales.*—O.S.F.S.
[1070]—*Redemptorist Fathers.*—C.SS.R.

RELIGIOUS INSTITUTES OF WOMEN REPRESENTED IN THE DIOCESE

[]—*Association of West Indian Franciscans.*—W.I.F.
[2710]—*Missionaries of Charity.*—M.C.
[2750]—*Missionary Sisters of the Immaculate Heart of Mary.*—I.C.M.
[0590]—*Sisters of Charity of Saint Elizabeth (Convent Station).*—S.C.
[1830]—*Sisters of the Good Shepherd.*—R.G.S.

NECROLOGY
(No Deaths)

PART III
Canada and Mexico

(Editor's Note: Not updated for the 2001 edition.)

APOSTOLIC NUNCIATURE

(For Canada)
Apostolic Pro-Nuncio:
Most Reverend Carlo Curis, Titular Archbishop of Medeli.
Counsellor-Rev. Msgr. Vito Rallo
Res., 724 Manor Ave., Rockcliffe Park, Ottawa, ON Canada, K1M OE3
Tel: 613-746-4914; Fax: 613-746-4786.

PROVINCE OF EDMONTON

Archdiocese of Edmonton; Dioceses of Calgary, and St. Paul.

PROVINCE OF GATINEAU-HULL

Archdiocese of Gatineau-Hull, Dioceses of Amos, Mont-Laurier and Rouyn-Noranda.

PROVINCE OF GROUARD-MCLENNAN

Archdiocese of Grouard-McLennan; Dioceses of Mackenzie-Fort Smith, Prince George, and Whitehorse.

PROVINCE OF HALIFAX

Archdiocese of Halifax; Dioceses of Antigonish, Charlottetown, and Yarmouth.

PROVINCE OF KEEWATIN-LE PAS

Archdiocese of Keewatin-Le Pas; Dioceses of Churchill-Baie D'Hudson, Moosonee, and Labrador City-Schefferville.

PROVINCE OF KINGSTON

Archdiocese of Kingston; Dioceses of Alexandria-Cornwall, Peterborough, and Sault Ste. Marie.

PROVINCE OF MONCTON

Archdiocese of Moncton; Dioceses of Edmundston, Bathurst, and St. John.

PROVINCE OF MONTREAL

Archdiocese of Montreal; Dioceses of Joliette, Saint-Jean-Longueuil, St. Jerome, and Valleyfield.

PROVINCE OF OTTAWA

Archdiocese of Ottawa; Dioceses of Hearst, Pembroke, and Timmins.

PROVINCE OF QUEBEC

Archdiocese of Quebec; Dioceses of Chicoutimi, Ste. Anne-de-la-Pocatiere, and Trois-Rivieres.

PROVINCE OF RIMOUSKI

Archdiocese of Rimouski; Dioceses of Baie Comeau, and Gaspe.

PROVINCE OF REGINA

Archdiocese of Regina; Dioceses of Prince Albert, and Saskatoon.

PROVINCE OF SHERBROOKE

Archdiocese of Sherbrooke; Dioceses of Nicolet, and St. Hyacinthe.

PROVINCE OF ST. BONIFACE

Archdiocese of St. Boniface.

PROVINCE OF ST. JOHN'S

Archdiocese of St. John's; Dioceses of Grand Falls, and St. George's.

PROVINCE OF TORONTO

Archdiocese of Toronto; Dioceses of Hamilton, London, St. Catharines, and Thunder Bay.

PROVINCE OF VANCOUVER

Archdiocese of Vancouver; Dioceses of Kamloops, Nelson, and Victoria.

ARCHDIOCESE OF WINNIPEG

(Immediately subject to the Holy See)

PROVINCE OF UKRAINIAN BYZANTINE RITE

Metropolitan See of Winnipeg; Ukrainian Eparchates of Edmonton, New Westminster, Saskatoon, and Toronto.

MILITARY ORDINARIATE

CANADIAN CONFERENCE OF CATHOLIC BISHOPS

SECRETARIAT OF THE CANADIAN HIERARCHY
(Established October 12, 1943)

Address: 90 Parent Ave., Ottawa, Ont. K1N 7B1. Tel: 613-241-9461; Fax: 613-241-5090 (Publications).

MEMBERS AND OFFICERS C.C.C.B. PERMANENT COUNCIL

Executive Committee and Permanent Council: President: His Eminence Cardinal Jean-Claude Turcotte (Montreal). Vice-President: Most Rev. Gerald Wiesner (Prince George).

Co-Treasurers: Most Rev. Anthony F. Tonnos (Hamilton); Rev. Msgr. Jacques Berthelet (Saint-Jean-Longueuil).

Programmes and Priorities Committee Representatives: Rev. Msgr. Andre Gaumond (Sherbrooke); Most Rev. Brendan O'Brien (Pembroke).

Representants Des Regions-Regional Representatives: Atlantic - Most Rev. James H. MacDonald; Ontario - Rev. Msgr. Gilles Cazabon (Saint Jerome); Quebec - Rev. Msgr. Martin Veillette (Quebec); West - Rev. Msgr. Raymond Roussin.

Representants Des Secteurs-Sector Representatives: Most Rev. Jacques Berthelet (Saint-Jean-Longueuil); Most Rev. Blaise Morand (Prince Albert); Rev. Msgr. Andre Richard (Bathurst); Most Rev. Anthony F. Tonnos (Hamilton); Most Rev. James Weisgerber (Saskatoon).

Membres De Droit-Ex Officio Members: His Eminence Cardinal Jean-Claude Turcotte (Montreal); Rev. Msgr. Maurice Couture (Quebec); Most Rev. Aloysius M. Ambrozic (Toronto); Most Rev. Michael Bzdel (Metropolitan, Winnipeg).

Programmes and Priorities Committee: Most Rev. Gerald Wiesner (Prince George); Rev. Msgr. Andre Gaumond (Sherbrooke); Rev. Msgr. Gilles Cazabon (Saint-Jerome); Most Rev. Francis J. Spence (Kingston); Most Rev. Terrence Prendergast (Toronto); Most Rev. Brendan O'Brien (Pembroke); Most Rev. Francois Thibodeau (Edmundston).

EPISCOPAL COMMISSIONS

The CCCB's twelve episcopal commissions are appointed by the Permanent Council to undertake study and projects in specific areas of pastoral work. Six Commissions serve nationally and six commissions relate to the French and English Sectors.

NATIONAL LEVEL

Social Affairs
Most Revs. Francois Thibodeau, Pres.; Bertrand Blanchet; Nicola De Angelis; Raymond Dumais; James Weisgerber.

Canon Law - Inter Rite
Most Revs. Francis J. Spence, Chm.; Joseph Khoury; James M. Wingle; Severian Yakymyshyn.

Commission for Relations with Associations of Clergy, Consecrated Life, and Laity
Most Revs. Terrence Prendergast, Chm.; Clement Fecteau; Jean-Guy Hamelin; Stephen Soroka.

Evangelization of Peoples
Most Revs. Andre Gaumond, Pres.; Vincent Cadieux; Denis Croteau; Faber MacDonald.

Ecumenism
Most Revs. Brendan O'Brien, Chm.; Michael Bzdel; Raymond Lahey; Vincent Masse; Jean-Louis Plouffe; Martin Veillette.

Theology
Most Revs. Gilles Cazabon, Pres.; Aloysius Ambrozic; Thomas Collins; Gerard Drainville; Cornelius Pasichny; Laurent Noel.

SECTOR LEVEL

English Sector

Social Communications
Most Revs. Frederick J. Colli, Chm.; Reynald Rouleau; John M. Sherlock; J. Edward Troy.

Christian Education
Most Revs. Eugene J. Cooney, Chm.; John S. Knight; John M. O'Mara; Vernon Fougere.

Liturgy
Most Revs. Marcel A. Gervais, Chm.; James H. MacDonald; Peter Novecosky; Douglas Crosby.

French Sector

Social Communications
Most Revs. Robert Lebel, Pres.; Pierre Morissette; Andre Richard; Andre Vallee.

Christian Education
Most Revs. Paul Marchand, Pres.; Jean-Pierre Blais; Ernest Leger; Raymond Roussin.

Liturgy
Most Revs. Antoine Hacault, Pres.; Jacques Berthelet; Paul-Andre Durocher; Gilles Lussier.

ARCHDIOCESES

Edmonton. *Archbishop*—Most Rev. Joseph N. MacNeil; *Vicar General*—Rt. Rev. Donald G. MacDonald; *Chancellor*—Rev. Michael McCaffery; *Chancery Office*—8421-101 Ave., Edmonton, AB T6A 0L1. Tel: 780-469-1010; Fax: 780-465-3003.

Gatineau-Hull. *Archbishop*—Most Rev. Roger Ebacher; *Vicars General*—Revs. Normand Carpentier; Marcel Wolfe; *Chancellor*—Mrs. Lucy Gorman McCoy; *Chancery Office*—180, boulevard Mont-Bleu, Hull, QC J8Z 3J5. Tel: 819-771-8391; Fax: 819-778-8969.

Grouard-McLennan. *Archbishop*—Vacant; *Chancellor*—Rev. Charles Lavoie; *Chancery Office*—Archbishop's Residence, P.O. Box 388, McLennan, AB T0H 2L0. Tel: 780-324-3002; Fax: 780-324-3952.

Halifax. *Archbishop*—Most Rev. Terrence Prendergast, S.J., D.D.; *Vicar General*—Rev. Msgr. Martin Curie; *Chancellor*—Deacon John F. MacNeil; *Chancery Office*—P.O. Box 1527, Halifax, N.S. B3J 2Y3. Tel: 902-429-9800; Fax: 902-423-5201.

Keewatin-Le Pas. *Archbishop*—Most Rev. Peter-Alfred Sutton; *Chancery Office*—Archbishop's Residence, 108-1st St. West, P.O. Box 270, The Pas, MB R9A 1K4. Tel: 204-623-2503; Fax: 204-623-6121.

Kingston. *Archbishop*—Most Rev. Francis Spence, D.D.; *Vicar General*—Rev. T. J. Raby; *Chancellor*—Rev. M.J. Lynch; *Chancery Office*—390 Palace Rd., Kingston, ON K7L 4T3. Tel: 613-548-4461; Fax: 613-548-4744.

Moncton. *Archbishop*—Most Rev. Ernest Leger; *Chancery Office*—452, rue Amirault, Dieppe, N.B., E1A 1G3. Tel: 506-857-9531; Fax: 506-857-9533.

Montreal. *Archbishop*—His Eminence Cardinal Jean-Claude Turcotte; *Auxiliary Bishops*—Most Revs. Jude Saint-Antoine; Andre Rivest. *Vicars General*—Rev. Msgrs. Robert Beaupre, P.H., V.G.; Anthony Mancini, C.S.S., V.G.; *Chancellor*—Rev. Msgr. Michel Parent, C.S.S., V.E.; *Chancery Office*—2000 Sherbrooke St. W., Montreal, QC H3H 1G4. Tel: 514-931-7311; Fax: 514-931-3432.

Ottawa. *Archbishop*—Most Rev. Marcel A. Gervais; *Auxiliary Bishops*—Most Revs. Paul Marchand; Fred J. Colli. *Vicars General*—Most Revs. Fred J. Colli; Paul Marchand; Roger Morin; *Chancellor*—Rev. Msgr. Roger Morin, P.A., V.G.; *Chancery Office*—1247, Kilborn Place, Ottawa, ON K1H 6K9. Tel: 613-738-5025; Fax: 613-738-0130.

Quebec. *Archbishop*—Most Rev. Maurice Couture, r.s.v.; *Auxiliary Bishops*—Most Revs. Jean-Pierre Blais; Jean Gagnon; Eugene Tremblay.; *Vicar General*—Most Rev. Jean-Pierre Blais; *Chancellor*—Sr. Lucienne Boisvert, S.C.S.L.; *Chancery Office*—1073, boul. Rene Levesque West, QC G1S 4R5. Tel: 418-688-1211; Fax: 418-688-1399.

Regina. *Archbishop*—Most Rev. Peter Joseph Mallon, D.D.; *Vicar General*—Very Rev. Kenneth E. Miller; *Chancellor*—Very Rev. John Ryan Prince; *Chancery Office*—445 Broad St. N., Regina, Sask. S4R 2X8. Tel: 306-352-1651; Fax: 306-545-0510.

Rimouski. *Archbishop*—Most Rev. Bertrand Blanchet; *Vicar General*—Raynald Brillant; *Chancellor*—Rev. Yves-Marie Melancon; *Chancery Office*—34, Eveche West, P.O. Box 730, Rimouski, P.Q. G5L 7C7. Tel: 418-723-3320; Fax: 418-722-8978.

St. Boniface. *Archbishop*—Most Rev. Antoine Hacault; *Vicar General*—Rev. Msgr. Albert Frechette, P.H.; *Chancellor*—Rev. Msgr. Roland Belanger; *Chancery Office*—151, Ave. de la Cathedrale, Saint-Boniface, MB R2H 0H6. Tel: 204-237-9851; Fax: 204-231-2652.

St. John's, Nfld. *Archbishop*—Most Rev. James H. MacDonald, C.S.C., D.D.; *Vicars General*—Rev. Msgrs. Francis A. Cody; John T. Wallis; *Chancellor*—Rev. Msgr. Francis A. Cody; *Chancery Office*—Pastoral Center, P.O. Box 1363, St. John's, NF A1C 5N5. Tel: 709-726-3660; Fax: 709-726-8021.

Sherbrooke. *Archbishop*—Most Rev. Andre Gaumond; *Vicar General*—Rev. Msgr. Jodoin, P.H.; *Chancellor*-Sr. Cecile Grenier, P.M.; *Archdiocesan Office*—130, rue de la Cathedrale, Sherbrooke, QC J1H 4M1. Tel: 819-563-9934; Fax: 819-562-0125.

Toronto. *Archbishop*—His Eminence Cardinal Aloysius M. Ambrozic; *Auxiliary Bishops*—Most Revs. John S. Knight, D.D.; Nicola De Angelis, C.F.I.C., D.D.; Anthony G. Meagher, D.D.; *Vicars General*—Most Revs. John S. Knight, D.D.; Nicola De Angelis, C.F.I.C., D.D.; Anthony G. Meagher, D.D.; Rev. John K. Murphy; *Chancellor*—Rev. John K. Murphy; *Chancery Office*—1155 Yonge, Toronto, ON M4T 1W2. Tel: 416-934-0606; Fax: 416-934-3433.

Vancouver. *Archbishop*—Most Rev. Adam Exner, O.M.I.; *Vicar General*—Rev. Msgr. David Monroe. P.H.; *Chancellor*—Rev. Msgr. Gregory N. Smith, P.H., J.C.L.; *Chancery Office*—150 Robson St., Vancouver, B.C., V6B 2A7. Tel: 604-683-0281; Fax: 604-683-4288.

Winnipeg. *Archbishop*—Most Rev. Leonard J. Wall, S.T.D., D.D.; *Vicar General*—Rev. Msgr. D. Ward Jamieson, P.H., V.G.; *Chancellor*—Rev. W. Richard Arsenault; *Chancery Office*—Catholic Center, 1495 Pembina Hwy., Winnipeg, MB R3T 2C6. Tel: 204-452-2227; Fax: 204-475-4409.

DIOCESES

Alexandria-Cornwall. *Bishop*—Most Rev. Eugene P. LaRocque, S.E.; *Chancellor*—Rev. Denis Vaillancourt; *Chancery Office*—220, Chemin Montreal, P.O. Box 1388, Cornwall, ON K6H 5V4. Tel: 613-933-1138; Fax: 613-937-4931.

Amos. *Bishop*—Most Rev. Gerard Drainville; *Vicar General*—Rev. Marcel Albert; *Chancellor*—Sr. Rejeanne Veillette; *Chancery Office*—450, rue Principale Nord, Amos, QC J9T 2M1. Tel: 819-732-6515; Fax: 819-732-7994.

Antigonish. *Bishop*—Most Rev. Colin Campbell; *Vicar General*—Rev. Angus B. MacDougall; *Chancellor*—Sr. Florence Steele, C.S.M; *Chancery Office*—P.O. Box 1330, Antigonish, NS B2G 2L7. Tel: 902-863-3335; Fax: 902-863-0037.

Baie-Comeau. *Bishop*—Most Rev. Pierre Morissette; *Vicar General*—Rev. Germain Gagnon; *Chancellor*—Sr. Jeanne-Mance Caron, S.C.I.M.; *Chancery Office*—639 rue de Bretagne, Baie-Comeau, QC G5C 1X2. Tel: 418-589-5744; Fax: 418-295-3145.

Bathurst. *Bishop*—Most Rev. Andre Richard, C.S.C.; *Vicar General*—Rev. Zoel Saulnier; *Chancellor*—Rev. Lionel Comeau; *Chancery Office*—645 Ave. Murray, P.O. Box 460, Bathurst, N. B. E2A 3Z4. Tel: 506-546-1420; Fax: 506-546-1423.

Calgary. *Bishop*—Most Rev. Frederick Henry, D.D.; *Vicar General*—Very Rev. J.G. Schuster; *Chancellor & Vicar for Matrimonial Affairs*—Sr. Rose-Anne Engel, O.S.U.; *Chancery Office*—Catholic Pastoral Centre, Room 285, The Iona Building, 120-17 Avenue, S.W., Calgary, AB, T2S 2T2. Tel: 403-218-5528; Fax: 403-264-0272.

Charlottetown. *Bishop*—Most Rev. Joseph Vernon Fougere; *Vicar General*—Rev. Arthur O'Shea; *Chancellor*—Rev. Lyndon P. Hogan; *Chancery Office*—P.O. Box 907 - 350 North River Rd., Charlottetown, PE CIA 7L9. Tel: 902-368-8005; Fax: 902-892-1253.

Chicoutimi. *Bishop*—Most Rev. Jean-Guy Couture; *Auxiliary Bishop*—Most Rev. Roch Pedneault; *Vicar General*—Rev. Yvan Tremblay; *Chancellor*—Sr. Marie-Berthe Demers, O.S.U.; *Chancery Office*—602 rue Racine Est., Chicoutimi, QC G7H 1V1. Tel: 418-543-0783; Fax: 418-543-2141.

Churchill-Hudson Bay. *Bishop*—Most Rev. Reynald Rouleau, O.M.I.; *Vicar General*—Robert Lechat, O.M.I.; *Bishop's Office*—242 La Verendrye, P.O. Box 10, Churchill, MB R0B 0E0. Tel: 204-675-2541; Fax: 204-675-2140.

Edmundston. *Bishop*—Most Rev. Francois Thibodeau, C.J.M.; *Vicar General*—Roger Dionne; *Chancellor*—Sr. Ronilla Sirois, R.H.S.J.; *Chancery Office*—Centre Diocesan, Edmundston, NB E3V 3K1. Tel: 506-735-5578; Fax: 506-735-4271.

Gaspe. *Bishop*—Most Rev. Raymond Dumais; *Vicar General*—Joseph Deschenes; *Chancellor*—Sr. Marie-Paule Couturier, F.M.A.; *Chancery Office*—P.O. Box 440, 172, rue Jacques-Cartier, Gaspe, QC G0C 1R0. Tel: 418-368-2274; Fax: 418-368-3772.

Grand Falls. *Bishop*—Vacant; *Vicar General*—Rev. Msgr. E.T. Bromley; *Chancellor*—Rev, Brian Dunn, J.C.D.; *Chancery Office*—P.O. Box 397, Grand Falls, Windsor, NF A2A 2J8. Tel: 709-489-4019. Fax: 709-489-6393.

Hamilton. *Bishop*—Most Rev. Anthony F. Tonnos, D.D.; *Auxiliary Bishop*—Most Rev. Matthew F. Ustrzycki, D.D.; *Vicar General*—Rev. Msgr. John H. Newstead; *Chancellor*—Rev. Gerard Bergie; *Chancery Office*—700 King St. W., Hamilton, ON L8P 1C7. Tel: 905-528-7988; Fax: 905-528-1088.

Hearst. *Bishop*—Most Rev. Andre Vallee, P.M.E.; *Vicar General*—Rev. Jean-Paul Decarie; *Chancellor*—Rev. Rene Grandmont; *Chancery Office*—P.O. Box 1330, 76-7th St., Hearst, ON P0L 1N0. Tel: 705-362-4903; Fax: 705-362-4421.

Joliette. *Bishop*—Most Rev. Gilles Lussier; *Chancellor*—Sr. Jacinthe Ricard; *Chancery Office*—2, rue Saint-Charles-Borromee nord, P.O. Box 470, Joliette, QC J6E 6H6. Tel: 450-753-7596; Fax: 450-759-0929.

Kamloops. *Bishop*—Most Rev. Lawrence Sabatini, C.S., D.D.; *Chancery Office*—635A Tranquille Rd., Kamloops, B.C., V2B 3H5. Tel: 250-376-3351; Fax: 250-376-3363.

Labrador City-Schefferville. *Bishop*—Most Rev. David Douglas Crosby, O.M.I.; *Vicar General*—Rev. Clarence Lavigne, O.M.I.; *Chancellor*—Mr. Patrick Furlong; *Chancery*—318 Elizabeth Ave., P.O. Box 545, Labrador City, NF A2V 2K7. Tel: 709-944-2046; Fax: 709-944-5798.

London. *Bishop*—Most Rev. John M. Sherlock, D.D.; *Vicar General*—Most Rev. Richard J. Grecco; *Chancellor*—Rev. J. Richard Boll; *Chancery Office*—1070 Waterloo St., London, ON N6A 3Y2. Tel: 519-433-0658; Fax: 519-433-0011.

Mackenzie-Fort Smith. *Bishop*—Most Rev. Denis Croteau, O.M.I.; *Vicar General*—Rev. Jean Pochat, O.M.I.; *Chancery Office*—5117, 52nd St., Yellowknife, NT, X1A 1T7. Tel: 867-920-2129; Fax: 867-873-9021.

Mont-Laurier. *Bishop*—Most Rev. Jean Gratton; *Vicar General*—Rev. Msgr. Jean Levert; *Chancellor*—Sr. Denise Savard, S.C.O.; *Chancery Office*—Bishop's Residence, 435, de la Madone, Mont-Laurier, QC J9L 1S1. Tel: 819-623-5530; Fax: 819-623-9523.

Moosonee. *Bishop*—Most Rev. Vincent Cadieux, O.M.I.; *Vicar General*—Rev. Rodrigue P. Vezina, O.M.I.; *Chancellor*—Vacant; *Chancery Office*—P.O. Box 40, Moosonee, ON P0L IY0. Tel: 705-336-2908; Fax: 705-336-2759.

Nelson. *Bishop*—Most Rev. Eugene J. Conney; *Judicial Vicar*—Rev. Wayne Phliger, J.C.L.; *Vicar General*—Rev. Charles Mulvihill; *Chancellor*—Rev. Peter Tompkins; *Chancery Office*—402 W. Richards St., Nelson, B.C., V1L 3K3. Tel: 250-352-6921; Fax: 250-352-1737.

Nicolet. *Bishop*—Most Rev. Raymond Saint-Gelais; *Vicars General*—Rev. Andre Genest; *Chancellor*—Rev. Msgr. Simon Heroux; *Chancery Office*—Bishop's Residence, 49, rue Mgr. Brunault, Nicolet, QC J3T 1X7. Tel: 819-293-4653; Fax: 819-293-4653.

Pembroke. *Bishop*—Most Rev. Brendan M. O'Brien; *Vicar General*—Rev. Msgr. Michael J. Barry; Mgr. Douglas N. Bridge; *Chancellor*—Rev. Msgr. Robert L. Borne, P.H.; *Chancery Office*—188 Renfrew St., P.O. Box 7, Pembroke, ON K8A 6X1. Tel: 613-735-7933.

Peterborough. *Bishop*—Most Rev. James L. Doyle; *Vicar General*—Rev. Msgr. Clayton O'Donoghue, P.A., J.C.D.; *Chancellor*—Sr. Gaudentia; *Chancery Office*—350 Hunter St. W., Box 175, Peterborough, ON K9J 6Y8. Tel: 705-745-5123; Fax: 705-745-2555.

Prince Albert. *Bishop*—Most Rev. Blaise Morand, D.D.; *Vicar General*—Very Rev. Ghislain Gaudet; *Chancellor*—Very Rev. Ghislain Gaudet; *Chancery Office*—1415 4th Ave. W., Prince Albert, SK S6V 5H1. Tel: 306-922-4747.

Prince George. *Bishop*—Most Rev. Gerald Wiesner, O.M.I.; *Vicar General*—Rev. Ivan McCormack, O.M.I.; *Chancellor*—Vacant; *Chancery Office*—2935 Highway 16 West, P.O. Box 7000, Prince George, BC V2N 3Z2. Tel: 250-964-4424; Fax: 250-964-2101.

Rouyn-Noranda. *Bishop*—Most Rev. Jean-Guy Hamelin, D.D.; *Vicar General*—Robert Charron; *Chancellor*—Sr. Rosia Douaire, N.D.A.; *Chancery Office*—515 Cuddihy Ave., Rouyn-Noranda, QC J9X 4C5. Tel: 819-764-4660; Fax: 819-764-3972.

St. Catharines. *Bishop*—Most Rev. John A. O'Mara, D.D., J.C.L.; *Vicar General*—Rev. Msgr. Dominic J. Pizzacalla, P.H., V.G.; *Chancellor*—Rev. Wayne Kirkpatrick, J.C.L.; *Chancery Office*—Catholic Center, P.O. Box 875, St. Catharines, ON 6Y3 4C2. Tel: 905-684-0154; Fax: 905-684-2185.

St. George's. *Bishop*—Most Rev. Raymond J. Lahey, Ph.D., D.D.; *Vicar General*—Rev. John Collins; *Chancellor*—Rev. Msgr. William J. Boone; *Chancery Office*—16 Hammond Dr., Corner Brook, Newfoundland, A2H 2W2. Tel: 709-639-8662; Fax: 709-639-8662.

St. Hyacinthe. *Bishop*—Most Rev. Francois Lapierre, p.m.e.; *Vicar General*—Rev. Andre Vincent; *Chancellor*—Rev. Msgr. Jean-Roch Choiniere, P.H., V.E.; *Chancery Office*—1900 rue Girouard West, P.O. Box 190, Girouard, St. Hyacinthe, QC J2S 7B4. Tel: 450-773-8581; Fax: 450-774-1895.

Saint-Jean-Longueuil. *Bishop*—Most Rev. Jacques Berthelet, C.S.V.; *Vicar General*—Rev. Msgr. Roland-Roch Martin; *Chancellor*—Rev. Jean-Pierre Camerlain; *Chancery Office*—740 boul. Ste. Foy, P.O. Box 40, Longueuil, QC J4K 4X8. Tel: 450-679-1100; Fax: 450-679-1102.

St. Jerome. *Bishop*—Most Rev. Gilles Cazabon, O.M.I.; *Auxiliary Bishop*—Most Rev. Vital Masse; *Vicars General*—Rev. Msgr. Vital Masse; Rev. Lue Cyr; *Chancellor*—Rev. Claude Massicotte, V.E.; *Chancery Office*—355 rue St. Georges, Saint Jerome, QC J7Z 5A9. Tel: 450-432-9742; Fax: 450-432-8155.

Saint John, N.B. *Bishop*—Most Rev. J. Faber MacDonald, D.D.; *Vicar General*—Vacant; *Chancellor*—Rev. John Keoughan; *Chancery Office*—1 Bayard Dr., St. John, N.B., E2L 3L5. Tel: 506-653-6802; Fax: 506-653-6812.

St. Paul in Alberta. *Bishop*—Most Rev. Thomas Christopher Collins; *Chancellor*—Rev. Msgr. Jean-Luc Pigeon, P.H., V.E., V.G.; *Chancery Office*—4410, 51st Ave., Saint Paul, AB, T0A 3A2. Tel: 403-645-3277; Fax: 403-645-6099.

Sainte-Anne-de-la-Pocatiere. *Bishop*—Most Rev. Clement Fecteau; *Chancellor*—Rev. Roland Picard, V.G.; *Chancery Office*—1200, 4th Ave., P.O. Box 430, La Pocatiere, QC G0R 1Z0. Tel: 418-856-1811; Fax: 418-856-5513.

Saskatoon. *Bishop*—Most Rev. V. James Weisgerber, D.D.; *Vicar General*—Very Rev. Ronald Beechinor; *Chancellor*—Very Rev. Paul Donlevy; *Chancery Office*—100, 5th Ave. N., Saskatoon, SK S7K 2N7. Tel: 306-242-1500; Fax: 306-244-6010.

Sault Ste. Marie. *Bishop*—Most Rev. Jean-Louis Plouffe; *Auxiliary Bishop*—Most Rev. Paul-Andre Durocher; *Chancellor*—Rev. Msgr. Normand F. Clement, P.H., V.G.; *Chancery Office*—387 Algonquin, P.O. Box 510, Station Main, North Bay, ON P1B 8J1. Tel: 705-476-1300; Fax: 705-476-9087; *Sudbury Office*—435, Ave. Notre Dame, Sudbury, ON P3C 5K6. Tel: 705-673-4566; Fax: 705-675-7593.

Thunder Bay. *Bishop*—Vacant; *Chancellor*—Sr. Shirley Grexton, C.S.J.; *Chancery Office*—P.O. Box 10400, Thunder Bay, ON P7B 6T8. Tel: 807-343-9313; Fax: 807-343-9114.

Timmins. *Bishop*—Vacant; *Diocesan Administrator*—Rev. Maurice Magnan; *Chancellor*—Sr. Gisele Roy, C.N.D.; *Chancery Office*—65 E. Jubilee Ave., Timmins, ON P4N 5W4. Tel: 705-267-6224; Fax: 705-267-6226.

Trois-Rivieres. *Bishop*—Most Rev. Martin Veillette; *Vicar General*—Rev. Yvon Leclerc; *Chancellor*—Rev. Guy Panneton; *Chancery Office*—362, rue Bonaventure, P.O. Box 879, Trois-Rivieres, QC G9A 5J9. Tel: 819-374-7022; Fax: 819-375-6382.

Valleyfield. *Bishop*—Most Rev. Robert Lebel; *Vicar General*—Rev. Gilles Bergeron; *Chancellor*—Mrs. Monique Boisvert; *Chancery Office*—11, rue de l'Eglise, Salaberry-de-Valleyfield, QC J6T 1J5. Tel: 450-373-8122; Fax: 450-371-0000.

Victoria. *Bishop*—Most Rev. Remi J. De Roo, S.T.D.; *Vicar General*—Rev. Sigismond Lajoie, O.F.M.; *Chancellor*—Rt. Rev. Michael W. Lapierre; *Chancery Office*—1, 4044 Nelthorpe St., Victoria, BC V8X 2A1. Tel: 250-479-1331; Fax: 250-479-5423.

Whitehorse. *Bishop*—Most Rev. Thomas Lobsinger, O.M.I.; *Vicar General*—Rev. Jean-Paul Tanguay, O.M.I.; *Chancellor*—Sr. Margaret Coyle, S.C.I.C., J.C.L.; *Chancery*—406 Steele St., Whitehorse, Yukon Y1A 2C8. Tel: 867-668-3826; Fax: 867-667-4713.

Yarmouth. *Bishop*—Most Rev. James M. Wingle; *Vicar General*—Rev. Gerald LeBlanc; *Chancellor*—Sr. Jeanne Cottreau, S.C.; *Chancery Office*—P.O. Box 278, 53 Park St., Yarmouth, NS B5A 4B2. Tel: 902-742-7163; Fax: 902-742-2465.

ABBEY

Abbey Nullius of St. Peter. *Abbot-Ordinary*—Rt. Rev. Peter Novecosky, O.S.B.; *Vicar General*—Rev. Leo Hinz, O.S.B.; *Chancellor*—Rev. Roman Schneider, O.S.B.; *Chancery Office*—St. Peter's Abbey, Muenster, SK, SOK 2YO. Tel: 306-682-1788; Fax: 306-682-1766.

UKRAINIAN CATHOLIC PROVINCE

Archeparchy and Metropolitan See of Winnipeg. *Archeparch Metropolitan*—Most Rev. Michael Bzdel, C.Ss.R.; *Auxiliary Bishop*—Most Rev. Stefan Soroka; *Chancellor*—Rev. Gregory Oliynek; *Chancery Office*—233 Scotia St., Winnipeg, MB R2V 1V7. Tel: 204-338-7801; Fax: 204-339-4006.

Eparchy of Toronto. *Eparch*—Most Rev. Cornelius John Pasichny, O.S.B.M.; *Chancellor*—Rev. Mitred Archpriest Myron Stasiw, V.G.; *Chancery Office*—143 Franklin Ave., Toronto, ON M6P 3Y9. Tel: 416-538-1436. Fax: 416-538-1639.

Eparchy For Slovaks. *Eparch*—Vacant; *Apostolic Administrator*—Very Rev. John Fetsco, C.Ss.R.; *Chancery Office*—223 Carlton Rd., Unionville, ON L3R 3M2. Tel: 905-477-4867; Fax: 905-887-1032.

Eparchy of Edmonton. *Eparch*—Most Rev. Lawrence Huculak, O.S.B.M.; *Chancellor*—Very Rev. Michael Kowalchyk; *Chancery Office*—9645, 108th Ave., Edmonton, AB T5H 1A3. Tel: 780-424-5496; Fax: 780-425-2330.

Eparchy of New Westminster. *Eparch*—Most Rev. Severian Yakymyshyn, O.S.B.M.; *Chancery Office*—502-5th Ave., New Westminster, BC V3L 1S2. Tel: 604-524-8824; Fax: 604-521-8015.

Eparchy of Saskatoon. *Eparch*—Most Rev. Cornelius Ivan Pasichny, O.S.B.M.; *Vicar General*—Rt. Rev. Msgr. Rudolph Luzney, P.H.; *Chancellor*—Rt. Rev. Vladimir Mudri; *Chancery Office*—866 SK Crescent E., Saskatoon, SK S7N 0L4. Tel: 306-653-0138; Fax: 306-655-2569.

Information for the Apostolic Exarchate for Catholic Armenians for Canada and the United States; Our Lady of Deliverance for Syriac Catholics in the United States and Canada; and the Hungarian Emigrants can be found by referring to the table of contents found at the beginning of the Directory.

MILITARY ORDINARIATE OF CANADA

Military Ordinary—Most Rev. Donald J. Theriault; *Chancellor*—Mrs. Anne Asselin; Tel: 613-998-8747; *Chancery Office*—1247, Kilborn Place, Ottawa, ON K1H 6K9. Tel: 613-990-7824; Fax: 613-991-1056. *Dir. of Chaplaincy Administration*—Colonel Rev. Murray Farwell; Tel: 613-996-5444; *Dir. of Pastoral Services*—Commander Richard Marchand; Tel: 613-992-1399; *Curia Address*—National Defense Headquarters, Ottawa, ON K1A 0K2. Tel: 613-992-1400; Fax: 613-992-6025.

UNITED STATES OF MEXICO

United States of Mexico

The United States of Mexico (Estados Unidos Mexicanos) are ecclesiastically divided into 14 Provinces (14 Archdioceses, 56 Dioceses, 7 Prelacies, and 1 Vicariate Apostolic).
Apostolic Nuncio—Most Rev. Justo Mullor Garcia, D.D., Res. Juan Pablo II No. 118, Col. Guadalupe Inn, Deleg. Alvaro Obregon, 01020 Mexico, D.F. (Apartado Postal 19-106, 03910 Mexico, D.F.) Tel: 525-663-3999; 663-4115; 663-4168; Fax: 525-663-5308.
Secretary—Rt. Rev. Msgr. Jose Spiteri.

PROVINCE OF ACAPULCO

ARCHDIOCESE OF ACAPULCO. Established March 18, 1958. Elevated to an archdiocese on February 10, 1983.
Archbishop—Most Rev. Rafael Bello Ruiz, D.D.; Apartado Postal 201, 39300 Acapulco, Guerrero. Tel: 5274-82-07-63; Fax: 5274-82-07-63.

DIOCESE OF CIUDAD LAZARO CARDENAS. Established in 1985.
Bishop—Most Rev. Salvador Flores Huerta, D.D.
Bishop Emeritus—Most Rev. Jesus Sahagun de la Parra, D.D.; Apartado Postal 500, 60950 Cd. Lazaro Cardenas, Michoacan. Tel: 52753-2-34-88; Fax: 52753-2-29-84.

DIOCESE OF CHILPANCINGO-CHILAPA. Established March 16, 1863. Chilapensis.
Bishop—Most Rev. Efren Ramos Salazar; Apartado Postal 185; 39000 Chilpancingo, Guerrero. Tel: 52747-1-05-92; 1-06-12; Fax: 52747-2-01-13.

DIOCESE OF CIUDAD ALTAMIRANO. Established October 27, 1964. Civitatis Altamirensis.
Bishop—Most Rev. Carlos Garfias Merlos, D.D. (Archbishop of Acapulco); Apartado Postal 17, 40660 Ciudad Altamirano, Guerrero. Tel: 52-767-2-00-37; 2-17-74; Fax: 52767-2-19-12.

DIOCESE OF TLAPA. Established 1994.
Bishop—Most Rev. Alejo Zavala Castro, D.D.; Anexo Catedral, Centro, 41300 Tlapa de Comonfort, Guerrero. Tel: 52-747-6-08-35; 6-09-02.

PROVINCE OF CHIHUAHUA

ARCHDIOCESE OF CHIHUAHUA. Established June 23, 1891. Created Archbishopric November 22, 1958. Chihuahuensis.
Archbishop—Most Rev. Jose Fernandez Arteaga, D.D.; *Archbishop Emeritus*—Most Rev. Adalberto Almeida Merino, D.D.; Apartado Postal 7, 31000 Chihuahua, Chihuahua. Tel: 52-14-10-32-02; 10-32-03; Fax: 5214-10-56-21.

DIOCESE OF CIUDAD JUAREZ. Established April 10, 1957. Civitatis Juarezensis.
Bishop—Most Rev. Renato Ascencio Leon, D.D.; *Bishop Emeritus*—Most Rev. Manuel Talamas Camandari, D.D.; Apartado Postal 188, 32000 Cd. Juarez, Chihuahua. Tel: 52-16-15-09-92; 15-09-82; Fax: 5216-15-00-24.

DIOCESE OF CUAUHTEMOC-MADERA. Established April 25, 1966. Civitatis Materiensis.
Bishop—Most. Rev. Juan Guillermo Lopez, S.,D.D. Apartado Postal 209; 31500 Cuauhtemoc, Chihuahua. Tel & Fax: 52-5-157-2-11-97.

PRELACY OF NUEVO CASAS GRANDES. Established April 13, 1977. Neograndicasensis.
Prelate—Most Rev. Hilario Chavez Joya, M.N.M., D.D., Bishop-Prelate of Nuevo Casas Grandes; Apartado Postal 198, 31700 Nuevo Casas Grandes, Chihuahua. Tel: 52-169-4-05-20; Fax: 52-169-4-36-15.

DIOCESE OF PARRAL.
Bishop—Most Rev. Jose Andres Corral Arredondo, D.D.; Apartado Postal 313, 33800 H. del Parral, Chihuahua. Tel & Fax: 52-152-2-03-71

DIOCESE OF TARAHUMARA.
Bishop—Most Rev. Jose Luis Dibildox Martinez, D.D.; Apartado Postal 11, 33190 Guachochi, Chihuahua. Tel: 52-154-3-02-07; Fax: 52-154-3-07-04.

PROVINCE OF DURANGO

ARCHDIOCESE OF DURANGO. Established September 17, 1620. Created Archbishopric June 23, 1891. Durangensis.
Archbishop—Most Rev. Jose Trinidad Medel Perez, D.D.; *Auxiliary Bishop*—Most Rev. Juan de Dios Caballero Reyes, D.D.; *Archbishop Emeritus*—Most Rev. Antonio Lopez Avina, D.D.; Apartado Postal 116, 34000 Durango, Durango. Tel: 52-18-11-42-42; 11-98-44; Fax: 52-18-12-88-81.

DIOCESE OF CULIACAN. Established May 24, 1883. Formerly Sinaloensis, as of February 16, 1959 became Culiacanensis.
Bishop—Most Rev. Benjamin Jimenez Hernandez, D.D.; *Bishop Emeritus*—Most Rev. Luis Rojas Mena, D.D.; Apartado Postal 666, 80220 Culiacan, Sinaloa. Tel: 52-67-12-32-72; 12-14-97; Fax: 52-67-12-14-97.

DIOCESE OF MAZATLAN. Established November 22, 1958. Mazatlanensis.
Bishop—Most Rev. Rafael Barraza Sanchez, D.D.; Apartado Postal 1, 82000 Mazatlan, Sinaloa. Tel: 52-69-81-33-52; Fax: 52-69-81-04-28.

DIOCESE OF TORREON. Established June 9, 1957. Torreonensis.
Bishop—Most Rev. Luis Morales Reyes, D.D.; *Bishop Emeritus*—Most Rev. Fernando Romo Gutierrez, D.D.; Apartado Postal 430, 27000 Torreon, Coahuila. Tel: 52-17-12-30-43; Fax: 52-17-12-57-81.

PRELACY OF EL SALTO. Established June 12, 1968. Saltensis in Mexico.
Bishop—Most Rev. Manuel Mireles Vaquera, D.D., Bishop-Prelate of El Salto; Apartado Postal 58, 34950, El Salto, Durango. Tel: 52-187-6-00-70 (Phone & Fax).

PROVINCE OF GUADALAJARA

ARCHDIOCESE OF GUADALAJARA. Established July 13, 1548. Created Archbishopric March 19, 1863. Formerly Compostellana now Guadalajarensis.
Archbishop—His Eminence Juan Cardinal Sandoval Iniguez, D.D.; *Auxiliary Bishops*—Most Rev. Ramon Godinez Flores; Most Rev. Javier Navarro Rodriguez, D.D.; Most Rev. J. Luis Chavez Botello, D.D.; Most Rev. Jose Trinidad Gonzalez r., D.D.; *Bishop Emeritus*—Most Rev. Antonio Sahagun Lopez; *Bishop Auxiliary Emeritus*—Most Rev. Adolfo Hernandez Hurtado, D.D.; Apartado Postal 1-331, 44100 Guadalajara, Jalisco. Tel: 52-3-614-55-04; Fax: 52-3-658-23-00.

DIOCESE OF AGUASCALIENTES. Established August 27, 1899. De Aguas Calientes.
Bishop—Most Rev. Rafael Munoz Nunez, D.D.; Apartado Postal 628, 20000 Aguascalientes, Aguascalientes. Tel: 52-49-15-32-61; Fax: 52-49-16-33-12.

DIOCESE OF AUTLAN. Established January 28, 1961. Rivoriensis.
Bishop—Most Rev. Lazaro Perez Jimenez, D.D

Apartado Postal 8, 48900 Autlan, Jalisco. Tel: 52-338-2-12-28 (Phone & Fax).

DIOCESE OF COLIMA. Established December 11, 1881. Colimensis.
Bishop—Most Rev. Gilberto Valbuena Sanchez, D.D.; *Bishop Emeritus*—Most Rev. Rogelio Sanchez Gonzalez, D.D.; Apartado Postal 1, 28000 Colima, Colima. Tel: 52-331-2-02-62; Fax: 52-331-2-43-44.

DIOCESE OF TEPIC. Established June 22, 1891. Tepicensis.
Bishop—Most Rev. Alfonso Humberto Robles Cota, D.D., Apartado Postal 15, 63137 Tepic, Nayarit. Tel: 52-321-4-46-45;4-46-47; Fax: 52-321-3-20-23.

DIOCESE OF ZACATECAS. Established January 26, 1863. Zacatecensis.
Diocesan Administrator—Very Rev. Fernando Chavez Ruvalcaba; *Bishop Emeritus*—Most Rev. Jose Pablo Rovalo Azcue, D.D., Apartado Postal 1, 98000 Zacatecas, Zacatecas. Tel: 52-492-2-65-37; 2-12-74; Fax: 52-492-2-23-42. *Archbishop Emeritus* —Most Rev. Javier Lozano Barragan, D.D., Pres.-Pontifical College for Health Agents, Via della Conciliazione 3, 00193 Rome, Italia. Tel: 39-6-698-3138; Fax: 39-698-3139.

PRELATURE OF JESUS MARIA OF NAYAR. Established May 24, 1962. Nayariana de Jesu et Maria.
Bishop—Most Rev. Antonio Perez Sanchez, O.F.M., D.D., Bishop-Prelate of Jesus Maria of Nayar; *Bishop Emeritus*—Most Rev. Manuel Romero Arvizu, D.D.; Apartado Postal 33-B, 63150 Tepic, Nayarit. Tel: 52-321-3-38-80; 2-14-21.

DIOCESE OF SAN JUAN DE LOS LAGOS. Established March 25, 1972. Sancti Ioannis a Lacubus.
Bishop—Most Rev. Jose Trinidad Sepulveda Ruiz-Velasco, D.D.; Apartado Postal 1, 47000 San Juan de los Lagos, Jalisco. Tel: 52-378-5-05-70; 5-06-57; 5-09-26; Fax: 52-378-5-29-71.

DIOCESE OF CIUDAD GUZMAN. Established March 25, 1972. Civitatis Gusmanopolitana.
Bishop—Most Rev. Serafin Vasquez Elizalde, D.D.; Apartado Postal 86, 49000 Cd. Guzman, Jalisco. Tel: 52-341-2-19-94; 2-05-28. Fax: 52-341-2-15-44.

PROVINCE OF HERMOSILLO

ARCHDIOCESE OF HERMOSILLO. Established May 7, 1779. Created Archbishopric September 4, 1963. Hermosillensis, formerly Sonorensis.
Archbishop—Most Rev. Jose Ulises Macias Salcedo, D.D.; *Archbishop Emeritus*—Most Rev. Carlos Quintero Arce, D.D.; Apartado Postal 1, 83260 Hermosillo, Sonora. Tel: 52-62-13-21-38; Fax: 52-62-13-13-27.

DIOCESE OF CIUDAD OBREGON. Established June 20, 1959. Civitatis Obregonensis.
Bishop—Most Rev. Vicente Garcia Bernal, D.D.; Apartado Postal 402, 85000 Cd. Obregon, Sonora. Tel: 52-641-3-20-98; Fax: 52-641-4-99-94.

DIOCESE OF LA PAZ. Established March 30, 1988. Paciensis in California Inferiori Meridionali.
Bishop—Most Rev. Braulio Rafael Leon Villegas, D.D.; Apartado Postal 25, 23000 La Paz, Baja California Sur. Tel: 52-112-2-25-96; 2-02-08; Fax: 52-112-2-82-72.

DIOCESE OF MEXICALI. Established April 12, 1966. Mexicalensis.
Bishop—Most Rev. Jose Isidro Guerrero G., D.D.; Apartado 3-547, 21100 Mexicali, Baja California Norte. Tel: 52-65-52-40-09; Fax: 52-65-52-45-96.

DIOCESE OF TIJUANA. Established June 13, 1963. Tigiuanaensis, formerly Vicariate Apostolic of Tijuana (July 13, 1957), formerly Californiae Inferioris (January 20, 1874).
Bishop—Most Rev. Rafael Romo Munoz; Apartado Postal 226, 22000 Tijuana, Baja California Norte. Tel: 52-66-84-84-11; 84-84-12; Fax: 52-66-84-76-83.

PROVINCE OF MEXICO

ARCHDIOCESE OF MEXICO. Established Sept. 2, 1530. Created Archbishopric February 12, 1546. Mexicana.
Archbishop Primate—His Eminence Most Rev. Norberto Cardinal Rivera Carrera, D.D.; *Auxiliary Bishops*—Most Rev. Luis Mena Arroyo, D.D.; Most Rev. Abelardo Alvarado Alcantara; Most Rev. Jose de Jesus Martinez Z., D.D.; *Archbishop Primate Emeritus*—His Eminence Most Rev. Ernesto Cardinal Corripio Ahumada, D.D.; *Bishop Auxiliary Emeritus*—Most Rev. Francisco Maria Aguilera Gonzalez, D.D.; Apartado Postal 24-433, 06700 Mexico, D.F. Tel: 52-5-525-1110; 208-3200; Fax: 52-5-208-5350.

DIOCESE OF ATLACOMULCO. Established December 27, 1984.
Diocesan Administrator—Very Rev. Rodrigo Guadarrama Rosas; Apartado Postal 22, 50450 Atlacomulco, Edo. de Mexico. Tel. & Fax: 52-712-2-05-53.

DIOCESE OF CUERNAVACA. Established June 23, 1891. Cuernavacensis.
Bishop—Most Rev. Luis Reynoso Cervantes, D.D.; Apartado Postal 13, 62000 Cuernavaca, Morelos. Tel: 52-73-18-45-90; 18-96-46; Fax: 52-73-18-63-18.

DIOCESE OF TOLUCA. Established June 4, 1950. Tolucensis.
Bishop—Most Rev. Francisco Robles Ortega, D.D.; Apartado Postal 82, 50000 Toluca, Edo. de Mexico. Tel: 52-72-15-25-35; 15-39-59; Fax: 52-72-14-69-55.

DIOCESE OF TULA. Established February 27, 1961. Tullanensis.
Bishop—Most Rev. Octavia Villegas Aguilar, D.D.; Apartado Postal 31, 42800 Tula de Allende, Hidalgo. Tel: 52-773-2-02-75 (Phone & Fax).

DIOCESE OF TULANCINGO. Established January 22, 1862. Tulancingensis.
Bishop—Most Rev. Pedro Aranda-Diaz Munoz, D.D.; Apartado Postal 14, 43600 Tulancingo, Hidalgo. Tel: 52-775-3-10-10 (Phone & Fax).

EPANTLA

ARCHDIOCESE OF TLALNEPANTLA. Established March 31, 1964. Tlalnepantlana. Established as Archdiocese June 28, 1989.
Archbishop—Most Rev. Ricardo Guizar Diaz, D.D.; Apartado Postal 268 y 270, 54000 Tlalnepantla, Edo. de Mexico. Tel: 52-5-565-39-44; 565-39-56; 565-82-90; Fax: 52-5-565-27-51.

DIOCESE OF TEXCOCO. Established April 30, 1960. Texcocensis.
Bishop—Most Rev. Carlos Aguiar Retes, D.D.; *Bishop Emeritus*—Magin C. Torreblanca Reyes, D.D.; Apartado 35, 56100 Texcoco, Edo. de Mexico. Tel: 52-595-4-02-82; 4-35-63. Fax: 52-595-4-08-69.

DIOCESE OF CUAUTITLAN. Established February 5, 1979.
Bishop—Most Rev. Manuel Samaniego Barriga, D.D.; Apartado Postal 14-21, 54800 Cuautitlan, Edo. de Mexico. Tel: 52-5-872-19-96; Fax: 52-5-872-3004.

DIOCESE OF NETZAHUALCOYOTL. Established May 1, 1979.
Bishop—Most Rev. Jose Maria Hernandez Gonzalez, D.D.; *Bishop Emeritus*—Most Rev. Jose Melgoza Osorio, D.D.; Apartado Postal 89, 57700 Cd. Netzahualcoyotl, Edo. de Mexico. Tel: 52-5-797-6132; 797-8301; Fax: 52-5-765-9804.

DIOCESE OF ECATEPEC.
Bishop—Most Rev. Onesimo Cepeda Silva, D.D.; Apartado Postal 95, 55000 Ecatepec de Morelos, Edo de Mexico. Tel: 52-5-116-0976; Fax: 52-5-882-4019.

PROVINCE OF MONTERREY

ARCHDIOCESE OF MONTERREY. Established December 15, 1777. Created Archbishopric June 28, 1898. Monterreyensis formerly Linarensis.
Archbishop—His Eminence Most Rev. Adolfo Antonio Cardinal Suarez Rivera, D.D.; *Auxiliary Bishops*—Most Rev. Jose Lizares Estrada, D.D.; Most Rev. Alfonso Hinojosa Berrones, D.D.; *Chancery*—Apartado Postal 7, 64000 Monterrey, Nuevo Leon. Tel: 52-83-45-24-66; 45-24-18; Fax: 52-83-45-35-57.

DIOCESE OF CIUDAD VALLES. Established November 27, 1960. Vallipolitana.
Bishop—Most Rev. Jose Guadalupe Galvan Galindo, D.D.; *Chancery*—Apartado Postal 170, 79000 Ciudad Valles, San Luis Potosi. Tel: 52-138-2-25-97; Fax: 52-138-2-47-96.

DIOCESE OF CIUDAD VICTORIA. Established December 21, 1964. Civitatis Victoriensis.
Bishop—Most Rev. Antonio Gonzalez Sanchez, D.D.; *Chancery*—Apartado Postal 335, 87000 Ciudad Victoria, Tamaulipas. Tel: 52-131-2-80-83; Fax: 52-131-6-48-11. *Bishop Emeritus*—Most Rev. Raimundo Lopez Mateos, D.D., Res., Roger Bacon College - Franciscan Friars, 2400 Marr St., El Pasto, TX 79903.

DIOCESE OF LINARES. Established April 30, 1962. Linarina.
Bishop—Most Rev. Ramon Calderon Batres, D.D.; Apartado Postal 70, 67700 Linares, Nuevo Leon. Tel: 52-821-2-00-54; Fax: 52-821-2-07-50.

DIOCESE OF MATAMOROS. Established February 16, 1958. Matamorensis.
Bishop—Most Rev. Francisco Javier Chavolla Ramos, D.D.; Apartado Postal 70, 87351 H. Matamoros, Tamaulipas. Tel: 52-88-13-36-58; Fax: 52-88-16-06-08.

DIOCESE OF NUEVO LAREDO. Established January 10, 1990. Nuevo Laredensis.
Bishop—Most Rev. Ricardo Watty Urquidi, M.Sp.S., D.D.; Apartado Postal 20-B, 88280 Nuevo Laredo, Tamaulipas. Tel: 52-871-5-29-28; 5-83-95; Fax: 52-871-5-57-99.

DIOCESE OF SALTILLO. Established June 23, 1891. Saltillensis.
Bishop—Most Rev. Francisco Raul Villalobos Padilla, D.D.; Apartado Postal 25, 25000 Saltillo, Coahuila. Tel: 52-84-12-37-84; Fax: 52-84-14-92-67.

DIOCESE OF TAMPICO. Established March 6, 1870. Tampicensis formerly Civitatis Victoriae or Tamaulipana.
Bishop—Most Rev. Rafael Gallardo Garcia, O.S.A., D.D.; Apartado Postal 545, 89000 Tampico, Tamaulipas. Tel: 52-12-12-28-10; 12-28-02; Fax: 52-12-12-67-81.

PROVINCE OF MORELIA

ARCHDIOCESE OF MORELIA. Established August 11, 1536. Created Archbishopric March 19, 1863. Moreliensis.
Archbishop—Most Rev. Alberto Suarez Inda, D.D.; *Bishop Emeritus*—Most Rev. Estanislao Alcaraz, F., D.D.; *Chancery*—Apartado Postal 17, 58000 Morelia, Michoacan. Tel: 52-43-12-05-23; 12-37-38; Fax: 52-43-12-37-44.

DIOCESE OF APATZINGAN. Established April 30, 1962. Apatzinganiensis.
Bishop—Most Rev. Miguel Patino Velazquez, M.S.F., D.D., Calle Esteban Vaca Calderon 100, 60600 Apatzingan, Michoacan. Tel: 52-453-4-17-87; Fax: 52-453-4-22-26.

DIOCESE OF TACAMBARO. Established July 26, 1913. Tacambarensis.
Bishop—Most Rev. Rogelio Cabrera Lopez, D.D. Apartado Postal 4, 61650 Tacambaro, Michoacan. Tel: 52-454-6-00-44; Fax: 52-454-6-07-30.

DIOCESE OF ZAMORA. Established January 26, 1862. Zamorensis.
Bishop —Most Rev. Carlos Suarez Cazarez, D.D.; *Chancery*—Apartado Postal 18, 59600 Zamora, Michoacan. Tel: 52-351-2-12-08; 2-04-82; Fax: 52-351-5-40-20.

PROVINCE OF OAXACA

ARCHDIOCESE OF OAXACA. Established 1535. Created Archbishopric June 23, 1981.
Archbishop—Most Rev. Hector Gonzalez Martinez, D.D.; *Auxiliary Bishop*—Most Rev. Miguel Angel Alba Diaz, D.D.; *Archbishop Emeritus*—Most Rev. Bartolome Carrasco Briseno, D.D.; Apartado Postal 31, 68000 Oaxaca, Oaxaca. Tel: 52-951-6-48-22; Fax: 52-951-4-13-48.

DIOCESE OF SAN CRISTOBAL DE LAS CASAS. Established March 19, 1539. S. Christophori de las Casas.
Bishop—Most Rev. Samuel Ruiz Garcia, D.D; *Bishop Coadjutor*—Most Rev. Raul Vera Lopez, O.P., D.D; *Chancery*—Av. 20 de Noviembre 1, Centro, 29200 San Cristobal de las Casas, Chiapas. Tel: 52-967-8-00-53; Fax: 52-967-8-31-36.

DIOCESE OF TAPACHULA. Established June 19, 1957. Tapacolensis.
Bishop—Most Rev. Felipe Arizmendi Esquivel, D.D.; Apartado Postal 70, 30700 Tapachula, Chiapas. Tel: 52-962-6-15-03; Fax: 52-962-6-50-24.

DIOCESE OF TEHUANTEPEC. Established June 23, 1891, in San Andres Tuxtla, State of Veracruz. Transferred May 23, 1959 to Tehuantepec, State of Oaxaca, Tehuantepecensis.
Bishop-Most Rev. Arturo Lona Reyes, D.D.; *Bishop Coadjutor*-Most Rev. Felipe Padilla Cardona, D.D.; Apartado Postal 93, 70760 Tehuantepec, Oaxaca. Tel: 52-971-5-00-60; Fax: 52- 971-5-14-42.

DIOCESE OF TUXTLA GUTIERREZ. Established October 27, 1964. Tuxtlensis.
Bishop—Most Rev. Felipe Aguirre Franco, D.D.; *Chancery*—Anexo a St. Domingo, 1a Poniente Norte 232, 29000 Tuxtla Gutierrez, Chiapas. Tel: 52-961-2-21-54; Fax: 52-961-1-35-67.

DIOCESE OF TUXTEPEC. Established January 8, 1979.
Bishop—Most Rev. Jose de Jesus Castillo Renteria, M.N.M., D.D.; Apartado Postal 9, 68300 Tuxtepec, Oaxaca. Tel: 52-287-5-00-42.

PRELACY OF MIXES. Decreed on December 21, 1964. Mixepolitana.
Bishop-Prelate—Most Rev. Braulio Sanchez Fuentes, S.D.B., D.D., Bishop-Prelate of Mixes; Res., Ayutla-Mixes, Oaxaca; Mailing Address: Av. H. Colegio Militar No. 721, Colonia Reforma, 70283 Ayutla-Mixes, Oaxaca. Tel: 52-951-5-25-56 (Phone & Fax).

PRELACY OF HUAUTLA. Decreed October 7, 1972. Huautlensis.
Bishop-Prelate—Most Rev. Hermenegildo Ramirez Sanchez, M.J., D.D.; Apartado Postal 2, 68500 Huautla de Jimenez, Oaxaca. Tel: 52-237-8-00-19 (Phone & Fax).

PROVINCE OF SAN LUIS POTOSI

ARCHDIOCESE OF SAN LUIS POTOSI. Established August 31, 1854. S. Ludovici Potesiensis.
Archbishop—Most Rev. Arturo Antonio Szymanski

Ramirez, D.D.; Apartado Postal 1, 78000 San Luis Potosi, S.L.P. Tel: 52-48-12-45-55; 12-22-50; Fax: 52-48-12-79-79.

DIOCESE OF CELAYA. Established October 13, 1973. Celayensis.
Bishop—Most Rev. Jesus Humberto Velazquez Garay, D.D.; Apartado Postal 207, 38000 Celaya, Guanajuato. Tel: 52-461-2-43-98 (Phone & Fax).

DIOCESE OF LEON. Established January 26, 1863. Leonensis.
Bishop—Most Rev. Jose Guadalupe Martin Rabago, D.D.; *Bishop Emeritus*—Most Rev. Anselmo Zarza Bernal, D.D.; *Chancery*—Pedro Moreno 312, 37000 Leon, Guanajuato. Tel: 52-47-13-27-47; Fax: 52-47-13-08-15.

DIOCESE OF QUERETARO. Established January 26, 1882. Queretarensis.
Bishop—Most Rev. Mario de Gasperin Gasperin, D.D.; Apartado Postal 49, 76000 Queretaro, Queretaro. Tel: 52-42-12-10-33; Fax: 52-42-12-18-45.

DIOCESE OF MATEHUALA.
Bishop—Most Rev. Rodrigo Aguilar M., D.D. Apartado Postal 140, 78700 Matehuala, San Luis Potosi. Tel: 52-488-2-35-05; Fax: 52-488-2-08-42.

PROVINCE OF PUEBLA DE LOS ANGELES

ARCHDIOCESE OF PUEBLA DE LOS ANGELES. Established October 13, 1525. Created Archbishopric August 11, 1903. Angelorum formerly Tlascalensis.
Archbishop—Most Rev. Rosendo Huesca Pacheco, D.D.; Apartado Postal 235, 72000 Puebla, Puebla. Tel: 52-22-32-62-12; Fax: 52-22-46-22-77.

DIOCESE OF HUAJUAPAN DE LEON. Established November 13, 1903. Huajuapanensis.
Diocesan Administrator—Most Rev. Felipe Padilla Cardona, D.D.; *Bishop Emeritus*—Most Rev. Jose De Jesus Aguilera Rodriguez, D.D.; Apartado Postal 43, 69000 Huajuapan de Leon, Oaxaca. Tel: 52-953-2-07-97; Fax: 52-953-2-06-36.

DIOCESE OF HUEJUTLA. Established November 24, 1922. Huejutlensis.
Bishop—Most Rev. Salvador Martinez Perez, D.D.; *Chancery*—Apartado Postal 8, 43000 Huejutla, Hidalgo. Tel: 52-129-6-01-85 (Phone & Fax).

DIOCESE OF TEHUACAN. Established January 13, 1962. Tehuacaniensis.
Bishop—Most Rev. Mario Espinosa Contreras, D.D.; Apartado Postal 137, 75700 Tehuacan, Puebla. Tel: 52-238-3-20-00; Fax: 52-238-3-14-68.

DIOCESE OF TLAXCALA. Established May 23, 1959. Tlaxcalensis.
Bishop—Most Rev. Luis Munive Escobar, D.D.; *Coadjutor Bishop*—Most Rev. Jacinto Guerrero Torres, D.D.; Apartado Postal 84, 90000 Tlaxcala, Tlaxcala. Tel: 52-246-2-07-23; Fax: 52-246-2-0739.

PROVINCE OF XALAPA

ARCHDIOCESE OF XALAPA. Established March 19, 1863. Created Archbishopric June 29, 1951. Jalapensis, formerly Verae Crucis.
Archbishop—Most Rev. Sergio Obeso Rivera, D.D.; Apartado Postal 359, 91000 Xalapa, Veracruz. Tel: 52-28-17-29-35; 52-28-17-55-78.

DIOCESE OF PAPANTLA. Established November 24, 1922. Papantlensis.
Bishop—Most Rev. Lorenzo Cardenas Aregullin, D.D.; *Bishop Emeritus*—Most Rev. Genaro Alamilla Arteaga, D.D.; *Chancery*—Apartado Postal 27, 73800 Teziutlan, Puebla. Tel: 52-231-2-01-69.

DIOCESE OF SAN ANDRES TUXTLA. Established May 23, 1959. On March 14, 1984, the Diocese of San Andres Tuxtla was divided into two jurisdictions: San Andres Tuxtla and the New Diocese of Coatzacoalcos, as a suffragan diocese of Jalapa.
Bishop—Most Rev. Guillermo Ranzahuer Gonzalez, D.D.; Constitucion y Morelos s/n, 95700 San Andres Tuxtla, Veracruz. Tel: 52-294-2-12-45; Fax: 52-294-2-03-74.

DIOCESE OF COATZACOALCOS. Established March 14, 1984. Coatzacoalsensis.
Bishop—Most Rev. Carlos Talavera Ramirez, D.D.; Apartado Postal 513, 96400 Coatzacoalcos, Veracruz. Tel: 52-921-2-59-03; Fax: 52-921-2-73-23.

DIOCESE OF TUXPAN. Established June 9, 1962. Tuxpaniensis.
Bishop—Most Rev. Luis Gabriel Cuara Mendez, D.D.; Juarez 30, Col. Centro, 92800 Tuxpan, Veracruz. Tel: 52-783-4-00-28 (Phone & Fax).

DIOCESE OF VERACRUZ. Established January 19, 1963. Verae Crucis.
Bishop—Most Rev. Jose Guadalupe Padilla Lozano, D.D.; Insurgentes Veracruzanos 470, Paseo del Malecon, 91700 Veracruz, Veracruz. Tel: 52-29-32-20-26; 52-29-31-24-13.

PROVINCE OF YUCATAN

ARCHDIOCESE OF YUCATANENSIS. Established December 16, 1561. Created Archbishopric November 11, 1906.
Archbishop—Most Rev. Emilio Carlos Berlie Belaunzaran, D.D.; *Archbishop Emeritus*—Most Rev. Manuel Castro Ruiz, D.D.; Calle 58, 501 Centro, 97000 Merida, Yucatan. Tel: 52-99-28-62-14.

DIOCESE OF CAMPECHE. Established July 25, 1845. Campecorensis.
Bishop—Most Rev. Jose Luis Amezcua, D.D.; *Bishop Emeritus*—Most Rev. Jesus Garcia Ayala, D.D.; Apartado Postal 127, 24000 Campeche, Campeche. Tel: 52-981-6-26-05; Fax: 52-981-6-03-39.

DIOCESE OF TABASCO. Established May 25, 1880. Tabasquensis.
Bishop—Most Rev. Florencio Olvera Ochoa, D.D.; Apartado Postal 97, 86000 Villahermosa, Tabasco. Tel: 52-93-12-13-97; Fax: 52-93-12—19-05.

PRELACY OF CANCUN-CHETUMAL. Established November 21, 1970. Chetumaliensis.
Bishop-Prelate—Most Rev. Jorge Bernal Vargas, L.C., D.D.; Apartado Postal 165, 77000 Chetumal, Quintana Roo. Tel: 52-983-2-06-38; Fax: 52-983-2-25-70.

EPARCHY OF NUESTRA SENORA DEL PARAISO (Melquite Greek Rite). *Bishop*—Most Rev. Antonio Mouhanna, D.D.; Iglesia de Porta Coeli, Venustiano Carranza 107, 06060 Mexico, D.F. Tel: 52-5-542-0225; Fax: 52-5-575-1687.

MEXICAN BISHOPS' CONFERENCE. Most Rev. Luis Morales Reyes, Bishop of Torreon, Pres.; Most Rev. Jose Guadalupe Martin Rabago, Bishop of Leon, Vice Pres.; Most Rev. Abelardo Alvarado Alcantara, Auxiliary Bishop of Mexico, Sec. Gral.; Most Rev. Gilberto Valbuena Sanchez, Bishop of Colima, Treas.; Most Rev. Jose Guadalupe Martin, Auxiliary Bishop of Guadalajara, First Vocal; Most Rev. Mario de Gasperin Gasperin, Second Vocal; Rev. Luis Guillermo Herrera Herrera, Exec. Sec.; Prolongacion Misterios 24-B, Col. Tepeyac Insurgentes, 07020 Mexico, D.F. Tel: 52-5-781-84-62; 577-54-01; 577-54-31. Fax: 52-5-577-5489.

SHRINE OF OUR LADY OF GUADALUPE. *Abbot*—Rt. Rev. Msgr. Guillermo Schulenburg; Very Rev. Carlos Warnholtz Bustillos; Basilica de N.S. de Guadalupe, Apartado 14-120, 07050 Mexico, D.F. Tel: 52-5-577-6022; 577-6088; Fax: 52-5-577-5038.

CONFERENCIA DE INSTITUTOS RELIGIOSOS DE MEXICO. Rev. Jose Morales Orozco, S.J., Pres.; Rev. Ruben Cabello Ramos, S.J., Sec. Gral.; Sr. Mariela Pena Kipper, R.S.C.J., Vice Pres.; Bro. Joaquin Flores Segura, S.M.S., Vice Pres.; Vocals: Sr. Constanza Aguilar Abril; Sr. Maria Luisa Chapa Urquidi, M.E.S.S.T.; Sr. Raquel Hernandez Garcia, H.J.; Sr. Delia Esther Peruyera Cruz, O.D.N.; Sr. Elena Andrade Moreno, F.M.M.; Rev. Jorge Ortiz Gonzalez, M.Sp.S.; Rev. Joaquin Azcona M., S.V.D.; Rev. Roberto Balmori Cinta, M.J.; Rev. Aaron J. Cahuantzi Bello, S.CH.P.; Rev. Miguel Conca Malo, O.P.; Av. Amores 1318, Col. del Valle, 03100 Mexico, D.F. Tel: 52-5-604-5414; Fax: 52-5-604-9555.

American Foreign Missions

Augustinian Missions (O.S.A.)

Foreign Missions of the Midwestern Provinces of the Order of St. Augustine (O.S.A.)

Foreign Missions

Provincial Headquarters

Province of Our Mother of Good Counsel (Midwestern): *Tolentine Center,* 20300 Governors Highway, Olympia Fields, IL 60461-1081. Tel: 708-748-5435; Fax: 708-481-2090. Very Rev. Robert F. Prevost, O.S.A. Ord: '82. Prov. Bro. John J. Stobba, O.S.A., Mission Procurator.

Midwestern Augustinian Religious serving in foreign missions: Most Rev. John C. McNabb, O.S.A., D.D. Ord: '52, Peru; Most Rev. Daniel T. Turley, O.S.A. Ord: '68, Peru; Revs. Alfred M. Burke, O.S.A. Ord: '57, Japan; Charles J. Bodden, O.S.A. Ord: '78, Peru; John J. Dowling, O.S.A. Ord: '68, Peru; Richard Palmer, O.S.A. Ord: '87, Peru; John P. Tasto, O.S.A. Ord: '67, Mexico; John A. Tyma, O.S.A. Ord: '59, Peru; Christopher C. Steinle, O.S.A. Ord: '98, Peru.

Province of St. Thomas of Villanova (Eastern): P.O. Box 340, Villanova, PA 19085-0340. Tel: 610-525-3330; Fax: 610-520-0618. Very Rev. John E. Deegan, O.S.A. Ord: '61, Prior Prov. Tel: 610-525-9962. Revs. Richard D. Appicci, O.S.A. Ord: '60, Dir. Missions; Anthony P. Burrascano, O.S.A. Ord: '79, Mission Procurator.

U.S. Religious serving in foreign missions: Revs. John J. Lydon, O.S.A. Ord: '84; Richard G. Mullen, O.S.A. Ord: '81; Maurice J. Mahoney, O.S.A. Ord: '60; Thomas P. Dwyer, O.S.A. Ord: '53; Aquilino D. Gonzalez, O.S.A. Ord: '72; Robert P. Terranova, O.S.A. Ord: '73; Michael J. Hilden, O.S.A. Ord: '73; Michael H. Stanley, O.S.A. Ord: '81; Edward V. Hattrick, O.S.A. Ord: '56; Thomas P. Purcell, O.S.A. Ord: '43.

American Benedictine Foreign Missions (O.S.B.)

American - Cassinese Congregation Foreign Missions

St. Vincent Archabbey: 300 Fraser Purchase Rd., Latrobe, PA 15650-2690. Tel: 724-532-6600. Rt. Rev. Douglas R. Nowicki, O.S.B. Ord: '72, Archabbot; Rev. Noel H. Rothrauff, O.S.B. Ord: '54, Mission Dir.

U.S. Religious serving Abroad: Bro. Nicholas Koss, O.S.B., Prior, Taiwan.

St. John's Abbey, Box 2015, Collegeville, MN 56321-2015. Fax: 320-363-3082.

U.S. Religious serving Abroad: Very Rev. Robert Pierson, O.S.B. Ord: '84, Prior, Nassau; Revs. Kieran Nolan, O.S.B. Ord: '59, Japan; Neal Henry Lawrence, O.S.B. Ord: '60, Japan; Mel Taylor, O.S.B. Ord: '67, Bahamas; Aloysius Michels, O.S.B. Ord: '39, Japan; Fintan Bromenshenkel, O.S.B. Ord: '45, Nassau; George Wolf, O.S.B. Ord: '44, Nassau; Anthony Hellenberg, O.S.B. Ord: '66, Nassau; Thomas Wahl, O.S.B. Ord: '58, Japan; Cyprian Weaver, O.S.B. Ord: '72, Taiwan; William Skudlarek, O.S.B. Ord: '64, Japan.

St. Benedict's Abbey, Atchison, KS 66002. Tel: 913-367-7853; Fax: 913-367-6230. Rt. Rev. Barnabas Senecal, O.S.B., Abbot.

U.S. Religious serving in Brazil: Most Rev. Herbert Hermes. Rev. Kieran McInerney, O.S.B. Ord: '52. Rev. Duane Roy, O.S.B. Ord: '67.

St. Procopius Abbey: 5601 College Rd., Lisle, IL 60532. Tel: 630-969-6410; Fax: 630-969-6426.

U.S. Religious serving in China: Very Rev. Alban Hrebic, O.S.B. Ord: '52, Prior.

Assumption Abbey: P.O. Box A, Richardton, ND 58652. Tel: 701-974-3315.

U.S. Religious serving in South America: Very Rev. Philip Vanderlin, O.S.B. Ord: '80, Prior; Revs. Gonzalo Blanco, O.S.B., Subprior; Efraim Villegas, O.S.B. Ord: '88; Carlos Suarez, O.S.B. Ord: '86; Francis Wehri, O.S.B. Ord: '61; Gonzalo Blanco, O.S.B. Ord: '92; Nicolas Cano Ord: '97; Milton Martinez Ord: '97; Bros. Fabio Mejia; Manuel Cely; Roberto Duarte; Alexander Narvaez.

Mount Angel Abbey: St. Benedict, OR 97373. Tel: 503-845-3030; Fax: 503-845-3594. Monks of Mount Angel Abbey (Benedictines).

U.S. Religious serving in Mexico: Very Rev. Konrad Shaefer, O.S.B. Ord: '80. Revs. Louis Charvet, O.S.B. Ord: '45; Bro. James Bartos, O.S.B.

Marmion Abbey: 850 Butterfield Rd., Aurora, IL 60504.

U.S. Religious serving in Central America: Very Rev. John Brahill, O.S.B. Ord: '82, Prior; Revs. Matthias Zinkan, O.S.B. Ord: '40; Gerald Benkert, O.S.B. Ord: '34.

Blue Cloud Abbey: Marvin, SD 57251. Tel: 605-398-9200; Fax: 605-398-9201. Rt. Rev. Thomas Hillenbrand Ord: '65, Supr. & Mission Dir.

U.S. Religious serving in Guatemala: Revs. Basil Dilger, O.S.B. Ord: '61; Cletus Miller, O.S.B. Ord: '44; Bernardine Ness, O.S.B. Ord: '64.

New Subiaco Abbey: Subiaco, AR 72865; Fax: 501-934-4328. Rt. Rev. Jerome Kodell, O.S.B., Supr.

U.S. Religious serving in Central America: Revs. Richard Walz, O.S.B. Ord: '67, Prior; Bruno Fuhrmann, O.S.B. Ord: '54; Bro. Tobias DeSalvo, O.S.B.

St. Paul's Abbey: Newton, NJ 07860. Tel: 973-383-2470; Fax: 973-383-5782.

U.S. Religious serving Abroad: Revs. Damian Milliken, O.S.B. Ord: '58, Tanzania; Peter W. Blue, O.S.B. Ord: '70, South Africa.

American Capuchin Missions (O.F.M.Cap.)

Missions of the American Provinces of the Order of Friars Minor Capuchin (The Capuchin Friars) in the United States and other countries

General Headquarters: Via Piemonte, 70, 00187, Rome, Italy. Most Rev. John Corriveau, O.F.M.Cap., Gen. Min.; Rev. Linus Faeh, O.F.M.Cap., Sec. Gen. for the Missions.

Provincial Headquarters

Capuchin Foreign Missions

Province of St. Joseph: 740 Mt. Elliott Ave., Detroit, MI 48207. Fax: 313-579-2275. Revs. Daniel Fox, O.F.M.Cap. Ord: '75, Prov. Minister; James Zelinski, O.F.M.Cap. Ord: '61, Mission Sec.

U.S. Religious serving Abroad: Revs. Charles Bantle, O.F.M.Cap. Ord: '48, Japan; Evarist Bertrand, O.F.M.Cap. Ord: '63, Nicaragua; Paul Craig, O.F.M.Cap. Ord: '66, Middle East; Francis Solanus Fary, O.F.M.Cap. Ord: '67, Nicaragua; Ralph Fellenz, O.F.M.Cap. Ord: '68, Panama; Carmel Flora, O.F.M.Cap. Ord: '53, Australia; Bro. Patrick Forton, O.F.M.Cap., Nicaragua; Revs. Glenn Gessner, O.F.M.Cap. Ord: '60, Nicaragua; Kevin Heagerty, O.F.M.Cap. Ord: '61, Panama; Walter Kasuboski, O.F.M.Cap. Ord: '74, Panama; Wilbert Lanser, O.F.M.Cap. Ord: '59, Nicaragua; Benjamin Markwell, O.F.M.Cap. Ord: '66, Middle East; John Myers, O.F.M.Cap. Ord: '54, Australia; Theodore Niehaus, O.F.M.Cap. Ord: '65, Nicaragua; John Francis Samsa, O.F.M.Cap. Ord: '61, Honduras; Most Rev. Paul Schmitz, O.F.M.Cap., Ord: '70, Bishop-Vicar Apostolic of Bluefields, Nicaragua; Revs. August Seubert, O.F.M.Cap. Ord: '57, Nicaragua; Gregory Smutko, O.F.M.Cap. Ord: '58, Costa Rica; Bernard Wagner, O.F.M.Cap. Ord: '63, Nicaragua; Lawrence Webber, O.F.M.Cap. Ord: '80, Costa Rica; Andre Weller, O.F.M.Cap. Ord: '63, Panama; Nicholas Widhammer, O.F.M.Cap. Ord: '63, Middle East; Joseph Wolf, O.F.M.Cap. Ord: '64, Nicaragua; David Zywiec, O.F.M.Cap. Ord: '74, Nicaragua.

Province of Mid-America: 3553 Wyandot St., Denver, CO 80211-2948. Tel: 303-477-0296; Fax: 303-477-6925. Revs. David Gottschalk, O.F.M.Cap. Ord: '69, Prov. Min.; John Lager, O.F.M.Cap. Ord: '79, Mission Sec.

U.S. Religious serving in Papua New Guinea (St. Michael the Archangel Vice Provice of Papua New Guinea and the Solomon Islands): Most Rev. Stephen Reichert, O.F.M.Cap. Ord: '69, Bishop of Mendi; Revs. Myron Flax, O.F.M.Cap. Ord: '64; Peter Meis, O.F.M.Cap. Ord: '67; Donald Debes, O.F.M.Cap. Ord: '70; Bro. Gerald Wintz, O.F.M.Cap.

Province of St. Augustine: 220 37th St., Pittsburgh, PA 15201. Tel: 412-682-6011; Fax: 412-682-0506. Very Rev. Paul Kuppe, O.F.M.Cap. Ord: '70, Prov. Min.; Rev. Francis Fugini, O.F.M.Cap. Ord: '54, Coord. of Missions.

U.S. Religious serving in Puerto Rico (St. John the Baptist Vice Province): Revs. John Bednarik, O.F.M.Cap. Ord: '68, Definitor Gen.; Mario Mastrangelo, O.F.M.Cap. Ord: '58; Leo Morgan, O.F.M.Cap. Ord: '44; Regis Schlick, O.F.M.Cap. Ord: '65.

U.S. Religious serving in Papua New Guinea (St. Michael the Archangel Vice Province of Papua New Guinea and the Solomon Islands): Revs. Allan Wasiecko, O.F.M.Cap. Ord: '68, Vice-Prov.; Emilio Biosca, O.F.M.Cap. Ord: '94; Samuel Driscoll, O.F.M.Cap. Ord: '59; William Fey, O.F.M.Cap. Ord: '68; Dunstan Jones, O.F.M.Cap. Ord: '61; Benjamin Madden, O.F.M.Cap. Ord: '58; Brian Newman, O.F.M.Cap. Ord: '61; Cyril Repko, O.F.M.Cap. Ord: '62; Bro. Raymond Ronan, O.F.M.Cap.; Revs. Colman Studeny, O.F.M.Cap. Ord: '61; Joseph Tuscan, O.F.M.Cap. Ord: '97; Roger White, O.F.M.Cap. Ord: '65; Jonathan Williams, O.F.M.Cap. Ord: '71.

Province of St. Mary: 30 Gedney Park Dr., White Plains, NY 10605. Tel: 914-761-3008. Very Rev. Bernard Smith, O.F.M.Cap. Ord: '64, Prov.; Rev. Peter Kaseta, O.F.M.Cap. Ord: '67, Mission Sec.

U.S. Religious serving in Guam: Revs. Lee G. Friel, O.F.M.Cap. Ord: '56, Guam; George Maddock, O.F.M.Cap. Ord: '64, Guam; Randolph Nowak, O.F.M.Cap. Ord: '52, Guam.

U.S. Religious serving in Japan: Revs. Wayne Berndt, O.F.M.Cap. Ord: '83; Louis Chiusano, O.F.M.Cap. Ord: '57; Roland Daigle, O.F.M.Cap. Ord: '84, Japan; Peter Von Essen, O.F.M.Cap. Ord: '56, Japan; John Szamreta, O.F.M.Cap. Ord: '81, Japan; Bartholomew Minson, O.F.M.Cap. Ord: '64, Japan; LaSalle Parsons, O.F.M.Cap. Ord: '57, Japan.

U.S. Religious serving in Central America: Revs. Roderick Brennan, O.F.M.Cap. Ord: '45, Nicaragua; Peter Danaher, O.F.M.Cap. Ord: '84, El Salvador; John Clermont, O.F.M.Cap. Ord: '53, Honduras; Raymond Richard, O.F.M.Cap. Ord: '72, Honduras; Jose McCarthy, O.F.M.Cap. Ord: '60, Puerto Rico.

The Seraphic Mass Association-Capuchin Mission Association: St. Mary's Province, 210 West 31st St., New York, NY 10001-2876.

This Association supports the Capuchin Foreign Mission.

American Carmelite Missions (O.Carm)

Carmelite Foreign Missions

Foreign Missions of the American Province of the Most Pure Heart of Mary

Provincial Headquarters: *Carmelite Provincial Office,* 1317 Frontage Rd., Darien, IL 60561. Fax: 630-971-0195. Very Rev. Leo McCarthy, O.Carm. Ord: '62, Prov.

Mission Office: Carmelite Missions, 1317 Frontage Rd., Darien, IL 60561. Very Rev. John Malley, O.Carm. Ord: '56, Mission Dir.

U.S. Religious serving in Peru: Revs. Gerald Payea, O.Carm. Ord: '70, Formation Dir.; Joseph Lucchesi, O.Carm. Ord: '84; Kevin Lafey, O.Carm. Ord: '72; Alban Quinn, O.Carm. Ord: '49; Joseph Cilia, O.Carm. Ord: '68; Salvador Bartolo, O.Carm. Ord: '52; Rev. Msgr. Michael LaFay, O.Carm. Ord: '60; Revs. Michael Brown, O.Carm. Ord: '93; James Geaney, O.Carm. Ord: '59; Enrique Laguna, O.Carm. Ord: '90; Michael Sgarioto, O.Carm. Ord: '85; Edward Adelmann, O.Carm. Ord: '75.

U.S. Religious serving in Mexico: Revs. John Hertel, O.Carm. Ord: '53; Thomas Jordan, O.Carm. Ord: '70; Joel Moelter, O.Carm. Ord: '51; William Smith, O.Carm. Ord: '54; Charles Countie, O.Carm. Ord: '78.

Comboni Missionaries (Verona Fathers) (M.C.C.J.)

Comboni Foreign Missions

Legal Title: Comboni Missionaries of the Heart of Jesus, Inc.

U.S. Headquarters: Comboni Mission Center, 8108 Beechmont Ave., Cincinnati, OH 45255-3194. Tel: 513-474-4997; Fax: 513-474-0382. E-mail: klcomboni@juno.com; Website: www.ComboniMissionaries.org. Revs. Dennis Conway, M.C.C.J. Ord: '68, Prov. Supr.; Joseph Bragotti, M.C.C.J. Ord: '62, Mission Dir. & Vice Prov.

U.S. Religious serving Abroad: Revs. Albert Anichini, M.C.C.J. Ord: '62, Uganda; Manuel Baeza, M.C.C.J. Ord: '96, South Africa; David Baltz, M.C.C.J. Ord: '67, Uganda; Michael Barton, M.C.C.J. Ord: '75, Sudan; David Bohnsack, M.C.C.J. Ord: '94, Sudan; Angel Camorlinga, M.C.C.J. Ord: '96, Ecuador; James Francez, M.C.C.J. Ord: '57, Mexico; Luis Monzon-Tapia, M.C.C.J. Ord: '95, Ecuador; Raymond Pax, M.C.C.J. Ord: '65, Sudan; John Converset, M.C.C.J. Ord: '71, South Africa.

American Conventual Franciscan Missions (O.F.M.Conv.)

Conventual Franciscan Foreign Missions

General Headquarters: Convento SS. XII Apostoli Piazza SS. Apostoli, 51, 00187, Roma, Italia. Most Rev. Enrique Montero, O.F.M.Conv., Sec. Gen. for the Missions.

Provincial Headquarters

Province of the Immaculate Conception: P.O. Box 629, 517 Washington Ave., Rensselaer, NY 12144. Very Rev. Canice Connors, O.F.M.Conv. Ord: '61, Prov. & Mission Dir. Tel: 518-472-1000.

U.S. Religious serving Abroad: Revs. Bertrand Hodes, O.F.M.Conv. Ord: '39; Maury Marhafer, O.F.M.Conv. Ord: '54; Most Rev. Elias Manning, O.F.M.Conv., Bishop of Valenca, Brazil.

Province of Saint Anthony of Padua: Provincial House & Office of Mission Procurator, 12300 Folly Quarter Rd., Ellicott City, MD 21042-1419. Tel: 410-531-9200; Fax: 410-531-4881. Very Rev. Mark L. Curesky, O.F.M.Conv. Ord: '75, Minister Prov.; Rev. Placido Kaczorek, O.F.M.Conv. Ord: '64, Mission Procurator.

Franciscan Mission Association: 185 West State St., Granby, MA 01033. Tel: 413-467-9196. Rev. Placid Kaczorek, O.F.M.Conv. Ord: '64, Mission Dir.

U.S. Religious serving Abroad: Revs. David Blowey, O.F.M.Conv. Ord: '87, Kenya; Timothy Dore, O.F.M.Conv. Ord: '92, Costa Rica; Vincent Lachendro, O.F.M.Conv. Ord: '63, Philippines; Jerome Lukaszewski, O.F.M.Conv. Ord: '48, Japan; Ron Roll, O.F.M.Conv. Ord: '80, Honduras; Bro. Mitchell Sawicki, O.F.M.Conv., Ghana; Revs. Dominic Slemba, O.F.M.Conv. Ord: '51, Ghana; Nicholas Swiatek, O.F.M.Conv. Ord: '68, Japan; Giles Zakowicz, O.F.M.Conv. Ord: '75, Ghana.

Province of Our Lady of Consolation: Provincial Office, Mt. St. Francis, IN 47146. Rev. Kent Biergans, O.F.M.Conv. Ord: '67, Min. Prov.

Religious serving Abroad: Revs. Juniper Cummings, O.F.M.Conv. Ord: '50, Vicar Custos; Kamil Wenzel, O.F.M.Conv. Ord: '66, Zambia; Bro. John Doyle, O.F.M.Conv., Zambia; Revs. Aloysius Jacoby, O.F.M.Conv. Ord: '47, Zambia; Efisio Steri, O.F.M.Conv. Ord: '60, Zambia; Werner Iten, O.F.M.Conv. Ord: '74, Zambia; Bro. Joseph Weissling, O.F.M.Conv., Guardian; Revs. Emil Cook, O.F.M.Conv. Ord: '66, Honduras; Ronald Roll, O.F.M.Conv. Ord: '80, Honduras; Pius Uitendaal, O.F.M.Conv. Ord: '63, Zambia; Terence Tobin, O.F.M.Conv. Ord: '55, Zambia; Mark Weaver, O.F.M.Conv. Ord: '77, Honduras; Bro. Anthony Droll, O.F.M.Conv., Zambia; Revs. Fritz O'Kelly, O.F.M.Conv. Ord: '56, Zambia; Jude Rochford, O.F.M.Conv. Ord: '55, Zambia.

Province of Saint Bonaventure: Provincial Office, 6107 N. Kenmore Ave., Chicago, IL 60660-2797. Tel: 773-274-7681; Fax: 773-274-9751. Very Rev. Anthony Labedis, O.F.M.Conv. Ord: '60, Minister Prov.

U.S. Religious serving Abroad: Revs. John Calgaro, O.F.M.Conv. Ord: '74, Mexico; Abraham Crisostomo, O.F.M.Conv. Ord: '96; Bros. Paschal Metzger, O.F.M.Conv., Mexico; Stanislaus Zabkiewicz, O.F.M.Conv., Zambia.

Crosier Fathers Missions (O.S.C.)

Crosier Foreign Missions

Crosier Fathers and Brothers (Canons Regular of the Order of the Holy Cross)

U.S. Address: Crosier Missions-Province of St. Odilia, 3510 Vivian Ave., Shoreview, MN 55126-3852. Tel: 651-486-7456; Fax: 651-486-7589. Very Rev. Thomas Carkhuff, O.S.C. Ord: '76, Prov.; Rev. David E. Gallus, O.S.C. Ord: '66, Mission Coord.

U.S. Religious serving Abroad: Very Rev. Glen Lewandowski, O.S.C. Ord: '74, Indonesia; Rev. Ernest Martello, O.S.C. Ord: '70, Congo; Bro. Clarence Neuner, O.S.C., Indonesia; Rev. Virgil Petermeier, O.S.C. Ord: '77, Indonesia; Robert Rossi, O.S.C Ord: '70, Congo; Most Rev. Alphonse Sowada, O.S.C., Indonesia; Rev. Gregory Poser, O.S.C. Ord: '75, Indonesia.

American Divine Word Missionaries (S.V.D.)

Society of the Divine Word Foreign Missions

Missions of the American Provinces of the Society of the Divine Word (S.V.D.) commonly known as Divine Word Missionaries

Latin: Societas Verbi Divini

Provincial Headquarters in the U.S.A.

Chicago Province: Society of the Divine Word-Province of Blessed Joseph Freinademetz, S.V.D., 1985 Waukegan Rd., P.O. Box 6038, Techny, IL 60082-6038. Tel: 847-272-2700; Fax: 847-272-2517. Very Rev. Stanley Uroda, S.V.D. Ord: '74, Prov. Supr.; Rev. Thomas A. Krosnicki, S.V.D. Ord: '66, Mission Dir. for all three Provinces.

Publication: *Divine Word Missionaries.*

Southern Province: Society of the Divine Word-Province of St. Augustine, 201 Ruella Ave., Bay St. Louis, MS 39520-4638. Tel: 228-467-4322. Very Rev. Clifton Labbe, S.V.D. Ord: '69, Prov. Supr.

Western Province: Society of the Divine Word, P.O. Box 77-F, Los Angeles, CA 90007. Tel: 213-483-3013. Very Rev. Eamonn Donnelly, S.V.D. Ord: '70, Prov. Supr.

American Divine Word Missionaries in Overseas Missions: Revs. Thomas Ascheman, S.V.D. Ord: '82, Italy; Daniel Bauer, S.V.D. Ord: '74, Taiwan; Francis Beemsterboer, S.V.D. Ord: '51, Ghana; Andrew Biller, S.V.D. Ord: '61, Philippines; Joseph Bisson, S.V.D. Ord: '63, Papua New Guinea; Michael Blume, S.V.D. Ord: '72, Rome; Bro. William Brennan, S.V.D., Australia; Revs. Francis Budenholzer, S.V.D. Ord: '72, Taiwan; Most Rev. John Bukovsky, S.V.D., Austria; Revs. Francis Bures, S.V.D. Ord: '53, Japan; Vincent Burke, S.V.D. Ord: '61, Ghana; Dennis Callan, S.V.D. Ord: '87, Korea; Thomas Cassidy, S.V.D. Ord: '45, Philippines; Richard Daschbach, S.V.D. Ord: '64, East Timor; Anthony Dugay, S.V.D. Ord: '62, Ghana; Elmer Elsbernd, S.V.D. Ord: '65, Papua New Guinea; Bro. Xavier Eshman, S.V.D., Paraguay; Revs. Lloyd Fiedler, S.V.D. Ord: '70, Philippines; Patrick Fincutter, S.V.D. Ord:. '55, Papua New Guinea; Kenneth Feehan, S.V.D. Ord: '59, Papua New Guinea; Dennis Flynn, S.V.D. Ord: '61, Philippines; Bro. Ronald Fratzke, S.V.D., Australia; Revs. Paul Gootee, S.V.D. Ord: '55, Indonesia; Robert Grochowski, S.V.D. Ord: '96, Japan; Lawrence Hambach, S.V.D. Ord: '61, Indonesia; James Heisig, S.V.D. Ord: '69, Japan; Edward Herberger, S.V.D. Ord: '60, Anguilla; Raymond Hober, S.V.D. Ord: '60, Philippines; Bro. Andre Hotchkiss, S.V.D., Kenya; Revs. Clement Hotze, S.V.D. Ord: '47, Ghana; Alan Jenkins, S.V.D. Ord: '73, Mexico; Robert Johnson, S.V.D. Ord: '92, Montserrat - Caribbean; Most Rev. Raymond Kalisz, S.V.D., Papua New Guinea; Bros. Stephen Kerekes, S.V.D., Papua New Guinea; Lawrence Kieffer, S.V.D., Papua New Guinea; Revs. Jon Kirby, S.V.D., Ord: '71, Ghana; Robert Kisala, S.V.D. Ord: '85, Japan; Ronald Lange, S.V.D. Ord: '71, Ghana; Paul LaForge, S.V.D. Ord: '58, Japan; Lawrence LaPlante, S.V.D. Ord: '67, Philippines; William Liebert, S.V.D. Ord: '57, Papua, New Guinea; James Liebner, S.V.D. Ord: '85, Taiwan; Michael Lindstrom, S.V.D. Ord: '82, Japan; Bro. Damien Lunders, S.V.D., Thailand; Revs. Matthew Lunzer, S.V.D. Ord: '45, Papua New Guinea; John Khien Luu, S.V.D. Ord: '92, Australia; Adam MacDonald, S.V.D. Ord: '00, Philippines; David Mayer, S.V.D. Ord: '66, Japan; Dennis McKillip, S.V.D. Ord: '47, Philippines; John McSherry, S.V.D. Ord: '61, Philippines; Peter Michael, S.V.D. Ord: '40, Philippines; Bro. Henry Miller, S.V.D., Antigua - Caribbean; Revs. Theodore Murnane, S.V.D. Ord: '59, Philippines; John Musinsky, S.V.D. Ord: '44, Rome; Paul Nadolny, S.V.D. Ord: '89, Mozambique; Lawrence Nemer, S.V.D. Ord: '60, England; Joseph Trong Nguyen, S.V.D. Ord: '91, Vietnam; Peter Sam Cao Nguyen, S.V.D. Ord: '86, Korea; Van Hiep Nguyen, S.V.D. Ord: '99, Ecuador; Cuong Hung Nguyen, S.V.D. Ord: '00, Argentina; Nick Hien Nguyen, S.V.D. Ord: '00, Taiwan; Michael Van Nhan Tran, S.V.D. Ord: '00, Argentina; Joseph Minh Vu Nguyen, S.V.D. Ord: '96, Australia; Donald O'Connor, S.V.D. Ord: '64, Papua New Guinea; Vincent Ohlinger, S.V.D. Ord: '68, Papua New Guinea; Stanley Plutz, S.V.D. Ord: '53, Philippines; Robert Pung, S.V.D. Ord: '44, Rome; Bro. Mark Rastall, S.V.D., Australia; Revs. Robert Riemer, S.V.D. Ord: '60, Japan; Roger Risse, S.V.D. Ord: '54, Indonesia; James Risse, S.V.D. Ord: '61, Philippines; Charles Scanlon, S.V.D. Ord: '54, Philippines; Bartley Schmitz, S.V.D. Ord: '44, Taiwan; Eugene Schmitz, S.V.D. Ord: '67, Indonesia; Charles Schneider, S.V.D. Ord: '46, Ghana; William Seifert, S.V.D. Ord: '67, Papua New Guinea; John Seland, S.V.D. Ord: '68, Japan; Werner Shadeg, S.V.D. Ord: '45, Papua New Guinea; Norbert Shadeg, S.V.D. Ord: '49, Indonesia; Otto Shelly, S.V.D. Ord: '42, Australia; Arnold Steffen, S.V.D. Ord: '57, Papua New Guinea; Victor Stevko, S.V.D. Ord: '57, Australia; Nicholas Strawn, S.V.D. Ord: '62, Indonesia; David Streit, S.V.D. Ord: '69, Rome; Richard Szippl, S.V.D. Ord: '81, Japan; Gerald Theis, S.V.D. Ord: '80, Papua New Guinea; Richard Thibeau, S.V.D. Ord: '57, Mexico; Frederick Timp, S.V.D. Ord: '71, Ghana; Joseph Huynh Tran, S.V.D. Ord: '93, Taiwan; Cong Bang Tran, S.V.D. Ord: '00, Togo; Peter Tam Tran, S.V.D. Ord: '98, Australia; Thomas Umbras, S.V.D. Ord: '81, Mexico; James Vorwek, S.V.D. Ord: '69, Argentina; Lawrence Wagner, S.V.D. Ord: '44, Mexico; Wilbert Wagner, S.V.D. Ord: '40, Mexico; John Wald, S.V.D. Ord: '43, Papua New Guinea; Joseph Tri Van Vu, S.V.D. Ord: '85, Vietnam; John Khien Mai Luu, S.V.D. Ord: '92, Vietnam.

American Dominican Missions (O.P.)

Dominican - Order of Preachers Foreign Missions

Foreign Missions of the American Provinces of the Order of Preachers

Provincial Headquarters

Province of St. Joseph (Eastern): 141 E. 65th St., New York, NY 10021. Tel: 212-734-4784. Very Rev. Norman Alfred Haddad, O.P. Ord: '61, Prov. Bro. Thomas-Aquinas Dolan, O.P., Mission Dir.

U.S. Religious serving in Pakistan: Revs. J. M. Connors, O.P. Ord: '51; T. C. McVey, O.P. Ord: '60; J. Nuttall, O.P. Ord: '69; L. L. Turon, O.P. Ord: '55; G. L. Sukovaty, O.P. Ord: '51.

Priests 7.

U.S. Religious serving in Peru: Revs. J. L. Dolan, O.P. Ord: '60; Thomas K. Kraft, O.P. Ord: '86.

U.S. Religious serving in Kenya: Very Rev. David D. Izzo, O.P. Ord: '94, Vicar Prov.; Revs. W. T. Sinkele, O.P. Ord: '73; M. B. Schepers, O.P. Ord: '56; L. M. Shea, O.P. Ord: '52; Edward Gorman, O.P. Ord: '92; T. R. Heath, O.P. Ord: '50; Kieran J. Healy, O.P. Ord: '61; Robert E. Bertrand, O.P. Ord: '58; Leon M. Martiny, O.P. Ord: '98.

U.S. Religious serving elsewhere: Revs. D. G. Doherty, O.P. Ord: '57, Philippines; Frank I.Sutman, O.P. Ord: '85, Russia; James J. Lenaghan, O.P. Ord: '95, Russia; Christopher Cardone, O.P. Ord: '86, Solomon Islands; Stanley Azaro, O.P. Ord: '75, Lithuania.

Province of St. Albert the Great (Central): 1909 S. Ashland Ave., Chicago, IL 60608-2994, Fax: 312-829-8471. Very Rev. Edward M. Ruane, O.P. Ord: '69, Prov.; Rev. Bede Jagoe, O.P. Ord: '60, Dir. St. Dominic Mission Society.

U.S. Religious serving in Bolivia: Revs. Patrick Reardon, O.P. Ord: '60; Thomas Lynch, O.P. Ord: '86; Chrysostom Geraets, O.P. Ord: '56; Daniel Roach, O.P. Ord: '56; James Spahn, O.P. Ord: '81; Mark Paraday, O.P. Ord: '83.

U.S. Religious serving in Kenya: Rev. Lewis M. Shea, O.P. Ord: '52.

U.S. Religious serving in Nigeria: Revs. Peter Otillio, O.P. Ord: '57; Joseph H. Kenny, O.P. Ord: '50; Thomas K. McDermott, O.P. Ord: '83; Justus Pokrzewinski, O.P. Ord: '60; Edward H. Riley, O.P. Ord: '60; Gilbert Thesing, O.P. Ord: '75; Ambrose Windbacher, O.P. Ord: '54; Bro. Stephen Lucas, O.P.

Province Of The Holy Name: (Western Dominican Province), 5877 Birch Court, Oakland, CA 94618. Very Rev. Daniel Syverstad, O.P. Ord: '82, Prov.

U.S. Religious serving in Guatemala: Rev. Timothy Conlan, O.P. Ord: '67; Bro. Raymond Bertheaux, O.P.

U.S. Religious serving in Mexico: Revs. David Bello, O.P. Ord: '81; Thomas Kraft, O.P. Ord: '86; Jose Ricardo Garcia, O.P. Ord: '72.

St. Martin de Porres Province: (Southern Dominican Province), 1421 N. Causeway Blvd., Ste. 200, Metairie, LA 70001-4144. Tel: 504-837-2129; Fax: 504-837-6604. Very Rev. Alberto Rodriguez, O.P. Ord: '71, Prov.; Rev. John Raymond Corr, O.P. Ord: '56, Dir. Southern Dominican Global Missions.

U.S. Religious serving abroad: Revs. James L. Dolan, O.P. Ord: '60, Peru; Emanuel

Camilleri, O.P. Ord: '37, Malta; Jesus Guerra, O.P. Ord: '57, Venezuela; Luis Roberto Aguilar Leal, O.P. Ord: '92, Honduras; Brian J. Pierce, O.P. Ord: '83, Honduras; Raphael Proenza, O.P. Ord: '96, Cuba.

American Franciscan Missions (O.F.M.)

Franciscan Foreign Missions

Missions of the American Provinces of the Order of Friars Minor (Franciscans) in the United States and other countries

Holy Name Province: 135 W. 31st St., New York, NY 10001-3439. Bro. Gordon Clark, O.F.M., Prov., Promoter of the Missions, Sec. Missionary Evangelization.

U.S. Religious serving in Japan: Revs. Jerome A. Donnelly, O.F.M. Ord: '39; Bede Fitzpatrick, O.F.M. Ord: '55; Campion Lally, O.F.M. Ord: '53; Bartholomew McMahon, O.F.M. Ord: '62; Donnan P. Murray, O.F.M. Ord: '56; Callistus Sweeney, O.F.M.; Stanislaus Widomski Ord: '62.

U.S. Religious serving Brazil: Most Rev. John Burke O.F.M.; Most Rev. Benedict D. Coscia, O.F.M.; Most Rev. Capistran F. Heim, O.F.M.; Revs. David J. Babcock, O.F.M. Ord: '53; Donald J. Chin, O.F.M. Ord: '67; Alexander F. Eustace, O.F.M. Ord: '50; Thomas J. Fox, O.F.M. Ord: '46; Berard J. Hanlon, O.F.M. Ord: '63; Juvenal F. Leahy, O.F.M. Ord: '58; Ignatius J. McGeady, O.F.M. Ord: '48; Aloysius Siracuse, O.F.M. Ord: '47.

U.S. Religious serving in Peru: Revs. Mariano Gagnon, O.F.M. Ord: '58; Mariano Guzman, O.F.M. Ord: '57; Christopher J. Dunn, O.F.M. Ord: '82; Bros. Declan McCabe, O.F.M.; Rev. Anthony Wilson, O.F.M. Ord: '87.

U.S. Religious serving in Taiwan: Rev. Pius Lui, O.F.M. Ord: '53.

U.S. Religious serving in Bolivia: Revs. Gavin P. Hanlon, O.F.M. Ord: '56; Ignatius Harding, O.F.M. Ord: '65; William R. Keenan, O.F.M. Ord: '56; Thomas J. Kornacki, O.F.M. Ord: '88; Bernardine Ward, O.F.M. Ord: '42.

U.S. Religious serving in Africa: Revs. Roy Corrigan, O.F.M. Ord: '55; Joseph B. Ehrhardt, O.F.M. Ord: '76; Finian A. Riley, O.F.M. Ord: '55; Charles A. Steen, O.F.M. Ord: '64.

U.S. Religious serving in Puerto Rico: Rev. Alfonso D. Guzman, O.F.M. Ord: '71.

Franciscan Province of the Immaculate Conception: 125 Thompson St., New York, NY 10012. Rev. Marion Cascino, O.F.M. Ord: '49, Sec./Missionary Evangelization & Franciscan Missionary Union.

Province-affiliated Religious serving in Honduras: Revs. Peter Paul Meilak, O.F.M. Ord: '49; Albert Gauci, O.F.M. Ord: '71; Bro. Guillermo Salgado, O.F.M.; Rev. Ubladimiro Rivera, O.F.M. Ord: '75; Most Rev. Maurice Muldoon, O.F.M.; Most Rev. Gerald Scarpone, O.F.M.; Revs. Roberto Camilleri, O.F.M. Ord: '75; Angelo Falzon, O.F.M. Ord: '84; Joseph Bonello, O.F.M. Ord: '85; Donald Salazar, O.F.M. Ord: '67; Valentine Gesuale, O.F.M. Ord: '65; Felix Mansueto, O.F.M. Ord: '55.

Province-affiliated Religious serving in Guatemala: Revs. Athanasius Iazzetta, O.F.M. Ord: '54; Rocco Famiglietti, O.F.M. Ord: '47; Ottaviano Battolini, O.F.M. Ord: '43; Robert Siguere, O.F.M. Ord: '73.

Province-affiliated Religious serving in El Salvador: Revs. Flavian Mucci, O.F.M. Ord: '63; Guy Vellardita, O.F.M. Ord: '58, San Pedro; Rafael Fernandez, O.F.M. Ord: '87.

Sacred Heart Province: 3140 Meramec St., St. Louis, MO 63118. Tel: 314-353-3421. Revs. John L. Doctor, O.F.M. Ord: '76, Prov.; Kenneth Capalbo, O.F.M. Ord: '74, Prov. Vicar; Thomas Gardner, O.F.M. Ord: '79, Promoter of the Missions.Franciscan Missionary Union. Tel: 314-353-7729.

U.S. Religious serving in Brazil: Revs. Michael Grawe, O.F.M. Ord: '70; Gregory Kemner, O.F.M. Ord: '55; Nestor Windolph, O.F.M. Ord: '55.

U.S. Religious serving in Alaska: Revs. William E. Cardy, O.F.M. Ord: '72; Joseph Hemmer, O.F.M. Ord: '54; Bro. Robert Ruzicka, O.F.M.

U.S. Religious serving Elsewhere: Bro. Jeffrey Haller, O.F.M., Taiwan; Revs. Albert Haase, O.F.M. Ord: '83, Taiwan; James Perluzzi, O.F.M. Ord: '65, Italy; Basil Tsung, O.F.M. Ord: '53, Taiwan; Jesus Aguirre Garza, O.F.M. Ord: '96, Taiwan.

St. Barbara Province: 1500 34th Ave., Oakland, CA 94601. Fax: 510-536-3970.

U.S. Religious serving Overseas: Revs. Camillus Cavagnaro, O.F.M. Ord: '46, Mexico; Elias Galvez, O.F.M. Ord: '56, Mexico; John Peterson Ord: '63, Mexico; Bros. Miguel Lozano, O.F.M., Mexico; Ivo Toneck, O.F.M., Mexico; Leo Gonzalez, O.F.M., Israel; Gerard Saunders, O.F.M., Peru.

Assumption B.V.M. Province: Pulaski, WI 54162. Tel: 920-822-5422; Fax: 920-822-5423. Revs. Thomas Luczak, O.F.M. Ord: '70, Minister Prov.; Hugh Zurat, O.F.M. Ord: '62.

Franciscan Evangelization Center - Assumption Province: Chicago, IL 60659. Tel: 773-539-4042; Fax: 773-539-9553.

Publication: *Mission Newsletter*.

U.S. Religious serving Abroad: Revs. Laurian Wegner, O.F.M. Ord: '78, Japan; Bro. Augustine Fraszczak, O.F.M., Philippines; Revs. Lyle Chrobak, O.F.M. Ord: '62, Mexico; Henry Howaniec, O.F.M. Ord: '56, Kazakhstan; Blase Karas, O.F.M. Ord: '59, Russia; Barnabas Gorski, O.F.M. Ord: '60, Morocco; Bro. Mario Nagy, O.F.M., Russia; Rev. James Heinsch, O.F.M. Ord: '67, Israel; Bro. John Brice, O.F.M., South Africa. Rev. Sergius Wroblewski, O.F.M. Ord: '46, South Africa.

Province of St. John the Baptist: 1615 Vine St., Cincinnati, OH 45210-1222. Tel: 513-721-4700; Fax: 513-421-9672. Bro. Scott Obrecht, O.F.M., Dir.-Secretariat for Missionary Evangelization & Franciscan Missionary Union

Publication: monthly newsletter, *Friarworks*.

U.S. Religious serving Abroad: Revs. Malachy Brogan, O.F.M. Ord: '57, Holy Land; Robert Bruno, O.F.M. Ord: '77, Germany; Henry Beck, O.F.M. Ord: '80, Jamaica, West Indies; Harold Geers, O.F.M. Ord: '60, Philippines; Carl Kemphues, O.F.M. Ord: '56, Philippines; Bro. Philip Wilhelm, O.F.M., Philippines; Revs. Humbert Moster, O.F.M. Ord: '57, Jamaica, West Indies; Louis Zant, O.F.M. Ord: '73, Jamaica, West Indies; James Fehrenbach, O.F.M. Ord: '71, Germany; Mark Gehret, O.F.M. Ord: '62, Jamaica, West Indies; Lawrence Landini, O.F.M. Ord: '61, South Africa; Bro. Roger Covero, O.F.M., Philippines; Revs. Daniel Kroger, O.F.M. Ord: '73, Philippines; John Quigley, O.F.M. Ord: '72, Geneva.

VI Slav-Byzantine Missions, U.S.A.

Custody of St. Mary of the Angels. Byzantine-Slavonic Rite (New Canaan, CT)

Established by decree of the Most Rev. Minister General of the Order of Friars Minor on November 7, 1947, with the approbation of the Sacred Congregation for the Oriental Church on October 28, 1947, among the peoples of the Byzantine Rite

Commissariats of the Holy Land: 1400 Quincy St. N.E., Washington, DC 20017. Tel: 202-526-6800; Fax: 202-529-9889. Bros. Callistus Welch, O.F.M., Commissary; David Wathen, O.F.M.; James Paul Brabandt, O.F.M.; Revs. Joshua Doyle, O.F.M.; Brian McTommoney, O.F.M. Ord: '53.

St. Anthony Friary: 3140 Meramec St., St. Louis, MO 63118. Rev. Thomas Gardner, O.F.M. Ord: '79, Commissary.

St. Joseph's Friary: 218 East 12th St., Los Angeles, CA 90015. Rev. Martial Luebke, O.F.M. Ord: '39, Commissary.

Custody of the Holy Land: Jordan, Israel, Lebanon, Syria, Cyprus, Egypt and Rhodes.

U.S. Religious serving Abroad: Bro. Aloysius Florio, O.F.M., Rome, Italy; Rev. Xavier Geiser, O.F.M. Ord: '55, Jerusalem, Israel; Bros. Michael Raum, O.F.M., Jerusalem, Israel; Thomas Courtney, O.F.M., Syria; Revs. Peter Vasko, O.F.M. Ord: '87, Jerusalem, Israel; Raphael Bonanno, O.F.M., Rome; George Lewett, O.F.M. Ord: '88, Bethlehem, Isreal; Athanasius Macora, O.F.M. Ord: '92, Jerusalem, Israel; Matthias Rendon, O.F.M. Ord: '92, Jerusalem, Israel; Danielmose Shroeder, O.F.M. Ord: '91, Jerusalem, Israel; Bros. Leo Gonzales, O.F.M., Mt. Tabor, Israel; Angel Beda Ison, O.F.M., Jerusalem, Israel.

Franciscan Friars Of The Atonement (S.A.)

General Headquarters: Graymoor, P.O. Box 300, Garrison, NY 10524. Tel: 914-424-2113; Fax: 914-424-2166. Rev. Thomas Orians, S.A. Ord: '92, Mission Coord. Office: P.O. Box 300, Graymoor, Garrison, NY 10524-0300. Tel: 914-424-3671, Ext. 2125.

For detailed information on the U.S. Religious working in foreign missions, please refer to the listings under the Archdiocese of New York section entitled "Monasteries and Residences of Priests and Brothers", Graymoor, Garrison, NY.

Holy Cross Mission Center (C.S.C.)

U.S. Headquarters and Procure: Holy Cross Mission Center for Cross-Cultural Ministries, P.O. Box 543, Notre Dame, IN 46556. Tel: 219-631-5477; Fax: 219-631-6813. Rev. James T. Rahilly, C.S.C. Ord: '64, . Dir.

Legal Title: Holy Cross Foreign Mission Society, Inc.

Holy Cross Foreign Missions

Indiana Province: Congregation of Holy Cross, 1304 East Jefferson, South Bend, IN 46617.

Midwest Province: Congregation of Holy Cross, Box 460, Notre Dame, IN 46556.

Eastern Province: Congregation of Holy Cross, 835 Clinton Ave., Bridgeport, CT 06604-2393.

South-West Province: Congregation of Holy Cross, 3001 S. Congress Ave., #1046, Austin, TX 78704-6489.

Eastern Province of Brothers: Congregation of Holy Cross, 85 Overlook Cir., New Rochelle, NY 10804-4501.

Southern Province of Priests: Congregation of Holy Cross, 2111 Brackenridge St., Austin, TX 78704-4322.

U.S. Religious serving in foreign missions: Revs. Robert R. Baker, C.S.C. Ord: '70, Peru; James T. Banas, C.S.C. Ord: '57, Bangladesh; Revs. Gerald R. Barmasse, C.S.C. Ord: '76, Chile; Rev. Thomas V. Bednar, C.S.C. Ord: '85, Chile; Bros. Thomas More Beere, C.S.C., Bangladesh; John Benesh, C.S.C., Peru; Richard Burgie, C.S.C., Brazil; Revs. William Blum, C.S.C. Ord: '65, Uganda; Arthur J. Colgan, C.S.C. Ord: '73, Peru; Charles A. Delaney, C.S.C. Ord: '49, Chile; Philip T. Devlin, C.S.C. Ord: '56, Peru; Joseph A. Dorsey, C.S.C. Ord: '57, Chile; Bro. Ronald Drahozal, C.S.C., Bangladesh; Rev. David E. Farrell, C.S.C. Ord: '68, Peru; Bros. John Flood, C.S.C., Uganda; William Gates, C.S.C., Ghana; Revs. Robert Gilbo, C.S.C. Ord: '67, Chile; Robert G. Gilmour, C.S.C. Ord: '68, Ghana; Bros. Vincent Gross, C.S.C., Ghana; Thomas Giumenta, C.S.C., Chile; Alan Gugel, C.S.C., Uganda; Alan Harrod, C.S.C., Uganda; Ronald Hein, C.S.C., Brazil; Alberic Houle, C.S.C., Bangladesh; Revs. Robert T. Hesse, C.S.C. Ord: '58, Uganda; Eugene E. Homrich, C.S.C. Ord: '55, Bangladesh; James W. Irwin, C.S.C. Ord: '65, Mexico; Malcolm D. Johnson, C.S.C. Ord: '59, Chile; Bros. Richard F. Johnson, C.S.C., Ghana; Thomas Keefe, C.S.C., Uganda; Bros. Joseph Kinsman, C.S.C., Brazil; Bernard Klim, Uganda; Revs. James Kelly, C.S.C. Ord: '58, Uganda; T. Daniel Kennerk, C.S.C. Ord: '53, Bangladesh; Bros. Jerome F. Kreotsch, C.S.C., Ghana; Donald Kuchenmeister, C.S.C., Chile; Dismas Lenzi, C.S.C., Brazil; Rev. Joseph Lehane, C.S.C. Ord: '57, Bangladesh; Bro. Norbert Lengerich, C.S.C., Brazil; Revs. L. Peter Logsdon, C.S.C. Ord: '68, Mexico; George Lucas, C.S.C. Ord: '72, Uganda; Revs. H. Thomas McDermott, C.S.C. Ord: '79, Uganda; Russell McDougall, C.S.C. Ord: '91, Uganda; Most Rev. Mark G. McGrath, C.S.C., Panama; Rev. Francis Murphy, C.S.C. Ord: '86, Uganda; Bros. Harold Naudet, C.S.C., Brazil; James Nichols, C.S.C., Uganda; Revs.; Daniel A. Panchot, C.S.C. Ord: '65, Mexico; Gerald T. Papen, C.S.C. Ord: '63, Chile; Joseph S. Peixotto, C.S.C. Ord: '61, Bangladesh; William Persia, C.S.C. Ord: '62, Peru; George F. Pope, C.S.C. Ord: '58, Bangladesh; Richard L. Potthast, C.S.C. Ord: '67, Uganda; Francis Quinlivan, C.S.C. Ord: '70, Bangladesh; Bros. Leonard Reeson, C.S.C., Brazil; Frank Robinson, C.S.C., Brazil; Rev. Cornelius J. Ryan, C.S.C. Ord: '56, Kenya; Bro. Paul Schaefer, C.S.C., Brazil; Most Rev. Charles A. Schleck, C.S.C. Ord: '51, Italy; Revs. Thomas Shea, C.S.C. Ord: '67, Peru; Robert G. Simon, C.S.C. Ord: '61, Chile; Thomas W. Smith, C.S.C. Ord: '72, Kenya; Frederick A. Schmidt, C.S.C. Ord: '37, Mexico; Bro. Sergio Stolf, C.S.C., Brazil; Rev. Richard E. Stout, C.S.C. Ord: '71, Kenya; Bros. J. Rodney Struble, C.S.C., Bangladesh; Nicholas Thielman, C.S.C., Bangladesh; Revs. Richard W. Timm, C.S.C. Ord: '49, Bangladesh; Robert Plasker, C.S.C. Ord: '57, Chile; Donald Fetters, C.S.C. Ord: '76, Chile; James J. Ferguson, C.S.C. Ord: '65, Uganda; Bros. Ernest Turk, C.S.C., Brazil; Robert Weinmann, C.S.C., Brazil; Matthew Lyons, C.S.C., Chile; Robert Nebus, C.S.C., Uganda; Joseph Walsh, C.S.C., Uganda; Thomas Dillman, C.S.C., Ghana; Revs. Gerald J. Whelan, C.S.C. Ord: '55, Chile; Richard J. Wunsch, C.S.C. Ord: '66, Uganda.

Priests 55; Brothers 43.

Holy Ghost Fathers (C.S.Sp.)

Holy Ghost Foreign Missions

U.S.A. - East Province: Holy Ghost Fathers, 6230 Brush Run Rd., Bethel Park, PA 15102. Fax: 412-831-0970. Very Rev. Christopher P. Promis, C.S.Sp. Ord: '72, Prov.

U.S. Religious serving Abroad: Revs. Remo J. Bonifazi, C.S.Sp. Ord: '45, Republic of South Africa; William H. Christy, C.S.Sp. Ord: '92, Arusha, Tanzania; Paul M. Flamm, C.S.Sp. Ord: '99, Kasulu-Kigoma; Adrien T. Hebert, C.S.Sp. Ord: '58, Verde, RSA; Francis A. Greff, C.S.Sp. Ord: '47, Arusha, Tanzania; Joseph M. Herzstein, C.S.Sp. Ord: '63, Arusha; Joseph L. Kelly, C.S.Sp. Ord: '50, Arusha, Tanzania; Richard J. LeClair, C.S.Sp. Ord: '51, Arusha, Tanzania; Edward T. Marchessault, C.S.Sp. Ord: '64, Arusha, Tanzania; Josaphat Msongore, C.S.Sp. Ord: '63, Arusha, Tanzania; Patrick A. Patten, C.S.Sp. Ord: '78, Arusha, Tanzania; Edward J. Raszewski, C.S.Sp. Ord: '47, Arusha, Tanzania; Bro. Francis Sullivan, C.S.Sp., Arusha, Tanzania; Rev. Vincent G. Stegman, C.S.Sp. Ord: '62, Ethiopia; Most Rev. Dennis V. Durning, C.S.Sp. Ord: '50, Karatu, Tanzania; Most Rev. Bernard M. Ngaviliau, C.S.Sp. Ord: '49, Arusha, Tanzania.

Jesuit Volunteers International (S.J.)

U.S. Headquarters: Jesuit Volunteers International, P.O. Box 3756, Washington, DC 20007. Tel: 202-687-1132; Fax: 202-687-5082. Mr. John Sealey, Acting Dir.

A Christian service organization offering young College educated lay men and women an opportunity to volunteer in a developing country in collaboration with Jesuits. Volunteers serve for two years without returning to the U.S.

Jesuit Missions (S.J.)

Jesuit Foreign Missions

Jesuit Mission Inc.: An official missionary organization of the Provinces of the United States Assistancy of the Society of Jesus.

National Headquarters: Jesuit Missions, 1616 P St., N.W., #400, Washington, DC 20036. Tel: 202-462-0400; Fax: 202-328-9212. Revs. James R. Stormes, S.J. Ord: '79, Pres.; David Nazar, S.J. Ord: '83, Sec.; Thomas H. Smolich, S.J. Ord: '86, Treas.; Richard J. Ryscavage, S.J. Ord: '77, Exec. Dir.

Provinces

Society of Jesus: California Province, 284 Stanyan St., San Francisco, CA 94118. Tel: 415-221-1588.

Legal Title: California Jesuit Missionaries; Revs. Thomas H. Smolich, S.J. Ord: '86, Prov.; Theodore T. Taheny, S.J. Ord: '56, Mission Dir.

U.S. Religious serving in foreign missions: Revs. Louis G. Aldrich, S.J. Ord: '86, Republic of China; William A. Ameche, S.J. Ord: '81, Mexico; Ferdinand T. Azevedo, S.J. Ord: '70, Brazil; Robert Becka, S.J. Ord: '60, Japan; Walter Brennan, S.J. Ord: '60, Japan; James Chevedden, S.J. Ord: '78, Republic of China; Robert Chiesa, S.J. Ord: '68, Japan; Robert Cunningham, S.J. Ord: '55, Philippines; Bro. Richard Devine, S.J., Japan; Revs. John R. Donahue, S.J. Ord: '79, Honduras; John Donald, S.J. Ord: '72, Honduras; Gustavo Fernandez, S.J. Ord: '67, Honduras; Thomas W. Franxman, S.J. Ord: '64, Philippines; Thomas E. Splain, S.J. Ord: '71, Fiji Islands; Fred Green, S.J. Ord: '58, Peru; Bro. Robert Griffin, S.J., Philippines; Revs. Robert B. Grimaldi, S.J. Ord: '68, Honduras; Kieth Barry Martinson, S.J. Ord: '75, Republic of China; George G. Martinson, S.J. Ord: '73, . Republic of China; Edward Murphy, S.J. Ord: '43, . Republic of China; Paul O'Brien, S.J. Ord: '38, Thailand; John B. Palm, S.J. Ord: '41, Republic of China; Paul Pollock, S.J. Ord: '73, Thailand; Bro. Donald Poetzl, S.J., Mexico; Revs. David Reed, S.J. Ord: '64, Republic of China; Robert Ronald, S.J. Ord: '65, Republic of China; Daniel Ross, S.J. Ord: '66, Republic of China; Richard Schneck, S.J. Ord: '72, Ecuador; Glen E. Smith, S.J. Ord: '63, Japan; Norman Walling, S.J. Ord: '61, Hong Kong; Charles Welsh, S.J. Ord: '72, Republic of China.

Priests 32; Brothers 3; Scholastics 2.

Society of Jesus: Chicago Province, 2050 N. Clark St., Chicago, IL 60614. Tel: 773-975-6363.

Legal title: Jesuit International Missions, (Formerly, Jesuits in Peru, Chicago Province, and Patna Jesuit Mission Society): Revs. Richard J. Baumann, S.J. Ord: '75, Prov.; George E. Von Kaenel, S.J. Ord: '58, Prov. Asst. Intl. Ministries.

U.S. Religious serving in foreign missions: Revs. Robert E. Beckman, S.J. Ord: '56, Peru; Theodore B. Bowling, S.J. Ord: '53, India; Lawrence V. Brooks, S.J. Ord: '74, Nepal; Patrick M. Casey, S.J. Ord: '72, Peru; Francis M. Chamberlain, S.J. Ord: '68, Peru; Terrence P. Charlton, S.J. Ord: '76, Kenya; Martin P. Coyne, S.J. Ord: '66, Nepal; Edwin J. Daly, S.J. Ord: '59, India; Robert M. Deiters, S.J. Ord: '58, Japan; Robert L. Dolan, S.J. Ord: '73, Peru; James J. Donnelly, S.J. Ord: '59, Nepal; Jerome F. Durack, S.J. Ord: '60, India; William J. Everett, S.J. Ord: '53, Japan; Kevin H. Flaherty, S.J. Ord: '83, Peru; Charles J. Fox, S.J. Ord: '44, India; Kevin E. Gallagher, S.J. Ord: '61, Peru; Anthony J. Grollig, S.J. Ord: '55, India; John J. Kenealy, S.J. Ord: '58, India; Jeffrey L. Klaiber, S.J. Ord: '74, Peru; Richard T. Lambert, S.J. Ord: '67, India; Charles A. Law, S.J. Ord: '64, Nepal; Roman B. Lewicki, S.J. Ord: '65, India; John K. Locke, S.J. Ord:

'64, Nepal; Charles L. Murtaugh, S.J. Ord: '69, Peru; James M. O'Leary, S.J. Ord: '91, Peru; John L. O'Malley, S.J. Ord: '63, Japan; Edward Schmidt, S.J. Ord: '71, Peru; Ludwig F. Stiller, S.J. Ord: '62, Nepal; Eugene L. Watrin, S.J. Ord: '52, Nepal; Joseph F. Willmes, S.J. Ord: '48, India.

Priests 44.

Detroit Province: 7303 West Seven Mile Rd., Detroit, MI 48221-2121. Tel: 313-861-7500.

Legal Title: Jesuit International Missions, (Formerly, Patna Jesuit Mission Society). Revs. John F. Libens, S.J. Ord: '70, Prov.; Richard H. Twohig, S.J. Ord: '65, Mission Dir.

U.S. Religious serving in foreign missions: Revs. Paul H. Besanceney, S.J. Ord: '56, Sudan; Leo P. Cachat, S.J. Ord: '66, Burma; Richard W. Cherry, S.J. Ord: '69, Tanzania; Bro. Richard L. Cure, S.J., Japan; Revs. Gerald A. Drinane, S.J. Ord: '62, India; Michael A. Evans, S.J. Ord: '83, Kenya; William G. Goudreau, S.J. Ord: '52, India; Eugene F. Hattie, S.J. Ord: '53, Uganda; Gregory J. Hyde, S.J. Ord: '98, Philippines; Paul S. Kehres, S.J. Ord: '51, India; James J. Kenney, S.J. Ord: '57, India; Norman Langenderfer, S.J. Ord: '54, India; Casper J. Miller, S.J. Ord: '64, Nepal; Joseph E. Mulligan, S.J. Ord: '73, Nicaragua; James J. Regan, S.J. Ord: '67, Peru; Robert H. Schmidt, S.J. Ord: '69, India; William A. Schock, S.J. Ord: '62, Philippines; John D. Smith, S.J. Ord: '59, India; Thomas F. Tobin, S.J. Ord: '65, India; Theodore W. Walters, S.J. Ord: '56, Tanzania; George M. Ziebert, S.J. Ord: '41, India.

Priests 25; Brothers 2.

Society of Jesus: Maryland Province, 5704 Roland Ave., Baltimore, MD 21210. Tel: 410-532-1400; Fax: 410-532-1419. Rev. James R. Stormes, S.J. Ord: '79, Prov.; Mr. Stephen J. Callahan, Asst. Prov. International Apostolate.

Legal Title: Jesuit Mission Bureau, Maryland Province, Inc.; Jesuit Jamshedpur Mission Society, Inc.

U.S. Religious serving in foreign missions: Revs. Eugene J. Barber, S.J. Ord: '63, Chile; Gerard S. Barry, S.J. Ord: '63, Japan; John K. Bingham, S.J. Ord: '58, China; Edward J. Brady, S.J. Ord: '59, Sudan; Vincent J. Capuano, S.J. Ord: '98, Argentina; Jeffrey G.L. Chang, S.J. Ord: '99, China; Robert F. Currie, S.J. Ord: '71, Nicaragua; William J. Currie, S.J. Ord: '67, Japan; Angelo D'Agostino, S.J. Ord: '66, Kenya; Edgar J. Debany, S.J. Ord: '84, Nigeria; John J. Deeney, S.J. Ord: '52, India; James M. Desjardins, S.J. Ord: '77, Russia; Carl L. Dincher, S.J. Ord: '57, India; Edward C.A. Dougherty, S.J. Ord: '72, South Africa; Thomas M. Gavin, S.J. Ord: '75, Chile; John F. Guidera, S.J. Ord: '56, India; Robert E. Hamm, S.J. Ord: '68, Nigeria; John F. Henry, S.J. Ord: '55, Chile; George A. Hess, S.J. Ord: '50, India; F. Scott Howell, S.J. Ord: '77, Japan; Richard A. Kenna, S.J. Ord: '57, India; Sigmund J. Laschenski, S.J. Ord: '55, Thailand; Richard S. McCouch, S.J. Ord: '93, Micronesia; Edward H. McGrath, S.J. Ord: '53, India; Edward H. Nash, S.J. Ord: '46, India; John J. Nissel, S.J. Ord: '56, Japan; Francis M. O'Connor, S.J. Ord: '69, Nigeria; George W. Quickley, S.J. Ord: '80, Nigeria; Eugene M. Rooney, S.J. Ord: '57, Chile; Dominic J. Totaro, S.J. Ord: '67, Nigeria; David L. Ungerleider, S.J. Ord: '77, Mexico; Donald M. Ward, S.J. Ord: '70, Tanzania; Eugene A. Welch, S.J. Ord: '60, India; Robert D. Wiesenbaugh, S.J. Ord: '71, Bolivia; Charles E. Wolf, S.J. Ord: '49, Philippines.

Priests 32.

Society of Jesus: Missouri Province, 4511 W. Pine Blvd., St. Louis, MO 63108. Tel: 314-361-7765; Fax: 314-758-7164.

Legal Title: The Jesuits of the Missouri Province. Revs. Frank Reale, S.J. Ord: '81, Prov.; John A. Apel, S.J. Ord: '69, Mission Dir.

U.S. Religious serving in foreign missions: Rev. Robert T. Costello, S.J. Ord: '63, Britain; Bro. Gerardino Diaz, S.J., Honduras; Revs. Leonard E. Dieckman, S.J. Ord: '62, Belize; Mauricio Gaborit, S.J. Ord: '78, El Salvador; Steven B. Hawkes-Teeples, S.J. Ord: '93, Canada; Vernon R. Heinsz, S.J. Ord: '73, Zimbabwe; Carl J. Heumann, S.J. Ord: '72, Belize; Charles T. Hunter, S.J. Ord: '45, Belize; John M. Hunthausen, S.J. Ord: '70, Italy; Robert J. Luchi, S.J. Ord: '93, France; John L. Maher, S.J. Ord: '74, Belize; Keith P. McMillan, S.J. Ord: '93, Britain; Donald J. Murphy, S.J. Ord: '61, Belize; Maurice M. Murray, S.J. Ord: '66, Belize; Bro. James O. O'Leary, S.J., Honduras; Revs. Robert F. O'Toole, S.J. Ord: '67, Italy; Raymond A. Pease, S.J. Ord: '68, Honduras; Richard D. Perl, S.J. Ord: '78, Belize; Donald W. Reck, S.J. Ord: '65, Spain; Jesus R. Riveroll, S.J. Ord: '88, Belize; Thomas M. Rochford, S.J. Ord: '76, Italy; James M. Short, S.J. Ord: '61, Belize; Robert A. Simms, S.J. Ord: '46, Belize; Ricardo Steinmetz, S.J. Ord: '55, Mexico; John J. Stochl, S.J. Ord: '54, Belize; Raymond L. Sullivant, S.J. Ord: '66, Spain; James H. Swetnam, S.J. Ord: '58, Italy; Bros. Karl D. Swift, S.J., Belize; Harold A. Teel, S.J., Belize; Revs. J. Timothy Thompson, S.J. Ord: '70, Belize; Jorge R. Toruno, S.J. Ord: '44, Guatemala; Bro. N. Aloysius Vogt, S.J., Belize; Revs. Robert D. Voss, S.J. Ord: '72, Honduras; Jarrell D. Wade, S.J. Ord: '65, Honduras; Francis K. Wallace, S.J. Ord: '46, Panama; John B. Warner, S.J. Ord: '74, Honduras; Leo F. Weber, S.J. Ord: '56, Belize; John J. Welch, S.J. Ord: '55, Italy; Robert A. White, S.J., Ord: '62, Italy; John H. Willmering, S.J. Ord: '68, Honduras; Stephen T. Yavorsky, S.J. Ord: '77, Rwanda-Burundi; John H. Zupez, S.J. Ord: '67, Nigeria.

Priests 36; Brothers 5.

Society of Jesus: New England Province, 771 Harrison Ave., Boston, MA 02118. Tel: 617-266-7233; Fax: 617-536-8074.

Legal Title: The Society of Jesus of New England. Revs. Robert J. Levens, S.J. Ord: '81, Prov.; James M. Hayes, S.J. Ord: '85, Mission Liaison.

U.S. Religious serving in foreign missions: Revs. John P. Banks, S.J. Ord: '51, Jamaica; Robert B. Campbell, S.J. Ord: '57, Lebanon; John A. Carty, S.J. Ord: '59, Egypt; Vincent F. Connolly, S.J. Ord: '70, Jamaica; John J. Donohue, S.J. Ord: '59, Lebanon; Thomas J. Fitzpatrick, S.J. Ord: '68, Jordan; Mr. Thomas J. Frink, S.J., Jamaica; Revs. Louis L. Grenier, S.J. Ord: '49, Jamaica; Richard P. Guerrera, S.J. Ord: '73, Mozambique; Donald L. Larkin, S.J. Ord: '66, Jamaica; Michael D. Linden, S.J. Ord: '80, Jamaica; Joseph A. MacWade, S.J. Ord: '61, Jamaica; Martin F. McDermott, S.J. Ord: '64, Lebanon; Joseph F. McHugh, S.J. Ord: '83, Jamaica; Gerald L. McLaughlin, S.J. Ord: '59, Jamaica; Oliver E. Nickerson, S.J. Ord: '54, Jamaica; Kevin G. O'Connell, S.J. Ord: '69, Jordan; Joseph V. Owens, S.J. Ord: '71, Honduras; William J. Raftery, S.J. Ord: '57, Bahamas; Francis J. Ryan, S.J. Ord: '56, Jamaica; Paul A. Schweitzer, S.J. Ord: '70, Brazil; David A. Skelskey, S.J. Ord: '80, Ethiopia; John E. Surette, S.J. Ord: '67, Jamaica; Thomas Vallamattam, S.J. Ord: '64, Jamaica.

Priests 23; Seminarians 1.

Society of Jesus: New Orleans Province, 211 Pere Marquette Bldg., New Orleans, LA 70112. Tel: 504-525-4043.

Legal Title: Jesuit Mission Bureau. Rev. Edward B. Arroyo, S.J. Ord: '75, Prov.

U.S. Religious serving in foreign missions: Revs. Donald G. Bahlinger, S.J. Ord: '59, Paraguay; Edward G. Benya, S.J. Ord: '84, Brazil; David C. Borbridge, S.J. Ord: '63, Brazil; Bro. Anthony S. Coco, S.J., Brazil; Revs. Fred Cooley, S.J. Ord: '54, Sri Lanka; Claude Daly, S.J. Ord: '43, Sri Lanka; Carlos E. de la Cruz, S.J. Ord: '75, Paraguay; Alfonso Del Marmol, S.J. Ord: '51, Sri Lanka; Edward J. Dougherty, S.J. Ord: '70, Brazil; A. Gerard Fineran, S.J. Ord: '50, Brazil; Bro. Robert E. Hollingsworth, S.J., Brazil; Revs. O. Kenneth Johnson Ord: '92, Zambia; Leo V. Leise, S.J. Ord: '94, Paraguay; Roland J. Lesseps, S.J. Ord: '65, Zambia; Lloyd Lorio, S.J. Ord: '56, Sri Lanka; Patrick S. Madigan, S.J. Ord: '83, Zimbabwe; Francis X. Mayer, S.J. Ord: '50, Sri Lanka; Joseph H. Meyer, S.J. Ord: '46, Sri Lanka; Harry Miller, S.J. Ord: '54, Sri Lanka; Harold J. Rahm, S.J. Ord: '50, Brazil; David H. Romero, S.J. Ord: '91, Brazil; Stephen C. Rowntree, S.J. Ord: '75, Kenya; John F. Schroder, S.J. Ord: '53, Belize; John Stacer, S.J. Ord: '63, Zimbabwe; Charles B. Thibodeaux, S.J. Ord: '59, Paraguay; Bro. Terence N. Todd, S.J., Micronesia; Rev. Harold J. Weber, S.J. Ord: '44, Sri Lanka.

Priests 27; Brothers 3; Scholastics 1.

Society of Jesus: New York Province, 39 E. 83rd St., New York, NY 10028. Tel: 212-774-5500. Revs. Kenneth J. Gavin, S.J. Ord: '75, Prov.; Thomas E. Smith, S.J. Ord: '74, Asst. Prov.-International Apostolates.

U.S. Religious serving in foreign missions: Rev. Gerald W. Aman, S.J. Ord: '73, Nigeria; Bro. David P. Antonelli, S.J., Micronesia; Revs. Charles J. Beirne, S.J. Ord: '69, Guatemala; Joseph E. Billotti, S.J. Ord: '63, Micronesia; Kenneth C. Bogart, S.J. Ord: '56, Philippines; J. Dean Brackley, S.J. Ord: '76; El Salvador; Gary J. Bradley, S.J. Ord: '75, Micronesia; Philip J. Calderone, S.J. Ord: '56, Philippines; John J. Carroll, S.J. Ord: '55, Philippines; Joseph A. Cavanagh, S.J. Ord: '62, Micronesia; John E. Chambers, S.J. Ord: '64, Philippines; Francis X. Clark, S.J. Ord: '43, Philippines; James P. Croghan, S.J. Ord: '85, Micronesia; John J. Curran, S.J. Ord: '59, Micronesia; Edgar J. Debany, S.J. Ord: '84, Nigeria; James P. Dunne, S.J., Philippines; Paul V. Finster, S.J. Ord: '45, Philippines; Thomas R. Fitzpatrick, S.J. Ord: '59, Micronesia; Robert J. Flynn, S.J. Ord: '50, Japan; Matthew N. Fullam, S.J. Ord: '42, Philippines; Joseph A. Galdon, S.J. Ord: '59, Philippines; Pasquale T. Giordano, S.J. Ord: '72, Philippines; Francis N. Glover, S.J. Ord: '58, Philippines; Very Rev. James C. Gould, S.J. Ord: '74, Micronesia, Pref. Apostolic, Marshall Islands; Revs. George R. Graziano, S.J. Ord: '59, Japan; Thomas H. Green, S.J. Ord: '63, Philippines; Leonard G. Hacker, S.J. Ord: '47, Micronesia; John J. Halligan, S.J. Ord: '61, Ecuador; Robert E. Hamm, S.J. Ord: '68, Nigeria; William L. Hayes, S.J. Ord: '44, Philippines; Gerald W. Healy, S.J. Ord: '46, Philippines; Victor J. Helly, S.J. Ord: '54, Philippines; Francis X. Hezel, S.J. Ord: '69, Micronesia; Revs. Kenneth J. Hezel, S.J. Ord: '66, Guam; Donald J. Hinfey, S.J. Ord: '63, Ghana; Robert C. Hogan, S.J. Ord: '64, Philippines; Raymond T. Holscher, S.J. Ord: '72, Philippines; Paul J. Horgan, S.J. Ord: '68, Micronesia; Joseph A. Johnston, S.J. Ord: '52, Australia; William P. Klintworth, S.J. Ord: '61, Philippines; John G. Krebs, S.J.

Ord: '65, Philippines; William H. Kreutz, S.J. Ord: '69, Philippines; Dennis M. Leder, S.J. Ord: '76, Guatemala; Paul J. Maher, S.J. Ord: '64, Nigeria; William J. Malley, S.J. Ord: '64, Philippines; John J. Madden, S.J. Ord: '69, Nigeria; Richard R. McAuliff, S.J. Ord: '92, Micronesia; Daniel F. McCoy, S.J. Ord: '45, Japan; Richard S. McCougch, S.J. Ord: '93, Micronesia; James A. McDonough, S.J. Ord: '42, Guam; William J. McGarry, S.J. Ord: '58, Micronesia; Thomas B. McGrath, S.J. Ord: '64, Guam; Gerald J. McIntyre, S.J. Ord: '74, Zimbabwe; James A. McKeough, S.J. Ord: '54, Philippines; Daniel J. McNamara, S.J. Ord: '80, Philippines; James T. Meehan, S.J. Ord: '63, Philippines; Michael D. Moga, S.J. Ord: '64, Philippines; John F. Moran, S.J. Ord: '57, Philippines; Gregory F. Muckenhaupt, S.J. Ord: '88, Micronesia; Daniel J. Mulhauser, S.J. Ord: '60, Guam; Ugo R. Nacciarone, S.J. Ord: '64, Zambia; Joseph F. O'Brien, S.J. Ord: '44, Philippines; James O'Donnell, S.J. Ord: '61, Philippines; Thomas H. O'Gorman, S.J. Ord: '63, Philippines; Thomas J. O'Shaughnessy, S.J. Ord: '44, Philippines; John J. Phelan, S.J. Ord: '58, Philippines; Calvin H. Poulin, S.J. Ord: '62, Philippines; Neil C. Poulin, S.J. Ord: '66, Micronesia; George W. Quickley, S.J. Ord: '80, Nigeria; William J. Rakowicz, S.J. Ord: '80, Micronesia; Francis E. Reilly, S.J. Ord: '53., Philippines; James B. Reuter, S.J. Ord: '46, Philippines; Robert A. Rice, S.J. Ord: '53, Philippines; Joseph L. Roche, S.J. Ord: '58, Philippines; Michael F. Rooney, S.J. Ord: '72, Philippines; Marc J. Roselli, S.J. Ord: '85, Nigeria; Robert T. Rush, S.J. Ord: '59, Japan; Patrick J. Ryan, S.J. Ord: '68, Nigeria; Very Rev. Ramon A. Salomone, S.J. Ord: '65, Regional Supr., Nigeria-Ghana; Revs. J. Peter Schineller, S.J. Ord: '70, Nigeria; Herbert Schneider, S.J. Ord: '70, Philippines; John N. Schumacher, S.J. Ord: '57, Philippines; Lawrence P. Searles, S.J. Ord: '87, Puerto Rico; Arthur F. Shea, S.J. Ord: '38, Philippines; John R. Sheehan, S.J. Ord: '92, Nigeria; Paul M. Sheehan, S.J. Ord: '52, Philippines; Joseph J. Smith, S.J. Ord: '57, Philippines; Edward A. Soucie, S.J. Ord: '62, Micronesia; Thomas B. Steinbugler, S.J. Ord: '61, Philippines; Robert J. Suchan, S.J. Ord: '56, Philippines; William T. Suchan, S.J. Ord: '58, Micronesia; William M. Sullivan, S.J. Ord: '66, Micronesia; Terence N. Todd, S.J., Micronesia; Dominic J. Totaro, S.J. Ord: '67, Nigeria; Juan C. Villegas, S.J. Ord: '75, Colombia; Charles E. Wolf, S.J. Ord: '49, Philippines; John H. Zupez, S.J. Ord: '67, Zimbabwe.

Priests 77; Brothers 2; Scholastics 1.

Society of Jesus: Oregon Province, 2222 N.W. Hoyt, Portland, OR 7210. Tel: 503-227-1174.

Legal Title: American Jesuits in Africa. Revs. Robert B. Grimm, S.J. Ord: '76, Prov.; Ignatius F. Ohno, S.J. Ord: '92, Mission Dir.

U.S. Religious serving in foreign missions: Revs. Joseph B. Danel, S.J. Ord: '52, Zambia; Peter J. Henriot, S.J. Ord: '70, Zambia; Ronald E. Hidaka, S.J. Ord: '74, Zambia; William J. Loyens, S.J. Ord: '58, Malawi; Gary N. Smith, S.J. Ord: '71, Uganda; Bro. Frederick O. Mercy, S.J., Uganda; James P. McGloin, S.J. Ord: '74, Zambia; John J. Morris, S.J. Ord: '50, Uganda; Bartholomew J. Murphy, S.J. Ord: '72, Tanzania; John J. O'Leary, S.J. Ord: '60, Zambia; Michael J. Schultheis, S.J. Ord: '65, Mozambique; Joseph H. Small, S.J. Ord: '60, Kenya; Roy W. Thaden, S.J. Ord: '73, Zambia; Peter R. Titland, S.J. Ord: '70, Zambia.

Priests 11; Brothers 1.

Society of Jesus: Wisconsin Province, 3400 W. Wisconsin Ave., P.O. Box 080288, Milwaukee, WI 53208-0288. Tel: 414-937-6949; Fax: 414-937-6950.

Legal Title: Jesuit Mission Service, Inc.: Revs. D. Edward Mathie, S.J. Ord: '68, Prov.; James E. Grummer, S.J. Ord: '82, Mission Dir.

U.S. Religious serving in foreign missions: Revs. Francis X. Buchmeier, S.J. Ord: '73, Korea; John V. Daly, S.J. Ord: '66, Korea; Emil J. Denemark, S.J. Ord: '81, Korea; Robert W. Dundon, S.J. Ord: '69, Zimbabwe; James A. Egan, S.J. Ord: '65, Uganda; Jonathan Haschka, S.J. Ord: '75, Kenya; Daniel J. Kenney, S.J. Ord: '63, Kenya; Robert J. Kelly, S.J. Ord: '52, Korea; John D. Mace, S.J. Ord: '68, Philippines; Peter E. Marchetti, S.J. Ord: '77, Honduras; Francis H. Mathy, S.J. Ord: '58, Japan; Robert K. McIntosh, S.J. Ord: '72, Korea; Albert J. DiUlio, S.J. Ord: '74, Ethiopa; Philip E. Pick, S.J. Ord: '50, Honduras; Basil M. Price, S.J. Ord: '54, Korea; Robert P. Raszkowski, S.J. Ord: '46, Belize; Donald F. Rauscher, S.J. Ord: '68, Zimbabwe; John R. Schak, S.J. Ord: '61, Argentina; Nicholas E. Schiel, S.J. Ord: '55, Honduras; Christopher A. Spalatin, S.J. Ord: '71, Korea; Anthony J. Wach, S.J. Ord: '72, Uganda.

Priests 24.

Maryknoll (M.M.)

A community of American secular priests and brothers. Established in 1911 by action of the United States Hierarchy. Authorized by Pope Pius X, with later approvals by Pope Benedict XV and Pope Pius XI

U.S. Foundation: Maryknoll Society Center & Administrative Offices. Catholic Foreign Mission Society of America, P.O. Box 303, Maryknoll, NY 10545-0303. Tel: 914-941-7590; Fax: 914-762-0316. Revs. Raymond J. Finch, M.M. Ord: '76, Supr. Gen. & Pres.; Jeremiah R. Burr, M.M. Ord: '67, Vicar Gen. & Vice Pres.; Thomas P. Henehan, M.M. Ord: '65, Asst. Gen.; Michael J. Snyder, M.M. Ord: '78, Asst. Gen.; Bro. Wayne J. Fitzpatrick, M.M., Asst. Gen.

The Society is incorporated in New York, under the legal title: Catholic Foreign Mission Society of America, Incorporated. It is also incorporated in California, Hawaii, Illinois, Massachusetts, Minnesota, Missouri, and New Jersey.

For detailed information regarding statistics, activities in the Archdioceses and Dioceses in the United States, Properties owned or sponsored and Houses in the United States, and the placement of the Maryknollers in the various Archdioceses and Dioceses, please refer to the sections for Religious Institutes of Men and the designated Archdioceses and Dioceses.

Maryknoll Foreign Missions

Maryknollers serving overseas:

Religious serving in Tanzania: Revs. John C. Sivalon, M.M. Ord: '75, Regional Supr.; James A. Conard, M.M. Ord: '56; William F. Daley, M.M. Ord: '56; Edward V. Davis, M.M. Ord: '61; James E. Eble, Jr., M.M. Ord: '88; John W. Eybel, M.M. Ord: '70; Paul E. Fagan, M.M. Ord: '60; John F. Felago, M.M. Ord: '68; J. Francis Flynn, M.M. Ord: '52; Herbert T. Gappa, M.M. Ord: '68; Edward A. Hayes, M.M. Ord: '59; Joseph G. Healey, M.M. Ord: '66; Richard A. Hochwalt, M.M. Ord: '51; James J. Kuhn, M.M. Ord: '51; Ramon J. McCabe, M.M. Ord: '56; Howard E. O'Brien, M.M. Ord: '55; Daniel F. Ohmann, M.M. Ord: '55; Edward J. Quinn, M.M. Ord: '51; Thomas J. Shea, M.M. Ord: '67; David A. Smith, M.M. Ord: '85; William S. Stanley, M.M. Ord: '92; Kenneth J. Sullivan, M.M. Ord: '57; Donald F. Sybertz, M.M. Ord: '55; Arthur H. Wille, M.M. Ord: '51; John W. Waldrep, M.M. Ord: '90; Richard W. Bauer Ord: '85.

Priests 24; Brothers 3; Priest Associates 1; Seminarians 1.

Religious serving in Bangladesh: Revs. Robert T. McCahill, M.M. Ord: '64, Unit Coord.; William J. McIntire, M.M. Ord: '67; Douglas F. Venne, M.M. Ord: '59.

Priests 3.

Religious serving in Bolivia: Revs. Denis P. Browne, M.M. Ord: '47; James W. Fitzgerald, M.M. Ord: '50; Gerard T. McCrane, M.M. Ord: '59; John F. Gorski, M.M. Ord: '63; Michael A. Gould, M.M. Ord: '54; Sigmund S. Jamroz, M.M. Ord: '66; Francis T. McGourn, M.M. Ord: '64, Regional Supr.; Paul A. O'Brien, M.M. Ord: '59; John J. Ogurchock, M.M. Ord: '54; Arthur J. Prall, M.M. Ord: '52; William Senger, M.M. Ord: '73.

Priests 11; Brothers 3.

Religious serving in Cambodia: Revs. John C. Barth, M.M. Ord: '91; James P. Noonan, M.M. Ord: '60; Charles R. Dittmeier, M.M. Ord: '70.

Religious serving in Brazil: Revs. Daniel F. McLaughlin Ord: '61; William F. Marley, M.M. Ord: '52; Dennis Moorman, M.M. Ord: '98; James L. Hilgeman, M.M., M.D. Ord: '65; Gerald M. Wickenhauser, M.M. Ord: '62, Unit Coord.

Priests 5.

Religious serving in Chile: Revs. Dale F. Barron, M.M. Ord: '65; Richard L. Brooker, M.M. Ord: '55; Joseph H. Cappel, M.M. Ord: '35; Stephen T. DeMott, M.M. Ord: '76; John J. Gallahue, M.M. Ord: '62; Thomas P. Golden, M.M. Ord: '51; Frederick J. Hegarty, M.M. Ord: '53; John A. Jensen, M.M. Ord: '44; Ernest C. Lukaschek, M.M. Ord: '64, Reg. Supr.; Elmer J. Meyer, M.M. Ord: '54; George F. Painter, M.M. Ord: '44; Richard J. Sammon, M.M. Ord: '56; J. Lawrence Schanberger, M.M. Ord: '49; Eugene W. Toland, M.M. Ord: '64; James R. Weckesser, M.M. Ord: '55.

Priests 15; Brothers 1; Seminarians 1.

Religious serving in Egypt: Rev. Douglas E. May, M.M. Ord: '86.

Religious serving in Ethiopia: Rev. Richard M. Baker, M.M. Ord: '71.

Religious serving in El Salvador: Revs. David C. Kelly, M.M. Ord: '57; Gerald J. Persha, M.M. Ord: '70; John H. Spain, M.M. Ord: '70.

Priests 3.

Religious serving in Guatemala: Revs. William J. Donnelly, M.M. Ord: '65, Reg. Supr.; Thomas R. Amarillas, M.M. Ord: '68; William F. Mullan, M.M. Ord: '62; Robert F. Crohan, M.M. Ord: '62; Thomas P. Fox, M.M. Ord: '56; Joseph W. Halpin, M.M. Ord: '52; James P. LaCoste, M.M. Ord: '56; Kevin A. Lynch, M.M. Ord: '61; John J. McGovern, M.M. Ord: '54; Joseph C. Nerino, M.M. Ord: '50; John J. Ruessmann, M.M. Ord: '79.

Priests 11; Brothers 2.

Religious serving in Honduras: Revs. Robert F. Coyne, M.M. Ord: '83; Richard C. Frank, M.M. Ord: '53; Thomas F. Goekler, M.M. Ord: '67; Paul D. Belliveau, M.M. Ord: '69; David E. LaBuda, M.M. Ord: '71; Ronald J. Potter, M.M. Ord: '61.

Priests 6.

Religious serving in Hong Kong: Revs. Sean P. Burke, M.M. Ord: '78, Reg. Supr.; John F. Ahearn, M.M. Ord: '73; Robert F. Astorino, M.M. Ord: '70; Peter J. Barry, M.M. Ord: '65; Robert C. Bayne, M.M. Ord: '63; Anthony V. Brennan, M.M. Ord: '61; John J. Casey, M.M. Ord: '56; Robert J. Carleton, M.M. Ord: '64; John A. Cioppa, M.M. Ord: '59; Vincent F. Corbelli, M.M Ord: '60; John P. Cuff, M.M. Ord: '69; Thomas E. Danaher, M.M. Ord: '62; John F. Felago, M.M. Ord: '68; Scott T. Harris, M.M. Ord: '78; Laurence A. Dugas, M.M. Ord: '54; Stephen B. Edmonds, M.M. Ord: '40; William Galvin, M.M. Ord: '56; John E. Geitner, M.M. Ord: '53; John P. Grady, M.M. Ord: '55; Adam B. Gudalefsky, M.M. Ord: '59; Denis J. Hanly, M.M. Ord: '59; Matthew H. Kelleher, M.M. Ord: '67; Timothy Kilkelly, M.M. Ord: '90; William T. Knipe, M.M. Ord: '58; Carmen G. LaMazza, M.M. Ord: '55; Lawrence J. Lewis, M.M. Ord: '75; Michael J. McKeirnan, M.M. Ord: '41; Edward F. Malone, M.M. Ord: '52; Thomas A. Peyton, M.M. Ord: '58; Lawrence D. Radice, M.M. Ord: '85; Ronald R. Saucci, M.M. Ord: '65; J. Edward Szendrey, M.M. Ord: '62; John J. Sullivan, M.M. Ord: '60; Eugene A. Thalman, M.M. Ord: '60; John C. Tynan, M.M. Ord: '62; Michael P. Walsh, M.M. Ord: '88; C. Thomas Wilcox, M.M. Ord: '51; Elmer P. Wurth, M.M. Ord: '56.

Priests 38; Brothers 3.

Religious serving in Indonesia: Revs. Robert F. Baudhuin, M.M. Ord: '54; Vincent P. Cole, M.M. Ord: '71.

Priests 2.

Religious serving in Japan: Revs. Patrick F. O'Donoghue, M.M. Ord: '50, Reg. Supr.; Roy C. Assenheimer, M.M. Ord: '65; Richard A. Aylward, M.M. Ord: '53; Gerald L. Beausoleil, M.M. Ord: '52; Anthony B. Brodniak, M.M. Ord: '54; Alfonso Kim, M.M. Ord: '97; Richard Czajkcwski, M.M. Ord: '61; LoXuan Dam, M.M. Ord: '00; Regis B. Ging, M.M. Ord: '66; James H. Gorman, M.M. Ord: '52; William J. Grimm, M.M. Ord: '77; Joseph L. Hamel, M.M. Ord: '85; Kevin J. Hanlon, M.M. Ord: '89; Joseph H. Hermes, M.M. Ord: '62; James R. Jackson, M.M. Ord: '58; Joseph V. Maynard, M.M. Ord: '48; James J. Mylet, M.M. Ord: '75; Robert V. Nehrig, M.M. Ord: '54; Bryce T. Nishimura, M.M. Ord: '56; James K. Nishimuta, M.M. Ord: '54; James W. O'Neill, M.M. Ord: '55; Francis A. Riha, M.M. Ord: '68; Kenneth C. Sleyman, M.M. Ord: '90; Donald J. Vittengl, M.M. Ord: '56; Clarence J. Witte, M.M. Ord: '35; Louis J. Wolken, M.M. Ord: '46; Robert R. Zahn, M.M. Ord: '55.

Priests 27; Brothers 1.

Religious serving in Kenya: Revs. John E. Conway, M.M. Ord: '73; Donald F. Donovan, M.M. Ord: '55; Robert A. Jalbert, M.M. Ord: '79; David A. Lemkuhl Ord: '79; William Fryda, M.M. Ord: '88; Carroll B. Houle, M.M. Ord: '62; Michael C. Kirwen, M.M. Ord: '63; John J. Lange, M.M. Ord: '58; Lance P. Nadeau, M.M. Ord: '90; Edward J. Phillips, M.M. Ord: '74; Richard J. Quinn, M.M. Ord: '54; Thomas A. Tiscornia, M.M. Ord: '73; Robert W. Vujs, M.M. Ord: '61; Maurice J. Zerr, M.M. Ord: '51.

Priests 12; Brothers 5; Priest Associate 1.

Religious serving in Korea: Most Rev. William J. McNaughton, M.M., D.D., Bishop of Inchon; Revs. Roman G. Theisen, M.M. Ord: '54; Richard Agustin, M.M. Ord: '85; Francis H. Beninati, M.M. Ord: '55; Brian Barrons, M.M. Ord: '84; Carl A. Costa, M.M. Ord: '71; Thomas R. Egan, M.M. Ord: '64; Gerald J. Farrell, M.M. Ord: '57; Russell J. Feldmeier, M.M. Ord: '80; Alfred J. Fleming, M.M. Ord: '60; James M. Gilligan, M.M. Ord: '55; Gerard E. Hammond, M.M. Ord: '60, Reg. Supr.; Robert M. Lilly, M.M. Ord: '60; Gerald P. O'Connor, M.M. Ord: '69; Fernand Paquet, M.M. Ord: '56; Robert R. Pellini, M.M. Ord: '59; David L. Pfeiffer, M.M. Ord: '66; Richard S. Rolewicz, M.M. Ord: '65; Joseph A. Slaby, M.M. Ord: '66; John F. Soltis, M.M. Ord: '62; Edward J. Whelan, M.M. Ord: '61; Michael O. Zunno, M.M. Ord: '53.

Priests 21; Bishops 1.

Religious serving in Nicaragua: Rev. Edward O. Custer, M.M. Ord: '72.

Religious serving in Mexico: Revs. Richard L. Clifford, M.M. Ord: '53; Thomas E. Lavelle, M.M. Ord: '55; John P. Lomasney, M.M. Ord: '43; John P. Martin, M.M. Ord: '66, Reg. Supr.; John R. McGuire, M.M. Ord: '43; Charles A. Murray, M.M. Ord: '51; Peter J. Petrucci, M.M. Ord: '49; Eugene A. Theisen, M.M. Ord: '53, Reg. Supr.; Robert E. Tobin, M.M. Ord: '57.

Priests 9; Brothers 1.

Religious serving in Mozambique: Revs. Jose Padin, M.M. Ord: '97; Kenneth F. Thesing, M.M. Ord: '69.

Priests 2.

Religious serving in Namibia: Rev. Richard P. Albertine, M.M. Ord: '66.

Religious serving in Nepal: Revs. Robert J. Lloyd, M.M. Ord: '62; John J. Corcoran, M.M. Ord: '63; Joseph L. Thaler, M.M. Ord: '77.

Priests 3.

Religious serving in Peru: Revs. Thomas J. Burns, M.M. Ord: '69; Bernard P. Byrne, M.M. Ord: '56; Charles H. Cappel, M.M. Ord: '44; Edmund L. Cookson, M.M. Ord: '65; Joseph J. Donovan, M.M. Ord: '79; Joseph M. Everson, M.M. Ord: '99; Joseph Fedora, M.M. Ord: '84; Stephen P. Judd, M.M. Ord: '78; James J. Madden, M.M. Ord: '60; Philip N. Erbland, M.M. Ord: '66; Thomas F. Garrity, M.M. Ord: '46; Robert E. Hoffman, M.M. Ord: '60; Robert A. Hurteau, M.M. Ord: '89; Richard G. Laszewski, M.M. Ord: '51; James Lynch, M.M. Ord: '74; James M. O'Brien, M.M. Ord: '49; James V. Roth, M.M. Ord: '54; James J. Stefaniak, M.M. Ord: '50; Kyungsu Son, M.M. Ord: '79.

Priests 19.

Religious serving in the Philippine Islands: Revs. James H. Kroeger, M.M. Ord: '75; Herman W. Cisek, M.M. Ord: '65; John F. Coholan, M.M. Ord: '46; Robert L. Depinet, M.M. Ord: '61; Francis J. Felter, M.M. Ord: '69; James T. Ferry, M.M. Ord: '56; Richard R. Fries, M.M. Ord: '76; William P. Heffernan, M.M. Ord: '55; James C. Kalchthaler, M.M. Ord: '56; Ralph S. Kroes, M.M. Ord: '58; William J. LaRousse, M.M. Ord: '80; James D. McAuley, M.M. Ord: '80; Donald P. McQuade, M.M. Ord: '65; Walter J. Maxcy, M.M. Ord: '47; John B. Northrop, M.M. Ord: '74; Edward D. Shellito, M.M. Ord: '80; J. David Sullivan, M.M. Ord: '60, Reg. Supr.; John D. Walsh, M.M. Ord: '56.

Priests 18; Brothers 2.

Religious serving in Russia: Revs. Emile E. Dumas, M.M. Ord: '67; Fernand L. Gosselin, M.M. Ord: '70; Robert J. Reiley, M.M. Ord: '59; Edward Schoellmann, M.M. Ord: '65; Benedict A. Zweber, M.M. Ord: '59.

Religious serving in Taiwan: Revs. Alan T. Doyle, M.M. Ord: '64; Kurt J. Anderson, M.M. Ord: '72, Reg. Supr.; James V. Buttino, M.M. Ord: '47; Michael G. Collins, M.M. Ord: '59; James A. Collignon, M.M. Ord: '53; Robert F. Crawford, M.M. Ord: '61; Richard M. Devoe, M.M. Ord: '56; Richard E. Downey, M.M. Ord: '44; Alan T. Doyle, M.M. Ord: '64; Clarence A. Engler, M.M. Ord: '59; Edward J. Flanigan, M.M. Ord: '56; Donald F. Glover, M.M. Ord: '70; Delos A. Humphrey, M.M. Ord: '54; John B. Keaney, M.M. Ord: '55; Raymond H. Kelley, M.M. Ord: '58; John F. Kennedy, M.M. Ord: '55; J. Donald McGinnis, M.M. Ord: '53; John P. McKernan, M.M. Ord: '52; James T. Manning, M.M. Ord: '48; Leonard J. Marron, M.M. Ord: '57; Eugene M. Murray, M.M. Ord: '58; Cuong H. Nguyen, M.M. Ord: '98; Nhuan D. Nguyen, M.M. Ord: '93; Brendan M. O'Connell, M.M. Ord: '63; Francis T. O'Donnell, M.M. Ord: '55; Norbert A. Pacheco, M.M. Ord: '79; Anthony V. Polyak, M.M. Ord: '62; Francis Rebol, M.M. Ord: '53; Louis B. Rost, M.M. Ord: '55; Francis F. Schexnayder, M.M. Ord: '64; R. Russell Sprinkle, M.M. Ord: '35; Peter A. Wu, M.M. Ord: '61; Richard E. Zeimet, M.M. Ord: '64.

Priests 33; Brothers 2; Seminarians 1.

Religious serving in Thailand: Revs. Michael Bassano, M.M. Ord: '75; Daniel A. Boyd, M.M. Ord: '82; Thomas J. Dunleavy, M.M. Ord: '75; Roberto T. Fuentes, M.M. Ord: '92; James W. Kofski, M.M. Ord: '91, Unit Coord.; William T. O'Leary, M.M. Ord: '61; Thomas E. Pesaresi, M.M. Ord: '85.

Priests 7; Brothers 2.

Religious serving in Samoa: Most Rev. J. Quinn Weitzel, M.M. Ord: '55.

Priests 1; Brothers 1.

Religious serving in Venezuela: Revs. Thomas Ahearn, M.M. Ord: '68, Unit Coord.; Joseph A. Heim, M.M. Ord: '61; Donald P. McNamara Ord: '61.

Priests 2; Priests Associates 1.

Religious serving in Vietnam: Revs. Charles P. Robak, M.M. Ord: '70, Unit Coord.; Thomas J. O'Brien, M.M. Ord: '74.

Religious serving in Italy: Revs. Joseph V. McCabe, M.M. Ord: '77; Edward M. Dougherty, M.M. Ord: '79, Procurator, Collegio Maryknoll, Via Sardegna 83, Rome, Italy 00187.

Priests 2.

Missionaries of Africa (M.Afr.)

Missionaries of Africa Foreign Missions

U.S. Headquarters: Province of North America, 1624-21 St. N.W., Washington, DC 20009-1055. Tel: 202-232-5154; Fax: 202-332-8640. Rev. William Moroney, M.Afr. Ord: '61, Asst. Prov.

U.S. Religious serving in Africa: Revs. Richard Archambault, M.Afr. Ord: '73; William Curran, M.Afr. Ord: '66; Rene Dionne, M.Afr. (Spain) Ord: '61; William Dyer, M.Afr. Ord: '70; Roger A. LaBonte, M.Afr. Ord: '62; Robert McGovern, M.Afr. Ord: '63; Michel J. Lavoie, M.Afr. Ord: '70; Thomas Reilly, M.Afr. Ord: '78; Richard Roy, M.Afr. Ord: '71; Bros. Vernon Zachman, M.Afr.; Martin Chapper, M.Afr.; James Heintz, M.Afr.

Missionaries of the Sacred Heart (M.S.C.)

Missionaries of the Sacred Heart Foreign Missions

Missionaries of the Sacred Heart: P.O. Box 270, 305 S. Lake St., Aurora, IL 60507. Tel: 630-892-2371; 892-8400 (Prov. Supr.); Fax: 630-892-1678. Very Rev. David Foxen, M.S.C. Ord: '67, Prov. Supr.; Revs. Gerald Paul, M.S.C. Ord: '60, Treas.; Raymond Diesbourg, M.S.C. Ord: '74, Sec. & Editor, M.S.C. Spotlite.

Publication: *M.S.C. Spotlite.*

Religious serving in Papua New Guinea: Rev. Hilary Fischer, M.S.C. Ord: '57; Bro. Anton Freitas, M.S.C.; Revs. Joseph Gleixner, M.S.C. Ord: '65; Bernard Miller, M.S.C. Ord: '59; Bros. James Miller, M.S.C.; Patrick O'Hara, M.S.C.; Daniel Rakow, M.S.C.; Joseph Tesar, M.S.C.; Revs. Leon Weisenberger, M.S.C. Ord: '59; Richard Kennedy, M.S.C. Ord: '67.

Religious serving in Colombia, South America: Very Rev. German Barona Monsalve, M.S.C. Ord: '86, Section Supr.; Revs. Wilson Tascon, M.S.C. Ord: '90; Michael Miller, M.S.C. Ord: '85; Howard Fath, M.S.C. Ord: '61; Tito Medina Mora, M.S.C. Ord: '92; Javier Bautista Pinillos, M.S.C. Ord: '95; Luis Alfonso Segura, M.S.C. Ord: '99.

Religious serving in Marshall Islands: Rev. James Campbell, M.S.C. Ord: '72.

Missionhurst (C.I.C.M.)

Missionhurst Foreign Missions

American Headquarters (1946): Congregation of the Immaculate Heart of Mary, 4651 N. 25th St., Arlington, VA 22207. Tel: 703-528-3800; Fax: 703-528-5355. E-mail: provcicm@missionhurst.com. Rev. Bill Quigley, C.I.C.M. Ord: '74, Prov. Supr.

Publication: *Missionhurst.*

U.S. Religious serving Abroad: Revs. Albert Verbeke, C.I.C.M. Ord: '46, Belgium; Roger Tshikele, C.I.C.M. Ord: '87, Prov. Supr., Cameronn; Joseph Leavens, C.I.C.M. Ord: '65, Prov. Supr., Kasayi; Roy Shea, C.I.C.M. Ord: '86, Brazil; Bro. Robert Dixon, C.I.C.M., Brazil; Revs. Tim Atkin, C.I.C.M. Ord: '74, Haiti; Alphonse Rigouts, C.I.C.M. Ord: '48, Guatemala; Stan Szarwark, C.I.C.M. Ord: '64, Dominican Republic; Paul Delaere, C.I.C.M. Ord: '43, Belgium; Gerard Rogmans, C.I.C.M. Ord: '55, Dominican Republic; Bro. Leon Delanoy, C.I.C.M., Dominican Republic; Revs. Herman Louwagie, C.I.C.M. Ord: '58, Supr., Mexico; Thomas Matondo, C.I.C.M. Ord: '82; Bro. Jerry Galloway, C.I.C.M., Kinshasa, Democratic Republic of Congo; Revs. Jules Spriet, C.I.C.M. Ord: '34, Belgium; Paul Van Houtteghem, C.I.C.M. Ord: '48, Belgium; Joseph Verswyvel, C.I.C.M. Ord: '52, Belgium; Vincent VandeWeyer, C.I.C.M. Ord: '48, Belgium; Victor De Clercq, .C.I.C.M. Ord: '37, Belgium; Marcel Josson, C.I.C.M. Ord: '36, Belgium; William Missinne, C.I.C.M. Ord: '54, Belgium; Luke Moortgat, C.I.C.M. Ord: '65, Philippines; Jos Bastiaensen, C.I.C.M. Ord: '64, Prov. Supr., Japan; John Raymaker, C.I.C.M. Ord: '64, Japan; Michael Hann, C.I.C.M. Ord: '73, Haiti; John B. Peters, C.I.C.M. Ord: '53, Brazil; Cyriel Stulens, C.I.C.M. Ord: '65, Prov. Supr., North Congo; Jean-Marie Mbombo, C.I.C.M. Ord: '91, Prov. Supr., Nigeria; Patrick Masschelein, C.I.C.M. Ord: '73, Prov. Supr., Sinica.

American Oblate Missions (O.M.I.)

Home and Foreign Missions of the American Provinces of the Missionary Oblates of Mary Immaculate (Oblate Fathers).

Oblate Conference of the U.S., 8818 Cameron St., Silver Spring, MD 20910. Tel: 301-565-0060; Fax: 301-589-2897. Rev. Seamus Finn, O.M.I. Ord: '76, National Coord.

Oblates Foreign Missions

Eastern Province: 391 Michigan Ave., N.E., P.O. Box 29152, Washington, DC 20017. Tel: 202-529-5958; Fax: 202-636-9444. Very Rev. David Kalert, O.M.I. Ord: '64, Prov.

Publication: *The Oblate World; Oblate Foreign Missions; Oblates.*

Southern Province: 7711 Madonna Dr., San Antonio, TX 78216. Tel: 210-349-1475; Fax: 210-349-7411. Very Rev. Eugene Canas, O.M.I. Ord: '64, Prov.

Publication: *Province Newsletter.*

Northern U.S. Province: 200 Lowell Rd., Hudson, NH 03051-4908. Tel: 603-883-3233; Fax: 603-883-6089. Very Rev. Arthur Obin, O.M.I. Ord: '64, Prov.; Rev. Charles Breault, O.M.I. Ord: '59, Treas.

Publication: *Oblate World.*

Oblate Foreign Missions: 46 Mt. Washington St., Lowell, MA 01854-3498. Tel: 978-458-4380; Fax: 978-454-5308. Bro. Augustin Cote, O.M.I., Dir. Revs. Bernard Belley, O.M.I. Ord: '54; Real Bourque, O.M.I. Ord: '54; Francis Dolan, O.M.I. Ord: '73, Treas.; Raymond Lacasse, O.M.I. Ord: '58.

Central Province: 267 E. 8th, St. Paul, MN 55101. Tel: 612-292-8622; Fax: 612-292-8769.

Publications: *Oblates,* 15 S. 59th St., Belleville, IL 62222.

U.S. Religious serving in the Philippines Islands: Most Rev. Philip Smith, O.M.I., Archbishop of Cotabato; Revs. Armand Carignan, O.M.I. Ord: '53; Maurice Hemann, O.M.I. Ord: '50; Richard Pommier, O.M.I. Ord: '66; Robert Sullivan, O.M.I. Ord: '41; Cletus Ternes, O.M.I. Ord: '61; Richard Weixelman, O.M.I. Ord: '65.

U.S. Religious serving in Haiti: Revs. Richard Bolduc, O.M.I. Ord: '64; Alfred Charpentier, O.M.I. Ord: '71; Real Corriveau, O.M.I. Ord: '61; Omer Duplessis, O.M.I. Ord: '43; Roger Hallee, O.M.I. Ord: '63, Prov.; John Henault, O.M.I. Ord: '63; Roland Gagnon, O.M.I. Ord: '51; Charles Heon, O.M.I. Ord: '64; Leroy Landry, O.M.I. Ord: '61; Albert Lirette, O.M.I. Ord: '45; Raymond Marquis, O.M.I. Ord: '74; Francis Mitchell, O.M.I. Ord: '44; Roger Paradis, O.M.I. Ord: '48; Mauril Rancourt, O.M.I. Ord: '60; John St. Cyr, O.M.I. Ord: 61; Andre Tanguay, O.M.I. Ord: '53; Joseph Vaillancourt, O.M.I. Ord: '46; Marc Boisvert, O.M.I. Ord: '84.

U.S. Religious serving in Tahiti: Rev. Roger Roy, O.M.I. Ord: '49.

U.S. Religious serving in Indonesia: Rev. Lucien Bouchard, O.M.I. Ord: '55.

U.S. Religious serving in Brazil: Very Rev. James Gibbons, O.M.I. Ord: '69; Revs. Roger Bergkamp, O.M.I. Ord: '64; Thomas Brown, O.M.I. Ord: '55; Peter Curran, O.M.I. Ord: '71; Thomas Delaney, O.M.I. Ord: '60; John Drexel, O.M.I. Ord: '62; Edward Figueroa, O.M.I. Ord: '60; Robert Fitzpatrick, O.M.I. Ord: '71; Bro. Daniel Hayes, O.M.I.; Rev. Bruce Heit, O.M.I. Ord: '64; Revs. James Kohmetscher, O.M.I. Ord: '55; Edmund Leising, O.M.I. Ord: '46; William Lindkugel, O.M.I. Ord: '45; Paul Medeiros, O.M.I. Ord: '64; Robert Mayer, O.M.I. Ord: '67; Daniel Meehan, O.M.I. Ord: '61; David O'Brien, O.M.I. Ord: '59; Thomas O'Brien, O.M.I. Ord: '55; William Reinhard, O.M.I. Ord: '61; Anthony Rendon, O.M.I. Ord: '67; William Sheehan, O.M.I. Ord: '42; James Sullivan, O.M.I. Ord: '53; Charles Tierney, O.M.I. Ord: '73.

U.S. Religious serving in Canada: Revs. Richard G. Cote, O.M.I. Ord: '60; Normand Bonneau, O.M.I. Ord: '76; Dale Schlitt, O.M.I. Ord: '69.

U.S. Religious serving in Japan: Revs. John Mahoney, O.M.I. Ord: '54; Raymond Bourgoin, O.M.I. Ord: '66; John Deely, O.M.I. Ord: '70; Francis Hahn, O.M.I. Ord: '72; Richard Harr, O.M.I. Ord: '52; Ronald Laframboise, O.M.I. Ord: '67; Thomas Maher, O.M.I. Ord: '57; William Maher, O.M.I. Ord: '66; Jerome Novotney, O.M.I. Ord: '68; Angelo Siani, O.M.I. Ord: '65; Bertram Silver, O.M.I. Ord: '54; Edward Williams, O.M.I. Ord: '57.

U.S. Religious serving in Mexico: Revs. Carlos DeAnta, O.M.I. Ord: '50; Jaime Dukowski, O.M.I. Ord: '67; Philip Ehrhardt, O.M.I. Ord: '27; Daniel Gagnon, O.M.I. Ord: '87; Robert Hickl, O.M.I. Ord: '79; Richard Junius, O.M.I. Ord: '56; Edwin Krzewinski, O.M.I. Ord: '52; Ernest Liekens, O.M.I. Ord: '61; Augustine Petru, O.M.I. Ord: '53; Gilberto Pinon, O.M.I. Ord: '71; Gregorio Ramos, O.M.I. Ord: '50; Lawrence Rosebaugh, O.M.I. Ord: '63, Guatemala; John Schwider, O.M.I. Ord: '40; Jose Torres, O.M.I. Ord: '74; Robert Ward, O.M.I. Ord: '61; George Protopapas, O.M.I. Ord: '43; Gerald Kapustka, O.M.I. Ord: '65, Guatemala.

Religious in Scandinavian Missions: Bros. Olof Asblom, O.M.I.; Daniel Bozek, O.M.I.; Revs. Michael Bradley, O.M.I. Ord: '66; Allen Courteau, O.M.I. Ord: '76; Frank Jobst, O.M.I. Ord: '72; Leo Kertz, O.M.I. Ord: '63; Paul Marx, O.M.I. Ord: '65; Carroll Parker, O.M.I. Ord: '61; Clyde Rausch, O.M.I. Ord: '68; John Schoeberle, O.M.I. Ord: '61.

U.S. Religious serving in Zambia: Most Rev. Paul Duffy, O.M.I. Ord: '62, Archbishop of Mongu; Revs. Patrick Gitzen, O.M.I. Ord: '75; Jack Joyce, O.M.I. Ord: '61; Ronald Larignan, O.M.I. Ord: '59; John Staak, O.M.I. Ord: '95; Ronald Walker, O.M.I. Ord: '61.

Oblates of St. Francis de Sales Missions (O.S.F.S.)

Oblates of St. Francis de Sales Foreign Missions

U.S. Mission Headquarters: *Office of the Mission Procurator Oblates of St. Francis de Sales,* 1801 N. Broom St., Wilmington, DE 19802. Revs. Francis D. Dougherty, O.S.F.S. Ord: '38, Procurator. Tel: 302-652-3202; John

J. Hurley, O.S.F.S. Ord: '68, Procurator. Tel: 302-654-2238; Francis J. Gross, O.S.F.S., Mission Procurator, Toledo-Detroit Prov., 69 O'Hara Rd., Tonawanda, NY 14150. Tel: 716-694-4950.

U.S. Religious serving in Africa & South America: Revs. Leon V. Bonikowski, O.S.F.S. Ord: '65; George J. Brownholtz, O.S.F.S. Ord: '69; Edward P. Canavan, O.S.F.S.; John J. Coyne, O.S.F.S. Ord: '71; Walter DeSa, O.S.F.S.; Walter J. Hartlove, O.S.F.S. Ord: '48; Peter J. Harvey, O.S.F.S. Ord: '60; Robert J. Hindley, O.S.F.S. Ord: '58. Most Rev. John B. Minder, O.S.F.S., D.D.; Revs. Michael Moore, O.S.F.S.; Edmund F. O'Rourke, O.S.F.S.; Harry J. Schlight, O.S.F.S. Ord: '44; Most Rev. Edward J. Schlotterback, O.S.F.S., D.D.; Revs. Alfred J. Smuda, O.S.F.S. Ord: '66; Joseph A. Travers, O.S.F.S.

American Passionist Missions (C.P.)

Passionist Foreign Missions

Home and Foreign Missions of the American Provinces of the Congregation of the Passion

General Motherhouse: SS. Giovanni e Paolo 13, Rome 00184, Italy. Most Rev. Ottaviano D/Egidio, C.P., Supr. Gen.

Provincial Headquarters U.S.A.

St. Paul of the Cross Province: Province Pastoral Center, 80 David St., South River, NJ 08882. Tel: 732-257-7177. Very Rev. Terence Kristofak, C.P. Ord: '69, Prov. Supr.; Very Rev. Gerald Laba, C.P. Ord: '73, Consultor & Mission Procurator; Very Rev. Joseph Jones, C.P. Ord: '65, Sec.

U.S. Religious serving abroad: Revs. Richard Award, C.P. Ord: '81, West Indies; Thomas Brislin, C.P. Ord: '68, Bahamas; Bertram Chin, C.P. Ord: '91, West Indies; Herbert Eberly, C.P. Ord: '58, Philippines; Richard Frechette, C.P. Ord: '79, Haiti; Henry Free, C.P. Ord: '58, Philippines; Aelred Lacomara, C.P. Ord: '57, Africa; Richard Leary, C.P. Ord: '46, West Indies; Bernard McEachern, C.P. Ord: '64, Philippines; Bro. Robert McKenna, C.P., Philippines; Revs. Dominic Papa, C.P. Ord: '60, Rome; Bro. Michael Stomber, C.P., West Indies; Revs. Jerome Vereb, C.P. Ord: '72, Rome; Hilarion Walters, C.P. Ord: '47, Philippines.

Priests 13; Brothers 3.

Mission Procurators

Eastern: Revs. Gerald Laba, C.P. Ord: '73, Dir., 80 David St., South River, NJ 08882; Rev. Sebastian Kolinovsky, C.P. Ord: '51; Passionist Missionaries, Monastery Pl., Union City, NJ 07087. Bro. Leo DiFiore, C.P. Passionist Overseas Missions, 148 Monastery Ave., Pittsburgh, PA 15203.

Canada: 2102 Kipling Ave., Rexdale, ON M9W 4K5.

Philippines: Rev. Bernard McEachern, C.P. Ord: '64, Procurator, P.O. Box 1290 MCCPO, Metro Manila 1252, Makati.

China: Passionist Mission Procurator, Maryknoll House, Stanley, Hong Kong.

Holy Cross Province (Western): Immaculate Conception Monastery, 5700 N. Harlem Ave., Chicago, IL 60631. Tel: 773-631-6336; Fax: 773-631-8059. Very Rev. Michael Higgins, C.P. Ord: '70, Prov.; Rev. Luke Connolly, C.P. Ord: '52, Mission Appeals

Mission Procurators

Western: Mr. Edward Scholl, Dir.; Rev. Luke Connolly, C.P. Ord: '52, Mission Appeals, Passionist Missions, Inc., 5700 N. Harlem Ave., Chicago, IL 60631. Tel: 773-631-1686; Procuration Office of Holy Cross Province-Passionist Missions, Inc.

Japan: Rev. Francis Horack, C.P. Ord: '42, Japan Passionist Missions, Passionist Community 10-1, Yamate-cho, Mefu Takarazuka-shi, Hyogo Prefecture 665, Japan. Tel: 011-81-797 84-3111.

India: Rev. Walter Kaelin, C.P. Ord: '42, 1924 Newburg Rd., Louisville, KY 40205.

U.S. Religious serving in Japan: Revs. Ward Biddle, C.P. Ord: '51; Gabriel Brecheteau, C.P. Ord: '48; Francis Horack, C.P. Ord: '42; Leonard Kosatka, C.P. Ord: '59; Denis McGowan, C.P. Ord: '55; Clement Paynter, C.P. Ord: '52; Matthew Vetter, C.P. Ord: '38.

Also serving in Japan are the Cloistered Passionist Nuns; Mother Marie Paul Asayama, C.P., Supr.

Sisters 15

U.S. Religious serving Elsewhere: Revs. Justin Bartoszek, C.P. Ord: '64, Korea; Richard Thomson, C.P. Ord: '69, Korea; Bro. Laurence Finn, C.P., Korea; Revs. Joseph Moons, C.P. Ord: '77, India; Joseph VanLeeuwen, C.P. Ord: '64, India.

American Redemptorist Fathers (C.Ss.R.)

Mission of the Provinces and Vice-Provinces in the United States and other countries and lands

Redemptorist Foreign Missions

Baltimore Province: Redemptorist Fathers of New York, 7509 Shore Rd., Brooklyn, NY 11209. Fax: 718-630-5666. Very Rev. George J. Keaveney, C.Ss.R. Ord: '66, Prov.

Publication: *Perpetual Help World*, 294 E. 150th St., New York, NY 10051.

U.S. Religious serving in Paraguay: Revs. Antonio Cannoles, C.Ss.R. Ord: '69; Robert Hopwood, C.Ss.R. Ord: '52.

U.S. Religious serving in St. Lucia, W.I.: Revs. David M. Grainson, C.Ss.R. Ord: '98; Edmund J. Faliskie, C.Ss.R. Ord: '91; John P. Gallagher, C.Ss.R. Ord: '95; Rodney J. Olive, C.Ss.R. Ord: '86; Matthew T. Allman, C.Ss.R. Ord: '00.

U.S. Religious serving in Dominica, W.I.: Revs. Jerome Moody, C.Ss.R. Ord: '73; Joseph F. Krastel, C.Ss.R. Ord: '64; John F. McLoughlin, C.Ss.R. Ord: '92;Henrique Schulterbrandt, C.Ss.R. Ord: '94.

Denver Province: P.O. Box 300399, Denver, CO 80203-0399. Tel: 303-370-0036; Fax: 303-370-0036. Very Rev. Richard Thibodeau, C.Ss.R. Ord: '76, Prov.; Rev. Charles Beierwaltes, C.Ss.R. Ord: '67, Dir.-Foreign Missions, P.O. Box 6, Glenview, IL 60025. Tel: 847-724-0425; Fax: 847-724-8953.

U.S. Religious serving in Brazil: Revs. Vince Aggeler, C.Ss.R. Ord: '58, Joseph Butz, C.Ss.R. Ord: '70; William Fitzgerald, C.Ss.R. Ord: '43; John Gouger, C.Ss.R. Ord: '65; Donnell Kirchner, C.Ss.R. Ord: '66; Patrick McBride, C.Ss.R. Ord: '85; John McCarthy, C.Ss.R. Ord: '62; Thomas McIntosh, C.Ss.R. Ord: '66; Most Rev. Alfred Novak, C.Ss.R., Bishop of Paranagua, Brazil; Most Rev. Gutemberg Regis, C.Ss.R., Bishop of Coari, Brazil; Bro. Leo Patin, C.Ss.R.; Revs. William Steiner, C.Ss.R. Ord: '54; Joseph Stenger, C.Ss.R. Ord: '57; Andrew Thompson, C.Ss.R. Ord: '81; Ronald Weninger, C.Ss.R. Ord: '49.

U.S. Religious serving in Thailand: Revs. Raymond Brennan, C.Ss.R. Ord: '59; Charles Cotant, C.Ss.R. Ord: '41; Francis Gautreaux, C.Ss.R. Ord: '50; Joseph Maier, C.Ss.R. Ord: '65; Robert Martin, C.Ss.R. Ord: '50; Patrick Morrissy, C.Ss.R. Ord: '55; Lawrence Patin, C.Ss.R. Ord: '63; Most Rev. George Phimphisan, C.Ss.R., Bishop of Udon Thani; Revs. Michael Shea, C.Ss.R. Ord: '64; Harold J. Thiel, C.Ss.R. Ord: '56; Leo Travis, C.Ss.R. Ord: '54; William Wright, C.Ss.R. Ord: '60.

U.S. Religious serving in Nigeria: Revs. William M. Cleary, C.Ss.R. Ord: '62; Joseph Dorcey, C.Ss.R. Ord: '74; William A. Peterson, C.Ss.R. Ord: '67; Richard Thiele, C.Ss.R. Ord: '54; John Willett, C.Ss.R. Ord: '61; Robert Wirth, C.Ss.R. Ord: '64.

St. Columban's Foreign Mission Society (S.S.C.) (THE COLUMBAN FATHERS)

Founded in 1918 with the approval of Pope Benedict XV. Placed under the patronage of St. Columban and made a Pontifical Society by Pope Pius XI.

Generalate: St. Columban's, Grange Rd., Donaghmede, Dublin 13, Ireland. Very Rev. Nicholas Murray, S.S.C. Ord: '62, Supr. Gen.

U.S. Foundation & Administration: Columban Fathers, St. Columbans, NE 68056. Tel: 402-291-1920. Very Rev. Brendan O'Sullivan, S.S.C. Ord: '70, Dir.; Rev. James J. Hastings, S.S.C. Ord: '72, Vice Dir.

Publication: *Columban Mission*.

Legal Title: St. Columban's Foreign Mission Society. The Society is incorporated in California, Illinois, Massachusetts, Nebraska, New York, Rhode Island, and Registered in Pennsylvania.

St. Columban's Foreign Mission

House of Post-Graduate Studies: Collegio Colombano, Corso Trieste, 57, Roma 00198, Italy. Very Rev. Padhraic O'Loughlin, S.S.C. Ord: '57, Procurator Gen.

U.S. Religious serving Overseas: Revs. Edward A. Allen, S.S.C. Ord: '30, Philippines; William D. Bourke, S.S.C. Ord: '54, Philippines; Thomas Browning, S.S.C. Ord: '90, Taiwan; John A. Buckley, S.S.C. Ord: '68, Brazil; Vincent J. Busch, S.S.C. Ord: '74, Philippines; Salvatore S. Caputo, S.S.C. Ord: '76, Korea; Francis P. Carroll, S.S.C. Ord: '62, Japan; David J. Clay, S.S.C. Ord: '62,

Philippines; John Comiskey, S.S.C. Ord: '68, Philippines; Neil Boyle, S.S.C. Ord: '43, Ireland; Charles Duster, S.S.C. Ord: '61, Fiji; William Hennessey, S.S.C. Ord: '35, Philippines; Michael Hoban, S.S.C. Ord: '70, Chile; Quentin F. Kalick, S.S.C. Ord: '42, Philippines; David Padrnos, S.S.C. Ord: '71, Japan; Ronald Kelso, S.S.C. Ord: '73, Japan; Donald Kill, S.S.C. Ord: '72, Philippines; Charles Lintz, S.S.C. Ord: '70, Korea; James J. McCaslin, S.S.C. Ord: '54, Hong Kong; Joseph McSweeny, S.S.C. Ord: '90, Taiwan; John P. Moran, S.S.C. Ord: '50, Philippines; Robert E. Mosher, S.S.C. Ord: '82, Chile; Richard L. Pankratz, S.S.C. Ord: '74, Philippines; Desmond Quinn, S.S.C. Ord: '54, Philippines; Edward I. Quinn, S.S.C. Ord: '55, Fiji; Francis A. Regan, S.S.C. Ord: '66, Britain; Paul Richardson, S.S.C. Ord: '54, Philippines; Michael O'Loughlin, S.S.C. Ord: '60, Ireland; Thomas Shaughnessy, S.S.C. Ord: '66, Philippines; David M. Sheehan, S.S.C. Ord: '53, Korea; Robert P. Sweeney, S.S.C. Ord: '59, Korea; Thomas Walsh, S.S.C. Ord: '57, Chile; Vincent J. Youngkamp, S.S.C. Ord: '59, Japan.

Priests 33.

Brothers of the Sacred Heart (S.C.)

Brothers of the Sacred Heart Foreign Missions

Provincial House: 685 Steere Farm Rd., Pascoag, RI 02859-4601. Tel: 401-568-3361; Fax: 401-568-1450. Bros. Robert F. Breault, S.C., Prov. Supr.; Paul Hebert S.C., Mission Procurator. The Brothers of the Sacred Heart have mission schools and stations in Kenya, Lesotho, Uganda, Zambia, and Zimbabwe.

Brothers 89; Brothers in Africa 50.

Salesians of Don Bosco (S.D.B.)

Salesians of Don Bosco Foreign Missions

Salesian Provincial House: 148 Main St., Box 639, New Rochelle, NY 10802-0639. Tel: 914-636-4225. Very Rev. Patrick Angelucci, S.D.B. Ord: '76, Prov.; Rev. Patrick Diver, S.D.B. Ord: '74, Procurator.

U.S. Religious serving Abroad: Revs. Henry Bonetti, S.D.B. Ord: '73, China; Dominic DeBlase, S.D.B. Ord: '61, Sierra Leone; Robert Falk, S.D.B. Ord: '63, Korea; Lawrence Gilmore, S.D.B. Ord: '84, Liberia; Edward Liptak, S.D.B. Ord: '59, Tanzania; Harry Peterson, S.D.B. Ord: '61, Chile; John Thompson, S.D.B. Ord: '79, Sierra Leone; John Trisolini, S.D.B. Ord: '67, Korea; Bro. John Cosgrove, S.D.B., Sierra Leone.

Salesian Provincial House: 1100 Franklin St., San Francisco, CA 94109. Tel: 415-441-7144; Fax: 415-441-7155. Very Rev. Nicholas J. Reina, S.D.B. Ord: '78, Prov.

U.S. Religious serving Abroad: Revs. Albert Mengon, S.D.B. Ord: '66, Sierra Leone; Christian Kot, S.D.B. Ord: '94, Sierra Leone; Bros. Joseph Reza, S.D.B., Ethiopia; William Regner, S.D.B., Sierra Leone.

Salvatorian Missions (S.D.S.)

Salvatorian Foreign Missions

U.S.A. Provincial Headquarters: *Salvatorian Provincial Residence,* 1735 Hi-Mount Blvd., Milwaukee, WI 53208-1720. Tel: 414-258-1735. Very Rev. Peter Schuessler, S.D.S. Ord: '80, Prov.

U.S.A. Procurator: 1735 Hi-Mount Blvd., Milwaukee, WI 53208-1720. Tel: 414-258-1735. Rev. Eric Middlecamp, S.D.S. Ord: '52, Mission Dir.

Publication: *The Salvatorian Newsletter.*

U.S. Religious serving in Tanzania: Revs. Carl Gleason, S.D.S. Ord: '56; Daniel Pekarsken, S.D.S. Ord: '90; James Weyker, S.D.S. Ord: '69; Bros. Donald Maurer, S.D.S.; Charles Kubat, S.D.S.

Society of African Missions (S.M.A.)

Society of African Missions

U.S. Provincial Headquarters: *Society of African Missions,* 23 Bliss Ave., Tenafly, NJ 07670. Tel: 201-567-0450, 567-9085; Fax: 201-567-7156, 541-1280. Rev. Ulick Bourke, S.M.A. Ord: '68, Prov. Supr.

U.S. Religious serving Abroad: Revs. Terrance Doherty, S.M.A. Ord: '70, Liberia; James Gessler, S.M.A. Ord: '63, Liberia; Thomas Hayden, S.M.A. Ord: '58, Liberia; Michael Moran, S.M.A. Ord: '81, Liberia; Frank Allen Wright, S.M.A. Ord: '93, Kenya.

Society of St. Edmund (S.S.E.)

Edmundite Foreign Missions

U.S. Foundation: Edmundite Generalate, 270 Winooski Park, Colchester, VT 05439. Tel: 802-654-3400; Fax: 802-654-3409. Very Rev. Richard M. Myhalyk, S.S.E. Ord: '71, Supr. Gen.

U.S. Religious serving Abroad: Revs. Edward J. Dubriske, S.S.E. Ord: '64, Venezuela; Philippe Simonnet, S.S.E. Ord: '52, France.

The Society of Mary (S.M.) MARIST FATHERS

Marist Foreign Missions

General Motherhouse: Via Alesandro Poerio, 63 00152, Rome, Italy. Very Revs. Joaquin Fernandez, S.M. Ord: '68, Supr. Gen.; Friedrich Arnold, S.M. Ord: '70, Vicar Gen.

U.S. Mission Promoter: Marist Missions, 29 Isabella St., Boston, MA 02116-5216. Tel: 617-482-0832; Fax: 617-482-1570. Rev. J. Armand Robichaud, S.M. Ord: '50, Dir.

Missions in Brazil, Fiji, Japan, New Caledonia, Norway, Papua New Guinea, Peru, Philippine Islands, Samoa, Senegal, Solomon Islands, Tonga, Vanuatu, Venezuela, Wallis & Futuna, Republic of Cameroon.

U.S. Religious serving Abroad: Revs. Raymond Coolong, S.M. Ord: '71, Peru; Paul Frechette, S.M. Ord: '76, Peru; John Galvin, S.M. Ord: '63, Solomon Islands; Roland Lajoie, S.M. Ord: '74, Senegal; Joseph J. McLaughlin, S.M. Ord: '72, Philippines; Louis Morosini, S.M. Ord: '56, Solomon Islands; Alfred Puccinelli, S.M. Ord: '66, Brazil; Joseph Pusateri, S.M. Ord: '65, Samoa; Bertrand Soucy, S.M. Ord: '53, Vanuatu; Neil Soucy, S.M. Ord: '62, New Caledonia; Bro. Matthew F. Wade, S.M., Peru.

Society of St. James the Apostle

Society of St. James the Apostle, Inc.: 24 Clark St., Boston, MA 02109. Tel: 617-742-4715; Fax: 617-723-7389. Revs. Gabriel Troy (BO) Ord: '66, Dir.; Milton Eggerling (OAK) Ord: '54.

Founded by His Eminence Richard Cardinal Cushing, in 1958 to recruit Diocesan Priest volunteers for South America.

Serving in Peru: Revs. John E. Davis (FAR) Ord: '69; Frank Fairbairn (BO) Ord: '69; George Flynn (BO) Ord: '56; Donald Gorski (CHR) Ord: '59; Kevin Hays (CHI) Ord: '77; Eugene K. Kirke (BO) Ord: '62; Paul Madden (JKS) Ord: '70; Joseph I. Martin (BO) Ord: '56; J. Joseph McCarthy (BO) Ord: '66; Philip McKenna (MOB); John O'Leary (MIA) Ord: '67; Gerard O'Meara (BO) Ord: '76; Hugh Joseph Shields (PH) Ord: '72; Raymond O'Sullivan (BO) Ord: '68; John J. Pashby (BO) Ord: '60; William Pearsall (BO) Ord: '53; Jules Roos (PIT) Ord: '56; Desmond Tynan (BO) Ord: '67.

Serving in Bolivia: Revs. Donald J. Bowen (FR) Ord: '64; James Coleman (P) Ord: '73; Raymond Cowell (CHI) Ord: '56; Thomas Domurat (BO) Ord: '79; Harold Holbrook (BGP) Ord: '57; Thomas Keyes (BO) Ord: '73; Paul M. Koch (DM) Ord: '61; Charles Stanley (BO) Ord: '71; John L. Sullivan (BO) Ord: '52; Thomas Oates (BO) Ord: '63; John Michael Ricker (TOL) Ord: '55.

Serving in Ecuador: Revs. James Cribbin (SD) Ord: '85; John Hendricks (TR) Ord: '52; John Gordon (MET) Ord: '85; John Grimes (BO) Ord: '71; Cornelius Kiely (BAK) Ord: '67; John J. Moriarty (JOL) Ord: '62; Robert Thomas (BO) Ord: '61.

Third Order Regular Missions (T.O.R.) Third Order Regular of St. Francis

T.O.R. Foreign Missions

Provincial Residence: Province of the Most Sacred Heart of Jesus, 128 Woodshire Dr., Pittsburgh, PA 15215-1714. Tel: 412-781-8333. Very Rev. Edmund F. Carroll, T.O.R. Ord: '57, Minister Prov.; Bro. Mark McBride, T.O.R., Prov. Dir. of Foreign Missions.

U.S. Religious serving Abroad: Revs. Gerald J. King, T.O.R. Ord: '71, Brazil; Paul R. Pavlik, T.O.R. Ord: '59, Brazil; Most Rev. Adrian J. Veigle, T.O.R., D.D. (Retired), Brazil.

Missionary Servants of the Most Holy Trinity (S.T.)

Trinity Missions

International Headquarters

Generalate: 1215 N. Scott St., Arlington, VA 22209-3097. Tel: 703-276-8646; Fax: 703-522-2656. Rev. Austin Walsh, S.T. Ord: '65, Supr. Gen.; Bro. Steven Vesely, S.T., Sec. Gen.

U.S. Religious serving abroad: Revs. Rudy Breunig, S.T. Ord: '65, Costa Rica; Charles Gordon, S.T. Ord: '67, Costa Rica; Louis E. Murphy, S.T. Ord: '60, Colombia; Kevin Nugent, S.T. Ord: '51, Costa Rica; Victor Santiago Mateo, S.T. Ord: '82, Colombia; Harold Stone, S.T. Ord: '59, Mexico; Bruce Ward, S.T. Ord: '60, Mexico; Guy Wilson, S.T. Ord: '78, Costa Rica.

American Vincentian Missions (C.M.)

Vincentian Foreign Missions

Provincial Headquarters

Eastern Province: *St. Vincent's Seminary,* 500 East Chelten Ave., Philadelphia, PA 19144. Tel: 215-848-1985; Fax: 215-844-2085. E-mail: cmphila88@aol.com. Very Rev. Thomas F. McKenna, C.M. Ord: '67, Prov.

U.S. Religiou sserving abroad: Revs. Elmer Bauer, III, C.M. Ord: '93,

Rome, Italy; Thomas M. Byrnes, C.M. Ord: '50, Balboa, Panama; John J. Carney, C.M. Ord: '82, Puerto Armuelles, Panama; Juan Chavarria, C.M. Ord: '95, Puerto Armuelles, Panama; Edison Famania, C.M. Ord: '94, Concepcion, Panama; Alcibiades Guerra, C.M. Ord: '90, Centro Vicentino, Panama; Jose Pio Jimenez, C.M. Ord: '68, Balboa, Panama; Teodoro Justavino, C.M. Ord: '90, Centro Vicentino, Panama City; John E. Kane, C.M. Ord: '70, Teologado Vicentino, Panama City; G. Edgardo Lopez, C.M. Ord: '99, Puerto Armuelles, Panama; Alan J. McLellan, C.M. Ord: '65, Colon, Panama; John J. MacGillivray, C.M. Ord: '76, Concepcion, Panama; Robert P. Maloney, C.M. Ord: '66, Rome; Francis Maguire, C.M. Ord: '51, Addis Ababa, Ethiopia; Michael T. Mazurchuk, C.M. Ord: '86, Concepcion, Panama; A. Alberto Mendoza, C.M. Ord: '96, Concepcion, Chiriqui, Panama; Emmet J. Nolan, C.M. Ord: '92, Concepcion, Panama; Rigoberto Pitti, C.M. Ord: '98, Centro Vicentino, Panama; John P. Prager, C.M. Ord: '82, Soloy, Panama; Teodoro A. Rios, C.M. Ord: '76, Concepcion, Panama; Francisco Samudio, C.M. Ord: '92, Centro Vicentino, Panama; Charles G. Schuster, C.M. Ord: '55, Puerto Armuelles, Panama; Harold G. Skidmore, C.M. Ord: '50, Balboa, Panama; Juan Wardrope, C.M. Ord: '89, Colon, Panama.

Midwest Province: Vincentian Fathers and Brothers, 13663 Rider Trail N., Earth City, MO 63045-1512. Tel: 314-344-1184; Fax: 314-344-2989. Very Rev. William E. Hartenbach, C.M. Ord: '64, Prov.

U.S. Religious serving in foreign missions: Revs. Gary A. Mueller, C.M. Ord: '95; Stephen Gallegos, C.M. Ord: '88; Very Rev. Robert Wood, C.M. Ord: '56, Supr.; Revs. Francis A. Gaydos, C.M. Ord: '47; W. Barry Moriarty, C.M. Ord: '67; Thomas G. O'Hern, C.M. Ord: '77; John T. Richardson, C.M. Ord: '49; Hugh F. O'Donnell, C.M. Ord: '61; Edward Gallagher, C.M. Ord: '78; Jacob Johnson, C.M. Ord: '47; Robert W. Chap, C.M. Ord: '66; Richard Preuss, C.M. Ord: '73.

Southern Province: Congregation of the Mission, 3826 Gilbert Ave., Dallas, TX 75219-4346. Tel: 214-526-0234 or 526-2421; Fax: 214-526-3477. E-mail: CongMissSP@aol.com. Very Rev. George J. Weber, C.M. Ord: '54, Prov.

Xaverian Missionary Fathers (S.X.)

Xaverian Foreign Missions

U.S. Foundation: *Xaverian Missionary Fathers,* 12 Helene Ct., Wayne, NJ 07470. Tel: 201-942-2975; Fax: 201-942-5012. Revs. Ivan Marchesin, S.X. Ord: '66, Prov.; Dario Maso, S.X. Ord: '82, Local Supr. & Dir.-Vocation Ministry; Frank B. Grappoli, S.X. Ord: '63, Treas. & Mission Dir.

Religious serving in Brasil: Revs. Francis Gugliotta, S.X. Ord: '52; Danilo Lago, S.X. Ord: '77; Mario Pezzotti, S.X. Ord: '59; Gino Nasini, S.X. Ord: '65.

Religious serving in Cameroon: Revs. Rene Lovat, S.X. Ord: '57; Pierino Zoni, S.X. Ord: '61.

U.S. Religious serving in Colombia: Revs. Mark Marangone, S.X. Ord: '84; Mauro Loda, S.X. Ord: '99.

U.S. Religious serving in Indonesia: Revs. Bruno Orru, S.X. Ord: '63; Franco Qualizza, S.X. Ord: '71.

U.S. Religious serving in Japan: Revs. Pio Devoti, S.X. Ord: '63; Paolo Gobbo, S.X. Ord: '94; Greg Holm, S.X. Ord: '87.

U.S. Religious serving in Mexico: Rev. Adolph Menendez, S.X. Ord: '68.

U.S. Religious serving in Philippines: Revs. Carl Chudy, S.X. Ord: '86; Kenneth Cannon, S.X. Ord: '97.

U.S. Religious serving in Sierra Leone: Most Rev. George Biguzzi, S.X.; Revs. Victor Mosele, S.X. Ord: '60; Luciano Peterlini, S.X. Ord: '63; Graziano Rossato, S.X. Ord: '66 ; James Tully, S.X. Ord: '75.

U.S. Religious serving in Taiwan: Revs. Joseph Matteucig, S.X. Ord: '84; Martino Roia, S.X. Ord: '82.

Missionary Activities

RELIGIOUS SOCIETIES ENGAGED IN MISSIONARY WORK

Augustinian Recollect Fathers: *Province of St. Nicholas of Tolentine U.S. Delegation,* 2800 Scurz Ave., Bronx, NY 10465. Phone: 718-823-0460. Rev. Jose Luis Duenas, O.A.R., Supr. Delegate.

Engaged in missionary work among Spanish-speaking people. Sustains mission personnel in the Archdiocese of New York, Newark and in the Dioceses of Las Cruces and El Paso.

Augustinian Recollect Fathers and Brothers (1944): *Province of St. Augustine,* 29 Ridgeway Ave., West Orange, NJ 07052. Very Rev. John A. Gruben, O.A.R. Prov. Supr.

Missionary work among Spanish-speaking people established in colonies throughout a notable part of the U.S. and active in cursillo and retreat work in the Archdiocese of New York.

Blessed Sacrament Fathers And Brothers: *Province of St. Ann,* 5384 Wilson Mills Rd., Cleveland, OH 44143.

Brothers of the Christian Schools: *U.S.A. & Toronto Regional Office of the De La Salle Christian Brothers Conference,* 4351 Garden City Dr., Ste. 200, Landover, MD 20785. Phone: 301-459-9410; Fax: 301-459-8056.

The missionary activities administered by The Christian Brothers Conference include Bethlehem University, West Bank; Kenya, Nigeria, South Africa; Eritrea/Ethiopia & St.Vincent Island, West Indies. Individual Province Mission responsibilities include San Francisco: Mexico, Tijuana; Toronto: The Grenadines. Christian Brothers also serve as missionaries in the Philippines & Central America.

*** Christian Foundation for Children and Aging:** One Elmwood Ave., Kansas City, KS 66103. Phone: 913-384-6500; 800-875-6564. Robert K. Hentzen, Pres.; Most Rev. James P. Keleher, Member of the Board; Louis Finocchario, Exec. Dir. & Contact Person.

Christian Foundation for Children and Aging (CFCA) is an international Catholic mission organization dedicated to raising mission consciousness here at home and helping the poor at Catholic mission sites abroad. Founded by Catholic lay people in 1981, CFCA's develops support through "sponsorship" — linking a child or aging friend in need with a sponsor in a mutually beneficial relationship. Sponsor assistance helps provide food, medical care, opportunity for education while at the same time permitting the sponsor to get to know the culture and life of their sponsored friend. CFCA currently works with over 40 missionary orders and the local church in 25 developing countries and also sponsors an extensive lay volunteer program.

Claretian Missionaries: *Headquarters of Western Province,* 1119 Westchester Pl., Los Angeles, CA 90019. Very Rev. Ralph Berg C.M.F., Prov. Phone: 323-734-1824; Fax: 323-737-0301.

Headquarters of Eastern Province, 400 N. Euclid Ave., Oak Park, IL 60302. Phone: 708-848-2076. Very Rev. Len Brown, C.M.F., Prov.

Please refer to the Religious Institutes of Men section for activities and representation in the United States

Publications: monthly magazine, *U.S. Catholic*; extensive line of Pamphlets and Paperback Books; bimonthly Newsletter; *Fides-Claretian.*

Claret Center, 5536 S. Everett Ave., Chicago, IL. Resources for Counseling and Spiritual Directions. Chicago, IL

Missions outside the United States entrusted to the Claretians: Guatemala, Cameroons.

Columban Sisters (1922 Ireland): 73 Mapleton St., Brighton, MA 02135. Phone: 617-782-5683; Fax: 617-789-3569. Sr. Maura Ryan, S.S.C., U.S. Area Coord.

The Missionary Sisters of Saint Columban are also known as the Columban Sisters. The Columban Sisters are religious women called to bring the good news of Christ to all in need, particularly the poor and the oppressed and those who have not yet had the Gospel proclaimed to them. The congregation strives to respond to the needs of the people by dedication to the work of evangelization through pastoral, educational, medical, and social ministries, and supporting the efforts of the local church where its members are sent. The congregation also endeavors, through programs of mission education and animation, to deepen an awareness of global vision and world justice.

Active in the U.S. in the Archdioceses of Boston, Los Angeles, and in the Diocese of Buffalo. Active outside the U.S. in Ireland, England, Scotland, Hong Kong, Korea, Philippines, Peru, Chile and Pakistan.

Comboni Missionaries of the Heart of Jesus, Inc. (Verona Fathers) Provincial Headquarters: *Comboni Mission Center,* 8108 Beechmont Ave., Cincinnati, OH 45255-3194. Phone: 513-474-4997. Revs. Dennis Conway, M.C.C.J., Prov.; Joseph Bragotti, M.C.C.J., Mission Dir.; Paul Donohue, M.C.C.J., Communications Dir. Foreign mission society, both priests and brothers, founded by Bishop Daniel Comboni, Vicar Apostolic of Central Africa.

Active in the Archdioceses of Chicago, Cincinnati, Los Angeles and Newark.

Comboni Missionaries work with local churches in: Africa—Benin, Central African Republic, Egypt, Eritrea, Ethiopia, Ghana, Kenya, Malawi, Mozambique, South Africa, Sudan, Chad, Togo, Uganda, Zambia and Democratic Republic of the Congo; Asia—Philippines, China; Latin America—Brazil, Chile, Colombia, Costa Rica, Ecuador, El Salvador, Guatemala, Mexico and Peru; North America—Canada and the United States.

Training Centers: Africa—Eritrea, Ethiopia, Kenya, Malawi, Mozambique, South Africa, Togo, Egypt, Sudan, Uganda, Democratic Republic of the Congo; Asia—Philippines; Europe—Austria, England, France, Germany, Italy, Poland, Portugal and Spain; Latin America—Brazil, Colombia, Costa Rica, Ecuador, Mexico and Peru; North America—United States.

Publications: *Comboni Press Network Newsletter; Comboni Press Feature Service; Comboni Mission Newsletter.*

Comboni Missionary Sisters: *American Headquarters,* 1307 Lakeside Ave., Richmond, VA 23228. Phone: 804-262-8827; Fax: 804-264-2906. Sr. Maria Teresa Goffi, Prov. Supr.

An international congregation of 1,800 sisters founded by Bishop Daniel Comboni in 1872 in Verona, Italy. Engaged in pastoral and catechetical work; education; social services; health services; building Christian communities; training of local church leaders in Africa, Latin America and Middle East.

The American Province recruits and trains sisters for the foreign mission, mission education, fundraising for missions, pastoral ministry among the poor, and day care centers.

Congregation of Alexian Brothers: *Immaculate Conception Province, U.S. Provincial Headquarters,* 600 Alexian Way, Elk Grove Village, IL 60007. Bro. Lawrence Krueger, Provincial

Missionary healthcare work in Davao City, Philippines directed by four Alexian Brothers. Please refer to the Religious Institutes of Men section for activities and representation in the United States.

Congregation of Christian Brothers: *Eastern American Province, United States Headquarters,* 21 Pryer Terr., New Rochelle, NY 10804. Bro. J. B. Moffett, C.F.C., Prov.; Bro. C. F. Miller, C.F.C., Mission Dir.

Missionary and educational work in Italy, Kenya, and Peru.

Congregation of the Holy Ghost and of the Immaculate Heart of Mary (1872): 6230 Brush Run Rd., Bethel Park, PA 15102. Phone: 412-831-0302; Fax: 412-831-0970. *Holy Ghost Fathers and Brothers (C.S.Sp.), Eastern Province,* Very Rev. Donald J. McEachin, C.S.Sp., Prov., *Western Province* (1963); 1700 W. Alabama St., Houston, TX 77098-2808. Phone: 713-522-2882; 713-522-2667; Fax: 713-522-8063. Very Rev. Donald S. Nesti, C.S.Sp., Prov.

Missionary work among the abandoned, including first evangelization, teaching, care of homeless children, and pastoral ministry.

Missionaries serve in 17 (arch)dioceses in the United States; the Archdiocese of San Juan and the Dioceses of Arecibo in Puerto Rico; the Dioceses of Ciudad Valles, Tampico, the Archdiocese of San Luis Potosi in Mexico; Archdiocese of Arusha, and Dioceses of Mbulu and Zanzibar in Tanzania. Nairobi in Kenya; Bethlehem in South Africa; and Awasa in Ethiopia. Other establishments in North and South America, Europe, Africa and Australia.

Missionaries of Our Lady of La Salette: *Province of Our Lady of Seven Dolors,* 915 Maple Ave., Hartford CT 06114-2330. Phone: 860-956-8870. Very Rev. James H. Kuczynski, M.S., Prov. Supr.; Rev. John R. Nuelle, M.S., Procurator, 85 New Park Ave., Hartford, CT 06106-2184.

Active in Archdioceses of Buenos Aires, Argentina; Cochabamba, Bolivia; Cordoba, Argentina; and Dioceses of Santiago del Estero.

Please refer to the Religious Institutes of Men section for activities and representation in the United States.

Congregation of the Missionaries of Our Lady of La Salette: 947 Park St., P.O. Box 2965, Attleboro, MA 02703-0965. Phone: 508-222-7171; Fax: 508-222-6178. *Immaculate Heart of Mary Province La Salette Provincial House.* Very Rev. Dennis Loomis, M.S., Prov. Supr., Rev. William Slight, M.S., Procurator. Phone: 508-226-7747.

The southern portion of Isabela, Diocese of Ilagan is entrusted to the care of the Province Ina ng Pag-asa, originating from the Immaculate Heart of Mary Province of the La Salette Missionaries. The La Salette Mission Seminary was established in 1962 in Santiago, Isabela, Philippines

Please refer to the Religious Institutes of Men section for representation and statistics in the United States. Also active in the Archdiocese of Montreal and the Dioceses of London, Ontario and Gatineau-Hull, Quebec, Canada; Manila, Imus and Ilagan, Philippines; Bangalore, Trivandrum and Irinjalakuda, Kerala, S. India.

Congregation of the Priests of the Sacred Heart, The: *U.S. Provincialate Offices,* P.O. Box 289, Hales Corners, WI 53130-0289. Phone: 414-425-6910. Very Rev. John Czyzynski, S.C.J., Prov. Supr.

Please refer to the Religious Institutes of Men section for other activities and representation in the United States.

Missionary work in the home and foreign missions; educational activities; welfare work, especially in industrial centers. Home Missions: Lower Brule and Cheyenne Indian Reservations, South Dakota; Black Missions, Diocese of Jackson, Mississippi; Spanish-speaking Apostolate, Dioceses of Brownsville, Galveston-Houston, and Archdiocese of San Antonio

Foreign Missions: Zaire, Cameroon, Mozambique, South Africa, Brazil, Argentina, Uruguay, Chile, Venezuela, India, Indonesia and Finland.

Congregation of the Resurrection: *Resurrection Catholic Missions of the South, Inc.,* 2815 Forbes Dr., Montgomery, AL 36110. Phone: 334-263-4221; Fax: 334-263-4999.

The Resurrection Catholic Missions ministries includes a home for handicapped and severely mentally retarded children, an early childhood development facility for preschoolers, a church and elementary school, a 20-bed geriatric nursing facility, as well as an outreach program to homebound elders and an addictions counseling/prevention program.

Please refer to the Religious Institutes of Men section for activities and representation in the United States. Active also in Australia, Brazil, Bolivia, Bulgaria, Canada, Germany, Jamaica, Mexico and Poland.

Consolata Missionaries (1901): *Provincial Headquarters,* 2301 Hwy. 27, P.O. Box 5550, Somerset, NJ 08875. Phone: 732-297-9191; Fax: 732-940-3121. Rev. Leonard DePasquale, I.M.C., Reg. Supr.

Legal Title: *Consolata Society for Foreign Missions.*

Serving in 20 countries around the world including the United States.

Publication: *Consolata Missionaries.*

Consolata Missionary Sisters (1910): 6801 Belmont Ave., N.E., P.O. Box 371, Belmont, MI 49306. Phone: 616-361-2072; Fax: 616-361-2049. Sr. Cecilia Clara Zamboni, M.C., Supr.

The congregation is committed to all types of missionary apostolate, primarily in African and South American countries.

Corpus Christi Carmelites: 516 Broadway, Newport, RI 02840. Sr. Teresa Winefride, O.Carm., Supr.

Sisters work as catechists and social workers in America and abroad; own and/or operate homes for the aged, girls, and sick children; hostels; day nurseries; do ministry work in prisons and hospitals and educational work in kindergartens, primary and secondary schools.

Crosier Fathers and Brothers: *Crosier Missions,* 3510 Vivian Ave., Shoreview, MN 55126-3852. Phone: 651-486-7456; Fax: 651-287-1130. Rev. David E. Gallus, O.S.C., Coord.

Legal Title: *Canons Regular of the Order of the Holy Cross.*

Missionary work among the Asmat tribes of Irian Jaya Indonesia, since 1958.

Publications: quarterly, *Crossview.*

Daughters of Mary Help of Christians: *St. Philip Apostle Province,* 655 Belmont Ave., Haledon, NJ 07508. Mother Judith Suprys, F.M.A., Prov.

Legal Title: *Missionary Society of the Salesian Sisters, Inc.*

Missionary work in home and foreign countries; catechetical, educational and training centers; social services; hostels, hospitals, clinics and dispensaries; mission centers, leper colonies and youth centers.
Active in U.S. within the Archdioceses of Newark, New Orleans, New York, Miami and the Dioceses of Paterson, St. Petersburg, and Birmingham.

Eucharistic Missionaries of St. Dominic: 3801 Canal Street, Suite 400, New Orleans, LA 70119. Phone: 504-486-1133; Fax: 504-486-6547. Sr. Dorothy Troclair, O.P., Pres.
Missionary work and ministry in religious education; diocesan offices; pastoral associates; social service; parish administrators; spirituality- retreat center; home & clinic nursing; hospital chaplaincy; counseling; pastoral care of the sick in homes; literacy ministry to Mayan immigrants

Franciscan Friars Of The Atonement-Generalate: *Graymoor,* P.O. Box 300, Garrison, NY 10524-0005. Phone: 914-424-2113; Fax: 914-424-2166.
Mission activities outside of the U.S.: Japan. Also staff parishes in Canada, England and the United States. The Friars mission of reconciliation is promoted through preaching of the Gospel, ecumenism and inter-religious activity and missionary activity.
Please refer to the Religious Institutes of Men section for activities and representation in the United States.

Franciscan Missionaries of Mary, The: *U.S. Provincial House,* 3305 Wallace Ave., Bronx, NY 10467. Phone: 718-547-4604; Fax: 718-547-4607. Sr. Mary Motte, F.M.M., Prov.
Founded in India in 1877, for the work of evangelization and development in non-Christian and de-Christianized countries. Active mission apostolate is centered in daily adoration of the Blessed Sacrament exposed.
This international congregation serves 856 missions in 56 provinces.
Missionary work of evangelization and development, catechetics, social work, nursing, community development programs, educational and public health programs, pastoral activity and various forms of ministry and service.

Franciscan Missionary Sisters for Africa: *American Headquarters Center for Promotion and Formation,* 172 Foster St., Box 35095, Brighton, MA 02135. Sr. Mary Jordan, O.S.F., Supr. Gen.
Missions in Kenya, Uganda, South Africa, Zambia and Zimbabwe.
Publication: *The Daystar*

Franciscan Mission Association: *Franciscan Mission House,* Washington Ave., Rensselaer, NY 12144. Phone: 518-465-0062; Fax: 518-465-3673. Bro. James Amrhein, O.F.M.Conv.; Dir.
The American branch of the Franciscan Mission Crusade founded in 1924, approved by Pope Pius XI to further the work of the Conventual Franciscan Missionary Apostolate. The purpose is to aid the Mission of the Order in every possible way. The revenues of the Association accrue from the annual and perpetual enrollments in the Association, bequests, other free-will offerings and donations, membership in monthly mission club appeal.

Franciscan Mission Association (1953): *Franciscan Missions,* 322 West St., Carey, OH 43316. Phone: 419-396-6455. Bro. Bryan Hoban O.F.M.Conv., Dir.
The purpose of the association, which part of the Province of Our Lady of Consolation, is to give financial and other material aid to the missionaries of Africa: the Dioceses of Ndola and Solwezi, Zambia; missionaries in the dioceses of Olancho, Tegucigalpa and Comayagua in Honduras and San Jose in Costa Rica; and missionaries of the Southwestern United States. Both living and deceased may be enrolled as members. Members of the laity have an active part in promoting the growth of the association as outlined in Vatican II.

Franciscan Mission Association, Inc.: *Province of St. Anthony of Padua,* 185 W. State St., Granby, MA 01033. Phone: 413-467-9196; Fax: 413-467-7944. Rev. Placid Kaczorek, O.F.M.Conv., Dir.
Founded to support the domestic and foreign missions of the Conventual Franciscans of St. Anthony Province.

Franciscan Sisters of Allegany: *St. Elizabeth Motherhouse,* Allegany, NY 14706. Sr. Margaret Mary Kimmins, O.S.F., Gen. Minister; Sr. Marie Dolores Gionta, O.S.F., Mission Society Dir.
Sisters serve in areas of education; health-care; pastoral ministry; migrant ministry in the U.S; missionary work in the archdiocese of Kingston and dioceses of Montego Bay, Mandeville, Jamaica; the archdioceses of Brazilia and Goiania, and LaPaz; dioceses of Anapolis, Ipameri, Jatai, Ruy Barbosa, Goias, Cristalandia, Brazil and Pando, Bolivia.
Congregation 421; foreign missions 97.
Publication: *Zeal*

Franciscan Sisters, Daughters of the Sacred Hearts of Jesus and Mary: *Province of St. Clara,* P.O. Box 667, Wheaton, IL 60189-0667. Phone: 630-462-7422; Fax: 630-462-7148. Sr. Margaret Grempka, O.S.F., Prov. Dir.
Active in U.S.-institutional and home health care; housing; education; pastoral ministry; care of elderly; wellness; long-term care; social services; spiritual direction and retreats in archdioceses of Milwaukee, St. Louis, Dubuque, Denver and Chicago; in dioceses of Joliet, Green Bay, LaCrosse, Springfield-Cape Girardeau and Gary. Outside the U.S.: Brazil, Nigeria.

Franciscan Sisters of Little Falls, MN: *Motherhouse,* Little Falls, MN 56345. Phone: 320-632-2981. Sr. Rose Margaret Schneider, Pres.
Serving in Catholic and non-sectarian hospitals; Catholic and non-sectarian nursing homes; group homes; apartments for the elderly; home health nursing; public health nursing; Catholic high schools; Catholic elementary schools; special education; Spirituality Farm, Native Americans; community colleges; state colleges and universities; religious education; parish ministry; liturgical music ministry; music center; holistic growth center; health and recreation center; retreat ministry; counseling; spiritual direction; social service; ministry to the poor; ministry to the migrants; clinics; consultant for healthcare & related organizations; art therapist, computer programmer; Pastoral ministry; Education, health, social services in Quito, Ecuador, S.A., Zanzibar, Africa.

Franciscan Sisters of the Poor: *Congregational Office,* 133 Remsen St., Brooklyn, NY 11201. Phone: 718-643-1919; Fax: 718-643-9710. Sr. Jeanne M. Glisky, S.F.P., Pres.
Sisters serve in healing ministry; health care; social welfare; pastoral ministry in the U.S.; pastoral ministry and health care in the Dioceses of Rome, Padua and Messina in Italy. Mission ministry is represented in the Archdiocese of Goiania and in the Dioceses of Jatai and Ipameri in Brazil and in Kaolack and Dakar in Senegal, West Africa.
Number in Congregation 178; Mission ministry 20

Glenmary Home Missioners (1939): *National Headquarters,* P.O. Box 465618, Cincinnati, OH 45246-5618. Rev. Jerry Dorn, Pres.
Glenmary is an apostolic society of priests and brothers, and the only home mission society dedicated exclusively to establishing the Catholic Church in small towns and rural areas of the United States where there is no effective Catholic presence. The Glenmary society employs every available technique in organizing viable and effective Catholic parishes in these areas. Priests, brothers and lay coworkers are engaged in radio and television work, youth programs, systematic home visits, and a wide variety of projects designed to achieve better social conditions. When it is practical, these programs are conducted ecumenically; *Glenmary Research Center,* 1312 Fifth Ave., N., Nashville, TN 37208. Phone: 615-256-1900. Dr. Kenneth Sanchagrin, Dir.; *Glenmary Department of Pastoral Services,* 1312 Fifth Ave., N., Nashville, TN 37208. Rev. Michael Langell, Dir.
Please refer to the Religious Institutes of Men section for activities and representation in the United States.
Publication: *Glenmary Challenge*

Glenmary Home Mission Sisters of America (1941): *Glenmary Sisters,* P.O. Box 22264, Owensboro, KY 42302-2264. Fax: 502-686-8759. Sr. Christine Beckett, Pres.
Glenmary is a community of women religious of diocesan right and the only home mission community dedicated to bringing mission presence and activity to the rural, small town areas of the United States. The sisters live and work among the poor, the sick, the oppressed and unchurched in Appalachia and the South in areas where less than 5% of the total population is Catholic. When possible the Sisters work in collaboration with the Glenmary Priests and Brothers and the Glenmary Co-Missioners. The Glenmary Sisters believe in a holistic approach to mission - the caring of the whole person - through their ministries of co-creating with local people a Catholic Christian faith community, ecumenism, evangelization, radio programs, pastoral outreach, religious education, home health, home visitations, and a wide variety of social services for the very poor.
Please refer to the Religious Institutes of Women section for activities in the United States.
Publication: *Kinship*

Institute of Charity (Rosminian Fathers): *Rosmini House,* 2327 W. Heading Ave., Peoria, IL 61604.
Active in the Dioceses of Peoria, and St. Petersburg
Missions and missionary work in Tanga, Tanzania; New Zealand; Venezuela; and Kerela, India.

Jesuit Volunteers International: P.O. Box 3756, Washington, DC 20007. Phone: 202-687-1132; Fax: 202-687-5082. Mr. John Sealey, Acting Dir.
A Christian service organization offering young college educated lay men and women an opportunity to volunteer in a developing country in collaboration with Jesuits. Volunteers serve for two years without returning to the U.S. in the interim.

Mariannhill, Congregation of Missionaries of (1882): 23715 Ann Arbor Tr., Dearborn Hts., MI 48127. Rev. Gervais Giguere, C.M.M., Provincial Supr.
The American-Canadian province recruits and trains young men as priests and lay brothers for foreign missions, secures funds for the foreign missions, and does a limited amount of pastoral work at home.
Active in the Archdiocese of Detroit.
Outside the U.S.: Austria, Canada, Germany, Kenya, Mozambique, Netherlands, Papua New Guinea, Poland, South Africa, Spain, Switzerland, Zambia and Zimbabwe.
Publication: *Leaves*
Worldwide membership: Bishops 2; Priests 203; Brothers 104; Students Professed 71; Total Members 380.

Marist Missionary Sisters: *North American Provincial Office,* 349 Grove St., Waltham, MA 02453. Phone: 781-893-0149; Fax: 781-894-7610. Sr. Mary Jane Kenney, S.M.S.M., Prov.; Sr. Claire Rheaume, S.M.S.M., Mission Promotor; Sr. Annemarie Woeste, S.M.S.M., Vocation Directress.
We were founded in France in 1845 for mission in the South Pacific. Today, we are an International Missionary Congregation of 595 sisters (in seven provinces), serving the people of God in 28 countries around the world. The American Province has 120 sisters working in Massachusetts, Tennessee, Texas, Florida, Alaska, California, New York and Jamaica, W.I. Our mission is to bring the good news of God's love through spiritual and corporal works of mercy; catechetical, medical, educational and social services; pastoral ministry; formation of laity for leadership and a great concern for the poorest and most neglected. We work by preference among people of different cultures and languages, to bring about greater understanding, dignity and mutual respect.
Our formation is international with a French-speaking novitiate in Senegal, an English-speaking novitiate in Australia and a Spanish-speaking novitiate in Peru.
Province headquarters are in the United States, Italy, Australia, New Zealand, Peru, France and New Caledonia.
Legal Title: *Missionary Sisters of the Society of Mary, Inc.*
Please refer to the Religious Institutes of Women section for activities and representation in the United States.

Maryknoll Sisters of St. Dominic, Inc.: P.O. Box 311, Maryknoll, NY 10545-0311. Sr. Helene O'Sullivan, M.M., Community Pres.; Sr. Patricia Ryan, M.M., Vice Pres.; Sr. Joan Mury, M.M., Gen. Sec.; Sr. Mary Lou Daoust, M.M., Team Member.
A Pontifical Institute under the jurisdiction of the Congregation for the Institutes of Consecrated Life. The purpose of the Maryknoll Sisters Congregation is to participate in the mission presence and activity of the universal Church so that God's reign of peace, justice and love may be proclaimed and witnessed to throughout the world. The Maryknoll Sisters embrace a plurality of ministries while giving a clear sign of Christian community; faith-sharing; self-gift in service through pastoral and catechetical work; basic ecclesial communities; education; social services; medical and health promotion work; services through hostels; services to refugees; and ministries that promote human rights, social justice and the dignity and equality of women.
Please refer to the Religious Institutes of Women section for activities in the United States.
Active in Bangladesh, Bolivia, Brazil, Cambodia, Central Pacific, Chile, Ecuador, El Salvador, Guatemala, Hong Kong, Indonesia, Japan, Kenya, Korea, Macau, Mexico, Nepal, Namibia, Nicaragua, Panama, Peru, Philippines, Sudan, Taiwan, Tanzania, Thailand, USA and Zimbabwe.

Medical Missionaries of Mary: *MMM Zonal Center,* 563 Minneford Ave., City Island, NY 10464-1118. Phone: 718-885-0945; Fax: 718-885-0010. Sr. Philomena Sheerin, M.M.M., Congregational Ldr.; Sr. Joanne Bierl, M.M.M., Zonal Coord.
Missionary work in hospitals, clinics and leprosy treatment; public health and pastoral ministry centers in Africa, South America and Clinchco, VA.
Please refer to the Religious Institutes of Women section for activities and representation in the United States. Active also in Angola, Nigeria, Uganda, Tanzania, Honduras, Kenya, Malawi, Ethiopia, England, Ireland and Brazil.
Publication: quarterly, *The Mini MMM.*

Medical Mission Sisters: *North American Headquarters,* 8400 Pine Rd., Philadelphia, PA 19111. Fax:

215-342-3948. Sr. Elizabeth Koonthanam, M.M.S., Society Coord.; Sr. Maria Horning, M.M.S., North American Sector Coord.; Monica M. McGinley, Pub. Rels. Dir.

Legal Title: *Society of Catholic Medical Missionaries, Inc., Society of Catholic Medical Missionaries Generalate, Inc.*, (effective 1991).

Medical Mission Sisters have the special call in the Church of "being a healing presence at the heart of a wounded world." Members commit themselves "to promote healing and wholeness in all aspects of life" in the spirit of Jesus. They share life with those who are sick and have been made poor, trying to help them to live fully as human beings. Medical Mission Sisters' healing presence today involves a full range of preventitive, curative and promotive health services; health training programs; and development and social justice activities in Ghana, Uganda, Kenya, Ethiopia, Malawi, Democratic Republic of Congo, Pakistan, India, Belgium, Venezuela, Brazil, Peru, Indonesia, Philippines, Italy, Holland, Germany, England, Mexico and the United States.

Medical Mission Houses in the United States are listed under the Religious Institutes of Women section.

Publication: *Medical Mission Sisters News.*

Mill Hill Missionaries: *St. Joseph's Missionary Society,* 222 W. Hartsdale Ave., Hartsdale, NY 10530. Phone: 914-682-0645; Fax: 914-682-0862. Very Rev. Terence J. Lee, M.H.M., Reg. Rep.; Very Rev. Theo M. Feldbrugge, M.H.M., Admin. & Reg. Bursar, Los Angeles.

An international society of priests and brothers, founded in 1866, devoted entirely to the missionary needs of the Church.

Active in the U.S., in the Archdioceses of New York, Los Angeles, and the Diocese of Portland (ME).

Active outside the United States. Canada: Diocese of Kingston, ONT. Cameroon: the Archdiocese of Bamenda and the Dioceses of Buea, Kumbo and Ngoundere. Kenya: Archdioceses of Kisumu, Nairobi, and the Dioceses of Bungoma, Garissa, Homa-Bay, Kakamega, Kericho, Kisii, Nakuru and Ngong. Sudan: Archdiocese of Khartoum, and the Dioceses of Malakal and Tombura-Yambio. Uganda: Archdiocese of Kampala, and the Dioceses of Jinja, Soroti and Tororo. South Africa: Diocese of Port Elizabeth. China: Diocese of Hong Kong. India: Archdioceses of Hyderabad, Bangalore, and the Dioceses of Jamma-Srinagar and Varanasi. Indonesia: Diocese of Irian Jaya. Pakistan: Dioceses of Islamabad-Rawalpindi and Hyderabad. Malaysia: Archdiocese of Kuching, and the Dioceses of Keningau, Kota Kinabalu, Miri and Sibu. Philippines: Archdioceses of Manila, Jaro, and the Dioceses of San Jose and Infanta. Australia: Diocese of Geraldton. New Zealand: Dioceses of Aukland and Hamilton. Bolivia: Archdiocese of Cochabamba. Brazil: Dioceses of Governador Valadares and Itaquai. Ecuador: Archdiocese of Guayaquil. Netherlands Antilles: Diocese of Willemstad. Peru: Diocese of Chimbote. Also active in the Falkland Islands, St. Helena; Ascension and Tristan da Cunha.

Mission Helpers of the Sacred Heart: 1001 W. Joppa Rd., Baltimore, MD 21204-3787. Phone: 410-823-8585; Fax: 410-825-6355. Sr. M. Judith Waldt, M.H.S.H., Pres.

A Pontifical, missionary congregation with principal work of evangelization and catechesis; adult religious education; instruction of youth and children; D.R.E. programs; pastoral ministers; pastoral associates; pastoral social ministers; special ministers of the Eucharist; ministry in homes and institutions; ministry to the elderly and infirm; catechesis of blind, deaf, retarded; campus ministry; Hispanic pastoral ministry to adults and youth; spiritual direction and retreat work.

Please refer to the Religious Institutes of Women for activities and representation in the United States. Activities also in the Archdioceses of Barquisimeto, Venezuela, and San Juan.

Publication: 3 times yearly, *The Mission Helper.*

Mission International, Inc.: 2301 Hwy. 27, Somerset, NJ 08873. Phone: 732-297-9191; Fax: 732-940-3121. Rev. Leonard DePasquale, Chm.

Missionaries of Africa (M.Afr.): *U.S. Province of North America Headquarters,* 1624 21st St., N.W., Washington, DC 20009-1003. Fax: 202-332-8640. Rev. Richard Roy, M.Afr., Asst. Prov.

International and interracial missionary society of priests and brothers working in teams almost exclusively in Africa.

Active in the Archdioceses of Chicago, Washington and the Diocese of St. Petersburg.

Training centers and mission promotion centers in Brazil, Canada, Belgium, France, Germany, Great Britain, Holland, India, Ireland, Italy, Mexico, Philippines, Poland, Spain and Switzerland.

Missionary work in Algeria, Burundi, Chad, Ethiopia, Ghana, Kenya, Malawi, Mali, Mozambique, Nigeria,Rwanda, Senegal, Sudan, Tanzania, Tunisia, Uganda, Burkina Faso, Democratic Republic of Congo, Zambia, South Africa, Ivory Coast, and Nigeria. Totaling 99 dioceses and archdioceses in Africa; also special team working in Jerusalem.

Publication: newsletter, *Missionaries of Africa Report.*

Missionaries of the Holy Apostles, Society of the: 24 Prospect Hill Rd., Cromwell, CT 06416. Phone: 860-632-3039; Fax: 860-635-4823. Very Rev. Raymond Halliwell, M.S.A., Prov. Animator

Apostolic works consist in the promotion and training of adults for Christian leadership and for the diocesan or religious priesthood.

Please refer to the Religious Institutes of Men section for activities and representation in the United States. Activities also in Brazil, Venezuela, Colombia, Canada, and Peru.

Missionary Benedictine Sisters: *Provincial Motherhouse & Novitiate-Immaculata Convent,* 300 N. 18th St., Norfolk, NE 68701-3687. Phone: 402-371-3438; Fax: 402-379-2877. Sr. M. Agnes Salber, O.S.B., Prioress.

Missionary work in elementary schools; catechetical programs; pastoral ministry; nursing homes; hospitals in the Archdiocese of Omaha and Diocese of New Ulm, Minnesota; Indian Mission, Northeast Nebraska; Hispanic ministry; Korean ministry.

Missionary work outside the U.S. the Philippine Islands, Korea, Brazil, Argentina, Australia, China, India, Tanzania, Namibia, Kenya, Angola, South Africa, Portugal, Germany, Italy, Spain, Switzerland, Bulgaria and Uganda.

Missionary Servants of the Most Blessed Trinity: *Motherhouse, Novitiate and Generalate,* 3501 Solly Ave., Philadelphia, PA 19136. Fax: 215-335-7559. Sr. Barbara De Moranville, M.S.B.T., Gen. Custodian.

The congregation's mission is the preservation of the faith. This involves nourishing the faithlife of those of the Roman Catholic tradition, cooperating in ecumenical endeavors, strengthening life-giving faith among all people, evangelization, actively promoting human development and social justice. The special apostolic intent is to advance and support the ministry of the laity in the mission of the Church, accomplished through the ministries of education, social work and health care on parish and diocesan levels.

Please refer to the Religious Institutes of Women section for activities and representation in the United States. Active also in the Archdiocese of San Juan and the Dioceses of Ponce, Caguas and Mayaguez in Puerto Rico as well as the Dioceses of Apatzingan and Texcoco in Mexico.

Missionary Servants of the Most Holy Trinity (Trinity Missions): 1215 N. Scott St., Arlington, VA 22209-3097. Phone: 703-276-8646; Fax: 703-522-2656. Rev. Austin Walsh, S.T., Gen. Custodian; Bro. Steven Vesely, S.T., Sec. Gen.; Rev. Domingo Rodriguez, S.T., Mission Procurator, P.O. Box 7130, Silver Spring, MD 20907-7130.

A clerical congregation of Pontifical Right founded for the preservation of the faith and missionary work wherever the Church directs. The major fields are the missionary areas of the southern United States and the Spanish-speaking people in the United States, Puerto Rico, Colombia, Costa Rica and Mexico. The principal work is the development of Catholic lay leaders. There is also training for the missionary priesthood and brotherhood of the congregation.

Please refer to the Religious Institutes of Men section for activities and representation in the United States.

Publication: *Trinity Missions.*

Missionary Sisters of Our Lady of Africa: *American Headquarters,* 47 W. Spring St., Winooski, VT 05404. Sr. Claire Bernier, Liaison.

Missionary activities in Africa and Yemen: catechetical, pastoral ministry, social work, education and health programs, and the founding and forming of African Religious Congregations.

Missionary Sisters of St. Columban are also known as the Columban Sisters - please see entry under Columban Sisters for details.

Missionary Sisters of St. Peter Claver (1894): *American Headquarters,* P.O. Box 401, 667 Woods Mill Rd., S. Chesterfield, MO 63006. Phone: 314-434-8084. Sr. Mary Irene Brahmakulath

The congregation is of Pontifical Jurisdiction, fostering interest in and obtaining funds and requisites for the missions. Apostolate of the press in Africa.

Legal Title: *The Sodality of St. Peter Claver for the African Missions*

Publications: monthly magazine, *Echo from Africa;* annual, *Claver Almanac.*

Missionary Sisters of Our Lady of the Holy Rosary: 205 Cricket Ave., Ardmore, PA 19003. Phone: 610-896-1786. Sr. Monica Devine, Congregational Ldr.; Sr. Bernadette Murdoch, M.S.H.R., Reg. Ldr.

Founded for the evangelization of people in Africa and Latin America through educational, medical, social, pastoral and catechetical work.

Active in the U.S. in the Archdiocese of Philadelphia.

Active outside the U.S. in England, Ireland, Scotland, Nigeria, Sierra Leone, Cameroon, Ethiopia, Kenya, South Africa, Zambia, Ghana, Mexico and Brazil.

Missionary Sisters of the Immaculate Conception of the Mother of God: *Generalate,* 48 Garden Ave., West Paterson, NJ 07424. Phone: 973-279-1484; Fax: 973-279-2991. Sr. Corona Chung, S.M.I.C., Coord. Gen.

Missionary work in homes for the aged, catechetical and social service centers, schools, dispensaries and hospitals.

Active in the U.S. in the Archdioceses of Newark, San Antonio and the Dioceses of Austin, Gallup, Galveston-Houston, Paterson, Portland, Steubenville, San Bernardino and Trenton.

Active outside the U.S. in Brazil, Germany, Namibia, Philippines and Taiwan.

Missionary Sisters of the Immaculate Heart of Mary (1919): 238 E. 15th St., New York, NY 10003. Phone: 212-677-2959. Sr. Alene Grothues, Dist. Supr.

Please refer to the Religious Institutes of Women section for further details.

Missionary Sisters Servants of the Holy Spirit (1901): Techny, IL 60082-6026. Fax: 847-441-5587. Sr. Margaret Anne Norris, Prov. Supr.; Sr. Mary Pardy, Supr.

Home and foreign missions including teaching, nursing and social work.

Please refer to the Religious Institutes of Women section for activities and representation in the United States. Also active in the Philippine Islands, New Guinea, China, Indonesia, Japan, India, Africa, Australia, Europe, Russia, South America, Taiwan, Mexico, Cuba and Korea.

Publication: *SSpS Mission.*

Operation Help, Inc.: P.O. Box 134, Hartly, DE 19953. Phone: 302-492-8985; Fax: 302-492-8360. Rev. Patrick Shaules, S.J., Pres.; Marcinda Haedge, Admin. For Contributions: P.O. Box 57, Hartly, DE 19953.

Operation Help, Inc., is an independently incorporated non-profit organization dedicated to helping Catholic priests and sisters bring spiritual and material salvation to the destitute poor. It offers advice and funding and places a special emphasis on Asian and African mission areas.

Our Lady of Victory Missionary Sisters: Victory-Noll, Box 109, Huntington, IN 46750. Phone: 219-356-0628. Sr. Jeanette Halbach, O.L.V.M., Pres.; Sr. Marjorie Curran, O.L.V.M., Gen. Sec.

Legal Title: *Our Lady of Victory Missionary Sisters, Inc.*

A Marian congregation proclaiming the Gospel in a personal, non-institutional way through pastoral ministry, religious education, social service and health-care programs in favor of the poor and oppressed.

Please refer to the Religious Institutes of Women section for activities and representation in the United States. Active also in foreign missions in Oruro, Bolivia.

Parish Visitors of Mary Immaculate: *Motherhouse Generalate and Novitiate-Marycrest,* P.O. Box 658, Monroe, NY 10950-0658. Phone: 845-783-2251. Sr. Carole Marie Troskowski, Gen. Supr.; Sr. Dolores Marie, Novice Dir.

Founded for the missionary visitation of families and individuals in the parish and for religious instruction of children and adults; assists parish priests in their ministry of evangelization, catechetical programs, spiritual surveys, census, follow-up religious counseling, religious social services, training laity.

Please refer to the Religious Institutes of Women section for activities and representation in the United States and overseas.

Publication: *The Parish Visitor.*

Passionist Sisters (1924): *Sisters of the Cross and Passion American Provincialate,* Holy Family Convent, One Wright Lane, North Kingstown, RI 02852. Sr. Ellen Downes, C.P.; Prov. Supr.

Diversified apostolic works according to the needs of the Church; catechetical, pastoral and social work; educational functions; retreats; missionary work in the United States and Africa, Argentina, Bosnia, Botswana, Europe, England, Ireland, Jamaica, Latin America Chile, Papua New Guinea, Peru, Romania, Scotland, Wales, and West Indies.

Please refer to the Religious Institutes of Women section for activities and representation in the United States.

Pontifical Institute for Foreign Missions, P.I.M.E., Inc.: *U.S. Region,* 17330 Quincy Ave., Detroit, MI 48221. Phone: 313-342-4066; Fax: 313-342-6816. Very Rev. Bruno Piccolo P.I.M.E., Prov. Supr.

Legal Title: *Pontifical Institute for Foreign Missions (P.I.M.E.), Inc.*

American Province recruits and trains priests and brothers for foreign missionary work; secures funds for foreign mission work and mission education activities.

Active in the Archdiocese of Detroit and the Dioceses of Columbus, Paterson and Palm Beach.

Outside the U.S. - Bangladesh, Brazil, Cambodia, Cameroon, Hong Kong, India, Ivory Coast, Japan, Guinea-Bissau, Mexico, Papua New Guinea, Philippines, Taiwan, and Thailand.

Publication: national magazine, *PIME World.*

St. Joseph's Society of the Sacred Heart (Josephites): *Headquarters,* 1130 North Calvert St., Baltimore, MD 21202. Phone: 410-727-3386; Fax: 410-727-1006. Very Rev. Robert M. Kearns, S.S.J., Supr. Gen.

An organization of priests and brothers doing missionary work in the African American community of the United States.

Publication: *The Josephite Harvest*

St. Patrick's Missionary Society: 70 Edgewater Rd., Cliffside Park, NJ 07010. Fax: 201-943-2946. Rev. James Barry, U.S. Supr.; Rev. Karl Langsdorf, Supr. Chicago, IL; Rev. S. Donohue, Supr. Saratoga CA.

A society of secular priests devoted entirely to the missionary needs of the Church.

Activities in the Archdioceses of Newark, Chicago, New Orleans, San Francisco and the Dioceses of San Jose, and Paterson. Outside the U.S. in Nigeria—Archdiocese of Lagos, Dioceses of Abakaliki, Calabar, Abuja, Minna, Ogoja, Warri, Port Harcourt and Missio Sui Juris Bomadi. Kenya—Archdiocese of Nairobi, Dioceses of Eldoret, Kitui, Lodwar and Nakuru. Sudan—Diocese of Torit. Malawi—Dioceses of Lilongwe, Chikwawa, Zomba and Mzuzu. Zambia—Archdiocese of Lusaka, Diocese of Chipata. Brazil—Archdioceses of Sao Paulo, Dioceses of Campo Limpo, Osasco, Santo Amaro, Sao Miguel Paulista and Campina Grande. Grenada—Diocese of St. George's. South Africa—Dioceses of Tzaneen and Witbank. Zimbabwe—Archdiocese of Harare and Diocese of Mutare. Cameroon—Archdiocese of Bamenda.

Publication: *Africa, St. Patrick's Mission.*

Salesian Missions: 2 Lefevre Ln., New Rochelle, NY 10801. Phone: 914-633-8344.

The Salesians were founded to help bring the Faith to all people, and contribute to their social and economic development through education, especially in trade and agricultural schools. The purpose of the society is the recruitment and preparation of vocations for the missions and the education of the American public on the needs of other people through lectures, mass media, direct mail and the magazine, Salesian. It is also the purpose of the society to educate the American public on the unique system of education developed by the society's founder, St. John Bosco, as well as to spread knowledge of his life and accomplishments. Funds are raised to implement the religious, educational and technical assistance projects of the society.

Please refer to the Religious Institutes of Men section for activities and representation in the United States. Represented in over 125 countries throughout the world.

Publication: *Salesian.*

School Sisters of Notre Dame: *Milwaukee Province,* 13105 Watertown Plank Rd., Elm Grove, WI 53122-2291. Phone: 262-782-9850; Fax: 262-782-5725. Sr. Marilyn Kesler, Prov. Leader.

Please refer to the Religious Institutes of Women section I.D.# [2970] for provinces, activities and representations in the United States and overseas.

Sisters of the Blessed Sacrament for Indians and Colored People (1891): *St. Mary Generalate,* Bensalem, PA 19020-8502. Phone: 215-244-9900; Fax: 215-244-8174. Sr. Monica Loughlin, Pres.

Missionary work in the educational, catechetical and social services among Black and Native Americans as well as Haitians in the U.S. and Haiti.

Please refer to the Religious Institutes of Women section for activities and representation in the United States.

Publications: *Mission; The Peacemaker.*

Society of African Missions: *SMA Fathers American Province,* 23 Bliss Ave., Tenafly, NJ 07670. Phone: 201-567-9085 & 567-0450; Fax: 201-567-7156 & 541-1280. Very Rev. Ulick Bourke, S.M.A., Prov.

Please refer to the Religious Institutes of Men section for activities and representation in the United States

Active also in: Liberia—Diocese of Cape Palmas, Archdiocese of Monrovia, Diocese of Gbarnga; Ivory Coast—Archdiocese of Abidjan; Dioceses of Abengourou, Bondoukou, Bouake, Daloa, Gagnoa, Katiola, Grand-Bassam, Korhogo, Odienne, Man, San Pedro, Yamoussoukro, and Yopougon; Ghana—Archdiocese of Cape Coast; Dioceses of Accra, Konongo-Mampong, Keta-Akatsi, Kumasi, Sekondi-Takoradi, Obuasi; Togo—Archdiocese of Lome; Dioceses of Kara, and Sokode; Benin—Archdiocese of Cotonou & Parakou; Dioceses of Abomey, Kandi, Djougou, Natitingou, Dassa-Zoume and Porto-Novo; Nigeria—Archdioceses of Kaduna, Abuja (Benin City)Jos, Lagos, Ibadan; Dioceses of Abeokuha, Bauchi, Ilorin, Issele-Uku, Kafanchan, Kano, Kontagor, Makurdi, Ondo and Warri; Niger—Diocese of Niamey; Central African Republic—Archdiocese of Bangui; Dioceses of Berberati. Zambia—Archdiocese of Lusaka, Dioceses of Ndola, Solwezi. Egypt—Vicarate Apostolic of Alexandria. Tanzania—Dioceses of Mwanza and Shinyanga. Kenya—Archdiocese of Nairobi; Diocese of Ngong & Lodwar. Argentina—Archdiocese of Cordoba. Australia—Archdiocese of Perth. South Africa—Diocese of Rustenburg, Archdiocese of Pretoria. Philippines—Archdiocese of Manila. South India: Tamil-Nadu. Poland—Warsaw. Morocco-Rabat; Congo-Kinshasa, Kikwit.

Society of Mary: *Cincinnati Province, Marianist Provincialate,* 4435 E. Patterson Rd., Dayton, OH 45430-1095. Phone: 937-429-0794; Fax: 937-429-3195. Bro. Joseph H. Kamis, S.M., Prov.

Missionary work in the following territories: Archdiocese of Nairobi, Mombasa, Kenya and the Dioceses of Karonga, Malawi, Lusaka, Zambia, Africa; Diocese of Yokohama, Japan.

Society of Mary: *St. Louis Province,* P.O. Box 23130, St. Louis, MO 63156. Phone: 314-367-0390; Fax: 314-361-3131. Rev. Timothy Dwyer S.M., Prov.

Educational, parish and development work in the following territories: (Peru) Archdioceses of Arequipa and Trujillo; (India) Archdiocese of Ranchi, Bangalore and the Diocese of Patna; (Mexico) Dioceses of Coatzacoalcos and Queretaro; Diocese of Dhaka, Bangladesh; Israel – Jerusalem, Pontifical Mission for Palestine.

Society of Mary: *Province of the Pacific (Marianists),* P.O. Box 1775, Cupertino, CA 95015-1775. Phone: 408-253-4841; Fax: 408-253-5280. Very Rev. John Russi, S.M., Prov.

Educational, social and parish work in mission territories.

Society of Mary: *New York Province,* 4301 Roland Ave. Baltimore, MD 21210-2793. Bro. Stephen Glodek, S.M., Prov.

Educational, social and parish work in the following mission territories: Archdiocese of San Juan and Diocese of Ponce, Puerto Rico. Also in Africa in Karonga, Malawi; Mzuzu, Malawi; Mombasa, Kenya; Nairobi, Kenya; and Lusaka, Zambia.

Society of St. Edmund: *Edmundite Generalate,* 270 Winooski Park, Colchester, VT 05439. Phone: 802-654-3400; Fax: 802-654-3409. Very Rev. Richard M. Myhalyk, S.S.E., Supr. Gen.

Legal Title: *Society of St. Edmund, Inc.*

Major missionary endeavors in the United States are in Selma, Alabama and surrounding areas, and in the inner city of New Orleans (LA).

See the Foreign Mission section for the list of priests serving abroad.

Publications: *Edmundite Missions; The Edmundite; Common Life; New Springtime.*

Society of the Precious Blood: *Cincinnati Province,* 431 E. Second St., Dayton, OH 45402. Fax: 937-228-6878. Very Rev. Angelo Anthony, C.PP.S., Prov. Dir.; Rev. Larry Hemmelgarn, C.PP.S., Prov. Sec.; Bro. Joseph J. Fisher, C.PP.S., Mission Procurator; Rev. William Nordenbrock, C.PP.S., Mission Coord.

Mission activities outside the U.S. in Chile, Peru, South America, Guatemala, Central America; missions in La Tinta, Tucuru, Santiago, Purranque, Valdivia, LaOroya, Lima, Guatemala City, La Labor.

Priests, brothers and deacons in foreign missions 33.

Publication: *C.PP.S. Today.*

Sons of Mary Missionary Society (1952): 567 Salem End Rd., Framingham, MA 01702-5599. Phone: 508-879-2541. Rev. John Murphy, F.M.S.I., Major Coord.; Bro. Kevin Courtney, F.M.S.I., Finance Coord.; Rev. John Coss, F.M.S.I., Councilor.

Dedicated to the ministry of healing: medical, catechetical and social apostolates in the home and foreign missions.

Legal Title: *Sons of Mary, Health of the Sick, Inc.*

Third Order Regular of St. Francis: *Province of the Most Sacred Heart of Jesus, Franciscan T.O.R. Missions,* P.O. Box 188, Loretto, PA 15940. Phone: 814-472-3348. Bro. Mark McBride, T.O.R., Prov., Dir. of Foreign Missions; Very Rev. Edmund Carroll, T.O.R., Minister Prov. Phone: 412-781-1232.

Secures missionaries and material aid to missions.

Active in the Archdioceses of Manaus and Sao Paulo; the Prelacy of Borba, Brazil; the Diocese of Bhagalpur, Bihar, India; and Diocese of Vice Province of Saint Joseph, Republic of South Africa.

Xaverian Missionary Fathers: *Provincial Headquarters,* 12 Helene Ct., Wayne, NJ 07470-2813. Phone: 973-942-2975; Fax: 973-942-5012. Very Rev. Ivan Marchesin, S.X.

A religious society of priests and brothers dedicated exclusively to foreign mission work and the training of candidates for missionary life.

Active in Brazil, Democratic Republic of Congo, Burundi, Chad, Cameroon, Bangladesh, Indonesia, Japan, Mexico, Sierra Leone, Colombia, Philippines, Mozambique, Taiwan, Italy, Spain and Great Britain.

Please refer to the Religious Institutes of Men section for activities and representation in the United States.

Publication: *Xaverian Mission Newsletter.*

Pontifical Missionary Societies.

A. The Pontifical Society for the Propagation of the Faith (1822): *National Office,* 366 Fifth Ave., New York, NY 10001. Phone: 212-563-8700; Fax: 212-563-8725. Website: www.propfaith.org e-mail zamcat@aol.com. Most Rev. William J. McCormack, National Dir. & Pres.; Rev. Msgr. James A. Moloney, Vice Pres.; Rev. Msgr. Bernard H. Sandheinrich, Treas.; Rev. Msgr.; Andrew F. Connell, Asst. Treas.; Rev. Msgr., Ferdinando D. Berardi, Sec.; Mr. James R. Borut, Asst. Sec.

International Officers: Jozef Cardinal Tomko, Prefect of the Congregation for Evangelization of Peoples; Most Rev. Charles A. Schleck, C.S.C., Pres., Rev. Bernard A. Prince, Sec. Gen., Vatican City.

The Propagation of the Faith, under the direction of the Congregation for the Evangelization of Peoples, is established in every country where the Church is free to operate; it has a two-fold goal of promoting a universal missionary spirit and encouraging prayer and financial support for the local churches of the missions.

Each diocese in the United States has a director appointed by the Ordinary to promote the work of the Society through programs such as World Mission Sunday (the next-to-last Sunday in October) and Membership, presentations in seminaries, lesson plans and materials for mission animation in schools (grades 7-12) and parishes, news media and personal contact with parishes and diocesan organizations.

Offerings received by the Propagation of the Faith in the United States are joined with offerings from all other countries and distributed annually to more than 1,000 mission dioceses and vicariates.

Publication: quarterly, *Mission,* Most Rev. William J. McCormack, Publisher.

B. The Society of St. Peter Apostle (1889): *National Office,* 366 Fifth Ave., New York, NY 10001. Phone: 212-563-8700. Most Rev. William J. McCormack, National Dir.

International Officers: Jozef Cardinal Tomko, Prefect of the Congregation for Evangelization of Peoples; Most Rev. Charles A. Schleck, C.S.C., Pres.; Rev. Jose Antonio S. Galvez, Sec. Gen., Vatican City.

The Society of St. Peter Apostle, under the direction of the Congregation for the Evangelization of Peoples, is established for the support of seminarians and novices in the missions. During 1999, there were 29,117 major seminarians, 49,952 minor seminarians and 9,734 novices receiving assistance from the Society of St. Peter Apostle. The Society also helps support local religious communities and retired native clergy. Each diocese in the United States has a local director who is also the Director of the Propagation of the Faith.

C. The Pontifical Missionary Union (1916): *National Office,* 366 Fifth Ave., New York, NY 10001. Phone: 212-563-8700. Most Rev. William J. McCormack, National Dir. & Pres.; Rev. Eugene LaVerdiere, S.S.S. National Sec.

International Officers: Jozef Cardinal Tomko, Prefect of the Congregation for Evangelization of Peoples; Most Rev. Charles A. Schleck, C.S.I., Pres.; Rev. Fernando Galbiati, P.I.M.E., Intl. Sec.

The Missionary Union, under the direction of the Congregation for the Evangelization of Peoples, is established to inspire, deepen and sustain a mission spirit among priests, deacons, religious, seminarians, candidates for the religious life and others in the pastoral ministry of the Church. The director in each diocese is also the Director of the Propagation of the Faith.

D. Holy Childhood Association: *National Office,* 1720 Massachusetts Ave. N.W., Washington, DC 20036. Phone: 202-775-8637; Fax: 202-429-2987. Very Rev. Francis W. Wright, C.S.Sp., Natl. Dir.; His Holiness Pope John Paul II, Supreme Head & Protector; Most Rev. Charles A. Schleck, C.S.C., Pres.; Rev. Msgr. Patrick Byrne, Sec. Gen., Vatican City.

Founded in 1843 by Bishop Charles de Forbin Janson. It is the official agency of the Church by which Catholic children of the world contribute through their prayers and sacrifices to the welfare of other children in more than 100 mission countries. Since its beginning, it has become the personal favorite of every Pope. In 1926, Pope Pius XI elevated the society to Pontifical rank. Holy Childhood endeavors to attain its ends through the united efforts of all Catholic children who are taught to recognize that sensitivity to others is an essential dimension of Christianity. Funds raised through children's efforts are directed to the Association's two-fold mandate, the majority being distributed annually to every part of the mission world by a Ponitifical Commission and a portion being directed to catechetical education of children in the United States.

The Education and Promotion Fund solicits adult donations for the purpose of underwriting HCA educational efforts so that a greater portion of children's donations reach children in need.

All allocations sent to the missions through the agency of the Holy Childhood are used solely in the interests of the children of these missions. The Association is officially established in all archdioceses and dioceses of the United States.

Missionary Societies, Mission Boards and their Diocesan Branches.

Committee on the Home Missions: 3211 Fourth St. N.E., Washington, DC 20017. Phone: 202-541-3011; Fax: 202-722-8752. Most Rev. Edward J. Slattery, Chm.; Dr. David M. Byers, Exec. Dir.

A committee of the National Conference of Catholic Bishops dedicated to support of the home missions. The CHM makes grants to extend the Church's presence as a means of salvation and to strengthen the Church's presence where it is weak. Grantees include dioceses, religious institutes and national, regional and interdiocesan Catholic organizations in the United States and its dependencies. The CHM funds a wide range of mission and evangelization activities; examples include parish support, seminary formation, lay ministry training, religious education, and Hispanic and African American ministry. Application materials are available October 1 of each year; the deadline for submission of completed applications is November 1. The CHM makes grant decisions once a year in March, and grants are disbursed in quarterly payments July through June. The CHM's funds come from the Catholic Home Missions Appeal.

American Conventual Franciscan Missions: Refer to the American Foreign Mission section of the Directory and the Religious Institutes of Men section I.D. #[0480] for detailed information on provinces and activties.

Bureau of Catholic Indian Missions (1874): 2021 H St., N.W., Washington, DC 24207. Phone: 202-331-8542; Fax: 202-331-8544. His Eminence Anthony Cardinal Bevilacqua, Pres.; His Eminence, Edward Cardinal Egan; His Eminence William Cardinal Keeler; Rev. Msgr., Paul A. Lenz, Exec. Dir.; Rev. Ted Zuern, S.J., Dir. of Legislation, Patricia L. O'Rourke, Asst. Sec. & Treas.

Collecting and distribution of funds for the support of American Indian missions. The Bureau represents the missions in Government relations, specifically in Washington, DC. Active throughout the United States, where American Indian, Eskimo and Aleute missions are present.

Publication: monthly newsletter.

Catholic Church Extension Society of the United States of America, The (1905): 150 S. Wacker Dr.- 20th Flr., Chicago, IL 60606-4200. Phone: 312-236-7240; Fax: 312-236-5276. His Eminence Francis E. George, O.M.I., Chancellor; Rev. Msgr. Kenneth Velo Pres.; Mr. Richard A. Ritter, Vice Pres. & Treas.

Catholic Extension is a Papal fund-raiser that helps to support the Church in rural, remote and poor areas of the United States and its protectorates. Catholic Extension raises money through freewill donations, charitable gift annuities, trusts and will bequests to support missionary work in America.

Requests for funds are submitted by bishops in designated America mission dioceses. Funding is for religious purposes: construction of chapels and other mission buildings; living expenses of priests, religious and lay people working for missions; seminarian education; campus ministry; scholarships in religious education at Fordham University to those working in mission catechetical programs; chapel furnishings; evangelization; religious education, including sponsorship of Extension Line radio show, parish calendars, videotapes on mission work in the U.S., and evangelization booklets.

Publications: *EXTENSION Magazine; Catholic Extension Parish Calendars.*

Catholic Medical Mission Board, Inc. (1928): 10 W. 17th St., New York, NY, 10011-5765. Members of the Board: Rev. Msgr. Ferdinando D. Berardi; Rev. William J. Scanlan, S.J.; John A. Donnelly; Sr. Marilyn Fischer, S.F.P., Rev. Msgr. Robert J. Fuhrman, Dr. Thomas G. Flynn, M.D.; Dr. Patricia Smith, M.D.; Mr. Thomas P. Melady; Most Rev. William Skylstad, Sr. Peggy Egan, O.S.F.; Mr. James A. Cunningham; Mr. Terry Kirch; Rev. Charles J. Casamento.

The Catholic Medical Mission Board (CMMB), founded in 1928, provides pharmaceuticals and health care supplies for organizations and clinical facilities that make healthcare available to the world's needy. In addition to its schedule of shipments, CMMB responds to health care emergencies. In 1999, over $43 million in medicines and related supplies were shipped to clinical facilites in 52 countries. Financial aid is also granted to students in accredited health care training programs. CMMB's Medical Volunteer Program places health providers interested in volunteering for short-term and long-term tours of service at selected clinical sites around the world. Catholic Medical Mission Board publishes "Medical Mission News", a quarterly magazine which provides in-depth information on its programs.

Catholic Missionary Union: 86-11 Midland Pkwy., Jamaica Estates, NY 11432. Phone: 718-291-5995. His Eminence Edward Cardinal Egan, Pres.; Rev. Edward Whitley, C.S.P., Sec. & Treas.

The corporation subsidizes missions to non-Catholics. Activities are in outlying districts of the South, particularly in those sections where there are few Catholics and facilities for practicing religion.

Catholic Near East Welfare Association (1926): 1011 First Ave., New York, NY 10022. His Eminence Edward Cardinal Egan, Pres. & Treas.; Most Rev. William H. Keeler, Vice Pres.; Rev. Msgr. Robert L. Stern, Sec. Gen.; Rev. Msgr. Denis Madden, Assoc. Sec. Gen.; Chorbishop John D. Faris, Asst. Sec. Gen.

A papal agency for humanitarian and pastoral support established by Pope Pius XI in 1926. It promotes awareness of the condition and the needs of the churches, institutions and persons under the jurisdiction of the Congregation for the Eastern Churches and the Permanent Interdiscasterial Commission for the Church on Eastern Europe. It raises and distributes funds to help meet the material and spiritual needs of the people it serves.

The Association works for people in those lands in which from ancient times the majority of Christians have been members of the various eastern churches. Its mandate extends to the churches and peoples of the Middle East, Northeast Africa, India and Eastern Europe. It encourages and provides assistance to projects and programs of pastoral support, humanitarian assistance, interfaith communication and public awareness.

Publication: bimonthly magazine, *Catholic Near East.*

Catholic Negro-American Mission Board (1907): 2021 H St., N.W., Washington, DC 24207. Phone: 202-331-8542. His Eminence Anthony Cardinal Bevilacqua, Pres.; His Eminence Edward Cardinal Egan; His Eminence William Cardinal Keeler, Rev. Msgr. Paul A. Lenz, Exec. Dir.; Patricia L. O'Rourke, Asst. Sec. & Treas.

Engaged in the support of priests and sisters throughout the states below Mason and Dixon Line, especially monthly support of sisters and lay teachers in poor black schools.

Active in the United States, particularly all states in the South.

Commissariat of the Holy Land: *Franciscan Monastery,* 14th and Quincy Sts., N.E., Washington, DC 20017. Phone: 202-526-6800; Fax: 202-529-9889. Bro. Fabian Adkins, O.F.M.

Collecting funds for support of the sacred places, educational and charitable institutions in the Holy Land through the Good Friday collection, and educating young men for the Missions of the Custody of the Holy Land in Syria, Jordan, Lebanon, Cyprus, Rhodes, Israel and Egypt.

Commissariat of the Holy Land: 3140 Meramec St., St. Louis, MO 63118-4339. Phone: 314-353-7729; Fax: 314-655-0563; Bro. Joseph Rogenski, O.F.M., Commissary.

Established for collecting and distributing funds for the support of the sacred places in the Holy Land. Regional Commissariat for the Ecclesiastical Provinces of Chicago, Cincinnati, Detroit, Dubuque, Indianapolis, Kansas City, Louisville, Milwaukee, Mobile, New Orleans, Oklahoma City, Omaha, St. Louis, St. Paul-Minneapolis and San Antonio.

Commissariat of the Holy Land: 218 E. 12th St., Los Angeles, CA 90015. Phone: 213-748-5394. Rev. Martial Luebke, O.F.M., Commissary; Rev. Warren Rouse, O.F.M., Vice Commissary.

Established to collect and distribute funds for support of the Sacred Shrines and educational and charitable institutions in the Holy Land. Assigned Territory: Ecclesiastical Provinces of Denver, Los Angeles, Portland (OR), San Francisco, Santa Fe and Seattle.

Commission for Catholic Missions Among the Colored People and the Indians (Black and Indian Mission Office) (1884): 2021 H St., N.W., Washington, DC 24207. Phone: 202-331-8542; Fax: 202-331-8544. Board of Directors: His Eminence Anthony Cardinal Bevilacqua, Pres.; His Eminence William Cardinal Keeler, His Eminence Edward Cardinal Egan; Rev. Msgr. Paul A. Lenz, Exec. Dir.; Patricia L. O'Rourke, Dir. Collection & Asst. Sec./Treas.

Organized by the Third Plenary Council as trustee of the funds collected in the churches for support of the Black and Indian mission work in the United States

Publication: annual, *Annual Report.*

Dominican Mission Secretariate: 141 E. 65th St., New York, NY 10021-6607. Phone: 212-861-3776; Fax: 212-639-9823. Bro. Thomas Aquinas Dolan, O.P., Dir.

Founded by the Order of Preachers (Dominican Friars), Province of St. Joseph for the purpose of promoting American Dominican activity in the foreign missions throughout the world. Presently the Secretariate aids and supports work in the Archdioceses of Karachi and Lahore, the dioceses of Multan, Faisalabad and Islamabad-Rawalpindi in Pakistan. The Archdioceses of Lima, Peru. Nairobi and Kisumu in Kenya. St. Petersburg, Russia; Vilnius, Lithuania; Calayan Island, Philippines, and the Solomon Islands.

Legal Title: *St. Jude Dominican Foreign Missions, Inc.* (formerly Rosary Foreign Mission Society, Inc.)

Assumption B.V.M. Province: *Holy Dormition Friary,* P.O. Box 270, Sybertsville, PA 18251. Fax: 717-788-2431. Rev. Carmen Sanderi, O.F.M., Guardian.

Preparing missionaries to work among the people of Slav origin in the Byzantine Church.

General Secretariat of the Franciscan Missions, Inc.: P.O. Box 130, Waterford, WI 53185. Phone: 414-534-5470. Revs. Sereno Baiardi, O.F.M., Dir.; Sante de Angelis, O.F.M., Assoc. Dir.

General American office for assistance to Franciscan Missions under the auspices of the General Minister of the Order of Friars Minor.

Catholic Network Of Volunteer Service: 1410 Q St., N.W., Washington, DC 20009. Phone: 202-332-6000; 800-543-5046; Fax: 202-332-1611. Most Rev. John J. Snyder, Episcopal Advisor; James G. Lindsay, Exec. Dir.

Catholic Network of Volunteer Service promotes, recruits and refers volunteers to missions in the United States and overseas. We represent nearly 200 faith-based volunteer programs worldwide and work with the U.S. dioceses, religious communities and the private sector to determine their needs for help. Catholic Network of Volunteer Service (CNVS) is committed to the goal that every Catholic man and woman be invited to consider a period of service in the missions, as a vital and important manifestation of the baptismal call of all Catholic people. Currently, 6,500 men and women are serving in CNVS member mission programs offering their gifts and abilities in full-time service to people in need and living their Catholic faith more fully than many had imagined possible. These volunteers are serving domestically for a summer, six months, a year or more, and they are serving internationally for two or more years at a time. They are single and married, recent college graduates and early retirees, doctors and teachers, parish ministers and social workers, community organizers, computer programmers, legal aides and more.

Gatherings: Annual Conference; Formation Workshops, Training Seminars.

Publications: annual, *Response: Directory of Volunteer Opportunities*; biweekly, How Can I Help?; quarterly, Lay Mission Handbook. *Awards: The Father George Mader Award, given annually during the Fall meeting of the NCCB to honor organizations and individuals who promote the value of lay mission service.*

Missionary Association of Catholic Women (1916): *National Office,* 3501 S. Lake Dr. – Box 070912, Milwaukee, WI 53207-0912. Phone: 414-769-3406. E-mail: wmo@archmil.org. Sr. Frances P. Cunningham, O.S.F. Contact Person.

Association providing material and financial aid to home and foreign missions.

Miva-America Missionary Vehicle Association Inc.: *National Office,* 1400 Michigan Ave., N.E., Washington, DC 20017. Phone: 202-635-3444; Fax: 202-526-0830. Rev. Philip DeRea, M.S.C., Natl. Dir.; Agnes McBryan, S.N.D., Sec.; Michele Marth, M.S.C., Development Personnel.

The Missionary Vehicle Association raises funds to provide vehicles (cars, trucks, jeeps, boats) to American Missionaries in developing and undeveloped countries, whose work depends on safe, adequate transportation to provide health care and education and preaching the Gospel.

Oblates of St. Francis de Sales (O.S.F.S.) (1906): *Wilmington-Philadelphia Province,* 2200 Kentmere Pkwy., Wilmington, DE 19806. Phone: 302-656-8529; Fax: 302-658-8052. Very Rev. Joseph G. Morrissey, O.S.F.S., Prov.;

Toledo-Detroit Province (1966), 2056 Parkwood Ave., Toledo, OH 43620. Phone: 419-243-5105. Very Rev. James F. Cryan, O.S.F.S., Prov., American Mission Director; Rev. John J. Hurley, O.S.F.S., 1600 Brinckle Ave., Wilmington, DE 19806.

Missionary work in Republic of South Africa, Diocese of Keimeos; Nambia, Diocese of Keetmamshoop; South America—Uruguay, Archdiocese of Montevideo; Brazil, Archdioceses of Rio de Janeiro and Porto Alegre (Rio Grande de Sol), Dioceses of Bage (RGS), Cruz Alta (RGS), Frederico Westphalen (RGS), and Senhor do Bofim (Bahia); India, Archdiocese of Bangalore (province of Kerala); Haiti—Diocese of Les Gonaives; Mexico—Archdiocese of Merida.

Please refer to the Religious Institutes of Men section for activities and representation in the United States

Provinces outside the United States: France, Germany, Austria, Switzerland, Italy, and Holland.

Pontifical Mission for Palestine (1949): 1011 First Ave., New York, NY 10022. Phone: 212-826-1480. Rev. Msgr. Robert L. Stern, Pres.; Rev. Denis Madden, Vice Pres.; Rev. Msgr. John F. McCarthy, Dir.-Vatican Office, Mr. Issam Bishara, Dir.-Beirut Office; Rev. Guido Gockel, Dir.-Jerusalem Office.

A papal agency for humanitarian and charitable assistance established by Pope Pius XII in 1949. Its mission is to assist, without regard to nationality or religion, all who suffer as a result of the repeated conflicts which have devastated Palestine and neighboring regions of the Middle East.

It encourages and supports projects and programs of relief, rehabilitation, development; collaboration with other agencies; and education.

St. Paul's Guild, Inc.: *Attn: Chancellors office,* 1011 First Ave., Rm. 1940, New York, NY 10022.

Formerly National Catholic Converts' League, now interested in assisting former Protestant clergymen and former Protestant religious.

Tekakwitha Conference National Center, The (1939): P.O. Box 6768, Great Falls, MT 59406. Phone: 406-727-0147; Fax: 406-452-9845.

Non-profit organization established for evangelization within the Catholic Church with American Indians, Eskimos and missionaries working together at the national level to develop a Native American identity voice and presence in the Catholic Church. Catechesis, liturgy, youth ministry, Inculturation and related areas within the Catholic Church are goals of the Conference.

Publication: 5 issues annually, *Cross & Feathers.*

United States Conference of Secular Institutes

U.S.C.S.I., Attn.: Ms. Carol Winkler, Pres., P.O. Box 4556, 12th St. N.E., Washington, DC 20017.

Members of the U.S.C.S.I. are Secular Institutes of Diocesan or Pontifical Right, canonically erected since 1947, following the promulgation of the Apostolic Constitution, "Provida Mater Ecclesia," by Pope Pius XII. The Institutes are listed on this page by the Congregation for the Institutes of Consecrated Life and for Societies of Apostolic Life. The purpose of the U.S.C.S.I., canonically erected by the Congregation as of its 1976 statutes, is to offer the Institutes an opportunity to exchange experiences, conduct research, and promote ways to make the vocation and Institutes known. The executive council includes: Carol Winkler, President (Schoenstatt); Rev. John F. Lorenz, Vice-President (Institute of the Heart of Jesus); Marjorie L. Baker, Secretary (Missionaries of the Kingship of Christ); Anita H. Plourde, Treasurer (Oblate Missionaries of Mary Immaculate).

Caritas Christi: P.O. Box 5162, River Forest, IL 60305. Mary Jane McCarthy, Natl. Sponsor. Forms and gives to the Church laywomen who according to their callings, talents and professional skills seek to respond to the love of Christ in their providential environment by following the demands of the Gospel.

Company of St. Paul: 52 Davis Ave., White Plains, NY 10605. Rev. Stuart Sandberg, Contact Person (Lay People and Priests).

Founded in Milan, Italy November 17, 1920, under the auspices of Cardinal Andrew Ferrari; approved as a Secular Institute of Pontifical Right on June 30, 1950.

Aim: The practice of evangelical counsels is the expression of consecration to God. Professional work becomes the main means of the apostolate.

Diocesan Laborer Priests: 3706 15th St. N.E.Washington, DC 20017 Tel: 202-832-4217 Fax: 202-526-5692. Rev. Rutilio J. del Riego, Delegate.

A Secular Institute of Pontifical Right founded in Spain in 1886.

The aim of the Institute is the promotion, sustenance and cultivation of apostolic, religious and priestly vocations.

St. Francis de Sales Secular Institute: 3503 Jean St. Fairfax, VA 22030. Tel: 703-591-5196. Joan Bereswill, Dir. (Laywomen).

Founded in Vienna, Austria; Pontifical Right 1964.

Aim: Personal sanctification of its members living in the world according to the spirituality of St. Francis de Sales. Open to women: single, widowed and divorced who wish to embrace the consecrated life by the profession of vows.

Don Bosco Volunteers: P.O. Box 588, Hawthorne, NJ 07507-0588. Cathy Sylvester, Contact Person.

Founded as a Secular Institute for Women by Blessed Philip Rinaldi, S.D.B., in Turin, Italy in 1917. Approved as an Institute of Pontifical Right in 1978. Existing in 35 countries, with over 1,200 members.

Aim: To live in the spirit of St. John Bosco, in a wide variety of apostolates in one's own environment, and in the service of the local church, particularly on behalf of youth. An Institute for Men was founded in Rome in November, 1994. For information, see address above.

Handmaids of Divine Mercy: 2410 Hughes Ave., Bronx, NY 10458.

A Secular Institute for women who, through the practice of the evangelical, counsel in a faithful imitation of Jesus Christ. The members commit themselves to the service of the Church by a parish- or diocesan-oriented apostolate under the leadership of and in collaboration with the clergy.

Institute of Secular Missionaries: 2710 Ruberg, Cincinnati, OH 45211. Evelyn Dilger, Contact Person (Women).

Founded in Vitoria, Spain in 1939, approved as Secular Institute in 1955. Working for the integral good of humankind, specifically for the poor who need and claim most of the Church's support at this time. This endeavor is taken within the spirit of the Beatitudes and in communion with the Church.

Missionaries of the Kingship of Christ: P.O. Box 34513, Bethesda, MD 20827. Under this title are included three distinct and juridically separate institutes following the spirituality of St. Francis of Assisi.

Women Missionaries of the Kingship of Christ.

Founded in Italy in 1919 and approved as an Institute of Pontifical Right in 1953. Existing in twenty-nine countries, the American branch began in 1950 and has spread to 25 states. Through a consecrated life in the world they work individually in professions and apostolates for the reign of Christ in the world. Rev. Dominic Monti, O.F.M., Ecclesiastical Asst., Gemelli House, 10400 Lorain Ave., Silver Spring, MD 20901. Tel: 301-593-4479.

Men Missionaries of the Kingship of Christ.

Founded in Italy in 1928 and approved as an institute of Pontifical Right in 1998. It was established in the United States in 1962. Their purpose is spreading the social reign of Christ through individual professions and occupations.

Priest Missionaries of the Kingship of Christ.

Approved as an Institute of Pontifical Right, July 15, 1978; established in the United States, 1954. Members are diocesan priests serving in the active ministry of their diocese while promoting the social reign of Jesus Christ.

Oblate Missionaries of Mary Immaculate: P.O. Box 303, Manville, RI 02838. Women: P.O. Box 764, Lowell, MA 01853.

Founded in Canada on July 2, 1952. Approved of Pontifical Right March 24, 1984.

International Membership. The members profess the evangelical counsels. Unique spirituality based on five attitudes of life: presence of God, absence of criticism and complaints, service and peacemaking.

Aim: Building and strengthening of the Kingdom of Christ in cooperation with the Church by bearing witness to the charity of Christ in the very midst of society.

Opus Spiritus M Sancti: 21 S.W. 3rd St., Pocahontas, IA 50574. Tel: 712-335-3242. Rev. Merle Kollasch, Regional Coord.

Pius X: Lynchville Park, Goffstown, NH 03045. Tel: 603-669-8614. (Men).

Founded in New Hampshire in 1940. Approved as a Secular Institute of Pontifical Right on Dec. 8, 1959.

Aim: The general end is the perfection of its members. The members strive to achieve this aim through the effective practice in the world of the three evangelical counsels of perfection, and by making the promise to dedicate themselves totally to the particular apostolate of the Institute. The Institute also admits married or unmarried men as associate members.

Secular Institute of Schoenstatt Fathers: W. 284 N. 746 Cherry Ln., Waukesha, WI 53188 (Priests). Rev. Hector R. Vega, Supr.

Founded by Father Joseph Kentenich in 1965, approved as a Secular Institute of Pontifical Right, June 24, 1988.

Aim: To aid the moral and religious renewal of society and the realization of the post-Vatican II mission of the Church, especially through priestly service to the International Schoenstatt Movement. About 230 ordained members in 20 nations worldwide.

Secular Institute of Schoenstatt Sisters of Mary (Women): W. 284 N. 404 Cherry Ln., Waukesha, WI 53188-9416. Tel: 262-542-4384 & 542-1544; Fax: 262-542-5730. E-mail: sijoan@execpc.com.

Founded in Germany in 1926 by Father Joseph Kentenich; approved as a Secular Institute of Pontifical Right in 1948

Aim: The moral and religious renewal of society. The members practice a Marian lay asceticism as a means of growing in love for God, and consecrating the world to Him. They are active within the Schoenstatt Movement and in a wide variety of professional spheres.

Servitum Christi (Women): Mailing Address, 1209 Greenwood Ave., Pueblo, CO 81003. 184 E. 76th St., New York, NY 10021. Ms. Elaine Kozlowski, Contact Person.

Origin inspired by St. Peter Julian Eymard (1868), founder of the Congregation of the Blessed Sacrament. Founded in Holland, 1952; approved as a Secular Institute of Diocesan Right May 8, 1963.

Aim: To live the mystery of the Eucharist fully as consecrated lay persons and to make known its meaning so that the reign of Christ may come and the glory of God be revealed to the world.

Society of Our Lady of the Way: 2339 N. Catalina St., Los Angeles, CA 90027. Additional Members in Cleveland, OH; San Francisco, CA; Bridgeport, CT; Green Bay, WI; Jersey City, NJ; Tokyo, Japan; and New Orleans.

Founded in Vienna, Austria in 1936; approved as a Secular Institute of Pontifical Right in 1953. To Christianize the secular order, members are consecrated to God through the vows of chastity, obedience and poverty. They pursue individual apostolates, seeking to manifest Christ in all the circumstances of their life and work. Spirituality is Marian and Ignatian.

Voluntas Dei Institute (1958): 370 Emerald Bay Cir., N-7, Naples, FL 34110. Rev. George F. Hazler, Contact Person.

Approved as a Secular Institute of Pontifical Right in 1987.

The Institute groups together within a common apostolic project both clerics and celibate laymen. The Institute directs its members to discover the will of God, adhere to it and cherish it through the profession of the vows of poverty, chastity, and obedience. The Institute also includes married couples as Associates Members. These commit themselves to live according to their state in life the same ideal and apostolic project as the clerics and celibate laymen, through commitment to living poverty, chastity and apostolic obedience. Members of the Institute regularly gather as a team which is the place for listening to the Word and discerning the Will of God.

Alphabetical Listing of Mission Churches in the United States

A

Aasu/Aoloau, AS, c/o Pago Pago, AS, St. Paul Church. (SPP)
Abernathy, TX, Hale Co., St. Isidore, c/o Petersburg, TX, Sacred Heart Church. (LUB)
Abeytas, NM, Socorro Co., San Antonio, c/o La Joya, NM, Our Lady of Sorrows Church. (SFE)
Abie, NE, Butler Co., SS. Peter and Paul, c/o Bruno, NE, St. Anthony Church. (LIN)
Abingdon, MD, St. Francis, c/o Baltimore, MD, Patronage of the Mother of God Church. (PSC)
Abo, NM, Torrance Co., c/o Mountainair, NM, St. Alice Church. (SFE)
Abram, TX, St. Mary Magdalene, c/o La Joya, TX, Our Lady, Queen of Angels Church. (BWN)
Absarokee, MT, St. Michael, c/o Columbus, MT, St. Mary's Church. (GF)
Acomita, NM, Cibola Co., St. Anne, c/o Acoma, NM, San Esteban, Acoma Catholic Indian Mission. (GLP)
Adel, GA, Cook Co., St. Margaret Mary, c/o Lakeland, GA, Queen of Peace Church. (SAV)
Adel, OR, St. Richard, c/o Lakeview, OR, St. Patrick's Church. (BAK)
Adona, AR, Conway Co., St. Elizabeth's, c/o Bigelow, AR, St. Boniface's Church. (LR)
Adrian, OR, Our Lady of Guadalupe, c/o Nyssa, OR, St. Bridget of Kildare Church. (BAK)
Afono, AS, c/o [10] Pago Pago, AS, Church of the Immaculate Conception. (SPP)
Afton, NY, Chenango Co., St. Agnes, c/o Bainbridge, NY, St. John the Evangelist Church. (SY)
Afton, WY, Lincoln Co., Holy Family, c/o Jackson, WY, Our Lady of the Mountains Church. (CHY)
Agafa Gumas, GU, Santa Bernadita Mission Chapel, c/o Yigo, GU, Our Lady of Lourdes Church. (AGN)
Aguas, PR, St. Martin, c/o Yauco, PR, Holy Rossary Church. (PCE)
Aguila, AZ, Our Lady of Guadalupe, c/o Wickenburg, AZ, St. Anthony of Padua Church. (PHX)
Aguirre, PR, La Milagrosa, c/o Aguirre, PR, Sacred Heart Church. (PCE)
Ak-Chin, AZ, St.Francis, c/o Laveen, AZ, St. John The Baptist Church. (PHX)
Alamillo, NM, Socorro Co., c/o Socorro, NM, San Miguel Church. (SFE)
Alapaha, GA, Berrien Co., St. Ann, c/o Tifton, GA, Our Divine Saviour Church. (SAV)
Albany, IL, Whiteside Co., St. Patrick, c/o Fulton, IL, Immaculate Conception Church. (RCK)
Albany, NY, Albany Co., Albany Medical Center, c/o [16] Albany, NY, St. Teresa of Avila Church. (ALB)
Albany, NY, Albany Co., Child's Hospital & Eden Park Nursing Home, c/o [8] Albany, NY, St. James Church. (ALB)
Alberton, MT, Mineral Co., St. Albert the Great, c/o Frenchtown, MT, St. John the Baptist Church. (HEL)
Albin, WY, Laramie Co., St. Joseph, c/o Pine Bluffs, WY, St. Paul's Church. (CHY)
Albuquerque, NM, Bernalillo Co., Monada de San Jose, c/o [23] Albuquerque, NM, St. Anne Church. (SFE)
Albuquerque, NM, Bernalillo Co., Our Lady of Mount Carmel, c/o [7] Albuquerque, NM, Nativity of the Blessed Virgin Mary Church. (SFE)
Albuquerque, NM, Bernalillo Co., San Jose de los Duranes, c/o [18] Albuquerque, NM, San Felipe de Neri Church. (SFE)
Alcalde, NM, Rio Arriba Co., c/o San Juan Pueblo, NM, St. John the Baptist Church. (SFE)
Alderson, WV, Greenbrier Co., St. Mary of the Greenbrier, c/o Hinton, WV, St. Patrick Church. (WH)
Alexander, ND, McKenzie Co., Our Lady of Consolation, c/o Watford City, ND, Epiphany Church. (BIS)
Alexandria, NE, Thayer Co., St. Mary's, c/o Fairbury, NE, St. Michael's Church. (LIN)
Algarrobos, PR, Our Lady of Fatima, c/o Yauco, PR, Holy Rossary Church. (PCE)
Algodones, NM, Sandoval Co., c/o Bernalillo, NM, Our Lady of Sorrows Church. (SFE)
Alice, ND, Cass Co., St. Henry, c/o Enderlin, ND, St. Patrick's Church. (FAR)
Alice, TX, Jim Wells Co., Sacred Heart, c/o Alice, TX, St. Joseph Church. (CC)
Alice, TX, Jim Wells Co., Santo Nino De Atocha, c/o Alice, TX, Our Lady of Guadalupe Church. (CC)
Allaben, NY, Ulster Co., Our Lady of Lourdes, c/o Phoenicia, NY, St. Francis de Sales Church. (NY)
Allagash Plantation, ME, St. Paul, c/o St. Francis, ME, St. Charles Church. (PRT)
Allen, SD, Bennett Co., St. John of the Cross, c/o Kyle, SD, Our Lady of Sorrows Church. (RC)
Allendale, SC, Barnwell Co., St. Mary, c/o Orangeburg, SC, Holy Trinity Church. (CHR)
Alma, GA, Bacon Co., St. Raymond, c/o Waycross, GA, St. Joseph's Church. (SAV)
Almacigo Alto, PR, S. Juan Macias, c/o Yauco, PR, Holy Rossary Church. (PCE)
Almacigo Bajo, PR, St. Martin de Porres, c/o Yauco, PR, Holy Rossary Church. (PCE)
Almont, ND, Morton Co., St. Mary, Queen of Peace, c/o New Salem, ND, St. Pius V Church. (BIS)
Alpine, CA, Nativity of BVM, c/o Lakeside, CA, Blessed Kateri Tekakwitha Church. (SD)
Alto, TN, Franklin Co., St. Margaret Mary, c/o Decherd, TN, Good Shepherd Church. (NSH)
Altona, NY, Jericho, St. Alexis, c/o Altona, NY, Holy Angels Church. (OG)
Alturas de Campo Rico, PR, Ntra. Sra. Del Carmen, c/o [5] Canovanas, PR, San Jose Church. (SJN)
Alturas de Mayaguez, PR, El Senor de Los Milagros, c/o [4] Mayaquez, PR, Church De El Buen Pastor Church. (MGZ)
Alturas de Rio Grande, PR, La Milagrosa, c/o Rio Grande, PR, Nuestra Senora del Carmen Church. (SJN)
Alvord, IA, Lyon Co., Sacred Heart, c/o Rock Valley, IA, St. Mary's Church. (SC)
Amado, AZ, Santa Cruz Co., Assumption Chapel, c/o Tubac, AZ, St. Ann Church. (TUC)
Amagansett, NY, Suffolk Co., St. Peter the Apostle, c/o East Hampton, NY, Most Holy Trinity Church. (RVC)
Amalia, NM, Taos Co., c/o Questa, NM, St. Anthony Church. (SFE)
Amaluia, AS, c/o [9] Pago Pago, AS, Church of the Holy Cross. (SPP)
Amelia, NE, Holt Co., St. Joseph, c/o O'Neill, NE, St. Patrick Church. (OM)
Amherst, NE, Buffalo Co., St. John Capistran, c/o Elm Creek, NE, Immaculate Conception Church. (GI)
Amherst, VA, St. Francis of Assisi, c/o Scottsville, VA, St. George Church. (RIC)
Amouli, AS, c/o [11] Pago Pago, AS, Church of Sacred Heart. (SPP)
Anaheim, CA, Orange Co., Maronite Catholic Community of Riverside, c/o Anaheim, CA, St. John Maron Mission. (OLL)
Anaheim, CA, Sacred Heart, c/o Anaheim, CA, St. Justin Martyr Church. (ORG)
Andes, NY, St. Ann, c/o Margaretville, NY, Sacred Heart Church. (ALB)
Andrews, SC, Georgetown Co., St. Leo the Great, c/o Georgetown, SC, St. Mary's Church. (CHR)
Andrus Cove, LA, Jefferson Davis Parish, St. Gertrude Chapel, c/o Lake Arthur, LA, Our Lady of the Lake Church. (LKC)
Aneta, ND, Nelson Co., Sacred Heart, c/o Cooperstown, ND, St. George's Church. (FAR)
Angoon, AK, c/o Sitka, AK, St. Gregory of Nazianzen Church. (JUN)
Anguilla, MS, Our Mother of Mercy, c/o Belzoni, MS, All Saints Church. (JKS)
Annapolis, MD, Anne Arundel Co., St. John Neuman, c/o Annapolis, MD, St. Mary Church. (BAL)
Anniston, AL, Calhoun Co., All Saints, c/o Anniston, AL, Sacred Heart of Jesus Church. (BIR)
Anones, PR, San Jose, c/o Las Marias, PR, Immaculate Heart of Mary Church. (MGZ)
Ansley, NE, Custer Co., Sacred Heart, c/o Broken Bow, NE, St. Joseph's Church. (GI)
Antelope, OR, St. Mary's, c/o Wasco, OR, St. Mary's Church. (BAK)
Anthony, KS, Harper Co., c/o Harper, KS, St. Joan of Arc Church. (WCH)
Anton, TX, Hockley Co., St. Anthony, c/o Shallowater, TX, St. Phillip Benizi Church. (LUB)
Antonito, CO, Conejos Co., St. Augustine, c/o Conejos, CO, Our Lady of Guadalupe Church. (PBL)
Antwerp, NY, Jefferson Co., St. Michael, c/o Evans Mills, NY, St. Mary Church. (OG)
Anza, CA, Riverside Co., Cahuilla Indian Reservation, c/o Anza, CA, Sacred Heart Church. (SB)
Anza, CA, Riverside Co., Our Lady of the Snows, c/o Anza, CA, Sacred Heart Church. (SB)
Anza, CA, Riverside Co., Santa Rosa Indian Mission, c/o Anza, CA, Sacred Heart Church. (SB)
Anza, CA, Riverside Co., Santa Rosa Reservation, c/o Anza, CA, Sacred Heart Church. (SB)
Aoa, AS, c/o [11] Pago Pago, AS, Church of Sacred Heart. (SPP)
Apache, OK, Caddo Co., Mother of Sorrows, c/o Elgin, OK, St. Ann Church. (OKL)
Aquasco, MD, Prince Georges Co., St. Dominic's, c/o Baden, MD, St. Michael Church. (WDC)
Arago, NE, Richardson Co., St. Mary's, c/o Rulo, NE, Immaculate Conception Church. (LIN)
Arapahoe, NE, Furnas Co., St. Germanus, c/o Cambridge, NE, St. John's Church. (LIN)
Arboles, CO, Archuleta Co., SS. Peter & Rose, c/o Ignacio, CO, St. Ignatius Parish Church. (PBL)
Arbuckle, CA, Colusa Co., Holy Cross, c/o Maxwell, CA, Sacred Heart Church. (SAC)
Ardoch, ND, Walsh Co., St. John the Baptist, c/o Minto, ND, Sacred Heart Church. (FAR)
Arenzville, IL, Cass Co., St. Fidelis, c/o Beardstown, IL, St. Alexius Church. (SFD)
Argusville, ND, Cass Co., St. William, c/o [1] Fargo, ND, St. Mary's Cathedral. (FAR)
Arivaca, AZ, Pima Co., St. Ferdinand, c/o Tubac, AZ, St. Ann Church. (TUC)
Arkadelpia, AR, Clark Co., St. Mary, c/o Hot Springs National Park, AR, St. John the Baptist Church. (LR)
Arlee, MT, Lake Co., Sacred Heart, c/o St. Ignatius, MT, St. Ignatius Mission. (HEL)
Armagh, MO, Franklin Co., St. Patrick, c/o Catawissa, MO, St. James Church. (STL)
Arnold, CA, Arnold Co., Our Lady of the Sierra, c/o Angels Camp, CA, St. Patrick Church. (STO)
Arnold, NE, Custer Co., St. Agnes, c/o Stapleton, NE, St. John the Evangelist Church. (GI)
Arnot, PA, Tioga Co., St. Stanislaus Kostka, c/o Blossburg, PA, St. Mary's Church. (SCR)
Arock, OR, Holy Family, c/o Jordan Valley, OR, St. Bernard's Church. (BAK)
Arroyo Hondo, NM, Taos Co., Nuestra Senora de Dolores, c/o Arroyo Seco, NM, La Santisima Trinidad Church. (SFE)
Arvada, CO, Coal Creek Catholic Community, c/o [2] Arvada, CO, St. Joan of Arc Church. (DEN)
Ashdown, AR, Little River Co., St. Elizabeth Ann Seton, c/o Texarkana, AR, St. Edward's Church. (LR)
Ashfork, AZ, St. Anne, c/o Seligman, AZ, St. Francis Church. (PHX)
Ashland, AL, Clay Co., St. Mark, c/o Alexander City, AL, St. John the Apostle Church. (BIR)
Ashland, NY, St. Joseph's Chapel, c/o Windham, NY, St. Theresa of Child Jesus Church. (ALB)
Ashley, ND, McIntosh Co., St. David, c/o Zeeland, ND, St. Andrew's Church. (FAR)
Ashtabula, OH, Ashtabula Co., Our Lady of Miracles (St. Joseph Mission), c/o Ashtabula, OH, St. Joseph's Church. (Y)
Ashton, NE, Sherman Co., St. Francis, c/o Farwell, NE, St. Anthony of Padua Church. (GI)
Ashuelot, NH, St. Michael, c/o Winchester, NH, St. Stanislaus Church. (MAN)
Aspen, CO, Snowmass in Snowmass Village, c/o Aspen, CO, St. Mary Church. (DEN)
Aspermont, TX, Stonewall Co., St. Mary, c/o Rotan, TX, St. Joseph Church. (LUB)
Asti, CA, Our Lady of Mt. Carmel, c/o Cloverdale, CA, St. Peter's Church. (SR)
Astor, FL, Lake Co., St. Hubert of the Forest, c/o [2] Ocala, FL, Our Lady of the Springs Church. (ORL)
Atalaya, PR, Ntra. Sra. de Altagracia, c/o Aguada, PR, St. Francis of Assisi Church. (MGZ)
Athena, OR, Sacred Heart, c/o Milton Freewater, OR, St. Francis of Assisi Church. (BAK)
Atlanta, GA, Fulton Co., San Felipe de Jesus, c/o [8] Atlanta, GA, Sacred Heart of Jesus Church. (ATL)
Atlanta, IL, Logan Co., St. Mary, c/o Lincoln, IL, Holy Family Church. (PEO)
Atlantic Mine, MI, Houghton Co., St. Mary, c/o Houghton, MI, St. Ignatius Loyola Church. (MAR)
Atoka, OK, Atoka Co., St. Patrick Church, c/o Durant, OK, St. William Church. (TLS)
Atwood, CA, Orange Co., St. Theresa Chapel, c/o Placentia, CA, St. Joseph Church. (ORG)

Aua, AS, c/o [10] Pago Pago, AS, Church of the Immaculate Conception. (SPP)
Auberry, CA, Infant Jesus of Prague, c/o [2] Fresno, CA, Holy Spirit Church. (FRS)
Auburn, CA, Placer Co., St. Teresa of Avila, c/o Auburn, CA, St. Joseph Church. (SAC)
Auburn, PA, Susquehanna Co., St. Bonaventure, c/o Meshoppen, PA, St. Joachim's Church. (SCR)
Augusta, MT, Lewis and Clark Co., St. Matthias, c/o Fairfield, MT, St. John Church. (HEL)
Ault, CO, Weld Co., Sacred Heart, c/o Greeley, CO, Our Lady of Peace Church. (DEN)
Ault, CO, Weld Co., St. Mary, c/o Greeley, CO, Our Lady of Peace Church. (DEN)
Aurora, NM, San Miguel Co., c/o Villanueva, NM, Our Lady of Guadalupe Church. (SFE)
Austin, NV, St. Augustine, c/o Battle Mountain, NV, St. John Bosco Church. (RNO)
Austin, PA, Potter Co., St. Augustine, c/o Coudersport, PA, St. Eulalia Church. (E)
Austwell, TX, Refugio Co., St. Anthony of Padua, c/o Tivoli, TX, Our Lady of Guadalupe Church. (CC)
Autrain, MI, Alger Co., St. Therese, c/o Trenary, MI, St. Rita Church. (MAR)
Ava, MO, Douglas Co., St. Leo the Great, c/o Mansfield, MO, Immaculate Heart of Mary Church. (SPC)
Avoca, NE, Cass Co., Holy Trinity, c/o Syracuse, NE, St. Paulinus Church. (LIN)
Avon, MT, Powell Co., St. Theodore, c/o Deer Lodge, MT, Immaculate Conception Church. (HEL)
Avondale, LA, Jefferson Civil Parish, Assumption of Mary, c/o [2] Marrero, LA, St. Agnes Le Thi Thanh Church. (NO)
Avondale, PA, Chester Co., Santa Maria, Madra de Dios, c/o West Grove, PA, Assumption B.V.M. Church. (PH)
Ayrshire, IA, Palo Alto Co., Sacred Heart, c/o Ruthven, IA, Sacred Heart Church. (SC)
Azle, TX, Tarrant Co., Holy Trinity, c/o [16] Fort Worth, TX, St. Thomas Church. (FWT)

B

Babb, MT, St. Mary, Queen of the World, c/o Browning, MT, Church of the Little Flower. (HEL)
Badger, MN, Roseau Co., St. Mary's, c/o Roseau, MN, Sacred Heart Church. (CR)
Baggs, WY, Carbon Co., Our Lady of the Sage, c/o Rawlins, WY, St. Joseph's Church. (CHY)
Bagley, MN, Clearwater Co., St. Joseph, c/o Fosston, MN, St. Mary's Church. (CR)
Bahner, MO, Pettis Co., St. John, c/o Sedalia, MO, Sacred Heart Church. (JC)
Bainville, MT, Sacred Heart, c/o Culbertson, MT, St. Anthony's Church. (GF)
Bajio, PR, Sagrada Familia, c/o Aguada, PR, St. Francis of Assisi Church. (MGZ)
Baker, CA, San Bernardino Co., Our Lady of the Desert, c/o Barstow, CA, St. Joseph Church. (SB)
Bakersfield, CA, Kern Co., Holy Spirit, c/o [1] Bakersfield, CA, Our Lady of Guadalupe Church. (FRS)
Bakersfield, CA, Kern Co., San Clemente, c/o [2] Bakersfield, CA, Our Lady of Perpetual Help Church. (FRS)
Bakersfield, CA, Kern Co., St. Jude, c/o [1] Bakersfield, CA, Our Lady of Guadalupe Church. (FRS)
Bald Knob, AR, White Co., St. Richard, c/o Searcy, AR, St. James Church. (LR)
Baldwin, IA, Jackson Co., Holy Trinity, c/o Maquoketa, IA, Sacred Heart Church. (DUB)
Ball Club, MN, Itasca Co., St. Joseph's, c/o Duluth, MN, Indian Missions Church. (DUL)
Ballantine, MT, Sts. Cyril & Methodius, c/o [4] Billings, MT, St. Bernard's Church. (GF)
Ballardville, MA, St. Joseph's, c/o Andover, MA, St. Augustine Church. (BO)
Baltimore, MD, Baltimore Co., Holy Redeemer Chapel, c/o [87] Baltimore, MD, Sacred Heart of Jesus Church. (BAL)
Baltimore, MD, Baltimore Co., St. Gerard's Chapel, c/o [87] Baltimore, MD, Sacred Heart of Jesus Church. (BAL)
Bancroft, WV, Putnam Co., St. Patrick, c/o Nitro, WV, Holy Trinity Church. (WH)
Banning, CA, Riverside Co., St. Mary, c/o Banning, CA, Precious Blood Church. (SB)
Banquete, TX, Nueces Co., St. Michael, c/o Agua Dulce, TX, St. Frances of Rome Church. (CC)
Barberville, FL, Volusia Co., San Jose Mission, c/o De Land, FL, St. Peter's Church. (ORL)
Bardstown, KY, Nelson Co., St. Mark, c/o Culvertown, KY, Immaculate Conception Church. (L)
Barinas, PR, St. James, c/o Yauco, PR, Holy Rossary Church. (PCE)
Barneston, NE, Gage Co., St. Joseph's, c/o Wymore, NE, St. Mary's Church. (LIN)
Barnesville, GA, Lamar Co., St. Ann, c/o Griffin, GA, Sacred Heart Church. (ATL)
Barnsdall, OK, Osage Co., St. Mary, c/o Pawhuska, OK, Immaculate Conception Church. (TLS)
Barnwell, SC, Barnwell Co., St. Andrew the Apostle, c/o Orangeburg, SC, Holy Trinity Church. (CHR)
Barriada Vietnam, Guaynabo, La Milagrosa, c/o [10] Guaynabo, PR, Santa Rosa de Lima Church. (SJN)
Barrineau Park, FL, Escambia Co., St. Elizabeth of Hungary, c/o Cantonment, FL, St. Jude Thaddeus Church. (PT)
Barrington, NH, Chapel of the Nativity, c/o Dover, NH, St. Joseph Church. (MAN)
Barrio Apeadero, PR, San Alfonso, c/o Villalba, PR, Our Lady of Mt. Carmel Church. (PCE)
Barrio Cecilia, Sector La Fe, PR, c/o Naguabo, PR, Nuestra Senora del Rosario Church. (CGS)
Barrio Hatillo, PR, Sagrada Familia, c/o Villalba, PR, Our Lady of Mt. Carmel Church. (PCE)
Barrio Indios, PR, San Juan Bosco, c/o Guayanilla, PR, Immaculate Conception Church. (PCE)
Barrio Jaguey, PR, Madre Cabrini, c/o Villalba, PR, Our Lady of Mt. Carmel Church. (PCE)
Barrio Rio, Sector Brazo Seco, PR, c/o Naguabo, PR, Nuestra Senora del Rosario Church. (CGS)
Barrio Semil, PR, Santa Cecilia, c/o Villalba, PR, Our Lady of Mt. Carmel Church. (PCE)
Barrio Sierra Baja, PR, Our Lady of Mt. Carmel, c/o Guayanilla, PR, Immaculate Conception Church. (PCE)
Barstow, TX, Our Lady of Refuge, c/o Pecos, TX, Santa Rosa Church. (ELP)
Bartolo, PR, Immaculate Conception, c/o Castaner, PR, Our Lady of the Miraculous Medal Church. (PCE)
Barton, MD, St. Gabriel, c/o Westernport, MD, St. Peter Church. (BAL)
Bartow, WV, Pocahontas Co., St. Mark the Evangelist, c/o Marlinton, WV, St. John Neumann Church. (WH)
Basile, LA, Evangeline Parish, Assumption, c/o Basile, LA, St. Augustine Church. (LAF)
Basin, WY, Big Horn Co., St. Philip, c/o Greybull, WY, Sacred Heart Church. (CHY)
Bass Lake, CA, Madera Co., St. Dominic Savio, c/o Bass Lake, CA, Our Lady of the Sierra Church. (FRS)
Bassett, NE, Rock Co., Holy Cross, c/o Ainsworth, NE, St. Pius X Church. (GI)
Basye, VA, Shenandoah Co., Our Lady of the Shenandoah, c/o Woodstock, VA, St. John Bosco Church. (ARL)
Batesville, TX, St. Patrick, c/o La Pryor, TX, St. Joseph Church. (LAR)
Baxley, GA, Appling Co., St. Rose of Lima, c/o Hazlehurst, GA, Good Shepherd Church. (SAV)
Bay Mills, MI, Chippewa Co., Blessed Kateri Tekakwitha, c/o Brimley, MI, St. Francis Xavier Church. (MAR)
Bay St. Louis, MS, Hancock Co., St. Joseph's Chapel, c/o Bay St. Louis, MS, Our Lady of the Gulf Church. (BLX)
Bayamon, PR, c/o [1] Bayamon, PR, San Agustin Church. (SJN)
Bayamon, PR, Sector Punta Brava, Convento Misioneras De La Caridad, c/o [24] Bayamon, PR, Santa Teresa de Jesus Church. (SJN)
Bayamon, PR, Sector La Morenita, Cristo Rey, c/o [15] Bayamon, PR, Ntra. Sra. de la Monserrate Church. (SJN)
Bayamon, PR, N. Sra. Del Carmen, c/o [18] Bayamon, PR, Santa Rita de Casia Church. (SJN)
Bayamon, PR, Sagrado Corazon, c/o [23] Bayamon, PR, Santa Maria Church. (SJN)
Bayamon, PR, Sagrado Corazon De Jesus, c/o [18] Bayamon, PR, Santa Rita de Casia Church. (SJN)
Bayamon, PR, San Gerardo de Mayela, c/o [23] Bayamon, PR, Santa Maria Church. (SJN)
Bayamon, PR, San Jose, c/o [18] Bayamon, PR, Santa Rita de Casia Church. (SJN)
Bayamon, PR, San Martin de Porres, c/o [1] Bayamon, PR, San Agustin Church. (SJN)
Bayamon, PR, San Martin de Porres, c/o [24] Bayamon, PR, Santa Teresa de Jesus Church. (SJN)
Bayamon, PR, Sector Pena, Santa Monica, c/o [15] Bayamon, PR, Ntra. Sra. de la Monserrate Church. (SJN)
Bayard, NE, Morrill Co., Sacred Heart, c/o Bridgeport, NE, All Souls Church. (GI)
Bayfield, CO, La Plata Co., St. Bartholemew, c/o Ignacio, CO, St. Ignatius Parish Church. (PBL)
Bayside, TX, Refugio Co., St. Mary, c/o Woodsboro, TX, St. Therese, The Little Flower Church. (CC)
Bda. Esperanza, PR, Guanica Co., La Providencia, c/o Guanica, PR, St. Anthony Abbot Church. (PCE)
Bda. Marin, PR, La Milagrosa, c/o Arroyo, PR, Our Lady of Mt. Carmel Church. (PCE)
Beach Haven, NJ, Ocean Co., St. Thomas Aquinas, c/o Brant Beach, NJ, St. Francis of Assisi Church. (TR)
Beach Lake, PA, Wayne Co., St. Bernard, c/o White Mills, PA, St. Joseph's Church. (SCR)
Beardsley, KS, Rawlins Co., St. John's, c/o St. Francis, KS, St. Francis Church. (SAL)
Beaulieu, MN, Mahnomen Co., St. Joseph, c/o Mahnomen, MN, St. Michael's Church. (CR)
Beaver, OK, Beaver Co., St. Frances Cabrini, c/o Woodward, OK, St. Peter's Church. (OKL)
Beaver Creek, CO, Eagle Co., Beaver Creek Chapel, c/o Edwards, CO, St. Clare of Assisi Church. (DEN)
Bechyne, ND, Walsh Co., SS. Peter & Paul, c/o Michigan, ND, St. Lawrence O'Toole Church. (FAR)
Becket, MA, Berkshire Co., St. Matthew, c/o Hinsdale, MA, St. Patrick's Church. (SPR)
Bedford, KY, Trimble Co., St. Matthew, c/o LaGrange, KY, Immaculate Conception Church. (L)
Bedford Hills, NY, Westchester Co., St. Matthias, c/o Katonah, NY, St. Mary of the Assumption Church. (NY)
Bee, NE, Seward Co., St. Wenceslaus, c/o Dwight, NE, Assumption Church. (LIN)
Beech Bottom, WV, Brooke Co., Holy Family, c/o Wellsburg, WV, St. John The Evangelist Church. (WH)
Bel Air, MD, Harford Co., St. Mary Magdalen, c/o Bel Air, MD, St. Margaret Church. (BAL)
Belaire Cove, LA, Sacred Heart, c/o Ville Platte, LA, Sacred Heart of Jesus Church. (LAF)
Belcourt, ND, St. Ann, c/o Turtle Mountain Reservation, ND, (Chippewa Indians) Church. (FAR)
Belcourt, ND, Rolette Co., St. Anthony Indian Mission, c/o Belcourt, ND, St. Ann Church. (FAR)
Belcourt, ND, Rolette Co., St. Benedict, c/o St. John, ND, St. John the Baptist Church. (FAR)
Belfair, WA, Mason Co., Prince of Peace, c/o Port Orchard, WA, St. Gabriel Church. (SEA)
Belgrade, MT, Valley of Flowers, c/o Three Forks, MT, Holy Family Church. (HEL)
Belgrade Lakes, ME, St. Helena, c/o Oakland, ME, St. Theresa Church. (PRT)
Bellevue, LA, St. Landry Parish, Christ the King, c/o Grand Coteau, LA, St. Charles Borromeo Church. (LAF)
Bellflower, IL, McLean Co., St. John, c/o Farmer City, IL, Sacred Heart Church. (PEO)
Bellwood, NE, Butler Co., St. Joseph's, c/o Bellwood, NE, St. Peter's Church. (LIN)
Bemidji, MN, Beltrami Co., Holy Spirit Newman Center, c/o Bemidji, MN, St. Philip's Church. (CR)
Ben Bolt, TX, Jim Wells Co., St. Peter's Church, c/o Alice, TX, St. Elizabeth Church. (CC)
Bena, MN, St. Anne's, c/o Ball Club, MN, St. Joseph's Church. (DUL)
Bennettsville, SC, Marlboro Co., St. Denis, c/o Cheraw, SC, St. Peter's Church. (CHR)
Bennington, NY, Wyoming Co., Our Lady Help of Christians, c/o Darien Center, NY, Our Lady of Good Counsel Church. (BUF)
Bensenville, IL, Polish Catholic Pastoral Mission, c/o Bensenville, IL, St. Charles Borromeo Church. (JOL)
Bent, NM, Our Lady of Guadalupe, c/o Mescalero, NM, St. Joseph Church. (LSC)
Benton, LA, Bossier Parish, Mary, Queen of Heaven, c/o Bossier City, LA, St. Jude Church. (SHP)
Benton, PA, Columbia Co., Christ the King, c/o Bloomsburg, PA, St. Columba Church. (HBG)
Benwood, MN, Roseau Co., St. Joseph, The Worker, c/o Roseau, MN, Sacred Heart Church. (CR)
Bergland, MI, Ontonagon Co., St. Ann, c/o White Pine, MI, St. Jude Church. (MAR)
Berino, NM, Immaculate Conception, c/o Anthony, NM, St. Anthony's Church. (LSC)
Bermuda, LA, St. Charles, c/o Isle Brevelle, LA, St. Augustine's Church. (ALX)
Berne, NY, Albany Co., St. Bernadette, c/o Altamont, NY, St. Lucy Church. (ALB)
Berrien Springs, MI, Berrien Co., St. Gabriel Mission , c/o Niles, MI, St. Mary Church. (KAL)
Berryville, AR, Carroll Co., St. Anne, c/o Eureka Springs, AR, St. Elizabeth of Hungary Church. (LR)
Berryville, VA, Clarke Co., St. Bridget of Ireland, c/o Winchester, VA, Sacred Heart of Jesus Church. (ARL)
Berthold, ND, Ward Co., St. Ann, c/o Foxholm, ND, St. Mary Church. (BIS)
Bertram, TX, Burnet Co., Holy Cross, c/o Burnet, TX, Our Mother of Sorrows Church. (AUS)
Betances, PR, Our Lady of Fatima, c/o Cabo Rojo, PR, St. Michael Church. (MGZ)
Bethel, ME, Oxford Co., Our Lady of the Snows, c/o Norway, ME, St. Catherine of Sienna Church. (PRT)
Bethlehem, MD, Caroline Co., Holy Child, c/o Secretary, MD, Our Lady of Good Counsel Church. (WIL)
Bethlehem, NH, Grafton Co., Christ the King, c/o Littleton, NH, St. Rose of Lima Church. (MAN)
Betterton, MD, Kent Co., Most Precious Blood, c/o Chestertown, MD, Sacred Heart Church. (WIL)
Beulah, CO, Pueblo Co., Our Lady of Lourdes, c/o [11] Pueblo, CO, St. Francis Xavier Church. (PBL)
Bevier, MO, Macon Co., Sacred Heart, c/o Macon, MO, Immaculate Conception Church. (JC)
Bibo, NM, Our Lady of Loretto, c/o Seboyeta, NM, Our Lady of Sorrows Church. (GLP)
Biddeford Pool, ME, York Co., St. Brendan, c/o Biddeford, ME, St. Mary's Church. (PRT)
Bieber, CA, Lassen Co., St. Stephen, c/o Burney, CA, St. Francis of Assisi Church. (SAC)
Big Bay, MI, Marquette Co., St. Mary, c/o [1] Marquette, MI, St. Peter Cathedral. (MAR)

Big Elbow Lake, MN, Becker Co., St. Francis Cabrini, c/o Waubun, MN, St. Ann Church. (CR)
Big Lake, AK, Our Lady of the Lake, c/o Wasilla, AK, Sacred Heart Church. (ANC)
Big Oak Flat, CA, Tuolumne Co., Our Lady of Mt. Carmel, c/o Sonora, CA, St. Patrick Church. (STO)
Big Pine, CA, Inyo Co., St. Stephen, c/o Bishop, CA, Our Lady of Perpetual Help Church. (FRS)
Big Piney, WY, Sublette Co., St. Anne, c/o Pinedale, WY, Our Lady of Peace Church. (CHY)
Big Sandy, TX, Upshur Co., Holy Spirit, c/o Longview, TX, St. Anthony Church. (TYL)
Big Spring, TX, Howard Co., St. Joseph, c/o Big Spring, TX, Immaculate Heart of Mary Church. (SAN)
Big Sur, CA, Monterey Co., St. Francis of the Redwoods, c/o Carmel, CA, San Carlos Borromeo Basilica . (MRY)
Big Wells, TX, St. Michael, c/o Asherton, TX, Immaculate Conception Church. (LAR)
Bigfoot, TX, Frio Co., Our Lady of Mt. Carmel, c/o Von Ormy, TX, St. Peter the Fisherman Church. (SAT)
Billings, OK, Noble Co., Sacred Heart, c/o Perry, OK, St. Rose of Lima Church. (OKL)
Binger, OK, Binger Co., Our Lady of the Most Holy Rosary, c/o Anadarko, OK, St. Patrick's Church. (OKL)
Bird City, KS, Cheyenne Co., St. Joseph's, c/o St. Francis, KS, St. Francis Church. (SAL)
Birmingham, AL, Jefferson Co., Holy Rosary (Gate City), c/o [9] Birmingham, AL, St. John Bosco Church. (BIR)
Bisbee, ND, Towner Co., c/o Rolette, ND, Sacred Heart Church. (FAR)
Biscoe, NC, Montgomery Co., Our Lady of the Americas, c/o Albemarle, NC, Our Lady of the Annunciation Church. (CHL)
Bismarck, MO, St. Francois Co., St. John, c/o Park Hills, MO, Immaculate Conception Church. (STL)
Black Canyon City, AZ, Yavapai Co., St. Philip Benizi, c/o Camp Verde, AZ, St. Frances Cabrini Church. (PHX)
Black Horse, PA, Montgomery Co., Our Lady of Mount Carmel, c/o [2] Norristown, PA, Holy Saviour Church. (PH)
Black Lake, LA, Our Lady of the Holy Rosary, c/o Campti, LA, Nativity of The Blessed Virgin Mary Church. (ALX)
Black Lake, NM, Colfax Co., St. Anthony, c/o Cimarron, NM, Immaculate Conception Church. (SFE)
Black Pipe-Corn Creek, SD, St. Joseph Hall, c/o Parmelee, SD, St. Agnes Church. (RC)
Blackduck, MN, Beltrami Co., St. Patrick, c/o Kelliher, MN, St. Patrick Church. (CR)
Blackville, SC, Barnwell Co., Sacred Heart, c/o Orangeburg, SC, Holy Trinity Church. (CHR)
Blackwater, AZ, Holy Family, c/o Bapchule, AZ, St. Peter's Church. (PHX)
Blackwell's Corner, CA, Kern Co., Nuestra Senora de la Paz, c/o Wasco, CA, St. John the Evangelist Church. (FRS)
Blaine, WA, Whatcom Co., St. Anne, c/o Ferndale, WA, St. Joseph Church. (SEA)
Blanca, CO, Costilla Co., St. James, c/o San Luis, CO, Sangre de Cristo Church. (PBL)
Blencoe, IA, Monona Co., St. Bernard, c/o Onawa, IA, St. John Church. (SC)
Blooming Grove, PA, Good Shepherd, c/o Lords Valley, PA, St. John Neumann Church. (SCR)
Bloomingburgh, NY, Sullivan Co., Our Lady of the Assumption, c/o Middletown, NY, Our Lady of Mt. Carmel Church. (NY)
Bloomington, NE, Franklin Co., Sacred Heart, c/o Alma, NE, St. Joseph's Church. (LIN)
Blowing Rock, NC, Epiphany, c/o Boone, NC, St. Elizabeth Church. (CHL)
Blue Hill, NE, Webster Co., Holy Trinity, c/o Campbell, NE, St. Anne Church. (LIN)
Blue Lake, CA, St. Joseph, c/o Arcata, CA, St. Mary's Church. (SR)
Blue Mountain Lake, NY, Hamilton Co., St. Paul, c/o Indian Lake, NY, St. Mary's Church. (OG)
Bluetown, TX, Cristo Rey, c/o Progreso, TX, Holy Spirit Church. (BWN)
Bluewater, NM, McKinley Co., Risen Savior, c/o Crownpoint, NM, St. Paul Church. (GLP)
Bly, OR, St. James the Apostle, c/o Chiloquin, OR, Our Lady of Mt. Carmel Church. (BAK)
Blythewood, SC, Transfiguration Catholic Community, c/o [5] Columbia, SC, St. John Neumann Church. (CHR)
Bo Barreal, PR, Cristo de la Salud, c/o Penuelas, PR, St. Joseph Church. (PCE)
Bo. Aceituna, PR, San Martin de Porres, c/o Moca, PR, Our Lady of Monserrate Church. (MGZ)
Bo. Aibonito Guerrero, PR, Ntra. Sra. del Carmen, c/o San Sebastian, PR, San Sebastian Martir Church. (MGZ)
Bo. Altozano, PR, Ntra. Sra. de Fatima, c/o San Sebastian, PR, San Sebastian Martir Church. (MGZ)
Bo. Alturita, PR, Cacao Co., Our Lady of Mt. Carmel, c/o Villalba, PR, Our Lady Mother of Divine Providence Church. (PCE)
Bo. Arenas de Guancia, PR, Guancia Co., S. Martin de Porres, c/o Yauco, PR, St. Martin de Porres Church. (PCE)
Bo. Atalaya, PR, El Cristo de la Reconciliacion, c/o Rincon, PR, St. Rose of Lima Church. (MGZ)
Bo. Barrancas, PR, La Monserrate, c/o Guayama, PR, St. Anthony of Padua Church. (PCE)
Bo. Bauta, PR, Bauta Abajo Co., N.S. del Rosario, c/o Villalba, PR, Our Lady Mother of Divine Providence Church. (PCE)
Bo. Belgica, PR, Guanica Co., Cristo Rey, c/o Guanica, PR, St. Anthony Abbot Church. (PCE)
Bo. Buena Vista, PR, Holy Family, c/o Penuelas, PR, Sacred Heart Church. (PCE)
Bo. Cacao, PR, Cacao Co., Imm. Concepcion, c/o Villalba, PR, Our Lady Mother of Divine Providence Church. (PCE)
Bo. Cain, PR, St. Martin de Porres, c/o San German, PR, St. Rose of Lima Church. (MGZ)
Bo. Calabazas, PR, San Gabriel de la Dolorosa, c/o San Sebastian, PR, San Sebastian Martir Church. (MGZ)
Bo. Calvache, PR, Santa Rosa, c/o Rincon, PR, St. Rose of Lima Church. (MGZ)
Bo. Calzada, PR, c/o Maunabo, PR, San Isidor Labrador Church. (CGS)
Bo. Camarones, PR, Jesus Crucificado, c/o Villalba, PR, Our Lady of Mt. Carmel Church. (PCE)
Bo. Camarones-Los Robles, PR, San Antonio, c/o Villalba, PR, Our Lady of Mt. Carmel Church. (PCE)
Bo. Cambute, PR, Divino Nino, c/o [18] Carolina, PR, Cristo Rey Church. (SJN)
Bo. Canonilla Abajo, PR, Maria Madre de la Iglesia, c/o Villalba, PR, Our Lady of Mt. Carmel Church. (PCE)
Bo. Canovanillas, PR, Maria Auxiliadora, c/o [18] Carolina, PR, Cristo Rey Church. (SJN)
Bo. Capa Barreto, PR, Virgen del Rosario, c/o Moca, PR, Our Lady of Monserrate Church. (MGZ)
Bo. Capa Bosque, PR, Cristo Salvador, c/o Moca, PR, Our Lady of Monserrate Church. (MGZ)
Bo. Carreras, PR, La Providencia, c/o Anasco, PR, St. Anthony Abbot Church. (MGZ)
Bo. Carretera Nueva, PR, La Asuncion, c/o Hormigueros, PR, Shrine of Our Lady of Monserrate Church. (MGZ)
Bo. Cerro Gordo, PR, Espiritu Santo, c/o Villalba, PR, Our Lady of Mt. Carmel Church. (PCE)
Bo. Cerro Gordo, PR, La Inmaculada, c/o Moca, PR, Our Lady of Monserrate Church. (MGZ)
Bo. Cerro Gordo, PR, Our Lady of Monserrat, c/o Anasco, PR, St. Anthony Abbot Church. (MGZ)
Bo. Cerro Gordo, PR, San Francisco de Asis, c/o Sabana Grande, PR, Church of San Isidro. (MGZ)
Bo. Cerro Gordo, PR, San Judas, c/o Moca, PR, Our Lady of Monserrate Church. (MGZ)
Bo. Chucillas Sabana, PR, Corazon de Jesus, c/o Moca, PR, Our Lady of Monserrate Church. (MGZ)
Bo. Collado, PR, Ponce Co., Our Lady of Monserrate, c/o [3] Ponce, PR, Church of the Resurrection. (PCE)
Bo. Corazon, PR, La Candelaria, c/o Guayama, PR, St. Anthony of Padua Church. (PCE)
Bo. Corcega, PR, La Milagrosa, c/o Rincon, PR, St. Rose of Lima Church. (MGZ)
Bo. Cordero, PR, Virgen Monserrate, c/o Moca, PR, Our Lady of Monserrate Church. (MGZ)
Bo. Corillo, PR, San Pedro, c/o Villalba, PR, Our Lady of Mt. Carmel Church. (PCE)
Bo. Corral Viejo, PR, Ponce Co., Cristo Rey, c/o [10] Ponce, PR, La Santisima Trinidad Church. (PCE)
Bo. Cruces, PR, Sagrado Corazon de Jesus, c/o Rincon, PR, St. Rose of Lima Church. (MGZ)
Bo. Cuatro Calles, PR, Ponce Co., St. Anthony, c/o [13] Ponce, PR, Santuario San Judas Tadeo Church. (PCE)
Bo. Cuchilla del Limon, PR, La Asuncion, c/o Villalba, PR, Our Lady of Mt. Carmel Church. (PCE)
Bo. Cuchillas La Salle, PR, Santos Guillermo y Mateo, c/o Moca, PR, Our Lady of Monserrate Church. (MGZ)
Bo. Cuchillas Loperena, PR, Virgen del Carmen, c/o Moca, PR, Our Lady of Monserrate Church. (MGZ)
Bo. Cuesta Blanca, PR, Ntra. Sra. de Monserrate, c/o Lajas, PR, De la Merced Parish Church. (MGZ)
Bo. Dajas, PR, N.S. del Carmen, c/o Villalba, PR, Our Lady of Mt. Carmel Church. (PCE)
Bo. Damian Abajo, PR, Damian Abajo Co., N.S. del Pilar, c/o Villalba, PR, Our Lady Mother of Divine Providence Church. (PCE)
Bo. El Bajo, Pastillas, PR, Pastillas Co., Cristo Rey, c/o Patillas, PR, Inmaculado Corazon de Maria Church. (PCE)
Bo. El Frio, PR, Ala de La Piedra Co., Nino de Praga, c/o Villalba, PR, Our Lady Mother of Divine Providence Church. (PCE)
Bo. El Hoyo, PR, La Virgen Milagrosa, c/o Sabana Grande, PR, Church of San Isidro. (MGZ)
Bo. El Hoyo, PR, Santa Rosa de Lima, c/o Hormigueros, PR, Shrine of Our Lady of Monserrate Church. (MGZ)
Bo. El Porvenir, PR, Ntra. Sra. de la Providencia (Rep. Masias), c/o [3] Mayaquez, Mayaguez, Ascension Church. (MGZ)
Bo. El Real, Pastillas, PR, Pastillas Co., San Guillermo, c/o Patillas, PR, Inmaculado Corazon de Maria Church. (PCE)
Bo. Espino, PR, St. Lawrence Martyr, c/o Anasco, PR, St. Anthony Abbot Church. (MGZ)
Bo. Fuig., PR, Monserrate, c/o Ensenada, PR, Sacred Heart Church. (PCE)
Bo. Guama, PR, N. Sra. de la Consolacion, c/o San German, PR, St. Rose of Lima Church. (MGZ)
Bo. Guamani, PR, Sgdo. Corazon, c/o Guayama, PR, St. Anthony of Padua Church. (PCE)
Bo. Guanajibo, PR, San Martin de Porres, c/o Hormigueros, PR, Shrine of Our Lady of Monserrate Church. (MGZ)
Bo. Guaragoa, PR, Ponce Co., San Andres, c/o [10] Ponce, PR, La Santisima Trinidad Church. (PCE)
Bo. Guaragoa, Arriba, PR, Ponce Co., Santa Ana, c/o [10] Ponce, PR, La Santisima Trinidad Church. (PCE)
Bo. Guaras, PR, Ntra. Sra. de Fatima, c/o Sabana Grande, PR, Church of San Isidro. (MGZ)
Bo. Guarderraya, Pastillas, PR, Pastillas Co., Madre Cabrini, c/o Patillas, PR, Inmaculado Corazon de Maria Church. (PCE)
Bo. Guerrero, PR, La Providencia, c/o Aguadilla, PR, San Jose Obrero Church. (MGZ)
Bo. Guineo, PR, Ala de La Piedra Co., Santa Ana, c/o Villalba, PR, Our Lady Mother of Divine Providence Church. (PCE)
Bo. Hatillo Viejo, PR, La Milagrosa, c/o Villalba, PR, Our Lady of Mt. Carmel Church. (PCE)
Bo. Hato Arriba, PR, San Patricio, c/o San Sebastian, PR, San Sebastian Martir Church. (MGZ)
Bo. Hato Arriba (Parcelas), PR, San Pablo de la Cruz, c/o San Sebastian, PR, San Sebastian Martir Church. (MGZ)
Bo. Higuero, PR, Santisimo Sacramento, c/o Villalba, PR, Our Lady of Mt. Carmel Church. (PCE)
Bo. Hoyamala, PR, San Jose Obrero, c/o San Sebastian, PR, San Sebastian Martir Church. (MGZ)
Bo. Hoyos, PR, Ponce Co., Santa Maria Virgen, c/o [17] Ponce, PR, Our Lady of Mt. Carmel Church. (PCE)
Bo. Jacaboa, Pastillas, PR, Pastillas Co., Carmen, c/o Patillas, PR, Inmaculado Corazon de Maria Church. (PCE)
Bo. Jagual, Pastillas, PR, Pastillas Co., Carmen, c/o Patillas, PR, Inmaculado Corazon de Maria Church. (PCE)
Bo. Jaguey, PR, San Jose, c/o Rincon, PR, St. Rose of Lima Church. (MGZ)
Bo. Jagueyes Arriba, PR, La Milagrosa, c/o Villalba, PR, Our Lady of Mt. Carmel Church. (PCE)
Bo. Jaquitas, PR, Ntra. Sra. de la Paz, c/o Hormigueros, PR, Shrine of Our Lady of Monserrate Church. (MGZ)
Bo. Juncal, PR, Santa Teresita, c/o San Sebastian, PR, San Sebastian Martir Church. (MGZ)
Bo. La Cuarta, PR, Ponce Co., San Pedro Nolasco, c/o [15] Ponce, PR, Church of the Sacred Heart. (PCE)
Bo. La Lechuza, PR, La Asuncion, c/o San Sebastian, PR, San Sebastian Martir Church. (MGZ)
Bo. La Luna, PR, Guanica Co., N. Sra Fatima, c/o Guanica, PR, St. Anthony Abbot Church. (PCE)
Bo. La Maquina, PR, Santa Ana, c/o Sabana Grande, PR, Church of San Isidro. (MGZ)
Bo. La Pica, PR, San Jose, c/o Sabana Grande, PR, Church of San Isidro. (MGZ)
Bo. La Plata, PR, Sagrado Corazon de Jesus, c/o Lajas, PR, Our Lady of the Purification Church. (MGZ)
Bo. La Torre, PR, Santa Catalina de Siena, c/o Sabana Grande, PR, Church of San Isidro. (MGZ)
Bo. La Yuca, PR, Ponce Co., Immaculate Heart of Mary, c/o [3] Ponce, PR, Church of the Resurrection . (PCE)
Bo. Lajas Arriba (La Tea), PR, Ntra. Sra. del Perpetuo Socorro, c/o Lajas, PR, Our Lady of the Purification Church. (MGZ)
Bo. Lajas Arriba (Parcelas), PR, San Pablo, c/o Lajas, PR, Our Lady of the Purification Church. (MGZ)
Bo. Las Palmas, PR, Virg. del Carmen, c/o Salinas, PR, Our Lady of Monserrat Church. (PCE)
Bo. Las Raices, PR, Ponce Co., Sagrado Corazon de Jesus, c/o [17] Ponce, PR, Our Lady of Mt. Carmel Church. (PCE)
Bo. Las Vallas, PR, Ponce Co., San Lucas, c/o [3] Ponce, PR, Church of the Resurrection. (PCE)
Bo. Las Vegas, PR, Our Lady of Perpetual Help, c/o [3] Mayaquez, Mayaguez, Ascension Church. (MGZ)
Bo. Lavadero, PR, Sagrado Corazon de Jesus, c/o Hormigueros, PR, Shrine of Our Lady of Monserrate Church. (MGZ)
Bo. Limon, PR, St. Teresita, c/o [3] Mayaquez, Mayaguez, Ascension Church. (MGZ)

Bo. Limon, PR, Virgen de la Amargura, c/o Villalba, PR, Our Lady of Mt. Carmel Church. (PCE)
Bo. Limon, PR, Virgen del Rosario, c/o Moca, PR, Our Lady of Monserrate Church. (MGZ)
Bo. Lizas, PR, c/o Maunabo, PR, San Isidor Labrador Church. (CGS)
Bo. Los Barros, Pastillas, PR, Pastillas Co., S. Juan Evangelista, c/o Patillas, PR, Inmaculado Corazon de Maria Church. (PCE)
Bo. Los Pollos, Pastillas, PR, Pastillas Co., Santa Rosa de Lima, c/o Patillas, PR, Inmaculado Corazon de Maria Church. (PCE)
Bo. Luna, PR, Guanica Co., San Judas, c/o Guanica, PR, St. Anthony Abbot Church. (PCE)
Bo. Madrigal, PR, Ponce Co., N.S. del Rosario, c/o [10] Ponce, PR, La Santisima Trinidad Church. (PCE)
Bo. Maginas, PR, Sagrado Corazon de Jesus, c/o Sabana Grande, PR, Church of San Isidro. (MGZ)
Bo. Maguayo, PR, Ntra. Sra. de la Monserrate, c/o Lajas, PR, De la Merced Parish Church. (MGZ)
Bo. Magueyes, PR, Ponce Co., San Juan de Mata, c/o [10] Ponce, PR, La Santisima Trinidad Church. (PCE)
Bo. Malezas, PR, La Milagrosa, c/o [6] Mayaquez, PR, Sacred Heart Church. (MGZ)
Bo. Marias, PR, St. Rita, c/o Anasco, PR, St. Anthony Abbot Church. (MGZ)
Bo. Marin Alto, Pastillas, PR, Pastillas Co., Perpetuo Socorro, c/o Patillas, PR, Inmaculado Corazon de Maria Church. (PCE)
Bo. Marueno, Arriba, PR, Ponce Co., N.S. Fatima, c/o [10] Ponce, PR, La Santisima Trinidad Church. (PCE)
Bo. Minillas Carretera, PR, Perpetuo Socorro, c/o San German, PR, St. Rose of Lima Church. (MGZ)
Bo. Minillas Valle, PR, Santa Monica, c/o San German, PR, St. Rose of Lima Church. (MGZ)
Bo. Miradero, PR, Ntro. Sra. de la Providencia, c/o Cabo Rojo, PR, St. Michael Church. (MGZ)
Bo. Mogote, PR, Santisima Tinidad, c/o Villalba, PR, Our Lady of Mt. Carmel Church. (PCE)
Bo. Molinas, PR, Ntra. Sra. de Monserrate, c/o Sabana Grande, PR, Church of San Isidro. (MGZ)
Bo. Naranjo, PR, Corazon de Jesus, c/o Moca, PR, Our Lady of Monserrate Church. (MGZ)
Bo. Olimpo, PR, Cristo Rey, c/o Guayama, PR, St. Anthony of Padua Church. (PCE)
Bo. Ollas, PR, Monserrate, c/o Santa Isabel, PR, St. James Church. (PCE)
Bo. Oveja, PR, Cristo Redentor, c/o Anasco, PR, St. Anthony Abbot Church. (MGZ)
Bo. Palmarejo, PR, San Jose, c/o Villalba, PR, Our Lady of Mt. Carmel Church. (PCE)
Bo. Palmarejo II, PR, San Juan Bautista, c/o Lajas, PR, Our Lady of the Purification Church. (MGZ)
Bo. Palmas, PR, Ntra Sra. de Fatima, c/o Arroyo, PR, Our Lady of Mt. Carmel Church. (PCE)
Bo. Paloseco, PR, c/o Maunabo, PR, San Isidor Labrador Church. (CGS)
Bo. Parcelas Guacio (Parcelas), PR, Santa Cruz, c/o San Sebastian, PR, San Sebastian Martir Church. (MGZ)
Bo. Parcelas Palmarejo, PR, San Judas Tadeo, c/o Lajas, PR, Our Lady of the Purification Church. (MGZ)
Bo. Parcelas Santa Rosa, PR, Santa Rosa de Lima, c/o Lajas, PR, Our Lady of the Purification Church. (MGZ)
Bo. Parguera, PR, San Pedro, c/o Lajas, PR, De la Merced Parish Church. (MGZ)
Bo. Paris, PR, Ntra Sra. del Perpetuo Socorro, c/o Lajas, PR, De la Merced Parish Church. (MGZ)
Bo. Paso Secos, PR, Virgen del Rosario, c/o Santa Isabel, PR, St. James Church. (PCE)
Bo. Pastillo, PR, Ponce Co., Inmaculada, c/o [10] Ponce, PR, La Santisima Trinidad Church. (PCE)
Bo. Penuelas, PR, Virgen del Rosario, c/o Santa Isabel, PR, St. James Church. (PCE)
Bo. Perchas 1, PR, Cristo Rey, c/o San Sebastian, PR, San Sebastian Martir Church. (MGZ)
Bo. Perchas 11, PR, La Pasion, c/o San Sebastian, PR, San Sebastian Martir Church. (MGZ)
Bo. Pinales, PR, La Immaculade, c/o Anasco, PR, St. Anthony Abbot Church. (MGZ)
Bo. Pitahaya, PR, Ntra Sra. del Carmen, c/o Arroyo, PR, Our Lady of Mt. Carmel Church. (PCE)
Bo. Placita, PR, c/o Juncos, PR, Inmaculada Concepcion Church. (CGS)
Bo. Playa, PR, Carmen, c/o Salinas, PR, Our Lady of Monserrat Church. (PCE)
Bo. Playita, PR, Virgen Milagrosa, c/o Salinas, PR, Our Lady of Monserrat Church. (PCE)
Bo. Pozas, PR, Damian Abajo Co., N.S. Monserrate, c/o Villalba, PR, Our Lady Mother of Divine Providence Church. (PCE)
Bo. Pozo Hondo, PR, Santa Rosa de Lima, c/o Anasco, PR, St. Anthony Abbot Church. (MGZ)
Bo. Providencia, Pastillas, PR, Pastillas Co., Providencia, c/o Patillas, PR, Inmaculado Corazon de Maria Church. (PCE)
Bo. Puente Jobos, PR, SS. Peter and Paul, c/o Guayama, PR, St. Anthony of Padua Church. (PCE)
Bo. Puerto Jobos, PR, San Francisco de Asis, c/o Guayama, PR, St. Anthony of Padua Church. (PCE)
Bo. Punta Brava, PR, San Pedro, c/o Moca, PR, Our Lady of Monserrate Church. (MGZ)
Bo. Puntas, PR, Nuestra Senora del Carmen, c/o Rincon, PR, St. Rose of Lima Church. (MGZ)
Bo. Quebrada Arenas, PR, c/o Maunabo, PR, San Isidor Labrador Church. (CGS)
Bo. Quebrado del Agua, PR, Ponce Co., La Milagrosa, c/o [16] Ponce, PR, Church of the Good Shepherd . (PCE)
Bo. Rayo Plata, PR, San Judas Tadeo, c/o Sabana Grande, PR, Church of San Isidro. (MGZ)
Bo. Real Anon Abajo, PR, Ponce Co., San Mateo, c/o [17] Ponce, PR, Our Lady of Mt. Carmel Church. (PCE)
Bo. Real Anon Arriba, PR, Ponce Co., San Martin de Porres, c/o [17] Ponce, PR, Our Lady of Mt. Carmel Church. (PCE)
Bo. Recio, Pastillas, PR, Pastillas Co., Sto. Cristo de Los Milagros, c/o Patillas, PR, Inmaculado Corazon de Maria Church. (PCE)
Bo. Retiro Tea, PR, Santa Rita, c/o San German, PR, St. Rose of Lima Church. (MGZ)
Bo. Rio Abajo, PR, Ceiba Co., N.S. del Perpetuo Socorro Bo. Rio Abajo, c/o Ceiba, PR, San Antonio de Padua Church. (CGS)
Bo. Robles, PR, Sagrado Corazon, c/o San Sebastian, PR, San Sebastian Martir Church. (MGZ)
Bo. Rocha Magueyes, PR, La Providencia, c/o Moca, PR, Our Lady of Monserrate Church. (MGZ)
Bo. Rosario Penon, PR, La Monserrate, c/o Rosario, PR, Rosary Church. (MGZ)
Bo. Salinas, PR, Ntra. Sra. del Carmen, c/o Lajas, PR, De la Merced Parish Church. (MGZ)
Bo. Salistral, PR, Ponce Co., Santa Marta, c/o [4] Ponce, PR, Our Lady of Mt. Carmel Church. (PCE)
Bo. Saltos, PR, San Judas Tadeo, c/o San Sebastian, PR, San Sebastian Martir Church. (MGZ)
Bo. Santa Juanita, PR, Guanica Co., N. Sra. Rosario, c/o Guanica, PR, St. Anthony Abbot Church. (PCE)
Bo. Santana Pichel, PR, Ntra. Sra. del Rosario, c/o Sabana Grande, PR, Church of San Isidro. (MGZ)
Bo. Santas Pascuas, PR, Ponce Co., Resurreccion, c/o [10] Ponce, PR, La Santisima Trinidad Church. (PCE)
Bo. Sierrita Caonillas, PR, Cristo de la Salud, c/o Villalba, PR, Our Lady of Mt. Carmel Church. (PCE)
Bo. Sta. Ana Moreno, PR, Sta Lucia, c/o Sabana Grande, PR, Church of San Isidro. (MGZ)
Bo. Susa, PR, Yauco Co., N.S. de La Monserrate, c/o Yauco, PR, St. Martin de Porres Church. (PCE)
Bo. Susa, PR, Guanica Co., N.S. de La Providencia, c/o Yauco, PR, St. Martin de Porres Church. (PCE)
Bo. Susa, PR, Yauco Co., S. Francisco de Asis, c/o Yauco, PR, St. Martin de Porres Church. (PCE)
Bo. Susa, PR, Guanica Co., Santa Rita, c/o Yauco, PR, St. Martin de Porres Church. (PCE)
Bo. Talante, PR, c/o Maunabo, PR, San Isidor Labrador Church. (CGS)
Bo. Talante (La Pica), PR, c/o Maunabo, PR, San Isidor Labrador Church. (CGS)
Bo. Vista Alegre, PR, Jesus Crucificado, c/o Villalba, PR, Our Lady of Mt. Carmel Church. (PCE)
Bo. Voladoras Lomas, PR, Espiritu Santo, c/o Moca, PR, Our Lady of Monserrate Church. (MGZ)
Bo. Voladoras Parcelas, PR, Sagrada Familia, c/o Moca, PR, Our Lady of Monserrate Church. (MGZ)
Bo. Yaurel Palmarejo, PR, San Jose, c/o Arroyo, PR, Our Lady of Mt. Carmel Church. (PCE)
Bo. Yaurel Santa Clara, PR, San Martin, c/o Arroyo, PR, Our Lady of Mt. Carmel Church. (PCE)
Bobtown, PA, Greene Co., Holy Family, c/o Bobtown, PA, St. Ignatius of Antioch Church. (PIT)
Bodega, CA, St. Teresa, c/o Occidental, CA, St. Philip Church. (SR)
Boiceville, NY, Ulster Co., Our Lady of La Salette, c/o Phoenicia, NY, St. Francis de Sales Church. (NY)
Boise City, OK, Cimarron Co., Good Shepherd, c/o Guymon, OK, St. Peter's Church. (OKL)
Boles Acres, NM, Our Lady of the Desert, c/o Alamogordo, NM, Immaculate Conception Church. (LSC)
Bolinas, CA, Marin Co., St. Mary Magdalen, c/o Olema, CA, Sacred Heart Church. (SFR)
Boling, TX, St. Joseph, c/o Wharton, TX, Holy Family Church. (VIC)
Bon Secour, AL, Baldwin Co., Our Lady of Bon Secour, c/o Magnolia Springs, AL, St. John the Baptist Church. (MOB)
Bonanza, OR, St. Frances Cabrini, c/o Merrill, OR, St. Augustine Church. (BAK)
Bongard, IL, Champaign Co., Immaculate Conception, c/o Philo, IL, St. Thomas Church. (PEO)
Bonhamtown, NJ, Middlesex Co., St. Margaret Mary Alacoque, c/o Edison, NJ, Guardian Angels Church. (MET)
Bonita Springs, FL, Lee Co., Hispanic Mission, c/o Bonita Springs, FL, St. Leo Church. (VEN)
Bonneau, SC, Berkeley Co., Our Lady of Peace, c/o Moncks Corner, SC, St. Philip Benizi Church. (CHR)
Booker, TX, St. Peter, c/o Perryton, TX, Immaculate Conception Church. (AMA)
Boomer, WV, Fayette Co., St. Anthony Shrine, c/o Montgomery, WV, Immaculate Conception Church. (WH)
Boone, CO, Pueblo Co., St. William, c/o Avondale, CO, Sacred Heart Church. (PBL)
Booneville, CA, Sonoma Co., St. Elizabeth Seton, c/o Ukiah, CA, St. Mary of the Angels Church. (SR)
Booneville, KY, Owsley Co., Booneville Catholic Church of the Holy Family, c/o Beattyville, KY, Queen of All Saints Church. (LEX)
Boonsboro, MD, Washington Co., St. James, c/o Hagerstown, MD, St. Mary Church. (BAL)
Boqueron, PR, St. Joseph, c/o Cabo Rojo, PR, St. Michael Church. (MGZ)
Borica, NM, Guadalupe Co., c/o Santa Rosa, NM, St. Rose of Lima Church. (SFE)
Borinquen, PR, Our Lady of Victory, c/o Aguadilla, PR, La Milagrosa Church. (MGZ)
Bosque, NM, Valencia Co., c/o Belen, NM, Our Lady of Belen Church. (SFE)
Boswell, OK, Choctaw Co., St. Jude, c/o Hugo, OK, Immaculate Conception Church. (TLS)
Boulder Valley, MT, Jefferson Co., St. John the Evangelist, c/o Boulder, MT, St. Catherine Church. (HEL)
Bowie, AZ, Cochise Co., Our Lady of Guadalupe, c/o Willcox, AZ, Sacred Heart Church. (TUC)
Bowling Green, FL, Hardee Co., Holy Child, c/o Wauchula, FL, St. Michael Church. (VEN)
Box Elder, MT, St. Anthony, c/o Big Sandy, MT, St. Margaret Mary Church. (GF)
Braddock, ND, Emmons Co., St. Katherine, c/o Hazelton, ND, St. Paul Church. (BIS)
Bradley, CA, Monterey Co., Our Lady of Guadalupe, c/o San Miguel, CA, San Miguel Church. (MRY)
Brainardsville, NY, Franklin Co., St. Jude, c/o Chateaugay, NY, St. Patrick Church. (OG)
Braithwaite, LA, Plaquemines Parish, Assumption of the Blessed Virgin, c/o Pointe a la Hache, LA, St. Thomas Church. (NO)
Branch, LA, French Parish, St. Edmund, c/o Robert's Cove, LA, St. Leo IV Church. (LAF)
Brant Lake, NY, Warren Co., St. Teresa of Avila, c/o Hague, NY, Blessed Sacrament Church. (ALB)
Bremen, ND, Wells Co., St. Joseph, c/o Fessenden, ND, St. Augustine's Church. (FAR)
Bridgeport, CA, Mono Co., Infant of Prague, c/o Mammoth Lakes, CA, St. Joseph Church. (STO)
Bridger, SD, Ziebach Co., Immaculate Conception, c/o Eagle Butte, SD, All Saints Church. (RC)
Bridger, SD, Ziebach Co., Immaculate Conception, c/o Eagle Butte, SD, Cheyenne River Reservation Church. (RC)
Bridport, VT, Addison Co., St. Bernadette, c/o Middlebury, VT, Assumption of the Blessed Virgin Mary Church. (BUR)
Brier Hill, NY, St. Lawrence Co., Our Lady of Grace, c/o Morristown, NY, St. John the Evangelist Church. (OG)
Brisbane, CA, San Mateo Co., Our Lady of Guadalupe, c/o [55] San Francisco, CA, Visitacion, Church of the . (SFR)
Bristol, CO, Prowers Co., St. Mary, c/o Holly, CO, St. Frances of Rome Church. (PBL)
Bristol, IL, Kendall Co., St. Patrick, c/o Plano, IL, St. Mary Church. (JOL)
Bristow, OK, Creek Co., St. Joseph, c/o Sapulpa, OK, Sacred Heart Church. (TLS)
Broadview, MT, Little Flower, c/o Roundup, MT, St. Benedict's Church. (GF)
Brocket, ND, Ramsey Co., St. Joseph, c/o Lakota, ND, St. Mary's Church. (FAR)
Brockton, MT, St. Thomas, c/o Poplar, MT, Our Lady of Lourdes Church. (GF)
Bromley, AL, St. John, c/o Daphne, AL, Shrine of the Holy Cross Church. (MOB)
Bronte, TX, Coke Co., St. James, c/o Ballinger, TX, St. Mary Star of the Sea Church. (SAN)
Brookline, NH, Hillsborough Co., Infant Jesus, c/o Milford, NH, St. Patrick Church. (MAN)
Brooklyn, NY, Queens Co., Our Lady of Mount Carmel, c/o [190] Queens, NY, St. Leo Church. (BRK)
Brooklyn, NY, Regina Pacis Votive Shrine, c/o [126] Brooklyn, NY, St. Rosalia-Regina Pacis Church. (BRK)
Brooks, MN, Red Lake Co., St. Joseph, c/o Red Lake Falls, MN, St. Joseph's Church. (CR)
Brown City, MI, Sanilac Co., Sacred Heart, c/o North Branch, MI, St. Mary's Burnside Church. (DET)
Brownlee, NE, Cherry Co., St. Joan of Arc, c/o Mullen, NE, St. Mary's Church. (GI)
Brownstown, IN, Jackson Co., Our Lady of Providence, c/o Seymour, IN, St. Ambrose Church. (IND)
Brownsville, OR, Linn Co., Holy Trinity, c/o Sweet Home, OR, St. Helen Church. (P)

Brownsville, TN, Haywood Co., c/o Jackson, TN, St. Mary's Church. (MEM)
Brownsville, TX, Cameron Co., Blessed Juan Diego de Guadalupe, c/o [2] Brownsville, TX, Christ the King Church. (BWN)
Brownsville, TX, Cameron Co., Sacred Heart, c/o [1] Brownsville, TX, Immaculate Conception Cathedral . (BWN)
Brownsville, TX, Cameron Co., St. Thomas, c/o [1] Brownsville, TX, Immaculate Conception Cathedral . (BWN)
Bruceton Mills, WV, Preston Co., Mary Help of Christians, c/o Cheat Lake, WV, St. Luke Church. (WH)
Bruni, TX, Webb Co., St. Bridget, c/o Hebbronville, TX, Our Lady of Guadalupe Church. (LAR)
Bruno, MN, Sacred Heart, c/o Sandstone, MN, St. Luke's Church. (DUL)
Brunswick, NE, Antelope Co., St. Ignatius, c/o Creighton, NE, St. Ludger Church. (OM)
Brunswick, OH, Medina Co., c/o Lorain, OH, St. John the Baptist Church. (SJP)
Bryan, TX, Brazos Co., San Salvador, c/o Bryan, TX, St. Anthony's Church. (AUS)
Bucarabones, PR, Sagrado Corazon, c/o Maricao, PR, St. John the Baptist Church. (MGZ)
Buchanan, ND, Stutsman Co., St. Margaret, c/o Jamestown, ND, The Basilica of St. James. (FAR)
Buckhead Ridge, FL, Glades Co., St. Theresa of the Child Jesus, c/o Moore Haven, FL, St. Joseph the Worker Church. (VEN)
Buckhorn, CA, Amador Co., Our Lady of the Pines, c/o Jackson, CA, St. Patrick's Church. (SAC)
Buena Vista, GA, Marion Co., St. Mary Magdalen, c/o [2] Columbus, GA, Our Lady of Lourdes Church. (SAV)
Buena Vista, PR, La Milagrosa, c/o Las Marias, PR, Immaculate Heart of Mary Church. (MGZ)
Buenavista, NM, Mora Co., c/o Mora, NM, St. Gertrude Church. (SFE)
Bueyeros, NM, Harding Co., c/o Roy, NM, Holy Family-St. Joseph Church. (SFE)
Buffalo, ND, Cass Co., St. Thomas, c/o Casselton, ND, St. Leo Church. (FAR)
Buffalo, OK, Harper Co., St. Joseph, c/o Woodward, OK, St. Peter's Church. (OKL)
Buffalo Creek, CO, Jefferson Co., St. Elizabeth, c/o Conifer, CO, Our Lady of The Pines Church. (DEN)
Buhach, CA, Merced Co., Immaculate Conception, c/o Atwater, CA, St. Anthony Church. (FRS)
Buhl, MN, Our Lady of the Sacred Heart, c/o Chisholm, MN, St. Joseph's Church. (DUL)
Bullhead, SD, Corson Co., St. Aloysius, c/o McLaughlin, SD, St. Bernard Church. (RC)
Bullhead, SD, Corson Co., St. Aloysius, c/o Standing Rock, SD, Standing Rock Reservation Church. (RC)
Bullville, NY, Orange Co., St. Paul, c/o Middletown, NY, Our Lady of Mt. Carmel Church. (NY)
Bunker, MO, Reynolds Co., Christ the King, c/o Salem, MO, Sacred Heart Church. (SPC)
Burchard, NE, Pawnee Co., Sacred Heart, c/o Steinauer, NE, St. Anthony Church. (LIN)
Bureau, IL, Bureau Co., St. Francis Xavier, c/o Granville, IL, Sacred Heart Of Jesus Church. (PEO)
Burkesville, KY, Cumberland Co., Holy Cross Catholic, c/o Albany, KY, Emmanuel Catholic Church. (L)
Burlington, TX, Milam Co., St. Michael's, c/o Rosebud, TX, St. Ann's Church. (AUS)
Burlington Junction, MO, Nodaway Co., St. Benedict Catholic Church, c/o Tarkio, MO, St. Paul the Apostle Church. (KC)
Burnstad, ND, Logan Co., St. Clara, c/o Napoleon, ND, St. Philip Neri Church. (FAR)
Burnsville, NC, Yancey Co., Sacred Heart, c/o Mars Hill, NC, St. Andrew the Apostle Church. (CHL)
Busby, MT, Christ the King, c/o Lame Deer, MT, Blessed Sacrament Church. (GF)
Bush, LA, St. Tammany Civil Parish, St. Michael the Archangel, c/o Abita Springs, LA, St. Jane de Chantal Church. (NO)
Butner, NC, St. Bernadette, c/o Roxboro, NC, SS. Mary and Edward Church. (R)
Butte La Rose, LA, St. Martin Parish, Sacred Heart, c/o Henderson, LA, Our Lady of Mercy Church. (LAF)
Buxton, NC, Dare Co., Our Lady of the Seas, c/o Kitty Hawk, NC, Holy Redeemer Church. (R)
Bylas, AZ, Graham Co., Blessed Kateri Tekakwitha, c/o San Carlos, AZ, San Carlos Catholic Mission. (TUC)

C

Cabezon, NM, Sandoval Co., San Jose, c/o Cuba, NM, Immaculate Conception Church. (GLP)
Cabool, MO, Texas Co., St. Michael, c/o Mountain Grove, MO, Sacred Heart Church. (SPC)
Cactus, TX, Our Lady of Guadalupe, c/o Dumas, TX, SS. Peter and Paul Church. (AMA)
Cade, LA, St. Anthony, c/o Broussard, LA, St. Joseph Church. (LAF)
Caimital, PR, Our Lady of Perpetual Help, c/o Guayama, PR, St. Anthony of Padua Church. (PCE)
Cainsville, MO, Harrison Co., St. Mary's, c/o Bethany, MO, Blessed Sacrament Church. (KC)
Cairo, GA, Grady Co., St. Elizabeth Ann Seton, c/o Thomasville, GA, St. Augustine Church. (SAV)
Caldwell, TX, Burleson Co., Holy Rosary, c/o Caldwell, TX, St. Mary's Church. (AUS)
Calhoun, LA, Ouachita Parish, St. Francis of Assisi, c/o West Monroe, LA, St. Paschal Church. (SHP)
California City, CA, Kern Co., Our Lady of Lourdes, c/o Boron, CA, St. Joseph Church. (FRS)
Callabo, PR, Bo. Callabo, San Ramon, c/o Juana Diaz, PR, St. Raymond Nonato Church. (PCE)
Callaway, MN, Becker Co., Assumption, c/o Lake Eunice Township, MN, St. Mary of the Lakes Church. (CR)
Calvert, TX, Robertson Co., St. Mary, c/o Hearne, TX, St. Mary's Church. (AUS)
Camaseyes, PR, Our Lady of Fatima, c/o Aguadilla, PR, La Milagrosa Church. (MGZ)
Cambalaches, PR, Our Lady of Perpetual Help, c/o Yauco, PR, Holy Rossary Church. (PCE)
Cambridge, IL, Henry Co., St. John Vianney, c/o Kewanee, IL, St. Francis of Assisi Church. (PEO)
Camden, AL, Wilcox Co., St. Joseph, c/o Monroeville, AL, Annunciation Church. (MOB)
Cameron, LA, Cameron Parish, St. Rose of Lima, c/o Creole, LA, Sacred Heart of Jesus Church. (LKC)
Camilla, GA, Mitchell Co., St. John Vianney, c/o Moultrie, GA, Immaculate Conception Church. (SAV)
Camp Sacramento, CA, El Dorado Co., Our Lady of the Sierras, c/o South Lake Tahoe, CA, St. Theresa Church. (SAC)
Camp Summit, NY, N.Y.S. Correctional Facility, c/o Summit, NY, St. Anna Church. (ALB)
Camp Summit, NY, S.U.N.Y. Cobleskill College, c/o Summit, NY, St. Anna Church. (ALB)
Camp Wood, TX, Real Co., St. Mary Magdalen, c/o Rocksprings, TX, Sacred Heart of Mary Church. (SAT)
Campbell, NY, Steuben Co., St. Joseph, c/o Bradford, NY, St. Stanislaus Church. (ROC)
Campbellton, TX, Atascosa Co., Sacred Heart, c/o Pleasanton, TX, St. Andrew Church. (SAT)
Campobello, ME, St. Timothy's, c/o Lubec, ME, Sacred Heart Church. (PRT)
Campton, KY, Wolfe Co., Catholic Church of the Good Shepherd, c/o Beattyville, KY, Queen of All Saints Church. (LEX)
Canaan, NH, Grafton Co., St. Mary, c/o Enfield, NH, St. Helena Church. (MAN)
Canaan, PA, Wayne Co., St. Patrick, c/o Waymart, PA, St. Mary's Church. (SCR)
Canadohta Lake, PA, Crawford Co., Our Lady of Fatima, c/o Union City, PA, St. Teresa of Avila Church. (E)
Canalizo, PR, Jayuya Co., La Milagrosa, c/o Jayuya, PR, Our Lady of Monserrate Church. (PCE)
Candelaria, TX, Our Lady of Peace, c/o Presidio, TX, Santa Teresa de Jesus Church. (ELP)
Canjilon, NM, Rio Arriba Co., St. Juan Nepumoceno, c/o Chama, NM, St. Patrick Church. (SFE)
Cannon Ball, ND, Sioux Co., St. Elizabeth, c/o Fort Yates, ND, St. Peter - Catholic Indian Mission . (BIS)
Canon de Vallecitos, NM, Rio Arriba Co., c/o El Rito, NM, San Juan Nepomuceno Church. (SFE)
Canoncito, NM, Mora Co., c/o Mora, NM, St. Gertrude Church. (SFE)
Canoncito, NM, Santa Fe Co., c/o Pecos, NM, St. Anthony Church. (SFE)
Canoncito, NM, Bernalillo Co., c/o Tijeras, NM, Holy Child Church. (SFE)
Canones, NM, Rio Arriba Co., c/o Abiquiu, NM, St. Thomas Apostle Church. (SFE)
Canovanas, PR, Capilla Cristo Salvador, c/o [4] Canovanas, PR, Santa Maria Madre de Dios Church. (SJN)
Canovanas, PR, Ntra. Sra. de la Providencia, c/o [2] Canovanas, PR, Resurreccion del Senior Church. (SJN)
Canovanas, PR, San Francisco Javier, c/o [1] Canovanas, PR, Nuestra Senora del Pilar Church. (SJN)
Canton, NC, Haywood Co., Immaculate Conception, c/o Waynesville, NC, St. John the Evangelist Church. (CHL)
Cantwell, AK, c/o Healy, AK, Holy Mary of Guadalupe Church. (FBK)
Canyon, NM, Sandoval Co., c/o Jemez Pueblo, NM, San Diego Indian Missions Church. (SFE)
Canyon Ferry, MT, Our Lady of the Lake, c/o East Helena, MT, SS. Cyril and Methodius Church. (HEL)
Capitan, NM, Sacred Heart, c/o Carrizozo, NM, St. Rita Church. (LSC)
Capulin, NM, Rio Arriba Co., c/o Abiquiu, NM, St. Thomas Apostle Church. (SFE)
Carbondale, CO, Garfield Co., St. Mary of the Crown, c/o Basalt, CO, St. Vincent Church. (DEN)
Carenage, VI, Chapel of St. Anne, c/o [1] St. Thomas, VI, Cathedral of Sts. Peter and Paul. (STV)
Carey, OH, Wyandot Co., Our Lady of Consolation, c/o Salem Twp., OH, St. Joseph Church. (TOL)
Carlisle, TX, Lubbock Co., St. Theresa, c/o Shallowater, TX, St. Phillip Benizi Church. (LUB)
Carmen, PR, Our Lady of Mt. Carmel, c/o Guayama, PR, St. Anthony of Padua Church. (PCE)
Carnation, WA, King Co., St. Anthony, c/o Snoqualmie, WA, Our Lady of Sorrows Church. (SEA)
Carnegie, OK, Caddo Co., St. Richard, c/o Anadarko, OK, St. Patrick's Church. (OKL)
Carnuel, NM, Bernalillo Co., Holy Child, c/o Tijeras, NM, Holy Child Church. (SFE)
Caroga Lake, NY, St. Barbara, c/o Gloversville, NY, St. Mary of Mt. Carmel Church. (ALB)
Carolina, PR, c/o [8] Carolina, PR, San Fernando Church. (SJN)
Carolina, PR, Cristo Rey, c/o [18] Carolina, PR, Cristo Rey Church. (SJN)
Carolina, PR, La Sagrada Familia, c/o [12] Carolina, PR, San Juan de Dios Church. (SJN)
Carolina, PR, Parque Boliviano 5-JL, c/o [3] Carolina, PR, Santa Clara de Asis Church. (SJN)
Carolina, PR, San Antonio, c/o [20] Carolina, PR, San Valentin Church. (SJN)
Carolina, PR, San Francisco de Asis, c/o [3] Carolina, PR, Santa Clara de Asis Church. (SJN)
Carpenter, WY, Laramie Co., St. Peter, c/o Pine Bluffs, WY, St. Paul's Church. (CHY)
Carrissa Plains, CA, San Luis Obispo Co., St. James Mission, c/o Santa Margarita, CA, Santa Margarita de Cortona Church. (MRY)
Carrizales, PR, Ntra. Sra. de las Mercedes, c/o Aguada, PR, St. Francis of Assisi Church. (MGZ)
Carrizales, PR, Our Lady of Montserrat, c/o Yauco, PR, Holy Rossary Church. (PCE)
Carroll, NH, Coos Co., St. Patrick, c/o Whitefield, NH, St. Matthew Church. (MAN)
Carroll Township, IA, St. Wenceslaus, c/o Clutier, IA, Immaculate Conception Church. (DUB)
Carson, MS, Jefferson Davis Co., St. Elizabeth, c/o Bassfield, MS, St. Peter Church. (BLX)
Cartersville, IA, St. John, c/o Rockwell, IA, Sacred Heart Church. (DUB)
Casa Colorada, NM, Valencia Co., c/o Tome, NM, Immaculate Conception Church. (SFE)
Cascade, CO, El Paso Co., Holy Rosary, c/o [8] Colorado Springs, CO, Sacred Heart Church. (COS)
Cascade, MT, Sacred Heart, c/o Fort Shaw, MT, St. Ann Church. (GF)
Cascade, PA, Lycoming Co., Assumption of the B.V.M., c/o [6] Williamsport, PA, St. Ann's Church. (SCR)
Castine, ME, Hancock Co, Our Lady of Holy Hope, c/o Stonington, ME, St. Mary Star of the Sea Church. (PRT)
Catano, PR, Sector La Cucharilla, Immaculada Concepcion, c/o Catano, PR, San Francisco de Sales Church. (SJN)
Catano, PR, Maria Auxiliadora, c/o Catano, PR, San Francisco de Sales Church. (SJN)
Catano, PR, San Jose Obrero, c/o Catano, PR, Nuestra Senora del Carmen Church. (SJN)
Catano, PR, San Judas Tadeo (Santuario), c/o Catano, PR, San Francisco de Sales Church. (SJN)
Catano, PR, San Martin de Porres, c/o Catano, PR, Nuestra Senora del Carmen Church. (SJN)
Catano, PR, Santo Domingo, c/o Catano, PR, San Francisco de Sales Church. (SJN)
Catarina, TX, St. Henry, c/o Asherton, TX, Immaculate Conception Church. (LAR)
Catatonk, NY, Tioga Co., St. Francis of Assisi, c/o Newark Valley, NY, St. John the Evangelist Church. (ROC)
Cathlamet, WA, Wahkiakum Co., St. Catherine, c/o Longview, WA, St. Rose de Viterbo Church. (SEA)
Cave Junction, OR, Josephine Co., St. Patrick, c/o Grants Pass, OR, St. Anne Church. (P)
Cayuga, ND, Sargent Co., Sts. Peter & Paul, c/o Forman, ND, St. Mary's Church. (FAR)
Cazadero, CA, St. Colman, c/o Guerneville, CA, St. Elizabeth Church. (SR)
Cebolla, NM, Rio Arriba Co., Santo Nino, c/o Chama, NM, St. Patrick Church. (SFE)
Cedar Bluffs, NE, Saunders Co., St. Mary, c/o Colon, NE, St. Joseph's Church. (LIN)
Cedar Brook, NJ, Camden Co., Sacred Heart, c/o Blue Anchor, NJ, St. Lucy's Church. (CAM)
Cedar Creek, AZ, St. Anthony, c/o Cibecue, AZ, St. Catherine Church. (GLP)
Cedar Hill, NE, Saunders Co., Sacred Heart, c/o Morse Bluff, NE, St. George Church. (LIN)
Cedar Hill, TN, Robertson Co., St. Michael, c/o Springfield, TN, Our Lady of Lourdes Church. (NSH)
Cedaredge, CO, Delta Co., St. Philip Benizi, c/o Delta, CO, St. Michael Church. (PBL)
Cedarville, CA, Modoc Co., St. James, c/o Alturas, CA, Sacred Heart Church. (SAC)
Ceiba, PR, Sagrado Corazon de Jesus, Bo. Saco, c/o Ceiba, PR, San Antonio de Padua Church. (CGS)
Ceiba, PR, Ceiba Co., N.S. del Carmen, c/o Ceiba, PR, San Antonio de Padua Church. (CGS)
Celina, TN, Clay Co., Divine Savior, c/o Cookeville, TN, St. Thomas Aquinas Church. (NSH)

Center, MO, Ralls Co., St. Paul (Historic Church), c/o Perry, MO, St. William Church. (JC)
Center Barnstead, NH, Belknap Co., St. Paul, c/o Alton, NH, St. Joan of Arc Church. (MAN)
Center Harbor, NH, Belknap Co., Our Lady of Victory, c/o Meredith, NH, St. Charles Church. (MAN)
Centermoreland, PA, Luzerne Co., Blessed Sacrament, c/o Carverton, PA, St. Frances Cabrini Church. (SCR)
Centerville, TX, Leon Co., St. Leo the Great, c/o Crockett, TX, St. Francis of the Tejas Church. (TYL)
Central City, CO, Gilpin Co., St. Mary of the Assumption, c/o Idaho Springs, CO, St. Paul's Church. (DEN)
Centreville, MI, St. Clare, c/o Three Rivers, MI, Immaculate Conception Church. (KAL)
Cerrito, NM, San Miguel Co., c/o Villanueva, NM, Our Lady of Guadalupe Church. (SFE)
Cerro, NM, Taos Co., c/o Questa, NM, St. Anthony Church. (SFE)
Cerro Gordo, PR, Buen Consejo, c/o Aguada, PR, St. Francis of Assisi Church. (MGZ)
Chacon, NM, Mora Co., c/o Mora, NM, St. Gertrude Church. (SFE)
Chalan Kanoa Village, MP, Mercedarian Missionary Sisters of Berriz, c/o Chalan Kanoa Village, MP, Cathedral of Our Lady of Mt. Carmel. (CHK)
Challenge, CA, Yuba Co., St. Anthony, c/o Downieville, CA, Immaculate Conception Church. (SAC)
Chama, CO, Costilla Co., Immaculate Conception, c/o San Luis, CO, Sangre de Cristo Church. (PBL)
Chama, CO, Huerfano Co., Our Lady of Guadalupe, c/o Walsenburg, CO, St. Mary Church. (PBL)
Chamisal, NM, Taos Co., Santa Cruz Mission, c/o Penasco, NM, San Antonio de Padua Church. (SFE)
Chamita, NM, Rio Arriba Co., c/o San Juan Pueblo, NM, St. John the Baptist Church. (SFE)
Chaparral, NM, St. Thomas More, c/o Anthony, NM, St. Anthony's Church. (LSC)
Chapmanville, WV, Logan Co., St. Barbara, c/o Madison, WV, St. Mary, Queen of Heaven Church. (WH)
Charco, TX, Our Lady of Guadalupe, c/o Goliad, TX, Immaculate Conception Church. (VIC)
Charlemont, MA, Franklin Co., St. Christopher, c/o Shelburne Falls, MA, St. Joseph's Church. (SPR)
Charlestown, RI, Washington Co., St. James, c/o Charlestown, RI, St. Mary Church. (PRO)
Charley Creek, MT, St. Bernard's, c/o Sidney, MT, St. Matthew Church. (GF)
Charlo, MT, Mount Lake Co., St. Joseph's, c/o Ronan, MT, Sacred Heart Church. (HEL)
Chatom, AL, Washington Co., St. Paul, c/o Butler, AL, St. John The Evangelist Church. (MOB)
Cherokee, NC, Swain Co., Our Lady of Guadalupe, c/o Bryson City, NC, St. Joseph Church. (CHL)
Cherokee, OK, Alfalfa Co., St. Cornelius, c/o Alva, OK, Sacred Heart Church. (OKL)
Cherry Creek, SD, Ziebach Co., St. Joseph, c/o Eagle Butte, SD, All Saints Church. (RC)
Cherry Creek, SD, Ziebach Co., St. Joseph, c/o Eagle Butte, SD, Cheyenne River Reservation Church. (RC)
Cherryfield, ME, St. Michael's, c/o Machias, ME, Holy Name of Jesus Church. (PRT)
Chesapeake City, MD, Cecil Co., St. Rose of Lima, c/o Middletown, DE, St. Joseph Church. (WIL)
Chester, CA, Plumas Co., Christ the King, c/o Westwood, CA, Our Lady of the Snows Church. (SAC)
Chester, MA, Hampden Co., St. John, c/o Huntington, MA, St. Thomas Church. (SPR)
Chester, PA, Delaware Co., Saint Katharine Drexel Center for Evangelization, c/o [2] Chester, PA, Saint Katharine Drexel Church. (PH)
Chester, PA, Delaware Co., St. Hedwig Chapel, c/o Clifton Heights, PA, Sacred Heart Church. (PH)
Chesterfield, NH, Cheshire Co., Our Lady of the Lake, c/o Keene, NH, St. Margaret Mary Church. (MAN)
Chicago, IL, Cook Co., Holy Redeemer Church, c/o Chicago, IL, Ss. Peter and Paul Mission. (ROM)
Chicago, IL, Cook Co., Sacred Heart, c/o [81] Chicago, IL, Holy Name of Mary Church. (CHI)
Chichiltah, NM, Good Shepherd Catholic Mission, c/o Chichiltah, NM, St. Patrick Church. (GLP)
Childersburg, AL, Talladega Co., Holy Name of Jesus, c/o Sylacauga, AL, St. Jude Church. (BIR)
Chilili, NM, Bernalillo Co., San Juan de Nepumoceno, c/o Tijeras, NM, Holy Child Church. (SFE)
China Lake, ME, St. Peter, c/o North Vassalboro, ME, St. Bridget's Church. (PRT)
Chino Valley, AZ, Yavapai Co., St. Catherine Laboure, c/o Prescott, AZ, Sacred Heart Church. (PHX)
Chippewa Lake, OH, Medina Co., Jesus Divine Redeemer, c/o Litchfield, OH, Our Lady Help of Christians Parish Church. (CLV)
Chireno, TX, Nacogdoches Co., Our Lady of Lourdes, c/o Nacogdoches, TX, Sacred Heart Church. (TYL)
Chocorua, NH, Carroll Co., Our Lady of Perpetual Help, c/o Center Ossipee, NH, St. Joseph Church. (MAN)
Choctaw, LA, St. James, c/o Kraemer, LA, St. Lawrence the Martyr Church. (HT)
Christine, TX, Ataseosa Co., St. Ignatius, c/o Jourdanton, TX, St. Matthew's Church. (SAT)
Christmas Valley, OR, Holy Family, c/o La Pine, OR, Holy Redeemer Church. (BAK)
Chualar, CA, Monterey Co., Chualar Mission, c/o Gonzales, CA, St. Theodore Church. (MRY)
Chugwater, WY, Platte Co., Mary Queen of Heaven, c/o Wheatland, WY, St. Patrick's Church. (CHY)
Cincinnatus, NY, Our Lady of Perpetual Help, c/o Marathon, NY, St. Stephen Church. (SY)
Citra, FL, Marion Co., Christ the King, c/o Candler, FL, Immaculate Heart of Mary Church. (ORL)
Clallam Bay, WA, Clallam Co., St. Thomas the Apostle, c/o Forks, WA, St. Anne Parish Church. (SEA)
Clancy, MT, St. John's, c/o East Helena, MT, SS. Cyril and Methodius Church. (HEL)
Clanton, AL, Chilton Co., Church of the Resurrection, c/o Montevallo, AL, St. Thomas the Apostle Church. (BIR)
Claremont, VA, St. Anne, c/o Hopewell, VA, St. James Church. (RIC)
Clark, WY, Park Co., Our Lady of the Valley, c/o Powell, WY, St. Barbara Church. (CHY)
Clarkdale, AZ, Yavapai Co., St. Cecilia, c/o Cottonwood, AZ, Immaculate Conception Church. (PHX)
Clarksville, MO, Pike Co., Mary Queen of Peace, c/o Louisiana, MO, St. Joseph Church. (JC)
Clatskanie, OR, Columbia Co., St. John the Baptist, c/o Rainier, OR, Nativity B.V.M. Church. (P)
Claudell, KS, Smith Co., St. Francis, c/o Phillipsburg, KS, SS. Philip and James Church. (SAL)
Claybanks, MI, St. John, c/o Montague, MI, St. James Church. (GR)
Claypool, AZ, Gila Co., St. Joseph, c/o Miami, AZ, Our Lady of the Blessed Sacrament Church. (TUC)
Clayton, AL, Barbour Co., Ventress Correctional Facility, c/o Eufaula, AL, Holy Redeemer Church. (MOB)
Clayton, GA, Rabun Co., St. Helena, c/o Clarkesville, GA, St. Mark Church. (ATL)
Clayton, OK, Pushmataha Co., Holy Trinity, c/o Antlers, OK, St. Agnes Church. (TLS)
Clear Lake, IN, Steuben Co., St. Paul Chapel, c/o Angola, IN, St. Anthony Church. (FTW)
Clear Spring, MD, Washington Co., St. Michael, c/o Williamsport, MD, St. Augustine Church. (BAL)
Clearmont, WY, Johnson Co., St. Mary, c/o Buffalo, WY, St. John the Baptist Church. (CHY)
Clendenin, WV, Kanawha Co., St. Anne, c/o Elkview, WV, Our Lady of the Hills Church. (WH)
Cleveland, GA, White Co., St. Paul the Apostle, c/o Blairsville, GA, St. Francis of Assisi Church. (ATL)
Cleveland, NM, Mora Co., c/o Mora, NM, St. Gertrude Church. (SFE)
Cleveland, OH, c/o [56] Cleveland, OH, Our Lady of Mount Carmel Church. (CLV)
Clifford, MI, Lapeer Co., St. Patrick's, c/o North Branch, MI, SS. Peter and Paul Church. (DET)
Clifton, AZ, Greenlee Co., St. Mary, c/o Clifton, AZ, Sacred Heart Church. (TUC)
Climax Springs, MO, Camden Co., Our Lady of the Snows, c/o Hermitage, MO, St. Bernadette Church. (JC)
Clinton Corners, NY, Dutchess Co., St. Joseph, c/o Bangall, NY, Immaculate Conception Church. (NY)
Clintonville, NY, St. Catherine of Sienna, c/o Keeseville, NY, Church of the Immaculate Conception. (OG)
Cloquet, MN, Carlton Co., Holy Family Church, c/o Duluth, MN, Indian Missions Church. (DUL)
Cloudcroft, NM, Sacred Heart, c/o Alamogordo, NM, Immaculate Conception Church. (LSC)
Cloverdale, OR, Tillamook Co., St. Joseph, c/o Tillamook, OR, Sacred Heart Church. (P)
Clyde, TX, Callahan Co., Sts. Joachim and Ann, c/o [1] Abilene, TX, Sacred Heart Church. (SAN)
Clyde Park, MT, St. Margaret, c/o Livingston, MT, St. Mary's Church. (GF)
Coabbey, PR, Jayuya Co., San Jorge, c/o Jayuya, PR, Our Lady of Monserrate Church. (PCE)
Coal Mine, TX, Atascosa Co., Immaculate Conception, c/o Lytle, TX, St. Andrew Church. (SAT)
Coalburg, WV, Kanawha Co., Good Shepherd, c/o Belle, WV, St. John Church. (WH)
Coaldale, PA, Schuylkill Co., St. Patrick (Seek), c/o Tamaqua, PA, St. Jerome Church. (ALN)
Coamo, PR, Coamo Co., Saint James, c/o Coamo, PR, St. Blase Church. (PCE)
Coamo Arriba, PR, Coamo Co., Sacred Heart, c/o Coamo, PR, St. Blase Church. (PCE)
Cochiti, NM, Sandoval Co., Indian Pueblo, c/o Pena Blanca, NM, Nuestra Senora De Guadalupe Church. (SFE)
Cochranton, PA, Crawford Co., Our Lady of Lourdes, c/o Frenchtown, PA, St. Hippolyte Church. (E)
Coco, PR, Santa Ana, c/o Salinas, PR, Our Lady of Monserrat Church. (PCE)
Cocodrie, LA, Our Lady of the Gulf, c/o Chauvin, LA, St. Joseph Church. (HT)
Coeburn, VA, Wise Co., St. Mary, c/o Norton, VA, St. Anthony Church. (RIC)
Coffman Cove, AK, c/o Craig, AK, St. John by the Sea Church. (JUN)
Cogswell, ND, Sargent Co., Our Lady of Mercy, c/o Forman, ND, St. Mary's Church. (FAR)
Cohasset, MN, St. Augustine, c/o Deer River, MN, St. Mary's Church. (DUL)
Cohoes, NY, Sacred Heart of Jesus, c/o [7] Cohoes, NY, St. Rita-Sacred Heart Church. (ALB)
Cokeville, WY, Lincoln Co., St. Dominic, c/o Kemmerer, WY, St. Patrick's Church. (CHY)
Cole Camp, MO, Benton Co., SS. Peter & Paul, c/o Warsaw, MO, St. Ann Church. (JC)
Collares, PR, Jayuya Co., Cristo Rey, c/o Jayuya, PR, Our Lady of Monserrate Church. (PCE)
Collegeville, AL, Jefferson Co., Sacred Heart, c/o [19] Birmingham, AL, Our Lady Queen of the Universe Church. (BIR)
Collores, PR, Bo. Jacaguas, La Milagrosa, c/o Juana Diaz, PR, St. Raymond Nonato Church. (PCE)
Collores, PR, Sacred Heart, c/o Yauco, PR, Holy Rossary Church. (PCE)
Colon, MI, St. Joseph Co., St. Barbara, c/o Bronson, MI, St. Mary's Church. (KAL)
Colonia Nueva, TX, Christ the King, c/o Donna, TX, St. Joseph Church. (BWN)
Colonia Villodos, PR, Perpetuo Socorro, c/o Guayama, PR, St. Anthony of Padua Church. (PCE)
Colonias, NM, Guadalupe Co., c/o Santa Rosa, NM, St. Rose of Lima Church. (SFE)
Colrain, MA, Franklin Co., St. John the Baptist, c/o Shelburne Falls, MA, St. Joseph's Church. (SPR)
Columbia, AL, Houston Co., Good Shepherd, c/o Dothan, AL, St. Columba Church. (MOB)
Columbia, CA, Tuolumne Co., St. Anne, c/o Sonora, CA, St. Patrick Church. (STO)
Columbia, KY, Adair Co., Good Shepherd, c/o Jamestown, KY, Holy Spirit Church. (L)
Columbia, LA, St. John, c/o Winnsboro, LA, St. Mary Church. (ALX)
Columbia, NC, Tyrrell, All Souls, c/o Edenton, NC, St. Anne Church. (R)
Comal, TX, Comal Co., St. Joseph, c/o New Braunfels, TX, SS. Peter and Paul Church. (SAT)
Commerce, GA, Jackson Co., St. Catherine Laboure, c/o Toccoa, GA, St. Mary's Church. (ATL)
Comstock, TX, Valverde Co., Mary, Queen of the Universe, c/o Del Rio, TX, Sacred Heart Church. (SAT)
Concepcion, TX, Duval Co., Immaculate Conception, c/o Premont, TX, St. Theresa of the Infant Jesus Church. (CC)
Concrete, WA, Skagit Co., St. Catherine, c/o Sedro Woolley, WA, Immaculate Heart of Mary Church. (SEA)
Conde Avila, PR, St. Martin de Porres, c/o Cabo Rojo, PR, St. Michael Church. (MGZ)
Conehatta, MS, St. Catherine, c/o Philadelphia, MS, Holy Rosary Church. (JKS)
Conesus, NY, Livingston Co., St. William, c/o Livonia, NY, St. Joseph Church. (ROC)
Congress Junction, AZ, Yavapai Co., Good Shepherd of the Desert, c/o Prescott, AZ, Sacred Heart Church. (PHX)
Consejo Alto, PR, La Monserrate, c/o Guayanilla, PR, Immaculate Conception Church. (PCE)
Constantia, NY, Oswego Co., St. Bernadette, c/o Cleveland, NY, St. Mary of the Assumption Church. (SY)
Contoocook, NH, Merrimack Co., St. Mary, c/o Henniker, NH, St. Theresa Church. (MAN)
Contreras, NM, Socorro Co., San Jose, c/o La Joya, NM, Our Lady of Sorrows Church. (SFE)
Conway, MA, Franklin Co., St. Mark, c/o South Deerfield, MA, St. James Church. (SPR)
Conway, ND, Walsh Co., St. Marks, c/o Pisek, ND, St. John Nepomucene Church. (FAR)
Conway, NH, Carroll Co., St. Charles Borromeo, c/o North Conway, NH, Our Lady of the Mountains Church. (MAN)
Cookson, OK, Cherokee Co., St. John the Evangelist, c/o Sallisaw, OK, St. Francis Xavier Church. (TLS)
Cooper, TX, Delta Co., St. Clare Mission, c/o Sulphur Springs, TX, St. James Church. (TYL)
Cooper Landing, AK, St. John Neumann Church, c/o Seward, AK, Sacred Heart Church. (ANC)
Copper Harbor, MI, Keweenaw Co., Our Lady of the Pines, c/o Ahmeek, MI, Our Lady of Peace Church. (MAR)
Coqui, PR, Our Lady of Perpetual Help, c/o Aguirre, PR, Sacred Heart Church. (PCE)
Coral, MI, St. Clara, c/o Sand Lake, MI, Mary Queen of Apostles Church. (GR)
Cordell, OK, Washita Co., St. Anne, c/o Clinton, OK, St. Mary's Church. (OKL)
Cordova, MD, Talbot Co., St. Joseph, c/o Easton, MD, SS. Peter and Paul Church. (WIL)
Cordova, NM, Rio Arriba Co., San Antonio, c/o Chimayo, NM, Holy Family Church. (SFE)
Corning, AR, Clay Co., St. Joseph, c/o Engelberg, AR, St. John the Baptist Church. (LR)
Corning, AR, Clay Co., St. Joseph, c/o Paragould, AR, St. Mary's Church. (LR)
Corona, NM, St. Therese of the Little Flower, c/o Carrizozo, NM, St. Rita Church. (LSC)

Corozal, PR, San Antonio, c/o Penuelas, PR, St. Joseph Church. (PCE)
Corpus Christi, TX, Nueces Co., Mary, Mother of the Church, c/o [4] Corpus Christi, TX, Holy Family Church. (CC)
Corpus Christi, TX, Nueces Co., Our Lady of Mount Carmel, c/o [7] Corpus Christi, TX, Our Lady of the Rosary Church. (CC)
Corpus Christi, TX, Nueces Co., St. Mary, c/o [19] Corpus Christi, TX, St. Peter Prince of Apostles Church. (CC)
Corral, PR, P. Socorro, c/o Juana Diaz, PR, St. Raymond Nonato Church. (PCE)
Costilla, NM, Taos Co., c/o Questa, NM, St. Anthony Church. (SFE)
Cotton City, NM, St. Jude, c/o Lordsburg, NM, St. Joseph Church. (LSC)
Cottonwood, CA, Shasta Co., St. Anne, c/o Anderson, CA, Sacred Heart Church. (SAC)
Cottonwood, MT, St. John the Baptist, c/o Havre, MT, St. Jude Thaddeus Church. (GF)
Cotuy, PR, Our Lady of Fatima, c/o San German, PR, San German de Auxerre Church. (MGZ)
Coulee City, WA, Grant Co., Holy Angels, c/o Hartline, WA, St. Patrick's Church. (YAK)
Coupeville, WA, Island Co., St. Mary, c/o Oak Harbor, WA, St. Augustine Church. (SEA)
Coushatta, LA, Red River Parish, St. George, c/o Bossier City, LA, Mary, Queen of Peace Church. (SHP)
Covelo, CA, Queen of Peace, c/o Willits, CA, St. Anthony Church. (SR)
Covington, KY, Kenton Co., St. Ann, c/o [6] Covington, KY, St. John Church. (COV)
Cox, SD, Harding Co., St. Agnes, c/o Buffalo, SD, St. Anthony Church. (RC)
Coyanosa, TX, Pecos Co., St. Isidore, c/o Fort Stockton, TX, St. Agnes Church. (SAN)
Coyote, NM, Rio Arriba Co., c/o Abiquiu, NM, St. Thomas Apostle Church. (SFE)
Craftsbury, VT, Orleans Co., Our Lady of Fatima, c/o Hardwick, VT, St. Norbert Church. (BUR)
Crane, OR, St. Thomas, c/o Burns, OR, Holy Family Church. (BAK)
Cranfield, MS, St. John the Baptist, c/o Natchez, MS, Holy Family Church. (JKS)
Crates, PA, Clarion Co., St. Nicholas, c/o New Bethlehem, PA, St. Charles Church. (E)
Crawfordsville, AR, Crittenden Co., Sacred Heart, c/o West Memphis, AR, St. Michael's Church. (LR)
Creede, CO, Mineral Co., Immaculate Conception, c/o Del Norte, CO, Holy Name of Mary Church. (PBL)
Crescent, OK, Logan Co., St. Margaret Mary, c/o Guthrie, OK, St. Mary's Church. (OKL)
Crescent City, IL, Iroquois Co., St. Joseph, c/o Watseka, IL, St. Edmund Church. (JOL)
Creswell, OR, Lane Co., St. Philip Benizi, c/o Cottage Grove, OR, Our Lady of Perpetual Help Church. (P)
Cripple Creek, CO, Teller Co., St. Peter's, c/o Woodland Park, CO, Our Lady of the Woods Church. (COS)
Cristo Rey, TX, La Victoria, c/o Grulla, TX, Holy Family Church. (BWN)
Crittenden, NY, Erie Co., St. Patrick, c/o Corfu, NY, St. Francis of Assisi Church. (BUF)
Crockett Co., TN, c/o Humboldt, TN, Sacred Heart Church. (MEM)
Croghan, NY, Belfort, St. Vincent de Paul, c/o Croghan, NY, St. Stephen Church. (OG)
Croghan, NY, New Bremen, St. Peter, c/o Croghan, NY, St. Stephen Church. (OG)
Cromwell-Wright, MN, Carlton Co., Immaculate Conception, c/o Floodwood, MN, St. Louis Church. (DUL)
Crook, CO, Logan Co., St. Peters, c/o Julesburg, CO, St. Anthony Church. (DEN)
Crosbyton, TX, Crosby Co., St. Joseph, c/o Ralls, TX, St. Michael Church. (LUB)
Cross City, FL, Dixie Co., Holy Cross, c/o Chiefland, FL, St. John the Evangelist Church. (STA)
Crosstown, MO, Perry Co., St. James, c/o Perryville, MO, St. Vincent De Paul Church. (STL)
Crows Landing, CA, Stanislaus Co., Immaculate Heart of Mary, c/o Patterson, CA, Sacred Heart Church. (STO)
Cruces, PR, Santa Monica, c/o Aguada, PR, St. Francis of Assisi Church. (MGZ)
Crystal, ND, Pembina Co., St. Patrick, c/o Park River, ND, St. Mary's Church. (FAR)
Crystal Beach, TX, Galveston Co., St. Therese of Lisieux, c/o Port Bolivar, TX, Our Mother of Mercy Church. (GAL)
Cuadrilla, TX, San Jose, c/o Fabens, TX, Our Lady of Guadalupe Church. (ELP)
Cuba, OH, Putnam Co., St. Isidore, c/o Kalida, OH, St. Michael Church. (TOL)
Cube Cove, AK, c/o Yakutat, AK, St. Ann Church. (JUN)
Cuchillo, NM, Sierra Co., St. Joseph, c/o Truth or Consequences, NM, Our Lady of Perpetual Help Church. (LSC)
Cuervo, NM, Guadalupe Co., c/o Santa Rosa, NM, St. Rose of Lima Church. (SFE)
Cummiskey, PA, Sullivan Co., St. Francis of Assisi, c/o Dushore, PA, St. Basil's Church. (SCR)
Cundiyo, NM, Rio Arriba Co., Santo Domingo, c/o Chimayo, NM, Holy Family Church. (SFE)
Cuny Table, SD, Shannon Co., St. Joseph, c/o Pine Ridge, SD, Holy Rosary Church. (RC)
Cupey, PR, San Martin de Porres, c/o [58] San Juan, PR, Santa Teresa Jornet Church. (SJN)
Cupey, PR, Virgen de la Salud, c/o [58] San Juan, PR, Santa Teresa Jornet Church. (SJN)
Curtis, MI, Mackinac Co., St. Timothy, c/o Grand Marais, MI, Holy Rosary Church. (MAR)
Custer, MT, St. Mary, c/o Hardin, MT, St. Joseph's Church. (GF)
Cuthbert, GA, Randolph Co., St. Luke, c/o Blakely, GA, Holy Family Church. (SAV)
Cygnet, OH, Wood Co., Sacred Heart, c/o North Baltimore, OH, Our Lady of the Miraculous Medal Church. (TOL)

D

Dahlia, NM, Guadalupe Co., c/o Anton Chico, NM, San Jose Church. (SFE)
Dallas, GA, Paulding Co., St. Vincent de Paul, c/o Lithia Springs, GA, St. John Vianney Church. (ATL)
Dallas City, IL, Hancock Co., Sacred Heart, c/o Nauvoo, IL, SS. Peter and Paul's Church. (PEO)
Dalton, NE, Cheyenne Co., St. Mary, c/o Bridgeport, NE, All Souls Church. (GI)
Danby, VT, Rutland Co., Holy Trinity, c/o East Dorset, VT, St. Jerome Church. (BUR)
Danby, VT, Rutland Co., Holy Trinity, c/o Manchester Center, VT, Conversion of St. Paul Church. (BUR)
Danforth, ME, St. Ann, c/o Lincoln, ME, St. Mary Church. (PRT)
Dansville, NY, Holy Family Catholic Community, c/o Dansville, NY, St. Mary Church. (ROC)
Danville, KS, Harper Co., c/o Harper, KS, St. Joan of Arc Church. (WCH)
Danville, VT, Caledonia Co., Our Lady Queen of Peace, c/o Lyndonville, VT, St. Elizabeth Church. (BUR)
Darby, MT, Ravalli Co., St. Philip Benizi, c/o Hamilton, MT, St. Francis Church. (HEL)
Dardanelle, AR, Yell Co., St. Augustine, c/o Atkins, AR, Assumption B.V.M. Church. (LR)
Darien, GA, McIntosh Co., Nativity of Our Lady, c/o Brunswick, GA, St. Francis Xavier Church. (SAV)
Darlington, SC, Darlington Co., St. Joseph the Worker, c/o Hartsville, SC, St. Mary the Virgin Mother Church. (CHR)
Darrington, WA, Snohomish Co., St. John Mary Vianney, c/o Arlington, WA, Immaculate Conception Church. (SEA)
David City, NE, Butler Co., Assumption, c/o David City, NE, St. Mary's Church. (LIN)
Dawsonville, GA, Dawson Co., Christ Redeemer, c/o Dahlonega, GA, St. Luke Catholic Church. (ATL)
Dayton, OR, Yamhill Co., St. Martin de Porres, c/o McMinnville, OR, St. James Church. (P)
Daytona Beach, FL, c/o Apopka, FL, St. Mary's Church. (SJP)
Dazey, ND, Barnes Co., St. Mary, c/o Sanborn, ND, Sacred Heart Church. (FAR)
De Bruce, NY, Sullivan Co., Sacred Heart, c/o Livingston Manor, NY, St. Aloysius Church. (NY)
De Ridder, LA, Beauregard Parish, St. Jude, c/o De Ridder, LA, St. Joseph's Church. (LKC)
Decatur, NE, Burt Co., Holy Family, c/o Tekamah, NE, St. Patrick Church. (OM)
Deerfield, KS, Kearny Co., Christ the King, c/o Garden City, KS, St. Mary Church. (DOD)
Deerwood, MN, St. Joseph, c/o Crosby, MN, St. Joseph's Church. (DUL)
Del City, OK, Mission Co., c/o [9] Oklahoma City, OK, St. Paul, Apostle Church. (OKL)
Del Rey, CA, Fresno Co., St. Katherine's, c/o Sanger, CA, St. Mary Church. (FRS)
Del Rio, TX, San Juan Diego Chapel, c/o Del Rio, TX, Our Lady of Guadalupe Church. (SAT)
Delhi, CA, Merced Co., Teresa of Calcutta, c/o Livingston, CA, St. Jude Thaddeus Church. (FRS)
Delhi, LA, Richland Parish, St. Theresa, c/o Rayville, LA, Sacred Heart Church. (SHP)
Dell City, TX, San Isidro, c/o Van Horn, TX, Our Lady of Fatima Church. (ELP)
Delmar, MD, Wicomico Co., Holy Redeemer, c/o Salisbury, MD, St. Francis De Sales Church. (WIL)
Delmas Dedeaux, MS, Harrison Co., Our Lady of Chartres, c/o [1] Gulfport, MS, St. Ann Church. (BLX)
Delta, UT, Millard Co., St. John Bosco, c/o Milford, UT, St. Bridget Church. (SLC)
Deming, NM, Luna Co., Holy Family, c/o Deming, NM, St. Ann's Church. (LSC)
Deming, WA, Whatcom Co., St. Peter, c/o Lynden, WA, St. Joseph Church. (SEA)
Denmark, WI, All Saints, c/o New Denmark, WI, Holy Trinity Church. (GB)
Denmark, WI, New Denmark, Holy Trinity, c/o Denmark, WI, All Saints Church. (GB)
Dennis Port, MA, Barnstable Co., Our Lady of the Annunciation, c/o West Harwich, MA, Holy Trinity Church. (FR)
Denton, MD, Caroline Co., St. Elizabeth, c/o Ridgely, MD, St. Benedict Church. (WIL)
Denton, MT, St. Anthony, c/o Stanford, MT, St. Rose of Lima Church. (GF)
Denver, CO, Denver Co., St. Elizabeth of Hungary, c/o [12] Denver, CO, Holy Ghost Church. (DEN)
Dermott, AR, Chicot Co., Nativity of the Blessed Virgin Mary, c/o McGehee, AR, St. Mary Church. (LR)
DeRuyter, NY, St. Lawrence, c/o Truxton, NY, St. Patrick Church. (SY)
Des Moines, IA, Polk Co., Our Lady of Guadalupe, c/o [13] Des Moines, IA, Visitation Church. (DM)
Des Moines, NM, Union Co., Our Lady of Guadalupe, c/o Clayton, NM, St. Francis Xavier Church. (SFE)
Detroit, OR, Marion Co., St. Christopher, c/o Sublimity, OR, St. Boniface Church. (P)
Deweese, NE, Clay Co., Assumption, c/o Lawrence, NE, Sacred Heart Church. (LIN)
Dexter, NY, Jefferson Co., St. Elizabeth Seton, c/o Brownville, NY, Immaculate Conception of the B.V.M. Church. (OG)
Dexter, OR, Lane Co., St. Henry, c/o Oakridge, OR, St. Michael Church. (P)
Dickey, ND, LaMoure Co., Assumption, c/o La Moure, ND, Holy Rosary Church. (FAR)
Diego Hdez, PR, St. Anthony, c/o Yauco, PR, Holy Rossary Church. (PCE)
Diener Ranch At Five Points, CA, Fresno Co., Holy Family Chapel, c/o Riverdale, CA, St. Ann Church. (FRS)
Dilia, NM, Guadalupe Co., c/o Anton Chico, NM, San Jose Church. (SFE)
Dilley, TX, Frio Co., St. Mary, c/o Dilley, TX, St. Joseph's Church. (SAT)
Dillon Valley, CO, Summit Co., Our Lady of Peace, c/o Breckenridge, CO, St. Mary Church. (DEN)
Dilworth, MN, Clay Co., St. Elizabeth, c/o Lake Park, MN, St. Francis Xavier's Church. (CR)
Dimmick Township, IL, Sacred Heart, c/o [3] La Salle, IL, Resurrection Church. (PEO)
Diomede, AK, St. Jude, c/o Nome, AK, St. Joseph Church. (FBK)
Dividing Ridge, KY, Pendleton Co., St. John's, c/o Williamstown, KY, St. William Church. (COV)
Dixfield, ME, St. Joseph, c/o Mexico, ME, St. Theresa Church. (PRT)
Dixon, NE, Dixon Co., St. Anne, c/o Laurel, NE, St. Mary Church. (OM)
Dobbins, CA, Yuba Co., Sacred Heart Church, c/o Marysville, CA, St. Joseph Church. (SAC)
Dobson, NC, Surry Co., Sacred Heart, c/o Mount Airy, NC, Holy Angels Church. (CHL)
Dockton, WA, King Co., St. Patrick, c/o Vashon, WA, St. John Vianney Church. (SEA)
Dodson, MT, Sacred Heart, c/o Malta, MT, St. Mary's Church. (GF)
Dodson, MT, St. Thomas, c/o Hays, MT, St. Paul's Indian Mission. (GF)
Doe Run, PA, Chester Co., St. Malachy, c/o Parkesburg, PA, Our Lady of Consolation Church. (PH)
Dolan Springs, AZ, Mohave Co., Our Lady of the Desert, c/o Kingman, AZ, St. Mary's Church. (PHX)
Dollar Bay, MI, Houghton Co., St. Francis of Assisi, c/o Hancock, MI, Resurrection Church. (MAR)
Dolores, CO, Montezuma Co., Our Lady of Victory Church, c/o Mancos, CO, St. Rita Church. (PBL)
Donalsonville, GA, Seminole Co., Church of the Incarnation, c/o Bainbridge, GA, St. Joseph's Church. (SAV)
Donken, MI, Houghton Co., Immaculate Heart of Mary, c/o Chassell, MI, St. Anne Church. (MAR)
Donnybrook, ND, Ward Co., St. Anthony, c/o Kenmare, ND, St. Agnes Church. (BIS)
Doraville, GA, Dekalb Co., Our Lady of the Americas, c/o [4] Atlanta, GA, Immaculate Heart of Mary Church. (ATL)
Dorothy, NJ, Atlantic Co., St. Bernard, c/o Mays Landing, NJ, St. Vincent de Paul Church. (CAM)
Dorrance, KS, Russell Co., St. Joseph, c/o Wilson, KS, St. Wenceslaus Church. (SAL)
Dorris, CA, Siskiyou Co., Our Lady of Good Counsel, c/o Tulelake, CA, Holy Cross Church. (SAC)
Douglas, NE, Otoe Co., St. Martin's, c/o Palmyra, NE, St. Leo's Church. (LIN)
Dove Creek, CO, Dolores Co., St. Jude, c/o Cortez, CO, St. Margaret Mary Church. (PBL)
Downey, CA, Los Angeles Co., Los Padrinos Juvenile Hall, c/o Downey, CA, St. Raymond Church. (LA)
Downey, CA, Los Angeles Co., Rancho Los Amigos Hospital, c/o Downey, CA, St. Raymond Church. (LA)
Downs, KS, Osborne Co., St. Mary's, c/o Osborne, KS, St. Aloysius Church. (SAL)

Downsville, NY, Delaware Co., Holy Family, c/o Walton, NY, St. John the Baptist Church. (ALB)
Doylesburg, PA, Franklin Co., Our Lady of Refuge, c/o Chambersburg, PA, Corpus Christi Church. (HBG)
Doyline, LA, Webster Parish, Mary, Queen of the Holy Rosary, c/o Bossier City, LA, Christ the King Church. (SHP)
Drain, OR, Douglas Co., St. John the Apostle, c/o Sutherlin, OR, St. Francis Xavier Church. (P)
Drake, ND, McHenry Co., St. Margaret Mary, c/o Anamoose, ND, St. Francis Xavier Church. (FAR)
Draper, SD, Jones Co., St. Anthony of Padua, c/o Presho, SD, Christ the King Church. (RC)
Drew, SD, Perkins Co., St. James, c/o Bison, SD, Blessed Sacrament Church. (RC)
Drewsey, OR, Our Lady of Loretto, c/o Burns, OR, Holy Family Church. (BAK)
Drifting, PA, Clearfield Co., St. Severin, c/o Frenchville, PA, St. Mary of the Assumption Church. (E)
Driftwood, PA, Cameron Co., St. James, c/o Emporium, PA, St. Mark Church. (E)
Driscoll, TX, Nueces Co., St. James, c/o Bishop, TX, St. James Church. (CC)
Drummond Island, MI, Chippewa Co., St. Florence, c/o DeTour, MI, Sacred Heart Church. (MAR)
Drumright, OK, Creek Co., St. Mary, c/o Cushing, OK, SS. Peter and Paul Church. (TLS)
Dubina, TX, Fayette Co., SS. Cyril and Methodius, c/o Weimar, TX, St. Michael Church. (VIC)
Dublin, NH, Our Lady of the Snows, c/o Harrisville, NH, St. Denis Church. (MAN)
Dubois, WY, Fremont Co., Our Lady of the Woods, c/o Riverton, WY, St. Margaret's Church. (CHY)
Dubuisson, MS, Harrison Co., St. Ann, c/o DeLisle, MS, The Catholic Church in DeLisle Church. (BLX)
Duchesne, UT, Duchesne Co., Holy Spirit, c/o Roosevelt, UT, St. Helen's Church. (SLC)
Duey, PR, Chapel of St. Augustin, c/o San German, PR, San German de Auxerre Church. (MGZ)
Duey, PR, Virgin of Mt. Carmel, c/o Yauco, PR, Holy Rossary Church. (PCE)
Dulce, NM, Rio Arriba Co., St. Anthony, c/o Lumberton, NM, St. Francis of Assisi Church. (GLP)
Dumas, AR, Desha Co., Holy Child, c/o McGehee, AR, St. Mary Church. (LR)
Duncannon, PA, Perry Co., St. Bernadette, c/o Marysville, PA, Our Lady of Good Counsel Church. (HBG)
Dundee, NY, Yates Co., St. Andrew, c/o Penn Yan, NY, St. Michael Church. (ROC)
Dungannon, VA, St. Patrick, c/o Gate City, VA, St. Bernard Church. (RIC)
Dupree, SD, Ziebach Co., Sacred Heart, c/o Eagle Butte, SD, All Saints Church. (RC)
Dupree, SD, Ziebach Co., Sacred Heart, c/o Eagle Butte, SD, Cheyenne River Reservation Church. (RC)
Dupuyer, MT, Pondera Co., Holy Cross, c/o Valier, MT, St. Francis Church. (HEL)
Duran, NM, Torrance Co., c/o Vaughn, NM, St. Mary Church. (SFE)
Durham, CA, Butte Co., St. James, c/o Chico, CA, St. John the Baptist Church. (SAC)
Duvall, WA, King Co., Holy Innocents, c/o Snoqualmie, WA, Our Lady of Sorrows Church. (SEA)

E

E. Huntsville, OH, Logan Co., St. George Chapel Marianists of Ohio, c/o Russells Point, OH, St. Mary of the Woods Church. (CIN)
Eagle, CO, Eagle Co., St. Mary, c/o Edwards, CO, St. Clare of Assisi Church. (DEN)
Eagle Harbor, MI, Keweenaw Co., Holy Redeemer, c/o Ahmeek, MI, Our Lady of Peace Church. (MAR)
Eagle Nest, NM, Colfax Co., St. Mel, c/o Cimarron, NM, Immaculate Conception Church. (SFE)
Eagles Mere, PA, Sullivan Co., St. Francis of Assisi, c/o Dushore, PA, St. Basil's Church. (SCR)
Eagles Mere, PA, Sullivan Co., St. Francis of Assisi, c/o Mildred, PA, St. Francis of Assisi Church. (SCR)
Eagleville, CT, Tolland Co., St. Joseph, c/o Coventry, CT, St. Mary Church. (NOR)
Earth, TX, Lamb Co., St. Mary Magdalen, c/o Muleshoe, TX, Immaculate Conception Church. (LUB)
Easley, SC, Anderson Co., St. Luke, c/o Pickens, SC, Holy Cross Church. (CHR)
East Barre, VT, Washington Co., St.Cecilia & St. Frances Cabrini, c/o Graniteville, VT, St. Sylvester Church. (BUR)
East Berkshire, VT, Franklin Co., Our Lady of Lourdes, c/o Richford, VT, All Saints Church. (BUR)
East Brewster, MA, Barnstable Co., Immaculate Conception, c/o Brewster, MA, Our Lady of the Cape Church. (FR)
East Dorset, VT, Bennington Co., St. Jerome, c/o Manchester Center, VT, Conversion of St. Paul Church. (BUR)
East Durham, NY, Greene Co., Our Lady of Knock Shrine, c/o Cairo, NY, Sacred Heart Church. (ALB)
East Durham, NY, Greene Co., St. Mary, c/o Cairo, NY, Sacred Heart Church. (ALB)
East Fairfield, VT, Franklin Co., St. Anthony-St. George, c/o Fairfield, VT, St. Patrick Church. (BUR)
East Glacier, MT, Church of the Ascension, c/o Browning, MT, Church of the Little Flower. (HEL)
East Highlands, CA, San Bernardino Co., St. John Bosco, c/o Highland, CA, St. Adelaide Church. (SB)
East Killingly, CT, Windham Co., Our Lady of Peace, c/o Danielson, CT, St. James Church. (NOR)
East Longmeadow, MA, Hampden Co., St. Joseph's, c/o [18] Springfield, MA, St. Paul Church. (SPR)
East Otto, NY, Cattaraugus Co., St. Isidore, c/o Cattaraugus, NY, St. Mary Church. (BUF)
East Quogue, NY, Suffolk Co., c/o Hampton Bays, NY, St. Rosalie's Church. (RVC)
East Raymond, ME, St. Raymond Chapel, c/o Windham, ME, Our Lady of Perpetual Help Church. (PRT)
East Sebago, ME, Our Lady of Sebago, c/o Gorham, ME, St. Anne Church. (PRT)
Eastman, GA, Dodge Co., St. Mark, c/o McRae, GA, Holy Redeemer Church. (SAV)
Eatonville, WA, Pierce Co., Our Lady of Good Counsel, c/o Puyallup, WA, Holy Disciples Church. (SEA)
Eddyville, NE, Custer Co., St. Patrick, c/o Elm Creek, NE, Immaculate Conception Church. (GI)
Eden, VT, Lamoille Co., St. Gabriel, c/o Morrisville, VT, Holy Cross Church. (BUR)
Eden, WY, Sweetwater Co., St. Christopher, c/o Pinedale, WY, Our Lady of Peace Church. (CHY)
Edenville, MI, Gladwin Co., St. Anne, c/o Coleman, MI, St. Philip Neri Church. (SAG)
Edgemont, SD, Fall River Co., St. James, c/o Hot Springs, SD, St. Anthony's Church. (RC)
Edgerly, LA, St. John Evangelist, c/o Vinton, LA, St. Joseph Church. (LKC)
Edgewater, FL, Volusia Co., St. Gerard, c/o New Smyrna Beach, FL, Sacred Heart Church. (ORL)
Edgewood, NM, Santa Fe Co., St. Elizabeth, c/o Moriarty, NM, Estancia Valley Catholic Parish Church. (SFE)
Edison, NJ, Middlesex Co., St. Therese of the Infant Jesus, c/o [7] New Brunswick, NJ, St. Mary of Mount Virgin Church. (MET)
Edisto Island, SC, Charleston Co., SS. Frederick & Stephen, c/o Yonges Island, SC, St. Mary Church. (CHR)
Edmeston, NY, Nativity of B.V.M., c/o Morris, NY, Holy Cross Church. (ALB)
Edroy, TX, San Patricio Co., Our Lady of Guadalupe, c/o Odem, TX, Sacred Heart Church. (CC)
Effie, LA, St. Winifred, c/o Deville, LA, St. John the Baptist Church. (ALX)
Egan, LA, Acadia Parish, St. Michael, c/o Iota, LA, St. Joseph Church. (LAF)
Ekalaka, MT, St. Joan of Arc, c/o Baker, MT, St. John the Evangelist Church. (GF)
El Alto, PR, San Antonio, c/o Penuelas, PR, St. Joseph Church. (PCE)
El Cajon, CA, Immaculate Conception of BVM, c/o Lakeside, CA, Blessed Kateri Tekakwitha Church. (SD)
El Carmen, NM, Mora Co., c/o Mora, NM, St. Gertrude Church. (SFE)
El Corozo, PR, Cristo Rey, c/o Cabo Rojo, PR, St. Michael Church. (MGZ)
El Duende, NM, Rio Arriba Co., c/o Espanola, NM, Sacred Heart Church. (SFE)
El Guache, NM, Rio Arriba Co., c/o Espanola, NM, Sacred Heart Church. (SFE)
El Guique, NM, Rio Arriba Co., c/o San Juan Pueblo, NM, St. John the Baptist Church. (SFE)
El Macho, NM, San Miguel Co., c/o Pecos, NM, St. Anthony Church. (SFE)
El Papayo, PR, Cristo Rey, c/o Sabana Grande, PR, Church of San Isidro. (MGZ)
El Paso, TX, El Paso Co., Santa Teresita, c/o [38] El Paso, TX, San Judas Tadeo Church. (ELP)
El Pueblo, NM, San Miguel Co., San Antonio de Padua, c/o Ribera, NM, San Miguel Del Vado Church. (SFE)
El Rancho, NM, Santa Fe Co., c/o Pojoaque, NM, N.S. de Guadalupe del Valle de Pojoaque Church. (SFE)
El Rio, CA, Ventura Co., Santa Clara Chapel, c/o [2] Oxnard, CA, Santa Clara Church. (LA)
El Rucio, PR, Penuelas Co., La Milagrosa, c/o Penuelas, PR, St. Joseph Church. (PCE)
El Santuario, NM, Santa Fe Co., El Santuario Shrine, c/o Chimayo, NM, Holy Family Church. (SFE)
El Sauz, TX, Our Lady of Guadalupe, c/o Escobares, TX, Sacred Heart Church. (BWN)
El Valle, NM, Taos Co., San Miguel Archangel, c/o Chimayo, NM, Holy Family Church. (SFE)
Elba, NE, Howard Co., St. Joseph, c/o Farwell, NE, St. Anthony of Padua Church. (GI)
Elberta, UT, Utah Co., San Isidro, c/o Provo, UT, St. Francis of Assisi Church. (SLC)
Elberton, GA, Elbert Co., St. Mary's, c/o Washington, GA, St. Joseph's Church. (ATL)
Elbridge, MI, St. Joseph Church, c/o Hart, MI, St. Gregory's Church. (GR)
Eleele, HI, Kauai Co., Sacred Heart, c/o Kalaheo, HI, Holy Cross Church. (HON)
Elfin Cove, AK, c/o Yakutat, AK, St. Ann Church. (JUN)
Elfrida, AZ, Cochise Co., St. Francis of Assisi, c/o Sunsites, AZ, St. Jude Thaddeus Church. (TUC)
Elizabeth, CO, Elbert Co., Our Lady of the Visitation, c/o Parker, CO, Ave Maria Church. (COS)
Elizabeth, IN, Harrison Co., St. Peter, c/o Corydon, IN, St. Joseph Church. (IND)
Elizabeth, LA, Allen Parish, St. Frances, c/o Oakdale, LA, Sacred Heart Church. (LKC)
Elizabeth, WV, Wirt Co., St. Elizabeth of Hungary, c/o Spencer, WV, Holy Redeemer Church. (WH)
Elizabethtown, NC, Bladen Co., Our Lady of the Snows, c/o Whiteville, NC, Sacred Heart Church. (R)
Elk, TX, McLennon Co., St. Joseph, c/o Tours, TX, St. Martin Church. (AUS)
Elka Park, NY, Greene Co., St. Francis de Sales, c/o Haines Falls, NY, Immaculate Conception Church. (ALB)
Elkhorn City, KY, Pike Co., St. Joseph the Worker, c/o Pikeville, KY, St. Francis of Assisi Church. (LEX)
Elkin, NC, Surry Co., St. Stephen, c/o North Wilkesboro, NC, St. John Baptist de LaSalle Church. (CHL)
Ellijay, GA, Gilmer Co., Good Samaritan, c/o Blue Ridge, GA, St. Anthony's Church. (ATL)
Elmer, LA, St. Peter, c/o Glenmora, LA, St. Louis Church. (ALX)
Elmwood, NE, Cass Co., St. Mary's, c/o Manley, NE, St. Patrick's Church. (LIN)
Elsie, NE, Perkins Co., Resurrection of Our Lord, c/o Wallace, NE, St. Mary's Church. (LIN)
Emanueli, PR, Coamo Co., Holy Family, c/o Coamo, PR, St. Blase Church. (PCE)
Eminence, KY, Henry Co., St. John Chrysostom, c/o Shelbyville, KY, Annunciation of the Blessed Virgin Mary Church. (L)
Eminence, MO, Shannon Co., St. Sylvester, c/o Mountain View, MO, St. John Vianney Church. (SPC)
Emmanuel, LA, Holy Rosary, c/o Cloutierville, LA, St. John the Baptist Church. (ALX)
Emory, TX, Rains Co., St. John the Evangelist, c/o Sulphur Springs, TX, St. James Church. (TYL)
Empire, LA, Plaquemines Parish, St. Ann, c/o Buras, LA, Our Lady of Good Harbor Church. (NO)
Empire, NV, St. Joseph the Worker, c/o Fernley, NV, St. Robert Bellarmine Church. (RNO)
Encinal, NM, Nativity of the Blessed Virgin Mary, c/o Laguna, NM, St. Joseph Church. (GLP)
Encino, NM, Torrance Co., c/o Vaughn, NM, St. Mary Church. (SFE)
Encino, TX, Brooks Co., St. Ann, c/o Falfurrias, TX, Sacred Heart Church. (CC)
England, AR, Lonoke Co., Holy Trinity, c/o Carlisle, AR, St. Rose of Lima Church. (LR)
Ensenada, NM, Rio Arriba Co., c/o Los Ojos, NM, San Jose Church. (SFE)
Eola, TX, Concho Co., St. Philip, c/o Eden, TX, St. Charles Church. (SAN)
Ephraim, UT, Sanpete Co., St. Jude, c/o Monroe, UT, St. Elizabeth's Church. (SLC)
Ericson, NE, Wheeler Co., St. Theresa of the Child Jesus, c/o Burwell, NE, Sacred Heart Church. (GI)
Erie, IL, Whiteside Co., St. Ambrose, c/o Prophetstown, IL, St. Catherine Church. (RCK)
Errol, NH, Coos Co., St. Pius X, c/o Colebrook, NH, St. Brendan Church. (MAN)
Erving, MA, Franklin Co., St. Blanche, c/o Millers Falls, MA, St. John's Church. (SPR)
Escalalute, UT, Wayne Co., St. Sylvester, c/o Cedar City, UT, Christ the King Church. (SLC)
Escobosa, NM, Bernalillo Co., San Isidro, c/o Tijeras, NM, Holy Child Church. (SFE)
Esopus, NY, Ulster Co., Sacred Heart, c/o Port Ewen, NY, Presentation of the Virgin Mary Church. (NY)
Esparto, CA, Yolo Co., St. Martin, c/o Winters, CA, St. Anthony Church. (SAC)
Estaca, NM, Rio Arriba Co., c/o San Juan Pueblo, NM, St. John the Baptist Church. (SFE)
Estancia, NM, Torrance Co., Sts. Peter & Paul, c/o Moriarty, NM, Estancia Valley Catholic Parish Church. (SFE)
Esther, LA, Vermilion Parish, St. James, c/o Henry, LA, St. John Church. (LAF)
Estherwood, LA, Acadia Parish, St. Margaret, c/o Mermentau, LA, St. John the Evangelist Church. (LAF)
Ethete, WY, Fremont Co., St. Joseph, c/o St. Stephens, WY, St. Stephen's Church. (CHY)
Etna, CA, Siskiyou Co., St. Mary's, c/o Fort Jones, CA, Sacred Heart Church. (SAC)
Ettal, FM, c/o Lukunor, FM, Sacred Heart Church. (CI)
Euclid, MN, Polk Co., St. Mary, c/o [1] Crookston, MN, Cathedral of the Immaculate Conception. (CR)
Eufaula, OK, McIntosh Co., St. Paul's, c/o Henryetta, OK, St. Michael Church. (TLS)
Eureka, CA, St. Joseph, c/o Eureka, CA, St. Bernard Church. (SR)

Eureka, UT, Utah Co., St. Patrick Parish, c/o Payson, UT, San Andres Church. (SLC)
Europa, MS, Webster Co., St. John, c/o West Point, MS, Immaculate Conception Church. (JKS)
Eutaw, AL, Greene Co., St. Mary, c/o Demopolis, AL, St. Leo Church. (BIR)
Everglades City, FL, Collier Co., Holy Family Mission, c/o Marco Island, FL, San Marco Church. (VEN)
Everly, IA, Clay Co., St. Mary's, c/o Royal, IA, St. Louis Church. (SC)
Expressway Heights, TX, Nuestra Senora de Guadalupe, c/o Weslaco, TX, San Martin de Porres Church. (BWN)

F

Fabius, NY, Onondaga Co., St. Paul, c/o Pompey, NY, Immaculate Conception Church. (SY)
Faga'alu, AS, c/o [2] Pago Pago, AS, Co-Cathedral of St. Joseph the Worker. (SPP)
Faga'itua, AS, c/o [8] Pago Pago, AS, Church of St. Peter and Paul. (SPP)
Fagasa, AS, c/o [2] Pago Pago, AS, Co-Cathedral of St. Joseph the Worker. (SPP)
Fair Haven, NY, Cayuga Co., St. Jude Chapel, c/o Red Creek, NY, St. Thomas the Apostle Church. (ROC)
Fairacres, NM, Dona Ana Co., San Jose Mission, c/o Mesilla, NM, St. Albino Church. (LSC)
Fairfield, AL, Jefferson Co., St. Mary's, c/o [7] Birmingham, AL, Holy Family Church. (BIR)
Fairford, AL, Washington Co., Our Lady of Sorrows, c/o Chastang, AL, St. Peter the Apostle Church. (MOB)
Fairplay, CO, Park Co., St. Joseph, c/o Buena Vista, CO, St. Rose of Lima Church. (COS)
Fairview, MT, Richland Co., St. Catherine, c/o Sidney, MT, St. Matthew Church. (GF)
Fairview, OK, Major Co., St. Ann, c/o Bison, OK, St. Joseph's Church. (OKL)
Falcon, TX, Santa Ana, c/o Zapata, TX, Our Lady of Lourdes Church. (LAR)
Falcon Heights, TX, Holy Trinity, c/o Roma, TX, Our Lady of Refuge Church. (BWN)
Faleniu, AS, c/o [6] Pago Pago, AS, St. Paul Church. (SPP)
Fall River Mills, CA, Shasta Co., Our Lady of the Valley, c/o Burney, CA, St. Francis of Assisi Church. (SAC)
Falls Village, CT, Litchfield Co., St. Patrick, c/o Canaan, CT, St. Joseph's Church. (HRT)
Falun, MN, Roseau Co., St. Philip, c/o Warroad, MN, St. Mary's Church. (CR)
Fannin, TX, Our Lady of Assumption, c/o Goliad, TX, Immaculate Conception Church. (VIC)
Farmersville, CA, Tulare Co., St. Anthony of Egypt, c/o Exeter, CA, Sacred Heart Church. (FRS)
Farmerville, LA, Union Parish, Our Lady of Perpetual Help, c/o West Monroe, LA, St. Paschal Church. (SHP)
Farnam, NE, Dawson Co., St. Joseph's, c/o Curtis, NE, St. James Church. (LIN)
Fashing, TX, Atascosa Co., St. Elizabeth, c/o Karnes City, TX, St. Cornelius Church. (SAT)
Fayette, AL, Fayette Co., Holy Family, c/o Winfield, AL, Holy Spirit Church. (BIR)
Faysville, TX, St. Theresa, c/o San Carlos, TX, St. Joseph the Worker Church. (BWN)
Faywood, NM, Luna Co., San Jose, c/o Hurley, NM, Infant Jesus Church. (LSC)
Federal Dam, MN, Sacred Heart, c/o Ball Club, MN, St. Joseph's Church. (DUL)
Federal Dam, MN, Sacred Heart, c/o Duluth, MN, Indian Missions Church. (DUL)
Fellsmere, FL, Indian River Co., c/o Fellsmere, FL, Our Lady of Guadalupe Mission. (PMB)
Fence Lake, NM, El Morro, c/o Tinaja, NM, San Lorenzo Church. (GLP)
Fierro, NM, Grant Co., St. Anthony, c/o Bayard, NM, Our Lady of Fatima Church. (LSC)
Fillmore, UT, Millard Co., Holy Family, c/o Milford, UT, St. Bridget Church. (SLC)
Fine, NY, St. Lawrence Co., St. Michael, c/o Star Lake, NY, St. Hubert Church. (OG)
Fingal, ND, Barnes Co., Holy Trinity, c/o Oriska, ND, St. Bernard's Church. (FAR)
Finlayson, MN, St. Joseph's, c/o Sandstone, MN, St. Luke's Church. (DUL)
Finley, ND, Steele Co., St. Olaf, c/o Hope, ND, St. Agatha's Church. (FAR)
Fish Creek, NY, SS. Peter & Paul, c/o West Leyden, NY, St. Mary's Nativity Church. (OG)
Fish Lake, NV, Esmeralda Co., Our Lady of Guadalupe, c/o Tonopah, NV, St. Patrick Church. (LAV)
Fisher, MN, Polk Co., St. Francis, c/o East Grand Forks, MN, Sacred Heart Church. (CR)
Fishville, LA, St. Edward, c/o Jena, LA, St. Mary Church. (ALX)
Fitchville, CT, New London Co., St. John, c/o [2] Norwich, CT, Sacred Heart Church. (NOR)
Fitzgerald, GA, Ben Hill Co., St. William, c/o Douglas, GA, St. Paul's Church. (SAV)
Fitzwilliam, NH, St. Joseph, c/o Troy, NH, Immaculate Conception Church. (MAN)
Flagler, CO, Kit Carson Co., St. Mary, c/o Limon, CO, Our Lady of Victory(1925) Church. (COS)
Flanagan, IL, Livingston Co., St. Joseph, c/o Minonk, IL, St. Patrick's Church. (PEO)
Flatwoods, LA, St. Cyril, c/o Boyce, LA, St. Margaret Church. (ALX)
Flaxville, MT, St. Louis, c/o Scobey, MT, St. Philip Bonitus Church. (GF)
Fleming, CO, Logan Co., St. Peter the Apostle, c/o Holyoke, CO, St. Patrick Church. (DEN)
Flint, MI, Genesee Co., c/o Troy, MI, St. Joseph Chaldean Parish Church. (EST)
Florence, MT, Ravalli Co., St. Joseph, c/o Stevensville, MT, St. Mary Church. (HEL)
Florian, MN, Marshall Co., Assumption, c/o Warren, MN, SS. Peter and Paul Church. (CR)
Florida, NY, Orange Co., St. Edward, c/o Warwick, NY, St. Stephen Church. (NY)
Floyd, VA, Floyd Co., Church of All Saints, c/o Woodlawn, VA, St. Joseph's Church. (RIC)
Folkston, GA, Charlton Co., St. Francis of Assisi, c/o St. Marys, GA, Our Lady Star of the Sea Church. (SAV)
Folly Beach, SC, Charleston Co., Our Lady of Good Counsel, c/o [11] Charleston, SC, Church of the Nativity. (CHR)
Folsom, NM, Union Co., St. Joseph, c/o Clayton, NM, St. Francis Xavier Church. (SFE)
Ford City, MO, Gentry Co., St. Patrick's, c/o Stanberry, MO, St. Peter's Church. (KC)
Fordyce, AR, Dallas Co., Good Shepherd, c/o Camden, AR, St. Louis Church. (LR)
Foreman, AR, Little River Co., Sacred Heart, c/o Texarkana, AR, St. Edward's Church. (LR)
Forest City, MO, Holt Co., St. Patrick, c/o Savannah, MO, St. Rose of Lima Church. (KC)
Forestville, MI, Sanilac Co., St. John Chrysostom, c/o Port Sanilac, MI, St. Mary Church. (SAG)
Forked Island, LA, Vermilon Parish, Immaculate Conception, c/o Cow Island, LA, St. Anne Church. (LAF)
Forrest, IL, Livingston Co., St. James, c/o Fairbury, IL, St. John the Baptist Church. (PEO)
Fort Adams, MS, St. Patrick, c/o Woodville, MS, St. Joseph Church. (JKS)
Fort Belknap Agency, MT, Sacred Heart, c/o Hays, MT, St. Paul's Indian Mission. (GF)
Fort Bridger, WY, Uinta Co., St. Helen, c/o Evanston, WY, St. Mary Magdalen Church. (CHY)
Fort Duchesne, UT, Uintah Co., Blessed Kateri Tekakwitha, c/o Roosevelt, UT, St. Helen's Church. (SLC)
Fort Garland, CO, Costilla Co., Holy Family, c/o San Luis, CO, Sangre de Cristo Church. (PBL)
Fort Meade, FL, Polk Co., St. Elizabeth Ann Seton, c/o Bartow, FL, St. Thomas Aquinas Church. (ORL)
Fort Mill, SC, York Co., St. Philip Neri, c/o Rock Hill, SC, St. Anne's Church. (CHR)
Fort Myers, FL, Lee Co., Our Lady of Perpetual Help, c/o [5] Fort Myers, FL, St. Francis Xavier Church. (VEN)
Fort Peck, MT, Our Lady of the Lake, c/o Glasgow, MT, St. Raphael's Church. (GF)
Fort Stanton, NM, Sacred Heart, c/o Ruidoso, NM, St. Eleanor Church. (LSC)
Fort Totten, ND, Benson Co., St. Jerome's, c/o Fort Totten Reservation, ND, (Sioux Indians) Church. (FAR)
Fort Totten Reservation, ND, Benson Co., Seven Dolors Indian Mission, c/o Fort Totten Reservation, ND, (Sioux Indians) Church. (FAR)
Fort Valley, GA, Peach Co., St. Juliana, c/o Perry, GA, St. Patrick Church. (SAV)
Fort Washakie, WY, Fremont Co., Blessed Sacrament, c/o St. Stephens, WY, St. Stephen's Church. (CHY)
Fort Yates, ND, Sioux Co., Sacred Heart, c/o Selfridge, ND, St. Philomena Church. (BIS)
Fossil, OR, St. Catherine, c/o Condon, OR, St. John's Church. (BAK)
Foster City, MI, Dickinson Co., St. Joseph, c/o Channing, MI, St. Rose Church. (MAR)
Fountain, FL, Bay Co., Our Lady Queen of Peace, c/o Bayou George, FL, Our Lady of the Rosary Church. (PT)
Fowler, CO, Otero Co., Mary Queen of Heaven, c/o Rocky Ford, CO, St. Peter Church. (PBL)
Frances, CO, Archuleta Co., St. Francis, c/o Pagosa Springs, CO, Immaculate Heart of Mary Church. (PBL)
Frances, WA, Pacific Co., Holy Family, c/o Pe Ell, WA, St. Joseph Church. (SEA)
Franconia, MN, Chisago Co., St. Francis Xavier, c/o Taylors Falls, MN, St. Joseph's Church. (STP)
Franconia, NH, Grafton, Our Lady of the Snows, c/o Littleton, NH, St. Rose of Lima Church. (MAN)
Franklin, NY, Delaware Co., St. Paul, c/o Sidney, NY, Sacred Heart Church. (ALB)
Franklin, VT, Franklin Co., St. Mary, c/o Sheldon Springs, VT, St. Anthony Church. (BUR)
Frankston, TX, Anderson Co., St. Charles Borromeo, c/o Palestine, TX, Sacred Heart Church. (TYL)
Frazer, MT, St. Joseph, c/o Wolf Point, MT, Immaculate Conception Church. (GF)
Frederick, MD, New Frederick County Mission, c/o Frederick, MD, St. John the Evangelist Church. (BAL)
Fredericksburg, TX, Gillespie Co., Our Lady of Guadalupe, c/o Fredericksburg, TX, St. Mary's Church. (SAT)
Freeburg, MN, St. Nicholas, c/o Brownsville, MN, St. Patrick's Church. (WIN)
Freeport, FL, Walton Co., Christ the King, c/o De Funiak Springs, FL, St. Margaret Church. (PT)
Freeport, ME, St. Jude's, c/o Yarmouth, ME, Sacred Heart Church. (PRT)
Freiburg, MI, Sanilac Co., St. Ignatius, c/o Argyle, MI, St. Joseph Church. (SAG)
French Camp, CA, San Joaquin Co., Good Shepherd, c/o [4] Stockton, CA, St. George Church. (STO)
French Village, MO, St. Francois Co., St. Anne, c/o Bonne Terre, MO, St. Joseph's Church. (STL)
Frenchtown, IN, Crawford Co., St. Joseph, c/o Frenchtown, IN, St. Bernard Church. (IND)
Fresno, CA, St. Francis, c/o [1] Fresno, CA, St. John Cathedral. (FRS)
Fried, ND, Stutsman Co., Sacred Heart, c/o Jamestown, ND, The Basilica of St. James. (FAR)
Friendship, NY, Allegany Co., Sacred Heart, c/o Cuba, NY, Our Lady of Angels Church. (BUF)
Frilot Cove, LA, St. Ann, c/o Plaisance, LA, St. Joseph Church. (LAF)
Froid, MT, Immaculate Conception, c/o Culbertson, MT, St. Anthony's Church. (GF)
Fromberg, MT, St. Joseph, c/o Bridger, MT, Sacred Heart Church. (GF)
Fronton, TX, Lamb of God, c/o Roma, TX, Our Lady of Refuge Church. (BWN)
Fryeburg, ME, Oxford Co., St. Elizabeth Ann Seton, c/o Bridgton, ME, St. Joseph Church. (PRT)
Fulda, ND, McHenry Co., St. Anselm, c/o Balta, ND, Our Lady of Mount Carmel Church. (FAR)
Fullerton, ND, Dickey Co., St. Patrick, c/o Ellendale, ND, St. Helena's Church. (FAR)
Fulton, MS, Itawamba Co., Christ the King, c/o Amory, MS, St. Helen Church. (JKS)
Futiga, AS, c/o [6] Pago Pago, AS, St. Paul Church. (SPP)

G

Gabbs, NV, St. Michael, c/o Hawthorne, NV, Our Lady of Perpetual Help Church. (RNO)
Gabriels, NY, Franklin Co., Assumption of the B.V.M., c/o Bloomingdale, NY, St. Paul Church. (OG)
Gackle, ND, Logan Co., St. Anne, c/o Windsor, ND, St. Mathias Church. (FAR)
Gainesville, MO, Ozark Co., St. William, c/o Mansfield, MO, Immaculate Heart of Mary Church. (SPC)
Galicia-Columbani, PR, Santo Tomas de Villanueva, c/o Aguada, PR, St. Francis of Assisi Church. (MGZ)
Galisteo, NM, Santa Fe Co., c/o Cerrillos, NM, St. Joseph Church. (SFE)
Gallatin, MO, Daviess Co., Mary Immaculate, c/o Hamilton, MO, Sacred Heart Church. (KC)
Gallegos, NM, Harding Co., c/o Roy, NM, Holy Family-St. Joseph Church. (SFE)
Gallina, NM, Rio Arriba Co., c/o Abiquiu, NM, St. Thomas Apostle Church. (SFE)
Gallinas, NM, San Miguel Co., Santo Nino, c/o Las Vegas, NM, Our Lady of Sorrows Church. (SFE)
Galveston, TX, Galveston Co., Queen of Peace Mission, c/o [4] Galveston, TX, St. Patrick Church. (GAL)
Galway, NY, St. Mary, c/o Broadalbin, NY, St. Joseph Church. (ALB)
Gamerco, NM, St. Joseph the Worker, c/o [2] Gallup, NM, St. Francis of Assisi Church. (GLP)
Garapan Village, District 11, MP, Maturana House of Prayer, c/o Garapan Village, District 11, MP, Kristo Rai Parish Church. (CHK)
Garapan Village, District 11, MP, Navy Hill, Commonwealth Health Center Chapel, c/o Garapan Village, District 11, MP, Kristo Rai Parish Church. (CHK)
Garcia, CO, Costilla Co., Sacred Heart of Jesus, c/o San Luis, CO, Sangre de Cristo Church. (PBL)
Gardiner, MT, St. William, c/o Livingston, MT, St. Mary's Church. (GF)
Gardner, CO, Huerfano Co., Sacred Heart, c/o Walsenburg, CO, St. Mary Church. (PBL)
Garrison, ND, St. Nicholas, White Shield, Sacred Heart, c/o Garrison, ND, St. Nicholas Church. (BIS)
Garrison, NY, Putnam Co., St. Joseph, c/o Cold Spring-on-Hudson, NY, Our Lady of Loretto Church. (NY)
Gary, IN, St. Hedwig, c/o [2] Merrillville, IN, St. Andrew Church. (GRY)
Garzas, PR, San Francisco, c/o Adjuntas, PR, St. Joachim Church. (PCE)
Genesee, PA, Potter Co., Sacred Heart, c/o Galeton, PA, St. Bibiana Church. (E)
Geneseo, ND, Sargent Co., St. Martin, c/o Lidgerwood, ND, St. Boniface's Church. (FAR)

Geneva, AL, Geneva Co., St. Mary, c/o Enterprise, AL, St. John Church. (MOB)
Gentilly, MN, Polk Co., St. Peter, c/o [1] Crookston, MN, Cathedral of the Immaculate Conception. (CR)
George West, TX, Live Oak Co., c/o George West, TX, St. George Church. (CC)
Georgetown, CA, El Dorado Co., St. James, c/o Placerville, CA, St. Patrick's Church. (SAC)
Georgetown, CO, Clear Creek Co., Our Lady of Lourdes, c/o Idaho Springs, CO, St. Paul's Church. (DEN)
Georgia, VT, Franklin Co., Ascension, c/o Fairfax, VT, St. Luke Church. (BUR)
Geraldine, MT, St. Margaret, c/o Fort Benton, MT, Immaculate Conception Church. (GF)
Germfask, MI, Schoolcraft Co., St. Therese, c/o Grand Marais, MI, Holy Rosary Church. (MAR)
Geyser, MT, St. Cyril, c/o Stanford, MT, St. Rose of Lima Church. (GF)
Gila, NM, Grant Co., St. Isidore, c/o Silver City, NM, St. Vincent de Paul Church. (LSC)
Gila Bend, AZ, San Lucy, c/o Laveen, AZ, St. John The Baptist Church. (PHX)
Gila River, AZ, Indian Care Center, c/o Laveen, AZ, St. John The Baptist Church. (PHX)
Gilbert, IL, Kane Co., St. Mary, c/o Dundee, IL, St. Catherine of Siena Church. (RCK)
Gilchrist, OR, Our Lady of the Snows, c/o La Pine, OR, Holy Redeemer Church. (BAK)
Gilman, VT, Essex Co., St. Theresa, c/o St. Johnsbury, VT, St. John the Evangelist Church. (BUR)
Giltner, NE, Hamilton Co., St. Joseph's, c/o Aurora, NE, St. Mary's Church. (LIN)
Gladstone, ND, Stark Co., St. Thomas the Apostle, c/o Lefor, ND, St. Elizabeth Church. (BIS)
Glasgo, CT, New London Co., St. Anne, c/o Voluntown, CT, St. Thomas Apostle Church. (NOR)
Glen Ullin, ND, Grant Co., St. Joseph, c/o Glen Ullin, ND, Sacred Heart of Jesus Church. (BIS)
Glenco, NM, San Ysidro, c/o Ruidoso, NM, St. Eleanor Church. (LSC)
Glencoe, LA, St. Joan of Arc, c/o Four Corners, LA, St. Peter the Apostle Church. (LAF)
Glendale, OR, Douglas Co., Holy Family, c/o Myrtle Creek, OR, All Souls Church. (P)
Glendale, RI, St. Louis Chapel, c/o [3] Burrillville, RI, St. Patrick Church. (PRO)
Glendo, WY, Platte Co., Our Lady of Lourdes, c/o Douglas, WY, St. James Church. (CHY)
Glenmont, OH, Holmes Co., SS. Peter and Paul, c/o Millersburg, OH, St. Peter Church. (COL)
Glenmore, NY, Oneida Co., St. Anne, c/o Taberg, NY, St. Patrick Church. (SY)
Glennon, MO, Bollinger Co., St. Anthony, c/o Advance, MO, St. Joseph Church. (SPC)
Glennville, GA, Tattnall Co., St. Jude, c/o Claxton, GA, St. Christopher Church. (SAV)
Glentana, MT, Holy Family, c/o Scobey, MT, St. Philip Bonitus Church. (GF)
Glenwood, NM, Catron Co., Santo Nino, c/o Alpine, AZ, St. Helena Church. (GLP)
Glidden, IA, Carroll Co., St. Elizabeth Seton Church, c/o Lidderdale, IA, Holy Family Church. (SC)
Glorieta, NM, Santa Fe Co., c/o Pecos, NM, St. Anthony Church. (SFE)
Gloster, MS, Amite Co., Holy Family, c/o Woodville, MS, St. Joseph Church. (JKS)
Gluckstadt, MS, St. Joseph, c/o Madison, MS, St. Francis of Assisi Church. (JKS)
Gnesen, MN, St. Joseph, c/o [9] Duluth, MN, St. John's Church. (DUL)
Gobles, MI, Van Buren Co., St. Jude's Church, c/o Paw Paw, MI, St. Mary Church. (KAL)
Gold Beach, OR, Curry Co., St. Charles Borromeo, c/o Brookings, OR, Star of the Sea Church. (P)
Goldcreek, MT, Powell Co., St. Mary, c/o Drummond, MT, St. Michael Church. (HEL)
Golden, NM, Santa Fe Co., c/o Cerrillos, NM, St. Joseph Church. (SFE)
Goldens Bridge, NY, Westchester Co., St. Michael, c/o Croton Falls, NY, St. Joseph Church. (NY)
Goldthwaite, TX, Mills Co., St. Peter's, c/o Lampasas, TX, St. Mary's Church. (AUS)
Golondrinas, NM, Mora Co., c/o Mora, NM, St. Gertrude Church. (SFE)
Goltry, OK, Alfalfa Co., St. Michael, c/o Enid, OK, St. Gregory the Great Church. (OKL)
Golva, ND, Golden Valley Co., St. Mary, c/o Beach, ND, St. John the Baptist Church. (BIS)
Gonzales, TX, Gonzales Co., Sacred Heart, c/o Gonzales, TX, St. James Church. (SAT)
Gonzales Ranch, NM, San Miguel Co., c/o Villanueva, NM, Our Lady of Guadalupe Church. (SFE)
Goodhue, MN, Goodhue Co., Holy Trinity, c/o Belle Creek, MN, St. Columbkill Church. (STP)
Goodridge, MN, Pennington Co., St. Ann, c/o Thief River Falls, MN, St. Bernards Church. (CR)
Gorum, LA, St. Margaret Mary, c/o Boyce, LA, St. Margaret Church. (ALX)
Goshen, NJ, Cape May Co., St. Elizabeth, c/o Woodbine, NJ, St. Casimir's Church. (CAM)
Gothenburg, NE, Dawson Co., Our Lady of Good Counsel, c/o Cozad, NE, Christ the King Church. (GI)
Goudeau, LA, St. Charles, c/o Evergreen, LA, Little Flower Church. (ALX)
Grady, AR, Lincoln Co., Blessed Sacrament, c/o Star City, AR, St. Justin's Church. (LR)
Granby, CO, Grand Co., Our Lady of the Snow, c/o Grand Lake, CO, St. Anne Church. (DEN)
Grand Chenier, LA, Cameron Parish, Immaculate Conception, c/o Grand Chenier, LA, St. Eugene Church. (LKC)
Grand Gorge, NY, Delaware Co., St. Philip Neri, c/o Stamford, NY, Sacred Heart Church. (ALB)
Grand Isle, VT, Grand Isle Co., St. Joseph, c/o South Hero, VT, St. Rose of Lima Church. (BUR)
Grand Junction, IA, Greene Co., St. Brigid, c/o Jefferson, IA, St. Joseph's Church. (SC)
Grand Portage, MN, Holy Rosary, c/o Grand Marais, MN, St. John's Church. (DUL)
Grand Portage, MN, Cook Co., Holy Rosary, c/o Duluth, MN, Indian Missions Church. (DUL)
Grand Ridge, IL, LaSalle Co., St. Mary, c/o Ransom, IL, St. Patrick's Church. (PEO)
Grand Saline, TX, Van Zandt Co., St. Celestine, c/o Mineola, TX, St. Peter the Apostle Church. (TYL)
Grandfalls, TX, Ward Co., St. Gertrude, c/o Monahans, TX, St. John the Apostle and Evangelist Church. (ELP)
Grandfield, OK, Tillman Co., Our Lady of Perpetual Help, c/o Frederick, OK, St. Helen Church. (OKL)
Grandin, MO, Carter Co., St. Anne, c/o Doniphan, MO, St. Benedict Church. (SPC)
Granite Falls, WA, Snohomish Co., Holy Cross, c/o Snohomish, WA, St. Michael Church. (SEA)
Granjeno, TX, Our Lady of Fatima, c/o [2] Mission, TX, Our Lady of the Holy Rosary Church. (BWN)
Grant, MI, Our Lady of Guadalupe Church, c/o Newaygo, MI, St. Bartholomew's Church. (GR)
Grantsville, WV, Calhoun Co., Jesus Christ, Prince of Peace, c/o Spencer, WV, Holy Redeemer Church. (WH)
Granville, ND, McHenry Co., Our Lady of Perpetual Help, c/o Towner, ND, St. Cecilia's Church. (FAR)
Grapeland, TX, Houston Co., St. Stephen, c/o Palestine, TX, Sacred Heart Church. (TYL)
Grass Flats, PA, Clearfield Co., SS. Peter & Paul, c/o Frenchville, PA, St. Mary of the Assumption Church. (E)
Grass Valley, OR, St. John the Baptist, c/o Wasco, OR, St. Mary's Church. (BAK)
Grassy Butte, ND, McKenzie Co., St. Peter Canisius, c/o Watford City, ND, Epiphany Church. (BIS)
Greasewood, AZ, Our Lady of the Rosary, c/o Ganado, AZ, All Saints Church. (GLP)
Great Falls, SC, Chester Co., St. Michael, c/o Lancaster, SC, St. Catherine's Church. (CHR)
Greeley, PA, Pike Co., Sacred Heart, c/o Shohola, PA, St. Ann's Church. (SCR)
Green Lake, ME, Our Lady of the Lake, c/o Ellsworth, ME, St. Joseph's Church. (PRT)
Green River, UT, Emery Co., St. Michael, c/o East Carbon, UT, Good Shepherd Church. (SLC)
Greene, ME, St. Francis, c/o Sabattus, ME, Our Lady of the Rosary Church. (PRT)
Greenfield, MO, Dade Co., St. Patrick, c/o Mount Vernon, MO, St. Susanne Church. (SPC)
Greensboro, AL, Hale Co., Our Lady of Lourdes, c/o Demopolis, AL, St. Leo Church. (BIR)
Greensboro, FL, Gadsen Co., Casa Guadalupe Catholic Center for Evangelization, c/o Quincy, FL, St. Thomas the Apostle Church. (PT)
Greensboro, FL, Gadsen Co., Juan Diego, c/o Quincy, FL, St. Thomas the Apostle Church. (PT)
Greensboro Bend, VT, Orleans Co., St. Michael, c/o Hardwick, VT, St. Norbert Church. (BUR)
Greenup, KY, St. Lawrence, c/o Ashland, KY, Holy Family Church. (LEX)
Greenville, CA, Plumas Co., St. Anthony, c/o Quincy, CA, St. John Church. (SAC)
Greenwich, CT, Fairfield Co., St. Timothy's, c/o [2] Greenwich, CT, St. Michael the Archangel Church. (BGP)
Greenwood, NE, Cass Co., St. Joseph's, c/o Ashland, NE, St. Mary's Church. (LIN)
Greig, NY, Lewis Co., St. Thomas, c/o Glenfield, NY, St. Mary Church. (OG)
Gripinas, PR, Jayuya Co., Buen Pastor, c/o Jayuya, PR, Our Lady of Monserrate Church. (PCE)
Gruver, TX, Hansford Co., Cristo Redentor, c/o Spearman, TX, Sacred Heart Church. (AMA)
Grygla, MN, Marshall Co., St. Clement, c/o Thief River Falls, MN, St. Bernards Church. (CR)
Guachupanque, NM, Rio Arriba Co., c/o Espanola, NM, Sacred Heart Church. (SFE)
Guadalupita, NM, Mora Co., c/o Mora, NM, St. Gertrude Church. (SFE)
Gualala, CA, Mary, Star of the Sea, c/o Point Arena, CA, St. Aloysius Church. (SR)
Guaniquilla, PR, Ntra. Sra. del Carmen, c/o Aguada, PR, St. Francis of Assisi Church. (MGZ)
Guayabal, PR, Bo. Guayabal, Our Lady of the Rosary, c/o Juana Diaz, PR, St. Raymond Nonato Church. (PCE)
Guayabo, PR, El Buen Pastor, c/o Aguada, PR, St. Francis of Assisi Church. (MGZ)
Guayama, PR, Bo. Carite, San Martin, c/o Guayama, PR, St. Anthony of Padua Church. (PCE)
Guaynabo, PR, Cristo del Perdon, c/o [4] Guaynabo, PR, San Juan M. Vianney Church. (SJN)
Guaynabo, PR, Dulce Nombre de Maria, c/o [4] Guaynabo, PR, San Juan M. Vianney Church. (SJN)
Guaynabo, PR, El Buen Pastor, c/o [7] Guaynabo, PR, Divino Nino Jesus Church. (SJN)
Guaynabo, PR, Jesus Nazareno, c/o [7] Guaynabo, PR, Divino Nino Jesus Church. (SJN)
Guaynabo, PR, La Milagrosa, c/o [4] Guaynabo, PR, San Juan M. Vianney Church. (SJN)
Guaynabo, PR, Ntra. Sra. del Carmen, c/o [3] Guaynabo, PR, Maria Madre de Mi Senor Church. (SJN)
Guaynabo, PR, Ntra. Sra. del Carmen, c/o [4] Guaynabo, PR, San Juan M. Vianney Church. (SJN)
Guaynabo, PR, San Rafael Arcangel, c/o [7] Guaynabo, PR, Divino Nino Jesus Church. (SJN)
Guaynabo, PR, Virgen de la Paz, c/o [9] Guaynabo, PR, Sagrados Corazones Church. (SJN)
Guilarte, PR, San Antonio, c/o Adjuntas, PR, St. Joachim Church. (PCE)
Gulf Breeze, FL, Santa Rosa Co., Our Lady of the Assumption, c/o Gulf Breeze, FL, St. Ann Church. (PT)
Gulliver, MI, Schoolcraft Co., Divine Infant of Prague, c/o Engadine, MI, Our Lady of Lourdes Church. (MAR)
Gulnare, CO, Las Animas Co., San Jose, c/o Aguilar, CO, St. Anthony Church. (PBL)
Gussetville, TX, Live Oak Co., St. Joseph, c/o George West, TX, St. George Church. (CC)
Gustavus, AK, c/o Yakutat, AK, St. Ann Church. (JUN)
Gwinner, ND, Sargent Co., St. Vincent De Paul, c/o Lisbon, ND, St. Aloysius Church. (FAR)

H

Hachita, NM, St. Catherine, c/o Lordsburg, NM, St. Joseph Church. (LSC)
Hackensack, MN, Sacred Heart, c/o Walker, MN, St. Agnes Church. (DUL)
Hagerman, NM, St. Catherine, c/o Dexter, NM, Immaculate Conception Church. (LSC)
Hagerstown, MD, St. Ann's, c/o Baltimore, MD, Patronage of the Mother of God Church. (PSC)
Hague, VA, Westmoreland Co., St. Paul, c/o Kilmarnock, VA, St. Francis de Sales Church. (ARL)
Haines Falls, NY, Greene Co., Wayside Shrine, c/o Haines Falls, NY, Immaculate Conception Church. (ALB)
Halaula, HI, Hawaii Co., Our Lady of Grace, c/o Hawi, HI, Sacred Heart Church. (HON)
Haleyville, AL, Winston Co., Our Lady of Guadalupe, c/o Jasper, AL, St. Cecilia Church. (BIR)
Halfway, OR, St. Therese, c/o [1] Baker, OR, Cathedral of St. Francis De Sales. (BAK)
Hallsville, TX, Harrison Co., Our Lady of Grace, c/o Longview, TX, St. Mary Church. (TYL)
Halstad, MN, Norman Co., Holy Family, c/o Ada, MN, St. Joseph's Church. (CR)
Hamburg, AR, Ashley Co., c/o Crossett, AR, Holy Cross Church. (LR)
Hamilton, IL, Hancock Co., St. Mary, c/o Warsaw, IL, Sacred Heart Church. (PEO)
Hamilton, KS, Greenwood Co., St. John, c/o Eureka, KS, Sacred Heart Church. (WCH)
Hamilton City, CA, Glenn Co., St. Mary, c/o Orland, CA, St. Dominic Church. (SAC)
Hamlin, TX, Jones Co., Holy Trinity, c/o Anson, TX, St. Michael's Church. (LUB)
Hammond, OR, Clatsop Co., St. Francis de Sales, c/o Astoria, OR, St. Mary, Star of the Sea Church. (P)
Hampton, CT, Windham Co., Our Lady of Lourdes, c/o Brooklyn, CT, Our Lady of La Salette Church. (NOR)
Hampton, IL, Rock Island Co., St. Mary, c/o Rapids City, IL, St. John the Baptist Church. (PEO)
Hampton, SC, Hampton Co., St. Mary, c/o Ridgeland, SC, St. Anthony's Church. (CHR)
Hanalei, HI, Kauai Co., St. William, c/o Kapaa, HI, St. Catherine Church. (HON)
Hanceville, AL, Cullman Co., St. Boniface, c/o Cullman, AL, Sacred Heart Church. (BIR)
Hanna, WY, Carbon Co., St. Joseph, c/o Saratoga, WY, St. Ann's Church. (CHY)
Hanover, NM, Grant Co., Holy Family, c/o Bayard, NM, Our Lady of Fatima Church. (LSC)
Happy Camp, CA, Siskiyou Co., All Saints, c/o Fort Jones, CA, Sacred Heart Church. (SAC)
Hardeeville, SC, Jasper Co., St. Anthony's, c/o Bluffton, SC, St. Gregory the Great Church. (CHR)
Hargill, TX, St. Frances Xavier Cabrini, c/o Raymondville, TX, Our Lady of Guadalupe Church. (BWN)

Harlem, MT, Blaine Co., St. Thomas the Apostle, c/o Chinook, MT, St. Gabriel's Church. (GF)
Harmon, NY, Westchester Co., Church of the Good Shepherd, c/o Croton-on-Hudson, NY, Holy Name of Mary Church. (NY)
Harmony, WA, Lewis Co., St. Yves, c/o Morton, WA, Sacred Heart Church. (SEA)
Harpswell, ME, Cumberland Co., St. Katharine Drexel, c/o Brunswick, ME, St. Charles Church. (PRT)
Harquahala Valley, AZ, San Isidoro Labrador, c/o Buckeye, AZ, Saint Henry Church. (PHX)
Harrington, DE, Kent Co., St. Bernadette, c/o Milford, DE, St. John the Apostle Church. (WIL)
Harrison, NE, Sioux Co., Church of the Nativity of the Blessed Virgin Mary, c/o Crawford, NE, St. John the Baptist Church. (GI)
Hart, TX, Castro Co., St. John's, c/o Dimmitt, TX, Immaculate Conception Church. (AMA)
Hartford, AR, Sebastian Co., St. Leo's, c/o Fort Smith, AR, Immaculate Conception Church. (LR)
Hartley, IA, O'Brien Co., St. Joseph's, c/o Sanborn, IA, St. Cecilia's Church. (SC)
Hartselle, AL, Morgan Co., Holy Family, c/o Decatur, AL, St. Ann's Church. (BIR)
Harvard, MI, Kent Co., St. Margaret, c/o Greenville, MI, St. Charles Church. (GR)
Harwood, PA, Luzerne Co., St. Michael, c/o West Hazleton, PA, St. Francis of Assisi Church. (SCR)
Haskell, TX, Haskell Co., St. George, c/o Stamford, TX, St. Ann Church. (LUB)
Hastings-on-Hudson, NY, Westchester Co., Andrus Nursing Home, c/o Hastings-on-Hudson, NY, St. Matthew Church. (NY)
Hato Rey, PR, San Juan, Sma. Trinidad, c/o [7] San Juan, PR, Ntr. Sra. de la Caridad del Cobre Church. (SJN)
Hawk Run, PA, Clearfield Co., SS. Peter & Paul, c/o Morrisdale, PA, St. Agnes Church. (E)
Hawkinsville, CA, Siskiyou Co., Immaculate Conception, c/o Yreka, CA, St. Joseph Church. (SAC)
Hawley, MN, Clay Co., St. Andrew, c/o Lake Park, MN, St. Francis Xavier's Church. (CR)
Hawthorne, FL, Alachua Co., St. Philip Neri, c/o [1] Gainesville, FL, St. Patrick's Church. (STA)
Haxtun, CO, Phillips Co., Christ the King, c/o Holyoke, CO, St. Patrick Church. (DEN)
Hay Springs, NE, Sheridan Co., Sacred Heart, c/o Hemingford, NE, St. Bridget Church. (GI)
Hay Springs, NE, Sheridan Co., St. Columbkille, c/o Gordon, NE, St. Leo's Church. (GI)
Hayales, PR, Coamo Co., Our Lady of Mt. Carmel, c/o Coamo, PR, St. Blase Church. (PCE)
Hayden, NM, Quay Co., Holy Trinity, c/o Clayton, NM, St. Francis Xavier Church. (SFE)
Hayes, LA, Calcasieu Parish, St. Daniel Chapel, c/o Bell City, LA, St. John Vianney Church. (LKC)
Hayesville, NC, Clay Co., Immaculate Heart of Mary, c/o Murphy, NC, St. William Church. (CHL)
Hayfork, CA, Trinity Co., Holy Trinity, c/o Weaverville, CA, St. Patrick Church. (SAC)
Haymarsh, ND, Morton Co., St. Clement, c/o Hebron, ND, St. Ann Church. (BIS)
Hazard, NE, Sherman Co., St. Gabriel, c/o Pleasanton, NE, St. Mary's Church. (GI)
Hazlehurst, MS, St. Martin, c/o Crystal Springs, MS, St. John Church. (JKS)
Hazleton, PA, Luzerne Co., St. Ladislaus, c/o [6] Hazleton, PA, St. Joseph's Church. (SCR)
He Dog, SD, St. Patrick Hall, c/o Parmelee, SD, St. Agnes Church. (RC)
Healdton, OK, Carter Co., St. Cecilia, c/o Ardmore, OK, St. Mary Church. (OKL)
Heart Butte, MT, Glacier Co., Holy Family Mission, c/o Heart Butte, MT, St. Anne Church. (HEL)
Heartwell, NE, Kearney Co., Holy Family, c/o Minden, NE, St. John's Church. (LIN)
Heber, CA, Imperial Co., Sacred Heart, c/o Imperial, CA, St. Anthony of Padua Church. (SD)
Heber City, UT, Wasatch Co., St. Lawrence, c/o Park City, UT, St. Mary of the Assumption Church. (SLC)
Heber Springs, AR, Cleburne Co., St. Albert, c/o Searcy, AR, St. James Church. (LR)
Hedgesville, WV, Berkeley Co., St. Bernadette, c/o Martinsburg, WV, St. Joseph's Church. (WH)
Heidelberg, KY, Lee Co., St. Therese, c/o Beattyville, KY, Queen of All Saints Church. (LEX)
Helena, TX, Karnes Co., St. Helena, c/o Panna Maria, TX, Immaculate Conception of the Blessed Virgin Mary Church. (SAT)
Henderson, NY, Jefferson Co., Queen of Heaven, c/o Sackets Harbor, NY, St. Andrew Church. (OG)
Henryville, IN, Clark Co., St. Francis Xavier, c/o Charlestown, IN, St. Michael Church. (IND)
Hermeleigh, TX, Scurry Co., St. John, c/o Snyder, TX, St. Elizabeth's Church. (LUB)
Hermosa, SD, St. Michael's, c/o [1] Rapid City, SD, Cathedral of Our Lady of Perpetual Help. (RC)
Hernandez, NM, Rio Arriba Co., c/o Espanola, NM, Sacred Heart Church. (SFE)
Hershey, NE, Lincoln Co., Our Lady of Guadalupe, c/o Sutherland, NE, Sacred Heart Church. (GI)
Hesperia, MI, Christ the King, c/o Brunswick, MI, St. Michael's Church. (GR)
Hessel, MI, Mackinac Co., Our Lady of the Snows, c/o Goetzville, MI, St. Stanislaus Kostka Church. (MAR)
Hibbing, MN, St .Louis Co., Immaculate Conception, c/o Hibbing, MN, Blessed Sacrament Church. (DUL)
Hibbing, MN, St. Louis Co., St. Leo's, c/o Hibbing, MN, Blessed Sacrament Church. (DUL)
Hickory Hill, LA, St. Richard, c/o Marksville, LA, Holy Ghost Church. (ALX)
High Falls, NY, Ulster Co., Our Lady Help of Christians, c/o Rosendale, NY, St. Peter Church. (NY)
Highland, MO, Perry Co., St. Joseph, c/o Perryville, MO, St. Vincent De Paul Church. (STL)
Highlands, NC, Macon Co., Our Lady of the Mountains, c/o Franklin, NC, St. Francis of Assisi Church. (CHL)
Hill Top, PA, Wayne Co., St. Cecilia, c/o Pleasant Mount, PA, St. James Church. (SCR)
Hillsboro, NM, Sierra Co., Our Lady of Guadalupe, c/o Garfield, NM, San Isidro Church. (LSC)
Hingham, MT, Our Lady of Ransom, c/o Chester, MT, St. Mary's Church. (GF)
Hinsdale, MT, St. Albert, c/o Glasgow, MT, St. Raphael's Church. (GF)
Hinton, OK, Caddo Co., Sacred Heart, c/o Weatherford, OK, St. Eugene's Church. (OKL)
Hobart, OK, Kiowa Co., Sts. Peter & Paul, c/o Mangum, OK, Sacred Heart Church. (OKL)
Hobart Bay, AK, c/o Yakutat, AK, St. Ann Church. (JUN)
Hobson, MT, Sacred Heart, c/o Stanford, MT, St. Rose of Lima Church. (GF)
Hochheim, TX, St. Ann, c/o Yoakum, TX, St. Joseph Church. (VIC)
Hoconuco, PR, Chapel of St. Joseph, c/o San German, PR, San German de Auxerre Church. (MGZ)
Hode, KY, Martin Co., St. John Neumann, c/o Louisa, KY, St. Jude Church. (LEX)
Hogares Seguros, PR, San Antonio Co., c/o Jayuya, PR, Our Lady of Monserrate Church. (PCE)
Hogeland, MT, Blaine Co., St. Thomas Aquinas, c/o Chinook, MT, St. Gabriel's Church. (GF)
Hollandale, MS, Immaculate Conception, c/o Leland, MS, St. James Church. (JKS)
Hollis, AK, c/o Craig, AK, St. John by the Sea Church. (JUN)
Hollis, OK, Harmon Co., Our Lady of Guadalupe, c/o Altus, OK, Prince of Peace Church. (OKL)
Holly Beach, LA, Holy Trinity, c/o Hackberry, LA, St. Peter Apostle Church. (LKC)
Holly Hill, SC, Orangeburg Co., St. Ann, c/o Summerton, SC, St. Mary's Church. (CHR)
Holman, NM, Mora Co., c/o Mora, NM, St. Gertrude Church. (SFE)
Holman, NM, Mora Co., c/o Mora, NM, St. Gertrude Church. (SFE)
Holman, TX, St. Wenceslaus, c/o Ammannsville, TX, St. John The Baptist Church. (VIC)
Holualoa, HI, Immaculate Conception, c/o Kailua-Kona, HI, St. Michael The Archangel Church. (HON)
Holyoke, MA, Hampden Co., Holyoke Soldier's Home Chapel, c/o [1] Holyoke, MA, Blessed Sacrament Church. (SPR)
Homer, IL, Champaign Co., St. Charles Borromeo, c/o Tolono, IL, St. Patrick's Church. (PEO)
Homer, LA, Claiborne Parish, St. Margaret, c/o Minden, LA, St. Paul Church. (SHP)
Homer, NE, Dakota Co., St. Cornelius, c/o South Sioux City, NE, St. Michael Church. (OM)
Hominy, OK, Osage Co., c/o Cleveland, OK, St. Joseph Church. (TLS)
Honalo, HI, St. Paul, c/o Kailua-Kona, HI, St. Michael The Archangel Church. (HON)
Honokahua (Kapalua), HI, Maui Co., Sacred Hearts of Jesus and Mary, c/o Lahaina, HI, Maria Lanakila Church. (HON)
Honomu, HI, Hawaii Co., Good Shepherd, c/o Papaikou, HI, Immaculate Heart of Mary Church. (HON)
Hooker, OK, Texas Co., Sacred Heart, c/o Guymon, OK, St. Peter's Church. (OKL)
Hopedale, IL, Tazewell Co., St. Joseph's, c/o Delavan, IL, St. Mary's Church. (PEO)
Hopeton, CA, St. John the Baptist, c/o Merced, CA, Our Lady of Mercy/St. Patrick's Church. (FRS)
Hopland, CA, St. Francis, c/o Ukiah, CA, St. Mary of the Angels Church. (SR)
Hornitos, CA, Mariposa Co., St. Catherine of Sienna, c/o Mariposa, CA, St. Joseph Church. (FRS)
Horse Cave, KY, Hart Co., Our Lady of the Caves Church, c/o Glasgow, KY, St. Helen Church. (L)
Horse Springs, NM, Catron Co., St. Anne, c/o Aragon, NM, Santo Nino Church. (GLP)
Horseshoe Lake, AR, Crittenden Co., St. Mary's of the Lake, c/o West Memphis, AR, St. Michael's Church. (LR)
Hostyn Hill, TX, Fayette Co., St. Mary's, c/o Fayetteville, TX, St. John's Church. (AUS)
Hot Springs, MT, Sacred Heart, c/o Plains, MT, St. James Church. (HEL)
Hot Springs, NC, Madison Co., Chapel of the Redeemer, c/o Mars Hill, NC, St. Andrew the Apostle Church. (CHL)
Hotchkiss, CO, Delta Co., St. Margaret Mary, c/o Paonia, CO, Sacred Heart Church. (PBL)
Houston, MS, Chickasaw Co., Immaculate Heart of Mary, c/o Aberdeen, MS, St. Francis of Assisi Church. (JKS)
Hoyo Planas, PR, Jayuya Co., Esp. Santo, c/o Jayuya, PR, Our Lady of Monserrate Church. (PCE)
Hubbard, NE, Dakota Co., St. Mary, c/o Jackson, NE, St. Patrick Church. (OM)
Hubbard, OR, Marion Co., St. Agnes, c/o Woodburn, OR, St. Luke Church. (P)
Hudson, WY, Fremont Co., Ascension, c/o Lander, WY, Holy Rosary Church. (CHY)
Huff, ND, Morton Co., St. Martin, c/o Mandan, ND, Christ the King Church. (BIS)
Huff, ND, Morton Co., St. Martin, c/o St. Anthony, ND, St. Anthony Church. (BIS)
Hugo, CO, Lincoln Co., St. Anthony of Padua, c/o Limon, CO, Our Lady of Victory(1925) Church. (COS)
Hulberton, NY, Orleans Co., St. Rocco, c/o Holley, NY, St. Mary Church. (BUF)
Hulett, WY, Crook Co., St. Matthew's, c/o Newcastle, WY, Corpus Christi Church. (CHY)
Huletts Landing, NY, Washington Co., Our Lady of Assumption, c/o Whitehall, NY, Our Lady of Hope Church. (ALB)
Humansville, MO, Polk Co., St. Catherine, c/o Bolivar, MO, Sacred Heart Church. (SPC)
Humarock, MA, St. Theresa's, c/o Marshfield, MA, St. Christine Church. (BO)
Hume, IL, Edgar Co., St. Michael's, c/o Villa Grove, IL, Sacred Heart Church. (SFD)
Hunter, ND, Cass Co., St. Agnes, c/o Mayville, ND, Our Lady of Peace Church. (FAR)
Hunter, TX, Comal Co., St. John, c/o New Braunfels, TX, Our Lady of Perpetual Help Church. (SAT)
Huntingdon, TN, Carroll Co., Holy Family Church, c/o Camden, TN, St. Mary Church. (MEM)
Huntington, OR, St. Joachim, c/o Ontario, OR, Blessed Sacrament Church. (BAK)
Huntington, UT, Emery Co., San Rafael, c/o Price, UT, Notre Dame de Lourdes Church. (SLC)
Huntsville, UT, Weber Co., St. Florence, c/o [3] Ogden, UT, St. Joseph's Church. (SLC)
Hurdsfield, ND, Wells Co., St. Patrick, c/o Sykeston, ND, St. Elizabeth's Church. (FAR)
Hurley, MS, Jackson Co., St. Ann, c/o Moss Point, MS, St. Joseph Church. (BLX)
Hurricane Branch, MO, Chariton Co., St. Joseph, c/o Marceline, MO, St. Bonaventure Church. (JC)
Hyannis, NE, Grant Co., All Saint's, c/o Mullen, NE, St. Mary's Church. (GI)
Hydaburg, AK, c/o Craig, AK, St. John by the Sea Church. (JUN)
Hyde Park, VT, Lamoille Co., St. Teresa, c/o Morrisville, VT, Holy Cross Church. (BUR)
Hysham, MT, St. Joseph, c/o Forsyth, MT, Immaculate Conception Church. (GF)

I

Imperial, TX, Pecos Co., Our Lady of Lourdes, c/o Fort Stockton, TX, St. Agnes Church. (SAN)
Independence, CA, Inyo Co., St. Vivian, c/o Lone Pine, CA, Santa Rosa Church. (FRS)
Indian Township, ME, St. Theresa's Chapel, c/o Indian Township, ME, St. Ann Church. (PRT)
Indian Village, LA, Sacred Heart Parish, Sacred Heart, c/o Kinder, LA, St. Philip Neri Church. (LKC)
Indiera Fria, PR, Santa Rosa, c/o Maricao, PR, St. John the Baptist Church. (MGZ)
Industry, TX, Austin Co., Immaculate Conception, c/o Bellville, TX, SS. Peter & Paul Church. (GAL)
Inglis, FL, Levy Co., St. Anthony the Abbot, c/o Williston, FL, Holy Family Church. (STA)
Interior, SD, Jackson Co., Holy Rosary, c/o Wall, SD, St. Patrick's Church. (RC)
Inverness, MT, Sacred Heart, c/o Chester, MT, St. Mary's Church. (GF)
Ione, CA, Amador Co., Mule Creek State Prison, c/o Ione, CA, Sacred Heart Church. (SAC)
Ione, CA, Amador Co., Preston School of Industry, California Youth Authority, c/o Ione, CA, Sacred Heart Church. (SAC)
Iowa, LA, Calcasieu Parish, St. Peter Claver, c/o Welsh, LA, St. Joseph Church. (LKC)
Iraan, TX, Pecos Co., St. Francis of Assisi, c/o McCamey, TX, Sacred Heart Church. (SAN)
Irasburg, VT, Orleans Co., St. John Vianney, c/o Orleans, VT, St. Theresa of Child Jesus Church. (BUR)
Irish Grove Rd., IL, Stephenson Co., St. Patrick, c/o Durand, IL, St. Mary Church. (RCK)
Irish Ridge, NY, Oneida Co., St. Mary, c/o Durhamville, NY, St. Francis Church. (SY)

Irishtown, MI, Gratiot Co., St. Patrick, c/o Shepherd, MI, St. Vincent De Paul Church. (SAG)
Isabel, SD, Dewey Co., St. Mary, c/o Timber Lake, SD, Holy Cross Church. (RC)
Island Heights, NJ, Ocean Co., St. Gertrude, c/o [1] Toms River, NJ, St. Joseph Church. (TR)
Isle La motte, VT, Grand Isle Co., St. Joseph, c/o Alburg, VT, St. Amadeus Church. (BUR)
Isle of Hope, GA, Our Lady of Good Hope, c/o [9] Savannah, GA, St. James Church. (SAV)
Isleboro, ME, St. Mary of the Isles, c/o Belfast, ME, St. Francis of Assisi Church. (PRT)
Islesford, ME, Our Lady Star of the Sea, c/o Northeast Harbor, ME, St. Ignatius Church. (PRT)
Italy, TX, Ellis Co., Epiphany, c/o Waxahachie, TX, St. Joseph Church. (DAL)
Iuka, MS, Tishomingo Co., St. Mary, c/o Booneville, MS, St. Francis of Assisi Church. (JKS)
Ivanhoe, CA, Tulare Co., San Felipe de Jesus, c/o Visalia, CA, Holy Family Church. (FRS)

J

Jacaquas, PR, Bo. Jacaguas, N.S. de Fatima, c/o Juana Diaz, PR, St. Raymond Nonato Church. (PCE)
Jackpot, NV, Elko Co., Our Lady of Guadalupe, c/o Elko, NV, St. Joseph's Church. (RNO)
Jackson, AL, Clarke Co., Visitation, c/o Grove Hill, AL, Sacred Heart Church. (MOB)
Jackson, GA, Butts Co., St. Mary's, c/o McDonough, GA, St. James The Apostle Church. (ATL)
Jackson, NJ, Ocean Co., Church of St. Monica, c/o New Egypt, NJ, Assumption Church. (TR)
Jacksonville, OR, Jackson Co., St. Joseph, c/o Medford, OR, Sacred Heart of Jesus Church. (P)
Jacumba, CA, San Diego Co., St. Mary Magdalene, c/o [2] El Cajon, CA, Our Lady of Grace Church. (SD)
Jaguey Chiquito, PR, San Augustin, c/o Aguada, PR, St. Francis of Assisi Church. (MGZ)
Jamaica Beach, TX, Galveston Co., Mary, Star of the Sea, c/o [5] Galveston, TX, St. Peter the Apostle Church. (GAL)
Jamestown, PA, Mercer Co., St. Margaret, c/o Greenville, PA, St. Michael Church. (E)
Jamestown, TN, Fentress Co., Mission Catholic Community of Fentress County, c/o Harriman, TN, Blessed Sacrament Church. (KNX)
Jarales, NM, Valencia Co., c/o Belen, NM, Our Lady of Belen Church. (SFE)
Jardines de Carolina, PR, Santa Rosa, c/o [20] Carolina, PR, San Valentin Church. (SJN)
Jardines de Rio Grande, PR, Ntra. Sra. de Guadalupe, c/o Rio Grande, PR, Nuestra Senora del Carmen Church. (SJN)
Jardines del Caribe, PR, Perpetuo Socorro, c/o [2] Mayaquez, PR, Our Lady of Mt. Carmel Church. (MGZ)
Jasper, FL, Hamilton Co., St. Therese of Jesus, c/o Live Oak, FL, St. Francis Xavier Church. (STA)
Jasper, GA, Pickens Co., Our Lady of the Mountains, c/o Canton, GA, Our Lady of LaSalette Church. (ATL)
Jauca, PR, San Ignacio de Loyola, c/o Santa Isabel, PR, St. James Church. (PCE)
Jayton, TX, Kent Co., Epiphany, c/o Spur, TX, St. Mary Church. (LUB)
Jefferson, NH, Coos, St. Agnes, c/o Lancaster, NH, All Saints Church. (MAN)
Jefferson, OR, Marion Co., St. Thomas, c/o Scio, OR, St. Bernard Church. (P)
Jeffrey City, WY, Freemont Co., St. Brendan, c/o Lander, WY, Holy Rosary Church. (CHY)
Jenny Lind, AR, Sebastian Co., Sts. Sabina and Mary's Church, c/o Van Buren, AR, St. Michael's Church. (LR)
Jessenland, MN, Sibley Co., St. Thomas, c/o Henderson, MN, St. Joseph Church. (NU)
Jessie, ND, Griggs Co., St. Lawrence, c/o Cooperstown, ND, St. George's Church. (FAR)
Jessup, PA, Lackawanna Co., St. Stanislaus, c/o Jessup, PA, St. James Church. (SCR)
Jobstown, NJ, Burlington Co., St. Andrew, c/o Mount Holly, NJ, Sacred Heart Church. (TR)
Jocko, MT, Lake Co., St. John Berchman's, c/o St. Ignatius, MT, St. Ignatius Mission. (HEL)
Johnson, VT, Lamoille Co., St. John the Apostle, c/o Morrisville, VT, Holy Cross Church. (BUR)
Johnson Bayou, LA, Our Lady of the Assumption, c/o Hackberry, LA, St. Peter Apostle Church. (LKC)
Johnson City, TX, Blanco Co., Good Shepherd, c/o Blanco, TX, St. Ferdinand's Church. (AUS)
Johnsonville, SC, Florence Co., St. Patrick, c/o Lake City, SC, St. Philip's Church. (CHR)
Joliet, MT, St. John, c/o Bridger, MT, Sacred Heart Church. (GF)
Jolon, CA, Monterey Co., South Shore of Lake San Antonio, c/o Jolon, CA, San Antonio Mission. (MRY)
Jones, OK, Oklahoma Co., St. Robert Bellarmine, c/o [5] Oklahoma City, OK, Corpus Christi Church. (OKL)
Jonesville, LA, St. Gerard, c/o Ferriday, LA, St. Patrick Church. (ALX)
Jordan, MT, St. John the Baptist, c/o Circle, MT, St. Francis Xavier Church. (GF)
Joyuda, PR, St. John the Baptist, c/o Cabo Rojo, PR, St. Michael Church. (MGZ)
Juana Diaz, PR, Divine Mercy, c/o Juana Diaz, PR, Santa Teresita Church. (PCE)
Juana Diaz, PR, Bo. Rio Cana Arriba, La Merced, c/o Juana Diaz, PR, St. Raymond Nonato Church. (PCE)
Juana Diaz, PR, San Martin de Porres, c/o Juana Diaz, PR, Santa Teresita Church. (PCE)
Judith Gap, MT, Wheatland Co., Immaculate Conception, c/o Harlowton, MT, St. Joseph Church. (HEL)
Julian, NE, Nemaha Co., St. Bernard's, c/o Paul, NE, St. Joseph's Church. (LIN)
Juniata, NE, Adams Co., Assumption, c/o Roseland, NE, Sacred Heart Church. (LIN)
Juntura, OR, St. Charles, c/o Vale, OR, St. Patrick's Church. (BAK)

K

Kahakuloa, HI, St. Francis Xavier, c/o Waihee, HI, St. Ann Church. (HON)
Kahaluu, HI, St. Peter, c/o Kailua-Kona, HI, St. Michael The Archangel Church. (HON)
Kake, AK, c/o Petersburg, AK, St. Catherine of Siena Church. (JUN)
Kalama, WA, Cowlitz Co., St. Joseph, c/o Woodland, WA, St. Philip Church. (SEA)
Kalaoa, HI, Holy Rosary, c/o Kailua-Kona, HI, St. Michael The Archangel Church. (HON)
Kalawao, HI, Molokai Co., St. Philomena, c/o Kalaupapa, HI, St. Francis Church. (HON)
Kalskag, AK, c/o Aniak, AK, St. Theresa Church. (FBK)
Kannapolis, NC, Cabarrus Co., St. Joseph, c/o Concord, NC, St. James Church. (CHL)
Kansas, OH, Seneca Co., St. James, c/o Millersville, OH, St. Mary Church. (TOL)
Kaplan, LA, Vermilion Parish, St. Frances Xavier Cabrini, c/o Kaplan, LA, Our Lady of the Holy Rosary Church. (LAF)
Karlsruhe, ND, McHenry Co., Sts. Peter & Paul, c/o Velva, ND, St. Cecilia's Church. (FAR)
Karlstad, MN, Marshall Co., St. Edward, c/o Greenbush, MN, Blessed Sacrament Church. (CR)
Kasaan, AK, c/o Craig, AK, St. John by the Sea Church. (JUN)
Kaumakani, HI, Kauai Co., St. Joseph, c/o Kekaha, HI, St. Theresa Church. (HON)
Kaupo, HI, Maui Co., St. Joseph, c/o Hana, HI, St. Mary Church. (HON)
Kaycee, WY, Johnson Co., St. Hubert, c/o Buffalo, WY, St. John the Baptist Church. (CHY)
Keaau, HI, Holy Rosary, c/o Mountain View, HI, St. Theresa Church. (HON)
Kealakekua, HI, Honaunau Co., c/o Honaunau, HI, St. Benedict Church. (HON)
Keanae, HI, Maui Co., St. Gabriel, c/o Haiku, HI, St. Rita Church. (HON)
Keenesburg, CO, Weld Co., Holy Family, c/o Roggen, CO, Sacred Heart Church. (DEN)
Keithsburg, IL, Mercer Co., St. Mary's, c/o Aledo, IL, St. Catherine's Church. (PEO)
Kelly, NM, Socorro Co., c/o Socorro, NM, San Miguel Church. (SFE)
Kelseyville, CA, St. Peter, c/o Lakeport, CA, St. Mary Church. (SR)
Kenel, SD, Corson Co., Assumption of the Blessed Virgin Mary Church, c/o Standing Rock, SD, Standing Rock Reservation Church. (RC)
Kenel, SD, Corson Co., Our Lady of the Assumption Parish, c/o McLaughlin, SD, St. Bernard Church. (RC)
Kenyon, MN, Goodhue Co., St. Michael, c/o Pine Island, MN, St. Michael Church. (STP)
Kerhonkson, NY, Ulster Co., Our Lady of Lourdes, c/o Ellenville, NY, St. Mary and St. Andrew Church. (NY)
Keshena, WI, St. Joseph of the Lake, South Branch, c/o Keshena, WI, St. Michael Church. (GB)
Keswick, IA, Keokuk Co., Our Lady of Lourdes, c/o Sigourney, IA, St. Mary's Church. (DAV)
Kettleman City, CA, St. Cecilia, c/o Avenal, CA, St. Joseph Church. (FRS)
Kewanna, IN, Fulton Co., St. Ann, c/o Rochester, IN, St. Joseph Church. (LFT)
Keyapaha, SD, Tripp Co., St. Ann, c/o Winner, SD, Immaculate Conception Church. (RC)
Keystone, SD, Pennington Co., Our Lady of Mt. Carmel, c/o [2] Rapid City, SD, Blessed Sacrament Church. (RC)
Kilauea, HI, Kauai Co., St. Sylvester, c/o Kapaa, HI, St. Catherine Church. (HON)
Killington, VT, Rutland Co., Our Lady of the Mountains, c/o Chittenden, VT, St. Robert Church. (BUR)
Kindred, ND, Cass Co., St. Maurice, c/o Wyndmere, ND, St. John the Baptist Church. (FAR)
King, NC, Stokes Co., Good Shepherd, c/o Winston-Salem, NC, St. Benedict the Moor Church. (CHL)
King George, VA, King George Co., St. Anthony's, c/o Colonial Beach, VA, St. Elizabeth Church. (ARL)
King Ranch, TX, Kleberg Co., Christ the King, c/o [4] Kingsville, TX, St. Martin Church. (CC)
Kingman, ME, St. James, c/o Lincoln, ME, St. Mary Church. (PRT)
Kings Beach, CA, Placer Co., Our Lady of the Lake, c/o Truckee, CA, Assumption of the Blessed Virgin Mary Church. (SAC)
Kings Mountain, NC, Cleveland Co., Christ the King, c/o Shelby, NC, St. Mary's Church. (CHL)
Kingston, NH, Rockingham Co., St. Frederick, c/o Newton, NH, Mary, Mother of the Church. (MAN)
Kingsville, TX, Kleberg Co., St. Thomas Aquinas Catholic Campus Center - Texas A & M, c/o [2] Kingsville, TX, St. Gertrude Church. (CC)
Kinnear, WY, Fremont Co., St. Edward, c/o Riverton, WY, St. Margaret's Church. (CHY)
Kintyre, ND, Emmons Co., St. Boniface, c/o Wishek, ND, St. Patrick Church. (FAR)
Kipahulu, HI, Maui Co., St. Paul, c/o Hana, HI, St. Mary Church. (HON)
Kirtland, NM, San Juan Catholic Center, c/o Waterflow, NM, Sacred Heart Church. (GLP)
Kit Carson, CO, Cheyenne Co., St. Augustine, c/o Cheyenne Wells, CO, Sacred Heart Church. (COS)
Kitzmiller, MD, Garrett Co., Immaculate Conception, c/o Oakland, MD, St. Peter the Apostle Church. (BAL)
Klagetoh, AZ, Apache Co., St. Anne, c/o Ganado, AZ, All Saints Church. (GLP)
Klamath, CA, St. Robert and Ann, c/o Crescent City, CA, St. Joseph Church. (SR)
Klawock, AK, c/o Craig, AK, St. John by the Sea Church. (JUN)
Knickerbocker, TX, Tom Green Co., Immaculate Conception, c/o Eldorado, TX, Our Lady of Guadalupe Church. (SAN)
Knippa, TX, Uvalde Co., St. Joseph, c/o Sabinal, TX, St. Patrick's Church. (SAT)
Knox, ND, Benson Co., St. Mary, c/o Leeds, ND, St. Vincent de Paul Church. (FAR)
Koeltztown, MO, St. Boniface, c/o Argyle, MO, St. Aloysius Church. (JC)
Kolin, LA, Sts. Francis and Anne, c/o Deville, LA, St. John the Baptist Church. (ALX)
Koontz Lake, IN, Starke Co., St. Dominic, c/o Hamlet, IN, Holy Cross Church. (GRY)
Kovar, TX, Bastrop Co., Sts. Peter and Paul, c/o Smithville, TX, St. Paul the Apostle Church. (AUS)
Kress, TX, Swisher Co., St. Paul the Apostle, c/o Tulia, TX, Church of the Holy Spirit. (AMA)
Kuttu, FM, c/o Lukunor, FM, Sacred Heart Church. (CI)
Kwajalein, MH, Santo, c/o Ebeye, MH, Queen of Peace Church. (MI)

L

L'Erable, IL, Iroquois Co., St. John the Baptist, c/o Ashkum, IL, Assumption of the Blessed Virgin Mary Church. (JOL)
La Bajada, NM, Sandoval Co., c/o Pena Blanca, NM, Nuestra Senora De Guadalupe Church. (SFE)
La Barge, WY, Lincoln Co., La Barge Catholic Community Center, c/o Kemmerer, WY, St. Patrick's Church. (CHY)
La Casita, TX, Our Lady of the Peace, c/o Grulla, TX, Holy Family Church. (BWN)
La Cienega, NM, Santa Fe Co., c/o [6] Santa Fe, NM, San Isidro Church. (SFE)
La Cueva, NM, Mora Co., c/o Mora, NM, St. Gertrude Church. (SFE)
La Grange, CA, Stanislaus Co., St. Louis, c/o Hughson, CA, St. Anthony Church. (STO)
La Grange, MO, Lewis Co., Notre Dame, c/o Canton, MO, St. Joseph Church. (JC)
La Honda, CA, San Mateo Co., Our Lady of Refuge, c/o Half Moon Bay, CA, Our Lady of the Pillar Church. (SFR)
La Isla, TX, San Luis, c/o Fabens, TX, Our Lady of Guadalupe Church. (ELP)
La Jara, CO, Conejos Co., Our Lady of the Valley, c/o Capulin, CO, St. Joseph Church. (PBL)
La Jara, NM, Sandoval Co., Santo Nino, c/o Cuba, NM, Immaculate Conception Church. (GLP)
La Lagunita, NM, San Miguel Co., c/o Ribera, NM, San Miguel Del Vado Church. (SFE)
La Luz, NM, Our Lady of the Light, c/o Alamogordo, NM, Immaculate Conception Church. (LSC)
La Madera, NM, Rio Arriba Co., c/o El Rito, NM, San Juan Nepomuceno Church. (SFE)
La Paloma, TX, Our Lady of Lourdes, c/o Ranchito, TX, St. Ignatius Church. (BWN)
La Pica, PR, San Patricio Co., c/o Jayuya, PR, Our Lady of Monserrate Church. (PCE)
La Piedra, PR, Ala de La Piedra Co., O.L. of Perp. Help, c/o Villalba, PR, Our Lady Mother of Divine Providence Church. (PCE)

La Playa, PR, Our Lady of Carmel, c/o Anasco, PR, St. Anthony Abbot Church. (MGZ)
La Puente, NM, Rio Arriba Co., c/o Los Ojos, NM, San Jose Church. (SFE)
La Puerta, TX, St. Paul, c/o Rio Grande City, TX, Immaculate Conception Church. (BWN)
La Sara, TX, St. Patrick, c/o Raymondville, TX, Our Lady of Guadalupe Church. (BWN)
La Union, NM, Our Lady of Refuge, c/o Anthony, NM, St. Anthony's Church. (LSC)
La Veta, CO, Huerfano Co., Christ the King, c/o Walsenburg, CO, St. Mary Church. (PBL)
La Villa, TX, Our Lady of Guadalupe, c/o Edcouch, TX, St. Theresa of the Infant Jesus Church. (BWN)
Lacassine, LA, Jefferson Davis Parish, St. John the Evangelist, c/o Iowa, LA, St. Raphael Church. (LKC)
Lacey, MI, Barry Co., Our Lady of Great Oak, c/o Delton, MI, St. Ambrose Church. (KAL)
Lackawaxen, PA, Pike Co., St. Mary, c/o Shohola, PA, St. Ann's Church. (SCR)
LaCrosse, IN, LaPorte Co., St. Martin, c/o Wanatah, IN, Sacred Heart Church. (GRY)
Laddonia, MO, Audrain Co., St. John, c/o Vandalia, MO, Sacred Heart Church. (JC)
Lafayette, LA, Lafayette Parish, Gift of Mary Chapel, c/o [11] Lafayette, LA, St. Genevieve Church. (LAF)
Lafayette, LA, Lafayette Parish, Our Lady of Good Hope, c/o [2] Lafayette, LA, St. Paul The Apostle Church. (LAF)
LaGrangeville, NY, Dutchess Co., Mission Church of Blessed Kateri Tekakwitha, c/o Hopewell Junction, NY, St. Columba Church. (NY)
Laguna, PR, Santa Rita, c/o Aguada, PR, St. Francis of Assisi Church. (MGZ)
Lajitas, TX, Lajitas Mission, c/o Presidio, TX, Santa Teresa de Jesus Church. (ELP)
Lake Arthur, NM, Our Lady of Guadalupe, c/o Dexter, NM, Immaculate Conception Church. (LSC)
Lake Bonaparte, NY, St. Rita, c/o Harrisville, NY, St. Francis Solanus Church. (OG)
Lake Carmel, NY, Putnam Co., Our Lady of the Lake, c/o Carmel, NY, St. James the Apostle Church. (NY)
Lake Charles, LA, Calcasieu Parish, Christ the King, c/o [8] Lake Charles, LA, Our Lady Queen of Heaven Church. (LKC)
Lake Charles, LA, Calcasieu Parish, Our Lady of Fatima Chapel, c/o [2] Lake Charles, LA, Immaculate Heart of Mary Church. (LKC)
Lake Charles, LA, Calcasieu Parish, St. Martin de Porres, c/o [8] Lake Charles, LA, Our Lady Queen of Heaven Church. (LKC)
Lake City, CO, Hinsdale Co., St. Rose of Lima, c/o Gunnison, CO, St. Peter Church. (PBL)
Lake Como, PA, Wayne Co., Assumption of the B.V.M., c/o Pleasant Mount, PA, St. James Church. (SCR)
Lake Hauto, PA, Sacred Heart Chapel, c/o Nesquehoning, PA, Sacred Heart Church. (ALN)
Lake Huntington, NY, Sullivan Co., Our Lady of the Lake, c/o Narrowsburg, NY, St. Francis Xavier Church. (NY)
Lake Peekskill, NY, Putnam Co., North American Martyrs, c/o Cortlandt Manor, NY, St. Columbanus Church. (NY)
Lake Titus, NY, Franklin Co., St. Mary, c/o Chasm Falls, NY, St. Helen Church. (OG)
Lake Wallenpaupack, PA, Pike Co., St. Veronica, c/o Hawley, PA, Blessed Virgin Mary, Queen of Peace Church. (SCR)
Lake Williams, ND, Kidder Co., Our Lady of the Lake, c/o Tappen, ND, St. Paul's Church. (FAR)
Lake Wylie, SC, York Co., All Saints, c/o York, SC, Divine Saviour Church. (CHR)
Lakeshore, MS, Hancock Co., St. John, c/o Clermont Harbor, MS, St. Ann Church. (BLX)
Lakeside, CA, Assumption of BVM, c/o Lakeside, CA, Blessed Kateri Tekakwitha Church. (SD)
Lakeside, SD, Meade Co., St. Margaret, c/o New Underwood, SD, St. John the Evangelist Church. (RC)
Lakeview, NY, Nassau Co., Chapel, c/o West Hempstead, NY, St. Thomas, the Apostle Church. (RVC)
Lakewood, NJ, Ocean Co., Holy Family Church, c/o Lakewood, NJ, St. Mary of the Lake Church. (TR)
Lambert, MT, Richland Co., St. Theresa, c/o Sidney, MT, St. Matthew Church. (GF)
Lamesa, TX, Dawson Co., Our Lady of Guadalupe, c/o Lamesa, TX, St. Margaret Mary Church. (LUB)
Lancaster, CA, Los Angeles Co., St. Elizabeth, c/o Lancaster, CA, Blessed Junipero Serra Church. (LA)
Lancaster, MN, Kittson Co., Holy Rosary, c/o Hallock, MN, St. Patrick's Church. (CR)
Lankin, ND, Walsh Co., St. Joseph, c/o Pisek, ND, St. John Nepomucene Church. (FAR)
Lansford, ND, Bottineau Co., St. John, c/o Glenburn, ND, St. Philomena Church. (BIS)
Lantana, FL, c/o Miami, FL, Assumption of B.V.M. Church. (SJP)
Laona, WI, St. Leonard, c/o Newald, WI, St. Hubert Church. (GB)
LaPorte, MN, Hubbard Co., St.Theodore, c/o Cass Lake, MN, St. Charles Church. (DUL)
Laporte, PA, Sullivan Co., Sacred Heart, c/o Dushore, PA, St. Basil's Church. (SCR)
Laporte, PA, Sullivan Co., Sacred Heart, c/o Mildred, PA, St. Francis of Assisi Church. (SCR)
Laredo, TX, Apostolate Missions in Northern Mexico, c/o [17] Laredo, TX, St. Patrick Church. (LAR)
Laredo, TX, Ntra. Sra. Del Rosario (Colonia Los Obispos), c/o [11] Laredo, TX, Santa Margarita de Escocia Independent Mission. (LAR)
Laredo, TX, Webb Co., Santa Cruz, c/o [6] Laredo, TX, Holy Redeemer Church. (LAR)
Las Colonias, NM, San Miguel Co., c/o Pecos, NM, St. Anthony Church. (SFE)
Las Colonias, NM, Taos Co., Santo Nino de Atocha, c/o Arroyo Seco, NM, La Santisima Trinidad Church. (SFE)
Las Flores, PR, Coamo Co., San Martin, c/o Coamo, PR, St. Blase Church. (PCE)
Las Mareas, PR, St. Judas, c/o Aguirre, PR, Sacred Heart Church. (PCE)
Las Margaritas, PR, Bo. Collores Arriba, Santiago, Ap., c/o Juana Diaz, PR, St. Raymond Nonato Church. (PCE)
Las Nutrias, NM, Socorro Co., San Isidro, c/o La Joya, NM, Our Lady of Sorrows Church. (SFE)
Las Ochenta, PR, Inmaculada Concepcion, c/o Salinas, PR, Our Lady of Monserrat Church. (PCE)
Las Palmas, PR, St. Rita, c/o Cabo Rojo, PR, St. Michael Church. (MGZ)
Las Palomas, NM, Sierra Co., San Ysidro, c/o Truth or Consequences, NM, Our Lady of Perpetual Help Church. (LSC)
Las Rucias, TX, Sacred Heart, c/o Ranchito, TX, St. Ignatius Church. (BWN)
Las Tablas, NM, Taos Co., c/o El Rito, NM, San Juan Nepomuceno Church. (SFE)
Las Vegas, PR, Sta. Teresita, c/o Yauco, PR, Holy Rossary Church. (PCE)
LaSal, UT, San Juan Co., Sacred Heart, c/o Moab, UT, St. Pius X Church. (SLC)
LaSalle, TX, St. Theresa, c/o Vanderbilt, TX, St. John Bosco Church. (VIC)
Lathrop, CA, San Joaquin Co., Our Lady of Guadalupe, c/o [4] Stockton, CA, St. George Church. (STO)
Latimer, MS, Jackson Co., Christ the King, c/o Vancleave, MS, Holy Spirit Catholic Church. (BLX)
Lattnerville, IA, Annunciation, c/o Peosta, IA, St. John the Baptist Church. (DUB)
Laupahoehoe, HI, c/o Papaaloa, HI, St. Anthony Church. (HON)
Laurens, SC, Laurens Co., Holy Spirit, c/o Joanna, SC, St. Boniface Church. (CHR)
Lavelle, PA, Schuylkill Co., St. Elizabeth, c/o Ashland, PA, St. Mauritius Church. (ALN)
Lawrence, NE, Nuckolls Co., St. Stephen's, c/o Lawrence, NE, Sacred Heart Church. (LIN)
Lawrenceville, VA, Greensville Co., St. Bernard, c/o Emporia, VA, St. Richard Church. (RIC)
LBJ Village, VI, U.S.V.I., Sacred Heart Chapel, c/o [2] Christiansted, VI, Church of the Holy Cross. (STV)
Le Bleu Settlement, LA, Calcasieu Parish, St. Joseph, c/o Iowa, LA, St. Raphael Church. (LKC)
Le Doux, NM, Mora Co., c/o Mora, NM, St. Gertrude Church. (SFE)
Le Grand, CA, Merced Co., Our Lady of Lourdes, c/o Planada, CA, Sacred Heart Church. (FRS)
Leakesville, MS, Perry Co., Holy Trinity, c/o Waynesboro, MS, St. Bernadette Church. (BLX)
Leakey, TX, Real Co., St. Raymond of Pennafort, c/o Rocksprings, TX, Sacred Heart of Mary Church. (SAT)
Leaton, MI, Isabella Co., St. Charles, c/o Rosebush, MI, St. Henry Church. (SAG)
Lebanon, PA, Lebanon Co., Our Lady of Fatima, c/o [1] Lebanon, PA, Assumption of the Blessed Virgin Mary Church. (HBG)
Lebanon Junction, KY, St. Clare, c/o Lebanon Junction, KY, St. Benedict Church. (L)
Ledgedale, PA, Wayne Co., St. Mary, c/o Lake Ariel, PA, St. Thomas More Church. (SCR)
Lee Vining, CA, Mono Co., Our Savior of the Mountains, c/o Mammoth Lakes, CA, St. Joseph Church. (STO)
Leeds, NY, St. Bridget, c/o Catskill, NY, St. Patrick Church. (ALB)
Leggett, CA, St. Cecilia, c/o Garberville, CA, Our Lady of the Redwoods Church. (SR)
Lehi, AZ, St. Paschal Baylon, c/o [4] Tempe, AZ, St. Margaret Church. (PHX)
Leicester, VT, Addison Co., St. Agnes, c/o Brandon, VT, St. Mary's Church. (BUR)
Leming, TX, Atascosa Co., Our Lady of Guadalupe, c/o Pleasanton, TX, St. Luke-Loire Church. (SAT)
Lemitar, NM, Socorro Co., c/o Socorro, NM, San Miguel Church. (SFE)
Lenorah, TX, Martin Co., St. Isidore, c/o Stanton, TX, St. Joseph's Church. (SAN)
Leroy, ND, Pembina Co., St. Joseph, c/o Walhalla, ND, St. Boniface's Church. (FAR)
Lesterville, MO, Reynolds Co., Our Lady of Sorrows, c/o Ironton, MO, Ste. Marie Du Lac Church. (SPC)
Lewes, DE, Sussex Co., Shrine of St. Jude, c/o Rehoboth, DE, St. Edmond Church. (WIL)
Lewisburg, WV, Greenbriar Co., St. Louis, King of France, c/o Ronceverte, WV, St. Catherine of Siena Church. (WH)
Lewiston, CA, Trinity Co., St. Gilbert, c/o Weaverville, CA, St. Patrick Church. (SAC)
Lexington, IL, McLean Co., St. Mary, c/o Chenoa, IL, St. Joseph's Church. (PEO)
Lexington, TX, Lee Co., Holy Family, c/o Dime Box, TX, St. Joseph's Church. (AUS)
Leyba, NM, San Miguel Co., c/o Villanueva, NM, Our Lady of Guadalupe Church. (SFE)
Liberty, KY, Casey Co., Sacred Heart, c/o Clementsville, KY, St. Bernard Church. (L)
Licking, MO, Texas Co., St. John The Baptist, c/o Houston, MO, St. Mark Church. (SPC)
Limani, PR, Inm. Corazon de Maria, c/o Adjuntas, PR, St. Joachim Church. (PCE)
Lincoln, MT, Lewis and Clark Co., St. Jude's, c/o Helmville, MT, St. Thomas Church. (HEL)
Lincoln, NM, San Juan, c/o Ruidoso, NM, St. Eleanor Church. (LSC)
Lindsay, OK, Garvin Co., St. Peter's, c/o Pauls Valley, OK, St. Catherine of Siena Church. (OKL)
Lindsborg, KS, McPherson, St. Bridget of Sweden, c/o McPherson, KS, St. Joseph Church. (WCH)
Linlithgo, NY, Nativity of Our Lord, c/o Germantown, NY, Resurrection Church. (ALB)
Linville, NC, Avery Co., St. Bernadette, c/o Spruce Pine, NC, St. Lucien Church. (CHL)
Lisco, NE, Garden Co., St. Gall, c/o Chappell, NE, St. Joseph's Church. (GI)
Litchfield, ME, Kennebec Co., St. Leo, c/o Richmond, ME, St. Ambrose Church. (PRT)
Litchfield, OH, Medina Co., Jesus the Christ Child, c/o Litchfield, OH, Our Lady Help of Christians Parish Church. (CLV)
Little Egg Harbor, NJ, Ocean Co., St. Michael, c/o Tuckerton, NJ, St. Teresa Church. (TR)
Little Italy, AR, Pulaski Co., St. Francis, c/o Bigelow, AR, St. Boniface's Church. (LR)
Little Orleans, MD, Allegany Co., St. Patrick's, c/o Hancock, MD, St. Peter's Church. (BAL)
Little River, KS, Rice Co., Holy Trinity, c/o Bushton, KS, Holy Name of Jesus Church. (WCH)
Little Valley, NY, Cattaraugus Co., St. Mary, c/o Cattaraugus, NY, St. Mary Church. (BUF)
Littleton, WV, Wetzel Co., Assumption of the Blessed Virgin Mary, c/o Mannington, WV, St. Patrick's Church. (WH)
Live Oak, CA, Sutter Co., Our Lady of Guadalupe, c/o Gridley, CA, Sacred Heart Church. (SAC)
Llano Largo, NM, Taos Co., San Acacio Mission, c/o Penasco, NM, San Antonio de Padua Church. (SFE)
Llano Quemado, NM, Taos Co., N.S. del Carmel, c/o Ranchos De Taos, NM, San Francisco de Asis Church. (SFE)
Llano San Juan, NM, Taos Co., San Juan Nepomuceno Mission, c/o Penasco, NM, San Antonio de Padua Church. (SFE)
Llanos, PR, Sector El Juicio, c/o Aibonito, PR, Church of St. Joseph. (CGS)
Llanos Tunas, PR, Our Lady of Good Counsel, c/o Cabo Rojo, PR, St. Michael Church. (MGZ)
Lluberas, PR, St. Joseph, c/o Yauco, PR, Holy Rossary Church. (PCE)
Lobatos, CO, Sagrada Familia, c/o Conejos, CO, Our Lady of Guadalupe Church. (PBL)
Loch Lomond, CA, Our Lady of the Lake, c/o Middletown, CA, St. Joseph Church. (SR)
Lockney, TX, Floyd Co., San Jose, c/o Plainview, TX, St. Alice Church. (LUB)
Loda, IL, Iroquois Co., St. Joseph, c/o Paxton, IL, St. Mary Church. (JOL)
Lodi, OH, Medina Co., Jesus Our Teacher, c/o Litchfield, OH, Our Lady Help of Christians Parish Church. (CLV)
Logan, NM, Quay Co., San Antonio, c/o Tucumcari, NM, St. Anne Church. (SFE)
Loiza, PR, La Milagrosa, c/o Loiza, PR, Santiago Apostol, El Mayor Church. (SJN)
Loiza, PR, La Providencia, c/o Loiza, PR, Santiago Apostol, El Mayor Church. (SJN)
Loiza, PR, N. Sra. De Fatima, c/o Loiza, PR, Santiago Apostol, El Mayor Church. (SJN)
Loiza, PR, Ntra. Sra. de Fatima, c/o Loiza, PR, San Patricio Church. (SJN)
Loiza, PR, Ntra. Sra. del Perpetuo Socorro, c/o Loiza, PR, San Patricio Church. (SJN)
Loiza, PR, Parcelas Suarez, Ntra. Sra. Perpetuo Socorro, c/o Loiza, PR, Santiago Apostol, El Mayor Church. (SJN)
Loiza, PR, San Antonio, c/o Loiza, PR, San Patricio Church. (SJN)
Loiza, PR, San Rafael, c/o Loiza, PR, San Patricio Church. (SJN)
Loiza, PR, Santa Rosa, c/o Loiza, PR, San Patricio Church. (SJN)

Loiza, PR, Santisima Trinidad, c/o Loiza, PR, San Patricio Church. (SJN)
Loleta, CA, St. Patrick, c/o Fortuna, CA, St. Joseph Church. (SR)
Lolo, MT, Missoula Co., Spirit of Christ, c/o [2] Missoula, MT, Holy Family Church. (HEL)
Lometa, TX, Lampasas Co., Good Shepherd Catholic Church, c/o Lampasas, TX, St. Mary's Church. (AUS)
Lomice, ND, Walsh Co., St. Catherine, c/o Michigan, ND, St. Lawrence O'Toole Church. (FAR)
London, CA, Tulare Co., Santa Cruz, c/o Kingsburg, CA, Holy Family Church. (FRS)
Long Beach, CA, Los Angeles Co., Our Lady of Mt. Carmel Cambodian Catholic Center, c/o [1] Long Beach, CA, St. Anthony Church. (LA)
Long Eddy, NY, Sullivan Co., St. Patrick, c/o Callicoon, NY, Holy Cross Church. (NY)
Long Island, ME, Great Diamond Island, c/o [8] Portland, ME, St. Christopher's Church. (PRT)
Longcreek, OR, St. Katherine, c/o John Day, OR, St. Elizabeth's Church. (BAK)
Lopeno, TX, San Pedro, c/o Zapata, TX, Our Lady of Lourdes Church. (LAR)
Lopezville, TX, Immaculate Conception, c/o San Juan, TX, St. John the Baptist Church. (BWN)
Loraine, TX, Mitchell Co., San Jose, c/o Colorado City, TX, St. Ann's Church. (SAN)
Lorenzo, TX, Crosby Co., San Lorenzo, c/o Idalou, TX, St. Philip Benizi Church. (LUB)
Loris, SC, Horry Co., Church of the Resurrection, c/o Conway, SC, St. James Church. (CHR)
Los Alamos, CA, Santa Barbara Co., St. Anthony's Church, c/o Santa Maria, CA, St. Louis de Montfort Church. (LA)
Los Angeles, CA, Old Co., Assumption, c/o [5] Los Angeles, CA, Assumption Church. (LA)
Los Angeles, CA, Los Angeles Co., La Purisima Chapel, c/o [32] Los Angeles, CA, Our Lady of the Rosary of Talpa Church. (LA)
Los Angeles, CA, Los Angeles Co., San Conrado, c/o [88] Los Angeles, CA, St. Peter Church. (LA)
Los Angeles, CA, Los Angeles Co., San Felipe, c/o [25] Los Angeles, CA, Our Lady of Guadalupe Church. (LA)
Los Angeles, CA, Los Angeles Co., Santo Nino, c/o [96] Los Angeles, CA, St. Vincent De Paul Church. (LA)
Los Angeles, CA, Los Angeles Co., St. John Bosco, c/o [84] Los Angeles, CA, St. Odilia Church. (LA)
Los Angeles, CA, Los Angeles Co., St. Turibius, c/o [73] Los Angeles, CA, St. Joseph Church. (LA)
Los Chavez, NM, Valencia Co., c/o Belen, NM, Our Lady of Belen Church. (SFE)
Los Cordovas, NM, Taos Co., San Isidro, c/o Ranchos De Taos, NM, San Francisco de Asis Church. (SFE)
Los Ebanos, TX, St. Michael, c/o La Joya, TX, Our Lady, Queen of Angels Church. (BWN)
Los Garcias Ranch, TX, Sacred Heart, c/o Rio Grande City, TX, Immaculate Conception Church. (BWN)
Los Hueros, NM, Mora Co., c/o Wagon Mound, NM, Santa Clara Church. (SFE)
Los Le Febres, NM, Mora Co., c/o Wagon Mound, NM, Santa Clara Church. (SFE)
Los Lentes, NM, Valencia Co., San Antonio, c/o Los Lunas, NM, St. Clement Church. (SFE)
Los Llanos, PR, Coamo Co., St. Anthony, c/o Coamo, PR, St. Blase Church. (PCE)
Los Martinez, NM, Our Lady of Guadalupe, c/o Blanco, NM, St. Rose of Lima Church. (GLP)
Los Saenz, TX, Holy Family, c/o Roma, TX, Our Lady of Refuge Church. (BWN)
Los Sauces, CO, St. Anthony, c/o Capulin, CO, St. Joseph Church. (PBL)
Los Valdeses, CO, Rio Grande Co., St. Francis of Assisi, c/o Del Norte, CO, Holy Name of Mary Church. (PBL)
Losap, FM, c/o Lukunor, FM, Sacred Heart Church. (CI)
Lott, TX, Falls Co., Sacred Heart, c/o Marlin, TX, St. Joseph's Church. (AUS)
Louise, TX, St. Procopius, c/o Hillje, TX, St. Andrew Church. (VIC)
Louisville, GA, Jefferson Co., St. Joan of Arc, c/o Waynesboro, GA, Sacred Heart Church. (SAV)
Loveladies, NJ, Ocean Co., St. Clare, c/o Brant Beach, NJ, St. Francis of Assisi Church. (TR)
Lovingston, VA, Nelson Co., St. Mary, c/o Scottsville, VA, St. George Church. (RIC)
Lowell, VT, Orleans Co., St. Ignatius Loyola, c/o Troy, VT, Sacred Heart of Jesus Church. (BUR)
Lower San Francisco, NM, Catron Co., San Isidro, c/o Aragon, NM, Santo Nino Church. (GLP)
Loyalton, CA, Sierra Co., Holy Rosary, c/o Portola, CA, Holy Family Church. (SAC)
Lozano, TX, St. Vincent de Paul, c/o Rio Hondo, TX, St. Helen Church. (BWN)
Lucedale, MS, George Co., St. Lucy, c/o Wiggins, MS, St. Francis Xavier Church. (BLX)
Lucerne, CA, Queen of the Rosary, c/o Clearlake, CA, Our Lady, Queen of Peace Church. (SR)
Lucerne, IN, Cass Co., St. Elizabeth of Hungary, c/o Logansport, IN, All Saints Church. (LFT)
Lucero, NM, Mora Co., c/o Mora, NM, St. Gertrude Church. (SFE)
Ludlow, IL, Champaign Co., Sacred Heart, c/o Thomasboro, IL, St. Elizabeth's Church. (PEO)
Luis Lopez, NM, Socorro Co., c/o Socorro, NM, San Miguel Church. (SFE)
Lull, TX, Capilla de San Jose, c/o Edinburg, TX, Sacred Heart Church. (BWN)
Lummi, WA, Whatcom Co., St. Joachim (Indian Reservation), c/o Ferndale, WA, St. Joseph Church. (SEA)
Lunenburg, VT, Essex Co., St. Leo, c/o St. Johnsbury, VT, St. John the Evangelist Church. (BUR)
Luquillo, PR, Ntra. Sra. del Cobre, c/o Luquillo, PR, San Jose Church. (SJN)
Luquillo, PR, San Judas, c/o Luquillo, PR, San Jose Church. (SJN)
Luther, MI, St. Ignatius, c/o Baldwin, MI, St. Ann's Church. (GR)
Luther, OK, Oklahoma Co., St. Theresa of the Infant Jesus, c/o Jones, OK, St. Robert Bellarmine Church. (OKL)
Lyden, NM, Rio Arriba Co., San Jose, c/o Dixon, NM, St. Anthony Church. (SFE)
Lyman, NE, Scotts Bluff Co., Sacred Heart, c/o Mitchell, NE, St. Theresa's Church. (GI)
Lyons, OR, Linn Co., St. Patrick, c/o Jordan, OR, Our Lady of Lourdes Church. (P)
Lyons Falls, NY, Lewis Co., St. John, c/o Port Leyden, NY, St. Martin Church. (OG)

M

Macana, PR, Fatima, c/o Penuelas, PR, St. Joseph Church. (PCE)
Macana Parcelas, PR, San Martin de Porres, c/o Guayanilla, PR, Immaculate Conception Church. (PCE)
Macana Rio, PR, Virgen de Fatima, c/o Guayanilla, PR, Immaculate Conception Church. (PCE)
MacDonaldton, PA, Somerset Co., St. Gregory, c/o Meyersdale, PA, SS. Philip and James Church. (ALT)
Macon, MS, Corpus Christi, c/o Starkville, MS, St. Joseph Church. (JKS)
Macy, NE, Thurston Co., Our Lady of Fatima, c/o Walthill, NE, St. Joseph Church. (OM)
Madawaska, ME, Aroostook Co., St. Michael's Chapel, c/o St. Agatha, ME, St. Agatha's Church. (PRT)
Maddock, ND, Benson Co., St. William, c/o Esmond, ND, St. Boniface Church. (FAR)
Madera, CA, Madera Co., St. Agnes, c/o Madera, CA, St. Joachim Church. (FRS)
Madera, PA, Clearfield Co., Immaculate Conception, c/o Houtzdale, PA, Christ the King Church. (E)
Madero, TX, Our Lady of Lourdes, c/o [2] Mission, TX, Our Lady of the Holy Rosary Church. (BWN)
Madill, OK, Marshall Co., Holy Cross, c/o Sulphur, OK, St. Francis Xavier Church. (OKL)
Madison, GA, Morgan Co., St. James, c/o Covington, GA, St. Augustine Church. (ATL)
Madison, KS, Greenwood Co., St. Teresa Of Avila, c/o Eureka, KS, Sacred Heart Church. (WCH)
Magas Arriba, PR, Perpetuo Socorro, c/o Guayanilla, PR, Immaculate Conception Church. (PCE)
Magdalena, NM, Socorro Co., c/o Socorro, NM, San Miguel Church. (SFE)
Mageetown, PA, Crawford Co., Immaculate Conception, c/o Titusville, PA, St. Titus Church. (E)
Magnolia, ID, St. Joseph's Chapel, c/o [1] Gloucester, MA, St. Ann Church. (BO)
Magnolia, MS, Pike Co., St. James, c/o Chatawa, MS, St. Teresa Church. (JKS)
Majuro Atoll, MH, Laura, c/o Majuro, MH, Cathedral of the Assumption. (MI)
Makoti, ND, Ward Co., St. Elizabeth, c/o Parshall, ND, St. Bridget Church. (BIS)
Malaga, CA, Fresno Co., Christ the King, c/o [8] Fresno, CA, St. Anthony Mary Claret Church. (FRS)
Malaga, NM, Cristo Rey, c/o Loving, NM, Our Lady of Grace Church. (LSC)
Malakoff, TX, Henderson Co., Mary Queen of Heaven, c/o Gun Barrel City, TX, St. Jude Church. (TYL)
Malpaso-Cesar Ruiz, PR, Immaculada Concepcion, c/o Aguada, PR, St. Francis of Assisi Church. (MGZ)
Malvern, AR, Hot Spring Co., c/o Hot Springs National Park, AR, St. John the Baptist Church. (LR)
Mamey, PR, Perpetuo Socorro, c/o Aguada, PR, St. Francis of Assisi Church. (MGZ)
Mameyes, PR, Jayuya Co., S. Antonio, c/o Jayuya, PR, Our Lady of Monserrate Church. (PCE)
Manassa, CO, Conejos Co., St. Therese of the Child Jesus, c/o Capulin, CO, St. Joseph Church. (PBL)
Mani, PR, Infant of Prague, c/o [2] Mayaquez, PR, Our Lady of Mt. Carmel Church. (MGZ)
Manito, IL, Mason Co., Immaculate Conception, c/o Havana, IL, St. Patrick's Church. (PEO)
Manitou Springs, CO, El Paso Co., Our Lady of Perpetual Help, c/o [8] Colorado Springs, CO, Sacred Heart Church. (COS)
Mankato, MN, Blue Earth Co., St. Francis Xavier, c/o [1] Mankato, MN, SS. Peter and Paul's Church. (WIN)
Mannford, OK, Creek Co., Our Lady of the Lake, c/o Sand Springs, OK, St. Patrick's Church. (TLS)
Manset, ME, St. Peter's, c/o Northeast Harbor, ME, St. Ignatius Church. (PRT)
Mansfield, WA, Douglas Co., St. Mary, c/o Bridgeport, WA, St. Anne's Church. (YAK)
Mantador, ND, Richland Co., Sts. Peter & Paul, c/o Mooreton, ND, St. Anthony's Church. (FAR)
Manton, KY, Washington Co., Holy Rosary, c/o [3] Springfield, KY, Holy Trinity Church. (L)
Manu'a Island, AS, Mary, Star of the Sea, c/o [1] Pago Pago, AS, Cathedral of the Holy Family. (SPP)
Many, LA, Sabine Parish, St. Terence, c/o Many, LA, St. John the Baptist Church. (SHP)
Many Farms, AZ, Apache Co., St. Anthony, c/o Chinle, AZ, Our Lady of Fatima Church. (GLP)
Manzano, NM, Torrance Co., c/o Mountainair, NM, St. Alice Church. (SFE)
Manzanola, CO, Otero Co., St. Joseph the Worker, c/o Rocky Ford, CO, St. Peter Church. (PBL)
Marak, TX, Milam Co., Ss. Cyril & Methodius, c/o Cyclone, TX, St. Joseph's Church. (AUS)
Marana, AZ, Pima Co., San Juan Bautista, c/o [2] Tucson, AZ, Blessed Kateri Tekakwitha Church. (TUC)
Marcellus, MI, Cass Co., St. Margaret Mary, c/o Mattawan, MI, St. John Bosco Church. (KAL)
Marenisco, MI, Gogebic Co., St. Catherine, c/o Wakefield, MI, Immaculate Conception of the Blessed Virgin Mary Church. (MAR)
Maresua, PR, Gruta de Lourdes, c/o San German, PR, San German de Auxerre Church. (MGZ)
Marian, TN, Marian Co., Virgin of the Poor Shrine, c/o South Pittsburg, TN, Our Lady of Lourdes Church. (KNX)
Marias, PR, Asuncion de Maria, c/o Aguada, PR, St. Francis of Assisi Church. (MGZ)
Maricopa, AZ, Pinal Co., St. Francis de Sales, c/o Casa Grande, AZ, St. Anthony of Padua Church. (TUC)
Marienville, PA, Forest Co., St. Anne, c/o Crown, PA, St. Mary Church. (E)
Marietta, OK, Love Co., Good Shepherd, c/o Ardmore, OK, St. Mary Church. (OKL)
Marion, NC, McDowell Co., Our Lady of the Angels, c/o Morganton, NC, St. Charles Borromeo Church. (CHL)
Marion, ND, LaMoure Co., St. Francis, c/o La Moure, ND, Holy Rosary Church. (FAR)
Marion, SC, Marion Co., Infant Jesus, c/o Dillon, SC, St. Louis Church. (CHR)
Marion, TX, Guadalupe Co., Immaculate Conception, c/o Schertz, TX, Church of the Good Shepherd . (SAT)
Markham, TX, St. Robert, c/o Blessing, TX, St. Peter's Church. (VIC)
Marlow, OK, Stephens Co., Immaculate Conception, c/o Duncan, OK, Assumption Church. (OKL)
Marmarth, ND, Slope Co., Immaculate Heart of Mary, c/o Bowman, ND, St. Charles Church. (BIS)
Marshall, OK, Logan Co., St. Camillus, c/o Hennessey, OK, St. Joseph's Church. (OKL)
Marshfield, VT, Washington Co., North American Martyrs, c/o Montpelier, VT, St. Augustine Church. (BUR)
Marysdale, OH, Defiance Co., Immaculate Conception, c/o The Bend, OH, St. Stephen Church. (TOL)
Marysville, Haiti, St. Thomas d'Aquin, c/o Marysville, OH, Our Lady of Lourdes Church. (COL)
Marysville, MT, Lewis and Clark Co., Our Lady of Lourdes, c/o [3] Helena, MT, Our Lady of the Valley Church. (HEL)
Masefau, AS, c/o [8] Pago Pago, AS, Church of St. Peter and Paul. (SPP)
Mason, TX, Mason Co., St. Joseph, c/o Llano, TX, Holy Trinity Church. (AUS)
Mason, WV, Mason Co., St. Joseph, c/o Point Pleasant, WV, Sacred Heart Church. (WH)
Mason City, IL, Mason Co., St. Columba, c/o Lincoln, IL, Holy Family Church. (PEO)
Mason City, NE, Custer Co., St. Thomas, c/o Broken Bow, NE, St. Joseph's Church. (GI)
Matador, TX, Motley Co., Our Lady of Guadalupe, c/o Floydada, TX, St. Mary Magdalen Church. (LUB)
Matrullas, PR, Cacao Co., Sacred Heart of Jesus, c/o Villalba, PR, Our Lady Mother of Divine Providence Church. (PCE)
Mattingly Settlement, OH, Muskingum Co., St. Mary, c/o Dresden, OH, St. Ann's Church. (COL)
Mattituck, NY, Suffolk Co., Our Lady of Good Counsel, c/o Cutchogue, NY, Sacred Heart Church. (RVC)
Matunuck, RI, Washington, St. Romuald, c/o South Kingstown, RI, St. Francis of Assisi Church. (PRO)
Maud, OK, Seminole Co., St. Cecelia, c/o Seminole, OK, Immaculate Conception Church. (OKL)
Maupin, OR, St. Mary's, c/o Dufur, OR, St. Alphonsus Church. (BAK)
Max, ND, McClean Co., Immaculate Conception, c/o Garrison, ND, St. Nicholas Church. (BIS)

Maxwell, NM, Colfax Co., c/o Springer, NM, St. Joseph Church. (SFE)
Mayaguez, PR, Corpus Christi, c/o [5] Mayaquez, PR, Nuestra Senora De Fatima Church. (MGZ)
Mayaguez, PR, Cristo Rey, c/o [5] Mayaquez, PR, Nuestra Senora De Fatima Church. (MGZ)
Mayaguez, PR, Espiritu Santo, c/o [5] Mayaquez, PR, Nuestra Senora De Fatima Church. (MGZ)
Mayaguez, PR, Maria Socorro de los Cristianos, c/o [1] Mayaquez, PR, Cathedral of Our Lady of Purification . (MGZ)
Mayaguez, PR, Santa Ana, c/o [1] Mayaquez, PR, Cathedral of Our Lady of Purification. (MGZ)
Mayer, AZ, St. Joseph, c/o Prescott Valley, AZ, St. Germaine Church. (PHX)
Maysville, MO, DeKalb Co., St. Aloysius, c/o Cameron, MO, St. Munchin Church. (KC)
Mayville, ND, Traill Co., State University Newman Club, c/o Mayville, ND, Our Lady of Peace Church. (FAR)
McCartys, NM, Cibola Co., Santa Maria de Acoma, c/o Acoma, NM, San Esteban, Acoma Catholic Indian Mission. (GLP)
McClellanville, SC, Charleston Co., McClellanville Mission, c/o Georgetown, SC, St. Mary's Church. (CHR)
McClusky, ND, Sheridan Co., Holy Family, c/o Sykeston, ND, St. Elizabeth's Church. (FAR)
McCook, NE, Red Willow Co., Sacred Heart, c/o McCook, NE, St. Patrick Church. (LIN)
McCook, NE, Red Willow Co., St. Ann's, c/o McCook, NE, St. Patrick Church. (LIN)
McCormick, SC, McCormick Co., Good Shepherd, c/o Abbeville, SC, Sacred Heart Church. (CHR)
McCrory, AR, Woodruff Co., St. Mary's, c/o Wynne, AR, St. Peter's Church. (LR)
McDade, TX, Bastrop Co., St. Christopher's, c/o Elgin, TX, Sacred Heart Church. (AUS)
McDermitt, NV, Humboldt Co., Sacred Heart, c/o Winnemucca, NV, St. Paul Church. (RNO)
McGill, NV, White Pine Co., St. Michael's, c/o Ely, NV, Sacred Heart Church. (LAV)
McHenry, ND, Foster Co., SS. Peter & Paul, c/o New Rockford, ND, St. John's Church. (FAR)
McIntosh, SD, Corson Co., St. Bonaventure, c/o McLaughlin, SD, St. Bernard Church. (RC)
McKee, KY, Jackson Co., St. Paul, c/o Berea, KY, St. Clare Church. (LEX)
McRoberts, KY, Letcher Co., Holy Angels, c/o Jenkins, KY, St. George Church. (LEX)
Mead, CO, Weld Co., Guardian Angels, c/o Frederick, CO, St. Theresa Church. (DEN)
Meadow Wood Acres, TX, Bexar Co., St. John Vianney, c/o LaCoste, TX, Our Lady of Grace Church. (SAT)
Meadowlands, MN, St. Mary's, c/o Floodwood, MN, St. Louis Church. (DUL)
Meadville, MS, Franklin Co., St. Ann, c/o Brookhaven, MS, St. Francis Church. (JKS)
Mechanic Falls, ME, Oxford Co., St. Mary, c/o Mechanic Falls, ME, Our Lady of Ransom Church. (PRT)
Mechanicsville, CT, Sacred Heart, c/o North Grosvenordale, CT, St. Joseph Church. (NOR)
Medanales, NM, Rio Arriba Co., c/o Abiquiu, NM, St. Thomas Apostle Church. (SFE)
Medicine Bow, WY, Carbon Co., St. Malachy, c/o Saratoga, WY, St. Ann's Church. (CHY)
Medicine Lane, MT, St. Patrick, c/o Plentywood, MT, St. Joseph's Church. (GF)
Medicine Root, SD, Shannon, St. Stephens, c/o Kyle, SD, Our Lady of Sorrows Church. (RC)
Medina, ND, Stutsman Co., St. Mary, c/o Windsor, ND, St. Mathias Church. (FAR)
Medina Lake, TX, Bandera Co., St. Victor's Chapel, c/o Bandera, TX, St. Stanislaus Church. (SAT)
Medora, ND, Billings Co., St. Mary, c/o Belfield, ND, St. Bernard Church. (BIS)
Meeker, OK, Lincoln Co., St. Michael, c/o Prague, OK, St. Wenceslaus, National Shrine of the Infant Jesus of Prague Church. (OKL)
Meekin's Neck, MD, Dorchester Co., St. Mary, Star of the Sea, c/o Cambridge, MD, St. Mary Refuge of Sinners Church. (WIL)
Meeteetse, WY, Park Co., St. Therese, c/o Cody, WY, St. Anthony Church. (CHY)
Meherrin, VA, Sacred Heart, c/o Crewe, VA, St. John the Baptist Church. (RIC)
Melbourne, FL, c/o Orlando, FL, St. Nicholas of Myra Church. (PSC)
Melendez, PR, Coamo Co., Our Lady of Fatima, c/o Coamo, PR, St. Blase Church. (PCE)
Melrose, MT, Silver Bow Co., St. John The Apostle, c/o Dillon, MT, St. Rose of Lima Church. (HEL)
Melrose, NM, Curry Co., c/o Clovis, NM, Sacred Heart Church. (SFE)
Melstone, MT, Our Lady of Mercy, c/o Roundup, MT, St. Benedict's Church. (GF)
Melvin, IL, Ford Co., St. George, c/o Gibson City, IL, Our Lady of Lourdes Church. (JOL)
Melvin, TX, McCullogh Co., St. Francis Xavier, c/o Brady, TX, St. Patrick's Church. (SAN)
Merced, CA, Merced Co., El Nido, c/o Merced, CA, Sacred Heart Church. (FRS)
Merced, CA, Merced Co., St. George, c/o Merced, CA, Sacred Heart Church. (FRS)
Mercersburg, PA, Franklin Co., St. Luke the Evangelist, c/o Greencastle, PA, St. Mark the Evangelist Church. (HBG)
Mereta, TX, Tom Green Co., Holy Family, c/o Wall, TX, St. Ambrose Church. (SAN)
Merkel, TX, Taylor Co., Our Mother of Mercy, c/o Sweetwater, TX, Holy Family Church. (SAN)
Merna, NE, Custer Co., St. Paul, c/o Anselmo, NE, St. Anselm's Church. (GI)
Merrill, IA, Plymouth Co., St. Joseph at Ellendale, c/o Merrill, IA, Assumption Church. (SC)
Merryville, LA, Beauregard Parish, St. Bridget, c/o De Ridder, LA, St. Joseph's Church. (LKC)
Mertzon, TX, Irion Co., St. Peter's, c/o Eldorado, TX, Our Lady of Guadalupe Church. (SAN)
Mesa de Poleo, NM, Rio Arriba Co., c/o Abiquiu, NM, St. Thomas Apostle Church. (SFE)
Mesita, NM, Sacred Heart, c/o Laguna, NM, St. Joseph Church. (GLP)
Mesquite, NM, Our Lady of Perpetual Help, c/o San Miguel, NM, San Miguel Church. (LSC)
Metip, FM, c/o Tamoroi, FM, Sacred Heart Church. (CI)
Metlakatla, AK, Holy Family, c/o Ketchikan, AK, Holy Name Church. (JUN)
Metter, GA, Candler Co., Holy Family, c/o Swainsboro, GA, Holy Trinity Church. (SAV)
Mexico Beach, FL, Bay Co., Our Lady of Guadalupe, c/o Panama City, FL, St. Dominic Church. (PT)
Miami, FL, La Milagrosa, c/o [3] Miami, FL, Corpus Christi Church. (MIA)
Miami, FL, La Purisima, c/o [25] Miami, FL, St. Kieran Church. (MIA)
Miami, FL, Nuestra Senora de Altagracia, c/o [3] Miami, FL, Corpus Christi Church. (MIA)
Miami, FL, San Francisco y Santa Clara, c/o [3] Miami, FL, Corpus Christi Church. (MIA)
Miami, FL, San Juan Bautista, c/o [3] Miami, FL, Corpus Christi Church. (MIA)
Michigan City, IN, La Porte Co., Maronite Catholic Community, c/o Hillside, IL, Our Lady of Lebanon Church. (OLL)
Michigan City, IN, Sacred Heart, c/o [1] Michigan City, IN, St. Mary of the Immaculate Conception Church. (GRY)
Mico, TX, Medina Co., St. Francis of Assisi (Medina Lake Chapel), c/o Castroville, TX, St. Louis Church. (SAT)
Middle River, MN, Marshall Co., St. Joseph, c/o Greenbush, MN, Blessed Sacrament Church. (CR)
Middlebourne, WV, Tyler Co., St. Lawrence, c/o Paden City, WV, Mater Dolorosa Church. (WH)
Middleport, PA, Schuylkill Co., Immaculate Heart of Mary Chapel, c/o New Philadelphia, PA, Sacred Heart Church. (ALN)
Middletown, IL, Logan Co., St. John the Baptist, c/o Elkhart, IL, St. Patrick Church. (PEO)
Middletown, PA, Susquehanna Co., St. Patrick, c/o Friendsville, PA, St. Francis Xavier's Church. (SCR)
Middleville, NY, St. Mary of the Assumption, c/o Newport, NY, St. John the Baptist Church. (ALB)
Midkiff, TX, Upton Co., St. Thomas, c/o St. Lawrence, TX, St. Lawrence Church. (SAN)
Midland, LA, St. Aloysius, c/o Morse, LA, Immaculate Conception Church. (LAF)
Midland, SD, Haakon Co., St. William, c/o Philip, SD, Sacred Heart Church. (RC)
Midwest, WY, Natrona Co., St. Francis Mission, c/o Casper, WY, St. Anthony of Padua Church. (CHY)
Mifflinburg, PA, Union Co., Saint George Church, c/o Lewisburg, PA, Sacred Heart of Jesus Church. (HBG)
Milagro, NM, Guadalupe Co., c/o Santa Rosa, NM, St. Rose of Lima Church. (SFE)
Milesville, SD, Haakon Co., St. Mary, c/o Philip, SD, Sacred Heart Church. (RC)
Milford Center, OH, Union Co., Sacred Heart, c/o Plain City, OH, St. Joseph Church. (COL)
Mill City, OR, Marion Co., St. Catherine of Siena, c/o Sublimity, OR, St. Boniface Church. (P)
Mill Rift, PA, Pike Co., Holy Family, c/o Matamoras, PA, St. Joseph's Church. (SCR)
Mill River, MA, Berkshire Co., Immaculate Conception, c/o Sheffield, MA, Our Lady of the Valley Church. (SPR)
Millcreek, FL, St. Johns Co., Our Lady of Good Counsel, c/o Elkton, FL, St. Ambrose Church. (STA)
Millen, GA, Jenkins Co., St. Bernadette, c/o Sylvania, GA, Our Lady of the Assumption Church. (SAV)
Millersview, TX, Concho Co., Our Lady of Guadalupe, c/o Eden, TX, St. Charles Church. (SAN)
Millersville, MD, Waugh Chapel Mission Community Inc., c/o Millersville, MD, Our Lady of the Fields Church. (BAL)
Millerton, NY, Dutchess Co., St. Patrick, c/o Amenia, NY, Immaculate Conception Church. (NY)
Milligan, NE, Fillmore Co., St. Wenceslaus, c/o Friend, NE, St. Joseph's Church. (LIN)
Millington, MI, Tuscola Co., St. Bernard, c/o Vassar, MI, St. Frances Xavier Cabrini Church. (SAG)
Millsboro, DE, Sussex Co., Mary Mother of Peace, c/o Georgetown, DE, St. Michael the Archangel Church. (WIL)
Millwood, NY, Westchester Co., Our Lady of the Wayside, c/o Briarcliff Manor, NY, St. Theresa Church. (NY)
Milnor, ND, Sargent Co., St. Arnold, c/o Forman, ND, St. Mary's Church. (FAR)
Milo, ME, St. Paul, c/o Brownville Junction, ME, St. Francis Xavier Church. (PRT)
Milolii, HI, Honaunau Co., c/o Honaunau, HI, St. Benedict Church. (HON)
Milton, ND, Cavalier Co., St. Clothilde, c/o Wales, ND, St. Michael's Church. (FAR)
Milton, NH, Strafford Co., Sacred Heart, c/o Sanbornville, NH, St. Anthony Church. (MAN)
Milwaukee, WI, Milwaukee Co., St. John's Chapel, c/o [6] Milwaukee, WI, All Saints Church. (MIL)
Minerva, KY, Mason Co., St. James, c/o Brooksville, KY, St. James Church. (COV)
Minnewauken, ND, Benson Co., St. James, c/o Leeds, ND, St. Vincent de Paul Church. (FAR)
Minot, ND, Ward Co., St. Michael, c/o Wilton, ND, SS. Peter and Paul Church. (STN)
Miraflores, PR, Chapel of Our Lady of Perpetual Help, c/o Anasco, PR, St. Anthony Abbot Church. (MGZ)
Mirando City, TX, Webb Co., Immaculate Conception, c/o Hebbronville, TX, Our Lady of Guadalupe Church. (LAR)
Mirasol, PR, La Virgen, c/o Castaner, PR, Our Lady of the Miraculous Medal Church. (PCE)
Mission, SD, Todd Co., St. Thomas, c/o St. Francis, SD, Rosebud Reservation Church. (RC)
Mitchell, WI, Sheboygan Co., St. Michael Chapel, c/o Armstrong, WI, Good Shepherd Church. (MIL)
Mobridge, SD, c/o Wilton, ND, SS. Peter and Paul Church. (STN)
Moch, FM, c/o Lukunor, FM, Sacred Heart Church. (CI)
Mojave, CA, Kern Co., St. Francis of Assisi Church, c/o Rosamond, CA, St. Mary Church. (FRS)
Mokelumne Hill, CA, Calaveras Co., St. Thomas Aquinas, c/o San Andreas, CA, St. Andrew Church. (STO)
Monacillos, PR, San Fernando, c/o [23] San Juan, PR, Inmaculado Corazon de Maria Church. (SJN)
Monarch, MT, St. Clement, c/o Belt, MT, St. Mark the Evangelist Church. (GF)
Moncla, LA, St. John the Baptist, c/o Fifth Ward, LA, Our Lady of Lourdes Church. (ALX)
Monet Ferry, LA, Holy Family, c/o Cloutierville, LA, St. John the Baptist Church. (ALX)
Mongaup Valley, NY, Sullivan Co., St. Joseph, c/o Monticello, NY, St. Peter Church. (NY)
Monmouth, ME, Kennebec Co., St. Stanislaus, c/o Winthrop, ME, St. Francis Xavier Church. (PRT)
Monroeville, AL, Dallas Co., Mission of Annunciation Parish, c/o Camden, AL, St. Joseph Church. (MOB)
Monte Alto, TX, Hidalgo Co., Christ the King, Holy Cross Catechetical Center, c/o Elsa, TX, Sacred Heart Church. (BWN)
Monte Aplanado, NM, Mora Co., c/o Mora, NM, St. Gertrude Church. (SFE)
Monte Grande, PR, St. Jude Thaddeus, c/o Cabo Rojo, PR, St. Michael Church. (MGZ)
Monte Rio, CA, St. Catherine, c/o Guerneville, CA, St. Elizabeth Church. (SR)
Montecello, NM, Sierra Co., St. Ignatius, c/o Truth or Consequences, NM, Our Lady of Perpetual Help Church. (LSC)
Monterey, MA, Berkshire Co., Our Lady of the Hills, c/o Sheffield, MA, Our Lady of the Valley Church. (SPR)
Montesano, WA, Grays Harbor Co., St. John, c/o Elma, WA, St. Joseph Church. (SEA)
Montezuma, GA, Macon Co., St. Michael, c/o Americus, GA, St. Mary Church. (SAV)
Montezuma, IN, Parke Co., Immaculate Conception, c/o Rockville, IN, St. Joseph Church. (IND)
Montgomery, AL, Montgomery Co., Resurrection Catholic Mission, c/o [8] Montgomery, AL, Resurrection Catholic Church. (MOB)
Montgomery, LA, St. Patrick, c/o Colfax, LA, St. Joseph Church. (ALX)
Montgomery Center, VT, Franklin Co., St. Isidore, c/o Richford, VT, All Saints Church. (BUR)
Monticello, MS, Lawrence Co., St. Lawrence, c/o Bassfield, MS, St. Peter Church. (BLX)
Monument, OR, St. Anne, c/o John Day, OR, St. Elizabeth's Church. (BAK)
Moody, TX, McLennan Co., Our Lady of San Juan, c/o McGregor, TX, St. Eugene Church. (AUS)
Moorcroft, WY, Crook Co., St. Patrick, c/o Gillette, WY, St. Matthew's Church. (CHY)
Moore, MT, St. Mathias, c/o Stanford, MT, St. Rose of Lima Church. (GF)
Moore, TX, Frio Co., St. Augustine, c/o Von Ormy, TX, St. Peter the Fisherman Church. (SAT)
Mooreland, OK, Woodward Co., Sacred Heart, c/o Woodward, OK, St. Peter's Church. (OKL)

Moorhead, MN, Clay Co., St. Thomas Newman Center, c/o Moorhead, MN, St. Joseph's Church. (CR)
Moquino, NM, Santa Rosalia, c/o Seboyeta, NM, Our Lady of Sorrows Church. (GLP)
Moral, TX, Nacogdoches Co., Immaculate Conception, c/o Nacogdoches, TX, Sacred Heart Church. (TYL)
Moravia, TX, Lavaca Co., Ascension of Our Lord, c/o St. John, TX, St. John the Baptist Church. (VIC)
Moretown, VT, Washington Co., St. Patrick, c/o Waitsfield, VT, Our Lady of the Snows Church. (BUR)
Moretown, VT, Washington Co., St. Patrick, c/o Waterbury, VT, St. Andrew Church. (BUR)
Morgan City, LA, St. Martin Parish, St. Rosalie, c/o Morgan City, LA, Holy Cross Church. (HT)
Morning View, KY, Kenton Co., Assumption of the Blessed Virgin, c/o Kenton, KY, St. Matthew Church. (COV)
Morrill, NE, Scotts Bluff Co., St. Ann, c/o Mitchell, NE, St. Theresa's Church. (GI)
Morris, CT, Litchfield Co., Our Lady of Hope, c/o Bantam, CT, Our Lady of Grace Church. (HRT)
Morris, PA, Tioga Co., Sacred Heart, c/o Wellsboro, PA, St. Peter's Church. (SCR)
Morris Run, PA, Tioga Co., St. Joseph, c/o Blossburg, PA, St. Mary's Church. (SCR)
Morristown, SD, Corson Co., Sacred Heart, c/o Lemmon, SD, St. Mary's Church. (RC)
Moses, NM, Union Co., Sacred Heart, c/o Clayton, NM, St. Francis Xavier Church. (SFE)
Mosquero, NM, Harding Co., c/o Roy, NM, Holy Family-St. Joseph Church. (SFE)
Mount Carmel, ND, Cavalier Co., Our Lady of Mount Carmel, c/o Wales, ND, St. Michael's Church. (FAR)
Mount Holly, VT, Rutland Co., St. Mary, c/o Wallingford, VT, St. Patrick Church. (BUR)
Mount Ida, AR, Montgomery Co., All Saints, c/o Mena, AR, St. Agnes Church. (LR)
Mount Olive, NC, Duplin Co., Posada Guadalupana, c/o Clinton, NC, Immaculate Conception Church. (R)
Mount Palatine, IL, Putnam Co., Immaculate Conception, c/o Hennepin, IL, St. Patrick's Church. (PEO)
Mount Pocono, PA, Monroe Co., St. Nicholas, c/o Old Forge, PA, St. Nicholas Church. (PSC)
Mount Pulaski, IL, Logan Co., St. Thomas Aquinas, c/o Elkhart, IL, St. Patrick Church. (PEO)
Mountain Iron, MN, Sacred Heart, c/o Virginia, MN, Sacred Heart Church. (DUL)
Mountain View, AR, Stone Co., St. Mary's, c/o Batesville, AR, St. Mary's Church. (LR)
Moxham, PA, Cambria Co., St. Anne's, c/o [18] Johnstown, PA, St. Therese of the Child Jesus Church. (ALT)
Mud Butte, SD, St. Joseph, c/o Belle Fourche, SD, St. Paul Church. (RC)
Mud Butte, SD, Meade Co., St. Joseph's Catholic Church, c/o Newell, SD, St. Mary Star of the Sea Church. (RC)
Mukilteo, WA, Snohomish Co., St. John, c/o Everett, WA, St. Mary Magdalen Church. (SEA)
Mulvey, LA, Vermilion Parish, St. David, c/o Gueydan, LA, St. Peter Church. (LAF)
Mumford, NY, Monroe Co., St. Patrick, c/o Caledonia, NY, St. Columba Church. (ROC)
Murdo, SD, Jones Co., St. Martin of Tours, c/o Presho, SD, Christ the King Church. (RC)
Murphys, CA, Murphys Co., St. Patrick, c/o Angels Camp, CA, St. Patrick Church. (STO)
Myrtle Point, OR, Coos Co., Sts. Ann and Michael, c/o Coquille, OR, Holy Name Church. (P)

N

N. Truro, MA, Our Lady of Perpetual Help,, c/o Provincetown, MA, St. Peter the Apostle Church. (FR)
Naco, AZ, Cochise Co., St. Michael, c/o Bisbee, AZ, St. Patrick Church. (TUC)
Nacogdoches, TX, Nacogdoches Co., Our Lady of Guadalupe, c/o Nacogdoches, TX, Sacred Heart Church. (TYL)
Nags Head, NC, Dare Co., Holy Trinity, c/o Kitty Hawk, NC, Holy Redeemer Church. (R)
Naknek, AK, St. Theresa, c/o Dillingham, AK, Holy Rosary Church. (ANC)
Nama, FM, c/o Lukunor, FM, Sacred Heart Church. (CI)
Nambe, NM, Santa Fe Co., c/o Pojoaque, NM, N.S. de Guadalupe del Valle de Pojoaque Church. (SFE)
Nambe Indian Pueblo, NM, Sante Fe Co., c/o Pojoaque, NM, N.S. de Guadalupe del Valle de Pojoaque Church. (SFE)
Namoluk, FM, c/o Lukunor, FM, Sacred Heart Church. (CI)
Nanticoke, PA, Luzerne Co., St. Joseph, c/o Wanamie, PA, St. Mary's Church. (SCR)
Naper, NE, Boyd Co., Sacred Heart, c/o Butte, NE, SS. Peter and Paul Church. (OM)
Naples, FL, c/o North Fort Myers, FL, All Saints Byzantine Catholic Church. (PSC)
Naponee, NE, Franklin Co., St. Mary, c/o Alma, NE, St. Joseph's Church. (LIN)
Nara Visa, NM, Quay Co., Sacred Heart, c/o Tucumcari, NM, St. Anne Church. (SFE)
Naranjo, PR, Santa Marta, c/o Salinas, PR, Our Lady of Monserrat Church. (PCE)
Naranjo, PR, St. Anthony, c/o Yauco, PR, Holy Rossary Church. (PCE)
Naranjo Militar, PR, Ntra. Sra. de Monserrate, c/o Aguada, PR, St. Francis of Assisi Church. (MGZ)
Naranjo-Guanabanas, PR, San Pablo, c/o Aguada, PR, St. Francis of Assisi Church. (MGZ)
Naschitti, NM, St. Anthony, c/o Tohatchi, NM, St. Mary Church. (GLP)
Nashua, MT, Queen of the Angels, c/o Glasgow, MT, St. Raphael's Church. (GF)
Nashville, AR, Howard Co., St. Martin, c/o De Queen, AR, St. Barbara's Church. (LR)
Nashville, GA, Berrien Co., St. Mary, c/o Lakeland, GA, Queen of Peace Church. (SAV)
Nashville, MI, Barry Co., St. Cyril, c/o Hastings, MI, St. Rose of Lima Church. (KAL)
Natalia, TX, Medina Co., St. John Bosco, c/o Lytle, TX, St. Andrew Church. (SAT)
Natural Bridge, NY, Jefferson Co., St. Henry, c/o Harrisville, NY, St. Francis Solanus Church. (OG)
Naubinway, MI, Mackinac Co., St. Stephen, c/o Engadine, MI, Our Lady of Lourdes Church. (MAR)
Naukati, AK, c/o Craig, AK, St. John by the Sea Church. (JUN)
Naytahwaush, MN, Mahnomen Co., St. Anne, c/o Waubun, MN, St. Ann Church. (CR)
Nebish, MN, Beltrami Co., St. John, c/o Red Lake, MN, St. Mary's Mission. (CR)
Neche, ND, Pembina Co., SS. Nereus and Achilleus, c/o Cavalier, ND, St. Bridget's Church. (FAR)
Nederland, CO, Boulder Co., St. Rita, c/o [1] Boulder, CO, Sacred Heart of Jesus Church. (DEN)
Nekoma, ND, Cavalier Co., St. Edwards, c/o Langdon, ND, St. Alphonsus Church. (FAR)
Neligh, NE, Antelope Co., St. Theresa, c/o Neligh, NE, St. Francis Church. (OM)
Nelson, NE, Nuckolls Co., Sacred Heart, c/o Superior, NE, St. Joseph's Church. (LIN)
Nenzel, NE, Cherry Co., St. Mary, c/o Valentine, NE, St. Nicholas Church. (GI)
Neobrara, NE, Knox Co., St. William, c/o Verdigre, NE, St. Wenceslaus Church. (OM)
Nephi, UT, Utah Co., Our Lady of Victory Mission, c/o Payson, UT, San Andres Church. (SLC)
Nett Lake, MN, St. Louis Co., Holy Cross, c/o Duluth, MN, Indian Missions Church. (DUL)
Nevis, MN, Hubbard Co., Immaculate Conception, c/o Akeley, MN, St. John's Church. (CR)
New Almelo, KS, Norton Co., St. Joseph's Church, c/o Norton, KS, St. Francis of Assisi Church. (SAL)
New Boston, IL, Mercer Co., St. Theresa of the Little Flower, c/o Aledo, IL, St. Catherine's Church. (PEO)
New Boston, TX, Bowie Co., Hooks Catholic Community, c/o New Boston, TX, St. Mary of the Cenacle Church. (TYL)
New Deal, TX, Lubbock Co., Our Lady Queen of Apostles, c/o [8] Lubbock, TX, St. Patrick Church. (LUB)
New Dorp Beach, NY, Richmond Co., Our Lady of Lourdes, c/o [219] Staten Island, NY, Our Lady, Queen of Peace Church. (NY)
New Germany, PA, Cambria Co., Immaculate Conception, c/o Summerhill, PA, St. John Church. (ALT)
New Haven, MO, Franklin Co., St. Gerald, c/o Port Hudson, MO, Holy Family Church. (STL)
New Hradec, ND, Dunn Co., SS. Peter and Paul, c/o [5] Dickinson, ND, St. Wenceslaus Church. (BIS)
New Iberia, LA, Iberia Parish, St. Jude, c/o [4] New Iberia, LA, St. Edward Church. (LAF)
New Leipzig, ND, Grant Co., St. John the Baptist, c/o Mott, ND, St. Vincent de Paul Church. (BIS)
New Marion, IN, Ripley Co., St. Mary Magdalen, c/o Osgood, IN, St. John Church. (IND)
New Middletown, IN, Harrison Co., Most Precious Blood, c/o Corydon, IN, St. Joseph Church. (IND)
New Milford, PA, Susquehanna Co., St. John, c/o Great Bend, PA, St. Lawrence's Church. (SCR)
New Orleans, LA, Orleans Civil Parish, Our Lady of Guadalupe, c/o [1] New Orleans, LA, St. Louis Cathedral. (NO)
New Orleans, LA, Orleans Civil Parish, Our Lady of La Vang, c/o [14] New Orleans, LA, Mary, Queen of Vietnam Church. (NO)
New Orleans, LA, Orleans Civil Parish, St. Joseph, c/o [2] Marrero, LA, St. Agnes Le Thi Thanh Church. (NO)
New River, AZ, Maricopa Co., Good Shepherd Mission, c/o [16] Phoenix, AZ, St. Luke Church. (PHX)
New Summerfield, TX, Cherokee Co., Our Lady of Guadalupe, c/o Jacksonville, TX, Our Lady of Sorrows Church. (TYL)
New Village, NJ, Warren Co., St. Christopher, c/o Phillipsburg, NJ, St. Philip & St. James Church. (MET)
New York, NY, Richmond Co., Christ the King, c/o [214] Staten Island, NY, St. Mary of the Assumption Church. (NY)
New York, NY, New York Co., Gift of Love, c/o [120] New York, NY, St. Veronica Church. (NY)
Newald, WI, Argonne Co., St. Hubert, c/o Laona, WI, St. Leonard Church. (GB)
Newell, SD, St. Mary, Star of the Sea, c/o Belle Fourche, SD, St. Paul Church. (RC)
Newfields, NH, Rockingham Co., Sacred Heart, c/o Newmarket, NH, St. Mary Church. (MAN)
Newfound Lake, NH, Grafton Co., Our Lady of Grace, c/o Bristol, NH, St. Timothy Church. (MAN)
Newfoundland, PA, Wayne Co., St. Anthony of Padua, c/o Gouldsboro, PA, St. Rita Church. (SCR)
Newport, AR, Jackson Co., St. Cecilia, c/o Batesville, AR, St. Mary's Church. (LR)
Newport, KY, Campbell Co., Corpus Christi, c/o [1] Newport, KY, Holy Spirit Church. (COV)
Newport, KY, Campbell Co., St. Francis de Sales, c/o [1] Newport, KY, Holy Spirit Church. (COV)
Newport, KY, Campbell Co., St. Stephen, c/o [1] Newport, KY, Holy Spirit Church. (COV)
Newport, KY, Campbell Co., St. Vincent de Paul, c/o [1] Newport, KY, Holy Spirit Church. (COV)
Newton, MS, St. Anne, c/o Forest, MS, St. Michael Church. (JKS)
Newton, PA, Lackawanna Co., St. Benedict, c/o Clarks Summit, PA, Our Lady of the Snows Church. (SCR)
Newton Falls, NY, St. Lawrence Co., St. Anthony of Padua, c/o Star Lake, NY, St. Hubert Church. (OG)
Ngcheangl, FM, c/o Koror, FM, Sacred Heart Church. (CI)
Ngulu, FM, c/o Ulithi and Neighboring Islands, FM, Queen of Heaven Church. (CI)
Nicasio, CA, Marin Co., St. Mary, c/o Lagunitas, CA, St. Cecilia Church. (SFR)
Nicolaus, CA, Sutter Co., St. Boniface, c/o Lincoln, CA, St. Joseph Church. (SAC)
Ninilchik, AK, St. Peter, c/o Homer, AK, St. John the Baptist Church. (ANC)
Nisswa, MN, St. Christopher's, c/o Pequot Lakes, MN, St. Alice's Church. (DUL)
No Water, SD, Shannon Co., Our Lady of Good Counsel, c/o Pine Ridge, SD, Holy Rosary Church. (RC)
Noble, LA, Sabine Parish, St. Catherine, c/o Noble, LA, St. Ann Church. (SHP)
Nocatee, FL, De Soto Co., Blessed Juan Diego, c/o Arcadia, FL, St. Paul Church. (VEN)
Noel, MO, McDonald Co., Nativity of Our Lord, c/o Neosho, MO, St. Canera Church. (SPC)
Noonan, ND, Divide Co., St. Luke, c/o Crosby, ND, St. Patrick Church. (BIS)
Norborne, MO, Carrollton Co., Sacred Heart, c/o Carrollton, MO, St. Mary's Church. (KC)
Norcross, GA, Gwinnett Co., Mary, Our Queen, c/o Dunwoody, GA, All Saints Catholic Church. (ATL)
Nordheim, TX, St. Ann's, c/o Yorktown, TX, Holy Cross Church. (VIC)
Norias Ranch, TX, Kenedy Co., Santa Elena, c/o Sarita, TX, Our Lady of Guadalupe Church. (CC)
Norris, SD, Mellette Co., Sacred Heart, c/o St. Francis, SD, Rosebud Reservation Church. (RC)
North Bangor, NY, Franklin Co., St. Edward, c/o North Bangor, NY, St. Augustine Church. (OG)
North Brookfield, NY, Madison Co., St. Mary, c/o Waterville, NY, St. Bernard Church. (SY)
North Creek, OH, Putnam Co., St. Joseph, c/o New Bavaria, OH, Sacred Heart of Jesus Church. (TOL)
North East, MD, Cecil Co., St. Jude, c/o Elkton, MD, Immaculate Conception Church. (WIL)
North Eastham, MA, Visitation Church, c/o Wellfleet, MA, Our Lady of Lourdes Church. (FR)
North Fork, CA, Madera Co., St. Joseph the Worker, c/o Bass Lake, CA, Our Lady of the Sierra Church. (FRS)
North Greenbush, NY, Rensselaer Co., Van Rensselaer Manor, County Welfare Home, c/o [8] Troy, NY, St. Michael the Archangel Church. (ALB)
North Haven, ME, Our Lady of Peace, c/o Camden, ME, Our Lady of Good Hope Church. (PRT)
North Hero, VT, Grand Isle Co., St. Benedict Joseph Labre, c/o South Hero, VT, St. Rose of Lima Church. (BUR)
North Hollywood, CA, Los Angeles Co., Our Lady of Zapopan, c/o Sun Valley, CA, Our Lady of the Holy Rosary Church. (LA)
North Powder, OR, St. Anthony, c/o [1] Baker, OR, Cathedral of St. Francis De Sales. (BAK)
North Pownal, VT, Our Lady of Lourdes, c/o Bennington, VT, Sacred Heart St. Francis de Sales Church. (BUR)
North Salem, NY, Westchester Co., St. John, c/o Croton Falls, NY, St. Joseph Church. (NY)
North San Juan, CA, Nevada Co., St. John, c/o Downieville, CA, Immaculate Conception Church. (SAC)
North Swanzey, NH, Cheshire Co., St. Stephen, c/o West Swanzey, NH, St. Anthony Church. (MAN)
Northland, MI, Marquette Co., St. Joseph, c/o Gwinn, MI, St. Anthony Church. (MAR)
Northome, MN, Koochiching Co., St. Michael, c/o Kelliher, MN, St. Patrick Church. (CR)

Northwood, NH, Rockingham Co., St. Joseph, c/o Pittsfield, NH, Our Lady of Lourdes Church. (MAN)
Norton, VT, Essex Co., St. Bernard, c/o Island Pond, VT, St. James the Greater Church. (BUR)
Nortonville, ND, LaMoure Co., Holy Spirit, c/o Edgeley, ND, Transfiguration Church. (FAR)
Norwich, VT, Windsor Co., St. Francis of Assisi, c/o Bradford, VT, Our Lady of Perpetual Help Church. (BUR)
Nova-Savannah, OH, Medina Co., Jesus the Good Shepherd, c/o Litchfield, OH, Our Lady Help of Christians Parish Church. (CLV)
Novinger, MO, Adair Co., St. Rose of Lima, c/o Kirksville, MO, Mary Immaculate Church. (JC)
Nowata, OK, Nowata Co., St. Catherine, c/o Bartlesville, OK, The Community of St. James Church. (TLS)
Noxon, MT, c/o Thompson Falls, MT, St. William Church. (HEL)
Nucla, CO, Montrose Co., Our Lady of Sorrows, c/o Telluride, CO, St. Patrick Church. (PBL)
Nuremberg, PA, Luzerne Co., St. Joseph, c/o Weston, PA, Sacred Heart Church. (SCR)

O

O'Connor, NE, Greeley Co., Our Lady of the Visitation, c/o Greeley, NE, Sacred Heart Church. (GI)
O'Connor Ranch, TX, Refugio Co., St. Dennis, c/o Tivoli, TX, Our Lady of Guadalupe Church. (CC)
Oak Beach, NY, Suffolk Co., c/o Babylon, NY, St. Joseph's Church. (RVC)
Oak Creek, CO, Routt Co., St. Martin of Tours, c/o Steamboat Springs, CO, Holy Name Church. (DEN)
Oak Forest, IN, Franklin Co., St. Cecilia of Rome, c/o St. Mary-of-the-Rock, IN, St. Mary-of-the-Rock Church. (IND)
Oak Grove, MO, Jackson Co., St. Jude the Apostle, c/o Odessa, MO, St. George Church. (KC)
Oak Ridge, MN, Immaculate Conception Chapel, c/o Rollingstone, MN, Holy Trinity Church. (WIN)
Oakland, CA, Alameda Co., Mary Help of Christians, c/o [9] Oakland, CA, St. Elizabeth's Church. (OAK)
Ocala National Forest, FL, Marion Co., St. Joseph of the Forest, c/o [2] Ocala, FL, Our Lady of the Springs Church. (ORL)
Ocate, NM, Mora Co., c/o Wagon Mound, NM, Santa Clara Church. (SFE)
Ocean City, MD, Worcester Co., Holy Saviour, c/o Ocean City, MD, St. Mary, Star of the Sea Church. (WIL)
Ocean Pines, MD, Worcester Co., St. John Neumann, c/o Ocean City, MD, St. Luke and St. Andrew Church. (WIL)
Oceano, CA, San Luis Obispo Co., St. Francis of Assisi, c/o Arroyo Grande, CA, St. Patrick Church. (MRY)
Oconto, NE, St. Mary, c/o Stapleton, NE, St. John the Evangelist Church. (GI)
Odell, NE, Gage Co., St. Mary's, c/o Wymore, NE, St. Mary's Church. (LIN)
Odessa, TX, Ector Co., Our Lady of San Juan, c/o [3] Odessa, TX, St. Elizabeth Ann Seton Church. (SAN)
Odessa, TX, Ector Co., St. Martin de Porres, c/o [4] Odessa, TX, St. Joseph Church. (SAN)
Ogilvie, MN, Kanabec Co., St. Kathryn, c/o Mora, MN, St. Mary's Church. (SCL)
Oglala, SD, Shannon Co., Our Lady of Sioux, c/o Pine Ridge, SD, Holy Rosary Church. (RC)
Ogunquit, ME, All Saints, c/o Wells, ME, St. Mary Church. (PRT)
Oilton, TX, Webb Co., St. Agnes, c/o Hebbronville, TX, Our Lady of Guadalupe Church. (LAR)
Ojo Armarillo, NM, Sacred Heart Missionary Cenacle, c/o Waterflow, NM, Sacred Heart Church. (GLP)
Ojo Caliente, NM, Rio Arriba Co., c/o El Rito, NM, San Juan Nepomuceno Church. (SFE)
Ojo Feliz, NM, Mora Co., c/o Mora, NM, St. Gertrude Church. (SFE)
Ojo Sarco, NM, Rio Arriba Co., Santo Tomas, c/o Chimayo, NM, Holy Family Church. (SFE)
Okemah, OK, Okfuska Co., St. Teresa, c/o Holdenville, OK, St. Stephen's Church. (TLS)
Oklee, MN, Red Lake Co., St. Francis Xavier, c/o Fosston, MN, St. Mary's Church. (CR)
Okmulgee, OK, Okmulgee Co., Uganda Martyrs, c/o Okmulgee, OK, St. Anthony's Church. (TLS)
Okolona, MS, Chickasaw Co., St. Theresa, c/o Aberdeen, MS, St. Francis of Assisi Church. (JKS)
Okreek, SD, Todd Co., St. Peter, c/o St. Francis, SD, Rosebud Reservation Church. (RC)
Okreek, SD, Todd Co., St. Peter's, c/o Mission, SD, St. Thomas the Apostle Church. (RC)
Olathe, CO, Montrose Co., Our Lady of Fatima, c/o Montrose, CO, St. Mary Church. (PBL)
Old River, LA, St. Anne, c/o Isle Brevelle, LA, St. Augustine's Church. (ALX)
Old Washington, TX, Washington Co., Blessed Virgin Mary Chapel, c/o Somerville, TX, St. Ann's Church. (AUS)
Olga, ND, Cavalier Co., Our Lady of the Sacred Heart, c/o Walhalla, ND, St. Boniface's Church. (FAR)
Olla, LA, St. William, c/o Winnfield, LA, Our Lady of Lourdes Church. (ALX)
Olmito, TX, Our Heavenly Father, c/o Los Fresnos, TX, St. Cecilia Church. (BWN)
Olton, TX, Lamb Co., St. Peter, Apostle, c/o Hale Center, TX, St. Theresa's Church. (LUB)
Olympic Valley, CA, Placer Co., Queen of the Snows, c/o Tahoe City, CA, Corpus Christi Church. (SAC)
Onarga, IL, Iroquois Co., Our Lady of Guadalupe, c/o Gilman, IL, Immaculate Conception Church. (JOL)
One Hundred Palms, CA, Riverside Co., San Felipe de Jesus, c/o Coachella, CA, Our Lady of Soledad Church. (SB)
Oneida, PA, Schuylkill Co., St. John the Baptist, c/o Sheppton, PA, St. Joseph Church. (ALN)
Oneop, FM, c/o Lukunor, FM, Sacred Heart Church. (CI)
Onset, MA, St. Mary Star of the Sea, c/o Buzzards Bay, MA, St. Margaret Church. (FR)
Oquawka, IL, Henderson Co., St. Andrew, c/o Monmouth, IL, Immaculate Conception Church. (PEO)
Oracle, AZ, Pinal Co., St. Helen, c/o San Manuel, AZ, St. Bartholomew Church. (TUC)
Orange Lake, NY, Orange Co., Our Lady of the Lake, c/o [1] Newburgh, NY, St. Patrick Church. (NY)
Orange Park, FL, Clay Co., Moosehaven Chapel, c/o Orange Park, FL, St. Catherine's Church. (STA)
Ordway, CO, Crowley Co., St. Peter Chapel, c/o Rocky Ford, CO, St. Peter Church. (PBL)
Orlando, FL, Orange Co., St. Ignatius Kim Korean Mission, c/o [1] Orlando, FL, St. James Cathedral . (ORL)
Orrin, ND, Pierce Co., Sacred Heart, c/o Balta, ND, Our Lady of Mount Carmel Church. (FAR)
Ortiga, PR, Bauta Abajo Co., San Mateo, c/o Villalba, PR, Our Lady Mother of Divine Providence Church. (PCE)
Orting, WA, Pierce Co., SS. Cosmas and Damian, c/o Sumner, WA, St. Andrew Church. (SEA)
Ortiz, CO, San Juan Nepomuceno y San Cayetano, c/o Conejos, CO, Our Lady of Guadalupe Church. (PBL)
Osceola, MO, St. Clair Co., St. Catherine's, c/o Clinton, MO, Holy Rosary Church. (KC)
Osceola, NE, Polk Co., St. Mary's, c/o Osceola, NE, St. Vincent Ferrer Church. (LIN)
Oshkosh, NE, Garden Co., St. Elizabeth, c/o Chappell, NE, St. Joseph's Church. (GI)
Oslo, MN, Marshall Co., St. Joseph, c/o Warren, MN, SS. Peter and Paul Church. (CR)
Osnabrock, ND, Cavalier Co., St. Joseph, c/o Wales, ND, St. Michael's Church. (FAR)
Otis, MA, Berkshire Co., St. Mary of the Lakes, c/o Lee, MA, St. Mary's Church. (SPR)
Otisco, NY, Onondaga Co., St. Patrick, c/o Tully, NY, St. Leo Church. (SY)
Oto, IA, Woodbury Co., St. Mary's, c/o Mapleton, IA, St. Mary's Church. (SC)
Otter Lake, NY, Oneida Co., St. Mary of the Snows, c/o Forestport, NY, St. Patrick Church. (SY)
Overton, NE, Dawson Co., Holy Rosary, c/o Elm Creek, NE, Immaculate Conception Church. (GI)
Overton, PA, Sullivan Co., St. Francis Xavier, c/o Dushore, PA, St. Basil's Church. (SCR)
Overton, TX, Rusk Co., Our Lady Queen of Angels, c/o Kilgore, TX, Christ the King Church. (TYL)
Owasco, NY, Cayuga Co., St. Ann, c/o [2] Auburn, NY, Sacred Heart Church. (ROC)
Owenton, KY, Owen Co., St. Edward, c/o Warsaw, KY, St. Joseph Church. (COV)
Owingsville, KY, Bath Co., St. Julie Billiart, c/o West Liberty, KY, Prince of Peace Church. (LEX)
Owl's Head, NY, Franklin Co., St. Joseph, c/o Chasm Falls, NY, St. Helen Church. (OG)
Oxford, NE, Furnas Co., St. Michael's, c/o Orleans, NE, St. Mary's Church. (LIN)
Oxnard, CA, Ventura Co., Christ the King, c/o [3] Oxnard, CA, Our Lady of Guadalupe Parish Church. (LA)

P

Paauilo, HI, Hawaii Co., St. Joseph, c/o Honokaa, HI, Our Lady of Lourdes Church. (HON)
Packing Town, OK, Oklahoma Co., Our Lady of Guadalupe, c/o [15] Oklahoma City, OK, Our Lady of Mount Carmel and St. Therese Little Flower Church. (OKL)
Paducah, TX, Cottle Co., St. Elizabeth, c/o Floydada, TX, St. Mary Magdalen Church. (LUB)
Page, ND, Cass Co., St. James, c/o Hope, ND, St. Agatha's Church. (FAR)
Pageland, SC, Chesterfield Co., St. Ernest, c/o Cheraw, SC, St. Peter's Church. (CHR)
Pago Pago, AS, c/o [2] Pago Pago, AS, Co-Cathedral of St. Joseph the Worker. (SPP)
Pagosa Junction, CO, Archuleta Co., St. John Baptist, c/o Pagosa Springs, CO, Immaculate Heart of Mary Church. (PBL)
Paguate, NM, St. Elizabeth, c/o Laguna, NM, St. Joseph Church. (GLP)
Pahrump, NV, c/o Pahrump, NV, Our Lady of the Valley Church. (LAV)
Painesdale, MI, Houghton Co., Sacred Heart, c/o Chassell, MI, St. Anne Church. (MAR)
Paisley, OR, St. John the Apostle, c/o Lakeview, OR, St. Patrick's Church. (BAK)
Palisade, CO, Mesa Co., St. Ann, c/o Grand Junction, CO, Immaculate Heart of Mary Church. (PBL)
Palisade, NE, Hitchcock Co., Holy Family, c/o Trenton, NE, St. James Church. (LIN)
Palito Blanco, TX, Jim Wells Co., St. Joseph, c/o San Diego, TX, St. Francis de Paula Church. (CC)
Palma Escrita, PR, N.S. de Fatima, c/o Las Marias, PR, Immaculate Heart of Mary Church. (MGZ)
Palma Sola, PR, Ntra. Sra. de la Asuncion, c/o [5] Canovanas, PR, San Jose Church. (SJN)
Palmarejo, PR, Coamo Co., Sacred Heart of Mary, c/o Coamo, PR, St. Blase Church. (PCE)
Palmas, PR, St. Gerard, c/o Guayama, PR, St. Anthony of Padua Church. (PCE)
Palmer, MI, Marquette Co., Our Lady Perpetual Help, c/o Negaunee, MI, St. Paul Church. (MAR)
Palmer, PR, Hato Rio Grande, La Milagrosa, c/o Rio Grande, PR, Cristo Rey Church. (SJN)
Palmer, PR, Rio Grande, Ntra. Sra. de la Providencia, c/o Rio Grande, PR, Cristo Rey Church. (SJN)
Palmetto, LA, St. Landry Parish, St. Thomas, the Apostle, c/o Melville, LA, St. John the Evangelist Church. (LAF)
Palo Blanco, NM, Colfax Co., c/o Springer, NM, St. Joseph Church. (SFE)
Panguitch, UT, Garfield Co., St. Gertrude, c/o Cedar City, UT, Christ the King Church. (SLC)
Paoli, IN, Orange Co., Our Lord Jesus Christ the King, c/o French Lick, IN, Our Lady of the Springs Church. (IND)
Paplin, NE, Howard Co., Our Lady of Mount Carmel, c/o Farwell, NE, St. Anthony of Padua Church. (GI)
Parachute, CO, Garfield Co., St. Brendan, c/o Rifle, CO, St. Mary's Church. (DEN)
Paradise, MI, Chippewa Co., Our Lady of Victory, c/o Newberry, MI, St. Gregory Church. (MAR)
Paradise Valley, NV, Humboldt Co., St. Alphonsus, c/o Winnemucca, NV, St. Paul Church. (RNO)
Paraje, NM, St. Mary Margaret, c/o Laguna, NM, St. Joseph Church. (GLP)
Paramount, CA, Los Angeles Co., Catholic Korean Community of St. Raphael, c/o Paramount, CA, Our Lady of the Rosary Church. (LA)
Parcelas de Marueno, PR, Ponce Co., San Antonio de Padua, c/o [10] Ponce, PR, La Santisima Trinidad Church. (PCE)
Parcelas Soledad, PR, Sta. Teresita, c/o [4] Mayaquez, PR, Church De El Buen Pastor Church. (MGZ)
Parcelas Vazquez, PR, Esp. Santo, c/o Salinas, PR, Our Lady of Monserrat Church. (PCE)
Parem, FM, c/o Fefan, FM, Sacred Heart Church. (CI)
Paris, MI, Mecosta Co., St. Anne, c/o Reed City, MI, St. Philip Neri Church. (GR)
Paris, MO, Monroe Co., St. Frances Cabrini, c/o Perry, MO, St. William Church. (JC)
Parishville, NY, St. Lawrence Co., St. Michael, c/o Colton, NY, St. Patrick Church. (OG)
Parks, LA, St. Louis, c/o Parks, LA, St. Joseph Church. (LAF)
Parmelee, SD, Todd Co., St. Agnes, c/o St. Francis, SD, Rosebud Reservation Church. (RC)
Parque Encuestre, PR, S. Francisco de Asis, c/o [18] Carolina, PR, Cristo Rey Church. (SJN)
Parsons, TN, Decatur Co., St. Regina, c/o Lexington, TN, St. Andrew Church. (MEM)
Parsons, WV, Tucker Co., Our Lady of Mercy, c/o Thomas, WV, St. Thomas Aquinas Church. (WH)
Pastillito, Manzanilla, PR, Our Lady of Carmel, c/o Juana Diaz, PR, Santa Teresita Church. (PCE)
Pastillo, PR, Cotopaso Co., Santiago Apostol, c/o Juana Diaz, PR, St. Raymond Nonato Church. (PCE)
Pastura, NM, Guadalupe Co., c/o Vaughn, NM, St. Mary Church. (SFE)
Patrick Springs, VA, Church of the Risen Lord, c/o Woodlawn, VA, St. Joseph's Church. (RIC)
Patten, ME, St. Paul, c/o Island Falls, ME, St. Agnes Church. (PRT)
Paul Smiths, NY, Franklin Co., St. Gabriel, c/o Lake Clear, NY, St. John in the Wilderness Church. (OG)
Pava'ia'i, AS, c/o [6] Pago Pago, AS, St. Paul Church. (SPP)
Pawnee, TX, Bee Co., Our Lady of Guadalupe, c/o Three Rivers, TX, Sacred Heart Church. (CC)
Paxton, NE, Keith Co., St. Patrick, c/o Sutherland, NE, Sacred Heart Church. (GI)
Peapack, NJ, Somerset Co., St. Brigid, c/o Far Hills, NJ, St. Elizabeth Church. (MET)
Pecan Island, LA, Vermilion Parish, Sacred Heart, c/o Cow Island, LA, St. Anne Church. (LAF)
Peck, MI, Sanilac Co., St. John, c/o Croswell, MI, St. Patrick Church. (SAG)
Pedro Garcia, PR, Coamo Co., Miraculous Virgin, c/o Coamo, PR, St. Blase Church. (PCE)
Peerless, MT, St. Ann, c/o Scobey, MT, St. Philip Bonitus Church. (GF)

Pejepscot, ME, Topsham Co., St. Andrew, c/o Brunswick, ME, St. John the Baptist Church. (PRT)
Pelican, AK, c/o Yakutat, AK, St. Ann Church. (JUN)
Pellejas, PR, Santa Rosa, c/o Adjuntas, PR, St. Joachim Church. (PCE)
Pellets Island (New Hampton), NY, Orange Co., St. Andrew Bobola, c/o Florida, NY, St. Joseph Church. (NY)
Pembina, ND, Pembina Co., Assumption, c/o Drayton, ND, St. Edward's Church. (FAR)
Pembroke, GA, Bryan Co., Holy Cross, c/o Claxton, GA, St. Christopher Church. (SAV)
Pembroke, ME, St. John the Evangelist, c/o Eastport, ME, St. Joseph Church. (PRT)
Pengilly, MN, St. Kevin, c/o Nashwauk, MN, St. Cecilia's Church. (DUL)
Penitas, TX, St. Anthony, c/o La Joya, TX, Our Lady, Queen of Angels Church. (BWN)
Pennington, MN, Beltrami Co., St. Charles, c/o Bemidji, MN, St. Philip's Church. (CR)
Pensacola, FL, Escambia Co., Church of Our Savior, c/o [13] Pensacola, FL, St. Paul Church. (PT)
Pentwater, MI, St. Vincent, c/o Weare Twp., MI, St. Joseph's Church. (GR)
Pep, TX, Hockley Co., St. Philip Neri, c/o Morton, TX, St. Ann Church. (LUB)
Perrineville, NJ, Monmouth Co., St. Joseph, c/o Englishtown, NJ, Our Lady of Mercy Church. (TR)
Perrinton, MI, Gratiot Co., St. Martin De Porres, c/o Ithaca, MI, St. Paul the Apostle Church. (SAG)
Perry Park, KY, Owen Co., Transfiguration, c/o Carrollton, KY, St. John the Evangelist Church. (COV)
Perryville, KY, Boyle Co., St. Mary, c/o Harrodsburg, KY, St. Andrew Church. (LEX)
Peru, NE, Nemaha Co., St. Clara, c/o Auburn, NE, St. Joseph's Church. (LIN)
Pescadero, CA, San Mateo Co., St. Anthony, c/o Half Moon Bay, CA, Our Lady of the Pillar Church. (SFR)
Petaca, NM, Taos Co., c/o El Rito, NM, San Juan Nepomuceno Church. (SFE)
Petersville, MD, Frederick Co., St. Mary's, c/o Brunswick, MD, St. Francis of Assisi Church. (BAL)
Petit Mamou, LA, Acadia Parish, St. Jules, c/o Evangeline, LA, St. Joseph Church. (LAF)
Petrolia, CA, St. Patrick, c/o Ferndale, CA, Church of the Assumption. (SR)
Petronila, TX, Nueces Co., St. Vivian, c/o [7] Corpus Christi, TX, Our Lady of the Rosary Church. (CC)
Phelps, KY, Pike Co., Jesus of the Mountains Catholic Church, c/o Pikeville, KY, St. Francis of Assisi Church. (LEX)
Philadelphia, MS, St. Theresa, c/o Philadelphia, MS, Holy Rosary Church. (JKS)
Philadelphia, NY, Jefferson Co., St. Joseph, c/o Evans Mills, NY, St. Mary Church. (OG)
Philadelphia, PA, c/o [48] Philadelphia, PA, St. Francis Xavier Church. (PH)
Philadelphia, PA, Philadelphia Co., Holy Redeemer Chinese Church, c/o [80] Philadelphia, PA, St. John the Evangelist Church. (PH)
Phillipsburg, KY, Marion Co., Our Lady of Fatima, c/o Calvary, KY, Holy Name of Mary Church. (L)
Philmont, NY, Pine Haven Home, c/o Philmont, NY, Sacred Heart Church. (ALB)
Philo, OH, Muskingum Co., St. Ann, c/o Zanesville, OH, St. Thomas Aquinas Church. (COL)
Phoenix, AZ, Maricopa Co., Our Lady of Fatima, c/o [7] Phoenix, AZ, SS. Anthony and Pius X Church. (PHX)
Phoenix, AZ, Maricopa Co., Santa Rosa Chapel, c/o [1] Phoenix, AZ, SS. Simon and Jude Cathedral. (PHX)
Phoenix, AZ, Maricopa Co., St. Philip the Deacon Catholic Center, c/o [17] Phoenix, AZ, St. Mark Church. (PHX)
Phoenix, AZ, Maricopa Co., St. Pius X, c/o [7] Phoenix, AZ, SS. Anthony and Pius X Church. (PHX)
Picacho, NM, St. Joseph, c/o Ruidoso, NM, St. Eleanor Church. (LSC)
Pickens, WV, Randolph Co., Sacred Heart, c/o Buckhannon, WV, Holy Rosary Church. (WH)
Pickerel, WI, St. Mary, c/o Elcho, WI, Holy Family Church. (GB)
Pickwick, TN, Our Lady of the Lake, c/o Savannah, TN, St. Mary's Church. (MEM)
Picuris Indian Pueblo, NM, Taos Co., San Lorenzo Mission, c/o Penasco, NM, San Antonio de Padua Church. (SFE)
Piedmont, AL, Calhoun Co., St. Joachim, c/o Jacksonville, AL, St. Charles Church. (BIR)
Piedras Blancas, PR, Ntra. Sra. Reina de la Paz, c/o Aguada, PR, St. Francis of Assisi Church. (MGZ)
Pigeon Forge, TN, Sevier Co., Holy Cross, c/o Gatlinburg, TN, St. Mary Church. (KNX)
Piis, FM, c/o Lukunor, FM, Sacred Heart Church. (CI)
Pilar, NM, Taos Co., Nuestra Senora de los Dolores, c/o Dixon, NM, St. Anthony Church. (SFE)
Pilottown, DE, Cecil Co., St. Patrick, c/o Perryville, MD, Church of the Good Shepherd. (WIL)
Pima, AZ, Graham Co., Pima Mission, c/o Safford, AZ, St. Rose of Lima Church. (TUC)
Pin Oak, TX, Bastrop Co., St. Mary's, c/o Giddings, TX, St. Margaret Church. (AUS)
Pine Bluff, AR, Jefferson Co., St. Raphael's, c/o Pine Bluff, AR, St. Peter's Church. (LR)
Pine Mountain, GA, Harris Co., Christ the King, c/o [3] Columbus, GA, St. Anne Church. (SAV)
Pine Point, ME, Scarborough Co., St. Jude, c/o Scarborough, ME, St. Maximilian Kolbe Church. (PRT)
Pine Springs, AZ, St. Rose, c/o Houck, AZ, St. John the Evangelist Church. (GLP)
Pinedale, CA, Fresno Co., St. Agnes, c/o [2] Fresno, CA, Holy Spirit Church. (FRS)
Pineville, KY, Bell Co., St. Anthony, c/o Middlesboro, KY, St. Julian Church. (LEX)
Pineville, WV, Wyoming Co., Holy Cross, c/o Mullens, WV, St. John the Evangelist Church. (WH)
Pingree, ND, Stutsman Co., St. Michael, c/o Jamestown, ND, The Basilica of St. James. (FAR)
Pinhook, IA, St. Bridget, c/o Sumner, IA, Immaculate Conception Church. (DUB)
Pinon, AZ, Navajo Co., St. Mary of the Rosary, c/o Chinle, AZ, Our Lady of Fatima Church. (GLP)
Pinos Altos, NM, Grant Co., Holy Cross, c/o Silver City, NM, St. Vincent de Paul Church. (LSC)
Pinos Wells, NM, Torrance Co., c/o Vaughn, NM, St. Mary Church. (SFE)
Pintada, NM, Guadalupe Co., c/o Santa Rosa, NM, St. Rose of Lima Church. (SFE)
Piru, CA, Ventura Co., San Salvador, c/o Fillmore, CA, St. Francis of Assisi Church. (LA)
Pittsburg, OK, Pittsburg Co., St. Edwards, c/o McAlester, OK, St. John Church. (TLS)
Pittsfield, MA, Berkshire Co., All Souls, c/o [3] Pittsfield, MA, Our Lady of Mt. Carmel Church. (SPR)
Placentia, CA, Orange Co., St. George, c/o [5] North Hollywood, CA, St. Paul Assyrian-Chaldean Church. (LA)
Placentia, CA, Orange Co., St. George, c/o North Hollywood, CA, St. Paul Assyrian-Chaldean Catholic Parish Church. (EST)
Placita, NM, Taos Co., Nuestra Senora de la Asuncion Mission, c/o Penasco, NM, San Antonio de Padua Church. (SFE)
Placitas, NM, Sandoval Co., c/o Bernalillo, NM, Our Lady of Sorrows Church. (SFE)
Placitas, NM, Rio Arriba Co., c/o El Rito, NM, San Juan Nepomuceno Church. (SFE)
Placitas, NM, Sierra Co., San Lorenzo, c/o Truth or Consequences, NM, Our Lady of Perpetual Help Church. (LSC)
Plains, TX, Yoakum Co., Sacred Heart, c/o Denver City, TX, St. William Church. (LUB)
Plainview, SD, Meade Co., Our Lady of Victory, c/o Faith, SD, St. Joseph Church. (RC)
Plaisance, LA, St. Landry Parish, St. Andrew, c/o Grand Prairie, LA, St. Peter Church. (LAF)
Plasi, NE, Saunders Co., SS. Cyril and Methodius, c/o Prague, NE, St. John's Church. (LIN)
Platteville, CO, Weld Co., St. Nicholas, c/o Fort Lupton, CO, St. William Church. (DEN)
Playas, NM, St. Augustine, c/o Lordsburg, NM, St. Joseph Church. (LSC)
Playita Cortada, PR, San Patricio, c/o Santa Isabel, PR, St. James Church. (PCE)
Plaza, ND, Mountrail Co., Sacred Heart, c/o Parshall, ND, St. Bridget Church. (BIS)
Plaza Blanca, NM, Rio Arriba Co., c/o Los Ojos, NM, San Jose Church. (SFE)
Pleasant Hill, MO, Cass Co., St. Bridget, c/o Harrisonville, MO, Our Lady of Lourdes Church. (KC)
Pleasant Valley, PA, Blair Co., Our Lady of the Assumption, c/o [7] Altoona, PA, Our Lady of Mt. Carmel Church. (ALT)
Pleasantville Park, NY, Westchester Co., Our Lady of Pompeii, c/o Pleasantville, NY, Holy Innocents Church. (NY)
Plena, PR, San Jose, c/o Salinas, PR, Our Lady of Monserrat Church. (PCE)
Plevna, MT, St. Anthony, c/o Baker, MT, St. John the Evangelist Church. (GF)
Plum Bayou, AR, Jefferson Co., St. Mary's, c/o Pine Bluff, AR, St. Joseph's Church. (LR)
Plum Island, MA, St. James, c/o Newburyport, MA, Immaculate Conception Church. (BO)
Plunketville, OK, McCurtain Co., St. Henry, c/o Idabel, OK, St. Francis De Sales Church. (TLS)
Plush, OR, St. Thomas, c/o Lakeview, OR, St. Patrick's Church. (BAK)
Plymouth, CA, Amador Co., St. Mary of the Mountains, c/o Sutter Creek, CA, Immaculate Conception Church. (SAC)
Plymouth Rock, IA, St. Agnes, c/o Cresco, IA, Notre Dame Church. (DUB)
Pocahontas, PA, Somerset Co., St. Mary's, c/o West Salisbury, PA, St. Michael's Church. (ALT)
Pocono Summit, PA, Monroe Co., St. Joan of Arc, c/o Mount Pocono, PA, St. Mary of the Mount Church. (SCR)
Point Blank, TX, St. Stephen the Martyr, c/o New Waverly, TX, St. Joseph Church. (GAL)
Point Comfort, TX, St. Ann, c/o Port Lavaca, TX, Our Lady of the Gulf Church. (VIC)
Polvadera, NM, Socorro Co., c/o Socorro, NM, San Miguel Church. (SFE)
Ponce, P.R., La Dolorosa, c/o [2] Ponce, PR, Christ the King Church. (PCE)
Ponce, PR, Our Lady of Carmel, c/o [3] Ponce, PR, Church of the Resurrection. (PCE)
Ponce, PR, Saint Joseph, c/o [3] Ponce, PR, Church of the Resurrection. (PCE)
Pond Creek, OH, Scioto Co., Holy Trinity, c/o West Portsmouth, OH, Our Lady of Sorrows Church. (COL)
Pond Creek, OK, Grant Co., St. Joseph's, c/o Medford, OK, St. Mary's Church. (OKL)
Pond Eddy, NY, Sullivan Co., Sacred Heart, c/o Yulan, NY, St. Anthony of Padua Church. (NY)
Ponderosa, NM, Sandoval Co., c/o Jemez Pueblo, NM, San Diego Indian Missions Church. (SFE)
Ponsford, MN, Becker Co., St. Theodore, c/o Ogema, MN, Most Holy Redeemer Church. (CR)
Pontiac, MI, Oakland Co., St. Vincent de Paul, c/o Pontiac, MI, St. Joseph Church. (DET)
Pontotoc, MS, Pontotoc Co., St. Christopher, c/o New Albany, MS, St. Francis of Assisi Church. (JKS)
Poplarville, MS, Pearl River Co., St. Joseph, c/o Lumberton, MS, Our Lady of Perpetual Help Church. (BLX)
Porcupine, ND, Sioux Co., St. James, c/o Fort Yates, ND, St. Peter - Catholic Indian Mission. (BIS)
Porcupine, SD, Shannon Co., St. Paul, c/o Porcupine, SD, Church of Christ the King. (RC)
Port Costa, CA, Contra Costa Co., St. Patrick, c/o Crockett, CA, St. Rose of Lima Church. (OAK)
Port Deposit, MD, Cecil Co., St. Teresa, c/o Perryville, MD, Church of the Good Shepherd. (WIL)
Port Norris, NJ, Cumberland Co., St. Anthony, c/o Cedarville, NJ, St. Michael's Church. (CAM)
Port O'Connor, TX, St. Joseph, c/o Port Lavaca, TX, Our Lady of the Gulf Church. (VIC)
Port Orford, OR, Curry Co., St. John the Baptist, c/o Bandon, OR, Holy Trinity Church. (P)
Port St. Joe, FL, Gulf Co., San Blas Catholic Mission, c/o Port St. Joe, FL, St. Joseph Church. (PT)
Portage, ME, Our Lady of the Lakes, c/o Ashland, ME, St. Mark's Church. (PRT)
Portal, ND, Burke Co., St. John the Baptist, c/o Bowbells, ND, St. Joseph Church. (BIS)
Portales, NM, Roosevelt Co., University Catholic Center, c/o Portales, NM, St. Helen Church. (SFE)
Porterville, CA, Our Lady of Guadalupe, c/o Porterville, CA, St. Anne Church. (FRS)
Portland, PA, Northampton Co., St. Vincent de Paul, c/o Bangor, PA, Our Lady of Good Counsel Church. (ALN)
Portola Valley, CA, San Mateo Co., Our Lady of the Wayside, c/o [2] Menlo Park, CA, St. Denis Church. (SFR)
Poston, AZ, Kateri Tekawitha Indian Mission, c/o Parker, AZ, Sacred Heart Church. (TUC)
Potash, LA, Plaquemines Parish, St. Joseph, c/o Port Sulphur, LA, St. Patrick Church. (NO)
Potato Creek, SD, Jackson Co., St. Henry, c/o Wanblee, SD, Ignatius Loyola Church. (RC)
Potawatomi Reservation, KS, Our Lady of Snows, c/o Holton, KS, St. Dominic's Church. (KCK)
Potter Place, NH, Merrimack Co., Immaculate Conception, c/o New London, NH, Our Lady of Fatima Church. (MAN)
Pottersville, NY, St. Pius X, c/o North Creek, NY, St. James Church. (ALB)
Power, MT, Guardian Angel, c/o Dutton, MT, St. William Church. (HEL)
Powers, OR, Coos Co., St. Bridget, c/o Coquille, OR, Holy Name Church. (P)
Powers Lake, ND, Burke Co., St. James, c/o Stanley, ND, Queen of the Most Holy Rosary Church. (BIS)
Prairie Center, NE, Buffalo Co., St. Mary, c/o Pleasanton, NE, St. Mary's Church. (GI)
Prairie Laurent, LA, St. Landry Parish, St. Jules, c/o Leonville, LA, St. Catherine Church. (LAF)
Prairie Ronde, LA, St. Landry Parish, Sacred Heart, c/o Lawtell, LA, St. Bridget Church. (LAF)
Prairie View, AR, Logan Co., St. Meinrad, c/o Scranton, AR, St. Ignatius Church. (LR)
Prentiss, MS, Jefferson Davis Co., St. Mary's, c/o Bassfield, MS, St. Peter Church. (BLX)
Primghar, IA, O'Brien Co., St. Anthony of Padua, c/o Sutherland, IA, Sacred Heart Church. (SC)
Primrose, NE, Boone Co., St. Mary, c/o Cedar Rapids, NE, St. Anthony Church. (OM)
Princeton, CA, Colusa Co., St. Joseph, c/o Colusa, CA, Our Lady of Lourdes Church. (SAC)
Princeton, MO, Mercer Co., Immaculate Heart of Mary Church, c/o Trenton, MO, St. Joseph's Church. (KC)
Proctorsville, VT, Windsor Co., Holy Name of Mary, c/o Chester, VT, St. Joseph Church. (BUR)
Promise, SD, Dewey Co., St. Catherine, c/o Eagle Butte, SD, All Saints Church. (RC)

Promise, SD, Dewey Co., St. Catherine, c/o Eagle Butte, SD, Cheyenne River Reservation Church. (RC)
Promised Land, PA, Monroe Co., Our Lady of Fatima, c/o Canadensis, PA, St. Bernadette Church. (SCR)
Prudence Island, RI, Our Lady of Prudence, c/o Bristol, RI, St. Mary Church. (PRO)
Puako, HI, Church of the Ascension, Puako, c/o Kamuela, HI, Church of the Annunciation. (HON)
Pueblitos, NM, Valencia Co., c/o Belen, NM, Our Lady of Belen Church. (SFE)
Pueblo West, CO, Pueblo Co., St. Paul the Apostle, c/o [16] Pueblo, CO, St. Pius X Church. (PBL)
Puerto de Luna, NM, Guadalupe Co., c/o Santa Rosa, NM, St. Rose of Lima Church. (SFE)
Puerto Nuevo, PR, Ntra. Sra. de la Caridad, c/o [43] San Juan, PR, San Pablo Church. (SJN)
Puerto Plata, PR, Jayuya Co., San Juan, c/o Jayuya, PR, Our Lady of Monserrate Church. (PCE)
Puerto Real, PR, Our Lady of Mt. Carmel, c/o Cabo Rojo, PR, St. Michael Church. (MGZ)
Pulaski, VA, Davis Co., St. Edward, c/o Wytheville, VA, St. Mary's Church. (RIC)
Pulguillas, PR, Coamo Co., Christ the King, c/o Coamo, PR, St. Blase Church. (PCE)
Punaluu, HI, Honolulu Co., St. Joachim, c/o Kahuku, HI, St. Roch Church. (HON)
Punta de Agua, NM, Torrance Co., c/o Mountainair, NM, St. Alice Church. (SFE)
Punto Oro, PR, Ponce Co., Ntra. Sra. del Pilar, c/o [11] Ponce, PR, San Jose Obrero Church. (PCE)
Puuiki, HI, Maui Co., St. Peter, c/o Hana, HI, St. Mary Church. (HON)

Q

Quartzsite, AZ, Queen of Peace, c/o Parker, AZ, Sacred Heart Church. (TUC)
Quebrada Ceiba, PR, Milagrosa, c/o Penuelas, PR, St. Joseph Church. (PCE)
Quebrada Honda, PR, Nuestra Senora, c/o Guayanilla, PR, Immaculate Conception Church. (PCE)
Quebrada Larga, PR, Sgdo. Corazon de Jesus, c/o Aguada, PR, St. Francis of Assisi Church. (MGZ)
Quebradas, PR, Sacred Heart, c/o Yauco, PR, Holy Rossary Church. (PCE)
Quebradas, PR, San Francisco de Asis, c/o Guayanilla, PR, Immaculate Conception Church. (PCE)
Queen Creek, AZ, Maricopa Co., Our Lady of Guadalupe, c/o Gilbert, AZ, St. Anne Church. (PHX)
Queensbury, NY, Warren Co., Our Lady of the Assumption, c/o Lake George, NY, Sacred Heart Church. (ALB)
Queenstown, MD, Queen Anne Co., St. Peter, c/o Centreville, MD, Our Mother of Sorrows Church. (WIL)
Quemado, TX, Our Lady of Guadalupe, c/o Eagle Pass, TX, Our Lady of Refuge Church. (LAR)
Quimby, IA, Cherokee Co., St. John the Baptist, c/o Holstein, IA, Our Lady of Good Counsel Church. (SC)
Quinault, WA, Grays Harbor & Jefferson Cos., Our Lady of the Olympics, c/o Hoquiam, WA, Our Lady of Good Help Church. (SEA)
Quinlan, TX, Hunt Co., Our Lady of Fatima, c/o Greenville, TX, St. William Church. (DAL)
Quitman, MS, Good Shepherd, c/o Meridian, MS, St. Patrick Church. (JKS)

R

Ragley, LA, Beauregard Parish, St. Pius X, c/o De Quincy, LA, Our Lady of La Salette Church. (LKC)
Rainsville, NM, Mora Co., c/o Mora, NM, St. Gertrude Church. (SFE)
Raleigh, MS, St. Paul, c/o Magee, MS, St. Stephen Church. (JKS)
Ralph, SD, Harding Co., St. Isidore, c/o Buffalo, SD, St. Anthony Church. (RC)
Ralston, PA, Lycoming Co., St. Aloysius, c/o Canton, PA, St. Michael Church. (SCR)
Ramey-Maleza, PR, Los Santos Reyes, c/o Aguadilla, PR, San Jose Obrero Church. (MGZ)
Ramirez, TX, Duval Co., Our Lady of Guadalupe, c/o Premont, TX, St. Theresa of the Infant Jesus Church. (CC)
Ranchester, WY, Sheridan Co., St. Edmund, c/o Sheridan, WY, Holy Name Church. (CHY)
Ranchito, TX, Fisher Co., Sacred Heart, c/o Rotan, TX, St. Joseph Church. (LUB)
Ranchitos, NM, Rio Arriba Co., c/o San Juan Pueblo, NM, St. John the Baptist Church. (SFE)
Rancho Murieta, CA, Sacramento Co., c/o Elk Grove, CA, St. Joseph Church. (SAC)
Randsburg, CA, Kern Co., Santa Barbara, c/o Ridgecrest, CA, St. Ann Church. (FRS)
Rangeley, ME, St. Luke, c/o Oquossoc, ME, Our Lady of the Lakes Church. (PRT)
Rangely, CO, Rio Blanco Co., St. Ignatius, c/o Meeker, CO, Holy Family Church. (DEN)
Rankin, TX, Upton Co., St. Thomas, c/o Big Lake, TX, St. Margaret of Cortona Church. (SAN)
Rapid City, SD, Pennington Co., Indian Health Service, Sioux San Hospital and Pennington County Jail, c/o [4] Rapid City, SD, St. Isaac Jogues Church. (RC)
Rasselas, PA, Elk Co., Holy Cross, c/o Wilcox, PA, St. Anne Church. (E)
Ray, ND, Williams Co., St. Michael, c/o Tioga, ND, St. Thomas Church. (BIS)
Raymond, CA, Madera Co., St. Anne, c/o Madera, CA, St. Joachim Church. (FRS)
Raymond, MS, Immaculate Conception, c/o Clinton, MS, Holy Savior Church. (JKS)
Raynesford, MT, St. Mary, c/o Belt, MT, St. Mark the Evangelist Church. (GF)
Reading, PA, Berks Co., Holy Rosary Chapel, c/o [6] Reading, PA, Holy Rosary Church. (ALN)
Realitos, TX, Dual Co., Sacred Heart, c/o Hebbronville, TX, Our Lady of Guadalupe Church. (LAR)
Rector, AR, Clay Co., St. Henry's, c/o Paragould, AR, St. Mary's Church. (LR)
Red Cliff, CO, Eagle Co., Our Lady of Mt. Carmel, c/o Minturn, CO, St. Patrick's Church. (DEN)
Red Feather Lakes, CO, Larimer Co., Our Lady of the Lakes, c/o [1] Fort Collins, CO, St. Joseph Church. (DEN)
Red Owl, SD, Meade Co., St. Anthony, c/o Faith, SD, St. Joseph Church. (RC)
Red River, NM, Taos Co., c/o Questa, NM, St. Anthony Church. (SFE)
Red Scaffold, SD, Ziebach Co., Sacred Heart, c/o Eagle Butte, SD, All Saints Church. (RC)
Red Scaffold, SD, Ziebach Co., Sacred Heart, c/o Eagle Butte, SD, Cheyenne River Reservation Church. (RC)
Red Shirt Table, SD, Shannon Co., St. Bernard, c/o Pine Ridge, SD, Holy Rosary Church. (RC)
Red Springs, NC, Robeson Co., St. Andrew, c/o Lumberton, NC, St. Francis De Sales Church. (R)
Reddick, IL, Kankakee Co., St. Mary, c/o Cabery, IL, St. Joseph Church. (JOL)
Redford, TX, San Jose, c/o Presidio, TX, Santa Teresa de Jesus Church. (ELP)
Redwood, TX, Guadalupe Co., St. Joseph, c/o Seguin, TX, Our Lady of Guadalupe Church. (SAT)
Redwood City, CA, San Mateo Co., San Jose Obrero (St. Joseph the Workman), c/o [1] Menlo Park, CA, St. Anthony Church. (SFR)
Reeder, ND, Adams Co., Sacred Heart, c/o Hettinger, ND, Holy Trinity Church. (BIS)
Reeves, LA, Sacred Heart Parish, St. Maurice, c/o Kinder, LA, St. Philip Neri Church. (LKC)
Reform, AL, Pickens Co., St. Robert, c/o Tuscaloosa, AL, St. Francis of Assisi University Parish Church. (BIR)
Regal, MN, Kandiyohi Co., St. Anthony, c/o Spicer, MN, Our Lady of the Lakes Church. (NU)
Regent, ND, Hettinger Co., St. Henry's, c/o New England, ND, St. Mary Church. (BIS)
Reidsville, GA, Tattnall Co., St. Andrew the Apostle, c/o Vidalia, GA, Sacred Heart Church. (SAV)
Remer, MN, St. Paul, c/o Longville, MN, St. Edward's Church. (DUL)
Reserve, NM, Catron Co., St. Francis, c/o Aragon, NM, Santo Nino Church. (GLP)
Retsof, NY, Livingston Co., St. Lucy, c/o Leicester, NY, St. Thomas Aquinas Church. (ROC)
Reva, SD, Harding Co., Our Lady of the Prairie, c/o Buffalo, SD, St. Anthony Church. (RC)
Rhame, ND, Bowman Co., St. Mel, c/o Bowman, ND, St. Charles Church. (BIS)
Rhinecliff, NY, Dutchess Co., St. Joseph, c/o Rhinebeck, NY, The Good Shepherd Church. (NY)
Ricardo, TX, Kleberg Co., Sacred Heart, c/o Vattman, TX, Our Lady of Consolation Church. (CC)
Rich Hill, MO, Bates Co., St. Bridget's, c/o Nevada, MO, St. Mary's Church. (KC)
Richardton, ND, Stark Co., St. Stephen, c/o Richardton, ND, St. Mary Church. (BIS)
Richey, MT, St. Francis de Sales, c/o Circle, MT, St. Francis Xavier Church. (GF)
Richgrove, CA, Tulare Co., St. Vincent, c/o Delano, CA, St. Mary's of the Miraculous Medal Church. (FRS)
Richland, NJ, Atlantic Co., St. Joseph, c/o [5] Vineland, NJ, St. Mary's Church. (CAM)
Richlands, VA, Buchanan Co., St. Joseph, c/o Richlands, VA, St. Mary Church. (RIC)
Richmond, KY, St. Stephen the Martyr, c/o Richmond, KY, St. Mark Church. (LEX)
Rico, CO, Dolores Co., Immaculate Heart of Mary Chapel, c/o Mancos, CO, St. Rita Church. (PBL)
Rideau Settlement, LA, St. Landry Parish, Sacred Heart, c/o Lebeau, LA, Immaculate Conception Church. (LAF)
Ridgebury, PA, Bradford Co., Our Lady of Perpetual Help, c/o Bentley Creek, PA, St. Ann's Church. (SCR)
Ridgefield, WA, Clark Co., St. Mary of Guadalupe, c/o Battle Ground, WA, Sacred Heart Church. (SEA)
Ridgeview, SD, Dewey Co., St. Joseph, c/o Eagle Butte, SD, All Saints Church. (RC)
Ridgeview, SD, Dewey Co., St. Joseph, c/o Eagle Butte, SD, Cheyenne River Reservation Church. (RC)
Riegelwood, NC, Columbus Co., Christ the King, c/o Wilmington, NC, St. Mark Church. (R)
Riley, NM, Socorro Co., c/o Socorro, NM, San Miguel Church. (SFE)
Rileyville, PA, Wayne Co., St. Joseph, c/o Honesdale, PA, St. John the Evangelist Church. (SCR)
Rimersburg, PA, Clarion Co., St. Richard, c/o East Brady, PA, St. Eusebius Church. (E)
Rincon, NM, Dona Ana Co., Our Lady of All Nations, c/o Hatch, NM, Our Lord of Mercy Church. (LSC)
Ringgold, LA, Bienville Parish, Blessed Sacrament, c/o Minden, LA, St. Paul Church. (SHP)
Rio Bravo, TX, Santa Monica Mission, c/o Rio Bravo, TX, Santa Rita de Casia Independent Mission. (LAR)
Rio Canas, PR, Rio Canas Abajo, San Judas, c/o Juana Diaz, PR, St. Raymond Nonato Church. (PCE)
Rio Chiquito, NM, Rio Arriba Co., Sagrado Corazon, c/o Chimayo, NM, Holy Family Church. (SFE)
Rio Chiquito, PR, Ponce Co., Nino Jesus de Praga, c/o [2] Ponce, PR, Christ the King Church. (PCE)
Rio Chiquito, PR, Ponce Co., San Vicente, c/o [14] Ponce, PR, San Vicente-Cantera Church. (PCE)
Rio en Medio, NM, Sante Fe Co., Our Lady of Sorrows, c/o [2] Santa Fe, NM, Our Lady of Guadalupe Church. (SFE)
Rio Grande, PR, Nuestra Senora de Fatima, c/o Rio Grande, PR, Nuestra Senora del Carmen Church. (SJN)
Rio Grande, PR, Perpetuo Socorro, c/o Aguada, PR, St. Francis of Assisi Church. (MGZ)
Rio Grande, PR, San Pedro, c/o Rio Grande, PR, Nuestra Senora del Carmen Church. (SJN)
Rio Grande-Playa, PR, Ntra. Sra. del Carmen, c/o Aguada, PR, St. Francis of Assisi Church. (MGZ)
Rio Hondo, PR, San Carlos y San Antonio, c/o [6] Mayaquez, PR, Sacred Heart Church. (MGZ)
Rio Jueyes, PR, Coamo Co., Our Lady of Lourdes, c/o Coamo, PR, St. Blase Church. (PCE)
Rio Lucio, NM, Taos Co., Sagrado Corazon Mission, c/o Penasco, NM, San Antonio de Padua Church. (SFE)
Rio Piedras, PR, N. Sra. Del Rosario, c/o [2] Trujillo Alto, PR, San Pio X Church. (SJN)
Rio Piedras, PR, N. Sra. Reina de la Paz, c/o [57] San Juan, PR, Santisimo Salvador Church. (SJN)
Rio Piedras, PR, San Jose de Calasanz, c/o [57] San Juan, PR, Santisimo Salvador Church. (SJN)
Rio Piedras, PR, Ba. Venezuela Co., Santa Teresita de Nino Jesus, c/o [47] San Juan, PR, Nuestra Senora del Pilar Church. (SJN)
Rio Prieto, PR, Milagrosa, c/o Castaner, PR, Our Lady of the Miraculous Medal Church. (PCE)
Rio Rancho, NM, Sandoval Co., Church of the Incarnation, c/o Rio Rancho, NM, St. Thomas Aquinas . (SFE)
Rio Rancho, NM, Sandoval Co., St. John Vianney, c/o Rio Rancho, NM, St. Thomas Aquinas Church. (SFE)
Rio Verde, AZ, St. Dominic, c/o Fountain Hills, AZ, Ascension Church. (PHX)
Rios, TX, Duval Co., St. Francis of Assisi, c/o Premont, TX, St. Theresa of the Infant Jesus Church. (CC)
Ripley, CA, Riverside Co., Our Lady of Guadalupe, c/o Blythe, CA, St. Joan of Arc Church. (SB)
Ripley, NY, Chautauqua Co., St. Thomas More, c/o Westfield, NY, St. James Church. (BUF)
Ripley, TN, Lauderdale Co., Ave Maria, c/o Covington, TN, St. Alphonsus Church. (MEM)
Rising Sun, MD, Cecil Co., St. Agnes, c/o Perryville, MD, Church of the Good Shepherd. (WIL)
Ritter, SC, Colleton Co., St. James, c/o Walterboro, SC, St. Anthony's Church. (CHR)
Riverdale, CA, Fresno Co., Our Lady of the Assumption, c/o Riverdale, CA, St. Ann Church. (FRS)
Riverside, CA, Riverside Co., Our Lady of Guadalupe, c/o [11] Riverside, CA, St. Thomas the Apostle Church. (SB)
Riverside, MT, Sacred Heart, c/o Wolf Point, MT, Immaculate Conception Church. (GF)
Riverton, NE, Franklin Co., St. Catherine's, c/o Red Cloud, NE, Sacred Heart Church. (LIN)
Riviera, TX, Kleberg Co., Our Lady of Guadalupe, c/o Vattman, TX, Our Lady of Consolation Church. (CC)
Roanoke, AL, Randolph Co., Immaculate Conception, c/o Lanett, AL, Holy Family Church. (BIR)
Robbins, IL, Cook Co., St. Peter Claver, c/o Blue Island, IL, St. Benedict Church. (CHI)
Robbins, NC, Moore Co., Blessed Juan Diego, c/o Pinehurst, NC, Sacred Heart Church. (R)
Robbinsville, NC, Graham Co., Prince of Peace, c/o Andrews, NC, Holy Redeemer Church. (CHL)
Robert Lee, TX, Coke Co., Our Lady of Guadalupe, c/o Ballinger, TX, St. Mary Star of the Sea Church. (SAN)
Roberts, IL, Immaculate Conception, c/o Piper City, IL, St. Peter Church. (JOL)
Robinson Township, MI, St. Anthony, c/o Grand Haven, MI, St. Patrick's Church. (GR)

Robstown, TX, Nueces Co., St. Mary, c/o Robstown, TX, St. Anthony Church. (CC)
Roby, MO, Texas Co., St. Vincent de Paul, c/o Houston, MO, St. Mark Church. (SPC)
Rochester, VT, Windsor Co., St. Elizabeth, c/o Bethel, VT, St. Anthony Church. (BUR)
Rociada Abajo, NM, San Miguel Co., Santo Nino, c/o Las Vegas, NM, Our Lady of Sorrows Church. (SFE)
Rock City Falls, NY, St. Paul, c/o Greenfield Center, NY, St. Joseph Church. (ALB)
Rock Hall, MD, Kent Co., St. John, c/o Chestertown, MD, Sacred Heart Church. (WIL)
Rock Lake, ND, Towner Co., Immaculate Heart of Mary, c/o Rolla, ND, St. Joachim's Church. (FAR)
Rock Point, MD, Charles Co., St. Francis de Sales, c/o Issue, MD, Holy Ghost Church. (WDC)
Rockvale, CO, Fremont Co., St. Patrick, c/o Florence, CO, St. Benedict Church. (PBL)
Rockville, MD, Montgomery Co., Our Lady of China, c/o [3] Rockville, MD, St. Mary Church. (WDC)
Rockville, NE, Sherman Co., St. Mary's, c/o Ravenna, NE, Our Lady of Lourdes Church. (GI)
Rockwood, ME, Somerset Co., St. Joseph's, c/o Greenville, ME, Holy Family Church. (PRT)
Rocky Boy Indian Reservation, MT, St. Mary, c/o Big Sandy, MT, St. Margaret Mary Church. (GF)
Rocky Mount, NC, Nash & Edgecombe Cos., Immaculate Conception, c/o Rocky Mount, NC, Our Lady of Perpetual Help Church. (R)
Rockyford, SD, Shannon Co., St. Peter's, c/o Manderson, SD, St. Agnes Church. (RC)
Rodarte, NM, Taos Co., Santa Barbara Mission, c/o Penasco, NM, San Antonio de Padua Church. (SFE)
Rodeo, NM, San Felipe, c/o Lordsburg, NM, St. Joseph Church. (LSC)
Rogers, TX, Bell Co., St. Matthew, c/o Temple, TX, St. Luke's Church. (AUS)
Rogue River, OR, Jackson Co., Rogue River Catholic Community, c/o Grants Pass, OR, St. Anne Church. (P)
Roland, OK, Sequoyah Co., Blessed Kateri Tekakwitha, c/o Sallisaw, OK, St. Francis Xavier Church. (TLS)
Romanum, FM, St. Joseph, c/o Udot, FM, St. Francis Assisi Church. (CI)
Romeo, CO, Conejos Co., Our Lady of the Immaculate Conception, c/o Capulin, CO, St. Joseph Church. (PBL)
Romero, PR, Sagrado Corazon, c/o Villalba, PR, Our Lady of Mt. Carmel Church. (PCE)
Roosevelt Lake, AZ, Gila Co., St. Theresa, c/o Miami, AZ, Our Lady of the Blessed Sacrament Church. (TUC)
Ropesville, TX, Hockley Co., San Francisco de Asis, c/o Brownfield, TX, St. Anthony's Church. (LUB)
Rosario, PR, Nuestra Senora del Rosario, c/o Rosario, PR, Rosary Church. (MGZ)
Rosario, PR, San Jose, c/o [6] Mayaquez, PR, Sacred Heart Church. (MGZ)
Roscoe, IL, Winnebago Co., Church of the Holy Spirit, c/o South Beloit, IL, St. Peter Church. (RCK)
Roscoe, NY, Sullivan Co., Gate of Heaven, c/o Livingston Manor, NY, St. Aloysius Church. (NY)
Roscoe, TX, Nolan Co., St. Albert the Great, c/o Sweetwater, TX, Immaculate Heart of Mary Church. (SAN)
Rosebud, SD, Todd Co., St. Bridget, c/o St. Francis, SD, Rosebud Reservation Church. (RC)
Roseton, NY, Orange Co., Our Lady of Mercy, c/o Marlboro, NY, St. Mary Church. (NY)
Rosita, TX, Santa Rosa de Lima, c/o Escobares, TX, Sacred Heart Church. (BWN)
Rossie, NY, St. Lawrence Co., St. Patrick, c/o Hammond, NY, St. Peter Church. (OG)
Rotten Bayou, MS, Harrison Co., St. William, c/o DeLisle, MS, The Catholic Church in DeLisle Church. (BLX)
Roulette, PA, Potter Co., St. Mary, c/o Port Allegany, PA, St. Gabriel the Archangel Church. (E)
Round Mountain, NV, Nye Co., St. Barbara, c/o Tonopah, NV, St. Patrick Church. (LAV)
Round Rock, AZ, Our Lady of Guadalupe, c/o Lukachukai, AZ, St. Isabel Church. (GLP)
Rouseville, PA, Venango Co., St. Venantius, c/o [1] Oil City, PA, Assumption of the Blessed Virgin Mary Church. (E)
Rowe, NM, San Miguel Co., c/o Pecos, NM, St. Anthony Church. (SFE)
Roxbury, CT, Litchfield Co., St. Patrick's, c/o Washington Depot, CT, Our Lady of Perpetual Help Church. (HRT)
Roxbury, NY, Our Lady of Good Counsel, c/o Margaretville, NY, Sacred Heart Church. (ALB)
Roxbury Pond, ME, St. Mary's Chapel, c/o Rumford, ME, St. Athanasius-St. John Church. (PRT)
Rubidoux, CA, Riverside Co., Our Lady of Guadalupe, c/o [8] Riverside, CA, St. John the Evangelist Church. (SB)
Rudyard, MT, Holy Family Center, c/o Chester, MT, St. Mary's Church. (GF)
Rush Springs, OK, Grady Co., St. Francis of Assisi, c/o Duncan, OK, Assumption Church. (OKL)
Rushville, NE, Sheridan Co., Immaculate Conception, c/o Gordon, NE, St. Leo's Church. (GI)
Rushville, NY, Ontario Co., St. Mary, c/o Stanley, NY, St. Theresa Church. (ROC)
Rusk, TX, Cherokee Co., Sacred Heart, c/o Jacksonville, TX, Our Lady of Sorrows Church. (TYL)
Russell, NY, St. Lawrence Co., St. Rene Goupil, c/o De Kalb Junction, NY, St. Henry Church. (OG)
Russian Mission, AK, Wade Hampton Co., Our Lady of Guadalupe Russian Mission, c/o Marshall, AK, Immaculate Heart of Mary Church. (FBK)
Rutherford, CA, Holy Family, c/o Yountville, CA, St. Joan of Arc Church. (SR)
Rutten, ND, Ramsey Co., St. Benedict, c/o Devils Lake, ND, St. Joseph's Church. (FAR)
Ryan, OK, Jefferson Co., San Jose, c/o Duncan, OK, Assumption Church. (OKL)
Rye, CO, Pueblo Co., St. Aloysius, c/o [3] Pueblo, CO, Holy Family Church. (PBL)
Ryegate, MT, St Mathias, c/o Roundup, MT, St. Benedict's Church. (GF)

S

Sa'ilele, AS, c/o [8] Pago Pago, AS, Church of St. Peter and Paul. (SPP)
Sabana, PR, San Jose, c/o Aguada, PR, St. Francis of Assisi Church. (MGZ)
Sabana Eneas, PR, San Judas Tadeo, c/o San German, PR, San German de Auxerre Church. (MGZ)
Sabana Llana, PR, Perpetuo Socorro, c/o Salinas, PR, Our Lady of Monserrat Church. (PCE)
Sabin, MN, Clay Co., St. Cecilia, c/o Barnesville, MN, Assumption Church. (CR)
Sabinal, NM, Socorro Co., San Antonio, c/o La Joya, NM, Our Lady of Sorrows Church. (SFE)
Sabinoso, NM, San Miguel Co., c/o Roy, NM, Holy Family-St. Joseph Church. (SFE)
Sacaton, AZ, St. Anthony, c/o Bapchule, AZ, St. Peter's Church. (PHX)
Sacaton Flats, AZ, Our Lady of Victory, c/o Bapchule, AZ, St. Peter's Church. (PHX)
Saco, MT, St. Francis of Assisi, c/o Malta, MT, St. Mary's Church. (GF)
Saegertown, PA, Crawford Co., St. Bernadette, c/o Meadville, PA, St. Agatha Church. (E)
Sagamore, MA, Barnstable Co., St. Theresa, c/o Sandwich, MA, Corpus Christi Church. (FR)
Saginaw, MN, St. Philip Neri, c/o Proctor, MN, St. Rose Catholic Church. (DUL)
Saguache, CO, Saguache Co., St. Agnes, c/o Center, CO, St. Francis Jerome Church. (PBL)
Sahuarita, AZ, Pima Co., St. Martin de Porres, c/o Green Valley, AZ, Our Lady of the Valley Church. (TUC)
St. Anne, IN, Jennings Co., St. Anne, c/o St. Joseph, IN, St. Joseph Church. (IND)
St. Anthony, ND, Rolette Co., St. Anthony, c/o Turtle Mountain Reservation, ND, (Chippewa Indians) Church. (FAR)
St. Anthony, ND, Morton Co., St. Anthony, c/o Mandan, ND, Christ the King Church. (BIS)
St. Augustine, FL, St. Johns Co., Prince of Peace, c/o [1] St. Augustine, FL, Cathedral of St. Augustine. (STA)
St. Augustine, FL, St. Johns Co., St. Benedict the Moor, c/o [1] St. Augustine, FL, Cathedral of St. Augustine . (STA)
St. Augustine, TX, San Augustine Co., San Augustine, c/o Hemphill, TX, St. Pius I Church. (TYL)
St. Boniface, PA, Cambria Co., St. Boniface Chapel, c/o Hastings, PA, St. Bernard Church. (ALT)
St. David, IL, Fulton Co., St. Michael, c/o Lewistown, IL, St. Mary's Church. (PEO)
St. Denis, IN, Jennings Co., St. Denis, c/o Millhousen, IN, Immaculate Conception Church. (IND)
St. Elmo, IL, Fayette Co., St. Mary, c/o Altamont, IL, St. Clare Church. (SFD)
St. Francis, SD, c/o St. Francis, SD, St. Charles Church. (RC)
St. Francis, SD, Todd Co., St. Charles, c/o St. Francis, SD, Rosebud Reservation Church. (RC)
Saint Helena Island, SC, Beaufort Co., Holy Cross, c/o Beaufort, SC, St. Peter's Church. (CHR)
St. James, MO, c/o St. James, MO, Immaculate Conception Church. (JC)
St. Landry, LA, St. Theresa, c/o Pine Prairie, LA, St. Peter Church. (LAF)
St. Mary, NE, Johnson Co., St. Mary's, c/o Tecumseh, NE, St. Andrew's Church. (LIN)
St. Michaels, AZ, St. Michael's Mission for Navajo Indians, c/o St. Michaels, AZ, St. Michael Church. (GLP)
St. Michaels, MD, Talbot Co., St. Michael, c/o Easton, MD, SS. Peter and Paul Church. (WIL)
St. Paul, MN, Mission of the Mother-Coredemptrix, c/o [28] Minneapolis, MN, St. Joseph Hien Church. (STP)
St. Paul, TX, San Patricio Co., St. Paul, c/o Sinton, TX, Sacred Heart Church. (CC)
St. Petersburg, FL, The Mercy of God Polish Mission, c/o [7] St. Petersburg, FL, St. Paul Church. (SP)
St. Petersburg, FL, Pinellas Co., Vietnamese Martyrs Mission, c/o [5] St. Petersburg, FL, St. Joseph Church. (SP)
St. Pius, IN, Ripley Co., St. Pius, c/o Milan, IN, St. Charles Borromeo Church. (IND)
St. Thomas, ND, Pembina Co., St. Thomas, c/o Drayton, ND, St. Edward's Church. (FAR)
St. Vincent de Paul, IN, c/o St. Vincent de Paul, IN, St. Vincent de Paul Church. (IND)
St. Xavier, MT, St. Francis Xavier, c/o Crow Agency, MT, St. Dennis Church. (GF)
Saipan, MP, Korean Catholic Community, c/o Chalan Kanoa Village, MP, Cathedral of Our Lady of Mt. Carmel. (CHK)
Saipan, MP, Santa Soledad Mission, c/o San Vicente Village, District 10, MP, San Vicente Parish Church. (CHK)
Salem, IN, Washington Co., St. Patrick, c/o Scottsburg, IN, American Martyrs Church. (IND)
Salem, OR, Marion Co., San Jose, c/o Salem, OR, St. Joseph Church. (P)
Salem Township, OH, Wyandot Co., St. Joseph, c/o Carey, OH, Our Lady of Consolation, Basilica-National Shrine. (TOL)
Saliente, PR, Jayuya Co., San Francisco, c/o Jayuya, PR, Our Lady of Monserrate Church. (PCE)
Salinas-Providencia, PR, Divina Providencia, c/o Ensenada, PR, Sacred Heart Church. (PCE)
Salineno, TX, St. Joseph, c/o Roma, TX, Our Lady of Refuge Church. (BWN)
Salon Usos Multiples-Urb. April Gardens, PR, Las Piedras, c/o Las Piedras, PR, Inmaculada Concepcion Church. (CGS)
Salt River Indian, AZ, St. Francis, c/o [4] Tempe, AZ, St. Margaret Church. (PHX)
Saltillo, MS, St. Thomas Aquinas, c/o Tupelo, MS, St. James Church. (JKS)
Salto, PR, Jayuya Co., Santos Reyes, c/o Jayuya, PR, Our Lady of Monserrate Church. (PCE)
Salton City, CA, Imperial Co., c/o Borrego Springs, CA, St. Richard Church. (SD)
San Acacio, CO, Costilla Co., San Acacio, c/o San Luis, CO, Sangre de Cristo Church. (PBL)
San Antonio, CO, San Antonio de Padua, c/o Conejos, CO, Our Lady of Guadalupe Church. (PBL)
San Antonio, NM, P.Sandia Park Co., c/o Moriarty, NM, Estancia Valley Catholic Parish Church. (SFE)
San Antonio, NM, Socorro Co., c/o Socorro, NM, San Miguel Church. (SFE)
San Antonio, NM, Bernalillo Co., c/o Tijeras, NM, Holy Child Church. (SFE)
San Antonio, NM, San Miguel Co., Los Vigiles (Our Lady of Refuge), c/o Las Vegas, NM, Immaculate Conception Church. (SFE)
San Antonio, TX, Bexar Co., Byzantine Catholic Mission, c/o Houston, TX, St. John Chrysostom Church. (PBR)
San Antonio, TX, Bexar Co., Purisima Concepcion, c/o [32] San Antonio, TX, St. Cecilia Church. (SAT)
San Antonio, TX, Bexar Co., San Francesco di Paola (Italian), c/o [1] San Antonio, TX, Cathedral of San Fernando. (SAT)
San Antonio, TX, Santa Maria Goretti, c/o [47] San Antonio, TX, St. Jude Church. (SAT)
San Antonio, TX, Bexar Co., St. Catherine, c/o [52] San Antonio, TX, St. Margaret Mary Church. (SAT)
San Antonio, TX, Bexar Co., St. Frances Cabrini, c/o [69] San Antonio, TX, San Francisco de la Espada Church. (SAT)
San Ardo, CA, Monterey Co., Our Lady of Ransom, c/o San Miguel, CA, San Miguel Church. (MRY)
San Benito, TX, St. Joseph, c/o San Benito, TX, Our Lady, Queen of the Universe Church. (BWN)
San Cristobal, NM, Taos Co., San Cristobal, c/o Arroyo Seco, NM, La Santisima Trinidad Church. (SFE)
San Diego, CA, San Diego Co., SDSU Newman Center, c/o [3] San Diego, CA, Blessed Sacrament Church. (SD)
San Diego, PR, Coamo Co., San Diego, c/o Coamo, PR, St. Blase Church. (PCE)
San Felipe, NM, Sandoval Co., Indian Pueblo, c/o Pena Blanca, NM, Nuestra Senora De Guadalupe Church. (SFE)
San Felipe, PR, St. Martin de Porres, c/o Aguirre, PR, Sacred Heart Church. (PCE)
San Felipe, TX, Austin Co., c/o [1] Harlingen, TX, Our Lady of the Assumption Church. (BWN)
San Francisco, CA, San Francisco Co., All Hallows Chapel, c/o [41] San Francisco, CA, Our Lady of Lourdes Church. (SFR)
San Francisco, CO, Costilla Co., St. Francis of Assisi, c/o San Luis, CO, Sangre de Cristo Church. (PBL)
San Ignacio, NM, Guadalupe Co., c/o Santa Rosa, NM, St. Rose of Lima Church. (SFE)
San Ignacio, TX, St. Ignatius, c/o Zapata, TX, Our Lady of Lourdes Church. (LAR)
San Ildefonso, NM, Sante Fe Co., Indian Pueblo, c/o [1] Santa Fe, NM, The Cathedral of San Francisco de Asis. (SFE)

San Isidro, CO, Costilla Co., St. Isidro, c/o San Luis, CO, Sangre de Cristo Church. (PBL)
San Isidro, NM, Dona Ana Co., San Isidro, c/o Dona Ana, NM, Our Lady of the Purification Church. (LSC)
San Isidro Norte, NM, San Miguel Co., c/o Ribera, NM, San Miguel Del Vado Church. (SFE)
San Isidro Sur, NM, San Miguel Co., c/o Ribera, NM, San Miguel Del Vado Church. (SFE)
San Joaquin, CA, Fresno Co., St. Vincent de Paul, c/o Tranquillity, CA, St. Paul Church. (FRS)
San Jon, NM, Quay Co., Our Lady of Guadalupe, c/o Tucumcari, NM, St. Anne Church. (SFE)
San Jose, AZ, Graham Co., San Jose, c/o Solomon, AZ, Our Lady of Guadalupe Church. (TUC)
San Jose, NM, San Miguel Co., c/o Ribera, NM, San Miguel Del Vado Church. (SFE)
San Jose, NM, Sierra Co., Arrey, c/o Garfield, NM, San Isidro Church. (LSC)
San Jose Ranch, TX, Duval Co., St. Joseph, c/o Benavides, TX, St. Rose of Lima Church. (CC)
San Juan, NM, San Miguel Co., c/o Ribera, NM, San Miguel Del Vado Church. (SFE)
San Juan, NM, Grant Co., San Juan, c/o Hurley, NM, Infant Jesus Church. (LSC)
San Juan, PR, Capilla San Conrado, c/o [18] San Juan, PR, San Francisco de Asis Church. (SJN)
San Juan, PR, Egida del Maestro, c/o [16] San Juan, PR, Ntra. Sra. de Fatima Church. (SJN)
San Juan, PR, Ermita N. Sra. Providencia, c/o [58] San Juan, PR, Santa Teresa Jornet Church. (SJN)
San Juan, PR, Jesus Nazareno, c/o [24] San Juan, PR, Jesus Maestro Church. (SJN)
San Juan, PR, Medalla Milagrosa, c/o [9] San Juan, PR, Santa Catalina Laboure Church. (SJN)
San Juan, PR, Sector Buenavista, Nra. Sra. del Altagracia, c/o [37] San Juan, PR, Maria Auxiliadora Church. (SJN)
San Juan, PR, Ntra. Senora de la Caridad del Cobre, c/o [38] San Juan, PR, Santa Maria de Los Angeles Church. (SJN)
San Juan, PR, Sector Ultimo Chance-Cerro, Ntra. Sra. de Fatima, c/o [37] San Juan, PR, Maria Auxiliadora Church. (SJN)
San Juan, PR, Ntra. Sra. de la Providencia, c/o [14] San Juan, PR, Nuestra Senora de la Esperanza Church. (SJN)
San Juan, PR, Ntra. Sra. del Rosario, c/o [28] San Juan, PR, San Juan Bosco Church. (SJN)
San Juan, PR, Nuestra Senora del Buen Consejo, c/o [4] San Juan, PR, San Antonio Church. (SJN)
San Juan, PR, Sagrada Familia, c/o [59] San Juan, PR, Santa Teresita Del Nino Jesus Church. (SJN)
San Juan, PR, Sector Buenavista, Sagrado Corazon, c/o [37] San Juan, PR, Maria Auxiliadora Church. (SJN)
San Juan, PR, Embalse Sector, San Antonio Ma. Claret, c/o [27] San Juan, PR, San Jose Obrero Church. (SJN)
San Juan, PR, San Francisco de Asis, c/o [30] San Juan, PR, San Juan Evangelista Church. (SJN)
San Juan, PR, San Martin de Porres, c/o [8] San Juan, PR, Nuestra Senora del Carmen Church. (SJN)
San Juan, PR, San Martin de Porres, c/o [28] San Juan, PR, San Juan Bosco Church. (SJN)
San Juan, PR, San Martin de Porres, Bitumul, c/o [27] San Juan, PR, San Jose Obrero Church. (SJN)
San Juan, PR, San Pablo, c/o [9] San Juan, PR, Santa Catalina Laboure Church. (SJN)
San Juan, PR, Santa Ana, c/o [42] San Juan, PR, Ntra. Sra. de la Monserrate Church. (SJN)
San Juan, PR, Santisima Trinidad, c/o [37] San Juan, PR, Maria Auxiliadora Church. (SJN)
San Juan, PR, Sector Santo Domingo, Santo Domingo, c/o [11] San Juan, PR, Corpus Christi Church. (SJN)
San Judas Tadeo, PR, Playuelas, c/o Aguadilla, PR, La Milagrosa Church. (MGZ)
San Lorenzo, NM, Grant Co., San Lorenzo, c/o Bayard, NM, Our Lady of Fatima Church. (LSC)
San Lucas, CA, Monterey Co., St. Luke, c/o King City, CA, St. John the Baptist Church. (MRY)
San Luis, NM, Sandoval Co., Saint Aloysius Gonzaga, c/o Cuba, NM, Immaculate Conception Church. (GLP)
San Luis Rey, CA, San Diego Co., San Luis Rey de Francia, c/o [1] Oceanside, CA, Mission San Luis Rey Church. (SD)
San Manuel, TX, St. Anne, c/o San Carlos, TX, St. Joseph the Worker Church. (BWN)
San Marcos, TX, Hays Co., Guadalupe Chapel, c/o San Marcos, TX, St. John the Evangelist Church. (AUS)
San Miguel, CO, San Miguel, c/o Conejos, CO, Our Lady of Guadalupe Church. (PBL)
San Patricio, NM, St. Jude Thaddeus, c/o Ruidoso, NM, St. Eleanor Church. (LSC)
San Patricio, TX, San Patricio Co., St. Patrick, c/o Mathis, TX, Sacred Heart Church. (CC)
San Pedro, CO, Costilla Co., SS. Peter and Paul, c/o San Luis, CO, Sangre de Cristo Church. (PBL)
San Pedro, TX, San Pedro, c/o [5] Brownsville, TX, Our Lady of Good Counsel Church. (BWN)
San Perlita, TX, St. Anne, Mother of Mary, c/o Raymondville, TX, St. Anthony Church. (BWN)
San Rafael, CA, Marin Co., St. Sylvester, c/o [3] San Rafael, CA, St. Raphael Church. (SFR)
San Rafael, CO, San Pedro y San Rafael, c/o Conejos, CO, Our Lady of Guadalupe Church. (PBL)
San Simon, AZ, Cochise Co., Our Lady of Perpetual Help, c/o Willcox, AZ, Sacred Heart Church. (TUC)
San Vicente Village, District 10, MP, Dominican Sisters of the Most Holy Rosary Convent, c/o San Vicente Village, District 10, MP, San Vicente Parish Church. (CHK)
San Ysidro, NM, Sandoval Co., c/o Jemez Pueblo, NM, San Diego Indian Missions Church. (SFE)
Sand Springs, IA, Immaculate Conception, c/o Hopkinton, IA, St. Luke's Church. (DUB)
Sandersville, GA, Washington Co., St. William, c/o Dublin, GA, Immaculate Conception Church. (SAV)
Sandia Indian Pueblo, NM, Sandoval Co., c/o Bernalillo, NM, Our Lady of Sorrows Church. (SFE)
Sandy Valley, NV, Clark Co., St. Catherine of Siena, c/o [2] Las Vegas, NV, Christ the King Church. (LAV)
Sangerville, ME, Holy Family, c/o Dover-Foxcroft, ME, St. Thomas Church. (PRT)
Santa Ana, NM, Sandoval Co., c/o Jemez Pueblo, NM, San Diego Indian Missions Church. (SFE)
Santa Ana, PR, Coamo Co., Santa Ana, c/o Coamo, PR, St. Blase Church. (PCE)
Santa Catalina, PR, Coamo Co., Miraculous Virgin, c/o Coamo, PR, St. Blase Church. (PCE)
Santa Catalina, PR, Coama Co., Sacred Heart, c/o Coamo, PR, St. Blase Church. (PCE)
Santa Clara, NM, Rio Arriba Co., Indian Pueblo, c/o [1] Santa Fe, NM, The Cathedral of San Francisco de Asis. (SFE)
Santa Clara, NY, St. Peter, c/o Saint Regis Falls, NY, St. Ann Church. (OG)
Santa Cruz, AZ, St. Catherine, c/o Laveen, AZ, St. John The Baptist Church. (PHX)
Santa Fe, NM, Santa Fe Co., Old Guadalupe, c/o [3] Santa Fe, NM, Cristo Rey Church. (SFE)
Santa Maria, AZ, Our Lady of Guadalupe, c/o Cashion, AZ, St. William Church. (PHX)
Santa Maria, TX, St. Margaret Ann, c/o Progreso, TX, Holy Spirit Church. (BWN)
Santa Monica, TX, Santa Monica, c/o Lyford, TX, Prince of Peace Church. (BWN)
Santa Rita, NM, San Miguel Co., c/o Ribera, NM, San Miguel Del Vado Church. (SFE)
Santan, AZ, St. Anne, c/o Bapchule, AZ, St. Peter's Church. (PHX)
Santiago-Talco, NM, Mora Co., c/o Mora, NM, St. Gertrude Church. (SFE)
Santo Domingo, NM, Sandoval Co., Indian Pueblo, c/o Pena Blanca, NM, Nuestra Senora De Guadalupe Church. (SFE)
Santurce, PR, La Milagrosa, c/o [28] San Juan, PR, San Juan Bosco Church. (SJN)
Sapello, NM, San Miguel Co., Our Lady of Guadalupe, c/o Las Vegas, NM, Our Lady of Sorrows Church. (SFE)
Sapphire Valley, NC, Transylvania Co., St. Jude, c/o Brevard, NC, Sacred Heart Church. (CHL)
Saragosa, TX, Our Lady of Guadalupe, c/o Balmorhea, TX, Christ the King Church. (ELP)
Saratoga Lake, NY, Saratoga Co., St. Isaac Jogues, c/o Stillwater, NY, St. Peter the Apostle Church. (ALB)
Sardis, MS, St. John the Baptist, c/o Batesville, MS, St. Mary Church. (JKS)
Sargent, NE, Custer Co., Assumption of the Blessed Virgin Mary, c/o Burwell, NE, Sacred Heart Church. (GI)
Sartwell, PA, McKean Co., St. Mary, c/o Eldred, PA, St. Raphael Church. (E)
Saspamco, TX, Bexar Co., Our Lady of Perpetual Help, c/o Elmendorf, TX, St. Anthony Church. (SAT)
Satin, TX, Satin Falls Co., Santa Rita, c/o [2] Waco, TX, St. Francis on the Brazos Church. (AUS)
Satowan, FM, c/o Lukunor, FM, Sacred Heart Church. (CI)
Savage, MT, Richland Co., St. Michael, c/o Sidney, MT, St. Matthew Church. (GF)
Savannah, NY, Wayne Co., St. Patrick, c/o Clyde, NY, St. John the Evangelist Church. (ROC)
Savoy, LA, St. Landry Parish, St. Thomas, c/o Richard, LA, St. Edward Church. (LAF)
Sawmill, AZ, Apache Co., St. Francis Mission, c/o Navajo, NM, St. Berard Church. (GLP)
Sawyer, MI, Berrien Co., St. Agnes, c/o Three Oaks, MI, St. Mary of the Assumption Church. (KAL)
Sawyer, MN, Carlton Co., SS. Mary & Joseph, c/o Cloquet, MN, Holy Family Church. (DUL)
Sawyer, MN, Carlton Co., SS. Mary and Joseph, c/o Duluth, MN, Indian Missions Church. (DUL)
Sawyer's Bar, CA, Siskiyou Co., St. Joseph, c/o Fort Jones, CA, Sacred Heart Church. (SAC)
Saxtons River, VT, Windham Co., St. Edmund of Canterbury, c/o Putney, VT, Our Lady of Mercy Church. (BUR)
Sayre, OK, Beckham Co., Queen of All Saints, c/o Elk City, OK, St. Matthew's Church. (OKL)
Schenectady, NY, Schenectady Co., St. Teresa Carmelite Monastery, c/o [11] Schenectady, NY, St. Luke Church. (ALB)
Schenevus, NY, Otsego Co., St. Mary, c/o Worcester, NY, St. Joseph Church. (ALB)
Schley, IA, Holy Cross, c/o Protivin, IA, Holy Trinity Church. (DUB)
Schodack Landing, NY, Assumption of B.V.M., c/o Castleton-on-Hudson, NY, Sacred Heart Church. (ALB)
Schodack Landing, NY, Shrine of St. Jude, c/o Castleton-on-Hudson, NY, Sacred Heart Church. (ALB)
Schoolcraft, NE, Madison Co., St. Francis de Sales, c/o Battle Creek, NE, St. Patrick's Church. (OM)
Scio, NY, Allegany Co., St. Joseph, c/o Belmont, NY, St. Mary Church. (BUF)
Scotia, NE, Greeley Co., St. Patrick, c/o Greeley, NE, Sacred Heart Church. (GI)
Scotland, CT, Windham Co., St. Margaret, c/o Willimantic, CT, St. Joseph Church. (NOR)
Scotland Neck, NC, Halifax Co., St. Anne, c/o Ahoskie, NC, St. Charles Borromeo Church. (R)
Scotts Mills, OR, Marion Co., Holy Rosary, c/o Mt. Angel, OR, St. Mary Church. (P)
Scranton, ND, Bowman Co., Sacred Heart, c/o Hettinger, ND, Holy Trinity Church. (BIS)
Scriba, NY, Sacred Heart, c/o [6] Oswego, NY, St. Peter Church. (SY)
Scribner, NE, Dodge Co., St. Lawrence, c/o Hooper, NE, St. Rose of Lima Church. (OM)
Seabrook Beach, NH, Rockingham Co., St. Elizabeth's, c/o Hampton, NH, Our Lady of the Miraculous Medal Church. (MAN)
Seadrift, TX, St. Patrick, c/o Port Lavaca, TX, Our Lady of the Gulf Church. (VIC)
Seagraves, TX, Gaines Co., St. Paul's, c/o Seminole, TX, St. James Church. (LUB)
Seama, NM, St. Anne, c/o Laguna, NM, St. Joseph Church. (GLP)
Seaside, OR, Clatsop Co., St. Peter the Fisherman, c/o Seaside, OR, Our Lady of Victory Church. (P)
Seat Pleasant, MD, St. Matthias, c/o Seat Pleasant, MD, St. Margaret Church. (WDC)
Seatonville, IL, Bureau Co., St. Gertrude, c/o Ladd, IL, St. Benedict's Church. (PEO)
Seattle, WA, Maronite Catholic Community, c/o Portland, OR, Saint Sharbel Church. (OLL)
Sebastian, TX, Willacy Co., St. Martin, c/o Lyford, TX, Prince of Peace Church. (BWN)
Seco Mines, TX, Our Lady of Lourdes, c/o Eagle Pass, TX, Our Lady of Refuge Church. (LAR)
Sedillo, NM, Bernalillo Co., San Isidro, c/o Tijeras, NM, Holy Child Church. (SFE)
Seeley, CA, Imperial Co., Holy Spirit, c/o Imperial, CA, St. Anthony of Padua Church. (SD)
Seeley Lake, MT, Missoula Co., Living Water Mission, c/o Bonner, MT, St. Ann Church. (HEL)
Segundo, CO, Las Animas Co., St. Ignatius, c/o Trinidad, CO, Most Holy Trinity, Trinidad Area Catholic Community (Trinidad Cluster) Church. (PBL)
Seiling, OK, Dewey Co., St. Thomas, c/o Okeene, OK, St. Anthony's Church. (OKL)
Seldovia, AK, St. James the Apostle, c/o Homer, AK, St. John the Baptist Church. (ANC)
Selinsgrove, PA, Snyder Co., Selinsgrove Center, c/o Selinsgrove, PA, St. Pius X Church. (HBG)
Selinsgrove, PA, Snyder Co., Snyder County Prison, c/o Selinsgrove, PA, St. Pius X Church. (HBG)
Selinsgrove, PA, Snyder Co., Susquehanna University, c/o Selinsgrove, PA, St. Pius X Church. (HBG)
Selz, ND, Pierce Co., c/o Harvey, ND, St. Cecilia's Church. (FAR)
Sena, NM, San Miguel Co., c/o Villanueva, NM, Our Lady of Guadalupe Church. (SFE)
Seneca, OR, St. Charles, c/o John Day, OR, St. Elizabeth's Church. (BAK)
Seneca, SC, Oconee Co., St. Paul the Apostle, c/o Clemson, SC, St. Andrew Church. (CHR)
Servilleta, NM, Taos Co., c/o El Rito, NM, San Juan Nepomuceno Church. (SFE)
Seville-Creston, OH, Medina Co., Jesus Emmanuel, c/o Litchfield, OH, Our Lady Help of Christians Parish Church. (CLV)
Shafter, TX, Sgdo. Corazon de Jesus, c/o Presidio, TX, Santa Teresa de Jesus Church. (ELP)
Shamrock, TX, St. Patrick, c/o Wellington, TX, Our Mother of Mercy Church. (AMA)
Sharon, GA, Talifero Co., Purification, c/o Washington, GA, St. Joseph's Church. (ATL)
Sharon Springs, NY, St. Mary, c/o Cobleskill, NY, St. Vincent de Paul Church. (ALB)
Sharpsburg, GA, Coweta Co., c/o Peachtree City, GA, Holy Trinity Catholic Church. (ATL)
Shasta Lake City, CA, Shasta Co., St. Michael, c/o Redding, CA, St. Joseph Church. (SAC)

Shattuck, OK, Ellis Co., Holy Name, c/o Woodward, OK, St. Peter's Church. (OKL)
Shawmut, MT, Wheatland Co., Blessed Sacrament, c/o Harlowton, MT, St. Joseph Church. (HEL)
Sheffield, TX, Pecos Co., Good Shepherd, c/o Ozona, TX, Our Lady of Perpetual Help Church. (SAN)
Shelby, IN, Lake Co., St. Theresa, c/o Lowell, IN, St. Edward Church. (GRY)
Sheldon, ND, Ransom, St. Mary, Our Lady of the Scapular, c/o Enderlin, ND, St. Patrick's Church. (FAR)
Sheldon Point, AK, St. Peter's, c/o Alakanuk, AK, St. Ignatius Church. (FBK)
Shelton, NE, Buffalo Co., Sacred Heart, c/o Wood River, NE, St. Mary's Church. (GI)
Sheridan, AR, Grout Co., Holy Cross, c/o Camden, AR, St. Louis Church. (LR)
Sherman Station, ME, Penobscot Co., St. Joseph's Church, c/o Benedicta, ME, St. Benedict's Church. (PRT)
Sherwood, ND, Renville Co., St. James, c/o Mohall, ND, St. Jerome Church. (BIS)
Shickley, NE, Fillmore Co., St. Mary, c/o Geneva, NE, St. Joseph's Church. (LIN)
Shidler, OK, Osage Co., St. Ann, c/o Pawhuska, OK, Immaculate Conception Church. (TLS)
Shingletown, CA, Shasta Co., Mary Queen of Peace, c/o Anderson, CA, Sacred Heart Church. (SAC)
Shoreham, VT, Addison Co., St. Genevieve, c/o Orwell, VT, St. Paul Church. (BUR)
Shoshone-Tecopa, CA, Inyo Co., St. John the Baptist, c/o Lone Pine, CA, Santa Rosa Church. (FRS)
Shoshoni, WY, Fremont Co., St. Joseph, c/o Riverton, WY, St. Margaret's Church. (CHY)
Shubert, NE, Richardson Co., St. Anne's, c/o Dawson, NE, St. Mary's Church. (LIN)
Sidnaw, MI, Houghton Co., St. Francis Xavier, c/o Ewen, MI, Sacred Heart Church. (MAR)
Sieper, LA, St. Jude, c/o Glenmora, LA, St. Louis Church. (ALX)
Sierra Alta, PR, St. Lucy, c/o Yauco, PR, Holy Rossary Church. (PCE)
Sierra Blanca, TX, Our Lady of Miracles, c/o Van Horn, TX, Our Lady of Fatima Church. (ELP)
Sierra City, CA, Sierra Co., St. Thomas, c/o Downieville, CA, Immaculate Conception Church. (SAC)
Sigel, PA, Jefferson Co., St. Dominic, c/o Brookville, PA, Immaculate Conception Church. (E)
Sile, NM, Sandoval Co., c/o Pena Blanca, NM, Nuestra Senora De Guadalupe Church. (SFE)
Siletz, OR, Lincoln Co., St. Mary, c/o Newport, OR, Sacred Heart Parish Church. (P)
Silt, CO, Garfield Co., Sacred Heart, c/o Rifle, CO, St. Mary's Church. (DEN)
Silver Lake, PA, Susquehanna Co., St. Augustine, c/o Friendsville, PA, St. Joseph's Church. (SCR)
Silverton, CO, San Juan Co., St. Patrick, c/o Ouray, CO, St. Daniel the Prophet Church. (PBL)
Silverton, TX, Briscoe Co., Our Lady of Loreto, c/o Tulia, TX, Church of the Holy Spirit. (AMA)
Sioux Center, IA, Sioux Co., Christ the King, c/o Rock Valley, IA, St. Mary's Church. (SC)
Slim Butte, SD, Shannon Co., Our Lady of Lourdes, c/o Pine Ridge, SD, Holy Rosary Church. (RC)
Smith Valley, NV, Lyon Co., St. John the Baptist, c/o Yerington, NV, Holy Family Church. (RNO)
Smithfield, NE, Gosper Co., St. John's, c/o Holdrege, NE, All Saints Church. (LIN)
Smiths Corners, MI, Huron Co., Holy Trinity, c/o Rapson, MI, St. Joseph Church. (SAG)
Smiths Creek, MI, St. Clair Co., Holy Rosary, c/o Columbus, MI, St. Philip Neri Church. (DET)
Smithville, TX, St. Paul the Apostle, c/o Kovar, TX, Sts. Peter and Paul Church. (AUS)
Sodus Point, NY, Wayne Co., St. Rose, c/o Sodus, NY, Epiphany Church. (ROC)
Soileau, LA, Allen Parish, St. Joseph, c/o Oberlin, LA, St. Joan of Arc Church. (LKC)
Solana Beach, CA, San Diego Co., St. Leo, c/o Solana Beach, CA, St. James Church. (SD)
Soldier Creek, SD, St. Rose, c/o Rosebud, SD, St. Bridget Church. (RC)
Soldier Creek, SD, Todd Co., St. Rose, c/o St. Francis, SD, St. Charles Church. (RC)
Soldier Creek, SD, Todd Co., St. Rose, c/o St. Francis, SD, Rosebud Reservation Church. (RC)
Soledad, CA, Monterey Co., Nuestra Senora de la Soledad, c/o Soledad, CA, Our Lady of Solitude Church. (MRY)
Somers, MT, St. Ann, c/o Bigfork, MT, St. Catherine Church. (HEL)
Sonoita, AZ, Santa Cruz Co., Our Lady of Angels, c/o Patagonia, AZ, St. Theresa Church. (TUC)
Sonsorol, FM, c/o Koror, FM, Sacred Heart Church. (CI)
South Byron, NY, Genesee Co., St. Michael, c/o Bergen, NY, St. Brigid Church. (BUF)
South Chatham, MA, Barnstable Co., Our Lady of Grace, c/o Chatham, MA, Holy Redeemer Church. (FR)
South Colton, NY, St. Lawrence Co., St. Paul, c/o Colton, NY, St. Patrick Church. (OG)
South Fork, CO, Rio Grande Co., Holy Family, c/o Del Norte, CO, Holy Name of Mary Church. (PBL)
South Hampton Twp., NJ, Vincentown Co., St. Jude, c/o Roebling, NJ, St. Nicholas Church. (PSC)
South Hartford, NY, St. Philip, c/o Fort Ann, NY, St. Ann Church. (ALB)
South Lee, MA, Berkshire Co., St. Francis of Assisi, c/o Lee, MA, St. Mary's Church. (SPR)
South Royalston, MA, Worcester Co., Our Lady Queen of Heaven, c/o Athol, MA, Our Lady Immaculate Church. (WOR)
South Royalton, VT, Windsor Co., St. Matthew, c/o Bethel, VT, St. Anthony Church. (BUR)
South Salem, NY, Westchester Co., South Salem Presbyterian Church, c/o Katonah, NY, St. Mary of the Assumption Church. (NY)
South Sterling, PA, Wayne Co., St. Mary Magdalene, c/o Gouldsboro, PA, St. Rita Church. (SCR)
South Strafford, VT, Orange Co., Our Lady of Light, c/o Bradford, VT, Our Lady of Perpetual Help Church. (BUR)
South Tucson, AZ, Pima Co., St. Nicholas Indian Center, c/o [2] Tucson, AZ, Blessed Kateri Tekakwitha Church. (TUC)
South Vallejo, CA, Solano Co., St. Louis Bertrand, c/o Vallejo, CA, St. Vincent Ferrer Church. (SAC)
Southton, TX, Bexar Co., St. Ann, c/o [71] San Antonio, TX, San Juan Capistrano Church. (SAT)
Southwest Oswego, NY, St. Joseph, c/o Hannibal, NY, Our Lady of the Rosary Church. (SY)
Spanish Lake, LA, St. Anne, c/o Powhatan, LA, St. Francis of Assisi Church. (ALX)
Sparta, NC, Alleghany Co., St. Frances of Rome, c/o Jefferson, NC, St. Francis of Assisi Church. (CHL)
Spartansburg, PA, Crawford Co., Our Lady of Victory, c/o Corry, PA, St. Elizabeth Church. (E)
Spelter, WV, Harrison Co., Holy Family, c/o Shinnston, WV, St. Ann's Church. (WH)
Spencer, OH, Medina Co., Jesus Our Savior, c/o Litchfield, OH, Our Lady Help of Christians Parish Church. (CLV)
Spencer Mountain, NC, Gaston Co., St. Helen, c/o [3] Charlotte, NC, Our Lady of Consolation Church. (CHL)
Spencerville, OH, Allen Co., St. Patrick, c/o Landeck, OH, St. John Baptist Church. (TOL)
Spiro, OK, Leflore Co., St. Elizabeth Seton, c/o Poteau, OK, Immaculate Conception Church. (TLS)
Split Rock, NY, Onondaga Co., St. Peter, c/o Onondaga Hill, NY, St. Michael Church. (SY)
Spofford Junction, TX, Kinney Co., St. Blaise, c/o Brackettville, TX, St. Mary Magdalen Church. (SAT)
Spring Creek, SD, Todd Co., St. Patrick, c/o St. Francis, SD, St. Charles Church. (RC)
Spring Creek, SD, Todd Co., St. Patrick, c/o St. Francis, SD, Rosebud Reservation Church. (RC)
Spring Lake, NJ, Monmouth Co., St. Margaret, c/o Spring Lake, NJ, St. Catharine Church. (TR)
Spring Lake Twp., MN, Scott Co., St. Catherine, c/o Cedar Lake, MN, St. Patrick Church. (STP)
Springfield, GA, St. Boniface, c/o Port Wentworth, GA, Our Lady of Lourdes Church. (SAV)
Springfield, SC, Orangeburg Co., St. Theresa, c/o Orangeburg, SC, Holy Trinity Church. (CHR)
Springfield Center, NY, Blessed Sacrament, c/o Cherry Valley, NY, St. Thomas the Apostle Church. (ALB)
Springhill, LA, Webster Parish, Sacred Heart, c/o Minden, LA, St. Paul Church. (SHP)
Spurlington, KY, Taylor Co., St. Frances de Sales, c/o Calvary, KY, Holy Name of Mary Church. (L)
Squaw Valley, CA, Fresno Co., St. Rita, c/o Orange Cove, CA, St. Isidore the Farmer Church. (FRS)
Staatsburg, NY, Dutchess Co., St. Paul, c/o Hyde Park, NY, Regina Coeli Church. (NY)
Staffordville, CT, Tolland Co., St. Joseph, c/o Stafford Springs, CT, St. Edward Church. (NOR)
Stamford, VT, Bennington Co., St. John Bosco, c/o Readsboro, VT, St. Joachim Church. (BUR)
Standish, NY, Clinton Co., St. Michael, c/o Lyon Mountain, NY, St. Bernard Church. (OG)
Stanfield, AZ, Pinal Co., St. Mary, c/o Casa Grande, AZ, St. Anthony of Padua Church. (TUC)
Stanton, KY, Powell Co., Our Lady of the Mountains, c/o Ravenna, KY, St. Elizabeth Church. (LEX)
Stapleton, NE, St. Boniface, c/o Stapleton, NE, St. John the Evangelist Church. (GI)
Starks, LA, St. Michael, c/o Vinton, LA, St. Joseph Church. (LKC)
Starkweather, ND, Ramsey Co., Assumption of the Blessed Virgin Mary, c/o Munich, ND, St. Mary's Church. (FAR)
Starr School, MT, Sacred Heart, c/o Browning, MT, Church of the Little Flower. (HEL)
Starrucca, PA, Wayne Co., St. Paul, c/o Jackson, PA, St. Martin of Tours Church. (SCR)
Staten Island, NY, Staten Island Co., St. Nicholas, c/o [230] Staten Island, NY, St. Teresa Church. (NY)
Steele, ND, Kidder Co., St. Francis de Sales, c/o Tappen, ND, St. Paul's Church. (FAR)
Steilacoom, WA, Pierce Co., Immaculate Conception, c/o Lakewood, WA, St. John Bosco Church. (SEA)
Stephentown, NY, St. Joseph's, c/o New Lebanon, NY, Immaculate Conception Church. (ALB)
Stepstone, KY, Pendleton Co., Immaculate Conception, c/o California, KY, Sts. Peter and Paul Church. (COV)
Sterling, CT, Windham Co., St. Joseph, c/o Moosup, CT, All-Hallows Church. (NOR)
Sterling, OK, Comanche Co., Our Lady of Perpetual Help, c/o Elgin, OK, St. Ann Church. (OKL)
Sterling City, TX, Sterling Co., St. Paschal Baylon, c/o Carlsbad, TX, St. Therese of the Child Jesus Church. (SAN)
Stevenson, WA, Skamania Co., Star of the Sea, c/o Camas, WA, St. Thomas Aquinas Church. (SEA)
Stevinson, CA, Merced Co., St. Mary, c/o Hilmar, CA, Holy Rosary Church. (FRS)
Stigler, OK, Haskell Co., St. Joseph, c/o Poteau, OK, Immaculate Conception Church. (TLS)
Stinnett, TX, St. Ann's, c/o Borger, TX, St. John the Evangelist Church. (AMA)
Stockton, CA, San Joaquin Co., Maronite Catholic Community of Stockton, c/o Millbrae, CA, Our Lady of Lebanon Church. (OLL)
Stockton, MO, Cedar Co., St. Peter the Apostle, c/o El Dorado Springs, MO, St. Elizabeth Church. (SPC)
Stockton, NJ, Hunterdon Co., St. Agnes, c/o Lambertville, NJ, St. John the Evangelist Church. (MET)
Stone City, IA, St. Joseph, c/o Anamosa, IA, St. Patrick's Church. (DUB)
Stoneham, CO, Morgan Co., St. John, c/o Brush, CO, St. Mary Church. (DEN)
Stonehan, TX, Grimes Co., St. Joseph, c/o Plantersville, TX, St. Mary Church. (GAL)
Stonewall, LA, DeSoto Parish, St. Ann's Chapel, c/o Mansfield, LA, St. Joseph Church. (SHP)
Stoney Point, TX, Travis Co., Blessed Juan Diego, c/o Kyle, TX, St. Anthony Marie De Claret Church. (AUS)
Stonyford, CA, Colusa Co., St. Mary of the Mountain, c/o Maxwell, CA, Sacred Heart Church. (SAC)
Story, WY, Sheridan Co., Our Lady of the Pines, c/o Sheridan, WY, Holy Name Church. (CHY)
Stowell, PA, Wyoming Co., St. Anthony, c/o Wyalusing, PA, St. Mary's Assumption Church. (SCR)
Stratford, CA, Kings Co., St. Joseph, c/o Lemoore, CA, St. Peter Church. (FRS)
Strathmore, CA, Tulare Co., St. James Catholic Church, c/o Lindsay, CA, Sacred Heart Church. (FRS)
Stratton, ME, St. John, c/o Oquossoc, ME, Our Lady of the Lakes Church. (PRT)
Stratton, NE, Hitchcock Co., St. Joseph's, c/o Benkelman, NE, St. Joseph's Church. (LIN)
Stratton Mountain, VT, Windham Co., Chapel of the Snows, c/o Putney, VT, Our Lady of Mercy Church. (BUR)
Strawn, IL, Livingston Co., St. Rose, c/o Colfax, IL, St. Joseph's Church. (PEO)
String Prairie, TX, Bastrop Co., Assumption of the Blessed Virgin Mary, c/o Rockne, TX, Sacred Heart Church. (AUS)
Stroud, OK, Lincoln Co., St. Louis, c/o Chandler, OK, Our Lady of Sorrows Church. (OKL)
Sturgeon Lake, MN, St. Isidore's, c/o Willow River, MN, St. Mary's Church. (DUL)
Sugar Island, MI, Chippewa Co., Sacred Heart, c/o [1] Sault Sainte Marie, MI, Holy Name of Mary Church. (MAR)
Sugarloaf Shores, FL, Sugarloaf Firehouse, c/o Big Pine Key, FL, St. Peter Church. (MIA)
Sugarloaf U.S.A., ME, Richard H. Bell Memorial Chapel, c/o Oquossoc, ME, Our Lady of the Lakes Church. (PRT)
Sullivan City, TX, St. William, c/o La Joya, TX, Our Lady, Queen of Angels Church. (BWN)
Sulphur, LA, Calcasieu Parish, St. Peter Claver, c/o [3] Sulphur, LA, Our Lady of Prompt Succor Church. (LKC)
Sun River, OR, Deschutes Co., Holy Trinity, c/o La Pine, OR, Holy Redeemer Church. (BAK)
Sunapee, NH, Sullivan Co., St. Joachim, c/o Newport, NH, St. Patrick Church. (MAN)
Sunburst, MT, St. Thomas Aquinas, c/o Shelby, MT, St. William Church. (HEL)
Sundance, WY, Crook Co., St. Paul, c/o Newcastle, WY, Corpus Christi Church. (CHY)
Sundown, TX, Hockley Co., San Isidro, c/o Levelland, TX, St. Michael's Church. (LUB)
Sunray, TX, Moore Co., Christ the King, c/o Dumas, TX, SS. Peter and Paul Church. (AMA)
Sunrise Beach, TX, Burnet Co., Our Lady of the Lake, c/o Kingsland, TX, St. Charles Borromeo Church. (AUS)
Superior, MT, St. Mary Queen of Heaven, c/o Frenchtown, MT, St. John the Baptist Church. (HEL)

Superior, WY, Sweetwater Co., St. Vivian, c/o Rock Springs, WY, Holy Spirit Catholic Community Church. (CHY)
Suquamish, WA, Kitsap Co., St. Peter, c/o Poulsbo, WA, St. Olaf Church. (SEA)
Surf City, NC, Pender Co., St. Mary, Gate of Heaven, c/o Hampstead, NC, St. Jude the Apostle Church. (R)
Surf City, NJ, Ocean Co., St. Thomas of Villanova, c/o Brant Beach, NJ, St. Francis of Assisi Church. (TR)
Susua, PR, La Resurreccion, c/o Sabana Grande, PR, Church of San Isidro. (MGZ)
Swartz, LA, Ouachita Parish, St. Lawrence, c/o [3] Monroe, LA, Our Lady of Fatima Church. (SHP)
Sweet Lake, LA, St. Patrick's, c/o Big Lake, LA, St. Mary of the Lake Church. (LKC)
Sweet Springs, MO, Saline Co., Holy Family, c/o Marshall, MO, St. Peter Church. (JC)

T

Ta, FM, c/o Lukunor, FM, Sacred Heart Church. (CI)
Tabor, MN, Polk Co., Holy Trinity, c/o East Grand Forks, MN, Sacred Heart Church. (CR)
Tabor, NE, Colfax Co., St. Mary, c/o Heun, NE, Holy Trinity Church. (OM)
Tache Indian Reservation, CA, Kings Co., St. Rosa, c/o Lemoore, CA, St. Peter Church. (FRS)
Taconite, MN, St. Joseph's, c/o Marble, MN, St. Mary's Church. (DUL)
Tahoka, TX, Lynn Co., St. Jude, c/o O'Donnell, TX, St. Pius X Church. (LUB)
Talihina, OK, Leflore Co., St. Catherine of Siena, c/o Hartshorne, OK, Holy Rosary Church. (TLS)
Tallaboa Alta, PR, Santa Ana St. Domingo, Carmen, c/o Penuelas, PR, St. Joseph Church. (PCE)
Talpa, NM, Taos Co., N.S. de San Juan de Los Lagos, c/o Ranchos De Taos, NM, San Francisco de Asis Church. (SFE)
Tampa, FL, Hillsborough Co., St. Joseph Vietnamese Mission, c/o [3] Tampa, FL, Epiphany Church. (SP)
Tampa, KS, Marion Co., Holy Redeemer, c/o Marion, KS, Holy Family Church. (WCH)
Tanama, PR, Sagrado Corazon, c/o Adjuntas, PR, St. Joachim Church. (PCE)
Taos, NM, Taos Co., St. Jerome, c/o Taos, NM, Nuestra Senora De Guadalupe Church. (SFE)
Taos Pueblo, NM, c/o Taos, NM, Nuestra Senora De Guadalupe Church. (SFE)
Tatum, NM, Our Lady of the Holy Rosary, c/o Lovington, NM, St. Thomas Aquinas Church. (LSC)
Tatum, TX, Panola Co., San Pedro the Fisherman, c/o Marshall, TX, St. Joseph Church. (TYL)
Taylorsville, KY, Spencer Co., All Saints Church, c/o Fairfield, KY, St. Michael Church. (L)
Taylorsville, NC, Alexander Co., Holy Trinity, c/o Lenoir, NC, St. Francis of Assisi Church. (CHL)
Teague, TX, Freestone Co., St. Mary, c/o Fairfield, TX, St. Bernard of Clairvaux Church. (TYL)
Tecolotito, NM, San Miguel Co., c/o Anton Chico, NM, San Jose Church. (SFE)
Tehama, CA, Tehama Co., St. Stanislaus, c/o Corning, CA, Immaculate Conception Church. (SAC)
Temple, PA, Berks Co., St. Anthony, c/o [5] Reading, PA, Holy Guardian Angels Church. (ALN)
Ten Sleep, WY, Washakie Co., St. Brigid's, c/o Worland, WY, St. Mary Magdalen Church. (CHY)
Tenakee Springs, AK, c/o Yakutat, AK, St. Ann Church. (JUN)
Tenino, WA, Thurston Co., St. Peter, c/o Yelm, WA, St. Columban Church. (SEA)
Tennessee, IL, McDonough Co., Sacred Heart, c/o Macomb, IL, St. Paul's Church. (PEO)
Terlingua, TX, Brewster Co., St. Mary, c/o Alpine, TX, Our Lady of Peace Church. (ELP)
Terra Alta, WV, Preston Co., St. Edward, c/o Kingwood, WV, St. Sebastian's Church. (WH)
Terra Bella, CA, Tulare Co., Blessed Miguel Agustin Pro, c/o Porterville, CA, St. Anne Church. (FRS)
Terry, MT, Sacred Heart, c/o Miles City, MT, Sacred Heart Church. (GF)
Tesuque, NM, Sante Fe Co., Indian Pueblo, c/o [1] Santa Fe, NM, The Cathedral of San Francisco de Asis. (SFE)
Tesuque, NM, Santa Fe Co., San Ysidro, c/o [2] Santa Fe, NM, Our Lady of Guadalupe Church. (SFE)
Texico, NM, Curry Co., c/o Clovis, NM, Our Lady of Guadalupe Church. (SFE)
Texline, TX, Dallum Co., St. Mary's, c/o Dalhart, TX, St. Anthony's Church. (AMA)
Thatcher, AZ, Graham Co., Neuman Center, c/o Safford, AZ, St. Rose of Lima Church. (TUC)
Thayer, MO, Oregon Co., Sacred Heart, c/o West Plains, MO, St. Mary Church. (SPC)
Thedford, NE, Thomas Co., St. Thomas of Canterbury, c/o Mullen, NE, St. Mary's Church. (GI)
Theresa, NY, Jefferson Co., St. Theresa of Avila, c/o Evans Mills, NY, St. Mary Church. (OG)
Thermal, CA, Riverside Co., El Senor de la Misericordia, c/o Coachella, CA, Our Lady of Soledad Church. (SB)
Thomas, OK, Custer Co., Blessed Sacrament, c/o Weatherford, OK, St. Eugene's Church. (OKL)
Thomaston, GA, Upson Co., St. John the Baptist, c/o Griffin, GA, Sacred Heart Church. (ATL)
Thomaston, ME, Knox Co., St. James, c/o Rockland, ME, St. Bernard's Church. (PRT)
Thomasville, AL, Clarke Co., St. Joseph, c/o Grove Hill, AL, Sacred Heart Church. (MOB)
Thompson, ND, Grand Forks Co., St. Jude, c/o Reynolds, ND, Our Lady of Perpetual Help Church. (FAR)
Thorne Bay, AK, c/o Craig, AK, St. John by the Sea Church. (JUN)
Thornhurst, PA, Luzerne Co., St. Mark, c/o Bear Creek Township, PA, St. Elizabeth Church. (SCR)
Thornton, CA, San Joaquin Co., Mater Ecclesiae, c/o Lodi, CA, St. Anne Church. (STO)
Thornwell, LA, Jefferson Davis Parish, St. Francis of Assisi Chapel, c/o Lake Arthur, LA, Our Lady of the Lake Church. (LKC)
Three Rivers, CA, Tulare Co., St. Clair, c/o Woodlake, CA, St. Frances Cabrini Church. (FRS)
Three Rivers, NM, Otero Co., St. Patrick, c/o Mescalero, NM, St. Joseph Church. (LSC)
Three Rocks, CA, Fresno Co., Our Lady of Lourdes, c/o Mendota, CA, Our Lady of Guadalupe Church. (FRS)
Throne Bay, AK, c/o Craig, AK, St. John by the Sea Church. (JUN)
Thunder Butte, SD, Ziebach Co., St. Luke, c/o Eagle Butte, SD, All Saints Church. (RC)
Thunder Butte, SD, Ziebach Co., St. Luke, c/o Eagle Butte, SD, Cheyenne River Reservation Church. (RC)
Tijeras, NM, Bernalillo Co., c/o Tijeras, NM, Holy Child Church. (SFE)
Tilden, TX, McMullen Co., St. Joseph, c/o Charlotte, TX, St. Rose of Lima Church. (SAT)
Timpson, TX, Shelby Co., Epiphany, c/o Center, TX, St. Therese Church. (TYL)
Tinaja, NM, Colfax Co., c/o Springer, NM, St. Joseph Church. (SFE)
Tioga, PA, Tioga Co., St. Mary, c/o Mansfield, PA, Holy Child Church. (SCR)
Tionesta, PA, Forest Co., St. Anthony, c/o Tidioute, PA, St. John Church. (E)
Tishomingo, OK, Johnston Co., St. Anthony, c/o Sulphur, OK, St. Francis Xavier Church. (OKL)
Toa Alta, PR, Cristo de los Milagros, c/o [3] Toa Alta, PR, San Jose Church. (SJN)
Toa Alta, PR, Cristo Rey, c/o [2] Toa Baja, PR, Ntra. Sra. de la Candelaria Church. (SJN)
Toa Alta, PR, La Resurreccion, c/o [5] Toa Alta, PR, N. Sra. de la Providencia Church. (SJN)
Toa Alta, PR, Sector Rincon, N. Sra. de Fatima, c/o [5] Toa Alta, PR, N. Sra. de la Providencia Church. (SJN)
Toa Alta, PR, Sector Del 7, N. Sra. Del Carmen, c/o [5] Toa Alta, PR, N. Sra. de la Providencia Church. (SJN)
Toa Alta, PR, Ntra. Sra. del Camino, c/o [3] Toa Alta, PR, San Jose Church. (SJN)
Toa Alta, PR, Nuestra Senora del Carmen, c/o [4] Toa Alta, PR, Nuestra Senora de la Medalla Milagrosa Church. (SJN)
Toa Alta, PR, S. Francisco De Asis, c/o [3] Toa Alta, PR, San Jose Church. (SJN)
Toa Alta, PR, S. Martin De Porres, c/o [6] Toa Alta, PR, San Judas Tadeo Church. (SJN)
Toa Alta, PR, Sector Marzan, Sagrada Familia, c/o [3] Toa Alta, PR, San Jose Church. (SJN)
Toa Alta, PR, Sagrada Familia, c/o [5] Toa Alta, PR, N. Sra. de la Providencia Church. (SJN)
Toa Alta, PR, Sector Los Mudos, Sagrado Corazon, c/o [3] Toa Alta, PR, San Jose Church. (SJN)
Toa Alta, PR, Sagrado Corazon de Jesus, c/o [4] Toa Alta, PR, Nuestra Senora de la Medalla Milagrosa Church. (SJN)
Toa Alta, PR, San Antonio, c/o [2] Toa Alta, PR, San Fernando Rey Church. (SJN)
Toa Alta, PR, Santa Teresa De Jesus, c/o [6] Toa Alta, PR, San Judas Tadeo Church. (SJN)
Toa Alta, PR, Santa Teresita, c/o [3] Toa Alta, PR, San Jose Church. (SJN)
Toa Baja, PR, Buen Pastor, c/o [2] Toa Baja, PR, Ntra. Sra. de la Candelaria Church. (SJN)
Toa Baja, PR, Divino Nino Jesus, c/o [1] Toa Baja, PR, Nuestra Senora de Covadonga Church. (SJN)
Toa Baja, PR, La Virgen de la Providencia, c/o [5] Toa Baja, PR, San Pedro Apostol Church. (SJN)
Toa Baja, PR, N. Sra. del Carmen, c/o [3] Toa Baja, PR, Espiritu Santo Church. (SJN)
Toa Baja, PR, Ntra. Sra. de Guadalupe, c/o [5] Toa Baja, PR, San Pedro Apostol Church. (SJN)
Toa Baja, PR, Ntra. Sra. de Lourdes, c/o [1] Toa Baja, PR, Nuestra Senora de Covadonga Church. (SJN)
Toa Baja, PR, Sector Los Bravos, Ntra. Sra. del Carmen, c/o [4] Toa Baja, PR, San Jose Obrero Church. (SJN)
Toa Baja, PR, San Jose, c/o [5] Toa Baja, PR, San Pedro Apostol Church. (SJN)
Toa Baja, PR, San Martin de Porres, c/o [1] Toa Baja, PR, Nuestra Senora de Covadonga Church. (SJN)
Toa Baja, PR, San Martin de Porres, c/o [4] Toa Baja, PR, San Jose Obrero Church. (SJN)
Toa Baja, PR, San Pablo, c/o [5] Toa Baja, PR, San Pedro Apostol Church. (SJN)
Toa Baja, PR, Santa Maria La Mayor, c/o [2] Toa Baja, PR, Ntra. Sra. de la Candelaria Church. (SJN)
Toa Baja, PR, Santisima Trinidad, c/o [2] Toa Baja, PR, Ntra. Sra. de la Candelaria Church. (SJN)
Toa Baja, PR, St. Teresita, c/o [5] Toa Baja, PR, San Pedro Apostol Church. (SJN)
Tobias, NE, Saline Co., St. Joseph's, c/o Wilber, NE, St. Wenceslaus Church. (LIN)
Tohono O'Odham, AZ, St. Lucy, Paloma Ranch, c/o Gila Bend, AZ, St. Michael Church. (PHX)
Tok, AK, Holy Rosary, c/o Delta Junction, AK, Our Lady of Sorrows Church. (FBK)
Tokio, ND, Benson Co., Christ the King, c/o Fort Totten, ND, Seven Dolors Church. (FAR)
Tokio, ND, Benson Co., Christ the King, c/o Fort Totten Reservation, ND, (Sioux Indians) Church. (FAR)
Tolna, ND, Nelson Co., St. Joseph, c/o Lakota, ND, St. Mary's Church. (FAR)
Tomales, CA, Marin Co., St. Helen, c/o Tomales, CA, Church of the Assumption. (SFR)
Tompkinsville, KY, Monroe Co., Christ the King, c/o Edmonton, KY, Christ the Healer Church. (L)
Tonyville, CA, St. Anthony Church, c/o Lindsay, CA, Sacred Heart Church. (FRS)
Tornillo, TX, Santa Rita, c/o Fabens, TX, Our Lady of Guadalupe Church. (ELP)
Torreon, NM, Torrance Co., c/o Mountainair, NM, St. Alice Church. (SFE)
Torrey, UT, Wayne Co., St. Anthony of the Desert, c/o Monroe, UT, St. Elizabeth's Church. (SLC)
Toston, MT, Broadwater Co., Immaculate Conception, c/o Townsend, MT, Holy Cross Church. (HEL)
Touhy, NE, Saunders Co., St. Vitus, c/o Weston, NE, St. John Nepomucene Church. (LIN)
Toulon, IL, Stark Co., St. John, c/o Wyoming, IL, St. Dominic's Church. (PEO)
Townsend, TN, Blount Co., St. Francis of Assisi, c/o Alcoa, TN, Our Lady of Fatima Church. (KNX)
Townshend, VT, Windham Co., Our Lady of the Valley, c/o Putney, VT, Our Lady of Mercy Church. (BUR)
Toyah, TX, St. Emily, c/o Pecos, TX, St. Catherine Church. (ELP)
Trail City, SD, Corson Co., Holy Rosary, c/o Timber Lake, SD, Holy Cross Church. (RC)
Trampas, NM, Taos Co., San Jose de Gracia, c/o Chimayo, NM, Holy Family Church. (SFE)
Trapper Creek, AK, St. Philip Benizi, c/o Talkeetna, AK, St. Bernard Church. (ANC)
Traver, CA, Tulare Co., St. John the Baptist Educational Center, c/o Kingsburg, CA, Holy Family Church. (FRS)
Tremonton, UT, Box Elder Co., Santa Ana, c/o Brigham City, UT, St. Henry Church. (SLC)
Trenton, ND, Williams Co., St. John the Baptist, c/o Williston, ND, St. Joseph Church. (BIS)
Tres de Jayuya, PR, Santa Teresita, c/o Adjuntas, PR, St. Joachim Church. (PCE)
Tres Piedras, NM, Taos Co., c/o El Rito, NM, San Juan Nepomuceno Church. (SFE)
Triadelphia, WV, Ohio Co., Our Lady of Seven Dolors, c/o [11] Wheeling, WV, St. Vincent de Paul's Church. (WH)
Trichel, LA, St. Joseph, c/o Campti, LA, Nativity of The Blessed Virgin Mary Church. (ALX)
Trinidad, CA, Holy Trinity, c/o McKinleyville, CA, Christ the King Church. (SR)
Trout Lake, MI, Chippewa Co., St. Mary, c/o Rudyard, MI, St. Joseph Church. (MAR)
Troy, MT, Immaculate Conception, c/o Libby, MT, St. Joseph Church. (HEL)
Troy, NY, Rensselaer Co., Hallmark Nursing Home, c/o [8] Troy, NY, St. Michael the Archangel Church. (ALB)
Troy, PA, Bradford Co., St. John Nepomucene, c/o Canton, PA, St. Michael Church. (SCR)
Truchas, NM, Rio Arriba Co., Holy Rosary, c/o Chimayo, NM, Holy Family Church. (SFE)
Trujillo, CO, Archuleta Co., St. James, c/o Pagosa Springs, CO, Immaculate Heart of Mary Church. (PBL)
Trujillo, NM, San Miguel Co., San Isidro, c/o Las Vegas, NM, Our Lady of Sorrows Church. (SFE)
Trujillo Alto, PR, El Divino Pastor, c/o [6] Trujillo Alto, PR, San Judas Tadeo Church. (SJN)
Trujillo Alto, PR, Espiritu Santo, c/o [4] Trujillo Alto, PR, San Francisco de Asis Church. (SJN)
Trujillo Alto, PR, La Inmaculada Concepcion, c/o [4] Trujillo Alto, PR, San Francisco de Asis Church. (SJN)
Trujillo Alto, PR, Ntra. Sra. del Carmen, c/o [6] Trujillo Alto, PR, San Judas Tadeo Church. (SJN)
Trujillo Alto, PR, San Jose de la Montana, c/o [4] Trujillo Alto, PR, San Francisco de Asis Church. (SJN)

Trujillo Creek, CO, Mount Carmel, c/o Aguilar, CO, St. Anthony Church. (PBL)
Tsaile, AZ, St. Ann, c/o Lukachukai, AZ, St. Isabel Church. (GLP)
Tsis, FM, c/o Fefan, FM, Sacred Heart Church. (CI)
Tucson, AZ, Pima Co., Cristo Rey, c/o [2] Tucson, AZ, Blessed Kateri Tekakwitha Church. (TUC)
Tucson, AZ, Pima Co., El Senor de los Milagros, c/o [2] Tucson, AZ, Blessed Kateri Tekakwitha Church. (TUC)
Tucson, AZ, Pima Co., Our Lady of Guadalupe, c/o [24] Tucson, AZ, Santa Cruz Church. (TUC)
Tucson, AZ, Pima Co., Santa Catalina, c/o [21] Tucson, AZ, Saint Odilia Church. (TUC)
Tucson, AZ, Pima Co., Santa Rosa, c/o [2] Tucson, AZ, Blessed Kateri Tekakwitha Church. (TUC)
Tucson, AZ, Pima Co., Santa Rosa, c/o [4] Tucson, AZ, Holy Family Church. (TUC)
Tucson, AZ, Pima Co., St. Anthony's Catholic Instruction Center and Capilla, c/o [24] Tucson, AZ, Santa Cruz Church. (TUC)
Tucson, AZ, Pima Co., St. Mary of the Desert, c/o [7] Tucson, AZ, Our Lady of Fatima Church. (TUC)
Tulalip, WA, Snohomish Co., Tulalip Indian Reservation, St. Anne, c/o Marysville, WA, St. Mary Church. (SEA)
Tule Indian Reservation, CA, Tulare Co., Mater Dolorosa, c/o Porterville, CA, St. Anne Church. (FRS)
Tullytown, PA, Bucks Co., Sacred Heart of Jesus, c/o Bristol, PA, St. Ann Church. (PH)
Tunica, MS, Tunica Co., St. Anthony of Padua, c/o Walls, MS, Sacred Heart Church. (JKS)
Tuolumne, CA, Tuolumne Co., St. Joseph, c/o Twain Harte, CA, All Saints Church. (STO)
Turquillo, NM, Mora Co., c/o Mora, NM, St. Gertrude Church. (SFE)
Turtle Lake, ND, McLean Co., St. Catherine, c/o Underwood, ND, St. Bonaventure Church. (BIS)
Tuscaloosa, AL, Tuscaloosa Co., St. John, c/o Tuscaloosa, AL, Holy Spirit Church. (BIR)
Tuscon, AZ, Pima Co., San Ignacio, c/o [2] Tucson, AZ, Blessed Kateri Tekakwitha Church. (TUC)
Tuscon, AZ, Pima Co., San Martin, c/o [2] Tucson, AZ, Blessed Kateri Tekakwitha Church. (TUC)
Twin Bridges, MT, Jefferson Co., Notre Dame, c/o Whitehall, MT, St. Teresa Church. (HEL)
Twin Buttes, ND, Dunn Co., St. Joseph, c/o Mandaree, ND, St. Anthony Church. (BIS)
Twin Sisters, TX, Blanco Co., Our Lady Help of Christians, c/o Blanco, TX, St. Ferdinand's Church. (AUS)
Twin Valley, MN, Norman Co., St. William, c/o Ada, MN, St. Joseph's Church. (CR)
Two Inlets, MN, Becker Co., St. Mary, c/o Park Rapids, MN, St. Peter's Church. (CR)
Tylertown, MS, Walthall Co., St. Paul the Apostle, c/o Columbia, MS, Most Holy Trinity Church. (BLX)
Tynan, TX, Bee Co., St. Francis Xavier, c/o Skidmore, TX, Immaculate Conception Church. (CC)

U

Ulster, PA, Bradford Co., Immaculate Conception, c/o Towanda, PA, SS. Peter and Paul Church. (SCR)
Ulupalakua, HI, Maui Co., St. James the Less, c/o Kula, HI, Our Lady Queen of the Angels Church. (HON)
Unadilla, NY, Otsego Co., St. Ambrose, c/o Sidney, NY, Sacred Heart Church. (ALB)
Unalaska, AK, St. Christopher, c/o Dillingham, AK, Holy Rosary Church. (ANC)
Union, WV, Monroe Co., St. Andrew the Apostle, c/o Ronceverte, WV, St. Catherine of Siena Church. (WH)
Union City, MI, Branch Co., Our Lady of Fatima, c/o Coldwater, MI, St. Charles Borromeo Church. (KAL)
Union Springs, AL, Bullock Co., Bullock County Correctional Facility, c/o Eufaula, AL, Holy Redeemer Church. (MOB)
Union Springs, AL, Bullock Co., St. Pius X, c/o Eufaula, AL, Holy Redeemer Church. (MOB)
Unionville, MO, Putnam Co., St. Mary, c/o Milan, MO, St. Mary Church. (JC)
Unionville, NY, Orange Co., Our Lady of the Scapular, c/o Middletown, NY, Holy Cross Church. (NY)
Unity, OR, St. Joseph's, c/o [1] Baker, OR, Cathedral of St. Francis De Sales. (BAK)
Universal, IN, Vermillion Co., St. Joseph, c/o Clinton, IN, Sacred Heart Church. (IND)
Upper Cutmeat, SD, Sacred Heart, c/o Parmelee, SD, St. Agnes Church. (RC)
Upper Cutmeat, SD, Todd Co., Sacred Heart, c/o St. Francis, SD, Rosebud Reservation Church. (RC)
Upper Little Caillou, LA, Our Lady of Prompt Succor, c/o Chauvin, LA, St. Joseph Church. (HT)
Upton, WY, Weston Co., St. Anthony, c/o Newcastle, WY, Corpus Christi Church. (CHY)
Urb. Santa Teresita, PR, Ponce Co., Santa Teresita, c/o [2] Ponce, PR, Christ the King Church. (PCE)
Uriah, AL, Monroe Co., Our Lady of Mount Carmel, c/o Monroeville, AL, Annunciation Church. (MOB)
Urich, MO, Henry Co., Holy Trinity, c/o Montrose, MO, Immaculate Conception Church. (KC)
Ute, IA, Monona Co., St. Mary's, c/o Charter Oak, IA, St. Boniface Church. (SC)
Utica, NE, Seward Co., St. Patrick's, c/o Beaver Crossing, NE, Sacred Heart Church. (LIN)
Utulei, AS, c/o [2] Pago Pago, AS, Co-Cathedral of St. Joseph the Worker. (SPP)

V

Vadito, NM, Taos Co., Nuestra Senora de los Dolores Mission, c/o Penasco, NM, San Antonio de Padua Church. (SFE)
Vado, NM, Dona Ana Co., San Pedro Del Cerro, c/o La Mesa, NM, San Jose Church. (LSC)
Vail, CO, Eagle Co., The Interfaith Chapel, c/o Minturn, CO, St. Patrick's Church. (DEN)
Valdez, NM, Taos Co., San Antonio de Padua, c/o Arroyo Seco, NM, La Santisima Trinidad Church. (SFE)
Valentine, TX, Sacred Heart, c/o Van Horn, TX, Our Lady of Fatima Church. (ELP)
Valiant, OK, McCurtain Co., Good Shepherd, c/o Idabel, OK, St. Francis De Sales Church. (TLS)
Vallecitos, NM, Rio Arriba Co., c/o El Rito, NM, San Juan Nepomuceno Church. (SFE)
Valley Falls, NY, Our Lady of Good Counsel, c/o Schaghticoke, NY, St. John the Baptist Church. (ALB)
Van Alstyne, TX, Grayson Co., Holy Family, c/o McKinney, TX, St. Michael Church. (DAL)
Van Buren, ME, Aroostook Co., St. Rose Chapel, c/o Van Buren, ME, St. Bruno - St. Remi Church. (PRT)
Van Buren, MO, Carter Co., St. George, c/o Piedmont, MO, St. Catherine of Siena Church. (SPC)
Vanceboro, ME, Guardian Angel, c/o Lincoln, ME, St. Mary Church. (PRT)
Vandalia, NY, Cattaraugus Co., St. John the Baptist, c/o Allegany, NY, St. Bonaventure Church. (BUF)
Vanderpool, TX, Bandera Co., St. Mary, c/o Sabinal, TX, St. Patrick's Church. (SAT)
Variadero, NM, San Miguel Co., Holy Family, c/o Las Vegas, NM, Our Lady of Sorrows Church. (SFE)
Vegas Abajo, PR, La Milagrosa, c/o Adjuntas, PR, St. Joachim Church. (PCE)
Vegas Arriba, PR, Sta. Ana, c/o Adjuntas, PR, St. Joachim Church. (PCE)
Veguita, NM, Socorro Co., San Juan, c/o La Joya, NM, Our Lady of Sorrows Church. (SFE)
Velarde, NM, Rio Arriba Co., Nuestra Senora de Guadalupe, c/o Dixon, NM, St. Anthony Church. (SFE)
Venice, LA, Plaquemines Parish, St. Anthony, c/o Buras, LA, Our Lady of Good Harbor Church. (NO)
Verdunville, LA, St. Mary Parish, Immaculate Conception, c/o Franklin, LA, St. Jules Church. (LAF)
Vernonia, OR, Our Lady of the Woods, c/o Vernonia, OR, St. Mary Church. (P)
Verona, ND, LaMoure Co., St. Raphael, c/o Oakes, ND, St. Charles Borromeo Church. (FAR)
Verona Beach, NY, Oneida Co., St. Mary, c/o North Bay, NY, St. John Church. (SY)
Versailles, MO, Morgan Co., St. Philip Benizi, c/o Laurie, MO, Shrine of St. Patrick Church. (JC)
Viburnum, MO, Iron Co., St. Philip Benizi, c/o Ironton, MO, Ste. Marie Du Lac Church. (SPC)
Victor, CO, Teller Co., St. Victor's, c/o Woodland Park, CO, Our Lady of the Woods Church. (COS)
Victoria, TX, Victoria Co., Holy Trinity, c/o [4] Victoria, TX, Our Lady of Sorrows Church. (VIC)
Vida, MT, St. Ann, c/o Wolf Point, MT, Immaculate Conception Church. (GF)
Vidrine, LA, Evangeline Parish, Holy Spirit, c/o Mamou, LA, St. Ann Church. (LAF)
Vigil, CO, Las Animas Co., St. Isidore, c/o Trinidad, CO, Most Holy Trinity, Trinidad Area Catholic Community (Trinidad Cluster) Church. (PBL)
Villa del Carmen, PR, Ponce Co., San Martin de Porres, c/o [4] Ponce, PR, Our Lady of Mt. Carmel Church. (PCE)
Vintondale, PA, Cambria Co., SS. Timothy & Mark Chapel, c/o Twin Rocks, PA, SS. Timothy & Mark Church. (ALT)
Viola, IL, Mercer Co., St. John, c/o Matherville, IL, St. Anthony's Church. (PEO)
Virginia Beach, VA, Virginia Beach Co., Our Lady of Perpetual Help, c/o Williamsburg, VA, Ascension of Our Lord Church. (PSC)
Volcano, CA, Amador Co., St. Bernard, c/o Jackson, CA, St. Patrick's Church. (SAC)
Vredenburgh, AL, Monroe Co., St. Martin de Porres, c/o Monroeville, AL, Annunciation Church. (MOB)

W

W. Claremont, NH, Sullivan Co., Old St. Mary, c/o Claremont, NH, St. Mary Church. (MAN)
Waco, TX, c/o [4] Waco, TX, St. John the Baptist Church. (AUS)
Waco, TX, McLennan Co., St. John the Baptist, c/o [7] Waco, TX, St. Mary of the Assumption Church. (AUS)
Wadena, IA, St. Joseph, c/o Elkader, IA, St. Joseph's Church. (DUB)
Wadesboro, NC, Anson Co., Sacred Heart, c/o Hamlet, NC, St. James Church. (CHL)
Wadsworth, TX, Sacred Heart, c/o Bay City, TX, Holy Cross Church. (VIC)
Waelder, TX, Gonzales Co., St. Patrick, c/o Gonzales, TX, St. James Church. (SAT)
Wahneta, FL, Polk Co., Our Lady of Guadalupe, c/o Bartow, FL, St. Thomas Aquinas Church. (ORL)
Waiakoa, HI, Maui Co., Holy Ghost, c/o Kula, HI, Our Lady Queen of the Angels Church. (HON)
Waikapu, HI, St. Joseph, c/o Waihee, HI, St. Ann Church. (HON)
Waimea, HI, Kauai Co., Sacred Hearts of Jesus & Mary, c/o Kekaha, HI, St. Theresa Church. (HON)
Waimea Bay, HI, Honolulu Co., SS. Peter and Paul, c/o Waialua, HI, St. Michael Church. (HON)
Waitsfield, VT, Washington Co., Our Lady of the Snows, c/o Waterbury, VT, St. Andrew Church. (BUR)
Wakefield, VA, Infant of Prague, c/o Franklin, VA, St. Jude Church. (RIC)
Wakita, OK, Grant Co., St. Mary's Assumption, c/o Medford, OK, St. Mary's Church. (OKL)
Wakpala, SD, Corson Co., St. Bede, c/o McLaughlin, SD, St. Bernard Church. (RC)
Wakpala, SD, Corson Co., St. Bede, c/o Standing Rock, SD, Standing Rock Reservation Church. (RC)
Walden, CO, Grand Co., St. Ignatius, c/o Kremmling, CO, St. Peter Church. (DEN)
Waldron, AR, Scott Co., St. Jude Thaddeus, c/o Mena, AR, St. Agnes Church. (LR)
Wales, MA, Hampden Co., St. Monica, c/o Brimfield, MA, St. Christopher's Church. (SPR)
Walhalla, SC, Oconee Co., St. Francis of Assisi, c/o Clemson, SC, St. Andrew Church. (CHR)
Walker, CA, Mono Co., Our Lady of the Valley, c/o Mammoth Lakes, CA, St. Joseph Church. (STO)
Walker, MN, Ah-Gwah-Ching State Nursing Home, c/o Duluth, MN, Indian Missions Church. (DUL)
Walker Valley, NY, Ulster Co., Our Lady of the Valley, c/o Pine Bush, NY, The Infant Saviour Church. (NY)
Wallace, KS, Wallace Co., St. Peter, c/o Sharon Springs, KS, Holy Ghost Church. (SAL)
Wallace, NC, Duplin Co., Transfiguration, c/o Burgaw, NC, St. Joseph Church. (R)
Wallkill, NY, Ulster Co., St. Benedict, c/o Walden, NY, Most Precious Blood Church. (NY)
Wallowa, OR, St. Pius X, c/o Enterprise, OR, St. Katherine's Church. (BAK)
Walnut Ridge, AR, Lawrence Co., Immaculate Heart of Mary, c/o Engelberg, AR, St. John the Baptist Church. (LR)
Walpole, NH, Cheshire Co., St. Joseph, c/o North Walpole, NH, St. Peter Church. (MAN)
Walters, OK, Cotton Co., St. Patrick, c/o Frederick, OK, St. Helen Church. (OKL)
Wamsutter, WY, Sweetwater Co., Catholic Community, c/o Rock Springs, WY, Holy Spirit Catholic Community Church. (CHY)
Wanette, OK, Pottawatomie Co., St. Mary, c/o Konawa, OK, Sacred Heart Church. (OKL)
Warba, MN, St. Paul's, c/o Hill City, MN, St. John Church. (DUL)
Wardsboro, VT, Windham Co., Our Lady of Hope, c/o Putney, VT, Our Lady of Mercy Church. (BUR)
Warm Springs, GA, Meriwether Co., St. Elizabeth Seton, c/o LaGrange, GA, St. Peter's Church. (ATL)
Warm Springs, OR, Jefferson Co., Blessed Kateri Tekakwitha, c/o Madras, OR, St. Patrick's Church. (BAK)
Warner Springs, CA, San Diego Co., St. Francis, c/o Santa Ysabel, CA, Santa Ysabel Indian Mission . (SD)
Warren, AR, Bradley Co., St. Luke, c/o Monticello, AR, St. Mark Church. (LR)
Warren, NH, Grafton Co., St. John Vianney, c/o Woodsville, NH, St. Joseph Church. (MAN)
Warrenton, NC, Warren Co., St. Joseph, c/o Henderson, NC, St. James the Greater Church. (R)
Warrenton, TX, Fayette Co., St. Martin's, c/o Fayetteville, TX, St. John's Church. (AUS)
Warrior, AL, Jefferson Co., St. Henry, c/o Gardendale, AL, St. Elizabeth Ann Seton Church. (BIR)
Washburn, ME, St. Catherine, c/o Ashland, ME, St. Mark's Church. (PRT)
Washburn, ND, Mercer Co., St. Edwin, c/o Center, ND, St. Martin Church. (BIS)
Washington, VA, Rappahannock Co., St. Peter, c/o Culpeper, VA, Precious Blood Church. (ARL)
Washoe Valley, NV, Washoe Co., Holy Spirit, c/o [5] Reno, NV, St. Rose of Lima Church. (RNO)
Waskom, TX, Harrison Co., St. Lawrence Brindisi, c/o Jefferson, TX, Immaculate Conception Church. (TYL)

Wataga, IL, Knoxville Co., St. Aloysius, c/o Alexis, IL, St. Theresa's Church. (PEO)
Watauga, SD, Corson Co., St. Michael, c/o Lemmon, SD, St. Mary's Church. (RC)
Waterproof, LA, St. Francis of Assisi, c/o St. Joseph, LA, St. Joseph Church. (ALX)
Watonga, OK, Blaine Co., St. Rose of Lima, c/o Okeene, OK, St. Anthony's Church. (OKL)
Watrous, NM, Mora Co., c/o Wagon Mound, NM, Santa Clara Church. (SFE)
Watson, MI, Allegan Co., Sacred Heart, c/o Dorr, MI, St. Stanislaus Church. (KAL)
Wauneta, NE, Chase Co., St. John's, c/o Imperial, NE, St. Patrick's Church. (LIN)
Waurika, OK, Jefferson Co., St. Thomas Aquinas, c/o Frederick, OK, St. Helen Church. (OKL)
Wayland, MO, Clark Co., St. Martha, c/o Kahoka, MO, St. Michael the Archangel Church. (JC)
Waynoka, OK, Woods Co., Our Mother of Mercy, c/o Alva, OK, Sacred Heart Church. (OKL)
Webbers Falls, OK, Muskogee Co., St. Joseph, c/o Sallisaw, OK, St. Francis Xavier Church. (TLS)
Weirs Beach, NH, St. Helena, c/o Lakeport, NH, Our Lady of the Lakes Church. (MAN)
Welch, OK, Craig Co., St. Ann, c/o Miami, OK, Sacred Heart Church. (TLS)
Welches, OR, Clackamas Co., St. John the Evangelist, c/o Sandy, OR, St. Michael the Archangel Church. (P)
Weldona, CO, Morgan Co., St. Francis of Assisi, c/o Fort Morgan, CO, St. Helena Church. (DEN)
Wellfleet, NE, Lincoln Co., St. William's, c/o Curtis, NE, St. James Church. (LIN)
Wells, NV, St. Thomas Aquinas, c/o Elko, NV, St. Joseph's Church. (RNO)
Wells, VT, Rutland Co., St. Paul, c/o Middletown Springs, VT, St. Anne Church. (BUR)
Wells River, VT, Orange Co., St. Eugene, c/o Bradford, VT, Our Lady of Perpetual Help Church. (BUR)
Wellton, AZ, Yuma Co., St. Joseph the Worker, c/o Yuma, AZ, Immaculate Conception Church. (TUC)
Wenden, AZ, St. John the Baptist, c/o Parker, AZ, Sacred Heart Church. (TUC)
Weslaco, TX, St. Jude Chapel, c/o Weslaco, TX, San Martin de Porres Church. (BWN)
West Alton, MO, St. Charles Co., Immaculate Conception, c/o Portage Des Sioux, MO, St. Francis of Assisi Church. (STL)
West Barnstable, MA, Barnstable Co., Our Lady of Hope, c/o Centerville, MA, Our Lady of Victory Church. (FR)
West Castleton, VT, Rutland Co., St. Matthew of Avalon, c/o Fair Haven, VT, Our Lady of Seven Dolors Church. (BUR)
West Charleston, VT, Orleans Co., St. Benedict Labre, c/o Derby Line, VT, St. Edward Church. (BUR)
West Columbia, TX, Brazoria Co., St. John the Apostle, c/o Sweeny, TX, Our Lady of Perpetual Help Church. (GAL)
West Covina, CA, Los Angeles Co., St. Christopher Korean Catholic Community, c/o West Covina, CA, St. Christopher Church. (LA)
West Forks, ME, SS. Philip & James, c/o Bingham, ME, St. Peter's Church. (PRT)
West Gilgo Beach, NY, Suffolk Co., c/o Babylon, NY, St. Joseph's Church. (RVC)
West Glacier, MT, Flathead Co., c/o Columbia Falls, MT, St. Richard Church. (HEL)
West Haven, CT, Our Lady of Mt. Carmel Chapel, c/o [5] West Haven, CT, St. Paul's Church. (HRT)
West Mount Vernon, AL, Mobile Co., St. Theresa, c/o Chastang, AL, St. Peter the Apostle Church. (MOB)
West Pawlet, VT, Rutland Co., St. Frances Cabrini, c/o Middletown Springs, VT, St. Anne Church. (BUR)
West Peru, NY, Clinton Co., St. Patrick, c/o Peru, NY, St. Augustine Church. (OG)
West Point, CA, Calaveras Co., Our Lady of Fatima, c/o San Andreas, CA, St. Andrew Church. (STO)
West Point, IL, Hancock Co., St. Mary, c/o Carthage, IL, Immaculate Conception Church. (PEO)
West Point, KY, Hardin Co., St. Patrick Church, c/o [2] Valley Station, KY, Our Lady Help of Christians Church. (L)
West Point, OH, Columbiana Co., St. Agatha, c/o Lisbon, OH, St. George Church. (Y)
West Ridge, IA, St. John the Baptist, c/o Waukon, IA, St. Patrick's Church. (DUB)
West Shokan, NY, Ulster Co., St. Augustine, c/o West Hurley-Woodstock, NY, St. John Church. (NY)
West Springfield, MA, Hampden Co., St. Ann, c/o [9] Springfield, MA, Our Lady of Mt. Carmel Church. (SPR)
West Wareham, MA, Plymouth Co., St. Anthony, c/o Wareham, MA, St. Patrick's Church. (FR)
West Yellowstone, MT, Big Sky, c/o West Yellowstone, MT, Our Lady of the Pines Church. (HEL)
Westfield, PA, Tioga Co., St. Catherine, c/o Elkland, PA, St. Thomas the Apostle Church. (SCR)
Westhoff, TX, St. Aloysius, c/o Meyersville, TX, SS. Peter & Paul Church. (VIC)
Westhope, ND, Bottineau Co., St. Andrew, c/o Bottineau, ND, St. Mark's Church. (FAR)
Westminster, CO, Adams Co., Our Lady of Visitation, c/o Westminster, CO, Holy Trinity Church. (DEN)
Westover, MD, Somerset Co., St. Elizabeth, c/o Pocomoke City, MD, Holy Name of Jesus Church. (WIL)
Westport, WA, Grays Harbor Co., St. Paul, c/o Aberdeen, WA, St. Mary Church. (SEA)
Westville, NY, Franklin Co., Our Lady of Fatima, c/o Constable, NY, St. Francis of Assisi Church. (OG)
Westway, TX, El Paso Co., Immaculate Heart of Mary, c/o Canutillo, TX, St. Patrick Church. (ELP)
Wetumpka, AL, Elmore Co., St. Mark's, c/o Millbrook, AL, St. Elizabeth Ann Seton Church. (MOB)
Wewahitchka, FL, Gulf Co., St. Lawrence, c/o Blountstown, FL, St. Francis of Assisi Church. (PT)
Wewahitchka, FL, Gulf Co., St. Lawrence Mission, c/o Port St. Joe, FL, St. Joseph Church. (PT)
Wewoka, OK, Seminole Co., St. Joseph, c/o Konawa, OK, Sacred Heart Church. (OKL)
Whale Pass, AK, c/o Craig, AK, St. John by the Sea Church. (JUN)
Wheat Ridge, CO, Jefferson Co., Immaculate Conception Community, c/o [1] Colorado Springs, CO, St. Mary's Cathedral. (COS)
Wheatfields, AZ, Our Lady of the Lake, c/o Lukachukai, AZ, St. Isabel Church. (GLP)
Wheatland, CA, Yuba Co., St. Daniel, c/o Lincoln, CA, St. Joseph Church. (SAC)
Wheatville, NY, Genesee Co., St. Patrick, c/o Oakfield, NY, St. Cecilia Church. (BUF)
Wheeler, TX, Collingsworth Co., St. Mary, c/o Canadian, TX, Sacred Heart Church. (AMA)
Wheelwright, MA, Hardwick Co., St. Augustine, c/o Barre, MA, St. Joseph's Church. (WOR)
Whetstone, AZ, Cochise Co., Good Shepherd, c/o Sierra Vista, AZ, St. Andrew Church. (TUC)
White Church, MO, Howell Co., St. Joseph, c/o Willow Springs, MO, Sacred Heart Church. (SPC)
White Earth, MN, Becker Co., St. Benedict, c/o Ogema, MN, Most Holy Redeemer Church. (CR)
White Horse, SD, Dewey Co., St. Therese, c/o Eagle Butte, SD, All Saints Church. (RC)
White Horse, SD, Ziebach Co., St. Therese, c/o Eagle Butte, SD, Cheyenne River Reservation Church. (RC)
White Horse Beach, MA, St. Catherine's Chapel, c/o [2] Plymouth, MA, St. Bonaventure Church. (BO)
White Lake, NY, Sullivan Co., St. Anne, c/o Monticello, NY, St. Peter Church. (NY)
White River, SD, Mellette Co., Sacred Heart, c/o St. Francis, SD, Rosebud Reservation Church. (RC)
White River, SD, Mellette Co., St. Ignatius, c/o St. Francis, SD, Rosebud Reservation Church. (RC)
White Rock, NM, Los Alamos Co., c/o Los Alamos, NM, Immaculate Heart of Mary Church. (SFE)
White Sulphur, KY, Scott Co., St. Francis de Sales, c/o Georgetown, KY, St. John's Church. (LEX)
Whitesboro, TX, Grayson Co., St. Francis of Assisi, c/o Sherman, TX, St. Mary Church. (DAL)
Whitesville, WV, Boone Co., St. Joseph the Worker, c/o Madison, WV, St. Mary, Queen of Heaven Church. (WH)
Whiteville, LA, Resurrection, c/o Morrow, LA, St. Peter Church. (LAF)
Whitewater, MT, St. John, c/o Malta, MT, St. Mary's Church. (GF)
Wibaux, MT, St. Peter, c/o Glendive, MT, Sacred Heart Church. (GF)
Wibaux, MT, St. Philip, c/o Glendive, MT, Sacred Heart Church. (GF)
Wichita Falls, TX, Wichita Co., The Assumption of Mary, c/o Wichita Falls, TX, Sacred Heart Church. (FWT)
Wiggins, CO, Morgan Co., Our Lady of Lourdes, c/o Roggen, CO, Sacred Heart Church. (DEN)
Wilburton, OK, Latimer Co., Sacred Heart, c/o Hartshorne, OK, Holy Rosary Church. (TLS)
Wildwood, FL, Sumter Co., St. Vincent de Paul Mission, c/o Bushnell, FL, St. Lawrence Church. (ORL)
Wilkeson, WA, Pierce Co., Our Lady of Lourdes, c/o Buckley, WA, St. Aloysius Church. (SEA)
Willacoochee, GA, Atkinson Co., Holy Family, c/o Douglas, GA, St. Paul's Church. (SAV)
Willard, NM, Torrance Co., c/o Mountainair, NM, St. Alice Church. (SFE)
Williams, CA, Colusa Co., Annunciation, c/o Maxwell, CA, Sacred Heart Church. (SAC)
Williams, MN, Lake of the Woods Co., St. Joseph, c/o Baudette, MN, Sacred Heart Church. (CR)
Williamsfield, IL, Knox Co., St. James, c/o Brimfield, IL, St. Joseph's Church. (PEO)
Williamstown, NY, St. Patrick, c/o Parish, NY, St. Ann Church. (SY)
Williamstown, PA, Dauphin Co., Sacred Heart of Jesus, c/o Lykens, PA, Our Lady Help of Christians Church. (HBG)
Williamstown, VT, Orange Co., St. Edward, c/o Northfield, VT, St. John the Evangelist Church. (BUR)
Williamsville, MO, Wayne Co., Our Lady of Sorrows, c/o Piedmont, MO, St. Catherine of Siena Church. (SPC)
Willow, AK, St. Christopher, c/o Talkeetna, AK, St. Bernard Church. (ANC)
Willow City, ND, Bottineau Co., Notre Dame, c/o Rolette, ND, Sacred Heart Church. (FAR)
Wills Point, TX, Van Zandt Co., St. Luke, c/o Canton, TX, St. Therese Church. (TYL)
Wilmington, NY, Essex Co., St. Margaret, c/o Keene, NY, St. Brendan Church. (OG)
Wilson, TX, Lynn Co., Blessed Sacrament, c/o Post, TX, Holy Cross Church. (LUB)
Wilton, MN, Beltrami Co., Sacred Heart, c/o Bemidji, MN, St. Philip's Church. (CR)
Windsor, CO, Weld Co., Our Lady of the Valley, c/o Johnstown, CO, St. John the Baptist Church. (DEN)
Windsor, MO, Henry Co., St. Bartholomew, c/o Clinton, MO, Holy Rosary Church. (KC)
Wingdale, NY, Dutchess Co., Our Lady of Solace Mission, c/o Dover Plains, NY, St. Charles Borromeo Church. (NY)
Winifred, MT, Holy Family, c/o Lewistown, MT, St. Leo's Church. (GF)
Winn, ME, Sacred Heart, c/o Lincoln, ME, St. Mary Church. (PRT)
Winn, MI, Isabella Co., St. Leo, c/o Shepherd, MI, St. Vincent De Paul Church. (SAG)
Winnboro, SC, Fairfield Co., St. Theresa, c/o [2] Columbia, SC, St. Joseph Church. (CHR)
Winnett, MT, St. Aloysius, c/o Roundup, MT, St. Benedict's Church. (GF)
Winnsboro, TX, Wood Co., St. Ann, c/o Sulphur Springs, TX, St. James Church. (TYL)
Winona, MS, Sacred Heart, c/o Lexington, MS, St. Thomas Church. (JKS)
Winston-Salem, NC, Forsyth Co., Our Lady of Fatima, c/o Winston-Salem, NC, Our Lady of Mercy Church. (CHL)
Winter Harbor, ME, St. Margaret, c/o Ellsworth, ME, St. Joseph's Church. (PRT)
Winter Park, CO, Grand Co., St. Bernard, c/o Grand Lake, CO, St. Anne Church. (DEN)
Winterhaven, CA, Imperial Co., St. Mary, c/o Winterhaven, CA, St. Thomas Church. (SD)
Wisdom, MT, Beaverhead Co., Our Lady of Wisdom, c/o Dillon, MT, St. Rose of Lima Church. (HEL)
Wolbach, NE, Greeley Co., St. Joseph's, c/o St. Libory, NE, St. Libory's Church. (GI)
Wolf Creek, MT, Lewis and Clark Co., Sacred Heart, c/o [3] Helena, MT, Our Lady of the Valley Church. (HEL)
Wolfforth, TX, Lubbock Co., St. Francis of Assisi, c/o Woodrow, TX, San Ramon Church. (LUB)
Wood, SD, Melette Co., Our Lady of Good Counsel, c/o White River, SD, St. Ignatius Church. (RC)
Wood, SD, Mellette Co., Our Lady of Good Counsel, c/o St. Francis, SD, Rosebud Reservation Church. (RC)
Woodland, WI, Dodge Co., St. Mary, c/o Neosho, WI, St. Matthew Church. (MIL)
Woodville, CA, Tulare Co., St. Francis of Assisi, c/o Tipton, CA, St. John The Evangelist Church. (FRS)
Woodville, FL, Leon Co., St. Stephen the Protomartyr, c/o Medart, FL, St. Elizabeth Ann Seton Church. (PT)
Woodward, IA, Dallas Co., St. Ann, c/o Granger, IA, Assumption of the Blessed Virgin Mary Church. (DM)
Woodward, IA, Dallas Co., St. John of God, c/o Madrid, IA, St. Malachy's Church. (SC)
Woodworth, LA, Mary, Mother of Jesus, c/o Lecompte, LA, St. Martin Church. (ALX)
Wounded Knee, SD, Shannon Co., Sacred Heart, c/o Manderson, SD, St. Agnes Church. (RC)
Wright, WY, Campbell Co., Blessed Sacrament, c/o Gillette, WY, St. Matthew's Church. (CHY)
Wrightsville, PA, York Co., Mother of Holy Purity, c/o Columbia, PA, St. Peter Church. (HBG)
Wyanet, IL, Bureau Co., St. Margaret Mary, c/o Sheffield, IL, St. Patrick's Church. (PEO)
Wykoff, MN, St. Kilian, c/o Spring Valley, MN, St. Ignatius Church. (WIN)
Wyola, MT, Blessed Kateri Tekakwitha, c/o Lodge Grass, MT, Our Lady of Loretto Church. (GF)

Y

Yacolt, WA, Clark Co., St. Joseph the Workman, c/o Battle Ground, WA, Sacred Heart Church. (SEA)
Yadkinville, NC, Yadkin Co., Cristo Rey Catholic Hispanic Center of Yadkin Valley, c/o Clemmons, NC, Holy Family Church. (CHL)
Yahuecas, PR, Virgen del Carmen, c/o Adjuntas, PR, St. Joachim Church. (PCE)

Yakima, WA, Yakima Co., Ahtanum, c/o [2] Yakima, WA, Holy Family Church. (YAK)

Yancy, TX, Medina Co., Immaculate Heart of Mary, c/o D'Hanis, TX, Holy Cross Church. (SAT)

Yarmouth Port, MA, Barnstable Co., Sacred Heart Chapel, c/o Hyannis, MA, St. Francis Xavier's Church. (FR)

Yarnell, AZ, Yavapai Co., St. Mary's, c/o Prescott, AZ, Sacred Heart Church. (PHX)

Yellowstone National Park, WY, Park Co., c/o Cody, WY, St. Anthony Church. (CHY)

Yellville, AR, Marion Co., St. Andrew's, c/o Mountain Home, AR, St. Peter the Fisherman Church. (LR)

Yolo, CA, Yolo Co., Our Lady of Guadalupe, c/o Woodland, CA, Holy Rosary Church. (SAC)

Yonkers, NY, Westchester Co., Holy Protection of the Mother of God, c/o Yonkers, NY, St. Michael Church. (STF)

York Beach, ME, St. Mary, Star of the Sea, c/o York Harbor, ME, St. Christopher-by-the-Sea Church. (PRT)

Yorktown, TX, San Luis, c/o Yorktown, TX, Holy Cross Church. (VIC)

Youngsville, NM, Rio Arriba Co., c/o Abiquiu, NM, St. Thomas Apostle Church. (SFE)

Yuma, AZ, Yuma Co., Our Lady of Guadalupe, c/o Yuma, AZ, Immaculate Conception Church. (TUC)

Z

Zama, PR, Jayuya Co., Santa Cecila, c/o Jayuya, PR, Our Lady of Monserrate Church. (PCE)

Zamora, CA, Yolo Co., St. Agnes, c/o Knights Landing, CA, St. Paul Church. (SAC)

Zapata, TX, Zapata Co., Ntra. Sra. Del Refugio, c/o Zapata, TX, Our Lady of Lourdes Church. (LAR)

Zia, NM, Sandoval Co., c/o Jemez Pueblo, NM, San Diego Indian Missions Church. (SFE)

Zolfo Springs, FL, Hardee Co., San Alfonso Catholic Center, c/o Wauchula, FL, St. Michael Church. (VEN)

Zortman, MT, St. Joseph, c/o Hays, MT, St. Paul's Indian Mission. (GF)

Index for Religious Institutes of Men

Religious Order Initials for Men

A.A.	Assumptionists	[0130]
B.C.S.	Brothers of Christian Service	[]
B.G.S.	Little Brothers of the Good Shepherd	[0580]
B.S.O.	Basilian Salvatorian Fathers	[0190]
C.F.A.	Alexian Brothers	[0120]
C.F.C.	Congregation of Christian Brothers	[0310]
C. F.M.M.	Brothers of Our Lady, Mother of Mercy	[0980]
C.F.P.	Brothers of the Poor of St. Francis	[0460]
C.F.R.	Franciscan Friars of the Renewal	[0535]
C.F.X.	Brothers of St. Francis Xavier	[1350]
C.I.C.M.	Missionhurst Congregation of the Immaculate Heart of Mary	[0860]
C.J.	Josephite Fathers	[0710]
C.J.M.	Congregation of Jesus and Mary	[0450]
C.M.	Congregation of the Mission	[1330]
C.M.C.	Congregation of Mother Coredemptrix	[]
C.M.F.	Claretian Missionaries	[0360]
C.M.I.	Carmelites of Mary Immaculate	[0275]
C.M.L.M.	The Congregation of Maronite Lebanese Missionaries	[0785]
C.M.M.	Congregation of Mananhill Missionaries, Marianhill Fathers & Brothers	[0750]
C. M.Vd.	Mekhitarist Fathers	[]
C.O.	Oratorians	[0950]
C.P.	Congregation of the Passion	[1000]
C.P.M.	Congregation of the Fathers of Mercy	[0820]
C.PP.S.	Society of the Precious Blood	[1060]
C.R.	Congregation of the Resurrection	[1080]
C.R.	Theatine Fathers	[1300]
C.R.I.C.	Canons Regular of the Immaculate Conception	[]
C.R.L.	Canons Regular of the Lateran	[0250]
C.R.M.	Adorno Fathers	[0100]
C.R.S.	Somascan Fathers	[1250]
C.R.S.P.	Clerics Regular of St. Paul	[0160]
C.S.	Missionaries of St. Charles Scalabrinians	[1210]
C.S.B.	Basilian Fathers	[0170]
C.S.C.	Brothers of the Congregation of Holy Cross	[0600]
C.S.C.	Priests of the Congregation of Holy Cross	[0610]
C.S.J.	Congregation of St. Joseph	[1150]
C.S.J.B.	Congregation of St. John the Baptist	[]
C.S.P.	Paulist Fathers	[1030]
C.S.P.X.	Brothers of Saint Pius X	[1180]
C.S.S.	Stigmatine Fathers and Brothers.	[1280]
C.S.Sp.	Holy Ghost Fathers	[0650]
C.SS.R.	Redemptorist Fathers	[1070]
C.S.V.	Clerics of St. Viator	[1320]
D.L.P.	Diocesan Labor Priests	[]
Er.Cam.	Camaldolese Hermits of the Congregation of Monte Corona	[0230]
F.C.	Brothers of Charity	[0290]
F.D.P.	Sons of Divine Providence	[0410]
F.F.I.	Franciscan Friars of the Immaculate	[0533]
F.F.S C.	Franciscan Brothers of the Holy Cross	[0510]
F.I.C.	Brothers of Christian Instruction	[0320]
F.J.	Congregation of St. John	[]
F.M.M.	Brothers of Mercy	[0810]
F.M.M.	Missionary Fraternity of Mary	[]
F.M.S.	The Marist Brothers	[0770]
F.M.S.I.	Sons of Mary Missionary Society	[1270]
F.P.M.	Presentation Brothers	[]
F.S.C.	Brothers of the Christian Schools	[0330]
F.S.E.	Brothers of the Holy Eucharist	[0620]
F.S.P.	Brothers of St. Patrick	[1160]
F.S.R.	Brothers of the Congregation of Our Lady of the Holy Rosary	[0960]
F.S.S.P.	Priestly Fraternity of St. Peter	[1065]
G.H.M.	The Glenmary Home Missioners	[0570]
H.J.D.	Los Hermanos de Juan Diego	[]
H.M.C.	Hermits of Mount Carmel	[]
I.C.	Institute of Charity	[0300]
I.C.	Incarnational Consecration	[]
I.H.M.	Brothers of the Immaculate Heart of Mary	[0680]
I.M.C.	Consolata Missionaries	[0390]
I.S.S.S.	Schoenstatt Institutė of Secular Priests	[]
L.B.S.F.	Little Brothers of Saint Francis	[1144]
L.C.	Legionaries of Christ	[0730]
M.Afr.	Missionaries of Africa	[0850]
M.C.B.S.	Missionary Congregation of the Blessed Sacrament	[]
M.C.C.J.	Comboni Missionaries of the Heart of Jesus (Verona)	[0380]
M.Des.	Mercedarios Descalzos	[]
M.E.P.	Paris Foreign Mission Society	[0897]
M.G.	Guadalupe Missioners	[]
M.H.M.	Mill Hill Missionaries	[0830]
M.I.C.	Congregation of Marians of the Immaculate Conception	[0740]
M.J.	Missionaries of St. Joseph (Mexico)	[]
M.M.	Maryknoll	[0800]
M.S.	The Missionaries of Our Lady of La Salette	[0720]
M.S.C.	Missionaries of the Sacred Heart	[1110]
M.S.F.	Congregation of the Missionaries of the Holy Family	[0630]
M.S.P.	Missionaries of St. Paul	[]
M.Sp.S.	Missionaries of the Holy Spirit	[0660]
M.Ss.A.	Missionaries of the Holy Apostles	[0590]
M.SS.CC.	Missionaries of the Sacred Hearts of Jesus and Mary	[1120]
O.A.R.	Order of the Augustinian Recollects	[0150]
O.Carm.	Carmelite Fathers and Brothers	[0270]
O.Cart.	Order of Carthusians	[0280]
O.C.D.	Discalced Carmelite Fathers	[0260]
O.Cist.	Cistercian Fathers	[0340]
O.C.S.O.	The Cistercian Order of the Strict Observance (Trappists)	[0350]
O.de.M.	Order of Our Lady of Mercy	[0970]
O.F.M.	Franciscan Friars	[0520]
O.F.M.Cap.	The Capuchin Friars	[0470]
O.F.M.Conv.	Conventual Franciscans	[0480]
O.H.	Hospitaller Brothers of St. John of God	[0670]
O.I.C.	Order of the Imitation of Christ	[]
O.L P.	Brothers of Our Lady of Providence	[]
O.M.	Minim Fathers	[0835]
O.Mar.	Congregation of Maronite Monks	[0790]
O.M.I.	Oblates of Mary Immaculate	[0910]
O.M.V.	Oblates of the Virgin Mary	[0940]
O.P.	Order of Preachers (Dominicans)	[0430]
O.Praem.	Canons Regular of Premontre	[0900]
O.R.C.	Operarios del Reina de Cristo	[]
O.S.A.	The Augustinians	[0140]
O.S.B.	Benedictine Monks	[0200]
O.S.B.Cam.	Camaldolese Hermits	[]
O S.B.M.	Order of St. Basil the Great	[0180]
O.S.C.	Canons Regular of the Order of the Holy Cross	[0400]
O.S.Cam.	Camillian Fathers and Brothers	[0240]
O.S.F.	Congregation of the Religious Brothers of the Third Order Regular of St Francis	[0490]
O.S.F.	Franciscan Brothers of Christ the King	[0500]
O.S.F.	Franciscan Brothers of the Third Order Regular	[0515]
O.S.F.	Franciscan Missionary Brothers of the Sacred Heart of Jesus	[0540]
O.S.F.S.	Oblates of St. Francis de Sales	[0920]
O.S.J.	Oblates of St. Joseph	[0930]
O.S.M.	Servites	[1240]
O.S.P.P.E.	Pauline Fathers	[1010]
O.Ss.S.	Brigittine Monks	[0895]
O.SS.T.	Order of the Holy Trinity	[1310]
P.I.M.E.	Pontifical Institute for Foreign Missions	[1050]
R.C.J.	Rogationist Fathers	[1090]
S.A.	Franciscan Friars of the Atonement	[0530]
S.A.C.	Society of the Catholic Apostolate	[0990]
S.C.	Brothers of the Sacred Heart	[1100]
S.C.	Servants of Charity	[1220]
S.Ch.	Society of Christ	[1260]
Sch.P.	Piarist Fathers.	[1040]
S.C.J.	Congregation of the Priests of the Sacred Heart	[1130]
S.D.B.	Salesians of Don Bosco	[1190]
S.D.S.	Society of the Divine Savior	[1200]
S.D.V.	Vocationist Fathers	[1340]
S.F.	Sons of the Holy Family	[0640]
S.F.M.	Scarboro Foreign Missions	[]
S.J.	Jesuit Fathers and Brothers	[0690]
S.M.	Society of Mary (Marianists)	[0760]
S.M.	Marist Fathers	[0780]
S.M.A.	Society of African Missions	[0110]
S.M.M.	Montfort Missionaries	[0870]
S.M.P.	Society of Our Mother of Peace	[]
S.O.Cist.	Cistercian Monks of the Strict Observance	[]
S.O.L.T.	Society of Our Lady of the Most Holy Trinity	[0975]
s.P.	Servants of the Paraclete	[1230]
S.P.S.	St. Patrick Missionary Society	[1170]
S.S.	Society of the Priests of Saint Sulpice	[1290]
S.S.C.	Society of St. Columban	[0370]
SS.CC.	Congregation of the Sacred Hearts of Jesus and Mary	[1140]
S.S.E.	Society of Saint Edmund	[0440]
S.S.J.	St. Joseph's Society of the Sacred Heart	[0700]
S.S.P.	Pauhne Fathers and Brothers	[1020]
S.S.S.	Congregation of the Blessed Sacrament	[0220]
S.S.T.	Missionary Society of St. Thomas the Apostle	[]
S.T.	Missionary Servants of the Most Holy Trinity	[0840]
S.X.	Xaverian Missionary Fathers	[1360]
S.V.D.	Society of the Divine Word	[0420]
T.O.R.	Third Order Regular of Saint Francis	[0560]
V.C.	Vincentian Congregation (India)	[]
V.D.C.	Verbum Dei Community	[]

Religious Institutes of Men

The Conference of Major Religious Superiors of Men, U.S.A., 8808 Cameron St., Silver Spring, MD 20910. Tel: 301-588-4030; Fax: 301-587-4575. An association of the major Superiors of religious communities and institutes for the purpose of promoting the spiritual and apostolic welfare of Priests and Brothers. Rev. Ted Keating, S.M., Exec. Dir; Bro. Stephen Glodek, S.M., Pres.; Rev. Kurt Hartrich, O.F.M., Vice Pres.; Rev. John Libens, S.J., Sec. & Treas.

[0100] (C.R.M.)—ADORNO FATHERS
(Clerics Regular Minor)

General Motherhouse: Via Alpi Apuane 1, 00141 Rome, Italy. Very Rev. Nello Morrea, C.R.M., Supr. Gen.

U.S. Foundation (1936): *St. Michael's Seminary,* 575 Darlington Ave., Ramsey, NJ 07446. Tel: 201-327-7375; Fax: 201-934-5826. Revs. Americo Salvi, C.R.M., U. S. Delegate; Michael Marotta, C.R.M., Supr.

Priests 7; Brothers 5

Represented in the Archdiocese of Newark and in the Diocese of Charleston.

[0110] (S.M.A.)—SOCIETY OF AFRICAN MISSIONS
(Societas Missionum ad Afros)

Founded Dec. 8, 1856 with the approval of Pope Pius IX. A clerical society of apostolic life.

General Motherhouse: Via della Nocetta 111 00164, Rome, Italy. Very Rev. Daniel Cardot, S.M.A. Revs. Kiernan O'Reilly, S.M.A., Vicar Gen.; Lorenzo Mandirola, S.M.A., Gen. Councillor.

American Province (1941): 23 Bliss Ave., Tenafly, NJ 07670. Tel: 201-567-0450; Fax: 201-541-1280. Very Rev. Ulick Bourke, S.M.A., Prov. Supr. Tel: 201-567-9085; Fax: 201-567-7156; Revs. Brendan Darcy, S.M.A., Vice Prov.; M.C. Yates, S.M.A., Prov. Councillor.

Legal Title: *Society of African Missions, Inc. N.J.*

Priests 39; Lay Missionary in temporary commitment 9; Lay Missionary in permanent commitment 1; Priest Associates 1; Seminarians 1.

Represented in the Archdioceses of Boston, Newark, and Washington.

[0120] (C.F.A.)—ALEXIAN BROTHERS
(Congregatio Fratrum Cellitarum seu Alexianorum)

Generalate: Signal Mountain, TN 37377. Tel: 423-886-2969. Bros. Edward Walsh, Supr. Gen.; Warren Longo, Asst. Gen., 3910 Ohio, St. Louis, MO 63118; Kamillus Bonn, Gen. Councillor: 52001 Aachen, Germany; Dominick Champagne, C.F.A. , Gen. Councillor: B-2530 Boechout, Belgium.

General Motherhouse: Congregation of Alexian Brothers, Aachen, Germany.

United States Province (1866): 600 Alexian Way, Elk Grove Village, IL 60007. Tel: 847-640-7550; Fax: 847-981-5561. Bro. Lawrence Krueger, C.F.A., Prov. Supr.; Prov. Councillors: Bros. Thomas Keusenkothen, C.F.A., Eugene Gizzi, C.F.A.; John Howard; Richard Lowe, C.F.A., Dir. Vocations; Bro. Daniel Pisano, C.F.A., Dir. of Novices, *Novitiate of Alexian Brothers,* 6007 North Kenmore Ave., Chicago, IL 60660.

Professed Brothers 43; Novice Brothers 1.

Properties owned and or sponsored: General Hospitals 2; Continuing Care Retirement Communities 3; Alzheimers Assisted Living Facility 1; Novitiates 2; Nursing Homes 2; Residential AIDS Facility 2; Mobile Clinic (Davao, Philippines) 1.

Represented in the Archdioceses of Chicago, Milwaukee and St. Louis and in the Dioceses of Knoxville. Also in Davao, Philippines.

[0130] (A.A.)—ASSUMPTIONISTS
(Augustinians of the Assumption)

General House: via San Pio V, 55, Rome, Italy 00165. Very Rev. Richard Lamoureux, A.A., Supr. Gen.

Province of North America (1946): 330 Market St., Brighton, MA 02135. Tel: 617-783-0400. Very Rev. John L. Franck, A.A., Prov. Supr.; Councillors: Revs. Philip Bonvouloir, A.A.; Dennis Gallagher, A.A.; Stephen Goguen, A.A., Prov. Treas.

Priests 55; Brothers 20.

Parishes 3; Shrines 1; Colleges 1; Formation Centers 1; Novitiates 1; Residences 8.

Represented in the Archdioceses of Boston and New York and in the Dioceses of St. Petersburg, Nashville and Worcester. Also in Jerusalem, Kenya, Mexico, Russia and Canada.

[0140] (O.S.A.)—THE AUGUSTINIANS
(Ordo Fratrum Sancti Augustini)

Founded in 1244, first American foundation 1796.

Generalate: Via Paolo VI, 25 00193, Rome, Italy. Most. Rev. Miguel Angel Orcasitas, O.S.A., Gen.

Province of St. Thomas of Villanova (1796): *Saint Augustine Friary,* 214 Ashwood Rd., P.O. Box 340, Villanova, PA 19085-0338. Tel: 610-527-3330. (The Brothers of the Order of Hermits of St. Augustine, a corporation in the state of Pennsylvania.) Very Rev. John E. Deegan, O.S.A., Prior Prov.; Revs. John E. Rotelle, O.S.A., Prov. Sec., Dir. Augustinian Press, Devel. Office & Augustinian Guild; Anthony P. Burrascano, O.S.A., Prov. Treas.; Prov. Councillors: Revs. Arthur D. Johnson, O.S.A.; Kail C. Ellis, O.S.A.; Bro. Robert M. Thornton, O.S.A.; Revs. Francis J. Horn, O.S.A.; James R. Flynn, O.S.A.; Peter M. Donohue, O.S.A.; Joseph S. Mostardi, O.S.A., Dir. Augustinian Volunteers; Richard D. Appicci, O.S.A., Dir. Mission Office; John J. Sheridan, O.S.A., Archivist; Joseph A. Genito, O.S.A., Dir. Augustinian Justice & Peace Office.

Legal Title: *The Brothers of the Order of Hermits of Saint Augustine.*

Priests 248; Students in Theology 9; Brothers 11; Permanent Deacon 1.

Parishes 23; (USA 19; Japan 4); Major Seminary 1; Colleges 1; Universities 1; Preparatory Schools and High Schools 3; Foreign Missions.

Represented in the Archdioceses of Boston, Miami, New York, Philadelphia and Washington and in the Dioceses of Albany, Orlando and Venice.

Province of Our Mother of Good Counsel (Order of St. Augustine) (1941): *Tolentine College & Center,* 20300 Governors Hwy., Olympia Fields, IL 60461-1081. Tel: 708-748-9500; Fax: 708-481-2090. Web site: www.midwestaugustinians.org. Very Rev. Robert F. Prevost, O.S.A., Prior Prov.; Rev. G. Jerome Knies, O.S.A., Asst. Prov. & Personnel Dir.; Bros. Kenneth D. Mehn, O.S.A., Prov. Sec.; Bruce A. Jendraszak, O.S.A., Prov. Treas. & Dir.-Tolentine Center; Rev. John D. Merkelis, O.S.A., Vocation Dir.

Fathers 99; Bishops 2; Permanent Deacons 1; Professed Brothers 22; Professed Students 2.

Parishes 13; High Schools 3; Retreat Centers 1; Residences 9.

Represented in the Archdioceses of Chicago, Detroit, Milwaukee, St. Louis and in the Dioceses of Fort Worth, Joliet, Kalamazoo, Lansing and Tulsa. Also in Hamilton, Ontario, Canada, and Peru.

Province of St. Augustine: 1605 28th St., San Diego, CA 92102-1417. Tel: 619-235-0247; 282-2028. Very Rev. Stephen M. Ochoa, O.S.A., Prov.; Counselors: Revs. Patrick Keane, O.S.A.; Gary C. Rye, O.S.A.; John D. Keller, O.S.A.; Kevin C. Mullins, O.S.A., Sec.

Priests 29; Deacons 1; Brothers 2.

Parishes 7; High Schools 2; Low-Income Housing 2; Orphanages 1.

Legal Holdings or Titles: *St. Augustine High School*, San Diego, CA; *Monica House* , San Diego, CA; *Tierra del Sol,* Boulevard, CA; *Rita de Cascia House,* San Francisco, CA; *Villanova Preparatory School,* Ojai, CA; *Austin House,* San Diego, CA.

Represented in the Archdioceses of Los Angeles and Portland (OR) and in the Dioceses of Oakland and San Diego.

Order of St. Augustine Province of St. Joseph: P.O. Box 333, King City, Ontario L0G 1K0, Canada.

U.S. Address: *Mother of Consolation Monastery,* 3103 Arlington Ave., Bronx, NY 10463. Tel: 718-548-0888. Revs. Cyril Smetana, O.S.A., Prov.; Leo Cameronosa, O.S.A.; Blaise Pelerine, O.S.A.; Lawrence MacQuarrie, O.S.A.; Othmar Mussmaecher, O.S.A.; S. K. Treu, O.S.A.; Arnold C. Diederich, O.S.A., Treas.

Priests 26; Professed Brothers 18; Seminarians 6.

Represented in the Archdiocese of New York.

Province of St. Thomas Villanova: *St. Augustine Preparatory School,* 611 Cedar Ave., P.O. Box 279, Richland, NJ 08350. Tel: 856-697-2600; Fax: 856-697-8389. Revs. Paul Galetto, O.S.A., Ph.D., Pres.; Ronald Hamaday, O.S.A., Prior.

St. Augustine Preparatory School.

Represented in the Archdiocese of Philadelphia and in the Diocese of Camden.

Region U.S.A. (1993): *Christo Rey Church,* 767 Ave. A, Beaumont, TX 77701. Tel: 409-835-7788. Rev. Luis Urriza, O.S.A., Reg. Delegate.

Fathers 6.

Represented in the Archdiocese of San Antonio and in the Diocese of Beaumont.

[0150] (O.A.R.)—ORDER OF THE AUGUSTINIAN RECOLLECTS
(Ordo Augustinianorum Recollectorum)

General Motherhouse: Rome, Italy, viale dell' Astronomia 27 (E.U.R.). Most Rev. Javier Guerra, O.A.R., Prior Gen.

Province of St. Augustine (1944): *Augustinian Recollects,* 29 Ridgeway Ave., West Orange, NJ 07052. Tel: 973-731-0616; Fax: 973-731-1033. Very Rev. John A. Gruben, O.A.R., Prior Prov. Revs. Gerard Cosgayon, O.A.R., 1st Councillor, Vicar of Prov.; Francis Cregan, O.A.R., 2nd Councillor; Bro.Joseph Gallardo, O.A.R., 3rd Councillor; Rev. Charles Huse, O.A.R., 4th Councillor.

Priests 40; Brothers 12; Professed Clerics 9; Novices 2; Prepostulants 12.

Represented in the Archdioceses of Los Angeles, Newark and New York and in the Diocese of Orange. Also in Mexico.

Province of St. Nicholas of Tolentine (U.S.A. Delegation): 2800 Schurz Ave., Bronx, NY 10465. Tel: 718-823-0460. Rev. Francisco Legarro, O.A.R., Prov. Delegate.

Priests 24

Represented in the Archdioceses of Newark and New York and in the Dioceses of El Paso and Las Cruces.

[0160] (C.R.S.P.)—CLERICS REGULAR OF ST. PAUL (Barnabite Fathers)
(Ordo Clericorum Regularium Sancti Pauli)

Founded in Milan, Italy in 1533. First foundation in the United States in 1952 in Buffalo, NY.

Historical Motherhouse: *Church of St. Barnabas*, Milan, since 1545.

General Motherhouse: Via Giacomo Medici, 15, Rome, Italy. Rt. Rev. Giovanni M. Villa, C.R.S.P., Supr. Gen.

North American Province: *Provincial Motherhouse,* 981 Swann Rd., Youngstown, NY 14174. Tel: 716-754-7489. Very Rev. Julio M. Ciavaglia, C.R.S.P., Prov.

Legal Title: *Barnabite Fathers, Inc.*

Priests 17.

Fathers staff and serve: Parishes 3; Marian Shrine 1; Colleges 1; Philippine Mission 1; Spiritual Center 1.

Properties Owned: *Our Lady of Fatima Shrine and Barnabite Fathers Seminary,* Youngstown, NY; *Barnabite Spiritual Center,* Bethlehem, PA.

Represented in the Dioceses of Allentown, Buffalo and San Diego. Also in Hamilton, Ontario, Canada and the Philippines.

[0170] (C.S.B.)—BASILIAN FATHERS
(Congregatio Presbyterorum a S. Basilio)

General Curia: *Cardinal Flahiff Basilian Centre,* 95 St. Joseph St., Toronto, Ont. M5S 3C2, Canada. Tel: 416-921-6674; Fax: 416-920-3413. Very Rev. Ronald P. Fabbro, C.S.B., Supr. General

Casa San Basilio, 1910 W. Alabama, Houston, TX 77098. Tel: 713-522-1736.

Eastern U.S.: 1910 W. Alabama, Houston, TX 77098. Rev. Alvin A. Sinasac, C.S.B., U.S. Gen. Councillor.

[0180] (O.S.B.M.)—ORDER OF ST. BASIL THE GREAT
(Ordo Sancti Basilii Magni)

General Superior "Protoarchimandrita": Rt. Rev. Dionysius Lachovicz, O.S.B.M., Rome, Italy 00153 (Aventino), Via San Giosafat 8.

American Province (1948): 29 Peacock Lane, Locust Valley, NY 11506. Tel: 516-609-3262; Fax: 516-609-3264. Very Rev. Mauricio Popadiuk, O.S.B.M., Prov.

Fathers 22; Scholastics 9; Brothers 3.

Parishes 6; Community Houses 6; House of Studies; Novitiate; Monasteries 3; Retreat House; Library

Represented in the Byzantine Rite Archdiocese of Philadelphia and in the Byzantine Rite Dioceses of Chicago, Parma, Passaic and Stamford.

[0190] (B.S.O.)—BASILIAN SALVATORIAN FATHERS

General Motherhouse: *Holy Savior Monastery,* Saida, Lebanon. Rt. Rev. Salim Ghazal, B.S.O., Supr. Gen.

American Headquarters: *Basilian Salvatorian Fathers,* 30 East St., Methuen, MA 01844. Rt. Rev. Gerasimos Murphy, B.S.O., J.C.D., Prov. Supr.; Revs. Simon Hage, B.S.O.; Lawrence Tumminelli, B.S.O.; John Jadaa, B.S.O.; Youssef Aziz, B.S.O.; Adib Badaoui, B.S.O.; George Dagher, B.S.O.; Eugene Mitchell, B.S.O., General Economos; Martin A. Hyatt, B.S.O., Local Supr.

Fathers in American Region 22.

Novitiate and House of Studies: *St. Basils Seminary;* Methuen, MA.

Parishes: Canada 4; U.S.A. 7.

Represented in the Archdioceses of Boston and Miami and the Dioceses of Cleveland, Manchester, Newton and Norwich.

[0200] (O.S.B.)—BENEDICTINE MONKS
(Ordo Sancti Benedicti)

American Cassinese Congregation (Established by Pope Pius IX, Aug. 24, 1855.)

Headquarters: *Newark Abbey,* 520 Dr. M.L. King Blvd., Newark, NJ 07102. Tel: 973-733-2822; Fax: 973-643-6922. Rt. Rev. Melvin J. Valvano, O.S.B., Abbot Pres.

President's Council: Rt. Rev. Douglas Nowicki, O.S.B., Saint Vincent Archabbey; Rt. Rev. Matthew Leavy, O.S.B., Saint Anselm Abbey; Revs. Claude Peifer, O.S.B., Saint Bede Abbey; Daniel Ward, O.S.B., Saint John Abbey; Roman Galiardi, O.S.B., Saint Procopius Abbey.

The Abbeys and Priories belonging to this Congregation are as follows:

St. Vincent Archabbey: 300 Fraser Purchase Rd., Latrobe, PA 15650-2686. Tel: 724-532-6600. Rt. Rev. Douglas R. Nowicki, O.S.B., Archabbot; Rt. Rev. Paul R. Maher, O.S.B., Archabbot (Resigned); Most Rev. Rembert G. Weakland, O.S.B., Archbishop of Milwaukee.

Legal Titles: T*he Benedictine Society of Westmoreland County; Saint Vincent College Corporation; The Wimmer Corporation; The Saint Vincent Cemetery Corporation.*

Priests 136; Deacons 4; Solemn Professed Choir-Monks 24; Junior Professed Monks 11; Brothers 6; Choir Novices 3.

Represented in the Archdiocese of Baltimore and in the Dioceses of Altoona-Johnstown, Erie, Greensburg, Harrisburg, Pittsburgh, Richmond and Savannah.

St. John's Abbey: P.O. Box 2015, Collegeville, MN 56321-2015. Tel: 320-363-2011; Fax: 320-363-3082.

Monastery founded in 1856 and raised to an Abbey in 1866. Rt. Rev. Timothy Kelly, O.S.B., Abbot; Very Rev. Geoffrey Fecht, O.S.B., Prior; Very Ven. Douglas Mullin, O.S.B., Subprior.

Fathers 144; Professed Brothers 61; Novices 3.

Abbeys 1; Dependent Priories 2; Parishes 18; Chaplaincies 11; Indian Mission Residences 1; Japanese Residences 2; School of Theology 1; University 1; High Schools 2; Novitiates 1.

Legal Holdings: *Saint John's Seminary; Saint John's University; Saint John's Preparatory School; Saint John's Abbey.*

Represented in the Archdiocese of St. Paul-Minneapolis and the Dioceses of Crookston, Duluth, Metuchen, New Ulm, St. Cloud and San Bernardino. Also in Japan, The Bahamas and Republic of China.

St. Benedict's Abbey: Atchison, KS 66002. Tel: 913-367-7853; Fax: 913-367-6230.

Founded in 1857 and raised to an Abbey in 1876. Rt. Rev. Barnabas Senecal, O.S.B., Abbot; Rt. Rev. Owen Purcell, O.S.B., Retired Abbot; Rt. Rev. Ralph Koehler, O.S.B., Retired Abbot; Very Rev. Michael Santa, O.S.B., Prior & Dir. Formation; Rev. Meinrad Miller, Subprior.

Bishops 1; Fathers 44; Brothers Professed 15.

Abbeys 1; Parishes 11; Missions 3; Foreign Missions 1; Chaplaincies 3; Colleges 1; High Schools 1.

Represented in the Archdiocese of Chicago, Kansas City in Kansas and the Diocese of Arlington. Also in Brazil.

St. Mary's Abbey: Delbarton, Morristown, NJ 07960. Tel: 973-538-3231; Fax: 973-538-7109. Web site: www.osbmok.org

Monastery founded in 1857 and raised to an Abbey in 1884. Rt. Rev. Thomas J. Confroy, O.S.B., Abbot; Very Rev. Elias R. Lorenzo, O.S.B. Prior; Rev. Patrick M. Hurley, O.S.B., Subprior.

Priests 42; Brothers 11.

Parishes 2; Schools Preparatory School; Retreat Center.

Represented in the Archdiocese of Newark and in the Dioceses of Paterson and Trenton.

Newark Abbey: 528 Dr. Martin Luther King, Jr. Blvd., Newark, NJ 07102. Tel: 973-643-4800; Fax: 973-643-6922.

Priory founded 1857, Abbey in 1884; title transferred from Newark to Morristown, N.J. in 1956; became Abbey again in 1968 and known as Newark Abbey under the patronage of the Immaculate Conception Rt. Rev. Melvin J. Valvano, O.S.B., Abbot; Very Revs. Mark M. Payne, O.S.B., Prior; Matthew Wotelko, O.S.B., Subprior.

Priests 19; Brothers 8.

Legal Holding: *St. Benedict Preparatory School,* Newark, NJ.

Abbeys 1; Dependent Priories 1; Parishes 1; Preparatory (High) School 1.

Represented in the Archdioceses of Indianapolis and Newark.

Belmont Abbey: 100 Belmont-Mount Holly Rd., Belmont, NC 28012-1802. Tel: 704-825-6675; Fax: 704-825-6680.

Monastery founded in 1876, raised to an Abbey in 1884 and erected into an Abbey Nullius in 1910; Abbey Nullius suppressed January 1, 1977 and incorporated into Diocese of Charlotte. Rt. Rev. Placid D. Solari, O.S.B., Abbott & 2nd Novicemaster; Rt. Rev. Oscar C. Burnett, O.S.B., Retired Abbot; Very Rev. Arthur J. Pendleton, O.S.B., Prior; Very Rev. David G. Brown, O.S.B., Subprior

Priests 17; Brothers 2; Novices 2;Postulants 1

Legal Title: *Southern Benedictine Society of North Carolina, Incorporated*

Properties owned or sponsored: *Belmont Abbey College,* Belmont, NC.

St. Bernard Abbey (1891): Cullman, AL 35055. Tel: 256-734-8291; Fax: 256-734-2925. Rt. Rev. Cletus D. Meagher O.S.B., Abbot; Very Rev. Thomas O'Connor, O.S.B., Prior; Ven. Bro. Leo Borelli, O.S.B., Subprior & Novicemaster;

Legal Title: *St. Benedictine Society of Alabama, Inc.*

Priests 16; Brothers 11.

Represented in the Archdiocese of Mobile and the Diocese of Birmingham.

St. Procopius Abbey: 5601 College Rd., Lisle, IL 60532. Tel: 630-969-6410; Fax: 630-969-6426.

Monastery founded in 1885 and raised to an Abbey in 1894. Rt. Rev. Hugh Anderson, O.S.B., Abbot; Very Ven. Columban Trojan, O.S.B., Prior; Revs. Thomas Chisholm, O.S.B., Subprior; Kevin Sheeran, O.S.B., Procurator & Business Mgr.

Legal Holdings or Titles: *Benedictine University,* Lisle, IL; *Benet Academy,* Lisle, IL; *Benedictine Chinese Mission,* Lisle, IL; *Slav Mission ,* Lisle, IL; *King of Martyrs Priory,* Fifield, WI; *St. Scholastica Mission House, Inc. ,* Naperville, IL; *St. Procopius Abbey Endowment,* Lisle, IL.

Bishops 1; Priests 35; Brothers 16; Oblates 3.

Represented in the Archdiocese of Denver and in the Dioceses of Alexandria, Joliet and Superior. Also in Taiwan.

St. Gregory's Abbey: Shawnee, OK 74804. Tel: 405-878-5491; Fax: 405-878-5189.

Monastery founded in 1875 and raised to an Abbey in 1896.

Legal Title: *Benedictine Fathers of Sacred Heart Mission, Inc.* Rt. Rev. Charles Massoth, O.S.B., Resigned Abbot; Rt. Rev. Philip Berning, O.S.B., Resigned; Rt. Rev. Adrian Vorderlandwehr, O.S.B., Resigned; Rt. Rev. Martin Lugo, O.S.B., Abbot; Very Rev. Patrick McCool, O.S.B., Prior Rev. Joachim Spexarth, O.S.B., Subprior.

Properties owned or sponsored: *National Shrine of the Infant of Prague,* Prague, OK; *Mabee-Gerrer Museum of Art,* Shawnee, OK; *St. Gregory's University,* Shawnee, OK.

Ministries in 7 Parishes

Priests 22; Brothers 13; Deacons 2.

Represented in the Archdiocese of Oklahoma City and in the Diocese of Tulsa.

St. Leo Abbey: P.O. Box 2350, Saint Leo, FL 33574. Tel: 352-588-8624; Fax: 352-588-5217. Founded in 1889 and raised to an Abbey in 1902. Rev. Simeon J. Thole, O.S.B., Apostolic Admin.

Legal Title: *Order of St. Benedict of Florida, Inc.*

Fathers 13; Brothers 16; Internal Oblates 1

Represented in the Dioceses of Charlotte, and St. Petersburg.

Assumption Abbey: P.O. Box A, Richardton, ND 58652. Tel: 701-974-3315.

Founded in 1893 and raised to an Abbey in 1903. Rt. Rev. Patrick Moore, O.S.B., Abbot; Rt. Rev. Lawrence Wagner, O.S.B., Resigned Abbot; Rt. Rev. Robert West, O.S.B., Resigned Abbot; Very Rev. Valerian Odermann, O.S.B., Prior; Bro. Basil Kirsch, O.S.B., Subprior; Bro. Alban Petesch, O.S.B., Formation Dir.

Priests 34; Brothers 23.

Properties owned or sponsored: Abbey; Dependent Priory; Parishes 8; Chaplaincies 4; Indian Mission.

Represented in the Dioceses of Bismarck, Fargo, Great Falls and Indianapolis. Also in Colombia.

St. Bede Abbey: Peru, IL 61354. Tel: 815-223-3140.

Monastery founded and raised to an Abbey in 1910. Rt. Rev. Marion Balsavich, O.S.B., Resigned Abbot; Rt. Rev. Roger Corpus, O.S.B., Abbot; Very Ven. Nathaniel Grossman, O.S.B., Prior; Very Rev. Claude Peifer, O.S.B., Subprior.

Priests 28; Brothers 6

Legal Title: *The Benedictine Society of Saint Bede.*

Properties owned or sponsored: Parishes 5.

Represented in the Archdiocese of Chicago and in the Diocese of Peoria.

St. Martin's Abbey: 5300 Pacific Ave. S.E., Lacey, WA 98503-1297.

Monastery founded in 1895 and raised to an Abbey in 1914. Rt. Rev. Neal G. Roth, O.S.B.; Rt. Rev. Conrad R. Rausch, O.S.B., Resigned Abbot; Rt. Rev. Adrian Parcher, O.S.B., Resigned Abbot; Very Revs. Alfred J. Hulscher, O.S.B., Prior; Rev. Nicholas Rausch, O.S.B., Subprior.

Legal Holdings or Titles: *St. Martin's Abbey; St. Martin's College.*

Priests 26; Brothers 11.

Represented in the Archdiocese of Seattle, and the Dioceses of San Bernadino, Spokane and Yakima.

Holy Cross Abbey: P.O. Box 1510, Canon City, CO 81215-1510. Tel: 719-275-8631.

Founded in 1886 and raised to an Abbey in 1925. Rt. Rev. Kenneth Hein, O.S.B., Abbot; Rev. Ignatius Smith, O.S.B., Prior.

Fathers 12; Brothers 4; Oblates 1.

Parishes 3; Chaplaincies 2; Missions 1.

Represented in the Archdiocese of Portland in Oregon and the Dioceses of Colorado Springs and Pueblo.

St. Anselm Abbey: 100 St. Anselm Dr., Manchester, NH 03102-1310. Tel: 603-641-7000; Fax: 603-641-7267.

Monastery founded in 1889 and raised to an Abbey in 1927. Rt. Rev. Matthew K. Leavy, O.S.B., Abbot; Most Rev. Joseph J. Gerry, O.S.B., 3rd Abbot, Tenth Bishop of Portland, ME; Rt. Rev. Gerald F. McCarthy, O.S.B., 2nd Abbot, Retired; Very Rev. William J. Sullivan, O.S.B., Prior; Very Rev. Peter J. Guerin, O.S.B., Subprior.

Legal Title: *Order of Saint Benedict of New Hampshire*

Bishops 1; Abbots 2; Fathers 31; Brothers 7.

Represented in the Archdiocese of San Francisco and the Diocese of Manchester.

St. Andrew Abbey: 10510 Buckeye Rd., Cleveland, OH 44104. Tel: 216-721-5300.

Founded in 1922 and raised to an Abbey in 1934. Rt. Rev. Roger Gries, O.S.B., Abbot; Very Rev. Anselm Zupka, O.S.B., Prior; Ven. Bro. Peter Ancell, O.S.B., Subprior.

Legal Holdings or Titles: *Benedictine Order of Cleveland; Benedictine High School.*

Priests 25; Brothers 11; Simple Vows 2.

Abbeys 1; Parishes 2; High School; Chaplaincies 5.

Represented in the Dioceses of Cleveland and Great Falls-Billings.

St. Maur Priory: 4615 N. Michigan Rd., Indianapolis, IN 46228. Tel: 317-925-9095. Very Rev. Charles W. Henry, O.S.B., Prior.

Priests 2; Professed Brothers 4.

Represented in the Archdiocese of Indianapolis.

Holy Trinity Monastery: P.O. Box 990, Butler, PA 16003. Tel: 724-287-4461. Rt. Rev. Leo R. Schlosser, O.S.B., Hegumen.

Monks 8.

Represented in the Byzantine Archdiocese of Pittsburgh.

Benedictine Priory: P.O. Box 13577, 6502 Seawright Dr., Savannah, GA 31406. Tel: 912-356-3520; Fax: 912-356-3527. Very Rev. Jude W. Brady, O.S.B., Prior.

Founded 1877, dependent priory of St. Vincent Archabbey, Latrobe, PA.

Priests 7; Brothers 3.

High Schools 1.

Represented in the Diocese of Savannah.

Woodside Priory: 302 Portola Rd., Portola Valley, CA 94028. Tel: 650-851-8220. Founded in 1956, erected as Conventual Priory 1958, became a dependent Priory upon St. Anselm's Abbey, Manchester, NH, 1976. Very Rev. Martin J. Mager, O.S.B., Supr.

Priests 4; Brothers 1.

Legal Title: *Benedictine Fathers of the Priory, Inc.*

High Schools 1; Middle Schools 1.

Represented in the Archdiocese of San Francisco.

Benedictine Abadia de San Antonio Abad: P.O. Box 729, Humacao, PR 00792. Tel: 787-852-1616; 852-1766; Fax: 787-852-1920. Rt. Rev. Oscar Rivera, O.S.B., Abbot; Rev. Eduardo Torrellas, O.S.B., Prior; Bro. Aristides Pacheco, Subprior.

Monastery founded in 1947 and became an abbey in 1984.

Priests 10; Brothers 8.

Mary Mother of the Church Abbey: 12829 River Rd., Richmond, VA 23233-7206. Tel: 804-784-3508; Fax: 804-784-2214. Community founded in 1911 and became an Abbey in 1989. Rt. Rev. Benedict R.

McDermott, O.S.B., Abbot & Novice Master; Rev. Donald F. Scales, O.S.B., Prior.
Priests 8; Brothers 6; Novices 5.
Abbeys 1; Chaplaincies 3; High Schools 1.
Legal Holdings: *Benedictine High School of Richmond; Mary Mother of the Church Abbey.*
Represented in the Diocese of Richmond.

Swiss-American Congregation

Founded by Pope Pius IX, 1870, and Pope Leo XIII, April 5, 1881.
The Abbeys and Priories belonging to this Federation are as follows:

St. Meinrad Archabbey: *Secretary to the Archabbot,* St. Meinrad, IN 47577. Tel: 812-357-6611; Fax: 812-357-6551.
Founded 1854; raised to an Abbey in 1870. Rt. Rev. Lambert Reilly, O.S.B., Archabbot; Rt. Rev. Bonaventure Knaebel, O.S.B., Retired Archabbot; Very Rev. Tobias Colgan, O.S.B., Prior.
Archbishops 1; Priests 89; Brothers 34; Novices 2.
Parishes 18; Schools of Theology 1; Chaplaincies 10.
Represented in the Archdioceses of Hartford, Indianapolis, Washington and in the Dioceses of Arlington, Baton Rouge, Belleville, Charleston, Evansville, Gary, Helena, Little Rock, Owensboro, Phoenix, Sioux Falls, and Springfield-Cape Girardeau.

Conception Abbey: Conception, MO 64433. Tel: 660-944-2211; Fax: 660-944-2800.
Founded December 8, 1873; Abbey April 5, 1881. Rt. Rev. Gregory Polan, O.S.B., Abbot; Very Rev. Kenneth Reichert, O.S.B., Prior; Bro. Bernard Montgomery, O.S.B., Subprior.
Legal Title: *Conception Abbey, Inc.*
Archbishops 1; Fathers 49; Brothers 19.
Parishes 13; Seminary College 1; Chaplaincies 6.
Represented in the Dioceses of Cheyenne, Dodge City, Jefferson City, Kansas City-St. Joseph, Salina and Springfield-Cape Girardeau.

Mount Michael Abbey: 22520 Mount Michael Rd., Elkhorn, NE 68022-3400. Tel: 402-289-2541; Fax: 402-289-4539. Rt. Rev. Theodore Wolff, O.S.B., Abbot; Bro. Jerome Kmiecik, Prior; Rev. Michael Liebl, O.S.B., Subprior.
Legal Holdings & Titles: *Benedictine Fathers, Inc.; Mount Michael Benedictine High School,* Elkhorn, NE; *Mt. Michael Foundation, Inc.*
Fathers 15; Brothers 9.
Monks serve & staff: Parishes 3.
Represented in the Archdiocese of Omaha and the Diocese of Pueblo.

Subiaco Abbey: Subiaco, AR 72865. Tel: 501-934-4295; Fax: 501-934-4328. Rt. Rev. Jerome Kodell, O.S.B., Abbot; Rev. David Bellinghausen, O.S.B., Prior; Bro. Ephrem O'Bryan, O.S.B., Subprior.
Legal Title: *Subiaco Abbey,* Subiaco, AR 72865.
Fathers 29; Perpetually Professed Brothers 29; Temporarily Professed Brothers 3.
Properties staffed or sponsored: Parishes 11; High School 1; Missions 1.
Represented in the Dioceses of Fort Worth and Little Rock. Also in Belize City-Belmopan.

St. Joseph Abbey: St. Benedict, LA 70457. Tel: 504-892-1800. Rt. Rev. Patrick Regan, O.S.B., Abbot; Very Rev. Justin Brown, O.S.B., Prior; Rev. Matthew R. Clark, O.S.B., Subprior.
Fathers 25; Brothers 16; Novices 3.
Legal Holdings: *St. Joseph Seminary College,* St. Benedict, LA.
Parishes 4; Novitiates 3; Seminary College 1.
Represented in the Archdiocese of New Orleans.

Mt. Angel Abbey: St. Benedict, OR 97373. Tel: 503-845-3030; Fax: 503-845-3594.
Founded on Oct. 30, 1882, from Engelberg in Switzerland and raised to an abbey on March 24, 1904. Rt. Rev. Joseph Wood, O.S.B., Abbot; Very Rev. Paul Thomas, O.S.B., Prior; Very Rev. Paschal Cheline, O.S.B., Subprior.
Legal Holdings or Titles: *Our Lady of the Angels,* Cuernavaca, Morelos, Mexico.
Finally Professed Monks: Priests 49; Brothers 23.
Temporarily Professed Monks: Brothers 12; Novices 7.

Marmion Abbey: 850 Butterfield Rd., Aurora, IL 60504. Tel: 630-897-7215.
Founded as Dependent Priory of St. Meinrad's Abbey, June 20, 1943; Abbey since March 21, 1947. Rt. Rev. Vincent de Paul Bataille, O.S.B., Abbot; Rt. Rev. Gerald Benkert, O.S.B., Abbot Emeritus; Rt. Rev. David J. Cyr, O.S.B., Abbot Emeritus. Very Rev. Kenneth Theisen, O.S.B., Prior; Rev. Joel Rippinger, O.S.B., Subprior.
Priests 31; Brothers 16.
Properties staffed or sponsored: Parishes 2; High Schools 2.
Represented in the Diocese of Rockford. Also in Quetzaltenango, Guatemala.

St. Benedict's Abbey: Benet Lake, WI 53102. Tel: 414-396-4311.
Monastery founded in 1945 and raised to an Abbey in 1952. Very Rev. Edmund Boyce, O.S.B., Admin.; Rt. Rev. Andrew Garber, O.S.B., Abbot Resigned; Rt. Rev. Robert Schoofs, O.S.B., Abbot Resigned; Rt. Rev. Leo Ryska, O.S.B., Abbot Resigned; Very Rev. Henry Nurre, O.S.B., Prior.
Legal Titles: *Benedictine Monks, Inc.; St. Benedict's Home Missionary Society.*
Priests 10; Brothers 11.
Represented in the Archdiocese of Milwaukee.

Glastonbury Abbey: 16 Hull St., Hingham, MA 02043. Tel: 781-749-2155; Fax: 781-749-7236. Rt. Rev. Nicholas J. Morcone, O.S.B., Abbot.
Property owned: *Lincoln School Apartments for the Elderly & Handicapped,* Hingham, MA.
Monks in Solemn Vows 11; Temporary Vows 2; Internal Oblate 1.
Represented in the Archdiocese of Boston.

Blue Cloud Abbey: P.O. Box 98, Marvin, SD 57251-0098. Tel: 605-398-9200; Fax: 605-398-9201.
Monastery founded June 24, 1950; raised to a Priory August 5, 1952; raised to an Abbey March 21, 1954. Rt. Rev. Thomas Hillenbrand, O.S.B., Abbot. Retired Abbots: Rt. Rev. Alan Berndt, O.S.B.; Rt. Rev. Denis Quinkert, O.S.B.; Rev. George Lyon, O.S.B., Prior.
Legal Title: *Blue Cloud Abbey, Inc.*
Priests 23; Brothers 21.
Represented in the Diocese of Sioux Falls. Also in Guatemala.

Corpus Christi Abbey: HCR 2, Box 6300, Sandia, TX 78383. Tel: 361-547-3257; Fax: 361-547-5184. Rt. Rev. Louis Hacker, O.S.B., Abbot; Bro. Simon Huggins, O.S.B., Prior.
Fathers 8; Professed Brothers 12.
Property owned: *Benedictine Retreat Center,* Sandia, TX.
Represented in the Diocese of Corpus Christi.

Prince Of Peace Abbey: 650 Benet Hill Rd., Oceanside, CA 92054. Tel: 760-430-1305; 430-1306. Rt. Rev. Charles Wright, O.S.B., Abbot.; Rt. Rev. Claude Ehringer, O.S.B., Abbot (Retired); Very Rev. Sharbel Ewen, O.S.B., Prior.
Fathers 11; Brothers 13; Postulants 3.

St. Benedict Abbey: 252 Still River Rd., P.O. Box 67, Still River-Harvard, MA 01467. Tel: 978-456-3221; Fax: 978-456-8181. Rt. Rev. Gabriel Gibbs, O.S.B., Abbot; Very Rev. Xavier Connelly, O.S.B., Prior.
Priests 8; Brothers 10; Oblates 1.
Represented in the Diocese of Worcester.

Congregation of St. Ottilien For Foreign Missions

St. Paul's Abbey: Newton, NJ 07860. Tel: 973-383-2470; Fax: 973-383-5782. (Benedictine Missionaries)
Monastery established March 15, 1924; elevated to an Abbey June 9, 1947. Rt. Rev. Joel P. Macul, O.S.B., Abbot; Rt. Rev. Justin E. Dzikowicz, O.S.B., Resigned Abbot; Rt. Rev. Augustine J. Hinches, O.S.B., Resigned Abbot.
Solemnly professed monks 12 (10 priests).
Represented in the Diocese of Paterson.

Christ The King Priory - Benedictine Mission House: Schuyler, NE 68661. Tel: 402-352-2177; Fax: 402-352-2176. Revs. Germar Neubert, O.S.B., Prior; Volker Futter, O.S.B.; Herman Kornbrust, O.S.B.; Thomas Leitner, O.S.B.
Fathers 4; Brothers 4.
Represented in the Archdiocese of Omaha.

Congregation of The Annunciation

St. Andrew's Abbey: Valyermo, CA 93563. Tel: 661-944-2178. Rt. Rev. Francis Benedict, O.S.B., Abbot; Revs. Simon O'Donnell, O.S.B., Prior; John Bosco Stoner, O.S.B., Subprior.
Monks solemn vows 20; Simple vows 3; Novices 1.
Represented in the Archdiocese of Los Angeles.

Houses Not In Congregations

Mount Saviour Monastery: 231 Monastery Rd., Pine City, NY 14871-9787. Tel: 607-734-1688; Fax: 607-734-1689. E-mail: msaviour@servtech.com
Monastery founded in 1950, raised to Independent Priory 1957. Very Rev. Martin Boler, O.S.B., Prior Rev. James Cronin, O.S.B., Subprior.
Professed Monks 16; Oblates 1.
Represented in the Diocese of Rochester.

Weston Priory (1953): 58 Priory Hill Rd., Weston, VT 05161. Tel: 802-824-5409; Fax: 802-824-3573. Very Rev. Richard Iaquinto, O.S.B., Prior.
Monks 15.
Represented in the Diocese of Burlington.

Camaldolese Benedictine Congregation

(Congregatio Camaldulensis Ordinis Sancti Benedicti)

General Motherhouse: *The Sacred Hermitage and Monastery of Camaldoli,* Arezzo, Italy. Most Rev. Emanuele Bargellini, O.S.B.Cam., Prior Gen.

U.S. Foundation (1958): *New Camaldoli Hermitage,* 62475 Coast Hwy. One, Big Sur, CA 93920. Tel: 831-667-2456. Very Rev. Daniel Hoffman, O.S.B.Cam., Prior.
Fathers 15; Professed Brothers 10.
Represented in the Dioceses of Monterey and Oakland.

English Benedictine Congregation

St. Anselm's Abbey: 4501 S. Dakota Ave. N.E., Washington, DC 20017. Tel: 202-269-2300; Fax: 202-269-2312. Rt. Rev. Aidan Shea, O.S.B., Abbot.
Legal Title: *Benedictine Foundation at Washington DC*
Solemnly Professed Monks 24.

Abbey of St. Gregory the Great: Cory's Ln., Portsmouth, RI 02871. Tel: 401-683-2000; Fax: 401-683-5888. Rt. Rev. Mark Serna, O.S.B., Abbot; Rt. Rev. Matthew Stark, O.S.B., Abbot Emeritus; Very Rev. Ambrose Wolverton, O.S.B., Prior.
Choir Religious 16.

Abbey of St. Mary and St. Louis: 500 S. Mason Rd., St. Louis, MO 63141-8500. Tel: 314-434-2557; Fax: 314-434-0795.
Founded as a dependent Priory 1955, granted independence 1973, raised to status of Abbey 1989. Rt. Rev. W. Thomas Frerking, O.S.B., Abbot.
Solemnly professed monks 17 (13 priests).
Simply professed monks 5; Novices 1; Oblates 1.

Benedictines—Sylvestrine Congregation

(Monachorum Silvestrinorum, O.S.B.)

General Motherhouse: Rome, Italy, S. Stefano del Cacco 26. Rt. Rev. Andrew Pantaloni, O.S.B., Abbot Gen.

Foundations in U.S. (1910): *Saint Benedict Priory,* 2711 E. Drahner Rd., Oxford, MI 48370. Tel: 248-628-2249. Very Rev. Daniel Homan, O.S.B., Conventual Prior, *St. Sylvester Monastery,* 17320 Rosemont Rd., Detroit, MI 48219. Tel: 313-532-6064. *Holy Face Monastery,* 1697 State Hwy. S-3, Clifton, NJ 07012. Tel: 201-778-1177.
Brothers 5; Priests 9.
Represented in the Archdiocese of Detroit and in the Diocese of Paterson.

Olivetan Benedictines

(Congregatio Sanctae Mariae Montis Oliveti Ordinis Sancti Benedicti)

General Motherhouse: *The Archabbey of Monte Oliveto Maggiore,* Monte Oliveto, Siena, Italy. Most Rev. Michelangelo M. Tiribilli, O.S.B., Abbot Gen.

U.S. Foundations: *Holy Trinity Monastery:* P.O. Box 298, St. David, AZ 85630. Tel: 602-720-4642. Revs. Henri Capdeville O.S.B., Prior; Alcuin Almasy, O.S.B.; Lawrence Fedor, O.S.B.; Alexander Mills, O.S.B.
Solemnly Professed 7; Postulants 1.
Represented in the Diocese of Tucson.

Our Lady of Guadalupe Abbey: P.O. Box 1080, Pecos, NM 87552-1080. Tel: 505-757-6415. Order of St. Benedict: Rt. Rev. James Liprie, O.S.B., Abbot; Rev. Paul Meaden, O.S.B., Claustral Prior.
Priests 9; Brothers 5.
Represented in the Archdiocese of Santa Fe.

Benedictine Monastery of Hawaii: 67-290 Farrington Hwy., P.O. Box 490, Waialua, HI 96791. Tel: 808-637-7887; Fax: 808-637-8601. Rev. David Barfknecht, O.S.B., Supr.
Priests 3; Brothers 2.

Benedictines Subiaco Congregation

Monastery of Christ in the Desert (1966): Abiquiu, NM 87510. Tel: 505-470-4515. Independent 1983; Abbey 1996. Rt. Rev. Philip Lawrence, O.S.B., Abbot.
Monks 51.
Represented in the Archdioceses of Chicago & Santa Fe. Also in Mexico.

Saint Mary's Monastery (1987): P.O. Box 345, Petersham, MA 01366. Tel: 978-724-3350. Dependent Monastery 1987. Rev. Dom Anselm Atkinson, O.S.B., Supr.
Monks 6
Represented in the Diocese of Worcester.

[0220] (S.S.S.)—CONGREGATION OF THE BLESSED SACRAMENT

(Congregatio Sanctissimi Sacramenti)

General Motherhouse: 46 Via Giovanni Battista de Rossi, Rome 00161, Italy. Very Rev. Fiorenzo Salvi, S.S.S., Supr. Gen.

Province of St. Ann (1931): 5384 Wilson Mills Rd., Cleveland, OH 44143. Tel: 440-442-6311. Very Rev. Anthony Schueller S.S.S., Prov.; Rev. Edward Stapleton, S.S.S., Consultor & Prov. Treas.; Consultors: Revs. Ernest Falardeau S.S.S., Vicar Provincial; Eugene LaVerdiere, S.S.S., Consultor for Formation; Michael Arkins, S.S.S.
Bishops 1; Priests 56; Permanent Deacons 1; Clerics 1; Brothers 18.
Properties staffed or owned: Parishes 8; Seminary 1; Community Houses 9; Novitiate 1.
Represented in the Archdioceses of Chicago, New York, San Antonio and Santa Fe and in the Dioceses of Cleveland, Green Bay, Galveston-Houston and Salt Lake City.

[0230] (Er. Cam.)—CAMALDOLESE HERMITS OF THE CONGREGATION OF MONTE CORONA
(Eremitae Camaldulenses Congregationis Montis Coronae)

General Motherhouse: *Sacro Eremo Tuscolano* 00044-Frascati (Roma), Italy. Rt. Rev. Lanfranco Longhi, Er. Cam., Father Major.
U.S. Foundation (1959): *Holy Family Hermitage,* 1501 Fairplay Rd., Bloomingdale, OH 43910-7971. Tel: 740-765-4511. Very Rev. Basil Corriere, Er. Cam., Prior.
Hermit Priests 2; Professed 2.
Represented in the Diocese of Steubenville.

[0240] (O.S.CAM.)—CAMILLIAN FATHERS AND BROTHERS or ORDER OF ST. CAMILLUS
(Order of the Servants of the Sick)
(Ordo Ministrantium Infirmis)

General Motherhouse: *Casa Generalizia,* Ministri degli Infermi, C.P. 643 00100, Roma Centro, Italy. Most. Rev. Angelo Brusco, O.S.Cam., Supr. Gen.; Very Rev. Richard O'Donnell, O.S.Cam., Vicar Gen.; Rev. Laurent Zougrana, O.S.Cam., Sec. of Formation; Rev. Anselmo Zambotti, O.S.Cam., Sec. of Missions; Rev. Ademar Rover O.S.Cam., Sec. of Ministry.
North American Province (1923): *Provincialate,* 10101 W. Wisconsin Ave., Wauwatosa, WI 53226. Tel: 414-259-4511; Fax: 414-258-4707. Very Rev. William F. Cronin, O.S.Cam., Prov.; Revs. Louis Lussier, O.S.Cam., Vicar Prov.; James Francis Kovarik, O.S.Cam., Asst. Prov.; Stephen E. Braddock, O.S.Cam., Ph.D, Chm. Bd.-St. Camillus Campus; Bro. Thomas Farrell, O.S.Cam.
Legal Titles: *St. Camillus Nursing Home,* Whitinsville, MA; *St. Camillus Institute,* Whitinsville, MA; *St. Camillus Health Center Inc.,* Wauwatosa, WI; *St. Camillus Institute,* Wauwatosa, WI; *San Camillo, Inc.,* Wauwatosa, WI; *St. Camillus Ministries Inc.,* Wauwatosa, WI; *St. Camillus Ministries Inc.,* Milwaukee, WI; *St. Camillus Formation House,* St. Francis, WI; *St. Camillus Communities Inc.,* Wauwatosa, WI.
Fathers 14; Professed Brothers 6; Temporary Professed 1; Novices 4.
Represented in the Archdiocese of Milwaukee and the Dioceses of Madison and Worcester.

[0250] (C.R.L.)—CANONS REGULAR OF THE LATERAN
(Ordo Canonicorum Regularium S. Augustini Congregations Ss. Salvatoris Lateranensis)

General House: *Curia Generalizia dei Canonicio Regolari Lateranensi,* Piazza S. Pietro in Vincoli, 4A 00184, Roma, Italy.
United States: *Canons Regular of the Lateran,* 2317 Washington Ave., Bronx, NY 10458. Tel: 212-295-9600. Rev. Jose L. Biain, C.R.L., Supr. Tel: 212-994-1477.
Priests 6; Brothers 4.
Represented in the Archdiocese of New York and in the Diocese of Arecibo.

[0260] (O.C.D.)—DISCALCED CARMELITE FRIARS
(Ordo Carmelitarum Discalceatorum)

Founded Mt. Carmel, Palestine in the 13th Century.
Generalate: *Carmelitani Scalzi,* Corso d'Italia, 38 00198, Rome, Italy. Very Rev. Camilo Maccise, O.C.D., Supr. Gen.
California-Arizona Province (1983): *Provincial House,* 926 E. Highland Ave., P.O. Box 2178, Redlands, CA 92373. Tel: 909-793-0424; Fax: 909-335-1304. Very Rev. Stephen Watson, O.C.D., Prov.
Legal Title: *Discalced Carmelite Province of California*.
Fathers 32; Brothers 2; Students 8; Novices 5; Postulants7.
Properties owned, staffed, or sponsored: Parishes 4; Retreat House; Novitiate; House of Studies; House of Prayer; Institute of Spirituality.
Represented in the Archdioceses of Los Angeles, Portland, Seattle and the Dioceses of San Jose, San Bernardino, Santa Rosa and Tucson.
Province of St. Therese of Oklahoma (1935): *Provincial House-Monastery of Marylake,* 5151 Marylake Drive, Little Rock, AR 72206-9424. Tel: 501-888-5827. Very Rev. Bonaventure Sauer, O.C.D., Prov.
Fathers 24; Brothers 1; Students of Philosophy 4; Students of Theology 4; Novices 1.
Properties staffed or sponsored: Parishes 3; Community Houses 1; Novitiate 1; Student House 1.
Represented in the Archdioceses of San Antonio, New Orleans and Oklahoma City and in the Dioceses of Dallas and Little Rock.
Washington Province of the Immaculate Heart of Mary (1947): *Discalced Carmelites-Prov. Office,* 1233 S. 45th St., Milwaukee, WI 53214-3693. Tel: 414-672-7212; Fax: 414-672-3138. Very Rev. Jude Peters, O.C.D., Prov.
Fathers 56; Brothers 12; Temporary Professed Brothers 8; Novices 3.
Properties owned or sponsored: Community Houses 7.
Represented in the Archdioceses of Boston, Chicago, Milwaukee, Washington and the Diocese of Wheeling-Charleston. Also in Nairobi, Kenya.
Polish Province of the Holy Spirit, Poland (1949): *Monastery of Our Lady of Mt. Carmel,* 1628 Ridge Rd., Munster, IN 46321. Tel: 219-838-7111; Fax: 219-838-7214. Rev. Sylwan Zielinski, O.C.D., Prior.
Priests 12; Brothers 1.
Represented in the Diocese of Gary.

[0270] (O.CARM.)—CARMELITE FATHERS & BROTHERS
(Ordo Fratrum Beatissimae Virginis Mariae de Monte Carmelo)

General Curia: 00184, Rome, Italy, Via Giovanni Lanza, 138. Most Rev. Joseph Chalmers, O.Carm., Prior Gen.
Province of the Most Pure Heart of Mary (1864): *Carmelite Provincial Office,* 1317 Frontage Rd., Darien, IL 60561. Tel: 630-971-0050; Fax: 630-971-0195. Very Rev. Leo McCarthy, O.Carm., Prior Prov.; Rev. Bernard Bauerle, O.Carm., Prov.-Midwest Commissary; Rev. William Harry, O.Carm., Prov.-Western Commissary; Rev. John Welch, O.Carm., Prov.-Eastern Commissary; Provincial Officers: Revs. Daniel O'Neill, O.Carm., Prov. Treas.; John Welch, O.Carm., Dir. of Education; Councillors: Revs. David Simpson, O.Carm.; Michael Sgarioto, O.Carm.; David McEvoy, O.Carm.; Frederick Tillotson, O.Carm.; Patrick McMahon, O.Carm., Lay Carmelite Dir.; Robert Colaresi, O.Carm., Dir. Little Flower Society; John Malley, O.Carm., Dir.-Carmelite Mission Office; William Harry, O.Carm., Prov. Communications Dir.
Priests 216; Clerics 9; Pre-Novitiates 15; Novices 3; Brothers 19.
Properties owned: Spiritual Centers 4; Shopping-center Chapels 2; Carefree Village, residence for senior citizens, Darien, IL; High Schools 5; Community Houses 38; House of Study 2.
Ministries in 30 Parishes
Represented in the Archdioceses of Boston, Chicago, Kansas City in Kansas, Los Angeles, Louisville, Newark, Washington and in the Dioceses of Galveston-Houston, Joliet, Pittsburgh, Phoenix, Sacramento, Tucson and Venice. Also in Canada and Lima.
Province of St. Elias (1931): P.O. Box 3079, Middletown, NY 10940-0890. Tel: 914-344-2223. Very Rev. Michael T. Driscoll, O.Carm., Prov.
Legal Holdings or Titles: *The Missionary Society of Our Lady of Mt. Carmel of the State of New York; The Carmelite Fathers, Inc. of New York; Carmelite Fathers, Inc. of the Commonwealth of Massachusetts; Mt. Carmel Hermitage; Order of Carmelites of Palm Beach, Inc.; National Shrine of Our Lady of Mount Carmel, Inc.*
Fathers 64; Clerics 7; Brothers 2; Novices 5; Pre-Novices 14.
Properties staffed, owned, or sponsored: Parishes 10; Priories 14; House of Study 2; Retreat Houses 1; Novitiate 1; High Schools 1; Hermitages 2; Shrines 1.
Represented in the Archdioceses of New York and Washington and the Dioceses of Albany, Brooklyn, Greensburg, Palm Beach, Rochester, Sioux Falls, Springfield (MA) and Trenton. Also in Trinidad.
Mt. Carmel Hermitage: R.D. 1, Box 330 C, Bolivar, PA 15923. Tel: 724-238-0423.
Founded in 1970, became dependent upon St. Elias Province in 1995. Revs. Bede Mulligan, O.Carm.; Simeon Marro, O.Carm.
Fathers 2; Novices 1.
Represented in the Diocese of Greensburg.

[0275] (C.M.I.)—CARMELITES OF MARY IMMACULATE
(Congregatio Fratrum Carmelitarum B.V. Mariae Immaculatae)

Founded by Blessed Kuriakose Elias Chavara and Companions at Mannanam, Kerala, India in 1831.
Generalate: *Prior General's House,* P.B. No. 1056 Ernakulam, Cochin 682 011, Kerala, India. Tel: 484-360-137. Very Rev. Alex Ukken, C.M.I., Prior Gen.
North American Headquarters: 21 Nassau Ave., Brooklyn, NY 11222. Tel: 718-388-4866. Rev. John Menonkari, C.M.I., Reg. Coord.
Legal Title: *Carmelites of Mary Immaculate, Inc.*
Priests in the United States and Canada 64.
Ministries in Parishes; Hospitals; Universities; Prisons; Mission to the Syro-Malabar catholics.
Represented in the Archdioceses of New York and Philadelphia and the Dioceses of Beaumont, Brooklyn, Joliet, Lafayette, Lake Charles, Nashville, Syracuse, Toledo and Tyler. Also in Canada.

[0280] (O.CART.)—ORDER OF CARTHUSIANS
(Ordo Cartusianorum)

Motherhouse: *Grande Chartreuse,* St. Pierre de Chartreuse (Isere), France. Rev. Father Marcellin Theeuwes, Supr. Gen.
U.S. Charterhouse of the Transfiguration (1951): *Carthusian Foundation,* 1800 Beartown Rd., Arlington, VT 05250. Tel: 802-362-2550; Fax: 802-362-3584. Rev. Lorenzo Maria T. De La Rosa, Jr., O.Cart., Prior.
In Community 12.
Legal Titles: *Carthusian Foundation in America, Inc.; Carthusian Foundation, Association Fraternelle Romande.*
Represented in the Diocese of Burlington.

[0290] (F.C.)—BROTHERS OF CHARITY
(Congregatio Fratrum Caritate)

General Motherhouse (1807): Via G.B. Pagano 35, C.P. 9082 00167, Rome, Italy. Bro. Rene Stockman, F.C., Supr. Gen.
American District (1963): *District of Our Lady of Charity,* 7720 Doe Ln., Laverock, PA 19038. Bro. Michael Lonsway, District Supr.
Represented in the Archdiocese of Philadelphia.

[0300] (I.C.)—INSTITUTE OF CHARITY
Rosminians
Institutum Charitatis

General Motherhouse: *Collegio Rosmini Via Porta,* Latina 17, Rome, Italy. Very Rev. James Flynn, I.C., Supr. Gen.
U.S. Foundation (1877): 2327 W. Heading Ave., Peoria, IL 61604. Tel: 309-676-6341. Very Rev. Christopher Fitzgerald, I.C., Prov.
Fathers in the U.S. 14.
Novitiate 1; Parishes 8.
Represented in the Dioceses of Peoria and St. Petersburg.

[0305] (I.C.)—INSTITUTE OF CHRIST THE KING-SOVEREIGN PRIEST
Institute of Christ the King-Sovereign Priest
Institutum Christi Regis Summi Sacerdotis

General Motherhouse and House of Formation: *Villa Martelli,* Via di Gricigliano 52, 50069, Sieci, Italy. Rev. Msgr. Gilles Wach, Prior Gen.
U.S. Mailing Address: *Institute of Christ the King-Sovereign Priest:* P.O. Box 5417, McLean, VA 22103-5417.
American Headquarters: *Immaculate Conception Priory,* 26400 CTH U, Cashton, WI 54619-9757. Tel: 608-823-7992; Fax: 608-823-7992. Rev. Timothy E. Svea, Prior/Supr.
Priory of Our Lady of the Sacred Heart: 1204 North Church St., Rockford, IL 61103. Tel: 815-965-5971; Fax: 815-965-6029. Rev. Brian A.T. Bovee, Prior.
Fathers in the U.S.: 2.
Represented in the Dioceses of La Crosse and Rockford.

[0310] (C.F.C.)—CONGREGATION OF CHRISTIAN BROTHERS
(Christian Brothers Institute)

Founded in Ireland in 1802. First foundation in the United States in 1906.
General Motherhouse: *Fratelli Cristiani,* Via Marcantonio Colonna 9, 00192, Rome, Italy. Very Rev. Bro. Edmund M. Garvey, C.F.C., Congregational Leader.
Eastern U.S. American Province (1916): 21 Pryer Terrace, New Rochelle, NY 10804. Tel: 914-636-6194. Bros. James B. Moffett, Prov.; Brian M. Walsh, Deputy Prov.; Consultors: Bros. Kevin G. Cawley; Vincent G. McNally; John P. Mostyn; Mr. Vincent J. Dougherty, Prov. Treas.
Brothers 200.
Properties owned, staffed, or sponsored: Colleges 1; High Schools 18; Grade Schools 4; Migrant Education Center; Care Center; Pastoral Ministry Center.
Represented in the Archdioceses of Boston, Miami, Newark, New York and in the Dioceses of Albany, Brownsville, Charlotte, Jackson, Orlando, Owensboro, Providence, Rochester, St. Petersburg and Venice.

Brother Rice Province: (Western United States): *Brother Rice Provincialate,* 958 Western Ave., Joliet, IL 60435-6954. Tel: 815-723-5464. Bros. Charles J. Gattone, Prov.; James R. Keane, Deputy Prov.; Councillors: Bros. Charles D. McKenna; D. Dominic Murray; Michael S. Segvich; Bros. Paul Ickes, Vocations; George A. Gremley, Prov. Bursar; James McDonald; James A. Houlihan.

Development Office: Christian Brothers Association, P.O. Box 42903, Evergreen Park, IL 60805-0903. Tel: 773-233-2949. Bro. Daniel F. McGovern, Dir.

Legal Title: *The Christian Brothers of Ireland, Inc.*

Properties administered: *Brother Rice High School - The Christian Brothers Institute of Michigan, Inc.,* Bloomfield Hills, MI; *Brother Rice High School, Inc.,* Chicago, IL; *Damien Memorial High School - The Congregation of Christian Brothers of Hawaii, Inc.,* Honolulu, HI; *Palma Junior-Senior High School - The Christian Brothers Institute of California, Inc.,* Salinas, CA; *St. Laurence High School, Inc.,* Burbank, IL.

Brothers under Vows: 92.

Represented in the Archdioceses of Chicago, Detroit, Seattle and in the Dioceses of Helena, Honolulu, Joliet, Monterey and Owensboro. Also in Peru.

[0320] (F.I.C.)—BROTHERS OF CHRISTIAN INSTRUCTION

La Mennais Brothers

(Institutum Fratrum Instructionis Christianae)

General Motherhouse: *Casa Generalizia,* Via della Divina Provvidenz, 44 00166, Rome, Italy. Tel: 66-41-5618; Fax: 66-41-5652. Rev. Jose Antonio Obeso Vega, F.I.C., Supr. Gen.

American Province (1946): *Notre Dame Province-Notre Dame Institute,* P.O. Box 159, Alfred, ME 04002. Tel: 207-324-0067. Bro. Francis Blouin, F.I.C., Prov.

Brothers 45

College 1; High Schools 2; Retreat Center 1.

Represented in the Dioceses of Fall River, Ogdensburg, Portland (ME) and Youngstown.

[0330] (F.S.C.)—BROTHERS OF THE CHRISTIAN SCHOOLS

(Fratres Scholarum Christianarum)

General Motherhouse: *Casa Generalizia,* Via Aurelia 476, CP 9099 00100, Rome, Italy. Bros. John Johnston, F.S.C., Supr. Gen.; Alvaro Rodriquez Echeverria, Vicar Gen.

Christian Brothers Conference: *USA / Toronto Region,* 4351 Garden City Dr., Ste. 200, Landover, MD 20785-2248. Tel: 301-459-9410. Bros. Kevin Gilhooly, F.S.C., Exec. Sec.; Robert Schieler, F.S.C., Dir. Education; Robert Carnaghi, F.S.C., Dir. Formation.

Organizations served by this office: *Regional Conference of USA-Toronto Brothers Provincial; Regional F.S.C. Education Board; Regional F.S.C. Finance Board; Regional F.S.C. Vocation and Formation Board; F.S.C. Publication Board.*

Organizations associated with this office: Christian Brothers Major Superiors.

Properties owned and or sponsored: Bethlehem University of the Holy Land, P.O. Box 9, Bethlehem, via Israel (Incorporated in the State of New Jersey).

Province of Baltimore (1845): *The Provincialate,* Box 29, Adamstown, MD 21710. Tel: 301-874-5188; Fax: 301-874-5674. Bros. Benedict Oliver, F.S.C., Prov., Visitor; Kevin Dalmasse, F.S.C., Auxiliary-Visitor; Timothy Froehlich, F.S.C., Dir. Finance; Patrick Ellis, F.S.C., Dir. Development; Thomas Chadwick, F.S.C., Dir. St. LaSalle Auxiliary; Robert Schaefer, F.S.C., Dir. Vocations; Martin Fahey, F.S.C., Sec.

Brothers 187.

Legal Holdings or Titles: *Christian Brothers of Frederick, Inc.; Ammendale Normal Institute of Prince George's County, Inc.; Christian Brothers Community Support Charitable Trust.*

Represented in the Archdioceses of Baltimore, Newark, Philadelphia and Washington and in the Dioceses of Camden and Pittsburgh.

Brothers Of The Christian Schools (Midwest Province - 1995): *Bro. Francis Carr, FSC,* 7650 S. County Line Rd., Burr Ridge, IL 60521-6950. Tel: 630-323-3725; Fax: 630-323-3779. E-mail: info@cbmidwest.org Bros. Thomas Johnson, F.S.C., Prov. Visitor; Francis Carr, F.S.C., Aux. Visitor; Michael Fehrenbach, F.S.C., Aux. Visitor; Leo F. Hirsch, F.S.C., Dir. Development; Joseph Saurbier, F.S.C., Dir. Finance; Thomas Sullivan, F.S.C., Dir. Vocations/Formation; Nicholas Schumer, F.S.C., Dir. St. La Salle Auxiliary.

Legal Titles: *The Christian Brothers of the Midwest, Inc.; The Christian Brothers of Illinois; Brothers of the Christian Schools of the St. Louis District; The Christian Brothers of Minnesota.*

Brothers 227; Aspirants 2.

Properties owned, staffed, or sponsored: Communities 33; Universities 3; High Schools 15; Middle Schools 2; Elementary Schools 1; Retreat Houses 3; Group Homes 1; Publishing House.

Represented in the Archdiocese of Chicago, St. Louis, St. Paul-Minneapolis, and in the Dioceses of Green Bay, Gaylord, Jefferson City, Joliet, Kansas City-St. Joseph, Memphis, Tulsa and Winona.

Province of New York (1848): *La Salle Provincialate Inc.,* 800 Newman Springs Rd., Lincroft, NJ 07738. Tel: 732-842-7420; Fax: 732-530-3504. Bros. Michael Corry, F.S.C., Prov. & Chm. Bd.; Stephen McCabe, F.S.C., Aux. Prov., Vice Pres.; Robert Carnaghi, F.S.C., Aux. Prov. & Vice Pres.; John Martin, F.S.C., Treas.; Edward Cleary, F.S.C., Sec.; William Martin, F.S.C., Dir.- St. La Salle Auxiliary & Dir.-Devel. Office, P.O. Box 228, Lincroft, NJ 07738. Direct all inquiries to: Bro. Michael Corry, F.S.C., Prov. All of these Brothers constitute the Board Members of St. Joseph Normal Institute, De La Salle Institute, Hillside Hall and De La Salle College.

Brothers 190.

Properties owned, staffed or sponsored: Colleges 1; High Schools 10; Elementary Schools 2; Welfare Schools 1; Community Houses 17; House of Study and Formation 1.

Represented in the Archdioceses of Detroit, Newark, New York and the Dioceses of Albany, Buffalo, Syracuse and Trenton.

Province of Long Island-New England (1957): *Christian Brothers' Center-Provincial Offices,* St. La Salle Auxiliary and Office of Public Information and Development, Narragansett, RI 02882-1314. Tel: 401-789-0244; Fax: 401-783-5303. Bros. Daniel Casey, F.S.C., Acting Prov.; Peter Iorlando, F.S.C., Vocation & Formation Counselor; Eugene O'Gara, F.S.C., Archivist.

Legal Titles: *Brothers of the Christian Schools; Province of the Long Island-New England, Inc.*

Organizations served by this office: The Familiares; Ocean Tides, Inc.

Brothers 94; Aspirants 3; Postulants 1.

Properties owned, staffed, or sponsored: High Schools 5; Elementary Schools 2; Community Houses 10.

Represented in the Dioceses of Brooklyn, Providence and Rockville Centre.

Province of San Francisco (1868): *Brothers of the Christian Schools Provincial Office,* P.O. Box 3720, Napa, CA 94558-0372. Tel: 707-252-0222. Bro. David Brennan, F.S.C., Prov.

Brothers 127.

Properties owned, staffed or sponsored: Colleges 1; High Schools 10; Elementary Schools 1; Community Houses 17; House of Study 1; Retreat & Conference Center 1.

Represented in the Archdioceses of Los Angeles, Portland (OR), San Francisco and the Dioceses of Monterey, Oakland, Sacramento, Santa Rosa and Yakima. Also in India, Italy, Israel, Mexico, Philippines, Kenya, Tijuana, and England.

Province of New Orleans-Santa Fe (1921): *De La Salle - Christian Brothers Provincialate,* 1522 Carmel Dr., Lafayette, LA 70501. Tel: 337-234-1973. Bros. Clarence Fioke, F.S.C., Prov.; James Brown, F.S.C., Auxiliary Prov. & Finance Dir.

Legal Holdings or Titles: *Brothers of the Christian Schools of Lafayette, LA., Inc.; St. La Salle Auxiliary; New Orleans-Santa Fe Retirement Plan; The Christian Brothers of J.K. Mullen High School; J.K. Mullen High School Corporation; Christian Brothers Foundation; Christian Brothers Retirement Trust.*

Brothers 112; Postulants 1.

Properties owned, staffed, or sponsored: College; High Schools 6; Elementary Schools 2.

Represented in the Archdioceses of Denver, New Orleans and Santa Fe and in the Dioceses of El Paso and Lafayette (LA).

[0340] (O.CIST.)—CISTERCIAN FATHERS

(Ordo Cisterciensis)

Headquarters: Piazza del Tempio di Diana 14 I-00153, Rome, Italy. Most Rev. Maurus Esteva, O.Cist., S.T.D., Abbot Gen.

Cistercian Abbey: *Our Lady of Spring Bank,* 17304 Havenwood Rd., Sparta, WI 54656. Tel: 608-269-8138; Fax: 608-269-2800. Web site: www.MonksOnline.org; E-Mail: Porter@MonksOnline.org. Very Rev. Robert Keffer, O.Cist., Prior; Rt. Rev. Blaise J. Fuez, O.Cist., Abbot Emeritus; Rt. Rev. Bernard McCoy, O.Cist., Subprior & Cellarer; Rev. Gregory Norman, O.Cist.

Solemnly Professed 4; Simply Professed 1; Postulants 2.

Cistercian Monastery: *Our Lady of Dallas,* 1 Cistercian Rd., Irving, TX 75039. Tel: 972-438-2044. Rt. Rev. Denis Farkasfalvy, O.Cist., Abbot; Revs. Peter Verhalen, O.Cist., Prior; Bernard Marton, O.Cist., Subprior.

Priests 19.

Staff: Universities 2; Preparatory School 1; Novitiate 1; Chaplaincies 1.

Properties owned: Abbey & Preparatory School.

Represented in the Dioceses of Dallas and Fort Worth.

Cistercian Monastery of Our Lady of Fatima: 564 Walton Ave., Mt. Laurel, NJ 08054. Tel: 609-235-1330. Revs. Lino Parente, O.Cist., Prior; Anselmo Florio, O.Cist.; Maurizio Nicoletti, O.Cist.; Teclezghi Ucbaghiorghis, O.Cist. Established in 1961 as a dependent Monastery of the Congregation of Casamari (Italy).

Property owned: *Fatima House and the Monastery.*

Cistercian Conventual Priory: *St. Mary's Priory,* R.D. No. 1, Box 206, New Ringgold, PA 17960. Tel: 570-943-2645; Fax: 570-943-3035. Very Rev. Luke Anderson, O.Cist., Ph.D., Prior.

Legal Title: *The Cistercian Monastery of Pennsylvania.*

Monks 3.

[0350] (O.C.S.O.)—THE CISTERCIAN ORDER OF THE STRICT OBSERVANCE (TRAPPISTS)

(Ordo Cisterciensium Strictioris Observantiae)

General Motherhouse: *Casa Generalizia,* O.C.S.O., 33 Viale Africa, Rome 00144, Italy. Most Rev. Dom Bernardo Olivera, O.C.S.O., Abbot Gen.

Abbey of Gethsemani (1848): Trappist, KY 40051. Tel: 502-549-3117. Rt. Rev. Damien Thompson, O.C.S.O., Abbot.

Priests 16; Brothers 55.

Abbey of Our Lady of New Melleray (1849): 6500 Melleray Cir., Peosta, IA 52068. Tel: 319-588-2319. Rt. Rev. Brendan Freeman, O.C.S.O., Abbot; Revs. Thomas MacMaster, O.C.S.O., Prior; Neil Paquette, O.C.S.O., Subprior.

Professed Monks 36 (Priests 20).

St. Joseph's Abbey (1825): 167 North Spencer Rd., Spencer, MA 01562-1233. Tel: 508-885-8700; Fax: 508-885-8701. Rt. Rev. Damian Carr, O.C.S.O., Abbot.

Legal Title: *Cistercian Abbey of Spencer, Inc.*

Total in community 84 (Priests 35); Solemnly Professed 76; Simply Professed 4; Novices 3.

Monastery of The Holy Spirit, Inc. (1944): 2625 Hwy. 212 S.W., Conyers, GA 30094. Tel: 770-483-8705; Fax: 770-760-0989. Rt. Rev. M. Basil Pennington, O.C.S.O., Abbot; Rt. Rev. Dom Augustin, O.C.S.O., Retired Abbot.

Professed Monks 46; Priests 28.

Represented in the Archdiocese of Atlanta.

Abbey of Our Lady of Guadalupe (1947): Lafayette, OR 97127. Tel: 503-852-7174; Fax: 503-852-7748. Rt. Rev. Peter McCarthy, O.C.S.O., Abbot; Very Rev. John-Baptist Hasbrouck, O.C.S.O., Prior; Bro. Phillip Wertman, O.C.S.O., Subprior.

Solemnly Professed 34; Priests 16; Simply Professed 1; Novices 2.

Abbey of Our Lady of the Holy Trinity (1947): Huntsville, UT 84317. Tel: 801-745-3784. Rt. Rev. Leander Dosch, O.C.S.O., Abbot.

Priests 12.

Abbey of The Genesee (1951): P.O. Box 900, Piffard, NY 14533. Tel: 716-243-0660. Rt. Rev. John Eudes Bamberger, O.C.S.O., Abbot; Rev. John Denburger, O.C.S.O., Prior; Bro. Anthony Weber, O.C.S.O., Novice Master. Retreat House. Tel: 716-243-2220.

Solemnly Professed 35; Simply Professed 3; Novices 2; Postulants 1; Oblates 1; Professed Priests 13.

Mepkin Abbey (1949): 1098 Mepkin Abbey Road, Moncks Corner, SC 29461. Tel: 843-761-8509; Fax: 843-761-6719. Rt. Rev. Francis Kline, O.C.S.O., Abbot; Bro. Stephen Petronek, O.C.S.O., Prior; Bro. Stan Gumula, O.C.S.O,, Business Mgr.; Rt. Rev. Christian Aidan Carr, O.C.S.O., (Retired Abbot).

Priests 9; Monks in Community 26.

Abbey of Our Lady of the Holy Cross (1950): 901 Cool Spring Ln., Berryville, VA 22611-2700. Tel: 540-955-1425; Fax: 540-955-1356. Rt. Rev. Robert Barnes, O.C.S.O., Abbot.

Legal Title: *Community of Cistercians of the Strict Observance, Inc.*

Solemnly Professed 22; Simply Professed 1; Novices 2; Priests 12.

Assumption Abbey: Rte. 5, Box 1056, Ava, MO 65608. Tel: 417-683-5110; Fax: 417-683-5658. Rev. Mark A. Scott, O.C.S.O., Supr. ad nutum; Rt. Rev. Robert Matter, O.C.S.O., Abbot (Retired); Rt. Rev. Cyprian Harrison, O.C.S.O., Abbot (Retired)

Priests 12; Professed 16.

Abbey of New Clairvaux (1955): *Trappist-Cistercian Abbey,* Vina, CA 96092. Tel: 530-839-2161. Rt. Rev. Thomas X. Davis, O.C.S.O., Abbot.
Legal Title: *Abbey of New Clairvaux, Inc.*
Solemn Vows 19; Simple Vows 1.

St. Benedict's Monastery (1956): 1012 Monastery Rd., Snowmass, CO 81654. Tel: 970-927-3311. Rt. Rev. Joseph Boyle, O.C.S.O., Abbot; Bros. Raymond Roberts, O.C.S.O., Prior; Charles Albanese, O.C.S.O., Subprior.
Professed Monks 15.

[0360] (C.M.F.)—CLARETIAN MISSIONARIES
Missionary Sons of the Immaculate Heart of Mary
(Congregatio Missionariorum Filiorum Immaculati Cordis Beatae Mariae Virginis.)

General Headquarters: Rome, Via Sacro Cuore di Maria 5, Italy. Very Rev. Aquilino Bocos, C.M.F., Supr. Gen.

Western Province: *Provincial Headquarters,* 1119 Westchester Pl., Los Angeles, CA 90019. Tel: 323-734-1824; Fax: 323-737-0301. Revs. Ralph Berg, C.M.F., Prov.
Legal Title: *Claretian Missionaries-Western Province, Inc.* A not-for-profit corporation under the laws of the State of California having as its purpose the support of any Roman Catholic benevolent, charitable, educational or missionary undertakings of the Claretian Missionaries - Western Province, Inc.
Other Corporations: *Dominguez Seminary, Inc.,* Compton, CA; *Claretian Educational and Renewal Center, Inc.,* Los Angeles, CA; *Claretian Tape Ministry, Inc.,* Los Angeles, CA.
Fathers 77; Brothers 8; Students 5; Deacons 1.
Ministries in the following areas: Newman Centers; Parishes; Novitiate; House of Study; Centers for Spanish Speaking; Renewal Centers; Education; Spiritual Direction.
Represented in the Archdioceses of Los Angeles, San Antonio and the Dioceses of Austin, Fresno, Lubbock and Phoenix.

Eastern Province: *Claretian Missionary Hdqtrs.,* 400 N. Euclid Ave., Oak Park, IL 60302. Tel: 708-848-2076; Fax: 708-848-2069. Very Rev. Leonard J. Brown, C.M.F., Prov. Supr.; Revs. Carl J. Quebedeaux, C.M.F., Vicar & Consultor; Mark J. Brummel, C.M.F., Treas. & Consultor; James F. Maloney, C.M.F., Sec. & Consultor; Bruce L. Wellems, C.M.F., Consultor.
Legal Holdings or Titles: *The Congregation of Sons of the Immaculate Heart of Mary of the Eastern Province, Inc.; Claret Center,* Chicago, IL; *Claretian Volunteer Program,* Chicago, IL; *Claretian Associates,* Chicago, IL; *Claretians, Inc.; St. Jude League, Inc.; St. Jude Seminary, Inc.*
Fathers 41; Brothers 4; Novices 4; House of Study 1
Represented in the Archdioceses of Atlanta and Chicago and in the Dioceses of Metuchen and Springfield-Cape Girardeau.

[0370] (S.S.C.)—SOCIETY OF ST. COLUMBAN
(Societas Sancti Columbani pro missionibus ad Exteros)

Central Administration (1918): *St. Columban's,* Grange Rd., Donaghmede, Dublin 13, Ireland. Very Rev. Nicholas Murray, S.S.C., Supr. Gen.
Members 599.

Region of the United States: *Society of St. Columban,* P.O. Box 10, St. Columbans, NE 68056. Tel: 402-291-1920. Very Rev. Brendan O'Sullivan, S.S.C., Dir.; Rev. James J. Hastings, S.S.C., Vice Dir.; Council: Revs. Mark Mengel, S.S.C., Rector - International Theologate; Thomas P. Reynolds, S.S.C., Education Coord.; William Morton, S.S.C.; Charles O'Rourke, S.S.C. Rev. William Sweeney, Reg. Treas.
Legal Titles: *St. Columban's Foreign Mission Society; The Columban Fathers.*
Fathers 108; Student Members and Candidates 3.
Represented in the Archdioceses of Boston, Chicago, Los Angeles, Omaha, and Washington, and in the Dioceses of Brooklyn, Orange, Providence, and San Bernadino.

[0380] (M.C.C.J.)—COMBONI MISSIONARIES OF THE HEART OF JESUS
(Verona Fathers)
Missionarii Comboniani Cordis Jesu
(A Pontifical World Missionary Congregation Of Priests And Brothers)

Founded by Blessed Bishop D. Comboni in 1867. First foundation in United States in 1939.

General Motherhouse: *Missionari Comboniani,* Via Luigi Lilio, 80 00142, Rome, Italy. Very Rev. Manuel Augusto Ferreira, M.C.C.J., Supr. Gen.

North American Province (1950): *Comboni Mission Center,* 8108 Beechmont Ave., Cincinnati, OH 45255-3194. Tel: 513-474-4997; Fax: 513-474-0382. Web site: www.ComboniMissionaries.org; E-Mail: klcomboni@juno.com Revs. Dennis Conway, M.C.C.J., Prov.; Paul Donohue, M.C.C.J., Editor Comboni Mission Newsletter & Comboni Press Feature Service, Joseph Bragotti, M.C.C.J., Mission Office Dir.
Legal Title: *Comboni Missionaries of the Heart of Jesus, Inc.*
Priests 37; Brothers 2; College Students 3; Scholastics 18.
Home Mission Parishes 4; Mission Centers 5.
Represented in the Archdioceses of Chicago, Cincinnati, Los Angeles and Newark.

[0390] (I.M.C.)—CONSOLATA MISSIONARIES
(Institutum Missionum a Consolata)

General Motherhouse: Rome, Viale delle Mura Aurelie, 11, Italy. Very Rev. Peter Trabucco, Supr. Gen.

Headquarters in the U.S.: P.O. Box 5550, 2301 Rte. 27, Somerset, NJ 08875. Tel: 732-297-9191; Fax: 732-940-3121. Rev. Leonard DePasquale, I.M.C., Reg. Supr.
Legal Title: *Consolata Society for Foreign Missions.*
Priests 21; Brothers 5.
Properties owned: Mission Community House 3; House of Studies.
Represented in the Archdiocese of Washington and the Dioceses of Buffalo, Metuchen, and San Bernardino.

[0400] (O.S.C.)—CANONS REGULAR OF THE ORDER OF THE HOLY CROSS
(Crosier Fathers and Brothers)
Canonici Regulares Ordinis Sanctae Crucis (Cruciferi)

Generalate: *Generalatus Ordinis S. Crucis,* Via del Velabro 19 00186, Rome, Italy. Most Rev. Rein Vaanhold, O.S.C., Master Gen.

United States Province: *Province of St. Odilia, Crosier National Headquarters,* 3510 Vivian Ave., Shoreview, MN 55126-3852. Tel: 651-486-7456; Fax: 651-287-1130. Very Rev. Thomas R. Carkhuff, O.S.C., Prov. Provincial Councillors: Revs. Steven Henrich, O.S.C.; Michael Van Sloun, O.S.C.; Timothy Conlon, O.S.C.; Thomas E. O'Brien, O.S.C., Prov. Econome.
Legal Titles: *Crosier Fathers and Brothers Province, Inc.; Canons Regular of the Order of the Holy Cross.*
Bishops 1; Fathers 78; Professed Clerics 6; Brothers 23.
Properties owned, sponsored, or staffed: Monasteries 5; Novitiates 2; Parishes 10; Chaplaincies 5; Foreign Mission 1.
Represented in the Archdioceses of Baltimore, Chicago, Detroit, St. Paul-Minneapolis, and the Dioceses of Duluth, Phoenix and St. Cloud. Also in Tokyo, Japan, Indonesia and the Democratic Republic of the Congo.

[0410] (F.D.P.)—SONS OF DIVINE PROVIDENCE
(Filiorum Divinae Providentiae)

General Motherhouse: Via Etruria 6 00183, Rome, Italy.
Founded in 1893 by Blessed Don Louis Orione. Very Rev. Roberto Simionato, F.D.P., Supr. Gen.

Delegation of Our Lady Queen of the Universe-U.S. Foundation (1953): III Orient Ave., E. Boston, MA 02128. Tel: 617-569-2100; Fax: 617-561-1138. Very Rev. Angelo Quadrini, F.D.P., Supr.
Priests 10.
Properties staffed or owned: Parishes 2; Nursing Home 2; Shrine 1.
Represented in the Archdioceses of Boston and New York and the Diocese of Evansville.

[0420] (S.V.D.)—SOCIETY OF THE DIVINE WORD
(Societas Verbi Divini)

General Motherhouse: *Collegio del Verbo Divino,* Via Dei Verbiti 1, Rome, Italy. Very Rev. Antonio Pernia, S.V.D., Supr. Gen.
Founded 1897, with Headquarters at St. Mary's Mission House (Divine Word Seminary) Techny, Illinois; later separating into four provinces. In 1985 the Eastern and Northern Provinces combined.

Chicago Province (1985): *Province of Blessed Joseph Freinademetz, S.V.D.* Province Center, 1985 Waukegan Rd., P.O. Box 6038, Techny, IL 60082-6038. Tel: 847-272-2700; Fax: 847-272-2517. Very Rev. Stanley Uroda, S.V.D., Prov.; Bro. Dennis Newton, S.V.D., Vice Prov.; Rev. Thomas Griffith, S.V.D., Treas.
Priests 195; Brothers 49; Theologians 43.
Minor Seminarians: College 80; Student Brothers 3; Novices 7; Associates 3.
Properties owned: Theologate; College; Retreat House; House of Studies; Conference Center. Chaplaincies 1; Retirement Homes 2.
Legal Title: *Divine Word Funds, Inc.,* 1835 Waukegan Rd., P.O. Box 6099, Techny, IL 60082-6099. Tel: 847-272-7600. Revs. Thomas Krosnicki, S.V.D., Pres.; Walter Bracken, S.V.D., Delegate Supr.-Missionaries on Leave.
Legal Titles: *Divine Word Missionaries, Inc.; S.V.D. Catholic Universities, Inc.; Divine Word International; Blessed Arnold Charitable Trust.*
Represented in the Archdioceses of Boston, Chicago, Dubuque, Indianapolis, Milwaukee, Newark, St. Louis, Washington and the Dioceses of Pittsburgh, Trenton and Wheeling-Charleston. Also in Canada, Jamaica and the West Indies.

Eastern Province: Amalgamated with Northern Province. See Chicago Province.

Southern Province (1940): *Southern Province of St. Augustine Provincial Residence,* 201 Ruella Ave., Bay St. Louis, MS 39520. Tel: 228-467-4322; 467-3815. Very Rev. Clifton Labbe, S.V.D., Prov.; Rev. Thomas James, S.V.D., Vice. Prov.; Bro. Richard Chanbers, S.V.D., Treas. Address applications for Retreats and Missions to: Rev. William Kelley, S.V.D.
Fathers 51; Brothers 8.
Parishes 23; Mission Stations 3; Elementary Schools 5.
Represented in the Archdiocese of New Orleans and in the Dioceses of Baton Rouge, Biloxi, Galveston-Houston, Jackson, Lafayette (LA) and Little Rock.

Western Province (1964): *Province of St. Therese of the Child Jesus,* 2181 West 25th St. - P.O. Box 77-F, Los Angeles, CA 90007. Tel: 323-735-8130; Fax: 323-735-8122. Very Rev. Eamonn Donnelly, S.V.D., Prov.; Revs. Melvin P. James, S.V.D., Vice Prov.; Gerard O'Doherty, S.V.D., Prov. Treas.
Fathers 51; Brothers 6.
Properties staffed, sponsored, or owned: High Schools 1; Parishes 5; Retreat Centers 1; House of Study 1.
Represented in the Archdiocese of Los Angeles, San Francisco and the Dioceses of Oakland, Orange, and San Bernardino.

[0430] (O.P.)—ORDER OF PREACHERS
Dominicans
Fratres Sacri Ordinis Praedicatorum

Generalitia: *Convento Santa Sabina,* Piazza Pietro d' Illiria, Aventino 00153, Rome, Italy. Most Rev. Timothy J. Radcliffe, O.P., Master of the Order; Very Rev. Carlos A. Azpiroz Costa, O.P., Procurator Gen.

Province of St. Joseph-Eastern Dominican Province (1805): 869 Lexington Ave., New York, NY 10021-6680. Tel: 212-737-5757; Fax: 212-861-4216.
Corporate Title: *Dominican Fathers Province of St. Joseph.* Very Revs. Norman A. Haddad, O.P., Prior Prov.; Kevin D. Robb, O.P., Vicar Prov. & Socius to Prov.; Revs. Albert A. Caprio, O.P., Prov. Econ. Admin.; Terence J. Keegan, O.P., Regent of Studies; John W. Burke, O.P., Dir.-Preaching; Bro. Ignatius Perkins, O.P., Dir.-Health Services; Revs. Matthew F. Morry, O.P., Dir.-Aging Services & Promoter-Rosary; John A. McMahon, O.P., Dir.-Center for Assisted Living; Joseph S. Tortorici, O.P., Dir.-Vocations; John S. Fitzhenry, O.P., Dir.-Continuing Formation; Joseph P. Allen, O.P., Dir.-Dominican Laity; Bro. Thomas Aquinas Dolan, O.P., Sec.-Missions & Dir.-Dominican Foreign Missions; Revs. Michael DeTemple, O.P., Dir.-Social Justice; George L. Concordia, O.P., Promoter-Holy Name Society. Raymond F. Halligan, O.P., Dir. Advancement & Dir.-Dominican Friars' Guild, Inc.; Deserving Poor Boys Priesthood Association, Inc.; St. Jude Dominican Missions, Inc.; St. Martin de Porres Guild, Inc.; Rosary Apostolate, Inc.; Kenneth A. France-Kelly, O.P., Dir.-Rosary Shrine of St. Jude (Washington); Joseph E. Fox, O.P., Dir.-Angelicum Fund.
Fathers 234; Cooperator Brothers 14; Professed Clerics 29; Novices 6.
Properties owned, staffed, or sponsored: Priories 12; Houses 5; Parishes 16; Campus Ministries 2; Colleges 1; House of Study 1; Retreat Houses 1; Novitiates 1; Foreign Missions 1.
Legal Titles: *Retirement Plan and Pension Plan; Dominican Fathers, Province of St. Joseph; Dominican Friars' Guilds, Inc.; Deserving Poor Boys Priesthood Association, Inc.; St. Jude Dominican Missions, Inc.; St. Martin de Porres Guild, Inc.; Dominican Foreign Missions; Handicapped Children's Fund,* Peru; *Rosary Shrine of St. Jude,* (Detroit); *Rosary Apostolate; Angelicum Fund.*
Represented in the Archdioceses of Boston, Cincinnati, Hartford, Louisville, Newark, New York, Washington and the Dioceses of Columbus, Metuchen, Providence, Richmond, and Youngstown.

Province of the Most Holy Name of Jesus-Western Dominican Province (1912): 5877 Birch Ct., Oakland, CA 94618-1626. Tel: 510-658-8722; Fax: 510-658-1061. Very Rev. Daniel Syverstad, O.P., Prior Prov.; Very

Rev. Jordan Bradshaw, O.P., Vicar Prov. & Socius; Revs. Michael Dodds, O.P., Vicar; Donald Bramble, O.P., Dir. Mission Foundation; Christopher Renz, O.P., Student Master & Sec.-Dominican Family; Richard Schenke, O.P., Regent of Studies; Jude Eli, O.P., Dir.-Preaching; Anthony G. Cordeiro, O.P., Treas.

Legal Title: *Province of the Holy Name, Inc.*

Fathers 121; Brothers 8; Professed Clerics 28; Novices 12; Donatus 1.

Parishes 11; Newman Centers/Personal Parishes 9; Retreat House; House of Studies; Novitiate.

Represented in the Archdioceses of Anchorage, Los Angeles, Portland in Oregon, San Francisco, Seattle, and the Dioceses of Norwich, Oakland, Phoenix, Providence, Sacramento, Salt Lake City, San Bernardino, San Diego, San Jose and Tucson. Also in Mexico, Kenya, Germany, Guatemala and Rome.

Province of St. Albert the Great-Central Dominican Province (1939): 1909 S. Ashland Ave., Chicago, IL 60608. Tel: 312-666-3244; Fax: 312-829-8471. Very Revs. Edward M. Ruane, O.P., Prov.; David F. Wright, O.P., Socius, Vicar Prov. – Archivist; Bro. Kevin W. Carroll, O.P., Vicar Prov.; Revs. Louis S. Morrone, O.P., Promoter of Vocations; Dennis C. Woerter, O.P., Promoter of Social Justice; Frank C. Quinn, O.P., Regent; Benjamin J. Russell, O.P., Dir. Society Vocational Support; Thomas J. Johnston, O.P., Prov. Rep. to Dominican Laity; Bede R. Jagoe, O.P., Dir. St. Dominic Mission Society & Shrine of St. Jude; John J. Meany, O.P., Dir. of Dominican Conference Center, 7200 W. Division St., River Forest, IL 60305.

Legal Titles: *Dominicans, Province of St. Albert the Great, U.S.A.; Shrine of St. Jude Thaddeus, Inc.; Society for Vocational Support, Inc.; St. Dominic Mission Society; Dominican Social Action Fund; Dominican Laity; Dominican Central Productions; Fra Angelico Art Foundation; The Bolivian Trust of the Dominicans, Office for Mission Advancement.*

Fathers 177; Professed Clerics 20; Novices 6; Brothers 22.

Properties owned, staffed, or sponsored: Parishes 8; Convents 8; Houses 12; Houses of Studies 2; Novitiate; High Schools 1.

Represented in the Archdioceses of Chicago, Denver, Detroit, Military Services, St. Louis, St. Paul-Minneapolis, Santa Fe and the Dioceses of Dallas, Des Moines, Fort Wayne-South Bend, Grand Rapids, Joliet, Madison, Pueblo, Springfield (IL), Superior, and Winona.

Southern Dominican Province of St. Martin de Porres (1979): 1421 N. Causeway Blvd., Ste. 200, Metairie, LA 70001-4144. Tel: 504-837-2129; Fax: 504-837-6604. Very Revs. Alberto Rodriguez, O.P., Prov.; Carl B. Trutter, O.P., Vicar Prov.; James A. McDonough, O.P., Econ. Admin.; Bruce B. Schultz, O.P., Promoter for Community Life and Permanent Formation; John J. Markey, O.P., Regent of Studies; Henry B. Groover, O.P., Promoter of Vocations.

Legal Holdings or Titles: *Southern Dominican Foundation; Retirement and Community Support Plan, Southern Province, U.S.A.; Shrine of St. Martin de Porres.*

Fathers 108; Professed Clerics 21; Brothers 9; Novices 13.

Properties owned, staffed, or sponsored: Parishes 13; Priories 6; Houses 6.

Represented in the Archdioceses of Los Angeles, Miami, New Orleans, St. Louis, San Antonio, Washington and the Dioceses of Austin, Baton Rouge, Birmingham, Dallas, El Paso, Galveston-Houston, Houma-Thibodaux, Knoxville, Memphis, Nashville, Raleigh, Tyler and Venice.

U.S. Foundation (1926): *Province of Spain,* P.O. Box 279, San Diego, TX 78384. Tel: 361-279-3596. Rev. Benito Retortillo, O.P.

Priests 2.

Represented in the Diocese of Corpus Christi.

[0440] (S.S.E.)—SOCIETY OF SAINT EDMUND

(Societas Sancti Edmundi)

General Motherhouse: *Edmundite Generalate,* 270 Winooski Park, Colchester, VT 05439. Tel: 802-654-3400; Fax: 802-654-3409. Very Rev. Richard M. Myhalyk, S.S.E., Supr. Gen. Councillors: Revs. David G. Cray, S.S.E.; Michael P. Cronogue, S.S.E.; Carroll W. Plourde, S.S.E.; Richard N. Berube, S.S.E.

Legal Titles: *Society of St. Edmund, Inc.*

Bishops 1; Fathers 45; Brothers 6.

Properties owned, staffed, or sponsored: Parishes 13; Missions 1; College 1; Retreat House; Novitiate; Middle School.

Represented in the Archdioceses of Detroit, Mobile, New Orleans and the Dioceses of Burlington, Norwich and Venice. Also Venzuela and France.

[0450] (C.J.M.)—CONGREGATION OF JESUS AND MARY

(Congregatio Jesu et Mariae)

(Eudist Fathers)

General Motherhouse: Via dei Querceti, 15 00184, Rome, Italy. Very Rev. Pierre Drouin, C.J.M., Supr. Gen.

North American Province: 6125 Premiere Ave., Charlesbourg, Quebec G1H 2V9, Canada. Tel: 418-626-6494. Very Rev. Aurele Godbout, C.J.M., Prov.

U.S. Region Eudist Community: 36 Flohr Ave., W. Seneca, NY 14224-1818. Tel: 716-825-4475.

Bishops 1; Fathers 98.

Represented in the Dioceses of Buffalo and San Diego.

[0460] (C.F.P.)—BROTHERS OF THE POOR OF ST. FRANCIS

(Congregatio Fratrum Pauperum)

Motherhouse: Aachen, Germany. Very Rev. Bro. Mark Gastel, C.F.P., Min. Gen.

Province of St. Joseph: *Provincial Office,* 324 Donham Ave. , Cincinnati, OH 45226-2116. Tel: 513-272-6347; Fax: 513-321-3293. Bro. Joel Stern, C.F.P., Prov. Minister.

Professed Brothers 23.

Brothers serve and staff: Development Office 2; High Schools 1; Elementary Schools 6; AIDS Social Service Agency; Homes for Senior Citizens 3; Group Homes; Literacy Program for the Inprisoned.

Brothers' Special Mission: Care & education of neglected youth; elementary & secondary education; human services.

Properties owned: *Morris School for Boys,* Searcy, AR.

Represented in the Archdioceses of Cincinnati, Newark and the Dioceses of Covington, Davenport, El Paso, and Little Rock.

[0470] (O.F.M.CAP.)—THE CAPUCHIN FRIARS

(Ordinis Fratrum Minorum Capuccinorum)

Generalate: *Curia Generalis Ord. Min. Cap.* via Piemonte 70, Rome, Italy 00187. Most Rev. John Corriveau, O.F.M.Cap., General Min.

Province of St. Joseph (1857): 1740 Mt. Elliott Ave., Detroit, MI 48207-3496. Tel: 313-579-2100; Fax: 313-579-2275. Revs. Daniel Fox, O.F.M.Cap., Prov. Minister; Perry McDonald, O.F.M.Cap., Prov. Vicar. Councillors: Rev. Daniel Anholzer, O.F.M.Cap.; Bros. John Scherer, O.F.M.Cap.; Robert Smith, O.F.M.Cap.; Mr. John Kook, Corp. Sec./Treas.; Bros. David Schwab, O.F.M.Cap., Sec.-Religious Affairs; T.L. Auman, O.F.M.Cap., Dir.-Publications; Revs. James Wolf, O.F.M.Cap., Dir.-Archives; Edward Foley, O.F.M.Cap., Dir.-Continuing Education; Richard Hart, O.F.M.Cap., Dir.-Preaching; Revs. Lloyd Thiel, O.F.M.Cap., Dir.-Public Relations/Devel.; James Zelinski, O.F.M.Cap., Dir.-JPE & Mission Sec.; Lester Bach, O.F.M.Cap., Prov. Asst.-Secular Franciscan Order; Bros. Richard Merling, O.F.M.Cap., Dir.-Solanus Guild; Leo Wollenweber, O.F.M.Cap., Vice Postulator-Cause of Ven. Solanus Casey; Rev. Michael H. Crosby, O.F.M.Cap., Corp. Responsibility Agent.

Legal Title: *Province of St. Joseph of the Capuchin Order, Inc.*

Priests 158; Perpetually Professed Lay Friars 45; Professed Friars in Temporary Vows 3.

Parishes, Hospitals, Nursing Homes, Hospices, Prisons, Retreat Centers, Soup Kitchens, Educational Institutions, and Foreign Missions

Represented in the Archdioceses of Chicago, Detroit, Los Angeles, Milwaukee, New York, St. Paul-Minneapolis and the Dioceses of Brooklyn, Fort Wayne-South Bend, Great Falls-Billings, Green Bay, LaCrosse, Las Cruces, Madison, Marquette, Oakland, Pittsburgh, Saginaw and San Bernardino. Also the vicariate of Bluefiels, Nicaragua and in dioceses of Panama, Guam, Japan, Australia, Costa Rica, Honduras and Brisbane.

Province of St. Augustine (1873): *Provincial Office,* 220 37th St., Pittsburgh, PA 15201. Tel: 412-682-6011; Fax: 412-682-0506. Very Rev. John Bednarik, O.F.M.Cap., Definitor Gen.; Very Rev. Paul Kuppe, O.F.M.Cap., Prov. Min.; Revs. John Pavlik, O.F.M.Cap., Vicar Prov.; John Petrikovic, O.F.M.Cap., Exec. Sec. & Sec. Communications; Definitors: Revs. Vernon Busch, O.F.M.Cap.; John Harvey, O.F.M.Cap.; Donald Lippert, O.F.M.Cap.; Richard Lubomski, Sec. Finances; Brendon Malloy, O.F.M.Cap., Communications/Newsletter.

Legal Title: *Province of St. Augustine of the Capuchin Order; Headquarters of Capuchin Franciscan Volunteer Corps., Inc.; Augustine Province of the Capuchin Order; National Headquarters of Archconfraternity of Christian Mothers; Mission Office of Seraphic Mass Association; Secular Franciscan Order of St. Augustine, Province; Capuchin Friars Sick and Elderly Trust Fund; St. Fidelis, Inc.; Capuchin Friars Formation and Education Trust Fund.*

Bishops 1; Priests 131; Brothers 37; Professed in Formation 8; Novices 3; Postulants 3.

Properties owned, staffed, or sponsored: Parishes 29; Formation Houses 2; Novitiate 1; Friaries 17; Postulancy Houses 3; Hospital Chaplains 12; Military Chaplain 1; Foreign Missions 2.

Represented in the Archdioceses of Baltimore, Philadelphia and Washington and in the Dioceses of Altoona-Johnstown, Cleveland, Columbus, Greensburg, Harrisburg, Pittsburgh and Wheeling-Charleston. Also in Papua New Guinea and Puerto Rico.

Province of St. Mary (1952): *St. Conrad Friary,* Attn: Rev. Jerome McHugh, O.F.M.Cap. 30 Gedney Park Dr., White Plains, NY 10605. Tel: 914-761-3008; Fax: 914-948-6429. Very Rev. Bernard Smith, O.F.M.Cap., Minister Prov. Definitors: Revs. Michael Banks, O.F.M.Cap.; Francis Gasparik, O.F.M.Cap.; David Couturier, O.F.M.Cap.

Legal Titles: *The Province of St. Mary of the Capuchin Order; Capuchin Friars International, Inc.; St. Francis of Assisi Foundation,* Development Office: St. John Friary, 210 W. 31st St., New York, NY 10001.

Bishops 2; Priests 135; Professed Clerical Brothers 5; Professed Lay Brothers 37; Postulants 8.

Properties staffed or sponsored: Parishes 13; Chaplaincies 26; Major Seminaries 1; Novitiate 1; Foreign Missions 3.

Represented in the Archdioceses of Agana, Boston and New York and the Dioceses of Bridgeport, Brooklyn, Honolulu, Manchester, Norwich, Portland (ME), Rochester, Rockville Centre. Also in Japan.

Province of the Sacred Stigmata of St. Francis (1918): *Our Lady of Guadalupe Friary,* 319 - 36th St., P.O. Box 809, Union City, NJ 07087. Tel: 201-865-0611; Fax: 201-866-7035. Revs. Robert Grix, O.F.M.Cap., Prov. Min.; Cyprian Rosen, O.F.M.Cap, Prov. Vicar; Definitors: Bro. Kellen Mears, O.F.M.Cap.; Revs. Vincent Fortunato, O.F.M.Cap.; Achilles Cassiere, O.F.M.Cap.; Francis Sariego, O.F.M.Cap., Prov. Sec.

Priests 47; Brothers 17; Temporary Professed 5; Novices 1; Postulants 3.

Parishes 10; Friaries 5; Retreat House 1; Hospital Chaplaincies 1

Represented in the Archdioceses of Newark, New York and the Dioceses of Charlotte, Paterson, St. Petersburg and Wilmington.

Our Lady of Angels, Western American Province: 1345 Cortez Ave., Burlingame, CA 94010. Rev. Ronald Talbott, O.F.M.Cap., Prov.; Definitors: Revs. Michael Mahoney, O.F.M.Cap.; Antonio Marti, O.F.M.Cap.; David Lapierre, O.F.M.Cap.; Matthew Elshoff, O.F.M.Cap.; Revs. Camillus MacRory, O.F.M.Cap., Spiritual Asst.-Secular Franciscans; Flavian Welstead, O.F.M.Cap., Dir.-Devel./Finances; Cyril Kelleher, O.F.M.Cap., Dir.-Foreign Missions; Enda Heffernan, O.F.M.Cap., Treas.; Miguel Angel Ortiz, O.F.M.Cap., Sec.

Priests 47; Brothers 14; Brothers in Formation 5; Novices 6; Postulants 6.

Ministries in Parishes, High Schools, Novitiates, Chaplaincies, House of Study, Retreats, Foreign Missions, Campus Ministry, Military Chaplaincy and Hospital Chaplaincy.

Represented in the Archdioceses of Los Angeles and San Francisco and in the Dioceses of Baker, Fresno and Oakland. Also in Mexico.

Province of SS. Stanislaus and Adalbert (1948): *St. Stanislaus Friary,* 2 Manor Dr., Oak Ridge, NJ 07438. Tel: 973-697-7757. Revs. Henry T. Krajewski, O.F.M.Cap., Supr.; Francis Z. Majewski, O.F.M.Cap., Asst. Supr.

Fathers 9.

Represented in the Dioceses of Metuchen, Paterson and Trenton.

Vice Province of Texas: *Capuchin Franciscan Friars of Texas,* 5604 Bernal Dr., Dallas, TX 75212. Tel: 214-631-1937; Fax: 214-631-6267. Rev. Ignacio Cizur, O.F.M.Cap., Vice Prov.

Fathers 16; Brothers 2.

Parishes 4; Cursillo Centers 2.

Represented in the Dioceses of Dallas and Fort Worth.

Province of Mid-America (1977): *St. Francis of Assisi Friary,* 3553 Wyandot St., Denver, CO 80211-2948. Tel: 303-477-5436; 477-5542; Fax: 303-477-6925.

Legal Titles: *Capuchin Province of Mid-America, Inc.; St. Francis Seminary Endowment Foundation, Inc.;* Revs. David Gottschalk, O.F.M.Cap., Prov.; Gene Emrisek, O.F.M.Cap., Vicar Prov.; Duane Reinert, O.F.M.Cap., Coord.-Ongoing Formation; Michael Scully, O.F.M.Cap., Councillor; Francis X. Grinko, O.F.M.Cap., Councillor & Coord.-Province Formation; Harvey P. Dinkel, O.F.M.Cap., Exec. Sec. & Treas.; John Lager, O.F.M.Cap., Sec.-Missions & Dir.-Devel.;

Jeff Ernst, O.F.M.Cap., Coord.-Initial Formation; John Schmeidler, O.F.M.Cap., Dir.-Vocation Programs; Blaine Burkey, O.F.M.Cap., Communications Dir. & Councillor; Christian Fey, O.F.M.Cap., Archivist.
Bishops 3; Priests 47; Students 1; Brothers 7.
Represented in the Archdioceses of Denver, Kansas City in Kansas and St. Louis and in the Diocese of Salina

Vice Province of St. John The Baptist (1905): *Vice Provincial Offices,* 216 Arzuaga St., P.O. Box 21350, Rio Piedras, PR 00928-1350. Tel: 787-764-3090; Fax: 787-764-4070. Bros. Alberto Figueroa Morales, O.F.M.Cap., Vice Prov. Min.; Roberto Marinez Rivera, O.F.M.Cap., First Councillor; Ramon J. Casellas Rivera, O.F.M.Cap., Second Councillor; Jorge Macias de Cespedes, O.F.M.Cap., Vice Prov. Sec. & Treas.; Joseph McCarthy, O.F.M.Cap., Dir. Capuchin Mass Assoc.
Legal Title: *Asociacion de Frailes Capuchinos, Inc.; Capuchin Formation Trust of Puerto Rico.*
Friars 27; Postulants 3.
Properties owned, staffed and sponsored: Formation Fraternites 3; Parishes 4; Retreat Center 1; Friaries 6; Mission Office 1.
Represented in the Archdiocese of San Juan and the Dioceses of Arecibo and Ponce.

[0480] (O.F.M.CONV.)—CONVENTUAL FRANCISCANS
(Friars Minor Conventual)
(Ordo Fratrum Minorum S. Francisci Conventualium)

General Curia: Piazza SS. Apostoli, 51, Rome 00187, Italy. Most Rev. Agostino Gardin, O.F.M.Conv.; Most Rev. William Robison, O.F.M.Conv., Asst. Gen.

Province of the Immaculate Conception B.V.M. (1852): *Provincial House-Immaculate Conception Friary,* Rensselaer, NY 12144. Very Rev. Canice Connors, O.F.M.Conv., Minister Prov. Rev. Paul Lininger, O.F.M.Conv., Treas.; Bros. John-Joseph Dolan, O.F.M.Conv., Guardian & Sec.; Andre Picotte, O.F.M.Conv., Dir.; Stephen Merrigan, O.F.M.Conv., Archivist & Dir. of Elder Care.
Legal Title: *Order of Friars Minor Conventual Immaculate Conception; Province Charitable Trust; Franciscorps, Inc.,* Rensselaer, NY; *The Franciscan Center for Spirituality, Inc.,* Albany, NY; *Franciscans in Collaborative Ministry, Inc.,* Rensselaer, NY.
Fathers 110; Professed Clerics 1; Professed Brothers 16.
Parishes 21; Friaries 17; Chaplaincies 8; Filial Houses 2.
Represented in the Archdioceses of Newark, New York, Philadelphia, and Washington, and in the Dioceses of Albany, Charlotte, Metuchen, Raleigh, Syracuse and Trenton.

Province of St. Anthony of Padua (1906): *Provincial House,* 12300 Folly Quarter Rd., Ellicott City, MD 21042-1419. Tel: 410-531-9200; Fax: 410-531-4881. Very Rev. Mark L. Curesky, O.F.M.Conv., Minister Prov. Revs. Gregory Moore, O.F.M.Conv., Vicar Prov.; Robert Twele, O.F.M.Conv., Prov. Sec. & Treas.; Definitors: Revs. Donald Grzymski, O.F.M.Conv.; Michael Kolodziej, O.F.M.Conv.; John Koziol, O.F.M.Conv.; Dennis Grumsey, O.F.M.Conv.
Legal Titles: *St. Francis High School of Athol Springs, NY, Inc.; The Father Justin Rosary Hour, Inc.; Franciscan Fathers Minor Conventuals of Buffalo, NY, Inc.; The Franciscan Center, Inc.; St. Anthony of Padua Province, Franciscan Fathers Minor Conventual, U.S.A., Inc.; The Friars Knights of the St. Francis High School, Inc.; Order of Friars Minor Conventual, Inc.; Conventual Franciscan Friars, St. Anthony of Padua Province, Franciscan Mission Association, Inc.; Franciscan Fathers Minor Conventual, St. Anthony of Padua Province U.S.A., MA. Inc.; Franciscan Friars, St. Anthony of Padua Province, Education Fund, Inc.; Franciscan Friars, St. Anthony of Padua Province, Fund for the Aged and Infirm, Inc.; Franciscan Minor Conventuals of Maryland, of Ellicott City, MD, Inc.; The Franciscan Fathers, Minor Conventuals, of St. Stanislaus Church of Baltimore City, MD. Inc.; St. Francis of Assisi Community, Inc.; Order of Friars Minor Conventual, St. Anthony of Padua Province, U.S.A., Inc.; St. Stanislaus Cemetery, Inc.*
Priests 160; Brothers in Solemn Vows 17; Clerics in Temporary Vows 2; Novices 3; Candidates 4.
Friaries 36; Filial Houses 5.
Apostolates owned, staffed, or sponsored: Novitiates 1; College 1; House of Study 1; Parishes 38; Campus Ministries 4; High Schools 3; Youth-Crisis Shelter 1; Sisters' Chaplaincies 2; Hospital-Nursing Home Chaplaincies 2; Apostolates Radio Apostolate; Healing Ministry; Preaching Apostolate; Foreign Missions 3; Candidate House; Youth Ministry.
Represented in the Archdioceses of Atlanta, Baltimore, Boston, Hartford and the Dioceses of Altoona-Johnstown, Birmingham, Bridgeport, Brooklyn, Buffalo, Erie, Fall River, Harrisburg, Norwich, Ogdensburg, Palm Beach, Paterson, Rochester, Savannah, Springfield (MA) and Trenton.

St. Bonaventure Province (1939): 6107 Kenmore Ave., Chicago, IL 60660-2797. Tel: 773-274-7681; Fax: 773-274-9751. Very Rev. Anthony Labedis, O.F.M.Conv., Min. Prov. ; Bro. Thomas Surmam, Treas.; Definitors: Revs. Patrick Greenough, O.F.M.Conv.; James Ciaramitaro, O.F.M.Conv., Sec.; Luke Poczworowski, O.F.M.Conv., Vicar Prov.; William Callahan, O.F.M.Conv.; Bro. Martin Schmidt, O.F.M.Conv.
Legal Titles: *Conventual Franciscans of St. Bonaventure Province; Franciscan Friars Educational Corp.; Conventual Franciscan Friars of Marytown; Shrine of St. Maximillian Kolbe; St. Hedwig Cemetery and Mausoleum; The Conventual Franciscans of Saint Bonaventure Province Charitable Continuing Care Trust Fund.*
Fathers 34; Professed Clerics 2; Brothers 20.
Properties owned or sponsored: Parishes 5; Chaplaincies; Marian Center; Shrine.
Represented in the Archdioceses of Chicago, Detroit and Milwaukee and in the Dioceses of Peoria and Rockford. Also in Mexico.

Province of Our Lady of Consolation (1926): 101 Anthony Dr., Mount St. Francis, IN 47146. Tel: 812-923-8444. Very Rev. Kent Biergans, O.F.M.Conv., Min. Prov. Rev. Richard Kaley, O.F.M.Conv., Vicar Prov. Bro. Jeff Hines, O.F.M.Conv., Sec.
Fathers 121; Brothers 30; Professed Clerics 2; Candidates 5; Novices 3.
Friaries 24; Parishes 22; Houses of Formation 2; Retreat-Renewal Centers 3; Missions 15; Chaplaincies 2.

Province of St. Joseph of Cupertino (1981): *St. Joseph of Cupertine Friary,* P.O. Box 820, Arroyo Grande, CA 93421-0820. Tel: 805-489-1012; Fax: 805-489-8303. Very Rev. Allen Ramirez, O.F.M.Conv., Min. Prov. Rev. Victor Abegg, O.F.M.Conv., Vicar Prov. Bro. James Reiter, O.F.M.Conv., Prov. Sec.; Revs. Paul Fazio, O.F.M.Conv., Custos Capitularis; Stephen Gross O.F.M.Conv., Prov. Spiritual Asst. for Secular Franciscan Order; Christopher Deitz, O.F.M.Conv., Definitor; John Heinz, O.F.M.Conv., Definitor
Legal Title: *Conventual Franciscans of California, Inc.*
Properties owned, staffed or sponsored: Parishes 8; Shrines 1; Chaplaincies 5; High Schools 2; Houses of formation 3.
Priests 44; Brothers 15; Clerics (Professed Seminarians) 13; Novices 3; Candidates 6.
Represented in the Archdiocese of Los Angeles, Military Archdiocese, Portland in Oregon, San Francisco and the Dioceses of Fresno, Monterey, Oakland, Reno, and San Bernardino.

[0490] (O.S.F.)—CONGREGATION OF THE RELIGIOUS BROTHERS OF THE THIRD ORDER REGULAR OF ST. FRANCIS
Franciscan Brothers of Brooklyn

Generalate (1858): *St. Francis Monastery,* 135 Remsen St., Brooklyn, NY 11201-4212. Tel: 212-858-8217; Fax: 718-858-8306. Bros. Kevin Smith O.S.F., Supr. Gen.; Councillors: Joseph Moloney O.S.F.; Patrick Murphy, O.S.F., Master of Novices; Robert Smith, O.S.F.; Campion Lally, O.S.F.; Joshua Di Mauro, O.S.F.
Legal Titles and Holdings: *St. Francis Monastery; Franciscan Brothers' Generalate; Franciscan Brothers, Inc.,* Brooklyn, NY; *Mount Alvernia, Inc.; St. Francis Center, Inc.,* Rockville Centre, NY.
Brothers 106.
Ministries in the field of Education at all levels; Pastoral Ministries, Social Services; Spirituality Centers.
Represented in the Archdiocese of New York, and the Dioceses of Brooklyn, Paterson, Raleigh, Rockville Centre and Springfield-Cape Girardeau.

[0500] (O.S.F.)—FRANCISCAN BROTHERS OF CHRIST THE KING

General Motherhouse and Novitiate (1961): 3737 N. Marybelle Ave., Peoria, IL 61615. Tel: 309-688-0094; 0093. Bro. Francis A. Skube, Supr. Gen.
Professed Brothers 4; Novices 1.
Represented in the Archdiocese of Peoria.

[0510] (F.F.S.C.)—FRANCISCAN BROTHERS OF THE HOLY CROSS

Generalate: *St. Josefshaus, Hausen,* Linz Rhein, West Germany. Bro. David Sarnecki, Supr. Gen.

American Region (1924): 2500 St. James Rd., Springfield, IL 62707. Tel: 217-544-4876, Ext. 222. Bros. John Francis Tyrrell, F.F.S.C., Pres.; Stephen Bissler, F.F.S.C., Vice Pres.; Joseph Havrilka, Board Member; Raphael Kreikemeier, Exec. Dir.; Joel Marc Roussea; Luke Morin.
Properties owned, staffed, or sponsored: Home for Mentally Handicapped; Adult Training Center for Mentally Handicapped; Schools Elementary School; Novitiate.
Brothers 17.
Represented in the Dioceses of Jefferson City, Madison and Springfield (IL).

[0512] (O.S.F.)—FRANCISCAN BROTHERS OF THE SACRED HEART

St. Francis Friary: *Franciscan Brothers of the Sacred Heart:* 705 13th Ave. North - P.O. Box 5072, Fargo, ND 58105-5072. Tel: 701-298-3009; Fax: 701-298-3010. Bros. Vincent Lomonaco, O.S.F., Supr.; Timothy Nelson, O.S.F., Anthony Keidl, O.S.F.
Brothers 3.
Represented in the Diocese of Fargo.

[0515] (O.S.F.)—FRANCISCAN BROTHERS OF THE THIRD ORDER REGULAR

Generalate: *Franciscan Brothers' Generalate,* Mountbellew, Ireland.

United States Region: 2117 Spyglass Trail W., Oxnard, CA 93030. Tel: 805-485-5002 & 323-644-2740; Fax: 323-644-2977. Mailing Address: 4522 Gainsborough Ave., Los Angeles, CA 90027. Bro. Hilarion O'Connor, Reg. Supr.
Brothers 8.
Ministries in the field of secondary education.
Represented in the Archdiocese of Los Angeles.

[0520] (O.F.M.)—FRANCISCAN FRIARS
(Ordinis Fratrum Minorum)

General Headquarters: Via S. Maria Mediatrice, 25 00165, Rome, Italy. Curia Generalizia dei Frati Minori. Most Rev. Giacomo Bini, O.F.M., Min. Gen. Tel: 011-39-6-684-91-203. Very Rev. Estevao Ottenbreit, O.F.M., Vicar Gen. Rev. Sean Collins, O.F.M., English-Speaking General Councillor. Tel: 011-39-6-68491290.

Order of Friars Minor: *English-Speaking Conference,* 1615 Vine St., Cincinnati, OH 45210-1200. Tel: 513-721-4700; Fax: 513-421-9672. Bro. Ronald Bolfeta, O.F.M., Exec. Dir.
Includes: Order of Friars Minor Provinces 12; Vice Province 1; Custodies 1: of the United States, Canada, England, Ireland and Malta. Associate Member: Commissariat of the Holy Land, Washington DC.

Province of St. John the Baptist (1844): 1615 Vine St., Cincinnati, OH 45210-1222. Tel: 513-721-4700; Fax: 513-421-9672. Revs. Fred Link, O.F.M., Prov. Min.; Jeffrey Scheeler, O.F.M., Prov. Vicar; Councillors: Revs. Thomas Richstatter, O.F.M.; Frank Jasper, O.F.M.; Gregory Friedman, O.F.M.; James Bok, O.F.M., Dir.-Devel.; Roger Bosse, O.F.M.; Bro. Mark Ligett, O.F.M.; Bro. Gene Mayer, O.F.M., Prov. Sec.; Revs. Kenan Freson, O.F.M., Prov. Treas; Maynard Tetreault, O.F.M., Bldg. Coord.; Nicholas Lohkamp, O.F.M., Coord. of Ministry of the Word; Francis Tebbe, O.F.M., Dir. Continuing Education/Formation. Tel: 313-432-5300. Henry Beck, O.F.M., Dir.-Office of Peace, Justice & Integrity of Creation Bros.; Scott Obrecht O.F.M., Dir.-Franciscan Missionary Union; David Crank, O.F.M., Dir.-Office of Senior Friars.; Revs. Daniel Anderson, O.F.M., Prov. Archivist & Librarian; Loren Connell, O.F.M., Prov. Spiritual Asst. for Secular Order; Stanley Bir, O.F.M., Personnel Advr. ; Vocation Dirs.: Revs. Norbert Bertram, O.F.M.; Edward Demyanovich, O.F.M.; Dennet Jung, O.F.M.
Priests 155; Temporary Professed 6; Deacons 2; Novices 1; Brothers 66.
Represented in the Archdioceses of Chicago, Cincinnati, Detroit, Indianapolis, Louisville, New Orleans, Santa Fe, Washington and the Dioceses of Baton Rouge, Brownsville, Buffalo, Gallup, Galveston-Houston, Gary, Houma-Thibodaux, Joliet, Lafayette (LA), Las Cruces, Lexington, Marquette, Peoria, Pittsburgh, Shreveport, St. Augustine, St. Petersburg, and Youngstown.

Province of The Sacred Heart (1858): 3140 Meramec St., St. Louis, MO 63118. Tel: 314-353-3421. Revs. John Doctor, O.F.M., Prov. Minister; Kenneth Capalbo, O.F.M., Prov. Vicar; Councillors: Revs. Arthur Anderson, O.F.M.; Fernand Cheri, III, O.F.M.; William Burton, O.F.M.; John Eaton, O.F.M.; Ralph Parthie, O.F.M.; Larry Nickels, O.F.M., Interim Dir.-Office of Ministries; Bro. Christopher Lambert, O.F.M., Prov. Sec.; Revs. Allan DaCorte, O.F.M., Prov. Treas.; Henry Willenborg, O.F.M., Prov. Dir. of Formation; Michael Fowler, O.F.M., Dir.-Franciscan Vocation Center, 4860 W. 29th St., Cicero, IL 60650; Thomas Gardner, O.F.M., Prov. Promoter of the Missions, Commissary of the Holy Land.
Legal Titles: *An Association of Franciscan Fathers of*

the State of Illinois; Franciscan Fathers of the State of Missouri; Friars Minor of the Order of St. Francis, Cleveland; Franciscan Fathers of the State of Wisconsin, Inc.; Franciscan Press; Franciscan Tertiary Province of the Sacred Heart, Incorporated; Mayslake Village; Franciscan Mayslake Village; Cloister Courts; Chariton Apartments; Employees of the Franciscan Orders.

Solemnly Professed: Priests 217; Brothers 78; Simply Professed: Brothers 8; Permanent Deacons 2.

Properties owned, sponsored or staffed: Friaries 40; Parishes 48; Missions 18; Institutional Chaplaincies 15; Chaplaincies for Religious 5; Formation Houses 2; Novitiates 1; Colleges 1; High Schools 2; Publishing House 1.

Represented in the Archdioceses of Chicago, Indianapolis, New Orleans, St. Louis, St. Paul-Minneapolis and San Antonio and in the Dioceses of Cleveland, Fairbanks, Fort Worth, Gaylord, Honolulu, Jefferson City, Joliet, Knoxville, Little Rock, Memphis, Nashville, Shreveport, Springfield (IL), Superior and Victoria.

Province of the Assumption of the Blessed Virgin Mary (1887): *Provincial Office,* Pulaski, WI 54162. Tel: 920-822-5422; Fax: 920-822-5423. Very Rev. Thomas Luczak, O.F.M., Prov.; Rev. Thomas Wojciechowski, O.F.M., Vicar; Definitors: Revs. Anthony Skurla, O.F.M.; John Cella, O.F.M., Comptroller; Placid Strolk, O.F.M.; Laurian Janicki, O.F.M.; Andrew Brophy, O.F.M.; Revs. Eliot Bacia, O.F.M., Prov. Sec.; Hugh Zurat, O.F.M., Dir. of Evangelization Center; James Carroll, Prov. Spiritual Asst. of Secular Franciscan Order.

Legal Holdings or Titles: *St. Mary of the Angels Friary,* Green Bay, WI; *Queen of Peace Friary,* Burlington, WI; *Our Lady of Lourdes Friary,* Cedar Lake, IN; *San Damiano Friary,* Cedar Lake, IN; *St. Stanislaus Friary,* Cleveland, OH; *St. Francis of Assisi School,* Greenwood, MS; *Francis and Clare House,* Milwaukee, WI; *Franciscan Pilgrimage Programs, Inc.,* Milwaukee, WI; *St. Anthony Friary and Mission House,* Pittsburgh (Ben Avon), PA; *St. Pius X Friary,* Philadelphia, PA.

Priests 137; Professed Clerics 1; Professed Brothers 53.

Properties owned or staffed: Parishes 29; Friaries 14.

Represented in the Archdioceses of Chicago, Detroit, Milwaukee, New York, Philadelphia, Ukrainian, Pittsburgh Byzantine, and the Dioceses of Brownsville, Burlington, Camden, Cleveland, Fort Wayne-South Bend, Gary, Gaylord, Green Bay, Jackson, Joliet, Parma, Pittsburgh, Rochester, Rockford, Saginaw, and St. Josaphat.

Province of Our Lady of Guadalupe (1985): *San Antonio Friary,* 1350 Lakeview Rd., S.W., Albuquerque, NM 87105. Tel: 505-877-5425; Fax: 505-877-1440. Very Rev. Larry C. Dunham, O.F.M., Min. Prov. Revs. Gino Correa, O.F.M., Prov. Vicar & Sec.-Formation & Studies; Councillors Bruce Michalek, O.F.M.; Ron Walters, O.F.M.; Ben Begin, O.F.M.; Charlie Martinez, O.F.M., Vocation Dir.; Duane Torisky, O.F.M., Sec. Prov. & Dir.-Communications; George Ward, O.F.M., Prov. Treas.; Bruce Michalek, O.F.M., Sec. Missionary Evangelization & Franciscan Partners Volunteer Program.

Legal Titles: *The Province of Our Lady of Guadalupe of the Order of Friars Minor, Inc.; Southwest Franciscan Missions, Inc.; Southwest Franciscan Services, Inc.*

Priests 54; Brothers 16; Postulants 1; Novices 1.

Represented in the Archdioceses of Denver and Santa Fe and the Dioceses of Gallup and Las Cruces. Also in Mexico and Peru.

Order of Friars Minor of the Province of the Most Holy Name (Legal Title) (1901): 126 West 32nd St., New York, NY 10001-3202. Tel: 212-967-6300; Fax: 212-967-6344. Very Rev. John M. Felice, O.F.M., Prov. Minister, Very Rev. Charles J. Miller, O.F.M., Prov. Vicar; Provincial Councillors; Revs. Peter Brophy, O.F.M.; David Hyman, O.F.M.; Daniel McLellan, O.F.M.; John O'Connor, O.F.M.; Ronald Pecci, O.F.M, Bros. Daniel Sulmasy, O.F.M.; F. Edward Coughlin, O.F.M., Prov. Sec.; Revs. Vincent Grogan, O.F.M., Canonical Counsel; Cassian A. Miles, O.F.M., Dir. Communications; Joseph Hertel, O.F.M., Dir. Office of Devel. & Public Rels.; Dennis Wilson, O.F.M., Treas.; Bro. Gordon (Denis) Clark, O.F.M., Promoter of the Missions & Sec.-Missionary Evangelization; Revs. Peter Brophy, O.F.M., Dir. Vocations; Matthew Gaskin, O.F.M., Prov. Spiritual Asst. for Secular Franciscan Order.

Solemn Profession: Bishops 3; Priests 359; Brothers 79; Permanent Deacons 3; Temporary Profession: Brothers 18; Clerics 6; Novices 5.

Properties owned or sponsored: Province Parishes 31; Missions 1; Urban Ministry Centers 4; University 1; Colleges 1; Community Houses-Residences 45; Houses of Formation 5; Shrine Churches 2; Chaplaincies 16; Military Chaplain 4; Campus Ministry 8.

Represented in the Archdioceses of Atlanta, Baltimore, Boston, Chicago, Denver, Hartford, Kansas City in Kansas, Miami, Military, Newark, New York, Philadelphia, San Juan, Washington and the Dioceses of Albany, Arlington, Bridgeport, Buffalo, Camden, Charleston, Charlotte, Fall River, Ogdensburg, Palm Beach, Paterson, Providence, Raleigh, Rockville Centre, San Diego, Scranton, St. Petersburg, Steubenville, Trenton, and Wilmington.

Province of St. Barbara (1915), The Franciscan Friars of California (1900): 1500 34th Ave., Oakland, CA 94601. Tel: 510-536-3722; Fax: 510-536-3970. Very Rev. Finian McGinn, O.F.M., Prov. Rev. Stephen Barnufsky, O.F.M., Vicar Prov.; Definitors: Revs. Ben Innes, O.F.M.; John Hardin, O.F.M. Bros.; Ed Dunn, O.F.M.; William Short, O.F.M.; Joseph Schwab, O.F.M.; John Kiesler, O.F.M.; Rev. Melvin A. Jurisich, O.F.M., Prov. Sec.

Legal Titles: *Franciscan Friars of California; Franciscan Fathers of Arizona; Franciscan Fathers of Oregon.*

Priests 145; Solemnly Professed Lay Brothers 71; Simply Professed Brothers 14; Novices 5; Pre-novitiate 4.

Represented in the Archdioceses of Los Angeles, Portland (OR), San Francisco and the Dioceses of Fresno, Gallup, Las Cruces, Monterey, Oakland, Orange, Phoenix, Las Vegas, Sacramento, San Diego, San Jose, Spokane and Tucson.

Province of the Immaculate Conception (Friars Minor of the Order of St. Francis) (1871): 125 Thompson St., New York, NY 10012. Tel: 212-674-4388. Very Rev. Robert M. Campagna, O.F.M., Prov. Rev. Patrick Boyle, O.F.M., Vicar Prov.; Definitors: Revs. Ralph Paonessa, O.F.M.; Armand Padula, O.F.M.; James Goode, O.F.M.; Ronald Gliatta, O.F.M.; Michael Bercik, O.F.M.; Simeon Distefano, O.F.M., Prov. Sec.; Claude Scrima, O.F.M., SFO Prov. Spiritual Asst.; Marion Cascino, O.F.M., Promoter of the Franciscan Missions; Madeline Bonnici, Exec. Dir., Franciscan Mission Associates, 274-280 W. Lincoln Ave., Mount Vernon, NY 10550; Rev. Robert M. Campagna, O.F.M., Pious League of St. Anthony.

Fathers 153; Bishops 3; Brothers 31; Permanent Deacons 3.

Properties owned or staffed: Parishes 40; Residences 20.

Represented in the Archdioceses of Boston, Hartford and New York and in the Dioceses of Albany, Bridgeport, Brooklyn, Fall River, Manchester, Metuchen, Pittsburgh, Portland (ME), Trenton, Wheeling-Charleston and Youngstown. Also in Toronto and Italy.

Commissariat of The Holy Cross (1912): 14246 Main St., P.O. Box 608, Lemont, IL 60439. Tel: 630-257-2494; Fax: 630-257-8559. Rev. Blase Chemazar, O.F.M., Pres.; Councillors: Revs. Vendelin Spendov, O.F.M.; Athanasius Lovrencic, O.F.M.; Bernard Karmanocky, O.F.M.

Legal Titles: *The Slovene Franciscan Fathers, Order of Friars Minor, Commissariat of the Holy Cross,* Lemont, IL; *St. Mary's Retreat House,* Lemont, IL.

Fathers 11.

Parishes 3; Monastery 1; Retreat House 1; Mission Center 1.

Represented in the Archdioceses of Chicago, New York and in the Diocese of Altoona-Johnstown.

Vice Province of the Holy Savior: *Provincial House-Holy Family Friary,* 232 S. Home Ave., Pittsburgh, PA 15202-2899. Tel: 412-761-2550; Fax: 412-761-2959. Revs. Fred Lin, O.F.M., Prov. Min.; Jeffrey Scheeler, O.F.M., Vicar Prov.; Councillors: Thomas Richstatter, O.F.M.; Frank Jasper, O.F.M.; Gregory Friedman, O.F.M.; James Bok, O.F.M.; Roger Bosse, O.F.M.; Bro. Mark Ligett, O.F.M.

Represented in the Dioceses of Allentown, Greensburg and Pittsburgh.

Franciscan Friars: *Mt. Alverna Friary,* 517 S. Belle Vista Ave., Youngstown, OH 44509. Tel: 330-799-1888. Revs. John Reiss, O.F.M., Vicar; Matthew J. Kiss, O.F.M., Guardian.

Represented in the Diocese of Youngstown.

Croatian Franciscan Custody of the Holy Family of U.S. & Canada (1926): 4848 S. Ellis Ave., Chicago, IL 60615. Tel: 773-536-0552; Fax: 773-536-2094. Rev. Slavko Soldo, O.F.M., Custos; Councillors: Revs. Lawrence Frankovich, O.F.M.; Joseph Galic, O.F.M.; Jozo Grbes, O.F.M.; Marko Puljic, O.F.M.

Fathers 37; Cleric 1.

Friaries 1; Parishes 9; Missions in Canada 7; Printery 1.

Represented in the Archdioceses of Chicago, Detroit, Milwaukee, New York and St. Louis and in the Dioceses of Allentown and Erie. Also in Canada.

Lithuanian Franciscan Vice-Province of St. Casimir: *Franciscan Friary,* 28 Beach Ave. - P.O. Box 980, Kennebunkport, ME 04046-0980. Tel: 207-967-2011; Fax: 207-967-5721. Very Rev. Placid Barius, O.F.M., Prov. Min.; Rev. Augustine Simanavicius, O.F.M., Prov. Vicar; Councillors: Revs. Francis Giedgaudas, O.F.M.; Raphael Sakalys, O.F.M.; John Bacevicius, O.F.M.; Benedict Jurcys, O.F.M.

Bishops 1; Fathers 34; Brothers 4; Seminarians 14.

Properties owned or sponsored: Parishes 4; Summer Camps 1; Guest House 1; Retreat House 1; Printery 1.

Represented in the Dioceses of Brooklyn, Portland (ME), and St. Petersburg. Also in Toronto, Canada.

U.S. Foundation (1940): *Province of the Holy Gospel Roger Bacon College,* 2400 Marr St., El Paso, TX 79903. Rev. Raul Vazquez, O.F.M.

Priests 3.

Represented in the Diocese of El Paso.

Commissariat of the Holy Land, Franciscan Monastery Of Mt. St. Sepulchre: 1400 Quincy St., N.E., Washington, DC 20017. Tel: 202-526-6800; Fax: 202-529-9889. Bros. Fabian Adkins, O.F.M., Guardian; Callistus Welch, O.F.M., Commissary of the Holy Land-Procurator; Revs. James Brabandt, O.F.M., Dir.-Postulants & Moderator-Knights; Stephen F. Sabbagh, O.F.M., Prov. Spiritual Asst. to the Secular Franciscan Order; Joshua Doyle, O.F.M.; Sabin Plechta, O.F.M.; Kevin Treston, O.F.M., Public Rels., Editor of Cursador's Almanac; Francis Sihuay, O.F.M. (Peru); Manuel Ybarra, O.F.M., Asst. Procurator; Patrick Flanigan, O.F.M.

Priests 9; Brothers 14; Solemnly Professed 23.

Represented in the Archdiocese of Washington.

Franciscan Custody of St. Mary of the Angels (Byzantine-Slavonic Rite): *Holy Dormition Friary,* P.O. Box 270-Rte. 93, Sybertsville, PA 18251-0270. Tel: 570-788-1212; Fax: 570-788-2431. Very Rev. Carmen Scuderi, O.F.M., Protohegumen.

Represented in the Byzantine Rite Dioceses of Passaic, Parma, Pittsburgh, St. Nicholas in Chicago, Philadelphia, Stamford and Van Nuys.

Academy of American Franciscan History: 1712 Euclid Ave., Berkeley, CA 94709.

Legal Title: *Academy of American Franciscan History.* Dr. John F. Schwaller, Dir.

Franciscan Vocational Conference (F.V.C.) (1944) *Assumption B.V.M. Province* P.O. Box 100, Pulaski, WI 54162-0100. Tel: 920-822-5833. Rev. Gregory Plata, O.F.M., Pres.

Franciscan Society organized nationally to promote cooperative and unified vocational effort in the Franciscan Provinces, Vice-Provinces and Custodies of the U.S.A.

National Fraternity of the Secular Franciscan Order, U.S.A. (formerly North American Federation, Third Order of St. Francis): 3307 Quail Meadows Dr., Santa Maria, CA 93455. William Wicks, S.F.O., Natl. Minister.

Founded by St. Francis of Assisi in 1209, to give secular, clergy and laity, an opportunity to live according to the Gospel through the observance of an approved rule of life. In 1921 the Fraternities in the United States united in Secular Franciscan Provinces, and are officially known as the National Fraternity of the Secular Franciscan Order, U.S.A. Present membership in the United States is 20,000 in 800 local fraternities and 33 regional fraternities.

[0530] (S.A.)—FRANCISCAN FRIARS OF THE ATONEMENT

(Societas Adunationis T.O.R.)

St. James Friary P.O. Box 5, Garrison, NY 10524-0005. Tel: 845-424-3539. Very Rev. Arthur M. Johnson, S.A., Minister Gen.; Bro. Gregory Lucrezia, S.A.

Motherhouse: *St. Paul's Friary,* P.O. Box 300, Graymoor, Garrison, NY 10524. Tel: 845-424-3671.

Legal Titles: *St. Chistopher's Inn; St. James Friary; St. Paul's Friary; St. Francis of Assisi Novitiate.*

Priests 87; Professed Seminarians 4; Professed Brothers 44.

Friaries 12; Novitiates 1; Parishes (U.S. and Canada) 7; Overseas Ministries: England, Italy, and Japan; Ecumenical Institute 1; Pastoral Center 1; Campus Ministries; Retreat and Conference Center 1; Rehabilitation Center for Alcoholics 1; Shelter for Homeless men; Military Chaplaincies 2.

Represented in the Archdioceses of Boston, Los Angeles, New York and Washington and in the Dioceses of Arlington, Ogdensburg and Raleigh.

[0533] (F.F.I.)—FRANCISCAN FRIARS OF THE IMMACULATE

General Motherhouse: Benevento, Italy. Founded 1990.

Our Lady's Chapel: *Marian Friary of Our Lady Queen of the Seraphic Order,* 600 Pleasant St., New Bedford, MA 02740-6299. Tel: 508-996-8274. P.O. Box 3003, New Bedford, MA 02741-3003. Rev. Peter Damian Mary Fehlner, F.F.I., American Supr.

Legal Title: *Marian Friary of Our Lady of Guadalupe,* Baltic, CT.

Represented in the Dioceses of Fall River, Norwich and Syracuse.

[0534] (O.F.M.I.)—FRANCISCAN FRIARS OF MARY IMMACULATE

Founded 1996.

Headquarters-Novitiate: *Saint Francis Friary,* 119 Clement Ave., Pisek, ND 58279. Tel: 701-284-6880; Fax: 701-284-6882. Revs. Steven Reiske, Episcopal Liaison; Joachim Mudd, O.F.M.I., Supr.

Legal Title: *Franciscan Friars of Mary Immaculate.*

Priests 4; Brothers 5; Novices 2; Candidates 5.

Represented in the Dioceses of Fargo and Norwich.

[0535] (C.F.R.)—FRANCISCAN FRIARS OF THE RENEWAL

Central House: *Saint Crispin Friary,* 420 E. 156th St., Bronx, NY 10455. Tel: 718-665-2441. Revs. Glenn Sudano, C.F.R., Community Servant; Robert Lombardo, C.F.R., Vicar; Counselors: Benedict J. Groeschel, C.F.R.; Andrew Apostoli, C.F.R.; Michael Kmiotek, C.F.R.; Richard Roemer, C.F.R.

Represented in the Archdiocese of New York.

[0540] (O.S.F.)—FRANCISCAN MISSIONARY BROTHERS OF THE SACRED HEART OF JESUS

(Fratres Missionarii sti Francisci de Sso. Corde Jesu)

Motherhouse (1927): *Our Lady of Angels Monastery,* St. Joseph Rd., Eureka, MO 63025. Tel: 314-587-3661. Bros. Matthew Gallagher, O.S.F., Dir. Gen.; Damien De Braekeleer, O.S.F., Asst. Dir. Gen.

Legal Holdings or Titles: *The Black Madonna Shrine and Grottos (Our Lady of Czestochowa); St. Joseph's Hill Infirmary, Inc.; Price Memorial,* Eureka, MO; *Merkle-Knipprath Nursing Home & Apartment Community,* Clifton, MO.

Brothers 13.

Represented in the Archdiocese of St. Louis and the Diocese of Joliet.

[0560] (T.O.R.)—THIRD ORDER REGULAR OF SAINT FRANCIS

(Tertius Ordo Regularis de Poenitentia)

General Motherhouse: *SS. Cosmas and Damian,* Via dei Fori Imperiali, 1, Rome, Italy. Very Rev. Bonaventure Midili, T.O.R., Minister Gen. Revs. Kevin Queally, T.O.R., Sec. Gen. Robert Sisk, T.O.R., Gen. Councillor & Sec. Gen. of Missions; Bro. John Paul McMahon, T.O.R., Staff.

Province of the Most Sacred Heart of Jesus (1910): *Provincial Residence,* 128 Woodshire Dr., Pittsburgh, PA 15215-1714. Tel: 412-781-8333; Fax: 412-781-1219. Very Rev. Edmund F. Carroll, T.O.R., Minister Prov. Rev. Thomas Bourque, T.O.R., Vicar Prov., Dir. Formation, Dir.-Continuing Education, Dir.-Post Novitiate Formation; Councillors: Revs. Michael Higgins, T.O.R., Terence Henry, T.O.R., Thomas Carapella, T.O.R., Dir.-Postulants; Richard Davis, T.O.R., Dir.-Vocations; Bros. James Boyle, T.O.R., Prov. Sec. National Spiritual Asst.; Mark McBride, T.O.R., Treas. & Dir.-Missions; Revs. Laurence Uhlman, T.O.R., Novice Master; Joseph Markalonis, T.O.R., Dir. Missions; Bernard Tickerhoof, T.O.R., Secular Franciscans Prov. Spiritual Asst.

Fathers 115; Professed Clerics 11; Brothers 26; Novices 11; Postulants 6.

Legal Title: *Province of the Most Sacred Heart of Jesus, Third Order Regular of Saint Francis (USA),* Loretto, PA.

Ministries in Parishes; Universities and Colleges; High School; Chaplaincies; Foreign Mission in Brazil; House of Study 1; Novitiates 1; Laymen's Retreat League.

Represented in the Archdioceses of Baltimore, Philadelphia, Washington and the Dioceses of Altoona-Johnstown, Arlington, Charlotte, Erie, Fort Worth, Pittsburgh, St. Augustine, St. Petersburg, Sioux Falls, Steubenville, Trenton, Venice, Wilmington, and Wheeling-Charleston.

Province of The Immaculate Conception: *San Pedro Center,* 2400 Dike Rd., Winter Park, FL 32792. Tel: 407-677-6406; Fax: 407-677-6489. Very Rev. Robert J. D'Aversa, T.O.R., Minister Prov. Very Rev. Carl Vacek, T.O.R., Vicar Prov. Revs. Frank A. Scornaienchi, T.O.R.; Patrick Quinn, T.O.R.; Anthony Criscitelli, T.O.R.; Bro. Regis J. Leonard, T.O.R.; Prov. Councillors: Bro. David Liedl, T.O.R., Prov. Sec. Most Rev. Bonaventure Midili, Minister Gen. of the Order, Rome, Italy; Bro. John A. Kerr, T.O.R., Bangladesh.

Legal Title: *Third Order Regular of St. Francis, Province of the Immaculate Conception (USA).*

Priests 52: Brothers 9; Permanent Deacons 1; Student Friars 1.

Represented in the Archdioceses of St. Paul-Minneapolis, Washington, and the Dioceses of Altoona-Johnstown, Davenport, Fort Worth, Orlando, Owensboro, Scranton, and Wheeling-Charleston.

U.S.A. Franciscan Commissariate T.O.R., of The Spanish Province (1924): 301 Jefferson Ave., Waco, TX 76701. Tel: 817-626-3065; Fax: 817-626-3050. Very Rev. Estaeban Jasso, T.O.R., Prov. Delegate; Rev. Lawrence Soler, T.O.R., Councillor.

Fathers 7

Parishes 4

Represented in the Dioceses of Austin and Fort Worth

[0570] (G.H.M.)—THE GLENMARY HOME MISSIONERS

(Societas Missionariorum Domesticorum Americas)

(The Home Missioners of America)

General Headquarters: P.O. Box 465618, Cincinnati, OH 45246-5618. Tel: 513-874-8900. Revs. Jerry Dorn, G.H.M., Pres.; Dan Dorsey, G.H.M., 1st Vice Pres.; Bro. Jack Henn, G.H.M., 2nd Vice Pres.; Mr. Bob Knueven, G.H.M., Treas.; Dennis Craig, G.H.M., House Dir.; Revs. Richard Kreimer, G.H.M., Dir.-Development; Dominic Duggins, G.H.M., Mgr.-MEMO Office; Gus Guppenberger, G.H.M., Assoc. House Dir.; Del Holmes, G.H.M., Senior Member; Bro. Vincent Wilmes, G.H.M.

Houses of Formation: *Vocation Center,* P.O. Box 465618, Cincinnati, OH 45246. Rev. Jerry Dorn, G.H.M., Dir. Vocations. *Glenmary Lay Pastoral Coordinators,* 1312 Fifth Ave. N., Nashville, TN 37208. Tel: 615-256-4348. Rev. Bob Dalton, Dir. *Glenmary Members' Personnel,* 1312 Fifth Ave. N., Nashville, TN 37208. Tel: 615-256-1900. Rev. Robert Hare, Dir. *Glenmary Department of Pastoral Services,* 1312 Fifth Ave. N., Nashville, TN 37208. Tel: 615-256-1900. Rev. Michael Langell, Dir. Assists in educational programs, teacher training, parish evaluations and long range planning. Maintains extensive library of publications and audio visuals. *Glenmary Research Center,* 1312 Fifth Ave., N., Nashville, TN 37208. Tel: 615-256-1900. Dr. Kenneth Sanchagrin, Dir. Works exclusively in the rural missionary apostolate, to serve the needs of the Catholic Church as a whole in small town and rural America.

Fathers 59; Candidates 3; Professed Brothers 18.

Properties owned, sponsored or staffed: Mission Bases 36; Houses of Study 1; Pastoral and Research Centers.

Represented in the Archdioceses of Atlanta, Cincinnati and Washington and in the Dioceses of Birmingham, Charlotte, Covington, Jackson, Knoxville, Lexington, Little Rock, Nashville, Owensboro, Richmond, Savannah, Tulsa, and Wheeling-Charleston.

[0580] (B.G.S.)—LITTLE BROTHERS OF THE GOOD SHEPHERD

Villa Mathias: *Foundation House:* Little Brothers of The Good Shepherd, 901 Bro. Mathias Pl. N.W., P.O. Box 389, Albuquerque, NM 87102. Tel: 505-243-4238; Fax: 505-764-9721.

General Headquarters (1987): *Good Shepherd Centre,* 412 Queen St. East, Toronto, Ontario, Canada M5A 1T3. Tel: 416-869-3619. Rev. Bros. David Lynch, B.G.S., Supr. Gen.; Gerard Sullivan, B.G.S., Vicar Gen.; Savio Charron, B.G.S., Sec. Gen.; Richard MacPhee, B.G.S., Gen. Treas.; Majella Marchand, B.G.S., Dir. of Novices.

Legal Holdings and Titles: *Caritas Deus, Inc. of New Mexico; Camillus House Inc. of Florida; Camillus Health Concern Inc. of Florida; Charity Unlimited, Inc. of New Mexico; BGS Charitable of Illinois; Brother Mathias Barrett Inc. of Illinois; Brother Mathias Barrett Inc. of New Mexico; Brothers of Good Sheperd Inc. of Pennsylvania; Brothers of Good Sheperd Inc. of Florida; Brothers of The Good Shepherd Inc. of New Mexico; Brother Mathias Barrett Inc. of New Mexico (Good Shepherd Manor); Good Shepherd Center Inc. of New Mexico; Good Shepherd Center Auxiliary Inc. of New Mexico; Good Shepherd Manor, Inc.,* Momence, IL; *Little Brothers of Good Sheperd Inc. of Illinois; Villa Mathia, Inc. of New Mexico; Brothers of the Good Sheperd Inc. of California,* Los Angeles, CA.

Properties owned and /or sponsored: temporary shelters for marginalized men & women 14; residences for the elderly 2; shelter for battered women & children 3; residences for persons with AIDS.

Professed Brothers 38; Novice Brothers 5.

Represented in the Archdioceses of Miami, Philadelphia and Santa Fe and the Diocese of Joliet.

[0590] (M.S.A.)—SOCIETY OF T THE MISSIONARIES OF THE HOLY APOSTLES

General Administration: *Society of the Missionaries of the Holy Apostles,* 8594 rue Berri, Montreal, (Quebec) Canada H2P 2G4. Tel: 514-387-2222; Fax: 514-387-0863. Very Rev. Yvon Archambault, M.S.A., Supr. Gen. Animator.

Society of Missionaries of the Holy Apostles: *Provincial Administration Headquarters,* 24 Prospect Hill Rd., Cromwell, CT 06416. Tel: 860-632-3039; Fax: 860-635-4823. Very Rev. Raymond Halliwell, M.S.A., Prov. Animator.

Priests 40; Brothers 8.

Properties owned, staffed, or sponsored: Holy Apostles College and Seminary; 2 Parishes; Hermitage; Hospital Chaplaincies.

Represented in the Archdioceses of Denver, Washington and the Dioceses of Norwich, Pennsacola-Tallahassee and Wheeling-Charleston.

[0600] (C.S.C.)—BROTHERS OF THE CONGREGATION OF HOLY CROSS

(Congregatio A Sancta Cruce)

Generalate: *Congregazione di Santa Croce,* Via Framura, 85 00168, Rome, Italy. Rev. Hugh W. Cleary, C.S.C., Supr. Gen.; Bro. John Gleason, C.S.C., First Asst. & Vicar; Rev. Robert P. Morin, C.S.C., Second Asst. & Procurator; Bro. Donald Blauvelt, C.S.C., Third Asst.; Rev. Arulraj Gali, C.S.C., Fourth Asst.

Midwest Province of the Brothers of Holy Cross (1841): *Province Administration,* 54515 State Rd. 933 North-P.O. Box 460, Notre Dame, IN 46556. Tel: 219-251-2222; Fax: 219-289-0487. Bros. Donald Gibbs, C.S.C., Prov. Supr.; Robert Fillmore, C.S.C., Asst. Prov. & Vicar; Jerome Meyer, C.S.C., Sec.; William Dygert, C.S.C., Steward & Treas.; Councillor: Kenneth Haders, C.S.C.; Donald Stabrowski, C.S.C.; Chester Freel, C.S.C.

Legal Title: *Notre Dame, Ind. Brothers of Holy Cross, Inc.*

Professed Brothers 215; Temporarily Professed 8; Novices 3; Aspirants 5.

Properties owned, staffed, or sponsored: Community Houses 2; Junior College; High Schools 9; Boarding Military Grade School; Scholasticates 2; Foreign Mission Schools 3.

Represented in the Archdioceses of Anchorage, Chicago, Detroit, Los Angeles, Miami, Milwaukee, New Orleans, Portland (OR), San Antonio and the Dioceses of Austin, Cleveland, Colorado Springs, Erie, Evansville, Fort Wayne-South Bend, Gary, Grand Rapids, Lansing, Nashville, Oakland, Phoenix, Providence, St. Petersburg, Savannah, Scranton, and Venice.

South-West Province of the Brothers of Holy Cross (1956): *Brother John Baptist Province Center,* St. Edward University, No. 1046, Austin, TX 78704. Tel: 512-442-7856. Bros. Richard Critz, C.S.C., Prov.; Stephen Walsh, C.S.C., Asst. Prov.; John McLaughlin, C.S.C., Sec.; Harold Ehlinger, C.S.C., Steward; Councillors: Bros. Stanley Culotta, C.S.C.; Richard Daly, C.S.C.

Professed Brothers 119; Temporarily Professed 5.

Properties owned, staffed, or sponsored: Colleges 1; High Schools 7; Home for Boys 1; Schools Foreign Mission Schools 2.

Represented in the Archdioceses of Los Angeles, Louisville, New Orleans, Portland (OR), San Antonio, Santa Fe and in the Dioceses of Austin, Beaumont, Cheyenne, Cleveland, Fort Wayne-South Bend, Knoxville, Oakland, San Jose and Savannah.

Eastern Province of the Brothers of Holy Cross (1956): 85 Overlook Cir., New Rochelle, NY 10804. Tel: 914-632-4468; 4469; Fax: 914-632-2490. Bros. George C. Schmitz, C.S.C., Prov.; William Zaydak, C.S.C., Vicar; Paul Bednarcyzk, C.S.C., Sec.; Councillors: Jerome Donnelly, C.S.C.; Joseph McDonnell, C.S.C.

Legal Title: *Brothers of Holy Cross of the Eastern Province of the United States of America, Inc.*

Professed Brothers 130; Temporarily Professed 18.

Properties owned, staffed or sponsored: High Schools 4; Foreign Mission Houses 6; Schools Middle School; Spiritual Life Center; Boys Home.

Represented in the Archdioceses of Hartford, New York, Washington and the Dioceses of Albany, Brooklyn, Savannah, and Wilmington.

[0610] (C.S.C.)—PRIESTS OF THE CONGREGATION OF HOLY CROSS

Congregatio a Sancta Cruce

Generalate: *Curia Generalizia di Santa Croce,* Via Framura 85 00168, Rome, Italy. Rev. Hugh W. Cleary, C.S.C., Supr. Gen., Bro. John Gleason, C.S.C., First Asst. & Vicar; Rev. Robert P. Morin, C.S.C., Second Asst. & Procurator; Bro. Donald Blauvelt, C.S.C., Third Asst.; Rev. Arulraj Gali, C.S.C., Fourth Asst.

Congregation of Holy Cross, Indiana Province (1841): *Provincial House,* 1304 E. Jefferson Blvd., South Bend, IN 46617. Tel: 219-289-6850. Revs. William E. Dorwart, C.S.C., Prov. Supr.; Robert L. Epping, C.S.C., First Asst. Prov.; Kenneth M. Molinaro,

C.S.C., Second Asst. Prov.; E. William Beauchamp, C.S.C., Steward; Prov. Councillors; Revs. David L. Guffey, C.S.C.; John A.Herman, C.S.C.; Peter A. Jarret, C.S.C.; Wilson D. Miscamble, C.S.C.; Robert S. Pelton, C.S.C.; David T. Tyson, C.S.C.; Bro. Edmund C. Luther, C.S.C.

Legal Title: *Priests of Holy Cross, Indiana Province, Inc.*

Fathers 298; Professed Clerics 5; Temporarily Professed Clerics 33; Novices 8; Candidates 55; Professed Brothers 21.

Properties owned, sponsored, or staffed: College Seminary; Theological Seminary; Novitiate; Mission Center; Provincial House; Postulate; Universities 2; Colleges 2; High Schools 2; Parishes 15; Chaplaincies 17; Publishing House; Retreat House.

Holy Cross Associates Lay Missionary Program, P.O. Box 668, Notre Dame, IN 46556. Mr. John Pinter, Dir.

Holy Cross Association, Box K, Notre Dame, IN 46556. Rev. Herbert C. Yost, C.S.C., Dir.

Represented in the Archdioceses of Anchorage, Chicago, Detroit, Los Angeles, New Orleans, New York, Portland (OR), San Antonio, San Francisco and in the Dioceses of Bridgeport, Cleveland, Colorado Springs, Erie, Fall River, Fort Wayne-South Bend, Gary, Kalamazoo, Monterey, Oakland, Orange, Phoenix, and San Bernardino.

Congregation of Holy Cross—Eastern Province, Inc. (1952): *Provincial Headquarters,* 835 Clinton Ave., Bridgeport, CT 06604. Tel: 203-367-7252; 367-1152; Fax: 203-366-7886. Revs. Arthur J. Colgan, C.S.C., Prov. Supr., James T. Preskenis, C.S.C., Asst. Prov. & Vicar; James Lackenmier, C.S.C., Treas & Steward; Prov. Councillors: Revs. Mark T. Cregan, C.S.C.; Anthony R. Grasso, C.S.C.; George B. Mulligan, C.S.C.; Laurence M. Olszewski, C.S.C.; John P. Phalen, C.S.C.; Peter J. Walsh, C.S.C.; Bro. Richard F. Kyle, C.S.C.

Fathers 122; Temporarily Professed Clerics 12; Candidates 12; Novices 4; Brothers Professed 18.

Properties owned, sponsored, or staffed: Colleges 2; Mission Houses; Parishes 11; Retreat House; Chaplaincies 22; Campus Ministry 8; Family Rosary Crusade; Family Theater.

Represented in the Archdioceses of Boston, Chicago, Hartford, Los Angeles, New York, Washington and the Dioceses of Albany, Bridgeport, Brooklyn, Burlington, Fall River, Fort Wayne-South Bend, Manchester, Norwich, Orlando, Portland (ME), Rochester, St. Petersburg, and Scranton.

Holy Cross Southern Province (1968): *Provincial House,* 2111 Brackenridge St., Austin, TX 78704. Tel: 512-443-3886; Fax: 512-416-1216. Revs. John S. Korcsmar, C.S.C., Prov. Supr., Bro. Thomas G. Krieter, C.S.C., Asst. Prov. & Steward; Revs. Jeffrey L. Allison, C.S.C., Prov. Sec.; Joseph A. Tomei, C.S.C., Prov. Councillor; L. Peter Logsdon, C.S.C., Prov. Councillor.

Legal Title: *Congregation of Holy Cross, Southern Province, Inc.*

Fathers 31; Professed Brothers 1; Temporarily Professed 6.

Ministries in Parishes; Foreign Missions; Chaplaincies; Social Service.

Represented in the Archdioceses of New Orleans, St. Louis and San Antonio and in Dioceses of Austin, Baton Rouge, Fort Wayne-South Bend, Lafayette (LA) and Las Cruces.

[0620] (F.S.E.)—BROTHERS OF THE HOLY EUCHARIST

Founded in the United States 1957.

General Motherhouse and Novitiate: P.O. Box 25, Plaucheville, LA 71362. Tel: 318-922-3630; 922-3401. Rev. Bro. Andre M. Lucia, F.S.E., Supr. Gen.

Represented in the Diocese of Alexandria.

[0630] (M.S.F.)—CONGREGATION OF THE MISSIONARIES OF THE HOLY FAMILY

(Congregatio Missionariorum a Sacra Familia)

General Motherhouse: Via Odoari Beccari, 41 I-00154, Rome, Italy. Tel: 011-39-6-57-55-192; Fax: 011-39-6-57-55-208. Very Rev. Wim van der Weiden, M.S.F., Supr. Gen.

General Mission Office - M.S.F., Inc.: P.O. Box 918 - 260 W. Euclid Blvd., West Point, VA 23181. Tel: 804-843-2622; Fax: 804-843-3182. Rev. John Brieffies, M.S.F., Exec. Dir.

MSF Center: *Provincialate USA of the Missionaries of the Holy Family,* 210 El Rancho Way, San Antonio, TX 78209. Tel: 210-826-9815; Fax: 210-826-3393. Very Rev. Robert E. O'Hara, M.S.F., Prov. Supr. Rev. John Dowling, M.S.F., Prov. Treas.

Fathers 52; Theology Students 4; Brothers 8.

Ministries in House of Study 2; Parishes 16.

Represented in the Archdioceses of St. Louis, San Antonio, and in the Dioceses of Brownsville, Corpus Christi, Duluth and Richmond. Also in Canada and Mexico.

[0640] (S.F.)—SONS OF THE HOLY FAMILY

(Congregatio Filiorum Sacrae Familiae)

General Motherhouse: Entenza 301, Barcelona 08029, Spain. Very Rev., Luis Picazo, S.F., Gen. Superior.

U.S. Foundation (1920): 401 Randolph Rd., P.O. Box 4138, Silver Spring, MD 20914. Tel: 301-622-1184. Rev. Francisco Gonzalez, S.F., Vice Prov.

Fathers 16.

Represented in the Archdioceses of Santa Fe, Washington, and the Archdiocese for the Military Services, U.S.A.

[0650] (C.S.SP.)—HOLY GHOST FATHERS

(Congregation of the Holy Ghost and of the Immaculate Heart of Mary)

Congregatio Sancti Spiritus sub tutela Immaculati Cordis Beatissimae Virginis Mariae)

Generalate: Clivo di Cinna 195, Rome 00136, Italy. Very Rev. Pierre Schouver, C.S.Sp., Supr. Gen.

Eastern Province of the United States (1872): 6230 Brush Run Rd., Bethel Park, PA 15102. Tel: 412-831-0302; Fax: 412-831-0970. Very Rev. Donald J. McEachin, C.S.Sp., Prov. Supr., Councillors: Revs. James P. McCloskey, C.S.Sp.; John P. Skaj, C.S.Sp.; David L. Smith, C.S.Sp.; Norman E. Bevan, C.S.Sp.; Jeffrey T. Duaime, C.S.Sp.

Legal Holdings: *Archconfraternity of the Holy Ghost; Provincial Residence; Duquesne University; Laval House; Holy Ghost Preparatory School; Bethel Holy Ghost Animation Center.*

Fathers in U.S. 76; Professed Brothers 1

Properties owned, sponsored, or staffed: Parishes 8; Retirement Residences 3.

Represented in the Archdioceses of Chicago, Cincinnati, Detroit, New York, Philadelphia, Washington and in the Dioceses of Arlington, Charlotte, Pittsburgh, Providence, and Venice. Also in Puerto Rico.

Western Province of the United States (1964): *Congregation of the Holy Ghost,* 1700 W. Alabama St., Houston, TX 77098-2808. Tel: 713-522-2882; Fax: 713-522-8063. Very Rev. Donald S. Nesti, C.S.Sp., Prov. Supr.; Prov. Councillors: Revs. Michael T. White, C.S.Sp., 1st Asst.; Thomas J. Byrne, C.S.Sp., 2nd Asst.; Albert J. McKnight, C.S.Sp. Bro. Michael E. Suazo, C.S.Sp., Prov. Sec.; Rev. Philip D. Evanstock, C.S.Sp., Prov. Bursar.

Priests 45; Professed Brothers 2; Candidates 4; Scholastics 10; Lay Associates 20.

Properties owned, sponsored, or staffed: *Holy Spirit Provincialate & Holy Ghost Hall,* Houston, TX; *Libermann House at Spiritan Renewal Center,* New Braunfels, TX; *Casa Laval and Holy Ghost Novitiate,* Hemet, CA; *Iglesia de Santa Ana; Maison Brottier,* Natchitoches, LA; *Mision San Juan Bautista.*

Staff: Parishes 13; Training Centers 3.

Represented in the Archdioceses of New Orleans, San Antonio and in the Dioceses of Alexandria, Galveston-Houston, Lafayette (LA), Little Rock, Oakland, Pittsburgh, Salt Lake City, San Bernardino, San Diego, and Tucson. Also in Guam, Mexico, and the Philippines.

Holy Ghost Fathers of Ireland (1971): 4849 37th St., Long Island City, NY 11101. Tel: 718-729-5273; Fax: 718-729-6949. Very Rev. Patrick Doody, C.S.Sp., Prov. Delegate U.S.A. East; Very Rev. Diarmud Casey, C.S.Sp., Prov. Delegate U.S.A. West, Tel: 650-961-8600; Fax: 650-968-5633. Very Rev. Matthias Moore, C.S.Sp., Prov. Delegate Louisiana, Tel: 504-344-0953. Councillors: Revs. Patrick Holohan, C.S.Sp.; Vincent O'Connell, C.S.Sp.; Noel O'Meara, C.S.Sp.; James Delaney, C.S.Sp.

Fathers 48.

Represented in the Archdioceses of Boston, Miami, New Orleans, New York and San Francisco and in the Dioceses of Brooklyn, Fargo, Metuchen, Palm Beach and St. Augustine.

[0660] (M.Sp.S.)—MISSIONARIES OF THE HOLY SPIRIT

General Motherhouse: Av. Universidad 1702 04010, Mexico, D.F., Mexico. Tel: 5-658-74-33; 5-658-7851. Very Rev. Jorge Ortiz, M.Sp.S., Supr. Gen.

American Headquarters: *Our Lady of Guadalupe,* 500 N. Juanita Ave., P.O. Box 1091, Oxnard, CA 93030. Tel: 805-483-0987.

Priests 17; Professed 17; Novices 16.

Parishes 3; House of Study 1; Novitiates 1; Theologate 1.

Represented in the Archdiocese of Los Angeles, Portland in Oregon and the Diocese of Fresno.

[0670] (O.H.)—HOSPITALLER BROTHERS OF ST. JOHN OF GOD

General Motherhouse: *Hospitaller Brothers of St. John of God,* via della Nocetta 263, Rome, Italy 00164. Most Rev. Bro. Pascual Piles, O.H., Prior Gen.

Order founded by St. John of God at Granada, Spain, in 1537.

American Province of Our Lady Queen of Angels (1970): *Villa Maria-Provincial Curia,* 2425 S. Western Ave., Los Angeles, CA 90018. Tel: 323-734-0233; 731-0641; Fax: 323-731-5987. Bro. Edward Francis McEnroe, O.H., Prov.

Brothers 29; Solemn Professed 28; Simple Professed 1; Priests 2.

Legal Holdings: *St. John of God Retirement and Care Center,* Los Angeles, CA; *St. Joseph Health & Retirement Center,* Ojai, CA; *St. John of God Health Care Services,* Victorville, CA.

Represented in the Archdiocese of Los Angeles and the Diocese of San Bernardino.

[0680] (I.H.M.)—BROTHERS OF THE IMMACULATE HEART OF MARY

General Motherhouse (1948): 609 N. 7th St., Steubenville, OH 43952. Tel: 740-283-2462. Bro. Dominic Carroll, I.H.M., Supr. Gen.; Bro. Anthony Motto, I.H.M., Novice Master.

Professed Brothers 4.

Ministries in: Novitiate; Bishop's Residence; CCD Center; Pastoral Associates 3.

Represented in the Diocese of Steubenville.

[0690] (S.J.)—JESUIT FATHERS AND BROTHERS

(Societas Jesu)

Generalate: Casella Postale 6139 00195, Rome, Italy. Very Rev. Peter-Hans Kolvenbach, S.J., Gen. Revs. Hans Zwiefelhofer, Sec.; Francis E. Case, S.J., U.S. Assistant.

Jesuit Conference: *The Society of Jesus in the United States National Offices,* 1616 P Street, Suite 400, Washington, DC 20036-1405. Tel: 202-462-0400; Fax: 202-328-9212. Revs. Bradley M. Schaeffer, S.J., Pres.; James A. Casciotti, S.J., Exec. Sec.; John F. Armstrong, S.J., Sec. Formation & Secondary Education; Richard J. Ryscavage, S.J., Sec.-Social & International Ministries and Dir.-Jesuit Refugee Services; British Robinson, Dir.-Social & International Ministries; Thomas C. Widner, S.J., Sec. for Communications; Walter C. Deye, S.J., Sec.-Pastoral Ministries.

Maryland Province (1833): 5704 Roland Ave., Baltimore, MD 21210. Tel: 410-532-1400; Fax: 410-532-1419. Very Rev. James R. Stormes, S.J., Prov., Revs. James A. Casciotti, S.J., Supr. & Socius to the Prov.; J. Donald Freeze, S.J., Treas.; Charles L. Currie, S.J., Asst. Prov. for Higher Ed.; Daniel K. Lahart, S.J., Asst. Prov. for Secondary Ed.; Clement J. Petrik, S.J., Asst. Prov. for Pastoral Min.; Thomas P. Gaunt, S.J., Asst. Prov. for Jesuit Students; Hugh A. Kennedy, S.J., Asst. Sec. to Prov.; Mr. Stephen J. Callahan, Asst. Prov.-Social & International Apostolates; Revs. Liborio J. LaMartina, S.J., Resident Archivist; William F. Lamm, S.J., Asst. Treas. & Sec.; Thomas P. Martin, S.J., Asst. Treas.; Francis H. McGauley, S.J., Health Care Coord.; William K. McGroarty, S.J., Asst. Treas. for Properties; Mr. James S. Schaefer, Bus. Mgr.; Mr. Kevin J. O'Brien, Dir.-Ignatian Apostolic Partnerships & Mission Bureau & Jesuit Seminary Guild, Maryland Province; Revs. Joseph M. Kennedy, S.J., Assoc. Dir.; Richard J. Colgan, S.J., Asst. Dir.- Mission Bureau & Jesuit Seminary Guild; Robert E. Reiser, S.J., Dir. Vocations; Gerald P. Fogarty, S.J., Archivist; James A. O'Brien, S.J., Promoter, Christian Life Communities; Brian O. McDermott, S.J., Tertian Instructor; Bruce A. Maivelett, S.J., Novice Dir.

Legal Title: *Corporation of the Roman Catholic Clergymen, Maryland; Jesuit Volunteer Corps, East,* 17th & Thompson Sts., Philadelphia, PA 19121.

Fathers 397; Scholastics 29; Brothers 23.

Properties owned, sponsored, or staffed: Parishes 12; Universities 4; Colleges 1; High Schools 5; Middle and Grammar Schools 2; Houses of Retreats 2; Residences 9.

Represented in the Archdioceses of Baltimore, Philadelphia and Washington and in the Dioceses of Allentown, Arlington, Camden, Charlotte, Erie, Raleigh, Richmond, Scranton, Wheeling-Charleston and Wilmington.

Province of New York (1943): 39 E. 83rd St., New York, NY 10028. Tel: 212-774-5500; Fax: 212-774-5510.

Legal Title: *The New York Province of the Society of Jesus,* New York, N.Y. Very Rev. Kenneth J. Gavin, S.J., Prov., Rev. James L. Dugan, S.J., Exec. Asst. to Prov.; Bro. Gilbert J. Scott, S.J., Asst. to the Prov.; Revs. J. Raymond Johnson, S.J., Prov. Treas.; Auditor & American Rep. for the Missions of the Society of Jesus, Vatican City; D. James French, S.J., Asst. Pastoral Ministries & Asst. for Formation; Frederick J. O'Brien, S.J., Asst. for Sec. Education; James F. Joyce, S.J., Asst. for Social & Pastoral Ministries; Thomas E. Smith, S.J., Asst. for Intl. Apostolate; Edward J. Quinnan, S.J., Asst.-Retreat Houses & Spirituality; Thomas D. Reiser, S.J., Dir. of Vocations; William J. Scanlon, S.J., Exec. Dir. of the Jesuit Seminary & Mission Bureau.

Fathers 498; Scholastics 84; Brothers 28.

Properties owned, sponsored, or staffed: Parishes 8; Universities 1; Colleges 3; High Schools 8; Houses for Laymen's Retreats 3; House of Study 1; Novitiates 2; Community Houses 4.

Represented in the Archdioceses of Newark and New York and in the Dioceses of Albany, Brooklyn, Buffalo, Paterson, Rochester, Rockville Centre and Syracuse. Also in Guam, the Caroline Islands, Chalan Kanoa, and the Prefecture Apostolic of Marshall Islands.

The Jesuits of the Missouri Province (Missouri Province of the Society of Jesus): *Province Offices,* 4511 W. Pine Blvd., St. Louis, MO 63108-2191. Tel: 314-361-7765; Fax: 314-758-7164. Very Rev. Frank Reale, S.J., Prov., Revs. Philip G. Steele, S.J., Socius & Asst. for Secondary Education; Robert F. Weiss, S.J., Treas.; John A. Apel, S.J., Asst. for Jesuits in Pastoral and Intl. Apostolates; William T. Oulvey, S.J., Prov. Asst.-Vocations & Asst.-Prov. Planning; L. Gene Martens, S.J., Assoc. Dir. Jesuit Devel. Office; David L. Fleming, S.J., Dir. of Publications & Editor Publication: *The Jesuit Bulletin.* Tel: 314-977-2631; William B. Faherty, S.J., Archivist Emeritus; William L. Mugan, S.J., Archivist.

Fathers 261; Students in Major Seminary 17; Novices 6; Brothers 27.

Legal Titles: *Regis Jesuit High School Corporation,* Aurora, CO; *Regis University,* Denver, CO; *Rockhurst University; Rockhurst High School,* Kansas City, MO; *The Province-The Jesuits of the Missouri Province; Bellarmine House of Studies - The Jesuits of the Missouri Province; Fusz Pavilion - The Jesuits of the Missouri Province; Institute of Jesuit Sources - The Jesuits of the Missouri Province; Jesuit Mission Bureau - The Jesuits of the Missouri Province; Review for Religious - The Jesuits of the Missouri Province; DeSmet Jesuit High School; Jesuit Community Corporation at St. Louis University; Saint Louis University; St. Louis University High School; The Sacred Heart Program, Inc.; White House Retreat, Inc.,* St. Louis, MO; *Society of Jesus in Belize, Inc.; St. John's College, Inc.,* Belize; *Jesuit Retreat House,* Sedalia.

Ministries in Parishes; Universities; High Schools; Middle Schools; Noviates; Curia; Retreat Houses.

Represented in the Archdioceses of Denver, Kansas City in Kansas and St. Louis and the Dioceses of Colorado Springs, Dodge City, Kansas City-St. Joseph, Pueblo, and Springfield in Illinois.

New Orleans Province (1907): 500 S. Jefferson Davis Pky., New Orleans, LA 70119-7192. Tel: 504-821-0334; Fax: 504-822-5322.

Legal Title: *Catholic Society of Religious and Literary Education, A Louisiana Corporation.* Very Rev. James P. Bradley, S.J., Prov.; Revs. James L. Lambert, S.J., Asst. for Parishes & Retreat Apostolate; Edward B. Arroyo, S.J., Asst. for Social Apostolate; Thomas H. Stahel, S.J., Socius; Paul Deutsch, S.J., Asst. for Secondary Education; Bro. Lawrence J. Lundin, S.J., Treas.

Fathers 215; Students in Major Seminary 27; Novices 8; Brothers 30.

Properties owned, sponsored, or staffed: Parishes 14; Universities 1; Colleges 1; High Schools 4; Novitiate 1; Houses of Retreat 4.

Represented in the Archdioceses of Atlanta, Miami, New Orleans, San Antonio and Santa Fe and in the Dioceses of Alexandria, Amarillo, Austin, Baton Rouge, Charleston, Corpus Christi, Dallas, El Paso, Fort Worth, Galveston-Houston, Gallup, Lafayette (LA), Las Cruces, Little Rock, Mobile, Nashville, Orlando, Palm Beach, Pensacola-Tallahassee, St. Augustine, St. Petersburg and Venice.

California Province (1909): Executive Assistant, 300 College Ave., P.O. Box 519, Los Gatos, CA 95031-0519. Tel: 408-354-6143.

Legal Title: *The California Province of the Society of Jesus.* Very Rev. Thomas H. Smolich, S.J., Prov. Revs. Alfred E. Naucke, S.J., Exec. Asst.; Anthony E. Sholander, S.J., Asst. for Planning & Dir. Vocations Formation; Robert V. Caro, S.J., Asst. for Secondary Education; John A. Baumann, S.J., Asst. for Social Ministries; John W. Chandler, S.J., Asst. for Pastoral Ministries; Paul A. Soukup, S.J., Dir. Studies; Robert L. St. Clair, S.J., Prov., Treas.; William J. Maring, S.J., Prov. Dir.-Devel; Bros. Daniel J. Peterson, S.J., Prov. Archivist; Jack A. Hughes, S.J., Asst. Sec.; Revs. William J. Wood, S.J., Tertian Instructor; Theodore T. Taheny, S.J., Dir.; California Jesuit Missionaries, 284 Stanyan St., San Francisco, CA 94118-4299. Tel: 415-221-1588. George M. Twigg-Porter, S.J., Apostleship of Prayer; Andrew F. Maginnis, S.J., Dir. Jesuit Seminary Association & Editor.

Fathers 379; Brothers 38; Scholastics 42; Scholastic Novices 12.

Properties owned, sponsored, or staffed: Parishes 13; Universities 3; High Schools 5; Novitiates 1; Theologate 1; Retreat Center 2.

Represented in the Archdioceses of Los Angeles and San Francisco and in the Dioceses of Fresno, Honolulu, Monterey, Oakland, Orange, Phoenix, Reno, Sacramento, Salt Lake City, San Bernardino, San Diego, San Jose, Santa Rosa, Stockton and Tucson.

New England Province (1926): 771 Harrison Ave., Boston, MA 02118-2311. Tel: 617-266-7233; Fax: 617-536-8074. Revs. Robert J. Levens, S.J., Prov.; John P. Murray, S.J.; Exec. Asst.-Secondary Education; David I. Donovan, S.J., Asst. Formation & Pastoral Ministries; Joseph R. Fahey, S.J., Asst. for Prov. Finances; James M. Hayes, S.J., Liaison-International Ministries & Co-Dir. Vocations; William C. McInnes, S.J., Prov. Liaison for Continuing Education; Richard J. Roos, S.J., Liaison for Ministry of Spiritual Exercises; Richard J. Stanley, S.J., Co-Dir. Vocations; Bro.George T. Williams, S.J., Prov. Coord.-Criminal Justice Ministry.

Legal Title: *The Society of Jesus of New England.*

Fathers 386; Scholastics 26; Brothers 20.

Parishes 3; Universities 2; Colleges 1; High Schools 3; Houses of Retreats 2; Seminaries 1; Novitiates 1; Residences 1.

Represented in the Archdioceses of Anchorage, Baltimore, Boston, Chicago, Hartford, Los Angeles, Louisville, Miami, Milwaukee, New Orleans, New York, Philadelphia, St. Louis, St. Paul-Minneapolis, Seattle, Washington, and the Dioceses of Albany, Allentown, Bridgeport, Buffalo, Cleveland, Fairbanks, Fall River, Gallup, Honolulu, Manchester, Nashville, Norwich, Oakland, Portland (ME), Rapid City, St. Augustine, St. Petersburg, San Jose, Scranton, Sioux Falls, Spokane, Tucson, Tulsa, Venice, Wheeling-Charlestown and Worcester.

Chicago Province - Society of Jesus (S.J.) (1928): 2050 N. Clark St., Chicago, IL 60614. Tel: 773-975-6363; Fax: 773-975-0230. Very Rev. Richard J. Baumann, S.J., Prov; Revs. Richard H. McGurn, S.J., Exec. Asst. & Asst. for Formation; Daniel L. Flaherty, S.J., Prov. Treas. and Asst. for Bus. and Finance; James A. Stoeger, S.J., Asst. Secondary Education; David S. Godleski, S.J., Asst. for Vocation Promotion; Paul V. Robb, S.J., Asst. Treas.; George E. Von Kaenel, S.J., Asst.-Intl. Apostolates; Dir.-Jesuit Intl. Missions; Asst.-Social Min.; William O. Madden, S.J., Asst. for Records & Research; James P. Gschwend, S.J., Asst. for Continuing Education & Asst. for Jesuits in Diaspora; John F. Costello, S.J., Coord.-Planned Giving; John J. Foley, S.J., Asst. to Devel. Dir. for Jesuit Seminary Assoc.; John A. McGrail, S.J., Dir. Apostleship of Prayer.

Jesuit Development Office, 2059 N. Sedgwick St., Chicago, IL 60614. Tel: 773-975-8181; Fax: 773-975-2042.

Quarterly Publication: *Company Magazine.* Offices, 1400 W. Devon Ave.-#511, Chicago, IL 60660-1312. Tel: 773-761-9432; Fax: 773-761-9443.

Legal Title: *Chicago Province of the Society of Jesus.*

Fathers 205; Scholastics 26; Brothers 15; Scholastic Novices 6.

Properties Sponsored: Parishes 3; Universities 2; High Schools 5; Retreat Houses 2; Diocesan Major Seminary 1; Residences 9; House of Writers 1.

Represented in the Archdioceses of Chicago, Cincinnati, Indianapolis and Louisville and in the Dioceses of Covington, Evansville, Fort Wayne-South Bend, Gary, Joliet, Lafayette (IN), Peoria and Rockford.

Oregon Province - Society of Jesus (1932): 2222 N.W. Hoyt, Portland, OR 97210. Tel: 503-226-6977. Very Rev. Robert B. Grimm, S.J., Prov; Revs. Brad R. Reynolds, S.J., Socius and Legal Sec. & Asst. for Formation; Ignatius F. Ohno, S.J., Treas., Exec. Asst. to Prov. & Liaison for International & Social Ministries.

Legal Titles: *Society of Jesus, Oregon Province,* Portland, OR; *The Pioneer Educational Society,* Spokane, WA; *Montana Catholic Missions, SJ.*

Fathers 223; Scholastics 34; Brothers 16.

Properties owned, sponsored, or staffed: Parishes 7; Universities 2; High Schools 4; Middle Schools 1; House of Study 1; Novitiates 1.

Represented in the Archdioceses of Anchorage, Portland in Oregon and Seattle and in the Dioceses of Baker, Boise, Fairbanks, Great Falls-Billings, Helena, Spokane and Yakima.

Detroit Province- Society of Jesus (S.J.) (1955): 7303 W. Seven Mile Rd., Detroit, MI 48221. Tel: 313-861-7500; Fax: 313-861-4230. Very Rev. John F. Libens, S.J., Prov. Supr.; Revs. Keith J. Esenther, S.J., Exec. Asst.; Walter L. Farrell, S.J., Treas.; Richard H. Twohig, S.J., Asst.-Intl. Apostolates & Secondary Education; John E. Dister, S.J., Asst.-for Social Ministries; Dennis T. Dillon, S.J., Asst. Formation; Robert J. Scullin, S.J., Asst. Pastoral Ministries; Daniel T. Reim, S.J., Asst. Vocation Promotion.

Fathers 156; Scholastics 12; Brothers 16.

Properties owned, sponsored, or staffed: Parishes 6; Universities 2; High Schools 5; Retreat Houses 3.

Legal Titles: *Detroit Province of the Society of Jesus; Colombiere Center,* Clarkston, MI; *Jesuit Retreat House of Cleveland, Ohio; Jesuit Seminary Association; Jesuit International Missions; John Carroll University of Cleveland, Ohio; John Carroll Jesuit Community Corporation; Loyola High School,* Detroit, MI; *Loyola of the Lakes Jesuit Retreat House, Inc.; Manresa Jesuit Retreat House; Patna Jesuit Mission Society, Inc.; St. Ignatius High School of Cleveland, Ohio; St. John's Jesuit High School of Toledo, Ohio; University of Detroit Mercy; The Jesuit Community Corporation at the University of Detroit; University of Detroit Jesuit High School and Academy; Walsh Jesuit High School.*

Represented in the Archdioceses of Boston, Chicago, Cincinnati, Detroit, New York, Washington and the Dioceses of Buffalo, Cleveland, Columbus, Davenport, Fort Wayne-South Bend, Lexington, Oakland, Richmond, Saginaw, Toledo, Wheeling-Charleston and Worcester.

Wisconsin Province- Society of Jesus (S.J.) (1955): 3400 W. Wisconsin Ave., P.O. Box 080288, Milwaukee, WI 53208-0288. Tel: 414-937-6949; Fax: 414-937-6950. Very Rev. D. Edward Mathie, S.J., Prov. & Coord. for Higher Education, Revs. James E. Grummer, S.J., Asst. Prov. & Asst. for Intl. Ministries; Asst. for Secondary Education; Richard P. Abert, S.J., Asst.-Formation & Cross-Cultural Ministries; Eugene M. Dutkiewicz, S.J., Asst.-Finance; David J. Haschka, S.J., Asst.-Pastoral & Retreat Ministries; Social & International Ministries; Richard A. McGarrity, S.J., Pres.-Jesuit; Partnership.

Legal Title: *Wisconsin Province of the Society of Jesus.*

Fathers 270; Novices 12; Brothers 19; Scholastics 7.

Properties owned, sponsored, or staffed: Parishes 5; Universities 2; High Schools 3; Middle Schools 2; Community Houses 19; Novitiate; Native American Missions 3; Ethnic Parishes 2; Retreat Houses 3.

Represented in the Archdioceses of Milwaukee, Omaha and St. Paul-Minneapolis and in the Dioceses of Green Bay, La Crosse, Rapid City, Winona, and Cheyenne.

Province of the Antilles (1947): *Correa y Cindron,* 28; P.O. Box 76, Santo Domingo, Dominican Republic. Tel: 809-532-5628.

U.S. Address: 13339 S.W. 9 Terrace, Miami, FL 33184. Very Rev. Benjamin Gonzalez-Buelta, S.J., Prov.; Rev. Victor Hernandez, S.J., Miami Reg. Supr.

Fathers 107; Scholastics 44; Brothers 17.

Properties owned, staffed or sponsored: High Schools: Loyola in Dominican Republic Belen Jesuit Prep in Miami; Novitiate 1; House of Retreat 3 in Santo Domingo; Juan Pablo II in Miami; Residences 2.

Represented in the Archdiocese of Miami. Also in Santo Domingo.

[0700] (S.S.J.)—ST. JOSEPH'S SOCIETY OF THE SACRED HEART

(The Josephites)

(Societas Sancti Joseph SSmi Cordis)

Central House of Administration: 1130 N. Calvert St., Baltimore, MD 21202. Tel: 410-727-3386; Fax: 410-727-1006. Very Rev. Robert M. Kearns, S.S.J., Supr. Gen.

Fathers 111; Brothers 9; Students in House of Studies 2; Seminarians 3.

Legal Title: *St. Joseph's Society of the Sacred Heart, Inc.*

Properties owned, staffed, or sponsored: Parishes 54; Elementary Schools 18; High School; House of Study; Major Seminary; Novitiate; Nigerian Missions.

Represented in the Archdioceses of Baltimore, Los Angeles, Mobile, New Orleans and Washington and in the Dioceses of Arlington, Baton Rouge, Beaumont, Biloxi, Birmingham, Fort Worth, Galveston-Houston, Lafayette (LA), Lake Charles, Jackson, and Wilmington. Also in Nigeria.

[0710] (C.J.)—JOSEPHITE FATHERS
(Congregatio Iosephitarum Gerardimontensium)
General Motherhouse: Geraardsbergen, Belgium. Very Rev. Richard Lear, C.J., Supr. Gen.
U.S. Foundation (1963): *St. Joseph Seminary, Provincialate and Novitiate,* 180 Patterson Road, Santa Maria, CA 93455. Tel: 805-937-5378; Fax: 805-937-5759. Very Rev. Charles Hofschulte, C.J., Prov. Supr.
Fathers 14; Brothers 1.
Ministry to: Parishes; Academic Education; Military Chaplaincy.
Represented in the Archdiocese of Los Angeles.

[0720] (M.S.)—THE MISSIONARIES OF OUR LADY OF LA SALETTE
(Congregatio Missionariorum Vulgo "De la Salette")
General House: Piazza Madonna Della Salette 3, Rome 00152, Italy. Very Rev. Isidro Perin, M.S., Supr. Gen.
American Region was established 1892; Canonically erected 1934; Divided into other Provinces in 1945, 1958, 1967and 2000.
Province of Our Lady of Seven Dolors (1934): 915 Maple Ave., Hartford, CT 06114-2330. Tel: 860-956-8870. Very Rev. Dennis J. Loomis, M.S., Prov.; Revs. James H. Kuczynski, M.S., Vicar; Peter D. Kohler, M.S., Asst.; Joseph M. O'Neil, M.S., Asst. & Treas.
Legal Titles: *Missionaries of LaSalette Corp.; Religious Trust of the Missionaries of Our Lady of La Salette; Province of Our Lady of Seven Dolors.*
Priests 88; Brothers 13; Oblate Brothers 1; Scholastics 1.
Represented in the Archdioceses of Atlanta, Boston, Hartford, New York, St. Paul-Minneapolis and Washington and in the Dioceses of Albany, Manchester, Norwich, Orlando, Raleigh, Springfield (MA) and Worcester.
Province of the Immaculate Heart of Mary (1945): *Missionaries of Our Lady of La Salette,* 947 Park St., P.O. Box 2965, Attleboro, MA 02703-0965. Tel: 617-222-7171; Fax: 508-222-6178. Very Rev. Dennis J. Loomis, M.S., Prov. Supr., Revs. Bernard B. Baris, M.S., Vicar; Roland S. Nadeau, M.S., Councillor & Sec; Bro. Claude Rheaume, M.S., Treas.
Priests 51; Brothers 20; Oblates 1.
Missionaries (priests and brothers) serve: Parishes 7; Shrines 2; Retreat House 1; Hospital Chaplaincies 3; College Chaplaincies.
Properties owned: *La Salette Shrine, Provincial House and Center for Christian Living,* Attleboro, MA; *La Salette Shrine,* Enfield, NH.
Represented in the Dioceses of Burlington, Fall River, Manchester and Tucson. Also in Canada.
Province of Mary Queen (1958): *La Salette Missionaries,* 4650 S. Broadway, St. Louis, MO 63111-1303. Tel: 314-353-5000; Fax: 314-353-4582. Very Rev. Dennis J. Meyer, M.S., Prov. Supr.; Revs. Peter D. Kohler, M.S., Prov. Vicar; Sec. & Treas.; Eduardo Nevares, M.S., Prov. Asst.
Legal Title: *Missionaries of La Salette Corporation of Missouri.*
Fathers 35; Professed Brothers 4; Oblate Brothers 2.
Parishes 14; Religious Houses 5; Chaplaincies 4.
Represented in the Archdiocese of St. Louis and in the Dioceses of Beaumont, Galveston-Houston, Jefferson City, Lake Charles, and Tyler.
Province of Mary, Queen of Peace (1967): P.O. Box 250, Twin Lakes, WI 53181. Tel: 414-877-3123. Revs. James Stajkowski, M.S., Prov.; Terrence Niziolek, M.S., Vicar; Bro. Adam Mateja, M.S., Councillor; Rev. Thaddeus Galuszka, M.S., Treas.
Priests 16; Missionary Brothers 4; Oblate Brothers 1.
Represented in the Archdiocese of Milwaukee and the Diocese of Peoria.

[0730] (L.C.)—LEGIONARIES OF CHRIST
Founded in Mexico 1941, first foundation in United States 1965.
General Headquarters: Via Aurelia 677, Rome, Italy. Tel: 011-39-06-664991; Fax: 011-39-06-66416553. Very Rev. Marcial Maciel, L.C., Founder and Supr. Gen.
U.S. Headquarters: Attn: Fr. John Curran, L.C. 393 Derby Ave., Orange, CT 06477. Tel: 203-795-2800; Fax: 203-795-2808. Rev. Anthony Bannon, L.C., Natl. Dir. *Novitiate and Juniorate,* 475 Oak Ave., Cheshire, CT 06410. Tel: 203-271-0805. Rev. Julio Marti, L.C., Rector.
Priests 66; Religious 68; Novices 55; Juniors 53.
Represented in the Archdioceses of Atlanta, Chicago, Denver, Detroit, Hartford, Los Angeles, New York, Washington and the Dioceses of Dallas, Lincoln, Manchester, Madison Providence and Sacramento.

[0740] (M.I.C.)—CONGREGATION OF MARIANS OF THE IMMACULATE CONCEPTION
(Congregatio Clericorum Marianorum sub titulo Immaculatae Conceptionis Beatae Mariae Virginis)
General Motherhouse: via Corsica no. 1, Rome, Italy. Very Rev. Mark Garrow, M.I.C.; Very Rev. Jan Rokosz, M.I.C., Vicar Gen.
American Province of St. Casimir (1913): 6336 S. Kilbourn Ave., Chicago, IL 60629-5588. Tel: 773-582-8191; Fax: 773-582-8961. Very Rev. Donald S. Petraitis, M.I.C., Prov., Revs. Jerome Zalonis, M.I.C.; Timothy Roth, M.I.C.; Bros. Brian Manian, M.I.C.; Donald Schaefer, M.I.C., Prov. Treas.
Fathers 30; Seminarians 4; Brothers 2.
Properties owned, staff or sponsored: Parishes 8; High School 1; Community Houses 8.
Represented in the Archdioceses of Chicago and Milwaukee and in the Dioceses of Joliet, Norwich and Worcester. Also in Argentina.
St. Stanislaus Kostka Province: 2 Prospect Hill Rd., Stockbridge, MA 01262-0951. Tel: 413-298-3931. Very Rev. Walter Dziordz, M.I.C., Prov. Supr.; Councilors: Revs. Joseph Roesch, M.I.C.; Seraphim Michalenko, M.I.C.; Bro. Andrew Maczynski, M.I.C., Dir. Marian Helpers Center; Rev. Daniel Papineau, M.I.C.
Legal Holdings: *Marian Helpers Center; Marian Scholasticate; Divine Mercy International; John Paul II Institute of Divine Mercy; National Shrine of the Divine Mercy.*
Fathers 23; Brothers 8; Seminarians 5; Novices 1; Postulants 2.
Properties owned, staffed or sponsored: 3 Community Houses; Novitiate; Filial House; Residence.
Represented in the Archdiocese of Washington and the Dioceses of Fairbanks, Portland (ME), Steubenville and Springfield. Also in Portugal.

[0750] (C.M.M.)—CONGREGATION OF MARIANNHILL MISSIONARIES, MARIANNHILL FATHERS AND BROTHERS
(Congregatio Missionariorum de Mariannhill)
Generalate: Via S. Giovanni Eudes 91 00163, Rome, Italy. Very Rev. Yves LaFontaine, C.M.M., Supr. Gen.
American-Canadian Province (1938): *Our Lady of Grace Monastery,* 23715 Ann Arbor Trail, Dearborn Hts., MI 48127. Tel: 313-561-7140; Fax: 313-561-9486. Revs. Thomas Heier, C.M.M., American Reg.; Thomas Szura, C.M.M., Procurator.
Fathers 11; Brothers 3.
Legal Holdings: *Mariannhill Retreat Center,* Dearborn Heights, MI.
Represented in the Archdiocese of Detroit.

[0760] (S.M.)—SOCIETY OF MARY
(Marianists—Brothers of Mary)
(Societas Mariae—Marianistae)
General Motherhouse: Via Latina 22 00179 Rome, Italy. Very Rev. David Fleming, S.M., Supr. Gen.
Province of Cincinnati (1849): *Marianist Provincialate,* 4435 E. Patterson Rd., Dayton, OH 45430-1095. Tel: 937-429-0794; Fax: 937-429-3195. Bro. Joseph H. Kamis, S.M., Prov. Supr.; Councillors: Revs. Joseph H. Lackner, S.M.; Joseph P. Tedesco, S.M.; Bros. Robert J. Metzger, S.M.; Bernard J. Ploeger, S.M.
Legal Holdings or Titles: *Mount St. John; Bergamo Center; University of Dayton; Chaminade-Julienne High School; Marianist Mission,* Dayton OH; *Governor's Island,* Huntsville, OH; *Marianist Communities* in: Cleveland, OH; Cincinnati, OH; Dayton, OH; Portage, MI; Pittsburgh, PA.
Fathers 56; Brothers 158; Brothers Perpetual Professed 131; Temporary Professed 25; Novices 11; Aspirants 3.
Properties owned, sponsored, or staffed: Universities 1; High Schools 5; Parishes 5; Apostolic Centers 1; Novitiates 2.
Represented in the Archdiocese of Cincinnati and the Diocese of Cleveland, Kalamazoo and Pittsburgh.
Province of St. Louis (1908): *Marianist Provincialate,* P.O. Box 23130, St. Louis, MO 63156. Tel: 314-367-0390; Fax: 314-361-3131. Rev. Timothy Dwyer, S.M., Prov., Supr.; Bros. Jerome Bommer, S.M., Asst. Prov.; Richard Dix, S.M., Temporalities; Rev. Alvin McMenamy, S.M., Religious Life.
Fathers 58; Brothers 177; Novices 35.
Members serve and staff: Parishes 6; University 1; High Schools 5; Retreat House 1; Missions in India & Mexico.
Properties owned: *St. Mary's University,* San Antonio, TX; *Central Catholic Marianist High School,* San Antonio, TX; *Chaminade Preparatory,* St. Louis, MO; *Vianney High School,* St. Louis, MO; *Marianist Retreat & Conference Center,* Eureka, MO.
Represented in the Archdioceses of Chicago, New Orleans, St. Louis and San Antonio and in the Dioceses of Belleville, Fort Worth and Galveston-Houston.
Province of the Pacific (1948): *Marianist Provincial Residence,* 22825 San Juan Rd., Cupertino, CA 95014-3934. Mailing Address:, P.O. Box 1775, Cupertino, CA 95015-1775. Tel: 408-253-4841; Fax: 408-253-5280. Very Rev. John Russi, S.M., Prov. & Religious Life; Bros. Gary Morris, S.M., Asst. Prov. & Dir.-Education; John Haster, S.M., Temporalities.
Legal Title: *Marianist Province of the Pacific, a Hawaii Corp.*
Fathers 25; Brothers 59; Parishes 2; University 1; High Schools 4; Middle Schools 1.
Legal Holdings: *Marianist Community,* Santa Clara, CA; *Marianist Community,* San Jose, CA; *Marianist Center; Villa St. Joseph; Marianist Provincialate,* Cupertino, CA.
Represented in the Archdioceses of Los Angeles, San Francisco and the Dioceses of Honolulu, Oakland, Monterey and San Jose. Also in Korea.
Province of New York (1961): *Marianist Provincial House,* 4301 Roland Ave., Baltimore, MD 21210. Tel: 410-366-1300. Bro. Stephen M. Glodek, S.M., Prov.; Rev. George J. Cerniglia, S.M., Asst. Prov. Councillors; Bros. Francisco Gonzalez, S.M.; Steven O'Neil, S.M.; Rev. Christopher Conlon, S.M.
Legal Titles & Holdings: *Marianist Society, Inc. - A Maryland Corporation; Marianist Society of Florida, Inc. - A Florida Corporation; Marianist Provincial House,* Baltimore, MD; *Marianist Community Residence,* Baltimore, MD; *Marianist Family Center,* Cape May Point, NJ; *Marianist Community Residence,* Vernon, CT; *Marianist Community Residence,* Hollywood, FL; *Chaminade / Madonna High School,* Hollywood, FL; *Mission Noell,* Villalba, PR; *Colegio San Jose,* Rio Piedras, PR.
Fathers 27; Brothers 59.
Properties owned, sponsored, or staffed: High Schools 2; Orphanage 1; Parishes 2; Apostolic Centers 3.
Represented in the Archdioceses of Baltimore, Boston, Hartford, Miami, Philadelphia, San Antonio, and the Dioceses of Brooklyn, Camden, Fort Wayne-South Bend, Norwich, Orange, Raleigh, and Rockville Centre. Also in the Archdiocese of San Juan and the Diocese of Ponce.
Province of Meribah (1976): *Marianist Provincial Residence,* 240 Emory Rd., Mineola, NY 11501. Tel: 516-742-5555. Very Rev. Thomas A. Cardone, S.M., Prov.; Bro. Kenneth M. Hoagland, S.M., Asst. Prov. & Asst. for Education; Rev. James C. Williams, S.M., Asst. for Religious Life; Bro. Richard J. Hughes, S.M., Asst. for Temporalities; Rev. Philip K. Eichner, S.M., Councillor; Bro. Thomas J. Cleary, S.M., Councillor.
Legal Holdings: *Chaminade High School,* Mineola, NY; *Kellenberg Memorial High School,* Uniondale, NY.
Fathers 7; Brothers 32.
Properties owned, sponsored, or staffed: High Schools 2; Retreat Houses 2.

[0770] (F.M.S.)—THE MARIST BROTHERS
(Fratres Maristae a Scholis)
Generalate: Rome, Italy. Rev. Bro. Benito Arbues, F.M.S., Supr. Gen.; Rev. Bro. Sean D. Sammon, F.M.S., Vicar Gen.
Province of Esopus (1959): *Provincial Office,* 1241 Kennedy Blvd., Bayonne, NJ 07002. Tel: 201-823-1115; Fax: 201-823-2232. Bros. Leo Shea, F.M.S., Prov.; Robert Clark, F.M.S., Asst. Prov.; Councillors: Bros. Patrick Hogan, F.M.S.; Roy George, F.M.S.; Stephen Schlitte, F.M.S.; Benjamin Consigli, F.M.S.; Kevin O'Neill, F.M.S., Prov. Treas.; Stephen Milan, F.M.S., Vocation Dir.
Brothers 140.
Represented in the Archdioceses of Boston, Miami, Newark, New York and in the Dioceses of Brooklyn, Brownsville, Rockville Centre, Savannah and Wheeling-Charleston. Also in West Africa.
Poughkeepsie Province (1959): *Provincial Administration,* 26 First Ave., Pelham, NY 10803. Tel: 914-738-0740. Bros. Donnell Neary, F.M.S., Prov.; Michael Flanigan, F.M.S., Vice Prov.; Kevin O'Neill, F.M.S., Prov. Treas.; Hugh Turley, F.M.S., Devel.; Patrick Tyrrell, F.M.S., Dir. Marist Foreign Missions; Councillors: Bros. Donald Bisson, F.M.S.; Richard Carey, F.M.S.; Thomas Long, F.M.S.
Brothers 106.
Properties owned, staff or sponsored: High Schools 8; Community Houses 19; Junior High School 1; community school located in Japan.
Represented in the Archdioceses of Boston, Chicago, Miami, New York and in the Diocese of Houma-Thibodau, Manchester and Wheeling-Charleston.

[0780] (S.M.)—MARIST FATHERS
(Societas Mariae)

General Motherhouse: via Alessandro Poerio 63, Rome 00151, Italy. Very Rev. Joaquin Fernandez, S.M., Supr. Gen. Rev. John Harhager, S.M., Treas. Gen.

The first Marist foundation in the United States was in 1863, St. Michael's in Convent, Louisiana. The first Marist Province in the United States was established in 1889 under the name of American Province. This Province was subdivided in 1924 into the Washington Province and the Boston Province; On January 1, 1962, the San Francisco Province was established. On January 1, 2000 the San Francisco and Washington Province merged. On September 8, 2000 the merged entity became the Atlanta Province. The Boston Province continues as a separate province.

Atlanta Province (2000): P.O. Box 81144, Atlanta, GA 30366-1144. Tel: 770-458-1435. Very Rev. Dennis J. Steik, S.M., Prov.; Revs. Richmond J. Egan, S.M., Vicar Prov. & Councilor; H. Joseph Wilhelm, S.M., Prov. Treas.; Timothy F. Sugrue, S.M., Business Mgr. & Mission Promoter; Francis Springer, S.M., Mission Promoter; William F. Rowland, S.M., Dir. Vocations; Charles Girard, S.M., Archivist; Edwin L. Keel, S.M., Promoter of Marist Laity; Prov. Council: Revs. J. Michael Seifert, S.M.; Paul Hachey, S.M.; Timothy G. Keating, S.M.; Rene J. Iturbe, S.M.

Legal Holdings & Titles: *Marist Society, Inc.; Marist College; Marist Provincial House,* Washington, DC; *Marist Society of OH,* Cleveland, OH; *Marist Society of LA; Marist Community,* New Orleans, LA; *Marist Society of PA,* Philadelphia, PA.

Fathers 90; Brothers 14; Scholastics 4.

Properties owned, sponsored, or staffed: Community Houses 4; Parishes 12; Seminaries/Houses of Study and High School.

Represented in the Archdioceses of Atlanta, Chicago, Miami, Military Services, New Orleans, New York, Philadelphia, St. Paul-Minneapolis, Washington and the Dioceses of Austin, Baton Rouge, Brooklyn, Brownsville, Honolulu, Monterey, Oakland, Orlando, St. Petersburg, and Wheeling-Charleston.

Boston Province (Marist Fathers) (1924): *Marist Provincial House,* 27 Isabella St., Boston, MA 02116-5216. Tel: 617-426-5297; Fax: 617-482-1570. Very Rev. Kenneth Thibodeau, S.M., Prov.; Rev. Albert DiIanni, S.M., Vicar Prov. & Prov. Dir. of Third Order of Mary & Vocation Dir.; Prov. Council: Revs. Philip Parent, S.M.; John Sajdak, S.M.; Gerard Demers, S.M.; Raymond Arsenault, S.M., Prov. Treas.; Robert Graham, S.M., Prov. Archivist; J. Armand Robichaud, S.M., Marist Missions & Council; Gerard Caron, S.M., Dir. Paratours Inc. & Lourdes Center. Tel: 617-247-2533.

Legal Titles: *Marist Fathers of Boston; Marist Fathers of Detroit, Inc.; Marist Fathers of New York.*

Fathers 72; Brothers 6; Seminarians 4.

Properties owned, sponsored, or staffed: Community Houses 7; Parishes 6; High Schools 2; Retreat House.

Represented in the Archdioceses of Boston, Hartford, Detroit and the Dioceses of Brooklyn, Burlington, and Portland (ME).

Third Order of Mary. Envisioned as the Third or Lay Branch of the Society of Mary by its Founder, Father Jean-Claude Colin. The Third Order of Mary was approved in 1850 for lay men and women, as well as for members of the Diocesan Clergy. The rule was written by Rev. Jean Claude Colin, founder of the Society of Mary, the Marist Fathers and Brothers. It was approved by the Holy See in 1836. There are confraternities throughout the world. New styles of confraternities are being formed to help evangelize the world after the spirit of Jesus and Mary. Information concerning this Third Order of Mary or the Marist Laity Movement may be obtained from: Third Order of Mary-Marist Laity, 518 Pleasant St., Framingham, MA 01701-2898. Tel: 508-875-6075; 879-1620; Fax: 508-879-0719. Rev. Albert Dilanni, S.M., Dir.

[0782] (O.M.M.)—MARONITE ORDER OF BLESSED VIRGIN MARY

Maronite Order of the Blessed Virgin Mary: 4405 Earhart Rd., Ann Arbor, MI 48105. Tel: 734-662-4822; Fax: 734-662-4822. Rev. Roger Chikri, O.M.M.; Paul Acaf, O.M.M.; Nahed Tarabay, O.M.M.

[0785] (C.M.L.M.)—THE CONGREGATION OF MARONITE LEBANESE MISSIONARIES

Founded at the Monastery of Kreim-Ghosta (Mountain of Lebanon), in the year 1865. Established in the United States March of 1991: Agreement between Archbishop Zayek of the Diocese of St. Maron and the Congregation to serve the parishes of San Antonio, Dallas and Houston.

U.S. Headquarters: *Our Lady of the Cedars Maronite Mission,* 11935 Bellford Village, Houston, TX 77031. Tel: 281-568-6800; Fax: 281-564-6961. Rev. Abdallah Zaidan, C.M.L.M. Supr.

Bishops 2; Priests 78; Brothers 2; Seminarians 19; Novices 3; Postulants 6.

Represented in the Dioceses of Our Lady of Lebanon.

[0790] (O.Mar.)—MONASTERY OF MARONITE MONKS

Monastery of the Most Holy Trinity: 67 Dugway Rd., Petersham, MA 01366. Tel: 978-724-3347. Rt. Rev. William J. Driscoll, O. Mar., Abbot; Revs. Giles R. Goyette, O. Mar., 1st Councillor; Michael Cermak, O. Mar., Vicar.

Priests 11; Brothers 6.

Monastery of the Holy Nativity (a dependency of Holy Trinity Monastery, Petersham, MA), Bethlehem, SD 57769-0170. Tel: 605-787-4606. Rev. Louis Marie Dauphinais, O.Mar., Supr.

Priests 2; Brothers 3.

Represented in the Diocese of St. Maron, Brooklyn.

[0800] (M.M.)—MARYKNOLL

Catholic Foreign Mission Society of America, Inc.

U.S. Foundation (1911): *Maryknoll Society Center & Admin. Offices,* Maryknoll, NY 10545-0305. Tel: 914-941-7590; Fax: 914-762-0316. Revs. Raymond J. Finch, M.M., Supr. Gen.; Jeremiah R. Burr, M.M., Vicar Gen.; Assts. General: Revs. Thomas P. Henehan, M.M.; Michael J. Snyder, M.M.; Bro. Wayne J. Fitzpatrick, M.M.

Legal Title: *Catholic Foreign Mission Society of America Incorporated,* Training Center; *Maryknoll Society Center,* Maryknoll, NY 10545.

Houses in Archdioceses and Dioceses:

Boston. *Maryknoll Fathers and Brothers,* 80 Emerson Rd., East Walpole, MA 02032. Tel: 508-668-6831; Fax: 508-660-0252.

Buffalo. *Maryknoll Fathers and Brothers,* 71 Jewett Pkwy., Buffalo, NY 14214-2396. Tel: 716-834-6065; 716-834-3478.

Chicago. *Maryknoll Fathers and Brothers,* 3600 Seeley Ave., Chicago, IL 60609-1148. Tel: 773-927-9257; Fax: 773-927-7305. Seminary Residence, 5508 S. Cornell Ave., Chicago, IL 60637. Tel: 773-288-3143; Fax: 773-288-3950

Cincinnati. *Maryknoll Fathers and Brothers,* 6930 Greenfield Dr., Cincinnati, OH 45224. Tel: 513-681-7888; Fax: 513-761-5887.

Cleveland. *Maryknoll Fathers and Brothers,* 10309 Edgewater Dr., Cleveland, OH 44102. Tel: 216-651-2121; Fax: 216-651-8242.

Denver. *Maryknoll Fathers and Brothers,* 4460 Federal Blvd., Denver, CO 80211. Tel: 303-455-5669; Fax: 303-455-5753.

Galveston-Houston. *Maryknoll Fathers and Brothers,* 2360 Rice Blvd., Houston, TX 77005. Tel: 713-529-1912; Fax: 713-529-0372.

New York. *Maryknoll Fathers and Brothers,* 121 E. 39th St., New York, NY 10016. Tel: 212-697-4470; Fax: 212-697-4472.

Los Angeles. *Maryknoll Fathers and Brothers,* 745 W. Adams Blvd., Los Angeles, CA 90007. Tel: 213-747-9676; Fax: 213-747-8923.

Philadelphia. *Maryknoll Fathers and Brothers,* 6367 Overbrook Ave., Philadelphia, PA 19151. Tel: 215-477-5892; Fax: 215-477-3088.

Rockville Centre. *Maryknoll Fathers and Brothers,* 813 Myrna Dr., West Hempstead, NY 11552. Tel: 516-489-7799.

St. Augustine. *Maryknoll Fathers and Brothers,* 2243 Saragossa Ave., Jacksonville, FL 32217-2685. Tel: 904-739-1112; Fax: 904-739-9083.

St. Louis. *Maryknoll Fathers and Brothers,* 4542 W. Pine Blvd., St. Louis, MO 63108. Tel: 314-361-7729; Fax: 314-361-0718.

St. Paul. *Maryknoll Fathers and Brothers,* 10345 Portland Ave. S., Minneapolis, MN 55420. Tel: 612-884-7743; Fax: 612-884-7744.

San Francisco. *Maryknoll Fathers and Brothers,* 2555 Webster St., San Francisco, CA 94115. Tel: 415-921-1100; Fax: 415-775-8261.

San Jose. *Maryknoll Residence,* 23000 Cristo Rey Dr., Los Altos, CA 94024. Tel: 650-967-3822; Fax: 650-965-3473.

Seattle. *Maryknoll Fathers and Brothers,* 958 16th Ave., E., Seattle, WA 98112. Tel: 206-322-8831; Fax: 206-324-6909.

Washington. *Maryknoll Fathers and Brothers,* 4834 16th St., N.W., Washington, DC 20011. Tel: 202-726-4252; 726-4281; Fax: 207-726-0466.

Priests 504; Students in Theology 17; Brothers 67; Priests Associates 4.

Properties owned or sponsored: Major Society Center; House of Formation; U.S. Community Houses 24.

Represented in the Archdioceses of Boston, Chicago, Cincinnati, Denver, Detroit, Los Angeles, New York, Philadelphia, St. Louis, St. Paul-Minneapolis, San Francisco, Seattle, Washington and in the Dioceses of Buffalo, Cleveland, Galveston-Houston and San Jose.

[0810] (F.M.M.)—BROTHERS OF MERCY

General Motherhouse: D-56412 Montabaur, Germany. Bro. Stephen Geisslen, F.M.M., Supr. Gen.

American Province: 4520 Ransom Rd., Clarence, NY 14031. Tel: 716-759-8341; Fax: 716-759-8341. Bros. Jude Holzfoerster, F.M.M., Prov. Supr.; Councillors: Bros. John McGrath, F.M.M.; Fidelis Verrall, F.M.M.

Brothers 16; Novices 1; Candidate 1.

Legal Holdings or Titles: *Brothers of Mercy Nursing Home Co., Inc.; Brothers of Mercy Housing Co., Inc.; Brothers of Mercy Sacred Heart Home, Inc.*

Represented in the Diocese of Buffalo.

[0820] (C.P.M.)—CONGREGATION OF THE FATHERS OF MERCY

(Congregatio Presbyterorum a Misericordia)

Generalate and Novitiate (1808): 806 Shaker Museum Rd., South Union, KY 42283. Tel: 270-542-4146; Fax: 270-542-4147. Web site: www.fathersofmercy.com Very Rev. William Casey, C.P.M., Supr. Gen.; Consultors: Revs. Joseph Burgdorf, C.P.M.; John O'Brien, C.P.M.; David Wilton, C.P.M.; Louis Caporiccio, C.P.M.

Priests 24; Novices 2; Students 11.

Represented in the Archdiocese of Louisville and in the Diocese Owensboro.

[0825] M.S.S.—MISSIONARIES OF THE BLESSED SACRAMENT

Missionaries of the Blessed Sacrament

Regional Headquarters: P.O. Box 4337, Corpus Christi, TX 78469. Tel: 512-881-5025; Fax: 512-883-1581. Rev. Martin V. Lucia, M.S.S., Supr.

Fathers 4.

Ministries in Special Apostolate: Promotion of perpetual Eucharistic adoration.

Represented in the Dioceses of Alexandria, Baton Rouge, Corpus Christi, Lafayette, and Lake Charles.

[0830] (M.H.M.)—MILL HILL MISSIONARIES

St. Joseph's Missionary Society of Mill Hill

International Headquarters: *St. Joseph's College,* Mill Hill, London NW7 4JX, England. Very Rev. Jac Hetsen, M.H.M., Supr. Gen.

American Headquarters: *Mill Hill Missionaries,* 222 W. Hartsdale Ave., Hartsdale, NY 10530-1667. Tel: 914-682-0645; Fax: 914-682-0862. Very Rev. Terence J. Lee, M.H.M., Reg. Rep.

Legal Title: *Mill Hill Fathers, Inc.*

Fathers 13; Brothers 2; Associates 1.

Represented in the Archdioceses of Los Angeles & New York.

[0835] (O.M.)—MINIM FATHERS

General Motherhouse: Via S. Andrea delle Fratte, 1 00184, Rome, Italy. Tel: 011-39-6-678-0407; Fax: 011-39-6-678-0752. Very Rev. Giuseppe Morosini, O.M., Supr. Gen.

North American Delegation (1970): 3431 Portola Ave., Los Angeles, CA 90032. Tel: 323-223-1101. Friar Constantino Mandarino, O.M., Delegate Gen.

Legal Title: *Minim Fathers.*

Priests 3.

Vocation Center, 6043 N. Barranca Ave., Azusa, CA 91702.

Represented in the Archdiocese of Los Angeles.

[0840] (S.T.)—MISSIONARY SERVANTS OF THE MOST HOLY TRINITY

(Missionarii Servi Sanctissimae Trinitatis)
(Trinity Missions)

Generalate-Missionary Servants of the Most Holy Trinity: 1215 N. Scott St., Arlington, VA 22209-3097. Tel: 703-276-8646; Fax: 703-522-2656. Rev. Austin Walsh, S.T., Gen. Custodian, Revs. John S. Edmunds, S.T., Vicar Gen.; Jesus Rivera, S.T., Gen. Councilor; Gary Banks, S.T., Gen. Councilor; Bros. Steven Vesely, S.T., Sec. Gen.; Jordan Baxter, S.T., Treas. Gen.; Paul Michalenko, S.T., Gen Councilor.

Legal Titles: *Missionary Servants of The Most Holy Trinity (a.k.a) Trinity Missions; Missionary Servants*

Charitable Trust; Father Judge Charitable Trust.
Priests 92; Brothers 32; Student Brothers 15; Novices 6; Candidates 37; Deacon 2.
Ministry in the following areas: Missionary Cenacles; Parishes; Missions; Stations and Specialized Apostolates; Lay Apostolate Secretariat; Halfway House; Auxiliary Military Chaplaincies; Counseling Centers; Hospitals and Rest Home Chaplains; AA Programs; Protective Institutions; Prison Chaplains; V.A. Chaplains; Community Centers; Elementary Schools.
Properties owned and or sponsored: Generalate, Arlington, VA; Parish, rectory and school, Holy Trinity, AL; Apostolic Center, New Orleans, LA, Philadelphia, PA, Rio Piedras, PR; Seminary and Fund Raising Office Buildings, Silver Spring, MD; School Buildings, Camden, MS; St. Joseph Shrine, Stirling, NJ; Trinity Ministries Center, Stirling, NJ; Former minor seminary building, Monroe, VA; Residences: Harpers Ferry, WV, Sound Beach, NY; Residence Senior Ministry Residence, Adelphi, MD; Residence Post-Novitiate Formation House, Adelphi, MD; Holy Trinity Missionary Cenacle, University Park, MD.
Represented in the Archdioceses of Baltimore, Chicago, Los Angeles, Military Services-USA, Mobile, Newark, New Orleans, Philadelphia, Washington and the Dioceses of Arlington, Biloxi, Boise, Cleveland, Jackson, Knoxville, Orange, Paterson, Pensacola-Tallahassee, San Bernardino, San Diego, Savannah, and Tucson. Also in Mexico, Puerto Rico, Colombia, and Costa Rica.

[0850] (M.AFR.)—MISSIONARIES OF AFRICA
(Societas Missionariorum Africae)

Generalate: 269 via Aurelia, C.P. 9078 I-00165, Rome, Italy. Rev. Francois Richard, M.Afr., Supr. Gen.
Province of North America: 1624 21st St. N.W., Washington, DC 20009-1055. Tel: 202-232-5154; Fax: 202-332-8640. Revs. William Moroney, M.Afr., Asst. Prov.; David J. Goergen, M.Afr., Treas.; Roger L. Bisson, M.Afr., Dir. of Planned Giving Dept.; George Markwell, M.Afr., Chap.; John Lynch, M.Afr., Asst. Treas.
Priests 32; Brothers 2.
Represented in the Archdioceses of Chicago, Los Angeles and Washington, and in the Diocese of St. Petersburg.

[0853] (M.S.C.)—MISSIONARY SERVANTS OF CHRIST

Founded in the United States in 1979
Headquarters and Novitiate: *Missionary Servants of Christ,* P.O. Box 1932, Ocean City, MD 21842. Tel: 410-250-3386; Fax: 410-250-3386. Bro. Edwin Baker, M.S.C., Supr.
Professed Brothers 10; Novices 2; Postulants 1.
Represented in the Diocese of Wilmington.

[0854] (M.S.P.)—MISSIONARY SOCIETY OF ST. PAUL OF NIGERIA

Generalate: *Gwagwalada,* P.O. Box 23, , Abuja, Nigeria. Very Rev. Felix Elosi, M.S.P., Supr. Gen.
U.S. Region: *Missionary Society of St. Paul, Inc.,* 3607 Meriburr Ln., Houston, TX 77021-1399. Tel: 713-747-1722; Fax: 713-741-0245. Web site: www.mspfathers.org Rev. Paul N. Ofoha, M.S.P., Local Supr. Tel: 713-747-7800.
Universal number of Priests 133; Priests in U.S. 18.
Legal Titles: *Missionary Society of St. Paul, Inc.,* Houston, TX.
Represented in the Diocese of Galveston-Houston.

[0855] (F.M.M.)—MISSIONARY FRATERNITY OF MARY

General Headquarters: 6A Calle 48-98, Zona 7-Apartado Postal 623-I, Zona 7, Guatemala, Central America. Rev. Msgr. Eduardo Aguirre-Oestmann, General Moderator.
U.S. Foundation (1991): 340 Pine St., Seaford, DE 19973. Tel: 302-629-5115. Revs. Ruben A. Soto, F.M.M., U.S. Regional Vicar; Juan Vicente Hidalgo, F.M.M.
Represented in the Diocese of Wilmington.

[0860] (C.I.C.M.)—MISSIONHURST CONGREGATION OF THE IMMACULATE HEART OF MARY
(Congregatio Immaculati Cordis Mariae)

Foreign and home missions.
Generalate: *Casa Generalizia C.I.C.M.,* Via S. Giovanni Eudes, 95 00163, Rome, Italy. Very Rev. Jozef Lapauw, C.I.C.M., Supr. Gen.
U.S. Province (1946): *Missionhurst,* 4651 N. 25th St., Arlington, VA 22207. Tel: 703-528-3800; Fax: 703-528-5355. Rev. Bill Quigley, C.I.C.M., Prov.
Legal Titles: *American I.H.M. Province, Inc.; Immaculate Heart Missions, Inc.; Missionhurst, Inc.*
Fathers 50; Students 5.
Ministries in Parishes; Prison Ministry and Hospital Pastoral Work.
Represented in the Archdioceses of Detroit, Hartford, New York, Philadelphia, San Antonio and in the Dioceses of Arlington, and Brownsville.

[0870] (S.M.M.)—MONTFORT MISSIONARIES
(Missionaries of the Company of Mary)
(Societas Mariae Montfortana)

Generalate: Viale Dei Monfortani 65, Rome 00135, Italy. Very Rev. William J. Considine, S.M.M.
United States Province (1948): *Montfort Missionaries,* 101-18 104th St., Ozone Park, NY 11416. Tel: 718-849-5885; Fax: 718-849-7518. Very Rev. Gerald J. Fitzsimmons, S.M.M.; Counselors: Revs. Thomas Poth, S.M.M.; Donald LaSalle, S.M.M.; George Werner, S.M.M.; Matthew Considine, S.M.M.
Legal Titles: *Missionaries of the Company of Mary.*
Fathers 29; Brothers 3.
Parishes 2; Community Houses 6; Scholastics 1.
Represented in the Archdioceses of Hartford, St. Louis and in the Dioceses of Brooklyn, and Rockville Centre.

[0895] (O.Ss.S.)—BRIGITTINE MONKS
(The Order of the Most Holy Savior)

Priory of Our Lady of Consolation: 23300 Walker Ln., Amity, OR 97101. Tel: 503-835-8080; Fax: 503-835-9662. E-Mail: monks@brigittine.org; Web site: www.brigittine.org Bro. Steven Vargo, O.Ss.S., Prior.
Professed Monks 9; Novices 1.
Represented in the Archdiocese of Portland in Oregon.

[0897] (M.E.P.)—PARIS FOREIGN MISSION SOCIETY
(Societas Parisiensis
Missionum Ad Exteros)

Society of secular priests, without vows, of Pontifical Right.
Headquarters: 128 Rue du Bac, Paris, France. Very Rev. Jean-Baptiste Etcharren, M.E.P., Supr. Gen.
U.S. Establishment: *Paris Foreign Mission Society,* 930 Ashbury St., San Francisco, CA 94117. Tel: 415-664-6747. Rev. Jacques R. Didier, M.E.P., Dir.
Legal Title: *American Auxiliary of Paris Foreign Missions, Inc.*
Priests 2.
Represented in the Archdiocese of San Francisco.

[0900] (O. PRAEM.)—CANONS REGULAR OF PREMONTRE
(Norbertines, Order of St. Norbert,
Premonstratensians)
(Ordo Canonicorum Regularium
Praemonstratensium)

Founded in France in the 12th century. First foundation in the United States in 1893. Abbot General Most Rev. Hermenegild J. Noyens, O.Praem.
Norbertine Generalate, 27 Viale Giotto 00153, Rome, Italy. Tel: 011-39-06-5746-979; 011-39-06-5742-397; Fax: 011-39-06-574-0241.
United States: *St. Norbert Abbey,* 1016 N. Broadway, De Pere, WI 54115-2697. Tel: 920-337-4300; Fax: 920-337-4328. Rt. Rev. E. Thomas De Wane, O.Praem., Abbot; Rt. Rev. Jerome G. Tremel, O.Praem., Abbot Emeritus; Rt. Rev. Benjamin T. Mackin, O.Praem., Abbot Emeritus; Very Rev. David M. Komatz, O.Praem., Prior; Ambrose J. Peeters, O.Praem., Sub Prior, Revs. James T. Baraniak, O.Praem., Vocation Coord.; Gary J. Neville, O.Praem., Provisor/Sec.-Treas.; John L. Bostwick, O.Praem., Dir.-Norbertine Center for Spirituality; Thomas O. Meulemans, O.Praem., Mission Procurator.
Legal Titles: *The Premonstratensian Fathers; NORBERT & CO., a nominee of The Premonstratensian Fathers; Norbertine Fathers; St. Norbert Abbey, Inc.; The Walnut Markets, Inc.; Los Amigos del Peru, Inc.; Norbertine Generalate, Inc.*
Fathers 74; Seminarians 5; Brothers 6.
Properties owned, staffed, or sponsored: Dependent Priories 4; House of Studies 1; Colleges 1; Chaplaincies 5; Parishes 11.
Represented in the Archdioceses of Boston, Chicago, Military Services, Santa Fe and the Dioceses of Green Bay, Jackson, Madison and Providence. Also in Peru.
Daylesford Abbey: *Norbertine Fathers and Brothers,* 220 S. Valley Rd., Paoli, PA 19301-1900. Tel: 610-647-2530; Fax: 610-651-0219. Rt. Rev. Ronald J. Rossi, O.Praem., Abbot; Revs. John J. Novielli, O.Praem., Prior; Stephen J. Albero, O.Praem, Vocation Dir.; Francis X. Cortese, O.Praem., Master of Novices; Joseph A. Serano, O.Praem., Treas.
Legal Title: *Norbertine Fathers, Inc.*
Fathers 24; Brothers 3.
Properties owned, staffed, or sponsored: Chaplaincies 1; Seminary; Parishes 3.
Represented in the Archdiocese of Philadelphia. Also in Peru.
St. Michael's Abbey: 19292 El Toro Rd., Silverado, CA 92676. Tel: 949-858-0222; Fax: 949-858-4583.
Legal Title: *The Norbertine Fathers of Orange, Inc.* Rt. Rev. Eugene J. Hayes, O.Praem., Abbot; Very Rev. Hugh Barbour, O.Praem., Prior; *Pious Association (Aid to the Church in Need, Inc.),* P.O. Box 819, El Toro, CA 92630. Tel: 949-858-0222.
Priests 42; Deacons 1; Juniors 12; Postulants 4; Novices 1.
Properties owned: St. Michael's College Preparatory High School, Orange, CA; Summer Camp, Orange, CA.
Represented in the Archdiocese of Los Angeles and in the Diocese of Orange.

[0910] (O.M.I.)—OBLATES OF MARY IMMACULATE

General House: *Oblati di Maria Immacolata,* C.P. 9061 00100, Roma-Aurelio-Italy. Most Rev. Marcello Zago, O.M.I., Supr Gen.; Very Rev. Daniel Corijn, O.M.I., Vicar Gen.
Southwest Area of the United States Province (1904): *Missionary Oblates of Mary Immaculate,* Provincial Admin. Office 7711 Madonna Dr., San Antonio, TX 78216-6696. Tel: 210-349-1475; Fax: 210-349-7411. Very Rev. Charles Banks, O.M.I., Prov.; Revs. Salvatore DeGeorge, O.M.I., Vicar Prov; Warren Brown, O.M.I., Consultor; F. Kelly Nemeck, O.M.I., Consultor; Robert Wright, O.M.I., Consultor & Prov. Archivist; Rufus Whitley, O.M.I., Bursar.
Fathers 131; Brothers 5; Scholastics 29.
Properties owned, staffed, or sponsored: Retreat Centers; Religious Residences & Houses.
Represented in the Archdiocese of San Antonio and the Diocese of Austin, Beaumont, Brownsville, Corpus Christi, Dallas, Galveston-Houston, and San Angelo.
Eastern American Province (1883): *Our Lady of Hope:* 391 Michigan Ave., N.E., Washington, DC 20017. Revs. William Sheehan, O.M.I., Prov.; William O'Donnell, O.M.I., Vicar Prov.; Councillors: Revs. Henry Lemoncelli, O.M.I.; Stephen Conserva, O.M.I.; Thomas Coughlin, O.M.I.; James Fee, O.M.I.; John Madigan, O.M.I.
Fathers 111; Brothers 8; Professed Clerics 9.
Staff and-or serve Parishes 21, Prisons 2; Hospitals 2; Community Houses 5.
Represented in the Archdioceses of Boston, Miami, New York, Washington and in the Diocese of Buffalo, Columbus, Juneau, Lexington, Palm Beach and Pensacola-Tallahassee. Also in Puerto Rico.
Northern U.S. Province (St. John the Baptist) (1921): 200 Lowell Rd., Hudson, NH 30351-4934. Tel: 603-883-3233; Fax: 603-883-6089. Very Rev. Arthur Obin, O.M.I., Prov.; Rev. Charles Breault, O.M.I., Treas.; Councillors: Revs. Roger E. Lamoureaux, O.M.I.; Daniel Nassaney, O.M.I.; Thomas Horan, O.M.I.; James Robichaud, O.M.I.
Legal Title: *Missionary Oblates of Mary Immaculate*
Fathers 75; Scholatics (Theology) 1; Brothers 9.
Ministries in Parishes; Retreat Houses; Hospital Chaplains; Men's Correctional Institutions; Nursing Home Res. Chaplains; Religious Community Resident Chaplains; Special Ministries; U.S. Military.
Legal Holdings: *Oblate Provincial House,* Hudson, NH; *Andre Garin Residence,* Lowell, MA; *Shrine of Our Lady of Grace,* Colebrook, NH; *Oblate Retreat House,* Hudson, NH; *Oblate Foreign Missions Office,* Lowell, MA; *Oblate Ministry Development Office,* Lowell, MA; *St. Joseph the Worker Shrine & Center,* Lowell, MA; *Immaculata Retreat House,* Willimantic, CT; *St. Joseph Cemetary,* East Chelmsford, MA; *St. Eugene House,* Lowell, MA.
Represented in the Archdioceses of Boston, Miami, New Orleans, Washington and the Diocese of Manchester, Norwich, Oakland, Ogdensburg, Portland (ME), Providence, Richmond. Also in Canada and French Polynesia.
Central U.S. Province: (1924) 267 E. 8th St., St. Paul, MN 55101. Tel: 651-292-8769. Revs. David A. Kalert, O.M.I., Prov.; Thomas J. Singer, O.M.I., Vicar Prov. & Personnel Dir.; William P. Clark, O.M.I.; James F. Allen, O.M.I.; Louis B. Studer, O.M.I.; Joseph H. Hitpas, O.M.I.; William L. Johnson, O.M.I.; Robert F. Moobrugger, O.M.I., Treas.

Priests 124; Brothers 17; Scholastics 8; Novices 1; Post College Seminarians 2.
Ministries in Parishes; House of Study and Retreat Houses.
Represented in the Archdioceses of Chicago, St. Paul-Minneapolis and St. Louis and in the Dioceses of Belleville, Crookston, Duluth, Green Bay, Superior, Sioux Falls, Springfield-Cape Girardeau and Springfield (IL).
OMI Pacific Area (1953): 290 Lenox Ave., Oakland, CA 94610-4625. Tel: 510-452-1550; Fax: 510-452-3421. Very Rev. Jose Arong, O.M.I., Prov.
Ministry in Parishes; Missions; Retreat Houses; Chaplaincies.
Represented in the Archdiocese of Los Angeles, Portland (OR), Seattle and the Diocese of Boise, Fresno, Monterey, Oakland and SanDiego. Also in Mexico.

[0920] (O.S.F.S.)—OBLATES OF ST. FRANCIS DE SALES

(Congregatio Oblatorum Sancti Francisci Salesii)
General Motherhouse: Via Dandolo 49, Rome, Italy.
In July 1966, the American Province divided into two provinces.
Wilmington-Philadelphia Province (1906): 2200 Kentmere Pkwy., Wilmington, DE 19806. Very Rev. Joseph G. Morrissey, O.S.F.S., Prov.; Provincial Councillors: Revs. Edward T. Fitzpatrick, O.S.F.S.; James E. Dalton, O.S.F.S.; James J. Behan, O.S.F.S.; James J. Greenfield, O.S.F.S.; Provincial Staff: Revs. Edward T. Fitzpatrick, O.S.F.S., Dir. Personnel; Robert A. Mancini, O.S.F.S., Treas.; Richard R. De Lillio, O.S.F.S., Dir. Development; John A. Hanley, O.S.F.S., Dir. Vocations; John J. Hurley, O.S.F.S., Dir. Missions; James R. Yeakel, O.S.F.S., Formation Advisor.
Fathers 200; Scholastics 1; Brothers 21.
Properties owned, staffed, or sponsored: Parishes 21; Colleges; Scholasticates; Novitiates; High Schools 6; Retreat Houses; Armed Forces; Chaplaincies 13; Foreign Missions.
Properties owned: *Provincial Residence,* Wilmington, DE; *Salesianum School,* Wilmington, DE; *DeSales House,* Wilmington, DE; *Center for New Life,* Childs, MD; *Oblate Novitiate,* Wyndmoor, PA; *Villa St. Joseph,* Newfield, NJ; *Oblate Residence,* Cape May, NJ; *DeSales Hall,* Washington, DC; *Deshairs House,* Washington, DC.
Represented in the Archdioceses of Philadelphia, Washington and Dioceses of Allentown, Arlington, Camden, Charlotte, Harrisburg, Raleigh, Trenton, Venice and Wilmington.
Toledo-Detroit Province (1966): 2056 Parkwood Ave., Toledo, OH 43620-1616. Tel: 419-243-5105; Fax: 419-243-8827. Very Rev. James F. Cryan, O.S.F.S., Prov.; Revs. John J. Loughran, O.S.F.S., Asst. Prov.; Kenneth N. McKenna, O.S.F.S., Treas. & Councillor; Ronald W. Olszewski, O.S.F.S., Councillor.
Legal Title: *Oblates of St. Francis de Sales, Inc.*
Priests 70; Brothers 12; Professed Scholastics 1.
Properties owned, staffed, or sponsored: *Provincial Residence,* Toledo, OH; *St. Francis de Sales High School,* Toledo, OH; *Oblate Residence,* Jackson, MI; *Oblate Residence,* Toronto, Canada; *Oblate Residence,* Lewiston, NY; *Oblate Residence,* Buffalo, NY.
Ministries in Parishes; Highschools; Chaplaincies; Missionaries; Armed forces; Senior Citizens Residence.
Represented in the Archdioceses of Detroit, Miami, Military Services, and Philadelphia, and in the Dioceses of Buffalo, Erie, Kalamazoo, Lansing, Oakland, Saginaw, Salt Lake City, Stockton and Toledo. Also in Canada and the Virgin Islands.

[0930] (O.S.J.)—OBLATES OF ST. JOSEPH

(Congregatio Oblatorum S. Joseph)
Founded in Italy in 1878. Founder: Blessed Bishop Joseph Marello (1844-1895). Cause of Beatification introduced May 28, 1948. Beatified 1993. First foundation in U.S. in 1929.
Motherhouse: Corso Alfieri 384, Asti, Italy.
General House: Via Boccea, 364, Rome, Italy. Very Rev. Lino Mela, O.S.J., Supr. Gen.; Very Rev. Sebastian Jacobi, O.S.J., Vicar Gen.; Very Rev. Giocondo Bronzini, O.S.J., Procurator Gen.
Oblates of St. Joseph Eastern Province: Rte. 315, R.R. 4, Box 14, Pittston, PA 18640. Fax: 717-654-8621. Rev. Gregory T. Finn, O.S.J., Prov.; Councillors: Revs. Paul A. McDonnell, O.S.J; Daniel Schwebs, O.S.J.
Priests 10. Parishes 4; Community Houses 5; Houses of Studies 1.
Properties owned: *St. Joseph's Oblate Seminary,* Pittston, PA.
Represented in the Dioceses of Norwich and Scranton.
California Province: 544 W. Cliff Dr., Santa Cruz, CA 95060. Tel: 831-457-1868; Fax: 831-457-1317. Rev. Philip Massetti, O.S.J., Prov.; Councillors: Revs. Larry Toschi, O.S.J.; Brian Crawford, O.S.J.
Legal Title: *Oblates of St. Joseph.*
Priests 15: Brothers 3; Novices 1; Students 1.
Parishes 4; Community Houses 6; Houses of Study 2; Shrines 1.
Properties owned: *St. Joseph House of Studies,* Berkeley, CA; *Mount St. Joseph Seminary,* Loomis, CA; *Shrine of St. Joseph, Guardian of the Redeemer,* Santa Cruz, CA; *Blessed Marello House of Studies,* Oxnard CA; *St. Joseph's Villa,* Soda Springs, CA.
Represented in the Archdiocese of Los Angeles and in the Dioceses of Fresno, Monterey and Sacramento.

[0940] (O.M.V.)—OBLATES OF THE VIRGIN MARY

(Congregation of the Oblates of the Virgin Mary)
(Congregatio Oblatorum Beatae Mariae Virginis)
Generalate: Viale XXX Aprile, 17 00153, Rome, Italy. Very Rev. Patrice Veraquin, O.M.V., Rector Major.
St. Ignatius Province: 2 Ipswich St., Boston, MA 02215-3607. Tel: 617-536-4141. Rev. Timothy Gallagher, O.M.V., Prov.
Priests in U.S. 36; Brothers 3.
Legal Holdings: *St. Clement's Eucharistic Shrine,* Boston, MA; *St. Joseph House,* Milton, MA; *St. Ignatius Province of the Oblates of the Virgin Mary, Inc.*, Boston, MA.
Ministries in Parishes; Hospital and Prison Chaplaincies; Retreats & Parish Missions; Novitiate; Community Houses; College Seminary Shrine Chaplaincies.
Represented in the Archdioceses of Boston and Los Angeles and in the Dioceses of Metuchen and Springfield. Also in the Philippines.

[0950] (C.O.)—ORATORIANS

(Confederatio Oratorii S. Philippi Nerii)
A Confederation of Autonomous Houses first founded in Rome, 1575.
General Confederation: *Confederazione dell'Oratorio S. Philippi Neri,* Via S. Girolamo della Carita 63 00186, Rome, Italy. Revs. Edoardo Cerrato, C.O., Procurator Gen.; Antonio Chavez Rios, C.O., Delegate of the Holy See: The Oratory, La Profesa, Isabel La Catolica, 21 Apartado Postal 7113, Mexico, DF 06000.
The Oratory of Rock Hill: P.O. Box 11586, Rock Hill, SC 29731. Tel: 803-327-2097. Very Rev. Joseph Wahl, C.O., Father Provost.
Fathers 9; Brothers 5; Novices 1.
Represented in the Diocese of Charleston.
The Oratorian Community of Monterey: P.O. Box 1688, Monterey, CA 93942. Tel: 408-373-0476. Very Rev. Peter C. Sanders, Provost & Major Supr.; Revs. Michael P. Drury, Vicar & Sec.; Thomas A. Kieffer, Treas.
Total in community 3.
Oratorian Foundation Inc., Arizona, P.O. Box 241, Yarnell, AZ 85362. An outreach of the Oratorian Community in Monterey.
Represented in the Diocese of Monterey.
The Pittsburgh Oratory: *Congregation of the Oratory of St. Philip Neri,* 4450 Bayard Street, Pittsburgh, PA 15213-1506. Tel: 412-681-3181. Very Rev. Bryan F. Summers, C.O., Provost; Revs. Drew P. Morgan, C.O., Vicar; David S. Abernethy, C.O., Treas.
Fathers 5; Novices 1.
Represented in the Diocese of Pittsburgh.
The Oratory of Pharr: *Mailing Address,* P.O. Box II, Pharr, TX 78577-1235. Tel: 956-843-8217; Fax: 956-843-2946. Residence, end of S. Jackson Rd., FM 2061, near Hidalgo. Very Rev. Leo Francis Daniels, C.O., Provost; Revs. Jose Encarnacion Losoya, C.O., Vicar & Treas.; Alberto Aviles, C.O., Sec.; David Garcia, C.O. Very Rev. Antonio Rios, C.O., Delegate of the Holy See.
Properties owned: *Casa Maria of the Oratory,* Pharr, TX; *Oratory Academy-Academia Oratoriana,* Pharr, TX; *Pharr Oratory of St. Philip Neri of Pontifical Right.*
Ministries in Parish work; Services to the poor; promotion of Mexican-American cultural services; Education at all levels; Spanish language communities.
Secular Oratory, Lay Institute founded by St. Philip Neri. Principal Work; Federacion Mexicana del Oratorio de San Felipi Neri, American Office, The Oratory, Rte. 1, Box 118, Pharr, TX 78577. Rev. Antonio Ortega, C.O., Natl. Procurator. The Pharr Oratory is a member of the Mexican Federation of Oratories, and at present serves as the American office of all eleven houses.
Represented in the Diocese of Brownsville. Also in Mexico and Costa Rica.
The Oratory of St. Philip Neri: 109 Willoughby St., Brooklyn, NY 11201. Tel: 718-875-2096; Fax: 718-875-4678. Very Rev. Dennis M. Corrado, C.O., Provost.
Fathers 3; Brothers 1; Deacons 1.

[0960] (F.S.R.)—BROTHERS OF THE CONGREGATION OF OUR LADY OF THE HOLY ROSARY

Founded in the United States in 1957
General Motherhouse and Novitiate: 232 Sunnyside Dr., Reno, NV 89503-3510. Tel: 775-747-4441. Bros. Philip Napolitano, F.S.R., Supr.; Matthew Cunningham, F.S.R., Asst. Supr.
Brothers 3.
Ministries in the field of Education and Pastoral Ministry.
Represented in the Diocese of Reno.

[0970] (O.de.M.)—ORDER OF OUR LADY OF MERCY

(Mercedarians Friars)
(Ordo de Beatae Mariae Virginis de Mercede)
(Founded in Barcelona, Spain on August 10, 1218)
Generalate: *Curia Generalizia dei PP. Mercedari,* Via Monte Carmelo 3 00166, Rome, Italy. Most Rev. Emilio Aguirre Herrera, O.de.M., Master Gen.
U.S. Vicariate: *St. Rocco Rectory,* 3205 Fulton Rd., Cleveland, OH 44109. Tel: 216-961-8331. Rev. Marino Frascati, O.de.M., Vicar Prov.
Priests 16; Brothers 4; Clerics 4; Novices 2.
Properties owned: *St. Raymond Nonnatus Novitiate,* Le Roy, NY; *Monastery of Our Lady of Mercy,* Philadelphia, PA; *Saint Peter Nolasco Residence,* St. Petersburg, FL.
Represented in the Archdiocese of Philadelphia and the Dioceses of Buffalo, Cleveland and St. Petersburg.

[0975] (S.O.L.T.)—SOCIETY OF OUR LADY OF THE MOST HOLY TRINITY

Headquarters: *Casa San Jose,* 109 W. Avenue F, P.O. Box 152, Robstown, TX 78380. Tel: 512-387-2754. Rev. Vincent Albano, S.O.L.T., Gen. Priest Servant.
Priests 75; Deacons 3; Novices 21; Seminarians 81.
Pastoral Ministries: Community House; House of Study-Novitiate; Migrant Ministry.
Represented in the Archdioceses of Hartford and Santa Fe and in the Dioceses of Albany, Cheyenne, Corpus Christi, Gallup, Kansas City-St. Joseph, Lafayette, Norwich and Wheeling-Charleston.

[0980] (C.F.M.M.)—BROTHERS OF OUR LADY, MOTHER OF MERCY

(Congregatio Fratrum Beatae Mariae Virginis, Matris Misericordiae)
Generalate: Gasthuisring 54 5041 DT, Tilburg, The Netherlands.
U.S. Region: 2336 S. C St., Oxnard, CA 93033. Tel: 805-486-3692. Bro. C. W. Gresnigt, C.F.M.M., Reg. Supr.
Brothers 6.
Represented in the Archdiocese of Los Angeles.

[0990] (S.A.C.)—SOCIETY OF THE CATHOLIC APOSTOLATE

(Pallottines)
Generalate: *Pallottines,* Piazza S.V. Pallotti 204 00186, Rome, Italy.
Province of the Immaculate Conception (Eastern) (1953): *Mailing Address,* P.O. Box 979, South Orange, NJ 07079. Tel: 201-762-2926. 204 Raymond Ave., South Orange, NJ 07079. Very Rev. Frank Amato, S.A.C., Prov. Revs. Peter T. Sticco, S.A.C., 1st Consultor; Frank Gaetano, S.A.C., Bursar & Consultor; Consultors: Revs. Bernard Carman, S.A.C.; Michael Salerno, S.A.C.
Fathers 21; Professed Clerics 1; Professed Brothers 3.
Properties owned, sponsored, or staffed: Parishes 4; Seminary; High School; Novitiate; *Shrine of St. Jude, Pallottine Center for Apostolic Causes.*
Represented in the Archdioceses of Baltimore, Newark and Washington and in the Dioceses of Brooklyn and Camden.
Mother of God Province (1946): *Pallottine Fathers and Brothers, Inc.,* 5424 W. Blue Mound Rd., Milwaukee, WI 53208. Tel: 414-259-0688; Fax: 414-258-9314. Very Rev. Robert V. Carney, S.A.C., Prov. Revs. Leon Martin, S.A.C., 1st Consultor; Richard J. Gunderman, S.A.C., Consultor & Prov. Treas..
Fathers 14; Brothers 1.

Ministries in Parishes; Retreat House; Hospital Chaplaincies; High School.
Represented in the Archdiocese of Milwaukee and the Diocese of Fargo.
Irish Province (1909): *Homestead*, Sandyford Rd., Dundrum, Dublin 16, Republic of Ireland. Very Rev. William Hanly, S.A.C., Prov.
U.S. Foundation: 3352 4th St., P.O. Box 249, Wyandotte, MI 48192. Very Rev. Philip McNamara, S.A.C., Prov. Delegate.
Fathers 20.
Parishes 19; Missions 10.
Represented in the Archdiocese of Detroit and in the Diocese of Fort Worth, Lubbock and Reno-Las Vegas.
Queen of the Apostles Province (1909): Via Giuseppe Ferrari, 1-Rome, Italy. Very Rev. Gaetano Ianni, S.A.C., Prov.
U.S. Foundation: *Our Lady of Mt. Carmel Shrine and Church,* 448 E. 116th St., New York, NY 10029. Tel: 212-534-0681.
Fathers 8.
Parishes 4.
Represented in the Archdiocese of New York and the Diocese of Albany and Pensacola-Tallahassee.
Infant Jesus Delegature of Christ The King Province: *Mission House and Infant Jesus Shrine,* 3452 Niagara Falls Blvd., North Tonawanda, NY 14120. Rev. John Posiewala, S.A.C., Supr. & Prov. Delegate. Motherhouse, Poznan, Poland. *Society of the Catholic Apostolate.*
Priests 10.
Represented in the Dioceses of Brooklyn and Buffalo.

[1000] (C.P.)—CONGREGATION OF THE PASSION

(Congregatio Passionis Jesu Christi)

Founded in Italy in 1720 by St. Paul of the Cross. First foundation in United States in 1853
General Motherhouse: *SS. Giovanni e Paolo Monastery,* Rome 00184, Italy. Most Rev. Ottaviano D'Egidio, C.P., Supr. Gen.
Eastern Province, Province of St. Paul of the Cross (1852): *Province Pastoral Center,* 80 David St., South River, NJ 08882. Tel: 732-257-7177. Very Revs. Terence Kristofak, C.P., Prov.; Gerald Laba, C.P., 1st Consultor; Joseph Jones, C.P., 2nd Consultor; Melvin Shorter, C.P., 3rd Consultor; Francis Finnigan, C.P., 4th Consultor.
Legal Titles: *St. Paul's Benevolent, Educational and Missionary Institute of West Hoboken, New Jersey; Passionist Missions, Inc.; Passionist Missionaries, Inc.*
Fathers 181; Professed Clerics 2; Brothers 29; Pre Novitiates 1.
Properties owned, sponsored, or staffed: Parishes 12; Community Houses 23; House of Study; Novitiate.
Represented in the Archdioceses of Atlanta, Baltimore, Boston, Hartford, Newark, New York and Philadelphia and in the Dioceses of Altoona-Johnstown, Brooklyn, Metuchen, Palm Beach, Pittsburgh, Raleigh, Rockville Centre, Scranton, Springfield (MA), Wheeling-Charleston and Worcester. Also in Canada
Western Province, Province of the Holy Cross: *Passionist Provincial Office,* 5700 N. Harlem Ave., Chicago, IL 60631. Tel: 773-631-6336.
Legal Title: *Congregation of the Passion, Holy Cross Province.* Very Rev. Michael Higgins, C.P., Prov.; Consultors: Revs. Donald Webber, C.P., Asst. Prov. ; James Strommer, C.P., Prov. Consultor; Alexander Steinmiller, C.P., Consultor; Richard Parks, C.P., Consultor.
Fathers 117; Brothers 18.
Properties owned or sponsored: *Passionist Provincial Office; Stauros International; Immaculate Conception Monastery; Daneo Hall; Passionist Community CTU; Immaculate Conception Parish,* Chicago, IL.
Represented in the Archdioceses of Chicago, Detroit, Los Angeles, Louisville, San Antonio and in the Dioceses of Birmingham, Galveston-Houston, Orlando and Sacramento.

[1010] (O.S.P.P.E.)—PAULINE FATHERS

(Ordo Sancti Pauli Primi Eremitae)

Founded in Hungary in the 13th Century. First foundation in the United States in 1953.
General Motherhouse: *Ojcowie Paulini - Jasna Gora ul.* Kordeckiego 2 42-200, Czestochowa, Poland. Most Rev. Stanislaw Turek, O.S.P.P.E., Supr. Gen.
American Provincial Motherhouse (1984): *Shrine of Our Lady of Czestochowa Monastery, Beacon Hill,* P.O. Box 2049, Ferry Rd., Doylestown, PA 18901. Tel: 215-345-0607; Fax: 215-345-8071. Very Rev. Lucius Turasinski, O.S.P.P.E., Prov.; Revs. Stephen Wozniczka, Shrine Dir.; John Kolmaga, O.S.P.P.E., Prior.
Priests in U.S. 19; Brothers 5.
Represented in the Archdioceses of New York, Philadelphia and in the Diocese of Greensburg and Norwich.

[1020] (S.S.P.)—PAULINE FATHERS AND BROTHERS

Society of St. Paul for the Apostolate of Communications.
General Motherhouse: Via della Fanella 39 00148, Rome, Italy. Very Rev. Pietro Campus, S.S.P., Supr. Gen. Very Rev. Abramo Parmeggiani, S.S.P., Vicar Gen.
United States Province (1932): *Pauline Fathers & Brothers,* P.O. Box 139, Ellsworth, OH 44416-0139. Tel: 330-533-7427. Very Rev. Matthew R. Roehrig, S.S.P., Prov. Supr. Bro.; Aloysius W. Milella, S.S.P., Vicar Prov.; Rev. Ignatius W. Staniszewski, S.S.P., Publishing Editor, Publication: *Alba House.* Tel: 718-761-0047; Rev. Matthew Roehrig, S.S.P., Editor; Publication: *Pastoral Life Magazine, Alba House.* Tel: 216-533-5503; Bro. Dismas Beique, S.S.P., Editor, Publication: *Alba House AV Communications.* Tel: 216-533-5503; Bro. Peter C. Lyne, S.S.P., Vocation Dir. Tel: 313-582-3798.
Priests 12; Brothers 24; Juniors 2.
Represented in the Archdioceses of Detroit, New York and the Diocese of Youngstown.
Los Angeles Province: 112 S. Herbert Ave., Los Angeles, CA 90063. Tel: 213-269-9814; 268-5010 (Bookstore); Fax: 213-268-4583. Revs. Gilberto Martinez, S.S.P., Supr.; Thomas Martinez, S.S.P., Vice Supr.; Valeriano Giachino, S.S.P.; Gonzalo Ponce, S.S.P.
Priests 4.

[1030] (C.S.P.)—PAULIST FATHERS

(Societas Missionaria a S. Paulo Apostolo)

Paulist Fathers Motherhouse (1858): 86-11 Midland Pkwy., Jamaica Estates, NY 11432. Tel: 718-291-5995. Very Rev. Frank P. DeSiano, C.S.P., Pres.
Legal Title: *Missionary Society of St. Paul the Apostle in the State of New York.*
Fathers 180; Students in Major Seminary 10; Novices 3.
Properties owned or sponsored: Newman Campus Chaplaincies; Information Centers; Paulist Press; Paulist Radio-TV-Film Communications Svcs.; Paulist National Catholic Evangelization Association; House of Study; Novitiate.
Represented in the Archdioceses of Boston, Chicago, Denver, Los Angeles, New York, Portland (OR), St. Paul-Minneapolis, San Francisco, Washington and the Dioceses of Austin, Brooklyn, Columbus, Grand Rapids, Knoxville, Memphis, Oakland, Paterson, and Tucson.

[1040] (SCH.P.)—PIARIST FATHERS

(Ordo Clericorum Regularum Pauperum Matris Dei Scholarum Piarum)

General Motherhouse: *San Pantaleo,* Piazza De Massimi, 4, Rome, Italy 00186. Most Rev. Joseph M. Balcells, Sch.P., Supr. Gen.
U.S. Province (1975): *Devon Preparatory School,* 363 Valley Forge Rd., Devon, PA 19333. Tel: 215-688-7337; 688-6807. Very Rev. Richard S. Wyzykiewicz, Sch.P., Prov. Supr.
Legal Titles and Holdings: *Piarist Fathers, Inc.; Order of the Pious Schools, Inc.; Piarist Fathers House of Studies,* Washington, DC; *Piarist Fathers Residence,* Derby, NY; *Piarist Fathers Residence,* Martin, KY; *Devon Preparatory School,* Devon, PA.
Priests 25.
Represented in the Archdioceses of Miami, Philadelphia and Washington and the Dioceses of Buffalo, Lexington and Paterson.
New York-Puerto Rico Vice Province: *Seminario Escolapio,* P.O. Box 118, Playa Sta., Ponce, PR 00734. Tel: 809-840-0610; Fax: 809-841-6861. Rev. Joseph Mateo, Sch.P., Vice Prov.
Priests 21; Cleric Students 1.
Houses 5; Parishes 3; High Schools 2; Schools 4.
Represented in the Archdioceses of New York and San Juan and the Diocese of Ponce. Also, Calasanzian Fathers and Padres Escolapios de P.R.
Californias' Vice Province Piarist Fathers: *Piarist Fathers,* 3940 Perry St., Los Angeles, CA 90063-1174. Tel: 323-261-1386; Fax: 323-269-0883. Rev. Antonio Tort, Sch.P., Vice Prov.
Properties owned, staffed, or sponsored: Parishes 5; Grammar Schools 2; House of Formation 4.
Priests 21; Novices 5; Prenovices 8; Seminarians 16.
Represented in the Archdiocese of Los Angeles.

[1050] (P.I.M.E.)—PONTIFICAL INSTITUTE FOR FOREIGN MISSIONS, INC.

General Motherhouse: Via F. D. Guerrazzi 11, Rome, Italy 00152. Very Rev. Franco Cagnasso, P.I.M.E., Supr. Gen.
U.S. Region: 17330 Quincy Ave., Detroit, MI 48221. Tel: 313-342-4066; Fax: 313-342-6816. Very Rev. Bruno Piccolo, P.I.M.E., Prov. Supr.
Fathers 25; Brothers 1; Seminarians 5.
Legal Titles and Holdings: *P.I.M.E. Mission Center,* Newark, OH; *PIME Missionaries - PIME Mission Center; PIME College Community,* Detroit, MI; *PIME Missionaries,* Wayne, NJ & Tequesta, FL.
Formation Communities 1; Mission Houses 4.
Represented in the Archdiocese of Detroit and the Dioceses of Paterson, Columbus and Palm Beach.

[1060] (C.PP.S.)—SOCIETY OF THE PRECIOUS BLOOD

(Congregatio Missionariorum Pretiosissimi Sanguinis Domini Nostri Jesu Christi)

General Motherhouse: Viale di Porta Ardeatina 66, Rome, Italy 1-00154. Very Rev. Barry Fischer, C.PP.S., Moderator.
Cincinnati Province: 431 E. Second St., Dayton, OH 45402. Tel: 937-228-9263. Very Rev. Angelo P. Anthony, C.PP.S., Prov. Dir.; Prov. Council: Revs. William O'Donnell, C.PP.S.; James Seibert, C.PP.S.; Thomas Hemm, C.PP.S.; Alfred Naseman, C.PP.S.; James Dugal, C.PP.S. Bro.; Joseph Fisher, C.PP.S., Treas. & Mission Procurator.
Fathers 168; Brothers 30; Students in Major Seminaries 8; Students in Preparatory Seminary 21.
Ministries in Parishes; Missions; Chaplaincies; Shrine; Education; Retreat Preaching; Community Houses; Houses of Study; Military Chaplains.
Represented in the Archdioceses of Chicago, Cincinnati, Detroit, Military Services and in the Dioceses of Cleveland, Columbus, Fort Wayne-South Bend, Gary, Harrisburg, Lafayette in Indiana, Orlando, Pensacola-Tallahassee, Steubenville, Toledo and Youngstown.
Kansas City Province: *Precious Blood Society Provincial Office,* P.O. Box 339, Liberty, MO 64069-0339. Tel: 816-781-4344; Fax: 816-781-3639. Very Rev. Mark Miller, C.PP.S., Prov. Dir.; Revs. William Walter, C.PP.S., 1st Consultor; Garry Richmeier, C.PP.S., 2nd Consultor & Prov. Sec.; Joseph Bathke, C.PP.S., 3rd Consultor; David Matz, C.PP.S., 4th Consultor; William Dineen, C.PP.S., Prov. Treas.
Bishops 1; Fathers 62; Brothers 4; Seminarians 1.
Ministries in Parishes; Missions; Houses of Study; Community House; Chaplaincies.
Represented in the Archdioceses of Chicago, Cincinnati, Denver, Indianapolis, Kansas City in Kansas and in the Dioceses of Belleville, Columbus, Davenport, Des Moines, Jefferson City, Kansas City-St. Joseph, Salina, San Angelo, Toledo and Wichita.
Province of the Pacific: *Society of the Precious Blood Province Center,* 2337 West Avenue 134th, San Leandro, CA 94577-4132. Tel: 510-357-4982; Fax: 510-357-4036. Very Rev. James D. Sloan, C.PP.S., Prov. Dir.; Councillors: Revs. Gregory Comella, C.PP.S., Vice Prov.; Jeffrey Keyes, C.PP.S., Sec.; Jerome Stack, C.PP.S.; Gary Luiz, C.PP.S., Vocation Dir.; Joseph Brown, C.PP.S., Treas.
Fathers 19
Ministries in Parishes; Chaplaincies; Community Houses; Center of Spirituality; Houses of Study.
Represented in the Archdioceses of Los Angeles, and the Dioceses of Monterey and Oakland. Also in Mexico City.
Atlantic Province: *Society of the Precious Blood, Provincial House,* 13313 Niagara Pkwy., Niagara Falls, Ontario L2E 6S6, Canada. Tel: 905-382-0865. Very Rev. Peter Nobili, C.PP.S., Prov.; Rev. Sam D'Agelo, C.PP.S., Sec.
Priests in the U.S. 9.
Represented in the Archdioceses of Miami, Washington and the Dioceses of Buffalo, Rochester and Youngstown. Also in Canada.

[1065] (F.S.S.P.)—PRIESTLY FRATERNITY OF ST. PETER

Founded in Switzerland in 1988. First foundation in United States in 1991
General Motherhouse: *Seminarium Internationale Sancti Petri,* Kirchstrasse 20 D-88145, Opfenbach-Wigratzbad, Germany. Tel: 49-0-8385/9539; Fax: 49-0-8385/9531. Very Rev. Josef Bisig, F.S.S.P., Supr. Gen.
U.S. Headquarters: *Our Lady of Guadalupe Seminary,* Griffin Rd. - P.O. Box 196, Elmhurst, PA 18416.

Tel: 717-842-4000; Fax: 717-842-4001. Revs. Arnaud J. Devillers, F.S.S.P., District Supr.; William Richardson, F.S.S.P., Sec. to District Supr.; John Melnick, F.S.S.P., Vocations Dir.; James McLucas, F.S.S.P., Major Gifts Dir.

House of Formation, Griffin Rd. - P.O. Box 188, Elmhurst, PA 18416. Tel: 717-842-6711; Fax: 717-842-6714. Revs. Karl Pikus, F.S.S.P., Rector; James B. Buckley, F.S.S.P., Dir.-Spirituality; Dennis M. Duvelius, F.S.S.P., Dir.-Admissions.

Priests 34; Deacons 3; Seminarians 62; Novices 12.

Properties owned or sponsored: Houses 12; Elementary & High Schools.

Represented in the Archdioceses of Atlanta, Denver, Indianapolis, Kansas City, Oklahoma City, Omaha, and the Dioceses of Corpus Christi, Dallas, Lincoln, Little Rock, Paterson, Rapid City, Sacramento, Scranton, Tulsa, and Youngstown. Also in Canada.

[1070] (C.SS.R.)—REDEMPTORIST FATHERS

(Congregatio Sanctissimi Redemptoris)

(Redemptorist Fathers and Brothers)

Generalate: *Sant'Alphonso,* Via Merulana 31. C.P. 2458 1-00100, Rome, Italy. Most Rev. Joseph Tobin, C.Ss.R., Supr. Gen.; Very Rev. George Darlix, C.Ss.R., Vicar Gen. Rev. Jose Sousa, C.Ss.R., Proc. Gen.

Province of Baltimore (1850): *Provincial Residence,* 7509 Shore Rd., Brooklyn, NY 11209. Tel: 718-833-1900. Very Rev. George J. Keaveney, C.Ss.R., Prov. Supr.; Revs. Patrick F. Woods, C.Ss.R., Prov. Vicar; Francis J. O'Rourke, C.Ss.R., Prov. Consultor; Very Rev. Francis Nelson, C.Ss.R., Prov. Procurator; Bro. Albert R. Schreiber, C.Ss.R., Prov. Sec.; Revs. Carl Hoegerl, C.Ss.R., Prov. Archivist; Gerard Knapp, C.Ss.R., Asst. Procurator.

Bishops 3; Priests 245; Brothers 25; Novices 3; Postulants 10.

Properties owned, staffed, or sponsored: Parishes 35; Residences 6; Retreat Houses 4; Community Houses 40.

Represented in the Archdioceses of Baltimore, Boston, Hartford, New York, Philadelphia and Washington and in the Dioceses of Albany, Brooklyn, Harrisburg, Rockville Centre, Toledo, Trenton and Wilmington. Also in St. Thomas, V.I. and West Indies.

Richmond Vice Province (1942): *Vice Provincial Headquarters,* 313 Hillman St., P.O. Box 1529, New Smyrna Beach, FL 32170. Tel: 904-427-3094. Very Rev. Edward J. Gray, C.Ss.R., Vice Prov.; Revs. Eugene S. Daigle, C.Ss.R., Vicar; Consultors: Joseph Majewski, C.Ss.R.; Michael Koncik, C.Ss.R., Vocation Dir.; Bro. Thomas Kuhn, C.Ss.R., Vice Prov. Procurator.

Legal Title: *Congregation of the Most Holy Redeemer.*

Priests 53; Brothers 2; Professed Students 3.

Properties owned, staffed, or sponsored: Parishes 9; Retreat Houses 2; Retirement Home 1; Residences 1; Missions 7.

Represented in the Archdiocese of Atlanta and the Dioceses of Charleston, Charlotte, Orlando, Richmond, St. Augustine, St. Petersburg and Venice.

The Redemptorist Denver Province (1875): *The Redemptorists Provincial Residence,* Box 300399, Denver, CO 80203-0399. Tel: 303-370-0035; Fax: 303-370-0036. Very Rev. Richard Thibodeau, C.Ss.R., Prov. Supr. Revs. J. Robert Fenili, C.Ss.R., Prov. Vicar; John Steingraeber, C.Ss.R., Co-Dir. - Office of Financial Svcs.; Bro. Tom Wright, C.Ss.R., Co-Dir. - Office of Financial Servs.

Total in community Priests 28; Brothers 2.

Properties owned, sponsored or staffed: Parishes 15; Retreat Houses 5; Residences 3; Community Houses 22.

Represented in the Archdioceses of Chicago, Denver, Los Angeles, Milwaukee, Omaha, St. Louis, St. Paul-Minneapolis, Seattle, and in Dioceses of Grand Rapids, Kansas City-St. Joseph Oakland, Tucson, and Wichita. Also in Foreign Missions.

Bangkok Vice-Province: *Redemptorists,* 123-19 Ruam Rudi Lane, Bangkok 10500, Thailand. Very Rev. Philip Banchong Chaiyara, C.Ss.R., Vice Prov.

Manaus Vice-Province: *Redentoristas,* Caixa Postal 217, 69.011 Manaus, Amazonas, Brazil, South America. Very Rev. Joseph Butz, C.Ss.R., Vice Prov.

New Orleans Vice-Province: *Redemptorist Fathers and Brothers,* 5354 Plank Rd.-P.O. Box 53900, Baton Rouge, LA 70892-3900. Tel: 504-355-2600; Fax: 504-355-6200. Very Rev. Thomas D. Picton, C.Ss.R., Vice Prov.; Revs. Samuel Maranto, C.Ss.R., Vice Prov. Consultor, Local Supr. & Archivist; Richard Luberti, C.Ss.R., Joseph Steffes, C.Ss.R.; Eugene E. Staub, C.Ss.R.; John C. Vargas, C.Ss.R., (Redemptorist Generalate - Rome); Bro. Steven E. Fruge, C.Ss.R., Vice Prov.-Sec.; Clement Fumo, C.Ss.R.

Priests 46; Brothers 7; Professed Students 2.

Properties owned, staffed, or sponsored: Parishes 6; Residences.

Represented in the Archdioceses of New Orleans, San Antonio and the Dioceses of Baton Rouge, Biloxi, Corpus Christi, Galveston-Houston, and Lafayette (LA).

[1080] (C.R.)—CONGREGATION OF THE RESURRECTION

(Congregatio a Resurrectione Domini Nostri Jesu Christi)

Generalate: Via San Sebastianello 11 00187, Rome, Italy. Very Rev. Sutherland MacDonald, C.R., Supr. Gen.

U.S. of America Province: 7050 N. Oakley Ave., Chicago, IL 60645. Tel: 773-465-8320. Very Rev. John H. Nowak, C.R., Prov. Supr.; Councillors: Revs. Joseph Glab, C.R.; Gary Hogan, C.R., Dir. of Vocations; Eugene Szarek, C.R.; Manuel Williams, C.R.; Steven Bartczyszyn, C.R.

Fathers 70; Brothers 6.

Ministries in Parishes; Missions; High Schools; Retreat House; Chaplaincies.

Represented in the Archdioceses of Chicago, Mobile, St. Louis and the Dioceses of Kalamazoo, Pensacola-Tallahassee, Rockford and San Bernardino. Also in Bermuda.

Ontario Kentucky Province U.S. Address: *St. Cecilia House,* 338 N. 25th St., Louisville, KY 40212. Tel: 502-772-3694; Fax: 502-772-3695. Rev. Wm. Joseph Scollard, C.R.; Deacon Philip Tremblay, C.R.; Provincialate: Resurrection College, Waterloo, Ontario, Canada N2L 3G7; Fax: 519-885-4951. Revs. Lory A. Keasey, C.R.; Charles Fedy, C.R.; Councillors: Revs. Robert Liddy, C.R.; Jerome Kroetsch, C.R.; Sam Restivo, C.R.; Bro. D. Taylor, C.R., Bursar; Deacon Brian Karley, C.R.

Properties owned, sponsored, or staffed: Resurrection College; Parishes 2; University; High Schools 3; Community Houses 15; House of Study.

Represented in the Archdiocese of Louisville.

[1090] (R.C.J.)—ROGATIONIST FATHERS

Congregatio Rogationis-a-Corde-Jesu

Generalate: via Tuscolana 167 00182, Rome, Italy. Very Rev. George Nalin, R.C.J., Supr. Gen.

U.S.A. Delegation: 2688 S. Newmark Ave., Box 37, Sanger, CA 93657. Tel: 209-875-5808; 875-2025; Fax: 209-875-1281. Rev. John Bruno, R.C.J., Delegation Supr.

U.S. Foundations: *St. Mary's Church,* 828 O St., P.O. Box 335, Sanger, CA 93657. Tel: 209-875-2025. Revs. Salvatore Ciranni, R.C.J.; John Bruno, R.C.J.; Vito DiMarzio, R.C.J. *Vocation Center,* 9815 Columbus Ave., North Hill, CA 91343. Tel: 818-894-2546. Revs. Rodolfo D'Agostino, R.C.J.; Vincent Buccheri, R.C.J.

Legal Title: *Congregation of Rogationists, Inc.*

Priests 7

Ministries in Parishes; Vocation Center; Formation House; Social Service Center.

Represented in the Archdiocese of Los Angeles and the Diocese of Fresno.

[1100] (S.C.)—BROTHERS OF THE SACRED HEART

(Societas Fratrum Sacris Cordis)

Founded in Lyons, France in 1821. First foundation in the United States in Mobile in 1847.

Generalate: *Piazza Sacro Cuore,* No. 3, Rome, Italy 00151. Bro. Bernard Couvillion, S.C., Supr. Gen. Provinces.

New Orleans Province (1847): *Provincial Office,* 4540 Elysian Fields Ave., New Orleans, LA 70122. Tel: 504-282-5693; Fax: 504-288-9920. Bro. Ivy LeBlanc, S.C., Prov.; Prov. Councillors: Bros. Richard Hingle, S.C.; Neal Golden, S.C.; Francis David, S.C.; Xavier Werneth, S.C.; Donnan Berry, S.C., Treas.

Perpetual Professed 65; Temporary Professed 2; Ordained Brothers 6.

Incorporated Schools: *Brother Martin High School,* New Orleans, LA; *Catholic High School,* Baton Rouge, LA; *Saint Stanislaus College,* Bay St. Louis, MS.

Legal Titles: *Brothers of the Sacred Heart, (a Louisiana Corporation); Brothers of the Sacred Heart Foundation of the New Orleans Province, Inc.*

Represented in the Archdioceses of Mobile and New Orleans and the Dioceses of Baton Rouge, Biloxi and Houma-Thibodaux.

New England Province (1945): *Provincial House - Brothers of the Sacred Heart,* 685 Steere Farm Rd., Pascoag, RI 02859-4601. Tel: 401-568-3361; Fax: 401-568-9810. Bro. Robert F. Breault, S.C., Prov. Supr.; Councillors: Bros. Robert Croteau, S.C.; Donald Tardif, S.C.; Raymond Reinsant, S.C.; Frederick U. Bouchard, S.C.; Edward Breault, S.C., Prov. Sec.; Louis Laperle, S.C., Exec. Asst. Finances; Paul Hebert, S.C., Missions Procurator; John L. Collignon, S.C., Dir.-Development; Roland Ouellette, S.C., Dir.-Vocation.

Brothers 89.

Properties owned: *Brothers of the Sacred Heart Provincial House,* Pascoag, RI; *Mt. St. Charles Academy,* Woonsocket, RI; *Bishop Guertin High School,* Nashua, NH; *St. John Residence,* Woonsocket, RI; *Brothers of the Sacred Heart Residence,* Nashua, NH.

Represented in the Archdiocese of Hartford and the Dioceses of Manchester and Providence. Also in England, Lesotho, Zambia, Zimbabwe, and Uganda, Kenya.

Province of New York (1960): *Brothers of the Sacred Heart Provincial House,* 141-11 123 Ave., South Ozone Park, NY 11436-1426. Tel: 718-322-3309; Fax: 718-529-6004. Bro. Joseph Rocco, S.C., Prov.

Final Professed Brothers 42; Temporary 2.

Ministries in the field of Education; Spiritual Centers; Kenya Missions.

Properties owned: *Sacred Heart Center,* Belvidere, NJ; *Msgr. McClancy High School,* East Elmhurst, NY; *St. Joseph High School,* Metuchen, NJ.

Represented in the Dioceses of Brooklyn, Metuchen and Rockville Center. Also in Kenya.

[1110] (M.S.C.)—MISSIONARIES OF THE SACRED HEART

(Societas Missionariorum Sacratissimi Cordis Jesu)

General Motherhouse: Via Asmara 11 00199, Rome, Italy. Very Rev. Michael Curran, M.S.C., Supr. Gen.

United States Province (1939): P.O. Box 270, 305 S. Lake St., Aurora, IL 60507. Tel: 630-892-8400; 892-2371; Fax: 630-892-3071. Very Rev. David Foxen, M.S.C., Prov. Supr.; Consultors: Revs. John Kavcak, M.S.C., Vice Prov.; Michael Camilli, M.S.C.; Raymond Diesbourg, M.S.C.; Earl Henley, M.S.C.; Mark Zacker, M.S.C.

Legal Title: *Society of the Missionaries of the Sacred Heart.*

Fathers 68; Brothers 22; Foreign Missionaries 18; Professed Students 3.

Properties owned, staffed, or sponsored: Renewal Centers 1; Residential Houses 6; Parishes 11; Chaplaincies 3; Foreign Missions 2.

Represented in the Archdioceses of Baltimore, Chicago, Philadelphia, Washington and the Dioceses of Allentown, Gary, Ogdensburg, Rockford, San Bernardino, Toledo, and Youngstown. Also in Colombia, Papua New Guinea, Namibia.

U.S. Section of the Irish Province for California and Southern States: *Sectional Headquarters,* 237 Magnolia Ave., San Antonio, TX 78212-2916. Tel: 210-737-6394; Fax: 210-737-0327. Rev. James Dudley, M.S.C.; Pat McGlanaghy, M.S.C.

Priests 20.

Represented in the Archdioceses of Los Angeles, San Antonio and the Dioceses of Beaumont, Charleston, Corpus Christi, Dallas San Angelo and Tyler.

[1120] (M.SS.CC.)—MISSIONARIES OF THE SACRED HEARTS OF JESUS AND MARY

(Missionarii a Sacris Cordibus Jesus et Mariae)

Founded in Italy in 1833.

General Motherhouse: Via dei Falegnami 23, Rome, Italy. Very Rev. Luigi Toscano, M.SS.CC., Supr. Gen.

American Headquarters: 2249 Shore Rd., Linwood, NJ 08221. Tel: 609-927-5600; Fax: 609-927-5262. Revs. Anthony Patrizio, M.SS.CC., Reg. Supr.; Robert McDade, M.SS.CC., Mission Procurator.

Legal Title: *Missionaries of the Sacred Heart of Jesus and Mary.*

Priests 10; Brothers 2.

Represented in the Dioceses of Camden and Harrisburg.

[1130] (S.C.J.)—CONGREGATION OF THE PRIESTS OF THE SACRED HEART

(Priests of the Sacred Heart)

(Congregatio Sacerdotum a Corde Jesu)

General Motherhouse: *Curia Generalizia,* S.C.J., Via Casale S. Pio v, no. 20 00165, Rome, Italy. Very Rev. Virginio Domingo Bressanelli, S.C.J., Supr. Gen.

United States Province (1933): *Provincialate Offices,* P.O. Box 289, Hales Corners, WI 53130-0289. Tel: 414-425-6910. Very Rev. John Czyzynski, S.C.J., Prov. Supr.

Bishops 2; Priests 97; Clerics 6; Brothers 21; Deacons 2.

Represented in the Archdioceses of Chicago, Milwaukee and San Antonio and in the Dioceses of Brownsville, Galveston-Houston, Green Bay, Jackson, Rapid City, St. Petersburg and Sioux Falls.

[1140] (SS.CC.)—CONGREGATION OF THE SACRED HEARTS OF JESUS AND MARY

(Congregatio Sacrorum Cordium)

General Motherhouse: *Casa Generalizia-Padri Dei Sacri Cuori-via,* Rivarone 85 00166, Rome, Italy. Very Rev. Enrique Losada, SS.CC., Supr. Gen.

Legal Title: *Congregation of the Sacred Hearts of Jesus and Mary.*

Eastern Province (1946): *Provincial House,* Box 111, Fairhaven, MA 02719-0111. Tel: 508-993-2442; Fax: 508-996-5499. Very Rev. Davide P. Reid, SS.CC., Prov. Revs. Finton D. Sheeran, SS.CC., Vicar Prov.; Councillors: Martin Gomes, SS.CC.; Robert Charlton, SS.CC.; Gerry Shanley, SS.CC.

Priests 63; Novices 6; Brothers 6.

Properties owned or staffed: Parishes 8; Community Houses 3; House of Studies 1.

Represented in the Archdiocese of Washington and the Dioceses of Brownsville, and Fall River.

Western United States Province (1970): *Congregation of the Sacred Hearts of Jesus and Mary,* 2150 Damien Ave., La Verne, CA 91750. Tel: 909-593-5441; Fax: 909-593-3971. Very Rev. Martin P. O'Loghlen, SS.CC., Prov.

Priests 20.

Ministries in the field of Religious and Academic Education; Parishes; Chaplaincies.

Represented in the Archdiocese of Los Angeles and the Dioceses of Oakland, and San Bernardino. Also in the Philippines.

Hawaii Province: *Sacred Hearts Center,* Box 797, Kaneohe, Oahu, HI 96744. Tel: 808-247-5035; Fax: 808-235-8849. Very Rev. Clyde Guerreiro, SS.CC., Prov.

Fathers 35; Brothers 7.

Properties owned, staffed, or sponsored: Churches 10; Mission 1; Chaplaincies 2.

[1144] (L.B.S.F.)—LITTLE BROTHERS OF SAINT FRANCIS

Founded in the United States in 1970 by Bro. James Curran, L.B.S.F.

Regional Fraternity and Novitiate (1970): 785-789 Parker St., Roxbury, MA 02120. Tel: 617-442-2556.

Legal Title: *Little Brothers of Saint Francis - Franciscan Fraternity of Peace and Love, Inc.*

Professed Brothers 4; Novices 2; Postulants 3.

Represented in the Archdiocese of Boston.

[1150] (C.S.J.)—CONGREGATION OF ST. JOSEPH

(Congregatio Sancti Joseph)

Founded in Turin, Italy in 1873. First foundation in United States in 1951.

General Motherhouse: Via Belvedere Montello 77 00166, Rome, Italy. Very Rev. Luigi Pierini, C.S.J., Supr. Gen.

U.S. and Mexico Vice Province: 338 N. Grand Ave., San Pedro, CA 90731. Tel: 310-547-2969. Rev. John Trimaglio, C.S.J., Prov. Supr.

Priests 25

Properties owned, staffed, or sponsored: Parishes 5; High Schools 2; Center for troubled youths.

Properties owned: *St. Leonard House,* Avon, OH.

Represented in the Archdiocese of Los Angeles and the Diocese of Cleveland. Also in Mexico.

[1160] (F.S.P.)—BROTHERS OF ST. PATRICK

(Patrician Brothers)

Founded in Ireland 1808 by Bishop Daniel Delaney.

U.S. Foundation (1948): *St. Patrick's Novitiate,* 7820 Bolsa Ave., Midway City, CA 92655. Tel: 714-897-8181; Fax: 714-898-9020. Bro. Aquinas Cassin, F.S.P., Prov.

Brothers 8.

Represented in the Archdiocese of Los Angeles and Diocese of Orange.

[1170] (S.P.S.)—ST. PATRICK'S MISSIONARY SOCIETY

(St. Patrick Fathers)

Founded March 17, 1932 with the approval of Pope Pius XI. A Pontifical Society of secular priests devoted entirely to the missionary needs of the Church.

International Headquarters: *St. Patrick's,* Kiltegan, Wicklow, Ireland. Very Rev. Kieran Birmingham, S.P.S., Supr. Gen. Rev. Sean Barry, S.P.S., Vicar Gen. Rev. James Bermingham, S.P.S., Proc. Gen.-Rome; Rev. James Barry, S.P.S., Supr. for North America.

Total number of Priests 380; Priests in the U.S. 19.

U.S. Foundations (1965): *St. Patrick's,* 70 Edgewater Rd., Cliffside Park, NJ 07010. Tel: 201-943-6575; Fax: 201-943-2946. Rev. James Barry, S.P.S., Supr.; *St. Patrick's (1967),* 19536 Eric Dr., Saratoga, CA 95070. Tel: 408-253-3135; Fax: 408-253-5433 Rev. Stephen Donohue, S.P.S., Supr.; *St. Patrick's (1968),* 1347 W. Granville Ave., Chicago, IL 60660. Tel: 773-973-3737. Tel: 773-973-6049. Rev. Karl Langsdorf, S.P.S., Supr.

Legal Title: *St. Patrick Missionary Society,* Camden, N.J.

Represented in the Archdioceses of Chicago, New Orleans, Newark , San Francisco and in the Dioceses of Paterson and San Jose.

[1180] (C.S.P.X.)—BROTHERS OF SAINT PIUS X

Founded in the United States in 1952

Motherhouse: P.O. Box 217, DeSoto, WI 54624. Tel: 608-648-2087. Bro. Charles Bisenius, Dir.

Ministries in the field of Religious and Academic Education; Health Care; Community services and Administration.

Represented in the Diocese of La Crosse.

[1190] (S.D.B.)—SALESIANS OF DON BOSCO

Societas Sancti Francisci Salesii

Generalate: *Salesian D. Bosco,* via Della Pisana, 1111, C.P. 00163, Roma-Aurelio, Italy. Very Rev. Juan Vecchi, S.D.B., Rector Major.

Province of St. Philip the Apostle (1902): 148 Main St., New Rochelle, NY 10802. Tel: 914-636-4225. Very Rev. Patrick Angelucci, S.D.B., Prov.; Revs. Francis X. Aracil, S.D.B., Sec. & Dir.-Social Communication; Joseph Santa-Bibiana, S.D.B., Prov. Economer & Councillor; James Heuser, S.D.B., Vice Prov.; Steven Shafran, S.D.B., Dir. of Formation & Councillor; Patrick Diver, S.D.B., Mission Procurator; Bro. Emile Dube, S.D.B., Dir. of Religious Education & Councillor.

Legal Title: *Salesian Society, Inc.,* New Rochelle, NY.

Fathers 150; Professed Clerics 15; Students in Major Seminaries 6; Coadjutor-Brothers 44.

Ministries in: Parishes; High Schools; Trade Schools; Technical Schools; Boys Clubs; Camps.

Represented in the Archdioceses of Boston, Chicago, Miami, Newark, New Orleans, New York and the Dioceses of Birmingham, Columbus, Palm Beach, Passaic, Paterson, St. Petersburg and Scranton. Also in Canada.

San Francisco Province (1926): *Salesian Society - San Francisco,* 1100 Franklin St., San Francisco, CA 94109. Tel: 415-441-7144; Fax: 415-441-7155. Very Rev. Nicholas Reina, S.D.B., Prov.; Rev. Ted Montemayor, S.D.B., Vice Prov.; Councillors: Revs. John Itzaina, S.D.B.; Mel Trinidad, S.D.B.; David Purdy , S.D.B.; Richard Presenti, S.D.B., Treas.

Fathers 90; Professed Clerics 15; Professed Brothers 26; Students in Seminaries 7.

Ministries in Parishes; High Schools; Retreat House; Youth Centers.

Represented in the Archdioceses of Los Angeles, Santa Fe, San Francisco and the Dioceses of Corpus Christi, Monterey, Oakland, San Bernardino, San Diego, Santa Rosa, Stockton. Also in Canada and Sierra Leone.

[1200] (S.D.S.)—SOCIETY OF THE DIVINE SAVIOR

Salvatorian Fathers and Brothers

(Salvatorians - Societas Divini Salvatoris)

General Headquarters: *Curia Generalizia dei Salvatoriani,* Via della Conciliazione 51 00193, Rome, Italy. Very Rev. Andrew Urbanski, S.D.S., Supr. Gen.

U.S.A. Province (1896): *Salvatorian Provincial Residence,* 1735 Hi-Mount Blvd., Milwaukee, WI 53208-1720. Tel: 414-258-1735; Fax: 414-258-1934. Very Rev. Peter Schuessler, S.D.S., Prov.; Revs. Joseph Rodriguez, S.D.S., Vicar; John Gorman, S.D.S., Dir. Personnel; Sean McLaughlin, S.D.S., Consultor.

Legal Titles: *Camp St. Charles, Inc.; Society of the Divine Savior; Society of the Divine Savior Ongoing Community Support Trust; Fund Raising and Public Relations Center; Salvatorian Center,* New Holstein, WI 53061.

Fathers 92; Brothers 42; Clerics 3; Novices 1; Candidates 1.

Properties owned, staffed, or sponsored: Parishes 18; Houses of Study and Formation 2.

Represented in the Archdioceses of Baltimore, Louisville, Milwaukee, New York, Portland, San Francisco, Washington and the Dioceses of Camden, Birmingham, Bismarck, Gallup, Green Bay, LaCrosse, Nashville, Oakland, Orlando, Phoenix, Sacramento, Savannah, Tucson, Venice, Wilmington and Richmond.

[1210] (C.S.)—MISSIONARIES OF ST. CHARLES-SCALABRINIANS

(Congregatio Missionariorum A Sancto Carolo)

General Motherhouse: Via Calandrelli, 42 00153, Rome, Italy. Very Rev. Gaetano Parolin, C.S., Supr. Gen.

Province of St. Charles Borromeo (1888): *Scalabrinians Provincial Curia,* 27 Carmine St., New York, NY 10014. Tel: 212-675-3993; Fax: 212-727-2866. Very Rev. Sergio Dall'Agnese, C.S., Prov. Supr.; Revs. Walter Tonelotto, C.S., Vicar & 1st Councillor; Vincenzo Ronchi, C.S., Sec. & 2nd Councillor; Alvirio Mores, C.S., 3rd Councillor; Alex Dalpiaz, C.S., 4th Councillor; Joseph Fugolo, C.S., Treas.

Legal Title: *The Pious Society of the Missionaries of St. Charles Borromeo, Inc.*

Fathers 97; Brothers 3.

Properties staffed or owned: Parishes 30; Missions 7; Homes for Aged 2; Seminaries 3; Center for Migration Studies; Assistance Agency for Migrants.

Represented in the Archdioceses of Boston, Hartford, Newark, New York, Washington and the Dioceses of Brooklyn, Buffalo, Palm Beach, Providence, Syracuse and Venice. Also in Eastern Canada, Venezuela, Colombia, the Dominican Republic and Haiti.

Province of St. John Baptist (1903): *Missionaries of St. Charles - Fathers of St. Charles,* 546 N. East Ave., Oak Park, IL 60302. Tel: 708-386-4430; Fax: 708-386-4457. Very Rev. Patrick Murphy, C.S., Prov.

Legal Titles: *The Fathers of Saint Charles; Scalabrinian Community Support Corp.; Scalabrinian Community Formation Corp.*

Fathers 72; Brothers 5.

Ministries in 23 Parishes; 2 Homes for the Aged; 3 Missions; 5 Seminaries; 5 Centers for Migrants and Refugees.

Represented in the Archdioceses of Chicago, Cincinnati and Los Angeles and the Dioceses of Galveston-Houston, Kansas City-St. Joseph, San Diego and San Jose. Also in Canada, Guatemala, and Mexico.

[1220] (S.C.)—SERVANTS OF CHARITY

(Guanellians)

(Congregatio Servorum a Charitate)

General Motherhouse: Vicolo Clementi 41, Rome, Italy. Very Rev. Nino Minetti, Supr. Gen.

U.S. Headquarters: *Servants of Charity,* 16195 Old U.S. 12, Chelsea, MI 48118-9646. Tel: 313-475-8430; Fax: 313-475-0310. Rev. Silvio De Nard, S.C., Supr. USA Province.

Priests 12; Brothers 1; Theologian 1; Novices 1.

Legal Titles: *Pious Union of St. Joseph.*

Publication: *Now and At the Hour.*

Ministry for the suffering and dying: Schools for mentally handicapped boys 2; Residences for mentally handicapped adults 2; Parishes 1; House of Formation 1; Group Home 1; Chaplaincies 1.

Represented in the Archdioceses of Chicago and Philadelphia and in the Dioceses of Lansing and Providence.

[1230] (s.P.)—SERVANTS OF THE PARACLETE

Generalate & U.S. Motherhouse (1952): *Fitzgerald Center,* P.O. Box 10, Jemez Springs, NM 87025-0010. Tel: 505-829-3586; Fax: 505-829-3706. Very Rev. Peter Lechner, s.P., Servant Gen.; Revs. John Murphy, s.P., Vicar Gen.; David Fitzgerald, s.P., Treas. Gen.; Paul Valley, s.P., Sec. Gen.; Raymond Gunzel, s.P., Asst. for the Apostolate.

Professed Priests 17; Professed Brothers 3; Novices 2.

Represented in the Archdioceses of St. Louis and Santa Fe and the Diocese of San Bernardino.

[1240] (O.S.M.)—SERVITES

Order of Friar Servants of Mary

(Ordo Fratrum Servorum Beatae Virginis Mariae)

Generalate: *Curia Generalizia dei Servi di Maria,* Piazza San Marcello al Corso, 5 00187, Rome, Italy.

Servite Friars (1967): *United States of America Province* 3121 W. Jackson Blvd., Chicago, IL 60612. Tel: 773-533-0360; Fax: 773-533-8307. Very Rev. Michael M. Guimon, O.S.M., Prior Prov. Revs. Peregrine M. Graffius, O.S.M., Prov.; Bro. Brian M. Fitzpatrick, O.S.M., Prov. Councillor; Revs. Gerald M. Horan, O.S.M., Prov. Councillor; Christopher M. Krymski, O.S.M., Prov. Councillor & Province St. Peregrine Ministry; Councillors: Bros. Joel A. Lechner, O.S.M., Prov. Councillor; Edmund M. Baran, O.S.M., Prov. Treas.; Michael M. Callary, O.S.M., Prov. & Corporate Sec.; Revs. Eugene M. Smith, O.S.M.; Conrad M.

Borntrager, O.S.M., Archivist & Historian; Walter M. Brennan, O.S.M., Cor-Dir.-Province Marian Center; Joseph M. Cheah, O.S.M., Co-Dir.-Province Marian Center; Paul M. Gins, O.S.M., Vocation Dir.; Bro. Martin Doherty, O.S.M., Sacristan; Revs. John Topper, O.S.M., Dir.-Sanctuary of Our Sorrowful Mother; Philip M. McGlynn, O.S.M., Prov. Devel. Dir.; Robert M. Warsey, O.S.M., Dir.-Formation; Vidal M. Martinez, O.S.M., Prov. Asst.-Servite Secular Order.

Legal Titles: *The Order of Friar Servants of Mary-U.S.A. Province, Inc.*, Chicago IL; *Retirement Plan of the Order of Friar Servants of Mary-U.S.A.*, Chicago IL; *Charitable Trust of the Order of Friar Servants of Mary-U.S.A. Province, Inc.*, Chicago, IL; *The Servite Fathers, A California Corporation; Sacntuary of Our Sorrowful Mother, Inc.*, Portland, OR.

Parishes 15; High Schools 1; Shrines 1; Residences 15; Hospital Chaplaincies 3; Prison Ministry 1; Sister Chaplaincies 1.

Priests 102; Professed Brothers 14; Temporary Professed Friars 2; Novices 2.

Represented in the Archdioceses of Chicago, Denver, Detroit, Los Angeles, Portland (OR), St. Louis, Santa Fe and the Dioceses of Oakland, Orange, Orlando, Tucson, and Springfield-Cape Girardeau. Also in Germany, Ireland, and South Africa.

[1250] (C.R.S.)—SOMASCAN FATHERS
(Clericorum Regularium Somaschensium)
Order of St. Jerome Aemilian

General Motherhouse: Via Casal Morena, 8 00040, Morena - Rome, Italy. Most Rev. Bruno Luppi, C.R.S., Ph.D., Father Gen.

U.S. Foundation: *Pine Haven Boys Center,* 133 River Rd.- P.O. 162, Suncook, NH 03275. Tel: 603-485-7141. Rev. Julian Gerosa, C.R.S., Supr.

Priests 9.

Represented in the Archdiocese of Hartford and in the Dioceses of Galveston-Houston and Manchester.

[1260] (S.Ch.)—SOCIETY OF CHRIST
(Societas Christi Pro Emigrantibus Polonis)

General Motherhouse: 60-962 Poznan Ulica Panny Marii 4, Poland. Very Rev. Tadeusz Winnicki, S.Ch., Supr. Gen. Rev. Marian Burniak, Procurator Gen.; Via Botteghe Oscure 15 00186, Rome, Italy.

American-Canadian Province: *Provincial Residence,* 3000 Eighteen Mile Rd., Sterling Heights, MI 48314. Tel: 810-939-5022. Very Rev. Andrzej Maslejak, S.Ch., Prov.; Revs. Stanislaw Kuczaik, S.Ch., Vice-Prov.; Gerald Grupczynski, S.Ch., Treas.

Priests 51.

Represented in the Archdioceses of Atlanta; Baltimore, Chicago, Detroit, Los Angeles, Miami, Portland (OR), St. Paul-Minneapolis, San Francisco, Seattle, Washington and the Dioceses of Dallas, Galveston-Houston, Joliet, Phoenix, San Diego, San Jose and Toledo. Also in Canada.

[1270] (F.M.S.I.)—SONS OF MARY MISSIONARY SOCIETY
Sons of Mary, Health of the Sick
(Filii Mariae Salutis Infirmorum)

General Headquarters: 567 Salem End Rd., Framingham, MA 01702. Tel: 508-879-6711. Rev. John Murphy, F.M.S.I., Major Coord.; Bro. Kevin Courtney, Financial Coord.; Rev. John Coss, Councilor.

Professed 12.

Represented in the Archdiocese of Boston. Also in the Philippines.

[1280] (C.S.S.)—STIGMATINE FATHERS AND BROTHERS
(Congregation of the Sacred Stigmata)

General Motherhouse: Via Mazzarino No. 16, Rome, Italy. Very Rev. Andrea Meschi, C.S.S., Supr. Gen. Rev. Joao Carlos Seneme, C.S.S., Vicar Gen.

North American Province (1940): 554 Lexington St., Waltham, MA 02452. Tel: 781-209-3100; Fax: 781-894-9785. Very Rev. Gregory J. Hoppough, C.S.S., Prov. Supr.

Priests 38; Brothers 1.

Legal Title: *Stigmatine Fathers & Brother, Inc.*

Properties owned, staffed, or sponsored: Parishes 6; Retreat & Conference Center.

Represented in the Archdioceses of Boston, New York, and the Dioceses of Springfield (MA) and Worcester.

[1290] (S.S.)—SOCIETY OF THE PRIESTS OF SAINT SULPICE
(Societas Presbyterorum a S. Sulpitio)

General Motherhouse: 6 rue du Regard, Paris 75006, France. Very Rev. Lawrence B. Terrien, S.S., Supr. Gen.

U.S. Provincial House: 5408 Roland Ave., Baltimore, MD 21210. Tel: 301-323-5070; Fax: 410-433-6524. Very Rev. Ronald D. Witherup, S.S., Prov.; Mr. Joseph M. Reynolds, Exec. Asst. to Prov.; Revs. Charles J.T. Talar, S.S., Prov. Treas.; Gerald D. McBrearity, S.S., Dir.-Formation; Thomas R. Ulshafer, S.S., Prov. Sec. & Dir. Discernment & Admissions.

Legal Title: *The Associated Sulpicians of the United States.*

Fathers 78.

Represented in the Archdioceses of Baltimore, San Antonio, San Francisco, Seattle, Washington and the Diocese of San Jose.

[1300] (C.R.)—THEATINE FATHERS
(Congregatio Clericorum Regularium)

General Motherhouse: *Sant' Andrea della Valle,* Piazza Vidoni, 6 00186, Rome, Italy. Most Rev. Gabriele Darida, C.R., Supr. Gen.

U.S. Headquarters: 1050 S. Birch St., Denver, CO 80222. Tel: 303-756-5522. Very Rev. Patrick Valdez, C.R.

Fathers 17; Clerics 5.

Parishes 9; House of Formation 1; Provincial House 1.

Represented in the Archdioceses of Denver and New York and in the Diocese of Pueblo.

[1310] (O.SS.T.)—ORDER OF THE MOST HOLY TRINITY
Holy Trinity Fathers, Inc.
(Ordo Sanctissimae Trinitatis; *The Trinitarians*)

Founded in France in 1198 by St. John De Matha for the ransom of Christian slaves. First settlement in the United States in 1911.

General Curia: Via Massimi, 114C 00136, Rome, Italy. Most Rev. Jose Hernandez Sanchez, Minister Gen.

U.S.A. Province (1950): *Province of the Immaculate Heart of Mary,* P.O. Box 5742 - 8400 Park Heights Ave., Baltimore, MD 21282-0742. Tel: 410-486-5171. Very Rev. Raul P. Rendon, O.SS.T., Minister Prov.;Very Rev. John L. Dorn, O.SS.T., Vicar Prov.; Revs. Thomas N. Cerlo, O.SS.T., Vicar Prov.; Revs. Joseph Gidaro, O.SS.T.; Damian Anuszewski, O.SS.T.; Albert Anuszewski, O.SS.T., Dir.-Vocation; Charles J. Flood, O.SS.T.; Thomas A. Morris, O.SS.T., Sec. Prov.; Bro. Richard Micka, O.SS.T., Treas.

Trinitarian Communities in the U.S. 14; Fathers 55; Brothers 12; Novices 2.

Ministries in 12 parishes; Seminary Facility Positions; High Schools; Prison Chaplaincies; Hospital Chaplaincies; Social Apostolate to the Homeless; India Foundation; Mission for Persecuted Christians.

Properties owned: *DeMatha Catholic High School,* Hyattsville, MD; *Holy Trinity Monastery,* Pikesville, MD; *Redeemer House,* Baltimore, MD; *Trinity House,* Victoria, TX; *Trinitarian Residence,* Ellicott, MD; *Trinitarian Residence,* Adelphi, MD.

Represented in the Archdioceses of Baltimore, Los Angeles, New Orleans, Philadelphia, New York, Washington and the Dioceses of Corpus Christi, Dallas, Newton, Rockville Centre, Savannah, Trenton and Victoria. Also in India.

[1320] (C.S.V.)—CLERICS OF ST. VIATOR (Congregatio Clericorum Sancti Viatoris)

General Motherhouse: Via Padre A. Paoli, 41, Rome, Italy. Casella Postale 10793 00144, Roma, Italia. Very Rev. Mark R. Francis, C.S.V., Supr. Gen.

Province of Chicago (1882): 1212 East Euclid St., Arlington Heights, IL 60004. Tel: 847-398-1354. Very Rev. Robert M. Egan, C.S.V., Prov.; Revs. Richard A. Rinn, C.S.V., Councillor and Asst. Prov.; Robert E. Erickson, C.S.V., Prov. Treas.

Fathers 87; Brothers 20.

Properties owned, staffed, or sponsored: Parishes 15; High Schools 4; Formation Houses 2.

Represented in the Archdioceses of Chicago, Kansas City in Kansas, and the Dioceses of Joliet, Manchester, Monterey, Oakland, Peoria, Las Vegas, Rockford, San Diego, San Jose, Springfield (IL) and Tucson. Also in Belize, Colombia and Italy.

[1330] (C.M.)—CONGREGATION OF THE MISSION
Vincentians
(Congregatio Missionis Sti. Vincentii a Paulo)

Founded in France in 1625. First foundation in the United States in 1818.

General Motherhouse: *Curia Generalizia,* Via dei Capasso, 30 00164, Roma, Italia. Very Rev. Robert P. Maloney, C.M., Supr. Gen.

Eastern Province of the U.S.A. (1888): *St. Vincent's Seminary,* 500 E. Chelten Ave., Philadelphia, PA 19144. Tel: 215-848-1985; Fax: 215-844-2085. Very Rev. Thomas F. McKenna, C.M., Prov.; Revs. Charles P. Strollo, C.M., Asst. Prov.; John W. Gouldrick, C.M., Prov. Treas.; Consultors: William W. Sheldon, C.M.; John Kettelberger, C.M.; Michael J. Carroll, C.M.; Patrick Griffin, C.M.; Charles Plock,C.M.

Legal Title: *Congregation of the Mission of St. Vincent de Paul in Germantown, Inc.*

Fathers 169; Brothers 11; Students in Major Seminaries 12; College Seminarians 10.

Properties owned, sponsored, or staffed: Parishes 15; Missions in Republic of Panama 9; Universities 2; Major Seminary Residences 2; Novitiates 2; Retreat Houses 2; Hospitals 1.

Represented in the Archdioceses of Baltimore, New York, Mobile, Philadelphia, Washington and the Dioceses of Albany, Allentown, Birmingham, Brooklyn, Buffalo, Charleston, Charlotte, Galveston-Houston, Grand Rapids, Metuchen, Rockville Centre, and St. Augustine.

Midwest Province - Vincentians (1888): 13663 Rider Trail N., Earth City, MO 63045-1512. Tel: 314-344-1184; Fax: 314-344-2989. (Motherhouse St. Mary's Seminary, Perryville, MO.) Very Rev. William E. Hartenbach, C.M., Prov.; Bro. F. Joseph Hess, C.M., Prov. Treas.

Priests 122; Brothers 18.

Serving in 18 (arch)dioceses; Universities; Foreign Mission Stations; Houses of Apostolic Activity.

Represented in the Archdioceses of Chicago, Denver, Kansas City in Kansas, San Francisco, St. Louis, and the Dioceses of Belleville, Cheyenne, Colorado Springs, Evansville, Galveston-Houston, Jefferson City, Kansas City-St. Joseph, Little Rock, Phoenix, Pueblo, and Springfield-Cape Girardeau. Also in Marsabit and Nairobi, Kenya.

The New England Province of the Vincentian Fathers (1975): *Vincentian Provincial House,* 234 Keeney Street, Manchester, CT 06040-7048. Tel: 860-643-2828; Fax: 860-533-9462. Very Rev. John S. Sledziona, C.M., Prov.

Fathers 33; Brothers 3.

Legal Title: *New England Province of the Congregation of the Mission, Inc.; Charitable Trust of the New England Province of the Congregation of the Mission.*

Represented in the Archdiocese of Hartford and the Dioceses of Brooklyn, and Manchester.

American Italian Branch (Naples, Italy) (1922): *Our Lady of Pompei Church,* 3600 Claremont St., Baltimore, MD 21224. Tel: 410-675-7790. Rev. Luigi Esposito, C.M., Supr.

Legal Title: *Vincentian Fathers of the Neapolitan Province of Maryland Charities, Inc.*

Fathers 3.

Represented in the Archdiocese of Baltimore.

Vincentian Fathers-(American Spanish Branch Barcelona, Spain): 234 Congress St., Brooklyn, NY 11201. Tel: 718-624-3425; Fax: 718-834-0380. Rev. Robin E. Rodriguez, C.M., Supr.

Fathers 5.

Represented in the Diocese of Brooklyn

American Spanish Branch (Zaragoza, Spain) (1926): *Holy Agony Church,* 1834 3rd Ave., New York, NY 10029. Tel: 212-289-5589; Fax: 212-289-8321. Revs. Victor Elia, C.M.; Candido Arrizurieta, C.M.; Santiago Lluch, C.M.

Legal Title: *Padres Paules Community - Vincentians Inc.*

Fathers 13.

Represented in the Archdioceses of Los Angeles, & New York.

(Vincentian) Province of the West (1975): 650 W. 23rd St., Los Angeles, CA 90007-2036. Tel: 213-749-1865; Fax: 213-749-1554. Very Rev. Bernard J. Quinn, C.M., Prov.

Fathers 50; Brothers 3; Permanent Deacons 2; Major Theologians 2.

Members serve and staff: Parishes 4, Seminaries 2, evanglization centers 2; community houses 11.

Legal Titles: *Congregation of the Mission in California, A Corporation; Vincentian Community Charitable Trust; Vincentian Foreign Mission Society; DePaul Center Corp. (Formerly St. Vincent's Seminary Corp.); Vincentians Province of the West Support Trust Fund.*

Properties owned: *DePaul Center,* Montebello, CA; *St. Mary's Seminary,* Santa Barbara, CA; *Amat House,* Los Angeles, CA; 2 Residences in California.

Represented in the Archdioceses of Chicago and Los Angeles, and the Dioceses of Fresno, Gallup, Phoenix, San Jose and Stockton. Also in Belgium.

The Congregation of the Mission Southern Province (1975): 3826 Gilbert Ave., Dallas, TX 75219-4346.

Tel: 214-526-2421 & 526-0234; Fax: 214-526-3477. Very Rev. George Weber, C.M., Prov.; Rev. Miles Heinen, C.M., Treas.

Priests 28; Brothers 1.

Properties owned, sponsored, or staffed: Parishes 9; Community Houses 5; Mission Churches 3.

Represented in the Archdioceses of New Orleans, St. Louis, San Antonio and the Dioceses of Alexandria, Dallas, and Little Rock.

[1335] (V.C.)—VINCENTIAN CONGREGATION
Vincentians

Founded by Rev. Fr. Varkey Kattarath at Thottakom, Kerala, India in 1904.

Generalate: *Vincentian Generalate,* P.B. No. 2250 - Edappally Kochi 682 024, Kerala, India. Very Rev. Antony Plackal, V.C., Supr. Gen.

St. Joseph Province: *Vincentian Provincial House,* S.H. Mouont P.O. 686 006, Kottayam, Kerala, India. Tel: 481-563-559. Very Rev. George Arackal, V.C., Prov. Supr.

North American Headquarters: *Vincentian House,* P.O. Box 252, Emery, SD 57332-0252. Revs. Joseph Thalanany, V.C., Reg. Coord.; Joseph J. Arackal, V.C., Mission Procurator.

Fathers 5.

Represented in the Archdioceses of St. Paul-Minneapolis and in the Dioceses of Sioux Falls, St. Cloud and Trenton.

[1340] (S.D.V.)—VOCATIONIST FATHERS
(Society of The Divine Vocations)

Generali: Via Cortina D'Ampezzo, 138 00135, Rome, Italy. Very Rev. Raffael Castiglione, S.D.V., Supr. Gen.

American Headquarters: 90 Brooklake Rd., Florham Park, NJ 07932. Tel: 973-966-6262. Revs. Mario Muccitelli, S.D.V., Delegate of Supr. Gen. for U.S.A.

U.S. Foundations: *Our Lady of Perpetual Help Center,* 170 Broad St., Newark, NJ 07104. Revs. Louis Caputo, S.D.V., Pastor-Religious Supr. & Vocation Dir.; Giosue DiCesare, S.D.V.; Felix Antonitti, S.D.V.; Bro. Harold Hernandez, S.D.V.; Revs. Antonio Da Silva, S.D.V.; Angelito Rosales, S.D.V.

Represented in the Archdiocese of Newark and the Diocese of Paterson.

[1350] (C.F.X.)—BROTHERS OF ST. FRANCIS XAVIER
(Congregatio Fratrum Xaverianorum)

Generalate - Xaverian Brothers: 4409 Frederick Ave., Baltimore, MD 21229. Tel: 410-644-0034; Fax: 410-644-2762. Bros. Matthew Burke, C.F.X., Supr. Gen.; Cornelius E. Hubbuch, C.F.X., Vicar; Lawrence Harvey, C.F.X., Dir. Xaverian Sponsored Schools; John Fox, C.F.X., Assoc. Xaverian Sponsored Schools; Richard Mazza, C.F.X., Dir. Pastoral Care; Thomas Morrissey, C.F.X., Dir.-Development; Mr. Michael Naccarato, Chief Fin. Officer.

Legal Titles: *Xaverian Brothers USA Inc.; American Northeastern Province of the Xaverian Brothers Inc.; Isadore Charitable Trust.*

Brothers 255.

Ministries in the field of: Religious and Academic Education at all levels; Diocesan Offices; Pastoral Ministry; Mission Schools; Communities; Houses and House of Formation.

Represented in the Archdioceses of Baltimore, Boston, Chicago, Los Angeles, Louisville, Milwaukee, Newark, New York, Santa Fe, Washington and the Dioceses of Arlington, Birmingham, Brooklyn, Charleston, Fairbanks, Fall River, Memphis, Norwich, Richmond, Rapid City, Scranton, St. Petersburg, Venice, Wilmington, and Worcester. Also in Bangladesh, Bolivia, Belgium, Canada, Congo, England, Haiti, Kenya, Lithuania and Uganda.

[1360] (S.X.)—XAVERIAN MISSIONARY FATHERS
Saint Francis Xavier Foreign Mission Society
(Pia Societas Sancti Francisci Xaverii pro Exteris Missionibus)

General Motherhouse: *Istituto Saveriano Missioni Estere,* Viale Vaticano 40 00165, Rome, Italy. Very Rev. Francesco Marini, S.X., Supr. Gen.

U.S. Province: *Xaverian Missionary Fathers,* 12 Helene Ct., Wayne, NJ 07470. Tel: 973-942-2975; Fax: 973-942-5012. Very Rev. Ivan Marchesin, S.X., Prov.

Fathers 21; Seminarians 7.

Mission Houses 2; Houses of Formation 2.

Represented in the Archdioceses of Boston, Chicago and Milwaukee and in the Diocese of Paterson.

Index for Religious Institutes of Women

(The initial D or P indicates Diocesan or Pontifical Jurisdiction.)

Religious Order Initials for Women

A.B.S.	Auxiliaries of the Blessed Sacrament	[]
A.C.J.	Handmaids of the Sacred Heart of Jesus	[1870]
A.D.	Sisters of the Lamb of God	[2260]
A.I.M.	Association of Mary Immaculate	[]
A.N.G.	A New Genesis	[]
A.P.	Nuns of Perpetual Adoration of Blessed Sacrament	[3190]
A.P.B.	Adorers of the Precious Blood	[0110]
A.P.G.	Sisters of Perpetual Adoration	[3195]
A.R.	Handmaids of the Sacred Heart of Jesus for Reparation	[1880]
A.R.	Augustinian Recollects	[]
A.S.C.	Adorers of the Blood of Christ	[0100]
A.S.C.J.	Apostles of the Sacred Heart of Jesus	[0130]
B.C.	Notre Dame du Bon Conseil (Quebec)	[]
Bethl.	Bethlemita Daughters of the Sacred Heart of Jesus	[0910]
B.V.M.	Sisters of Charity of Blessed Virgin Mary	[0430]
B.V.M.C.	Blessed Virgin Missionaries of Carmel	[]
C.ach.	Carmeilte Sisters of Charity	[0340]
Carmel.D.C.J.	Carmelite Sisters of the Divine Heart of Jesus	[0360]
C.B.S.	Congregation of Bon Secours	[0270]
C.C.	Carmel Community	[0310]
C.C.V.I.	Sisters of Charity of Incarnate Word	[0460]
C.C.V.I.	Sisters of Charity of Incarnate Word (Houston, TX)	[0470]
C.C.W.	Carmelite Community of the Word	[0315]
C.D.P.	Sisters of Divine Providence	[0990]
C.D.P.	Sisters of Divine Providence of Kentucky	[1000]
C.D.P.	Sisters of Divine Providence of San Antonio, TX	[1010]
C.D.P.	Capuchin Sisters (Spain)	[]
C.D.S.	Congregation of Divine Spirit	[1040]
C.F.M.M.	Minim Daughters of Mary Immaculate	[2675]
C.F.P.	Feminine Congregation of the Passion	[]
C.F.P.	Mexican Passionist Sisters	[]
C.G.S.	Contemplatives of Good Shepherd	[1830]
C.H.F.	Sisters of Holy Faith	[1940]
C H.M.	Congregation of Humility of Mary	[2100]
C.H.S.	Community of the Holy Spirit	[2020]
C.I.C.	Sisters of Immaculate Conception	[2120]
C.I.J.	Congregation of Infant Jesus	[2230]
C.J.C.	Poor Sisters of Jesus Crucified and Sorrowful Mother	[3240]
C.K.	School Sisters of Christ the King	[]
C.L.H.C.	Congregation of Our Lady Help of the Clergy	[3090]
C.M.C.	Congregation of Mother of Carmel	[]
C.M.R.	Congregation of Mary Queen	[]
C.M.S.	Comboni Missionary Sisters	[0690]
C.M.S.	Cashel Mercy Sisters	[2515]
C.M.S.T.	Missionary Carmelites of St. Teresa	[0390]
C.N.D.	Congregation of Notre Dame	[2980]
C.O.C.	Companions of Christ	[]
C.P.	Religious of the Passion of Jesus Christ	[3170]
C.P.	Sisters of the Cross and Passion	[3180]
C.P.C.	Capuchin Poor Clares	[]
C.P.C.	St. Clare Capuchin Sisters	[]
C.P.P.S.	Sisters of the Precious Blood Dayton, Ohio	[3260]
C.P.P.S.	Sisters of the Most Precious Blood, (O'Fallon, MO)	[3270]
C.P.S.	Missionary Sisters of the Precious Blood	[2850]
C.R.	Sisters of the Resurrection	[3480]
C.S.	Company of the Savior	[0710]
C.S.	The Christian Sisters (Pious Union)	[]
C.S.A.	Sisters of Charity of St. Augustine	[0580]
C.S.A.	Sisters of St. Agnes	[3710]
C.S.A.	Albertine Sisters (Krakow, Poland)	[]
C.S.A.C.	Sisters of the Catholic Apostolate (Pallottine)	[3140]
C.S.B.	Congregation of St. Brigid	[3735]
C.S.C.	Congregation of Sisters of Holy Cross	[1920]
C.S.C.	Sisters of Holy Cross	[1930]
C.S.C.	Sisters of Holy Cross and Seven Dolors	[]
C.S.E.	Carmelite Sisters of the Eucharist	[]
C.S.F.N.	Sisters of Holy Family of Nazareth	[1970]
C.S.J.	Sisters of St. Joseph (Boston, Brighton)	[3830-01]
C.S.J.	Sisters of St. Joseph (Chicago, Lagrange Park)	[3830-02]
C.S.J.	Sisters of St. Joseph (Orange)	[3830-03]
C.S.J.	Sisters of St. Joseph (Rockville Centre, Brentwood)	[3830-05]
C.S.J.	Sisters of St. Joseph (Cleveland)	[3830-08]
C.S.J.	Sisters of St. Joseph (Lafayette, IN)	[3830-10]
C.S.J.	Sisters of St. Joseph (Pittsburgh, Baden)	[3830-13]
C.S.J.	Sisters of St. Joseph (Salina, Concordia)	[3830-15]
C.S.J.	Sisters of St. Joseph (Wichita)	[3830-18]
C.S.J.	Sisters of St. Joseph of Carondelet	[3840]
C.S.J.	Sisters of St. Joseph of Chambery	[3850]
C.S.J.	Sisters of St. Joseph (Lyons, France)	[3870]
C.S.J.	Sisters of St. Joseph of Medaille	[3880]
C.S.J.B.	Sisters of St. John the Baptist	[3820]
C.S.J.P.	Sisters of St. Joseph of Peace	[3890]
C.S.M.	Sisters of St. Martha of Antigonish N.S	[3937]
C.S.N.	Congregation of Sisters of Nazareth	[]
C.S.R.	Sisters of Holy Redeemer	[2000]
C.S.S.F.	Felician Sisters	[1170]
C.S.Sp.	Sisters of Holy Spirit	[2030]
C.S.S.T.	Carmelite Sisters of St. Teresa	[]
C.S.T.	Carmelite Sisters of St. Therese of Infant Jesus	[0380]
C.V.D.	Sisters of Bethany	[0250]
C.V.I.	Congregation of Incarnate Word and Blessed Sacrament	[2190]
C.V.I.	Religious of the Incarnate Word	[3449]
D.C.	Daughters of Charity of St. Vincent de Paul	[0760]
D.C.	Daughters of the Cross	[0770]
D.C.M.	Diocesan Carmelites of Maine	[]
D.C.P.B.	Daughters of Charity of Most Precious Blood	[0740]
D.H.M.	Daughters of Heart of Mary	[0810]
D.H.S.	Daughters of the Holy Spirit	[0820]
D.L.F.	Daughters of Our Lady of Fatima	[]
D.L.J.C.	Disciples of the Lord Jesus Christ	[0965]
D.M.	Daughters of Mary of the Immaculate Conception	[0860]
D.M.	Daughters of Our Lady of Mercy	[0890]
D.M.I.	Daughters of Mary Immaculate (Chaldean)	[]
D.M.J.	Daughters of Mary and Joseph	[0880]
D.O.M.	Daughters of Mercy (Croatian)	[]
D.S.F.	Daughters of St. Francis of Assisi	[0920]
D.S.M.P.	Daughters of St. Mary of Providence	[0940]
D.W.	Daughters of Wisdom	[0960]
E.F.M.S.	Eucharistic Franciscan Missionary Sisters	[1150]
E.M.S.	Eucharistic Missionary Society	[]
F.A.S.	Franciscan Apostolic Sisters	[]
F.C.	Daughters of the Cross of Liege	[0780]
F.C.J.	Society of Sisters Faithful Companions of Jesus	[4048]
F.C.S.C.J.	Daughters of Charity of the Sacred Heart of Jesus	[0750]
F.D.C.	Daughters of Divine Charity	[0790]
Fd.CC.	Canossian Daughters of Charity	[0730]
F.D.L.P.	Daughters of Providence	[]
F.D.N.S.C.	Daughters of Our Lady of the Sacred Heart	[0900]
F.D.P.	Daughters of Divine Providence	[0800]
F.D.Z.	Daughters of Divine Zeal	[0795]
F.H.I.C.	Franciscan Hospitaller Sisters of the Immaculate Conception	[1270]
F.H.M.	Franciscan Handmaids of the Most Pure Heart of Mary	[1260]
F.H.M.	Franciscan Sisters Daughters of Mercy	[1235]
F.I.	Daughters of Jesus	[0840]
F.J.	Congregation of the Daughters of Jesus	[0830]
F.L.G.	Franciscan Sisters of Our Lady of Grace	[]
F.M.A.	Daughters of Mary Help of Christians	[0850]
F.M.D.C.	Franciscan Missionaries of the Divine Child	[1340]
F.M.I.	Congregation of the Daughters of Mary Immaculate (Marianist Sisters)	[0870]
F.M.I.	Franciscan Sisters of Mary Immaculate of the Third Order of St. Francis of Assisi	[1500]
F.M.I.J.	Franciscan Missionaries of the Infant Jesus	[1365]
F.M.M.	The Franciscan Missionaries of Mary	[1370]
F.M.S.C.	Franciscan Missionary Sisters of the Sacred Heart	[1400]
F.M.S.J.	Mill Hill Sisters	[1410]
F.M.S.R.	Daughters of Our Lady of Holy Rosary	[]
F.N.S.S.C.	Franciscan Sisters of Our Lady of the Sacred Heart	[]
F.S.E.	The Institute of the Franciscan Sisters of the Eucharist	[1250]
F.S.J.	Religious Daughters of St. Joseph	[0930]
F.S.M.	Franciscan Sisters of Mary	[1415]
F.S.O.L.	Franciscan Sisters of Our Lady	[]
F.S.P.	Pious Society Daughters of St. Paul	[0950]
F.S.P.	Franciscan Sisters of Peace	[1425]
F.S.P.A.	Congregation of the Sisters of the Third Order of St. Francis of Perpetual Adoration	[1780]
F.S.R.	Franciscan Sisters of Ringwood	[1420]
F.S.S.C.	Franciscan Sisters of St. Clare (Pious Union)	[]
F.S.S.E.	Franciscan Sisters of St. Elizabeth	[1460]
F.S.S.J.	Franciscan Sisters of St. Joseph	[1470]
F.S.S.J.	Franciscan Sisters of St. Joseph	[1480]
F S.S.M.	Franciscan Sisters of the Sorrowful Mother	[]
F.S.Sp.J.	Franciscan Sisters of the Spirit of Jesus	[]
G.H.M.S.	Home Mission Sisters of America (Glenmary)	[2080]
G.N.S.H.	Grey Nuns of the Sacred Heart	[1840]
H.B.S.	Hermanas Contemplativas del Buen Pastor	[]
H.C.G.	Hermanas Catequistas Guadalupanas	[1900]
H.F.deS.J.	Franciscan Sisters of St. Joseph (Mexico City)	[]
H.G.S.	Congregation de Hermanas Guadalupanas de la Salle	[]

H.H.S.	Society of Helpers	[1890]
H.J.	Hermanas Josefinas	[1910]
H.J.D.	Las Hermanas de Juan Diego	[]
H.M.	Sisters of the Humility of Mary	[2110]
H.M.C.	Hermits of Mount Carmel	[]
H.M.S.S.	Mercedarian Sisters of the Blessed Sacrament	[2590]
H.M.S.S.	Religious Sisters of the Apostolate of the Blessed Sacrament	[3370]
H.O.Carm.	Hermits of Our Lady of Mt. Carmel	[]
H.P.B.	Congregation of the Handmaids of the Precious Blood	[1860]
H.R.F.	Sisters of the Holy Rosary of Fatima (Mexico)	[]
H.S.H.	Handmaids of the Sacred Heart of Pohang	[]
H.S.M.	Hermit Sisters of Mary	[]
H.Sp.S.	Daughters of the Holy Spirit Nazareth of the Good Shepherd	[]
H.S.S.	Hermanas del Servicio Social	[]
H.S.S.R.	Hermit Sisters of Romuald	[]
H.T.	Handmaids of the Most Holy Trinity	[]
H.V.M.	Sisters, Home Visitors of Mary	[2090]
I.B.V.M.	Institute of the Blessed Virgin Mary (Loretto Sisters)	[2370]
I.B.V.M.	Institute of the Blessed Virgin Mary (Loretto Sisters)	[2380]
I.C.	Vietnamese Sisters Incarnational Consecration	[]
I.C.M.	Missionary Sisters of the Immaculate Heart of Mary	[2750]
I.H.M.	Sisters of the Immaculate Heart of Mary at Mirinae	[2182]
I.H.M.	Sisters Servants of the Immaculate Heart of Mary	[2150]
I.H.M.	Sisters Servants of the Immaculate Heart of Mary	[2160]
I.H.M.	Sisters Servants of the Immaculate Heart of Mary	[2170]
I.H.M.	Sisters Servants of the Immaculate Heart of Mary	[2180]
I.H.M.	The California Institute of the Sisters of the Most Holy and Immaculate Heart of the Blessed Virgin Mary	[2930]
I.H.M.	Sisters of the Immaculate Heart of Mary of Wichita	[2185]
I.J.	Sisters of the Infant Jesus	[2240]
I.M.	Sisters of Charity of the Infant Mary	[]
I.S.S.M.	Secular Institute of Schoenstatt Sisters of Mary	[]
I.W.B.S.	Congregation of the Incarnate Word and Blessed Sacrament	[2200]
I.W.B.S.	Congregation of the Incarnate Word and Blessed Sacrament	[2205]
J.S.O.P.	Dominican Oblates of Jesus (Spain)	[]
L.B.	Ladies of Bethany	[]
L.C.M.	Sisters of the Little Company of Mary	[2270]
L.H.C.	Lovers of the Holy Cross Sisters	[2390]
L.M.S.C.	Little Missionary Sisters of Charity	[2290]
L.S.	Lasallian Sisters (Vietnam)	[]
L.S.A.	Little Sisters of the Assumption	[2310]
L.S.G.	Little Sisters of the Gospel (France)	[]
L.S.I.C.	Little Servant Sisters of the Immaculate Conception	[2300]
L.S.J.	Little Sisters of Jesus	[2330]
L.S.J.M.	Little Sisters of Jesus and Mary	[2331]
L.S.P.	Little Sisters of the Poor	[2340]
M.C.	Consolata Missionary Sisters	[0720]
M.C.	Missionaries of Charity	[2710]
M.C.	Poor Clare Missionary Sisters	[2840]
M.C.D.P.	Missionary Catechists of Divine Providence, San Antonio, TX	[2690]
M.C.M.	Cordi Marian Sisters	[]
M.C.P.	Missioneras Catequestas de los Pobres	[]
M.C.S.	Missionary Sisters of the Sacred Side	[]
M.C.S.J.M.	Congregation of Missionary Catechists of the Sacred Heart of Jesus and Mary	[]
M.D.	Mothers of the Helpless	[]
M.D.P.V.M.	Missionary Daughters of the Most Pure Virgin Mary	[]
M.E.	Missionary Ecumenical (Rome)	[]
M.C.SS.CC.J.M.	Missionary Catechists of the Sacred Hearts of Jesus and Mary	[2700]
M.E.S.S.T.	Eucharistic Missionaries of the Most Holy Trinity	[]
M.E.S.T.	Eucharistic Missionaries of St. Theresa (Mexico)	[]
M.F.P.	Franciscan Missionaries Our Lady of Peace	[]
M.G.Sp.S.	Guadalupan Missionaries of the Holy Spirit	[1845]
M.H.S.	Sisters of the Most Holy Sacrament	[2940]
M.H.S.H.	Mission Helpers of the Sacred Heart	[2720]
M.I.C.	Missionary Sisters of the Immaculate Conception (Canada)	[]
M.J.	Missionary Sisters of Jesus	[]
M.J.M.J.	Missionaries of Jesus, Mary and Joseph	[2770]
M.M.	Maryknoll Sisters of St. Dominic	[2470]
M.M.D.	Servite Missionary Sisters of the Sorrowful Mother	[]
M.M.M.	Medical Missionaries of Mary	[2480]
M.M.S.	Medical Mission Sisters	[2490]
M.O.M.	Missionary Sisters of Our Lady of Mercy	[2830]
M.P.F.	Religious Teachers Filippini	[3430]
M.P.H.	Missionary Sisters of Our Lady of Perpetual Help	[]
M.P.S.	Misioneras del Perpetual Socorro	[]
M.P.S.	Missionary Sisters of Our Lady of Perpetual Help	[]
M.P.V.	Religious Venerini Sisters	[4180]
M.R.	Marianist Sisters	[]
M.S.	Marian Sisters of the Diocese of Lincoln	[2400]
M.S.B.T.	Missionary Servants of the Most Blessed Trinity	[2790]
M.S.C.	Congregation of the Marianites of the Holy Cross	[2410]
M.S.C.	Missionary Sisters of the Most Sacred Heart of Jesus of Hiltrup	[2800]
M.S.C.	Missionary Sisters of the Sacred Heart	[2860]
M.S.C.Gpe.	Missionaries of the Sacred Heart of Jesus and of Our Lady of Guadalupe	[2865]
M.S.C.K.	Missionary Sisters of Christ the King	[2715]
M.S.F.	Missionary Sisters of the Holy Family	[]
M.S.H.F.	Missionary Sisters of the Holy Family (Poland)	[]
M.S.H.R.	Missionary Sisters of the Holy Rosary	[2730]
M.S.J.	Medical Sisters of St. Joseph	[2500]
M.S.K.C.P.	Missionary Sisters of Christ the King of Polonia	[]
M.S.M.G.	Missionary Sisters of Mother of God	[2810]
M.S.O.L.A.	Missionary Sisters of Our Lady of Africa	[2820]
M.S.S.A.	Missionary Servants of St. Anthony	[2890]
M.S.S.C.B.	Missionary Sisters of St. Charles Borromeo	[2900]
M.S.S.J.	Missionary Servants of St. Joseph (Spain)	[]
M.S.Sp.	Mission Sisters of the Holy Spirit	[2740]
M.SS.S.	Missionary Sisters of the Most Blessed Sacrament	[2780]
M.T.G.	Adorers of the Holy Cross	[4155]
M.X.Y.	The Yarumal Foreign Mission Institute (Colombia)	[]
N.A.U.-O.L.C.	North American Unions of Sisters of Our Lady of Charity	[3070]
N.D.	Notre Dame Sisters	[2960]
N.D.S.	Congregation of Notre Dame de Sion	[2950]
O.A.R.	Augustinian Recollect Sisters	[]
O.B.T.	Sisters Oblates to the Blessed Trinity	[3020]
O.C.A.	Carmelite Vietnamese of Our Lady of Mt. Carmel	[]
O.Carm.	Calced Carmelites	[0300]
O.Carm.	Carmelite Nuns of the Ancient Observance	[0320]
O.Carm.	Carmelite Sisters for Aged and Infirm	[0330]
O.Carm.	Carmelite Sisters (Corpus Christi)	[0350]
O.Carm.	Congregation of Our Lady of Mt. Carmel	[0400]
O.Carm.	Institute of the Sisters of Our Lady of Mt. Carmel	[0410]
O.C.D.	Carmelite Sisters of the Most Sacred Heart of Los Angeles	[0370]
O.C.D.	Discalced Carmelite Nuns	[0420]
O.C.D.	Carmelitas del Sagrado Corazon	[]
O.Cist.	Cistercian Nuns	[0680]
O.C.S.O.	Cistercian Nuns of the Strict Observance	[0670]
O.D.N.	Company of Mary	[0700]
O.L.C.	Sisters of Our Lady of Charity	[3071]
O.L.C.	Sisters of Our Lady of Charity	[3073]
O.L.G.	Sisters of Our Lady of the Garden	[]
O.L.L.	Sisters of Our Lady of Lourdes	[]
O.L.M.	Sisters of Charity of Our Lady of Mercy	[0510]
O.L.S.	Sisters of Our Lady of Sorrows	[3120]
O.L.V.M.	Our Lady of Victory Missionary Sisters	[3130]
O.M.M.I.	Oblate Missionaries of Mary Immaculate	[]
O.M.O.	Oblates of the Mother of Orphans	[3035]
O.P.	Dominican Contemplative Nuns (Cloistered)	[1050]
O.P.	Dominican Contemplative Sisters (Cloistered)	[1060]
O.P.	Dominican Sisters (St. Catharine, KY)	[1070-01]
O.P.	Dominican Sisters (Columbus, OH)	[1070-02]
O.P.	Dominican Sisters (Sinsinawa, WI)	[1070-03]
O.P.	Dominican Sisters (San Rafael, CA)	[1070-04]
O.P.	Dominican Sisters (Amityville, NY)	[1070-05]
O.P.	Dominican Sisters (Newburgh, NY)	[1070-06]
O.P.	Dominican Sisters (Nashville, TN)	[1070-07]
O.P.	Dominican Sisters (New Orleans, LA)	[1070-08]
O.P.	Dominican Sisters (Racine, WI)	[1070-09]
O.P.	Dominican Sisters (Springfield, IL)	[1070-10]
O.P.	Dominican Sisters (Sparkill, NY)	[1070-11]
O.P.	Dominican Sisters (San Jose, CA)	[1070-12]
O.P.	Dominican Sisters (Adrian, MI)	[1070-13]
O.P.	Dominican Sisters (Grand Rapids, MI)	[1070-14]
O.P.	Dominican Sisters (Blauvelt, NY)	[1070-15]
O.P.	Dominican Sisters (Ossining, NY)	[1070-16]
O.P.	Dominican Sisters (Media, PA)	[1070-17]
O.P.	Dominican Sisters (Caldwell, PA)	[1070-18]
O.P.	Dominican Sisters (Houston, TX)	[1070-19]
O.P.	Dominican Sisters (Tacoma, WA)	[1070-20]
O.P.	Dominican Sisters (Edmonds, WA)	[1070-21]
O.P.	Dominican Sisters (Fall River, MA)	[1070-22]
O.P.	Dominican Sisters (Hawthorne, NY)	[1070-23]
O.P.	Dominican Sisters (Great Bend, KS)	[1070-24]
O P.	Dominican Sisters (Kenosha, WI)	[1070-25]
O.P.	Dominican Sisters (Oxford, MI)	[1070-26]
O.P.	Dominican Sisters (Justice, IL)	[1070-27]
O.P.	Dominican Sisters (Akron, OH)	[1070-28]
O.P.	Dominican Sisters (Spokane, WA)	[1070-29]
O.P.	Dominican Sisters (Oxford, South Africa)	[1070-30]
O.P.	Marian Society of Dominican Catechists	[1090]
O.P.	Dominican Sisters of Charity of the Presentation of the Blessed Virgin	[1100]
O.P.	Dominican Sisters of Our Lady of the Rosary and of Saint Catherine of Siena, Cabra	[1110]
O.P.	Dominican Sisters of the Roman Congregation	[1120]

O.P.	Dominican Rural Missionaries	[1130]
O.P.	Eucharistic Missionaries of St. Dominic	[1140]
O.P.	Dominican Sisters of Carondelet	[]
O.P.	Religious Missionaries of St. Dominic (Spanish Prov.)	[]
O.P.	Dominican Sisters of Mt. Thabor	[]
O.P.	Dominican Sisters of Our Lady of the Most Holy Rosary	[]
O.P.	Dominican Sisters (Vietnam)	[]
O.P.	Dominican Contemplative Sisters	[]
O.P.	Dominican Sisters (Colombia)	[]
O.P.	Dominican Sisters (Ecuador)	[]
O.P.	Hermanas Dominicanas de la Doctrine Cristiana	[]
O.S.A.	Augustinian Nuns of Contemplative Life	[0160]
O.S.A.	Congregation of Augustinian Sisters Servants of Jesus and Mary	[2145]
O.S.A.	Sisters of St. Rita	[4010]
O.S.A.	Sisters of St. Augustine	[]
O.S.A.	Augustinian Sisters of Our Lady of Consolation	[]
O.S.B.	Benedictine Nuns of the Congregation of Solesmes	[0170]
O.S.B.	Benedictine Nuns of the Primitive Observance	[0180]
O.S.B.	Benedictine Sisters	[0190]
O.S.B.	Benedictine Sisters	[0200]
O.S.B.	Missionary Benedictine Sisters	[0210]
O.S.B.	Congregation of the Benedictine Sisters of Perpetual Adoration of Pontifical Jurisdiction	[0220]
O.S.B.	Benedictine Sisters of Pontifical Jurisdiction	[0230]
O.S.B.	Benedictine Nuns	[0233]
O.S.B.	Olivetan Benedictine Sisters	[0240]
O.S.B.	Congregation of Jesus Crucified	[2250]
O.S.B.	Benedictine Congregation of Our Lady of Monte	[]
O.S.B.	Benedictine Sisters of Sacred Heart	[]
O.S.B.	Contemplative Sisters of St. Benedict	[]
O.S.B.	Benedictine Sisters of Liberty	[]
O.S.B.	Congregation of the Benedictine Sisters of the Sacred Heart	[]
O.S.B.Cam.	Camaldolese Benedictine Sisters	[]
O.S.B.M.	Sisters of the Order of St. Basil the Great	[3730]
O.S.B.S.	Oblate Sisters of the Blessed Sacrament	[3010]
O.S.C.	Order of St. Clare	[3760]
O.S.C.	Sisters of St. Clare	[3770]
O.S.C.Cap.	Capuchin Poor Clares	[3765]
O.S.F.	Franciscan Sisters of Allegany New York	[1180]
O.S.F.	The Franciscan Sisters of Baltimore	[1200]
O.S.F.	Franciscan Sisters of Chicago	[1210]
O.S.F.	Franciscan Sisters of Christian Charity	[1230]
O.S.F.	Franciscan Sister, Daughters of the Sacred Hearts of Jesus and Mary	[1240]
O.S.F.	Franciscan Sisters of the Immaculate Conception	[1280]
O.S.F.	Franciscan Sisters of the Immaculate Conception and St. Joseph for the Dying	[1300]
O S.F.	Franciscan Sisters of Little Falls, Minnesota	[1310]
O.S.F.	Franciscan Missionary Sisters for Africa	[1320]
O.S.F.	Franciscan Missionary Sisters of the Immaculate Conception	[1350]
O.S.F.	Missionary Franciscan Sisters of the Immaculate Conception	[1360]
O.S.F.	Franciscan Missionaries of Our Lady	[1380]
O.S.F.	Franciscan Missionary Sisters of Our Lady of Sorrows	[1390]
O.S.F.	Franciscan Sisters of Our Lady of Perpetual Help	[1430]
O.S.F.	Franciscan Sisters of the Sacred Heart	[1450]
O.S.F.	Franciscan Sisters of St. Paul	[1485]
O.S.F.	Sisters of the Third Franciscan Order	[1490]
O.S.F.	St. Francis Mission Community	[1505]
O.S.F.	Sisters of St. Francis	[1510]
O.S.F.	Sisters of St. Francis of Christ the King	[1520]
O.S.F.	Sisters of St. Francis of the Congregation of Our Lady of Lourdes, Sylvania, Ohio	[1530]
O.S.F.	Sisters of Saint Francis, Clinton, Iowa	[1540]
O.S.F.	Sisters of St. Francis of the Holy Cross	[1550]
O.S.F.	Sisters of St. Francis of the Holy Eucharist	[1560]
O.S.F.	Sisters of St. Francis of the Holy Family	[1570]
O.S.F.	Sisters of St. Francis of the Immaculate Conception	[1580]
O.S.F.	Sisters of St. Francis of the Immaculate Heart of Mary (Hankinson, North Dakota)	[1590]
O.S.F.	Sisters of St. Francis of the Martyr St. George	[1600]
O.S.F.	Sisters of Saint Francis of Millvale, Pennsylvania	[1620]
O.S.F.	Sisters of St. Francis of Penance and Christian Charity	[1630]
O.S.F.	Sisters of St. Francis of Perpetual Adoration	[1640]
O.S.F.	The Sisters of St. Francis of Philadelphia	[1650]
O.S.F.	Sisters of Saint Francis of the Providence of God	[1660]
O.S.F.	Sisters of St. Francis of Savannah, MO	[1670]
O.S.F.	School Sisters of St. Francis	[1680]
O.S.F.	School Sisters of the Third Order of St. Francis (Pittsburgh, PA)	[1690]
O.S.F.	School Sisters of the Third Order of St. Francis (Panhandle, TX)	[1695]
O.S.F.	School Sisters of the Third Order of St. Francis (Bethlehem, PA)	[1700]
O.S F.	The Sisters of St. Francis of Assisi	[1705]
O.S.F.	Congregation of the Third Order of St. Francis of Mary Immaculate (Joliet, IL)	[1710]
O.S.F.	Sisters of the Third Order Regular of St. Francis of the Congregation of Our Lady of Lourdes	[1720]
O.S.F.	Congregation of the Sisters of the Third Order of St. Francis (Oldenburg, IN)	[1730]
O.S.F.	Sisters of the Third Order of St. Francis of Penance and Charity	[1760]
O.S.F.	Sisters of the Third Order of St. Francis (Peoria, IL)	[1770]
O.S.F.	Sisters of St. Francis of the Third Order Regular (Williamsville, New York)	[1800]
O.S.F.	Bernardine Sisters of the Third Order of St. Francis	[1810]
O.S.F.	Hospital Sisters of the Third Order of St. Francis	[1820]
O.S.F.	Servants of the Holy Infancy of Jesus	[1980]
O.S.F.	Consolation Sisters (Highland, CA)	[]
O.S.F.	Franciscan Sisters of Christ the Divine Teacher	[]
O.S.F.	St. Francis Mission Community	[]
O.S.F.S.	Oblate Sisters of St. Francis de Sales	[3060]
O.S.H.J.	Oblate Sisters of the Sacred Heart of Jesus	[3050]
O.S.M.	Mantellate Sisters, Servants of Mary of Blue Island	[3570]
O.S.M.	Servants of Mary	[3580]
O.S.M.	Servants of Mary (Servite Sisters)	[3590]
O.S.M.	Oblates of St. Martha	[]
O.S.P.	Oblate Sisters of Providence	[3040]
O.S.S.	Sacramentine Nuns	[3490]
O.SS.R.	Order of the Most Holy Redeemer	[2010]
O.SS.R.	Oblates of the Most Holy Redeemer	[3030]
O.SS.S.	The Brigittine Sisters	[0280]
O.SS.T.	Sisters of the Most Holy Trinity	[0260]
O.S.U.	Ursuline Nuns (Roman Union)	[4110]
O.S.U.	Ursuline Nuns of the Congregation of Paris (St. Martin, OH)	[4120]
O.S.U.	Ursuline Nuns of the Congregation of Paris (Cincinnati, OH)	[4120-01]
O.S.U.	Ursuline Nuns of the Congregation of Paris (Kansas City, KS)	[4120-02]
O.S.U.	Ursuline Nuns of the Congregation of Paris (Louisville, KY)	[4120-03]
O.S.U.	Ursuline Nuns of the Congregation of Paris (Cleveland, OH)	[4120-04]
O.S.U.	Ursuline Nuns of the Congregation of Paris (Owensboro, KY)	[4120-05]
O.S.U.	Ursuline Nuns of the Congregation of Paris (Toledo, OH)	[4120-06]
O.S.U.	Ursuline Nuns of the Congregation of Paris (Youngstown, OH)	[4120-07]
O.S.U.	Ursuline Sisters of the Congregation of Tildonk, Belgium	[4130]
O.S.U.	Ursuline Sisters of Belleville	[4140]
O.S.U.	Irish Ursuline Union	[4150]
P.B.V.M.	Presentation of the Blessed Virgin Mary Sisters	[3280]
P.B.V.M.	Sisters of the Presentation of the B.V.M	[3320]
P B.V.M.	Union of the Sisters of the Presentation of the Blessed Virgin Mary	[3330]
P.C.C.	Order of St. Clare	[3760]
P.C.I.	Pax Christi Institute	[]
P.C.J.	Sisters of the Poor Child Jesus	[3220]
P.C.P.A.	Poor Clares of Perpetual Adoration	[3210]
P.D.D.M.	Pious Disciples of the Divine Master	[0980]
P.F.M.	Franciscans of Mary	[2280]
P.H.J.C.	Poor Handmaids of Jesus Christ	[3230]
P.M.	Sisters of the Presentation of Mary	[3310]
P.O.S.C.	Little Workers of the Sacred Heart	[2345]
P.S.N.	Poor Sisters of Nazareth	[3242]
P.S.S.F.	The Little Sisters of the Holy Family	[2320]
P.S.S.J.	Poor Sisters of St. Joseph	[3250]
P.V.M.I.	The Parish Visitors of Mary Immaculate	[3160]
Q.M.H.C.	Quinhon Missionary Sisters of the Holy Cross	[]
R.A.	Religious of the Apostolate of the Sacred Heart	[3380]
R.A.	Religious of the Assumption	[3390]
R.A.	Antonine Sisters	[]
R.A.D.	Sisters of the Love of God	[]
R.C.	Congregation of Our Lady of Retreat in the Cenacle	[3110]
R.C.D.	Sisters of Our Lady of Christian Doctrine	[3080]
R.C.E.	Religious of Christian Education	[3410]
R.C.M.	Sisters of the Immaculate Conception	[2130]
R.C.S.C.J.	Sisters of the Cross of the Sacred Heart of Jesus (Mexico)	[]
R.D.C.	Sisters of the Divine Compassion	[0970]
R.E.	Religious of the Eucharist	[3420]
R.F.	Sisters of St. Philip Neri Missionary Teachers	[]
R.F.R.	Sisters of Our Lady of Refuge	[]
R.G.S.	The Sisters of the Good Shepherd	[1830]
R.H.S.J.	Religious Hospitallers of Saint Joseph	[3440]
R.J.M.	Religious of Jesus and Mary	[3450]
R.M.	Marianitas	[]
R.M.I.	Claretian Missionary Sisters	[0685]
R.M.I.	Religious of Mary Immaculate	[3460]
R.M.M.	Mercedarian Sisters	[]
R.O.D.A.	Sisters Oblates to Divine Love	[]
R.O.L.C.	Our Lady of Charity of Refuge	[3072]
R.S.C.	Religious Sisters of Charity	[3400]
R.S.C.J.	Society of the Sacred Heart	[4070]
R.S.H.M.	Religious of the Sacred Heart of Mary	[3465]
R.S.J.	Religious of St. Joseph of Australia	[]
R.S.M.	Religious Sisters of Mercy of Alma, Michigan	[2519]
R.S.M.	Sisters of Mercy	[2520]
R.S.M.	Sisters of Mercy of Ardagh & Clonmacnois	[2523]
R.S.M.	Sisters of Mercy (Galway)	[2535]
R.S.M.	Sisters of Mercy	[2540]
R.S.M.	Sisters of Mercy (Sligo)	[2549]
R.S.M.	Sisters of Mercy	[2550]
R.S.M.	Sisters of Mercy of the Americas	[2575]
R.S.M.	Sisters of Mercy (Ballyshannon, Ireland)	[]
R.S.M.	Sisters of Mercy (Mayo, Ireland)	[]
R.S.M.	Sisters of Mercy of Mississippi, Inc.	[]
R.S.M.	Sisters of Mercy of Portland	[2655]

R.S.M.	Diocesan Sisters of Mercy	[]
R.S.R.	Congregation of Our Lady of the Holy Rosary	[3100]
R.T.	Theatine Sisters of the Immaculate Conception	[]
R.V.M.	Religious of the Blessed Virgin Mary	[]
S.A.	Franciscan Sisters of the Atonement	[1190]
S.A.A.	Sisters Auxillaries of the Apostolate	[0140]
S.A.B.	Sisters of St. Anne Bangalone	[]
S.A.C.	Sisters of the Guardian Angel	[1850]
S.A.C.	Pallottine Missionary Sisters Queen of Apostles Prov	[3150]
S.A.S.V.	Sisters of the Assumption	[0150]
S.B.S.	The Sisters of the Blessed Sacrament for Indians and Colored People	[0260]
S.C.	Sisters of Charity of Cincinnati, Ohio	[0440]
S.C.	Sisters of Charity of Seton Hill, Greensburg, PA	[0570]
S.C.	Sisters of St. Elizabeth, Convent Station	[0590]
S.C.	Sisters of Charity of St. Vincent de Paul, Halifax	[0640]
S.C.	Sisters of Charity of St. Vincent de Paul, New York	[0650]
S.C.C.	Sisters of Christian Charity	[0660]
Sch.P.	Sisters of the Pious Schools	[3200]
S.C.I.C.	Sisters of Charity of the Immaculate Conception of Ivrea	[0450]
S.C.I.M.	Servants of the Immaculate Heart of Mary	[3550]
S.C.K.	Sisters of Christ the King	[]
S.C.L.	Sisters of Charity of Leavenworth, Kansas	[0480]
S.C.M.C.	Sisters of Charity of Our Lady, Mother of the Church	[0530]
S.C.M.M.	Sisters of Charity of Our Lady Mother of Mercy	[0520]
S.C.M.M.	Medical Mission Sisters	[2490]
S.C.N.	Sisters of Charity of Nazareth	[0500]
S.C.O.	Sisters of Charity of Ottawa (Grey Nuns of the Cross)	[0540]
S.C.O.	Sisters of Charity of Quebec (Grey Nuns)	[0560]
S.C.R.H.	Sisters of Charity of Rolling Meadows	[]
S.C.S.J.A.	Sisters of Charity of St. Joan Antida	[0600]
S.C.S.L.	Sisters of Charity of St. Louis	[0620]
S.C.S.H.	Sisters of Charity of St. Hyacinthe (Grey Nuns)	[0610]
S.deP.	Sister Servants of the Poor	[]
S.D.R.	Sisters of the Divine Redeemer	[1020]
S.D.S.	Sisters of the Divine Saviour	[1030]
S.D.S.H.	Sisters of the Society Devoted to the Sacred Heart	[4050]
S.D.V.	Vocationist Sisters	[4210]
S.E.	Sisters of Emanuel	[]
S.E.C.	Sisters of the Eucharistic Covenant	[]
S.F.C.C.	Sisters for Christian Community	[]
S.F.M.A.	Franciscan Missionary Sisters of Assisi	[1330]
S.F.p.	Franciscan Sisters of the Poor	[1440]
S.G.M.	Sisters of Charity of Montreal (Grey Nuns)	[0490]
S.G.S.	Hermanas del Buen Pastor	[]
S.H.C.J.	Society of the Holy Child Jesus	[4060]
S.H.F.	Sisters of the Holy Family	[1960]
S.H.J.M.	Sisters of the Sacred Hearts of Jesus and Mary	[3680]
S.H.S.	Sisters of the Holy Spirit	[2040]
S.H.Sp.	Sisters of the Holy Spirit and Mary Immaculate	[2050]
S.I.M.	Missionaries of the Kingship of Chnst	[]
S.I.W.	Sisters of the Incarnate Word and the Blessed Sacrament	[2210]
S.J.	Servants of Jesus	[3560]
S.J.A.	Sisters of Ste. Jeanne D'Arc	[3815]
S.J.B.	Sisters of St. John Bosco (Taylor, TX)	[]
S.J.C.	Sisters of St. Joseph of Cluny	[3860]
S.J.S.	Servants of the Blessed Sacrament	[3499]
S.J.S M.	Sisters of St. Joseph of St. Mark	[3910]
S.J.W.	Sisters of St. Joseph the Worker	[3920]
S.L.	Sisters of Loretto at the Foot of the Cross	[2360]
S.L.T.	Pious Society of Our Lady of the Most Holy Trinity	[]
S.L.W.	Sisters of the Living Word	[2350]
S.M.	Marist Sisters Congregation of Mary	[2430]
S.M.	Sisters of Mercy	[2516]
S.M.	Sisters of Mercy	[2518]
S.M.	Sisters of Mercy	[2570]
S.M.	Sisters of Mercy (Cork and Ross)	[2600]
S.M.	Misericordia Sisters	[2680]
S.M.	Sisters Servants of Mary	[3600]
S.M.	Sisters of Mercy (Loughrea, Ireland)	[]
S.M.	Sisters of Mercy of Tralee	[]
S.M.D.C.	Sisters of Mercy of Christian Charity of St. Vincent de Paul of Hungary	[2610]
S.M.G.	Poor Servants of the Mother of God	[3640]
S.M.I.	Sisters of Mary Immaculate	[2440]
S.M.I.C.	Missionary Sisters of the Immaculate Conception of the Mother of God	[2760]
S.M.M.G.	Sisters of Mary, Mother of God	[]
S.M.M.I.	Sisters Minor of the Mary Immaculate	[]
S.M.M.S.	Society of Mary Missionary Sisters	[]
S.M.P.	Sisters of Mary of the Presentation	[2450]
S.M.P.	Daughters of Our Mother of Peace	[]
S.M.P.	Society of Our Mother of Peace	[]
S.M.R.	Society of Mary Reparatrix	[2560]
S.M.S.H.	Sisters of Saint Marthe (of St. Hyacinthe)	[3940]
S.M.S.M.	Marist Missionary Sisters	[2420]
S.N.D.	Sisters of Notre Dame	[2990]
S.N.D.deN.	Sisters of Notre Dame de Namur	[3000]
S.N.J.M.	Sisters of the Holy Names of Jesus and Mary	[1990]
S.O.L.M.	Sisters of Our Lady of Mercy	[2670]
S.O.L.P.H.	Sisters of Our Lady of Perpetual Help	[]
S.O.L.T.	Our Lady of the Most Holy Trinity Convent	[3105]
S.P.	Sisters of Providence	[3340]
S.P.	Sisters of Providence	[3350]
S.P.	Sisters of Providence of Saint Mary-of-the-Woods, IN	[3360]
S.P.C.	Sisters of St. Paul of Chartres	[3980]
S.R.	Sisters of Reparation of the Sacred Wounds of Jesus	[3475]
S.R.C.	Servants of Our Lady, Queen of Clergy	[3650]
S.R.C.M.	Sisters of Reparation of the Congregation of Mary	[3470]
S.S.A.	Sisters of St. Ann	[3718]
S.S.A.	Sisters of St. Anne	[3720]
S.S.C.	Missionary Sisters of St. Columban	[2880]
S.S.C.	Sisters of St. Casimir	[3740]
S.S.C.	Society of the Sisters of the Church	[]
SS.CC.	Congregation of the Sacred Hearts and of Perpetual Adoration	[3690]
S.S.Ch.	Sisters of St. Chretienne	[3750]
S.S.C.J.	Servants of the Most Sacred Heart of Jesus	[3630]
S.S.C.J.	Sisters of the Sacred Heart of Jesus of Saint Jacut	[3670]
S.S.C.K.	Sisters Servants of Christ the King	[3510]
S.S.C.M.	Servants of the Holy Heart of Mary	[3520]
SS.C.M.	Sisters of Saints Cyril and Methodius	[3780]
S.S.D.	Institute of the Sisters of St. Dorothy	[3790]
S.S.E.	Sisters of St. Elizabeth	[3800]
S.S.F.	Congregation of the Sisters of the Holy Family	[1950]
S.S.H.	Sisters Servants of the Most Sacred Heart	[]
S.S.H.J.P.	Servants of the Sacred Heart of Jesus and of the Poor	[3660]
S.S.J.	Servants of St. Joseph	[3595]
S.S.J.	Sisters of St. Joseph (Buffalo)	[3830-06]
S.S.J.	Sisters of St. Joseph (Burlington)	[3830-07]
S.S.J.	Sisters of St. Joseph (Erie)	[3830-09]
S.S.J.	Sisters of St. Joseph (Kalamazoo, Nazareth)	[3830-11]
S.S.J.	Sisters of St. Joseph (Ogdensburg)	[3830-12]
S.S.J.	Sisters of St. Joseph (Rochester)	[3830-14]
S.S.J.	Sisters of St. Joseph, (Springfield, MA)	[3830-16]
S.S.J.	Sisters of St. Joseph (Wheeling, Eng)	[3830-17]
S.S.J.	Sisters of Saint Joseph of Chestnut Hill, Philadelphia	[3893]
S.S.J.	Sisters of St. Joseph of St. Augustine, Florida	[3900]
S.S.J.C.	Sisters of St. Joseph Benedict Cottolengo	[]
S.S.J.-T.O.S.F.	Sisters of St. Joseph of the Third Order of St. Francis	[3930]
S.S.L.	Congregation of the Sisters of St. Louis, Juilly-Monaghan	[3935]
S.S.LOG.	Seton Sisters of Our Lady of Guadalupe, Tucson	[]
S.S.M.	Sisters of the Sorrowful Mother (Third Order of St. Francis)	[4100]
S.S.M.I.	Sisters Servants of Mary Immaculate	[3610]
S.S.M.I.	Sisters Servants of Mary Immaculate	[3620]
S.S.M.N.	Sisters of Saint Mary of Namur	[3950]
S.S.M.O.	Sisters of St. Mary of Oregon	[3960]
S.S.N.D.	School Sisters of Notre Dame	[2970]
S.S.P.C.	Missionary Sisters of St. Peter Claver	[3990]
S.Sp.S.	Missionary Sisters Servants of the Holy Spirit	[3530]
S.Sp.S.deA.P.	Sister Servants of the Holy Spirit of Perpetual Adoration	[3540]
S.S.S.	Servants of the Blessed Sacrament	[3500]
S.S.S.	Sisters of Social Service of Los Angeles, Inc.	[4080]
S.S.S.	Sisters of Social Service	[4090]
S.S.S.F.	School Sisters of St. Francis	[1680]
S.S.T.V.	Congregation of Sisters of St. Thomas of Villanova	[4030]
S.T.J.	Society of St. Teresa of Jesus	[4020]
S.U.	Society of St. Ursula	[4040]
S.U.S.C.	Sisters of the Holy Union	[2070]
S.V.M.	Sisters of the Visitation of the Congregation of the Immaculate Heart of Mary	[4200]
V.D.C.	Verbum Dei Community	[]
V.H.M.	Visitation Nuns	[4190]
V.S.	Vestiarski Sisters	[]
V.S.C.	Vincentian Sisters of Charity	[4160]
V.S.C.	Vincentian Sisters of Charity	[4170]
V.Z.	Sisters of Charity of St. Vincent de Paul	[0630]
X.M.M.	Xaverian Missionary Society of Mary, Inc.	[4230]
X.S.	Catholic Mission Sisters of St. Francis Xavier	[3810]

Religious Institutes of Women

Leadership Conference of Women Religious of the United States of America—National Office: 8808 Cameron St., Silver Spring, MD 20910. Tel: 301-588-4955; Fax: 301-587-4575. Sr. Mary Christine Fellerhoff, C.S.A., Exec. Dir.; Sr. Nancy Sylvester, Pres.; Sr. Mary Mollison, C.S.A., Pres.; Sr. Mary Bernadette McNulty C.S.J., Treas. Council Major Superiors of Women Religious in the United States of America—1211 Lawrence St., N.E., P.O. Box 4467, Washington, DC 20017-0467. Tel: 202-832-2575; Fax: 202-832-6325. Mother Mary McGreevy, R.S.M., Chm.

(The initial D or P indicates Diocesan or Pontifical Jurisdiction)

[0100] (A.S.C.)—ADORERS OF THE BLOOD OF CHRIST P

Founded in Acuto, Italy, in 1834. First foundation in the United States in 1870.

General Motherhouse: Via Beata Maria De Mattias 10, Rome, 00183 Italy. Sr. Giuseppina Fragasso, A.S.C., Supr. Gen.

Province of Ruma (1876): *Provincial House,* 2 Pioneer Ln., Red Bud, IL 62278. Tel: 618-282-3848; 282-6229. Sr. Margaret Mary Kopish, A.S.C., Prov. Supr.

Professed Sisters 205.

Sisters serve and staff: Colleges, Secondary & Elementary Schools, Special and Religious Education; Hospitals; Pastoral Care; Nursing Homes; Domestic Service in Communities and Institutions; Administration in Religious Orders and Parishes; Prayer Ministry; Retreat Ministry; Social Service; Pastoral and Chaplaincy Ministries; Prison and Minority Ministries.

Properties owned: *St. Clement Hospital,* Red Bud, IL; *St. Vincent Memorial Hospital,* Taylorville, IL; *MariaCare,* Red Bud, IL.

Represented in the Archdioceses of St. Louis, and San Antonio and the Dioceses of Belleville, Dodge City, Fort Wayne-South Bend, Gallup, Harrisburg, Jefferson City, Joliet, Springfield-Cape Girardeau, Oakland, Springfield (IL) and Tucson.

Province of Wichita (1929): *Provincial House,* 1400 S. Sheridan, Wichita, KS 67213-1394; Tel. 316-943-1203. Sr. Charlotte Rohrbach, A.S.C., Prov. Supr., Sr. Joyce Suellentrop, Community Archivist.

Finally Professed Sisters 206; Scholasticates 5; Novices 1.

Sisters Serve and Staff: College and Universities; High Schools; Elementary Schools; CCD-Parish Ministry; Social Work; Diocesan Offices; Hospitals-Clinics; Homes for the Aged; Foreign Missions.

Properties owned: *Villa Maria,* Mulvane, KS; *Newman University,* Wichita, KS; *St. Joseph's Villa,* David City, NE.

Represented in the Archdioceses of Kansas City in Kansas, Oklahoma City, St. Louis, San Antonio, Washington and the Dioceses of Arlington, Brownsville, Dodge City, El Paso, Fort Wayne-South Bend, Fort Worth, Gallup,Jefferson City, Lincoln, Oakland, Owensboro, Salina, San Diego, Springfield (IL), and Wichita.

Province of Columbia (1925): *Adorers of the Blood of Christ (Provine Center),* 3950 Columbia Ave., Columbia, PA 17512-9714. Tel: 717-285-4536. Sr. Agatha Marie Groft, A.S.C., Prov. Coord.

Legal Title:*Adorers of the Blood of Christ, Province of Columbia, PA, Inc.*

Total number in community 73.

Ministry in the field of Academic and Religious Education through College; Home for the Aged; Home Nursing; Independent Living Retirement Village; Retreat House; Pastoral Assistants; Hospital Chaplaincy; Ministry to the homeless.

Properties owned: *St. Joseph Convent-Provincial House; Precious Blood Spiritual Center; St. Anne's Home for the Aged, Inc.; De Mattias Residence; St. Anne's Independent Living Retirement Village,* Columbia, PA.

Represented in the Archdioceses of Chicago, New York, Newark, St. Louis and the Dioceses of Altoona-Johnstown, Alexandria, Harrisburg, Wilmington and Youngstown. Also in Guatemala.

[0110] (A.P.B.)—THE SISTERS ADORERS OF THE PRECIOUS BLOOD P (Cloistered Contemplative Order)

American Federation: Consisting of six autonomous monasteries:400 Pratt St., Watertwon, NY 13601-4238. Sr. Marilyn McGillan, A.P.B.,Pres. American Federation.

New York: 54th & Ft. Hamilton Pkwy.,Brooklyn, NY 11219. Tel: 718-438-6371.

New Hampshire: 700 Bridge St., Manchester, NH 03104 Tel: 603-623-4264.

Indiana: 1106 State St., Lafayette, IN 47905. Tel: 317-742-8227.

New York: 400 Pratt St., Watertown, NY 13601. Tel: 315-788-1669.

Maine: 166 State St., Portland, ME 04101. Tel: 207-774-0861.

Canada: 9415 - 165th St., Edmonton, Alberta, Canada T5R 2S5. Tel: 403-484-6691.

Professed Sisters 75; Novices 8;Postulants 2.

Represented in the Dioceses of Brooklyn, Lafayette (IN), Manchester, Ogdensburg and Portland (ME).

[0130] (A.S.C.J.)—APOSTLES OF THE SACRED HEART OF JESUS P

Founded in Italy in 1894. First foundation in United States 1902.

General Motherhouse: *Via Germano Sommeiller,* No. 38 Rome, Italy. Mother Auxiliadora deGodoy, Supr. Gen.; Sr. Leopoldina Euclidi, Archivist.

U.S. Provincial Motherhouse: *Mt. Sacred Heart,* 265 Benham St., Hamden, CT 06514. Tel: 203-248-4225; Fax: 203-230-8341.

Professed Sisters 175.

Ministry in the field of Education, Health Care, Parishes and Adult Day Care.

Properties owned: *Mary, Mother of the Church Convent,* Hamden, CT; *Mount Sacred Heart College for Sisters; Sacred Heart Academy; Sacred Heart Manor; Sacred Heart Manor Kindergarten and Nursery; Clelian Adult Day Care,* Hamden, CT; *Sacred Heart on the Lake,* Higganum, CT; *Cor Jesu Academy, Sacred Heart Villa Nursery,* St. Louis, MO; *Our Lady Queen of Apostles (Convent & Nursery),* Imperial, MO; *Clelian Heights School for Exceptional Children,* Greensburg, PA; *Sacred Heart Private Elementary School,* Bronx, NY.

Represented in the Archdioceses of Hartford, Newark, New York and St. Louis and in the Dioceses of Bridgeport, Greensburg, Metuchen, Norwich, Palm Beach, Pensacola-Tallahassee, Pittsburgh, and Providence. Also in Taiwan.

[0150] (S.A.S.V.)—SISTERS OF THE ASSUMPTION P

Founded in Saint-Gregoire, P.Q., Canada in 1853. First foundation in the United States in 1891.

General Motherhouse: Nicolet, P.Q., Canada. Sr. Aline Vadnais, S.A.S.V., Supr. Gen.

United States Region: *Regional Office,* 316 Lincoln St., Worcester, MA 01605. Tel: 508-856-9450. Sr. Lorraine Normand, S.A.S.V., Reg. Treas.

Total in Region and Professed 102.

Ministry in all levels of education.

Legal Holdings: *Assumption Residence of the Sisters of the Assumption of the Blessed Virgin,* Petersham, MA; *Harper Residence,* Worcester, MA.

Represented in the Archdioceses of Boston, Hartford and the Dioceses of Fall River, Manchester, Portland in Maine, Providence, Springfield (MA) and Worcester. Missions in Japan, Brazil and Ecuador.

[0160] (O.S.A.)—AUGUSTINIAN NUNS OF CONTEMPLATIVE LIFE P

Augustinian Contemplative Nuns: *Mother of Good Counsel Convent,* 440 Marley Rd., New Lenox, IL 60451. Sr. Mary Grace, O.S.A., Prioress.

Total number in community 5.

Legal Title: *Augustinian Cloistered Nuns, Inc.*

Represented in the Diocese of Joliet.

[0170] (O.S.B.)—BENEDICTINE NUNS OF THE CONGREGATION OF SOLESMES P

Order originated in Italy, c.529. Congregation of Solesmes formed in France in 1837.

U.S. Establishment (1981): *Monastery of the Immaculate Heart of Mary,* 4103 VT Rte 100, Westfield, VT 05874. Tel: 802-744-6525. Rev. Mother Marguerite Derome, O.S.B., Prioress.

Total in Congregation 261; Total in community 16.

Represented in the Diocese of Burlington.

[0180] (O.S.B.)—BENEDICTINE NUNS OF THE PRIMITIVE OBSERVANCE P

First founded in Italy in about 529. First United States establishment in 1948.

Abbey of Regina Laudis: Bethlehem, CT 06751. Tel: 203-266-7727; Fax: 203-266-5915. Rt. Rev. Mother Benedict Duss, O.S.B., Abbess.

Professed Nuns 28; Sisters in First Vows 5; Novices 3; Postulants 3.

[0190] (O.S.B.)—BENEDICTINE SISTERS P

First founded in Italy c.529. Founded in the United States in 1931 from St. Walburg Abbey, Eichstatt, Bavaria, Germany.

The Sisters of St. Benedict of Westmoreland County: *St. Emma Monastery,* 1001 Harvey Ave., Greensburg PA 15601-1494. Tel: 724-834-3060; Fax: 724-834-5772. Mother Mary Anne Noll, O.S.B., Prioress.

Professed Sisters 17, Postulants 2.

Ministry is Monastic Life; Benedictine hospitality extended through adjacent St. Emma Retreat House.

Represented in the Diocese of Greensburg.

Benedictine Nuns: *Abbey of St. Walburga,* 32,109 N. U.S. Highway 287, Virginia Dale, CO 80536-8942. Tel: 970-472-0612; Fax: 970-484-4342. Mother Maria-Thomas Beil, O.S.B., Abbess.

Sisters 21.

Represented in the Archdiocese of Denver.

[0200] (O.S.B.)—BENEDICTINE SISTERS D (Regina Pacis)

The Congregation of Benedictine Sisters of Kaunas, Lithuania was founded in 1621.

General Motherhouse: Benediktiniu 6-7, LT-3000 Kaunas Lithuania. Mother Regina Petkeviciute, O.S.B., Supr. Gen.

U.S. Foundation (1957): *Benedictine Sisters of Regina Pacis,* 333 Wallace Rd., Bedford, NH 03110. Tel: 603-472-3239. Sr. Gertrude Luksaite, O.S.B., Supr.

Represented in the Diocese of Manchester.

[0210] (O.S.B.)—MISSIONARY BENEDICTINE SISTERS P

The Congregation of Missionary Benedictine Sisters is of Pontifical Jurisdiction. Its Constitutions were approved by Rome on June 25, 1934; Revised approval June 29, 1983.

Generalate: Rome, Italy.

Provincial Motherhouse and Novitiate: *Immaculata Convent,* (1923), 300 N. 18th St., Norfolk, NE 68701-3687. Tel: 402-371-3438; Fax: 402-379-2877. Sr. M. Agnes Salber, O.S.B., Prioress.

Professed Sisters 51; Juniorates 1; Postulants 1; Novices 3.

Minstry in the fields of Education;Health & Hospitals; Social Services with Hispanics; Nursing Homes.

Legal Holdings or Titles: *Missionary Benedictine Sisters, Inc.,* Norfolk, NE; *Our Lady of Lourdes Hospital, Inc.,* Norfolk, NE; *St. Joseph Nursing Home, Inc.,* Norfolk, NE; *Providence Medical Center, Inc.,* Wayne, NE; *Graceville Missionary Benedictine Sisters, Inc.,* dba *Holy Trinity Hospital - Grace Home,* Graceville, MN.

Represented in the Archdiocese of Omaha and the Diocese of New Ulm.

[0220] (O.S.B.)—CONGREGATION OF THE BENEDICTINE SISTERS OF PERPETUAL ADORATION OF PONTIFICAL JURISDICTION P

Founded from Maria Rickenbach, Switzerland, in 1874 with first monastery at Clyde, MO. Congregation erected by decree of the Holy See on June 16, 1936. Generalate, Novitiate and Healthcare community transferred to St. Louis in 1966.

General Motherhouse: *Benedictine Monastery of Perpetual Adoration,* 8300 Morganford Rd., St. Louis, MO 63123. Tel: 314-638-6427. Sr. Mary Jane Romero, Prioress Gen., General Council; Sr. M. Bede Luetkemeyer; Sr. Sarah Schwartzberg; Sr. Joan Therese Anderson; Sr. Cathleen Marie Timberlake, Public Rels. Dir.

Total number in community: Professed 119.

Interdependent Monasteries: R.R. 1, Box 101, Clyde MO 64432. 800 N. Country Club Rd., Tucson, AZ 85716. Osage Monastery, 18701 W. Monastery Rd., Sand Springs, OK 74063. Mailing Address: San Benito Monastery, Box 520, Dayton, WY 82836.

Ministry in Monastic/Contemplative/Eucharistic Apostolate of Prayer; Liturgy of the Hours four times daily in Choir; Contemplative Prayer and Monastic Atmosphere Shared with Others; Prayer Days and Retreats for Sisters; Editing and Publishing Bi-monthly Magazine: Spirit & Life; Production and

Distribution of Altar Breads; Liturgical Vestments; Correspondence.
Represented in the Archdiocese of St. Louis and the Dioceses of Cheyenne, Kansas City-St. Joseph, Tucson and Tulsa.

[0230] (O.S.B.)—BENEDICTINE SISTERS OF PONTIFICAL JURISDICTION P

(I) The Federation of St. Scholastica:
Erected by Decree of the Holy See, Feb. 25, 1922, with final approbation by Decree of June 10, 1930. Twenty Motherhouses in the United States and two in Mexico. Total number in the Federation 1,130; Sr. Esther Fangman, O.S.B., Pres., residing at: Benedictines of Pontifical Jurisdiction, 3741 Forest Ave., Kansas City, MO 64109. Tel: 816-753-2514.

Benedictine Sisters of Baltimore, Inc.: *Emmanuel Monastery*, 2229 W. Joppa Rd., Lutherville, MD 21093. Tel: 410-821-5792. Sr. Patricia Kirk, O.S.B., Prioress.
Total number in community 16.
Ministry in the field of Education; Parish Ministry; Retreats and Spiritual Direction; Justice Ministry; Social Services; Administrative Services; Hospital Service Ministry.
Represented in the Archdioceses of Baltimore and Newark.

Benedictine Sisters of the Byzantine Rite (1969): *Queen of Heaven Monastery,* 8640 Squires Ln., N.E., Warren, OH 44484. Tel: 330-856-1813. Sr. Margaret Mary Schima, O.S.B., Prioress.
Professed Sisters 10.
Ministry in the field of Religious and Academic Education; Pastoral Ministry; Administration.
Represented in the Archdiocese of Pittsburgh Byzantine Rite.

Mount St. Scholastica, Inc. (1863): *Motherhouse of the Sisters of St. Benedict*, 801 S. Eighth St., Atchison, KS 66002-2778. Tel: 913-360-6200; Fax: 913-360-6190. Sr. Mary Collins, O.S.B., Prioress.
Total number in community 215.
Legal Holdings: *Dooley Center, Inc., The Mount Community Center, Inc., Mount St. Scholastica, Inc.*, Atchison, KS.
Ministry in the field of Academic Education at all levels; Special Education; Music Conservatory; Pastoral Ministry; Counseling; Retreats; Spirituality Center; Spiritual Direction; Social Services; Diocesan Offices; Ministry to the Aged; Hospitality; Community Center Work; Special Services to the needy; Ministry to the sick; Missionary Work in Brazil.
Represented in the Archdioceses of Chicago, Kansas City in Kansas, St. Louis, Washington and the Dioceses of Des Moines, Kansas City-St. Joseph, Arlington, and Tulsa. Also in Brazil.

Sisters of Benedict of Colorado, Inc.: 4264 W. Ponds View Dr., Littleton, CO 80123. Tel: 303-795-2378. Sr. Judith Elms, O.S.B., Supr.

Benedictine Sisters of Elk Co. (1852): *St. Joseph Monastery,* St. Marys, PA 15857. Tel: 814-834-2267. Sr. Raphael Baker, O.S.B., Prioress.
Professed Sisters 36.
Ministry in the fields of Academic and Religious Education; Pastoral Ministry; Retreats.
Represented in the Diocese of Allentown.

Benedictine Sisters (1998): *Transfiguration Monastery,* 526 Fairview St., Emmaus, PA 18049-3837. Tel: 610-965-6818. Sr. Martina Revak, O.S.B., Supr.
Professed Sisters 3.
Ministry in the fields of Education; Pastoral Ministry; Hospitality and Spirituality.
Represented in the Diocese of Allentown.

Benedictine Sisters of Erie (1856): *Mt. St. Benedict Monastery*, 6101 East Lake Rd., Erie, PA 16511. Tel: 814-899-0614, Fax: 814-898-4004. Sr. Christine Vladimiroff, O.S.B., Prioress.
Total in congregation 133; Professed sisters 132; In formation 1.
Sisters serve and staff: High Schools; Elementary Schools; Colleges; Day Care Centers; Residence for Elderly and Handicapped; Hospitals; Social Services; Diocesan Offices; Pastoral Ministry; Religious Education.
Properties owned: *Mount Saint Benedict Monastery; Glinodo Center; St. Benedict Education Center; Benet Center; 8 community houses.*
Represented in the Archdiocese of Milwaukee and the Dioceses of Cleveland, Dodge City, Erie, Orlando and Syracuse. Also in Mexico and Columbia.

Benedictine Sisters of Chicago O.S.B. (1861): *St. Scholastica Monastery*, 7430 Ridge Blvd., Chicago, IL 60645. Tel: 773-764-2413. Sr. Jane Smith, Prioress; Sr. Vivian Ivantic, Community Archivist.
Professed Sisters 78.
Ministry in Graduate Programs; High Schools; Pastoral Ministry; Religious Education; University staff; Management Consultant; Campus Ministry; Spiritual Direction; Peace and Shelter Ministry; Community Center Work; Social Service Counseling.
Properties owned: *St. Scholastica Monastery,* Chicago, IL; *St. Scholastica Academy*, Chicago, IL; *St. Scholastica Academy*, Canon City, CO.
Represented in the Archdioceses of Chicago and the Diocese of Pueblo.

Benedictine Sisters of the Sacred Heart O.S.B. (1895): *Sacred Heart Monastery*, 1910 Maple Ave., Lisle IL. Tel: 60532-2164, 630-969-7040. Sr. Judith Ann Heble, O.S.B., Prioress.
Legal Title: *Benedictine Sisters of the Sacred Heart Charitable Trust.*
Professed Sisters 49.
Sisters serve and staff: High Schools; Elementary Schools; Colleges; Queen of Peace Retirement Center; Religious Education; Pastoral Ministry; Nurses Administration; P.A.D.S.; Independent Positions involving Secretarial, Counseling, Liturgical Works, Occupational Therapy, Internal Ministry and Altar Bread Baking.
Represented in the Diocese of Joliet.

Benedictine Sisters of Elizabeth, NJ O.S.B. (1868): *St. Walburga Monastery and Novitiate,* 851 N. Broad St., Elizabeth, NJ 07208. Tel: 201-352-4278. Sr. Louise Garley, O.S.B., Prioress.
Professed Sisters 66.
Legal Holdings and Titles: Benedictine Hospital, Kingston, NY; Benedictine Academy, Elizabeth, NJ; Bender Memorial Academy, Elizabeth, NJ.
Represented in the Archdioceses of New York, Newark and the Diocese of Paterson.

Benedictine Sisters of Pittsburgh, PA. O.S.B. (1870): *St. Benedict Monastery,* 4530 Perrysville Ave., Pittsburgh, PA 15229-2296. Tel: 412-931-2844. Sr. Roberta Campbell, O.S.B., Prioress.
Professed Sisters 77.
Ministry in the field of Education in all levels; Religious and Special Education; Pastoral Ministry; Childcare; Social Service; Campus Ministry; Hospital Chaplaincy; Art Education; Ministry Resource; Outreach with Poor; Benedictine Center for Senior Citizens; Adult Day Care.
Represented in the Dioceses of Greensburg, Lexington and Pittsburgh.

Sisters of Benedict O.S.B. (1968): *Red Plains Monastery,* 728 Richland Rd., S.W., Piedmont, OK 73078. Tel: 405-373-4565, Fax: 405-373-3392. Sr. Marie Ballmann, O.S.B., Prioress.
Professed Sisters 11.
Ministry in the fields of Education, CCD and Adult Religious Education; Spiritual Formation; Spiritual Direction; Retreats.
Properties owned: *Benedictine Spirituality Center*, Piedmont, OK.
Represented in the Archdiocese of Oklahoma City.

Benedictine Sisters O.S.B. (1879): *St. Joseph Monastery, Priory and Novitiate,* 2200 S. Lewis, Tulsa, OK 74114-3100. Tel: 918-742-4989. Sr. Barbara Austin, O.S.B., Prioress.
Professed Sisters 35; In Formation 1.
Ministry in the field of Academic Education; Catechetics; Evangelization; Nursing; Pastoral Ministry; Social Civic & Ecumenical Group Work; Counselling & Spiritual Direction; Prison Ministry; Religious Education & Religious Formation.
Legal Titles & Holdings: *Congregation of the Benedictine Sisters of the Sacred Hearts; Monte Cassino School.*
Represented in the Archdiocese of Oklahoma City and the Dioceses of Lincoln, Tulsa and Wichita.

Benedictine Sisters of Pontifical Jurisdiction O.S.B. (1857): *St. Gertrude Monastery,* 14259 Benedictine Ln., Ridgely, MD 21660. Tel: 410-634-2497.
Professed Sisters 39.
Ministry in Special Schools and Elementary & Secondary Education; Job Training Center for the Mentally Handicapped; Open Community Houses for Mentally Handicapped; Do-It-Yourself Retreat Facility: Berg Center; Outreach facility for the poor: St. Martin's Barn.
Legal Holdings & Titles: *The Benedictine School for Exceptional Children; Berg Retreat Facility; St. Martin's Barn; St. Martin House*, Ridgely, MD; *St. Benedict*, Wilmington, DE.
Represented in the Archdiocese of Washington and the Dioceses of Wilmington.

St. Walburg Monastery of Benedictine Sisters of Covington, KY O.S.B. (1859): *St. Walburg Monastery,* 2500 Amsterdam Rd., Villa Hills, KY 41017-5316. Tel: 859-331-6324; Fax: 859-331-2136. Motherhouse and Novitiate. Sr. Rita Brink, O.S.B., Prioress. Sr. Teresa Wolking, O.S.B., Community Archivist.
Professed Sisters 93.
Sisters serve and staff: Diocesan Offices; Hospitals; Pastoral and Social Ministry; Home or Public Health Care; Seminary; all levels of academic education.
Legal titles & holdings: *Madonna Manor Nursing-Senior Citizens Home; Villa Madonna Early Learning Center; Villa Madonna Academy; Villa Madonna Center - Spirituality Center.*
Represented in the Archdiocese of Cincinnati and the Dioceses of Covington, Lexington and Pueblo.

Benedictine Sisters (1902): *Sacred Heart Monastery*, P.O. Box 2040, Cullman, AL 35056. Tel: 256-734-2199; 734-4622; Fax: 256-734-3835. Sr. Veronica Ryan, O.S.B., Prioress; Sr. Benedicta Karter, O.S.B., Community Archivist.
Professed Sisters 62.
Sisters staff and serve: in all levels of Academic Education; Pastoral Ministry; Diocesan Offices; Retirement Homes; Conference Centers.
Properties owned: *Benedictine Spirituality and Conference Center; Benedictine Manor Retirement Home.*
Represented in the Archdioceses of Atlanta, and the Dioceses of Birmingham and Orlando.

Benedictine Sisters of Virginia O.S.B. , (1868): *St. Benedict Monastery*, Bristow, VA 20136-1217. Tel: 703-361-0106. Sr. Andrea Verchuck, O.S.B., Prioress.
Total Professed Sisters 40.
Legal Holdings and Titles: Benedictine Sisters of Virginia, Inc.; *St. Gertrude High School*, Richmond, VA; *Linton Hall School*; *Benedictine Pastoral Center*; *Benedictine Counseling Services*, Bristow, VA.
Represented in the Dioceses of Arlington and Richmond.

Benedictine Sisters (1911): *St. Scholastica's Monastery and Novitiate,* 416 W. Highland Dr., Boerne, TX 78006; Tel: 830-249-2645; Fax: 830-249-4728. Sr. Mary Agnes Zinni, O.S.B., Prioress.
Total number in community 21.
Properties owned: *St. Scholastica Monastery*; *St. Albert Early Learning Center*, Boerne, TX; *Omega Retreat Center*, Boerne, TX; *Benedictine Sisters Charitable Trust I*; *Benedictine Sisters Charitable Trust II*; *Benedictine Resource Center*, San Antonio, TX.
Represented in the Archdiocese of San Antonio, and the Dioceses of Austin and Gallup.

Benedictine Sisters of St. Lucy's Priory Inc. O.S.B. (1956): *St. Lucy's Priory,* 19045 E. Sierra Madre Ave., Glendora, CA 91741; Tel: 626-335-1682. Sr. Elizabeth Brown, O.S.B., Prioress.
Professed Sisters 24.
Sisters serve & staff: all levels of Academic Education; Continuing Education; Home for Developmentally Disabled Adults; Pastoral Ministry.
Legal Holdings: *St. Lucy's Priory High School*; *St. Lucy's Benedictine Child Development Center*.
Represented in the Archdiocese of Los Angeles and the Diocese of San Diego.

Benedictine Sisters of Florida (1889): *Holy Name Monastery*, P.O. Box 2450, St. Leo, FL 33574-2450. Tel: 352-588-8320; Fax: 352-588-8319. Sr. Mary Clare Neuhofer, O.S.B., Prioress; Sr. M. Dorothy Neuhofer, O.S.B., Community Archivist.
Professed Sisters 24; Temporary Professed 2; Postulants 1.
Represented in the Diocese of St. Petersburg.

Sisters of St. Benedict (1963): *Benet Hill Monastery-Motherhousem*, 2555 N. Chelton Rd., Colorado Springs, CO 80909-1399. Tel: 719-633-0655; Fax: 719-471-0403. Sr. Rose Ann Barmann, O.S.B., Prioress; Sr. Diane Liston, Community Archivist.
Total number in community 47.
Properties owned: *Benet Hill Center; Benet Pines Retreat Center.*
Represented in the Archdiocese of Denver, Santa Fe and the Dioceses of Colorado Springs, Grand Island, Salina, and Pueblo. Also in Jamaica.

Benedictine Sisters O.S.B. (1989): *Queen of Angels Monastery,* 23615 N.E. 100th St., Liberty, MO 64068. Tel: 816-750-4618; Fax: 816-750-4621. Sr. Imelda Koch, O.S.B., Prioress.
Professed Sisters 7; Temporary Professed 2; Pre-Novitiate 3.
Ministry in Companioning, food for the hungry & thrift stores.
Represented in the Diocese of Kansas City-St. Joseph.

(II) The Federation of St. Gertrude
Erected by Decree of the Apostolic See on April 14, 1937, with final approbation by Decree of April 4, 1950. *Federation Office*, Monastery Immaculate Conception (1867), 802 E. 10th St., Ferdinand, IN 47532-9239. Tel: 812-367-1411; Fax: 812-367-2313. Sr. Kathryn Huber, O.S.B., Federation Pres.
Total in the Federation 1,055. Eighteen member monasteries form this Federation as follows:

Sisters of St. Benedict of Beech Grove, Ind., Inc.: *Our Lady of Grace Monastery* (1956), 1402 Southern Ave., Beech Grove, IN 46107. Tel: 317-787-3287; Fax: 317-780-2368. Sr. Rachel Best, O.S.B., Prioress.
Total Professed Sisters 76.

Ministry in Education; Parish Ministries; Retirement Home; Educational Center; Religious Education; Hospitals.
Properties owned and sponsored: *Our Lady of Grace Monastery; Benedictine Inn Retreat and Conference Center; St. Paul Hermitage Regina Retreat.*
Legal Title: *Sisters of St. Benedict of Beech Grove, Ind., Inc.; Charitable Trust of the Monastery of Our Lady of Grace; Sisters of the Order of St. Benedict.*
Represented in the Archdioceses of Cincinnati and Indianapolis and the Diocese of Evansville.

Benedictine Sisters of Belcourt O.S.B.: *Queen of Peace Monastery (1963)*, P.O. Box 370, Belcourt, ND 58316. Tel: 701-477-6167; Fax: 701-477-5575. Sr. Judith Emge, O.S.B., Prioress.
Professed Sisters 6.
Ministry inCounseling; Religious Education; Parish Ministry and Administration; Home Ministry; Educational Center; Indian Ministry.

Benedictine Sisters O.S.B.: *Our Lady of Peace Monastery,* 3710 West Broadway, Columbia, MO 65203-0116. Tel: 573-446-2300; Fax: 573-446-2312. Sr. Rose Maria Birkenfeld, O.S.B., Prioress.
Professed Sisters 11.
Ministry in Education; Home Health Care; Pastoral Care; Parish & Social Ministries; Counseling.
Represented in the Dioceses of Jefferson City, and Springfield-Cape Girardeau.

Monastery of St. Gertrude (1882): HC 3 Box 121, Cottonwood, ID 83522-9408. Tel: 208-962-3224; Fax: 208-962-7212.
Legal Title: *Idaho Corporation of Benedictine Sisters;* Sr. Jean Lalande, O.S.B., Prioress.
Professed Sisters 73.
Sisters serve in Education; Parish Ministry; Health Care; Retreat Ministry; Social Work; Counseling; St. Gertrude's Museum.
Represented in the Archdioceses of Indianapolis, Los Angeles, Portland (OR) , Seattle and the Dioceses of Boise, St. Cloud, and Spokane.

Sisters of St. Benedict of Crookston O.S.B.: *Mount St. Benedict Monastery (1919),* 620 E. Summit Ave., Crookston, MN 56716-2799. Tel: 218-281-3441; Fax: 218-281-6966. Sr. Catherine Merck, O.S.B., Prioress.
Professed Sisters 132.
Sisters serve and staff: Elementary, High Schools, Colleges; Nursing Homes; Board, Care and Assisted Living Home; Religious Education Center; Adult Education; Parish Ministry; Pastoral Care; Retreat Centers & Social Services; Child Care; Nursery School.
Legal Holding: *Villa St. Vincent,* Crookston, MN.
Represented in the Dioceses of Brownsville, Crookston, New Ulm and St. Cloud.

Benedictine Sisters O.S.B.: *Monastery Immaculate Conception (1867),* 802 E. 10th St., Ferdinand, IN 47532-9239. Tel: 812-367-1411; Fax: 812-367-2313. Sr. Joella Kidwell, O.S.B., Prioress.
Professed Sisters 220.
Legal Title: *Sisters of St. Benedict of Ferdinand, Indiana, Inc.*
Sisters serve and staff on all levels of Academic Education; Religious Education Centers; Parish Ministry; Special Education Centers; Hospitals; Public Health-Social Service Agencies; Diocesan Offices; Foreign Missions; Retreat House.
Sisters Sponsor: *Kordes Enrichment Center,* Ferdinand, IN.
Represented in the Archdioceses of Indianapolis, Louisville, and the Dioceses of Evansville, Fort Wayne-South Bend, Joliet, Lexington, Memphis, and Owensboro.

Benedictine Sisters, O.S.B. of St. Scholastica Monastery: *St. Scholastica Monastery (1879),* P.O. Box 3489, Fort Smith, AR 72913. Tel: 501-783-4147; Fax: 501-782-4352. Sr. Elise Forst, O.S.B., Prioress.
Professed Sisters 105.
Ministry in the fields of Elementary and Religious Education; Retreat Center; Parish Ministry; Hospital Chaplaincy; House of Prayer; Spiritual Direction.
Dependent Monastery: *St. Benedict Monastery,* Canyon, TX.
Represented in the Dioceses of Amarillo, Little Rock, and Tulsa.

Sisters of St. Benedict of Riverside, California, Inc.: *Holy Spirit Monastery (1972)*, 22791 Pico St., Grand Terrace, CA 92313-5725. Tel: 909-783-4446; Fax: 909-783-3525. Sr. Mary Ann Scheperss, O.S.B., Prioress.
Professed Sisters 12.
Ministry in Religious Education; Parish and Diocesan Ministry Counseling and Spiritual Direction; Hospital Chaplaincy; Work with the Elderly; Retreat Centers; Educating the Handicapped.
Represented in the Diocese of San Bernardino.

Benedictine Sisters: *Spirit of Life Monastery,* 10760 W. Glennon Dr., Lakewood, CO 80226. Tel: 303-986-9234. Sr. Katherine Wawersich, O.S.B., Prioress.
Corporate Ministry: *Spirit of Life Center*.
Sisters serve in Retreat and Prayer Ministry; Counseling and Spiritual Direction.
Professed Sisters 2.
Represented in the Archdiocese of Denver.

Sisters of St. Benedict of Madison, Wisconsin, Inc.: *Monastery of St. Benedict Center (1897)*, P.O. Box 5070, Madison, WI 53705-0070. Tel: 608-836-1631; Fax: 608-836-5586. Sr. Mary David Walgenbach, O.S.B., Prioress.
Professed Sisters 6.
Sisters serve Community Building, Prayer, Education, Retreat and Conference Ministries.
Corporate Ministries: *St. Benedict Center*.
Legal Titles: *Sisters of St. Benedict*, Sioux City, Iowa, Inc.; *Sisters of St. Benedict of Madison*, Wisconsin, Inc.
Represented in the Dioceses of Madison and Sioux City.

Benedictine Sisters of Mt. Angel, Oregon: *Queen of Angels Monastery (1882),* 840 S. Main St., Mt. Angel OR 97362. Tel: 503-845-6141; Fax: 503-845-6585. Sr. Dorothy Jean Beyer, O.S.B., Prioress.
Professed Sisters 55.
Sisters serve Elementary and High Schools; Colleges; Parish Ministry; Retreat and Prayer Ministry; Nursing; Counseling and Spiritual Direction; Work with Handicapped and Aging; Home Health Care; Hospital Chaplaincy; Ministry to Poor and Hispanics.
Corporate Ministries: *Shalom Prayer Center*; *St. Joseph's Shelter*, Mt. Angel, OR.
Represented in the Archdiocese of Portland (OR) and the Diocese of Boise, Fresno and Honolulu.

Benedictine Convent of St. Martin: *St. Martin Monasatery (1889),* 2110-C St. Martin's Dr., Rapid City, SD 57702-9660. Tel: 605-343-8011; Fax: 605-399-2723. Sr. Lorane Coffin, O.S.B., Prioress.
Professed Sisters 36.
Properties owned: *St. Martin's Academy Learning Center and Community Center.*
Ministry in Religious Education; Parish Ministry; Chancery; Hospital Chaplaincies, Nursing and Child Care.
Dependent Monastery: *Epiphany Monastery,* Columbia Falls, MT.
Charitable Trust: *Benedictine Convent of St. Martin Retirement Trust.*
Represented in the Archdiocese of Seattle and Dioceses of Great Falls-Billings, Helena, and Rapid City.

Benedictine Sisters of Richardton, O.S.B.: *Sacred Heart Monastery (1916),* P.O. Box 364, Richardton, ND 58652. Tel: 701-974-2121; Fax: 701-974-2124. Sr. Paula Larson, O.S.B., Prioress.
Professed Sisters 37.
Ministry in the fields of Academic Education; Summer Vacation Schools; Hospital Chaplaincy; Indian ministry; Parish ministry; Health Care.
Legal Titles or Holdings: *St. Vincent's Nursing Home, Inc., Marillac Manor, Inc., Subiaco Manor Inc., Sacred Heart Benedictine Foundation.*
Represented in the Diocese of Bismarck.

The Benedictine Sisters of Mother of God Monastery O.S.B.: *Mother of God Monastery (1961),* 110 S.E. 28th Ave., Watertown, SD 57201. Tel: 605-882-6600; Fax: 605-882-6658. Sr. Judith Fischer, O.S.B., Prioress.
Professed Sisters 72
Sisters serve and staff in Elementary and College Education; Religious Education Centers; Parish Ministry; Social Services; Hospitals and Hospices; Retreat Center; Homes for Aged; Juvenile Services; Home Health Care; Native American Ministeries; Hispanic Ministries; Libraries & Archives; and Congregate Housing for Elderly.
Legal Titles: *The Benedictine Sisters of Mother of God Monastery,* Watertown, SD; *St. Ann's Corporation* (includes Benet Place), Watertown, SD; *Evergreen Assisted Living*, Watertown, SD; *Retirement Trust*, Watertown, SD.
Represented in the Archdioceses of Chicago, San Antonio, St. Paul-Minneapolis and the Dioceses of Arlington, Bismarck, Crookston, Fargo, Lincoln, Madison, New Ulm, Sioux Falls, Tyler, and Yakima.

St. Benedict's Monastery (1912): 225 Masters Ave., Winnipeg, Manitoba, Canada R4A 2A1. Tel: 204-338-4601; Fax: 204-339-1705. Sr. Irene Burzynski, O.S.B., Prioress.
Professed Sisters 42.
Ministry in Retreat & Conference Center; Education; Health Care; Pastoral Care.
Represented in the Dioceses of Calgary, and Winnipeg Canada.

Benedictine Convent of the Sacred Heart: *Sacred Heart Monastery (1880)*, 1005 W. 8th St., Yankton, SD 57078. Tel: 605-668-6000; Fax: 605-668-6153. Sr. Jacquelyn Ernster, O.S.B., Prioress.
Professed Sisters 156.
Sisters serve and staff in Health Care Institutions; all levels of Academic Education; Social Services; Parish Ministry; Pastoral Care; Diocesan Offices; Counseling & Religious Education.
Represented in the Archdiocese of Omaha and the Dioceses of Bismarck, Lincoln, Pueblo, and Sioux Falls.

Benedictine Sisters, O.S.B.: *The Dwelling Place Monastery (1993),* 150 Mt. Tabor Rd., Martin, KY 41649. Tel: 606-886-9624. Sr. Judy Yunker, O.S.B., Prioress.
Professed Sisters 5.
Sisters serve and staff Elementary and Adult Education; Mentally Handicapped; Retreat Center; Parish; Social Outreach; Volunteer Program.
Represented in the Diocese of Lexington.

Benedictine Sisters of Nanaimo: *House of Bread Monastery (1993),* 2329 Arbot Rd., Nanaimo, British Columbia, Canada V9R 6S8. Tel: 250-753-1763; Fax: 250-753-6742. Sr. Jean Ann Berning, O.S.B., Prioress.
Sisters serve: Counselling; Retreat and Prayer Ministry; Nursing; Artist;
Corporate Ministries: Bethlehem Retreat Centre; Bethlehem Counselling Centre.
Represented in the Diocese of Victoria, Canada.
Professed Sisters 9.

(III) The Federation of St. Benedict:
Erected by decree of the Holy See March 24, 1947; *St. Benedict Monastery*, 104 Chapel Lane, St. Joseph, MN. Tel: 56374-0220, 320-363-7070; Fax: 320-363-7130. Sr. Colleen Haggerty, O.S.B., Federation Pres.
Legal Title: *Federation of St. Benedict*.
Total number of Sisters in Federation 900. Twelve monasteries form this Federation; In addition to the eight American monasteries listed, three autonomous monasteries exist: Japan, St. Benedict's Monastery (1985) Sapporo, Hokkaido; Taiwan, St. Benedict Monastery (1988) Tanshui, Taipei; Bahamas, Saint Martin Monastery (1994)Nassau.

Sisters of St. Benedict (1994): *Mount Benedict Monastery,* 6000 South 1075 East, Ogden, UT 84405-4945. Tel: 801-479-6030. Sr. Mary Zenzen, O.S.B., Prioress.
Professed sisters 10.
Sisters serve and staff: Health Care; Campus Ministry; Diocesan: Offices—Retreat Center, Vocation Director.
Represented in the Diocese of Salt Lake City.

Sisters of the Order of Saint Benedict-O.S.B. (1857): *Monasterio Santa Escolastica*, Apartado 8526, Humacao, PR 00792. Tel: 787-852-4222. Sr. Mary Ruth Santana, O.S.B., Prioress.
Total Sisters 12.
Legal Title: *Sisters of the Order of Saint Benedict*, St. Joseph, MN.
Ministry in the field of Education at all levels; Parish Ministry; Social Work; Counseling.
Represented in the Dioceses of Caguas.

Sisters of the Order of Saint Benedict-O.S.B. (1857): St. Benedict's Monastery-Motherhouse and Novitiate, St. Joseph, MN 56374-0220. Tel: 320-363-7100. Sr. Ephrem Hollermann, O.S.B., Prioress; Sr. Ruth Boedigheimer, O.S.B., Archivist.
Total Sisters in Congregation 390.
Legal Title: *Sisters of the Order of Saint Benedict,* St. Joseph, MN.
Ministry in the field of Education at all levels; Indian Missions; Hospitals; Nursing Homes; Individual Apostolates; Diocesan Marriage Tribunal; Parish Ministry; Social Work; Counseling.
Represented in the Archdioceses of Mobile, St. Paul-Minneapolis, and the Dioceses of Crookston, Duluth, Manchester, New Ulm, St. Cloud, San Diego and Santa Rosa.

Sisters of St. Benedict - St. Scholastica Monastery O.S.B. (1892): 1001 Kenwood Ave., Duluth, MN 55811. Tel: 218-723-6555. Sr. Kathleen Hofer, O.S.B., Prioress; Sr. Aelred Roehl, Archivist.
Total number in community 152.
Ministry in the field of Academic Education at all levels; Religious Education; Indian Ministry; Residence for Elderly; Nursing Homes; Hospitals; Pastoral Care and Parish Ministries; Prison Ministry; Peace and Justice; Retreat Center.
Properties owned and/or sponsored: *McCabe Renewal Center,* Duluth, MN; *College of St. Scholastica; St. Mary's Medical Center*, Duluth, MN; *Benedictine Foundation, Inc.; Benedictine Living Communities, Inc.*, Duluth, MN; *Benedictine Health Center; Polinsky Rehabilitation Center*, Duluth MN; *St. Joseph's Medical Center*, Brainerd, MN; *St. Mary's Regional Health Center*, Detroit Lakes, MN; *St. Francis Regional Medical Center*, Shakopee, MN; *St. Mary's Hospital*, Cottonwood, ID; *Tekakwitha Nursing Center, Inc.*, Sisseton, ND; *Madonna Towers of Rochester, Inc.*, Rochester, MN; *St. Benedict's Health Center; Prince of Peace Care Center; Benedictine Living Center of Garrison; St. Rose Care Center; St. Catherine's Living Center,* ND; *Aber-*

deen Living Center, SD; *Benedictine Sisters Benevolent Association, Benedictine Health System,* Duluth, MN; *St. Gertrude's Health Center,* Shakopee, MN; *Trinity Hospital,* Farmington, MN; *Benedictine Health Dimensions,* Cambridge, MN; *St. Mary's Hospital,* Superior, WI; *St. Anne Hospice,* Winona, MN; *St. Mary's Care Center,* Winsted, MN; *Mount Carmel Health & Rehabilitation Center,* Milwaukee, WI.

Represented in the Archdioceses of Chicago, Milwaukee, St. Paul-Minneapolis, Seattle, and the Dioceses of Bismarck, Boise, Crookston, Duluth, Fargo, New Ulm, Phoenix, St. Cloud, Superior, Sioux Falls, and Winona.

St. Bede Priory (1948): 1190 Priory Rd., P.O. Box 66 Eau Claire, WI 54702. Tel: 715-834-3176. Sr. Margaret Michaud, O.S.B., Prioress; Sr. Lorayne Andre, O.S.B., Archivist.

Total number in community 45.

Properties owned and sponsored: *St. Bede Priory Motherhouse; St. Bede Retreat and Conference Center.*

Represented in the Archdiocese of San Antonio and the Dioceses of La Crosse and Springfield-Cape Girardeau. Also in Jamaica.

Sisters of the Order of St. Benedict O.S.B. (1874): *St. Mary Monastery,* P.O. Box 128, Nauvoo, IL 62354-0128. Tel: 217-453-2227. Sr. Ruth Ksycki, O.S.B., Prioress; Sr. Rita Cain, Archivist.

Total number in community 71.

Ministry in the field of Religious and Academic Education; Pastoral Care; Parish Ministry.

Represented in the Dioceses of Davenport, Gary, and Peoria.

Benedictine Sisters of the Annunciation, BVM (1947): *Annunciation Monastery,* 7520 University Dr., Bismarck, ND 58504-9653. Tel: 701-255-1520. Sr. Susan Berger, O.S.B., Prioress.

Professed Sisters 89.

Ministry in Hospitals; Parish Ministry and Catechetical Work; Education and Health Care.

Represented in the Dioceses of Bismarck and Fargo.

Sisters of St. Benedict (1948): *St. Paul's Monastery,* 2675 Larpenteur Ave. E., St. Paul, MN 55109. Tel: 651-777-8181; Fax: 651-777-4442. Sr. Marie Fujan, O.S.B., Prioress.

Professed Sisters 76.

Sisters serve and staff School on all levels; Hospitals; Homes for the Aged; Business, Child Care; Retreat Center; Parish Ministry; Social Service and various other apostolic work.

Represented in the Archdiocese of St. Paul-Minneapolis and the Dioceses of Great Falls, and Superior.

Sisters of St. Benedict O.S.B. (1952): *St. Placid Priory,* 500 College St., N.E., Lacey, WA 98516-5338. Tel: 360-438-1771. Sr. Laura Swan, O.S.B., Prioress.

Professed Sisters 23.

Sisters serve in the field of Education; Spirituality Centers.

Represented in the Archdiocese of Seattle.

[0233] (O.S.B.)—BENEDICTINE NUNS Subiaco Congregation

St. Scholastica Priory, Benedictine Nuns (Cloistered), Box 606, 271 N. Main St., Petersham, MA 01366-0606. Tel: 978-724-3213; Fax: 978-724-3216. Very Rev. Mother Mary Clare Vincent, O.S.B., Prioress; Sr. Mary Frances Wynn, O.S.B., Sub-Prioress.

Nuns in Solemn vows 9; Simple vows 2; Novices 1; Claustral Oblates 1.

[0235] (O.S.B.Cam.)—CAMALDOLESE BENEDICTINE SISTERS Camaldolese Congregation

First founded in Italy in the 11th century, affiliated with monastery in Rome founded in 1722; United States foundation in 1988.

Transfiguration Monastery: *Camaldolese Benedictine Sisters,* 701 NY Rte 79, Windsor, NY 13865. Tel: 607-655-2366. Sr. Donald Corcoran, O.S.B.Cam., Prioress.

Professed Nuns 4.

Monastic life and Benedictine hospitality.

Represented in the Diocese of Syracuse.

[0240] (O.S.B.)—OLIVETAN BENEDICTINE SISTERS D

Established in the Diocese of Little Rock in 1887.

Motherhouse and Novitiate (1887): *Holy Angels Convent,* P.O. Drawer 130, Jonesboro, AR 72403-0130. Tel: 870-935-5810; Fax: 870-935-4210. Sr. M. Eileen Schneider, O.S.B., Prioress.

Professed Sisters 48.

Sisters serve and staff High Schools; Grammar Schools; Diocesan Ministries; CCD Centers & Parish Services.

Properties owned: *Little Angels Day Care Center,* Little Rock, AR; *St. Bernards Healthcare, Inc.,* Jonesboro, AR; *St. Bernards Development Foundation, Inc.,* Jonesboro, AR; *Homecare Pharmarcy, Inc.,* Jonesboro, AR.

Represented in the Dioceses of Fort Worth and Little Rock.

[0250] (C.V.D.)—SISTERS OF BETHANY P

Founded in El Salvador in 1928.

General Motherhouse: *Instituto Bethania,* Santa Tecla, El Salvador, C.A. Mother Dolores de Maria Zea, Mother Foundrees; Madre Luz Elena Ordonez, Supr. Gen.

U.S. Address (1949): Bethany House, 850 N. Hobart Blvd., Los Angeles, CA 90029. Tel: 213-669-9411; 665-6937. Sr. Leticia Gomez, C.V.D., Supr.

Professed Sisters 14.

Ministry in Social Service Centers; Parish Work.

Represented in the Archdiocese of Los Angeles.

[0260] (S.B.S.)—THE SISTERS OF THE BLESSED SACRAMENT FOR INDIANS AND COLORED PEOPLE P

Founded in the United States in 1891.

General Motherhouse: *St. Elizabeth's Convent,* Bensalem, PA 19020-8502. Tel: 215-244-9900. Sr. Monica Loughlin, Pres.

Professed Sisters 244.

Sisters serve and staff in the field of Education on all levels; Catechetical Schools; Houses for Catechetical; Adult Education and Social Service; House of Prayer; Spiritual Center; Evangelization Center.

Properties owned: *St. Catherine Indian School,* Santa Fe, NM; *St. Michael Indian School,* St. Michael's, AZ; *Xavier Prep,* New Orleans, LA.

Represented in the Archdioceses of Atlanta, Boston, Chicago, Los Angeles, New Orleans, New York, Philadelphia, Santa Fe and the Dioceses of Birmingham, Evansville, Gallup, Lafayette (LA), Palm Beach, Savannah and Tucson. Also in Haiti.

[0270] (C.B.S.)—CONGREGATION OF BON SECOURS P

Founded in France in 1824. First foundation in the United States in 1881.

Generalate: *Maison Mere du Bon Secours,* 20, rue N.D. des Champs, 75006 Paris, France. Sr. Nancy Glynn, C.B.S., Congregational Leader.

United States Province: *Provincial House and Novitiate,* 1525 Marriottsville Rd., Marriottsville, MD 21104. Tel: 410-442-1333; Fax: 410-442-1394. Sr. Anne Marie Mack, Pres.

Total Sisters in U.S. Province 42.

Sisters own, sponsor and operate: *Bon Secours Spiritual Center, Bon Secours Health System, Inc.,* and its subsidiaries.

Represented in the Archdioceses of Baltimore, Detroit, Miami, Newark, New York, Philadelphia and the Dioceses of Altoona-Johnstown, Charleston, Covington, Richmond, St. Petersburg and Venice.

[0280] (O.SS.S.)—THE BRIGITTINE SISTERS P

Founded in Sweden in 14th century.

Motherhouse: Rome, Italy.

Convent and Novitiate (1957): *Convent of St. Birgitta Vikingsborg,* 4 Runkenhage Rd., Darien, CT 06820. Tel: 203-655-1068. Sr. M. Sabina Kavanadi, O.SS.S., Supr. Monastic tradition, more contemplative than active.

Legal Title: *Order of the Most Holy Savior of St. Bridget.*

Professed Sisters 8.

Represented in the Diocese of Bridgeport.

[0300] (O.CARM.)—CALCED CARMELITES P

Carmelite Nuns of the Ancient Observance, Strictly Cloistered, belonging to the Second Order of Carmel.

Founded in Naples, Italy in 1536. First foundation in the United States in 1931.

Carmelite Monastery of St. Therese: *Little Flower of Jesus and St. M. Magdalen Di Pazzi,* St. Therese's Valley, 3551 Lanark Rd., Coopersburg, PA 18036-9324. Mother Marie Charlette, O.Carm., Prioress.

Professed Sisters 11.

Legal Title: *The Carmelite Sisters of St. Therese's Valley, Inc.*

Represented in the Dioceses of Allentown, Fargo, San Angelo and Superior.

[0315] (C.C.W.)—CARMELITE COMMUNITY OF THE WORD D

Motherhouse & Novitiate (1971): 394 Bem Rd., Gallitzin, PA 16641. Fax: 814-886-4098. Sr. Marilyn Welch, C.C.W., Gen. Admin.

Total number in the community 21.

Ministries in Diocesan Administration; the field of Religious and Academic Education at all levels; Pastoral Care to the Imprisoned, Institutionalized, E lderly, Mentally Handicapped, Family Life Support Groups and the Poor; Parish Ministry; Mission activity in Appalacia.

Represented in the Diocese of Altoona-Johnstown.

[0320] (O.CARM.)—CARMELITE NUNS OF THE ANCIENT OBSERVANCE P

Carmelite Nuns of the Ancient Observance

Strictly Cloistered, belonging to the Second Order of Carmel.

Founded in Guelder, Holland, in 1453. First Foundation in the United States in 1930.

Carmel Of Mary (1954): 17765 78th St., S.E., Wahpeton, ND 58075. Tel: 701-642-2360. Mother Margaret Mary of the Sacred Heart, O.Carm., Prioress.

Total number in community 12.

Represented in the Diocese of Fargo.

Monastery of Our Lady of Grace (1989): 1 Via Maria, Christoval, TX 76935. Tel: 915-853-1722.

Professed Sisters 5; Junior Professed 1.

Represented in the Diocese of San Angelo.

Carmel Of The Sacred Heart (1963): 430 Laurel Ave., Hudson, WI 54016. Tel: 715-386-2156. Sr. Mary O'Neill, O.Carm., Prioress; Sr. Lucia LaMontagne, O.Carm., Archivist.

Professed Sisters 5.

Legal Title: *Carmelite Nuns of the Diocese of Superior, Inc.*

Represented in the Diocese of Superior.

[0330] (O.CARM.)—CARMELITE SISTERS FOR THE AGED AND INFIRM P

Founded in 1929 in New York. Foundress: Mother M. Angeline Teresa, O.Carm.

Motherhouse and Novitiate: *St. Teresa's Motherhouse and Novitiate,* 600 Woods Rd., Avila on the Hudson, Germantown, NY 12526. Mother Mary Suzanne, O.Carm., Supr. Gen.

Professed Sisters 259; Novices 3

Legal Holdings: *St. Patrick Home,* Bronx, NY; *Sacred Heart Manor,* Philadelphia, PA; *Villa Teresa,* Harrisburg, PA; *St. Raphael Home,* Columbus, OH; *St. Rita's Home,* Columbus, OH; *St. Margaret's Hall,* Cincinnati, OH; *Carmel Manor,* Fort Thomas, KY; *Kahl Home for the Aged,* Davenport, IA; *St. Patrick's Manor,* Framingham, MA; *Marian Manor,* Boston, MA; *St. Patrick's Residence,* Naperville, IL; *Lourdes - Noreen McKeen Residence,* West Palm Beach, FL; *Avila Institute of Gerontology; Our Lady's Manor,* Dublin, Ireland.

Represented in the Archdioceses of Boston, Cincinnati, New York and Philadelphia and the Dioceses of Albany, Altoona-Johnstown, Bridgeport, Brooklyn, Columbus, Covington, Davenport, Fall River, Joliet, Harrisburg, Palm Beach, Scranton and Syracuse.

[0340] (C.aCh.)—CARMELITE SISTERS OF CHARITY P

Founded in 1826.

Motherhouse: Vic, Spain.

Generalate: Carlo Zucchi, 12, 00165 Rome, Italy 06-662-03-52.

Provincial/Formation House: *Carmelite Sisters of Charity,* 701 Beacon Rd., Silver Spring, MD 20903. Tel: 301-434-6344. Sr. Maria Pilar Chamorro, Prov.

Ministry in Health Clinics; Parishes; Higher Education; Immigrants, Hispanics and Homeless, Educational Centers.

Properties owned or sponsored: *Mount Carmel House, Formation House.*

Represented in the Archdiocese of Washington and the Diocese of Brooklyn.

[0350] (O.CARM.)—CARMELITE SISTERS (CORPUS CHRISTI) P

First foundation in the United States in 1920.

General Motherhouse: Tunapuna, Trinidad, West Indies. Sr. Antoinette Dickie, O.Carm., Supr. Gen.

U.S. Address: *Mount Carmel Home-Keens' Memorial, 412 W. 18th St.,* Kearney, NE 68847. Tel: 308-237-2287. Sr. Delphine, O.Carm., Reg. Supr.

Professed Sisters 105.

Ministry in Home and foreign missions; Academic and Religious Education; Social Work.

Represented in the Dioceses of Grand Island and Providence.

[0360] (Carmel D.C.J.)—CARMELITE SISTERS OF THE DIVINE HEART OF JESUS P

Founded in Germany in 1891. First Convent in the United States in 1912.

General Motherhouse: Sittard, Netherlands. Mother M. Katharina, Supr. Gen.

Northern Province: 1230 Kavanaugh Pl., Milwaukee,

WI 53213. Tel: 414-453-4040; Fax: 414-453-6503. Sr. Maria Giuseppe, Prov. Supr.

Central Province: 10341 Manchester Rd., St. Louis, MO 63122. Tel: 314-965-7616. Sr. M. Lydia Ann, Prov. Supr.

South Western Province: 8585 La Mesa Blvd., La Mesa CA 92041. Tel: 619-466-3116. Sr. Mary Fatima, Prov. Supr.

Professed Sisters Worldwide 457.

Total in U.S. 70; Novices 59; Postulants 34.

Sisters minister to Homes for Children 2; Homes for the Aged 9; Day Nurseries 4; Mission work in Africa, Nicaragua, Venezuela & Brazil.

Represented in the Archdioceses of Detroit, Milwaukee, St. Louis and San Antonio and the Dioceses of Gary, Grand Rapids, Jefferson City, Owensboro and San Diego.

[0370] (O.C.D.)—CARMELITE SISTERS OF THE MOST SACRED HEART OF LOS ANGELES P

General Motherhouse & Novitiate: *Carmelite Sisters of the Most Sacred Heart of Los Angeles*, 920 E. Alhambra Rd., Alhambra, CA 91801. Tel: 626-289-1353; Fax: 626-308-1913. Mother Regina Marie Gorman, O.C.D., Supr. Gen.

Total number in community 141.

Legal Title: *Carmelite Sisters of the Most Sacred Heart of Los Angeles*; *Carmelite Educational Centers, Inc.*, dba *Sacred Heart Retreat House*; *Mount Carmel in the Desert Retreat House and Day Care Center*; *St. Joseph Center*, Alhambra, CA; *Little Flower Center, Inc.*, dba *Little Flower Missionary House*, Los Angeles, CA; *Avila Gardens Residence for Seniors*, Duarte, CA; *Santa Teresita Hospital*, Duarte, CA; *Santa Teresita Clinic*, Asuza, CA.

Sisters serve and staff Religious and Academic Education; General Hospital; Skilled Nursing Facility for the care of the Aged; Nursery Schools With Day Care Centers and Kindergarten; Retreat House; Directors of Religious Education; Ministry to elderly, sick and convalescents.

Represented in the Archdioceses of Los Angeles, Miami and the Diocese of Tucson.

[0380] (C.S.T.)—CARMELITE SISTERS OF ST. THERESE OF THE INFANT JESUS D

Founded in the United States in 1917 at Bentley, OK.

General Motherhouse: *Villa Teresa*, 1300 Classen Dr., Oklahoma City, OK 73103-2447. Tel: 405-232-7926. Sr. Maria Francesca Forst, C.S.T., Gen. Supr.

Legal Title: *Carmelite Sisters of St. Therese of the Infant Jesus Motherhouse.*

Properties owned and sponsored: *Villa Teresa School*, Oklahoma City, OK; *Villa Teresa Moore,* Oklahoma City, OK.

Total number in community 29.

Ministry in the field of Academic Education; Religious Education and Parish Ministry; Archdiocese of Oklahoma City.

[0390] (C.M.S.T.)—MISSIONARY CARMELITES OF ST. TERESA P

Founded in Mexico City in 1903.

General Motherhouse: Fresno 150, 06400, Mexico, D.F. Mother Edith Lucia Frias De la Rosa, C.M.S.T., Supr. Gen.

U.S. Holy Family Province (1983): 9548 Deer Trail Dr., Houston, TX 77038. Tel: 281-445-5520; Fax: 281-445-5748. Sr. Maria del Rosario Martinez, C.M.S.T., Prov. Supr.

Professed Sisters 66.

Ministry in Pastoral; Hospital Chaplaincy; Domestic and Retreats.

Represented in the Archdioceses of Los Angeles, St. Louis, Oklahoma City and the Dioceses of Corpus Christi, Galveston-Houston, and Little Rock.

[0397] (C.M.R.)—CONGREGATION OF MARY, QUEEN P

Founded in Vietnam in 1670 by Bishop Pierre Lambert de la Motte. First foundation in the United States in 1979 at Springfield MO.

U.S. Regional: 625 South Jefferson Ave., Springfield, MO 65806. Tel: 417-869-9842; Fax: 417-832-0852. Sr. Marguerite A. Tran, C.M.R., Reg. Leader.

Professed Sisters 31.

Legal Title: *Congregation of Mary, American Region.*

Represented in the Archdiocese of St. Louis and the Dioceses of Kansas City-St. Joseph, Springfield-Cape Girardeau.

[0400] (O.CARM.)—CONGREGATION OF OUR LADY OF MOUNT CARMEL P

Founded in France in 1824. First foundation in the United States in 1833.

Generalate: P.O. Box 476, Lacombe, LA 70445. Tel: 504-524-2398; Fax: 504-524-5011. Sr. Rose Marie Penouilh, O.Carm., Pres.; Sr. Therese Gregoire, O.Carm., Archivist; Sr. M. Hyacinth Breaux, O.Carm., Asst. Archivist; Sr. Andree Marie Bindewald, O.Carm., Devel. Dir.

Professed Sisters 95.

Ministry in the field of Education on all levels; Hospitals; Social Service; Religious Education; Pastoral Ministry and Retreat Work.

Represented in the Archdiocese of New Orleans, Washington and the Dioceses of Joliet, and Lafayette (LA). Also in the Philippines.

[0410] (O.CARM.)—INSTITUTE OF THE SISTERS OF OUR LADY OF MOUNT CARMEL P (Istituto delle Suore di Nostra Signora del Carmelo)

Founded in Italy in 1854, First foundation in the United States, 1947.

General Motherhouse: *Istituto di Nostra Signora del Carmelo,* Via dei Baglioni 10, Roma, Italy.

U.S. Headquarters: *Carmelite Sisters,* 5 Wheatland St., Peabody, MA 01960. Tel: 978-531-4733. Sr. Benedetta Zaccardi, Supr.

Professed Sisters 8.

Ministry in Holy Childhood Nursery and Kindergarten.

Represented in the Archdioceses of Boston and Washington.

[0420] (O.C.D.)—DISCALCED CARMELITE NUNS P

Founded in Spain in 1562. First foundation in the United States in 1790 in Charles County, Maryland; later this monastery was moved to Baltimore.

The Monasteries listed here are strictly contemplative and belong to the Order of Discalced Carmelites.

Carmelite Monastery (1790): 1318 Dulaney Valley Rd., Towson, Baltimore MD 21286-1399. Tel: 410-823-7415. Sr. Colette Ackerman, O.C.D., Prioress; Sr. Constance FitzGerald, O.C.D., Community Archivist.

Professed Sisters 14.

Legal Title: *Carmelite Sisters of Baltimore.*

Carmel of St. Joseph (1863): 9150 Clayton Rd., St. Louis, MO 63124-1898. Tel: 314-993-6899; Fax: 314-993-5039. Mother Mary Joseph of Divine Providence, O.C.D., Prioress.

Professed Cloistered Nuns 8; Professed Extern sisters 1; Novices 4; Postulants 1.

Monastery of St. Joseph and St. Teresa (1877): *Discalced Carmelite Nuns,* 73530 River Rd., Covington, LA 70435-2206.

Carmelite Nuns, Discalced (O.C.D.): Mother Mary Alice Grace, O.C.D., Prioress.

Total number in community 11.

Discalced Carmelite Monastery (1890): 61 Mt. Pleasant Ave., Boston, MA 02119. Tel: 617-442-1411; Fax: 617-442-0203. Sr. Mary Teresa Wisniewski, O.C.D., Prioress.

Total number in community 11.

Carmelite Monastery (1902): 66th Ave. and Old York Rd. (Oak Lane), Philadelphia, PA 19126. Tel: 215-424-6143; Fax: 215-424-6143/5. Mother Barbara of the Holy Ghost, O.C.D., Prioress.

Professed Nuns 8.

Monastery of Our Lady of Mt. Carmel (1907): *The Chancery*, P.O. Box C, Brooklyn, NY 11202. Tel: 718-399-5900. Sr. Jane Ann Scanlon, C.N.D., Vice Chancellor (Diocese of Brooklyn).

Carmelite Monastery of the Infant Jesus (1908): 1000 Lincoln St., Santa Clara CA 95050. Tel: 408-296-8412. Sr. Emmanuel of Bethlehem, O.C.D., Prioress.

Sisters Solemn Vows 19, Novices 3.

St. Joseph's Carmelite Monastery (1908): 2215 N.E. 147th, Shoreline, WA 98155. Tel: 206-363-7150; Fax: 206-365-7335. Sr. Marie Therese, O.C.D., Prioress.

Professed Sisters 8; Novices 1.

Legal Title: *Carmelite Monastery of Seattle.*

Carmel of the Queen of Heaven (Formerly known as Regina Coeli Monastery) (1911): 17937 250th St., Eldridge, IA 52748. Tel: 319-285-8387; Fax: 319-285-7467. Sr. Catherine Luth, O.C.D., Prioress.

Professed Sisters 16; Novices 2.

Discalced Carmelite Nuns (1930): *Monastery of Mary Immaculate and St. Joseph*, 1740 Newburg Rd., Louisville, KY 40205. Tel: 502-451-6796. Mother Francis Prioress; Sr. Clare, Archivist.

Professed Sisters 10; Novices 1; Postulants 1.

Legal Title: *Carmelite Monastery of Louisville, Inc.*

Order of Discalced Carmelites O.C.D. (1913): *Carmel of St. Teresa of Los Angeles, Inc.,* 215 E. Alhambra Rd., Alhambra CA 91801. Tel: 626-282-2387; Fax: 626-282-2053. Mother Maria, O.C.D., Prioress.

Total number in community 16.

Carmelite Monastery (1916): 4300 Mount Carmel Dr. N.E., Ada (Parnell), MI 49301. Mother Agnes Therese, O.C.D., Prioress.

Professed Nuns 17; Novices 1; Externs 2.

Discalced Carmelite Nuns (1920): *Carmelite Monastery,* 89 Hiddenbrooke Dr., Beacon, NY 12508-3599. Sr. Michael Ann Cladek, O.C.D., Prioress.

Total number in community 26.

Discalced Carmelite Monastery of St. Therese of the Child Jesus (1920): 75 Carmel Rd., Buffalo, NY 14214. Tel: 716-837-6499. Mother Miriam of Jesus, O.C.D., Prioress.

Cloistered Professed Sisters 16; Extern Professed Sisters 2; Novices 2.

Monastery of Discalced Carmelites (1922): 2500 Cold Spring Rd., Indianapolis, IN 46222. Tel: 317-926-5654. Sr. Joanne Dewald, O.C.D., Prioress.

Legal Title: *Monastery of the Resurrection, Discalced Carmelites; Sisters of Our Lady of Mount Carmel Carmelite Monastery.*

Contemplative Professed Nuns 15.

Carmel of the Holy Family (1923): 3176 Fairmount Blvd., Cleveland Heights, OH 44118-4199. Tel: 216-321-6568. Sr. Mary Lavin, O.C.D., Prioress.

Contemplative Professed Nuns 15; Vowed Religious Transfer Sisters in Formation 1.

Discalced Carmelite Nuns of Schenectady, NY, Inc. (1923): *Monastery of St. Teresa of Jesus*, 428 Duane Ave., Schenectady, NY 12304. Mother Mary St. John of the Cross, O.C.D., Prioress.

Professed Nuns 12.

Discalced Carmelites of the Order of Our Lady of Mount Carmel O.C.D. (1925): *Monastery of Our Lady and St. Therese,* 27601 Hwy. 1, Carmel, CA 93923. Tel: 831-624-3043; Fax: 831-624-5495. Mother Mercedes of Mary Immaculate, O.C.D., Prioress.

Professed Sisters 14.

Legal Title: *Carmelite Monastery of Carmel*, California, Inc.

Discalced Carmelites O.C.D. (1926): *Monastery of the Most Blessed Virgin Mary of Mount Carmel,* 189 Madison Ave., Morristown, NJ 07960. Mother Mary Michael, O.C.D., Prioress.

Professed Sisters 7; Novices 1.

Order of Discalced Carmelites O.C.D. (1926): *Carmelite Monastery of the Trinity,* 5158 Hawley Blvd., San Diego, CA 92116. Tel: 619-280-5424. Sr. Yvonne Hanke, O.C.D., Prioress.

Professed Nuns 14.

Monastery of St. Therese of the Child Jesus (1926): 35750 Moravian Dr., Clinton Township, MI 48035-2138. Tel: 810-790-7255. Mother Mary Elizabeth, O.C.D., Prioress.

Professed Nuns 8; Professed Extern Sisters 3; Novices 1.

Carmel of St. Therese of Lisieux, Inc. (1927): *Discalced Carmelite Nuns,* P.O. Box 57, Loretto, PA 15940-0057. Tel: 814-472-8620. Mother John of the Cross, O.C.D., Prioress.

Solemn Professed Nuns 10; Temporary Professed Nuns 1; Novices 1; Extern Sisters 1.

Discalced Carmelite Nuns O.C.D. (1928): *Carmelite Monastery of Cristo Rey*, 721 Parker Ave., San Francisco, CA 94118-4297. Mother Mary Joseph, O.C.D., Prioress; Sr. Maria de la Immaculada, O.C.D., Archivist.

Total number in community 17.

Monastery of Discalced Carmelites (1928): 600 Flowers Ave., Dallas, TX 75211. Reverend Mother Prioress, O.C.D.

Professed Nuns 9.

Discalced Carmelite Nuns (1930): *Monastery of Our Lady and St. Joseph,* 1931 W. Jefferson Rd., Pittsford, NY 14534. Tel: 716-427-7094. Mother Miriam of the Angels, Prioress.

Professed Nuns with Solemn Vows 8; Professed Extern Sisters 1; Novices 1; Simply Professed 1.

Legal Title: *Carmelite Monastery of Rochester*.

Monastery of Discalced Carmelites O.C.D. (1930): *Monastery of Our Lady of Mount Carmel and St. Therese of the Child Jesus,* 25 Watson Ave., Barrington, RI 02806. Tel: 401-245-3421. Sr. Vilma Seelaus, O.C.D., Prioress.

Total number in community 15.

Discalced Carmelite Nuns O.C.D. (1934): *Monastery of the Infant Jesus of Prague and Our Lady of Guadalupe,* 6301 Culebra & St. Joseph Way, San Antonio, TX 78238-4909. Tel: 210-680-1834. Mother Therese Leonard, Prioress.

Total number in community 9.

Carmel of the Holy Family and St. Therese (1935): 6981 Teresian Way, P.O. Box 1720, Georgetown, CA 95634. Tel: 530-333-1617. Mother Christine, Prioress.

Total number in community 13.

Discalced Carmelite Nuns O.C.D. (1936): *Monastery of Mary, Mother of Grace,* 1250 Carmel Ave., Lafayette, 70501. Tel: 337-232-4651. Mother Mary John Billeaud, O.C.D., Prioress.
Total number in community 21.

Discalced Carmelite Nuns O.C.D. (1939): *Carmel of St. Joseph,* 20,000 N. County Line Rd., Piedmont, OK 73078. Sr. Monica Lotter, O.C.D., Prioress.
Total number in community 12.

Discalced Carmelite Nuns of Milwaukee O.C.D. (1940): *Carmel of the Mother of God,* W267 N2517, Meadowbrook Rd., Pewaukee, WI 53072. Tel: 262-691-0336. Sr. Mary Agnes Kramer, Prioress.
Total number in community 8.

Discalced Carmelite Nuns of Alexandria, South Dakota, Inc.-O.C.D.: *Monastery of Our Mother of Mercy,* 221 5th St., W., P.O. Box 67, Alexandria, SD 57311-0067. Tel: 605-239-4382. Mother Marie Therese of the Child Jesus, Prioress.
Total number in community 11.

Carmelite Monastery (1943): 716 Dauphin Island Pkwy., Mobile, AL 36606. Fax: 334-471-3991. Mother Marie Therese, Prioress.
Solemnly Professed Nuns 4.

Discalced Carmelite Monastery (1945): 49 Mount Carmel Rd., Santa Fe, NM 87501-4552. Tel: 505-983-7232. Mother Rose Teresa, O.C.D., Prioress.
Total number in community 13.

Discalced Carmelite Monastery (1946): 275 Pleasant St., Concord, NH 03301-2590. Tel: 603-225-5791. Sr. Emmanuel Sache, O.C.D., Prioress.
Solemnly Professed Nuns 11; Novices 1.

Monastery of Discalced Carmelites O.C.D. (1947): *Monastery of St. Joseph,* 59 Allendale, Terre Haute, IN. Tel: 812-299-1410; Fax: 812-299-5820. Mother Mary Clare Trolley, O.C.D., Prioress.
Professed Nuns 11; Novices 2; Postulants 1.

Discalced Carmelite Nuns of Colorado, Inc. (1948): *Carmel of Holy Spirit,* 6138 S. Gallup St., Littleton, CO. Tel: 80120-2702, 303-798-4176. Mother Judith of the Immaculate Heart, D.C., Prioress.
Professed Nuns 9.

Carmel of St. Joseph of Santa Ynez Valley, Inc. O.C.D. (1949): 1883 Ringsted Dr., P.O. Box 379, Solvang, CA 93463. Tel: 805-686-4292. Mother Mary Veronica Arakaki, O.C.D., Prioress.
Professed Sisters 11.

Order of Discalced Carmelites O.C.D. (1949): *Carmel of Mary Immaculate and St. Mary Magdalen,* 26 Harmony School Rd., Flemington, NJ 08822. Mother Anne of Christ, O.C.D., Prioress.
Total in community 14.

Discalced Carmelite Nuns O.C.D. (1950): *Monastery of the Infant Jesus of Prague,* 3501 Silver Lake Rd., Traverse City, MI 49684-8949. Tel: 231-946-4960. Mother Celine of the Cross, O.C.D., Prioress and Archivist.
Total number in community 10.

Carmelite Monastery of Christ, the Exiled King (1950): 68 Rincon Rd., Kensington, CA 94707. Sr. Mary Prioress.
Professed Nuns of Solemn Vows 5.

Discalced Carmelite Nuns O.C.D. (1951): *Monastery of the Holy Cross,* Hwy. U.S. 2, P.O. Box 397, Iron Mountain, MI 49801. Tel: 906-774-0561. Mother Maria of Jesus, O.C.D., Prioress.
Total number in community 18.

Discalced Carmelite Nuns O.C.D.: *Monastery of the Holy Name of Jesus,* 4047 Chapel Dr., New Franken, WI 54229-9768. Tel: 920-866-1815. Mother Mary Elizabeth, O.C.D., Prioress.

Discalced Carmelite Nuns O.C.D. (1950): *Monastery of the Immaculate Heart of Mary,* 94 Main St. -P.O. Box F, Montepelier, VT 05601-1455. Tel: 914-831-5572. Sr. Jeanne Gonyon, O.C.D., Prioress.
Total number in community 10.

Discalced Carmelite Nuns O.C.D. (1950): *Monastery of St. Teresa of Jesus,* 7201 W. 32nd St. Little Rock, AR 72204-4716. Tel: 501-565-5121. Sr. Joan Monkhouse, O.C.D., Prioress.
Professed Sisters 12.
Legal Title: *Discalced Carmelite Nuns of Little Rock.*

Discalced Carmelite Nuns O.C.D. (1951): *Monastery of Our Lady of Mount Carmel and The Little Flower,* 2155 Terry Rd., Jackson, MS 39204. Tel: 601-373-1460. Sr. Dona Marie Degnan, O.C.D., Prioress.
Professed Nuns 5.

Carmel of the Immaculate Heart of Mary (1952): 5714 Holladay Blvd., Salt Lake City, UT 84121-1599. Tel: 801-277-6075. Mother Margaret Mary Miller, O.C.D., Prioress. Sr. Mary Ann Krajicek, O.C.D., Archivist.
Solemn Vows 6; Finally Professed Externs 1.

Discalced Carmelite Nuns (1952): *St. Joseph's Monastery,* 89 Hiddenbrook Dr., Beacon, NY 12508-3599. Tel: 914-831-5579; Fax: 914-831-5579. Sr. Michael Ann Cladek, O.C.D., Prioress.
Total number in community 26.

Discalced Carmelite Nuns of St. Paul (1952): *Carmel of Our Lady of Divine Providence,* 8251 De Montreville Trail N. Lake Elmo, MN 55042-9547. Tel: 651-777-3882. Sr. Rose of the Sacred Heart, O.C.D., Prioress.
Professed Sisters 11; Novices 1; Postulants 1.

Discalced Carmelite Nuns O.C.D. (1953): 70 Monastery Rd., Elysburg, PA 17824-9697. Tel: 570-672-2935; Fax: 570-672-0278. Sr. Christine O'Brien, O.C.D., Prioress; Sr. Joan Lundy, O.C.D., Archivist; Sr. Patricia Boyd, O.C.D., Vocation Dir.
Professed Sisters 16.

Discalced Carmelite Nuns O.C.D. (1954): *Monastery of Our Lady of the Mountains,* 1950 La Fond Dr., Reno, NV 89509-3099. Tel: 775-323-3236; Fax: 775-322-1532. Sr. Ann Weber, O.C.D., Prioress.
Professed Nuns 14.

Carmel of Maria Regina O.C.D. (1957): 87609 Green Hill Rd., Eugene, OR 97402. Tel: 541-345-8649. Mother Maria Teresa, O.C.D., Prioress; Mother Maria Teresa, O.C.D., Community Archivist.
Total number in community 10.

Monastery of the Holy Family (1957): 510 E. Gore Rd., Erie, PA 16509. Mother Emmanuel of the Mother of God, Prioress.
Professed Sisters 5; Novices 1.

Discalced Carmelite Nuns (1958): *Coffee Bluff,* 11 W. Back St., Savannah, GA 31419-3219. Tel: 912-925-8505. Sr. Carmela Marolda, O.C.D., Prioress.
Total number in community 6.

Monastery of the Most Holy Trinity (1958): 5801 Mt. Carmel Dr., Arlington, TX 76017. Tel: 817-468-1781. Mother Anne Teresa of Jesus Kulinski, O.C.D., Prioress.
Total number in community 11.

Discalced Carmelite Nuns O.C.D. (1958): *Carmel of the Most Holy Trinity,* 1100 Parthenon Pl., Roman Forest, New Caney, TX 77357. Sr. Angel Teresa Sweeney, O.C.D., Prioress; Sr. Mary Ann Harrison, O.C.D., 1st Council Sister.
Total number in community 10.

Monastery of Discalced Carmelites (1959): 1101 N. River Rd., Des Plaines IL 60016. Tel: 847-298-4241. Mother Marie Andre of the Holy Spirit, Prioress.
Total number in community 17.

Order of Discalced Carmelites O.C.D. (1958): *Carmel of St. Therese,* 15 Mt. Carmel Rd., Danvers, MA 01923-3796. Tel: 978-774-3008. Mother Michael of Christ the King, O.C.D., Prioress.
Total number in community 16.
Legal Title: *Discalced Carmelite Nuns of Danvers.*

Discalced Carmelite Nuns O.C.D. (1960): *Monastery of The Sacred Heart and St. Joseph,* 2201 W. Main St., Jefferson City, MO 65109. Tel: 573-636-3364. Mother Therese, O.C.D., Prioress.
Solemnly Professed Nuns 8; Novices 1; Postulants 3.

Carmel of the Assumption (1961): R.D. 6, Box 28, Center Dr., Latrobe, PA 15650. Tel: 724-539-1056. Sr. Marie Elizabeth Krug, O.C.D., Prioress.
Professed Sisters 14.

Discalced Carmelite Nuns, Inc. (1962): *Monastery of the Discalced Carmelite Nuns,* 2901 S. Cecelia St., Sioux City, IA 51106-3299. Tel: 712-276-1680. Mother Therese of the Spirit of Love, O.C.D., Prioress.
Total number in community 11.

Carmelite Monastery of the Mother of God (1965): 530 Blackstone Dr., San Rafael, CA 94903. Tel: 415-479-6872; Fax: 415-491-4964. Mother Anna Marie, O.C.D., Prioress.
Total number in community 7.

Discalced Carmelite Nuns O.C.D. (1965): *Carmel of St. Anne,* 424 E. Monastery St., Springfield, MO 65807. Tel: 417-881-2115. Mother Mary Charles, O.C.D., Prioress.
Total number in community 5.

Carmel of the Holy Trinity: 6301 Pali Hwy., Kaneohi, HI 96744. Tel: 808-261-6542. Mother Mary Agnes Tse, O.C.D., Prioress.
Total number in community 8.

Discalced Carmelite Nuns of the Byzantine Rite (1980): *Holy Annunication Monastery,* R.R. No. 1, Box 1336, Sugarloaf, PA 18249. Tel: 570-788-1205; Fax: 570-788-3329. Mother Marija of the Holy Spirit, O.C.D., Prioress.
Professed Nuns 13.
Represented in the Diocese of Passaic.

Carmel of Port Tobacco: 5678 Mt. Carmel Rd., La Plata, MD 20646.
Founded 1790 and refounded 1976; Mother Mary Joseph, O.C.D., Prioress.
Professed 13; Simple Professed 1; Novices 1; Postulants 1.

[0430] (B.V.M.)—SISTERS OF CHARITY OF THE BLESSED VIRGIN MARY P

Founded in America in 1833.

BVM Center: *Mount Carmel,* 1100 Carmel Dr., Dubuque, IA 52003. Tel: 319-588-2351; Fax: 319-588-4832. Sr. Joellen McCarthy, B.V.M., Pres.
Total number in Congregation 811.
Sisters staff and serve in the field of Academic Education on all levels; Health Care-Aging; Religious Education;Chaplaincies; Pastoral Ministry; Diocesan School Offices; Diocesan Services-Administration; Social Work; Homeless Shelters; Aids Ministry; Social Justice; Extended Day Care.
Represented in the Archdioceses of Atlanta, Boston, Chicago, Denver, Dubuque, Indianapolis, Los Angeles, Omaha, Miami, Milwaukee, Mobile, Portland (OR), St. Louis, St. Paul-Minneapolis, San Francisco, Seattle and the Dioceses of Baton Rouge, Belleville, Brooklyn, Biloxi, Dallas, Davenport, Des Moines, Fort Wayne-South Bend, Fresno, Green Bay, Helena, Honolulu, Jackson, Joliet, Kansas City-St. Joseph, Knoxville, Lafayette, Lexington, Memphis, Oakland, Orange, Orlando, Peoria, Pensacola-Tallahassee, Phoenix, Reno-Las Vegas, Rockford, Rockville Centre, San Diego, San Bernardino, San Jose, Santa Rosa, Sioux City, Springfield-Cape Girardeau, Springfield (IL), Stockton, Tucson, Venice, Wichita and Winona. Also in Africa, Ecuador, Philippines and Guatemala.

[0440] (S.C.)—SISTERS OF CHARITY OF CINCINNATI, OHIO P

Founded by Saint Elizabeth Ann Seton, Emmitsburg, MD 1809. The Cincinnati Community became independent in 1852, Papal approval in 1939.

General Motherhouse (1852): *Mount St. Joseph,* Mt. St. Joseph, OH 45051. Tel: 513-347-5201; Fax: 513-347-5228. Sr. Mary Ellen Murphy, Pres.
Legal Title: *Sisters of Charity,* Cincinnati, OH.
Professed Sisters 596.
Sisters serve and staff Colleges; Secondary and Elementary Schools; Parishes Healthcare Facilities and School of Nursing; Foreign Missions; Home for Profoundly Challenged Children; Senior Care Services; Social Services; Congregational Services.
Represented in the Archdioceses of Baltimore, Boston, Chicago, Cincinnati, Denver, Detroit, Indianapolis, Louisville, Newark, New Orleans, New York, St. Louis, St. Paul-Minneapolis, San Francisco, Santa Fe, Washington and the Dioceses of Brownsville, Cleveland, Colorado Springs, Columbus, Covington, El Paso, Helena, Kalamazoo, Knoxville, Las Cruces, Lansing, Lexington, Little Rock, Memphis, Oakland, Orlando, Palm Beach, Phoenix, Pueblo, Raleigh, Rapid City, Saginaw, Savannah, St. Petersburg, Toledo, Wichita and Wilmington. Also in Armenia, Ecuador, Poland, and Gautemala.

[0450] (S.C.I.C.)—SISTERS OF CHARITY OF THE IMMACULATE CONCEPTION OF IVREA P

Founded in Italy in the 18th Century. First Foundation in the United States in 1961.

General Motherhouse: della Renella 85, Rome, Italy, 396-5818145. Sr. Grazia Raffaella Rossi, Supr. Gen.
Total number in Congregation 1,387.

U.S. Foundation (1961): *Immaculate Virgin of Miracles Convent,* R.D. 2, Box 348, Mount Pleasant, PA 15666. Tel: 412-887-6753. Sr. Letizia Garrubai, Reg. Supr. Tel: 412-887-0220.
Professed Sisters in the U.S.A. 15.
Sisters serve and staff Kindergarten and Elementary Schools; Parish Services; Religious Education; Pastoral Ministry.
Properties owned: *Verna Montessori Children's House & Elememtary School; Immaculate Virgin of Miracles Convent,* Mt. Pleasant, PA.
Represented in the Diocese of Greensburg and Norwich.

[0460] (C.C.V.I.)—CONGREGATION OF THE SISTERS OF CHARITY OF THE INCARNATE WORD P

Founded in 1869 at San Antonio, Texas.

Generalate: 4503 Broadway, San Antonio, TX 78209-6297. Tel: 210-828-2224; Fax: 210-828-9741. Sr. Teresa Stanley, C.C.V.I., Gen. Supr.

Incarnate Word Provincialate - U.S. Province: P.O. Box 15378, San Antonio, TX 78209-0290. Tel: 210-734-8310; Fax: 210-734-8369. Sr. Helena Monahan, C.C.V.I., Prov. Coord.

Incarnate Word Retirement Community: 4707 Broadway, San Antonio, TX 78209-6299. Tel: 210-829-7561; Fax: 210-828-0020. Mr. Richard Boyd, Exec. Dir.
Universal Total in Congregation 491; U.S. Province 285.
Properties owned and sponsored: Universities 1; High

schools 3; Hospitals (co-sponsored) 27; Temporary shelter for homeless women & children 2; Retirement Center 1; Center for Spirituality and the Arts; Foster Home.

Ministry in the field of Education at all levels; Hospitals and Health Service Agencies; Nursing Homes; Pastoral Ministries; Diocesan Offices; Social Service Agencies.

Represented in the Archdioceses of Chicago, New Orleans, St. Louis, San Antonio, and the Dioceses of Amarillo, Brownsville, Corpus Christi, El Paso, Fort Worth, Jefferson City, Springfield-Cape Girardeau, San Angelo, Spokane, and Tucson. Also in Mexico, and Peru.

[0470] (C.C.V.I.)—CONGREGATION OF THE SISTERS OF CHARITY OF THE INCARNATE WORD, HOUSTON, TEXAS P

Founded in the United States in 1866, St. Mary's Infirmary, Galveston, Texas.

Motherhouse: *Villa de Matel*, 6510 Lawndale Ave., P.O. Box 230969, Houston, TX 77223-0969. Tel: 713-928-6053; Fax: 713-928-8148. Sr. Olive Bordelon, Gen. Supr.

Total number in congregation 226.

Legal Title: *Incarnate Word Charitable Trust.*

Sisters serve and staff Hospitals, Homes for Aged, Elementary Schools, Social Services.

Represented in the Archdiocese of Los Angeles and the Dioceses of Alexandria, Beaumont, Brownsville, Galveston-Houston, Lake Charles, Little Rock, Salt Lake City, San Bernardino, Shreveport and Tyler. Also in Ireland, Guatemala, San Salvador and Kenya.

[0480] (S.C.L.)—SISTERS OF CHARITY OF LEAVENWORTH, KANSAS P

Founded in the United States in 1858.

Community Offices and Motherhouse: 4200 S. Fourth St., Leavenworth, KS 66048-5054. Tel: 913-758-6501; Fax: 912-682-2128. Sr. Joan Sue Miller, S.C.L., Community Dir.; Sr. Helen Forge, Archivist.

Total number in community 413.

Properties owned and sponsored: *Saint Mary College*, Leavenworth, KS. Residential and Day Treatment Centers for Children: *Mount St. Vincent Home*, Denver, CO; *Saint John's Child Study Center*, Santa Monica, CA. Health Facilities: *Sisters of Charity of Leavenworth Health Services Corporation*, *Cantwell Hall*, Leavenworth, KS; *Saint John's Hospital & Health Center*, Santa Monica, CA; *Saint Joseph Hospital*, Denver, CO; *St. Mary's Hospital & Medical Center*, Grand Junction, CO; *Saint John Hospital*, Leavenworth, KS; *St. Francis Hospital and Medical Center*, Topeka, KS; *Saint Vincent Hospital & Health Center*, Billings, MT; *St. James Community Hospital*, Butte, MT; *Holy Rosary Health Center*, Miles City, MT; *Marian Clinic*, Topeka, KS; *Marillac Clinic*, Grand Junction, CO; *Providence Medical Center*, Kansas City, KS; *Bethany Medical Center*, Kansas City, KS; *Caritas Clinic, Inc.*, Kansas City, KS.

Sisters serving in Elementary, Secondary, and Higher Education; Nursing Education; Special Education; Religious Education; Ministry Training; Hospitals; Latin American Missions; Diocesan Offices; Parish Administration and Pastoral Ministry; Liturgy-Music Ministry; Campus Ministry; Spiritual Direction; Communications; Social Justice; Housing.

Ministries to AIDS Victims; Cross-culture; Elderly; Prisoners, Handicapped Adults and Youth; Health Service Agencies; Mental Health; Native Americans; and Social Service Agencies.

Represented in the Archdioceses of Denver, Kansas City in Kansas, Los Angeles, Oklahoma City, Omaha, Santa Fe, San Antonio, St. Louis, Seattle and the Dioceses of Cheyenne, Dodge City, Gallup, Great Falls-Billings, Helena, Jefferson City, Kansas City-St. Joseph, Oakland, Orange, Pueblo, San Diego, St. Cloud, and Tucson. Also in Peru.

[0490] (S.G.M.)—SISTERS OF CHARITY OF MONTREAL (Grey Nuns) P

Founded in 1737 by Saint Marguerite d'Youville at Montreal, Canada. First foundation in the United States 1855.

Generalate: *General Administration*, 138 Rue Saint-Pierre, Montreal, Quebec H2Y 2L7, Canada. Tel: 514-842-9411. Sr. Aurore Larkin, S.G.M., Supr. Gen.

St. Joseph Province - U.S.A.: *Provincial Administration*, 10 Pelham Rd.-Ste. 1000, Lexington, MA 02421-8499. Tel: 781-862-4700. Sr. June Ketterer, S.G.M., Prov. Supr.; Sr. Helene Georges, S.G.M., Dir.-Formation.

Legal Title: *The Grey Nuns Charities, Inc.*

Total number in community 60.

Ministry in Hospitals; Schools of Nursing; Nursing Homes;Parish Ministry; Adult Day Health Care; Social Day Care; Social Justice; Pastoral Care; Foreign Missions; Housing for the Elderly & Handicapped; Nutrition Programs for Poor; Elder Health Center; Assisted Living Residence; Shelter for Homeless; Emergency Satellite Facilities.

Represented in the Archdiocese of Boston and the Dioceses of Manchester, Portland (ME) and Toledo. Also in Argentina.

[0500] (S.C.N.)—SISTERS OF CHARITY OF NAZARETH P

Founded in the United States in 1812.

SCN Center: P.O. Box 172, Nazareth, KY 40048. Tel: 502-348-1555; Fax: 502-348-1502. Sr. Maria Vincent Brocato, S.C.N., Pres.

Legal Title: *Nazareth Literary & Benevolent Institution.*

Total number in Congregation 744.

Properties owned or sponsored: *Nazareth Hospital*; *Mokama India Educational Facilities*; *Our Lady of Nazareth Academy*, Wakefield, MA; *Nazareth Montessori Children's Center*. Retreat Facilities: *Catherine Spalding Center*, Nazareth, KY; *Bethany Spring*, New Haven, KY; *Camp Maria*, Leonardtown, MD. Facilities for the Elderly and Handicapped: *Nazareth Village I*, *Nazareth Village II*, Nazareth, KY; *Nazareth Home*, Louisville, KY. Missions: *SCN Missions*.

Louisville Region: *Regional Office*, 676 Atwood, P.O. Box 17545, Louisville, KY 40217. Tel: 502-636-0411. Sr. Elizabeth Blandford, S.C.N., Reg. Rep.

Final professed sisters 221.

Sisters serve and staff the field of Academic Education on all levels; Special Educational Services; Social Services; Public Library; Counseling; Campus Ministry; Archdiocesan Offices; Health Care Institutions; Pastoral Ministry; Literacy Council and Retirement Center.

Represented in the Archdioceses of Indianapolis, Louisville and the Diocese of San Jose.

Southern Region: P.O. Box 187, Nazareth, KY 40048. Tel: 502-331-4071. Sr. Marlenea Lehmkuhl, S.C.N., Reg. Rep.

Final professed sisters 247.

Sisters serve and staff in the field of Academic Education on all levels; Literacy Program; Parish Ministry; Diocesan Centers; Social Services; Retirement Centers; Retreat Centers; Peace & Justice Center; Department of Human Resources; Counseling; Health Care Agencies.

Represented in the Archdioceses of Chicago, Cincinnati, Louisville and the Dioceses of Baton Rouge, Covington, Charleston, Jackson, Little Rock, Lexington, Memphis, Nashville, Owensboro, Palm Beach, and St. Petersburg. Also in Belize City, Independence, Belize and Nicaragua.

Northern Region: *Regional House*, 169 Fenno St., Quincy, MA 02170. Tel: 617-479-4909. Sr. Gwen McMahon, S.C.N., Reg. Rep.

Final professed sisters 59.

Sisters serve and staff in the field of Academic Education on all levels; Social Services; Parish Ministry; Diocesan Center; Health Care Institutions; Retreat Centers; Retirement Centers and Seminary.

Represented in the Archdioceses of Boston, Philadelphia and Washington and the Dioceses of Columbus, Richmond, Steubenville, and Wilmington.

India Region: *Regional House*, E. Boring Canal Rd., Post Box 219, Patna, Bihar 800-001, India. Tel: 011-91-612-2341-21. Sr. Teresa Kotturan, S.C.N., Prov.

Final professed sisters 147. Central Leadership Team: Final professed sisters 3

[0510] (O.L.M.)—SISTERS OF CHARITY OF OUR LADY OF MERCY D

Founded in Charleston, South Carolina in 1829.

Generalate and Motherhouse: 424 Fort Johnson Rd. - P.O. Box 12410, Charleston, SC 29422. Tel: 843-795-2866; Fax: 843-795-6083. Sr. Anne Francis Campbell, O.L.M., Gen. Supr.

Total number in community 29.

Sisters serve and staff: Parishes; Elementary Schools; Social Services.

Legal Title: *The Sisters of Charity of Our Lady of Mercy Charitable Trust.*

Properties owned: *Motherhouse, May Forest*, Charleston, SC; *Our Lady of Mercy Convent*, John's Island, SC; *Our Lady of Mercy Community Outreach Services, Inc.*, Johns Island, SC.

Represented in the Diocese of Charleston.

[0520] (S.C.M.M.)—SISTERS OF CHARITY OF OUR LADY, MOTHER OF MERCY P

Founded in Holland 1832. First foundation in the United States in 1874.

General Motherhouse: *Den Bosch*, Netherlands. Universal number in Congregation 1,100

U.S. Provincial House: 520 Thompson Ave., East Haven CT 06512. Tel: 203-469-7872. Sr. Mary Ellen Ryley, S.C.M.M., Prov.

Total number in community 20.

Represented in the Archdioceses of Chicago, Detroit, Hartford and St. Paul-Minneapolis and the Dioceses of Bridgeport and San Diego.

[0530] (S.C.M.C.)—SISTERS OF CHARITY OF OUR LADY, MOTHER OF THE CHURCH D

First foundation in the United States in 1970.

General Motherhouse: Baltic, CT 06330. Tel: 860-822-8241; Fax: 860-822-9842. Mother M. Anthony Lemire, Supr. Gen.

Professed Sisters 77; Junior Professed 5; Novices 1.

Properties owned, staffed or sponsored: High Schools 1; Nursing Home 1; Elementary Schools 8; Home for Aged 2; Home for Dependent Children 1; Catechetical Schools 18; Domestic Help; Shelter for the Homeless 1; Hispanic Ministry 1.

Represented in the Archdiocese of Hartford and the Dioceses of Manchester, Madison and Norwich.

[0540] (S.C.O.)—SISTERS OF CHARITY OF OTTAWA (Grey Nuns of the Cross) P

Founded in Ottawa, Canada, in 1845. First foundation in the United States in 1857.

General Motherhouse: 9 Bruyere St., Ottawa, Ontario K1N 5C9, Canada. Mother Claire Malette, S.C.O., Gen. Supr.

Total number of Sisters in Congregation based in Ottawa 800.

American Province (1950): *St. Joseph*, 975 Varnum Ave., Lowell, MA 01854. Tel: 978-453-4993. Sr. Gabrielle L. Jean, S.C.O., Prov. Supr.; Sr. Jeannine Bernier, S.C.O., Archivist.

Professed U.S. Sisters 44.

Sisters staff Grammar Schools; CCD Parish Services; Health Care and Pastoral Ministries; Apostolate of Aging.

Properties owned: *D'Youville Senior Care, Inc., Bachand Hall Emmaus, St. Joseph Residence,* Lowell, MA.

Legal Title: *Sisters of Charity of Ottawa.*

Represented in the Archdioceses of Boston and Newark.

[0560] (S.C.Q.)—SISTERS OF CHARITY OF QUEBEC (Grey Nuns) P

Founded in Quebec in 1849. First United States foundation in 1890.

General Motherhouse: 2655 Le Pelletier St., Beauport, Quebec GIC 3X7, Canada. Tel: 418-628-8860. Sr. Denise Marcoux, S.C.Q., Supr. Gen.

U.S. House (1908): *Franco - American School,* 357 Pawtuckert St., Lowell, MA 01854. Tel: 978-937-8672. Sr. Lorraine Richard, S.C.Q., Supr.

U.S. House (1917): *Sacred Heart Home, Inc.*, 359 Summer St., New Bedford, MA 02740. Tel: 508-996-6751. Sr. Blandine D'Amours, S.C.Q., Supr.

Professed U.S. Sisters 6.

Sisters serve and staff the field of education and care of the elderly; Franco American School, Lowell, MA; Sacred Heart Home, New Bedford, MA.

Represented in the Archdiocese of Boston and the Diocese of Fall River.

[0570] (S.C.)—SISTERS OF CHARITY OF SETON HILL, GREENSBURG, PENNSYLVANIA P

Foundation from Cincinnati, Ohio to Altoona, Pennsylvania in 1870.

Generalate: *DePaul Center*, Mount Thor Rd., Greensburg, PA 15601. Tel: 724-836-0406; Fax: 724-836-8280. Sr. Gertrude Foley, S.C., Pres.; Sr. Mary Catherine Seli, S.C., Archivist.

Total number in the community 518.

Ministry in the field of Academic Education at all levels; Day Care Centers; Community Service Center; Adult Day Care Center; Special Education for persons with Handicaps.

Properties owned: *Elizabeth Seton Center,* Pittsburgh, PA.

Represented in the Archdioceses of Chicago, Cincinnati, Hartford, Los Angeles, Washington and the Dioceses of Altoona-Johnstown, Brooklyn, Erie, Greensburg, Orlando, Phoenix, Pittsburgh, Raleigh, St. Petersburg, Steubenville, Tucson, and Wheeling-Charleston. Also in South Korea, Israel and Uganda

[0580] (C.S.A.)—SISTERS OF CHARITY OF ST. AUGUSTINE D

Founded in Cleveland, Ohio in 1851.

Motherhouse: *Mount Augustine*, 5232 Broadview Rd.,

Richfield, OH 44286. Sr. Nancy Hendershot, C.S.A., Congregational Leader; Sr. Mary Denis Maher, C.S.A., Archivist.
Total number in Congregation 88.
Properties owned and sponsored: *CSA Health Network,* Cleveland, OH; *Providence Hospital,* Columbia, SC; *Regina Health Center,* Richfield, OH; *Saint Ann Foundation,* Cleveland, OH; *Saint Augustine Academy,* Lakewood, OH; *St. Vincent Charity Hospital,* Cleveland, OH; *Sisters of Charity of St. Augustine Health System, Inc.,* Cleveland, OH; *Mercy Medical Center,* Canton, OH; *Westlake Health Campus Association* dba *St. John West Shore Hospital,* Westlake, OH.
Represented in the Doceses of Charleston, Cleveland and Youngstown.

[0590] (S.C.) —SISTERS OF CHARITY OF SAINT ELIZABETH, CONVENT STATION P
Founded in Newark, New Jersey in 1859.
General Motherhouse: *Convent of St. Elizabeth*-Administration Building, P.O. Box 476, Convent Station, NJ 07961-0476. Tel: 973-290-5000; 290-5450 (Admin.); Fax: 973-290-5335. Sr. Barbara Conroy, Gen. Supr.; Sr. Elizabeth McLoughlin, Archivist; Sr. Miriam Teresa, League of Prayer.
Legal Titles and Properties: *Sisters of Charity of Saint Elizabeth Academy of Saint Elizabeth,* Convent Station, NJ; *Saint Vincent Academy,* Newark, NJ; *Academy of the Sacred Heart,* Hoboken, NJ; *Saint Frances Residence,* Paterson, NJ.
Total number in Congregation 612.
Sisters serve and staff: Academies; High Schools 2; Elementary Schools 17; Hospitals 2; C.C.D. 7; Parish Work 21; Social Work 5; Health Services 22; College Teaching 13.
Represented in the Archdioceses of Boston, Hartford, Newark, New York, Omaha, St. Louis, Washington, and the Dioceses of Camden, Charlotte, El Paso, Fairbanks, Fall River, Galveston-Houston, Jackson, Metuchen, Paterson, Palm Beach, Providence, Pensacola-Tallahassee, Richmond, Rochester, St. Petersburg, Syracuse, Trenton, Tucson, Venice, Wheeling-Charleston and Wilmington. Also in St. Thomas, Virgin Islands.

[0600] (S.C.S.J.A.)—SISTERS OF CHARITY OF ST. JOAN ANTIDA P
Founded in France in 1799 by Saint Joan Antida Thouret. First foundation in the U.S. 1932.
General Motherhouse: *Suore della Carita di Santa Giovanna Antida,* Via S. Maria in Cosmedin 5, 00153 Roma, Italia. Sr. M. Luisa Colombo, Supr. Gen.
North American Province (1976): *Regina Mundi Provincial House,* 8560 N. 76th Pl., Milwaukee, WI 53223. Tel: 414-354-9233; Fax: 414-355-6463. Sr. Jennifer L. Daul, S.C.S.J.A., Prov.
Total number in Congregation 45.
Properties owned and sponsored: *St. Joan Antida High School, Inc.; St. Joan Antida Home, Inc.; Hope Nursing Home, Inc.; Guardian Angel Learning Center, Inc.; St. Joan Antida Day Care Center, Inc.; St. Joan Antida High School Foundation, Ltd.*
Ministry in prisons; neighborhood services and parishes.
Represented in the Archdiocese of Milwaukee and the Diocese of Amarillo.

[0610] (S.C.S.H.)—SISTERS OF CHARITY OF ST. HYACINTHE (Grey Nuns) P
Founded in 1840 in St. Hyacinthe, P.Q., Canada. First United States foundation in 1878.
Legal Title: *The Society of the Sisters of Charity,* Lewiston, ME.
General House: 16470 Avenue Bourdages, SUD, St. Hyacinthe, P.Q., Canada J2T 4J8. Sr. Diane Beaudoin, S.C.S.H., Supr. Gen.; Sr. Claudette Jacques, S.C.S.H., Gen. Sec.
Universal number in Congregation 226.
U.S. Regional Administration: *Sisters of Charity of St. Hyacinthe,* 98 Campus Ave., Lewiston, ME 04240-6076. Tel: 207-797-8607. Sr. Diane Beaudoin, Pres.; Sr. Marguerite Carignan, Sec.
Total number in U.S. 12.
Properties owned: *St. Peter's Home,* Manchester, NH.
Represented in the Dioceses of Manchester and Portland (ME). Also in Canada and Haiti.

[0620] (S.C.S.L.)—SISTERS OF CHARITY OF ST. LOUIS P
Founded in France in 1803. First foundation in the United States in 1910.
Generalate: 5169 Avenue MacDonald, Montreal, (Quebec) H3X 2V9, Canada. Sr. Geraldine Hagel, Supr. Gen.
Total universal number in Congregation 779.
American Region: 4907 S. Catherine St., Plattsburgh, NY 12901. Tel: 518-563-0383; Fax: 518-563-0383. Sr. Louisee Marceau, Reg. Supr.
Total number in community 15.
Properties owned and sponsored: *Our Lady of Victory Convent,* Albany, NY.
Represented in the Dioceses of Albany and Ogdensburg.

[0630] (V.Z.)—SISTERS OF CHARITY OF ST. VINCENT DE PAUL OF ZAGREB P
Founded in Croatia (Austria-Hungary) in 1845. First U.S. Foundation in 1955.
General Motherhouse: Zagreb, Croatia. Mother Maria Agneta Tadic-Sutra, Supr. Gen.
U.S. Foundation: *Sisters of Charity Convent,* 171 Knox Ave., West Seneca, NY 14224. Tel: 716-825-5859. Sr. M. Stella Simetich, V.Z., Supr.
Professed Sisters 17.
Sisters staff Nursery Schools; CCD Centers and Parish Services; Hospital & Health Services.
Properties owned: *Nursery School.*
Represented in the Diocese of Buffalo.

[0640] (S.C.) SISTERS OF CHARITY OF ST. VINCENT DE PAUL, HALIFAX P
Founded by Saint Elizabeth Ann Seton, Emmitsburg, Maryland in 1809. Congregation at Halifax became independent in 1856, Papal approval in 1908.
Motherhouse: *Mount Saint Vincent,* 150 Bedford Hwy., Halifax, N.S B3M 3J5, Canada. Tel: 902-457-3500; Fax: 902-457-3506. Sr. Mary Louise Brink, Congregation Leader; Sr. Marie Gillen, Archivist.
Legal Title: *Sisters of Charity* (Halifax)
Total universal number in Congregation 725.
Commonwealth of Massachusetts: *Boston Branch Office,* 26 Phipps St., Quincy, MA 02169-6626. Tel: 617-773-6085; Fax: 617-472-7179. Sr. Esther Plefka, S.C., Congregation Councillor. Tel: 617-773-6076; Fax: 617-472-7179.
Legal Title: *Sisters of Charity (Halifax) Corporate Mission, Inc.,* 26 Phipps St., Quincy, MA 02169-6626. Tel: 617-773-6085; Fax: 617-773-7179. Sr. Mary Louise Brink, Congregational Leader.
Legal Title: *Sisters of Charity (Halifax) Supporting Corporation,* 125 Oakland St., Wellesley Hills, MA 02481-5338. Tel: 781-237-2161; Fax: 781-237-8152. Sr. Mary Louise Brink, Congregational Leader.
Mount St. Vincent Retirement Community: 125 Oakland St., Wellesley Hills, MA 02481-5338. Tel: 781-237-2161; Fax: 781-237-8152. Community Leadership Team: Sr. Ann Marie Barry; Sr. Elizabeth Groome; Sr. Ann Regan.
Legal Titles and Holdings: *Marillac Residence, Inc.,* Wellesley Hills, MA; *Elizabeth Seton Residence, Inc.,* Wellesley Hills, MA.
State of New York: *New York Branch Office,* 84-32 63rd Ave., Middle Village, NY 11379-1967. Tel: 718-651-1685; Fax: 718-651-5645. Sr. Joan Holmberg, Congregational Councillor. Tel: 718-779-6284; Fax: 718-651-5645. Sr. Judith Park, Congregational Councillor. Tel: 718-426-6502; Fax: 718-205-3662.
Ministering in education at all levels; homes for the aging; hospitals; parish ministry; spiritual direction/retreats/houses of prayer; social services; pastoral ministry; administration.
Represented in the Archdiocese of Boston and the Dioceses of Brooklyn, and Rockville Centre. Also in Canada, Bermuda, Dominican Republic and Peru.

[0650] (S.C.)—SISTERS OF CHARITY OF ST. VINCENT DE PAUL, OF NEW YORK D
Founded in Emmitsburg, MD in 1809 by Saint Elizabeth Ann Seton.
General Motherhouse: *Sisters of Charity Center, Mount Saint Vincent-on-Hudson,* 6301 Riverdale Ave., Bronx, NY 10471. Tel: 718-549-9200; Fax: 718-884-3013. Sr. Elizabeth A. Vermaelen, Pres.
Total number in Congregation 515.
Sisters serve and staff Colleges; High Schools; Elementary Schools; Secretarial Science School; Child Caring Homes; General Hospitals; Foundling Hospital; Schools of Nursing; Residence for Senior and Invalid Sisters; Mental Health Divisions, Rest House for Community use; Housing for Homeless.
Represented in the Archdioceses of Atlanta, Baltimore, Newark, New York, Washington and the Dioceses of Albany, Bridgeport, Brooklyn, Camden, Gary, Oakland, Rockville Centre, and Shreveport. Also in the Bahamas, and Guatemala.

[0660] (S.C.C.)—SISTERS OF CHRISTIAN CHARITY P
Daughters of the Blessed Virgin Mary of the Immaculate Conception
Founded in Germany in 1849. First foundation in the United States in 1873.
Generalate: *Suore della Carita Cristiana Casa Generalizia,* Largo XXI Aprile, 10 00162, Roma, Italia. Tel: 011-3906-8622011. Sr. Gregoris Michels, Supr. Gen.
Total universal number in congregation 853.
North American Eastern Province (1927): *Mallinckrodt Convent Div. of North American Province,* Mendham, NJ 07945. Tel: 973-543-6528. Sr. Mary Edward Spohrer, S.C.C., Prov.; Sr. Mary Pierre Koesters, S.C.C., Archivist.
Professed Sisters 298.
Ministry in Academic Education; Retreat House; Catechetical Centers; Religion Coordinators; Health care & Parish Ministry.
Properties owned and/or sponsored: *Villa Pauline, Retreat House,* Mendham, NJ; *Divine Providence Hospital,* Williamsport, PA; *Holy Spirit Hospital,* Camp Hill, PA; *Mallinckrodt Convent Motherhouse,* Mendham, NJ; *Holy Family Convent, Home for Aged and Retired Sisters,* Danville, PA; *Muncy Valley Hospital,* Muncy, PA.
Represented in the Archdioceses of Newark, New York and Philadelphia and in the Dioceses of Allentown, Camden, Harrisburg, Metuchen, Paterson and Scranton.
North American Western Province: *Sisters of Christian Charity - Daughters of the Blessed, Virgin Mary of the Immaculate Conception,* 2041 Elmwood Ave., Wilmette, IL 60091-1431, 847-920-9341; Fax: 847-920-9346. Sr. M. Judith Moran, Prov.; Sr. Joann Kelzer, Archivist.
Professed Sisters 127.
Ministry in the field of Academic Education at all levels; Abused and Neglected Children; Religious Education; Parish Ministry; Ministry to Aged; Prayer Ministry; Ministry to the Poor; Multi-Cultural Ministry.
Properties owned and sponsored: *Maria Immaculata Convent, Sacred Heart Convent,* Wilmette, IL; *Josephinum High School and Convent,* Chicago, IL; *Mallinckrodt College of the North Shore,* Wilmette, IL.
Represented in the Archdioceses of Chicago, New Orleans, St. Louis, Santa Fe and the Dioceses of Jefferson City, Lansing, Rapid City and Tucson.

[0670] (O.C.S.O.)— CISTERCIAN NUNS OF THE STRICT OBSERVANCE P
Founded at Citeaux, France, in 1125. First foundation in the United States in 1949.
Generalate: Viale Africa 33, 00144, Rome, Italy.
Total universal number of nuns in Order 1,863. Contemplative.
U.S. Establishments:
Mount St. Mary's Abbey: 300 Arnold St., Wrentham, MA 02093-1799. Tel: 508-528-1282. Rev. Mother M. Agnes Day, O.C.S.O., Abbess.
Total number in community 46.
Represented in the Archdiocese of Boston.
Our Lady of the Mississippi Abbey: 8400 Abbey Hill Road, Dubuque, IA 52003. Tel: 319-582-2595; Fax: 319-582-5511. Rev. Mother Gail Fitzpatrick, O.C.S.O., Abbess.
Total number in community 24.
Legal Title: *Trappistine Nuns, Inc., Iowa Cistercians of the Strict Observance.*
Represented in the Archdiocese of Dubuque.
Santa Rita Abbey: HC 1, Box 929, Sonoita, AZ 85637-9705. Tel: 520-455-5595. Mother Miriam Pollard, O.C.S.O., Prioress.
Legal Title: *Cistercian Nuns of the Strict Observance.*
Total number in community 13.
Represented in the Diocese of Tucson.
Our Lady of the Redwoods Abbey: 18104 Briceland Thorn Rd., Whitethorn, CA 95589. Tel: 707-986-7419. Sr. Kathy DeVico, O.C.S.O., Abbess.
Total number in community 9.
Represented in the Diocese of Santa Rosa.
Our Lady of the Angels Monastery: 3365 Monastery Dr., Crozet, VA 22932. Tel: 804-823-1452; Fax: 804-823-6379. Mother Marion Rissetto, O.C.S.O., Prioress.
Legal Title: *Cistercian Nuns of the Strict Observance in Virginia, Inc.*
Total number in community 8.
Represented in the Diocese of Richmond.

[0680] (O.CIST.)—CISTERCIAN NUNS P
Headquarters: *Piazza del Tempio di Diana,* 14, Roma, Italia 00153. Most Rev. Maurus Esteva, O.Cist., Abbot General.
U.S. Headquarters: *Valley of Our Lady Monastery,* E. 11096 Yanke Dr., Prairie du Sac, WI 53578-9737. Tel: 608-643-3520; Fax: 608-643-0684. Rev. Mother Paula Hannah, O.Cist., Prioress.
Total number in community 15.

[0685] (R.M.I.)—CLARETIAN MISSIONARY SISTERS P
Religious of Mary Immaculate Claretian Missionary Sisters
Founded in Santiago de Cuba, August 25, 1855. Established in the United States in 1956.

Generalate: Via Calandrelli 16, 00153, Roma, Italy. Eusebia Pizarro, Supr. Gen.

U.S. Delegation: 9600 W. Atlantic Ave., Delray Beach, FL 33446. Sr. Regina Tutzo, R.M.I., Local Supr.

Sisters in the World 600; Sisters in Florida 11.

Legal Title: *Claretian Missionary Sisters of Florida, Inc.*

Ministry in Religious Education; Theological formation in Pastoral Institutes and Seminaries; Social Ministries; Parish and Diocesan Ministries.

Represented in the Archdiocese of Miami and the Diocese of Palm Beach.

[0690] (C.M.S.)—COMBONI MISSIONARY SISTERS P

Founded in Italy in 1872. An international congregation of 1,800 sisters serving in the mission fields of Africa, Latin America and the Middle East. First United States Foundation in 1950.

Generalate: Rome, Italy. Mother Adele Brambilla, C.M.S., Supr. Gen.

American Headquarters: 1307 Lakeside Ave., Richmond, VA 23228. Tel: 804-262-8827; Fax: 804-264-2906. Sr. Maria Teresa Goffi, Prov. Supr.

Legal Titles & Holdings: *Provincial House, Holy Angels Day Care Center, Comboni Missionary Sisters, Inc.*, Richmond, VA

Represented in the Archdiocese of Philadelphia and the Diocese of Richmond.

[0700] (O.D.N.)—COMPANY OF MARY P

Founded in Bordeaux, France, April 7, 1607, by St. Jeanne de Lestonnac. First foundation in the United States in 1926, in Douglas, Arizona.

General Motherhouse: Rome, Italy. Sr. Margarita Maria Pedraz, O.D.N., Supr. Gen.

Universal number in Congregation 1,930.

U.S. Motherhouse (1926): *Company of Mary Provincial House*, 16791 E. Main St. Tustin, CA 92780. Tel: 714-541-3125. Sr. Mary Salud Estrada, O.D.N., Prov. Supr.; Sr. Kathy Schneider, O.D.N., Community Archivist.

Total number in U.S. 53.

Sisters serve and staff Pre-Schools—Kindergartens; Grammar Schools; Religious Instruction Centers; Residences; Parishes & Retreat Centers.

Properties owned: *St. Jeanne de Lestonnac Kindergarten & Day Nursery*, Los Angles, CA; *Divine Providence Kindergarten & Day Nursery*, Los Angeles, CA; *St. Joseph Residence for Women*, Los Angeles, CA; *St. Jeanne De Lestonnac School*, Tustin, CA; *Vina de Lestonnac Ministry Center-Retreat*; *Lestonnac Kindergarten & Day Nursery*, Douglas, AZ.

Represented in the Archdiocese of Los Angeles and the Dioceses of Orange, San Bernardino, and Tucson.

[0710] (C.S.)—THE COMPANY OF THE SAVIOR D

Founded in Spain in 1952. First United States foundation in 1962.

General Motherhouse: Aravaca Madrid-23, Spain. Mother Amelia Lora-Tamayo, Supr. Gen.

U.S. Foundation: 820 Clinton Ave., Bridgeport, CT 06604. Tel: 203-368-1875.

Professed Sisters 62; Novices 3; Postulants 4.

Represented in the Diocese of Bridgeport.

[0720] (M.C.)—CONSOLATA MISSIONARY SISTERS P

Founded in Italy in 1910. First foundation in United States in 1954.

Motherhouse: *Istituto Suore Missionarie della Consolata*, Via Cassia Km. 37, 01036 Nepi, Viterbo, Italy. Mother Gabriella Bono, Supr. Gen.

Total universal number in congregation is approximately 928.

U.S. Headquarters: *Consolata Missionary Sisters*, 6801 Belmont Rd.-P.O. Box 371, Belmont, MI 49306. Tel: 616-361-2072; Fax: 616-361-2049. Sr. Cecilia Clara Zamboni, M.C., Supr.

Total number in community 20.

Sisters serve and staff Elementary and High Schools; Apostolate among Minorities; Catechetical and Pastoral Work.

Represented in the Dioceses of Birmingham and Grand Rapids.

[0725] (M.C-M.)—CORDI-MARIAN MISSIONARY SISTERS CONGREGATION P

Founded in Mexico City in 1921. First United States foundation in 1926.

General Motherhouse: Apdo. Postal #1109, Toluca, Mexico C.P., 50091. Sr. Evangelina Perez, M.C-M., Supr. Gen.

U.S. Provincial House: 11624 FM 471, Apt. 402, San Antonio, TX 78253. Tel: 210-688-3889. Sr. Celestina Castro, M.C-M., Prov. Supr.

Total number in Congregation 122; Total number in U.S. community 38.

Properties Owned: *Cordi-Marian Villa—Retreat Center and Provincial House*, San Antonio, TX; *East St. Louis Catholic Day Care Center and Convent*, East St. Louis, IL.

Ministry in Catechetical Centers; Pastoral Ministry Programs; Elementary Education; Kindergarten and Day Care Centers; Retreat Center; Social Service; Migrant Ministry; Prison Ministry; Vestment and Banner Making.

Represented in the Archdioceses of Kansas City, San Antonio and the Dioceses of Austin and Laredo.

[0730] (Fd.CC.)—CANOSSIAN DAUGHTERS OF CHARITY P
Canossian Sisters

Founded in Verona, Italy in 1808.

General Motherhouse: via della Stazione di Ottavia 70, Rome, Italy 00135.

U.S. Provincial House: *Cristo Rey-Canossian Sisters*, 5625 Isleta Blvd., S.W., Albuquerque, NM 87105. Tel: 505-873-2854. Sr. E. Chaambers, Prov. Supr.

Sisters in U.S. 43.

Ministry in Evangelization; Spirituality Center, Integral Promotion of the Person; Parish Pastoral Ministry; Pastoral care of the sick; Intermediate Care Facility for Handicapped Children; Youth Detention Center.

Represented in the Archdioceses of San Francisco and Santa Fe and the Diocese of Sacramento. Also in Canada and Mexico.

[0740] (D.C.P.B.)—DAUGHTERS OF CHARITY OF THE MOST PRECIOUS BLOOD P

Founded in Pagani, Italy in 1872. First foundation in United States in 1908.

Generalate: Via Vigna Fabbri 45, Rome, Italy. Sr. Ofelia Marzocca, Mother Gen.

U.S. Address: *Daughters of Charity of the Most Precious Blood*, 1482 North Ave., Bridgeport, CT 06604. Tel: 203-334-7000. Sr. Rosaria Carlino, D.C.P.B., Supr.

Total number in community 18.

Represented in the Dioceses of Albany, Bridgeport and Paterson.

[0750] (F.C.S.C.J.)—DAUGHTERS OF THE CHARITY OF THE SACRED HEART OF JESUS P

First founded in France at La Salle de Vihiers in 1823. First founded in the United States at Newport, Vermont in October 1905

Generalate: Montgeron, France.

General Motherhouse: La Salle de Vihiers, France. Sr. Collette Lussier, Supr. Gen.

Mount Sacred Heart Provincial House: *Daughters of the Charity of the Sacred Heart of Jesus* (1949), 226 Grove St. - P.O. Box 642, Littleton, NH 03561-0642; Tel: 603-444-5346; Fax: 603-444-3970; 603-444-5348. Sr. Jeannette Roy, F.C.S.C.J., Prov.; Sr. Lucille Grandpre, F.C.S.C.J., Local Supr.; Sr. Yvette Beloin, F.C.S.C.J., Local Supr.

Total number in province 64.

Sisters serve and staff Grammar Schools and Kindergarten; Catechetical Centers; Spiritual Directors; Pastoral Ministry; Preschools; Foreign Missions.

Represented in the Archdiocese of Boston and the Dioceses of Burlington, Fall River, Lafayette, LA, Manchester, Ogdensburg and Portland (ME).

[0760] (D.C.)—DAUGHTERS OF CHARITY OF ST. VINCENT DE PAUL P

Founded in France in 1633. First foundation in the United States in 1809 by Saint Elizabeth Ann Seton, Emmitsburg, Md.

General Motherhouse: Paris, France. Sr. Juana Elizondo, Supr. Gen.

Emmitsburg Province (Southeast) (1809): *St. Joseph's Provincial House*, Emmitsburg, MD 21727. Tel: 301-447-3121; Fax: 301-447-6038. Sr. Elyse Staab, D.C., Prov.

Legal Title: *Sisters of Charity of St. Joseph's.*

Total number in province 247.

Sisters serve and staff High Schools; Elementary Schools; Medical Clinics; Hospitals; Nursing Homes; Homes for unmarried Mothers; Child Caring Homes; Retreat Center; Dining Facilities for the homeless; Social Service Centers; Catholic Charities; Parish Ministries; Hispanic Ministry.

Represented in the Archdioceses of Baltimore and Washington and in the Dioceses of Arlington, Charleston, Pensacola-Tallahassee, Raleigh, Richmond, Savannah, St. Augustine, St. Petersburg, and Wheeling-Charleston.

West Central Province (1910): *Marillac Provincial House*, 7800 Natural Bridge Rd., St. Louis, MO 63121-4694. Tel: 314-382-2800; Fax: 314-382-8392. Sr. Marie Therese Sedgwick, Prov.; Sr. Genevieve Keusenkothen, Archivist.

Total number in the community 231.

Ministry in the field of Religious and Academic Education at all levels; Seminary Education; Hospitals; Leprosarium; Psychiatric Hospitals; Parish Ministry; Social Service Centers; Schools of Nursing; Day Care Centers; Clinics; Homes for Children and Young Women; Housing for the Homeless; Catholic Charities Offices; Housing; Peace and Justice; Diocesan Offices; Hospice; State Health Care; Home Health Care; Emergency Relief Centers; Spiritual Direction and Retreats.

Sponsors: Clinics—*Centro San Vicente*, El Paso, TX; *Daughters of Charity Services of New Orleans*; *Daughters of Charity Services of San Antonio, Inc.*; *Daughters of Charity Services of San Antonio-El Carmen Div.*, San Antonio, TX; *Daughters of Charity Services of San Antonio*-De Paul Div., San Antonio, TX; *Daughters of Charity Community Services of El Paso (DCCS-EP)*; *Daughters of Charity Health Services of Austin - Seton East*, Austin, TX; *Daughters of Charity Health Services of Austin - Seton South*, Austin, TX. Hospitals—*Seton Medical Center*, Austin, TX; *Seton Northwest*, Austin, TX; *De Paul Center*, Waco, TX; *Providence Health Center*, Waco, TX; *Daughters of Charity Services of Arkansas – DePaul Health Center*, Dumas, AR; *Ascension Health*, St. Louis, MO.

Represented in the Archdioceses of Kansas City in Kansas, New Orleans, St. Louis, San Antonio and the Dioceses of Austin, Amarillo, Baton Rouge, Brownsville, Dallas, El Paso, Kansas City-St. Joseph, Little Rock, San Angelo and Springfield-Cape Girardeau.

East Central Province - Evansville (1969): *Daughters of Charity of St. Vincent de Paul of Indiana, Inc.*, 9400 New Harmony Rd., Evansville, IN 47720; Tel: 812-963-3341; Fax: 812-963-7589. Sr. Catherine Madigan, D.C., Prov. Supr.; Sr. Lois Martin, D.C., Archivist.

Total number in the community 179.

Sponsored Works: Home for Retired Sisters; General Hospitals; Skilled Nursing Facilities; Clinics; Home Health Care; Day Care Centers and Neighborhood Services; Childrens' Residence; Services to Elderly.

Sponsored Organizations: *Daughters of Charity National Health System, Inc., Daughters of Charity Regional Information Services, Inc.* Local Development Corporations. Shared ownership in Health Maintenance Organizations and Preferred Provider Organizations.

Legal Title: *Mater Dei Provincialate, Inc.*

Ministries of Insertion Religious and Academic Education at all levels; Campus Ministry; Parish Ministry; Social Services in parishes; Catholic Charities Office; Prison Ministry; Missionary work in Haiti and with the native Americans; Shelters for homeless; Residences for Elderly.

Represented in the Archdioceses of Chicago, Detroit, Indianapolis, Milwaukee, Mobile and the Dioceses of Belleville, Birmingham, Evansville, Lafayette (IN), Nashville, Jackson, Peoria, Saginaw and Springfield (IL).

Northeast Province (1969): *De Paul Provincial House*, 96 Menands Rd., Albany, NY 12204-1499. Sr. Louise Gallahue, Prov. Supr.; Sr. Margaret Ahl, Archivist.

Total number in the community 214.

Ministry in the field of Academic Education at all levels; Hospital; Specialized Hospitals; Homes for Unmarried Mothers; Child Caring Homes; Day Care Centers; Social Service Centers; Parish Centers.

Represented in the Archdioceses of Boston, New York, Philadelphia and in the Dioceses of Albany, Allentown, Bridgeport, Brooklyn, Buffalo, Greensburg, Metuchen, Ogdensburg, Rochester, Syracuse and Wilmington. Also in Canada.

Province of the West (Los Altos Hills) (1969): *Seton Provincialate*, 26000 Altamont Rd., Los Altos Hills, CA 94022-4317. Tel: 650-941-4490; Fax: 650-949-3874. Sr. Margaret Keaveney, D.C., Prov.

Total number in the community 148.

Properties owned and sponsored: *Seton Medical Center*, Daly City, CA; *Seton Provincialate*, Los Altos Hills, CA; *St. Vincent Medical Center*, Los Angeles, CA; *St. Vincent's Senior Citizen Nutrition Program*, Los Angeles, CA; *St. Francis Medical Center*, Lynwood, CA; *Maryvale*, Rosemead, CA; *Mount St. Joseph-St. Elizabeth*, San Francisco, CA; *O'Connor Hospital*, San Jose, CA; *Villa Siena*, Mountain View, CA; *St. Louise Regional Hospital*, Gilroy, CA; *St. Vincent's*, Santa Barbara, CA; *Robert F. Kennedy Medical Center*, Hawthorne, CA.

Represented in the Archdioceses of Anchorage, Los Angeles, San Francisco and in the Dioceses of Fresno, Gallup, Monterey, Oakland, Phoenix, Salt Lake City, and San Jose.

[0770] (D.C.)—DAUGHTERS OF THE CROSS D

Founded in France in 1640. First foundation in the United States in 1855.

Motherhouse: *Daughters of the Cross Motherhouse,* 411 E. Flournoy-Lucas Rd., Shreveport, LA 71115-3901. Tel: 318-797-0887. Sr. Mary Louise Parisy, Supr. Gen.
Total number in community 6.
Represented in the Diocese of Shreveport.

[0780] (F.C.)—DAUGHTERS OF THE CROSS OF LIEGE P
Founded in Liege, Belgium in 1833. First foundation in the United States in 1958.
Principal House: *St. Bernard Convent,* 165 W. Eaton Ave., Tracy, CA 95376. Sr. M. Eugene Hagan, F.C., Supr.
Total number in community 8.
Represented in the Diocese of Stockton.

[0790] (F.D.C.)—DAUGHTERS OF DIVINE CHARITY P
Founded in Austria on Nov. 21, 1868. First founded in the United States on Oct. 8, 1913, in New York City.
General Motherhouse: Grottaferrata, Rome, Italy. Sr. Nicolina Hendges, Supr. Gen.
St. Joseph Province (1921): *St. Joseph Provincialate,* 205 Major Ave., Staten Island, NY 10305. Tel: 718-720-4377. Sr. Josita DiVita, F.D.C., Prov.; Sr. Helen Bay, F.D.C., 1st Prov. Councilor.
Total number universally 1,488.
Ministry in Education; Nursing; Residences for Women; Working with the Homeless and the Elderly.
Properties owned: *St. Mary's Residence,* New York, NY; *St. Joseph Hill Academy,* Staten Island, NY; *Villa Madonna,* Hackettstown, NJ.
Represented in the Archdioceses of Newark and New York and the Dioceses of Bridgeport, Metuchen, San Bernardino and San Diego.

[0793] (D.D.L.)—DAUGHTERS OF DIVINE LOVE
Founded in Ukpor, Nigeria in 1969. First United States Foundation in 1990.
General House: Fifth Avenue, P.O. Box 546, Enugu, Enugu State, Nigeria. Tel: 042-559071; 042-554450. Rev. Mother Ifechukwu Udorah, D.D.L., Mother Gen.
Total Professed Sisters 653.
U.S. Regional House: 140 North Ave., Highwood, IL 60040. Tel: 847-432-9003; Fax: 847-681-8974. Sr. Maria Uche Chukwu, D.D.L., Reg. Supr.
Professed Sisters in U.S. 45.
Ministry in the field of Administration; Religious and Academic Education at all levels; Special Education; Health Services; Parish and Diocesan Services; Retreat Work; Social Work.
Represented in the Archdioceses of Chicago, and the Dioceses of Brooklyn, Brownsville, Gavelston-Houston, Fargo, and Springfield, IL.

[0794] (F.D.P.)—DAUGHTERS OF DIVINE PROVIDENCE
General Motherhouse: *Daughters of Divine Providence,* Via Matteo Bartoli 255, 00143, Rome, Italy. Mother Damiana DiLauro, F.D.P., Supr. Gen.
U.S. Delegation: *Daughters of Divine Providence,* 3100 Mumphrey Rd., Chalmette, LA 70043. Tel: 504-279-4617; Fax: 504-279-4617. Sr. Piercarla Barone, F.D.P., Local Supr.
Total number in community 6.
Represented in the Archdiocese of New Orleans and the Diocese of Alexandria.

[0795] (F.D.Z.)—DAUGHTERS OF DIVINE ZEAL
Founded in Messina, Italy in 1887 by Blessed Hannibal Maria DiFrancia. First foundation in the United States in 1951.
Generalate: *Figlie Del Divino Zelo,* Circonvallazione Appia 144, 00179, Rome, Italy. Mother M. Diodata Guerrera, F.D.Z., Supr. Gen.
Total universal number in the congregation 1,000.
U.S. Headquarters: *Hannibal House Spiritual Center,* 1526 Hill Rd., Reading, PA 19602; Tel: 610-375-1738 & 375-9072; Fax: 610-375-2188. Sr. Marita A. Olango, F.D.Z., Supr.
Total number in community 6.
Ministry in the field of Religious and Academic Education; Parish and Youth Ministry; Retreat, Vocation, Prayer and Apostolate.
Represented in the Diocese of Allentown.
St. Mary Province (1950): *Provincial Motherhouse and Novitiate,* 39 N. Portage Path, Akron, OH 44303-1183. Tel: 330-867-4960. Sr. Christine Cochenet, Prov. Supr.
Total number in community 22.
Ministry in the field of Education; Home for Working Girls; Home for elderly senior Women and Men.
Properties owned: *Daughters of Divine Charity, Inc., Leonora Hall Convent, Leonora Hall Residence, Francesca Residence.*
Represented in the Archdioceses of Miami, Milwaukee and the Dioceses of Cleveland.

Holy Trinity Province (1972): *Provincial House,* 39315 N. Woodward Ave., Bloomfield Hills, MI 48304. Tel: 248-645-5318. Sr. M. Paschal Grand, Prov. Supr.
Professed Sisters 26.
Ministry in Education; Foster Care Residence; Homes for the Aged.
Represented in the Archdiocese of Detroit and the Diocese of Fort Wayne-South Bend.

[0810] (D.H.M.)—DAUGHTERS OF THE HEART OF MARY P
Founded in France in 1790. First United States foundation in 1851.
Generalate: 39 rue Notre Dame des Champs, 75006, Paris, France.
Provincialate: 1339 Northampton St., Holyoke, MA 01040-1913. Tel: 413-532-7406; Fax: 413-533-4217. Sr. Miriam Najimy, D.H.M., Prov.
Properties owned: *Marian Center & Residence,* Holyoke, MA; *Mary Hill,* St. Paul, MN; *Nardin Academy,* Buffalo, NY; *Heart of Mary Center,* St. Louis, MO; *St. Isaac Jogues Center,* Philadelphia, PA; *Regina Maria Retreat House,* Plattsburgh, NY; *St. Joseph's School for the Deaf,* Bronx, NY; *Ephpheta Center,* Oak Park, IL.
Professed Sisters 92; Novices 3.
Represented in the Archdioceses of Chicago, New York, Philadelphia, St. Louis and St. Paul-Minneapolis and the Dioceses of Buffalo, Ogdensburg, Springfield (MA) and Trenton.

[0820] (D.H.S.)—DAUGHTERS OF THE HOLY SPIRIT P
Founded in France in 1706. First foundation in the U.S. in 1902.
General Motherhouse: *St. Brieuc,* Cotes du Nord, Bretagne, France. Sr. Yvette LeGrand, F.S.E., Supr. Gen.
Provincial House: *Daughters of the Holy Spirit, Inc.,* 72 Church St., Putnam, CT 06260. Tel: 860-928-0891. Sr. Bonnie Morrow, D.H.S., Prov.
Total number in the community 183.
Ministry in the field of Academic Education at all levels; Home for Aged; Home/District Nursing; Health care center for Daughters of the Holy Spirit; and various social and pastoral ministries of service.
Represented in the Archdioceses of Boston, Hartford, Mobile, New York, Philadelphia and in the Dioceses of Birmingham, Bridgeport, Burlington, Fall River, Fresno, Norwich, Ogdensburg, Providence, Richmond, Sacramento, Springfield (MA), Stockton and Worcester.

[0830] (F.J.)—CONGREGATION OF THE DAUGHTERS OF JESUS (LES FILLES DE JESUS) P
Founded in France in 1834. First foundation in the U.S. in 1903.
Motherhouse: Kermaria, 56500, Locmine, France.
Generalate: 11, rue d'Arras, 75005, Paris, France. Sr. Ellen Martin, Supr. Gen.
Total universal number in Congregation 2,138.
Western Province (1902): 9040 84th Ave., Edmonton, Alberta T6C 1E4, Canada. Tel: 403-466-6527. Sr. Irene Magnan, Prov. Supr.
U.S. Address: 4209 3rd Ave. S., Great Falls, MT 59405. Tel: 406-452-7231.
Total number in community 3.
Represented in the Diocese of Great Falls.

[0840] (F.I.)—DAUGHTERS OF JESUS P
Founded in Spain in 1871. First foundation in the U.S. in 1950.
General Motherhouse: Rome, Italy.
U.S. Foundation: 2021 Stuart Ave., Baton Rouge, LA 70808. Tel: 225-344-7131. Sr. Carmen Maria Rodriguez, F.I., Prov.
Professed Sisters 4.
Represented in the Diocese of Baton Rouge.

[0850] (F.M.A.)—DAUGHTERS OF MARY HELP OF CHRISTIANS P
Salesian Sisters of St. John Bosco
Founded in Mornese, Italy, in 1872. First foundation in the U.S. in 1908 at Paterson, New Jersey.
General Motherhouse: Via Ateneo Salesiano, 81, 00139, Rome, Italy. Very Rev. Mother Antonia Colombo, F.M.A., Mother Gen.
Total universal number in Congregation 15,835.
Province of St. Philip, Apostle: *Provincial House,* 655 Belmont Ave., Haledon, NJ 07508-2398. Tel: 973-790-7963. Mother Judith Suprys, F.M.A., Prov.
Legal Title: *Missionary Society of the Salesian Sisters, Inc., Salesian Sisters of Tampa, Inc.*
Properties owned: *Provincial House,* Haledon, NJ; *Mary Help of Christians Academy,* North Haledon, NJ; *Sacred Heart Center,* Newton, NJ; *Villa Madonna School-Salesian Sisters of Tampa, Inc.,* Tampa, FL; *Camp Auxilium Learning Center,* Newton, NJ.
Total number in the community 128.
Ministry in the field of academic and religious Education at all levels; Youth Ministry.
Represented in the Archdioceses of Miami, Newark, New Orleans, New York and the Dioceses of Birmingham, Paterson and St. Petersburg.
Province of Mary Immaculate: *FMA Provincial House,* 6019 Buena Vista, San Antonio, TX 78237. Tel: 210-432-0090; Fax: 210-432-4016. Sr. Phyllis Neves, F.M.A., Prov.
Legal Titles: *Institute of the Daughters of Mary Help of Christians - Salesian Sisters of St. John Bosco,* San Antonio, TX; *Salesian Sisters - Mary Help of Christians Youth Center, Inc.,* Corralitos, CA.
Properties owned: *FMA Provincial House & St. John Bosco School,* San Antonio, TX; *Mary Help of Christians School,* Laredo, TX; *Salesian Sisters School - Salesian Sisters: MHC Youth Center, Inc.,* Corralitos, CA.
Total number in community 109.
Ministry in Education; Youth Ministry and Religious Education.
Represented in the Archdioceses of Los Angeles, New Orleans, San Antonio and San Francisco and the Dioceses of Austin, Laredo, Monterey and Phoenix.

[0860] (D.M.)—DAUGHTERS OF MARY OF THE IMMACULATE CONCEPTION P
Founded in New Britain in 1904.
General Motherhouse: 314 Osgood Ave., New Britain, CT 06053. Tel: 860-225-9406. Mother Mary Mark, Supr. Gen.
Total number in community 62.
Legal Title: *Congregation of the Daughters of Mary of the Immaculate Conception, Inc.*
Ministry in the field of Education; Home for the Aged; Homes for Working Girls and Students; Skilled Care Facilities.
Properties owned: *St. Lucian's Home; Marian Educational Clinic; Monsignor Bojnowski Manor; Mary Immaculate Academy; Motherhouse and Novitiate Complex,* New Britain, CT; *St. Joseph's Home,* NY; *St. Agnes Residence,* NY; *Our Lady's Guild House,* Boston, MA; *Sancta Maria Nursing Facility,* Cambridge, MA.
Represented in the Archdioceses of Boston, Hartford and New York and in the Diocese of Springfield (MA).

[0870] (F.M.I.)—CONGREGATION OF THE DAUGHTERS OF MARY IMMACULATE P
Marianist Sisters
Founded in France in 1816.
Motherhouse: Rome, Italy. Mother M. Blanca Jamar, Supr. Gen.
U.S. Foundation (1949): *Our Lady of the Pillar Convent,* 251 W. Ligustrum Dr., San Antonio, TX 78228. Tel: 210-433-5501; Fax: 210-431-9611. Sr. Evangeline Escobar, Prov. Supr.
Total number in community 19.
Properties owned: *Our Lady of the Pillar Convent,* San Antonio, TX; *Novitiate,* Dayton, OH.
Represented in the Archdioceses of Cincinnati and San Antonio.

[0880] (D.M.J.)—DAUGHTERS OF MARY AND JOSEPH P
Founded in Belgium in 1817. First U.S. Foundation in 1926.
Generalate: Via Garibaldi, 28 00153, Rome, Italy. Sr. Agnes Charles, Supr. Gen.
Novitiate: 5300 Crest Rd., Rancho Palos Verdes, CA 90275. Tel: 310-377-9968; Fax: 310-541-5967. Sr. Pauline Knapp, Formation Dir.
Provincialate: 5300 Crest Rd., Rancho Palos Verdes, CA 90274. Tel: 310-377-9968. Sr. Linda Webb, Prov.
Professed Sisters 70.
Legal Title: *Daughters of Mary and Joseph,* California.
Sisters staff: Grammar & High Schools; Parish Ministry; Health Ministry; Missionary Work; Detention Ministry; Retreat Work.
Represented in the Archdioceses of Los Angeles and San Francisco and in the Dioceses of Orange, San Bernardino and San Diego.

[0890] (D.M.)—DAUGHTERS OF OUR LADY OF MERCY P
Founded in Italy in 1837 by Saint Mary Joseph Rossello. First foundation in the United States in 1919.
Generalate: Via Monte Grappa, No. 7., Savona, Italy. Rev. Mother M. Giovannina Lusso, Supr. Gen.
Provincialate and Novitiate: *Villa Rossello,* 1009 Main Rd., Newfield, NJ 08344. Tel: 856-697-2983. Sr. Grace Marie Scandale, Mother Prov.; Sr. Loretta Marie Stevens, D.M., Community Archivist.

Total number in community 66.
Ministry in the field of Education; Health Services; Day Nursery; Convalescent Hospital; C.C.D. and Parish Work.
Legal Holdings: *Misericordia Convalescent Home*, York, PA; *Holy Child Nursery*, York, PA; *Our Lady of Mercy Academy*, Newfield, NJ.
Represented in the Dioceses of Camden, Harrisburg, Scranton and Springfield (MA).

[0895] (F.M.S.R.)—DAUGHTERS OF OUR LADY OF THE HOLY ROSARY P

Founded in 1946 in Trung Linh, Bui Chu, North Vietnam by Bishop Dominic May Ho Ngoc Can. First foundation in the United States in 1967. Motherhouse in Vietnam. Sr. Mary Cecile Vu thi Thanh, F.M.S.R.
U. S. Provincial Office: *Queen of Peace Convent*, 1492 Moss St., New Orleans, LA 70119-2904. Sr. Mary John Bosco Dinh Thi Kim Thanh, F.M.S.R., Prov. Supr.
Total number in community 46.
Ministry in the field of Education; Health Services; Pastoral Ministry.
Properties Owned: 6 Residences
Represented in the Archdiocese of New Orleans, and the Dioceses of Biloxi and Houma-Thibodeaux.

[0900] (F.D.N.S.C.)—DAUGHTERS OF OUR LADY OF THE SACRED HEART P

Founded in France in 1882.
Motherhouse: Via Casale S. Pio. V, 37, Rome, Italy. Sr. Mary Ringnalda, Supr. Gen.
U.S. Foundation (1955): *St. Francis de Sales Convent*, 424 E. Browning Rd., Bellmawr, NJ 08031. Tel: 856-931-8973; Fax: 856-931-7018.
Professed Sisters in U.S. 14.
Represented in the Archdiocese of Philadelphia and the Dioceses of Camden.

[0910] (Bethl.)—BETHLEMITA, DAUGHTER OF THE SACRED HEART OF JESUS P

Founded in Guatemala in 1861. First foundation in United States in Dallas, Texas.
Motherhouse: Bogota, Colombia, S.A.
U.S. Foundation: *St. Joseph Residence, Inc.*, 330 W. Pembroke St., Dallas, TX 75208. Tel: 214-948-3597. Sr. Adelaide Bocanegra, Admin.
Professed Sisters 7.
Represented in the Diocese of Dallas.

[0920] (D.S.F.)—CONGREGATION OF THE DAUGHTERS OF ST. FRANCIS OF ASSISI P

Founded in Austro, Hungary, 1894. First foundation in United States in 1946.
Motherhouse: *St. Joseph's Convent*, 507 N. Prairie St., Lacon, IL 61540. Tel: 309-246-2175. Sr. M. Vaclava Ballon, D.S.F., Prov. Supr.
Professed Sisters 34.
Legal Title: *Congregation of the Daughters of St. Francis of Assisi, American Province.*
Represented in the Dioceses of Davenport, Peoria and Springfield-Cape Girardeau. Also in Mexico.

[0930] (F.S.J.)—RELIGIOUS DAUGHTERS OF ST. JOSEPH P

Founded in Gerona, Spain in 1875.
General Motherhouse: *General Asensio Cabanillas*, 18, Madrid, 28003, Spain. Mother Carmen Vela, Supr. Gen.
Total universal number in Congregation 880.
Provincial House, Calzada Ermita Istapalapa, Mexico. Sr. Pilar Soto, Prov.
U.S. Foundation: *Santa Marta Hospital*, 319 N. Humphreys Ave., Los Angeles, CA 90022. Sr. Eulalia Yepez, F.S.J., Supr.
Legal Title: *Daughters of St. Joseph of California, Inc.*
Total number in community 8.
Represented in the Archdiocese of Los Angeles.

[0940] (D.S.M.P.)—DAUGHTERS OF ST. MARY OF PROVIDENCE P

Founded in Italy in 1881. First foundation in the U.S. in 1913.
Generalate: Rome, Italy. Mother Giustina Valicenti, D.S.M.P., Supr. Gen.
Novitiate: *Daughters of St. Mary*, 24955 North Highway 12, Lake Zurich, IL 060047. Tel: 847-438-5050.
Provincialate: *Daughters of St. Mary of Providence*, 4200 N. Austin Ave., Chicago, IL 60634. Tel: 773-545-2596. Sr. Bernardine Kauffmann, Prov.
Professed Sisters 100.
Represented in the Archdioceses of Boston, Chicago, Detroit and Philadelphia and the Dioceses of Camden, Gary, Lansing, New Ulm, and Sioux Falls.

[0950] (F.S.P.)—PIOUS SOCIETY DAUGHTERS OF ST. PAUL P

(Missionary Sisters of the Media of Communications)
Founded in Alba, Piedmont, Italy, on June 15, 1915. First founded in the United States on June 28, 1932, in New York.
General Motherhouse: Rome, Italy. Sr. Giovanna Maria Carrara, Supr. Gen.
Total universal number in Congregation 2,607.
Provincial House, Novitiate, Publishing House: 50 St. Paul's Ave., Boston, MA 02130. Tel: 617-522-8911. Sr. Germana Santos, F.S.P., Prov. Supr.; Sr. M. Sophie Stewart, F.S.P., Local Supr.
Legal Title: *Daughters of St. Paul, Inc.*
Properties owned: *St. Paul Book and Media Centers*, found in 18 locations throughout the States (see list of (Arch)Dioceses where represented); *Provincialate*, Boston, MA; *St. Thecla Retreat House*, Billerica, MA.
Total number in community 147
Represented in the Archdioceses of Boston, Chicago, Los Angeles, Miami, New Orleans, New York, Philadelphia, St. Louis, San Antonio, San Francisco and the Dioceses of Arlington, Charleston, Cleveland, Honolulu, Memphis, Metuchen and San Diego. Also in Canada.

[0960] (D.W.)—DAUGHTERS OF WISDOM P

Founded in France in 1703. First foundation in the United States in 1904.
General Motherhouse: St. Laurent-sur-Sevre, Vendee, France. Superior General Headquarters located in Rome, Italy.
U.S. Province (1949): *Provincial House*, 385 Ocean Ave., Islip, NY 11751-4600. Tel: 631-277-2660; Fax: 631-277-3274. Sr. Evelyn Eckhardt, D.W., Prov.
Professed Sisters 140.
Ministry in all levels of Education; Retreat House; Hospital & Health Services; Orphanage; Social Work; Pediatrics Clinic.
Properties owned: *Wisdom House Center for Spirituality*, Litchfield, CT; *Our Lady of Perpetual Help Convent* (Rest Home for Sisters), Sound Beach, NY; *Provincial House*, Islip, NY; *Our Lady of Wisdom Convent*, St. Agatha, ME.
Represented in the Archdioceses of Hartford, Mobile, Washington and the Dioceses of Arlington, Brooklyn, Burlington, Charleston, Portland (ME), Raleigh, Richmond, Rockville Centre, St. Augustine, St. Petersburg and Wheeling-Charleston.

[0965] (D.L.J.C.)—DISCIPLES OF THE LORD JESUS CHRIST D

Founded in the United States in 1972.
Motherhouse: P.O. Box 17, Channing, TX 79018. Tel: 806-534-2312; Fax: 806-534-2223. Mother Bernadette Beamsley, Supr. Gen.
Total number in community 28.
Legal Holdings and Titles: *Prayertown Emmanuel Retreat House*, Channing, TX; *House of Prayer*, Alexandria, LA.
Ministry in Retreat Work and Evangelization.
Represented in the Dioceses of Alexandria and Amarillo. Also in Mexico.

[0970] (R.D.C.)—SISTERS OF THE DIVINE COMPASSION D

Founded in the United States in 1886.
General Motherhouse: *Good Counsel Convent*, 52 N. Broadway, White Plains, NY 10603. Tel: 914-949-2950; Fax: 914-949-5169. Sr. Alice Feeley, R.D.C., Pres.
Total number in community 113.
Legal Holdings and Titles: *Academy of Our Lady of Good Counsel High School and Elementary School*, White Plains, NY; *Preston High School*, New York, NY; *Divine Compassion Center for Spiritual Renewal*, NY; *Migrant Ministry*, Goshen, NY; *Residence*, Hampton Bays, NY; *RDC Center for Counselling and Human Development.*
Ministry in Preschool, Elementary, Secondary, College and University Education; Religious Education; Educational Consultation; Adult Education; Special Education; Pastoral Ministry; Retreat Work and Spiritual Direction; Counseling; Social Services; Migrant Ministry; Health Services; Administration and Business Services.
Represented in the Archdiocese of New York.

[0980] (P.D.D.M.)—PIOUS DISCIPLES OF THE DIVINE MASTER P

Founded in 1924. First foundation in the United States in 1948.
General Motherhouse: Rome, Italy. Mother Mary Paola Mancini, Supr. Gen.
Universal number in Congregation 1,400
U.S. Headquarters: 60 Sunset Ave., Staten Island, NY 10314. Tel: 718-494-8597; Fax: 718-494-2123. Sr. M. Josephine Fallon, P.D.D.M., Reg. Supr.
Total number in region 47.
Ministry is a Three Dimensional Mission: Eucharistic, Priestly, Liturgical.
Represented in the Archdioceses of Boston, Los Angeles, and New York and the Dioceses of Fresno and San Jose.

[0990] (C.D.P.)—SISTERS OF DIVINE PROVIDENCE P

Founded in Germany in 1851. First foundation in United States in 1876.
General Motherhouse: *Mother of Providence Convent*, 12 Christopher St., Wakefield, RI 02879. Tel: 401-782-1785; Fax: 401-782-6967. Sr. Myra Rodgers, C.D.P., Gen. Supr.
St. Peter's Province (1876): *Provincial House*, 9000 Babcock Blvd., Allison Park, PA 15101. Tel: 412-931-5241; Fax: 412-635-5416. Sr. Mary Ellen Rufft, Prov.
Total number in community 253.
Properties owned and sponsored: *La Roche College*, Pittsburgh, PA; *Providence Heights Alpha*, Allison Park, PA; *Transfiguration House of Prayer*, Butler, PA; *Kearns Spirituality Center*, Allison Park, PA; *Providence Connections, Inc.*; *Providence Child Care Center - South*, Castle Shannon, PA; *Providence Child Care Center, North*, Pittsburgh, PA; *Providence Family Support Center*, Pittsburgh, PA; *Amelia House - Safe House*, Clarion, PA.
Ministry in the fields of Education; Social Services; Pastoral Ministry; and Health Care Services.
Represented in the Archdioceses of Baltimore, Chicago, Denver, Detroit, Kansas City in Kansas, New York, Philadelphia, Santa Fe and the Dioceses of Altoona-Johnstown, Bismarck, Charlotte, Cleveland, Columbus, Crookston, Davenport, Erie, Greensburg, Orlando, Phoenix, Pittsburgh, Raleigh, Wheeling-Charleston, Yakima and Youngstown. Also in Puerto Rico, and the Dominican Republic.
St. Louis Province (1930): *Provincial Center - Sisters of Divine Providence*, 3415 Bridgeland Dr., Bridgeton, MO 63044. Tel: 314-209-9181; Fax: 314-209-9207. Sr. Janet Folkl, C.D.P., Prov. Dir.
Total number in community 52.
Properties owned and sponsored: *Room at the Inn*, St. Louis, MO; *La Posada Providencia*, San Benito, TX; *Sisters of Divine Providence of Missouri; St. Elizabeth Medical Center*, Granite City, IL; *St. Elizabeth Health Foundation*, Granite City, IL; *Providence Ministry Corporation*, Bridgeton, MO; *Providence Charitable Trust*, Bridgeton, MO.
Ministry in the fields of Education; Health Services; Parish Ministry; Social Work; Services to Refugees and Homeless People.
Represented in the Archdioceses of Chicago, St. Louis and the Dioceses of Brownsville, Jefferson City, La Crosse, Nashville, Springfield-Cape Girardeau, and Springfield (IL).
Our Lady of Divine Providence Province (1957): 363 Bishops Hwy., Kingston, MA 02364. Tel: 781-585-1745. Sr. Claudia Ward, C.D.P., Prov. Supr.
Total number in the community 45.
Sisters minister in the field of Education at all levels; Hospital and other Health Services; Parish Ministries; Diocesan Administration; Elderly Care; Education for Mentally Handicapped; Alcohol Rehabilitation Ministry.
Properties owned: *Provincial Residence; Sacred Heart Junior-Senior High School; Sacred Heart Elementary and Pre-primary School; Visitation Camp Mishannock*, Kingston, MA.
Represented in the Archdiocese of Boston and the Dioceses of Jackson and Richmond.

[1000] (C.D.P.)—CONGREGATION OF DIVINE PROVIDENCE, MELBOURNE, KENTUCKY P

Founded in France in 1762. First foundation in the United States in 1889.
General Motherhouse: *St. Jean de Bassel*, 57930 Fenetrange, France. Sr. Marie Therese Seyler, Supr. Gen.
American Provincial House (1889): *St. Anne Convent*, Melbourne, KY 41059. Tel: 606-441-0679. Sr. Lynn Stenken, C.D.P., Prov. Supr.; Sr. Mary Joan Dohmen, C.D.P., Archivist.
Total number in community 170.
Ministry in the field of Academic Education at all levels; Montessori Schools; Home for Working Women; Retreat Center; Religious Education & Pastory Ministry; Health & Social Services.
Represented in the Archdioceses of Cincinnati, Louisville, New York and Washington and the Dioceses of Charleston, Covington, Duluth, Lafayette in Indiana, Lexington, and Toledo. Also in West Africa.

[1010] (C.D.P.)—CONGREGATION OF DIVINE PROVIDENCE, SAN ANTONIO, TEXAS P

Founded in France in 1762. First Foundation in the United States in 1866.

The Generalate: P.O. Box 197, 18811 Scenic Loop Rd., Helotes, TX 78023. Tel: 210-695-8721; Fax: 210-695-6033. Sr. Antoinette Billeaud, Supr. Gen. Councilors: Sr. Diane Langford; Sr. Mary Christine Morkovsky; Sr. Patrice Sullivan; Sr. Catherine Parent; Sr. Margaret Riche, Archivist; Sr. Antoinette Keiser, Treas.
Legal Titles & Holdings: *Congregation of Divine Providence, Inc.; Providence Trust,* Helotes, TX.
Novitiate and Formation: *Formation / Vocation Office,* 515 S.W. 24th St., San Antonio, TX 78207-4600. Tel: 210-434-1866.
Total number in community 292.
Properties owned: *The Generalate,* Helotes, TX; *Moye Center*, Castroville, TX; *Our Lady of the Lake Retirement Center*, San Antonio, TX.
Ministry in all levels of Education; Catechetical Centers; Hospitals, Clinics; Diocesan Offices; Retreat Houses; Spiritual Direction-Counseling; Pastoral; Social Work; Chaplaincies in Public Institutions; Home-Health Care; Administration.
Represented in the Archdioceses of Chicago, Denver, Los Angeles, Milwaukee, New Orleans, Oklahoma City, St. Louis, San Antonio, San Francisco, Seattle, Washington and in the Dioceses of Alexandria, Austin, Baton Rouge, Brownsville, Colorado Springs, Corpus Christi, Dallas, El Paso, Fort Wayne-South Bend, Fort Worth, Fresno, Galveston-Houston, Lafayette (LA), Lake Charles, Raleigh, St. Petersburg, San Angelo, Springfield-Cape Giradeau, Tucson, Tulsa and Victoria. Also in Ghana, and Mexico.

[1020] (S.D.R.)—SISTERS OF THE DIVINE REDEEMER P

Founded in 1849 at Niederbronn, France. First founded in the United States on Oct. 6, 1912 at McKeesport, Pennsylvania.
Generalate: Rome, Italy. Sr. M. Julia Zarembova, Supr. Gen.
American Province (1922): *Divine Redeemer Motherhouse,* 999 Rock Run Rd., Elizabeth, PA 15037. Tel: 412-751-8600; Fax: 412-751-0355. Sr. M. Monica Kosztolnyik, Prov. Supr.; Sr. Bernard Szeman, Archivist.
Total number in province 52.
Legal Titles and Holdings: *Sisters of the Divine Redeemer Charitable Trust; Divine Redeemer Health Care Ministries Corp.,* Elizabeth, PA.
Sisters serve and staff Elementary School; Personal Care Home; CCD Centers; Parish Ministry; Nursing Home.
Represented in the Archdiocese of Philadelphia and the Diocese of Pittsburgh.

[1030] (S.D.S.)—SISTERS OF THE DIVINE SAVIOR P

Founded in Tivoli, Italy, in 1888. First foundation in the United States in 1895.
General Motherhouse: Rome, Italy, Viale Mura Gianicolensi 67. Sr. Jean Schafer, Supr. Gen.
North American Province: *Sisters of the Divine Savior,* 4311 N. 100 St., Milwaukee, WI 53222-1393. Tel: 414-466-0810; Fax: 414-466-4335. Sr. Sheila Novak, S.D.S., Prov. Supr.; Sr. Aquin Gilles, S.D.S., Archivist.
Total number in U.S. Community 125.
Ministry in Novitiate; all levels of Education; Pastoral and Social Services; Health Care; and Homes for the Aged.
Properties owned or sponsored: *St. Anne's Home for the Elderly; St. Mary's Nursing Home; Divine Savior Holy Angels High School,* Milwaukee, WI; *Divine Savior Hospital and Nursing Home*, Portage, WI; *Divine Savior Holy Angels High School Endowment Foundation, Inc.,* Milwaukee, WI; *St. Mary's Convent*, St. Nazianz, WI.
Represented in the Archdioceses of Atlanta, Baltimore, Chicago, Milwaukee and the Dioceses of Birmingham, Green Bay, Jackson, La Crosse, Madison, Phoenix, Rapid City, Sioux Falls and Tucson.

[1040] (C.D.S.)—CONGREGATION OF THE DIVINE SPIRIT D

First foundation in Erie, Pennsylvania in 1956.
Motherhouse: 409 W. Sixth St., Erie, PA 16507. Tel: 814-455-3590. Mother Patricia O'Connor, Supr. Gen.
Membership 40.
Sisters serve and staff Parochial Schools 1; CCD Activities 1; Home for Aged 1; Social Work.
Represented in the Dioceses of Erie and Youngstown.

[1050] (O.P.)—DOMINICAN CONTEMPLATIVE NUNS P
(The Nuns of the Order of Preachers)

Founded in France in 1206. First foundation in the United States in 1880. Monastic contemplative branch of the Order of Preachers. Papal cloister
Monastery of St. Dominic: 375 13th Ave., Newark, NJ 07103. Tel: 973-622-6622. Sr. Mary Joseph, O.P., Prioress.
Total number in community 15.
Nuns of the Order of Preachers O.P.: *Corpus Christi Monastery,* 1230 Lafayette Ave., Bronx, NY 10474. 718-328-6996; Fax: 718-328-1974. Sr. Maria Pia, O.P., Prioress.
Total number in community 18.
Monastery of the Blessed Sacrament: *Nuns of the Order of Preachers,* 29575 Middlebelt, Farmington Hills, MI 48334-2311. Tel: 248-626-8321/8253; Fax: 248-626-8724. Sr. Mary Rose Figura, O.P., Prioress.
Dominicans (Contemplative, Cloistered) Perpetual Adoration.
Cloistered Professed Nuns 32; Extern Professed Sisters 2; Extern Novices 1.
Monastery of the Angels: *Cloistered Dominican Nuns of Perpetual Adoration,* 1977 Carmen Ave., Los Angeles, CA 90068. Tel: 323-466-2186. Sr. Mary Raymond, O.P., Prioress.
Sisters 23.
Legal Title: *The Monastery of the Angels.*
Daughter Houses:
Monastery of the Angels: Karachi, Pakistan. Mother Mary Augustine, O.P., Prioress.
Sisters 13.
Queen of Angels Monastery: Bocaue, Bulacan, Philippines. Sr. Mary of Jesus, O.P., Prioress.
Sisters 20.
Corpus Christi Monastery: 215 Oak Grove Ave., Menlo Park, CA 94025. Tel: 650-322-1801; Fax: 650-322-6816. Sr. Mary of the Holy Family, O.P., Prioress.
Cloistered Total number in community 21.
Dominican Nuns O.P.: *Monastery of the Mother of God,* 1430 Riverdale St., West Springfield, MA 01089-4698. Tel: 413-736-3639; Fax: 413-736-0850. Sr. Mary St. John, O.P., Prioress.
Total number in community 23.
Dominican Contemplative Nuns - O.P.: *Monastery of Our Lady of the Rosary,* 335 Doat St., Buffalo, NY 14211-2199. Tel: 716-892-0066; Fax: 716-897-1566. Mother Rose of St. Mary, O.P., Prioress.
Legal Title: *Dominican Nuns of the Perpetual Rosary.*
Professed 30; Junior Professed 2; Novices 4; Postulants 6.
Monastery of Our Lady of Grace: North Guilford, CT 06437-1099. Tel: 203-457-0599. Sr. Lee, O.P., Prioress.
Legal Title: *Dominican Nuns of North Guilford, CT Inc.*
Total number in community 43.
Monastery of the Infant Jesus: *Dominican Contemplative Nuns O.P.,* 1501 Lotus Ln., Lufkin, TX 75904. Tel: 936-634-4233; Fax: 936-634-2156. Sr. Mary John, O.P., Prioress.
Professed 20; Novices 3.
Monastery of Our Lady of the Rosary (Rosary Shrine): Morris Ave. & Springfield Ave., Summit, NJ 07901. Tel: 908-273-1228. Sr. Mary Joseph Fox, O.P., Vicaress.
Professed Choir Sisters 18.
Nuns of the Order of Preachers O.P.: *Monastery of Mary the Queen,* 1310 W. Church St., Elmira, NY 14905. Tel: 607-734-9506; Fax: 607-734-1452. Sr. Mary of the Sacred Heart, O.P., Prioress.
Total number in community 14
Monastery of the Dominican Nuns of the Perpetual Rosary (Cloistered): 14th St. & West St., Union City, NJ 07087. Tel: 201-866-7004. Mother Mary Clare, O.P., Prioress.
Professed Sisters 8; Aspirants 2.
Monastery of the Perpetual Rosary: 1500 Haddon Ave., Camden, NJ 08103. Mother M. Immaculate Heart, O.P., Prioress.
Professed Nuns 7.
St. Dominic's Monastery (Contemplative): 4901 16th St. N.W., Washington, DC 20011-3839. Sr. Mary Paul, O.P., Prioress.
Nuns 11.
The Dominican Nuns of the Perpetual Rosary (Cloistered-Contemplative): *Monastery of the Immaculate Heart of Mary,* 1834 Lititz Pike, Lancaster, PA 17601-6585. Tel: 717-569-2104; Fax: 717-569-1598. Mother Mary Veronica, O.P., Prioress.
Solemnly Professed 12; Postulants 1.
Dominican Monastery of the Perpetual Rosary: 802 Court St., Syracuse, NY 13208. Tel: 315-471-6762. Sr. Mary Augustine, O.P., Prioress, Solemn Vows, Papal enclosure.
Total number in community 11.
Dominican Monastery of St. Jude: P.O. Box 170, Marbury, AL 36051. Tel: 205-755-1322. Dominican Nuns of Perpetual Rosary and Adoration; Mother Mary Aimee of the Holy Spirit, O.P., Prioress.
Professed Nuns 7.

[1060] (O.P.)—DOMINICAN CONTEMPLATIVE SISTERS D
(Cloistered Contemplative)

Founded in Calais, France in 1880.
Monastery of the Dominican Sisters of the Perpetual Rosary (Cloistered): 217 N. 68th St., Milwaukee, WI 53213. Tel: 414-258-0579. Mother Miriam Leonard, O.P., Prioress.
Professed Sisters 13.

[1070] (O.P.)—DOMINICAN SISTERS

There are thirty Congregations of the Dominican Sisters of the Third Order of St. Dominic in the United States. The list of General Motherhouses follows in the order of seniority. If the Congregation is known under a more familiar name, that name is given under the name of the Congregation.

[1070-01] CONGREGATION OF ST. CATHARINE OF SIENA (1822) P

The first American Foundation of the Dominican Sisters in the United States founded in Kentucky in 1822.
General Motherhouse: *Congregational Offices of St. Catharine of Siena,* 2645 Bardstown Rd., St. Catharine, KY 40061. Tel: 606-336-9303; Fax: 606-336-9306. Sr. Joan Scanlon, O.P., Pres.; Sr. Louise Quinlan, O.P., Archivist.
Legal Title: *The Literary Society of Saint Catharine of Siena.*
Total number in community 262
Sisters serve and staff Colleges and Universities; High Schools; Elementary Schools; Foreign Missions; Health Care-Facilities; Diocesan Offices; Pastoral Associates-Assistants; Parish Ministry; Chaplain-Pastoral Care; Directors Religious Education, and Human Services.
Properties owned: *Rosary Manor,* Watertown, MA; *Dominican Sisters,* Plainville, MA; *St. Mel Independent School,* Gloucester, MA; *Sansbury Memorial Infirmary; St. Catharine Motherhouse; St. Catharine College,* St. Catharine, KY; *St. Agnes Academy-St. Dominic School,* Memphis, TN.
Represented in the Archdioceses of Boston, Chicago, Louisville, New York, Omaha, and the Dioceses of Brooklyn, Brownsville, Fort Wayne-South Bend, Grand Island, Jackson, Joliet, Lincoln, Lubbock, Memphis, Rockford, and Saginaw. Also in Vietnam.

[1070-02] DOMINICAN SISTERS, ST. MARY OF THE SPRINGS (1830) P

General Motherhouse: *Dominican Sisters - St. Mary of the Springs,* 2320 Airport Dr., Columbus, OH 43219-2098. Tel: 614-252-2137; Fax: 614-252-7435. Sr. Mary Faith Geelan, O.P., Prioress.
Legal Title: *Dominican Sisters, St. Mary of the Springs,* Columbus, Ohio.
Total number in community 315.
Properties owned and sponsored: *Dominican Academy,* New York, NY; *Ohio Dominican College,* Columbus, OH; *Albertus Magnus College,* New Haven, CT; *Mohun Health Care Center,* Columbus, OH.
Ministry in Diocesan Offices; the field of Academic Education at all levels; Religious Education; Adult Education Programs; Congregational Infirmary; Art and Ecological/Environment; Hospitals; Home Health Care Agencies; Care of the Elderly; Parish Ministry; Pastoral Care; Justice and Peace Ministry; Family Care; Liturgy Preaching and Spirituality Programs; Research Programs; Missionaries; Counseling and Canon Law Ministry; Campus Ministry; Social Work.
Represented in the Archdioceses of Baltimore, Cincinnati, Denver, Detroit, Hartford, New Orleans, New York, Santa Fe, Seattle, Washington and the Dioceses of Brooklyn, Bridgeport, Columbus, Fort Wayne-South Bend, Gary, Green Bay, Pittsburgh, Steubenville, St. Petersburg, Venice and Wheeling-Charleston. Also in Peru, Italy and Honduras.

[1070-03] SINSINAWA DOMINICAN CONGREGATION OF THE MOST HOLY ROSARY (1847) P

Generalate: Sinsinawa, WI 53824-9700. Tel: 608-748-4411. Sr. Antoinette Harris, O.P., Prioress of the Congregation.
Interdependent Provinces (1987):
Eastern Province, 7200 W. Division St., River Forest, IL 60305. Tel: 708-366-0282. Sr. Mary Ellen Green, O.P., Prov.
Southern Province, Casa San Jose, 360 Travino Ave., St. Augustine, FL 32086-7369. Tel: 904-797-7011. Sr. Christa Cunningham, O.P., Prov.
Western Province, 3916 N. Farwell Ave., Milwaukee, WI 53211. Tel: 414-332-1997. Sr. Mary Ann Nelson, O.P., Prov.; Sr. Marjorie Buttner, O.P., Archivist.
Total number in community 829.
Novitiate: Overland, MO. Tel: 314-423-7328.
Properties owned or Institutions sponsored: *Sinsinawa Dominicans, Inc.; Dominican University,* River Forest, IL; *Bethlehem Academy,* Faribault, MN; *Dominican High School,* Whitefish Bay, WI; *Queen of Peace High School,* Burbank, IL; *Trinity High School,* River Forest, IL; *Dominican Motherhouse,* Sinsinawa, WI;

St. Dominic Villa, Sinsinawa, IA; *Camp We-Ha-Kee,* Winter, WI; *The Bridge,* Denmark, WI; *Edgewood Campus School; Edgewood High School; Edgewood College,* Madison, WI.

Ministry in a variety of cultures in Preaching & Evangelization; Elementary, Secondary and Higher Education; Medical, Legal and Social Services; Adult and Religious Education; Diocesan and Parish Administration, Spiritual Direction and Counseling; Rural, Migrant and Native American Services; Writing Research.

Represented in the Archdioceses of Anchorage, Atlanta, Boston, Chicago, Denver, Dubuque, Indianapolis, Los Angeles, Miami, Milwaukee, Mobile, New Orleans, New York, Omaha, Portland (OR), St. Louis, St. Paul-Minneapolis, San Antonio, San Francisco, Santa Fe, Seattle, Washington and the Dioceses of Altoona-Johnstown, Austin, Baker, Birmingham, Boise, Brownsville, Camden, Charleston, Charlotte, Cheyenne, Colorado Springs, Columbus, Crookston, Dallas, Des Moines, Fairbanks, Fort Wayne-South Bend, Gallup, Gaylord, Grand Rapids, Great Falls-Billings, Green Bay, Helena, Honolulu, Jackson, Joliet, Juneau, Kansas City-St. Joseph, La Crosse, Lexington, Madison, Memphis, Monterey, Nashville, Oakland, Ogdensburg, Orange, Orlando, Owensboro, Palm Beach, Pensacola-Tallahassee, Peoria, Phoenix, Rapid City, Rockford, Sacramento, Saginaw, San Angelo, San Diego, San Jose, St. Augustine, St. Cloud, St. Petersburg, Santa Rosa, Spokane, Superior, Tucson, Tulsa, Winona, and Venice. Also in Bolivia, Guatemala, Switzerland, and Trinidad.

[1070-04] CONGREGATION OF THE MOST HOLY NAME (1850) P

Generalate: *Dominican Sisters of San Rafael,* 1520 Grand Ave., San Rafael, CA 94901. Tel: 415-453-8303; Fax: 415-453-8367. Sr. Patricia Simpson, O.P., Prioress Gen.

Total number in community 150.

Legal Holdings and Titles: *Justin Siena High School,* Napa, CA; *San Domenico School,* San Anselmo, CA; *Santa Sabina Retreat Center,* San Rafael, CA; *St. Rose Academy,* San Francisco, CA; *St. Joseph's Regional Health System; St. Joseph's Housing Corporation,* Stockton, CA; *St. Mary's Health Network; Sisters of St. Dominic, Congregation of the Most Holy Name,* San Rafael, CA; *Mission Holding Corporation,* San Rafael, CA.

Represented in the Archdioceses of Los Angeles, San Francisco and in the Dioceses of Charleston, Monterey, Oakland, Reno, Sacramento, San Jose, Santa Rosa and Stockton. And also in Canada and Mexico.

[1070-05] CONGREGATION OF THE HOLY CROSS (1853) D

General Motherhouse: *Queen of the Rosary Motherhouse,* Albany Ave., Amityville, NY 11701. Tel: 631-842-6000; Fax: 631-842-0240. Sr. Mary Hughes, O.P., Prioress; Sr. Margaret Clines, O.P., Archivist.

Total number in community 703.

Sisters are engaged in the ministry of Education at all levels; Catechetical Schools; Handicapped, Adult and Continuing Education; Hospitals; Homes for the Aged; Residence for Senior Citizens; Spiritual Life Centers; Chaplaincy; Advocacy; Communications; Social Service Institutions; Shelters; Pastoral Services; Prison ministry; Retreats; Health Services; ministry to AIDS Victims; Environmental Education Ministry.

Represented in the Archdioceses of Baltimore, Hartford, Newark, New York, St. Louis, and in Dioceses of Albany, Brooklyn, Kalamazoo, Nashville, Paterson, Providence, Rochester, Rockville Centre, St. Augustine, and Trenton. Also in Puerto Rico, and Colombia.

[1070-07] CONGREGATION OF ST. CECILIA (1860) P

General Motherhouse: *St. Cecilia Convent,* 801 Dominican Dr., Nashville, TN 37228-1909. Tel: 615-256-5486; Fax: 615-726-1333. Mother Rose Marie Masserano, O.P., Prioress Gen.; Sr. Marian Sartain, O.P., Archivist.

Professed sisters in community 152; Novices 9; Postulants 20.

Ministry in the field of Academic Education at all levels.

Legal Holdings and Titles: *Aquinas College,* Nashville, TN.

Represented in the Archdioceses of Baltimore, Chicago, Cincinnati, Denver, Washington and the Dioceses of Arlington, Birmingham, Knoxville, Memphis, Nashville and Richmond.

[1070-08] CONGREGATION OF ST. MARY (1860) P

General Motherhouse: *Dominican Sisters,* 7300 St. Charles Ave., New Orleans, LA 70118. Tel: 504-861-8183; Fax: 504-861-8184. Sr. Mary Jordan Langenhennig, O.P., Prioress.

Total number in community 65.

Ministry in Education and Social Apostolates.

Legal Holdings: *St. Mary's Dominican High School,* New Orleans, LA; *Dominican Conference Center,* New Orleans, LA; *Rosaryville Retreat Center,* Ponchatoula, LA.

Represented in the Archdiocese of New Orleans, Dioceses of Baton Rouge and Houma-Thibodeaux.

[1070-09] CONGREGATION OF ST. CATHERINE OF SIENA (1862) P

General Motherhouse: *Convent of St. Catherine,* Siena Center, 5635 Erie St., Racine, WI 53402-1900. Tel: 262-639-4100; Fax: 262-639-9702. Sr. Jean Ackerman, O.P., Pres.; Sr. Diane Kenel, Archivist.

Total number in community 235.

Sisters minister in the areas of Elementary, Secondary, Higher and Music-Cultural Education; Adult Education; Religious Education; Administration; Parish and Pastoral Ministry; Prison Ministry; Social Justice; Campus Ministry; Social Services, Hospital and Health Services; Writing-Research; Hospital Chaplains; Diocesan Services; Retreats-Prayer Programs; Community Services.

Legal Holdings and Titles: *Sisters of St. Dominic,* Racine, WI; *Dominican College of Racine, Inc.,* Racine, WI; *St. Catherine's High School of Racine, Inc.,* Racine, WI; *Racine Dominican Ministries, Inc.,* Racine, WI; *St. Catherine's Infirmary, Inc.,* Racine, WI.

Properties sponsored by the Franciscan Sisters, Daughters of the Sacred Hearts of Jesus and Mary, Wheaton, IL and the Sisters of St. Dominic, Racine, WI; Catherine Marian Housing, Inc.; Villa St. Anna, Inc., Racine, WI.

Represented in the Archdioceses of Chicago, Detroit, Indianapolis, Milwaukee, Newark, New York, St. Louis, Santa Fe, and in the Dioceses of Brownsville, Gallup, Jackson, Green Bay, La Crosse, Las Cruces, Las Vegas, Lansing, Marquette, Nashville, Rapid City, Superior, Toledo and Winona.

[1070-10] DOMINICAN SISTERS OF SPRINGFIELD IN ILLINOIS (1873) P

General Motherhouse: *Sacred Heart Convent,* 1237 W. Monroe St., Springfield, IL 62704-1680. Tel: 217-787-0481; Fax: 217-787-8169. Sr. Mary Jean Traeger, O.P., Prioress Gen.

Total number in community 314.

Ministry in elementary, secondary schools and college religious & academic education; daycare and learning center; hospices, hospitals, nursing homes, congregations' infirmary, and retirement centers; retreat & renewal centers; administrative positions in parishes and diocesan offices; parish liturgist/musician & pastoral associates; prison ministry; social services; and foreign missions.

Legal Holdings or Titles: *Dominican Sisters of Springfield, Illinois, Inc.; Dominican Sisters of Springfield in Illinois Charitable Trust,* Springfield, IL; *Benincasa-Dominican Renewal Center,* Riverton, IL; *Marian Catholic High School,* Chicago Heights, IL; *Rosary High School,* Aurora, IL; *Sacred Heart-Griffin High School,* Springfield, IL; *St. Dominic-Jackson Memorial Hospital,* Jackson, MS.

Represented in the Archdioceses of Chicago and St. Paul-Minneapolis and the Dioceses of Baton Rouge, Belleville, Duluth, Great Falls-Billings, Little Rock, Jackson, Joliet, Peoria, Rockford, Springfield (IL) and Toledo. Also in Peru.

[1070-11] CONGREGATION OF OUR LADY OF THE ROSARY (1876) D

General Motherhouse and Novitiate: *Dominican Convent of Our Lady of the Rosary,* Sparkill, NY 10976. Tel: 914-359-6400. Sr. Kathleen Kane, O.P., Pres.

Legal Title: *Dominican Congregation of Our Lady of the Rosary.*

Total number in community 455.

Ministry in High Schools and Elementary Schools; Adult Education/Literacy; Parishes; Pastoral; Colleges; House of Prayer; Housing and Community Centers; Foreign Missions; Substance Abuse Recovery.

Properties Sponsored: *Aquinas High School,* New York, NY; *Albertus Magnus High School,* Bardonia, NY; *Thorpe Family Residence,* Bronx, NY.

Represented in the Archdioceses of Chicago, New York, Newark, St. Louis and the Dioceses of Belleville, Bridgeport, Brooklyn, Charleston, Great Falls-Billings, Helena, Jefferson City, Metuchen, Oakland, Phoenix, Rockville Centre, Rockford, San Diego, St. Petersburg, Scranton, Trenton and Wilmington.

[1070-12] CONGREGATION OF THE QUEEN OF THE HOLY ROSARY (1876) P

General Motherhouse: *Dominican Convent,* P.O. Box 3908, Mission San Jose, CA 94539. Tel: 510-657-2468; Fax: 510-657-1734. Sr. Rose Marie Hennessy, Prioress Gen.; Sr. M. Evangela Balde, Community Archivist.

Legal Title: *Dominican Sisters of Mission San Jose, a Corporation; Queen of the Holy Rosary College,* a Corporation, Mission San Jose, CA; *St. Catherine's Military School,* a Corporation, Anaheim, CA; *Immaculate Conception Academy,* a Corporation, San Francisco, CA; *Flintridge Sacred Heart Academy,* a Corporation, La Canada-Flintridge, CA; *Pia Backes Support Trust,* Fremont, CA.

Total number in community 297.

Ministry in Parishes; Colleges; High Schools and Elementary Schools; Kindergarten and Music School.

Represented in the Archdioceses of Los Angeles, Portland (OR) and San Francisco and the Dioceses of Oakland, Orange, and Tucson. Also in Germany and Mexico.

[1070-13] CONGREGATION OF THE MOST HOLY ROSARY (1892) P

General Motherhouse: 1257 Siena Heights Dr., Adrian, MI 49221. Tel: 517-266-3400; Fax: 517-266-3545. Sr. Janet Capone, O.P., Prioress.

Mission Chapters (1982):

Florida Mission Chapter, 810 N. Olive Ave., West Palm Beach, FL 33401. Tel: 561-832-6521. Sr. Mary Ann Caulfield, O.P., Chapter Prioress.

Great Lakes Mission Chapter, 9400 Courville, Detroit, MI 48224. Tel: 313-882-8484. Sr. Joan Lawrence Sustersic, O.P., Chapter Prioress.

Mid-Atlantic Mission Chapter, P.O. Box 17087, Raleigh, NC 27619. Tel: 919-844-8369. Sr. Marilyn Winter, O.P., Chapter Prioress.

Midwest Dominican Mission Chapter, 8000 Linder Ave., Burbank, IL 60459. Tel: 708-636-7566. Sr. Sarah Ann Fergus, O.P., Chapter Prioress.

Motherhouse Mission Chapter, 1257 Siena Heights Dr., Adrian, MI 49221. Tel: 517-266-4107. Sr. Celestine Dunne, O.P., Chapter Prioress.

Nokomis Mission Chapter, 9400 Courville St., Detroit, MI 48224. Tel: 313-343-0573. Sr. Margaret O'Flynn, O.P., Chapter Prioress.

Rosa de Lima Mission Chapter, c/o 1257 Siena Heights Dr., Adrian, MI 49221. Tel: 809-533-0272. Sr. Rose Ann Schlitt, O.P., Chapter Prioress.

Pacific West Mission Chapter, P.O. Box 2235, Santa Cruz, CA 95063. Tel: 831-457-7117. Sr. Jane Robert Stuckel, O.P., Chapter Prioress.

South East Adrian Mission Chapter, 28650 Eleven Mile Rd., Farmington Hills, MI 48336. Tel: 248-426-9185. Sr. Lorraine Mordenski, O.P., Chapter Prioress.

Southwest Mission Chapter, 1983 S. Broadway, Grand Junction, CO 81503. Tel: 970-241-6152. Sr. Barbara Stanek, O.P., Chapter Prioress.

Upper Midwest Mission Chapter, 8000 Linder Ave., Burbank, IL 60459. Tel: 708-636-8178. Sr. Mary Margaret Mannard, O.P., Chapter Prioress.

Total number in community 1,070.

Legal Holdings or Titles: *Dominican Sisters of Adrian, MI, Inc.,* Adrian, MI; *Camilla Madden Charitable Trust,* Adrian, MI; *Adrian Dominican Sisters Office of Development,* Adrian, MI; *Dominican High School,* Detroit, MI; *Dominican Santa Cruz Hospital,* Santa Cruz, CA; *Dominican Life Center,* Adrian, MI; *Regina Dominican High School,* Wilmette, IL; *Rosarian Academy,* West Palm Beach, FL; *Siena Heights University,* Adrian, MI; *St. Joseph Academy,* Adrian, MI; *St. Rose Dominican Hospital,* Henderson, NV; *Adrian Dominican Sisters House of Preachers,* Garner, NC; *Weber Retreat Center,* Adrian, MI.

Sisters minister in the areas of Formal Education - as administrators, teachers and consultants at elementary, secondary, college, state and diocesan levels; Pastoral Ministry - parishes, hospitals and campuses; Religious Education - coordinators and teachers; Social Services - case workers, administrators, counselors, therapists, consultants, care-givers for elderly and staff for retirement centers; Health Services - administrators, nurses, therapists, doctors, physician assistants, psychologists, technologists, pharmacists and dietitians;Business Services - directors, accountants, secretaries, administrative assistants, typists, bookkeepers, office managers, office staff, drivers and housekeeping staff; Spiritual Direction - retreat work, formation, Congregation leadership and as diocesan Vicars for Religious; Social Justice - coordinators, staff and community organizers; other ministries including research, law, science, public relations, art, communications and full-time study.

Represented in the Archdioceses of Atlanta, Boston, Chicago, Cincinnati, Detroit, Los Angeles, Louisville, Miami, New Orleans, New York, Oklahoma City, Philadelphia, St. Louis, San Antonio, San Francisco, Santa Fe, Washington and the Dioceses of Austin, Birmingham, Charleston, Charlotte, Cleveland, Columbus, El Paso, Evansville, Fresno, Fort Wayne-South Bend, Gallup, Galveston-Houston, Gary, Gaylord, Green

Bay, Helena, Jackson, Joliet, Kalamazoo, Las Vegas, La Crosse, Lansing, Lexington, Madison, Marquette, Monterey, Oakland, Orange, Orlando, Palm Beach, Pensacola-Tallahassee, Peoria, Phoenix, Pittsburgh, Providence, Pueblo, Raleigh, Rapid City, Richmond, Rockford, Saginaw, St. Augustine, St. Petersburg, San Bernardino, San Diego, San Jose, Santa Rosa, Spokane, Toledo, Tucson, and Venice. Also in Canada, Dominican Republic, Mexico, and Puerto Rico.

[1070-14] CONGREGATION OF OUR LADY OF THE SACRED HEART (1877) P

General Motherhouse: *Marywood,* 2025 E. Fulton St., Grand Rapids, MI 49503. Tel: 616-459-2910; Fax: 616-454-6105. Sr. Maribeth Holst, O.P., Prioress; Sr. Michael Ellen Carling, O.P., Archivist.

Legal Holdings or Titles: *Sisters of the Order of St. Dominic of Grand Rapids; Marywood Academy; Sisters of St. Dominic of the Congregation of Our Lady of the Sacred Heart Charitable Trust.*

Total number in community 328.

Sisters are involved in Academic and Religious Education at all levels; Liturgy; Pastoral Ministry and Administration; Diocesan Offices; Food Service; Health Care; Congregational Services; Social Work; Sabbatical Volunteer; Public Education and Study; Foreign Missions; Justice Advocacy.

Represented in the Archdioceses of Baltimore, Chicago, Detroit, Louisville, Mobile, New Orleans, Omaha, St. Louis, Santa Fe, Seattle, and in the Dioceses of Albany, Colorado Springs, Gaylord, GrandRapids, Greensburg, Kalamazoo, Lansing, Lexington, Monterey, Providence, Saginaw, Sioux Falls, Toledo and Wheeling-Charleston. Also in Peru and Honduras.

[1070-15] CONGREGATION OF SAINT DOMINIC (1878) D

General Motherhouse: *Sisters of Saint Dominic of Blauvelt, New York,* 496 Western Hwy., Blauvelt, NY 10913-2097; Tel: 914-359-5600; Fax: 914-359-5773. Sr. Barbara Werner, O.P., Pres.; Sr. Judith Campbell, O.P., Archivist.

Total number in community 225.

Sisters serve and staff Elementary; Secondary; Higher Education; Special Education; Hospital Care; Pastoral Care; Parish Ministry; Retreat Work; Child Care; Neighborhood Services; Services to Migrants; Services to Chemically Dependent.

Represented in the Archdioceses of Newark and New York and in the Dioceses of Orlando, Paterson, Providence, Rockville Centre and San Bernardino. Also in Jamaica.

[1070-16] DOMINICAN SISTERS OF THE SICK POOR—CONGREGATION OF THE IMMACULATE CONCEPTION (1879) D

General Motherhouse: *Mariandale - Queen of the Rosary Convent,* 299 N. Highland Ave., Ossining, NY 10562. Tel: 914-941-4455. Sr. Kathleen Hebbeler, O.P., Pres.

Total number in community 53.

Legal Titles and Holdings: *Dominican Sisters of the Sick Poor Ministry Trust.*

Sisters minister in low income areas providing health, social, community and pastoral services.

Represented in the Archdioceses of Cincinnati, Denver, Detroit, Newark, New York, Philadelphia and Washington and the Dioceses of Allentown, Jackson, Richmond and Rockville Centre.

[1070-17] CONGREGATION OF ST. CATHERINE DE RICCI (1880) P

General Motherhouse: *Fanjeaux,* 750 Ashbourne Rd., Elkins Park, PA 19027-2596. Tel: 215-635-6027. Sr. Mary Ellen Bennett, O.P., Pres.

Professed Sisters 88.

Sisters serve and staff Retreat Houses; Religious Education Centers and Parish Services; Hospital; Pastoral Ministry; College; Diocesan Offices; Residence for Women; Campus Ministry; Special Services; Residence for Women; Spiritual Direction; Counselling Center; Liturgical Art Studio.

Properties owned: *Dominican Retreat House / Convent of Our Lady of Prouille,* Elkins Park, PA; *St. Dominic Hall,* Elkins Park, PA; *Dominican Retreat, Immaculate Heart of Mary Convent,* McLean, VA; *Dominican Retreat House / Our Lady of Grace Convent,* Niskayuna, NY; *Dominican Retreat House / Queen of Apostles Convent,* Miami, FL; *The Lucy Eaton Smith Residence,* Philadelphia, PA; *St. Catherine Hall,* Elkins Park, PA.

Represented in the Archdioceses of Baltimore, Cincinnati, Detroit, Miami, Philadelphia, Santa Fe and the Dioceses of Albany, Arlington, Biloxi, Camden, Harrisburg, Orlando, Palm Beach, Providence, Raleigh, St. Petersburg, and Scranton.

[1070-18] SISTERS OF ST. DOMINIC OF THE AMERICAN CONGREGATION OF THE SACRED HEART OF JESUS (1881) D

Dominican Motherhouse: 1 Ryerson Ave., Caldwell, NJ 07006. Tel: 973-403-3331; Fax: 973-228-9611. Sr. Joan Doyle, O.P., Prioress; Sr. Helen Marguerite, O.P., Archivist.

Total number in community 203.

Legal Title: *Sisters of St. Dominic of Caldwell, N.J.*

Properties owned: *Caldwell College,* Caldwell, NJ; *Mount Saint Dominic Academy,* Caldwell, NJ; *St. Dominic Academy,* Jersey City, NJ; *Lacordaire Academy,* Upper Montclair, NJ.

Ministry in Education at all levels; Pastoral Ministry; Health and Human Services.

Represented in the Archdioceses of Baltimore, Boston, Louisville, Newark, Portland, and the Dioceses of Metuchen, Orange, Paterson, Savannah, Springfield (IL) and Trenton. Also in the Dominican Republic.

[1070-19] DOMINICAN SISTERS OF HOUSTON, TEXAS (CONGREGATION OF THE SACRED HEART) (1882) P

General Motherhouse & Novitiate: *Dominican Sisters,* 6501 Almeda Rd., Houston, TX 77021. Tel: 713-747-3310; Fax: 713-747-4707. Sr. Heloise Cruzat, O.P., Prioress.

Legal Title: *Dominican Sisters of Houston, Texas, Inc.* (aka *Sacred Heart Convent of Houston*).

Total number in community 134.

Properties owned and sponsored: *St. Agnes Academy; St. Agnes Academy Foundation; St. Pius X High School; St. Pius X High School Foundation, Inc.; The Sacred Heart Convent Retirement Trust.*

Ministry in the field of Academic Education at all levels and Parish Ministry.

Represented in the Archdioceses of Baltimore, Los Angeles, San Antonio, St. Louis, Seattle and the Dioceses of Austin, Beaumont, Brownsville, Corpus Christi, Galveston-Houston, Lake Charles, San Angelo, San Bernardino, San Jose, Tyler and Victoria. Also in Guatemala.

[1070-20] CONGREGATION OF ST. THOMAS AQUINAS (1888) P

Motherhouse: *Tacoma Dominican Center,* 935 Fawcett Ave. S., Tacoma, WA 98402-5605. Tel: 253-272-9688; Fax: 253-272-8790. Sr. Kathleen Reilly, O.P., Pres.

Total number in community 84.

Ministry in a variety of apostolacies.

Legal Holdings and Titles: *Sisters of St. Dominic, Tacoma Dominican Center; Sisters of St. Dominic - Tacoma Charitable Trust.*

Represented in the Archdioceses of Los Angeles, San Francisco, Seattle and the Dioceses of Baker, Fresno, St. Augustine, San Diego, San Bernardino, and Yakima. Also in Canada.

[1070-21] DOMINICAN SISTERS CONGREGATION OF HOLY CROSS (1890) P

General Motherhouse & Novitiate: *Rosary Heights,* P.O. Box 280, Edmonds, WA 98020. Tel: 206-542-7511; 542-3212. Sr. Michele Kopp, O.P., Prioress.

Total number in community 62.

Sisters minister in Elementary, Secondary and University Education; Arts; Diocesan, Parish and Hospital Pastoral Ministry; Health Care; Mental Health; Detention; Political; Direct Service and Advocacy with Women and Children; Housing; Peace and Justice; Community Service.

Represented in the Archdioceses of Los Angeles, Portland in Oregon, San Francisco, Santa Fe, Seattle and the Dioceses of Boise, Dodge City and San Diego.

[1070-23] CONGREGATION OF ST. ROSE OF LIMA (1900) D THE SERVANTS OF RELIEF FOR INCURABLE CANCER IN THE U.S.

General Motherhouse: *Rosary Hill Home,* Hawthorne, NY 10532. Tel: 914-769-0114. Mother Marie Edward, O.P., Mother Gen.

Total number in community 80.

The work of these sisters is confined entirely to the incurable cancerous poor.

Represented in the Archdioceses of Atlanta, New York, Philadelphia and St. Paul-Minneapolis and in the Dioceses of Cleveland and Fall River.

[1070-24] DOMINICAN SISTERS OF GREAT BEND (1902) P

Motherhouse & Novitiate: *Immaculate Conception Convent,* 3600 Broadway, Great Bend, KS 67530. Tel: 316-792-1232. Sr. Gemma Doll, O.P., Prioress.

Total number in community 124.

Legal Title: *The Nuns of the Third Order of St. Dominic.*

Sisters serve in Grade Schools; Colleges; Special Education; Religious Education Centers and Centers for Retreats and Spirituality; Hospitals; Nursing Homes; Infirmary; Home Health Services; Health Care Ministries; Foreign Missions; Ministry to Minorities; Ministry to Aging; Housing; Music Ministry; Parish Ministry; Office of Mission and Ministry.

Properties owned: *Hospitality House,* Wichita, KS; several residential convents; *Heartland Farm,* Pawnee Rock, KS; *Novitiate House,* Great Bend, KS.

Properties owned and sponsored: *Heartland Center for Spirituality,* Great Bend, KS; *St. Martin de Porres Association Dominican Retreat Center,* Great Bend, KS; *Cedar Park Place, Inc.* (low- and middle-income housing for the elderly and handicapped), Great Bend, KS; *Heartland Center for Wholistic Health Association,* Great Bend, KS; *Office of Mission and Ministry,* Great Bend, KS; *Art of Learning Center,* Wichita, KS; co-sponsor of Catholic Health initiatives.

Represented in the Archdioceses of Chicago, Denver, Kansas City in Kansas, St. Louis, St. Paul-Minneapolis and in the Dioceses of Dodge City, Phoenix, Pueblo, Salina, San Angelo and Wichita. Also in Africa.

[1070-25] CONGREGATION OF THE DOMINICAN SISTERS OF ST. CATHERINE OF SIENA OF KENOSHA (1911) P

General Motherhouse & Novitiate: P.O. Box 1288, Kenosha, WI 53141. Tel: 262-694-2067; Fax: 262-694-6542. Sr. Susan Anne Snyder, O.P., Prioress.

Legal Title: *Congregation of the Dominican Sisters of St. Catherine of Siena of Kenosha, Inc.*

Total number in community 29.

Properties owned: *Holy Rosary Medical Center,* Ontario, OR; *Our Lady of Fatima Villa,* Saratoga, CA; *Mercy Hospital,* Merced, CA.

Represented in the Archdioceses of Milwaukee and San Francisco and the Dioceses of Baker, Columbus, and Fresno. Also in Ecuador.

[1070-26] CONGREGATION OF ST. ROSE OF LIMA (1923) D

General Motherhouse: *St. Joseph's Convent,* 775 Drahner Rd., Oxford, MI 48371-4866. Tel: 248-628-2872. Sr. Frances Mary Kernasovich, O.P., Pres.; Sr. Teresita Lipar, O.P., Vice Pres.; Sr. Susan McMahon, O.P., Vice Pres.

Total number in community 46.

Properties owned and sponsored: *St. Mary's Retreat House,* Oxford, MI; *St. Jude Home,* Waterford, MI; *Dominican Center* (retreat house for teenagers), Oxford, MI; *Lourdes Nursing Home; Fox Manor,* Waterford, MI; *Dominican Sisters of Oxford Charitable Trust,* Oxford, MI.

Sisters minister in Elementary Schools; Nursing Homes; Retreat House; Parish Ministry; Religious Education; Senior Citizens Residence; Hospital Ministry; Pastoral Assistant.

Represented in the Archdioceses of Chicago, Detroit and the Dioceses of Gary, Lansing and Saginaw.

[1070-27] CONGREGATION OF THE IMMACULATE CONCEPTION (1929) D

Provincial House: *Immaculate Conception Provincial House,* 9000 W. 81st. St., Justice, IL 60458. Tel: 708-458-3040. Mother M. Natalie, O.P., Prov. Supr.

Total number in community 29.

Represented in the Archdioceses of Chicago, Milwaukee and the Diocese of Little Rock. Also in Canada.

[1070-28] CONGREGATION OF THE SISTERS OF ST. DOMINIC OF THE IMMACULATE HEART OF MARY (1929) D

General Motherhouse: *Our Lady of the Elms Convent,* 1230 W. Market St., Akron, OH 44313-7108. Tel: 330-836-4908; Fax: 330-836-5913. Sr. Bernadine Baltrinic, O.P., Pres.; Sr. Rebecca Betz, O.P., Archivist.

Total number in community 97.

Properties owned: *Our Lady of the Elms School; Crown Point Ecology Center,* Bath, OH.

Represented in the Archdioceses of Anchorage, Milwaukee, Portland, Seattle, and the Dioceses of Alexandria, Cleveland, Fort Wayne-South Bend, Lansing, Phoenix, St. Augustine, St. Petersburg, Toledo and Youngstown. Also in Central America.

[1070-29] DOMINICAN SISTERS OF SPOKANE D

Dominican Center: W. 3102 Ft. George Wright Dr., Spokane, WA 99224. Tel: 509-328-8033; Fax: 509-325-9877. Sr. Judith Nilles, O.P., Prioress.

Total number in community 36.

Legal Holdings or Titles: *Dominican Outreach Services; Dominican Outreach Foundation.*
Represented in the Diocese of Spokane.

[1070-30] DOMINICAN SISTERS OF OAKFORD P
U.S. Regional Center: *Dominican Sisters of Oakford,* 980 Woodland Ave., San Leandro, CA 94577. Tel: 510-638-2822; Fax: 510-633-9734. Sr. Nicolina Kohler, O.P., Reg. Supr.
Total number in community 22.
Ministries in Teaching; Spiritual Direction; Counselling; Parish Work; Adult Education; Care for the Elderly; Community Services and Nursing.
Properties owned: 3 residences in California; *Formation House,* San Leandro, CA; *St. Catherine's Convent,* Sunnyvale, CA.
Represented in the Dioceses of Oakland, Phoenix and San Jose.

[1100] (O.P.)—DOMINICAN SISTERS OF CHARITY OF THE PRESENTATION OF THE BLESSED VIRGIN P
Founded in France in 1696. First foundation in the United States in 1906.
Motherhouse: 15 Quai Portillon, 37023, Tours Cedex, France.
Universal total in Congregation 3,377.
Provincial House: 3012 Elm St., Dighton, MA 02715. Tel: 508-669-5425; 669-5023. Sr. Joanna Fernandes, O.P., Prov. Supr.
Total number in province 42.
Ministry in Hospitals; Homes For the Aged; Residence for Working Women & Students; Dispensaries; Migrant Clinic; Education; Pastoral Ministry.
Represented in the Archdiocese of Washington and the Dioceses of Brownsville, Fall River and Providence. Also in India, Haiti, Korea, Peru, Bolivia, Columbia and Mexico.

[1105] (O.P.)—DOMINICAN SISTERS OF HOPE P
Founded July 20, 1995, as a merging of three former Congregations: Dominican Sisters of the Congregation of the Most Holy Rosary of Newburgh, NY; Dominican Sisters of the Sick Poor of Ossining, NY and Congregation of Catherina of Siena, of Fall River, MA.
General Administrative Offices: *Dominican Sisters of Hope,* 299 N. Highland Ave., Ossining, NY 10562. Tel: 914-941-4420; Fax: 914-941-1125. Sr. Philomena Marie McCartney, O.P., Prioress.
Total number in community 302.
Legal Titles and Holdings: *Dominican Sisters of Hope Ministry Trust.*
Ministry in Religious & Academic Education at all levels; Health, social, community and pastoral services in low income area; Parish service, counseling, retreats and spiritual direction.
Represented in the Archdioceses of Cincinnati, Denver, Detroit, Hartford, Newark, New York, Oklahoma City, Philadelphia, Washington and the Dioceses of Albany, Allentown, Arlington, Bridgeport, Brooklyn, Burlington, Camden, Fall River, Gallup, Jackson, Lexington, Metuchen, Ogdensburg, Palm Beach, Paterson, Providence, Richmond, Rockville Centre.

[1110] (O.P.)—DOMINICAN SISTERS OF OUR LADY OF THE ROSARY AND OF SAINT CATHERINE OF SIENA, CABRA P
Founded in Ireland in 1644.
General Motherhouse: Cabra, Dublin 7, Ireland.
Region of Louisiana established in 1978
Regional House: *Dominican Sisters,* Cabra, 1930 Robert E. Lee, New Orleans, LA 70122. Tel: 504-288-1593. Sr. Elizabeth Ferguson, O.P., Reg. Prioress.
Total number in local community 11.
Ministry in Academic and Religious Education; Parish Ministry; Neighborhood Social Service Agency; Diocesan Tribunal; Prison Ministry; Adult Education; Social Apostolate; Retreats; Spiritual Direction.
Represented in the Archdiocese of New Orleans and the Dioceses of Fort Worth and Houma-Thibodeaux.

[1120] (O.P.)—DOMINICAN SISTERS OF THE ROMAN CONGREGATION P
Founded in France in 1621. First United States foundation in 1904.
General Motherhouse: Rome, Italy. Sr. Rosario de Meer, Supr. Gen.
Universal total in Congregation 639.
U.S. Provincial Office: 123 Dumont Ave., Lewiston, ME 04240-6107. Tel: 207-782-3535; 782-0435. Sr. Monique Belanger, O.P., Prov. Prioress.
Total number in community 27.
Properties owned: *Retreat House;* Residences 5.
Ministry in the field of Religious & Academic Education; Adult Education; Indian Reservation; Pastoral Ministry; Health Care; Social Work.
Represented in the Archdioceses of Chicago, New York and Portland (OR) and in the Dioceses of Davenport, Gallup, Phoenix and Portland (ME).

[1140] (O.P.)—EUCHARISTIC MISSIONARIES OF ST. DOMINIC D
Founded in Louisiana in 1927. Eucharistic Missionaries of St. Dominic.
General Motherhouse: 3801 Canal St. - Suite 400, New Orleans, LA 70119. Tel: 504-486-1133; Fax: 504-486-6547. Sr. Dorothy Trosclair, O.P., Pres.
Perpetually Professed Sisters 43; Missions 24.
Properties owned: *Regina Coeli Retreat Center,* Covington, LA; houses in New Orleans & Tucson, AZ.
Sisters Staff and Serve: Parish and Diocesan Religious Education; Parish and Diocesan Social Services; Parish Administrators; Home Health Nursing; Literacy ministry to immigrants; Hospital Chaplaincy and Parish ministry.
Represented in the Archdiocese New Orleans and the Dioceses of Baton Rouge, Beaumont, Biloxi, Houma-Thibodeaux, Lafayette (LA), Palm Beach, and Tucson.

[1145] (O.P.)—RELIGIOUS MISSIONARIES OF ST. DOMINIC
General Motherhouse: Via di Val Cannuta 138, 00166, Rome, Italy. Mother Catalina Civit, O.P., Supr. Gen.
U.S. Provincial Office: 2237 Waldron Rd., Corpus Christi, TX 78418. Tel: 361-939-8102; Fax: 361-939-8203. Sr. Esperanza C. Manas, O.P., Delegate of the Supr. Gen.
Total number in congregation 626; Sisters in the United States 31.
Represented in the Archdiocese of Los Angeles, and the Dioceses of Corpus Christi, and Galveston-Houston.

[1150] (E.F.M.S.)—EUCHARISTIC FRANCISCAN MISSIONARY SISTERS D
Founded in Mexico in 1943. Mother Maria Gemma de Jesus Aranda, Founderess.
Motherhouse: *Our Lady's Convent,* 943 S. Soto St., Los Angeles, CA 90023. Tel: 323-264-6556. 1421 Cota Ave., Torrance, CA 90501. Tel: 310-328-6725. Mother Rose Seraphim, E.F.M.S., Supr. Gen.; Sr. Gloria de Jesus, E.F.M.S., Gen. Sec.
Total number in community 26.
Legal Title: *Eucharistic Franciscan Missionary Sisters of Los Angeles.*
Sisters serve and staff: The field of Education; Missionary Activities; Catechetics; Social Work; Diocesan and Administration offices.
Represented in the Archdiocese of Los Angeles and the Diocese of Stockton, and Tyler.

[1170] (C.S.S.F.)—FELICIAN SISTERS P
(Congregation of Sisters of St. Felix of Cantalice, of the III Order of St. Francis)
Founded in Poland in 1855. First foundation in the United States in 1874.
General Motherhouse: Via del Casaletto 540, 00151, Rome, Italy. Sr. Mary Raymond Kasprzak, C.S.S.F., Min. Gen.
Presentation of the B.V.M. Province (1874): *Motherhouse and Novitiate-Provincialate,* 36800 Schoolcraft Rd., Livonia, MI 48150. Tel: 734-591-1730; Fax: 734-591-1710. Sr. Mary Renetta Rumpz, C.S.S.F., Prov. Min.
Professed 226; Novices 1.
Ministry in the Field of Academic Education at all levels; Catechetical Center; CCD Programs; Archival and Secretarial Services in Seminary; Diocesan Nursing Home; Youth Ministry Center; Pastoral Ministry Programs; DRE Offices; Hospital; Health Care Centers; Nursing Homes; Assisted Living; Archdiocesan Tribunal and Office of Delegate for Religious; Hospice Inpatient and Home Care Program; Day Care Centers; Retreat Centers; House of Prayer; Senior Clergy Residence.
Properties owned: *Madonna University, Ladywood High School, Montessori Center of Our Lady St. Mary Mercy Hospital,* Livonia, MI; *St. Joseph Day Care; Presentation Prayer Center,* Jackson, MI; *Maryville Center,* Holly, MI; *Angela Hospice Home Care and Inpatient Facility, Marian Professional Building,* Livonia, MI.
Represented in the Archdiocese of Detroit and the Dioceses of Fort Wayne-South Bend, Gaylord, Lansing, Saginaw and Toledo.
Immaculate Heart of Mary Province (1900): *Novitiate-Villa Maria,* 600 Doat St., Buffalo, NY 14211. Tel: 716-892-4141. Sr. Mary Raymond Kasprzak, C.S.S.F., Prov. Minister; Sr. Mary Simplicia Wytrwal, C.S.S.F., Prov. Archivist.
Total number in community 331.
Ministry in the field of Academic Education on all levels; Day Care Center; School for Mentally and Multiply Handicapped; Institute of Music; Religious Education Centers; Outreach Centers; Diocesan Office.
Properties owned: *Villa Maria College of Buffalo, Villa Maria Academy, Villa Maria Institute of Music,* Buffalo, NY.
Represented in the Dioceses of Buffalo, Charleston, Erie, Syracuse and Wilmington. Also in Canada, and Italy.
Mother of Good Counsel Province (1910): *Mother of Good Counsel Provincialate, Novitiate, & Convent,* 3800 W. Peterson Ave., Chicago, IL 60659. Tel: 773-463-3020. Sr. Mary Barbara Ann Bosch, C.S.S.F., Prov. Minister; Sr. M. Adolphine Ksioszk, C.S.S.F., Community Archivist.
Total number in the community 259.
Ministry in the field of Academic and Religious Education at all levels; Homes for Aged; Independent Living for the Elderly; Assisted Living for the Elderly; Pastoral Ministry; Social Workers; Family Therapists; Day Care Centers; Hospitals; Infirmary for Sisters; Foreign Missions; Recreation House for Children.
Represented in the Archdioceses of Chicago and Milwaukee and the Dioceses of Belleville, Green Bay, Joliet, La Crosse and Rockford.
Immaculate Conception Provincial House (1913): *Motherhouse and Novitiate-Immaculate Conception Convent,* 260 S. Main St., Lodi, NJ 07644-2196. Tel: 973-473-7447; Fax: 973-473-7126. Sr. Mary Antonelle Chunka, C.S.S.F., Prov. Minister; Sr. Mary Alicia Adametz, Prov. Sec.; Sr. Mary Raphael Monczewska, Archivist.
Total number in community 222.
Properties sponsored: *Immaculate Conception High School; Felician College; Felician College Day Care Center; Felician School for Exceptional Children,* Lodi, NJ; *Felician Retreat Center; Our Lady of Grace Home; St. Ignatius Nursing Home.*
Sisters Serve and Staff: Colleges; High Schools; Elementary Schools; Hospitals; Home for Neglected Children; Home for Aged; Infirmary for Sisters; Day Care Center; School for Exceptional Children; Religious Education; Parish Ministries.
Represented in the Archdioceses of Newark and Philadelphia and the Dioceses of Camden, Metuchen, Paterson, Trenton and Wilmington.
Our Lady of the Sacred Heart Province (1921): *Provincial House and Novitiate, Felician Sisters of Pennsylvania,* 1500 Woodcrest Ave., Coraopolis, PA 15108. Tel: 412-264-2890; Fax: 412-264-7047. Sr. Mary Cabrini Procopio, C.S.S.F., Prov. Min.
Total number in community 130.
Ministry in the field of Academic Education at all levels; Religious Education; CCD Centers; Youth and Pastoral Ministry; Home for Mentally Retarded Children; Infirmary and Home for Aged; Missionary Work.
Legal Holdings and Titles: *Felician Sisters of Pennsylvania; Our Lady of the Sacred Heart High School.*
Represented in the Dioceses of Altoona-Johnstown, Charleston, Greensburg, Harrisburg, and Pittsburgh. Also in Kenya.
Our Lady of the Angels Province (1932): *Felician Sisters Provincial Hse./Novitiate, Our Lady of the Angels Convent,* 1315 Enfield St., Enfield, CT 06082-4929. Tel: 860-745-7791; Fax: 860-741-0819. Sr. Mary Laureann Alexandrowicz, C.S.S.F., Prov. Minister.
Universal total 2,500; Sisters in province 126.
Properties owned and sponsored: *Montessori School; Felician Adult Day Care,* Enfield, CT; *St. Joseph Hospital,* Bangor, ME.
Ministry in the field of Religious and Academic Education; Pastoral Ministry; Social Services; Healthcare.
Represented in the Archdioceses of Boston, Hartford, New York and the Dioceses of Albany, Manchester, Norwich, Portland (ME), Providence, Springfield (MA) and Worcester.
Assumption of the B.V.M. Province (1953): *Provincial House – Novitiate,* 4210 Meadowlark Ln., S.E., Rio Rancho, NM 87124-1021. Sr. Rosemarie Goins, C.S.S.F., Prov. Min.
Total number in community 73.
Legal Titles and Holdings: *Felician Sisters of the Southwest, Inc.; St. Felix Pantry Inc.*
Sisters serve and staff: High Schools; Elementary Schools; Foreign and Rural Missions; Religious Education Centers & Classes; Health Care; Pastoral Care; Food & Clothing Pantry; Youth Ministry; Adult Education.
Represented in the Archdioceses of Los Angeles, San Antonio, Santa Fe and the Dioceses of Fort Worth and San Bernardino. Also in Mexico.

[1180] (O.S.F.)—FRANCISCAN SISTERS OF ALLEGANY, NEW YORK P
Founded in the United States in 1859.
General Motherhouse (1859): *St. Elizabeth Motherhouse,* Allegany, NY 14706. Tel: 716-373-0200;

Fax: 716-372-5774. Sr. Margaret Mary Kimmins, O.S.F., Gen. Minister; Sr. Noella Lachat, O.S.F., Local Minister.
Total number in community 419.
Legal Titles and Holdings: *Franciscan Sisters of Allegany, NY, Inc.; Franciscan Center, Inc.,* Tampa, FL; *Dwelling Place, Inc.,* New York, NY; *St. Joseph Villa, Inc.,* Catskill, NY; *St. Francis Respite Program, Inc.,* Allegany, NY; *St. Elizabeth Mission Society, Inc.,* Allegany, NY.
Ministry to Evangelization in all levels of Education; Health Care; Social Services; Pastoral and Campus Ministries; Spiritual Ministries and Social Advocacy.
Represented in the Archdioceses of Boston, Hartford, Miami, Newark, New York, Philadelphia and the Dioceses of Albany, Brooklyn, Buffalo, Camden, Fall River, Metuchen, Palm Beach, Providence, Rochester, Rockville Centre, St. Petersburg, Shreveport, Spokane, Springfield(MA), Syracuse, Trenton, Venice and Wilmington. Also in Bolivia, Brazil and Jamaica.
Region I Office: *Franciscan Sisters of Allegany (1984),* 115 E. Main St., Allegany, NY 14706. Tel: 716-373-1888. Sr. Roberta Frances Brunner, O.S.F., Region I Minister.
Represented in the Dioceses of Albany, Buffalo, Rochester, Spokane, and Syracuse. Also in Bolivia.
Region II: *Franciscan Sisters of Allegany (1984),* 282 Suffolk St., Lowell, MA 01854. Tel: 978-452-2823. Sr. Mary Lou Lafferty, O.S.F., Region II Minister.
Represented in the Archdioceses of Boston, Hartford, Newark, New York, Philadelphia and the Dioceses of Brooklyn, Camden, Fall River, Metuchen, Providence, Rockville Centre, Springfield (MA), Trenton and Wilmington.
Region III: *Franciscan Sisters of Allegany (1984),* 631 - 11th St., No., St. Petersburg, FL 33705. Tel: 727-824-0857. Sr. Marie Kathleen Stagnaro, O.S.F., Region III Minister.
Represented in the Archdiocese of Miami and in Dioceses of Palm Beach, Shreveport, St. Petersburg and Venice. Also in Bolivia.
Region IV: *Franciscan Sisters of Allegany,* 152 Constant Spring Rd., Box 1654, Kingston, Jamaica, West Indies. Tel: 876-925-1973. Sr. Teresita Marie De Souza, O.S.F., Region IV Minister.
Region V: *Franciscan Sisters of Allegany,* C.P. 322, 75001-970 Anapolis, Goias, Brazil, South America. Tel: 011-55-62-321-0805. Sr. Maria do Socorro Rabelo, O.S.F., Region V Minister.

[1190] (S.A.)—FRANCISCAN SISTERS OF THE ATONEMENT P

Founded in the United States in 1898.
Motherhouse: *St. Francis Convent-Graymoor,* 41 Old Highway Trnpk., Garrison, NY 10524. Tel: 845-424-3623; Fax: 845-424-3298. Sr. Diane Bernier, S.A., Congregational Min.; Sr. Mary Annunciata Griffitts, S.A., Archivist.
Total number in community 212.
Properties owned: *St. Francis Convent - Complex,* Garrison, NY; *Mother Lurana House,* Garrison, NY; *Washington Retreat House,* Washington, DC.
Represented in the Archdioceses of Boston, Detroit, Newark, New York, Washington and the Dioceses of Albany, Brooklyn, Bridgeport, Burlington, Fresno, Manchester, Metuchen, Monterey, Norwich, Ogdensburg, Pittsburgh, Raleigh, Reno-Las Vegas, Sacramento, Salt Lake City, Syracuse and Trenton. Also in Canada, Brazil, Ireland, Italy, Japan and South Africa.

[1200] (O.S.F.)—THE FRANCISCAN SISTERS OF BALTIMORE P

Founded in England in 1868. First foundation in the United States in 1881.
General Motherhouse: 3725 Ellerslie Ave., Baltimore, MD 21218. Tel: 410-235-0139; Fax: 410-243-2569. Sr. Mary Therese White, O.S.F., Dir. Gen.
Total number in community 46
Legal Title: *Franciscan Sisters of Baltimore, Inc.*
Sisters serve and staff: Parochial Schools; Schools of Special Education; Emergency Welfare Center; Youth Center; Religious Education Centers; Pastoral Ministry; Lay Volunteer Program; Chaplaincy Programs; Retreat Centers; Infant Aids Programs; Hispanic & African-American Evangelization.
Properties owned: *St. Elizabeth School, Inc.; Francis House, Inc.; Franciscan Center, Inc.; General Motherhouse,* Baltimore, MD.
Represented in the Archdioceses of Baltimore, New York, San Antonio, Washington and the Dioceses of Brownsville and Trenton.

[1210] (O.S.F.)—FRANCISCAN SISTERS OF CHICAGO P

Founded in Chicago, Illinois in 1894 by Mother Mary Theresa (Josephine Dudzik) Venerable Servant of God.
General Motherhouse: *Our Lady of Victory Convent;* 14700 Main St., Lemont, IL 60439-0956. Tel: 630-257-7776; Fax: 630-257-7887. Sr. M. Francis Clare Radke, O.S.F., Gen. Minister; Sr. Diane Marie Collins, O.S.F., Archivist.
Total number in community 114.
Sisters serve and staff: Elementary Schools; CCD Programs.
Properties owned: *Madonna High School,* Chicago, IL; *St. Anthony Home, Inc.,* Crown Point, IN; *St. Joseph Home of Chicago, Inc.,* Chicago IL; *Mount Alverna Home, Inc.; Mount Alverna Home Annex, Inc.,* Parma, OH; *Mother Theresa Home, Inc.; Franciscan Village,* Lemont, IL; *St. Francis House of Prayer; Franciscan Sisters of Chicago Service Corp.; Our Lady of Victory Convent,* Lemont IL.
Represented in the Archdiocese of Chicago and the Dioceses of Cleveland and Gary.

[1230] (O.S.F.)—FRANCISCAN SISTERS OF CHRISTIAN CHARITY P

Founded in the United States in 1869.
Motherhouse: *Holy Family Convent,* 2409 S. Alverno Rd., Manitowoc, WI 504220. Tel: 920-682-7728; Fax: 920-682-4195. Sr. Paula Vanden Hogen, Community Dir.; Sr. Donna Marie Kessler, Community Archivist.
Total number in community 468.
Properties owned or sponsored: *Holy Family Convent,* Manitowoc, WI; *Holy Family Convent of Franciscan Sisters of Christian Charity, Inc.,* Manitowoc, WI; *Holy Family Memorial, Inc.,* Manitowoc, WI; *The Retirement Trust of the Franciscan Sisters of Christian Charity,* Manitowoc, WI; *St. Francis Memorial Hopital,* West Point, NE; *Good Samaritan Medical Center,* Zanesville, OH; *St. Joseph Retirement Community,* West Point, NE; *St. Paul Villa,* Kaukauna, WI; *St. Paul Home,* Kaukauna, WI; *St. Paul Manor,* Kaukauna, WI; *Silver Lake College,* Manitowoc, WI; *Franciscan Sisters of Christian Charity HealthCare Ministry, Inc.,* Manitowoc, WI; *Holy Family Conservatory of Music,* Manitowoc, WI; *St. Clare Convent,* Manitowoc, WI; *St. Francis Convent,* Manitowoc, WI; *San Damiano Convent,* Slinger, WI.
Represented in the Archdioceses of Chicago, Los Angeles, Milwaukee, Omaha and in the Dioceses of Columbus, Green Bay, Jackson, Honolulu, Lexington, Marquette, Phoenix, Steubenville, Superior, and Tucson. Also in Peru.

[1235] (F.H.M.)—FRANCISCAN SISTERS DAUGHTERS OF MERCY
Franciscanas Hijas de la Misericordia

Founded in Pina, Mallorca, Spain in 1856. First U.S. establishment in 1962.
General Motherhouse: Calle Moral 4, 07001 Palma de Mallorca, Spain. Sr. Antonia Barrilero Canadas, Supr. Gen.
Universal number in Congregation 447.
U.S. Regional Delegation: 612 N. 3rd St., Waco, TX 76701. Tel: 817-753-5565. Sr. Rose Moreno, F.H.M., Reg. Delegate.
Professed Sisters 9.
Ministry in Kingergarten; Catechetical Work; Pastoral Work.
Represented in the Diocese of Austin.

[1240] (O.S.F.)—FRANCISCAN SISTERS, DAUGHTERS OF THE SACRED HEARTS OF JESUS AND MARY P

Founded in Germany in 1860. First foundation in the United States in 1872.
Generalate: *Via di Sant' Alessio,* 22-24, 00153, Rome, Italy. Sr. Carola Thomann, O.S.F., Gen. Dir.
Universal number in Congregation 839.
St. Clara's Province (1877): *Convent of Our Lady of the Angels, Motherhouse and Novitiate,* P.O. Box 667, Wheaton, IL 60189. Tel: 630-462-7422. Sr. Margaret Grempka, O.S.F., Prov. Dir.
Total number in province 119.
Sisters serve and staff: Hospitals; Housing Development; Parish Ministry; Spirituality Center; Home Health Care; Corporate Offices; System Ministries; Long-term Care; Social Services; Wellness; Spiritual Direction; Campus Ministry; Foreign Mission.
Legal Holdings and Titles: *Affinity Health System,* Oshkosh, WI; *All Saints Visiting Nurse Association & Hospice of Racine, Inc.; All Saints Healthcare Foundation, Inc.,* Racine, WI; *All Saints Healthcare System, Inc.,* Racine, WI; *Assisi Homes of Neenah, Inc.,* Neenah, WI; *Assisi Homes - Batavia Apartments, Inc.,* Batavia, IL; *Assisi Homes - Colony Park, Inc.,* Carol Stream, IL; *Assisi Homes - Constitution House, Inc.,* Aurora, IL; *Assisi Homes of Gurnee, Inc.,* Gurnee, IL; *Assisi Homes of Illinois, Inc.,* Wheaton, IL; *Assisi Homes of Wisconsin, Inc.; Assisi Homes - Elor Manor, Inc.,* Tomah, WI; *Assisi Homes - Gateway, Inc.,* Fort Atkinson, WI; *Assisi Homes - Jefferson Court, Inc.; Assisi Homes - Kenosha, Inc.,* Kenosha, WI; *Assisi Homes - Mabess Manor, Inc.; Assisi Homes - Rock View, Inc.,* Jefferson, WI; *Assisi Homes - Saxony, Inc.,* Kenosha, WI; *Assisi Homes of Milwaukee, Inc.,* Milwaukee, WI; *Canticle Place Ministries, Inc.,* Wheaton, IL; *Canticle Place, Inc.,* Wheaton, IL; *Clare Gardens, Inc.,* Denver, CO; *Clare of Assisi Homes - Westminster, Inc.,* Westminster, CO; *Clara Pfaender Fund, Inc.,* Wheaton, IL; *Covenant Community Foundation, Inc.; Covenant Medical Center, Inc.; Covenant Healthcare System, Inc.,* Milwaukee, WI; *Covenant Home Health Services, Inc.; Covenant Foundation, Inc.; Convenant Health System, Inc.,* Waterloo, IA; *Convenant Rehabilitation, Inc.; Dayspring Villa, Inc.,* Denver, CO; *Elmbrook Memorial Hospital,* Brookfield, WI; *Franciscan Care and Rehabilitation Center, Inc.,* Appleton, WI; *Franciscan Shared Laboratory, Inc.,* Wauwatosa, WI; *Franciscan Seniors, Kenosha, Inc.,* Kenosha, WI; *Franciscan Ministries, Inc.,* Wheaton, IL; *Francis Heights, Inc.,* Denver, CO; *Franciscan Health and Education Corporation, Inc.,* Wheaton, IL; *Francis of Assisi Foundation of Colorado, Inc.,* Denver, CO; *Marianjoy, Inc.,* Wheaton, IL; *Marian Catholic Center, Inc.; Marian Center of Racine, Inc.,* Racine, WI; *Marian Franciscan Center, Inc.; Marian Housing Center, Inc.,* Racine, WI; *Marian Park, Inc.; Mercy Hospital of Franciscan Sisters, Inc.; Oak Park Hospital,* Oak Park, IL; *O.S.F. Services, Inc.; Ridgeway Place, Inc.,* Waterloo, IA; *Rosalie Manor, Inc.; Sartori Memorial Hospital, Inc.,* Cedar Falls, IA; *St. Catherine's Hospital, Inc.; St. Elizabeth Hospital Inc.,* Appleton, WI; *St. Elizabeth Hospital Community Foundation, Inc.,* Appleton, WI; *St. Joseph's Hospital of Franciscan Sisters of Milwaukee, Inc.,* Milwaukee, WI; *St. Michael Hospital of Franciscan Sisters of Milwaukee, Inc.,* Milwaukee, WI; *St. Michael Hospital Community Foundation, Inc.,* Milwaukee, WI; *St. Mary's Medical Center, Inc.,* Racine, WI; *S.E.T. Ministry, Inc.; Villa St. Anna, Inc.; Villa St. Clare, Inc.,* Neenah, WI; *Villa St. Theresa, Inc.; Villa Maria, Inc.,* Westminster, CO; *Wheaton Franciscan Sisters Corp.; Wheaton Franciscan Sisters Religious Charitable Trust; Wheaton Franciscan Services, Inc.*
Represented in the Archdioceses of Chicago, Denver, Dubuque, Milwaukee and St. Louis and the Dioceses of Green Bay, Joliet, La Crosse, Madison, Rockford and Springfield-Cape Girardeau. Also in Brazil, Italy and Nigeria.

[1250] (F.S.E.)THE INSTITUTE OF THE FRANCISCAN SISTERS OF THE EUCHARIST P

Founded December 2, 1973.
Motherhouse: *John Lateran Center,* 405 Allen Ave., Meriden, CT 06451. Tel: 203-237-0841. Team Members: Mother Rosemae Pender, Mother Gen.; Mother Shaun Vergauwen, Mother Asst.; Mother Mary Ann Schmitz; Mother Mona Brunner; Mother Suzanne Gross; Mother Barbara Johnson.
Total number in community 78.
Legal Title: *Franciscan Sisters of the Eucharist, Inc.*
Schools and programs operated under: Franciscan Life Center Network, Incorporated.
Represented in the Archdioceses of Hartford, Portland (OR), Seattle, Washington, and the Dioceses of Boise, Duluth, Galveston-Houston and Grand Rapids. Also in Israel and Italy.

[1260] (F.H.M.)—FRANCISCAN HANDMAIDS OF THE MOST PURE HEART OF MARY D

Founded in the United States in 1916.
General Motherhouse: 15 W. 124th St., New York, NY 10027. Tel: 212-289-5655.
Novitiate, 444 Woodvale Ave., Pleasant Plains, Staten Island, NY 10309. Sr. Maria Goretti, Congregation Minister. Sr. Loretta Theresa, Dir. Formation. Sr. Jacqueline, Community Archivist.
Total number in community 23.
Properties owned: *St. Benedict Day Nursery; Camp Saint Edward; Franciscan Handmaids of Mary Novitiate; Franciscan Handmaids of Mary Motherhouse.*
Ministry in the field of Education, Social Work and Pastoral Care.
Represented in the Archdiocese of New York.

[1270] (F.H.I.C.)—FRANCISCAN HOSPITALLER SISTERS OF THE IMMACULATE CONCEPTION P

Founded in Portugal in 1876.
General Motherhouse: *Linda-a-Pastora,* Portugal. Sr. Maria Isilda Freitas, F.H.I.C., Supr. Gen.
U.S. Foundation (1960): *St. Joseph Novitiate,* 300 S. 17th St., San Jose, CA 95112-2245. Tel: 408-998-2896; Fax: 408-998-3407. Sr. Lucinda D. Fonseca, Supr.
Total number in community 20.

Sisters serve and staff: Parishes; Schools; Hospitals; Social Work.
Represented in the Dioceses of Fresno, Monterey and San Jose.

[1280] (O.S.F.)—FRANCISCAN SISTERS OF THE IMMACULATE CONCEPTION P
First foundation in United States in 1928.
General Motherhouse: *Kloster Bonlanden,* Germany. Sr. M. Veronica Mang, O.S.F., Supr. Gen.
Province of the Blessed Virgin Mary: 291 North St., Buffalo, NY 14201. Fax: 716-881-1578. Sr. M. Bernard, O.S.F., Prov.
Professed Sisters 7.
Represented in the Archdiocese of New York and the Diocese of Buffalo.

[1300] (O.S.F.)—FRANCISCAN SISTERS OF THE IMMACULATE CONCEPTION AND ST. JOSEPH FOR THE DYING D
Founded in the United States in December, 1919 at San Carlos Parish, Monterey, California.
General Motherhouse: *St. Joseph's Convent,* 485 Church St., Monterey, CA 93940. Tel: 408-372-3579. Sr. M. Constance, O.S.F., Supr. Gen.; Sr. M. Bernadette, O.S.F., Archivist.
Total number in community 7.
Legal Holding: *Ave Maria Convalescent Hospital,* Monterey, CA.
Represented in the Diocese of Monterey

[1310] (O.S.F.)—FRANCISCAN SISTERS OF LITTLE FALLS, MINNESOTA P
Founded in the United States in 1891.
General Motherhouse: *St. Francis' Convent,* Little Falls, MN 56345. Tel: 320-632-2981. Sr. Rose Margaret Schneider, O.S.F., Pres.; Sr. Judi Welle, O.S.F., Dir-Archives.
Total number in community 238.
Ministry in the field of Academic Education at all levels; Health Care in Nursing Homes, Hospitals, Apartment for the Elderly, Children's Home, Clinics; Religious Education; Parish Ministry; Retreat Ministries; Liturgical Music; Music Center; Wholistic Growth Center; Ministry to Refugees; Health and Recreation Center; Diocesan Offices; Social Services; Counseling; Spiritual Direction; Consulting; Ministry to the Poor; Ministry to Migrants; Ministry to the Hearing Impaired; Altar Bread-making, and Craft Activities; Ministry in Ecology; Social Justice and Nonviolent Activities; Spirituality Farm; Native Americans.
Properties owned or sponsored: *Wholistic Growth Resources Program; St. Francis Music Center; St. Francis Health & Recreation Center; Clare's Well.*
Represented in the Archdioceses of Chicago, Los Angeles, Milwaukee, New York, St. Louis, St. Paul-Minneapolis, Sante Fe, San Antonio, and the Dioceses of Arlington, Birmingham, Buffalo, Des Moines, Fargo, Jackson, La Crosse, Madison, Manchester, Memphis, New Ulm, Oakland, Phoenix, St. Cloud, St. Petersburg, San Diego, Scranton, Sioux Falls, Spokane, Toledo, Tucson, and Winona. Also in Ecuador and Tanzania.

[1320] (O.S.F.)—FRANCISCAN MISSIONARY SISTERS FOR AFRICA P
Generalate: *Franciscan Missionary Sisters for Africa,* 34a Gilford Rd., Sandymount, Dublin 4, Ireland. Tel: 011-353-1-283876; Fax: 011-353-1-2602049.
American Headquarters: 172 Foster St., P.O. Box 35095, Brighton, MA 02135. Tel: 617-254-4343. Sr. Helen Hennessy, O.S.F.
Total number in community 7.
Represented in the Archdiocese of Boston.

[1330] (S.F.M.A.)—FRANCISCAN MISSIONARY SISTERS OF ASSISI P
General Motherhouse: Via San Francesco 13, Assisi, Italy. Sr. Serena Picchio, Mother Gen.
U.S. Foundation (1961): *St. Francis Convent,* 1039 Northampton St., Holyoke, MA 01040. Tel: 413-532-8156; Fax: 413-534-7741.
Total number in community 16.
Represented in the Archdiocese of New York and the Dioceses of Buffalo and Springfield (MA)

[1340] (F.M.D.C.)—FRANCISCAN MISSIONARY SISTERS OF THE DIVINE CHILD D
First founded in the United States on August 15, 1927 in Buffalo, New York.
Motherhouse: *Franciscan Missionary Sisters of the Divine Child Motherhouse,* 6380 Main St., Williamsville, NY 14221. Tel: 716-632-3144; Fax: 716-626-1332. Sr. Concetta DeFelice, F.M.D.C., Minister Gen.
Total number in community 28.
Sisters serve and staff: Catechetical Centers; CCD Coordinators; Education in Elementary, High School and College; Parish Ministry; Vocation Formation Director.
Represented in the Archdiocese of Newark, Miami and the Diocese of Buffalo.

[1350] (O.S.F.)—FRANCISCAN SISTERS OF THE IMMACULATE CONCEPTION P
Founded in Mexico in 1874. First foundation in the United States in 1926.
Provincial House: 11320 Laurel Canyon Blvd., San Fernando, CA 91340. Tel: 818-365-2582. Sr. Maria de la Paz Ulloa, O.S.F., Prov. Supr.; Sr. Mary Gabriel De Leon, O.S.F., Community Archivist.
Total number in community 118.
Legal Holdings and Titles: *Franciscan Missionary Sisters of the Immaculate Conception, Inc.; Poverello of Assisi Retreat House,* San Fernando, CA; *St. Francis Home,* Santa Ana, CA; *Mother Gertrude Balcazar Home,* San Fernando, CA.
Ministry in the field of Education and Religious Education to Children and Adults; Health Care in Hospitals and Home Visitation to the Sick.
Represented in the Archdiocese of Los Angeles and the Dioceses of Gallup and Orange. Also in Mexico.

[1360] (M.F.I.C.)—MISSIONARY FRANCISCAN SISTERS OF THE IMMACULATE CONCEPTION P
Founded in the United States in 1873 in Belle Prairie, Minnesota.
General Motherhouse: Rome, Italy. Sr. Marian Bandille, M.F.I.C., Gen. Minister.
Provincialate: *Immaculate Conception Province,* 790 Centre St., Newton, MA 02458-2530. Tel: 617-527-1004; Fax: 617-527-2528. Sr. Mary Michele Craig, M.F.I.C., Prov.
Total number in province 252.
Represented in the Archdioceses of Boston, Newark, New York, Philadelphia, and the Dioceses of Bridgeport, Brooklyn, Charleston, Providence, Savannah, Syracuse and Venice. Also in Peru and Bolivia.

[1365] (F.M.I.J.)—FRANCISCAN MISSIONARY SISTERS OF THE INFANT JESUS P
Founded in Aquila, Italy in 1879 by Sr. Maria Giuseppa Micarelli. First Foundation in the U.S. in 1961.
Generalate: Piazza Nicoloso da Recco 13, Rome, Italy 00154; Tel: 6-575-8358. Mother Maria Felicita Decio, F.M.I.J., Supr. Gen.
U.S. Province and Novitiate: 1215 Kresson Rd., Cherry Hill, NJ 08003. Tel: 609-428-7930; Fax: 609-428-7930. Sr. Chiara Lilia Ferrario, F.M.I.J., Delegate Supr.
Ministry in Ministries of Evangelization; Education; Health Care; Social-Pastoral Services.
Professed Sisters 19.
Represented in the Dioceses of Arlington, Camden and Trenton.

[1370] (F.M.M.) THE FRANCISCAN MISSIONARIES OF MARY P
Founded in India in 1877. First foundation in the United States in 1904.
General Motherhouse: 12 via Giusti, Rome, Italy. Sr. Christiane Megarbane, F.M.M., Supr. Gen.
Franciscan Missionaries of Mary—U.S. Province (1920): 3305 Wallace Ave., Bronx, NY 10467-6599. Tel: 718-547-4604. Sr. Mary Motte, F.M.M., Prov.
Total number in community 193.
Ministry in Educational Projects among Minority Group of Immigrants; Child Care Agencies; Cardiac and General Hospital; General Pediatric Hospital with Rehabilitation Specialty; Chaplaincy; Retreat Work; Day Care for Elderly; Catechetics; Mission Animation & Formation; Home Visiting & Community Development.
Represented in the Archdioceses of Boston, Chicago, New York, St. Louis, San Francisco and in the Dioceses of Las Cruces, Providence, Rockville Centre, Savannah, and St. Petersburg.

[1380] (O.S.F.)—FRANCISCAN MISSIONARIES OF OUR LADY P
Founded in Calais, France in 1854. First U.S. foundation in 1913.
General Motherhouse: Paris, France.
Generalate: Paris, France.
Provincial and Novitiate House: *Maryville Novitiate,* 4200 Essen Ln., Baton Rouge LA 70809. Tel: 225-926-1627; Fax: 225-925-5268. Sr. Brendan M. Ronayne, Supr.
Total number in community 27.
Properties owned and sponsored: *Our Lady of the Lake Regional Medical Center, Inc.,* Baton Rouge, LA; *Ollie Steele Burden Manor, Inc.,* Baton Rouge, LA; *Our Lady of Lourdes Regional Medical Center, Inc.,* Lafayette, LA; *St. Francis Medical Center, Inc.,* Monroe, LA; *FMOL Health System, Inc.,* Baton Rouge, LA; *Haiti Project, Inc.,* Baton Rouge, LA.
Represented in the Dioceses of Baton Rouge, Lafayette (LA) and Shreveport.

[1390] (O.S.F.)—FRANCISCAN MISSIONARY SISTERS OF OUR LADY OF SORROWS D
Founded in Hunan China in 1939. First United States foundation in 1950.
Community Headquarters: *Our Lady of Peace Retreat House,* 3600 S.W. 170th Ave., Beaverton, OR 97006. Tel: 503-649-7127; Fax: 503-649-8382. Sr. Anne Marie Warren, O.S.F., Supr. Gen.
Total number in community 53.
Legal Titles and Holdings: *Our Lady of Peace Retreat,* Beaverton, OR; *St. Clare Retreat House,* Soquel, CA; *Our Lady of Mt. Carmel Group Home,* Gallup, NM.
Ministry in religious and academic education; retreat houses, group homes, and foreign missions.
Represented in the Archdiocese of Portland (OR), and the Dioceses of Gallup and Monterey.

[1400] (F.M.S.C.)—FRANCISCAN MISSIONARY SISTERS OF THE SACRED HEART P
Founded in Italy in 1861. First foundation in the U.S. in New York City (1865).
General Motherhouse: Rome, Italy. Sr. Ermenegilda Cavasin, Supr. Gen.
St. Francis Province (1869): *Mt. St. Francis,* 250 South St., Peekskill, NY 10566. Tel: 914-737-5409; Fax: 914-736-9614. Sr. M. Rose Cecilia Bozzo, F.M.S.C., Prov.
Universal number in Congregation 782; Number in United States Province 59.
Legal Title: *Missionary Sisters of the Third Order of St. Francis.*
Ministry in Religious and Academic Education; Health Care for Retired Sisters; Pastoral Ministry; Prison Apostolate; Hospital Ministry.
Represented in the Archdioceses of Newark, New York and in Dioceses of Brooklyn.

[1410] (F.M.S.J.)—MILL HILL SISTERS P
Franciscan Missionaries of St. Joseph
Founded in 1883. First United States foundation in 1952.
Generalate: *St. Joseph's Convent,* Worsley Manchester, England. Sr. Joan O'Gorman, F.M.S.J., Supr. Gen.
American Headquarters: *Franciscan House,* 1006 Madison Ave., Albany, NY 12208. Tel: 518-482-1991. Sr. Joan Kerley, F.M.S.J., Reg Supr.
Legal Title: *Mill Hill Sisters–New York Charitable Trust.*
Total number in community 12.
Represented in the Dioceses of Albany and Norwich.

[1415] (F.S.M.)—FRANCISCAN SISTERS OF MARY P
Founded in the United States in 1872.
Administrative Offices & Novitiate: *Franciscan Sisters of Mary,* 1100 Bellevue Ave., St. Louis, MO 63117-1883. Tel: 314-768-1824; Fax: 314-768-1880. Sr. Jacqueline Motzel, F.S.M., Pres.
Total number in community 185.
Properties owned or sponsored: *St. Mary of the Angels,* St. Louis, MO.
Ministry in Hospitals; Skilled Nursing Facilities; Rehabilitation Unit; Hospice; Foreign Missions; Woman's Center; Social Services; Birthing Centers; Pastoral Services; Wholistic Health Services; Consultation Services.
Represented in the Archdioceses of Chicago, Cincinnati, Milwaukee, Oklahoma City, St. Louis and the Dioceses of Albany, Belleville, Brownsville, Charleston, Jefferson City, Kansas City-St. Joseph, Lexington, Madison, and Springfield-Cape Girardeau. Also in Brazil.

[1420] (F.S.R.)—FRANCISCAN SISTERS OF RINGWOOD D
Founded in the United States in Passaic, New Jersey on Nov. 21, 1929.
General Motherhouse and Novitiate: *Mt. St. Francis,* Ringwood, NJ 07456. Tel: 973-962-7411; Fax: 973-962-0445. Sr. Annette Lucchese, Gen. Coord.
Total number in community 30.
Ministry in the field of academic and religious education and as pastoral associates.
Represented in the Archdioceses of Newark and the Diocese of Paterson.

[1425] (F.S.P.)—FRANCISCAN SISTERS OF PEACE D
Sisters of St. Francis of Peace: *Congregation Center,* 20 Ridge St., Haverstraw, NY 10927. Tel: 845-429-2527; Fax: 845-942-8141. Sr. Margaret Gaffikin, F.S.P., Congregation Minister.

Total number in the community 83.
Legal Titles and Holdings: *Our Lady of Hope Convent*, Cortlandt Manor, NY; *Congregation Center*, Haverstraw, NY.
Ministry in Youth; Care for the Aged; Pastoral; Education; Nursing; Catechetical; Social Work; Prison Ministry; Ministry to Unwed mothers; Evangelization; Social Services; Chaplaincies.
Represented in the Archdioceses of Chicago, Newark, New York, San Francisco and the Diocese of Albany, Brooklyn, Camden, Charlotte, Gallup, Paterson, Pueblo, Rockville Centre and Tucson.

[1430] (O.S.F.)—FRANCISCAN SISTERS OF OUR LADY OF PERPETUAL HELP P

Founded in the United States in 1901.
Motherhouse and Novitiate: *Villa St. Joseph*, 201 Brotherton Ln., St. Louis (Ferguson), MO 63135. Tel: 314-522-6800. Sr. Monica Marie Laws, O.S.F., Supr. Gen.
Total number in community 148.
Legal Holdings and Titles: *Villa St. Joseph Motherhouse and Novitiate*, St. Louis, MO; *St. Francis Health Care Centre*, Green Springs, OH; *Perpetual Help Charitable Trust*, St. Louis, MO.
Ministry in Education; Nursing Homes; Rehabilitation Hospital; Indian Missions.
Represented in the Archdioceses of Chicago, Kansas City in Kansas, Milwaukee, St. Louis, Santa Fe and the Dioceses of Belleville, El Paso, Las Cruces, Phoenix, Portland (ME), Shreveport, Toledo and Wichita.

[1440] (S.F.P.)—FRANCISCAN SISTERS OF THE POOR P

Founded in Aachen, Germany in 1845. First foundation in the United States in 1858.
Congregational Office: 133 Remsen St., Brooklyn, NY 11201. Tel: 718-643-1919; Fax: 718-643-9710. Sr. Jeanne M. Glisky, S.F.P., Congregational Min.
Total number in community 181.
Congregation Sponsors: *Franciscan Health Partnership, Inc.; The Franciscan Sisters of the Poor, Inc.*
U.S. Region: 60 Compton Rd., Cincinnati, OH 45215. Tel: 513-761-9040; Fax: 513-761-6703. Sr. Marilyn Trowbridge, S.F.P., Reg. Min.
Congregation sponsors: *St. Joseph Franciscan House, Inc.*, Brooklyn, NY; *Franciscan Sisters of the Poor Foundation, Inc.; Franciscan Sisters of the Poor Health System, Inc.*, Brooklyn Heights, NY; *St. Leonard Center*, Centerville, OH; *Franciscan Health System of Dayton, Inc.*; Co-Sponsors: *St. Anthony Medical Center, Inc.*, Columbus, OH; *West Park Retirement Community, Inc.*, Cincinnati, OH; *St. Raphael Social Service Center, Inc.*, Hamilton, OH; *West Park II, Inc.; St. John Social Service Center, Inc.; Franciscan Health System of Cincinnati, Inc.*—Subsidiaries: St. Clare Retirement Community, Inc. Parent:—Subsidiaries: *Mary Black Schroder Home for the Aging, Inc.*, Hamilton, OH; *Brazil Regional House and Frascati Complex*, Italy.
Represented in the Archdioceses of Cincinnati, Detroit, Newark, New York, Philadelphia and the Dioceses of Brooklyn, Charleston, Columbus, Gallup, Lansing, Lexington, Phoenix and Springfield (IL). Also in Italy, Senegal and Brazil.

[1450] (O.S.F.)—FRANCISCAN SISTERS OF THE SACRED HEART P

Congregation of the Franciscan Sisters of the Sacred Heart. Founded in Germany 1866. Established in the United States in 1876.
Motherhouse, Novitiate, Postulancy & Portiuncula Center for Prayer: *St. Francis Woods*, 9201 W. St. Francis Rd., Frankfort, IL. Tel: 60423-8335, 815-469-4895; Fax: 815-464-3809. Sr. Mary Elizabeth Imler, Gen. Supr.
Legal Titles: *An Association of Franciscan Sisters of the Sacred Heart; The Franciscan Sisters of the Sacred Heart in California.*
Legal Titles for Health Care entities: *Franciscan Sisters Health Care Corporation; St. Anne's Maternity Home; St. Francis Medical Center of Santa Barbara Franciscan Foundation.*
Sisters sponsor: *St. Joseph Medical Center*, Joliet, IL; *St. Joseph Hospital*, Elgin, IL; *St. Francis Medical Center*, Santa Barbara, CA; *St. Joseph College of Nursing*, Joliet, IL; *Villa Franciscan*, Joliet, IL; *Sacred Heart Home*, Avilla, IN; *LaVerna Terrace*, Avilla, IN; *St. Anne's Maternity Home*, Los Angeles, CA; *United Samaritans Medical Center, Logan Campus*, Danville, IL; *United Samaritans Medical Center, Sager Campus*, Danville, IL; *St. Therese Medical Center*, Waukegan, IL; *Franciscan Foundation*, Frankfort, IL.
Total number in community 139.
Sisters serve and staff: Elementary Schools; High School; Religious Education Centers; Neighborhood Health Care Centers; Foreign Mission Centers; Direct Domestic Work at Retreat Houses; Canon Lawyer; Diocesan Offices; Retreat Centers; Clinics, Home Health Agencies, Health Care Systems, Hospitals, Schools of Nursing, Nursing and Retirement Homes; Home for Unwed Mothers; Apartments-Well Elderly; Parish & Youth Ministry; Hispanic Ministry; Liturgical Ministry; Social Work; Congregate Care Facility.
Represented in the Archdioceses of Chicago, Los Angeles and the Dioceses of Fort Wayne-South Bend, Gary, Joliet, Peoria and Rockford. Also in Brazil.

[1460] (F.S.S.E.)—FRANCISCAN SISTERS OF ST. ELIZABETH P
(Suore Francescane Elisabettine)

First founded in Naples, Italy, 1865. Founded in United States in Newark, New Jersey in 1919.
General Motherhouse: Via Marsico Nuovo 35, Rome, Italy. Mother Clara Capaso, Supr. Gen.
Delegate House: 499 Park Rd., Parsippany, NJ 07054. Tel: 973-539-3797. Mother Gina Maria Amico, Delegate Gen.
Total number in U.S. 54; Total in Community 300.
Ministry in Day Nurseries; Mission Houses; Elementary Schools and Montessori Schools.
Sisters serve Christ in the person of the poor in Schools & Day Nursery Schools; Catechetical Instruction; Hospitals; Homes for the Poor, Aged, and Disabled.
Represented in the Archdiocese of Newark and the Diocese of Paterson. Also in India, Italy, Panama, Philippines and Africa.

[1470] (F.S.S.J.)—FRANCISCAN SISTERS OF ST. JOSEPH P

Founded in the United States in 1897.
General Motherhouse: *Immaculate Conception Convent*, 5286 S. Park Ave., Hamburg, NY 14075. Tel: 716-649-1205; Fax: 716-649-5958. Sr. Mary Paulette Tirone, F.S.S.J., Gen. Min.
Total number in community 174.
Properties owned: *St. Clare Convent*, Hamburg, NY; *Immaculata Academy*, Hamburg, NY; *Hilbert College*, Hamburg, NY; *Marycrest Manor*, Livonia, MI; *St. Joseph Hospital*, Cheektowaga, NY.
Ministry in Education; Health Care; Parish Ministries.
Represented in the Archdioceses of Baltimore, Detroit, Milwaukee and in the Dioceses of Bridgeport, Brooklyn, Buffalo, Harrisburg, Norwich, Savannah, Springfield (MA) and Trenton.

[1480] (F.S.S.J.)—FRANCISCAN SISTERS OF ST. JOSEPH D

Founded in Mexico.
Motherhouse: Ave. Revolucion No. 431, Delegacion Benito Juarez, Mexico, D.F. 03801. Tel: 277-29-66. Rev. Madre Eva Juana Perez, H.F.J.
U.S. Address: *St. Paul's College*, 3015 4th St., N.E., Washington, DC 20017-1199. Tel: 202-832-6262; 269-2515.
Total number in community 5.
Ministry in domestic areas.
Represented in the Archdiocese of Washington.

[1485] (O.S.F.)—FRANCISCAN SISTERS OF ST. PAUL, MN. P
Franciscan Sisters of the Blessed Virgin Mary of the Holy Angels
(Beatae Mariae Virginis Angelorum)

Founded in Germany in 1863. First foundation in the United States in St. Paul in 1923.
General Motherhouse (1863): *St. Marienhaus*, Waldbreitbach, bei Neuwied, Rhine, Germany. Sr. Basina Kloos, O.S.F., Supr. Gen.
Universal total in Congregation 475.
U.S Foundation: *Franciscan Regional Center*, 1388 Prior Ave. S., St. Paul, MN 55116. Tel: 516-690-1501; Fax: 516-690-2509. Sr. Mary Wolfe, Prov.
Total number in community 12.
Represented in the Archdiocese of St. Paul-Minneapolis.

[1490] (O.S.F.)—SISTERS OF THE THIRD FRANCISCAN ORDER P

Founded in the United States in 1860.
Generalate Offices: *Sisters of the Third Franciscan Order*, 2500 Grant Blvd., Syracuse, NY 13208-1794. Tel: 315-425-0115; Fax: 315-425-0610. Sr. Marion Kikukawa, Gen. Supr.
Motherhouse: *St. Anthony Convent*, 1024 Court St., Syracuse, NY 13208-1794.
Total number in community 321.
Ministry in Academic Education at all levels; Hospitals; Schools of Nursing; Religious Education & Pastoral Ministry; Retreat House; Rehabilitation Centers; Home for Dying; Adult & Child Day Care.
Legal Holding: *Sisters of the Third Franciscan Order-Retirement Trust Fund.*
Properties Owned and/or Sponsored: *Sister Patricia Ann Preschool dba Gingerbread House*, Syracuse, NY; *St. Anthony Convent and Motherhouse*, Syracuse, NY; *St. Joseph's Hospital Health Center*, Syracuse, NY; *St. Elizabeth Hospital*, Utica, NY; *Stella Maris Retreat Center*, Skaneateles, NY; *St. Francis Social Adult Day Service*, Syracuse, NY; *St. Francis Health Care System*, Honolulu, HI; *St. Francis School*, Honolulu, HI; *Mercy Health and Rehabilitation Center*, Auburn, NY.
Represented in the Archdioceses of Boston, Cincinnati, Los Angeles, Miami, Newark, San Antonio, Washington and the Dioceses of Albany, Camden, Gallup, Harrisburg, Honolulu, Orange, Orlando, Richmond, Rochester, San Diego, St. Petersburg, Scranton, Syracuse, Trenton, and Venice. Also in Peru.

[1500] (F.M.I.)—FRANCISCAN SISTERS OF MARY IMMACULATE OF THE THIRD ORDER OF ST. FRANCIS OF ASSISI P

Founded in Switzerland in the 16th Century. First founded in the United States on Aug. 15, 1932 at Amarillo, Texas.
General Motherhouse: Carrera 79 No. 40A-20 - Apartado Aereo 98892, Bogota, Colombia, South America. Sr. Ana Margarita Untersander, F.M.I., Supr. Gen.
Universal total in congregation 598.
U.S. Provincial House and Novitiate (1964): *St. Francis Convent* (1932), 4301 N.E. 18th Ave., Amarillo, TX 79107-7220. Tel: 806-383-5769; Fax: 806-383-6545. Sr. Geraldine Duran, F.M.I., Prov. Supr.
Total number in community 40.
Represented in the Archdioceses of Los Angeles, Santa Fe and the Diocese of Amarillo.

[1505] (O.S.F.)—ST. FRANCIS MISSION COMMUNITY

Established 1981 in the United States of America in Amarillo, Texas, as an autonomous province of the Franciscan Sisters of Mary Immaculate.
General Motherhouse: *St. Francis Convent*, 4305 54th St., Lubbock, TX 79413-4617. Tel: 806-793-9859. Sr. Mary Jane Alaniz, O.S.F., Mission Community Coord.
Professed Sisters 22.
Ministry in the field of Religious and Academic Education in Elementary and Middle Schools; Parish Work; Pastoral Care in Hospitals.
Properties owned: *La Verna Convent*, Amarillo, TX; *St. Francis Convent*, Lubbock, TX; 50 acres of real estate.
Represented in the Archdiocese of Los Angeles and the Dioceses of Amarillo and Lubbock. Also in Mexico.

[1510] (O.S.F.)—SISTERS OF ST. FRANCIS D

Sisters of St. Francis of the Mission of the Immaculate Virgin. Founded in New York in 1893.
General Motherhouse: *Sisters of St. Francis-Immaculate Conception Motherhouse*, 49 Jackson Ave., Hastings-on-Hudson, NY 10706-3217. Tel: 914-478-3930; Fax: 914-478-5470. Sr. Roberta Stark Smith, Gen. Minister.
Total number in community 76.
Properties sponsored: *St. Francis Hospital*, Poughkeepsie, NY; *Nazareth Day Nursery*, New York, NY.
Ministry in Education; Day Nurseries; Hospitals and Parishes.
Represented in the Archdiocese of New York.

[1520] (O.S.F.)—SISTERS OF ST. FRANCIS OF CHRIST THE KING P

Founded in Austria in 1869. First founded in the United States at Kansas City, Kansas, in 1909.
General Motherhouse: Rome, Italy. Sr. Natalija Palac, Supr. Gen.
Universal number in congregation 1,200.
St. Francis of Assisi of Christ the King Province (1926): *Mt. Assisi Convent*, 13900 Main St., Lemont, IL 60439. Tel: 630-257-7495. Sr. M. Paula Nasenbeny, O.S.F., Prov. Supr.
Total number in community 71.
Properties owned and sponsored: *Mount Assisi Convent and Academy*, Lemont, IL; *Alvernia Manor*, Lemont, IL.
Ministry in Education and Care in Homes for the Aged.
Represented in the Archdioceses of Chicago and the Diocese of Joliet.

[1530] (O.S.F.)—SISTERS OF ST. FRANCIS OF THE CONGREGATION OF OUR LADY OF LOURDES SYLVANIA, OHIO P

Founded in the United States in 1916 at Sylvania, Ohio. Foundation from Rochester, Minnesota.
General Motherhouse: *Convent and Novitiate*, 6832 Convent Blvd., Sylvania, OH 43560-2897. Tel: 419-882-2016; Fax: 419-885-8643. Sr. Ruth Marie Kachelek, Minister Gen.
Total number in the Congregation 291.

Properties owned and sponsored: *Lourdes College,* Sylvania, OH; *Franciscan Services Corp., Hospital System,* Sylvania, OH. Sponsored Facilities: *St. Francis Health Center,* Madisonville, TX; *Providence Hospital, Inc.,* Sandusky, OH; *Burleson St. Joseph Health Center,* Caldwell, TX; *Trinity Community Medical Center,* Brenham, TX; *St. Joseph Regional Health Center,* Bryan, TX; *Franciscan Shelters (Bethany House),* Toledo, OH; *Franciscan Center,* Sylvania, OH; *Convent Park Apartments,* Sylvania, OH; *Providence Care Center,* Sandusky, OH; *The Commons of Providence,* Sandusky, OH; *Trinity Medical Center East and Trinity Medical Center West,* Steubenville, OH.

Ministry in the field of Religious and Academic Education at all levels; Healthcare; Communications, Media, Producing; Counseling; Parish Ministries; Retreat Center; Social Services.

Represented in the Archdioceses of Atlanta, Detroit, Los Angeles, New Orleans, Portland (OR), St. Paul-Minneapolis, Santa Fe, Washington and the Dioceses of Austin, Biloxi, Cleveland, Columbus, Dallas, Grand Rapids, Jackson, Knoxville, Lansing, Lafayette, Pueblo, Raleigh, Richmond, St. Cloud, Sioux City, Springfield-Cape Girardeau, Shreveport, Steubenville, Toledo, Wheeling-Charleston, and Winona.

[1540] (O.S.F.)—SISTERS OF SAINT FRANCIS, CLINTON, IOWA P

Founded in the United States in 1866.

General Motherhouse: *Administrative Center,* 588 N. Bluff Blvd., Clinton, IA 52732. Tel: 319-242-7611; Fax: 319-243-0007. Sr. Marilyn Huegerich, O.S.F., Pres.

Total number in community 101.

Legal Holdings and Properties: *Mount St. Clare College; The Alverno Health Care Facility; Mount St. Clare Speech and Hearing Center; Sisters of St. Francis, Clinton, Iowa Charitable Trust,* Clinton, IA; *The Canticle,* Clinton, IA.

Ministry in the field of Academic Education at all levels; Home Health Care; Health Care in Centers and Homes for the aged; Hospitals; Pastoral Ministry; Hospital Chaplaincy; Religious Education and Spiritual Direction; Prison Ministry; Ministry to the Poor in Legal Aid and Housing as well as to Persons with AIDS.

Represented in the Archdioceses of Chicago, Detroit, Dubuque, Indianapolis, Louisville, St. Louis and the Dioceses of Belleville, Charleston, Davenport, Des Moines, Joliet, Lexington, Kansas City-St. Joseph, Oakland, Orange, Peoria, Portland, Phoenix, San Bernardino, San Diego, and Sioux City. Also in Peru.

[1550] (O.S.F.)—SISTERS OF ST. FRANCIS OF THE HOLY CROSS D

Founded in Wisconsin in 1881.

Motherhouse and Novitiate: *St. Francis Convent,* 3025 Bay Settlement Rd., Green Bay, WI 54311-7301. Tel: 920-468-1828; Fax: 920-468-1207. Sr. Sally Ann Brickner, O.S.F., Pres.

Total number in community 86.

Legal Title: *Sisters of St. Francis of the Holy Cross, Inc.*

Ministries in the following areas: Education; Pastoral Ministry and Religious Education; Ministry to the Elderly; Health Care; Hospital Chaplaincy; Retreat Work; Foreign Missions.

Represented in the Archdioceses of Milwaukee, Washington and the Diocese of Green Bay. Also in Nicaragua.

[1560] (O.S.F.)—SISTERS OF ST. FRANCIS OF THE HOLY EUCHARIST D

Founded in Grimmenstein, Switzerland in 1378. First foundation in United States in 1892.

Motherhouse, Novitiate and Prayer Center: *St. Francis Convent,* 2100 N. Noland Rd., Independence, MO 64050. Tel: 816-252-1673; Fax: 816-252-5574. Sr. M. Connie Boulch, O.S.F., Sister Servant; Sr. M. Lucy Lang, O.S.F., Vicar.

Total number in community 18.

Ministry in the following areas: Education at all levels; Retreat; Evangelization; Pastoral; Health Care.

Legal Title: *Franciscan Prayer Center,* Independence, MO; *Sisters of St. Francis of the Holy Eucharist Foundation,* Independence, MO.

Represented in the Archdiocese of Kansas City in Kansas and the Diocese of Kansas City-St. Joseph.

[1570] (O.S.F.)—SISTERS OF ST. FRANCIS OF THE HOLY FAMILY P

Founded in Germany in 1864. First foundation in the United States in 1875.

Motherhouse and Novitiate: *Mount St. Francis,* 3390 Windsor Ave., Dubuque, IA 52001-1311. Tel: 319-583-9786; Fax: 319-583-3250. Sr. Dorothy Heiderscheit, Pres.; Sr. Elvira Kelley, Community Archivist.

Total number in community 424.

Ministry in Ministry in the following areas: Elementary and High Schools; Intercommunity High Schools; Religious Education-Parish Ministry; Health-Pastoral Care; Diocesan Offices; Social Service-Social Justice Centers; Food Service-Dietary; Communication Centers; Clerical Work-Business; Administration; Campus Ministry; Deaf Ministry; Art Studios; International Missions.

Properties owned and sponsored: *Briar Cliff College,* Sioux City, IA; *Stonehill Care Center; Alverno Apartments; Shalom Retreat Center and Mercy Health Center* (co-sponsors), Dubuque, IA; *Sisters of St. Francis of the Holy Family Charitable Trust,* Dubuque, IA.

Represented in the Archdioceses of Anchorage, Chicago, Detroit, Dubuque, Indianapolis, Milwaukee, Omaha, Philadelphia, Portland (OR), St. Paul-Minneapolis, San Antonio, San Francisco, Santa Fe, and the Dioceses of Austin, Bismarck, Charleston, Charlotte, Colorado Springs, Columbus, Davenport, Des Moines, Fort Wayne-South Bend, Gary, Jackson, Joliet, Las Cruces, Lafayette, Lexington, Little Rock, Madison, Manchester, New Ulm, Owensboro, Phoenix, Providence, Pueblo, Rapid City, Richmond, Rockford, St. Petersburg, Santa Rosa, Sioux City, Springfield-Cape Girardeau, Springfield (IL), Tucson, Tulsa, Tyler and Winona. Also in Central America & Africa.

[1580] (O.S.F.)—SISTERS OF ST. FRANCIS OF THE IMMACULATE CONCEPTION D

Founded in the United States in 1891.

Motherhouse: *Immaculate Conception Convent Inc.,* 2408 W. Heading Ave., West Peoria, IL 61604-5096. Tel: 309-674-6168. Sr. Mary Barbara Buckley, Pres.; Sr. Mary Virginia Butkovich, Archivist.

Total number in community 54.

Properties owned and sponsored: *Immaculate Conception Convent,* Peoria, IL; *St. Joseph's Home of Peoria; St. Joseph's Home of Springfield in Illinois.*

Represented in the Dioceses of Joliet, Peoria, Rapid City and Springfield (IL).

[1590] (O.S.F.)—SISTERS OF ST. FRANCIS OF THE IMMACULATE HEART OF MARY (HANKINSON, NORTH DAKOTA) P

Founded in 1241 in Bavaria. First founded in the United States in 1913 at Collegeville, Minnesota.

General Motherhouse: Dillingen, Germany. Sr. Ann Marie Friederichs, Supr. Gen.

Province of Hankinson (1928): *Sisters of St. Francis Motherhouse,* Hankinson, ND 58041. Tel: 701-242-7195. Sr. Donna Welder, O.S.F., Prov. Supr.

Professed Sisters 60; Novices 2.

Legal Holdings or Titles: *St. Gerard's Community Nursing Home,* Hankinson, ND; *St. Anne's Guest Home,* Grand Forks, ND.

Ministry in the field of Religious and Academic Education; Health Care in Hospitals; Homes for the Aged.

Represented in the Diocese of Fargo.

[1600] (O.S.F.)—SISTERS OF ST. FRANCIS OF THE MARTYR ST. GEORGE P

Founded in Thuine, Germany. First United States foundation in 1923.

General Motherhouse: Thuine, Germany. Mother M. Carmen Droste, O.S.F., Supr. Gen.American Province St. Elizabeth

Provincial Motherhouse: *St. Francis Convent and Novitiate,* 2120 Central Ave., P.O. Box 9020, Alton, IL 62002-9020. Tel: 618-463-2750; 463-2755. Mother M. Ingeborg Rohner, O.S.F., Prov.

Worldwide Total 1,800. Total in American Province 170

Properties owned and sponsored: *Saint Anthony's Hospital,* Alton, IL; *St. Francis Day Care Center,* Alton, IL; *Mother of Good Counsel Home,* St. Louis, MO; *Saint Clare Hospital,* Alton, IL.

Sisters serve and staff: Hospitals; Homes for Chronically ill; Foreign Missions; Day Care Center; Retirement Homes for the Aged; Grade & High Schools; Retirement Homes for Priests.

Represented in the Archdioceses of St. Louis and Washington and the Dioceses of La Crosse, Lincoln, Metuchen, Peoria, Springfield (IL) and Tulsa.

[1620] (O.S.F.)—SISTERS OF SAINT FRANCIS OF MILLVALE, PENNSYLVANIA P

Motherhouse and Novitiate (1871): *St. Francis Convent,* Mt. Alvernia, 146 Hawthorne Rd., Millvale P.O. Pittsburgh, PA 15209. Tel: 412-821-2200; Fax: 412-821-3318. Sr. Eileen Magill, O.S.F., Community Min.; Sr. M. Thomasita Heller, O.S.F., Community Archivist; Sr. Marilyn Joyce, O.S.F., Community Archivist.

Total number in community 207.

Properties owned: *Mt. Alvernia High School,* Millvale, PA; *Mt. Alvernia Day Care & Learning Center,* Pittsburgh, PA.

Sponsored or managed facilities: *St. Francis Health System; St. Francis Hospital,* New Castle, PA.

Ministry in the following areas: Academic High Schools; Hospitals; Consolidated Elementary Schools; Schools of Nursing; Day Care and Learning Center; Montessori School.

Represented in the Archdioceses of Baltimore, Buffalo, Chicago, Indianapolis, Los Angeles, Miami, Newark, Philadelphia, Santa Fe, San Juan, Washington and the Dioceses of Altoona-Johnstown, Caguas, Erie, Greensburg, La Crosse, Lubbock, Pittsburgh, Savannah, Sioux Falls, and Steubenville. Also in Canada and Nigeria.

[1630] (O.S.F.)—SISTERS OF ST. FRANCIS OF PENANCE AND CHRISTIAN CHARITY P

(aka Sisters of St. Francis of the Holy Name Province)

Founded in Holland in 1835. First Foundation in the U.S. in 1874.

General Motherhouse: Rome, Italy. Sr. Anisia Margareta Schneider, Gen. Min.

Universal number in Congregation 2,224.

Holy Name Province (1928): *Sisters of St. Francis,* 4421 Lower River Rd., Stella Niagara, NY 14144. Tel: 716-754-4312; Fax: 716-754-7657. Sr. Mary McCarrick, O.S.F., Prov. Minister.

Total number in community 202.

Legal Holdings: *Stella Niagara Education Park,* Stella Niagara, NY; *Buffalo Academy of the Sacred Heart,* Eggertsville, NY; *Francis Center,* Niagara Falls, NY; *St. Francis of Holy Name Province, Inc.,* Stella Niagara, NY.

Ministry in the field of Academic Education at all levels; Foreign Mission Work; Health and Hospital Care; Social Work; Pastoral Ministry.

Represented in the Archdioceses of Chicago, Cincinnati, Louisville, Miami, Sante Fe and the Dioceses of Buffalo, Columbus, Orlando, Paterson, St. Petersburg, Steubenville, Trenton, Venice, and Wheeling-Charleston. Also in Canada.

Sacred Heart Province (1939): *Provincial Motherhouse-Marycrest,* 2851 W. 52nd Ave., Denver, CO 80221; Tel: 303-458-6270. Sr. Gloria Shuffer, Prov. Minister.

Total number in community 78.

Sisters Serve and Staff: High Schools; Parish Ministries; Apostolate of Aging; Diocesan Biblical School; Hospital Pastoral Ministry; Emergency Housing; Home for Neglected Children; Retreat Ministry; Formation Programs; Administrative.

Legal Holdings or Titles: *Marycrest Motherhouse; Marycrest Franciscans Development, Inc.; Queen of Peace Convent, House of Prayer; Damen House - Home for Single Women & Children; Marycrest Health System; Sisters of St. Francis Foundation-Sacred Heart Province,* Denver, CO; *St. Francis Home,* (Home for Abused Native American Children), Manderson, SD; *Marian Residence, Convent for Retired Sisters,* Alliance, NE; *St. Francis Convent; St. Clare Convent,* Alliance, NE.

Represented in the Archdioceses of Denver, Omaha, Sante Fe and the Dioceses of Bismarck, Grand Island, and Las Vegas.

St. Francis Province (1939): *Mt. Alverno,* 3910 Bret Harte Dr., P.O. Box 1028, Redwood City, CA 94064. Tel: 650-369-1725. Sr. Maria Elena Martinez, Prov. Minister.

Total number in community 100.

Legal Title: *Sisters of St. Francis Charitable Trust; Sisters of St. Francis - Mount Alverno.*

Ministry in the following areas: Grammar Schools; Formation House; Colleges; Diocesan Offices; Parish Ministry; Pastoral Ministry; Catholic Social Services Agencies; Secondary Education; Hospitals; Residence for Retired Men and Women; Day Home; CCD Centers; Retreat-Conference Centers; Apostolic Projects; ESL.

Represented in the Archdioceses of Los Angeles, Portland (OR), San Francisco, Seattle and the Dioceses of Monterey, Oakland, Phoenix, Sacramento, San Diego, San Jose and Stockton.

[1640] (O.S.F.) SISTERS OF ST. FRANCIS OF PERPETUAL ADORATION P

Founded in Germany in 1863. First foundation in the United States in 1875.

Generalate: Olpe, Westfalen, Germany. Sr. Mediatrix Neis, Supr Gen.

Universal total in congregation 745.

Province of the Immaculate Heart of Mary (1875): *Provincial House and Novitiate, St. Francis Convent,* Box 766, Mishawaka IN 46546-0766. Tel: 219-259-5427. Sr. M. Blanche Rausch, O.S.F., Prov.

Total number in community 154.
Ministry in the field of Academic Education at all levels; Health Care in Hospitals.
Properties owned: *Sisters of St. Francis of Perpetual Adoration, Inc.; St. Francis Convent,* Mishawaka, IN; *University of St. Francis, Inc.,* Fort Wayne, IN; *Sisters of St. Francis Health Services, Inc.; Alverno Clinical Laboratories, Inc.,* Mishawaka, IN; *Sisters of St. Francis Health Services, Inc., Corporate Office,* Mishawaka, IN, owns the following: *Catholic Health Midwest, Inc.,* Mishawaka, IN; *St. Anthony Medical Center of Crown Point,* Crown Point, IN; *St. Anthony Memorial Health Center,* Michigan City, IN; *St. Elizabeth Healthcare Center,* Delphi, IN; *St. Francis Hospital & Health Centers,* Beech Grove, IN; *St. James Hospital and Health Centers,* Chicago Heights, IL; *St. Margaret Mercy Health Care Centers, North Campus,* Hammond, IN; *St. Margaret Mercy Health Care Centers, South Campus,* Dyer, IN; *St. Elizabeth Hospital Medical Center,* Lafayette, IN; *St. James-Hospital Medical Clinic,* Beecher, IL; *Alverno Administrative Services,* Beech Grove, IN.
Represented in the Archdioceses of Chicago, Indianapolis, Louisville and New Orleans and the Dioceses of Fort Wayne-South Bend, Gary, Joliet, Lafayette (IN) and Memphis.
Province of St. Joseph (March 19, 1932): *Provincial House and Formation House-Mt. St. Francis,* 7665 Assisi Heights, Colorado Springs, CO 80919. Tel: 719-598-5486. Sr. Clarice Gentrup, Prov.
Professed Sisters 105.
Ministry in Education; Hospitals; Homes for the Aged; Parish/Pastoral Ministry; Religious Education Centers.
Represented in the Archdioceses of Denver, Omaha, Santa Fe and the Dioceses of Colorado Springs, Grand Island, and Lincoln.

[1650] (O.S.F.)—THE SISTERS OF ST. FRANCIS OF PHILADELPHIA P

Founded in the United States in 1855.
Congregational Motherhouse: *Convent of Our Lady of Angels,* Aston, PA 19014. Tel: 215-459-4125. Sr. Marie Lucey, O.S.F., Congregational Min.; Sr. Esther Anderson, O.S.F., Asst. Congregational Min.; Sr. Eileen Valerie Kulacz, O.S.F., Congregational Sec.; Sr. M. Andrew, O.S.F., Archivist.
Total number in community 786.
Properties owned: *Formation House,* Puerto Rico; *Sisters of St. Francis,* Sea Isle City, NJ; *Franciscan Residence,* Hamilton Square, NJ; *Bay House,* Tacoma, WA; *Marion House,* Tacoma, WA; *St. Ann Convent,* Tacoma, WA; *Neumann College,* Aston, PA; *Assisi House,* Aston, PA; *Catholic Health Initiatives,* Denver, CO; *Portiuncula Convent,* Aston, PA; *St. Mary Convent,* Langhorne, PA; *St. Francis Convent,* Lancaster, PA; *Franciscan Residence,* Langhorne, PA; *St. Agnes Convent,* Philadelphia, PA; *Neumann Convent,* Reading, PA; *The Catholic High School of Baltimore,* Baltimore, MD; *St. Joseph Counseling Center,* Spokane, WA; *Franciscan Renewal Center,* Portland, OR; *Sisters of St. Francis of Philadelphia, Canticle House,* Philadelphia, PA *Sisters of St. Francis of Philadelphia, TAU Convent,* Aston, PA; *St. Clare Renewal Center,* Aston, PA; *Sisters of St. Francis of Philadelphia, Our Lady of the Valley,* Aston, PA *Mt. Alvernia Convent,* Aston, PA; *St. Clare Convent,* Trenton, NJ.
Ministry in Health Care; Eldercare; Academic and Religious Education at all Levels; Specialized Education; Parish Ministry; Social Services; Family Centers; Renewal Centers; Diocesan Offices; Retreat Ministry; National Organizations.
Represented in the Archdioceses of Atlanta, Baltimore, Boston, Hartford, Los Angeles, Mobile, New Orleans, New York, Philadelphia, Portland (OR), San Francisco, San Juan, Santa Fe, Seattle, Washington and the Dioceses of Allentown, Baker, Birmingham, Buffalo, Caguas (PR), Camden, Charleston, Cheyenne, El Paso, Fairbanks, Fort Wayne-South Bend, Gallup, Harrisburg, Honolulu, Lexington, Metuchen, Oakland, Orange, Orlando, Owensboro, Pensacola-Tallahassee, Pittsburgh, Raleigh, Reno, San Bernardino, San Diego, Spokane, Trenton, Venice, Wheeling-Charleston and Wilmington. Also in Ireland, Central America, England, Zambia, Kenya, Ethiopia, West Indies and Dominican Republic

[1660] (O.S.F.)—SISTERS OF SAINT FRANCIS OF THE PROVIDENCE OF GOD P

Founded in Pittsburgh in 1922.
Motherhouse: *St. Francis Convent,* 3603 McRoberts Rd., Pittsburgh, PA 15234-2398. Tel: 412-882-9911; Fax: 412-885-7210. Sr. Joanne Brazinski, O.S.F., Gen. Minister.
Total professed 107.
Properties owned and sponsored: *Sisters of St. Francis of the Providence of God; Sisters of St. Francis, Mt. Vernon Ill., Inc.; Sisters of St. Francis of the Providence of God Ministries Corporation; St. Francis Academy Franciscan Child Day Care Center; Franciscan Spirit and Life Center.*
Ministry in the field of Education; Health Care; Social Service; Pastoral, Parish & Retreat Ministries; Retreat Directors; Prison Chaplains; Foreign Mission work in Brazil & Lithuania.
Represented in the Archdiocese of Newark and the Dioceses of Albany, Bridgeport, Buffalo, Grand Rapids, Paterson, and Pittsburgh.

[1670] (O.S.F.)—SISTER OF ST. FRANCIS OF SAVANNAH, MO P

Founded in Austria, 1850. Founded in the United States, August 22, 1922.
Provincial House and Novitiate: 104 E. Park La Verna Heights, Box 488, Savannah, MO 64485-0488. Tel: 816-324-3179; Fax: 816-324-7264. Sr. Kathleen Reichert, Prov. Supr.
Total number in community 22.
Ministry in long-term care for the elderly and infirm; Academic and Religious education; Hospice care for persons; Housing for Elderly, Persons with Aids, Pastoral Care; Food Pantry.
Legal Holdings and Titles: *Sisters of St. Francis of Savannah, Inc.; Maintenance and Custodial Care Trust of the Franciscan Sisters of Savannah; La Verna Village Apartment Units for Senior Citizens and Handicapped; La Verna Village Nursing Home, Inc.; La Verna Heights Provincial House and Retirement Center.*
Represented in the Diocese Kansas City-St. Joseph.

[1680] (O.S.F.)—SCHOOL SISTERS OF ST. FRANCIS P

Founded in the United States in 1874.
General Motherhouse: 1501 S. Layton Blvd., Milwaukee, WI 53215; Tel: 414-384-4105; Fax: 414-645-7198. Sr. Joan Puls, O.S.F., Pres.; Sr. Alida Lopez, O.S.F., First Vice Pres.; Sr. Toni Anne Gradisnik, O.S.F., Vice Pres.; Sr. Anna Marie Tharakan, O.S.F., Vice Pres.; Sr. Charlita Foxhoven, Treas.; Sr. Constance Halbur, Archivist.
Total in Congregation 1,415; Total in U.S. 918.
Properties owned: *St. Joseph Convent,* Milwaukee, WI; *School Sisters of St. Francis, Inc.*
U.S. Province: 1515 S. Layton Blvd., Milwaukee, WI 53215. Tel: 414-384-1515. Provincial Team: Sr. Therese Thoenen; Sr. Adelia Milligan; Sr. Kathleen Kunze.
Sisters serve and staff: Universities, Colleges, Seminaries, High Schools, Grade Schools, Preschools, Adult and Special Education; National and Diocesan Offices; Hospitals and Nursing Homes; School & Parish Musicians; Retreat and Spiritual Direction; Social Ministries; Campus Ministry; Psychotherapy; Home Health Care Service; Religious Education and CCD; Pastoral Ministry; Pastoral Associate; Health Pastoral Care; Retirement Homes; Overseas Missions; Mission Projects; Special Service to Women; Fine Arts; Home Missions.
Properties owned and sponsored: *Alverno College,* Milwaukee, WI; *Clement Manor, Inc.,* Greenfield, WI; *Maryhill Manor,* Niagra, WI; *New Cassel,* Omaha, NE; *Clare Towers I,* Milwaukee, WI; *Clare Towers II,* Milwaukee, WI; *Telos, Inc.,* Milwaukee, WI; *St. Clare Management, Inc.,* Milwaukee, WI; *Marian Hall,* Milwaukee, WI; *Sacred Heart Center,* Milwaukee, WI; *St. Joseph Convent,* Campbellsport, WI; *School Sisters of St. Francis Foundation, Inc.,* Omaha, NE; *School Sisters of St. Francis of St. Joseph's Convent,* Milwaukee, Wisconsin, Inc.; *Convergence, Inc.,* Milwaukee, WI; *Vision Ministries,* Milwaukee, WI; *The School Sisters of Saint Francis of St. Joseph's Convent, Milwaukee, Wisconsin, Inc. - Congregational Support Charitable Trust,* Milwaukee, WI.
Represented in the Archdioceses of Anchorage, Chicago, Denver, Dubuque, Milwaukee, New York, Oklahoma City, Omaha, St. Louis, St. Paul-Minneapolis, San Antonio, Santa Fe, Washington and the Dioceses of Buffalo, Davenport, Des Moines, El Paso, Green Bay, Jackson, Jefferson City, Joliet, Kansas City-St. Joseph, La Crosse, Lexington, Lincoln, Madison, Nashville, New Ulm, Orange, Phoenix, Rockford, San Bernardino, San Diego, Springfield (IL), St. Petersburg, Superior, Tucson, Venice, Wheeling-Charleston and Winona.

[1690] (O.S.F.)—SCHOOL SISTERS OF THE THIRD ORDER OF ST. FRANCIS (PITTSBURGH, PA.) P

First foundation in the U.S. in 1913.
General Motherhouse: Rome, Italy.
Motherhouse and Novitiate: *Mount Assisi Convent,* 934 Forest Ave., Bellevue, Pittsburgh, PA 15202. Tel: 412-761-6004. Sr. Elaine Hromulak, O.S.F., Prov. Minister. Tel: 412-761-2855.
Total number in community 82.
Legal Title: *School Sisters of the Third Order of St. Francis; School Sisters of the Third Order of St. Francis, of Texas.*
Ministry in the following areas: the field of academic education at all levels; CCD Centers; Pastoral Ministry; Pastoral Associate; Residence Home for Aged Women; Mission Work in Chile & South Africa; Hospital Ministry; Campus Ministry; Social Ministry; House of Prayer.
Represented in the Archdiocese of San Antonio and the Dioceses of Austin, Erie, Greensburg, Phoenix, Pittsburgh and San Angelo. Also in South Africa and Chile.

[1695] (O.S.F.)—SCHOOL SISTERS OF THE THIRD ORDER OF ST. FRANCIS (PANHANDLE, TEXAS) P

Founded in Austria, 1723; The Vienna Foundation in 1845. First founded in the United States, 1931.
General Motherhouse: Vienna, Austria.
American Center and Novitiate: P.O. Box 906, Panhandle, TX 79068. Tel: 806-537-3182. Mother M. Bernadette Black, O.S.F., Reg. Supr.
Total number in U.S. 24.
Ministry in the following areas: Grammar Schools; Confraternity Classes; Home for the Aged.
Represented in the Dioceses of Amarillo and Victoria.

[1700] (O.S.F.)—SCHOOL SISTERS OF THE THIRD ORDER OF ST. FRANCIS (BETHLEHEM, PA.) P

Founded in Austria, 1843. First founded in the United States, 1913.
General Motherhouse: Rome, Italy.
Bethlehem Province and Novitiate: 395 Bridle Path Rd., Bethlehem, PA 18017. Tel: 610-866-2597; Fax: 610-861-7478. Sr. M. Rosaria Shina, O.S.F., Prov. Supr.
Sisters 60.
Properties owned: *St. Francis Academy Kindergarten; St. Francis Day Care; St. Francis Center for Renewal,* Bethlehem, PA.
Represented in the Archdioceses of Newark, Philadelphia and the Dioceses of Allentown, Manchester, Metuchen, Paterson, Springfield (MA), and Trenton. Also in Chile, India, South Africa and Rome, Italy.

[1705] (O.S.F.)—THE SISTERS OF ST. FRANCIS OF ASSISI (Sisters of Penance and Charity)

Founded in the United States in 1849.
General Motherhouse: *St. Francis Convent,* 3221 S. Lake Dr., St. Francis, WI 53235-3799. Tel: 414-744-1160; Fax: 414-744-7193. Sr. Marcia Lunz, O.S.F, Dir.
Total number in community 333.
Legal Titles: *The Sisters of St. Francis of Assisi; The Ongoing Community Support Fund of the Sisters of St. Francis.*
Goals of the Congregation are: to bring the healing, teaching, reconciling and liberating power of Jesus into the human situations in which we live and minister; to be in solidarity with the poor through the work of justice and peace; to appreciate and affirm and to encourage the development of each community member and each community apostolate for the sake of full effectiveness in the ministry of the Church; and to work effectively toward implementing co-responsibility, subsidiarity and accountability at all levels within the Congregation
Sponsored Corporations: *St. Ann Center for Intergenerational Care, Inc.,* Milwaukee, WI; *St. Mary's Academy, Inc.,* Milwaukee, WI; *Cardinal Stritch University, Inc.,* Milwaukee, WI; *St. Coletta's of Wisconsin, Inc.,* Jefferson, WI; *St. Coletta School Foundation of Jefferson Charitable Trust,* Jefferson, WI; *St. Coletta's of Illinois,* Palos Park, IL; *St. Coletta's of Illinois Foundation, Inc.,* Palos Park, IL; *St. Coletta's of Massachusetts: Cardinal Cushing School and Training Center,* Hanover, MA; *Cushing Residence, Inc.,* Hanover, MA; *Cardinal Cushing School Foundation of Hanover Charitable Trust,* Hanover, MA; *St. Coletta Day School,* Braintree, MA. Services to the Elderly: *Alverno Housing Corporation,* Jefferson, WI; *Canticle Court, Inc.; Juniper Court, Inc.,* St. Francis, WI.
Represented in the Archdioceses of Baltimore, Boston, Chicago, Denver, Los Angeles, Milwaukee, Philadelphia, St. Paul-Minneapolis, San Antonio, San Francisco, Santa Fe and the Dioceses of Birmingham, Boise, Buffalo, Cheyenne, Des Moines, Duluth, Fall River, Joliet, Gary, Gallup, Green Bay, La Crosse, Madison, Peoria, Phoenix, Reno, Rockford, San Diego, Santa Rosa, Springfield, Steubenville, Superior, Tucson and Winona. Also in Taiwan.

[1710] (O.S.F.)—CONGREGATION OF THE THIRD ORDER OF ST. FRANCIS OF MARY IMMACULATE, JOLIET, IL P

Founded in the United States, Joliet, Illinois, in 1865.
General Motherhouse: *St. Francis Convent,* 520 Plainfield, Ave., Joliet, IL 60435. Tel: 815-727-3686.

Sr. Maria Pesavento, O.S.F., Pres.; Sr. Marian Voelker, O.S.F., Community Archivist.
Total number in community 329.
Legal Title: *Congregation of the Third Order of St. Francis of Mary Immaculate*, Joliet, IL; *Retirement Plan Trust of the Congregation of the Third Order of St. Francis of Mary Immaculate*, Joliet, IL.
Ministry in the following areas: School and Adult Education; Home for Emotionally Disturbed Children; Retirement Home; House of Prayer. Also engaged in Religious Education; Social Services; Spiritual Direction; Nursing and Health Services; Hospital and Parish Ministry; Food Service; and Prison ministry.
Represented in the Archdioceses of Boston, Chicago, Cincinnati, Denver, Los Angeles, Miami, Milwaukee, Omaha, St. Louis, Washington, and the Dioceses of Cleveland, Colorado Springs, Columbus, Fort Wayne-South Bend, Gary, Joliet, Lansing, Palm Beach, Phoenix, Peoria, Rockford, St. Cloud, San Diego, St. Petersburg, Springfield-Cape Girardeau, Springfield (IL), Stockton, Superior, Toledo, Tucson, and Youngstown. Also in Agana, Guam and Brazil.

[1720] (O.S.F.)—SISTERS OF THE THIRD ORDER REGULAR OF ST. FRANCIS OF THE CONGREGATION OF OUR LADY OF LOURDES P

Founded in the United States in 1877.
Administration Center: *Assisi Heights*, 1001 14th St., N.W., Suite 100, Rochester, MN 55901. Tel: 507-282-7441; Fax: 507-282-7762. Sr. Dolores M. Rockers, O.S.F., Pres./Community Min. Tel: 507-529-3535. Sr. Mary Lonan Reilly, Community Archivist.
Total number in community 367.
Properties owned and sponsored: *Holy Spirit Retreat Center*, Janesville, MN; *Tau Center*, Winona, MN; *Assisi Heights*, Rochester, MN.
Ministry in the following areas: Education Services; Pastoral Concerns Development; Religious Life Development; Spiritual Life Development; Community Life Development; Social Concerns Development; Business Services; Health Care Services; Support Services.
Represented in the Archdioceses of Baltimore, Chicago, Denver, Dubuque, Indianapolis, Milwaukee, Omaha, St. Paul-Minneapolis, San Francisco, Santa Fe, Seattle and Washington and the Dioceses of Brownsville, Charleston, Charlotte, Columbus, Colorado Springs, Gallup, Great Falls-Billings, Helena, Joliet, La Crosse, Las Cruces, Lexington, New Ulm, Oakland, Owensboro, Pueblo, St. Cloud, San Bernardino, San Diego, Sioux Falls, Springfield-Cape Girardeau, Steubenville, Superior, Tucson and Winona. Also in Colombia.

[1730] (O.S.F.)—CONGREGATION OF THE SISTERS OF THE THIRD ORDER OF ST. FRANCIS, OLDENBURG, IN. P

Founded in U.S., Oldenburg, Indiana in 1851.
General Motherhouse and Novitiate: *Convent of the Immaculate Conception*, Oldenburg, IN 47036. Tel: 812-934-2475. Sr. Jean Marie Cleveland, O.S.F., Congregational Minister.
Total number in community 325.
Sisters serve & staff: Liberal Arts College, Academy, High Schools, Elementary Schools; Navajo, Crow Indian and Cheyenne Missions; Religious Education Centers; Hospital & Parish Ministry; Apostolate of Aging; Diocesan Offices; Retreat & Counseling Ministry; Hispanic Ministry; Justice & Peace Offices; Clerical Staff; Social Services; Foreign Missions: New Guinea.
Properties owned: *Marian College*, Indianapolis, IN; *Oldenburg Academy*, Oldenburg, IN.
Represented in the Archdioceses of Chicago, Cincinnati, Detroit, Indianapolis, Los Angeles, Miami, New York, St. Louis and the Dioceses of Charleston, Cleveland, Columbus, Covington, El Paso, Evansville, Gallup, Great Falls-Billings, Helena, Jefferson City, Lexington, Peoria, Springfield-IL, St. Augustine, St. Petersburg and Wheeling-Charleston. Also in Korea and Mexico.

[1760] (O.S.F.)—SISTERS OF THE THIRD ORDER OF ST. FRANCIS OF PENANCE AND OF CHARITY P

Founded in Tiffin, Ohio in 1869.
General Motherhouse: *St. Francis Convent*, St. Francis Ave., Tiffin, OH 44883. Tel: 419-447-0435; Fax: 419-448-1612. Sr. Virginia Welsh, O.S.F., Community Minister.
Total number in community 136.
Legal Title: *Sisters of St. Francis of Tiffin*, OH.
Properties owned or sponsored: *St. Francis Villas, Inc.; St. Francis Home, Inc.*, Tiffin, OH.
Ministry in the following areas: Parochial Schools; Ministry to the Aged; Parish Ministry; Retreat and Renewal Centers; Diocese Offices; Health Care; Health-Pastoral Care; Administration.
Represented in the Archdioceses of Cincinnati, Detroit, Milwaukee, Santa Fe and the Dioceses of Evansville, Cleveland, Columbus, Charlotte, Davenport, Lansing, Lexington, Owensboro, Rockford, Toledo, and Wheeling-Charleston. Also in Mexico

[1770] (O.S.F.)—THE SISTERS OF THE THIRD ORDER OF ST. FRANCIS (EAST PEORIA, ILLINOIS) P

Founded in the United States in 1877.
Motherhouse: 1175 St. Francis Lane, East Peoria, IL 61611-1299. Tel: 309-699-7215. Sr. Mary Ellen Flannery, Major Supr.
Total number in community 64.
Properties owned and sponsored: *Saint Francis Medical Center*, Peoria, IL; *St. Joseph Medical Center*, Bloomington, IL; *St. Mary Medical Center*, Galesburg, IL; *Saint James Hospital*, Pontiac, IL; *Saint Anthony Medical Center*, Rockford, IL; *Saint Francis Hospital*, Escanaba, MI; *St. Francis Continuation Care and Nursing Home Center*, Burlington, IA; *St. Anthony's Continuing Care Center*, Rock Island, IL; *St. Mary of the Angels Convent*, Rock Island, IL; *OSF Healthcare System*, Peoria, IL; *OSF Healthcare Foundation*, Peoria, IL; *Motherhouse*, East Peoria, IL; *Saint Clare Home*, Peoria Heights, IL.
Represented in the Dioceses of Davenport, Marquette, Peoria and Rockford.

[1780] (F.S.P.A.)—CONGREGATION OF THE SISTERS OF THE THIRD ORDER OF ST. FRANCIS OF PERPETUAL ADORATION P
(Francisan Sisters of Perpetual Adoration)

Founded in the United States in 1849.
Generalate - Motherhouse and Novitiate: *St. Rose Convent*, 912 Market St., La Crosse, WI 54601-8800. Tel: 608-782-5610; Fax: 608-782-6301. Sr. Marla Lang, F.S.P.A., Pres.; Sr. Jolyce Greteman, F.S.P.A., Archivist.
Total number in Congregation 463.
Properties owned and sponsored: *St. Joseph Memorial Hospital, Inc.*, Hillsboro, WI; *St. Anthony Regional Hospital, Inc.*, Carroll, IA; *Viterbo College, Inc.*, La Crosse, WI; *Villa St. Joseph*, La Crosse, WI; *Fransican Skemp Healthcare*, La Crosse, WI; *Clare Center*, Spokane, WA; *Fransican Spirituality Center*, La Crosse, WI; *Prairiewoods - Franciscan Spirituality Center*, Hiawatha, IA; *Marywood -Fransican Spirituality Center*, Arbor Vitae, WI.
Represented in the Archdioceses of Agana, Chicago, Denver, Dubuque, Los Angeles, Milwaukee, Mobile, Portland in Oregon, San Antonio, Santa Fe, Seattle, St. Louis, St. Paul-Minneapolis, and the Dioceses of Amarillo, Boise, Davenport, El Paso, Gallup, Green Bay, Helena, Honolulu, Jackson, Joliet, La Crosse, Lexington, Madison, Oakland, Peoria, Phoenix, Reno, Las Vegas, Phoenix, Rockford, San Jose, Savannah, Tucson. Also in Mexico and Europe.

[1800] (O.S.F.)—SISTERS OF ST. FRANCIS OF THE THIRD ORDER REGULAR (WILLIAMSVILLE, NEW YORK) P

Motherhouse: *St. Mary of the Angels Convent of Perpetual Adoration*, P.O. Box 275, Williamsville, NY 14231. Tel: 716-632-2155; Fax: 716-632-0339. Sr. Patricia Burkard, Gen. Minister.
Total number in community 128.
Sisters serve and staff: Universities; High Schools; Grammar Schools; Hospitals; Nursing Homes & Homes for the Aged; Pastoral Ministry in Parishes; Diocesan Offices.
Properties owned and/or sponsored: *Mount St. Mary's LTC Facility, Inc.*, Niagara Falls, NY; *Holy Family Home*, Williamsville, NY.
Represented in the Archdioceses of Chicago, and the Dioceses of Buffalo, Charleston, Oakland, Ogdensburg, Pittsburgh, Rochester, and Syracuse. Also in Africa.

[1810] (O.S.F.)—BERNARDINE FRANCISCAN SISTERS P

Founded in the United States in 1894.
Generalate: 403 Allendale Rd., King of Prussia, PA 19406. Tel: 610-337-3864; Fax: 610-337-4359. Sr. Madonna Marie Harvath, O.S.F., Gen. Min.
Total number in community 518.
Bernardine Sisters OSF—Bernardine Franciscan Sisters: United States Province Offices, 460 St. Bernardine St., Reading, PA 19607-1737. Tel: 610-777-4174; Fax: 610-777-3973. Sr. Danielle Marie Kubelsky, O.S.F., Prov. Minister; Sr. Shaun Patrice Malone, O.S.F., Prov. Minister; Sr. Mary Sninsky, O.S.F., Prov. Minister.
Total number in province 401.
Ministry in the field of academic education at all levels —preschool to college; religious education of children & adults; hospitals, health & home care; retreat work; social work.
Represented in the Archdiocese of Boston, Detroit, Kansas City, Los Angeles, Newark, Philadelphia, San Antonio, San Juan, Washington, and the Dioceses of Allentown, Arlington, Bridgeport, Lexington, Metuchen, Providence, Richmond, Saginaw, Scranton, Trenton and Tucson. Also in Poland and West Africa.
Our Lady of Grace Convent: 106 S. Seventh Ave., West Reading, PA 19611-1022. Tel: 610-372-3390; Fax: 610-372-2786. Sr. Mary Sninsky, O.S.F., Prov. Minister; Sr. Danielle Marie Kubelsky, O.S.F., Prov. Minister; Sr. Shaun Patrice Malone, O.S.F., Prov. Minister.

[1820] (O.S.F.)—HOSPITAL SISTERS OF THE THIRD ORDER OF ST. FRANCIS P

Founded in Germany in 1844. First foundation in the United States in 1875.
General Motherhouse: Muenster in Westphalia, Germany. Sr. Mary Ann Minor, O.S.F., Gen. Supr.
American Province (1875): *St. Francis Convent, Motherhouse and Novitiate*, Box 19431, Springfield, IL 62794. Tel: 217-522-3386. Sr. Joan Winkler, O.S.F., Prov. Supr.; Sr. Maureen O'Connor, O.S.F., Prov. Sec. & Contact Person.
Total number in the community 190.
Sisters serve and staff: Hospitals; Home Health Services; Catechetical; Care of Chemically Dependent; Social Ministries; Pastoral Ministries; Overseas Missions.
Properties owned or sponsored: Residence 18; *St. Francis Convent, Motherhouse, Novitiate*, Springfield, IL; *Hospital Sisters Services, Inc.; Hospital Sisters of St. Francis Foundation; Hospital Sisters Health System; St. John's Hospital; St. John's College of Nursing*, Springfield, IL; *St. Mary's Hospital*, Decatur, IL; *St. Anthony Memorial Hospital*, Effingham, IL; *St. Joseph's Hospital*, Highland, IL; *St. Francis Hospital*, Litchfield, IL; *St. Elizabeth's Hospital*, Belleville, IL; *St. Joseph's Hospital*, Breese, IL; *St. Mary's Hospital Medical Center; St. Vincent Hospital*, Green Bay, WI; *St. Joseph's Hospital; L.E. Phillips Treatment Center for the Chemically Dependent; Hospital Sisters Health Care West, Inc.; Transitus House*, Chippewa Falls, WI; *Sacred Heart Hospital; St. Francis Apartments*, Eau Claire, WI; *St. Nicholas Hospital*, Sheboygan, WI; *St. Mary's Hospital*, Streator, IL.
Represented in the Archdioceses of Dubuque, Milwaukee, St. Louis, and the Dioceses of Belleville, Green Bay, La Crosse, Peoria and Springfield (IL). Also in Africa, Taiwan, Japan and Haiti.

[1830] (R.G.S. - C.G.S.)—THE SISTERS OF THE GOOD SHEPHERD P
Congregation of Our Lady of Charity of the Good Shepherd

Founded in France in 1835. First foundation in the United States in Louisville, KY 1842.
Generalate for the Provinces: *Suore del Buon Pastore*, via Raffaello Sardiello 20, 00165, Rome, Italy. Sr. Liliane Tauvette, Supr. Gen.
Province of Mid-North America (2000): *Provincialate*, 7654 Natural Bridge Blvd., St. Louis, MO 63121. Tel: 314-381-3400; Fax: 314-381-7102. Sr. Barbara Beasley, Prov.
Legal Title: *Sisters of the Good Shepherd Province of Mid-North America; The Sisters of the Good Shepherd, Cincinnati Province; The Congregation of Our Lady of Charity of the Good Shepherd Community Support Trust*, Cincinnati, OH; *Sisters of the Good Shepherd of the City of Washington, D.C.; Sisters of the Good Shepherd St. Louis Province; Pelletier Trust, a Charitable Trust of the Sisters of the Good Shepherd; Sisters of the Good Shepherd, St. Paul Province.*
Professed Sisters 235.
Properties owned and staffed: *Good Shepherd Shelter* (for battered women with children), Los Angeles, CA; *Gracenter* (Women in Need), San Francisco, CA; *Droste Residence* (Women in need), St. Louis, MO; *Good Shepherd Services* (after-school program), New Orleans, LA; *DeNeuville Learning Center*, Memphis, TN; *House of the Good Shepherd* (Battered women with children), Chicago, IL; *Immaculate Heart Convent* (Retired Good Shepherd Sisters), St. Louis, MO; *Good Shepherd Provincialate*, St. Louis, MO.
Contemplative Sisters of the Good Shepherd:
Properties Owned and Staffed: *Gilead House and Good Shepherd Pelletier, Inc.*, Cincinnati, OH; *Sisters of the Good Shepherd*, Grand Rapids, MI; *Sisters of the Good Shepherd of Detroit aka Vista Maria*, Dearborn Heights, MI; *Sisters of the Good Shepherd of the City of Cleveland aka Marycrest*, Independence, OH; *House of the Good Shepherd of Columbus aka Rosemont*, Columbus, OH; *Good Shepherd Corporation*, Clarks Summit, PA; *Lourdesmont Good Shepherd Youth &*

Family Services, Clarks Summit, PA; *CORA Services, Inc.,* Philadelphia, PA; *Euphrasia House, Inc.,* Philadelphia, PA; *Good Shepherd Corporation,* Philadelphia, PA; *Good Shepherd Neighborhood House,* Mediation Program, Philadelphia, PA; *House of the Good Shepherd,* Baltimore, MD; *Sisters of the Good Shepherd,* A Corporation, Baltimore, MD; *Sisters of the Good Shepherd of the City of Washington, DC; Good Shepherd Corporation dba Shepherd's Dwelling,* Washington, DC; *Good Shepherd Services,* Atlanta, GA; *Good Shepherd Corporation of Orlando, Inc.; ALEE Shelter and Children's Shetler,* Agana, GU; *Projecto Nino,* Washington, DC; *Good Shepherd Shelter,* Los Angeles, CA; *Gracenter,* San Francisco, CA; *Droste Residence,* St. Louis, MO; *Good Shepherd Services,* New Orleans, LA; *DeNeuville Learning Center,* Memphis, TN; *House of the Good Shepherd,* Chicago, IL; Immaculate Heart Convent, St. Louis, MO; *Good Shepherd Provincialate,* St. Louis, MO; *Convent of the Good Shepherd Inc.,* St. Paul, MN; *Home of the Good Shepherd Inc.,* St. Paul, MN

02*Contemplatives of the Good Shepherd:*

Professed sisters 98.

Represented in the Archdioceses of Baltimore, Detroit, Philadelphia, St. Louis, St. Paul-Minneapolis and the Diocese of Cleveland.

Province of New York (1857): *Sisters of the Good Shepherd,* 82-31 Doncaster Pl., Jamaica, NY 11432. Tel: 718-380-3270; Fax: 718-591-9376. Sr. Helene Hayes, Prov.

Legal Title: *Sisters of the Good Shepherd,* Province of New York.

Professed Active Sisters 90; Contemplative Sisters 63.

Ministry in Counseling Centers; Social Service Agencies; Special Education Schools; Neighborhood Family Services; Adolescent Residential Programs; Human Services Workshops; Pastoral Ministry; Prison Ministry; Hospital Chaplaincy.

Legal Holdings or Titles: *Sisters of the Good Shepherd,* New York, NY; *Sisters of the Good Shepherd,* Albany, NY; *Sisters of the Good Shepherd,* Huntington, NY; *House of the Good Shepherd in the City of Hartford,* Hartford, CT; *The Gathering Place,* Waltham, MA; *Good Shepherd Volunteers,* Brooklyn, NY; *Madonna Hall,* Marlboro, MA; *Global Women's Exchange, Inc.,* Jamaica, NY; *Maria Droste Services (Madonna Hall).*

Programs Sponsored: *Good Shepherd Services,* New York, NY; *Maria Droste Services,* New York, NY; *Global Women's Exchange, Inc.; The Gathering Place; Collier Services,* Wickatunk, NJ; *Good Shepherd Volunteers.*

Represented in the Archdioceses of Boston, New York and the Dioceses of Albany, Brooklyn, Fall River, Metuchen, Rockville Centre, and Trenton

[1840] (G.N.S.H.)—GREY NUNS OF THE SACRED HEART P

General Motherhouse (1921): 1750 Quarry Rd., Yardley, PA 19067-3998. Tel: 215-968-4236; Fax: 215-968-6656. Sr. Marlene G. Butler, G.N.S.H., Pres.; Sr. R. Patricia Smith, Archivist. Sr. Mary O'Connell, Dir. Congregational Advancement Office.

Total number in community 174.

Sisters staff: College, Secondary and Elementary Education; Hospitals; Nursing Homes; Rehabilitation Care of Aging; Pastoral Care; Personal Care Home; CCD-Parish Services; Diocesan Offices; Campus Ministry; Prison Ministry; Homeless Housing.

Properties owned: *Holy Angels Academy,* Buffalo, NY; *Motherhouse Complex,* Yardley, PA.

Represented in the Archdioceses of Anchorage, Atlanta, Baltimore, Newark, Philadelphia and the Dioceses of Brooklyn, Buffalo, Erie, Manchester, Ogdensburg, Paterson, Richmond, Rochester, Rockville Centre and Trenton. Also in Canada.

[1845] (M.G.Sp.S.)—GUADALUPAN MISSIONARIES OF THE HOLY SPIRIT P

(Misioneras Guadalupanas del Espiritu Santo)

Founded in Morelia, Michoacan, Mexico in 1930 by Rev. Felix de Jesus Rougier, M.Sp.S.

General Motherhouse: Hidalgo #7, Tlalpan 14000 Mexico, D.F., Mexico. Mother Felicitas Almanza, Supr. Gen.

U.S. Delegation Headquarters: 2483 S.W. 4th St., Miami, FL 33135-2907. Tel: 305-642-9544.

U.S. Novitiate: 758 S. Dunsmuir Ave., Los Angeles, CA 90036-3811. Tel: 213-936-0135.

Legal Title: *Missionary Guadalupanas of the Holy Spirit, Inc.*

Total Sisters in U.S. 44

Ministry in Religious Education; Pastoral and Parish Ministries.

Represented in the Archdiocese of Denver, Los Angeles, Miami and the Dioceses of Fall River, Palm Beach Pueblo, and Savannah. Also in San Juan, Puerto Rico.

[1850] (S.A.C.)—SISTERS OF THE GUARDIAN ANGEL

Founded in Quillan, France in 1839.

General Motherhouse: Avda, del Valle, 42, Madrid 3, Spain. Sr. Sagrario Escudero, S.A.C., Supr. Gen.

U.S. Foundation: 1245 S. Van Ness, Los Angeles, CA 90019. Tel: 213-732-7881.

Represented in the Archdiocese of Los Angeles.

[1860] (H.P.B.)—HANDMAIDS OF THE PRECIOUS BLOOD P

Founded in Jemez Springs, New Mexico in 1947.

Motherhouse and Novitiate: *Cor Jesu Monastery,* P.O. Box 90, Jemez Springs, NM 87025. Tel: 505-829-3906. Mother John Paul, Prioress.

Professed Sisters 33.

Ministry in as Contemplative, Life of Eucharistic Adoration (Perpetual) for the sanctification of priests and for the entire world.

Represented in the Archdioceses of Chicago and Santa Fe. Also in Italy.

[1870] (A.C.J.)—THE HANDMAIDS OF THE SACRED HEART OF JESUS P

Founded in Spain in 1877. First Foundation in the United States in 1926.

General Motherhouse: *Largo dei Monti Parioli,* 3, 00197, Rome, Italy. Sr. Rita Burley, Supr. Gen.

Universal total in Congregation 1,700

Provincial Motherhouse: 1242 S. Broad St., Philadelphia, PA 19146. Tel: 215-468-6368; Fax: 215-271-1488. Sr. Gloria Petrone, A.C.J., Prov. Supr.

Total number in community 40.

Sisters serve and staff: Elementary Schools; Retreat Center; Mission Center; Parish Ministry; CCD; Diocesan Offices; Hispanic Pastoral Ministry; Vietnamese & Cambodian Pastoral Ministry; Hospital Chaplaincy.

Properties owned: *St. Raphaela Center,* Haverford, PA; *Ancillae Assumpta Academy,* Wyncote, PA; *Handmaids of Sacred Heart of Jesus Provinical Residence,* Philadelphia, PA.

Represented in the Archdioceses of Atlanta, Miami, Philadelphia and the Diocese of Beaumont.

[1880] (A.R.)—HANDMAIDS OF REPARATION OF THE SACRED HEART OF JESUS P

Founded in Messina, Italy in 1918.

U.S. Foundation (1958): *Sacred Heart Villa,* 36 Villa Dr., Steubenville, OH 43953-7129. Tel: 614-282-3801. Sr. Rosalba Putrino, A.R., Supr.

Total number in U.S. 6.

Ministry in Apostolic Work in Religious & Academic Education; Education All Levels; Religious Education; Parish and Diocesan Ministry; CCD Work; Orphanages; Missionary Work in Africa, Brazil and Poland.

Represented in the Dioceses of Arlington and Steubenville. Also in Africa, Brazil, Italy and Poland.

[1890] (H.H.S.)—SOCIETY OF HELPERS P

Founded in France in 1856. First foundation in the U.S. in 1892.

Generalate: 16 rue St. J. Baptiste de la Salle, Paris, France, 75006. Sr. Silvia Conde, Supr. Gen.

American Provincial Office (1921): 3206 S. Aberdeen, Chicago, IL 60608. Tel: 773-523-8638. Sr. Margaret Nimbley, Prov. Supr.

Total number in U.S. province 42.

Legal Title: *Society of the Helpers of the Holy Souls; Helpers of the Holy Souls; Province of the Helpers of the Holy Souls in the United States.*

Represented in the Archdioceses of Chicago, New York, St. Louis, San Francisco and the Diocese of San Jose.

[1900] (H.C.G.)—HERMANAS CATEQUISTAS GUADALUPANAS P

Founded in Saltillo, Coahuila, Mexico in 1923. First United States foundation in 1950.

Motherhouse and Novitiate: Saltillo, Coahuila, Mexico.

U.S. Address: *Hermanas Catequistas Guadalupanas Convents,* 4110 S. Flores, San Antonio, TX 78214. Tel: 210-532-9344. Sr. Martha Ruiz, Reg. Delegate.

Total number in the U.S. 18.

Represented in the Archdioceses of Oklahoma City, San Antonio and the Diocese of Fort Worth.

[1910] (H.J.)—HERMANAS JOSEFINAS P

General Motherhouse: Condor 336, Col. las Aguilas, Delg. Alvaro Obregon, 01710, Mexico D.F. Mother Cointa Quijas, H.J., Supr. & Mother Gen.

U.S. Address: *Assumption Seminary,* 2600 W. Woodlawn Ave., P.O. Box 28240, San Antonio, TX 78284. Tel: 210-734-0039.

Sisters 8.

Represented in the Archdioceses of Chicago, Denver, Los Angeles and San Antonio and the Diocese of El Paso.

[1920] (C.S.C.)—CONGREGATION OF THE SISTERS OF THE HOLY CROSS P

Founded at Le Mans, France in 1841. First foundation in the U.S. in 1843.

General Administration: *Sisters of the Holy Cross Generalate,* Bertrand Hall-Saint Mary's, Notre Dame, IN 46556. Tel: 219-284-5550; Fax: 219-284-5779. Sr. Aline Marie Steuer, C.S.C., Pres.; Sr. M. Veronique Wiedower, C.S.C., Gen. Sec.

Professed Members 613; Temporarily Professed 23; Novices 5; Candidates 13.

Legal Title: *Sisters of the Holy Cross, Inc.; Sisters of the Holy Cross, Inc. dba CSC Consultation Services; Holy Cross Services Corporation; Holy Cross Ministry Net-Work, Inc.; Sisters of the Holy Cross of California,* Ventura, CA; *The Academy of the Holy Cross, Inc.,* MD; *The Corporation of Saint Mary's College,* Notre Dame, IN; *Sociedade Civil Irmas da Santa Cruz,* Brasil; *Society of the Congregation of the Sisters of the Holy Cross,* Bangladesh.

Areas and Coordinators:

Area I - USA West, Los Angeles, CA. Tel: 323-732-5662. Sr. Patricia McGee, C.S.C., Coord.

Area II - USA Midwest, Notre Dame, IN. Tel: 219-284-5902; Fax: 219-284-5900. Sr. Kathryn Callahan, C.S.C., Coord.

Area III - USA South & Mexico, Austin, TX. Tel: 301-549-1556. Sr. Mary Louise Full, C.S.C., Coord.

Area IV - USA East, Wheaton, MD. Tel: 301-236-4967. Sr. M. Geraldine Blume, C.S.C., Coord.

Area V - USA Retired, Notre Dame, IN. Tel: 812-623-4901; Fax: 812-623-3670. Sr. Eileen Flavin, C.S.C., Coord.

Area VI - South America, Sao Paulo, Brazil. Tel: 011-55-11-5632-0191; Fax: 011-55-11-522-7148. Sr. Anne Veronica Horner Hoe, C.S.C., Coord.

Area VII - West Africa, Takaradi Ghana, West Africa. Tel: 011-233-31-21645; Fax: 011-233-31-21645. Sr. M. Jane Chantal Method, C.S.C., Coord.

Area VIII Asia, Dhaka, Bangladesh. Tel: 011-880-2-912-9600; Fax: 011-880-2-912-9600. Sr. Marian Teresa Gomes, C.S.C., Coord.

Sisters staff and serve: Colleges; High Schools; Grade Schools; Adult Education Centers; Social Service Centers; Prayer Centers; Counseling Centers; Human Rights Centers; Women's Development Center; Hospitals and other Health Ministries including Administration of Health Systems, Primary Health Care and Long Term Health Care; Parish Ministry; Diocesan Catechetical Services; Other Parish and Diocesan Ministries; Retirement Homes; Senior Citizen Residences; Pastoral Ministry with the Deaf.

Represented in the Archdioceses of Baltimore, Boston, Chicago, Cincinnati, Denver, Indianapolis, Los Angeles, Louisville, Newark, Portland (OR), San Antonio, San Francisco, Santa Fe, Seattle, Washington and the Dioceses of Arlington, Austin, Boise, Brownsville, Columbus, Colorado Springs, Corpus Christi, Covington, Des Moines, Fall River, Fort Wayne-South Bend, Fresno, Gary, Harrisburg, Joliet, Kalamazoo, Knoxville, Lafayette (IN), Lansing, Lexington, Monterey, Oakland, Orange, Palm Beach, Peoria, Raleigh, Richmond, Rockford, Rockville Centre, St. Cloud, St. Petersburg, Salt Lake City, San Diego, Stockton, and Tucson. Also in Brasil, Peru, Ghana, Uganda, Mexico, Bangladesh, India, and Lebanon.

[1930] (C.S.C.)—SISTERS OF HOLY CROSS P

Founded in Le Mans, France in 1841. First foundation in Canada in 1847.

General Administration: 905 rue Basile-Moreau, St-Laurent, Montreal, Quebec H4L 4A1, Canada. Sr. Liette Finnerty, C.S.C., Supr. Gen.

Universal total in congregation 1,036.

American Regional Office: 377 Island Pond Rd., Manchester, NH 03109. Tel: 603-622-9504. Sr. Louise Auclair, C.S.C., Reg. Rep.

Total number in region 186.

Ministry in the field of Academic Education at all levels; Religious Education Centers; Social and Family Services; Counselor-Therapist; Parish Ministry; Youth and Hospital Chaplaincies; Administrative Positions; Diocesan Services; Hispanic Ministry; Ministry to Abused Women and Children; Social Work and Elderly Assistance.

Properties owned: *Notre Dame College; Holy Cross Kindergarten,* Manchester, NH; *St. George Manor,* Manchester, NH; *Our Lady of the Sacred Heart Convent,* West Franklin, NH; *Londonderry House,* Londonderry, NH; *Sisters of the Holy Cross,* 454 Island Pond Rd., Manchester, NH 03109; 136 Lynwood Ln., Manchester, NH 03109; 113 Wedgewood Ln.,

Manchester, NH 03109; 969 & 971 Chestnut St., Manchester, NH 03104; 377 Island Pond Rd., Manchester, NH; Fairview Rd., R.R. 1, Box 191, Pittsfield, NH 03263.
Represented in the Archdioceses of Boston and New York and the Dioceses of Burlington, Fall River, Manchester, Norwich, Rochester and St. Petersburg. Also in Bangladesh, Cameroon, Chile, Haiti, Mali, Rome, and Peru.

[1940] (C.H.F.)—CONGREGATION OF THE SISTERS OF THE HOLY FAITH P

Founded in Ireland in 1856. First foundation in U.S. in 1953. St. John of God School, 13817 Pioneer Blvd., Norwalk, California, 90650.
Motherhouse: Glasnevin, Dublin, Ireland.
U.S. Province: 12322 S. Paramount Blvd., Downey, CA 90242. Tel: 562-869-6092; Fax: 562-869-4609. Sr. Miriam Harney, C.H.F., Reg. Supr.
Total number in community 240.
Represented in the Archdioceses of Los Angeles, New Orleans and San Francisco and the Diocese of Sacramento.

[1950] (S.S.F.)—CONGREGATION OF THE SISTERS OF THE HOLY FAMILY P

Founded in the New Orleans, Louisiana, in 1842.
Motherhouse: 6901 Chef Menteur Hwy., New Orleans, LA 70126. Tel: 504-242-8315. Sr. Sylvia Thibodeaux, S.S.F., Supr. Gen.
Total number in community 168.
Ministry in Secondary and Elementary Schools; Day Care Centers; Pastoral and Social Services; Nursing Home and Apartments for the Elderly, Disabled and Handicapped.
Represented in the Archdioceses of Los Angeles, New Orleans and Washington and in the Dioceses of Galveston-Houston, Lafayette (LA) and Memphis. Also in Belize, Central America

[1960] (S.H.F.)—SISTERS OF THE HOLY FAMILY P

Founded in San Francisco, California, in 1872.
General Motherhouse: P.O. Box 3248, Fremont, CA 94539. Tel: 510-624-4500; Fax: 510-624-4537. Sr. Sharon Flannigan, Congregational Pres.
Total number in community 126.
Ministry in the following areas: Child Care; Primary Education in Schools; School Counseling; Prison Chaplaincy; Religious Education and Pastoral Care; Social Service Agencies related to Child Protective Services; Hospital Chaplaincy; Parish Administration.
Properties owned: *St. Elizabeth's Day Home,* San Jose, CA; *Holy Family Renewal Center,* Pleasant Hill, CA.
Represented in the Archdioceses of Anchorage, Los Angeles, Louisville, San Antonio, San Francisco, and the Dioceses of Fresno, Honolulu, Las Vegas, Oakland, Reno, Sacramento, Salt Lake City, Santa Rosa, San Diego, San Jose and Stockton

[1970] (C.S.F.N.)—SISTERS OF THE HOLY FAMILY OF NAZARETH P

Founded in Italy in 1875. First foundation in the United States in 1885.
General Motherhouse: Rome, Italy. Mother Maria Teresa Jasionowicz, Supr. Gen.
Sacred Heart Province (1885): 310 N. River Rd., Des Plaines, IL 60016-1211. Tel: 847-298-6760; Fax: 847-803-1941. Sr. Marie Kelanowicz, C.S.F.N., Prov. Supr.; Sr. M. Gemma, C.S.F.N., Archivist.
Total number in province 143.
Properties owned: *St. Mary of Nazareth Hospital Center; Holy Family Medical Center; Holy Family Health Center Nazarethville.*
Ministry in Academic Education; Hospitals and Health Care.
Represented in the Archdiocese of Chicago.
Blessed Frances Siedliska Province (1962): Sisters of The Holy Family of Nazareth, 1814 Egyptian Way, Box 530959, Grand Prairie, TX 75053. Tel: 972-641-4496; Fax: 972-641-1668. Sr. M. Ancilla Sojka, Prov. Supr.
Total number in community 45.
Legal Holdings or Titles: *United Regional Health Care System-11th Street Campus,* Wichita Falls, TX; *Holy Family of Nazareth Health Ministry of Wichita Falls,* Wichita Falls, TX; *Trinity Mother Frances Health System,* Tyler, TX; *Blessed Frances Siedliska Province Charitable Trust Fund,* Dallas, TX.
Ministry in Education; Health Care; Parish Ministry; Religious Education.
Represented in the Dioceses of Dallas, Fort Worth and Tyler.
Immaculate Conception BVM Province (1918): *Sisters of the Holy Family of Nazareth Provincial House and Academy,* 4001 Grant Ave., Philadelphia, PA 19114-2999. Tel: 215-637-6464; Fax: 215-637-8475. Sr. M. Michaelann Delaney, Prov. Supr.; Sr. Mary Rosella, Community Archivist.
Total number in community 164.
Properties owned: *Holy Family College Nazareth Academy Mount Nazareth,* Philadelphia, PA; *St. Mary Villa,* Ambler, PA; *Villa Nazareth,* Meadowbrook, PA.
Ministry in the field of Academic Education at all levels; Child-caring Institution; Hospitals; Nursing Homes; Sisters Retirement Home.
Represented in the Archdioceses of Philadelphia, San Juan and the Dioceses of Allentown and Scranton.
Saint Joseph Province (1918): 285 Bellevue Rd., Pittsburgh, PA 15229-2195. Tel: 412-931-4775; Fax: 412-931-9746. Sr. Michele Collins, C.S.F.N., Prov. Supr.
Professed sisters in provincialate 34; Professed sisters 149.
Sisters serve and staff: High Schools; Elementary Schools; Religious Education Centers; Hospitals; Parish Pastoral Ministry; Housing Counseling; Low-Income Home Ownership; Family Counseling; Family Life Education; Senior Citizen Apartments; Home for the Elderly; Home for Children; Learning Centers.
Legal Holdings and Titles: *Mt. Nazareth Center, Inc.,* Pittsburgh, PA; *Holy Family Institute,* Emsworth, PA; *St. Leonard's Home, Inc.,* Hollidaysburg, PA; *The Holy Family Foundation,* Emsworth, PA; *Bon Secours-Holy Family Regional Health System,* Altoona, PA; *Nazareth Family Foundation,* Pittsburgh, PA.
Represented in the Archdiocese of Detroit and the Dioceses of Altoona-Johnstown, Cleveland, Erie, Pittsburgh and Steubenville.
Immaculate Heart of Mary Province (1959): *Sisters of Holy Family of Nazareth Provincial Residence - Marian Heights,* 1428 Monroe Turnpike, Monroe, CT 06468. Tel: 203-268-7646; Fax: 203-452-9947. Sr. M. Agnese Palczynski, Prov. Supr.
Legal Title: *C.S.F.N. Congregation of the Sisters of the Holy Family of Nazareth.*
Total number in Province 102.
Ministry in Education; Child Care; Health Care; Religious Education; Retreat Work; House of Prayer; Pastoral Ministry and Hospital Chaplaincy; Prison Ministry.
Represented in the Archdioceses of Hartford, New York and the Dioceses of Bridgeport, Brooklyn, Rockville Centre, Syracuse, Trenton and Worcester.

[1980] (O.S.F.)—CONGREGATION OF THE SERVANTS OF THE HOLY CHILD JESUS OF THE THIRD ORDER REGULAR OF SAINT FRANCIS P

Founded in Germany in 1855. First founded in the United States on April 9, 1929, at Staten Island, New York.
General Motherhouse (1855): Kloster Oberzell, Wuerzburg, Germany. Mother M. Reginarda Holzer, Supr. Gen.
Regional House: Villa Maria, 641 Somerset St., North Plainfield, NJ 07060-4909. Tel: 908-757-3050. Sr. M. Dominic Ritter, Reg. Supr.
Total in American region 31.
Properties owned: *Villa Maria Sanitarium, Inc.,* North Plainfield, NJ.
Ministry in Social Work; Health Care; Teaching.
Represented in the in the Archdiocese of Newark and Diocese of Metuchen.

[1990] (S.N.J.M.)—SISTERS OF THE HOLY NAMES OF JESUS AND MARY P

Founded by Marie Rose Durocher, in Longueuil, Quebec, Canada in 1843. First foundation in the U.S. in 1859.
Generalate: 80, rue Saint-Charles Est, Longueuil, Quebec, Canada J4H 1A9. Tel: 450-651-8104. Sr. Mary Pat LeRoy, Supr. Gen.
Oregon Province (1859): *Provincial Administration,* Box 25, Marylhurst, OR 97036. Tel: 503-635-3621. Sr. Lynda Thompson, Prov. Dir.
Total number in community 212.
Properties owned: *Provincial House,* Marylhurst, OR; *St. Mary's Academy,* Portland, OR; **Mary's Woods at Marylhurst, Inc.,* Marylhurst, OR.
An international congregation of 1,655 religious women with missions in Lesotho, Mexico, Nicaragua, Haiti and Brazil. Congregational sponsored works include colleges; adult centers; secondary, elementary and preschools; continuing care retirement community and health clinics.
Ministry in Sisters ministering in works sponsored by other institutions/agencies include Formal Education in Universities, Secondary, Elementary and Preschools; Adult Basic Education/Literacy; Administration in Diocesan Offices; Campus Ministry; Pastoral Ministry; Religious Education, Health Care and Social Services.
Represented in the Archdioceses of Detroit, Los Angeles, Portland (OR), San Francisco, Seattle and Washington and the Dioceses of Albany, Baker, Fairbanks, Jackson, Monterey, Oakland, Orlando, Palm Beach, Richmond, San Jose, Spokane, St. Petersburg, Venice and Yakima.
California Province (1868): Provincial Administration, P.O. Box 907, Los Gatos, CA 95031. Tel: 408-395-5150. Sr. Margaret Spiller, S.N.J.M., Prov.
Total number in community 250.
Properties owned or sponsored: *Provincial House,* Los Gatos, CA; *Holy Names College; Holy Names High School,* Oakland, CA; *Ramona Convent Secondary School,* Alhambra, CA; *Villa Maria Del Mar,* Santa Cruz, CA; *Next Step Learning Center,* Oakland, CA.
New York Province (1865): *Provincial Administration,* 1061 New Scotland Ave., Albany, NY 12208. Tel: 518-489-5469; Fax: 518-489-5804. Sr. Grace R. Diaz, Prov. Dir.
Total number in community 106.
Properties owned: *Provincial Center; Academy of the Holy Names,* Albany, NY; *Sisters of the Holy Names,* Silver Spring, MD; *Academy of the Holy Names,* Tampa, FL.
Washington Province (1962): *Provincial Administration,* 2911 W. Fort Wright Dr., Spokane, WA 99224. Tel: 509-328-7470; Fax: 509-328-9824. Sr. Ann Pizelo, S.N.J.M., Prov. Dir.
Total number in community 188.
Properties owned: *Provincial House,* Spokane, WA; *Holy Names Academy,* Seattle, WA.

[2000] (C.S.R.)—SISTERS OF THE HOLY REDEEMER P

First foundation in the United States on March 19, 1924 in Baltimore, Maryland.
General Motherhouse (1866): Wuerzburg, Germany. Sr. M. Veronika Stauch, Supr. Gen.
American Province of the Immaculate Conception: 521 Moredon Rd., Huntingdon Valley, PA 19006. Tel: 215-914-4100; Fax: 215-914-4171. Sr. M. Regina Heilman, C.S.R., Prov. Supr.
Legal Holdings and Titles: *Holy Redeemer Health Care Corporation and Foundation; Holy Redeemer Health System; Holy Redeemer Hospital and Medical Center; Redeemer Center; St. Joseph's Manor; The Lafayette-Redeemer; Holy Redeemer Home Health and Hospice Services; Holy Redeemer Transitional Care Unit; Holy Redeemer Managed Care Organization; Holy Redeemer Physician and Ambulatory Services; Holy Redeemer Visiting Nurse Agency, Inc.,* NJ; *Redeemer Village & Redeemer Village II; Drueding Center; HRH Management Corporation; Redeemer Medical Supply Co., Inc. Convents— Provincialate; Emmaus Convent; Angelus Convent; Emmanuel Convent; Our Lady of Peace Convent; St. Elizabeth Convent.*
Represented in the Archdiocese of Philadelphia and the Dioceses of Camden and Trenton.

[2010] (O.SS.R.)—ORDER OF THE MOST HOLY REDEEMER P (Redemptoristine Nuns)

Founded 1731 by St. Alphonsus de Liguori and Ven. Marie Celeste. (Contemplative).
Rule approved 1750 by Pope Benedict XIV.
First United States Monastery (1957) Esopus, New York.
Mother of Perpetual Help Monastery: *Remptoristine Nuns,* P.O.Box 220, Esopus, NY 12429-0220. Tel: 845-384-6533; Fax: 845-384-6533. Sr. Maura Quinn, O.SS.R., Prioress Solemn Vows, Papal Enclosure.
Total number in community 10.
Monastery of St. Alphonsus (1960): *Order of the Most Holy Redeemer,* 200 Liguori Dr., Liguori, MO 63057. Tel: 636-464-1093; Fax: 636-464-9446. Sr. Mary Ann Phillipps, O.Ss.R., Prioress.
Total number in community 16.
Represented in the Archdioceses of New York and St. Louis.

[2020] (C.H.S.)—COMMUNITY OF THE HOLY SPIRIT D

U.S. Foundation (1970): 6151 Rancho Mission Rd. - #205, San Diego, CA 95108. Tel: 619-584-0809. Sr. Susann Kernaghan, C.H.S., General Coord.
Total number in community 17.
Ministry in the field of Education; Health Care; and Social Services.
Represented in the Dioceses of Oakland, Orange, Portland (OR), Reno-Las Vegas, San Diego and San Jose.

[2030] (C.S.Sp.)—SISTERS OF THE HOLY SPIRIT D

Founded in the United States 1929; Decree of Establishment 1932.
Motherhouse and Novitiate: 10102 Granger Rd., Garfield Heights, OH 44125. Sr. Mary Assumpta, Supr. Gen.
Total number in community 9.
Represented in the Diocese of Cleveland.

[2040] (S.H.S.)—SISTERS OF THE HOLY SPIRIT D

Founded in the United States in 1913 at Donora, Pennsylvania.

Motherhouse: 5246 Clarwin Ave., Ross Township, Pittsburgh, PA 15229-2208. Tel: 412-931-1917. Sr. Marita Juras, S.H.S., Gen. Supr.

Total number in community 59.

Sisters serve and staff: Elementary Schools; Religious Education; Health and Social Services; Retreat Services; Child Day Care; Care Facility for the Aged.

Facilities owned and staffed: *Corporation of Sisters of the Holy Spirit of Pittsburgh; Marian Manor, Corp.; Martina Spiritual Renewal Center Inc.*

Represented in the Dioceses of Greensburg, and Pittsburgh.

[2050] (S.H.Sp.)—SISTERS OF THE HOLY SPIRIT AND MARY IMMACULATE P

Founded in America in 1893. Papal Approbation 1930; final Approbation, 1938.

General Motherhouse: *Convent of the Holy Spirit and Mary Immaculate,* 301 Yucca St., San Antonio, TX 78203. Tel: 210-533-5149. Sr. Anne Finnerty, S.H.Sp., Gen. Supr.

Professed Sisters 115.

Legal Holdings: *Holy Spirit Trust; Holy Spirit Motherhouse; Healy Murphy Center, Inc., San Antonio, TX; Mother of Perpetual Help Nursing Home,* Brownsville, TX.

Ministry in the following areas Education; Health Care; Pastoral Ministry; Catechetical Ministry; Social Service; Retreats.

Represented in the Archdioceses of New Orleans and San Antonio and the Dioceses of Beaumont, Biloxi, Brownsville, Corpus Christi, Dallas, Fort Worth, Galveston-Houston, Houma-Thibadoux, Jackson, and Lafayette (LA). Also in Mexico and Zambia.

[2060] (O.SS.T.)—SISTERS OF THE MOST HOLY TRINITY P

Founded in Rome in 1198. First foundation in the United States in 1920.

General Motherhouse: Rome, Italy.

Provincial House: *Immaculate Conception Province,* 21281 Chardon Rd., Euclid, OH 44117. Tel: 216-481-8232; Fax: 216-481-6577. Sr. M. Valentine, Reg. Delegate.

Total number in community 27.

Properties owned: *Our Lady of Lourdes Shrine,* Euclid, OH.

Represented in the Archdiocese of Philadelphia and the Diocese of Cleveland.

[2070] (S.U.S.C.)—HOLY UNION SISTERS P

Founded in France in 1826. First foundation in the United States in 1886.

Generalate: Rome, Italy. Sr. Carol Regan, S.U.S.C., Supr. Gen.

United States Province: *Provincial Office,* P.O. Box 410–444 Centre St., Milton, MA 02186-0006; Tel: 617-696-8765; Fax: 617-696-8571. Province Mission Team: Sr. Mary Catherine Duerr, S.U.S.C., Sr. Theresa M. Horvath, S.U.S.C.; Sr. Mary Louise Sullivan, S.U.S.C., Co-Archivists; Sr. Grace Donovan, S.U.S.C.; Sr. Rita Beaudoin, S.U.S.C.

Total number in community 171.

Legal Title: *Holy Union Sisters, Inc.*

Properties owned: *Holy Union Spiritual Life Center,* Groton, MA; *Holy Union Asian Center,* Lowell, MA; *Holy Union African Center,* Lowell, MA; *Holy Union House of Hospitality,* Tiverton, RI.

Ministry in the field of Religious and Academic Education; Social Services; Pastoral Care; Pastoral Ministry; Spiritual Renewal; Day Care; Ministry Education; Family Ministry; Nursing; Peace & Justice; Spanish Apostolate; Ministry to the Handicapped; Ministry to Immigrants and Refugees; Clerical & Secretarial services; Diocesan Administrative Services; Foreign Mission work in Tanzania.

Represented in the Archdioceses of Baltimore, Boston, Detroit, Miami, New York, and the Dioceses of Albany, Brooklyn, Fall River, Harrisburg, Lexington, Orlando, Pensacola-Tallahassee, Providence, and Rockville Centre.

[2080] (G.H.M.S.)—HOME MISSION SISTERS OF AMERICA (Glenmary Sisters)

Founded July 16, 1952.

Motherhouse: *Glenmary Sisters - Glenmary Center,* P.O. Box 22264, Owensboro, KY 42304-2264. Tel: 270-686-8401. Sr. Christine Beckett, Pres.

Total number in community 11.

Ministry in Social Outreach; Evangelization and Catechesis; Promotional Center.

Represented in the Dioceses of Lexington, Owensboro and Savannah.

[2090] (H.V.M.)—SISTERS HOME VISITORS OF MARY D

Founded in Detroit, Michigan in 1949.

Motherhouse: 121 E. Boston Blvd., Detroit, MI 48202. Tel: 313-869-2160

Total number in community 18.

Ministry in Urban Parishes; Senior Citizen; Prisons; Sojourner Spiritual Affirmation Center; Seminary Staff; Intercultural Center; Preschools; Religious Education, RCIA.

Represented in the Archdiocese of Detroit.

[2100] (C.H.M.)—CONGREGATION OF THE HUMILITY OF MARY P

Founded in France in 1854. First United States foundation in 1864.

Motherhouse: *Humility of Mary Center,* Davenport, IA 52804. Tel: 319-323-9466; Fax: 319-323-5209. Sr. Jude Fitzpatrick, Pres.

Legal Title: *Congregation of the Humility of Mary; Humility of Mary Shelter, Inc.; Congregation of the Humility of Mary Charitable Trust.*

Total number in community 168

Ministry in Schools and Colleges; Religious Education Centers; Migrant Programs; Pastoral Ministry; Social Services; Inner City Programs; Health Services; and Ministry to the Elderly.

Represented in the Archdioceses of Chicago, Denver, Dubuque, Los Angeles, Seattle Washington and the Dioceses of Biloxi, Davenport, Des Moines, Great Falls-Billings, Helena, Jackson, Kansas City, Lexington, Peoria, Richmond, Rockford, St. Cloud, San Angelo, Tulsa, Tyler, Wheeling-Charleston and Yakima. Also in Mexico.

[2110] (H.M.)—SISTERS OF THE HUMILITY OF MARY P

Founded in France in 1854. First foundation in the United States in 1864 at Villa Maria, Lawrence County, Pennsylvania, 16155.

Motherhouse: *Villa Maria Community Center,* P.O. Box 914, Villa Maria, PA 16155-0914. Tel: 724-964-8861; Fax: 724-964-8082. Sr. Ruthmary Powers, H.M., Major Supr., Sr. Mary-Joanna Huegle, H.M., Community Archivist.

Total number in community 238.

Ministry in the field of Academic and Religious Education at all levels; Hospitals and Nursing Home, Assisted Living; Parish and Pastoral Ministries; Publishing of Education Materials; Diocesan Offices; Legal Services; Social Services; Ministry to Native Americans, Migrants, Hispanics, Haitians; Housing Ministry to Rural Poor, Single Parents, Independent Elderly; Ministry to Deaf and to Prisoners; Retreat Ministry; Spirituality and Counseling; Advocacy for Eco-justice; Marketing of Creative Arts.

Legal Holdings and Titles: *Sisters of the Humility of Mary (Motherhouse),* Villa Maria, PA; *Sisters of the Humility of Mary Charitable Trust,* Villa Maria, PA; *HM Health Services,* Youngstown, OH; *The Assumption Village,* North Lima, OH; *Community Health Partners of Ohio,* Lorain, OH; *Community Health Partners Foundation,* Lorain, OH; *Laurel Lake Retirement Community,* Hudson, OH; *Magnificat High School,* Rocky River, OH; *Villa Montessori Center,* Cleveland, OH; *The Center for Learning,* Villa Maria, PA; *Villa Maria Education Center,* Villa Maria, PA; *Humility of Mary Housing, Inc.,* Akron, OH; *HM Housing Development Corporation,* Akron, OH; *HM Life Opportunity Services,* Akron, OH; *Villa Residential Services (Villa Maria Apartments),* Villa Maria, PA; *Heartbeats,* Rocky River, OH; *Common Ground Center for Community Renewal,* Oberlin, OH.

Represented in the Archdioceses of Chicago, Cincinnati, San Antonio, Washington and the Dioceses of Charleston, Cleveland, Erie, Grand Island, Lansing, Palm Beach, Pittsburgh, Richmond, Spokane, Trenton, Tucson, Venice, Wheeling-Charleston and Youngstown.

[2120] (C.I.C.)—SISTERS OF THE IMMACULATE CONCEPTION D

Founded in the United States in 1874.

General Motherhouse and Convent of the Immaculate Conception: P.O. Box 50426, New Orleans, LA 70185-0426. Tel: 504-486-7426. Sr. Ada Missler, C.I.C., Contact Person.

Total number in community 17.

Ministry in Pastoral Ministry.

Represented in the Archdiocese of New Orleans and the Diocese of Houma-Thibodaux.

[2130] (R.C.M.)—SISTERS OF THE IMMACULATE CONCEPTION P

Founded in Spain in 1892.

General Motherhouse: Princesa 19 y 21, 28008, Madrid, Spain. Mother Maria Luz Martinez, Mother Gen.

U.S. Delegation House (1962): 2230 Franklin, San Francisco, CA 94109. Tel: 415-474-0159.

Represented in the Archdiocese of San Francisco and the Diocese of Fresno.

[2140] SISTERS OF THE IMMACULATE CONCEPTION OF THE BLESSED VIRGIN MARY (LITHUANIAN) D

Founded in Marijampole, Lithuania in 1918. First foundation in the United States in 1936.

American Headquarters: *Immaculate Conception Convent and Novitiate,* 600 Liberty Hwy., Putnam, CT 06260-2503. Tel: 860-928-7955; Fax: 860-928-1930. Sr. Mary Paul Savickas, Prov. Supr.

Total number in community 28.

Ministry in Nursing Homes; Retreat House; Catechetical Work in Parishes; Summer Camp for Children and Young Adults.

Legal Titles & Holdings: *Immaculate Conception Convent; Matulaitis Nursing Home,* Putnam, CT; *Camp Neringa,* Marlboro, VT.

Represented in the Archdiocese of Chicago and the Dioceses of Burlington and Norwich. Also in Canada.

[2145] (O.S.A.)—CONGREGATION OF AUGUSTINIAN SISTERS SERVANTS OF JESUS AND MARY P

Generalate: via Nomentana 514, Rome, Italy. Mother Atanasia Buhagiar, Gen.

Malta Province: 208 Fleur-de-Lys, B'Kara, Malta. Mother Miriam Grech, Mother Prov.

U.S. Foundation: *St. John School,* 513 E. Broadway, Brandenburg, KY 40108. Sr. Lydia Falzon, Supr.

Total number in community 4.

Represented in the Archdiocese of Louisville.

[2150] (I.H.M.)—SISTERS, SERVANTS OF THE IMMACULATE HEART OF MARY P

Founded in the United States in 1845.

SSIHM Leadership Council: 610 W. Elm, Monroe, MI 48162-7909. Tel: 734-240-9700; Fax: 734-240-9784. Sr. Virginia Pfau, I.H.M., Pres.; Sr. Jane Farrell, Archivist.

Total number in Congregation 666.

Ministry in Academic and Religious Education at all levels; Pastoral Ministry (parish, healthcare, campus and prison settings); Diocesan and Parish Administration; Peace and Justice; Social Service and Counseling; Spiritual Growth and Development; Overseas Ministries.

Legal Titles: *Marygrove College,* Detroit, MI; *Immaculate Heart of Mary High School,* Westchester, IL; *Marian High School,* Bloomfield Hills, MI; *St. Mary Center,* Monroe, MI; *Visitation House of Prayer,* Monroe, MI; Co-Sponsor: *Groundwork for a Just World,* Detroit, MI.

Represented in the Archdioceses of Atlanta, Boston, Chicago, Cincinnati, Detroit, Indianapolis, Louisville, Miami, Milwaukee, Mobile, New York, Oklahoma City, Philadelphia, St. Louis, St. Paul-Minneapolis, San Antonio, San Juan, Santa Fe, Washington and the Dioceses of Albany, Austin, Buffalo, Cleveland, Duluth, Fort Wayne-South Bend, Galveston-Houston, Gaylord, Grand Rapids, Joliet, Kalamazoo, Kansas City-St. Joseph, Lansing, Lexington, Marquette, Oakland, Palm Beach, Pensacola-Tallahassee, Phoenix, Raleigh, Richmond, Rockville Centre, Saginaw, St. Augustine, St. Petersburg, San Diego, Toledo, Venice, and Wichita. Also in Brazil, Canada, Italy, Honduras, London, Mexico, Uganda, South Africa.

[2160] (I.H.M.)—SISTERS, SERVANTS OF THE IMMACULATE HEART OF MARY P

Founded in 1845. Established in Scranton, Pennsylvania in 1871.

General Motherhouse: *Immaculate Heart of Mary Center,* 2300 Adams Ave., Scranton, PA 18509. Tel: 570-342-6850; Fax: 570-346-5439. Sr. Anne Munley, I.H.M., Pres.

Total number in community 617.

Properties owned: *IHM Center Marian Convent; Marywood University,* Scranton, PA; *Marian Community Hospital,* Carbondale, PA; *St. Joseph's Center,* Scranton, PA; *Our Lady of Grace Center, Manhasset,* NY.

Ministry in the field of Academic Education; Hospitals; Early Childhood Education Centers; Congregation Retirement and Health Care Centers; Spiritual Renewal Center; Directors of Religious Education; Pastoral Ministries; Social Services; Campus Ministry; Peace and Justice Center; Volunteer Services; Family Ministry; Drug and Alcohol Counseling; Ministry to Hispanics; Diocesan Offices; Vicar for Religious; Ministry to Persons with AIDS.

Represented in the Archdioceses of Baltimore, Boston, Los Angeles, Miami, Newark, New York, Philadelphia, Santa Fe, Washington and the Dioceses of Albany, Altoona-Johnstown, Bridgeport, Brooklyn, Camden, Harrisburg, Jackson, Pittsburgh, Raleigh, Rockville Centre, St. Augustine, St. Petersburg, Scranton, Syracuse, Trenton, Venice, Wheeling-Charleston, Wilmington, Worcester and Yakima. Also in Canada and Peru.

[2170] (I.H.M.)—SISTERS, SERVANTS OF THE IMMACULATE HEART OF MARY P

Founded in 1845. Established in West Chester, Pennsylvania in 1872.

General Motherhouse: *Villa Maria,* Immaculata, PA 19345. Tel: 610-647-2160; Fax: 610-889-4874. Sr. Rose Marie DeCarlo, I.H.M., Gen. Supr.

Total number in congregation 1,215.

Ministry in the field of Academic Education at all levels in the U.S., as well as Peru and Chile and Infirmary work.

Represented in the Archdioceses of Atlanta, Boston, Hartford, Miami, Philadelphia and the Dioceses of Allentown, Camden, Harrisburg, Metuchen, Richmond, San Jose, Savannah and Trenton.

[2180] (I.H.M.)—SISTERS OF THE IMMACULATE HEART OF MARY P

Founded in Spain in 1848. First foundation in United States in 1871.

General Motherhouse: Rome, Italy.

U.S. Province: 4100 Sabino Canyon Rd., Tucson, AZ 85750-6503. Tel: 520-886-4273. Sr. Alice M. Martinez, Prov. Supr.; Sr. M. Julian Valdez, Sec. & Community Archivist.

Total number in community 29.

Ministry in the field of Academic and Religious Education.

Represented in the Dioceses of Oakland and Tucson.

[2182] (I.H.M.)—SISTERS OF THE IMMACULATE HEART OF MARY AT MIRINAE D

Founded in 1976 by Rev. Francis Haengman Tiyeng, Marinae, Diocese of Suwon, Korea, under the motto, "to the Most Holy Trinity through the Immaculate Heart of Mary".

Motherhouse: Mirinae, Korea.

U.S. Foundation: *St. Mary Pre School,* 423 South Commonwealth Ave., Los Angeles, CA 90020; Mailing Address: P.O. Box 75867, 90075. Sr. Mary John Shin, I.H.M, Supr.

Ministry in retreat work, school, youth and care for the aged.

Properties owned: *Sisters of the Immaculate Heart of Mary at Mirinae* , Los Angeles, CA.

Represented in the Archdiocese of Los Angeles.

[2185] (I.H.M.)—SISTERS OF THE IMMACULATE HEART OF MARY OF WICHITA

Founded in Olot, Spain, in 1848. First foundation in United States in 1871. Wichita foundation in 1979.

Motherhouse: 605 N. Woodchuck, Wichita, KS 67212. Tel: 316-722-9316. Mother Marie Bernadette Mertens, I.H.M., Gen. Supr.

Total number in community 15.

Apostolate: Contemplation of the Word and the spread of His Message of salvation through the various works and levels of education and retreat work.

Represented in the Diocese of Wichita.

[2190] (C.V.I.)—CONGREGATION OF THE INCARNATE WORD AND BLESSED SACRAMENT P

Founded in France in 1625. First foundation in the United States in 1853.

Motherhouse and Novitiate: *Incarnate Word Convent,* 3400 Bradford Pl., Houston, TX 77025-1398. Tel: 713-668-0423. Sr. Brigid Cummins, Supr.; Sr. Dympna Lyons, Archivist; Sr. Brendan O'Donnell, Archivist.

Total number in community 61.

Ministry in the field of Academic and Religious Education; Social Service; Administration; Hispanic Ministry; Diocesan Ministry (Department of Aging, Pastoral Care); Parish Ministry; Renewal Work.

Represented in the Dioceses of Austin, Beaumont and Galveston-Houston.

[2200] (I.W.B.S.)—CONGREGATION OF THE INCARNATE WORD AND BLESSED SACRAMENT P

Founded in France in 1625. First founded in the United States in 1853.

Motherhouse and Novitiate: *Incarnate Word Convent,* 1101 N.E. Water St., Victoria, TX 77901-9298. Tel: 361-575-2266; Fax: 361-575-2165. Sr. M. Evelyn Korenek, I.W.B.S., Supr. Gen.; Sr. Mary Virginia Sheblak, I.W.B.S., Community Archivist.

Total number in commuity 115.

Legal Titles: *Sisters of the Incarnate Word and Blessed Sacrament, Victoria, Texas, Inc.; Sisters of the Incarnate Word and Blessed Sacrament of Victoria, Texas Medical and Retirement Trust,* Victoria, TX.

Properties owned or sponsored: *Nazareth Academy,* Victoria, TX; *Blessed Sacrament Academy,* San Antonio, TX.

Ministry in the field of Education; CCD Centers; Hospitals.

Represented in the Archdiocese of San Antonio and the Dioceses of Austin, Beaumont, Dallas, Galveston-Houston and Victoria. Also in Africa.

[2205] (I.W.B.S.)—SISTERS OF THE INCARNATE WORD AND BLESSED SACRAMENT P

Founded in France in 1625. First Founded in the United States in 1853.

Motherhouse and Novitiate: *Incarnate Word Convent,* 2930 S. Alameda St., Corpus Christi, TX 78404. Tel: 361-882-5413; Fax: 361-880-4152. Sr. Marie Irma Gonzalez, Supr. Gen.

Legal Title: *Convent Academy of the Incarnate Word; Incarnate Word Academy Foundation.*

Sisters 68.

Sisters serve and staff: Private High Schools; Private Kindergartens; Montessori; Private Middle Schools; Parochial and Private Elementary Schools; Other ministries include Religious Education; Hospital Ministry; Vocation Ministry; Diocesan Offices; Adult Education; General Administration; Retreat Ministry; Parish Ministry.

Represented in the Dioceses of Brownsville, Corpus Christi, Beaumont, Galveston-Houston and Laredo.

[2210] (S.I.W.)—SISTERS OF THE INCARNATE WORD AND BLESSED SACRAMENT D

Founded in France in 1625. First foundation in the United States in 1853.

Motherhouse and Novitiate: 6618 Pearl Rd., (Parma Heights-U.S. Rd. 42), Cleveland, OH 44130. Tel: 216-886-6440. Sr. Carol Tobler, S.I.W., Congregational Leader.

Total number in community 37.

Ministry includes Evangelization; Elementary and Religious Education; Spiritual Ministry (Retreat and Spiritual Direction).

Pastoral Ministry in Parishes, Hospitals and Nursing Homes.

Represented in the Diocese of Cleveland.

[2230] (C.I.J.)—CONGREGATION OF THE INFANT JESUS D

Founded in France in 1835. First foundation in the United States in 1905.

General Motherhouse: 310 Prospect Park W., Brooklyn, NY 11215. Tel: 718-965-7300, 516-823-3800, 516-594-0476. Sr. Dolores Castellano, C.I.J., Supr. Gen.

Total number in community 76.

Corporate Title: *Nursing Sisters of the Sick Poor Inc.* Congregation sponsors one Hospital and one Home Health Agency.

Ministry in the fields of Nursing; Social Work; Physical Therapy; Services to Disabled Persons; Pastoral Care; Chaplains; Retreat Work; Teaching; Parish Ministry; and other works related to Health Services.

Represented in the Dioceses of Brooklyn and Rockville Centre.

[2245] (S.J.S.)—SISTERS OF JESUS THE SAVIOR D

Founded in Elele, Nigeria in 1985.

U.S. Foundation: *St. Scholastica Convent,* 17305 Ashton Rd., Detroit, MI 48219. Tel: 313-541-4368.

Professed Sisters 10.

Ministry in Education and Social Assistance.

Represented in the Archdiocese of Detroit.

[2250] (O.S.B.)—CONGREGATION OF BENEDICTINES OF JESUS CRUCIFIED P

Founded in France in 1930. First foundation in the United States in 1955.

General Motherhouse: Brou-sur-Chantereine, France. Mother Godefrieda Bouwman, O.S.B., Prioress Gen.

U.S. Foundations: *Regina Mundi Priory,* 550 S. Waterloo Rd., Devon, PA 19333-1798. Tel: 610-688-5130; Fax: 610-995-0477. Sr. Marie Rita Syn, O.S.B., Prioress.

St. Paul's Priory, Newport, RI 02840, Sr. Marie-Agathe Karunaratne, O.S.B., Prioress; Sr. Marie-Zita Wenker, O.S.B., Vocation Dir.

Total number in the U.S. 29.

Represented in the Archdiocese of Philadelphia and the Diocese of Providence.

[2260] (A.D.)—SISTERS OF THE LAMB OF GOD D

Founded in France 1945.

General Motherhouse: *Institute of the Lamb of God,* 85 Rt du Vieux Saint Marc, Brest, France 29283. Sr. Claire Marie Ducraux, A.D., Supr. Gen.

U.S. Foundation (1958): *House of Formation,* 2063 Wyandotte Ave., Owensboro, KY 42301. Tel: 502-281-5450, Sr. Mary Raymande, Supr.; Sr. Audrey Gold, Formation Dir.

Sisters 5; Novices 3.

Other Address: 9534 Ky. 144, Philpot KY, 42366. Tel: 502-281-5450. Sr. Mary Raymonde, Supr.

Sisters 4.

Represented in the Diocese of Owensboro.

[2270] (L.C.M.)—SISTERS OF THE LITTLE COMPANY OF MARY P

Founded in England in 1877. First foundation in the United States in 1893.

Generalate: *Little Company of Mary Generalate,* 28 Trinity Crescent, Tooting Bec London, England SW17 7AE.

Universal total for the congregation 443.

Provincial Office: *Province of the Immaculate Conception, The Little Company of Mary,* 9350 S. California Ave., Evergreen Park, IL 60805. Tel: 708-422-0130. Sr. Carol Pacini, L.C.M., Prov.

Total number in community 28.

Properties owned: *Little Company of Mary Hospital and Health Care Centers,* Evergreen Park, IL; *Bay Harbor Hospital,* Harbor City, CA; *Memorial Hospital and Health Care Center,* Jasper, IN; *Little Company of Mary Health Services (Little Company of Mary Hospital,* Torrance, CA and *San Pedro Peninsula Hospital,* San Pedro, CA).

Ministry in Hospitals and Health Care; Pastoral/Parish areas.

Represented in the Archdioceses of Chicago, Los Angeles and the Dioceses of Evansville, Orange and Toledo.

[2280] (P.F.M.)—LITTLE FRANCISCANS OF MARY (U.S.) P

Founded in the United States in 1889.

General Motherhouse: *Baie St. Paul,* (Charlevoix), Diocese of Quebec, P.Q. Canada. Sr. Carmen Gravel, Supr. Gen.

American Region: *St. Francis,* 55 Moore Ave., Worcester, MA 01602. Tel: 508-755-0878. Sr. Rena Mae Gagnon, Reg. Supr.

Total number in congregation including Canada and the United States 264.

Represented in the Dioceses of Portland (ME) and Worcester.

[2300] (L.S.I.C.)—LITTLE SERVANT SISTERS OF THE IMMACULATE CONCEPTION P

Founded in Poland on May 3, 1850. First founded in the United States in Reading, Pennsylvania on December 8, 1926.

General Motherhouse: *Stara Wies,* 460, 36-201 Stara Wies k., Brzozow woj. Podkarpackie, Poland. Mother Mariola Karas, L.S.I.C., Supr Gen.

Universal total in Congregation 1,445.

Holy Trinity Province: *Little Servants Sisters of the Immaculate Conception Provincialate-Novitiate,* 1000 Cropwell Rd., Cherry Hill, NJ 08003. Tel: 856-424-1962; Fax: 856-424-5333. Mother Mary M. Leonarda, L.S.I.C., Prov.; Sr. M. Philomena Nowicka, L.S.I.C., Archivist.

Legal Titles: *Congregation of the Little Servant Sisters of the Blessed Virgin Mary of the Immaculate Conception, Immaculate Conception Convent, Provincialate-Novitiate,* Cherry Hill, NJ; *St. Joseph's Catholic Nursing Homes,* Woodbridge, NJ; *St. Joseph's Residences,* Woodbridge, NJ; *Edmund Child Education Center,* Cherry Hill, NJ.

Professed Sisters 76; Novices 2.

Ministry in Early Childhood Education; Religious and Academic Education; Visiting Home Nursing Services; Senior Day Care Center; Senior Residential Homes & Assisted Living Homes, Nursing Homes; Guest House and Retreat House; Prayer Groups & Youth Ministry; Pastoral Services in hospitals and prisons.

Represented in the Archdioceses of Newark, Philadelphia and Diocese of Camden.

[2310] (L.S.A.)—LITTLE SISTERS OF THE ASSUMPTION P

Founded in France in 1865. First foundation in the United States in 1891.

General Motherhouse: Paris, France. Sr. Mercedes Martinez, Supr. Gen., 57 rue Violet, Paris, France 75015.
United States Province: *Little Sisters of the Assumption Provincialate,* 100 Gladstone Ave., Walden, NY 12586. Tel: 914-778-0667. Sr. Jean McCormack, Prov. Coord.
Total number in community 45.
Ministry in Home Health; Community Development Supportive Family Services Located in Poverty Areas; Services are predominantly provided in the Home Setting.
Represented in the Archdioceses of Boston, New York and Philadelphia and in the Diocese of Worcester.

[2315] (L.S.G.)—LITTLE SISTERS OF THE GOSPEL D
Founded in 1963 in France by Rev. Rene Voillaume. First foundation in the United States in 1972 in New York.
Generalate: *La Courneuve,* France 93120. Tel: 1-48361814.
U.S. House: Box 305, Mott Haven Sta., Bronx, NY 10454. Tel: 718-292-2867.
Residence: 340 Willis Ave., Bronx NY, 10454.
Professed Sisters 78; Novices 6.
Ministry in Prison Ministry; Service to the Poor and Underserved.
Represented in the Archdiocese of New York.

[2320] (P.S.S.F.)—THE LITTLE SISTERS OF THE HOLY FAMILY P
Les Petites Soeurs de la Sainte Famille
Founded in Canada in 1880. First foundation in the United States in 1900.
General Motherhouse: *Mont Sainte-Famille,* 1820 Ouest, Rue Galt, Sherbrooke, Quebec, Canada J1K 1H9. Tel: 819-823-0345. Sr. Jeannine Ferland, Supr. Gen.
U.S. Headquarters: *Marie Leonie Residence,* 285 Andover St., Lowell, MA 01852-1446. Tel: 508-454-7481. Sr. Gabrielle Paille, P.S.S.F., Supr.
Total number in U.S. 22.
Ministry in Sisters dedicated to the service of priests by prayer and domestic work in rectories.
Represented in the Archdioceses of Boston, Chicago, and the Diocese of Manchester.

[2330] (L.S.J.)—LITTLE SISTERS OF JESUS P
Founded in the Sahara in 1939. First foundation in the United States in 1952.
General Motherhouse: Rome, Italy. Sr. Raymonde Andree, Prioress Gen.
Universal total in congregation 1,324.
U.S. Regional House: 400 N. Streeper St., Baltimore, MD 21224-1230. Tel: 410-327-7863. Sr. Anne-Marie Boucher, L.S.J., Reg. Dir.
Total number in U.S. 26.
Represented in the Archdioceses of Anchorage, Baltimore, Chicago, Washington and the Dioceses of Altoona-Johnstown, and Fairbanks.

[2331] (L.S.J.M.)—LITTLE SISTERS OF JESUS AND MARY D
Founded in the United States in 1974. Sr. Mary Elizabeth, Foundress.
Joseph House: P.O. Box 1755, Salisbury, MD 21802. Tel: 410-543-1645. Sr. Mary Elizabeth Gintling, Dir.
Total in the community 8.
Represented in the Diocese of Wilmington.

[2340] (L.S.P.)—LITTLE SISTERS OF THE POOR P
Founded in France in 1839. First foundation in the United States in 1868.
General Motherhouse: *La Tour St. Joseph,* St. Pern, France 35190. Mother Celine de la Visitation, Supr. Gen.
Universal total in congregation 3,460.
Province of Brooklyn (1868): *Queen of Peace Residence,* 110-30 221st St., Queens Village, NY 11429. Sr. Genevieve Regina, Prov.
Total number in province 158.
Ministry in Homes for the Aged.
Represented in the Archdioceses of Boston, Hartford, Philadelphia and New York and the Dioceses of Albany, Brooklyn, Metuchen, Paterson, Providence and Scranton. Also in Montreal.
Province of Baltimore: *Little Sisters of the Poor,* 601 Maiden Choice Ln., Baltimore, MD 21228-3698. Tel: 410-744-9367; Fax: 410-747-0601. Sr. Mary Bernard du St. Esprit., Prov.
Total number in province 143.
Ministry in Homes for the Aged.
Represented in the Archdioceses of Baltimore, Cincinnati, Indianapolis, Mobile, New Orleans and Washington and the Dioceses of Cleveland, Pittsburgh, Richmond, Toledo and Wilmington.
Province of Chicago: *Little Sisters of the Poor, Chicago Province,* Inc., 80 W. Northwest Hwy., Palatine, IL 60067-3582. Tel: 847-358-5700; Fax: 847-934-6852. Sr. Margaret Regina, Prov.
Total number in province 140.
Ministry in Homes for the Aged.
Represented in the Archdioceses of Chicago, Denver, Los Angeles, Louisville, St. Louis, St. Paul-Minneapolis and San Francisco and the Dioceses of Evansville, Gallup, and Kansas City-St. Joseph.

[2345] (P.O.S.C.)—LITTLE WORKERS OF THE SACRED HEARTS P
Founded in Italy in 1892. First Foundation in the U.S. in 1948.
General House: Via dei Pamphili 3, 00152, Rome, Italy
Motherhouse and Novitiate: *Our Lady of Grace Convent,* 635 Glenbrook Rd., Stamford, CT 06906. Tel: 203-348-5531. Mother Lillian Cairo, P.O.S.C., Supr.
Ministry in Day Care Centers; Catechetics.
Represented in the Archdioceses of Philadelphia and Washington and the Diocese of Bridgeport.

[2350] (S.L.W.)—SISTERS OF THE LIVING WORD D
Founded in the United States in 1975.
General Motherhouse: *The Living Word Center,* 800 N. Fernandez Ave. B, Arlington Heights, IL 60004-5316. Tel: 847-577-5972; Fax: 847-577-5980. Sr. Lea Woll, S.L.W., Coord. of Spiritual Life.
Total number in community 77.
Ministry in the field of Academic and Religious Education; Hospitals; Parish Ministry and Social Services.
Represented in the Archdioceses of Chicago, Detroit, New Orleans, St. Louis, St. Paul-Minneapolis and the Dioceses of Biloxi, Cleveland, Jackson, Lansing, Rockford, San Angelo and Sioux City.

[2360] (S.L.)—SISTERS OF LORETTO AT THE FOOT OF THE CROSS P
Founded in America in 1812.
General Motherhouse & Novitiate: *Loretto Motherhouse and Novitiate,* Nerinx, KY 40049. Tel: 270-865-5811.
Administrative Office: 300 E. Hampden Ave., Suite 400, Englewood, CO 80110-2661. Tel: 303-783-0450; Fax: 303-783-0611. Sr. Mary Catherine Rabbitt, S.L., Pres.
Legal Titles: *Loretto Literary and Benevolent Institution Havern Center,* Littleton, CO.
Total number in congregation 371.
Ministry in the field of Academic and Religious Education at all levels; Seminaries; Specialized Education; Health Care-Aging; Community Administration; Pastoral Ministry; Social Justice-Social Service; Administration; Diocesan Offices; Medicine and Nursing; Prayer Retreats; Clerical Offices; Consultants; Spirituality Center.
Represented in the Archdioceses of Baltimore, Chicago, Denver, Indianapolis,Los Angeles, Louisville, Mobile, New Orleans, New York, St. Louis, San Antonio, Santa Fe, Seatte, Washington and the Dioceses of Cheyenne, Colorado Springs, El Paso, Galveston-Houston, Kansas City-St. Joseph, Knoxville, Lexington, Oakland, Orange, Orlando, Pueblo, Rockford, San Bernardino, San Diego, San Jose, Wheeling-Charleston and Worcester.

[2370] (I.B.V.M.)—INSTITUTE OF THE BLESSED VIRGIN MARY (LORETTO SISTERS) P
Founded in St. Omer, Belgium, 1609. First foundation in Canada in 1847; in the United States in 1880.
General Motherhouse North America: *Loretto Abbey,* 101 Mason Blvd., Toronto, Ontario, Canada M5M 3E2. Sr. Maria Bierer, Gen. Supr.
Universal total in congregation 224.
Regional Office Canada: *Canadian Regional Government, Loretto College,* 70 St. Mary St., Toronto, Ontario, Canada M5S 1J3. Sr. Evanne Hunter, Reg. Supr.-Canada.
Regional Office United States: *American Regional Administration, Loretto Convent,* P.O. Box 508, Wheaton, IL 60189. Tel: 630-665-3814; Fax: 630-653-4886. Sr. Ellen Enright, Reg. Supr.
Total number in community 91.
Properties owned: *Loretto High School,* Sacramento, CA; *Loretto Development Office; Loretto Convent,* Wheaton, IL; *Loretto Early Childhood Center,* Wheaton, IL; *Loretto Sisters Novitiate,* Ontario, Canada; *Loretto Conference Center,* Wheaton, IL.
Sisters serve and staff: High Schools; Grammar Schools; Missionary Work; Correspondence School; University; Pastoral Ministry; Adult Education; Social Work; Retreat Ministry; Diocesan Office; Director of Religious Education.
Represented in the Archdiocese of Chicago and the Dioceses of Joliet, Marquette, Fairbanks, Phoenix, Sacramento and Venice.

[2380] (I.B.V.M.)—INSTITUTE OF THE BLESSED VIRGIN MARY (LORETO SISTERS) P
Founded in St. Omer, Belgium, in 1609. Foundation in Arizona, 1954 from the diocese of Meath, Ireland.
Generalate: Viale Appio Claudio, 10, Rome, Italy. Sr. Noni Mitchell, Supr. Gen.
Total number in congregation 988.
U.S. Regional: *Mary Ward House,* 2521 W. Maryland Ave., Phoenix, AZ 85017. Tel: 602-433-0659. Sr. Raphael Quinn, I.B.V.M., Reg. Supr.
Total number in community 18.
Represented in the Diocese of Phoenix.

[2390] (L.H.C.)—LOVERS OF THE HOLY CROSS SISTERS D
Founded in 1670 in Viet Nam by Bishop Pierre Lambert de la Motte. First foundation in the United States in 1976. Established as an autonomous institute of Consecrated Life of Diocesan Right in 1992.
General Motherhouse: *Holy Cross Convent,* 14700 South Van Ness Ave., Gardena, CA 90249. Tel: 310-768-1906 or 516-0271; Fax: 310-352-6435. Sr. Monica Phi Tran, L.H.C., Supr. Gen.
Legal Title: *Lovers of the Holy Cross Sisters, Inc.*
Sisters 47; Novices 9; Postulants 7; Aspirants 15; Oblates 2.
Represented in the Archdioceses of Los Angeles and the Diocese of Orange and San Bernardino.

[2400] (M.S.)—MARIAN SISTERS OF THE DIOCESE OF LINCOLN D
Marycrest Motherhouse: *Marian Center,* R.R. No. 1, Box 108, Waverly, NE 68462. Tel: 402-786-2750; Fax: 402-786-7256. Sr. Bernadette Radek, M.S., Major Supr.
Total number in community 38.
Ministry in the field of Education; Specialized Education; Health Care; Catechetics.
Represented in the Diocese of Lincoln.

[2410] (M.S.C.)—CONGREGATION OF THE MARIANITES OF HOLY CROSS P
Founded in France in 1841. First foundation in the United States in 1843.
Congregational Administration Headquarters: 1011 Gallier St., New Orleans, LA 70117. Tel: 504-945-1620. Sr. Mary Kay Kinberger, M.S.C., Congregational Leader.
Total number in North America 185.
Legal Holdings or Titles: *Our Lady of Holy Cross Convent,* New Orleans, LA; *Our Lady of Holy Cross College,* New Orleans, LA; *Prompt Succor Nursing Home,* Opelousas, LA; *C'est la Vie (Senior Citizen Independent Living Units),* Opelousas, LA.
Ministry in Parishes; Social & Health Services; and the field of Education.
Represented in the Archdioceses of New Orleans, New York, and the Dioceses of Alexandria, Baton Rouge, Biloxi, Camden, Dallas, Galveston-Houston, Houma-Thibodeaux, Lafayette (LA), Lake Charles, Manchester, Paterson, and Trenton. Also in Bangladesh, Haiti, and Canada.

[2420] (S.M.S.M.)—MARIST MISSIONARY SISTERS (MISSIONARY SISTERS OF THE SOCIETY OF MARY) INC. P
Founded in France in 1845-1857. First foundation in the United States in Boston, Massachusetts 1922.
Motherhouse: Via Cassia, 1243, Roma, Italia, 00189.
Universal total in congregation 609.
North American Province: *Provincial Office,* 349 Grove St., Waltham, MA 02453-6018. Tel: 781-893-0149; Fax: 781-894-7610. Sr. Mary Jane Kenney, S.M.S.M., Prov. Vocation Promotion House, 1515 Boxwood Ave., San Leandro, CA 94579. Sr. Annemarie Woeste, S.M.S.M.
Represented in the Archdioceses of Boston, San Francisco and the Dioceses of Austin, Fairbanks, Memphis, St. Petersburg, Rochester, and Venice.

[2430] (S.M.)—MARIST SISTERS/ CONGREGATION OF MARY P
Founded in France 1824 by Venerable John Claude Colin and Jeanne Marie Chavoin.
General Motherhouse: Via Aurelia 292, Rome, Italy 00165. Sr. Gail Reneker, S.M., Supr. Gen.
Universal total in Congregation 500.
U.S. Foundation (1956): *Marist Sisters - Congregation of Mary,* 810 Peach, Abilene, TX 79602. Tel: 915-675-5806; Fax: 915-675-5127. Sr. Andrena Mulligan, S.M., Prov. Supr.
Total number in the community 18.

Ministry in Elementary & Adult Education; Pastoral Ministry; Counseling; Pastoral Care in Hospitals; Physical Therapy; Seminary Formation; Social Ministry.
Represented in the Archdioceses of Chicago, Detroit and the Dioceses of Saginaw, San Angelo and Wheeling-Charleston.

[2440] (S.M.I.)—SISTERS OF MARY IMMACULATE P
Catechist Sisters of Mary Immaculate, Help of Christians.
Founded in India in 1948 by the late Bishop Louis LaRavoire Morrow, Bishop of Krishnagar, India.
General Motherhouse: Krishnagar, Nadia Dist., West Bengal, India 741 101. Sr. Marie Pothanamala, Supr. Gen.
Universal total in Congregation 482.
U.S. Foundation(1981): *Sisters of Mary Immaculate,* R.D. No.5, Box 1231, Leechburg, PA 15656. Tel: 724-845-2828; 836-0449. Sr. Gratia Kuttianickal, S.M.I., Delegation Supr.; Sr. Tracy Vattakuzhiyil, S.M.I., Supr.
Total number in the community 6.
Legal Holdings & Titles: *St. Joseph Hall Convent,* Greensburg, PA; *Bishop Morrow Personal Care Home,* Leechburg, PA.

[2450] (S.M.P.)—SISTERS OF MARY OF THE PRESENTATION P
Founded in France. First foundation in the United States in 1903.
General Motherhouse: *Broons,* Cotes-du-Nord, France. Sr. Anne Grall, Supr. Gen.
U.S. Provincial House & Novitiate At Maryvale: 11550 River Rd., Valley City, ND 58072. Tel: 701-845-2864. Sr. Marlyss Dionne, S.M.P., Prov.
Total number in the community 57.
Properties owned: *St. Margaret's Hospital,* Spring Valley, IL; *Prairieland Home Health Agency,* Fargo, ND;
Ministry in the field of Religious and Academic Education at all levels; Parish Ministry; Hospitals and Home Health Agencies.
Represented in the Archdiocese of Chicago and the Dioceses of Cheyenne, Fargo, and Peoria.

[2460] (S.M.R.)—SOCIETY OF MARY REPARATRIX P
Founded in France in 1857. First foundation in the United States in 1908. Total International Membership: 974 Sisters.
Generalate: *Society Di Maria Riparatrice,* Via dei Lucchesi 3, Roma, Italia 00187. Sr. Mary Henihan, Supr. Gen.
U.S. Province: 17320 Grange Rd., Riverview, MI 48192. Tel: 734-285-4510; Fax: 734-285-8147. Sr. Margaret Hoey, S.M.R., Prov.
Total number in the community 32.
Represented in the Archdioceses of Detroit, Miami, New York and the Diocese of Brooklyn.

[2470] (M.M.)—MARYKNOLL SISTERS OF ST. DOMINIC P
Founded in New York 1912.
Center: *Maryknoll Sisters Center,* Maryknoll, NY 10545-0311. Tel: 914-941-7575. Sr. Helene O'Sullivan, M.M., Community Pres.; Sr. Carol Hassey, M.M., Center Coord.; Sr. Mary Anne O'Donnell, M.M.; Center Coord.; Sr. Miedal Stone, M.M., Center Coord.
Orientation Program: *Maryknoll Sisters.* Co-Dirs.: Sr. Susan Glass, M.M., Sr. Christelle Zabalerio, M.M.
Legal Titles and Holdings: *Maryknoll Sisters of St. Dominic, Inc.; Maryknoll Mission Institute.*
Total number in the Congregation 660.
Represented in the Archdioceses of Baltimore, Boston, Chicago, Cincinnati, Detroit, Hartford, Los Angeles, Louisville, Newark, New York, Philadelphia, Portland (OR), St. Louis, San Francisco, Washington and the Dioceses of Albany, Baker, Brownsville, Brooklyn, Gallup, Honolulu, Galveston-Houston, Kansas City-St. Joseph, Las Cruces, Madison, Manchester, Oakland, Palm Beach, Phoenix, Providence, Raleigh, Rochester, Rockville Centre, Sacramento, St. Augustine, St. Petersburg, San Bernardino, San Diego, San Jose, Scranton, Springfield, Stockton and Winona. Also in Samoa.

[2480] (M.M.M.)—MEDICAL MISSIONARIES OF MARY P
Founded in Ireland in 1937. First United States Foundation in 1950.
General Motherhouse: *Rosemount,* Booterstown Ave., Blackrock, Co. Dublin, Ireland. Mother Mary Martin, M.M.M., Foundress; Sr. Philomena Sheerin, Congregational Leader.
Zonal Center: 563 Minneford Ave., City Island, NY 10464-1118. Tel: 718-885-0945; Fax: 718-885-0010. Sr. Joanne Bierl, M.M.M., Zonal Coord.
Total number in the Congregation 430.
Represented in the Archdioceses of Boston, Chicago and New York and the Dioceses of Richmond and San Diego.

[2490] (M.M.S.)—MEDICAL MISSION SISTERS P
Generalate: London, England. Sr. Elizabeth Koonthanam, M.M.S., Society Coord.
Universal total in the Congregation 671.
North American Headquarters (1925): 8400 Pine Rd., Philadelphia, PA 19111. Tel: 215-742-6100; Fax: 215-342-3948. Sr. Maria Hornung, M.M.S., North American Coord.
Legal Titles: *Society of Catholic Medical Missionaries, Inc.; Society of Catholic Medical Missionaries Generalate, Inc.*
Total number in North America 144
Represented in the Archdioceses of Anchorage, Baltimore, Boston, Chicago, Cincinnati, Hartford, Louisville, New York, Philadelphia, St. Louis, Seattle, Washington and the Dioceses of Arlington, Harrisburg, Las Cruces, Memphis, Palm Beach, Richmond, St. Petersburg, San Jose, San Diego, Savannah, Trenton, and Tucson. Also in Mexico.

[2500] (M.S.J.)—MEDICAL SISTERS OF ST. JOSEPH P
Founded in Kerala, South India, 1946.
General Motherhouse: *Dharmagiri,* P.O. Kothamangalam, Kerala, South India 686691. Mother Nora, M.S.J., Supr. Gen.
U.S. Foundation (1985): *Medical Sisters of St. Joseph,* 3435 E. Funston, Wichita, KS 67218. Tel: 316-686-4746. Sr. Audrey, M.S.J.,Supr.
Total number in Congregation 700.
Ministry in as Health Care Apostolates.
Represented in the Diocese of Wichita.

[2515] (C.M.S.)—CASHEL MERCY SISTERS D
U.S. Foundation (St. Mel's Convent): *Congregation of the Sisters of Mercy of Ireland,* P.O. Box 1180, Fair Oaks, CA 95628. 916-967-9504. Sr. Kathleen O'Dwyer, Contact Person.
Represented in the Diocese of Sacramento.

[2516] (S.M.)—SISTERS OF MERCY P
Founded in Ireland in 1831.
Motherhouse: *Convent of Mercy,* Carrick-on-Suir, Ireland.
U.S. Foundation (1956): *St. John's Convent of Mercy,* 11154 San Pablo Ave., El Cerrito, CA 94530. Tel: 415-233-6769.
Other U.S. Convents (1960): *St. Nicholas Convent,* 12816 S. El Monte Ave., Los Altos Hills CA, 94022. Tel: 415-948-0775.
Professed Sisters 10.
Represented in the Dioceses of Oakland, San Jose, Santa Rosa and Sioux Falls.

[2517] SISTERS OF MERCY P
Founded in Dublin, 1831.
Headquarters: Dublin, Ireland.
Holy Infant Convent: 239 Nancy Pl., Ballwin, MO 63021. Tel: 314-391-1528. Sr. Agnes Nolan, Facilitator.
Total number in the community 4.
Legal Title: *Sisters of Mercy, Ireland.*
Ministry in Education & Pastoral Ministries.
Represented in the Archdiocese of St. Louis.

[2519] (R.S.M.)—RELIGIOUS SISTERS OF MERCY OF ALMA, MICHIGAN P
The Religious Sisters of Mercy of Alma was officially founded on September 1, 1973; Diocesan approval on Jan. 25, 1974; Constitutions of Community approved March 17, 1978; Pontifical Status fully approved June 18, 1982. Final approval of constitution May 31, 1991.
Motherhouse and Novitiate: *Religious Sisters of Mercy,* 1835 Michigan Ave., Alma, MI 48801. Tel: 517-463-6035. Mother Mary Quentin Sheridan, R.S.M.
Total number in the community 57
Represented in the Archdioceses of Denver, Hartford, Portland (OR), Washington and the Dioceses of Lansing, Saginaw, Tulsa and Winona. Also in Canada, Germany and Italy.

[2520] (R.S.M.)—SISTERS OF MERCY P
Founded in the United States in 1960.
General Motherhouse: *Congregation of the Sisters of Mercy,* Elblana Ave., Dun Laoghlaire, Dublin 01-2800448. Ireland. Sr. Breege O'Neill, Supr. Gen.
U.S. Foundation: *St. Joan of Arc,* 500 S.W. Fourth Ave., Boca Raton, FL 33432. Tel: 561-368-6655. Sr. Kathleen Sweeney, Communications Coord.
Professed Sisters 4.
Represented in the Diocese of Palm Beach.

[2523] (R.S.M.)—SISTERS OF MERCY OF ARDAGH & CLONMACNOIS
Sisters of Mercy (1971): 5392 S.W. 33rd Ave., Ft. Lauderdale, FL 33312. Tel: 954-989-8291. Sr. Teresa O'Connell, Prov. Supr.
Total number in the community 10.
Ministry in the field of Education; Parish Work.
Represented in the Archdiocese of Miami and the Diocese of Palm Beach.
U.S. Address: 2766 Navajo Rd., El Cajon, CA 92020. Tel: 619-465-2233.
Ministry in Hospital, Schools and Parishes.
Professed Sisters 3.
Represented in the Diocese of San Diego.

[2530] SISTERS OF MERCY D
Founded in Dublin, Ireland in 1831.
Mercy Generalate: Dundalk Co. Louth, Ireland. Sr. M. Rosarii Carville.
U.S. Foundation: *Mailing Address:* P.O. Box 360937, Melbourne, FL 32936-0937; Ascension School, P.O. Box E.G. 937, Melbourne, FL 32935. Sr. M. Joseph Barden, Local Supr.
Represented in the Diocese of Orlando.

[2549] (R.S.M.)—SISTERS OF MERCY (SLIGO) P
Founded in Ireland in 1846. First foundation in United States in 1956.
Generalate: *St. Peter's Convent,* Athlone Roscommon, Ireland. Sr. Patricia Kelly, Supr. Gen.
American Region: 4825 H St., San Bernardino, CA 92447. Tel: 909-886-6172; Fax: 909-883-5954. Sr. Maura Feeley, Reg. Supr.
Total number in the community 25.
Ministry in the field of Religious and Academic Education; Parishes; Social Services; Diocesan Offices.
Represented in the Dioceses of Orange, San Bernardino and San Diego.

[2560] SISTERS OF MERCY D
Founded in Ireland.
General Motherhouse: *Sisters of Mercy - U.S. Province Redlands, CA 92374.*
U.S. Address (1963): *St. James School,* 603 West Ave., Gulfport, MS 39507. Tel: 288-896-6631. Sr. Teresa O'Connell, Prov.
Total number in the community 7.
Represented in the Diocese of Biloxi.

[2575] (R.S.M.)—SISTERS OF MERCY OF THE AMERICAS
Catherine McAuley founded the Sisters of Mercy in Dublin, Ireland, in 1831. Ten years later, she received confirmation of the Rule by Pope Gregory XVI. In 1843 the Sisters of Mercy established their first U.S.A. foundation in Pittsburgh. In 1929 several of the independent congregations amalgamated to form the Sisters of Mercy of the Union. In 1991 the members of the nine provinces of the Union and of 16 other Mercy congregations founded the Sisters of Mercy of the Americas, with its 25 regional communities.
Universal total in the Congregation 5,469.
Institute Administrative Offices: 8300 Colesville Rd., #300, Silver Spring, MD 20910-3243. Tel: 301-587-0423; Fax: 301-587-0533. Sr. Marie Chin, R.S.M., Pres.
Mercy Action, Inc. is separately incorporated to foster innovative works of mercy.
McAuley Institute, Inc. is separately incorporated to foster the development of low-income housing ministry as a work of mercy.
Mercy Corps, Inc. is separately incorporated to conduct a volunteer lay ministry program to further the works of mercy.

Albany P
Regional Community of Albany (1863): 310 S. Manning Blvd., Albany, NY 12208. Tel: 518-437-3000; Fax: 518-437-3030. Sr. Margaret J. Straney, R.S.M., Pres.
Total number in the community 159.
Properties owned or sponsored: Maria College; St. Peter's Hospital; McAuley Living Services.
Ministry in the field of Education; Health Services; Pastoral Ministry; Social Services.
Represented in the Archdioceses of Anchorage, Hartford, New York, Washington and the Dioceses of Albany, Rochester, and Syracuse.

Auburn P
Auburn Regional Community: *Institute of the Sisters of Mercy of the Americas,* 535 Sacramento St., Auburn, CA 95603. Tel: 530-887-2000. Sr. Sheila Browne, R.S.M., Pres.
Total number in the community 83.
Properties owned, staffed or sponsored: *Our Lady of Mercy Convent,* Auburn, CA; *McAuley Convent; Russell*

House; Mercy Convent, Sacramento, CA; *Mercy Convent,* Redding, CA; *Mercy San Juan Convent,* Fair Oaks, CA; *Mercy Convent,* Folsom, CA; *Mercy Convent,* Carmichael, CA.
Ministry in the field of Education; Parishes; Diocesan Offices; Health Care; Pastoral Ministries; Housing; Social Ministries.
Represented in the Diocese of Sacramento.

Baltimore P
Sisters of Mercy, Regional Community of Baltimore: 1322 E. Northern Pkwy, Baltimore, MD 21239-1998. Tel: 410-435-4400. Sr. Barbara Wheeley, R.S.M., Pres.
Total number in community 218.
Legal Holdings and Titles: *Sisters of Mercy, Baltimore, Inc.; The Villa, Inc.,* Baltimore, MD.
Sisters serve and staff: Elementary Schools; High Schools; Institutions of Higher Education; Multi-Level Long-Term Care Facility & Health Systems; Diocesan Child Care Homes; Pastoral Ministry Programs in Parishes; Diocesan Ministries; National Conference of Catholic Bishops; United States Catholic Conference.
Properties Owned or Sponsored: High Schools 3; Hospitals 4; Retirement Facilities for Sisters 4; Leisure-Retreat Houses for Sisters 3; Residential Program for Homeless Women; Theological Center; Neighborhood Center for Families.
Represented in the Archdioceses of Atlanta, Baltimore, Mobile and Washington and the Dioceses of Birmingham, Pensacola-Tallahassee, Savannah and Wilmington. Also in Belize & Guyana.

Brooklyn P
Brooklyn Regional Community (1855): 273 Willoughby Ave., Brooklyn, NY 11205. Tel: 718-622-5750. Sr. Camille D'Arienzo, Pres.
Total number in the community 254.
Properties Owned or Sponsored: Angel Guardian Children and Family Services; Mercy Home for Children; Catherine McAuley H.S., Brooklyn, NY; St. Mary's Children and Family Services; Our Lady of Mercy Academy, Syosset, NY; Mercy H.S., Riverhead, NY.
Sisters serve and staff: Elementary and High Schools; Institutions of Higher Education; Child Care Institutions; Pastoral Ministry Programs and Spirituality and Retreat Programs.
Represented in the Archdioceses of Baltimore, New Orleans and the Dioceses of Brooklyn, Fall River, Orlando, Rockville Centre, and Toledo. Also in Panama.

Buffalo P
Regional Community of Buffalo: 625 Abbott Rd., Buffalo, NY 14220. Tel: 716-826-5051; Fax: 716-826-1518. Sr. Nancy Hoff, R.S.M., Pres.
Total number in the community 189.
Legal Holdings and Titles, Sponsored Works: *Trocaire College; Mount Mercy Academy,* Buffalo, NY. Co-sponsor: *Catholic Health System,* Buffalo, NY; *Catholic Health East,* Radnor, PA.
Ministry in the field of Education at all levels; Catholic Charities; Parish & Pastoral Ministry; Health Care; Community Table.
Represented in the Archdiocese of Washington and the Dioceses of Buffalo, Providence and Rochester. Also in the Philippine Islands.

Burlingame P
Regional Community of Burlingame (1854): 2300 Adeline Dr., Burlingame, CA 94010-5599. Tel: 650-340-7410; Fax: 650-347-2550. Sr. Judith Carle, Pres.; Sr. Marilyn Gouailhardou, Archivist
Total number in the community 198.
Legal Title: *Sisters of Mercy,* Burlingame.
Ministry in Health Care; Religious and Academic Education; Spirituality and Conference Center; Foreign Missions; Social Services including housing; Retreats; Diocesan Offices.
Represented in the Archdioceses of Los Angeles and San Francisco and the Dioceses of Fresno, Oakland, Orange, Phoenix, Sacramento, San Diego, San Jose and Santa Rosa. Also in Peru & Romania.

Cedar Rapids P
Regional Community of Cedar Rapids: *Sacred Heart Convent Motherhouse,* 1125 Prairie Dr., N.E., Cedar Rapids, IA 52402-4737. Tel: 319-364-5196; Fax: 319-364-7383. Sr. Susan O'Connor, R.S.M., Pres.; Sr. Delores Marie Hannon, R.S.M., Vice Pres.
Total number in the community 100.
Ministry in the field of Academic and Religious Education at all levels; Parish Ministry; Pastoral Care; Foreign Mission work; Social Services; Hospitals; Literacy Programs; Transitional Housing; Social Justice Ministries; Home for Aged.
Properties owned or sponsored: *Mount Mercy College; Mercy Medical Center; Sisters of Mercy Charitable Trust; Catherine McAuley Center for Women,* Cedar Rapids, IA.
Represented in the Archdioceses of Baltimore, Cincinnati, Dubuque, Indianapolis, Milwaukee, New York, St. Louis, Washington and the Dioceses of Crookston, Davenport, Des Moines, Helena, Sioux City, St. Cloud, Wheeling-Charleston, Winona.

Chicago P
Regional Community of Chicago: *Administrative Center,* 10024 S. Central Park Ave., Chicago, IL 60655-3132. Tel: 773-779-6011; Fax: 773-779-6094. Sr. Joy Clough, R.S.M., Pres.
Total number in community 303.
Sisters serve and staff: Education at all Levels; Social Services; Pastoral Services; Health Care; Spirituality; Foreign Missions.
Legal Holdings and Titles: *Sisters of Mercy of the Americas, Regional Community of Chicago; Mercy Housing Corporation,* Chicago, IL; *Sisters of Mercy of the Americas, Regional Community of Chicago Charitable Trust.*
Properties owned and sponsored: University 1; High Schools 1; Hospitals 1; Residence 1; Retreat Houses 1; Health System 1; co-sponsors Provena Health.
Represented in the Archdioceses of Baltimore, Boston, Chicago, Milwaukee, St. Louis and the Dioceses of Charleston, Colorado Springs, Davenport, Des Moines, El Paso, Joliet, Knoxville, Peoria, Phoenix, Rockford, St. Petersburg, Savannah, and Springfield (IL). Also in Honduras.

Cincinnati P
Regional Community of Cincinnati: 2335 Grandview Ave., Cincinnati, OH 45206. Tel: 513-221-1800; Fax: 513-221-0207. Sr. Marjorie Rudemiller, R.S.M., Pres.
Total number in community 363.
Sisters staff and serve: Academic Education at all levels; Parish & Diocesan Ministry; Health and Child-Care; Hospitals and Schools of Nursing; Homes for the Aged; Retreat and Renewal Center; Special Education.
Represented in the Archdioceses of Cincinnati, Detroit, Louisville, Newark, St. Louis, Washington and the Dioceses of Amarillo, Brooklyn, Brownsville, Charlotte, Cleveland, Knoxville, Lansing, Las Cruces, Lexington, Memphis, Nashville, Oakland, Orlando,Owensboro, Portland, Richmond, and Youngstown. Also in Jamaica, West Indies.

Connecticut P
Regional Community of Connecticut: *Sisters of Mercy of the Americas,* 249 Steele Rd., West Hartford, CT 06117. Tel: 860-232-8602; Fax: 860-233-0065. Sr. Judith A. Carey, R.S.M., Reg. Pres.; Sr. Dolores Liptak, Archivist.
Total number in the community 258.
Legal Title: *Sisters of Mercy of Connecticut, Inc.*
Properties owned and sponsored: *Mercyknoll, Inc.; Saint Mary Home, Inc.; McAuley Center, Inc.; The Academy of Our Lady of Mercy - Lauralton Hall, Inc.; Saint Joseph College, Inc.; Our Lady of Mercy School, Inc.; Mercy Housing and Shelter, Inc.; Mercy Center, Inc.; Mercy Community Health, Inc.; Mercy Community Homecare, Inc.*
Ministry in the field of Religious and Academic Education at all levels; School for Exceptional Children; Spirituality and Retreat Work; Social Services and; Health Care.
Represented in the Archdioceses of Boston, Hartford, New York, and the Dioceses of Bridgeport, Burlington, Lexington, Corpus Christi, Manchester, Norwich, Pittsburgh, Providence, Springfield, Wheeling-Charleston, Wichita, and Worcester. Also in Belize, Guatemala and Haiti.

Dallas P
Regional Community of Dallas: *Administrative Office,* P.O. Box 369, Dallas, PA 18612-0369. Tel: 570-675-1966; Fax: 570-675-9051. Sr. Catherine McGroarty, R.S.M., Pres.; Sr. Susan Marie Nowalis, R.S.M., Community Archivist.
Total number in community 333.
Properties owned or sponsored: *Mercy Center College; Misericordia Mount Aloysius College; Mercy Center Preschool; Catherine McAuley Center; Neuman Housing Services, Inc.; Project REMAIN.*
Ministry in the field of Education; Hospital & Health Care; Art; Communications; Retirement Homes; Housing; Pastoral Services; Social Services; South American Ministries; European Ministries (overseas ministry).
Represented in the Archdioceses of Baltimore, Newark, New York, Philadelphia, St. Louis, and the Dioceses of Altoona-Johnstown, Brooklyn, Camden, Charlotte, Greensburg, Harrisburg, Madison, Pittsburgh, Rockville Centre, St. Cloud, St. Petersburg, Scranton, Springfield-Cape Girardeau and Wheeling-Charleston. Also in Guatemala, Guyana, & Honduras.

Detroit P
Regional Community of Detroit: *Sisters of Mercy,* 29000 Eleven Mile Rd., Farmington Hills, MI 48336. Tel: 248-476-8000; Fax: 248-476-4222. Sr. Linda Werthman, R.S.M., Pres.; Sr. Michaeline Lewandowski, R.S.M., Archivist.
Total number in community 261.
Legal Title: *Sisters of Mercy - Regional Community of Detroit; Sisters of Mercy of the Americas, Regional Community of Detroit, Charitable Trusts I and II.*
Properties Sponsored: *Mercy High School,* Farmington Hills, MI; *Colegio Santa Ethnea,* Bella Vista, Agentina; *Mercy Center,* Farminton Hills, MI; *Mercy Education Project,* Detroit, MI. Properties Co-Sponsored: *University of Detroit Mercy,* Detroit, MI; *Our Lady of Guadalupe Middle School,* Detroit, MI. Participating Entity: *Catholic Health Ministries,* Novi, MI.
Represented in the Archdioceses of Baltimore, Chicago, Detroit, Dubuque, Hartford, Louisville, Milwaukee, San Antonio, Washington and the Dioceses of Charlotte, Cleveland, Columbus, Gaylord, Grand Rapids, Kalamazoo, LaCrosse, Lansing, Lexington, Orlando, Owensboro, Saginaw, and St. Petersburg. Also in Argentina, & Chile.

Erie P
Regional Community of Erie: 444 E. Grandview Blvd., Erie, PA 16504. Tel: 814-824-2516; Fax: 814-824-2127. Sr. JoAnne Courneen, Reg. Pres.; Sr. Edith Langiotti, Archivist.
Total number in the community 75.
Legal Title: *Institute of the Sisters of Mercy of the Americans - Regional Community of Erie.*
Properties owned and or sponsored: *Mercyhurst College; Mercyhurst Preparatory School; Mercy Center for the Arts, (Preschool); Mercy Center on Aging; Mercy Terrace Apartments, (Housing for Elderly); Mercy Center for Women.*
Ministry in the field of Religious and Academic Education at all levels; Prison Ministry; Health Care Ministry; Diocesan Marriage Tribunal; Social Services.
Represented in the Archdioceses of Detroit, Washington and the Dioceses of Erie and Savannah.

Merion P
Regional Community of Merion: *Motherhouse of The Sisters of Mercy,* Merion, PA 19066. Tel: 610-664-6650; Fax: 610-664-3429. Sr. Christine McCann, R.S.M., Reg. Pres.; Sr. Juliet Ferrari, R.S.M., Local Coord.
Total number in the community 444.
Legal Title: *Sisters of Mercy of Merion, PA.*
Properties owned, staffed, or sponsored: *Gwynedd Mercy College; McAuley Convent; Merion Mercy Academy; Waldron Mercy Academy; Gwynedd Mercy Academy; Mercy Vocational High School; St. Mary Residence; Walsingham Academy Mercy Health System.*
Sisters serve and staff: Religious and academic education at all levels; Hospices; House of Prayer; Social service organizations.
Represented in the Archdioceses of Anchorage, Atlanta, Baltimore, Cincinnati, Miami, New York, Philadelphia, St. Louis, Washington and the Dioceses of Allentown, Biloxi, Buffalo, Camden, Gallup, Grand Rapids, Orlando, Raleigh, Richmond, Scranton, Toledo, Trenton, Tucson, Wheeling-Charleston and Wilmington. Also in Italy, Peru, Bolivia and Canada.

New Hampshire P
Motherhouse of the Sisters of Mercy Inc.: *Sisters of Mercy of the Americas-Regional Community of New Hampshire, (1858),* 21 Searles Rd., Windham, NH 03087-1297. Tel: 603-893-6550; Fax: 603-893-2413. Sr. Patricia Sullivan, Pres.
Total number in the community 168.
Properties owned or sponsored: *Marian Court College,* Swampscott, MA; *Mt. St. Mary Academy,* Manchester, NH; *Manchester Convent of the Sisters of Mercy; Mount Saint Mary Corporation of the Sisters of Mercy Frances Warde House, Inc.,* Manchester, NH; *Warde Health Center, Inc.,* Windham, NH; *McAuley Commons, Inc.,* Windham, NH.
Ministry in the field of Academic Education at all levels; Nursing Homes; Hospitals.
Represented in the Archdioceses of Baltimore, Boston, and the Dioceses of Brooklyn, Fall River, Orlando, Manchester, Portland (ME), Providence, Pueblo, and St. Augustine.

New Jersey P
Regional Community of New Jersey: 1645 U.S. Hwy 22, W., Watchung, NJ 07069-6587. Tel: 908-756-0994; Fax: 908-754-0164. Sr. Diane Szubrowski, R.S.M., Reg. Pres.; Sr. Innocent Dolan, R.S.M., Archivist.
Total number in the community 297.
Legal Title: *Sisters of Mercy of New Jersey.*
Properties owned or sponsored: *McAuley Hall; McAuley School for the Exceptional Child,* Watchung, NJ; *Geor-*

gian Court College of the Sisters of Mercy, Lakewood, NJ; *Mount Saint Mary Academy,* Watchung, NJ; *Mount Saint Mary House of Prayer Mercy Center,* Asbury Park, NJ.
Ministry in the field of Religious and Academic Education at all levels; Health Care and Hospital Chaplaincy; Diocesan and Tribunal Administration; Parish and Prison Ministry; School for Special Education; Day Center for Senior Citizens; Child Day Care Center; House of Prayer.
Represented in the Archdioceses of New York, Newark, Philadelphia, Washington and the Dioceses of Camden, Charlotte, Las Cruces, Metuchen, Paterson, Rochester, Santa Rosa and Trenton.

New York **P**
Regional Community of New York: *Sisters of Mercy,* 150 Ridge Rd., Hartsdale, NY 10530. Tel: 914-328-3200; Fax: 914-328-3761. Sr. Suzanne Elliott, R.S.M., Reg. Pres.
Total number in community 181.
Legal Title: Sisters of Mercy, Inc.
Properties owned and sponsored: *Our Lady of Victory Academy,* NY; *St. Catharine Academy,* NY; *Nazareth Home for Boys,* Leicester, MA; *Uihlein Mercy Center (Skilled Nursing Facility),* Lake Placid, NY; *Mercy Healthcare Center, Inc.,* Tupper Lake, NY; *St. Joseph's Home,* Worcester, MA; *Mercy Center,* Bronx, NY.
Ministry in the field of Academic Education at all levels; Health and Child care; Special Education; Social Services; Spirituality and Counseling centers; Catechetical services; Pastoral Ministry.
Represented in the Archdioceses of Boston, Hartford, Los Angeles, New York and the Dioceses of Ogdensburg, Rockville Centre, St. Petersburg and Worcester.

North Carolina **P**
Sisters of Mercy of the Americas - Regional Community of North Carolina: *Mercy Administration Center,* 101 Mercy Dr., Belmont, NC 28012. Tel: 704-829-5260; Fax: 704-829-5267. Sr. Mary Rosalind Picot, R.S.M., Pres.; Sr. Mary Andrew Ray, R.S.M., Community Archivist.
Total number in the community 123.
Legal Title: *Sisters of Mercy of NC, Inc.*
Ministry in the field of Religious and Academic Education at all levels; Aids Ministry; Pastoral Ministry; Health Care Ministry; Developmental Center for Handicapped Children; Social Work; Daycare and Preshool Centers; Transitional Housing for homeless women and children; Psycho-Spiritual Programs.
Represented in the Archdiocese of Agana, Miami and the Dioceses of Caroline Islands, Chalan Kanoa, Charlotte, Orlando, Pensacola-Tallahassee, and Wheeling-Charleston.

Omaha **P**
Regional Community of Omaha: *Sisters of Mercy Regional Office,* 7262 Mercy Rd., Omaha, NE 68124. Tel: 402-393-8225; Fax: 402-393-8145. Sr. Patricia Forret, R.S.M., Pres.; Sr. Rita Connell, R.S.M., Community Archivist.
Total number in community 238; Associates 116.
Ministry in the field of Education at all levels; Hospitals; Nursing Centers and Long Term Care Facilities for the Aged; Diocesan and Parish programs & services; Social Service; Housing for Families and Elderly.
Properties owned or sponsored: *Knowles Mercy Center,* Waterloo, NE; *Mercy High School,* Omaha, NE; *Health and Retirement Plan of the Sisters of Mercy of the Americas Health System of Mercy,* Omaha, NE; *McAuley Fund,* Omaha, NE; *Regional Community of Omaha.* Co-sponsor: *Catholic Health Initiatives,* Denver, CO; *Mercy Housing Inc.,* Denver, CO.
Represented in the Archdioceses of Chicago, Denver, Detroit, Dubuque, Kansas City in Kansas, Omaha, Portland (OR), Santa Fe, Seattle, St. Louis, St. Paul-Minneapolis, San Francisco, Washington and the Dioceses of Bismarck, Boise, Colorado Springs, Des Moines, Fargo, Fresno, Great Falls-Billings, Kansas City-St. Joseph, Las Cruces, Lincoln, Oakland, Orange, Phoenix, Rochester, Sacramento, Salt Lake City, San Diego, and Springfield-Cape Girardeau. Also in Mexico.

Pittsburgh **P**
Regional Community of Pittsburgh (1843): 3333 Fifth Ave., Pittsburgh, PA 15213. Tel: 412-578-6225; Fax: 412-578-6180. Sr. Gerogine Scarpino, R.S.M., Pres.; Sr. Patricia Hodge, R.S.M., Community Archivist.
Total number in the community 190.
Ministry in the field of Education and Health Services.
Legal Titles & Holdings: *Carlow College; Pittsburgh Mercy Health System, Inc.; The Mercy Hospital of Pittsburgh; Pittsburgh Mercy Foundation; St. Joseph Nursing and Health Care Center, Inc.; St. Pius X Residence,* Pittsburgh, PA; *Holy Cross Health Ministries, Inc.; Holy Cross Hospital,* Fort Lauderdale, FL.
Represented in the Archdioceses of Boston, Hartford, Miami, and the Dioceses of Charleston, Erie, Greensburg, Orlando, Pittsburgh, and Richmond. Also in Honduras, Peru and Puerto Rico.

Portland **P**
Regional Community of Portland: *St. Joseph's Convent Motherhouse,* 605 Stevens Ave., Portland, ME 04103. Tel: 207-797-7861; Fax: 207-797-0146. Sr. Jean Little, R.S.M., Pres.; Sr. Mary Shaun Sevigny, R.S.M., Community Archivist.
Total number in the community 124.
Ministry in the field of Education; Health Services; Diocesan & Pastoral Services; Social Services.
Represented in the Archdiocese of New York and the Diocese of Portland (ME). Also in the Bahamas and Peru.

Providence **P**
Regional Community of Providence: *Sisters of Mercy of the Americas,* 15 Highland View Rd., Cumberland, RI 02864-1124. Tel: 401-333-6333; Fax: 401-333-6450. Sr. Patricia Combies, R.S.M., Pres., Sr. Catherine Felton, R.S.M., Community Archivist.
Total number in community 382.
Sisters serve and staff: Houses of Prayer; Hospitality Houses; Transitional House; Literacy Centers; Nursing Home; University; High Schools; Elementary Schools; Office of Peace and Justice; Diocesan Offices; Preschool and Day Care; Education for Special Groups; Health Services; Pastoral Care; Religious Education; Parish Ministry Centers; Social Service; Spirituality and Counseling Services; Foreign Missionary work.
Legal Holdings or Titles: *Sisters of Mercy of Providence, Inc.; Mount St. Rita Health Centre, Inc.; Mercymount Country Day School; Mercy Lodge House of Hospitality,* Cumberland, RI; *St. Mary Academy,* East Providence, RI.; *Salve Regina University,* Newport, RI; *McAuley House McAuley Village,* Providence, RI.
Represented in the Archdioceses of Baltimore, Boston, Chicago, Hartford, Philadelphia, St. Louis, Washington and the Dioceses of Fall River, Ogdensburg, Phoenix, Pittsburgh, Providence, Richmond and St. Petersburg. Also in Australia, Belize, and Honduras.

Rochester **P**
Regional Community of Rochester (1857): 1437 Blossom Rd., Rochester, NY 14610. Tel: 716-228-2710; Fax: 716-288-2756. Sr. Sheila Stevenson, R.S.M., Pres.
Total number in the community 207.
Properties owned: *Our Lady of Mercy High School,* Rochester, NY; *Mercy Prayer Center,* Rochester, NY; *Mercy Motherhouse,* Rochester, NY.
Ministry in the field of Education at all levels; Inner City and Urban Renewal Programs; Religious Education Coords.; Parish Associates; Campus Ministry; Social Work; Rural Ministry; Prayer Ministry; Ministry with the Aging; Hospital Ministry; Parish Visitation; Health Apostolates; AIDS Ministry; Foreign Missions (Chile); Care of Foster Children; Ministry to Pregnant Women.
Represented in the Archdioceses of Atlanta, Washington and the Dioceses of Buffalo, Jackson, Palm Beach, Rochester, St. Petersburg, San Jose, Toledo and Venice. Also in Chile.

St. Louis **P**
Regional Community of St. Louis: *Sisters of Mercy,* 2039 N. Geyer Rd., St. Louis, MO 63131-3399. Tel: 314-966-4313. Sr. Richard Mary Burke, R.S.M., Reg. Pres.
Total number in community 303.
Ministry in the following areas: Hospitals; Ambulatory Health Care Center; Long Term Care; Social Work Centers; Education Centers; Care and Counseling; Ministry to Elderly; Parish Ministry-Pastoral Care-Lay Ministry; Universities and Colleges; High Schools; Elementary Schools; Education Research Programs; Schools for Exceptional Children; Adult Education; Parish Directors of Religious Education-Coordinator of Religious Education; staffing of Diocesan Offices; Conference/Retreat; On-Going Development Vocation/incorporation ministry; Novitiate; Creative Spirituality Department/Office of Mercy/Associates-Volunteers.
Properties owned or sponsored: *Mercy Center,* St. Louis, MO; *Sisters of Mercy Health System, St. Louis, Inc.* Hospitals: *St. Edward Health Facilities of Logan County-dba North Logan Mercy Hospital,* Paris, AR; *St. Edward Mercy Medical Center,* Fort Smith, AR; *St. Edward Health Facilities of Franklin County dba Mercy Hospital / Turner Memorial,* Ozark, AR; *Harbor View Mercy Hospital,* Fort Smith, AR; *Saint Joseph's Regional Health Center, Inc.,* Hot Springs, AR; *St. Edward Health Facilities of Scott County-dba Mercy Hospital of Scott County; Mercy Village,* Waldron, AR; *Mercy Hospitals of Kansas, Inc.-dba Mercy Hospital of Fort Scott,* Fort Scott, KS; *Mercy Health System of Kansas, Inc.,* Independence, KS; *Mercy Health System of Kansas, Inc.,* Fort Scott, KS; *Mercy Memorial Health Center,* Ardmore, OK; *St. Francis Hospital-Mountain View,* Mountain View, MO; *St. John's Mercy Medical Center,* St. Louis, MO; *St. John's Regional Health Center,* Springfield, MO; *St. John's Mercy Hospital,* Washington, MO; *St. Mary-Rogers Memorial Hospital,* Roger, AR; *Mercy Health Center, Inc.,* Oklahoma City, OK; *Mercy Hospital of Laredo dba Mercy Health Center,* Laredo, TX; High Schools: *Mount St. Mary Academy,* Little Rock, AR; *Mount St. Mary High School,* Oklahoma City, OK; *Mercy Crest Housing, Inc.,* Barling, AR; *Sisters of Mercy Ministries,* New Orleans, LA; *St. Clement Health Services,* Red Bud, IL.
Convent Corporations: *Sisters of Mercy of the St. Louis Regional Community, Inc.; Sisters of Mercy Education System, St. Louis, Inc.*
Represented in the Archdioceses of Chicago, Hartford, New Orleans, Oklahoma City, St. Louis, San Antonio, Washington, and in the Dioceses of Baton Rouge, Biloxi, Brownsville, Colorado Springs, Houma-Thibodaux, Jackson, Lafayette (LA), Laredo, Little Rock, Lubbock, Metuchen, Providence, Portland, Springfield-Cape Girardeau and Wichita. Also in London, Ghana, South Africa, Georgetown, Guyana.

Vermont **P**
Regional Community of Vermont: *Mt. St. Mary Motherhouse and Novitiate,* 100 Mansfield Ave., Burlington, VT 05401. Tel: 802-863-6835. Sr. Jeannine Mercure, R.S.M., Pres.
Total number in the community 79.
Properties owned or sponsored: *Trinity College of Vermont, Inc.; Institute for Spiritual Development; Mater Christi School Inc.,* Burlington, VT.
Ministry in the field of Education; Parish Ministry.
Represented in the Archdiocese of Hartford and the Dioceses of Burlington, & Las Cruces.

[2590] (H.M.S.S.)—MERCEDARIAN SISTERS OF THE BLESSED SACRAMENT P
(Mercedarian Sisters of the Blessed Sacrament)
Founded in Mexico in 1910. First foundation in the United States in 1926.
General Motherhouse: Fernandez Leal #130, Coyoacan 04330, Mexico. Mother Maria De La Luz Acosta Bustos, H.M.S.S., Supr. Gen.
Regional House: *Blessed Sacrament Convent,* 222 W. Cevallos St., San Antonio, TX 78204. Tel: 210-223-5013; 222-1354; Fax: 210-222-0275. Sr. Guadalupe Rosales, H.M.S.S., Reg. Supr.
Professed Sisters in U.S. 32.; Novices 1.
Represented in the Archdiocese of San Antonio and the Dioceses of Cleveland, Corpus Christi, and San Diego.

[2600] (S.M.)—SISTERS OF MERCY (CORK AND ROSS) D
U.S. Address: *Sacred Heart Convent,* 6240 105th St., Jacksonville, FL 32244. Tel: 904-771-3858. Sr. Patricia O'Hea, Contact Person.
Represented in the Diocese of St. Augustine.

[2610] (S.M.D.C.)—SISTERS OF MERCY DAUGHTERS OF CHRISTIAN CHARITY OF ST. VINCENT DE PAUL OF (HUNGARY) P
Founded in Hungary in 1842. Mother M. Klara Both, Supr. Gen.
U.S. Foundation: *St. Joseph Home and Convent and Novitiate,* Rte. 1, Box 353 A, 240 Longhouse Dr., Hewitt, NJ 07421. Tel: 973-853-7212. Sr. Mary Louise Horvath, Supr.
Represented in the Diocese of Paterson.

[2630] (S.C.S.C.)—SISTERS OF MERCY OF THE HOLY CROSS P
Founded in Switzerland in 1856. First foundation in the U.S. in 1912.
General Motherhouse: Ingenbohl, Switzerland. Sr. Louise-Henri Kolly, S.C.S.C., Supr. Gen.
U.S. Provincial Residence: *Holy Cross Sisters,* 501 South Center Ave., Merrill, WI 54452. Fax: 715-539-5012. Sr. Pat Cormack, S.C.S.C., Prov.
Total number in community 45.
Legal Title: *Bell Tower Residence, Inc.; Sisters of Mercy of the Holy Cross of Merrill, WI, Inc.*
Ministry in the following areas: Schools; Hospitals; Home Nursing; Social Ministries; Parishes and Diocesan Offices; Retirement Homes; Adult Education; Campus Ministries.

Represented in the Archdioceses of Cincinnati, Milwaukee, New Orleans, St. Paul-Minneapolis and the Dioceses of Belleville, Baton Rouge, Gaylord, Green Bay, La Crosse, Steubenville, Superior and Winona.

[2655] SISTERS OF MERCY OF PORTLAND D

Motherhouse: *Diocesan Sisters of Mercy of Portland,* 265 Cottage Rd., South Portland, ME 04106. Tel: 207-767-5804. Sr. Eunice Boyd, R.S.M.

[2670] (S.O.L.M.)—SISTERS OF OUR LADY OF MERCY
(Mercedarians)

General Motherhouse: via Ostriana 24, Rome, Italy. Mother Luisa Sanchez, Supr. Gen.

Brooklyn: *Most Precious Blood,* 133 27th Ave., Brooklyn, NY 11214. Sr. Doloretta, Supr.

Sisters 4.

St. Edward, Pine Hill, NJ 08021. Sr. Leonilla, Supr.

Sisters 6.

Represented in the Dioceses of Brooklyn and Camden.

[2675] (C.F.M.M.)—MINIM DAUGHTERS OF MARY IMMACULATE P

Founded in Leon, Guanajuato, Mexico 1886. Came to the United States in 1926.

U.S. Regional House: *Minim Daughters of Mary Immaculate,* 555 Patagonia Hwy., Nogales, AZ 85628. Tel: 520-287-3377; Fax: 520-287-2910. Sr. Rosa Maria Ruiz, C.F.M.M., Reg. Supr.

Ministry in Academic and Religious Education and Health Care.

Properties owned: *Our Lady of Lourdes High School,* Nogales, AZ.

Total Sisters in the U.S. 23.

Represented in the Diocese of Tucson.

[2677] (S.M.M.I)—SISTERS MINOR OF MARY IMMACULATE D

First foundation in the United States June 13, 1989. Active- contemplative Franciscan Religious Congregation following the spirituality of St. Maximilian Mary Kolbe, O.F.M.Conv. and St. Terese of Liseux.

Central Motherhouse & Novitiate: Via Germanico 198, 00192 Rome, Italy. Tel: 011-39-6-324-2036. Mother Maria Elisabetta Patrizi, S.M.M.I., Foundress & Mother Gen.

American Headquarters - St. Francis Villa: 138 Brushy Hill Rd., Danbury, CT 06810-8431. Tel: 203-744-8041. Sr. Theresa Marie Kovacs, S.M.M.I., U.S. Custos/Delegate.

Legal Title: *Sisters Minor of Mary Immaculate.*

Ministry in the field of Academic and Religious Education; Health Care; Pastoral Care; Care to the elderly, youths, widows and immigrants.

Represented in the Archdiocese of Hartford and the Dioceses of Bridgeport, and Springfield (MA).

[2680] (S.M.)—MISERICORDIA SISTERS P

Founded in Canada in 1848. First foundation in the United States in 1887.

General Motherhouse: 12435 Misericorde Ave., Montreal, Que, Canada H4J 2G3. Tel: 514-332-0550. Sr. Monique Lallier, S.M., Supr. Gen.

U.S. Address: 225 Carol Ave., Pelham, NY, 10803.

Represented in the Archdiocese of New York.

[2690] (M.C.D.P.)—MISSIONARY CATECHISTS OF DIVINE PROVIDENCE, SAN ANTONIO, TEXAS P

Autonomy with Pontifical status granted December 12, 1989.

Administrative House: *St. Andrew's Convent,* 2318 Castroville Rd., San Antonio, TX 78237. Tel: 210-432-0113; Fax: 210-432-1709. Sr. Guadalupe Ramirez, M.C.D.P., Supr.

Properties owned or sponsored: Benitia Family Center, San Antonio, TX.

Total number in community 525; Candidates 1.

Represented in the Archdiocese of Anchorage, Omaha, San Antonio and the Dioceses of Austin, Brownsville, Corpus Christi, Dallas, Fort Worth, Fresno, Galveston-Houston, Laredo and Tucson.

[2700] (M.C.S.H.)—MISSIONARY CATECHISTS OF THE SACRED HEARTS OF JESUS AND MARY D

Founded in Mexico City, D.F. in 1918. U.S. foundation in 1943 in Victoria, Texas.

Central House: Mexico City, Mexico. Sr. Hermila Pena, Supr. Gen.

Immaculate Heart of Mary Province: 805 S. Liberty St., Victoria, TX 77901. Tel: 361-578-9302; Fax: 361-580-2181. Sr. Miriam Perez, M.C.S.H., Prov. Supr.

Total number in U.S. Region 57.

Ministry in Catechetical family ministry in parishes and missions.

Represented in the Dioceses of Fort Worth, Galveston-Houston, Lubbock, Metuchen, and Victoria.

[2710] (M.C.)—MISSIONARIES OF CHARITY P

Founded in India, 1950.

General Motherhouse: 54A AJC Bose Rd., Calcutta 700016, India. Sr. M. Nirmala, M.C., Supr. Gen.

U.S. Foundation & Office (1971): *Missionaries of Charity,* 335 E. 145th St., Bronx, NY 10451. Tel: 718-292-0019. Sr. M. Dominga, M.C., Reg. Supr.

Professed sisters in congregation 4,500.

Legal Title: *Missionaries of Charity, Inc.*

Sisters serve and staff: Soup Kitchens; Emergency Shelters for Women; Homes for Unwed Mothers; Shelters for Unwed Mothers; Shelters for Men; Religious Education Programs; After-School and Summer Camp Programs for Children; Homes for AIDS Patients; Prison Ministry; Nursing Homes; Hospital and Shut-in Ministry; Family Counseling and Ministry; Home for Infants for Adoption; Foreign Missionary Work.

Represented in the Archdioceses of Atlanta, Baltimore, Boston, Chicago, Denver, Detroit, Los Angeles, Miami, New York, Newark, Philadelphia, San Francisco, St. Louis, Washington and the Dioceses of Baton Rouge, Brooklyn, Charlotte, Dallas, Fall River, Gallup, Gary, Lafayette, Lexington, Little Rock, Memphis, Peoria, Phoenix and Trenton. Also in Canada and Mexico.

[2715] (M.CHR.)—MISSIONARY SISTERS OF CHRIST THE KING FOR POLONIA P

Founded in Poland on November 21, 1959 by Father Ignacy Posadzy. First foundation in the U.S. 1978.

General Motherhouse: *Siostry Misjonarki Chrystusa Krola,* ulica Siostr Misjonarek 10, 61-680 Poznan, 50 Poland. Sr. Teresa Ambroza, M.Chr., Supr. Gen.

Delegation Superior in the U.S.: (residing at) *St. James Parish,* 2441 N. Menard Ave., Chicago, IL 60639-2334. Tel: 773-637-9187; Fax: 773-637-2183. Sr. Weronika E. Ilnicka, M.Chr., Delegate Gen. Supr.; Sr. Dorota Galewska, M.Chr., Sec.; Sr. Beata Koltun, M.Chr., Treas.

Legal Title: *Missionary Sisters of Christ the King for Polonia.*

Total in Congregation 198; Professed in U.S. and Canada 26.

Ministry among Polish immigrants and people of Polish heritage.

Represented in the Archdioceses of Chicago, Detroit, Los Angeles and in the Diocese of San Jose. Also in Toronto, Canada.

[2717] (M.D.P.V.M.)—MISSIONARY DAUGHTERS OF THE MOST PURE VIRGIN MARY P

Founded in Mexico. First foundatioin in the United States in the Diocese of Corpus Christi 1916.

General Motherhouse: *Heroe de Nacocariz,* 721 Sur Aguascalientes, Mexico. Mother Maria Christina Duran Hererra, M.D.P.V.M., Supr. Gen.

Missionary Daughters of the Most Pure Virgin Mary: 919 N. 9th St., Kingsville, TX 78363. Tel: 512-595-1087. Sr. Rafaela Valadez, M.D.P.V.M., Supr.; Sr. Rosario Armendariz, M.D.P.V.M., Sec.; Sr. Vicenta Aquilar, M.D.P.V.M., Treas.

Legal Title: *Missionary Daughters of the Most Pure Virgin Mary.*

Total in Congregation 500; Present in U.S. 27.

Ministry in the field of Religious and Academic Education at the elementary level; Pastoral Ministry.

Represented in the Diocese of Camden, Corpus Christi, Brownsville, and Yakima.

[2720] (M.H.S.H.)—MISSION HELPERS OF THE SACRED HEART P

Founded in the United States in 1890.

Mission Helper Center: 1001 W. Joppa Rd., Baltimore, MD 21204-3787. Tel: 410-823-8585; Fax: 410-825-6355. Sr. M. Judith Waldt, M.H.S.H., Pres.

Total number in community 100.

Legal Title: *Institute of Mission Helpers of Baltimore City.*

Represented in the Archdioceses of Baltimore, Boston, Cincinnati, Detroit, Indianapolis, New York, San Juan (PR), San Francisco, Washington and the Dioceses of Erie, Norwich, Orlando, Raleigh, Pensacola-Tallahassee, Pittsburgh, Rochester, St. Petersburg, Tucson, and Youngstown. Also in Venezuela.

[2730] (M.S.H.R.)—MISSIONARY SISTERS OF THE HOLY ROSARY P

Generalate (1924): 23 Cross Ave., Blackrock County, Dublin, Ireland. Sr. Monica Devine, Supr. Gen.

U.S. Regional Headquarters (1954): *Missionary Sisters of the Holy Rosary,* 741 Polo Rd., Bryn Mawr, PA 19010. Tel: 610-520-1974. Sr. Bernadette Murdoch, M.S.H.R., Reg. Leader.

Total number in community 385.

Represented in the Archdiocese of Philadelphia.

[2740] (M.S.Sp.)—MISSION SISTERS OF THE HOLY SPIRIT D

Motherhouse and Novitiate: 1030 N. River Rd., Saginaw, MI 48609. Tel: 517-781-0934. Sr. Mary Lou Owczarzak, Community Coord.

Total number in community 12.

Legal Title: *Society of the Mission Sisters of the Holy Spirit of the Diocese of Saginaw Holy Spirit Sisters Charitable Trust,* Saginaw, MI.

Ministry in Social Services; Religious Education at all levels including Mentally Retarded; Pastoral Ministry; Pastoral Administrator.

Represented in the Diocese of Saginaw.

[2750] (I.C.M.)—MISSIONARY SISTERS OF THE IMMACULATE HEART OF MARY P

Founded in India in 1897. First foundation in the United States in 1919.

Generalate: Via Filogaso 40, Rome, Italy 00173. Sr. M. Josee Cleymans, I.C.M., Supr. Gen.

Universal total of congregation 933.

American Province: 238 E. 15th St., New York, NY 10003. Tel: 212-677-2959. Sr. Alene Grothues, I.C.M., Prov.

Total number in community 29.

Missionaries Minister in Education; Catechetical; Pastoral and Social Ministry; Health Care; Ecology; Leprosaria; International Justice and the Promotion of Human Dignity.

Represented in the Archdioceses of Los Angeles, New York and the Dioceses of Albany and Brownsville. Also in Belgium, Brazil, Burundi, Cameroon, Guatemala, Hong Kong, India, Italy, Philippines, Taiwan, Mongolia, Chad, Virgin Islands, West Indies and Congo.

[2760] (S.M.I.C.)—MISSIONARY SISTERS OF THE IMMACULATE CONCEPTION OF THE MOTHER OF GOD P

Founded in Brazil in 1910. First foundation in the United States in 1922.

Generalate: 48 Garden Ave., West Paterson, NJ 07424-3325. Tel: 973-279-1484. Sr. Corona Chung, S.M.I.C., Coord. Gen.

U.S. Province (1960): *Provincialate of the Immaculate Conception,* P.O. Box 3026, Paterson, NJ 07509-3026. Tel: 973-279-3790; Fax: 973-742-8231. Sr. Eleanor Geokler, S.M.I.C., Prov. Coord.

Professed Sisters 50.

Sisters serve and staff: Elementary Schools; Universities, Religious Education; Pastoral Ministries; Health and Social Services.

Represented in the Archdioceses of Newark, San Antonio, Washington and the Dioceses of Austin, El Paso, Gallup, Galveston-Houston, Paterson, Portland (ME), San Bernardino, and Trenton.

[2770] (M.J.M.J.)MISSIONARY SISTERS OF JESUS, MARY AND JOSEPH P

Founded in Spain in 1942. First foundation in United States in 1956. Mother Maria Dolores de la Cruz Domingo, Foundress.

Motherhouse: Plaza Inmaculada Concepcion 1, Madrid, Spain 28019. Sr. Maria Amparo Munoz, M.J.M.J., Supr. Gen.

Delegation Headquarters and Formation House: 12940 Leopard St., Corpus Christi, TX 78410. Tel: 361-241-1955. Sr. Raquel D. Gomez, M.J.M.J., Delegation Supr.; Sr. Angela Berrozpe, M.J.M.J., Local Supr.

Sisters 25.

Properties owned: *Joseph of the Valley Preschool,* El Paso, TX.

Represented in the Archdiocese of San Antonio and the Dioceses of Corpus Christi, and El Paso. Also in Mexico.

[2780] (M.SS.S.)—MISSIONARY SISTERS OF THE MOST BLESSED SACRAMENT P

General Motherhouse: San Lucas 7, Madrid, Spain. Mother Socorro Mugueta, Mother Gen.

U.S. Foundation: *Convent of Mary Immaculate,* 1111 Wordin Ave., Bridgeport, CT 06605. Sr. Nirma Rodriguez, M.SS.S., Prov.

Formation Center: 1109-1111 Wordin Ave., Bridgeport, CT 06605.

Represented in the Archdioceses of Boston and Newark and the Diocese of Bridgeport.

[2790] (M.S.B.T.)—MISSIONARY SERVANTS OF THE MOST BLESSED TRINITY P
Founded in United States in 1912.
Motherhouse-Generalate-Novitiate and Candidacy: 3501 Solly Ave., Philadelphia, PA 19136. Tel: 215-335-7550. Sr. Barbara DeMoranville, M.S.B.T., Gen. Custodian.
Total number in community 223.
Properties owned and sponsored: *Blessed Trinity Mother Missionary Cenacle,* Philadelphia, PA; *Blessed Trinity Shrine Retreat Cenacle,* Holy Trinity, AL; *Trinita Ecumenical Retreat Center,* New Hartford, CT; *Blessed Trinity Missionary Cenacle,* Stirling, NJ; *Blessed Trinity Mother Missionary Cenacle,* Philadelphia, PA.
Represented in the Archdioceses of Boston, Chicago, Hartford, Newark, Mobile, New York and Philadelphia and the Dioceses of Arlington, Biloxi, Birmingham, Brooklyn, Charleston, Camden, Charlotte, Fall River, Gallup, Owensboro, Paterson, Pensacola-Tallahassee, Phoenix, Raleigh, Richmond, Rockford, Wilmington and Yakima. Also in Puerto Rico and Mexico.

[2800] (M.S.C.)—MISSIONARY SISTERS OF THE MOST SACRED HEART OF JESUS (OF HILTRUP) P
Founded in Germany in 1899. First foundation in the United States in 1908.
Generalate: Via Martiri di Via Fani, Sutri (Viterbo), Italy. Sr. MaryAnne Bigos, M.S.C.
American Province-Motherhouse (1908): *St. Michael's Convent,* 51 Seminary Ave., Reading, PA 19605. Tel: 610-929-5751.
Sr. Joanne Leblanc, M.S.C., Coord.
MSC Province Center: 2811 Moyers Ln., Reading PA, 19605. Tel: 610-929-5944. Sr. Marie Clark, M.S.C., Prov.
Total number in U.S. Province 117.
Legal Title: *Missionary Sisters of the Most Sacred Heart of Jesus, Inc.*
Ministry in Education; Health Care; Home Health Care; Parish Ministry; Pastoral Ministry to people on the move; Prison Ministry; Counseling; Social Ministry; Spiritual Ministry.
Properties owned or sponsored: *MSC Province Center; St. Michael Convent,* Reading, PA.
Represented in the Archdioceses of Atlanta, Philadelphia, and the Dioceses of Allentown, Galveston-Houston, Harrisburg, Jackson, Venice and Wheeling-Charleston. Also in Mexico.

[2810] (M.S.M.G.)—MISSIONARY SISTERS OF MOTHER OF GOD D
(ByzantineUkrainianRite-Stamford)
Motherhouse: 711 N. Franklin St., Philadelphia, PA 19123. Tel: 215-627-7808.
Novitiate: 111 W. North St., Stamford, CT 06902. Tel: 203-323-1237. Sr. Josepha Kruchinsky, M.S.M.G., Admin.
Professed Sisters 12.
Ministry in the field of Education.
Represented in the Ukrainian Archdiocese of Philadelphia and in the Ukrainian Diocese of Stamford.

[2820] (M.S.O.L.A.)—MISSIONARY SISTERS OF OUR LADY OF AFRICA P
(Sisters of Africa)
Founded in Algiers, N. Africa, in 1869. First foundation in the United States in 1929.
General Motherhouse: Rome, Italy. Sr. Marie McDonald, Supr. Gen.
Universal total in congregation 1,227.
American Headquarters: 47 West Spring St., Winooski, VT 05404. Tel: 802-655-4003. Sr. Marie Claire Bernier, M.S.O.L.A., District Supr.
Total number in U.S. 17.
Represented in the Archdiocese of Washington and the Diocese of Burlington.

[2830] (M.O.M.)—MISSIONARY SISTERS OF OUR LADY OF MERCY D
Founded in Piaui, Brazil in 1938. First foundation in United States at Lackawanna, New York 1955.
General Motherhouse: Salvador, Bahia, Brazil. Mother Felicidade Santos, M.O.M., Supr. Gen.
U.S. Headquarters: *Rainbow K,* 388 Franklin St., Buffalo, NY 14202. Tel: 716-854-5198. Sr. M. Neves, M.O.M., Supr.
Total number in community 3.
Represented in the Diocese of Buffalo.

[2840] (M.C.)—POOR CLARE MISSIONARY SISTERS P
Founded in Mexico by Mother Maria Ines Teresa Arias
General Motherhouse: Via Cardinale Garampi 17, Pineta Sachetti, Rome, Italy. Mother Maria Teresa Botello, Gen. Supr.
U.S. Foundation: *Regional House and Novitiate,* 1019 N. Newhope, Santa Ana, CA 92703.
Total number in community 42.
Ministry in Day Nurseries; Schools and; Retreat House.
Represented in the Archdiocese of Los Angeles and the Diocese of Orange.

[2850] (C.P.S.)—MISSIONARY SISTERS OF THE PRECIOUS BLOOD P
Founded in South Africa on Sept. 8, 1885. First founded in the United States at Princeton, New Jersey on August 15, 1925.
Generalate: *Casa Generalizia, Suore Missionarie del Preziosissimo Sangue Mariannhill,* Via San Giovanni Eudes 93, Roma, Italia 00163.
Universal number in congregation 980.
North American Province: *Precious Blood Convent,* P.O. Box 97 – 1094 Welsh Rd., Reading, PA 19607-0097. Tel: 610-777-1624. Sr. Eva A. Janning, C.P.S., Prov. Supr.
Total number in province 50.
Represented in the Dioceses of Allentown and Gallup. Also in Canada.

[2860] (M.S.C.)—MISSIONARY SISTERS OF THE SACRED HEART OF JESUS P
(Cabrini Sisters)
Founded in Italy in 1880, by Saint Frances Xavier Cabrini. First foundation in the United States 1889.
Motherhouse: Viale Cortina D'Ampezzo, 269, Rome, Italy 00135. Sr. Lina Colombini, M.S.C., Supr. Gen.
Provincial Office: 222 E. 19th St., 5B, New York, NY 10003. Sr. Diane Dalle Molle, M.S.C., Prov. Supr.
Professed Sisters 480; Total in Congregation 500.
Ministry in the field of Education; Hospitals; Nursing Home; Child Care; Parish Ministry; Pastoral Work; Parish Work.
Represented in the Archdioceses of Chicago, Denver, New Orleans, New York, Philadelphia and Seattle. Also in Argentina, Australia, Brazil, Central America, England, France, Italy, Philippines, Portugal, Spain, and Swaziland.

[2865] (M.S.C.Gpe.)—MISSIONARIES OF THE SACRED HEART OF JESUS AND OUR LADY OF GUADALUPE
National Address: 1212 E. Euclid Ave., Arlington Heights, IL 60004. Tel: 708-398-1350. Sr. Piedad Fernandez, Pres.; Sr. Esperansa Hernandez, Sec.; Sr. Zoila Alcala, Treas.
Ministry in Schools; Nursing Homes; Seminaries and Foreign Missions.
Represented in the Archdiocese of Boston, Chicago, San Francisco and Washington and the Diocese of Rockford.

[2880] (S.S.C.)—MISSIONARY SISTERS OF ST. COLUMBAN P
(Columban Sisters)
Founded in Ireland in 1922. First Foundation in the United States in 1930.
General Motherhouse: Wicklow, Ireland. Sr. Kathleen Geaney, Congregational Leader.
U.S. Region: *Missionary Sisters of St. Columban,* 73 Mapleton St., Brighton, MA 02135. Tel: 617-782-5683; Fax: 617-789-3569. Sr. Maura Ryan, S.S.C., U.S. Area Coord.
Professed Sisters 27.
Represented in the Archdioceses of Boston, Los Angeles, and the Diocese of Buffalo.

[2890] (M.S.S.A.)—MISSIONARY SERVANTS OF ST. ANTHONY D
Founded in the United States in 1929.
General Motherhouse: 100 Peter Baque Rd., San Antonio, TX 78209-1805. Tel: 210-824-4553. Sr. Mary Ann Domagalski, M.S.S.A., Supr. Gen.
Total number in community 5.
Represented in the Archdiocese of San Antonio.

[2900] (M.S.C.S.)—MISSIONARY SISTERS OF ST. CHARLES BORROMEO
(Scalabrini Sisters)
Founded in Italy in 1895. First United States in 1941.
Motherhouse: Via Monte del Gallo 68, Rome, Italy 00165. Sr. Lice Maria Signor, M.S.C.S., Gen.
Universal total in congregation 804.
North American Provincial House: *Bishop Scalabrini Community and Provincial House,* 1414 N. 37th Ave., Melrose Park, IL 60160. Tel: 708-343-2162; Fax: 708-343-6452. Sr. Marissonia Daltoe, M.S.C.S., Prov.
Total number in community 69.
Ministry in the fields of Education; Pastoral Care of the Sick; Catechesis; Social Service.
Represented in the Archdioceses of Chicago, New York and Washington. Also in Canada, Mexico and the Philippines.

[2920] (M.D.)—MOTHERS OF THE HELPLESS D
Founded in Malaga, Spain in 1881. Founded in the United States in 1916.
General Motherhouse: Avda. San Jose de la Montana No.15, Valencia, Spain 46008. Mother Esperanza Ordonez, Supr. Gen.
U.S. Address: *Sacred Heart Residence,* 432 W. 20th St., New York, NY 10011. Mother Guadalupe Sordo, M.D., Dir.
Professed Sisters in U.S. 9.
Properties owned and sponsored: *San Jose De La Montana Day Nursery; Sacred Heart Residence; San Jose Day Nursery,* New York, NY.
Represented in the Archdiocese of New York.

[2930] (I.H.M.)—THE CALIFORNIA INSTITUTE OF THE SISTERS OF THE MOST HOLY AND IMMACULATE HEART OF THE BLESSED VIRGIN MARY P
Founded in Spain in 1848. First foundation in the United States in 1871.
Generalate, Novitiate and Retreat House: 3431 Waverly Dr., Los Angeles, CA, 90027. Tel: 213-664-1124.
Professed Sisters 21.
Properties staffed: High Schools; Grammar Schools 2.
Represented in the Archdiocese of Los Angeles.

[2940] (M.H.S.)—SISTERS OF THE MOST HOLY SACRAMENT P
Founded in France in 1851. First foundation in the United States in 1872. Pontifical Approbation 1935.
Generalate: *Sisters of the Most Holy Sacrament,* 313 Corona Dr., P.O. Box 90037, Lafayette, LA 70509-0037. Tel: 337-981-8475. Sr. Judine Theriot, M.H.S. Major Supr.
Total number in community 39.
Legal Title: *St. Augustine Trust Fund,* Lafayette, LA; *Bethany Health Care Center,* Lafayette, LA.
Ministry in the field of Education; Homes for the Aged; Pastoral Care.
Represented in the Archdiocese of New Orleans and the Dioceses of Baton Rouge, Biloxi, Gallup, and Lafayette (LA).

[2950] (N.D.S.)—CONGREGATION OF NOTRE DAME DE SION P
Founded in France in 1850. First foundation in the United States in 1892.
Generalate: Rome, Italy. Sr. Mechthild Vahle, N.D.S., Supr. Gen.
Universal Total in Congregation 800.
Notre Dame de Sion: 3823 Locust St., Kansas City, MO 64109. Tel: 816-531-1374.
Represented in the Archdiocese of Chicago and the Dioceses of Brooklyn and Kansas City-St. Joseph.

[2960] (N.D.)—NOTRE DAME SISTERS P
Founded in Czechoslovakia, Europe, in 1853. First foundation in the United States in 1910.
General Motherhouse: Hradec Kralove, Czech Republic. Mother Miriam Baumrukova, N.D., Supr. Gen.
U.S. Provincial Motherhouse: *Notre Dame Convent,* 3501 State St., Omaha, NE 68112-1709. Tel: 402-455-2994; Fax: 402-455-3974. Sr. Margaret Hickey, N.D., Prov. Supr.
Total number in community 64.
Sisters staff and serve: all levels of academic education; Hispanic Ministry; Pastoral Care; Housing for low income elderly; Social Work; Religious Education; Youth Ministry; Chemical Dependency Counseling; Health Care; TEC; Adult Education; Family Life-Diocesan Offices; Community Administration and Services.
Represented in the Archdioceses of Denver, Dubuque, Kansas City in Kansas, Omaha and the Dioceses of Davenport, Kansas City-St. Joseph, Lincoln, Pueblo, Rapid City and Springfield-Cape Girardeau.

[2970] (S.S.N.D.)—SCHOOL SISTERS OF NOTRE DAME P
Founded in Germany in 1833. First foundation in the United States in 1847.
General Motherhouse: Rome, Italy. Sr. Rosemary Howarth, Supr. Gen.
Milwaukee Province (1850) Milwaukee; (1959) Mequon; (1983) Milwaukee: *Milwaukee Province, Motherhouse,* 13105 Watertown Plank Rd., Elm Grove, WI 53122-2291. Tel: 262-782-9850; Fax: 262-782-5725. Sr. Marilyn Kesler, S.S.N.D., Leader.
Total number in community 528.
Legal Title: *School Sisters of Notre Dame Milwaukee Province, Inc.; School Sisters of Notre Dame at Milwaukee, Wisconsin, Inc. Charitable Trust.*
Properties owned: *Mount Mary College,* Milwaukee, WI; *Notre Dame of Elm Grove,* Elm Grove, WI; *Our Lady of Mt. Carmel Convent,* Mt. Calvary, WI.

Ministry in Various ministries to Women, Youth, the Poor, Sick and Elderly; all levels of Academic Education; D.R.E.s; Pastoral Associates.

Represented in the Archdioceses of Chicago, Detroit, Milwaukee, St. Paul-Minneapolis, Seattle, St. Louis, and the Dioceses of Baker, Davenport, Fort Wayne-South Bend, Gary, Gallup, Grand Rapids, Green Bay, Jefferson, La Crosse, Lafayette (IN), Lexington, Madison, Marquette, New Ulm, Phoenix, Rockford, Saginaw, Springfield, Steubenville, and Wheeling-Charleston. Also in Africa, Caroline-Marshall Islands, Central America and Guam.

Baltimore Province (1876): *School Sisters of Notre Dame,* 6401 N. Charles St., Baltimore, MD 21212-1099. Tel: 410-377-7774; Fax: 410-377-5363. Sr. Jane Burke, S.S.N.D., Prov. Leader.

Total number in community 389.

Legal Titles and Properties Owned: *School Sisters of Notre Dame in the City of Baltimore; Maria Health Care Center, Inc.; Villa Assumpta-Motherhouse of Baltimore Province; College of Notre Dame of Maryland; Notre Dame Preparatory School; Institute of Notre Dame,* Baltimore, MD.

Ministries to the Needy and Elderly; Teaching and Administering in the field of Academic Education at all levels; D.R.E.'s and Pastoral Associates.

Represented in the Archdioceses of Baltimore, Boston, Chicago, Los Angeles, Miami, Milwaukee, Newark, Philadelphia, St. Louis, San Antonio, Washington and the Dioceses of Arlington, Bridgeport, Camden, Charleston, Gary, Harrisburg, Jackson, Lexington, Little Rock, Paterson, Palm Beach, Pittsburgh, Richmond, Rockville Centre, St. Petersburg, Trenton, Tucson, Venice and Wilmington. Also in Boliva, Ghana, Kenya, Vienna, and Nigeria.

St. Louis Province (1895): *School Sisters of Notre Dame,* 320 E. Ripa Ave., St. Louis, MO 63125. Tel: 314-544-0455; Fax: 314-544-6754. Sr. Joanne Hanrahan, Prov. Supr.

Legal Title: *The School Sisters of Notre Dame of St. Louis.*

Total number in community 633.

Represented in the Archdioceses Baltimore, Boston, Denver, Louisville, Los Angeles, Milwaukee, Oklahoma City, Omaha, St. Louis, St. Paul-Minneapolis, San Antonio, Washington and the Dioceses of Albany, Austin, Belleville, Bismarck, Charleston, Dallas, Davenport, Evansville, Fresno, Jefferson City, Knoxville, Little Rock, La Crosse Monterey, Oakland, Orange, Peoria, Rapid City, San Angelo, San Diego, Shreveport, Sioux City, Springfield-Cape Girardeau, Springfield in Illinois, Tucson, and Venice. Also in Ghana, Kenya, Nigeria, Honduras, Italy, Japan, Nepal, Guam and Korea.

Mankato Province (1912): *School Sisters of Notre Dame,* 170 Good Counsel Dr., Mankato, MN 56001-3138. Tel: 507-389-4200; Fax: 507-345-6679. Sr. Katherine Du Val, Prov. Sr. Irene Feltz, Community Archivist.

Total number in community 438.

Legal Title: *School Sisters of Notre Dame at Mankato, Minnesota, Inc.; School Sisters of Notre Dame at Mankato, Minnesota, Inc. - Charitable Trust; School Sisters of Notre Dame Cooperative Investment Fund.*

Represented in the Archdioceses of Chicago, Dubuque, Milwaukee, New Orleans, New York, St. Louis, St. Paul-Minneapolis, Seattle, Washington and the Dioceses of Albany, Alexandria, Bismarck, Brownsville, Bridgeport, Charlotte, Crookston, Dallas, Duluth, Fargo, Forth Worth, New Ulm, Phoenix, Richmond, Rockford, Sioux Falls, Superior, St. Cloud, Tyler, and Winona. Also in Ghana, Guatemala, Kenya, and Tanzania.

Northeastern Province (1957): *School Sisters of Notre Dame,* Wilton, CT 06897. Tel: 203-762-1220; Fax: 203-762-9434. Sr. Marie Jeannette Blatz, Prov. Leader.

Total number in community 366.

Legal Holdings and Titles: *The Northeastern Province of the School Sisters of Notre Dame in the State of Connecticut; Motherhouse and Lourdes Health Care Center,* Wilton, CT; *Academy of the Holy Angels,* Demarest, NJ.

Represented in the Archdioceses of Baltimore, Boston, Hartford, Miami, Newark, New York, Philadelphia, Washington and the Dioceses of Albany, Bridgeport, Brooklyn, Manchester, Norwich, Paterson, Rochester, Rockville Centre and Venice. Also in Chile, Ghana, Paraguay, Peru and Puerto Rico.

Dallas Province (1961): *Notre Dame of Dallas - School Sisters of Notre Dame,* P.O. Box 227275, Dallas, TX 75222. Tel: 214-330-9152; Fax: 214-330-9197. Sr. Elizabeth Newman, Prov. Leader.

Total number in community 178.

Legal Title: *School Sisters of Notre Dame of Dallas Charitable Trust.*

Represented in the Archdioceses of New Orleans, San Antonio and in the Dioceses of Alexandria, Austin, Biloxi, Baton Rouge, Brownsville, Dallas, El Paso, Fort Worth, Galveston-Houston, Houma-Thibodaux, Jackson, Lafayette (LA), Little Rock, Phoenix, San Angelo, and Victoria. Also in Guatemala, Honduras, and West Africa.

Chicago Province: *School Sisters of Notre Dame,* 1431 Euclid Ave., Berwyn, IL 60402. Tel: 708-749-1380. Sr. Catherine Sarther, S.S.N.D., Prov. Leader.

Total number in the community 134.

Properties Owned: *Academy of Our Lady,* Chicago, IL.

Ministry in the field of Academic, Special and Religious Education; Day Care Centers; Foreign Mission work; Nurses; Pastoral Work; Apostolate of the Aging; Vicar for Women Religious.

Represented in the Archdioceses of Baltimore, Chicago, Los Angeles, Miami, Milwaukee, Washington and the Dioceses of Joliet, Orange, Peoria and Rockford. Also in Brazil, Japan, Nepal and Paraguay.

[2980] (C.N.D.)—SISTERS OF THE CONGREGATION DE NOTRE DAME P

Founded in Canada in 1653. First Foundation in United States in 1860. American Novitiate established at Ridgefield, Connecticut.

General Motherhouse: 4873 Westmount Ave., Montreal, Quebec, Canada.

Generalate: 2330 Sherbrooke St., W., Montreal, Quebec, Canada. Sr. Lorraine Caza, C.N.D., Congregational Leader.

U.S. Province (1946): *Blessed Sacrament Province,* 223 W. Mountain Rd., Ridgefield, CT 06877. Tel: 203-438-5282; Fax: 203-894-9686. Sr. Anne Leonard, C.N.D., Prov. Leader.

Total number in the U.S. Province 193.

Represented in the Archdioceses of Boston, Chicago, Hartford and New York and the Dioceses of Albany, Bridgeport, Brooklyn, Brownsville, Charlotte, Fall River, Joliet, Gallup, Pensacola-Tallahassee, Providence, Rapid City, and Scranton.

[2990] (S.N.D.)—SISTERS OF NOTRE DAME P

Founded in Germany in 1850. First foundation in the United States in 1874.

Generalate: Rome, Italy. Sr. Mary Sujita Kallupurakkathu, S.N.D., Supr. Gen.

Universal total in congregation 2,571.

Cleveland Province (1874): *Notre Dame Educational Center - Provincial Center, Juniorate, & Novitiate,* 13000 Auburn Rd., Chardon, OH 44024-9331. Tel: 440-286-7101; Fax: 440-286-3377. Sr. Melannie Svoboda, Prov. Supr.; Sr. M. Helen Louise Kist, Prov. Sec.

Legal Titles: *The Corporation of the Sisters of Notre Dame of Cleveland, Ohio; The Sisters of Notre Dame Charitable Trust.*

Total number in community 430.

Properties owned and sponsored: *Notre Dame Cathedral Latin School,* Chardon, OH; *Notre Dame College of Ohio,* South Euclid, OH; *Notre Dame Elementary School,* Chardon, OH; *Notre Dame Pre School,* Chardon, OH; *Regina High School,* Cleveland, OH; *Julie Billiart School,* Lyndhurst, OH.

Ministry in the field of Academic Education at all levels; Special Education for Exceptional Children; Foreign Mission Work; Religious Education; Pastoral Ministry; Community Service; Diocesan and National Offices; Pastoral Associate and D.R.E.; Adult Literacy; Spiritual Life Ministries; Hispanic & Refugee Outreach; Sick and Elderly in Hospitals and Nursing Homes; Youth Ministry; Campus Ministry; Writing; Liturgy and Music.

Represented in the Archdioceses of Boston, Washington and the Dioceses of Arlington, Cleveland, Orlando, Raleigh, Saginaw, St. Petersburg, St. Augustine, Springfield-Cape Girardeau, Superior, Venice and Youngstown. Also in Uganda and the Philippines.

Covington Province (1924): *Provincial House and Novitiate of the Sisters of Notre Dame,* 1601 Dixie Hwy., (St. Joseph Heights), Covington, KY 41011. Tel: 606-291-2040; Fax: 606-291-1774. Sr. Mary Shauna, S.N.D., Prov.

Total number in the community 171.

Legal Title: *Sisters of Notre Dame of Covington, KY, Inc.*

Ministry in the field of Education; Hospital and Health Care Services; Child Care.

Properties sponsored and owned: *St. Claire Medical Center,* Morehead, KY; *St. Charles Care Center and Village,* Covington, KY; *Notre Academy,* Covington, KY.

Represented in the Archdiocese of Cincinnati and the Dioceses of Birmingham, Covington and Lexington. Also in Hoima, Uganda, and East Africa.

Province of Toledo (1924): *Notre Dame Provincialate, Juniorate & Novitiate,* 3837 Secor Rd., Toledo, OH 43623. Tel: 419-474-5485. Sr. Constance Marie Suchala, S.N.D., Prov. Supr.

Total number in community 281.

Properties owned and sponsored: *Notre Dame Academy; Ladyfield School; Maria Child Care; Mary Immaculate School; Notre Dame School of Music,* Toledo, OH; *Lial Elementary School; Convent & Renewal Center,* Whitehouse, OH; *Holy Trinity Mission,* Papua, New Guinea.

Ministry in the field of Education; Specialized Education; Foreign Mission Work; Vocational School.

Represented in the Archdioceses of Chicago, Detroit and the Dioceses of Fort Wayne-South Bend, Grand Rapids, Joliet, Lafayette (IN), Orlando, St. Augustine and Toledo.

Province of Los Angeles (1924): *Notre Dame Provincialate,* 1776 Hendrix Ave., Thousand Oaks, CA 91360. Tel: 805-496-3243; Fax: 805-379-3616. Sr. Mary Amy, Prov. Supr.

Total number in province 78.

Legal Title: *Corporation of the Sisters of Notre Dame of Los Angeles; Notre Dame Academy High School; Notre Dame Academy Elementary School,* Los Angeles, CA; *Notre Dame Center; La Reina High School,* Thousand Oaks, CA; *Providence House,* Long Beach, CA.

Ministry in the field of Education and Parish Ministry; Catechetics; Foreign Mission Work.

Represented in the Archdiocese of Los Angeles.

[3000] (S.N.D.deN.)—SISTERS OF NOTRE DAME DE NAMUR P

Founded in France in 1804. First foundation in the United States in 1840.

Generalate: *Suore di Nostra Signora di Namur,* Via Raffaello Sardiello 20, 00165, Rome, Italy 011-39-06-6641-8704. Sr. Ellen Gielty, S.N.D.deN., Gen. Moderator.

U.S. Notre Dame Congregational Center: *Generalate Offices,* 30 Jeffreys Neck Rd., Ipswich, MA 01938. Tel: 978-356-2159; Fax: 978-356-2118. Sr. Marie Kelly, S.N.D.deN.

Boston Province (1973): *Sisters of Notre Dame de Namur,* 351 Broadway, Everett, MA 02149. Tel: 617-387-2500; Fax: 617-387-1303. Prov. Team: Sr. Lorraine Connell, S.N.D.deN.; Sr. Patricia Conner, S.N.D.deN.; Sr. Noel Doyle, S.N.D.deN.

Total number in community 235.

Legal Title: *The Boston Province of the Sisters of Notre Dame de Namur, Inc.*

Properties owned and sponsored: *Notre Dame Academy,* Worcester, MA; *Notre Dame Children's Class,* Wenham, MA.

Ministry in the field of Academic Educational at all levels; Adult Education Programs; Parish Ministries; Religious Education Programs; and Social Services.

Represented in the Archdioceses of Boston, Hartford, Louisville, New York and Washington and the Dioceses of Albany, Fall River, Gallup, Galveston-Houston, Honolulu, Manchester, Orlando, Portland (ME), Saginaw, Springfield (MA) and Worcester.

Ipswich Province (1973): *Sisters of Notre Dame de Namur Provincialate,* 30 Jeffrey's Neck Rd., Ipswich, MA 01938. Tel: 978-356-4381; Fax: 978-356-9759. Prov. Admin. Team: Sr. Mary M. Farren, S.N.D.deN.; Sr. Marie A. McDonald, S.N.D.deN.; Sr. Therese J. Fitzmaurice, S.N.D.deN.

Total number in community 236.

Legal Title: *Notre Dame Training School, Inc.*

Ministry in all fields of Education; Pastoral Ministry; Health, Social and Community Services; Retreat Work.

Properties owned and sponsored: *Academy of Notre Dame,* Tyngsboro, MA; *Julie Country Day School,* Leominster, MA; *Notre Dame Academy,* Hingham, MA; *Notre Dame Long Term Health Care Facility,* Worcester, MA; *Notre Dame Education Center,* Lawrence, MA; *Cuvilly Arts and Earth Center,* Ipswich, MA; *Notre Dame du Lac,* Worcester, MA.

Represented in the Archdiocese of Boston, Washington, and the Dioceses of Baton Rouge, Jackson, Manchester and Worcester.

Connecticut Province (1959): *The Connecticut Province of the Sisters of Notre Dame de Namur, Inc., Sisters of Notre Dame de Namur Province Center,* 468 Poquonock Ave., Windsor, CT 06095-2473. Tel: 860-688-1832. Prov. Admin. Team: Sr. Joan Farley, S.N.D.; Sr. Elizabeth McLaughlin, S.N.D.; Sr. Marilyn Pechillo, S.N.D.

Total number in community 153.

Sisters Serve and Staff: Colleges, High Schools, Grammar Schools.

Sisters Engaged in Specialized Educational Programs: Pastoral Ministry and Religious Education, Social Health and Community Services, Diocesan Offices.

Represented in the Archdioceses of Boston, Hartford, Washington, and the Dioceses of Bridgeport, Norwich, Oakland, Providence, St. Augustine, Springfield (MA) and Worcester.

Baltimore Province (1934): *Sisters of Notre Dame de Namur, Maryland Province Center,* 1531 Greenspring

Valley Rd., Stevenson, MD 21153. Tel: 410-486-5599. Sr. Marian Schaechtel, S.N.D., Prov. Moderator. Leadership: Sr. Jeanne McGlone, S.N.D.; Sr. Patricia Loome, S.N.D.
Total in community 138.
Properties owned and sponsored: *Trinity School,* Ellicott City, MD; *Maryland Province Center,* Stevenson, MD; *Villa Julie Infirmary,* Stevenson, MD; *Maryvale Preparatory School,* Brooklandville, MD; *Notre Dame Academy,* Villanova, PA; *The Development Center, a joint activity of the Maryland, Chesapeake & Notre Dame Base Communities Provinces.*
Represented in the Archdioceses of Baltimore, Philadelphia, Washington and the Dioceses of Brooklyn, Portland (ME), Rockville Centre and Wilmington. Also in Italy.

Chesapeake Province (1990): *Sisters of Notre Dame de Namur Provincial Offices,* 305 Cable St., Baltimore, MD 21210-2511. Tel: 410-243-1993; Fax: 410-243-2279. Administrative Team: Sr. Margaret Shawn Scanlan; Sr. Louann Sciubba.
Total number in community 79.
Represented in the Archdioceses of Baltimore, Cincinnati, Miami, New York, Philadelphia and Washington and the Dioceses of Brooklyn, Fort Wayne-South Bend, Metuchen, Raleigh, Richmond, and Wheeling-Charleston. Also in Brazil, Kenya, Mexico, Peru, Dem. Republic of Congo and South Africa.

Ohio Province (1840): *Sisters of Notre Dame de Namur Provincal House,* 701 E. Columbia Ave., Cincinnati, OH 45215. Tel: 513-821-7448. Sr. Elizabeth Marie Bower, Prov.
Total number in community 243.
Legal Title: *St. Mary's Educational Institute at Cincinnati; Sisters of Notre Dame de Namur - Ohio Province; Sisters of Notre Dame de Namur, Ohio Province, Charitable Trust.*
Ministry in the field of Education at all levels; Montessori; Reading Centers; Pastoral Ministry; Administration and Services; Social Services; Communication; Health Care; Community Services.
Represented in the Archdioceses of Boston, Chicago, Cincinnati, Detroit, Indianapolis, Louisville and St. Louis and the Dioceses of Austin, Buffalo, Columbus, Covington, Gallup, Joliet, Lafayette, Palm Beach, Phoenix, Saginaw, Sioux Falls, and Tucson. Also in Brazil, Nicaragua, Nigeria, Rome and Zimbabwe.

California Province (1851): *Provincial House Sisters of Notre Dame de Namur,* 14800 Bohlman Rd., Saratoga, CA 95070. Tel: 408-741-0324; Fax: 408-741-5809. Provincial Team: Sr. Mary Laxague, S.N.D.deN.; Sr. Nancy O'Shea, S.N.D.deN.; Sr. Virginia Unger, S.N.D.deN.
Total number in community 156.
Legal Title: *Sisters of Notre Dame de Namur California Province.*
Ministries Include: Counselors; Convalescent Hospital Ministry; Diocesan Administrative Positions; Directors of Religious Education; Health Ministry; Missionary Work; Parish Ministry; Education at all levels; Religious Education for Adults; Retreat Work; Social Services.
Represented in the Archdioceses of Los Angeles, San Francisco, Seattle and the Dioceses of Burlington, Des Moines, Fairbanks, Honolulu, Lincoln, Monterey, Oakland, Sacramento, San Jose, Stockton and Wheeling-Charleston.

Base Communities Province (1989): *Sisters of Notre Dame de Namur Base Communities Province Office,* 3037 Fourth St., N.E., Washington, DC 20017. Tel: 202-832-8770. Communications Network: Sr. Christina Murphy; Sr. Mary Murphy; Sr. Mary Suplee.
Total in Province 49.
Legal Titles: *Sisters of Notre Dame de Namur Base Communities, Inc.; S.N.D.B.C. Charitable Trust.*
Ministry in Formal Education; Health Care; Social Services/Community Development; Pastoral Ministry.
Represented in the Archdioceses of Baltimore, Boston, Hartford, Philadelphia, Washington and the Dioceses of Brooklyn, Charleston, Harrisburg, Orlando, Richmond, Rockville Centre, and Wilmington.

[3010] (O.S.B.S.)—OBLATE SISTERS OF THE BLESSED SACRAMENT D

Founded in 1935 by Rev. Sylvester Eisenman, O.S.B.
Motherhouse: *St. Sylvester's Convent,* P.O. Box 217, Marty, SD 57361. Tel: 605-384-3305. Sr. Patricia Mylott, O.S.B.S., Supr.
Kateri Convent: 624 Adams St., Rapid City, SD 57701 Tel: 605-343-6261.
Total number in community 7.
Represented in the Dioceses of Rapid City and Sioux Falls.

[3020] (O.B.T.)—SISTERS OBLATES TO THE BLESSED TRINITY D

Founded in Italy in 1923. First foundation in the United States in 1987.
General House: New York, NY.
U.S. Novitiate: *St. Aloysius Gonzaga Novitiate,* Beekman Rd., Hopewell Junction, NY 12533. Tel: 914-226-5671. Mother Gloria Castro, Supr. Gen.
Total number in community 42.
Represented in the Archdiocese of New York and the Diocese of Madison. Also in Archdiocese of San Juan and the Diocese of Ponce, PR.

[3030] (O.SS.R.)—OBLATES OF THE MOST HOLY REDEEMER P

Founded in Madrid in 1864.
Motherhouse: *Ciempozuelos,* Madrid, Spain, Analita Albani, Mother Gen.
U.S. Foundation: *Our Lady of the Way Residence,* 60-80 Pond St., Jamaica Plain, MA, 02130. Tel: 617-524-1640. Sr. Aurea Rendon, Supr.
Total number in community 3.
Represented in the Archdioceses of Boston and New York. Also in Puerto Rico.

[3035] (O.M.O.)—OBLATES OF THE MOTHER OF ORPHANS P

Founded in Italy on September 8, 1945.
General Motherhouse: via Amundsen 10, Milano, Italy. Sr. Lucilla Passoni, General Supr.
Universal Total in Congregation 200.
U.S. Address: 20 E. 72nd St., New York, NY 10021. Sr. Maria Isabel Reina, O.M.O., Supr.
Total in community 3.
Represented in the Archdiocese of New York. Also in Cameroon, Colombia, El Salvador, Guatemala and Italy.

[3040] (O.S.P.)—OBLATE SISTERS OF PROVIDENCE P

Founded in the United States in 1829.
General Motherhouse: *Our Lady of Mount Providence Convent,* 701 Gun Rd., Baltimore, MD 21227. Tel: 410-242-8500. Sr. Mary Claudina Sanz, O.S.P., Supr. Gen.; Sr. Mary Alexis Fisher, O.S.P., Asst. Supr. Gen.; Sr. Crescentia Proctor, O.S.P., Sec. Gen.; Sr. Sharon Young, O.S.P., Treas. Gen.
Professed Sisters 104.
Legal Title: *The Oblate Sisters of Providence of the City of Baltimore.*
Sisters serve as Pastoral Ministry-Associates in the field of Education; Reading Centers; Day Care Centers; Teaching; Counseling; Hispanic & Migrant ministry.
Represented in the Archdioceses of Baltimore, Chicago, Mobile, Washington and the Diocese of Buffalo. Also in Costa Rica and the Dominican Republic.

[3050] (O.S.H.J.)—OBLATE SISTERS OF THE SACRED HEART OF JESUS P

Founded in 1894. First foundation in the United States in 1949.
General Motherhouse: Rome, Italy.
American Headquarters: *Villa Maria Teresa,* 50 Warner Rd., Hubbard, OH 44425. Tel: 330-759-9329; Fax: 330-759-7290. Sr. Teresina Rosa, O.S.H.J., Supr.
Total number in the community 20.
Represented in the Diocese of Youngstown.

[3060] (O.S.F.S.)—OBLATE SISTERS OF ST. FRANCIS DE SALES P

Founded in France in 1866. First foundation in the United States in 1951.
General Motherhouse: 10 rue des Terrasses, Troyes, France.
American Headquarters: *Villa Aviat Convent,* Childs, MD 21916. Tel: 410-398-3699. Sr. Anne Elizabeth, O.S.F.S., Supr.
Total number in the community 16.
Ministry in the field of Academic and Religious Education; Summer Camp.
Represented in the Archdiocese of Philadelphia and the Dioceses of Arlington, Wilmington.

[3070] (N.A.U.-O.L.C.)—NORTH AMERICAN UNION SISTERS OF OUR LADY OF CHARITY P

Founded in Caen, France in 1641, by St. John Eudes. First foundation in the United States in 1855.
The primary work of the Sisters of Our Lady of Charity, is to devote themselves to the needs of women and girls in residential and non-residential settings, also nursing homes, people with AIDS, day care centers, teaching, pastoral ministries, CCD program, parish ministry, English and Spanish speaking.
The Autonomous Houses were Federated in 1944 and March 21, 1979 the North American Union of the Sisters of Our Lady of Charity was established and approved by Rome.
Legal Title: *North American Union of the Sisters of Our Lady of Charity, Inc.*

Administration Office & Canonical Formation: 154 Edgington Ln., Wheeling, WV 26003-1535. Tel: 304-242-0042; Fax: 304-242-8981. Sr. Deana Kohlman, Supr. Gen.

Green Bay

General Motherhouse and Administrative Centre: 2560 Shawano Ave., Green Bay, WI 54307-2295. Tel: 304-242-0042; Fax: 304-242-8981.
Total Sisters Membership 119.
Legal Title: *North American Union of the Sisters of Our Lady of Charity, Inc.*
Canonical Formation Wheeling, WV.
North American Union Sisters of Our Lady of Charity, 1930 Illion St., San Diego, CA 92110. Tel: 619-275-0764. Sr. Celia Robledo, Local Supr.
North American Union Sisters of Our Lady of Charity, St. Andrew's Retreat House, 257 St. Andrew's Rd., Walden, NY 12586. Tel: 845-778-5941; Fax: 845-778-5099. Sr. Rose Marie Levesque, Local Supr.
North American Union Sisters of Our Lady of Charity, 140 Cottage St., Fort Myers, FL 33901. Tel: 941-337-4550. Sr. Mary John Franey, Coord.
Represented in the Archdioceses of New York and San Antonio and the Dioceses of Buffalo, El Paso, Erie, Green Bay, Pittsburgh, Rochester, San Diego, Steubenville, Venice and Wheeling-Charleston. Also in Canada and Mexico.

Buffalo

North American Union of the Sisters of Our Lady of Charity: 3800 Howard Rd., Hamburg, NY 14075. Tel" 716-648-4988; Fax: 716-648-3062. Sr. Bernard Clement, Local Supr.
Legal Title: *Sisters of Our Lady of Charity of Refuge, Inc.*

El Paso

North American Union of Our Lady of Charity: 415 N. Glenwood Dr., El Paso, TX 79905. Tel: 915-722-0737. Sr. Yolanda Martinez, Local Supr.
San Juan Day Care Centre, Inc., 5636 Frutas Ave., El Paso, TX 79905. Tel: 915-772-1681.
Legal Title: *North American Sisters of Our Lady of Charity, Inc.*

Erie

North American Union of the Sisters of Our Lady of Charity (1934): 4635 East Lake Rd., Erie, PA 16511. Tel: 814-899-1052; Fax: 814-899-1573. Sr. Rosemary Toth, Local Supr.
Legal Title: *Gannondale Residential Center for Girls,* Erie, PA; *North American Union Sisters of Our Lady of Charity, Inc.*

Green Bay

North American Union of the Sisters of Our Lady of Charity: 2560 Shawano Ave. - P.O. Box 10357, Green Bay, WI 54307. Tel: 920-434-8208; Fax: 920-662-0047. Sr. Patrick Dolan, Local Supr.
Legal Title: *Sisters of Our Lady of Charity of the North American Union, Inc. McClosky Program, Inc.,* Green Bay, WI.

Pittsburgh

North American Union of the Sisters of Our Lady of Charity: *Nativity Convent,* 4100 Vinceton St., Pittsburgh, PA 15214. Tel: 412-931-2299; Fax: 412-931-6044. Sr. Lynn Reid, Local Supr.
Legal Title: *North American Union Sisters of Our Lady of Charity, Inc.; Eudes Institute.*

Rochester

North American Union Sisters of Our Lady of Charity: 1280 Winton Rd. N., Rochester, NY 14609. Tel: 716-654-8600; Fax: 716-654-8601. Sr. Zita Toto, Local Supr.
Legal Title: *Sisters of Our Lady of Charity of Refuge, Inc.*

San Antonio

North American Union Sisters of Our Lady of Charity (1897): 1900 Montana St., San Antonio, TX 78203. Tel: 210-475-9390; Fax: 210-475-9373. Sr. Agnes O'Mahony, Local Supr.
Legal Title: *North American Union Sisters of Our Lady of Charity, Inc.; Our Lady of Victory School.*

Steubenville

North American Union Sisters of Our Lady of Charity: 620 Roswell Rd., N.W., - P.O. Box 158, Carrollton, OH 44615-0158. Tel: 330-627-7647; Fax: 330-627-4411. Sr. Carol Pregno, Local Supr.
Legal Title: *North American Union Sisters of Our Lady of Charity, Inc.*

Walden

North American Union of the Sisters of Our Lady of Charity: *St. Andrews Retreat House,* 257 St. Andrew's Rd., Walden, NY. Tel: 845-778-5941; Fax: 845-778-5099.

Legal Title: *North American Union Sisters of Our Lady of Charity, Inc.*

Wheeling

North American Union Sisters of Our Lady of Charity: 141 Edgington Ln., Wheeling, WV 26003. Tel: 304-242-7070; Fax: 304-242-8221. Sr. Cruz Celia Gomez, Local Supr.

Legal Title: *North American Union Sisters of Our Lady of Charity, Inc.*

[3071] (O.L.C.)—SISTERS OF OUR LADY OF CHARITY P

Mt. St. Michael Convent of Our Lady of Charity: 4500 W. Davis St., Dallas, TX 75211. Tel: 214-331-1754. Sr. Margaret McCaffrey, Major Supr.

Total number in the community 11.

Legal Holding: *Mt. St. Michael Spiritual Life Center.*

[3072] (R.O.L.C.)—OUR LADY OF CHARITY OF REFUGE P

Monastery of Our Lady of Charity of Refuge: 1125 Malvern Ave., Hot Springs, AR 71901. Tel: 501-623-9651. Sr. Mary Theresa Dionne, R.O.L.C., Supr.

Total number in the community 14.

[3080] (R.C.D.)—SISTERS OF OUR LADY OF CHRISTIAN DOCTRINE D

Founded in New York in 1910 for the work of religious education and social service.

Central Office: *Visitation House,* 629 North Midland Ave., Nyack, NY 10960. Tel: 914-358-7733. Sr. Virginia Johnson, R.C.D., Supr.

Total number in the community 38.

Ministry in the field of Religious Education in Parish Centers and Parishes; Social Work and Counseling.

Represented in the Archdioceses of Chicago and New York and the Diocese of Manchester. Also in the Dominican Republic.

[3090] (C.L.H.C.)—CONGREGATION OF OUR LADY, HELP OF THE CLERGY D

Maryvale Sisters

Founded in the United States in 1961.

Motherhouse: *Maryvale Motherhouse,* 2522 June Bug Rd., Vale, NC 28168. Tel: 704-276-2626. Mother Mary Louis, Supr.

Total number in the community 5.

Represented in the Diocese of Charlotte.

[3100] (R.S.R.)—CONGREGATION OF OUR LADY OF THE HOLY ROSARY P

Founded in Rimouski, P.Q., Canada, in 1874. First Foundation in the United States in 1899.

General Motherhouse: 300 Alle du Rosaire, Rimouski, P.Q., Canada, G5L 3E3. Tel: 418-724-5940. Sr. Ida Cote, R.S.R., Supr. Gen.

U.S. Address: *Our Lady of the Holy Rosary,* 20 Thomas St., Portland, ME 04102. Tel: 207-774-3756; 772-3130 (Office). Sr. Carole Jean Lappa, R.S.R., Reg. Supr.

Total number in the region 9.

Our Lady of the Holy Rosary Regional House: 25 Portland Ave., Old Orchard Beach, ME, 04064. Tel: 207-934-0592.

Ministry in the fields of Education; Diocesan Ministry; Retreat Ministry.

Represented in the Diocese of Portland (ME).

[3105] (S.O.L.T.)— OUR LADY OF THE MOST HOLY TRINITY CONVENT D

General Mother House: P.O. Box 189, Skidmore, TX 78389. Tel: 361-287-3146. Sr. Mary of the Trinity Vaughan, S.O.L.T., Gen. Sister Servant.

Professed Sisters 70; Novices 12; Candidates 12.

Represented in the Archdiocese of Santa Fe and in the Dioceses of Corpus Christi and Kansas City-St. Joseph.

[3110] (R.C.)—CONGREGATION OF OUR LADY OF THE RETREAT IN THE CENACLE P

Founded in France in 1826. First foundation in the United States in 1892.

Generalate: Piazza Madonna del Cenacolo, 15, Rome, Italy 00136.

North American Province (1946): *Congregation Of Our Lady of the Cenacle,* 513 Fullerton Pkwy., Chicago, IL 60614-5999. Tel: 773-528-6300; Fax: 773-549-0554. Sr. Mary Peters, R.C., Prov.

Total number in community 175.

Properties owned and sponsored: *Cenacle Center for Spiritual Renewal,* Brooklyn, NY; *Cenacle Convent, Inc.,* Chicago, IL; *Cenacle Convent, Inc.,* Houston, TX; *Convent of Our Lady of the Cenacle,* Metairie, LA; *The Religious of Our Lady of the Cenacle of New Brunswick, NJ,* Metuchen, NJ; *The Cenacle Convent of Palm Beach Co., Inc.,* Palm Beach, FL; *Ronkonkoma Cenacle, Inc.,* Rockville Centre NY; *Warrenville Cenacle Retreat House,* Warrenville, IL.

Represented in the Archdioceses of Atlanta, Boston, Chicago, Denver, Milwaukee, New Orleans, New York, St. Louis and the Dioceses of Arlington, Brooklyn, Colorado Springs, Gavleston-Houston, Joliet, Madison, Metuchen, Oakland, Palm Beach, Palm Beach, Paterson, Providence, Rochester, Rockville Centre, St. Augustine, St. Petersburg, Santa Rosa, Tucson and Wheeling-Charleston. Also in Canada.

[3120] (O.L.S.)—SISTERS OF OUR LADY OF SORROWS P

Founded in Italy in 1839. First foundation in the United States in 1947.

General Motherhouse: Viale Vaticano 90, Rome, Italy 00165. Mother Lina Rossi, O.L.S., Supr. Gen.

American Headquarters: *Sisters of Our Lady of Sorrows Convent,* 9894 Norris Ferry Rd., Shreveport, LA 71106. Fax: 318-797-7003. Sr. Seraphine Ricci, O.L.S., Supr.

Total number in community 31 universal number 371.

Ministry in the field of Education; Work with people with mental retardation; Outreach to the poor; Pastoral Ministry; CCD & Adult Education.

Represented in the Dioceses of Alexandria and Shreveport.

[3130] (O.L.V.M.)—OUR LADY OF VICTORY MISSIONARY SISTERS P

Founded in the United States in 1922.

Motherhouse: *Victory Noll,* Box 109, Huntington, IN 46750. Tel: 219-356-0628; Fax: 219-358-1504. Sr. Jeanette Halbach, Pres.

Total number in the community 181.

Legal Holding: *Victory Noll Sisters Community Support Trust.*

Represented in the Archdioceses of Chicago, Cincinnati, Denver, Detroit, Dubuque, Los Angeles, Louisville, Miami, Oklahoma City, Omaha, San Antonio, Santa Fe and the Dioceses of Austin, Belleville, Cheyenne, Cleveland, Fort Wayne-South Bend, Gary, Kansas City-St. Joseph, Las Cruces, Lubbock, Oakland, Orlando, Phoenix, Salt Lake City, San Bernardino, San Diego, Sioux Falls, Toledo and Tucson.

[3140] (C.S.A.C.)—SISTERS OF THE CATHOLIC APOSTOLATE (PALLOTTINE) P

Founded in Italy in 1835. First foundation in the United States in 1889.

General Motherhouse: Viale Kennedy No. 62, Grottaferrata, Rome, Italy. Mother M. Ivete Garlet, C.S.A.C., Supr. Gen.

Universal total in congregation 520.

Provincial Motherhouse in America: *St. Patrick's Villa,* Harriman Heights, P.O. Box 118, Harriman, NY 10926. Tel: 914-783-9007. Sr. Michele Ruggiero, C.S.A.C., Prov. Moderator.

Novitiate Pallottine House of Formation, Box 350, Harriman, NY 10926. Tel: 914-774-7585.

Total number in the community 65.

Ministry in the field of Academic and Religious Education at Elementary and Secondary Levels; Pastoral Services.

Represented in the Archdioceses of Newark and New York and the Diocese of Brooklyn.

[3150] (S.A.C.)—PALLOTTINE MISSIONARY SISTERS - QUEEN OF APOSTLES PROVINCE P

(Missionary Sisters of the Catholic Apostolate)

Founded in Rome, Italy, in 1838. First founded in the United States in 1912.

General Motherhouse: Rome, Italy. Sr. Stella Holitz, S.A.C., Supr. Gen.

American Provincialate: *Pallottine Renewal Center,* 15270 Old Halls Ferry Rd., Florissant, MO 63034. Tel: 314-837-7100; Fax: 314-837-1041. Sr. M. Elisabeth Heptner, S.A.C., Prov.; Sr. Marian Ruth Creamer, S.A.C., Community Archivist.

Total number in the community 686.

Properties Owned: *Pallottine Renewal Center,* Florissant, MO; *Frascati Convent,* Londell, MO; *St. Mary's Hospital & Convent,* Huntington, WV; *Vincent Pallotti House,* Huntington, WV; *St. Joseph's Hospital & Convent,* Buckhannon, WV; *St. Vincent Pallotti Convent, High School & Child Care Center,* Laurel, MD.

Sisters minister in the fields of Health Care; Child Day Care; Education; Retreat and Renewal Ministry; Social Services; Counseling; Parish and Pastoral Work.

Represented in the Archdioceses of St. Louis and Washington and the Diocese of Wheeling-Charleston.

[3160] (P.V.M.I.)—PARISH VISITORS OF MARY IMMACULATE P

Founded in New York City in 1920 for family visitation and religious education. A contemplative-missionary community serving the Church by person-to person evangelization.

Motherhouse, Juniorate and Novitiate: *Marycrest,* P.O. Box 658, Monroe, NY 10950-0658. Tel: 845-783-2251. Sr. Carole Marie Troskowski, Gen. Supr; Sr. Rita Mairelenes, Juniorate Dir.; Sr. Dolores Marie, Novice Dir; Sr. Ann Marie, Postulant Dir.

Total number in community 68.

Ministry in evangelization, catechetics, & spiritual counseling; liaison for social services.

Represented in the Archdiocese of New York and the Dioceses of Brooklyn, Scranton and Syracuse. Also in Nigeria.

[3170] (C.P.)—RELIGIOUS OF THE PASSION OF JESUS CHRIST P

(Passionist Nuns)

Founded in Italy in 1771, by St. Paul of the Cross. First foundation in the United States in 1910.

Our Lady of Sorrows Convent of the Passionist Nuns (Contemplative): 2715 Churchview Ave., Pittsburgh, PA 15227. Tel: 412-881-1155. Mother Joyce Foga, C.P., Supr.

Professsed 9.

The Religious of the Passion of Jesus Christ (Contemplative) (1926): *St. Gabriel's Monastery,* 631 Griffin Pond Rd., Clarks Summit, PA 18411. Tel: 570-586-2791; Fax: 570-586-8210. Sr. Mary Regina, C.P., Supr.

Professed Sisters 10.

Legal Holding: *St. Gabriel's Monastery and Retreat Center.*

Sisters serve and staff: Retreats and other Programs for Women and Men of all Faiths; Clergy and Religious; Ecumenical Groups; Business and Civic Groups.

Passionist Nuns (Cloistered Contemplative) (1946): *St. Joseph's Monastery,* 8564 Crisp Rd., Whitesville, KY 42378. Tel: 270-233-4571. Mother Mary Agnes, C.P., Supr.

Professed Nuns 17.

Passionist Nuns (Contemplative) (1947): *Monastery of the Sacred Passion,* 1151 Donaldson Hwy., Erlanger, KY 41018. Tel: 606-371-8568. Sr. Margaret Mary, C.P., Supr.

Legal Title: *Passionist Nuns of Covington, KY.*

Total number in community 9.

Passionist Nuns (Cloistered) (1948): *Passionist Monastery,* 15700 Clayton Rd., Ellisville, MO 63011-2300. Tel: 636-227-3550. Mother Mary Veronica, C.P., Supr.

Total number in community 10.

[3180] (C.P.)—SISTERS OF THE CROSS AND PASSION P

(Passionist Sisters)

Founded in 1852. First foundation in the United States 1924. Generalate located at Parkmount, 458 Bury New Rd., Salford M7 4LH England. Sr. Patricia Denny, C.P., Supr. Gen.

Motherhouse-American Provincial Office: *Holy Family Convent,* One Wright Ln., North Kingstown, RI 02852. Tel: 401-294-3554. Sr. Ellen Downes, C.P., Prov.

Professed Sisters 44.

Sisters minister in Retreat Houses; Elementary and Secondary Education; Hospital Chaplaincy; Parish Ministry; Religious Education; Social Services.

Properties owned and operated: *Our Lady of Calvary Retreat,* Farmington, CT.

Represented in the Archdioceses of Hartford, New York, Washington and the Dioceses of Memphis, Providence and Rockville Centre. Also in Jamaica, West Indies.

[3190] (A.P.)—NUNS OF THE PERPETUAL ADORATION OF THE BLESSED SACRAMENT P

Founded in Rome in 1807. First foundation in United States in 1925.

El Paso: *Expiatory Shrine of Christ the King and Monastery of Perpetual Adoration,* 145 N. Cotton Ave., El Paso, TX 79901. Tel: 915-533-5323. Mother Maria de Jesus, A.P., Supr.

Sisters 20.

Represented in the Archdioceses of Anchorage and San Francisco and the Diocese of El Paso.

San Francisco: *Monastery of Perpetual Adoration,* 771 Ashbury St., San Francisco, CA 94117. Tel: 415-566-2743. Mother Rosalba Maria, A.P., Supr.

Sisters 20.

Represented in the Archdiocese of San Francisco. Also in Africa, Chile, Mexico and Spain.

[3195] (A.P.G.)—SISTER OF PERPETUAL ADORATION OF GUADALUPE, INC. P

U.S. Foundation: 2403 W. Travis, San Antonio, TX 78207. Tel: 210-227-5546. Mother Luz del Carmen Sanchez, A.P.G., General Counsel.

Total number in community 9.

[3200] (Sch.P.)—SISTERS OF THE PIOUS SCHOOLS (Escolapias) P

Founded in Figueras, Spain in 1829.
Universal total in congregation 844.
General Motherhouse: Via Crescenzio 77, Rome, Italy 00193. Mother Isolina Vasquez, Sch.P., Supr. Gen.
U.S. Headquarters (1954): 17601 Nordhoff St., Northridge, CA 91325. Tel: 818-882-5265; Fax: 818-718-6752. Sr. Maria Jesus Jurado, Sch.P., Vice Prov.
Total number in community 25.
Ministry in Religious Education; Parish Schools.
Represented in the Archdiocese of Los Angeles.

[3210] (P.C.P.A.)—POOR CLARES OF PERPETUAL ADORATION P

Founded in France, 1854. First foundation in the United States at Cleveland, Ohio, 1921.
Poor Clares of Perpetual Adoration, cloistered, contemplative, solemn vows. Object: Perpetual Adoration in spirit of Praise and Thanksgiving, and Gospel living. Solemn Exposition day and night. Each monastery is autonomous.
Sancta Clara Monastery (1946): 4200 N. Market Ave., Canton, OH 44714. Sr. Kay Marie Abbess.
Total number in community 12.
Saint Joseph Adoration Monastery (1956): 2311 Stockham Ln., Portsmouth, OH 45662-3049. Tel: 740-353-4713. Mother M. Agnes Abbess.
Total number in community 6.
Legal Holdings and Titles: *Poor Clares of Perpetual Adoration; St. Joseph Adoration Monastery.*
Adoration Monastery (1921): 4108 Euclid Ave., Cleveland, OH, 44103. Tel: 216-361-0783. Mother Mary James, P.C.P.A., Abbess.
Total number in community 19.
Poor Clares of Perpetual Adoration (1954): *Our Lady of the Most Blessed Sacrament Monastery,* 3900 13th St., N.E., Washington, DC 20017. Tel: 202-526-6808; Fax: 202-526-0678. Mother Margaret Mary, P.C.P.A., Abbess.
Total number in community 9.
Our Lady of the Angels Monastery: *Shrine of the Most Blessed Sacrament,* 3222 County Rd. 548, Hanceville, AL 35077. Tel: 256-352-6267; Fax: 256-352-1843. Mother M. Angelica, P.C.P.A., Abbess & Pres.
Total number in community 32; Novices 4; Postulants 3.
Represented in the Diocese of Birmingham.

[3220] (P.C.J.)—SISTERS OF THE POOR CHILD JESUS P

Founded on February 2, 1844 in Germany. First founded in the United States on July 2, 1924 at Parkersburg, West Virginia.
General Motherhouse: *Haus Loreto,* Simpelveld, Netherlands. Rev. Mother Clare Angela, P.C.J., Supr. Gen.
Universal number in congregation 850.
American Region and Novitiate: *Our Lady of Bethlehem Convent,* 4567 Olentangy River Rd., Columbus, OH 43214. Tel: 614-451-3900; Fax: 614-451-4745. Sr. Frances Teresa Holzberger, P.C.J., Reg. Supr.
Total number in community 7.
Ministry in the field of Education.
Properties owned: Kindergarten and a Day Care Center.
Represented in the Dioceses of Columbus and Wheeling-Charleston.

[3230] (P.H.J.C.)—POOR HANDMAIDS OF JESUS CHRIST P (The Ancilla Domini Sisters)

Founded in Germany in 1851. First foundation in the United States in 1868.
General Motherhouse: Dernbach, Westerwald, Germany. Sr. M. Germaine Hustedde, P.H.J.C., Supr. Gen.
American Province-Provincialate: *Convent Ancilla Domini,* Donaldson, IN 46513. Tel: 219-936-9936; Fax: 219-935-1785. Sr. Jolise May, P.H.J.C., Prov. Councilors: Sr. Mary Josef Shingler, P.H.J.C.; Sr. Shirley Bell, P.H.J.C.; Sr. Joetta Huelsmann, P.H.J.C.; Sr. Margaret Anne Henss, P.H.J.C.; Treas.; Ms. Mary Chudzynski, Dir. Devel.; Sr. M. Cecelia Bianchino, P.H.J.C.; Archivist.
Professed Sisters 178.
Properties owned or sponsored: *Ancilla Domini College; Convent Ancilla Domini; Maria Center; Catherine Kasper Life Center, Inc.; Lindenwood Retreat & Ministry Center; Earthworks, Inc.; Poor Handmaids of Jesus Christ Community Support Trust,* Donaldson, IN; *Ancilla Domini Convent,* Milwaukee, WI; *Ancilla Domini Hospitals; Self Insurance Trust; St. Catherine Convent,* East Chicago, IN; *Annunciation Convent,* Hoffman Estates, IL; *Poor Handmaids of Jesus Christ,* 1916 S. Clarence Ave., Berwyn, IL 60402; *Mary Katherine Convent,* Cairo, IL; *Marian Convent,* Fort Wayne, IN; *Beacon House,* Burlington, IA; *St. Mary Hospital; St. Mary Convent,* East St. Louis, IL; *Ancilla Systems, Inc.; St. Mary Medical Center,* Hobart, IN. *St. Elizabeth Hospital,* Chicago, IL; *St. Catherine Hospital,* East Chicago, IL.
Ministry in the field of Academic Education at all levels; Hospitals; Parish Ministries; Retreat Ministries; Child Care Institutions; and Retirement Homes.
Represented in the Archdioceses of Chicago, Cincinnati, Milwaukee, and the Dioceses of Belleville, Fort Wayne-South Bend, Gary, Savannah, Springfield (IL), and Springfield-Cape Girardeau. Also in Africa, Brazil, Germany and Mexico.

[3240] (C.J.C.)—POOR SISTERS OF JESUS CRUCIFIED AND THE SORROWFUL MOTHER D

Founded in the United States in 1924.
General Motherhouse and Novitiate: *Our Lady of Sorrows Convent,* 261 Thatcher St., Brockton, MA 02302-3997. Sr. Mary Valliere, C.J.C., Gen. Supr.
Total number in community 48.
Properties owned: *St. Joseph Manor Health Care, Inc.; Mater Dei Adult Day Health Program; Our Lady of Sorrows Convent,* Brockton, MA; *St. Mary's Villa Nursing Home,* Elmhurst, PA; *St. Peter's Convent,* South Boston, MA.
Ministry in Nursing Homes; Education Center; Elementary Schools; Assisted Living facilities; and Pastoral Ministry.
Represented in the Archdiocese of Boston and in the Diocese of Scranton.

[3242] (P.S.N.)—POOR SISTERS OF NAZARETH P

Founded in England by Mother St. Basil.
Motherhouse: *Nazareth House,* Hammersmith, London, W6 8DB, England. Sr. St. Hilary, Supr. Gen.
U.S. Region and Novitiate (1924): 3333 Manning Ave., Los Angeles, CA 90064. Tel: 310-839-2361. Sr. John Berchmans, Supr.
Professed Sisters 35.
Represented in the Archdioceses of Los Angeles and San Francisco and the Dioceses of Fresno, Madison and San Diego. Also in American Samoa.

[3250] (P.S.S.J.)—POOR SISTERS OF ST. JOSEPH P

Founded in Buenos Aires, Argentina, 1880.
General Motherhouse: Leon Gallardo 734, Muniz, Buenos Aires, Argentina. Mother Agueda Magdalena Padros, Mother Gen.
U.S. Foundation: *Casa Belen,* 305 E. Fourth St., Bethlehem, PA 18015. Tel: 610-867-4030.
U.S. Motherhouse: *St. Gabriel Convent,* 4319 Sano St., Alexandria, VA 22312. Tel: 703-354-0395.
Casa Nazareth: 532 Spruce St., Reading, PA 19602. Tel: 610-378-1947.
Total number in community 14.
Represented in the Dioceses of Allentown and Arlington.

[3260] (C.PP.S.)—SISTERS OF THE PRECIOUS BLOOD (DAYTON, OHIO) P

Founded in Switzerland in 1834. First foundation in the United States in 1844.
Generalate: 4000 Denlinger Rd., Dayton, OH 45426. Tel: 937-837-3302; Fax: 937-837-8825. Sr. Maryann Bremke, C.PP.S., Pres.; Sr. Nancy Raley, C.PP.S., Vice Pres. & Councilor; Sr. M. Elise Calmus, C.PP.S., Sec. & Councilor; Sr. Nadine Kaschalk, C.PP.S.; Councilor; Sr. Benita Volk, C.PP.S., Councilor; Sr. Barbara Brown, C.PP.S.; Treas.; Sr. Noreen Jutte, C.PP.S.; Archivist.
Total Membership 275.
Properties owned and sponsored: *Generalate,* Dayton, OH; *Salem Heights Convent,* Dayton, OH; *Maria Stein Center,* Maria Stein, OH; *San Luis Rey Academy, Inc.,* San Luis Rey, CA.
Ministry in Universities, High Schools, Elementary Schools & Seminaries; Diocesan Offices; Pastoral Ministry in Hospitals and Long-term Care Centers; Religious and Adult Education; Nursing Care; Homemaking Services in Homes for the Aged; Ethnic Minorities and Marginalized Peoples; Retreat and Music Ministry; Missionary and Volunteer Services.
Represented in the Archdioceses of Cincinnati, Denver, Detroit, Kansas City in Kansas, Los Angeles, Philadelphia, Washington and the Dioceses of Cleveland, Columbus, Covington, Dallas, Gallup, Grand Rapids, Kalamazoo, Lafayette (IN), Lansing, Lexington, Marquette, Phoenix, Saginaw, San Bernardino San Diego, Toledo and Tucson. Also in Chile, and Guatemala.

[3270] (C.PP.S.)—SISTERS OF THE MOST PRECIOUS BLOOD (O'FALLON, MO.) P

Founded in Switzerland in 1845. First foundation in the United States in 1870.
General Motherhouse: *St. Mary's Institute,* 204 N. Main St., O'Fallon, MO 63366-2299. Tel: 636-240-3420; Fax: 636-272-5031. Sr. Susan Borgel, C.PP.S., Supr. Gen. Gen. Councilors: Sr. Rosemary Russell; Sr. Nadine Flott; Sr. Ruth Kertz; Sr. Virginia Jaskiewicz, Treas. & Councilor; Sr. Charlene Grieshaber, Sec.; Sr. Virginia Volkerding, Community Archivist.
Total number in community 270.
Properties Owned: *St. Mary's Institute, Inc.,* O'Fallon, MO; *Charitable Trust, Sisters of the Most Precious Blood of O'Fallon, MO,* O'Fallon, MO; *Linda Vista Catholic School,* Chesterfield, MO; *St. Elizabeth Academy,* St. Louis, MO; *St. Elizabeth Adult Day Care Center,* St. Louis, MO; *Centers for Professional and Pastoral Services,* O'Fallon, MO.
Ministry in the field of Education; Care of the Elderly; Pastoral and Parish Ministry; Ecclesiastical Art; Foreign Missions; Social Services; Prayer/Presence.
Represented in the Archdioceses of Anchorage, Baltimore, Chicago, St. Louis, Washington and the Dioceses of El Paso, Jefferson City, Las Cruces, Lincoln, Nashville, Sioux City, Springfield-Cape Girardeau, Springfield (IL) and Wheeling-Charleston.

[3310] (P.M.)—SISTERS OF THE PRESENTATION OF MARY P

Founded in France in 1796. First foundation in the United States in 1873.
General Motherhouse: *Presentazione di Maria,* Viale PIO XI, 29 C.P. 104, Castelgandolfo, Italy 00040. Mother Angele Dion, Supr. Gen.
Inter-Provincial Novitiate: 180 Lowell Rd., Hudson, NH 03051. Sr. Suzette Tanguay, Dir. Tel: 603-880-8186.
Manchester Province: *Provincial Administration,* 495 Mammoth Rd., Manchester, NH 03104-5494. Tel: 603-669-1080. Sr. Suzanne Bourret, Prov. Supr.
Sisters 210.
Ministry in the field of Education at all levels; Pastoral Ministry; Youth Ministry; Ministry for Persons with Disabilities.
Properties owned: *Rivier College,* Nashua, NH; *Presentation of Mary Academy,* Hudson, NH; *Provincial House; St. Joseph Residence; St. Marie Residence,* Manchester, NH; *Our Lady of Hope House of Prayer,* New Ipswich, NH; *Bethany House,* Manchester, NH; *Trinity House; Presentation of Mary Novitiate,* Hudson, NH; *Emmanuel House,* Woonsocket, RI.
Represented in the Dioceses of Fall River, Galveston-Houston, Manchester and Providence.
Methuen Province: *Provincial Administration, Sisters of the Presentation of Mary,* 209 Lawrence St., Methuen, MA 01844. Tel: 978-687-1369; 685-0980. Sr. Helene Bissonnette, P.M., Prov.
Total number in Province 147.
Ministry in High Schools; Elementary Schools; Montessori Kindergartens; Montessorri Day Nurseries; Religious Instruction Centers; Spiritual Retreat Center.
Properties owned: *Montessori Kindergartens; Montessori Day Nurseries; Marie Joseph Spiritual Center,* Biddeford, ME; *Presentation of Mary Academy,* Methuen, MA.
Represented in the Archdiocese of Boston and the Dioceses of Portland (ME), Springfield (MA) and Worcester.

[3320] (P.B.V.M.)—SISTERS OF THE PRESENTATION OF THE B.V.M. P

Founded in Ireland in 1775. First foundation in San Francisco CA in 1854.
Represented in the United States in the following Archdioceses and Dioceses.

Dubuque P

Mt. Loretto Convent, Motherhouse and Novitiate: 2360 Carter Rd., Dubuque, IA 52001-2997. Tel: 319-588-2008; Fax: 319-588-4463. Sr. Joy Peterson, P.B.V.M., Pres.
Legal Title: *Sisters of the Presentation of the B.V.M.,* Dubuque, IA.
Total number in community 159.
Ministry in the field of Religious and Academic Education; Hospital & Prison Chaplaincy; Elder Care; Parish & Campus Ministries; South American Mission; Mission in Guatemala; Diocesan/Metropolitan Offices; Retreat & Spiritual Direction; Food Service; Mission in Tanzania.
Represented in the Archdioceses of Chicago, Denver Dubuque, Kansas City (KS), St. Paul-Minneapolis, Washington and the Dioceses of Birmingham, Brownsville, Covington, Davenport, Jackson, Knoxville, New Ulm, Orlando, Rapid City, Sioux City and Winona. Also in Bolivia, Tanzania, and Guatemala.

New York P

Mt. St. Joseph Administration Center: *Sisters of the Presentation of the Blessed Virgin Mary,* 880 Jackson

Ave., New Windsor, NY 12553. Tel: 914-564-0513; Fax: 914-567-0219. Sr. Catherine Cleary, C.PP.S., Pres.; Sr. Luke Mulraney, C.PP.S., Community Archivist.
Total number in community 190.
Ministry in the field of Academic Education at all levels; Pastoral Services; Health Care, and Social Services.
Represented in the Archdioceses of Boston, Newark, New York, Washington, and the Dioceses of Brooklyn, Manchester, Metuchen, Norwich, Paterson, Providence and Worcester. Also in Bolivia and Ghana.
Our Lady of the Presentation, Motherhouse and Novitiate: 419 Woodrow Rd., Staten Island, NY 10312. Tel: 718-356-2121. Sr. Catherine Quinn, Congregation Leader.
Professed Sisters 26.
Ministry in Elementary and High Schools; University; Campus Ministry; Pastoral Counseling; Adult Education; Healing & Parish Ministry.
Represented in the Archdioceses of New York, Philadelphia and the Diocese of Sioux Falls.

San Francisco P
Presentation Convent-Motherhouse: 2340 Turk Blvd., San Francisco, CA 94118. Tel: 415-751-0406. Sr. Ann Therese Lynch, P.B.V.M., Acting Pres.; Sr. Kathleen Griffin, Archivist.
Legal Title: *Sisters of the Presentation of the Blessed Virgin Mary.*
Total number in community 131.
Ministry in the field of Religious and Academic Education at all levels; Parish Ministry; Social and Health Ministry; College and University Teaching; Retreat Work; Church Related Administrative Positions; Missionary Work; Internal Ministry.
Represented in the Archdioceses of Los Angeles, San Francisco and the Dioceses of Monterey Oakland, San Jose, San Diego and Santa Rosa.

Albany P
St. Colman's Presentation Convent, Motherhouse and Novitiate: *Sisters of the Presentation of the Blessed Virgin Mary PVBM,* Watervliet, NY 12189. Tel: 518-273-4911; Fax: 518-273-3312. Mother Mary Carmel, Supr.
Total number in community 46.
Ministry in the field of Academic Education; Day Care Center; Child Caring Institution; Resident School for Autistic & Emotionally Disturbed Children; Parish Ministry; Residential School for Mentally Retarded; Preschool Handicapped Program.
Represented in the Diocese of Albany.

Fargo P
Sacred Heart Convent, Motherhouse and Novitiate: *Sisters of Presentation of the Blessed Virgin Mary PBVM,* 1101 32nd Ave., S., Fargo, ND 58103. Tel: 701-237-4857. Sr. Paula Ringuette, Pres.; Sr. Mary Jo Hasey, Archivist.
Total number in community 62.
Sponsored Ministries: *Presentation Prayer Center,* Fargo, ND; *Riverview Place,* Fargo, ND; *Presentation Center,* Fargo, ND; *Friendship,* Fargo, ND; *St. Ansgar's Hospital,* Park River, ND; *Carrington Health Center,* Carrington, ND.
Represented in the Archdioceses of Dubuque, and the Dioceses of Columbus, Fargo, Jackson, Knoxville, Lexington, Rapid City, Sioux Falls, and Springfield-Cape Girardeau. Also in Peru.

Sioux Falls P
Presentation Convent, Motherhouse and Novitiate: *Sisters of the Presentation of the Blessed Virgin Mary,* Aberdeen, SD 57401. Tel: 605-229-8419. Sr. Virginia McCall, Pres.; Sr. Lois Ann Sargent, Congregation Archivist.
Total number in community 147.
Ministry in the field of Academic Education; Hospitals; Homes for the Aged; Parish Pastoral Ministry; Missionary Ministry in Bolivia and Gautemala.
Represented in the Diocese of Sioux Falls.

Worcester P
Presentation Convent of the Presentation of the B.V.M.: 99 Church St., Leominster, MA 01453. Sr. Catherine Cleary, Pres.
Total number in community 182.
Sisters Staff or Sponsor: Elementary and High School Education; Spanish Apostolate; Pastoral Ministry; Social Services; Nursing.
Represented in the Archdiocese of Boston, Newark, New York, Washington, and the Dioceses of Brooklyn, Manchester, Metuchen, Norwich, Paterson, Providence, Rockville Centre, Trenton, and Worcester. Also in Bolivia and Ghana.

[3330] (P.B.V.M.)—UNION OF SISTERS OF THE PRESENTATION OF THE BLESSED VIRGIN MARY P
The Congregation of the Presentation was founded in Cork, Ireland, 1775. By decree of the Sacred Congregation for Religious, the Union of Sisters of the Presentation was established in Ireland in 1976. First U.S.A. Province in 1989.
Generalate: Monasterevan Co. Kildare, Ireland, 045-525-335. Sr. Wiona Engel, P.B.V.M., Supr. Gen.
Provincialate: 729 W. Wilshire Dr., Phoenix, AZ 85007. Tel: 602-271-9687. Sr. Catherine Burke, P.B.V.M., Prov.; Sr. Betty O'Dowd, P.B.V.M., Treas.
Novitiate: 5151 Evergreen Ave., Cypress, CA 90630. Tel: 714-527-4844.
Perpetual Profession 93.
Sisters serve and staff: Elementary and Religious Education; Parish Ministry; Health & Hospital Services; Social Services.
Represented in the Archdioceses of Los Angeles, Mobile, New Orleans, San Antonio and San Francisco and the Dioceses of Birmingham, Biloxi, Oakland, Orange, Phoenix, Sacramento, San Bernadino, Savannah and Tucson.

[3340] (S.P.)—SISTERS OF PROVIDENCE D
Founded in Kingston, Canada in 1861. First foundation in the United States in 1873. Became independent, diocesan foundation in 1892.
Providence Motherhouse: 5 Gamelin St., Holyoke, MA 01040-4081. Tel: 413-536-7511; Fax: 413-536-7917. Sr. Ruth McGoldrick, S.P., Congregation Pres.
Professed Sisters 104.
Legal Holdings and Titles: *Sisters of Providence, Inc.,* Holyoke, MA; *Sisters of Providence Health System, Inc.,* Springfield, MA; *Hospitals: Mercy Hospital,* Springfield, MA; *Providence Hospital,* Holyoke, MA; *Sisters of Providence Care Centers, Inc. including: Queen of Peace Centennial House; Beaven Kelly Home; St. Luke's Home, Inc.; Mt. St. Vincent Nursing Home,* Holyoke, MA; *Farren Care Center, Inc.,* Turners Falls, MA; *St. Joseph of the Pines Hospital, Inc.,* Southern Pines, NC; *Brightside for Children & Families, Inc.,* West Springfield, MA; *Family Services: Providence Ministries for the Needy, Inc.,* Holyoke, MA. *Retreat House: Genesis Spiritual Life Center,* Westfield, MA; *Providence Place, Inc.,* Holyoke, MA.
Represented in the Dioceses of Raleigh, Springfield (MA) and Worcester.

[3350] (S.P.)—SISTERS OF PROVIDENCE P
Founded in Montreal in 1843. First foundation in the United States in 1856.
General Motherhouse and Novitiate: 12055 Grenet St., Montreal, Quebec, Canada H4J 2J5. Sr. Gloria Keylor, Supr. Gen.
Mother Joseph Province (2000): *Sisters of Providence,* 506 Second Ave - Ste. 1200, Seattle, WA 98104-2329. Tel: 206-464-3386. Sr. Barbara Schamber, S.P., Prov. Supr. Tel: 509-474-4884. Loretta Zwolak Greene, Archivist. Tel: 206-937-4600.
Novitiate-Vocation House: 1016 N. Superior, Spokane, WA 99202-2096. Tel: 509-487-7644.
Total number in community 1,236; Sisters in Mother Joseph Province 214.
Ministry in the field of Academic Education; Health Care Services; Hospitals & Skilled Nursing Facilities; Outpatient Health Care Services; Home, Health and Hospice; Retirement Homes; Children's Nursing Centers; Senior and Handicapped Housing Facilities; Shelters for Homeless Women with Children; Transitional Housing for Women; Assisted Living facilities; Health Plans; Health Care Clinics; Child and Family Services; Prison Ministry.
The Providence Housing Association dba Vincent House, Seattle, WA; *Providence Health System - System Office:* P.O. Box 11038, Seattle, WA 98111-9038. Tel: 206-464-3355. Sr. Karin Dufault, S.P., Chm. Bd; Mr. Henry Walker, Pres. & CEO.
Properties, entities and divisions owned or operated: *Sisters of Providence – Mother Joseph Province —St. Joseph Residence,* Seattle, WA; *Providence-Pariseau Association—Providence Hospitality House,* Seattle, WA; *Sojourner Place,* Seattle, WA; *Woman Spirit Center,* Issaquah, WA; *The Gamelin Association dba—Providence House,* Yakima, WA; *The Gamelin-Oregon Association dba—Emilie House,* Portland, OR; *The Gamelin-California Association—Providence House,* Oakland, CA; *Providence Health Systems - Washington; Providence Alaska Medical Center,* Anchorage, AK; *Providence Extended Care Center,* Anchorage, AK; *Providence Horizon House,* Anchorage, AK; *Providence Seward Medical Center,* Seward, AK; *Providence Kodiak Island Medical Center,* Kodiak, AK; *Mary Conrad Center, Anchorage, AK; Providence General Medical Center, Everett,* WA; *Providence Holy Cross Medical Center,* Mission Hills, CA; *Providence St. Elizabeth Care Center,* North Hollywood, CA; *Providence Home Care and Hospice of Snohomish County,* Everett, WA; *Heritage House at the Market (leased),* Seattle, WA; *Hospice of Seattle,* Seattle, WA; *Providence Mount St. Vincent,* Seattle, WA; *Providence St. Peter Hospital,* Olympia, WA; *Providence Mother Joseph Care Center,* Olympia, WA; *Providence Marianwood,* Issaquah, WA; *Providence Centralia Hospital,* Centralia, WA; *Providence Sound HomeCare,* Olympia, WA; *Providence St. Francis Association dba St. Francis House,* Olympia, WA; *St. Luke Association dba-Providence Place,* Chehalis, WA; *Providence Blanchet Association dba Providence Blanchet House,* Centralia, WA; *Providence Rossi Association dba Providence Rossi House,* Centralia, WA; *Providence Yakima Medical Center,* Yakima, WA; *Providence Hospital,* Toppenish, WA; *Sisters of Providence in Oregon— Oregon Regional Office; Providence St. Vincent Medical Center; Providence Portland Medical Center ; Providence Child Center,* Portland, OR; *Providence Milwaukie Hospital,* Milwaukie, OR; *Providence Newberg Hospital,* Newberg, OR; *Providence Seaside Hospital (leased),* Seaside, OR; *Providence Medford Medical Center,* Medford, OR. *Sisters of Providence in California—Providence High School; Providence Saint Joseph Medical Center,* Burbank, CA; *Sisters of CA.*
Represented in the Archdioceses of Anchorage, Los Angeles, Portland (OR) and Seattle and the Dioceses of Oakland and Yakima.
Mount St. Joseph (1891): *Sisters of Providence,* 12 W. Ninth Ave., Spokane, WA 99204-2309. Tel: 509-838-2594; Fax: 509-838-3220. Sr. Eileen Croghan, S.P., Prov. Supr.; Sr. Ida Mae Marceau, S.P., Supr.
Total number in province 24.
Properties owned or sponsored: *Novititate –Vocation House,* Spokane, WA; *Providence Services,* Spokane, WA; *St. Mary Medical Center,* Walla Walla, WA; *Dominican Health Services dba Holy Family Hospital,* Spokane, WA; *Dominican Health Services dba Mount Carmel Hospital,* Colville, WA; *Dominican Health Services dba St. Joseph's Hospital,* Chewelah, WA; *Sacred Heart Medical Center,* Spokane, WA; *Holy Family Adult Day Centers,* Spokane, WA; *Dominicare,* Chewelah, WA; *Spokane Visiting Nurse Association,* Spokane, WA; *Caritas Services,* Spokane, WA; *St. Joseph Care Center,* Spokane, WA; *Deer Park Health Center & Hospital,* Deer Park, WA; *Mount St. Joseph,* Spokane, WA.
Represented in the Archdioceses of Anchorage, Los Angeles, Portland (OR) and the Diocese of Spokane.

[3360] (S.P.)—SISTERS OF PROVIDENCE OF SAINT MARY-OF-THE-WOODS, INDIANA P
Founded in France in 1806. First foundation in the United States in 1840.
General Administration: *Sisters of Providence– Owens Hall,* St. Mary-of-the-Woods, IN 47876-1089. Tel: 812-535-4193. Sr. Diane Ris, S.P., Gen. Supr.; Sr. Eileen Ann Kelley, S.P., Congregation Archivist.
Legal Titles and Sponsored Institutions: *Mother Theodore Guerin High School,* River Grove, IL; *Saint Mary-of-the-Woods College,* Saint Mary-of-the-Woods, IN; *Woods Day Care / Preschool, Inc.,* St. Mary-of-the-Woods, IN; *Providence Self-Sufficency Ministries, Inc.,* New Albany, IN; *Hispanic Education Center, Inc.,* Indianapolis, IN.
Sisters of Providence Community Support Trust (1969): Foundation to provide support for the aged and infirm members of the Congregation.
Total Number Professed Sisters 581.
Ministry in the fields of Education at all levels; Diocesan Offices; Parish and Pastoral Ministry; Health Care and Retirement Facilities; Congregation Administration; Social Services; Therapeutic/Rehabilitative/Mental Health Services.
Represented in the Archdioceses of Boston, Chicago, Cincinnati, Indianapolis, Louisville, Los Angeles, Mobile, Omaha, Portland in Oregon, St. Paul-Minneapolis, San Antonio, San Francisco, Washington and the Dioceses of Arlington, Belleville, Cleveland, Corpus Christi, Davenport, Evansville, Fort Wayne-South Bend, Galveston-Houston, Gary, Helena, Jackson, Joliet, Lafayette (LA), Lafayette (IN), Lexington, Manchester, Ogdensburg, Oklahoma, Orange, Owensboro, Peoria, St.Petersurg, San Bernadino, Springfield, Trenton, Venice, and Worcester. Also in China, and Mexico.
Area of Taiwan: *Providence University,* 200 Chung Chi Rd., Shalu 433, Taichung County, Taiwan, Republic of China. Tel: 011-886-4-631-1182. Sr. Rose Chiu, S.P., Area Rep.
Total number in community 8.
Ministry in the field of Education; Opportunity Center for Mentally Handicapped.
Represented in the Archdiocese of Taipei and the Dioceses of Taichung and Tainan.

[3390] (R.A.)—RELIGIOUS OF THE ASSUMPTION P

Founded in France in 1839. Established in the United States of America in 1919.

Generalate: 17 rue de l'Assomption, 75016, Paris, France. Universal total in Congregation 1,350.

Represented in the 31 countries through Europe, Africa, Asia, North America, Central America, and South America.

North American Province: *Provincial House,* 227 N. Bowman Ave., Merion Station, PA 19066. Tel: 610-664-3074. Sr. Clare Teresa Tjader, R.A., Prov. Supr.

Total number in province 25.

Represented in the Archdiocese of Philadelphia and the Diocese of Worcester.

Ministry in Spiritual Formation; Counselling; Campus Ministry; Pastoral and Social Ministry; Education.

[3400] (R.S.C.)—RELIGIOUS SISTERS OF CHARITY P

Founded in Dublin, Ireland in 1815. Sisters in entire congregation 650.

Motherhouse: *Caritas,* 15 Gilford Rd., Sandymount, Dublin 4, Ireland. Sr. Una O'Neill, Supr. Gen.

U.S. Headquarters & Novitiate (1953): *Regional Residence,* 10664 St. James' Dr., Culver City, CA 90230. Tel: 310-559-0176; Fax: 213-559-3530. Sr. Carmel Noone, R.S.C., Reg. Supr.

Total in U.S. community 31.

Represented in the Archdiocese of Los Angeles.

[3410] (R.C.E.)—RELIGIOUS OF CHRISTIAN EDUCATION P

Founded in France in 1817. First foundation in the United States in 1905.

General Motherhouse: France.

Provincial Residence: 55 Parkwood Dr., Milton, MA 02186. Tel: 617-696-7732; Fax: 617-696-9405. Sr. Martha Brigham, R.C.E., Prov. Supr.

Total number in community 35.

Legal Title: *Religious of Christian Education, Inc.*

Ministry in Religious Education Centers; Pastoral Associates; Teaching; Home Care.

Represented in the Archdiocese of Boston and the Dioceses of Fall River and Springfield, MA.

[3420] (R.E.)—RELIGIOUS OF THE EUCHARIST P

(formerly Society of Perpetual Adoration)

Founded in Belgium in 1857. First Foundation in U.S. in 1900.

General Motherhouse: Watermael, near Brussels, Belgium. Very Rev. Mother, Marie Virginie, Supr. Gen.

American Foundation: *Convent of the Religious of the Eucharist,* 2907 Ellicott Terrace, N. W., Washington, DC 20008. Tel: 202-966-3111. Sr. Patricia, Supr.

Ministry in the fields of Education; General.

Professed Sisters 5.

Represented in the Archdiocese of Washington.

[3430] (M.P.F.)—RELIGIOUS TEACHERS FILIPPINI P
(Maestre Pie Filippini)

Founded in Italy in 1692. First foundation in the United States in 1910.

General Motherhouse: *Villa Maria Regina,* Via Stazione Ottavia, 72, Rome, Italy. Sr. Mary DeBacco, M.P.F., Supr. Gen.

St. Lucy Filippini Province: *Villa Walsh,* Morristown, NJ, 07960-4928. Tel: 973-538-2886. Sr. Frances Lauretti, Prov. Supr.; Sr. Clare Testa, Community Archivist.

Total number in community 264.

Properties owned and sponsored: *Villa Walsh,* Morristown, NJ; *Villa Victoria,* Trenton, NJ; *St. Joseph by The Sea,* South Mantoloking, NJ.

Ministry in the field of Religious and Academic Education in elementary and secondary schools; Child Care Centers; Parish Ministry; Pastoral Care; Foreign Mission Work; House of Prayer; Retreat House.

Represented in the Archdioceses of Newark, Philadelphia, Santa Fe and the Dioceses of Brooklyn, Cleveland, Camden, Metuchen, Paterson, Pittsburgh, Scranton and Trenton.

Queen of Apostles Province: Religious Teachers Filippini M.P.F., 474 East Rd., Bristol, CT 06010. Tel: 860-584-2138. Sr. Christine Spirito, M.P.F., Prov.; Sr. Josephine Riccio, M.P.F., Community Archivist.

Total number in community 39.

Ministry in the field of Education; Pastoral Ministry; Catechetical Centers; Youth Retreats; Foreign Mission Work.

Represented in the Archdioceses of Hartford and Washington and the Dioceses of Bridgeport, Norwich, Orlando and Providence.

[3449] (C.V.I.)—RELIGIOUS OF THE INCARNATE WORD P

Founded in Lyon, France, in 1625. First foundation in United States in 1853, in Mexico 1894.

General Motherhouse: Mexico City, Industria #1-Col.Toriello Guerra, Deleg. Tlalpan, Mexico, D.F. 14050. Sr. Marta Patricia Ochoa, C.V.I., Gen. Supr.

U.S. Vice Provincial House: 153 Rainier Ct., Chula Vista, CA 91911. Tel: 619-420-0231. Sr. Camille Crabbe, C.V.I., Vice Prov.

Total number in Congregation 490.

Ministry in Parishes; Schools; Diocesan Offices and Missions.

Represented in the Diocese of San Diego. Also in Africa, Argentina, France, Guatemala, Mexico & Spain.

[3450] (R.J.M.)—RELIGIOUS OF JESUS AND MARY P

Founded at Lyons, France, 1818. First foundation in the U.S. in 1877.

Motherhouse: Via Nomentana 325, Rome, Italy. Rev. Mother, Aurora Trallero, R.J.M., Supr. Gen.

Universal number in Congregation 1,634.

United States Province Provincialate: 3706 Rhode Island Ave., Mount Rainier, MD 20712. Tel: 301-277-3794; Fax: 301-277-8656. Sr. Rosemary Mangan, R.J.M., Prov.; Sr. Yvette Beaulieu, R.J.M., Archivist.

Legal Title: *Religious of Jesus and Mary, Inc.*

Total in community 138.

Ministry in the field of Academic and Religious Education; Pastoral Ministry; Social Services; QUEST Volunteer Program.

Represented in the Archdioceses of Boston, Los Angeles, New York, Washington and the Dioceses of El Paso, Fall River, Manchester, Providence and San Diego. Also in Haiti and Mexico.

[3460] (R.M.I.)—RELIGIOUS OF MARY IMMACULATE P

Founded in Madrid, Spain in 1876.

Motherhouse: Madrid, Spain.

Generalate: Rome, Italy.

U.S. Foundation (1954): *Villa Maria,* 719 Augusta St., San Antonio, TX 78215. Tel: 210-226-0025; Fax: 210-226-3305. Sr. Ada Mabel Mier, Local Supr.

Total number in community 13.

Headquarters: *Centro Maria,* 539 West 54th St., New York, NY 10019. Tel: 212-581-5273. Sr. Clara Echeverra, Local Supr.

Total number in community 7.

Represented in the Archdioceses of New York, San Antonio and Washington.

[3465] (R.S.H.M.)—RELIGIOUS OF THE SACRED HEART OF MARY P

Founded in France in 1849. First foundation in the United States in 1877.

Generalate: Via Adelaide Ristori 26, Curia Generalizia, Rome, Italy 00197. Sr. Catherine Dolan, R.S.H.M., Gen. Supr.

Universal number in Congregation 1,041.

Eastern American Province (1907): 50 Wilson Park Dr., Tarrytown, NY 10591. Tel: 914-631-8872. Sr. Letizia Pappalardo, R.S.H.M., Prov.

Total number in community 230.

Ministries including Education; Pastoral Ministry; Retreat and Spiritual Direction; Health Care and Social Work.

Represented in the Archdioceses of Baltimore, New York and St. Louis and the Dioceses of Arlington, Brooklyn, Norwich, Oakland, Palm Beach, Richmond, Rockville Centre, Trenton, Venice and Winona. Also in Africa and Europe.

Western American Province (1959): *Religious of the Sacred Heart of Mary R.S.H.M., R.S.H.M. Provincial Center,* 441 N. Garfield Ave., Montebello, CA 90640-2901. Tel: 323-887-8821; Fax: 323-887-8952. Sr. Mary Milligan, R.S.H.M., Prov.

Total number in province 84.

Legal Titles or Holdings: *Religious of the Sacred Heart of Mary, Western American Province, a California corporation; Marymount School, a California corporation.*

Ministry in the field of Academic Education at all levels; Diverse Pastoral Ministries.

Represented in the Archdioceses of Los Angeles, San Francisco and the Dioceses of San Bernardino, San Diego and San Jose. Also in Mexico.

[3470] (S.R.C.M.)—SISTERS OF REPARATION OF THE CONGREGATION OF MARY, INC. D

Motherhouse and Novitiate: *St. Zita's Villa,* Monsey, NY 10952. Tel: 914-356-2011. Sr. Maureen Francis, S.R.C.M.

Total number in the community 11.

Represented in the Archdiocese of New York.

[3475] (S.R.)—SISTERS OF REPARATION OF THE SACRED WOUNDS OF JESUS D

Founded in 1959 in New York by Mother Mary Rose Therese, S.R. Established in the Diocese of San Diego in 1959. Motherhouse and Novitiate transferred to the Archdiocese of Portland in Oregon.

General Motherhouse and Novitiate: *Sacred Wounds of Jesus Convent,* 2120 S.E. 24th Ave., Portland, OR 97214. Tel: 503-236-4207; Fax: 503-236-3400. Mother Mary of the Angels, S.R., Supr.

Sisters 3; Donne members 90.

Legal Title: *Sisters of Reparation of the Sacred Wounds of Jesus,* Portland, OR.

Ministry in Health Care; Education; Pastoral Animation.

Represented in the Archdiocese of Portland in Oregon.

[3480] (C.R.)—SISTERS OF THE RESURRECTION P

Founded in Rome, Italy, in 1891. First foundation in the United States in 1900.

General Motherhouse: Via Marcantonio Colonna 52A, Rome, Italy. Rev. Mother Dolores Stepien, C.R., Supr. Gen.

Universal total in Congregation 586.

Western Province Provincialhouse and Novitiate: 7432 Talcott Ave., Chicago, IL 60631. Tel: 773-792-6363. Sr. Mary Barbara Sniegowski, C.R., Prov. Supr.

Total number in community 72.

Properties owned or sponsored: *Resurrection Medical Center; Our Lady of Resurrection Medical Center; Resurrection Nursing and Rehabilitation Center; Resurrection Retirement Community; Resurrection Day Care Center; Resurrection High School; Resurrection Health Care Corporation; Queen of Resurrection House of Prayer.*

Represented in the Archdioceses of Chicago, Milwaukee and Mobile.

Eastern Province Provincialhouse and Novitiate: *Sisters of the Resurrection - Mount St. Joseph,* 35 Boltwood Ave., Castleton-on-Hudson, NY 12033. Tel: 518-732-2226; Fax: 518-732-2898. Sr. Jeanne Marie Harla, C.R., Prov. Supr.

Total number in community 71.

Legal Title: *Sisters of the Resurrection, New York, Inc.*

Ministry in Nursing Homes; Elementary Schools; Christian Doctrine Centers; High School for Girls; Day Care Centers; Preschools.

Represented in the Archdiocese of New York and the Dioceses of Albany, Fall River and Trenton.

[3490] (O.S.S.)—RELIGIOUS OF THE ORDER OF THE BLESSED SACRAMENTAND OF OUR LADY P

Sacramentine Nuns

Cloistered Contemplative.

Founded in France in 1639. First foundation in the United States in 1912. The Sisters devote their lives to the perpetual adoration of Christ in the Eucharist.

Blessed Sacrament Monastery: 86 Dromore Rd., Scarsdale, NY 10583-1706. Tel: 914-722-1657. Sr. Mary Veronica, O.S.S., Prioress.

Professed sisters 13.

Monastery of Perpetual Adoration (1951): 2798 U.S. 31 N., - P.O. Box 86, Conway, MI 49722-0086. Tel: 231-347-0447. Sr. Rosalie, O.S.S., Prioress.

Professed Sisters 4.

Represented in the Archdiocese of New York and the Diocese of Gaylord.

[3499] (S.J.S.)—SISTERS SERVANTS OF THE BLESSED SACRAMENT P

Founded in Mexico in 1904. First foundation in the United States in 1926.

General Motherhouse: Juan Bernardino 650, Guadalajara, Jalisco, Mexico, 45000. Sr. M. Concepcion Cervantez, S.J.S., Supr. Gen.

U.S. Vice Province: 215 Lomita St., El Segundo, CA 90245. Tel: 310-615-0766; Fax: 310-615-0571. Sr. Ana Rosa Aceves, S.J.S., Vice Prov.

Total number in the community 59.

Legal Title: *Sisters Servants of the Blessed Sacrament, Inc.*

Ministry in the field of Education.

Represented in the Archdiocese of Los Angeles and the Diocese of Fresno, Sacramento and San Diego.

[3500] (S.S.S.)—SERVANTS OF THE BLESSED SACRAMENT P

Founded in France in 1858; First foundation in the United States in 1947.

General Motherhouse: Via Aurelia, 145-Int. C-2, Rome, Italy 00165.

U.S. Address: *St. Mary Help of Christian Parish,* 311 E. Mesa Ave., Pueblo, CO 81006. Tel: 719-545-7729; Fax: 719-542-3094. Sr. Josephine Roney, S.S.S., Prov.

Total number in the community 21.

Represented in the Dioceses of Portland (ME) and Pueblo.

[3510] (S.S.C.K.)—SISTER SERVANTS OF CHRIST THE KING D

Founded in the United States in 1936.

General Motherhouse: *Loretto Convent,* N. 8114 Calvary St., Mt. Calvary, WI 53057. Tel: 920-753-3211. Mother Mary Rose, Supr.

Professed Sisters 9.

Represented in the Archdiocese of Milwaukee and the Diocese of Fargo.

[3520] (S.S.C.M.)—SERVANTS OF THE HOLY HEART OF MARY P

Founded in Paris, France in 1860. First foundation in the United States in 1889.

Generalate: 2029 rue Holy Cross, Montreal, Quebec, Canada H4E 2A4. Sr. Fernande Dionne, S.S.C.M., Gen. Supr.

United States Region-Holy Family Province: *Provincialate,* 485 W. Merchant St., Kankakee, IL 60901. Tel: 815-937-2380. Sr. Kathleen Mulchay, S.S.C.M., Prov. Supr.

Total number in region 59.

Legal Title: *Servants of the Holy Heart of Mary; cosponsor: Provena Health.*

Ministry in Grammar Schools; Nursing Homes; Health Care; Education; Pastoral Ministry; Parishes; Ministry to the Aged; and Home Missions.

Represented in the Archdiocese of Chicago and the Dioceses of Joliet, Peoria and Rockford.

[3530] (S.Sp.S.)—MISSIONARY SISTERS SERVANTS OF THE HOLY SPIRIT P

Founded in Holland in 1889. First foundation in the United States in 1901.

General Motherhouse: *Convento dello Spirito Santo,* Via Cassia 645, Roma, Italy 00189. Sr. Agada Brand, S.Sp.S., Supr. Gen.

Universal total in Congregation 3,629.

American Motherhouse (1901): *Convent of the Holy Spirit,* Techny, IL, 60082-6026. Tel: 847-441-0126; Fax: 847-441-5587. Sr. Margaret Anne Norris, S.Sp.S., Prov.

Total number in the community 107.

Legal Title: *Missionary Sisters Sponsorship, Inc.,* Techny, IL; *Arnold Janssen Foundation,* Techny, IL; *Helena Stollenwerk Foundation,* Techny, IL.

Ministry in Schools; Catechetical Work; Parish Ministry & Administration.

Represented in the Archdiocese of Chicago.

[3540] (S.Sp.S.deA.P.)—SISTER-SERVANTS OF THE HOLY SPIRIT OF PERPETUAL ADORATION P

Cloistered Contemplative.

Founded in Holland in 1896. First foundation in the United States in 1915.

Generalate: *Convent of the Most Holy Trinity,* Bad Driburg, Germany. Mother Mary Aurora, S.Sp.S.deA.P., Supr. Gen.

U.S. House of Formation: *Mount Grace Convent,* 1438 E. Warne Ave., St. Louis, MO. Tel: 314-381-5686. Sr. Mary Gemma, S.Sp.S.deA.P., Supr.

Professed Sisters 10.

Convent of Divine Love: 2212 Green St., Philadelphia, PA 19130. Tel: 215-567-0123. Sr. Mary Catherine, S.Sp.S.deA.P., Supr.

Professed Sisters 28; Novices 2.

Convent of the Blessed Sacrament: 4105 Ocean Dr., Corpus Christi, TX 78411. Tel: 512-852-6212. Sr. Mary Margaret, S.Sp.S.deA.P., Supr.

Professed Sisters 10.

Adoration Convent of Christ the King Church: 1040 S. Cotner Blvd., Lincoln, NE 68510. Tel: 402-489-0765. Sr. Mary Henrita, S.Sp.S.deA.P., Supr.

Professed Sisters 98.

[3550] (S.C.I.M.)—SERVANTS OF THE IMMACULATE HEART OF MARY P

Good Shepherd Sisters of Quebec.

Founded in Canada in 1850. First foundation in the United States in 1882.

Generalate: 2550, rue Marie-Fitzbach, Ste-Foy, Quebec, Canada. Sr. Helen Pelletier, S.C.I.M., Supr. Gen.

Universal total in Congregation 857.

Provincial House: *St. Joseph Province at Bay View,* 313 Seaside Ave., Saco, ME 04072. Tel: 207-283-3433; Fax: 207-282-7376. Sr. Theresa Rounds, S.C.I.M., Prov. Supr.

Total number in community 109.

Ministry in Grammar Schools; Adoption Agency; Group Homes for Unmarried Mothers; Group Home for Troubled Adolescents; C.C.D. Centers; Youth (Retreat Work); Apostolate to the Elderly and Homeless.

Represented in the Archdiocese of Boston and the Diocese of Portland (ME).

[3570] (O.S.M.)—MANTELLATE SISTERS, SERVANTS OF MARY OF BLUE ISLAND P

Founded in Italy in 1861. First foundation in the United States in 1916.

Generalate and Novitiate: Rome, Italy.

U.S. Motherhouse & Novitiate: *Convent of Our Mother of Sorrows,* 13811 S. Western Ave., Blue Island, IL 60406. Tel: 708-385-2103. Sr. M. Eleanor Carella, O.S.M., Reg. Supr.

Professed Sisters 16.

Represented in the Archdiocese of Chicago.

[3572] (O.S.M.)—MANTELLATE SISTERS SERVANTS OF MARY OF PLAINFIELD

Founded October 6, 1861 in Treppi, Italy. First founded in the United States 1916.

Universal number of Mantellate Sisters 700.

Mantellate Sisters Servants of Mary of Plainfield (1977): 16949 S. Drauden Rd., Plainfield, IL 60544-9219. Tel: 815-436-5796. Sr. Francis Gresser, O.S.M., Reg. Supr.

Sisters 9.

Ministry in the field of Academic Education; Parish Ministry; Social Work; Nursing; Homes for the Aged; Foreign Missions.

Represented in the Archdiocese of Chicago and the Diocese of Joliet.

[3580] (O.S.M.)—SERVANTS OF MARY P

Founded in Italy in the 13th Century. First foundation in the United States in 1893.

General Motherhouse: *St. Juliana's Convent,* 2a, Woodstock Rd. West, Begbroke, Oxen, 0X5 1RZ England. Sr. M. Felicity McKeon, O.S.M., Prioress Gen.

American Province (1893): *Provincial Motherhouse, Convent of Our Lady of Sorrows,* 7400 Military Ave., Omaha, NE 68134-3398. Tel: 402-571-2547; Fax: 402-573-6055. Sr. Jean Morrow, O.S.M., Prov.

Total number in community 111.

Ministry in the field of Religious and Academic Education at all levels; Parishes; Social Service Agencies; Diocesan Offices; Hospital Pastoral Care; Counseling Agencies; Peace and Justice Offices; Campus Ministry; Hospice; Health Care Services; Medical Research; Consulting; Spiritual Direction; Retreat Work; Missionary Work in Foreign Countries and in the United States.

Properties owned: *Marian High School,* Omaha, NE; *Our Lady of Sorrows Convent,* Omaha, NE.

Represented in the Archdioceses of Denver, Detroit, Omaha, Portland (OR), and the Dioceses of Des Moines, Grand Island, Lexington, Metuchen, Ogdensburg, St. Cloud, Sioux City, and Tucson. Also in Jamaica, West Indies.

[3590] (O.S.M.)—SERVANTS OF MARY (SERVITE SISTERS) D

Founded in Italy in the 13th Century. First United States foundation in 1912.

General Motherhouse: *Servants of Mary,* 1000 College Ave. W., Ladysmith, WI 54848. Tel: 715-532-3364; Fax: 715-532-6153. Sr. Theresa H. Sandok, O.S.M., Pres.

Total number in community 79.

Ministry in the field of Academic Education; Parish and Pastoral Ministry; Health Care; Social Services, Law; and Administration.

Represented in the Archdioceses of Boston, Chicago, Los Angeles, Milwaukee and St. Paul-Minneapolis and the Dioceses of Fresno, Joliet, La Crosse, Orange, Orlando, Superior, St. Petersburg, Tucson and Wheeling-Charleston.

[3595] (S.S.J.)—SERVANTS OF ST. JOSEPH P

Founded in Spain in 1874.

Motherhouse: Salamanca, Spain.

General House: Rome, Italy. Mother Josefa Somoza, Supr. Gen.

U.S. Address (1957): 203 Falls Church, VA 22046. Tel: 703-533-8441; 703-534-9549.

Total number in community 16.

Represented in the Archdiocese of Newark and Diocese of Arlington.

[3600] (S.M.)—SISTERS SERVANTS OF MARY (Ministers to the Sick) P

Founded in Madrid, Spain by St. Maria Soledad Torres, August 15, 1851. First foundation in the United States in 1914.

Total Membership 1,950 Sisters.

General Motherhouse: via Antonio Musa 16, Rome, Italy. Mother Josefa Oyarzabal, S.M., Supr. Gen.

Provincial Motherhouse: 800 N. 18th St., Kansas City, KS 66102. Sr. Alfonsa Bellido, S.M., Prov. Supr.; Sr. Mercedes Rodriguez, S.M., Locale Supr.; Sr. Carmela Sanz, S.M., Community Archivist; Sr. Victoria P. Villarreal, S.M., Treas.

Total number in the province 251.

Represented in the Archdioceses of Kansas City in Kansas, Los Angeles, New Orleans and New York.

[3610] (S.S.M.I.)—SISTERS SERVANTS OF MARY IMMACULATE P

Founded in Zuzel, Ukraine on August 28, 1892. Approved by the Holy See, 1932. Arrived in the United States on August 15, 1935 at Stamford, Connecticut.

Generalate: Via Cassia Antica 104, Rome, Italy 00191. Sr. Janice Soluk, S.S.M.I., Supr. Gen.

Sisters Servants of Mary Immaculate: *Sisters Servants Ln.,* 9 Emmanuel Dr., P.O. Box 6, Sloatsburg, NY 10974-0006. Tel: 845-753-2840. Sr. Michele Yakymovitch, S.S.M.I., Prov. Supr.; Sr. Thadea Nykolayow, S.S.M.I., Prov. Archivist.

Total number in community 47.

Properties owned: *Immaculate Conception Provincialate & Novitiate; St. Joseph's Home (for the aged); Saint Mary's Villa Spiritual, Cultural and Educational Center,* Sloatsburg, NY.

Ministry in the field of Education; Parish and Pastoral ministry; Health Care; Administration; Hospitality; Holy Dormition Pilgrimage.

Represented in the Ukrainian and Byzantine Rite Catholic Dioceses of the United States.

[3620] (S.S.M.I.)—SISTERS SERVANTS OF MARY IMMACULATE P

First founded in Poland 1878.

General Motherhouse: Mariowka-Opoczynska, Poland. Mother Danuta Wrobel, Mother Gen.

Universal total in Congregation 1,100.

American Province (1935): 1220 Tugwell Dr., Catonsville, MD 21228. Tel: 410-747-1353. Sr. Bernadette Kozyra, S.S.M.I., Prov. Supr.; Sr. Marianna Danko, Community Archivist.

Total in the community 33.

Represented in the Archdioceses of Baltimore and Washington and the Diocese of Cleveland.

[3630] (S.S.C.J.)—SERVANTS OF THE MOST SACRED HEART OF JESUS P

Founded in Poland in 1894.

General Motherhouse: Garncarska St., Cracow, Poland. Mother Szczesna Niemiec, Supr. Gen.

Sister Servants of the Most Sacred Heart of Jesus (1959): *Sacred Heart Province,* 866 Cambria St., Cresson, PA 16630-1713. Sr. Theresa Marie, S.S.C.J., Prov. Supr.

Total number in U.S. Province 32.

Represented in the Archdiocese of Philadelphia and the Dioceses of Altoona-Johnstown and Metuchen.

[3640] (S.M.G.)—POOR SERVANTS OF THE MOTHER OF GOD P

Founded in London, England in 1869. First foundation in the United States in 1947.

General Motherhouse: Maryfield, Roehampton, London S.W. 15, England. Sr. Rosarii O'Connor, S.M.G., Supr. Gen.

American Foundations: *Maryfield Nursing Home,* High Point, NC 27260. Tel: 336-886-2444. Sr. Elizabeth Crehan, S.M.G., Reg. Supr.

Total number in the community 25.

Ministry in Hospitals; Nursing Homes; Schools; Retreat House.

Represented in the Archdiocese of Philadelphia and the Dioceses of Charlotte, Metuchen, and Richmond.

[3658] (S.S.H.J.)—SISTERS OF THE SACRED HEART OF JESUS P

Founded in Ragusa, Italy in 1889. First foundation in the United States in 1951.

Generalate House: *Instituto Sacro Cuore di Ragusa,* Via Cassia 1714, 00123 Rome, Italy.

Universal total in Congregation 620.

Motherhouse: *Instituto Sacro Cuore,* Via Suor Maria Schinina 2, 97100 Ragusa, Italy.

American Headquarters: *Sacred Heart Villa School & Convent,* 5269 Lewiston Rd., Lewiston, NY 14092. Tel: 716-284-8273. Sr. M. Ambrogia Alderuccio, S.S.H.J., Supr.

Legal Title: *Sacred Heart Villa School & Convent,* Lewiston, NY; *Saint Frances Cabrini Nursery and Convent,* North Haven, CT.

Ministry in the field of Religious and Academic Education at all levels; Hospitals; Homes for the Aged; Orphanages; Parish Ministry; Youth Ministry; Foreign Missions; Social Services.

Represented in the Archdiocese of Hartford and the Diocese of Buffalo.

[3660] (S.S.H.J.P.)—SERVANTS OF THE SACRED HEART OF JESUS AND OF THE POOR P

Founded in Leon, Gto., Mexico in 1885. First foundation in U.S. in 1907.

Motherhouse: Apartado 92, Puebla, Pue, Mexico. Tel: 01152-22-42-1869. Mother Guadalupe Lucia Bertoglio, Mother Gen.

U.S. Address: *Sacred Heart Children's Home Convent,* 3310 S. Zapata Hwy., Laredo, TX 78046. Tel: 956-723-3343; Fax: 956-723-3409. Mother Aurora Teresa Navarro, S.S.H.J.P., Major Supr.; Sr. Maria Teresa Grajeda, S.S.H.J.P., Admin.

Professed Sisters in U.S. 46.

Ministry in academic and religious education at all levels; Children's Home.

Represented in the Dioceses of Corpus Christi and El Paso.

[3670] (S.S.C.J.)—SISTERS OF THE SACRED HEART OF JESUS OF SAINT JACUT P

Founded in France in 1816. First foundation in the United States in 1903.

Generalate: Paris, France.

Motherhouse: *St. Jacut,* Brittany, France.

USA\Mexico Province (1916): *Provincialate Offices,* 11931 Radium St., San Antonio, TX 78216. Tel: 210-344-7203; Fax: 210-341-0721. Sr. Juana Villescas, S.S.C.J., Prov.

Total number in community 61.

Properties owned or sponsored: *Mount Sacred Heart School,* San Antonio, TX; *Casa Angelique, Mexico Casa San Antonio,* San Antonio, TX.

Ministry in Education; Pastoral Work; Schools of Religion; Health Care; Mexico Missions.

Represented in the Archdioceses of San Antonio and Santa Fe and the Dioceses of Brownsville and Galveston-Houston. Also in Mexico City.

[3680] (S.H.J.M.)—SISTERS OF THE SACRED HEARTS OF JESUS AND MARY P

Founded in France in 1866. First foundation in United States in 1953.

Motherhouse: Essex, England.

Regional House: 2150 Lake Shore Ave., Oakland, CA 94606. Tel: 510-832-2935; Fax: 510-839-5256. Sr. Lorna Walsh, S.H.J.M., Reg. Prov.

Universal Number 259; U.S. Community 15.

Ministry in Pastoral Care; Adult Education; Counseling.

Represented in the Dioceses of Oakland, Sacramento and Stockton.

[3690] (SS.CC.)—CONGREGATION OF THE SACRED HEARTS AND OF PERPETUAL ADORATION P

Founded in France in 1800 as a Congregation of men and women. Members are consecrated to the Hearts of Jesus and Mary. Special Ministries are Perpetual Adoration, the education of youth, especially the poor, parish work and foreign missions. First Catholic missionaries to Hawaii in 1827: Sisters started Catholic Schools for girls in Hawaii 1859. First foundation in the continental United States in 1908.

Generalate: Via Aurelia 145, Scala C-Int 10-14-00165, Rome, Italy. Mother Jeanne Cadiou, SS.CC., Supr. Gen.

Pacific Province: *Sisters of the Sacred Hearts,* 1120 Fifth Ave., Honolulu, HI 96816. Tel: 808-737-5822. Sr. Regina Mary Jenkins, SS.CC., Prov.

Total number in community 39.

Legal Holdings and Titles: *Sisters of the Sacred Hearts Corporation; Regina Pacis Convent; Sacred Hearts Academy Corporation; Saint Anthony Home Corporation; Malia O Ka Malu Community,* Honolulu, HI.

East Coast Region: *Sisters of the Sacred Hearts of Jesus and Mary and of Perpetual Adoration,* 35 Huttleston Ave., Fairhaven, MA 02719-3154. Tel: 508-994-9341; Fax: 508-990-1967. Sr. Dolores Pavao, SS.CC., Reg. Supr.

Total number in region 10.

Represented in the Diocese of Fall River.

[3710] (C.S.A.)—CONGREGATION OF SISTERS OF SAINT AGNES P

Founded in the United States in 1858.

General Motherhouse: *St. Agnes Convent,* 1755 E. Johnson St., Fond du Lac, WI 54935. Tel: 920-923-2121. Sr. Mary Mollison, C.S.A., Gen. Supr.; Sr. Patricia Hayes, C.S.A., Gen. Vicar. Councillors: Sr. Anita Henning, C.S.A.; Sr. Deborah Walter, C.S.A.

Total number in congregation 374.

Properties owned or sponsored: *Hazotte Ministries, Inc.; Marian College of Fond du Lac; Agnesian HealthCare of Fond du Lac, WI, Inc.; St. Francis Home,* Fond du Lac, WI; *Waupun Memorial Hospital,* Waupun, WI; *The Monroe Clinic,* Monroe, WI.

Ministry in the field of Academic and Religious Education; Hospitals; Homes for Aged; Parish Ministry; Foreign Missions; Social Services; Healthcare.

Represented in the Archdioceses of Chicago, Milwaukee, Mobile, New York, Portland in Oregon, St. Paul-Minneapolis, Washington, and the Dioceses of Allentown, Altoona-Johnstown, Columbus, Dodge City, Fort Wayne-South Bend, Gallup, Gary, Green Bay, Harrisburg, Jackson, Joliet, Madison, Manchester Marquette, Memphis, Raleigh, Rockford, Salina, St. Petersburg, Superior, Toledo, Tucson and Wichita. Also in Honduras, Nicaragua, and Russia.

[3718] (S.S.A.)—SISTERS OF ST. ANN P

Founded in Italy in 1834.

General Motherhouse: V.d. Aldobrandeschi, 100-00163, Rome, Italy. Franceschina Milanesio, S.S.A., Supr. Gen.

Universal total in Congregation 1,500.

U.S. Delegation (1952): *Mount St. Ann,* P.O. Box 328, Ebensburg, PA 15931. Tel: 814-472-9354; Fax: 814-472-9354. Sr. Anna Maria Lorenzon, S.S.A., Delegate; Sr. Melany Pereira, S.S.A., Community Archivist.

Total number in Community 9.

Ministry in the field of Education; Retreat Ministry; Foreign Mission; Pastoral Ministry.

Represented in the Dioceses of Altoona-Johnstown and Corpus Christi.

[3720] (S.S.A.)—SISTERS OF SAINT ANNE P

Founded in Vaudreuil, Province of Quebec, Canada, 1850. First foundation in the United States in 1866.

Legal Title: *The Community of the Sisters of St. Anne.*

General Motherhouse: 1950 Provost St., Lachine, Quebec, Canada. Sr. Mary Ellen King, S.S.A., Congregational Leader.

Saint Marie Province (1887): 720 Boston Post Rd. East, Marlboro, MA 01752. Tel: 508-485-3791. Prov. Leaders: Sr. Yvette Dargy, S.S.A.; Sr. Paulette Gardner, S.S.A. Tel: 508-481-4934.

Total number in province 156; In Community 900.

Properties owned: *Saint Anne Convent; Mary Martha House,* Marlboro, MA; *Emmanuel House,* Wayland, MA; *Esther House,* Worcester, MA; *Marie Esther Health Center, Inc.,* Marlboro, MA.

Ministry in the field of Academic and Religious Education at all levels; Center for Spiritual Renewal; Campus Ministry; Various Apostolates; Retreat Work; Pastoral Ministry; Ministry to the Aged, Shut-ins and the Poor; Hospital and Infirmary Nursing; Hospital Chaplaincies; Foreign Missions.

Represented in the Archdioceses of Boston and Washington and the Dioceses of Fall River, Manchester, Norwich, Providence, Springfield (MA), Venice, Wheeling-Charleston and Worcester.

[3730] (O.S.B.M.)—SISTERS OF THE ORDER OF ST. BASIL THE GREAT P (International Byzantine Rite)

Founded in Cappadocia in the 4th Century by St. Basil the Great and his sister St. Macrina. First foundation in the United States in 1911.

Basilian Generalate: Via San Alessio 26, Roma, Italy 00153. Sr. M. Dia Stasiuk, Gen. Supr.

Philadelphia-Ukrainian Byzantine Rite

Provincial and Motherhouse: 710 Fox Chase Rd., Fox Chase Manor, PA 19046. Tel: 215-379-2817; 663-9153; Fax: 215-728-6129. Sr. Dorothy Ann Busowski, O.S.B.M., Prov.

Solemnly Professed Sisters 67.

Ministry in Education at all levels; Pastoral Ministry.

Represented in the Ukrainian Archdiocese of Philadelphia and the Ukrainian Dioceses of Chicago, Parma and Stamford.

Pittsburgh Ruthenian Byzantine Rite

Motherhouse and Novitiate: *Mount St. Macrina,* 500 W. Main St., P.O. Box 878, Uniontown, PA 15401. Tel: 724-438-8644. Sr. Ruth Plante, O.S.B.M., Prov.

Professed Sisters 92.

Sisters serve in Diocesan, Parish and Religious Education Ministry; Health Care; Pastoral Ministry.

Legal Title: *Declaration of the Sisters of the Order of St. Basil the Great Endowment Trust; Declaration of Trust of the Sisters of the Order of St. Basil the Great Community Support Program; St. Macrina Cemetery, Inc.,* Uniontown, PA.

Represented in the Byzantine Archdiocese of Pittsburgh and the Dioceses of Parma, Passaic and Van Nuys.

[3735] (C.S.B.)—CONGREGATION OF ST. BRIGID P

Founded in Ireland in 1807.

U.S. Foundation (1953): *St. Brigid's Convent,* 5118 Loma Linda Dr., San Antonio, TX 78201. Tel: 210-733-0701. Sr. Teresa Carter, C.S.B., Reg. Coord.

Total number in community 16.

Properties owned: *Regional House; St. Brigid's Kindergarten,* San Antonio, TX.

Pastoral Ministry in Seminary, Detention and Hospitals; Academic Education at all levels; Ministry among immigrants and overseas; Music Ministry.

Represented in the Archdioceses of Boston and San Antonio.

[3740] (S.S.C.)—SISTERS OF ST. CASIMIR P

Founded by Mother Maria Kaupas in the United States in 1907.

General Motherhouse: 2601 W. Marquette Rd., Chicago, IL 60629. Tel: 773-776-1324; Fax: 773-776-8755. Sr. M. Immacula Wendt, S.S.C., Gen. Supr.; Sr. Margaret Mary Mazgelis, S.S.C., Gen. Sec.; Sr. M. Christella, S.S.C., Archivist.

Total number in community 165.

Properties owned: *Maria High School; Holy Cross Hospital,* Chicago, IL; *Villa Joseph Marie High School,* Holland, PA; *St. Joseph Home for the Aged,* Holland, PA.

Ministry in the field of Academic Education; Foreign Missions; Hospitals; Homes for the Aged; Pastoral Ministry.

Represented in the Archdioceses of Chicago, Philadelphia and Washington and the Dioceses of Allentown, Joliet and Las Cruces. Also in Argentina.

[3750] (S.S.Ch.)—SISTERS OF ST. CHRETIENNE P

Founded in France in 1807. First foundation in the United States in 1903.

General Motherhouse: Metz (Moselle), 57000, France.

Provincial House: 297 Arnold St., Wrentham, MA 02093-1798. Tel: 508-384-8066; Fax: 508-384-3170. Sr. Suzanne Beaudoin, S.S.Ch., Prov. Supr. Tel: 508-384-7841.

Total number in Province 67.

Legal Titles: *St. Chretienne Educational Institute, Inc.,* Marlboro, MA; *St. Chretienne Educational Institute Trust,* Wrentham, MA.

Properties Owned: *Our Lady Preschool Learning Center,* Marlboro, MA.

Represented in the Archdiocese of Boston and the Dioceses of Lexington, Manchester, Portland (ME), Providence, and St. Petersburg.

[3760] (P.C.C. or O.S.C.)—ORDER OF ST. CLARE P

Poor Clares—Poor Clares of the Primitive Observance—

Founded in Assisi, Italy in 1212. First foundation in the United States in 1875.

Motherhouse: Monastery of St. Clare, Assisi, Italy, is called the Motherhouse of the Order, but the Abbess of said Monastery has no jurisdiction over other Communities of Poor Clares. Some Monasteries, such as those at Omaha, Evansville, New Orleans, Memphis, Jamaica Plain, Greenville, Lowell and Spokane, are subject to a Father General and to the Provincial of the Franciscan Province in which the Monastery is located. Monasteries at Aptos, Cleveland, Kokomo. Los Altos Hills, Newport News, Rockford, Roswell and Santa Barbara are Colettines.

Franciscan Monastery of St. Clare: 3626 N. 65th Ave., Omaha, NE 68104-3299. Tel: 402-558-4916; Fax: 402-558-5046. Sr. Mary Clare Brown, O.S.C., Abbess.

Solemnly Professed Sisters 8; Novices 1.

St. Clare's Monastery of the Blessed Sacrament O.S.C.: 720 Henry Clay Ave., New Orleans, LA 70118. Tel: 504-895-2019. Sr. Marianne L. Zadrozny, O.S.C., Abbess.

Cloistered. Total number in community 12.

Franciscan Monastery of St. Clare O.S.C.: 6825 Nurrenbern Rd., Evansville, IN 47712. Tel: 812-425-4396. Sr. Jeanne A. Maffet, O.S.C., Supr.; Sr. Mary Martha, O.S.C., Community Archivist.

Total number in community 16.

Monastery of St. Clare (1932): 1310 Dellwood Ave., Memphis, TN 38127. Tel: 901-357-6662. Sr. Mary Marguerite, O.S.C., Abbess.

Solemnly Professed Cloistered. Total number in community 13.

The Franciscan Monastery of St. Clare: 920 Centre St., Jamaica Plain, MA 02130. Tel: 617-524-1760. Sr. Teresa J. Dericks, O.S.C., Abbess.

Total number in community 20.

Monastery of St. Clare O.S.C.: 327 S. Broad St., Trenton, NJ 08608. Tel: 609-392-7673; Fax: 609-392-9233. Sr. Mary McCourt, O.S.C., Abbess.

Total number in community 13.

Franciscan Monastery of Saint Clare: 1271 Langhorne-Newtown Rd., Langhorne, PA 19047-1297. Tel: 215-968-5775; Fax: 215-968-6254. Sr. Evelyn L. Eynan, O.S.C., Abbess.

Total number in community 14.

Franciscan Monastery of St. Clare, Spokane, Washington: *Poor Clare Nuns,* 4419 N. Hawthorne St., Spokane, WA 99205. Tel: 509-327-4479. Solemn Vows, Papal Enclosure Franciscan Province of Santa Barbara. Mother Bentivoglio Federation of Poor Clares; Sr. Mary Rita Dolan, O.S.C., Abbess; Sr. Patricia Proctor, O.S.C., Community Archivist.

Professed Nuns 8.

Monastery of St. Clare: 86 Mayflower Ave., New Rochelle, NY 10801-1615. Tel: 914-632-5227; Fax: 914-

632-5227. Sr. Mary Bernadette Quinn, O.S.C., Abbess, Solemn Vows, Papal Enclosure.
Total number in community 12.

St. Clare's Monastery: 421 S. Fourth St., Sauk Rapids, MN 56379. Tel: 320-251-3556. Mother Mary Peter, O.S.C., Abbess.
Total number in community 19.

St. Clare's Monastery of the Infant Jesus (1953): *Franciscan Poor Clare Nuns,* 8650 Russell Ave. S., Minneapolis, MN 55431-1998. Tel: 612-881-4766. Sr. Frances Getchell, O.S.C., Abbess.
Legal Title: *Franciscan Poor Clare Nuns.*
Total number in community 12.

Monastery of Poor Clares: *Order of St. Clare-Poor Clare Colettine Nuns P.C.C.,* 3501 Rocky River Dr., Cleveland, OH 44111-2998. Tel: 216-941-2820. Mother Mary St. Paul, P.C.C., Abbess. Poor Clare Nuns (Colettines), observing the Primitive Rule of St. Clare. Strictly cloistered, Solemn Vows, Perpetual Exposition of the Most Blessed Sacrament.
Total number in community 28.

Franciscan Monastery of St. Clare: *Order of St. Clare-Poor Clare Colettine Nuns P.C.C.,* 1505 Miles Rd., Cincinnati, OH 45231-2427. Tel: 513-825-7177; Fax: 513-825-4071. Sr. Dianne Short, O.S.C., Abbess. Solemn vows; papal enclosure.
Total number in community 6.

St. Joseph Monastery of the Poor Clares Colettines P.C.C.: 1671 Pleasant Valley Rd., P.O. Box 160, Aptos, CA 95001-0160. Tel: 831-761-9659. Mother Mary Clare, Abbess, (Reform of St. Colette) Daily Exposition of the Most Blessed Sacrament.
Total number in community 15; Juniors 2.

Corpus Christi Monastery (Solemn Vows, Papal Enclosure): *Poor Clare Colettines P.C.C.,* 2111 S. Main St., Rockford, IL 61102. Tel: 815-963-7343. Mother Mary Regina, P.C.C., Abbess.
Cloistered. Total number in community 21.

Annunciation Monastery: *Poor Clare Colettines P.C.C.,* 6200 E. Minooka Rd., Minooka, IL 60447-9458.

Monastery of Poor Clares-P.C.C. (1928): 215 E. Los Olivos St., Santa Barbara, CA 93105. Tel: 805-682-7670. Mother M. Clare of Jesus, Abbess.
Total number in community 15.

Monastery of St. Clare: 460 River Rd., Andover, MA 01810-4260. Tel: 978-851-6743; Fax: 978-851-2320. Sr. Therese Lacroix, O.S.C., Abbess.
Cloistered. Total number in community 14.

Poor Clare Monastery of Our Lady of Guadalupe: 809 E. 19th St., Roswell, NM 88201. Tel: 505-622-0868. Mother M. Francis, Abbess.
Legal Title: *Community of the Poor Clares of New Mexico, Inc.*
Cloistered. Total number in community 35.

Immaculate Heart Monastery of Poor Clares: 28210 Natoma Rd., Los Altos Hills, CA 94022. Tel: 650-948-2947. Mother Maura, P.C.C., Abbess.
Total number in community 15.

Monastery of St. Clare: 1916 N. Pleasantburg Dr., Greenville, SC 29609-4080. Tel: 864-244-4514; Fax: 864-268-9379. Sr. Rucia Rauton, O.S.C., Abbess.
Cloistered. Total number in community 18.

Monastery of Poor Clares Colettine P.C.C.: 28 Harpersville Rd., Newport News, VA 23601. Tel: 757-596-5942. Solemn Vows. Mother Mary Colette, P.C.C. Abbess; Sr. Mary Agnes, P.C.C., Archivist.
Cloistered. Total number in community 15.

Maria Regina Mater Monastery P.C.C.: *Poor Clare Nuns,* 1175 N., 300 W., Kokomo, IN 46901. Tel: 765-457-5743. Mother Miriam, Abbess.
Cloistered. Total number in community 12.

Christ the King Monastery of St. Clare O.S.C.: 3900 Sherwood Blvd., Delray Beach, FL 33445. Tel: 561-498-3294. Sr. Mary Veronica Butler, O.S.C., Abbess.
Total number in community 12.

Monastery of St. Clare of the Immaculate Conception O.S.C.: *Poor Clares,* 200 Marycrest Dr., St. Louis, MO 63129. Tel: 314-846-2618. Mother Mary Leo Hoffmann, O.S.C., Abbess.
Legal Title: *Nuns of the Order of St. Clare of St. Louis.*
Total number in community 9.

Monastery of St. Clare (Solemn Vows, Papal Enclosure): 6029 Estero Blvd., Fort Myers Beach, FL 33931-4325. Tel: 941-463-5599; Fax: 941-463-4993. Sr. Mary Emmanuel Kilkenny, O.S.C., Abbess.
Cloistered Sisters 4.

Monastery of St. Clare: 9300 Hwy 105, Brenham, TX 77833. Tel: 409-836-2444; Fax: 409-836-9652. Sr. Mary Angela Chandler, O.S.C., Abbess.
Sisters in Community 10.

[3765] (O.S.C.CAP.)—CAPUCHIN POOR CLARES P

Federation of Our Lady of the Angels in North America (1991): *Monastery of the Blessed Sacrament,* 4201 N.E. 18th St., Amarillo, TX 79107. Tel: 806-383-6771; Fax: 806-383-9877. Mother Catalina de Maria Banuelos, Pres.

[3770] (O.S.C.)—SISTERS OF ST. CLARE P

Generalate: 63 Harold's Cross Rd., Dublin 6W, Ireland. Sr. Helen Conway, O.S.C., Abbess Gen.

U.S. Foundation (California): Santa Clara, 1974 Cherrywood St., Vista, CA 92083. Tel: 760-945-0981. Sr. Madeline Fitzgerald, O.S.C., Contact Person; Sr. Sarah Shrewsbury, O.S.C., Reg. Supr.-California; Sr. Maria Lucia Brady, O.S.C., Reg. Supr.-Florida.
Ministry in the Fields of Academic and Religious Education at All Levels; Pastoral & Youth Ministry; Retreats; Ministry to the Sick and Poor.
Represented in the Dioceses of Orange, St. Petersburg, San Bernadino and San Diego. Also in Albania, Australia, El Salvador, England, Ireland and Wales.

[3780] (SS.C.M.)—SISTERS OF SAINTS CYRIL AND METHODIUS P

Founded in the United States in 1909.

General Motherhouse: *Villa Sacred Heart,* Danville, PA 17821-1698. Tel: 570-275-3581; Fax: 570-275-5997. Sr. Pam Smith, Gen. Supr.
Total number in community 170.
Properties owned or sponsored: *St. Cyril Academy; Villa Sacred Heart; Sacred Heart Institute; Maria Hall; Maria Joseph Manor; The Meadows at Maria Joseph Manor,* Danville, PA; *Villa St. Cyril,* Highland Park, IL.
Ministry in the field of Education; Parish Ministry and Religious Education; Retreat/Spiritual Direction; Hospital Chaplaincy; Prison Ministry; Deaf Apostolate; Homes for the Aged; Music Conservatory; Continuing Care Retirement Community.
Represented in the Archdioceses of Chicago, Detroit, and the Dioceses of Allentown, Bridgeport, Charleston, Gary, Harrisburg, Joliet, Scranton, Syracuse and Wilmington.

[3790] (S.S.D.)—INSTITUTE OF THE SISTERS OF ST. DOROTHY P

Founded in Italy in 1834. First foundation in the United States in 1911.

General Motherhouse: Via del Gianicolo 4-a, Rome, Italy 00165. Sr. Teresa Lopez, Gen. Coord.

Province of United States of America (1920): *Mt. St. Joseph,* 13 Monkeywrench Lane, Bristol, RI 02809. Tel: 401-253-7835. Sr. Dorothy Schwarz, S.S.D., Prov. Coord.
Universal number 1,200; Total number in the U.S. 48.
Properties owned or sponsored: *Villa Fatima,* Taunton, MA; *Mt. St. Joseph,* Bristol, RI; *Our Lady of Fatima High School,* Warren, RI; *St. Dorothy Academy,* Staten Island, NY.
Ministry in the fields of Education; Spiritual Life Centers; Hospital Chaplaincies;Social work with immigrants.
Represented in the Archdiocese of New York and the Dioceses of Brownsville, Fall River and Providence.

[3810] (X.S.)—SOCIETY OF CATHOLIC MISSION SISTERS OF ST. FRANCIS XAVIER, INC. D (Xavier Sisters)

Founded in the United States in 1946.

Convent: 37179 Moravian Dr., Clinton Township, MI 48036. Tel: 810-465-5082. Sr. Miriam Kennedy, Coord.
Total number in community 2.
Represented in the Archdiocese of Detroit.

[3820] (C.S.J.B.)—SISTERS OF ST. JOHN THE BAPTIST P

Founded in Italy in 1878. First foundation in the United States in 1906.
Legal Title: *Sisters of St. John the Baptist, Inc.*

General Motherhouse: Rome, Italy. Mother John Marie White, C.S.J.B., Supr. Gen.

U.S. Provincial House: 3308 Campbell Dr., Bronx, NY 10465-1358. Tel: 718-518-7820. Sr. John Agnes Barone, C.S.J.B., Prov. Supr.
Total number in community 120.
Legal Titles and Holdings: *Mt. St. John Convent,* Purchase, NY; *St. John Villa Academy,* Staten Island, NY; *Providence Rest Nursing Home,* Bronx, NY; *St. Lucy School,* Newark, NJ; *Mt. St. John Convent,* Gladstone, NJ; *St. Joseph Villa,* Peapack, NJ.
Ministry in the field of Education; Health Care for Aged Women & Men; Child Day Care; Private Guest House.
Represented in the Archdioceses of Newark, New York and the Dioceses of Albany, Metuchen and Paterson.

[3830] (C.S.J. or S.S.J.)—SISTERS OF ST. JOSEPH

The Independent Motherhouses of the Sisters of St. Joseph are represented in the United States in the following Archdioceses and Dioceses:

[3830-01] BOSTON D

Motherhouse of the Congregation of the Sisters of St. Joseph of Boston-CSJ (1873): 637 Cambridge St., Brighton, MA 02135. Tel: 617-783-9090; Fax: 617-783-8246. Sr. Joan Duffy, C.S.J., Pres.; Sr. Therezon Sheerin, C.S.J., Community Archivist.
Total number in community 651.
Legal Holdings or Titles: *Motherhouse of the Sisters of Saint Joseph of Boston,* Brighton, MA; *Bethany Health Care Center, Inc.,* Framingham, MA; *Bethany Hill School, Inc.,* Framingham, MA; *Fontbonne Hall,* Framingham, MA; *Retreat Center,* Cohasset, MA; *The Merrimack Montessori School,* Haverhill, MA; *Walnut Park Montessori School,* Newton, MA; *Jackson School Continuous Progress Elementary,* Newton, MA; *Fontbonne Academy,* Milton, MA; *Mount Saint Joseph Academy,* Brighton, MA; *Regis College,* Weston, MA; *Corporation for the Sponsored Ministries of the Sisters of St. Joseph of Boston,* Brighton, MA; *CSJ Ministries Connection, Inc.,* Brighton, MA.
Ministry in the field of Education at all levels; Health and Hospital services; Human Services and Pastoral Ministries.
Represented in the Archdioceses of Boston and Santa Fe.

[3830-02] CHICAGO D

Sisters of St. Joseph of La Grange CSJ(1899): 1515 W. Ogden Ave., La Grange Park, IL 60526. Tel: 708-354-9200. Leadership Team: Sr. Marianne Race, C.S.J., Pres.; Sr. Kathleen Lucas, C.S.J.; Sr. Jean Anne McGrath, C.S.J.; Sr. Patricia Bergen, C.S.J.; Sr.; Mary Schaefer, C.S.J.
Total number in community 106.
Ministry in the field of Education; School Administration; Nursing; Pastoral Care in Hospitals; Nursing Homes; Work with the Elderly; Parish Ministry; Archdiocesan Administration; Spiritual Direction and Retreats.
Legal Titles and Holdings: *Nazareth Academy; Sisters of St. Joseph of LaGrange Charitable Trust,* LaGrange Park, IL.
Represented in the Archdioceses of Chicago, Milwaukee and the Dioceses of Fort Wayne-South Bend, Jackson, Joliet, New Ulm, Rockford and Springfield-Cape Girardeau.

[3830-03] ORANGE P

Sisters of St. Joseph of Orange –Motherhouse: 480 S. Batavia St., Orange, CA 92868. Tel: 714-633-8121; Fax: 714-744-3165. Sr. Nancy O'Connor, Gen. Supr.; Sr. Annette Bachand, C.S.J., Community Archivist.
Total number in community 214.
Ministry in the field of Education; Health & Hospital Services; Pastoral and Social Services.
Legal Holdings and Titles: *St. Joseph Hospital of Orange,* Orange, CA; *St. Joseph Health System, A Sisters of St. Joseph of Orange Corporation,* Orange, CA; *St. Jude Medical Center,* Fullerton, CA; *Center for Spiritual Development,* Orange, CA; *St. Joseph College,* Orange, CA; *Santa Rosa Memorial Hospital,* Santa Rosa, CA; *St. Joseph Hospital of Eureka,* Eureka, CA *Redwood Memorial Hospital,* Fortuna, CA; *Queen of the Valley Hospital of Napa,* Napa, CA; *St. Mary of the Plains Hospital,* Lubbock, TX; *St. Joseph Health System Foundation,* Orange, CA; *St. Jude Memorial Foundation,* Fullerton, CA; *Redwood Memorial Foundation,* Fortuna, CA; *St. Jude Hospital Yorba Linda,* Yorba Linda, CA; *Sisters of St. Joseph Healthcare Foundation,* Orange, CA; *Mission Hospital Regional Medical Center,* Mission Viejo, CA; *St. Mary Medical Center,* Apple Valley, CA.
Represented in the Archdioceses of Los Angeles, San Francisco and the Dioceses of Colorado Springs, Las Cruces, Lubbock, Oakland, Orange, San Bernardino, San Diego and Santa Rosa. Also in El Salvador, Mexico, Hungary, Israel and Australia.

[3830-05] ROCKVILLE CENTRE D

St. Joseph's Convent - Congregation of the Sisters of Saint Joseph of Brentwood, NY CSJ: Brentwood, NY 11717. Tel: 516-273-4531. Sr. Jean Amore, Pres.; Sr. Edna McKeever, Community Archivist.
Total number in community 880.
Ministry in the field of Education; Health & Hospital Services.
Represented in the Dioceses of Brooklyn and Rockville Centre. Also in Puerto Rico, Dominican Republic and Brazil.

[3830-06] BUFFALO P

Generalate - Congregation of the Sisters of St. Joseph SSJ: 23 Agassiz Cir., Buffalo, NY 14214. Tel: 716-838-4400; Fax: 716-838-4102. Sr. Bea Manzella, Pres.; Sr. Mary Anne Butler, S.S.J., Community Archivist.
Total number in community 146.
Properties owned or sponsored: *Mt. St. Joseph Academy Administrative Office; Sisters of St. Joseph Residence.*
Ministry in the field of Education at all levels; Hospital; Infant Home; School for Deaf; Youth Ministry; Justice Ministry; Pastoral Ministry; Hospital Chaplaincy; Prison Ministry; Spirituality Center.

Represented in the Archdioceses of Cincinnati, Detroit and the Dioceses of Buffalo, Great Falls-Billings, and Pensacola-Tallahassee.

[3830-07] BURLINGTON D
Sisters of St. Joseph SSJ: 7 Clement Rd., Rutland, VT 05701. Tel: 802-775-0665. Sr. Miriam Francis Freedom, Pres.
Total number in community 42.
Properties owned or sponsored: *St. Joseph Residence; Kervick Home; Fontbonne Hall; St. Francis Residence\Avila Hall; Marion Hall Residence; Mt. St. Joseph Academy,* Rutland, VT.
Ministry in the field of Education; Pastoral Ministry; Health Care; Social Services.
Represented in the Diocese of Burlington.

[3830-08] CLEVELAND D
St. Joseph Convent - Sisters of St. Joseph CSJ: 3430 Rocky River Dr., Cleveland, OH 44111. Tel: 216-252-0440. Executive Team: Sr. Mary Brinkman; Sr. Pat Kozak; Sr. Mary Schrader; Sr. Ruth Rogers, Community Archivist.
Total number in community 145.
Legal Holdings & Titles: *Saint Joseph Academy; Sisters of Saint Joseph Community Support Charitable Trust Fund.*
Ministry in the field of Academic and Religious Education at all levels; Parish and Pastoral Ministry; Deaf Apostolate; Parish Team Member; Justice Work; Health Care; Social Services; Bookstore and Radio; Social Concerns; Retreat Work.
Represented in the Archdiocese of Chicago, Washington and the Dioceses of Cleveland, Columbus, Galveston-Houston, St. Augustine, and Venice.

[3830-09] ERIE D
Sisters of St. Joseph SSJ: *Villa Maria,* 5031 W. Ridge Rd., Erie, PA 16506-1249. Tel: 814-838-4100; Fax: 814-838-5167. Sr. Ricarda Vincent, Pres.
Total number in the community 161.
Legal Title: *Sisters of St. Joseph of Northwestern Pa.*
Institutions sponsored: *Saint Vincent Health Center; St. Mary's Home of Erie; Villa Maria Elementary; Villa Maria Academy; Villa Maria Center;Sisters of St. Joseph Neighborhood Network, Inc.*
Ministry in the field of Education at all levels; Social Ministries; Nursing Home; Health Care; Pastoral Work and other Diocesan Ministries.
Represented in the Archdioceses of Louisville, Miami, Washington and the Dioceses of Arlington, Buffalo, Cleveland Memphis, and Pittsburgh.

[3830-10] LAFAYETTE-IN-INDIANA D
Sisters of St. Joseph of Tipton CSJ: 1440 W. Division Rd., Tipton, IN 46072. Tel: 765-675-6203; Fax: 765-675-7471. Sr. Martin McEntee, C.S.J., Pres.
Total number in community 45.
Ministry in Education; Health Care; Pastoral Ministry; Social Service; Evangelization.
Represented in the Archdiocese of Indianapolis, Louisville and the Dioceses of Baker, Lafayette, Lansing, and St. Cloud. Also in Haiti.

[3830-11] KALAMAZOO P
Motherhouse and Novitiate - Sisters of St. Joseph of Nazareth SSJ: Nazareth, MI 49074. Tel: 616-381-6290; Fax: 616-381-4909. Leadership Team: Sr. Janet Fleischhacker, Pres.; Sr. Christine Parks; Sr. Rita Ann Teichman; Sr. Judy Schroeder.
Total number in community 309.
Properties owned or sponsored: Hospitals; Holding Companies for Health Service Corporation; Nursing Homes; Day Care Center for handicapped and senior citizens; Residence for Senior Citizens; Home Health Care Organizations; Ambulatory Care Services; Residential Treatment Center; Family Clinic; Gerontology Research Center; Outpatient Mental Health Clinic.
Ministry in the field of Educational; Social Services; Parish and Church-related Ministries; Foreign Missions.
Represented in the Archdioceses of Detroit, Los Angeles, New Orleans, Sante Fe, and the Dioceses of Gary, Gaylord, Grand Rapids, Jackson, Kalamazoo, Lafayette in Indiana, Lansing, Phoenix, Saginaw, and St. Petersburg. Also in Peru and France.

[3830-12] OGDENSBURG D
Motherhouse of the Society of the Sisters of St. Joseph SSJ: 1425 Washington St., Watertown, NY 13601-4533. Tel: 315-782-3460. Sr. Annunciata Collins, Major Supr.; Sr. Mary Joseph Meichelbeck, Community Archivist.
Total number in community 67.
Ministry in the field of Education at all levels; Parish and Diocesan Administration; Social Word.
Represented in the Diocese of Fairbanks, Ogdensburg and Syracuse.

[3830-13] PITTSBURGH P
Sisters of St. Joseph CSJ-Motherhouse: *St. Joseph Convent:* 1020 State St., Baden, PA 15005. Tel: 724-869-2151; Fax: 724-869-3336. Leadership Team: Sr. Sharon Costello; Sr. Paula Drass; Sr. Anna Marie Gaglia; Sr. Marguerite Kropinak; Sr. Patricia Tittler; Sr. Helen Marie Shrift, Community Archivist.
Total number in community 287.
Properties owned: *Motherhouse* and 14 residences for sisters.
Ministry in the field of Religious and Academic Education; Health Care; Social Services; Spiritual Development; Prison Ministry; Missionaries; Diocesan Administrative Services.
Represented in the Archdioceses of Baltimore, Boston, Chicago, Detroit, Hartford, Mobile, New York, St. Louis, Washington and the Dioceses of Altoona-Johnstown, Arlington, Buffalo, Charlotte, Cheyenne, Columbus, Erie, Fresno, Gallup, Greensburg, Harrisburg, Jackson, Memphis, Pittsburgh, Richmond, Salina, San Bernardino, Tucson, and Wheeling-Charleston. Also in Jamaica.

[3830-14] ROCHESTER P
Sisters of St. Joseph SSJ – Motherhouse: 4095 East Ave., Rochester, NY 14618-3798. Tel: 716-586-1000; Fax: 716-586-1193. Sr. Janice Morgan, Congregational Pres.; Sr. Jeanne Agnes Michaud, Archivist.
Total number in community 395.
Properties owned and sponsored: *Nazareth Academy; Nazareth Hall; Nazareth Academy Convent Motherhouse; St. Joseph Convent Infirmary.*
Ministry in the field of Education at all levels; Homes for Aging; Health Care; Pastoral Ministry;School for Special Children and Adults; Homes for Emotionally Disturbed Children; Parish and Diocesan Evangelization; College Campus Ministry; Social Service; Justice and Peace Office; Drug Dependency Programs; Retreats & Spiritual Direction; AIDS Ministry; Prison Ministry.
Sisters sponsor: Foster Care Homes, Food Kitchens, Spirituality Center, and Community Neighborhood Center.
Represented in the Archdiocese of Mobile and the Dioceses of Albany, Buffalo, Charlotte, Ogdensburg, Pensacola-Tallahassee, Rochester, Venice, and Syracuse. Also in Brazil.

[3830-15] SALINA P
General Administration Office (1884): *Nazareth Motherhouse - Sisters of St. Joseph of Concordia CSJ,* 215 Court St., P.O. Box 279, Concordia, KS 66901. Tel: 785-243-2149. Sr. Patricia McLennon, Pres.
Motherhouse: *Sisters of St. Joseph,* 1300 Washington St., Concordia, KS 66901. Tel: 785-243-2113.
Total sisters in community 222; Novices 2; Postulants 1.
Properties owned: *Medaille Center,* Salina, KS; *Manna House of Prayer,* Concordia, KS; *Saint Joseph Foundation for Apostolic and Charitable Purposes, Inc.*
Ministries: Care for Elderly; Homeless; Education; Parish and Diocesan Evangelization; Social Services; Justice and Peace Offices; Marriage and Family Counseling; Youth Formation; Healthcare; College Campus Ministry; Drug Dependency Programs; Prisons; Consultants; Refugees; Continuous Prayer.
Represented in the Archdioceses of Atlanta, Boston, Denver, Kansas City in Kansas, New York, St. Paul-Minneapolis, and the Dioceses of Davenport, Dodge City, El Paso, Grand Island, Jackson, Jefferson City, Kansas City, Las Cruces, Marquette, Phoenix, Pueblo, Rockford, St. Cloud, Salina and Wichita.

[3830-16] SPRINGFIELD (MA) D
Motherhouse: *Mont Marie - Sisters of St. Joseph of Springfield SSJ,* Holyoke, MA 01040. Tel: 413-536-0853; Fax: 413-533-3275. Sr. Jane Morrissey, Pres.; Sr. Mary Lavelle, Archivist.
Total number in community 367.
Legal Holdings and Titles: *Mont Marie Child Care Center, Inc.; Mont Marie Health Care Center, Inc.; Mont Marie Conference Center,* Holyoke, MA.
Ministry in the field of Religious & Academic Education; Parish Ministry; Cross-Cultural; Diocesan Administration; Chaplaincy; Refugee Resettlement; Research and Study; Restorative Justice; AIDS Ministry; Creative Arts.
Represented in the Archdioceses of Hartford, Washington and the Dioceses of Bridgeport, Fall River, Lake Charles, Norwich, Providence, Springfield (MA), Worcester and Youngstown. Also in Tanzania and Kenya.

[3830-17] WHEELING D
Motherhouse: *Mt. St. Joseph-Sisters of St. Joseph of Wheeling SSJ,* 137 Mount St. Joseph Rd., Wheeling, WV 26003. Tel: 304-232-8160. Sr. Marguerite O'Brien, Pres.; Sr. Mary Thomas Camilletti, Community Archivist.
Total number in community 100.
Properties owned and sponsored: *Sisters of St. Joseph of Wheeling Foundation, Inc.; A.B.L.E. Families, Inc.; Holy Family Child Care Center, Inc.; Sisters of St. Joseph House of Hospitality, Inc.; Sisters of St. Joseph Health System, Inc.; St. Joseph Hospital of Parkersburg, Inc.; Saint Francis Health System, Inc.; Saint Francis Hospital, Inc.; Sisters of St. Joseph Charitable Fund, Inc.; Sisters of St. Joseph Ministries Support Fund, Inc.*
Ministry in the following areas: Parish Ministry; Pastoral Services; Elementary, Secondary, College Education; Health Care; Social Services; Spiritual Formation, Direction and Retreat Ministries; Diocesan; Administration and Service.
Represented in the Diocese of Wheeling-Charleston.

[3830-18] WICHITA P
Motherhouse: *Mt. St. Mary Convent - Sisters of St. Joseph of Wichita, CSJ,* 3700 E. Lincoln St., Wichita, KS 67218. Tel: 316-686-7171; Fax: 316-689-4056. Sr. Helene Lentz, Pres.; Sr. Denise Sevart, Archivist.
Total number in community 1796.
Legal Holdings and Titles: Properties owned and sponsored: *The Sisters of St. Joseph of Wichita, Kansas and the Sisters of the Sorrowful Mother – U.S. Carribean Province, Inc.,* co-sponsor The Marian Health System which owns and operates organizations that provide acute, long term, and other health care services. *Marian Health System includes - Via Christi Health System, Inc., (Parent organization) for: Via Christi Regional Medical Center, Inc.; St. Francis Campus; St. Joseph Campus; Via Christi Rehabilitation Hospital, Inc. - Lourdes Campus GeorgeTown Village, Inc.,* Wichita, KS; *Mount Carmel Medical Center, Inc. Parent organization for: Mount Carmel Foundation,* Pittsburg, KS; *Mount Joseph Senior Community, Inc.,* Concordia, KS; *St. Joseph Senior Community, Inc.,* Manhattan, KS; *St. Joseph Regional Medical Center of Northern Oklahoma, Inc.,* Ponca City, OK; *Westminster Village, Inc.,* Ponca City, OK; *Hayward Sisters Hospital, dba St. Rose Hospital, Parent organization for: St. Rose Medical Building, Inc.; St. Rose Hospital Foundation,* Hayward, CA.
Ministry in the fields of Religious and Academic Education; Adult Religious Correspondence Courses; Diocesan Program for the Handicapped; School of Special Education; Day Nursery; Home for Aged; Pro-Life Ministry to Women; ESL Language School; G.E.D. Program; Home Hospice; Hospital and Clinical Care; Pastoral Ministry; Campus Ministry.
Represented in the Archdioceses of Kansas City in Kansas, Oklahoma City and the Dioceses of Oakland, Salina and Wichita. Also in Japan.

[3840] (C.S.J.)—SISTERS OF ST. JOSEPH OF CARONDELET P
Founded in France in 1650. First foundation in the United States in 1836.
Congregational Offices: 2307 S. Lindbergh Blvd., St. Louis, MO 63131. Sr. Helene Wilson, C.S.J., Congregational Dir. for the Provinces and Vice Province listed below.
Province of St. Louis (1836): *St. Joseph's Provincial House,* 6400 Minnesota Ave., St. Louis, MO 63111. Tel: 314-481-8800; Fax: 314-481-2366; 351-3111. Sr. Barbara Dreher, C.S.J., Prov. Dir. Team Members: Sr. Paulette Gladis, C.S.J.; Sr. Suzanne Giblin, C.S.J.
Total number in community 574.
Sponsored Institutions: Colleges 2; Academies 2; Hospitals 3; Institute for the Deaf 1; Long Term Care Facility 1.
Legal Title: *Sisters of St. Joseph of Carondelet, St. Louis Province.*
Ministries in the field of Academic Education; Pastoral Ministries; Diocesan Offices; Health Care; Child Care; Geriatric Care; Foreign Missions; Social Servies; Community Services; Special Services; Fine Arts.
Represented in the Archdioceses of Atlanta, Boston, Chicago, Denver, Indianapolis, Kansas City in Kansas, Los Angeles, Miami, Mobile, New Orleans, Oklahoma City, St. Louis, St. Paul-Minneapolis, Seattle and the Dioceses of Brownsville, Charleston, Colorado Springs, El Paso, Evansville, Green Bay, Helena, Jackson, Kansas City-St. Joseph, Marquette, Palm Beach, Peoria, Reno-Las Vegas, St. Petersburg, San Diego, San Jose, Savannah, Shreveport, Springfield-Cape Girardeau, Steubenville, Tucson, and Venice. Also in Canada.
Province of St. Paul (1851): *St. Joseph's Administration Center,* 1884 Randolph Ave., St. Paul, MN 55105. Tel: 651-690-7000; Fax: 651-690-7039. Province Leadership Team: Sr. Chris Ludwig, C.S.J.; Sr. Susan Oeffling, C.S.J.; Sr. Dolore Rochon, C.S.J.; Sr. Mary Kraft, C.S.J., Archivist.

Total number in community 423.
Legal Holdings or Titles: *St. Joseph of Carondelet - St. Paul Province Provincial House; The College of St. Catherine; Bethany Convent for Retired Sisters,* St. Paul, MN.
Ministry in the fields of Education; Health; Social Services; Spirituality.
Represented in the Archdioceses of Portland (OR), St. Paul-Minneapolis, Seattle and the Dioceses of Brownsville, Charlotte, Duluth, El Paso, Fargo, Jackson, Jefferson City, Kalamazoo, New Ulm, Pittsburgh and Superior.

Province of Albany (1858): *St. Joseph's Provincial House,* 385 Watervliet-Shaker Rd., Latham, NY 12110-4799. Tel: 518-783-3500. Leadership Team: Sr. Danielle Bonetti, C.S.J.; Sr. Laura Bufano, C.S.J.; Sr. Mary Catherine Ryan, C.S.J.; Sr. Christine Partisano, C.S.J.; Sr. Miriam Ukeritis, C.S.J.; Sr. Lauren VanDermark, C.S.J.; Sr. Anne L. Clark, C.S.J., Prov. Archivist.
Total number in community 563.
Novitiate, 369 Watervliet-Shaker Rd., Latham, NY 12110. Tel: 518-783-3536.
Ministry in the fields of Academic and Special Education at all levels; Hospital and Infirmary Services; Hospital Pastoral Ministries; Parish Ministry and Religious Education; Diocesan Offices; Youth Ministry; Counseling; Retreat and Spiritual Direction; Social and Community Services; Fine Arts.
Represented in the Archdioceses of Anchorage, Atlanta, Boston, Cincinnati, Detroit, Indianapolis, Los Angeles, New York, St. Louis, St. Paul-Minneapolis, Seattle, San Francisco, Washington and the Dioceses of Albany, Arlington, Birmingham, Brooklyn, Buffalo, Charleston, Erie, Fall River, Harrisburg, Honolulu, Kansas City-St. Joseph, Ogdensburg, Orlando, Palm Beach, Pensacola-Tallahassee, Pittsburgh, Providence, Rochester, Rockville Centre, Scranton, Shreveport, Spokane, Syracuse, Trenton, Tucson, and Worcester. Also in Chile, Japan and Peru.

Province of Los Angeles (1878): *St. Mary's Provincialate and Carondelet Center,* 11999 Chalon Rd., Los Angeles, CA 90049-1524. Tel: 310-889-2100; Fax: 310-476-8735. Sr. Maureen O'Connor, C.S.J., Prov. Supr.; Sr. Mary Ellen Sprouffske, C.S.J., Archivist.
Professed Sisters 460.
Legal Titles or Holdings: *Sisters of St. Joseph in California; Sisters of St. Joseph in Arizona; Sisters of St. Joseph Ministerial Services.*
Sisters serve in the fields of Education, Health Services; Social Services; Pastoral Ministry.
Represented in the Archdioceses of Baltimore, Boston, Los Angeles, St. Louis, San Francisco, Seattle and the Dioceses of Boise, Fresno, Honolulu, Little Rock, Monterey, Oakland, Orange, Phoenix, Portland, Sacramento, San Bernardino, San Diego, San Jose, Santa Rosa, Spokane, Stockton, Tucson and Yakima.

Hawaii Vice-Province (1956): *Sisters of St. Joseph of Carondelet, Carondelet Center,* 5311 Apo Dr., Honolulu, HI 96821-1829. Tel: 808-373-2096. Sr. Brenda Lau, C.S.J., Dir.
Legal Title: *Sisters of St. Joseph of Carondelet-Hawaii Vice-Province.*
Professed Sisters 40.
Ministries Include: Elementary and Secondary Schools; Pastoral Associates; Prayer & Spirituality; Administering Diocesan Offices; Religious Education Directors; Campus Ministry; Couseling and social work to the physically impaired; Social Ministry.
Represented in the Diocese of Honolulu. Also in Chile & Japan.

[3850] (C.S.J.)—SISTERS OF ST. JOSEPH OF CHAMBERY P

Founded in France in 1650. First foundation in United States in 1885.
Generalate: Via Calandrelli 7, 00153, Rome, Italy. Sr. Lorraine Delaney, C.S.J., Supr. Gen.
Provincial House: *Convent of Mary Immaculate,* 27 Park Rd., West Hartford, CT 06119. Tel: 860-233-5126; 232-8252. Sr. Mary Kelly, C.S.J., Prov. Supr.
Total number in community 176
Legal Title: *Sisters of St. Joseph Corporation.*
Ministry in the field of Academic and Religious Education at all levels; Social Services; Pastoral and Parish Ministries; Prisons; Law and Business; Child Day Care Center; Foreign Missions; Hospitals and Health Care.
Represented in the Archdioceses of Hartford, Miami, Mobile, and the Dioceses of Bridgeport, El Paso, Fairbanks, Lexington, Norwich, Springfield (MA) and Trenton.

[3860] (S.J.C.)—SISTERS OF ST. JOSEPH OF CLUNY P

Founded in France in 1807.
Generalate: Paris, France. Sr. Morag Collins, Supr. Gen.
American Novitiate: *Mary Immaculate Queen Novitiate,* 20955 Halldale Ave., Torrance, CA 90501. Tel: 310-328-1807.
Provincialate: Brenton Rd., Newport, RI 02840. Tel: 401-846-4757. Sr. Marie Cooper, S.J.C., Prov. of U.S. & Canada.
Professed Sisters in U.S. & Canada 40.
Legal Title: *Sisters of St. Joseph of Cluny, Inc.*
Ministry in outreach ministry; education.
Represented in the Archdiocese of Los Angeles and the Dioceses of Little Rock, Providence and Wheeling-Charleston. Also in Canada.

[3870] (C.S.J.)—SISTERS OF ST. JOSEPH OF LYONS, FRANCE P

Founded in France October 15, 1650. First foundation in United States in 1906 in Jackman, Maine.
General Motherhouse: Lyons, France. Sr. Janet Gagnon, Supr. Gen.
Maine Province: *Sisters of St. Joseph,* 93 Halifax: St., Winslow, ME 04901. Tel: 207-873-4512; Fax: 207-873-1976. Sr. Laurette Levasseur, Prov.
Total number in community 49.
Properties owned and sponsored: *Mount St. Joseph Nursing Home,* Waterville, ME; *St. Joseph Child Care Center,* Auburn, ME.
Ministry in Catechesis; Holistic Care; Spirituality and Ecology; Pastoral Ministry; Education; Pastoral Care; Mental Illness, social work, and canon law; Work with Migrants and Communities.
Represented in the Dioceses of Brownsville, El Paso, Manchester and Portland (ME). Also in Mexico.

[3880] (C.S.J.)—SISTERS OF ST. JOSEPH OF MEDAILLE P

Founded in France in 1650. First foundation in the United States in 1855. Classified as an American Congregation November 30, 1977.
Central Office: *Congregation of the Sisters of Saint Joseph of Medaille,* 1821 Summit Rd., Suite 210, Cincinnati, OH 45237. Tel: 513-761-2888; Fax: 513-761-9957. Sr. Lucy Silvio, Pres.; Sr. Maria Hill, Vice Pres.; Sr. Mary Ann Farris, Gen. Councilor; Sr. Caroline Benken, Gen. Councilor.
Total number in community 181.
Legal Title: *Sisters of St. Joseph of Medaille, Ohio Corporation.*
Ministry in the field of Academic Education at all levels; Hospital and Clinic Care; Pastoral Ministry; Religious Education; Foreign Missions; Social Service; Centers for Christian Renewal; Services to Poor and Minorities; Community Service; Diocesan Offices; Activities Programs for Retired-Elderly; Chemical Dependency; Adult Mentally Retarded; Care for Retired Sisters.
Represented in the Archdioceses of Cincinnati, New Orleans, St. Paul-Minneapolis and the Dioceses of Baton Rouge, Covington, Crookston, El Paso, Fargo, Fort Wayne-South Bend, Green Bay, Houma-Thibodaux.

[3890] (C.S.J.P.)—SISTERS OF ST. JOSEPH OF PEACE P

Founded in England 1884. First United States foundation 1885.
Generalate: *Sisters of St. Joseph of Peace Generalate, Inc.,* 3043 Fourth St. N.E., Washington, DC 20017. Tel: 202-832-5333; Fax: 202-832-5327. Sr. Ann Rutan, C.S.J.P., Congregation Leader; Sr. Mary McLeod, C.S.J.P., Asst. Congregation Leader.
Total number in the community 326.
St. Joseph Province-Eastern Province (1885): Sr. Mary Rattigan, C.S.J.P., Prov.; Sr. Nora Molyneux, C.S.J.P., Vice Prov.
Total number in the Eastern Province 157.
Ministry in the field of Education; Health and Social Services.
Properties owned or sponsored: *St. Joseph's Home for the Blind; St. Ann's Home for The Aged; St. Mary's Residence; St. Joseph's Home; The Nurturing Place (York Street Child Development Center).*
Represented in the Archdioceses of Baltimore, Los Angeles, Newark, New York and Washington and the Dioceses of Camden, Metuchen, Paterson, St. Petersburg and Trenton.
Our Lady Province (Western) (1909): *St. Mary's Provincialate,* 1663 Killarney Way, Box 248, Bellevue, WA 98009-0248. Tel: 425-451-1770; Fax: 425-462-9760. Sr. Kathleen Pruitt, C.S.J.P., Prov. Leader.
Properties owned: *St. Mary's Residence and Novitiate,* Bellevue, WA; *Prospect House,* Seattle, WA; *St. Theres Residence,* Seattle, WA; *Grace House,* Seattle, WA; *Alicia Park House,* Seattle, WA; *Eugene Residence,* Eugene, OR.
Corporate Titles: *Sisters of St. Joseph of Peace, Our Lady Province (Western); Sisters of St. Joseph of Peace Charitable Trust,* Bellevue, WA.
Total number in community 96.
Ministry in the field of Education; Social Services; Religious Education; Parish Ministry, Retreat Ministry, Social and Minority Ministry.
Represented in the Archdioceses of Anchorage, Los Angeles, Portland (OR), San Francisco and Seattle and the Dioceses of Juneau, San Diego, Spokane and Yakima. Also in Canada.

[3893] (S.S.J.)—SISTERS OF SAINT JOSEPH OF CHESTNUT HILL, PHILADELPHIA P

Founded in France in 1650. First foundation in Philadelphia in 1847.
Motherhouse (1847): *Mount St. Joseph Convent,* Chestnut Hill, Philadelphia, PA 19118-2694. Tel: 215-248-7200. Sr. Patricia Kelly, Supr. Gen; Sr. Lawrence Joseph Murphy, Community Archivist.
Total number in congregation 1,252.
Legal Holdings or Titles: *Saint Joseph Villa; Saint Joseph Guild; Bethlehem Retirement Village,* Flourtown, PA; *Academy Village,* McSherrystown, PA; *Saint Joseph Housing Corporation; Saint Mary by-the-Sea Convent,* Cape May Point, NJ; *Cecilian Academy,* Philadelphia, PA; *Mount Saint Joseph Academy,* Flourtown, PA; *Norwood-Fontbonne Academy for Boys and Girls,* Philadelphia, PA; *Holy Family Academy,* Bayonne, NJ; *Chestnut Hill College,* Philadelphia, PA; *Saint Joseph Academy,* McSherrystown, PA; *The Convent of the Sisters of St. Joseph,* Chestnut Hill, PA.
Ministry in the field of Academic and Religious Education at all levels; Institutes for Dependent Children; Pastoral Ministry; Campus Ministry; Care of the Aged; Social Services; Prison Ministry; Health Care; Psychologists; Hospice Ministry; Hospital Chaplaincy; Spiritual Directors; Drug and Alcohol Counsellors; Legal Services Ministry; Delegates for Religious.
Represented in the Archdioceses of Baltimore, Boston, Mobile, Newark, Philadelphia, San Antonio, Washington and the Dioceses of Albany, Allentown, Arlington, Belleville, Bridgeport, Camden, Charlotte, Corpus Christi, Fort Wayne-South Bend, Harrisburg, Jackson, Juneau, Lexington, Metuchen, Paterson, Raleigh, Rockville Centre, St. Petersburg, Savannah, Trenton and Wilmington. Also in Canada, Gautemala, and Peru.

[3900] (S.S.J.)—SISTERS OF ST. JOSEPH OF ST. AUGUSTINE, FLORIDA D

Founded in France in 1650. First foundation in the United States in 1866. Classified as an American Congregation in 1899.
Motherhouse: *St. Joseph Convent,* 241 St. George St. P.O. Box 3506, St. Augustine, FL 32085. Tel: 904-824-1752. Sr. Florence Bryan, S.S.J., General Supr.; Sr. Thomas Joseph McGoldrick, S.S.J., Community Archivist.
Legal Title: *The Sisters of St. Joseph Continuing Community Support Trust Fund.*
Total number in community 100.
Ministry in Hospital-Health Care Services; Social Services; Hospital Pastoral Care; Care of Aged; Academic and Religious Education at all levels; Parish Ministry; Diocesan Office Administration; Architectural Liturgical Design; Retreat Ministry; Ministry to the Handicapped.
Represented in the Archdiocese Miami and the Dioceses of Orlando, Palm Beach, Pensacola-Tallahassee, St. Augustine and St. Petersburg.

[3910] (S.J.S.M.)—SISTERS OF ST. JOSEPH OF ST. MARK D

Founded in France in 1845. First foundation in the United States in October, 1937.
Generalate: Colmar, France. Sr. Sophie Moog, Gen. Supr.
Universal total number in Congregation 249.
General Motherhouse (Cleveland) (1939): 21800 Charden Rd., Euclid, OH 44117. Mother Mary Therese Trunk Supr. Gen.
Youngstown Diocese: *Sisters of St. Joseph of St. Mark, Community Center,* 2308 Reno Dr., Louisville, OH 44641. Tel: 330-875-5946. Sr. Mary Ann Duplain, S.J.S.M., Supr.
Total number in U.S. 8.
Represented in the Diocese of Cleveland and Youngstown.

[3920] (S.J.W.)—SISTERS OF ST. JOSEPH THE WORKER D

General Motherhouse: *St. William Convent,* 1 St. Joseph Ln., Walton, KY 41094. Mother Ellen Curran, S.J.W., Supr.
Total number in the community 19.
Properties owned and operated: *Taylor Manor Nursing Home,* Versailles, KY; 16-acre property in Walton, KY: *Motherhouse Formation House.*
Represented in the Dioceses of Covington and Lexington.

[3930] (SSJ-TOSF)—SISTERS OF ST. JOSEPH OF THE THIRD ORDER OF ST. FRANCIS P

Founded in the United States in 1901.
Corporate Office: P.O. Box 305 - 1300 Maria Dr., Stevens Point, WI 54481-0305. Tel: 715-341-8457; Fax: 715-341-8830. Sr. Jeanne Conzemius, S.S.J.-T.O.S.F., Pres.; Sr. Katherine Wyszynski, S.S.J.-T.O.S.F., Vice Pres.; Sr. Mary Alice Jarosz, S.S.J.-T.O.S.F., Vice Pres.; Sr. Valerie Kulbacki, S.S.J.-T.O.S.F., Vice Pres.
Total number in the Congregation 465.
Ministries in the following areas: Academic Education at all levels; Pastoral Ministry; Health Care Services; Ministry abroad in South Africa, South America and Puerto Rico; 8th Day Center for Justice; Social Services.
Sponsors: 1 Learning Center; 3 High Schools; 1 Health Care Facility.
Represented in the Archdioceses of Chicago, Detroit, Hartford, Los Angeles, Milwaukee, St. Paul-Minneapolis and the Dioceses of Cleveland, Fort Wayne-South Bend, Gary, Grand Island, Green Bay, Harrisburg, Jackson, Joliet, Kalamazoo, Knoxville, La Crosse, Lansing, Madison, Norwich, Oakland, Paterson, Phoenix, Rockford, Superior, and Toledo.

[3935] (S.S.L.)—THE CONGREGATION OF THE SISTERS OF ST. LOUIS, JUILLY - MONAGHAN P

Founded in France in 1842. First foundation in the United States in 1949.
General Motherhouse: *Louisville Monaghan,* Ireland. Sr. Maud Murphy, S.S.L., Supr. Gen.
Regional House: *Louisville Convent,* 22300 Mulholland Dr., Woodland Hills, CA 91364. Tel: 818-883-1678. Sr. Donna Hansen, S.S.L., Reg. Supr.
Legal Title: *Sisters of St. Louis (Monaghan), Inc.*
Finally Professed Sisters 73.
Ministry in the field of Education; Pastoral and Social Ministries.
Represented in the Archdioceses of Chicago, Los Angeles, Washington and the Dioceses of Oakland, Orange, Raleigh, Salt Lake City, San Diego and Santa Rosa.

[3950] (S.S.M.N.)—SISTERS OF SAINT MARY OF NAMUR P

Founded in Namur, Belgium, in 1819. First foundation in the United States in 1863.
General Motherhouse: Namur, Belgium. Sr. Marie Julianne Farrington, Gen. Supr.
Universal Total in Congregation 421.
Eastern Province: *Provincial House,* 250 Bryant, Buffalo, NY 14222. Tel: 716-884-8221; Fax: 716-884-2950. Sr. Maureen Quinn, S.S.M.N., Prov. Supr.
Total number in community 110.
Legal Holdings or Titles: 7 Residences.
Ministry in the field of Religious and Academic Education; Pastoral Ministry; Social Services; Diocesan and Health related services; Refugee Assistance.
Represented in the Archdiocese of Boston and the Dioceses of Buffalo, Charleston, Savannah and Syracuse. Also in Canada.
Western Province: *Provincial House - Our Lady of Victory Center,* 909 W. Shaw St., Fort Worth, TX 76110. Tel: 817-923-8393. Sr. Joan Markey, Prov. Supr.
Total number in community 63.
Properties owned or sponsored: *Our Lady of Victory Center,* Fort Worth, TX; *Our Lady of Victory Elementary School,* Fort Worth, TX; *Sisters of St. Mary of Namur,* Fort Worth, TX; *Notre Dame Convent; Mercy Convent,* Wichita Falls, TX.
Ministry in the field of Religious and Academic Education; Diocesan Offices; Pastoral Ministry; Social Services; Health Care.
Represented in the Dioceses of Dallas, Fort Worth, Galveston-Houston, and Richmond.

[3960] (S.S.M.O.)—SISTERS OF ST. MARY OF OREGON P

Founded in Oregon in 1886.
General Motherhouse: *St. Mary of the Valley,* 4440 S.W. 148th Ave., Beaverton, OR 97007. Tel: 503-644-9181. Sr. Delores Adelman, Supr. Gen.
Total number in Congregation 92.
Properties owned or sponsored: *St. Mary of the Valley School & Convent; Valley Catholic School; Maryville Nursing Home; Little Flower Development Center,* Beaverton, OR.
Ministry in the field of Education; Nursing Homes; and Parish Services.
Represented in the Archdioceses of Los Angeles, Portland (OR), Seattle and the Dioceses of Baker, and Helena.

[3980] (S.P.C)—SISTERS OF SAINT PAUL DE CHARTRES P

Founded in France in 1696.
General House: 193 Via della Vignaccia, Rome, I-00163, Italy. Sr. Anne-Marie Audet, S.P.C., Supr. Gen.
Universal total in Congregation 4,000.
U.S. Province: 1300 County Rd. 492, Marquette, MI 49855-9632. Tel: 906-226-3932; 226-2139. Sr. Mary Ann Laurin, S.P.C., Prov. Supr.
Total number in community 20.
Legal Holding: *Bishop Noa Home for Senior Citizens,* Escanaba, MI.
Ministry in the field of Academic and Religious Education; Campus Ministry; Hospital Chaplaincy; Pastoral Associates; Counseling; Ministry to the Aged & Impaired.
Represented in the Archdiocese of Washington and the Diocese of Marquette.

[3990] (S.S.P.C.)—MISSIONARY SISTERS OF ST. PETER CLAVER P

Founded in 1894. First Foundation in the United States, 1914.
Legal Title: *The Sodality of St. Peter Claver for the African Missions -Missionary Sisters of St. Peter Claver.*
General House: 16 via dell' Olmata, Rome, Italy. Mother M. Elizabeth Adamiak, S.S.P.C., Supr. Gen.
American Headquarters: 667 Woods Mill Rd. S., P.O. Box 401, Chesterfield, MO 63006-0401. Tel: 314-434-8084. Sr. M. Irene Brahmakulath, S.S.P.C., Supr.
Total number in community 20.
Represented in the Archdioceses of Chicago, St. Louis and St. Paul-Minneapolis.

[4010] (O.S.A.)—SISTERS OF ST. RITA D

General Motherhouse: F. Spee Str., Wurzburg, 87. Germany. Sr. M. Dolores Schneider, Gen.
Universal total in Congregation 190.
U.S. Address: *St. Monica's Convent,* 3920 Green Bay Rd., Racine, WI 53404. Tel: 414-639-1766. Sr. Hanika Supr.
Represented in the Archdiocese of Milwaukee.

[4020] (S.T.J.)SOCIETY OF ST. TERESA OF JESUS (Teresian Sisters) P

Founded in Spain in 1876. First foundation in the United States in 1910. Total Membership 1,745.
Generalate: Via Valcannuta, 134, Rome, 00166, Italy.
Provincial House: *St. Francis de Sales Province,* 18080 St. Joseph's Way, Covington, LA 70435-5624. Tel: 504-893-1470; Fax: 504-893-2476.
Formation House: 18158 St. Joseph's Way, Covington, LA 70435-5623. Tel: 504-893-1557. Sr. Martha L. Gonzalez, Community Archivist.
Total number in community 46.
Ministry in the field of Academic Education at all levels; Education in underdeveloped areas; Youth Ministry.
Properties owned: *St. Teresa's Academy,* San Antonio, TX; *Henry de Osso Convent,* San Antonio, TX; *Provincialate,* Covington, LA.
Represented in the Archdioceses of Miami, New Orleans and San Antonio.

[4030] (S.S.T.V.)—CONGREGATION OF SISTERS OF ST. THOMAS OF VILLANOVA P

Founded in France in 1661. First foundation in the United States in 1948.
General Motherhouse: 52 Blvd. d'Argenson, Neuilly-sur-Seine, France.
Universal total in Congregation 300.
Sisters of St. Thomas of Villanova Convent: Rocks Rd., Norwalk, CT 06851. Tel: 203-847-2885. Mother Edmond, Supr.
Total number in the community 4.
Properties owned: *Notre Dame Convalescent Home.*
Represented in the Dioceses of Bridgeport.

[4040] (S.U.)—SOCIETY OF ST. URSULA P

Founded in Dole, France, in 1606. First foundation in the United States in 1901.
General Motherhouse: St. Cyr-Loire, France. Sr. Marie Bernard, Supr. Gen.
Provincialate: *American Regional Ctr.,* 50 Linwood Rd., Rhinebeck, NY 12572. Tel: 845-876-2557; 845-876-4512. Sr. Mary Isaac Jogues Koenig, Prov.
Total number in the community 34.
Ministry in the field of Education; Parish Ministry; Social Work.
Represented in the Archdioceses of Boston, New York, Washington and the Dioceses of Providence and Raleigh.

[4048] (F.C.J.)—SOCIETY OF THE SISTERS, FAITHFUL COMPANIONS OF JESUS P

Founded in France in 1820. First founded in United States 1895.
General Motherhouse: *Stella Maris Convent,* Northforeland, Broadstairs Kent, England.
American Province: *St. Philomena Convent,* Cory's Ln., Portsmouth, RI 02871. Tel: 401-683-2222. Sr. Paula Terroni, F.C.J., Supr. Gen.; Sr. Susan Donohue, F.C.J., Prov. Supr.; Sr. Imelda Toomey, Novice Dir.
Sisters 26.

[4050] (S.D.S.H.)—SISTERS OF THE SOCIETY DEVOTED TO THE SACRED HEART D

Founded in Hungary in 1940.
Motherhouse (1956): 9814 Sylvia Ave., Northridge, CA 91324. Tel: 818-772-9961; Fax: 818-772-2742. Sr. Lucia Tu, Supr. Gen.; Sr. Ida Peterfy, Foundress.
Novitiate House: 10480 Winnetka, Chatsworth, CA 91313. Tel: 818-831-9710; Fax: 818-831-0790.
Total number in community 51.
Ministry in Parish Religious Education Centers; Catechist Formation Centers; Camp for year-round Retreats and summer Family Retreats Camps; Catechesis; Youth Leadership Programs; Day Retreat Center for Children and Adults; Catechesis in Parochial Schools and Catholic High Schools; "Sacred Heart Kids' Club" Video Catechesis; Hispanic, Chinese and Korean Catechetical Centers; Catechetical Programs on Military Bases; Catechetical Missions to Dioceses; Far East Mission in Taiwan; Mission in Hungary.
Properties owned: *Heart of Jesus Retreat Center,* Santa Ana, CA; *Sacred Heart Retreat Camp,* Big Bear Lake, CA; *Sacred Heart Novitiate,* Chatsworth, CA.
Represented in the Archdiocese of Los Angeles and Dioceses of Orange, and San Bernardino. Also in Taiwan and Hungary.

[4060] (S.H.C.J.)—SOCIETY OF THE HOLY CHILD JESUS P

Founded in England in 1846. First foundation in the United States in 1862.
Motherhouse: Via della Maglianella 379, Rome, Italy 00166. Sr. Geraldine MacCarthy, S.H.C.J., Society leader.
American Province: *Provincial Offices,* 460 Shadeland Ave., Drexel Hill, PA 19026-2312. Tel: 610-626-1400. Sr. Marcia Sichol, Prov. Leader; Sr. Helena Mayer, Archivist, 1341 Montgomery Ave., Rosemont, PA 19010.
Total number in province 246.
Properties owned or sponsored: *Connelly School of the Holy Child,* Potomac, MD; *Cornelia Connelly School,* Anaheim, CA; *Mayfield Junior School of the Holy Child Jesus; Mayfield Senior School of the Holy Child Jesus,* Pasadena, CA; *Oak Knoll School of the Holy Child,* Summit, NJ; *Old Westbury School of the Holy Child,* Old Westbury, NY; *Rosemont School of the Holy Child,* Rosemont, PA; *School of the Holy Child,* Drexel Hill, PA; *School of the Holy Child,* Rye, NY; *Providence Center,* Philadelphia, PA; *Cornelia Connelly Center for Education; Holy Child Middle School,* New York, NY.
Sisters minister in a variety of Educational and Pastoral Work.
Represented in the Archdioceses of Baltimore, Boston, Chicago, Los Angeles, Milwaukee, Newark, New Orleans, New York, Philadelphia, Portland (OR) and Washington and the Dioceses of Baker, Brooklyn, Camden, Charlotte, Las Cruces, Metuchen, Orange, Paterson, Pueblo, Richmond, Rockville Centre, Sacramento, San Diego, Trenton, Venice, Wheeling-Charleston, and Wilmington.

[4070] (R.S.C.J.)—SOCIETY OF THE SACRED HEART P

Founded in France in 1800. First foundation in the United States in 1818.
Generalate: Via Tarquinio Vipera, 16, 00152, Rome, Italy. Sr. Clare Pratt, Supr. Gen.
United States Provincial House: 4389 W. Pine Blvd., St. Louis, MO 63108. Tel: 314-652-1500; Fax: 314-534-6800. Sr. Kathleen Hughes, Prov.; Sr. Margaret Phelan, Prov. Archivist.
Total number in the Province 491.
Province Corporations: *California Province of the Society of the Sacred Heart, Inc.; Society of the Sacred Heart, Chicago Province, Inc.; Religious of the Sacred Heart, Washington Province, Inc.; Religious of the Sacred Heart, New York Province, Inc.; Ladies of the Sacred Heart, MO; Religious of the Sacred Heart in Massachusetts, Inc.*
Network of Sacred Heart Schools, Inc.: 860 Beacon St., Newton, MA 02459-1879. Tel: 617-244-9260.
Ministry in the field of Religious and Academic Education at all levels; Adult Education; Parish, Pastoral, Social and Health Care Ministries.
Represented in the Archdioceses of Boston, Chicago, Detroit, Miami, New Orleans, New York, Omaha, St. Louis, San Francisco, Seattle and Washington and the Dioceses of Albany, Bridgeport, Galveston-Houston, Lafayette (LA), Richmond, San Diego, San Jose, Trenton and Venice.

[4080] (S.S.S.)—SISTERS OF SOCIAL SERVICE OF LOS ANGELES, INC. P

Founded in Hungary. Established in the United States at Los Angeles, California in 1926.

General Motherhouse: 2303 S. Figueroa Way, Los Angeles, CA 90007. Tel: 213-746-2117; Fax: 213-747-4499. Sr. Michele Walsh, Gen. Dir.

Total number in the community 100.

Legal Title: *Sisters of Social Service of Los Angeles; Sisters of Social Service Support Trust Fund.*

Social Service Work in Parishes and in Diocesan Agencies; Leadership Training of Youth and Adults; Summer Camps for Children and Families; Programs for the Elderly; Peace and Justice Work; Religious Education; Settlement Houses; Health Programs; Low Cost Legal Services; Family Counseling Services; International houses in Mexico, Philippines and Taiwan.

Represented in the Archdioceses of Boston, Los Angeles, Portland (OR), San Francisco and Seattle and the Dioceses of Oakland, Sacramento and San Diego.

[4090] (S.S.S.)—SISTERS OF SOCIAL SERVICE D

Founded in Budapest, Hungary in 1923; Sr. Margaret Slachta, Foundress.

U.S. Residence: 296 Summit Ave., Buffalo, NY 14214. Tel: 716-834-0197. Sr. Agnes Pataki, S.S.S., District Moderator.

Total number in the United States 19.

Social Work in private and public agencies; Religious Education; Parish Ministry; Health Care; Ministry for Justice and Human Rights.

Represented in the Archdioceses of Miami, Washington and the Dioceses of Buffalo and Ponce, PR.

[4100] (S.S.M.)—SISTERS OF THE SORROWFUL MOTHER (THIRD ORDER OF ST. FRANCIS) P

Founded in Italy in 1883. First foundation in the United States in 1889.

General Motherhouse: *Casa Generalizia della Suore dell'Addolorata,* Via Paolo III, 7-9, I-00165, Roma, Italy. Sr. Helen Malolepsy, S.S.M., General Superior.

U.S./Caribbean Province: *Our Lady of Sorrows Convent,* 17600 E. 51st St., Broken Arrow, OK 74012. Tel: 918-355-1148; Fax: 918-355-3534. Sr. Dorothy Ann M. Dirkx, S.S.M., Prov. Supr.

Total number in the U.S. community 195.

Legal Holding: *Sisters of the Sorrowful Mother - US Health System, Inc.; Sisters of the Sorrowful Mother - US / Caribbean Province, Inc.*

Ministry in the fields of Religious and Academic Education; Nursing Homes; Social Work; Hospitals and Hospital Administration.

Represented in the Archdiocese of Milwaukee and the Dioceses of El Paso, Green Bay, La Crosse, Paterson, Superior, Tulsa, Wichita and Winona. Also in Dominican Republic, Trinidad, Grenada and Castries.

[4110] (O.S.U.)—URSULINE NUNS (Roman Union) P

Founded in Italy in 1535. First foundation in the United States New Orleans, Louisiana in 1727.

Generalate: Via Nomentana, 236, Rome, 00162, Italy. Mother Colette Lignon, O.S.U., Prioress Gen.

Eastern Province of the U.S. (1900): *Ursuline Provincialate-St. Mary's Hall,* 323 E. 198th St., Bronx, NY 10458. Tel: 718-365-7410; Fax: 718-733-4498. Sr. Marie-Celine Miranda, O.S.U., Prov.

Total number in the province 198.

Legal Title: *Ursuline Provincialate, Eastern Province of the United States, Inc.; Marian Residence Fund, Bronx, NY; OSU Charitable Trust,* Bronx, NY.

Ministry in the field of Academic Education at all levels; varied Pastoral and Social Services.

Represented in the Archdioceses of Baltimore, New York, Washington and the Dioceses of Ogdensburg, Orlando, Paterson, Raleigh, and Wilmington.

Central Province of the U.S.: *Ursuline Provincialate,* 210 Glennon Heights Rd., Crystal City, MO 63019. Tel: 636-937-6206; Fax: 636-937-7627. Sr. Pauline Lorch, O.S.U., Prov. Prioress.

Total number in the community 188.

Ministry in the field of Religious and Academic Education.

Represented in the Archdioceses of Cincinnati, New Orleans, St. Louis, St. Paul-Minneapolis, San Antonio and the Dioceses of Brownsville, Dallas, Galveston-Houston, Juneau, Laredo, Peoria, Springfield-Cape Girardeau and Springfield (IL).

Western Province U.S. (1932): *Ursuline Provincialate,* 639 Angela Dr., Santa Rosa, CA 95403-1793. Tel: 707-545-6811; Fax: 707-579-8571. Sr. Francis Xavier Porter, O.S.U., Prov. Prioress.

Total number in the province 46.

Ministry in the field of Elementary and Secondary Education; Work with the Eskimos, American Indians, & Hispanics; Parish Ministry; Catechetical Coordinators; Blind Apostolate; Spiritual Direction; Spiritual Growth Center; Counseling Services.

Represented in the Archdioceses of Anchorage, Los Angeles, San Francisco and the Dioceses of Boise, Fairbanks, Great Falls-Billings, Juneau, San Jose and Santa Rosa.

Northeastern Province: *Ursuline Provincialate,* 45 Lowder St., Dedham, MA 02026-4200. Tel: 781-326-6219; Fax: 781-326-7296. Sr. Angela Krippendorf, O.S.U., Prov.

Total number in the community 49.

Ministry in the field of Education.

Represented in the Archdiocese of Boston and the Diocese of Portland (ME).

[4120] (O.S.U.)—URSULINE NUNS, OF THE CONGREGATION OF PARIS P

Founded in Italy in 1535. First foundation in the United States in New Orleans, Louisiana in 1727.

Motherhouse (1845): *Immaculate Heart of Mary Convent,* 20860 St. Rte. 251, St. Martin, OH 45118-9705. Tel: 513-875-2020; Fax: 513-875-2311. Sr. Nancy Vollman, O.S.U., Supr.

Total number in the community 40.

Ministry in the field of Academic Education at all levels; Special Education; Adult Education; Catechetical Instruction; Administration; Retreats; Counseling; Organization Consultation; Social-Inner City & Rural; Hospital; Senior Services; Campus and Parish Ministry.

Legal Title: *St. Ursula Literary Institute; Ursulines of Brown County; Ursuline Academy of Cincinnati; Chatfield College.*

Represented in the Archdiocese of Cincinnati and the Dioceses of Covington, and Toledo.

[4120-01] Cincinnati P

Motherhouse: *Ursulines of Cincinnati, St. Ursula Convent,* 1339 E. McMillan St. (Walnut Hills), Cincinnati, OH 45206. Tel: 513-961-3410. Sr. Elizabeth Lang, O.S.U., Supr.

Total number in the community 26.

Legal Title: *Ursulines of Cincinnati.*

Ministry in the field of Academic Education at all levels; Adult Education; Pastoral Ministry; Catholic Social Services.

Represented in the Archdiocese of Cincinnati and the Diocese of Covington.

[4120-02] Kansas City in Kansas D

Ursuline Convent of Our Lady of Lourdes: 901 E. Miami St., Paola, KS 66071. Tel: 913-557-2349. Sr. Pat Lynch, O.S.U., Supr.

Total number in the community 36.

Legal Title: *Ursuline Sisters, Inc.; Ursuline Sisters Charitable Trust.*

Ministry in the field of Academic Education at all levels; Parish and Diocesan Services.

Represented in the Archdioceses of Chicago, Kansas City in Kansas and the Dioceses of Kansas City-St. Joseph and Sacramento.

[4120-03] Louisville P

Ursuline Motherhouse of the Immaculate Conception: 3115 Lexington Rd., Louisville, KY 40206. Tel: 502-893-0125; Fax: 502-896-3913. Sr. Sarah Stauble, O.S.U., Pres.; Sr. Amelia Dues, O.S.U., Community Archivist.

Total number in the community 206.

Legal Title: *Ursuline Society and Academy of Education aka Ursuline Sisters.*

Properties owned and sponsored: *Sacred Heart Academy; Sacred Heart Model School; Ursuline Montessori; Ursuline Child Development Center; Ursuline School of Music & Drama Marian Home,* Louisville, KY.

Ministry in the field of Academic Education; Child Care; Pastoral Ministry; Social Services; Health Care.

Represented in the Archdioceses of Baltimore, Cincinnati, Indianapolis, Louisville, Philadelphia, San Francisco and the Dioceses of Charleston, Cheyenne, Davenport, Evansville, Grand Island, Jackson, Lexington, Madison, Pittsburgh, St. Petersburg and Wheeling-Charleston.

[4120-04] Cleveland P

Ursuline Motherhouse and Educational Center: 2600 Lander Rd., Cleveland, OH 44124. Fax: 440-449-3588. Sr. Virginia DeVinne, O.S.U., Supr. Gen.; Sr. Joann Kessler, O.S.U., Community Archivist.

Total number in the community 253.

Legal Title: *The Ursuline Academy of Cleveland; The Ursuline Sisters of Cleveland.*

Properties sponsored: *Ursuline College; Beaumont High School; Ursuline Sophia Center.*

Ministry in the field of Academic Education at all levels; Parish Ministry; Diocesan Offices; Seminary; Social Service Agency; Hospital and Health Care Ministry; Spiritual Direction and Retreat Ministry; Foreign Mission.

Represented in the Archdioceses of Boston, Chicago, Indianapolis, New York, and the Dioceses of Buffalo, Cleveland, Columbus, Kansas City-St. Joseph, Lexington, Manchester, New Ulm, Richmond, Pittsburgh and Youngstown.

[4120-05] Owensboro P

Mt. St. Joseph Ursuline Motherhouse: Maple Mount, KY 42356. Tel: 270-229-4103; Fax: 270-229-4127. Sr. Rose Marita O'Bryan, O.S.U., Major Supr.

Total number in community 202.

Legal Holdings & Titles: *St. Joseph Female Ursuline Academic, Inc.; Brescia University,* Owensboro, KY; *Mount Saint Joseph Conference and Retreat Center,* Maple Mount, KY.

Ministry in Colleges; High Schools; Elementary Schools; Pastoral Ministries; Retreat Care; Pastoral Care; Social Services; Chancellor, Diocesan Offices.

Represented in the Archdioceses of Boston, Louisville, New York, St. Louis, Santa Fe, Washington and the Dioceses of Beaumont, Brownsville, Evansville, Gallup, Kansas City-St. Joseph, Lincoln, Memphis, Owensboro, Shreveport, Springfield (IL) and Springfield-Cape Girardeau. Also in Chile.

[4120-06] Toledo P

Ursuline Convent of the Sacred Heart Offices: 4045 Indian Rd., Toledo, OH 43606. Tel: 419-536-9587. Sr. Nancy Mathias, Gen. Supr.

Total number in the community 90; Associates 134.

Legal Title: *Ursuline Convent of the Sacred Heart.*

Properties owned or sponsored: *St. Ursula Academy,* Toledo, OH.

Ministry in the field of Administration; Religious and Academic Education; Health Care; Counseling Services; Diocesan Education Office; Pastoral Ministry; Pastoral Care; Retreat Work; Spiritual Direction; Education in Music; Home Health Care.

Represented in the Archdiocese of Washington and the Dioceses of Fresno and Toledo. Also in Lima, Peru.

[4120-07] Youngstown P

Motherhouse: *Ursuline Motherhouse and Educational Center,* 4250 Shields Rd., Canfield, OH 44406. Tel: 330-792-7636. Sr. Nancy Dawson, Gen. Supr.

Total number in the community 71.

Legal Title: *Ursuline Sisters of Youngstown.*

Properties owned: *Ursuline Motherhouse; Ursuline Center; Ursuline Preschool & Kindergarten; Beatitude House.*

Ministry in the field of Religious and Academic Education at all levels; Parish Ministry; Diocesan Offices; Social Services; Hospital Services; Single Parenting; AIDS Ministry; Preschool; Kindergarten; Nursing Home Administration; Nursing Home Service; Audiology; Speech Pathology; Music.

Represented in the Dioceses of Brownsville, Cleveland, and Youngstown.

[4130] (O.S.U.)—URSULINE SISTERS OF THE CONGREGATION OF TILDONK, BELGIUM P

International Congregation.

Founded in Italy in 1535 by St. Angela Merici (Ursulines). Congregation of Tildonk founded in Belgium in 1832. First foundation in the United States in Ozone Park, New York, in 1924.

Generalate: Brussels, Belgium. Sr. Judith O'Connor, O.S.U., Gen. Supr.

Ursuline Provincialate: 81-15 Utopia Pkwy., Jamaica, NY 11432. Tel: 718-591-0681. Sr. Catherine Talia, O.S.U., Prov. Supr.

Properties owned: *St. Ursula Center, (Convent & Retreat Center),* Blue Point, NY; *Ursuline Provincialate,* Jamaica, NY.

Total number in the province 64.

Ministry in the field of Education in all its aspects.

Represented in the Archdioceses of Hartford, New York and the Dioceses of Bridgeport, Brooklyn, Burlington, and Rockville Centre.

[4140] (O.S.U.)—URSULINE SISTERS OF BELLEVILLE D

Founded in Italy in 1535. First foundation in the United States in 1910. Newly established as Diocesan Community August 13, 1983.

Central House: 1026 N. Douglas Ave., Belleville, IL 62220-4198. Tel: 618-235-3444. Sr. Dorothy Helbling, O.S.U., Community Leader.

Total number in the community 15.

Ministry in the field of Religious and Academic Education; Retreat Work; Hospice; Pastoral Ministry.

Represented in the Dioceses of Belleville and Springfield (IL).

[4155] (M.T.G.)—ADORERS OF THE HOLY CROSS P

Founded in 1670 in Vietnam by Bishop Pierre Lambert de la Motte. First foundation in the U.S. 1976.

General Motherhouse: *Holy Cross Convent,* 7408 S.E. Adler, Portland, OR 97215. Tel: 503-254-3284. Sr. Agatha Thuy-Hang Tran, M.T.G., Supr.

Sisters 23; Novices 1; Candidates 10.

Represented in the Archdiocese of Portland, OR and the Diocese of Arlington.

[4160] (V.S.C.)—VINCENTIAN SISTERS OF CHARITY P

First foundation in the United States in 1902.

General Motherhouse and Novitiate: *St. Vincent Hill,* 8200 McKnight Rd., Pittsburgh, PA 15237. Tel: 412-364-3000; Fax: 412-364-9055. Sr. Charlene Reebel, Major Supr.

Professed sisters 166.

Properties owned or sponsored: *Vincentian Child Care Center; Vincentian High School; Vincentian Home, Inc.; Villa de Marillac Nursing Home; Regency Hall Nursing Home and Adult Day Care; St. Louise De Marillac Mission Convent,* Talara, Peru.

Ministry in the Field of Education at All Levels; Health Care in Nursing Homes; Child Care Center; Adult Day Care; Catechetical Centers; Social Apostolates; Pastoral Ministries.

Represented in the Archdiocese of Mobile and in Dioceses of Altoona-Johnstown, Greensburg, Pittsburgh, Springfield-Cape Girardeau, Steubenville, Venice, and Youngstown. Also in Canada, Peru.

[4170] (V.S.C.)—VINCENTIAN SISTERS OF CHARITY D

Founded in Bedford in 1928.

Motherhouse & Novitiate: *Villa San Bernardo,* 1160 Broadway, Bedford, OH 44146-4523. Tel: 440-232-4755; Fax: 440-232-7832. Sr. Christine Rody, Gen. Supr.; Sr. Dorothy Ann Blatnica, Dir. Formation; Sr. Margaret Mach, Vocation Contact Person.

Professed 67.

Ministry in the field of Education at Elementary & College levels; Pastoral Ministry and Counseling; Social Services; Nursing; Care of the Elderly; Marian Shrine and Poustinia; Hospice; Poor in Appalachia; Facility for Elderly - Independent and Assisted Living; Light of Hearts Villa (Assisted Living Facility).

Represented in the Archdiocese of Seattle, and the Dioceses of Cleveland, and Lexington.

[4180] (M.P.V.)—RELIGIOUS VENERINI SISTERS P

Founded in Italy in 1685. First foundation in the United States in 1909.

General Motherhouse: via Gioachino Belli 31, Rome, Italy. Rev. Mother Marcella Lorenzetti, Supr. Gen.

Universal total in Congregation 422.

Provincialhouse for the U.S.: 23 Edward St., Worcester, MA 01605. Sr. Hilda Ponte, Prov.

Total number in the community 32.

Legal Holdings: *Venerini Academy,* Worcester, MA.

Ministry in the field of Education; Health Care; Social Services; Parish and Diocesan Ministry; Foreign Missions.

Represented in the Dioceses of Albany, Fall River, St. Petersburg, and Worcester.

[4190] (V.H.M.)—VISITATION NUNS P

Founded in France in 1610. First foundation in the United States in Georgetown, Washington, DC in 1799.

First Federation of North America

Major pontifical enclosure. Mother Margaret Mary McGuire, Federation Pres., residing at the Monastery of Visitation, Rockville, Virginia

Listed in the Order of Foundation established.

Monastery of the Visitation (1833): 2300 Springhill Ave., Mobile, AL 36607-3202. Tel: 334-473-2321. Sr. Jane De Chantal Word, V.H.M., Supr.

Total number in the community 10.

Monastery of the Visitation: 14 Beach Rd.-P.O. Box 432m, Tyringham, MA 01264. Tel: 413-243-3995. Mother Mary Ruth Dolch, V.H.M., Supr.

Legal Title: *Visitation of Holy Mary.*

Total number in the community 18.

Monastery of the Visitation: 12221 Bienvenue Rd., Rockville, VA 23146. Tel: 804-749-4885. Mother Mary Paula Zemienieuski, V.H.M., Supr.

Legal Title: *Visitation of Holy Mary.*

Professed Sisters 17; Novices 1.

Monastery of the Visitation: 5820 City Ave., Philadelphia, PA 19131-1295. Tel: 215-473-5888. Mother Antoinette Marie Walker, V.H.M., Supr.

Legal Title: *Sisters of the Visitation of Philadelphia.*

Professed Sisters Cloistered 10; Postulants 1; Externs 1.

Monastery of the Visitation (Contemplative): 1745 Parkside Blvd., Toledo, OH 43607-1599. Tel: 419-536-1343. Mother Jane Frances Rohen, V.H.M., Supr.

Legal Title: *The Contemplative Order of the Visitation of Toledo, Ohio.*

Professed Sisters 15; In formation 4.

Monastery of the Visitation (Strictly Cloistered): 2055 Ridgedale Dr., Snellville, GA 30078. Tel: 770-972-1060. Mother Mary Jozefa Kowalewski, V.H.M., Supr.

Legal Title: *Order of the Visitation.*

Professed Sisters 13; Novices 1.

Second Federation of North America

Monastery of the Visitation of Georgetown: 1500 35th St., N.W., Washington, DC 20007. Tel: 202-337-0305; Fax: 202-965-3845. Mother Mary de Sales McNabb, Supr.; Sr. Mada-anne Gell, Community Archivist.

Legal Titles & Holdings: *Sisters of the Visitation of Georgetown; Georgetown Visitation Preparatory School.*

Total number in the school community 459; Total number in religious community 20.

Monastery of the Visitation (1833): 3020 N. Ballas Rd., St. Louis, MO 63131. Tel: 314-432-5353. Sr. Mary Veronica Haronik, Supr.

Total number in the community 24.

Ministry in Education.

Legal Holdings: *Visitation Academy of St. Louis County; Monastery of the Visitation,* St. Louis, MO.

Monastery of the Visitation (1846): 200 E. Second St., Frederick, MD 21701. Tel: 301-622-3322. Mother Marguerite Therese Leary, V.H.M., Supr.

Total number in the community 6.

Legal Holdings or Titles: *Monastery of the Visitation - Frederick, Maryland; Frederick Academy of the Visitation Cloistered Contemplative Order with Elementary School as Apostolate.*

Sisters of the Visitation of Holy Mary of Mount de Chantal, Inc. (1848): Wheeling, WV 26003. Tel: 304-232-1283. Sr. Mary Grace Flynn, V.H.M., Supr.

Total number in the community 23.

Legal Holdings or Titles: *Sisters of the Visitation of Holy Mary of Mount de Chantal, Inc.; Mount de Chantal Visitation Academy, Inc.*

Ministry in the field of Education.

Monastery of the Visitation (1855): 8902 Ridge Blvd., Brooklyn, NY 11209-5716. Tel: 718-745-5151; Fax: 718-745-3680. Mother Marie de ChantalMannino, V.H.M., Supr.

Professed Sisters 18.

Villa de Chantal Monastery of the Visitation Mailing Address: 2936 36th St., Rock Island, IL 61201. Sr. Mary Veronica Haronik, V.H.M., Pres.

Monastery located at 2000 16th Ave., Rock Island, IL 61201. Tel: 314-432-5353.

Legal Title: *Sisters of the Visitation.*

Ministry in Spiritual and Educational Center.

Monastery of the Visitation: 2455 Visitation Dr., Mendota Heights, MN 55120. Tel: 651-683-1700. Sr. Marie Therese Conaty, V.H.M., Supr.

Total number in the community 18.

Ministry in Prayer and Education.

[4200] (S.V.M.)—SISTERS OF THE VISITATION OF THE CONGREGATION OF THE IMMACULATE HEART OF MARY D

Founded in France in 1610. First foundation in the United States in 1799.

Visitation Convent: 2950 Kaufmann Ave., Dubuque, IA 52001-1631. Tel: 319-556-2440. Sr. Bernadine Curoe, Pres.

Total number in community 7.

Ministry in Elementary & Higher Education; Adult Education; Parish Ministry.

Represented in the Archdiocese of Dubuque and the Dioceses of Fort Wayne-South Bend and Oakland.

[4210] (S.D.V.)—VOCATIONIST SISTERS P (Sisters of the Divine Vocations)

Founded in Italy in 1921. First established in the United States in 1967.

General Motherhouse: *Corso Duca D'Aosta,* 22 Pianura, 80126, Naples, Italy. Sr. Giannina Di Francia, S.D.V., Mother Supr. Gen.

U.S. Foundation: *Perpetual Help Day Nursery,* 172 Broad St., Newark, NJ 07104. Tel: 973-484-3535. Sr. Romilda Borges, S.D.V., Supr.

Total number in community 6.

Ministry in Nursery Schools & Kindergartens; CCD Program and Parish Services.

Represented in the Archdiocese of Newark.

Sister Joanna Formation House: 88 Brooklake Rd., Florham Park, NJ 07932. Tel: 201-966-9762. Sr. Anna Maria Mancino, Delegate & Supr.

Total number in community 10.

Ministry in Nursery School; Formation House.

Represented in the Diocese of Paterson.

[4230] (X.M.M.)—XAVERIAN MISSIONARY SOCIETY OF MARY, INC. P

Founded in Italy in 1945. First established in the United States in 1954.

General Motherhouse: *Missionarie Saveriane Di Maria,* Via Omero 4, Parma, Italy. Sr. Giuseppina Caccia, X.M.M., Supr. Gen.

Total Membership 250.

U.S. Headquarters: *Xaverian Missionary Society of Mary,* 242 Salisbury St., Worcester, MA 01609. Tel: 508-757-0514. Sr. Stefanina Loi, X.M.M., Gen. Delegate.

Ministry to Hispanics; Elderly; Families; CCD Programs and Mission Education.

Represented in the Archdiocese of New York and the Diocese of Worcester.

COLLEGES AND UNIVERSITIES

ALABAMA

Mobile
Archdiocese of Mobile

Spring Hill College (1830)
4000 Dauphin St.
Mobile, AL 36608
Tel: 334-380-4000; Fax: 334-460-2195
Web Site: www.shc.edu
Revs.:
GREGORY LUCEY, S.J., Pres.
DONALD A. HAWKINS, S.J., Rector of Jesuit Community
FREDERICK W. GUNTI (LR)
J. WILLIAM HARMLESS, S.J.
WALTER L. FURMAN, S.J.
DAVID BORBRIDGE, S.J.
STEVEN J. SAUER, S.J.
GERALD T. REGAN, S.J (Wisconsin)
ROBERT B. RIMES, S.J.
JESUS RODRIGUEZ, S.J.
MICHAEL A. WILLIAMS, S.J (Maryland)
STEPHEN CAMPBELL, S.J.
CHRISTOPHER J. VISCARDI, S.J.
Bro. FERRELL BLANK
Priests of Faculty 9
Brothers 1
Lay Teachers 56
Students 1003

CALIFORNIA

Belmont
Archdiocese of San Francisco

College of Notre Dame
1500 Ralston Ave.
Belmont, CA 94002
Tel: 650-593-1601; Fax: 650-508-3736
E-mail: gwhite@cnd.edu
Web Site: www.cnd.edu
Sisters of Notre Dame de Namur
Dr. JOHN B. OBLAK, Pres.
LUCILLE H. SANSING, Ph.D., Vice Pres., Academic Affairs
ROBERT MALLON, Dir. Campus Ministry
Priests 1
Sisters 4
Lay Faculty 62
Students 1,670

Fremont
Diocese of Oakland

Queen of the Holy Rosary College
Mailing Address:
P.O. Box 3908
Mission San Jose, CA 94539
Tel: 510-657-2468; Fax: 510-657-1734
Web Site: www.msjdominicans.org/college/html
Legal Title: *Queen of the Holy Rosary College*
Dominican Sisters of Mission San Jose
Sr. ROSE MARIE HENNESSY, O.P., Pres.
Sr. MARY PAUL MEHEGAN, O.P., Dean
Priests 1
Sisters 15
Lay Teachers 3
Total Enrollment 199

Los Angeles
Archdiocese of Los Angeles

Loyola Marymount University
7900 Loyola Blvd.
Los Angeles, CA 90045-2699
Tel: 310-338-2700
Web Site: www.lmu.edu
Sponsored by the Society of Jesus (Jesuit Fathers), Religious of Sacred Heart of Mary, Sisters of St. Joseph of Orange
Revs.:
ROBERT B. LAWTON, S.J., Pres.
DONALD P. MERRIFIELD, S.J., Chancellor
PATRICK J. CAHALAN, S.J., Assoc. Chancellor
Dr. JOSEPH G. JABBRA, Academic Vice Pres.
Mr. JOHN R. OESTER, Vice Pres. Business and Finance
Mr. CHARLES RASBERRY, Acting Vice Pres. University Relations
Dr. LANE BOVE, Vice Pres. Student Affairs
Rev. RICHARD A. ROBIN, S.J., Asst. to the Pres.
Mr. DAVID G. TRUMP, Vice Pres. Facilities Mgmt.
Mr. DAVID W. BURCHAM, Dean, Law School
Ms. ROSENIA ST. ONGE, Registrar
Dr. JOSEPH A. MERANTE, Assoc. Vice Pres. Academic Affairs
Mr. MATTHEW FISSINGER, Dir. Admissions
Ms. DONNA PALMER, Dir. Financial Aid
Mr. FRANK MONTALVO, Dir. Human Resources
Mr. FERNANDO D. MORENO, Dir. Campus Ministry
Dr. JOHN T. WHOLIHAN, Dean of Business Admin.
Dr. GERALD S. JAKUBOWSKI, Dean of Science and Engrg.
THOMAS KELLY, Dean of Communication & Fine Arts
Dr. KENYON CHAN, Dean, Liberal Arts
Jesuit Community
P.O. Box 45041
Los Angeles, CA 90045-8427
Tel: 310-338-7445
Very Rev. PAUL BERNADICOU, S.J., Rector
Rev. TERRANCE L. MAHAN, S.J., Min.
In res.,
Revs.:
CLINTON E. ALBERTSON, S.J.
JAMES ARENZ, S.J.
JOSE IGNACIO BADENES, S.J.
JOHN L. BOYLE, S.J.
Bro. MICHAEL E. BREAULT, S.J.
Revs.:
CURTIS BRYANT, S.J.
ROBERT I. BURNS, S.J.
PATRICK J. CAHAHAN, S.J.
WILLIAM F. CAIN, S.J.
ROBERT V. CARO, S.J.
JOHN COLEMAN, S.J.
JOHN P. DALY, S.J.
TRI M. DINH, S.J.
MICHAEL E. ENGH, S.J.
Bro. WILLIAM C. FARRINGTON, S.J.
Revs.:
D. THEODORE FISHER, S.J.
WILLIAM J. FULCO, S.J.
THOMAS P. HIGGINS, S.J.
FLOYD A. JENKINS, S.J.
FELIX JUST, S.J.
JAMES H. KEENE, S.J.
JOHN F. KILLEEN, S.J.
JOSEPH LABRIE, S.J.
ROBERT B. LAWTON, S.J.
ROBERT W. MCCHESNEY, S.J.
JOHN MCMANAMON, S.J.
TERRANCE L. MAHAN, S.J.
DONALD P. MERRIFIELD, S.J.
WAYNE NEGRETE, S.J.
THOMAS POWERS, S.J.
LUIS PROENCA, S.J.
THOMAS P. RAUSCH, S.J.
RICHARD A. ROBIN, S.J.
RICHARD W. ROLFS, S.J.
HERBERT J. RYAN, S.J.
EDWARD J. SIEBERT, S.J.
ERNEST S. SWEENEY, S.J.
ROBERT H. TAYLOR, S.J.
Bros.:
RAYMOND W. UPTON, S.J.
JAMES SANDERS
Revs.:
RICHARD P. VAUGHAN, S.J.
CLARENCE J. WALLEN, S.J.
HANFORD E. WECKBACH, S.J.
ROBERT J. WELCH, S.J.
JAMES FREDERICKS
ALBERT P. KOPPES, O.Carm.
ROBERT W. SCHOLLA, S.J.
THOMAS P. SHERMAN, S.J.
Bros.:
JOHN GREVER, C.F.M.M.
ANTHONY SMULDERS, C.F.M.M.
Priests 46
Brothers 6
Sisters 10
Lay Teachers 290
Total Staff 708
Students 5,332
The Sacred Heart of Mary and Sisters of St. Joseph of Orange
7900 Loyola Blvd.
Los Angeles, CA 90045
Tel: 310-338-2700; 641-4682
Legal Title: *Communities of the Religious of the Sacred Heart of Mary and Sisters of St. Joseph of Orange*
Loyola School of Law
919 S. Albany St., P.O. Box 15019
Los Angeles, CA 90015
Tel: 213-736-1000
Students 1,027
DAVID W. BURCHAM, Dean

Mount St. Mary's College
Tel: 310-954-4010; Fax: 310-954-4019
E-mail: jpdoud@msmc.la.edu
Web Site: www.msmc.la.edu
Chalon Campus
12001 Chalon Rd.
Los Angeles, CA 90049-1599
Tel: 310-954-4000; Fax: 310-954-4019
Web Site: www.msmc.la.edu
Doheny Campus
10 Chester Pl.
Los Angeles, CA 90007
Tel: 213-477-2500; Fax: 213-477-2519
Conducted by the Sisters of St. Joseph of Carondelet
Resident and non-resident students.
Dr. JACQUELINE POWERS DOUD, Pres.
Dr. JANE LINGUA, Vice Pres. for Student Affairs
Mr. LARRY SMITH, Assoc. Provost for Info. Support Services
Sr. MARY WILLIAMS, Provost
Mr. NEIL YONEJI, Interim Vice Pres. for Admin. & Finance
Dr. KAREN JENSEN, Asst. Vice Pres. Hope & Graduate Programs
Mr. JOSEPH ZARETTA, Vice Pres. for Institutional Advancement
Ms. KATY MURPHY, Asst. Provost for Enrollment
Sr. JANET DUFFY, Dean of Traditional AA Prog.
Sisters 6
Priests 2
Lay Teachers 69
Students 1,398

Moraga
Diocese of Oakland

St. Mary's College
Moraga, CA 94575
Tel: 510-631-4000; Fax: 925-376-1847
Web Site: www.stmarys-ca.edu
Legal Title: *Saint Mary's College of California*
Brothers of the Christian Schools
Coed. Resident and Non-Resident Students.
Bros.:
CRAIG J. FRANZ, F.S.C., Pres.
JACK CURRAN, F.S.C., Vice Pres., Student Affairs
MICHAEL MEISTER, F.S.C., Asst. Academic Vice Pres.
Saint Mary's College Community:
Bros.:
DOMINIC BERADELLI, F.S.C., Dir.
MARTIN FALLIN, F.S.C., Sub-Dir.
Alemany Community:
Bro. CHARLES HILKEN, F.S.C., Dir.
Campus Ministers:
Sr. INGRID CLEMMENSEN, O.P., Dir. Campus Ministry
Faculty:
Rev. OWEN CARROLL (Canada)
Rev. Msgr. EDGAR P. MCCARREN (RVC)
Revs.:
JOHN MORRIS, O.P.
MICHAEL A. RUSSO (NEW)
Bros.:
MICHAEL S. AVILA, F.S.C.
WILLIAM BEATIE, F.S.C.
KENNETH W. CARDWELL, F.S.C., (On Leave)
CAMILLUS CHAVEZ, F.S.C.
CRAIG J. FRANZ, F.S.C.
RONALD GALLAGHER, F.S.C., (On Leave)
THEOPHANE NGUYEN VAN KE, F.S.C., (Retired)
JAMES J. LEAHY, F.S.C., (On Leave)
BRENDEN MADDEN, F.S.C.
MICHAEL F. MEISTER, F.S.C.
JOHN O'NEILL, F.S.C.
RAPHAEL PATTON, F.S.C.
O. DESALES PEREZ, F.S.C.
T. JEROME WEST, F.S.C., (Retired)
MARTIN YRIBARREN
Sr. CLARE WAGSTAFFE
Sr. CAROLYN KROHN, R.S.M.
Priests 4
Sisters 2
Brothers 12
Professors 456
Total Enrollment 4,060

Oakland
Diocese of Oakland

Holy Names College (1868)
3500 Mountain Blvd.
Oakland, CA 94619
Tel: 510-436-1000; Fax: 510-436-1199
Web Site: www.hnc.edu
Chartered 1880. Resident and Non-Resident Students.
Sisters of the Holy Names of Jesus and Mary
Legal Title: *Sisters of the Holy Names of Jesus and Mary, A Corporation*
Legal Title: *Holy Names College, A Corporation*
Administration:
Sr. ROSEMARIE NASSIF, S.S.N.D., Pres.

DAVID J. FIKE, Vice Pres. for Academic Affairs
Sr. CAROL SELLMAN, S.N.J.M., Vice Pres. for Mission Effectiveness
JOHN MCCREADY, Vice Pres. Finance & Administration
JOANN BERRIDGE, Dean Undergraduate Admissions & Financial Aid
DANITA NELMS, Dir. Adult & Graduate Programs
BITTA FARAHMAND, Dir., Residence Life
CLAIRE OLIVARES, Dir., Development
JEANETTE HONSTEIN TOBLER, Registrar
JOYCE MCLEAN, Dir., Library Services
ERIK STILLING, Dir of Continuing Education
Sr. SHARON CASEY, O.P., Dir., Campus Ministry
Sr. ELIZABETH ADAMS, S.N.J.M.
Sr. MARY ANDERSON, S.N.J.M.
Sr. MARGARET CAMPBELL, S.N.J.M.
Sr. DEBORAH CHURCH, S.N.J.M.
Rev. JAMES CONLON
Sr. MARCIA FRIDEGER, S.N.J.M.
Sr. MAUREEN HESTER, S.N.J.M.
Sr. DONNA MAYNARD, S.N.J.M.
Rev. HENRY ORMOND, O.Carm.
Sr. JOANNE QUINLIVAN, S.N.J.M.
Sr. DELORES RASHFORD, S.N.J.M.
Sr. NANCY TESKEY, S.N.J.M.
Sr. CHRISTINE PATRINOS, S.N.J.M.
Sr. IRENE WOODWARD, C.F.C.
Religious Staff:
Sr. SYLVIA BARTHELD, S.N.J.M.
Sr. ETHEL MARY TINNEMANN, S.N.J.M.
Sr. FRANCESCA CABRINI WEBER, S.N.J.M.
Sr. MARY CHRISTINE FLEITZ, S.N.J.M.
Sr. JUNE KEARNEY, S.N.J.M.
Priests 2
Sisters 18
Lay Professors 37
Students 947

Orange
Diocese of Orange in California

St. Joseph College, Orange
480 S. Batavia St.
Orange, CA 92868
Tel: 714-633-8121; Fax: 714-744-3165
Branch Campus of University of San Francisco; St. Joseph College Library.

Rancho Palos Verdes
Archdiocese of Los Angeles

Marymount College, Palos Verdes, California
30800 Palos Verdes Dr., E.
Rancho Palos Verdes, CA 90275-6299
Tel: 310-377-5501; Fax: 310-265-0642
E-mail: shart@marymountpv.edu
Web Site: www.marymountpv.edu
An Independent and Catholic Co-Educational Two-Year Liberal Arts College; Resident and Non-Resident.
Dr. THOMAS M. MCFADDEN, Pres.
Dr. ROBERT MATTHES, Dean of Academic Affairs
Mr. JAMES REEVES, Vice Pres. of College Opererations & Student Svcs.
Rev. Msgr. ANTHONY LEUER
Priests 1
Sisters 1
Lay Teachers 78
Students 739

Rosemead
Archdiocese of Los Angeles

Don Bosco Technical Institute
(Junior College)
1151 San Gabriel Blvd.
Rosemead, CA 91770-4299
Tel: 626-307-6500; Fax: 626-280-9316
E-mail: malvarez@netdbti.boscotech.tec.ca.us
Web Site: www.boscotech.tec.ca.us
Two-year college program leading to Associate in Science degree in eight technical areas. (Staffed by Salesians of St. John Bosco).
Revs.:
CARMINE VAIRO, S.D.B., Pres.
MICHAEL GERGEN, S.D.B., Admin. Vice Pres.
PETER BUI, S.D.B.
ZBIGNIEW BARAN, S.D.B.
Bros.:
PATRICK BARBARIOL, S.D.B.
JOHN RASOR, S.D.B.
GENE MYLAN, S.D.B.
Priests 4
Brothers 3
Lay Teachers 39
Students 148

Don Bosco High School
Tel: 626-940-2000; Fax: 626-940-2001
Mr. MICHAEL ALVAREZ, Prin.
Priests 4
Brothers 6
Sisters 1
Lay Teachers 73
Students 1,122

San Diego
Diocese of San Diego

Austin House
1605 28th St.
San Diego, CA 92102-1417
Tel: 619-233-9141
E-mail: osa-west@k-online.com
Very Rev. STEVEN M. OCHOA, O.S.A., Prior Prov., Tel: 619-235-0247; Fax: 619-231-2814
Revs.:
WALTER P. VOGEL, O.S.A., Prior
JEROME BEVILACQUA, O.S.A.
Deacon RICHARD HARDICK, O.S.A.

University of San Diego
5998 Alcala Park
San Diego, CA 92110-2492
Tel: 619-260-4600
Dr. ALICE BOURKE HAYES, Pres.
Dr. FRANCIS M. LAZARUS, Vice Pres. & Provost
Rev. Msgr. DANIEL DILLABOUGH, Vice Pres. Missions & Ministry
Mr. PAUL BISSONNETTE, Vice Pres. Finance & Admin.
Mr. THOMAS BURKE, Vice Pres. Student Affairs
Mr. JOHN MCNAMARA, Vice Pres University Rels.
Dr. PATRICK DRINAN, Dean, College of Arts & Sciences
Dr. CURTIS COOK, Dean, School of Business Administration
Dr. PAULA CORDEIRO, Dean, School of Education
Dr. DANIEL RODRIGUEZ, Dean, School of Law
Dr. JANET RODGERS, Dean, Hahn School of Nursing & Health Science
University Ministers:
Rev. JOHN D. KELLER, O.S.A., Dir. of Univ. Ministry
VICTOR CRUZ, Asst.
Sr. IRENE CULLEN, R.S.C.J., Assoc.
AMY GUALTIERI, Sacristan
MARY KRUER, Assoc.
MARY LORINGER, Asst.
JUDY MCDONALD, Asst.
MIKE MCINTYRE, Assoc.
CARA MCMAHON, Assoc.
CHRIS NICHOLS, Asst.
Revs.:
J. J. O'LEARY, S.J., Asst. to Vice Pres.
JOSE PIMENTAL, O.P., Assoc.
Sr. VIRGINIA RODEE, R.S.C.J., Asst. to Vice Pres.
Bro. TOM THING, O.F.M., Assoc.
ANNETTE WALSH, Assoc.
Rev. MICHAEL WHITE, C.S.Sp., Chap.
Faculty:
Revs.:
STEPHEN DUNN
DENNIS KROUSE
JAMES MCGRAY
NORBERT RIGALI, S.J.
Rev. Msgr. WILLIAM SHIPLEY
Rev. MATTHEW SPAHR
Priests 14
Sisters 11
Brothers 1
Lay Faculty 614
Students 6,806
Graduate Division:
Students 1,118
Msgr. John Portman Chair of Roman Catholic Systematic Theology
Most Rev. JOHN QUINN
Center for the Study of Latino/Latina Catholicism
Rev. ORLANDO ESPIN, Dir.
Institute for Christian Ministries
Dr. M. JANE GORMAN, Dir.
Practical Theology Program
Rev. RON PACHENCE (SAV) Dir.
Pastoral Care and Counseling Program
Rev. RON PACHENCE (SAV)
Values Institute
Dr. LARRY HINMAN
School of Law:
DANIEL RODRIGUEZ, Dean
Lay Teachers 59
Students 1,117
University:
Priests 14
Sisters 11
Brothers 1
Lay Teachers 573
Total Staff 614
Students 6,806

San Francisco
Archdiocese of San Francisco

**University of San Francisco*
2130 Fulton St.
San Francisco, CA 94117-1080
Tel: 415-422-5555; Fax: 415-422-2303
Jesuit Fathers
Established 1855; Chartered by State, 1859.
Revs.:
JOHN P. SCHLEGEL, S.J., Pres.
JOHN J. LOSCHIAVO, S.J., Chancellor
CHARLES W. DULLEA, S.J., Chancellor Emeritus
JOHN W. CLARK, S.J., Provost & Vice Pres. Academic Affairs
ROBERT F. CURRAN, S.J., Vice Pres. for Legal Affairs
PHILIP P. CALLAGHAN, S.J., Sec. of the Univ.
Dr. CARMEN A. JORDAN-COX, Vice Pres. Student Affairs
Mr. WILLARD H. NUTTING, Vice Pres. Business & Finance
Mr. ALFRED P. ALESSANDRI, Vice Pres. Univ. Rels.
Mr. DAVID F. MACMILLAN, Vice Pres. Devel.
MAUREEN L. PRYOR, Dir. of Campus Ministry
The following are the Schools and Colleges that compose the University:
College of Arts and Sciences—
Dr. STANLEY D. NEL, Dean
School of Business and Management—
Dr. GARY G. WILLIAMS, Dean
School of Nursing—
Dr. JOHN M. LANTZ, Dean
School of Education—
Dr. PAUL B. WARREN, Dean
School of Law—
JEFFREY S. BRAND, Dean
College of Professional Studies—
Dr. LAWRENCE G. BREWSTER, Dean
Priests 11
Sisters 3
Lay Faculty 300
Students 7,948

San Rafael
Archdiocese of San Francisco

Dominican University of California
50 Acacia Ave.
San Rafael, CA 94901-2298
Tel: 415-457-4440; Fax: 415-485-3205
E-mail: enroll@dominican.edu
Web Site: www.dominican.edu
An Independent and Catholic Coeducational International Teaching University.
Dr. JOSEPH R. FINK, Pres.
Dr. DENISE LUCY, Vice Pres. for Academic Affairs
Resident and non-resident students.
Sisters 5
Lay Teachers 195
Students 1,480

Santa Clara
Diocese of San Jose in California

Santa Clara University
500 El Camino Real
Santa Clara, CA 95053-0001
Tel: 408-554-4000; Fax: 408-554-2700
E-mail: username@scu.edu
Web Site: www.scu.edu
Mission Santa Clara. Founded in 1777. University established in 1851 and chartered by the State in 1855.
Society of Jesus
Administrators:
Rev. PAUL L. LOCATELLI, S.J., Pres.
Ms. DENISE CARMODY, Interim Provost
Mr. ROBERT WARREN, Vice Pres. Finance Admin.
Mr. JAMES M. PURCELL, V.P. Univ. Relations
Dr. PETER A. FACIONE, Dean, College of Arts and Sciences
Dr. BARRY POSNER, Dean, Leavey School of Business Administration
Dr. TERRY E. SHOUP, Dean, School of Engrg.
Dr. MACK A. PLAYER, Dean, School of Law
Rev. MARIO J. PRIETTO, S.J., Dir. Campus Ministry
Priest Teachers 31
Brothers 1
Sisters 3
Scholastics 1
Lay Teachers 379
Students 7,668
Jesuit Community
500 El Camino Real
Santa Clara, CA 95053-1600
Tel: 408-554-4124; Fax: 408-554-4795
Legal Title: *Jesuit Community at Santa Clara University, Inc.*

Revs.:
DENNIS R. PARNELL, S.J., Rector
PETER F. FILICE, S.J., Min. & Contact
EDWARD T. BURKE, S.J.
LUIS F. CALERO, S.J.
MARTIN J. CALKINS, S.J.
PAUL G. CROWLEY, S.J.
WILLIAM F. DONNELLY, S.J.
JAMES W. FELT, S.J.
PAUL J. FITZGERALD, S.J.
PAUL J. GODA, S.J.
JOHN HUGH GRAY, S.J., In Res.
CARL H. HAYN, S.J.
ARTHUR F. LIEBSCHER, S.J.
PAUL L. LOCATELLI, S.J.
GERALD L. MCKEVITT, S.J.
GERDENIO M. MANUEL, S.J.
NORMAN F. MARTIN, S.J.
CHARLES T. PHIPPS, S.J.
MARIO J. PRIETTO, S.J.
MARK A. RAVIZZA, S.J.
THEODORE J. RYNES, S.J.
THOMAS E. SHANKS, S.J.
GREGORY C. SHARKEY, S.J.
FRANCIS R. SMITH, S.J.
DENNIS C. SMOLARSKI, S.J.
PAUL A. SOUKUP, S.J.
ROBERT L. ST. CLAIR, S.J.
GERALD P. SULLIVAN, S.J.
SALVATORE A. TASSONE, S.J.
FREDERICK P. TOLLINI, S.J.
EDWARD V. WARREN, S.J.
MICHAEL F. WEILER, S.J.
TENNANT C. WRIGHT, S.J.
MICHAEL A. ZAMPELLI, S.J.
Bro. THOMAS C. BRACCO, S.J.
Mr. JOSEPH A. THOMAS, S.J., Scholastic
Mr. ANH Q TRAN, S.J., Scholastic
Priests 37
Brothers 1
Scholastics 1

Santa Paula
Archdiocese of Los Angeles

Thomas Aquinas College
10000 N. Ojai Rd.
Santa Paula, CA 93060
Tel: 805-525-4417; Fax: 805-525-0620
E-mail: admissions@thomasaquinas.edu
Web Site: www.thomasaquinas.edu
Four-year undergraduate program in the Liberal Arts leading to the B.A. Degree; Coeducational.
Dr. THOMAS E. DILLON, Pres.
Dr. R. GLEN COUGHLIN, Dean
Mr. PETER L. DELUCA, III, Vice Pres. Finance and Admin.
Mr. DANIEL J. GRIMM, Vice Pres. Devel.
Chaplains:
Revs.:
BARTHOLOMEW DE LA TORRE, O.P.
MICHAEL U. PEREA, O.Praem.
WILFRED F. BORDEN, O.M.I.
Lay Teachers 27
Students 277

COLORADO

Denver
Archdiocese of Denver

Regis University
3333 Regis Blvd.
Denver, CO 80221-1099
Tel: 303-458-4100; Fax: 303-458-4921
Web Site: www.regis.edu
A university conducted under the auspices of the Society of Jesus.
Mr. WILLIAM J. FORTUNE, Chm. Board of Trustees
Revs.:
MICHAEL J. SHEERAN, S.J., Pres.
DAVID M. CLARKE, S.J., Chancellor
Dr. ALLAN L. SERVICE, Vice Pres. Academic Affairs
Dr. JAMES R. SCHOEMER, Vice Pres. Admin.
Dr. THOMAS E. REYNOLDS, Vice Pres. Student Life
Mr. JOHN A. ALEXANDER, Vice Pres. Devel. & Public Affairs
Dr. STEPHEN DOTY, Dean, Regis College
Dr. WILLIAM J. HUSSON, Dean, School for Professional Studies
Dr. PATRICIA A. LADEWIG, Dean, School for Health Care Professions
Mr. ANDREW D. SCRIMGEOUR, Dean Libraries
Ms. KATHLEEN M. SCHAEFER, Dir. Campus Ministry
Priests 16
Sisters 3
Lay Teachers 500
Students 11,240

CONNECTICUT

Bridgeport
Diocese of Bridgeport

St. Vincent's College
2800 Main St.
Bridgeport, CT 06606
Tel: 203-576-5235; Fax: 203-576-5893
E-mail: jnolanfaye@aol.com
Web Site: www.stvincentscollege.edu
ANNE T. AVALLONE, Ed.D., Pres.
BARBARA B. DAVIS, Ed.D., Dean/Provost
ROBERT S. TROJANOWSKI, M.B.A., J.D., CFO
JANICE NOLAN FAYE, Dir. Admin. Svcs.
JO ANN LOFTUS, B.S., Registrar
ANITA K. MCCAIN, Ed.D., Assoc. Dean of Academic Svcs.
MARY L. RICH, Fin. Aid Officer
JOAN MCTAGGART KAYSER, B.A., Dir. of Admissions & Marketing
Students 275

Fairfield
Diocese of Bridgeport

**Fairfield University*
(Coed)
1073 N. Benson Rd.
Fairfield, CT 06430-5195
Tel: 203-254-4000; Fax: 203-254-4101
Web Site: www.fairfield.edu
The Society of Jesus. College of Arts and Sciences; School of Business; School of Continuing Education; School of Nursing; School of Engineering; Graduate School of Education & Allied Professions; Graduate Program in Financial Management; Graduate Program in Nursing; Masters in Business Administration; Graduate Programs in Engineering and Masters in American Studies.
Revs.:
ALOYSIUS P. KELLEY, S.J., Pres.
JOHN HIGGINS, S.J., Rector
CHARLES H. ALLEN, S.J., Exec. Asst. to Pres.
Mr. L. WILLIAM MILES, Vice Pres. Admin.
Dr. ORIN L. GROSSMAN, Academic Vice Pres.
Mr. ROBERT C. RUSSO, University Registrar
Mr. STEPHEN P. JAKAB, Assoc. Vice Pres. Admin.
Rev. W. LAURENCE O'NEIL, S.J., Dir. Student Support Svcs.
Dr. WALTER RYBA, Dean School of Business
Dr. ANN MANTON, Dean School of Nursing
Dr. BEVERLY KAHN, Dean of Arts & Sciences
Dr. EVANGELOS HADJIMICHAEL, Dean, School of Engrg.
Dr. EDNA WILSON, Acting Dean of Continuing Education
Dr. MARGARET DEIGNAN, Dean of Graduate School of Education & Allied Professions
Dr. DEBNAM CHAPPELL, Acting Dean of Freshmen
Ms. MARY SPIEGEL, Dir. Admissions
Mrs. SUSAN KADIR, Dir. of Financial Aid
Mr. JAMES ESTRADA, Vice Pres. for Information Resources and Svcs. & Univ. Librarian
Mr. WILLIAM P. SCHIMPF, Vice Pres. Student Svcs.
Dr. GWENDOLYN M. VENDLEY, Dean of Students Asst. Vice Pres. Student Svcs.
Mr. JAMES D. FITZPATRICK, Asst. Vice Pres. for Students Svcs. Operations
Dr. SUSAN BIRGE, Dir. Counseling Svcs.
Mr. MATTHEW DINAN, Assoc. Dean of Students & Dir. University Activities
Rev. PAUL E. CARRIER, S.J., University Chap.
Ms. KATE CARTER, Asst. University Chap.
Revs.:
GREGG H. GROVENBURG, S.J., Asst. Chap.
RICHARD A. DESHAIES, S.J., Asst. Chap.
Mr. GEORGE E. DIFFLEY, Vice Pres. Advancement
Mr. DOUGLAS WHITING, Assoc. Vice Pres. for Public Rels.
Ms. JANET CANEPA, Dir. Alumni Rels.
Mr. FREDRIC WHEELER, Assoc. Vice Pres. Devel.
Mr. WILLIAM J. LUCAS, Vice Pres. Finance
Mr. MICHAEL S. MACCARONE, Controller
Revs.:
MARK J. CONNELLY, S.J.
FRANCIS T. HANNAFEY
JOHN W. ELDER, S.J.
FRANCIS W. LEWIS, S.J.
JOSEPH F. MACDONNELL, S.J.
JAMES J. MAYZIK, S.J.
THOMAS J. REGAN, S.J.
Jesuits 14
Sisters 1
Lay Teachers 198
Students 5,127
(See separate listing for Fairfield College Prep).

**Sacred Heart University*
5151 Park Ave.
Fairfield, CT 06432-1000
Tel: 203-371-7999; Fax: 203-365-7652
E-mail: QUINNM@sacredheart.edu
Web Site: sacredheart.edu
Coeducational and Comprehensive University. Courses offered year round, day & evening.
Dr. ANTHONY J. CERNERA, Pres.
Dr. THOMAS FORGET, Provost & Vice Pres. for Academic Affairs
Dr. DONNA DODGE, S.C., Vice Pres. Mission & Planning
Mr. JAMES M. BARQUINERO, Vice Pres. Enrollment, Planning & Student Affairs
Dr. PAUL K. MADONNA, Vice Pres. Admin. & Finance
Mr. LUKE DOYLE, Vice Pres. Institutional Advancement
Priests 3
Sisters 3
Lay Teachers 408
Students 5,637

Hamden
Archdiocese of Hartford

Mt. Sacred Heart College
265 Benham St.
Hamden, CT 06514-2801
Tel: 203-248-4225; Fax: 203-230-8341
E-mail: srpasej@aol.com
Chartered by the State of Connecticut for Sisters of Community of Apostles of the Sacred Heart of Jesus.
Sr. DEBORAH LOPEZ, A.S.C.J., Pres. & Dean

New Haven
Archdiocese of Hartford

Albertus Magnus College
700 Prospect St.
New Haven, CT 06511-1189
Tel: 203-773-8550; Fax: 203-785-8652
E-mail: admissions@albertus.edu
Web Site: www.albertus.edu
Dominican Sisters (St. Mary of the Springs, Columbus, OH)
Dr. JULIA M. MCNAMARA, Pres.
Sr. CHARLES MARIE BRANTL, O.P., Vice Pres.
JEANNE MANN, Treas.
EILEEN PERILLO, Registrar
MAUREEN MORRISON, Dean Student Svcs.
Sisters 2
Lay Teachers 27
Total Enrollment 2,065

West Hartford
Archdiocese of Hartford

Saint Joseph College
1678 Asylum Ave.
West Hartford, CT 06117
Tel: 860-232-4571; Fax: 860-233-5695
E-mail: info@mercy.sjc.edu
Web Site: www.sjc.edu
Women.
Sisters of Mercy
Chartered by the State of Connecticut.
WINIFRED E. COLEMAN, M.A., Pres.
Dr. CLARK HENDLEY, Ph.D., Vice Pres. Academic
Dr. MAUREEN REARDON, Exec. Vice Pres. & COO & Contact
MARY C. DEMO, Dean of Students
KAREN KINGSTON, Registrar
Revs.:
DAVID CINQUEGRANI, C.P.
JOHN J. STACK, S.T.D.
CHARLES J. TOPPER, Ed.D.
AIDAN DONAHUE, S.T.M., S.T.L.
Priests 4
Sisters 12
Lay Teachers 83
Students 1,823
Undergraduates:
Women 1,191
Men 35
Graduates Coed 597
School for Young Children 134
Gengras Center for Exceptional Children 124

DISTRICT OF COLUMBIA

Washington
Archdiocese of Washington

Catholic University of America, The (1887)
Nugent Hall/Executive Offices
Washington, DC 20064
Tel: 202-319-5000; Fax: 202-319-4441
E-mail: webmaster@cua.edu

Web: www.cua.edu
Most Rev. THEODORE E. MCCARRICK, Chancellor (Ex Officio)
His Eminence BERNARD CARDINAL LAW, Chm., Bd. of Trustees
Very Rev. DAVID M. O'CONNELL, C.M., J.C.D., Pres.
JOHN J. CONVEY, Ph.D., Provost
RALPH H. BEAUDOIN, M.B.A., Vice Pres. Finance and Treas.
SUSAN D. PERVI, M.A., Vice Pres. Admin.
Rev. ROBERT M. FRIDAY, S.T.D (PIT) Vice Pres. Student Life
FRANK G. PERSICO, M.A., Gen. Sec.
Revs.:
STEPHEN HAPPEL, Ph.D., Interim Dean, School of Religious Studies
KURT PRITZL, O.P., Interim Dean, School of Philosophy
ANTANAS SUZIEDELIS, Ph.D., Dean, School of Arts and Sciences
WILLIAM E. KELLY, D. Civil Eng., Dean, School of Engrg.
ROBERT A. DESTRO, J.D., Interim Dean, Columbus School of Law
Dr. ANN MARIE T. BROOKS, Ph.D., Dean, School of Nursing
ELAINE R. WALTER, Ph.D., Dean, Benjamin T. Rome School of Music
PETER LIEBSCHER, Ph.D., Dean, School of Library and Information Science
Sr. ANN PATRICK CONRAD, D.S.W., Dean, National Catholic School of Social Svc.
GREGORY K. HUNT, A.I.A., Dean, School of Architecture and Planning
STEPHEN J. WESLEY, Dean, Metropolitan College
Rev. HOWARD P. BLEICHNER, S.S., D.Th., Rector, Theological College
INGRID MERKEL, Ph.D., Vice Provost & Dean of Undergraduate Studies
PETER CIMBOLIC, Ph.D., Vice Provost & Dean of Graduate Studies
PETER MURRAY, Ed.D., Vice Provost for Information Technologies
JAMES W. MAYO, Ph.D., Assoc. Provost for Sponsored Research
Rev. ROBERT SCHLAGETER, O.F.M.Conv., S.T.L., Univ. Chap. & Dir. Campus Ministry
ADELE CHWALEK, M.S.L.S., Dir. Libraries
ARTHUR CAVANAGH, M.A., Registrar
VICTOR NAKAS, Exec. Dir., Office of Public Affairs
DAVID J. MCGONAGLE, Dir., CUA Press
DALE M. HEROLD, Dean, Enrollment Mgt.
Priests Associated with the University Full-Time:
Revs.:
JOHN P. BEAL, J.C.D.
CHRISTOPHER T. BEGG, S.T.D., Ph.D.
HOWARD P. BLEICHNER, S.S., D.Th.
WILLIAM CENKNER, O.P., Ph.D.
RAYMOND F. COLLINS, S.T.D.
FRANCIS W. DANELLA, O.S.F.S., D.Min.
ALEXANDER A. DI LELLA, O.F.M., Ph.D.
JOHN T. FORD, C.S.C., S.T.D.
ROBERT M. FRIDAY, S.T.D (PIT)
JOHN P. GALVIN, D.Th (BO)
FRANCIS T. GIGNAC, S.J., D.Phil.
PATRICK GRANFIELD, O.S.B., J.D., Ph.D., S.T.D.
THOMAS J. GREEN, J.C.D (BGP)
JACQUES GRES-GAYER, Dr.Th (France)
SIDNEY H. GRIFFITH, S.T., Ph.D.
THOMAS P. HALTON, Ph.D (Ireland)
DONALD J. HEET, O.S.F.S., D.Min.
STEPHEN W. HAPPEL, S.T.D., Ph.D.
KEVIN W. IRWIN, S.T.D (NY)
JOSEPH JENSEN, O.S.B., S.T.D.
DAVID W. JOHNSON, S.J., Ph.D.
THOMAS C. KANE, O.P., S.T.D.
ROBERT T. KENNEDY, J.U.D (NY)
JOSEPH A. KOMONCHAK, Ph.D (NY)
LOUIS M. LAFAVIA, C.PP.S., Ph.D.
JOHN E. LYNCH, C.S.P., Ph.D.
BERARD L. MARTHALER, O.F.M.Conv., Ph.D., S.T.D.
FRANK J. MATERA, Ph.D (HRT)
RAYMOND C. O'BRIEN, J.D.
PETER C. PHAN, Ph.D., S.T.D (DAL)
DAVID N. POWER, O.M.I., S.T.D.
KURT PRITZL, O.P., Ph.D.
BRIAN J. SHANLEY, O.P., Ph.D.
ROBERT S. SOKOLOWSKI, Ph.D (HRT)
RAYMOND STUDZINSKI, O.S.B., Ph.D.
Rev. Msgr. ROBERT F. TRISCO, H.E.D (CHI) Prof. Emeritus, Church History
Rev. TIMOTHY FRIEDRICHSEN, Ph.D.
Rev. Msgr. JOHN WIPPEL, Ph.D (STU)
Revs.:
JAMES A. WISEMAN, O.S.B., S.T.D.
NEIL J. ROY, M.A.
DOMINIC F. SERRA, S.T.D.
Priests Associated with the University Part-Time:
Very Rev. SEELY BEGGIANI, S.T.D (SAM)
Rev. JOSEPH A. FITZMYER, S.J., Ph.D., Prof. Emeritus, Biblical Studies
Rev. Msgr. GEORGE G. HIGGINS, Ph.D (CHI)
Rev. Msgr. ROBERT PAUL MOHAN
Revs.:
RAYMOND H. POTVIN, Ph.D (SPR) Prof. Emeritus, Sociology
JOHN F. SMOLKO (BGP)
Clerical Members, Board of Trustees:
Most Rev. Robert J. Banks; His Eminence, Anthony Cardinal Bevilacqua; Rev. Msgr. Michael Bransfield; Most Rev. Daniel M. Buechlein; Most Rev. Charles J. Chaput; Most Rev. Thomas V. Daily; Most Rev. Harry J. Flynn; His Eminence Francis Cardinal George; His Eminence, James Cardinal Hickey, Chancellor (Ex-Officio); His Eminence, William Cardinal Keeler; His Eminence, Bernard Cardinal Law, Chm.; Most Rev. William J. Levada; Most Rev. William E. Lori; His Eminence, Adam Cardinal Maida; Most Rev. Theodore E. McCarrick; Most Rev. Robert E. Mulvee; Most. Rev. William Francis Murphy; Most Rev. Daniel E. Pilarczyk; Most Rev. Frances B. Shulte; Most Rev. Terry J. Steib; Most Rev. Donald W. Wuerl; Most Rev. Philip M. Hannan, (Emeritus); His Eminence Roger Cardinal Mahony; Most Rev. Justin F. Rigali; His Eminence Edward M. Egan.
Priests 55
Sisters 16
Lay Teachers 1,390
Students 5,930

**Georgetown University* (1789)
37th and O Sts., N.W.
Washington, DC 20057
Tel: 202-687-0100
E-mail: umhoferm@gunet.georgetown.edu
Web Site: www.georgetown.edu
Rev. LEO J. O'DONOVAN, S.J., Pres.
DOROTHY M. BROWN, Ph.D., Provost
SAM WIESEL, M.D., Exec. Vice Pres. & Exec. Dean, Medical Center
JUDITH C. AREEN, Vice Pres., Law Center Affairs & Dean of the Law Center
JOHN J. DEGIOIA, Ph.D., Senior Vice Pres.
EDWARD M. QUINN, Univ. Sec.
NICOLE MANDEVILLE, Vice Pres. & Treas.
MICHAEL GOODWIN, Vice Pres., Alumni & Univ. Relations
JUAN C. GONZALEZ, Ph.D., Vice Pres., Student Affairs
DANIEL R. PORTERFIELD, Ph.D., Vice Pres., Communications & Public Affairs
H. DAVID LAMBERT, Vice Pres. for Information Services & Chief Information Officer
JANE E. GENSTER, Vice Pres. & Gen. Counsel
Rev. ADAM E. BUNNELL, O.F.M., University Chap., Campus Ministry
MICHAEL D. MCGUIRE, Exec. Dir., Planning & Inst. Research
The following are the Schools and Colleges which compose the University: Georgetown College (1789)
JANE DAMMEN MCAULIFFE, Ph.D., Dean
Graduate School of Arts & Sciences (1789)
JOSEPH SERENE, Ph.D., Dean
School of Medicine (1851)
3900 Reservoir Rd., N.W.
Washington, DC 20007
RAY MITCHELL, M.D., Senior Assoc. Dean, Academic Affairs
Law Center (1870)
600 New Jersey Ave., N.W.
Washington, DC 20001
JUDITH C. AREEN, J.D., Dean
School of Nursing & Health Studies (1903)
3700 Reservoir Rd., N.W.
Washington, DC 20007
BETTE KELTNER, R.N., FAAN, Ph.D., Dean
Edmund A. Walsh School of Foreign Service (1919).
HON. ROBERT L. GALLUCCI, Ph.D., Dean Robert Emmett McDonough School of Business (1957)
CHRISTOPHER PUTO, Ph.D., Dean School for Summer and Continuing Education (1974)
MICHAEL J. COLLINS, Ph.D., Dean
Undergraduate Admissions
CHARLES A. DEACON, M.A., Dean
Joseph Mark Lauinger Library
SUSAN K. MARTIN, Ph.D., Librarian
Office of the University Registrar
JOHN Q. PIERCE, IV, M.A., University Registrar
Office of Alumni & University Relations
Georgetown University, Box 571253
Washington, DC 20057
Tel: 202-687-4111
Affirmative Action Programs
G-10 Darnall Hall, 37th St. & O St., N.W.
Washington, DC 20057
Tel: 202-687-4798; Fax: 202-687-7778
ROSEMARY KILKENNY, J.D., Special Asst. to Pres. for AAP
Jesuits 19
Sisters 1
Lay Teachers 1,064
Total Enrollment 11,178

Trinity College
Michigan Ave. and Franklin St., N.E.
Washington, DC 20017
Tel: 202-939-5000
Sisters of Notre Dame de Namur
PATRICIA A. MCGUIRE, Pres.
Sr. CATHERINE MARIE LEE, S.N.D., Community Rep.
Dr. PATTY WEITZEL-O'NEILL, Vice Pres. Academic Affairs
Priests 2
Sisters 6
Lay Professors 44
Students 1,450

FLORIDA

Miami
Archdiocese of Miami

Barry University
President's Office
11300 N.E. 2nd Ave.
Miami, FL 33161
Tel: 305-899-3000; Fax: 305-899-3018
E-mail: jolaughlin@mail.barry.edu
Web Site: www.barry.edu
Sisters of St. Dominic (Adrian, MI)
Sr. JEANNE O'LAUGHLIN, O.P., Ph.D., Pres.
Sr. PEGGY ALBERT, O.P., Ph.D., Exec. Vice Pres.
Dr. J. PATRICK LEE, Ph.D., Provost & Senior Vice Pres. Academic Affairs
Sr. ARLENE SCOTT, O.P., Dir. of Mission & Ministry
Ms. DEBRA WEYMAN, Registrar
Mr. TIMOTHY H. CZERNIEC, Senior Vice Pres. Business & Finance
Dr. MICHAEL GRIFFIN, Ph.D., Senior Vice Pres. Student Svcs.
Sr. LORETTA MULRY I.H.M., Ed.D., Dean School of Adult & Continuing Education
Dr. EILEEN MCDONOUGH, Assoc. Vice Pres. Student Svcs.
Revs.:
MARK WEDIG, O.P.
DANIEL P. MADDEN, O.P.
PEDRO A. SUAREZ, S.J.
JOHN F. O'GRADY, S.S.D., S.T.D (ALB)
JOHN E. LYDON, O.P.
JOHN MARKEY, O.P.
Sr. EVELYN PICHE, O.P., Ph.D., Dean of School of Education
Sr. JOHN KAREN FREI, O.P., Ph.D., Assoc. Vice Pres. Research & Dean School of Natural & Health Science
CHESTER A. EVANS, D.P.M., Assoc. Vice Pres. & Dean, School of Podiatric Medicine
JACK SCARBOROUGH, Ph.D., Dean, School of Business
LAURA S. ARMESTO, Ph.D., Assoc. Vice Pres. Undergraduate Studies & Dean, School of Arts & Sciences
NANCY MAXWELL, M.S.L.S., Dir., Library
JUDITH A. BALCERSKI, Ph.D., Dean, School of Nursing
STEPHEN M. HOLLOWAY, Ph.D., Assoc. Vice Pres. Graduate Studies & Dean, School of Social Work
WILLIAM FENTON, Vice Pres., Institutional Advancement & Chm. Capital Campaign
Sr. SARAH CAVANAUGH, O.P., M.S., Assoc. Vice Pres. Institutional Advancement
G. JEAN CERRA, Ph.D., Vice Provost Enrollment & Academic Svcs. & Dean, School of Human Performance
Sr. CANDACE INTROCASO, C.D.P.
Priests 7
Sisters 30
Lay Teachers 301
Students 8,300

Opa Locka
Archdiocese of Miami

St. Thomas University
(Coed)
16400 N.W. 32nd Ave.
Opa Locka, FL 33054
Tel: 305-625-6000; Fax: 305-628-6511
Web Site: www.stu.edu
Board of Trustees:
Most Revs.:
GILBERTO FERNANDEZ
THOMAS G. WENSKI
PAMELA ADAMS
CARL BUCCELLATO
Bro. RICHARD J. DEMARIA
H. MICHAEL DYE

Thomas J. Flood
Arthur J. Furia, Esq.
Diane Saulney Gaines, Esq.
James McDonald, Esq.
Robert J. McKee, Esq.
Carlos Planas
Gus Robayna
Uriel Mendieta
Benjamin Leon
Maria Elena Torano
Thomas A. Bastian, C.P.A.
Robert V. Glaser
Ronald E. Frazier
William O. Cullom
Frank R. Esposito, Trustee Emeritus
George Goldbloom
Rev. Msgr. William J. Hennessey
Very Rev. Tomas M. Marin
Samuel L. Higginbottom
Maria C. Leiva
Ann P. Machado, Chair
Victor H. Mendelson
Dr. P. Alan Smurfit, Trustee Emeritus
The Member:
Most Rev. John Clement Favalora
Of Counsel:
J. Patrick Fitzgerald
Administration:
Rev. Msgr. Franklyn M. Casale, Pres.
John Makdisi, Dean & Interim Vice Pres. for Academic Affairs
Mr. Norman Blair, Vice Pres. for Admin. & Treas.
Beverly Bachrach, Vice Pres. University Advancement
Dr. Sarah Shumate, Vice Pres. Student Affairs
Dr. Joseph Iannone, Dean of the School of Graduate Studies
John Makdisi, Dean of the School of Law
Rev. Edward A. Blackwell, Dir. of Campus Ministry
Dr. Fred Holman, Dean of Adult & Continuing Educ.
Clergy and Religious Full-Time Faculty:
Revs.:
Jorge Sardinas
Daniel Kent
James L. MacDougall, O.S.A.
Dr. Helen Rosenthal, R.S.C.J.
Sr. Mary Tindell
Priests 4
Sisters 1
Lay Teachers 86
Students 3,339

Saint Leo
Diocese of St. Petersburg

Saint Leo University, University Ministry
P.O. Box 6665, MC 2186
Saint Leo, FL 33574-6665
Tel: 352-588-8200; 8331; Fax: 352-588-8885
E-mail: michael.coopersj@saintleo.edu
Web Site: www.saintleo.edu
An Independent and Catholic Coeducation Liberal Arts University
Dr. Arthur F. Kirk, Jr., Pres.
Revs.:
Michael Cooper, S.J., S.T.D., Asst. to Pres. for University Ministry
Anthony Kissel, Ph.D., S.T.D., Assoc. Professor of Religious Studies
Legal Title: *Saint Leo University, Inc.*
Legal Title: *Saint Leo University Educational Fund, Inc.*
Priests 1
Lay Teachers 68
Total Enrollment 8,270

HAWAII

Honolulu
Diocese of Honolulu

**Chaminade University of Honolulu*
3140 Waialae Ave.
Honolulu, HI 96816
Tel: 808-735-4711; Fax: 808-735-7748
E-mail: cuhadm@lava.net
Web Site: www.chaminade.edu
Dr. Sue Wesselkamper, Pres.
Campus Ministry:
Rev. Herman Gomes, SS.CC.
Bros.:
Thomas Heinle, S.M.
Thomas Spring, S.M.
Mrs. Catherine Agor
Brothers 7
Lay Teachers 56
Students 2,712
Total Staff 155
Total Enrollment 8,454

ILLINOIS

Chicago
Archdiocese of Chicago

De Paul University
One E. Jackson Blvd.
Chicago, IL 60604
Tel: 312-362-8000
Web Site: www.depaul.edu
Sponsored by the Priests of the Congregation of the Mission (Vincentian Fathers and Brothers)
Campuses: Downtown, Lincoln Park, Oak Forest, O'Hare, Naperville, Lake Forest, Rolling Meadows, Lake County, Schaumburg.
Revs.:
John P. Minogue, C.M., Pres.
John T. Richardson, C.M., Chancellor
Dr. Richard J. Meister, Exec. Vice Pres. Academic Affairs
Rev. Edward R. Udovic, C.M., Senior Exec. Univ. Mission
Mr. Kenneth A. McHugh, Exec. Vice Pres. for Opers.
Ms. Elaine M. Watson, Sec. Univ. & Vice Pres. Admin.
Administrative Officers of the University:
Rev. Edward R. Udovic, C.M., Senior Exec. for Univ. Mission
Ms. Maryann Ahamd, Spec. Asst. to Pres. on Diversity
Mr. Judson Mitchell, Vice Pres. Human Resources
Mr. James R. Doyle, Vice Pres. Student Affairs
Mr. Robert Janis, Vice Pres. Facilities
Mr. David O. Justice, Vice Pres. Lifelong Learning & Suburban Campuses
Mr. David Kalsbeek, Vice Pres. Enrollment Mgmt.
Mr. Steven R. Loevy, Assoc. Vice Pres. Devel.
Mr. Frank Mares, Gen.Counsel
Mr. Judson C. Mitchell, Vice Pres. Human Resources
Mr. David Soria, Acting Treas.
Mr. Ophir Trigalo, Vice Pres. Information Svcs.
Mr. Steven Loevy, Assoc. Vice Pres. Devel.
Ms. Susan H. Wallace, Vice Pres. Finance
Mr. Ophir Trigalo, Vice Pres. Information Svcs.
Mr. David O. Justice, Vice Pres. Lifelong Learning & Suburban Campuses
College of Liberal Arts and Sciences
2320 N. Kenmore Ave.
Chicago, IL 60614
Dr. Michael L Mezey, Dean
College of Law
931 Lewis Center, 25 E. Jackson Blvd.
Chicago, IL 60604
Dr. Teree E. Foster, Dean
College of Commerce
7103 DePaul Center, One E. Jackson Blvd.
Chicago, IL 60604
Arthur Kraft, Dean
Academic Officers of the University:
School of Music
200 Music Bldg., 804 W. Belden
Chicago, IL 60614
Dr. Donald E. Casey, Dean
School for New Learning
212 Lewis Center, 25 E. Jackson Blvd.
Chicago, IL 60604
Dr. Susanne M. Dumbleton, Dean
School of Computer Science, Telecommunication and Information Systems
450 CS & T Center, 243 S. Wabash Ave.
Chicago, IL 60604-2302
Dr. Helmunt P. Epp, Dean
The Theatre School
214 Theatre School Bldg., 2135 N. Kenmore Ave.
Chicago, IL 60614
John Culbert, Acting Dean
School of Education
317 Schmitt Academic Center, 2320 N. Kenmore Ave.
Chicago, IL 60614
Quintin Vargas, III, Dean
Faculty 660
Undergraduates 8,200
Graduates 12,300
Total Students 20,500

Jesuit Community at Loyola University of Chicago
Jesuit Residence, 6525 N. Sheridan Rd.
Chicago, IL 60626
Tel: 773-508-8800; Fax: 773-508-2098
E-mail: jocalla@luc.edu
Web Site: www.luc.edu
Legal Title: *The Jesuit Community Corporation at Loyola University*
Revs.:
John J. O'Callaghan, S.J., Rector
Dennis P. Ahern, S.J.
M. Selvan Augustine, S.J.
Bonaventura Balige, S.J.
Raymond C. Baumhart, S.J.
Frans J. van Beeck, S.J.
Fred F. Bergewisch, S.J.
Robert L. Bireley, S.J.
Bruno Brantschen, S.J.
Donald E. Brugger, S.J.
Bro. Brutus J. Clay, S.J.
Revs.:
David J. Collins, S.J.
Richard F. Costigan, S.J.
William E. Creed, S.J.
Matthew E. Creighton, S.J.
Eugene F. Dwyer, S.J.
Ronald J. Ferguson, S.J.
Kevin T. FitzGerald, S.J.
David A. Godleski, S.J.
Bro. Michael J. Grace, S.J.
Revs.:
Paul F. Harman, S.J.
Daniel F. Hartnett, S.J.
John C. Haughey, S.J.
William H. Hogan, S.J.
Dennis R. Karamitis, S.J.
John J. Kilgallen, S.J.
Allan F. Kirk, S.J.
Isaac Kiyaka, S.J.
Walter P. Krolikowski, S.J.
Francis V. Kuriakose, S.J.
Peter Lah, S.J.
Carlos Llagas, S.J.
Robert W. Mulligan, S.J.
John P. Murphy, S.J.
Daniel C. O'Connell, S.J.
Sean A. O'Sullivan, S.J.
Jerome T. Overbeck, S.J.
Gene D. Phillips, S.J.
John J. Piderit, S.J.
Eduardo Pinzon, S.J.
John J. Powell, S.J.
Ross T. Pribyl, S.J.
John E. Reilly, S.J.
John H. Reinke, S.J.
Lawrence Reuter, S.J.
Paul V. Robb, S.J.
Charles E. Ronan, S.J.
Donald F. Rowe, S.J.
Robert T. Sears, S.J.
Maria Augustine Selvan, S.J.
Myles N. Sheehan, S.J.
William J. Spine, S.J.
J. Michael Sparough, S.J.
J. David Stewart, S.J.
James A. Stoeger, S.J.
Leo C. Sweeney, S.J.
Ephrem Thomas, S.J.
Thomas H. Tobin, S.J.
Theodore J. Tracy, S.J.
J. Richard VandeVelde, S.J.
Joseph Vilakkunnel, S.J.
George E. Von Kaenel, S.J.
Earl A. Weis, S.J.
Priests 37
Brothers 5
Sisters 12
Lay Teachers 1,024
Total Enrollment 12,612

Loyola University-Chicago
Tel: 312-915-6000; 773-274-3000
Web Site: www.luc.edu
President's Office
820 N. Michigan Ave.
Chicago, IL 60611
Tel: 312-915-6400; Fax: 312-915-6414
Web Site: http://www.luc.edu
Legal Title: *Loyola University of Chicago, Illinois*
Michael R. Quinlan, Chm. Bd.
Rev. John J. Piderit, S.J., Pres.
Dr. Anthony L. Barbato, Pres. & C.E.O, Loyola Univ. Medical Center
Dr. Joseph Sandman, Vice Pres. Advancement
Dr. Sherri Coe-Perkins, Vice Pres. Student Affairs
Mr. Jerry Sanders, Acting Vice Pres. Information Technologies
Rev. Lawrence Reuter, S.J., Vice Pres. University Ministry
Dr. Larry Braskamp, Senior Vice Pres. Academic Affairs
Ms. Janet Gribbs, Senior Vice Pres. Finance
Dr. Marjorie Beane, Senior Vice Pres. Admin.
Mr. David Meagher, Vice Pres. Investments & Treas.
Mr. Wayne Magdziarz, Senior Vice Pres. Oper.
Mrs. Ellen Kane Munro, Vice Pres. and General Counsel

The following are the Schools and Colleges which compose the University:
The College of Arts and Sciences (1870)
Tel: 773-508-3500; Fax: 773-508-3514
Lake Shore Campus
6525 N. Sheridan Rd.
Chicago, IL 60626
Tel: 773-274-3000
Dr. JOHN SMARRELLI, Dean, Tel: 773-508-3500
The School of Law (1908)
1 E. Pearson St.
Chicago, IL 60611
Tel: 312-915-7120; Fax: 312-915-7201
NINA APPEL, Dean
The Stritch School of Medicine (1909)
2160 S. First Ave.
Maywood, IL 60153
Tel: 708-216-3223; Fax: 708-216-4305
Dr. STEPHEN SLOGOFF, Dean
School of Social Work (1914)
820 N. Michigan Ave.
Chicago, IL 60611
Tel: 312-915-7005; Fax: 312-915-7645
Dr. JOSEPH WALSH, Dean
Mundelein College of Loyola
6525 N. Sheridan Rd.
Chicago, IL 60626
Tel: 773-508-8000; Fax: 773-508-8008
Dr. STEPHEN FREEDMAN, Dean
The School of Business Administration (1922)
820 N. Michigan Ave.
Chicago, IL 60611
Tel: 312-915-6113; Fax: 312-915-6118
Dr. HENRY VENTA, Dean
The Graduate School (1926)
6525 N. Sheridan Rd.
Chicago, IL 60626
Tel: 773-508-3396; Fax: 773-508-2460
Dr. WILLIAM YOST, Acting Dean
The School of Nursing (1935)
6525 N. Sheridan Rd.
Chicago, IL 60626
Tel: 773-508-3249; Fax: 773-508-3241
Dr. SHEILA HAAS, Dean
The School of Education (1969)
Mallinkrodt Campus, 1041 Ridge Rd.
Wilmette, IL 60091
Tel: 847-853-3000; Fax: 847-853-3375
Dr. MARGARET FONG, Dean
Total University Enrollment 12,604
Total full-time faculty 540
St. Joseph's Seminary
6551 N. Sheridan Rd.
Chicago, IL 60626
Tel: 773-973-9700; Fax: 773-973-9718
Rev. PATRICK RUGEN, Academic Dean
Mallinckrodt Campus
1041 Ridge Rd.
Wilmette, IL 60091
Tel: 847-853-3000

Saint Xavier University
3700 West 103rd St.
Chicago, IL 60655
Tel: 773-298-3000
Dr. RICHARD A. YANIKOSKI, Pres.
Sisters of Mercy of the Union in the U.S. 10
Order of St. Francis 1
Sisters of Charity of Blessed Virgin Mary 1
Lay Teachers 262
Students 4,100

Joliet
Diocese of Joliet in Illinois

University of St. Francis
500 N. Wilcox
Joliet, IL 60435
Tel: 815-740-3360; Fax: 815-740-4285
Web Site: www.stfrancis.edu
A coed resident and commuter school.
Dr. JAMES A. DOPPKE, Pres.
Sr. ROSEMARY SMALL, O.S.F., Dir. of Mission Integration
Priests 1
Sisters of St. Francis of Mary Immaculate 6
Lay Teachers 71
Students 4,321
Total Staff 289

Lake Forest
Archdiocese of Chicago

Barat College
700 E. Westleigh Rd.
Lake Forest, IL 60045
Tel: 847-234-3000; Fax: 847-615-5000
E-mail: dimengo@barat.edu
Web Site: www.barat.edu
Dr. LUCY S. MORROS, Pres.
DEBORAH L. HOLMES, Exec. Vice Pres.
Religious of the Sacred Heart 2
Lay Teachers 136
Students 830

Lisle
Diocese of Joliet in Illinois

Benedictine University
5700 College Rd.
Lisle, IL 60532-0900
Tel: 630-829-6000; Fax: 630-960-1126
Web Site: www.ben.edu
Rt. Rev. HUGH R. ANDERSON, O.S.B., Chancellor
Dr. WILLIAM J. CARROLL, Pres.
Ms. BARBARA DWYER, Vice Pres., Community Devel.
CHARLES GREGORY, Vice Pres., University Svcs.
Dr. MARY DALY-LEWIS, Provost & Vice Pres. for Academic Affairs
Revs.:
DAVID TURNER, O.S.B., Univ. Chap.
KEVIN J. SHEERAN, O.S.B., Sec. & Treas.
PHILIP S. TIMKO, O.S.B.
CHRISTIAN W. CEPLECHA, O.S.B.
MICHAEL E. KOMECHAK, O.S.B.
ODILO CRKVA, O.S.B.
THEODORE D. SUCHY, O.S.B.
JOHN PALMER, C.S.V.
JULIAN VON DUERBECK, O.S.B.
JAMES FLINT, O.S.B.
Bro. ROBERT SUM, O.S.B.
Fathers 10
Brothers 1
Sisters 1
Lay Teachers 202
Administrators 177
Students 2,860

Quincy
Diocese of Springfield in Illinois

Quincy University (1860)
1800 College Ave.
Quincy, IL 62301
Tel: 217-222-8020; 228-5318
Web Site: www.quincy.edu
Franciscan Friars, Sacred Heart Province
Revs.:
EUGENE R. KOLE, OFM.Conv (NY), Pres.
VICTOR KINGERY, O.F.M.
LOUIS DAVINO, O.F.M.
JAMES EDMISTON, O.F.M.
Bro. JACK HARDESTY, O.F.M.
Revs.:
PHILIBERT HOEBING, O.F.M.
RICHARD M. JESKE, O.F.M., Chap., Illinois Veteran's Home
WILLIAM BURTON, O.F.M.
JOHN J. LAKERS, O.F.M.
Bro. THOM SMITH O.F.M., Campus Min.
Revs.:
DENNIS SCHAFER, O.F.M.
ADRIAN FISCHER, O.F.M.
GEORGE WINDOLPH, O.F.M.
JOSEPH ZIMMERMAN, O.F.M.
Bros.:
JACK CARNAGHI, O.F.M.
JOHANNES ZONG YUEWANG, O.F.M.
SCOTUS REN, O.F.M.
JOSE MARTINEZ VALENZUELA, O.F.M.
Rev. IRENAEUS KIMMINAU, O.F.M.
Priests 13
Brothers 6
Lay Faculty - Administrators 109
Students 1,182

River Forest
Archdiocese of Chicago

Dominican University (Formerly Rosary College)
7900 W. Division St.
River Forest, IL 60305
Tel: 708-366-2490; Fax: 708-524-5990
E-mail: webmaster@email.dom.edu
Web Site: www.dom.edu
Legal Title: *Dominican University*
Dominican Sisters of Sinsinawa, WI
Dr. DONNA M. CARROLL, Pres.
Sr. PATRICIA DOERR, O.P., Prioress
Dr. NORMAN CARROLL, Vice Pres. of Academic Affairs
Rosary College of Arts and Sciences at Dominican University
Tel: 708-524-6816; Fax: 708-524-5990
Dr. HUGH MCELWAIN, Dean
School of Business
Tel: 708-524-6826; Fax: 708-524-6939
Dr. MOLLY BURKE, Dean
School of Education
Tel: 708-524-6830; Fax: 708-524-6665
Sr. COLLEEN MCNICHOLAS, Dean
Graduate School of Library and Information Science
Tel: 708-524-6472; Fax: 708-524-6657
Dr. PRUDENCE DALRYMPLE, Dean
Graduate School of Social Work
Tel: 708-524-6495; Fax: 708-524-5990
Dr. VIMALA PILLARI, Dean
Institute for Adult Learning
Tel: 847-562-8810; Fax: 847-562-0494
BRYAN WATKINS, Exec. Dir.
Sisters 9
Lay Teachers 68
Total Enrollment 2,360
Sisters 9
Lay Teachers 68
Students 2,360

Romeoville
Diocese of Joliet in Illinois

Lewis University
(Coed University)
One University Pkwy.
Romeoville, IL 60446
Tel: 815-838-0500; Fax: 815-838-1267
E-mail: wassbeca@lewis.edu
Web Site: www.lewisu.edu/
Bros.:
JAMES GAFFNEY, F.S.C., Pres.
ROBERT MURPHY, O.Carm., Dir. University Ministry
Priests 5
Sisters 2
Brothers of the Christian Schools 17
Lay Teachers 147
Students 4,289

Springfield
Diocese of Springfield in Illinois

Springfield College in Illinois
1500 N. Fifth St.
Springfield, IL 62702
Tel: 217-525-1420; Fax: 217-789-1698
E-mail: rappe@sci.edu
Web Site: www.sci.edu
ROBERT J. BUCCINO, Pres.
Rev. DAVID S. LANTZ, Dir.
Ursuline Sisters 1
Lay Teachers 19
Students 308

INDIANA

Donaldson
Diocese of Fort Wayne - South Bend

Ancilla Domini College
Tel: 219-936-8898; Fax: 219-935-1773
Web Site: www.ancilla.edu
Mailing Address:
P.O. Box 1
Donaldson, IN 46513
Poor Handmaids of Jesus Christ (Ancilla Domini Sisters)
Dr. WILLIAM J. SHUSTOWSKI, JR., Pres.
RAYMOND GIRRES, Business Officer
DIANNE RASCH, Academic Dean
SHARON BLUBAUGH, Registrar
JEFFREY MEECE, Dir. Enrollment Mgmt.
GLENDA BOCKMAN, Head Librarian
THOMAS SIBAL, Assoc. Dir. Inst. Advancement
Sisters 4
Lay Teachers 46
Students 473

Fort Wayne
Diocese of Fort Wayne - South Bend

University of Saint Francis
2701 Spring St.
Fort Wayne, IN 46808-3994
Tel: 219-434-3100; Fax: 219-434-3183
E-mail: ekriss@sf.edu
Web Site: www.sf.edu
Conducted by Sisters of St. Francis of Perpetual Adoration.
Sr. M. ELISE KRISS, O.S.F., Pres.
Rev. JAMES SAPP (WH) Residence Chap.
Priests 1
Sisters 8
Lay Teachers 96
Students 1,629
Total Staff 141

Indianapolis
Archdiocese of Indianapolis

Marian College
(Coed)
3200 Cold Spring Rd.
Indianapolis, IN 46222
Tel: 317-955-6000; Fax: 317-955-6048

Web Site: www.marian.edu
Sisters of the Third Order Regular of St. Francis
Sr. NORMA ROCKLAGE, O.S.F., Ph.D., Senior Vice Pres. Mission Effectiveness & Planning
CONNIE WESNER, Acting Dean
ROBERT M. ABENE, Ph.D., Pres.
Revs.:
FRANCIS E. BRYAN
LEOPOLD KEFFLER, O.F.M.Conv.
Priests 2
Sisters 6
Lay Teachers 64
Students 1,787

Notre Dame
Diocese of Fort Wayne - South Bend

Holy Cross College, Holy Cross College, Inc.
54515 State Rd., 933 N.
Notre Dame, IN 46556-0308
Tel: 219-239-8400; Fax: 219-233-7427
E-mail: rgilman@hcc-nd.edu
Web Site: www.hcc-nd.edu
Legal Title: *Holy Cross College, Inc.*
Bro. RICHARD GILMAN, C.S.C., Pres.
R. DOUGLAS IRVINE, Dir. Financial Aid
MARK P. MULLANEY, Vice Pres. Finance
Bro. CHARLES GREGG, C.S.C., Librarian
JOSEPH GOEPFRICH, Vice Pres. Advancement
RICHARD J. SULLIVAN, Registrar
VINCENT M. DUKE, Dir. Admissions
ROBERT KLOSKA, Dir. Campus Ministry
TINA HOLLAND, Vice Pres. Student Affairs
DANIEL COCHRAN, Dir. Residence Life
WILLIAM MANGAN, Vice Pres. Academic Affairs
Bro. CHRIS DREYER, C.S.C., Dir. Student Support Svcs.
Priests 5
Sisters 4
Brothers 11
Lay Professors 27
Students 485

Saint Mary's College
Notre Dame, IN 46556
Tel: 219-284-4556; Fax: 219-284-4707
E-mail: 1hitch@saintmarys.edu
Web Site: www.saintmarys.edu
An institution of higher education for women.
Sisters of the Holy Cross
MARILOU ELDRED, Pres.
Sisters 2
Lay Professors 106
Students 1,458

**University of Notre Dame Du Lac* (1842)
Provost Office, 300 Main Bldg.
Notre Dame, IN 46556
Tel: 219-631-5000; 631-5090 (Provost); Fax: 219-631-6897
E-mail: hubbard.4@nd.edu
Web Site: www.nd.edu
The Graduate School (29 departments). The Law School. The Undergraduate School (four colleges, 36 departments). Institutes and Radiation Laboratory, Center for Study of Man, Institute for Urban Studies and Institute for International Studies.
Officers Group:
Revs.:
EDWARD A. MALLOY, C.S.C., Pres. & C.S.C. Faculty
LARRY FORD, O.F.M., Interim Dir. Mendoza College of Business
NATHAN O. HATCH, Ph.D., Provost
Revs.:
TIMOTHY R. SCULLY, C.S.C., Exec. Vice Pres.
JOHN I. JENKINS, C.S.C., Vice Pres. & Assoc. Provost
MARK L. POORMAN, C.S.C., Vice Pres. Student Affairs
CHANDRA JOHNSON, Asst. to the Pres.
JEFFREY C. KANTOR, Ph.D., Vice Pres. & Assoc. Provost
CAROL A. MOONEY, J.D., Vice Pres. & Assoc. Provost
Dr. WILLIAM P. SEXTON, Vice Pres. Univ. Rels.
JAMES L. MERZ, Ph.D., Vice Pres. Graduate Studies & Research
Rev. WILLIAM D. SEETCH, C.S.C., Rel. Supr.
JAMES J. LYPHOUT, Assoc. Vice Pres. for Business Operations
SCOTT C. MALPASS, Assoc. Vice Pres. for Finance
CAROL C. KAESEBIER, J.D., Vice Pres. & General Counsel
LOUIS NANNI, Exec. Asst. to Pres.
Rev. RICHARD V. WARNER, C.S.C., Counselor to the Pres., Dir. of Campus Ministry
Administrative Group:
Dr. ANTHONY HYDER, Assoc. Vice Pres. Graduate School
Dr. THOMAS L. SWEENEY, Asst. Vice Pres. Research
Dr. JAMES H. POWELL, Asst. Vice Pres. & Dir. Summer Session
DANIEL J. SARACINO, Asst. Provost for Enrollment
JENNIFER YOUNGER, Dir. Univ. Libraries
RICHARD NUGENT, Asst. Vice Pres. for Human Resources
KEVIN M. WHITE, Dir. Athletics
RICHARD W. CONKLIN, Assoc. Vice Pres. Univ. Rels.
IRIS OUTLAW, Dir. Minority Students
WILLIAM W. KIRK, Asst. Vice Pres. for Residence Life
Sr. JEAN LENZ, O.S.F., Asst. Vice Pres. for Student Affairs
Sr. MARY L. GUDE, C.S.C., Asst. Vice Pres. Student Affairs
DAVID MOSS, Asst. Vice Pres. Student Affairs
JENNIFER MONAHAN, Asst. to the Vice Pres. Student Affairs
WILLIAM HOYE, Assoc. Vice Pres & Counsel
Assistant Vice Presidents and Counsels:
JILL BODENSTEINER
TIMOTHY J. FLANAGAN
TRACY MAGINN
MARY E. PUGEL, Exec. Asst. to the Provost
MICHAEL J. FRANCIS, Asst. Provost for Information Technologies
LARRY RAPAGNANI, Assoc. Vice Pres. for Information Technologies
PETER DIFFLEY, Assoc. Dean Graduate School
TERRANCE J. AKAI, Assoc. Dean Graduate School
DIANE WILSON, Asst. Dean Graduate School
BARBARA TURPIN, Assoc. Dean Graduate School
JANICE POORMAN, Asst. Dean Graduate Admissions
HAROLD L. PACE, Registrar
JOSEPH A. RUSSO, Dir. Financial Aid
KEVIN WHITE, Dir. Athletics
CHARLES F. LENNON, JR., Asst. Vice Pres. University Rels.
DENNIS K. MOORE, Dir. Public Rels. & Information
C.S.C. Faculty & Personnel:
Revs.:
ROBERT J. AUSTGEN, C.S.C.
NICHOLAS AYO, C.S.C.
LEONARD N. BANAS, C.S.C.
ERNEST J. BARTELL, C.S.C.
MICHAEL J. BAXTER, C.S.C.
E. WILLIAM BEAUCHAMP, C.S.C.
THOMAS V. BEDNAR, C.S.C.
THOMAS E. BLANTZ, C.S.C.
RICHARD S. BULLENE, C.S.C.
DAVID B. BURRELL, C.S.C.
GARY CHAMBERLAND, C.S.C.
AUSTIN I. COLLINS, C.S.C.
JOHN E. CONLEY, C.S.C.
MICHAEL CONNORS, C.S.C.
RAYMOND F. COUR, C.S.C.
ALFRED F. D'ALONZO, C.S.C.
PAUL F. DOYLE, C.S.C.
THOMAS P. DOYLE, C.S.C.
JOHN S. DUNNE, C.S.C.
CLARENCE R. DURBIN, C.S.C.
CARL EBEY, C.S.C.
MARK J. FITZGERALD, C.S.C.
JAMES F. FLANIGAN, C.S.C.
JAMES K. FOSTER, C.S.C.
PATRICK GAFFNEY, C.S.C.
THOMAS E. GAUGHAN, C.S.C.
JAMES GILLIS, C.S.C.
Bro. FRANCIS GORCH, C.S.C.
Revs.:
CHARLES GORDON, C.S.C.
EUGENE GOESKI, C.S.C.
GREGORY A. GREEN, C.S.C.
DANIEL GROODY, C.S.C.
Bro. EDWARD HAGUS
Revs.:
JOHN HERMAN, C.S.C.
THEODORE M. HESBURGH, C.S.C.
Bro. LOUIS HURCIK, C.S.C.
Revs.:
WILLIAM D. SEETCH, C.S.C., Religious Supr.
EDMUND P. JOYCE, C.S.C.
JAMES KING, C.S.C.
THOMAS P. KING, C.S.C.
JEROME E. KNOLL, C.S.C.
JOHN LAHEY, C.S.C.
Bro. EDWARD LUTHER, C.S.C.
Revs.:
PATRICK H. MALONEY, C.S.C.
JAMES J. MCGRATH, C.S.C.
DONALD P. MCNEILL, C.S.C.
JOSE M. MARTELLI, C.S.C.
LEON J. MERTENSOTTO, C.S.C.
Bros.:
DENNIS MEYERS, C.S.C.
JEROME MEYER, C.S.C.
Revs.:
MATTHEW M. MICELI, C.S.C.
WILSON D. MISCAMBLE, C.S.C.
FELIPE MOREL, C.S.C.
ROBERT H. MOSS, C.S.C.
MICHAEL J. MURPHY, C.S.C.
PAT NEARY, C.S.C.
MARTIN LAM NGUYEN, C.S.C.
EDWARD D. O'CONNOR, C.S.C.
JOHN H. PEARSON, C.S.C.
ROBERT S. PELTON, C.S.C.
HERMAN R. REITH, C.S.C.
JAMES L. RIEHLE, C.S.C.
JAMES A. RIGERT, C.S.C.
JOHN RILEY, C.S.C.
PETER ROCCA, C.S.C.
GEORGE A. ROZUM, C.S.C.
Bro. BEATUS SCHLENKER, C.S.C.
Revs.:
DAVID J. SCHEIDLER, C.S.C.
WILLIAM SIMMONS, C.S.C.
JOHN STEELE, C.S.C.
THOMAS G. STREIT, C.S.C.
MICHAEL BRUCE SULLIVAN, C.S.C.
THOMAS TALLARIDA, C.S.C.
MARK THESING, C.S.C.
MERWYN J. THOMAS, C.S.C.
Bro. THOMAS TUCKER, C.S.C.
Revs.:
WILLIAM A. WACK, C.S.C.
JOSEPH L. WALTER, C.S.C.
CHARLES F. WEIHER, C.S.C.
OLIVER F. WILLIAMS, C.S.C.
GEORGE C. WISKIRCHEN, C.S.C.
Non-C.S.C. Religious Faculty:
Rev. JOSEPH P. AMAR (SAM)
Sr. ELEANOR BERNSTEIN, C.S.J.
Rev. PAUL F. BRADSHAW
Sr. KATHLEEN CANNON, O.P.
Sr. DEBORAH M. CERULLO, S.S.N.D.
Sr. REGINA COLL, C.S.J.
Revs.:
BRIAN DALEY, S.J.
MICHAEL DRISCOLL
Sr. MARY CATHERINE HILKERT, O.P.
Rev. MAXWELL E. JOHNSON
Sr. JEAN LENZ, O.S.F.
Revs.:
RICHARD P. MCBRIEN
ERNAN MCMULLIN
JOHN A. MELLOH, S.M.
JOHN P. MEIER
Sr. MARY ANN MUENINGHOFF, O.P.
Revs.:
JEROME H. NEYREY, S.J.
MARVIN R. O'CONNELL
THOMAS O'MEARA, O.P.
HUGH H. PAGE
FREDERICK W. PFOTENHAUER
ROBERT E. SULLIVAN
JOSEPH E. WEISS, S.J.
D. REGINALD WHITT, O.P.
Priests 53
Sisters 6
Total Staff 1,415
Total Enrollment 10,654

Rensselaer
Diocese of Lafayette in Indiana

Saint Joseph's College
P.O. Box 909
Rensselaer, IN 47978
Tel: 219-866-6000; Fax: 219-866-6100
Web Site: www.saintjoe.edu
The Society of the Precious Blood
Dr. ALBERT SHANNON, Ph.D., Pres.
Revs.:
DOMINIC B. GERLACH, C.PP.S.
PHILIP F. GILBERT, C.PP.S.
LAWRENCE F. HEIMAN, C.PP.S.
LEONARD J. KOSTKA, C.PP.S., (Retired)
EDWARD P. MCCARTHY, C.PP.S., (Retired)
TIMOTHY D. MCFARLAND, C.PP.S.
CHARLES J. ROBBINS, C.PP.S., (Retired)
CHARLES R. RUEVE, C.PP.S.
WILLIAM J. STANG, C.PP.S.
RALPH C. VERDI, C.PP.S.
PAUL R. WHITE, C.PP.S., (Retired)
Bros.:
TIMOTHY P. HEMM, C.PP.S., Religious Supr.
JAVIER SOTO, C.PP.S.
Sr. CATHERINE FAY, B.V.M.
Sr. PATRICIA ROBINSON, B.V.M.
Priests 11
Sisters 2
Lay Teachers 74
Brothers 2
Total Staff 200
Students 848

Saint Mary-of-the-Woods
Archdiocese of Indianapolis

Saint Mary-of-the-Woods College
Saint Mary-of-the-Woods, IN 47876
Tel: 812-535-5151; Fax: 812-535-4613
E-mail: smeier@woods.smwc.edu
Web Site: www.smwc.edu
Dr. JOAN LESCINSKI, C.S.J., Pres.
Priests 1
Sisters of Providence 4
Sisters of St. Francis 1
Lay Teachers 56
Students 1,439

Whiting
Diocese of Gary

Calumet College of St. Joseph
2400 New York Ave.
Whiting, IN 46394
Tel: 219-473-7770; Fax: 219-473-4259
Web Site: www.ccsj.edu
Dr. DENNIS RITTENMEYER, Pres.
Rev. ERNEST KRANTZ, C.PP.S., Chap.
Bros.:
BENJAMIN BASILE, C.PP.S., Faculty
JAMES BALLMANN, C.PP.S., Religious Supr.; Computer Svcs.
GABRIEL BRIDGES, C.PP.S., Campus Ministry
Priests 1
Brothers 3
Sisters 2
Lay Teachers 65
Total Staff 110
Enrollment 978

IOWA

Cedar Rapids
Archdiocese of Dubuque

Mount Mercy College
1330 Elmhurst Dr., N.E.
Cedar Rapids, IA 52402-4797
Tel: 319-363-8213; Fax: 319-368-6492
E-mail: admission@mmc.mtmercy.edu
Web Site: www.mtmercy.edu
Dr. ROBERT W. PEARCE, Pres.
LORI HEYING, Registrar
Dr. SUSAN E. PAULY, Vice Pres. Academic Affairs
Sisters 2
Lay Teachers 66
Students 1,363

Clinton
Diocese of Davenport

Mt. St. Clare College
(Coed)
400 Bluff Blvd., P.O. Box 2967
Clinton, IA 52733-2967
Tel: 319-242-4023
E-mail: admissns@clare.edu
Web Site: www.clare.edu
Sisters of St. Francis, Clinton, IA
MALCOLM T. MYERS, Interim Pres.
Sisters 3
Lay Teachers 57
Total Staff 60

Davenport
Diocese of Davenport

St. Ambrose University
Davenport, IA 52803-2898
Tel: 319-333-6300; Fax: 319-333-6243
E-mail: admit@sau.edu
Web Site: www.sau.edu/
EDWARD ROGALSKI, Ph.D., Pres.
DONALD J. MOELLER, Provost
ANN FREEBERG, Ph.D., Vice Pres. Inst. Research
DANIEL F. OSBERGER, Vice Pres. Finance
Very Rev. DRAKE R. SHAFER, Asst. to Pres. for Diocesan Rels.
Dr. EDWARD G. LITTIG, Vice Pres. for Advancement
JAMES P. LOFTUS, Vice Pres. Enrollment Mgmt.
Revs.:
CHARLES A. ADAM, Campus Chap.
ROBERT L. GRANT, Campus Min.
Sr. AUDREY CLEARY, O.S.B., Dir., Prayer & Spirituality Center
SHEILA FUNDERBURK, Campus Min. Dir.
Ms. JENNIFER NOEL, Campus Min.
Priest Faculty:
Revs.:
CHARLES A. ADAM
EDWARD A. BOTKIN
WILLIAM F. DAWSON, Ph.D.
JOSEPH DE FRANCISCO, Ph.D (BEA)
EDMOND J. DUNN, Ph.D.
ROBERT L. GRANT
GEORGE MCDANIEL, Ph.D.
DRAKE R. SHAFER
BRIAN MICLOT, Ph.D.
JOSEPH E. KOKJOHN, (Retired)
WILLIAM J. STRATMAN, (Retired)
Priests 11
Sisters 1
Lay Teachers 116
Total Staff 257
Students 3,011

Des Moines
Diocese of Des Moines

Mercy College of Health Sciences
928-6th Ave.
Des Moines, IA 50309-1239
Tel: 515-643-3180; Fax: 515-643-6698
E-mail: admissions@mchs.edu
Web Site: www.mchs.edu
Sponsored by Sisters of Mercy of the Americas (Omaha Province).
DEANNE M. REMER, Ph.D., Pres.
HUGH B. HANSEN, M.S., Academic Dean
KATHLEEN CLAUSON, Ph.D., Dean of Students
BRIAN TINGLEFF, B.A., Dir. Inst. Advancement
Lay Teachers 25
Students 432

Dubuque
Archdiocese of Dubuque

Clarke College
1550 Clarke Dr.
Dubuque, IA 52001
Tel: 563-588-6300; Fax: 563-588-6789
Web Site: www.clarke.edu
Liberal Arts College. (Coed)
Conducted by Sisters of Charity, B.V.M.
Sr. CATHERINE DUNN, B.V.M., Ph.D., Pres.
Sr. REGINA QUALLS, B.V.M., Registrar
Sr. MARGARET FELDNER, O.S.F., Vice Pres. Academic Affairs
LOUISE OTTAVI, Assoc. Academic Dean
KATE ZANGER, Vice Pres. Student Life
GAIL NAUGHTON, Vice Pres. Institutional Advancement
EUGENE KIRSCHBAUM, M.B.A., Vice Pres. Business & Finance
LAURA KESTNER, Dir. Career Svcs.
JULIE TEBBE, Dir. Campus Ministry
NANCY VAN MILLIGEN, M.A., Vice Pres. Adult & Continuing Formation
OMAR CORREA, Exec. Dir. Admissions & Fin. Aid
Sisters 22
Lay Teachers 60
Students 1,249

Loras College
1450 Alta Vista St., P.O. Box 178
Dubuque, IA 52004-0178
Tel: 563-588-7100; Fax: 563-588-7964
E-mail: jfroehli@loras.edu
(Accredited by the North Central Assoc. of Colleges and Secondary Schools)
Dr. JOACHIM FROEHLICH, Pres.
Dr. JOHN BURNEY, Vice Pres. Academic Affairs
Dr. MARY JOHNSON, Vice Pres. Student Devel.
JAMES COLLINS, Senior Vice Pres. Inst. Advancement
STEPHEN S. SCHMALL, C.P.A., Vice Pres. Finance & Admin. Svcs.
Mr. JON CHRISTY, Registrar
Rev. DAVID H. O'CONNOR, Chap.
JOHN C. WALDMEIR, Ph.D., Assoc. Vice Pres. Academic Affairs & Dean of Experimental Learning
MICHAEL J. BOYD, Ph.D, Dir. Campus Ministry
College Faculty:
Revs.:
ROBERT R. BECK, D.Min.
DENNIS J. COLTER
MARK A. RESSLER, Ph.D.
DOUGLAS O. WATHIER, S.T.D.
In res.,
Rev. Msgr. ROBERT R. VOGL, M.A., (Retired)
Revs.:
JOHN C. FRIEDELL, (Retired)
WILLIAM E. WILKIE, Ph.D., (Retired)
PHILLIP G. GIBBS
Priests 9
Sisters 1
Lay Teachers 106
Students 1,725

Sioux City
Diocese of Sioux City

Briar Cliff College
3303 Rebecca St., P.O. Box 2100
Sioux City, IA 51104-2100
Tel: 712-279-5405; Fax: 712-279-5410
E-mail: wielandt@briarcliff.edu
Web Site: www.briarcliff.edu
Sisters of St. Francis of the Holy Family of Dubuque, Iowa
Liberal Arts College. Coed. Day and Resident Students.
Dr. JACK CALARESO, Pres.
JULIE SCOTT, Registrar
SHARISUE WILCOXON, Vice Pres. of Enrollment Mgmt.
Revs.:
ALFRED E. MCCOY
ROBERT M. CONDON
Priests 2
Sisters 12
Lay Teachers 47
Lay Admins. & Staff 94
Students 949

KANSAS

Atchison
Archdiocese of Kansas City in Kansas

Benedictine College
Atchison, KS 66002
Tel: 913-367-5340; Fax: 913-367-3673
E-mail: peylar@raven.benedictine.edu
Web Site: www.benedictine.edu
DANIEL J. CAREY, Ph.D., Pres.
SHERRIE KUNECKE, Controller
BEV MCCONAUGHEY, Registrar
Revs.:
DENIS MEADE, O.S.B.
BLAINE SCHULTZ, O.S.B.
EUGENE DEHNER, O.S.B., (Retired)
MARK BROSKI, O.S.B.
MEINRAD MILLER, O.S.B., Campus Ministry Dir.
JAMES ALBERS, O.S.B.
BRENDAN ROLLINS, O.S.B.
STEPHEN MCCANN, O.S.B.
Bro. LAWRENCE BRADFORD, O.S.B.
Coed College of St. Benedict's & Mount St. Scholastica.
Priests 8
Brothers 1
Benedictine Sisters 9
Laypeople 40
Students 1,430

Kansas City
Archdiocese of Kansas City in Kansas

Donnelly College
608 N. 18th St.
Kansas City, KS 66102
Tel: 913-621-6070; Fax: 913-621-0354
E-mail: kgibson@donnelly.cc.ks.us
Web Site: www.Donnelly.cc.ks.us
Dr. KEN GIBSON, Pres.
Sr. MARY AGNES PATTERSON, Vice Pres.
FRANCES SANDERS, Dean
Sr. FRAN CROSS, Registrar
Benedictine Sisters 6
Other Order Sisters 3
Lay Teachers 42
Students 600

Leavenworth
Archdiocese of Kansas City in Kansas

Saint Mary College
Leavenworth, KS 66048
Tel: 913-682-5151; Fax: 913-758-6140
E-mail: admis@hub.smcks.edu
Web Site: www.smcks.edu
Rev. RICHARD MUCOWSKI, O.F.M., Ph.D., Pres.
Dr. SANDRA VAN HOOSE, Academic Vice Pres.
Sisters of Charity of Leavenworth 15
Lay Teachers 92
Students 780

Wichita
Diocese of Wichita

Newman University
3100 McCormick Ave.
Wichita, KS 67213-2097
Tel: 316-942-4291; Fax: 316-942-4483
Web Site: www.newmanu.edu
AIDAN O. DUNLEAVY, Ph.D.
ALTON BEAVER, Interim Vice Pres., Academic Affairs
MARK DRESSELHAUS, Vice Pres. Finance & Admin.
KIM MILLER JACOBS, Vice Pres. Student Affairs
SHIRLEY RUEB, Registrar

Coeducational liberal arts college, founded in 1933 by the Sisters Adorers of the Blood of Christ. (Accredited by the North Central Association of Colleges and Secondary Schools).
Sisters 4
Lay Teachers 72
Total Staff 187
Students 1,005

KENTUCKY

Covington
Diocese of Covington

Thomas More College
(Coed)
333 Thomas More Pkwy. Crestview Hills
Covington, KY 41017-3495
Tel: 859-341-5800; Fax: 859-344-3649
E-mail: william.cleves@thomasmore.edu
Web Site: www.thomasmore.edu
Rev. William F. Cleves, Ph.D., Pres.
Mr. John R. Parker, Vice Pres. Admin. & Finance
Dr. Dale K. Myers, Vice Pres. Academic Affairs
Ms. Judith Kinman, Dir. of Campus Ministry
Mr. James McKellogg, Dir. Library
Ms. Patsy Kenner, Registrar
Mr. Timothy Ring, Dir. Financial Aid
Ms. Barbara Davis, Dir. Student Support Svcs.
Sr. Rita Marie Mueller, S.N.D., Dir. Inst. Research
Priests 2
Lay Teachers 70
Sisters 2
Administration:
Priests 1
Lay People 24
Students 1,274

Louisville
Archdiocese of Louisville

Bellarmine University
2001 Newburg Rd.
Louisville, KY 40205-0671
Tel: 502-452-8211; Fax: 502-452-8033
Web Site: www.bellarmine,edu
Administration Officers:
Most Rev. Thomas C. Kelly, O.P., J.C.D., Archbishop of Louisville, Chancellor
Dr. Joseph J. McGowan, Jr., Pres.
Mr. Robert L. Zimlich, Vice President for Business Affairs
Dr. Fred W. Rhodes, Vice Pres. Student Affairs & Dean of Students
Mr. Vince Maniaci, Vice Pres. Inst. Advancement
Dr. Susan Davis, Dean of the Lansing School of Nursing
Mr. Tim Sturgeon, Dean of Admission and Financial Aid
Dr. John Oppelt, Provost and Dean of the College
Dr. Dan Bauer, Dean of the Rubel School of Business
Dr. Doris Tegart, Vice Pres. Enrollment Mgmt.
Revs.:
Clyde F. Crews
W. Frederick Hendrickson
George A. Kilcourse
Eugene L. Zoeller
Priests 4
Sisters 3
Students 2,214

Spalding University
851 S. 4th St.
Louisville, KY 40203
Tel: 502-585-9911; Fax: 502-585-7158
Web Site: www.spalding.edu
Dr. Thomas R. Oates, Pres.
Sharon Hoffman, Sr. Vice Pres. Academic Affairs
Larry Romine, Vice Pres. for Finance
Deborah Tillett, Senior Mgr., Enrollment Svcs.
Phyllis Passafiume, Dean, College of Arts & Sciences
Judith Plawecki, Dean, College of Professional Svcs.
Maggie McCullough, Assoc. Dean, School of Business
Betty Lindsey, Assoc. Dean, School of Education
Dr. Cynthia Crabtree, Assoc. Dean, School of Nursing & Health Sciences
Jillian Johnson, Assoc. Dean, School of Social Work
Jackie Hinshaw, Dir. Library
Dr. Deborah A. Ford, Vice Pres. Student Affairs & Dean, Students
Jeffrey L. Ashley, Vice Pres., Univ. Advancement
Brian Kesse, Dir. Strategic Planning
Lisa Flack, Dir. Student Financial Aid
Priests 1
Sisters 4
Brothers 1
Lay Teachers 77
Students 1,606

Owensboro
Diocese of Owensboro

Brescia University
717 Frederica St.
Owensboro, KY 42301
Tel: 270-685-3131; 800-264-1234; Fax: 270-686-4266
E-mail: brescia.edu
Web Site: www.brescia.edu
Sr. Vivian Marie Bowles, O.S.U., Pres.
Kathleen H. McKee, Ph.D., Dean
Sr. Helena Fischer, O.S.U., Registrar
Revs.:
Larry Hostetter, Campus Min.
Leonard J. Alvey
Anthony J. Shonis
Pat Ryan (STL)
Priests 3
Sisters 7
Lay Teachers 34
Students 750

St. Catharine
Archdiocese of Louisville

St. Catharine College
2735 Bardstown Rd.
St. Catharine, KY 40061
Tel: 606-336-5082; Fax: 606-336-5031
Web Site: www.scky.edu
Dominican Sisters
Mr. Bill Huston, Pres.
Sr. Marina Gibbons, O.P., Vice Pres. & Academic Dean
Sisters 1
Lay Teachers 25
Students 509

LOUISIANA

Baton Rouge
Diocese of Baton Rouge

Our Lady of the Lake College
5345 Brittany Dr.
Baton Rouge, LA 70808-4398
Tel: 225-768-1710; Fax: 225-768-1726
E-mail: msmith@ololcollege.edu
Web Site: www.ololcollege.edu
Dr. Michael Smith, Pres.
Lay Teachers 75
Students 1,047

New Orleans
Archdiocese of New Orleans

Loyola University New Orleans (1912)
6363 St. Charles Ave.
New Orleans, LA 70118-6195
Tel: 504-865-2011; Fax: 504-865-3851
E-mail: RAMAGOS@LOYNO.EDU
Revs.:
Bernard P. Knoth, S.J., Pres.
James C. Carter, S.J., Chancellor
Dr. David C. Danahar, Provost & Vice Pres. for Academic Affairs
Revs.:
Robert S. Gerlich, S.J., Rector
Christopher Lockard, S.J., Regent
Ronald Schmidt, S.J., Regent
Bentley Anderson, S.J.
John F. Armstrong, S.J.
Edward B. Arroyo, S.J.
Thomas Clancy, S.J.
Harold F. Cohen, S.J.
Gregory F. Curtin, S.J.
Stephen Duffy, S.T.D.
Gerald M. Fagin, S.J.
Ernest Ferlita, S.J.
Alvin J. Holloway, S.J.
Theodore M. Kalamaja, S.J.
Marvin C. Kitten, S.J.
Clyde LeBlanc, S.J.
C. Franklyn Lynette, S.J.
Lawrence Moore, S.J.
Leo A. Nicoll, S.J.
Charles E. O'Neill, S.J.
Robert J. Ratchford, S.J.
Peter S. Rogers, S.J.
Edwin L. Gros, S.J., Min.
Peter J. Bernardi, S.J.
Bro. Charles J. Blouin, S.J., Treasurer
Revs.:
James P. Bradley
Edward P. Buvens, S.J.
M. Deshotels S.J.
William J. Farge, S.J.
Bro. Gebhard R.M. Frohlich, (Retired)
Michael A. Kane, S.J., Regent
Bros.:
Lawrence J. Lundin, S.J.
Francis J. Riedinger, S.J., (Retired)
Joseph E. Schneeweis, S.J.
Revs.:
Thomas J. Sheehan, S.J.
John B. Weling, S.J.
Dr. David A. Boileau
Dr. Kenneth P. Keulman
Dr. Bernard J. Lee, S.M.
Dr. Frank Scully, Dean, College of Arts and Sciences
Dr. Edward Kvet, Dean, School of Music
Dr. J. Patrick O'Brien, Dean, College of Business Admin.
Dr. Marcel Dumestre, Dean, City College
James Klebba, Interim Dean, Law School
Priests 27
Brothers 1
Lay Teachers 330
Students 5,400

Our Lady of Holy Cross College
4123 Woodland Dr.
New Orleans, LA 70131-7399
Tel: 504-394-7744; Fax: 504-391-2421
E-mail: lmelancon@olhcc.edu
Web Site: www.olhcc.edu
Rev. Thomas E. Chambers, C.S.C., Ph.D., Pres.
Dr. Gerald F. DeLuca, Vice Pres. Academic Affairs
Mr. Thomas O. Porteous, Jr., Vice Pres. Business Affairs
Sr. Ann Martinez, Registrar
Rev. Thomas Ellerman, S.M., Chap.
Priests 2
Brothers 1
Congregation of the Sisters Marianites of Holy Cross 6
Sisters 7
Lay Teachers 36
Students 1,233
Total Staff 154

Xavier University of Louisiana
One Drexel Dr.
New Orleans, LA 70125-1098
Tel: 504-486-7411; Fax: 504-485-7904
Web Site: www.xula.edu
(Coed)
Dr. Norman C. Francis, Pres.
Dr. Deidre Labat, Vice Pres. Academic Affairs
Mrs. Lisa Lewis McClain, Dir., Office of Campus Ministry
Priests 1
Brothers 1
Sisters of the Blessed Sacrament 5
Lay Teachers 219
Students 3,787

MAINE

Standish
Diocese of Portland (In Maine)

Association of Mercy Colleges and Universities
278 Whites Bridge Rd.
Standish, ME 04084-5263
Tel: 207-893-7711; Fax: 207-893-7867
Dr. David B. House, Treas.
Sponsor: Colleges and Universities run by the Sisters of Mercy throughout the U.S.A.

Saint Joseph's College
278 Whites Bridge Rd.
Standish, ME 04084-5263
Tel: 207-893-7711; Fax: 207-893-7867
Web Site: www.sjcme.edu
Dr. David B. House, Pres.
Dr. Daniel P. Sheridan, Vice Pres. for Academic Affairs and Dean
Dr. Timothy O'Leary, Vice Pres. for Student Affairs
Sr. Mary George O'Toole, R.S.M., Vice Pres. Sponsorship & Mission Integration
Sr. Mary Kneeland, R.S.M., Treas.
Rev. John Tokaz, O.F.M.Cap., Chap.
Sr. Sylvia Comer, R.S.M., Campus Min.
Deacon John McAuliffe, Jr.
William Morgan, Vice Pres., Finance & Admin.
Robert Sullivan, Vice Pres., Institutional Advancement
William Dunfrey, Vice Pres., Enrollment Management
Priests 1
Sisters 13

Deacons 1
Lay Professors 100
Undergraduate Students in Distance Education 2,610
Graduate Students 1,331
Total Students 3,941

MARYLAND

Baltimore
Archdiocese of Baltimore

College of Notre Dame of Maryland
4701 N. Charles St.
Baltimore, MD 21210
Tel: 410-435-0100; Fax: 410-532-5791
Web Site: www.ndm.edu
School Sisters of Notre Dame
Sr. JANE BURKE, S.S.N.D., Chm. of the Bd. of Trustees
Dr. MARY PAT SEURKAMP, Ph.D., Pres.
Dr. MARIE HELENE GIBNEY, Vice Pres. Academic Affairs
KAREN HORNIG, Vice Pres. Enrollment Mgmt.
RICHARD STAISLEFF, Vice Pres. Financial Affairs
JULIA THOMAS, Registrar
Dr. JEANNE ORTIZ, Vice Pres. Student Affairs
PATRICIA BOSSE, Vice Pres. for Inst. Advancement
Sr. EILEEN O'DEA, Vice Pres. Institutional Planning
MARGARET BRACK, Campus Min.
Sisters 14
Lay Professors 67
Students 3,193
Residents 355
Total Staff 235

**Loyola College in Maryland*
4501 N. Charles St.
Baltimore, MD 21210
Tel: 410-617-2000; Undergraduate Admissions: Ext 5012; Fax: 410-617-2176
Web Site: www.loyola.edu
Loyola Graduate Center-Columbia Campus
7135 Minstrel Way
Columbia, MD 21045-5245
Tel: 410-617-7600; Fax: 410-617-7643
Loyola Graduate Center -Timonium Campus
2034 Greenspring Dr.
Timonium, MD 21093
Tel: 410-617-1500; Fax: 410-617-1518
Other locations at which courses are offered: Anne Arundel County, Bel Air, Cecil County, Eastern Shore.
For additional information call Graduate Admissions: Tel: 410-617-2000, Ext. 5064
College Established 1852. Combined with Mt. St. Agnes College 1971.
Legal Title: *Loyola College in Maryland, Inc.*
Rev. HAROLD E. RIDLEY, S.J., Pres.
Dr. DAVID HADDAD, Vice Pres. Academic Affairs
Dr. JOHN HOLLWITZ, Dean, College of Arts and Sciences
Dr. PETER LORENZI, Dean, Sellinger School of Business & Mgmt.
Dr. SUSAN DONOVAN, Vice Pres. & Dean, Students
JOHN PALMUCAL, Vice Pres. Admin & Finance, Treasurer
MICHAEL GOFF, Vice Pres. Development & College Relations
FRANCIS J. CUNNIGHAM, Ph.D., Assoc. Vice Pres. Academic Affairs
WILLIAM BOSSEMEYER, Dean, Admissions
ILONA MCGUINESS, Ph.D., Dean, Freshmen
Revs.:
RONALD J. ANTON, S.J.
JEFFREY P. BAERWALD, S.J.
CHARLES BORGES, S.J.
MICHAEL L. BRADEN, S.J.
TIMOTHY B. BROWN, S.J.
JOHN L. BRUNETT, S.J.
EDWIN H. CONVEY, S.J.
WILLIAM M. DAVISH, S.J.
PATRICK F. EARL, S.J.
MICHAEL D. FRENCH, S.J.
C. KEVIN GILLESPIE, S.J.
TEODULO P. GONZALEZ, S.J.
EDGAR B. GRAHAM, S.J.
JOHN H. GRAY, S.J.
FRANK R. HAIG, S.J.
HANK HILTON, S.J.
JOSEPH M. KENNEDY, S.J.
WILLIAM K. MCGROARTY, S.J.
FRANCIS G. MCMANAMIN, S.J.
FRANCIS J. NASH, S.J.
LEO PETER PRENGAMAN, S.J.
HAROLD E. RIDLEY, S.J.
JOSEPH S. ROSSI, S.J.
PETER F. RYAN, S.J.
JAMES F. SALMON, S.J.
WILLIAM J. SNECK, S.J.
STEVE SPAHN, S.J.
LAWRENCE YOM, S.J.
Students 6,133
Undergraduate Division 3,171
Graduate Division 2,962
Priests 27
Sisters 6
Total Faculty 432
Jesuit Community of Loyola College, Inc.
Revs.:
PATRICK F. EARL, S.J., Rector
JOHN H. GRAY, S.J., Asst. to the Rector
EDGAR B. GRAHAM, S.J., Treas.
Mount St. Agnes College (Merged with Loyola College.)
Sisters of Mercy of the Americas
Sr. MARGARET BEATTY, R.S.M., Pres. Sisters of Mercy Baltimore Region
Priests 11
Sisters 1
Lay Teachers 223
Total Staff 1,055
Total Enrollment 6,073

Emmitsburg
Archdiocese of Baltimore

Mount Saint Mary's College (1808)
Emmitsburg, MD 21727
Tel: 301-447-6122; Fax: 301-447-5755
E-mail: communications@msmary.edu
Web Site: www.msmary.edu
GEORGE R. HOUSTON, JR., Pres.
Dr. STEPHEN ROCKWOOD, Librarian
Sr. PAULA MARIE BULEY, Vice Pres. Finance and Admin.
Mr. DAVID C. REEDER, Dir. Financial Aid
Dr. CAROL L. HINDS, Provost
Dr. STANLEY J. WERNE, Dean of Academic Svcs.
Mr. STEPHEN P. NEITZ, Dir. Admissions
Mr. JOHN C. GILL, Registrar
Dr. MICHAEL ZOLL, Dean of Student Devel.
Rev. KEVIN C. RHOADES, Rector of the Seminary
Rev. Msgr. HUGH J. PHILLIPS, Chap. of the Grotto Shrine and Pres. Emeritus
Revs.:
RAYMOND L. HARRIS, JR., Chap.
DANIEL C. NUSBAUM (ALB)
PAUL V. REDMOND (ALB)
DAVID W. SHAUM, Ph.D.
CARL J. FIVES (SCR)
JAMES DONOHUE, C.R.
Priests 1
Sisters 1
Lay Teachers 87
Total Enrollment 1,716

MASSACHUSETTS

Boston
Archdiocese of Boston

Emmanuel College
400 The Fenway
Boston, MA 02115
Tel: 617-735-9715; Fax: 617-735-9877
E-mail: johnsonp@emmanuel.edu
Web Site: www.emmanuel.edu
Sr. JANET EISNER, S.N.D., Ph.D., Pres. Sisters of Notre Dame de Namur
Sr. PATRICIA MCSHARRY, S.N.D., Dir. Campus Min.
Priests 1
Sisters 9
Lay Teachers 44
Students 1,630

Chestnut Hill
Archdiocese of Boston

**Boston College*
(Coed)
Chestnut Hill, MA 02467
Tel: 617-552-8000; Fax: 617-522-8828
Web Site: www.bc.edu
Rev. WILLIAM P. LEAHY, S.J., Pres.
Dr. JOHN NEUHAUSER, Academic Vice Pres.
Students 14,419
College of Arts and Sciences.
Students 5,741
JOSEPH QUINN, Dean
Summer Session.
Students 3,960
Rev. JAMES A. WOODS, S.J., Dean
Graduate School of Arts and Sciences.
Students 1,027
Dr. MICHAEL A. SMYER, Dean
School of Law.
Students 805
JOHN H. GARVEY, Dean
College of Advancing Studies.
Students 868
Rev. JAMES A. WOODS, S.J., Dean
Graduate School of Social Work.
Students 467
Dr. ALBERTO GODENZI, Dean
School of Management.
Students 2,187
Dr. HELEN F. PETERS, Dean
Graduate School of Management.
Students 956
School of Nursing.
Students 217
Dr. BARBARA HAZARD MUNRO, Dean
School of Education.
Students 785
Priests 37
Sisters 3
Lay Teachers 606
Dr. MARY M. BRABECK, Dean
Graduate School of Nursing
Students 165
Dr. BARBARA HAZARD MUNRO, Dean
Graduate School of Education
Students 1,028
Dr. MARY M. BRABECK, Dean

Chicopee
Diocese of Springfield in Massachusetts

College of Our Lady of the Elms
Chicopee, MA 01013
Tel: 413-594-2761; Fax: 413-592-4871
E-mail: keating@elms.edu
Web Site: www.elms.edu
Sisters of St. Joseph
Most Rev. THOMAS L. DUPRE, Bishop of Springfield
Sr. KATHLEEN C. KEATING, S.S.J., Pres.
Dr. ANNE HARRISON, Academic Dean
Sisters 22
Professors 46
Lay Teachers 39
Total Staff 130
Students 1,013

Easton
Diocese of Fall River

Villa Nazareth USA, Inc.
320 Washington St.
Easton, MA 02537
Tel: 508-230-5738; Fax: 508-565-1420
E-mail: rrossi@stonehill.edu
RICK ROSSI, Dir.

North Andover
Archdiocese of Boston

Merrimack College
North Andover, MA 01845
Tel: 978-837-5000
Web Site: www.merrimack.edu
Revs.:
ROBERT M. BURKE, O.S.A., Treas., Our Mother of Good Counsel Monastery
THOMAS M. CASEY, O.S.A.
KEVIN F. DWYER, O.S.A.
GEORGE R. MORGAN, O.S.A.
JOSEPH F. GILLIN, O.S.A.
JOSEPH L. FARRELL, O.S.A.
SCOTT C. NESS, O.S.A.
JAMES WENZEL, O.S.A.
Priests 8
Lay Teachers 120
Students 2,100
Continuing Education 800
Our Mother of Good Counsel Monastery (1947)
Tel: 978-837-5168
In res.,
Revs.:
THOMAS C. KENNY, O.S.A., Prior
JOHN V. CASEY, O.S.A.
CARMEN J. COLETTA, O.S.A., (Chicago Prov.)
ALBERT P. MACPHERSON, O.S.A.
WILLIAM J. WYNNE, O.S.A., Librarian
JOSEPH X. O'CONNOR, O.S.A., Sacristan

North Easton
Diocese of Fall River

Holy Cross Fathers Religious
480 Washington St.
North Easton, MA 02356
Tel: 508-238-5942; Fax: 508-230-7455
E-mail: bbeaupre@stonehill.edu
Revs.:
R. BRADLEY BEAUPRE, C.S.C., Supr.
JOHN J. MURPHY, C.S.C., Asst. Supr.
GENARO P. AGUILAR, C.S.C.
DAVID J. ARTHUR, C.S.C.
THOMAS C. BERTONE, C.S.C.
FOSTER J. BURBANK, C.S.C.
JOSEPH F. CALLAHAN, C.S.C.
THOMAS L. CAMPBELL

RUDOLPH V. CARCHIDI, C.S.C.
JAMES W. CHICHETTO, C.S.C.
Bro. STEPHAN CLARKE, C.S.C.
Revs.:
MARK T. CREGAN, C.S.C.
JOHN F. DENNING, C.S.C.
PAUL J. DUFF, C.S.C.
HARRY B. EICHORN, C.S.C.
THOMAS M. FEELEY
JAMES FENSTERMAHER, C.S.C.
RICHARD E. GRIBBLE, C.S.C.
THOMAS M. HALKOVIC, C.S.C.
FRANCIS J. HURLEY, C.S.C.
LAWRENCE A. JERGE, C.S.C.
ROBERT J. KRUSE, C.S.C.
THOMAS E. LAWTON, C.S.C.
Bro. JAMES W. MADIGAN, C.S.C.
Revs.:
LOUIS A. MANZO, C.S.C.
JOHN E. MCCARTHY, C.S.C.
JOHN J. MURPHY, C.S.C.
GEORGE B. MULLIGAN, C.S.C.
LEO POLSELLI, C.S.C.
Bro. PAUL RAHAIM, C.S.C.
Revs.:
RICHARD J. SEGREVE, C.S.C.
KEVIN P. SPICER, C.S.C.
JAMES E. TOBIN, C.S.C.
FRANCIS M. WALSH, C.S.C.
PETER J. WALSH, C.S.C.

Stonehill College
North Easton, MA 02357
Tel: 508-565-1000; Fax: 508-238-1297
E-mail: bbeaupre@stonehill.edu
Web Site: www.stonehill.edu
Revs.:
R. BRADLEY BEAUPRE, C.S.C., Supr., Tel: 508-565-1058; Fax: 508-565-1492
FRANCIS M. WALSH, C.S.C.
MARK T. CREGNAN, C.S.C., Pres.
KEVIN SPICER, C.S.C.
GEORGE B. MULLIGAN, C.S.C.
F. JAMES BURBANK, C.S.C.
RUDOLPH V. CARCHIDI, C.S.C.
JAMES W. CHICHETTO, C.S.C.
HARRY B. EICHORN, C.S.C.
THOMAS P. GARIEPY, C.S.C., (sabbatical)
THOMAS M. HALKOVIC, C.S.C.
FRANCIS J. HURLEY, C.S.C.
ROBERT J. KRUSE, C.S.C.
JOHN E. MCCARTHY, C.S.C.
LOUIS A. MANZO, C.S.C.
GENARO P. AGUILAR, C.S.C.
JOHN F. DENNERG, C.S.C., College Chap.
BARTLEY MACPHAIDIN, C.S.C.
Bro. PAUL RAHAIM C.S.C.
Priests 181
Lay Teachers 119
Students 2,165

Paxton
Diocese of Worcester

Anna Maria College
Sunset Lane
Paxton, MA 01612
Tel: 508-849-3300; Fax: 508-849-3334
E-mail: jprice@annamaria.edu
Web Site: www.annamaria.edu
A Coeducational Catholic College.
Sisters of St. Anne
WILLIAM MCGARRY, Pres.
Sr. ROLLANDE QUINTAL, S.S.A., Registrar
Lay Teachers 37
Total Staff 365
Students 1,267

Weston
Archdiocese of Boston

Regis College
235 Wellesley St.
Weston, MA 02493-1571
Tel: 781-768-7000; Fax: 781-768-8339
E-mail: postmaster@regiscollege.edu
Web Site: www.regiscollege.edu
Sr. SHEILA E. MEGLEY, Ph.D., Pres.
Sr. MILDRED CROWLEY, S.C., Campus Min.
Sisters of St. Joseph 20
Lay Teachers 129
Students 1,200

Worcester
Diocese of Worcester

Assumption College
500 Salisbury St.
Worcester, MA 01615-0005
Tel: 508-767-7000; Fax: 508-756-1780
E-mail: info@ave.assumption.edu
Web Site: www.assumption.edu
A Catholic Liberal Arts College under the Auspices of the Augustinians of the Assumption (Assumptionists).
Dr. THOMAS R. PLOUGH, Pres.
Revs.:
WILFRID J. DUFAULT, A.A., Chancellor
LOUIS F. DION, A.A., Vice Chancellor
FRANCIS P. GURLEY, Exec. Vice Pres.
MARY LOU ANDERSON, Interim Provost
Vice Presidents:
J. RICHARD CHRISTIANSEN, Vice Pres. Student Life
Rev. DENNIS GALLAGHER, Vice Pres. Mission
THOMAS E. RYAN, Vice Pres. Inst. Advancement
Priests 5
Sisters 1
Lay Teachers 122
Students 2,766

College of the Holy Cross, Inc.
Worcester, MA 01610
Tel: 508-793-2011; Fax: 508-793-3030
Web Site: www.holycross.edu
A College for Boarders and Day Scholars.
Rev. MICHAEL C. MCFARLAND, S.J., Pres.
Sisters 1
Lay Teachers 256
Students 2,801
Jesuit Teachers 11

MICHIGAN

Adrian
Diocese of Lansing

Siena Heights University
1247 E. Siena Heights Dr.
Adrian, MI 49221-1796
Tel: 517-263-0731; Fax: 517-264-7702
Web Site: www.sienahts.edu
RICHARD B. ARTMAN, Ph.D., Pres.
Sr. SHARON R.. WEBER, O.P., Ph.D., Academic Dean
Sisters 16
Brothers 1
Faculty 65
Staff 112
Students 1,994
Sponsored by the Adrian Dominican Sisters.

Ann Arbor
Diocese of Lansing

Ave Maria School of Law
3475 Plymouth Rd.
Ann Arbor, MI 48105-2550
Tel: 734-930-4408
E-mail: avemarialaw.edu
BERNARD DOBRANSKI, Dean

Detroit
Archdiocese of Detroit

Marygrove College
8425 W. McNichols Rd.
Detroit, MI 48221
Tel: 313-927-1200
(Coed)
Dr. GLENDA PRICE, Pres.
Dr. JOHN R. NOVAK, Vice Pres., Academic Affairs & Dean of Faculty
Dr. LISA JONES BROWN, Vice Pres., Student Affairs
Mr. JAMES MCKINNEY, Vice Pres., Finance & Admin.
Sr. CAROL QUIGLEY, I.H.M., Vice Pres., Inst. Advancement
Faculty:
I.H.M. Sisters 7
Sisters 2
Priests 1
Lay 240
Students 4,906
Incorporated.
Sisters, Servants of the Immaculate Heart of Mary

University of Detroit Mercy
McNichols Campus, 4001 W. McNichols Rd. at Livernois
Detroit, MI 48219-0900
Tel: 313-993-1000; Fax: 313-993-1534
Outer Drive Campus
8200 W. Outer Dr.
Detroit, MI 48219-0900
Law School
851 E. Jefferson
Detroit, MI 48226
Dental School
8200 E. Outer Dr.
Detroit, MI 48219-0900
Dr. MAUREEN FAY, O.P., Pres.
Dr. GEORGE F. LUNDY, S.J., Vice Pres. Academic Affairs & Provost
Dr. BETH TRIPLETT, Vice Pres. for Enrollment
Mr. DALE TUCKER, Vice Pres. Business & Finance
Ms. BARBARA MILBAUER, Vice Pres. University Advancement
Dr. KENNETH HENOLD, Vice Pres. Student Affairs
Priests 11
Sisters 7
Lay 280
Students 6,500

Grand Rapids
Diocese of Grand Rapids

Aquinas College
1607 Robinson Rd., S.E.
Grand Rapids, MI 49506
Tel: 616-459-8281, Ext. 4417; Fax: 616-732-4589
HARRY J. KNOPKE, Ph.D., Pres.
C. EDWARD BALOG, Ph.D., Provost & Dean of Faculty
MICHAEL C. KELLER, M.S.A., Vice Pres. Planning & Analysis
Mr. WILLIAM SHEFFERLY, Vice Pres. Finance & Oper.
JULIE RIDENOUR, B.A., Vice Pres. Devel.
Sr. M. AQUINAS WEBER, O.P., M.A., Chancellor
Dr. LARRY PFAFF, Dean of School Mgmt.
Dr. V. JAMES GAROFALO, Dean School Educ.
Dr. SHIRLEY LEWIS, Dean School Arts & Sciences
Ms. PAULA MEEHAN, Dean Admissions
Mr. BRADFORD WINKLER, Dean Student Afffairs
Ms. ELIZABETH JONES, Dir. Inst. Mktg.
LOIS B. KLAMAN, B.A., Registrar
Mr. DAVID J. STEFFEE, Dir. Fin. Aid
Sisters 10
Lay Teachers 95
Students 2,605

Livonia
Archdiocese of Detroit

Madonna University
36600 Schoolcraft Rd.
Livonia, MI 48150
Tel: 734-432-5300; Fax: 734-432-5393
Coeducational, resident and non-resident.
Conducted by the Felician Sisters.
Sr. M. FRANCILENE VAN DE VYVER, C.S.S.F., Pres.
Sr. M. LAURIANA GRUSZCZYNSKI, C.S.S.F., Vice Pres. Univ. Advancement
Dr. ERNEST NOLAN, Vice Pres. Academic Affairs
Sr. NANCY MARIE JAMROZ, C.S.S.F., Vice Pres. Student Life
Ms. KATHLEEN GRENDA, Registrar
Mr. LEONARD WILHELM, Vice Pres. Finance
Mr. FRANK KRIBAR, Dir. Enrollment Mgmt.
Ms. DONNA BERRY, Dir. Admin. Computer Center & Inst. Research
Mr. CHRIS ZIEGLER, Dir. Financial Aid
Deacon EUGENE DESJARLAIS, Dir. Campus Ministry
Priests 8
Sisters 21
Lay Staff 509
Students 3,868

Orchard Lake
Archdiocese of Detroit

Saint Mary's College
3535 Indian Trail
Orchard Lake, MI 48324
Tel: 248-683-0521; Fax: 248-683-0433
(Coed, resident and non-resident)
Rev. Msgr. STANLEY E. MILEWSKI, Chancellor of the Orchard Lake Schools and Centers
THADDEUS C. RADZILOWSKI, Pres.
THOMAS GLADSKY, Ph.D., Academic Dean
MICHAEL LOEFFLER, Business Office
Rev. Msgr. FRANCIS B. KOPER (WIL) Dir. Prog. of Priestly Formation
JAMES BASS, Dir. Financial Aid & Dir. Admissions
SARAH COOMER, Dean of Students
Rev. JAMES K. MAZUREK (PIT) Exec. Sec. Natl. Alumni Assn.
NANCY WARD, Dir. Library
LINDA MARIO, Registrar Faculty
Faculty 34
Students 326

Ypsilanti
Diocese of Lansing

Ave Maria College
300 W. Forest Ave.
Ypsilanti, MI 48197
Tel: 734-482-4180; 1-877-285-9072 (Toll Free); Fax: 734-482-2140
E-mail: admissions@avemaria.edu
Web Site: www.avemaria.edu
NICHOLAS J. HEALY, JR., Pres.
Students 124

MINNESOTA

Collegeville
Diocese of St. Cloud

St. John's University (1857)
(Men)
Collegeville, MN 56321-2000
Tel: 320-363-2011; Fax: 320-363-2504
E-mail: nthorburn@csbsju.edu
Web Site: www.csbsju.edu
Sponsored by the Collegeville Benedictine Monks as a division of the corporate Order of St. Benedict, Collegeville, MN.
The Graduate School of Theology (Coed)/Saint John's Seminary (Men): M.A. in Theology, Liturgical Studies, Liturgical Music, Pastoral Ministry and a Master of Divinity. The Undergraduate College of Liberal Arts and Sciences (Men), in full coordinate academic relation with the College of St. Benedict, St. Joseph (Women), offers forty departments, ten pre-professional and ten special academic programs.
Rt. Rev. JOHN KLASSEN, O.S.B., Ph.D., Abbot, Chancellor
Sponsored Programs: The Hill Monastic Manuscript Library, the Interfaith Sexual Trauma Institute, the Saint John's Pottery.
Officers Group:
Bro. DIETRICH REINHART, O.S.B., Pres.
Dr. NEIL THORBURN, Provost, Academic Affairs
Dr. GAR KELLOM, Vice Pres., Student Devel.
Mr. WARREN JANZEN, Vice Pres., Admin. Svcs.
Mr. ROB CULLIGAN, Vice Pres., Institutional Advancement
MARY MILBERT, Dean of Admissions
Bro. BENEDICT LEUTHNER, O.S.B., Corp. Treas.
Dr. WILLIAM CAHOY, Dean, School of Theology
Dr. CHERYL KNOX, Dean of the College
Administrative Group:
Rev. ALBERIC CULHANE, O.S.B., Exec. Asst. to the Pres. for Univ. Rels.
Mr. HERB TRENZ, Dir. Human Resources
Mr. JAMES HARDWICK, Assoc. Dean of Students
Bro. ISAAC CONNOLLY, O.S.B., Dean of Students
Rev. TIMOTHY BACKOUS, O.S.B., Chap., Dir. Campus Ministry
Dr. BERNARD EVANS, The Butler Family's Virgil Michel Ecumenical Chair in Rural Social Ministries
Dr. DANIEL RUSH FINN, The William & Virginia Clemens Chair in Economics and the Liberal Arts
Dr. THORPE RUNNING, The Michael Blecker Professorship
BARRY CYTRON, Rabbi, The Jay Phillips Center for Jewish-Christian Learning
Mr. RONALD BOSROCK, The John and Elizabeth Myers Chair in Mgmt.
Dr. NICHOLAS P. HAYES, The McNeely Chair in Critical Thinking
Mr. MICHAEL WHITE, Dir. Financial Aid
Dr. DAVID BENNETTS, Dir. Summer Academic Prog.
Mr. MICHAEL KATHMAN, Dir. Libraries and Media
Mr. JAMES KOENIG, Dir. Computing Svcs.
Ms. JULIE GRUSKA, Registrar
Revs.:
- LUKE STEINER, O.S.B., Rector, St. John's Seminary
- ERIC HOLLAS, O.S.B., Dir. Hill Monastic Manuscript Library
- ROMAN PAUR, O.S.B., Dir. Interfaith Sexual Trauma Institute

Mr. RICHARD BRESNAHAN Potter, The St. John's Pottery
Ms. MICHELLE HARRIS, Dir. of Intercultural Programs
Mr. JAMES SMITH, Dir. Athletics
Mr. GREGORY HOYE, Exec. Dir. Comm. & Mktg.
Mr. JOHN YOUNG, Dir. Devel. and Univ. Rels.
Bros.:
- LINUS ASCHEMAN, O.S.B., Dir. Buildings and Grounds
- DAVID KLINGEMAN, O.S.B., Archivist

Priests 28
Brothers 4
Sisters 4
Faculty 185
Administrators 161
Students 2,020

Duluth
Diocese of Duluth

College of St. Scholastica
1200 Kenwood Ave.
Duluth, MN 55811
Tel: 218-723-6000; Fax: 218-723-6290
A coed Benedictine college for resident and day students.
Dr. LARRY GOODWIN, Pres.
Sr. MARY ODILE CAHOON, O.S.B., Senior Vice Pres.
STEVE LYONS, Dean of Student Affairs
Sisters 7
Lay Faculty 100
Students 2,100

Minneapolis
Archdiocese of St. Paul and Minneapolis

The College of St. Catherine-Minneapolis
601 25th Ave. S.
Minneapolis, MN 55454
Tel: 651-690-7702; Fax: 651-690-7849
E-mail: mkmclaughlin@stkate.edu
Web Site: www.stkate.edu
MARGARET MCLAUGHLIN, Ph.D., Dean Health Professions
ANDREA LEE, IHM Pres.
Coed Health Occupation Human Service and Continuing Education Programs.
Total Staff 65
Students 969

St. Joseph
Diocese of St. Cloud

College of St. Benedict (1913)
(Women)
37 S. College Ave.
St. Joseph, MN 56374-2099
Tel: 320-363-5407 (Inst. Mktg. & Communications); Fax: 320-363-5136 (Inst. Mktg. & Comm.)
E-mail: cms@csbsju.edu
Web Site: www.csbsju.edu
Legal Title: *College of Saint Benedict*
Affiliation: Roman Catholic, established for the undergraduate education of women by the Sisters of the Order of Saint Benedict.
Sisters of the Order of St. Benedict
Partnership: The College of St. Benedict is a private, nationally recognized women's, residential, liberal arts, Catholic, Benedictine college of 1,900 students, located in St. Joseph, MN joined in a coeducational mission with St. John's University for men. As the only Catholic all women's Baccalaureate I college, St. Benedict's is unique in its commitment to gender specfic education within a coeducational environment.
Officers Group:
MARY E. LYONS, Pres.
NEIL THORBURN, Provost, Academic Affairs
MARY GELLER, Vice Pres. Student Devel.
SUSAN PALMER, Vice Pres. of Fin.
DAVID HOFFMAN, College Advancement
MARY MILBERT, Dean of Admission
RITA KNUESEL, Dean of the College
Administrative Group:
HERB TRENZ, Dir. Human Resources
MARY GELLER, Dean of Students
JODY TERHAAR, Dir. of Residence Life & Housing
MARY CATHERINE HOLICKY, O.S.B., Dir. Campus Ministry
JANE HAUGEN, Dir. of Fin. Aid
MICHAEL KATHMAN, Dir. of Libraries and Media
JAMES KOENIG, Dir., Info. Tech. Svc.
JOHN MCGEE, Vice Pres. Institutional Planning, Research & Comm.
JULIE GRUSKA, Registrar
SUSAN DOUMA, Dir. of Academic Advising
STEPHEN BURMEISTER-MAY, Dir. of Intl. Education
CAROL HOWE-VEENSTRA, Dir. of Athletics
MARY HARLANDER-LOCKE, Dir. of Career Svcs.
GREG HOYE, Exec. Dir Comm. & Mktg Svc.
JOANN SHROYER, Asst. Dir. Comm & Mktg. Svc.
KAY BUYTAERT, Dir. of Publications
MIKE DURBIN, Dir. of Sports Information
JIM FREDRICKS, Chief Physical Plant & Facilities Mgr.
Sisters 17
Faculty 169
Administrators 119
Students 2,024

St. Paul
Archdiocese of St. Paul and Minneapolis

College of St. Catherine
2004 Randolph Ave.
St. Paul, MN 55105
Tel: 651-690-6000; Fax: 651-690-6024
E-mail: admissions@stkate.edu
Web Site: www.stkate.edu
ANDREA J. LEE, I.H.M., Pres.
MARY MARGARET SMITH, Ph.D., Vice Pres. Academic Affairs & Dean of Faculty
MARY DESROCHES, Vice Pres. Business and Financial Affairs
PATRICIA HUIDSTUN, Vice Pres. Institutional Advancement (Interim)
COLLEEN HEGRANES, Vice Pres. Student Affairs
JAN CZECHOWSKI, Dean of Arts & Sciences
SUSAN HAMES, C.S.J., Co-Dir. Campus Ministry
CATHY STEFFENS, C.S.J., Co-Dir. Campus Ministry
SUSAN COCHRANE, Dean of Professional Studies
MARGARET MCLAUGHLIN, Dean of Health Professions
BRIAN BRUCSS, Dean of Students
Sisters of St. Joseph of Carondelet 4
Total Staff 552
Students 4,491

University of St. Thomas
2115 Summit Ave.
St. Paul, MN 55105
Tel: 651-962-5000; Fax: 651-962-6504
Web Site: www.stthomas.edu
Rev. DENNIS J. DEASE, Pres.
Rev. Msgr. TERRENCE J. MURPHY, Chancellor
Dr. JUDITH DWYER, Exec. Vice Pres.
Dr. SUSAN ALEXANDER, Assoc. Vice Pres. Academic Affairs (Interim)
Dr. NANCY H. ZINGALE, Exec. Asst. to the Pres.
Dr. THOMAS CONNERY, Dean of the College & Dean of Graduate School of Arts and Sciences
Dr. RALPH PEARSON, Vice Pres. Academic Affairs
Mr. TERRENCE O'CONNOR, Vice Pres., Finance and Admin.
Mr. GREGORY ROBERTS, Vice Pres. Students Affairs
Dr. GENE SCAPANSKI, Dean, School of Continuing Studies
Dr. TED FREDRICKSON, Dean, Graduate School of Business
Mr. QUENTIN J. HIETPAS, Senior Vice Pres. External Affairs
Dr. NONA MASON, Dir., Masters in Business Communications
Dr. BERNICE FOLZ, Dir., Graduate Program in Software Design
Dr. ALAN SICKBERT, Dean of Student Life
Dr. RONALD BENNETT, Dir., Manufacturing Systems Engineering Dept.
JEAN WALSTROM HALEY, Assoc. Vice Pres. for Info. Technology
Dr. JAMES P. DANIEL, Vice Pres. Devel.
Mr. DAVID LINK, Dean School of Law & Assoc. Vice Pres. Academic Affairs
Rev. PHILLIP J. RASK, Vice Pres. & Rector of St. Paul Seminary School of Divinity
Dr. JEANNE MCLEAN, Dean, St. Paul Seminary School of Divinity
Dr. MIRIAM Q. WILLIAMS, Interim Dean, School of Education
Dr. BARBARA SHANK, Dean, School of Social Work
Dr. BURTON NOLAN, Dir., Graduate Program in Professional Psychology
Rev. Msgr. WILLIAM L. BAUMGAERTNER, Prof. Emeritus, School of Divinity
Rev. Msgr. HENRI DULAC, (Retired), Philosophy
Rev. Msgr. JAMES HABIGER, Campus Ministry
Rev. Msgr. ELLSWORTH KNEAL, Prof. Emeritus School of Divinity
Rev. Msgr. JAMES M. LAVIN, Alumni Affairs
Rev. Msgr. ROBERT L. PROBST, Computing & Communication Svcs.
Rev. Msgr. JOHN P. SANKOVITZ, Theology Dept. (Retired)
Revs.:
- RONALD BOWERS, J.C.D., Assoc. Prof. of Canon Law, Vice Rector
- WILLIAM J. BAER, Rector, St. John Vianney Seminary
- MICHAEL BYRON, Instructor in Theology
- THOMAS J. CONROY, Asst. Prof. Theology (Retired)
- DOUGLAS E. DANDURAND (SC) Assoc. Dir. Spiritual Formation
- JEROME M. DITTBERNER, S.T.D., Prof. Dogmatic Theology
- JOHN ECHERT, S.S.L., Asst. Prof. Sacred Scripture
- PAUL F. FEELA, M.A., Instructor, Sacramental Theology & Liturgy; Dir. Worship
- PETER E. FELDMEIER, Ph.D., Asst. Prof. Spirituality
- JEFFREY HUARD, Dir. Campus Ministry
- LEO R. HUBER, (Retired)
- JAN MICHAEL JONCAS, Asst. Prof. Theology
- ARTHUR L. KENNEDY (BO) Prof. Theology
- DAVID W. KOHNER, Dir. Spiritual Formation
- PETER LAIRD, M.Div, Instructor in Moral Theology
- ROY LEPAK, (Retired), Philosophy
- JOHN M. MALONE, Asst. Prof. Business
- JAMES R. MOTL, O.P., Ph.D., Assoc. Prof. Homiletics
- WILLIAM O'NEILL, C.PP.S., Ph.D., (Retired), Assoc. Prof. Psychology
- THADEUS J. POSEY, O.F.M.Cap., Assoc. Prof. of Theology
- PATRICK QUINN, T.O.R., Asst. Prof. of Dogmatic Theology
- JAMES E. REIDY, (Retired), English Dept.
- JOHN F. RILEY, Theology Dept. (Retired)
- GEORGE SSERWANGA, Visiting Asst. Prof., Philosophy
- DOMINIC SERRA, Assoc. Prof. Sacramental Theology & Liturgy (On leave)

Donald DeGrood, Spiritual Dir., St. John Vianney Seminary
James Perkl, Spiritual Dir., St John Vianney Seminary
David W. Smith, Prof. Theology
James S. Stromberg, Philosophy Dept. (Retired)
Xavier Thelakkatt, Spiritual Dir. St. John Vianney Seminary
Robert B. Wellisch, Ph.D., Assoc. Prof. English
George A. Welzbacher, (Retired), Dept. of History
James W. Whalen, (Retired), Asst. Prof. Journalism
Priests 15
Sisters 2
Brothers 1
Lay Teachers 362
Students 11,435

Winona
Diocese of Winona

Saint Mary's University of Minnesota
(Coed)
700 Terrace Hts.
Winona, MN 55987-1399
Tel: 507-452-4430; 800-635-5987; Fax: 507-457-1633
E-mail: admissions@smumn.edu
Web Site: www.smumn.edu
DeLaSalle Christian Brothers
Bro. Louis De Thomasis, F.S.C., Pres.
Dr. Jeffrey Highland, Vice Pres., Academic Affairs & Dean, College of Liberal Arts
Mr. Anthony Piscitiello, Exec. Vice Pres., Admissions
Sharon Goo, Vice Pres., Student Devel.
Dr. Mary C. Fox, Vice Pres. Univ. Rels.
Cynthia Marek, Vice Pres., Financial Affairs
Loras Sieve, Vice Pres., Corporate and Community Rels.
Tim Burchill, Pres., Metanoia
Ann Merchlewitz, Vice Pres., General Counsel
Dr. James Towers, Dean, School of Education
Lawrence Gorrell, Dean, School of the Arts
James Bedtke, Vice Pres. Graduate & Special Programs
Revs.:
William M. Becker Tel: 507-457-6625
Andrew C. Fabian, O.P.
Priests 3
Brothers 15
Sisters 3
Lay Faculty 107
Students 1,364

MISSOURI

Kansas City
Diocese of Kansas City-St. Joseph

Avila College
11901 Wornall Rd.
Kansas City, MO 64145-1698
Tel: 816-942-8400; Fax: 816-942-3362
Web Site: www.avila.edu
Thomas F. Gordon, J.D., LL.M., Pres.
Joseph W. Deighton, J.D., Vice Pres. & Dean for Student Affairs
Sr. Marie Joan Harris, C.S.J., Ph.D., Vice Pres. & Dean for Academic Affairs
John M. Scarpitti, Ed.D., Vice Pres. for Fiscal Affairs
Mary Ellen Clark, Acting Vice Pres. Advancement
Stephen Huber, Dir. Campus Ministry
Sisters 1
Lay Teachers 57
Students 1,412

Rockhurst University
1100 Rockhurst Rd.
Kansas City, MO 64110-2561
Tel: 816-501-4000; Fax: 816-501-4293
E-mail: cathy.dubois@rockhurst.edu
Web Site: www.rockhurst.edu
Terrence P. Dunn, Chm. Bd. of Trustees
Rev. Edward Kinerk, S.J., Pres.
Ms. Robin Harris, Vice Pres. Inst. Advancement
Roger McCoy, Vice Pres. Finance
Mark Kopenski, Vice Pres. Enrollment
Elizabeth Brent, Vice Pres. Student Devel.
Jeanne Langdon, Dir. of the Library
Jo Adams, Controller
College of Arts & Sciences:
William Haefele, Dean
School of Professional Studies:
Nancy Evanson, Dean
School of Management:
Earl Walker, Dean
Research College of Nursing:
Nancy DeBasio, Pres./Dean
2316 E. Meyer Blvd.
Kansas City, MO 64123
Tel: 816-276-4700; Fax: 816-276-3526
Rockhurst College Continuing Education Center/ National Seminars Group:
Mark Truitt, Exec. Dir.
Gary Truitt, Mng. Dir.
6901 West 63rd St.
Kansas City, KS 66205
Tel: 913-432-7755; Fax: 913-432-2031
Revs.:
Martin J. Bredeck, S.J.
Edward K. Burger, S.J.
Luke J. Byrne, S.J.
John J. Callahan, S.J.
Thomas J. Casey, S.J.
Thomas F. Denzer, S.J.
Edward Kinerk, S.J.
Wilfred L. LaCroix, S.J.
Robert J. Mahoney
Timothy M. McMahon, S.J.
Louis J. Oldani, S.J.
James D. Wheeler, S.J.
Bros.:
E. Glenn Kerfoot, S.J.
John R. Olson, S.J.
Sisters 2
Priests 14
Lay Professors 160
Students 3,751

St. Louis
Archdiocese of St. Louis

Fontbonne College
6800 Wydown Blvd.
St. Louis, MO 63105
Tel: 314-862-3456; Fax: 314-889-1451
E-mail: sking@fontbonne.edu
Web Site: www.fontbonne.edu
Dennis C. Golden, Ed.D., Pres.
Sisters 7
Lay Teachers 55
Students 2,060

Saint Louis University
Corporate Title: Saint Louis University
221 N. Grand Blvd., DB 351
St. Louis, MO 63103-2097
Tel: 314-977-2222; Fax: 314-977-3874
Web Site: www.slu.edu
Mr. Michael F. Shanahan, Sr., Chm. Bd. of Trustees
Rev. Lawrence H. Biondi, S.J., Pres.
Sandra Johnson, Provost
James R. Kimmey, M.D., M.P.H., Dir., Institute for Urban Health Policy
Revs.:
Paul C. Reinert, S.J., Chancellor Emeritus
J. Barry McGannon, S.J., Chancellor
Vice Presidents:
Robert Altholz, Vice Pres. Business & Finance
Donald J. Whelan, Jr., Interim Vice Pres. Devel. & Univ. Rels.
Kathleen T. Brady, Vice Pres. Facilities Mgmt. & Civic Affairs
William R. Kauffman, J.D., Vice Pres. & General Counsel
Kathy G. Hagedorn, Vice Pres. Human Resource Mgmt.
Rick L. Chaney, Ph.D., Vice Provost
Rev. A. James Blumeyer, S.J., Vice Provost
Edwin B. Harris, Ph.D., Assoc. Provost Enrollment & Academic Svcs.
Robert M. Swanson, Ph.D., Assoc. Provost
Celerstine B. Johnson, Ed.D., Asst. Provost Academic Svcs. & Retention
Deans:
Allied Health Professions, School of
Tel: 314-577-8501; Fax: 314-577-8513
Joan Hrubetz, Interim Dean
Arts and Sciences, College of
Tel: 314-977-7205; Fax: 314-977-3649
Shirley M. Dowdy, Ph.D., Dean
Business and Administration, School of
Tel: 314-977-3833; Fax: 314-977-3897
Neil E. Seitz, Ph.D., Dean
Graduate School
Tel: 314-977-2244; Fax: 314-977-3943
Donald C. Brennan, Ph.D., Dean
Medicine, School of
Tel: 314-577-8201; Fax: 314-577-8645
Patricia L. Monteleone, M.D., Dean
Nursing, School of
Tel: 314-577-8910; Fax: 314-577-8949
Joan Hrubetz, Ph.D., R.N., Dean
Parks College of Engineering and Aviation
Tel: 314-977-8203; Fax: 314-577-8403
Charles C. Kirkpatrick, Ph.D., Dean
Philosophy and Letters, College of
Tel: 314-977-2701; Fax: 314-977-1602
Garth L. Hallett, S.J., Dean
Professional Studies, School of
Tel: 314-977-3409; Fax: 314-977-1482
Robert L. Hasenstab, Ph.D., Dean
Public Health, School of
Tel: 314-977-8111; Fax: 314-977-8150
Richard S. Kurz, Ph.D., Dean
Social Service, School of
Tel: 314-977-2730; Fax: 314-977-2731
Susan C. Tebb, Ph.D., Dean
Academic Services
Tel: 314-977-2370; Fax: 314-977-1424
John G. Severson, Ph.D.
College of Public Services
Tel: 314-977-3292; Fax: 314-977-3290
James F. Gilsinan, Ph.D., Dean
Pius XII Memorial Library
Tel: 314-977-3100; Fax: 314-977-3108
Frances Benham, Ph.D.
Student Educational Services Center
Tel: 314-977-2930; Fax: 314-977-3315
Celerstine B. Johnson, Ed.D.
Other Jesuits Associated with the University:
Revs.:
James H. Baker, S.J.
Michael D. Barber, S.J.
Bernard John Barry, S.J.
Stephen M. Belt, S.J.
Bro. William Biernatzki
Revs.:
Joseph E. Brown, S.J.
Robert A. Brungs, S.J.
Francis X. Cleary, S.J.
Anthony C. Daly, S.J.
Denis E. Daly, S.J.
Lowrie J. Daly, S.J.
Terrence E. Dempsey, S.J.
Michael J. Doody, S.J.
Robert S. Flack, S.J.
John B. Foley, S.J.
Garth L. Hallett, S.J.
W. Charles Heiser, S.J.
William J. Hutchison, S.J.
John J. Kavanaugh, S.J.
Thomas E.J. Kelly, S.J.
Edwin Lisson, S.J.
Michael Maher, S.J.
Michael K. May, S.J.
J. Barry McGannon, S.J.
Frederick G. McLeod, S.J.
Maurice McNamee, S.J.
John J. Mueller, S.J.
Claude N. Pavur, S.J.
Robert L. Phillips, S.J.
Robert Poirer, S.J.
Donald W. Reck, S.J.
Bro. William R. Rehg, S.J.
Revs.:
Paul C. Reinert, S.J.
Ralph C. Renner, S.J.
Albert C. Rotola, S.J.
James A. Sebesta, S.J.
Paul V. Stark, S.J.
James V. Veltrie, S.J.
James K. Voiss, S.J.
Pastoral Care Dept. of Saint Louis University Hospital:
Mary Lou Bennett, Dir.
Revs.:
Scott K. Davis, Supvr. Assoc. Clinical Pastoral Education
John Rausch, O.F.M.
Gregory G. Kirsch
Robert Hartmann
Sr. Virginia Geniesse, O.P.
Sr. Ann Johnston, O.P.
Elisabeth Price
Sandra Spencer
Helen Lombardo, Resident Student
Kathy Herron, Pastoral Care Asst.
Deacon Louis A. Menard
Monica Lee Donahue, Parish Nurse
Priests 29
Brothers 5
Sisters 6
Lay Teachers 1,259
Total Staff 1,299
Total Enrollment 11,112

MONTANA

Great Falls
Diocese of Great Falls - Billings

University of Great Falls (1932)
1301 20th St. S.
Great Falls, MT 59405
Tel: 406-761-8210; Fax: 406-791-5393
E-mail: adminrec@ugf.edu
Web Site: www.ugf.edu
Sponsored by the Sisters of Providence

Dr. FREDERICK GILLIARD, Pres.
DENNIS ALLAN OLSON, Academic Vice Pres. & Provost
CLAYTON SMITH, Vice Pres., Enrollment Mgmt.& Student Svcs.
JAMES B. WASHBURN, JR., Vice Pres. Admin. & Finance
HEIDI MCCORMICK, Campus Min.
Rev. JAMES R. SIKORA, Chap.
KIM FALCON, Grants Coord.
Assoc. Professors of Religious Studies:
Revs.:
JAMES R. SIKORA
JON TAYLOR, A.B.D.
Sr. MARY KAYE NEALEN, S.P.
Priests 2
Lay Teachers 41
Students 1,054

Helena
Diocese of Helena

Carroll College (1909)
1601 N. Benton Ave.
Helena, MT 59625
Tel: 406-447-4300; Fax: 406-447-4533
Four year Diocesan College of Liberal Arts and Sciences.
Revs.:
STEPHEN ROWAN (SEA) Interim Pres.
JEFFREY FLEMING, Chap. & Campus Min.
Dr. JAMES TRUDNOWSKI, Vice Pres. Academic Affairs
Ms. LYNN ETCHART, Vice Pres. Business Affairs
Mr. THOMAS J. MCCARVEL, Vice Pres. Inst. Advancement
Mr. ROBERT PASTOOR, Vice Pres. Student Affairs
Revs.:
WILLIAM GREYTAK
DANIEL P. HILLEN
JEREMIAH LOWNEY
J. EUGENE PEOPLES
DANIEL B. SHEA
JEREMIAH T. SULLIVAN
In res.,
Rev. Msgr. JOSEPH D. HARRINGTON
Rev. JOHN F. HUNTHAUSEN, (Retired)
Priests 8
Lay Professors 65
Students 1,292
Total Staff 115

NEBRASKA

Omaha
Archdiocese of Omaha

College of St. Mary
1901 S. 72nd St.
Omaha, NE 68124
Tel: 402-399-2400; Fax: 402-399-2342
E-mail: enroll@csm.edu
Web Site: www.csm.edu
Sr. MARYANNE STEVENS, R.S.M., Pres.
Dr. JUAN GARCIA, Vice-Pres. for Academic Affairs
Friar ROBERT GASS, Chap.
JAYNE SCHRAM, Media Relations Coord.
Sisters 7
Lay Teachers 54
Students 981

**Creighton University*
2500 California Plaza
Omaha, NE 68178
Tel: 402-280-2700; Fax: 402-280-2727
E-mail: jpschlegel@creighton.edu
Web Site: www.creighton.edu
Rev. JOHN P. SCHLEGEL, S.J., Pres. & Contact
The University is comprised of the following schools:
College of Arts and Sciences—
Rev. ALBERT A. AGRESTI, S.J., Ph.D., Dean
College of Business Administration—
Dr. ROBERT E. PITTS, Dean
Graduate School—
Dr. BARBARA J. BRADEN, Dean
School of Law—
PATRICK BORCHERS, J.D., Dean
University College/Summer Sessions—
Dr. C. TIMOTHY DICKEL, Dean
School of Dentistry—
Dr. WAYNE W. BARKMEIER, Dean
School of Medicine—
Dr. M. ROY WILSON, Dean
School of Nursing—
Dr. EDITH K. KITCHENS, Dean
School of Pharmacy and Allied Health Professions—
Dr. SIDNEY J. STOHS, Dean
Priests 11
Sisters 2
Lay Teachers 632
Students 6,237
Total Staff 1,503

NEW HAMPSHIRE

Manchester
Diocese of Manchester

Notre Dame College
2321 Elm St.
Manchester, NH 03104
Tel: 603-222-7100; Fax: 603-222-7101
E-mail: info@notredame.edu
Web Site: www.notredame.edu
Founded by Sisters of Holy Cross.
Rev. ANTHONY J. DECONCILIIS, C.S.C., Ph.D.
Sr. EDIE DALY, S.N.D.deN., Dir. Campus Ministry
Sisters 11
Lay Teachers 85
Students 1,121

Saint Anselm College
Manchester, NH 03102
Tel: 603-641-7000; Fax: 603-641-7284
E-mail: jdefelic@anselm.edu
Web Site: www.anselm.edu
Order of St. Benedict
Rt. Rev. MATTHEW K. LEAVY, O.S.B., Ph.D., Chancellor
Rev. JONATHAN P. DEFELICE, O.S.B., J.C.L., Pres. Admin. & Faculty
Priests 7
Brothers 1
Sisters 2
Lay Teachers 114
Students 1,985

Merrimack
Diocese of Manchester

The Thomas More College of Liberal Arts
6 Manchester St.
Merrimack, NH 03054
Tel: 603-880-8308; Fax: 603-880-9280
E-mail: thomaemorae@earthlink.com
Web Site: www.thomasmorecollege.edu
PETER V. SAMPO, Pres.
Total Staff 8
Students 75

Nashua
Diocese of Manchester

Rivier College
Nashua, NH 03060
Tel: 603-888-1311; Fax: 603-897-8883
E-mail: poneil@rivier.edu
Web Site: www.rivier.edu
Sisters of the Presentation of Mary
Sr. LUCILLE C. THIBODEAU, P.M., Ph.D., Pres.
Rev. PAUL R. DEMERS, S.C., Chap.
Presentation Sisters 27
Teaching Sisters 5
Teaching Priests 2
Lay Teachers 197
Students 2,572

Warner
Diocese of Manchester

Magdalen College
511 Kearsarge Mountain Rd.
Warner, NH 03278-9206
Tel: 603-456-2656; Fax: 603-456-2660
E-mail: admissions@magdalen.edu
Web Site: www.magdalen.edu
JEFFREY J. KARLS, Pres.
TERESA K. RUDKINS, Dean of Students
Dr. GEORGE N. STANCIU, Academic Dean
Rev. JACQUES DOLBEC
Lay Teachers 7
Total Staff 21
Students 75

NEW JERSEY

Caldwell
Archdiocese of Newark

Caldwell College
9 Ryerson Ave.
Caldwell, NJ 07006
Tel: 973-618-3000; Fax: 973-618-3600
E-mail: admissions@caldwell.edu
Web Site: www.caldwell.edu
Incorporated under the laws of the State of New Jersey with full power to confer degrees.
College Faculty:
Sr. PATRICE WERNER, O.P., Ph.D., Pres.
Dr. PAUL R. DOVILLARD, Ph.D., Vice Pres., Dean for Academic Affairs
Rev. THOMAS ORIANS, S.A., Coord. of Campus Ministry
Priests 2
Sisters 9
Sisters of St. Dominic 7
Lay Teachers 59
Students 2,104

Haledon
Diocese of Paterson

Salesian College
655 Belmont Ave.
Haledon, NJ 07508
Tel: 973-790-7963; Fax: 973-790-6484
E-mail: secretarysua@aol.com
Sr. JUDITH SUPRYS, F.M.A., Pres., Dean
Sr. CATHERINE ALTAMURA, F.M.A., Registrar
Students 9

Jersey City
Archdiocese of Newark

Saint Peter's College
2641 Kennedy Blvd.
Jersey City, NJ 07306-5997
Tel: 201-915-9000; Fax: 201-451-0036
E-mail: nieves_l@spcvxa.spc.edu
Web Site: www.spc.edu
Rev. JAMES N. LOUGHRAN, S.J., Pres.
EILEEN L. POIANI, Vice Pres. Student Affairs
Dr. ALEXANDRA GREGORY, Academic Vice Pres.
Mr. FRANK J. BARLETTA, Vice Pres. Finance and Admin. Svcs.
Mr. MARK L. MONTY, Vice Pres. Advancement
Dr. EUGENE CORNACCHIA, Acting Academic Dean, Day Session
Mr. JAMES ROBSON, Dean of Freshmen & Asst. Academic Dean, Day Session
Ms. BARBARA PENNIPEDE, Assoc. Dean, Englewood Cliffs Campus
Dr. RICHARD J. HAMILTON, Dean, Undergraduate Evening and Summer Sessions
Mr. WILLIAM MORRISON, Asst. Dean-Evening Session
RICHARD K. MULLIN, Assoc. Vice Pres. for Enrollment
Mr. BEN SCHOLZ, Dir. Admissions Svcs.
Ms. SUSAN E. NELSON, Registrar
Sr. DOROTHY GILOLEY, S.S., Dir. Campus Ministry
Priests 32
St. Peter's College Jesuit Community
Gothic Towers, 50 Glenwood Ave.
Jersey City, NJ 07306-4606
Tel: 201-433-2527; Fax: 201-432-7397
Jesuit Center
St. Peter Hall, 2652 Kennedy Blvd.
Jersey City, NJ 07306
Tel: 201-433-2527; 2528 (Rector's Office); Fax: 201-433-7139
Web Site: www.spc.edu
Revs.:
THOMAS C. BLESSIN, S.J.
EDWARD W. BRANDE, S.J.
JOHN M. BUCKLEY, S.J.
LAURENCE L. CASSIDY, S.J.
JAMES A. CATALANO, S.J.
MARK T. DESTEPHANO, S.J.
JUAN DIAZ VILAR
JAMES F. DOLAN
MARTIN DOYLE, S.J.
Bro. PATRICK T. FLANAGAN
Revs.:
CHARLES A. GALLAGHER, S.J.
EDWARD J. HEAVEY, S.J.
JOSEPH A. KELLY, S.J.
ROBERT E. KENNEDY, S.J.
JAMES N. LOUGHRAN, S.J.
JOSEPH W. LUX, S.J.
T. PATRICK LYNCH
DONAL T. MACVEIGH, S.J.
OSCAR G. MAGNAN
WILLIAM F.X. MAHER, S.J.
EDMUND W. MAJEWSKI, S.J.
ROBERT E. MCCARTY, S.J.
WILLIAM A. MCKENNA, S.J.
AIDAN C. MCMULLEN
JOSEPH A. NOVAK, S.J.
JOHN J. O'BRIEN
JOHN P. RUANE, S.J.
PATRICK H. SAMWAY, S.J.
JOHN P. ST. GEORGE, S.J.
RAYMOND A. SCHROTH, S.J.
DAVID X. STUMP, S.J.
THOMAS L. SHERIDAN, S.J.
JOHN P. WRYNN
Full Time Faculty:
Priests 14
Lay Teachers 98
Students 3,280

Lakewood
Diocese of Trenton

Georgian Court College
900 Lakewood Ave.
Lakewood, NJ 08701-2697
Tel: 732-364-2200; Fax: 732-367-3920
Web Site: www.georgian.edu
Sisters of Mercy
Dr. LOUIS C. VACCARO, Pres.
Dr. RITA CARNEY, Dean of Academic & Student Affairs
Rev. NORMAN DEMECK, C.P.
Priests 2
Sisters 23
Lay Teachers 125
Students 2,420

Lodi
Archdiocese of Newark

Felician College
Tel: 201-559-6000; Fax: 201-559-6188
E-mail: admissions@inet.felician.edu
Web Site: www.felician.edu
Lodi Campus:
262 Main St.
Lodi, NJ 07644
Rutherford Campus:
223 Montrose Ave.
Rutherford, NJ 07070
Sr. THERESA MARY MARTIN, C.S.S.F., Pres.
Dr. CHARLES J. ROONEY, Exec. Vice Pres. for Administration & Finance
R. DAVID CHANCEY, Exec. Vice Pres. & Rutherford Campus Admin.
Sr. PATRICIA A. MORRIS, O.P., Vice Pres. for Academic Affairs
Sr. MARY TARCILIA JUCHNIEWICZ, C.S.S.F., Vice Pres. for Student Affairs
JULIO IZQUIERDO, Vice Pres. for Business & Finance
SUSAN M. CHAFLIN, Assoc. Vice Pres. for Enrollment Mgmt.
Sr. MARY FIRMINA LAJEWSKI, C.S.S.F., Coord. Planning & Institutional Research
Dr. DONNA M. BARRON, Dir. Division of Teacher Education
Dr. MURIEL M. SHORE, Dir. of the Division of Health Sciences
Dr. GERARD P. O'SULLIVAN, Dir. Division of Arts & Sciences
Revs.:
DAMIAN COLICCHIO, O.F.M.Cap., Dir. Campus Ministry
JOHN P. O'NEILL, Assoc. Dir. Campus Ministry
Sr. MARIA MAGDALENA VALLELLANES, C.S.S.F., Assoc. Dir. Campus Ministry
CYNTHIA SIEVEWRIGHT, Dir. Undergraduate Admission
ROSALIE SANTANIELLO, Dir. Adult & Graduate Admission
JUNE FINN, Registrar
NORMA BETZ, Dir. Financial Aid

Mendham
Diocese of Paterson

Assumption College for Sisters
Mendham, NJ 07945
Tel: 973-543-6528; Fax: 973-543-9459
E-mail: socc@nac.net
Web Site: www.acscollegeforsisters.org
Conducted by Sisters of Christian Charity.
Sr. JULITTA HEINEN, S.C.C., Pres.
Sr. HELEN MARIE CRONIN, S.C.C., Academic Dean & Registrar
Sr. JOANNE BEDNARD, S.C.C., Treas.
Religious 10
Students 33

Morristown
Diocese of Paterson

College of Saint Elizabeth
2 Convent Rd.
Morristown, NJ 07960-6989
Tel: 973-290-4000; Fax: 973-290-4488
E-mail: smgeorge@112a.st-elizabeth.edu
Web Site: www.st-elizabeth.edu
Sisters of Charity
Sr. FRANCIS RAFTERY, S.C., Pres.
Dr. JOHANNA GLAZEWSKI, Vice Pres. for Academic Affairs and Dean of Studies
MARIA CAMMARATA, Vice Pres. for Finance & Admin. and Treas.
Mrs. ROSEMARIE GENCO, Comptroller
LAIPENG SPAGNOLETTI, Régistrar
Mrs. DONNA YAMANIS, Dean of Admissions and Financial Aid
Rev. ANTHONY J. CIORRA, O.F.M.Cap., Chap.
Tel: 973-290-4210
Full-time Admin. and Faculty:
Priests 3
Religious 20
Lay Teachers 161
Students 1,810

South Orange
Archdiocese of Newark

Seton Hall University (1856)
400 South Orange Ave.
South Orange, NJ 07079
Tel: 973-761-9000; Fax: 973-275-2361
Web Site: shu.edu
Rev. Msgr. ROBERT T. SHEERAN, S.T.D., Pres.
Officers of University:
MARY MEEHAN, Vice Pres. & Asst. to the Pres.
MEL J. SHAY, Acting Provost
JOHN H. SHANNON, J.D., Vice Pres. University Affairs
LAURA A. WANKEL, Ed.D., Vice Pres. Student Affairs
DENNIS GARBINI, M.B.A., Vice Pres., Finance & Technology
CATHERINE KIERNAN, J.D., Vice Pres. & University Counsel
Administrators:
FRANCISCO MORALES, Dir. Special Academic Programs
KING MOTT, Ph.D., Dean, Freshman Studies
ARTHUR W. HAFNER, Ph.D., Dean University Libraries
DEBORAH RAIKES-COLBERT, Assoc. Vice Pres. Human Resources
HELEN CUNNING, Asst. Vice Pres. Univ. Advancement
Dr. ROBERT HALLISSEY, Dir. Grants & Contracts
JEFF FOGELSON, Dir. University Athletics
Revs.:
JAMES M. CAFONE, S.T.D., Min. to Priest Community
JAMES F. SPERA, M.Div., Dir. Campus Ministry
ROBERT S. MEYER, S.T.L., Asst. to Vice Pres. Student Affairs
Rev. Msgr. ANDREW T. CUSACK, Ph.D., Dir. National Inst. for Clergy Formation
College of Arts and Sciences
JAMES VAN OOSTING, Ph.D., Dean, Tel: 973-761-9022
School of Business
KAREN E. BOROFF, Ph.D., Acting Dean, Tel: 973-761-9013
College of Education and Human Services
RICHARD OGNIBENE, Ed.D., Acting Dean, Tel: 973-761-9025
College of Nursing
PHYLLIS HANSELL, Ed.D., Dean, Tel: 973-761-9014
School of Law
PATRICK E. HOBBS, J.D., L.L.M., Dean
One Newark Center
Newark, NJ 07102
Tel: 973-642-8750
School of Theology
Rev. Msgr. ROBERT F. COLEMAN, J.C.D., Rector & Dean, Tel: 973-761-9016
School of Graduate Medical Education
JOHN PATERSON, D.D.S., Dean, Tel: 973-761-9710
College Seminary
Rev. Msgr. ROBERT F. COLEMAN, J.C.D.
School of Diplomacy and Intl. Rels.
CLAY CONSTANTINOU, J.D., L.L.M., Dean, Tel: 973-375-2515
Priest Community:
Rev. JOHN F. MORLEY, Ph.D.
Rev. Msgr. ROBERT F. COLEMAN, J.C.D.
Rev. Msgr. ANDREW T. CUSACK, Ph.D.
Rev. Msgr. WILLIAM N. FIELD, M.L.S., M.A.
Rev. Msgr. EDWARD J. FLEMING, Ph.D., (Retired)
Rev. Msgr. JOHN W. FLESEY, S.T.D.
Rev. Msgr. WILLIAM C. HARMS, D.Min.
Rev. Msgr. RICHARD M. LIDDY, Ph.D.
Rev. Msgr. ROBERT T. SHEERAN, S.T.D.
Rev. Msgr. EDWIN V. SULLIVAN, Ph.D., (Retired)
Rev. Msgr. JAMES C. TURRO, S.T.L.,S.S.L.,M.A.,Ph.D., (Retired)
Rev. Msgr. ROBERT J. WISTER, S.T.M.
Revs.:
JOHN M. BALLWEG, M.A.
W. JEROME BRACKEN, Ph.D.
ALFRED V. CELIANO, Ph.D., (Retired)
GABRIEL B. COSTA, Ph.D.
EUGENE J. COTTER, D.Lett
WALTER A. DEBOLD, M.A., (Retired)
ARNOLD P. DE ROSA, Ph.D.
LAWRENCE E. FRIZZELL, D.Phil.
FRANCIS T. GAVIN, M.A., (Retired)
NICHOLAS S. GENGARO, S.T.D.
THOMAS G. GUARINO, S.T.D.
KEVIN M. HANBURY, Ed.D.
PAUL A. HOLMES, S.T.D.
CHRISTOPHER J. HYNES, Ed.S.
PETER F. LENNON, Ph.D.
GERALD H. MCCARREN, S.T.D.
ROBERT S. MEYER, S.T.L.
JOHN F. MORLEY, Ph.D.
RICHARD M. NARDONE, Ph.D.
ROBERT P. NESTOR, Ed.D.
MARTIN F. O'BRIEN, M.S.
LAWRENCE B. PORTER, O.P., Ph.D.
JOHN J. RANIERI, Ph.D.
HENRY J. SCHREITMUELLER, Ed.D.
ARTHUR J. SERRATELLI, S.T.D.
WILLIAM P. SHERIDAN, M.Div.
DONALD C. SMITH, M.A.
JAMES F. SPERA, M.Div.
C. ANTHONY ZICCARDI, S.T.L., S.S.L.
In res.,
Revs.:
JOSEPH R. CHAPEL, S.T.D.
DOUGLAS J. MILEWSKI, S.T.L.
THOMAS P. NYDEGGER, M.Div.
JOSEPH F. WORTMANN, M.A.
Priests 50
Lay Teachers 350
Students 9,760

NEW MEXICO

Santa Fe
Archdiocese of Santa Fe

College of Santa Fe (1947)
(Coed Four Year Liberal Arts College)
1600 St. Michaels Dr.
Santa Fe, NM 87505
Tel: 505-473-6011
Brothers of the Christian Schools
Dr. JAMES FRIES, Pres.
Dr. JIM LAWRENCE, Sr. Vice Pres. & Dean of the College
DALE REINHART, Dir. Admissions and Enrollment Mgmt.
Ms. YVONNE RUSSELL, Dean of Students
Revs.:
WANDA KILE, Dir. Campus Ministry
JAMES CRONIN
Brothers 7
Lay Teachers 160
Students 1,700

NEW YORK

Albany
Diocese of Albany

The College of Saint Rose
(Corporate Name)
432 Western Ave.
Albany, NY 12203
Tel: 518-454-5111; 800-657-8556; Fax: 518-458-5447
Founded by the Sisters of St. Joseph of Carondelet in 1920.
Dr. MARK SULLIVAN, Pres.
Dr. WILLIAM LOWE, Acting Vice Pres. for Academic Affairs
KATHLEEN M. SINEL, Vice Pres. for Finance & Admin.
Ms. JEANNE KOBUSZEWSKI, Vice Pres. Institutional Advancement
CHARLES E. GREENE, JR., Assoc. Vice Pres. for Administration
JUDITH A. KELLY, Registrar
MARGARET KIRWIN, Assoc. Vice Pres. for Acadamic Affairs
DENNIS MCDONALD, Dean of Student Svcs.
MARY GRONDAHL, Assoc. Vice Pres. for Enrollment Planning and Undergraduate Admissions
Revs.:
CHRISTOPHER DEGIOVINE, Chap. & Dir. of Campus Ministry
ANTHONY D. GULLEY, Non-Resident Priest
Priests 2
Sisters 7
Lay Teachers 125
Students 4,031

Maria College
700 New Scotland Ave.
Albany, NY 12208
Two Year College
Sr. LAUREEN FITZGERALD, Pres.
Sr. JOSEPHINE REYNOLDS, Dean for Academic Affairs
Ms. LAURIE GILMORE, Dir. Admissions
Ms. DEBORAH CORRIGAN, Dean Students
Mrs. FRANCES BERNARD, Dir. Business Affairs

Revs.:
MICHAEL HOGAN
PAUL R. SMITH
THOMAS F. BERARDI
Sisters of Mercy 14
Sisters of the Holy Names of Jesus and Mary (SNJM) 1
Lay Teachers 34
Students 815

St. Bernard's Institute at Albany
Extension Program of St. Bernard's Institute, Rochester, NY.
40 N. Main Ave.
Albany, NY 12203
Tel: 518-453-6760; Fax: 518-453-6793
E-mail: stbernardsinstitute@rcda.org
Graduate School of Theology & Ministry Studies.
Dr. JOSEPH PICCOLINO, Dir.

Bronx
Archdiocese of New York

**Fordham University* (1841)
Fordham Rd.
Bronx, NY 10458
Fax: 718-817-4925
Web Site: www.fordham.edu
Second campus and Branch campus at Lincoln Center, New York, NY 10023 and Marymount College, Tarrytown, NY 10591. Chartered by the Legislature of the State of New York.
Rev. JOSEPH A. O'HARE, S.J., Pres.
Mr. JOHN J. LORDNN, Sr. Vice Pres., Chief Fin. Officer & Treasurer
Dr. JOHN C. HOLLWITZ, Vice Pres. Academic Affairs
Mr. BRUNO M. SANTONOCITO, Vice Pres. Devel. & Univ. Rels.
Mr. CHARLES H. HODULIK, Vice Pres. Lincoln Center
Mr. JEFFREY L. GRAY, Vice Pres. Students Affairs
Dr. BRIAN BYRNE, Vice Pres. Admin.
Dr. PETER STACE Vice Pres. for Enrollment
Dr. NANCY BUSCH, Dean of Graduate School of Arts and Sciences
Rev. JEFFREY VON ARX, S.J., Dean of Fordham College at Rose Hill
Dr. SHARON SMITH, Dean of College of Business Admin.
Dr. ERNEST SCALBERG, Dean of Graduate School of Business Admin.
Dr. REGIS D. BERNHADT, Dean of Graduate School of Education
JOHN D. FEERICK, LL.B., Dean of School of Law
Dr. PETER B. VAUGHAN, Dean of Graduate School of Social Service
Rev. ROBERT R. GRIMES, S.J., Dean of Fordham College at Lincoln Center
Dr. MICHAEL GILLAN, Dean of Fordham College of Liberal Studies
Rev. VINCENT M. NOVAK, S.J., Dean of Graduate School of Religion and Religious Education
Priests 27
Sisters 3
Lay Teachers 567
Total Staff 597
Total Enrollment 14,000

Manhattan College
Manhattan College Pkwy.
Bronx, NY 10471
Tel: 718-862-7200; 800-MC2-XCEL; Fax: 718-862-8019
E-mail: admit@manhattan.edu
Web Site: www.manhattan.edu
Bro. THOMAS SCANLAN, F.S.C., Pres.
Priests 1
Brothers 4
Sisters 2
Lay Staff 162
Total Staff 169
Total Enrollment 2,622

Brooklyn
Diocese of Brooklyn

**St. Francis College*
180 Remsen St.
Brooklyn, NY 11201
Tel: 718-489-5200
Dr. FRANK MACCHIAROLA Pres.
Brothers 4
Sisters 1
Students 2,505

**St. Joseph's College*
245 Clinton Ave.
Brooklyn, NY 11205
Tel: 718-636-6800; Fax: 718-636-7245
E-mail: fburns@sjcny.edu
Branch Campus
155 West Roe Blvd.
Patchoque, NY 11772
Tel: 516-447-3200; Fax: 718-636-7245
Under supervision of Board of Trustees.
Sr. ELIZABETH A. HILL, C.S.J., Pres.
Sr. MARY FLORENCE BURNS, C.S.J., Ph.D., Academic Vice Pres.
Sr. MARGARET BUCKLEY, C.S.J., Ed.D., Academic Dean, School of Arts & Science
THOMAS G. TRAVIS, Ph.D., Vice Pres. & Dean, School of Adult & Professional Education
Sisters 19
Lay Teachers 44
Students 1,352

Buffalo
Diocese of Buffalo

Canisius College
2001 Main St.
Buffalo, NY 14208-1098
Tel: 716-883-7000; Fax: 716-888-2525
E-mail: cookev@canisius.edu
Web Site: www.canisius.edu
Revs.:
VINCENT M. COOKE, S.J., Pres.
JAMES P. HIGGINS, S.J., Sec., Bd. Trustees
RICHARD R. GALLIGAN, S.J., Dir. Campus Min.
Dr. ELLEN O. CONLEY, Vice Pres. for Student Affairs
Mr. JOHN J. HURLEY, Vice Pres. for College Relations & Gen. Counsel
Dr. LAURENCE W. FRANZ, Vice Pres. of Business & Finance & Treas.
Dr. HERBERT J. NELSON, Vice Pres. for Academic Affairs
Dr. JAMES P. MCDERMOTT, Dean College of Arts & Sciences
Dr. RICHARD A. SHICK, Dean, Wehle School of Business
Dr. KEITH R. BURICH, Dean, School of Educ. & Human Svcs.
Dr. JOEL A. COHEN, Dir., Assoc. Vice Pres. for Library & Information Services
Priests 15
Lay Teachers 187
Total Enrollment 4,861

**D'Youville College*
320 Porter Ave.
Buffalo, NY 14201
Tel: 716-881-3200; Fax: 716-881-7780
E-mail: Brayjd@dyc.edu
Web Site: www.dyc.edu
Grey Nuns of the Sacred Heart.
Sr. DENISE A. ROCHE, G.N.S.H., Ph.D., Pres.
Rev. ANTHONY RIGOLI, O.M.I., Chap. (Dir. Campus Ministry)
Priests 1
Sisters 4
Lay Teachers 158
Total Staff 318
Students 2,397

Trocaire College
360 Choate Ave.
Buffalo, NY 14220
Tel: 716-827-2423; Fax: 716-828-6109
E-mail: hurleyp@trocaire.edu
Web Site: www.trocaire.edu
PAUL B. HURLEY, JR., Ph.D., Pres.
Sisters 7
Lay Teachers 65
Students 746
Total Staff 48

Villa Maria College of Buffalo
240 Pine Ridge Rd.
Buffalo, NY 14225-3999
Tel: 716-896-0700; Fax: 716-896-0705
Web Site: www.villa.edu
Sr. MARCELLA MARIE GARUS, Pres.
NATALIE J. MOUDGIL, Ph.D., Vice Pres. Academic Affairs
Sr. MARY DE ANGELIS NOWAK, Vice Pres. Business Affairs
Sr. MARY MARCINE BOROWIAK, Vice Pres. Devel.
Sr. MARY LOUIS RUSTOWICZ, Vice Pres. Student Affairs
Sisters 3
Lay Teachers 56
Students 408
Total Staff 132

Hamburg
Diocese of Buffalo

Hilbert College
5200 S. Park Ave.
Hamburg, NY 14075
Tel: 716-649-7900; Fax: 716-649-0702
E-mail: edmunette@hilbert.edu
Web Site: www.hilbert.edu/
Franciscan Sisters of Saint Joseph
Sr. EDMUNETTE PACZESNY, F.S.S.J., Pres.
Rev. BERNARD OLSZEWSKI, O.F.M.Conv., Chap.
Sr. JACQUELINE BENBENEK, C.S.S.F., Campus Min.
Priests 2
Sisters 4
Lay Teachers 79
Students 893
Total Staff 137

Jamaica
Diocese of Brooklyn

St. John's University
8000 Utopia Pkwy.
Jamaica, NY 11439
Tel: 718-990-6161; Fax: 718-990-5723
Web Site: www.stjohns.edu
Sponsored by the Vincentian Priests and Brothers Eastern Province of the Congregation of the Mission.
Rev. DONALD J. HARRINGTON, C.M., Pres.
Officers of Administration:
ROBERT J. CRIMMINS, Exec. Vice Pres.
TONY H. BONAPARTE, Ph.D., Provost
Rev. MICHAEL J. CARROLL, C.M., Vice Pres. Univ. Ministry & Graduate Center, Rome, Italy
CECILIA S. CHANG, Ed.D., Vice Pres. Intl. Rels.
JOHN P. CONNOLLY, JR., Vice Pres. Administrative Svcs.
Rev. JOSEPH V. DALY, C.M., Ombudsman & Asst. to the Pres.
SUSAN L. EBBS, Ed.D., Senior Vice Pres. Student Life
DOROTHY E. HABBEN, Ph.D., Vice Pres., Univ. Sec. & Chief Assessment Officer
SUZANNE M. HALPIN, Vice Pres. Office of External Affairs
Rev. JAMES F. KIERNAN, C.M., Senior Vice Pres., Staten Island Campus
DENNIS P. MCAULIFFE, Vice Pres. Univ. Affairs
JAMES P. PELLOW, Senior Vice Pres. & Treas.
JOSEPH A. SCIAME, Vice Pres. Govt. & Community Rels.
FRANK J. SIRIANNI, Ph.D., Vice Pres. & Chief Information Officer
Rev. BERNARD M. TRACEY, C.M., Vice Pres. Inst. Advancement
Priests 20
Sisters 3
Lay Teachers 566
Total Enrollment 18,523 (undergraduate and graduate of Queens Staten Island campuses and Rome)
Queens campus enrollment 15,593

Loudonville
Diocese of Albany

Siena College
Loudonville, NY 12211
Tel: 518-783-2300; Fax: 518-783-4293
Web Site: www.siena.edu
Founded in 1937 by the Franciscan Friars, Order of Friars Minor, Province of the Most Holy Name of Jesus.
Revs.:
KEVIN E. MACKIN, Pres.
JAMES TOAL, Vice Pres.
Dr. TIMOTH LEDERMAN, Vice Pres. Academic Affairs
ANTHONY PONDILLO, Vice Pres. Finance & Admin.
Dr. GREGORY STAHL, Vice Pres. for Inst. Advancement
Dr. CHITRA RAJAN, Vice Pres. Planning
NOEL HOGAN, Dean of Enrollment Mgmt.
NED JONES, Dir. of Admissions
Rev. JOHN C. FRAMBES, O.F.M., Vice Pres. for Student Affairs
SUZANNE ALLEGRETTI, Dir. of Continuing Education
Rev. JAMES SABAK, O.F.M., Chap.
ANN WHITE, Dir. Financial Aid
WILLIAM KELLEY, Dir. of Physical Plant
JAMES A. SERBALIK, Registrar
GARY B. THOMPSON, Dir. of Library
THOMAS DENHAM, Dir. of Career Center
Legal Title: *Siena College*
Students 3,011
The Friary:
Rev. DANIEL P. DWYER, O.F.M.
Bro. THOMAS CONWAY, Vicar
Rev. CALLISTUS M. BAMBERG, O.F.M., Dir. St. Francis Chapel
Bros.:
ROMUALD CHINETSKY, O.F.M.
GARY MACIAG, O.F.M.
MICHAEL HARLAN, O.F.M.
Revs.:
MATTHEW T. CONLON, O.F.M.
JULIAN A. DAVIES, O.F.M.
WILLIAM DEBIASE, O.F.M.

JAMES FALDUTI, O.F.M.
PETER A. FIORE, O.F.M.
JOHN C. FRAMBES, O.F.M.
CAPISTRAN HANLON, O.F.M.
KEVIN E. MACKIN, O.F.M.
HENRY L. MADDEN, O.F.M.
WILLIAM E. MCCONVILLE, O.F.M.
DANIEL C. NELSON, O.F.M.
LUKE A. O'CONNELL, O.F.M.
KENNETH PAULLI, O.F.M.
LAURENCE P. RAINVILLE, O.F.M.
REGINALD J. REDDY, O.F.M.
BLAISE R. REINHART, O.F.M.
EVAN ROCHE, O.F.M.
JAMES SABAK, O.F.M.
SENNEN C. SAN FRATELLO, O.F.M.
DENNIS TAMBURELLO, O.F.M.
JAMES TOAL, O.F.M.
JOHN E. VAN HOOK, O.F.M.

New Rochelle
Archdiocese of New York

**College of New Rochelle*
29 Castle Pl.
New Rochelle, NY 10805
Tel: 914-654-5000; Fax: 914-654-5980
E-mail: info@cnr.edu
Web Site: www.cnr.edu
Founded in 1904 by the Religious of the Order of St. Ursula. Chartered by the Regents of the University of the State of New York. The College is composed of four schools: School of Arts and Sciences (Women); Graduate School; School of New Resources; School of Nursing (Coed).
Dr. STEPHEN SWEENY, Pres.
Dr. JOAN BAILEY, Senior Vice Pres. Academic Affairs
Dr. ROSE MARIE HURRELL, Dean, School of Arts and Sciences
Dr. LAURA ELLIS, Dean, Graduate School
Dr. DONNA DEMAREST, Dean, School of Nursing
Dr. BESSIE BLAKE, Dean of School of New Resources
WALTER MCCARTHY, Vice Pres. Financial Affairs
Rev. JOHN RATHSCHMIDT, O.F.M.Cap., Chap.
Mrs. MARY NAUGHTON, Dir., Campus Ministry
Rev. BASILIO MONTERO Academic Admin. (facilities in Rockville Diocese)
Priests 2
Sisters 8
Lay Teachers 475
Students 6,514

Iona College
715 North Ave.
New Rochelle, NY 10801
Tel: 914-633-2000
E-mail: webmaster@iona.edu
Web Site: www.iona.edu
(Coed)
Branch Orangeburg Campus
One Dutch Hill Rd.
Orangeburg, NY 10962
Tel: 914-359-2252
Branch Manhattan Campus
St. Michael High School, 425 W. 33rd St.
New York, NY 10001
Tel: 212-630-0270
Education in the tradition of the Christian Brothers. Independent College.
Bro. JAMES A. LIGUORI, Ed.D., Pres.
Dr. JUDSON R. SHAVER, Vice Pres. for Academic Affairs/Provost
Mr. JOHN BRAUNSTEIN, Vice Provost for Enrollment Management
Dr. MICHAEL MCGRATH, Vice Provost for Student Devel.
Ms. DIXIE K. NORRIS, Vice Pres. Finance & Administration
Mr. JAMES LINK, Vice Pres. for Advancement
Dr. WARREN ROSENBERG, Dean of School of Arts & Sciences
Dr. NICHOLAS BEUTELL, Dean of the Hagan School of Business
Ms. JOY COLLINS, Dir. of Libraries
Priests 3
Brothers 27
Sisters 11
Lay Teachers 468
Students 4,897

New York
Archdiocese of New York

College of Mount Saint Vincent
(Coed)
6301 Riverdale Ave.
New York, NY 10471-1093
Tel: 718-405-3200; Fax: 718-549-2603
E-mail: cfinegan@cmsv.edu
Web Site: www.cmsv.edu
Founded by the Sisters of Charity of Saint Vincent de Paul. Chartered by the University of the State of New York.
CHARLES L. FLYNN, JR., Ph.D., Pres.
MICHAEL J. MCGOVERN, Ed.D., Vice Pres., Academic Affairs
THERESA D. WHITESELL, C.F.R.E., Vice Pres. Institutional Advancement
Brothers 1
Sisters 5
Lay Faculty 65
Total Enrollment 1,515

Marymount Manhattan College
Chartered by the Univ. of the State of NY.
221 E. 71st St.
New York, NY 10021
Tel: 212-517-0400
E-mail: vdorgan@mmm.edu
Web Site: www.mmm.edu
Dr. REGINA S. PERUGGI, Pres.
ANN JABLON, Acting Vice Pres. Academic Affairs
TOBY SIMON, Vice Pres. Student Affairs
PAUL CIRAULO, Vice Pres. Business & Financial Affairs
MARY KAY DEMETRY-JEYNES, Dean Courses for Adults
JEANNE EVANS, Dir. College Rels. & Inst. Advancement
Sr. VIRGINIA DORGAN, R.S.H.M., Campus Min.
Sisters 3
Students 2,330

Newburgh
Archdiocese of New York

Mt. St. Mary College (1954)
Leslie Reggero
Newburgh, NY 12550
Tel: 914-561-0800; Fax: 914-562-6762
E-mail: coyne@msmc.edu
Web Site: www.msmc.edu
(Coed)
Sr. ANN SAKAC, O.P., Pres.
Sr. AGNES BOYLE, O.P., Academic Dean
GERALD JILBERT, Registrar
Rev. MARK CONNELL, Chap.
Divisions: Arts & Letters; Education; Business; Nursing; Natural Sciences; Mathematics & Computer Science; Philosophy & Religious Studies; Social Sciences.
Sisters 4
Lay Teachers 49
Students 2,011

Niagara University
Diocese of Buffalo

Niagara University
Lewiston Rd.
Niagara University, NY 14109-2015
Tel: 716-285-1212; Fax: 716-286-8355
E-mail: jbm@niagara.edu
Web Site: www.niagara.edu
Revs.:
JOSEPH L. LEVESQUE, C.M., Pres.
DENNIS H. HOLTSCHNEIDER, C.M., Exec. Vice Pres. & CEO
SUSAN E. MASON, Ph.D., Vice Pres. for Academic Affairs
MICHAEL S. JASZKA, Vice Pres. for Admin.
Rev. FRANCIS X. PRIOR, C.M., Vice Pres. Devel. & Univ. Rels., Emeritus
SHEILA L. HAUSRATH, M.S.Ed., Vice Pres. for Student Life
RICHARD S. HOPKINS, B.S., Vice Pres. for Univ. Advancement
Rev. VINCENT J. O'MALLEY, C.M., Senior Asst. to the Pres. for Mission
JUDITH S. WILLARD, Ph.D., Asst. Pres. for Planning
DOLORES A. BOWER, R.N., Ph.D., Dean, College of Nursing
NANCY E. MCGLEN, Ph.D., Dean, College of Arts & Science
KEITH T. MILLER, Ph.D., Dean, College of Business Administration
Dr. DEBRA A. COLLEY, Dean, College of Education
GEORGE C. PACHTER, JR., M.S.Ed., Dean of Admissions
MARK D. LAROACH, M.S., Dir. of External Programs
PATRICIA G. KINNER, M.A., Dir., Academic Support
DAVID M. SCHOEN, M.L.S., Dir. Library
SANDRA H. OLSEN, Ph.D., Dir. Castellani Art Museum
MAUREEN SALFI, M.S.Ed., Dir. Fin. Aid
JOHN B. STRANGES, Ph.D., Univ. Prof.
DAVID J. BOYDA, M.S.Ed., Dir., Campus Activities
MARY BETH COATES, M.S., Dir. Campus Min.
JOSEPH H. CUDA, M.A., Dean Student Affairs
ILONA YUNGBLUT, Dir. Health Svcs.
DAVID BLACKBURN, Dir. Multicultural Student Affairs
THOMAS MCDERMOTT, M.S., Dir. Counseling Svcs.
MARTHA E. TROIA, M.S., Dir. Career Dev.
KIMBERLY J. ZUKOWSKI, M.S.Ed., Dir. University Housing
SANDRA MANN ORMSBY, B.A., Alumni Dir.
LINUS L. ORMSBY, M.S.Ed., Dir. Public Relations
JEANNINE BROWN MILLER, M.A., Dir. Human Resources
Revs.:
WILLIAM M. ALLEGRETTO, C.M., Campus Ministry
JOSEPH G. HUBBERT, C.M., Asst. Prof. Rel. Studies
JOHN A. KETTELBERGER, C.M., Supr. of Vincentian Community & Campus Min.
GREGORY L. KLEIN, O.Carm., Asst. Prof. of Rel. Studies
THOMAS P. MCGOURTY, C.M., Adjunct Prof. of Rel. Studies
LOUIS P. TROTTA, C.M., Asst. Pres. Alumni Relations
Bros.:
STEPHEN J. KENNEDY, C.M., Dir. St. Vincent de Paul
MARTIN SCHNEIDER, C.M., Coordinator Conv.
AUGUSTINE D. TOWEY, C.M., Prof. of English and Theatre Studies
Meade Hall:
In res.,
Revs.:
MICHAEL J. TUMULTY, C.M.
MARTIN J. SLEASMAN, C.M.
THOMAS P. MALLAGHAN, C.M.
WILLIAM L. GREEN, C.M.
Priests 5
Brothers 2
Lay Teachers 117
Sisters 2
Students 3,146
Total Staff 599
Founded in 1856 by the Congregation of the Mission (Vincentian Community of Priests & Brothers). Niagara University is composed of the College of Arts & Sciences; Business Administration; Education; Nursing; and The Institute of Travel & Hotel-Restaurant Administration.

Orangeburg
Archdiocese of New York

Dominican College
470 Western Hwy.
Orangeburg, NY 10962
Tel: 845-359-7800; Fax: 845-359-2313
E-mail: admissions@dc.edu
Web Site: www.dc.edu
Chartered by University of the State of New York.
Sr. MARY EILEEN O'BRIEN, O.P., Pres.
Sr. KATHLEEN SULLIVAN, O.P., Chancellor
Dr. LEIGH HOLT, Vice Pres. Academic Affairs & Academic Dean
DOHN HARSHBARGER, Vice Pres. Student Devel. & Dean of Students
CATHLEEN KENNY, Vice Pres. Fin. Affairs & Chief Fiscal Officer
DOROTHY FILORAMO, Vice Pres. Institutional Advancement
BRIAN FERNANDES, Vice Pres. Enrollment Mgmt.
Sr. M. NOEL DWYER, O.P., Registrar
Dr. MICHAEL HAINES, Institutional Research
Mr. JOSEPH CLINTON, Athletics
Sr. BARBARA MCENEANY, Campus Min.
Divisions:
Dr. BERYL HERDT, Allied Health
Dr. WILLIAM HURST, Arts & Sciences
Mr. JOHN SPILLNER, Business Admin.
Dr. MAUREEN CREEGAN, Nursing
Dr. BARBARA SOCOR, Social Sciences
Dr. MARIE PAGLIARO, Teacher Educ.
Sisters 18
Lay Teachers 54
Students 1,700

Patchogue
Diocese of Rockville Centre

**St. Joseph's College*
155 W. Roe Blvd.
Patchogue, NY 11772-2399
Tel: 631-447-3200; Fax: 631-654-1782
E-mail: lmcgrann@sjcny.edu
Web Site: www.sjcny.edu
Mailing Address:
245 Clinton Ave.
Brooklyn, NY 11205-3688
Sr. LORETTA MCGRANN, C.S.J.
Priests on Faculty:
Revs.:
JOHN GILVEY, O.S.F.S (NY Archdiocese)
KENNETH GRANDE

FRANK PIZZARELLI, S.M.M., Part-time
Priests 1
Sisters 9
Lay Teachers 79
Students 3,234

Poughkeepsie
Archdiocese of New York

Marist College
(Coed)
Poughkeepsie, NY 12601-1328
Tel: 914-575-3000
E-mail: hmaltmi@marista.marist.edu
Web Site: www.marist.edu
DENNIS J. MURRAY, Ph.D., Pres.
Rev. LUKE W. MCCANN, Ph.D., Chap.
Priests 2
Brothers 8
Lay Teachers 160
Students 4,300
Marist Foreign Missions
Bro. PAUL AMBROSE, F.M.S.

Rochester
Diocese of Rochester

St. Bernard's Institute
1100 S. Goodman St.
Rochester, NY 14620
Tel: 716-271-3657; Fax: 716-271-2045
Web Site: www.sbi.edu
Dr. PATRICIA A. SCHOELLES, S.S.J., Pres.
Dr. JOSEPH R. PICCOLINO, Dir. at Albany
THOMAS MCDADE CLAY, Dir. Admissions
Dr. CY YOUNG, Dir. of Development
JUDITH ANN KOLLAR, Dir. Continuing Education
Ms. MARY ANN LACOUR, Dir. Business Affairs
Dr. DEVADASAN PREMNATH, Interim Dean
Rev. JOHN COLACINO, Dir. Certification
Priests 2
Sisters 2
Lay Teachers 2
Total Staff 14
Total enrollment 135

Rockville Centre
Diocese of Rockville Centre

Molloy College
1000 Hempstead Ave.
Rockville Centre, NY 11571-5002
Tel: 516-678-5000; 888-4-MOLLOY
Web Site: www.molloy.edu
Dr. VALERIE COLLINS, Ph.D., Acting Pres.
Sr. DOROTHY ANNE FITZGIBBONS, O.P., Ed.D., Exec. Asst. to Pres.
Sr. JOAN GARVEY, O.P., Dir. Campus Ministries
CATHERINE C. KREIN, M.A., Vice Pres. External Affairs
ANTHONY MANCALUSO, C.F.O. & Treas.
ROCHELLE SAGER, M.L.S., Vice Pres. Information Resources & Dir. Library
WAYNE F. JAMES, M.S., Assoc. Vice Pres. Enrollment Management
JAMES A. O'REILLY, JR., M.A., Registrar
LISA KANDELL, Dir. Financial Aid
Sr. DORIS NEVITT, O.P., M.A., Dir. Student Financial Svcs.
Rev. JOHN A. MADIGAN, O.P., M.A., Chap. for Sisters
Priests 2
Brothers 1
Ministers 4
Sisters of St. Dominic (Amityville Community) 29
Lay Teachers 251
Students 2,252

Sparkill
Archdiocese of New York

St. Thomas Aquinas College
Sparkill, NY 10976
Tel: 914-398-4000; Fax: 914-359-8136
Web Site: www.stac.edu
Founded by Dominican Sisters of Sparkill in 1952. Senior coed college, chartered by Univ. of the State of New York.
Sr. MARGARET M. FITZPATRICK, S.C., Ed.D., Pres.
Dr. LEE BADGETT, Provost & Vice Pres. Academic Affairs
Priests 1
Sisters 9
Lay Professors 65
Students 2,200

St. Bonaventure
Diocese of Buffalo

St. Bonaventure University
St. Bonaventure, NY 14778
Tel: 716-375-2000; Fax: 716-375-2055
E-mail: fstorms@sbu.edu
Web Site: www.sbu.edu
Franciscan Friars, Province of the Holy Name, Order of Friars Minor.
School of Arts and Sciences, School of Education, School of Business, School of Journalism/Mass Communication; School of Franciscan Studies and the Franciscan Institute; Graduate Studies.
Administration:
ROBERT J. WICKENHEISER, Ph.D., Pres.
DAVID E. COOK, Ph.D., Vice Pres. Academic Affairs & Graduate Studies
DONALD L. ZEKAN, Ed.D., Vice Pres. Business & Finance
GEORGE F. SOLAN, M.S., Vice Pres. Student Life
ROGER W. SOROCHTY, Ph.D., Vice Pres. Univ. Advancement
BARBARA L. SOROCHTY, M.S., Vice Pres. Public Relations
Rev. FRANCIS STORMS, O.F.M., M.A., Asst. to Pres.
JAMES P. WHITE, Ph.D., Dean, School of Arts & Sciences
Sr. MARGARET CARNEY, O.S.F., S.T.D., Dean, School of Franciscan Studies & Dir. Franciscan Institute
MICHAEL J. FISCHER, Ph.D., Dean, School of Business
CAROL ANNE PIERSON, Ph.D., Dean, School of Education
LEE COPPOLA, J.D., Dean, Russel J. Jandoli School of Journalism & Mass Communication
MICHAEL V. CHIARIELLO, Ph.D., Dean, Clare College
JON J. BOECKENSTEDT, B.A., Vice Pres. Enrollment
JAMES M. DIRISIO, B.A., Acting Dir. Admissions
MARY K. PICCIOLI, M.B.A., Dir. Financial Aid
BARBARA RUSSELL, M.S., Registrar & Dir. of Institutional Research
STEPHEN PLESAC, M.S., Dir. Student Activities
MICHELLE RUSSELL, Dir. Residence Life
JOSEPH V. FLANAGAN, M.S., Dir. Alumni Services
JUNE T. SOLAN, M.S., Dir. Human Resources
MARGARET T. BRYNER, M.S., Dir. Higher Educ. Opportunities Program (HEOP)
JEAN T. EHMAN, M.A., Dir. The Teaching & Learning Center
JOHN P. KEENAN, Ph.D., Dean, School of Leadership & Human Devel.
ALICE F. SAYEGH, M.S., Advisor, International Student Advisement
JOHN A. LYMPANY, M.Ed., Dir. Technology Svcs.
PAUL J. SPAETH, M.L.S., M.A., Dir. Library
CONSTANCE F. WHITCOMB, M.S.Ed., Dir. Career Devel.
Sr. MARY KATHRYN DOUGHERTY, O.S.F., M.A., Vice Pres. University Ministries
Rev. THOMAS D. BLOW, O.F.M., M.A., M.Div., Guardian of the Friary
Priests 23
Brothers 10
Sisters 5
Lay Professors 147
Students 2,800
Friar Community
St. Bonaventure, NY 14778
Tel: 716-375-2416; Fax: 716-375-2424
Bros.:
ZACHARY ELLIOT, O.F.M.
DAVID HAACK, O.F.M.
ANTHONY J. LOGALBO, O.F.M.
SALVADOR MIRANDA, O.F.M.
MICHAEL MONTGOMERY, O.F.M.
JAMES V. PISTO, O.F.M.
ADRIAN A. RIESTER, O.F.M.
JULIAN RIESTER, O.F.M.
BASIL VALENTE, O.F.M.
Revs.:
DAVID D. BLAKE, O.F.M.
MICHAEL BLASTIC, O.F.M.Conv.
THOMAS D. BLOW, O.F.M., Guardian
J. GREGORY BRENNAN, O.F.M.
MICHAEL CUSATO, O.F.M.
REGIS A. DUFFY, O.F.M.
RICHARD C. FLAHERTY, O.F.M.
DAVID FLOOD, O.F.M.
ROBERT KARRIS, O.F.M.
PETER SCHNEIBLE, O.F.M.
XAVIER J. SEUBERT, O.F.M., Vicar
ROBERT STEWART, O.F.M.
FRANCIS STORMS, O.F.M.
ALPHONSUS A. TRABOLD, O.F.M.
JAMES VACCO, O.F.M.
ALLEN WEBER, O.F.M.
WILLIAM J. WEIKSNAR, O.F.M.
ROBERT H. WHITE, O.F.M.
GERVASE F. WHITE, O.F.M.
ALLAN WOLTER, O.F.M.
Holy Peace Friary
Mt. Irenaeus
West Clarksville, NY 14786-0100
Tel: 716-973-2470; Fax: 716-973-2400
Bro. JOSEPH A. KOTULA, O.F.M.
Revs.:
DANIEL A. HURLEY, O.F.M.
LOUIS M. MCCORMICK, O.F.M.
DANIEL P. RILEY, O.F.M., Guardian, Dir.

Staten Island
Diocese of Brooklyn

St. John's University, Staten Island Campus
300 Howard Ave.
Staten Island, NY 10301
Tel: 718-390-4545; Fax: 718-816-4520
Web Site: www.stjohns.edu
Sponsored by the Vincentian Priests and Brothers Eastern Province of the Congregation of the Mission.
Rev. DONALD J. HARRINGTON, C.M., Pres.
Officers of Administration:
ROBERT J. CRIMMINS, Exec. Vice Pres.
TONY H. BONAPARTE, Ph.D., Provost
Rev. MICHAEL J. CARROLL, C.M., Vice Pres. Campus Ministry & Rome Campus
CECILIA S. CHANG, Ed.D., Vice Pres. Intl. Rels.
JOHN P. CONNOLLY, JR., Vice Pres. Administrative Svcs.
Rev. JOSEPH V. DALY, C.M., Asst. to the Pres.
SUSAN L. EBBS, Ed.D., Vice Pres. Student Life
DOROTHY E. HABBEN, Ph.D., Vice Pres. & Univ. Sec.
SUZANNE M. HALPIN, Vice Pres. Communications
Rev. JAMES F. KIERNAN, C.M., Senior Vice Pres., Staten Island Campus
JAMES P. PELLOW, Vice Pres. Finance & Treas.
JOSEPH SCIAME, Vice Pres. Govt. & Community Rels.
Rev. BERNARD M. TRACEY, C.M., Vice Pres. Inst. Advancement
Priests 21
Sisters 2
Lay Teachers 559
Staten Island Campus Enrollment 2,382
Total Undergraduate & Graduate Enrollment 18,500

Archdiocese of New York

St. John's University Staten Island Campus
300 Howard Ave.
Staten Island, NY 10301
Tel: 718-390-4545; Fax: 718-816-4520
Vincentian Community
Very Rev. DONALD J. HARRINGTON, C.M., Pres.
Rev. JAMES F. KIERNAN, C.M., Senior Vice Pres.-Staten Island
Sr. MARGARET JOHN KELLY, D.C., Academic Dean & Dean of Faculty St. John's College
DONNA NARDUCCI, Asst. Dean & Dir. Programs Colleges of Business
KATHLEEN MACDONALD, Dean St. Vincent's College
Dr. STEPHEN KUNTZ, Asst. Dean, School of Education, Graduate Div.
Mr. JAMES R. GUILBERT, Dean, Office of Student Life

Syracuse
Diocese of Syracuse

Le Moyne College
1419 Salt Springs Rd.
Syracuse, NY 13214-1399
Tel: 315-445-4100; Fax: 315-445-4540
Rev. CHARLES J. BEIRNE, S.J., Pres.
Dr. KURT F. GEISINGER, Academic Vice Pres.
Dr. MICHAEL W. YOST, Vice Pres. Student Life
Ms. GENEVIEVE R. SAYA, Vice Pres. Campus Svcs. & Asst. to Pres.
Mr. THOMAS E. O'NEIL, Vice Pres. for Finance & Treasurer
Mrs. BARBARA M. MAYLONE-KARPER, Assoc. Dean Student Life & Dir. Campus Activities
Mr. MARK G. GODELSKI, Dir. Residence Life & Coord. Judicial Affairs
Rev. EDMUND G. RYAN, S.J., Special Asst. to the Pres. for Mission & Planning
Dr. MARCIA RUWE, Academic Dean
Mr. CHRISTOPHER KNAUER, Registrar
Mr. DENNIS R. DEPERRO, Dean of Enrollment Management
Jesuits 17
Brothers 1
Lay Teachers 114
Total Enrollment 3,129

Tarrytown
Archdiocese of New York

Marymount College
Tarrytown, NY 10591
Tel: 914-631-3200

E-mail: admiss@mmt.marymt.edu
Web Site: www.marymt.edu
Founded by the Religious of the Sacred Heart of Mary. Women resident and non-resident.
Sr. BRIGID DRISCOLL, R.S.H.M., Ph.D., Pres.
ROBERTA MATTHEWS, Ph.D., Vice Pres. Academic Affairs & Dean of Faculty
Sisters 3
Lay Teachers 55
Students 842

Thornwood
Archdiocese of New York

Legion of Christ College, Inc.
584 Columbus Ave.
Thornwood, NY 10594
773 Armonk Rd.
Mount Kisco, NY 10549
Tel: 914-773-1368; Fax: 914-773-1438
Bro. SCOTT MADGEY, L.C., Contact Person

NORTH CAROLINA

Belmont
Diocese of Charlotte

**Belmont Abbey College*
100 Belmont-Mount Holly Rd.
Belmont, NC 28012-1802
Tel: 704-825-6700; Fax: 704-825-6670
E-mail: schup@crusader.bac.edu
Web Site: belmontabbeycollege.edu
(Coed) Liberal Arts Senior College.
Dr. ROBERT A. PRESTON, Pres.
Rt. Rev. PLACID D. SOLARI, O.S.B., Chancellor
DEAN DE LA MOTTE, Ph.D., Academic Dean
MARGARET SKIDMORE, Registrar
KATY VOLPONI, Dir. Campus Ministry
KAREN VAN NORMAN, Dean, Student Life
Mr. JAMES SCHUPPENHAUER, Vice Pres. Admin. & Finance
Mr. DENIS M. STOKES, Vice Pres. Enrollment Mgmt.
DONALD BEAGLE, Dir. Library
Priests 6
Sisters 2
Lay Teachers 31
Students 925
The Ecumenical Institute of Wake Forest University and Belmont Abbey College
Tel: 704-825-6700; Fax: 704-825-6670
Ecumenical Institute
Wake Forest University, P.O. Box 7363
Winston-Salem, NC 27109
Tel: 336-759-5800

Sacred Heart College
100 Mercy Dr.
Belmont, NC 28012-4805
Tel: 704-829-5100; Fax: 704-829-5137
Sisters of Mercy
Sr. M. ROSALIND PICOT, R.S.M., Pres.
College ceased academic operation, effective August 1987. Corporation intact.

NORTH DAKOTA

Bismarck
Diocese of Bismarck

University of Mary
7500 University Dr.
Bismarck, ND 58504-9652
Tel: 701-255-7500; Fax: 701-255-7687
E-mail: marauder@umary.edu
Web Site: www.umary.edu
Sr. THOMAS WELDER, O.S.B., Pres.
Dr. DIANE FLADELAND, Vice Pres. Academic Affairs
Revs.:
DANIEL MALONEY, O.S.B.
DENIS FOURNIER, O.S.B.
VICTOR FESER, O.S.B.
BONIFACE MUGGLI, O.S.B.
VALERIAN ODERMANN, O.S.B., Chap.
Priests 2
Sisters 5
Lay Teachers 86
Students 2,115

OHIO

Cincinnati
Archdiocese of Cincinnati

College of Mount St. Joseph
5701 Delhi Rd.
Cincinnati, OH 45233-1670
Tel: 513-244-4200; Fax: 513-244-4601
E-mail: greg_grady@mail.msj.edu
Web Site: www.msj.edu
Coed. Chartered by the State of Ohio.
Sr. FRANCIS MARIE THRAILKILL, O.S.U., Pres.
Sr. JOHN MIRIAM JONES, Ph.D., Academic Dean
Rev. ANGELO A. DELLA PICCA (Italy)
Sisters 11
Lay Teachers 110
Students 5,741

Xavier University
3800 Victory Pkwy. at Dana Ave.
Cincinnati, OH 45207
Tel: 513-745-3000; Fax: 513-745-4223
Web Site: www.xu.edu
Rev. MICHAEL J. GRAHAM, S.J., Pres.
Vice Presidents:
Rev. J. LEO KLEIN, S.J.
Dr. JAMES E. BUNDSCHUH
Dr. RONALD SLEPITZA
Dr. J. RICHARD HIRTE
Mr. JOHN F. KUCIA
Mr. GARY R. MASSA
Rev. RICHARD W. BOLLMAN, S.J., Pastor & Rector, Bellarmine Chapel
Mr. ALLEN COLE, Registrar
VALERIE WITHIAM, Assoc. V.P. for Marketing
Dr. JANICE WALKER, Dean, College of Arts & Sciences
Rev. THOMAS P. KENNEALY, S.J., Assoc. Dean, College of Arts & Sciences and College of Social Sciences
Dr. MICHAEL WEBB, Dean, Williams College of Business
Dr. JAMES BRODZINSKI, Assoc. Dean, Williams College of Business
Dr. NEIL R. HEIGHBERGER, Dean, College of Social Sciences
Ms. SUSAN G. WIDEMAN, Dean, Center for Adult and Part-Time Students
Enrollment: College of Arts & Sciences:
Students 1,889
College of Business Administration:
Students 936
College of Social Sciences:
Students 994
Center for Adult and Part-Time Students:
Students 200
Graduate Programs:
Students 2,504
Permanent Staff:
Priests 10
Sisters 2
Faculty (full-time):
Priests 7
Lay Teachers 251

Cleveland
Diocese of Cleveland

John Carroll Jesuit Community
E-mail: jesuits@jcu.edu
John Carroll University
University Heights
Cleveland, OH 44118
Tel: 216-397-1886; Fax: 216-397-4228
Web Site: www.jcu.edu/jesuit
Revs.:
STEPHEN T. KRUPA, S.J., Acting Rector
JOHN A. KNAPEK, S.J., Min.
WILLIAM M. BICHL, S.J.
CASIMIR R. BUKALA, S.J.
EMMANUEL M. CARREIRA, S.J. (Spain)
PETER J. FENNESSY, S.J., Sabbatical
CHRISTOPHER S. FRONK, S.J.
HARRY J. GENSLER, S.J.
EDWARD GLYNN, S.J.
GREGORY N.P. KONZ, S.J.
MICHAEL D. KURIMAY, S.J.
FRANCIS P. LIHVAR, S.J.
DANIEL T. REIM, S.J.
FRANCIS X. RYAN, S.J.
GERALD J. SABO, S.J.
RICHARD P. SALMI, S.J.
JOSEPH O. SCHELL, S.J.
THOMAS L. SCHUBECK, S.J.
FRANCIS J. SMITH, S.J.
ERNEST G. SPITTLER, S.J.
Bro. MICHAEL L. NUSBAUM, S.J.
Priests 20
Brothers 1

John Carroll University
20700 N. Park Blvd.
Cleveland, OH 44118
Tel: 216-397-1886; Fax: 216-397-4256
Web Site: www.jcu.edu
Revs.:
EDWARD GLYNN, S.J., Pres.
RICHARD P. SALMI, S.J., Vice Pres. Student Affairs
Mr. PETER ANAGNOSTOS, Vice Pres. Devel. & Alumni Rels.
Mr. JONATHAN IVEC, Vice Pres. Finance & Administrative Svcs.
Dr. FREDERICK F. TRAVIS, Provost and Academic Vice Pres.
Dr. DAVID M. LAGUARDIA, Assoc. Academic Vice Pres.
JOHN GLADSTONE, Assoc. Academic Vice Pres. for Enrollment Svcs.
Dr. FRANK J. NAVRATIL, Dean, Boler School of Business
Dr. NICK BAUMGARTNER, Dean, College of Arts & Sciences
Dr. THOMAS ZLATOPER, Dean of Graduate School
Dr. JOSEPH B. MILLER, Assoc. Dean, College of Arts & Sciences
Rev. WILLIAM M. BICHL, S.J., Asst. Dean, College of Arts & Sciences
SOPHIE KUS-PATENA, Asst. Dean, College of Arts & Sciences
Dr. JAMES DALEY, Assoc. Dean, Boler School of Business
Dr. ANDREW BUYNACEK, Asst. Dean, Boler School of Business
Mrs. MARSHA DALEY, Asst. Dean, Graduate School
PATRICK ROMBALSKI, Dean of Students
WILLIAM FICHTER, Dir. Campus Ministry
Priests 11
Sisters 1
Lay Faculty 218
Students 4,384
Total Staff 625

Notre Dame College of Ohio
4545 College Rd.
South Euclid, OH 44121
Tel: 216-381-1680; Fax: 216-381-3802
E-mail: ndc.edu
Web Site: www.ndc.edu
ANNE L. DEMING, Ph.D., Pres.
Sr. MARGARET GORMAN, S.N.D., Exec. Vice Pres.
MARILYN JONES, Ph.D., Vice Pres. Academic Affairs
Priests 1
Sisters of Notre Dame 4
Lay Teachers 22
Total Staff 27
Students 813

Ursuline College
2550 Lander Rd.
Pepper Pike, OH 44124
Tel: 440-449-4200; Fax: 440-646-8102
Web Site: www.ursuline.edu
DIANA STANO, O.S.U., Ph.D., Pres.
JOANNE PODIS, Ph.D., Vice Pres. Academic Affairs
DAVID STEINER, CFO
DEANNE HURLEY, Dean of Students
Sr. ANNA MARGARET GILBRIDE, O.S.U., Ph.D., Asst. to the Pres.
CATHERINE HACKNEY, Ph.D., Dean Graduate Studies
Ursuline Sisters of Cleveland 12
Lay Professors 53
Students 1,253

Columbus
Diocese of Columbus

Ohio Dominican College
1216 Sunbury Rd.
Columbus, OH 43219
Tel: 614-253-2741; Fax: 614-252-0776
E-mail: admissions@odc.edu
Web Site: www.odc.edu
Dominican Sisters of the Third Order of St. Dominic
Sr. MARY ANDREW MATESICH, O.P., Pres.
ANDREW KEOGH, Vice Pres. Academic Affairs
JAMES SAGONA, Vice Pres. Admissions & Student Affairs
MICHAEL D. BROMBERG, Vice Pres. Business Affairs
LYNDA HUEY, Vice Pres. College Advancement
JAMES GROVE, Dir. Campus Ministry & Lecturer in Theology Studies
Rev. DANIEL L. TORSON, C.PP.S., Chap.
Sisters 10
Lay Teachers 105
Students 2,135

Dayton
Archdiocese of Cincinnati

The University of Dayton (1850)
(Coed)
300 College Park Ave.
Dayton, OH 45469-1624
Tel: 937-229-1000
Web Site: www.udayton.edu
Bro. RAYMOND L. FITZ, S.M., Pres.
Rev. JAMES L. HEFT, S.M., Chancellor & Prof. of Faith and Culture
Dr. JOHN O. GEIGER, Senior Vice Pres. for Academics and Provost

Dr. Patrick F. Palermo, Assoc. Provost, Faculty & Academic Affairs
Mr. Christopher Munoz, Assoc. Provost, Enrollment Mgmt.
Bro. Bernard J. Ploeger, S.M., Senior Vice Pres.-Admin.
Mr. Thomas E. Burkhardt, Vice Pres. for Financial Affairs & Treas.
Mr. Ted L. Kissell, Vice Pres. & Dir. of Athletics
Dr. William C. Schuerman, Vice Pres. Student Devel. & Dean of Students
Rev. J. Eugene Contadino, S.M., Rector
Ms. Lisa Rismiller, Exec. Asst. to the Pres.
Mr. Richard T. Ferguson, Asst. to the Pres. for Regional & Government Relations
Mr. Richard G. Perales, Dir. Facilities Mgmt.
Mr. Thomas J. Westendorf, Registrar
Mr. Myron H. Achbach, Dir. Admissions
Mrs. Joyce J. Wilkins, Dir. Financial Aid
Revs.:
Norbert C. Burns, S.M.
Gerald T. Chinchar, S.M.
Matthew F. Kohmescher, S.M.
William P. Frost
Joseph F. Kozar, S.M.
Robert J. Hater
James L. Heft, S.M.
Paul F. Vieson, S.M.
Thomas A. Schroer, S.M.
John S. Putka, S.M.
Bertrand A. Buby, S.M.
James F. Fitz, S.M., Dir., Campus Ministry
John A. McGrath, S.M.
Johann B.G. Roten, S.M.
Joseph D. Massucci
Kenneth A. Templin, S.M.
Sr. Nancy H. Bramlage, S.C.
Sr. Laura M. Leming, F.M.I., (On Leave)
Sr. Kathleen A. Rossman, O.S.F.
Sr. Judith G. Martin, S.S.J.
Sr. Jody O'Neil, S.P.
Sr. Pamela L. Thimmes, O.S.F.
Sr. Frances M. Trampiets, S.C.
Sr. Angela Ann Zukowski, M.H.S.H.
Sr. Mary Louise Foley, F.M.I.
Society of Mary (Marianists)
College of Arts and Sciences
Tel: 937-229-2611; Fax: 937-229-2615
Dr. Paul J. Morman, Dean
Dr. Fred P. Pestello, Assoc. Dean
Dr. Mary Jo Vesper, Assoc. Dean
Mr. Sam F. Johnson, Asst. Dean
Mrs. Rae Ellen Huff, Asst. Dean
Professors 218
Students 3,207
Graduate Studies and Research
Tel: 937-229-2390; Fax: 937-229-4545
Dr. Gordon A. Sargent, Vice Pres. Graduate Studies & Research, Dir of UDRI and Dean of Graduate School
Dr. Katy E. Marre, Assoc. Dean of the Grad. School
Ms. Carol M. Shaw, Dir. Center for Competitive Change
Students 2,784
School of Business Administration
Tel: 937-229-3731; Fax: 937-229-3301
Dr. Sam Gould, Dean
Dr. John E. Rapp, Assoc. Dean
Dr. Charles E. Wells, Assoc. Dean & Dir., MBA Prog.
Dr. Thomas W. Ferratt, Assoc. Dean Learning Tech. of Faculty Development
Professors 39
Students 1,315
School of Education
Tel: 937-229-3146; Fax: 937-229-3199
Dr. Thomas J. Lasly, Dean
Dr. C. Daniel Raisch, Assoc. Dean Admin.
Dr. James R. Biddle, Dir. of Doctoral Studies
Professors 44
Students 946
School of Engineering
Tel: 937-229-2736; Fax: 937-229-2756
Dr. Blake E. Cherrington, Dean
Dr. Donald L. Moon, Assoc. Dean for Graduate Programs, Research and Technology
Dr. Richard J. Kee, Asst. Dean of Undergrad Programs
Professors 63
Students 1,323
School of Law
Tel: 937-229-3211; Fax: 937-229-4769
Francis J. Conte, Dean
Mr. Richard P. Perna, Assoc. Dean for Academic Affairs
Mr. Timothy P. Stonecash, Asst. Dean of Law School Development and Alumni Affairs
Professors 19
Students 427
Libraries and Information Technologies
Tel: 937-229-4265
Dr. Edward D. Garten, Dean of Libraries and Information Technology
Total Enrollment 10,170
Faculty 383
The Marian Library / International Marian Research Institute (IMRI)
Tel: 937-229-4124; Fax: 937-229-4258
Revs.:
Johann B.G. Roten, S.M., S.T.D., Dir.
Thomas A. Thompson, S.M., Dir. & Curator
Theodore A. Koehler, S.M., S.T.D., Dir. Emeritus
University of Dayton
Dayton, OH 45469-1390
Tel: 937-229-4214

North Canton
Diocese of Youngstown

Walsh University
(Coed)
2020 Easton St., N.W.
North Canton, OH 44720-3396
Tel: 330-490-7090; Fax: 330-490-7165
E-mail: admissions@walsh.edu
Web Site: www.walsh.edu
Brothers of Christian Instruction
Rev. Donald A. Miller, O.F.M., Ph.D., (St. John the Baptist Province), Dir. Campus Ministry
Kenneth N. Hamilton, Jr., Ph.D., Pres.
Mr. Dale Howard, Vice Pres. for Student Affairs
Brett Freshour, Dean, Enrollment Mgmt.
John Wray, Vice Pres., Business & Finance
Rick Russell, Vice Pres., Devel. & Univ. Rels
Priests 1
Brothers 3
Lay Teachers 66
Total Staff 177
Students 1,580

Saint Martin
Archdiocese of Cincinnati

Chatfield College
Brown County Ursulines, 20918 State Rte. 251
Saint Martin, OH 45118
Tel: 937-875-3344; Fax: 937-875-3912
E-mail: margaret@chatfield.edu
Web Site: www.chatfield.edu
Sr. Margaret Anne Dougherty, R.S.M., Pres.
Students 452

Steubenville
Diocese of Steubenville

Franciscan University of Steubenville
1235 University Blvd.
Steubenville, OH 43952
Tel: 740-283-3771; Fax: 740-283-6472
E-mail: admissions@franuniv.edu
Web Site: www.franuniv.edu
Revs.:
Terence Henry, T.O.R., Pres.
Michael Scanlon, T.O.R., Chancellor
Mr. David Skiviat, Vice Pres. Finance & Admin.
Dr. Steven Miletic, Dean of Faculty
Mr. Michael Campbell, Vice Pres. Univ. Rels.
Mr. John Madigan, Vice Pres. Community Rels.
Mr. Randall Cirner, Dean of Students
Mr. Joel Recznik, Dean of Human Resources & Strategic Planning
Miss Mary Kay Lacke, Dean of Evangelization
Ms. Sharon Kilzer, Sec. of the Univ.
Revs.:
Bevil Bramwell, O.M.I., Asst. Prof.
Brian Cavanaugh, T.O.R., Student Svcs.
Augustine Donegan, T.O.R.
Dennis Gang, T.O.R.
Conrad Harkins, O.F.M., Assoc. Prof.
Stanley Holland, T.O.R., Dir. of Works of Mercy
Joseph Lehman, T.O.R., Res. Hall Chap.
James Morman, Religious Admin.
Daniel Pattee, T.O.R, Lecturer
David Pivonka, T.O.R., Asst. to Pres.
Dominic Scotto, T.O.R., Univ. Chap.
Samuel Tiesi, T.O.R.
Laurence Uhlman, T.O.R., Chap.
Joseph Yelenc, T.O.R., Biology Prof.
Priests 14
Brothers 2
Lay Teachers 99
Students 2,131

Sylvania
Diocese of Toledo

Lourdes College
6832 Convent Blvd.
Sylvania, OH 43560
Tel: 419-885-3211; Fax: 419-882-3987
E-mail: pmazur@lourdes.edu
Web Site: www.lourdes.edu
Sisters of St. Francis of the Congregation of Our Lady of Lourdes, (O.S.F.).
Dr. George C. Matthews, Pres.
Sr. M. Cabrini Warpeha, O.S.F., Vice Pres. Academic Affairs
Nick Ulrich, C.P.A., Vice Pres. Finance & Admin.
Dr. Robert Turek, Vice Pres. Student Svcs.
Mary Arquette, Vice Pres. Inst. Advancement
Michelle Rable, Registrar
Franciscan Care Centers
6832 Convent Blvd.
Sylvania, OH 43560
Tel: 419-882-8373
E-mail: director@franciscancenter.org
Web Site: www.franciscancenter.org
Total Staff 14
John W. O'Connell, Pres.
Mary Arquette, Contact Person
Sisters 18
Full-time faculty 66
Lay instructors 48
Enrollment 1,356

OKLAHOMA

Shawnee
Archdiocese of Oklahoma City

St. Gregory's University
(Coed)
Shawnee, OK 74804
Tel: 405-878-5100; Fax: 405-878-5170
E-mail: frlawrence@sgc.edu
Web Site: www.sgc.edu/
Liberal Arts and Sciences.
Benedictine Monks
Rev. Lawrence Stasyszen, O.S.B., S.T.D., Pres.
Priests 6
Brothers 1
Sisters 2
Lay Teachers 36
Students 755

OREGON

Marylhurst
Archdiocese of Portland in Oregon

Marylhurst University
Marylhurst, OR 97036
Tel: 503-636-8141; Fax: 503-636-9526
E-mail: president@marylhurst.edu
Web Site: www.marylhurst.edu
Dr. Nancy Wilgenbusch, Pres.
John Freed, Vice Pres. Academic Affairs & Contact Person
Peggy Medina, Contact Person
Sisters 21
Lay Teachers 366
Students 1,876

Portland
Archdiocese of Portland in Oregon

**University of Portland*
5000 N. Willamette Blvd.
Portland, OR 97203
Tel: 503-943-7911; Fax: 503-943-7401
E-mail: webmaster@up.edu
Web Site: www.up.edu
Endowed by the Congregation of Holy Cross; established 1901.
Exec. Officers of the Univ.:
Rev. David T. Tyson, C.S.C., Pres.
Dr. Arthur A. Schulte, Jr., Special Asst. to the Pres. & Exec. Vice Pres. Emeritus
Bro. Donald J. Stabrowski, C.S.C., Academic Vice Pres.
Mr. Anthony J. DiSpigno, Vice Pres. Univ. Rels.
Dr. John Goldrick, Vice Pres. Student Svcs.
Dr. Roy Heynderickx, Financial V.P.
Madeline Doll, Contact Person
Faculty Staff:
Revs.:
Robert Antonelli, C.S.C.
James Connelly, C.S.C.
Michael M. DeLaney, C.S.C., Religious Supr.
John Donato, C.S.C.
Thomas Hosinski, C.S.C.
William Hund, C.S.C.
John Kurtzke, C.S.C.
James Lackenmier, C.S.C.
Edwin Obermiller, C.S.C.
Dennis P. O'Hare, C.S.C.
Claude Pomerleau, C.S.C.
Richard Rutherford, C.S.C.
Charles D. Sherrer, C.S.C.
Ronald Wasowski, C.S.C.
Arthur F. Wheeler, C.S.C.

In res.,
Revs.:
FREDERICK BARR, C.S.C.
GEORGE C. BERNARD, C.S.C.
THOMAS BILL, C.S.C.
BARRY J. HAGAN, C.S.C.
CHESTER PRUSYNSKI, C.S.C.
ADRIEN STE. MARIE, C.S.C.
ARTHUR SCHOENFELDT, C.S.C.
Bros.:
KEN ALLEN, C.S.C.
FULGENCE DOUGHERTY, C.S.C.
FREDERICK WILLIAMS, C.S.C.
SHAWN PRIGGEL, C.S.C.
Priests 23
Brothers 5
Sisters 7
Lay Teachers 156
Adjunct Faculty 103
Students 2,673
Following is the Academic Structure of the University:
College of Arts and Sciences—
Dr. MARLENE MOORE, Dean
School of Nursing—
Dr. TERRY MISENER, Dean
School of Business Administration—
Dr. RONALD HILL, Dean
School of Engineering—
Dr. ZIA J. YAMAYEE, Dean
School of Education—
Sr. MARIA CIRIELLO, O.P., Dean
Graduate School—
Dr. PATRICIA CHADWICK

PENNSYLVANIA

Aston
Archdiocese of Philadelphia

Neumann College
One Neumann Dr.
Aston, PA 19014-1298
Tel: 610-459-0905; Fax: 610-459-1370
E-mail: neumann@neumann.edu
Web Site: www.neumann.edu
Opened September 1965.
Sponsored by the Sisters of St. Francis of Philadelphia
Dr. ROSALIE M. MIRENDA, D.N.Sc., Pres.
Rev. JUDE MICHAEL KRILL, O.F.M.Conv., Chap.
Priests 2
Sisters 24
Administrators 35
Faculty and Staff 157
Adjuncts 120
Lay Teachers 48
Students 1,659

Center Valley
Diocese of Allentown

Desales University
2755 Station Ave.
Center Valley, PA 18034-9568
Tel: 610-282-1100; Fax: 610-282-2255
E-mail: admiss@desales.edu
Web Site: www.desales.edu
Coeducational liberal arts college conducted by the Oblates of St. Francis de Sales (1965); Accredited.
Very Rev. BERNARD F. O'CONNOR, O.S.F.S., Ph.D., Pres.
Rev. ALEXANDER T. POCETTO, O.S.F.S., Ph.D., Senior Vice Pres.
Dr. TIM FITZGERALD, Dean Students
Mr. GERARD JOYCE, Dean Enrollment Mgmt.
Mr. THOMAS MANTONI, Registrar
Mr. WILLARD CRESSMAN, Vice Pres. Admin., Finance & Technology
Mr. TOM CAMPBELL, Vice Pres. Devel.
Dr. MOHAMED A.S. LATIB, Vice Pres. Program & Strategic Devel.
Dr. KAREN DOYLE WALTON, Vice Pres. Academic Affairs & Provost
Dr. CARMINA MAGNUSEN CHAPP, Dir. Campus Ministry
ROBERT SNYDER, Assoc. Vice Pres. Finance & Treas.
Revs.:
JOHN F. HARVEY, O.S.F.S., S.T.D.
JAMES P. FINNEGAN, O.S.F.S., Ph.D.
GERARD H. SCHUBERT, O.S.F.S., Ph.D.
BERNARD F. DONAHUE, O.S.F.S., Ph.D.
PETER J. LEONARD, O.S.F.S., M.A.
A. ROBERT MCGILVARY, O.S.F.S., Ph.D.
THOMAS F. DAILEY, O.S.F.S., S.T.L.
DANIEL G. GAMBET, O.S.F.S., Ph.D.
JOHN F. MCGINLEY, O.S.F.S., M.A.
JOSEPH F. DIMAURO, O.S.F.S., M.A.
DOUGLAS BURNS, O.S.F.S., M.S.
JOSEPH P. BECKER, O.S.F.S., M.A.
CHRISTOPHER J. HUDGIN, O.S.F.S., M.A.
Priests on Faculty 9
Lay Teachers 106
Students 1,272

Cresson
Diocese of Altoona-Johnstown

Mount Aloysius College
7373 Admiral Peary Hwy.
Cresson, PA 16630
Tel: 814-886-4131; Fax: 814-886-2978
E-mail: cmiller@mtaloy.edu
Web Site: www.mtaloy.edu
Sisters of Mercy
Sr. MARY ANN DILLON, R.S.M., Pres.
Sr. VIRGINIA BERTSCHI, Asst. to the Pres. for Administrative Svcs.
Mr. MICHAEL M. MACEKURA, Dean Enrollment Mgmt.
Dr. DANIEL FREDRICKS, Academic Dean
Dr. DANE R. FOUST, Dean of Students
RONALD J. MCCONNELL, Dean Inst. Advancement
Rev. JOHN SLOVIKOVSKI, M.A., M.Div., Chap.
Priests 1
Sisters 2
Lay Teachers 51
Total Staff 113
Students 2,000

Dallas
Diocese of Scranton

College Misericordia
Dallas, PA 18612
Tel: 570-674-6400; Fax: 570-675-2441
Web Site: www.miseri.edu
Religious Sisters of Mercy of the Americas.
Administration:
MICHAEL A. MACDOWELL, Ed.D., Pres.
Mr. JOHN RISBOSKIN, Vice Pres. of Financial & Admin.
Rev. MICHAEL M. BRYANT, M.Th., Chap.
Sr. MARY GLENNON, R.S.M., Ed.D., Vice Pres. of Academic Affairs & Dean of the College
Ms. SUSAN HELWIG, Vice Pres. Institutional Advancement
Sr. JEAN MESSAROS, R.S.M., Dean of Students
Mrs. JANE DESSOYE, M.S., Exec. Dir., Admissions & Financial Aid
Mr. EDWARD LAHART, M.S., Registrar
Mr. MICHAEL BALDIGA, Dir., Career Svcs.
Ms. JACQUELINE GHORMOZ, M.S., Dir., Counseling Svcs.
Mr. JOSEPH MACK, M.B.A., Dir., Mgmt. Information Svcs.
Sr. MARY SHARON GALLAGHER, R.S.M., M.S.L.S., Dir., Library Svcs.
Ms. KATHLEEN A. FOLEY, B.S., M.S., Asst. Dean of Students
Mr. RONALD HROMISIN, C.P.A., Comptroller
Mr. JAMES ROBERTS, Dir. of Public Communication
Priests 1
Sisters Teaching 3
Students 1,640

Erie
Diocese of Erie

Gannon University
University Square
Erie, PA 16541
Tel: 814-871-7000
Web Site: www.gannon.edu
THOMAS S. OSTROWSKI, Ph.D., Acting Pres.
Rev. Msgr. ADDISON YEHL, M.S.
Rev. Msgr. GERALD L. ORBANEK, M.A.
Rev. Msgr. MICHAEL D. MCGRAW
Very Rev. JOSEPH C. GREGOREK, V.F.
Revs.:
JOHN P. SCHANZ, Censor Librorum
SCOTT P. DETISCH, Ph.D.
GILIO L. DIPRE, Ph.D.
ROBERT G. FIN, Ph.D., (Retired)
EDWARD C. KRAUSE, C.S.C., Ph.D.
ROBERT J. LEVIS, Ph.D.
JAMES MCCULLOUGH, M.S.
NICHOLAS J. ROUCH
ROBERT P. SUSA, M.A.
CASIMIR J. WOZNIAK
MICHAEL KESICKI
CHRISTOPHER HAMLETT
RONALD E. GMEREK
GEORGE E. STROHMEYER, M.A.
Priests 20
Sisters 9
Lay Teachers 279
Students 3,289

Mercyhurst College
501 E. 38th St.
Erie, PA 16546
Tel: 814-824-2000
E-mail: igower@mercyhurst.edu
Web Site: www.mercyhurst.edu
Dr. WILLIAM P. GARVEY, Pres.
Dr. JOSEPH F. GOWER, Dean & Vice Pres. Academic Affairs
Rev. JAMES PISZKER, Chap.
Priests 3
Sisters 11
Lay Teachers 119
Students 3,026

Greensburg
Diocese of Greensburg

Seton Hill College
Greensburg, PA 15601
Tel: 724-834-2200; Fax: 724-830-4611
E-mail: admit@setonhill.edu
Web Site: www.setonhill.edu
Sisters of Charity of Seton Hill
Dr. JOANNE W. BOYLE, Pres.
MARY ANN GAWELEK, Ed.D., Vice Pres. Academic Affairs & Dean of College
Sisters 5
Lay Teachers 59
Students 1,328

Gwynedd Valley
Archdiocese of Philadelphia

Gwynedd-Mercy College
Gwynedd Valley, PA 19437
Tel: 215-646-7300; Fax: 215-641-5573
E-mail: hoffman.r@gmc.edu
Web Site: www.gmc.edu
Rev. JOSEPH B. SMITS, C.I.C.M., Chap.
Sisters of Mercy: 6 Faculty, 8 Staff
Lay Teachers 57
Students 1,819

Immaculata
Archdiocese of Philadelphia

Immaculata College (1920)
Immaculata, PA 19345
Tel: 610-647-4400; Fax: 610-251-1668
Web Site: www.immaculata.edu
Conducted by Sisters, Servants of the Immaculate Heart of Mary
Sr. MARIE ROSEANNE BONFINI, I.H.M., Pres.
Sr. M. CARROLL ISSELMANN, I.H.M., Vice Pres. for Academic Affairs
Sr. CATARIN P. CONJAR, I.H.M., Vice Pres. for Student Affairs
Dr. THOMAS FORD, Vice Pres. for Financial Affairs
Dr. LINDA HOPKINS, Vice Pres. for Institutional Advancement
JANICE BATES, Registrar
Dr. ELKE FRANKE, Dean, College of Lifelong Learning
KENNETH RASP, Undergrad. Enrollment Svcs.
Sr. ANN HEATH, I.H.M., Dean, College of Graduate Studies
Dr. JANET KANE, Dean, Women's College
MARIE MOUGHAN, Exec. Dir. Public Rels. & Mktg.
PETER LYSIONEK, Dir. Financial Aid
Rev. HANS A.L. BROUWERS, M.A., Chap.
Priests 1
Sisters 29
Total Staff 220
Enrollment 2,800

Jenkintown
Metropolitan Archdiocese of Philadelphia Ukrainian

Manor College
700 Fox Chase Rd.
Jenkintown, PA 19046
Tel: 215-885-2360; Fax: 215-576-6564
E-mail: scecilia@mail.manor.edu
Web Site: www.manor.edu
Approved by the Commonwealth of Pennsylvania and accredited by the Middle States Association of Colleges and Secondary Schools.
Sisters of St. Basil the Great
Sr. M. CECILIA JURASINSKI, O.S.B.M., Pres.
SALLY MYDLOWEC, Academic Dean
OLGA UDVARI, Contact Person

Latrobe
Diocese of Greensburg

Saint Vincent College
300 Fraser Purchase Rd.
Latrobe, PA 15650-2690

Tel: 724-539-9761; Fax: 724-537-4587
Legal Title: *Saint Vincent College Corporation*
Rt. Rev. DOUGLAS R. NOWICKI, O.S.B., Chancellor
JAMES F. WILL, Pres.
Bro. NORMAN W. HIPPS, O.S.B., Provost
Priests 18
Brothers 6
Lay Teachers 60
Students 1,206

Loretto
Diocese of Altoona-Johnstown

St. Francis College
P.O. Box 600
Loretto, PA 15940-0600
Tel: 814-472-3000; Fax: 814-472-3044
Web Site: www.sfcpa.edu
Rev. CHRISTIAN R. ORAVEC, T.O.R., Pres.
Dr. RICHARD CRAWFORD, Asst. to the Pres.
Dr. KATHLEEN OWENS, Vice Pres. Academic Affairs
Dr. F. DENNIS RIEGELNEGG, Vice Pres. Student Devel.
Mr. EVAN LIPP, Dean Enrollment Mgmt.
Mr. KEVIN O'FLAHERTY, Vice Pres. Finance
Ms. MARY ANN JACOBS, Dir. Continuing Education
Mr. RAYMOND PONCHIONE, Dir. Devel.
Mr. RANDY FRYE, Dir. M.B.A. Prog.
Dr. WILLIAM DURYEA, Dir. M.M.S. Prog.
Ms. GLENDA GRIFFITH, Dir. Residence Life
Ms. PATRICIA SEROTKIN, Dir. Library
Mr. MICHAEL SARAKA, Dir. Career Devel.
Mr. GEORGE PYO, Dir. Computer Svcs.
Dr. PHILIP BENHAM, Dir. Graduate School Human Resource Mgmt./Industrial Rels.
Mr. DOMINICK PERUSO, Dir. Student Activities
Ms. DENISE KOVACH, Dir. Learning Resource Center
Mr. JEFFREY EISEN, Dir. Athletics
Mr. DAVID WILSON, Dir. Counseling
Revs.:
BEDE F. HINES, T.O.R.
EMIL C. RESCONICH, T.O.R., (Retired)
OLIVER J. HEBERT, T.O.R.
MICHAEL HIGGINS, T.O.R.
JOHN MARK KLAUS, T.O.R.
DAVID MORRIER, T.O.R.
ANDRE STRITTMATTER, T.O.R.
PATRICK DONAHOE, T.O.R.
EDWARD STAFFORD, T.O.R.
Priests 9
Lay Professors 76
Students 1,321

Philadelphia
Archdiocese of Philadelphia

Chestnut Hill College
9601 Germantown Ave.
Philadelphia, PA 19118-2693
Tel: 215-248-7000; Fax: 215-248-7155
E-mail: apply@chc.edu
Web Site: www.chc.edu
Sr. CAROL JEAN VALE, S.S.J., Ph.D., Pres.
Sisters 19
Lay Teachers 36
Students 1,536

Holy Family College (1954)
Grant and Frankford Aves.
Philadelphia, PA 19114
Tel: 215-637-7700; Fax: 215-637-3787
E-mail: fonley@hfc.org
Web Site: www.hfc.edu
Congregation of the Sisters of the Holy Family of Nazareth
Sr. FRANCESCA ONLEY, C.S.F.N., Pres.
Rev. ALBERT J. SMITH, O.S.F.S., Chap. & Campus Minister
In res.,
Rev. JAMES J. COLLINS, S.O.E.D., Dept. of Religious Studies
Priests 9
Sisters 14
Lay Faculty 215
Undergraduate Students 1,831
Graduate 636

LaSalle University
1900 W. Olney Ave.
Philadelphia, PA 19141
Tel: 215-951-1000; Fax: 215-951-1783
(Incorporated under the auspices of the Brothers of the Christian Schools)
Bros.:
JOSEPH F. BURKE, F.S.C., Ph.D., Pres.
DANIEL C. PANTALEO, Ph.D., Provost
RAYMOND P. HEATH, Ph.D., Vice Pres. Student Affairs
DAVID C. FLEMING, M.B.A., Vice Pres. Business Affairs
FRED J. FOLEY, JR., Ph.D., Vice Pres. Devel.
RAYMOND A. RICCI, Ed.M., Vice Pres. Enrollment Svcs.
BARBARA C. MILLARD, Ph.D., Dean of the School of Arts and Sciences
JOSEPH A. KANE, Ph.D., Dean of the School of Business Admin.
MARYANNE R. BEDNAR, Ph.D., Interim Dean, School of Continuing Studies
Bros.:
CHRISTOPHER LYDON, Dir., Admissions
CHARLES ECHELMEIER, F.S.C., Dir. Campus Ministry
GLORIA A. DONNELLY, Ph.D., Dean, School of Nursing
Brothers 24
Priests 5
Sisters 1
Lay Teachers 194
Students 5,376

St. Joseph's University
5600 City Ave.
Philadelphia, PA 19131
Tel: 610-660-1000; Fax: 610-660-1201
Web Site: www.sju.edu
Jesuit Fathers
Tel: 610-660-1400
Under the direction of the Jesuit Fathers. Incorporated January 29, 1851.
Revs.:
NICHOLAS J. RASHFORD, S.J., Pres.
JAMES W. MOORE, S.J., Assoc. Dean College of Arts and Sciences
JOSEPH A. ARROYO, S.J., (Spain) Assoc. Dean, College of Business and Admin.
JOHN E. BENNETT, S.J., Campus Min.
ANTHONY J. BERRET, S.J.
H. CORNELL BRADLEY, S.J.
FRANCIS F. BURCH, S.J.
JOSEPH F. CHORPENNING, O.S.F.S., S.T.D., Ph.D.
DONALD G. CLIFFORD, S.J.
JEROME B. COLL, S.J.
JOSEPH J. FEENEY, S.J.
GERALD F. FINNEGAN, S.J.
VINCENT J. GENOVESI, S.J.
JOSEPH J. GODFREY, S.J.
HOWARD J. HEIM, S.J.
FREDERICK A. HOMANN, S.J.
ALBERT H. JENEMANN, S.J.
JOSEPH M. KAKALEC, S.J.
JOSEPH L. LOMBARDI, S.J.
MICHAEL A. MCELWEE, S.J.
DENNIS E. MCNALLY, S.J.
MARTIN R. TRIPOLE, S.J.
Bro. JOHN J. MCLANE S.J.
Sr. ANN BERNADETTE, G.N.S.H.
Sr. FRANCES HART, S.S.J.
Sr. ELIZABETH ANN LINEHAN, R.S.M.
Priests 26
Sisters 3
Lay Teachers 200
Students 6,350

Pittsburgh
Diocese of Pittsburgh

Carlow College
3333 5th Ave.
Pittsburgh, PA 15213
Tel: 412-578-6005; Fax: 412-578-6048
Web Site: www.carlow.edu
Sisters of Mercy
Sr. GRACE ANN GEIBEL, R.S.M., Ph.D., Pres.
GARY SMITH, Ph.D., Vice Pres. for Academic Affairs
Sisters 2
Lay Teachers 58
Students 2,000

Duquesne University of the Holy Ghost
600 Forbes Ave.
Pittsburgh, PA 15282
Tel: 412-396-6000; Fax: 412-396-4334
Web Site: www.duq.edu
Dr. JOHN E. MURRAY, JR., Pres.
Holy Ghost Fathers
Revs.:
DAVID T. COTTINGHAM, C.S.Sp.
REGINALD DEFOUR, C.S.Sp.
FRANCIS HANLEY, C.S.Sp.
WILLIAM R. HEADLEY, C.S.Sp.
J. CLIFTON HILL, C.S.Sp.
SEAN M. HOGAN, C.S.Sp., Exec. Vice Pres. Student Life
MATHIAS IDYU, C.S.Sp.
SEAN KEALY, C.S.Sp.
RAYMOND D. FRENCH, C.S.Sp.
DAVID L. SMITH, C.S.Sp.
EDMUND R. SUPPLE, C.S.Sp.
JOCELYN GREGORIE, C.S.Sp.
MICHAEL GREY, C.S.Sp.
Priests 20
Lay Teachers 405
Students 10,000
The University is coeducational and comprises the following Colleges and Schools and Institutes:
College of Liberal Arts—
Dr. CONSTANCE RAMIREZ, Dean, College & Graduate School of Liberal Arts
School of Business Administration—
JAMES C. STALDER, Dean
School of Music—
EDWARD KOCHER, Dean
School of Law—
NICHOLAS CAFARDI, Dean
Division of Continuing Education—
Dr. BENJAMIN HODES, Dean
School of Education—
Dr. JAMES E. HENDERSON, Dean
School of Nursing—
Dr. MARY DE CHESNAY, Dean
School of Pharmacy—
Dr. R. PETE VANDERVEEN, Dean
School of Health Sciences—
Dr. JEROME L. MARTIN, Dean
Dr. DAVID W. SEYBERT, Interim Dean, School of Natural & Environmental Sciences
Dr. MICHAEL P. WEBER, Provost and Academic Vice Pres.
Mr. ISADORE R. LENGLET, Executive Vice Pres., Mgmt. and Business
Dr. PAUL J. PUGLIESE, Librarian
Mr. FRANK YINING LIU, Law Librarian

La Roche College
9000 Babcock Blvd.
Pittsburgh, PA 15237
Tel: 412-367-9300; Fax: 412-536-1038
E-mail: admsas@laroche.edu
Web Site: www.laroche.edu
Sisters of Divine Providence
Rev. Msgr. WILLIAM A. KERR, Ph.D., Pres.
DAN SOLLER, Exec. Vice Pres., Admin.
Sr. CAROLYN WINSCHEL, C.D.P., Ph.D., Senior Vice Pres., Mission & Planning
Rev. W. PETER HORTON, M.A., M.Div., Campus Minister
BETTY E. TAYLOR, Ph.D., Vice Pres. Academic Affairs & Graduate Dean
ROGER CAROTHERS, Asst. Vice Pres. Facilities Mgmt.
JOHN GLONINGER, Vice Pres., Business & Finance
Rev. PATRICK O'BRIEN, S.T.D., M.S.Ed., Dept. Chair Religious Studies
Priests 3
Sisters 9
Lay Teachers 199
Students 1,875

Radnor
Archdiocese of Philadelphia

Cabrini College (1957)
610 King of Prussia Rd.
Radnor, PA 19087-3698
Tel: 610-902-8100; Fax: 610-902-8309
E-mail: nancy.gardner@cabrini.edu
Web Site: www.cabrini.edu
Missionary Sisters of the Sacred Heart
Dr. ANTOINETTE IADAROLA, Pres.
Campus Ministers:
JOHN DIMUCCI
Dr. MARY LOVER
Lay Teachers 194
Students 2,534

Reading
Diocese of Allentown

Alvernia College
Reading, PA 19607
Tel: 610-796-8200; Fax: 610-796-8324
E-mail: mazzela@alvernia.edu
Web Site: www.alvernia.edu
Bernardine Sisters of the Third Order of St. Francis
LAURENCE W. MAZZENO, Ph.D., Pres.
Priests 1
Sisters 1
Lay Teachers 61
Students 2,033

Rosemont
Archdiocese of Philadelphia

Rosemont College of the Holy Child Jesus
Rosemont, PA 19010-1699
Tel: 610-526-2984; Fax: 610-527-0341
E-mail: jtrogers@rosemont.edu
Web Site: www.rosemont.edu
MARGARET M. HEALY, Pres.
KATHY RONEY, Campus Minister
Sisters of the Holy Child Jesus 5
Full Time Lay Teachers 42
Part Time Lay Teachers 93
Students 1,198

Scranton
Diocese of Scranton

Marywood University
Scranton, PA 18509
Tel: 570-348-6211; Fax: 570-340-6014
E-mail: mreap@ac.marywood.edu
Web Site: www.marywood.edu
Sisters, Servants of the Immaculate Heart of Mary
Sr. MARY REAP, I.H.M., Ph.D., Pres.
Sr. PATRICIA ANN MATTHEWS, I.H.M., Ph.D., Vice Pres., Academic Affairs
Mr. LEO J. DANYLAK, M.B.A., Vice. Pres., Business Affairs
Dr. CLAYTON N. PHEASANT, Vice Pres., University Advancement
Dr. RAYMOND P. HEATH, Vice Pres., Student Life
Dr. JOHN C. ALESSIO, Dean, Undergraduate School
Dr. LOIS K. DRAINA, Dean, Graduate School of Arts & Sciences
Dr. WILLIAM H. WHITAKER, Dean, School of Social Work
Dr. JOANN SMITH, Dean, School of Continuing Educ.
ANN BOLAND-CHASE, M.A., Registrar
MARY ANNE FEDRICK, M.S.L.S., M.A., Asst. Vice Pres., Academic Affairs
Dr. BARBARA R. SADOWSKI, Asst. to Pres. for Planning & Institutional Research
Faculty:
Sisters 16
Lay Teachers 111
Students 2,903

University of Scranton
(Society of Jesus)
18510
Tel: 570-941-7533; Fax: 570-941-6340
Web Site: www.scranton.edu
Rev. JOSEPH M. MCSHANE, S.J., Pres.
Dr. THOMAS P. HOGAN, Provost & Academic Vice Pres.
Rev. BRENDAN G. LALLY, S.J., Rector of the Jesuit Community
Mr. DAVID E. CHRISTIANSEN, Vice Pres., Finance & Treas.
Mr. ROBERT J. SYLVESTER, Vice Pres., Inst. Advancement
Rev. THOMAS D. MASTERSON, S.J., Vice Pres., Univ. Ministries
Dr. JOSEPH H. DREISBACH, Dean of the College of Arts and Sciences
Dr. RONALD D. JOHNSON, Dean of the Kania School of Mgmt.
Dr. SHIRLEY M. ADAMS, Dean of Dexter Hanley College
Dr. ROSE SEBASTIANELLI, Acting Dean of the Graduate School
Mr. ROBERT FETTERHOFF, Registrar
Dr. JAMES J. PALLANTE, Dean, J.A. Panuska, S.J. College Professional Studies
Dr. VIRGINIA SCHWALM, Dean Student Development & Dir., Counseling Center
Dr. JAMES T. BRYAN, Vice Pres., Student Affairs
Dr. LAWRENCE J. MORTON, Asst. to Vice Pres., Student Affairs
Mr. MARTIN L. LANGAN, Assoc. Vice Pres., Admin. Svcs.
Mr. CHARLES E. KRATZ, Dir., Library
Mr. GERALD C. ZABOSKI, Exec. Asst. to the Pres.
Ms. ABIGAIL BYMAN, Sec. of the University & Gen. Counsel
Revs.:
JOHN J. BEGLEY, S.J.
PAUL R. BEINING, S.J.
TIMOTHY J. CADIGAN, S.J.
HENRY C. COSTER, S.J.
ROYDEN B. DAVIS, S.J., Subminister, Campion Hall
JOHN H. DUGGAN, S.J.
JOSEPH M. HAMERNICK, S.J.
WILLIAM B. HILL, S.J.
MICHAEL A. HRICKO, S.J.
JOSEPH M. KAKALEC, S.J.
HERBERT B. KELLER, S.J., Pres., Scranton Prep
FRANCIS J. KOWNACKI, S.J.
BRENDAN G. LALLY, S.J.
JOHN W. LANGE, S.J.
JOHN J. LEVKO, S.J.
FRANCIS J. MACENTEE, S.J.
LEONARD A. MARTIN, S.J.
THOMAS D. MASTERSON, S.J.
WILLIAM J. MCGRATH, S.J.
BERNARD R. MCILHENNY, S.J., Min. Jesuit Community
RONALD H. MCKINNEY, S.J.
NEIL P. MCLAUGHLIN, S.J.
JOSEPH M. MCSHANE, S.J.
ROBERT J. MCTEIGUE, S.J.
J. PATRICK MOHR, S.J.
G. DONALD PANTLE, S.J.
EDWARD R. POWERS, S.J.
JOHN J. QUINN, S.J.
JOSEPH L. QUINN, S.J.
RICHARD W. ROUSSEAU, S.J.
THOMAS F. SABLE, S.J.
JOHN J. SHEA, S.J.
TERRENCE TOLAND, S.J.
Bros.:
DARRELL J. BURNS, S.J.
JAMES C. LEMON, S.J.
Mr. CHARLES A. FREDERICO, Scholastic
Mr. GUSTAVO PALLAMARES, Scholastic
Priests 34
Students 4,615
Center for Eastern Christian Studies
University of Scranton
Scranton, PA 18510
Tel: 570-941-6116; Fax: 570-941-4030
Revs.:
JOHN J. LEVKO, S.J., Dir.
THOMAS F. SABLE, S.J., Editor Diakonia
Sr. JOAN L. ROCCASALVO, C.S.J., Coord. & Mng. Editor

Villanova
Archdiocese of Philadelphia

Villanova University
Villanova, PA 19085
Tel: 610-519-7499; Fax: 610-519-5333
E-mail: Stephen.Merritt@Villanova.edu
Founded 1842 by the Augustinians, Province of St. Thomas of Villanova. Colleges of Liberal Arts and Sciences, Engineering, Commerce and Finance, Nursing, Part-time and Continuing Education, Graduate Studies and the School of Law and Continuing Education.
Board of Trustees:
Revs.:
EDMUND J. DOBBIN, O.S.A., Pres.
GEORGE F. BURNELL, O.S.A.
JAMES R. FLYNN, O.S.A.
JOHN E. DEEGAN, O.S.A.
JOHN M. DRISCOLL, O.S.A.
KEVIN F. DWYER, O.S.A.
WILLIAM T. GARLAND, O.S.A.
DONALD F. REILLY, O.S.A.
JOSEPH F. WIMMER, O.S.A.
EDSON J. WOOD, O.S.A.
JAMES A. ANDERSON, Ph.D.
HERBERT F. ASPBURY, Esq.
Mr. LAWRENCE E. BATHGATE, II, Esq.
JAMES R. BIRLE
ROBERT M. BIRMINGHAM, Chair
GERALD S.J. CASSIDY, ESQ.
GERALD CLARK
JOHN G. DROSDICK
WILLIAM B. FINNERMAN
ROSA M. GATTI
JOHN G. GILFILLAN, III, ESQ.
HARRY R. HALLORAN, JR.
HAZEL W. JOHNSON-BROWN, Ph.D.
ANDREW J. MARKEY, JR.
MAUREEN H. MCCULLOUGH, Esq.
MICHAEL P. MONACO
MICHAEL B. PICOTTE
ANTHONY T. RANDAZZO
EMILY C. RILEY
MARGUERITE K. SCHLAG, Ed.D.
Dr. MARIELLEN WHELAN
Administration:
Dr. JOHN R. JOHANNES, Vice Pres. Academic Affairs
Dr. HELEN K. LAFFERTY, Univ. Vice Pres.
Revs.:
WILLIAM A. MCGUIRE, O.S.A., Senior Vice Pres. Admin.
JOHN P. STACK, O.S.A., Vice Pres. Student Life
Mr. JOHN M. ELIZANDRO, Vice Pres. Inst. Advancement
Dr. MARK A. SARGENT, Dean School of Law
Mr. VINCENT NICASTRO, Dir. Athletics
Ms. DOROTHY A. MALLOY, Vice Pres. University Counsel
Rev. GEORGE F. RILEY, O.S.A., Special Asst. to Pres. External Affairs
Mr. KENNETH G. VALOSKY, Chief Fin. Officer
Dr. THOMAS F. MONAHAN, Dean College of Commerce & Finance
Dr. ROBERT D. LYNCH, Dean College of Engineering
Rev. KAIL C. ELLIS, O.S.A., Dean of Liberal Arts and Sciences
Mr. PAUL PUGH, Dean of Students
Dr. M. LOUISE FITZPATRICK, Dean College of Nursing
Mr. STEPHEN R. MERRITT, Dean Office of Enrollment Mgmt.
Revs.:
RICHARD O'LEARY, O.S.A., Campus Ministry
T. SHAWN TRACY, O.S.A., Campus Ministry
GORDON E. MARCELLUS, O.S.A., Dir. Development
JOHN P. BETONI, O.S.A., Asst. Registrar
JOHN F. MCATEE, O.S.A., Campus Ministry
Revs.:
THOMAS MURNANE, O.S.A., Office of University Admission
DENNIS J. GALLAGHER, O.S.A., Archivist
THOMAS J. MAHONY, O.S.A., Facilities Mgmt.
Clerical Faculty:
Revs.:
DONALD X. BURT, O.S.A.
JAN H. BUSCH, O.S.A.
ARTHUR B. CHAPPELL, O.S.A.
RICHARD G. CANNULI, O.S.A., Dir., Art Gallery
FRANK E. CHAMBERS, O.S.A., Office of University Admission
PETER M. DONOHUE, O.S.A.
DANIEL E. DOYLE, O.S.A.
FRANCIS A. EIGO, O.S.A.
EDWARD J. ENRIGHT, O.S.A.
JOHN J. FARRELL, O.S.A.
JOHN J. HAGEN, O.S.A.
RICHARD JACOBS, O.S.A.
CHARLES P. LAFERTY, O.S.A.
MARTIN LAIRD, O.S.A.
BERNARD A. LAZOR, O.S.A.
JOSEPH LOYA, O.S.A.
LEE J. MAKOWSKI, O.S.A.
THOMAS F. MARTIN, O.S.A.
JAMES J. MCCARTNEY, O.S.A.
NEIL J. MCGETTIGAN, O.S.A.
JOHN J. MCKENZIE, O.S.A.
ROBERT J. MURRAY, O.S.A.
JOSEPH RYAN, O.S.A.
MICHAEL J. SCANLON, O.S.A.
RALPH C. SHURER, O.S.A.
Bro. JOHN STAGLIANO, O.S.A.
Total Staff 523
Full-Time Enrollment 6,354
Part-Time Enrollment 346
Total Enrollment 10,019
Priests 22
Brothers 1
Lay Teachers 500
Students 10,019

Wilkes-Barre
Diocese of Scranton

**Kings College*
Wilkes-Barre, PA 18711
Tel: 570-208-5900; Fax: 570-825-9046
Web Site: www.kings.edu
Officers of the College:
Rev. THOMAS J. O'HARA, C.S.C., Ph.D., Pres.
Dr. DONALD W. FARMER, Vice Pres., Academic Affairs
Mr. STEVEN H. SEITCHIK, Vice Pres., Business Affairs & Treas.
Ms. JANET MERCINCAVAGE, Vice Pres., Student Affairs
Mr. TERRENCE F. MECH, Vice Pres., Information & Instructional Technologies & Dir., Corgan Library
Mr. FRANK J. PASQUINI, Vice Pres., Development
Revs.:
JOHN R. GERACCI, C.S.C., College Chap. & Dir., Campus Ministry
DONALD J. GRIMES, C.S.C., Assoc. Vice Pres. for Academic Affairs
Mr. RUSSELL J. SINGER, Dean of the William J. McGowan School of Business
Dr. WILLIAM A. SHERGALIS, Dean of the College of Arts and Sciences
Ms. SUSAN MCGARRY-HANNON, Dir. Admissions
Mr. DANIEL T. CEBRICK, Registrar
Rev. ANTHONY R. GRASSO, C.S.C., Religious Supr.
Holy Cross Community
Revs.:
THOMAS F. CARTEN, C.S.C.
ROBERT E. DE LEON, C.S.C.
JOHN R. GERACCI, C.S.C.
ANTHONY R. GRASSO, C.S.C.
DONALD J. GRIMES, C.S.C.
CHARLES J. KOCIOLEK, C.S.C.
THOMAS P. LOONEY, C.S.C.
THOMAS J. O'HARA, C.S.C.
WILLIAM R. RIBANDO, C.S.C.
JOHN J. RYAN, C.S.C.
JOSEPH A. SIDERA, C.S.C.
Bros.:
RICHARD F. KYLE, C.S.C.
JEROME MATTHEWS, C.S.C.
JAMES H. MILLER, C.S.C.
THOMAS SAWYER, C.S.C.
In res.,
Revs.:
JAMES J. DOYLE, C.S.C.
JOSEPH J. LONG, C.S.C.
PATRICK J. SULLIVAN, C.S.C.
Bro. HAROLD J. ROGAN, C.S.C.
Priests 13
Brothers 5
Lay Teachers 95
Students 2,207

PUERTO RICO

Ponce

Diocese of Ponce, Puerto Rico

The Pontifical Catholic University of Puerto Rico
2250 Avenida de las Americas
Ponce, PR 00717-0777
Tel: 787-841-2000; Fax: 787-840-4295
Web Site: www.pucpr.edu
The University is composed of the following: College of Arts and Humanities and Graduate Studies in Hispanic Studies; College of Business Administration and Graduate Studies; College of Education and Graduate Studies; College of Science and Graduate Studies; School of Law; Institute of Graduate Studies in Behavioral Science and Community Affairs; Institute of Social Doctrine of the Church; Program for Special Services; Post-Baccalaureate Achievement Program; Upward Bound Program.
Administration:
Most Revs.:
FREMIOT TORRES OLIVER, D.D., Chancellor
RICARDO A. SURINACH, Vice Chancellor
Mr. JOSE ALBERTO MORALES, ESQ., Pres.
Mrs. MARCELINA VELEZ DE SANTIAGO, Vice Pres. for Academic and Student Affairs
Mr. CARL SAUDER, Vice Pres. Institutional Commitment
Mrs. IRMA RODRIGUEZ, Assoc. Vice Pres. for Academic Affairs
Mrs. CARIDAD C. DE FRAU, Assoc. Vice Pres. for Student Affairs
Rev. FELIX LAZARO, Sch.P., Dean, College of Arts and Humanities
Mr. JAIME SANTIAGO CANET, Dean, College of Business Admin.
Dr. LILLIAN NEGRON, Dean, College of Education
Miss CARMEN L. VELAZQUEZ, Interim Dean, College of Science
CHARLES R. CUPRILL, ESQ., Dean, School of Law
Mr. IVAN E. DAVILA, Registrar
Mrs. ANA BONILLA DE SANCHEZ, Dir., Admissions
Mrs. IREM C. POVENTUD, Dir. Devel.
Mrs. CARMEN GONZALEZ, Dir., Guidance Ctr.
Mrs. ESTHER IRIZARRY, Dir. Libraries
Mrs. NOELIA PADUA, ESQ., Dir. Law Library
Faculty:
Rev. Msgr. HERMINIO DE JESUS
Rev. Msgr. ROBERTO GARCIA
Rev. Msgr. JESUS R. DIEZ ANTONANZAS
Rev. Msgr. ABEL A. DIMARCO
Rev. Msgr. ELIAS MORALES
Revs.:
TOSELLO GIANGIACOMO, C.S.Sp.
EDUARDO TORRES
FELIX LAZARO, Sch.P.
JOSE LUIS LARREATEGUI, Sch.P.
PERFECTO ALVAREZ, O.S.A.
JOSE M. HERRERO
BRIAN W. HARRISON, O.S.
MOISES NAVASCUES, Sch.P.
ADALIN RIVERA
ALVARO HUERGA, O.P.
ESTEBAN SANTAELLA
ALFREDO ALVAREZ LACRUZ
JOSE DIEGO RODRIGUEZ
Ponce:
Revs.:
ALEXIO JOSE DE ARMAS, O.C.D.
SEGISMUNDO CINTRON
CARMELO DE JESUS, O.C.D.
JUAN RODRIGUEZ
VICENTE SALAS, O.M.
JULIO ROLON
JOSE LUIS ALONSO, O.P.
JESUS PACHO
Guayama:
Revs.:
FELIX E. ALVARADO
ANTONIO A. HERNANDEZ, C.SS.R.
JOSE C. VARGAS OLIVERAS
Priests 29
Sisters 3
School of Law 29
Lay Teachers 404
Students 10,365

RHODE ISLAND

Newport

Diocese of Providence

Salve Regina University
Newport, RI 02840-4192
Tel: 401-847-6650; Fax: 401-847-0372
E-mail: sruadmis@salve.edu
Web Site: www.salve.edu
Legal Title: *Salve Regina University*
Sisters of Mercy of the Americas
Dr. M. THERESE ANTONE, R.S.M., Pres.
Dr. BARBARA KATHE, Vice Pres. for Academic Affairs
WILLIAM B. HALL, Vice Pres. for Business and Financial Affairs
THOMAS P. FLANAGAN, Vice Pres. for Admin./Services and Community Relations
JOHN J. ROK, Vice Pres. for Student Life
LAURA E. MCPHIE, Vice Pres. Enrollment Svcs.
FREDERICK C. PROMADES, Dir. Institutional Research
AIDA MIRANTE, Dir. Financial Aid
MICHAEL SEMENZA, Vice Pres. Institutional Advancement
KATHLEEN BOYD, Dir. Library Svcs.
JOHN QUINN, Dean of Students
THOMAS H. BRENNAN, Dir. of Information Systems
Revs.:
PETER D'AMBROSIA
MICHAEL T. MALONE, C.S.Sp.
JOHN LAVIN
Priests 3
Brothers 4
Sisters 15
Lay Teachers 92
Students-Men 762
Women 1,489

Providence

Diocese of Providence

Providence College
River Ave. & Eaton St.
Providence, RI 02918
Tel: 401-865-1000; Fax: 401-865-2057
E-mail: pcadmiss@providence.edu
Web Site: www.providence.edu
Legal Title: *Providence College*
Conducted by the Dominican Friars.
Revs.:
PHILIP A. SMITH, O.P.
TERENCE KEEGAN, O.P., Exec. Vice Pres.
THOMAS L. CANAVAN, O.P., Vice Pres. Academic Admin.
Mr. MICHAEL V. FRAZIER, Vice Pres. Finance & Business
Rev. J. STUART MCPHAIL, O.P., Vice Pres. Student Svcs.
Mr. JOSEPH P. BRUM, Vice Pres. Alumni/Devel.
Mr. EDWARD J. CARON, Vice Pres. College Relations
Rev. MARK S. NOWEL, O.P., Dean Undergraduate Studies
JOSEPH G. MARINA, Dean School of Continuing Education
Revs.:
ROBERT J. HENNESSEY, O.P., Dir. Academics for Graduate Religious Studies Prog.
JAMES A. DRISCOLL, O.P., Dir. Promotions and Publicity of the Grad. School of Rel. & Biblical Studies
THOMAS ERTLE, O.P., Acting Chap.
HARVEY VARNET, Dir. Library
Dominican Priests Teaching 32
Diocesan Priests Teaching 3
Sisters Teaching 4
Lay Professors 302
Enrollment-Day School:
Men 1,567
Women 2,184
Graduate School:
Men 345
Women 592
Evening Division:
Men 286
Women 468

SOUTH DAKOTA

Aberdeen

Diocese of Sioux Falls

Presentation College
Aberdeen, SD 57401
Tel: 605-225-1634; Fax: 605-229-8430
E-mail: lorhale@presentation.edu
Web Site: www.presentation.edu
Sisters of the Presentation of the B.V.M.
Dr. LORRAINE M. HALE, P.B.V.M., Pres.
Rev. JOSEPH SHEEHAN, O.Carm., Chap.
Priests 1
Sisters 3
Lay Teachers 23
Students 462

Yankton

Diocese of Sioux Falls

Mount Marty College
1105 W. 8th St.
Yankton, SD 57078
Tel: 800-658-4552; Fax: 605-668-1357
E-mail: bzhang@mtmc.edu
Web Site: www.mtmc.edu
Benedictine Sisters
Dr. MARK HURTUBISE, Pres.
Sisters 7
Lay Teachers 30
Students 1,125

TENNESSEE

Memphis

Diocese of Memphis

**Christian Brothers University* (1871)
(Coed)
650 E. Parkway S.
Memphis, TN 38104
Tel: 901-321-3000; Fax: 901-321-3494
Legal Title: *Christian Brothers Univ. (of Memphis, Tenn.)*
Bro. STANISLAUS SOBCZYK, F.S.C., Pres.
Four-Year university with Schools of Business, Engineering, Liberal Arts, and Science-Mathematics. Graduate programs in Business and Engineering, and Education.
Dr. MARK SMITH, Vice Pres. Academic Affairs
Mr. DAN WORTHAM, Vice Pres. Admin. Affairs
Mr. NICK SCULLY, Vice Pres. Institutional Advance & Student Affairs
LISA BELL, Dir. of Media Relations
Ms. BETTY MCWILLIE, Dir. Career Devel. & Placement
Bro. JOHN EDWARD DOODY, F.S.C., Dir. Grants & Proposals
Mr. THOMAS COCHRAN, Dir. of Foundations; Business Office Mgr.
Sr. DOLORES MONTINI, C.S.J., Campus Minister
Brothers 33
Sisters 2
Lay Teachers 145
Students 2,055

Nashville

Diocese of Nashville

Aquinas College
4210 Harding Rd.
Nashville, TN 37205
Tel: 615-297-7545; Fax: 615-297-7970
Web Site: www.aquinas-tn.edu
Dominican Sisters of St. Cecilia Congregation
Mother ROSE MARIE MASSERANO, O.P., Chm.
Sr. MARY EVELYN POTTS, O.P., Pres.
Sr. MARY JUSTIN HALTOM, Academic Dean
Sisters 6
Lay Teachers 23
Students 306

TEXAS

Austin

Diocese of Austin

St. Edward's University
Established in 1878 by the Congregation of Holy Cross and chartered by the state in 1885.
3001 S. Congress Ave.
Austin, TX 78704-6489
Tel: 512-448-8400; Fax: 512-448-8492
E-mail: seu.admit@admin.stedwards.edu
Web Site: www.stedwards.edu
Officers:
Dr. GEORGE E. MARTIN, Pres.
Sr. DONNA M. JURICK, S.N.D., Exec. Vice Pres.
DAVID A. DICKSON, JR., Vice Pres. Financial Affairs
Mr. KEN WILLIAMS, Interim Vice Pres., Univ. Rels.
ANNE E. PROVINCE, Assoc. Vice Pres. Planning/Information Svcs.
Dr. J. D. LEWIS, Vice Pres. Undergraduate College
Bro. JOSEPH M. BARRY, C.S.C., Dir. Campus Ministry
Dr. MARIANNE F. HOPPER, Dean, Behavioral Social Science
Dr. FRANK KRAFKA, Dean, Business Admin.
Dr. FRANK SMITH, Dean, School of Education
Mrs. MARCIA KINSEY, Dean, School of Humanities
WILLIAM J. QUINN, Interim Dean, School of Natural Sciences
H. RAMSEY FOWLER, Dean of New College
Ms. EILEEN SHOCKET, Librarian
Dr. LANCE HAYES, Registrar
Dr. SANDRA L. PACHECO, Assoc. Vice Pres. for Student Affairs.
Dr. JOHN HOUGHTON, Vice Pres. College of Professional and Graduate Studies
Ms. MARSHA C. KELLIHER, Interim Dean, MBA Prog.
Dr. JAMES A. JOHNSON, Interim Dean, MAHS Prog.

Rev. RICHARD S. WILKENSON, C.S.C., Assoc. Campus Min.
Bros.:
ANDREW ANGERMEIRER, C.S.C.
LAWRENCE ATKINSON, C.S.C.
ROMARD BARTHEL, C.S.C.
THOMAS CHADY, C.S.C.
LOUIS COE, C.S.C.
RICHARD DALY, C.S.C.
WILLIAM DUNN, C.S.C.
EAGAN HUNTER, C.S.C.
GEORGE KLAWITTER, C.S.C.
THOMAS MCCULLOUGH, C.S.C.
VICTOR MONETTE, C.S.C.
HOWARD METZ, C.S.C.
GERALD MULLER, C.S.C.
JOHN PAIGE, C.S.C.
JOHN PERRON, C.S.C.
EDWIN REGGIO, C.S.C.
DONALD STEFFERS, C.S.C.
Faculty:
Priests 1
Holy Cross Brothers 12
Sisters 1
Lay Professors 275
Total Staff 288
Students 3,669

Houston
Diocese of Galveston—Houston

**University of St. Thomas*
3800 Montrose Blvd.
Houston, TX 77006-4696
Tel: 713-522-7911; Fax: 713-525-2125
E-mail: president@stthom.edu
Web Site: www.stthom.edu
Founded in 1947, Graduate Division (Four Schools). Undergraduate Division (21 Departments). Center for Thomistic Studies. Center for International Studies. Center for Business Ethics Studies.
Rev. J. MICHAEL MILLER, C.S.B., Pres.
Dr. JEROME A. KRAMER, Vice Pres., Academic Affairs
Rev. WILLIAM J. YOUNG, C.S.B., Pres. Emeritus; Dir. Community Svcs. of the Univ.
Ms. MARY PATSATZIS, Registrar
Mrs. ELSIE BIRON, Dean, Admissions
Mr. JAMES PICCININNI, Dir., Doherty Library
Rev. LOUIS T. BRUSATTI, C.M., Dean School of Theology
Dr. YHI-MIN HO, Dean, Cameron School of Business
Dr. RUTH STRUDLER, Dean, School of Education
Dr. RONALD HATCHETT, Dir., Center for Intl. Studies
Ms. LINDA BALLARD, Dir., Financial Aid
Mr. JACK HANK, Vice Pres. for Student Affairs
Rev. JEFFERSON THOMPSON, C.S.B., Dir. Campus Ministry
Ms. SUSAN GREENSAGE, Dir., Alumni Relations
Rev. EDWARD A. BADER, C.S.B., Curator, University Art Collection
Dr. COLLEEN HESTER, Vice Pres. Strategic Planning, Institutional Research and Evaluation
Mr. JAMES BOOTH, Vice Pres., Finance
Dr. MARY CATHERINE SOMMERS, Dean, Arts & Sciences
Dr. JANICE GORDON-KELTER, Dean Special Sessions & Prog.
Ms. MARIE-PIERRE STIEN, Dir., Human Resources
Dr. ROSE SIGNORELLO, Dir., Counseling and Testing Services
Dr. DANIEL MCINERNY, Dir., Center for Thomistic Studies
Mr. GARY MCCORMACK, Vice Pres. for Information Technology
Mr. KEN DEDOMINICIS Vice Pres. for Institutional Advancement
Mr. MATTHEW PRASIFKA, Dir., Recreation & Sports Svcs.
Mr. LANCE JONES, Dir., Security
Ms. DORITA HATCHETT, Dir., Student Activities
Ms. ELLIE COLLIER, Dir. Office of Volunteer Opportunities
Mr. HOWARD ROSE, Asst. Vice Pres. Facilities Opers.
Ms. KAREN BURNS, Controller
Ms. SUSAN BYFORD, Treas.
Mr. ADAM MARTINEZ, Dir., Major Gifts
Rev. DONALD NESTI, C.S.Sp., Dir., Center for Faith & Culture
Dr. DARYL KOEHN, Dir., Center for Business Ethics
Ms. PATRICIA MCKINLEY, Dir., Career Svcs. & Testing
Mr. PAUL HARASIM, Dir., Public Affairs
Ms. MARIONETTE MITCHELL, Dir., Publications
Ms. GAYLE MONGAN, Dir., Advancement Projects
Ms. SUSAN BRADFORD, Exec. Dir., Inst. Advancement
Mr. FRANK SOUTO, Dir., Network & Campus Computing
Ms. CHRISTINE BARRY, Dir., Central Computing Svcs.
Ms. JOANNA PALASOTA, Dir., Administrative Computing Svcs.
Mr. TIM MURPHY, Dir., Instructional Technology & Media Svcs.
Ms. BOBBE AMES, Vice Pres., Enrollment Svcs.
Priests 8
Sisters 3
Lay Professors 101
Total Staff 113
Students 2,897

Irving
Diocese of Dallas

University of Dallas
President's Office, 1845 E. Northgate
Irving, TX 75062
Tel: 972-721-5000; Fax: 972-721-5017
Administrative Officers:
Most Rev. CHARLES V. GRAHMANN, D.D., Grand Chancellor
Rev. Msgr. MILAM JOSEPH, Pres.
Mr. ROBERT GALECKE, Vice Pres. Admin.
Dr. GLEN E. THUROW, Provost & Dean
Dr. PAULA HUGHES, Dean of Graduate School of Management
Mrs. SYBIL NOVINSKI, Assoc. Provost
Dr. FRED ZUKER, Dean of Students
Rev. SEAN MARTIN
Most Rev. JOSEPH GALANTE
Diocesan Priests:
Revs.:
JOHN COLLET
MITCHELL PACWA, S.J.
Cistercian Priests:
Revs.:
DAVID BALAS, O.Cist.
ROBERT BRADLEY
FREDERICK CAMPBELL
JAMES LEHRBERGER, O.Cist.
ROBERT MAGUIRE, O.Cist.
Sr. ST. JOHN BEGNAD
Rev. JAMES COVLEY
Lay Teachers 205
Students 3,738

San Antonio
Archdiocese of San Antonio

Oblate School of Theology (1903)
(Coed) (Graduate Theology)
285 Oblate Dr.
San Antonio, TX 78216-6693
Tel: 210-341-1366; Fax: 210-341-4519
Web Site: www.ost.edu
Conducted by the Missionary Oblates of Mary Immaculate
Rev. J. WILLIAM MORELL, O.M.I., M.Div., Pres.
Dr. MARCELLA HOESL, M.M., Academic Dean
Mr. SCOTT WOODWARD, M.A., Assoc. Academic Dean
Mrs. CHRISTIANE B. SCHEEL, Dir. Admissions, Registrar
Mr. HECTOR RODRIGUEZ, Dir. Faculty and Personnel
Rev. CHARLES BREAULT, O.M.I., Dir. of Finance
Ms. ELVA RUIZ, Admin. Asst. Pres.
Faculty:
Revs.:
GERALD BROWN, S.S.
WARREN BROWN, O.M.I., L.C.L., M.C.L.
ROBERT A. BUSCH, Ph.D (AMA)
KEVIN COLLINS, O.M.I., M.Div., Dir. Oblate Renewal Center
GILBERT A. ENDERLE, C.Ss.R., Ph.D.
MARK A. GARRETT, O.S.A.
KEN HANNON, O.M.I., Ph.D.
JAN HEEMROOD, O.M.I., S.S.L.
RON E. JENKINS, J.C.D (AUS)
DONALD J. JOYCE, O.M.I., M.Div., Dir. Library
JOHN KEMPER, S.S., D.Min., Dir.
JAN PIOTR KLAK
JOSEPH T. LA BELLE, O.M.I., S.T.L.
JOSE A. LOPEZ
JOHN M. MAKOTHAKAT, Ph.D., J.C.D., S.T.D.
JOHN RAY MEREK, O.M.I., D.Min (Canada)
FRANCIS KELLY NEMECK, O.M.I., S.S.D.
LEOPOLDO G. PEREZ, O.M.I., S.T.D., Co-Dir. M.Div.
FREDERICK SACKETT, O.M.I., J.C.D.
STEPHEN K. SHERWOOD, C.M.F., S.T.D.
JAMES K. SULLIVAN, M.A (SPC) Dir. Ministry to Ministers Prog.
ROBERT E. WRIGHT, O.M.I., Ph.D.
RONALD W. YOUNG, O.M.I., S.T.D.
Sr. SARAH ANN SHARKEY, O.P., Ph.D.
Ms. MARGARET ESCOBEDO, M.T.S., Dir. Lay Ministry
Mr. FRANK SPINNER, Dir. Devel.
Priests 25
Sisters 4
Lay Professors 11
Students 268

**Our Lady of the Lake University*
411 S.W. 24th
San Antonio, TX 78207-4689
Tel: 210-434-6711; Fax: 210-436-0824
E-mail: mahos@lake.OLLUSA.edu
Web Site: www.ollusa.edu
Sponsored by Sisters of Divine Providence
SALLY MAHONEY, M.S., Pres.
Dr. JAMES L. GEARITY, Ph.D., Provost
ALLEN R. KLAUS, B.B.A., C.P.A., Vice Pres. Finance and Facilities
MARY ELLEN SMITH, M.S., Vice Pres. & Dean of Student Life
Ms. LORETTA A. SCHLEGEL, M.Ed., Vice Pres. Enrollment Mgmt.
FRED D. SCOTT, M.A., Inst. Research Dir.
Mr. MORLEY GLICKEN, Ph.D., Dean, Worden School of Social Svcs.
Sr. ISABEL BALL, C.D.P., Ph.D., Dean, College of Arts & Sciences
Dr. LOIS GRAFF, Ph.D., Dean, School of Business
Dr. JACQUELYN ALEXANDER, Ph.D., Dean, School of Education & Clinical Studies
Campus Ministry Team:
Rev. MIGUEL BRISENO, O.F.M.Conv., Chap.
WAYNE ROMO, M.T.S., Dir.
GLORIA URRUBAZO, L.M.S.W., M.A., Assoc. Dir.
Sisters 15
Full-time Faculty 106
Lay Teachers 240
Students 3,474

St. Mary's University of San Antonio, Texas (1852)
(Coed)
One Camino Santa Maria
San Antonio, TX 78228-8572
Tel: 210-436-3011; Fax: 210-436-3500
E-mail: jmoder@alvin.stmarytx.edu
Web Site: www.stmarytx.edu
Conducted by the Society of Mary
Dr. CHARLES COTRELL, Pres.
Dr. DAVID MANUEL, Acting V.P., Academic Affairs
Ms. KATHERINE SISOIAN, Vice Pres. Student Devel.
Mr. DANIEL J. WHITE, Vice Pres. Admin. & Finance
Dr. JANET DIZINNO, Dean, School of Humanities and Social Sciences
Dr. SUSANNE CORY, Acting Dean, School of Business
Dr. ANTHONY J. KAUFMANN, Dean, School of Science, Engrg. and Technology
Dr. RONALD MERRELL, Dean, Graduate School
Mr. R. WILLIAM PIATT, Dean, School of Law
Ms. LOUISA AVITUA-TREVINO, Registrar
Mr. RICHARD CASTILLO, Dir. Admissions
Dr. H. PALMER HALL, Dir. Academic Library
Mr. BERNARD REAMS, Dir. Law Library
Revs.:
WILLIAM MEYER, S.M., Dir. Campus Ministry
NORBERT C. BROCKMAN, S.M.
LAWRENCE DOERSCHING, S.M.
CHRISTIAN JANSON, S.M.
CONRAD J. KACZKOWSKI, S.M.
JOHN A. LEIES, S.M.
J. WILLIS LANGLINAIS, S.M.
GEORGE MONTAGUE, S.M.
CHARLES H. MILLER, S.M.
JOHN RECHTEIN, S.M.
W. FRANZ SCHORP, S.M.
Priests 11
Brothers 13
Sisters 5
Lay Teachers 160
Students 4,137

The United Colleges of San Antonio
(A Consortium of Catholic Colleges in San Antonio)
285 Oblate Dr.
San Antonio, TX 78216
Tel: 210-341-1366; Fax: 210-341-4519
Rev. J. WILLIAM MORELL, O.M.I.
CHARLES L. COTRELL, Ph.D.
Dr. LOUIS AGNESE, JR., Ph.D.
Ms. SALLY MAHONEY, M.S.

University of the Incarnate Word
4301 Broadway
San Antonio, TX 78209
Tel: 210-829-6000; Fax: 210-829-3901
E-mail: douge@universe.uiwtx.edu
Web Site: www.uiw.edu
Dr. LOUIS J. AGNESE, JR., Ph.D., Pres.
Sr. MARGARET PATRICE SLATTERY, C.C.V.I., Ph.D., Chancellor
Dr. EDUARDO PADERON, Ph.D., Provost
DOUGLAS B. ENDSLEY, M.B.A, Vice Pres. Business & Finance
THOMAS PLOFCHAN, M.A., Vice Pres. Inst. Advancement
FRANK AYALA, Ph.D., Dean Academic Progress
DAVID JURENOVICH, Ph.D., Vice Pres. Admin.
GILBERT HINOJOSA, Ph.D., Dean Graduate Studies/Research
PATRICIA WATKINS, Ed.D., Dean of Education
DENISE DOYLE, Ph.D., Vice Pres. Academic & Student Affairs
RENEE MOORE, Dean of Campus Life

ANDREA CYTERSKI, Dir. of Admissions
Ms. KATHERINE RUIZ, Dir. Campus Ministry
Sr. EILISH RYAN, Th.D., Dir. Pastoral Institute
BOBBYE FRY, Registrar
DONNA ARONSON, Ph.D, Dean Humanities, Arts & Sciences
PATRICIA BURR, Ph.D., Dean Business, Applied Arts & Sciences
Dr. REGINALD TRAYLOR, Ph.D., Dean Math, Science & Engineering
KATHLEEN LIGHT, Dean Nursing & Health Professionals
MENDAL MORGAN, Dean Library
EDITH COGDELL, C.P.A., Comptroller
Priests 1
Sisters of the Incarnate Word 15
Lay Faculty 412
Students 3,702

VERMONT

Burlington
Diocese of Burlington

Trinity College of Vermont
President's Office, 208 Colchester Ave.
Burlington, VT 05401
Tel: 802-658-0337; Fax: 802-846-7003
E-mail: kieslich@trinityvt.edu
Web Site: www.trinityvt.edu
Sr. JACQUELINE KIESLICH, Pres.
Sisters 1
Lay Teachers 11
Students 200

Colchester
Diocese of Burlington

St. Michael's College
Winooski Park
Colchester, VT 05439
Tel: 802-654-2000; 654-2386; Fax: 802-654-2701
E-mail: mcormier@smcvt.edu
Web Site: www.smcvt.edu
Dr. MARC A. VANDERHEYDEN, Pres.
Mr. PETER R. WORRELL, Chm. of the Board
Ms. MARILYN CORMIER, Asst. to Pres.
Dr. JANET SHEERAN, Vice Pres. Academic Affairs
Mr. MICHAEL D. SAMARA, Vice Pres. for Student Affairs
Mr. NEAL ROBINSON, Vice Pres. Finance
Ms. BARBARA WESSEL, Vice Pres. Institutional Advancement
Dr. JOHN P. KENNEY, Dean of the College
Mr. JERRY E. FLANAGAN, Vice Pres. for Enrollment & Mktg.
Mr. JOHN D. SHEEHEY, Registrar
Dr. BONNIE TANGALOS, Dean of Intl. Studies
Dr. EDWARD MAHONEY, Chm. Graduate Theology & Pastoral Ministry Prog.
Rev. MARCEL R. RAINVILLE, S.S.E., Dir. Edmundite Campus Min.
Ms. ANN GIOMBETTI, Dir. of Volunteer Programs
Priests 3
Lay Teachers 137
Students 2,635

Rutland
Diocese of Burlington

College of St. Joseph in Vermont
71 Clement Rd.
Rutland, VT 05701-3899
Tel: 802-773-5900; Fax: 802-773-5900, Ext. 3
E-mail: fmiglorie@csj.edu
Web Site: www.csj.edu
Dr. FRANK G. MIGLORIE, JR., Pres.
Lay Teachers 14
Students 517

VIRGINIA

Arlington
Diocese of Arlington

Marymount University
2807 N. Glebe Rd.
Arlington, VA 22207
Tel: 703-522-5600; Fax: 703-522-0349
E-mail: admissions@marymount.edu
Web Site: www.marymount.edu
Religious of the Sacred Heart of Mary
Resident and Non-resident coed students.
Sr. EYMARD GALLAGHER, R.S.H.M., Pres.
Rev. KEVIN B. WALSH, Chap.
Sisters 8
Lay Faculty & Staff 642
Students 3,675

Front Royal
Diocese of Arlington

Christendom College
134 Christendom Dr.
Front Royal, VA 22630
Tel: 540-636-2900; Fax: 540-636-1655
Resident and Non-resident students.
TIMOTHY T. O'DONNELL, S.T.D., Pres.
In res.,
Revs.:
ROBERT L. KINCL
ANTHONY J. MASTROENI
Priests 2
Lay Teachers 24
Students 286

WASHINGTON

Lacey
Archdiocese of Seattle

St. Martin's College
5300 Pacific Ave., S.E.
Lacey, WA 98503
Tel: 360-438-4311; Fax: 360-459-4124
E-mail: admissions@stmartin.edu
Web Site: www.stmartin.edu
Order of St. Benedict College of Liberal Arts and Sciences.
Dr. DAVID R. SPANGLER, Pres.
Dr. JACQUELINE JOHNSON, Vice Pres. Academic Affairs
Resident and non-resident students.
Main Campus 974
Extension Campuses 515
Total Staff 175
Priests 5
Brothers 2
Lay Teachers 66

Seattle
Archdiocese of Seattle

Seattle University
900 Broadway
Seattle, WA 98122
Tel: 206-296-6000; Fax: 206-296-6200
E-mail: mafcseattleu.edu
Web Site: www.seattleu.edu
Revs.:
STEPHEN V. SUNDBORG, S.J., Pres.
MICHAEL S. BAYARD, S.J.
ALEXIUS W. BYRNE, S.J.
PHILIP L. BOROUGHS, S.J., Rector
EMMETT H. CARROLL, S.J.
GERALD T. COBB, S.J.
PETER B. ELY, S.J.
JOHN F. FOSTER, S.J.
RONALD R. FUNKE, S.J.
ROGER S. GILLIS, S.J.
JAMES M. HARBAUGH, S.J.
ANTON J. HARRIS, S.J.
STEPHEN M. HESS, S.J.
PATRICK J. HOWELL, S.J.
PAUL A. JANOWIAK, S.J.
MICHAEL M. KELLIHER, S.J.
WILLIAM F. LEROUX, S.J.
DAVID J. LEIGH, S.J.
FRANCIS A. LOGAN, S.J.
PHILIP J. LUCID, S.J.
JOSEPH O. MCGOWAN, S.J.
THOMAS R.E. MURPHY, S.J.
PATRICK B. O'LEARY, S.J.
LAMMERT B. OTTEN, S.J.
JAMES B. REICHMANN, S.J.
RICHARD R. ROACH, S.J.
JOSEF V. VENKER, S.J (MIS)
JOSEPH R. STOCKING, S.J.
WILLIAM J. SULLIVAN, S.J.
MICHAEL J. TAYLOR, S.J.
L. JOHN TOPEL, S.J.
CHARLES A. WOLLESEN, S.J.
THEODORE E. ZEMBAL, S.J.
Bro. WAYNE M. GSELL, S.J.
Mr. JAMES R. NOLTE, Scholastic
Mr. JAMES (VIET) T. TRAN, Scholastic
Priests 17
Sisters 2
Scholastics 2
Lay Teachers 294
Students 5,829

Spokane
Diocese of Spokane

Gonzaga University
Spokane, WA 99258
Tel: 509-328-4220
College of Arts and Sciences, and Schools of Law, Engineering, Education, Business Administration, Graduate School. Professional Studies Education conducted by the Fathers of the Society of Jesus.
Revs.:
PATRICK J. FORD, S.J., Academic Vice Pres.
ROBERT J. ARAUJO, S.J.
DONALD R. CADDEN, S.J.
J. ALFRED CARROLL, S.J.
TIMOTHY R. CLANCY, S.J.
JOSEPH C FORTIER, S.J.
SCOTT W. COBLE, S.J.
MICHAEL J. CONNOLLY, S.J (New England)
MICHAEL L. COOK, S.J.
FRANK B. COSTELLO, S.J.
BERNARD J. COUGHLIN, S.J (Missouri)
ROBERT R. DORIN, S.J (New England)
ROBERT J. EGAN, S.J.
JOHN J. EVOY, S.J.
GERALD R. GORDON, S.J.
DONALD E. HIGHBERGER, S.J (Missouri)
CLIFFORD KOSSEL, S.J.
KENNETH R. KRALL, S.J.
STEPHEN R. KUDER, S.J.
WALTER F. LEEDALE, S.J.
ANTHONY LEHMANN, S.J.
ROBERT LYONS, S.J.
JAMES M. MCDONOUGH, S.J.
WILLIAM C. HAUSMANN, S.J.
J. PATRICK HURLEY, S.J.
ALFRED MORISETTE, S.J.
GEORGE O. MORRIS, S.J.
JOHN P. MOSSI, S.J (California)
STEPHEN CHANTRY, S.J.
JAMES G. POWERS, S.J.
WILLIAM F. RYAN, S.J.
FREDRIC SCHLATTER, S.J.
LEONARD F. SITTER, S.J.
M. DELMAR SKILLINGSTAD, S.J.
ROBERT J. SPITZER, S.J., Pres.
MICHAEL TRELEAVEN, S.J.
FRANK D. MASTERSON, S.J.
WILLIAM M. O'MALLEY, S.J.
JOHN J. ROCK, S.J.
MICHAEL T. SHANNON, S.J.
ROBERT L. WHELAN, S.J.
BERNARD J. TYRRELL, S.J.
GARY D. UHLENKOTT, S.J.
ANTHONY P. VIA, S.J.
J. KEVIN WATERS, S.J.
WILLIAM M. WATSON, S.J.
JOHN H. WRIGHT
Bros.:
DONALD A. JELLISON, S.J.
EDWARD S. JENNINGS, S.J.
MAURICE C. PAQUET, S.J.
STEPHEN J. SOUZA, S.J.
ADAM C. WEISGERBER, S.J.
Priests 48
Brothers 5
Sisters 4
Lay Teachers 282
Students 4,515

The Ministry Institute
(at Gonzaga University)
E. 405 Sinto Ave.
Spokane, WA 99202-1849
Tel: 509-328-8332; Fax: 509-325-4011
Full Time Enrollment 18
ROBERT TROMAN, Ph.D.
DONNE CROW, Formation Dir.
DIANE IMES, Bus. Mgr.
JOLIE MONASTERIO, Sabbatical Coord.

Toppenish
Diocese of Yakima

**Heritage College*
(Interdenominational University with an Independent Board)
3240 Fort Rd.
Toppenish, WA 98948
Tel: 509-865-2244; Fax: 509-865-4469
Web Site: www.heritage.edu
Sisters 5
Lay Teachers 29
Students 1,185

WEST VIRGINIA

Wheeling
Diocese of Wheeling-Charleston

Wheeling Jesuit University
316 Washington Ave.
Wheeling, WV 26003-6243
Tel: 304-243-2000; Fax: 304-243-4349
E-mail: gflundy@wju.edu
Web Site: www.wju.edu
Jesuit Fathers
Web Site: www.wju.edu

Very Rev. JOSEPH J. HAYDEN, S.J., Rector, Jesuit Community
Revs.:
GEORGE F. LUNDY, S.J., Pres., University
LOUIS A. BONACCI, S.J.
FRANK C. BOURBON, S.J.
WALTER A. BUCKIUS, S.J.
W. NORRIS CLARKE, S.J.
JOHN J. COLL, S.J.
JOSEPH A. BURKE, S.J.
PAUL JESURAJA, S.J.
EDWARD A. JARVIS, S.J.
JOHN J. KARWIN, S.J.
JOSEPH E. KOLB, S.J.
VINCENT J. LAGOMARSINO, S.J.
JAMES A. O'BRIEN, S.J.
DOUGLAS F. PEDUTI, S.J.
DONALD M. SERVA, S.J.
MICHAEL F. STELTENKAMP, S.J.
Priests 16
Scholastics 2
Lay Teachers 100
Students 1,515

WISCONSIN

De Pere
Diocese of Green Bay

St. Norbert College
De Pere, WI 54115-2099
Tel: 920-337-3181; Fax: 920-403-4096
E-mail: kinnae@mail.snc.edu
Web Site: www.snc.edu
Legal Title: *St. Norbert College, Inc.*
Dr. WILLIAM J. HYNES, Pres.
Dr. THOMAS J. TREBON, Vice Pres. Academic Affairs & Dean of College
Ms. NANCY KIN, Vice Pres., Business & Finance
Dr. RICHARD RANKIN, Vice Pres. Student Life
Mr. DONALD L. SALMON, Vice Pres., Institutional Advancement
Revs.:
GERY G. MEEHAN, O.Praem, Dir. Campus Min. & Pastor St. Norbert College Parish
DANE RADECKI, O.Praem., Asst. to the Pres. on Mission and Heritage
Faculty:
Revs.:
ROBERT J. CORNELL, O.Praem.
JOHN P. KASTENHOLZ, O.Praem.
DAVID M. KOMATZ, O.Praem.
JAY M. FOSTNER, O.Praem.
MICHAEL F. FRISCH, O.Praem
JOHN BOSTWICK, O.Praem
Priests 3
Sisters 1
ROTC 1
Lay Teachers 112
Students 2,000
St. Norbert College Summer School
Tel: 920-403-3051; Fax: 920-403-4096
Dr. JOHN SUTTON, Assoc. Dean Instructional Svcs.

Fond du Lac
Archdiocese of Milwaukee

Marian College of Fond du Lac
45 S. National Ave.
Fond du Lac, WI 54935
Tel: 920-923-7600; Fax: 920-923-8087
E-mail: admissions@mariancollege.edu
Web Site: www.mariancollege.edu
Dr. RICHARD I. RIDENOUR, Pres.
SHERYL AYALA, Acting Academic Dean
Sr. MARIE SCOTT, C.S.A., Campus Min.
Sisters of the Congregation of St. Agnes 3
Lay Teachers 69
Students 2,243
Total Staff 129

La Crosse
Diocese of La Crosse

Viterbo University
815 Ninth St. South
La Crosse, WI 54601-8802
Tel: 608-796-3000; Fax: 608-796-3050
E-mail: admission@viterbo.edu
Web Site: www.viterbo.org
A Catholic four-year coed liberal arts university founded by the Franciscan Sisters of Perpetual Adoration in 1890.
WILLIAM J. MEDLAND, Ph.D., Pres.
JOHN F. HAVERTAPE, Academic Vice Pres.
S. JEAN MOORE, F.S.P.A., Ph.D., Vice Pres. Student Devel.
TODD M. ERICSON, C.P.A., Vice Pres. Finance
KENNA CHRISTIANS, Vice Pres. Inst. Advancement
PATRICK G. KERRIGAN, Dir. Marketing & Communications
JANET LINDERBAUM, Registrar
ROLAND NELSON, Ph.D., Dir. Admissions
Rev. THOMAS M. O'NEILL, Chap. & Dir. Campus Ministry, Tel: 608-796-3804
Priests 1
Sisters 6
Lay Teachers 120
Students 2,106

Madison
Diocese of Madison

Edgewood College
1000 Edgewood College Dr.
Madison, WI 53711
Tel: 608-663-4861; Fax: 608-663-6717
Dominican Sisters, Sinsinawa, WI
Dr. JAMES A. EBBEN, Pres.
Sr. MAUREEN MCDONNELL, O.P., Campus Minister
Sr. MARGARET HOPKINS, O.P., Dir., Office of Dominican Mission
STEPHEN BULLOCK, Campus Ministry
Sisters 14
Lay Teachers 164
Students 1,909

Manitowoc
Diocese of Green Bay

Silver Lake College of the Holy Family
2406 S. Alverno Rd.
Manitowoc, WI 54220-9319
Tel: 920-684-6691; Fax: 920-684-7082
E-mail: silver.sl.edu
Web Site: www.sl.edu
Connected with Holy Family Motherhouse of Franciscan Sisters of Christian Charity.
Sr. MAUREEN ANNE SHEPARD, O.S.F., Pres.
Priests 4
Sisters 46
Lay Teachers 110
Students 4,455

Milwaukee
Archdiocese of Milwaukee

Alverno College
3400 S. 43rd St., P.O. Box 343922
Milwaukee, WI 53234-3922
Tel: 414-382-6000; Fax: 414-362-6354
Web Site: www.alverno.edu
GARY P. GRUNAU, Chm., Bd. of Trustees
Sr. JOEL READ, O.S.F., Pres.
Sr. KATHLEEN O'BRIEN, O.S.F., Vice Pres. Academic Affairs
Mr. JAMES OPPERMANN, Vice Pres., Finance & Mgmt. Svcs.
Sisters 10
Lay Teachers 87
Students 1,940
Total Staff 220

Cardinal Stritch University
6801 N. Yates Rd.
Milwaukee, WI 53217
Tel: 414-410-4000; Fax: 414-410-4239
Web Site: www.stritch.edu
Conducted by Sisters of St. Francis of Assisi
Sr. MARY LEA SCHNEIDER, O.S.F., Pres.
Dr. MARNA BOYLE, Vice Pres. Academic Affairs
Revs.:
JAMES E. LOBACZ, Office of Campus Ministry
TRINETTE MCCRAY, Office of Camp. Ministry
MARGARET WILHITE, Sociology Dept.
Sisters 10
Lay Teachers 80
Students 5,658
Total Staff 754

Marquette University
P.O. Box 1881
Milwaukee, WI 53201-1881
Tel: 414-288-7250
Web Site: www.marquette.edu
Legal Title: *Marquette University*
Opened in 1881. Conducted under the auspices of the Society of Jesus.
Major University Officers:
Rev. ROBERT A. WILD, S.J., Pres.
Mr. DAVID A. STRAZ, JR., Chm. Bd. of Trustees
Dr. JERRY A. VISCIONE, Exec. Vice Pres.
Rev. DANIEL C. MCDONALD, S.J., Exec. Dir., University Mission and Identity
Dr. DAVID R. BUCKHOLDT, Vice Pres. Academic Affairs
Mr. GREGORY GARBER, Treas., V.P. Finance
Mr. JOHN L. HOPKINS, Vice Pres., Communication
Ms. CYNTHIA M. BAUER, Vice Pres. & Gen. Counsel
Ms. RANA ALTENBURG, Vice Pres., Governmental & Community Relations
Mr. GREGORY J. KLIEBHAN, Vice Pres., Admin.
Rev. ANDREW J. THON, S.J., Vice Pres., Student Affairs
Dr. JAMES P. LYDDY, Vice Pres., University Advancement
Deans:
Dr. MICHAEL A. MCKINNEY, Acting Dean, College of Arts & Science
Dr. DAVID L. SHROCK, Dean, College of Bus. Admin.
Dr. WILLIAM R. ELLIOTT, Dean, College of Communication
Dr. WILLIAM K. LOBB, Dean, School of Dentistry
Dr. JOHN J. AUGENSTEIN, Interim Dean, School of Educ.
Dr. DOUGLAS M. GREEN, Dean, College of Engrg.
Dr. LYNN E. MINER, Interim Dean, Grad. School
Dr. JACK C. BROOKS, Dean, College of Health Sciences
Mr. HOWARD B. EISENBERG, Dean, Law School
Dr. NICHOLAS C. BURCKEL, Dean, Libraries
Dr. MADELINE WAKE, Dean, College of Nursing
Dr. ROBERT J. DEAHL, Dean, College of Professional Studies
Dr. JAMES P. MCMAHON, Asst. Vice Pres. & Dean, Residence Life
Dr. MARK D. MCCARTHY, Asst. Vice Pres.& Dean, Student Devel.
Mr. ROBERT BLUST, Acting Dean, Undergraduate Admissions
Additional Department Heads:
SUSAN MOUNTAIN, Interim Dir., University Ministry
Priests 46
Sisters 8
Lay Staff 2,209
Total Staff 2,263
Students 10,780

Mount Mary College
2900 N. Menomonee River Pkwy.
Milwaukee, WI 53222-4545
Tel: 414-258-4810; Fax: 414-256-1224
Web Site: www.mtmary.edu
Sponsored by the School Sisters of Notre Dame
PATRICIA D. O'DONOGHUE, Pres.
Sisters 33
Lay Teachers 59
Students 1,319
Total Staff 270

HOSPITALS

ALABAMA

Birmingham
Diocese of Birmingham

St. Vincent's Hospital
P.O. Box 12407
Birmingham, AL 35202-2407
Tel: 205-939-7000; Fax: 205-930-2157
E-mail: apurdy@stv.org
Web Site: www.stv.org
810 St. Vincent's Dr.
Birmingham, AL 35205
Sponsored by Daughters of Charity
CURTIS JAMES, Pres. & CEO
Sisters 6
Full-Time Nurses 330
Patients assisted annually 143,898
Beds 338

Seton Health Corporation of North Alabama
P.O. Box 12407
Birmingham, AL 35202-2407
Tel: 205-939-8600
Daughters of Charity
CURTIS JAMES, Pres. & CEO
Full-Time Nurses 71
Patients assisted annually 242,431

Mobile
Archdiocese of Mobile

Providence Foundation
6701 Airport Blvd., B. 227, P.O. Box 850429
Mobile, AL 36608
Tel: 334-639-2050; Fax: 334-639-2052
BETH MCFADDEN ROUSE, Chm. of the Board
GAVIN J. BENDER, Sec.
FRANK J. LOTT, JR., Treas.
Patients assisted annually 215,039
Total Staff 1,919
Nurses 511

Providence Healthcare Services
6801 Airport Blvd., P.O. Box 850429
Mobile, AL 36685
Tel: 334-633-1000; Fax: 334-633-1679
Sr. MARY FRANCES LOFTIN, D.C., Chm.
Mr. CLARK P. CHRISTIANSON, Pres. & CEO
KENNETH J. BLOCH, Sec. & Treas.
Patients assisted annually 215,039
Nurses 511
Total Staff 1,919

Providence Hospital
6801 Airport Blvd., P.O. Box 850429
Mobile, AL 36608
Tel: 334-633-1000; Fax: 334-633-1679
Web Site: www.providencehospital.org
Mr. CLARK P. CHRISTIANSON, Pres. & CEO
Sr. MARY FRANCES LOFTIN, D.C., Chm.
Rev. LEO WEISHAAR, Chap.
Daughters of Charity of St. Vincent de Paul 8
Beds 349
Patients assisted annually 215,039
Nurses 511
Total Staff 1,919

Seton Health Corp. of South Alabama
6801 Airport Blvd., P.O. Box 850429
Mobile, AL 36608
Tel: 334-633-1660; Fax: 334-633-1679
Sr. MARY FRANCES LOFTIN, D.C., Chm. Bd.
Mr. CLARK P. CHRISTIANSON, Pres. & CEO
Sr. MARY LOUISE YEEND, D.C., Sec.
Patients assisted annually 215,039
Nurses 511
Total Staff 1,919

Seton Medical Management, Inc.
6701 Airport Blvd., Suite D-439
Mobile, AL 36608
Tel: 334-639-2660; Fax: 334-639-2664
Sr. MARY FRANCES LOFTIN, D.C., Board Chair
Mr. CLARK P. CHRISTIANSON, Interim Pres. & CEO
Mr. ROBERT B. ANDREWS, Sec. & Treas.
Patients assisted annually 213,206
Nurses 562
Total Staff 2,083

ALASKA

Anchorage
Archdiocese of Anchorage

Providence Alaska Medical Center
3200 Providence Dr., P.O. Box 196604
Anchorage, AK 99519
Tel: 907-562-2211; Fax: 907-261-3041
Mr. GENE O'HARA, Admin.
MONICA ANDERSON, Mission & Spiritual Care
Sr. KAYE BELCHER, S.P., Mission Integration Svcs.
Properties, entities, and divisions owned or operated: Providence Health System—Washington; Providence Alaska Medical Center, Anchorage, AK, Providence Extended Care Center, Anchorage, AK, Providence Health System Housing* dba Providence Horizon House, Anchorage, AK, Mary Conrad Center, Anchorage, AK.
Bed Capacity 391
Patients assisted annually 403,479
Staff 2,672

Ketchikan
Diocese of Juneau

Ketchikan General Hospital
3100 Tongass
Ketchikan, AK 99901
Tel: 907-225-5171; Fax: 907-228-8334
EDWARD F. MAHN, Admin.
Licensed Bed Capacity 92
Patients assisted annually 50,133
Island View Nursing Home

ARIZONA

Nogales
Diocese of Tucson

Holy Cross Hospital, Inc.
Div. of Carondelet Health Care Corporation,
1171 W. Target Range Rd.
Nogales, AZ 85621
Tel: 520-287-2771; Fax: 520-287-8015
WILLIAM FINLAYSON, Pres.
CAROL A. FIELD, C.P.A., Senior Corp. Dir. & Admin.
Sr. CLAUDIA RUSHLOW, S.C., Chap.
Beds 31
Patients assisted annually 43,000
Holy Cross Geriatric Center
1171 W. Target Range
Nogales, AZ 85621
Tel: 520-287-2771; Fax: 520-397-5909
Patients assisted annually 77
Total Acute Patients Days 4,396
Admissions 1,819

Phoenix
Diocese of Phoenix

St. Joseph's Hospital and Medical Center
350 W. Thomas Rd., P.O. Box 2071
Phoenix, AZ 85001
Tel: 602-285-3000
Chaplaincy Services:
Sr. MARGARET MCBRIDE, R.S.M., Dir.
Sr. MICHAELLE HENNESSEY, R.S.M., Dir.
Revs.:
MILTON N. ADAMSON, C.S.C.
CORNELIUS DRAVES-ARPAIA
REX STANCIL
Sr. DOLORES TRINGL, O.L.V.M.
MICHAEL HUNDEMER
BETTY DALY
FRANCES LOZON
SUSAN WINTZ
JUDITH QUATRANI
Sisters of Mercy 7
Beds 477
Patients assisted annually 415,019
Total Staff 5,588

Tucson
Diocese of Tucson

Carondelet Health Network
1601 W. St. Mary's Rd.
Tucson, AZ 85745-2682
Tel: 520-622-5833; Fax: 520-620-5483
E-mail: srsjwillert@carondelet.org
WILLIAM FINLAYSON, Pres.
St. Joseph and St. Mary Hospitals and Health Centers
1601 W. St. Mary's Rd.
Tucson, AZ 85745-2682
Tel: 520-622-5833; Fax: 520-620-5483
GREG ANGLE, C.F.O.
St. Joseph Hospital Div. of Carondelet Health Network.
350 N. Wilmot Rd., P.O. Box 12069
Tucson, AZ 85711-2678
Tel: 520-296-3211; Fax: 520-620-5483
WILLIAM FINLAYSON, Pres.
Revs.:
JAMES A. FREEMAN
ISAAC A. FYNN
Mrs. BETH BEBEE, Dir. Chaplain Svcs.
Sisters of St. Joseph of Carondelet 8
Beds 340
Bassinets 30
Patients assisted annually 124,000
St. Mary's Hospital Div. of Carondelet Health Network.
1601 W. St. Mary's Rd.
Tucson, AZ 85745-2682
Tel: 520-622-5833; Fax: 520-620-5483
WILLIAM FINLAYSON, Pres.
Revs.:
JOSEPH SABA
JAMES MODEEN
Sisters of St. Joseph 15
Beds 394
Bassinets 29
Patients assisted annually 190,000
Carondelet Foundation
140 N. Tuscon Blvd.
Tucson, AZ 85732-3170
Tel: 520-319-5001
Mr. CHARLES CAJERO, Chm.
Sisters of St. Joseph in Arizona
1601 W. St. Mary's Rd.
Tucson, AZ 85745
Tel: 520-620-4940; Fax: 520-620-5483
Sr. MAUREEN O'CONNOR, C.S.J., Pres.

St. Elizabeth of Hungary Out-Patient Clinic
140 W. Speedway Blvd.
Tucson, AZ 85705
Tel: 520-628-7871; Fax: 520-205-8461
E-mail: stelizccs@aol.com
Sr. BARBARA ANNE STOWASSER, C.S.J., Exec. Dir., Admin.
Patients assisted annually 36,803

ARKANSAS

Fort Smith
Diocese of Little Rock

Northside Community Health Center
3202 North 6th
Fort Smith, AR 72904
Tel: 501-782-1456; Fax: 501-782-1462
Operated and sponsored by St. Edward Mercy Medical Center
Total Staff 4
Total Assisted 3,260

St. Edward Mercy Medical Center
7301 Rogers Ave.
Fort Smith, AR 72917
Tel: 501-484-6000; Fax: 501-452-1770
Web Site: www.StEdwardMercy.com
Mr. MICHAEL MORGAN, Pres. & CEO
Total Staff 1,793
Beds 343
Patients assisted annually 144,467
St. Edward Mercy Foundation
5401 Ellsworth Rd.
Fort Smith, AR 72903
Tel: 501-478-1133

St. Edward Mercy Medical Center, dba Harbor View Mercy Hospital and Counseling Center
10301 Mayo Rd., P.O. Box 17000
Fort Smith, AR 72917-7000
Tel: 501-484-5550
Web Site: www.StEdwardMercy.com
Mr. MICHAEL MORGAN, Pres. & CEO
Total Staff 231
Beds 80
Patients assisted annually 1,070

Hot Springs National Park
Diocese of Little Rock

St. Joseph's Regional Health Center
P.O. Box 29001
Hot Springs National Park, AR 71903-9001
Tel: 501-622-1000; Fax: 501-622-1199
E-mail: tmcvey@htsp.smhs.com
Web Site: www.saintjosephs.com

RANDALL J. FALE, Pres. & CEO
Rev. ALAN ROSENAU, Priest Chap.
Total Staff 1,281
Patients assisted annually 340,385
Bed Capacity 317
Sisters of Mercy of St. Joseph Convent of Hot Springs, Arkansas, Inc.
Tel: 501-321-1554

Jonesboro
Diocese of Little Rock

St. Bernard's Regional Medical Center
224 E. Matthews St.
Jonesboro, AR 72401
Tel: 870-972-4100; Fax: 870-974-5112
E-mail: ldalford@sbrmc.org
Web Site: SBRMC.com
BEN E. OWENS, Pres.
Rev. NICHOLAS FUHRMAN, O.S.B., Chap.
Olivetan Benedictine Sisters 11
Total Staff 1,398
Patients assisted annually 189,896
Beds 375

St. Bernards Behavioral Health Servies, Inc.
2712 E. Johnson Ave.
Jonesboro, AR 72401
Tel: 870-932-2800
JAMES P. STANZELL, Legal Counsel
Beds 68
Staff 112
Patients assisted annually 1,155

Little Rock
Diocese of Little Rock

St. Vincent Doctors Hospital
6101 St. Vincent Cir.
Little Rock, AR 72205
Tel: 501-660-3564
E-mail: Kellyv@exchange.svimc.com

St. Vincent Infirmary Medical Center
No. 2 St. Vincent Circle
Little Rock, AR 72205
Tel: 501-660-3571; Fax: 501-671-4014
E-mail: coleenh@exchange.SVIMC.com
Rev. IGNATIUS GOMES, S.F.X., Chap.
Sisters 3
Total Staff 2,640
Beds 973
Patients assisted annually 219,947
Catholic Health Initiatives

Morrilton
Diocese of Little Rock

St. Anthony's Hospital Association
#4 Hospital Dr.
Morrilton, AR 72110-4510
Tel: 501-977-2300; Fax: 501-354-2830
E-mail: ceosmith@swbell.net
Legal Title: *St. Anthony's Hospital Association*
JOHNSON L. SMITH, Admin.
Sponsored by St. Vincent Health System, a division of Catholic Health Initiatives.
Total Staff 291
Patients assisted annually 26,188
Beds 49

Ozark
Diocese of Little Rock

St. Edward Health Facilities of Franklin County, dba Mercy Hospital / Turner Memorial
801 W. River St.
Ozark, AR 72949
Tel: 501-667-4138; Fax: 501-667-4751; 667-9778 (Admin.)
E-mail: jmaddox@ftsm.smhs.com
Mr. MICHAEL MORGAN, CEO
Mr. JIM MADDOX, Admin.
Total Staff 45
Patients assisted annually 7,527
Beds 39

Paris
Diocese of Little Rock

St. Edward Health Facilities of Logan Co., dba North Logan Mercy Hospital
500 E. Academy
Paris, AR 72855
Tel: 501-963-6101; Fax: 501-963-6155
Mr. MICHAEL MORGAN, CEO
JIM L. MADDOX, Admin., Tel: 501-963-6101, FAX: 501-963-6155
Total Staff 42
Patients assisted annually 11,615
Beds 16

Rogers
Diocese of Little Rock

St. Mary-Rogers Memorial Hospital
72756
Tel: 501-636-0200, Ext. 705; Fax: 501-936-2906
Web Site: www.mercyhealthnwa.smhs.com
Rev. LEO MICHAEL, S.D.B., Chap.
SUSAN BARRETT, CEO
1119 W. Poplar St.
Rogers, AR,
Tel: 501-636-2548
Sisters of St. Dominic 9
Total Staff 800
Beds 165
Patients assisted annually 109,365
St. Mary Hospital Foundation
Tel: 501-636-0200; Fax: 501-936-2906

Sherwood
Diocese of Little Rock

St. Vincent Medical Center / Sherwood
2215 Wildwood Ave.
Sherwood, AR 72120
Tel: 501-660-3564
E-mail: Kellyv@exchange.svimc.com

Waldron
Diocese of Little Rock

St. Edward Health Facilities of Scott County dba Mercy Hospital
Hwy. 71 & 80, Box 2230
Waldron, AR 72958
Tel: 501-637-4135; Fax: 501-637-3523
JIM MADDOX, Admin.
DOROTHY "DEDE" O'BAR, Asst. Admin.
Mr. MICHAEL L. MORGAN, CEO
Total Staff 43
Patients assisted annually 30,000
Beds 20

Wynne
Diocese of Little Rock

St. Bernards Community Hospital Corporation dba Crossridge Community Hospital
310 S. Falls Blvd.
Wynne, AR 72396
Tel: 870-238-3300
Beds 15
Staff 124
Patients assisted annually 16,500

CALIFORNIA

Apple Valley
Diocese of San Bernardino

St. Mary Medical Center
18300 Hwy. 18
Apple Valley, CA 92307.
Tel: 760-946-8195; Fax: 760-242-2994
Rev. PETER GELFER, O.H., Chap.
St. Joseph Health System
Sisters 4
Brothers 1
Beds 186
St. Mary Medical Center Auxiliary
Tel: 760-242-2311; Fax: 760-242-9750
St. Mary Hospital Foundation
Tel: 760-242-2311; Fax: 760-242-9750
Beds 186
Patients assisted annually 74,478

Bakersfield
Diocese of Fresno

Catholic Healthcare West Central California
2215 Truxtun Ave.
Bakersfield, CA 93301
Tel: 661-632-5000; Fax: 661-327-2592
Web Site: www.chw.edu
Mailing Address:
P.O. Box 119
Bakersfield, CA 93302
BERNARD J. HERMAN, Regl. Pres.
Mercy Southwest Hospital
400 Old River Rd.
Bakersfield, CA 93311
Tel: 661-663-6000
Mailing Address:
P.O. Box 119
Bakersfield, CA 93302
Friends of Mercy Foundation
2215 Truxtun Ave.
Bakersfield, CA 93301
Tel: 661-632-5683
Mailing Address:
P.O. Box 119
Bakersfield, CA 93302
STEPHANIE WEBER, Exec. Dir.
Patients assisted annually 200,000
Beds 261
Sisters 2
Staff 1,500

Burbank
Archdiocese of Los Angeles

Providence Health System
(San Fernando Valley Service Area)
501 S. Buena Vista St.
Burbank, CA 91505
Tel: 818-843-5111; Fax: 818-843-0641
Web Site: www.providence.org
Sponsored by the Sisters of Providence and the Sisters of the Little Company of Mary
GEORGIANNE JESSEN, CEO
Sr. COLLEEN SETTLES, O.P.D. Min., Regional Dir., Mission Leadership
Chaplains:
Rev. M. STUART BAER, Dir. Spiritual Care
BETH BOYD, CPE Supvr.
Revs.:
JAMES TOAL
JESS LABONTE
Sr. MARY PRENDERGAST
STEPHEN ELIAS
MARGARET BURDGE
Bed Capacity 455
Sisters 3
Patients assisted annually 315,786
Total Staff 2,307
Providence St. Elizabeth Care Center
10425 Magnolia Blvd.
N. Hollywood, CA 91601
Tel: 818-980-3872; Fax: 818-980-6349
Bed Capacity 52
Patients assisted annually 52
Total Staff 52
Providence Holy Cross Medical Center
15031 Rinaldi St.
Mission Hills, CA 91345
Tel: 818-365-8051; Fax: 818-898-4569
Chaplains:
Bro. JOE MCTAGGART, C.S.C.
JEFF FLEMING
Bed Capacity 257
Patients assisted annually 112,269
Total Staff 1,155

Providence Saint Joseph Medical Center
501 S. Buena Vista
Burbank, CA 91505
Tel: 818-843-5111; Fax: 818-843-0641
Conducted by the Sisters of Providence Health System
Revs.:
M. STUART BAER, Dir.
JAMES TOAL
JESS LABONTE
DAN HUDSON, (Protestant)
Sr. MARY PRENDERGAST, S.S.L.
Rev. BRENDA MITCHELL
BETH BOYD, Chap.
Bed Capacity 455
Patients assisted annually 190,000
Total Staff 2,306

Carmichael
Diocese of Sacramento

Mercy American River / Mercy San Juan Hospital / Mercy American River Campus
6501 Coyle Ave.
Carmichael, CA 95608
Tel: 916-537-5000; Fax: 916-537-5111
E-mail: mhs@mercysacramento.org
Web Site: www.mercysacramento.org
Affiliated with Mercy Healthcare Sacramento.
MICHAEL UBOLDI, Vice Pres. & COO
NORM HARRIS, Dir. Ancillary & Support Svcs.
KATHY RICHERSON, Dir. Inpatient Svcs.
Sr. CLARE DALTON, R.S.M., Mission Svcs. & Chaplaincy
Sisters of Mercy 5
Beds 284
Nurses 350
Inpatients 78,674

Daly City
Archdiocese of San Francisco

Seton Medical Center
1900 Sullivan Ave.
Daly City, CA 94015-2229
Tel: 650-992-4000; Fax: 650-991-6024
E-mail: MBaez@chw.edu
Daughters of Charity of St. Vincent de Paul
BERNADETTE M. SMITH, COO
JOAN EVANS, Dir. Spiritual Care
Daughters of Charity 10
Patients assisted annually 316,651
Member of Catholic Healthcare West
Seton Health Services Foundation
San Francisco Heart Institute

Duarte
Archdiocese of Los Angeles

Santa Teresita Hospital
819 Buena Vista St.
Duarte, CA 91010
Tel: 626-359-3243; Fax: 626-357-7166
E-mail: sth@santa-teresita.org
Web Site: www.santa-teresita.org
MICHAEL COSTELLO, CEO
Mother REGINA MARIE, O.C.D., Pres. Bd. Directors
Chaplains:
Revs.:
CORNELIUS M. BUCKLEY, S.J.
ROBERT LEONARD, S.J.
Bed Capacity 253
Sisters 44
Total Staff 400
Patients assisted annually 47,000

Eureka
Diocese of Santa Rosa in California

St. Joseph Hospital of Eureka
2700 Dolbeer St.
Eureka, CA 95501
Tel: 707-445-8121; Fax: 707-269-3897
Web Site: www.sjhshumboldtcounty.org
Sisters of St. Joseph of Orange
MIKE PURVIS, Pres. & CEO
KEN MEECE, Area Dir. of Pastoral Care
Bed capacity 140
Sisters 3
Employees 850
Patients assisted annually 171,630

Folsom
Diocese of Sacramento

Mercy Hospital of Folsom
1650 Creekside Dr.
Folsom, CA 95630
Tel: 916-983-7400; Fax: 916-983-7406
E-mail: mhs@mercysacramento.org
Web Site: www.mercysacramento.org
DON HUDSON, Vice Pres. & COO
Sisters of Mercy 2
Beds 95
Nurses 150
Patients assisted annually 35,140
Attended by St. John the Baptist, Folsom.
Corporate Name: Mercy Hospital of Folsom

Fortuna
Diocese of Santa Rosa in California

Redwood Memorial Hospital
3300 Renner Dr.
Fortuna, CA 95540
Tel: 707-725-3361; Fax: 707-725-7212
Sisters of St. Joseph of Orange
MIKE PURVIS, Pres. & CEO
Sisters 2
Staff 184
Bed capacity 46
Patients assisted annually 8,539
Redwood Memorial Foundation
DENNIS LEONARDI, Pres.

Fresno
Diocese of Fresno

Saint Agnes' Medical Center
1303 E. Herndon
Fresno, CA 93720
Tel: 559-449-3000; Fax: 559-449-5699
Sisters of the Holy Cross
Sr. RUTH MARIE NICKERSON, C.S.C., Pres. & CEO
Mr. JOHN C. HARRIS, Chm., Bd. of Trustees
Sisters 9
Nurses 645
Bed Capacity 326
Patients assisted annually 455,635

Professional Office Corporation
Saint Agnes Medical Center, 1303 E. Herndon Ave.
Fresno, CA 93720
Tel: 559-449-3000; Fax: 559-449-2143
Sr. RUTH MARIE NICKERSON, C.S.C., CEO
THOMAS MAC MICHAEL, Chm. Bd. of Trustees

Fullerton
Diocese of Orange in California

St. Jude Medical Center
101 E. Valencia Mesa Dr.
Fullerton, CA 92835-3875
Tel: 714-871-3280; Fax: 714-446-5067
Web Site: www.stjudemc.com
LOURENE MONEY, R.N., Vice Pres. Clinical Svcs.
Chaplains:
Revs.:
JOSEPH MILLER, S.V.D.
WILLIAM PATRICK
RAYMUNDUS BHIA WEA, S.V.D.
MARY JANE STEED, B.C.C.
Revs.:
JEAN WATKINS
JIM ERIXSON
Beds 331
Nurses 627
Total Staff 2,049
Total Assisted Inpatient & Outpatient 139,409

Gilroy
Diocese of San Jose in California

St. Louise Regional Hospital
Admin. Office, 9400 N. Name Uno
Gilroy, CA 95020
Tel: 408-848-2000; Fax: 408-842-2155
E-mail: tfox@chw.edu
Web Site: www.chw.edu
Member of Catholic Healthcare West
Sr. PAULA BAKER, P.B.V.M., Contact Person
THEODORE P. FOX, Regional V.P./COO
Sisters 1
Staff 400
Beds 93
Patients assisted annually 47,309

Hawthorne
Archdiocese of Los Angeles

**Hawthorne Community Hospital, Inc. dba Robert F. Kennedy Medical Center*
Part of Catholic Healthcare West
4500 W. 116th St.
Hawthorne, CA 90250

Robert F. Kennedy Medical Center
4500 W. 166th St.
Hawthorne, CA 90250
Tel: 310-973-1711
PETER APRATO, Pres.
Bro. RICHARD HIRBE, B.F.C.C., Dir., Spiritual Healthcare Services
Catholic Healthcare West Southern California Region
Patients assisted annually 46,956
Bed Capacity 274
Total Staff 575

Hayward
Diocese of Oakland

St. Rose Hospital 1962
27200 Calaroga Ave.
Hayward, CA 94545-4383
Tel: 510-264-4000; Fax: 510-887-7421
E-mail: smurray@strosehospital.org
Web Site: www.strosehospital.org
Affiliated with Via Christi Health System, Inc.
Sisters of St. Joseph of Wichita, Kansas
Jointly sponsored by the Sisters of the Sorrowful Mother and the Sisters of St. Joseph of Wichita, Kansas.
Mr. MICHAEL MAHONEY, Pres. & CEO
Sr. MARY ALICE GIRRENS, C.S.J., Dir. of Mission Services
Chaplains:
Revs.:
ROY V. ECO
BRUCE J. KLIKUNAS, O.S.M.
Sr. DONALDA WINFREY, C.S.J.
RUTHANNE VIHINEN
SALLY HUSSEY
JOAN M. SILVA
Religious 5
Beds 175
Total Staff 733
Patients assisted annually 100,150
St. Rose Medical Office Bldg., Inc.
27200 Calaroga
Hayward, CA 94545
Tel: 510-264-4000; Fax: 510-887-7421
St. Rose Hospital Foundation
Sr. ANTOINETTE YELEK, C.S.J., Exec. Dir.
27200 Calaroga Ave.
Hayward, CA 94545-4383
Tel: 510-264-4008; Fax: 510-887-7421
Silva Pediatric Clinic
680 W. Tennyson Rd.
Hayward, CA 94544
Tel: 510-782-4470
Dental Clinic
Tel: 510-780-9119; Fax: 510-780-9211

Inglewood
Archdiocese of Los Angeles

Daniel Freeman Memorial Hospital
Division of Daniel Freeman Hospitals
333 N. Prairie Ave.
Inglewood, CA 90301
Tel: 310-674-7050; 678-0361; Fax: 310-419-8273
Web Site: www.danielfreeman.org
Sponsored by Sisters of St. Joseph of Carondelet in California.
JOSEPH W. DUNN, Ph.D., CEO
NANCY J. LEE, R.N., M.S.N., COO
Sr. REGINA CLARE SALAZAR, C.S.J., Corp. Vice Pres. Sponsorship and Mission
DANIEL J. AHEARN, M.D., Vice Pres. & Medical Dir.
WILLARD F. WORTHEN, M.D., Chief of Staff
Rev. FRANCIS X. CHRYSOSTOM (Sri Lanka) Chap.
Sr. LORETTA FLOOD, C.S.J., Dir. of Pastoral Care
Sisters of St. Joseph of Carondelet 11
Sisters from Other Communities 5
Bed Capacity 364
Patients assisted annually 102,115
Total Staff 1,643
Sisters of St. Joseph of Carondelet in California
Sr. KATHLEEN MARY MCCARTHY, C.S.J., Chm.
Freeman Hospitals Foundation
Tel: 310-419-8292; Fax: 310-419-8248
Sr. MARY ESTHER MCCANN, C.S.J., Pres. Emeritus
BRIAN GAUTHIER, Vice Pres.
BERNIE SKLAR, Chm.

Long Beach
Archdiocese of Los Angeles

St. Mary Medical Center
1050 Linden Ave.
Long Beach, CA 90813
Tel: 562-491-9000
TOMI HADFIELD, Pres.
Sr. MARY MCCLUSKEY, C.C.V.I., Dir. of Spiritual Care
Catholic Healthcare West Southern California
Patients assisted annually 126,336
Bed Capacity 576
Total Staff 1,896

St. Mary Medical Center Foundation
P.O. Box 887
Long Beach, CA 90801
Tel: 562-491-9225; Fax: 562-491-9888
Bed Capacity 539
Total Assisted Annually 77,566
Total Staff 1,775

St. Mary Professional Building, Inc.
1045 Atlantic Ave.
Long Beach, CA 90813
JAMES RIEDEL, Sec., Tel: 310-491-9010
TAMMIE MCMANN BRAILSFORD, Pres.

Los Angeles
Archdiocese of Los Angeles

St. Vincent Medical Center
2131 W. 3rd St.
Los Angeles, CA 90057
Tel: 213-484-7111
WILLIAM D. PARENTE, Pres.
Rev. FRANCISCO AYLA
Patients assisted annually 42,993
Bed Capacity 380
Total Staff 1,097
Catholic Healthcare West Southern California Region

Santa Marta Hospital
319 N. Humphreys Ave.
Los Angeles, CA 90022
Tel: 323-266-6500; Fax: 213-260-8641 (Admin.)
Web Site: www.santamarta.org
Mr. HARRY E. WHITNEY, Pres. & CEO
Sr. LOUISE BERNSTEIN, Vice Pres. Mission
Sponsored by Carondelet Health System, which is Sponsored by Sisters of St. Joseph of Carondelet.
Bed Capacity 110
Patients assisted annually 31,000
Total Staff 430

Lynwood
Archdiocese of Los Angeles

St. Francis Medical Center
3630 E. Imperial Hwy.
Lynwood, CA 90262
Tel: 310-603-6000
PETER APRATO, Pres.
Bro. RICHARD HIRBE, B.F.C.C., Dir. Spiritual Healthcare Services
Revs.:
JAMES CLEARY, O.F.M., Assoc. Chap.
BOCTOR BISHARA, Assoc. Chap.
Sponsered by the Daughters of Charity of St. Vincent de Paul. (Member of CHW Southern California Region)
Patients assisted annually 134,668
Bed Capacity 328
Total Staff 1,663
Catholic Healthcare West Southern California Region

Manteca
Diocese of Stockton

St. Dominic's Hospital
(Sub. of St. Joseph's Regional Health System) Member of Catholic Healthcare West
1777 W. Yosemite Ave., P.O. Box 1307
Manteca, CA 95337
Tel: 209-825-3500; Fax: 209-825-3524
Web Site: www.chw.edu/manteca
Acute care community hospital.
EDWARD G. SCHROEDER, Pres. & CEO
Beds 77
Staff 370
Patients assisted 36,014

Marina Del Rey
Archdiocese of Los Angeles

Daniel Freeman Marina Hospital
Division of Daniel Freeman Hospitals, Inc.
4650 Lincoln Blvd.
Marina Del Rey, CA 90292
Tel: 310-823-8911; Fax: 310-574-7854
Web Site: www.danielfreeman.org
Sponsored by Sisters of St. Joseph of Carondelet in California.
Mailing Address:—c/o Daniel Freeman Hospitals
333 N. Prairie Ave.
Inglewood, CA 90301
JOSEPH W. DUNN, Ph.D., CEO, Daniel Freeman Hospitals
NANCY LEE, R.N., M.S.N., COO
Sr. REGINA CLARE SALAZAR, C.S.J., Corp. Vice Pres., Sponsoship & Mission
DANIEL J. AHEARN, M.D., Vice Pres. & Medical Dir.
LAWRENCE J. COHEN, M.D., Chief of Staff
Revs.:
LAWRENCE MURPHY, S.J.
JOSE MEJIA
Sr. JOAN HAGEN, Dir., Pastoral Care
Sr. KATHLEEN MARY MCCARTHY, C.S.J., Chm.
Sisters of St. Joseph of Carondelet 1
Sisters from other Communities 1
Total Staff 463
Bed Capacity 166
Patients assisted annually 41,170

Merced
Diocese of Fresno

Mercy Hospital & Health Services
2740 M St.
Merced, CA 95340
Tel: 209-384-6444; Fax: 209-722-2902
Mr. EDWARD G. SCHROEDER, Pres.
JOHN HEADDING, Chief Admin. Officer
Catholic Healthcare West and San Joaquin-Sierra Region
Sacramental Ministry by Priests of Merced.
Sponsored by the Sisters of St. Catherine of Siena of Kenosha, Wisconsin.
Mercy Home Care
Annually assisted 11,000
Sisters 2
Beds 101
Patients assisted annually 88,000

Mission Viejo
Diocese of Orange in California

Mission Hospital Regional Medical Center
27700 Medical Center Rd.
Mission Viejo, CA 92691
Tel: 949-364-1400; Fax: 949-364-2056
E-mail: srma@0103.stjoe.org
Web Site: www.mhrmc.com
Sponsored by Sisters of St. Joseph of Orange
PETER BASTONE, Pres. & CEO
Staff 1,850
Patients assisted: Inpatient days 66,677
Outpatients 122,123
Bed Capacity 271

Moss Beach
Archdiocese of San Francisco

Seton Medical Center Coastside
600 Marine Blvd.
Moss Beach, CA 94038
Tel: 650-563-7100; Fax: 650-728-5314
E-mail: kinnerst@cww.edu
Daughters of Charity of St. Vincent de Paul, a Catholic Health Care West organization.
BERNADETTE M. SMITH, COO
KATY INNERST, R.N., DON-SNF
Religious 1
Patients assisted annually 10,724
Member of Catholic Healthcare West.

Mt. Shasta
Diocese of Sacramento

Mercy Hospital of Mount Shasta dba Mercy Medical Center Mt. Shasta
914 Pine St., P.O. Box 239
Mt. Shasta, CA 96067
Tel: 530-926-6111; Fax: 530-926-0517
Web Site: ntmhn1.mercy.org
Mr. RICK J. BARNETT, Exec. Vice Pres. & COO
Beds 80
Patients assisted annually 33,000
Staff 336

Napa
Diocese of Santa Rosa in California

Queen of the Valley Hospital of Napa
1000 Trancas St.
Napa, CA 94558
Tel: 707-252-4411; Fax: 707-257-4173
E-mail: PHaley@qvh.stjoe.org
Web Site: www.thequeen.org
Sisters of St. Joseph of Orange, California
DENNIS SISTO, Pres. & CEO
Chaplains:
Revs.:
GERARD HEINTZELMAN (HBG)
JIM WARNOCK, Lutheran Min.
DENISE TITTLE, Baptist Min.
Sr. DARLEEN CHMIELEWSKI
Priests 1
Sisters 5
Lay Staff 1,150
Bed Capacity 166
Patients assisted annually 245,635

Orange
Diocese of Orange in California

St. Joseph Hospital of Orange
1100 W. Stewart Dr., P.O. Box 5600
Orange, CA 92868-3995
Tel: 714-771-8000, Ext. 8020; Fax: 714-744-8600
LARRY AINSWORTH, Pres. & CEO
Rev. ELLY S. TAVARRO
Patients assisted annually 100,500
Beds 472
Other Employees 2,179
Nurses 979

Oxnard
Archdiocese of Los Angeles

St. John's Regional Medical Center
1600 N. Rose Ave.
Oxnard, CA 93030
Tel: 805-988-2500; Fax: 805-981-4440
Web Site: www.stjohnshealth.com
CHARLES PADILLA, COO & Admin.
TINA PICCHI, Dir. Mission Svcs.
ELIZABETH COOK, Clinical Pastoral Education Mgr.
Sisters of Mercy 4
Bed Capacity 264
Patients assisted annually 88,377
Total Staff 1,334
St. John's Pleasant Valley Hospital
2309 Antonio Ave.
Camarillo, CA 93010
Tel: 805-389-5800
BILL CLEARWATER, Vice Pres., Site Admin. S.J.P.V.H.
Sisters 4
Acute Beds 81
Skilled Nursing 99
Patients assisted annually 48,266
Total Staff 549

Pasadena
Archdiocese of Los Angeles

Catholic Healthcare West Southern California
Regional Office, 251 S. Lake Ave., 8th Fl.
Pasadena, CA 91101-4842
Tel: 626-744-2300
Web Site: www.chwsocalregion.org
BETH O'BRIEN, CEO
(Parent Company: Catholic Healthcare West Coporate Office, 1700 Montgomery St, Suite 300, San Francisco, CA 94111-1024. Tel: 415-397-9000)
Sponsored by the Sisters of Mercy of Burlingame; Sisters of Mercy of Auburn; Adrian Dominican Sisters; Daughters of Charity, Province West; Congregation of the Sisters of Charity of the Incarnate Word, Houston, TX; Dominican Sisters of San Raphael; Dominican Sisters of St. Catherine of Siena of Kenosha, WI; Franciscan Sisters of the Sacred Heart of Frankfort, IL; Sisters of St. Francis of Penance and Christian Charity of Redwood City, CA.
Operating Divisions:
Robert F. Kennedy Medical Center
Tel: 310-973-1711; Fax: 310-219-3745
St. Bernadine Medical Center (San Bernadino Diocese)
Tel: 909-883-8711; Fax: 909-881-4546
St. Francis Medical Center
Tel: 310-900-8900; Fax: 310-604-0864
St. Mary Medical Center
Tel: 562-491-9000; Fax: 562-436-6378
St. Vincent Medical Center
Tel: 213-484-7111; Fax: 213-484-9304

Petaluma
Diocese of Santa Rosa in California

Petaluma Valley Hospital
400 N. McDowell Blvd.
Petaluma, CA 94954
Tel: 707-778-1111
Sisters of St. Joseph of Orange

Rancho Cordova
Diocese of Sacramento

Mercy Healthcare Sacramento
10540 White Rock Rd.
Rancho Cordova, CA 95670
Tel: 916-851-2000; Fax: 916-851-2727
E-mail: mhs@mercysacramento.org
Web Site: www.mercysacramento.org
MICHAEL ERNE, Pres.
(Parent Company - Catholic Healthcare West)
Corporate Office
1700 Montgomery St., Ste. 300
San Francisco, CA 94111
Tel: 415-397-9000; Fax: 415-438-5724
LLOYD DEAN, Pres. & CEO
Sponsored by Sisters of Mercy of Burlingame; Sisters of Mercy of Auburn; Adrian Dominican Sisters; Daughters of Charity, Province of the West; Congregation of the Sisters of Charity of the Incarnate Word, Houston, Texas; Dominican Sisters of San Rafael; Dominican Sisters of St. Catherine of Siena of Kenosha, WI; Franciscan Sisters of the Sacred Heart of Frankfort, IL; Sisters of St. Francis of Penance and Christian Charity of Redwood City, CA.
This organization provides regional management and support functions for the following affiliated non-profit organizations: Mercy General Hospital of Sacramento; Mercy San Juan Hospital, Carmichael; Mercy Hospital of Folsom; and the subsidiary corporations of Mercy McMahon Terrace and Mercy Medical Foundation.

Red Bluff
Diocese of Sacramento

Catholic Healthcare West North State dba St. Elizabeth Community Hospital
2550 Sr. Mary Columba Dr.
Red Bluff, CA 96080-4397
Tel: 530-529-8000; Fax: 530-529-8009
Mr. GEORGE A. GOVIER, Regl. Pres. & CEO, Catholic Healthcare West North State
Mr. THOMAS F. GRIMES, Exec. Vice Pres. & COO, St. Elizabeth Community Hospital
Sisters of Mercy 2
Nurses 157
Beds 61
Patients assisted annually 50,000
Total Staff 474
Attended by Sacred Heart, Red Bluff.

Redding
Diocese of Sacramento

Catholic Healthcare West North State dba Mercy Medical Center Redding
Tel: 530-225-6000; Fax: 530-225-6125
Web Site: www.mercy.org
Mailing Address:
P.O. Box 496009
Redding, CA 96049-6009
2175 Rosaline Ave.
Redding, CA 96001
Tel: 530-225-6000; Fax: 530-225-6125
Mr. GEORGE A. GOVIER, Rgnl. Pres. & CEO, Catholic Healthcare West North State
Mr. JOHN DI PERRY, JR., Exec. Vice Pres. & COO, Mercy Medical Center Redding
Rev. MICHAEL BRENNAN, C.P., Chap.
Sisters of Mercy 1
Beds 269
Total Staff 1,375
Patients assisted annually 146,338

Sacramento
Diocese of Sacramento

Mercy General Hospital
4001 J St.
Sacramento, CA 95819
Tel: 916-453-4545; Fax: 916-453-4587
E-mail: mhs@mercysacramento.org
Web Site: www.mercysacramento.org
Mr. THOMAS A. PETERSEN, Vice Pres. & COO
SUE KELMAN, Dir. Cardiovascular Svcs.
Rev. JOHN J. HEALY, Chap.
Sisters of Mercy 14
Sisters of St. Francis 1
Nurses 689
Patients assisted annually 76,874
Beds 395
MercyCare
862 39th St.
Sacramento, CA 95819
Tel: 916-733-6500; Fax: 916-452-6071
Patients assisted annually 95

San Bernardino
Diocese of San Bernardino

St. Bernardine Medical Center
2101 N. Waterman Ave.
San Bernardino, CA 92404
Tel: 909-883-8711; Fax: 909-881-4546
STEVEN BARRON, Pres.
Rev. BARNABAS LAUBACH, O.S.B., Chap. & Dir. Spiritual Care
Sisters 4
Beds 443
Patients assisted annually 81,244

San Francisco
Archdiocese of San Francisco

St. Mary's Medical Center
450 Stanyan St.
San Francisco, CA 94117
Tel: 415-668-1000; Fax: 415-750-5608
ROSEMARY FOX, Vice Pres. & COO
Chaplains:
Bro. GEORGE CHERRIE, O.F.M.Conv., Dir.
Revs.:
MICHAEL GREENWELL, O.Carm.
EDWARD K. MURRAY
Priests 2
Religious 9
Volunteers 20
Patients assisted annually 185,000

San Jose
Diocese of San Jose in California

O'Connor Hospital
2105 Forest Ave.
San Jose, CA 95218
Tel: 408-947-2500; Fax: 408-947-2819
Web Site: www.chwbay.org
Legal Title: *Catholic Healthcare West- Bay Area dba O'Connor Hospital*
Member of Catholic Healthcare West
JOAN A. BERO, Regl. Vice Pres. & COO
Revs.:
ROBERT CARY, Chaplain Svcs.
RORY MURPHY, Capetown, South Africa
BASIL ROYSTON
Mr. DAN OLIVIERI, Chap.
Total Staff 990
Beds 360
Patients assisted annually 148,129

O'Connor Foundation
2105 Forest Ave.
San Jose, CA 95128
Tel: 408-947-2717; Fax: 408-947-2649
RICK SPRAGUE, Dir.

San Pedro
Archdiocese of Los Angeles

San Pedro Peninsula Hospital
(Affiliate of Little Company of Mary Health Services)
1700 W. Seventh St.
San Pedro, CA 90732
Tel: 310-832-3311; Fax: 310-514-5314
E-mail: smbabcock@lcmhs.org
Bed Capacity 587
Patients assisted annually 40,600
Total Staff 1,200

Santa Barbara
Archdiocese of Los Angeles

St. Francis Medical Center of Santa Barbara
601 E. Micheltorena St.
Santa Barbara, CA 93102
Tel: 805-962-7661; Fax: 805-568-5704
E-mail: cbowman@chw.edu
Web Site: www.saintfrancis.org
Franciscan Sisters of the Sacred Heart
Mr. RON BISCARO, Admin.
Rev. Msgr. JOHN A. RAWDEN, Chap.
CAROL DETRANA, Coord. Spiritual Care Svcs.
P.O. Box 40289
Santa Barbara, CA 93102
Sisters 6
Bed Capacity 87
Patients assisted annually 26,117
Total Staff 446

Santa Cruz
Diocese of Monterey in California

Dominican Santa Cruz Hospital
1555 Soquel Dr.
Santa Cruz, CA 95065
Tel: 831-462-7700; Fax: 831-462-7555
Web Site: www.dominicanhospital.org
Sisters of St. Dominic (Adrian, MI)
Sr. JULIE HYER, O.P., Pres. & CEO
Rehabilitation Services
610 Frederick St.
Santa Cruz, CA 95062
Tel: 831-462-7700; Fax: 831-462-7555
Bed Capacity 375
Total Assisted in Hospital 116,693
Total Staff 1,300

Santa Maria
Archdiocese of Los Angeles

Marian Medical Center
1400 E. Church St.
Santa Maria, CA 93454
Tel: 805-739-3000
Sponsored by Sisters of St. Francis of Penance and Christian Charity
DANIEL HERLINGER, CEO
CHARLES J. COVA, Exec. Vice Pres.
Deacon ZENON L. NAWROCIK, Dir. Pastoral Care
Sisters 9
Bed Capacity 130
Patients assisted annually 57,977
Total Staff 1,030
Marian Medical Center Extended Care Facility
Skilled Nursing Facility.
Beds 95
Marian Medical Center Day Care Facility for Children
Capacity 52
Marian Residence Retirement Home
124 S. College Dr.
Santa Maria, CA 93454
Tel: 805-922-7731
Marian Medical Center Foundation
1406 E. Main St., Ste. E.
Santa Maria, CA 93454
Tel: 805-349-9486

Santa Monica
Archdiocese of Los Angeles

Saint John's Health Center
1328 22nd St.
Santa Monica, CA 90404
Tel: 310-829-5511; Fax: 310-315-6134
Sisters of Charity of Leavenworth
Sr. MARIE MADELEINE SHONKA, Pres.
Mr. BRUCE LAMOUREUX, C.E.O.
Rev. PATRICK COMERFORD, Chap.
Sisters 8
Bed Capacity 233
Patients assisted annually 200,000
Total Staff 1,440
Saint John's Health Center Foundation
The Michael Burke Foundation
The Hope Guild
The Irene Dunne Guild

Santa Rosa
Diocese of Santa Rosa in California

Santa Rosa Memorial Hospital
1165 Montgomery Dr.
Santa Rosa, CA 95405
Tel: 707-546-3210
Sisters of St. Joseph of Orange Corporation
Mr. DAVID AMEEN, Pres. & CEO
Rev. MARK G. O'LEARY, O.P., Chap.
Rev. Msgr. PATRICK MCCOY (England) Chap.
Priests 2
Sisters 5
Employees 1,297
Bed capacity 233
Patients assisted annually 96,152

Stockton
Diocese of Stockton

Catholic Healthcare West System San Joaquin-Sierra Region
1800 N. California St., P.O. Box 213008
Stockton, CA 95213-9008
Tel: 209-943-2000; Fax: 209-461-5199
Web Site: www.chwanjoaquin.com
Sponsored by the Sisters of Mercy, Auburn and Burlingame Regional Communities; Adrian Dominican Sisters; Daughters of Charity, Province of the West; Sisters of Charity of the Incarnate Word of Houston, Texas; Dominican Sisters of San Rafael; Dominican Sisters of St. Catherine of Siena of Kenosha, Wisconsin; Franciscan Sisters of the Sacred Heart, Frankfort, Illinois; Sisters of St. Francis of Redwood City, California
Mr. EDWARD G. SCHROEDER, Pres. & CEO
This organization provides regional management and support functions for the following affiliated non-profit organizations: St. Joseph's Medical Center of Stockton; St. Dominic's Hospital of Manteca; Mark Twain St. Joseph's Hospital of San Andreas; St. Joseph's Behavioral Health Center of Stockton and Mercy Hospital and Health Services of Merced.
Active Medical Staff 434
Licensed Acute Beds 479
Full-Time Employees 2,589
Total Annually Assisted 325,323

St. Joseph's Behavioral Health Center
(Sub. of St. Joseph's Regional Health System)
2510 N. California St.
Stockton, CA 95204
Tel: 209-948-2100; Fax: 209-464-2270
Web Site: www.stjosephscanhelp.org
Psychiatric and chemical dependency care hospital.
EDWARD G. SCHROEDER, Pres. & CEO
Beds 35
Staff 100
Patients assisted 2,447

St. Joseph's Medical Center of Stockton
(Sub. of St. Joseph's Regional Health System) Member of Catholic Healthcare West
1800 N. California St., P.O. Box 213008
Stockton, CA 95213-9008
Tel: 209-943-2000; Fax: 209-461-3299
Web Site: www.stjosephscares.org
Acute care community hospital.
EDWARD G. SCHROEDER, Pres. & CEO
Beds 294
Staff 2,233
Patients assisted 286,500

Torrance
Archdiocese of Los Angeles

Little Company of Mary Hospital
4101 W. Torrance Blvd.
Torrance, CA 90503
Tel: 310-540-7676; Fax: 310-540-7659
Conducted By: Sisters of Little Company of Mary.
Sr. CAROL PACINI, L.C.M., Chm.
MARK COSTA, Pres.
Sr. DOLORES MIKULA, S.S.J.-T.O.S.F., Mgr. Pastoral Care
Chaplains:
Revs.:
THOMAS HAMILTON, O.F.M.Conv.
CHRIS ONYENOBI
Deacon RICHARD PRUITT
Rev. JASON CUSICK, (Protestant)

Bed Capacity 291
Bassinets 35
Pavilion - Little Company of Mary Hospital skilled nursing facility.
4320 Maricopa St.
Torrance, CA 90503
Tel: 310-543-5900; Fax: 310-793-0928
Conducted By: Sisters of Little Company of Mary
DOROTHY GIRLEY-BRADSHAW, Admin. Dir.
Sr. DOLORES MIKULA, S.S.J.-T.O.S.F., Mgr. Pastoral Care
Rev. DOUGLAS JUDSON, Chap. (Episcopal)
Bed Capacity 121
San Pedro Peninsula Hospital
1300 W. 7th St.
San Pedro, CA 90732
Tel: 310-832-3311; Fax: 310-514-5314
Conducted By: Sisters of Little Company of Mary
JOHN M. WILSON, Pres.
Sr. DOLORES MIKULA, S.S.J.-T.O.S.F., Mgr. Pastoral Care
Chaplains:
Revs.:
FRANCIS L. SHIGO, S.V.D.
FRANK GORDILLO, (Protestant)
Bed Capacity 210
Total Staff 889
American Province of Little Company of Mary Sisters
San Pedro Peninsula Hospital Foundation
San Pedro Peninsula Pavilion
Peninsula Diagnostic Center
Peninsula Recovery Center
Pavilion - San Pedro Peninsula Hospital skilled nursing facility.
1322 W. Sixth St.
San Pedro, CA 90732
Tel: 310-514-5270; Fax: 310-514-5332
JULIE THEIRING, Administrative Dir.
Sr. DOLORES MIKULA, S.S.J.-T.O.S.F., Mgr. Pastoral Care
Chaplains:
Revs.:
FRANCIS L. SHIGO, S.V.D.
FRANK GORDILLO, (Protestant)
Bed Capacity 128
Bay Harbor Hospital West skilled nursing facility.
3620 W. Lomita Blvd.
Torrance, CA 90505
Tel: 310-378-8587; Fax: 310-791-4514
Conducted By: Sisters of Little Company of Mary.
LA VERNA MCMILLER, Admin. Dir.
Sr. DOLORES MIKULA, S.S.J.-T.O.S.F., Mgr. Pastoral Care
MARGARET O'LEARY
Bed Capacity 212
Total Staff 3,700

Victorville
Diocese of San Bernardino

St. John of God Health Care Services
P.O. Box 2457
Victorville, CA 92392
Tel: 760-241-4917; Fax: 760-241-8911
Bro. RICHARD GAULE, O.H., CEO
Brothers 3
Licensed Beds 66
Total Assisted Annually 27,740

West Covina
Archdiocese of Los Angeles

Citrus Valley Health Partners, Queen of the Valley Campus
1115 S. Sunset Ave., P.O. Box 1980
West Covina, CA 91790
Tel: 818-962-4011; Fax: 818-814-2482
E-mail: vip.pm@cvhp.org
Web Site: cvhp.com
Rev. ERIC A. LEWIS
Mr. PETER MAKOWSKI, CEO
Bed Capacity 269
Patients assisted annually 169,001
Staff 1,269

COLORADO

Canon City
Diocese of Pueblo

Centura Health-St. Thomas More Hospital
An operating unit of Catholic Health Initiatives Mountain Region (an affiliate of Catholic Health Initiatives).
1338 Phay Ave.
Canon City, CO 81212
Tel: 719-269-2000; Fax: 719-269-2016
C. RAY HONAKER, CEO
Chaplains:
Rev. BERNARD GERVAIS, O.S.B.
Sr. LADONNA PINKELMAN, O.S.F.
Beds 245
Patients assisted annually 72,252

Colorado Springs
Diocese of Colorado Springs

Penrose-St. Francis Health Services
2215 N. Cascade Ave., P.O. Box 7021
Colorado Springs, CO 80907
Tel: 719-776-5000; Fax: 719-776-2770
E-mail: LucilleKrippel@centura.org
Web Site: www.centura.org
Sr. LUCILLE KRIPPEL, O.S.F., Dir., Mission & Ministry
Penrose Hospital Sponsored by Catholic Health Initiatives.
2215 N. Cascade Ave.
Colorado Springs, CO 80907
Tel: 719-776-5000; Fax: 719-776-2770
Revs.:
GERALD H. BRUGGEMAN, Sacramental Min.
ALAN FILIPPI, Protestant Chap.
TOM STELLA
JAMES H. GUNN, Protestant Chap.
Chaplains:
MICHAEL CRINO
Sr. JANE GROSHEIDER, S.C.
Sr. LUCILLE KRIPPEL, O.S.F., Dir. Spiritual Care
Sr. IMMACULATA PARK, O.S.F.
JOHN ZAY
Sisters 3
Penrose Community Hospital Sponsored by Catholic Health Initiatives.
3205 N. Academy Blvd.
Colorado Springs, CO 80917
Tel: 719-776-5000; Fax: 719-591-3477
Sr. JOAN CROCKER, S.C.
Beds 522
Patients assisted annually 265,232
Staff 2600

Penrose-St. Francis Healthcare Foundation
A division of Catholic Health Initiatives Mountain Region Foundation.
961 E. Colorado at Centerpoint
Colorado Springs, CO 80903
Tel: 719-634-2046; Fax: 719-630-0832
Web Site: www.JerryBogg@Centura.com
St. Francis Health Center Sponsored by Catholic Health Initiatives.
825 E. Pikes Peak Ave.
Colorado Springs, CO 80903
Tel: 719-776-5000; Fax: 719-776-8767
Chaplains:
GENGER MORGAN
MARY JO BAY
SARAH PARINO
Staff 12

Denver
Archdiocese of Denver

**Centura Health*
1601 Lowell Blvd.
Denver, CO 80204
Tel: 303-825-2190; Fax: 303-899-5160
Gardens at St. Elizabeth
2835 W. 32nd Ave.
Denver, CO 80211
Tel: 303-477-4442; Fax: 303-964-2340
An operating unit of Sisters of Charity Health Services Colorado.
Centura Senior Life Center
1601 Lowell Blvd.
Denver, CO 80204
Tel: 303-825-2190; Fax: 303-899-5059
An operating unit of Sisters of Charity Health Services Colorado.
Centura Adult Day Care
4165 Eaton St.
Denver, CO 80033
Tel: 303-422-9000
An operating unit of Catholic Health Initiatives Mountain Region.
KRIS ORDELHEIDE, Sr. Vice Pres. General Counsel

Centura Health St. Anthony Central Hospital
4231 W. 16th Ave.
Denver, CO 80204
An operating unit of Catholic Health Initiatives Mountain Region.

Centura Health St. Anthony Hospital North
2551 W. 84th Ave.
Denver, CO 80030
An operating unit of Catholic Health Initiatives Mountain Region.

Centura Senior LIfe Center
1601 Lowell Blvd.
Denver, CO 80204
An operating unit of Catholic Health Initiatives Mountain Region.
KRIS ORDELHEIDE, Sr. Vice Pres. General Counsel

Provenant Acute Long Stay Hospital
1601 Lowell Blvd.
Denver, CO 80204
Affiliate of Catholic Health Initiatives Mountain Region.

Provenant Home Health and Eldercare Services
1560 Meade St.
Denver, CO 80204
Affiliate of Catholic Health Initiatives Mountain Region.

St. Joseph Hospital
1835 Franklin St.
Denver, CO 80218
Tel: 303-837-7111
JEFFREY SELBERG, Pres. & CEO
Sr. CHARLOTTE WHITE, S.C.L., Vice Pres. Mission
Chaplains:
Revs.:
FRANK GOLD
PATRICK TIERNEY
Sisters of Charity of Leavenworth 13
Bed Capacity 602
Patients assisted annually 116,503
Outpatients assisted annually 113,008

The Villas at Sunny Acres
An operating unit of Catholic Health Initiatives Mountain Region.
2501 E. 104th Ave.
Denver, CO 80233
Tel: 303-452-4181; Fax: 303-457-9885
E-mail: steverigsby@centura.org

Durango
Diocese of Pueblo

Centura Health-Mercy Medical Center
An affiliate of Catholic Health Initiatives.
375 E. Park Ave.
Durango, CO 81301
Tel: 970-247-4311; Fax: 970-382-1082
E-mail: kirkdignum@mercydurango.org
Web Site: www.mercydurango.org
Mr. KIRK DIGNUM, Pres. & CEO
Chaplains:
Rev. MICHAEL L. MCCLEARY
Sr. SHARON EKLER, Vice Pres., Mission & Ministry
Beds 111
Patients assisted annually 239,925
Total Staff 844

Grand Junction
Diocese of Pueblo

Marillac Clinic, Inc.
2333 N. 6th St.
Grand Junction, CO 81501
Tel: 970-243-7803; Fax: 970-255-1711
E-mail: jcameron@stmarygj.com
Ms. JANET K. CAMERON, Exec. Dir.
Legal Title: *Sisters of Charity of Leavenworth, Health Services Corp.*
Total Staff 40
Total Assisted 15,006

St. Mary Hospital and Medical Center
P.O. Box 1628
Grand Junction, CO 81502
Tel: 970-244-2273; Fax: 970-244-7510
Mr. ROBERT W. LADENBURGER, Pres. & CEO
Rev. ALOYSIUS J. BERTRAND, Chap.
Ms. M.J. MALLON, Exec. Asst.
Sisters of Charity of Leavenworth, Kansas 10
Beds 346
Patients assisted annually 350,440
Total Staff 1,637

Pueblo
Diocese of Pueblo

Centura Health-St. Mary-Corwin Medical Center
An operating unit of Catholic Health Initiatives Mountain Region (an affiliate of Catholic Health Initiatives).
1008 Minnequa Ave.
Pueblo, CO 81004
Tel: 719-560-4000; Fax: 719-560-4646
E-mail: chaplainsmc@centura.org
Web Site: www.stmarycorwin.org
Mr. THOMAS E. ANDERSON, CEO

Chaplains:
Revs.:
Joseph Williams, C.M.
Ervin J. Schmitt
Mrs. Irene Behling, Dir. Spiritual Care
Sr. Darleen Mahoney, O.S.F.
Beds 235
Patients assisted annually 236,676

CONNECTICUT

Bridgeport
Diocese of Bridgeport

St. Joseph Medical Center Foundation, Inc.
Diocese of Bridgeport, 238 Jewett Ave.
Bridgeport, CT 06606-2852

St. Vincent's Development Corporation
2800 Main St.
Bridgeport, CT 06606
Tel: 203-576-5459; Fax: 203-576-5345
Web Site: www.stvincents.org
Mr. William Riordan, Chm.
Mr. Richard D'Aquila, Pres. & CEO

St. Vincent's Health Services Corporation
2800 Main St.
Bridgeport, CT 06606
Tel: 203-576-5455; Fax: 203-576-5345
Web Site: www.stvincents.org
Sr. Margaret John Kelly, D.C., Chm.
Mr. William J. Riordan, Pres. & CEO

St. Vincent's Medical Center
2800 Main St.
Bridgeport, CT 06606
Tel: 203-576-6000; Fax: 203-576-5345
Web Site: www.stvincents.org
Daughters of Charity of St. Vincent de Paul (Albany, NY)
Sr. Margaret John Kelly, D.C., Chm.
Mr. William J. Riordan, Pres. & CEO
Revs.:
J. Dennis McCann, Ph.D.
Natalie Shiras
Daniel Kennelly
Thomas Elliott, C.S.C.
St. Vincent's College
Tel: 203-576-5578; Fax: 203-576-5893
Students 201
Saint Vincent's Special Needs Center, Inc.
95 Merritt Blvd.
Trumbull, CT 06611
Tel: 203-375-6400; Fax: 203-380-1190

St. Vincent's Medical Center Foundation
2800 Main St.
Bridgeport, CT 06606
Tel: 203-576-5451; Fax: 203-576-5880
Mr. William Carroll, Chm.
Mr. Ronald J. Bianchi, Pres.

Hartford
Archdiocese of Hartford

Saint Francis Hospital and Medical Center
114 Woodland St.
Hartford, CT 06105-1299
Tel: 860-714-4000; Fax: 860-714-7809
E-mail: pastoralcare@stfranciscare.org
Web Site: www.stfranciscare.org
Dr. David D'Eramo, Pres. & CEO
Chaplains:
Revs.:
Liam C. Casey, Dir. Pastoral Care
Mark Bonsignore
Thomas Puthiyadom
Licensed Beds 617
Bassinets 65
Out-Patient Visits 299,456
In-Patient Visits 28,880
Staff 3,850
The Women's Auxiliary of Saint Francis Hospital and Medical Center
Tel: 860-714-4558; Fax: 860-714-7809
Mrs. Carol Proom, Pres.
Asylum Hill Family Medicine Center, Inc.
Tel: 860-714-4212; Fax: 860-714-8079
Woodland Physician Associates, Inc.
Camillus Corporation
The One Thousand Corporation
Tel: 860-714-4793
One Thousand One Corporation
Saint Francis Hospital and Medical Center Foundation, Inc.
114 Woodland St.
Hartford, CT 06105-1299
Tel: 860-714-4901; Fax: 860-714-8069
Peter G. Kelly, Esq., Pres.
Richard Popilowski, Senior Vice Pres. Philanthropy
The Rehabilitation Hospital of Connecticut, Inc.
480 Blue Hills Ave.
Hartford, CT 06112
Tel: 860-714-4000; Fax: 860-714-8550

New Haven
Archdiocese of Hartford

Hospital of St. Raphael
1450 Chapel St.
New Haven, CT 06511
Tel: 203-789-3000; Fax: 203-789-3107
E-mail: mcanavan@srhs.org
Web Site: www.srhs.org
Sisters of Charity (Convent Station)
David W. Benfer, Pres.
Sr. Mary Canavan, S.C., Admin. & Contact
Chaplains:
Sr. Colette Hanlon, S.C., Dir. Pastoral Care
Sr. Marjorie Crean, S.C.
Revs.:
Chacko K. Kumplam
Gregory M. Altermatt
Augustine Mangalath
Jacob Atuahene-Nsowaah, United Methodist
William West, UCC
Sandy Augustine Belcher, Episcopal Priest
Rabbi Steve Steinberg
Chaplains 9
Sisters 12
Bed Capacity 511
Bassinets 22
Patients assisted annually 300,000
Staff 3,500
CPE Residents 16
Legal Holdings: Saint Raphael Healthcare System; Saint Raphael Foundation, Inc.; DePaul Health Services Corporation; Saint Regis Health Center, Inc. (Non-profit charitable corporations affiliated with the Hospital of Saint Raphael).

Saint Regis Health Center, Inc.
1354 Chapel St.
New Haven, CT 06511
Tel: 203-867-8300; Fax: 203-867-8370
E-mail: rhellrige@grhs.org
Robert Hellrigel, Exec. Dir. & Contact
125-bed skilled nursing facility.
Annually assisted 45,000
Staff 165

Waterbury
Archdiocese of Hartford

St. Mary Hospital
56 Franklin St.
Waterbury, CT 06706
Tel: 203-574-6000; Fax: 203-597-3238
Web Site: stmh.org
Sisters of St. Joseph of Chambery
Sr. Marguerite Waite, C.S.J., Pres.
Revs.:
Edmund Aku
Stanley R. Staron
Sisters 14
Bed Capacity 194
Licensed 347
Bassinets 24
Neonatal ICU 9
Patients assisted annually 198,266
Staff 1,718
The Slocum Corporation-St. Mary's Hospital Foundation, Inc., Non-profit corporations for the exclusive benefit of St. Mary Hospital.

West Hartford
Archdiocese of Hartford

McAuley Center, Inc.
275 Steele Rd.
West Hartford, CT 06117
Tel: 860-920-6300; Fax: 860-232-4077
Stephen Surprenant, Exec. Dir. & Contact
Continuing care retirement community; Sisters of Mercy. 229 residential apartment units for individuals age 62 and over. Nursing care at St. Mary's Home included.

DELAWARE

Wilmington
Diocese of Wilmington

St. Francis Hospital, Inc.
7th and Clayton Sts., P.O. Box 2500
Wilmington, DE 19805-0500
Tel: 302-575-8301; Fax: 302-575-8320
E-mail: juliekeegan@chi-east.org
Web Site: www.stfrancishealthcare.org
M. Eileen Schmitt, M.D., Pres./Chief Exec. Officer
Sr. Julie Keegan, O.S.F., V.P. Mission & Ministry
Revs.:
John Finn, O.S.F.S.
Joseph J. McKenna, O.S.F.S.
Chaplains:
Sr. Seton Connolly, S.S.C.M.
Jane Connolly
Sr. Margaret Culbert, S.S.J.
Beds 395
Staff 1,122
Patients assisted annually 217,707

DISTRICT OF COLUMBIA

Washington
Archdiocese of Washington

Center for Life of Providence Hospital
1150 Varnum St., N.E.
Washington, DC 20017
Non-Profit Corporation to Render Service, Support and Assistance in the Provision of Community Services Which Foster Human Dignity, Family Unity and Respect for Life. Services Include: Reduced Fee Maternity Programs.
Total Assisted 109,400
Total Staff 1,571

De Paul Foundation, Inc.
1150 Varnum St., N.E.
Washington, DC 20017
De Paul Foundation, Inc. was Organized to Provide Fund Development, Financial and Other Assistance to Provide Hospital and Other Subsidiaries of De Paul Foundation for the Health Care, Medical, Educational and Human Needs of the District of Columbia and Vicinity, by Functioning as a Charitable Nonprofit, Nonstock Corporation.
Providence Health Foundation
1150 Varnum St., N.E.
Washington, DC 20017
Providence Health Foundation, Inc. (PHF), a District of Columbia Charitable Nonprofit Corporation, was Organized to Support the Mission of Providence Hospital by Conducting Fundraising and Development Activities, by Receiving and Managing Donations, by Making Grants, and by Promoting Educational Activities and Scientific Research.

Georgetown University Hospital
3800 Reservoir Rd., N.W.
Washington, DC 20007
Tel: 202-784-3000; Fax: 202-784-3095
E-mail: sheamj@gunet.georgetown.edu
Web Site: www.georgetown.edu
Joy Drass, M.D., Pres.
Rev. James M. Shea, S.J., Dir. Pastoral Care
Chaplains:
Sr. Patricia Parachini, S.N.J.M.
Revs.:
Joy Alappat
Gustaaf M. Keppens, S.J.
Bed Capacity 535
Total Staff 3,773
Patients assisted annually 164,300

Providence Health Services, Inc.
1150 Varnum St., N.E.
Washington, DC 20017
Ambulatory-Outpatient Care, Promote Wellness and Carry Out of Educational Activities and Scientific Research.

Providence Hospital
1150 Varnum St., N.E.
Washington, DC 20017
Tel: 202-269-7000; Fax: 202-269-7160
E-mail: srcarol@provhosp.org
Web Site: www.provhosp.org
Daughters of Charity of St. Vincent de Paul
Sr. Carol Keehan, D.C., Pres.
Sr. Regina Loughlin, D.C., Dir. Pastoral Care
Chaplains:
Revs.:
Phelim Jordan, S.V.D. (Ireland)
Carlo Napoli, T.O.R.
Sisters 17
Bed Capacity 240
Patients assisted annually 106,000
Total Staff 2,317

FLORIDA

Clearwater
Diocese of St. Petersburg

St. Michael's Housing, Inc. dba Casa Miguel
Independent Living.
2285 State Rd. #580
Clearwater, FL 33763
Tel: 727-797-8551
Mrs. JoAnn Lungaro, Admin.
Total Staff 5
Residents 82

The Tepeyac Corporation dba La Clinica Guadalupana
1215 Drew St., Ste. 7B
Clearwater, FL 33755
Tel: 727-461-7730; Fax: 727-462-8117
E-mail: laclinica@compuserve.com
Dr. Jay E. Carpenter, M.D., Pres.
Annually Assisted 1,200
Staff 1

Fort Lauderdale
Archdiocese of Miami

Holy Cross Hospital
4725 N. Federal Hwy.
Fort Lauderdale, FL 33308
Tel: 954-771-8000; Fax: 954-351-5947
E-mail: john.johnson@holy-cross.com
Web Site: holy-cross.com
John C. Johnson, Pres. & CEO
Chaplains:
Revs.:
William Muniz
J. William Houran
Robert Monti
John Mullet
Michael Warthen, (Baptist)
Sr. Rita Levaseur, R.S.M.
Sr. Ann Driscoll, R.S.M.
Sr. Ann Hostovich R.S.M.
Sr. Margaret Ritchie, R.S.M.
Alex Garvey
Ms. Barbara Ouellette
Sisters of Mercy 12
Staff 2,400
Bed Capacity 577
Patients assisted annually 526,666 (includes Home Health & Holy Cross Medical Group Visits)
Holy Cross Health Ministries, Inc.
Tel: 954-492-5796; Fax: 954-351-5947
Holy Cross Hospital, Inc.
Tel: 954-492-5796; Fax: 954-351-5947
Holy Cross Long Term Care, Inc.
Tel: 954-492-5796; Fax: 954-351-5947

Jacksonville
Diocese of St. Augustine

St. Vincent's Medical Center, Inc.
Member Baptist/St. Vincent's Health System.
1800 Barrs St., P.O. Box 2982
Jacksonville, FL 32203
Tel: 904-308-7300; Fax: 904-308-7326
E-mail: jlogue@stvincentshealth.com
Daughters of Charity of St. Vincent de Paul
Revs.:
Robert Galchus, O.M.
Edward McQuillan, C.M.
Lester DeMott, C.M., Chap.
Nurses 755
Total Staff 3,450
Beds 528
Bassinets 15
Outpatients 206,224
Inpatients 23,372
St. Vincent's Foundation, Inc.
Tel: 904-308-7306; Fax: 904-308-7573
St. Vincent's Ambulatory Care, Inc.
Tel: 904-308-2110; Fax: 904-396-3646
St. Catherine Laboure Manor, Inc.
Tel: 904-308-4702; Fax: 904-308-2987

Miami
Archdiocese of Miami

Mercy Hospital
3663 S. Miami Ave.
Miami, FL 33133
Tel: 305-854-4400; Fax: 305-285-2114
E-mail: sisterliz@mercymiami.org
Web Site: www.mercymiami.com
Sponsored by the Sisters of St. Joseph of St. Augustine, FL
Sr. Elizabeth Anne Worley, S.S.J., Chm. Board of Trustees, Contact
Sr. Edith Gonzalez, S.S.J., Dir. Mission and Ministry
Mercy Mission Services (Subsidiary of Mercy Hospital)
Tel: 305-285-2121; Fax: 305-285-2114
Chaplains:
Revs.:
Carl T. Morrison
Joseph Fishwick
Fabio Arango
Anthony Acevedo
Sisters 9
Staff 1,582
Bed Capacity 512
Patients assisted annually 249,628

Pensacola
Diocese of Pensacola-Tallahassee

The Mother Seton Guild of Sacred Heart Hospital, Inc.
Pensacola, FL 32504
Mr. Donald Holland, Pres.

Sacred Heart Foundation, Inc.
4475 Bayou Blvd.
Pensacola, FL 32503
P.O. Box 2700
Pensacola, FL 32513-2700
Charles Alcott, III, Pres.

Sacred Heart Hospital of Pensacola
5151 N. Ninth Ave.
Pensacola, FL 32504
Tel: 850-416-7000; Fax: 850-416-6119
E-mail: pmadden@shhpens.org
Web Site: sacred-heart.org
Patrick J. Madden, Pres. & CEO
Annual Admissions 20,269
Total Staff 3,147
Total Assisted 276,936
Beds 431

Port Charlotte
Diocese of Venice

Bon Secours-St. Joseph Hospital
2500 Harbor Blvd.
Port Charlotte, FL 33952
Tel: 941-766-4122; Fax: 941-766-4140
E-mail: art_schute@bshsi.com
Web Site: www.bonsecours.org/florida
Mr. Michael Harrington, CEO
Sisters 3
Beds 212
Total Staff 960
Patients assisted annually 19,243
Bon Secours-St. Joseph Healthcare Group, Inc.
2500 Harbor Blvd.
Port Charlotte, FL 33952
Tel: 941-766-4122; Fax: 941-766-4140
Sr. Mary Catherine Rogers, C.B.S., Senior Vice Pres., Sponsorship
Mr. Michael Harrington, CEO
Chaplains:
Revs.:
Otmar Gallagher, O.F.M.Cap.
Paul A. Ortner, S.S.J., (Retired)
Arthur B. Schute, NACC Cert., Dir.
Karen Riley, Chap. & Coord. Parish Nurse, NACC Cert.

**Bon Secours-St. Joseph Healthcare Group Foundation, Inc.*
Tel: 941-766-4285; Fax: 941-766-4287
Bon Secours-St. Joseph Nursing and Rehabilitation Center
Tel: 941-766-4400; Fax: 941-624-3963
Bon Secours Place (ALF)
Tel: 941-766-8900; Fax: 941-766-8224
Sr. Kathleen Moroney, C.B.S., NACC Cert.
Hospice of Southwest Florida
Tel: 941-627-0848; Fax: 941-627-1875
Bon Secours-St. Joseph Home Health Agency, Inc.
Tel: 941-485-5570, Ext. [;] Fax: 941-423-5100
Bon Secours-North Port HealthPark
Tel: 941-423-5000; Fax: 941-423-4771
Bon Secours Care-A-Van
Tel: 941-766-4191; Fax: 941-627-5002
Bon Secours Clinica de Ayuda (Arcadia)
Tel: 863-491-5100; Fax: 863-766-4486
Bed Capacity 426
Total Annually Assisted 179,883
Total Staff 1,230

St. Petersburg
Diocese of St. Petersburg

Bethlehem Housing, Inc.
c/o Diocese of St. Petersburg, P.O. Box 40200
St. Petersburg, FL 33743-0200
Tel: 727-344-1611; Fax: 727-345-2143

Blessed Trinity Housing, Inc.
c/o Diocese of St. Petersburg
St. Petersburg, FL 33743-0200
Tel: 727-344-1611; Fax: 727-345-2143

**Bon Secours-Maria Manor Nursing Care Center, Inc.*
10300 Fourth St. N.
St. Petersburg, FL 33716
Tel: 727-576-1025; Fax: 727-576-1447
Sisters of Bon Secours
Mr. Michael Ward, Admin.
Sr. Karla Bognar, S.N.D., Dir. Pastoral Care
Rev. Peter Zemanick, O.C.S.O., Chap., Tel: 727-576-6370
Bed Capacity 274
Total Annually Assisted 300
Total Staff 300

Holy Cross Housing dba Casa Santa Cruz
7825 54th Ave. N.
St. Petersburg, FL 33709
Tel: 727-541-2631; Fax: 727-547-6741
E-mail: barb0113@aol.com
Mr. Joseph A. DiVito, Registered Agent
Total Staff 4
Total in Residence 81

St. Anthony's Hospital, Inc.
1200 Seventh Ave. N.
St. Petersburg, FL 33705
Tel: 727-825-1100; Fax: 727-825-1704
E-mail: al.hall@baycare.org
Web Site: www.bsahealth.org
Chaplains:
Revs.:
Terence K. Fleming
Jim Jones, O.F.M.
Franciscan Sisters of Allegany
Licensed Beds 405
Employees 913
Patients assisted annually 73,466
Inpatient Admissions 11,551
Outpatient Visits 47,528
Legal Title: *St. Anthony's Hospital, Inc.*
Legal Title: *St. Anthony's Ancillary Services, Inc.*
Legal Title: *St. Anthony's Professional Buildings and Services, Inc.*
Legal Title: *St. Anthony's Health Care Foundation, Inc.*

Tampa
Diocese of St. Petersburg

Christ the King Housing II, Inc. dba Kings Manor
2946 W. Columbus Dr.
Tampa, FL 33607
Tel: 813-875-0139; Fax: 813-875-6061
E-mail: Betsy0545@aol.com
Betsy Rowen, Admin.
Residents 110
Total Staff 3

Christ the King Housing, Inc. dba Kings Arms
4125 N. Lincoln Ave.
Tampa, FL 33607
Tel: 813-873-0234
Mrs. Yari Lopez, Mgr.
Total Staff 2
Total in Residence 95

Epiphany Housing of Tampa, Inc. dba Epiphany Arms
2508 E. Hanna Ave.
Tampa, FL 33610
Tel: 813-232-2693; Fax: 813-232-2984
E-mail: epiparms@aol.com
Hector Buria, Pres.
Total Staff 9
Residents 76

St. Joseph's Hospital, Inc.
3001 W. Martin Luther King Blvd.
Tampa, FL 33607
Mailing Address:
P.O. Box 4227
Tampa, FL 33677
Tel: 813-870-4000
Chaplains:
Revs.:
Kenneth Gerth, M.C.C.J.
John Beckley, S.M.
Franciscan Sisters of Allegany
Legal Title: *St. Joseph's Hospital, Inc.*
Legal Title: *St. Joseph's Ancillary Services, Inc.*
Legal Title: *St. Joseph's Community Care, Inc.*
Legal Title: *St. Joseph's Enterprises, Inc.*
Legal Title: *St. Joseph's Health Care Center, Inc.*
Legal Title: *St. Joseph's Hospital of Tampa Foundation, Inc.*
Legal Title: *St. Joseph's Speciality Services, Inc.*
Legal Title: *John Knox Village of Tampa Bay, Inc.*

Legal Title: *Franciscan Properties, Inc.*
Legal Title: *San Damiano Enterprises, Inc.*

St. Patrick's Housing Corporation dba Patrician Arms
4516 S. Manhattan Ave.
Tampa, FL 33611
Tel: 813-835-8227
Total Staff 4
Total in Residence 85

Venice
Diocese of Venice

Bon Secours-Venice Healthcare Corp.
540 The Rialto
Venice, FL 34285
Tel: 941-483-7773; Fax: 941-483-7699
E-mail: Michael_Guley@bshsi.com
Web Site: www.bshsi-florida.com
Sr. MARY CATHERINE ROGERS, C.B.S., Pres.
Mr. MICHAEL G. GULEY, F.A.C.H.E., CEO
Sisters 1
Acute Care Beds 342
LTC Beds 120
ALF Beds 104
Total Staff 1,500
Patients assisted annually 254,499

West Palm Beach
Diocese of Palm Beach

St. Mary's Foundation of Palm Beach County, Inc.
901 45th St.
West Palm Beach, FL 33407-2495
Tel: 561-881-2894; Fax: 561-881-2864
Mailing Address:
P.O. Box 24620
West Palm Beach, FL 33416-4620
Chaplains:
Rev. Msgr. RONALD N. BESHARA, Dir. Pastoral Care & Mission Integration
Revs.:
EMMETT MULLIGAN, O.F.M.
RICHARD SCHAEFER
JOHN MULLET (SAG)
Franciscan Sisters of Allegany 9
Beds 460
Patients assisted annually 230,000
Total Discharges 15,500
Affiliated Support Organizations:
St. Mary's Medical Center, Inc.
St. Mary's Hospital Foundation, Inc.
St. Mary's Ancillary Services, Inc.
St. Mary's Imaging Center, Inc.
St. Mary's Care Services, Inc.
St. Mary's Pain Center, Inc.
St. Mary's A.S.C., Inc.
St. Mary's Women's Health Services
Mid-County Medical Center, Inc.

GEORGIA

Athens
Archdiocese of Atlanta

St. Mary's Hospital
1230 Baxter St.
Athens, GA 30606-3791
Tel: 706-354-3033; Fax: 706-354-3197
E-mail: efechtel@stmarysathens.org
Web Site: www.stmarysathens.org
Sisters of Mercy, Regional Community of Baltimore
Mr. EDWARD J. FECHTEL, JR., Pres. & CEO
Sr. M. MARGUERITE, M.S.C., Community Care Coord.
Nursing Sisters 3
Other Sister Personnel 3
Nurses 321
Beds 196
Patients assisted annually 91,723

Atlanta
Archdiocese of Atlanta

Saint Joseph's Hospital of Atlanta, Inc.
5665 Peachtree Dunwoody Rd., N.E.
Atlanta, GA 30342
Tel: 404-851-7001; Fax: 404-851-5770
Web Site: www.st.josephsatlanta.org
Sisters of Mercy of Americas, Baltimore Regional Community.
RONALD P. HOGAN, CEO
Rev. STEVEN L. YANDER, Resident Chap.
Sisters 13
Total Staff 2,762
Bed Capacity 346
In Patients 18,066
Patients assisted annually 153,000

Augusta
Diocese of Savannah

St. Joseph Center For Life, Inc.
2260 Wrightsboro Rd.
Augusta, GA 30904-4726

St. Joseph Hospital, Augusta, GA, Inc.
2260 Wrightsboro Rd.
Augusta, GA 30904-4726
Tel: 706-481-7400; Fax: 706-481-7599
Dr. ANDREW A. LASSER, Pres./CEO
Deacon GREGORY BERNARD, Dir. Pastoral Care
Rev. MIGUEL GRAVE DE PERALTA, Chap.

Columbus
Diocese of Savannah

St. Francis Hospital
2122 Manchester Expwy., P.O. Box 7000
Columbus, GA 31908-7000
Tel: 706-596-4000
MICHAEL E. GARRIGAN, FACHE Pres.
Rev. JOHN B. HARTMAN, D.Min., Dir. Pastoral Svcs.
Beds 376
Patients assisted annually 93,200

Savannah
Diocese of Savannah

St. Joseph's Hospital
11705 Mercy Blvd., P.O. Box 60129
Savannah, GA 31419-1791
Tel: 912-925-4100
Mr. PAUL P. HINCHEY, Pres. & C.E.O., Tel: 912-927-5404

HAWAII

Honolulu
Diocese of Honolulu

St. Francis Healthcare System of Hawaii
P.O. Box 29380
Honolulu, HI 96820
Tel: 808-547-6883; Fax: 808-547-6616
Web Site: www.sfhs.hi.org
Sr. BEATRICE TOM, O.S.F., CEO & Pres.
Total Staff 170
St. Francis Medical Center
2230 Liliha St.
Honolulu, HI 96817
Tel: 808-547-6011; Fax: 808-547-6616
Sr. GRETCHEN GILROY, O.S.F., CEO
Chaplains:
Revs.:
MARIO RAQUEPO
JOSEPH E. SPECHT, S.J.
Sr. CANDIDA OROC, O.S.F.
Bed Capacity 291
Patients assisted annually 318,090
Total Staff 1,129
Women's Addiction Treatment Center
2230 Liliha St.
Honolulu, HI 96817
Tel: 808-547-6490; Fax: 808-547-6714
Patients assisted annually 109
Bed Capacity 14
St. Francis Medical Center - West
91-2141 Fort Weaver Rd.
Ewa Beach, HI 96706
Tel: 808-678-7000; Fax: 808-678-7054
Sr. GRETCHEN GILROY, O.S.F., CEO
Revs.:
GORDON COMBS, O.F.M.Cap., Chap.
THOMAS GRIFFIN-SMOLENSKI, S.J.
Bed Capacity 102
Patients assisted annually 46,142
Total Staff 685
St. Francis Healthcare Foundation of Hawaii
P.O. Box 30100
Honolulu, HI 96820
Tel: 808-547-6877; Fax: 808-547-6872
Mr. EUGENE TIWANAK, Pres.
Total Staff 5
St. Francis Community Health Service
P.O. Box 29380
Honolulu, HI 96820
Tel: 808-547-6175; Fax: 808-547-6891
HIRAM L.K.H. YOUNG, M.D., Pres.
Total Staff 41
The Sister Maureen Keleher Center (Hospice)
24 Puiwa Rd.
Honolulu, HI,
Tel: 808-595-7566; Fax: 808-595-6996
Sr. FRANCINE GRIES, O.S.F., Dir.
Bed Capacity 12
Patients assisted annually 699
Sister Maureen Intergenerational Learning Environment
2715 Pamoa Rd.
Honolulu, HI 96822
Tel: 808-988-5678; Fax: 808-988-1179
The Maurice J. Sullivan Family Hospice Center
91-2127 Fort Weaver Rd.
Ewa Beach, HI 96706
Tel: 808-678-7580; Fax: 808-678-7597
Bed Capacity 24333
Health Services for Senior Citizens
333 N. King St. Rm 103
Honolulu, HI 96817
Tel: 808-536-1837; Fax: 808-526-1254
Patients assisted annually 28,906

IDAHO

Boise
Diocese of Boise

St. Alphonsus Regional Medical Center, Inc.
1055 N. Curtis Rd.
Boise, ID 83706
Tel: 208-378-2121
SANDRA BENNETT BRUCE, Pres. & CEO
Sisters of the Holy Cross 4
Bed Capacity 298
Patients assisted annually 302,000
Legal Title: *St. Alphonsus Regional Medical Center.*
Legal Title: *St. Alphonsus Building Co., Inc.*
Legal Title: *St. Alphonsus Diversified Care.*

Cottonwood
Diocese of Boise

St. Mary's Hospital
(Sub. of Benedictine Health System)
701 N. Lewiston St., P.O. Box 137
Cottonwood, ID 83522
Tel: 208-962-3251; Fax: 208-962-3722
Mrs. CASEY UHLING, Admin.
Rev. MEINRAD SCHALLBERGER, Chap.
IRIS HAWLEY, D.N.S., Dir., Nursing
Sponsored by Sisters of St. Benedict, Duluth, MN
Sisters 1
Bed Capacity 28
Patients assisted annually 28,000

Jerome
Diocese of Boise

St. Benedict's Family Medical Center
709 N. Lincoln
Jerome, ID 83338
Tel: 208-324-4301; Fax: 208-324-3878
LYNNE M. MATTISON, Admin.
Sponsored by Sisters of St. Benedict, Cottonwood, ID
Sisters 1
Bed Capacity 80
Patients Assisted Annually 46,000
Skilled Nursing Facility in connection with Medical Center.

Lewiston
Diocese of Boise

St. Joseph Regional Medical Center
415 6th St., P.O. Box 816
Lewiston, ID 83501
Tel: 208-743-2511
HOWARD A. HAYES, Admin.
Sisters of St. Joseph of Carondelet 1
Bed Capacity 161
Patients assisted annually 105,000
Nursing Education is in affiliation with Lewis-Clark State College and with Walla-Walla Community College, Clarkston Branch.

Nampa
Diocese of Boise

Mercy Medical Center
1512 12th Avenue Rd.
Nampa, ID 83686
Tel: 208-467-1171
JOSEPH A. MESSMER, Pres. & CEO
MARK BEKKEDAHL, Vice Pres. Mission
Rev. JOSEPH NEWCOMER, Chap.
Sr. ALICE MARIE SCHMID, O.P.
JIM HOFF, Dir. Spiritual Care Resources
Sr. MAURA CLARK, R.S.M.
Sisters 2
Bed Capacity 152
Patients assisted annually 133,000

ILLINOIS

Alton
Diocese of Springfield in Illinois

Saint Anthony's Health Center
Saint Anthony's Way, P.O. Box 340
Alton, IL 62002-0340
Tel: 618-465-2571; Fax: 618-465-4569
Web Site: www.sahc.org
Three Campuses: Saint Anthony's Hospital, Saint Clare's Hospital and St. Anthony's Medical Mall.
WILLIAM E. KESSLER, Pres. & CEO
Rev. JOHN WYKES, O.M.V., Chap.
Sisters of St. Francis of the Martyr St. George 17
Bed Capacity 296
Patients assisted annually 141,546
Staff 831

Aurora
Diocese of Rockford

Provena Mercy Center
1325 N. Highland Ave.
Aurora, IL 60506
Tel: 630-859-2222; Fax: 630-859-9014
Legal Title: *Provena Hospitals dba Provena Mercy Center.*
JACK BARTO, Pres.
Sr. HELEN SCHILL, O.S.F., Dir. Pastoral Care
Chaplains:
Rev. JOSEPH M. LESSARD (PHX)
Mrs. D. VAN DYKE
Beds 338
Patients assisted annually 102,818
Total Staff 1,118

Belleville
Diocese of Belleville

St. Elizabeth Hospital
211 S. Third St.
Belleville, IL 62220-1998
Tel: 618-234-2120; Fax: 618-222-4650
Web Site: www.steliz.org
Hospital Sisters of the Third Order of St. Francis
Clinically Affiliated with St. Louis University School of Medicine.
Mr. GERALD M. HARMAN, Exec. Vice Pres.
Sisters 5
Bed Capacity 498
Patients assisted annually 148,000

Bloomington
Diocese of Peoria

OSF St. Joseph Medical Center
2200 E. Washington
Bloomington, IL 61701
Tel: 309-662-3311; Fax: 309-662-7143
Web Site: www.osfstjoseph.org
Mr. KENNETH J. NATZKE, Admin.
Sr. M. GRACE, O.S.F., Supr.
Rev. DONALD SCHLADEN
Sisters of the Third Order of St. Francis 2
Beds 182
Annually Assisted 101,530
Total Staff 960

Blue Island
Archdiocese of Chicago

St. Francis Hospital and Health Center
12935 S. Gregory St.
Blue Island, IL 60406
Tel: 708-597-2000; Fax: 708-389-9489
Web Site: www.stfrancisblueisland.com
Member of SSM Health Care
Mr. JAY KREUZER, Pres.
Chaplains:
Sr. DORIS ASHCRAFT, F.S.M.
Sr. VIRGINIA CONWAY, O.P.
Sr. RITA CORKERY, R.S.M.
H. KAY ERNST, R.N., M.P.C.
Revs.:
JOSEPH VARKEY KATTACKAL
P. T. THOMAS (India)
Bro. PATRICK VARILLA, C.F.C.
Mr. KARL B. WILSON, SR.
JEANETTE ARTHUR, Dir. Mission Services
Sisters 3
Bed Capacity 410
Patients assisted annually 95,617
Total Staff 1,589

Breese
Diocese of Belleville

St. Joseph Hospital
9515 Holy Cross Ln.
Breese, IL 62230
Tel: 618-526-4511; Fax: 618-526-8022
Web Site: www.stjoebreese.com
Hospital Sisters of the Third Order of St. Francis
JACOLYN M. SCHLAUTMAN, Exec. Vice Pres.
Sr. VIRGINIA KLEIN, S.C.S.C., Pastoral Care
Sisters 2
Bed Capacity 85
Patients assisted annually 71,000

Centralia
Diocese of Belleville

**St. Mary's Hospital*
400 N. Pleasant Ave.
Centralia, IL 62801
Tel: 618-532-6731
Mr. JAMES W. MCDOWELL, Pres. & CEO
Sisters 5
Bed Capacity 276
Patients assisted annually 153,263

Chicago
Archdiocese of Chicago

Columbus Hospital
Ascension Health & Missionary Sisters of the Sacred Heart of Jesus.
2520 N. Lakeview Ave.
Chicago, IL 60614
Legal Title: *Catholic Health Partners Services.*
Mr. PETER FAXIO, Board Chm.
Mr. ARNOLD KIMMEL, Interim Pres. & CEO
Ms. MARGARET MCDERMOTT, C.O.O.
Revs.:
THEODORE PLOPLIS, Dir. Pastoral Care Dept.
RICHARD B. BARTZ, Chap.
Sisters 9
Bed Capacity 121
Patients assisted annually 50,404
Chicago Institute for Neuro Surgery & Neuro Research (Affiliate)
420 W. Deming Pl.
Chicago, IL 60614
Tel: 773-883-8585
LEONARD CERULLO, M.D., Dir.

Holy Cross Hospital
2701 W. 68th St.
Chicago, IL 60629
Tel: 312-471-8000
Legal Title: *Holy Cross Hospital*
Sisters of St. Casimir of Chicago.
MARK C. CLEMENT, Pres. & CEO
ALICE KILGALLON, Dir. Pastoral Care
Chaplains:
Rev. ARUBRAJ AMBROSE
Sr. DOLORES CAVALLI, O.P.
Revs.:
ERWIN J. DODGE, O.S.A.
THOMAS GRIFFIN, O.S.A.
MARK MENZEL, S.S.C.
THOMAS A. MORRISON, O.P.
DONNA MULVENNA
Revs.:
PABLO MORA, S.J.
GERALD VAN OVERBEEL, O.S.A.
ARTURO PEREZ
MICHAEL HOGAN, O.S.A.
Sr. AGNESE CHAPP, Patient Visitor
Sisters 26
Licensed Beds 400
Patients assisted annually 185,123
Holy Cross Hospital and Sisters of St. Casimir Foundation

Mercy Hospital and Medical Center
2525 S. Michigan Ave.
Chicago, IL 60616
Tel: 312-567-5544; Fax: 312-567-6575
Web Site: www.mercy-chicago.org
Sr. SHEILA LYNE, R.S.M. Tel: 312-567-2580; Fax: 312-567-6575
Rev. MARTIN J. HEBDA, Vice Pres., Spirituality & Community, Tel: 312-567-2045; Fax: 312-328-7741
Sisters 11
Bed Capacity 383
Bassinets 30
Patients assisted annually 334,878
Affiliates:
Mercy Diagnostic & Treatment Center
Mercy Health Care Corp.
Mercy Services Corp.
Mercy Foundation, Inc.
Mercy Health Care & Rehabilitation Center
Mercy Medical at Presidential Towers (Outpatient Satellite Facility & Alcohol-Drug Dependency Program)
Tower Three, 614 W. Madison St.
Chicago, IL 60606
Tel: 312-902-4000
Mercy Medical in Chinatown (Outpatient Satellite Facility)
2347 S. Wentworth
Chicago, IL 60616
Tel: 312-842-0100
Mercy Medical in Justice (Ambulatory Care & Alcohol-Drug Dependency Program)
81st & Kean Ave.
Chicago, IL 60458
Tel: 708-594-3500
Mercy Medical on Pulaski (Outpatient Satellite Facility & Alcohol-Drug Dependency Program)
5635 S. Pulaski
Chicago, IL 60629
Tel: 312-585-1955
St. Patrick's Family Health Center (Outpatient Satellite Facility)
3344 S. Halsted
Chicago, IL 60608
Tel: 312-523-9550
Mercy Medical in Chicago Ridge (Outpatient Satellite Facility)
9830 S. Ridgeland
Chicago, IL 60415
Tel: 708-636-8200
Mercy Medical in Little Village (Outpatient Satellite Facility)
3649 W. 26th St.
Chicago, IL 60623
Tel: 312-521-2080
Mercy Medical on Michigan (Outpatient Satellite Facility)
2930 S. Michigan Ave.
Chicago, IL 60616
Tel: 312-808-0400
Mercy Medical in Mt. Greenwood, Chicago
11055 S. St. Louis Ave.
Chicago, IL 60655
Tel: 312-445-5800
Mercy Works on Ashland
3316 S. Ashland
Chicago, IL 60608
Tel: 312-890-2489
Arlington Heights (Alchohol, Drug Dependency Program)
115 S. Wilke Rd., Ste. 101
Arlington Heights, IL 60005
Tel: 708-398-0045
Hazel Crest (Alcohol, Drug Dependency Program)
17577 S. Kedzie Ave., Ste. 204
Hazel Crest, IL 60429
Tel: 708-922-1983
Mercy Medical in Lincoln Park, Chicago
990 W. Fullerton, Ste. 495
Chicago, IL 60616
Tel: 312-327-8848
Mercy Medical in Chatham
8529-33 S. State St.
Chicago, IL 60619
Bryn Mawr
8610 W. Bryn Mawr
Chicago, IL 60631
Tel: 312-380-0400

**Our Lady of the Resurrection Medical Center*
5645 W. Addison
Chicago, IL 60634
Tel: 773-282-7000; Fax: 773-794-7671
Web Site: www.reshealth.org
Sisters of the Resurrection
JOSEPH F. TOOMEY, Pres.
RONALD STRUXNESS, CEO
Chaplains:
Revs.:
ROBERT WALSH
JEROME ANDRACKI, C.R.
Sr. HEDWIG KUCZYNSKI, C.R.
Sr. LYDIA MARY YOKIEL, C.R.
Sr. MARY ANN POPPLER, S.C.C.
CAROL ANNE JARECKI, Coord., Spiritual Services
Sisters 3
Bed Capacity 286
Patients assisted annually 66,987

Resurrection Medical Center
7435 Talcott Ave.
Chicago, IL 60631
Tel: 773-774-8000; Fax: 773-792-9926
Web Site: www.reshealth.org
Sisters of the Resurrection
JOSEPH F. TOOMEY, Pres.
Sr. DONNA MARIE, C.R., CEO
Sr. MARY LEONETTE, C.R., Supr.
Chaplains:
Revs.:
WILLIAM BILINSKY
ROBERT KOWNACKI (SAT)

GORDON VAN HOOF, O.S.C.
Sisters 12
Bed Capacity 434
Patients assisted annually 184,645
Student Nurses affiliated with Nurses-Triton College 40
Students Nurses, Oakton Community College 20
Chicago Board of Education 12
Affiliates:
Resurrection Health Care Corporation
Resurrection Ambulatory Care Services
Resurrection Development Foundation

St. Anthony Hospital
Ascension Health & Missionary Sisters of the Sacred Heart of Jesus.
2875 W. 19th St.
Chicago, IL 60623
Tel: 773-521-1710
Legal Title: *Catholic Health Partners Services*
Mr. PETER FAXIO, Board Chm.
Mr. ARNOLD KIMMEL, Interim Pres. & CEO
Ms. KATHLEEN DEVINE, C.O.O.
Rev. THEODORE PLOPLIS, Dir. Pastoral Care Dept.
Chaplains:
Rev. ROBERT LUCAS, C.M.
Sr. BENIGNA MORAIS, M.S.C.
Sisters 4
Bassinets 26
Bed Capacity 163
Patients assisted annually 62,072

St. Basil Health Service - Free People's Clinic
1850 W. Garfield
Chicago, IL 60609
Tel: 773-436-4758; Fax: 773-436-2749
Patients assisted annually 5,000

St. Bernard Hospital & Health Care Center
326 W. 64th St.
Chicago, IL 60621
Tel: 773-962-3900
Legal Title: *St. Bernard Hospital*
Religious Hospitallers of St. Joseph
Sr. JANET WAHLEITHNER, R.H.S.J., Supr.
Sr. ELIZABETH VAN STRATEN, R.H.S.J., Pres. & CEO
Sr. JANET WAHLEITHMER, R.H.S.J., Dir. Pastoral Care Dept.
Sisters 2
Bed Capacity 233
Patients assisted annually 101,000

St. Elizabeth's Hospital
1431 N. Claremont Ave.
Chicago, IL 60622
Tel: 773-278-2000
Legal Title: *St. Elizabeth's Hospital of Chicago, Inc.*
Operated by the Ancilla Systems, Inc.
Sponsored by The Poor Handmaids of Jesus Christ.
JOANN BIRDZELL, CEO
Sisters 5
Bed Capacity 276
Patients assisted annually 149,172

St. Joseph Hospital
Missionary Sisters of the Sacred Heart of Jesus.
2900 N. Lake Shore Dr.
Chicago, IL 60657
Tel: 773-665-3000
Legal Title: *Catholic Health Partners Services*
Mr. PETER FAXIO, Board Chm.
Mr. ARNOLD KIMMEL, Pres. & CEO
Ms. MARGARET MCDERMOTT, C.O.O.
Rev. THEODORE PLOPLIS, Dir. Pastoral Care Dept.
Chaplains:
Revs.:
ANTHONY J. ADDUCCI
KEVIN R. FANE, O.P.
Deacon MICHAEL ROMANO
Sr. CYRILLA ZAREK, O.P.
Sr. ALVERDA BONIFAS, O.P.
Rabbi NORMAN LEWISON
Ms. SHARON BARCHAM
Sisters 8
Bassinets 31
Bed Capacity 352
Patients assisted annually 67,831

St. Mary of Nazareth Hospital Center
2233 W. Division
Chicago, IL 60622
Tel: 312-770-2000; Fax: 312-770-3391
Web Site: stmaryofnazareth.org
Sisters of the Holy Family of Nazareth
Sr. MICHAEL MARIE FRANCZAK, C.S.F.N., Supr.
Sr. SALLY MARIE KIEPURA, C.S.F.N., Pres. & CEO
Rev. JOHN KOBUS
Most Rev. ENRIQUE RIVERA HERNANDEZ
Rev. ABRAHAM MILLER
Sisters 18
Bed Capacity 387
Bassinets 32
Patients assisted annually 182,031

Chicago Heights
Archdiocese of Chicago

Alverno Lakeside Corporation
1423 Chicago Rd.
Chicago Heights, IL 60411
Sisters 2

St. James Hospital and Health Centers
1423 Chicago Rd.
Chicago Heights, IL 60411
Tel: 708-756-1000; Fax: 708-756-6863
Web Site: www.stjameshhc.org
20201 S. Crawford Ave.
Olympia Fields, IL 60461
Tel: 708-747-4000; Fax: 708-503-3270
Legal Title: *Sisters of St. Francis Health Services, Inc., Mishawaka, Indiana*
Chicago Heights
Sisters of St. Francis of Perpetual Adoration
Mr. PETER J. MURPHY, Pres. & CEO
Sr. MARLENE SHAPLEY, O.S.F., Vice Pres.
Rev. RONALD L. KONDZIOLKA, Chap.
Sisters 4
Bed Capacity 561
Patients assisted annually 179,770
Total Staff 2,208

Danville
Diocese of Peoria

Provena United Samaritans Medical Center
812 N. Logan
Danville, IL 61832
Tel: 217-443-5000; Fax: 217-443-1965
Legal Title: *Provena Hospitals.*
JAMES W. POPE, Pres.
Rev. ROBERT G. MANN, Chap.
Sisters 2
Capacity 308
Patients assisted annually 305,351
Staff 1,144
Provena Samaritan Health Partners

Decatur
Diocese of Springfield in Illinois

St. Mary's Hospital
1800 E. Lake Shore Dr.
Decatur, IL 62521
Tel: 217-464-2966; Fax: 217-464-1616
Web Site: www.stmarys-hospital.com
KEITH L. CALLAHAN, Exec. Vice Pres.
Hospital Sisters of the Third Order of St. Francis 5
Patients assisted annually 105,106
Bed Capacity 371
Staff 1,230

Des Plaines
Archdiocese of Chicago

Holy Family Medical Center
100 N. River Rd.
Des Plaines, IL 60016
Tel: 847-297-1800; Fax: 847-297-1863
Web Site: chicagotribune.com/link/holyfamily
Legal Title: *Holy Family Medical Center*
Sisters of the Holy Family of Nazareth
Sr. PATRICIA ANN KOSCHALKE, C.S.F.N., Pres. & CEO
Revs.:
ROBERT MILLER, O.P.
HALDANE MYSLIWIEC
Sisters 8
Bed Capacity 252
Patients assisted annually 85,359

East St. Louis
Diocese of Belleville

St. Mary's Hospital
129 N. 8th St.
East St. Louis, IL 62201
Tel: 618-274-1900; Fax: 618-482-7015
E-mail: ascott@ancilla.org
Web Site: www.ancilla.org/stmaryesl.htm
Sponsored by the Poor Handmaids of Jesus Christ.
Affiliate of Ancilla Systems, Inc.
RICHARD MARK, Pres. & CEO
Sisters 2
Bed Capacity 169
Patients assisted annually 93,075

Effingham
Diocese of Springfield in Illinois

St. Anthony's Memorial Hospital
503 N. Maple St.
Effingham, IL 62401
Tel: 217-342-2121; Fax: 217-347-1563
E-mail: hospital@effingham.net
Web Site: www.stanthonyshospital.org
DANIEL J. WOODS, Admin.
Rev. ALEXIS PRUEMER, O.F.M., Chap.
Hospital Sisters of the Third Order of St. Francis 3
Bed Capacity 146
Patients assisted annually 72,338
Staff 566

Elgin
Diocese of Rockford

Provena St. Joseph Hospital
77 N. Airlite St.
Elgin, IL 60123
Tel: 847-695-3200; Fax: 847-888-5475
E-mail: edhunter@provena.org
Web Site: www.provenasaintjoseph.org
Legal Title: *Provena Hospitals dba Provena St. Joseph Hospital.*
Mr. LARRY NARUM, Pres.
EDWARD J. HUNTER, Dir., Pastoral Care
Sisters 4
Beds 264
Patients assisted annually 238,963
Provena Lake in the Hills Medical Center, Lake in the Hills
Tel: 847-854-5511; Fax: 847-854-5531
Provena Wellness Center
100 S. Hawthorne
Elgin, IL 60123

Elk Grove Village
Archdiocese of Chicago

Alexian Brothers Medical Center
800 Biesterfield Rd.
Elk Grove Village, IL 60007-3397
Tel: 847-437-5500
E-mail: SchwartM@HBEG.HBOCWIN.COM
Web Site: http://www.wswwalexian.org
Congregation of Alexian Brothers, Immaculate Conception Province
Associated with Stritch School of Medicine of Loyola University.
MICHAEL J. SCHWARTZ, Pres. & CEO
Chaplains:
Sr. SUSAN HART, O.P., Chap. Supvr.
Revs.:
STAN FERNANDO
WILLIAM E. VEITH
Brothers 13
Licensed Beds 483
Lay Staff 2,200
Patients assisted annually 175,000
Parent: Alexian Brothers of Illinois

Evanston
Archdiocese of Chicago

Saint Francis Hospital
355 Ridge Ave.
Evanston, IL 60202
Tel: 847-316-4000; Fax: 847-316-7733
KENNETH W. WOOD, CEO
Spiritual Svcs. Dept.
Rev. ROMULO S. MANCHING, Coord.
Chaplains:
Revs.:
DANIEL J. COLLINS
JAMES E. DUNLAP
GERY W. STEFANSKI
WAYNE SCHIMMELMAN
THOMAS C. VAYALIL
HERBERT MAXWELL
RABBI ILENE MELEMAD
Bed Capacity 300
Patients assisted annually 250,000

Evergreen Park
Archdiocese of Chicago

Little Company of Mary Hospital and Health Care Centers
2800 W. 95th St.
Evergreen Park, IL 60805
Tel: 708-422-6200; Fax: 708-425-9756
Web Site: www.lcmh.org
Legal Title: *The Little Company of Mary Hospital and Health Care Centers*
Sr. KATHLEEN MCINTYRE, L.C.M., Chm. Bd.
DENNIS REILLY, Pres.
Ms. ROSEANN KELLER, Dir. Pastoral Care Svcs.

Chaplains:
Revs.:
LAMBERT KEMPKES, C.M.M.
ANTHONY ADEBUSUYI
JAMES R. GALLAGHER
DALE LAWSON, Baptist Min.
Sr. CHRISTA HENRICH, S.L.W.
Deacon GREG PRICE
Sr. JEAN STICKNEY, L.C.M.
Deacon RICHARD WARFIELD
MARGARET SCHNEIDER
Sr. SHARON ANN WALSH, L.C.M.
Sisters of the Little Company of Mary 28
Bed Capacity 302
Bassinets 24
Patients assisted annually 233,226
Affiliates:
Little Company of Mary Auxiliary
2800 W. 95th St.
Evergreen Park, IL 60805
Tel: 708-229-5447
Little Company of Mary Affiliated Services, Inc.
2800 W. 95th St.
Evergreen Park, IL 60805
Tel: 708-422-6200, Ext. 5100
Oak Lawn Care Station
5660 W. 95th St.
Oak Lawn, IL 60453
Tel: 708-499-2273; Fax: 708-857-3705
Burbank Care Station
4901 W. 79th St.
Burbank, IL 60459
Tel: 708-424-2273; Fax: 708-857-3713
Mary Potter Pavilion
2850 W. 95th St.
Evergreen Park, IL 60805
Tel: 708-857-9524
Little Company of Mary Hospital Foundation
2800 W. 95th St.
Evergreen Park, IL 60805
Tel: 708-229-5022; Fax: 708-229-6525
MARY JO MAY, Exec. Dir.

Frankfort
Diocese of Joliet in Illinois

Provena Health (Jol)
9223 West St. Francis Rd.
Frankfort, IL 60423
Tel: 815-469-4888; Fax: 815-469-4864
Web Site: www.Provena.Org

Provena Hospitals (Jol)
9223 West Saint Francis Rd.
Frankfort, IL 60423
Tel: 815-469-4888
Web Site: www.Provena.Org

Galesburg
Diocese of Peoria

St. Mary Medical Center
3333 N. Seminary St.
Galesburg, IL 61401-1299
Tel: 309-344-3161; Fax: 309-344-9494
Sr. M. JOAN, O.S.F., Supr.
Rev. MICHAEL R. VAN ACKER, Chap.
Sisters of the Third Order of St. Francis 2
Capacity 156
Patients assisted annually 35,000
Total Staff 485
The Galesburg St. Mary Medical Center Foundation
3333 N. Seminary St.
Galesburg, IL 61401

Granite City
Diocese of Springfield in Illinois

St. Elizabeth Medical Center
2100 Madison Ave.
Granite City, IL 62040
Tel: 618-798-3000; Fax: 618-798-3508
Sr. M. THOMAS, C.D.P., Chm. Bd.
TED EILERMAN, Pres.
Rev. FINIAN MCMULLIN, O.F.M., Chap.
Sisters of Divine Providence, IL 8
Patients assisted annually 210,000
Staffed Beds 229
Total Staff 840

Harrisburg
Diocese of Belleville

Harrisburg Medical Center
100 Hospital Dr., P.O. Box 428
Harrisburg, IL 62946
Tel: 618-253-7671; Fax: 618-252-7274
E-mail: cchatt@intrnet.net
Web Site: www.harrisburgmedicalcenter.com
Sponsored by the Daughters of Charity.
CLAUDE CHATTERTON, Admin.
Bed Capacity 80

Highland
Diocese of Springfield in Illinois

St. Joseph's Hospital
1515 Main St.
Highland, IL 62249
Tel: 618-654-7421; Fax: 618-654-2012
E-mail: mkorte@sjh.hshs.org
Web Site: stjosephs-highland.org
Hospital Sisters of the Third Order of St. Francis 4
Patients assisted annually 39,131
Bed Capacity 106
Staff 280

Hoffman Estates
Archdiocese of Chicago

Alexian Brothers Behavioral Health Hospital
1650 Moon Lake Rd.
Hoffman Estates, IL 60194
Tel: 847-882-1600; Fax: 847-755-8060
Web Site: abbhh.org
Congregation of Alexian Brothers, Immaculate Conception Province
MARK A. FREY, Pres. & CEO
Rev. DOROTHY S. SYMOND, Chap.
Brothers 1
Licensed Beds 100
Parents:
Alexian Brothers Health System
Tel: 847-981-0627; Fax: 847-981-5561
Alexian Brothers of Illinois
Tel: 847-640-7551

St. Alexius Medical Center
1555 N. Barrington Rd.
Hoffman Estates, IL 60194
Tel: 847-843-2000
E-mail: dmcaneiro@yahoo.com
Congregation of Alexian Brothers, Immaculate Conception Province
EDWARD M. GOLDBERG, Pres. & CEO
Chaplains:
Rev. DENIS CARNEIRO (India)
Sr. LAURETTE BETZ
Rev. MARK TABBOT
Mr. LARRY KANCLER
Brothers 1
Licensed Beds 344
Lay Staff 1,122
Patients assisted annually 66,456
Parents:
Alexian Brothers Health System
Alexian Brothers of Illinois

Joliet
Diocese of Joliet in Illinois

Provena Saint Joseph Medical Center
333 N. Madison St.
Joliet, IL 60435-6595
Tel: 815-741-7236; Fax: 815-741-7579
E-mail: name@provena.org
Web Site: www.provenasaintjoe.org
Legal Title: *Provena Hospitals dba Provena St. Joseph Medical Center*
THOMAS A. REITINGER, Pres. & CEO
Deacon ED PETAK, Dir. Pastoral Care
Sisters 10
Chaplains 10
Bed Capacity 543
Patients assisted annually 493,384
Total Staff 2,342
Provena City Center Health Care, Joliet
Tel: 815-726-0311
Provena Family Health Center, Coal City
Tel: 815-634-4545; Fax: 815-726-0520
Provena Family Health Center, Lockport
Tel: 815-834-1903
Provena Family Health Center, Mokena
Tel: 708-479-5442; Fax: 708-479-7837
Provena Family Health Center, Naperville
Tel: 630-904-1220; Fax: 630-904-0967
Provena Family Health Center, New Lenox
Tel: 815-485-2541; Fax: 815-485-2667
Provena Family Health Center, Plainfield
Tel: 815-436-1400; Fax: 815-436-1656
Provena Family Health Center, Romeoville
Tel: 630-378-9070; Fax: 630-378-4775
Provena Industrial Rehabilitation Center, Joliet
Tel: 815-436-4545
Provena Medical Specialty & Physical Therapy Ctr., Frankfort
Tel: 815-469-2123
Provena Physical Rehab & Sports Injury Center, Joliet
Tel: 815-741-7114
Provena Physical Therapy, New Lenox
Tel: 815-485-8495
St. Joseph/Morris Health Network
Tel: 815-741-7236

Kankakee
Diocese of Joliet in Illinois

Provena St. Mary's Hospital
500 West Court St.
Kankakee, IL 60901
Tel: 815-937-2490; Fax: 815-937-8772
Legal Title: *Provena Hospitals dba Provena St. Mary Hospital*
Sr. VIRGINIA MARIE DERK, Dir. Pastoral Care, Tel: 815-937-2384
Ms. PAULA JACOBI, Pres.
Rev. EDWARD POFF, Chap.
Bed Capacity 210
Patients assisted annually 172,772
Staff 1,049
Chaplains 1
Sisters (SSCM) 4
Sisters (Holy Family) 3
Bourbonnais Med Centre, Bourbonnais
Provena County Westmedcentre, Herscher
Med Centre West, Kankakee
Med Centre East, Kankakee
Provena Manteno MedCentre, Manteno
Provena Momence MedCentre, Momence
Provena Peotone MedCentre, Peotone
Provena Home Care, Bourbonnais

Litchfield
Diocese of Springfield in Illinois

St. Francis Hospital
1215 Franciscan Dr., P.O. Box 1215
Litchfield, IL 62056
Tel: 217-324-2191
MICHAEL SIPKOSKI, Admin.
Rev. THEODOSIUS A. SCHELICH, O.F.M., Chap.
Sr. MARY FLYNN, O.S.F., Religious Coord.
Hospital Sisters of the Third Order of St. Francis 1
Patients assisted annually 65,000
Bed Capacity 138
Staff 380

Maywood
Archdiocese of Chicago

Foster G. McGaw Hospital of Loyola University of Chicago
2160 S. First Ave.
Maywood, IL 60153
Tel: 708-216-9056; Fax: 708-216-1121
MARIE COGLIANESE, M.P.S., Dir. Pastoral Care
Revs.:
THOMAS M. HESKIN, O.S.M.
JOHN P. COAKLEY, S.J.
Mr. JERRY KAELIN, M.Div., M.A.
Revs.:
ALLAN F. KIRK, S.J.
JAMES J. CREIGHTON, S.J., CPE Supvr.
Ms. LINDA BRONERSKY, M.P.S., C.P.E. Mgr. & Supvr.
Mr. DAVID CORCORAN, M.Ed.
JOELLA DOGGETT, M.P.S.
Deacon ALBIN WEGNER
Rev. JOSEPH D. CALDERONE, O.S.A.
Ms. KATHLEEN BRANNNIGAN, M.T.S.
Mr. JOHN GRUBBA, M.Div., M.A.
Mrs. ADRIENNE ZERVOS, M.P.S.
Bed Capacity 537
Patients assisted annually 275,000

Mount Vernon
Diocese of Belleville

**Good Samaritan Regional Health Center*
605 N. 12th St.
Mount Vernon, IL 62864
Tel: 618-242-4600
Member of SSM Health Care.
LEO F. CHILDERS, JR., Pres.
Sr. DENISE SHARP, S.S.J., Chap.
Sisters 3
Bed Capacity 175
Patients assisted annually 91,000

Murphysboro
Diocese of Belleville

St. Joseph Memorial Hospital
2 S. Hospital Dr.
Murphysboro, IL 62966
Tel: 618-684-3156; Fax: 618-684-6243
Web Site: www.sih.net
A service of Southern Illinois Healthcare.
Adorers of the Blood of Christ.
Ms. BETTY GAFFNEY, Senior Vice Pres. & Admin.

Sr. MILDRED GROSS, A.S.C., Corporate Dir. of Spritual Care
Sr. MARY BEDE, A.S.C., Dir. of Pastoral Care
Sr. CLARA TERNES, A.S.C., Corporate Dir. of Missions, Values & Ethics
Sisters 3
Bed Capacity 59
Patients assisted annually 23,325

Oak Park
Archdiocese of Chicago

Oak Park Hospital
520 S. Maple Ave.
Oak Park, IL 60304
Tel: 708-383-9300; Fax: 708-660-6658
Legal Title: *Oak Park Hospital*
Wheaton Franciscan Sisters
Mr. BRUCE M. ELEGANT, Pres. & CEO
Chaplains:
Rev. BERNARD KENNEDY, O.F.M.
Bro. MICHAEL MAY, O.F.M.
SYLVIA FROMME
Bed Capacity 176
Patients assisted annually 78,154
Oak Park Hospital Endowment Fund Affiliate.

Peoria
Diocese of Peoria

OSF Healthcare System
800 N.E. Glen Oak Ave.
Peoria, IL 61603-3200
Tel: 309-699-2852; Fax: 309-655-6869
Web Site: www.osfhealthcare.org
OSF Healthcare Foundation
800 N.E. Glen Oak Ave.
Peoria, IL 61603-3200
Tel: 309-655-4817
Mr. KEVIN SCHOEPLEIN, Pres.
Total Annually Assisted 1,492,939
Total Staff 9,588
Bed Capacity 1,717

St. Francis' Medical Center
530 N.E. Glen Oak Ave.
Peoria, IL 61637
Tel: 309-655-2000; Fax: 309-655-2347
E-mail: keith.e.steffen@osfhealthcare.org
Mr. KEITH STEFFEN, Admin.
Sr. M. ILDEFONSA, O.S.F., Supr.
Rev. MICHAEL BLISS, Dir.
Capacity:Beds 570
Patients assisted annually 760,000
Staff 3,626

Pontiac
Diocese of Peoria

Saint James Hospital
610 E. Water
Pontiac, IL 61764
Tel: 815-842-2828; Fax: 815-842-4912
Web Site: www.osfstjames.org
DAVID T. OCHS, Admin.
Sr. M. GAUDENTIA, O.S.F., Supr.
Rev. DAVID ROCHE, Chap.
Sisters of the Third Order of St. Francis 5
Capacity 81
Patients assisted annually 75,590
Total Staff 400

Red Bud
Diocese of Belleville

St. Clement Health Services
One St. Clement Blvd.
Red Bud, IL 62278
Tel: 618-282-3831; Fax: 618-282-6101
Adorers of the Blood of Christ; Sisters of Mercy Health Care
MARY SALOIS, Dir. of Pastoral Care
Mr. MICHAEL MCMANUS, Pres.
Sisters 2
Bed Capacity 87
Patients assisted annually 1,926

Rockford
Diocese of Rockford

Saint Anthony College of Nursing
5658 E. State St.
Rockford, IL 61108
Tel: 815-395-5090; Fax: 815-395-2275
E-mail: Terriburch@sacn
Web Site: www.sacn.edu
TERESE A. BURCH, Ph.D., R.N., Dean
Students 74

Saint Anthony Medical Center
5666 E. State St.
Rockford, IL 61108
Tel: 815-226-2000; Fax: 815-395-5449
E-mail: info@osfhealth.com
Web Site: osfhealth.com
Mr. DAVID SCHERTZ, Admin.
Rev. WILLIAM R. WENTINK, Chap. & Dir., Pastoral Care
Sisters of the Third Order of St. Francis (East Peoria, IL) 3
Beds 259
Patients assisted annually 157,825
Total Staff 1,710

Spring Valley
Diocese of Peoria

St. Margaret's Hospital
600 E. First St.
Spring Valley, IL 61362
Tel: 815-664-5311; Fax: 815-664-1335
E-mail: admin@st.margarets.com
Web Site: http://www.St.Margarets.com
TIMOTHY MUNTZ, Pres.
Sr. MARY JO ZACKER, Chap.
Sisters of Mary of the Presentation 5
Bed Capacity 123
Patients assisted annually 178,679
Total Staff 585

Springfield
Diocese of Springfield in Illinois

St. John's Hospital
800 E. Carpenter St.
Springfield, IL 62769
Tel: 217-544-6464; Fax: 217-535-3989
E-mail: rcarlson@st-johns.org
RICHARD J. CARLSON, Acting Admin.
SUSAN LIED, Dir. Pastoral Care
Patients assisted annually 233,568
Bed Capacity 606
Staff 3,615
St. John's College of Nursing
Tel: 217-544-6464, Ext. 45165; Fax: 217-757-6870
JANE SCHACHTSIEK, R.N., Ph.D., Chancellor
Students 60

Streator
Diocese of Peoria

St. Mary's Hospital
111 E. Spring St.
Streator, IL 61364
Tel: 815-673-2311; Fax: 815-673-4541
Hospital Sisters of St. Francis.
MARK S. O'HALLA, Executive Vice Pres.
THOMAS WHELAN Asst. Admin.
Sisters 1
Patients assisted annually 42,654
Bed Capacity 251
Bassinets 28
Total Staff 565

Taylorville
Diocese of Springfield in Illinois

St. Vincent Memorial Hospital
201 E. Pleasant St.
Taylorville, IL 62568
Tel: 217-824-3331; Fax: 217-824-2099
Adorers of the Blood of Christ 5
Patients assisted annually 29,000
Bed Capacity 129
Bassinets 8
Extended care facility 50
Staff 440

Urbana
Diocese of Peoria

Provena Covenant Medical Center
1400 W. Park St.
Urbana, IL 61801
Tel: 217-337-2000; Fax: 217-337-4541
E-mail: dianehfriedman@provenahealth.com
Web Site: www.provenahealth.com
Legal Title: *Provena Hospitals.*
Sr. CHARLENE CESARIO, S.S.C.M., Supr.
Ms. DIANE FRIEDMAN, Pres. & CEO
Chaplains:
Sr. MARY ROBERT MORTON, S.S.C.M., Dir.
VERA DUNCANSON
GINNY CONRON
PETER DYCK
BOB MULLIGAN
HARRY LITZENBERG
Provena Family Care Network
Tel: 217-762-3011
St Joseph
Tel: 217-379-2161
Paxton
Tel: 217-379-2161
Tuscola
Tel: 217-253-2013
Sisters 7
Capacity 268
Patients assisted annually 185,000
Total Staff 970

Waukegan
Archdiocese of Chicago

Provena Saint Therese Medical Center
2615 Washington St.
Waukegan, IL 60085
Tel: 847-249-3900; Fax: 847-249-5897
TIMOTHY SELZ, Pres.
Sr. JEANETTE PIERCE, Dir. Pastoral Care
Chaplains 3
Bed Capacity 386
Patients assisted annually 156,000
Provena Physical Medicine
222 S. Greenleaf Ave.
Gurnee, IL 60031
Tel: 847-599-0400; Fax: 847-599-1054
Provena Work Power Center
1005 Butterfield Rd.
Vernon Hills, IL 60061
Tel: 847-816-9998; Fax: 847-816-4771
Bed Capacity 386
Patients assisted annually 150,000

INDIANA

Anderson
Diocese of Lafayette in Indiana

Saint John's Health System
2015 Jackson St.
Anderson, IN 46016
Tel: 765-646-8745; Fax: 765-646-8373
Mr. JERRY D. BRUMITT, Pres. & CEO
Mr. TONY PINTO, Dir. Center for Spiritual Care
Sisters of the Holy Cross 5
Bed Capacity 332
Total Assisted 386,600
Total Staff 1,500

Beech Grove
Archdiocese of Indianapolis

St. Francis Hospital and Health Centers
1600 Albany St.
Beech Grove, IN 46107
Tel: 317-787-3311; Fax: 317-782-6731
Web Site: www.stfrancishospitals.org
Sisters of St. Francis Health Services, Inc.
Mr. ROBERT J. BRODY, Pres. & CEO
Sr. CORITA LAST, Vice Pres., Mission Svcs., Supr.
Chaplains:
Revs.:
FREDERICK J. DETERS
RUTA A. CABAZI (Tanzania)
JOHN H. MANNION (LFT)
Sisters 7
Staff 4,146
Beds 600
Patients assisted annually 209,000

Carmel
Diocese of Lafayette in Indiana

St. Elizabeth Ann Seton Hospital of Central Indiana, Inc.
13500 N. Meridian St.
Carmel, IN 46032
Tel: 317-582-8560; Fax: 317-582-8565
E-mail: phalexan@stvincent.org
Mr. PETER H. ALEXANDER, Exec. Dir.
Bed Capacity 38
Patients assisted annually 300
total Staff 175

Crown Point
Diocese of Gary

St. Anthony Medical Center of Crown Point
1201 S. Main St.
Crown Point, IN 46307-8483
Tel: 219-738-2100; Fax: 219-757-6242
Sisters of St. Francis Health Services, Inc.
Mrs. NORDSTROM LOPEZ, Pres.
Pastoral Care Team:
Rev. ANTHONY F. JANIK, O.F.M.
Sister of St. Francis of Perpetual Adoration 1
Franciscan Sisters of Chicago 15
Beds 411
Total Staff 1,181
Patients assisted annually 114,037

Dyer
Diocese of Gary

St. Margaret Mercy Healthcare Centers, South Campus
(Div. of the Sisters of St. Francis Health Services, Inc.)
24 Joliet
Dyer, IN 46311
Tel: 219-865-2141
Rev. Ron Kondziolka
Sisters of St. Francis of Perpetual Adoration 2
Beds 360
Bassinets 20
Total Staff 798
Patients assisted annually 203,952

East Chicago
Diocese of Gary

St. Catherine Hospital
4321 Fir St.
East Chicago, IN 46312
Tel: 219-392-1700; Fax: 219-392-7002
Web Site: www.StCatherineHospital.org
Sponsored by the Poor Handmaids of Jesus Christ.
Affiliates of Ancilla Systems.
Joann Birdzell, Pres. & CEO
Mark Rogers, Chief Oper. Officer & Chief Fin. Officer
Sr. Nora Hahn, P.H.J.C., Vice Pres. Mission Effectiveness
Sisters 5
Beds 190
Bassinets 9
Total Staff 963
Patients assisted annually 84,794
St. Catherine Hospital Foundation, Inc.
Tel: 219-392-7009; Fax: 219-392-7037
Transitional Care Unit (TCU)
Tel: 219-392-7530; Fax: 219-392-7540
Nazareth Home
Tel: 219-392-7009; Fax: 219-392-7037

Elwood
Diocese of Lafayette in Indiana

St. Vincent Mercy Hospital, Inc.
1331 South A St.
Elwood, IN 46036-1942
Tel: 765-552-4600; Fax: 765-552-4700
E-mail: rjcoughl@stvincent.org
Rosemary J. Coughlin, C.S.J., Chap.
Daughters of Charity National Health System
Tel: 765-552-4622; Fax: 765-552-4700
Bed Capacity 40
Patients assisted annually 30,700
Staff 182

Evansville
Diocese of Evansville

St. Mary's Medical Center of Evansville, Inc.
3700 Washington Ave.
Evansville, IN 47750
Tel: 812-485-4000; Fax: 812-485-4927
Web Site: www.stmarys.org
Jay Kasey, Interim Pres. & CEO Missions Svcs.
Sr. Jane Burger, D.C., Vice Pres. Mission Svcs.
Daughters of Charity of St. Vincent de Paul 4
Beds 380
Patients assisted annually 255,131

Hammond
Diocese of Gary

St. Margaret Mercy Healthcare Centers - North Campus
5454 Hohman Ave.
Hammond, IN 46320
Tel: 219-932-2300
Sisters of St. Francis Health Services, Inc.
Rev. Gregory Holicky
Sisters of St. Francis of Perpetual Adoration 5
Beds 487
Bassinets 45
Total Staff 1,425
Patients assisted annually 148,243

Hobart
Diocese of Gary

St. Mary Medical Center
1500 S. Lake Park Ave.
Hobart, IN 46342
Tel: 219-942-0551; Fax: 219-947-6037
Web Site: www.stmary-hobart.com
Sponsored by the Poor Handmaids of Jesus Christ.
Affiliate of Ancilla Systems, Inc.
Milton Triana, CEO
Sr. Mary Ellen Goeller, PHJC, Vice Pres. Mission Effectiveness
Rev. Joseph Kelchak, Chap.
Sisters 3
Beds 184
Bassinets 12
Total Staff 885
Patients assisted annually 76,235
St. Mary Medical Center Foundation, Inc.
Tel: 219-947-6011; Fax: 219-947-6037
The Linden House of Hobart, Inc.
Tel: 219-942-9440; Fax: 219-947-9338

Indianapolis
Archdiocese of Indianapolis

St. Vincent Hospital and Health Care Center, Inc.
2001 W. 86th St.
Indianapolis, IN 46260
Tel: 317-338-7000; Fax: 317-338-7005
E-mail: jbford@stvincent.org
Web Site: www.stvincent.org
Daughters of Charity of St. Vincent de Paul.
Sr. Lucille Marie Beauchamp, D.C., Chairperson
Vincent C. Caponi, C.E.O., Central Indiana Health System, Inc.
Marsha J. Casey, Pres., St. Vincent Hospital and Health Care Center, Inc.
Sr. Sharon Richardt, D.C., Vice Pres. Mission Svcs.
Revs.:
Charles W. Henry, O.S.B.
George F. Plaster (LAF)
Joseph F. Rautenberg (IND)
William H. Hubmann
Ms. Joan M. Bumpus, Dir. Pastoral Care
Sisters 8
Bed Capacity 833
Total Staff 6,598
Inpatient Admissions 36,919
Outpatient Visits 953,495
Emergency Visits 60,049
Chaplains 21

**St. Vincent New Hope, Inc.*
8405 N. Payne Rd.
Indianapolis, IN 46268
Tel: 317-872-4210; Fax: 317-338-4532
Daughters of Charity of St. Vincent de Paul.
Bed Capacity 69
Total Annually Assisted 184
Total Staff 415

Seton Health Corporation of Central Indiana
2001 W. 86th St.
Indianapolis, IN 46260
Tel: 317-338-7000; Fax: 317-338-7005
E-mail: jbford@stvincent.org
Web Site: www.stvincent.org
Daughters of Charity of St. Vincent de Paul.
Marsha J. Casey, Pres.
Sr. Lucille Marie Beauchamp, D.C., Chm.

**St. Vincent Cardiac Services, Inc.*
2001 W. 86th St.
Indianapolis, IN 46260
Tel: 317-338-7000; Fax: 317-338-7005
M. Lynne O'Day, Chm.

Jasper
Diocese of Evansville

Memorial Hospital and Health Care Center, Little Company of Mary of Indiana, Inc.
800 W. Ninth St.
Jasper, IN 47546
Tel: 812-482-2345; Fax: 812-482-0672
Ray Snowden, Pres. & CEO
Sr. M. Adrian Davis, L.C.M., Bd. Chairperson
Sr. Maura Beckman, O.S.B., Chap.
Sisters of the Little Company of Mary 2
Beds 131
Patients assisted annually 5,843
Palliative Care Patients 22

Memorial Hospital Foundation, Inc.
Jasper, IN 47546
Tel: 812-482-0671; Fax: 812-482-0672
William Rubino, Pres.
Michael A. Jones, Exec. Dir.

Kokomo
Diocese of Lafayette in Indiana

St. Joseph Hospital & Health Center of Kokomo, Indiana, Inc.
1907 W. Sycamore St.
Kokomo, IN 46901
Tel: 765-452-5611
Web Site: www.stjhhc.org
Mailing Address:
P.O. Box 9010
Kokomo, IN 46904-9010
Kathleen M. Korbelak, Pres. & CEO
Joan Bumpus, Dir. Pastoral Care
Total Staff 875
Sisters 1
Bed Capacity 167
Patients assisted annually 87,140
Saint Joseph Foundation of Kokomo, Indiana, Inc.
Tel: 765-456-5308; Fax: 765-456-5824

Lafayette
Diocese of Lafayette in Indiana

St. Elizabeth Medical Center
1501 Hartford St., P.O. Box 7501
Lafayette, IN 47903
Tel: 765-423-6011; Fax: 765-423-6040
E-mail: pr@glhsi.org
Web Site: www.ste.org
Legal Title: *Sisters of St. Francis Health Services, Inc., Mishawaka, IN*
Mr. John R. Walling, CEO
Mr. Douglas W. Eberle, COO
Sr. Marilyn Oliver, O.S.F., Vice Pres. Corporate Mission
Revs.:
Donald Vernon
Paul Graf
Sisters of St. Francis of Perpetual Adoration 3
Operational Beds 183
Patients assisted annually 194,000
Staff 1,050
School of Nursing
Tel: 765-423-6408; Fax: 765-423-6385
Students 100

Michigan City
Diocese of Gary

St. Anthony Memorial Health Centers
301 W. Homer St.
Michigan City, IN 46360
Tel: 219-879-8511; Fax: 219-877-1409
E-mail: SAMHC.ORG
Web Site: www.SAMHC.ORG
Sisters of St. Francis Health Services, Inc.
Sisters of St. Francis of Perpetual Adoration 5
Beds 200
Bassinets 14
Total Staff 1,011
Patients assisted annually 203,306

Mishawaka
Diocese of Fort Wayne - South Bend

**St. Joseph Community Hospital*
215 W. 4th St.
Mishawaka, IN 46544
Tel: 219-259-2431; Fax: 219-257-2831
E-mail: khabgood@skynet.net
Web Site: http://www.ancillahealthcare.org
Poor Handmaids of Jesus Christ
Affiliate of Ancilla Systems Incorporated.
Mary Roos, Pres. & CEO
Sr. Pauline Bridegroom, P.H.J.C., Vice Pres. Mission Effectiveness
Bed Capacity 125
Total Staff 729
Patients assisted annually 64,182

Plymouth
Diocese of Fort Wayne - South Bend

Saint Joseph's Regional Medical Center - Plymouth Campus
1915 Lake Ave., P.O. Box 670
Plymouth, IN 46563
Tel: 219-936-3181; Fax: 219-935-2235
Sponsored by Congregation of Sisters of the Holy Cross
Robert L. Beyer, CEO & Pres.
Brian Dietz, Exec. Vice Pres.
Mark Lorenz, Vice Pres. Support Svcs.
Margaret Shaw, N.A.C.C. Cert., Chap.
Lori Price, Vice Pres. Clinical Patient Care Svcs.
Staff 300
Bed Capacity 58
Patients assisted annually 106,957

South Bend
Diocese of Fort Wayne - South Bend

Our Lady of Peace Hospital, Inc.
801 E. LaSalle Ave.
South Bend, IN 46617
Tel: 219-237-7457
E-mail: voordec@sjrmc.com
Christine T. Voorde, C.E.O.

Sr. GERTRUDE DOLORES, C.S.C., Pres.
PAUL GUENTERT, M.D., Vice Pres.

Saint Joseph's Regional Medical Center
801 E. LaSalle St.
South Bend, IN 46617
Tel: 219-237-7111; Fax: 219-271-7077
E-mail: breedenm@sjrmc.com
Web Site: www.sjmed.com
ROBERT L. BEYER, Pres. & CEO
MARTIN G. BREEDEN, Vice Pres., Mission Integration
ALAN BOWMAN, Center for Spiritual Care
Bed Capacity 339
Staff 2,783
Patients assisted annually 194,305

St. Mary's Medical Plaza
2515 E. Jefferson Blvd.
South Bend, IN 46615
Tel: 219-288-8311; Fax: 219-257-2831
E-mail: khobgood@skynet.net
Web Site: http://www.ancillahealthcare.org
Poor Handmaids of Jesus Christ (Affiliate of Ancilla Systems Incorporated)
Tel: 219-288-8311; Fax: 219-257-2831
MARY ROOS, Pres. & CEO
Sr. PAULINE BRIDEGROOM, P.H.J.C., Vice Pres. Mission Effectiveness
Total Assisted 24,885
Total Staff 80

IOWA

Carroll
Diocese of Sioux City

St. Anthony Regional Hospital
Carroll, IA 51401
Tel: 712-792-3581; Fax: 712-792-2124
E-mail: stanthony@netins.net
Web Site: stanthonyhospital.org
GARY P. RIEDMANN, Pres.
Rev. THOMAS MUNN, Chap.
Franciscan Sisters of Perpetual Adoration 3
Bed Capacity 99
Patients assisted annually 79,600
Total Staff 440
St. Anthony Regional Nursing Home
Tel: 712-792-3581; Fax: 712-792-2124
Orchard View, Inc.
S. Clark St.
Carroll, IA 51401
Tel: 712-792-3581; Fax: 712-792-2124

Cedar Rapids
Archdiocese of Dubuque

Mercy Medical Center, Cedar Rapids, Iowa, Endowment Foundation, Inc.
701 Tenth St., S.E.
Cedar Rapids, IA 52403
Tel: 319-398-6278
Sr. JAMES MARIE DONAHUE, Pres.

Mercy Medical Center-Cedar Rapids
(Sisters of Mercy-Regional Community of Cedar Rapids)
701 Tenth St., S.E.
Cedar Rapids, IA 52403
Tel: 319-398-6011
E-mail: mercylib@crpl.cedar-rapids.lib.ia.us
Web Site: http://www.mercycare.org
Sponsored by the Sisters of Mercy, Cedar Rapids Regional Community.
A. JAMES TINKER, CEO
Rev. JOHN R. GALLAGHER, Res. Chap.
Sr. MARY LOU PODZIMEK, R.S.M., Dir. Pastoral Care Office
Chaplains:
Sr. MARGARET MURPHY
Sr. BERNICE KURT, R.S.M.
Sr. CHERYL MCCULLOUGH
Staff 1,295
Bed Capacity Acute 355
Skilled Nursing 29
Patients assisted annually 176,907

Mercycare Service Corporation
(Parent Corp.)
701 10th St., S.E.
Cedar Rapids, IA 52403
Tel: 319-398-6011
Sponsored by the Sisters of Mercy, Cedar Rapids Regional Community.
A. JAMES TINKER, CEO

Centerville
Diocese of Davenport

Mercy Medical Center - Centerville
One St. Joseph's Dr.
Centerville, IA 52544
Tel: 641-437-4111; Fax: 641-437-3304
E-mail: stjocvil@se-iowa.net
WILLIAM C. ASSELL, Pres.
Rev. JOSEPH BATHKE, C.PP.S., Chap.
Owned by Mercy Hospital Medical Center, Des Moines.
Attended from St. Mary's, Centerville.
Legacies, The Foundation of St. Joseph's Mercy Hospital
Tel: 614-437-3434; Fax: 641-437-3304
Beds 54
Patients assisted annually 65,364
Total Staff 255

Clinton
Diocese of Davenport

Mercy Medical Center - Clinton
A subsidiary of Mercy Health Services.
1410 N. Fourth St.
Clinton, IA 52732
Tel: 319-244-5555; Fax: 319-244-5592
Web Site: www.mercyclinton.com
THOMAS J. HESSELMANN, Pres.
Revs.:
HORST HEHR, Chap.
JOHN J. STACK
Beds 201
Staff 1,049
Annually Assisted 145,188
Mercy Services for Aging
Bluff Terrace Nursing Home, 638 S. Bluff Blvd.
Clinton, IA 52732
Tel: 319-244-3888; Fax: 319-244-3882
Beds 87
Wyndcrest Nursing Home
600 14th Ave. N.
Clinton, IA 52732
Tel: 319-244-2888; Fax: 319-244-3882
Beds 95

Corning
Diocese of Des Moines

Mercy Midlands: Mercy Hospital
Rosary Dr., P.O. Box 368
Corning, IA 50841
Tel: 515-322-3121; Fax: 515-322-4872
JAMES C. RUPPERT, Admin.
Rev. DANIEL E. SIEPKER, Chap.
Patients assisted annually: Inpatient 545
Outpatient 9,440

Council Bluffs
Diocese of Des Moines

Bergan Mercy-Alegent Health System: Mercy Hospital
800 Mercy Dr.
Council Bluffs, IA 51502
Tel: 712-328-5306; Fax: 712-325-2432
Web Site: www.alegent.com
Catholic Health Initiatives
The Mercy Center
Tel: 712-328-5000; Fax: 712-325-2425
Mercy Medical Office Bldgs., Inc.
Tel: 712-328-5000; Fax: 712-325-2425
GERALD CONIGLIO, Chap.
Chaplains 1
Beds:
Acute 178
Behavorial 82
Long Term Care 24
Patients assisted annually 43,229

Des Moines
Diocese of Des Moines

Mercy Medical Center
1111 Sixth Ave.
Des Moines, IA 50314
Tel: 515-247-3121; Fax: 515-247-4259
Web Site: www.mercydesmoines.org
Sisters of Mercy of the Americas (Omaha Prov.)
DAVE VELLINGA, Pres.
Sr. PAULINE TURSI, C.H.M., Dir., Pastoral Care
Chaplains:
Revs.:
ROBERT J. AUBREY
DANIEL KRETTEK
FELIX ONUORA, C.S.Sp.
PAUL SOLOMIA (Philippines)
BRAULIO TOLOSA (Philippines)
Sisters 6
Patients assisted annually 1,020,561

Mercy Clinics, Inc.
Mercy Court
Mercy College of Health Sciences
Clark Street House of Mercy

Dubuque
Archdiocese of Dubuque

Mercy Medical Center-Dubuque
(A Division of Mercy Health Services-Iowa)
250 Mercy Dr.
Dubuque, IA 52001
Tel: 563-589-8000; Fax: 563-589-8073
RUSSELL KNIGHT, Pres.
PATRICK CONLON, Dir. Pastoral Care Dept.
Chaplains:
Rev. STEPHEN A. LUNDGREN
Sr. ROSALYN ULFERS, P.B.V.M.
Sr. GABRIELLE HOEFER, R.S.M.
Sr. MARILYN SCHLOSSER, O.P.
Sr. JEANNE WICKHAM, O.S.F.
JOAN HAUG, Pastor
Bed Capacity 402
Total Staff 1,126
Patients assisted annually 42,397

Dyersville
Archdiocese of Dubuque

Mercy Medical Center-Dubuque (Dyersville)
(A Division of Mercy Health Services Iowa)
1111 Third St., S.W.
Dyersville, IA 52040
Tel: 563-875-7101; Fax: 563-875-2957
RUSSELL KNIGHT, Pres.
Bed Capacity 49
Total Staff 59
Patients assisted annually 5,185

Estherville
Diocese of Sioux City

Holy Family Hospital
826 N. Eighth St.
Estherville, IA 51334
Tel: 712-362-2631; Fax: 712-362-2636
E-mail: info@avera-holyfamily.org
Sisters of the Presentation of the B.V.M. (Aberdeen, SD)
Bed Capacity 58
Patients assisted annually 30,397
Total Staff 132
Holy Family Hospital Foundation.
Tel: 712-362-2631; Fax: 712-362-2636

Iowa City
Diocese of Davenport

Mercy Hospital
500 E. Market St.
Iowa City, IA 52245-2689
Tel: 319-339-0300; Fax: 319-339-7800
E-mail: mercyoncall@mercyic.org
Web Site: www.mercyic.org
RONALD R. REED, Admin.
Chaplains:
Revs.:
ANDREW E. KELLY
TIM BURNEMANN
BENEDICT OKONKWO
Sr. NORA WELTER
Sr. THERESA KURMEL
DAVID OAKLAND
Sisters 3
Beds 234

Mason City
Archdiocese of Dubuque

Mercy Medical Center-North Iowa
(Member of Mercy Health Network)
1000 4th St., S.W.
Mason City, IA 50401
Tel: 641-422-7000; Fax: 641-422-7827
JAMES J. SEXTON, Pres. & CEO
Chaplains:
Rev. KENNETH B. GEHLING
Sr. EMILY DEVINE, R.S.M.
ROSE SCHLEUTER
Rev. KIRK JOHNSON, (Protestant)
BARBARA MCCAULLEY, (Protestant)
Rev. RON STEIN, (Protestant)
Bed Capacity 350
Staff 2,468
Patients assisted annually 910,282

New Hampton
Archdiocese of Dubuque

Mercy Medical Center-New Hampton
(Member of Mercy Health Network)
308 N. Maple Ave.
New Hampton, IA 50659
Tel: 641-394-4121; Fax: 641-394-5628
CAROLYN MARTIN-SHAW, Pres. & CEO
RON DIDDY, Chm. Board, Member Organization Board
Rev. JOHN HARPEL, S.V.D., Chap.
Staff 155
Bed Capacity 49
Patients assisted annually 23,260

Oelwein
Archdiocese of Dubuque

Mercy Hospital of Franciscan Sisters
201 - 8th Ave., S.E.
Oelwein, IA 50662
Tel: 319-283-6000; Fax: 319-283-6004
Franciscan Sisters. Daughters of the Sacred Hearts of Jesus and Mary, Wheaton, IL
RICHARD SCHRUPP, Pres. & C.E.O.
MAAUREEN NOLAN, Contact Person
Chaplains:
Sr. ALICE MAIERS, R.S.M.
Rev. FREDERICK FANGMAN
Bed Capacity 64
Patients assisted annually 23,246
Staff 137

Sioux City
Diocese of Sioux City

Mercy Medical Center - Sioux City
801 Fifth St.
Sioux City, IA 51101
Tel: 712-279-2010; Fax: 712-279-2034
E-mail: brehanyj@trinity-health.org
Web Site: www.mercy-siouxcity.com
Trinity Health, Catholic Health Minitires
Ms. DEBORAH VANDENBROECK, Pres. & CEO
Chaplains:
JOHN F. BREHANY, Ph.D., S.T.L., Dir. of Mission Services & Ethics
Rev. RICHARD A. SITZMANN
Sr. MARLYS BECKER, O.S.F.
Rev. DENNIS GROHN, Lutheran Chap.
Sisters 1
Total Staff 1,500
Bed Capacity 484
Patients assisted annually 325,000

Waterloo
Archdiocese of Dubuque

Covenant Health System, Inc.
3421 W. Ninth St.
Waterloo, IA 50702
Tel: 319-272-7302

Covenant Medical Center, Inc.
3421 W. Ninth St.
Waterloo, IA 50702
Tel: 319-272-8000; Fax: 319-272-7313
Franciscan Sisters. Daughters of the Sacred Hearts of Jesus and Mary, Wheaton, IL
Mr. RAYMOND BURFEIND, Pres.
Rev. PAUL C. MCMANUS, Chap.
Covenant Foundation, Inc.
3421 W. Ninth St.
Waterloo, IA 50702
Tel: 319-236-4030
DON L. HOTH, Exec. Dir.
Sartori Memorial Hospital, Inc. (Formerly known as S.F.H., Inc.)
515 College St.
Cedar Falls, IA 50613
Tel: 319-268-3000
Total Staff 263
Bed Capacity 101
Patients assisted annually 1,928
DAN WOODS, Pres.
Staff 2,594
Bed Capacity 346
Patients assisted annually 12,281

KANSAS

Columbus
Diocese of Wichita

Maude Norton Memorial Hospital (MNMCH, Inc.)
220 N. Pennsylvania St.
Columbus, KS 66725
Tel: 316-429-2545; Fax: 316-429-1984
E-mail: cneely@stj.com
CYNTHIA NEELY, Admin.
Bed Capacity 25
Patients assisted annually 9,466
Total Staff 55

Fort Scott
Diocese of Wichita

Mercy Health System of Kansas, Inc.
821 Burke St.
Fort Scott, KS 66701
Tel: 316-223-7057; Fax: 316-223-5327
SUSAN BARRETT, Admin.
Sisters of Mercy 19
Lay Staff 463
Bed Capacity 110
Bassinets 15
Patients assisted annually 39,141
Home Health Visits 28,310

Garden City
Diocese of Dodge City

St. Catherine Hospital
410 E. Walnut
Garden City, KS 67846-5672
Tel: 316-272-2222; Fax: 316-272-2566
Web Site: www.stcath-hosp.org
Affiliated with Catholic Health Initiatives.
MARK STEADHAM, Pres. & CEO
LEANNE IRSIK, Sr. Vice Pres.
SUSAN RUTTER, Chap. & Exec. Dir. Missions Min.
CAROLYN ALLEN, CFO
VICTOR HAWKINS, Exec. Dir. / Mktg.
JOHN OSTROM, Exec. Dir. Human Resources
TERRY STOFFERSON, Vice Pres. Clinical & Ancillary Services
Chaplains:
DOUG WILLIAMS
Sr. ELEANOR UNREIN
SHANNON BORCHERT
Bed Capacity 100
Patients assisted annually 44,348
Total Staff 527

Great Bend
Diocese of Dodge City

Central Kansas Medical Center
3515 Broadway
Great Bend, KS 67530
Tel: 316-792-2511; Fax: 316-786-6298
E-mail: ckmc@greatbend.com
Web Site: www.ckmc.org
Sisters of the Third Order of St. Dominic
Member-Catholic Health Initiatives.
TOM SOMMERS, Pres. & CEO
JUDY SCOTT, Vice Pres. Fiscal Svcs.
LUCY FLANNAGAN, Dir. Human Resources
Sr. JEAN MARIE LEHTINEN, O.P., Dir. Mission Effectiveness
Sisters 5
Bed Capacity 184
Total Staff 631
Patients assisted annually 53,270

Independence
Diocese of Wichita

Mercy Health Systems of Kansas, Inc.-Independence
800 W. Myrtle St., P.O. Box 388
Independence, KS 67301
Tel: 316-331-2200; Fax: 316-332-3270
E-mail: abrau@mhsk.smhs.com
Web Site: terraworld.net/mercy/
JERRY STEVENSON, CEO
Sisters of Mercy 4
Total Staff 266
Bed Capacity 93
Patients assisted annually 38,429

Kansas City
Archdiocese of Kansas City in Kansas

Bethany Medical Center, Inc.
51 N. 12th St.
Kansas City, KS 66102
Tel: 913-281-8400; Fax: 913-281-8494
E-mail: scbones@pmc-sjh.org
Web Site: www.pmc-sjh.org
An affiliate of the Sisters of Charity of Leavenworth

Providence Medical Center
8929 Parallel Pkwy.
Kansas City, KS 66112
Tel: 913-596-4000; Fax: 913-596-4098
An affiliate of the Sisters of Charity of Leavenworth Health System, Inc.
Mr. FRANK CREEDEN, Pres. & CEO
Sisters 3
Bed Capacity 400
Bassinets 13
Employees 970
Physicians 300
Patients assisted annually 68,516

Larned
Diocese of Dodge City

Central Kansas Medical Center, St. Joseph Campus
923 Carroll St.
Larned, KS 67550
Tel: 316-285-3161; Fax: 316-285-8883
TOM SOMMERS, Pres. & CEO
Bed Capacity 78
Total Staff 90

Leavenworth
Archdiocese of Kansas City in Kansas

Saint John Hospital
3500 S. 4th St.
Leavenworth, KS 66048
Tel: 913-680-6000; Fax: 913-680-6013
Mr. MARK JAEGER, Senior Exec. Officer
Sisters of Charity of Leavenworth 3
Bed Capacity 76
Patients assisted annually 50,379

Oswego
Diocese of Wichita

Oswego Health Center, Inc.
800 Barker Dr.
Oswego, KS 67356-9461
Tel: 316-795-2921; Fax: 316-795-4903
E-mail: kathym@oswego.net
Ms. KATHY MOYER, Admin.
Total Staff 5
Bed Capacity 6
Patients assisted annually 300

Pittsburg
Diocese of Wichita

Mount Carmel Medical Center; Mount Carmel Foundation
1102 E. Centennial
Pittsburg, KS 66762
Tel: 316-231-6100; Fax: 316-232-0493
DAN LINGOR, Pres. & CEO
Sisters of St. Joseph 3
Sisters of Sorrowful Mother 1
Total Staff 724
Bed Capacity 188
Patients assisted annually 79,752

Topeka
Archdiocese of Kansas City in Kansas

St. Francis Hospital and Medical Center
1700 W. 7th St.
Topeka, KS 66606
Tel: 785-295-8000
Sr. LORETTO MARIE COLWELL, S.C.L., Pres.
Sisters of Charity of Leavenworth 2
Bed Capacity 378
Total Staff 1,317
Patients assisted annually 304,486

Wichita
Diocese of Wichita

Via Christi Regional Medical Center, Inc.
Web Site: www.Via-Christi.org
Mr. RANDALL G. NYP, Pres. & CEO
Vice Presidents Mission Svcs.:
Sr. SHERRI MARIE KUHN, S.S.M.
Sr. MARIE VERONICA JANOUSEK
St. Francis Campus
929 N. St. Francis
Wichita, KS 67124
Tel: 316-268-5000
Rev. DAN VACCA, Chap., Tel: 316-268-8540
St. Joseph Campus
3600 E. Harry
Wichita, KS 67218
Tel: 316-685-1111
Rev. PETER LEIGH, Chap., Tel: 316-689-5323
Bed Capacity 1,532
Outpatients assisted annually 320,000
Inpatients assisted annually 40,000
Total Staff 4,000
Licensed Beds 1,532
In Patients 40,560
Out Patients 213,365
Total Staff 4,774

Via Christi Rehabilitation Center, Inc.
Our Lady of Lourdes Campus, 1151 N. Rock Rd.
Wichita, KS 67206
Tel: 316-634-3400; Fax: 316-634-1141
Web Site: www.via-christi.org
Mr. ANTHONY ISAAC, Chm.
Ms. LAURIE LABARCA, COO
Mr. TIM LYTLE, Pastoral Svcs.
Staff 252
Bed Capacity 60
Patients assisted annually 8,511

KENTUCKY

Ashland
Diocese of Lexington

BS-OLBH, Inc.
St. Christopher Dr.
Ashland, KY 41101
Tel: 606-833-3333
(Member of Bon Secours Kentucky Health System, Inc.)

Our Lady of Bellefonte Hospital, Inc.
St. Christopher Dr.
Ashland, KY 41101
Tel: 606-833-3333; Fax: 606-833-3695
E-mail: rmaker@olbh.com
Web Site: www.olbh.com
(Member of Bon Secours Kentucky Health System, Inc.)
Rev. JOHN P. NOE, Chap.
Franciscan Sisters of the Poor 3
Beds 204
Patients assisted annually 159,177

Bardstown
Archdiocese of Louisville

Flaget Memorial Hospital
201 Cathedral Manor
Bardstown, KY 40004
Tel: 502-348-3923, Ext. 4641; Fax: 502-349-4643
Catholic Health Initiatives
BRUCE KLOCKARS, Interim Pres. & CEO
Sisters 5
Bed Capacity 52
Bassinets 8
Patients assisted annually 62,428
Attended from St. Joseph Church.

Covington
Diocese of Covington

St. Elizabeth Medical Center, North
401 E. 20th St.
Covington, KY 41014-1585
Tel: 859-292-4000; Fax: 859-292-4487
Web Site: www.stelizabeth.com
Mr. JOSEPH W. GROSS, Pres. & CEO
Mr. MARC A. HOFFMAN, Senior Vice Pres. & COO
Ms. JANE SWAIN, Vice Pres. Nursing
Mr. DAVID PURCELL, Vice Pres. Finance
Mr. THOMAS HORTON, Vice Pres. Human Resources
Mr. LEN PUTHOFF, Vice Pres. General Svcs.
Mr. THOMAS E. SAALFIELD, Vice Pres. Professional Svcs.
Mr. MICHAEL J. WALTERS, Vice Pres. Systems Devel.
Mr. ALLEN ZOBAY, M.D., Vice Pres. Medical Affairs
Chaplains:
Rev. ROBERT J. ROSS, S.J., Dir. Pastoral Care
Res.,
2028 Mackoy St.
Covington, KY 41014-1543
Rev. ROBERT C. ROSING
Res.,
Marydale Retreat Center, 945 Donaldson Hwy.
Erlanger, KY 41018-1093
Beds 111
Patients assisted annually 64,516
St. Elizabeth Medical Center Foundation, Inc.
Tel: 859-344-3920; Fax: 859-344-3968

Edgewood
Diocese of Covington

St. Elizabeth Medical Center, South
One Medical Village Dr.
Edgewood, KY 41017-3441
Tel: 859-344-2000; Fax: 859-344-3968
Web Site: www.stelizabeth.com
Mr. JOSEPH GROSS, Pres. & CEO
Mr. MARC A. HOFFMAN, Senior Vice Pres. & COO
Chaplains:
Revs.:
ROBERT J. ROSS, S.J., Dir. Pastoral Care
JOHN P. WERNER
ROBERT C. ROSING
Beds 345
Patients assisted annually 267,184

Frenchburg
Diocese of Lexington

Menifee Medical Center
HCR 71, Box 220, Kentucky 36
Frenchburg, KY 40322
Tel: 606-768-2191
(Div. of St. Claire Medical Center).
CHRIS M. GODDARD, Vice Pres., Regional Network Development
Patients assisted annually 15,534

Irvine
Diocese of Lexington

Marcum and Wallace Memorial Hospital
60 Mercy Ct.
Irvine, KY 40336
Tel: 606-723-2115; Fax: 606-723-2951
(Member of Mercy Health System, Cincinnati, OH).
JAMES HEITZENRAPER, Admin.
Beds 25
Patients assisted annually 46,059

Lexington
Diocese of Lexington

St. Joseph Health Care, Inc. dba St. Joseph East
150 N. Eagle Creek Dr.
Lexington, KY 40509
Tel: 859-268-3750

St. Joseph Hospital
1 St. Joseph Dr.
Lexington, KY 40504
Tel: 859-278-3436
(Member of Catholic Health Initiatives)
BILL HENDRICKSON, Pres. & CEO
Revs.:
HERB OSBORNE, Dir. Chap. Svcs.
JOSEPH E. WHALEN (GI) Chap.
Sisters of Charity of Nazareth 12
Bed Capacity 468
Patients assisted annually 61,314

London
Diocese of Lexington

London, Marymount dba Marymount Medical Center
310 E. Ninth St.
London, KY 40741
Tel: 606-878-6520; Fax: 606-877-3707
E-mail: ljones@marymount.com
Web Site: marymount.com
(Member of Catholic Health Initiatives)
Mr. LOWELL JONES, Pres. & CEO
KEVIN LOFTON, Pres., Southeast Region
Bed Capacity 100
Patients assisted annually 197,665

Louisville
Archdiocese of Louisville

Caritas Medical Center
1850 Bluegrass Ave.
Louisville, KY 40215
Tel: 502-361-6000; Fax: 502-361-6799
Web Site: www.caritas.com
Catholic Health Initiatives
Rev. JOSEPH H. STOLTZ, Chap.
Sisters 9
Bed Capacity 331
Patients assisted annually 123,000

Martin
Diocese of Lexington

Our Lady of the Way Hospital, Inc.
Box 910
Martin, KY 41649
Tel: 606-285-5181; Fax: 606-285-6422
Web Site: www.olwh.org
Members of Catholic Health Initiatives
Mr. LOWELL JONES, CEO
KEVIN LOFTON, CHI, COO
Beds 39
Patients assisted annually 38,448

Morehead
Diocese of Lexington

Saint Claire Medical Center
Morehead, KY 40351
Tel: 606-783-6500; Fax: 606-783-6503
E-mail: mneff@st-claire.com
Web Site: st-claire.com
Sisters of Notre Dame
Mr. MARK NEFF, Pres. & CEO
Sisters 5
Beds 159
Bassinets 10
Patients assisted annually 427,003
Patients with Primary Care Centers 80,868

Olive Hill
Diocese of Lexington

Carter County Medical Clinic
P.O. Box 1268, 155 Bricklayer St.
Olive Hill, KY 41164
Tel: 606-286-4152; Fax: 606-286-2385
(Div. of St. Claire Medical Center).
KELLY FURBEE, Vice Pres.
Patients assisted annually 18,936

Owingsville
Diocese of Lexington

Bath County Medical Clinic
632 Slate Ave.
Owingsville, KY 40360
Tel: 606-674-6386; Fax: 606-674-3096
(Div. of St. Claire Medical Center).
KELLY FURBEE, Vice Pres.
Patients assisted annually 23,807

Paducah
Diocese of Owensboro

Lourdes Hospital
1530 Lone Oak Rd., P.O. Box 7100
Paducah, KY 42002-7100
Tel: 270-444-2444; Fax: 270-444-2980
E-mail: mmoore@lourdes-pad.org
Sisters of Mercy of the Americas, Region of Cincinnati.
ROBERT P. GOODWIN, Pres.
Sr. MARIE MOORE, Vice. Pres. of Mission Svcs.
McAuley Manor, Inc. Housing for Elderly.
Tel: 270-575-0050
Mercy Manor, Inc. Apartments for Elderly.
Tel: 270-575-0050
Lourdes Foundation, Inc.
1530 Lone Oak Rd.
Paducah, KY 42002-7100
Tel: 270-444-2115; 444-2101; Fax: 270-444-2980
ROBERT P. GOODWIN, Pres. & CEO
Mercy Regional Emergency Medical Services, Inc. Ambulance Service.
Tel: 270-443-6529
Legal Title: *Mercy Health Partners - Lourdes, Inc.*
Beds 389
Patients assisted annually 300,000

Sandy Hook
Diocese of Lexington

Elliot County Medical Clinic
P.O. Box 748
Sandy Hook, KY 41171
Tel: 606-738-5155
(Div. of St. Claire Medical Center).
CHRIS M. GODDARD, Vice Pres.
Patients assisted annually 13,132

Williamstown
Diocese of Covington

St. Elizabeth Medical Center, Grant County
238 Barnes Rd.
Williamstown, KY 41097-9482
Tel: 859-824-2400; Fax: 859-824-2418
Mr. JOSEPH GROSS, Pres. & CEO
Mr. MARC A. HOFFMAN, Senior Vice Pres. & COO
Mr. CHRIS CARLE, Admin.
Rev. ROBERT J. ROSS, S.J., Chap. & Dir. Pastoral Care
Beds 30
Patients assisted annually 17,591

LOUISIANA

Alexandria
Diocese of Alexandria

Christus Health Central Louisiana dba St. Frances Cabrini Hospital
3330 Masonic Dr.
Alexandria, LA 71301
Tel: 318-487-1122; Fax: 318-448-6754
Web Site: www.cabrini.org
Mr. STEPHEN WRIGHT, CEO
Rev. CHRISTUDAS NAYAK (India) Dir. Pastoral Care
Sisters of Charity of the Incarnate Word 6

Bed Capacity 265
Patients assisted annually 108,102
Christus St. Frances Cabrini Hospital Foundation of Alexandria, Inc.
3330 Masonic Dr.
Alexandria, LA 71301

The Dubuis Hospital for Continuing Care
3330 Masonic Dr.
Alexandria, LA 71301
Tel: 318-448-4960; Fax: 318-448-4941
Mr. OSWALD A. FERRY, Ed.D., Admin.
Bed Capacity 35
Patients assisted annually 388

Baton Rouge
Diocese of Baton Rouge

Our Lady of the Lake Regional Medical Center
5000 Hennessy Blvd.
Baton Rouge, LA 70808-4398
Tel: 225-765-6565; Fax: 225-766-5645
Franciscan Missionaries of Our Lady (North American Province)
Sr. BRENDAN MARY RONAYNE, O.S.F., Supr.
Mr. ROBERT C. DAVIDGE, CEO
Mrs. KATHY MYERS, Dir. Pastoral Care
Chaplains:
Revs.:
ANTHONY WALTER, O.F.M.
TIMOTHY J. KERNER, C.Ss.R.
CLEMENT J. MONROE, C.Ss.R.
Bed Capacity 852
Sisters 13
Patients assisted annually 208,184
Tau Center
8080 Margaret Ann Dr.
Baton Rouge, LA 70809-3444
Tel: 225-767-1320; Fax: 225-767-1327

Coushatta
Diocese of Shreveport

Christus Coushatta Health Care Center
1635 Marvel St.
Coushatta, LA 71019
Tel: 318-932-2000; Fax: 318-932-2198
Sr. LAUREEN MARIE PAINTER, O.S.F., Pres. & CEO
MICHAEL SHEEDY, Chap.
Christus Health West Central Louisiana.

Gonzales
Diocese of Baton Rouge

St. Elizabeth Hospital
1125 W. Hwy. 30
Gonzales, LA 70737-5000
Tel: 225-647-5071
K. SCOTT WESTER, Pres. & CEO

Lafayette
Diocese of Lafayette

Our Lady of Lourdes Regional Medical Center, Inc.
611 St. Landry St., P.O. Box 4027
Lafayette, LA 70502
Tel: 337-289-2100; Fax: 337-289-2574
Web Site: www.lourdes.net
Mr. ROBERT EDDY, JR., Chm. of the Governing Board
RON WEBB, Pres. & CEO
Revs.:
THOMAS KAMENSKI, O.F.M.
LAWRENCE N. ABARA
Franciscan Missionaries of Our Lady 2
Beds 266
Total Staff 1,580
Patients assisted annually 105,986
St. Mary's Imaging Center, Inc.
411 St. Landry St.
Lafayette, LA 70506
Tel: 337-233-6288; Fax: 337-289-2782
Patients assisted annually 20,716
A wholly owned, nonprofit subsidiary of Our Lady of Lourdes Regional Medical Center, Inc. Operating as an outpatient diagnostic facility.
Occupational Medicine Clinic of Acadiana Incorporated
611 St. Landry St.
Lafayette, LA 70506
Tel: 337-289-2100; Fax: 337-289-2574
Corporate Health Services Incorporated
611 St. Landry St.
Lafayette, LA 70506
Tel: 337-289-2100; Fax: 337-289-2574

Lake Charles
Diocese of Lake Charles

CHRISTUS St. Patrick Hospital of Lake Charles
524 S. Ryan St.
Lake Charles, LA 70601
Tel: 337-436-2511; Fax: 337-430-4300
Owned and operated by the Sisters of Charity of the Incarnate Word (Houston, TX).
JAMES GARDNER, Admin.
Rev. BRIAN MADISON KING, Dir. Pastoral Care & Chap.
Sisters 6
Beds 392
Patients assisted annually 117,653
Total Staff 1,181

Metairie
Archdiocese of New Orleans

Sisters of Mercy Ministries
(Mercy Family Center)
4444 York St., Ste 101
Metairie, LA 70001
Tel: 504-779-5500; Fax: 504-779-5505
839 Heavens Dr.
Mandeville, LA 70471
Tel: 985-792-1833; Fax: 985-792-1051
Mr. BERNARD A. DUCO, Pres.
STEWART J. CLARK, Exec. Dir.
Total Assisted 912
Staff 14

Monroe
Diocese of Shreveport

St. Francis Medical Center
P.O. Box 1901
Monroe, LA 71210-1901
Tel: 318-327-4000; Fax: 318-327-4142
E-mail: hoganr@stfran.com
Web Site: www.stfran.com
Mr. H. GERALD SMITH, Pres. & CEO
Rev. WILLIAM CAREY, Ph.D., Dir. Pastoral Ministries
Chaplains:
Revs.:
JOSEPH PUTHUPPALLY
SEBASTIAN KALLARACKAL, C.M.I. (India)
BOBY MANNAMPLACKAL ALEX (India)
JOHN D. KENNEDY
Non-Catholic Chaplains:
Revs.:
RANDY FARMER
EDDY SHOEMAKER
EVERETT SLACK
Franciscan Missionaries of Our Lady 4
Beds 365
Patients assisted annually 111,680
Total Staff 1,650
Hospice & Ancillary Care
30,163
Total Staff 204

**St. Francis Specialty Hospital* (1995)
309 Jackson St., P.O. Box 1532
Monroe, LA 71210
Tel: 318-327-4600; Fax: 318-327-4082
E-mail: hightob@stfran.com
Web Site: www.specialtyhospital.com
Mr. BILL HIGHTOWER, Pres. & CEO
Licensed Beds 50
Physicians 153
Employees 180
Patient admissions 488

**St. Patrick Psychiatric Hospital, Inc.*
309 Jackson St., P.O. Box 1901
Monroe, LA 71210-1901
Tel: 318-327-4686; Fax: 318-327-4951
E-mail: rogersc@stfran
Web Site: www.stpatricks.net
CINDY J. ROGERS, CEO
Franciscan Missionaries of Our Lady Health System.
Beds 28
Patients assisted annually: Inpatients 450
Outpatients 200
Total Staff 52

New Orleans
Archdiocese of New Orleans

Daughters of Charity Services of New Orleans
3900 S. Carrollton Ave.
New Orleans, LA 70118-4712
Tel: 504-482-2080; Fax: 504-483-6016
E-mail: dward@dcsno.org
Mr. DAVID J. WARD, Pres. & CEO
Daughters of Charity Health Center at Carrollton
3900 S. Carrollton Ave.
New Orleans, LA 70118-4712
Tel: 504-482-0084; Fax: 504-483-6018
E-mail: dsimpson@dcsno.org
DOLLY M. SIMPSON, Exec. Dir.
Daughters of Charity Neighborhood Health Partnership
8326 Apricot St.
New Orleans, LA 70118-3198
Tel: 504-866-4978; Fax: 504-866-4676
E-mail: rarnaud@dcsno.org
Ms. ROSLYN ARNAUD, Dir.
Seton Resource Center for Child Development
4310 Chestnut St.
New Orleans, LA 70115
Tel: 504-896-8235; Fax: 504-899-4083
E-mail: src@bellsouth.net
Mr. HAL ROARK, Dir.
Vincentian Ministries
8326 Apricot St.
New Orleans, LA 70118-3198
Tel: 504-866-4978; Fax: 504-866-4676
E-mail: kflahert@dcsno.org
Sr. KAREN FLAHERTY, D.C., Dir.

Shreveport
Diocese of Shreveport

Christus Schumpert Health System (1907)
One St. Mary Pl., P.O. Box 21976
Shreveport, LA 71120-1976
Tel: 318-681-4500; Fax: 318-681-4177 (Administration)
Operated by Christus Health Northern Louisiana
Sr. ROSE MARIE MCDERMOTT, Senior Vice Pres., Mission
BETSY WILLIAMS, Chap., Dir. Spiritual Care
Chaplains:
Rev. Msgr. NORMAN C. BUVENS
Revs.:
GONZALO FERRER, T.O.R. (Spain)
PETER PULIVELIL, C.M.I. (India)
Sisters 7
Beds 817
Patients assisted annually 556,901
Total Staff 2,500
Christus Schumpert Bossier (Sub. of Christus Schumpert Health System)
2105 Airline Dr.
Bossier City, LA 71111
Tel: 318-741-6000
Mr. GARY KERR, Admin.
BETSY WILLIAMS, Dir. Spiritual Care
Rev. GONZALO FERRER, T.O.R., (Spain) Chap.
Christus Schumpert Highland (Sub. of Christus Schumpert Health System)
1453 E. Bert Kouns Industrial Loop
Shreveport, LA 71105
Tel: 318-798-4300
Mr. MARK KERLIN, Admin.
BETSY WILLIAMS, Dir. Spiritual Care
Rev. PETER PULIVELLI, C.M.I., (India) Chap.

MAINE

Bangor
Diocese of Portland (In Maine)

St. Joseph Hospital
360 Broadway
Bangor, ME 04401
Tel: 207-262-1000
Sr. MARY EDITH, C.S.S.F., Supr.
Sr. MARY NORBERTA, C.S.S.F., Pres./CEO
Felician Sisters 9
Nursing Sisters 1
Lay Nurses 198
Patients assisted annually 54,273
Pastoral Care Dept.
360 Broadway
Bangor, ME 04401
Revs.:
RICHARD V. ROKOS
PAUL R. MARQUIS

Bucksport
Diocese of Portland (In Maine)

Bridgewell, Inc.
Box 836
Bucksport, ME 04416
Tel: 207-469-7616; Fax: 207-469-7616
Sr. MIRIAM DEVLIN, Contact Person
Health Care Facility.

Lewiston
Diocese of Portland (In Maine)

Community Clinical Services, Inc.
(Formerly: Metropolitan Rehabilitation Institute)
100 Campus Ave, Ste. #1
Lewiston, ME 04240
Tel: 207-777-8841
Sr. M Dir.

Sisters of Charity Health System, Inc.
97 Campus Ave.
Lewiston, ME 04240
Tel: 207-777-8802; Fax: 207-777-8595
JAMES E. CASSIDY, Pres. & CEO
Lifeline
Tel: 207-777-8827
Serving 550
Covenant 50
Tel: 207-777-8823; Fax: 207-777-8570
Subscribers 9,000
Genesis Residential Treatment Facility Facility for Adolescent Boys.
Tel: 207-753-5437; Fax: 207-777-8944
Renaissance House Residential Program for Children 3 months to 12 years old.
Tel: 207-753-5437
WorkMed Occupational Health Program.
Tel: 207-777-8816; Fax: 207-753-0873
Health & Wellness Program
Tel: 207-777-8898; Fax: 207-753-0873

**St. Mary's Regional Medical Center*
Campus Ave., P.O. Box 291
Lewiston, ME 04243-0291
Tel: 207-777-8100; Fax: 207-777-8595
Chaplains:
Sr. HUGUETTE ALLARD, S.G.M.
Sr. MADELEINE NORMAND, P.M.
Sr. SHARON LEAVITT, S.C.I.M.
SALLY A. BROCHU, Dir.
KENN RANCOURT
Rev. LOUIS F. BERUBE, Sacramental Min.
Sisters 2
Nurses 186
LPN 6
CNA 34
Beds 233
Patients assisted annually 82,682

Portland
Diocese of Portland (In Maine)

**Mercy Hospital*
144 State St.
Portland, ME 04101
Tel: 207-879-3000
Mr. HOWARD R. BUCKLEY, Pres.
Rev. DONALD MCALLISTER, Chap.
Lay Nurses (RN's and LPN's) 305
Beds 200
Patients assisted annually 78,360
School of Radiology Students 17

MARYLAND

Baltimore
Archdiocese of Baltimore

Bon Secours Baltimore Health Corporation, Inc.
2000 W. Baltimore St.
Baltimore, MD 21223
Tel: 410-362-3000; Fax: 410-362-3126
E-mail: phyllis_reese@bshsi.com
Web Site: www.bonsecours.org
Sisters of Bon Secours
PERCY ALLEN, II, CEO
Sr. ALICE TALONE, CBS, Pres.
Sr. MARY SKOPAL, S.S.J., Dir. of Pastoral Care
Sisters 7
Beds 208
Patients assisted annually 180,000
Total Staff 1,274
Bon Secours Hospital Baltimore, Inc.
Tel: 410-362-3000; Fax: 410-362-3450
Bon Secours Community Health Services, Inc.
Tel: 410-362-3560; Fax: 410-362-3443
Bon Secours Facilities, Inc.
Tel: 410-362-3000; Fax: 410-362-3450
Bon Secours Housing, Inc.
Tel: 410-362-3185; Fax: 410-362-3443
Bon Secours Housing II, Inc.
Tel: 410-362-3185; Fax: 410-362-3443
Bon Secours Fayette House
Tel: 410-566-0550; Fax: 410-566-5451
Unity Properties, Inc.
Tel: 410-362-3185; Fax: 410-362-3443
Bon Secours of Maryland Foundation, Inc.
Tel: 410-362-3185; Fax: 410-362-3443
Primary Care:
Bon Secours Family Care Center
Tel: 410-362-3079; Fax: 410-362-3321
Imani Center
Tel: 410-383-4030; Fax: 410-383-4498
Bon Secours Park Circle Health Center
Tel: 410-225-9696; Fax: 410-383-4471
Bon Secours Washington Village Community Medical Center
Tel: 410-539-3360; Fax: 410-539-5302
Community Health Services:
Bon Secours Renal Dialysis Center (Baltimore)
Tel: 410-362-3094; Fax: 410-362-3408
Bon Secours Renal Dialysis Center (Glen Burnie)
Tel: 410-760-7100; Fax: 410-787-9217
Bon Secours Renal Dialysis Center (Charing Cross)
Tel: 410-747-9356; Fax: 410-747-0603
Bon Secours Renal Dialysis Center (Ravenwood)
Tel: 410-837-2011; Fax: 410-837-2018
Bon Secours Dialysis at North Charles
Tel: 410-467-8236; Fax: 410-467-8385
Community Institute of Behavorial Services (CIBS)
Tel: 410-383-4900; Fax: 410-669-0450
New Hope Treatment Center
Tel: 410-945-7706; Fax: 410-945-8767
New Phases
Tel: 410-523-4400; Fax: 410-225-7056
Next Passage
Tel: 410-728-8901; Fax: 410-728-7817
Community Outreach:
Bon Secours Apartments
Tel: 410-566-2701; Fax: 410-566-7813
Bon Secours Hollins Terrace (Apts. for the Elderly)
Tel: 410-566-2701; Fax: 410-566-7813
Bon Secours Benet House (Apts. for the Elderly)
Tel: 410-566-0701; Fax: 410-566-1275
Bon Secours Senior Apartments at Liberty Village
Tel: 410-523-1113; Fax: 410-523-4494
Bon Secours Community Support Center
Tel: 410-362-3629; Fax: 410-362-3649
Bon Secours Women's Resource Center
Tel: 410-362-3547; Fax: 410-362-3637; 362-3389
St. Jerome's Head Start
Tel: 410-685-1700; Fax: 410-685-2546
Urban Medical Institute (UMI)
Tel: 410-383-4550; Fax: 410-383-4285
Bed Capacity 208
Total Assisted Annually 180,000
Total Staff 1,274

Good Samaritan Hospital of Maryland Inc.
320 Cathedral St.
Baltimore, MD 21201

Mercy Health Services Inc.
301 St. Paul Pl.
Baltimore, MD 21202
Tel: 410-332-9000; Fax: 410-962-1303
E-mail: srmanella@mercymed.com
Web Site: www.mercymed.com
Institute of the Sisters of Mercy of the Americas
Chaplains:
Revs.:
THEODORE E.A. BRADY, S.J.
BERNARD A. SUPPE, S.J.
FRANCIS L. DUFFY, S.J.
Sr. MARY HARPER, R.S.M.
Sisters 15
Employees 2,100
Patients assisted annually 466,628
Subsidiaries: Mercy Medical Center Inc.; St. Paul Place Specialists, Inc.; Mercy Southern; Mercy Little Italy; Healthcare for the Homeless; Mercy Family Care; New Song Health Center; South Baltimore Health Center (Cherry Hill); Mercy Transitional Care; Stella Maris Hospice at Mercy; Stella Maris, Inc.; Cardinal Shehan Center, Inc.
Bed Capacity 285
Patients assisted annually 466,628
Total Staff 2,100

St. Agnes HealthCare, Inc.
900 Caton Ave.
Baltimore, MD 21229-5299
Tel: 410-368-6000; Fax: 410-368-2109
E-mail: info@stagnes.org
Web Site: www.stagnes.org
Ascension Health
Sr. BARBARA WORN, S.N.D., Dir. Pastoral Care
ROBERT W. ADAMS, Pres. & CEO
Revs.:
SIMON RAJ, Chap.
PAUL TSAU, Chap.
Sisters 11
Bed Capacity 284
Patients assisted annually 215,070
Total Staff 3,104
St. Agnes Foundation, Inc. (Subsidiary of St. Agnes HealthCare, Inc.)
Tel: 410-368-3155; Fax: 410-368-3533

Cumberland
Archdiocese of Baltimore

Sacred Heart Hospital of the Western Maryland Health System
900 Seton Dr.
Cumberland, MD 21502
Tel: 301-723-4200; Fax: 301-723-5583
E-mail: webmaster@wmhs.com
Web Site: www.wmhs.com
Daughters of Charity of St. Vincent de Paul
FRANCIS A. POMMETT, JR., Exec. Dir.
Sr. MARY PATRICIA WINTERS, D.C.
Rev. ALFRED CUTAJAR, S.J., Chap.
Beds 240
Sisters 10
Nurses 250
Patients assisted annually 119,014
Total Staff 1,000

Silver Spring
Archdiocese of Washington

Holy Cross Hospital of Silver Spring, Inc.
1500 Forest Glen Rd.
Silver Spring, MD 20910
Tel: 301-754-7000; Fax: 301-754-7413
E-mail: holycrosshealth.org
Web Site: www/holycrosshealth.org
Sisters of the Holy Cross
Mr. KEVIN SEXTON, CEO
Sr. VIRGINIA MCLAUGHLIN, C.S.C., Dir. Pastoral Care
Revs.:
ELIOT NITZ, S.D.S.
LAMBERTO PASION, O.P.
Sisters 14
Bed Capacity 340
Patients assisted annually 193,000
Total Staff 2,743

Towson
Archdiocese of Baltimore

St. Joseph Medical Center, Inc.
7601 Osler Dr.
Towson, MD 21204
Tel: 410-337-1000; Fax: 410-337-1024
E-mail: nancyconner@chi-east.org
Web Site: www.sjmcmd.org
Sisters of St. Francis of Philadelphia
JAMES CULLEN, Pres. & CEO
Sr. ANNE PATRICE HEFNER, O.S.F., V.P. Mission & Ministry
NANCY CONNER, Dir. Spiritual Care
Chaplains:
Revs.:
JOSEPH LERCH, S.J.
GILBERTO LIBORONI-PIEROZZI
Sr. EVELYN JANE GRUDZA, O.S.F.
Sr. ANNE CONRAD KOERNER, O.S.F.
JOAN MANNING
PAMELA WICKLEIN
MAUREEN O'BRIEN
SUSAN BROCATO
JANETTE SILVA
Sisters 25
Nurses 727
Beds 460
Patients assisted annually 220,000
Total Staff 2,200
Affiliate of Catholic Health Initiatives.

MASSACHUSETTS

Boston
Archdiocese of Boston

Daughters of Charity National Health System - Boston, Inc.
(Formerly The Carney Hospital)
2100 Dorchester Ave.
Boston, MA 02124
Tel: 617-296-4000
MATTHIAS D. MAGUIRE, Pres.
Sr. DECHANTAL LAROW, D.C., Chm. Bd.
Rev. LUCIEN A. SAWYER, O.M.I.
Daughters of Charity of St. Vincent de Paul 12
Bed Capacity 285
Patients treated during the year 111,326

St. Elizabeth's Hospital of Boston
736 Cambridge St.
Brighton, MA 02135
Tel: 617-789-3900
E-mail: shagop@aol.com
Web Site: www.semc.org
Bed Capacity 350
Bassinets 50
Patients treated during the year 175,000
Mr. MICHAEL F. COLLINS, M.D., Pres.

Revs.:
PHILIP CONROY
YAROSLOV NALYSNK
MATTHEW PERUMPIL, O.S.C.
GARRETT J. THOMPSON
Sr. IVAN CADIGAN, C.S.J.
Sr. MARYANNE GALLAGHER, O.S.F.
Sr. SUSAN KEATING, S.S.G.
Sr. CATHERINE O'CONNOR, C.S.B.

Brockton
Archdiocese of Boston

Good Samaritan Medical Center
235 N. Pearl St.
Brockton, MA 02401
Tel: 508-427-3000; 427-3151
FRANK J. LARKIN, Pres. & CEO
Sisters of Charity of Nazareth 1
Sisters of Jesus Crucified 1
Holy Union Sisters 1
Revs.:
RICHARD W. VISBISKY, Chap. & Dir. of Pastoral Care
SUZANNE HIGGINS, (Congregational)
Mr. RICHARD MESSING, (Rabbi)
Total Assisted 107,500
Total Staff 1,350

Dorchester
Archdiocese of Boston

The Carney Hospital, Inc.
2100 Dorchester Ave.
Dorchester, MA 02124-5666
Tel: 617-723-1100
Mr. WILSON D. ROGERS, JR., Esq., Contact Person

Fall River
Diocese of Fall River

Saint Anne's Health Care Management Services, Inc.
795 Middle St.
Fall River, MA 02721-1798
Tel: 508-674-5741; Fax: 508-675-5647
MICHAEL W. METZLER, Pres.

Saint Anne's Health Care System, Inc.
795 Middle St.
Fall River, MA 02721-1798
Tel: 508-674-5741; Fax: 508-675-5647
MICHAEL W. METZLER, Pres.

Saint Anne's Hospital
795 Middle St.
Fall River, MA 02721-1798
Tel: 508-674-5741; Fax: 508-675-5647
Dominican Sisters of Charity of the Presentation of the Blessed Virgin Mary
MICHAEL W. METZLER, Pres.
Rev. ROBERT A. ROCHON
Sisters 6
Total Staff 1,057
Bed Capacity 139
Patients assisted annually 85,270

Lowell
Archdiocese of Boston

Saints Memorial Health System, Inc.
Tel: 978-458-1411; Fax: 978-458-8369
E-mail: info@stmmc.org
Web Site: www.saints-memorial.org
One Hospital Dr.
Lowell, MA 01852
Tel: 978-458-1411; Fax: 978-458-8369
THOM CLARK, Pres. & CEO
Sisters of Charity of Ottawa
Bed Capacity 218
Total Assisted 214,000
Total Staff 1,352

Methuen
Archdiocese of Boston

Holy Family Hospital and Medical Center
70 East St.
Methuen, MA 01844-4597
Tel: 978-687-0151; Fax: 978-688-7689
Web Site: www.holyfamilyhosp.org
WILLIAM L. LANE, Pres.
Rev. JOHN T. CRABB, S.J., Chap.
Bed Capacity 222
Bassinets 30
Patients assisted annually 183,000
Total Staff 1,396
Affiliating Hospital for: St. Anselm's Collegiate School of Nursing; Northern Essex Community College; UMass, Lowell; Salem State College; Boston University School of Public Health; Essex Agricultural School; New Hampshire Technical School; Massachusetts Bay Community College; Northeastern University; Rivier College; Woodmill Nursing Home; Greater Lowell Vocational School; Whittier Regional Vocational Technical School; Greater Lawrence Vocational School; and Salem High School.
Priests 1
Holy Family Hospital Auxiliary
70 East St.
Methuen, MA 01844-4597
Tel: 978-687-0156, Ext. 4023; Fax: 978-688-7689
Holy Family Hospital Men's Guild
70 East St.
Methuen, MA 01844-4597
Tel: 978-687-0156, Ext. 2304; Fax: 978-688-7689

Springfield
Diocese of Springfield in Massachusetts

CHE - The Mercy Hospital, Inc.
271 Carew St., Box 9012
Springfield, MA 01102-9012
Tel: 413-748-9000; Fax: 413-781-7217
VINCENT J. MCCORKLE, Pres.
Mr. EDMOND PLUMMER, CEO
Sr. MARGARET M. MCCARTHY, S.N.D., Dir. Dept. of Pastoral Care
Chaplains:
Revs.:
HERBERT C. BALOGA, O.F.M.Conv.
WILLIAM J. DOHERTY, M.S.
STEPHEN SCOTT
Sr. MADELINE JOY, S.P.
SANDRA MATTUCCI
BEVERLY KILEY MATAKAETIS
Sisters of Providence 4
Beds 271
Patients assisted annually 197,000
Total Staff (Mercy Hospital) 1,612
Nurses:
RNs 305
LPNs 12
Providence Hospital Campus of Mercy Hospital
1233 Main St.
Holyoke, MA 01040
Tel: 413-536-5111; Fax: 413-539-2992
Pastoral Care Dept. 1
Beds 104
Staff 398
Sr. THERESE DUBE, S.A.S.V.

Turners Falls
Diocese of Springfield in Massachusetts

Farren Care Center, Inc.
340 Montague City Rd.
Turners Falls, MA 01376
Tel: 413-774-3111; Fax: 413-774-7049
WILLIAM E. CASPER, Pres.
JAMES CLIFFORD, Admin.
Beds 122
Total Staff 210
Total Assisted 150

Worcester
Diocese of Worcester

Compassion House
36 King St.
Worcester, MA 01610
Tel: 508-756-2713
Rev. THOMAS B. FLEMING, Dir.
Mrs. NANCY PRICE, House Mgr.

Our Lady of Mercy Health Care Center, Inc.
101 Barry Rd.
Worcester, MA 01609
Tel: 508-798-3727; Fax: 508-757-9415
E-mail: olmhcc@aol.com
Sr. SUZANNE ELLIOTT, R.S.M., Board Chair
Sr. ANNA MARIA TAG, R.S.M., Licensed Admin.

Pernet Family Health Service
237 Millbury St.
Worcester, MA 01610
Tel: 508-755-1228; Fax: 508-797-3477
Mission of the Little Sisters of the Assumption.
Certified Home Health and Social Service Agency. Focus of services toward the parent and young child. Parenting groups, family activities available, Early Childhood Development services also available.
SHEILAH DOOLEY, Exec. Dir.
Total Staff 40
Little Sisters of the Assumption 3
Total Volunteers 7

Saint Vincent Hospital, Inc.
25 Winthrop St.
Worcester, MA 01604
Tel: 508-798-1234; Fax: 508-798-1240
E-mail: beap01@svh-worc.com
Mr. ROBERT E. MAHER, JR., Pres. & CEO
Rev. PETER R. BEAULIEU, Dir. Pastoral Care
Chaplains:
Rev. FRANCIS J. ROACH
Sr. MARY O'LEARY, S.P.
Deacon JOHN ALISKEVICZ
Sisters 1
Beds 329
Patients assisted annually 100,000
Saint Vincent Healthcare System, Inc.
25 Winthrop St.
Worcester, MA 01604

MICHIGAN

Ann Arbor
Diocese of Lansing

Ascension Health Great Lakes Division
455 E. Eisenhower, Ste. 300
Ann Arbor, MI 48108
Tel: 734-741-1700; Fax: 734-623-7240
E-mail: jnusbaum@ascensionhealth.org

Catherine McAuley Health Services Corporation
(Subsidiary of Mercy Health Services)
5305 E. Huron River Dr., P.O. Box 992
Ann Arbor, MI 48106
Tel: 734-712-3791; Fax: 734-712-5459
Health Care Center, Ancillary Care Systems: (Primary Care Physician Practices)
Staff 237
Patients assisted annually 191,924

St. Joseph Mercy Health System
(A Member of Trinity Health)
5305 E. Huron River Dr., Box 992
Ann Arbor, MI 48106
Tel: 734-734-4986; Fax: 734-712-5459
GARRY C. FAJA, Pres. & CEO
Gen. Hospitals 3
Beds 763
Staff 5,010
Annually Assisted 1,288,248

St. Joseph Mercy Hospital
5301 E. Huron River Dr., P.O. Box 995
Ann Arbor, MI 48106
Tel: 734-712-3791; Fax: 734-712-5459
Mr. GARRY C. FAJA, CEO
Sr. FRANCES GERHARD, R.S.M., Senior Advisor, Mission Services
Chaplains:
Revs.:
TIMOTHY DOMBROWSKI
WILLIAM LANPHEAR, O.S.F.S.
Gen. Hospitals 1
Beds 472
Total Staff 3,398
Patients assisted annually 586,193

Battle Creek
Diocese of Kalamazoo

Battle Creek Health System
300 North Ave.
Battle Creek, MI 49016
Tel: 616-966-8000; Fax: 616-966-8010
Div. of Mercy Health Services
Mr. PATRICK R. GARRETT, Pres. & CEO
Bed Capacity 490
Patients assisted annually 145, 289

Cadillac
Diocese of Gaylord

Mercy Hospital
Mercy Health Services North, Division of Sisters of Mercy Health Corp., Sisters of Mercy Detroit Prov.
400 Hobart St.
Cadillac, MI 49601
Tel: 231-779-7200
Mr. JACK HARRIFF, CEO
Bed Capacity 174
Patients assisted annually 63,797

Clinton Township
Archdiocese of Detroit

Mercy Mount Clemens Corporation
(Acting under the assumed name of St. Joseph's Mercy of Macomb or St. Joseph's Mercy Hospitals and Health Services). A subsidiary of Trinity Health-Michigan.
15855 Nineteen Mile Rd.
Clinton Township, MI 48038
Tel: 810-263-2300; Fax: 810-263-2614
Provides acute care hospital services, home health

care services, outpatient medical center services, hospice care services, long term service and fund-raising services.
JACK WEINER, Pres. & C.E.O.
DEBORA MURRAY, Dir., Spiritual Care Svcs.
Bed Capacity 512 acute care
St. Joseph's Mercy - West
15855 Nineteen Mile Rd.
Clinton Township, MI 48038
Tel: 810-263-2300; 263-2330; Fax: 810-263-2614
St. Joseph's Mercy - East
215 North Ave.
Mt. Clemens, MI 48043
Tel: 810-466-9300
St. Joseph's Mercy - North
80650 Van Dyke
Romeo, MI 48065
Tel: 810-752-3551
Additional divisional operations:
St. Joseph's HomeCare
St. Joseph's Medical Centers
St. Joseph's Mercy Foundation
St. Joseph's Mercy Healthier Image

Detroit
Archdiocese of Detroit

Mercy-Family Practice Center, St. Joseph Center, Chandler Center, Mercy-Nurse Managed Center, Gratiot Center.

St. John Hospital and Medical Center
(Subsidiary of St. John Health System)
22101 Moross Rd.
Detroit, MI 48236
Tel: 313-343-4000
ANTHONY R. TERSIGNI, Ed.D., FACHE, Pres. & CEO
Sr. SUZANNE ZIESKE, S.S.J., Vice Pres. Sponsorship
Sisters of Saint Joseph (Nazareth, Michigan) 12
Bed Capacity 607
Patients assisted annually 154,939
Outpatients 66,007
Affiliates:
Eastwood Community Clinics
Affilated Health Services, Inc.
St. John Senior Community
St. John Northeast Community Hospital
4777 E. Outer Dr.
Detroiy, MI 48234
St. John Oakland Hospital
St. John River District Hospital

Dowagiac
Diocese of Kalamazoo

Lee Memorial Hospital
420 W. High St.
Dowagiac, MI 49047
Tel: 616-782-8681; Fax: 616-782-7611
Mr. FRITZ FAHRENBACHER, CEO
Bed Capacity 74
Patients assisted annually 41,000

Escanaba
Diocese of Marquette

O.S.F. St. Francis Hospital
Escanaba, MI 49829
Tel: 906-786-3311; Fax: 906-786-4004
O.S.F. Healthcare System.
Mr. ROGER BURGESS, Admin.
Sisters 3
Patients assisted annually 80,043
Beds 110

Flint
Diocese of Lansing

Center for Gerontology
An affiliate of Genesys Health System.
3919 Beecher Rd.
Flint, MI 48532
Tel: 810-762-4550; Fax: 810-762-4576
E-mail: ssstevens@genesys.org
Provides adult day care, care management programs, and educational training.
Patients assisted annually 540
Total Staff 33

Genesys Ambulatory Health Services, Inc.
An affiliate of Genesys Health System.
3935 Beecher Rd.
Flint, MI 48532
Tel: 810-762-4340; Fax: 810-762-4283
E-mail: dcaudle@genesys.org
Provides private duty home care services and manages shared services. Also provides outpatient psychiatric services.
Annually Assisted 6,915
Total Staff 419

Genesys Home Health & Hospice
An affiliate of Genesys Health System.
3933 Beecher Rd.
Flint, MI 48532
Tel: 810-762-4600; Fax: 810-762-0027
Provides professional home care and rehabilitation services.

Goodrich
Diocese of Lansing

Genesys Hospice
(Affiliate of Genesys Health System)
7280 S. State Rd.
Goodrich, MI 48438
Tel: 810-636-5000; Fax: 810-636-5019
E-mail: lmccombs@coenesys.org
LAVERNE MCCOMBS, Admin. & Contact Person
Provides in-home and residential hospice care. Inpatient hospice care for symptom management and respite care.
Beds 30
Patients assisted annually 267 (Care Center)
Patients assisted annually 395 (Home Program)
Total Staff 65

Grand Blanc
Diocese of Lansing

Genesys Health System
One Genesys Pkwy.
Grand Blanc, MI 48439
Tel: 810-606-6600; Fax: 810-606-6605
E-mail: atucker@genesys.org
Mr. ELLIOT JOSEPH, Pres. & CEO
Sr. ELIZABETH GRANGER, S.S.J., Vice Pres., Mission Effectiveness

Genesys Regional Medical Center
An affiliate of Genesys Health System.
One Genesys Pkwy.
Grand Blanc, MI 48439
Tel: 810-606-6600; Fax: 810-606-6605
E-mail: atucker@genesys.org
ELLIOT JOSEPH, Pres. & CEO
Beds 379
Annually Assisted 343,619
Total Staff 2,944

Grand Rapids
Diocese of Grand Rapids

St. Mary's Health Services
200 Jefferson, S.E.
Grand Rapids, MI 49503
Tel: 616-752-6090
Religious Sisters of Mercy (Detroit Regional Community)
PHILIP MCCORKLE, Pres. & CEO
Rev. AYUB NASAR
Beds 330
Patients assisted annually 189,222
Mercy Central School of Nursing
Affiliation with U of D Mercy, Detroit.

Grayling
Diocese of Gaylord

Mercy Hospital
Mercy Health Services North, Division of Sisters of Mercy Health Corp., Sisters of Mercy Detroit Prov.
1100 E. Michigan Ave.
Grayling, MI 49738
Tel: 989-348-5461; Fax: 989-348-0479
STEPHANIE J. RIEMER-MATUZAK, CEO
Bed Capacity 130
Patients assisted annually 96,515

Grosse Pointe
Archdiocese of Detroit

**Bon Secours Cottage Health Services*
468 Cadieux Rd.
Grosse Pointe, MI 48230
Tel: 313-343-1900

Bon Secours Hospital
468 Cadieux Rd.
Grosse Pointe, MI 48230
Tel: 313-343-1000
RICHARD VAN LITH, CEO
DAVID G. ZILLI, Chief Finance Officer
Sr. ANNE LUTZ, C.B.S., V.P. Mission Effectiveness
MARY ALICE PURCELL, Dir. of Pastoral Care
Sisters of Bon Secours 3
Sisters 1
Registered Nurses 505
Practical Nurses 65
Bed Capacity 290
Bassinets 28
Patients assisted annually 145,000

**Bon Secours of Michigan Health Care System, Inc.*
Bon Secours of Michigan Foundation
MICHAEL SERILLA, Vice Pres. Operation

Howell
Diocese of Lansing

McPherson Hospital
(A unit of St. Joseph Mercy Health System)
620 Bryon Rd.
Howell, MI 48843-1093
Tel: 517-545-6000; Fax: 517-545-6192
PATRICIA CLAFFEY, R.N., Exec. Dir.
Beds 136
Gen. Hospitals 1
Patients assisted annually 290,768
Total Staff 478

Kalamazoo
Diocese of Kalamazoo

Borgess Medical Center
1521 Gull Rd.
Kalamazoo, MI 49048-1640
Tel: 616-226-7000; Fax: 616-226-7396
E-mail: rstasik@borgess.com
Mr. RANDALL STASIK, Pres. & CEO
Rev. ROBERT D. DENTZMAN, O.F.M., Chap.
936 Lake St.
Kalamazoo, MI 49001
Sisters of St. Joseph 4
Bed Capacity 424
Patients assisted annually 415,039

Livonia
Archdiocese of Detroit

Marian Village Corporation
36475 Five Mile Rd.
Livonia, MI 48154
Tel: 734-665-4800, Ext. 2301
Sr. MARY RENETTA RUMPZ, C.S.S.F., Pres. & C.E.O.
Marybrook Manor (Assisted Living)
36975 W. Five Mile Rd.
Livonia, MI 48154
Tel: 734-464-9667; Fax: 734-464-4846
Sr. ELIZABETH ANN MARIE SCHILLING, C.S.S.F.
Marywood Nursing Care Center
36975 W. Five Mile Rd.
Livonia, MI 48154
Tel: 734-464-0600; Fax: 734-464-4846

St. Mary Hospital
36475 W. Five Mile Rd.
Livonia, MI 48154
Tel: 734-655-4800; Fax: 734-655-1620
Sr. MARY RENETTA, C.S.S.F., Pres.
Revs.:
LOUIS TUFFOUR
CELEDONIO MELICOR
Sisters 16
Bed Capacity 304
Patients assisted annually 144,529
RN's 358
LPN's 19
Congregation of the Sisters of St. Felix Felician Sisters
36800 Schoolcraft
Livonia, MI 48150

Muskegon
Diocese of Grand Rapids

Mercy Hospital
1500 E. Sherman Blvd., P.O. Box 358
Muskegon, MI 49443
Tel: 231-739-9341; Fax: 231-733-0957
Sisters of Mercy (Detroit Regional Community)
ROGER SPOELMAN, Pres. & CEO
LYNNE GORDON, Dir. Pastoral Care
Sisters 2
Beds 322
Patients assisted annually 208,152

Pontiac
Archdiocese of Detroit

St. Joseph Mercy - Oakland
(Div. of Trinity Health-Michigan)
900 Woodward Ave.
Pontiac, MI 48341-2985
Tel: 248-858-3000
Sponsored Work of the Sisters of Mercy Regional Community of Detroit.
A community healthcare system comprised of: Mercy Bellbrook Living Center, Rochester Hills; Alexander Living Center, Royal Oak; Orchard Hills

Living Center, Pontiac; Amicare, West Bloomfield; Mercy Cranbrook Hospice, West Bloomfield; Seven Clinics & St. Joseph Mercy Hospital, Pontiac, MI.
THOMAS L. FEURIG, Pres. & CEO
RICHARD L. BROCHU, B.A., Th.M., Dir. Mission/ Values & Ethics
Chaplains:
Revs.:
JOSEPH SZEWCZYK
DONALD WORTHY
JAMES VON DREHLE
FREDERICK B. MOORE
Sr. DIANE RONDEAU, R.S.M.

Port Huron
Archdiocese of Detroit

Mercy Hospital of Port Huron
(Div. of Trinity Health-Michigan)
2601 Electric
Port Huron, MI 48060-6518
Tel: 810-985-1500; Fax: 810-985-1508
MARY R. TRIMMER, Pres. & CEO
Chaplains:
Rev. C. PAUL HIGDON
Sr. MARY MERCITA LOGAN, R.S.M.
Sr. HELEN RUHL, R.S.M.
Bed Capacity 119
Patients assisted annually 26,409

Saginaw
Diocese of Saginaw

St. Mary's Medical Center of Saginaw, Inc.
800 S. Washington
Saginaw, MI 48601-2594
Daughters of Charity of St. Vincent de Paul, East Central Province, Evansville, IN
FREDERIC L. FRAIZER, Pres. & CEO
Sr. DINAH WHITE, D.C., Vice Pres. Mission Svcs.
Chaplains:
Revs.:
JAMES MARTIN
TIMOTHY HASTINGS
Sr. ADELAIDE CURTIS, D.C., Patient Rep.
DELMAR SMOLINSKI
WILLIAM RABIOR
DIANE SMILEY
Sisters 3
Beds 268
Patients assisted annually 262,330
Field Neurosciences Institute
830 S. Jefferson Ave.
Saginaw, MI 48601
FREDERIC L. FRAIZER, Chm.

Saline
Diocese of Lansing

Saline Community Hospital
(A unit of St. Joseph Mercy Health System)
400 W. Russell
Saline, MI 48176
Tel: 734-429-1600; Fax: 734-429-4662
GARRY FAJA, CEO
Gen. Hospitals 1
Beds 82
Patients assisted annually 167,680
Total Staff 291

Southfield
Archdiocese of Detroit

Providence Hospital
(A unit of Ascension Health/St. John Health System)
16001 W. Nine Mile Rd., P.O. Box 2043
Southfield, MI 48037
Tel: 248-424-3000; Fax: 248-424-3035
Mr. ROBERT CASALOU, Pres.
Sr. CATHERINE KELLY, D.C., Vice Pres., Mission/ Ethics Services
Chaplains:
Revs.:
ROBERT F. GARDELLA, O.S.A., Dir. Pastoral Care
JOHN GAGALA
FELIX ALSOLA
Mrs. RITA MCEACHEN-NEAL
Daughters of Charity of St. Vincent de Paul 4
Bed Capacity 459
Bassinets 65
Lay Staff 3,160
Patients assisted annually 809,721
Medical and Surgical Residences.

Tawas City
Diocese of Gaylord

St. Joseph Health System
200 Hemlock, M-55
Tawas City, MI 48764-0659
Tel: 989-362-3411; 362-4611; Fax: 989-362-7277
Mr. PATRICK J. MURTHA, Pres. & CEO
Sr. MARGOT EDER, S.S.J., Chap.
Sr. PATRICIA MULLEN, S.S.J., Vice Pres. Sponsorship
Sisters of St. Joseph (Nazareth, MI) 2
Bed Capacity 49
Patients assisted annually 209,053

MINNESOTA

Albany
Diocese of St. Cloud

Albany Area Hospital
300 Third Ave.
Albany, MN 56307
Tel: 320-845-2121; Fax: 320-845-4707
BEN KOPPELMAN, Admin.
Chaplains:
DEBORAH ROBINSON
Sisters of St. Francis 2
Beds 17
Patients assisted annually 10,775

Baudette
Diocese of Crookston

Lakewood Health Center
600 South Main
Baudette, MN 56623
Tel: 218-634-2120; Fax: 218-634-1307
SHARRAY PALM, Pres. & CEO
Sisters 2
Bed Capacity: Acute 15
Long term care 52
Staff 145
Patients assisted annually 15,984
Affiliate of Catholic Health Initiatives.
Lakewood Care Center
410 Third Ave. S.E.
Baudette, MN 56623
Tel: 218-634-1588; Fax: 218-634-1589
Sisters 1
Beds 52
Staff 52
Residents assisted annually 118
Affiliate of Catholic Health Initiatives.

Brainerd
Diocese of Duluth

St. Joseph's Medical Center
523 N. Third St.
Brainerd, MN 56401
Tel: 218-829-2861; Fax: 218-828-3103
E-mail: care@stjosephsmedicalctr.com
Web Site: www.stjosephsmedicalctr.com
Sr. JANI WIEBOLT, V.P. Operations
VERN BROUGHTON, Dir. Spiritual Care
Nurses 247
Patients assisted annually 15,048
Beds 162

Breckenridge
Diocese of St. Cloud

St. Francis Medical Center
415 Oak St.
Breckenridge, MN 56520
Tel: 218-643-3000; Fax: 218-643-7502
E-mail: nancywhitney@chi-midwest.org
DAVID NELSON, Pres.
Sr. MARY ROGER ANDERT, Vice Pres. Mission
Rev. ANTHONY KROLL, Chap.
Sisters 3
Beds 47
Patients assisted annually 21,115

Detroit Lakes
Diocese of Crookston

**St. Mary's Regional Health Center*
(Sub. of Benedictine Health System)
1027 Washington Ave.
Detroit Lakes, MN 56501
Tel: 218-847-5611; Fax: 218-847-7674
THOMAS R. THOMPSON, CEO
Chaplains:
TIM COOK
Sr. LENORE PASCHKE, O.S.B.
St. Mary's EMS (Sub. of St. Mary's Regional Health Center)
1240 Washington Ave., P.O. Box 1410
Detroit Lakes, MN 56502
Tel: 218-847-1631; Fax: 218-847-0673
THOMAS R. THOMPSON, CEO
Beds: Acute 87
Long Term Care 100
Nursing Home Residents 100
Patients assisted annually 15,967

Duluth
Diocese of Duluth

St. Mary's Medical Center
407 E. Third St.
Duluth, MN 55805
Tel: 218-786-4000; Fax: 218-786-4383
E-mail: shofer@smdc.org
Web Site: www.smdc.org
Sr. KATHLEEN HOFER, O.S.B., Pres.
JOHN GIBBS, M.Div., Dir. of Chaplaincy Svcs.
Sisters 5
Nurses 891
Patients assisted annually 284,087
Beds 287
Bassinets 43

Farmington
Archdiocese of St. Paul and Minneapolis

Trinity Hospital
3410 - 213th St., West
Farmington, MN 55024
Tel: 651-460-1169
DAVID GRUNDSTROM, Pres. & CEO

Graceville
Diocese of New Ulm

Graceville Health Center dba Holy Trinity Hospital and Grace Home
115 W. 2nd St.
Graceville, MN 56240-0157
Tel: 320-748-7223; Fax: 320-748-7225
E-mail: gracehc@info-link.net
Hospital:
Beds 22
Inpatients 289
Outpatients 6,708
Clinic Patients 6,255
Staff 49
Home Health Visits 1,882
Patients assisted annually 13,425

Hastings
Archdiocese of St. Paul and Minneapolis

Regina Medical Center
1175 Nininger Rd.
Hastings, MN 55033
Tel: 651-480-4100; Fax: 651-480-4212
Web Site: www.reginamedical.com
STEWART W. LAIRD, Admin.
Rev. JAMES J. DUNNE, S.S.C., Chap.
A part of Regina Healthcare
Bed capacity 57
Patients assisted annually 27,330
Other Sister Personnel 1
Personnel 610

Ivanhoe
Diocese of New Ulm

Divine Providence Health Center
312 E. George St., P.O. Box 136
Ivanhoe, MN 56142-0136
Tel: 507-694-1414; Fax: 507-694-1191
Schoenstatt Sisters of Mary (Waukesha, WI)
PATRICK BRANCO, Admin.
Rev. MARION G. CASEY, Chap.
Sisters 4
Aged Workers & Other Nurses 134
Aged Residents 47
Bed Capacity 18
Patients assisted annually 194

Little Falls
Diocese of St. Cloud

St. Gabriel's Hospital
815 S.E. Second St.
Little Falls, MN 56345
Tel: 320-632-5441; Fax: 320-632-1190
MARY B. BOBERTZ, Co-Interim Pres. & CEO
LARRY NOVAKOSKE, Co-Interim Pres. & CEO
BEA BRITZ, Chap.
Sisters 1
Beds 49
Bassinets 10
Patients assisted annually 30,335

New Prague
Archdiocese of St. Paul and Minneapolis

Queen of Peace Hospital
302 Second St., N.E.
New Prague, MN 56071
Tel: 612-758-4431; Fax: 612-758-5009
E-mail: sjean@qofp.org

Web Site: www.np.k12.mn.us/[]qofp.htm
Sr. JEAN JUENEMANN, O.S.B., Admin.
Mr. LOY J. JEFFREY, Dir. Pastoral Care, Chap.
ANN SCHOENBAUER, Chap.
Sisters 3
Bed Capacity 56
Bassinets 6
RNs 68
LPNs 14
Other Personnel 185
Patients assisted annually 34,404

Park Rapids
Diocese of Crookston

St. Joseph Area Health Services
600 Pleasant Ave.
Park Rapids, MN 56470
Tel: 218-732-3311; Fax: 218-732-1368
Mr. PETER JACOBSON, Pres. & CEO
Sisters 3
Bed Capacity 50
Patients assisted annually 29,633
Affiliate of Catholic Health Initiatives.

Rochester
Diocese of Winona

**Saint Mary's Hospital*
Rochester, MN 55902-1970
Tel: 507-255-5123; Fax: 507-255-3125
JOHN PANICEK, Admin.
Revs.:
JAMES H. KUNZ Tel: 507-285-5123
JAMES F. BURYSKA Tel: 507-285-5123
Sisters of the Third Order Regular of St. Francis of the Congregation of Our Lady of Lourdes 32
Bed Capacity 1,157
Patients assisted annually 48,303

Shakopee
Archdiocese of St. Paul and Minneapolis

St. Francis Regional Medical Center
1455 St. Francis Ave.
Shakopee, MN 55379-3380
Tel: 612-403-3000; Fax: 612-403-3820
Subsidiary of Benedictine Health System. Benedictine and Allina Sponsorship.
VENETIA KUDRLE, Pres.
Sr. ANTONICE DELURY, O.S.F., Pastoral Care Mgr.
MARY BECKFELD, Chap.
Sisters of St. Francis 1
Nurses 163
Bed Capacity 40
Patients assisted annually 49,000

St. Cloud
Diocese of St. Cloud

St. Cloud Hospital
1406 Sixth Ave. N.
St. Cloud, MN 56303
Tel: 320-251-2700; Fax: 320-255-5711
Web Site: www.stcloudhospital.com
JOHN FROBENIUS, Pres.
BRET REUTER, Dir. Mission and Spiritual Care
Chaplains:
Rev. ROGER BOTZ, O.S.B.
Sr. JOYCE ITEN, O.S.B.
Sr. JOAN FELLING, O.S.B.
ANN BATES
Sisters of St. Benedict 3
Students 36
Beds 395
Bassinets 40
Patients assisted annually 152,786

Wabasha
Diocese of Winona

St. Elizabeth's Hospital of Wabasha, Inc.
1200 Fifth Grant Blvd., W.
Wabasha, MN 55981
Tel: 651-565-4531; Fax: 651-565-2482
Web Site: www.ministryhealth.com
Corporate sponsor: Ministry Health Care, Inc. (Milwaukee, WI); Sponsored by Sisters of the Sorrowful Mother
RONALD E. MOHOREK, Esq. & Contact
Mr. THOMAS CROWLEY, Pres.
Rev. Msgr. JOSEPH R. MCGINNIS
Sisters of the Third Order of St. Francis of the Sorrowful Mother 1
Beds 31
Patients assisted annually 22,900
Staff 140

MISSISSIPPI

Glendora
Diocese of Jackson

Glendora Clinic (Satellite of Tutwiler Clinic)
Gipson & Westbrook Sts.
Glendora, MS 38928
Tel: 662-375-8878
Patients assisted annually 1,306

Jackson
Diocese of Jackson

St. Dominic-Jackson Memorial Hospital
969 Lakeland Dr.
Jackson, MS 39216
Tel: 601-982-0121; Fax: 601-364-6800
E-mail: charbarger@stdom.com
Web Site: www.stdom.com
Sr. MARY KAREN O'KELLY, Prioress
Mr. CLAUDE W. HARBARGER, Pres.
Rev. ROBERT OLIVIER, Res. Chap.
Sisters of St. Dominic of Springfield, IL 10
Beds 571
Patients assisted annually 85,799

Tutwiler
Diocese of Jackson

Tutwiler Clinic, Inc.
205 Alma St., P.O. Box 462
Tutwiler, MS 38963-0462
Tel: 662-345-8334; Fax: 662-345-8336
Sr. ANNE BROOKS, S.N.J.M., D.O., Dir.
Patients assisted annually 7,965

MISSOURI

Blue Springs
Diocese of Kansas City-St. Joseph

St. Mary's Hospital of Blue Springs
201 W. R.D. Mize Rd.
Blue Springs, MO 64014
Tel: 816-228-5900; Fax: 816-655-5408
Sponsored by the Sisters of St. Joseph of Carondelet. Acute care facility, having medical, surgical, obstetrical and pediatric services.
GORDON DOCKING, CEO
Sisters 4
Bed Capacity 129
Patients assisted annually 77,315
Staff 625

Bridgeton
Archdiocese of St. Louis

SSM De Paul Health Center
12303 De Paul Dr.
Bridgeton, MO 63044
Tel: 314-344-6000
Member of SSM Health Care.
ROBERT G. PORTER, Pres.
Chaplains:
Revs.:
LAWRENCE F. ASMA, C.M.
FREDERICK LENCZYCKI, Mgr.
CHARLENE RAITT
ANGIE VORHOLT
JAMES WEIR
Sisters 3
Patients assisted annually 113,337
Staff 1,216
DePaul General Hospital Division
(Operating) Excluding Nursery-Including 14 Bed Acute Rehabilitation Unit 345
(Licensed) Excluding Nursery-Including 14 Bed Acute Rehabilitation Unit 440
St. Anne Division
12303 De Paul Dr.
Bridgeton, MO 63044
Tel: 314-344-6000
Skilled Nursing Facility, Certified for Medicare, for Men and Women.
Operating 30
Licensed 84
St. Vincent Division
12303 De Paul Dr.
Bridgeton, MO 63044
Tel: 314-344-6000
Pre-Adolescent, Adolescent, Adult & Gero Psychiatric Care and Chemical Dependency.
Operating 98
Licensed 98

Cape Girardeau
Diocese of Springfield-Cape Girardeau

**Saint Francis' Medical Center*
211 St. Francis Dr.
Cape Girardeau, MO 63703-8399
Tel: 573-331-5128
Owned and operated by a lay board with Diocesan sponsorship.
Mr. STEVEN C. BJELICH, FACHE, Pres. & CEO
Chapel St. Francis
Sisters 2
Bed Capacity 264
Inpatients 7,781
Outpatients 113,534
Rev. JOHN CANTORE, C.M., Chap.
St. Francis Medical Center
211 St. Francis Dr.
Cape Girardeau, MO 63703
St. Francis Foundation
211 St. Francis Dr.
Cape Girardeau, MO 63703
St. Francis Hospital of Franciscan Sisters
211 St. Francis Dr.
Cape Girardeau, MO 63703

Creve Coeur
Archdiocese of St. Louis

St. John's Mercy Medical Center
615 S. New Ballas Rd.
Creve Coeur, MO 63141
Tel: 314-569-6000; Fax: 314-569-6910
Conducted by the Religious Sisters of Mercy of the Americas-St. Louis Region
(See Branch Unit under Washington, MO)
Mr. MARK F. WEBER, Pres. & CEO
Chaplains:
Revs.:
DAVID D. SULLIVAN
LOWRIE J. DALY, S.J.
PHILIP G. KRAHMAN
Deacon KEN POTZMAN
Sisters 25
Other Nurses 984
Bed Capacity 892
Patients assisted annually 482,015
Capacity Includes: Chemical Dependency Unit of 35 beds
Skilled Nursing facility of 120 Beds

Jefferson City
Diocese of Jefferson City

St. Marys Health Center
100 St. Marys Medical Plaza
Jefferson City, MO 65101
Tel: 573-761-7000
MARK R. TAYLOR, Pres.
Chaplains:
Rev. JAMES CARTER, American Baptist Min., APC Certified Chap.
Mrs. MARGE DOYLE, NACC Certified
Rev. ROBERT FIELDS
Mrs. PEGGY VAN GUNDY
Sr. EVELYN MARIE PETERMAN, F.S.M.
Rev. HARVEL SANDERS, Episcopalian
Member of SSM Health Care
Bed Capacity 167
Patients assisted annually 281,999
Clinics 14
Clinic visits 149,012
Home health visits 33,366

Joplin
Diocese of Springfield-Cape Girardeau

St. John's Regional Medical Center; Mercy Lifecare Systems, Inc.
Affiliates of Catholic Health Initiatives.
2727 McClelland Blvd.
Joplin, MO 64804-1694
Tel: 417-781-2727; Fax: 417-625-2910
Sisters of Mercy (Omaha)
Mr. GARY L. ROWE, Pres.
Rev. BENEDICT W. HARTER, Chap.
Sisters 6
Bed Capacity 367
Inpatients 15,003
Outpatients 101,000
Emergency Room Patients 48,000
Mercy Regional Health Foundation, Inc.
2727 McClelland Blvd.
Joplin, MO 64804

Kansas City
Diocese of Kansas City-St. Joseph

Saint Joseph Health Center
1000 Carondelet Dr.
Kansas City, MO 64114
Tel: 816-942-4400; Fax: 816-943-2840
Web Site: www.carondelethealth.org
Sponsored by the Sisters of St. Joseph of Carondelet.
MICHELE SCHAEFER, CEO
TERESA RUDLOFF, Chap.
Sisters 6
Bed Capacity 300
Nurses 246
Total Staff 1,181
Patients assisted annually 153,549
Parent Corporation:
Carondelet Health
P.O. Box 8510
Kansas City, MO 64114
Tel: 816-943-5678; Fax: 816-943-2840
Parent Co. Sponsored by the Sisters of St. Joseph of Carondelet.
GEORGE A. ZARA, Pres. & CEO
Divisions:
Saint Joseph Health Center Foundation
1000 Carondelet Dr.
Kansas City, MO 64114
Tel: 816-942-4400; Fax: 816-943-2786
Sponsored by the Sisters of St. Joseph of Carondelet.
JACK KITCHIN, Chm.
GEORGE A. ZARA, Pres. & CEO
Carondelet Home Care Services Inc.
11050 Roe Ave., Ste. 120
Overland Park, KS 66211
Tel: 816-943-4700; Fax: 913-345-9129
KAREN STEFFEN, Admin.
Home health agency affiliated with Carondelet Health.

Kirkwood
Archdiocese of St. Louis

SSM St. Joseph Hospital of Kirkwood
525 Couch Ave.
Kirkwood, MO 63122
Tel: 314-966-1601; Fax: 314-966-1681
Member of SSM Health Care.
CARLA S. BAUM, Pres.
Revs.:
MARK L. FULLER, Supr. & Chap.
JAMES A. KRINGS, Dir. Mission Svcs.
Bed Capacity 269
Sisters 2
Nurses 300
Patients assisted annually 50,000

Lake St. Louis
Archdiocese of St. Louis

SSM St. Joseph Hospital West
100 Medical Plaza
Lake St. Louis, MO 63367
Tel: 314-625-5200; Fax: 314-625-5314
Member of SSM Health Care.
KEVIN F. KAST, Pres.
Mr. DAVID FITZGERALD, Dir. Pastoral Care
Bed Capacity 97
Patients assisted annually 48,190
Staff 427

Maryville
Diocese of Kansas City-St. Joseph

St. Francis Hospital & Health Services
2016 S. Main
Maryville, MO 64468
Tel: 660-562-2600; Fax: 660-562-7911
A member of the SSM Health Care. Sponsored by Franciscan Sisters of Mary, St. Louis, MO. Acute care facility.
MICHAEL BAUMGARTNER, Pres.
Priests of the deanery serve as chaplains.
Sisters 1
Bed Capacity 90
Total Staff 360
Patients assisted annually 32,500

Mountain View
Diocese of Springfield-Cape Girardeau

St. Francis Hospital
P.O. Box 82
Mountain View, MO 65548
Tel: 417-934-2246; Fax: 417-934-6024
Daughters of St. Francis of Assisi
GARY W. JORDAN, Pres.
Sisters 6
Bed Capacity 42
Inpatients 642
Outpatients 20,148
The Sister Cornelia Blasko Foundation, Inc.
100 W. Hwy. 60
Mountain View, MO 65548
Tel: 417-934-2246

Springfield
Diocese of Springfield-Cape Girardeau

St. John's Regional Health Center
1235 E. Cherokee
Springfield, MO 65804
Tel: 417-885-2000; Fax: 417-888-8730
Member of St. John's Health System, Inc.
Sisters of Mercy Health System (St. Louis)
Mr. JAY W. ECKERSLEY, Pres. & CEO
Rev. ANTHONY SHIDLER, O.S.B., Chap.
Sisters 9
Bed Capacity 866
Inpatients 28,419
Outpatients 238,853

St. Charles
Archdiocese of St. Louis

SSM St. Joseph Health Center
300 First Capitol Dr.
St. Charles, MO 63301
Tel: 314-947-5000; Fax: 314-947-5090
Member of SSM Health Care.
KEVIN F. KAST, Pres.
Mr. DAVID FITZGERALD, Dir. Pastoral Care
Rev. RAY HAMPE
Sisters 3
Bed Capacity 316
Patients assisted annually 87,988
Staff 1,288

St. Louis
Archdiocese of St. Louis

Alexian Brothers Hospital
3933 S. Broadway
St. Louis, MO 63118
Tel: 314-865-3333; Fax: 314-865-7938
Legal Title: *Alexian Brothers Hospital*
Congregation of The Institute of the Sisters of Mercy of the Americas, Regional Community of St. Louis
DAVID SEIFERT, Pres.
Bed Capacity 203
Patients assisted annually 60,446
Total Staff 717

St. Anthony's Medical Center
10010 Kennerly Rd.
St. Louis, MO 63128
Tel: 314-525-1000; Fax: 314-525-4485
Web Site: www.stanthonymedcenter.com
RITA S. MCSHEA, Dir. Pastoral Care Dept.
Rev. J. ANTHONY MEIS, Chap.
Beds 794
Patients assisted annually 189,579
Staff 4,011

SSM St. Mary's Health Center
6420 Clayton Rd.
St. Louis, MO 63117
Tel: 314-768-8000; Fax: 314-768-8011
Member of SSM Health Care
KENNETH W. LUKHARD, Pres.
Rev. JACK HACKEM, Chap.
Franciscan Sisters of Mary 5
Bed Capacity 622
Patients assisted annually 135,482
Total Staff 1,903

Washington
Archdiocese of St. Louis

St. John's Mercy Hospital
200 Madison Ave.
Washington, MO 63090
Tel: 314-239-8000; Fax: 314-569-6733
MICHAEL ZILM, Admin.
Sr. LOUISE EGGEN, O.S.B., Mgr.
Chaplains:
Rev. TIMOTHY J. TOOHEY
Sr. MICHAELANNE ESTOUP, R.S.M.
Rev. TOM HALLER, (Protestant)
Beds 185
Total Assisted 1,075
Staff 775
(See Listing Under Creve Coeur, MO)

MONTANA

Billings
Diocese of Great Falls - Billings

St. Vincent Healthcare
1233 N. 30th St., P.O. Box 35200
Billings, MT 59107-5200
Tel: 406-657-7000; Fax: 406-237-3078
E-mail: 11arson@svhhc.org
Web Site: www.svhhc.org
Sisters of Charity of Leavenworth, Kansas
Mr. PATRICK M. HERMANSON, Pres.
Pastoral Care:
LUKE LARSON, Dir.
Revs.:
MARTIN FISHER
ANTHONY J. OZIMEK, O.S.B.
ROBERT H. KOERNER
Sisters 6
Beds 314
Patients assisted annually 63,629

Butte
Diocese of Helena

St. James Healthcare, Sisters of Charity of Leavenworth Healthcare Corporation
400 S. Clark St.
Butte, MT 59701
Tel: 406-723-2500; Fax: 406-723-2443
Web Site: www.sj-mt.org
Mailing Address:
P.O. Box 3300
Butte, MT 59702
ROBERT ROGERS, Admin.
Pastoral Care:
Sr. MARY AGNES HOGAN, S.C.L., Dir.
Sr. JOY DUFF, S.C.L.
Rev. GREGORY BURKE, Chap.
Bed Capacity 168
Sisters of Charity of Leavenworth 6
Lay Staff 535
Patients assisted annually 47,314

Great Falls
Diocese of Great Falls - Billings

Benefis Health Care
500-15th Ave. S., P.O. Box 5013
Great Falls, MT 59403
Tel: 406-455-5000; Fax: 406-455-4587
E-mail: benefis@benefis.org
Web Site: www.benefis.org
Sisters of Providence
Rev. JAMES E. BIRKMAIER, Chap.
LLOYD V. SMITH, FACHE-Pres. & CEO
Sisters 2
Student Nurses 60
Patients assisted annually 94,000

Miles City
Diocese of Great Falls - Billings

Holy Rosary Healthcare
2600 Wilson St.
Miles City, MT 59301
Tel: 406-233-2600; Fax: 406-233-2611
Sponsored by Sisters of Charity of Leavenworth.
Mr. JAMES RISER, Senior Exec. Officer
Sisters 1
Beds: Acute Care 44
Extended Care 107
Patients assisted annually 16,000
Home Care 2,400

Missoula
Diocese of Helena

St. Patrick Hospital and Health Sciences Center, Sisters of Providence of Montana Corporation
500 W. Broadway
Missoula, MT 59802
Tel: 406-543-7271; Fax: 406-329-5693
E-mail: white@saintpatrick.org
Web Site: www.saintpatrick.org
Mailing Address:
P.O. Box 4587
Missoula, MT 59806
Mr. LAWRENCE L. WHITE, JR., Pres.
Revs.:
ROGER E. BLANCHETTE, S.J., Chap.
EMMETT KELLY
Pastoral Care:
Sr. MARIE L. CORR, B.V.M.
Sr. ELIZABETH OLSEN, B.V.M.
Sr. CATHERINE PALMATIER, S.P.
Sisters 3
Lay Staff 1,300

Bed Capacity 213
Patients assisted annually 63,900

Polson
Diocese of Helena

St. Joseph Hospital Corporation
#6 Thirteenth Ave. E., P.O. Box 1010
Polson, MT 59860
Tel: 406-883-5377; Fax: 406-883-8488
Web Site: saintjoes.org
JOHN W. GLUECKERT, Admin.
Deacon WES VERT
JOAN CHRISTENSEN, Pastoral Care
Bed Capacity 24
Lay Staff 110
Patients assisted annually 20,827

NEBRASKA

Grand Island
Diocese of Grand Island

Saint Francis Medical Center
2620 W. Faidley Ave., P.O. Box 9804
Grand Island, NE 68802
Tel: 308-384-4600; Fax: 308-389-5589
E-mail: dsanders@sfmc-gi.org
Web Site: www.sfmc-gi.org
Mr. MICHAEL GLOOR, Pres.
Catholic Health Initiatives.
Beds 194
Bassinets 17
Patients assisted annually 105,473
Total Staff 1,058

Kearney
Diocese of Grand Island

Good Samaritan Health Systems dba Good Samaritan Hospital
10 E. 31st St., P.O. Box 1990
Kearney, NE 68848-1990
Tel: 308-865-7100
KEN TOMLON, Pres. & CEO
Sisters 2
Total Staff 1,568
Beds 220
Patients assisted annually 58,000
Richard H. Young Hospital
4600 17th Ave.
Kearney, NE 68847
Tel: 308-865-2000
Beds 80
Patients assisted annually 1,000

Lincoln
Diocese of Lincoln

St. Elizabeth Regional Medical Center
555 S. 70th St.
Lincoln, NE 68510
Tel: 402-489-7181; Fax: 402-486-8973
E-mail: blanik@stez.org
Web Site: www.stez.org
Mr. ROBERT LANIK, Pres.
Rev. PATRICK MURPHY, B.A., Chap.
Priests 2
Sisters 3
Beds 197
Patients assisted annually 175,343
Affiliate of Catholic Health Initiatives.

Nebraska City
Diocese of Lincoln

St. Mary's Hospital
1314 3rd Ave.
Nebraska City, NE 68410
Tel: 402-873-3321; 873-9033
E-mail: dkelly@stez.org
DANIEL J. KELLY, CEO, Admin.
Beds 38
Patients assisted annually 26,546
Affiliate of Catholic Health Initiatives.

Norfolk
Archdiocese of Omaha

Faith Regional Health Services
1500 Koenigstein Ave.
Norfolk, NE 68701
Tel: 402-644-7205; Fax: 402-644-7468
E-mail: proche@frhs.org
Web Site: www.frhs.org
The Missionary Benedictine Sisters
Sr. MARY PAULA LIECK, O.S.B., Pres.
Sr. M. AGNES SALBER, O.S.B., Prioress
PATRICK ROCHE, Contact & Vice Pres. for Mission Effectiveness
Chaplains:
Revs.:
GERALD A. CONNEALY
TIMOTHY J. LANGE
Beds 166
Patients assisted annually 64,052
New Born 854

O'Neill
Archdiocese of Omaha

St. Anthony's Hospital
2nd and Adams St.
O'Neill, NE 68763
Tel: 402-336-2611; Fax: 402-336-2815
RONALD J. CORK, Admin.
JOHN T. PORTER, Pres. & CEO
Beds 29
Bassinets 10
Patients assisted annually 18,513
Attended by St. Patrick Church.

Omaha
Archdiocese of Omaha

Alegent Health - Bergen Mercy Health System
1010 N. 96th St., Ste. 200
Omaha, NE 68114
Tel: 402-343-4430; Fax: 402-343-4337
Web Site: www.alegent.com
Sr. NORITA COONEY, R.S.M., Board Chair
Affiliate of Catholic Health Initiatives.
General Hospitals 3
Nursing Home 1
Total Staff 3,200
Patients assisted annually 193,000

**Archbishop Bergan Mercy Medical Center*
7500 Mercy Rd.
Omaha, NE 68124
Tel: 402-398-6060; Fax: 402-398-6920
RICHARD A. HACHTEN, II, Pres.
MICHAEL MORAN, C.O.D.
Chaplains:
Sr. ELAINE ABELS, R.S.C.J.
KATHY KASHER
SHEILA BURKE
MARY SUE STURGEON
Deacon TOM MURPHY
LORETTA SIEGALE, Dir. Pastoral Care
MARY EILEEN ANDREASEN, Congregational Nurse Min.
MARIAN STANDEVEN, Operations Leader Mission Svcs./Community Affairs
PEGGY O'MALLEY, Coord. Health Ministry Prog.
Sisters 4
Bed Capacity 400
Patients assisted annually 147,728
Affiliate of Catholic Health Initiatives.
Bergan Mercy Foundation, Inc.
RICHARD A. HACHTEN, II, Pres.
MARIAN STANDEVEN, Contact

Boys Town National Research Hospital
555 N. 30 St.
Omaha, NE 68131
Tel: 402-498-6511; Fax: 402-498-6357
Dr. PATRICK BROOKHOUSER, Dir.
Bed Capacity 42
Total Annually Assisted 27,425
Staff 460

Wayne
Archdiocese of Omaha

Providence Medical Center
1200 Providence Rd.
Wayne, NE 68787
Tel: 402-375-3800; Fax: 402-375-7989
E-mail: MThomas@midlands.net
Missionary Benedictine Sisters
MARCILE THOMAS, Admin.
Sr. KEVIN HERMSEN, Asst. Admin.
Sr. MONICA BACKES, Supr.
Sr. GERTRUD MARIE WOLFER, O.S.B., Pastoral Care
Sr. KEVIN HERMSEN, Contact
Beds 34
Patients assisted annually 10,900

West Point
Archdiocese of Omaha

Franciscan Care Services, Inc., dba St. Francis Memorial Hospital
430 N. Monitor St.
West Point, NE 68788-1595
Tel: 402-372-2404; Fax: 402-372-2360
E-mail: fc70656@navix.net
Franciscan Sisters of Christian Charity
RONALD O. BRIGGS, CEO & Contact
Deacon VINCE MALY, Chap.
Sisters 6
Bed Capacity 25
Patients assisted annually 63,030

NEVADA

Henderson
Diocese of Las Vegas

St. Rose Dominican Hospital
102 Lake Mead Dr.
Henderson, NV 89015
Tel: 702-564-2622; Fax: 702-564-4699
E-mail: vdalesan@chw.edu
Sisters of the Third Order of St. Dominic, Congregation of the Most Holy Rosary (Adrian, MI)
Mr. ROD A. DAVIS, Pres. & CEO
Affiliated with the University of Nevada-Las Vegas School of Nursing Affiliated with the University of Nevada-Las Vegas School of Nursing-Paramedic Program-Vo-Tech. & Community College of South Nevada.
Sisters 11
Beds 143
Total Staff 1,222
Patients assisted annually 101,528

Reno
Diocese of Reno

St. Mary's Central Nevada Health Care Corp.
235 W. Sixth St.
Reno, NV 89520-0108
Tel: 775-770-3554; Fax: 775-770-3621
JEFF K. BILLS, Pres.

St. Mary's Foundation
235 W. Sixth St.
Reno, NV 89520-0108
Tel: 775-789-3020; Fax: 775-770-3545
E-mail: stephanie.hauk@saintmarysreno.com
STEPHANIE HAUK, Vice Pres.
Total Staff 7

St. Mary's Health Care Corp., dba St. Mary's Health Network
235 W. Sixth St.
Reno, NV 89520-0108
Tel: 775-770-3004
Web Site: www.saintmarysreno.com
Sisters of St. Dominic, Congregation of the Most Holy Name (Dominican Sisters, San Rafael)
Sr. JEREMY CARMODY, O.P., Congregational Representative
JEFF K. BILLS, Pres. & CEO
BENEDICT DASHER, Chm.

St. Mary's Regional Medical Center
235 W. Sixth St.
Reno, NV 89520-0108
Tel: 775-323-2041; Fax: 775-770-3963
Sisters of the Third Order of St. Dominic, Congregation of the Most Holy Name (San Rafael, CA)
Sr. JEREMY CARMODY, O.P., Congregational Rep.
JEFF K. BILLS, Pres. & CEO, Tel: 775-770-3004
BENEDICT DASHER, Chm.
GINGER AVALA, Vice Pres. & CEO
BOBBIE FLOWERS, M.A., Mgr. Spiritual Care
Revs.:
IVES ANIBAN, Chaplaincy Svcs.
MAXWELL OKOLIE
ALPHONSE VAN GUILDER, O.F.M.Conv.
BILL BARTHOFF, Chaplain
Sr. MARIANNA HARRISON, O.P.
Sr. DIANE CARROLL, O.P.
Sisters 4
Total Staff 1,742
Beds 367
Patients assisted annually 199,234

NEW HAMPSHIRE

Manchester
Diocese of Manchester

Catholic Medical Center of Manchester, NH, Inc.
100 McGregor St.
Manchester, NH 03102
Tel: 603-668-3545; Fax: 603-663-6850
Web Site: www.catholicmedicalcenter.org
ALYSON PITMAN GILES, Pres. & CEO
Sisters 7
Beds 330
Inpatient Admissions 7,558
Outpatient Admissions 72,018

Nashua
Diocese of Manchester

St. Joseph Hospital
172 Kinsley St.
Nashua, NH 03061
Tel: 603-882-3000; Fax: 603-598-3344
E-mail: cdescoteaux@sjh_nh.org
Web Site: www.stjosephhospital.com
PETER B. DAVIS, Pres. & CEO
Sr. CAROL J. DESCOTEAUX, C.S.C., Ph.D., Vice Pres.
Deacon JOHN MARTIN, Staff Chap.
Grey Nuns 1
Beds 208
Total Staff 1,030
Patients assisted annually 2,299
Rivier-St. Joseph School of Nursing
Fax: 603-897-8813

NEW JERSEY

Camden
Diocese of Camden

Our Lady of Lourdes Medical Center, Inc.
(Formerly Our Lady of Lourdes Hospital).
1600 Haddon Ave.
Camden, NJ 08103
Tel: 856-757-3500; Fax: 856-757-3611
Web Site: www.lourdesnet.org
Revs.:
WARREN RECTOR, O.F.M.
ARTHUR T. ANDERSON
Our Lady of Lourdes Associates Foundation, Inc.
1600 Haddon Ave.
Camden, NJ 08103
Tel: 856-757-3301; Fax: 856-757-3745
Lourdes HomeHealth Services, Inc.
900 Haddon Ave., Ste. 316
Collingswood, NJ 08108
Tel: 856-869-0900; Fax: 856-869-0311
Osborn Family Health Center, Inc.
1601 Haddon Ave.
Camden, NJ 08103
Tel: 856-757-3700; Fax: 856-365-7972
Our Lady of Lourdes School of Nursing, Inc.
1565 Vesper Blvd.
Camden, NJ 08103
Tel: 856-757-3730; Fax: 856-757-3393
Our Lady of Lourdes Medical Center, Inc. Auxiliary
1600 Haddon Ave.
Camden, NJ 08103
Tel: 856-757-3301; Fax: 856-757-3745
Our Lady of Lourdes Health Care Services, Inc.
1600 Haddon Ave.
Camden, NJ 08103
Tel: 856-757-3500; Fax: 856-757-3611
Patients assisted annually 205,291
Staff 1,663
Beds 377

Saint Luke's Catholic Medical Services, Inc.
511 State St.
Camden, NJ 08102
Tel: 856-365-4642; Fax: 856-365-0539
LESLY A. D'AMBOLA, M.D., Medical Dir.
Patients assisted annually 7,000
Staff 8

Denville
Diocese of Paterson

Saint Clare's Community Care, Inc. dba Saint Clare's Health Services
c/o 25 Pocono Rd.
Denville, NJ 07834
Tel: 973-989-3124; Fax: 973-989-3195
E-mail: jmccaffrey@stclares.org
Web Site: www.stclares.org
Mr. JACK E. COOK, Chm.
Ms. KATHRYN J. MCDONAEH, Pres. & CEO
Affiliates:
St. Clare's Hospital, Inc.
St. Clare's Foundation, Inc.
St. Francis Life Care Corporation
St. Francis Assisted Living Corporation
St. Clare's Management Services, Inc.
St. Francis Health Resort, Inc.
St. Clare's Home Care, Inc.
Wallkill Valley Health Care Foundation, Inc.
Visiting Nurse Association of Sussex County
Sisters of the Sorrowful Mother Housing Corporation I, Inc.
Sisters of the Sorrowful Mother Housing Corporation II, Inc.

Saint Clare's Hospital, Inc.
25 Pocono Rd.
Denville, NJ 07834
Tel: 973-625-6000; Fax: 973-625-0416
E-mail: jmccaffrey@saintclares.org
Web Site: www.saintclares.org
(Parent Corp.: St. Clare's Health Services)
Mr. JACK E. COOK, Chm.
Ms. KATHRYN MCDONAGH, Pres. & CEO
Campuses:
Saint Clare's Hospital-Denville
Tel: 973-625-6000; Fax: 973-625-0416
Saint Clare's Hospital-Boonton Township
Tel: 973-316-1808; Fax: 973-316-1839
Saint Clare's Hospital-Sussex
Tel: 973-702-2770; Fax: 973-702-2893
Saint Clare's Hospital-Dover
Tel: 973-989-3000; Fax: 973-989-3290
Pastoral Care Department:
Rev. CHARLES LOVATO
Sr. DIANE DUPREY, S.S.M.
Sr. MARY ELLEN JOYCE, S.S.M.
Sr. MARY LAETARE NIEBERLE, S.S.M.
Sr. MARY JOAN PHILLIPS, S.S.M.
Patients assisted annually 340,000
Beds 927

Elizabeth
Archdiocese of Newark

Trinitas Hospital
Jersey Street Campus, 925 E. Jersey St.
Elizabeth, NJ 07201
Tel: 908-629-8065; Fax: 908-629-8073
Web Site: www.trinitashospital.com
Sisters of Charity of Saint Elizabeth
DAVID A. FLETCHER, Pres.
Sr. DOROTHY APPRICH, S.S.J., Dir. Mission Effectiveness
Sisters 12
Total Staff 2,483
Bed Capacity 836
Bassinets 16
Patients assisted annually 412,402
Trinitas Hospital
Williamson Street Campus, 225 Williamson St.
Elizabeth, NJ 07207
Trinitas Hospital
New Point Campus, 655 E. Jersey St.
Elizabeth, NJ 07206

**Marillac Corp.*
240 Williamson St.
Elizabeth, NJ 07207
Tel: 908-527-5122; Fax: 908-820-0554
DAVID A. FLETCHER, Pres.

Montclair
Archdiocese of Newark

Montclair Community Hospital
120 Harrison Ave.
Montclair, NJ 07042
Parent Corporation: Cathedral Healthcare System, Inc.

New Brunswick
Diocese of Metuchen

St. Peter's University Hospital
254 Easton Ave., P.O. Box 591
New Brunswick, NJ 08903-0591
Tel: 732-745-8600; Fax: 732-247-9888
E-mail: inforasaintpetersuh.com
Web Site: www.saintpetersuh.com
JOHN E. MATUSKA, Pres. & CEO
Chaplains:
Revs.:
CECILIO E. SIPACO (Philippines)
JAMES DE VRIES, Dir.
RAYNARD SMITH
Sr. BREDA BOYLE, C.S.J.P.
Sr. CLAIRE MACDONALD, O.P.
Sr. JACQUELINE ROTTEVEEL
Sr. BARBARA ORTMANN, O.P.
Beds 420
Bassinets 77
Neonatal Intensive Care Bassinetts 35
Intermediate Care Bassinetts 19
Patients assisted annually 223,473

Newark
Archdiocese of Newark

Cathedral Affiliated Group at Montclair, Inc.
219 Chestnut St.
Newark, NJ 07105-1558
Parent Corporation: Cathedral Healthcare System, Inc.

Cathedral Affiliated Group at Orange, Inc.
219 Chestnut St.
Newark, NJ 07105-1558
Parent Corporation: Cathedral Healthcare System, Inc.

Catholic Community Services (C.C.S.) Mt. Carmel Guild Hospital
1160 Raymond Blvd.
Newark, NJ 07102
Tel: 973-596-4084
Rev. Msgr. DENNIS J. MAHON, Exec. Dir., C.C.S.
RONALD FINCH, Ed.D., Dir. Healthcare
Bed Capacity 20
Staff 32
Patients assisted annually 451

St. James Hospital
155 Jefferson St.
Newark, NJ 07105
Tel: 973-589-1300; Fax: 973-465-2861
E-mail: stjames@cathedralhealthcare.org
CEU CIRNE-NEVES, Admin.
ROBERT E. DEL GUIDICE, Vice Pres. Operations
Chaplains:
Sr. DOLORES CERVI
Rev. KENNETH MARTIN
VITT LENG, M.D., Pres. Medical Staff
Bed Capacity 189
Bassinets 23
Staff 550
Patients assisted annually 44,800
Division of Cathedral Health Services, Inc.

Saint Michael's Medical Center
268 Dr. Martin Luther King. Jr. Blvd.
Newark, NJ 07102-9880
Tel: 973-877-5411; Fax: 973-877-5672
BARBARA J. LOUGHNEY, Admin.
Rev. Msgr. MANUEL CRUZ, Mgr. Pastoral Care
NICHOLAS BARANETSKY, M.D., Pres. Medical Staff
Division of Cathedral Health Services, Inc.
Bed Capacity 337
Sisters 3
Admissions 11,303
Outpatient Visits 32,898
Total Staff 1,529

Orange
Archdiocese of Newark

**Orange Mountain Healthcare, Inc.*
Affiliated with Cathedral Healthcare System, Inc.
188 S. Essex Ave.
Orange, NJ 07050

Saint Mary Life Center, Inc. - Pope John Paul II Pavilion
Skilled nursing facility, comprehensive personal care.
135 S. Center St.
Orange, NJ 07050
Tel: 973-266-3000; Fax: 973-266-3094
DAVID RUMFORD, Admin.
Skilled nursing facility, comprehensive personal care.

**The Hospital Center at Orange*
Affiliated with Cathedral Healthcare System, Inc.
188 S. Essex Ave.
Orange, NJ 07050

Passaic
Diocese of Paterson

St. Mary's Hospital
211 Pennington Ave.
Passaic, NJ 07055
Tel: 973-470-3000
E-mail: petersonp@smh-passaic.org
Web Site: www.smh-passaic.org
PATRICIA PETERSON, Pres. & CEO
Rev. VINCENT LIUZZO, O.F.M.Cap., Dir. Pastoral Care
Sisters of Charity of St. Elizabeth, NJ 10
Bed Capacity 206
Patients assisted annually 113,752
St. Mary's Health Corporation

Paterson
Diocese of Paterson

St. Joseph's Hospital and Medical Center
703 Main St.
Paterson, NJ 07503
Tel: 973-754-2000; Fax: 973-754-3273
Mr. PATRICK R. WARDEL, Pres. & CEO
KATHLEEN SILARD, Vice Pres. & COO
Sr. ANN STANGO, S.C., Vice Pres., Mission
Revs.:
WILLIAM N. CRAMER, Dir. Pastoral Care
JANUSZ RZADGA
MARTIN ROONEY
Sisters of Charity of St. Elizabeth, NJ 40
Bed Capacity 792
Patients assisted annually 315,607

Teaneck
Archdiocese of Newark

Holy Name Hospital
718 Teaneck Rd.
Teaneck, NJ 07666
Tel: 201-833-3000; Fax: 201-833-3230
Sisters of St. Joseph of Peace
MICHAEL MARON, Pres. & CEO
Bed Capacity 361
Bassinets 36
School of Nursing
Sr. CLARE TYNAN C.S.J.P., Senior Vice Pres.
Pastoral Care:
Sr. LOIS JABLONSKI, S.S.J., M.S., Dir.
Chaplains:
Rev. PATERNO GOROSPE
CONSTANCE FORCILLO, R.N.
MARY ELLEN DORAN, M.S.
JANE SELINSKE, Ed.D., M.S.W.
Sisters 12

Trenton
Diocese of Trenton

St. Francis Medical Center
601 Hamilton Ave.
Trenton, NJ 08629
Tel: 609-599-5000; Fax: 609-695-2744
E-mail: johnbilik@chi-east.org
Web Site: www.sfme-healthytimes.com
Affiliate of Catholic Health Initiatives.
Sisters of St. Francis of Philadelphia 12
Bed Capacity 274
Patients assisted annually 139,705
Bassinets 24
Schools for Nurses
Tel: 609-599-5190; Fax: 609-599-5799
JUDITH M. PERSICHILLI, Pres. & C.E.O.
BONNIE ROSS, Dir. School of Nursing
Rev. JOEL F. SZYDLOWSKI, O.F.M., Dir. Pastoral Care
Student Nurses 40

NEW MEXICO

Albuquerque
Archdiocese of Santa Fe

St. Joseph Healthcare Foundation
500 Walter, N.E.
Albuquerque, NM 87102
Tel: 505-727-2709; Fax: 505-727-7034
E-mail: conem@sjhs.org
Affiliate of Catholic Health Initiatives.
Total Staff 4

St. Joseph Healthcare System
Tel: 505-727-2709; Fax: 505-727-7034
E-mail: ConeM@SJHS.ORG
Mailing Address:
P.O. Box 25555
Albuquerque, NM 87125-0555
601 Dr. Martin Luther King Jr. Ave., N.E.
Albuquerque, NM 87120
Tel: 505-727-2804; Fax: 505-727-9467
Affiliate of Catholic Health Initiatives.
ARTHUR T. DUNN, Interim CEO
Sr. MARIE RAPHAEL MORELL, O.P., Dir. Spiritual Care
Priests 1
Chaplains 6
Patients assisted annually 13,806
Beds 529
Total Staff 1,761

St. Joseph Medical Center
Tel: 505-727-2709; Fax: 505-727-7034
E-mail: ConeM@SJHS.ORG
Mailing Address:
P.O. Box 25555
Albuquerque, NM 87125-0555
601 Dr. Martin Luther King Jr. Ave., N.E.
Albuquerque, NM 87102
Tel: 505-727-2804; Fax: 505-727-9467
Affiliate of Catholic Health Initiatives.
ARTHUR T. DUNN
Sr. MARIE RAPHAEL MORELL, O.P., Dir. Spiritual Care
Priests 1
Chaplains 3
Beds 254
Patients assisted annually 8,300
Total Staff 748

St. Joseph Northeast Heights Hospital
Tel: 505-727-2709; Fax: 505-727-7034
E-mail: ConeM@SJHS.ORG
Mailing Address:
P.O. Box 25555
Albuquerque, NM 87125-0555
4701 Montgomery, N.E.
Albuquerque, NM 87109
Tel: 505-727-2804; Fax: 505-727-9467
Affiliate of Catholic Health Initiatives.
TONY STRUTHERS, Admin.
Sr. MARIE RAPHAEL MORELL, O.P., Dir. Spiritual Care
Priests 1
Chaplains 1
Beds 114
Patients assisted annually 3,746
Total Staff 218

St. Joseph Physician Group
7850 Jefferson, N.E., Ste. 100
Albuquerque, NM 87109
Tel: 505-727-2709; Fax: 505-727-7034
E-mail: conem@sjhs.org
Affiliate of Catholic Health Initiatives.
Total Staff 159

St. Joseph Rehabilitation Hospital
Tel: 505-727-2709; Fax: 505-727-7034
E-mail: ConeM@SJHS.ORG
Mailing Address:
P.O. Box 25555
Albuquerque, NM 87125-0555
505 Elm St., N.E.
Albuquerque, NM 87102
Tel: 505-727-2804; Fax: 505-727-9467
Affiliate of Catholic Health Initiatives.
SHERI S. MILONE
Sr. MARIE RAPHAEL MORELL, O.P., Dir. Spiritual Care
Priests 1
Chaplains 1
Beds 62
Patients assisted annually 1,172
Total Staff 234

St. Joseph West Mesa Hospital
Tel: 505-727-2709; Fax: 505-727-7034
E-mail: ConeM@SJHS.ORG
Mailing Address:
P.O. Box 25555
Albuquerque, NM 87125-0555
10501 Golf Course Rd., N.W.
Albuquerque, NM 87114
Tel: 505-727-2804; Fax: 505-727-9467
Affiliate of Catholic Health Initiatives.
TONY STRUTHERS, Admin.
Sr. MARIE RAPHAEL MORELL, O.P., Dir. Spiritual Care
Chaplains & Priests available 2
Beds 99
Patients assisted annually 588
Total Staff 126

NEW YORK

Albany
Diocese of Albany

Mercycare Corporation, St. Peter's Hospital
315 S. Manning Blvd.
Albany, NY 12208
Tel: 518-454-1540
Mr. STEVEN P. BOYLE, Pres. & CEO
Rev. JOHN TALLMAN, Chap.
Bed Capacity 437
Patients assisted annually 193,077
Hospice
Tel: 518-454-1563
Sr. JEAN ROCHE, R.S.M., Contact Person
Hospice of Rensselaer Co.
258 Broadway
Albany, NY 12180
Tel: 518-271-1901
Sr. MARLENE HORRIGAN, C.S.J., Contact Person
Our Lady of Mercy Life Center
2240 Western Ave.
Guilderland, NY 12084
Tel: 518-464-8100
WESLEY I. HALE, Exec. Dir.

St. Peter's Health Care Services
315 S. Manning Blvd.
Albany, NY 12208
Tel: 518-454-1084; Fax: 518-454-1520
E-mail: sboyle@stpetersburghealthcare.org

Amsterdam
Diocese of Albany

St. Mary's Hospital
427 Guy Park Ave.
Amsterdam, NY 12010
Tel: 518-842-1900; Fax: 518-842-0107
E-mail: capobiancop@SMHA.org
Mr. PETER E. CAPOBIANCO, Pres. & CEO
Rev. JOSEPH J. DWORAK, Chap.
Sisters of St. Joseph of Carondelet 14
Bed Capacity 143
Patients assisted annually 191,673

Auburn
Diocese of Rochester

Mercy Health & Rehabilitation Center Nursing Home Co., Inc. (1972)
St. Anthony St.
Auburn, NY 13021
Tel: 315-253-0351; Fax: 315-258-3904
E-mail: mercy@tds.net
Sr. MARY NORBERT STANG, Dir. Pastoral Care
Sr. LINDA ANN PALMISANO, CEO
Sisters of the Third Franciscan Order
Nursing Facility Beds 297

Beacon
Archdiocese of New York

St. Francis Hospital
11 Hastings Dr.
Beacon, NY 12508
Tel: 914-831-3500; Fax: 904-831-8131
LAWRENCE M. WITTE, FACHE
This Facility is a 100 bed facility for the treatment of chemical dependency, and is a division of St. Francis Hospital, North Rd., Poughkeepsie, NY.
Bed Capacity 100
Total annually Assisted 2000
Total Staff 147

Binghamton
Diocese of Syracuse

Our Lady of Lourdes Memorial Hospital
169 Riverside Dr.
Binghamton, NY 13905
Tel: 607-798-5111; Fax: 607-798-7681
Web Site: lourdes.com
Mr. JOHN D. O'NEIL, Pres.
Daughters of Charity of St. Vincent de Paul 9
Beds 277
Patients assisted annually 316,481

Brooklyn
Diocese of Brooklyn

St. Mary's Hospital of Brooklyn
70 Buffalo Ave.
Brooklyn, NY 11213
Tel: 718-221-3000
Rev. Msgr. AUSTIN P. BENNETT, Chm.
Affiliated with Catholic Medical Centers.
Beds 285

Buffalo
Diocese of Buffalo

Catholic Health System, Inc.
Marian Professional Center
515 Abbott Rd., Ste. 508
Buffalo, NY 14220
Tel: 716-828-2750; Fax: 716-828-2703
E-mail: webmaster@WNYCHS.org
DALE S. ST. ARNOLD, Pres. & CEO
Bed Capacity 868
Patients assisted annually 1.4 Million
Total Staff 8,060

McAuley Mercy Corporation
515 Abbott Rd.
Buffalo, NY 14220
Tel: 716-828-2750
Sr. SALLY MALONEY, R.S.M., Chairperson
Sponsored by the Catholic Health System, Inc.

Mercy Hospital
565 Abbott Rd.
Buffalo, NY 14220
Tel: 716-826-7000; Fax: 716-828-2700
E-mail: JPD@whychs.org
Sponsored by the Catholic Health System, Inc.
JOHN P. DAVANZO, Pres. & CEO
MARY BETH FARRUGGIO, Nursing Svcs.
Sisters of Mercy 4
Patients assisted annually 263,744
Outpatients 247,374
Admissions 16,370
Beds 349
Skilled Nursing Beds 74
Bassinets 60
Total Staff 1,883

Sisters Hospital Foundation, Inc.
2130 Main St.
Buffalo, NY 14214
Tel: 716-862-2533; Fax: 716-835-8643
E-mail: jhazzan@wnychs.org

Sisters of Charity Hospital of Buffalo, NY
2157 Main St.
Buffalo, NY 14214
Tel: 716-862-1000; Fax: 716-862-1899
E-mail: mdougherty@wnychs.org
Web Site: http://www.sisters-buffalo.org81
Sponsored by the Catholic Health System, Inc.
Chaplains:
Revs.:
LOUIS S. KLEIN
RICHARD E. ZAJAC
Sr. MARGARET DOUGHERTY, D.C., Dir., Pastoral Care
Sr. ANN PAUL CHENARD, D.C.
Sr. KATHLEEN SIMPSON, D.C.
Rev. ERNEST WILLIAMS
Ms. JUDITH MILLER
Ms. TERESA MAIKISCH
Ms. CAROL WILLE
Daughters of Charity of St. Vincent de Paul 12
Bed Capacity 216
Bassinets 60
Patients assisted annually 604,126
Total Staff 1,860

Cheektowaga
Diocese of Buffalo

McAuley-Seton Home Care
14 Appletree Business Park
Cheektowaga, NY 14227
Tel: 716-685-4870; Fax: 716-651-9613
MARCIA REISSIG, Pres. & CEO
Patients assisted annually 1,500

St. Joseph Hospital
2605 Harlem Rd.
Cheektowaga, NY 14225-4097
Tel: 716-891-2400; Fax: 716-891-2616
Sponsored by the Catholic Health System, Inc.
Franciscan Sisters of St. Joseph
Bed Capacity 208
Patients assisted annually 192,020
Total Staff 743

Elmira
Diocese of Rochester

St. Joseph's Hospital
55 E. Market St.
Elmira, NY 14902
Tel: 607-733-6541; Fax: 607-737-7837
E-mail: srmarie@stjosephs.org
Web Site: www.stjosephs.org
Sisters of St. Joseph
Skilled Nursing Facility.
Sr. MARIE CASTAGNARO, Pres.
Total Staff 1,056
Bed Capacity 224
Skilled Nursing Facility 71
Patients assisted annually 119,462

St. Joseph's Hospital Foundation, Inc.
200 Madison Ave., Ste. 1c
Elmira, NY 14901
Tel: 607-737-7004; Fax: 607-324-8115
E-mail: dsullivan@stjosephs.org
DAVID P. SULLIVAN, Pres.

Hornell
Diocese of Rochester

St. James Mercy Health System
411 Canisteo St.
Hornell, NY 14843
Tel: 607-324-8000; Fax: 607-324-8115
WILLIAM CONNORS, Pres. & CEO
Sr. ANN MILLER, Vice Pres. Mission Svcs.
Sisters of Mercy 2
Sisters of St. Joseph 1
Total Staff 973
Bed Capacity 225
Patients assisted annually 244,930

Jamaica
Diocese of Brooklyn

Catholic Medical Centers of Brooklyn & Queens
88-25 153rd St.
Jamaica, NY 11432
Tel: 718-558-6900; Fax: 718-558-7286
Corporate Staff:
Most Rev. JOSEPH M. SULLIVAN, Chm. Bd., Tel: 718-558-6921
WILLIAM D. MCGUIRE, Pres. & CEO, Tel: 718-558-6921
Ms. KATHLEEN GALVIN, COO, Tel: 718-558-6959
ROBERT NOLAN, Vice Pres. Human Resources, Tel: 718-459-4417
DANIEL J. RINALDI, CFO, Tel: 718-558-6940
KATHRYN ANASTOS, M.D., Vice Pres. Ambulatory Care, Tel: 718-558-5962
ANTHONY FERANTE, Vice Pres. Home Health Care, Tel: 718-459-4600
STEVEN WIRTH, Vice Pres. Mission Svcs., Tel: 718-558-7102
STEPHEN MCCLELLAN, Ph.D., Vice Pres. Public Relations & Marketing, Tel: 718-558-6925
G. MALCOLM MURRAY, Vice Pres. Information Systems, Tel: 718-558-7048
MILDRED A. SHANLEY, LL.D., Sr. Vice Pres., Chief Legal Officer, Tel: 718-558-6939
MARGARET FERNANDEZ, Administrative Asst. to the Pres., Tel: 718-558-6920
Mary Immaculate Hospital Division
152-11 89th Ave.
Jamaica, NY 11432
Tel: 718-558-2000; Fax: 718-558-2524
St. John's Queens Hospital Division
90-02 Queens Blvd.
Elmhurst, NY 11373
Tel: 718-558-1000; Fax: 718-558-1818
St. Joseph's Hospital Division
158-40 79th Ave.
Flushing, NY 11366
Tel: 718-558-6200; Fax: 718-558-6209
St. Mary's Hospital of Brooklyn Affiliate
170 Buffalo Ave.
Brooklyn, NY 11213
Tel: 718-221-3000; Fax: 718-221-3971
Mary Immaculate Hospital Home Health Agency
95-25 Queens Blvd.
Rego Park, NY 11374
Tel: 718-830-4500
CATHERINE BARBERA, Dir., Home Care Agency
St. Mary's Hospital of Brooklyn Home Health Agency
170 Buffalo Ave.
Brooklyn, NY 11213
Tel: 718-221-3844
CATHERINE BARBERA, Dir., Home Care Agency
St. Mary's Hospital of Brooklyn Long Term Home Health Program
170 Buffalo Ave.
Brooklyn, NY 11213
Tel: 718-221-3844
CATHERINE BARBERA, Dir., Home Care Agency
St. Anthony Health Professions & Nursing Institute
175-05 Horace Harding Expwy.
Fresh Meadows, NY 11365
Tel: 718-357-0500, Ext. 104
JOSEPH SKARZYNSKI, M.D., Dir. Allied Health & Pre-Hospital Care
Catholic Medical Center Physician Assistant Program
175-05 Horace Harding Expwy.
Fresh Meadows, NY 11365
Tel: 718-805-7599
JOANN DEASY, M.P.H., PA-C, Dir.
Catholic Medical Center School of Nursing
175-05 Horace Harding Expwy.
Fresh Meadows, NY 11365
Tel: 718-805-5602
GENEVIEVE JENSEN, R.N., M.S., Dir.
Catholic Medical Centers Program of Medical Technology
175-05 Horace Harding Expwy.
Fresh Meadows, NY 11365
Tel: 718-357-0500, Ext. 111
ANN PAULA ZERO, Dir.
Catholic Medical Centers Program of Radiography
175-05 Horace Harding Expwy.
Fresh Meadows, NY 11365
Tel: 718-357-0500, Ext. 112
ALBERT KISH, Dir.
Catholic Medical Centers Emergency Medical Services Institute
175-05 Horace Harding Expwy.
Fresh Meadows, NY 11365
Tel: 718-357-0500, Ext. 181
MICHAEL TRETOLA, Mgr. Allied Health Educ.
Catholic Medical Centers Pathology Assistants Program
152-11 89th Ave.
Jamaica, NY 11432
Tel: 718-558-6731
USHA RUDER, M.D., Dir.
Catholic Medical Centers Catholic Hospital Administration Personnel (CHAP) Program
175-05 Horace Harding Expwy.
Fresh Meadows, NY 11365
Tel: 718-357-0500, Ext. 173
Sr. ANNELLE FITZPATRICK, C.S.J., Ph.D., Dir.
Co-sponsored with St. John's University.

Kenmore
Diocese of Buffalo

Kenmore Mercy Foundation Inc.
2950 Elmwood Ave.
Kenmore, NY 14217
Tel: 716-447-6204; Fax: 716-447-6052
E-mail: swierskikaren@netscape.net

Kenmore Mercy Hospital
2950 Elmwood Ave.
Kenmore, NY 14217
Tel: 716-447-6100; Fax: 716-447-6090
Sponsored by the Catholic Health System, Inc.
PATRICK J. WILES, CEO
Chaplains:
Rev. VINCENT J. FERRARO
DONNA KROPIDLOWSKI, Dir.
Bed Capacity 184
Total Staff 815
Outpatient Visits 162,140
Admissions 6,872

Kingston
Archdiocese of New York

Benedictine Hospital
105 Mary's Ave.
Kingston, NY 12401
Tel: 914-338-2500; Fax: 914-334-3149
Web Site: www.benedictine.org
Sr. MARY FEEHAN, O.S.B., Senior Vice Pres., Mission Effectiveness
Sr. MARY DOROTHY HUGGARD, O.S.B., Dir., Pastoral Care
Rev. LIONEL G. TRUDEL, M.M.
Sisters of St. Benedict (Federation of St. Scholastica) 6
Capacity 222
Patients assisted annually 68,605
Total Staff 863

Lackawanna
Diocese of Buffalo

Our Lady of Victory Hospital
55 Melroy at Ridge Rd.
Lackawanna, NY 14218
Tel: 716-825-8000; Fax: 716-825-4681
Sponsored by the Catholic Health System, Inc.
Mr. JOHN P. DAVANZO, Pres. & CEO
Revs.:
ROBERT J. MCARTNEY, Dir. Pastoral Care
RAYMOND MAHAR
Sisters of St. Joseph 3
Capacity 41
Patients assisted annually 30,500
Total Staff 620

Our Lady of Victory Hospital Auxiliary
55 Melroy at Ridge Rd.
Lackawanna, NY 14218
Tel: 716-825-8000

Lewiston
Diocese of Buffalo

Mount St. Mary's Hospital of Niagara Falls
5300 Military Rd.
Lewiston, NY 14092-1997
Tel: 716-297-4800; Fax: 716-298-2333 (Gen.);716-298-2001 (Pres.)
Ascension Health, St. Louis, MO
ANGELO G. CALBONE, Pres. & CEO
Rev. MARK J. FRIEL, Chap.
Sr. MAUREEN HUET, O.S.F., Dir.
Sr. DIANE LOUTTIT, D.C., Dir.
Capacity 175
Bassinets 22
Patients assisted annually 157,850
Total Staff 764

Lockport
Diocese of Buffalo

Niagara Homemaker Services, dba Mercy Home Care of Western New York
111 Main St.
Lockport, NY 14094
Tel: 716-434-2388; Fax: 716-434-2621
E-mail: bholmesdo@aol.com
MARCIA REISSIG, Admin.
Patients assisted annually 1,400
Total Staff 325

Melville
Diocese of Rockville Centre

Catholic Health Services of Long Island
One Huntington Quadrangle, Ste. 4C04
Melville, NY 11714
Tel: 631-396-5600; Fax: 631-396-5040
Legal Title: *Catholic Heath System of Long Island, Inc.*
RONALD R. ALDRICH, Pres. & CEO
DONNA M. O'BRIEN, Exec. Vice-Pres. & CAO
GEORGE F. RICE, ESQ., Board Chair
Rev. Msgr. ALAN J. PLACA, Corp. Sec.
Rev. TERENCE G. DALY, Treas. & CFO
Rev. Msgr. DENNIS M. REGAN, Senior Vice-Pres. for Mission & Ministry
592 Middle Neck Rd.
Great Neck, NY 11023
Tel: 516-829-2370; Fax: 516-482-2424
Rev. Msgr. ALAN J. PLACA, Sec. to the Bishop for Healthcare Apostolate
Sr. EILEEN DONOVAN, O.P., Dir. of Chaplaincy Services, Tel: 516-678-5800 Ext. 521
Hospitals
St. Charles Hospital and Rehabilitation Center
200 Belle Terre Rd.
Port Jefferson, NY 11777
Tel: 631-474-6000
ROBERTA SAUNDERS-GRAY, Pres. & CEO
Mercy Medical Center
1000 N. Village Ave.
Rockville Centre, NY 11570
Tel: 516-255-0111
VINCENT DIRUBBIO, Pres. & CEO
St. Francis Hospital The Heart Center.
100 Port Washington Blvd.
Roslyn, NY 11576
Tel: 516-562-6000
ALAN D. GUERCI, M.D., Pres. & CEO
St. Catherine of Siena Medical Center
50 Route 25A
Smithtown, NY 11787
Tel: 631-862-3000
JAMES M. WILSON, Pres. & CEO
DONNA M. O'BRIEN, Pres.
Good Samaritan Hospital Medical Center
1000 Montauk Hwy.
West Islip, NY 11795
Tel: 631-376-3000
RICHARD J. MURPHY, Pres. & CEO
Nursing Homes and Sub-Acute Care
Good Samaritan Nursing Home
101 Elm St.
Sayville, NY 11782
Tel: 631-244-2400
MIKHAEL KEIFITZ, Admin.
St. Catherine of Siena Nursing Home
52 Rte. 25A
Smithtown, NY 11787
Tel: 631-862-3905
JEFFREY ROGOFF, Admin.
Our Lady of Consolation Geriatric and Rehabilitative Care Center
111 Beach Dr.
West Islip, NY 11795
Tel: 631-587-1600
Sr. AUDREY HARSEN, O.P., Pres. & CEO
Hospice and Palliative Care Services
CHS Hospice at Good Samaritan
655 Deer Park Ave.
Babylon, NY 11702
Tel: 631-376-3850
KATHLEEN COFFEY, Exec. Dir.
CHS Hospice
4747-12 Nesconset Hwy.
Port Jefferson Station, NY 11776
Tel: 631-474-4040
MARY ANN GILLEN, Pres. & CEO
CHS Hospice at St. Charles
CHS Hospice at St. Francis
CHS Hospice at St. Catherine of Siena
CHS Hospice at Mercy Medical Center
St. Pius X Service Center, 1220 Front St.
Uniondale, NY 11553
Tel: 516-485-3060
EDITH MEOZZI, Admin.
Community-Based Programs
Maryhaven Center of Hope
1010 Rte. 112
Port Jefferson Station, NY 11776
Tel: 631-474-4120
LEWIS GROSSMAN, Pres. & CEO
Siena Village Senior Housing
2000 Bishop's Rd.
Smithtown, NY 11787
Tel: 631-360-6000
JANET STEVENSON, Admin.
Home Care Agency
Nursing Sisters Home Care
1600 Stewart Ave., Ste. 201
Westbury, NY 11590
Tel: 516-683-1300
KEITH KERTLAND, Pres. & CEO
Ambulance
CHS Ambulance Service
315 Smith St.
Farmingdale, NY 11735
Tel: 631-777-5600
DOUGLASS C. WATOFF, Dir.
Foundations
St. Charles Foundation
Maryhaven Foundation
Mercy Medical Center Foundation
St. Catherine of Siena Foundation
St. Francis Hospital Foundation
Nursing Sisters Foundation
Good Samaritan Foundation
Our Lady of Consolation Foundation
Miscellaneous Entities
CHS Services, Inc.
Maryhaven School
Under the auspices of Maryhaven Center of Hope
St. Charles Education and Treatment Center
Under the auspices of The St. Charles Corporation
The St. Charles Corporation
Maryhaven Transportation Services
Riverhead Hostel Holding Corporation
Under the auspices of Maryhaven Center of Hope.
Supportive Home Care
Under the auspices of St. Charles Hospital and Rehabilitation Center.
Supportive Home Care
Under the auspices of Nursing Sisters Home Care.
Suffolk Hearing and Speech
Under the auspices of Good Samaritan Hospital Medical Center.
The Samaritan Corporation
St. Francis Research and Education Corporation
Under the auspices of St. Francis Hospital.
The St. Francis-Mercy Corporation

New York
Archdiocese of New York

Cabrini Medical Center (Cabrini Development Council, Inc.)
227 E. 19th St.
New York, NY 10003
Tel: 212-995-6000; Fax: 212-995-6568
Mr. PAUL CANDINO, Pres. & CEO
Sr. ARLENE PRIMUS, M.S.C., Asst. to the Pres. for Mission & Chaplaincy Svcs.
Bed Capacity Acute Hospital 519
Skilled nursing facility at Dobbs Ferry 304
Home Care 349
New York City, Beds 240 (Cabrini Nursing Home)
Missionary Sisters of the Sacred Heart 10
Patients assisted annually 57,352
Cabrini Hospice Program (home care) 856
Total Staff 1844
Stuyvesant Polyclinic, Inc.
Tel: 212-674-0220
Patients assisted annually 42,981

Our Lady of Mercy Medical Center
Tel: 718-920-9000; Fax: 718-920-9245
Web Site: www.ourladyofmercy.com
233rd St. Division
600 E. 233 St.
Bronx, NY 10466
Tel: 718-920-9000; Fax: 718-920-9245
Florence D'Urso Pavilion
1870 Pelham Pkwy. S.
Bronx, NY 10461
Tel: 718-430-6000; Fax: 718-430-6071
Acute Care General Hospital.
Mr. GARY S. HORAN, Pres. & CEO
Rev. Msgr. FREDERICK J. BECKER, Vice Pres. Pastoral Svcs.
Revs.:
THOMAS P. D'ANGELO, Catholic Chap.
BERNARD IHEOHA, Catholic Chap.
Capacity 612
Patients assisted annually 281,304
Total Staff 2,273
Rosalie Hall Shelter for Unwed Mothers
Tel: 718-290-9800; Fax: 718-920-9896
DIANE PRUSINSKI, S.M., Dir.
Bed Capacity 612
Total Assisted Annually 281,304
Total Staff 2,273

St. Clare's Hospital and Health Center
415 W. 51st St.
New York, NY 10019
Tel: 212-586-1500
JAMES A. RUTHERFORD, Pres. & CEO
Rev. JOHN J. DONAHUE, C.S.C., Chap.
Bed Capacity 250
Patients assisted annually 15,903

St. Vincents Catholic Medical Centers of New York
153 West 11 St.
New York, NY 10011
Tel: 212-604-7554; 604-2300; Fax: 212-604-7533
Web Site: svcmc.org
MARK ACKERMANN, Chief Admin.
St. Vincent's Manhattan
153 West 11th St.
New York, NY 10011
St. Vincent's Staten Island
355 Bard Ave.
Staten Island, NY 10310
Tel: 718-876-2413; Fax: 718-876-2293
Bayley Seton Campus
75 Vanderbilt Ave.
Staten Island, NY 10304
Tel: 718-354-6000; Fax: 718-354-6011
Mary Immaculate
152-11 89th Ave.
Jamaica, NY 11432
Tel: 718-558-2000; Fax: 718-558-2425
St. John's Queens
90-02 Queens Blvd.
Elmhurst, NY 11373
Tel: 718-558-1000; Fax: 718-558-1818
St. Joseph's
158-40 79th Ave.
Flushing, NY 11366
Tel: 718-558-6200; Fax: 718-558-6209
St. Mary's Brooklyn
170 Buffalo Ave.
Brooklyn, NY 11213
Tel: 718-221-3000; Fax: 718-221-3971
St. Vincent's Westchester
275 North St.
Harrison, NY 10528
Tel: 914-967-6500; Fax: 914-925-5157
Bed Capacity 2,600
Total Annually Assisted 500,929
Total Staff 15,000

Sisters of Charity Health Care System Corp.
Tel: 1-800-CARE-421
Web Site: www.schsi.org
75 Vanderbilt Ave.
Staten Island, NY 10304
Tel: 718-354-5080
Web Site: http://www.schcs.com
Bayley Seton Campus
Tel: 718-354-6000; Fax: 718-876-1234
St. Vincent's Medical Center of Richmond
Bed Capacity 866
Total Annually Assisted 29,794
Total Staff 4000

Port Jervis
Archdiocese of New York

Mercy Community Hospital
160 E. Main St.
Port Jervis, NY 12771
Tel: 914-856-5351; Fax: 914-858-5402
E-mail: mercycommunityhosp.org
MICHAEL A. PARMER, M.D., Site Admin.
THOMAS R. BRUNELLE
Capacity 141
SNF Beds 46
Patients assisted annually 68,964
Total Staff 472

Poughkeepsie
Archdiocese of New York

St. Francis Hospital
North Rd.
Poughkeepsie, NY 12601
Tel: 914-471-2000
Sisters of St. Francis of Hastings-on-Hudson
DONALD F. MURPHY, Exec. Vice Pres.
Sr. M. ANN ELIZABETH, O.S.F., Pres.
Rev. THOMAS A. MCDONALD, Dir. Pastoral Care
Capacity 295
St. Francis Health Care Foundation
North Rd.
Poughkeepsie, NY 12601
Sr. M. ANN ELIZABETH, Pres.
Saint Francis Hospital, Beacon
Delavan Ave.
Beacon, NY 12538
Tel: 914-831-3500
LAWRENCE M. WITTE, Exec. Dir.
Capacity 116 beds
Total Annually Assisted 150,000
Total Staff 1,300

Schenectady
Diocese of Albany

St. Clare's Holding Company, Inc.
600 McClellan St.
Schenectady, NY 12304
Tel: 518-347-5660; Fax: 518-347-5522
E-mail: jowens@stclares.org
Web Site: stclares.org

St. Clare's Hospital
600 McClellan St.
Schenectady, NY 12304
Tel: 518-382-2000; Fax: 518-347-5522
E-mail: jowens@stclares.org
Web Site: stclares.org
PAUL CHODKOWSKI, Pres. & CEO
Rev. RICHARD J. LESKOVAR, Chap., Dir. Pastoral Care
Sr. MARY ELIZABETH S.N.J.M.
Sr. THERESA HANSEN, S.S.N.D.
Sr. MIRIAM NATALE, O.S.F.
Bed Capacity 200
Patients assisted annually 166,165

Smithtown
Diocese of Rockville Centre

Siena Village, Inc.
52 Rte. 25 A
Smithtown, NY 11787-1346
Tel: 516-396-5600
DONNA M. O'BRIEN, Pres.

Suffern
Archdiocese of New York

Good Samaritan Hospital of Suffern
Suffern, NY 10901
Tel: 914-368-5000
JAMES A. MARTIN, Pres.
Sr. MARGARET STRAUCH, S.S.N.D., Dir. Pastoral Care
Chaplains:
Revs.:
GEORGE MATTIONI, O.A.R.
FRANCIS A. CREGAN, O.A.R.
Sr. SHEILA M. MULLINS, O.P.
Sisters of Charity of St. Elizabeth 2
Capacity 370
Patients assisted annually 165,000
Total Staff 1,575

Syracuse
Diocese of Syracuse

St. Joseph's Hospital Health Center
301 Prospect Ave.
Syracuse, NY 13203
Tel: 315-448-5111; Fax: 315-448-6161
E-mail: lavalt57@sjsyr.org
Web Site: www.sjhsyr.org
Mr. THEODORE M. PASINSKI, Pres. & CEO
Rev. MICHAEL TAYLOR, Chap.
Sisters of the Third Franciscan Order 16
Bed Capacity 431
Patients assisted annually 120,000
School for Nurses
Students 180

Troy
Diocese of Albany

Seton Health System, Inc.
1300 Massachusetts Ave.
Troy, NY 12180
Tel: 518-268-5000; Fax: 518-268-5257
E-mail: info@setonhealth.org
Web Site: setonhealth.org
Daughters of Charity of St. Vincent de Paul
Dr. MARK DONOVAN, Pres. & CEO
KELLY A. GORMAN, Dir. Spiritual Care
Deacon ALBERT G. SCHREMPF, Chap.
Sr. DE CHANTAL LAROW, D.C., Chm. Bd. of Dir.
Sisters 11
Bed Capacity 201
Patients assisted annually 315,000
Legal Title: *Seton Health System, Inc.*

Utica
Diocese of Syracuse

St. Elizabeth Hospital
2209 Genesee St.
Utica, NY 13501
Tel: 315-798-8100; Fax: 315-734-3092
E-mail: svincent@STEMC.org
Web Site: www.stemc.org
Sr. ROSE VINCENT GLEASON, CEO
Sr. M. JOHANNA DELELYS, COO
Rev. JOHN H. COMESKEY
Sisters of the Third Franciscan Order 19
Beds 201
Total Staff 1,114
Patients assisted annually 331,189
College of Nursing
Students 130

Warwick
Archdiocese of New York

St. Anthony Community Hospital, Inc.
Franciscan System of Warwick, Inc.
15-19 Maple Ave.
Warwick, NY 10990
Tel: 914-986-2276
JAMES GIORDANO, Site Admin.
LEAH CERKVENIK, R.N., Vice Pres. Mission
Sr. ROSEMARY CORK, O.P., Dir. Pastoral Care
Rev. EDWARD SULLIVAN, O.F.M., Chap.
Capacity 73
Patients assisted annually 34,262

White Plains
Archdiocese of New York

St. Agnes Hospital and Children's Rehabilitation Center
305 North St.
White Plains, NY 10605
Tel: 914-681-4500; Fax: 914-681-4974
Web Site: www.saintagneshospital.com
GARY S. HORAN, Pres. & CEO
Sr. MARY VIRGINIA R.D.C., Dir. Pastoral Care
Capacity 184
Childrens Rehabilitation Center 68,061
Hospital 34,921
Total Staff 765

Yonkers
Archdiocese of New York

St. Joseph's Medical Center
127 S. Broadway
Yonkers, NY 10701
Tel: 914-378-7000; Fax: 914-965-4838
E-mail: SJMCgen@interactive.net
Web Site: http://saintjosephs.org
Mr. MICHAEL J. SPICER, Pres.
Rev. THOMAS MURPHY, O.F.M.Cap.
Sr. CAROLYN PARKER, Dir. of Pastoral Care
Beds 194
Nursing Home Beds 200
Sisters of Charity of St. Vincent de Paul 9
Patients assisted annually 11,400
Total Staff 1300

NORTH CAROLINA

Asheville
Diocese of Charlotte

ARP/Phoenix
129 Biltmore Ave.
Asheville, NC 28801
Tel: 828-254-2700

Sisters of Mercy Services Corporation
345 Biltmore Ave.
Asheville, NC 28801
Tel: 828-281-1268; Fax: 828-254-4102
G. JOHN COLI, Ph.D., Pres. & COO

Sisters of Mercy Urgent Care, Inc.
345 Biltmore Ave.
Asheville, NC 28801
Tel: 828-281-2598; Fax: 828-254-4102
E-mail: bill@somse.org
Patients assisted annually 235,000

Southern Pines
Diocese of Raleigh

St. Joseph of the Pines
590 Central Dr.
Southern Pines, NC 28387-2899
Tel: 910-295-3920; Fax: 910-695-2371
Web Site: www.sjp.org
Legal Title: *St. Joseph of the Pines, Inc.*
Mr. GEORGE KECATOS, Pres. & CEO
Beds 176
Staff 225

NORTH DAKOTA

Bismarck
Diocese of Bismarck

St. Alexius Medical Center
P.O. Box 5510
Bismarck, ND 58506-5510
Tel: 701-530-7000; Fax: 701-530-7284
Web Site: www.st.alexius.org
Sisters of St. Benedict
RICHARD A. TSCHIDER, Admin. & CEO
Sr. RENEE ZASTOUPIL, Dir. Pastoral Care
Priests 1
Sisters 14
Bed Capacity 308
Total Staff 1,763
Patients assisted annually 127,141

Bottineau
Diocese of Fargo

St. Andrew's Health Center
316 Ohmer St.
Bottineau, ND 58318
Tel: 701-228-2255; Fax: 701-228-2255
E-mail: sahc@ndak.net
Web Site: bottineau.com/health.htm
Sr. CORINNE S.M.P., Supr.
KEITH KORMAN, Pres.
Sisters of Mary of the Presentation 3
Beds 57
Staff 105
Patients assisted annually 5,600

Carrington
Diocese of Fargo

Carrington Health Center
Catholic Health Initiatives.
800 N. Fourth St.
Carrington, ND 58421
Tel: 701-652-3141
BRIAN J. MCDERMOTT, CEO
Acute Beds 30
LTC Beds 30
Staff 143
Patients assisted annually 690

Devils Lake
Diocese of Fargo

Mercy Hospital
1031 Seventh St.
Devils Lake, ND 58301-2798
Tel: 701-662-2131; Fax: 701-662-9651
E-mail: marlenekrein@chi-midwest.org
MARLENE KREIN, Pres.
In res.,
Rev. DENNIS L. SCHUE
Sisters of Mercy of the Americas 2
Staff 202
Beds 50
Bassinets 7
Patients assisted annually 15,678

Dickinson
Diocese of Bismarck

St. Joseph's Hospital and Health Center
30 W. Seventh St.
Dickinson, ND 58601
Tel: 701-264-4271; Fax: 701-264-4800
Web Site: stjoeshospital.org
GREG HANSON, Pres. & CEO
Nurses 190
Total Staff 338
Beds 109
Patients assisted annually 40,222

Fargo
Diocese of Fargo

Prairie Psychiatric Center
501 4th St. S.
Fargo, ND 58102
Tel: 701-476-7200
MARSHALL KORMAN, CEO
Rev. JOHN EVAN, II, Chap.
Beds 41
Patients assisted annually 918
Staff 182

Garrison
Diocese of Bismarck

Garrison Memorial Hospital
P.O. Box 39
Garrison, ND 58540

Tel: 701-463-2275; Fax: 701-463-2886
E-mail: dgoebel@primecare.org
DENNIS GOEBEL, Admin.
Sisters of St. Benedict (Bismarck & Sacred Heart, Richardton) 3
Nurses 50
Total Staff 105
Bed Capacity 46
Patients assisted annually 5,625

Harvey
Diocese of Fargo

St. Aloisius Medical Center
325 E. Brewster St.
Harvey, ND 58341
Tel: 701-324-4651; Fax: 701-324-4651
E-mail: ruolk@stacoisius.com
Web Site: www.stacoisius.com
Sisters of Mary of the Presentation.
RONALD J. VOLK, Admin./Pres.
SHEILA ERICKSON, CFO
Staff 272
Beds 25
Nursing Home 116
Patients assisted annually 8,295

Oakes
Diocese of Fargo

Oakes Community Hospital
314 S. Eighth St.
Oakes, ND 58474
Tel: 701-742-3291
E-mail: bradburris@chi-midwest.org
Sr. M. DIANNA HELL, O.S.F., Supr.
BRADLEY D. BURRIS, CEO & Pres.
Sisters of St. Francis of the Immaculate Heart of Mary (Hankinson, ND) 4
Total Staff 92
Beds 30
Bassinets 4
Patients assisted annually 19,548

Rolla
Diocese of Fargo

Presentation Medical Center
213 Second Ave., N.E., P.O. Box 759
Rolla, ND 58367
Tel: 701-477-5564
E-mail: pmc@utma.com
KIMBER L. WRAALSTAD, Pres. & CEO
Sisters of Mary of the Presentation 3
Total Staff 175
Beds 54
Patients assisted annually 9,610

Valley City
Diocese of Fargo

Mercy Hospital
Catholic Health Initiatives.
570 Chautauqua Blvd.
Valley City, ND 58072
Tel: 701-845-6400; Fax: 701-845-6413
E-mail: janeabissel@chi-midwest.org
JANE BISSEL, Pres. & CEO
Beds 74
Bassinets 15
Patients Assisted 17,212
Staff 170

Williston
Diocese of Bismarck

Mercy Medical Center - Affiliate of Catholic Health Initiatives
1301 15th Ave. W.
Williston, ND 58801
Tel: 701-774-7400; Fax: 701-774-7479
M. THOMAS MITCHELL, Pres.& CEO
Beds 87
Patients assisted annually 35,362
Total Staff 498

Mercy Medical Foundation
1301 15th Ave. W.
Williston, ND 58801
Tel: 701-774-7404; Fax: 701-774-7479
E-mail: dougblack@chi-midwest.org
Total Staff 3

OHIO

Batavia
Archdiocese of Cincinnati

The Sisters of Mercy Of Clermont County, Ohio dba Mercy Hospital Clermont
3000 Hospital Dr.
Batavia, OH 45103
Tel: 513-732-8200; Fax: 513-732-8537
FRED L. KOLB, Pres.
Sr. KATHY GREEN, R.S.M., Vice Pres., Mission Svcs.
Bed Capacity 157
Patients assisted annually 10,398

Canton
Diocese of Youngstown

**CSAHS/UHHS - Canton, Inc.,*
Mercy Medical Center, 1320 Mercy Dr., N.W.
Canton, OH 44708
Tel: 330-489-1000; Fax: 330-489-1312
E-mail: mail@cantonmercy.com
Web Site: www.thequalityhospital.com
CHRISTOPHER M. DADLEZ-FACHE, Pres. & CEO
Beds 476
Bassinets 47
Total Staff 1,819

Cincinnati
Archdiocese of Cincinnati

Good Samaritan Hospital
375 Dixmyth Ave.
Cincinnati, OH 45220
Tel: 513-872-1400; Fax: 513-872-3435
Web Site: trihealth.com
Catholic Health Initiative (CHI).
Mr. JOHN PROUT, Pres. & CEO
Revs.:
GERALD R. NIKLAS
EUGENE J. NEVINS, S.J.
BRODIE HENRY, (Protestant)
Bed Capacity 614
Bassinets 62
Long-term Care 15
Patients assisted annually 200,000
Registered Training School for Nurses
Tel: 513-872-2631; Fax: 513-872-3572
Students 250

Mercy Health Plaza dba Mercy Franciscan Hospital-Western Hills
A member of the Mercy Health Partners.
3131 Queen City Ave.
Cincinnati, OH 45238
Tel: 513-389-5000; Fax: 513-389-9207
CHARLES LOBECK, Pres.
Sr. ARLENE MCGOWAN, Vice Pres. Social Svs. Outreach Min.
DON ROHLING, Dir. Spiritual Care
Chaplains:
Sr. JOANNE BURKHART, S.F.P.
Sr. ADRIENNE COLSON, O.P.
Sr. LAURENE HAGMAN, O.P.
Mrs. JOAN OWENS
Ms. ALBERTA UTRUP
Revs.:
PAUL WALSMAN, O.F.M.
AQUINAS SCHNEIDER, O.F.M.
Sisters 1
Beds 281
Patients assisted annually 86,466

Mercy Health Plaza dba Mercy Franciscan Hospital-Mt. Airy
A member of the Mercy Health Partners.
4340 Glendale-Milford Rd.
Cincinnati, OH 45242
Tel: 513-853-5000; Fax: 513-853-5910
STEVE GRINNELL, Pres.
Sr. KATHY GREEN, R.S.M., Vice Pres. Mission
DON ROHLING, Dir. Mission
Chaplains:
Rev. MICHAEL PARANIUK
CAROL SAYGERS
Sr. DONNA DE MANGE, O.S.F.
Sr. YVONNE FACKLER, S.F.P.
Sisters 3
Beds 331
Patients assisted annually 115,947
Total Staff 1,298

Mercy Hospital Anderson
7500 State Rd.
Cincinnati, OH 45255
Tel: 513-624-4500
Sisters of Mercy
FRED L. KOLB, Pres.
Sr. KATHY GREEN, R.S.M., Vice Pres., Mission Svcs.
Rev. DAVID J. KELLEY, Chap.
Bed Capacity 188
Patients assisted annually 8,387

Cleveland
Diocese of Cleveland

Marymount Hospital, Inc.
12300 McCracken Rd.
Cleveland, OH 44125
Tel: 216-581-0500; Fax: 216-587-8212
E-mail: ttrudell@marymount.org
Web Site: www.marymount.org
Mr. THOMAS J. TRUDELL, Pres.
JUDITH SHEMKOVITZ, Dir. Pastoral Care
Rev. JOSEPH O'DONNELL, Priest Chap. & Coord. Sacramental Svcs. & Priest Chaplains
Staff Chaplains:
Sr. ANNE MASLANKA, S.S.J.-T.O.S.F.
Sr. BERNICE THERESE, S.S.J.-T.O.S.F.
Sisters of St. Joseph of Third Order of St. Francis 5
Beds 312
Med/surg 259
Skilled Nursing 20
Rehab Unit 15
Bassinets 18
Patients assisted annually 145,971
Total Staff 1,427

St. John Hospital
2351 E. 22nd St.
Cleveland, OH 44115
Tel: 216-696-5560; Fax: 216-696-2204
Web Site: www.csahealthsystem.org
Sr. MARY PATRICIA BARRETT, C.S.A., Chm. Bd. Trustees
Sr. JUDITH ANN KARAM, Pres. & CEO

Columbus
Diocese of Columbus

Mohun Health Care Center
2320 Airport Dr.
Columbus, OH 43219
Tel: 614-253-8517; Fax: 614-251-0338
E-mail: jacquelinebaum@usa.net
Web Site: columbusdominicans.org
Sr. JACQUELINE BAUM, O.P., Admin.
Total Staff 113
Bed Capacity 75
Patients assisted annually 91

Mount Carmel Health System
793 W. State St.
Columbus, OH 43222
Tel: 614-234-5423; Fax: 614-234-5985
Web Site: mountcarmelhealth.com
JOSEPH CALVARUSO, Pres. & CEO
Beds 915
Staff 6,600
Patients assisted annually 909,625
Legal Holdings:
Mount Carmel Health System
Tel: 614-234-5423; Fax: 614-234-1359
Mount Carmel West (General Hospital)
Tel: 614-234-5000; Fax: 614-234-5756
Mount Carmel East (General Hospital)
Tel: 614-234-6000; Fax: 614-234-6408
Mount Carmel Care Continuum Businesses
Tel: 614-234-5105; Fax: 614-234-5756
Mount Carmel College of Nursing
Tel: 614-234-5800; Fax: 614-234-2875
Mount Carmel St. Ann's (General Hospital)
Tel: 614-898-4000; Fax: 614-898-8668
Mount Carmel Health System Foundation
Tel: 614-234-5290; Fax: 614-234-1920

Trinity Continuing Care, dba Saint Angela Nursing and Rehabilitation Center
5700 Karl Rd.
Columbus, OH 43229
Tel: 614-846-5420; Fax: 614-846-3247
KAY LAKHI, Admin.
Bed Capacity 260
Total Staff 232
Patients assisted annually 510

Dayton
Archdiocese of Cincinnati

Franciscan Medical Center - Dayton Campus
One Franciscan Way
Dayton, OH 45408
Tel: 937-229-6000
Sponsored by Franciscan Sisters of the Poor.

Good Samaritan Hospital
2222 Philadelphia Dr.
Dayton, OH 45406
Tel: 937-278-2612
Affiliate with Catholic Health Initiative.

Mr. Douglas Deck, Pres.
Bed Capacity 560
Patients assisted annually 200,000

Fairfield
Archdiocese of Cincinnati

Mercy Health Plaza
2990 Mack Rd.
Fairfield, OH 45242
Tel: 513-874-6440

Hamilton
Archdiocese of Cincinnati

The Sisters of Mercy of Hamilton, Ohio dba Mercy Hospital of Hamilton-Fairfield
100 Riverfront Plaza, P.O. Box 418
Hamilton, OH 45011
Tel: 513-867-6400; Fax: 513-867-9043
3000 Mack Rd.
Fairfield, OH 45014
Tel: 513-870-7000; Fax: 513-870-7065
Sisters of Mercy of Hamilton, OH
Mr. David A. Ferrell, Pres.
Sr. Sharon Wiedmar, Dir. of Mission Svcs.
Sisters 8
Bed Capacity 351
Patients assisted annually 7,424

Lima
Diocese of Toledo

St. Rita's Medical Center
730 W. Market St.
Lima, OH 45801
Tel: 419-227-3361; Fax: 419-226-9750
Web Site: www.stritas.org
Mr. James P. Reber, Pres.
Mr. Kenneth G. Payne, Vice Pres. Finance
Mr. Mark Skaja, Vice Pres. Mission Svcs.
Chaplains:
Revs.:
Vincent Hoying, C.PP.S.
Greta Wagner
Sr. Noel Frey, R.S.M.
Deacon Walt Miller
Sisters 1
Bed Capacity 424
Patients assisted annually 267,854
Total Staff 2,380

Lorain
Diocese of Cleveland

Community Health Partners Health System
Tel: 440-233-1053; Fax: 440-246-5390
E-mail: karen_yacobucci@hmis.org
(West Campus)
3700 Kolbe Rd.
Lorain, OH 44053-1697
Tel: 440-960-4000; Fax: 440-960-4630
(East Campus)
205 W. 20th St.
Lorain, OH 44052
Tel: 440-233-1053; Fax: 440-246-5390
Mr. Brian C. Lockwood, Pres. & CEO
Bed Capacity 326
Patients assisted annually 330,000
Total Staff 2,069

Oregon
Diocese of Toledo

St. Charles Mercy Hospital
2600 Navarre Ave.
Oregon, OH 43616
Tel: 419-696-7200; Fax: 419-696-7328
Web Site: www.mercyweb.org
Mercy Health Partners.
Cathleen K. Nelson, Pres. & CEO
Chaplains:
Revs.:
Charles J. Denny
Don Corbin, Pastoral Care Dir.
Sisters 4
Bed Capacity 333
Patients assisted annually 132,403
Total Staff 1,507

Sandusky
Diocese of Toledo

Providence Hospital Inc.
1912 Hayes Ave.
Sandusky, OH 44870
Tel: 419-621-7000; Fax: 419-621-7077
E-mail: snl@providencehealth.com
Sisters of St. Francis of Sylvania, Ohio
Sr. Nancy Linenkugel, O.S.F., EDM, Pres. & CEO
Rev. Philip Svehier, O.S.B., Chap.
Providence Hospital School of Nursing
Tel: 419-621-7114; Fax: 419-621-7116
Student Nurses 82
Providence Hospital School of Radiology
Tel: 419-621-7124; Fax: 419-625-7439
Student Radiology Technicians 12
Providence Care Centers
2025 Hayes Ave.
Sandusky, OH 44870
Tel: 419-627-2273; Fax: 419-627-0092
Sisters 2
Bed Capacity 138
Patients assisted annually 236
Total Staff 150
Rick G. Ryan, Pres. & CEO
Amie Gohlike, Admin.
Rev. Benedict E. Ringholz, Chap.
The Commons of Providence Apartment assisted living facility
5000 Providence Dr.
Sandusky, OH 44870
Tel: 419-624-1171; Fax: 419-624-1175
Bed Capacity 56
Residents 68
Total Staff 24
Lori Fleming, Admin.
Sisters 5
Bed Capacity 270
Patients assisted annually 55,053
Total Staff 720

Springfield
Archdiocese of Cincinnati

Mercy Health System - Western Ohio
1343 N. Fountain Blvd.
Springfield, OH 45501-1380
Tel: 937-390-5000; Fax: 937-890-5507
E-mail: sdarch@health-partners.org
Sisters of Mercy
Mr. Andrew McCulloch, Pres. & CEO
Sr. Betty Anne Darch, Mission Services
Rev. Marvin R. Hackman, Chap.
Patrick O'Connor, Ph.D., Regl. Dir., Spiritual Care
Sisters 5
Bed Capacity 329
Patients assisted annually 130,000

Steubenville
Diocese of Steubenville

Trinity Health System
Tel: 740-283-7212; Fax: 740-283-7104
Trinity Medical Center, West
4000 Johnson Rd.
Steubenville, OH 43952
Tel: 740-264-8000; Fax: 740-283-7104
Rev. John McCoy, Chap.
Trinity Medical Center, East
380 Summit Ave.
Steubenville, OH 43952
Tel: 740-283-7000; Fax: 740-283-7104
Chaplains:
Sr. Maria Consuelo, O.S.F.
Rev. John McCoy
Trinity Time, Inc.
Prime Time, 380 Summit Ave.
Steubenville, OH 43952
Tel: 740-283-7841; Fax: 740-283-7838
Trinity Health System Foundation
380 Summit Ave.
Steubenville, OH 43952
Tel: 740-283-7128; Fax: 740-283-7104
Beds 632
Sisters 5
RNs 408
LPNs 30
Nurse Anesthetists 12
Patients Assisted Annually:
Admissions 11,641
Outpatients 190,415
Emergency Room 54,176
Births 584

Tiffin
Diocese of Toledo

Mercy Hospital
485 W. Market St.
Tiffin, OH 44883
Tel: 419-447-3130; Fax: 419-448-3138
Web Site: www.mercyweb.org
Mark Shugarman, Pres. & CEO
Sisters of Mercy of the Americas
Sisters 4
Bed Capacity 74
Patients assisted annually 86,422
Total Staff 445

Toledo
Diocese of Toledo

Mercy Hospital
2200 Jefferson Ave.
Toledo, OH 43624-9988
Tel: 419-259-1500; Fax: 419-251-1509
Web Site: www.mercyweb.org
Sisters of Mercy of the Americas
Cathleen K. Nelson, Pres.
Sisters 4

Riverside Mercy Hospital
1600 N. Superior St.
Toledo, OH 43604
Tel: 419-729-6074; Fax: 419-729-6031
E-mail: scott_shook@mhsnr.org
Web Site: www.mhsnr.org
Scott E. Shook, Pres. & CEO
Beds 271
Patients assisted annually 101,985
Total Staff 905

St. Vincent Mercy Medical Center
2213 Cherry St.
Toledo, OH 43608-2691
Tel: 419-251-3232; Fax: 419-251-3810
Web Site: www.mercyweb.org
Grey Nuns
Affiliated with Mercy Health Partners.
Mr. Steven L. Mickus, Pres. & CEO
Chaplains:
William Foster, Dir. Pastoral Care
Rev. Joel R. Buchman
Deacon Michael Pence, Resident Chap.
Sharon Belisle
Ann Krause
Sr. Michelle Gillespie
Sisters 4
Total Staff 4,220
Patients assisted annually 317,199
Bed Capacity 465
Mercy College of Northwest Ohio
2238 Jefferson Ave.
Toledo, OH 43624
Tel: 415-251-1279; Fax: 419-251-1570
Sisters of Mercy of the Americas 5
Student Nurses 157
Total Staff 56
Sr. Patricia Ann Dalke, Pres.

Urbana
Archdiocese of Cincinnati

Mercy Memorial Hospital
904 Scioto St.
Urbana, OH 43078
Tel: 937-653-5231; Fax: 937-652-1866
E-mail: kzalar@health-partners.org
Sisters of Mercy
Sisters 2
Bed Capacity 73
Total Assisted 4,392

Warren
Diocese of Youngstown

St. Joseph Health Center
667 Eastland Ave., S.E.
Warren, OH 44484
Tel: 330-841-4000; Fax: 330-841-4019
Mr. Robert W. Shroder, Exec. Vice Pres. Oper.
Rev. George Popovich, Chap.
Ms. Beth Jacob, Mgr. Mission Integration
Sisters of the Humility of Mary 4
Bed capacity 202
Bassinets 17
Patients assisted annually 140,091
Total Staff 860

Willard
Diocese of Toledo

Mercy Hospital of Willard
110 E. Howard St.
Willard, OH 44890
Tel: 419-933-2931; Fax: 419-935-8966
Web Site: www.mercyweb.org
Sisters of Mercy of the Americas
Mr. Dale E. Thornton, Pres. & CEO
Sisters 1
Bed Capacity 39
Total Staff 221
Patients assisted annually 48,114

Youngstown
Diocese of Youngstown

Humility of Mary Health Partners
5211 Mahoning Ave.
Youngstown, OH 44515
Tel: 330-480-3776; Fax: 330-480-4548
MICHAEL ROWAN, Pres. & CEO
HM Hospice
5211 Mahoning Ave.
Youngstown, OH 44511
Tel: 330-480-4595; Fax: 330-480-4548
5211 Mahoning Ave.
Austintown, OH 44515
Tel: 330-480-3776; Fax: 330-480-4548
2460 Elm Rd.
Warren, OH 44483
Tel: 330-372-0259; Fax: 330-372-5035
Patients assisted annually 66,885
Total Staff 197

Humility of Mary Health Partners, St. Elizabeth Health Center
1044 Belmont Ave., Box 1790
Youngstown, OH 44501
Tel: 330-746-7211; Fax: 330-480-7974
MICHAEL ROWAN, Pres. & CEO
ROBERT SHRODER, Exec. Vice Pres., Oper.
Sisters of the Humility of Mary 8
Bed Capacity 580
Bassinets 60
Patients assisted annually 273,780
Total Staff 2,627

Zanesville
Diocese of Columbus

Genesis Healthcare System
800 Forest Ave. & 2951 Maple Ave
Zanesville, OH 43701
Tel: 740-454-4638; Fax: 740-455-4914
Mr. THOMAS L. SIEBER, Pres.
Franciscan Sisters of Christian Charity 7
Bed Capacity 433
Total Staff 2,634
Patients assisted annually 364,800

OKLAHOMA

Ardmore
Archdiocese of Oklahoma City

Mercy Memorial Health Center, Inc. (MMHC)
1011 14th Ave., N.W.
Ardmore, OK 73401
Tel: 580-221-6611; Fax: 580-220-6580
E-mail: BThompson@OKLA
Mr. BOBBY THOMPSON, Pres. & CEO
Total Staff 915
Beds 250
Patients assisted annually 98,806

Oklahoma City
Archdiocese of Oklahoma City

Hillcrest Health Center, Inc.
2129 S.W. 59th St.
Oklahoma City, OK 73119
Tel: 405-685-6671; Fax: 405-680-2817
E-mail: ray_brazier@ssmhc.com
Mr. RAY BRAZIER, Pres.
A member of SSM Health Care.
Total Staff 580
Beds 193
Patients assisted annually 85,342

Mercy Health Center
4300 W. Memorial Rd.
Oklahoma City, OK 73120
Tel: 405-755-1515; Fax: 405-752-3811
E-mail: 1ryan@okla.smhs.com
Owned and operated by Sisters of Mercy Health System, St. Louis.
MICHAEL J. PACKNETT, Pres. & CEO
Rev. CLETUS BASH
Sisters 2
Sister Volunteers 3
Beds 392
Patients assisted annually 201,144
Chaplains 7
Total Staff 2,165

St. Anthony Hospital
1000 N. Lee St., P.O. Box 205
Oklahoma City, OK 73101
Tel: 405-272-7000; Fax: 405-272-7075
E-mail: valinda_rutledge@ssmhc.com
Web Site: www.saintsok.com
Ms. VALINDA RUTLEDGE, Pres.
Rev. JOSEPH S. VAS, Chap.
A member of SSM Health Care.
Sisters 3
Beds 659
Patients assisted annually 188,624

Ponca City
Archdiocese of Oklahoma City

St. Joseph Regional Medical Center
1900 N. 14th
Ponca City, OK 74602
Tel: 580-765-3321; Fax: 580-765-0341
E-mail: susan_nolan@via-christi.org
Web Site: sjrmcpc.com
Sisters of St. Joseph of Wichita/Sisters of the Sorrowful Mother of Broken Arrow, OK
JAMES MCFADDEN, Interim Pres. & CEO
Sr. CLARITA WANER, C.S.J., Dir. Pastoral Care
Sr. NORA PHELAN, Vice Pres. Mission Svcs.
Sisters 2
Total Staff 525
Beds 169
Patients assisted annually 68,000
(Sub. of Via Christi Health System, Inc.)
1900 N. 14th, P.O. Box 1270
Ponca City, OK 74602-1270
Tel: 580-765-0500; Fax: 580-765-0341

Tulsa
Diocese of Tulsa

Marian Health System, Inc.
P.O. Box 4753
Tulsa, OK 74159-0753
Tel: 918-742-9988; Fax: 918-744-2716
Sr. M. THERESE GOTTSCHALK, Pres.

Saint Francis Hospital, Inc.
6161 S. Yale Ave.
Tulsa, OK 74136
Tel: 918-494-2200; Fax: 918-494-7175
Mr. WILLIAM E. WEEKS, Pres. & CEO
Ms. ANDREA L. HYATT, Vice Pres. Mission Effectiveness
Revs.:
DENIS CASEY, Dir. Pastoral Care
JOSEPH THOONKUZHY
JOSEPH W. HOWELL
Beds 868
Bassinets 50
Patients assisted annually 191,091

St. John Health System, Inc.
1923 S. Utica
Tulsa, OK 74104
Tel: 918-744-2180; Fax: 918-744-2716
Sr. M. THERESE GOTTSCHALK, Pres.

St. John Medical Center, Inc.
1923 S. Utica Ave.
Tulsa, OK 74104
Tel: 918-744-2345; Fax: 918-744-2716
Web Site: www.sjmc.org
Sisters of the Sorrowful Mother (Third Order of St. Francis)
DAVID PYNN, Pres.
Chaplains:
Revs.:
GARY SHERMAN
JOHN WADE
LAWRENCE P. COURTRIGHT
Sisters 11
Beds 572
Patients assisted annually 45,954

OREGON

Baker City
Diocese of Baker

St. Elizabeth Health Services, Inc.
3325 Pocahontas Rd.
Baker City, OR 97814
Tel: 541-523-6461 (Hospital); 523-4452 (Nursing Care); Fax: 541-523-1794
E-mail: johnperushek@chiwest.com
JOHN PERUSHEK, Pres. & CEO
Sisters of St. Francis of Philadelphia 3
Bed Capacity 36
Nursing Home Beds 120
Patients assisted annually 18,100
Nursing Home 110

Bend
Diocese of Baker

St. Charles Medical Center
2500 N.E. Neff Rd.
Bend, OR 97701
Tel: 541-382-4321; Fax: 541-388-7723
Web Site: www.scmc.org
Sisters of St. Joseph
Sr. CATHERINE HELLMANN, C.S.J., Pres. Emeritus
Mr. JIM LUSSIER, Pres., CEO
KARON HACK, D.Min., Pastoral Care Mgr.
Bed Capacity 181
Patients assisted annually 131,652

Eugene
Archdiocese of Portland in Oregon

**Sacred Heart Medical Center*
1255 Hilyard St., P.O. Box 10905
Eugene, OR 97440
Tel: 541-686-7300; Fax: 541-686-7391
Div. of Peace Health.
Sisters of St. Joseph of Peace
JUDY HODGSON, Admin., S.H.M.C.
ALAN YORDY, CEO, Peace Health OR
Chaplains:
ROBERT V. SCHERI, Dir. Pastoral Care
Revs.:
J. NOEL HICKIE (BAK)
KEN OLSEN
Sr. CAROL LEE, S.N.J.M.
Sr. VIVIAN RIPP, S.N.J.M.
Sisters 5
Bed Capacity 437
Total Staff 2,097
Patients assisted annually 269,976

Florence
Archdiocese of Portland in Oregon

Peace Harbor Hospital
400 Ninth St.
Florence, OR 97439
Tel: 541-997-8412; Fax: 541-997-9155
Acute care hospital owned and operated by Peace Health, Bellevue, WA.
JAMES BARNHART, Regional CEO
Sr. NOREEN TERRAULT, C.S.J.P., Pastoral Care
PEGGY BYERS, Contact Person
Bed Capacity 21
Total Staff 315
Patients assisted annually 92,294

Hood River
Diocese of Baker

Providence Hood River Memorial Hospital
811 13th St.
Hood River, OR 97031
Tel: 541-386-3911; Fax: 541-387-6462
E-mail: gyoung@providence.org
Web Site: www.providence.org
LARRY BOWE, CEO
Total Staff 266
Bed Capacity 32

Medford
Archdiocese of Portland in Oregon

Providence Medford Medical Center
1111 Crater Lake Ave.
Medford, OR 97504-6225
Tel: 541-732-5000; Fax: 541-732-5872
Legal Title: *Providence Health System*
Mr. CHARLES T. WRIGHT, Chief Executive, Southern Oregon Service Area
Mr. BARTHOLOMEW C. RODRIGUES, Dir. Mission Integration, Ethics & Spiritual Care
Rev. JOSEPH E. SHIREY, S.J., (Part-time)
Sr. THERESE KOHLES, S.P., Sr. Representative to Foundation Board (on call)
Sr. MARY GRONDIN, S.P., Rep. to Community Board
Sr. PATRICIA MARIE LANDIN, S.S.M.O., Chap.
Sisters 3
Bed Capacity 168
Total Staff 671
Patients assisted annually 67,000

**Providence Community Health Foundation, Medford*
Tel: 541-732-5193

Milwaukie
Archdiocese of Portland in Oregon

**Providence Milwaukie Hospital*
10150 S.E. 32nd Ave.
Milwaukie, OR 97222
Tel: 503-513-8300; Fax: 503-513-8463
Legal Title: *Providence Health System in Oregon.*
CAMELIA HANEMANN, Dir. Pastoral Care
Bed Capacity 56 (Acute Care), 29 (Skilled Nursing)
Total Staff 430
Patients assisted annually 70,000

**Providence Milwaukie Foundation, Milwaukie*
Tel: 503-513-8625; Fax: 503-513-8319

Newberg
Archdiocese of Portland in Oregon

Providence Newberg Hospital
501 Villa Rd.
Newberg, OR 97132
Tel: 503-537-1701; Fax: 503-537-1811
MARK MEINERT, CEO
JACK R. SUMNER, Dir. Finance & Contact Person
Bed Capacity 35
Total Staff 300
Patients assisted annually 98,689

Ontario
Diocese of Baker

The Dominican Sisters of Ontario, Inc. dba Holy Rosary Medical Center
351 S.W. Ninth St.
Ontario, OR 97914
Tel: 541-881-7000; Fax: 541-881-7184
Web Site: holyrosary-ontario.org
Mr. BRUCE JENSEN, CEO & Team Leader
LEROY CAMMACK, Chm. Bd.
Rev. CLETUS KIRKPATRICK, Chap.
Deacon HUGH POLENSKY, Pastoral Care
Dominican Sisters of St. Catherine of Siena (Kenosha, WI) 2
Bed Capacity 92
Patients assisted annually 67,055

Pendleton
Diocese of Baker

St. Anthony Hospital
1601 S.E. Court Ave.
Pendleton, OR 97801
Tel: 541-276-5121; Fax: 541-278-3227
E-mail: usimonton@chiwest.com
JEFFREY DROP, Pres.
Sisters of St. Francis of Philadelphia 6
Bed Capacity 49
Patients assisted annually 25,148

Portland
Archdiocese of Portland in Oregon

Providence Portland Medical Center
4805 N.E. Glisan St.
Portland, OR 97213
Tel: 503-215-1111; 215-6833; Fax: 503-215-5619
Legal Title: *Providence Health Systems, Oregon Region*
Revs.:
HERBERT WHEATLEY, O.F.M.
JON BUFFINGTON (EST)
JOHN WIRONEN, C.S.C.
JOHN HUBBARD, Presbyterian Chap.
SANDRA J. WALKER, E.L.C.A.
REBECCA GURNEY
Sr. KATHLEEN KIRCHER, S.N.J.M., Dir. Pastoral Care & Contact Person
Sr. ROSALIE ORR, S.N.J.M., Geriatrics
Sr. MAUREEN NIEDERMEYER, O.S.B., Cardiology
Sr. MARY COAKLEY, O.S.F., Chap.
Sr. BRIGID CAREY, P.B.V.M., Staff Chaplain
Lay Chaplains:
MICHELE SAKURAI, Oncology
JOSEPH JOYCE, Addiction Treatment
KATHRYN ANNE, Hospice Home Health (Protestant)
Sisters 8
Bed Capacity 483
Total Staff 2,324
Patients assisted annually 350,469
Providence Medical Foundation
4805 N.E. Glisan
Portland, OR 97213
Tel: 503-215-6187; Fax: 503-215-6858
BRYCE STRANG, Exec. Dir.

Providence St. Vincent Medical Center
9205 S.W. Barnes Rd.
Portland, OR 97225
Tel: 503-297-4411; Fax: 503-291-2468
Providence Health System.
Legal Title: *Providence Health System.*
RUSS DANIELSON, Admin. Health Care Oper., Providence Health System
DONALD S. ELSOM, Admin., Providence St. Vincent Medical Center
Sr. FARROEL RICHARDSON, S.N.J.M., Dir. Pastoral Svcs.
Revs.:
EDWARD P. MCTIGHE, S.J., Chap.
ELDON J. MCKAMY
Bro. LARRY ESCHWEILER, O.H.
Sr. MARY LOUISE OLBERDING, O.S.B.
Ms. SHIELA SCHAEFFER, Catholic Chap.
Mr. TIMOTHY G. SERBAN, Catholic Chap.
Ms. JOANNE FLANNIGAN, Catholic Chap.
Ms. THERESA VITHAYATHIL, Catholic Chap.
Sr. PATRICIA VALENTINE, S.N.J.M., Catholic Chap.
Ms. CHRISTINE WALLACE, Episcopal Chap.
Ms. SUNDAY BLACKMON, Protestant Chap. (Friends)
Sisters 3
Brothers 1
Bed Capacity 451
Patients assisted annually 836,508

**St. Vincent Medical Foundation, Portland*
Tel: 503-216-2227

Roseburg
Archdiocese of Portland in Oregon

Mercy Medical Center, Inc.
2700 Stewart Pkwy.
Roseburg, OR 97470
Tel: 541-673-0611; Fax: 541-677-4830
VICTOR J. FRESOLONE, Pres. & CEO
JANET BUCHANAN, Vice Pres., Mission Services
Bed Capacity 126
Total Staff 800
Patients assisted annually 212,647
Mercy Healthcare, Inc.
2700 Stewart Pkwy.
Roseburg, OR 97470
Tel: 541-673-0611; Fax: 541-677-4830
SANDRA R. PEARSON, Exec. Asst., Tel: 541-677-2467
Mercy Foundation, Inc.
2700 Stewart Pkwy.
Roseburg, OR 97470
Tel: 541-677-4818; Fax: 541-677-4891
Linus Oakes, Inc.
2700 Stewart Pkwy.
Roseburg, OR 97470
Tel: 541-677-4800; Fax: 541-677-2106
Mercy Rehabilitation and Care Center
525 W. Umpqua
Roseburg, OR 97470
Tel: 541-677-2199; Fax: 541-677-2126

Seaside
Archdiocese of Portland in Oregon

Providence Seaside Hospital
725 S. Wahanna Rd.
Seaside, OR 97138-7735
Tel: 503-717-7000; Fax: 503-717-7505
E-mail: jrenner@providence.org
Web Site: www.providence.org/northcoast
WILLIAM SEXTON, Admin.
Sr. JERI RENNER, O.P., Spiritual Care
Legal Title: *Sisters of Providence in Oregon.*
Bed Capacity 34
Extended Care 22
Total Staff 246
Patients assisted annually 66,000

**Providence Seaside Hospital Foundation, Inc.*
Tel: 503-717-7761; Fax: 503-717-7505

PENNSYLVANIA

Allentown
Diocese of Allentown

Sacred Heart Hospital
421 Chew St.
Allentown, PA 18102-3490
Tel: 610-776-4500; Fax: 610-776-5141
Web Site: shh.org
JOSEPH M. CIMEROLA, Pres. & CEO
Rev. MICHAEL J. VASTI, M.S.C., Chap. & Dir. Pastoral Care
Sisters 5
Beds 241
Skilled Nursing Beds 23
Total Staff 1,275
Patients assisted annually 565,835

Altoona
Diocese of Altoona-Johnstown

Bon Secours - Holy Family Regional Health System
2500 Seventh Ave.
Altoona, PA 16602
Tel: 814-944-1681; Fax: 814-949-5880
E-mail: Davecuz@aol.com
Web Site: www.bonsecoursholyfamily.org
BARBARA BIEHNER, CEO
Patients assisted annually 115,851
Total Staff 725
Bed Capacity 182

Camp Hill
Diocese of Harrisburg

Holy Spirit Hospital and Community Mental Health Center
503 N. 21st St.
Camp Hill, PA 17011-2288
Tel: 717-763-2100; Fax: 717-763-2183
E-mail: jfegan@hsh.org
Web Site: www.hsh.org
Sisters of Christian Charity
Sr. ROMAINE NIEMEYER, S.C.C., Pres.
Legal Title: *Sisters of Christian Charity Health Care Corporation.*
Legal Title: *Comfort Care of Holy Spirit Hospital, Inc.*
Legal Title: *Holy Spirit Ventures, Inc.*
Legal Title: *Holy Spirit Corporation.*
Legal Title: *West Shore ALS, Inc.*
Legal Title: *Holy Spirit Hospital.*
Legal Title: *Spirit Physician Services, Inc.*
Patients assisted annually 15,021
Bed Capacity 317
Bassinets 14
Sisters 22
Total Staff 1,768

Carbondale
Diocese of Scranton

Marian Community Hospital
100 Lincoln Ave.
Carbondale, PA 18407
Tel: 570-281-1000; Fax: 570-282-7177
E-mail: Prdept@marian.hcrn.com
Sr. JEAN COUGHLIN, I.H.M., Pres. & CEO
Rev. LEO P. CUMMINGS, Chap.
Sisters, Servants of the Immaculate Heart of Mary
Bed Capacity 112
Patients assisted annually 61,195
Sisters 11

Maxis Foundation
100 Lincoln Ave.
Carbondale, PA 18407
Tel: 570-281-1000; Fax: 570-282-4730

Maxis Medical Services
100 Lincoln Ave.
Carbondale, PA 18407
Tel: 570-281-1000

Cranberry Township
Diocese of Pittsburgh

St. Francis Hospital Cranberry
(Affiliate of St. Francis Health System)
One St. Francis Way
Cranberry Township, PA 16066
Tel: 412-772-5300
JACK L. SMEDLEY, Exec. Dir.
Bed Capacity 32
Total Staff 159
Patients assisted annually 64,344

St. Francis Nursing Center Cranberry
(Affiliate of St. Francis Health System)
5 St. Francis Way
Cranberry Township, PA 16066
Tel: 724-772-5350
Dr. JOHN L. SPIELER, Dr.P.H., Admin.
Rev. JOHN GALLAGHER, Chap.
Bed Capacity 150
Total Staff 104
Patients assisted annually 177

Darby
Archdiocese of Philadelphia

Mercy Catholic Medical Center
19023
Mercy Fitzgerald Hospital
1500 Lansdowne Ave.
Darby, PA 19023-1291
Tel: 610-237-4000; Fax: 610-237-4202
Opened July 1, 1933. Incorporated May 1, 1969.
Sr. CHRISTINE MCCANN, R.S.M., Chm. Bd.
MARY C. MORRISON, Sr. Vice Pres. and CEO
Chaplains:
Revs.:
LAWRENCE H. HANSEN
SELVAN ALBERT, O.Praem.
JOSEPH C. LAENEN, O.Praem.
Sisters of Mercy 7
Bed Capacity 391
Admissions 15,512
Total Outpatient and ED Visits 176,313

Erie
Diocese of Erie

**Saint Vincent Health Center*
232 W. 25th St.
Erie, PA 16544
Tel: 814-452-5000; Fax: 814-452-5102
Sr. CATHERINE MANNING, S.S.J., Corp. Leader

Revs.:
RAYMOND GRAMATA, Chap.
DENNIS A. MARTIN, Chap.
Saint Vincent Health System
Sr. CATHERINE MANNING, S.S.J., Pres. & CEO, St. Vincent Health System

Havertown
Archdiocese of Philadelphia

Mercy Community Hospital
2000 Old W. Chester Pike
Havertown, PA 19083
Tel: 610-853-7000; Fax: 610-449-0415
Opened Haverford Hospital in 1958; Haverford Community Hospital in 1977; Mercy Community Hospital June 28, 1991.
GEORGE F. MCLAUGHLIN, CEO
Attended by Local Parishes.
Sisters of Mercy
Bed Capacity 107
Patients assisted annually 27,208

Hazleton
Diocese of Scranton

Hazleton-Saint Joseph Medical Center
687 N. Church St.
Hazleton, PA 18201
Tel: 570-501-6000; Fax: 570-501-6203
E-mail: brudegair@ghha.org
Web Site: www.ghha.org
Mr. BERNARD C. RUDEGEAIR, Pres.
Sr. M. FRANCESCA, O.S.F., Supr.
Rev. AUSTIN E. FLANAGAN, Chap.
Bernardine Sisters of the Third Order of St. Francis 11
Beds 111
Patients assisted annually 157,434

Huntingdon Valley
Archdiocese of Philadelphia

Holy Redeemer Health Care Corporation and Foundation
521 Moredon Rd.
Huntingdon Valley, PA 19006
Tel: 215-914-4000; Fax: 215-914-4020
Web Site: www.holyredeemer.com
Subsididary of Holy Redeemer Health System; Sponsor: Sisters of the Holy Redeemer, C.S.R.
Marketing & Public Affairs Department
c/o 1602 Huntingdon Pike
Meadowbrook, PA 19046
Tel: 215-938-3226; Fax: 215-938-3232
Foundation solicits and manages funds for future growth and development.
Total Staff 3,487
Total Assisted 212,000

HRH Management Corporation
667 Welsh Rd.
Huntingdon Valley, PA 19006
Tel: 215-938-4650; Fax: 215-938-4671
Web Site: www.holyredeemer.com
Subsidiary of Holy Redeemer Health System. Sponsor: Sisters of the Holy Redeemer, C.S.R.
Marketing & Public Affairs Department
c/o 1602 Huntingdon Pike
Meadowbrook, PA 19046
Tel: 215-938-3226; Fax: 215-938-3232

Jeannette
Diocese of Greensburg

Jeannette District Memorial Hospital
Jefferson Ave.
Jeannette, PA 15644
Tel: 724-527-3551; Fax: 724-527-9430
E-mail: ram1@jdmh.org
Web Site: jdmh.org
Mr. ROBERT J. BULGER, Pres. & CEO
Revs.:
DOMINIC J. PETROY, O.S.B., Chap.
JUSTIN WITHROW, O.S.B., Assoc. Chap.
Sisters of Charity of Seton Hill 4
Bed Capacity 159

Johnstown
Diocese of Altoona-Johnstown

Good Samaritan Medical Center
1020 Franklin St.
Johnstown, PA 15905
Tel: 814-533-1000; Fax: 814-539-0264
E-mail: stucker@conemaugh.org
Mr. STEVEN E. TUCKER, Pres.
Rev. BERNARD V. GRATTAN
Skilled Nursing Care Center Beds 73
Patients assisted annually 200
Total Staff 43

Langhorne
Archdiocese of Philadelphia

St. Mary Medical Center
Langhorne-Newton Rd.
Langhorne, PA 19047
Tel: 215-750-2000
Sisters of St. Francis of Philadelphia 18
Bed Capacity 287
Total Staff 1,164
Patients assisted Annually 83,000
Opened February 21, 1973.
Sr. CLARE CARTY, O.S.F., Pres.
Rev. GEORGE WALLACE, S.M., Chap.
Affiliate of Catholic Health Initiatives.
Langhorne MRI, Inc.
Langhorne-Newton Rd.
Langhorne, PA 19047
Tel: 215-750-5280; Fax: 215-750-5287

Meadowbrook
Archdiocese of Philadelphia

Holy Redeemer Hospital and Medical Center
1648 Huntingdon Pike
Meadowbrook, PA 19046
Tel: 215-947-3000
Web Site: www.holyredeemer.com
Subsidiary of Holy Redeemer Health System, Inc.
Sponsor: Sisters of the Holy Redeemer, C.S.R.
GAIL LATIMER, COO
Chaplains:
Revs.:
MICHAEL C. BOLESTA
JAMES J. COONAN
TIMOTHY M. JUDGE
Acute care community hospital, providing broad spectrum of services, including preventive, rehabilitative, emergency and obstetrical care plus pastoral counseling.
Bed Capacity 283
Total Assisted 11,800
Total Staff 1,200

Muncy
Diocese of Scranton

Muncy Valley Hospital
215 E. Water St.
Muncy, PA 17756
Tel: 570-546-8282; Fax: 570-546-4150
E-mail: Lcioffi:@shscares.org
KIRBY O. SMITH, Pres.
Sr. SHARON HARTMAN, S.C.C., Dir., Pastoral Care
Capacity 184
Patients assisted annually 74,308

Nanticoke
Diocese of Scranton

Mercy Special Care Hospital
128 W. Washington St.
Nanticoke, PA 18634
Tel: 570-735-5000; Fax: 570-740-5220
ROBERT D. WILLIAMS, Admin.
Bed Capacity 68
Patients assisted annually 20,000

New Castle
Diocese of Pittsburgh

St. Francis Hospital of New Castle
(Affiliate of St. Francis Health System)
1000 S. Mercer St.
New Castle, PA 16101
Tel: 724-658-3511
Sr. PATRICIA FOGLE, O.S.F., CEO
Bed Capacity (includes 45 skilled nursing beds) 187
Patients assisted annually 100,933
Schools:
Nursing 69
Radiology 20
St. Francis Hospice of New Castle:
Total Staff 4
Patients assisted annually 4,005
St. Francis Home Health of New Castle:
Total Staff 25
Patients assisted annually 13,333

Philadelphia
Archdiocese of Philadelphia

Mercy Hospital of Philadelphia
501 S. 54th St.
Philadelphia, PA 19143
Tel: 215-748-9000
Opened July 2, 1918. Incorporated May 1, 1969.
Sr. CHRISTINE MCCANN, Chm. Bd.
PLATO A. MARINAKOS, Pres. & CEO Mercy Health System
BERNADETTE M. MANGAN, Senior Vice Pres. & CEO Mercy Hospital of Philadelphia
Chaplains:
Revs.:
LAWRENCE H. HANSEN, Dir. Pastoral Care
MATTHEW MICHAEL
Sisters of Mercy 14
Bed Capacity 266
Patients assisted annually 37,500

Nazareth Hospital
2601 Holme Ave.
Philadelphia, PA 19152
Tel: 215-335-6000; Fax: 215-335-6598
GREGORY T. WOZNIAK, Pres. & CEO
Revs.:
EDWARD V. AVERY
JOSEPH J. SWEENEY
Affiliate of Catholic Health Initiatives.
Bed Capacity 249
Total Staff 1,000
Patients assisted annually 162,000

St. Agnes Medical Center
1900 S. Broad St.
Philadelphia, PA 19145
Tel: 215-339-4100
Opened May 15, 1888.
Sr. MARGARET T. SULLIVAN, O.S.F., Pres.
Chaplains:
Revs.:
JOHN BRADLEY
JOSEPH MCCLOSKEY
Affiliate of Catholic Health Initiatives.
Bed Capacity 153
Total Staff 645
Annually Assisted 112,648

Pittsburgh
Diocese of Pittsburgh

Mercy Hospital of Pittsburgh
(Affiliate of Pittsburgh Mercy Health System)
1400 Locust St.
Pittsburgh, PA 15219
Tel: 412-232-8111; Fax: 412-232-7380
Web Site: www.mercylink.org
PENN KRAUSE, Exec. Vice Pres. & COO
Bed Capacity 411
Patients assisted annually 244,325
Total Staff 1,993

Mercy Providence Hospital
(Affiliate of Pittsburgh Mercy Health System)
1004 Arch St.
Pittsburgh, PA 15212
Tel: 412-323-5600; Fax: 412-323-5685
E-mail: ksweeney@mercy.pmhs.org
Sr. PATRICIA MARY HESPELEIN, Vice Pres. Mission Council
Rev. ROBERT MELLOTT, Chap.
Sisters 3
Bed Capacity 146
Patients assisted annually 268,000

Pittsburgh Mercy Foundation
1709 Blvd. of the Allies, Ste. 100
Pittsburgh, PA 15219-5947
Tel: 412-232-7504; Fax: 412-232-7810
E-mail: dbalcom@mercy.pmhs.org
Web Site: www.mercylink.org
Bed Capacity 604
Patients assisted annually 255,000
Total Staff 3,000

Pittsburgh Mercy Health System, Inc.
1400 Locust St.
Pittsburgh, PA 15219
Tel: 412-232-8111; Fax: 412-232-7380
Web Site: www.mercylink.org
Mr. GREGG G. ZOLLER, Pres. & CEO
Beds 722
Patients assisted annually 410,730
Staff 2,574
Parent company of the following subsidiaries:
Coolock Enterprises, Inc.
Tel: 412-232-8111; Fax: 412-232-7380
Mercy Primary Care, Inc.
Tel: 412-232-8111; Fax: 412-232-7380
The Mercy Hospital of Pittsburgh
Tel: 412-232-8111; Fax: 412-232-7380
Pittsburgh Mercy Foundation
Tel: 412-232-5583; Fax: 412-232-7810
Mercy Life Center Corporation
Tel: 412-232-8111; Fax: 412-232-7380
Mercy Senior Care: St. Joseph's
Tel: 412-232-8111; Fax: 412-232-7380
St. Pius X Residence, Inc.
Tel: 412-232-8111; Fax: 412-232-7380

Mercy Providence Hospital (Formerly Divine Providence Hospital of Pittsburgh)
Tel: 412-323-5600; Fax: 412-323-5685

St. Francis Medical Center
(Affiliate of St. Francis Health System)
400 45th St.
Pittsburgh, PA 15201
Tel: 412-622-4343
JOSEPH A. RUFFOLO, Acting CEO
Sr. ANN BREMER, O.S.F., COO
Schools:
Professional Nursing 38
Practical Nursing 16
Anesthesia 17
Respiratory Care 8
Sisters 4
Sisters of St. Francis of Millvale 23
Bed Capacity 588
Total Staff 2,200
Patients assisted annually 227,191

St. Francis Nursing Center-East
(Affiiate of St. Francis Health)
745 N. Highland Ave.
Pittsburgh, PA 15206
Tel: 412-362-6622
Sr. BARBARA JEAN DONOVAN, Admin.
Rev. EDWARD L. HOFFMAN, Chap.
Sisters of St. Francis of Whitehall 1
Sisters of St. Francis of Millvale 1
Bed Capacity 150
Total Staff 95
Patients assisted annually 187

**St. Francis Health System*
4401 Penn Ave.
Pittsburgh, PA 15224-1380
Tel: 412-622-4343; Fax: 412-622-4858
Web Site: www.sfhs.edu
Sr. FLORENCE BRANDT, O.S.F., Pres. & CEO
Parent company for the following affiliates:
St. Francis Medical Center
Tel: 412-622-4343; Fax: 412-622-4858
St. Francis Nursing Center-North
Tel: 724-772-5350; Fax: 724-772-5356
St. Francis Nursing Center-East
Tel: 412-362-6622; Fax: 412-362-5436
St. Francis Hospital of New Castle
Tel: 724-658-3511; Fax: 724-656-6181

**St. Francis Health Foundation*
Tel: 412-622-4343; Fax: 412-622-7163

**St. Francis Financial Corporation*
Tel: 412-622-4343; Fax: 412-622-8029

**St. Francis Health Care Services*
Tel: 412-622-4343; Fax: 412-688-3419
Beds 1,048
Total Assisted 392,722
Total Staff 2,636

Pottsville
Diocese of Allentown

Good Samaritan Regional Medical Center
700 E. Norwegian St.
Pottsville, PA 17901
Tel: 717-621-4000; Fax: 717-622-7950
Mr. GINO J. PAZZAGLINI, Pres.
Rev. JAMES MORGAN, Chap.
Daughters of Charity 10
Total Staff 700
Beds 221
Bassinets 20
Patients assisted annually 129,555
Good Samaritan Health Corporation
700 E. Norwegian St.
Pottsville, PA 17901
Tel: 717-621-4003
Good Samaritan Foundation, Inc.
700 E. Norwegian St.
Pottsville, PA 17901
Tel: 717-621-4252
Good Samaritan Regional Medical Center Auxiliary
700 E. Norwegian St.
Pottsville, PA 17901
Tel: 717-621-4242
Seton Medical Group, Inc.
700 E. Norwegian St.
Pottsville, PA 17901
Tel: 717-621-4003

Reading
Diocese of Allentown

Bornemann Health Corporation
c/o Saint Joseph Hospital, 12th St. & Walnut St., P.O. Box 316
Reading, PA 19603-0316
Tel: 610-358-4269; Fax: 610-358-4299
Mr. JOHN MORAHAN, Pres. & CEO
Total Staff 81
Bed Capacity 92
Total Assisted 32,940

Community Campus of St. Joseph Medical Center
215 N. 12th St., Box 316
Reading, PA 19603
Tel: 610-358-4215
Mr. PATRICK F. ROCHE, Pres.

Saint Joseph Medical Center
215 N. 12th St., P.O. Box 316
Reading, PA 19603
Tel: 610-378-2000; Fax: 610-378-2798
E-mail: bridgetmcnamara@chi-east.org
Opened Aug. 26, 1873.
JOHN R. MORAHAN, Pres.
Sr. BRIDGET MCNAMARA, O.S.F., Vice Pres., Mission & Ministry
Sisters 13
Total Staff 1,374
Beds 301
Bassinets 16
Patients assisted annually 267,432

Scranton
Diocese of Scranton

Mercy Hospital
Mercy Health Partners
746 Jefferson Ave.
Scranton, PA 18501
Tel: 570-348-7100; Fax: 570-348-7639
E-mail: spetula@mhs.nepa.com
JOHN L. NESPOLI, Pres. & CEO
SUE PETULA, Pres.
Sr. JOMARIE KACZANOWSKI, R.S.M., Local Coord.
Rev. JOHN C. RUTH, Chap.
Mercy Foundation
746 Jefferson Ave.
Scranton, PA 18501
Tel: 570-348-7024; Fax: 570-348-7639
JAMES E. O'BRIEN, ESQ.
Sisters of Mercy 13
Bed Capacity 274
Bassinets 18
Total Capacity 292
Patients assisted annually 252,996

Mercy Med-Care, Inc.
746 Jefferson Ave.
PA 18501
Tel: 570-348-7074; Fax: 570-348-7021

Wilkes-Barre
Diocese of Scranton

Mercy Hospital
Mercy Health Partners
25 Church St.
Wilkes-Barre, PA 18765
Tel: 570-826-3100; Fax: 570-831-8989
JOHN L. NESPOLI, Pres. & CEO
V. GAIL BLAUM, Pres.
Sr. CAROL GALLAGHER, R.S.M., Sisters Liasion
Rev. JOSEPH C. STREIT, Chap.
Sisters of Mercy 1
Bed Capacity 215
Bassinets 15
Patients assisted annually 312,000

Williamsport
Diocese of Scranton

Divine Providence Hospital of the Sisters of Christian Charity
1100 Grampian Blvd.
Williamsport, PA 17701
Tel: 570-326-8000; Fax: 570-326-8902
E-mail: Lcioffi@shscares.org
Web Site: shscarcs.org
KIRBY O. SMITH, Pres.
Sr. GRACE KEREKES, S.C.C., Supr.
Rev. JOSEPH B. WILSON, Chap.
Bed Capacity 167
Patients assisted annually 38,439

Providence Health System Foundation, Inc.
1100 Grampian Blvd.
Williamsport, PA 17701
Tel: 570-320-7010; Fax: 570-326-8902
E-mail: Lcioffi@shscares.org
Web Site: www.shscares.org
Sr. JEAN MOHL, S.C.C., Pres.

Sisters of Christian Charity Healthcare Corporation
1100 Grampian Blvd.
Williamsport, PA 17701
Tel: 570-326-8181; Fax: 570-326-8902
E-mail: Lcioffi@shscares.org
Web Site: www.shscares.org

**Susquehanna Regional Home Health Services*
1100 Grampian Blvd.
Williamsport, PA 17701
Tel: 570-320-7690; Fax: 570-323-0716
E-mail: Lcioffi@shscares.org
Web Site: www.shscares.org
Patients assisted annually 39,122

PUERTO RICO

Rio Piedras
Archdiocese of San Juan, Puerto Rico

Hospital del Maestro
Calle Flamboyanes #218, Hyde Park
Rio Piedras, PR 00929
Tel: 787-763-8383
Rev. Msgr. ANGEL VALDES, Chap.

San German
Diocese of Mayaguez, Puerto Rico

Hospital of the Immaculate Conception
Box 285
San German, PR 00683
Sisters of Charity
Sr. MARIA TERESA DIAZ BIRD, Supr.
Rev. FERNANDO PALACIO SALAZAR, Chap.
JAIME MAESTRE, Admin.
Sisters 9
Beds 135
Patients Assisted Annually:
Admission 8,640
Emergency Visits 38,400

San Juan
Archdiocese of San Juan, Puerto Rico

Casa La Providencia, Inc.
Drug Rehabilitation Center.
Tel: 787-725-5358; Fax: 787-725-0058
E-mail: info@casalaprovidencia.org
Web Site: casalaprovidencia.org
Mailing Address:
P.O. Box 9020614
San Juan, PR 00902-0614
Tel: 787-725-5358; Fax: 787-725-0058
Sisters Oblates of the Most Holy Redeemer 4
Bed Capacity 36
Annually Assisted 110
Total Staff 23

Centro Medico de P.R.
Calle 10 #1030, Puerto Nuevo, 00920
Apdo. 347
San Juan, PR 00936
Tel: 787-763-7272
Revs.:
FRANCISCO ARONA, Chap., Hospital Oncologico, Tel: 787-251-6466
PEDRO L. ZABALLA, Chap., Hospital Universitario, Tel: 787-754-3535
MANUEL GARCIA, Chap. Hospital Municipal, Tel: 787-796-3418
JUAN PATRON, Chap., Hospital Industrial, Tel: 787-752-1149
BARTOLOME VANRELL, Chap., Hospital Cardiovascular, Tel: 787-754-8500

VA Medical Center
One Veterans Plaza
San Juan, PR 00927-5800
Tel: 787-641-7582, Ext. 12167
Revs.:
JOSE E. COLON, Chief Chap. Serv.
HECTOR DIAZ ESTRADA, Chap.

RHODE ISLAND

North Providence
Diocese of Providence

St. Joseph Health Services of Rhode Island - Our Lady of Fatima Hospital
200 High Service Ave.
North Providence, RI 02904
Tel: 401-456-3000
Web Site: www.fatimahospital.com
Mr. H. JOHN KEIMIG, Pres.
Rev. JOHN PETROCELLI, Dir. Pastoral Care
Chaplains:
Revs.:
JOHN N. DONDAPATI (India)
VARGHESE THEKKATTAYIL (India)

Miss ELIZABETH DECOSTA, R.N., Dir. School of Nursing
Student Nurses 100
Beds 262
Patients assisted annually 201,000
Total Staff 1,800

Providence
Diocese of Providence

St. Joseph Health Services of Rhode Island - St. Joseph Hospital for Specialty Care
21 Peace St.
Providence, RI 02907
Tel: 401-456-4080; Fax: 401-456-4089
Web Site: www.stjosephri.com
Mr. H. JOHN KEIMIG, Pres.
Rev. C. LEON KACHEL, Chap.
Beds 104
Includes:
Southern New England Rehabilitation Center
Tel: 401-456-4500; Fax: 401-456-4501
JON A. MUKAND, M.D., Ph.D., Medical Dir.
A joint venture of St. Joseph Hospital and Rhode Island Hospital.
Corporate Care Occupational Health and Safety Services
Tel: 401-456-4020; Fax: 401-456-4203
JACQUELINE HESS, M.D., Medical Dir.
St. Joseph Center for Health & Human Services
Tel: 401-456-4321; Fax: 401-456-4089
MUNAWAR AZAM, M.D., Medical Dir.
St. Joseph Center for Psychiatric Services
Tel: 401-456-4437; Fax: 401-456-4078
RONALD GOBEIL, D.O., Medical Dir.

SOUTH CAROLINA

Charleston
Diocese of Charleston

Bon Secours St. Francis Hospital
2095 Henry Tecklenburg Dr.
Charleston, SC 29414
Tel: 843-402-1000
Sponsored by the Sisters of Bon Secours, Marriottsville, MD.
Sr. ANNE MARIE MACK, C.B.S., Pres., Sisters of Bon Secours USA
Mr. ALLEN P. CARROLL, Admin.
Sr. MARY GEMMA NEVILLE, C.B.S., Dir. Pastoral Svcs. & Clinical Pastoral Education
Sr. KATHLEEN OWEN, O.P., Assoc. Dir. Pastoral Svcs.
Bed Capacity 141
Staff 998
Patients assisted annually 80,957

**St. Francis Xavier Home Health Care, Inc.*

Greenville
Diocese of Charleston

**Bon Scours St. Francis Health System, Inc.*
One St. Francis Dr.
Greenville, SC 29601
Tel: 864-255-1000; Fax: 864-255-1034

**St. Francis Hospital, Inc.*
Tel: 864-255-1000; Fax: 864-255-1034
Mr. RICHARD NEUGENT, CEO
NINA BAGWELL, Supvr.
Sisters of Bon Scours 1
Bed Capacity 319
Patients assisted annually 300,668

SOUTH DAKOTA

Aberdeen
Diocese of Sioux Falls

Avera St. Luke's
Aberdeen, SD 57401
Tel: 605-622-5000
DALE STEIN, Pres. & CEO
Rev. CHARLES EMEZIE (Nigeria)
ELAINE VAN DOVER, Dir. Pastoral Care
Presentation Sisters of the B.V.M.(Aberdeen, SD) 16
Bed Capacity 225
Bassinets 20
Annually Assisted 174,418
Total Staff 892
Sponsored by Sisters of the Presentation of the B.V.M. of Aberdeen, SD, and Benedictine Sisters of Sacred Heart Monastery, Yankton, SD.
Avera St. Luke's dba Avera Mother Joseph Manor Retirement Community
1002 N. Jay St.
Aberdeen, SD 57401
Tel: 605-622-5850; Fax: 605-622-5851
E-mail: tom.snyder@averastlukes.org
TOM SNYDER, Admin.
Rev. CHARLES EMEZIE (Nigeria)
Presentation Sisters of the B.V.M. (Aberdeen, SD) 4
Residents 81
Units for Apartment Living 58
Assisted Living Beds 34
Total Staff 130
Adult Day Care, Community Outreach, Respite Care, Health Screening Clinics, and Family Support Council.

Gettysburg
Diocese of Sioux Falls

Gettysburg Medical Center
57442
Tel: 605-765-2488
MARK C. SCHMIDT, Exec. Dir.
Gettysburg Day Care Center
700 E. Garfield
Gettysburg, SD 57442
Tel: 605-765-2541; Fax: 605-765-2704
Staff 4
Children 25
BETTY BROWN, Dir.
Beds 67
Assisted Living Units 16
Residential Living Units 12

Milbank
Diocese of Sioux Falls

St. Bernard Providence Hospital
901 E. Virgil Ave.
Milbank, SD 57252
Tel: 605-432-4538; Fax: 605-432-5412
Rev. RAY OTTO, O.S.B., Chap.
Sr. GENEVIEVE KARELS, D.S.M.P., Supr.
Daughters of St. Mary of Providence 5
Bed Capacity 35
Staff 90
Patients assisted annually 4,000

Mitchell
Diocese of Sioux Falls

Avera Queen of Peace
525 N. Foster
Mitchell, SD 57301
Tel: 605-995-2000; Fax: 605-995-2441
E-mail: ron.jacobson@averaqueenofpeace.org
Web Site: www.averaqueenofpeace.org
RON JACOBSON, Pres. & CEO
Sisters 6
Beds 256
Staff 695
Patients assisted annually 60,000
Sponsored by Sisters of the Presentation of the B.V.M., Aberdeen, SD, and Benedictine Sisters of Sacred Heart Monastery, Yankton, SD.
Avera Queen of Peace dba Avera Brady Health & Rehabilitation, Avera Brady Assisted Living
500 S. Ohlman
Mitchell, SD 57301
Tel: 605-966-7701; Fax: 605-995-6134
Mrs. ROBERTA CLARK, Admin.
Rev. THOMAS J. MCPHILLIPS, Chap.
Presentation Sisters of the B.V.M. 1
Skilled Nursing Care Units 84
Senior Residences 9
Assisted Living 130
Total Staff 119
Sponsored by Sisters of the Presentation of the B.V.M., Aberdeen, SD, and Benedictine Sisters of Sacred Heart Monastery, Yankton, SD.
Bishop Hoch Villa
Units for Congregate Living 6
Additional Senior Units 3
Sisters 6
Beds 256
Staff 695
Patients assisted annually 60,000

Parkston
Diocese of Sioux Falls

St. Benedict Health Care Center dba Avera St. Benedict Health Center
Parkston, SD 57366
Tel: 605-928-3311; Fax: 605-928-7368
E-mail: sbhc@santel.net
GALE N. WALKER, Admin.
Benedictine Sisters (Yankton, SD) 2
Bed Capacity 105

Pierre
Diocese of Sioux Falls

St. Mary's Foundation
800 E. Dakota
Pierre, SD 57501
Tel: 605-224-3451; Fax: 605-224-3459
E-mail: ellenlee@chi-midwest.org
Web Site: www.St_Marys.com
ELLEN J. LEE, Exec. Dir.

St. Mary's Healthcare Center of Pierre, South Dakota
800 E. Sioux Ave.
Pierre, SD 57501
Tel: 605-224-3100; Fax: 605-224-3439
E-mail: jimrussell@chi-midwest.org
Web Site: www.St_Mary's.com
JAMES D.M. RUSSELL, CEO
Benedictine Sisters 1
Beds 86
Annually Assisted 27,758
Staff 400
Includes: Maryhouse Residential Nursing Facility and Parkwood Retirement Apartments.

Sioux Falls
Diocese of Sioux Falls

Avera McKennan
Sioux Falls, SD 57110-5045
Tel: 605-322-8000; Fax: 605-322-7822
Web Site: www.mckennan.org
Mr. FREDRICK W. SLUNECKA, Pres. & CEO
Rev. GARY TERNES, Chap.
Sponsored by Sisters of the Presentation of the B.V.M. of Aberdeen, S.D., and Benedictine Sisters of Sacred Heart Monastery, Yankton, S.D.
Avera McKennan dba Avera Prince of Peace Retirement Community
4500 S. Prince of Peace Pl.
Sioux Falls, SD 57103
Tel: 605-322-5600; Fax: 605-322-5622
Presentation Sisters of B.V.M. 1
Nursing Home Beds 90
Congregate Apartments 74
Assisted Living Apartments 32
Total Assisted 204
Total Staff 128
Sisters of the Presentation of the B.V.M. (Aberdeen, SD) 7
Bed Capacity 429
Total Staff 3,000
Patients assisted annually 220,000

Tyndall
Diocese of Sioux Falls

St. Michael's Hospital
Tyndall, SD 57066
Tel: 605-589-3341
CAROL DEURMIER, CEO
Bed Capacity 25
Nursing Home Beds 9
Annually Assisted 6,500
Total Staff 90

Yankton
Diocese of Sioux Falls

Sacred Heart Health Services dba Avera Sacred Heart Hospital
501 Summit
Yankton, SD 57078
Tel: 605-668-8000; Fax: 605-665-0170
PAMELA REZAC, Pres & CEO
Sisters 5
Beds 144
Sacred Heart Health Services dba Avera Sister James Nursing Homes
501 Summit
Yankton, SD 57078
Tel: 605-668-8000; Fax: 605-665-0170
Beds 113

TENNESSEE

Chattanooga
Diocese of Knoxville

Memorial Hospital (1952)
(Div. of Sisters of Charity of Nazareth Health Corp., S.C.N.H.C.)
2525 DeSales Ave.
Chattanooga, TN 37404
Tel: 423-495-2525
Web Site: memorial.org
Mr. CLARK TAYLOR, Pres. & CEO
JAMES W. ABLES, Asst. Dir.
2500 Citico Ave.
Chattanooga, TN 37404

Sisters 6
Bed Capacity 420
Patients assisted annually 400,030
Total Staff 2,371
Memorial Health Care System Foundation, Inc.
2525 DeSales Ave.
Chattanooga, TN 37404

Knoxville
Diocese of Knoxville

St. Mary's Health System, Inc. (1930)
900 E. Oak Hill Ave.
Knoxville, TN 37917
Tel: 865-545-8000; Fax: 865-545-6732
E-mail: rwilliams@stmaryshealth.com
Web Site: www.stmaryshealth.com
Conducted by Sisters of Mercy of the Americas
RICH WILLIAMS, Pres.
Rev. BERTRAND DEMERS, Chap.
Sisters 6
Bed Capacity 473
Patients assisted annually 216,902
Total Staff 2,152
St. Mary's Health System, Inc.

Nashville
Diocese of Nashville

St. Thomas Hospital (1898)
4220 Harding Rd.
Nashville, TN 37205
Tel: 615-222-2111; Fax: 615-222-6502
E-mail: nshlsthl.stthomas.org
Web Site: saintthomas.org
Legal Title: *St. Thomas Hospital.*
Daughters of Charity of St. Vincent de Paul, (East Central Prov., Evansville, IN)
THOMAS BEEMAN, Pres. & CEO
Sr. PRISCILLA GRIMES, D.C., Supr.
Sisters 7
Lay Staff 3,690
Beds 541
Chaplains 8
Patients assisted annually 204,113
Saint Thomas Foundation
Tel: 615-222-6800; Fax: 615-222-6159
St. Thomas Health Services
Tel: 615-222-2111; Fax: 615-222-6502
Covenant Care, Inc.
Tel: 615-222-2111; Fax: 615-222-6502
Calhoun S.T.H.S., Inc.,
Tel: 615-222-2111; Fax: 615-222-6502

TEXAS

Alice
Diocese of Corpus Christi

CHRISTUS Spohn Hospital Alice
Mailing Address:
1702 Santa Fe
Corpus Christi, TX 78404
700 N. Airport
Alice, TX 78322
Tel: 361-661-8000; Fax: 361-661-8074
E-mail: dominic_dominguez@iwhs.org
DOMINIC DOMINGUEZ, Vice Pres. & Admin.
Sr. RACHEL CASTILLO, M.C.D.P., Chap.
Beds 49
Staff 227
Patients assisted annually 41,778

Amarillo
Diocese of Amarillo

**Baptist St. Anthony's Health System*
1600 Wallace Blvd.
Amarillo, TX 79106
Tel: 806-212-2000; Fax: 806-212-2277
E-mail: loark@bsahs.org
Sisters of Charity of the Incarnate Word (C.C.V.I.)
Mr. LEE ROARK, Dir. Pastoral Care
Sr. ANN MILLER, S.F.C.C., Coord. Mission & Ministry

**Baptist St. Anthony's Hospital - St. Anthony's Campus*
200 N.W. Seventh St., P.O. Box 950
Amarillo, TX 79176
Tel: 806-212-2000; Fax: 806-212-6547

**The Auxiliary of St. Anthony's Hospital, Inc.*
Tel: 806-212-5404

**Baptist St. Anthony's Health System*
Tel: 806-212-6042

St. Anthony's Hospice and Life Enrichment Center
600 N. Tyler, P.O. Box 950
Amarillo, TX 79176
Tel: 806-378-6777; Fax: 806-378-5031
SHARON HUTCHINSON, Dir.

Austin
Diocese of Austin

Seton McCarthy Community Health Center
2811 E. Second St.
Austin, TX 78702
Tel: 512-324-4929; Fax: 512-324-4948
RICH PARSELLS, Site Mgr.
Total clients assisted annually 38,331

Seton Medical Center
1201 W. 38th St.
Austin, TX 78705
Tel: 512-324-1000; Fax: 512-459-5629
E-mail: mdigenan@seton.org
Web Site: www.goodhealth.com
Daughters of Charity Health Services of Austin
Mr. CHARLES J. BARNETT, Pres. & CEO
Rev. JIM DENHAM, Dir. Pastoral Care
Chaplains:
Revs.:
DON OLIVER WEERAKKODY
JOSEPH GENIESSE
LAWRENCE J. STEHLING
Daughters of Charity of St. Vincent de Paul 17
Bed Capacity 1,296
Patients assisted annually 484,098

Seton Northwest Hospital
11113 Research Blvd.
Austin, TX 78759
Tel: 512-324-6000; Fax: 512-324-6924
E-mail: cdurant@seton.org
Web Site: www,goodhealth.com
Daughters of Charity Health Services of Austin
CHARLES E. DURANT, JR., Vice Pres., Admin.
JIM DENHAM, Dir. Pastoral Care
Bed Capacity 92
Patients assisted annually 60,500
Staff 358

Seton South Community Health Center
3706 S. First St.
Austin, TX 78704
Tel: 512-324-4940
Mr. LARRY MEJIA, Dir.
Patients assisted annually 18,404

Seton Topfer Community Clinic
8913 Collingfield Dr.
Austin, TX 78758
Tel: 512-324-6850
GARY COE, Admin.

Beaumont
Diocese of Beaumont

CHRISTUS St. Elizabeth Hospital
2830 Calder Ave., P.O. Box 5405
Beaumont, TX 77726-5405
Tel: 409-892-7171; Fax: 409-899-8191
Operated by CHRISTUS Health Southeast Texas
Mr. ED MYERS, CEO
Sisters 7
Bed Capacity 461
Patients assisted annually 234,684

Beeville
Diocese of Corpus Christi

CHRISTUS Spohn Hospital Beeville
Mailing Address:
1702 Santa Fe
Corpus Christi, TX 78404
1500 E. Houston Hwy.
Beeville, TX 78102
Tel: 361-354-2000; Fax: 361-358-9322
E-mail: david_wagner@iwhs.org
DAVID S. WAGNER, Vice Pres. & Admin.
Sr. SARA M. CARTER, Pastoral Staff
Total Staff 3,904
Beds 69
Patients assisted annually 41,778

Brenham
Diocese of Austin

Trinity Community Medical Center of Brenham
700 Medical Pkwy.
Brenham, TX 77833
Tel: 979-836-6173; Fax: 979-830-2277
Web Site: trinitymed.org
JOHN SIMMS, Admin.
Sr. GERALDINE PALUSZAK, O.S.F., Dir. Pastoral Care/ Mission

Trinity Care Center
400 Sayles
Brenham, TX 77833
Tel: 979-836-9770
Sisters of St. Francis of Sylvania, OH 1
Bed Capacity 120
FLORENCE JULIAN, Exec. Dir.
Sr. WINIFRED TEMPLIN, O.S.F., Dir. Pastoral Care
Sisters of St. Francis of Sylvania, OH 3
Bed Capacity 60
Patients assisted annually 27,000
Staff 275

Bryan
Diocese of Austin

Burleson St. Joseph Health Center of Caldwell, Texas
2801 Franciscan Dr.
Bryan, TX 77802
Tel: 409-776-2599; Fax: 409-774-4590
E-mail: info@mail.st-joseph.org
Web Site: www.st-joseph.org
WILLIAM F. HYER, JR., Sec.
Patients assisted annually 13,765
Total Staff 63

St. Joseph Regional Health Center
2801 Franciscan Dr.
Bryan, TX 77802
Tel: 979-776-3777; Fax: 979-774-4590
E-mail: dbuch@mail.st-joseph.org
Web Site: http://www.st-joseph.org
DANIEL L. BUCHE, CEO
Rev. Msgr. JOHN C. MALINOWSKI, Chap.
Dr. JAMES W. STEGALL, Chm. Bd.
Bed Capacity 313
Patients assisted annually 247,000
Total Staff 1,535
Sisters of St. Francis of Sylvania, OH 6

St. Joseph Services Corp.
2801 Franciscan Dr.
Bryan, TX 77802
Tel: 979-776-3777; Fax: 979-774-4590
E-mail: info@mail.st-joseph.org
Web Site: http://www.st-joseph.org
Sr. GRETCHEN KUNZ, O.S.F., CEO
Dr. BILL H. MAGEE, Chm. Bd.
Bed Capacity 387
LTC Beds 208
Patients assisted annually 308,500
LTC Staff 159
Total Staff 1,930
Sisters of St. Francis of Sylvania, OH 8

Corpus Christi
Diocese of Corpus Christi

CHRISTUS Spohn Health System
1702 Santa Fe
Corpus Christi, TX 78404
Tel: 361-881-3400; Fax: 361-885-0566
E-mail: jake_henry@iwhs.org
Beds 1,145
Total Annually Assisted 605,193

CHRISTUS Spohn Hospital Shoreline
Mailing Address:
1702 Santa Fe
Corpus Christi, TX 78404
600 Elizabeth St.
Corpus Christi, TX 78404
Tel: 361-881-3148; Fax: 361-881-3149
E-mail: andy_harris@iwhs.org
ANDREW HARRIS, Admin.
Pastoral Staff:
Revs.:
JOSE GUITERREZ
DAVID SAENZ
EDWARD SALAZAR, S.J.
Sr. MARJORIE MULDOWNEY
Total Staff 1,374
Beds 370
Sisters of the Incarnate Word 7
Patients assisted annually 133,878

CHRISTUS Spohn Hospital Memorial
Mailing Address:
1702 Santa Fe
Corpus Christi, TX 78404
2606 Hospital Blvd.
Corpus Christi, TX 78405
Tel: 361-902-4000; Fax: 361-902-4949
E-mail: reese_jackson@iwhs.org
Mr. REESE JACKSON, Admin.
Pastoral Staff:
LYNNE BLACKLER, Chap.
Rev. MEDICUS RENTZ
Total Staff 1,174
Beds 397
Patients assisted annually 204,844

CHRISTUS Spohn Hospital South
Mailing Address:
1702 Santa Fe
Corpus Christi, TX 78404
5950 Saratoga Blvd.
Corpus Christi, TX 78414
Tel: 361-959-5000; Fax: 361-985-5109
E-mail: nora_fraiser@iwhs.org
Sisters of Charity of the Incarnate Word (San Antonio, TX)
NORA FRASIER, Vice Pres. & Admin.
Sr. JUNE SOUDER, S.S.J., Chap.
A member of the Spohn Health System.
Sisters 1
Total Staff 424
Beds 98
Patients assisted annually 60,694

Dallas
Diocese of Dallas

St. Paul Medical Center
5909 Harry Hines Blvd.
Dallas, TX 75235
Tel: 214-879-1000
Mr. FRANK TIEDEMANN, Pres.
Sr. NOREEN CREAN, D.C., Vice Pres. Mission Affairs & Ethics
Department of Chaplain Services,
Revs.:
F. PATRICK HANSER, C.M., Dir.
JOHN ALPHONSO (India)
RUDY RENTERIA (FWT)
ROYCE TAYLOR, Baptist Chap.
Sr. EDITH THOMPSON, D.C., Volunteer
Sr. MICHAEL FRIEBE, D.C., Volunteer
Sr. MARY ANGELYN PERA, D.C., Volunteer
Daughters of Charity of St. Vincent de Paul 11
Total Staff 1,200
Bed Capacity 554
Patients assisted annually 155,216

St. Paul Medical Center
5909 Harry Hines Blvd.
Dallas, TX 75235
(Texas Non-Profit Corp.)
Staff 1,200
Patients assisted annually 17,530

St. Paul Medical Center Foundation Inc.
5909 Harry Hines Blvd.
Dallas, TX 75235
Tel: 214-879-2000; Fax: 214-879-2019
(Texas Non-Profit Corp.)
MARY LOVE (BITSY) HENDERSON, Pres.
Support Organization for St. Paul Medical Center.

El Paso
Diocese of El Paso

Centro San Vicente
(Affiliated with Daughters of Charity National Health System)
8061 Alameda
El Paso, TX 79915
Tel: 915-859-7545
JIM C. PARKER, Exec. Dir.
Legal Title: *Centro San Vicente*
Community Oriented Primary Health Care Center (Medical Care).
Total Assisted 32,000

La Clinica Guadalupana, Inc.
901 Ascencion
El Paso, TX 79927
Tel: 915-852-3328; Fax: 915-852-4246
E-mail: guadalupana@juno.com
Sr. PEGGY DENEWETH, Contact Person
Sr. JANET GILDEA, M.D., Staff Physician & Medical Dir.

Houston
Diocese of Galveston—Houston

CHRISTUS Health
2600 N. Loop W.
Houston, TX 77092
Tel: 713-680-4835; Fax: 713-812-6867
Web Site: www.christushealth.org
THOMAS C. ROYER, M.D., Pres. & CEO
CHRISTUS Health Service Center
2600 N. Loop W.
Houston, TX 77092
Tel: 713-680-4835; Fax: 713-812-6867
CHRISTUS Health Corporate Office
2600 N. Loop W.
Houston, TX 77092
Tel: 713-680-4835; Fax: 713-812-6867

CHRISTUS Health Gulf Coast
1919 LaBranch
Houston, TX 77002
Tel: 713-756-5008; Fax: 713-657-7123
Web Site: CHRISTUShealth.org
SALLY JEFFCOAT, Pres.
CHRISTUS St. Joseph Hospital
1919 La Branch
Houston, TX 77002
Tel: 713-757-1000; Fax: 713-657-7123
Bed Capacity 792
Patients 311,978
Staff 2,200
SALLY JEFFCOAT, CEO
CHRISTUS St. Catherine Health & Wellness Center
701 S. Fry Rd.
Katy, TX 77450
Tel: 281-599-5700; Fax: 281-492-0936
Beds 58
Patients assisted annually 10,794
Staff 313
DAN BROWN, CEO
CHRISTUS Southwest Community Health Center
Tel: 713-779-6400; Fax: 713-779-9872
CHRISTUS Galveston Ministries
Tel: 409-795-2401; Fax: 409-795-2409
CHRISTUS New Horizons
Tel: 409-765-1479; Fax: 409-763-5924
CHRISTUS St. John Hospital
18300 St. John Dr.
Massau Bay, TX 77058
Tel: 281-333-8898; Fax: 281-333-8891
TOM PERMETTI, CEO
Bed Capacity 135
Patients assisted annually 123,487
Total Staff 683

Sisters of Charity of the Incarnate Word, Houston, Texas
6510 Lawndale Ave.
Houston, TX 77223-0969
Tel: 713-928-6053; Fax: 713-928-8148
E-mail: obordelon@ccvi-vdm.org
Sr. OLIVE BORDELON, Pres. & CEO
6510 Lawndale Ave.
Houston, TX 77023
Tel: 713-928-6053; Fax: 713-928-8148

Irving
Diocese of Dallas

CHRISTUS Health Irving System Office
6363 N. Hwy. 161, Ste. 450
Irving, TX 75038
Tel: 877-980-0100; Fax: 214-492-8550
Web Site: www.Christushealth.org
THOMAS C. ROYER, M.D., Pres. & CEO

Jasper
Diocese of Beaumont

CHRISTUS Jasper Memorial Hospital
1275 Hancock Dr.
Jasper, TX 75951
Operated by CHRISTUS Health Southeast Texas.
GEORGE MILLER, Admin.
Bed Capacity 81
Patients assisted annually 33,674

Kingsville
Diocese of Corpus Christi

CHRISTUS Spohn Hospital Kleberg
Mailing Address:
1702 Santa Fe
Corpus Christi, TX 78404
E-mail: buddyFlores@iwhs.org
1311 General Cavazos Blvd.
Kingsville, TX 8363
Tel: 631-595-1661; Fax: 361-595-9888
E-mail: buddy)flores@iwhs.org
Mr. ERNESTO FLORES, Vice Pres. & Admin.
Sr. ELIZABETH SMITH, Pastoral Care
Operated by the Sisters of Charity of the Incarnate Word (San Antonio, TX).
Total Staff 435
Beds 100
Patients assisted annually 76,959

Laredo
Diocese of Corpus Christi

Mercy Regional Medical Center
1515 Logan, P.O. Box 2068
Laredo, TX 78044
Tel: 210-718-6222; Fax: 210-718-6904
Web Site: www.mhst.smhs.com
MARK STAUDER, Pres. & CEO
Chaplains:
Sr. CECILIA BARANOWSKI, R.S.M.
Sisters of Mercy of the Americas 3
Beds 324
Staff 1,580
Patients assisted annually 94,000

Diocese of Laredo

Mercy Hospital of Laredo dba Mercy Health Center
1700 E. Saunders St.
Laredo, TX 78041
Tel: 956-796-5000; Fax: 956-793-3173
Web Site: www.mercylaredo.com

Lubbock
Diocese of Lubbock

St. Mary of the Plains Hospital
4000 24th St.
Lubbock, TX 79410-1894
Tel: 806-796-6000; Fax: 806-796-6081
Sisters of St. Joseph of Orange, CA
Mr. CHARLEY TRIMBLE, CEO
DAVID HARTMAN, Dir. Pastoral Care
Sr. MARY C. GERRIOR, O.P., CPE Supvr.
Rev. GEORGE THEKKEDAM, Chap.
Sisters 6
Bed Capacity 420
Total Staff 2,448
Patients assisted annually 391,647

Madison
Diocese of Tyler

Madison Acquisition Company dba Madison St. Joseph Health Center
P.O. Box 698 - 100 W. Cross St.
Madison, TX 77864-0698
WILLIAM F. HYER, JR., Trustee & Contact Person

Paris
Diocese of Tyler

Christus Home Health Services of North Texas
165 S.E. 6th St.
Paris, TX 75460
Tel: 903-737-3622
MONTY E. MCLAURIN, Pres. & CEO
Ms. DIANA SHEFTS, Contact Person

Christus St. Joseph Health Sytstem
820 Clarksville St., P.O. Box 9070
Paris, TX 75461
Tel: 903-785-4521; Fax: 903-737-3848
E-mail: monty_mclaurin@iwhs.org
Mr. MONTY MCLAURIN, Pres./CEO
Sisters 3
Beds 211
Patients assisted annually 18,283
Staff 784
Health Care Centers, Ancillary Care Systems 3
Patients Assisted Annually at St. Joseph's Family Clinics:
3,041 at Cooper, TX
1,609 at Honey Grove, TX
2,006 at Paris, TX
St. Joseph's Foundation of Paris, Texas
Tel: 903-737-3695; Fax: 903-783-0677

Port Arthur
Diocese of Beaumont

CHRISTUS St. Mary Hospital
3600 Gates Blvd., P.O. Box 3696
Port Arthur, TX 77643
Tel: 409-985-7431; Fax: 409-985-9404
Operated by CHRISTUS Health Southeast Texas.
ALICE BAKER, CEO
Sr. MAURA THERIOT, C.C.V.I., Treas.
Rev. DONALD E. DONAHUGH (RCK) Chap.
Sisters 8
Bed Capacity 242
Patients assisted annually 118,000

San Antonio
Archdiocese of San Antonio

Christus Santa Rosa Children's Hospital
519 W. Houston St.
San Antonio, TX 78207-3198
Tel: 210-704-2011; Fax: 210-704-3632
Owned and operated by Christus Health, Santa Rosa Health Care Corp.
RICHARD WAYNE, MD, CEO
Licensed Beds 191
Patients assisted annually 100,000

Christus Santa Rosa Health Care Corporation
519 W. Houston St.
San Antonio, TX 78207-3198
Tel: 210-704-2011; Fax: 210-704-3632
Web Site: www.santarosahealth.org
JAMES P. HOUSER, Pres. & CEO
RICH WOODLEY, Dir. Pastoral Ministry

Revs.:
MICHAEL NORTON, C.PP.S.
PALMER MAXWELL, O.C.D.
MARK SCHEFFLER, C.SS.R.
Health related activities.
Sisters 14
Nurses 1,097 (Full time registered & licensed)
Beds 801
Patients assisted annually 138,123

Christus Santa Rosa Hospital
519 W. Houston St.
San Antonio, TX 78207-3198
Tel: 210-704-2011
JAMES P. HOUSER, Pres. & CEO
Owned and operated by Christus Health, Santa Rosa Health Care Corp.
Licensed Beds 422
Patients assisted annually 39,189

Christus Santa Rosa Medical Center
2827 Babcock Rd.
San Antonio, TX 78229
Tel: 210-705-6300
Owned and operated by Christus Health, Santa Rosa Health Care Corp.
RICH WOODLEY, Dir. Pastoral Ministry
Licensed Beds 196
Patients assisted annually 19,120
Christus Santa Rosa Rehabilitation Hospital
2827 Babcock
San Antonio, TX 78229
Tel: 210-705-6100
Owned and operated by Christus Health, Santa Rosa Health Care Corp.
Beds 50

Incarnate Word Health System
4500 Broadway
San Antonio, TX 78209
Tel: 210-828-2224
PETER F. MADDOX, Pres.

Texarkana
Diocese of Tyler

Christus St. Michael Health System
2600 St. Michael Dr.
Texarkana, TX 75503
Tel: 903-614-1000; Fax: 903-614-2541
E-mail: whited@smit.sch.org
Web Site: www.christusstmichael.org
DON A. BEELER, CEO
Operated by Christus Health (merged 2/1/1999).
General Hospital
Annually Assisted 11,407
Staff 1,232
Bed Capacity 239
St. Michael Rehabilitation Hospital
2400 St. Michael Dr.
Texarkana, TX 75503
Tel: 903-614-4000; Fax: 903-614-4064
Web Site: www.christusstmichael.org
CLAUDIA EISENMANN, Admin.
Operated by Christus Health, Houston Texas Health Care Centers, Ancillary Care Systems:
Total Staff 256
Bed Capacity 80
Patients assisted annually 1,130

Tyler
Diocese of Tyler

Trinity Mother Frances Health System
800 E. Dawson St.
Tyler, TX 75701
Tel: 903-593-8441; Fax: 903-531-4067
Mr. J. LINDSEY BRADLEY, JR., Pres.
Rev. Msgr. JOHN BRENNAN, V.G., Chap.
Sisters of the Holy Family of Nazareth 8
Bed Capacity 358
Staff 2,707
Annually Assisted 693,240

Waco
Diocese of Austin

Providence Health Center
6901 Medical Pkwy., P.O. Box 2589
Waco, TX 76702-2589
Tel: 254-751-4764; Fax: 254-751-4769
E-mail: kkeahey@phn-waco.org
Web Site: prov-waco.org
KENT A. KEAHEY, Pres.
Sr. ROSEMARY BURKE, C.C.V.I., Dir. Chaplain Services
Sr. CECILE MATUSHEK, D.C., V.P. Mission
Medical/Surgical/OB/Pediatrics acute care; DePaul Center - Psychiatric care; St. Catherine's Center - Long Term care; Providence Clinics; Providence Home Health/Hospice; Providence Health Alliance.
Daughters of Charity of St. Vincent de Paul 5
Bed Capacity 427
Patients assisted annually 182,887
Total Staff 1,430

Wichita Falls
Diocese of Fort Worth

United Regional Health Care System
Eleventh Street Campus, 1600 Eleventh St.
Wichita Falls, TX 76301
Tel: 940-723-4111
E-mail: dwitcker@urhcs.org
Web Site: www.urhcs.org
Sisters of the Holy Family of Nazareth
Mr. DAVID D. WHITAKER, FACHE, Pres. & CEO
Sr. M. IRENA, C.S.F.N., Supr.
Rev. AIDAN DONLON, S.A.C., Chap.
Sisters 5
Bed Capacity 542
Patients assisted annually 160,000

VIRGINIA

Newport News
Diocese of Richmond

Mary Immaculate Hospital
2 Bernardine Dr.
Newport News, VA 23602-4499
Tel: 757-886-6600; Fax: 757-886-6751
Web Site: www.bonsecourshamptonroads.com
CYNTHIA B. FARRAND, Exec. Vice Pres. & Admin., Tel: 757-886-6768; Fax 757-886-6751
Sr. BERNARD MARIE MAGILL, O.S.F., M.S., Dir. Pastoral Care Dept.
Rev. JAMES GEIGER, C.SS.R.
Bernardine Franciscan Sisters Foundation, Inc.
3 Bernardine Dr.
Newport News, VA 23602
Tel: 757-886-6025; Fax: 757-886-6881
The Bernardine Sisters of the Third Order of St. Francis 15
Beds 110
Nurses 259
Staff 656
Patients assisted annually 154,545

Norfolk
Diocese of Richmond

Bon Secours De Paul Medical Center, Inc.
150 Kingsley Ln.
Norfolk, VA 23505
Tel: 757-889-5000; Fax: 757-889-5837
Sisters of Bon Secours
DAVID J. MCCOMBS, Exec. Vice Pres. & Admin.
Clinic is connected with hospital.
Sisters 1
Staff 835
Beds 238
Patients assisted annually 6,954
Legal Title: *Bon Secours DePaul Medical Center*
Legal Title: *Bon Secours DePaul Health Foundation*
Legal Title: *Bon Secours Bayley Properties*

Norton
Diocese of Richmond

St. Mary's Hospital, Inc.
P.O. Box 620
Norton, VA 24273
Tel: 540-679-9100; Fax: 540-679-7549
E-mail: alester@st_maryshospital.com
Web Site: www.st_maryshospital.com
Poor Servants of the Mother of God
GARY L. DELFORGE, Admin.
Sisters 6
Beds 133
Patients assisted annually 80,068
Nurses 185
Staff 432

Portsmouth
Diocese of Richmond

Maryview Medical Center
3636 High St.
Portsmouth, VA 23707
Tel: 757-398-2200; Fax: 757-398-2359
Legal Title: *Maryview Hospital*
Sisters of Bon Secours
DOMINICK CALGI, Exec. Vice Pres./Admin.
RICHARD CHASSE, Dir. Pastoral Care
Chaplains:
Rev. PANTALEON O. MANALO
Sr. GRACE MALONZO
KATHY KOFRON
Beds 346
Patients assisted annually 143,237

Maryview Psychiatric Hospital
3636 High St.
Portsmouth, VA 23707
ALLAN D. ERBE, Admin.
Beds 54

Richmond
Diocese of Richmond

St. Mary's Hospital
5801 Bremo Rd.
Richmond, VA 23226
Tel: 804-285-2011; Fax: 804-283-8327
Sisters of Bon Secours
PETER BERNARD, Senior Vice Pres.
Sisters 3
Beds 391
Patients assisted annually 234,782
Bon Secours-Maryview Health Corporation
Tel: 757-398-2200

**Bon Secours-Maryview Foundation, Inc.*
Tel: 757-398-2200
Bon Secours-St. Mary's Health Care Foundation
Tel: 804-342-1528
Bon Secours-Stuart Circle Hospital
Tel: 804-354-1121
Bon Secours-Richmond Community Hospital
Tel: 804-225-1701
Bon Secours-Richmond Health System
Tel: 804-281-8317

WASHINGTON

Bellingham
Archdiocese of Seattle

The Martin Center
(A children's mental health hospital)
2806 Douglas Ave.
Bellingham, WA 98225
Tel: 206-733-5804
Total Staff 50
Children 14

St. Joseph Hospital
2901 Squalicum Pkwy.
Bellingham, WA 98225
Tel: 360-734-5400; Fax: 360-738-6393
Sisters of St. Joseph of Peace and PeaceHealth
NANCY BITTING, Admin.
Sr. JUDY TRALNES, C.S.J.P., Dir. Mission & Values & Spiritual Care
Sisters 4
Total Staff 1,600
Beds 253
Patients assisted annually 21,344

Centralia
Archdiocese of Seattle

Providence Centralia Hospital
914 S. Scheuber Rd.
Centralia, WA 98531
Tel: 360-736-2803; Fax: 360-330-8614
E-mail: burdick@psph.providence.org
Web Site: providence. org
Legal Title: *Sisters of Providence - Mother Joseph Province*
STEVEN BURDICK, Admin.
Sisters 2
Beds 206
Patients assisted annually 120,000

Chewelah
Diocese of Spokane

St. Joseph's Hospital of Chewelah
E. 500 Webster
Chewelah, WA 99109
Tel: 509-935-8211; Fax: 509-935-5257
GARY V. PECK, CEO
Pastoral Care:
Sr. HUMILITAS LAMBER, O.P.
Sr. ALBERTA NETT, O.P.
Sr. MARY TOECKES, O.P.
DAVID VERWOLF
Sisters 3
Bed Capacity 65
Patients assisted annually 18,730

Colville
Diocese of Spokane

Mount Carmel Hospital
982 E. Columbia, Box 351
Colville, WA 99114
Tel: 509-684-2561
GLORIA P. COOPER, CEO
Sisters 3
Total Staff 209
Bed Capacity 55
Patients assisted annually 30,841

Deer Park
Diocese of Spokane

Deer Park Health Center and Hospital
Mailing Address:
5633 N. Lidgerwood
Spokane, WA 99207
CATHY J. SIMCHUK, R.N., COO
Total Staff 70
Bed capacity 26
Patients assisted annually 7,309

Everett
Archdiocese of Seattle

Providence Everett Medical Center
1321 Colby Ave., P.O. Box 1147
Everett, WA 98206
Tel: 425-261-2000
Web Site: www.providence.org/everett/
Mr. RAYMOND F. CRERAND, CEO
Mr. MEL PYNE, Admin.
Sr. DOROTHY KLINGELE, S.P., Sister Representative
Sisters 3
Beds 475
Patients assisted annually 117,581

Federal Way
Archdiocese of Seattle

St. Francis Hospital of Federal Way
34515 9th Ave. S.
Federal Way, WA 98003-6761
Tel: 253-927-9700; 838-9700; Fax: 253-952-7988
Web Site: fhshealth.org
Sisters of St. Francis of Philadelphia
Total Staff 560
Beds 110
Patients assisted annually 74,077

Lakewood
Archdiocese of Seattle

St. Clare Hospital
11315 Bridgeport Way S.W.
Lakewood, WA 98499
Tel: 253-588-1711; Fax: 253-584-3001
Web Site: www.fhshealth.org
Sisters of St. Francis of Philadelphia
SYD BERSANTE, Chief Oper. Officer
DIANNA KIELIAN, Vice Pres., Mission & Ministry
Total Staff 543
Beds 106
Patients assisted annually 62,212

Longview
Archdiocese of Seattle

PeaceHealth, St. John Medical Center
1615 Delaware St., P.O. Box 3002
Longview, WA 98632
Tel: 360-414-2000; Fax: 360-414-7550
Web Site: www.peacehealth.org
Sisters of St. Joseph of Peace and PeaceHealth
MARK MCGOURTY, Regl. CEO
Sisters of St. Joseph of Peace 3
Beds 346
Patients assisted annually 130,000
Total Staff 1,500

Olympia
Archdiocese of Seattle

Providence St. Peter Hospital
413 Lilly Rd., N.E.
Olympia, WA 98506
Tel: 360-491-9480
Legal Title: *Sisters of Providence - Mother Joseph Province*
Mr. SCOTT BOND, Admin.
Rev. KIERAN P. CUNNINGHAM, O.S.B., Chap.
Beds 390
Patients assisted annually 166,382

Pasco
Diocese of Spokane

Lourdes Medical Center
520 N. Fourth Ave., P.O. Box 2568
Pasco, WA 99302
Tel: 509-547-7704; Fax: 509-546-2291
JAMES F. DOVER, Fache Pres. & CEO
In res.,
Rev. JOHN BIRK
Sisters of St. Joseph of Carondelet 5
Total Staff 612
Bed capacity 132
Patients assisted annually 134,926

Richland
Diocese of Yakima

Lourdes Counseling Center
1175 Carondelet Dr.
Richland, WA 99352
Tel: 509-943-9104; Fax: 509-943-7206
E-mail: bmead@lourdesonline.org
Web Site: lourdesonline.org
BARBARA MEAD, Asst. Admin., Behavorial Health
Beds 32
Patients assisted annually 30,504
Total Staff 141

Spokane
Diocese of Spokane

Holy Family Adult Day Health
6018 N. Astor
Spokane, WA 99207
Tel: 509-482-2475; Fax: 509-482-2490
Mrs. MARIE RASCHKO, Exec. Dir.
Purpose: to perform and provide adult day health care services, including rehab & nursing, to the elderly and disadvantaged.

Holy Family Hospital
N. 5633 Lidgerwood St.
Spokane, WA 99207
Tel: 509-482-0111
Mr. THOMAS CORLEY, Pres. & CEO
Mr. RICHARD SPINAL, Dir. Pastoral Care
Chaplains 8
Sisters 2
Bed capacity 272
School of Radiology
Students 10

Sacred Heart Medical Center
W. 101 Eighth Ave., TAF-C9
Spokane, WA 99220
Tel: 509-455-3131
Mr. RYLAND P. DAVIS, Pres.
Priest Chaplains:
Revs.:
BOB DORAN, S.J.
GERALD R. GORDON, S.J.
MICHAEL D. VENNERI
Chaplains 19
Total Staff 4,125
Bed Capacity 623
Patients assisted annually 194,230

Tacoma
Archdiocese of Seattle

St. Joseph Medical Center
1717 S. J St., P.O. Box 2197
Tacoma, WA 98405-2197
Tel: 253-627-4101; Fax: 253-591-6880
E-mail: annemcnamara@chiwest.com
Sisters of St. Francis of Philadelphia
JOSEPH WILCZEK, CEO
HELEN BATIE, Mgr. Pastoral Care
Revs.:
URBAN FEUCHT, O.S.P.
JAMES E. POOLE, S.J.
Sisters 5
Total Staff 1,780
Beds 320
Patients assisted annually 260,166

Toppenish
Diocese of Yakima

Providence Hospital
504 W. 4th Ave., P.O. Box 672
Toppenish, WA 98948
Tel: 509-865-3105; Fax: 509-865-1519
Web Site: www.providence.org
LARRY ANTHONY, Admin.
Sr. BETTY KANE, C.S.J.P., Dir. Spiritual Care
Patients assisted annually 55,000
Beds 63
Total Staff 193

Walla Walla
Diocese of Spokane

St. Mary Medical Center
401 W. Poplar St.
Walla Walla, WA 99362
Tel: 509-525-3320; Fax: 509-522-5950
Sisters of Providence
Mr. JOHN A. ISELY, Pres.
Total Staff 820
Bed capacity 146
Patients assisted annually 61,230

Yakima
Diocese of Yakima

Providence Yakima Medical Center
110 S. 9th Ave.
Yakima, WA 98902
Tel: 509-575-5000; Fax: 509-454-6193
EARL CHRISTISON, CEO
Rev. JUSTIN D. MCCREEDY, O.S.B.
Sisters of Providence 1
Patients assisted annually 219,802
Beds 226
Total Staff 1,280

WEST VIRGINIA

Buckhannon
Diocese of Wheeling-Charleston

St. Joseph's Hospital of Buckhannon, Inc.
1 Amalia Dr.
Buckhannon, WV 26201
Tel: 304-473-2000; Fax: 304-472-6620
Web Site: www.stj.net
Mr. WAYNE B. GRIFFITH, Admin.
Sisters of the Pallottine Missionary Society 4
Bed Capacity 95
Patients assisted annually 58,134
Home Health Care & Hospice Patients 472
Total Staff 268
Attended by Marist Fathers
St. Joseph's Foundation of Buckhannon, Inc.
1 Amalia Dr.
Buckhannon, WV 26201

Huntington
Diocese of Wheeling-Charleston

Pallottine Health Services, Inc.
2900 First Ave.
Huntington, WV 25702
Tel: 304-526-8915; Fax: 304-526-8918
E-mail: srcelest@st-marys.org
Web Site: www.st-marys.org
Sponsored by the Pallottine Missionary Sisters.
Parent Corp. for:
St. Mary's Hospital of Huntington, Inc.
2900 First Ave.
Huntington, WV 25702
Tel: 304-526-1270; Fax: 304-526-1538
St. Joseph's Hospital of Buckhannon, Inc.
1 Amalia Dr.
Buckhannon, WV 26201
Tel: 304-473-2111; Fax: 304-472-6620
Bed Capacity 535
Total Annually Assisted 217,691
Total Staff 2,311

St. Mary's Hospital of Huntington, Inc.
2900 First Ave.
Huntington, WV 25702
Tel: 304-526-1234; Fax: 304-526-1538
Web Site: www.st-marys.org
MICHAEL G. SELLARDS, Exec. Dir.
Pallottine Missionary Sisters 13
Bed Capacity 440
Patients assisted annually 139,953
School of Nursing
Tel: 304-526-1415; Fax: 304-526-1517
Student Nurses 121
Total Staff 1,951

Pineville
Diocese of Wheeling-Charleston

Children's Health Care, Inc.
Pineville Children's Clinic, Box 430
Pineville, WV 24874
Tel: 304-732-7069; Fax: 304-732-7098
E-mail: ecatters@marshall.edu
Sr. EILEEN CATTERSON, D.W.M.D., Dir.
Total Annually Assisted 6,040
Total Staff 13

Rhodell
Diocese of Wheeling-Charleston

Rhodell Health Clinic
P.O. Box 158
Rhodell, WV 25915
Tel: 304-683-4318
Legal Title: *Appalachian Health Cooperative, Inc.*

Wheeling
Diocese of Wheeling-Charleston

Bishop Joseph H. Hodges Continuous Care Center
Medical Park
Wheeling, WV 26003
Tel: 304-243-3800; Fax: 304-243-3398
MICHAEL J. CARUSO, Admin.
Bed Capacity 144
Total Annually Assisted 360
Total Staff 158
Skilled and Intermediate Care.

Wheeling Hospital
Medical Park
Wheeling, WV 26003
Tel: 304-243-3000
DONALD H. HOFREUTER, M.D., Admin.
Sr. MARY ANN ROSENBAUM, S.S.J., Dir. of Pastoral Care Dept.
Chaplains:
Rev. RICHARD CHIRICHIELLO, O.S.B.
Sr. MAIREAO SCANLON, S.S.J.
Sisters of St. Joseph 2
Bed Capacity 276
Patients assisted annually 237,110

WISCONSIN

Antigo
Diocese of Green Bay

Langlade Memorial Hospital
112 E. 5th Ave.
Antigo, WI 55409
Tel: 715-623-2331; Fax: 715-623-9359
Religious Hospitallers of St. Joseph
Sr. DOLORES DEMULLING, R.H.S.J., Supvr., Mission and Philosophy Advocate & Trustee, Dir. of Le-Royer Hospice
Mr. DAVID SCHNEIDER, Exec. Dir.
Sr. JEAN BRICCO, Dir. Pastoral Care, Trustee & Contact Person
Sr. ADELE DEMULLING, Coord. LeRoyer Hospice
Rev. OMER C. KELLEY, Part-time Chap.
Sisters Res.
644 Longlade Rd.
Antigo, WI 55409
Tel: 715-623-4615
Sisters 3
Priests 1
Bed Capacity 49
Patients assisted annually 48,724

Appleton
Diocese of Green Bay

St. Elizabeth Hospital
1506 S. Oneida St.
Appleton, WI 54915-1305
Tel: 920-738-2000; Fax: 920-738-8913
E-mail: Bturner@affinityhealth.org
Legal Title: *St. Elizabeth Hospital, Inc.*
KEVIN NOLAN, Pres.
BOB TURNER, COO
Chaplains:
Rev. JAMES M. GILSOUL
JOSEPH MARCO
LUANNE VANDENBERG
Sr. DONNA SIEGL, O.S.F.
Priests 1
Franciscan Sisters, Daughters of the Sacred Hearts of Jesus and Mary (Wheaton, IL) 4
Bed Capacity 146
Total Staff 902
Patients assisted annually 210,784

Arcadia
Diocese of La Crosse

Franciscan Skemp Healthcare, Mayo Health System, Arcadia Campus Hospital
464 S. St. Joseph Ave.
Arcadia, WI 54612
Tel: 608-323-3341; Fax: 608-323-3694
Franciscan Sisters of Perpetual Adoration and Mayo Foundation
ROBERT TRACEY, Admin.
Chaplains:
Rev. ROBERT F. POLCYN, O.F.M.
Sr. ARLENE MELDER, F.S.P.A.
Total Staff 80
Bed Capacity 26
Patients assisted annually 16,425

Baraboo
Diocese of Madison

St. Clare Hospital and Health Services
707 14th St.
Baraboo, WI 53913
Tel: 608-356-1400
Web Site: www.stclare.com
Member of the SSM Health Care.
DAVID JORDAHL, Pres.
WILLIAM BEERS, Ph.D.
Franciscan Sisters of Mary (St. Louis, MO) 3
Bed Capacity 100
Patients assisted annually 45,000
Staff 310

Brookfield
Archdiocese of Milwaukee

Elmbrook Memorial Hospital, Inc.
19333 W. North Ave.
Brookfield, WI 53045
Tel: 262-785-2000; Fax: 262-785-2444
Franciscan Sisters, Daughters of the Sacred Hearts of Jesus and Mary (Wheaton, IL)
KIMRY A. JOHNSRUD, Pres.
LINDA PIOTOWSKI, Chap.
Bed Capacity 166
Patients assisted annually 87,698
Total Staff 657

Chippewa Falls
Diocese of La Crosse

St. Joseph's Hospital
2661 County Hwy. I
Chippewa Falls, WI 54729
Tel: 715-723-1811; Fax: 715-726-3204
Web Site: www.stjoeschipfalls.com
Hospital Sisters Health System.
Hospital Sisters of the Third Order of St. Francis
DAVID B. FISH, Exec. Vice Pres.
Sr. FRANCES E. SCHMITZ, O.S.F., Local Coord.
Sisters 3
Bed Capacity 84
Patients assisted annually 89,668

Eau Claire
Diocese of La Crosse

Sacred Heart Hospital
900 W. Clairemont Ave.
Eau Claire, WI 54701-6122
Tel: 715-839-4121; Fax: 715-839-8417
E-mail: shec.hshs/org
Web Site: www.sacredhearthospital-ec.org
STEPHEN F. RONSTROM, Exec. Vice Pres.
Rev. EDMUND J. KLIMEK, Chap.
Sr. AUGUSTA SPERL, O.S.F., Dir. Pastoral Care
Hospital Sisters of the Third Order of St. Francis 5
Bed Capacity 344
Patients assisted annually 108,732

Fond du Lac
Archdiocese of Milwaukee

Agnesian HealthCare, Inc.
430 E. Division St.
Fond du Lac, WI 54935
Tel: 920-929-2300; Fax: 920-926-4866
E-mail: fale@agnesian.com
Mr. ROBERT A. FALE, Pres. & CEO
Sisters 8
Bed Capacity 190, (18 TCU)
Patients assisted annually 212,846
Total Staff 1,414

Green Bay
Diocese of Green Bay

Libertas Treatment Center for Chemically Dependent
1701 Dousman St.
Green Bay, WI 54303-3282
Tel: 920-498-8600; Fax: 920-496-2027
Hospital Sisters Health System.
Hospital Sisters of the Third Order of St. Francis
DAVID B. FISH, Exec. Vice Pres.
PATRICK W. RYAN, Prog. Dir.
Bed Capacity 24
Patients assisted annually 6,889
Total Staff 30

St. Mary's Hospital-Medical Center
1726 Shawano Ave.
Green Bay, WI 54303-3282
Tel: 920-498-4200; Fax: 920-498-1861
Web Site: www.stmgb.org
Hospital Sisters of Third Order of St. Francis
Mr. JAMES G. COLLER, Admin.
DAVID J. SCHMIDT, Dir. Pastoral Care & Social Svc. Depts.
Deacon NICK WILLIAMS, Pastoral Care Assoc.
Bed Capacity 158
Staff 796
Patients assisted annually 85,921

St. Vincent Hospital
P.O. Box 13508
Green Bay, WI 54307-3508
Tel: 920-433-0111; 433-8162; Fax: 920-431-3275
E-mail: mbush@stvgb.org
Mr. JOSEPH J. NEIDENBACH, Exec. Vice Pres. & CEO
MARY J. BUSH, Dir. Pastoral Care
Chaplains:
Rev. JAY M. FOSTNER, O.Praem.
Sr. PAULETTE HUPFAUF, O.S.F.
Sr. MONICA BONGERT, O.S.F.
Sr. MARILYN HERR, O.S.F.
Hospital Sisters of the Third Order of St. Francis 3
Bassinets 25
Beds 547
Patients assisted annually 127,586
Total Staff 1,763

Hillsboro
Diocese of La Crosse

St. Joseph's Memorial Hospital, Inc.
400 Water Ave., P.O. Box 527
Hillsboro, WI 54634
Tel: 608-489-2211
Franciscan Sisters of Perpetual Adoration
Rev. JAMES E. ENNIS, Chap.
Sisters 1
Bed Capacity 34
Patients assisted annually 3,440
Connected with the hospital is a home for the aged. Under care 65 infirm and aged men and women.

Kenosha
Archdiocese of Milwaukee

St. Catherine's Hospital
3556 Seventh Ave.
Kenosha, WI 53140
Tel: 414-656-3011; Fax: 414-656-3804
Sponsored by Franciscan Sisters and Daughters of the Sacred Hearts of Jesus and Mary, Wheaton, IL
RICHARD O. SCHMIDT, JR., Pres. & CEO
MARY BECKER, Dept. Head, Pastoral Care
Legal Title: *St. Catherine's Hospital, Inc.*
Patients assisted annually 43,200
Total Staff 405

Kewaunee
Diocese of Green Bay

St. Mary Kewaunee Area Memorial Hospital
810 Lincoln St.
Kewaunee, WI 54216
Tel: 920-388-2210; Fax: 920-388-1166
CATHIE KOCOUREK, Admin.
HEATHER SCHROEDER, Site Dir.
Staff 45
Patients assisted annually 23,261

La Crosse
Diocese of La Crosse

Franciscan Skemp Healthcare, Mayo Health System, La Crosse Campus Medical Center
700 West Ave. S.
La Crosse, WI 54601-4796
Tel: 608-785-0940; Fax: 608-791-9429
GLENN FORBES, M.D., CEO
Rev. PAUL L. SANKOORIKAL, Chap.
Franciscan Sisters of Perpetual Adoration and Mayo Foundation
Sisters 7
Total Staff 1,200
Bed Capacity 345
Patients assisted annually 118,000

Madison
Diocese of Madison

St. Marys Hospital Medical Center
707 S. Mills St.
Madison, WI 53715
Tel: 608-251-6100; Fax: 608-258-6731
Member of SSM Health Care.
Franciscan Sisters of Mary (St. Louis, MO)
Mr. GERALD W. LEFERT, Pres.
Sisters 2
Capacity 440
Patients assisted annually 79,250
Pastoral Care Department Chaplains:
Revs.:
GARRETT KEEGSTRA, O.F.M.Cap.
TED LINDQUIST, Lutheran Minister, Evangelical Lutheran Church of America
KENNETH SMITS, O.F.M.Cap.
LEO PETRIMOULX, O.F.M.Cap.
GARY HEIN, Lutheran Min., Evangelical Lutheran Church of America
Sr. MARY ELLEN LEWIS, F.S.M.

Sr. Pamela Moehring, S.S.N.D.
Sr. Clement Sabol, V.S.C.
Julia Weaver
Paula McKenzie, Dir.
Liz Allen

Manitowoc
Diocese of Green Bay

Holy Family Memorial, Inc.
2300 Western Ave., P.O. Box 1450
Manitowoc, WI 54221-1450
Tel: 920-684-2011; Fax: 920-684-2522
E-mail: services@hfmhealth.org
Web Site: www.hfmhealth.org
Mr. Daniel McGinty, Pres.
Rev. Richard Klingeisen, Dir. Pastoral Care
Chaplains:
Rev. Richard H. Klingeisen
Deacon Rahlf Proulx
Sr. Jean Herman Dykstra
Molly La Fond
Franciscan Sisters of Christian Charity Sisters 7
Licensed Beds 216
Bassinets 26
Patients assisted annually 194,583
Total Staff 1,450

Marshfield
Diocese of La Crosse

Saint Joseph's Hospital of Marshfield, Inc.
611 St. Joseph Ave.
Marshfield, WI 54449
Tel: 715-387-1713; Fax: 715-387-8601
Web Site: www.ministryhealth.org
Michael Schmidt, Pres. & CEO
Chaplains:
Revs.:
Donald F. Wilger
Todd A. Mlsna
Nicolas Husain
Mary Ella Collins, Catholic Lay Chap.
Rita Austin, Catholic Lay Chap.
Robert Cassidy, Catholic Lay Chap.
Protestant Chaplains:
Revs.:
Steven E. Sutterer
Linden Nelson
Corporate Sponsor: Ministry HealthCare, Inc. (Milwaukee, WI); Sponsored by the Sisters of the Sorrowful Mother.
Sisters of the Sorrowful Mother 3
Bed Capacity 524
Patients assisted annually 103,623
Training School for Nurses (Affiliated with U.W.-Eau Claire).

Mequon
Archdiocese of Milwaukee

St. Mary's Hospital Ozaukee, Inc.
13111 N. Port Washington Rd.
Mequon, WI 53097
Tel: 414-243-7300; 800-848-2844; Fax: 414-243-7416
Therese Pandl, Sr. Vice Pres.
Rev. John R. Paczesny, Chap.
Ascension Health System
Bed Capacity 89
Patients assisted annually 176,769
Total Staff 918

Merrill
Diocese of Superior

Good Samaritan Health Center of Merrill, Wisconsin, Inc.
601 S. Center Ave.
Merrill, WI 54452
Tel: 715-536-5511; Fax: 715-539-2170
Michael Hammer, Pres. & CEO
Bed Capacity 73
Patients assisted annually 33,700

Milwaukee
Archdiocese of Milwaukee

Ministry Health Care, Inc.
11925 W. Lake Park Dr.
Milwaukee, WI 53224
Tel: 414-359-1060; Fax: 414-359-1656
Web Site: www.ministryhealth.org
Nicholas Desien, Pres. & CEO
Hospitals:
Door County Memorial Hospital
Mercy Medical Center, Inc.
Sacred Heart-St. Mary's Hospitals, Inc. Tomahawk and Rhinelander, WI
St. Elizabeth's Hospital's of Wabasha, Inc.
Saint Joseph's Hospital of Marshfield, Inc.
St. Michael's Hospital of Stevens Point, Inc.
Victory Medical Center, Inc.
Affinity Health System
Agape Community Center of Milwaukee, Inc.
Ministry Behavioral Health of St. Michael's Hospital, Inc.
Ministry Home Care, Inc.
Ministry Medical Group, Inc.
Saints, Inc.

St. Francis Hospital
3237 S. 16th St.
Milwaukee, WI 53215
Tel: 414-647-5000; Fax: 414-647-5565
E-mail: mworley@covhealth.org
Sponsored by the Congregation of the Sisters of St. Felix of Cantalice of the United States of America, Chicago Province (Felician Sisters).
Daniel Bonk, Pres. & CEO
Chaplains:
Revs.:
Joseph L. Bisoffi, O.S.Cam.
George Balderrama, S.C.J.
Sisters 7
Chaplains 6
Bed Capacity 260
Patients assisted annually 139,622
Total Staff 1,460

St. Joseph's Hospital of Franciscan Sisters, Milwaukee, Inc.
5000 W. Chambers St.
Milwaukee, WI 53210
Tel: 414-447-2000; Fax: 414-874-4393
Web Site: www.covhealth.org
Pat Kaldor, Pres.
Chaplains:
Revs.:
David J. Hanser
Richard Weeden, ELCA Lutheran
Norman R. Schwartz
Corporate title: St. Joseph Hospital of Franciscan Sisters, Milwaukee, Inc.
Franciscan Sisters, Daughters of the Sacred Hearts of Jesus and Mary (Wheaton, IL) 8
Bed Capacity 567
Patients assisted annually 178,064
Total Staff 2,686

St. Mary's Hospital of Milwaukee
2323 N. Lake Dr., P.O. Box 503
Milwaukee, WI 53201-0503
Tel: 414-291-1000; Fax: 414-291-1444
Susan Henckel, COO
Chaplains:
Revs.:
John R. Paczesny
Russell F. Tikalsky
Eugene Pocernich
Sr. Rosalynn Dzikonski, O.S.F.
Sr. Margaret Wenzel, F.S.P.A.
Sr. Margaret Ann Arnold, S.S.S.F.
Corporate title: St. Mary's Hospital of Milwaukee.
Ascension Health System
Bed Capacity 294
Patients assisted annually 376,483
Total Staff 2,162

St. Michael Hospital of Franciscan Sisters of Milwaukee, Inc.
2400 W. Villard Ave.
Milwaukee, WI 53209
Tel: 414-527-8000; Fax: 414-527-8461
Mr. Jeffrey K. Jenkins, Pres.
Linda Piotrowski, Regional Dir. Spiritual Care
Corporate title: St. Michael Hospital of Franciscan Sisters, Milwaukee, Inc.
Franciscan Sisters, Daughters of the Sacred Hearts of Jesus and Mary (Wheaton, IL) 6
Bed Capacity 405
Patients assisted annually 216,362
Total Staff 1,234

Monroe
Diocese of Madison

The Monroe Clinic, Inc.
515 22nd Ave.
Monroe, WI 53566
Tel: 608-324-1000; Fax: 608-324-1471
E-mail: Tom_Huber@themonroeclinic.org
Web Site: www.themonroeclinic.org/
Sisters of the Congregation of St. Agnes
Kenneth E. Blount, Pres. & CEO
Chaplains:
Rev. Thomas F. Campion
Sr. Agnes Kircher
Bed Capacity 100
Nurses 187
Patients assisted annually 235,000
Staff 1,014

New Richmond
Diocese of Superior

Holy Family Hospital
535 Hospital Rd.
New Richmond, WI 54017
Tel: 715-246-2101; Fax: 715-243-7203
E-mail: hfhjneed@pressenter.com
Jean Needham, Pres.
Sr. Marian Schmit C.S.J., Pastoral Care
Bed Capacity 40
Patients assisted annually 16,258

Oshkosh
Diocese of Green Bay

Mercy Medical Center
500 S. Oakwood Rd., P.O. Box 3370
Oshkosh, WI 54902-3370
Tel: 920-236-2000; Fax: 920-223-0508
E-mail: kphillip@affinityhealth.org
Mr. Kevin Nolan, CEO
Kay Phillips, COO
Chaplains:
Revs.:
Kevin Ori
Karin Derenne, E.L.C.A.
Sr. Johnette Marek, S.S.M.
Sr. Rita Schmidt, S.S.J.
Sisters of the Sorrowful Mother 1
Bed Capacity 157
Staff 1,177
Bassinets 14
Patients assisted annually 343,586

Portage
Diocese of Madison

Divine Savior Healthcare, Inc.
1015 W. Pleasant St., P.O. Box 387
Portage, WI 53901
Tel: 608-742-4131; Fax: 608-742-6098
Sisters of the Divine Savior
Mr. Michael Decker, Pres. & CEO
Chaplains:
Levonne Tappa, Dir. Spiritual Care
Sr. Mary Rouse, S.D.S.
Sisters 3
Bed Capacity 60
Patients assisted annually 62,000

Racine
Archdiocese of Milwaukee

St. Mary's Medical Center, Inc.
3801 Spring St.
Racine, WI 53405
Tel: 262-687-4011; Fax: 262-687-8039
E-mail: kbuser@allsaintshealthcare.org
Web Site: allsaintshealth.com
Mr. Kenneth R. Buser, Pres. & CEO
Rev. William J. Dietzler, Dir. Pastoral Care & Chap.
Corporate Title: St. Mary's Medical Center, Inc.
Franciscan Sisters, Daughters of the Sacred Hearts of Jesus and Mary Wheaton, IL 4
Bed Capacity 217
Patients assisted annually 253,000
Total Staff 1,300
Ambulatory Clinics
Patients assisted annually 540,000
Total Staff 715
All Saints Medical Group-Northwestern Campus
2405 Northwestern Ave.
Racine, WI 53404
Tel: 262-687-6000; Fax: 262-687-6422
All Saints Medical Group-Spring St. Campus
3807 Spring St.
Racine, WI 53405
Tel: 262-687-2011; Fax: 262-687-8089
All Saints Medical Group- Union Grove Campus
1120 Main St.
Union Grove, WI 53182
Fax: 262-687-8591
All Saints Medical Group- Northside
2408 Four Mile Rd.
Racine, WI,
Tel: 262-687-5900; Fax: 262-687-5950

Rhinelander
Diocese of Superior

Sacred Heart-St. Mary's Hospitals, Inc.
Corporate Sponsor: Ministry Health Care, Inc. (Milwaukee, WI);Sponsored by Sisters of the Sorrowful Mother
1044 Kabel Ave.
Rhinelander, WI 54501
Tel: 715-369-6600; Fax: 715-369-6441
Mr. Kevin J. O'Donnell, Pres.

Bed Capacity 99
Patients assisted annually 39,631

Sheboygan
Archdiocese of Milwaukee

St. Nicholas Hospital
1601 N. Taylor Dr.
Sheboygan, WI 53081
Tel: 920-459-8300; Fax: 920-452-8336
E-mail: al4425@stnicholashospital.org
Web Site: www.stnicholashospital.org
MICHAEL J. STENGER, Exec. Vice Pres. & Admin.
Sr. RENELLE BRUEGGEMANN, O.S.F., Rel. Coord.
BARBARA MULCAHY, Dir. Spiritual Devel.
Hospital Sisters of the Third Order of St. Francis 2
Bed Capacity 185
Patients assisted annually 74,112
Total Staff 506

Sparta
Diocese of La Crosse

Franciscan Skemp Healthcare, Mayo Health System, Sparta Campus Hospital
310 W. Main St.
Sparta, WI 54656-2142
Tel: 608-269-2132
Franciscan Sisters of Perpetual Adoration and Mayo Foundation
WILLIAM P. SEXTON, M.H.A., Admin.
Total Staff 144
Bed Capacity 25
Patients assisted annually 35,574

Stanley
Diocese of La Crosse

**Victory Medical Center, Inc.*
230 E. Fourth Ave.
Stanley, WI 54768
Tel: 715-644-5571; Fax: 715-644-5665
Web Site: www.ministryhealth.org
Mrs. CYNTHIA EICHMAN, CEO

Sr. PAT BELONGIA, Dir. Spiritual Svcs.
Corporate Sponsor: Ministry Healthcare, Inc. (Milwaukee, WI); Sponsored by Sisters of the Sorrowful Mother.
Hospital 41
Nursing Home 65
Patients assisted annually 26,528

Stevens Point
Diocese of La Crosse

St. Michael's Hospital of Stevens Point, Inc.
900 Illinois Ave.
Stevens Point, WI 54481
Tel: 715-346-5000; Fax: 715-346-5077
E-mail: jm@smhosp.org
Web Site: www.ministryhealth.org
Mr. JEFFREY L. MARTIN, Pres. & CEO
Rev. GEORGE BROCKE
Mr. DAVID C. BAKER, Dir. Spiritual Services
Mrs. JANET JACOBY, Spiritual Services
Sr. MARY LOU SLOWEY, S.S.M., Patient Concerns Rep.
Mrs. MARGE SCHUMANN, Chap.
Corporate Sponsor: Ministry Healthcare, Inc. (Milwaukee, WI); Sponsored by Sisters of the Sorrowful Mother.
Bed Capacity 181
Patients assisted annually 99,000

Sturgeon Bay
Diocese of Green Bay

**Door County Memorial Hospital*
323 S. 18th Ave.
Sturgeon Bay, WI 54235
Tel: 920-743-5566; Fax: 920-743-8165
E-mail: gworrick@dcmh.org
Web Site: www.ministryhealth.org
GERALD M. WORRICK, Pres.
JOAN CARLSON, Dir. of Pastoral Care, Tel: 920-746-3745
Corporate sponsor: Ministry Health Care, Inc.(Milwaukee, WI); sponsored by Sisters of the Sorrowful Mother.

Beds 77
Patients assisted annually 40, 191
Total Staff 465

Superior
Diocese of Superior

St. Mary's Hospital of Superior
3500 Tower Ave.
Superior, WI 54880
Tel: 715-392-8281; Fax: 715-392-8395
E-mail: tjacobson@smdl.org
Web Site: www.smdc.org
Mr. TERRY R. JACOBSON, Admin.
Bed Capacity 42
Patients assisted annually 24,974

Tomahawk
Diocese of Superior

Sacred Heart-St. Mary's Hospitals, Inc.
Corporate Sponsor: Ministry Health Care, Inc. (Milwaukee, WI);Sponsored by Sisters of the Sorrowful Mother.
216 N. 7th St.
Tomahawk, WI 54487
Tel: 715-453-7700; Fax: 715-453-7716
Corporate Sponsor: Ministry Health Care, Inc. (Milwaukee, WI)
Mr. KEVIN J. O'DONNELL, Pres. & CEO
Bed Capacity 60
Patients assisted annually 8,871

Waupun
Archdiocese of Milwaukee

Waupun Memorial Hospital
Waupun, WI 53963
Tel: 920-324-5581; Fax: 920-324-2085
JAMES E. BAER, Pres. & CEO
Bed Capacity 40
Patients assisted annually 29,213
Staff 192
Corporate title: Waupun Memorial Hospital, Inc.

SPECIAL CARE FACILITIES

ALABAMA

Daphne
Archdiocese of Mobile

Mercy Medical
A Corporation.
P.O. Box 1090
Daphne, AL 36526
Tel: 334-626-2694; Fax: 334-626-0315
E-mail: dennis@mercymedical.com
Web Site: www.mercymedical.com
Sr. Mary Eileen Wilhelm, R.S.M., Admin.
Rev. Msgr. J. Edwin Stuardi, Chap.
Acute Rehabilitation Hospital, Hospice, Home Health, LTC, SNF Service.
Carroll Place—An assisted living facility.
McAuley Place—An assisted living facility.
Portier Place—An independent living facility.
Sisters of Mercy 4
Nursing Sisters 1
Professional Nurses 200
Beds 162
Daughters of Wisdom 1
Congregation of St. Joseph 1
Patients assisted annually 4,000
Residential Care Units 161

Marbury
Archdiocese of Mobile

Resurrection Catholic Nursing Home
165 County Rd. 20 E., P.O. Box 89
Marbury, AL 36051-0089
Skilled Nursing Facility.
Rev. Manuel Williams, C.R., Dir.
Registered Nurses 1
Licensed Practical Nurses 4
Beds 20
In-Patients 20

Mobile
Archdiocese of Mobile

Allen Memorial Home Skilled Nursing Facility
735 S. Washington Ave.
Mobile, AL 36603
Tel: 334-433-2642; Fax: 334-431-6044
E-mail: allenmhome@aol.com
Sr. Marilyn Moore, D.C., Admin.
Daughters of Charity of St. Vincent de Paul 4
Beds 119
Patients assisted annually 174
Total Staff 124

Cathedral Place
351 Conti St.
Mobile, AL 36602
Tel: 334-434-1590; Fax: 334-434-1562
E-mail: jscan41974@aol.com
Mrs. Lorene Lami, Mgr.
Ve An Davis, Soc. Dir.
Sr. Delphine Fleming, D.C., Asst. Social Dir.
Residents 154
Total Staff 8

Little Sisters of the Poor, Home For the Aged, Inc.
Sacred Heart Residence, 1655 McGill Ave.
Mobile, AL 36604
Tel: 334-476-6335; Fax: 334-478-6519
Rev. Andrew Stauter, Chap.
Mother Marcel Joseph McCanless, Supr.
Rev. Msgr. George C. Royer
Rev. Michael Finbar Desmond
Sisters 11
Residents 84

St. Mary's Home
4350 Moffat Rd.
Mobile, AL 36618
Tel: 334-344-7733
Mr. Phillip A. Wynne, Admin.
Dependent Children 48

Montgomery
Archdiocese of Mobile

City of St. Jude, Inc., The
2048 W. Fairview Ave.
Montgomery, AL 36108
Tel: 334-265-6791; Fax: 334-269-1988
Rev. Matthew A. Sindik, Dir.
Mr. Michael G. McCormack, Exec. Dir.
Includes:
Father Purcell Memorial Exceptional Children's Center
St. Jude Administration Building
St. Jude Church and Rectory
St. Jude Elementary and High School
St. Jude Exceptional Children's Center
St. Jude Head Start
St. Jude Social Services Center
Vincentian Sisters' Convent
The Old Convent
Central Alabama Laubach Literacy
St. Jude Apartments

Father Purcell Memorial Exceptional Children Center
2048 W. Fairview Ave.
Montgomery, AL 36108
Tel: 334-834-5590; Fax: 334-834-5592
Mr. Sam Palomaria, Admin.
Bed Capacity 58
Patients assisted annually 59

Father Walter Memorial Center for Handicapped Children
2815 Forbes Dr.
Montgomery, AL 36199
Tel: 334-262-6421; Fax: 334-262-2265
Rev. Manuel Williams, C.R., Dir.
Mrs. Betty A. Thomas, Admin.
Kim K. Johnson, Asst. Admin.
A skilled nursing facility for the mentally and physically handicapped child. Operated by The Resurrection Catholic Missions.
R.N. 7
L.P.N. 8
Beds 54
Patients assisted annually 54
Total Staff 73

Laboure Complex Foundation
P.O. Box 3074
Montgomery, AL 36109
Tel: 334-277-5213; Fax: 334-272-1788
E-mail: smcarol@aol.com
Web Site: www.laboure.org
Board of Directors:
Larry Neuhoff, Pres.
Barbara Duke, Vice Pres.
Edward Azar, Sec. & Treas.

Resurrection Early Childhood Center
2815 Forbes Dr.
Montgomery, AL 36110
Tel: 334-265-4615; Fax: 334-265-4568
Sr. Rita Washington, S.F.C.C., Prin.
Licensed by Alabama State Dept. of Human Resources for 45 Students, Ages 2 1/2 to 5 years.

St. Bede's Children's Center
3840 Atlanta Hwy.
Montgomery, AL 36109
E-mail: klangston@school.stbede.org
Total Assisted 54
Total Staff 12

Seton Haven
3721 Wares Ferry Rd.
Montgomery, AL 36109
Tel: 334-272-4000; Fax: 334-272-1788
E-mail: sh36109@aol.com
Sr. Mary Carol Mautemps, D.C., Admin.
Residents 114
Total Staff 14

Prichard
Archdiocese of Mobile

Queen's Court I Apartments
Mailing Address:
c/o Archdiocese of Mobile, P.O. Box 1966
Mobile, AL 36633
W. Clark Ave.
Prichard, AL 36610
Tel: 334-434-1585

ALASKA

Anchorage
Archdiocese of Anchorage

Mary Conrad Center
9100 Centennial Dr.
Anchorage, AK 99504
Tel: 907-333-8100; Fax: 907-338-6789
Mr. Karl Garber, Admin.
Sr. Maria Bouleris, C.S.J., Spiritual Care Coord.
Patients assisted annually 90
Staff 143
A long term care facility for the elderly, owned by Cook Inlet Housing Development Corporation and managed by Sisters of Providence in Washington.

Providence Extended Care Center
4900 Eagle St.
Anchorage, AK 99503
Tel: 907-562-2281
Ronarl Bergstrom, Admin.
Sr. Patricia Collins, R.S.M., Mission Integration
Legal Title: *Sisters of Providence in Washington.*
Patients assisted annually 372
Staff 340
Bed Capacity 224

Juneau
Diocese of Juneau

St. Ann's Care Center, Inc.
415 Sixth St.
Juneau, AK 99801
Tel: 907-586-3883
Skilled and intermediate care facility.
Bed Capacity 45

ARIZONA

Avondale
Diocese of Phoenix

Vianney Villas Apartments
(Retirement)- HUD Rent Subsidized
750 S. Fourth St.
Avondale, AZ 85323
Tel: 623-932-2036

Kingman
Diocese of Phoenix

Kingman Heights Apartments
(Retirement)- HUD Rent Subsidized
1020 Detroit Ave.
Kingman, AZ 86401
Tel: 520-753-2425

Lake Havasu City
Diocese of Phoenix

Becket House Apartments
(Retirement)
865 Cashmere Dr.
Lake Havasu City, AZ 86403
Tel: 520-855-7178

Phoenix
Diocese of Phoenix

Desert Crest Apartments
(Retirement)
2101 E. Maryland Ave.
Phoenix, AZ 85016
Tel: 602-264-6427

Guadalupe Senior Village
222 W. Thomas Rd., Ste. 214
Phoenix, AZ 85103
Tel: 602-406-6218; Fax: 602-406-4119
Web Site: www.mercyhousing.org
Cherie Kerschbaum, Pres.

Mesa Senior Meadows
222 W. Thomas Rd., Ste. 214
Phoenix, AZ 85013
Tel: 602-406-6218; Fax: 602-406-4119
Web Site: www.mercyhousing.org
Cherie Kerschbaum, Pres.

Senior Village
3541 W. Vogel
Phoenix, AZ 85051
Tel: 602-843-3008

Sweetwater Gardens Apartments
(Handicapped)
2035 E. Sweetwater
Phoenix, AZ 85022
Tel: 602-867-4549

Wickenburg
Diocese of Phoenix

Padua Hills Apartments
(Retirement)- HUD Rent Subsidized
460 S. West Rd.
Wickenburg, AZ 85390
Tel: 520-684-7034

OUR MISSION

Guest House for Women Religious

At Guest House, we understand that sisters, just like the general population, are not immune from addictions. They need help too. So we welcome them here to begin the process of regaining their physical and emotional health along with their spirituality and commitment to their ministry.

Indeed, we are dedicated to the compassionate care of Catholic women religious and women in formation with the disease of alcoholism, chemical or other addictions, and related problems. Our services include care and treatment for the following:

- Alcoholism
- Chemical Addictions (such as to prescription drugs)
- Compulsive Overeating
- Gambling Addictions
- Spending Addictions

In addition, Guest House staff are available to assist in the intervention process.

GuestHouse®
For Women Religious

1840 W. Scripps Road • P.O. Box 68 • Lake Orion, Michigan 48361

1-800-626-6910 • Website: **www.guesthouse.org**

The problem is the disease, not the priest.

Alcoholism and addiction breed isolation, confusion, anger, and despair. The chemically dependent clergyman or religious is often very defensive and resistant to accepting help. He will put the blame for his problems on everything but the substance that he abuses. His disease tells him he cannot live without it. And he believes his disease. That's why he can't seem to change. He needs professional help in a safe, affirming environment.

Guest House treats both the problem and the priest.

- The Guest House program is designed to effectively treat chemical dependency in an atmosphere which affirms the special nature of the priesthood.
- We base our treatment on the 12-step recovery program of Alcoholics Anonymous.
- Our recovery rate is outstanding. A recent study shows that more than 90% of those who undergo primary treatment at Guest House are still abstinent after 18 months (Chart 1). A majority of vicars and superiors rate the Guest House experience as excellent (Chart 2).
- We provide an evaluation for any Catholic priest or religious in order to determine the extent of an addiction – or if indeed there is an addiction.
- We use the medical resources of the world-renowned Mayo Clinic.
- **No priest is turned away because of the inability to pay.**

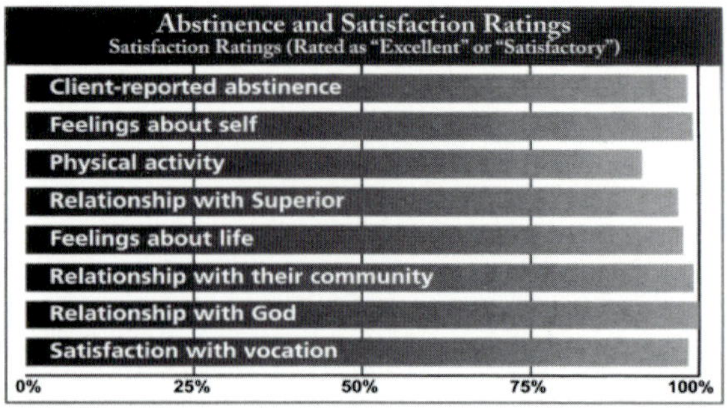

Chart 2.

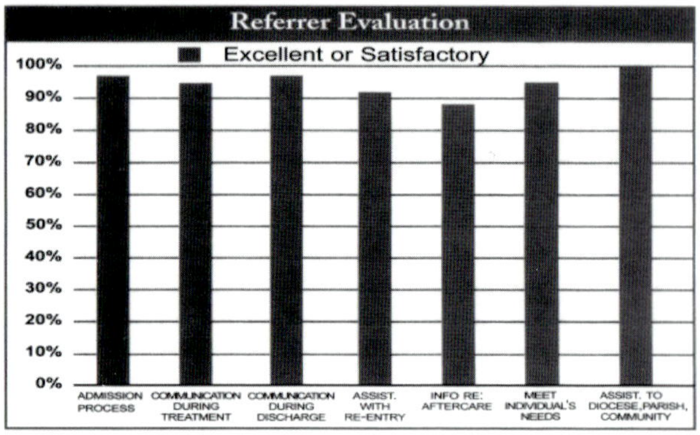

The Staff: The treatment team includes certified chemical dependency counselors, physicians, nurses, psychiatrists, psychologists, a dietician, and an exercise instructor.

The facility: Our environment is friendly, non-threatening, and spiritually affirming. The grounds and buildings are attractive and non-clinical. The atmosphere of quiet serenity is conducive to recovery.

The Mission: For more than four decades we have been dedicated to treating clergy and religious for addictive disease and restoring them to productive, spirit-filled lives.

Interventions:

Before confronting an alcoholic or an addict, you should get professional advice. Interventions can be difficult for all involved. But they can save lives and vocations. We have the expertise to advise and help you.

Call us 24 hours a day, 7 days a week at:

1-800-634-4155

GuestHouse®

Williams
Diocese of Phoenix

St. Agnes Apartments
(Retirement)
200 S. Ninth
Williams, AZ 86046
Tel: 520-635-2913

ARKANSAS

Barling
Diocese of Little Rock

Mercy Crest of Arkansas, Inc.
1300 Strozier Ln.
Barling, AR 72923
Tel: 501-478-3000; Fax: 501-452-8382
E-mail: jarnold@ftsm. smns.com
Web Site: www.mercycrest.com
Sponsored by the Religious Sisters of Mercy.
Retirement Facility:
Total Staff 26
Beds 60
Patients assisted annually 60
Residential Care Facility for the Elderly.

Hot Springs National Park
Diocese of Little Rock

Monastery of Our Lady of Charity of Refuge (Good Shepherd)
1125 Malvern Ave.
Hot Springs National Park, AR 71901
Tel: 501-623-9651; Fax: 501-623-1509
Sr. MARY THERESA DIONNE, Supr.
In res.,
Rev. BENOIT PICARD, O.F.F.
Sisters 14
Total Staff 20

St. Michael's School
1125 Malvern Ave.
Hot Springs National Park, AR 71901
Tel: 501-623-9651; Fax: 501-623-1509
E-mail: smichael@ipa.net
Web Site: www.LightofMary.org
Sr. MARY THERESA DIONNE, Supr.
Sisters of Our Lady of Charity of Refugee (Good Shepherd) 14
Elementary students 51
Kindergarten 12
Day Care Center 64

Little Rock
Diocese of Little Rock

ABBA House, Missionaries of Charity
1014 S. Oak St.
Little Rock, AR 72204
Tel: 501-666-9718
Home for expectant mothers.
Missionaries of Charity 4
Patients assisted annually 227

AS

Pago Pago
Diocese of Samoa-Pago Pago

Nazareth House
P.O. Box 1510
Pago Pago, AS 96799
Tel: 684-699-2101; Fax: 684-699-1459
Conducted by Poor Sisters of Nazareth.
Sr. SHEILA COLLINGBORN, Admin.
Sisters 34
Aged Residents 15
Special Care Children 11
Montessori Early Education 80
Day Care Center 95
Total Staff 60

CALIFORNIA

Chatsworth
Archdiocese of Los Angeles

Rancho San Antonio
21000 Plummer St.
Chatsworth, CA 91311
Tel: 818-882-6400; Fax: 818-882-6404
Sponsored by Catholic Archdiocese of Los Angeles.
Directed by the Brothers of Holy Cross.
Bro. JOHN CROWE, C.S.C., Exec. Dir.
In res.,
Rev. JAMES BLANTZ, C.S.C.
Brothers 4
Boys (13-17 yrs.) 102
Families Assisted 242

Culver City
Archdiocese of Los Angeles

Marycrest Manor, Convalescent Home
10664 St. James Dr.
Culver City, CA 90230-5498
Tel: 310-838-2778; Fax: 310-838-9647
Religious Sisters of Charity.
Skilled Nursing Facility attended by priests from Loyola University and St. Augustine Parish.
Sr. MAURITA DILLON, Admin.
Sr. FRANCIS MARIA, Plant & Risk Mgr.
Pastoral Care Sisters 2
Bed Capacity 57
Residents 57
Total Staff 99

Fresno
Diocese of Fresno

Nazareth House
2121 N. First St.
Fresno, CA 93703
Tel: 559-237-2257; Fax: 559-237-1958
E-mail: PSNRose@earthlink.net
Sr. ANTIONETTE FARRELL, P.S.N., Supr.
Rev. PIUS KURERA
Poor Sisters of Nazareth of Fresno Inc. 6
Residential Care 65
Skilled Nursing 39
Total Staff 92

La Mesa
Diocese of San Diego

Little Flower Haven
8585 La Mesa Blvd.
La Mesa, CA 91941
Tel: 619-466-3163; Fax: 619-466-9642
Sr. BARBARA LEARY, D.C.J., Admin.
Rev. PHILIP BRONK, S.T., Chap.
Total Staff 25
Aged Residents 85

Los Angeles
Archdiocese of Los Angeles

Convent of the Good Shepherd-Good Shepherd Shelter
2561 Venice Blvd.
Los Angeles, CA 90019
Tel: 323-737-6111; Fax: 323-737-6113
E-mail: rgslai@aol.com
Conducted by Sisters of the Good Shepherd.
Shelter for Battered Women and Their Children.
Sisters 12
Women Assisted Annually 24
Children 108

Franciscan Health Center
2859 Glassell St.
Los Angeles, CA 90026
Tel: 213-413-1050
ROSIE ORTEGA, Clinic Mgr.
Community Clinic Offering Surgical, Medical, OB-GYN, Optometry, Ophthalmology, Pediatrics, & Dental patients. Payment based on ability to pay.
A United Way Agency. Sponsored by Franciscan Sisters of the Sacred Heart.
Patients assisted annually 5,700

Knights of Malta Free Clinic, Inc.
2222 W. Ocean View #112
Los Angeles, CA 90057
Tel: 213-384-4323; Fax: 213-384-4097
E-mail: freemed112@aol
Conducted by Knights of Malta Free Clinic, Inc.
Primary Health Care for the frail elderly, the working poor and medically underserved children.
DAVID FRELINGER, M.D., K.M., Medical Dir.
DAVID JOHNSON, Admin.
Visitation 7,229
Total Staff 18

Little Flower Missionary House
2434 Gates St.
Los Angeles, CA 90031-2824
Tel: 323-221-9248; Fax: 323-221-9831
E-mail: littleflowercarmel@netzero.net
Web Site: www.geocities.com/athens/acropolis/7053
Sr. MARINA, O.C.D., Supr., Admin.
Mrs. CATHERINE CATANO, Dir. & Prin.
Attended by Salesian priests.
Child and Kindergarten Care Center.
Sisters 6
Lay Teachers 10
Capacity 197
Kindergarten Capacity 50
Total Staff 29

Missionary Brothers of Charity
1345 Alvarado Ter.
Los Angeles, CA 90006
Tel: 213-251-9707
Day Center and Residence for Homeless Youth.

Nazareth House
3333 Manning Ave.
Los Angeles, CA 90064
Tel: 310-839-2361; Fax: 310-839-4204
E-mail: naz-la@pacbell.net
Web Site: www.nazarethouse.org
Conducted by the Poor Sisters of Nazareth.
Sr. FINTAN KEAVENEY, Supr.
In res.,
Sisters 8
Retired Priests 20
Total Staff 85
Residents 123

St. Anne's
155 N. Occidental Blvd.
Los Angeles, CA 90026
Tel: 213-381-2931; Fax: 213-381-7804
E-mail: stannes@stannes.org
Web Site: www.stannes.org
Residential care and community counseling programs for pregnant and parenting adolescents.
Sponsored by the Franciscan Sisters of the Sacred Heart
TOM OWENSON, Pres. & CEO
Beds Licensed for Children Under 18 years of age 102
Children Served Annually in Residential Care 250
St. Anne's also provides counseling to pregnant/parenting young women in their homes and pregnancy prevention (abstinence) classes in schools.
Support groups include:
St. Anne's Foundation
St. Anne's Guild
St. Anne's Junior Guild
Mabel Mosler Auxiliary
Loretta Young Auxiliary
Sister Winifred Auxiliary
Residential 250
Prevention Education 2,000
Total Staff 109

St. John of God Retirement and Care Center
2035 W. Adams Blvd.
Los Angeles, CA 90018
Tel: 323-731-0641; Fax: 323-731-1452
JOHN WILLIAMS, Admin.
Bros.:
PETER GELFER, O.H., Prior
EDWARD FRANCIS MCENROE, O.H., Prov.
STEPHEN DE LA ROSA, O.H., Novice Master
Brothers 14
Bed Capacity 215
SNF 131
Residential Care 33
Independent Living 51
Patients assisted annually 258
Supporting Organizations:
Hospitaller Foundation of California, Inc.
Tel: 323-731-7141; Fax: 323-731-5717
Bro. PATRICK CORR, O.H., Pres.
Women's League of St. John of God, Inc., Helpers Club of St. John of God, Inc.
Tel: 323-731-7141; Fax: 323-731-5717

Los Banos
Diocese of Fresno

New Bethany
1441 Berkeley Dr. 93635
Los Banos, CA,
Tel: 209-827-8933
E-mail: JDF2003@grid.com
Directors:
Sr. HELEN PETROVICH, F.H.I.C., Skilled Nursing
Sr. JULIA FONSECA, F.H.I.C., Residential Care
Sr. LUCINDA FONSECA, F.H.I.C., Community Rep.
Rev. MANUEL SOARES, Chap.
Franciscan Hospitaller Sisters of the Immaculate Conception 13
Residential Care 76
Skilled Nursing 35
Total Staff 59
Capacity 111

Monterey
Diocese of Monterey in California

Ave Maria Convalescent Hospital
1249 Josselyn Canyon Rd.
Monterey, CA 93940
Tel: 831-373-1216; Fax: 831-373-2238
Rev. FELIX MIGLIAZZO, Chap.

Franciscan Sisters of the Immaculate Conception 7
Bed Capacity 31
Patients assisted annually 50
Total Staff 46

Mountain View
Diocese of San Jose in California

Villa Siena
1855 Miramonte Ave.
Mountain View, CA 94040
Tel: 650-961-6484; Fax: 650-961-6254
Residential Care and Skilled Nursing Facility.
Mrs. CORINE BERNARD, Exec. Dir.
Sr. JOAN GIBSON, D.C., Pres. & Bd. Chm.
Rev. SALVATORE M. DINARDO, D.C., Chap.
Daughters of Charity of St. Vincent de Paul.
Professed Sisters 3
Residents 66
In Nursing Care 20
Nursing Staff 28
Total Staff 52

Newbury Park
Archdiocese of Los Angeles

Mary Health of the Sick Convalescent and Nursing Hospital
2929 Theresa Dr.
Newbury Park, CA 91320
Tel: 805-498-3644; Fax: 805-498-5112
E-mail: health@ftel.net
Sisters Servants of Mary
Skilled Nursing Facility.
Sr. PURIFICACION FERRERO, S.M., Supr./Exec. Dir.
Sisters 15
Bed Capacity 61
Residents Assisted Annually 90
Total Staff 91

Oakland
Diocese of Oakland

Bishop Begin Villa
(Retired Priests)
3418 E. 18th St.
Oakland, CA 94601
Tel: 510-536-0719; Fax: 510-536-3561
Rev. Msgr. MARTIN E. WALSH
Revs.:
EDMUND L. HAYBURN
JOHN R. KENNY
THOMAS B. GALLAGHER
JAMES C. CLIFT
JOSEPH A. FERREIRA
Residents 6
Total Assisted 6

Mercy Retirement and Care Center
(Affiliated with Elder Care Alliance)
3431 Foothill Blvd.
Oakland, CA 94601
Tel: 510-534-8540; Fax: 510-261-7551
Sr. PATRICIA CREEDON, Admin.
Sponsored by the Sisters of Mercy.
Sisters of Mercy 4
Sisters of the Holy Names 2
Employees 160
Convalescent Hospital - Skilled Nursing Facility
Residential Care & Assisted Living.
Bed capacity 59
Retirement Facility for Priests in the Oakland Diocese Extensive community services.

Ojai
Archdiocese of Los Angeles

St. Joseph's Health and Retirement Center
2464 E. Ojai Ave., P.O. Box 760
Ojai, CA 93024
Tel: 805-646-1466; Fax: 805-646-1013
Hospitaller Brothers of St. John of God.
Bros.:
MICHAEL BASSEMIER, Prior
ANDRE ARCULETTA, O.H., Res. Mgr.
Rev. CARROLL LAUBACHER, S.J.
Capacity 28
Independent Living 25
Total Staff 53

Palm Desert
Diocese of San Bernardino

La Paz Villas
P.O. Box 1962
Palm Desert, CA 92261
Tel: 760-772-1382; Fax: 760-360-6638
E-mail: brallo@aol.com
Units 24

Rosemead
Archdiocese of Los Angeles

Maryvale
P.O. Box 1039
Rosemead, CA 91770-1003
Tel: 626-280-6510; 323-283-9311; Fax: 626-288-8903
E-mail: maryvalel/@aol.com
Sr. LINDA ANN CAHILL, D.C., Exec. Dir.
Daughters of Charity of St. Vincent de Paul 6
Children:
Residential Treatment 85
Foster Family 6
Day Care 152
The Los Angeles Orphan Asylum
7600 E. Graves Ave.
Rosemead, CA 91770
Tel: 626-280-6510; Fax: 626-288-8903
Los Angeles Orphanage Guild
7600 E. Graves Ave.
Rosemead, CA 91770
Tel: 626-280-6510; Fax: 626-288-8903
Total Assisted 250
Total Staff 210

Sacramento
Diocese of Sacramento

Mercy-McMahon Terrace
3865 J St.
Sacramento, CA 95816
Tel: 916-733-6510; Fax: 916-733-6515
E-mail: mfgexcalibur@aol.com
Web Site: www.mercysacramento.org
MARY FRANCIS GIAMMONA, Admin.
Licenced Units 189
Total Assisted 118
Total Staff 45

San Bernardino
Diocese of San Bernardino

St. Bernardine Plaza
550 W. Fifth St.
San Bernardino, CA 92401
Tel: 909-888-0153; Fax: 909-381-1589
Staff 4
Units 150

San Diego
Diocese of San Diego

Cathedral Plaza
1551 Third Ave.
San Diego, CA 92101
Tel: 619-234-0093; Fax: 619-234-5168
E-mail: cathplaza@aol.com
Legal Title: *Cathedral Plaza Development Corp. A California Nonprofit Corporation*
Res. Mgrs.:
IRIS BARRETT
BRUCE BARRETT
Total Staff 5
Total Assisted 172
Apartments 222
In Residence 256
Total Staff 5

Guadalupe Plaza
4142 42nd St.
San Diego, CA 92105
Tel: 619-584-2414; Fax: 619-584-2886
E-mail: GDplaza@aol.com
Legal Title: *Guadalupe Plaza Development Corp., A California Nonprofit Corporation*
JERRY LYNN SCRIVEN, Resident Mgr.
Apartments 126
In Residence 140

Nazareth House Retirement Home
6333 Rancho Mission Rd.
San Diego, CA 92108
Tel: 619-563-0480; Fax: 619-624-9215
E-mail: fmack@cts.com
Retired Priests Residential and Nursing
Rev. GEORGE BYRNE
Sr. FIDELIS MCCORMACK, P.S.N., Admin.
Capacity 139
Priests 20
Poor Sisters of Nazareth of San Diego 8

St. John's Plaza
8150 Broadway
Lemon Grove, CA 91945
Tel: 619-466-5354; Fax: 619-466-6643
E-mail: STJPlaza@aol.com
Legal Title: *Calexico Plaza Development Corp., A California Nonprofit Corporation*
Res. Mgrs.:
BETTY JOHNSON
MILTON JOHNSON
Residences 99
Total In Residence 106
Total Staff 6

San Fernando
Archdiocese of Los Angeles

Mother Gertrude Home for Senior Citizens
(Franciscan Missionary Sisters of the Immaculate Conception, Inc.)
11320 Laurel Canyon Blvd.
San Fernando, CA 91340
Tel: 818-898-1546; Fax: 818-365-3159
Capacity 98
Total Staff 19
Total in Residence 36

San Francisco
Archdiocese of San Francisco

Alexis Apartments of St. Patrick's Parish
390 Clementina St.
San Francisco, CA 94103
Tel: 415-495-3690; Fax: 415-495-3629
E-mail: alexisapts@aol.com
756 Mission St.
San Francisco, CA 94103
BRENDA THOMAS, Exec. Dir.
Residents 240

The Good Shepherd Gracenter
1310 Bacon St.
San Francisco, CA 94134
Tel: 415-337-1938; Fax: 415-586-0355
Residential treatment program for women recovering from drug and alcohol addiction.
Sisters 6
Lay Staff 9
Residence capacity 13
Total Assisted 38

Home for the Aged of the Little Sisters of the Poor
St. Anne's Home, 300 Lake St.
San Francisco, CA 94118
Tel: 415-751-6510; Fax: 415-751-0650
Sr. MARIA CHRISTINE LYNCH, l.s.p., Supr.
In res.,
Rev. Msgr. EDWIN J. KENNEDY
Revs.:
MICHAEL STRANGE, S.S., Res. Chap.
JOSEPH JASZOVSKY
ANTHONY LEE
LIAM O'BYRNE
GEORGE M. TWIGG-PORTER, S.J.
ALBERT CHAN, S.J.
Religious 12
Residents 90

Madonna Residence
350 Golden Gate Ave.
San Francisco, CA 94102
Tel: 415-592-2864; Fax: 415-928-5867
E-mail: CKoger@St.AnthonySF.org
CATHY KOGER, Mgr.
Total in Residence 51
Nonprofit residence for women over 60 on S.S.I.. Meal program, social services program.

Mercy Terrace Corporation Apartments
333 Baker St.
San Francisco, CA 94117
Tel: 415-931-2325; Fax: 415-931-7206
E-mail: mercyterrace@msn.com
Ms. ROSE NATAN, Admin.
The purpose of this corporation is to develop, construct, own, and operate housing for low and moderate income persons and families.
Units 157

Mount St. Joseph-St. Elizabeth (1976)
100 Masonic Ave.
San Francisco, CA 94118
Tel: 415-567-8370; Fax: 415-351-5531
E-mail: sreileendc@aol.com
Web Site: www.mountsjse.org
Sr. EILEEN KENNY, D.C., Exec. Dir.
Successor Corporation to Mount St. Joseph Home for Girls and St. Elizabeth Infant Hospital.
Sisters 3
Lay Staff 126
Total Assisted 323
Mount St. Joseph Program-Benita House Residential care for abused and neglected girls, ages 13-17, with emotional and behavioral problems.
Number assisted 34
St. Elizabeth Adolescent Parenting Program Residential care for pregnant teens, ages 13-17, teen mothers, and their children.
Girls 34
Babies 24

Simpatico School On-site non-public junior-senior high school offering basic education and vocational training to school-age residents of our group home and adolescent parenting programs.
Tel: 415-351-4056; Fax: 415-440-5033
Students 40
Epiphany Center for Families in Recovery
1. Comprehensive drug treatment, parenting and reunification services.
Families Served 60
2. Epiphany In-Home Services for Families at Risk.
Tel: 415-351-4052
Families Served by In-Home Services 85
3. Epiphany Residential Infant Program for infants prenatally exposed to drugs.
Individuals Assisted 26
4. Epiphany House—Transitional living for women and children.
Individuals Assisted 26

San Jose
Diocese of San Jose in California

Giovanni Center, Inc.
85 S. Fifth St.
San Jose, CA 95112
Tel: 408-288-7436; Fax: 408-288-7264
E-mail: alaujdm@aol.com
Web Site: hometown.aol.com/alaujdm/myhomepage/business.html
ALVIN LAU, Admin.
Lay Staff 3
Residents 40
A California nonprofit charitable, public-benefit, housing project for low-income elderly. Sponsored by the Roman Catholic Bishop of San Jose, a corporation sole.

Jeanne d'Arc Manor
85 S. Fifth St.
San Jose, CA 95112
Tel: 408-288-7421; Fax: 408-288-7264
E-mail: alaujdm@aol.com
Web Site: hometown@aol.com/alaujdm/myhomepage/business-html
Housing project for low-income elderly and handicapped. Sponsored by the Roman Catholic Bishop of San Jose, A Corporation Sole.
ALVIN LAU, Admin.
Lay Staff 12
Residents 145
Units 87

San Pedro
Archdiocese of Los Angeles

Little Sisters of the Poor
Jeanne Jugan Residence, 2100 S. Western Ave.
San Pedro, CA 90732
Tel: 310-548-0625; Fax: 310-548-4504
Sr. MARIE ANNE, Supr.
Legal Title: *Little Sisters of the Poor of Los Angeles. A Corporation*
Sisters 11
Residents 105
Total Staff 94

San Rafael
Archdiocese of San Francisco

Nazareth House
245 Nova Albion Way
San Rafael, CA 94903
Tel: 415-479-8282; Fax: 415-479-8824
Sr. MARY ANTOINETTE FARRELL, P.S.N., Supr.
Rev. WARREN WOODS, Chap.
Poor Sisters of Nazareth 5
Residents 151
In res.,
Rev. Msgr. THOMAS I. KENNEDY, (Retired)
Rev. Msgr. GEORGE MONAGHAN
Rev. Msgr. ANDRE TOURNEIR, (Retired)
Revs.:
HENRY FAUCHER, (Retired)
MARTIN AVIA, (Retired)

Santa Barbara
Archdiocese of Los Angeles

St. Vincent Residence
4200 Calle Real, P.O. Box 669
Santa Barbara, CA 93102-0669
Tel: 805-683-6381; Fax: 805-967-7508
For female youthful offenders, ages 12-17.
Daughters of Charity of St. Vincent de Paul Sisters 5
Residents 7
Total Assisted 15
Total Staff 20

Santa Maria
Archdiocese of Los Angeles

Marian Residence
124 S. College Dr.
Santa Maria, CA 93454
Tel: 805-922-7731; Fax: 805-922-9834
Conducted by Sisters of St. Francis of Penance and Christian Charity.
Sisters 27
Residents 32
Total Staff 41

Santa Rosa
Diocese of Santa Rosa in California

**Vigil Light Apartments (The Vigil Light, Inc.)*
1945 Long Dr.
Santa Rosa, CA 95405
Tel: 707-544-2810; Fax: 707-544-1219
E-mail: VIGILLIGHT@MINSPRING.COM
Sr. MARY ANN BREIDENICH, O.P., Mgr.
Sisters 1
Residents 53

Saratoga
Diocese of San Jose in California

Our Lady of Fatima Villa
20400 Saratoga-Los Gatos Rd.
Saratoga, CA 95070
Tel: 408-741-2950; Fax: 408-741-4930
E-mail: ourlady@earthlink.com
Provides skilled nursing care for aged women and men and Special Alzheimer's Unit.
Affiliate: Catholic Health Initiative
PRESTON WISNER, Admin.
SUSAN SNYDER, O.P., Prioress
Sr. ANDREA MENDOZA, S.N.D.deN., Pastoral Care
Sr. GERTRUDE BORACCA, S.N.D.deN.
Sisters 6
Residents 77
Total Staff 96

Spring Valley
Diocese of San Diego

Noah Homes
12526 Campo Rd.
Spring Valley, CA 91978
Tel: 619-660-6200; Fax: 619-660-1481
E-mail: NoahHomesSKJ@aol.com
Sr. KATHRYN JENNINGS, O.S.B., Exec. Dir.
Total Assisted 61
Total Staff 42

Stockton
Diocese of Stockton

Casa Manana Inn
3700 N. Sutter St.
Stockton, CA 95204
Tel: 209-466-4046
REBECCA WILLIAMS, Mgr.
Total in Residence 162
Total Staff 4

Garden Oaks
3334 Wagner Heights Rd.
Stockton, CA 95209
Tel: 209-956-3401; Fax: 209-956-3494
E-mail: info@oconnorwoods.org
Assisted living facility.
Sisters of the Third Order of St. Dominic, Congregation of the Most Holy Name.
PENNY LEAL-MALLETTE, Dept. Mgr.
Total Staff 20
Units 40

St. Joseph's Regional Housing Corp.
1805 N. California St., Ste. 407
Stockton, CA 95204
Tel: 209-467-6312; Fax: 209-952-6201
E-mail: info@oconnorwoods.org
O'Connor Woods Housing Corp. dba Garden Oaks
3334 Wagner Heights Rd.
Stockton, CA 95209
Tel: 209-956-3400; Fax: 209-952-6201
O'Connor Woods, A Calif. Corp.
3400 Wagner Heights Rd.
Stockton, CA 95209
Tel: 209-956-3400; Fax: 209-952-6201
St. Joseph's Regional Health System provides regional management and support functions for St. Joseph's Regional Housing Corp. Sponsored by the Sisters of the Third Order of St. Dominic, Congregation of the Most Holy Name, this non-profit Corp. provides a residential community for seniors offering a variety of living arrangements from active to assisted, and coordinates skilled nursing and rehabilitation services with St. Joseph's Medical Center's subsidiary operation, MEADOWOOD.
SCOTT SINCLAIR, Exec. Dir.
Total Assisted 322
Total Staff 90

Sun Valley
Archdiocese of Los Angeles

Villa Scalabrini
10631 Vinedale St.
Sun Valley, CA 91352
Tel: 818-768-6500; Fax: 818-768-0684
E-mail: nazzani@aol.com
Retirement Center and Special Care Unit.
Missionary Fathers of St. Charles
Rev. ERMETE NAZZANI, C.S., Exec. Dir. & Admin.
Sisters of the Poor of St. Catherine of Siena.
Bed Capacity 188
Retirement Center 140
Skilled Nursing Unit 58
Total Staff 110

COLORADO

Canon City
Diocese of Pueblo

Centura Health-Progressive Care Center
An operating unit of Catholic Health Initiatives Mountain Region (an affiliate of Catholic Health Initiatives).
1338 Phay Ave.
Canon City, CO 81212
Tel: 719-269-2000; Fax: 719-269-2016
E-mail: barbaracarochi@centura.org
BARBARA CAROCHI, Admin.
Beds 135

Colorado Springs
Diocese of Colorado Springs

Centura Health-Namaste Alzheimer Center
Sponsored by Catholic Health Initiatives.
2 Penrose Blvd.
Colorado Springs, CO 80906
Tel: 719-776-8500; Fax: 719-520-9709
Beds 64

The Medalion (East)
Sponsored by Catholic Health Initiatives.
1719 E. Bijou St.
Colorado Springs, CO 80909
Tel: 719-471-4800; Fax: 719-471-4807
Skilled Nursing 45
Assisted Living 25
Apartments 79
Rev. LEONARD WEEKS

The Medalion (West)
Sponsored by Catholic Health Initiatives.
417 E. Kiowa St.
Colorado Springs, CO 80903
Tel: 719-471-2578; Fax: 719-471-4807
Assisted Living 32
Apartments 89
Rev. LEONARD WEEKS

**St. Francis Nursing Center*
7550 Assisi Heights
Colorado Springs, CO 80919
Tel: 719-598-1336; Fax: 719-598-6472
Sisters of St. Francis of Perpetual Adoration
KENNETH M. SMITH, Admin.
Staff 90
Beds 110

Denver
Archdiocese of Denver

Archdiocesan Housing Committee
1544 Pearl St.
Denver, CO 80203
Tel: 303-830-0215; Fax: 303-830-2885
E-mail: HMSAHCI@aol.com
Archdiocesan Family Housing, Inc., Housing for Low-Income Families:
1544 Pearl St.
Denver, CO 80203
ANNA STROBL, Contact Person
3700 Humboldt
Denver, CO 80205
1900 S. Raritan
Denver, CO 80223
1300 S. Irving
Denver, CO 80219
800 S. Monaco
Denver, CO 80224

Cathedral Plaza Inc.
1544 Pearl St.
Denver, CO 80203
Tel: 303-837-1424
ANNA STROBL, Contact Person
Housing for Low-Income Elderly:
Holy Family Plaza, Inc.
1544 Pearl St.
Denver, CO 80212
Tel: 303-455-4433
ANNA STROBL, Contact Person
Marian Plaza, Inc.
1544 Pearl St.
Denver, CO 80203
Tel: 303-837-1818
ANNA STROBL, Contact Person
Higgins Plaza, Inc.
1380 Detroit St.
Denver, CO 80206
Tel: 303-320-4990
Madonna Plaza, Inc.
6275 Kearney St.
Commerce City, CO 80022
Tel: 303-289-2626
St. Martin Plaza, Inc.
1300 Bruce Randolph Ave.
Denver, CO 80205
Tel: 303-297-1414
Colorado Affordable Catholic Housing Corporation
1544 Pearl St.
Denver, CO 80203
Tel: 303-830-0215

Clare Gardens, Inc.
2626 Osceola St.
Denver, CO 80212
Tel: 303-433-6268; Fax: 303-455-5359
Franciscan Sisters, Daughters of the Sacred Hearts of Jesus and Mary (Wheaton, IL)
Rev. DECLAN A. MADDEN, O.F.M., Chap.
BARRY WEAVER, Prop. Mgr.
Housing Ministry, low-income family units.
Housing Units 128
Residents 600

Damen House
P.O. Box 11580
Denver, CO 80211
Tel: 303-433-4280; Fax: 303-433-8225
Shelter and Safehouse for Homeless Women and Children.
Sr. DONNA BAIOCCO, Contact person
Total Staff 11
Total Assisted 57

Dayspring Villa, Inc.
3777 W. 26th Ave.
Denver, CO 80211
Tel: 303-455-5066; Fax: 303-455-8966
DIANE JAEGER, Admin.
Total Assisted 56
Total Staff 20

Francis Heights, Inc.
2626 Osceola St.
Denver, CO 80212
Tel: 303-433-6268; Fax: 303-455-5359
Franciscan Sisters, Daughters of the Sacred Hearts of Jesus and Mary, (Wheaton, IL).
Rev. DECLAN A. MADDEN, O.F.M., Chap.
BARRY WEAVER, Property Mgr.
Housing Ministry, Senior Citizens and Handicapped.
Housing Units 384
Residents 411

**Gardens at St. Elizabeth*
(Men and Women)
2835 W. 32nd Ave.
Denver, CO 80211
Tel: 303-964-2005; Fax: 303-964-2340
E-mail: jackieleech@centura.org
Web Site: www.centura.org
An operating unit of Catholic Health Initiatives Mountain Region.
Sisters of St. Francis of Colorado Springs (O.S.F.)
BETH BREEN, Admin.
Sr. JACQUELINE LEECH, Chap.
Sisters 8
Aged Residents 320

Hospice of Peace
2420 W. 26th Ave., 200-D
Denver, CO 80211
Tel: 303-561-5000
E-mail: deemueller@centura.org
Home Hospice Care.
ANN LUKE, Dir.

Housing Management Services, Inc.
1544 Pearl St.
Denver, CO 80203
Tel: 303-830-0215; Fax: 303-830-2885

Little Sisters of the Poor Mullen Home for the Aged
3629 W. 29th Ave.
Denver, CO 80211
Tel: 303-433-7221; Fax: 303-455-9184
Sr. MARY MICHAEL NICKLES, L.S.P., Admin.
Rev. Msgr. WILLIAM H. JONES, Chap.
Little Sisters of the Poor 11
Aged Residents 70

St. Raphael Catholic Center, Inc.
1300 S. Steele St.
Denver, CO 80210
Tel: 303-715-2000
DENNIS RUSSELL, Sec. of Finance, Administration & Planning
To acquire, develop, maintain, operate and dispose of real and personal property for the purpose of providing retirement, assisted living and long term care facilities for retired priests of the Archdiocese of Denver and other persons.

Florence
Diocese of Pueblo

Centura Health-St. Joseph Manor
An operating unit of Catholic Health Initiatives Mountain Region (an affiliate of Catholic Health Initiatives).
600 W. 3rd St.
Florence, CO 81226-1117
Tel: 719-784-4893; Fax: 719-784-4308
Ms. ANN GENOVA, N.H.A.

Pueblo
Diocese of Pueblo

Villa Pueblo
An operating unit of Catholic Health Initiatives Mountain Region (an affiliate of Catholic Health Initiatives).
1111 Bonforte Blvd.
Pueblo, CO 81001
Tel: 719-545-5911; Fax: 719-544-1354
Rev. RAY HAWKINS, Chap.

Westminster
Archdiocese of Denver

Clare of Assisi Homes - Westminster, Inc.
2451 W. 82 Pl.
Westminster, CO 80003
Tel: 303-427-4406; 462-9271 (Corporate)

Villa Maria, Inc.
2461 W. 82nd Pl.
Westminster, CO 80031-4065
Tel: 303-426-1518; Fax: 303-426-4301
CINDY FRICK, Admin.
Total Assisted 40

CONNECTICUT

Bethel
Diocese of Bridgeport

Augustana Homes/Bishop Curtis Homes
Simeon Rd.
Bethel, CT 06801
Tel: 203-743-2508
BERNARD E. REIDY, K.C.S.G., Exec. Dir.
CLAIRE HIPP, Project Mgr.

Bridgeport
Diocese of Bridgeport

Augustana Homes/Bishop Curtis Homes
525 Palisade Ave.
Bridgeport, CT 06610
Tel: 203-366-4333; Fax: 203-366-4756
Mr. JAMES J. CASEY, Manager
Mrs. LILLIAN ARAUJO, Site Mgr.

Augustana Homes/Bishop Curtis Homes
280 Jewett Ave.
Bridgeport, CT 06606
Tel: 203-374-5346
Mr. JAMES J. CASEY, Mgr.
Mrs. NILDA ALAMO, Site Mgr.

Augustana Homes/Bishop Curtis Homes - East Bridgeport
238 Jewett Ave.
Bridgeport, CT 06606
Tel: 203-372-4301; Fax: 203-371-8698
Mr. LARRY W. ARSZYLA, Contact Person

Bridgeport Diocesan Health Care Corporation
238 Jewett Ave.
Bridgeport, CT 06606
Tel: 203-372-4301; Fax: 203-372-1817
E-mail: nygs@aol.com
Mr. MICHAEL R. BIRD, Exec. Dir.

The Pope John Paul II Foundation, Inc.
238 Jewett Ave.
Bridgeport, CT 06606
Tel: 203-797-9300; Fax: 203-797-9300

Roncalli Apartments
430 Grant St.
Bridgeport, CT 06610
Tel: 203-384-9984
Rev. EDWARD C. DOHERTY, M.SS.A., Pres.
MARIANN CALLAHAN, L.P.N., Admin.
Affiliate of the Roncalli Institute, Supervised Apartments for the Elderly & Handicapped.

St. Camillus Home Foundation, Inc.
238 Jewett Ave.
Bridgeport, CT 06606
Tel: 203-325-0200; Fax: 203-353-0550

Danbury
Diocese of Bridgeport

Augustana Homes Bishop Curtis Homes - Danbury
88 Main St.
Danbury, CT 06810
Tel: 203-791-8510; Fax: 203-791-8513
LARRY W. ARSZYLA, Exec. Dir.

The Pope John Paul II Center for Health Care, Inc.
33 Lincoln Ave.
Danbury, CT 06810
Tel: 203-797-9300; Fax: 203-790-4645
E-mail: onedee98@aol,com
Mrs. DIANE A. PIMENTEL, Admin.
Sr. FRANCES SMALKOWSKI, C.F.S.N., Co-Dir. Pastoral Care

Deep River
Diocese of Norwich

Mount St. John
135 Kirtland St.
Deep River, CT 06417-1816
Tel: 860-526-5391; Fax: 860-526-1636
E-mail: exdir@mountsaintjohn.org
Web Site: mountsaintjohn.org
Bro. K. PAUL MCGLADE, C.F.C., C.S.W.M., Exec. Dir.
Mrs. LESLIE CAMPOS, Prin.
ROXANNE T. O'BRIEN, C.S.W.M., Assoc. Dir. & Dir. Treatment Svcs.
Lay Staff 130
Boys 90
Total Assisted 183
Total Staff 166

Enfield
Archdiocese of Hartford

The Home for the Aged of the Little Sisters of the Poor
Incorporated Operating as St. Joseph's Residence
1365 Enfield St.
Enfield, CT 06082-4900
Tel: 860-741-0791; Fax: 860-741-3982
Rev. ANDREW J. SCOPP, S.J.
Little Sisters of the Poor 14
Residents 85
Senior Day Center 10
Total Assisted 95

Fairfield
Diocese of Bridgeport

Augustana Homes/Bishop Curtis Homes
1677 Post Rd.
Fairfield, CT 06430
Mr. JAMES J. CASEY, Manager, Tel: 203-576-0823

Meriden
Archdiocese of Hartford

Franciscan Family Care Center
267 Finch Ave.
Meriden, CT 06451
Tel: 203-237-8084; Fax: 203-639-1333
Legal Title: *Franciscan Family Care Center, Inc.*

Sr. SHAUN VERGAUWEN, F.S.E., Dir.
Sr. SUZANNE GROSS, F.S.E., Dir. Franciscan Home Care & Contact, Tel: 203-238-1441; Fax: 203-686-0807
Franciscan Sisters of the Eucharist 8
Total Assisted 495
Total Staff 90

New Britain
Archdiocese of Hartford

Marian Educational Clinic
314 Osgood Ave.
New Britain, CT 06053
Tel: 860-223-0501
Daughters of Mary of the Immaculate Conception
Sr. MARY EDMUNDA, D.M., Dir. & Contact
Sisters 2

Monsignor Bojnowski Manor, Inc.
50 Pulaski St.
New Britain, CT 06053
Tel: 860-229-0336; Fax: 860-229-3252
E-mail: dblados@snet.net
Web Site: mbmanor.org
Owned and operated by the Daughters of Mary of the Immaculate Conception.
Sr. MARY DEBORAH, D.M., Exec. Dir.
Sr. M. HONORATA, D.M., Contact
Skilled Nursing Beds 60
Total Staff 110

St. Lucian's Residence, Inc.
532 Burritt St.
New Britain, CT 06053-3699
Tel: 860-223-2123; Fax: 860-612-0321
Daughters of Mary of the Immaculate Conception
Rev. GILBERT WDZIECZNY, O.F.M.Conv., Chap.
Sisters 2
Residents 42

New Haven
Archdiocese of Hartford

St. Francis Home for Children, Inc.
651 Prospect St.
New Haven, CT 06511
Tel: 203-777-5513; Fax: 203-777-0644
Residential extended day treatment, group home, special education, and theraputic preschool.
Mr. PETER T. SALERNO, Exec. Dir. & Contact
Sisters 1
Lay Staff 120
Children 52
Extended Day Treatment 25
Preschool 25

Norwalk
Diocese of Bridgeport

Notre Dame Convalescent Home
76 W. Rocks Rd.
Norwalk, CT 06851
Tel: 203-847-5893; Fax: 203-849-1959
Sisters of St. Thomas of Villanova
Mother EDMOND, S.S.T.V., Supr.
Mr. KENNETH B. HUGO, Admin.
Rev. ALBERT W. WATTS, Chap.
Sisters 4
Patients assisted annually 60

Riverside
Diocese of Bridgeport

Augustana Homes of Greenwich / Bishop Curtis Homes
1040 E. Putnam Ave.
Riverside, CT 06878
Mr. JAMES J. CASEY, Manager, Tel: 203-576-0823

Stamford
Diocese of Bridgeport

Augustana Homes / Bishop Curtis Homes - Glenbrook
352 Glenbrook Rd.
Stamford, CT 06902
Tel: 203-576-0823
Mr. JAMES J. CASEY, Manager

St. Camillus Health Center
494 Elm St.
Stamford, CT 06902
Tel: 203-325-0200; Fax: 203-353-0550
Web Site: www.stcamillushealth.org
Mr. JOHN J. FARLING, Admin.
Mrs. ELIZABETH STEA, Asst. Admin.
Rev. CARLOS RODRIGUES, Chap.
St. Camillus Auxiliary Committee
494 Elm St.
Stamford, CT 06902
Tel: 203-325-0200; Fax: 203-353-0550

St. Camillus Adult Day Care
494 Elm St.
Stamford, CT 06902
Tel: 203-325-0200
CHRISTOPHER GALLO, Dir.

Trumbull
Diocese of Bridgeport

Carmel Ridge
6454 Main St.
Trumbull, CT 06611
Tel: 203-261-2229
Mr. PETER CADY, Site Mgr.

St. Joseph's Housing Corporation
Teresian Towers & Carmel Ridge Estates, 6448 Main St.
Trumbull, CT 06611
Tel: 203-261-2229
Mr. PETER CADY, Site Mgr.

St. Joseph's Manor
6448 Main St.
Trumbull, CT 06611
Tel: 203-268-6204; Fax: 203-268-5271
E-mail: saint.joseph.manor@snet.net
Web Site: www.stjosephsmanor.org
Sr. MICHELLE ANNE REHO, O.Carm., Admin.
Revs.:
ALFRED E. RUSSO, Chap.
CHARLES L. HEWITT (HRT)
PATRICK J. SPEER (HRT)
Carmelite Sisters for the Aged and Infirm 8
Capacity 297

West Hartford
Archdiocese of Hartford

Saint Agnes Home, Inc.
104 Mayflower St.
West Hartford, CT 06110
Tel: 860-521-7516; Fax: 860-521-6160
E-mail: safc@aol.com
For adolescent single mothers and their infants
M. KEEGAN, Exec. Dir.
Bed Capacity 16
Patients assisted annually 58
Total Staff 37

Saint Mary Home
2021 Albany Ave.
West Hartford, CT 06117
Tel: 860-570-8200; Fax: 860-570-8205
Mrs. PATRICIA ORSE Admin.
Mrs. PAT DUCLOS-MILLER, R.N., Dir. Nursing Svcs.
Rev. HERBERT CLARKIN, Res. Chap.
Sisters of Mercy 8
Sisters in Res. 2
Residents 107
Patients assisted annually 217

Willimantic
Diocese of Norwich

Holy Family Home and Shelter, Inc.
88 Jackson St., P.O. Box 884
Willimantic, CT 06226-0884
Tel: 860-423-7719; Fax: 860-423-3770
E-mail: holyfamily@neca.com
BONNIE REILEIN, Exec. Dir.
Sr. M. PETER, S.C.M.C., Dir. Public Rels.
In res.,
Rev. STEPHEN FRONCKEWICZ, O.S.B.
Residents 23
Total Assisted 165
Total Staff 9

Windham
Diocese of Norwich

St. Joseph Living Center
14 Club Rd.
Windham, CT 06280-1000
Tel: 860-456-1107; Fax: 860-450-7114
PATRICIA HAMILL, M.S., Admin.
Dr. MICHAEL KEENAN, Medical Dir.
PATRICIA DUFFY, R.N., Dir. Nursing Svcs.
VALERIE OLIVER, R.N., Case Mgr.
PAULA HANEY, Dir. Rehabilitation Svcs.
JANET GRISWOLD, Dir. Day Care
Sisters 1
Lay Staff 188
Capacity 120
Total Assisted 120
Total Staff 189

DELAWARE

Claymont
Diocese of Wilmington

Children's Home, Inc.
2901 Green St.
Claymont, DE 19703
Tel: 302-798-0601; Fax: 302-798-0604
Ms. FRITZ JONES, Dir. of Children's Svcs.
Capacity:
Children (Ages 9 - 18) 24
Total Assisted 25
Total Staff 15

Hockessin
Diocese of Wilmington

Franciscan Health System / Care at Brackenville
100 St. Clare Dr.
Hockessin, DE 19707
Tel: 302-234-5420; Fax: 302-234-5424
A 100-bed skilled nursing facility
Rev. PHILIP P. SHEEKEY

Newark
Diocese of Wilmington

Jeanne Jugan Residence
185 Salem Church Rd.
Newark, DE 19713
Tel: 302-368-5886; Fax: 302-738-5610
Conducted by the Little Sisters of the Poor
Sr. EDWARD MARIE, L.S.P., Supr.
Rev. ANTHONY T. SCHELICH, O.S.F.S.
Residents 80
Sisters 10

Marydale Retirement Village
135 Jeandell Dr.
Newark, DE 19713
Tel: 302-368-2784; Fax: 302-731-0584
E-mail: rpierce384@aol.com
Mr. RONALD PIERCE, Admin.
Sr. MARY SHEEHAN, I.H.M., Pastoral Care Coord.
Apartments for Elderly
Apartments 108
Residents 118
Total Assisted 35

Our Lady of Grace Home for Children, Inc.
487 E. Chestnut Hill Rd.
Newark, DE 19713
Tel: 302-738-4658; 737-6650; Fax: 302-369-1395
Sr. MARY ANTONEA SLOWIK, C.S.S.F., Admin. & Supr.
Sr. MARY CHARLOTTE WSZOLEK, C.S.S.F., Supr.
Felician Sisters 6
Children 14
Total Assisted 26

Wilmington
Diocese of Wilmington

The Antonian
1701 W. 10th St.
Wilmington, DE 19805
Tel: 302-421-3758
Mrs. CHRISTINE T. SPAGNOLO, Mgr.
Rev. MARIO BUGLIOSI, O.S.F.S., Chap.
Congregate Housing for the Elderly
Residents 143
Apartments 136

Franciscan Health System / Care at Wilmington
801 N. Broom St.
Wilmington, DE 19806
Tel: 302-652-3861
Rev. PHILIP P. SHEEKEY, Chap.

Home of Divine Providence, Inc.-Bayard House
300 Bayard Ave.
Wilmington, DE 19805
Tel: 302-654-1184; Fax: 302-654-8570
JANELLE VON BARGEN, Dir.
Pregnant Teens & Women (12-35)
Residents 25
Staff 14
Total Assisted Annually 400

Ministry of Caring, Inc.
506 N. Church St.
Wilmington, DE 19801-4812
Tel: 302-652-5523; Fax: 302-652-1919
E-mail: mail@ministryofcaring.org
RICHARD GIACCO, Pres., Board of Dir.
Rev. RONALD GIANNONE, O.F.M.Cap., Exec. Dir.
Ms. LOUISA TEOLI, Exec. Personal Asst.
DEBBE DUNPHY, Sr. Exec. Asst.
JAMES VAN ALSTINE, Staff Writer
ROBERT JACKSON, Co-Dir. Human Resources

Our Lady of Guadalupe
1801 W. 6th St.
Wilmington, DE 19805
Tel: 302-428-3702; Fax: 302-428-3705
Sr. CAROL SUKITZ, I.H.M., Deputy Dir. Program Svcs.
Sr. FIDES MILWICZ, C.S.S.F., Co-Dir. of Human Resources
JACKIE NELSON, CFO
Child Care Center
221 N. Jackson St.
Wilmington, DE 19805-3649
Tel: 302-652-8992; Fax: 302-652-8945
E-mail: childcarecenter@ministryofcaring.org
Child care for homeless children, from infancy to 4 years old.
RUTH DWYER, Dir.
St. Clare Medical Outreach
7th & Clayton Sts.
Wilmington, DE 19805-3156
Tel: 302-575-8218
Mobile medical van which provides health services for the poor.
THOMAS SCOTT, D.O., Medical Dir.
NAN CREWS, M.D.
MARYANN FAGAN, R.N.
Mary Mother of Hope House Transitional Residence
818-820 Jefferson St.
Wilmington, DE 19801-1432
Tel: 302-427-9170; Fax: 302-594-9434
E-mail: hopehouseI@ministryofcaring.org
Transitional residence for single women.
Sr. MARY ANNE MATARESE, O.S.B., Dir.
Capacity 12
House of Joseph II
7-9 W. 18th St.
Wilmington, DE 19802-4833
Tel: 302-594-9473; Fax: 302-594-9494
E-mail: houseofjosephII@ministryofcaring.org
Hospice for people with AIDS.
Bro. KEVIN O'LOUGHLIN, O.F.M. Cap., Dir.
Capacity 8
Pierre Toussaint Dental Office
830 Spruce St.
Wilmington, DE 19801-4205
Tel: 302-652-8947; Fax: 302-652-8994
E-mail: pierretoussaint@ministryofcaring.org
Dental office for the homeless.
Angela Merici House
1105 W. 8th St.
Wilmington, DE 19806-4605
Tel: 302-655-4817
Residence for Sisters of St. Francis.
Sisters of St. Francis 2
St. Francis Transitional Residence
103-107 & 111 N. Jackson St.
Wilmington, DE 19805-3648
Tel: 302-652-1935; Fax: 302-594-9475
E-mail: hopehouseII@ministryofcaring.org
Transitional living for women and children.
EMMA TERRELL, Dir.
House of Joseph Transitional Residence
704 West St.
Wilmington, DE 19801-1523
Tel: 302-652-0904; Fax: 302-652-9472
E-mail: houseofjosephI@ministryofcaring.org
Transitional residence for men.
JOHN TEOLI, Dir.
Samaritan Outreach
1410 N. Claymont St.
Wilmington, DE 19802-5227
Tel: 302-594-9476; Fax: 303-594-9478
E-mail: samaritanoutreach@ministryofcaring.org
Bro. MICHAEL ASCIONE, O.F.M.Cap., Dir.
Social outreach for the homeless.
Mary Mother of Hope House I
1103 W. 8th St.
Wilmington, DE 19806-4605
Tel: 302-652-8532; Fax: 302-594-9434
E-mail: hopehouseI@ministryofcaring.org
Sr. MARY ANNE MATARESE, O.S.B., Dir.
Emergency shelter for homeless women.
Capacity 21
Mary Mother of Hope House II
121 N. Jackson St.
Wilmington, DE 19805-3670
Tel: 302-652-1935; Fax: 302-594-9475
E-mail: hopehouseII@ministryofcaring.org
Emergency shelter for women with children.
Capacity 23
Mary Mother of Hope House III
515 N. Broom St.
Wilmington, DE 19805-3114
Tel: 302-652-0970; Fax: 302-594-9496
E-mail: hopehouseIII@ministryofcaring.org
Ms. LINDA MYRIE, Mgr.
Emergency shelter for women with children.
Capacity 21
Job Placement Center
1100 Lancaster Ave.
Wilmington, DE 19805-4009
Tel: 302-652-5518; Fax: 302-652-0917
E-mail: jobplacementcenter@ministryofcaring.org
Ms. ANGELA SANTOS, Dir.
Employment agency to assist the poor.
House of Joseph I
1328 W. Third St.
Wilmington, DE 19805-3662
Tel: 302-652-0904; Fax: 302-594-9496
E-mail: houseofjosephI@ministryofcaring.org
JOHN TEOLI, Dir.
Shelter for homeless employable men who are seeking employment.
Capacity 13
Emmanuel Dining Room, West
121 N. Jackson St.
Wilmington, DE 19805-3670
Tel: 302-652-3228; Fax: 302-652-2576
E-mail: emmanueldiningroom@ministryofcaring.org
Bro. ROBERT LONGO, O.F.M.Cap., Dir.
Emmanuel Dining Room, East
226 N. Walnut St.
Wilmington, DE 19801-3934
Tel: 302-652-2577; Fax: 302-652-2576
Mr. ODELL PARKER, Mgr.
Emmanuel Dining Room, South
500 Rogers Rd.
New Castle, DE 19720
Tel: 302-577-2951; Fax: 302-652-2576
Ms. EMMA MITCHELL, Mgr.
Ministry of Caring Distribution Center
1410 N. Claymont St.
Wilmington, DE 19802-5227
Tel: 302-652-0969; Fax: 302-594-9478
Mr. EUGENE McLAUGHLIN, Dir.
Ministry of Caring Guild
506 N. Church St.
Wilmington, DE 19801
VIRGINIA GRIMM, Pres.
Sacred Heart Housing, Inc.
506 N. Church St.
Wilmington, DE 19801
Tel: 302-652-5523; Fax: 302-652-1919
SUSAN CANNING, Pres., Board of Directors
Sacred Heart Oratory, Inc.
917 N. Madison St.
Wilmington, DE 19801
Tel: 302-428-3658; Fax: 302-594-9439
Bro. RONALD GIANNONE, O.F.M.Cap., Pres., Board of Directors
Guardian Angel Child Care
1000 Wilson St.
Wilmington, DE 19801
Tel: 302-428-3620; Fax: 302-428-3622
E-mail: guardianangel@ministryofcaring.org
PEGGY SUDLER, Dir.
Nazareth House I
106 N. Broom St.
Wilmington, DE 19805
Tel: 302-652-0790; Fax: 302-594-9496
E-mail: nazarethhouse@ministryofcaring.org
EMMA TERRELL, Dir.
Capacity 3 Families
Bethany House
601 N. Jackson St.
Wilmington, DE 19805-3241
Tel: 302-594-9458
E-mail: hopehouseI@ministryofcaring.org
Sr. MARY ANNE MATARESE, O.S.B., Dir.
Transitional residence for single women
Capacity 6
Nazareth House II
898 Linden St.
Wilmington, DE 19805-4423
EMMA TERRELL, Dir.
Transitional residence for families.
Capacity 4 Families
Nazareth House III
203 N. Jackson St.
Wilmington, DE 19805-3649
EMMA TERRELL, Dir.
Transitional residence for families.
Capacity 1 Family
Nazareth House IV
807 W. 6th St.
Wilmington, DE 19805
Transitional residence for families.
Capacity 1 Family

St. Patrick's House, Inc.
115 E. 14th St.
Wilmington, DE 19801
Tel: 302-654-6908
Rev. JAMES F. TRAINOR, Chm. of Board
Affiliated with St. Patrick Parish. Congregate Independent Living Facility for the elderly
Capacity 15
Total in Residence 15
Total Staff 3

Seton Villa, Inc.
800 Bellevue Rd.
Wilmington, DE 19809
Tel: 302-762-2982; Fax: 302-762-3187
Ms. FRITZ JONES, Dir. of Children's Svcs.
Capacity:
Children (ages 12 -18) 13
Total Assisted 18
Total Staff 15

Siena Hall, Inc.
2307 Kentmere Pkwy.
Wilmington, DE 19806
Tel: 302-656-2183; Fax: 302-658-2189
Ms. FRITZ JONES, Dir. of Children's Svcs.
Capacity:
Children (ages birth -18) 11
Total Assisted 24
Total Staff 16

Vianney House
905 Milltown Rd.
Wilmington, DE 19808
Tel: 302-636-0200
MARYANN BLATT, Dir.
Rev. CHRISTOPHER H. PLOKHOOY, Diocesan Liaison
Residents 5

DISTRICT OF COLUMBIA

Washington
Archdiocese of Washington

Cardinal O'Boyle Residence for Priests
1150 Varnum St., N.E.
Washington, DC 20017
Tel: 202-269-7100; Fax: 202-269-7820
In res.,
Rev. Msgr. LEONARD F. HURLEY, Chap., Carroll Manor
Rev. Msgr. JOSEPH W. HARTMAN
Rev. Msgr. ARMANDO JIMENEZ
Rev. Msgr. JOSEPH L. TELETCHEN
Revs.:
ROGER P. GALLAGHER
JAMES J. POWDERLY
JOSEPH BUI-TRANG-NGHIEM, Tribunal

Jeanne Jugan Residence-St. Joseph's Villa
4200 Harewood Rd., N.E.
Washington, DC 20017-1554
Tel: 202-269-1831; Fax: 202-269-1134
Little Sisters of the Poor
Sr. CHRISTINE KREUPER, L.S.P., Admin.
Rev. GEORGE WILSON, Chap.
Sisters 20
Residents 72
Apartments 23
Total Staff 72

FLORIDA

Daytona Beach
Diocese of Orlando

Casa San Pablo
401 N. Ridgewood Ave.
Daytona Beach, FL 32114
Tel: 904-253-2828; Fax: 904-253-0842
E-mail: bobbie0110@aol.com
ROBERTA RYAN, Admin.
Total Staff 12
Total in Residence 64

Fort Myers
Diocese of Venice

Villa Francisco
2140 Cottage St.
Fort Myers, FL 33901
Tel: 941-332-3229; Fax: 941-332-4178
Very Rev. THOMAS M. ANGLIM, V.G., Pres.
Sr. MARIE VINCENT CHIARAVALLE, O.S.F., Admin.
Total in Residence 74
Total Staff 2

Jacksonville
Diocese of St. Augustine

All Saints Nursing Home & Rehabilitation Center, Inc.
5888 Blanding Blvd.
Jacksonville, FL 32244
Tel: 904-772-1220; Fax: 904-772-6334
E-mail: fish6@bellsouth.net
ALICE WILBUR, Admin.
Deacon JOE JOHNSON, Chap.
Physical Therapy, Speech Therapy & Occupational Therapy Available.
Total Assisted 42,664

Casa San Pedro
P.O. Box 24000
Jacksonville, FL 32241-4000
Tel: 904-262-3200; Fax: 904-262-9270
Rev. KEITH R. BRENNAN, Chancellor

St. Catherine Laboure Manor
1750 Stockton St.
Jacksonville, FL 32204
Tel: 904-308-4700; Fax: 904-308-2987
E-mail: stvincentshealth.com
Long term health care Skilled Nursing Facility.
Beds 240
Sisters 3
Total Staff 239
Patients assisted annually 884

Melbourne
Diocese of Orlando

Ascension Manor
2960 Pineapple Ave.
Melbourne, FL 32935
Tel: 321-757-9828; Fax: 321-752-9437
E-mail: manorgang@aol.com
DONNA RAFANELLO, Mgr.
Total Staff 8
Total in Residence 85

Miami
Archdiocese of Miami

Camillus House, Inc.
P.O. Box 11829
Miami, FL 33101-1829
Web Site: camillus.org
336 N.W. 5th St.
Miami, FL 33128
Tel: 305-374-1065; Fax: 305-372-1402
Bro. RAPHAEL MIESZALA, B.G.S., Exec. Dir., Contact
Provides services to the homeless: emergency services, substance abuse rehabilitation, transitional housing
Camillus Health Concern, Inc.
P.O. Box 12408
Miami, FL 33101-2408
336 N.W. 5th St.
Miami, FL 33128
Tel: 305-577-4840; Fax: 305-372-1408
Provides medical and social services to the homeless and indigent.
Charity Unlimited of Florida, Inc.
Provides buildings and grounds for charitable works.
Brothers of the Good Shepherd, Inc.
A religious congregation
Brothers 5
Total Staff 85
Grand Total Assisted 427,294

Gift of Hope, Missionaries of Charity
724 N.W. 17 St.
Miami, FL 33136
Tel: 305-326-0032
Sr. NIRMALA, Supr. Gen.
Women's and Children's Shelter
Tel: 305-326-0032
Total Women Assisted 222
Total Children Assisted 85
Soup Kitchen for Men
Tel: 305-326-0032
Total Assisted 45,461
Total Staff 6

Ocala
Diocese of Orlando

Trinity Villas I, Inc.
3728 N.E. 8th Pl.
Ocala, FL 34470-1093
Tel: 352-694-5507; Fax: 352-694-1434
DEBRA CRAWFORD, Mgr.
Total Staff 5
Total in Residence 98

Trinity Villas II, Inc.
3728 N.E. 8th Pl.
Ocala, FL 34470-1093
Tel: 352-694-5507; Fax: 352-694-7434
DEBRA CRAWFORD, Mgr.
Total Staff 3
Total in Residence 64

Orlando
Diocese of Orlando

Bishop Grady Villas
954 Leigh Ave.
Orlando, FL 32804-2299

Monsignor Bishop Manor Apts., Inc.
824 Borders Cir.
Orlando, FL 32808
Tel: 407-293-3339; Fax: 407-293-0085
E-mail: BishopMano@aol.com
Web Site: www.orlandodawn.com/monsignorBishop Manor
Total Staff 4
Total in Residence 172

Ormond Beach
Diocese of Orlando

Prince of Peace Housing, Inc. dba Prince of Peace Villas
664 S. Nova Rd.
Ormond Beach, FL 32174
Tel: 904-673-5080; Fax: 904-673-2008
E-mail: popvillas@aol.com
SUE TYSON, Mgr.
Total in Residence 70
Total Staff 3

Pensacola
Diocese of Pensacola-Tallahassee

Haven of Our Lady of Peace
5203 N. Ninth Ave.
Pensacola, FL 32504
Tel: 850-477-0531; Fax: 850-477-6782
E-mail: mfox@shhpens.org
Daughters of Charity of St. Vincent de Paul
Mr. MICHAEL FOX, Admin.
Guests 89
Total Staff 99

Port Charlotte
Diocese of Venice

Bon Secours-St. Joseph Nursing Care Center, Inc.
2370 Harbor Blvd.
Port Charlotte, FL 33952
Tel: 941-624-5966; Fax: 941-624-3963
DANIEL FREED, Admin.
Total Staff 150
Patients assisted annually 37,960

St. Charles Housing I, Inc.
(aka Villa San Carlos)
2550 Easy St.
Port Charlotte, FL 33952
Tel: 941-624-2266; Fax: 941-624-2283
E-mail: dixie0940@aol.com
LYNN STEPHENS, Pres.
Total in Residence 53
Total Staff 3

St. Charles Housing II, Inc.
(dba Villa San Carlos II)
22250 Vick St.
Port Charlotte, FL 33980
Tel: 941-624-4404; Fax: 941-624-5556
E-mail: fran0941@aol.com
Sr. FRANCES KOWALSKI, O.S.F., Resident Mgr.
Ms. LYNN STEPHENS, Pres.
Residents 56
Total Staff 6

Port Orange
Diocese of Orlando

Epiphany Manor
4792 S. Ridgewood Ave.
Port Orange, FL 32127
Tel: 904-767-2556; Fax: 904-761-0490
Total Staff 3
Total in Residence 73

Sarasota
Diocese of Venice

St. Martha's Housing II, Inc.
(Casa Santa Marta II)
800 N. Lemon Ave.
Sarasota, FL 34236
Tel: 941-365-7913; Fax: 941-365-8887
E-mail: corab0116@aol.com
Rev. FAUSTO STAMPIGLIA, S.A.C., Pres.
CORA BEALS, Site Mgr.
Total in Residence 55
Total Staff 2

St. Martha's Housing, Inc.
(Casa Santa Marta)
1576 Eighth St.
Sarasota, FL 34236
Tel: 941-366-4448; Fax: 941-366-2544
E-mail: dorth0115@aol.com
Rev. FAUSTO STAMPIGLIA, S.A.C., Pres.
Total in Residence 82
Total Staff 3

Tallahassee
Diocese of Pensacola-Tallahassee

Casa Calderon, Inc.
800 W. Virginia St.
Tallahassee, FL 32304
Tel: 850-222-4026; Fax: 850-561-6868
E-mail: karkoel@aol.com.
Rev. Msgr. JAMES AMOS, V.G., Pres.
Mrs. CONNIE BROWN, Mgr.
Total Assisted 111
Total Staff 5

West Palm Beach
Diocese of Palm Beach

Noreen McKeen Residence for Geriatric Care
315 Flagler Dr. S.
West Palm Beach, FL 33401
Tel: 561-655-8544; Fax: 561-650-8952
Sr. DIANE M. MACK, O.Carm., Admin.
Rt. Rev. EDWARD CAMPBELL, O.S.B.

Winter Haven
Diocese of Orlando

Episcopal Catholic Apartments
500 Ave. L, N.W.
Winter Haven, FL 33881
Tel: 863-299-4481; Fax: 863-299-5719
E-mail: BethW0345@aol.com
BETH WIESE, Admin.
Total Staff 13
Total in Residence 199

GEORGIA

Atlanta
Archdiocese of Atlanta

Our Lady of Perpetual Help Home
760 Pollard Blvd., S.W.
Atlanta, GA 30315
Tel: 404-688-9515; Fax: 404-588-9568
Sisters of St. Dominic
Legal Title: *Servants of Relief for Incurable Cancer*
Nursing Home for Free Care of Cancer Patients.
Sr. M. FLORENCE GILMORE, O.P., Supr.
Rev. RICHARD LOPEZ, Res. Chap.
Sisters 8
Total Staff 32
Bed Capacity 48
Patients assisted annually 176

Saint Joseph's Mercy Care Services
60 Eleventh St.
Atlanta, GA 30309-3970
Tel: 404-249-8600
Division of Saint Joseph's Health System. Operates Mercy Mobile Health Care (Atlanta, Georgia). Operates Mercy Senior Care (Rome, Georgia).
Total Staff 102
Sisters 1
Total Assisted 20,000

Rome
Archdiocese of Atlanta

Mercy Senior Care, Inc.
212 W. Third St.
Rome, GA 30165
Tel: 706-291-0100; Fax: 706-295-5953
E-mail: rlawler@sjha.org
Sr. ANGELA MARIE EBBERWEIN, R.S.M., Vice Pres.
RITA LAWLER, Dir.
Total Staff 30
Total Assisted 275

Savannah
Diocese of Savannah

St. Mary's Home
2170 E. Victory Dr., P.O. Box 3627-B
Savannah, GA 31414
Tel: 912-236-7164; Fax: 912-236-9699
E-mail: STMARYHOME@aol.com
Sisters of Mercy of the Americas
Sr. MARY ALVIN SEUBOTT, R.S.M., Admin.
Summer Program
Total Assisted 51
Total Staff 35
Sisters 3
Lay Staff 32
Residents 45
Total Assisted 51

HAWAII

Kalaupapa
Diocese of Honolulu

Kalaupapa Settlement
Molokai
Kalaupapa, HI 96742
Tel: 808-567-6911; Fax: 808-567-6916
Operated by the State Dept. of Health for treatment of Leprosy.
Mrs. FE AUSTRIA-SCHWIND, Nursing Supvr.
Dr. W. PHILIP JONES, Settlement Medical Dir.
Rev. JOSEPH HENDRIKS, SS.CC., Pastor
Franciscan Sisters of the Third Order 3
Bed Capacity 14
Patients assisted annually 43
CareHome nursing care/assistance and home visits annually 16,016

ILLINOIS

Alton
Diocese of Springfield in Illinois

Catholic Children's Home
1400 State St.
Alton, IL 62002
Tel: 618-465-3594; Fax: 618-465-4023
E-mail: cch1400@ezl.com
Mr. STEVEN ROACH, Exec. Dir.
Ms. CANDACE LUMETTA, Admin.
Children under care 140
Total Staff 120

Marian Heights Apartments
20 Marian Heights Dr.
Alton, IL 62002
Tel: 618-462-0363; Fax: 618-462-0366
E-mail: marianhgtsapt@alton.net
Residence for the Elderly.
Sr. M. CARISTA, O.S.F., Supr.
SUSAN E. BARNETT, Operations Mgr.
Rev. DONALD SEDERWALL, Chap.
Sisters of St. Francis of the Martyr St. George 2
Residents 130
Total Staff 7

Aurora
Diocese of Rockford

Provena Fox Knoll
421 N. Lake St.
Aurora, IL 60506
Tel: 630-844-0380; Fax: 630-844-0702
Legal Title: *Provena Senior Services dba Provena Fox Knoll.*
Sr. DOROTHY BURNS, R.S.M., Admin.
Total Staff 53
Total in Residence 168
Independent Living 97
Assisted Living 68

Bartlett
Archdiocese of Chicago

Bartlett Learning Center
801 W. Bartlett Rd.
Bartlett, IL 60103
Tel: 630-289-4221; Fax: 630-289-4390
Legal Title: *Barlett Learning Center, Inc.*
SAMUELA BOVELLI-EMRICH, Admin.
Sisters 7
Lay Staff 73
Students 128
Day school program for developmentally delayed and multiple handicapped individuals ages 3 to 21. Accept youth identified LD, BD, EMH, & TMH, Speech/Language Impaired, Autistic.
Sponsored by the Sisters of St. Joseph, Third Order of St. Francis.

Belleville
Diocese of Belleville

Charles and Bertha Hincke Residence for Priests and Sense Residence
2620 Lebanon Ave.
Belleville, IL 62221
Tel: 618-234-5722; Fax: 618-234-5792
Owned by Diocese of Belleville.
ROBERT L. WEBER, Admin.
Guests 21

Meredith Memorial Home
16 S. Illinois St.
Belleville, IL 62220
Tel: 618-233-8780; Fax: 618-233-9602
Owned by the Diocese of Belleville.
Mr. ROBERT L. WEBER, Admin.
Rev. Msgr. LEONARD A. BAUER, Chap., Tel: 618-234-2773
Guests 86

Our Lady of the Snows Apartment Community Retirement Home
726 Community Dr.
Belleville, IL 62223
Tel: 618-397-6700; Fax: 618-394-9051
D. ROBERT McCARDLE, Exec. Vice Pres.
CATHY KNOWLTON, Dir. of Pastoral Care
Rev. ANDREW G. CHALKEY, O.M.I.
Guests 201

Bourbonnais
Diocese of Joliet in Illinois

Provena Our Lady of Victory
20 Briarcliff Ln.
Bourbonnais, IL 60914
Tel: 815-937-2022; Fax: 815-936-3231
Legal Title: *Provena Senior Services*
FREDDIE FRANKEN, Admin.
Rev. JOSEPH TREMONTI, C.S.V., Chap.
Bed Capacity 107

Chicago
Archdiocese of Chicago

Big Sisters
721 N. LaSalle St., Room 434
Chicago, IL 60610
Tel: 312-751-0111; Fax: 312-751-1085
Ms. MARY A. COURTNEY, Pres.
Dr. JOAN E. O'MALLEY, Past Pres.

Catholic Home Care
721 N. LaSalle St.
Chicago, IL 60610
Tel: 312-655-7415
Home health agency, Medicare certified, JCAHO accredited, providing health care to individuals in their homes in Cook and Lake Counties.

Catholic Home Care Home Services
721 N. LaSalle St.
Chicago, IL 60610
Tel: 312-655-7415
Home health agency, private duty, JCAHO accredited

Cortland Manor Retirement Home
1900 N. Karlov
Chicago, IL 60639
Tel: 773-235-3670
Catholic Charities Housing Development Corporation.
MAUREEN SCHOLLE, Admin.
Capacity 48

House of the Good Shepherd
1114 W. Grace St.
Chicago, IL 60613
Tel: 773-935-3434; Fax: 773-935-3523
Legal Title: *House of the Good Shepherd*
Sisters of The Good Shepherd
Sisters 6
Part time social workers 4
Capacity: 14 Families
Shelter for abused women with children.

Jugan Terrace
2300 N. Racine
Chicago, IL 60614
Tel: 773-935-9600; Fax: 773-935-4291
Legal Title: *Little Sisters of the Poor, North Side Chicago, Inc., (HUD subsidized)*
Sr. MARCEL JOSEPH, L.S.P., Admin.
Senior Housing Apts. 50

**L'Arche Chicago*
1049 S. Austin Blvd.
Chicago, IL 60644
Tel: 773-287-8249
E-mail: larchechicago@juno.com
Sr. MARIA ZEIMEN, O.S.F., Dir.
A Christian Community concerned with life sharing between persons with a developmental disability and persons who assist them.

Little Sisters of the Poor Center for the Aging
2325 N. Lakewood Ave.
Chicago, IL 60614
Tel: 773-935-9600; Fax: 773-935-9614
Legal Title: *Little Sisters of the Poor of Chicago, Inc.*
Sr. PATRICIA FRIEL, L.S.P., Supr.
Rev. WALTER HUPPENBAUER, Chap.
Sisters 12
Residents 74
Intermediate and skilled care facility.

Misericordia Home South
2916 W. 47th St.
Chicago, IL 60632
Tel: 773-254-9595; Fax: 773-254-6856
Sr. ROSEMARY R.S.M., Dir.
Sisters of Mercy 9
Patients assisted annually 110
Respite Beds 2
Handicapped children under 22 years of age: Bed Capacity for Children 110

Misericordia / Heart of Mercy Center
6300 N. Ridge
Chicago, IL 60660
Tel: 773-973-6300; Fax: 773-973-5214
Children and adults with Developmental disabilities.
Sr. ROSEMARY CONNELLY, R.S.M., Exec. Dir.
Sisters 27
Residents 550

Resurrection Retirement Community
7262 W. Peterson Ave.
Chicago, IL 60631
Tel: 773-792-7930; Fax: 773-792-8316
Division of Resurrection Health Care Corporation.
KAY F. CHOYINSKI, Dir. Oper.
Apartments 472

St. Joseph Home of Chicago, Inc.
2650 N. Ridgeway Ave.
Chicago, IL 60647
Tel: 773-235-8600; Fax: 773-235-2933
Legal Title: *St. Joseph Home of Chicago, Inc.*
Franciscan Sisters of Chicago
RICHARD BRACKEN, Admin.
Rev. CHARLES MROWINSKI, C.R., Chap.
Sisters 6
Licensed Beds 173

St. Joseph's Carondelet Child Center
739 E. 35th St.
Chicago, IL 60616
Tel: 773-624-7443; Fax: 773-624-7676
E-mail: jbmc@stjccc.org
Legal Title: *St. Joseph's Carondelet Child Center*
Treatment, rehabilitation and education of the dependent emotionally disturbed children and youth.
Sisters of St. Joseph of Carondelet
Mr. JAMES B. McLAUGHLIN, Pres. & CEO
Rev. CHARLES T. RUBEY, Chap.
Sisters 1
Children 157

St. Mary of Providence
4200 N. Austin Ave.
Chicago, IL 60634
Tel: 773-545-8300; Fax: 773-545-8035
E-mail: srpatmc@aol.com
Operated by the Daughters of St. Mary of Providence.
Sr. BETH ANN DILLON, Admin.
Sr. PATRICIA McCAFFERTY, Dir.
Rev. THOMAS A. MULCRONE, Chap.
Sisters 12
Staff 190
Students 70
Adults 96
Legal Title: *Daughters of St. Mary of Providence*
Education and residential care of developmentally disabled boys, girls and young adults.

Clifton
Diocese of Joliet in Illinois

Merkle-Knipprath Countryside Home
1190 E. 2900 N Rd.
Clifton, IL 60927-7103
Tel: 815-694-2306
Bro. DAMIEN DEBRAEKELEER, O.S.F., Admin.
Religious 4
Total in Nursing Care 100
Apartment Living 30
Apartment Community and Nursing Center.

Crete
Diocese of Joliet in Illinois

St. James Manor & Villas
Sponsored by Franciscan Sisters of Chicago
1251 Richton Rd.
Crete, IL 60417
Tel: 708-672-6700; Fax: 708-672-4939
E-mail: dstrutynski@franciscancommunities.com
DIANNE STRUTYNSKI, Exec. Dir.
Beds 181

Total Assisted Annually 35,770
Total Staff 150
Care of the Elderly.

Darien
Diocese of Joliet in Illinois

Carmelite Carefree Retirement Village
8419 Bailey Rd.
Darien, IL 60561-5361
Tel: 630-960-4060; Fax: 630-960-4071
Rev. ROY ONTIVEROS, O.Carm., Dir.
Residents 98

Des Plaines
Archdiocese of Chicago

Holy Family Health Center
2380 Dempster
Des Plaines, IL 60016
Tel: 847-296-3335
Sr. M. ELIZABETH, C.S.F.N., Admin.
Rev. RONALD E. SCARLATA, Chap.
Licensed Bed Capacity 362
Intermediate and skilled nursing care facility.
Sponsored by the Sisters of the Holy Family of Nazareth

Nazarethville
300 N. River Rd.
Des Plaines, IL 60016
Tel: 847-297-5900; Fax: 847-297-0504
Sr. M. LUCILLE MADURA, C.S.F.N., Admin.
Rev. DENNIS SANDERS, C.R., Chap.
Total under care 83
Sponsored by the Sisters of the Holy Family of Nazareth

Freeport
Diocese of Rockford

Provena St. Joseph Adult Day Care Services
659 E. Jefferson St.
Freeport, IL 61032
Tel: 815-266-8067; Fax: 815-232-6143
Mrs. KELLY SCHLEICH, Prog. Dir.
Rev. CLARENCE J. THENNES, Chap.
Sisters 4
Total Staff 10
Total Assisted 10,080

Provena St. Joseph Center
659 E. Jefferson St.
Freeport, IL 61032
Tel: 815-232-6181; Fax: 815-232-6143
Legal Title: *Provena Senior Services dba Provena St. Joseph Center.*
Mr. RICHARD RIMKUS, Admin.
Rev. CLARENCE J. THENNES, Chap.
Sisters 4
Aged Residents 120
Total Staff 150
Total Assisted 33

Geneva
Diocese of Rockford

Provena Geneva Care Center
1101 E. State St.
Geneva, IL 60134
Tel: 630-232-7544; Fax: 630-232-4409
Legal Title: *Provena Senior Services dba Provena Geneva Care Center.*
LINDA SHANNON, Admin.
Beds 107
Total Staff 100

Glenview
Archdiocese of Chicago

Maryhaven Inc.
1700 East Lake Ave.
Glenview, IL 60025
Tel: 847-729-1300; Fax: 847-729-9202
Legal Title: *Maryhaven Inc.*
Home for Aged, intermediate and skilled care facilities, Medicare, Therapy.
Mr. PAUL M. ASSELIN, Admin.
Rev. JOHN E. FLAVIN, Pres.
Capacity 138

Homewood
Archdiocese of Chicago

Mercy Health Care and Rehabilitation Center
19000 S. Halsted St.
Homewood, IL 60430
Tel: 708-957-9200; Fax: 708-799-4787
Affiliate of Mercy Hospital and Medical Center.
Sponsored by the Religious Sisters of Mercy
JANICE L. PODWIKA, Admin.
Pastoral Care:
Sr. GEORGINE SCHLEPER, P.H.J.C.
Bed Capacity 259
Total under care 215

Joliet
Diocese of Joliet in Illinois

Guardian Angel Home
1550 Plainfield Ave.
Joliet, IL 60435
Tel: 815-729-0930; Fax: 815-744-6087
E-mail: sas726@aol.com
Web Site: www.guardianangelhome.org
Sponsored by the Sisters of St. Francis of Mary Immaculate.
Child and family welfare agency: residential treatment, therapeutic school, foster care, domestic violence shelter, child abuse prevention center, and counselling.

Our Lady of Angels Retirement Home
1201 Wyoming
Joliet, IL 60435
Tel: 815-725-6631; Fax: 815-725-1451
Sisters of St. Francis of Mary Immaculate
Rev. JOSEPH MAISONNEUVE, O.Carm., Chap.
Sr. PHYLLIS PITZ, O.S.F., Admin.
In res.,
Sr. DAVID ANN HOY, Local Coord.
Sister Staff 14
Lay Employees 185
Retired Sisters 75
Residents 102

Provena Villa Franciscan
210 N. Springfield
Joliet, IL 60435
Tel: 815-725-3400; Fax: 815-725-2160
Legal Title: *Provena Senior Services*
CHERYL STOUT, Admin.
Bed Capacity 176
Extended, Intermediate, and Skilled Care, Respite Care, Alzheimer Unit.

St. Elizabeth Home
704 W. Marion St.
Joliet, IL 60436
Tel: 815-727-0125; Fax: 815-723-3452
Sr. ELLEN THOMAS, R.C., Senior Prog. Dir.
In Residence 11

Justice
Archdiocese of Chicago

Rosary Hill Home
9000 W. 81st St.
Justice, IL 60458
Tel: 708-458-3040; Fax: 708-458-7230
E-mail: rosaryhill@cometlink.com
Operated by the Dominican Sisters of Chicago
Sr. M. NATALIE, O.P., Supr.
Rev. JOSEPH MIKA, O.F.M., Chap.
Sisters 10
Bed Capacity 48
Number under care 48

Kankakee
Diocese of Joliet in Illinois

Provena Heritage Village
901 North Entrance Ave.
Kankakee, IL 60901
Tel: 815-939-4506; Fax: 815-939-4761
Legal Title: *Provena Senior Services d/b/a Provena Heritage Village*
CAROL MCINTYRE, Admin.
Bed Capacity 87

Provena Meadowview Lodge
995 North Entrance Ave.
Kankakee, IL 60901
Tel: 815-939-4506; Fax: 815-939-4761
Legal Title: *Provena Senior Services d/b/a Provena Meadowview Lodge*
CAROL MCINTYRE, Admin.
Provena Senior Services (Jol), Kankakee
Bed Capacity 26

Lacon
Diocese of Peoria

St. Joseph's Nursing Home
401 Ninth St.
Lacon, IL 61540
Tel: 309-246-2175; Fax: 309-246-3609
Daughters of St. Francis of Assisi
Mr. THOMAS BECHER, Admin.
Rev. HAROLD F. SCHMITT, Chap.
Sisters 7
Bed Capacity 93
Total Staff 83

Lake Zurich
Archdiocese of Chicago

Mt. St. Joseph Home
24955 North Hwy. 12
Lake Zurich, IL 60047
Tel: 847-438-5050; Fax: 847-438-1561
Intermediate care for developmentally developed women.
Operated by the Daughters of St. Mary of Providence.
Sr. JANET KOSMAN, Admin.
Rev. ALOYSIUS ROMANSKI, O.F.M.Conv.
Sisters 7
Lay Assistants 175
Residents 122

Lemont
Archdiocese of Chicago

Alvernia Manor
13950 Main St.
Lemont, IL 60439
Tel: 630-257-7721; Fax: 630-257-0338
E-mail: am13950@aol.com
Sr. GEORGINE HROMA, O.S.F., Admin.
Sisters of St. Francis of Christ King 6
Guests 50

Holy Family Villa
12375 McCarthy Rd.
Lemont, IL 60439
Sisters of St. Casimir
ROBERTA MAGURANY, Admin.
Sisters 3
Residents 99

Mother Theresa Home
1270 Franciscan Dr.
Lemont, IL 60439
Tel: 630-257-5801; Fax: 630-257-1328
E-mail: tkolaz@fv.fsoc.com
Sponsored by the Franciscan Sisters of Chicago.
THERESA D. KOLAZ, Admin.
Sisters 5
Residents 150

Lisle
Diocese of Joliet in Illinois

Villa St. Benedict
1920 Maple Ave.
Lisle, IL 60532
Tel: 630-852-5360; Fax: 630-852-3196
E-mail: glenntrem@aol.com
Web Site: www.Qopc.net
Retirement home.
Mr. GLENN TREMBLEY, Admin.
Lay Staff 9
Residents 32

Momence
Diocese of Joliet in Illinois

Good Shepherd Manor
P.O. Box 260
Momence, IL 60954
Tel: 815-472-6492; Fax: 815-472-2160
E-mail: gsm@keynet.net
Web Site: www.GoodShepherdManor.Org.
Adult Male DD-MR.
Dr. JAMES CZERWIONKA, Pres.
DORIS WILLIAMSON, Admin.
Bro. ALPHONSUS BROWN, B.G.S., Asst. Admin.
Brothers of the Good Shepherd 3
Bed Capacity 120
Permanent Residents 120

Naperville
Diocese of Joliet in Illinois

St. John Vianney Villa
1464 Green Trails Dr.
Naperville, IL 60540-8372
Tel: 630-983-0533; Fax: 630-983-6375
Retirement home for priests.
Revs.:
PATRICK MORAN
WILLIAM RYAN
THOMAS CORLEY
THOMAS FLEMING
ROBERT F. EMERSON
Residents 5

St. Patrick's Residence
1400 Brookdale Rd.
Naperville, IL 60563-2125
Tel: 630-416-6565; Fax: 630-416-8755
E-mail: stpatres@earthlink.net
Web Site: Stpatricksresidence.org
Sr. M. ANTHONY DELOURDES, O.Carm., Admin.
Rev. PHILIP DEDERA, Chap.
Carmelite Sisters 9
Beds 210
Residents 210
Total Assisted 290
Total Staff 373

Niles
Archdiocese of Chicago

St. Andrew Home for the Aged
7000 N. Newark Ave.
Niles, IL 60714-4497
Tel: 847-647-8332
Felician Sisters
JUDY PITZEK, Admin.
Sr. MARY AGNES, C.S.S.F., Supr.
Sisters 13
Number under care 177

St. Benedict Home for the Aged
6930 W. Touhy Ave.
Niles, IL 60714
Tel: 847-647-0003; Fax: 847-647-1936
Legal Title: *St. Benedict Home for the Aged (Catholic Charities of Chicago)*
Sisters of St. Benedict (Lisle, IL)
PETER E. GOSCHY, Admin.
Priests 18
Sisters 3
Residents 99

Northlake
Archdiocese of Chicago

Villa Scalabrini
480 N. Wolf Rd.
Northlake, IL 60164-1667
Tel: 708-562-0040
Missionaries of St. Charles Scalabrinians
SALLY MYERS, Admin.
Rev. JOHN DIVITO, C.S., Chap.
Sisters 10
Residents 259

Oak Brook
Diocese of Joliet in Illinois

Mayslake Village
1801 35th St.
Oak Brook, IL 60521
Tel: 630-850-8232; Fax: 630-850-8233
E-mail: mayslakvlg@aol.com
Web Site: www.mayslake.com
Including Mayslake Villas, Mayslake Manor, and Cloisters Courts.
Senior Citizen Retirement Community.
Rev. LARRY DREFFEIN, O.F.M., Pres.
Mr. MICHAEL A. FRIGO, Admin.
Units 630
Residents 750
Total Staff 45

Oak Park
Archdiocese of Chicago

Ephpheta Center and Hearing Conservation Service
119 S. Harvey Ave.
Oak Park, IL 60302
Legal Title: *Ephpheta Center and Hearing Conservation Service*
Under the direction of the Daughters of the Heart of Mary.

Olympia Fields
Archdiocese of Chicago

Mercy Residence at Tolentine Center
20300 Governors Hwy.
Olympia Fields, IL 60461
Tel: 708-748-9500; Fax: 708-481-2090
Sr. CONLETH FOLEY, R.S.M., Admin.
Sisters 4
Residents 48
Senior citizen housing.

Palatine
Archdiocese of Chicago

St. Joseph's Home for the Elderly
80 W. Northwest Hwy.
Palatine, IL 60067
Tel: 847-358-5700; Fax: 847-358-5763
Legal Title: *Little Sisters of the Poor, Palatine, Inc.*
Operated by the Little Sisters of the Poor
Sr. MARY ANTHONY POWER, Supr.
Sisters 16
Guests 61

Palos Park
Archdiocese of Chicago

St. Coletta's of Illinois
123rd and Wolf Rd.
Palos Park, IL 60464
Tel: 708-448-6520; Fax: 708-923-3532
Sponsored by the Sisters of St. Francis of Assisi. Residential care, education, job training & job placement for developmentally disabled children and adults.
Mr. WAYNE A. KOTTMEYER, Exec. Dir.
Residents 182
Students 100
Job Training Clients 165
Divisions:
Lt. Joseph P. Kennedy Jr. School, Palos Hills
Tel: 708-923-3584
Kennedy Job Training Center, Bedford Park
Tel: 708-923-3583
St. Coletta's of Illinois Foundation Affiliate
Tel: 708-923-3524; Fax: 708-923-3532

Park Ridge
Archdiocese of Chicago

Resurrection Nursing and Rehabilitation Center
1001 N. Greenwood
Park Ridge, IL 60068
Tel: 847-692-5600; Fax: 847-692-2305
Legal Title: *Resurrection Health Care*
NORMA WILSON, Admin.
Skilled Care Bed Capacity 295

Peoria
Diocese of Peoria

St. Augustine Manor
1301 N.E. Glendale Ave.
Peoria, IL 61603
Tel: 309-674-7069; Fax: 309-494-6547
Mr. DICK LANGJAHR, Admin.
In res.,
Rev. Msgr. BERNARD A. RENDER
Revs.:
E. C. BLOUGH
GEORGE RAYMOND SPRAGUE
Residents 80
Total Staff 30
Total Assisted 101

St. Joseph's Home of Peoria
2223 W. Heading Ave.
Peoria, IL 61604
Tel: 309-673-7425; Fax: 309-673-7430
Sisters of St. Francis of the Immaculate Conception
Co-Administrators:
Sr. MARY PAUL MAZZORANA
Sr. MARY DRIES
Rev. JOHN C. ANDERSON, Chap.
In res.,
Rev. Msgr. JOSEPH J. O'DEA
Rev. FRANCIS J. RYAN
Sisters 11
Residents 170
Retired Sisters 10
Total Assisted 195
Total Staff 110

Peoria Heights
Diocese of Peoria

Saint Clare Home
5533 N. Galena Rd.
Peoria Heights, IL 61614
Tel: 309-682-5428
Sponsored and owned by the Sisters of the Third Order of St. Francis.
Ms. LISA J. DENNING, Admin.
Skilled nursing facility.
Total Staff 94
Bed capacity 98

Red Bud
Diocese of Belleville

Maria Care
350 W. South First St.
Red Bud, IL 62278
Tel: 618-282-3891; Fax: 618-282-4070
Under the Co-sponsorship of the Adorers of the Blood of Christ & Sisters of Mercy.
BARBARA WAGNER, Admin.
MARY SALOIS, Dir. of Pastoral Care
Guests 158

Rock Island
Diocese of Peoria

St. Anthony's Continuing Care Center
767 30th St.
Rock Island, IL 61201
Tel: 309-788-7631
Rev. RAPHAEL FABISH
Sisters 3
Beds 120
Total Assisted 91
Total Staff 99

Rockford
Diocese of Rockford

Provena Cor Mariae Center
3330 Maria Linden Dr.
Rockford, IL 61114
Tel: 815-877-7416; Fax: 815-877-4299
E-mail: cormariaectr@aol.com
Legal Title: *Provena Senior Services dba Provena Cor Mariae Center.*
Rev. HARLAN CLAPSADDLE, Sacramental Min.
TERESA WESTER-PETERS, Admin.
Total Beds 146
Total Staff 110
Total Assisted 61

Provena St. Anne Center
4405 Highcrest Rd.
Rockford, IL 61107
Tel: 815-229-1999; Fax: 815-229-1560
Legal Title: *Provena Senior Services dba Provena St. Anne Center.*
Ms. JUDY K. LARSON, Admin.
Total Staff 165
Beds 179

St. Anne Place
4444 Brendenwood Rd.
Rockford, IL 61107
Tel: 815-399-6167; Fax: 815-399-6169
E-mail: eric@stanneplace.org
Web Site: www.stanneplace.org
Owned by the Rockford Diccese, managed by Provena Senior Services.
ERIC VANDENBERGH, Admin.
Total Staff 35
Total in Residence 120

Vianney Oaks
7712 E. McGregor Rd.
Rockford, IL 61102
Tel: 815-965-0910
Office:
1245 N. Court St., P.O. Box 7044
Rockford, IL 61126
Tel: 815-962-3709
A retirement home for priests conducted by the Diocese of Rockford.
Total in Residence 6

Springfield
Diocese of Springfield in Illinois

Brother James Court
2500 St. James Rd.
Springfield, IL 62707
Tel: 217-544-4876
E-mail: bjcicfdd@aol.com
Web Site: ffsc.net
Residence for Mentally Retarded Male Adults.
Franciscan Brothers of the Holy Cross
Bros.:
RAPHAEL KREIKEMEIER, F.F.S.C., Exec. Dir.
JOHN FRANCIS TYRRELL, Supr.
Franciscan Brothers of the Holy Cross 3
Bed Capacity 93
Residents 93

Pope John Paul Apartments
One Pope John Paul Plaza
Springfield, IL 62703
Tel: 217-528-1771; Fax: 217-528-5110
E-mail: polly@dio.org
Web Site: www.dio.org
Residence for the Elderly.
Sr. M. BARBARA, O.S.F., Supr.
NORMA JEAN CAPRANICA, Proj. Mgr.
Mr. THOMAS E. REISER, Admin.
Sisters of St. Francis of the Martyr St. George 2
Residents 160
Staff 5

St. Joseph's Home
3306 S. Sixth St. Rd.
Springfield, IL 62703

Tel: 217-529-5596
Residence for the Elderly.
Sr. JUDITH MORRIS, O.S.F., Admin.
Sr. M. PATRICIA MASTERSON, O.S.F., Asst. Admin.
Sisters of St. Francis of the Immaculate Conception 5
Residents 110
Staff 95

St. Monica's Center
109 E. Lawrence Ave.
Springfield, IL 62704
Tel: 217-523-7922; Fax: 217-525-8241
Maternity Home For Care of Unwed Mothers & Residential Care for Adolescent Women.
JOE CAIN, Program Dir.
Bed Capacity 12
Patients assisted annually 58
Staff 12

St. Charles
Diocese of Rockford

Provena Pine View Care Center
611 Allen Ln.
St. Charles, IL 60174
Tel: 630-377-2211; Fax: 630-377-4352
Web Site: Provenahealth.com
Legal Title: *Provena Senior Services dba Provena Pine View Care Center.*
ANN DODGE, Admin.
Bed Capacity 120
Residents 104
Total Staff 103

West Peoria
Diocese of Peoria

Catholic Social Service Foster Care Program
2900 W. Heading Ave.
West Peoria, IL 61604
Tel: 309-671-5700; Fax: 309-671-1046
Ms. PEGGY A. ARIZZI, Exec. Dir.
Ms. TRISH FOX, Asst. Dir. for Child Welfare
Clients placed in Foster Care during year 2,078
Total Staff 604

Guardian Angel Home
2900 W. Heading Ave.
West Peoria, IL 309-671-5760
Fax: 309-673-3405
PEGGY ARIZZI, Exec. Dir.
Treatment for Abused and Neglected Youth.
Staff 45
Capacity 22
Served 55

Wheaton
Diocese of Joliet in Illinois

Marian Park, Inc.
2126 W. Roosevelt Rd.
Wheaton, IL 60187
Tel: 630-665-9100; Fax: 630-665-9357
Mailing Address:—Franciscan Ministries, Inc.
26 W. 171 Roosevelt Rd., P.O. Box 667
Wheaton, IL 60189-0667

Diocese of Rockford

Assisi Homes-Batavia Apartments, Inc.
26 W. 171 Roosevelt Rd.
Wheaton, IL 60189
Tel: 708-462-9271
GARTH SEEHAWER, Contact

Wheeling
Archdiocese of Chicago

**Addolorata Villa*
555 McHenry Rd.
Wheeling, IL 60090-3899
Tel: 847-537-2900; Fax: 847-215-5805
Sponsored by the Franciscan Sisters of Chicago
Home for the aged and independent living apartments.
Mr. GERALD B. KINNEY, CFACHCA, CEO & Pres.
Sr. PATRICIA A. FERGUSON, O.S.M., Asst. Admin.
Mrs. BETTY SKONIECZNY, Pastoral Care Dir.
Rev. MARION J. SNIEG, Chap.
Servants of Mary 20
Skilled 88
Intermediate 10
Sheltered 42
Independent Living Apartments 100

INDIANA

Avilla
Diocese of Fort Wayne - South Bend

Provena LaVerna Terrace
517 N. Main St.
Avilla, IN 46710
Tel: 219-897-2093; Fax: 219-897-2086
Conducted by Franciscan Sisters Health Care Corp. whose sole member is Provena Health.
Legal Title: *LaVerna Terrace Housing Corp.*
LINDA A. SIMON, System Vice Pres. Mktg. & Planning
SHARON MCKINLEY, Mgr.
In res.,
Rev. DANIEL LEEUW Tel: 219-897-3922
Total Staff 2
Apartments 51
Total Assisted 51

Provena Sacred Heart Home
515 N. Main St.
Avilla, IN 46710-9602
Tel: 219-897-2841; Fax: 219-897-3724
Legal Title: *Provena Senior Services*
CRAIG PROKUPEK, Admin.
Sr. CORDE MIRANDA, O.S.F., Religious Leader
Rev. DANIEL LEEUW, Chap.
Staff 160
Residents 133

Beech Grove
Archdiocese of Indianapolis

St. Paul Hermitage
501 N. 17th Ave.
Beech Grove, IN 46107
Tel: 317-786-2261; Fax: 317-782-1411
E-mail: sphherm@indyweb.net
Legal Title: *Sisters of St. Benedict of Beech Grove, Ind., Inc.*
Sr. SHARON BIERMAN, O.S.B., Admin.
Rev. RALPH LYNCH, O.S.B.
Sisters 9
Total Staff 95
Residents 116

Crown Point
Diocese of Gary

Franciscan Home Care Services, Inc.
203 Franciscan Dr.
Crown Point, IN 219-757-6423
Sr. M. MADONNA ROUGEAU, O.S.F., Corp. Sec.

Franciscan Homes & Community Services, Inc.
203 Franciscan Dr.
Crown Point, IN 46307-4824
Tel: 219-757-6281; Fax: 219-757-6236
Web Site: www.franciscancommunities.com
STEPHEN J. BARDOCZI, Pres.
Rev. MYRON LOWISZ, O.F.M., Pastoral Care
Priests 1
Franciscan Sisters of Chicago 14
Total Staff 550
Residents 229
St. Anthony Home
Tel: 219-757-6281; Fax: 219-757-6236
Residents 200
St. Anthony Assisted Living Apartments
Tel: 219-757-5880
Residents 60
St. Anthony Hospice
Tel: 219-757-6423; Fax: 219-757-6278
HouseCall Private Duty Services
Tel: 219-757-6423; Fax: 219-757-6278
Caritas Adult Day Health Services
Tel: 219-681-6820; Fax: 219-757-6236
Capacity 25
Holy Family Child Care Center
Tel: 219-681-6880
Children 210

Delphi
Diocese of Lafayette in Indiana

St. Elizabeth Healthcare Center
701 Armory Rd.
Delphi, IN 46923
Tel: 765-564-6380; Fax: 765-564-6384
E-mail: SEHC@gte.net
Web Site: www.franciscanservices.com
Rev. RICHARD W. PUETZ, Chap.
Owned by Franciscan Sisters of Chicago.
Total Assisted 192
Total Staff 105

East Chicago
Diocese of Gary

Carmelite Home for Girls
4840 Grasselli Ave.
East Chicago, IN 46312
Tel: 219-397-1085; Fax: 219-392-3574
Sr. MARIA GIUSEPPE MOXLEY, Supr.
Carmelite Sisters of the Divine Heart of Jesus 3
Total Staff 34
Girls 48

Evansville
Diocese of Evansville

The Regina Continuing Care Center
3900 Washington Ave.
Evansville, IN 47714
Tel: 812-485-4226; Fax: 812-485-4732
Mrs. ANN M. MORROW, Admin.
Beds 137
Nursing Patients 137

St. John's Home for the Aged
1236 Lincoln Ave.
Evansville, IN 47714
Tel: 812-464-3607; Fax: 812-464-2141
Sr. MARGUERITE KEMP, L.S.P., Admin.
Rev. Msgr. CLARENCE LINDAUER, Chap.
Little Sisters of the Poor 12
Residents 70

Seton Residence
9200 New Harmony Rd.
Evansville, IN 47720-8918
Tel: 812-963-7600; Fax: 812-963-7654
Home for the Senior Sisters of the Daughters of Charity of St. Vincent de Paul.
Sr. ANTHONY PRUGGER, Admin.
Sr. GERTRUDE BASTNAGEL, Supr.
Rev. PATRICK HARRITY, C.M., Chap. pro tem
Senior Sisters 57

Fort Wayne
Diocese of Fort Wayne - South Bend

Saint Anne Home & Retirement Community
1900 Randallia Dr.
Fort Wayne, IN 46805
Tel: 219-484-5555; Fax: 219-482-8929
E-mail: sah1900@aol.com
Web Site: www.saintannehome.com
A Service of the Fort Wayne-South Bend Diocese, Inc.
MARY E. HAVERSTICK, Admin.
Rev. FRANK KRONEWITTER, Chap.
In res.,
Revs.:
ROBERT TRAUB
ROBERT HAMMOND
Staff 218
Residents 254

St. Anne Home of the Diocese of Fort Wayne - South Bend, Inc.
1900 Randalia Dr.
Fort Wayne, IN 46805
Tel: 219-484-5555; Fax: 219-482-8929
E-mail: sah1900@aol.com
Web Site: www.stannehome.com
Rev. Msgr. JAMES J. WOLF, Contact Person
Purpose: Nursing Home, Independent Living Units and Assisted Living
Total Staff 218
Total in residence 254

Hammond
Diocese of Gary

Albertine Home
1501 Hoffman St.
Hammond, IN 46327
Tel: 219-937-0575
E-mail: albertineusa@aol.com
Sr. LORETTA SOJA, Dir.
Albertine Sisters 12
Guests 35

St. Joseph's Home for Boys, Inc.
4007 Sheffield Ave.
Hammond, IN 46327
Tel: 219-931-6451; Fax: 219-931-2241
E-mail: stjoseph@netnitco.net
Total Staff 40
Boys 40

Indianapolis
Archdiocese of Indianapolis

St. Augustine Home, Little Sisters of the Poor
2345 W. 86th St.
Indianapolis, IN 46260
Tel: 317-872-6420; Fax: 317-875-9883
Sr. CHARLES MARIE, L.S.P.
Rev. ADRIAN FIGUEROLA, Chap.
Sisters 12
Total Staff 87
Residents 92

Jasper
Diocese of Evansville

Providence Home, Nursing Home for the Needy
520 W. Ninth St.
Jasper, IN 47546
Tel: 812-482-6603; Fax: 812-481-1778
Conducted by the Sons of Divine Providence.
Mr. ROBERT HAGAN, Admin.
Rev. ANGELO QUADRINI, Supr.
Priests 4
Residents 60

Lafayette
Diocese of Lafayette in Indiana

St. Anthony Health Care
1205 N. 14th St.
Lafayette, IN 47904
Tel: 765-423-4861; Fax: 765-742-8790
Rev. JOHN A. BACH, Chap.
Total Staff 147
Bed Capacity 120
Residents 115

New Albany
Archdiocese of Indianapolis

Mercy Long Term Care Initiatives dba Mercy Providence Village
4915 Charlestown Rd.
New Albany, IN 47150
Tel: 812-945-5221; Fax: 812-945-2614
Sisters of Mercy
JANE F. COOK, Admin.
Priests 1
Sisters 1
Total Staff 160
Residents 172
Adult Day Care clients 32

Notre Dame
Diocese of Fort Wayne - South Bend

University Health Services
Notre Dame, IN 46556
Tel: 219-239-8013; Fax: 219-631-6047
E-mail: Ann.E.Thompson.49@nd.edu
Rev. ROBERT J. AUSTGEN, C.S.C., Health Center Chap.
Total Staff 47
Patients assisted annually 20,000

San Pierre
Diocese of Gary

Holy Cross Care Services dba Little Company of Mary Health Facility, Inc.
7520 S. U.S. Hwy. 421
San Pierre, IN 46374-4275
Tel: 219-828-4111; Fax: 219-828-4275
Comprehensive Nursing Care Home.
JAMES MAY, Admin.
Rev. WILLIAM J. SPRANGER, Chap.
Priests 1
Beds 200
Patients assisted annually 214

Terre Haute
Archdiocese of Indianapolis

Gibault School for Boys
6301 S. U.S. Hwy. 41, P.O. Box 2316
Terre Haute, IN 47802-0316
Tel: 812-299-1156; Fax: 812-299-0019
E-mail: gibault@gibault.org
Web Site: www.gibault.org
School for delinquent boys, sponsored by the Knights of Columbus of Indiana.
Mr. JAMES M. SINCLAIR, M.S.S.W.; J.D., Exec. Dir.
Boys 147
Total Staff 220

IOWA

Burlington
Diocese of Davenport

St. Francis Continuation Care and Nursing Home
210 S. 5th St.
Burlington, IA 52601
Tel: 319-752-4564
Sr. BERNADETTE DUMAN, C.D.P., Admin.
Sr. M. DOLORITA, O.S.F., Supr.
Sisters of the Third Order of St. Francis 2
Bed Capacity 88
Independent Living Unit 12
Patients assisted annually 120

**Young House Family Services, Inc.*
Central Office, 724 N. 3rd St., P.O. Box 845
Burlington, IA 52601
Tel: 319-752-4000; Fax: 319-752-6933 or 758-6650
E-mail: younghse@interl.net
JACK ESCORCIA, Admin.
CYNTHIA FOSTER, Controller
Woodlands Treatment Center
Sullivan Slough Rd.
Burlington, IA 52601
Tel: 319-753-0700
JOHN KORB, Coord.

**Christamore Family Treatment Center*
905 S. Iris
Mount Pleasant, IA 52641
Tel: 319-385-2906
Total Assisted 2500
Total Staff 180

Carroll
Diocese of Sioux City

St. Anthony Nursing Home
406 E. Anthony St.
Carroll, IA 51401
Tel: 712-792-3581; Fax: 712-792-8288
E-mail: stanthony@netins.net
Web Site: www.netins.net/showcase/sarh/
GARY RIEDMANN, Admin.
Rev. THOMAS MUNN, Chap.
Total Staff 54
Residents 79

Cedar Rapids
Archdiocese of Dubuque

Hallmar-Mercy Medical Center
701 Tenth St., S.E.
Cedar Rapids, IA 52403
Sisters of Mercy
Cedar Rapids Regional, owned and operated by Mercy Medical Center. Home for Aged.
Mr. A. JAMES TINKER, CEO
Total Assisted 24
Total Staff 32
Residents 54

Clinton
Diocese of Davenport

The Alverno Health Care Facility
Clinton, IA 52732
Tel: 319-242-1521; Fax: 319-243-3016
E-mail: ruthcox@sanasys.com
Web Site: www.achcamembers.org/alverno
Sr. RUTH A. COX, O.S.F., Pres. & CEO
Sisters of St. Francis, Clinton, IA 2
Bed Capacity 138
Total Assisted 212
Total Staff 194

Arch, L'Arche in Clinton
Box 278
Clinton, IA 52733-0278
Tel: 319-243-9035; Fax: 319-243-9035
E-mail: larchia@clinton.net
JO ANNE HORSTMANN, Exec. Dir.
Arch I
402 S. Fourth St.
Clinton, IA 52732
Tel: 319-243-3980
Arch II
734 Fifth Ave. S.
Clinton, IA 52732
Tel: 319-242-5082
Arch III
505 7th Ave. S.
Clinton, IA 52732
Tel: 319-242-8740
Total Assisted 18
Total Staff 10

Cresco
Archdiocese of Dubuque

Elder Hospitality of Iowa, Inc.
(Village Apartments)
Franciscan SKEMP Healthcare, 301 First Ave.
Cresco, IA 52136
Tel: 563-547-3325; 608-791-9505
RICHARD BERENDES, Admin./Extended Care
Franciscan Sisters of Perpetual Adoration, La Crosse, Wisconsin and Mayo Foundation, Rochester, MN
Elderly housing for low income. HUD section 202.
Units 12
Elder Hospitality of Iowa II, Inc. (Village Apartments)
Franciscan SKEMP Healthcare, 509 Goose Island Dr.
Decorah, IA 52101
Tel: 563-382-2863; Fax: 608-791-9505
RICHARD BERENDES, Admin./Extended Care
Franciscan Sisters of Perpetual Adoration, La Crosse, Wisconsin and Mayo Foundation, Rochester, MN.
Elderly housing for low income. HUD section 202.
Units 24

Davenport
Diocese of Davenport

Kahl Home for the Aged and Infirm
1101 W. Ninth St.
Davenport, IA 52804
Tel: 319-324-1621; Fax: 319-324-1723
Carmelite Sisters for the Aged and Infirm
Sr. M. PAUL ANTHONY, O.Carm., Supr. & Admin.
Rev. JOSEPH ROGERS, Chap.
In res.,
Rev. Msgr. CLETUS P. MADSEN
Revs.:
PASQUALE L. FERRARA
HERMAN A. STRUB
RICHARD J. VON AH
Sisters 4
Beds 134
Total Assisted 134
Total Staff 135

Des Moines
Diocese of Des Moines

House of Mercy
1409 Clark St.
Des Moines, IA 50314-1964
Tel: 515-643-6500; Fax: 515-643-6598
E-mail: tbeveridge@mercydesmoines.org
Mr. TODD BEVERIDGE, Dir.

Dubuque
Archdiocese of Dubuque

Holy Family Hall Infirmary
3340 Windsor Ave.
Dubuque, IA 52001-1300
Tel: 563-583-9786; Fax: 563-583-6080
E-mail: mtstfran@mwci.net
Web Site: www.osfdbg.org
Sisters of St. Francis, Dubuque
Rev. HAROLD J. DREXLER, Chap.
Sr. EILEEN MILLER, O.S.F., Dir. Sister Support Svcs.
Bed Capacity 98
Professed Sisters 85
Patients assisted annually 42

Marian Hall Infirmary
1050 Carmel Dr.
Dubuque, IA 52003
Tel: 563-556-5474; Fax: 563-588-1975
E-mail: bvmcong.org
Web Site: www.bvmcong.org
Sr. MARY AGNES O'CONNOR, B.V.M., Admin.
Rev. Msgr. ROBERT R. VOGL, Chap.
Professed Sisters 94
Bed Capacity 118
Staff 175
Caritas Center
1130 Carmel Dr.
Dubuque, IA 52003-7911
Tel: 563-556-3240; Fax: 563-557-1349
E-mail: mhouse@bvm.org
SUSAN M. HOSTERT, Central Admin.
Professed Sisters 53
Bed Capacity 53
Staff 23
Mount Carmel Continuing Care Retirement Community.

St. Dominic Villa
600 Mazzuchelli Heights
Dubuque, IA 52001-7399
Tel: 563-582-7273; Fax: 563-583-1421
Sr. ROBERT MARY WILKE, Admin.

Stonehill Franciscan Services, Inc.
3485 Windsor Ave.
Dubuque, IA 52001-1312
Tel: 563-557-7180; Fax: 563-557-8934
E-mail: stonehill@mwci.net
JOHN SCHMIDT, Chm.
Sr. DOLORES ULLRICH, O.S.F., Pres./C.E.O.
Sisters of St. Francis of the Holy Family 9
Staff 242
Residents-Nursing Home 250
Residents-Retirement Units 51
Adult Day Care Program 42

Stonehill Benevolent Foundation
Sr. Mary Clare O'Toole, O.S.F., Chair, Stonehill Benevolent Foundation Board
Sponsored by Sisters of St. Francis of the Holy Family.

Villa Raphael
1235 Mt. Loretta Ave.
Dubuque, IA 52003
Tel: 563-583-4904; Fax: 563-556-5464
E-mail: dbqvilla@arch.pvt.k12.ia.us
Administered by the Archdiocese of Dubuque.
Patricia Flores, Dir.
Accommodations for 16 priests.
Total Staff 4
Total in Residence 9

Dyersville
Archdiocese of Dubuque

Mercy Medical Center-Dubuque-Dyersville-Oakcrest Manor
(A Division of Mercy Health Services - Iowa)
1111 Third St., S.W.
Dyersville, IA 52040
Tel: 563-875-7101; Fax: 563-875-2957
Web Site: www.mercydubuque.com
Russell Knight, Pres.
Bed Capacity 40
Total Staff 27
Patients assisted annually 55

Fort Dodge
Diocese of Sioux City

The Marian Home
2400 Sixth Ave. N.
Fort Dodge, IA 50501
Tel: 515-576-1138; Fax: 515-576-5009
Mr. Gerald Bruening Admin.
Rev. Eugene F. Walding
Guests 97
Total in Residence 29
Total Staff 110

Johnston
Diocese of Des Moines

Bishop Drumm Retirement Center
(Affiliate of Catholic Health Initiatives, Mercy Health Network & Mercy Medical Center-Des Moines)
5837 Winwood Dr.
Johnston, IA 50131-1651
Tel: 515-270-1100; Fax: 515-276-1714
Mr. Brian E. Farrell, Pres. & CEO
In res.,
Rev. Thomas M. DeCarlo, Res. Chap.
Sisters of Mercy of the Americas (Omaha Province) 8
Care Center Residents 150
Apartment Residents 81
McAuley Terrace Apts.
5921 Winwood Dr.
Johnston, IA 50131-1689
Tel: 515-270-6640
Sr. Sue Sellers, C.H.M.
Martina Place Assisted Living Residence
5815 Winwood Dr.
Johnston, IA 50131-1666
Tel: 515-251-7999; Fax: 515-331-8860
Residents 64
Mrs. Catherine Berry, Dir.

Sioux City
Diocese of Sioux City

Holy Spirit Retirement Home
1701 W. 25th St.
Sioux City, IA 51103
Tel: 712-252-2726
Patrick J. Tomscha, Admin.
Rev. Gerald A. Hartz
Total in Residence 125
Total Assisted 141
Total Staff 120

KANSAS

Concordia
Diocese of Salina

Mount Joseph Senior Community
1110 West 11th St.
Concordia, KS 66901
Tel: 785-243-1347; Fax: 785-243-1907
Owned & operated by the Sisters of St. Joseph of Wichita, via Christi, Inc., Wichita, KS & Sisters of the Sorrowful Mother.
Janet G. Chapman, CEO & Admin.
Rev. Henry Kieffer, Chap.
Sisters 2
Nursing Facility Residents 75
Retirement Apartments 16

Hays
Diocese of Salina

St. John's New Horizons
2225 Canterbury
Hays, KS 67601
Tel: 785-628-8742
Susan Jacobs, Admin.
Sr. Vera Bittel
Residents 47
Independent Living Apartments 10
Assisted Living Units 43

Kansas City
Archdiocese of Kansas City in Kansas

Marian Hall
1920 Tauromee
Kansas City, KS 66102
Tel: 913-621-4302; Fax: 913-621-1824
Lynne Serrano, Admin.
Total in Residence 45
Total Staff 10

Providence Place
8909 Parallel
Kansas City, KS 66112
Tel: 913-596-4200; Fax: 913-596-4901
E-mail: tallin@medmgmt.com
Tim Allin, Admin.
Sisters 1
Total Staff 60
Total Residents 77

Manhattan
Diocese of Salina

St. Joseph Senior Community, Inc.
2423 Kimball Ave.
Manhattan, KS 66502
Tel: 785-539-7671; Fax: 785-539-9125
E-mail: dfrihart@via.christi.org
Web Site: www.manhattan-ks.org/sjsc
Owned & operated by the Via Christi Health System of Wichita.
Total Staff 90
Residents 85

Mulvane
Diocese of Wichita

Villa Maria
116 S. Central
Mulvane, KS 67110
Tel: 316-777-1129; Fax: 316-777-4406
E-mail: chmathis@hotmail.com
Charlene Mathis, Admin.
Home for Aging Men and Women.
Adorers of the Blood of Christ 2
Total Staff 61
Guests 64
Total Assisted 103

Olathe
Archdiocese of Kansas City in Kansas

Villa St. Francis, Inc.
16600 W. 126th St.
Olathe, KS 66062
Tel: 913-829-5201; Fax: 913-829-5390
Mrs. Nancy Allenbrand, Admin.
Owned and operated by Villa St. Francis, Inc.
Skilled nursing care and independent boarding.
In res.,
Most Rev. Marion F. Forst
Rev. Msgr. Stanley Loncaric
Sisters of Charity of Leavenworth 3
Total Staff 200
Total Residents 200

Overland Park
Archdiocese of Kansas City in Kansas

Villa St. Joseph Nursing Home
11901 Rosewood
Overland Park, KS 66209
Tel: 913-345-1745; Fax: 913-345-1346
Ms. Katharine Ensign, Admin.
Total Staff 140
Total Assisted 118

Victoria
Diocese of Salina

St. John's Rest Home
701 Seventh St.
Victoria, KS 67671
Tel: 785-735-2208
Rev. Frank X. Grinko, O.F.M.Cap., Chap.
Residents 90

Wichita
Diocese of Wichita

Catholic Care Center, Inc.
6700 E. 45th St. N.
Wichita, KS 67226
Tel: 316-744-2020; Fax: 316-744-2182
Thomas Church, Admin.
Sisters 10
Total Staff 160
Residents 178
Total Assisted 248
Operated by Catholic Diocese of Wichita & the Via Christ Health System.

Georgetown Village, Inc.
1655 Georgetown St.
Wichita, KS 67218
Tel: 316-685-0400; Fax: 316-685-0174
Staff 12
Total Assisted 30

KENTUCKY

Cold Spring
Diocese of Covington

Campbell Lodge Boys Home
150 Skyline Dr.
Cold Spring, KY 41076-2099
Tel: 859-781-1214; Fax: 859-442-3473
E-mail: Mschroth@execs.com
Web Site: www.CampbellLodgeboyshome.org
Mr. Michael Schroth, M.S.W., Exec. Dir.
Staff 9
Boys 60

Covington
Diocese of Covington

Diocesan Catholic Children's Home
Orphanage Rd., P.O. Box 17007
Fort Mitchell, KY 41017-2730
Tel: 859-331-2040; Fax: 859-344-5021
E-mail: dcch@msn.com
Web Site: www.dccttome.org
Sisters of Notre Dame 4
Lay Staff 65
Children in Residence 32
Students 28
Sr. Jean Marie Hoffman, S.N.D., Exec. Dir.
Sr. M. Ann Christine Kathman, S.N.D., Prin.

Madonna Manor, Inc.
2344 Amsterdam Rd.
Villa Hills, KY 41017-3712
Tel: 859-341-3981; Fax: 859-578-7475
E-mail: smcconn@iglou.com
Web Site: www.re.net/covington.walburg
Patients assisted annually 60
49 Independent living apartments with 54 residents
Mrs. Susan McConn, Admin.

St. Charles Care Center, Inc.
500 Farrell Dr.
Covington, KY 41011-3798
Tel: 859-331-3224; Fax: 859-578-2065
E-mail: smluann@msn.com
Web Site: www.stcharlescare.org
Sr. Mary Luann Bender, S.N.D., Admin.
Sisters of Notre Dame 7
Beds 149
Assisted Living Apartments 60
Independent Living Apartments 12
Independent Living Cottages 44
Total Assisted 506
Adult Day Health Program & Licensed Physical Therapy Department.

Fort Thomas
Diocese of Covington

Carmel Manor
100 Carmel Manor Rd.
Fort Thomas, KY 41075-2395
Tel: 859-781-5111; Fax: 859-781-2337
Carmelite Sisters for the Aged and Infirm

Sr. TERESA KENNEDY, O.Carm., Admin.
Staff 142
Residents 145

Regina Cleri Home for Retired Priests
100 Carmel Manor Rd.
Fort Thomas, KY 41075-2395
Tel: 859-781-5111; Fax: 859-781-2337
Carmelite Sisters for the Aged and Infirm
Sr. TERESA KENNEDY, O.Carm., Admin.
Residents 1

Knottsville
Diocese of Owensboro

Bishop Soenneker Home
9545 Kentucky 144
Knottsville, KY 42366
Tel: 270-281-4881
Sr. MARY RAYMONDE CARRAT, A.D., Admin.
Residents 55
Staff 27
Residential Care of the Handicapped. Total Assisted 14

Louisville
Archdiocese of Louisville

Boys' Haven
2301 Goldsmith Ln.
Louisville, KY 40205
Tel: 502-458-1171; Fax: 502-451-2161
E-mail: boyshaven@win.net
Web Site: www.boyshaven.org
For dependent, neglected, or abused boys, 12 to 18 years of age.
Mr. JERRY A. WEBER, Exec. Dir.
Number of Boys in Home 30

Caritas Peace Center
2020 Newburg Rd.
Louisville, KY 40205
Tel: 502-451-3330; Fax: 502-473-1797
Web Site: www.caritas.com
Hospital for Psychiatric Illness.
Sisters 5
Bed Capacity 270
Patients assisted annually 2,400

Franciscan Health Care Center
3625 Fern Valley Rd.
Louisville, KY 40219
Tel: 502-964-3381; Fax: 502-964-3395
SUZANNE RINNE, Admin.
Rev. FLORIAN TIEL, O.F.M. Conv., Chap.
Nursing Facility Beds 150
Legal Title: *Franciscan Elder Care Services/Ill., Inc. dba Franciscan Health Care Center*

Marian Home
3105 Lexington Rd.
Louisville, KY 40206
Tel: 502-893-0121; Fax: 502-896-3925
Sr. ASSUMPTA DEVINE, O.S.U., Admin.
Rev. JOSEPH T. MERKT, Chap.
Staff Sisters 6
Residents 69

Nazareth Home
2000 Newburg Rd.
Louisville, KY 40205
Tel: 502-459-9681; Fax: 502-456-9077
E-mail: Jdencz@Nazhome.org
Web Site: Nazhome.org
Sisters of Charity of Nazareth
JOYCE DENCZEK, CEO & Admin.
Rev. GERMAIN LEGERE, C.P., Chap.
Staff Sisters 10
Residents 131

Sacred Heart Village, Inc.
(Rudd-Taylor Memorial)
2120 Payne St.
Louisville, KY 40206
Tel: 502-895-9888; 895-9425; Fax: 502-894-9619
Sisters of Mercy
Catholic Healthcare Partners, Cincinnati, OH.
LESLIE A. WILSON, Pres.
Rev. LOUIS MILLER, Chap.
Sisters 8
Residents 154
Capacity 249
Mercy Assoc. 3

St. Joseph Catholic Orphan Society
2823 Frankfort Ave.
Louisville, KY 40206
Tel: 502-893-0241; Fax: 502-896-2394
E-mail: sjkid@aol.com
Web Site: www.sjkids.org
Mr. ROBERT BEAM, Pres., Board of Directors

St. Joseph Children's Home
2823 Frankfort Ave.
Louisville, KY 40206
Tel: 502-893-0241; Fax: 502-896-2394
E-mail: sjkids@aol.com
Web Site: www.sjkids.org
Mr. DENNIS DAVIS, Exec. Dir.
Ursuline Sisters 1
Sisters of Charity 1
Children 70

St. Joseph Home for the Aged
15 Audubon Plaza Dr.
Louisville, KY 40217
Tel: 502-636-2300; Fax: 502-636-2239
Sr. ROSE MARIE MAYOCK, Admin.
In res.,
Revs.:
MARK SANFORD, O.F.M.
MAXIMILIAN KORECKI, O.F.M.Conv.
Legal Title: *Home for the Aged of the Little Sisters of the Poor*

St. Thomas Orphan Society, Inc.
P.O. Box 1073
Louisville, KY 40201

St. Vincent's Orphan Society, Inc.
P.O. Box 1073
Louisville, KY 40201

Owensboro
Diocese of Owensboro

Carmel Home
2501 Old Hartford Rd.
Owensboro, KY 42303
Tel: 270-683-0227; Fax: 270-688-0630
Carmelite Sisters of the Divine Heart of Jesus
Sr. ANDREA NIEHAUS, Carmel.D.C.J., Supr.
Rev. JOHN SPEAKS, Chap.
Sisters 4
Residents 101

Versailles
Diocese of Lexington

Taylor Manor Nursing Home
300 Berry Ave.
Versailles, KY 40383
Tel: 606-873-4201
Sr. MARY CHRISTINA MURRAY, S.J.W., Admin.
Rev. MAURICE J. BRINKER, Chap.
Sisters of St. Joseph the Worker 4
Patients assisted annually 82

LOUISIANA

Alexandria
Diocese of Alexandria

Our Lady of Sorrows Community Homes
347 Browns Bend Rd.
Alexandria, LA 71303
Tel: 318-487-8897; Fax: 318-487-9987
Congregation of the Sisters of Our Lady of Sorrows of the U.S.A., Inc.
Sisters 4
Lay Staff 21
Beds 20
Residents 20

Our Lady's Manor, Inc.
402 Monroe St.
Alexandria, LA 71301
Tel: 318-473-2560; Fax: 318-443-2449
Ms. BARBARA ROBBINS, Admin.
Apartments 114

St. Mary's Residential Training School, Inc.
P.O. Box Drawer 7768
Alexandria, LA 71306
Tel: 318-445-6443; Fax: 318-449-8520
E-mail: A2greco@aol.com
Congregation of the Sisters of Our Lady of Sorrows of the U.S.A., Inc.
Sr. MARY COLEMAN, O.L.S., Admin.
Sisters 3
Lay Staff 270
Beds 152
Students 152

Baton Rouge
Diocese of Baton Rouge

Elderly Housing of Our Lady of the Lake Medical Center
5000 Hennessy Blvd.
Baton Rouge, LA 70808-4398
Tel: 225-765-6565
Mr. ROBERT C. DAVIDGE, Pres. & CEO
Assisi Village, Inc., of Our Lady of the Lake Medical Center
7585 Bishop Ott Dr.
Baton Rouge, LA 70806-8922
Tel: 225-927-5070
Housing facilities for elderly persons.
Calais House, Inc., of Our Lady of the Lake Medical Center
7545 Bishop Ott Dr.
Baton Rouge, LA 70806-8900
Tel: 225-927-1889
Housing facilities for elderly persons.
Villa St. Francis, Inc., of Our Lady of the Lake Medical Center
7575 Bishop Ott Dr.
Baton Rouge, LA 70806-8906
Tel: 225-927-0070
Housing facilities for elderly and handicapped persons.

Ollie Steele Burden Manor
4250 Essen Ln.
Baton Rouge, LA 70809-2196
Tel: 225-926-0091; Fax: 225-926-4937
Our Lady of the Lake Regional Medical Center, Our Lady of the Lake Pastoral Care.
Staff 170
Bed Capacity 184

Belle Chasse
Archdiocese of New Orleans

Padua Pediatric Residential Program
200 Beta St.
Belle Chasse, LA 70037-1499
Tel: 504-392-0502; Fax: 504-392-5411
Residential Facility for Severely-Profoundly Retarded and Multihandicapped Children
Ms. RONNA TRAGER, Pro. Dir.

La Place
Archdiocese of New Orleans

Place Dubourg, Inc.
201 Rue Dubourg
La Place, LA 70068-2433
Tel: 985-652-1981; Fax: 985-651-6147
E-mail: chpalmisano@christopherhomesinc.org
Ms. CHRISTINE PALMISANO, Admin.
Units 115
Total Staff 8
Total in Residence 119

Lafayette
Diocese of Lafayette

Bethany M.H.S. Health Care Center
P.O. Box 2308
Lafayette, LA 70502
Tel: 337-234-2459; Fax: 337-234-9483
Sisters of the Most Holy Sacrament 8
Bed Capacity 42

Village du Lac, Inc.
1404 Carmel Ave.
Lafayette, LA 70501
Tel: 337-234-5106
Community housing for the handicapped and elderly with low income. Sponsored by the Diocese.
Mr. J. BERNEL FONTENOT, Dir.
Residents 200

Mandeville
Archdiocese of New Orleans

Rouquette Lodge
St. Tammany Manor, Inc.
4300 Hwy. 22
Mandeville, LA 70448-2824
Tel: 985-626-5217; Fax: 985-626-9226
Residence for Senior Citizens
Bro. HAROLD EHLINGER, C.S.C., Admin.
Residential Units 119
Total in Residence 119
Total Staff 7
Rouquette II
4300 Hwy. 22
Mandeville, LA 70448-2824
Tel: 985-626-5217; Fax: 985-626-9226
Residential Units 51
Total in Residence 51
Total Staff 3

Marrero
Archdiocese of New Orleans

Hope Haven Center (1925)
1101 Barataria Blvd.
Marrero, LA 70072-3085
Tel: 504-347-5581; Fax: 504-340-2075
Residential Treatment Center and School
Mr. ROBERT GUASCO, Admin.

Villa D'Ames Apartments
6305 Fourth St.
Marrero, LA 70072-1513
Tel: 504-347-0474; Fax: 504-347-0451
Ms. YVONNE STEWART, Admin.
Total Staff 9
Units 200
Total Assisted 200

Wynhoven Apartments and Wynhoven II
4600-10th St.
Marrero, LA 70072-3048
Tel: 504-347-8442; Fax: 504-340-6076
Private Non-Profit Residence for Senior Citizens Sponsored by the Archdiocese
DIANE JOHNSON, Admin.
LYNN RICHARD, Asst. Admin.
Residents 375
Total Staff 14

Wynhoven Health Care Center
1050 Medical Center Blvd.
Marrero, LA 70072-3170
Tel: 504-347-0777; 347-3443 (Convent); Fax: 504-341-7240
E-mail: wynhoven@msn.com
Mr. JOHN TIEPERMAN, Admin.
Total Assisted 190
Total Staff 173

Meraux
Archdiocese of New Orleans

St. Bernard Manor, St. Bernard II, and St. Bernard III
2400 Archbishop Hannan Blvd.
Meraux, LA 70075-2640
Tel: 504-277-2441; Fax: 504-277-6300
Mrs. PAMELA SHANEYFELT, Admin.
Residents 235
Total Staff 11

Metairie
Archdiocese of New Orleans

Metairie Manor, Metairie II, and Metairie III
4929 York St.
Metairie, LA 70001-1013
Tel: 504-456-1467; Fax: 504-887-3718
Sr. MARY ALOYSIUS OTT, O.P., Admin.
Sr. MARY GRIGNON BAUDOUIN, O.P., Asst. Admin.
Rev. JOHN A. POWERS, O.P., Chap.
Residential Units 287

Monroe
Diocese of Shreveport

Christus St. Joseph Home
2301 Sterlington Rd., P.O. Box 6057
Monroe, LA 71211-6057
Tel: 318-323-3426; Fax: 318-387-7157
Operated by Christus Health Monroe.
Rev. Msgr. PATRICK MURPHY (ALX) Chap.
Mrs. JOY HUFF, Admin.
Licensed capacity nursing care 132
Assisted living 60
Sisters 2
Total Staff 150

Moreauville
Diocese of Alexandria

St. John's Village
116 Beridon St.
Moreauville, LA 71355-3004
Tel: 318-985-2948
Rev. Msgr. JOHN TIMMERMANS, Admin.
Apartments 50

New Iberia
Diocese of Lafayette

Consolata Home
2319 E. Main St.
New Iberia, LA 70560
Tel: 337-365-8226; Fax: 337-365-8626
E-mail: HDLANDRY@aisp.Net
Mr. DAVID LANDRY, Admin.
Rev. RAYMOND ROBITAILLE, Chap., Tel: 318-365-7477
Residents 114
Bed Capacity 114
Total Staff 108

New Orleans
Archdiocese of New Orleans

The 1540 House
1540 N. Johnson St.
New Orleans, LA 70116-1721
Tel: 504-945-0253
Mr. MATTHEW ROBINSON, III, Admin.
Residents 12

Annunciation Inn
1220 Spain St.
New Orleans, LA 70117-8369
Tel: 504-944-0512; Fax: 504-944-0514
Residence for Elderly
Sr. HELEN I. BREAUX, S.F.C.C., Admin.
Units 106
Total Staff 8
Residents 111

Boys Hope
4128 Baudin St.
New Orleans, LA 70119-6815
Tel: 504-486-6030; Fax: 504-484-6120
E-mail: rallanach@bhgh.org
Web Site: www.boyshopegirlshope.org
4500 So. Carrollton Ave.
New Orleans, LA 70119-6714
Tel: 504-486-5223; Fax: 504-484-6120
2726 Esplanade
New Orleans, LA 70119-3333
Tel: 504-484-7744; Fax: 504-484-6120
Group Homes for Boys. Jesuit Program for Living and Learning
Rev. ROBERT C. ALLANACH, O.M.I., Ph.D., Dir.
Total Staff 11
Boys 16

Chateau de Notre Dame
2832 Burdette St.
New Orleans, LA 70125-2596
Tel: 504-866-2741; Fax: 504-866-6769
Residence and Nursing Home
Ms. PATRICIA ANN GAUTREAUX, Admin.
Rev. EDWARD J. LAWLOR, S.S.J., Chap.
Residential Units 98
Nursing Beds 178
Residential units with assistance 9
Priests 1
Sisters 4
Lay Staff 215

Christopher Inn Apts.
2110 Royal St.
New Orleans, LA 70116-1693
Tel: 504-949-0312; Fax: 504-945-2634
Private Non-Profit Residence for Senior Citizens Sponsored by the Archdiocese
Ms. EVANGELINE WASHINGTON, Acting Admin.
Residents 144
Total Staff 6

**Covenant House*
611 N. Rampart St.
New Orleans, LA 70112-3540
Tel: 504-584-1111; 800-999-9999 (Hotline); Fax: 504-584-1171
E-mail: khyrii@bellsouth.net
Web Site: covenanthouseno.org
Home for Runaway, Abused & Homeless Youth
Mrs. MAUDELLE CADE, Exec. Dir.

DeLille Inn
6924 Chef Menteur Hwy.
New Orleans, LA 70126-5260
Tel: 504-241-4877; Fax: 504-241-1828
E-mail: srtekawitha@christopherhomesinc.org
Sr. M. TEKAKWITHA VEGA, S.S.F., Admin.
Total Staff 5
Residents 52

Haydel Heights Apartments
4402 Reynes St.
New Orleans, LA 70126
Tel: 504-242-4438; Fax: 504-242-4061
Ms. LINDA CHAPMAN, Admin.
Units 65
Total Assisted 225
Total Staff 2

Josephine Apartments
1410 St. Andrew St., Apt. #4
New Orleans, LA 70130-5344
Tel: 504-522-5425; Fax: 504-522-5446
Mrs. ROSALYN W. TRIPPS, Mgr.
Residents 93

Lafon Nursing Home of the Holy Family
6900 Chef Menteur Hwy.
New Orleans, LA 70126-5296
Tel: 504-246-1100; Fax: 504-241-6672
Sisters of the Holy Family
Sr. AUGUSTINE MCDANIEL, S.S.F., Admin.
Sisters 8
Residents 171
Total Staff 154

Mary-Joseph Residence for the Elderly (1868)
4201 Woodland Dr.
New Orleans, LA 70131-7398
Tel: 504-394-2200; Fax: 504-391-3347
Sr. JOSEPH GRENON, L.S.P., Supr.
Rev. FRANCIS WHATLEY, O.SS.T., Chap.
Sisters 11
Total Staff 127
Residents 87
Independent Living 20

Nazareth II
9640 Hayne Blvd.
New Orleans, LA 70127-4725
Tel: 504-246-9640; Fax: 504-240-6686
Mr. ALVIN C. HARRISON JR., Asst. Adm.
Apartments 120
Total Staff 5
Total in Residence 122

Nazareth Inn
9630 Hayne Blvd.
New Orleans, LA 70127-1260
Tel: 504-241-9630; Fax: 504-241-9631
Legal Title: *Nazareth Manor, Inc.*
Mrs. SANDRA M. DALEO, Admin.
Apartments 150
Total Staff 9
Total in Residence 158

Our Lady of Wisdom Health Care Center
(Inter-Community Health Care, Inc.)
5600 Gen. deGaulle Dr.
New Orleans, LA 70131
Tel: 504-394-5991; Fax: 504-304-5421
E-mail: ourladyofwisdom@netscape.net
Sr. MARJORIE HEBERT, M.S.C., Exec. Dir.
WENDY LOCCO, Admin.
Total Staff 138
Bed Capacity 138

St. John Berchmans Manor
3400 St. Anthony St.
New Orleans, LA 70122-3098
Tel: 504-943-9343; Fax: 504-947-6090
Sr. M. DE CHANTAL ST. JULIEN, S.S.F., Admin.
Rev. VINCENT THEOBALD, S.V.D., Chap., Tel: 504-948-4425
Units 150
Residents 158
Total Staff 11

St. Margaret's Daughters' Home
6220 Chartres St.
New Orleans, LA 70117-1595
Tel: 504-279-6414; Fax: 504-277-1834
E-mail: stmargaretsl.org
DOROTHY H. ABBA, Exec. Dir.
Residents 115
Total Staff 109
Total Assisted 139

St. Martin Manor
1501 N. Johnson St.
New Orleans, LA 70116-1720
Tel: 504-945-7728; Fax: 504-945-7726
Sr. M. CAMILLUS DURALD, S.S.F., Admin.
Residential Units 140
Total Staff 12
Total in Residence 145

Villa St. Maurice
500 St. Maurice Ave.
New Orleans, LA 70117-1568
Tel: 504-277-8477; Fax: 504-277-8493
Residence for Senior Citizens & Handicapped
Mrs. CAROL MOTEN, Admin.
Residential Units 110
Residents 193
Total Staff 10

Villa St. Maurice II (Villa Additions)
6101 Douglas St.
New Orleans, LA 70117-2100
Tel: 504-277-8731; Fax: 504-277-8493
Residence for Senior Citizens & Handicapped.
Mrs. RAMONA ROUSSELL, Asst. Admin.
Residential Units 75
Residents 80
Total Staff 2

Opelousas
Diocese of Lafayette

C'est La Vie Center of the Sisters Marianites of Holy Cross
960 E. Prudhomme St.
Opelousas, LA 70570
Tel: 337-942-8154; Fax: 337-942-8279
E-mail: olpsnh@eatel.net
Independent living for the elderly and handicapped.
Sr. Kay Kinberger, M.S.C., Pres.
Harriet Fisher, Coord.
Michael Purser, Admin.
Sisters 2
Total Staff 2
Patients assisted annually 34

Our Lady of Prompt Succor Home
954 E. Prudhomme St.
Opelousas, LA 70570
Tel: 337-948-3634; Fax: 337-942-8279
E-mail: olpsnh@eatel.net
Michael Purser, Admin.
Sisters 6
Patients assisted annually 80

Shreveport
Diocese of Shreveport

Holy Angels Residential Facility
10450 Ellerbe Rd.
Shreveport, LA 71106-7712
Tel: 318-797-8500; 797-9070; Fax: 318-798-0159
E-mail: scrider@prysm.net
Sisters of Our Lady of Sorrows
Sr. Concetta Scipione, O.L.S., Admin.
Sr. Gemma Forlani, O.L.S., Supr.
Most Rev. William B. Friend, D.D., Pres.
Sisters 4
Lay Personnel 265
Residents 184

MAINE

Bangor
Diocese of Portland (In Maine)

St. Xavier's Home
119 Somerset St.
Bangor, ME 04401
Tel: 207-942-4815
Mailing Address:—St. John Parish
207 York St.
Bangor, ME 04401-5442
Gerard G. Gosselin, Contact Person
Units 19

Biddeford
Diocese of Portland (In Maine)

St. Andre Health Care & Rehab Center
407 Pool St.
Biddeford, ME 04005-9716
Tel: 207-282-5171; Fax: 207-282-5372
Sr. Madeleine D'Anjou, Admin.
Sponsored by Servants of the Immaculate Heart of Mary S.C.I.M. Good Shepherd, Quebec, Canada
Beds 96

Lewiston
Diocese of Portland (In Maine)

Maison Marcotte
(Formerly: Marcotte Congregate Housing)
100 Campus Ave.
Lewiston, ME 04240
Tel: 207-786-0062
Cecile Y. Mathieu, Dir.
Total In Residence 128
Total Staff 4

**St. Marguerite d'Youville Pavilion*
(Formerly: Marcotte Nursing Home)
102 Campus Ave.
Lewiston, ME 04240
Tel: 207-777-4200
Dana Larson, Admin.
Rev. Raymond Corriveau, O.P., Chap.
Beds 280

Portland
Diocese of Portland (In Maine)

Deering Pavilion Apartment House for Senior Citizens
880 Forest Ave.
Portland, ME 04103
Tel: 207-797-8777; Fax: 207-797-8963
E-mail: oren@maine.rr.com
Mr. Oren W. Schroeder, Admin.
Residents 232
Apartments 200

St. Joseph's Manor
1133 Washington Ave.
Portland, ME 04103
Tel: 207-797-0600; Fax: 207-797-4168
Most Rev. Joseph J. Gerry, O.S.B., Pres.
Mr. Ronald G. Tardif, Dir.
Faith Stilphen, R.N., Dir. Nurses
Bed Capacity 184

Waterville
Diocese of Portland (In Maine)

Mt. St. Joseph Holistic Care Community
Highwood St.
Waterville, ME 04901
Tel: 207-873-0705; Fax: 207-873-6626
E-mail: msj@mtsj.org
Web Site: www.mtsj.org
Gail Hillstrom, Admin.
Sisters of St. Joseph of Lyons, C.S.J.
Nursing Facility 148
Assisted Living 39

Seton Village Inc.
1 Carver St.
Waterville, ME 04901
Tel: 207-873-0178; Fax: 207-873-1233
Most Rev. Joseph J. Gerry, Bishop of Portland, Pres.
David P. Twomey, Treas.
Daniel Bard, Chm.
Mr. Harlan Cooper, Admin.
Units 140
Guests 150

MARYLAND

Baltimore
Archdiocese of Baltimore

Dismas House East
1415 N. Caroline St.
Baltimore, MD 21213
Tel: 410-539-2520
Mailing Address:—Dismas House of Baltimore, Inc.
Charles, R. Muskauski, Exec. Dir., P.O. Box 4435
Baltimore, MD 21223-0435
Charles R. Muskauski, Exec. Dir.
Non-Sectarian-Use Diocesan Property Rehabilitation center under contract to the Maryland Division of Corrections to provide inmate svcs.
Total Staff 1
Total in Residence 45
Total Assisted

Dismas House West
105 S. Mount St.
Baltimore, MD 21223-0435
Tel: 410-566-9400; Fax: 410-233-1622
Mailing Address:
Charles R. Muskauski, Exec. Dir., P.O. Box 4435
Baltimore, MD 21223-0435
Charles R. Muskauski, Exec. Dir
Non-Sectarian-Use Diocesan Property Rehabilitation center under contract to the Maryland Division of Corrections to provide inmate services.
Total Staff 2
Total in Residence 45
Total Assisted 172

Good Samaritan Nursing Center Inc.
320 Cathedral St.
Baltimore, MD 21201

St. Charles Villa
603 Maiden Choice Ln.
Baltimore, MD 21228
Tel: 410-747-1211; Fax: 410-747-2460
E-mail: wtokss@aol.com
Revs.:
Lawrence A. Bender, S.S.
John W. Bowen, S.S.
James H. Brennan, S.S.
Charles P. Dillon, S.S.
Claude H. Dukehart, S.S.
James J. Healy, S.S.
Raymond F. Hesler, S.S.
William J. Lee, S.S.
John F. Mattingly, S.S.
Vincent deP. McMurry, S.S.
William S. Morris, S.S.
William T. O'Keeffe, S.S., Supr. & Dir.
John H. Oliver, S.S.
John A. Ward, S.S.
J. Paul Welch, S.S.
Joseph L. White, S.S.
Total in Residence 16
Total Staff 10

St. Elizabeth Rehabilitation and Nursing Center
3320 Benson Ave.
Baltimore, MD 21227-1035
Tel: 410-644-7100; Fax: 410-644-2154
E-mail: info@catholiccharities-md.org
Web Site: www.catholiccharities-md.org
Legal Title: *The Jenkins Memorial Nursing Home, Inc.*
Sponsored by Associated Catholic Charities.
Ms. Christine Mour, Admin.
Sisters 3
Beds 162
Total Assisted 375
Total Staff 215

St. Joseph's Nursing Home
1222 Tugwell Dr.
Baltimore, MD 21228
Tel: 410-747-0026; Fax: 410-747-0386
Legal Title: *Sisters Servants of Mary Immaculate, Inc.*
Rev. Jaroslaw Gamrot, M.I.C., Chap.
Admin.:
Sr. Carolyn Carne
Sr. Krystyna Mroczek
Sisters 9
Residents 40
Total Assisted 49
Total Staff 51

St. Martin's Home for Aged, Little Sisters of the Poor
601 Maiden Choice Ln.
Baltimore, MD 21228
Tel: 410-744-9367; Fax: 410-747-0835
Rev. John J. Abrahams, Chap.
Sisters 20
Intermediate Care Beds 62
Assisted Living 22
Apartments 18
Aged Residents 104
Total Staff 130
Total Assisted 104

Beltsville
Archdiocese of Washington

Ammendale Normal Institute of Prince George's County-La Salle Hall (1880)
6001 Ammendale Rd.
Beltsville, MD 20705
Tel: 301-210-7443; Fax: 301-210-0614
Brothers of the Christian Schools
Bros.:
Kevin Erb, F.S.C., Dir.
Robert Wise, F.S.C., Assoc. Dir.
Residence for Retired and Convalescent Brothers.
Brothers 19

Ellicott City
Archdiocese of Baltimore

St. Agnes Nursing and Rehabilitation Center
(Subsidiary of St. Agnes HealthCare)
3000 N. Ridge Rd.
Ellicott City, MD 21043
Tel: 410-461-7577; Fax: 410-461-6695
Web Site: stagnes.org
Ascension Health
Barbara Gustke, Admin.
Pastoral Care:
Sr. Genevieve Kureth, Coord.
Francis Gollery, Chap.
Sisters 1
Beds 182
Total Assisted 550
Total Staff 172

Emmitsburg
Archdiocese of Baltimore

Villa St. Catherine, Inc.
331 S. Seton Ave.
Emmitsburg, MD 21727
Tel: 301-447-7000; Fax: 301-447-7015
Sponsored by Ascension Health
Mr. Joseph P. Lydon, Admin. & CEO
Beds 69
Total Staff 80

Hyattsville
Archdiocese of Washington

Sacred Heart Home Inc.
5805 Queens Chapel Rd.
Hyattsville, MD 20782
Tel: 301-277-6500; Fax: 301-277-3181
E-mail: sacredhearthome@erols.com
Sisters, Servants of Mary Immaculate

REBECCA M. PERRY, Admin.
Rev. ROBERT MERTES, S.V.D.
Sisters 3
Residents 102

St. Ann's Infant and Maternity Home
4901 Eastern Ave.
Hyattsville, MD 20782
Tel: 301-559-5500; Fax: 301-853-6985
E-mail: questions@saint-anns.com
Web Site: www.saint-anns.com
Daughters of Charity
Sr. JOSEPHINE MURPHY, D.C., Admin.
Sr. PAULA Local Supr.
Sisters 7
Residential Children 57
Maternity Program 18
Day Care 85
After Care Program:
Mothers 14
Infants 14

Mitchellville
Archdiocese of Washington

Villa Rosa Nursing Home, Inc.
3800 Lottsford Vista Rd.
Mitchellville, MD 20721-4026
Tel: 301-459-4700; Fax: 301-459-0754
Rev. DOMINIC RODIGHIERO, C.S., Dir.
Mr. EUGENE L. ZIBRAT, Admin.
Sr. TEOLIDE CECAGNO, M.S.C.S., Supr.
Sisters 6
Residents 100
Comprehensive Care Nursing Facility.

Ridgely
Diocese of Wilmington

St. Martin's Ministries
14259 Benedictine Ln.
Ridgely, MD 21660
Tel: 410-634-2497; Fax: 410-634-1410
E-mail: corta@juno.com
Sisters of St. Benedict
Sr. PATRICIA GAMGORT, O.S.B., Exec. Dir.
St. Martin's Barn
Tel: 410-634-1140; Fax: 410-634-2684
14376 Benedictine Ln.
Ridgely, MD 21660
Tel: 410-634-1140; Fax: 410-634-2684
Volunteers 22
Staff 5
Total Assisted 9,838
BILL REEP, Dir.
St. Martin's House
14374 Benedictine Ln.
Ridgely, MD 21660
Tel: 410-634-2537; Fax: 410-634-1293
Volunteers 5
Staff 5
Total Assisted 38
Sr. VERONICA DANIELS, O.S.B.

Timonium
Archdiocese of Baltimore

Stella Maris
2300 Dulaney Valley Rd.
Timonium, MD 21093
Tel: 410-252-4500; 560-9675 (Admissions); Fax: 410-560-9675
E-mail: STELLA@erols.com
Web Site: www.stellamarisinc.com
Sr. KAREN MCNALLY, R.S.M., Chief Admin. Officer
Rev. LAWRENCE M. JOHNSON, Dir. of Pastoral Care
The management corporation for all programs of the Center. Long-term care; subacute care; home health; rehabilitative services; hospice services; hospice inpatient; home/hospice care; outreach ministries program; independent living; group home; and counseling/bereavement services for adults and children. All applications for the facilities of the Center are processed directly through the Admissions Office at Stella Maris.
Lay Personnel 680
Sisters 12
Residents 416
Saint John Hall-Long Crandon
Tel: 410-252-4500, Ext. 251
Rev. Msgr. EDWARD J. LYNCH
Rev. Msgr. HENRY F. ZERHUSEN
Revs.:
GERALD BRODERICK
JOHN C. COLLOPY
PAUL F. DOLAN
JOSEPH A. KAISER
JOSEPH A. KENNEY
CHARLES L. LAFFERTY
MYLES MULLER
CHARLES H. QUINN

Stella Maris
Tel: 410-252-4500; Fax: 410-560-9675
Rev. CONRAD MILLER, O.F.M.Conv.
St. Elizabeth Hall
Rev. Msgr. ROBERT A. BOZEL
Rev. Msgr. THOMAS J. FANNON
Rev. Msgr. CHARLES MEISEL
Rev. JAMES BRADY
Cardinal Shehan Center, Inc.

MASSACHUSETTS

Boston
Archdiocese of Boston

Don Orione Nursing Home
111 Orient Ave.
East Boston, MA 02128-1006
Tel: 617-569-2100; Fax: 617-561-1138
E-mail: donorione@aol.com
Revs.:
LAWRENCE TOSATTO, F.D.P., Supr., Dir. and Admin.
ROCCO CRESCENZI, F.D.P., Vicar & Treas.
GINO MARCHESANI, F.D.P., Counselor
Sons of Divine Providence (Don Orione Fathers) 3
Guests 190
Total Assisted 185
Total Staff 230

Franciscan Children's Hospital and Rehabilitation Center
Tel: 617-254-3800; Fax: 617-779-1119
30 Warren St.
Brighton, MA 02135
Tel: 617-254-3800; Fax: 617-779-1119
E-mail: fch@fch.com
Web Site: www.fch.com
General Pediatrics, Rehabilitation, Special Education, Mental Health Services & Home Care.
PAUL DELLA ROCCO, Pres. & C.E.O.
Bed Capacity 100
Number under care 59,000
Day Program 90
Total Staff 750

Marian Manor (1954)
Web Site: www.marianmanor.org
130 Dorchester St.
South Boston, MA 02127
Tel: 617-268-3333; Fax: 617-268-4589
Sr. PAULINE ROSS, Admin.
Revs.:
JOSEPH M. KANE, Chap.
HERBERT J. CLEARY, S.J., Assoc. Chap.
Priests 2
Carmelite Sister for the Aged and Infirm 13
Guests 366

St. Joseph Nursing Care Center
321 Centre St.
Dorchester, MA 02122
Tel: 617-825-6320; Fax: 617-825-7410
PAUL F. SHANNON, Admin.
Rev. JOHN J. JENNINGS, Chap.
Member, Caritas Christi Healthcare System.
123 Bed Nursing Care Center.
St. Joseph Nursing Care Center, Inc.
Sisters 2
Total Staff 190
Total Assisted 191

St. Mary's Women and Infants Center
90 Cushing Ave.
Dorchester, MA 02125
Center for pregnant women.
(See Guidance Centers for more information.)

Brighton
Archdiocese of Boston

St. John of God Hospital
296 Allston St.
Brighton, MA 02135
Tel: 617-277-5750; Fax: 617-731-3094
WILLIAM K. BRINKERT, Pres.
Rev. JOSEPH K. COLEMAN, Chap., Dir. Pastoral Care, Chronic and Rehabilitation Hospital.
A member of Caritas Christi, the Catholic Health Care System of the Archdiocese of Boston.
Bed Capacity 58
Total Staff 120
Total Assisted 575

Brockton
Archdiocese of Boston

St. Joseph Manor Health Care Inc.
215 Thatcher St.
Brockton, MA 02402-3999
Tel: 508-583-5834; Fax: 508-583-8551
E-mail: ateri@stjosephmanor.com
THOMAS J. BROWN, CEO
ANNE M. TERI, Admin.
Adult Day Health Center
Tel: 508-583-8313
Total Assisted 40
Total Staff 6
Sisters of Jesus Crucified and the Sorrowful Mother 9
Residents 118

Cambridge
Archdiocese of Boston

Sancta Maria Nursing Facility
799 Concord Ave.
Cambridge, MA 02138
Tel: 617-868-2200; Fax: 617-864-2801
Daughters of Mary of the Immaculate Conception
Sr. MARY MARK, D.M., Admin.
In-Patients/Residents 141
Bed Capacity 141
Sisters 3
Total Staff 215

**Youville Hospital & Rehabilitation Center, Inc.*
1575 Cambridge St.
Cambridge, MA 02138-4398
Tel: 617-876-4344; Fax: 617-547-5501
Mr. DANIEL LEAHEY, Pres. & CEO
Ms. PATRICIA KENNEDY, Dir. Mission Integration
Chaplains:
Rev. RONALD PAQUIN
Ms. PATRICIA KENNEDY, Dir. Pastoral Care Services
Ms. ELIZABETH WALSH, Chap.
Ms. GEORGIA LEINER, Chap.
Priests 1
Sisters of Charity (Grey Nuns) 1
Member of Youville Lifecare, Inc.
Bed Capacity 146
Patients assisted annually 2,285
Staff 517

Fairhaven
Diocese of Fall River

Our Lady's Haven of Fairhaven Inc.
71 Center St.
Fairhaven, MA 02719
Tel: 508-999-4561; Fax: 508-997-0254
Web Site: www.dhfo.org
MANUEL BENEVIDES, Admin.
Rev. MATTHEW SULLIVAN, SS.CC., Chap.
Sr. MARIA CRAVEDI, M.P.V., Dir. Pastoral Care
Residents 117
Total Staff 159

Fall River
Diocese of Fall River

Catholic Memorial Home Inc.
2446 Highland Ave.
Fall River, MA 02720-4599
Tel: 508-679-0011; Fax: 508-672-5858
Sr. MARY ROBERT ROMANO, O.Carm., Supr. & Admin.
Rev. WILLIAM P. BLOTTMAN
Sr. CATHERINE DONOVAN, R.S.M., Dir. Pastoral Care
Carmelite Sisters 5
Total Assisted 300
Total Staff 425

Rose Hawthorne Lathrop Home
(Servants of Relief for Incurable Cancer)
1600 Bay St.
Fall River, MA 02724
Tel: 508-673-2322; Fax: 508-679-5830
Dominican Sisters of the Congregation of St. Rose of Lima
Total Assisted 102
Sisters 6
Total Staff 20
Bed Capacity 35
Patients assisted annually 102

Framingham
Archdiocese of Boston

Carmel Terrace
933 Central St.
Framingham, MA 01701
Tel: 508-788-8000; Fax: 508-626-1603
Sr. M. JOSEPH AUGUSTINE, Dir.
Carmelite Sisters for the Aged and Infirm 3
Apartments for Assisted Living of the Elderly 62
Total Assisted 70
Total Staff 38

St. Patrick's Manor, Inc.
863 Central St.
Framingham, MA 01701
Tel: 508-879-8000; Fax: 508-626-1604
Sr. SEAN DAMIEN FLYNN, Admin.
Rev. JOHN FENTON FOLEY, S.J., Chap.
Carmelite Sisters for the Aged and Infirm 30
Total Staff 460

Holyoke
Diocese of Springfield in Massachusetts

Mont Marie Health Care Center, Inc.
34 Lower Westfield Rd.
Holyoke, MA 01040
Tel: 413-536-0853; Fax: 413-533-4505
E-mail: MMHCC92@aol.com
Sr. ELIZABETH SULLIVAN, S.S.J., Admin.
In res.,
Revs.:
FRANCIS DUDA
AUGUSTINE PAUL HENNESSY, C.P.
RINALDO RIBEZZI
Total Staff 91
Total Resident Days 21,634
Total Census 81 residents

Providence Place, Inc.
5 Gamelin St.
Holyoke, MA 01040
Tel: 413-534-9700; Fax: 413-534-9782
Web Site: ProvidencePlace.org
Sisters of Providence
RICHARD PELLAND, Exec. Dir.
In res.,
Revs.:
EDWARD M. KENNEDY
RICHARD F. MEEHAN
Total in Residence 79
Total Staff 28

Sisters of Providence Care Centers, Inc.
35 Holy Family Rd.
Holyoke, MA 01040-2758
Tel: 413-532-3246; Fax: 413-532-0309
Mr. WILLIAM E. CASPER, Pres. & CEO
Beaven Kelly Home
25 Brightside Dr.
Holyoke, MA 01040
Tel: 413-532-4892; Fax: 413-535-2355
Residents 55
Sr. SHEILA MCGUIRK, S.S.J., Pastoral Care Coord.
Mrs. CYNTHIA BROWN, Admin.
Mount St. Vincent Nursing Home
35 Holy Family Rd.
Holyoke, MA 01040-2758
Tel: 413-532-3246; Fax: 413-532-0309
Persons under care 125
In res.,
Revs.:
EUGENE F. OZIMEK
CASIMIR S. SWITALSKI (SPR)
Sr. JEAN PIERRE, S.N.D., CNA (Staff)
Sr. MARY HORGAN, S.P., M.Div., Chap. (Staff)
Mr. DENNIS K. MCKENNA, Admin.
St. Luke's Home
85 Spring St.
Springfield, MA 01105
Tel: 413-736-5494; Fax: 413-746-5075
Residents 89
Sr. DOROTHY YOUNG, S.P., Pastoral Care Dir. (Staff)
Sr. GERALDINE NOONAN, S.P., Admin.
In res.,
Sr. GRACE LANE, O.P.
Center for Rehabilitation and Nursing Care
217 Westfield St.
West Springfield, MA 01089
Tel: 413-746-0390; Fax: 413-746-0309
Residents 120
DAVID IANACONE, Admin.
Sr. MARY DOLORETTA, S.P., Pastoral Care Coord. & Chap.
In res.,
Revs.:
JOHN SEXTON
JOSEPH MULLIGAN
Providence Care Center of Washington
1462 Lovers Ln.
Washington, MA 01223
Tel: 413-627-2660; Fax: 413-627-3085
Residents 69
ERIKO UMANA, Admin.
Providence Care Center of Springfield
370 Pine St.
Springfield, MA 01105
Tel: 413-731-5318; Fax: 413-731-5384
Residents 136
Sr. SHEILA MCGUIRK, S.S.J., Pastoral Care Coord.
Ms. CONSTANCE HENNING, Admin.
Total Staff 546
Total Assisted 594

Lawrence
Archdiocese of Boston

**M.I. Adult Day Health Center, Inc.*
189 Maple St.
Lawrence, MA 01841
Tel: 978-682-7575; Fax: 978-691-5374
E-mail: lori_barrett@mihs.com
Sisters of Charity of Montreal (Grey Nuns)
BARBARA E. GRANT, Pres. & C.E.O.
LORI BARRETT, RN, Program Dir.
Adult day health care for Senior Citizens; also, bilingual/bicultural (spanish) adult day health care.
Total in Residence 70
Total Staff 12

M.I. Nursing-Restorative Center, Inc.
172 Lawrence St.
Lawrence, MA 01841
Tel: 978-685-6321; Fax: 978-975-0050
Covenant Health Systems
BARBARA E. GRANT, Pres. & CEO
MICHAEL D. TURPIN, Admin.
Multi-level Skilled Nursing Facility.
Member of Convenant Health System, Lexington, MA. Unit of: Mary Immaculate Health Care Services.
Residents 250
Total Staff 300

M.I. Residential Community II, Inc.
191 Maple St.
Lawrence, MA 01841
Tel: 978-682-7575; Fax: 978-691-5374
Covenant Health Systems
BARBARA E. GRANT, Pres. & CEO
VIRGINIA LYNCH, Mgr.
Independent & assisted living for Elderly and Handicapped.
Units 106
Total in Residence 120
Total Staff 35

M.I. Residential Community III, Inc.
193 Maple St.
Lawrence, MA 01841
Tel: 978-682-7575; Fax: 978-691-5374
Sisters of Charity of Montreal (Grey Nuns)
BARBARA E. GRANT, Pres. & CEO
VIRGINIA LYNCH, Mgr.
Independent & assisted living for Elderly and Handicapped.
Units 88
Total in Residence 95
Total Staff 35

M.I. Residential Community, Inc.
189 Maple St.
Lawrence, MA 01841
Tel: 978-682-7575; Fax: 978-691-5374
Covenant Health Systems
BARBARA E. GRANT, Pres. & CEO
VIRGINIA LYNCH, Housing Mgr.
Independent & assisted living for Elderly and Handicapped.
Units 110
Total in Residence 121
Total Staff 35

**M.I. Transportation, Inc.*
189 Maple St.
Lawrence, MA 01841
Tel: 978-682-7575; Fax: 978-975-0050
Sisters of Charity of Montreal (Grey Nuns)
BARBARA E. GRANT, Pres. & CEO
VIRGINIA LYNCH, Mgr.
Total Assisted 75
Total Staff 5

Leominster
Diocese of Worcester

Presentation Health Care Center
99 Church St.
Leominster, MA 01453-3147
Tel: 978-537-7856; Fax: 978-840-1564
Sr. CATHERINE CLEARY, P.B.V.M., Pres.
Total in Residence 19
Total Staff 30
Purpose: To operate and maintain a nursing home for aged and/or infirmed persons at Presentation Convent.

Lowell
Archdiocese of Boston

D'Youville Manor
981 Varnum Ave.
Lowell, MA 01854
Tel: 978-454-5681; Fax: 978-459-7002
E-mail: dyouvill@dyouville.com
Web Site: www.dyouville.com
Sisters of Charity of Ottawa (Grey Nuns of the Cross)
STEVE JOHNSON, CEO
Rev. FRANK DOLAN, O.M.I., Chap.
Priests 4
Sisters 5
Total Assisted 208
Total Staff 300
Adult Day Health Care Capacity 22
Total Staff 6

Marlboro
Archdiocese of Boston

Marie Esther Health Center, Inc.
720 Boston Post Rd.
Marlboro, MA 01752
Tel: 508-485-3791; Fax: 508-229-2294
E-mail: mehci@ibm.net
Total Assisted 56
Total Staff 45

Millbury
Diocese of Worcester

Providence House Nursing Home of Millbury
29 Main St.
Millbury, MA 01527
Tel: 508-865-6106
Member of St. Vincent Healthcare System, Inc.
Beds 138
Total Assisted 138
Total Staff 180

New Bedford
Diocese of Fall River

Sacred Heart Home
359 Summer St.
New Bedford, MA 02740
Tel: 508-996-6751; Fax: 508-992-3145
Web Site: www.dhfo.org
JEAN M. GOLITZ, R.N., M.S.
Sisters of Charity of Quebec 3
Total Staff 324
Residents 217

North Attleboro
Diocese of Fall River

Madonna Manor Inc.
85 N. Washington St.
North Attleboro, MA 02760
Tel: 508-699-2794; Fax: 508-699-0481
E-mail: ekanuse@dhfo.org
Web Site: www.dhfo.org
Mrs. ERIN E. KANUSE, Admin.
Rev. RAYMOND MOQUIN, M.S.
Sr. MARY DUFFY, S.S.J., Dir. of Pastoral Care
Total Staff 180
Residents 129

Somerville
Archdiocese of Boston

Jeanne Jugan Pavilion
190 Highland Ave.
Somerville, MA 02143
Tel: 617-776-4420; Fax: 617-623-0707
Mailing Address:
186 Highland Ave.
Somerville, MA 02143
Apartments for the Elderly 24
Residents 30
Total Staff 3

Jeanne Jugan Residence
186 Highland Ave.
Somerville, MA 02143
Tel: 617-776-4420; Fax: 617-623-0707
Rev. JOSEPH J. DOWNEY, Chap.
Senior Citizen Total in Residence 84
Total Staff 100
Little Sisters of the Poor 16
Residents 84

Springfield
Diocese of Springfield in Massachusetts

St. Michael's Residence
86 Wendover Rd.
Springfield, MA 01118
Tel: 413-783-6773
In res.,
Rev. Msgr. ROGER VIAU
Rev. Msgr. JOHN F. HARRINGTON, P.A.

Revs.:
THOMAS S. GREENE
PETER G. LOUGHRAN
FRANCIS J. SULLIVAN
JOHN TOKARZ
Total Staff 2
Total in Residence 5

Taunton
Diocese of Fall River

Bethany House Adult Day Care
72 Church Green
Taunton, MA 02780
Tel: 508-822-9200
Mr. THOMAS F. HEALY, Admin.
Total Staff 6
Total Assisted 75

Marian Manor Inc.
33 Summer St.
Taunton, MA 02780
Tel: 508-822-4885; Fax: 508-677-4361
Mr. THOMAS F. HEALY, Admin.
Rev. BERNARD VANNASSE, Chap.
Sr. PAULINA CARDENAS, O.P., Dir. Pastoral Care
Dominican Sisters of Charity of the Presentation of the Blessed Virgin Mary 6
Total Staff 159

Waltham
Archdiocese of Boston

Maristhill Nursing & Rehabilitation Center
66 Newton St.
Waltham, MA 02453-6063
Tel: 781-893-0240; Fax: 781-894-6330
JANET C. MURPHY, Admin.
A member of Covenant Health Systems, offering skilled and rehabilitative nursing care.
Priests 3
Sisters 10
Residents 123
Total Staff 154

West Springfield
Diocese of Springfield in Massachusetts

Brightside, Inc.
Private, Non-Profit Agency.
2112 Riverdale St.
Springfield, MA 01089
Tel: 413-788-7366; Fax: 413-747-0182
Sisters of Providence
Mr. VINCENT J. MCCORKLE, Pres.
Mr. JONATHON CHASEN, M.D., CEO
Children in Residence 100
Children in Day Treatment Program 50
Placement Services:
Children in Foster Homes 10
Adoption Services 108
Pregnant Parenting Youth Services 100
Outpatient Mental Health Clinic 5,600
Family Stabilization Team 175

Whitinsville
Diocese of Worcester

St. Camillus Hospice, Inc.
447 Hill St.
Whitinsville, MA 01588
Tel: 508-234-7306; Fax: 508-234-7597
Rev. JOHN J. GALLAGHER, O.S.Cam.
Bro. THOMAS J. FARRELL, O.S.Cam., Treas.

St. Camillus Nursing Home Inc.
447 Hill St.
Whitinsville, MA 01588
Tel: 508-234-7306
Mr. DAVID C. TURNER
Bro. THOMAS FARRELL, O.S.Cam., Dir. Pastoral Care
Priests 1
Brothers 2
Beds 123
Patients assisted annually 43,070
St. Camillus Institute
497 Hill St.
Whitinsville, MA 01588
St. Camillus Rectory
495 Hill St.
Whitinsville, MA 01588
Rev. JACK GALLAGHER, O.S.Cam.

Worcester
Diocese of Worcester

Providence Extended Care Center
119 Providence St.
Worcester, MA 01604
Tel: 508-860-5000; Fax: 508-860-5109
Member of Saint Vincent Healthcare System, Inc.
Rev. THOMAS M. BARRY, Chap.
Beds 160
Patients assisted annually 1,000
Total Staff 200

Saint Francis Home
101 Plantation St.
Worcester, MA 01604
Tel: 508-755-8605; Fax: 508-798-0625
E-mail: admin@saintfrancishome.org
Sr. ANNA MARIE TAG, R.S.M., Admin.
Beds 137
Employees 225

Vianney House
222 June St.
Worcester, MA 01602
Tel: 508-791-0311
Retired Priests' Home.
Rev. Msgr. THOMAS J. DALEY
Rev. Msgr. EDMOND G. HADDAD
c/o 49 Elm St.
Worcester, MA 01609
Revs.:
WILLIAM W. MCGOVERN
CYRIL A. LEBEAU
JOHN F. CAHILL, Admin.
JOSEPH H. ASH
Total Staff 3

MICHIGAN

Allen Park
Archdiocese of Detroit

Little Sisters of the Poor
P.O. Box 610
Allen Park, MI 48101
Tel: 734-462-2809
Sr. JUDITH L.S.P., Supr.

Battle Creek
Diocese of Kalamazoo

Mercy Pavilion Skilled Nursing Home and Senior Care Residence
80 N. 20 St.
Battle Creek, MI 49015
Tel: 616-964-5400; Fax: 616-964-5559
Sub. of Battle Creek Health System.
Mr. MICHAEL C. RICHARDS, Admin.
Bed Capacity 77
Senior Care Residence Beds 64

Bloomfield Hills
Archdiocese of Detroit

St. Elizabeth's Briarbank
39315 Woodward Ave.
Bloomfield Hills, MI 48304
Tel: 248-644-1011; Fax: 248-644-1596
Daughters of Divine Charity
Sr. M. CELESTE, Admin.
Sisters 15
Aged Residents 44

Clinton Twp.
Archdiocese of Detroit

A Friends House Adult Day Care Center
16931 19 Mile Rd., Ste. 140
Clinton Twp., MI 48038
Tel: 810-412-8494; Fax: 810-412-8084
Daytime care for older adults. Support services for care giving families. A service of Catholic Services of Macomb.
SUZANNE SZCZEPANSKI-WHITE, Dir. of Senior Svcs.

Dearborn Heights
Archdiocese of Detroit

Vista Maria
20651 W. Warren Ave.
Dearborn Heights, MI 48127
Tel: 313-271-3050; Fax: 313-271-6250
Mr. CAMERON HOSNER, Exec. Dir.
Residential and community-based treatment programs for adolescent girls in conflict. Sponsored by the Sisters of the Good Shepherd.
Sisters 2
Girls Residential 145
Lay Staff 270
S.F.C. 41
Independent Living 6

Detroit
Archdiocese of Detroit

Christ Child House
15751 Joy Rd.
Detroit, MI 48228
Tel: 313-584-6077; Fax: 313-584-1148
JOHN YABLONKY, ACSW, Exec. Dir.

Don Bosco Hall, Inc.
2340 Calvert
Detroit, MI 48206
Tel: 313-869-2200; Fax: 313-869-8220
CHARLES SMALL, Dir.
Residential treatment center for boys, ages 12-17, in need of care, guidance and therapy.
Lay Staff 75
Residents 41
Emergency Shelter Program 20
Transitional Services 180
Mentoring Program 155

St. Catherine's House
1641 Webb Ave.
Detroit, MI 48206
Tel: 313-868-4505
MARY CONNORS, Mgr.
For elderly-ambulatory & younger disabled ambulatory women.
Capacity 12

St. Joseph's Home
4800 Cadieux Rd.
Detroit, MI 48224
Tel: 313-882-3800; Fax: 313-882-6944
Carmelite Sisters of the Divine Heart of Jesus
Sr. MARY MAGDALENE, Admin.
Sisters 5
Lay Staff 68
Aged Residents 104

St. Mary's Residence
2120 Orleans St.
Detroit, MI 48207
Tel: 313-259-6874; 259-0459
Sr. M. FIDELIS, F.D.C., Admin.
Rev. WILLIAM LUNNON
A residence for women desiring home-like surroundings.
Daughters of Divine Charity
Sisters 6
Residents 60

Dimondale
Diocese of Lansing

Dimondale Nursing Center
4000 N. Michigan Rd. (M-99)
Dimondale, MI 48821-9744
Tel: 517-646-6258; Fax: 517-646-0405
ROSEMARY ZIVIC, Admin.
Chaplains:
Rev. STANLEY CZARNOTA, in res., Tel: 517-646-0408; Fax: 517-646-7578
CAROLYN HUDSON, Chap., Tel: 517-646-6258
Nursing Home Residents 178
Total Staff 250
Total Assisted 178

Dowagiac
Diocese of Kalamazoo

Dowagiac Nursing Home
610 Uneta St.
Dowagiac, MI 49047
Tel: 616-782-3471; Fax: 616-782-1681
JUDITH HOESE, Admin.
Total Staff 110
Bed Capacity 108

Escanaba
Diocese of Marquette

Bishop Noa Home for Senior Citizens
2900 3rd Ave. S.
Escanaba, MI 49829
Tel: 906-786-5810; Fax: 906-786-5372
Sisters of St. Paul de Chartres
In res.,
Revs.:
EMIL J. BEYER, Assoc. Chap.
GILBERT N. NEUROHR, Chap.
Sisters of St. Paul de Chartres 5
Residents 123

Farmington Hills
Archdiocese of Detroit

Marillac Programs
A Division of St. Vincent and Sarah Fisher Center, 22255 Greenfield, Ste. 330
Southfield, MI 48334
Tel: 248-559-2272; Fax: 248-559-2226
JEAN VICKERS, Exec. Dir.
JACKIE DUNN BELL, Program Mgr.

Sr. WANDA SHEBER, D.C., Division Dir., Residential Svcs.
Outreach case management and counseling services for pregnant and parenting teens and young families in the tri-county area. Nine beds for the transitional housing of teen mothers 16-18 years of age who are wards of the state and nine homeless babies 0-18 months of age.

St. Vincent and Sarah Fisher Center
27400 W. Twelve Mile Rd.
Farmington Hills, MI 48334
Tel: 313-538-6000; 810-626-7527
JEAN M. VICKERS, Exec. Dir.
Licensed capacity for: Residential care 60 (ages 4-15), Specialized Foster Care 120 (ages 0-17), Seton Preschool & Child Care Center 49 (ages 2 weeks-5 yrs.).
Pregnancy and Parenting For Teen Parents (Ages 16-19)
Outreach Program:
Residential 41

Seton Nursery School and Infant-Toddler Child Care Center
29475 Inkster Rd.
Farmington Hills, MI 48018
Tel: 810-626-6990
ANN COYLE Dir.
Center licensed for 80 children, 8 weeks-5.5 years.
In Day Care 68
Legal Title: *Seton Nursery School and Infant-Toddler Child Care Center - St. Vincent Sara Fisher Center*

Trinity Continuing Care Services
P.O. Box 9185
Farmington Hills, MI 48331-9185
Tel: 248-305-7600; Fax: 248-305-7933
KAREN STRUVE, Pres. & CEO

Grand Blanc
Diocese of Lansing

Genesys Convalescent Center, Grand Blanc, Inc.
An affiliate of Genesys Health System.
8481 Holly Rd.
Grand Blanc, MI 48439-1899
Tel: 810-694-1711; Fax: 810-694-9717
E-mail: r.stevens@genesys.org
Nursing Home
Beds 140
Patients assisted annually 222
Total Staff 170

Grand Rapids
Diocese of Grand Rapids

St. Ann's Home
2161 Leonard St., N.W.
Grand Rapids, MI 49504
Tel: 616-453-7715; Fax: 616-453-7359
Carmelite Sisters of the Divine Heart of Jesus
Sisters 5
Residents 140
Adult Day Care 145

Kalamazoo
Diocese of Kalamazoo

Borgess Nursing Home
537 Chicago Ave.
Kalamazoo, MI 49048
Tel: 616-382-2392; Fax: 616-382-0843
DONNA MENCHINGER, Admin.
Total Staff 120
Total Assisted 121

Lake Orion
Archdiocese of Detroit

Guest House for Women Religious
1840 W. Scripps Rd., Box 68
Lake Orion, MI 48360
Tel: 248-391-3100; Fax: 248-391-1553
A state licensed and JCAHO accredited endorsed residential treatment center for Catholic sisters and women in formation.
Sr. MAE KIERANS, C.S.J., Prog. Dir.
Bed Capacity 20
Central Admissions Office, from U.S. & Canada call: 800-626-6910.
Office of Guest House, Inc. Management Services Offices
1601 Joslyn Rd., P.O. Box 420
Lake Orion, MI 48361
Tel: 248-391-4445; Fax: 248-391-0210
Mr. DANIEL A. KIDD, Pres. & CEO

Livonia
Archdiocese of Detroit

Marybrook Manor
36975 W. Five Mile Rd.
Livonia, MI 48154
Tel: 734-464-9667; Fax: 734-464-4846
Sr. ELIZABETH ANN C.S.S.F., N.H.A., Admin.
Residents 29

Marycrest Manor
15475 Middlebelt Rd.
Livonia, MI 48154
Tel: 734-427-9175; Fax: 734-427-9520
Sr. M. INNOCENT, F.S.S.J., Admin. Skilled nursing facility
Ownership: Franciscan Sisters of St. Joseph.
Sisters 2
Residents 55
Served by Marianhill Fathers.

Marywood Nursing Care Center
36975 W. Five Mile Rd.
Livonia, MI 48154
Tel: 734-464-0600; Fax: 734-464-4846
Long-term care Facility.
Sr. ELIZABETH ANN C.S.S.F., N.H.A., Admin.
Sisters 3
Capacity 91

Ryan Senior Residences of the Archdiocese of Detroit, Inc.
Central Office, 36800 Schdolcraft
Livonia, MI 48150
Tel: 313-953-5873
EDEL DUNNE O'TOOLE, Exec. Dir.
Madonna Villa
17825 Fifteen Mile Rd.
Clinton Township, MI 48035
Tel: 810-792-0358
Total Staff 14
Number of Units 86
Number of Persons Served in 12 Month Period 1,032
SUZANNE SZCZEPANSKI-WHITE, Admin.
Casa Maria
600 Maple Vista
Imlay City, MI 48444
Tel: 810-724-6300
Total Staff 19
Number of Units 84
Number of Persons Served in 12 Months Period 1,080
PAUL WALKER, Admin.
Villa Marie
15131 Newburgh
Livonia, MI 48154
Tel: 734-464-9494
Total Staff 15
Number of Units 86
Number of Persons Served in 12 Month Period 1,080
Sr. LUCILLE BLIZMAN, O.P., Admin.
Marian Place
408 W. Front St.
Monroe, MI 48161
Tel: 734-241-2414
Total Staff 11
Number of Units 53
Number of Persons Served in 12 Month Period 636
KAREN MORRIN, Admin.
Kundig Center
3300 Jeffries Fwy.
Detroit, MI 48208
Tel: 313-894-0555
Total Staff 18
Number of Units 160
Number of Persons Served in 12 Month Period 1,680
PAMELA ALEXANDER, Admin.
Stapleton Center
9341 Agnes
Detroit, MI 48214
Tel: 313-822-0397
Total Staff 11
Number of Units 59
Number of Persons Served in 12 Month Period 1,108
JENNIE BOYD, Admin.
Marian Oakland-West
29250 W. Ten Mile Rd.
Farmington Hills, MI 48336
Tel: 248-474-7204
Total Staff 14
Number of Units 87
Number of Persons Served in 12 Month Period 1,080
ELAINE MCDERMOTT, Admin.
Marydale Center
3147 Tenth Ave.
Port Huron, MI 48060
Tel: 810-985-9683
Total Staff 20
Number of Units 56
Number of Persons Served in 12 Month Period 672
Sr. ANN CHRISTINE CHARRON, Admin.

Maryhaven
11350 Reeck Road
Southgate, MI 48195
Tel: 734-287-2111
Total Staff 20
Number of Units 90
Number of Persons Served in 12 Month Period 700
Sr. PAULA COONEY, I.H.M., Admin.

Mount Clemens
Archdiocese of Detroit

St. Joseph Mercy Living Care Center
A Division of Mercy Mt. Clemens Corp.
37700 Harper
Mount Clemens, MI 48043
Tel: 810-468-0827
ROBERT L. BEYER, Pres.
Bed Capacity 264

Nazareth
Diocese of Kalamazoo

Dillon Complex for Independent Living, Inc.
Nazareth, MI 49074
Tel: 616-342-0263; Fax: 616-342-1814
E-mail: rheynssj@complink.net
Sponsored by the Sisters of St. Joseph
Sr. RUTH A. HEYN, S.S.J., Mgr.
Total In Residence 95
Total Staff 4
Residents 80

Northville
Archdiocese of Detroit

Our Lady of Providence Center
16115 Beck Rd.
Northville, MI 48167
Tel: 734-453-1300; Fax: 734-453-0266
Sr. LINDA WILLETTE, Supr., Admin.

Otsego
Diocese of Kalamazoo

Otsego Senior Apts., Inc.
Baraga Manor, 301 Washington St.
Otsego, MI 49078
Tel: 616-694-9711; Fax: 616-694-5857
Mrs. DONNA M. HOLMES, Mgr.
Managed by Catholic Family Services, Diocese of Kalamazoo.
1819 Gull Rd.
Kalamazoo, MI 49048
Apartments 48

Saginaw
Diocese of Saginaw

St. Francis Nursing Home
915 N. River Rd.
Saginaw, MI 48609
Fax: 517-781-3791
Sr. JANE MARIE LEBIEDZINSKI, C.S.S.F., Admin.
Felician Sisters (Livonia, MI) 3
Total Staff 150
Residents 100

St. Vincent Home-Boysville of Michigan, Inc.
925 N. River Rd.
Saginaw, MI 48609
Tel: 517-781-2780; Fax: 517-781-5422
RICK BOONE, M.S.W., C.S.W., Regl. Dir.
Mr. JOE MARTINUS, Pastoral Min.
Youth 60
Residential and community based treatment programs for troubled youth and families with facilities located throughtout the state of Michigan and one in Ohio, under the auspices of the Brothers of the Holy Cross at Notre Dame.
Holland House
614 E. Holland Ave.
Saginaw, MI 48601
Tel: 517-755-5396; Fax: 517-755-1616
Boys 14
Boysville's Family & Community Support Program
705 Hoyt St.
Saginaw, MI 48601
Tel: 517-752-5622; Fax: 517-752-6033
Includes Specialized Foster Care, Supervised Independent Living, In-Home Treatment, Families First, and Nokomis Challenge.
Curtis House
P.O. Box 309
Frankenmuth, MI 48734
Tel: 517-652-3212; Fax: 517-652-3214
Boys 14

Southfield
Archdiocese of Detroit

Boysville of Michigan, Inc.
Community Resource Office, 17117 W. Nine Mile Rd., Ste. 1111
Southfield, MI 48075
Tel: 248-569-6630; Fax: 248-569-8171
Residential and communtiy based treatment programs for troubled youth and families with facilities located throughout the state of Michigan and one in the state of Ohio under the auspices of the Brothers of Holy Cross at Notre Dame.
Bro. FRANCIS BOYLAN, C.S.C., Exec. Dir.
Associate Executive Directors:
EDWARD J. OVERSTREET
PAUL S. NEITMAN
LOREN BROWN
Andre House
7001 Burlingame
Detroit, MI 48204
Tel: 313-935-0769; Fax: 313-935-7930
Boys 18
Bowman House / Boysville of Michigan, Inc.
17200 Rowe St.
Detroit, MI 48205
Tel: 313-372-7320; Fax: 313-372-8623
Girls 19
Boysville's Family & Community Support Program
19403 W. Chicago
Detroit, MI 48228
Tel: 313-838-7500; Fax: 313-838-7584
Includes specialized foster care, supervised independent living, in-home family treatment.
Bro. FRANCIS BOYLAN, C.S.C., Exec. Dir.
LYNNE ALEXANDER, Regl. Dir.
Cabrini Center / Boysville of Michigan, Inc.
23915 Elmira
Redford, MI 48239
Tel: 313-537-7868; Fax: 313-838-7584
Girls 16
Hitchcock Center / Boysville of Michigan, Inc.
5675 Larkins
Detroit, MI 48210
Tel: 313-895-5119; Fax: 313-895-5135
Boys 13
Holy Cross Center / Boysville of Michigan, Inc.
5690 Cecil
Detroit, MI 48210
Tel: 313-895-2200; Fax: 313-895-4010
Day treatment, education, recreation program for Detroit region.
Johnson House / Boysville of Michigan, Inc.
7798 W. Fort St.
Detroit, MI 48209
Tel: 313-554-1700; Fax: 313-554-1748
Boys 111
King House / Boysville of Michigan, Inc.
24455 Crocker Blvd.
Mt. Clemens, MI 48043
Tel: 810-463-7130; Fax: 810-962-3426
Boys 22
Moreau Center / Boysville of Michigan, Inc.
3500 Comboni Way
Monroe, MI 48162
Tel: 734-242-5898; Fax: 734-242-6828
Boys 73
GEORGE BIRKAM, Reg. Dir.
Kennedy House / Boysville of Michigan, Inc.
7001 Burlingame St.
Detroit, MI 48204
Tel: 313-372-7320; Fax: 313-935-0605
Boys 17
St. Thomas Assessment Center / Boysville of Michigan, Inc.
8333 Townsend
Detroit, MI 48213
Tel: 313-579-1600; Fax: 313-579-1691
Sisters 1
Boys 214
Xavier Center / Boysville of Michigan, Inc.
27652 W. Outer Dr.
Ecorse, MI 48229
Tel: 313-381-5845; Fax: 313-381-0197
Boys 23

St. Francis Family Services
17500 W. Eight Mile Rd.
Southfield, MI 48075
Tel: 248-552-0750; Fax: 248-552-9019
RITA MONTGOMERY GREZLIK, Exec. Dir.
Foster home respite & adoption services for infants through 17 years.

Sheltering Arms
18310 W. 12 Mile
Southfield, MI 48076
Tel: 248-557-7373; Fax: 248-559-2309
2177 Orchard Lake Rd.
Sylvan Lake, MI 48320
Tel: 248-334-9680; Fax: 248-334-9690
Adult day care for the elderly. A service of Catholic Social Services of Oakland County.
Lay Staff 8
Volunteers 35
Patients assisted annually 71

St. Clair Shores
Archdiocese of Detroit

Sisters of Bon Secours Nursing Care Center
26001 E. Jefferson
St. Clair Shores, MI 48081
Tel: 810-779-7000
ANNE SADLER, Admin.
A member of the Bon Secours of Michigan Healthcare Systems, Inc. operated by the Sisters of Bon Secours. The center provides short and long term nursing, residential care and rehabilitative services for older adults.
Bed Capacity 200

Waterford
Archdiocese of Detroit

Fox Manor, Inc.
2350 Watkins Lake Rd.
Waterford, MI 48328
Tel: 248-674-9590
Dominican Sisters
Residential facility for independent senior citizens of moderate or limited means.
Sr. VIRGINIA BERAK, Admin.

Lourdes Assisted Living Corporation
2300 Watkins Lake Rd.
Waterford, MI 48328
Tel: 248-674-2241; Fax: 248-674-1211
Sr. SUE MCMAHON, O.P., Admin.

Lourdes Nursing Home
Dominican Sisters of Oxford, MI
2300 Watkins Lake Rd.
Waterford, MI 48328
Tel: 248-674-2241; Fax: 248-674-1211
Ms. JEANETTE REICHNER, Admin.
Rev. JEROME L. KRIEG, Res. Chap.
Skilled & basic nursing facility for men and women; 24 hour nursing care.
Residents 108

St. Jude Home, Inc.
2300 Watkins Lake Rd.
Waterford, MI 48328
Tel: 248-673-5179
SAM YAKER, Pres.
Dominican Sisters residential facility for those over 60 years of age requiring supervisory care, but not skilled nursing.
Religious 1
Lay Staff 6
Residents 6
McFadden Home
2150 Watkins Lake Rd.
Waterford, MI 48328
Tel: 248-673-3347
Religious 2
Lay Staff 2
Residents 6

MINNESOTA

Albany
Diocese of St. Cloud

Mother of Mercy Nursing Home and Retirement Center
Box 676
Albany, MN 56307
Tel: 320-845-2195; Fax: 320-845-7092
E-mail: mother@albanytel.com
BOB WIKAN, Admin.
Guests 169

Austin
Diocese of Winona

Burr Oak Care Center
116-Bed Long Term Care Facility
400 10th Ave., NW, P.O. Box 429
Austin, MN 55912
Tel: 507-433-7391
BILL LINDBERG, Interim Admin & CEO
DENNIS ACREA, Pres.
BERT NORMAN, CFO & Treas.
A subsidiary of St. Gertrude's Health Care Center of Shakopee, MN. (Benedictine Health System, sponsored by Sisters of St. Scholastica Monastery)

Sacred Heart Care Center, Inc.
1200 Twelfth St., S.W.
Austin, MN 55912
Tel: 507-433-1808
REBECCA MATHEWS HALVERSON, Admin.
Rev. FRANK E. ENRIGHT, Chap.
Sisters of the Third Order of St. Francis of the Congregation of Our Lady of Lourdes 1
Bed Capacity 59
Residents 59
Assisted Living Apartments (filled) 26
Adult Day Care (client days) 4,100
Alzheimer's Day Program (client days) 2,800
Total Staff 150

Breckenridge
Diocese of St. Cloud

St. Francis Home
Breckenridge, MN 56520
Tel: 218-643-7661
E-mail: davidnelson@chi-midwest.org
DAVID NELSON, CEO
Rev. ANTHONY KROLL, Chap.
Residents 124

Cannon Falls
Archdiocese of St. Paul and Minneapolis

Our Lady of the Angels Care Center
300 N. Dow St.
Cannon Falls, MN 55009-1899
Tel: 507-263-4658; Fax: 507-263-4127
E-mail: angel@cannon.net
JOSEPH STANISLAV, Pres. & CEO
MIKI GEMMEL, COO
Sr. PATRICIA FRITZ, Coord. Spiritual Care
Long Term Care Facility Residents 84

Clinton
Diocese of New Ulm

Graceville Health Center dba Clinton Providence Center
Clinton Providence Center
Clinton, MN 56225
Tel: 320-325-5414
Sr. PIA ROTTINGHAUS, O.S.B., Pres.
Beds 32
Patients assisted annually 45
Staff 50

Cold Spring
Diocese of St. Cloud

Assumption Court
615 First St. N.
Cold Spring, MN 56320
Tel: 320-685-4110; Fax: 320-685-7044
JAN LUTHENS, Admin.
Rev. JULIAN SCHMEISING, O.S.B., Chap.
Residents 34

Assumption Home
715 First St. N.
Cold Spring, MN 56320
Tel: 320-685-3693; Fax: 320-685-7044
JAN LUTHENS, Admin.
Rev. JULIAN SCHMEISING, O.S.B., Chap.
Sisters of St. Benedict 2
Residents 95

Bethany Home
13 Eighth Ave. S.
Cold Spring, MN 56320
Tel: 320-685-7899
Mr. STEVEN P. BRESNAHAN, Exec. Dir,
JOHN KRUEGER, Dir. Residential Svcs.
Supervised Living Situation for Persons with Developmental Mental Disabilities
Residents 4

John Paul Apartments
200 Eighth Ave. N.
Cold Spring, MN 56320
Tel: 320-685-4429; Fax: 320-685-7044
E-mail: jpa@cloudnet.com
Pioneer Housing Development, Inc.
JAN LUTHENS, Admin.
Rev. JULIAN SCHMEISING, O.S.B., Chap.
Apartments 61

Mother Teresa Home
101 Tenth Ave.
Cold Spring, MN 56320
Tel: 320-685-8626; Fax: 320-685-8626
Mr. STEVEN P. BRESNAHAN, Exec. Dir.
JOHN KRUEGER, Dir. Residential Svcs.
Supervised Living Situation for Persons with Developed Mental Disabilities
Residents 4

St. Ann's Home
103 10th Ave. N.
Cold Spring, MN 56320
Tel: 320-685-7898; Fax: 320-685-8626
Mr. STEVEN P. BRESNAHAN, Exec, Dir,
JOHN KRUEGER, Dir. Residential Svcs.
Supervised Living Situation for Persons with Developmental Disabilities
Residents 4

St. Luke's Home
411 Eighth Ave. N.
Cold Spring, MN 56320
Tel: 320-685-7750
Mr. STEVEN P. BRESNAHAN, Exec. Dir.
JOHN KRUEGER, Dir. Residential Svcs.
Adults with mild to moderate developmental disabilities.
Residents 4

Crookston
Diocese of Crookston

Villa St. Vincent
516 Walsh St.
Crookston, MN 56716
Tel: 218-281-3424; Fax: 218-281-4755
Mr. MICHAEL SIEKAS, Admin.
Sisters of St. Benedict 2
Board and Care Beds 34
Assisted Living Beds 27
Skilled Nursing Beds 80
Alzheimer's Beds 24
Residents 132
Co-sponsored by the Benedictine Sisters of Crookston, Mt. St. Benedict Monastery and the Benectine Health System.

Detroit Lakes
Diocese of Crookston

St. Mary's Nursing Center
Detroit Lakes, MN 56501
Mr. THOMAS R. THOMPSON, CEO
Residents 100
Attended by Staff of St. Mary's Regional Health Center.

Duluth
Diocese of Duluth

Benedictine Health Center
(Sub. of Benedictine Health System)
935 Kenwood Ave.
Duluth, MN 55811
Tel: 218-723-6408; Fax: 218-723-6449
Sr. DIANE HUNKER, C.S.J., Dir. of Chaplaincy Svcs.
Chaplains:
Rev. BERNARD BRENNAN
JOANN MORK
Rehabilitation services and respite care.
Permanent Guests 120
Day Care:
Adults 46
Children 70

St. Ann's Senior Residence
330 E. Third St.
Duluth, MN 55805
Tel: 218-727-8831; Fax: 218-727-8833
Web Site: www.stanns.com
Sisters of St. Benedict 2
Residents 185

Fergus Falls
Diocese of St. Cloud

Catholic Charities Intensive Treatment Unit
P.O. Box 1006
Fergus Falls, MN 56538-1006
Tel: 218-739-9325; Fax: 218-739-2242
Mr. STEVEN BRESNAHAN, Exec. Dir. in St. Cloud
JOHN KRUEGER, Dir. Residential Svc. in St. Cloud
Children 19
Total Persons 57

Graceville
Diocese of New Ulm

Graceville Health Center dba Trinity Hospital and Grace Hospital
116 W. 2nd St.
Graceville, MN 56240-0157
Tel: 320-748-7261; Fax: 320-748-7225
E-mail: gracehc@info-link.net
Nursing Home
Beds 60
Patients assisted annually 90
Staff 80

Hastings
Archdiocese of St. Paul and Minneapolis

Regina Convalescent and Nursing Care and Retirement Center
Hastings, MN 55033
Tel: 651-480-4336; Fax: 651-480-4212
Web Site: www.reginamedical.com
Rev. JAMES J. DUNNE, S.S.C., Res. Chap.
Regina Healthcare
Tel: 651-480-4100; Fax: 651-480-4212
Number under care 161
Nursing Care 61
Assisted living 134
Total Staff 134
A part of Regina Medical Center

Ivanhoe
Diocese of New Ulm

Divine Prividence Health Center
312 E. George St., P.O. Box G
Ivanhoe, MN 56142-0136
Tel: 507-694-1414; Fax: 507-694-1191
PATRICK BRANCO, Admin.
Rev. MARION G. CASEY, Chap.
Sisters 4
Lay Workers & Other Nurses 134
Aged Residents 51

Little Falls
Diocese of St. Cloud

Alverna Apartments
(An Affiliate of Catholic Health Initiatives.)
300 Eighth Ave., S.E.
Little Falls, MN 56345
Tel: 320-632-1246; Fax: 320-632-1190
BEA BRITZ, Chap.
Residents 63

St. Camillus Place
1100 S.E. Fourth St.
Little Falls, MN 56345
Tel: 320-632-1212; Fax: 320-632-1383
CORY GLAD, Admin.
BARBARA A. MILLER, Dir.
BEA BRITZ, Chap.
Beds 13

St. Otto's Care Center
920 S.E. 4th St.
Little Falls, MN 56345
Tel: 320-632-9281; Fax: 320-632-1120
CORY GLAD, Vice Pres.
SHARON RUHLAND, Chap.
Residents 150

Minneapolis
Archdiocese of St. Paul and Minneapolis

City of Lakes Care Center
110 E. 18th St.
Minneapolis, MN 55403
Tel: 612-879-2800
Mr. PAUL JENSEN, Admin. & CEO

St. Joseph's Home for Children
1121 E. 46th St.
Minneapolis, MN 55407
Tel: 612-827-6241
Mr. CHARLIE LAWLER, Admin.
In res.,
Rev. Msgr. J. JEROME BOXLEITNER
Intake; Emergency Shelter; Diagnostic and Assessment; Serving 4,000 Children Yearly; Residential Treatment (services 81); Day Treatment (services 49); Family Stability (outreach) Serving 120 Families Yearly; 3 Community Homes Serving 115 Yearly.
Lay persons 205

Morris
Diocese of St. Cloud

Villa of St. Francis Nursing Home
1001 Scott Ave.
Morris, MN 56267
Tel: 320-589-1133; Fax: 320-589-3005
E-mail: vosf@info.link.net
CAROL ABELE, Admin.
Guests 114

Parkers Prairie
Diocese of St. Cloud

St. William's Living Center
P.O. Box 30
Parkers Prairie, MN 56361
Tel: 218-338-4671; Fax: 218-338-5917
E-mail: pbaer@midwestinfo.net
PAUL BAER, Admin.
Guests 90

Pierz
Diocese of St. Cloud

St. Mary's Villa Inc.
Pierz, MN 56364
Tel: 320-468-6405
Revs.:
GERALD DALSETH, Chap.
RONALD DOCKENDORF, Chap.
LOREE A. BESSER, Admin.
Guests 83

Rochester
Diocese of Winona

Guest House
4800 48th St., N.E., P.O. Box 954
Rochester, MN 55903
Tel: 800-634-4155; 507-288-4693
E-mail: ghousemn@infonet.isl.net
Web Site: www.ic.net/fighouse/ghouse.html
WILLIAM C. MORGAN, Dir.
A State licensed, JCAHO accredited and ecclesiastically endorsed residential treatment center for priests, brothers, deacons and seminarians. (Corporate headquarters located in Lake Orion, MI 48361)
Bed Capacity 39
Total Assisted 106

Madonna Towers of Rochester, Inc.
4001 19th Ave., N.W.
Rochester, MN 55901
Tel: 507-288-3911; Fax: 507-288-0393
E-mail: mccairns@BHShealth.org
Subsidiary of Benedictine Health System.
MARK CAIRNS, Admin.
Guests 170
Total Staff 170
Chapel of St. Benedict and Chapel of St. Scholastica
Tel: 507-288-3911; Fax: 507-288-0393
Health Care Endowment Fund
4001 19th Ave., N.W.
Rochester, MN 55901
Tel: 507-288-3911; Fax: 507-288-0393

Shakopee
Archdiocese of St. Paul and Minneapolis

St. Gertrude's Health Center
1850 Sarazin St.
Shakopee, MN 55379
Tel: 612-403-3499
LEE LARSON, Admin.
JAMES O'BRIEN, Chairperson
GINI ANDERSON, Treas.

Sleepy Eye
Diocese of New Ulm

Divine Providence Community Home & Lake Villa Maria Senior Apts.
700 3rd Ave. N.W.
Sleepy Eye, MN 56085-1099
Tel: 507-794-3011; 794-5333; Fax: 507-794-3020
E-mail: divine@prairie.lake.com
Daughters of St. Mary of Providence
Sr. SHARON WILLIAMS, D.S.M.P., Admin. & Supr.
Sisters 4
Lay Workers 86
Aged Residents 58
Tenants 26
Total Assisted 84

St. Cloud
Diocese of St. Cloud

Caritas Family Services, Catholic Charities Community Services
305 N. Seventh Ave.
St. Cloud, MN 56303
Tel: 320-650-1660; Fax: 320-252-4508
Web Site: www.stcdio.org/cc/
Mr. STEVEN P. BRESNAHAN, Exec. Dir.

Community Services of Catholic Charities
205 Seventh Ave. N.
St. Cloud, MN 56303
Tel: 320-650-3337; Fax: 320-240-3339
Web Site: www.stcdio.org/cc/
Community Service of Catholic Charities: SILS (Semi-Independent Living Skills), Community Support for Mentally Ill and Related Services to Persons with Disabilities.
Mr. STEVEN P. BRESNAHAN, Exec. Dir.

Day Programs Services
1726 Seventh Ave. S.
St. Cloud, MN 56301
Tel: 320-650-1590; Fax: 320-203-1173
E-mail: nwebster@gw.stcdio.org
Mr. STEVEN P. BRESNAHAN, Exec. Dir.
JOHN KRUEGER, Dir. Residential Svcs.
Students 34

In-Home Family Services, Catholic Charities Community Services
700 Mall Germain
St. Cloud, MN 56302
Tel: 320-251-1404; Fax: 320-252-8180
Web Site: www.stcdio.org/cc/
Mr. STEVEN P. BRESNAHAN, Exec. Dir.

LaPaz Community Inc.
1730 Seventh Ave. S.
St. Cloud, MN 56301
Tel: 320-253-9470; Fax: 320-253-7464
Mr. STEVEN P. BRESNAHAN, Exec. Dir.
HARVEY SCHMITT, Dir. Housing Svcs.

St. Benedict's Senior Community
1810 Minnesota Blvd., S.E.
St. Cloud, MN 56304
Tel: 320-252-0010; Fax: 320-654-2351
LINDA DOERR, Exec. Dir.
DOUG ARETZ, Admin. Care Center
Sr. SUSAN RUDOLPH, O.S.B., Chap. & Dir of Pastoral Care
Rev. MEINRAD DINDORF, O.S.B., Chap.
Corporate Division of the St. Cloud Hospital. Operated under the auspices of the local Catholic Church of St. Cloud.
Residential Homes for residents with Alzheimers. All Benedict Homes are managed by St. Benedict's Senior Community. A division of the St. Cloud Hospital. Operated under the auspices of the local Catholic Church of St. Cloud.
Residents 198
Benedict Village
2000 15th Ave., S.E.
St. Cloud, MN 56304
Tel: 320-252-4380; Fax: 320-654-2351
LINDA DOERR, Exec. Dir.
ROBIN THEIS, Admin., Housing and Community Svcs.
Rev. MEINRAD DINDORF, O.S.B., Chap.
Managed by St. Benedict's Senior Community. A Division of the St. Cloud Hospital. Operated under the auspices of the local Catholic Church of St. Cloud.
Residents 115
Benedict Homes
Ruth House
1342 Minnesota Blvd., S.E.
St. Cloud, MN 56304
Tel: 320-252-0010
Residents 5
Rebekah House
1346 Minnesota Blvd., S.E.
St. Cloud, MN 56304
Tel: 320-252-0010
Residents 5
Daniel House
1344 Minnesota Blvd., S.E.
St. Cloud, MN 56304
Tel: 320-252-0010
Residents 5
Timothy House
1348 Minnesota Blvd., S.E.
St. Cloud, MN 56304
Tel: 320-252-0010
Residents 5
Residential Homes for residents with Alzheimers. All Benedict Homes are managed by St. Benedict's Senior Community. A division of the St. Cloud Hospital. Operated under the auspices of the local Catholic Church of St. Cloud.
Benedict Court
1980 15 Ave., S.E.
St. Cloud, MN 56304
Tel: 320-252-0010
Assisted living apartments-39.
Residents 40
LINDA DOERR, Exec. Dir.
ROBIN THEIS, Admin., Housing and Community Svcs.
Managed by St. Benedict's Senior Community. A Division of the St. Cloud Hospital. Operated under the auspices of the local Catholic Church of St. Cloud.

**Benet Place*
1420 Minnesota Blvd., S.E.
St. Cloud, MN 56304
Tel: 320-252-2557
Subsidized apartments with supportive services for older adults only. Managed by St. Benedict's Senior Community.
Tenants 40
Benet Place South
1975-15th Ave., S.E.
St. Cloud, MN 56304
Tel: 320-529-8700
Tenants 36

St. Cloud Children's Home of the Diocese of St. Cloud
1726 Seventh Ave. S.
St. Cloud, MN 56301
Tel: 320-650-1500; Fax: 320-251-3198
Mr. STEVEN P. BRESNAHAN, Exec. Dir.
JOHN KRUEGER, Dir. Residential Svcs.
Children 78
Youth Learning Center
374 Fourth Ave. S.
St. Cloud, MN 56301
Tel: 320-253-6614

St. Elizabeth Home
306 15th Ave. N.
St. Cloud, MN 56303
Tel: 320-252-8350; Fax: 320-252-8350
E-mail: dtupy@gw.stcdio.org
Mr. STEVEN P. BRESNAHAN, Exec. Dir.
JOHN KRUEGER, Dir. of Residential Svcs.
Board and Lodging Home for Functionally Impaired Adults.
Residents 18

St. Paul
Archdiocese of St. Paul and Minneapolis

Bethany Convent for Retired Sisters
1870 Randolph
St. Paul, MN 55105
Tel: 651-696-2500; Fax: 651-696-2501
Sr. MARY CALDER, C.S.J., Dir. of Community
Sr. GEORGE ANN BOHL, C.S.J., Assoc. Dir. of Community
Sisters of St. Joseph of Carondelet
Total Staff 95
Total in Residence 132

Franciscan Health Community
1925 Norfolk Ave.
St. Paul, MN 55116
Tel: 651-696-8400
JOSEPH STANISLAV, Pres. & CEO
Clergy:
Rev. Msgr. FRANCIS J. FLEMING
Revs.:
MARTIN M.P. FLEMING
JOHN R. FLEMING (NU)
Sisters 4
Aged Residents 223

Good Shepherd Care Center, Inc.
324 Johnson Pkwy.
St. Paul, MN 55106
Tel: 651-774-9737; Fax: 651-774-9641
DENNIS ACREA, Pres.
Patients assisted annually 184

Holy Family Residence
330 S. Exchange St.
St. Paul, MN 55102
Tel: 651-227-0336; Fax: 651-227-7321
Sr. MARGUERITE MCCARTHY, Supr.
Little Sisters of the Poor 12
Aged Residents 73
Apartments 32
Total Staff, all facilities 125

Our House of Minnesota, Inc. I
1846 Dayton Ave.
St. Paul, MN 55104
Tel: 651-644-6650; Fax: 651-646-1104
Office
Tel: 615-646-1104; Fax: 615-646-1104
DENNIS HOLMAN, Admin.
Staff 20
Mentally Handicapped Adults 6
Total Assisted 12

Our House of Minnesota, Inc. II
1846 Portland
St. Paul, MN 55104
Tel: 651-644-2411; Fax: 651-646-1104
Office:
Tel: 615-646-1104; Fax: 615-646-1104
DENNIS HOLMAN, Admin.
Staff 14
Mentally Handicapped Adults 6

Our Lady of Good Counsel Home
2076 St. Anthony Ave.
St. Paul, MN 55104
Tel: 651-646-2797; Fax: 651-646-7884
Sisters of St. Dominic. Servants of Relief for Incurable Cancer
Sr. ANNE MARIE, O.P., Supr.
Sr. MARY DENISE, O.P., Admin.
Rev. JAMES W. JACKSON
Nursing Sisters 7
Bed capacity 40
Patients assisted annually 175
Total Assisted 170
Total Staff 34

Staples
Diocese of St. Cloud

Mary Rondorf Retirement Home of Sacred Heart Parish
Staples, MN 56479
Tel: 218-894-2124; Fax: 218-894-3067
Mrs. VIRGINIA ROLLINS, Admin.
Assisted 26

Wabasha
Diocese of Winona

St. Elizabeth's Health Care Center
626 Shields Ave.
Wabasha, MN 55981
Tel: 651-565-4581
Web Site: www.ministryhealth.org
(Conducted in connection with St. Elizabeth's Hospital of Wabasha, Inc.)
RONALD E. MOHOREK, Esq. & Contact
THOMAS CROWLEY, Admin.
Rev. Msgr. JOSEPH R. MCGINNIS
Skilled Beds 90
Admissions 125
Total Assisted 200
Staff 80
St. Elizabeth's Nursing Home
1200 Fifth Grant Blvd., W.
Wabasha, MN 55981
Tel: 651-565-4531; Fax: 651-565-5679
(Conducted in connection with St. Elizabeth's Hospital of Wabasha, Inc.)
THOMAS CROWLEY, Admin.
Rev. Msgr. JOSEPH R. MCGINNIS
Beds 30
Residents 25
Admissions 25
Total Assisted 55
Staff 20

Waite Park
Diocese of St. Cloud

St. Francis Home
25 Second St. N.
Waite Park, MN 56387
Tel: 320-251-7630
Supervised Living Situation for Persons with Developmental Disabilities
Mr. STEVEN P. BRESNAHAN, Exec. Dir.
JOHN KRUEGER, Dir. Residential Svcs.
Residents 4

West St. Paul
Archdiocese of St. Paul and Minneapolis

Guild Incorporated
1025 Dodd Rd.
West St. Paul, MN 55118
Tel: 612-450-2220
Programs owned by The Guild of Catholic Women. A variety of housing and support services for adults who have experienced serious and persistant mental illness. Apartments and group living available.
Capacity for clients:
St. Paul 160
Total Assisted 435
Total Staff 52

Winona
Diocese of Winona

Franciscan Skemp Behavioral Health
725 W. Broadway
Winona, MN 55987
Tel: 507-454-7711; Fax: 507-452-0325
STEVEN MIDTHUNE, Dir.
Amethyst House
428 W. Broadway
Winona, MN 55987
Tel: 507-452-8877
A 14-bed residential treatment facility for alcohol and chemical abuse
Hiawatha Hall
725 W. Broadway
Winona, MN 55987
Tel: 507-454-7711
A 13-bed mental health residential treatment facility.

Wenonah Hall
221 E. Fourth St.
Winona, MN 55987
Tel: 507-452-1191
10-bed capacity for the mentally ill.
Total Assisted 114
Total Staff 22

St. Anne Retirement Community, Inc.
1347 W. Broadway
Winona, MN 55987
Tel: 507-454-3621; Fax: 507-452-2556
Subsidiary of Benedictine Health Systems.
FRANK MIEZIO, Admin.
Sr. JUNE MARIE TACHENY, Chap.
Bed Capacity 133
Residents 133
Nursing Care for the aged, chronically ill or invalid (resident days) 48,507
Total Staff 200
Callista Court Independent and assisted living for seniors.
1455 W. Broadway
Winona, MN 55987
Tel: 507-457-3810; Fax: 507-494-5117
Units 75
Residents 75
Total Staff 40
Benedictine Adult Day Center
Tel: 507-457-3810; Fax: 507-494-5117
Guest Days 2,600

Winsted
Diocese of New Ulm

St. Mary's Care Center
551 4th St., N, P.O. Box 750
Winsted, MN 55395-0750
Tel: 320-485-2151; Fax: 320-485-4241
E-mail: jdhess@healthdimensions.com
Web Site: www.bhshealth.org
Rev. MARTIN RATH, O.S.B., Chap.
JILL HESS-KOLLASCH, Admin.
Bed Capacity 90

MISSISSIPPI

Bay St. Louis
Diocese of Biloxi

Notre Dame de la Mer Retirement Apartments
292 Hwy. 90
Bay St. Louis, MS 39520
Tel: 228-467-2885; Fax: 228-466-6300
Ms. MICHELE TINE, Mgr.
Total Staff 3
Total in Residence 61

Biloxi
Diocese of Biloxi

Gabriel Manor
2321 Atkinson Rd.
Biloxi, MS 39531
Tel: 228-388-1013; Fax: 228-388-1176
E-mail: gab.apt@worldnet.att.net
Ms. BRENDA MULVANEY, Mgr.
Total Staff 3
Total in Residence 51

Santa Maria Retirement Apartments
674 Beach
Biloxi, MS 39530
Tel: 228-432-1289; Fax: 228-435-0380
E-mail: santamar@datasync.com
Ms. SHARON BALLOW, Mgr.
Total Staff 7
Total in Residence 223

Gulfport
Diocese of Biloxi

Carlow Manor
15195 Barbara Dr.
Gulfport, MS 39503
Tel: 228-539-0707; Fax: 228-539-0704
E-mail: carlowmanor@digiscape.com
ALBERTA VANCE, Mgr.
Total Staff 2
Total in Residence 40

Jackson
Diocese of Jackson

D'Evereaux Hall Home, Inc.
P.O. Box 2248
Jackson, MS 39225
Tel: 601-355-8634
Mrs. LINDA RAFF

St. Mary Orphan Home, Inc.
P.O. Box 2248
Jackson, MS 39225
Tel: 601-355-8634
Mrs. LINDA RAFF

Ocean Springs
Diocese of Biloxi

Samaritan House
642 Jackson Ave.
Ocean Springs, MS 39564
Tel: 228-875-1087; Fax: 228-872-9500
E-mail: samhouse@ametro.net
PATTY ROBERTS, Mgr.
Total Staff 2
Total in Residence 53

Villa Maria Retirement Apartments
921 Porter Ave.
Ocean Springs, MS 39564
Tel: 228-875-8811; Fax: 228-875-8889
E-mail: villacindy@aol.com
Mrs. CINDY A. LADNIER, Mgr.
Total Staff 15
Total in Residence 225

Petal
Diocese of Biloxi

Caritas Manor
145 W. 10th Ave.
Petal, MS 39465
Tel: 601-545-7744; Fax: 601-545-7740
Total Staff 2
Total in Residence 32

MISSOURI

Blue Springs
Diocese of Kansas City-St. Joseph

St. Mary's Manor
111 Mock Ave.
Blue Springs, MO 64014
Tel: 816-228-5655; Fax: 816-228-8480
E-mail: pkelley@carondelet.com
PAT KELLEY, Admin.
Rev. Msgr. TOM O'BRIEN
Revs.:
RONALD VERHAEGHE
MARTIN DEMEULENAERE
Long term care facility with skilled nursing care and residential care.
Skilled care 145
Residential care 57

Cameron
Diocese of Kansas City-St. Joseph

St. Patrick's Manor
514 Northland Dr.
Cameron, MO 64429
Tel: 816-632-1684; Fax: 816-632-7624
GLENNA LYKINS, Mgr.
NEAL D. COLBY, JR., Diocesan Dir.
A 31-unit apartment residence for the elderly and disabled.
Total Staff 2

Eureka
Archdiocese of St. Louis

Price Memorial
Forby Rd., P.O. Box 476
Eureka, MO 63025
Tel: 636-587-3200; Fax: 636-938-2266
Bro. JOHN SPILA, O.S.F., Admin.
A skilled nursing facility conducted by the Franciscan Missionary Brothers of St. Joseph's Hill Infirmary.
Brothers 3
Residents 120

St. Joseph Hill Infirmary, Inc. dba St. Joseph Hill Infirmary
St. Joseph Rd.
Eureka, MO 63025
Tel: 636-587-3661; Fax: 636-938-6398
Bro. BERNARDO TROSA, O.S.F., Admin.
A skilled nursing facility conducted by the Franciscan Missionary Brothers of the Sacred Heart of Jesus.
Brothers 11
Residents 127
Total Assisted 120
Total Staff 55

Florissant
Archdiocese of St. Louis

Father Dunne's News Boys Home
853 Dunn Rd.
Florissant, MO 63031
Tel: 314-837-0513; Fax: 314-837-0883
E-mail: cblake@archstl.org
Corporate Title: Father Dunne's Newsboys' Home and Protectorate
CHRISTOPHER M. BLAKE, Exec. Dir. & CEO
Emergency and long-term residential care & treatment for homeless, neglected and abused boys, status offenders and boys with family problems. Ages 12-21.
Monthly Residents 24
Total in Residence 64
Total Assisted 276
Total Staff 24

Marygrove Services, Inc.
2705 Mullanphy Ln.
Florissant, MO 63031
Tel: 314-837-1702; Fax: 314-830-6263
E-mail: mgrove@swb.net
Owned and operated under the auspices of Catholic Charities.
Sr. HELEN NEGRI, D.C., Admin.
Residential treatment for emotionally disturbed males and females (ages 6-21). Special education, therapy and medical services. Overnight emergency care: males and females (Birth-21).
Bed Capacity 97
Total Assisted 4,172
Total Staff 140
Sequoia House - Mullanphy
Tel: 314-837-1702; Fax: 314-830-6260
Beds 10
Group Home for Females Ages 17-21.
Sequoia Apartment Services
Tel: 314-837-1702
Sycamore House
Tel: 814-830-1329
Bed Capacity 3
Overnight Emergency Care: Bed Capacity 8

Jefferson City
Diocese of Jefferson City

St. Joseph's Home
1306 W. Main St.
Jefferson City, MO 65109
Tel: 573-635-0166; Fax: 573-635-1405
Conducted by the Carmelite Sisters of the Divine Heart of Jesus.
GRACE HOFFMANN, Admin.
Sr. M. BERNADETTE NIEHAUS, Supr.
DENISE SOMMERER, Dir. Nurses
Rev. Msgr. CHARLES PATTERSON, Chap.
Sisters 3
Residents 90

Villa Marie Skilled Nursing Facility
1030 Edmonds St.
Jefferson City, MO 65109
Tel: 573-761-6700
Member of SSM Health Care
JOHN H. SCHULTE, Admin.
Ms. BARBARA L. LOWRY, Dir. Nursing Svcs.
Franciscan Sisters of Mary, St Louis 4
Bed Capacity 120

Kansas City
Diocese of Kansas City-St. Joseph

Brighton Place
2429 Brighton
Kansas City, MO 64127
Tel: 816-483-8299
JERRY NAYLOR, Mgr.
A 31-unit residence for the elderly and disabled.

Carondelet Manor
621 Carondelet Dr.
Kansas City, MO 64114
Tel: 816-943-4777
DIANNE DOCTOR, Admin.
Bed Capacity 180
Legal Title: *Carondelet Long Term Care Facilities, Inc.*
Owned and operated by Carondelet Long Term Care Facilities, Inc. Sponsored by Sisters of St. Joseph of Carondelet.

Cathedral Square Towers
444 W. 12th St.
Kansas City, MO 64105
Tel: 816-471-6555; Fax: 816-421-1279
Apartment residence for the elderly and handicapped.
JAN CARSON, Mgr.

Mr. NEAL D. COLBY, JR., Diocesan Liaison
Units 156
Total in Residence 167
Total Staff 10

Columbus Park Plaza
801 Pacific
Kansas City, MO 64106
Tel: 816-472-0887; Fax: 816-472-6105
E-mail: columbus@planetkc.com
SANDY SCHAEFER, Mgr.
Mr. NEAL D. COLBY, Diocesan Liaison
Apartment residence for elderly and handicapped.
Units 56
Total in Residence 55
Total Staff 2

Jeanne Jugan Center
8745 James A. Reed Rd.
Kansas City, MO 64138
Tel: 816-761-4744; Fax: 816-761-4724
Legal Title: *Little Sisters of the Poor*
Little Sisters of the Poor
Sr. ANDREA MUNARRIZ, Supr.
Rev. JOHN MCCORMACK, Chap.
Sisters 11
Apartments 33
Beds 76
Total in Residence 95
Total Staff 94

Marlborough Manor
1818 E. 79th St.
Kansas City, MO 64132
Tel: 816-333-7761; Fax: 816-523-2388
E-mail: marlborough@planetKC.com
LOUISE SHEPHERD, Mgr.
Rental housing for low income (a 31-unit apartment residence for the elderly and disabled).
Total in Residence 31
Total Staff 2

Red Bridge Place
11300 Colorado
Kansas City, MO 64137
Tel: 816-761-4667; Fax: 816-761-4769
LINDA BARBER, Mgr.
Total in Residence 46
Total Staff 3

Tremont Place
6161 N. Chatham
Kansas City, MO 64151
Tel: 816-587-7707; Fax: 816-587-7637
E-mail: tremont@crn.org
DONNA QUICK, Mgr.
A 50-unit apartment residence for the elderly and disabled.

Kirkwood
Archdiocese of St. Louis

St. Agnes Home for the Elderly
10341 Manchester Rd.
Kirkwood, MO 63122
Tel: 314-965-7616; Fax: 314-965-3179
Sr. M. ANGELINA Finnel, Carmel.D.C.J., Admin.
Rev. Msgr. BERNARD GRANICH
Conducted for Elderly Ladies, Gentlemen and Couples by the Carmelite Sisters of the Divine Heart of Jesus.
Legal Title: *Carmelite Sisters of the Divine Heart of Jesus of Missouri*
Sisters 10
Guests 124
Total Staff 110

Liberty
Diocese of Kansas City-St. Joseph

Immacolata Manor
2101 Hughes Rd.
Liberty, MO 64068-9397
Tel: 816-781-4332; Fax: 816-781-8820
E-mail: immanor@crn.org
Residential and day habilitation services for women with developmental disabilities.
NANCY MILLER, Exec. Dir.
WILLIAM WEBB, Pres.
Operated by the Immacolata Board of Directors.
Residents 25
Total Staff 34

Our Lady of Mercy Country Home
2205 Hughes Rd.
Liberty, MO 64068
Tel: 816-781-5711; Fax: 816-781-7276
Web Site: ourladyofmercy.net
Mercedarian Missionaries of Berriz
Sr. BETTY PRESTON, M.M.B., Pres.
Guests 100
Sisters 19

Normandy
Archdiocese of St. Louis

Maria Droste Residence
7660 Natural Bridge Rd.
Normandy, MO 63121
Tel: 314-383-5553; Fax: 314-382-5294
Sisters of the Good Shepherd
For Women in Need.
Capacity 11
Total Assisted 70
Total Staff 6

St. Vincent Home for Children
7401 Florissant Rd.
Normandy, MO 63121
Tel: 314-261-6011; Fax: 314-385-1467
Legal Title: *The German St. Vincent Orphan Association*
Mr. WILLIAM J. DONLEY, Exec. Dir.
Children 48
Total Assisted 66
Total Staff 72
Chapel of the Sacred Heart.

Savannah
Diocese of Kansas City-St. Joseph

La Verna Heights Retirement Center, Inc.
104 E. Park Ave., P.O. Box 488
Savannah, MO 64485-0488
Tel: 816-324-3179; Fax: 816-324-6512
E-mail: osf@ccp.com
MICHAEL BURAK, Admin.
Sisters of St. Francis of Savannah
Guest Capacity 39
Total Assisted 54
Total Staff 48

La Verna Village Apartments
1000-1005 Hall Ave.
Savannah, MO 64485
Tel: 816-324-3179; Fax: 816-324-7264
Sisters of St. Francis of Savannah
Rev. ALEXANDER LUETKEMEYER, O.S.B.
DOYLE MCCUSH, Mgr.
Apartments for the elderly and handicapped.
Units 20
Total in Residence 23
Total Staff 1

La Verna Village Nursing Home
904 Hall Ave., P.O. Box 279
Savannah, MO 64485
Tel: 816-324-3185; Fax: 816-324-4097
MICHAEL BURAK, Admin.
Sisters of St. Francis of Savannah
Guest Capacity 120
Total Assisted 201
Total Staff 127

Springfield
Diocese of Springfield-Cape Girardeau

St. John's Mercy Villa
1100 E. Montclair
Springfield, MO 65807
Tel: 417-888-8500; Fax: 417-888-8532
Sisters of Mercy Healthcare System (St. Louis)
Skilled Care of Long Term Nursing Home, for the Aged and Chronically Ill.
Mr. GENE VESTAL, Admin.
Rev. WAYNE J. BARRON, C.M.F., Chap.
Bed Capacity 147

St. Charles
Archdiocese of St. Louis

St. Joseph Carmelite Home
723 First Capitol Dr.
St. Charles, MO 63301
Tel: 314-946-4140; Fax: 314-218-1104
E-mail: stjoseph@carmelitedcj.org
Web Site: carmelitedcj.org
Rev. ALBERT F. DANTER, Chap.
Conducted by the Carmelite Sisters of the Divine Heart of Jesus
Legal Title: *Carmelite Sisters of the Divine Heart of Jesus of Missouri*
Sisters 7
Guests 110
Total Staff 117

St. Louis
Archdiocese of St. Louis

Alexian Brothers Lansdowne Village
4624 Lansdowne
St. Louis, MO 63116
Tel: 314-351-6888; Fax: 314-351-5825
Total Assisted 390
Total Staff 170

Alexian Brothers Sherbrooke Village
4005 Ripa Ave.
St. Louis, MO 63125
Tel: 314-544-1111; Fax: 314-544-5134
C. MICHAEL ROTH, Pres.
Total in Residence (Assisted Living) 43
Total Assisted (Nursing Care) 113
Total Staff 130

Boys Hope/Girls Hope of St. Louis, Inc.
755 S. New Ballas Rd., Ste. 120
St. Louis, MO 63141
Tel: 314-692-7477; Fax: 314-692-7810
E-mail: sbrock@bhgh.org
Web Site: www.boyshopegirlshope.org/stlouis.htm
JULIE SHERIDAN, Exec. Dir.
Residential Care for Adolescent Boys and Girls, Troubled by Family Disruptions, who are Capable of College Preparatory High School Work. Ages 7-18.
Total Assisted 17
Total Staff 6

Cathedral Tower
325 N. Newstead Ave.
St. Louis, MO 63108
Tel: 314-531-0511, Ext. 114; Fax: 314-533-6073
E-mail: nrichter@archstl.org
Ms. RUTH RAITHEL, Admin.
Building which houses several agencies of Catholic Charities: Queen of Peace Center; St. Elizabeth Hall; Marion Hall; Catholic Community Services and Dial Help.
Residents 100

Chariton Apartments
4249 Michigan Ave.
St. Louis, MO 63111
Tel: 314-352-7600; Fax: 314-352-0022
Retirement Home for the Elderly, Conducted by the Third Order of St. Francis, Franciscan Tertiary Province of Missouri, Inc.
Total Staff 4
Residents 110
Apartments 122

Father Dempsey's Hotel, Inc.
3427 Washington Ave.
St. Louis, MO 63103
Tel: 314-535-7221
Rev. Msgr. CHARLES A. MOTTIN, Dir.
Total in Residence 49
Total Staff 4

Father Jim's Home
3427 Washington Ave.
St. Louis, MO 63103
Tel: 314-535-7221
Rev. Msgr. CHARLES A. MOTTIN, Gen. Mgr.
Under Care 81
Total in Residence 49
Total Staff 4

Fusz Pavilion
3601 Lindell Blvd.
St. Louis, MO 63108
Tel: 314-534-1201; Fax: 314-977-7211
A Retirement Home for Jesuits.
Rev. ALBERT C. ROTOLA, S.J., Rector
Bro. ROBERT L. AUG, S.J., Asst. Rector
Revs.:
PHILIP D. KRAUS, S.J., Aide to Rector
LAWRENCE E. BARRY, S.J.
JOHN E. BLEWETT, S.J.
JULES M. BRADY, S.J.
JOHN C. CHOPPESKY, S.J.
DARYL G. CORNISH, S.J.
CHESTER E. GAITER, S.J.
JOSEPH E. GOUGH, S.J.
JOHN G. FLANNIGAN, S.J.
JOSEPH M. FREEMAN, S.J.
EDWARD D. HARRIS, S.J.
ROBERT F. HOULIHAN, S.J.
WILLIAM J. KANE, S.J.
EUGENE D. KELLY, S.J.
HARRY R. KLOCKER, S.J.
EDWARD P. MANHARD, S.J.
J. PAUL O'CONNOR, S.J.
WALTER J. ONG, S.J.
FREDERICK E. SCHULLER, S.J.
BERNARD C. SCHULTE, S.J.

THOMAS F. THRO, S.J.
Bros.:
LAWRENCE W. EILERT, S.J.
JOSEPH L. GOCKEL, S.J.
Priests 22
Brothers 3
Total Assisted 22
Total Staff 3

Little Sisters of the Poor, Home for the Aged
3225 N. Florissant Ave.
St. Louis, MO 63107
Tel: 314-421-6022; Fax: 314-436-9069
Sr. MARY SYLVIA KARL, L.S.P., Supr.
Chaplains:
Revs.:
SIMON BRZOZOWSKI, M.S.F.
EUGENE RONAN, M.S.F.
Sisters 13
Residents 100
Total Assisted 112
Total Staff 110

Marian Hall Agencies
1340 Partridge Ave.
St. Louis, MO 63130
Tel: 314-726-3339; Fax: 314-726-3470
E-mail: srclarke@archstl.org
Sr. ANNE CLARKE, O.P., Admin.
Residential Care to Homeless, Neglected and Abused Adolescent Girls (ages 11-18) with Emotional and/or Behavioral Problems.
Legal Title: *Managers of the Roman Catholic Orphan Asylums of St. Louis*
Sisters 2
Lay Staff 25
Capacity 24
Total Assisted 657

Marian Hall Emergency Shelter
325 N. Newstead
St. Louis, MO 63108
Tel: 314-531-0511; Fax: 314-531-2993
Emergency Shelter in a Residential Setting for Runaway, Homeless or Abused Adolescent Girls (ages 11-18), with Emotional and/or Behavioral Problems.
Legal Title: *Managers of the Roman Catholic Orphan Asylums of St. Louis*
Total Staff 10
Capacity 10
Total Assisted 150

Mary, Queen and Mother Center
7601 Watson Rd.
St. Louis, MO 63119
Tel: 314-961-8000; Fax: 314-961-1548
E-mail: rmantia@archstl.org
Web Site: cardinalcarberry.org
RONALD MANTIA, Admin.
Skilled Nursing Facility.
Total Staff 201
Total in Residence 230
A part of Cardinal Carberry Living Center

Mother of Good Counsel Home
6825 Natural Bridge Rd., (St. Louis Co.)
St. Louis, MO 63121
Tel: 314-383-4765
Sr. M. STEPHANIE BELGERI, O.S.F., Admin.
Rev. ARTHUR BROMSCHWIG
Skilled Nursing Facility for Men and Women.
Conducted by Sisters of St. Francis of the Martyr St. George
Sisters 13
Residents 114
Total Staff 156

Mother of Perpetual Help Residence
7609 Watson Rd.
St. Louis, MO 63119
Tel: 314-961-8000; Fax: 314-961-1934
E-mail: swesley@archstl.org
Sr. SUZANNE WESLEY, Exec. Dir.
KAREN LEDBETTER, Admin.
Total Assisted 111
Total Staff 36
A part of Cardinal Carberry Living Center

Nazareth Living Center
2 Nazareth Ln.
St. Louis, MO 63129
Tel: 314-487-3950; Fax: 314-487-8001
E-mail: lwesthoff@nlccsj.com
Residential and Skilled Nursing Care Facility.
Sisters of St. Joseph of Carondelet and General Public
Sr. AUDREY OLSON, C.S.J., Supr.
Rev. THOMAS GRAHAM, Chap.
LOLA J. WESTHOFF, Exec. Dir.
Total Assisted 272
Total Staff 279

Our Lady of Life Apartments, Inc.
7655 Watson Rd.
St. Louis, MO 63119
Tel: 314-968-9447
E-mail: jschwaegel@archstl.org
Total Assisted 252
Total Staff 67
A part of Cardinal Carberry Living Center.

Queen of Peace Center
325 N. Newstead Ave.
St. Louis, MO 63108
Tel: 314-531-0511; Fax: 314-531-1458
E-mail: cneumann@archstl.org
CONSTANCE S. NEUMANN, Admin.
Comprehensive substance abuse treatment and rehabilitation for women and their children, including in-patient/outpatient. Licensed by DMH and accredited by COA. Licensed day care, infant care, development center and licensed comprehensive psychiatric services, licensed by SMH, St. Louis City Health Department, Missouri Department of Health and accredited by COA. Transitional housing and therapeutic services for drug-affected, homeless city women and their children, accredited by COA. Housing subsidy for the disabled homeless.
Beds 86
Outpatient 250
Total Assisted 3,000
Total Staff 86

Regina Cleri Residence
7850 Kenrick Rd.
St. Louis, MO 63119
Tel: 314-968-2240; Fax: 314-968-1049
E-mail: reginacleri@earthlink.net
A Residence for Retired Diocesan Priests of the Archdiocese of St. Louis. Conducted by the Archdiocese of St. Louis.
Sr. GERALDINE VOGEL, C.PP.S., Admin.
Sisters of the Most Precious Blood of O'Fallon, MO 4
Franciscan Sisters of Our Lady of Perpetual Help 2
Priests 30
Total Staff 24
Total Assisted 40

Rosati Group Home, Inc.
4532 Lindell Blvd.
St. Louis, MO 63108
Tel: 314-367-5500; Fax: 314-367-2982
RICHARD J. VEHIGE, Pres.
Group Home and Stabilization Center for homeless mentally ill adults.
Total Assisted 50
Total Staff 10

Rosati Stabilization Center
4224 N. Grand Ave.
St. Louis, MO 63107
Tel: 314-534-6624; Fax: 314-535-4394
Residential Transitional Facility for Mentally Ill Homeless.
Managed by the St. Patrick Center.
Capacity 15
Total Assisted 83
Total Staff 12

St. Joseph's Home for Boys
4753 S. Grand Blvd.
St. Louis, MO 63111-1459
Tel: 314-481-9121; Fax: 314-481-5605
E-mail: bbradley@archstl.org
Web Site: www.stjosephhome.org
BRUCE B. BRADLEY, Exec. Dir.
Emergency and Long-Term Residential Treatment Center for Young Men (ages 6-14) with Moderate to Severe Behavioral, Emotional, Family, and/or Educational Problems. Majority are Survivors of Neglect and/or Abuse. Day Treatment Program for Grades 1-8, Residents and Day Students.
Legal Title: *Managers of the Roman Catholic Orphan Asylums of St. Louis*
Sisters of St. Joseph of Carondelet 1
Lay Staff 25
Residential 46
Day Treatment 30
Total Assisted 76

St. Martha's Hall
P.O. Box 4950
St. Louis, MO 63108
Tel: 314-533-1313; Fax: 314-533-2035
MICHELLE SCHILLER-BAKER, Dir.
Provides Shelter, Advocacy and Support to Abused Women & their Children.
Capacity 25
Total Assisted 241

St. Philippine Duchesne Shelter
1015 Goodfellow Blvd.
St. Louis, MO 63112
Tel: 314-454-1012; Fax: 314-367-7455
Transitional housing for drug affected homeless city women and their children.
Total Assisted 45
Total Staff 9

SSM Cardinal Glennon Children's Hospital
1465 S. Grand Blvd.
St. Louis, MO 63104
Tel: 314-577-5600; Fax: 314-268-6468
E-mail: Doug_Ries@ssmhc.com
Web Site: www.cardinalglennon.com
Mr. DOUGLAS A. RIES, Pres.
Member of SSM Health Care.
Sisters 4
Bed Capacity (for Children) 190
Patients assisted annually 183,944
Total Staff 1,374

SSM Rehab
6420 Clayton Rd., Exec. Offices
St. Louis, MO 63117-1861
Tel: 314-768-5300; Fax: 314-768-5355
Web Site: www.ssmrehab.com
Member of SSM Health Care.
MELINDA CLARK, Pres.
For rehabilitation of pediatrics, adolescents and adults
Bed Capacity:
SSM St. Mary's Health Center, St. Louis 60
SSM St. Joseph Health Center, St. Charles 20
Outpatient Locations 14

Villa Maria Center
2647 Ohio Ave.
St. Louis, MO 63118
Tel: 314-664-4715; Fax: 314-664-4970
Ms. SUZANNE KING, L.C.S.W., Dir.
Under the Auspices of Catholic Services for Children and Youth. Comprehensive Residential Program for Pregnant and Parenting Teenage Girls; Provides Individual, Family and Group Counseling, Arranges Obstetrical and Pediatric Care, Provides Educational Services Including Academic and Personal Growth and Development, Training in Parenting and Living Skill.
Capacity 15 Teens and 9 Children
Total Assisted 50
Total Staff 20

NEBRASKA

Boys Town
Archdiocese of Omaha

**Father Flanagan's Boys' Home*
Boys Town, NE 68010
Tel: 402-498-1000; Fax: 402-498-1010
E-mail: peterv@boustown.org
Web Site: www.boystown.org
Rev. VALENTINE J. PETER, Exec. Dir.
Dr. PATRICK MCGINNIS, Dir. Education
Rev. EUGENE MCREYNOLDS, O.S.B.
High School:
Dr. RICHARD LOHMEIER, Prin.
Teachers 28
Students 489
Grade School:
CATHY DESALVO, Prin.
Teachers 13
Students 133
Boys Town USA
Tel: 402-498-1928; Fax: 402-498-1010
CAROLYN NOVICOFF, Assoc. Exec. Dir., U.S.A.
Dr. JERRY DAVIS, Assoc. Exec. Dir. (Prog. & Staff Devel.)
Dr. DAN DALY, Assoc. Exec. Dir., Home Campus
Boys Town National Research & Training Center
Tel: 402-498-1560; Fax: 402-498-1500
RUBY ASUGHA, Assoc. Exec. Dir.
BOB PICK, Dir. of Operations
Boys Town National Research Hospital for Children
Tel: 402-498-6501; Fax: 402-498-6357
Dr. PATRICK BROOKHOUSER, Dir.
Boys Town Crisis Hotline
Tel: 800-448-3000; Fax: 402-498-6357
DEE KOHLER, Coord.
Boys Town Religious Education Program
Tel: 402-498-1885; Fax: 402-498-1010
KATHY SORENSEN, Assoc. Dir.
Total Assisted 33,601
Total Staff 2,254

David City
Diocese of Lincoln

St. Joseph's Villa, Inc.
927 7th St.
David City, NE 68632
Tel: 402-367-3045; Fax: 402-367-3730

E-mail: st33446@navix.net
Sisters Adorers of the Blood of Christ (Wichita, KS)
JOYCE STEWART, Admin.
Residents 64

Kearney
Diocese of Grand Island

Mount Carmel Home-Keens' Memorial
412 W. 18th St.
Kearney, NE 68847
Tel: 308-237-2287; Fax: 308-236-9380
E-mail: marycarmelite@hotmail.com
Web Site: www.carmelites.org/corpuschristi.htm
Sr. DELPHINE NAPOLEONI, O.Carm., Supr.
Carmelites 14
Guests 75
Total Staff 95

Lincoln
Diocese of Lincoln

Bonacum House
3301 Sheridan Blvd.
Lincoln, NE 68506
Tel: 402-483-0391
Residence for retired priests.
Rev. Msgr. CHARLES J. KEENAN
Rev. Msgr. JEROME E. MURRAY
Rev. Msgr. CLARENCE P. REISDORFF
Revs.:
JOHN J. GLAVES
PATRICK J. LYONS
JOHN W. KELLY
JOHN A. ZASTROW

Madonna Rehabilitation Hospital
5401 South St.
Lincoln, NE 68506
Tel: 402-489-7102; Fax: 402-483-9460
E-mail: feedback@madonna.org
Web Site: www.madonna.org
Physical Medicine and Rehabilitation, Outpatient Services, Long-Term Care, Adult Day Care, and Supportive Inpatient Hospice Care.
Rev. PAUL J. RUTTEN, Chap.
Sisters 9
Beds 252
Patients assisted annually 5,123

Norfolk
Archdiocese of Omaha

St. Joseph Nursing Home
401 N. 18th St.
Norfolk, NE 68701
Tel: 402-371-9404
E-mail: bdisch@frhs.org
BILL DISCH, Admin. & Contact
Missionary Benedictine Sisters 1
Aged Residents 99

Omaha
Archdiocese of Omaha

**Bergan Mercy Care Center*
1870 S. 75th St.
Omaha, NE 68124
Tel: 402-398-8500
Sisters of Mercy of the Americas
SHEILA BURKE, Contact Person
S. DOTTIE BROWN, Operations Dir.
Subacute Care/Skilled Nursing Facility.
Beds 217
Average Daily Census 210
Total Assisted 1,730
Affiliate of Catholic Health Initiatives.

Mercy Villa
1845 S. 72nd St.
Omaha, NE 68124
Tel: 402-391-6224; Fax: 402-391-1872
E-mail: johneenO@mercyoma.org
Retirement Home for the Sisters of Mercy of the Americas for the Omaha Region
Sr. JOHNEEN OWENS, R.S.M., Coord.
Rev. EDWARD SCHAD, Chap.
Resident Sisters 48
Total Assisted 38
Total Staff 55

New Cassel Retirement Center
900 N. 90th St.
Omaha, NE 68114
Tel: 402-393-2277; Fax: 402-393-3784
Web Site: www.newcassel.org
School Sisters of St. Francis
Mr. JOSEPH H. SCHULTE, Dir.
Rev. JAMES R. TIEGS
MARY KERRES, Dir. Pastoral Care
JOSEPH H. SCHULTE, Contact
Sisters 1
Aged Residents 165
Total Staff 73

West Point
Archdiocese of Omaha

Franciscan Care Services, Inc., (dba St. Joseph Retirement Community)
320 E. Decatur
West Point, NE 68788
Tel: 402-372-3477; Fax: 402-372-6600
Sr. ANGELINE HENSEN, Admin. & Contact
Franciscan Sisters of Christian Charity, Manitowoc, WI 6
Residents 90
Total Assisted 10735

NEW HAMPSHIRE

Allenstown
Diocese of Manchester

Pine Haven Boys Center
River Rd., P.O. Suncook
Allenstown, NH 03275
Tel: 603-485-7141; Fax: 603-485-7142
Somascan Fathers
Revs.:
JOHN VITALI, C.R.S., M.Ed., Dir.
GIULIANO GEROSA, C.R.S., M.A., Supr.
PAOLO RIVA, C.R.S.
ZANATTA REMO, C.R.S.
Total Staff 38
Children 20

Berlin
Diocese of Manchester

St. Vincent de Paul Nursing Home
29 Providence Ave.
Berlin, NH 03570-3199
Tel: 603-752-1820; Fax: 603-752-7149
JEFFREY MARTIN, Admin.
New Hampshire Catholic Charities.
Total Staff 112
Residents 76

Dover
Diocese of Manchester

St. Ann Home
195 Dover Point Rd.
Dover, NH 03820-4693
Tel: 603-742-2612; Fax: 603-743-3055
Rev. KAREN PAINTER, Admin.
New Hampshire Catholic Charities.
Total Staff 75
Residents 54
Bishop Gendron Apartments
Total Staff 1
Apartments 31
CATHY MEATTEY-STAWARZ, Apartment Mgr.

Jaffrey
Diocese of Manchester

Good Shepherd Nursing Home
20 Plantation Dr.
Jaffrey, NH 03452-1935
Tel: 603-532-8762; Fax: 603-532-6057
JUDITH A. LEBLANC, Admin.
Rev. JOHN H. BRYSON, Chap.
New Hampshire Catholic Charities.
Total Staff 115
Total Assisted 83

Laconia
Diocese of Manchester

Bishop Bradley Apartments
406 Court St.
Laconia, NH 03246
Total Staff 2
Aged residents 27
Apartments 25

St. Francis Health Care Facility
406 Court St.
Laconia, NH 03246-3000
Tel: 603-524-0466; Fax: 603-527-0884
Mrs. JULIEANN R. FAY, Admin.
Rev. ANDRE J. GAGNON, Chap.
New Hampshire Catholic Charities.
Total Staff 70
Residents 51
Bishop Bradley Apartments
Total Staff 2
Apartments 25
MARLENE MAKOWSKI, Apartment Mgr.

Manchester
Diocese of Manchester

Carpenter Center, Inc.
323 Franklin St.
Manchester, NH 03101
Tel: 603-625-5422; Fax: 603-625-1014
E-mail: dbhinc@grolen.com
CAROL HAEBLER, Mgr.
Apartments 96
DBH Shelter, Inc.
Tel: 603-625-5422; Fax: 603-625-1014
DBH Shelter II, Inc.
Apartments 8
DBH Shelter III, Inc.
Apartments 28
DBH Management, Inc.
Total Staff 10
Total Assisted 132

Frances Warde House, Inc.
435 Union St.
Manchester, NH 03103
Residents 26

Mt. Carmel Nursing Home
235 Myrtle St.
Manchester, NH 03104-4399
Tel: 603-627-3811; Fax: 603-626-4696
STEPHEN FULCHINO, Admin.
Rev. MAURICE LAGUEUX, Chap.
New Hampshire Catholic Charities.
Total Staff 140
Residents 120

St. Peter's Home
300 Kelley St.
Manchester, NH 03102-3093
Tel: 603-625-9313; Fax: 603-625-1910
Sr. FLORENCE THERRIEN, S.C.S.H., Dir.
Mrs. DONNA M. VACHON, Asst. Dir.
Sr. RITA BEAULIEU, S.C.S.H., Treas.
Sisters of Charity (Grey Nuns) 4
Total Staff 75
Children 309

St. Teresa's Manor
519 Bridge St.
Manchester, NH 03104-5396
Tel: 603-668-2373; Fax: 603-668-0059
MONIQUE DOSOGNE, Admin.
Rev. J. KIERAN O'CONNOR, Chap.
New Hampshire Catholic Charities.
Total Staff 72
Aged Residents 51
Bishop Primeau Apartments
Total Staff 3
Apartments 25
LINDA ILLG, Apt. Mgr.

Nashua
Diocese of Manchester

Marguerite's Place
87 Palm St.
Nashua, NH 03060
Tel: 603-598-1582; Fax: 603-598-7574
E-mail: margplace@aol.com
Sr. MARY SHARON WALSH, G.N.S.H., CEO
Total Staff 15
Total in Residence 25

Rochester
Diocese of Manchester

St. Charles Children's Home
19 Grant St.
Rochester, NH 03867-3099
Tel: 603-332-4768; Fax: 603-332-3948
Sisters of Charity of Our Lady, Mother of The Church
Mother M. PAUL MARIE, Admin.
Rev. MAURICE R. BOULANGER, Chap.
New Hampshire Catholic Charities.
Sisters 7
Dependent Children 25

Windham
Diocese of Manchester

Warde Health Center
21 Searles Rd.
Windham, NH 03087-1297
Tel: 603-890-1290; Fax: 603-890-1293
Sisters of Mercy
Sr. JANICE TURNER, Admin.
Managed by New Hampshire Catholic Charities.

Total Staff 37
Residents 28
Total Assisted 40

NEW JERSEY

Caldwell
Archdiocese of Newark

St. Catherine of Siena
7 Ryerson Ave.
Caldwell, NJ 07006
Tel: 973-226-1577; Fax: 973-226-3977
Sr. Marge Jaros, Pres.
Sr. Veritas Picardi, Treas.
Sr. Joan Doyle, Sec.

Cape May
Diocese of Camden

Victorian Towers Associates
608 Washington St.
Cape May, NJ 08204
Tel: 609-884-5883; Fax: 609-884-5625
E-mail: victoriantowers@snip.net
Total in Residence 262
Total Staff 7

Cedar Grove
Archdiocese of Newark

St. Vincent's Nursing Home
(Div. of St. Joseph's Hospital and Medical Center)
315 E. Lindsley Rd.
Cedar Grove, NJ 07009
Tel: 973-754-4800; Fax: 973-746-2362
E-mail: pintod@sjhmc.org
Conducted by Sisters of Charity of St. Elizabeth
Mr. Thomas P. Sheehy, Jr., Admin.
Sisters 5
Capacity: Long term care beds 141
Patients assisted annually 220
Total Staff 200

Cherry Hill
Diocese of Camden

The Manor at St. Mary's
220 St. Mary's Dr.
Cherry Hill, NJ 08003
Tel: 856-424-3817; Fax: 856-424-5128
Sr. Frances Szymanska, L.S.I.C., Admin.
Total in Residence 81
Total Staff 47

Marian Residence
1000 Cropwell Rd.
Cherry Hill, NJ 08003
Tel: 856-424-1131; Fax: 856-424-5333
Sr. M. Melchior, L.S.I.C., Supvr.
Total in Residence 5
Total Staff 2

St. Mary's Nursing Home
210 St. Mary's Dr.
Cherry Hill, NJ 08003
Tel: 856-424-9521; Fax: 856-424-5143
Little Servant Sisters of the Immaculate Conception
Sr. Mary Frances Szymanska, Supr.
Sr. M. Beatrix Wieczorek, Admin.
Mr. James J. Heinz, Assoc. Admin.
Rev. Gerald Clements, Chap.
Sisters 8
Residents 215
Total Staff 240
Total Assisted Annually 292

Village Apartments of Cherry Hill, NJ, Inc.
212 Lourdes Ct.
Cherry Hill, NJ 08003
Tel: 856-424-7913; Fax: 856-424-9211
Mr. James Sweeney, Supt.
Total in Residence 168
Total Staff 7

Denville
Diocese of Paterson

Franciscan Oaks Independent Living Units & Health Center
21 Pocono Rd.
Denville, NJ 07834
Tel: 973-586-5000; Fax: 973-586-5039
Sponsored by Sisters of the Sorrowful Mother.

St. Francis Residential Community
Denville, NJ 07834
Fax: 973-625-9245
E-mail: billmili@aol.com
Rest and Residential Home
Mr. William Milianes, Admin.
Rev. William J. Freeswick, Chap.
Sisters of the Sorrowful Mother 16
Bed Capacity 100
Apartments 63
Guests 150

Hoboken
Archdiocese of Newark

Good Counsel, Inc. (St. Francis Home)
303 Madison St.
Hoboken, NJ 07030
Tel: 201-798-9059; 795-0637; 800-723-8331 (Hotline); Fax: 201-795-0809
E-mail: cxbell@aol.com
Rev. Benedict J. Groeschel, C.F.R., Chm.
Christopher R. Bell, Exec. Dir.
Housing, counseling and referrals for single women who are pregnant or single mothers with children.
Good Counsel, Inc.
P.O. Box 6068
Hoboken, NJ 07030
Tel: 201-795-0637
Residences for single mothers and children.
Rev. Benedict J. Groeschel, C.F.R., Chm.
Christopher R. Bell, Exec. Dir.
Patients assisted annually 347
Total Staff 72

Hopewell
Diocese of Trenton

St. Michael's Orphanage and Industrial School
Mailing Address:—c/o the Diocese of Trenton
701 Lawrenceville Rd.
Trenton, NJ 08648

Jersey City
Archdiocese of Newark

St. Ann's Home for the Aged
198 Old Bergen Rd.
Jersey City, NJ 07305
Tel: 201-433-0950; Fax: 201-433-6554
E-mail: paix2@aol.com
Sr. Norah Clarke, C.S.J.P., LNHA Admin.
Henry Wojtowicz, Pastoral Care
Sisters of St. Joseph of Peace 5
Total Staff 185
Under Care 116

St. Joseph's Home
81 York St.
Jersey City, NJ 07302
Tel: 201-413-9280
Sr. Kristin Funari, C.S.J.P., Dir.
Total Staff 32
Total Assisted 221
Transitional housing for homeless women and children.
The Nurturing Place
Sr. Barbara Moran, C.S.J.P., Dir., Tel: 201-413-1982
Total Staff 19
Total Assisted 110
A developmental child care center for disadvantaged youngsters.

St. Joseph's Home for the Blind
537 Pavonia Ave.
Jersey City, NJ 07306
Tel: 201-653-8300; Fax: 201-653-7705
E-mail: sjhb@compuserv.com
Sisters of St. Joseph of Peace
Sr. Ann Taylor, C.S.J.P., Admin.
Rev. John Cavanaugh, M.SS.CC., Chap.
Sisters 3
Total Staff 140
Nursing Home Patients 129

St. Mary's Residence for Business and Professional Women
240 Washington St.
Jersey City, NJ 07302
Tel: 201-432-6289; Fax: 201-451-0952
Sisters of St. Joseph of Peace
Sr. Mary Donohue, C.S.J.P., Admin.
Total Staff 7
Total Assisted 38

Kearny
Archdiocese of Newark

New Jersey Boystown
499 Belgrove Dr.
Kearny, NJ 07032
Tel: 201-991-3770
Family Counseling Services.
Revs.:
Janis Orlafsky, Dir.
Francis T. Malone, Clients Rights Advocate/ Pastoral Care Coord., Tel: 973-297-4749

Lawrenceville
Diocese of Trenton

Morris Hall-Saint Lawrence, Inc.
Morris Hall - St. Mary's Residence & Assisted Living.
1 Bishops' Dr.
Lawrenceville, NJ 08648-2050
Tel: 609-896-0006; Fax: 609-896-8037
E-mail: info@morrishall.org
Web Site: www.morrishall.org
Mr. Charles L. Brennan, CEO
Mrs. Susan Goldberg, L.N.H.A., C.A.L.A., Admin.
In res.,
Rev. Msgr. James Foley
Revs.:
Edward P. Atzert
Justin J. Herbst, Chap.
Edwin Dzienkiewicz
Guests 71
Beds 78

Morris Hall / Saint Lawrence, Inc.
St. Lawrence Rehabilitation Center.
2381 Lawrenceville Rd.
Lawrenceville, NJ 08648
Tel: 609-896-9500; Fax: 609-895-0242
E-mail: communityrelations@slrc.org
Web Site: www.slrc.org
Mr. Charles L. Brennan, Admin.
Rev. Justin J. Herbst, Chap.
Sr. Claire DeStefano, S.S.J., Dir. Pastoral Care
Bed Capacity 116
Bed Licensure 116

Morris Hall / Saint Lawrence, Inc.
Morris Hall - St. Joseph's Nursing Center
1 Bishops' Dr.
Lawrenceville, NJ 08648-2050
Tel: 609-896-0006; Fax: 609-896-8037
E-mail: info@morrishall.org
Web Site: www.morrishall.org
Susan Goldberg, L.N.H.A., C.A.L.A., Admin.
Skilled Nursing Care Facility for the Chronically Ill.
Residences and Assisted Living for Senior Citizens
Bed Capacity 120
Total in Residence 114

Montclair
Archdiocese of Newark

Mother Seton Residence
51 Washington St.
Montclair, NJ 07042
Tel: 973-783-1400; Fax: 973-783-1402
Sisters of Charity of St. Elizabeth
Sr. Marian Therese Boudreau, Admin.
Residents 23
Total Staff 10

Newark
Archdiocese of Newark

Queen of Peace
60 Jay St.
Newark, NJ 07103
Tel: 973-481-9056
Total Staff 4
Total Assisted 330
Missionaries of Charity

Newfield
Diocese of Camden

Mater Dei Nursing Home
176 Rte. 40
Newfield, NJ 08344
Tel: 856-358-2061; Fax: 856-358-0403
Marianites of Holy Cross
Sr. Anne Ebersold, Admin.
Rev. Sebastian V. Annino, Chap.
Sisters 4
Bed Capacity 64
Total Staff 100

North Plainfield
Diocese of Metuchen

Villa Maria Sanitarium
641 Somerset St.
North Plainfield, NJ 07060-4909
Tel: 908-757-3050; Fax: 908-754-4939
E-mail: www.villamariahome.com
Home for the aged (with infirmary).
Administration: Franciscan Sisters

Rev. SEVERIN DIETRICH, O.F.M.Conv., Chap., Tel: 908-757-3050
Patients and Residents 86

Paramus
Archdiocese of Newark

Mount St. Andrew Villa
55 W. Midland Ave.
Paramus, NJ 07652
Tel: 201-261-5950
Sr. JOANN BROMLEY, S.C.
Sisters of Charity of St. Elizabeth 2
Residents 55

Paterson
Diocese of Paterson

St. Joseph Rest Home for Aged Women
Conducted by Daughters of Charity of the Most Precious Blood
46 Preakness Ave.
Paterson, NJ 07522
Tel: 973-956-1921; Fax: 973-956-1582
Sr. MARIA GORETTI CHALOUX, Supr.
Residents 35

Pleasantville
Diocese of Camden

Our Lady's Residence
1100 Clematis Ave.
Pleasantville, NJ 08232
Tel: 609-646-2450; Fax: 609-646-7569
Hospitaler Sisters of Mercy
ANNA TOSTI, Acting Admin.
Sr. THRESIAMMA THADAHIL, H.S.M., Supr.
Rev. FREDERICK CLEMENT, M.SS.CC., Chap.
Sisters 7
Beds 214
Patients assisted annually 214
Total Staff 236

Red Bank
Diocese of Trenton

Collier Group Home
180 Spring St.
Red Bank, NJ 07701
Tel: 732-842-8337; Fax: 732-530-7096
E-mail: colliersgs@monmouth.com
Mr. PAUL DESANTIS, Dir.
24 Hour Program-Therapy and Educational Services. Provided Under the Supervision of the Sisters of the Good Shepherd.
Capacity 10

Saddle River
Archdiocese of Newark

Villa Marie Claire
12 W. Saddle River Rd.
Saddle River, NJ 07458
Tel: 201-327-1325; Fax: 201-327-6647
E-mail: vcmoshea@aol.com
Residence for retired, independent men & women.
Sisters of St. Joseph of Peace 11
Residents 30

Somerset
Diocese of Metuchen

McCarrick Care Center
15 Dellwood Ln.
Somerset, NJ 08873
Tel: 732-545-4200
JAMES F. CARON, Admin.
Rev. MAURICE T. CARLTON, Chap.
In res.,
Rev. WILLIAM A. ROOS
Sisters 2
Patients assisted annually 142

Totowa
Diocese of Paterson

St. Joseph's Home for the Elderly
140 Shepherd Ln.
Totowa, NJ 07512
Tel: 973-942-0300; Fax: 973-942-7201
Conducted by Little Sisters of the Poor
Sr. MARY VINCENT, L.S.P.
Rev. RAYMOND BEACH, O.F.M., Chap.
Sisters 18
Residents 134

Trenton
Diocese of Trenton

Cathedral Square Housing, Inc.
26 W. Hanover Pl.
Trenton, NJ 08608
Tel: 609-392-1111; Fax: 609-322-4107
Most Rev. JOHN M. SMITH, Dir.
Senior Citizen Housing Project.

Sister Georgine School
544 Chestnut Ave.
Trenton, NJ 08611
Tel: 609-396-5444; Fax: 609-396-0989
E-mail: srgeorgine@aol.com
Web Site: hometown.aol.com/srgeorgine/index.html
Sisters of St. Francis
Sr. BARBARA FURST, Prin.
Staff 10
Students 17

Vineland
Diocese of Camden

Bishop McCarthy Residence
1045 E. Chestnut Ave.
Vineland, NJ 08360
Tel: 856-692-2850; Fax: 856-696-5770
E-mail: bmr02@aol.com
Hospitaler Sisters of Mercy
Sr. LUCIA MAROOR, L.N.H.A., Admin.
Sr. ELETTA FELLI, Supr.
Rev. CARMEL F. POLIDANO, Chap.
Sisters 5
Beds 182
Patients assisted annually 182

Wickatunk
Diocese of Trenton

Collier Services
Collier High School, Conover Rd.
Wickatunk, NJ 07765
Tel: 732-946-4771; Fax: 732-946-3519
E-mail: info@collierservices.com
Web Site: www.collierservices.com
Ms. AIDEEN BUGLER, Program Dir.
Sr. ELLEN KELLY, Exec. Dir.
Adolescent Boys and Girls.
Capacity 150
Mr. EDWARD MARGOTTI, Prog. Dir. of Kateri Center, Tel: 732-946-9694
Mrs. LYNDA SHERIDAN, Prog. Dir., Shepherd Center for Child Care, Tel: 732-946-4323
Full-day Early Childhood Program for children 6 weeks through age 12. Full-day Kindergarten. School Age Care for Summer.
Capacity 98

Woodbridge
Diocese of Metuchen

St. Joseph Assisted Living Residence
One St. Joseph Terr.
Woodbridge, NJ 07095
Tel: 732-634-0004; Fax: 732-634-4586
Sr. MARY LOUISE, L.S.I.C., Admin.
Little Servant Sisters 15
Residents 60

NEW MEXICO

Albuquerque
Archdiocese of Santa Fe

Casa Angelica
5629 Isleta Blvd., S.W.
Albuquerque, NM 87105
Tel: 505-877-5763; Fax: 505-873-2786
The Daughters of Charity of Canossa
Home for developmentally disabled children.
Sisters 1
Residents 16
Lay Staff 49
Total Assisted 16
Total Staff 46

Good Shepherd Center, Inc.
218 Iron St., S.W., P.O. Box 749
Albuquerque, NM 87103
Tel: 505-243-2527; Fax: 505-243-2207
Direct Service Agency for the Homeless.
R. J. SCHAEFER, Pres.
Total Assisted 190,000
Total Staff 8

Good Shepherd Manor
10127 Guadalupe Tr., N.W., P.O. Box 10248
Albuquerque, NM 87184
Tel: 505-898-0177; Fax: 505-898-9756
Bro. SAVIO CHARRON, B.G.S., M.H.A., Admin.
Sponsored by Bro. Mathias Barrett, Inc. of New Mexico. Shelter Care Facility for aged adults.
Residents 40
Staff 21

Marie Amadea Shelter for Unwed Mothers
(Alternative to Abortion)
P.O. Box 708
Albuquerque, NM 87103
Tel: 505-242-1516; Fax: 505-243-0402
Mrs. DOROTHY WICKENS, Dir.
Home for unwed expectant women.
Total Assisted 19
Total Staff 6

Carlsbad
Diocese of Las Cruces

St. Mary's Health Care Center
(Sub. of St. Mary of the Plains Hospital)
2330 West Pierce
Carlsbad, NM 88220
Tel: 505-887-0516; Fax: 505-885-8239
STEVE RACCHITO, Dir.

Hobbs
Diocese of Las Cruces

St. Mary Medical Center
(Sub. of St. Mary of the Plains Hospital)
2410 North Fowler
Hobbs, NM 88240
Tel: 505-392-5572; Fax: 505-392-4848
STEVE RACCHITO, Dir.

St. Mary's Family Health Care Center
(Sub. of St. Mary of the Plains Hospital)
515 East Main
Hobbs, NM 88240
Tel: 505-393-1096; Fax: 505-393-3758
STEVE RACCHITO, Dir.

Santa Fe
Archdiocese of Santa Fe

Villa Therese Catholic Clinic
219 Cathedral Pl.
Santa Fe, NM 87501
Tel: 505-983-8561; Fax: 505-983-8561
E-mail: vtcc@juno.com
Sr. PATRICK MARIE BERNARD, S.C., Dir.
Sisters of Charity of Cincinnati, Ohio 1
Total Staff 3
Patients assisted annually 6,646

NEW YORK

Albany
Diocese of Albany

Arbor House
302 Western Ave.
Albany, NY 12203
Tel: 518-489-6030
Legal Title: *Arbor House, Inc.*

Bishop Broderick Apartments Housing Development Fund Co., Inc.
50 Prescott St.
Albany, NY 12205
Tel: 518-869-7441; Fax: 518-869-0443
Senior Citizen and Handicapped Housing.
GEORGE WALKO, Dir.

C.S.C. Housing Development Fund Co., Inc., dba Sanderson Court Senior Apts./ De Paul Housing Management
E-mail: mkscsa@aol.com
6 Carondelet Dr.
Watervliet, NY 12189
Tel: 518-459-0185; 782-1123; Fax: 518-782-1125
E-mail: mkscsac@aol.com
MICHELE KRAMM, Dir.

Cusack Community Service Corporation
40 N. Main Ave.
Albany, NY 12203
Tel: 518-453-6650
Sr. MAUREEN JOYCE, O.F.M., Contact Person

DePaul Housing Management Corp.
41 N. Main Ave.
Albany, NY 12203
Tel: 518-459-0183; Fax: 518-459-0202
E-mail: ddobdep@aol.com
DEBORAH DAMM O'BRIEN, Exec. Dir.
JILL MCLELLAN PHELPS, Dir. Oper.
Managing diocesan sponsored housing for persons who are elderly or mobility impaired.

LaSalle School, Inc.
391 Western Ave.
Albany, NY 12203
Tel: 518-242-4731; Fax: 518-242-4747

E-mail: information@lasalle-school.org
Web Site: www.lasalle-school.org
Brothers of the Christian Schools 8
Mr. WILLIAM WOLFF, Exec. Dir.
Residential and day programs, independent living program, sexual victim/offender program, licensed substance abuse treatment program, and preventative services for boys (ages 12-18) and their families in New York State. Registered New York State Junior and Senior High School and certified School of Special Education.
Prevention Families 60
Resident Students 100
Day Students 30
The La Salle School Foundation of Albany

McAuley Living Services
310 S. Manning Blvd.
Albany, NY 12208
Tel: 518-437-8400; Fax: 518-437-8418
E-mail: mhulihan@stpetershealthcare.org
Sisters of Mercy of the Americas - Albany Regional Community.
Sr. MARIA HULIHAN, R.N.M.S., Exec. Dir.

Saint Anne Institute
160 N. Main Ave.
Albany, NY 12206
Tel: 518-437-6500; Fax: 518-437-6555
RICHARD C. RICCIO, Exec. Dir.
Residential and Community-based Preventive Service Center. Regents accredited and certified junior and senior H.S. for the emotionally handicapped and Preschool program for 3-4 year olds who are speech impaired and emotionally disturbed. Residential care and Day Treatment for young women ages 12-18. Family Services, Vocational Training, Sex Abuse Prevention and Juvenile Sex Offender Programs for male and female adolescents in crisis and their families.
Capacity:
Residential 129
Day Treatment 40
Juvenile Sex Offender & Sex Abuse Prevention Families 90

Saint Catherine's Center for Children
40 N. Main Ave.
Albany, NY 12203
Tel: 518-453-6700; Fax: 518-453-6712
Web Site: www.st-cath.org
Ms. HELEN HAYES, Exec. Dir.
Residential and day treatment, group homes and foster family programs for children with special needs. Community based prevention programs; Parent aides; Parent Training; Transitional Program for Homeless Families.
Individuals assisted 1,250
The Foundation for St. Catherine's Center for Children

St. Vincent Apartments Housing Development Fund Co., Inc.
475 Yates St.
Albany, NY 12208
Tel: 518-482-8915; Fax: 518-489-1220

Teresian House (1974)
200 Washington Ave. Ext.
Albany, NY 12203
Tel: 518-456-2000; Fax: 518-456-1142
E-mail: info@teresianhouse.com
Web Site: www.teresianhouse.com
Corporate Title: Teresian House Nursing Home Co., Inc.
Carmelite Sisters for the Aged and Infirm
Sr. PAULINE BRECANIER, O.Carm., Admin.
Sr. JOAN LEWIS, O.Carm., Coord. Pastoral Care
Rev. JOHN MALECKI, Chap.
Bed Capacity 300
Teresian House Foundation

Villa Mary Immaculate
301 Hackett Blvd.
Albany, NY 12208
Tel: 518-482-3363; Fax: 518-482-8136
E-mail: rcassano@mercycare.com
S.N.F. and long term skilled care nursing home.
Sponsored by Mercycare.
Member of Catholic Health East
RENEE P. CASSANO, Exec. Dir.
Sr. BARBARA DUDLEY, R.S.M.
Sr. JOYCE BLANEY, C.S.J.
Sr. MARY BRUCE, C.S.J.
Sisters 3
Bed Capacity 160
Patients assisted annually 250

Amityville
Diocese of Rockville Centre

Dominican Village, Inc.
565 Albany Ave.
Amityville, NY 11701
Tel: 631-842-6091; Fax: 631-842-6131
E-mail: dv@dominicanvillage.org
Sr. HELEN BUTLER, Pres. & CEO
Sr. VIRGINIA MAGUIRE, Vice Pres.
Housing Units 266
Total Assisted 66
Total Staff 115

Amsterdam
Diocese of Albany

Mt. Loretto Nursing Home
302 Swart Hill Rd.
Amsterdam, NY 12010
Tel: 518-842-6790; Fax: 518-843-5993
Health Care Facility, 24 Hour Skilled Nursing Care, Hospice, IV Therapy & Rehab. Conducted by the Sisters of the Resurrection.
Sr. PATRICIA ANNE CORBETT, C.R., Admin.
Sr. MARY LUCILLE BOROWSKI, C.R., Supr. & Chap.
Rev. RAYMOND S. PIECHOCKI, Priest In Res.
Capacity 120

Auburn
Diocese of Syracuse

Mercy Housing Development Fund Co., Inc.
Mercy Apartments, 1 Thornton Ave.
Auburn, NY 13021
Tel: 315-253-2015; Fax: 315-258-8516
E-mail: dmechowski@christopher-community.org
40 one bedroom units for the elderly and handicapped. Christopher Community, Inc., (Managing Agent).

Baldwinsville
Diocese of Syracuse

Smokey Hollow Housing Development Fund Company, Inc.
Mailing Address:—St. Mary's Apartments c/o Christopher Community
1654 W. Onondaga St.
Syracuse, NY 13204
Tel: 315-424-1821
Christopher Community, Inc., (Managing Agent).

Batavia
Diocese of Buffalo

St. Luke Manor
17 Wiard St.
Batavia, NY 14020
Tel: 716-343-8806; Fax: 716-343-0959
SHEILA A. PERRY, Admin.
Bed Capacity 20
Patients assisted annually 30

Bayside
Diocese of Brooklyn

Ozanam Hall of Queens Nursing Home, Inc.
42-41 201st St.
Bayside, NY 11361
Tel: 718-423-2000; Fax: 718-224-7598
E-mail: ozanamgen@chcn.org
Sr. M. PHILIP ANN, O.Carm., Admin.
Rev. JAMES M. KELLY, Chap.
Carmelite Sisters for the Aged and Infirm
Sisters 19
Residents 432

Blauvelt
Archdiocese of New York

St. Dominic Home
10913
Tel: 914-359-3400; Fax: 914-359-4253
Web Site: www.st.dominichome.org
Sr. JOSEPH MARY, O.P., Exec. Dir.
Capacity: Boys 12
Girls 12
In Foster Homes 610
Group Homes 67
Boys 17
Girls 50
AOBH Girls 6
Sisters 8
New York Offices
343 E. 137th St.
Bronx, NY 10454
Tel: 718-993-5765; Fax: 718-402-8202
Special education program for emotionally disturbed mentally ill children ages 6-15.
Capacity 72
Preschool ages 3-5
Capacity 48
Community residences for developmentally disabled
Capacity 86
Community residences for emotionally handicapped
Capacity 46
TORCH (To Reach Children)
2340 Andrews Ave.
Bronx, NY 10463
Tel: 718-365-7238; Fax: 718-584-3057
Friends of St. Dominic
500 Western Hwy.
Blauvelt, NY 10913
Tel: 914-359-3400; Fax: 914-398-0466
Sr. JOSEPH MARY MAHONEY, O.P.

Brewerton
Diocese of Syracuse

Bartell Road Housing Development Fund Co., Inc.
Bartell Rd.
Brewerton, NY 13029
c/o Christopher Community
1654 W. Onondaga St.
Syracuse, NY 13204
20 units, one bedroom apartments. Christopher Community, Inc., (Managing Agent).

Bronx
Archdiocese of New York

Bon Secours New York Health System, Inc.
2975 Independence Ave.
Bronx, NY 10463-4699
Tel: 718-548-1700; Fax: 718-601-3384
E-mail: tbrooks@fhsny.org
Web Site: scherviercares.org
JEANNE LEE, CEO
Sr. SHEILA MORONEY, P.B.V.M., Dir. of Pastoral Care
Legal Title: *Schervier Nursing Care Center*
Legal Title: *Frances Schervier Housing Development Fund Corporation*
Legal Title: *Schervier Nutrition Services, Inc.*
Legal Title: *Schervier Long Term Home Health Care Program*
Bon Secours Health System, Inc.
1505 Marriottsville Rd
Marriottsville, MD 21104
Tel: 518-783-5257; Fax: 410-442-5511
Total Assisted 950
Total Staff 480

Jeanne Jugan Residence
142 Hollywood Ave., P.O. Box 1002
Bronx, NY 10465
Tel: 718-464-1800; Fax: 718-464-0254
Sr. BERNICE MARIE WALL, L.S.P., Pres.

Medical Missionaries of Mary
563 Minneford Ave.
Bronx, NY 10464-1118
Tel: 718-885-0945; Fax: 718-885-0010
E-mail: mmmci@aol.com
Web Site: www.mmmusa.org
Sr. PHILOMENA SHEERIN, M.M.M., Supr. Gen.
Sr. JOANNE BIERL, M.M.M., Zonal Coord. of the Americas

Pius XII Youth and Family Services, Inc.
188 W. 230th St.
Bronx, NY 10463
JOHN G. KELLY, Acting CEO
Central Offices.
The Victor J. Riley Jr. Center for Human Services
188 W. 230th St.
Bronx, NY 10463
Tel: 718-561-2073; Fax: 718-562-4538
Provides foster care, community and family services, work force development, employee assistance and chemical dependence services.
Non-Secure Detention and Group Homes
11 King Center
Middletown, NY 10940
Tel: 914-343-7487; Fax: 914-343-1842
Temporary group care provided at 3 homes in Middletown and Poughkeepsie.
Foster Boarding Homes & Adoption
Tel: 718-562-7855; Fax: 718-562-1815
188 W. 230th St.
Bronx, NY 10463
Foster care and adoption services for 500 infants, children and adolescents in the Bronx. Program provides services and medical care to natural families, children and foster parents and recruitment of new foster parents. Adoptive parents are sought for children freed for adoption.

Community Services:
North Bronx Family Service Center
2190 University Ave.
Bronx, NY 10453
Tel: 718-365-1400; Fax: 718-365-1411
Preventive services center for local community.
Bronx Community Services
Tel: 718-822-2325
1967 Turnbull Ave.
Bronx, NY 10473
Tel: 718-931-2611
University Heights Day Care
2167 University Ave.
Bronx, NY 10453
Tel: 718-584-6400; Fax: 718-584-2724
On-site day care for preschool children and after-school care for school-age children. Office for family day care that provides in-home services for families.
Children 101
Goshen Early Learning Center
59 St. John St.
Goshen, NY 10924
Tel: 914-294-7502; Fax: 914-294-9619
Montessori-based day care for 60, ages 3-5.
Employment Training and Youth Development Services
Snow House
135 Hall of Fame Terr.
Bronx, NY 10453
Tel: 718-365-7755; Fax: 718-365-7756
Training and placement in auto mechanics, word processing and secretarial skills. Special family support and resource program which coordinates job training with family services. After-school education and recreational services.
Student Services - Dropout Prevention
Theodore Roosevelt High School
500 E. Fordham Rd.
Bronx, NY 10458
Tel: 718-365-5051
Morris High School
166th St. & Boston Rd.
Bronx, NY 10456
Tel: 718-542-3700, Ext. 1003
P.S. 79
125 E. 181st St.
Bronx, NY 10453
Tel: 718-584-5158
Intergenerational program between Jewish Home Hospital and P.S. 79.
Adlai Stevenson High School
1980 Lafayette Ave.
Bronx, NY 10473
Tel: 718-918-2700, Ext. 560
Walton High School
West 196 St. & Reservoir Ave.
Bronx, NY 10468
Tel: 718-365-6215
Counseling services to identified population of students considered high risk for dropping out of school.
After School Programs
Family Service Center
2190 Unviersity Ave.
Bronx, NY 10453
Supervised Latch-key program of classes, workshops and recreation for 6-18 year olds. Teen Program for adolescents provides recreational program year round.
"Aimin' High Family Service Center
One hundred at-risk teens involved in sports and education programs with added community service.
Beacon Program
Middle School 45, 2502 Lorillard Pl.
Bronx, NY 10458
Tel: 718-584-1952
Community Center serving youths, children and adults in educational, recreational and social services after school, evenings, and weekends.
Tutoring for students 6-18 who are one year or more behind grade level. G.E.D. program for high school equivalency. English as a second language classes.
Chemical Dependency Services:
Administrative Office
224 Main St.
Goshen, NY 10924
Tel: 845-294-5124; Fax: 845-294-1369
Chemical Dependency Clinics:
224 Main St.
Goshen, NY 10924
Tel: 914-294-5888; Fax: 845-294-1402
62 Grand St.
Newburgh, NY 12550
Tel: 845-562-8255; Fax: 845-562-4140
10 Orchard St.
Middletown, NY 10940
Tel: 845-343-7675; Fax: 845-343-2501
520 Rte. 17M
Monroe, NY 10950
Tel: 845-782-0295; Fax: 845-782-5164
146 Pike St.
Port Jervis, NY 12771
Tel: 845-856-8440
Medically supervised outpatient clinics for chemically dependent adults and their families.
Alcohol Clinic
440 Rte. 17M
Monroe, NY 10950
Tel: 845-782-6600; Fax: 845-782-4408
Specialized clinic for the treatment of alcoholics and their families.
School-based Services
Alternatives
14 Scotchtown Ave., Box 87
Goshen, NY 10924
Tel: 845-294-3501; Fax: 845-294-3501
Chemical dependency awareness and prevention program. Taught to school districts in Orange County. Summer and year-round programs in chemical dependency, AIDS, coping with behavioral problems and others.
Gateway Center
46 Roe St.
Newburgh, NY 12550
Tel: 845-569-0034; Fax: 845-569-0047
Chemical dependency outpatient clinic for Newburgh high school students, located on school grounds.
Student Assistance Services.
Employee Assistance Services Office
Tel: 845-294-2501; Fax: 845-294-9932
Box 87
Goshen, NY 10924
Tel: 845-294-3501; Fax: 845-294-9932
Marie Smith Urban Street Academy
2900 Exterior St.
Bronx, NY 10463
Tel: 718-561-7842; Fax: 718-561-5283
Employment Training Program, GED Program, Computer Classes and ESOL Program.
Total Assisted 21,848
Total Staff 400

Providence Rest
3304 Waterbury Ave.
Bronx, NY 10465
Tel: 718-931-3000; Fax: 718-863-0185
E-mail: providencerest@aol.com
Web Site: www.chcn.org/providence
Sr. Seline Mary Flores, Admin.
Sr. Margaret Mary
Sisters of St. John the Baptist 20
Bed Capacity 200
Total Assisted 180
Total Staff 242

Saint Dominic's Home - Prevention Program (ASTAAN)
2345 University Ave.
Bronx, NY 10468
Tel: 718-584-4407
Parent Aide Counseling Advocacy Information and Referral.
Families 100
Families Served 200

St. Patrick's Home for the Aged and Infirm
66 Van Cortlandt Park S.
Bronx, NY 10463
Tel: 718-519-2800; Fax: 718-519-2817
E-mail: stpatrickhome@aol.com
Web Site: www.hometown.aol.com/stpatshome/stp/index.htm
Carmelite Sisters for the Aged and Infirm
Sr. M. Patrick Michael, O.Carm., Admin.
Rev. Gerard A. Orlando, C.P., Dir. Pastoral Care
Sisters 16
Bed Capacity 264
Total Assisted 380
Total Staff 350

St. Vincent de Paul Residence
900 Intervale Ave.
Bronx, NY 10459
Tel: 718-589-6965; Fax: 718-589-7010
E-mail: svdpres@chcn.org
Web Site: www.svdpres.org
Mr. Jorge Vasquez, Dir.

Brooklyn
Diocese of Brooklyn

Holy Family Home
1740 84th St.
Brooklyn, NY 11214
Tel: 718-232-3666; Fax: 718-259-9180
Affiliated with Catholic Medical Center.
Mary Anne Rose, Admin.
Sr. Patricia Murphy, Dir. Pastoral Care Office
Deacon Frank Rosati
Total Staff 284
Total Assisted 200

SS. Joachim & Anne Residence, Inc.
2720 Surf Ave.
Brooklyn, NY 11224
Tel: 718-714-4800
Marie Ferrara, Admin.

Buffalo
Diocese of Buffalo

The Franciscan Center, Inc.
1910 Seneca St.
Buffalo, NY 14210-1842
Tel: 716-822-8017; Fax: 716-822-8537
Emergency & Transitional Shelters for Adolescent Males 16-20.
Rev. Joseph Bayne, O.F.M.Conv., Exec. Dir. & Guardian
Total Assisted 130 (Shelter), 600 (Non-resident)
Total Staff 21
St. Joseph, Foster Parent, Friary
Tel: 716-826-6714; Fax: 716-822-8537

German Roman Catholic Orphan Home
795 Main St.
Buffalo, NY 14203
Inactive.

Nazareth Nursing Home
291 North St.
Buffalo, NY 14201
Tel: 716-881-2323; Fax: 716-881-1578
Sr. M. Bernard Keane, O.S.F., Board Pres.
Mr. Kevin B. Kennedy, Admin.
Franciscan Sisters of the Immaculate Conception 7
Bed Capacity 125
Patients assisted annually 125
Total Staff 220
Legal Title: *Nazareth Nursing Home of the Franciscan Sisters of the Immaculate Conception*
Chapel attended by Oblate Fathers of Holy Angels Church.

St. Francis Geriatric and Healthcare Services, Inc.
(Formerly known as St. Francis Hospital).
2787 Main St.
Buffalo, NY 14214
Tel: 716-837-4200; Fax: 716-837-4218
Sr. Jeanne Weisbeck, O.S.F., CEO
Rev. Robert Mack, Chap.
Sr. Marilyn Perkins, D.C., Chm. & Prov. Supr.
Sisters of St. Francis 2
Patients assisted annually 250
Bed Capacity 120
Total Assisted 288
Total Staff 188

Castleton
Diocese of Albany

Resurrection Nursing Home
(Corporate Name: Resurrection Nursing Home, Inc.)
Castleton, NY 12033
Tel: 518-732-7617; Fax: 518-732-4211
E-mail: rnh@ix.netcom.com
Nursing Home (Established 1962).
Conducted by Sisters of Resurrection
Bed Capacity 80

Catskill
Diocese of Albany

St. Joseph's Villa
38 Prospect Ave.
Catskill, NY 12414
Tel: 518-943-5701; Fax: 518-943-5033
Carla Erhartic, Admin.
An Adult Care Facility for Men and Women.

Cicero
Diocese of Syracuse

Cicero Housing Development Fund Company Inc.
Mailing Address:
1654 W. Onondaga St.
Syracuse, NY 13204
Tel: 315-424-1821
Sacred Heart Apartments
Cicero, NY 13039
Christopher Community, Inc., (Managing Agent).

Clarence
Diocese of Buffalo

Brothers of Mercy Housing Co., Inc.
10500 Bergtold Rd.
Clarence, NY 14031
Tel: 716-759-2122

Ms. LENORE MAURER, Admin.
Bro. JUDE HOLZFOERSTER, Pres.
Bed Capacity 110
Total in Residence 110
Total Staff 4

Brothers of Mercy Nursing & Rehabilitation Center
10570 Bergtold Rd.
Clarence, NY 14031
Tel: 716-759-6985; Fax: 716-759-6223
E-mail: BOMNRC@aol.com
Web Site: www.BrothersOfMercy.org
Mr. RICHARD C. CLELAND, Admin.
Bro. JUDE HOLZFOERSTER, F.M.M., Pres.
Rev. JOHN J. SARDINA, Chap.
In res.,
Sr. JEAN THOMSON, O.S.F., Dir. Spiritual Care
Bed Capacity 240
Total assisted annually 1,100
Staff 500

Brothers of Mercy Sacred Heart Home, Inc.
4520 Ransom Rd.
Clarence, NY 14031
Tel: 716-759-2644; Fax: 716-759-6433
E-mail: BOMSHH@aol.com
SUSAN C. REILLY, Admin.
Bro. JUDE HOLZFOERSTER, F.M.M., Pres. of Board
Rev. JOHN J. SARDINA, Chap.
Bed Capacity 80
Total in Residence 80
Total Staff 56

Clifton Park
Diocese of Albany

Halfmoon Housing Development Fund Co., Inc.
dba Bishop Hubbard Senior Apartments/De Paul Housing Management Corp.
54 Katherine Dr.
Clifton Park, NY 12065
Tel: 518-383-2705; Fax: 518-383-6350
E-mail: jmsbhsa@aol.com
JEANNE M. SPEANBURG, Dir.

Dobbs Ferry
Archdiocese of New York

St. Cabrini Nursing Home
115 Broadway
Dobbs Ferry, NY 10522
Tel: 914-693-6800; Fax: 914-693-1731
PATRICIA KRASNAUSKY, Exec. Dir.
Rev. EDWIN ROBINSON, O.F.M., Dir. Pastoral Care
Missionary Sisters of the Sacred Heart 5
Bed Capacity 304
Home Health Care 250
Total Staff 437

Dunkirk
Diocese of Buffalo

St. Vincent's Home for the Aged
319 Washington Ave.
Dunkirk, NY 14048
Tel: 716-366-2066; Fax: 716-366-0545
E-mail: stvhome@netsync.net
Catholic Charities of Buffalo, Inc.
BART SIENER, Admin.
Residents 40
Total Staff 25

Fayetteville
Diocese of Syracuse

Redfield South Housing Development Fund Co., Inc.
Redfield Village Apartments, 380 Salt Springs Rd.
Fayetteville, NY 13066
Tel: 315-637-8280; Fax: 315-637-2376
50 one bedroom units. Christopher Community, Inc., (Managing Agent).
Total Assisted 50
Total Staff 2

Garrison
Archdiocese of New York

St. Christopher's Inn
P.O. Box 150
Garrison, NY 10524-0150
Tel: 914-424-3616; Fax: 914-424-3786
Web Site: atonementfrairs.org
Temporary shelter for homeless men.
Atonement Friars
Rev. BERNARD PALKA, S.A., Dir.
Total Assisted 1,200
Total Staff 28

Germantown
Diocese of Albany

Avila Institute of Gerontology, Inc.
600 Woods Rd.
Germantown, NY 12526
Tel: 518-537-5000; Fax: 518-537-4579
Carmelite Sisters for the Aged and Infirm
Sr. M. MARK LOUIS ANNE, O.Carm., Pres.
Sr. M. PETER LILLIAN, O. Carm., Dir.

Harrison
Archdiocese of New York

St. Vincent's Hospital and Medical Center Westchester Branch
275 North St.
Harrison, NY 10528
Tel: 914-967-6500; Fax: 914-925-5157
BRIAN L. FITZSIMMONS, Ph.D.
Psychiatric Hospital.
Clergy Consultation Program
Women Religious Program.
Services for pre/post partum women. Inpatient and outpatient mental health and substance abuse services for adults, adolescents, children and their families. Sites in Harrison, Tuckahoe and Hawthorne. Services available in Spanish.
Capacity 133
Patients assisted annually 2,891
Sisters of Charity of St. Vincent de Paul 3
All outpatient program admissions 4,452
Partial Hospital 270
Methadone Maintenance Treatment Program 43

Hawthorne
Archdiocese of New York

Rosary Hill Home
Hawthorne, NY 10532
Tel: 914-769-0114; Fax: 914-769-3916
Legal Title: *The Servants of Relief for Incurable Cancer*
Free home for incurable cancer patients.
Sr. M. BRIGID, O.P, Admin.
Sr. DAMIEN, O.P., Supr.
Rev. JOHN PROPPE, O.F.M.Cap., Chap.
Professed Sisters of St. Dominic 24
Capacity 72
Patients assisted annually 234

Huntington
Diocese of Rockville Centre

St. Joseph's Guest Home for the Aged, Inc.
350 Cuba Hill Rd.
Huntington, NY 11743
Tel: 631-368-9528; Fax: 931-266-1015
Missionary Sisters of St. Benedict
Sr. M. JOACHIMA MYSTKOWSRA, O.S.B., Admin.
In res.,
Rev. Msgr. JOSEPH LAWLOR
Rev. Msgr. FRANCIS X. GLIMM
Rev. Msgr. WALTER C. GALUSZKA (BRK)
Revs.:
MALACHY C. GLACHERTY, O.F.M.Cap.
JOHN R. CURLEY, S.M.M.

Jamaica
Diocese of Brooklyn

Msgr. James H. Fitzpatrick Pavilion for Skilled Nursing Care
152-11 89th Ave.
Jamaica, NY 11432
Tel: 718-558-2800; Fax: 718-558-2476
St. Vincent's Catholic Medical Centers of NY
MICHELL A. EDWARDS, Admin.
Total Staff 115
Total Assisted 115
Residents 115

Kenmore
Diocese of Buffalo

Kenmore Mercy Homes, Inc. (dba McAuley Residence)
Administrative Offices, 2950 Elmwood Ave.
Kenmore, NY 14217
Tel: 716-447-6101; Fax: 716-447-6090
Residential Health Care Facility
Sponsored by the Catholic Health System, Inc.
Bed Capacity 160
Total Assisted 160
Total Staff 150

Lackawanna
Diocese of Buffalo

Baker Victory Services
(formerly known as Baker Hall, Our Lady of Victory Infant Home, St. Joseph Orphanage and St. John's Protectory)
780 Ridge Rd.
Lackawanna, NY 14218
Tel: 716-828-9500; 888-287-9986; Fax: 716-828-9526
E-mail: baker@buffnet.net
Web Site: www.bakervictoryservices.org
Rev. Msgr. ROBERT C. WURTZ, Pres. of the Board
JAMES J. CASION, C.E.O.
JOSEPH J. COZZO, C.O.O.
J. BRENT HERMAN, Personnel Dir.
Staff 800
Total Assisted 3,000
Educational Services:
Early Intervention (ages birth to 7)
Tel: 716-828-9560; Fax: 716-828-9460
Therapeutic Preschool (ages 3-5)
Tel: 716-828-9560; Fax: 716-828-9460
Baker Hall School (ages 12-21)
Tel: 716-828-9737; Fax: 716-828-9798
Edward Street School (ages 12-21)
Tel: 716-887-9478; Fax: 716-887-3844
Residential Services:
Dorothy Miler House (mother & child group residence)
Tel: 716-828-9500; Fax: 716-828-9526
Foster Family Boarding Home Care
Tel: 716-828-9500; Fax: 716-828-9526
Residential Treatment Facilities (phychiatric adolescent and young adult residence)
Tel: 716-828-9500; Fax: 716-828-9526
Special Services Program
Tel: 716-828-9500; Fax: 716-828-9526
Institutional Program
Tel: 716-828-9500; Fax: 716-828-9526
Group / Boarding Home Program
Tel: 716-828-9500; Fax: 716-828-9526
Services For The Developmentally Disabled:
Residential Services
Tel: 716-828-9500; Fax: 716-828-9526
Respite Program
Tel: 716-828-9500; Fax: 716-828-9526
Care Management
Tel: 716-828-9500; Fax: 716-828-9526
Other Services:
Family Pointe Evaluation Center Early Identification of delays in ages birth to five.
Tel: 716-892-9323; Fax: 716-892-9307
Prenatal Care Assistance Program
Tel: 716-828-9500; Fax: 716-828-9526
Postpartum Aftercare Program
Tel: 716-828-9500; Fax: 716-828-9526
Domestic and International Adoption Services
Tel: 716-828-9500; Fax: 716-828-9526
Preventive Services
Tel: 716-828-9755; Fax: 716-828-9745
Outpatient Clinic
Tel: 716-828-9700; Fax: 716-828-9745
Day Treatment Program
Tel: 716-828-9700; Fax: 716-828-9745
Baker Victory Healthcare Center (Fully owned subsidiary of Baker Hall) General medicine, pediatrics, ob/gyn and dental services.
Tel: 716-828-9454; Fax: 716-828-9526

Lake Placid
Diocese of Ogdensburg

St. Margaret Convent
420 Old Military Rd.
Lake Placid, NY 12946
Tel: 518-523-2929; Fax: 518-523-1401
Sisters of Mercy
Sr. M. CAMILLUS O'KEEFE, R.S.M., Supr.

Uihlein Mercy Center
420 Old Military Rd.
Lake Placid, NY 12946
Tel: 518-523-2464; Fax: 518-523-1401
Web Site: muhc.org
Institute of the Sisters of Mercy of the Americas, Regional Community of New York.
DOUGLAS MENZIES, Admin.
Rev. PATRICK J. O'REILLY, Chap.
Skilled Nursing Facility.
Sisters 2
Total Staff 198
Total Assisted 215

Lancaster
Diocese of Buffalo

St. Elizabeth's Home
5539 Broadway
Lancaster, NY 14086
Tel: 716-683-5150; Fax: 716-683-4049

CAROL A. WANTUCH, Admin.
Sisters of the Third Order of St. Francis 1
Residents 117
Total Staff 56

Latham
Diocese of Albany

Our Lady of Hope Residence
Little Sisters of the Poor
Jeanne Jugan Ln.
Latham, NY 12110
Tel: 518-785-4551; Fax: 518-785-3331
Rev. FIRMIN FINN, O.F.M.Conv.
Nursing Facility 70
Adult Care 30
Apartments for the Elderly 17

Lincolndale
Archdiocese of New York

Lincoln Hall
P.O. Box 600
Lincolndale, NY 10540
Tel: 914-248-7474; Fax: 914-248-8391
E-mail: pt.lincolnhall@worldnet.att.net
JOHN MICHAEL CHIARAVALLOTI, Acting Exec. Dir.
City Office
220 E. 23rd St.
New York, NY 10010
Capacity Boys 207
Total Staff 351
Total Assisted 421

Lockport
Diocese of Buffalo

St. Clare Manor
543 Locust St.
Lockport, NY 14094
Tel: 716-434-4718; Fax: 716-434-5900
Conducted by Catholic Charites of the Diocese of Buffalo.
SHEILA A. PERRY, Admin.
Residents 28

Middletown
Archdiocese of New York

St. Teresa's Nursing Home
120 Highland Ave.
Middletown, NY 10940
Tel: 914-342-1033; Fax: 914-344-5631
Bed Capacity 98
Total Assisted 98
Total Staff 120

Millbrook
Archdiocese of New York

Cardinal Hayes Home for Children
St. Joseph Dr., P.O. Box CH
Millbrook, NY 12545
Tel: 845-677-6363; Fax: 845-677-6691
Web Site: www.cardinalhayeshome.org
FRED APERS, Exec. Dir.
Residential care for developmentally disabled children and young adults.
Franciscan Missionaries of Mary 5
Capacity of residential facilities:
Millbrook Intermediate Care Facility 45
Community Intermediate Care Facilities 50
Total Assisted 100
Total Staff 225
In-home Respite Services.

Montrose
Archdiocese of New York

Kolping-on-Hudson
95 Montrose Point Rd.
Montrose, NY 10548
Tel: 914-737-9547
(Catholic Kolping Society New York, Inc.)
Total Assisted 2,000
Total Staff 10

Nanuet
Archdiocese of New York

St. Agatha Home of the New York Foundling Hospital
135 Convent Rd.
Nanuet, NY 10954
Tel: 914-623-3461
(Residential.)
Sisters of Charity of St. Vincent de Paul of New York.
KATHLEEN MCGLADE, Ph.D., Dir.
Rev. MICHAEL F. GANNON, Chap.
Bed Capacity 126
Diagnostic Facilities 26
In Foster Homes 38
Group Homes 81
Non-secure Detention 8 beds
Adult Intermediate Care facilities 65 beds
Family Support/Respite 10 beds
Runaway Youth Program.
Refugee Assistance Program.
Ulster County Prevention.

Nesconset
Diocese of Rockville Centre

Cleary Deaf Child Center, Inc.
301 Smithtown Blvd.
Nesconset, NY 11767
Tel: 631-588-0530 (Voice and TTY); Fax: 631-588-0016
E-mail: catherinef@clearyschool.org
Web Site: www.clearyschool.org
Directed by Catholic Charities.
Day School (Infants thru 21 years).
Sr. CATHERINE FITZGIBBON, C.S.J., Supt.
Students 70

New York
Archdiocese of New York

Cabrini Center for Nursing & Rehabilitation
542 E. 5th St.
New York, NY 10009
Tel: 212-358-3000; Fax: 212-358-6269
E-mail: mdevlin@ccnr.cabrininy.org
MARY DEVLIN, Admin.
Total SNF Beds 240
Total Staff 250

Calvary Hospital
1740 Eastchester Rd.
Bronx, NY 10461
Tel: 718-863-6900
For advanced cancer patients.
FRANK A. CALAMARI, Exec. Dir.
Rev. Msgr. MICHAEL J. ALESSANDRO, Chap.
MARY TERESA O'NEILL, Asst. Admin. & Dir. Pastoral Services
Pastoral Staff 16
Accommodations for 200
Patients assisted annually 3,300

Catholic Charities Department of Mental Health Services
1011 First Ave.
New York, NY 10022
Tel: 212-371-1000, Ext. 2040; Fax: 212-317-8719
E-mail: robert.pagliari@archny.org
MARJORIE STUCKLE, Ph.D., Interim Dir., Mental Health
Inwood/Washington Hts.:
652 E. 187th St.
New York, NY 10033
Tel: 212-795-6860; Fax: 212-928-4351
KATHRYN HOWARD, Admin. Supervisor
Bronx:
2380 Belmont Ave.
Bronx, NY 10458
Tel: 718-364-7700; Fax: 718-364-1513
Dr. MARJORIE STUCKLE, Admin. Supervisor
Yonkers:
4 St. Mary's St.
Yonkers, NY 10701
Tel: 914-476-2700; Fax: 914-965-4241
Peekskill:
1045 Park St.
Peekskill, NY 10566
Tel: 914-737-7338; Fax: 914-737-1050
Mrs. SUZANNE SANTANA-DELASHO, Admin. Supervisor
Hudson Valley Counseling Corps:
Rockland County
Tel: 845-942-5791; Fax: 845-429-2938
Orange County
Tel: 845-561-3452; Fax: 845-561-2825
Dutchess County
Tel: 845-452-1400; Fax: 845-452-3336
Sullivan County
Tel: 845-791-6023; Fax: 845-791-6104
Ulster County
Tel: 845-340-9170; Fax: 845-340-9596

Catholic Guardian Society
1011 First Ave.
New York, NY 10022
Tel: 212-371-1000
Mr. JOHN FREIN, Exec. Dir.
Intermediate care facilities, individual residential alternatives and family support programs for mentally retarded, developmentally disabled adults. Group home program for boys and girls, ages 13-21 years; agency operated boarding homes and adoption services for boys and girls ages 0-16; provides foster homes for boys and girls ages 0-21; and specialized foster homes for children with AIDS.
Total Assisted 1,075
Total Staff 506

Catholic Guild for the Blind
1011 First Ave., 6th Floor
New York, NY 10022
Tel: 212-371-1000, Ext. 2017; Fax: 212-826-8377
A THERESE SNYDER, Exec. Dir.
Independent Vendors 5
Total Staff 6

Catholic Home Bureau
1011 First Ave.
New York, NY 10022
Tel: 212-371-1000; Fax: 212-755-4110
E-mail: 6269xx@dfa.state.ny.us
PHILIP GEORGINI, Exec. Dir.
Placement of dependent and neglected boys and girls ages birth-18 in foster and adoptive homes and agency-operated boarding homes. Three shelters serve 45 homeless women with 26 preschool children. Family day car program serves 285 yearly. Maternity Services Program provides free, confidential counseling, medical & shelter care to single and married parents seeking help in planning for their unborn children. Toll-free hotline 1-800-592-HELP.
Total Assisted 2,770
Total Staff 202

Centro Maria, Inc.
539 W. 54th St.
New York, NY 10019
Tel: 212-581-5273; Fax: 212-307-5687
E-mail: cenmariany@mindspring.com
Web Site: rmi.world.org
For young students and working women.
Sr. CLARA ECHEVERRIA, R.M.I., Supr.
Religious of Mary Immaculate 7
Bed Capacity 54

Cor Mariae
c/o 1011 First Ave., Rm. 1130
New York, NY 10022
Tel: 212-371-1000, Ext. 2435
Residence for formerly homeless senior women.

Covenant House Under 21
460 W. 41st St.
New York, NY 10036
Tel: 212-613-0300; Fax: 212-629-3756
(Runaway and Homeless Youth.)
Sr. MARY ROSE MCGEADY, D.C., Pres.
BRUCE J. HENRY, Exec. Dir.
Total Assisted 8,593
Total Staff 539

The Dwelling Place
409 W. 40th St.
New York, NY 10018
Tel: 212-564-7887; Fax: 212-695-3642
E-mail: thedwellingplace@juno.com
For homeless women.
Sr. NANCY CHIARELLO, O.S.F., Admin.
Shelter: 18 Women Daily
Dinner Program: 60 Daily
Total Assisted: 22,000
Total Staff: 6

El Carmelo Residence
249 W. 14th St.
New York, NY 10011
Tel: 212-242-8224
Sr. MODESTA PEREZ, Supr.

Good Shepherd Services
305 7th Ave., 9th Floor
New York, NY 10001
Tel: 212-243-7070; Fax: 212-929-3412
E-mail: plomonaco@goodshepherds.org
Web Site: www.goodshepherds.org
Sr. PAULETTE LOMONACO, Exec. Dir.
Provides foster care and adoption services (formerly McMahon Services for Children) and five residential programs for troubled adolescents, a training program for social service workers and a comprehensive range of neighborhood family services to individuals and youth from the South Brooklyn community. These services include educational support, employment, counseling, crisis intervention, literacy, skills training and advocacy services.
Total Assisted 10,000
Total Staff 430

Guild of the Infant Savior
1011 First Ave., Room 1150
New York, NY 10022
Tel: 212-371-1000, Ext. 2440

The Jeanne d'Arc Residence
253 W. 24th St.
New York, NY 10011
Tel: 212-989-5952; Fax: 212-691-0257
E-mail: jdr253@juno.com
Women 18 to 40.
Sr. ROSE ANN MENKE, Admin.
Accommodations for 140 Residents
Sisters of Divine Providence 8
Lay Staff 12

Kateri Residence
150 Riverside Dr.
New York, NY 10024-2201
Tel: 212-769-0744; Fax: 212-873-0658
E-mail: 1bond@chcn.org
Web Site: www.chcn.org/kateri
Skilled Nursing Care/Residential Health Care Facility for the Elderly.
LASCELLES L. BOND, Exec. Vice Pres. & Admin.
ROBERT G. SUSSINGHAM, Assoc. Admin.
PATRICIA E. SCHNEIDER, R.N., Ph.D., Asst. Admin.
BRUCE L. ADLER, CFO
DORIS HUNG, Controller
WELLINGTON Y. LIU, M.D., Medical Dir.
JANET LEVINE, R.N., Dir., Nursing Svcs.
MARY J. HEALY, R.N., Dir., Resident Assessment
ROBERT HOLZER, Dir., Admissions
ROBERT J. GEIER, Dir., Recreation Therapy
RUTH PAPPELIS, Dir., Volunteers & Devel.
Sr. PATRICIA GEOGHEGAN, P.B.V.M., Dir. Pastoral Care
Sr. MIRIAM POVEDA, R.S.H.M., Pastoral Care Assoc.
Sr. PADRAIC MARY MCGUINNESS, O.P., Pastoral Care Assoc.
In res.,
Rev. VINCENT MELE, O.F.M (Immaculate Conception Prov.)
Rev. Msgr. JAMES J. HANLON
Sisters In Residence:
Sr. MARGARET MARY NIZIOL, S.R.C.M.
Sr. MARY MICHAEL MULLANEY, S.R.C.M.
Bed Capacity 520
Total Assisted 768
Total Staff 610

Kennedy Child Study Center
151 E. 67th St.
New York, NY 10021
Tel: 212-988-9500; Fax: 212-570-6690
E-mail: k.c.s.c@worldnet.att.net
ANN WILLIAMS, Ph.D., Exec. Dir.
Preschool Special Education 85
Infant/Parent Services 40
Case Management Services
Tel: 212-988-9500; Fax: 212-327-2601
Family Support Services 40
Clinic Program 400
Bronx Site
1028 E. 179th St.
Bronx, NY 10460
Tel: 718-842-0200; Fax: 718-842-1328
Preschool Special Education 125
Infant/Parent Services 50
Case Management Services
Tel: 718-842-0200; Fax: 718-842-1328
Family Support Services 40

Kolping Society of New York Men's Residence (Catholic Kolping Society New York, Inc.)
165 E. 88th St.
New York, NY 10128
Tel: 212-369-6647; Fax: 212-987-5652
For young Catholic men.
ERNST ENDRICH, Mgr.
Total in Residence 88
Total Staff 11

Kolping-on-Concourse
2916 Grand Concourse
Bronx, NY 10458
Tel: 718-733-6119
JORGE PARIS, Mgr.
(Catholic Kolping Society New York, Inc.)
Total in Residence 96
Total Staff 11

The Leo House
332 W. 23rd St.
New York, NY 10011
Tel: 212-929-1010; Fax: 212-366-6801
For the Clergy, Sisters & Laity.
THOMAS E. FREEBURN, Exec. Dir.
Senior Citizens in Residence 5
Total Staff 41
Catholic Hotel for Travelers 12,755

Mary Manning Walsh Home
1339 York Ave.
New York, NY 10021
Tel: 212-628-2800; Fax: 212-861-4178
E-mail: mmwhome@msn.com
Carmelite Sisters for the Aged and Infirm.
Sr. SEAN WILLIAM O'BRIEN, Admin.
Rev. Msgr. JAMES J. MURRAY, Chap.
Rev. MATTHEW MANALEL, Asst. Chap.
Total Staff 530
Total Assisted 362

Mission of the Immaculate Virgin
Mount Loretto
Staten Island, NY 10309
Tel: 718-317-2600; Fax: 718-317-2830
STEPHEN RYNN, Exec. Dir.
In res.,
Rev. Msgr. JOSEPH C. ANSALDI
Rev. MICHAEL P. REILLY
Legal Title: *Mission of the Immaculate Virgin for the Protection of Homeless and Destitute Children*
Intermediate Care Facility:
Capacity 12
Community Residence:
Capacity 4
Day Care Center:
Capacity 45
Individual Residential Alternatives:
St. Matthew Cottage:
Capacity 8
108 Bedell St.:
Capacity 6
6532 Amboy Rd.:
Capacity 7
Residential & Day Care
Total Assisted 82
Total Staff 104

New York Catholic Deaf Center
1011 First Ave., Room 670
New York, NY 10022
Tel: 212-371-1000 Ext. 2011 (Voice); 212-758-3045 (TTY); Fax: 212-317-8719
Rev. Msgr. PATRICK P. MCCAHILL, Dir.
Ms. JENNIFER RESTUCCI, Interpreter Advocate
Total Staff 5
Total Assisted 2200

New York Foundling Charitable Corp.
590 Avenue of the Americas
New York, NY 10011
Tel: 212-633-9300
Sr. ELIZABETH VERMAELEN, S.C., Pres.

New York Foundling Hospital for Pediatric, Medical and Rehabilitative Care, Inc.
590 Avenue of the Americas
New York, NY 10011
Tel: 212-633-9300; Fax: 212-886-4091
E-mail: carolb@nyfoundling.org
MICHAEL GARBER, Exec. Dir.
RUTH MULLER, Admin.
Sponsored by Sisters of Charity of St. Vincent de Paul of New York.
Children 136

New York Foundling Hospital, The
590 Avenue of the Americas
New York, NY 10011
Tel: 212-633-9300; Fax: 212-741-7516
E-mail: ritan@nyfoundling.org
(Children from Infancy to 21)
Mr. MICHAEL GARBER, Exec. Dir.
Children cared for during the year
In the institution 236
In foster homes 867
In adoptive homes 286
Mothers cared for in St. Mary's Maternity Residence 93
Group residences 415
Diagnostic reception centers 241
Sisters of Charity of St. Vincent de Paul of New York 15
Family day care 800 children & families
Group day care 128 children
Mother and abusing parent and child program
Families 560 children and families
Mother and child program 55 mothers and 55 babies
Community-based services
Families 700
Children 1,400
Programs for handicapped children 204
Foster Boarding Home Program 867
Children with AIDS 21
Total Assisted 7,843
Total Staff 1,700

Padre Pio Shelter for Homeless Men
419 E. 155th St.
Bronx, NY 10455
Tel: 718-292-3713
Total Assisted 18/night
Bro. SHAWN O'CONNOR, C.F.R., Dir.

Pelletier School & Services
147 W. 70th St.
New York, NY 10023
MARY ELLEN MURPHY, Program Dir.
Day School-Day Treatment Program for girls and boys 13-17.
Bed Capacity 50

Sacred Heart Residence
432 W. 20th St.
New York, NY 10011
Tel: 212-929-5790; Fax: 212-924-0891
Congregation of Mothers of the Helpless
Working or studying young ladies ages 19-29.
Sr. GUADALUPE SORDO ECHEVERRIA, Admin.
Capacity 30
Total Staff 3

St. Agnes' Residence
237 W. 74th St.
New York, NY 10023
Tel: 212-874-1361
For students and working women.
Sr. MARY PIUS FRIEL, R.S.M., Admin.
Daughters of Mary of the Immaculate Conception 2
Accommodations for 99
Total Assisted 101
Total Staff 6
Franciscan Fathers of St. Francis Monastery.

St. Joseph's Immigrant Home
425 W. 44th St.
New York, NY 10036-4402
Tel: 212-246-5363
For students and working women.
Sr. MARY CELINE, D.M., Admin.
Daughters of Mary of the Immaculate Conception 2
Accommodations for 90

St. Mary's Residence
225 E. 72nd St.
New York, NY 10021
Tel: 212-249-6850; Fax: 212-249-4336
For students and young working women.
Sr. M. PERPETUA KODBA, F.D.C., Admin.
Miss LISA REINWALD, Dir. of Admissions
Daughters of Divine Charity 6
Accommodations for 145

St. Rose's Home
71 Jackson St.
New York, NY 10002
Tel: 212-677-8132; Fax: 212-982-3485
Legal Title: *The Servants of Relief for Incurable Cancer*
Free home for incurable cancer patients.
Sr. M. LUCY O.P., Supr.
Sr. M. BARBARA O.P., Admin.
Rev. ANDREW DREW, O.F.M.Cap., Chap.
Dominican Sisters of the Congregation of St. Rose of Lima 9
Bed Capacity 60
Patients assisted annually 160

St. Zita's Home for Adults
143 W. 14th St.
New York, NY 10011
Tel: 212-243-7200
Home for Women.
Sr. ANTHONY MARIE Supr.
Sisters of Reparation of the Congregation of Mary 11
Accommodations for 46 Women
Total Assisted 22

Terence Cardinal Cooke Health Care Center
1249 Fifth Ave.
New York, NY 10029
Tel: 212-360-1000; Fax: 212-289-2739
E-mail: tcchcc@chcsnet.org
Web Site: www.catholichealthcaresystem.org/tcc
Mr. JAMES D. CAMERON, Pres. & CEO
Hospital for developmentally disabled.
Bed Capacity 50
Developmental Disabilities Clinic
1249 Fifth Ave.
New York, NY 10029
Tel: 212-360-3703
Comprehensive Outpatient medical, therapeutic and educational services.
Patients assisted annually 44,000
Hemodialysis
1249 Fifth Ave.
New York, NY 10029
Tel: 212-360-3860
22 End Stage Renal Dialysis Stations
Patients assisted annually 22,000
(For information concerning nursing home see Homes for Aged category.)

Terence Cardinal Cooke Health Care Center
1249 Fifth Ave.
New York, NY 10029
Tel: 212-360-1000; Fax: 212-289-2739

JAMES D. CAMERON, Pres. & CEO
Sr. MARY ANN DALY, S.C.
Skilled nursing facility.
Bed Capacity 523
Skilled Nursing Facility AIDS Program.
Bed Capacity 156
(See Special Hospitals Category for additional services offered from this Health Care Center.)

Thorpe Family Residence, Inc.
2252 Crotona Ave.
New York, NY 10457
Tel: 718-933-7312; Fax: 718-933-7311
E-mail: srbarbter@aol.com
Sr. BARBARA LENNIGER, O.P., Exec. Dir.
The Crotona-Thorpe Housing Development Fund Corporation (Sub of Thorpe Family Residence, Inc.),
Tel: 914-359-6400; Fax: 914-359-6503
Sr. MURIEL COONEY, O.P., Pres.
Residents 65
Total Assisted 130
Total Staff 10

Vincent J. Fontana Center for Child Protection
590 Ave. of the Americas
New York, NY 10011
Tel: 212-633-9300; Fax: 212-886-4008
E-mail: michaelg@nyfoundliving.org
MICHAEL GARLEEN, Contact Person

Niagara Falls
Diocese of Buffalo

Mount St. Mary's LTC Facility, Inc.
2600 Main St.
Niagara Falls, NY 14305
Tel: 716-285-9155; Fax: 716-285-4558
E-mail: MSMLTCF@aol.com
THOMAS LOSTRACCO, Admin.
BONNIE GIFFORD, Dir. Nursing Svcs.
Sponsored by the Sisters of St. Francis.
Bed Capacity 131
Patients assisted annually 190
Total Staff 190

St. Mary's Manor
515 Sixth St.
Niagara Falls, NY 14301
Tel: 716-285-3236; Fax: 716-285-4199
JOHN M. DUNN, Admin.
THERESA A. THOMAS, Dir. Nursing Svcs.
Bed Capacity 119
Patients assisted annually 179
Total Staff 160

North Greenbush
Diocese of Albany

S.J. Housing Development Fund Company, Inc. dba St. Jude's Apartments
50 Dana Ave.
Wynantskill, NY 12198
Tel: 518-283-5690; Fax: 518-283-5893
VIRGINIA HORDINES, Dir.
Nonprofit housing facility for elderly and handicapped persons of very low income.
Apartments 49

North Syracuse
Diocese of Syracuse

Pitcher Hill-Christopher Housing Development Fund Co., Inc.
114 Elbow Rd.
North Syracuse, NY 13212
Tel: 315-454-0697; Fax: 315-454-0053
Engaged in the construction and operation of nonprofit housing facilities for elderly and handicapped persons of low income. 100 units, one bedroom apartments. Christopher Community, Inc., (Managing Agent).
Total Assisted 99
Total Staff 3

Ogdensburg
Diocese of Ogdensburg

St. Joseph's Home
420 Lafayette St.
Ogdensburg, NY 13669
Tel: 315-393-3780; Fax: 315-393-3847
E-mail: stjh@gisco.net
Web Site: www.stjh.org
WILLIAM L. O'REILLY, Admin.
Total Staff 97
Total Assisted 117

Olean
Diocese of Buffalo

St. Joseph Manor
2211 W. State St.
Olean, NY 14760
Tel: 716-372-7810; Fax: 716-373-4375
E-mail: stjmanor@eznet.net
MARILYN J. GIBBIN, Admin.
Bed Capacity 22
Total Assisted 30
Total Staff 40

Orchard Park
Diocese of Buffalo

W.N.Y. Catholic LongTerm Care, Inc. dba Father Baker Manor
6400 Powers Rd.
Orchard Park, NY 14127
Tel: 716-667-0001; Fax: 716-667-0028
E-mail: bakermanor@aol.com
Nursing facility sponsored by the Catholic Health System, Inc.
JOHN DURNO, Admin.
Bed Capacity 160
Total Assisted 160
Total Staff 235

Ossining
Archdiocese of New York

The Cardinal McCloskey Emergency Residential School
155 N. Highland Ave.
Ossining, NY 10562
Tel: 914-762-5302; Fax: 914-762-7844
E-mail: eesaunders@aol.com

Oswego
Diocese of Syracuse

Saint Luke's Health Care Services
299 E. First St.
Oswego, NY 13126
Tel: 315-342-3166; Fax: 315-343-6531
E-mail: stluke@global2000.net
Web Site: www.stlukehs.com
Mr. TERRENCE GORMAN, Admin.
Total Staff 260

St. Luke's Housing Development Fund Co., Inc.
St. Luke's Apartments, W. First St.
Oswego, NY 13126
Engaged in the construction and operation of a non-profit housing facility for elderly and handicapped persons of low income. 100 units, one bedroom apartments. Christopher Community, Inc., (Managing Agent).

Port Jefferson Station
Diocese of Rockville Centre

Maryhaven Center of Hope
Administrative Offices, 1010 Rte. 112
Port Jefferson Station, NY 11776
Tel: 631-474-4120; Fax: 631-474-4110
Web Site: www.maryhaven.org
Mr. LEWIS GROSSMAN, CEO
Maryhaven provides services to approximately 2,000 mentally and physically challenged children and adults.
Adult Day Services (over age 18):
Vocational Training/Supported Work/Sheltered Workshop
Tel: 631-924-5900; Fax: 631-924-2464
Participants develop skills necessary to obtain employment within an array of community-based options, or within the agency's workshop.
Day Treatment
Tel: 631-924-5900; Fax: 631-924-0411
Participants receive assistance with learning skills necessary for independent living.
Day Habilitation
Tel: 631-474-4100; Fax: 631-474-4156
Individuals receive intensive therapeutic services along with increased community integration.
Adult Residential Services:
Adult Residences
Tel: 631-474-4100; Fax: 631-474-9014
The agency operates a variety of housing alternatives within community-based settings.
Home Touch
Tel: 631-474-4100; Fax: 631-474-9014
Individuals still living at home receive assistance in accessing needed support services.
Mental Health Services:
Case Management
Tel: 631-474-4100; Fax: 631-474-4156
Staff offer individuals assistance with accessing supports and services, advocacy and individual follow-up.
Continuing Day Treatment/Intensive Psychiatric Rehabilitation Treatment
Tel: 631-727-4044; Fax: 631-727-6531
These day programs work to develop individual skills to improve a person's living, working and social situations.
Children Services (Ages 5-21):
Maryhaven School
Tel: 631-474-3400; Fax: 631-474-4181
Progressive educational programming for children with developmental disabilities. The school is committed to the IEP diploma recipient and has a specialization in autism.
Children's Residences
Tel: 631-474-3400; Fax: 631-474-4181
Provides 24-hour programming for students requiring greater support than can be provided at home.

Queens Village
Diocese of Brooklyn

Queen of Peace Residence
110-30 221st St.
Queens Village, NY 11429
Tel: 718-464-1800
Legal Title: *Home for the Aged, Little Sisters of the Poor*
Sr. GERTRUDE MARY, L.S.P., Admin.
Rev. Msgr. WILLIAM J. RODGERS, Chap.
In res.,
Revs.:
JOHN F. HUGHES
JAMES MEADE
ALFRED J. WEINLICH
ANTHONY E. MUELLER
CHARLES F. HARTH
Sisters 19

Rensselaer
Diocese of Albany

East Greenbush Housing Development Fund Co., Inc. dba Branson Manor Senior Apartment
3 Grandview Dr.
Rensselaer, NY 12144
Tel: 518-283-8280; Fax: 518-283-8292

Rhinebeck
Archdiocese of New York

Astor Home for Children, The
36 Mill St., P.O. Box 5005
Rhinebeck, NY 12572-5005
Tel: 845-876-4081; Fax: 845-876-2020
E-mail: rlogan@ustorservices.org
Web Site: www.ustorservices.org
Sr. ROSE LOGAN, D.C., Exec. Dir.
Rev. GEORGE J. KUHN, Chap.
Daughters of Charity 4
Residential Treatment Facility for severe emotionally disturbed-mentally ill boys and girls, ages 5-12.
Bed Capacity 20
Residential Treatment Center (Rhinebeck):
Bed Capacity 55
Therapeutic Foster Boarding Homes 24
Family-Based Treatment 10
Child Guidance Clinics: Rhinebeck, Poughkeepsie, Beacon, Bronx, ages birth-18.
Capacity: unlimited
Day treatment programs ages 3-12:
Capacity Dutchess Co. 65
Bronx 160
Therapeutic Nursery, Bronx 40
Adolescent Day Treatment 120
School-Based Clinic 50
School-Based Services
unlimited
Intensive Parenting Program, Bronx, ages birth-18:
Capacity 90 families
Head Start-Day Care Centers: Poughkeepsie, Beacon, Red Hook, Millerton, Wingdale/Wappingers Falls
Capacity 384
Day Care Centers: Beacon, Red Hook, Millerton.
Capacity 35
Special Class Integrated Services, ages 3-5.
Capacity 58
Early Head Start.
Capacity 125
Total Assisted 5,809
Total Staff 575

Astor Learning Center, The
36 Mill St., P.O. Box 5005
Rhinebeck, NY 12572-5005
Tel: 914-876-4081; Fax: 914-876-2020
Special Education Program for emotionally disturbed, mentally ill children ages 6-13 in the Residential Treatment Center and local community.

Capacity 75
Total Assisted 107
Total Staff 38

Ferncliff Nursing Home
21 Ferncliff Dr.
Rhinebeck, NY 12572
Tel: 845-876-2011; Fax: 845-876-4810
Carmelite Sisters for the Aged and Infirm
Sr. M. BERNADETTE THERESE REILLY, Admin.
Rev. PETER J. SMITH, Chap.
Bed Capacity 328
Total Assisted 400
Total Staff 450

Rochester
Diocese of Rochester

St. Ann's Home for the Aged
1500 Portland Ave.
Rochester, NY 14621
Tel: 716-342-1700; Fax: 716-342-9585
Web Site: www.stannsrochester.org
BETTY MULLIN, Pres. & CEO
Rev. PETER T. BAYER, Dir. of Pastoral Care
ROSEMARIE ZLOTNICK, Pastoral Care Coord.
Residents 354

St. Ann's Nursing Home Co., Inc.
(The Heritage)
1450 Portland Ave.
Rochester, NY 14621
Tel: 716-342-1700; Fax: 716-342-9585
Web Site: www.stannsrochester.org
BETTY MULLIN, Pres. & CEO
Rev. PETER T. BAYER, Dir. of Pastoral Care
ROSEMARIE ZLOTNICK, Pastoral Care Coord.
Residents 237

Rome
Diocese of Syracuse

C.N.C. Inc.
W. Thomas St.
Rome, NY 13440
Tel: 315-735-7545
Mailing Address:
Utica Catholic Charities, 1408 Genese St.
Utica, NY 13502
Facility for ten deinstitutionalized chronically mentally ill individuals living in a group home.

Rome Mall Housing Development Fund Company, Inc.
Mailing Address:
1654 W. Onondaga St.
Syracuse, NY 13204
Tel: 315-424-1821
Rome Mall Apts.
Rome, NY 13440
40 one bedroom units for the elderly. Christopher Community, Inc., (Managing Agent).

Saranac Lake
Diocese of Ogdensburg

St. Joseph's Rehabilitation Center, Inc.
99 Glenwood Estates, P.O. Box 470
Saranac Lake, NY 12983
Tel: 518-891-3950; 891-4135 (Admissions); Fax: 518-891-3986
E-mail: stjoes@northnet.org
Alcoholism & Substance Abuse Rehab.
Revs.:
DANIEL P. CALLAHAN, S.A., Chap.
CARMEN GUILIANO, S.A.
Bros.:
ALAN LEMAY, S.A.
PASCHAL STEEN, S.A.
Franciscan Friars of the Atonement.
Priests 2
Brothers 2
Residents 62

Silver Creek
Diocese of Buffalo

St. Columbans on the Lake, Home for the Aged
2546 Lake Rd.
Silver Creek, NY 14136
Tel: 716-934-4515; Fax: 716-934-3919
Sr. CORONA COLLEARY, Admin.
In res.,
Revs.:
PATRICK CASHMAN, S.S.C.
PETER CRONIN, S.S.C.
EDMUND BAHL, S.S.C.
Columban Sisters 10
Aged Residents 50
Total Staff 35

Slingerlands
Diocese of Albany

Marie-Rose Manor HDFCI
100 Marquis Dr.
Slingerlands, NY 12159
Tel: 518-459-0204; Fax: 518-459-0527

Sloatsburg
Ukrainian Catholic Diocese of Stamford

St. Joseph's Home
125 Sisters Servants Ln., Box 25
Sloatsburg, NY 10974-0025
Tel: 845-753-2555; Fax: 845-753-6910
Sr. CHARLOTTE PIPPING, S.S.M.I., Admin.
Sisters Servants of Mary Immaculate 11
Residents 28
Staff 11

Springfield Gardens
Diocese of Brooklyn

Martin De Porres Group Homes
136-25 218th St.
Springfield Gardens, NY 11413
Tel: 718-527-0606; Fax: 718-528-7475
Bro. PHILIP ROFRANO, F.S.C., Exec. Dir.

Staten Island
Archdiocese of New York

Carmel Richmond Nursing Home, Inc.
88 Old Town Rd.
Staten Island, NY 10304-4299
Tel: 718-979-5000; Fax: 718-979-8027
Carmelite Sisters for the Aged and Infirm
Sr. M. STEPHEN MCBRIDE, O.Carm., Admin.
Rev. ERIC KYLE, O.F.M., Chap.
Bed Capacity 300
Friends of Carmel Richmond, Inc.
Tel: 718-979-5000; Fax: 718-979-8027
Total Assisted 300
Total Staff 352

Syosset
Diocese of Rockville Centre

St. Mary's Children and Family Services
525 Convent Rd.
Syosset, NY 11791-3864
Tel: 516-921-0808; Fax: 516-921-4542
E-mail: stmlg@cs.com
Web Site: stmaryscfs.com
Under the sponsorship of the Sisters of Mercy
LIZ GIORDANO, Exec. Dir.
Residential treatment center, non-secure detention, group homes, foster boarding homes, diagnostic assessment prog., preventive svc. prog. in Nassau Co. Residential treatment facility for mentally ill children. Abuse treatment & prevention program for males.
Total Staff 315
Total Assisted 892

Syracuse
Diocese of Syracuse

Bernardine Apartments, Inc.
417 Churchill Ave.
Syracuse, NY 13205
Tel: 315-469-7786
Mr. JAMES INTRONE, Pres.
TIM CARROLL, Mgr.

Christopher Community, Inc.
1654 W. Onondaga St.
Syracuse, NY 13204
Tel: 315-424-1821
Professional management and consultants of housing programs for the elderly, families and special populations.
Mr. PETER WHITE, Exec. Dir.
FRED ZOLNA, Housing Devel. Specialist

Churchill Manor, Inc.
750 E. Brighton Ave.
Syracuse, NY 13205
Tel: 315-492-1329; Fax: 315-492-6076
E-mail: cahika@lorettosystem.org
A non-profit corporation founded to provide housing for low and moderate income families and individuals.

Harbor View Housing Development Fund Co., Inc.
c/o 1654 W. Onondaga St.
Syracuse, NY 13204
Tel: 315-424-1822

Hawley Winton Housing Development Fund, Inc.
Walter Ludovico Apts., 340 Winton St.
Syracuse, NY 13203
Tel: 315-422-0475; Fax: 315-471-1554
32 one bedroom units occupied. Christopher Community, (Managing Agent).

Loretto
700 E. Brighton Ave.
Syracuse, NY 13205
Tel: 315-469-5561; Fax: 315-469-6558
Legal Title: *Loretto Rest Nursing Home Company, Inc.*
Mr. MITCHELL MARSH, Admin. Cunningham Bldg.
Deacon CHARLES O'CONNOR, Chap.

Loretto Geriatric Community Residences, Inc.
5018 S. Salina St.
Syracuse, NY 13205
Tel: 315-492-0896
4810 S. Salina St.
Syracuse, NY 13205
Tel: 315-469-8562
50 Syracuse St.
Baldwinsville, NY 13027
Tel: 315-635-1647
8659 Carpenter Rd.
Baldwinsville, NY 13027
Tel: 315-635-1763

Loretto Rest, Inc.
750 E. Brighton Ave.
Syracuse, NY 13205
Tel: 315-469-5061
Adult Home.
Mr. PATRICK DEPTULA, Exec. Vice Pres.
Deacon CHARLES O'CONNOR, Chap.

Ludden Housing Development Fund Company, Inc.
1654 W. Onondaga St.
Syracuse, NY 13204
Tel: 315-424-1821
Fifty one bedroom apartments for the elderly and handicapped. Christopher Community Inc., (Managing Agent).

Marcellus Apartments Housing Development Fund Company, Inc.
Mailing Address:
1654 W. Onondaga St.
Syracuse, NY 13204
Tel: 315-424-1821
Christopher Community, Inc., (Managing Agent).

Miller Road Housing Development Co., Inc.
(Brewerton)
Mailing Address:
1654 W. Onondaga St.
Syracuse, NY 13204
Tel: 315-424-1821
Housing for well elderly.

Mother Marianne Cope Housing Development Fund Co., Inc.
1654 W. Onondaga St.
Syracuse, NY 13204
Tel: 315-424-1821
E. Fayette St.
Syracuse, NY,
24 Units for HIV+ patients.

Mount St. James Corporation
1654 W. Onondaga St.
Syracuse, NY 13204
Tel: 315-424-1821
Engaged in the operation of a non-profit housing facility known as Mount St. James Apartments, at 338 Jamesville Ave., for persons of low to moderate income. Christopher Community, Inc., (Managing Agents).

Pompei Housing Development Fund Company, Inc.
c/o Christopher Community, Inc.
1654 W. Onondaga St.
Syracuse, NY 13204
Tel: 315-424-1821
50 one bedroom apartments for the elderly and handicapped. Christopher Community, Inc., (Managing Agent).

Pond St. Housing Development Fund Co., Inc.
Bishop Harrison Apartments, Pond St.
Syracuse, NY 13208
Tel: 315-476-8630; Fax: 315-474-0806
E-mail: slucas@christopher-community.org
Operation of 47 units, one bedroom apartments for the elderly and handicapped. Christopher Community Inc., (Managing Agent).

Providence House Apartments
1700 W. Onondaga St.
Syracuse, NY 13204
Tel: 315-471-8427; Fax: 315-474-1224
Senior citizen housing, 100 units. Christopher Community, (Managing Agent).

St. Camillus Health & Rehabilitation Center
813 Fay Rd.
Syracuse, NY 13219
Tel: 315-488-2951; Fax: 315-488-3255
Web Site: www.st-camillus.org
Mrs. AILEEN M. BALITZ, Pres.
Ms. PAM BUDNIKAS, Dir. Social Svcs.
Total Staff 590
St. Camillus Foundation
813 Fay Rd.
Syracuse, NY 13219
Tel: 315488-2951, Ext. 257
Mr. MICHAEL BYRNE, Foundation Chm.
MAUREEN CHARLAND, Exec. Dir.

St. Peter's Italian Church Housing Development Fund Co., Inc. Villa Scalabrini Apts.
709 James St.
Syracuse, NY 13203
RAYMOND A. BANACH, Vice Pres. & Treas.
MARIO ROSSI, Sec.
Operation of a non-profit housing facility for aged, well persons of low income at the 800 Block of E. Willow St. in Syracuse. 120 units, one-bedroom apartments. Christopher Community, Inc., (Managing Agent).

Stoneleigh Housing Development Fund Co., Inc.
Stoneleigh Apartments, 400 Lamb Ave., Canastota
Syracuse, NY 13032
Engaged in the construction and operation of a non-profit housing facility for elderly and handicapped persons of low income. 100 units, one bedroom apartments. Christopher Community, Inc., (Managing Agent).

Tyson Place Housing Development Fund Company, Inc.
(40 apartments for the elderly)
Mailing Address:—St. Joseph Manor
1654 W. Onondaga St.
Syracuse, NY 13204
Tel: 315-424-1821
Christopher Community, Inc., (Managing Agent).

Thornwood
Archdiocese of New York

Catholic World Mission, Inc.
582 Columbus Ave.
Thornwood, NY 10594
Tel: 914-749-3900; Fax: 914-749-3939
Rev. THOMAS MOYLAN, Contact Person

Town of Gates
Diocese of Syracuse

Steger Housing Development Fund Co., Inc.
4100 Lyell Rd.
Town of Gates, NY,
1654 W. Onondaga St.
Syracuse, NY 13204
Tel: 315-424-1821
56 apartments for well elderly.

Troy
Diocese of Albany

St. Mary's Woodland Village, Inc.
Upper Tibbits Ave.
Troy, NY 12180
Tel: 518-273-2040; Fax: 518-273-1542
Mrs. ROBIN SAGE, Admin.
Bed Capacity 155

Tupper Lake
Diocese of Ogdensburg

Mercy Healthcare Center, Inc.
114 Wawbeek Ave.
Tupper Lake, NY 12986
Tel: 518-359-3355; Fax: 518-359-9044
E-mail: jpeters@muhc.org
Web Site: muhc.org
Sr. JANET PETERS, R.S.M., V.P., Mission Svcs.
Skilled Nursing Facility.
Sisters of Mercy of the Americas (Hartsdale) 1
Capacity 80 Beds

Utica
Diocese of Syracuse

Catherine St. Housing Development Fund Company, Inc.
Mailing Address:—Mt. Carmel Apartments
1654 W. Onondaga St.
Syracuse, NY 13201-0511
Tel: 315-424-1821
Christopher Community, Inc., (Managing Agent).

St. Joseph Nursing Home
2535 Genesee St.
Utica, NY 13501
Tel: 315-797-1230; Fax: 315-797-5171
E-mail: frank@stjosephnh.org
Web Site: www.stjosephnh.org
Sr. BARBARA CONNOLLY, O.Carm., Admin.
Total Staff 182

Wading River
Diocese of Rockville Centre

Little Flower Children's Services of New York
Wading River, NY 11792
Tel: 631-929-6200; Fax: 631-929-6121
Web Site: www.LittleFlowerNY.org
Directed by the Diocese of Brooklyn. Foster care, adoption & post-adoption svcs., intermediate care facilities, residential treatment center, Special Act school district, family day care, family care for MR/DD clients, foster homes for teen mothers & their babies. Therapeutic foster boarding homes.
Rev. Msgr. JOHN T. FAGAN, Exec. Vice Pres. (CEO)
Mrs. MARY G. RYDER, Exec. Dir. (COO)
Sisters of the Holy Family of Nazareth
Sr. RITA WASILEWSKI, C.S.F.N., Supr.
Total Assisted 2,436

Warwick
Archdiocese of New York

Villa Frances at the Knolls
Franciscan Health Partner, Inc.
22 Van Duzer Pl.
Warwick, NY 10990
Tel: 914-987-5717; Fax: 914-986-1231
JEANNE LEE, Senior Vice Pres. Long Term Care & Tri State Health System
Rev. JOHN PIERCE, Chap.
Capacity 120

Watervliet
Diocese of Albany

Carondelet Commons Senior Apartments
Delatour Housing Development Fund Company, Inc. dba, Carondelet Commons Senior Apartments.
2 Carondelet Dr.
Watervliet, NY 12189
Tel: 518-783-0444; Fax: 518-783-0456
DORIS SEIP, Building Dir.

Fontbonne Manor Housing Development Fund Company, Inc.
c/o DePaul Management, 10 Carodelet Dr.
Watervliet, NY 12189
Tel: 518-782-2780; Fax: 518-782-2778
MICHELE KRAMM, Bldg. Dir.

Italian-American Housing Development Fund Co., Inc. dba Cabrini Acers Senior Apts.
4 Carondelet Dr.
Watervliet, NY 12189
Tel: 518-785-0050; Fax: 518-785-0110
DORIS SEIP, Building Dir.

St. Colman's Home
Watervliet, NY 12189
Tel: 518-273-4911; Fax: 518-273-3312
Sisters of the Presentation of the B.V.M.
Sr. M. VIRGINIA, P.B.V.M., Dir.
Rev. KENNETH GREGORY, Chap.
Children 50

West Islip
Diocese of Rockville Centre

Our Lady of Consolation Geriatric Care Center
Short & long term nursing & rehabilitative care.
111 Beach Dr.
West Islip, NY 11795
Tel: 631-587-1600; Fax: 631-587-5960
E-mail: olcl@villagenet.com
Web Site: ourladyofconsolation.org
Member of Catholic Health Services of LI.
Under the supervision of the Sisters of St. Dominic
Sr. AUDREY HARSEN, O.P., Pres. & CEO
Rev. ROBERT A. HYATT, Chap.
Bed Capacity 450
Total Assisted 994
Total Staff 787

West Park
Archdiocese of New York

St. Cabrini Home
West Park, NY 12493
Tel: 845-384-6500; Fax: 845-384-6001
E-mail: cabrini@ulster.net
Web Site: cabrinihome.com
JAMES J. LAVELLE, Exec. Dir.
Children 80
Agency Operated Boarding Home 2
Group Homes 13
Missionary Sisters of Sacred Heart 5
Served by Redemptionist Fathers
Cabrini-on-Hudson
Tel: 845-384-6720; Fax: 845-384-6002
An adult community.
Residents 60

White Plains
Archdiocese of New York

Cardinal McCloskey Services
Two Holland Ave.
White Plains, NY 10603
Tel: 914-997-8000; Fax: 914-997-2166
E-mail: mmcloughlin@cardinalmccloskey.org
Mrs. MARJORIE MCLOUGHLIN, Exec. Dir.
Sisters 3
In Foster Homes 500
In Group Homes 18
In Family Day Care:
Site I: Capacity 540
Site II: Capacity 115
Site III: Capacity 145
Cardinal McCloskey Emergency Residential School
155 N. Highland Ave.
White Plains, NY 10562
Tel: 914-762-5302; Fax: 914-762-7844
Capacity 20
Clients in Preventative Services 270
Total Assisted 2000
Total Staff 415

Williamsville
Diocese of Buffalo

Holy Family Home
410 Mill St.
Williamsville, NY 14221
Tel: 716-634-5400; Fax: 716-634-5730
Sr. VIRGINIA BALK, O.S.F., CEO
Sisters of St. Francis of the Third Order Regular 8
Residents 85
Total Staff 54

St. Francis Home of Williamsville
147 Reist St.
Williamsville, NY 14221
Tel: 716-633-5400; Fax: 716-663-6404
Legal Title: *St. Francis Home of Williamsville*
Skilled Nursing Facility
JAMES A. WALSH, Ph.D., Admin.
Rev. Msgr. HENRY J. GUGINO
Residents 142
Total Assisted 204
Total Staff 194

Yonkers
Archdiocese of New York

St. Eleanora's Home for Convalescents
127 S. Broadway
Yonkers, NY 10471
Tel: 718-378-7000; 549-9200; Fax: 718-884-3013
E-mail: scny@scny.org
Unit of St. Joseph's Nursing Home (Yonkers).

NORTH CAROLINA

Belmont
Diocese of Charlotte

**Holy Angels, Inc.*
6600 Wilkinson Blvd., P.O. Box 710
Belmont, NC 28012
Tel: 704-825-4161; Fax: 704-825-0553
E-mail: info@holyangelsnc.org
Web Site: www.holyangelsnc.org
Mrs. REGINA P. MOODY, M.Ed., Pres. & CEO
Sisters of Mercy 4
Capacity (All Programs) 174
Residential and developmental programs and services for children and adults with mental retardation and physical disabilities.
Holy Angels Specialized Community Residential Center (Children 0-20)

Little Angels Child Development Center
On-site integrated day care.
Great Adventures Social Club
Adults with mental retardation.
South Point
Children/Adult group home.
Belhaven
Adult group home.
Lakewood
Adult group home.
Fox Run ICF/MR Group Homes
Beds 18
Life Choices Vocational Program (Age 18+)
Cherubs Cafe, Gifts & Candy Bouquets by Holy Angels (Age 18+)
Tel: 704-825-0418; Fax: 704-825-0416
Job coaching, work options.
Supported Living (Age 18+)
Camp Hope
Integrated Day Camp for Children/Adults with Developmental Disabilities.
Carrabaun
Adult group home.
Gary Home
Adult/Children group home.

High Point
Diocese of Charlotte

Maryfield Nursing Home
1315 Greensboro Rd.
High Point, NC 27260
Tel: 336-886-2444; Fax: 336-886-4036
E-mail: srlucy@hpe_infi.net
Web Site: www.greensboro.com/mnh
Sr. LUCY HENNESSY, S.M.G., Admin.
Poor Servants of the Mother of God 7
Beds 115

Rosman
Diocese of Charlotte

**Frances Warde Health Service*
Star Rte. 1, Box 581
Rosman, NC 28772
Tel: 828-884-7990; Fax: 828-966-9609
E-mail: jdewarrsm@juno.com
Sr. GRETCHEN HERMANNY, R.S.M., M.D., Medical Dir.
Sisters 4
Total Assisted 3,600

NORTH DAKOTA

Bismarck
Diocese of Bismarck

Emmaus Place
1020 N. 26th St.
Bismarck, ND 58501
Tel: 701-258-2618
Priests retirement home.
Revs.:
THEODORE F. GUSTIN
PETE A. KRAMER
JOHN O'LEARY
WILLIAM J. FAHNLANDER
JOHN H. KUHN
ALBERT R. LEARY
WILLIAM A. RUSHFORD
JACOB J. SCHUMACHER
Total Staff 6
Total Assisted 8
Total in Residence 8

Marillac Manor
1016 N. 28th St.
Bismarck, ND 58501
Tel: 701-258-8702; Fax: 701-223-3127
E-mail: phoebeosb@hotmail.com
Sr. PHOEBE SCHWARTZE, O.S.B., Admin.
Retirement Apartments 78
Total Staff 10
Total in Residence 84

St. Vincent's Care Center, Inc.
1021 N. 26 St.
Bismarck, ND 58501-3199
Tel: 701-223-6888; Fax: 701-223-3015
E-mail: lblakeman@att.global.net
LYNN BLAKEMAN, Admin.
Sisters of St. Benedict 1
Total Staff 159
Resident Patients 101

Edgeley
Diocese of Fargo

Manor St. Joseph
404 Fourth Ave.
Edgeley, ND 58433
Tel: 701-493-2477; Fax: 701-493-2477
TAMMY JANGULA, Admin.
Sister Servants of Christ the King 2
Guests 40
Bed Capacity 40
Staff 33

Ellendale
Diocese of Fargo

Prince of Peace Care Center
201 8th St. N.
Ellendale, ND 58436
Tel: 701-349-3312; Fax: 701-349-3944
Operated by Benedictine Living Communities, Inc.
Mr. TONY HANSON, Admin.
Bed Capacity 74
Staff 94

Fargo
Diocese of Fargo

Riverview Place
5300 12th St. S.
Fargo, ND 58103
Tel: 701-237-4700; Fax: 701-235-5738
E-mail: riverjerry@juno.com
JERRY LINGEN, Admin.
Rev. Msgr. JOHN ANDERSON, (Retired)
Revs.:
PETER W. GRADY, (Retired)
WILLIAM J. MEHOK, S.J., (Retired)
JOHN MOORE, (Retired)
Residents 180
Staff 60

Villa Nazareth dba Friendship, Inc.
3004 S. 11th St.
Fargo, ND 58103
Tel: 701-235-8217; Fax: 701-235-7538
Presentation Sisters (P.B.V.M.). Catholic Health Initiatives
A community-based facility providing an array of educational, social and clinical services for children and adults with mental retardation and other developmental disabilities.
Total Assisted 220
Total Staff 300

Grand Forks
Diocese of Fargo

St. Anne's Guest Home
524 N. 17th St.
Grand Forks, ND 58203
Tel: 701-746-9401; Fax: 701-795-7825
E-mail: stannes@corpcomm.net
Sr. ELAINE MARIE ROGGENBUCK, O.S.F.
Sr. REBECCA METZGER, O.S.F., Admin.
Sisters of St. Francis of the Immaculate Heart of Mary (Hankinson, ND) 8
Staff 36
Guests 86

Hankinson
Diocese of Fargo

St. Gerard Community Nursing Home
613 First Ave. S.W.
Hankinson, ND 58041
Tel: 701-242-7891; Fax: 701-242-7896
Rev. PAUL L. KOEHLER, Chap.
Sr. ROSE MARIE FREUND, O.S.F., Admin.
Sisters of St. Francis of the Immaculate Heart of Mary (Hankinson, ND) 2
Beds 37
Patients assisted annually 54
Independent Living Unit Beds 12
Staff 70

La Moure
Diocese of Fargo

St. Rose Care Center
Hwy. 13, P.O. Box 627
La Moure, ND 58458
Tel: 701-883-5363; Fax: 701-883-5711
E-mail: tchanson@bhshealth
Operated by Benedictine Living Communities, Inc.
Mr. TONY HANSON, Admin.
Bed Capacity 60
Staff 82

Rolette
Diocese of Fargo

Presentation Care Center
304 John St.
Rolette, ND 58366
Tel: 701-246-3786
KIMBER WRAALSTAD, Pres. CEO
Beds 48
Patients Assisted 65
Staff 75

Sentinel Butte
Diocese of Bismarck

Home On The Range
16351 I-94
Sentinel Butte, ND 58654-9500
Tel: 701-872-3745; Fax: 701-872-3748
E-mail: hotr@beach.midstate.net
Mr. PATRICK J. PETERMANN, Exec. Dir.
Rev. DAVID G. MORMAN, Chap.
Total Staff 113
Total Assisted 169

Wahpeton
Diocese of Fargo

St. Catherine's Living Center
1307 N. Seventh St.
Wahpeton, ND 58075
Tel: 701-642-6667; Fax: 701-642-2485
Operated by Benedictine Living Communities, Inc.
BRIGID STEELE, Admin.
Residents 180
Long-term Care Beds 164
Basic Care Beds 16
Staff 200

OHIO

Akron
Diocese of Cleveland

Francesca Residence
39 N. Portage Path
Akron, OH 44303
Tel: 330-867-6334; Fax: 330-867-6334
Sr. M. MARTIN GREEN, F.D.C., Admin.
Rev. THOMAS F. SULLIVAN, Chap.
Daughters of Divine Charity 7
Total Under Care 42
Total in Residence 34
Total Staff 12

Leonora Hall
39 N. Portage Path
Akron, OH 44303
Tel: 330-867-1752; Fax: 330-867-6334, Ext. 330
E-mail: smpakron@aol.com
Residence for Young Women.
Sr. M. ANTOINETTE, F.D.C., Exec. Dir.
Daughters of Divine Charity 2
Residents 21

Austintown
Diocese of Youngstown

Humility House
755 Ohltown Rd.
Austintown, OH 44515
Tel: 330-505-0411; Fax: 330-544-5694
Total Staff 120
Nursing Home Residents 70
Assisted Living Residents 32

Beachwood
Diocese of Cleveland

Villa Sancta Anna Home for the Aged, Inc.
25000 Chagrin Blvd.
Beachwood, OH 44122-5665
Tel: 216-464-9250; Fax: 216-464-9274
LINDA SCHERGER, R.N., Admin.
3
Residents 68
Total Assisted 68
Total Staff 91

Bedford
Diocese of Cleveland

Light of Hearts Villa, Inc.
283 Union St.
Bedford, OH 44146
Tel: 216-232-1991; Fax: 440-232-1782
E-mail: lightofhearts@worldnet.att.net
Web Site: home.att.net/lightofhearts/
Sr. HELEN THERESE SCASNY, V.S.C., Exec. Dir.

BARBARA HAMMREL, Asst. Dir.
Total in Residence 86
Total Staff 61
Total Assisted 89

Canton
Diocese of Youngstown

House of Loreto
2812 Harvard Ave., N.W.
Canton, OH 44709
Tel: 330-453-8137; Fax: 330-453-8140
Administered by the Congregation of the Divine Spirit.
Sr. GLADYS SPENGLER, C.D.S., Exec. Dir.
Sr. CLAIRE BATTERSON, C.D.S., Admin.
In res.,
Rev. NORBERT R. WEST
Sisters of the Congregation of the Divine Spirit 18
Residents 57
Total Staff 61

Centerville
Archdiocese of Cincinnati

The Franciscan at St. Leonard
8100 Clyo Rd.
Centerville, OH 45458
Tel: 937-433-0480; Fax: 937-439-7165
A facility of the Franciscan Health System of the Ohio Valley, sponsored by the Franciscan Sisters of the Poor Health System, Inc. A residence for Senior Citizens.
Revs.:
JAMES VAN VURST, O.F.M., Dir. Pastoral Care
FRANCIS B. PILLIOD, Staff Chap.
ANTHONY GIANNAMORE, Moderator & Chap., Sunday Community
PHILIP C. HOELLE, S.M., (Retired)
Residents 738

Cincinnati
Archdiocese of Cincinnati

Archbishop Leibold Home for the Aged
476 Riddle Rd.
Cincinnati, OH 45220-2493
Tel: 513-281-8001; Fax: 513-281-4943
The Little Sisters of the Poor
Revs.:
MICHAEL LENZ, O.F.M., Chap.
JOVIAN C. WEIGEL, O.F.M.
AUGUST J. KNIEPP
BERARD GERBUS, O.F.M.
CHARLES MILLER, O.F.M.
CARL STEINBICKER
Sr. CECILIA SARTORIUS, L.S.P., Supr.
Sisters 14
Residents 100
Total Staff 80

Mercy Franciscan Senior Health and Housing Services Inc. dba Mercy St. Theresa Center
7010 Rowan Hill Dr.
Cincinnati, OH 45227
Tel: 513-271-7010; Fax: 513-527-0143
JAMIE J. HOUSEMAN, Exec. Dir.
Rev. STEPHEN J. EMERICK, Chap.
Sisters 3
Permanent Residents 160

Mercy Franciscan Senior Health and Housing Services, Inc. dba Mercy Franciscan Terrace
100 Compton Rd.
Cincinnati, OH 45215
Tel: 513-761-9036; Fax: 513-761-5199
BRIAN FORSCHNER, Pres.
BETH A. LUKEN, Admin.
Pastoral Care Dept.:
JOAN OWENS
Residents 157
Retired Sisters 15
Retired Brothers 4
Retired Priests 4
Other Residents 134

Mercy Franciscan Senior Health and Housing Services, Inc. dba Mercy Franciscan at West Park
2950 West Park Dr.
Cincinnati, OH 45238
Tel: 513-451-8900; Fax: 513-451-3728
BRIAN FORSCHNER, Pres.
TIMOTHY C. DRESSMAN, Admin.
DON ROHLING, Dir. Mission Svcs.
Ms. ALBERTA UTRUP, Chaplain
Residents 340

St. Aloysius Orphanage
4721 Reading Rd.
Cincinnati, OH 45237
Tel: 513-242-7600; Fax: 513-242-2845
E-mail: bclevenger@staloysiuscincinnati.org
Web Site: www.staloysiuscincinnati.org
Treatment group home for boys ages 9-17.
DONNA SAUNDERS, Exec. Dir.
LLOYD REEVES, Dir. Educ.
Children 66

St. Joseph Infant and Maternity Home dba St. Joseph Home
10722 Wyscarver Rd.
Cincinnati, OH 45241
Tel: 513-563-2520; Fax: 513-563-1958
E-mail: smvanvurst@sjh-cincy.com
Web Site: www.sjh-cincy.com
Sisters of Charity of Cincinnati, OH
Sr. MARIANNE VAN WURST, Admin.
Children and young adults with severe/profound mental and motor disabilities 47
Respite Beds 5

St. Joseph Orphanage
Archdiocesan Children's Residential Center.
5400 Edalbert Dr.
Cincinnati, OH 45239-7695
Tel: 513-741-3100; Fax: 513-741-5656
E-mail: sjoe@one.net
Web Site: www.stjosephorphanage.org
ROBERT J. WEHR, Ph.D., Exec. Dir.
A.C.T. Child Case Management
5400 Edalbert Dr.
Cincinnati, OH 54239
Tel: 513-245-9944; Fax: 513-245-9401
ROBERT J. WEHR, Ph.D., Exec. Dir.
Employees 68
Children Served 459
St. Joseph Villa
5400 Edalbert Dr.
Cincinnati, OH 45239
Tel: 513-741-3100; Fax: 513-741-5686
Residential Treatment Children 6-18.
ROBERT J. WEHR, Ph.D., Exec. Dir.
Staff 294
Residents 295
Altercrest
274 Sutton Rd.
Cincinnati, OH 45230
Tel: 513-231-5010; Fax: 513-231-8651
Residential Treatment for Boys ages 12-18.
ROBERT J. WEHR, Ph.D., Exec. Dir.
Staff 78
Residents 146
C.A.R.E. Child Case Management
90 Lawn Ave.
Hamilton, OH 45013
Tel: 513-887-2100; Fax: 513-887-2101
ROBERT J. WEHR, Ph.D., Exec. Dir.
Staff 11
Children Served 278
Family Ties Therapeutic Foster Care
5400 Edalbert Dr.
Cincinnati, OH 45239
Tel: 513-741-3100; Fax: 513-741-5686
ROBERT J. WEHR, Ph.D., Exec. Dir.
Staff 15
Total Assisted 155
In-Home Workers
2105 Grandin Ave.
Cincinnati, OH 45208
Tel: 513-924-0070; Fax: 513-924-0115
Dr. ROBERT J. WEHR, Ph.D., Exec. Dir.
Staff 32
Total Assisted 51

St. Margaret Hall
1960 Madison Rd.
Cincinnati, OH 45206-1896
Tel: 513-751-5880; Fax: 513-751-9813
Sr. ANN M. DAILEY, O.Carm., Admin.
Rev. RODNEY MCDANIEL, Chap.
Carmelite Sisters for the Aged and Infirm 8
Residents 133

Sisters of Charity Senior Care Corp., dba Bayley Place
990 Bayley Place Dr.
Cincinnati, OH 45233
Tel: 513-347-5500; Fax: 513-347-5553
E-mail: bayleyplace@srcharitycinti.org
Web Site: www.bayleyplace.org
Also includes Eldermount Adult Day Program and The Village at Bayley Place.
Sr. JEANNE ROACH, Pres. & CEO
Total Assisted 85
Independent Cottages 82

Cleveland
Diocese of Cleveland

Christ Child - DePaul Day Care Center
2320 E. 24th St.
Cleveland, OH 44115
Tel: 216-687-0007; Fax: 216-687-0403
Day Care program sponsored by Catholic Charities Services Corp. Funded by United Way & Catholic Charities.
ELBERT W. CLARK, JR., M.A., L.S.W., Dir. of Early Childhood Ed. Programs
DEBORAH BAKER, Day Care Admin.
Students 102
Total Staff 17
Total Assisted 189

Holy Family Home
6707 State Rd.
Cleveland, OH 44134
Tel: 440-885-3100; Fax: 440-885-0644
E-mail: www.holyfamilyhome.com
Free nursing home for terminal cancer patients who are unable to pay.
Legal Title: *The Servants of Relief for Incurable Cancer*
Administered by Dominican Sisters of the Third Order, Congregation of St. Rose of Lima.
Sr. M. CHRISTOPHER, O.P., Supr.
Rev. JOSEPH F. CIOLEK, Chap., Tel: 440-842-1436
Sisters 10
Total Staff 55
Bed Capacity 50
Patients assisted annually 203

Jennings Hall Center for Older Adults
10204 Granger Rd.
Cleveland, OH 44125
Tel: 216-581-2900; Fax: 216-581-4505; 216-581-1517
E-mail: jenninghal@aol.com
Mrs. MARTHA M. KUTIK, Pres. & Exec. Dir.
Rev. KESTUTIS ZEMAITIS (Vilnius) Chap., Tel: 216-581-2900
Residential Long-Term Care Facility. Under Diocesan Auspices.
Sisters 5
Residents 156
Total Assisted 285
Total Staff 200

Mount St. Joseph
21800 Chardon Rd.
Cleveland, OH 44117
Tel: 216-531-7426; Fax: 216-531-4033
E-mail: mountstjoe@aol.com
Sr. M. CECILIA ILLIG, NHA
Conducted by Sisters of St. Joseph of St. Mark - Mount St. Joseph.
Sisters 17
Bed Capacity 100
Residents 100
Total Assisted 100
Total Staff 160

Rose Mary, The Johanna Grasselli Rehabilitation and Education Center
19350 Euclid Ave.
Cleveland, OH 44117
Tel: 216-481-4823; Fax: 216-481-4154
Ms. PATRICIA A. COLOMBO, Pres. & CEO
Sisters of the Humility of Mary 1
Children 42
Residents 86
Bed Capacity 88
Total Staff 250

St. Augustine Manor
7801 Detroit Ave.
Cleveland, OH 44102
Tel: 216-634-7400; Fax: 216-634-7483
E-mail: p.gareau@worldnet.att.net
Web Site: www.staugustinemanor.org
Affiliated with Catholic Charities. Provider of rehabilitation services, subacute care, skilled nursing, assisted living and child day care.
Mr. ERIC SCHREIBER, Chm., Board of Trustees
Mr. PATRICK GAREAU, Pres. & CEO
Rev. JOSEPH A. ROMANSKY, Residence Chap.
Bed Capacity 347
Patients assisted annually 750
Total in Residence 340
Total Staff 450
Coterie of St. Augustine Manor, The
7801 Detroit Ave.
Cleveland, OH 44102
Tel: 216-634-7400
(Operates the Coterie Boutique)
Mrs. MARGARET LYNCH, Pres.

Sts. Mary and Joseph Home for the Aged
4291 Richmond Rd.
Cleveland, OH 44122-6199
Tel: 216-464-1222; Fax: 216-591-9255
Little Sisters of the Poor
Mother MARIE EDWARD, I.S.P.

In res.,
Revs.:
LEO A. BOYLE
EDWARD CORRIGAN, S.M.
CLAUDE GAEBELEIN
JOHN J. GERRITY
PAUL DUZINSKI, O.F.M.Conv.
GEORGE L. VITUJ
Sisters 12
Fraternity Members 1
Bed Capacity 122

Columbus
Diocese of Columbus

Nazareth Towers
300 E. Rich St.
Columbus, OH 43215
Tel: 614-464-4780; Fax: 614-464-1733
Sr. MARY LOIS SCHMELTZER, O.P., Admin.
Total in Residence 215
Total Staff 7

St. Raphael Home for the Aged, Inc.
1550 Roxbury Rd.
Columbus, OH 43212
Tel: 614-486-0436; Fax: 614-486-1640
E-mail: st50raph@aol.com
Carmelite Sisters for the Aged and Infirm
Sr. KATHLEEN DOMINICK, O.Carm., Admin. & Supr.
Rev. LARRY NOLAN, Chap.
Residents 78
Total Skilled 78
Total Staff 105

St. Rita Home
880 Greenlawn Ave.
Columbus, OH 43223
Tel: 614-443-9433; Fax: 614-443-1196
Sr. M. JACQUELINE O.Carm., Supr. & Admin.
Rev. THOMAS J. CADDEN, Chap.
Carmelite Sisters for the Aged and Infirm 5
Total Staff 200
Guests 100
Total Assisted 145

Seton South Columbus, Inc.
155 Highview Blvd.
Columbus, OH 43207
Tel: 614-492-9944; Fax: 614-861-8022
JUDY WARSCHAUER, Mgr.
Total in Residence 63
Total Staff 2

Seton Square North
1776 Drew Ave.
Columbus, OH 43235
Tel: 614-451-1995; Fax: 614-451-1995
CINDY FISHER, Gen. Mgr. Seton Projects
ALINE TAYLOR, Mgr.
Total in Residence 240
Total Staff 3

Seton Square, West
3939 Clime Rd.
Columbus, OH 43228
Tel: 614-451-8750
CINDY FISHER, Contact Person

Coshocton
Diocese of Columbus

Seton Coshocton, Inc.
377 Clow Ln.
Coshocton, OH 43812
Tel: 330-343-3611; Fax: 330-343-4473
E-mail: setondover@juno.com
377 Clow Ln.
Coshocton, OH 43812
Tel: 330-343-3611; Fax: 330-343-4473
E-mail: setondover@juno.com
Apartments 40
Total in Residence 39
Total Staff 3
CHARLES ERBE, Co-Mgr.
MYRTLE ERBE, Co-Mgr.
Apartment 40
Total in Residence 39
Total Staff 3

Dayton
Archdiocese of Cincinnati

The Maria Joseph Living Care Center
4830 Salem Ave.
Dayton, OH 45416
Tel: 937-278-2692; Fax: 937-278-9016
E-mail: mariajoseph@mariajoseph.org
Web Site: www.mariajoseph.org
Skilled Nursing-Intermediate Nursing; Independent Living.
BONNIE G. LANGDON, Pres. & CEO
Sr. ALICE SCHOETTELKOTTE, C.PP.S., Spiritual Care Coord.
Licensed/Certified Nursing Care 384
Independent Living 56
Staff 500
Total Assisted 792

Mercy Siena Springs
6215 N. Main St.
Dayton, OH 45415
Tel: 937-274-4790; Fax: 937-274-9812
Apartments, Independent Living for the Elderly. Sponsored by the Sisters of Mercy
Sr. PATRICIA CONNOLLY, R.S.M., Mgr.
Residents 45
Total Staff 2

Mercy Siena Woods
235 W. Orchard Springs Dr.
Dayton, OH 45415
Tel: 937-278-8211; Fax: 937-278-8046
E-mail: shayes@health-partners.org
Nursing Home, nonsectarian. A member of Catholic Healthcare Partners. Specialized Alzheimer's Center, Skilled Nursing Center. Sponsored by the Religious Sisters of Mercy. 58 years of ministry.
SUSAN M. HAYES, Admin. & CEO
Rev. FRANCIS A. MASSARELLA, Res. Chap.
Sisters 1
Residents 99

Dover
Diocese of Columbus

Seton Square Dover, I, Inc.
501 James St.
Dover, OH 44622
Tel: 330-343-3611; Fax: 330-343-4473
E-mail: setondover@juno.com
CHARLES ERBE, Co-Mgr.
MYRTLE ERBE, Co-Mgr.
Total in Residence 50
Total Staff 3

Seton Square Dover, II, Inc.
139 Fillmore St.
Dover, OH 44622
Tel: 330-343-3611; Fax: 330-343-4473
E-mail: setondover@juno.com
CHARLES ERBE, Co-Mgr.
MYRTLE ERBE, Co-Mgr.
Total in Residence 41
Total Staff 3

Fairlawn
Diocese of Cleveland

St. Edward Home dba The Village at St. Edward Nursing Care and Assisted Living
3131 Smith Rd.
Fairlawn, OH 44333
Tel: 330-666-1183; Fax: 330-666-2721
JOHN J. HENNELLY, Pres. & CEO
Rev. JOHN F. FLOOD, Chap.
Sisters 3
Nursing Care Residents 100
Assisted Living Residents 26
Total Staff 131
St. Edward Home dba The Village at St. Edward Independent Living
3125 Smith Rd.
Fairlawn, OH 44333
Tel: 330-668-2828; Fax: 330-666-6636
JOHN J. HENNELLY, Pres. & CEO
Rev. JOHN F. FLOOD, Chap.
Total in Residence 160
Total Staff 28

Green Springs
Diocese of Toledo

St. Francis Health Care Centre
401 N. Broadway St.
Green Springs, OH 44836
Tel: 419-639-2626; Fax: 419-639-6225
E-mail: emarker@sfhcc.org
Owned by Franciscan Sisters of Our Lady of Perpetual Help (St. Louis, MO)
Operated by Franciscan Sisters of Our Lady of Perpetual Help of Ohio Corp.
DANIEL P. SCHWANKE, Exec. Dir.
CHARLES HULL, M.D., Medical Dir.
Rev. RAYMOND A. FISHER, Chap.
Sisters 4
Bed capacity 186
Total Assisted 600
Total Staff 220

Hamilton
Archdiocese of Cincinnati

Mercy Franciscan Senior Health and Housing Services, Inc. dba Mercy Franciscan at Schroder
1302 Millville Ave.
Hamilton, OH 45013
Tel: 513-867-1300; Fax: 513-867-1415
E-mail: m/morgan@health-partners.org
A Facility of the Mercy Health Partners. Sponsored by the Catholic Healthcare Partners. Special unit for Alzheimer Treatment.
Ms. MARCY MORGAN, Exec. Dir.
Residents 125

Hubbard
Diocese of Youngstown

Villa Maria Teresa
50 Warner Rd.
Hubbard, OH 44425
Tel: 330-759-9329 (Villa); 875-4635 (Emmaus House); Fax: 330-759-7290
E-mail: jcoblate@aol.com
Web Site: www.oblatesistersofshj.com
Retired Priests' Residence.
Villa Residents 5
Emmaus House Residents 5
Total Assisted 15
Total Staff 4

Independence
Diocese of Cleveland

Marycrest
8010 Brookside Rd.
Independence, OH 44131
Tel: 216-524-5280; Fax: 216-524-2127
Residential treatment and transitional living for adolescent girls and adolescent mothers and babies. Foster homes and Adoptions, and out-patient are also available.
Sisters 4
Total Assisted 286
Total Staff 125

Kenton
Diocese of Columbus

Seton Kenton, Inc.
699 Morningside Dr.
Kenton, OH 43326
Tel: 419-673-7202; Fax: 419-673-7202
MARY LOU SWEET, Mgr.
Total in Residence 52
Total Staff 2

Lancaster
Diocese of Columbus

Seton Lancaster, Inc.
232 Gay St.
Lancaster, OH 43130
Tel: 740-681-1403; Fax: 740-681-9178
DONNA PARLETTE, Mgr.
Total in Residence 35
Total Staff 2

London
Diocese of Columbus

Seton London, Inc.
350 Cambridge Dr.
London, OH 43140
Tel: 740-852-4233
LINDA HATMACHER, Mgr.
Total in Residence 51
Total Staff 2

Louisville
Diocese of Youngstown

Emmaus House
1515 California Ave.
Louisville, OH 44641
Tel: 330-875-4635
E-mail: rsacred@neo.rr.com
Rev. WILLIAM B. KRAYNAK, Admin.
Retired Priests' Residence.
Residents 5

St. Joseph Care Center
2308 Reno Dr.
Louisville, OH 44641
Tel: 330-875-5562; Fax: 330-875-8947
E-mail: sjcc@neo.rr.com
JOHN T. BANKS, Admin.
Sisters of St. Joseph of St. Mark 4
Sisters of the Humility of Mary 1

Total Staff 170
Nursing Home Residents 100
Assisted Living Residents 40
Sisters of St. Joseph of St. Mark 4
Sisters of the Humility of Mary 1
Nursing Home 100 residents
Assisted Living 40 residents
Total Staff 170

Marion
Diocese of Columbus

Seton Square Marion, Inc.
255 Richland Rd.
Marion, OH 43302
Tel: 740-389-4746; Fax: 740-389-9780
DEBRA J. ERWIN, Mgr.
Total in Residence 109
Total Staff 3

North Lima
Diocese of Youngstown

The Assumption Village
9800 Market St.
North Lima, OH 44452
Tel: 330-549-0740; Fax: 330-549-0701
Sponsorship: Sisters of the Humility of Mary
Member: Catholic Healthcare Partners.
CHRISTOPHER MCLAUGHLIN, Admin.
SHELLY MAZERIK, R.N., Dir. Nursing
Special Care Unit for residents with Alzheimer's or Dementia.
Residents 120
Total Staff 25
Skilled Nursing Unit with Subacute Care Program
Total Assisted 42
Total Staff 20
Intermediate Care
Total Assisted 65
Total Staff 20

The Assumption Village
9800 Market St.
North Lima, OH 44452
Tel: 330-549-0740; Fax: 330-549-0701
Sponsorship: Sisters of the Humility of Mary
Member: Catholic Healthcare Partners.
CHRISTOPHER MCLAUGHLIN, Admin.
SHELLY MAZERIK, R.N., Dir. Nursing
Skilled Nursing Unit with Subacute Care Program
Total Assisted 120
Total Staff 25
Special Care Unit for residents with Alzheimer's or cognitive impairment
Residents 42
Total Staff 25
Intermediate Care
Total Assisted 65
Total Staff 20

Oregon
Diocese of Toledo

Sacred Heart Home
4900 Navarre Ave.
Oregon, OH 43616-3599
Tel: 419-698-4331; Fax: 419-698-1109
Little Sisters of the Poor
Sr. JUDITH MARY MEREDITH, L.S.P.
Rev. Msgr. ROBERT J. YATES
Revs.:
JOVAN MALANYAON (Philippines)
RICHARD G. MILLER
Sisters 11
Aged Residents 98
Independent Living Apartments 20
Total Staff 135

Parma
Diocese of Cleveland

CCSC/Parmadale
6753 State Rd.
Parma, OH 44134
Tel: 440-845-7700; Fax: 440-845-5910
E-mail: pdale@mail.cle-dioc.org
Web Site: www.cle-dioc.org
ANNE MENGERINK, Dir.
Rev. JOSEPH J. SEMINATORE, Chap.
In res.,
Rev. JAMES R. SEMONIN
Specialized Residential Services; Intensive Treatment Services; Partial Hospitalization; Community Flexible Clinical Response; Specialized Foster Care; Wrap-Around Services; Whole Family Treatment; In-Home Services; Outpatient Services; Day Care; Training and Consultation Services; and Volunteer Program; Adoption Services.
Total Capacity 102

Total Staff 280
Children in Foster Care 170
Total Assisted 2,386

Franciscan Communities - Mount Alverna Home
6765 State Rd.
Parma, OH 44134
Tel: 440-843-7800; Fax: 440-843-7107
Web Site: www.franciscancommunities.com/facilities/mtalverna
ROBERT J. SHERRIN, Admin.
Rev. ERIC GAUCHAT, O.F.M.Cap.
Capacity 203
Residents 203
Total Assisted 203
Total Staff 319

Reynoldsburg
Diocese of Columbus

Seton Square East, Inc.
12235 Briarcliff Rd.
Reynoldsburg, OH 43068
Tel: 614-861-4860; Fax: 614-861-8022
JUDY WARSCHAVER, Mgr.
Total in Residence 107
Total Staff 3

Richfield
Diocese of Cleveland

Regina Health Center
5232 Broadview Rd.
Richfield, OH 44286-9608
Tel: 216-659-4161; Fax: 216-659-5113
E-mail: bflannery@reginahealthcenter.org
Sr. NANCY HENDERSHOT, C.S.A., Pres.
Sponsored by Sisters of Charity of St. Augustine.
Nursing Home Beds 81
Assisted Living Units 74
Total in Residence 126
Total Assisted 48
Total Staff 155

Springfield
Archdiocese of Cincinnati

Oakwood Village Retirement Community
1500 Villa Rd.
Springfield, OH 45503
Tel: 937-390-9000; Fax: 937-390-9333
E-mail: razechiel@health-partners.org
Total in Residence 200

Tiffin
Diocese of Toledo

St. Francis Home Inc.
182 St. Francis Ave.
Tiffin, OH 44883
Tel: 419-447-2723; Fax: 419-448-1337
E-mail: doretta@bascom.bright.net
Sr. DORETTA MEIER, O.S.F., Pres. & CEO
Mr. TIM SACKSTEDER, Chm., Board of Trustees
Residents 171
Total Staff 220

Toledo
Diocese of Toledo

St. Anthony Villa/Boysville of Michigan, Inc.
2740 W. Central Ave.
Toledo, OH 43606
Tel: 419-473-1353; Fax: 419-473-2963
Web Site: www.boysville.org
Residential and community-based treatment programs for troubled youth and families with facilities located throughout the state of Michigan and three facilities in the state of Ohio under the auspices of the Brothers of Holy Cross at Notre Dame
Bro. FRANCIS BOYLAN, C.S.C., Exec. Dir.
Rev. PETE DEANE, S.J.
Sisters 2
Lay Staff 80
Residential 61

Urbana
Archdiocese of Cincinnati

Mercy McAuley Center-Mercy Health Systems
906 Scioto St.
Urbana, OH 43078
Tel: 937-653-5432; Fax: 937-652-2072
E-mail: kzalar@health-partners.org
KARL P. ZALAR, JR., Admin.
Residents 129
Total Staff 130

Warren
Metropolitan Archdiocese of Pittsburgh, Byzantine

Infant of Prague Manor
169 Kenmore, N.E.
Warren, OH 44483
Tel: 330-372-4700; Fax: 330-372-5965
E-mail: smm@netdotcom.com
Web Site: www.stspeterandpaulbyz.org
Sr. MARGARET MARY, O.S.B., Admin.
Apartments 46
Staff 4
In Residence 40
Housing for the elderly.

Washington Court House
Diocese of Columbus

Seton Washington Court House, Inc.
400 N. Glenn Ave.
Washington Court House, OH 43160
Tel: 740-335-2292; Fax: 740-335-2291
400 N. Glenn Ave.
Washington Court House, OH 43160
Tel: 740-335-2292; Fax: 740-335-2291
Total in Residence 41
Total Staff 2
LINDA HATMACHER, Mgr.
Total in Residence 41
Total Staff 2

Wellston
Diocese of Columbus

Seton Square Wellston, Inc.
570 W. First St.
Wellston, OH 45692
Tel: 740-384-6174
LINDA HATMACHER, Mgr.
Total in Residence 48
Total Staff 2

Zanesville
Diocese of Columbus

Seton Housing, Inc.
516 Sheridan St.
Zanesville, OH 43701
Tel: 740-453-4422
DONNA PARLETTE, Mgr.
Total in Residence 46
Total Staff 2

OKLAHOMA

Oklahoma City
Archdiocese of Oklahoma City

Bone and Joint Hospital
1111 North Dewey Ave.
Oklahoma City, OK 73103
Tel: 405-272-9671; Fax: 405-551-9197
E-mail: cathy_mckinney@ssmhc.com
Web Site: www.boneandjoint.com
Mr. JAMES A. HYDE, Pres.
Rev. JOSEPH S. VAS, Chap.
Member of SSM Health Care
Beds 102
Patients assisted annually 19,884

St. Ann's Home Inc.
9400 St. Ann's Dr.
Oklahoma City, OK 73162
Tel: 405-728-7888; Fax: 405-728-1302
E-mail: stann@swbell.net
Mr. ROBERT O'CONNOR, Admin.
Rev. DONALD C. MOORE, Chap.
Sisters 2
Total Staff 95
Beds 120
Total Assisted 108

St. Ann's Retirement Village, Inc.
7501 N.W. Expwy., P.O. Box 32180
Oklahoma City, OK 73123
Tel: 405-721-5651; Fax: 405-721-5210
Mr. DAVID J. JOHNSON, Business Mgr.

Trinity Place Apartments
Catholic Charities, 3825 N.W. 19th St.
Oklahoma City, OK 73107
Tel: 405-523-3000; Fax: 405-523-3030
E-mail:
TOCONNOR@CATHOLICCHARITIESOK.ORG
Mr. TIMOTHY O'CONNOR, Contact Person
1501 N. Classen
Oklahoma City, OK 73106

58 low income apartments for senior citizens.
Residents 56

Villa Isenbart, Inc.
c/o Catholic Charities, 1501 Classen Blvd.
Oklahoma City, OK 73106
Tel: 405-523-3000; Fax: 405-523-3030
E-mail: tooconnor@catholiccharitiesok.org
3801 N.W. 19th St.
Oklahoma City, OK 73107
Tel: 405-947-4143; Fax: 405-947-4199
Mr. Timothy O'Connor, Dir.
40 Apartment Residences for Low-Income Elderly.
Residents 41

Ponca City
Archdiocese of Oklahoma City

St. Mary's Housing Foundation
408 S. 8th St.
Ponca City, OK 74601
Tel: 580-765-7794; Fax: 580-765-1327
E-mail: stmarys@poncacity.net
Rev. John J. Michalicka, Pres.
Senior Citizens Residences 6

Westminster Village, Inc.
1601 Academy Rd.
Ponca City, OK 74604
Tel: 580-762-0927; Fax: 580-762-0933
Via Christi Health System.
Norma Vanman, CEO
Nursing Care for Aged.
Residents 131
Total Assisted 360
Total Staff 1,056

Tulsa
Diocese of Tulsa

Frances Streitel Senior Care Corporation
1923 S. Utica Ave.
Tulsa, OK 74104
Tel: 918-744-2471

St. John Villas, Inc.
1923 S. Utica
Tulsa, OK 74104
Tel: 918-744-2180; Fax: 918-744-2716
Retirement Residence and Health Care Center for Intermediate Nursing Care.
Sisters of the Sorrowful Mother
Sr. Catherine Marie Hanegan, Pres.
Chaplains:
Revs.:
Stephen A. MacAuley
Lawrence P. Courtright
Beds 170
Apartments 111
Residents 262
Total Staff 195

OREGON

Beaverton
Archdiocese of Portland in Oregon

Maryville Nursing Home
14645 S.W. Farmington Rd.
Beaverton, OR 97007
Tel: 503-643-8626; Fax: 503-520-1435
Sr. Geraldine Bernards, Admin.
Rita Williams, R.N., Dir. Nurses
Rev. John M. Domin, Chap.
Sisters 8
Lay Workers 200
Guests 233
Little Flower Development Center
4415 S.W. 148th Ave.
Beaverton, OR 97007
Tel: 503-520-0214; Fax: 503-626-6220
Children 229

Mount Angel
Archdiocese of Portland in Oregon

Providence Benedictine Nursing Center
540 S. Main St.
Mount Angel, OR 97362-9523
Tel: 503-845-6841; Fax: 503-845-9229
Sisters of Providence Health System.
Emily Dazey, Exec. Dir.
Chaplains:
Sr. Joseph Fennimore
Revs.:
Marion Del Monaco
Dana McBrien, Inter-faith Chap.
Providence Benedictine Orchard House Personalized Living Center (ALF).
Tel: 503-845-2544; Fax: 503-845-2560
Assisted 75
Providence Benedictine Garden Homes Adult Foster Care.
Tel: 503-845-2544; Fax: 503-845-2560
Assisted 20
Home Health Agency
Tel: 503-845-9226; Fax: 503-845-9880
Staff 32
Patients assisted annually 600
Sisters 2
Patients assisted annually 504

North Bend
Archdiocese of Portland in Oregon

Evergreen Court for Retirement Living, Inc.
451 O'Connell St.
North Bend, OR 97459
Tel: 541-756-4466; Fax: 541-756-5669
David T. Darling, Pres. & CEO
Affiliate of Catholic Health Initiatives.

St. Catherine's Residence and Nursing Center
3959 Sheridan Ave.
North Bend, OR 97459
Tel: 541-756-4151; Fax: 541-756-5669
David T. Darling, Pres. & CEO
Affiliate of Catholic Health Initiatives.
Sisters 5
Patients assisted annually 420
Bed Capacity 200

Portland
Archdiocese of Portland in Oregon

Mt. St. Joseph, Inc.
3060 S.E. Stark St.
Portland, OR 97214-3099
Tel: 503-535-4700; Fax: 503-797-6702
Operated by the Sisters of Mercy, Omaha Regional Community.
Bill Sherer, Pres. & CEO
Alexis Greshom, Dir. Pastoral Care
Affiliate of Catholic Health Initiatives.
Sisters 8
Residents 341

PENNSYLVANIA

Allison Park
Diocese of Pittsburgh

Vincentian Regency
9399 Babcock Blvd.
Allison Park, PA 15101
Tel: 412-366-8540; Fax: 412-369-9789
Web Site: www.vcs.org
Vincentian Sisters of Charity
Sr. Dorothy Dolak, V.S.C., Admin.
Revs.:
David C. Dixon
Paul G. Spisak
Beds 143
Total Staff 200

Ambler
Archdiocese of Philadelphia

St. Mary's Villa for Children
701 Bethlehem Pike, P.O. Box 388
Ambler, PA 19002-0388
Tel: 215-643-7676; Fax: 215-542-9219
Sr. M. Rita Fanning, C.S.F.N., M.S., Admin.
Provides services for dependent-neglected children with emotional problems 4-10 and their families.
Sisters of the Holy Family of Nazareth 7
Capacity 70
Total Staff 85
Total Assisted 95

Aston
Archdiocese of Philadelphia

Assisi House
600 Red Hill Rd.
Aston, PA 19014
Tel: 215-459-8990; Fax: 610-558-5344
E-mail: jmmcdevi@osfphila.org
Home for retired Sisters of St. Francis of Philadelphia.
Sr. Jean Margaret McDevitt, O.S.F., Admin.
Rev. Edward Henning, O.F.M.Cap.
Total Assisted 126
Total Staff 117

Audubon
Archdiocese of Philadelphia

St. Gabriel's Hall
Box 7280
Audubon, PA 19407-7280
Tel: 215-247-2776 (Philadelphia); 610-666-7970 (Audubon)
Bro. Robert Kinzler, F.S.C., A.C.S.W., Exec. Dir.
Mr. Augustine Keirans, Dir.
Offers residential treatment for court-committed delinquent boys, ages 12-18.
Capacity 201
Total Staff 230
Total Assisted 200

Baden
Diocese of Pittsburgh

**Villa St. Joseph of Baden, Inc.*
1030 State St.
Baden, PA 15005
Tel: 724-869-6300; Fax: 724-869-6399
Sr. Anna Marie Gaglia, C.S.J., Pres. & Contact Person
Sr. Michelle Prah, C.S.J., N.H.A., Admin.
Purpose: to operate a 120 bed skilled/intermediate care licensed nursing home, striving to address not only medical needs, but to also maximize opportunities for physical activity, social interaction and spiritual development - holistic care.
Beds for Patients with Dementia or Alzheimers 30
Total Staff 175

Bensalem
Archdiocese of Philadelphia

St. Francis Homes for Boys
857 Langstroth Ln.
Bensalem, PA 19020-5735
Tel: 215-638-9310
Francis E. Swiacki, Jr., L.S.W., Admin.
Provides residential treatment in four campus-based group homes and seven community-based group homes for boys, ages 12 to 18; also Supervised Living for boys 17 and older.
Total Assisted 175
Capacity 118
Total Staff 145

St. Joseph's House for Boys
857 Langstroth Ln.
Bensalem, PA 19020-5735
Tel: 215-244-8690; Fax: 215-244-8694
Francis Swiacki, Exec. Dir.
Provides community-based group home residential treatment for boys 8-18.
Capacity 40
Total Staff 45
Total Assisted 56

Bethlehem
Diocese of Allentown

Grace Mansion Assisted Living Residence of Holy Family Manor
1200 Spring St.
Bethlehem, PA 18018
Tel: 610-865-6748
Rev. Msgr. Dennis A. Rigney, Pres. & CEO
Karen Abruzzese, Admin.
Mr. Jim Polaski, Dir. Residential Svcs.
Personal care/assisted living facility for 25 elderly.
Total in Residence 23
Total Staff 12

Holy Family Apartments
330-338 13th Ave.
Bethlehem, PA 18018
Tel: 610-866-4603; Fax: 610-866-1622
E-mail: hfabeth@nni.com
Rev. Msgr. Dennis A. Rigney, Pres.
Judy Kern, Mgr.
Catholic housing for the elderly.
Total Staff 2
Apartments 50
Residents 51

Holy Family Manor
1200 Spring St.
Bethlehem, PA 18018
Tel: 610-865-5595; Fax: 610-865-5866
Rev. Msgr. Dennis A. Rigney, M.Div., L.S.W., A.C.S.W., Pres. & CEO
Sr. Priscilla Lahovski, N.H.A., Admin.
Rev. Joseph A. Rock, Th.F., Chap.
Nursing Care for the Aged, Chronically Ill, or Invalid.
Capacity 208
Total Assisted 382

Total Staff 280
Skilled and intermediate care facility.
Total Assisted 382
Total Staff 280

Trexler Pavilion, Assisted Living Residence of Holy Family Manor
1220 Prospect Ave.
Bethlehem, PA 18018
Tel: 610-868-7776
Rev. Msgr. DENNIS A. RIGNEY, Pres. & CEO
KAREN ABRUZZESE, Admin.
Mr. JAMES POLASKI, Dir. Residential Svcs.
Personal care/assisted living facility for 23 elderly.
Total in Residence 30
Total Staff 12

Columbia
Diocese of Harrisburg

St. Anne's Home
3952 Columbia Ave.
Columbia, PA 17512-9715
Tel: 717-285-5443; Fax: 717-285-5950
E-mail: stannadm@supernet.com
Adorers of the Blood of Christ
Sr. M. CARMELA GUITO, A.S.C., Admin.
Sisters 19
Total Staff 214 (includes Personal Care)
Personal Care Staff 8
Residents 121
Cottages 36
Residents in Retirement Village 45
Personal Care 18

Dallas
Diocese of Scranton

Mercy Center Nursing Unit, Inc.
Lake St., Box 370
Dallas, PA 18612
Tel: 570-675-2131; Fax: 570-674-7606
Sr. SARA SWEENEY, R.S.M., Admin.
SHEILA HECK, Dir. of Nursing
Rev. FRANCIS G. KULIG, Chap.

Danville
Diocese of Harrisburg

Holy Family Convent and Infirmary
One Montour St.
Danville, PA 17821
Tel: 717-275-3141
Home for the Aged Sisters of Christian Charity.
Sr. PIETRA CASH, S.C.C., Supr.
Rev. THADDEUS STRZELEC, Chap., Tel: 717-275-0103
Sisters of Christian Charity 85

Maria Hall
Maria Hall Dr.
Danville, PA 17821
Tel: 570-275-1120; Fax: 570-275-1134
E-mail: sscmarhl@aol.com
Home for retired Sisters of SS. Cyril and Methodius.
Sr. CELESTE MARIE, SS.C.M., Admin.
Rev. FRANCIS X. MALINOWSKI
Sisters 66
Total Assisted 26
Total Staff 46

Maria Joseph Manor
875 Montour Blvd.
Danville, PA 17821
Tel: 570-275-4221; Fax: 570-275-4711
E-mail: meadows@mail.ptdprolog.net
Sr. M. JEANETTE, SS.C.M., Exec. Dir.
Sr. M. MARGUERITE, SS.C.M., Admin.
Rev. TRI LUONG Tel: 570-275-8740
Nursing Home Beds 60
Personal Card Beds 45(licensed) 36(occupied)
Sisters 15
The Meadows at Maria Joseph Manor
875 Montour Blvd.
Danville, PA 17821
Tel: 570-271-1000; Fax: 570-275-4711
Sr. ELIZABETH ANN MATONAK, SS.C.M., Dir.
Independent Living Units 100
Total Staff 5
Residents 135

Darby
Archdiocese of Philadelphia

Little Flower Manor
1201 Springfield Rd.
Darby, PA 19023
Tel: 610-534-6000; Fax: 610-534-6039
Staffed by Sisters of the Divine Redeemer
All Skilled Nursing Care.
Rev. EDWARD J. CASEY, Chap.
Total Staff 185
Patients assisted annually 180

St. Francis Country House
1412 Lansdowne Ave.
Darby, PA 19023-1218
Tel: 610-461-6510; Fax: 610-461-3558
Opened June 30, 1913.
Mrs. CYNTHIA O'BRIEN, Admin.
Rev. EDWARD J. KENNEDY, Chap.
Total Assisted 444
Total Staff 325

Villa Saint Joseph
1436 Lansdowne Ave.
Darby, PA 19023-1298
Tel: 610-586-8535; Fax: 610-586-2810
Home for aged, infirm and convalescent priests of the Archdiocese of Philadelphia.
Rev. Msgr. FRANCIS A. MENNA, Rector
Rev. EDWARD J. CASEY, Asst. Rector
Sisters 1
Total Staff 43
Residents 62

Villa St. Teresa
1215 Springfield Rd.
Darby, PA 19023
Tel: 610-583-0700; Fax: 610-583-5011
Staffed by Sisters of the Divine Redeemer Residential.
Sr. M. ANNE ANGELCYK, S.D.R., Admin.
Sr. M. COLOMBIERE HOFSTEDDER, S.D.R., Supr.
Total Staff 32
Total Assisted 112
Residents 54

Downingtown
Archdiocese of Philadelphia

St. John Vianney Center
151 Woodbine Rd.
Downingtown, PA 19335
Tel: 610-269-2600; Fax: 610-873-8028
Web Site: sjvcenter.org
Center for Healing for Priests, Brothers, and Sisters.
Rev. CHARLES R. O'HARA, Chap.
Bed Capacity 54
Total Assisted 235
Total Staff 52

St. Martha Manor
470 Manor Ave.
Downingtown, PA 19335
Tel: 610-873-8490; Fax: 610-873-5927
COLLEEN PATRICIA FRANKFIELD, N.H.A., Admin.
Capacity 128
Total Staff 298
Total Assisted 188

Du Bois
Diocese of Erie

Christ the King Manor, Inc.
1100 W. Long Ave.
Du Bois, PA 15801
Tel: 814-371-3180; Fax: 814-371-4101
E-mail: etkm@penn.com
Rev. MARK S. SWOGER, Chap.
Residents 160

Easton
Diocese of Allentown

Antonian Towers
2405 Hillside Ave.
Easton, PA 18042
Tel: 610-258-2033; Fax: 610-258-6541
E-mail: antonian@nni.com
Total in Residence 50
Total Staff 2
Very Rev. WILLIAM CAMPION, Pres.
Mrs. JUDITH KERN, Mgr.
Catholic housing for the elderly.
Apartments 50

Elmhurst
Diocese of Scranton

St. Mary's Villa Nursing Home
18416
Tel: 570-842-7621; Fax: 570-842-2953
COLLEEN M. LANDO, N.H.A., Campus CEO
Sr. SEBASTIAN C.J.C., Convent Supr., Tel: 570-842-7466
Rev. JOSEPH C. OSTROWSKI, Chap.
St. Mary's Villa Residence
One Pioneer Pl.
Elmhurst, PA 18416
Tel: 570-842-5274; Fax: 570-842-3472
Residents 64
Total Staff 42
SANDRA BOZEK, R.N., Personal Care Home Admin.
Rev. JOSEPH C. OSTROWSKI, Chap.
Poor Sisters of Jesus Crucified and the Sorrowful Mother 4
Residents 140
Total Staff 240

Elverson
Archdiocese of Philadelphia

St. Mary of Providence Center
227 Isabella Rd.
Elverson, PA 19520
Tel: 610-942-4166; Fax: 610-942-4268
Sr. BERNADINE UGOLINI, D.S.M.P., Supr.
Rev. GERARD J. HOFFMAN, Chap.
Residence for Senior Citizens. Center of Spirituality, Retreats and Days of Recollection.
Sisters 5
Capacity 39
Overnight and day retreats 110
Total Staff 15
Total in Residence 52

Emsworth
Diocese of Pittsburgh

Holy Family Institute
8235 Ohio River Blvd.
Emsworth, PA 15202
Tel: 412-766-4030; Fax: 412-766-5434
E-mail: schott.sandra@hfi-pgh.org
Web Site: www.hfi-pgh.org
Sisters of the Holy Family of Nazareth
Sr. LINDA YANKOSKI, Exec. Dir.
Holy Family Institute is committed to helping children, preserving families and strengthening communities by providing a network of services including in-home counseling, residential treatment, summer day camp, foster care, and outpatient mental health services. Holy Family provides special education and alternative education for grades K through 12. The Bellefonds Method serves K through 12 as well as the adult population. This method uses a technique of assessment and re-education for learning difficulties due to developmental disabilities, stroke, brain trauma or infection. Volunteer opportunities are also available at Holy Family Institute.
Sisters 1
Total Assisted: Children 4,931
Families 2,001
Total Staff 420

Erie
Diocese of Erie

Bishop Michael J. Murphy Residence for Retired Priests
400 E. Gore Rd.
Erie, PA 16509
Tel: 814-825-0680
Rev. Msgr. ROBERT J. SMITH, J.C.L., Dir.

Gannondale, Inc.
4635 E. Lake Rd.
Erie, PA 16511
Tel: 814-899-7659; Fax: 814-898-4266
E-mail: gannondale@aol.com
North American Union of Sisters of Our Lady of Charity-Erie
Sr. ROSEMARY TOTH, O.L.C., Supr.
Mr. LOUIS J. GRANDE, A.C.S.W., Exec. Dir.
Residents 45

Mercy Center for Women
1039 E. 27th St.
Erie, PA 16504
Tel: 814-453-3668
TISH DONZE, Exec. Dir.

Mercy Terrace Apartments
430 E. Grandview Blvd.
Erie, PA 16504
Tel: 814-825-6791; Fax: 814-824-2127
E-mail: mta@erie.net
Sr. M. FELICE DUSKA, R.S.M., Mgr.
Sisters of Mercy of Erie

St. Mary's Home of Erie
607 E. 26th St.
Erie, PA 16504
Tel: 814-459-0621; Fax: 814-454-0909
Sr. ANASTASIA VALIMONT, S.S.J., Admin.
Rev. Msgr. JOSEPH V. WARDANSKI, Chap.

Sisters 17
Residents 131
Patients-Nursing Home 228

St. Patrick Haven, Inc.
147 E. 12th St.
Erie, PA 16501
Tel: 814-454-7219; 838-5430
Sr. MARIE EILEEN MOYER, Admin.

Flourtown
Archdiocese of Philadelphia

Bethlehem Retirement Village
100 W. Wissahickon Ave.
Flourtown, PA 19031
Tel: 215-233-0998; Fax: 215-233-9052
E-mail: JoanGrelis@aol.com
Staffed by the Sisters of St. Joseph
Sr. JOAN GRELIS, S.S.J., Mgr.
Apartments 100
Total Staff 4
Total in Residence 113

St. Joseph Villa
110 W. Wissahickon Ave.
Flourtown, PA 19031-1898
Tel: 215-836-4179; Fax: 215-248-7802
E-mail: rudegeairm@stjosephvilla.org
Chaplains:
Rev. GERARD M. DUFF, O.S.A.
Sr. MARIE RUDEGEAIR, S.S.J., N.H.A., Admin.
Bed Capacity 324
Total Assisted 525
Total Staff 275

Sisters of St. Joseph of Philadelphia, St. Joseph Villa Staff Visitation Community
110 W. Wissahickon Ave.
Flourtown, PA 19031-1898
Tel: 215-836-4179; Fax: 215-248-7802
Sr. LILLIAN DEVLIN, S.S.J., Contact

Greensburg
Diocese of Greensburg

Neumann House
2900 Seminary Dr.
Greensburg, PA 15601
Tel: 724-834-7350; Fax: 724-834-7351
E-mail: jbertig@dioceseofgreensburg.org
Residence for retired Priests.
In res.,
Rev. Msgr. ROBERT A. HANICAK Tel: 724-834-7991
Revs.:
ALOYSIUS J. BAHLEDA Tel: 724-834-5953
LOUIS W. CHEATHAM Tel: 724-850-7619
EDWARD V. CURRY Tel: 724-850-7647
ROBERT F. BRANNON Tel: 724-853-4307
MICHAEL A. BIENIA Tel: 724-836-1017

St. Anne Home
685 Angela Dr.
Greensburg, PA 15601
Tel: 724-837-6070; Fax: 724-837-6099
Rev. EDWARD J. KRETZ, Chap.
Sr. BERNICE M. FIEDOR, C.S.S.F., Admin.
In res.,
Revs.:
EDWIN H. HIRT Tel: 724-837-9443
ANDREW J. CHARNOKI Tel: 724-853-8935
Rev. Msgr. JOHN L. GARRED
Rev. ANDREW B. HORVATH
Felician Sisters 8
Capacity 125

Harborcreek
Diocese of Erie

**Benetwood Apartments for Persons Elderly and Handicapped*
641 Troupe Rd.
Harborcreek, PA 16421-1048
Tel: 814-899-0088
Sr. PATRICIA HAUSE, O.S.B., Admin.
Benedictine Sisters of Erie
Residents 80

Harborcreek Youth Services
5712 Iroquois Ave.
Harborcreek, PA 16421
Tel: 814-899-7664; Fax: 814-899-3075
E-mail: gmcclelland@hys-erie.org
Ms. GRACE MCCLELLAND, Exec. Dir.
Children 125

Harrisburg
Diocese of Harrisburg

Villa Teresa Nursing Home
1051 Avila Rd.
Harrisburg, PA 17109
Tel: 717-652-5900; Fax: 717-652-5941
E-mail: villateresa@panetwork.com
Carmelite Sisters
Sr. JEAN A. DAVIS, Admin.
Rev. EDWARD R. LAVELLE, Chap.
Sisters 6
Bed Capacity 184
Total Staff 228

Hermitage
Diocese of Erie

John XXIII Home
2250 Shenango Fwy.
Hermitage, PA 16148
Tel: 724-981-3200; Fax: 724-981-1677
E-mail: j23@pathway.net
KIRK L. HAWTHORNE, Admin.
Rev. Msgr. RAYMOND MEIER, Coord.
Residents 142

Holland
Archdiocese of Philadelphia

St. Joseph Home for the Aged
1182 Holland Rd.
Holland, PA 18966
Tel: 215-357-5511; Fax: 215-357-1701
Sisters of St. Casimir
CECILE F. SHOCKET, Admin.
Rev. JOHN A. CANNON, Chap.
Personal Care and Licensed Nursing facility.
Senior Residents 47
Total Staff 7
Nursing Care Total Assisted 38
Total Staff 33

Hollidaysburg
Diocese of Altoona-Johnstown

Dmitri Manor Priests' Residence
St. Mary's Ln.
Hollidaysburg, PA 16648
Tel: 814-696-4698
Rev. Msgr. GEORGE FLINN, V.G.
Aged Residents 6
Staff 1

Garvey Manor
128 Logan Blvd.
Hollidaysburg, PA 16648
Tel: 814-695-5571; Fax: 814-695-8516
Sr. M. JOACHIM ANNE FERENCHAK, O.Carm., Admin.
Carmelite Sisters for the Aged and Infirm 9
Aged Residents 150
Patients assisted annually 230
Total Staff 210

St. Leonard's Home, Inc.
601 N. Montgomery St.
Hollidaysburg, PA 16648
Tel: 814-695-9581; Fax: 814-695-2606
Legal Title: *St. Leonard's Home, Inc.*
Sr. DOROTHY M. PAWLUS, C.S.F.N., Admin.
Sisters of the Holy Family of Nazareth 1
Aged Residents 30
Total Staff 14

Huntingdon Valley
Archdiocese of Philadelphia

Redeemer Village - Redeemer Village II
1551 Huntingdon Pike
Huntingdon Valley, PA 19006
Tel: 215-947-8168
Web Site: www.holyredeemer.com
Mailing Address:—Marketing/Public Affairs Department
Holy Redeemer Health System, c/o 1602 Huntingdon Pike
Meadowbrook, PA 19046
Subsidiary of Holy Redeemer Health System. Low income housing for the elderly or handicapped, subsidized by HUD.
Sisters of the Holy Redeemer, C.S.R.
FRANCIS G. HAMEL, Mgr., Redeemer Village
Apartments 151
Redeemer Village II
1551 Huntingdon Pike
Huntingdon Valley, PA 19006
Tel: 215-947-8168
Subsidiary of Holy Redeemer Health System, Inc. Low income housing for the elderly or handicapped, subsidized by HUD.
Sisters of the Holy Redeemer, C.S.R.
Apartments 49

Immaculata
Archdiocese of Philadelphia

Camilla Hall Nursing Home
P.O. Box 100
Immaculata, PA 19345-0100
Tel: 610-644-1152; Fax: 610-695-0691
Sisters, Servants of the Immaculate Heart of Mary
Sr. MARGARET GRADL, I.H.M., Admin.
Mother MARIE GENEVIEVE, Supr.
Chaplains:
Rev. MICHAEL L. WALSH
Rev. Msgr. CHARLES V. GALLEN
Bed Capacity 248
Residents 190

Lansdale
Archdiocese of Philadelphia

St. Mary Manor
701 Lansdale Ave.
Lansdale, PA 19446
Tel: 215-368-0900; Fax: 215-362-2891
Immaculate Heart of Mary Sisters
JOHN T. CHAPMAN, Admin.
Rev. JOSEPH F. MCCAFFERTY, Chap.
Total Staff 200

Merion Station
Archdiocese of Philadelphia

McAuley Convent
517 Montgomery Ave.
Merion Station, PA 19066
Tel: 610-667-2775
Infirmary for Religious Sisters of Mercy.
Sr. THERESA MONAGHAN, R.S.M., Supr.
Sr. MARY BONAVENTURE, R.S.M., Dir.
Total Staff 40
Total Assisted 36

Nanticoke
Diocese of Scranton

Mercy Health Care Center
(Skilled Care Nursing Facility)
Newport St.
Nanticoke, PA 18634
Tel: 570-735-7300
ROBERT D. WILLIAMS, Vice Pres. of Aging Svcs.
DIANE MORRIS, Admin.
Rev. Msgr. BERNARD A. TOLOCZKO, Chap.
Bed Capacity 110
Patients assisted annually 170

New Philadelphia
Diocese of Allentown

Holy Family Apartments
Valley St. & Clay St.
New Philadelphia, PA 17959
Tel: 570-429-0699; Fax: 570-429-2368
Apartments 11
Total Staff 2

Orwigsburg
Diocese of Allentown

Holy Family Adult Day Care at St. Francis Center
900 W. Market St.
Orwigsburg, PA 17961
Tel: 570-366-2924; Fax: 570-366-2301
Rev. Msgr. DENNIS A. RIGNEY, Pres. & CEO
Mrs. LINDA HERB, Dir.
Day care for the elderly.
Total Staff 7
Clients 42

Holy Family Assisted Living Residence
900 W. Market St.
Orwigsburg, PA 17961
Tel: 570-366-2912; Fax: 570-366-7781
Rev. Msgr. DENNIS A. RIGNEY, Pres. & CEO
PATRICIA MISKE, Admin.
Mr. JAMES POLASKI, Dir. Residential Svcs.
Personal care/assisted living facility for 58 elderly of Holy Family Manor.
Total in Residence 85
Total Staff 22

Holy Family Home Health and Hospice Care
Schuylkill County and Admin. Office, 900 W. Market St.
Orwigsburg, PA 17961
Tel: 570-366-2912
PATRICIA MISKE, Admin.
Patients assisted annually 1,641

Philadelphia
Archdiocese of Philadelphia

Holy Family Home
5300 Chester Ave.
Philadelphia, PA 19143-4993

Tel: 215-729-5153
Little Sisters of the Poor
Mother PAUL L.S.P., Supr.
Rev. DOUGLAS M. MCKAY, Chap.
Total Staff 120
Residents 105

Immaculate Mary Home
2990 Holme Ave.
Philadelphia, PA 19136-1829
Tel: 215-335-2100; Fax: 215-331-1016
Opened March 1976.
STUART K. SKINNER, N.H.A., Admin.
Total Staff 317
Total Assisted 472

Mount Nazareth
2755 Holme Ave.
Philadelphia, PA 19152
Tel: 215-338-8992; Fax: 215-338-8752
Sisters of the Holy Family Of Nazareth
Home for retired and infirm sisters.
Sr. MARGARET MARY MACHOWSKI, C.S.F.N., Supr.
Rev. Msgr. CHARLES J. SCHAEFLEIN, Chap.
Resident Sisters 50
Total Staff 14
Total Assisted 42

Sacred Heart Free Home for Incurable Cancer
1315 W. Hunting Park Ave.
Philadelphia, PA 19140
Tel: 215-329-3222; Fax: 215-329-4197
Opened April 27, 1930.
Dominican Sisters of Hawthorne
Sr. M. JUDE, O.P., Supr.
Sr. MARY JOSEPH, O.P., Admin.
Legal Title: *The Servants of Relief for Incurable Cancer*
Bed Capacity 45
Total Staff 45
Total Assisted 75
Attended by Oblates of St. Francis de Sales.

Sacred Heart Manor
6445 Germantown Ave.
Philadelphia, PA 19119
Tel: 215-438-5268; Fax: 215-951-0798
E-mail: michaelshm@aol.com
Carmelite Sisters for the Aged and Infirm
Sr. M. PATRICIA MICHAEL, O.Carm., Admin.
Revs.:
JOHN S. HEIM, Chap.
EDUARDO G. MONTERO, Chap.
Nursing Care Residents 171
Independent Living Residents 48
Personal Care Boarding Home 48

St. Gabriel's System
Administrative Offices, 117 S. 17th St., Ste. 1701
Philadelphia, PA 19103
Tel: 215-665-8777; Fax: 215-665-8821
Bro. DENNIS MALLOY, F.S.C., Exec. Dir.
Administrative and Intake services for residential treatment; Group Home care and Day Treatment for Court-committed delinquent boys, ages 12-17. (See St. Gabriel's Hall, De LaSalle in Towne, De LaSalle Vocational and De LaSalle Aftercare).
Total Staff 430
Total Assisted 2,000

St. Ignatius Nursing Home
4401 Haverford Ave.
Philadelphia, PA 19104
Tel: 215-349-8800; Fax: 215-222-3078
Sr. MARY AGATHA CEBULA, C.S.S.F., N.H.A., Admin.
Attended from St. Ignatius Church.
Felician Sisters 6
Bed Capacity 176
Total Assisted 250
Total Staff 245
Total in Residence 176

St. John Neumann Nursing Home
10400 Roosevelt Blvd.
Philadelphia, PA 19116
Tel: 215-698-5600; Fax: 215-698-5755
E-mail: adminsec.sjnh@erols.com
Sisters of the Holy Famly of Nazareth
Beds 226
Total Staff 291

St. Joseph Catholic Home for Children
5238 N. Broad St.
Philadelphia, PA 19141
Tel: 215-324-2610; Fax: 215-457-8240
E-mail: srlouise@adphila.org
Sr. LOUISE KANE, S.S.J., L.S.W., Admin.
Provides Therapeutic Group Home Care; Maternity Home Care; Mother/Baby Residential Care; Supervised Independent Living; Outreach School Social Work for Adolescent Girls. Mental Health services available on site for all residents.
Sisters of St. Joseph 3
Capacity 60

St. Joseph Housing Corporation
Tel: 215-248-7200; Fax: 215-248-7277
E-mail: msvc19118@aol.com
Web Site: www.ssjphila.org
Mount St. Joseph Convent
Philadelphia, PA 19118-2694
Tel: 215-248-7200; Fax: 215-248-7277
E-mail: msvc19118@aol.com
Web Site: www.ssjphila.org
Total Staff 4
Total in Residence 107
Staffed by the Sisters of St. Joseph.

St. Vincent's Orphanage Tacony
7201 Milnor St.
Philadelphia, PA 19135
Tel: 215-624-5600
Revs.:
ENGELBERT G. MICHEL, Pres., Bd. of Mgrs.
EDUARDO G. MONTERO, J.C.L., Chap.
Provides Family Oriented residential care for children 2-12 years of age.
Residential program with 84 beds that provides comprehensive emergency shelter to over 450 boys and girls annually.
Capacity 84
Total Staff 105

Metropolitan Archdiocese of Philadelphia Ukrainian

Ascension Manor, Inc.
911 N. Franklin St.
Philadelphia, PA 19123
Tel: 215-922-1116
Most Rev. STEPHEN SULYK, D.D., S.T.L., Pres.
Rev. Msgr. JAMES MELNIC, Exec. Vice Pres.
Rev. Archpriest JOHN FIELDS, Sec. & Treas.
Directors:
DR. JAROSLAW JARYMOWYCH
JEANNE KARBIWNYK
IHOR SHUST
MARIE J. HANUSEY, Gen. Mgr.
Ascension Manor I
911 N. Franklin St.
Philadelphia, PA 19123
Tel: 215-922-1116; Fax: 215-922-3735
ANNA SIWAK, Mgr.
Ascension Manor II
970 N. Seventh St.
Philadelphia, PA 19123
Tel: 215-923-3907; Fax: 215-922-3735
TARAS HANKEWYCZ, Mgr.

Pittsburgh
Diocese of Pittsburgh

Franciscan Child Day Care Center
1401 Hamilton Rd.
Pittsburgh, PA 15234-2399
Tel: 412-882-5085; Fax: 412-885-7210
E-mail: srsosfprov@aol.com
Web Site: www.srsosfprov.org
CAROL A. UNRUE, Dir.
Sr. MARIAN BLODIS, O.S.F., Pres.
Total Assisted 100
Total Staff 35

Little Sisters of the Poor Home for the Aged
1028 Benton Ave.
Pittsburgh, PA 15212
Tel: 412-761-5373; Fax: 412-734-1030
E-mail: littlesisters1@mindspring.com
Sr. MARGARET BANAR, Supr. & Admin.
Rev. ALVIN GUTIERREZ
Sisters 12
Total Staff 100
Residents 40
Total Assisted 40

Marian Hall Home, Inc.
934 Forest Ave.
Pittsburgh, PA 15202-1118
Tel: 412-761-1999; Fax: 412-761-2556
Sr. MARIAN SGRICCIA, O.S.F.
Purpose: to provide programs, facilities, and services, including, but not limited to, residential personal care, and long-term care homes for the elderly, ill, or disabled, including supportive services.
Total in Residence 41
Total Staff 31

Marian Manor Corp.
2695 Winchester Dr.
Pittsburgh, PA 15220-4099
Tel: 412-563-6866 (Admin.); 563-1244 (Nursing Service); Fax: 412-563-1250
E-mail: marianmanr@aol.com
Web Site: www.marianmanor.com
Sr. EILEEN CHLEBOWSKI, N.H.A., Admin.
Rev. ROBERT R. WERTHMAN
Sisters of the Holy Spirit 14
Total Staff 280
Residents 194
Total Assisted 271

Mercy Senior Care: St. Joseph's
(Affiliate of Pittsburgh Mercy Health System)
5324 Penn Ave.
Pittsburgh, PA 15224-1798
Tel: 412-665-5100; Fax: 412-665-4627
BARBARA LLOYD, Admin.
Beds 153
Patients assisted annually 186

Mt. Alvernia Day Care & Learning Center
146 Hawthorne Rd.
Pittsburgh, PA 15209
Tel: 412-821-4302; Fax: 412-821-3318
Web Site: www.millvaleFranciscans.org
Provides infant care as well as before- and after-school care for school age children.
Total Assisted 131
Total Staff 29

Providence Connections, Inc.
Corporate Office, 3113 Brighton Rd.
Pittsburgh, PA 15212-2456
Tel: 412-766-3860; Fax: 412-766-6775
Sr. MARIA FEST, Exec. Dir.
Providence Child Care Center, North
200 Ridge Ave.
Pittsburgh, PA 15212-5239
Tel: 412-231-6190
Total Assisted 24 Families
Total Staff 8
Providence Child Care Center, South
400 Hoodridge Ave.
Pittsburgh, PA 15234-1793
Tel: 412-531-3360; Fax: 412-531-3360
Total Assisted 43 Families
Total Staff 11
Providence Family Support Center
3113 Brighton Rd.
Pittsburgh, PA 15212-2456
Tel: 412-766-6730; Fax: 412-766-6775
Total Assisted 107 Families
Total Staff 8
Amelia House
Tel: 814-226-6682
Total Assisted 22
Total Staff 1
Purpose: To engage in educational activities and operation of day care centers and other related services to women and children in need.

St. Pius X Residence, Inc.
(Affiliate of Pittsburgh Mercy Health System)
2681 Waddington Ave.
Pittsburgh, PA 15226
Tel: 412-563-5040; Fax: 412-563-3776
MARY JO HUMMEL, Admin.
Total in Residence 33
Total Staff 20

Vincentian Child Care, Inc.
8200 McKnight Rd.
Pittsburgh, PA 15237
Tel: 412-366-8588; Fax: 412-366-8588
Web Site: vincentiansrspgh.org/childcare/index.html
Sr. GEORGINE BIRES, V.S.C., Contact Person
Purpose: to engage in educational activities; operating a day care program; to perform any lawful acts to effectuate purposes of this corporation and in this pursuit to apply funds or incomes exclusively for charitable, religious, scientific, literary, and educational purposes.
Total Assisted 140 (per year)
Total Staff 28

Vincentian de Marillac
5300 Stanton Ave.
Pittsburgh, PA 15206
Tel: 412-361-2833; Fax: 412-361-2833
E-mail: villa@sgi.net
Non-sectarian, skilled nursing home.
ANNE TRZECIAK, N.H.A., Contact
Rev. THOMAS MURPHY, Chap.
Vincentian Sisters of Charity 3
Total Staff 75
Bed Capacity 52
Total Assisted 95

Vincentian Home Inc.
111 Perrymont Rd.
Pittsburgh, PA 15237
Tel: 412-366-5600; Fax: 412-366-1408
Vincentian Sisters of Charity

Sr. Anne Kull, V.S.C., Admin.
Revs.:
Paul G. Spisak
David C. Dixon
Sisters 11
Total Staff 258
Bed Capacity 217
Patients assisted annually 217

Pottsville
Diocese of Allentown

Queen of Peace Apartments
777 Water St.
Pottsville, PA 17901
Tel: 570-628-4504; Fax: 570-628-4712
E-mail: qpeace@voicenet.com
Rev. Msgr. William E. Jones, Pres.
Mrs. Hazel Black, Mgr.
Catholic housing for the elderly.
Apartments 62
Total in Residence 65
Total Staff 4

Reading
Diocese of Allentown

Queen of Angels Apartment
22 Rothermel St., Hyde Park
Reading, PA 19605
Tel: 610-921-3115; Fax: 610-921-8576
E-mail: qangels@voicenet.com
Rev. Dennis T. Hartgen, Pres.
Hazel C. Black, Mgr.
Catholic housing for the elderly.
Apartments 45
Total in Residence 47
Total Staff 2

Rosemont
Archdiocese of Philadelphia

St. Edmond's Home for Children
320 S. Roberts Rd.
Rosemont, PA 19010
Tel: 610-525-8800; Fax: 610-525-2693
Daughters of St. Mary of Providence
Mary O'Neill, Admin.
Rev. Romano DiRuscio, S.C., Chap.
Licensed I.C.F/M.R. care for severely/profoundly impaired, physically handicapped boys and girls ages 2-21.
Capacity 40
Total Staff 100

Saint Clair
Diocese of Allentown

Neumann Apartments
25 N. Nichols St.
Saint Clair, PA 17970
Tel: 570-429-0699; Fax: 570-429-2368
Rev. Ronald V. Jankaitis, Pres.
Mr. John T Stiles, Mgr.
Catholic housing for the elderly.
Total in Residence 24
Total Staff 2
Apartments 24
Total in Residence 24
Total Staff 2

Scranton
Diocese of Scranton

Home for Aged of the Little Sisters of the Poor, Holy Family Residence
2500 Adams Ave.
Scranton, PA 18509
Tel: 570-343-4065; 346-5788; Fax: 570-346-1196
Sr. Alice Marie Jones, p.s.d.p., Supr.
Rev. Joseph F. Meighan, Chap.
Little Sisters of the Poor 13
Aged Residents 55
Residents in Independent Living Apts. 22

St. Joseph's Center
2010 Adams Ave.
Scranton, PA 18509
Tel: 570-342-8379; Fax: 570-342-6080
E-mail: wecare@stjosephscenter.org
Web Site: www.stjosephcenter.org
Sr. Vincentia Dorsey, I.H.M., Admin.
Rev. William B. Pickard, Chap.
Sisters, Servants of the Immaculate Heart of Mary 11
Bed Capacity 144
Patients assisted annually 150

Uniontown
Metropolitan Archdiocese of Pittsburgh, Byzantine

Mt. Macrina Manor
520 W. Main St.
Uniontown, PA 15401-2602
Tel: 724-437-1400; Fax: 724-430-1095
Danette Loposky, R.N., N.H.A., Admin.
Brothers of the Holy Spirit 1
Sisters of St. Basil the Great 3
Beds 141

Ventnor
Archdiocese of Philadelphia

Villa St. Joseph by the Sea
114 S. Princeton Ave.
Ventnor, PA 08406
Tel: 609-822-7184
Summer residence for aged, infirm, and convalescent priests of the Archdiocese of Philadelphia.
Rev. Msgr. Francis A. Menna
Rev. Edward J. Casey, Asst. Rector

Warminster
Archdiocese of Philadelphia

Regina Coeli Residence for Priests
685 York Rd.
Warminster, PA 18974
Tel: 215-441-4642
Rev. James D. Beisel, Admin.
Home for retired priests of the Archdiocese of Philadelphia.
Total Staff 5
Total in Residence 13

Wilkes-Barre
Diocese of Scranton

Little Flower Manor of the Diocese of Scranton
200 S. Meade St.
Wilkes-Barre, PA 18702
Tel: 570-823-6131; Fax: 570-823-5171
Sr. M. Jeanette Lindsay, O.Carm., Supr. & Admin.
Rev. Edward J. Williams, Chap.
Conducted by the Carmelite Sisters for the Aged and Infirm.
St. Therese Residence
260 S. Meade St.
Wilkes-Barre, PA 18702
Tel: 570-823-6131; Fax: 570-208-0143
Residents 60
Total Staff 19
Sr. Kevin Patricia O'Brien, O.Carm., Admin.
Rev. Edward J. Williams
Conducted by the Carmelite Sisters for the Aged and Infirm.
Sisters 5
Aged Residents 133
Total Staff 230

Yardley
Archdiocese of Philadelphia

D'Youville Manor
1750 Quarry Rd.
Yardley, PA 19067
Tel: 215-579-1750; Fax: 215-579-3054
Operated by Grey Nuns of the Sacred Heart. Assisted living retirement residence for the elderly.
Sr. Jacqueline Weigle, G.N.S.H., Dir.
Capacity 51
Total Staff 27
Total in Residence 49

York
Diocese of Harrisburg

Misericordia Convalescent Home
998 S. Russell St.
York, PA 17402
Tel: 717-755-1964; Fax: 717-840-0010
E-mail: misericordia@computerlynx.net
Daughters of Our Lady of Mercy
Sr. Carmel Marie, D.M., Admin.
Sisters 7
Bed Capacity 53
Total Assisted 73
Total Staff 60

PUERTO RICO

Arecibo
Diocese of Arecibo, Puerto Rico

Hogar de Ancianos San Vicente
Mailing Address:
P.O. Box 4196
Vega Baja, PR 00694
Bo. Almirante Sur-Carr 645 Km. 6.6
Vega Baja, PR 00763
Tel: 787-855-0487
Guests 48

Hogar Sta. Maria Eufrasia
Mailing Address:
P.O. Box 1909
Arecibo, PR 00612
Fax: 787-880-2632
Calle Andres Garcia, No. 10
Arecibo, PR 00612
Tel: 787-878-5166
House for Unwed Mothers.
Good Shepherd Sisters 5
Unwed Mothers 12

La Milagrosa Home for Orphan Girls
Cotto Ave., No. 987
Arecibo, PR 00612
Tel: 809-878-6231
Sisters of Charity 7
Girls 12

San Rafael Home for Aged
00612
Hogar Geriatrico San Rafael
Calle Cervantes
Arecibo, PR 00612
Tel: 787-878-3813
Sisters of Charity 5
Guests 37

Bayamon
Archdiocese of San Juan, Puerto Rico

Hogar Del Nino "Elave Maria"
(For Abused Children)
Carpetera 861, km 2.0, Bo. Pajaros Americanos
Bayamon, PR,
Tel: 787-797-2382; 279-3003
Mailing Address:
P.O. Box 3367
Bayamon, PR 00958-3367
Rev. Pedro Gorena, O.SS.T., Dir.

Hogar Escuela Sop Maria Rafaela
(Girls with Problems)
Carpetera 871, km 1.0, Bo. El Volcan, Hato Tejas
Bayamon, PR,
Tel: 787-785-9586; Fax: 787-785-9586
Mailing Address:
P.O. Box 3024
Bayamon, 00960
Sr. Nelida Gonzalez, Dir.

Hogar Fatima
Ave. Santa Juanita Final, Camino Esteban Cruz
Bayamon, PR,
Mailing Address: (Adolescent Girls 11-18 years)
P.O. Box 4228
Bayamon Garden Sta., PR 00958-1218
Sr. Maria Saez, Dir.

Canovanas
Archdiocese of San Juan, Puerto Rico

Hogar Teresa Toda
(For Girls)
P.O. Box 868
Canovanas, PR 00729
Tel: 787-886-2060
Calle 5-A, R-14, Villas De Loiza
Loiza, PR 00729
Sr. Ines Pena, Dir.

Dorado
Archdiocese of San Juan, Puerto Rico

Santuario del Espiritu Santo
Box 187
Dorado, PR 00646-0187
Tel: 787-796-2798
E-mail: orlycssp@coqui.net
Revs.:
Eduardo Caron, C.S.Sp.
Augustine Nnamdi Nwosu, C.S.Sp.
Jonas Rivera Martinez, C.S.Sp.
P. Orlando Camacho, Torres

Isabela
Diocese of Arecibo, Puerto Rico

Hogar Infantil Jesus Nazareno, Inc.
P.O. Box 1671
Isabela, PR 00662
Residential Care of Children 25

Lares
Diocese of Arecibo, Puerto Rico

Fundacion Irma Fe
Calle Comerio No. 52
Lares, PR 00669
Tel: 787-897-6090
Charity Sisters of St. Joseph (Mexico) 6
Guests 25

Ponce
Diocese of Ponce, Puerto Rico

Home for Aged and Infirm
Barrio Sabenetas, P.O. Box 2127
Ponce, PR 00731
Tel: 787-840-7575
Sr. ARACELI VILLA, Supr.
Rev. PERFECTO ALVAREZ, O.S.A., Chap.
Total Staff 16
Residents 197

Puerta De Tierra
Archdiocese of San Juan, Puerto Rico

Asylum For The Aged and Infirm
Hogar de la Providencia, Stop 5
Puerta De Tierra, PR 00906
Tel: 787-722-1331
Mailing Address:
P.O. Box 9066571
San Juan, PR 00906-6571
Sisters of the Poor
Sr. ANA MARIA HIDALGO, Supr.
Rev. OVIDIO ORTEGA, Chap.
Sisters 19
Patients assisted annually 275

Rio Piedras
Archdiocese of San Juan, Puerto Rico

Asylum For Orphan Girls
107 Jose de Diego St. S.
Rio Piedras, PR 00925
Tel: 787-765-6114
Daughters of Charity
Sr. VIRGINIA TORRES, H.C., Supr.
Rev. HIGINIO MADRAZO, C.M., Chap.
Sisters 15
Beds 70

Centro N. Sra. de la Providencia
Sisters of Notre Dame.
R.F.D. #2, Box 16T
Rio Piedras, PR 00928
Tel: 787-761-0273

Centro Santa Luisa
(Day Care Center for the Elderly)
Carpetera 842, Camino Los Romeros km 1.9, Bo. Caimito
Rio Piedras, PR,
Tel: 787-720-2764; Fax: 787-731-7795
Mailing Address:
RR6, Box 9492
San Juan, PR 00926
Sr. CATERINA SANCHEZ, H.C., Dir.

Hogar Carmelitano
Julian Bengochea Final;
Urb. San Martin
Rio Piedras, PR 00924
Tel: 787-769-6510; 769-3110; Fax: 787-768-1240
Carmelite Sisters (Spain)
Sr. MARIBELLE MEJIAS MUNIZ, Admin.
Beds 224
Patients assisted annually 163
Total Staff 74

Hogar Santa Teresa Jornet for the Aged
Cupey Alto, Km. 3, Hm. 8, Box 21012
Rio Piedras, PR 00928
Tel: 787-761-5805; Fax: 787-755-5575
Sisters of the Poor
Sr. CARMEN VASQUEZ, Mother Supr.
Rev. JOSE MARIA LOPEZ, Chap.
Sisters 20
Beds 220
Residents 223
Total Staff 84

San Juan
Archdiocese of San Juan, Puerto Rico

Casa La Providencia
(Drug Addicted Women)
Blvd. Del Valle 2000
San Juan, PR,
Tel: 787-725-5358
Mailing Address:
P.O. Box 614
San Juan, PR 00902
Sr. AIDA CRUZ, Dir.

Hogar Fatima
(Single Mothers)
Floral Park, 20 C. Matienzo Citron
San Juan, PR 00919
Tel: 787-250-6323

Santurce
Archdiocese of San Juan, Puerto Rico

Casa Manuel Fernandez Juncos
(Orphans and Abused Boys)
Calle Villa Verde Esq. Refugio, PDA 11, Miramar
Santurce, PR,
Tel: 787-724-2904;725-6328; Fax: 787-724-0908
Mailing Address:
P.O. Box 9020163
San Juan, PR 00902-0163
Deacon LUIS G. FERNANDEZ

Toa Alta
Archdiocese of San Juan, Puerto Rico

Hogar Santisima Trinidad
(Drug Addiction Rehabilitation Home)
Lote A y Loted, km 7.0, Bo Mucarabones
Toa Alta, PR,
Tel: 787-799-6208
Mailing Address:
P.O. Box 3367
Bayamon, PR 00958-3367
Rev. PEDRO GORENA, O.SS.T.

Vega Alta
Diocese of Arecibo, Puerto Rico

Mision Juan XXIII
00692
Centro Geriatrico Juan de los Olivos
HC-91, Box 8983
Vega Alta, PR 00692-9606
Tel: 787-883-2370
Sisters of Charity 3
Guests 43

RHODE ISLAND

Cumberland
Diocese of Providence

Mount St. Rita Health Centre
15 Sumner Brown Rd.
Cumberland, RI 02864
Tel: 401-333-6352
E-mail: mail@mountstrita.org
Web Site: www.mountstrita.org
Legal Title: *Mount St. Rita Health Centre Inc.*
Licenced Nursing Home.
JULIE RICHARD, Admin.
Residents 98
Total Staff 163

Newport
Diocese of Providence

St. Clare Home
309 Spring St.
Newport, RI 02840
Tel: 401-849-3204; Fax: 401-849-5780
E-mail: clarehome@rcn.com
Legal Title: *The Saint Clare Home*
Nursing Facility.
MARY BETH DAIGNEAULT, Admin.
Rev. RICHARD A. WALSH, Chap.
Daughters of the Holy Spirit 4
Lay Nurses 12
Lay Employees 73
Residents 47

North Kingstown
Diocese of Providence

Scalabrini Villa
860 N. Quidnessett Rd.
North Kingstown, RI 02852
Tel: 401-884-1802; Fax: 401-884-4727
E-mail: villa@efortress.com
Web Site: www.freeyellow.com/members3/scalabrini/
Legal Title: *Scalabrini Villa Inc.*
Full Skilled Nursing Facility.
Rev. EDWARD J. MARINO, C.S., Admin., Tel: 401-884-1802
Sr. TERESITA TAUYAN, F.A.S., Supr., Tel: 401-884-4594
In res.,
Rev. Msgr. OSCAR A. GUILBAULT Tel: 401-884-1426
Franciscan Apostolic Sisters 4
Residents 120
Total Staff 126

North Smithfield
Diocese of Providence

St. Antoine Residence
400 Mendon Rd.
North Smithfield, RI 02896
Tel: 401-767-3500; Fax: 401-769-5249
E-mail: Antoine@tiac.net
Legal Title: *Saint Antoine Residence*
MARY ANN ALTRUI, Admin.
Rev. DONAT A. BARRETTE, Chap.
Residents 260
Total Staff 348

The Villa at Saint Antoine
400 Mendon Rd.
North Smithfield, RI 02896-6999
Tel: 401-767-2574; Fax: 401-767-2581
Legal Title: *The Frassati Residence*
Mr. JOHN HENDERSON, Dir.

Pawtucket
Diocese of Providence

Jeanne Jugan Apartments
310 Sayles Ave.
Pawtucket, RI 02860
Mailing Address:
964 Main St.
Pawtucket, RI 02860
Apartments for elderly 27
Residents 30
Total Staff 1

Jeanne Jugan Residence
964 Main St.
Pawtucket, RI 02860
Tel: 401-723-4314; Fax: 401-727-2885
Legal Title: *Jeanne Jugan Residence of the Little Sisters of the Poor*
Rev. Msgr. WILLIAM I. VARSANYI, J.C.D., Chap.
In res.,
Rev. Msgr. PAUL A. LLOYD
Rev. OVILA T. DOUCET
Little Sisters of the Poor 15
Residents 74
Total Staff 95

Providence
Diocese of Providence

St. Joseph Living Center
153 Dean St.
Providence, RI 02903
Tel: 401-272-3335
DIANE E. EVANS, R.N., B.S.N., Exec. Dir.
Assisted and independent living and respite care facility, a division of St. Joseph Health Services of Rhode Island.
Residents 60

Woonsocket
Diocese of Providence

Saint Francis House
167 Blackstone St.
Woonsocket, RI 02895
Tel: 401-762-5255; Fax: 401-767-2911
E-mail: st.francis@fortress.com
Legal Title: *Saint Francis House, Woonsocket RI*
HELEN STRADONE, Dir.
Rev. JOSEPH D. SHANLEY, Chap.
Residents 59
Total Staff 27

SOUTH CAROLINA

Charleston
Diocese of Charleston

Carter-May Home
1660 Ingram Rd.
Charleston, SC 29407
Tel: 843-556-8314; Fax: 843-402-9071
Mrs. JANINE N. BAUDER, Admin.
Residents 15

SOUTH DAKOTA

Aberdeen
Diocese of Sioux Falls

Aberdeen Living Center
(Operated by Benedictine Health System-Benedictine Living Communities, Inc.)
1700 N. Hwy. 281
Aberdeen, SD 57401
Tel: 605-225-7315; Fax: 605-225-0078
JEANETTE QUINTON, Admin.
Total Assisted 172
Total Staff 140

Milbank
Diocese of Sioux Falls

St. William Home for the Aged
901 E. Virgil Ave.
Milbank, SD 57252
Tel: 605-432-4538; Fax: 605-432-5412
Conducted by Daughters of St. Mary of Providence, Milbank
Rev. RAY OTTO, O.S.B.
Guests 60
Angela Hall Assisted Living Center
Guests 22
Sisters 5

Sisseton
Diocese of Sioux Falls

Tekakwitha Nursing Center, Inc.
(sub. of Benedictine Health System)
6 E. Chestnut
Sisseton, SD 57262
Tel: 698-693-7693; Fax: 605-698-3091
PATRICK J. RAFFERTY, Admin.
Sr. COLETTA VAN HEEK, O.S.B., Dir. Pastoral Care
Beds 85
Total Staff 101
(Owned and operated by: Benedictine Health System)
Rainbow Daycare Center

TENNESSEE

Dyersburg
Diocese of Memphis

St. Joseph Manor
885 Hwy. 51, Byp. W.,
Dyersburg, TN 38024
Tel: 901-285-8560; Fax: 901-285-8562
E-mail: stjoseph@usit.net
BEVERLY BATES, Mgr.

St. Joseph Village
885 Hwy. 51 Byp. W., Box 151
Dyersburg, TN 38024
Tel: 901-285-8560; Fax: 901-285-8562
E-mail: stjoseph@usit.net
BEVERLY BATES, Mgr.

Humboldt
Diocese of Memphis

St. Matthew Manor
2575 Viking Dr.
Humboldt, TN 38343
Tel: 901-784-7229
Mr. JIM BUTLER, Mgr.

St. Matthew Manor - West
2575 Viking Dr.
Humboldt, TN 38343
Tel: 901-824-3793
Mr. JIM BUTLER, Mgr.

Jackson
Diocese of Memphis

St. Mary Manor
1771 Hwy. 45 By-Pass
Jackson, TN 38305
Tel: 901-668-5633; Fax: 901-668-9252
ANNE M. SAIN, Mgr.

Knoxville
Diocese of Knoxville

Columbus Home, Inc.
119 Dameron Ave.
Knoxville, TN 37917
Tel: 865-971-3570; Fax: 865-546-0433
E-mail: inglecolumbus@aol.com
Rev. RAGAN SCHRIVER, Exec. Dir.
Total Assisted 320
Total Staff 28

Memphis
Diocese of Memphis

Diocese of Memphis Housing Corp.
P.O. Box 41705
Memphis, TN 38174-1705
Tel: 901-722-4761; 722-4772; Fax: 901-722-4791
E-mail: davidf@cathchar.org ; michelle@cathchar.org
Web Site: www.cathchar.org
Mr. DAVID FIELD, Dir. of Housing

St. Peter Home for Children (1852)
3060 Baskin St.
Memphis, TN 38127-7799
Tel: 901-354-6300; Fax: 901-354-6343

St. Peter Manor
108 N. Auburndale
Memphis, TN 38104
Tel: 901-278-8200; Fax: 901-278-8210
E-mail: mtwig@mecca32.mecca.org
Sr. MARILYN TERWILLIGER, S.S.J., Mgr.
St. Peter Chapel & Activity Center
Tel: 901-278-8200; Fax: 901-278-8210

St. Peter Villa
141 N. McLean
Memphis, TN 38104-2644
Tel: 901-276-2021; Fax: 901-725-3564
E-mail: kae@cathchar.org
Diocesan Nursing Home.
Mrs. KAE WERKHOVEN, Admin.

Moscow
Diocese of Memphis

St. Mark Village Apartments
85 St. Mark Cove
Moscow, TN 38057
Tel: 901-877-3456
Ms. GEORGIA LAUGHTER, Mgr.

Nashville
Diocese of Nashville

St. Mary Villa Child Development Center
30 White Bridge Rd.
Nashville, TN 37205
Tel: 615-356-6336; Fax: 615-356-6421
E-mail: jchase@edge.net
JOANNE CHASE, Exec. Dir.
Staff 45
Children 221

St. Mary Villa, Inc.
30 White Bridge Rd.
Nashville, TN 37205
Tel: 615-356-6336; Fax: 615-356-6421

**St. Bernard After School Program*
2020 24th Ave. S.
Nashville, TN 37212
Tel: 615-298-1298; Fax: 615-783-0241
BRENDA DYE, Dir.
Lay Staff 17
Students 120

Villa Maria Manor, Inc. dba Villa Maria Manor
32 White Bridge Rd.
Nashville, TN 37205
Tel: 615-352-3084; Fax: 615-352-0553
E-mail: thevilla@bellsouth.net
Mr. DAVID GLASCOE, Mng. Agent
Residents 230

Signal Mountain
Diocese of Knoxville

Alexian Village Health Care Center (1938)
100 James Blvd.
Signal Mountain, TN 37377
Tel: 423-886-0100; Fax: 423-886-0470
E-mail: AVTCEO@aol.com
Web Site: www.alexianvillage.com
Licensed Skilled & Intermediate Care Nursing Home.
Bro. EDWARD YOCHIM, C.F.A., Dir. of Community
Rev. MARO CANNON, C.F.A., Chap.
Mrs. CHRIS TARZIERS, Admin.
Total Assisted 189
Total Staff 94
Brothers 8
Bed Capacity 114
Patients assisted annually 184
Assisted Living 75

Alexian Village of Tennessee
100 James Blvd.
Signal Mountain, TN 37377
Tel: 423-886-0100; Fax: 423-886-0470
E-mail: AVTCEO@aol.com
Web Site: www.alexianvillage.com
Life Care Residences and Nursing Home.
Mr. SENECA S. FOOTE, CEO/Pres.
Rev. LOUIS J. JUNOD, Assoc. Chap.
Life Care Units 277
Total In Residence 513
Total Staff 145

TEXAS

Arlington
Diocese of Fort Worth

Nuestro Hogar, Inc. Catholic Charities
709 Magnolia St.
Arlington, TX 76012
Tel: 817-261-0608
E-mail: nuestrol@flash.net
Web Site: www.ccdofw.org
65 unit apartment complex for the elderly and disabled.
Total in Residence 63
Total Staff 5

Boerne
Archdiocese of San Antonio

Childrens' Inn
216 W. Highland Dr.
Boerne, TX 78006
Tel: 830-249-9456; Fax: 830-249-3327
E-mail: childrensinn@netscape.net
Co-Directors:
Sr. KATHLEEN KEAN, S.S.J.
MARILYN HAIDER
Provides foster care for children with special needs in a holistic setting.
Total Assisted 7

Brenham
Diocese of Austin

Trinity Care Center
400 E. Sayles
Brenham, TX 77833
Tel: 979-836-9770
E-mail: fjulian@mail.st-joseph.org
Web Site: TRINITYMED.ORG
FLORENCE JULIAN, Exec. Dir.
Sr. WINIFRED TEMPLIN, O.S.F., Dir. of Pastoral Care
Bed Capacity 120
Total Assisted 110
Total Staff 110

Brownsville
Diocese of Brownsville

Mother of Perpetual Help Nursing Home, Inc.
519 A East Madison St.
Brownsville, TX 78520
Tel: 956-546-6745; Fax: 956-546-0711
Owner: Sisters of the Holy Spirit and Mary Immaculate.
Mr. LAMON FURR, Admin.
Beds 38
Chapel attended from Immaculate Conception Cathedral.

Bryan
Diocese of Austin

St. Joseph Manor
2801 Franciscan Dr.
Bryan, TX 77802
Tel: 979-821-7590
Sr. ALICE WARRICK, O.S.F., Contact Person

Caldwell
Diocese of Austin

Burleson St. Joseph Manor
1022 Presidential Corridor, Hwy. 21E
Caldwell, TX 77836
Tel: 979-821-7590; Fax: 979-567-4811
E-mail: hcottrell@mail.st-joseph.org
Sr. ALICE WARRICK, Pres.
Beds 96
Sisters 1
Staff 75

Corpus Christi
Diocese of Corpus Christi

Casa San Lucas
222 Ocean View
Corpus Christi, TX 78411
Tel: 512-857-5758
Priests 3

Mount Carmel Home
4130 S. Alameda St.
Corpus Christi, TX 78411
Tel: 512-855-6243; Fax: 512-854-8513
Sr. MARY TERESA, Supr.
Rev. ARNOLD ANDERS, Chaplain
Sisters 7
Residents 82
Total Staff 25

Villa Maria, Inc.
3146 Saratoga Blvd.
Corpus Christi, TX 78415
Tel: 361-857-6171; Fax: 361-857-6173
Apartment complex for senior adults.
Total Staff 4
Total in Residence 55

Crowley
Diocese of Fort Worth

St. Francis Village, Inc.
1 Chapel Plaza
Crowley, TX 76036
Tel: 817-292-5786; Fax: 817-294-2989
Web Site: www.saintfrancisvillage.com
Residence village, on shores of Lake Benbrook near Fort Worth, for retirees and the elderly sponsored by Franciscan Tertiary Provinces Foundation & SFV, Inc. (Illinois).
Revs.:
J. MICHAEL EWERT, O.F.M., Chm. Bd.
LAMBERT LEYKAM, O.F.M., Chap.
In res.,
Rev. Msgr. W. ROBERT JOHNSON
Revs.:
RAYMAR BOBBER, O.F.M., (Retired)
PETER FRITZ, O.F.M., (Retired)
DONALD WERR, O.F.M., (Retired)
RONALD J. AXEN, (Retired)
MATHIAS KIEMEN, O.F.M., (Retired)
AUGUSTINE HEALEY, O.C.D.
BART LANDWERMEYER
Bros.:
ALLEN HAIAR, O.F.M.
CAMILLUS SMITH, O.F.M.
Residents 420
Franciscan Tertiary Provinces Foundation
1 Chapel Plaza
Crowley, TX 76036
Tel: 817-292-5786
Sponsor corporation of St. Francis Village (retirement village) in Crowley, TX.
Rev. J. MICHAEL EWERT, O.F.M., Chm.
Total Staff 15

El Paso
Diocese of El Paso

El Paso Diocese Home for the Aged
920 S. Oregon St.
El Paso, TX 79901
Tel: 915-533-5152
Home for Aged Women and Men.
Sr. MARY ANN HAMOR, C.S.J., Dir.
Women Residents 17
Men Residents 6

Nazareth Hall
4614 Trowbridge
El Paso, TX 79903
Tel: 915-565-4677; Fax: 915-566-7530

Fort Worth
Diocese of Fort Worth

Casa del Cor, Inc.
2701 Burchill Rd. N.
Fort Worth, TX 76105
Tel: 817-534-0814; Fax: 817-535-8779
E-mail: webmaster@ccdofw.org
Web Site: www.ccdofw.org

Casa, Inc. Housing for the Elderly and Handicapped
3201 Sondra Dr.
Fort Worth, TX 76107
Tel: 817-332-7276
E-mail: casal@flash.nt
Web Site: www.ccdofw.org
Units 200

Total in Residence 181
Total Staff 7

Hillje
Diocese of Victoria in Texas

Czech Catholic Home For The Aged
Rte. 3, Box 4
El Campo, TX 77437
Tel: 979-648-2628; Fax: 979-648-2884
E-mail: czechome@wcnet.net

Houston
Diocese of Galveston—Houston

Casa de Esperanza, De Los Ninos, Inc.
Mailing Address: P.O. Box 66581
Houston, TX 77266-6581
Tel: 713-529-0639; Fax: 713-529-9179
E-mail: casa@casahope.org
Homes for children in crisis situations, foster care, adoption, HIV family services.
KATHLEEN FOSTER, Dir.
Mr. WILLIAM JONES, Assoc. Dir.
Sisters 5
Served 2,000
Total Assisted 200
Total Staff 46

Casa Juan Diego
4818 Rose
Houston, TX 77007
Tel: 713-869-7376; Fax: 713-864-4994
E-mail: info@cjd.org
Web Site: www.cjd.org
Mr. MARK ZWICK, Dir.
Houses 16
Patients assisted annually 263,700

Casa Maria de Guadalupe Medical Clinic and Social Service Center
(Catholic Worker)
6101 Edgemoor
Houston, TX 77081
Tel: 713-995-9414; Fax: 713-864-4994
E-mail: info@cjd.org
Web Site: www.cjd.org
Mailing Address:
P.O. Box 70113
Houston, TX 77270
Patients assisted annually 229,300
Total Staff 10

Covenant House Texas
1111 Lovett Blvd.
Houston, TX 77006
Tel: 713-523-2231; Fax: 713-523-6904
E-mail: RRobinson@ghg.net
Web Site: covenanthousetx.org
Sr. MARY ROSE MCGEADY, Pres.
RONDA G. ROBINSON, Exec. Dir./CEO
PIERRE MATTA, Pastoral Min.
Total Assisted 2,677
Total Staff 97

St. Dominic Village
2401 Holcombe Blvd.
Houston, TX 77021-2099
Tel: 713-741-8701; Fax: 713-741-9811
RUTH WHIGHAM, Dir.
Pope John Paul XXIII Priests' Residence
2407 Holcombe Blvd.
Houston, TX 77021-2023
Tel: 713-748-4608
Revs.:
GABRE-TINSAYE ADHANA, (Retired), Tel: 713-748-4425
NICHOLAS C. ANTLE, (Retired), Tel: 713-748-1553
LEROY H. BRADEN, (Retired), Tel: 713-440-7540
PETER CHU, (Retired), Tel: 713-747-8774
THOMAS A. DONOVAN, (Retired), Tel: 713-741-9471
EUGENE E. GILLECE, (Retired), Tel: 713-748-7201
JACK B. JONES, (Retired), Tel: 713-747-1746
FRANK A. LAGANA, (Retired), Tel: 713-748-7022
LAWRENCE LEE, (Retired), Tel: 713-741-7267
JAMES J. MADDEN, (Retired), Tel: 713-748-1761
JAMES NELSON, (Retired), Tel: 713-748-8144
JOSEPH T. O'MALLEY, (Retired), Tel: 713-842-2728
LAWRENCE PEGUERO, (Retired), Tel: 713-741-8326
GEORGE V. RHEIN, (Retired), Tel: 713-747-7308
CHARLES K. SCHOEPPE, (Retired), Tel: 713-748-4596
GARY F. WANZONG, (Retired), Tel: 713-748-0957
Total Residents 16
Total Staff 2
St. Dominic Nursing Home
2409 Holcombe Blvd.
Houston, TX 7721-2023
Tel: 713-741-8701; Fax: 713-741-9811
RUTH WHIGHAM, Admin.
Aged Residents 267
Total Staff 125
St. Dominic Residence Hall
2401 Holcombe Blvd.
Houston, TX 77021-2023
Tel: 713-741-8700; Fax: 713-748-8305
RUTH WHIGHAM, Admin.
Total Residents 112
Total Staff 26

Santa Maria Hostel
807 Paschall St.
Houston, TX 77009
Tel: 713-228-0125; Fax: 713-222-0595
E-mail: cempey@hotmail.com
Intensive residential treatment (substance abuse) for women ages 18 and above.
Ms. CHERYL EMPEY, Exec. Dir.
Residents 23
Patients assisted annually 200
Total Staff 17

Kenedy
Archdiocese of San Antonio

John Paul II Nursing Home
209 S. 3rd St., P.O. Box 359
Kenedy, TX 78119
Tel: 830-583-9841; Fax: 830-583-9458
Sr. ELIZABETH DUBICKA, S.O.L.S., Admin.
Seraphic Sisters of Our Lady of Sorrows 4
Residents 64

Laredo
Diocese of Corpus Christi

Sacred Heart Children's Home
3310 S. Zapata Hwy.
Laredo, TX 78046
Tel: 956-723-3343; Fax: 956-723-3409
Servants of the Sacred Heart of Jesus and of the Poor
Mother MARIA TERESA GRAJEDA, Supr.
Sisters 22
Children 58

Diocese of Laredo

Sacred Heart Children's Home
3310 S. Zapata Hwy.
Laredo, TX 78046
Tel: 956-723-3343; Fax: 956-723-3409
Sr. MARIA TERESA GRAJEDA, Supr. & Admin.
Sisters 24
Children 57

Panhandle
Diocese of Amarillo

St. Ann's Nursing Home
P.O. Box 1179
Panhandle, TX 79068
Tel: 806-537-3194; Fax: 806-537-3003
Rev. Msgr. MONROE J. MATTHIESEN, Dir.
Rev. Msgr. JAMES SONDERMAN, Pastor Emeritus
Rev. Msgr. RICHARD VAUGHAN
Sr. JEAN MARIE LARA, Admin.
School Sisters of St. Francis
Residents 56

St. Joseph's Home for Retired Priests
P.O. Box 1179
Panhandle, TX 79068
Rev. Msgr. CLIFTON J. CORCORAN, Pastor Emeritus
Rev. Msgr. MONROE J. MATTHIESEN, Dir. & Pastor Emeritus
Rev. DALE GUIDRY

San Antonio
Archdiocese of San Antonio

Casa De Padres
8520 Cross Mountain Tr., P.O. Box 100
San Antonio, TX 78255
Fax: 830-981-9192
E-mail: jengberg@gutc.com
Mrs. JEANNINE ENGBERG, Dir, Tel: 210-698-0175
Home for retired Priests of San Antonio.
Rev. Msgr. ALOIS J. GOERTZ, No. 402, Tel: 210-698-9067
Rev. Msgr. J. LEROY MANNING, No. 1102, Tel: 210-698-3183
Rev. Msgr. PATRICK PALMER, No. 1101, Tel: 210-698-3276
Rev. PABLO PANIAGUA, No. 401, Tel: 210-698-8036
Rev. Msgr. ROY RIHN, No. 301, Tel: 210-698-0287
Rev. Msgr. SHERRILL SMITH, No. 201, Tel: 210-698-8819
Rev. Msgr. VINCENT FECHER, No. 302, Tel: 210-698-3923
Rev. Msgr. RAMON GARCIA, No. 202, Tel: 210-698-9079
Rev. Msgr. DAVID MEURER, No. 1001, Tel: 210-698-0175

Rev. Msgr. ALBERT HUBERTUS, No. 1002, Tel: 210-698-3183
In res.,
Rev. Msgr. JOSEPH PETSCH, No. 702, Tel: 210-698-7055
Rev. Msgr. TERENCE NOLAN, No. 701, Tel: 201-698-0349

Father Flanagan's Boys' and Girls' Town of San Antonio
503 Urban Loop
San Antonio, TX 78204
Tel: 210-271-1010; Fax: 210-271-3333
E-mail: morales@boystown.org
Web Site: www.boystown.org
Mr. RONALDO E. MORALES, Site Dir.
Staff 60
Bed Capacity 50
Children Under Care 46
Residential Center (For Children under 18)
8400, 8401, 8402, 8405, 8406 Flanagan St.
San Antonio, TX 78249
Tel: 210-271-1010; Fax: 210-271-3333
Staff 22
Bed Capacity 30
Youth Shelter
503 Urban Loop
San Antonio, TX 78204
Tel: 210-271-3131; Fax: 210-271-9407
Staff 22
Bed Capacity 20
Total Assisted 300
Family Preservation Services
503 Urban Loop
San Antonio, TX 78204
Tel: 210-271-1010; Fax: 210-271-3333
Staff 6
Families Assisted 50

Incarnate Word Retirement Community
4707 Broadway
San Antonio, TX 78209
Tel: 210-829-7561; Fax: 210-828-0020
For lay persons also.
Mr. RICHARD BOYD, Exec. Dir.
Rev. Msgr. THOMAS A. FRENCH, Chap.
Total in Residence 201

Marianist Residence: Skilled Nursing
520 Fordham Ln.
San Antonio, TX 78228-4821
Tel: 210-436-3771 (Nurses' Station); Fax: 210-431-4240
E-mail: jjaeckle@stmarytx.edu
Home for Infirm Marianist Brothers and Priests.
Bros.:
JOSEPH GRIESHABER, S.M., Dir.
JAMES JAECKLE, S.M., Sub Dir., Health Care Oper.
LAWRENCE JORDAN, S.M.
NORBERT MOELLERING, S.M. Tel: 210-436-3150
Revs.:
LOUIS REILE, S.M. Tel: 210-436-3764
THOMAS M. SCHELBLE, S.M.
JAMES YOUNG, S.M. Tel: 210-431-5014
Infirm Brothers 18
Infirm Priests 5
Total Assisted 30
Staff 43

Oblate Madonna Residence
5722 Blanco Rd.
San Antonio, TX 78216
Tel: 210-341-2350
Home for retired Priests and Brothers.
Missionary Oblates of Mary Immaculate
Revs.:
PATRICK GUIDON, O.M.I., Dir.
JOHN SOKOLSKI, Supr.
JOSE AZPIAZU, O.M.I.
CLIFFORD BLACKBURN, O.M.I.
CHARLES BORGERS, O.M.I.
ALAN BRELIVET, O.M.I.
JOHN BUSCH, O.M.I.
JAMES P. DELANEY, O.M.I.
LAURENT DUPUIS, O.M.I.
MAXIMO FUENTE, O.M.I.
LEO GAUVIN, O.M.I.
RICHARD A. HOULAHAN, O.M.I.
ALFRED LAVOIE, O.M.I.
JOSEPH LYONS, O.M.I.
JOHN MCGRATH, O.M.I.
SEBASTIAN MOZOS, O.M.I.
EDWARD MURRAY, O.M.I.
GEORGE O'CONNELL, O.M.I.
WILLIAM D. O'CONNOR, O.M.I.
RAYMOND POMAVILLE, O.M.I.
ALFRED PRADO, O.M.I.
FRANCIS SCHOUTTETEN, O.M.I.
MICHAEL SLATTERY, O.M.I.
ANTONIO STRANO, O.M.I.
JOSE VELASCO, O.M.I.
ROBERT VRETEAU, O.M.I.
WILLIAM ZAPALAC, O.M.I.
Bro. JOSEPH PALAZZO, O.M.I.
In res.,
Most Rev. THOMAS FLANAGAN, D.D.
Priests 27
Brothers 1

Padua Place
80 Peter Baque Rd.
San Antonio, TX 78209
Tel: 210-826-7721; Fax: 210-824-4554
E-mail: paduaplace@aol.com.
Home for infirm and retired Priests and Brothers.
Sr. ROSE MARY MARTINEZ, M.S.S.A., Admin.
In res.,
Revs.:
THEODORE CLERX, C.I.C.M.
JAMES COLEMAN (SAN)
EUGENE JANSON (VIC)
CHARLES LARUE (SAN)
JAMES MEUREE, C.I.C.M.
FRANCIS NELAN, M.S.C.
DANIEL O'BRIEN (VIC)
ROBERT TIMPERMAN, C.I.C.M.
PETER VERGAUWEN (SAN)
EDWARD ZABOROWSKI, M.S.F.
CHARLES ZEYEN, M.S.F.
Rev. Msgr. ANTHONY J. COSTANTINO (SAT)
Rev. Msgr. RODOLFO GALINDO (SD)
Rev. Msgr. KEVIN HEYBURN (SAN)
Rev. Msgr. BERNARD MULLANEY (SAT)
Rev. Msgr. CHARLES PUGH
Rev. Msgr. VICTOR SCHMIDTZINSKY (VIC)
Bro. EDWARD KINSLEY, M.S.F.
Priests 16
Brothers 1

Providence Home & Family Services, Inc.
(Foster Home and Childcare for HIV Positive Children)
2650 Castroville Rd.
San Antonio, TX 78237
Tel: 210-434-2111; Fax: 210-433-2806
E-mail: cbovarice@compuserve.com
Ms. CAROLE BOVA-RICE, Exec. Dir.
Sisters 4

St. Francis Nursing Home
630 W. Woodlawn
San Antonio, TX 78212
Tel: 210-736-3177; Fax: 210-783-2221
Home for the Aged and Convalescents.
Seraphic Sisters of Our Lady of Sorrows
Rev. JASPER MAUSS, O.F.M.
Sr. ALFONSA BOBEK, S.O.L.S., Pres. of Corp.
Sr. AGNES BOCHENEK, S.O.L.S., Admin.
Sisters 9
Bed Capacity 152
Total Staff 134

St. Peter & Joseph Childrens Home
919 Mission Rd.
San Antonio, TX 78210
Tel: 210-533-1203; Fax: 210-533-6177
E-mail: sbomlaski@stpjhom.org
SUSAN H. BOMALASKI, Ph.D., L.P.C., Exec. Dir.
House Parent Staff 17
Administrative & Support Staff 16
Bed Capacity 72
Children Under Care (ages 2-18) 60
Total Assisted 98

Seton Home for Homeless, Pregnant Young Women
1115 Mission Rd.
San Antonio, TX 78210
Tel: 210-533-3504; Fax: 210-533-3467
TOM HARRELL, Interim Dir.
Bed Capacity 24
Total Assisted 55

The South Texas Catholic Retirement Center, Inc.
P.O. Box 15378
San Antonio, TX 78212-8578
Tel: 210-734-8310; Fax: 210-734-8369
E-mail: coughlin@universe.uiwtx.edu
Sr. KATHLEEN COUGHLIN, C.C.V.I., Chm.
Purpose: A collaborative effort of 16 Religious Congregations, men and women, to provide a facility for elderly religious and lay men and women who are economically disadvantaged.

Visitation Hospitality House of San Antonio, Texas and Interconnections
945 W. Huisache
San Antonio, TX 78201
Tel: 210-735-6910; Fax: 210-738-8794
E-mail: visitprog@aol.com
Web Site: www.visitationhouseministries.org
A non-profit corporation chartered under the laws of the State of Texas.
Operated by the Sisters of Charity of the Incarnate Word of San Antonio, TX
Sr. YOLANDA TARANGO, C.C.V.I., Dir.
Provides transitional housing for homeless women and children on a temporary basis.
Interconnection: Education and Research Project
Tel: 210-653-7492; Fax: 210-653-7559

San Juan
Diocese of Brownsville

San Juan Hospice
300 Virgen de San Juan Blvd., P.O. Box 2359
San Juan, TX 78589
Tel: 956-782-0333; 800-816-6625; Fax: 956-782-0335

San Juan Nursing Home
300 Virgen de San Juan Blvd., P.O. Box 1238
San Juan, TX 78589
Tel: 956-787-1771; Fax: 956-787-8091
Legal Title: *San Juan Nursing Home, Inc., of the Diocese of Brownsville, a Texas Non-Profit Corporation*
Most Rev. RAYMUNDO J. PENA
Mrs. OLGA NAVARRO, Admin.
Board of Directors:
HERMILA ANZALDUA
Rev. LOUIS BRUM
Dr. BENJAMIN BUJANDA, M.D.
JANICE KLINE
RICARDO MARTINEZ
Rev. IVAN ROVIRA, Moderator of the Curia
CALIXTRO VILLARREAL, JR.
Mrs. OLGA NAVARRO, Staff
Bed Capacity 127

Stephenville
Diocese of Fort Worth

CASA Brendan & CASA II, Inc. Catholic Charities
1300 Hyman
Stephenville, TX 76401
Tel: 254-965-6964
E-mail: casab@our-town.net
Web Site: www.ccdofw.org
86 unit apartment complex for the elderly and handicapped.
Total in Residence 83
Total Staff 8

Waco
Diocese of Austin

CHRISTUS, The Regis Retirement Home & St. Elizabeth Nursing Home
400 Austin Ave., P.O. Box 1909
Waco, TX 76703
Tel: 254-756-5441; Fax: 254-754-0133
E-mail: doug35@aol.com
Web Site: members.aol.com/regisst
DOUGLAS F. WUENSCHEL, Admin.
Sisters of Charity of the Incarnate Word (Houston) 1
Residents 250
Total Assisted 445
Total Staff 228

DePaul Center
301 Londonderry Dr.
Waco, TX 76712
Tel: 254-776-5970; 1-800-777-5043
Psychiatric Hospital
Sr. MARY ANN RYAN, Dir. Pastoral Care
Dr. KEITH M. HANKINS, Ed.D., Admin.; Vice Pres.
Daughters of Charity of St. Vincent de Paul
Daughters of Charity 1
Bed Capacity 48
Patients assisted annually 1,900

UTAH

Salt Lake City
Diocese of Salt Lake City

Christus Halth Utah d.b.a. Christus St. Joseph Villa
451 Bishop Federal Ave.
Salt Lake City, UT 84115
Tel: 801-487-7557; Fax: 801-487-1112
Web Site: www.stjosephvilla.com
GALEN EWER, Pres. & Admin.

CHRISTUS St. Joseph Villa
451 Bishop Federal Ln.
Salt Lake City, UT 84115-2295
Tel: 801-487-7557; Fax: 801-487-1112
Web Site: www.stjosephvilla.com
Operated by CHRISTUS Health.
GALEN K. EWER, Pres. & CEO
Residents 300

Total in Residence 287
Total Assisted 750
Total Staff 280

VERMONT

Burlington
Diocese of Burlington

St. Joseph's Home
243 N. Prospect St.
Burlington, VT 05401
Tel: 802-864-0264; Fax: 802-864-5640
Operated by Vermont Catholic Charities.
Mrs. MARY M. MCNAMARA, Dir.
ESTHER MACPHERSON, Admin.
Rev. Msgr. EDWARD J. GELINEAU
Revs.:
EDWARD J. HART
THOMAS J. BEARY
Guests 34

Derby Line
Diocese of Burlington

Michaud Memorial Manor
Derby Line, VT 05830
Tel: 802-873-3152; Fax: 802-873-9206
E-mail: manor@together.net
Web Site: www.vermontcatholic.org
Conducted by Vermont Catholic Charities.
Mrs. MARY M. MCNAMARA, Dir.
RACHEL DUCHARME, Admin.
Guests 34

Rutland
Diocese of Burlington

Loretto Home for Aged
Rutland, VT 05701
Tel: 802-773-8840; Fax: 802-773-9638
E-mail: lhometc@sover.net
Conducted by Vermont Catholic Charities.
Mrs. MARY M. MCNAMARA, Dir.
Mrs. TERRY DION CAVACAS, Admin.
Rev. RAYMOND E. WALSH, Res. Chap.
Guests 57

St. Joseph Residence / Kervick Home
131 Convent Ave.
Rutland, VT 05701
Tel: 802-775-5133
Sr. MIRIAM FRANCIS PREDOM, S.S.J., Pres.
Sr. MARY POLWORTH, S.S.J., Vice. Pres.
Conducted by Covenant Health Systems, Inc.
Guests 47

VIRGINIA

Charlottesville
Diocese of Richmond

Our Lady of Peace
751 Hillsdale Dr.
Charlottesville, VA 22901
Tel: 804-973-1155; Fax: 804-973-3397
Web Site: our-lady-of-peace
DAVID L. RAWLINGS, Admin.
Nursing Bed Capacity 30
Independent Units 32
Assisted Units 92

Hampton
Diocese of Richmond

Seton Manor
215 Marcella Rd.
Hampton, VA 23666
Tel: 757-827-6512
Ms. REAGAN WEBER, Mgr.
Residents 112

Lynchburg
Diocese of Richmond

McGurk House Apartments
2425 Tate Springs Rd.
Lynchburg, VA 24501
Tel: 804-846-2425; Fax: 804-847-5046
E-mail: mcgurkhouse@worldnet.att.net
Independent Living for adults 62 yrs. or older, or mobility impaired.
HANNAH HERWARD, Dir.
Apartments 89

Newport News
Diocese of Richmond

St. Francis Nursing Center
4 Ridgewood Pkwy.
Newport News, VA 23602
LORRAINE MEADOWS, Admin., Tel: 757-886-6500
Bed Capacity 115
Total Assisted 1,339

Norfolk
Diocese of Richmond

Madonna Home
814 W. 37th St.
Norfolk, VA 23508
Tel: 757-623-6662; Fax: 757-623-4966
CHARLENE DAVIS, Dir.
Total Staff 7
Residents 16

St. Mary's Home for Disabled Children
317 Chapel St.
Norfolk, VA 23504
Tel: 757-622-2208
WILLIAM M. JOLLY, Admin.
Long term care for multiple handicapped children birth to eleven years old.
Daughters of Wisdom 2
Beds 88

Richmond
Diocese of Richmond

Marywood Apartments
1261 Marywood Ln.
Richmond, VA 23229
Tel: 804-740-5567; Fax: 804-740-9016
E-mail: marywood@MSN.com
PATRICIA SCOTT, Res. Mgr.
Residents 126

Our Lady of Hope Health Center, Inc.
13700 N. Gayton Rd.
Richmond, VA 23233
Tel: 804-360-1960
MATTHEW FARMER, Admin.
Residents 127

St. Francis Home, Inc.
2511 Wise St.
Richmond, VA 23225-3952
Tel: 804-231-1043; Fax: 804-231-1065
Mr. DAVID CRAN, Dir.
Total Staff 34
Bed Capacity 63

St. Joseph's Home for the Aged
1503 Michael Rd.
Richmond, VA 23229
Tel: 804-288-6245; Fax: 804-288-8906
Sr. REGINA MARIE LOFTUS, L.S.P., Supr.
Rev. THOMAS W. STUMPF, O.S.B., Chap.
Little Sisters of the Poor 12
Guests 72
Attended by Benedictine Fathers.

St. Joseph's Villa
8000 Brook Rd.
Richmond, VA 23227-1338
Tel: 804-553-3200; Fax: 804-553-3259
RAMON E. PARDUE, CEO
Children in Res. 15
Children in Day Care 200
Children in Extended Day Services 15
Children in Special Education 50
Children in Alternative Education 30
Children in Transitional Housing 80

St. Joseph's Villa Housing Corp.
8000 Brook Rd.
Richmond, VA 23227-1399
Tel: 804-553-3283; Fax: 804-553-3259
Mr. RAMON E. PARDUE, Exec Dir.
Apartments for Physically Challenged Adults.
Apartments 60
St. Joseph's Villa Housing Corp., II

St. Mary Wood's
1257 Marywood Ln.
Richmond, VA 23229
Tel: 804-741-8624; Fax: 804-740-7912
E-mail: stmw@mindspring.com
RANDY SCOTT, Admin.
Units 118
Independent Units 54
Total Staff 56
Total Assisted 64

Roanoke
Diocese of Richmond

De Paul Family Services, Inc.
5650 Hollins Rd.
Roanoke, VA 24019
Tel: 540-265-8923; Fax: 540-265-7663
Treatment Foster Care.
HERB BESKAR, Exec. Dir.
Total Assisted 450

Our Lady of the Valley Retirement Community
650 N. Jefferson St.
Roanoke, VA 24016
Tel: 540-345-5111; Fax: 540-985-6561
Web Site: ourladyofthevalley.com
Ms. MICHELE CRIGGER, Admissions Coord.
Assisted Living Units 86
Beds 30

Suffolk
Diocese of Richmond

Bon Secours-Maryview Nursing Care
4775 Bridge Rd.
Suffolk, VA 23435
Tel: 757-686-0488
DIANA L. JARRETT, Admin.
Bed Capacity 120
Martha W. Davis Cancer Center
Maryview Employee Assistance Program
Maryview MedCare Centers (Urgent Care)
Maryview Wellspring Home Health Agency
Maryview Hospice Program

Virginia Beach
Diocese of Richmond

Marian Manor
5345 Marian Ln.
Virginia Beach, VA 23462
Tel: 757-456-5018; Fax: 757-497-7561
LORYN DUNCAN-MARCIL, Admin.
Units 117

Our Lady of Perpetual Help Health Center, Inc.
4560 Princess Anne Rd.
Virginia Beach, VA 23462-7905

Russell House
900 First Colonial Rd.
Virginia Beach, VA 23454
Tel: 757-481-0770; Fax: 757-496-0859
E-mail: russellhouse@erols.com
ELEANOR OLSEN, Admin.
Total Staff 6
Units 119
Residents 126

WASHINGTON

Bellevue
Archdiocese of Seattle

Champion House
1800 145th Pl. S.E.
Bellevue, WA 98007-6209
Tel: 425-644-4477; Fax: 425-746-0438
E-mail: championhse@aol.com
Total Staff 13
Total Assisted 8

Elbert House
16000 N.E. 8th St.
Bellevue, WA 98008
Tel: 206-747-5111

Halcyon
1200 134th Ave. N.E.
Bellevue, WA 98005
Tel: 206-643-7806; Fax: 206-746-0438

Bothell
Archdiocese of Seattle

Franciscan Health System, Care Center at Bothell
10909 N.E. 185th St.
Bothell, WA 98011
Tel: 425-486-7174; 483-9905; Fax: 425-486-4962
CHI-Catholic Health Initiatives.
KEN BLOOMSTINE, Admin.
Total Staff 130
Beds 110

Chehalis
Archdiocese of Seattle

Providence Place
350 S.E. Washington Ave.
Chehalis, WA 98532
Tel: 360-740-8389; Fax: 360-740-6504
Sponsored by The Sisters of Providence.
Residents 60

Chewelah
Diocese of Spokane

DominiCare
303 E. King St., P.O. Box 1070
Chewelah, WA 99109
Sr. SHARON STANGLER, O.P., CEO
A home care/chore service in Stevens County.

Clarkston
Diocese of Spokane

Austen Manor
1222 Chestnut St.
Clarkston, WA 99403
CHARLES GRASSESCHI, Mgr.
30 apartments for senior citizens and mobility handicapped.

Lewis and Clark District Council of St. Vincent de Paul
Office
604 Second St.
Clarkston, WA 99403
Tel: 509-758-7061; Fax: 509-758-9545
Stores:
609 Third St.
Clarkston, WA 99403
3138 5th St.
Lewiston, ID 83501

Colville
Diocese of Spokane

The Rhodena, A Washington Non-profit Organization
Mailing Address:
P.O. Box 1453
Spokane, WA 99210-1453
A six unit affordable housing complex for families living in Colville, WA.

Dayton
Diocese of Spokane

St. Vincent de Paul Store
257 E. Main St.
Dayton, WA 99328
Tel: 509-382-4146
Mailing Address:
112 S. First St.
Dayton, WA 99328-1307

Everett
Archdiocese of Seattle

Providence Home Care and Hospice of Snohomish County
2731 Wetmore Ave., #520
Everett, WA 98201
Tel: 425-261-4800
Staff 120
Served 2,714

Issaquah
Archdiocese of Seattle

Providence Marianwood
3725 Providence Point Dr., S.E.
Issaquah, WA 98029
Tel: 425-391-2800; Fax: 425-391-5440
E-mail: leedaniels@providence.org
Web Site: www.providencemarianwood.org
Sisters of Providence Health System
Ms. ANN E. HUGHES, Admin.
MARY GOULD, Pastoral Care Svcs.
Total Staff 275
Bed Capacity 120

Olympia
Archdiocese of Seattle

Providence Mother Joseph Care Center
3333 Ensign Rd., N.E.
Olympia, WA 98506
Tel: 360-493-4900; Fax: 360-493-4948
E-mail: wildenhausb@psph.providence.org
Mr. ROBERT WILDENHAUS, Admin.
BEVERLY JENDEN, Pastoral Care
Total Staff 265
Patients assisted annually 750

Providence Sound Home Care and Hospice
3706 Griffin Ln., S.E.
Olympia, WA 98501
Tel: 800-869-7062; 360-459-8311
Staff 205
Patients assisted annually 4,935

Pasco
Diocese of Spokane

St. Vincent de Paul Store
1120 W. Sylvester
Pasco, WA 99301
Tel: 509-547-2341; Fax: 509-547-7804

Pullman
Diocese of Spokane

Pioneer Square
S.E. 220 Kamiaken
Pullman, WA 99163
Capacity 45

Redmond
Archdiocese of Seattle

Emma McRedmond Manor
7960 169th N.E.
Redmond, WA 98052
Tel: 206-869-2424

Seattle
Archdiocese of Seattle

Broadway House
2609 Broadway Ave. E.
Seattle, WA 98102
Tel: 206-860-4272

Chancery Place
910 Marion
Seattle, WA 98104
Tel: 206-343-9415

The Franciscan
15237 21st Ave. S.W.
Seattle, WA 98166
Tel: 206-431-8001

Providence Mount St. Vincent
4831 35th Ave. S.W.
Seattle, WA 98126
Tel: 206-937-3700; Fax: 206-938-8999
E-mail: cboyd@providence.org
Legal Title: *Sisters of Providence - Mother Joseph Province*
Ms. CHARLENE BOYD, Admin.
Rev. BRIAN J. MCGOVERN, Chap.
Sisters 3
Bed Capacity 174
Apartments 111

Providence Mount St. Vincent
4831 35th Ave. S.
Seattle, WA 98126
Tel: 206-937-3700
Rev. BRIAN J. MCGOVERN, Chap.
Total Staff 479
Total Assisted 580
Residents 174

Spruce Park Apartments
155 21st Ave.
Seattle, WA 98122
Tel: 206-322-0450

Vincent House
1423 First Ave.
Seattle, WA 98101
Tel: 206-682-9307; Fax: 206-682-0548
Sponsored by the Sisters of Providence.
Staff 3
Residents 60

The Westlake
2008 Westlake Ave.
Seattle, WA 98121
Tel: 206-340-0410; Fax: 206-682-8843
Total Staff 12
Total in Residence 65

Spanaway
Archdiocese of Seattle

Norm Fournier Court
112 S. 127th
Spanaway, WA 98444
Tel: 253-531-5087

Spokane
Diocese of Spokane

Cathedral Plaza Apartments
W. 1120 Sprague Ave.
Spokane, WA 99204
Capacity 150

Catholic Charities, Inc.
W. 1023 Riverside Ave., P.O. Box 1453
Spokane, WA 99210-1453
Tel: 509-358-4250; Fax: 509-358-4259
Mrs. DONNA HANSON, Bishop's Sec. for Social Ministries & Catholic Charities Diocesan Dir.

The Delaney
W. 242 Riverside Ave.
Spokane, WA 99201
Capacity 83

Fahy Garden Apartments
W. 1403 Dean Ave.
Spokane, WA 99201
Capacity 31

Fahy West Apartments
W. 1523 Dean Ave.
Spokane, WA 99201
Capacity 54

Guse Summit View
Housing for single parents with children.
Mailing Address:
P.O. Box 1453
Spokane, WA 99210-1453
820 N. Summit Blvd.
Spokane, WA 99210
E-mail: sumview@gntech.net

House of Charity
32 W. Pacific, P.O. Box 1453
Spokane, WA 99210-1453
Tel: 509-624-7821
ED MCCARRON, Dir.
Total Assisted 57,901 Hospitality house for homeless men.

Miryam's House
W. 1805 Ninth St.
Spokane, WA 99204
Total Staff 9
Total Assisted 81
A long-term residence for women in transition.

Morning Star Boys' Ranch, Inc.
P.O. Box 8087
Spokane, WA 99203
Tel: 509-448-1411
Rev. JOSEPH M. WEITENSTEINER, Dir.
Total Staff 25
Children in residence 23
Total Assisted 38

The O'Malley
E. 707 Mission Ave.
Spokane, WA 99202
Capacity 100

Rockwood Lane / Court
E. 221 Rockwood Blvd.
Spokane, WA 99202
Capacity 106
Residents 140

St. Anne's Children's Home
N. 707 Cedar St.
Spokane, WA 99201-1999
Tel: 509-325-7672
BONNIE DIEBLER, Acting Dir.
Therapeutic child care for abused/neglected children and assistance to their parents through parent education and counseling.

St. Joseph Care Center
(A Non-profit Corporation)
E. 17 Eighth Ave.
Spokane, WA 99202
Tel: 509-474-5678
Sisters of Providence
ALICE ANDERSON, Admin.
Beds 165

St. Joseph's Counseling Center
N. 1016 Superior St.
Spokane, WA 99202
Tel: 509-483-6495
E-mail: sjfc@icehouse.net
Sr. LYNN LAVIN, O.S.F., Dir., St. Joseph Family Center
Sisters of St. Francis of Philadelphia 6

St. Margaret's Shelter
P.O. Box 1453
Spokane, WA 99210
Tel: 509-624-9288; Fax: 509-624-1461
NADINE VAN HORN, Dir.
Total Staff 7
Total Assisted 54
Emergency shelter for single women & children.

St. Vincent de Paul Social Service Office
E. 2901 Trent Ave.
Spokane, WA 99202
Tel: 509-534-2824 (Social Svc.); 535-2491 (Main Store & Office)
GEORGE VASIL, Pres.
JURGEN WIGEN, Operations Mgr.
Total Staff 45
Total Assisted
55,428
Legal Title: *St. Vincent de Paul Social Service Office and Main Store St. Business Office*

St. Vincent de Paul Society
Spokane District Council
E. 2901 Trent Ave.
Spokane, WA 99202
Tel: 509-534-2824
GEORGE VASIL, Pres.

Senior Citizen Housing
W. 242 Riverside Ave.
Spokane, WA 99201
Tel: 509-624-6060
Mr. RICHARD CUNNINGHAM, Dir.

Transitional Living Center
3128 N. Hemlock
Spokane, WA 92204
E-mail: tlc@cet.com
Mailing Address:
3120 W. Fort George Wright Dr.
Spokane, WA 99224
Tel: 509-328-6702
Housing for homeless women & children.

Women's Drop In Center
218 S. Howard
Spokane, WA 92204-1419
Mailing Address:
3120 W. Fort George Wright Dr.
Spokane, WA 99224
Tel: 509-328-6702
A safe place for women at risk.

Tacoma
Archdiocese of Seattle

Franciscan Health System, Care Center at Tacoma
6220 S. Alaska
Tacoma, WA 98408
Tel: 253-473-2273; Fax: 253-475-2921
CHI-Catholic Health Initiatives.
LINDA LARSON, Admin.
Total Staff 150
Licensed skilled beds 123

Tumwater
Archdiocese of Seattle

Tumwater Apartments
5701 6th Ave., S.W.
Tumwater, WA 98501
Tel: 360-352-4321; Fax: 360-352-3557
E-mail: tumwater@bilbo.w.linknet

Walla Walla
Diocese of Spokane

Catholic Children and Family Service
5 W. Alder St., Ste. 333
Walla Walla, WA 99362
Tel: 509-525-0572; Fax: 509-525-0576
RICHARD A. GARCIA, M.S.W., Dir.

Garden Court Apartments
Sixth & Alder Sts.
Walla Walla, WA 99362
Capacity 20

Mike Foye Apartments
Mailing Address:
P.O. Box 1453
Spokane, WA 99210
Sixth & Alder Sts.
Walla Walla, WA 99362
Capacity 27

St. Vincent de Paul Store
308 W. Main St.
Walla Walla, WA 99362
Tel: 509-525-3903 (Store); 529-6778 (Office)
TERRY ADAMS, Store Mgr.
ALBERT TORRETTA, Society Pres.

WEST VIRGINIA

Clarksburg
Diocese of Wheeling-Charleston

Madonna Day Care Center
444 E. Pike St.
Clarksburg, WV 26031
Tel: 304-622-4453
Total Staff 6

Wheeling
Diocese of Wheeling-Charleston

Good Shepherd Nursing Home
159 Edgington Ln.
Wheeling, WV 26003
Tel: 304-242-1093; Fax: 304-242-1121
Mr. DONALD R. KIRSCH, Admin.
Rev. JOHN WEIGLEIN, S.M., Chap.
Sisters 2
Bed Capacity 192
Total Staff 220

Holy Family Child Care Center, Inc.
161 Edgington Ln.
Wheeling, WV 26003
Tel: 304-242-5222
E-mail: drp6713@aol.com
DEBRA PONSETTI, Exec. Dir.
Total Assisted 107
Total Staff 28

St. John's Home for Children
141 Key Ave.
Wheeling, WV 26003-7412
Tel: 304-242-5633; Fax: 304-243-4911
E-mail: stjohns@hgo.net
TERENCE A. MCCORMICK, Exec. Dir.
Children 8
Total Assisted 20

Welty Home for the Aged, Inc.
21 Washington Ave.
Wheeling, WV 26003-6261
Tel: 304-242-5233; Fax: 304-242-1312
Sr. SHEILA ROONEY, O.L.C., Admin.
Sisters 1
Residents 48
Welty Trust, Inc.
P.O. Box 230
Wheeling, WV 26003
Trustees:
Most Rev. BERNARD W. SCHMITT, Pres.
Very Rev. JOHN R. GALLAGHER, V.G., Vice Pres. & Sec.
RICHARD G. HERNDON, ESQ., Treas.
Welty Retirement Apartments
1276 National Rd.
Wheeling, WV 26003
Tel: 304-242-5820

WISCONSIN

Appleton
Diocese of Green Bay

**Franciscan Care and Rehabilitation Center, Inc.*
2915 N. Meade St.
Appleton, WI 54911-1598
Tel: 920-831-8700; Fax: 920-731-3206
E-mail: nbassett@affinityhealth.org
TODD GREENEWAY, Admin.
Residents 200
Total Staff 260

Arcadia
Diocese of La Crosse

Franciscan Skemp Healthcare, Mayo Health System, Arcadia Campus Nursing Home
464 S. St. Joseph Ave.
Arcadia, WI 54612
Tel: 608-323-3341; Fax: 608-323-3694
Franciscan Sisters of Perpetual Adoration and Mayo Foundation.
DARLENE GOEHNER, Admin.
Chaplains:
Rev. ROBERT F. POLCYN, O.F.M. Cap.
Sr. ARLENE MELDER, F.S.P.A.
Bed Capacity 75
Patients assisted annually 125
Total Staff 75

Baraboo
Diocese of Madison

St. Clare Meadows Care Center
1414 Jefferson St.
Baraboo, WI 53913
Tel: 608-356-5764; Fax: 608-356-5441
Member of the SSM Health Care.

Eau Claire
Diocese of La Crosse

St. Francis Apartment
851 University Dr.
Eau Claire, WI 54701
Tel: 715-834-1388
DAVID B. FISH, Chm.
Legal Title: *Hospital Sisters Health Care-West, Inc.*
Units 60
Total in Residence 65

Fond du Lac
Archdiocese of Milwaukee

Nazareth Center-Nazareth Court
375 Gillett St.
Fond du Lac, WI 54935
Tel: 920-923-7993; Fax: 920-907-6800
E-mail: lccsa@vbe.com
Retirement Home Sponsored by the Congregation of Sisters of St. Agnes.
Sr. IRENE KOHNE, C.S.A., Admin.
Sisters 78

St. Francis Home for Aged
33 Everett St.
Fond du Lac, WI 54935
Tel: 920-923-7980; Fax: 920-923-7995
E-mail: stfran@vbe.com
Sisters of St. Agnes, C.S.A.
Sr. M. IRENE KOHNE, C.S.A., Admin.
Rev. JOACHIM STRUPP, O.F.M.Cap., Chap.
Sisters 2
Residents 106
St. Clare Terrace
Tel: 920-923-7996; Fax: 920-923-7995
Residents 36
Independent Elderly Apartments 30
Total Staff 3
St. Francis Terrace
Tel: 920-923-7980; Fax: 920-923-7995
Residents 14
Assisted Living Units 13
Total Staff 5

Green Bay
Diocese of Green Bay

McClosky Program, Inc.
2560 Shawano Ave., P.O. Box 10357
Green Bay, WI 54313
Tel: 920-434-8208; Fax: 920-662-0047
Sr. BARBARA JEAN ARNSMEYER, O.L.C., Dir.
A Community based residential facility for women 18 years old and over who are pregnant or in a crisis situation and in need of transitional supervision and guidance. Needs addressed are personal and family problems. Also, shelter offered during crisis or unemployment.
Total Staff 3
Total Assisted 10

The McCormick Memorial Home for the Aged
212 Iroquois Ave.
Green Bay, WI 54301-1918
Tel: 920-437-0883; Fax: 920-437-2696
JAMES GENRICH, Admin.
Rev. THADDEUS J. KOSZAREK, Chap.
Sisters of St. Francis of the Holy Cross 1
Lay Helpers 28
Residents 60

Our Lady of Charity Center, Inc.
2560 Shawano Ave., P.O. Box 10357
Green Bay, WI 54313
Tel: 920-434-8208; Fax: 920-662-0047
Sr. PATRICK DOLAN, O.L.C., Admin.
Total Staff 4
Total Assisted 20

Greenfield
Archdiocese of Milwaukee

Clement Manor Health Center
3939 S. 92nd St.
Greenfield, WI 53228
Tel: 414-321-1800; Fax: 414-546-7333
Sponsored by School Sisters of St. Francis
Corporate Title: Clement Manor, Inc.
RICHARD RAU, Pres. & CEO
Mr. DENNIS FERGER, Admin.
Rev. DANIEL T. MURPHY, Chap.
Sisters 3
Residents 162
Adult Day Care 35
Child Day Care 30

Clement Manor Retirement Community
9339 W. Howard
Greenfield, WI 53228
Tel: 414-546-7374; Fax: 414-546-7357
Corporate Title: Clement Manor, Inc. Sponsored by the School Sisters of St. Francis
Mr. GREG SZPAK
DANIEL T. MURPHY, Chap.
Sisters 3
Residents 235
Apartments 201

Hillsboro
Diocese of La Crosse

St. Joseph's Nursing Home
P.O. Box 527
Hillsboro, WI 54634
(See Hospital Listing.)

Janesville
Diocese of Madison

St. Elizabeth Home
502 St. Lawrence Ave.
Janesville, WI 53545
Tel: 608-752-6709; Fax: 608-752-1724
Rev. RAY ASHENBRENNER, O.P.
Aged Residents 43

Kaukauna
Diocese of Green Bay

St. Paul Elder Services, Inc.
316 E. Fourteenth St.
Kaukauna, WI 54130
Tel: 920-766-6020; Fax: 920-766-7945
Web Site: stpaulelders.org
JAMES J. FETT, Admin.
d/b/a:
St. Paul Home
1211 Oakridge Ave.
Kaukauna, WI 54130
Tel: 920-766-6020; Fax: 920-766-7945
Residents 129
St. Paul Villa
312 E. Fourteenth St.
Kaukauna, WI 54130
Tel: 920-766-6020; Fax: 920-766-7945
Residents 34
St. Paul Manor
509 W. Wisconsin Ave.
Kaukauna, WI 54130
Tel: 920-766-6027; Fax: 920-766-6035
Residents 27

Kenosha
Archdiocese of Milwaukee

St. Joseph's Adult Day Care Center, Inc.
9244 29th Ave.
Kenosha, WI 53144
Tel: 414-694-6000; Fax: 414-694-0148
E-mail: sjoseph@net
Web Site: www.stjoseph.com
Ms. JOYCE MITCHELL, Dir.
Sponsored by: Carmelite Sisters of the Divine Heart of Jesus
Total Assisted 150
Total Staff 20

St. Joseph's Home for the Aged
9244 29th Ave.
Kenosha, WI 53143
Tel: 262-694-0080; Fax: 262-694-7325
E-mail: sjoseph@acronet.net
Web Site: www.sjosephs.com
Corporate Title: Carmelite Sisters of the Divine Heart of Jesus.
Sr. MARY EMMANUEL APANITES, D.C.J., Admin.
Sr. M. JACINTA CUSUMANO, D.C.J., Supr.
Rev. BRONISLAW SLODOWSKI
Sisters 5
Residents 93
Adult Day Care 45
Total Staff 150
St. Joseph's Villa, Independent living units
Apartments 44

La Crosse
Diocese of La Crosse

Bethany-St. Joseph Care Center
2501 Shelby Rd.
La Crosse, WI 54601
Tel: 608-788-5700
THOMAS RAND, Admin.
Rev. THOMAS J. SMITH, Chap., Tel: 608-788-4555
Bed Capacity 226
Patients assisted annually 247

Elder Care of North La Crosse, Inc. (Village on St. James)
800 St. James St.
La Crosse, WI 54603
Tel: 608-791-9784
RICHARD BERENDES, Admin. Extended Care
Units 24

Franciscan Elder Care, Inc.
800 West Avenue S.
La Crosse, WI 54601-4796
Tel: 608-791-9505; Fax: 608-782-2779
JOSEPH KRUSE, Vice Pres.
RICHARD BERENDES, Admin. Extended Care
Total Staff 17
Subsidized Units 132
Village on Cass
225 S. 24th St.
La Crosse, WI,
Tel: 608-791-9487; Fax: 608-782-2779
Village on 9th
621 S. 9th St.
La Crosse, WI,
Tel: 608-791-9505; Fax: 608-782-2779
Village on St. James
800 St. James St.
La Crosse, WI,
Tel: 608-791-9505; Fax: 608-782-2779
Village Apartments
Tel: 608-791-9505; Fax: 608-782-2779
Village Apartments
Tel: 608-791-9505; Fax: 608-782-2779
Village Apartments
Tel: 608-791-9505; Fax: 608-782-2779

Franciscan Skemp Healthcare, Mayo Health System, La Crosse Campus Nursing Home
620 S. 11th St.
La Crosse, WI 54601
Tel: 608-791-9787; Fax: 608-791-9716
ROBERTA MESSER, Admin.
Bed Capacity 95
Patients assisted annually 315

St. Joseph's Nursing Home
2902 East Ave. S.
La Crosse, WI 54601
Tel: 608-788-9870
Operated by Catholic Residential Services, Inc., Diocese of La Crosse.
JAMES S. BIALECKI, Admin.
Rev. THOMAS J. SMITH, Chap., Tel: 608-788-4555
Patients assisted annually 80
Units 80

Madison
Diocese of Madison

St. Marys Care Center
1347 Fish Hatchery Rd.
Madison, WI 53715
Tel: 608-257-0781; Fax: 608-257-9420
Member of the SSM Health Care.
WILLIAM BENDER, Admin.

Manitowoc
Diocese of Green Bay

Felician Village Inc.
1700 S. 18th St.
Manitowoc, WI 54220
Tel: 920-683-8811; Fax: 920-683-9292
Sr. MARY CLAUDE SZYPERSKI, C.S.S.F., Dir.
Total Staff 25
Apartments 134
Villagers 180

St. Mary's Home for the Aged
2005 Division St.
Manitowoc, WI 54220-5699
Tel: 920-684-7171; Fax: 920-684-0240
E-mail: stmarys@lakefield.net
Sr. NOEL MARIE GABRIEL, C.S.S.F., Admin.
Rev. THOMAS WOJCIECHOWSKI, O.F.M., Chap.
Sisters 23
Aged Residents 266

Milwaukee
Archdiocese of Milwaukee

Alexian Village of Milwaukee, Inc.
9301 N. 76th St.
Milwaukee, WI 53223
Tel: 414-355-9300; Fax: 414-357-5106
E-mail: marketing@alexianvillage.org
Web Site: www.alexianvillage.org
Congregation of Alexian Brothers, Immaculate Conception Province
Mr. GARY MOHN, CEO
Rev. JOE JAGODENSKY, S.D.S., Chap.
Continuing Care Retirement Community
Units 310
Residents 550
Brothers 6
Total Staff 325

Catholic Charities Adult Day Services and Resource Center
1919 N. 60th St.
Milwaukee, WI 53208
Tel: 414-771-5026, Ext. 162; Fax: 414-771-9115
E-mail: catholiccharities@ccmke.org
Web Site: www.ccmke.org
CATHY YOUNG, Dir.
Catholic Charities Adult Day Services
New Hope Center, 4033 W. Good Hope Rd.
Milwaukee, WI 53209
Tel: 414-771-5026, Ext. 162; Fax: 414-352-3042
Sponsored by Catholic Charities of the Archdiocese of Milwaukee
Catholic Charities Adult Day Services National Regency
13700 W. National Ave.
New Berlin, WI 53151
Tel: 262-782-0740

Daystar, Inc.
P.O. Box 2130
Milwaukee, WI 53201-2130
Tel: 414-385-0334; Fax: 414-385-0336
Transitional living program for formerly battered women without children, for up to two years.
Residents 10
Total Staff 5
Total Assisted 18

Hope Nursing Home, Inc.
8560 N. 76th Pl.
Milwaukee, WI 53223
Tel: 414-354-9233; Fax: 414-355-6463

**Marian Franciscan Center, Inc.*
9632 W. Appleton Ave.
Milwaukee, WI 53225
Tel: 414-461-8850; Fax: 414-461-9570
JAMES D. GRESHAM, Pres.
Franciscan Sisters, Daughters of the Sacred Hearts of Jesus and Mary, Wheaton, IL
Residents 310
Total Staff 387

MCC Liquidation Corp.
9632 W. Appleton Ave.
Milwaukee, WI 53225
Tel: 414-461-8850; Fax: 414-461-9570
Corporate Title: Marian Catholic Center Liquidation Corp.
Sponsored by Franciscan Sisters, Daughters of the Sacred Hearts of Jesus and Mary, Wheaton, IL.
JAMES GRESHAM, Reg. Vice Pres.

Milwaukee Catholic Home
2462 N. Prospect Ave.
Milwaukee, WI 53211-4462
Tel: 414-224-9700; Fax: 414-224-1666
E-mail: info@milwaukeecatholichome.org
Web Site: milwaukeecatholichome.org
Mr. PAUL J. CONNOLLY, N.H.A., Exec. Dir.
Rev. CHARLES R. KEEFE, Dir. Pastoral Care
Corporate Title: Milwaukee Catholic Home, Inc.
Retirement Home Residents 157
Retirement Home Total Staff 47
Nursing Home Residents 120
Nursing Home Total Staff 131
Day Care (Adult) 12
Assisted Living 29

Mount Carmel Health and Rehabilitation Center (Mount Carmel, LLC)
5700 W. Layton Ave.
Milwaukee, WI 53220
Tel: 414-281-7200; Fax: 414-281-0744
E-mail: lathomson@bhshealth.org
LISA A. THOMSON, N.H.A., Admin. & CEO

Rosalie Manor Community & Family Services, Inc.
4803 W. Burleigh St.
Milwaukee, WI 53210
Tel: 414-449-2868; Fax: 414-449-2870
E-mail: rosaliemanor@aeronet
ROSEMARIE FISHER, Dir.
Community Programs for Single and First-Time Parents and an abstinence-based pregnancy prevention program for youth.
Franciscan Sisters Daughters of the Sacred Hearts of Jesus & Mary of Wheaton, IL.
Total Assisted 2,957 families per year
Total Staff 64

Sacred Heart Rehabilitation Institute, Inc.
2350 N. Lake Dr.
Milwaukee, WI 53211
Tel: 414-298-6700; Fax: 414-298-6712
Ascension Health System
NANCY KUELZ, Adm.
Sr. MARGARET ANN ARNOLD, Chap.
Sisters 1
Bed Capacity 67
Patients assisted annually 19,269
Total Staff 215
Satellite Locations:
St. Mary's Hospital of Milwaukee
Milwaukee, WI 53211
Sacred Heart Rehabilitation Institute
Memorial Hosp. at Oconomowoc, 791 E. Summit Ave.
Oconomowoc, WI 53066
Tel: 414-569-0640; Fax: 414-569-0653

St. Ann Center for Intergenerational Care, Inc.
2801 E. Morgan Ave.
Milwaukee, WI 53207
Tel: 414-977-5000; Fax: 414-977-5050
Sr. EDNA LONERGAN, O.S.F., Dir.
Sisters of St. Francis of Assisi, St. Francis, WI
Total Assisted 500
Total Staff 100

St. Ann Rest Home
2020 S. Muskego Ave.
Milwaukee, WI 53204-3522
Tel: 414-383-2642; Fax: 414-383-2642
E-mail: stann2@execpc.com
Conducted by the Dominican Sisters (Congregation of the Immaculate Conception)
Rev. CANTIUS J. KOBAK, O.F.M., Pastoral Care Min.
Sr. M. COLUMBA, O.P., Admin.
Sisters 8
Residents 50
Total Staff 47

St. Anne's Home for the Elderly
3800 N. 92nd St.
Milwaukee, WI 53222
Tel: 414-463-7570; Fax: 414-463-2311
E-mail: mah@execpc.com
Web Site: www.wahsa.org/st.anne/index.html
Sisters of the Divine Savior
Ms. LYNN VOGT, Admin.
Rev. NEIL DURHAM, S.D.S., Chap.
Assisted Living Apartments 25
Residents 106
Total Staff 170

St. Charles Youth and Family Services, Inc.
151 S. 84th St., P.O. Box 14005
Milwaukee, WI 53214
Tel: 414-476-3710; Fax: 414-778-5985
E-mail: mstaz@execpc.com
Web Site: www.st-charle.org
Ms. CATHY CONNOLLY, Pres.
Residents 78
Girls in Knoernschild Girl's Development Center 12
Total Assisted 950
Total Staff 320

St. Joan Antida Home, Inc.
8560 N. 76th Pl.
Milwaukee, WI 53223
Tel: 414-354-9233; Fax: 414-355-6463

St. Mary's Nursing Home
3515 W. Hadley St.
Milwaukee, WI 53210
Tel: 414-873-9250; Fax: 414-873-6876
Corporate Title: St. Mary's Nursing Home of Milwaukee, Inc.
Sisters of the Divine Savior
Mr. MICHAEL BERRY, Admin.
Deacon DENNIS FERENCE, Chap.
In res.,
Rev. DANIEL CARROLL, S.D.S.
Bros.:
BOOKER ASHE, O.F.M.Cap.
BONIFACE PAPKE, S.D.S.
Residents 97
Total Staff 163

The Terrace at St. Francis, Inc.
3200 S. 20th St.
Milwaukee, WI 53215
Tel: 414-389-3200; Fax: 414-389-3300
Sponsored by the Congregation of the Sisters of St. Felix of Cantalice of the United States of America, Inc., Chicago Province (Felician Sisters).
Skilled Nursing Facility for Transitional & Extended Subacute Care.
Sr. M. RAMONA DOMBROWSKI, C.S.S.F., Pres.
Beds 81
Total Assisted 762
Total Staff 139

Villa St. Francis, Inc.
1910 W. Ohio Ave.
Milwaukee, WI 53215
Tel: 414-649-2888; Fax: 414-649-2880
Sr. MARY RAMONA DOMBROWSKI, C.S.S.F., Pres.
Sponsored by the Congregation of the Sisters of St. Felix of Cantalice of the United States of America, Inc. Chicago Province (Felician Sisters)
Independent & Assisted Living Facility
Resident Apartments 142
Total Assisted 63
Total Staff 57

Mount Calvary
Archdiocese of Milwaukee

Cristo Rey Ranch, Inc.
N8102 Calvary St.
Mount Calvary, WI 53057
Tel: 920-753-2026; 753-3211; Fax: 920-753-3100
E-mail: villasisters@netscape.net
Sister Servants of Christ the King
Provides weekend respite services to families caring for emotionally/behaviorially challenged children and adolescents. Program emphasis on pet therapy. Some day and evening programs thru County Social Services Department.
Total Assisted 50
Total Staff 5

Villa Loretto Nursing Home
N8114 Calvary St.
Mount Calvary, WI 53057
Tel: 920-753-3211; Fax: 920-753-3100
E-mail: villasisters@netscape.net
Sr. MARY ROSE, Supr.
Sisters 6
Residents 52
Total Assisted 78
Total Staff 82
Corporate Title: Sister Servants of Christ the King, Inc. dba Villa Loretto.

Neenah
Diocese of Green Bay

Assisi Homes of Neenah, Inc.
210 Byrd Ave.
Neenah, WI 54956
Tel: 920-722-5100; Fax: 920-722-5171
(An independent living community for Seniors.)
Total Staff 4
Total in residence 38
Total Assisted 45

Villa Saint Clare, Inc.
130 Byrd Ave.
Neenah, WI 54946
Tel: 920-722-5100; Fax: 920-722-5171
SHERRI BEYER, Mgr.
Special care facility, affordable housing with supportive accommodations in an independent setting for seniors 55+.
Total in Residence 45
Total Assisted 50
Staff 12

New London
Diocese of Green Bay

St. Joseph Residence, Inc., New London
107 E. Beckert Rd.
New London, WI 54961
Tel: 920-982-5354; Fax: 920-982-5420
E-mail: sjradm@athenet.net
Mr. DANIEL W. ORR, CEO
Total in Residence 63
Staff 23
Nursing Care Staff 170

Niagara
Diocese of Green Bay

Maryhill Manor (SNF)
501 Madison Ave.
Niagara, WI 54151
Tel: 715-251-3178; Fax: 715-251-1200
Sponsored by School Sisters of St. Francis, Milwaukee.
JANA CLEMENT, Admin.
Nursing Care:
Residents 75
Staff 90

Onalaska
Diocese of La Crosse

Franciscan Skemp Healthcare, Mayo Health System, Onalaska Nursing Home
1600 Main St.
Onalaska, WI 54650
Tel: 608-783-4681
LARRY ALENS, Admin.
Beds 112
Patients assisted annually 260
Total Staff 160

Oshkosh
Diocese of Green Bay

The Convent Project, Inc.
471 High Ave.
Oshkosh, WI 54901
Tel: 920-233-1894
For victims of domestic abuse
BARBARA BAKER, Pres.
Total Assisted 46

Portage
Diocese of Madison

Divine Savior Nursing Home
715 W. Pleasant St.
Portage, WI 53901
Tel: 608-742-4131; Fax: 608-742-3463
(See Divine Savior Hospital, Portage.)
Aged Residents 124

Racine
Archdiocese of Milwaukee

Marian Housing Center, Inc
4105 Spring St.
Racine, WI 53405
Tel: 262-633-5807

St. Monica's Senior Citizens Home, Inc.
3920 N. Green Bay Rd.
Racine, WI 53404
Tel: 262-639-5050; Fax: 262-639-5673
Non-Profit Corp.
Sr. IRENE HANIKA, O.S.A., Supr. and Admin.
Rev. THADDEUS BRYL
Sisters of St. Rita 7
Residents 110
Total Staff 45

South Milwaukee
Archdiocese of Milwaukee

Franciscan Villa of South Milwaukee, Inc.
3601 S. Chicago Ave.
South Milwaukee, WI 53172
Tel: 414-764-4100; Fax: 414-764-0706
Web Site: www.franciscanvilla.org
ROGER L. DEMARK, Pres. & CEO
Catholic Health Initiatives
Residents 150
Alzheimer's Assisted Living 64
Adult Day Care 30
Child Day Care 36
Affiliate of Catholic Health Initiatives.

Sparta
Diocese of La Crosse

Elder Care of Sparta, Inc.
622 S. Court
Sparta, WI 54656
Tel: 608-791-9505
RICHARD BERENDES, Admin. Extended Care Units 24

Franciscan Skemp Healthcare, Mayo Health System, Sparta Campus Nursing Home
310 W. Main St., P.O. Box 529
Sparta, WI 54656-2142
Tel: 608-269-2132; Fax: 608-269-1017
SUSAN STEIVANG, Admin.
Bed Capacity 30
Patients assisted annually 60
Total Staff 27

St. Francis
Archdiocese of Milwaukee

Canticle Court, Inc.
3201 S. Lake Dr.
St. Francis, WI 53235
Tel: 414-744-9959; Fax: 414-744-7636
E-mail: jcpres@seii.com
An Apartment building sponsored by the Sisters of St. Francis of Assisi funded by HUD for low income elderly persons who can live independently
Units 48
Total in Residence 49
Total Staff 2

Juniper Court, Inc.
3209 S. Lake Dr.
St. Francis, WI 53235-3702
Tel: 414-744-5878; Fax: 414-744-7636
E-mail: jcpres@seii.com
Sr. ANNE MARY RISCHAR, O.S.F., Pres.
An apartment building with congregate meal site for persons of low to moderate income who can live independently.
Sponsored by the Sisters of St. Francis of Assisi, St. Francis, WI.
Total in Residence 55
Total Units 53
Total Staff 2

Stoughton
Diocese of Madison

Nazareth House
814 Jackson St.
Stoughton, WI 53589
Tel: 608-873-6448; Fax: 608-873-0829
Poor Sisters of Nazareth
Sr. MARGARET BRODY, P.S.N., Supr.
Sisters 5
Aged Residents 99

Superior
Diocese of Superior

St. Francis Home, Inc.
1416 Cumming Ave.
Superior, WI 54880
Tel: 715-394-5591; Fax: 715-394-6617
BRIAN SOLAND, Acting CEO

Two Rivers
Diocese of Green Bay

Sisters Treatment Group Home
3904 Martin Ln.
Two Rivers, WI 54241
Tel: 920-794-1524; Fax: 920-794-1524
Co-Directors:
Sr. IRMINA BULA, S.S.J.-T.O.S.F.
Sr. EDMUND ANTONIEWICZ, S.S.J.-T.O.S.F.
For physically and mentally handicapped children.
Children 5
Adults 4
Staff 5
Total Assisted 9

Wausau
Diocese of La Crosse

Marywood Convalescent Center
1821 N. 4th Ave.
Wausau, WI 54401
Tel: 715-675-9451; Fax: 715-675-9051
SCOTT W. RUSCH, Admin.
Operated by Catholic Residential Services, Inc.
Units 90
Patients assisted annually 131

Wauwatosa
Archdiocese of Milwaukee

St. Camillus Health Center, Inc.
10101 W. Wisconsin Ave.
Wauwatosa, WI 53226
Tel: 414-258-1814
Skilled Nursing Home
Order of the Servants of the Sick (Order of St. Camillus)
Rev. LOUIS LUSSIER, O.S.Cam., M.S.W., Pres.
RICK JOHNSON, Pres. & CEO
Chaplains:
Revs.:
CARLO NOTARO, O.S.Cam.
LOYOLA AMALRAJ
Bro. MARIO CRIVELLO, O.S.Cam.
Ms. SALLY REDMOND
In res.,
Revs.:
GEORGE A. KOLANDA
PETER T. AMRHEIN
VICTOR BARTELT
MARTIN JAUTZ
MARK LYONS
PETER MILLER
BERNARD PORTZ
JEROME ROHRER
JOSEPH SCALLION
THOMAS SWICOX
ALBIN SOWINSKI
Patients assisted annually 386
Total Staff 638

San Camillo, Inc.
10200 W. Blue Mound Rd.
Wauwatosa, WI 53226
Tel: 414-259-6300
Order of the Servants of the Sick (Order of St. Camillus)
Rev. LOUIS LUSSIER, O.S.Cam., Pres.
MARIE D'AMICO, Vice Pres. Housing
Rev. CARLO NOTARO, O.S.Cam., Chap.
Independent living facilities for older adults.
Residents 340
Total Assisted 106
Total Staff 638

WYOMING

Casper
Diocese of Cheyenne

St. Anthony Manor
211 E. Sixth St.
Casper, WY 82601
Tel: 307-237-0843; Fax: 307-237-3516
Rev. MICHAEL CARR
JUDY GRIFFIN, Admin.
Total Staff 6
Total in Residence 64

Cheyenne
Diocese of Cheyenne

Holy Trinity Manor
2516 E. 18th St.
Cheyenne, WY 82001
Tel: 307-778-8850; Fax: 307-778-8850
E-mail: htscl@cheyenneweb.com
Sr. RUTH ANN HEHN, S.C.L., Admin.
Total Staff 1
Total in Residence 32
Total Assisted 39

Torrington
Diocese of Cheyenne

St. Joseph's Children's Home
Box 1117
Torrington, WY 82240-1117
Tel: 307-532-4197; Fax: 307-532-8405
E-mail: stjch@prairieweb.com
ROBERT C. MAYOR, Exec. Dir.
Children 62
Total Staff 120
Total Assisted 181

An Alphabetical List of Diocesan and Religious Priests of the United States

REPORTED TO THE PUBLISHERS FOR THIS ISSUE
(Cardinals, Archbishops, Bishops, Archabbots and Abbots are listed in previous section)

ABBREVIATIONS

aa.a. Assumptionists.
b.g.s. Little Brothers of the Good Shepherd.
b.s.o. Basilian Salvatorian Fathers.
c.f.a. Alexian Brothers.
c.f.c. Congregation of Christian Brothers.
c.f.m.m. Brothers of the Poor of St. Francis.
c.f.p. Brothers of the Poor of St. Francis.
c.f.r. Franciscan Friars of the Renewal.
c.f.x. Brothers of St. Francis Xavier.
c.i.c.m. Missionhurst Congregation of the Immaculate Heart of Mary.
c.j. Josephite Fathers.
c.j.m. Congregation of Jesus and Mary, Eudist Fathers.
c.m. Congregation of the Mission, Vincentian Fathers.
c.m.c. Congregation of Mother Coredemptrix.
c.m.f. Claretian Missionaries, Missionary Sons of the Immaculate Heart of Mary.
c.m.i. Carmelites of Mary Immaculate.
c.m.m. Congregation of Mariannhill Missionaries, Mariannhill Fathers and Brothers.
c.m.vd. Mekhitarist Fathers.
c.o. Oratorians.
c.p. Congregation of the Passion, Passionist Fathers.
c.p.m. Congregation of the Fathers of Mercy.
c.pp.s. Society of the Precious Blood.
c.r. Congregation of the Resurrection, Resurrectionist Fathers.
c.r. Theatine Fathers.
c.r.i.c. Canons Regular of the Immaculate Conception.
c.r.l. Canons Regular of the Lateran.
c.r.m. Adorno Fathers.
c.r.s. Somascan Fathers, Order of St. Jerome Aemilian.
c.r.s.p. Clerics Regular of St. Paul, Barnabite Fathers.
c.s. Missionaries of St. Charles-Scalabrinians.
c.s.b. Basilian Fathers.
c.s.c. Priests and Brothers of the Congregation of Holy Cross.
c.s.j. Congregation of St. Joseph.
c.s.p. Paulist Fathers.
c.s.p.x. Brothers of Saint Pius X.
c.s.s. Stigmatine Fathers and Brothers, Congregation of the Sacred Stigmata.
c.s.sp. Holy Ghost Fathers, Congregation of the Holy Ghost.
c.ss.r. Redemptorist Fathers.
c.s.v. Clerics of St. Viator, Viatorian Fathers.
d.l.p. Diocesan Labor Priests.
er.cam. Camaldolese Hermits of the Congregation of Monte Corona.
f.c. Brothers of Charity.
f.d.p. Sons of Divine Providence.
f.f.i. Franciscan Friars of the Immaculate
f.f.s.c. Franciscan Brothers of the Holy Cross.
f.i.c. Brothers of Christian Instruction.
f.j. Congregation of St. John.
f.m.j. The Monastic Fraternity of Jerusalem.
f.m.m. Brothers of Mercy.
f.m.s. Marist Brothers.
f.m.s.i. Sons of Mary Missionary Society.
f.s.c. Brothers of the Christian Schools.
f.s.e. Brothers of the Holy Eucharist.
f.s.p. Brothers of St. Patrick.
f.s.r. Brothers of the Congregation of Our Lady of the Holy Rosary.
glmy. The Glenmary Home Missioners.
i.c. Institute of Charity.
i.h.m. Brothers of the Immaculate Heart of Mary.
i.m.c. Consolata Missionaries.
l.b.s.f. Little Brothers of Saint Francis.
l.c. Legionaries of Christ.
m.afr. Missionaries of Africa.
m.c.b.s. Missionary Congregation of the Blessed Sacrament.
m.c.c.j. Comboni Missionaries of the Heart of Jesus.
m.d. Mercedarios Descalzos.
m.e.p. Paris Foreign Mission Society.
m.g. Guadalupe Missioners.
m.h.m. Mill Hill Missionaries.
m.i.c. Congregation of Marians of the Immaculate Conception.
m.j. Missionaries of St. Joseph.
m.m. Maryknoll Fathers, Catholic Foreign Mission Society of America.
m.s. The Missionaries of Our Lady La Salette.
m.s.c. Missionaries of the Sacred Heart.
m.s.c. Missionary Servants of Christ.
m.s.f. Congregation of the Missionaries of the Holy Family.
m.s.p. Missionaries of St. Paul.
m.sp.s. Missionaries of the Holy Spirit.
m.ss.a. Missionaries of the Holy Apostles.
m.ss.cc. Missionaries of the Sacred Hearts of Jesus and Mary.
o.a.r. Order of the Augustinian Recollects.
o.carm. Carmelite Fathers and Brothers.
o.cart. Order of Carthusians.
o.c.d. Discalced Carmelite Friars.
o.cist. Cistercian Fathers.
o.c.s.o. The Cistercians Order of the Strict Observance, Trappists.
o.de.m. Order of Our Lady of Mercy.
o.f.m. Franciscan Friars, Order of Friars Minor.
o.f.m.cap. The Capuchin Friars, Franciscan Fathers.
o.f.m-.conv. Conventual Franciscans, Friars Minor Conventual.
o.h. Hospitaller Brothers of St. John of God.
o.i.c. Order of the Imitation of Christ.
o.l.c. Brothers of Our Lady of Providence.
o.m. Minim Fathers.
o.mar. Congregation of Maronite Monks.
o.m.i. Oblates of Mary Immaculate.
o.m.v. Oblates of the Virgin Mary.
o.p. Order of Preachers, Dominican Fathers.
o.praem. Canons Regular of Premontre, Premonstratensians, Norbertines.
o.r.c. Operarios del Reina de Cristo.
o.s.a. The Augustinians.
o.s.b. Benedictine Monks, Olivetan Benedictines, Sylvestrine Benedictines.
o.s.b.cam. Camaldolese Hermits.
o.s.b.m. Order of St. Basil the Great.
o.s.c. Canons Regular of the Order of the Holy Cross, Crosier Fathers.
o.s.cam. Camillian Fathers and Brothers.
o.s.f. Religious Brothers of the Third Order Regular of St. Francis.
o.s.f. Franciscan Brothers of Christ the King.
o.s.f. Franciscan Brothers of the Third Order Regular.
o.s.f. Franciscan Missionary Brothers of the Sacred Heart of Jesus.
o.s.f.s. Oblates of St. Francis de Sales.
o.s.j. Oblates of St. Joseph.
o.s.m. Servite Fathers.
o.s.p.p.e. Pauline Fathers.
o.ss.s. Brigittine Monks.
o.ss.t. Order of the Most Holy Trinity, Trinitarian Fathers.
p.i.m.e. Pontifical Institute for Foreign Missions.
r.c.j. Rogationist Fathers.
s.a. Franciscan Friars of the Atonement.
s.a.c. Society of the Catholic Apostolate, Pallottine Fathers.
s.c. Brothers of the Sacred Heart.
s.c. Servants of Charity.
s.ch. Society of Christ.
sch.p. Piarist Fathers.
s.c.j. Congregation of the Priests of the Sacred Heart of Jesus.
s.d.b. Salesians of Don Bosco.
s.d.s. Society of the Divine Savior.
s.d.v. Vocationist Fathers, Society of the Divine Vocations.
s.f. Sons of the Holy Family.
s.f.c. Society of the Brothers of Charity.
s.f.m. Scarboro Foreign Missions.
s.j. Jesuit Fathers and Brothers, Society of Jesus.
s.l.t. Servants of Our Lady of the Most Holy Trinity.
s.m. Society of Mary, Marianists.
s.m. Marist Fathers.
s.m.a. Society of African Missions.
s.m.m. Montfort Missionaries.
s.m.p. Society of Our Mother of Peace.
s.o.cist. Cistercian Monks of the Strict Observance.
s.o.l.t. Society of Our Lady of the Most Holy Trinity.
s.p. Servants of the Paraclete.
s.p.s. St. Patrick's Missionary Society.
s.s. Society of the Priest of Saint Sulpice, Sulpician Fathers.
s.s.c. Society of St. Columban, St. Columban's Foreign Mission Society.
ss.cc. Congregation of the Sacred Hearts of Jesus and Mary.
s.s.e. Society of Saint Edmund.
s.s.j. St. Joseph's Society of the Sacred Heart, Josephite Fathers.
s.s.p. Pauline Fathers and Brothers, Society of St. Paul for the Apostolate of Communications.
s.s.s. Congregation of the Blessed Sacrament.
s.s.t. Missionary Society of St. Thomas the Apostle.
s.t. Missionary Servants of the Most Holy Trinity.
s.v.d. Society of the Divine Word.
s.x. Xaverian Missionary Fathers, St. Francis Xavier Mission Society.
t.o.r. Third Order Regular of Saint Francis.
v.c. Vincentian Congregation.

The letters in parentheses designate the diocese. See the "Diocesan Abbreviations". Numbers in brackets designate the numerical order of the Church in cities in which there are four or more Catholic Churches listed. Letters in brackets designate categories in the Institution Section.

A

Aaron, Andrew (BAL) Millersville, MD Our Lady of the Fields Church.

Aaron, James L. '54 (PIT) [78] Pittsburgh, PA Most Holy Name of Jesus Church; Retired.

Aaron, Robert *o.m.i.* '72 (BEL) [H] Belleville, IL King's House Retreat and Renewal Center.

Abad, Jose Antonio P. '82 (AGN) Tamuning, GU St. Anthony and St. Victor Church.

Abalon, Jose M. '00 (NEW) Secaucus, NJ Immaculate Conception Church.

Abano, Edgardo D. '85 (MET) Piscataway, NJ St. Frances Cabrini Church.

Abara, Lawrence N. '78 (LAF) On Special Assignment; [F] Lafayette, LA Our Lady of Lourdes Regional Medical Center, Inc.

Abarrategui, Leandro *o.f.m.* '54 (SJN) [3] Carolina, PR Santa Clara de Asis Church.

Abarratelegui, Leanadro *o.f.m.* '68 (SJN) [3] Carolina, PR Santa Clara de Asis Church.

Abas, Peter '86 (NY) [185] Bronx, NY St. Raymond Church.

Abate, Anthony *o.f.m.* '56 (NY) [DD] New York, NY Padua Friary.

Abaya, Francisco (NY) Manhattan, NY New York University Medical Center.

Abayomi, Augustine '93 (LA) Pico Rivera, CA St. Mariana de Paredes Church.

Abba, Yousif Mansour '75 (OLD) Toronto, St. Joseph Church.

Abbaticchio, Damian *o.s.b.* '45 (RIC) [5] Virginia Beach, VA St. Gregory the Great Church.
Abbatiello, Robert *o.f.m.cap.* '90 (NY) [DD] Garrison, NY St. Francis Friary.
Abbot, Walter M *s.j.* '56 (BO) [W] Weston, MA Campion Jesuit Community.
Abbott, Donald S. '73 (BO) Wilmington, MA St. Dorothy Church.
Abbott, Donald S. '73 (CHR) On Duty Outside the Diocese.
Abbott, Eugene J. '57 (STP) Minneapolis, MN Minnesota Soldiers' Home; Retired.
Abbott, Kerry *o.f.m.conv.* '90 (MRY) [F] Arroyo Grande, CA St. Joseph Cupertino Province, Provincial Center.
Abdella, Peter *c.s.p.* (OAK) [2] Berkeley, CA Holy Spirit Parish/Newman Hall Church.
Abdoo, Louis *i.m.c.* '73 (SB) [7] Riverside, CA St. Francis de Sales Church.
Abdulmasih, Yousif '75 (OLD) [1] Newark, NJ Our Lady of Deliverance Church.
Abe, John Adam '84 (RIC) Staunton, VA St. Francis of Assisi Church.
Abegg, Victor *o.f.m.conv.* '74 (MRY) [F] Arroyo Grande, CA St. Joseph Cupertino Province, Provincial Center.
Abel, Robert M. '73 (L) Payneville, KY St. Mary Magdalen of Pazzi Church; Rhodelia, KY St. Theresa Church.
Abele, Alan Carl '73 (ANC) Retired.
Abele, Joseph P. '49 (GI) Retired.
Abell, Donald E. '76 (BEL) Eldorado, IL St. Mary Church.
Abell, Edward '67 (GAL) [A] Houston, TX St. Mary's Seminary.
Abella, Ray *o.s.f.s.* '93 (STO) Jamestown, CA Sierra Conservation Center.
Abernethy, David S. *c.o.* '94 (PIT) [O] Pittsburgh, PA Congregation of the Oratory of St. Philip Neri; [R] Pittsburgh, PA Office for Campus Ministry; [R] Pittsburgh, PA Office for Campus Ministry; [R] Pittsburgh, PA Office for Campus Ministry.
Abert, Richard P. *s.j.* '76 (MIL) [P] Milwaukee, WI Jesuit Provincial Office, Wisconsin Province.
Abesamis, Gil-Romeo '80 (SJ) Morgan Hill, CA St. Catherine of Alexandria Church.
Abgali, Anthony '95 (DET) Detroit, MI Harper Hospital and Rehabilitation Center.
Abi-Khalil, Issam (BO) [5] Newton, MA Mary Immaculate of Lourdes Church.
Abi-Sarkis, Elias '75 (SAM) Unassigned.
Abichedid, Elie '85 (SAM) Jacksonville, FL St. Maron Maronite Church.
Ablahad, Najor '43 (EST) Retired.
Abler, Lawrence *o.f.m.cap.* '64 (DET) [K] Detroit, MI St. Mary's Friary; [T] St. Clair Shores, MI Catholic Kolping Society of America, Detroit Branch, Inc.
Ablino, John C. '90 (NY) [222] Staten Island, NY St. Patrick Church.
Ablog, Frederico-Joseph G. *s.s.s.* '90 (GAL) [25] Houston, TX Corpus Christi Church.
Aboh, Chinoye Bede '88 (CLV) [58] Cleveland, OH Our Lady of Peace Church.
Aboody, Charles '62 (NTN) Retired.
Aboumoussa, Richard A. '98 (WDC) [5] Washington, DC St. Anthony Church.
Abracinskas, Albert C. '40 (BO) Senior Priests.
Abraham, Andrew J. '00 (NSH) Franklin, TN St. Matthew Church; Old Hickory, TN St. Stephen Church.
Abraham, Benedict *s.a.c.* '65 (VEN) [4] Sarasota, FL St. Martha Church.
Abraham, Johnson C. '88 (OAK) Newark, CA St. Edward's Church.
Abraham, Joseph C. '90 (RNO) Hawthorne, NV Our Lady of Perpetual Help Church.
Abraham, Mussie *m.c.c.j.* '81 (CHI) [N] Chicago, IL Comboni Missionaries Theologate (M.C.C.J.), Verona Fathers.
Abraham, Philip *s.j.* '93 (MIL) [P] Milwaukee, WI Jesuit Community at Marquette University.
Abraham, Sebastian *c.m.i.* '91 (BEA) [9] Beaumont, TX St. Jude Thaddeus Church.
Abraham, Thaddeus '90 (BRK) [178] Queens, NY Holy Family Church.
Abraham, Thomas J. '66 (LC) Hatley, WI St. Florian Church.
Abrahams, John J. '79 (BAL) Special Assignment; [O] Baltimore, MD St. Martin's Home for Aged, Little Sisters of the Poor.
Abrahim, Jirjis '67 (EST) Troy, MI St. Joseph Chaldean Church.
Abramovic, Joseph M. *o.f.m.* '60 (STL) [44] St. Louis, MO St. Joseph Church.
Abramowicz, Richard B. '86 (MET) Retired.
Abramowicz, Msgr. Sylvester '46 (NEW) Retired.
Abrams, John L. '51 (BRK) Retired; [V] Douglaston, NY Bishop Mugavero Residence.
Abreu, John E. '74 (PRO) [5] Warren, RI St. Thomas the Apostle Church.
Abreu, Jose Sergio *s.d.b.* '86 (LAR) [9] Laredo, TX San Luis Rey Church.
Abreu, Sergio *s.d.b.* '86 (SFE) [20] Albuquerque, NM San Jose Church.
Abruzzese, Msgr. John A. '74 (BO) On Duty Outside the Archdiocese.
Abruzzese, Joseph A. '93 (PRO) Absent on Leave.
Abts, Cletus '44 (LC) Retired.
Abts, John *o.f.m.* '90 (SAT) [70] San Antonio, TX San Jose y San Miguel Church.
Abuan, Antonio *m.s.* '84 (SB) Moreno Valley, CA St. Christopher Church.
Abucewicz, Msgr. John A. '44 (BO) Senior Priests.
Abugel, Alexander '80 (BRK) [206] Queens, NY Our Lady of the Angelus Church.
Acaba, Jose A. '82 (ARE) [6] Vega-Baja, PR Our Lady of Lourdes Church.
Accardi, Joseph V. '90 (PH) Newtown, PA St. Andrew Church.
Acciarito, Anthony J. '78 (BRK) [131] Brooklyn, NY Sacred Hearts of Jesus and Mary and St. Stephen Church.
Acebo, Jeff '12 (OAK) [3] Oakland, CA St. Anthony's Church.
Acerbi, Luigi *p.i.m.e.* '50 (PAT) [M] Wayne, NJ P.I.M.E. Missionaries Residence.
Acevedo, Anthony '73 (MIA) [G] Miami, FL Mercy Hospital.
Acevedo, Bertulfo '55 (ARE) [5] Utuado, PR Our Lady of Sorrows Church.
Acevedo, Edward '97 (MGZ) Sabana Grande, PR Church of San Isidro.
Acevedo, Jaime H. '99 (MIA) [11] Fort Lauderdale, FL St. Mark Church.
Acevedo, Joaquin *o.f.m.* '60 (ELP) [B] El Paso, TX St. Anthony's School of Theology.
Acevedo, Luis H. '51 (ELP) Retired.
Acevedo, Natividad *o.p.* '86 (SJN) [2] Toa Alta, PR San Fernando Rey Church.
Achandy, Thomas *c.m.i.* '73 (PH) [125] Philadelphia, PA Our Lady of Mt. Carmel Church.
Achi, Stephen *m.s.p.* '86 (WDC) [B] Washington, DC St. Joseph's Seminary.
Acker, Karl H. '63 (MIL) Saukville, WI Immaculate Conception Church.
Acker, Thomas S. *s.j.* '63 (DET) [K] Detroit, MI Jesuit Provincial Office-Detroit Province of the Society of Jesus.
Ackeret, Dennis R. '68 (MIL) [2] Wauwatosa, WI Christ King Church.
Ackerman, Donald K. '61 (EVN) Ireland, IN Annunciation of the Blessed Virgin Mary Church.
Ackerman, James Thomas, Jr. '97 (BIR) [17] Birmingham, AL Our Lady of Sorrows Church; [A] Birmingham, AL John Carroll Catholic High School.
Ackerman, Phillip '78 (FAR) [2] Fargo, ND Holy Spirit Church; Fargo, ND Veterans Administration Facility.
Ackerman, Ray '91 (OKL) [K] Norman, OK Campus Ministry for the Archdiocese of Oklahoma City.
Ackerman, Raymond K. '91 (OKL) Ada, OK St. Joseph Church.
Ackerman, Raymond K. '91 (TLS) Coalgate, OK Blessed Sacrament Church.
Ackerson, Msgr. Francis A. '46 (ALT) Retired.
Acklin, Thomas *o.s.b.* '80 (GBG) [A] Latrobe, PA St. Vincent Seminary; [H] Latrobe, PA Saint Vincent Archabbey.
Aclan, Alex '93 (LA) Norwalk, CA St. John of God Church.
Acosta, Carlos Lopez '60 (NY) [139] Bronx, NY St. Francis of Assisi Church.
Acosta, Edgardo '83 (MGZ) Sabana Grande, PR Church of San Isidro.
Acosta, Francisco '70 (BWN) [1] McAllen, TX Our Lady of Perpetual Help Church.
Acquaro, Philip A. *c.s.b.* '70 (PHX) Special Assignment.
Acquaro, Philip A. *c.s.b.* '70 (VNN) Gilbert, AZ St. Thomas the Apostle Church; [A] Phoenix, AZ Congregation of Saint Basil.
Acquavia, Msgr. Paschal L. '48 (BUF) Retired.
Acri, John A. '65 (HBG) Enola, PA Our Lady of Lourdes Church.
Acton, Msgr. John A. (LA) Retired.
Acton, Msgr. John A. '48 (LA) Glendora, CA St. Dorothy Church.
Acton, Thomas M. '57 (LA) Gardena, CA Maria Regina Church.
Adackapara, Matthew '60 (TR) Freehold, NJ St. Robert Bellarmine Church.
Adaickalam, Michael *s.s.s.* (CHI) Maywood, IL St. Eulalia Church.
Adam, Charles A. '86 (DAV) [A] Davenport, IA St. Ambrose University Seminary; [B] Davenport, IA St. Ambrose University; [B] Davenport, IA St. Ambrose University.
Adam, John *s.j.* '61 (NY) [HH] Bronx, NY Saint Jutta Foundation, Inc.
Adam, Nicholas '76 (DAV) Mount Pleasant, IA St. Alphonsus Church.
Adam, Richard A. '88 (SC) Absent on Leave.
Adamcik, Bryan F.J. '96 (NEW) Emerson, NJ Church of the Assumption.
Adamec, Joseph *c.ss.r.* '52 (BO) [53] Boston, MA Our Lady of Perpetual Help Church.
Adamiak, Leo '46 (SJP) Youngstown, OH Holy Trinity Church.
Adamiak, Stephen (SJP) Retired.
Adamich, Albert R. '48 (CHI) Evergreen Park, IL Most Holy Redeemer Church; Retired.
Adamik, Adrian '96 (SAT) Panna Maria, TX Immaculate Conception of the Blessed Virgin Mary Church.
Adamik, Adrian '98 (SAT) Karnes City, TX St. Cornelius Church.
Adamko, Msgr. Cyril A. '53 (Y) Retired.
Adamo, Joseph A. '73 (WOR) [2] Worcester, MA Ascension Church.
Adamo, Joseph P. '42 (NY) Retired; [DD] New York, NY Our Lady of Consolation Residence.
Adamo, Robert B. '98 (BRK) [242] Queens, NY St. Stanislaus Kostka Church.
Adamo, Msgr. Salvatore J. '45 (CAM) Retired.
Adams, Alvin J. '67 (PIT) [4] Munhall, PA St. Rita Church; [C] Pittsburgh, PA Canevin Catholic High School.
Adams, Archie H. '55 (MAD) Absent on Sick Leave.
Adams, Benjamin *o.f.m.cap.* '57 (GB) [I] Appleton, WI St. Fidelis Friary.
Adams, Charles F. *o.f.m.* '40 (SP) [O] St. Petersburg, FL St. Anthony Friary.
Adams, Daniel '80 (P) On Duty Outside the Archdiocese.
Adams, Daniel '80 (SFR) [6] San Francisco, CA St. Benedict Parish at St. Francis Xavier Church.
Adams, David A. '88 (TR) Highlands, NJ Our Lady of Perpetual Help Church.
Adams, David C. '61 (KAL) Benton Harbor, MI Ss. John & Bernard Church.
Adams, Edmond F. '52 (SC) Retired.
Adams, Msgr. George J. '50 (STU) Retired.
Adams, Harry J. '68 (NO) [60] New Orleans, LA St. Simon Peter Church.
Adams, Harry J., Jr. *s.c.* '68 (NO) [R] Ponchatoula, LA Magnificat Center of the Holy Spirit.
Adams, J.K. '95 (SPK) [E] Spokane, WA Gonzaga Preparatory School.
Adams, James P. '82 (ATL) On Duty Outside the Archdiocese.
Adams, Joel K. *s.j.* '95 (P) [L] Portland, OR Jesuit Provincial Office (Society of Jesus, Oregon Prov.).
Adams, John '69 (WDC) [U] Washington, DC Community of Christ.
Adams, John *o.p.* '74 (SEA) [22] Seattle, WA Blessed Sacrament Church.
Adams, John E. '69 (WDC) Special Ministries.
Adams, Msgr. Michael '46 (CC) Retired.
Adams, Michael J. '59 (CHI) [128] Chicago, IL St. Mary, Star of the Sea Church.
Adams, Michael T. '68 (MRY) On Duty Outside the Diocese.
Adams, Patrick *o.f.m.* '42 (SP) [O] St. Petersburg, FL St. Anthony Friary.
Adams, Msgr. Raymond A. '51 (BUR) Retired.
Adams, Richard T. '65 (NY) Goshen, NY St. John the Evangelist Church.
Adams, Msgr. Robert (OAK) Livermore, CA St. Michael Church.
Adams, Msgr. Robert '45 (OAK) Retired.
Adams, Rodney T. '91 (OM) [27] Omaha, NE St. Margaret Mary Church.
Adams, Scott '95 (OKL) Guymon, OK St. Peter's Church; [K] Norman, OK Campus Ministry for the Archdiocese of Oklahoma City.
Adams, Stephen E. '81 (DEN) Johnstown, CO St. John the Baptist Church; Windsor, CO Our Lady of the Valley Church.
Adams, T. Edmund *o.s.b.* '89 (PRO) [P] Portsmouth, RI Abbey of St. Gregory the Great.
Adams, Terrance *t.o.r.* '67 (PIT) [O] McKeesport, PA Franciscan Friars.
Adams, Thomas J '64 (OM) [41] Omaha, NE St. Rose Church.
Adams, Walter C. '84 (NY) [E] New York, NY Cardinal Spellman High School.
Adams, William *s.v.d.* '45 (SB) [A] Riverside, CA Divine Word Seminary.
Adams, William *c.ss.r.* '63 (LA) Whittier, CA St. Mary of the Assumption Church; [Q] Whittier, CA Redemptorist Fathers Mission House.
Adams, William '78 (VEN) Arcadia, FL St. Paul Church.
Adamski, Donald J. *o.f.m.conv.* '75 (LSC) Hobbs, NM St. Helena Church.
Adamski, John S. '71 (ATL) [7] Atlanta, GA Our Lady of Lourdes Church.
Adamsky, Raymond J. '58 (MIL) Retired.
Adamson, Joseph '90 (CAM) [5] Cherry Hill, NJ St. Thomas More Church.
Adamson, Milton N. *c.s.c.* '66 (PHX) [D] Phoenix, AZ St. Joseph's Hospital and Medical Center; [G] Phoenix, AZ Holy Cross Congregation/Casa Santa Cruz.
Adan, Aurelio '69 (CGS) [B] Aibonito, PR Casa Manresa.
Adarve, Hernan '61 (SJN) [12] Bayamon, PR Nuestra Senora de la Milagrosa Church.
Adducci, Anthony J. '76 (CHI) [J] Chicago, IL St.

Joseph Hospital.
Adebusuyi, Anthony '89 (CHI) [J] Evergreen Park, IL Little Company of Mary Hospital and Health Care Centers.
Adebusuyui, Anthony O. '89 (CHI) [91] Chicago, IL Immaculate Conception of the Blessed Virgin Mary Church.
Adejoh, Patrick '95 (CIN) [3] Dayton, OH St. Albert the Great Church.
Adelman, Norbert '56 (ORL) Longwood, FL Church of the Nativity.
Adelmann, Edward *o.carm.* '75 (FgM) Carmelite Foreign Missions.
Adelmann, Edward *o.carm.* '75 (JOL) [J] Darien, IL Carmelite Provincial Office.
Adeniji, Michael '86 (NY) [185] Bronx, NY St. Raymond Church.
Adessa, Msgr. Dominick J. '47 (BRK) Retired.
Adessa, Msgr. Dominick J. '47 (RVC) [N] Amityville, NY Queen of the Rosary, Motherhouse.
Adewoye, John (CHI) [41] Chicago, IL St. Clotilde Church.
Adhana, Gabre-Tinsaye '47 (GAL) [N] Houston, TX St. Dominic Village.
Adibe, Anthony *c.s.sp.* '91 (DM) [6] Des Moines, IA St. Augustin's Church.
Adiletta, David C. *o.p.* '98 (NEW) [28] Jersey City, NJ Sacred Heart Church.
Adolf, Gregory P. '91 (TUC) Sierra Vista, AZ St. Andrew Church.
Adolfo, Hermengildo '68 (FRS) Tehachapi, CA California Correctional Institution.
Adonizio, Joseph J. '56 (SCR) Retired.
Adorno, Anibal '92 (DAL) [21] Dallas, TX St. Monica Church.
Adragna, Joseph J. '65 (STL) Gardenville, MO St. George Church.
Adrian, Stephen '39 (PHX) Gilbert, AZ St. Anne Church.
Adrian, Stephen J. '39 (NU) Retired.
Adrian, Stephen J. '68 (STP) [28] St. Paul, MN St. Matthew Church.
Adrians, Thomas M. '67 (PBL) [2] Pueblo, CO Christ the King Church.
Aduba, John '81 (LAN) [3] Flint, MI Christ the King Church.
Aduba, Peter '79 (TOL) [16] Toledo, OH St. Agnes Church.
Adversario, Efren '89 (AGN) Dededo, GU Santa Barbara Church; On Duty Outside the Archdiocese.
Aelavanthara, Antony '68 (ALX) St. Joseph, LA St. Joseph Church.
Aerts, Daniel C. '77 (GR) Reed City, MI St. Philip Neri Church.
Affanoso, Joseph L. '56 (NEW) [1] East Orange, NJ Holy Name of Jesus Church; Retired.
Affelt, Francis *o.f.m.* '52 (FTW) [K] Mishawaka, IN St. Francis Provincialate.
Affonso, Alexander '68 (SJ) Los Altos, CA St. Simon Church.
Afunugo, Emmanuel *d.d.* '83 (AMA) On Duty Outside the Diocese.
Agan, Msgr. Jose '70 (NEW) Kearny, NJ St. Cecilia's Church; Newark, NJ St. Michael Medical Center.
Aganbi, Isaac (NY) Mount Vernon, NY Mount Vernon Hospital.
Agapito, John *c.p.m.* '89 (WH) [F] Morgantown, WV Our Lady of Good Counsel Franciscan Friary.
Agar, Bartholomew A. *o.praem.* '58 (GB) [I] De Pere, WI St. Norbert Abbey.
Agbakwuru, Emmanuel C. '73 (PIT) Duquesne, PA St. Joseph Church.
Agbor, Emmanuel *m.s.p.* '95 (BR) Napoleonville, LA St. Benedict the Moor Church.
Ageas, Cesar '83 (SAC) [11] Sacramento, CA St. Charles Borromeo Church.
Agede, Kenneth '88 (PIT) [4] Donora, PA Our Lady of the Valley Church.
Ager, Fay W. '79 (OG) Chateaugay, NY St. Patrick Church.
Aggeler, Vince *c.ss.r.* '58 (FgM) Redemptorist Foreign Missions.
Aggrey, Michael '92 (RVC) Rockville Centre, NY Mercy Medical Center.
Aggrey, Michael N. '92 (NY) [127] Bronx, NY St. Anthony Church.
Agirembabazi, Nestorio B.K. *a.j.* (NY) [124] Bronx, NY St. Angela Merici Church.
Agliardo, Michael *s.j.* '94 (SD) [4] San Diego, CA Christ the King Church.
Agnew, Francis H. *c.m.* '60 (STL) Sereno, MO Our Lady of Victory Church.
Agnew, John '90 (CHI) [W] Chicago, IL Prelature of the Holy Cross and Opus Dei.
Agostinelli, Gianni *c.s.* '86 (BRK) [71] Brooklyn, NY St. Joseph Patron of the Universal Church.
Agostini, Sixtus *m.c.c.j.* '71 (CHI) [N] La Grange Park, IL Comboni Mission Center.
Agostini, Sixtus *m.c.c.j.* '71 (CIN) [V] Cincinnati, OH The Comboni Lay Missionaries Association.
Agostino, Emil *o.carm.* '68 (KCK) Richmond, KS St. Therese Church; Scipio, KS St. Boniface Church.
Agostino, Joseph V. *c.m.* '83 (BRK) [66] Brooklyn, NY St. John the Baptist Church; [V] Brooklyn, NY St. John the Baptist Rectory.
Agostino, Steven J. *s.j.* '93 (CLV) [D] Cleveland, OH St. Ignatius High School.
Agresti, Albert A. *s.j.* '80 (BO) [W] Boston, MA The Society of Jesus of New England-Provincial Offices.
Agresti, Albert A. *s.j.* '80 (OM) [A] Omaha, NE Creighton University; [K] Omaha, NE Jesuit Community at Creighton University.
Agudo, Moises '97 (SFR) [12] San Francisco, CA St. Charles Borromeo Church.
Agudo, Teodoro *o.f.m.cap.* '54 (NO) [62] New Orleans, LA St. Theresa of Avila Church.
Aguggia, Steven J. '93 (BRK) [81] Brooklyn, NY St. Mary Mother of Jesus Church.
Aguilar, A. *s.s.c.* '84 (OM) [K] St. Columbans, NE St. Columban's Foreign Mission Society.
Aguilar, Benjamin *o.carm.* '94 (CHI) [D] Chicago, IL Mt. Carmel High School.
Aguilar, Genaro P. *c.s.c.* '83 (FR) [A] North Easton, MA Stonehill College; [A] North Easton, MA Holy Cross Fathers Religious.
Aguilar, J. Ernest *c.s.p.* '00 (NY) [41] New York, NY Good Shepherd Church.
Aguilar, Jose '96 (NY) [160] Bronx, NY St. Luke Church.
Aguilar, Ricardo '95 (AUS) Temple, TX Our Lady of Guadalupe Church.
Aguilar, Rogelio Mur *o.carm.* '56 (MGZ) Anasco, PR St. Anthony Abbot Church.
Aguilar Leal, Luis Roberto *o.p.* '92 (FgM) Dominican - Order of Preachers Foreign Missions.
Aguilarleal, Luis Roberto *o.p.* '92 (NO) [P] New Orleans, LA Dominican Friars, Southern Dominican Province of St. Martin de Porres.
Aguilera, George '83 (LA) [41] Los Angeles, CA St. Aloysius Gonzaga Church.
Aguilera, Salvador '84 (ELP) On Duty Outside of Diocese.
Aguirre, Emilson (BO) [5] Lawrence, MA Holy Rosary Church.
Aguirre, Ignacio *o.s.b.* '53 (CGS) Humacao, PR Maria Reina de la Paz Church.
Aguirre, Juan Carlos '99 (TUC) Nogales, AZ Sacred Heart Church.
Aguirre, Nery *o.f.m.* '74 (NY) [DD] New York, NY Franciscan Province of the Immaculate Conception.
Aguirre, Osmar '93 (YAK) Sunnyside, WA St. Joseph's Church.
Aguirre, Robert G. '72 (CHI) Wauconda, IL Transfiguration Church.
Aguirre-Garza, Jesus *o.f.m.* '96 (STL) [P] St. Louis, MO Franciscan Friary of St. Anthony of Padua.
Agustin, Richard *m.m.* '85 (FgM) Maryknoll Foreign Missions.
Ahearn, Donald J. '51 (CHI) [109] Chicago, IL St. Juliana Church; Retired.
Ahearn, John F. *m.m.* '73 (FgM) Maryknoll Foreign Missions.
Ahearn, John S. *o.f.m.* '50 (PAT) [M] Butler, NJ St. Anthony Friary.
Ahearn, Richard F. '60 (BO) Senior Priests.
Ahearn, Thomas *m.m.* '68 (FgM) Maryknoll Foreign Missions.
Ahearn, Thomas '94 (BRK) [B] Elmhurst, NY Cathedral Preparatory Seminary of the Immaculate Conception.
Ahern, Bernard '54 (ALB) Retired.
Ahern, Dennis P. *s.j.* '70 (CHI) [C] Chicago, IL Jesuit Community at Loyola University of Chicago.
Ahern, Msgr. John B. '54 (NY) [88] New York, NY Our Lady of Loreto Church; [I] New York, NY The Catholic Charities of the Archdiocese of New York.
Ahern, John J. '48 (CHI) Retired.
Ahern, John J. '49 (CHI) Retired.
Ahern, John J. '79 (BO) [5] Brookline, MA St. Mary of the Assumption Church.
Ahern, John S. '54 (HRT) Norfolk, CT Immaculate Conception Church.
Ahern, John V. '67 (SY) [2] Liverpool, NY Immaculate Heart of Mary Church.
Ahern, Richard *c.s.s.* '54 (BO) [Z] Waltham, MA Stigmatine Fathers and Brothers.
Ahern, Thomas '54 (SJ) Retired.
Ahern, Thomas W. '48 (NOR) Old Lyme, CT Christ the King Church; Retired.
Aherne, Greg *s.j.* '60 (SFR) [49] San Francisco, CA Star of the Sea Church.
Aherne, James J. '73 (HRT) [8] Hartford, CT St. Anne-Immaculate Conception Church; [M] Hartford, CT Missionaries of LaSalette, Provincial Secretary.
Aherne, John '57 (MOB) Semmes, AL Holy Name of Jesus Church.
Aherne, P. Vincent *c.m.* '52 (STL) [P] St. Louis, MO Vincentian Residence.
Ahlbach, William J. '62 (SFR) [3] San Mateo, CA St. Matthew Church.
Ahlemeyer, Richard J. '77 (BRK) [227] Queens, NY St. Pius V Church; [229] Queens, NY Presentation of the Blessed Virgin Mary Church.
Ahler, Richard H. *s.j.* '61 (MIL) [P] Milwaukee, WI Jesuit Community at Marquette University.
Ahles, Donald M. '71 (RCK) Cary, IL SS. Peter & Paul Church.
Ahles, Jerry *o.f.m.* '44 (MRY) [F] San Miguel, CA Franciscan Friars, O.F.M.
Ahlin, Robert J. '71 (PIT) Brentwood, PA St. Sylvester Church.
Ahlstrom, Michael P. '69 (CHI) Rolling Meadows, IL St. Colette Church.
Aho, Charles A. '70 (SY) Liverpool, NY Developmental Center; Special Assignment; [S] Syracuse, NY St. Pius X Home, Inc.
Ahrens, Noel *o.carm.* '53 (JOL) [J] Darien, IL Carmelite Provincial Office.
Ahrens, Noel *o.carm.* '53 (NEW) Englewood, NJ St. Cecilia's Church.
Ahrens, William B. '51 (STL) Concord Village, MO St. Simon the Apostle Church.
Ahrensfield, Michael E. '80 (ALN) Shillington, PA St. John Baptist de la Salle Church.
Ahumanda, Jose E. *c.s.c.* '83 (FTW) [J] South Bend, IN Congregation of Holy Cross, Indiana Province, Provincial House.
Aiardi, Reno *i.m.c.* '65 (SB) [7] Riverside, CA St. Francis de Sales Church; Special or Other Diocesan Assignment.
Aichele, Raymond P. '58 (CIN) Retired.
Aidoo, Hilary (NY) [214] Staten Island, NY St. Mary of the Assumption Church.
Aidoo, Thomas '85 (NY) Bronx, NY Montefiore Medical Center.
Aidoo, Thoms '85 (RVC) Stony Brook, NY Stony Brook University Hospital.
Aiello, Anthony '69 (DM) [2] Des Moines, IA All Saints Church.
Aiello, John D. '69 (MIL) Special Assignment.
Aiello, Louis F. '77 (SY) Tully, NY St. Leo Church.
Aigner, Edward M. '72 (WIL) Salisbury, MD St. Francis De Sales Church.
Aigner, Edward M., Jr. '72 (WIL) Westover, MD Eastern Correctional Institution.
Aiken, Lloyd E. '70 (BAL) Glyndon, MD Sacred Heart Church.
Aiken, Richard J. '70 (MIL) Greendale, WI St. Alphonsus Church.
Aiken, Msgr. Roy F. '46 (CHR) Retired.
Aime, Moise '54 (RVC) Plainview, NY St. Pius X Church.
Aineto, Luis *s.d.b.* '61 (PMB) Belle Glade, FL St. Philip Benizi Church.
Ainikkal, Jose *c.m.i.* '82 (PH) [84] Philadelphia, PA St. Katherine of Siena Church.
Aitcheson, William M. '88 (ARL) Woodstock, VA St. John Bosco Church.
Aitsebaomo, Martin *o.p.* (HBG) Hershey, PA St. Joan of Arc Church.
Ajamie, Albert '50 (IND) Retired.
Ajiki, Pius T. '84 (WDC) [31] Washington, DC Nigerian Catholic Community Church.
Ajuria, Cruz *o.f.m.* '57 (SJN) [51] San Juan, PR Resurreccion del Senor Church.
Akamike, Romanus A. '89 (SAN) [1] Abilene, TX Sacred Heart Church.
Akata, Gerald '94 (BRK) [84] Brooklyn, NY St. Mary, Star of the Sea Church.
Akers, Bert *s.j.* '51 (WDC) [20] Washington, DC Holy Trinity Church.
Akiki, Joseph G. '87 (SAM) Olean, NY St. Joseph Church.
Akiona, Lane K. *ss.cc.* '81 (HON) [11] Honolulu, HI St. Patrick Church.
Akkim, Florentinus '93 (CI) Fefan, FM Sacred Heart Church.
Akkin, Florentinus '93 (CI) Tolowas, FM St. Anthony's Church.
Akordor, Edmund '80 (NO) New Orleans, LA Touro Infirmary.
Akpabio, Felix '78 (BRK) [238] Queens, NY Sacred Heart Church.
Akpagher, Iordepuun J. *c.s.sp.* '97 (PIT) Emsworth, PA Sacred Heart Church.
Akpen, Thomas '93 (PIT) Glade Mills, PA Holy Sepulcher Church.
Akpunonu, Peter Damian *s.s.l.* '66 (CHI) [A] Mundelein, IL University of St. Mary of the Lake-Mundelein Seminary.
Aksamit, Stanley J. '77 (SPR) Greenfield, MA Sacred Heart Church; Turners Falls, MA St. Mary's Church; Turners Falls, MA St. Anne Church.
Aku, Edmund '00 (HRT) [I] Waterbury, CT St. Mary Hospital.
Akwue, Francis *c.s.sp.* '71 (MIA) [7] Pompano Beach, FL St. Henry Church.
Al-Badwi, Alfred '91 (OLL) Dayton, OH Saint Ignatius Church.
Al-Nahal, Jean *m.l.m.* '93 (OLL) San Antonio, TX St. George Maronite Church.
Al-Nahal, John *m.l.m.* '93 (OLL) [A] Houston, TX The Congregation of Maronite Lebanese Missionaries.

Alabart, Francis X. '40 (FRS) Retired.
Alagia, Vincent P. *s.j.* '58 (CHL) [J] Charlotte, NC Jesuit Community.
Alaharasan, V. Antony '65 (NOR) North Stonington, CT St. Thomas More Church.
Alam, Alam '81 (NTN) Boston, MA Annunciation Church; North Hollywood, CA St. Anne Church.
Alamo, Emiliano '66 (PCE) Villalba, PR Our Lady of Mt. Carmel Church.
Alamo, Jose *c.s.sp.* '85 (ARE) Orocovis, PR Our Lady of Fatima Church.
Alapide, Eduardo *o.p.* (NEW) [4] Hackensack, NJ Church of St. Francis of Assisi.
Alappat, Joy '81 (WDC) [K] Washington, DC Georgetown University Hospital.
Alarcon, Felix '63 (RVC) Priests Released from Diocesan Assignment.
Alava, Andres *o.a.r.* (LSC) La Mesa, NM San Jose Church.
Alava, Andres *o.a.r.* '63 (LSC) [B] Mesilla, NM Augustinian Recollect Fathers.
Alayon, Hermenegildo '79 (CGS) [13] Barrio Rio Canas, PR Maria Madre de la Iglesia Church.
Alba, Msgr. Jose M. '48 (NEW) Retired.
Albacete, Msgr. Lorenzo '73 (NY) [A] Yonkers, NY St. Joseph's Seminary.
Albacete, Msgr. Lorenzo '73 (WDC) On Duty Outside the Archdiocese.
Albaladejo, Juan A. '85 (MET) [H] Raritan, NJ Clairvaux House; [K] Raritan, NJ Shrine Chapel of the Blessed Sacrament.
Albamonti, Richard J. '76 (NOR) Westbrook, CT St. Mark Church.
Albano, Arturo '74 (SFR) Colma, CA Holy Angels Church.
Albano, George M. '44 (TR) [4] Toms River, NJ St. Maximilian Kolbe Church; Retired.
Albano, Michael '90 (SD) [33] San Diego, CA St. Michael Church.
Albano, Peter J. *c.m.* '68 (BRK) [V] Jamaica, NY Vincentian Residence.
Albano, Vincent *s.o.l.t.* '72 (CC) Robstown, TX St. Anthony Church; [H] Robstown, TX Society of Our Lady of the Most Holy Trinity.
Albarano, Richard '68 (LA) Burbank, CA St. Francis Xavier Church.
Albee, Paul M. '84 (LA) [1] Los Angeles, CA Cathedral Residence Church.
Albensius, Paul M. '97 (OM) [24] Omaha, NE St. John Vianney Church.
Alber, Thomas L. '85 (JC) Canton, MO St. Joseph Church; St. Patrick, MO The Shrine of St. Patrick Church; [A] Hannibal, MO St. Thomas Aquinas Seminary.
Alberg, Leo W. '91 (LA) El Monte, CA Nativity Church.
Albero, Steven J. *o.praem.* '92 (PH) [B] Paoli, PA Daylesford Abbey; [AA] Paoli, PA Daylesford Abbey.
Albers, Austin *o.f.m.* '64 (SFD) Teutopolis, IL St. Francis of Assisi Church; [K] Quincy, IL St. Francis Solanus Friary.
Albers, Edwin O. *o.f.m.* '61 (SFD) Bishop Creek, IL St. Aloysius Church; Dieterich, IL Immaculate Conception Church; Island Grove, IL St. Joseph Church; [K] Teutopolis, IL St. Francis Assisi Friary.
Albers, George *c.pp.s.* '62 (CIN) [B] Carthagena, OH St. Charles.
Albers, James *o.s.b.* '00 (KCK) [A] Atchison, KS Benedictine College; [H] Atchison, KS St. Benedict's Abbey.
Albers, Paul C. '37 (DAV) Retired.
Albers, Robert J. *s.a.c.* '48 (MIL) [P] Milwaukee, WI Pallotti House.
Albers, Thomas *c.pp.s.* '67 (JC) Sedalia, MO St. Patrick Church.
Albers, Thomas L. *c.pp.s.* '67 (JC) Sedalia, MO Sacred Heart Church.
Albert, Andrew *s.m.* (BO) [8] Lowell, MA St. Margaret Church.
Albert, Claude A. '64 (PRT) Springvale, ME Notre Dame Church.
Albert, Claude J. '64 (PRT) Sanford, ME Holy Family Church; Sanford, ME St. Ignatius Martyr Church.
Albert, James R. '86 (PRT) Eagle Lake, ME St. Mary's Church; Wallagrass, ME St. Joseph's Church.
Albert, Msgr. Louis W. '34 (WDC) Retired.
Albert, Patrick L. '92 (SCR) Forest City, PA Sacred Heart of Jesus Church.
Albert, Selvan *o.praem.* '91 (PH) [U] Darby, PA Mercy Catholic Medical Center.
Albert, Timothy J. '91 (PRT) Springvale, ME Notre Dame Church.
Alberte, Carl P. '58 (MIL) [1] Pewaukee, WI Queen of Apostles Church; Retired.
Alberth, Regis R. '80 (PIT) Beaver, PA SS. Peter and Paul Church; Beaver County, PA McGuire Memorial Home.
Albertine, Richard P. *m.m.* '66 (FgM) Maryknoll Foreign Missions.
Alberto, Gerardo *m.sp.s.* 00 (P) Hillsboro, OR St. Matthew Church.
Alberts, Edward T. '75 (NSH) Brentwood, TN Holy Family Church.
Alberts, Keith '94 (CLV) Absent on Leave.
Albertson, Clinton E. *s.j.* '49 (LA) [C] Los Angeles, CA Loyola Marymount University.
Albertson, Eric J. '86 (ARL) On Duty Outside the Diocese; Military Chaplains.
Albertson, Lawrence '65 (KCK) [1] Overland Park, KS Church of the Ascension.
Albietz, Henry F. '74 (CIN) Bellefontaine, OH St. Patrick's Church.
Albino, Brian '79 (FR) [24] Fall River, MA Santo Christo Church.
Albino, Ramon E. (MGZ) [A] Aquadilla, PR Corpus Christi College.
Albino, Ramon E. '84 (MGZ) Aguadilla, PR La Milagrosa Church.
Albosta, John T. '64 (SCR) Waymart, PA St. Mary's Church.
Albrecht, Craig L. '95 (SAG) Merrill, MI Sacred Heart Church; Ryan, MI St. Patrick Church.
Albrecht, G.R. Keith '77 (CIN) Leave of Absence.
Albrecht, James W. '58 (NEW) [M] South Orange, NJ Opus Dei.
Albrecht, James W. '58 (NY) [II] New York, NY Prelature of the Holy Cross and Opus Dei.
Albrecht, Louis Henry '86 (BAK) La Grande, OR Our Lady of the Valley Church.
Albrecht, Walter H. '43 (SAC) Retired and in Senior Ministry.
Albright, Charles W. *c.s.p.* '49 (NY) [DD] Jamaica Estates, NY Paulist Fathers Generalate.
Albright, Charles W. *c.s.p.* '49 (SFR) [32] San Francisco, CA Old St. Mary's Church.
Albright, R. Gerard *s.j.* '58 (DET) [K] Detroit, MI Jesuit Community at the University of Detroit.
Albright, Robert E. '72 (BAL) Special Assignment; [U] Baltimore, MD Archdiocesan Office-Newman Center; [U] Baltimore, MD Archdiocesan Office-Newman Center.
Alcantara, Michael B. '65 (CHI) River Grove, IL St. Cyprian Church.
Alcaraz, Ramon Cisneros '99 (ORG) San Juan Capistrano, CA Mission Basilica Church.
Alcazar, Emanuel '89 (ELP) [29] El Paso, TX St. Paul the Apostle Church.
Alciati, Paul J. '77 (SY) [6] Binghamton, NY St. John the Evangelist Church.
Alcocer, Jose '60 (ELP) [36] El Paso, TX San Jose Church.
Alcoser, E. Michael *c.s.c.* '87 (OAK) [N] Berkeley, CA Holy Cross Fathers-Holy Cross Center.
Alcuin, William *o.f.m.cap.* '52 (GB) [I] Appleton, WI St. Fidelis Friary.
Alcuino, Miguel '88 (ELP) Pecos, TX Santa Rosa Church.
Aldana, Antonio '53 (NY) [169] Bronx, NY Our Lady of Angels Church.
Aldasoro, Msgr. Francisco '47 (SD) Retired.
Aldegunde, Jose R. '58 (BRK) [201] Queens, NY St. Michael Church.
Alder, Ronald J. '69 (DET) Dundee, MI St. Irene Church.
Alderson, George K. '71 (GBG) Freeport, PA St. Mary Church.
Alderson, John *o.f.m.* '66 (BUF) [59] Buffalo, NY SS. Rita & Patrick Church.
Aldrich, Louis G. *s.j.* '86 (FgM) Provinces.
Aldrich, Ralph '53 (PEO) Retired.
Aldridge, William J. *o.p.* '46 (BR) [J] Ponchatoula, LA Rosaryville/Spirit Life Center.
Aldworth, Thomas *o.f.m.* '74 (CHI) [164] Chicago, IL St. Peter's Church; [N] Chicago, IL St. Peter's Friary.
Alecio, Freddy '91 (SJN) [11] Carolina, PR Jesus Mediador Church; [C] San Juan, PR Seminario Menor San Jose.
Alegria, P. Gregorio *c.m.* '68 (SJN) [60] San Juan, PR San Vicente de Paul Church.
Alejunas, Richard '89 (NY) [F] New Rochelle, NY Salesian High School; [F] New Rochelle, NY Salesian High School; [DD] New Rochelle, NY Salesian Provincial House.
Aleksonis, Vladas '34 (FAR) Retired.
Alenchery, Joseph '87 (RVC) Selden, NY St. Margaret of Scotland Church.
Alesandro, Msgr. John A. '66 (RVC) Garden City, NY St. Joseph's Church; East Meadow, NY Nassau County Police Department.
Aleska, Thomas M. '75 (E) [7] Erie, PA Mount Calvary Church.
Alessandro, Msgr. Michael J. '44 (NY) Retired; [X] New York, NY Calvary Hospital.
Alex, Boby Mannamplackal '94 (SHP) [4] Monroe, LA St. Joseph Church; [B] Monroe, LA St. Francis Medical Center.
Alexander, Andrew *s.j.* '79 (OM) [K] Omaha, NE Jesuit Community at Creighton University.
Alexander, Anthony F. '45 (CLV) Perry, OH St. Cyprian Church; Retired.
Alexander, F. Leon '66 (WH) South Charleston, WV Blessed Sacrament Church.
Alexander, Fred *o.c.d.* '82 (MIL) Holy Hill, WI St. Mary of the Hill Church; [P] Holy Hill, WI Discalced Carmelite Monastery.
Alexander, Jim *s.c.j.* '44 (MIL) [P] Franklin, WI Villa Maria.
Alexander, John D. *s.j.* (NY) [HH] New York, NY Brooklyn Prep Alumni Association.
Alexander, John D. *s.j.* '54 (NY) [DD] New York, NY Jesuit Community at Fordham University.
Alexander, Jon *o.p.* '86 (PRO) [P] Providence, RI St. Thomas Aquinas Priory at Providence College.
Alexander, Joseph J. '73 (LAF) Eunice, LA St. Anthony of Padua Church.
Alexander, Marc R. '85 (HON) [13] Honolulu, HI Sacred Heart Church; [16] Honolulu, HI St. Pius X Church.
Alexandrunas, Albert *o.f.m.cap.* '65 (WH) Belle, WV St. John Church; [M] Charleston, WV Capuchins-St. Anthony Friary.
Alexius, Vincentius *s.v.d.* (LAF) [4] Lafayette, LA Immaculate Heart of Mary Church.
Alfaro, Juan '62 (SAT) [64] San Antonio, TX St. Rose of Lima Church.
Alfonso, San Juan *c.p.* '60 (SAC) [H] Citrus Heights, CA Christ the King Retreat.
Alia, Hyacinth (BRK) [208] Queens, NY Our Lady of the Cenacle Church; Queens, NY Jamaica Hospital - Trump Pavilion.
Alicea, Adrian (BRK) [15] Brooklyn, NY St. Barbara Church.
Alicea, Adrian *s.s.s.* '90 (CGS) [5] Caguas, PR Santisimo Sacramento Church.
Alicea, Luis Antonio '96 (CGS) Maunabo, PR San Isidor Labrador Church.
Alilonu, Augustine '00 (FAR) Rugby, ND St. Therese, Little Flower Church.
Alisauskas, Peter J. '43 (SCR) Retired.
Alkire, Thomas *o.carm.* '63 (JOL) [J] Darien, IL Carmelite Provincial Office.
Alkire, Timothy M. '85 (LFT) [3] Lafayette, IN St. Boniface Church.
Allaire, Barry J. '61 (BUF) [D] Olean, NY Archbishop Walsh High School.
Allaire, Barry J. '72 (BUF) Hinsdale, NY St. Helen Church.
Allaire, Robert A. '61 (PRO) Absent on Leave.
Allala, Patrick Nicanda '94 (CLV) [7] Akron, OH St. Hilary Church.
Allanach, Robert C. *o.m.i.* '80 (NO) [K] New Orleans, LA Boys Hope; [S] New Orleans, LA Jesuit Program for Living and Learning of New Orleans, Inc.
Allard, George L. '60 (PRO) [2] West Warwick, RI Christ the King Church.
Allard, Msgr. John C. '75 (PRO) [1] Woonsocket, RI St. Agatha Church; [11] Woonsocket, RI Precious Blood Church.
Allard, John E. *o.p.* '86 (BO) [W] Dover, MA St. Stephen Priory; [Y] Dover, MA St. Stephen Priory Spiritual Life Center.
Allard, Marcel M. '65 (MAN) [13] Manchester, NH Our Lady of Perpetual Help Church.
Allega, Ernest (WOR) South Barre, MA St. Thomas-A-Becket Church.
Allegra, John Christopher '70 (L) [3] Springfield, KY Holy Trinity Church; [M] St. Catharine, KY Sansbury Care Center.
Allegretto, William M. *c.m.* '85 (BUF) [C] Niagara University, NY Niagara University; [O] Niagara University, NY Vincentian Community at Niagara University; [R] Alfred, NY Campus Ministry.
Alleman, Msgr. C. J. '49 (GAL) Retired.
Allen, A. Christopher '81 (PMB) Stuart, FL St. Joseph Church.
Allen, Charles H. *s.j.* '73 (BGP) [B] Fairfield, CT Fairfield University; [P] Fairfield, CT The Fairfield Jesuit Community-Fairfield University.
Allen, David (DEN) [32] Denver, CO St. James Church.
Allen, David E. '78 (BR) [13] Baton Rouge, LA St. Jude the Apostle Church.
Allen, David G. *s.j.* '79 (BAL) [S] Baltimore, MD Jesuit Fathers and Brothers Maryland Provincial Curia.
Allen, Donald L. *m.m.* '69 (NY) [DD] Maryknoll, NY Maryknoll Fathers and Brothers; [GG] New York, NY University Apostolate.
Allen, Edward A. *s.s.c.* '30 (FgM) St. Columban's Foreign Mission.
Allen, Francis J. *s.m.m.* '51 (RVC) [M] Bay Shore, NY Montfort Missionaries.
Allen, Francis R. *s.j.* '56 (BGP) [P] Fairfield, CT The Fairfield Jesuit Community-Fairfield University.
Allen, Frederick J. *m.m.* '65 (NY) [DD] Maryknoll, NY Maryknoll Fathers and Brothers.
Allen, James *o.m.i.* '68 (MIA) Miramar, FL St. Stephen Church.
Allen, John Andrew '90 (CHL) Gastonia, NC St. Michael Church.
Allen, John G. '70 (HBG) [7] Harrisburg, PA St. Margaret Mary Alacoque Church.
Allen, Joseph '53 (FAR) Veseleyville, ND St. Luke Church.
Allen, Joseph A. '53 (BIS) On Duty Outside the Diocese.
Allen, Joseph A. '53 (GR) Retired.

Allen, Joseph C. '50 (BIR) Athens, AL St. Paul's Church.
Allen, Joseph P. *o.p.* '67 (Y) [13] Youngstown, OH St. Dominic's Church.
Allen, Joseph P. '91 (CHI) Other Assignments.
Allen, Joseph P. '91 (SFD) Arcola, IL St. John the Baptist Church.
Allen, Loren '94 (SR) Eureka, CA St. Bernard Church.
Allen, Michael '71 (EVN) [18] Evansville, IN St. Joseph Church; [21] Evansville, IN St. Theresa Church.
Allen, Peter A. '71 (RVC) Cutchogue, NY Sacred Heart Church.
Allen, Philip J. '58 (WCH) Aleppo, KS Immaculate Conception Church; Garden Plain, KS St. Anthony Church.
Allen, Philip T. '59 (OG) Redford, NY Assumption of the B.V.M. Church.
Allen, Msgr. Richard F. '56 (CHL) Retired.
Allen, Richard J. '70 (SP) [3] Largo, FL St. Matthew Church.
Allen, Richard J. '97 (E) [16] Erie, PA St. George Church.
Allen, Richard L. '61 (GB) Neenah, WI St. Gabriel Church.
Allen, S. William *f.s.s.p.* '90 (SCR) [M] Elmhurst, PA Priestly Fraternity of St. Peter (F.S.S.P.), North American District Headquarters.
Allen, Shawn '99 (BO) [1] Arlington, MA St. Agnes Church.
Allen, Terry E. '61 (ALX) Pineville, LA Sacred Heart Church.
Allende, Santiago Rivera '83 (MGZ) Moca, PR Our Lady of Monserrate Church.
Allender, Raymond P. *s.j.* '75 (SJ) [D] San Jose, CA Bellarmine College Preparatory.
Allender, Thomas G. *s.j.* '71 (SJ) [L] Los Gatos, CA Sacred Heart Jesuit Center.
Aller, Domingo *o.s.a.* '61 (SJN) [A] Bayamon, PR Bayamon Central University.
Allessandro, Michael J. '44 (NY) [127] Bronx, NY St. Anthony Church.
Alletto, Nicholas P. '45 (ROC) Retired.
Alleyne, Msgr. Edward D. '60 (CAM) [6] Cherry Hill, NJ Queen of Heaven Church.
Allgaier, Rob A. '98 (OM) Norfolk, NE Sacred Heart Church.
Allgaier, Sebastian *o.s.b.* '99 (KC) [A] Conception, MO Conception Seminary College; [J] Conception, MO Conception Abbey.
Alliata, Peter R. '61 (WDC) Mount Rainier, MD St. James Church.
Allie, Robert *o.m.i.* '51 (STP) [27] St. Paul, MN St. Mary Church; St. Paul, MN St. Paul-Ramsey Hospital; St. Paul, MN Gillette Children's Hospital.
Allie, Stanley J. '58 (ALB) On Duty Outside the Diocese.
Alliegro, Msgr. Michael J. '73 (MET) East Brunswick, NJ St. Bartholomew Church; [N] Metuchen, NJ The Catholic Lawyers Guild of the Diocese of Metuchen, Inc.
Allin, R. Benedict *o.s.b.* '67 (STL) [1] Creve Coeur, MO St. Anselm Church; [P] St. Louis, MO The Abbey of St. Mary and St. Louis.
Alling, James '92 (PHX) Kingman, AZ St. Mary's Church.
Allison, Msgr. Bruce '61 (E) [C] Erie, PA Cathedral Preparatory School; [C] Erie, PA Cathedral Preparatory School.
Allison, Bruce R. '61 (E) [9] Erie, PA Our Lady of Mt. Carmel Church.
Allison, Jeffrey *c.s.c.* '96 (AUS) [13] Austin, TX St. Ignatius Martyr Church.
Allison, Joseph C. '56 (CIN) Retired.
Allison, Michael P. '91 (E) [4] Erie, PA Holy Rosary Church.
Allman, Mark '96 (ALB) Leave of Absence.
Allman, Matthew T. *c.ss.r.* '00 (FgM) Redemptorist Foreign Missions.
Allmaras, Alfred '59 (FAR) Retired.
Allt, John F. '73 (TUC) [17] Tucson, AZ St. Joseph Church.
Almade, Frank D. '78 (PIT) [P] Allison Park, PA The Sisters of Divine Providence; [S] Pittsburgh, PA Christ Child Society of Pittsburgh.
Almagno, R. Stephen *o.f.m.* '65 (PIT) [60] Pittsburgh, PA St. Pamphilus Church.
Almarza, Juan *o.a.r.* '65 (LSC) Anthony, NM St. Anthony's Church.
Almasy, Alcuin M. *o.s.b.* '60 (TUC) [F] St. David, AZ Holy Trinity Monastery.
Almazan, Humberto *m.s.a.* '66 (NOR) [F] Cromwell, CT Society of the Missionaries of the Holy Apostles.
Almazan, Jose A. *c.m.* '63 (CC) Gregory, TX Immaculate Conception Church.
Almeida, George F. '65 (FR) [4] Swansea, MA Our Lady of Fatima Church.
Almendra, Leoncio T. '60 (NOR) Retired.
Almendras, Joel '75 (MRY) Soledad, CA Correctional Training Facility; Special Assignment.
Alminde, Joseph M. *s.j.* '62 (OAK) [N] Berkeley, CA Jesuit Community at Jesuit School of Theology at Berkeley.
Almodovar, Ivan *o.p.* '88 (SJN) [8] Bayamon, PR Invencion de la Santa Cruz Church.
Almonte, Alfred P. *c.s.* '61 (PRO) [4] Johnston, RI St. Rocco Church.
Almonte, Antonio '97 (NY) [53] New York, NY Incarnation Church.
Almy, Augustin '74 (BRK) [109] Brooklyn, NY Our Lady of Refuge Church.
Alonso, Armando '90 (MIA) [33] Miami, FL St. Timothy Church.
Alonso, Ignacio *c.m.* (SJN) [47] San Juan, PR Nuestra Senora del Pilar Church.
Alonso, Jose A. *l.c.* '64 (PRO) [U] Smithfield, RI Domus Mariae Formation Center ("Mater Ecclesiae").
Alonso, Msgr. Jose A. '68 (PAT) Absent on Leave.
Alonso, Jose Luis *o.p.* '61 (PCE) Yauco, PR Holy Rossary Church; [B] Ponce, PR The Pontifical Catholic University of Puerto Rico.
Alonso, Oscar *sch.p.* '68 (MIA) [C] Fort Lauderdale, FL Cardinal Gibbons High School.
Alonso, Santiago '50 (ELP) [35] El Paso, TX San Antonio Church.
Alookaran, Charles '90 (NEW) Scotch Plains, NJ Immaculate Heart of Mary Church.
Alookaran, Joy '80 (NEW) Scotch Plains, NJ St. Bartholomew Church.
Alosanaya, Michael *s.j.* '74 (BO) [W] Chestnut Hill, MA The Jesuit Community at Boston College.
Alphonse, Anthony '92 (TYL) Paris, TX Our Lady of Victory Church.
Alphonso, John '68 (DAL) [G] Dallas, TX St. Paul Medical Center.
Alsola, Felix '86 (DET) [H] Southfield, MI Providence Hospital.
Alt, Clement *c.pp.s.* '51 (CIN) [B] Carthagena, OH St. Charles.
Alt, Kenneth G. *c.pp.s.* '78 (CIN) Fort Recovery, OH St. Peter Church; St. Anthony, OH St. Anthony Church.
Altamira, Francisco *m.sp.s.* '39 (LA) [3] Oxnard, CA Our Lady of Guadalupe Church.
Altavilla, Philip A. '92 (SCR) Taylor, PA Immaculate Conception Church.
Altavista, Salvatore D. *m.s.* '64 (HRT) [M] Hartford, CT Missionaries of LaSalette, Provincial Secretary.
Altenbaugh, Richard L. '60 (PT) [9] Pensacola, FL St. John the Evangelist Church.
Altermatt, Gregory M. '76 (HRT) [1] West Haven, CT Our Lady of Victory Church; [I] New Haven, CT Hospital of St. Raphael.
Althoff, Arthur J. '55 (STL) Retired.
Altier, Robert J. '89 (STP) [12] St. Paul, MN St. Agnes Church.
Altine, Richard L. '95 (KAL) Byron Center, MI St. Mary's Visitation Church.
Altman, David *o.c.s.o.* '79 (SLC) [F] Huntsville, UT Abbey of Our Lady of the Holy Trinity of the Order of Cistercians.
Altman, Joseph W. '76 (CHI) Harvey, IL Ascension-St. Susanna Church.
Altmann, George '44 (BAL) Retired.
Altmann, Robert T. '62 (LC) Middle Ridge, WI St. Peter Church; Saint Joseph Ridge, WI St. Joseph Church.
Altrui, Ronald '81 (NY) Absent on Sick leave.
Altrui, Ronald P. '81 (NY) [DD] New York, NY Our Lady of Consolation Residence.
Altstock, Edward D. '59 (P) [N] Gold Hill, OR St. Rita's Retreat Center.
Altuna, Javier *s.j.* '66 (LA) Inglewood, CA St. John Chrysostom Church.
Alukal, Jos *c.m.i.* '75 (BEA) [8] Beaumont, TX St. Pius X Church; Beaumont, TX Memoral Hermann Baptist Hospital.
Alvar, Zosimo C., Jr. '89 (SFR) [45] San Francisco, CA St. Peter Church; San Francisco, CA San Francisco General Hospital.
Alvarado, Felix E. '90 (PCE) [B] Ponce, PR The Pontifical Catholic University of Puerto Rico.
Alvarado, John Paul '88 (MET) South Plainfield, NJ Sacred Heart Church.
Alvarado, Robert *c.m.f.* '39 (SAT) [12] San Antonio, TX Immaculate Heart of Mary Church.
Alvarado, Roberto '89 (ELP) [23] El Paso, TX St. Francis Xavier Church; Kermit, TX St. Thomas & St. Joseph Church.
Alvares, Augustine '50 (P) Retired.
Alvarez, Abel *o.s.a.* '58 (NY) [49] New York, NY Holy Rosary Church; Bronx, NY Lincoln Medical and Mental Health Center.
Alvarez, Antonio M. '93 (MET) [3] New Brunswick, NJ Our Lady of Mt. Carmel Church.
Alvarez, Armando '72 (SJN) [45] San Juan, PR Ntra. Sra. del Perpetuo Socorro Church.
Alvarez, Eduardo *s.j.* '74 (MIA) [D] Miami, FL Belen Jesuit Preparatory School; [H] Miami, FL Villa Javier.
Alvarez, Fred *s.a.* '61 (NY) [DD] Garrison, NY Franciscan Friars of the Atonement.
Alvarez, Isaias *o.s.a.* '76 (SJN) [42] San Juan, PR Ntra. Sra. de la Monserrate Church.
Alvarez, Javier *o.f.m.* '98 (SJ) [18] San Jose, CA Our Lady of Guadalupe Church.
Alvarez, John J. '81 (STL) [Q] Kirkwood, MO Prelature of the Holy Cross and Opus Dei.
Alvarez, Miguel *sch.p.* '61 (PCE) [4] Ponce, PR Our Lady of Mt. Carmel Church.
Alvarez, Miguel '97 (ORG) Brea, CA St. Angela Merici Church.
Alvarez, Milton *c.m.f.* '77 (ATL) Stone Mountain, GA Corpus Christi Church.
Alvarez, Pablo D. *f.s.s.p.* '86 (PCE) On Duty Outside the Diocese.
Alvarez, Perfecto *o.s.a.* '52 (PCE) [15] Ponce, PR Church of the Sacred Heart; [B] Ponce, PR The Pontifical Catholic University of Puerto Rico; [D] Ponce, PR Home for Aged and Infirm.
Alvarez, Pompilio '60 (NY) [130] Bronx, NY St. Athanasius Church.
Alvarez, Porfirio '69 (LA) [25] Los Angeles, CA Our Lady of Guadalupe Church.
Alvarez, Ramon (DAL) [N] Dallas, TX Cathedral Preservation Fund, Inc.
Alvarez, Ramon '82 (DAL) [1] Dallas, TX Cathedral-Santuario de Guadalupe Church.
Alvarez, Victor *s.s.p.* '83 (CHI) [A] Mundelein, IL University of St. Mary of the Lake-Mundelein Seminary.
Alvarez, Xavier '73 (AMA) Absent on Leave.
Alvarez-Garcia, Julio '75 (WDC) Piscataway, MD St. Mary Church.
Alvernaz, Dennis M. '71 (FRS) Yosemite National Park, CA Our Lady of the Snows Church.
Alves, Elvio Nery *c.s.sp.* '99 (GAL) [69] Houston, TX St. Philip Neri Church.
Alves, Eugene L. '61 (BO) [2] Gloucester, MA Our Lady of Good Voyage Church.
Alves, Francis *s.j.* '95 (WDC) [M] Washington, DC The Jesuit Community at Georgetown University.
Alves, Msgr. Joseph T. '53 (BO) Senior Priests.
Alves, Ronald *c.m.f.* '72 (FRS) [8] Fresno, CA St. Anthony Mary Claret Church.
Alvey, J. Paul '53 (SC) Retired.
Alvey, Leonard J. '58 (OWN) Non-Parochial Assignments; [A] Owensboro, KY Brescia University.
Alwell, Juniper *o.f.m.conv.* '56 (NY) [B] Staten Island, NY St. Francis Friary.
Alzate, Alberto '77 (LAV) [6] Las Vegas, NV St. Anne Church.
Alzugaray, Msgr. Joseph '67 (SR) Petaluma, CA St. James Church.
Amabile, Patsy C. '73 (CAM) [2] Vineland, NJ Sacred Heart Church.
Amadeo, Michael A. '92 (DM) Elkhart, IA St. Mary/Holy Cross Church; On Special Assignment.
Amadi, Dominic U. '73 (RVC) Deer Park, NY SS. Cyril and Methodius Church.
Amador, Alfonso *c.ss.r.* (CGS) Fajardo, PR Santiago Apostol Church.
Amaechi, Jerome '94 (SY) North Syracuse, NY St. Rose of Lima Church.
Amaldoss, '78 (NO) Pointe a la Hache, LA St. Thomas Church.
Amalfitano, Joseph A. '63 (PH) Marcus Hook, PA Immaculate Conception Church.
Amaliri, Paul O. '00 (TLS) Broken Arrow, OK St. Benedict Church.
Amalraj, Loyola (MIL) [N] Wauwatosa, WI St. Camillus Health Center, Inc.
Aman, Gerald W. *s.j.* '73 (FgM) Provinces.
Amanchukwu, Emeka Godfrey '88 (NY) Amenia, NY Immaculate Conception Church.
Amandolare, Msgr. Ronald A. '61 (PAT) Chatham, NJ St. Patrick's Church.
Amann, John J. '66 (BRK) [161] Queens, NY St. Catherine of Sienna Church.
Amann, Msgr. Robert A. '50 (CIN) Retired.
Amann, Steven J. '74 (MIL) New Berlin, WI St. Elizabeth Ann Seton Church.
Amann, William '54 (ROC) [34] Rochester, NY Our Lady of Lourdes Church.
Amann, William '61 (ROC) Retired.
Amantegui, Carmelo *s.j.* '53 (NY) [152] Bronx, NY St. Jerome's Church.
Amanzeh, Augustine '74 (SAT) San Antonio, TX San Antonio State Hospital.
Amar, Joseph P. '74 (FTW) [B] Notre Dame, IN University of Notre Dame Du Lac.
Amar, Joseph P. '74 (SAM) On Duty Outside the Diocese.
Amar, Mubarak Anwar '91 (PEO) Depue, IL St. Mary's Church.
Amaral, Angelo '91 (TR) Keansburg, NJ St. Ann Church.
Amaral, Stephen P. '78 (PRO) Coventry, RI Our Lady of Czenstochowa Church.
Amarillas, Thomas R. *m.m.* '68 (FgM) Maryknoll Foreign Missions.
Amaro, Arlindo A. *c.s.sp.* '56 (PRO) [4] Pawtucket, RI Immaculate Heart of Mary Church.
Amasekera, Giles '73 (AUS) Killeen, TX St. Joseph Church.

Amato, Antonio '61 (PRT) Mechanic Falls, ME Our Lady of Ransom Church.
Amato, Benet *o.s.b.* '79 (IND) Cannelton, IN St. Michael Church; Tell City, IN St. Paul Church; Troy, IN St. Pius Church; [J] St. Meinrad, IN St. Meinrad Archabbey.
Amato, Frank *s.a.c.* '88 (BRK) [110] Brooklyn, NY Our Lady of the Rosary of Pompeii Church.
Amato, Joseph '59 (ALB) Retired.
Amato, Msgr. Nicholas P. '70 (BAL) Parkton, MD Our Lady of Grace Church.
Amato, Salvatore '69 (BRK) [233] Queens, NY Resurrection-Ascension Church.
Amberger, Frank '96 (CIN) [11] Dayton, OH St. Henry Church.
Ambert, Jorge *s.j.* '66 (SJN) [22] San Juan, PR San Ignacio de Loyola Church; [D] San Juan, PR Renovacion Conyugal.
Ambosta, Dawson '75 (NY) Bronxville, NY St. Joseph Church.
Ambre, John T. '75 (GRY) [14] Gary, IN St. Mark Church; [N] Gary, IN Indiana University Northwest.
Ambrogi, James J. '64 (PH) Malvern, PA St. Patrick Church.
Ambrose, (STN) [A] Eagle Harbor, MI Skete of Holy Transfiguration Monastery.
Ambrose, Arubraj (CHI) [J] Chicago, IL Holy Cross Hospital.
Ambrose, C. '88 (NY) Mamaroneck, NY St. Vito Church.
Ambrose, Malcolm '72 (LA) Santa Clarita, CA Our Lady of Perpetual Help Church.
Ambrosio, Joseph '74 (NEW) [28] Newark, NJ Our Lady of Mt. Carmel Church.
Ambrosy, David J. '85 (DUB) [1] Cedar Rapids, IA Immaculate Conception Church.
Ameche, William A. *s.j.* '81 (FgM) Provinces.
Amedee, Francis '48 (HT) Retired.
Amedzi, Emmanuel K. '94 (CLV) [9] Akron, OH St. John the Baptist Church.
Ameling, Richard H. '66 (GRY) [2] Michigan City, IN Notre Dame Church.
Amen, Maurice *c.s.c.* '61 (FTW) [J] Notre Dame, IN Congregation of Holy Cross, Midwest Province.
Amen, Maurice E. *c.s.c.* '61 (FTW) [J] South Bend, IN Congregation of Holy Cross, Indiana Province, Provincial House.
Amengual, Miguel '46 (LA) Retired.
Ament, Richard J. '66 (DUB) [4] Cedar Rapids, IA St. Jude Church.
Ament, Robert J. '52 (DUB) Retired.
Amerando, Gerald '84 (FRS) [10] Fresno, CA St. Helen Church.
Amerando, Jerry '84 (FRS) On Special Assignment.
Amershek, Charles M., Jr. '75 (ALT) [8] Johnstown, PA St. Rochus Church.
Ames, Gregory K. '86 (DEN) Greeley, CO St. Peter Church; [P] Greeley, CO University of Northern Colorado (Greeley).
Ames, John J. '82 (PH) Conshohocken, PA St. Matthew Church.
Amesse, Michael *o.m.i.* '84 (NO) [1] New Orleans, LA St. Louis Church; [17] New Orleans, LA Our Lady of Guadalupe /International Shrine of St. Jude Church.
Amey, Robert G. '69 (WDC) [4] Silver Spring, MD St. Catherine Laboure Church.
Amezaga, Louis (LSC) Absent On Leave.
Amezcua, Pedro E. '86 (LA) [16] Los Angeles, CA Immaculate Conception Church.
Amico, Alexander D. '73 (E) Coalport, PA St. Basil the Great Church.
Amico, Charles R. '52 (BUF) [A] East Aurora, NY Christ the King Seminary.
Amico, Francis A. *c.s.b.* '75 (GAL) [Q] Sugar Land, TX Basilian Mission Center.
Amico, Nicholas H. '51 (DET) Oak Park, MI Our Lady of Fatima Church.
Amico, Msgr. Richard S. '60 (BUF) [5] Niagara Falls, NY St. Joseph Church.
Amidon, Philip R. *s.j.* '74 (OM) [23] Omaha, NE St. John Church; [K] Omaha, NE Jesuit Community at Creighton University.
Amiot, Ronald J. *s.j.* '78 (BO) [W] Weston, MA Campion Jesuit Community; [W] Weston, MA Campion Health Center, Inc.
Amiro, Raymond M. '43 (SFE) Retired.
Amissah, Kofi '79 (ALB) [6] Albany, NY St. George Church.
Ammering, Bruce '54 (ROC) Retired.
Ammering, Bruce F. '54 (ROC) [8] Rochester, NY Blessed Sacrament Church.
Ammerling, Bruce (ROC) [J] Rochester, NY St. Joseph Convent Infirmary.
Ammonpantana, John Wirach *c.ss.r.* (NY) [150] Bronx, NY Immaculate Conception Church.
Amo, Steven C. '92 (SPR) [16] Springfield, MA St. Mary's Church.
Amora, Silvano '77 (TR) Tuckerton, NJ St. Teresa Church.
Amoros, Juan Maria *o.carm.* '55 (MGZ) Anasco, PR St. Anthony Abbot Church.
Amos, Msgr. James '54 (PT) [3] Pensacola, FL Holy Spirit Church; [E] Tallahassee, FL Casa Calderon, Inc.
Amos, Msgr. John R. '73 (MOB) Mon Luis Island, AL St. Rose of Lima Church.
Amos, Martin J. '68 (CLV) Shaker Heights, OH St. Dominic Church.
Amponsah, Peter (BEL) Carterville, IL Church of the Holy Spirit.
Amponsah, Peter '89 (BEL) Carbondale, IL St. Francis Xavier Church.
Amrhein, Peter T. '48 (MIL) Retired; [N] Wauwatosa, WI St. Camillus Health Center, Inc.
Amrhein, Quentin *c.p.* '53 (HRT) [M] West Hartford, CT Holy Family Monastery/Retreat.
Amrhein, Raphael *c.p.* '62 (PMB) [H] North Palm Beach, FL Our Lady of Florida Spiritual Center.
Amrhein, Robert *o.f.m.conv.* '62 (SY) [2] Syracuse, NY Assumption B.V.M. Church; Syracuse, NY St. Joseph's Hospital Health Center.
Amritharaj, Andrews '90 (OAK) [1] Berkeley, CA St. Ambrose Church.
Amsberry, John '95 (P) [17] Portland, OR Holy Redeemer Church.
Amul, Salagunla Xavier '91 (NY) [1] New Rochelle, NY Blessed Sacrament Church.
Amundsen, Robert L. '69 (DEN) [3] Fort Collins, CO John XXIII University Church; [P] Fort Collins, CO Colorado State University (Fort Collins).
Amy, Msgr. Peter L. '64 (LA) Sylmar, CA St. Didacus Church.
Amyot, Andrew J. '64 (OG) Norfolk, NY Visitation of the B.V.M. Church.
An, Andrew (ROC) [6] Rochester, NY St. Anthony of Padua Church.
An, Dominic G. (NEW) Demarest, NJ St. Joseph Church.
An Ninh, Vincent Nguyen '71 (DET) [4] Eastpointe, MI Our Lady of Grace Vietnamese Church.
Anable, Richard J. *s.j.* '45 (PAT) [I] Morristown, NJ Loyola House of Retreats.
Anadore, Msgr. Charles E. '50 (BO) [1] Milton, MA St. Agatha Church; Senior Priests.
Anaele, Ignatius I. '98 (CHI) Calumet City, IL St. Victor Church.
Anaeto, Dominic (SFD) [2] Decatur, IL Our Lady of Lourdes Church.
Anandappa, Mahendra *s.s.s.* '85 (CC) [7] Corpus Christi, TX Our Lady of the Rosary Church.
Anania, Alexis *o.f.m.* '58 (PIT) [60] Pittsburgh, PA St. Pamphilius Church.
Anastasia, Thomas '91 (SP) Pinellas Park, FL Sacred Heart Church.
Anastasio, Thomas '58 (BRK) [115] Brooklyn, NY St. Patrick Church.
Ancharski, John J. '83 (TUC) Solomon, AZ Our Lady of Guadalupe Church; Safford, AZ Conservation Center; Fort Grant Rural Station, AZ Fort Grant Training Center; Solomon, AZ Our Lady of Guadalupe.
Ancheril, Jose '86 (BEL) Stonefort, IL St. Francis de Sales Church; Vienna, IL St. Paul Church.
Ancona, Msgr. Gaspar F. '63 (GR) Byron Center, MI St. Sebastian's Church.
Anctil, Leo '43 (SUP) Retired.
Anctil, Peter Claude *o.s.b.* '67 (BUR) [E] Weston, VT Priory of Benedictine Monks.
Andalikiewicz, Charles '58 (KCK) [6] Kansas City, KS Sacred Heart Church; [12] Kansas City, KS St. John the Evangelist Church.
Andary, Edward J. '69 (PBL) Ignacio, CO St. Ignatius Church.
Andary, John S. '51 (SAM) Retired.
Andary, Thomas M. '41 (MAR) Retired.
Andel, David '95 (SB) On Duty Outside the Diocese.
Anderl, Henry *o.s.b.* '45 (SCL) [I] Collegeville, MN St. John's Abbey, of the Order of St. Benedict.
Anderlonis, Msgr. Joseph J. *s.t.d.* '69 (PH) [50] Philadelphia, PA St. George Church.
Anders, Arnold (CC) Retired.
Anders, Arnold '50 (VIC) Absent on Sick Leave.
Anders, Arnold '88 (CC) [F] Corpus Christi, TX Mount Carmel Home.
Anderson, Alexander R. '75 (STL) Eureka, MO Sacred Heart Church.
Anderson, Anthony *s.o.l.t.* '91 (CC) [H] Robstown, TX Society of Our Lady of the Most Holy Trinity; [J] Corpus Christi, TX Our Lady of Corpus Christi Catholic Undergraduate Liberal Arts.
Anderson, Arthur *o.f.m.* '83 (CHI) [N] Chicago, IL St. Joseph Interprovincial Post-Novitiate Formation House.
Anderson, Arthur C. '62 (RVC) Brookville, NY St. Paul the Apostle Church.
Anderson, Arthur T. '58 (CAM) [9] Camden, NJ Sacred Heart Church; [H] Camden, NJ Our Lady of Lourdes Medical Center, Inc.
Anderson, Basil J. *o.s.b.* '54 (MIL) [P] Benet Lake, WI St. Benedict's Abbey.
Anderson, Bentley *s.j.* '96 (NO) [C] New Orleans, LA Loyola University New Orleans.
Anderson, Bertil J. '74 (PRO) [8] Warwick, RI St. Rita Church.
Anderson, Daniel J. *o.f.m.* '76 (CIN) [M] Cincinnati, OH Pleasant Street Friary.
Anderson, David '83 (STN) Ukiah, CA Ukrainian Catholic Church.
Anderson, David *s.j.* '97 (FBK) Nightmute, AK Our Lady of Perpetual Help Church.
Anderson, David J. *s.j.* '97 (FBK) Toksook Bay, AK St. Peter the Fisherman Church; Tununak, AK St. Joseph Church; [E] St. Marys, AK Brother Joe Prince Jesuit Community.
Anderson, Emil '64 (E) Retired.
Anderson, Ernie '82 (B) Twin Falls, ID St. Edward The Confessor Church; [F] Twin Falls, ID College of Southern Idaho.
Anderson, Gabriel C. '89 (DUB) Urbana, IA St. Mary Church; Walker, IA Sacred Heart Church.
Anderson, George M. *s.j.* '73 (NY) [80] New York, NY Nativity Church.
Anderson, Gregory H. *o.p.* '47 (SFR) [14] San Francisco, CA St. Dominic Church; [N] San Francisco, CA St. Dominic Priory.
Anderson, James *m.s.a.* '77 (NOR) [F] Cromwell, CT Society of the Missionaries of the Holy Apostles.
Anderson, Msgr. James '78 (GAL) [74] Houston, TX St. Rose of Lima Church.
Anderson, Joe *o.s.b.* (LSC) Special Assignment.
Anderson, Msgr. John '62 (FAR) [E] Fargo, ND Riverview Place.
Anderson, John C. '59 (PEO) Special Assignment; [L] Peoria, IL St. Joseph's Home of Peoria; [M] Henry, IL Christ the King Retreat Center - Diocese of Peoria.
Anderson, John C. '93 (SUP) Hawkins, WI St. Mary of Czestowchowa Church; Ladysmith, WI Our Lady of Sorrows Church; Tony, WI St. Anthony de Padua Church.
Anderson, John D. '62 (FAR) Retired.
Anderson, John E. '66 (LSC) [2] Las Cruces, NM Holy Cross Church.
Anderson, John F. '50 (CLV) Chesterland, OH St. Anselm Church; Retired.
Anderson, John R. '96 (ATL) Buford, GA Prince of Peace Church.
Anderson, Msgr. John V. (DEN) [12] Denver, CO Holy Ghost Church.
Anderson, Msgr. John V. '52 (DEN) [1] Denver, CO Cathedral of the Immaculate Conception.
Anderson, Jordan S. *o.praem.* '96 (ORG) [D] Silverado, CA St. Michael's College Preparatory High School; [I] Silverado, CA Norbertine Fathers of Orange Inc.
Anderson, Joseph G. '63 (MIL) New Berlin, WI Holy Apostles Church.
Anderson, Joseph W. '62 (PEO) [2] La Salle, IL St. Hyacinth's Church.
Anderson, Jude *o.s.b.* '94 (B) [C] Jerome, ID Monastery of the Ascension.
Anderson, Kenneth J. '87 (RCK) Dixon, IL St. Anne Church.
Anderson, Kenneth Joseph '98 (COL) [5] Columbus, OH St. Andrew Church.
Anderson, Kevin '83 (SCL) [10] St. Cloud, MN Christ Church; [L] St. Cloud, MN Newman Center, Inc.
Anderson, Knute *o.s.b.* '56 (SCL) [I] Collegeville, MN St. John's Abbey, of the Order of St. Benedict.
Anderson, Kurt J. *m.m.* '72 (FgM) Maryknoll Foreign Missions.
Anderson, Louis L. '63 (GR) [17] Grand Rapids, MI St. Mary Magdalen Church.
Anderson, Luke *s.o.cist.* '54 (ALN) [K] New Ringgold, PA Cistercian Conventual Priory, St. Mary's Priory.
Anderson, Msgr. Marcel '57 (ALX) Retired.
Anderson, Michael F. '83 (STP) [15] St. Paul, MN St. Bernard Church.
Anderson, Richard W. *s.j.* '66 (CIN) [P] Milford, OH Milford Spiritual Center.
Anderson, Robert Kevin *o.c.s.o.* '55 (WOR) [N] Spencer, MA St. Joseph's Abbey.
Anderson, Robert L. *s.j.* '50 (NO) [P] New Orleans, LA Ignatius Residence.
Anderson, Robert M. *o.s.m.* '65 (CHI) [N] Chicago, IL Order of Friar Servants of Mary (Servites) United States of America Province, Inc.
Anderson, Ronald '72 (DET) Milford, MI St. Mary, Our Lady of the Snows Church.
Anderson, Ronald *s.j.* '84 (BO) [W] Chestnut Hill, MA The Jesuit Community at Boston College.
Anderson, Stephen A. '86 (E) Conneaut Lake, PA Our Lady Queen of the Americas Church.
Anderson, Terry '84 (SFS) Aberdeen, SD Sacred Heart Church.
Anderson, Thomas S. *s.j.* '98 (MIL) [P] Milwaukee, WI Jesuit Provincial Office, Wisconsin Province.
Anderson, William A. '63 (WH) Elkins, WV St. Brendan Church.
Anderson, William C. '52 (TR) Holmdel, NJ St. Benedict Church.
Anderson, William R. '42 (BO) Senior Priests.
Andert, Thomas *o.s.b.* '75 (SCL) [I] Collegeville, MN St. John's Abbey, of the Order of St. Benedict.
Andonian, Raphael *o.mech.* '65 (ARM) Boston, MA Holy

Cross Church.
Andracki, Jerome *c.r.* (CHI) [189] Chicago, IL St. Stanislaus, Bishop and Martyr Church; [J] Chicago, IL Our Lady of the Resurrection Medical Center.
Andrade, Anthony *o.s.b.* (STP) [26] St. Paul, MN St. Mark Church.
Andrade, Antonio L. '63 (BO) Hudson, MA St. Michael Church.
Andrade, Bernardino '65 (OAK) Oakley, CA St. Anthony Church.
Andrade, David M. '86 (FR) [6] Fall River, MA Holy Trinity Church.
Andrade, Joseph A. '92 (STP) St. Paul, MN United Hospitals, Inc.
Andrade, Joseph Anthony '92 (STP) [34] St. Paul, MN St. Thomas The Apostle Church.
Andrade, Richard G. '83 (FR) Absent on Leave.
Andrae, Henry C. '78 (E) Stoneboro, PA St. Columbkille Church.
Andraschko, Msgr. James '59 (SFS) [I] Sioux Falls, SD St. Mary/Holy Spirit School Endowment Trust.
Andraschko, Msgr. James F. '59 (SFS) [3] Sioux Falls, SD Holy Spirit Church.
Andre, Leonard J. '61 (MIL) Retired.
Andre, Msgr. Ludwig M. '57 (SJ) Los Altos, CA St. Simon Church.
Andreano, Michael A. '00 (NEW) Ridgewood, NJ Our Lady of Mount Carmel Church.
Andreatta, Msgr. Tullio '38 (SB) Retired.
Andree, Daniel H. *c.ss.r.* '80 (WCH) [14] Wichita, KS St. Joseph Church; [F] Wichita, KS Redemptorist Mission House.
Andree, John Paul *c.ss.r.* '68 (CHI) [133] Chicago, IL St. Michael Church; [X] Chicago, IL Co-Redemptorist Association Office.
Andrejek, Michael J. '98 (PEO) Moline, IL Sacred Heart Church; [B] Rock Island, IL Alleman High School.
Andres, James *o.f.m.cap.* (DET) [4] Clinton Twp., MI St. Ronald Church.
Andres, James R. *o.f.m.cap.* '63 (DET) [P] Washington, MI Capuchin Retreat.
Andres, Joseph P. '48 (CIN) Retired.
Andres, Juan Ramon *l.d.* '97 (PCE) [18] Ponce, PR Church Santisimo Sacramento Church.
Andres, Napoleon '85 (HON) [3] Honolulu, HI St. Anthony Church.
Andres, Timothy P. *o.carm.* '86 (JOL) [C] Joliet, IL Joliet Catholic Academy; [J] Joliet, IL St. Elias Carmelites.
Andreu, Ramon R. *s.j.* '55 (LA) [74] Los Angeles, CA St. Kevin Church.
Andrews, Alexander *o.s.b.* '69 (SCL) [I] Collegeville, MN St. John's Abbey, of the Order of St. Benedict.
Andrews, Dennis M. '65 (MIL) Brookfield, WI St. John Vianney Church.
Andrews, Dennis M. *c.s.b.* '70 (GAL) [Q] Houston, TX Residence of the Basilian Fathers of the University of St. Thomas.
Andrews, Edward *o.s.a.* (FWT) Gainesville, TX St. Mary Church.
Andrews, Edward *o.s.a.* '59 (CHI) [D] Chicago, IL St. Rita High School.
Andrews, Eric P. *c.s.p.* '95 (KNX) [4] Knoxville, TN John XXIII University Parish/Catholic Center Church; [J] Knoxville, TN UT-Knoxville, Newman Foundation, Inc.
Andrews, Gregory J. '76 (SP) [1] Clearwater, FL All Saints Church.
Andrews, John F. '62 (FR) Wellfleet, MA Our Lady of Lourdes Church.
Andrews, John S. '96 (OM) Hartington, NE Holy Trinity Church.
Andrews, Lawrence W. '78 (OG) Absent on Leave.
Andrews, Mark W. *s.j.* '92 (CHI) [N] Chicago, IL Chicago Province of the Society of Jesus-Provincial Office.
Andrews, Mark W. *s.j.* '92 (DET) [B] Berkley, MI Loyola House.
Andrews, Peter J. '88 (PRO) [4] Tiverton, RI St. Theresa Church.
Andrews, Philip *c.ss.r.* '74 (SJN) [2] San Juan, PR San Agustin Church.
Andrews, Robert F. *o.s.a.* '54 (NY) [216] Staten Island, NY Our Lady of Good Counsel Church.
Andrey, Roberto '83 (SFR) [3] South San Francisco, CA St. Augustine Church.
Andrie, Donald A. *c.s.p.* '94 (STP) [29] Minneapolis, MN St. Lawrence Church; [N] Minneapolis, MN Paulist Fathers; [V] Minneapolis, MN Newman Center at St. Lawrence.
Andriekus, Leonard *o.f.m.* '40 (PRT) [I] Kennebunkport, ME St. Anthony's Friary.
Andries, John W. '96 (ALX) Boyce, LA St. Margaret Church.
Andrietta, Reginald '83 (BAL) [62] Baltimore, MD St. Michael Church; [78] Baltimore, MD St. Patrick Church.
Andrus, Albin A. '73 (PRT) [1] Portland, ME Cathedral of the Immaculate Conception; Portland, ME Maine Medical Center.
Andrus, Charles *s.s.j.* '76 (LA) [52] Los Angeles, CA St. Brigid's Church.
Andrus, David L. *s.j.* '79 (LAF) Grand Coteau, LA St. Charles Borromeo Church.
Andrus, Richard *s.v.d.* '83 (CHI) [51] Chicago, IL St. Elizabeth Church.
Andrushkiw, Vladimir '36 (STF) Retired.
Andujar, J. Iriarte *o.p.* '86 (PRO) [P] Providence, RI St. Thomas Aquinas Priory at Providence College.
Anemelu, Charles (NEW) Berkeley Heights, NJ Runnells County Hospital.
Angadiath, Jacob '72 (CHI) Bellwood, IL Syro-Malabar Catholic Mission of the Archdiocese of Chicago Church.
Angadiath, Joseph *c.m.i.* '69 (LKC) [4] Lake Charles, LA St. Henry Church.
Angeles, Joey F. '00 (BR) [9] Baton Rouge, LA St. George Church.
Angelicchio, Paul F. '77 (SY) Fairmount, NY Holy Family Church.
Angelini, Joseph '69 (MIA) [35] Miami, FL Visitation Church.
Angelini, Joseph Barry *o.f.m. conv.* '65 (CHL) Winston-Salem, NC Our Lady of Mercy Church.
Angell, Charles *s.a.* '60 (NY) [DD] Garrison, NY Franciscan Friars of the Atonement; [DD] Garrison, NY St. Christopher's Friary.
Angella, Ludovico '47 (NY) Middletown, NY St. Joseph Church.
Angelle, Msgr. Robert G. '56 (LAF) Retired.
Angelo, Girard F. '55 (SCR) Harleigh, PA Sacred Heart of Jesus Church.
Angelo, Thomas M. '85 (NOR) On Duty Outside the Diocese; Military Chaplains.
Angeloni, Michael '75 (WIL) Ogletown, DE Holy Family Church.
Angeloni, Owen *o.f.m.* '62 (ALB) [A] Catskill, NY St. Anthony Friary.
Angelov, Kiril '89 (STF) Ludlow, MA SS. Peter and Paul Church; South Deerfield, MA Holy Ghost Church.
Angelovic, Michael '65 (SEA) Seahurst, WA St. Francis of Assisi Church.
Angelucci, Patrick *s.d.b.* '76 (FgM) Salesians of Don Bosco Foreign Missions.
Angelucci, Patrick *s.d.b.* '76 (NY) [DD] New Rochelle, NY Salesian Provincial House.
Anger, Raymond G. '57 (WOR) Retired.
Angers, Joseph *o.p.* '48 (NSH) [I] Nashville, TN St. Cecilia Convent.
Angert, James *t.o.r.* '71 (ARL) Herndon, VA St. Joseph Church.
Angi, Steven J. '85 (CIN) On Duty Outside the Archdiocese.
Angilella, Joseph T. *s.j.* '65 (SFR) [N] San Francisco, CA Jesuit Community at University of San Francisco.
Anginoli, Joseph T. '75 (PAT) Green Pond, NJ St. Simon the Apostle Church.
Angkel, Julio '83 (CI) Neepwukos, FM Holy Family Church; [C] Tunnuk, Chuuk, FM Vicariate Residence.
Angle, Camillus *t.o.r.* '54 (ALT) [F] Newry, PA St. Bernardine Monastery.
Angles, Sebastian '44 (BRK) Retired.
Angles, Sebastian '44 (ORL) Retired.
Anglim, Ronald H. '65 (CHI) Antioch, IL St. Peter Church.
Anglim, Thomas M. '54 (VEN) [5] Fort Myers, FL St. Francis Xavier Church; [F] Fort Myers, FL Villa Francisco; [K] Fort Myers, FL St. Francis Xavier School Foundation.
Anglin, John *o.f.m.* '81 (BO) [W] Boston, MA Ministry of the Word.
Angotti, Joseph A. '91 (GRY) On Duty Outside the Diocese.
Anguiano, James '66 (LA) Van Nuys, CA St. Bridget of Sweden Church.
Anguiano, James '82 (LA) [D] Mission Hills, CA Alemany High School.
Angulo, Raul '85 (MIA) [8] Miami, FL Mother of Christ Church.
Anh, Anthony *s.j.* '90 (P) [L] Portland, OR Jesuit Provincial Office (Society of Jesus, Oregon Prov.).
Anholzer, Daniel *o.f.m.cap.* '80 (SAG) [14] Saginaw, MI St. Joseph Church.
Aniban, Ives '66 (RNO) [B] Reno, NV St. Mary's Regional Medical Center.
Anich, Kenneth *s.v.d.* '73 (DUB) [B] Epworth, IA Divine Word College.
Anichini, Albert *m.c.c.j.* '62 (FgM) Comboni Foreign Missions.
Aniello, Frederick M. '79 (HRT) [13] Hartford, CT St. Luke Church.
Anifer, Jeffrey '67 (DET) Melvindale, MI St. Mary Magdalen Church.
Aniszczyk, Leon S. '73 (MET) Spotswood, NJ Immaculate Conception Church.
Ankenbrandt, Thomas F. *s.j.* '60 (DET) [P] Clarkston, MI Colombiere Center.
Ankenbrandt, Thomas W. '56 (TOL) Retired.
Anleu, Saul '92 (RIC) Amherst, VA St. Francis of Assisi Church; Lovingston, VA St. Mary Church.
Annese, Joseph P. '62 (LAV) Boulder City, NV St. Andrew's Church.
Annie, Frederick P. '78 (WH) [1] Wheeling, WV St. Joseph's Church.
Annino, Sebastian V. '61 (CAM) Rosenhayn, NJ St. Mary's Church; [I] Newfield, NJ Mater Dei Nursing Home.
Annunziato, Michael *ss.cc.* '53 (BWN) Edinburg, TX Sacred Heart Church.
Anoia, John '57 (SP) New Port Richey, FL Our Lady Queen of Peace Church.
Anoia, John '57 (SPR) Retired.
Anonuevo, Salvador '86 (NY) Pearl River, NY St. Margaret Church.
Anosike, Donatus U. *m.s.p.* '90 (GAL) [53] Houston, TX St. Nicholas Church; [T] Houston, TX Texas Southern University Catholic Newman Hall.
Anosike, Gabriel (NY) Manhattan, NY New York University Medical Center.
Anosike, Gabriel '89 (NY) [52] New York, NY Immaculate Conception Church.
Ansaldi, Msgr. Joseph C. '62 (NY) [F] New York, NY St. Joseph by the Sea, High School; [S] New York, NY Mission of the Immaculate Virgin.
Ansaloni, Edmond *o.f.m.* (SP) [O] Clearwater Beach, FL St. Paul Friary.
Ansbro, Msgr. Francis J. '51 (NY) Peekskill, NY Assumption Church.
Anschutz, Larry '82 (SFD) Mount Olive, IL Ascension Church; Mount Olive, IL Holy Trinity Church.
Anselment, Joseph '61 (ALB) Queensbury, NY Our Lady of the Annunciation Church.
Anselmi, Albert J. (ALT) West Salisbury, PA St. Michael's Church.
Anselmi, Victor J. '74 (ALN) Ringtown, PA St. Mary Church; [7] Shenandoah, PA St. Stephen Church.
Anson, Cesar '77 (TR) [2] Trenton, NJ Blessed Sacrament Church.
Anstiss, Arthur '60 (SFE) Retired.
Anta, Antonio '55 (NEW) Retired.
Antal, Andras '68 (CLV) [21] Cleveland, OH St. Elizabeth Church.
Antall, Richard C. '80 (CLV) El Salvador, C.A., OH Parroquial de Nuestra Senora de Guadalupe.
Antao, Msgr. John S. '60 (NEW) [15] Elizabeth, NJ Our Lady of Fatima Church.
Antczak, John '63 (JOL) Bradley, IL St. Joseph Church; Kankakee, IL Riverside Medical Center.
Antczak, Robert '64 (NEW) [26] Jersey City, NJ St. Paul's Church.
Antekeier, Charles R. '62 (GR) Retired.
Anthamatten, Joseph *c.pp.s.* '43 (CIN) [B] Carthagena, OH St. Charles.
Anthony, Angelo *c.pp.s.* '89 (CIN) [M] Dayton, OH Provincial Office of the Cincinnati Province of the Society of the Precious Blood.
Anthony, Joseph L. '80 (LAV) [12] Las Vegas, NV St. Joseph, Husband of Mary Church.
Anthony, Msgr. Paul G. '61 (STL) Warson Woods, MO Ste. Genevieve Du Bois Church.
Anthony, Walter *c.s.p.* '56 (NY) [DD] Jamaica Estates, NY Paulist Fathers Generalate.
Antillon, William '79 (RCK) Dundee, IL St. Catherine of Siena Church.
Antinarelli, Ronald A. '73 (ROC) Penfield, NY Holy Spirit Church.
Antipas, Douglas *o.f.m.cap.* (AGN) [F] Agana Heights, GU St. Fidelis Friary.
Antiporek, James '81 (JOL) Warrenville, IL St. Irene Church.
Antl, Louis B. *o.f.m.* '48 (JOL) [11] Joliet, IL St. John the Baptist Church; [J] Joliet, IL St. John the Baptist Friary.
Antle, Nicholas C. '59 (GAL) Retired; [N] Houston, TX St. Dominic Village.
Antoine, James *o.f.m.cap.* '67 (GF) Lodge Grass, MT Our Lady of Loretto Church.
Antolini, Vincenzo *o.m.v.* '58 (BO) [B] Boston, MA Oblate Provincialate.
Anton, Ronald J. *s.j.* '83 (BAL) [B] Baltimore, MD Loyola College in Maryland; [S] Baltimore, MD Jesuit Community of Loyola College, Inc.
Antonanzas, Msgr. Jesus R. Diez '57 (PCE) [A] Ponce, PR Diocesan Seminary.
Antoncic, Msgr. John J. '68 (BRK) [200] Queens, NY St. Mel Church.
Antonelli, Msgr. Louis '49 (CHK) Rota, MP San Isidro Church; Songsong Village, MP San Isidro Church.
Antonelli, Robert *c.s.c.* '65 (P) [B] Portland, OR University of Portland; [L] Portland, OR Holy Cross Fathers & Brothers, C.S.C. - University of Portland.
Antonellis, Joseph A. '72 (BO) [2] Revere, MA Immaculate Conception Church.
Antonicelli, Charles V. '93 (WDC) Pastoral Center Special Ministries.
Antonio, William '88 (WDC) [M] Washington, DC Oblate College/Center for Mission Studies Community.
Antonucci, Richard J. *o.praem.* '72 (PH) [AA] Philadelphia, PA St. Norbert Priory; [AA] Paoli, PA Daylesford Abbey.

Antony, Charles '70 (NY) Absent on Leave.
Antony, John K. *j.c.l.* (LR) [6] Little Rock, AR St. Edward Church; [L] Little Rock, AR The Guadalupe Prenatal Clinic.
Antony, Wilson Paul '92 (MIL) [19] Milwaukee, WI St. Catherine Church.
Antos, Paul J. '54 (ALB) [2] Watervliet, NY Immaculate Conception Church.
Antoun, Msgr. Elie '80 (SAM) Retired.
Antram, Cormac *o.f.m.* '54 (GLP) Houck, AZ St. John the Evangelist Church.
Antunez, Roy *s.j.* '71 (P) [19] Portland, OR St. Ignatius Church.
Antus, Lawrence T. *o.m.i.* '58 (DUL) Cook, MN St. Mary's Church; Orr, MN Holy Cross Church; Duluth, MN Indian Missions Church.
Antus, Roland '62 (DUL) Longville, MN St. Edward's Church.
Antweiler, Donald J. '73 (JC) St. Thomas, MO St. Thomas the Apostle Church.
Antwi-Boasiako, Dominic (VIC) Meyersville, TX SS. Peter & Paul Church.
Anuka, Damien '77 (FTW) New Haven, IN St. John the Baptist Church.
Anumudu, Alphonsus '73 (NY) [89] New York, NY Our Lady of Lourdes Church.
Anuszewski, Albert M. *o.ss.t.* '91 (WDC) [M] Hyattsville, MD St. John de Matha Monastery, Order of Most Holy Trinity.
Anuszewski, Damian *o.ss.t.* '78 (WDC) [M] Hyattsville, MD St. John de Matha Monastery, Order of Most Holy Trinity.
Anuzis, Stanislovas '83 (LA) [55] Los Angeles, CA St. Casimir Church.
Anyanwu, Celestine '83 (BRK) [170] Queens, NY St. Gabriel Church.
Anyanwu, Celestine C. '83 (RVC) Freeport, NY Our Holy Redeemer Church.
Anyanwu, Christopher '80 (NEW) [18] Jersey City, NJ St. Nicholas Church; Jersey City, NJ Christ Hospital.
Anyanwu, Innocent *c.s.sp.* '80 (PIT) Port Vue, PA St. Mark Church.
Anziano, James J. '81 (PH) [21] Philadelphia, PA St. Bartholomew Church.
Anzoategui, Francisco J. *s.x.* '88 (BO) [3] Peabody, MA St. John the Baptist Church.
Apassa, Cyril '71 (RNO) [6] Reno, NV St. Therese Church of the Little Flower.
Apel, John A. *s.j.* '69 (FgM) Provinces.
Apel, John A. *s.j.* '69 (STL) [P] St. Louis, MO Bellarmine House of Studies; [P] St. Louis, MO The Jesuits of the Missouri Province.
Apfelbeck, Keith B. '99 (LC) [3] Wausau, WI St. Anne Church.
Apfelbeck, Kurt J. '99 (LC) [4] Eau Claire, WI Sacred Heart of Jesus-St. Patrick Church; Fall Creek, WI St. Raymond of Penafort Church.
Apochi, Michael '86 (WDC) [B] Washington, DC St. Joseph's Seminary.
Apolinar, Moises '81 (LA) [7] Long Beach, CA Holy Innocents Church.
Apolinares, Jaime G. '77 (NO) [44] New Orleans, LA St. Maria Goretti Church.
Aponte, Eliud '86 (ARE) [1] Camuy, PR St. Joseph Church.
Aponte, Eliud '86 (PCE) On Duty Outside the Diocese.
Apostol, Moises '78 (RCK) Algonquin, IL St. Margaret Mary Church.
Apostoli, Andrew D. *c.f.r.* '67 (NY) [A] Yonkers, NY St. Joseph's Seminary; [DD] Yonkers, NY St. Felix Friary.
Apparcel, Gregora *c.s.p.* '83 (NY) [DD] Jamaica Estates, NY Paulist Fathers Generalate.
Appelby, Gerald J. '59 (ROC) Pittsford, NY Church of the Transfiguration.
Appelt, Francis '52 (GRY) [J] Cedar Lake, IN Our Lady of Lourdes Friary.
Appiah, John '98 (KNX) [4] Chattanooga, TN St. Stephen Church.
Appiasi, Samuel '83 (VIC) Blessing, TX St. Peter's Church.
Appicci, Richard D. *o.s.a.* '60 (FgM) Foreign Missions.
Appicci, Richard D. *o.s.a.* '60 (PH) [AA] Villanova, PA Provincial Offices of the Order of St. Augustine, Province of St. Thomas of Villanova; [AA] Villanova, PA St. Thomas Monastery.
Applegate, Gary '81 (KCK) [2] Leavenworth, KS Sacred Heart of Jesus Church; [3] Leavenworth, KS St. Casimir's Church.
Appleyard, Msgr. George '68 (SJP) Austintown, OH St. Anne Church.
Appleyard, Joseph A. *s.j.* '62 (BO) [W] Chestnut Hill, MA The Jesuit Community at Boston College.
Appuhamy, Roger '87 (TYL) Longview, TX St. Anthony Church.
Apura, Nilo '75 (TR) [4] Toms River, NJ St. Maximilian Kolbe Church.
Apuzzo, Pasquale '76 (RIC) [10] Richmond, VA St. Elizabeth Church; On Special or Other Diocesan Assignment.
Aquila, Samuel J. (DEN) [A] Denver, CO St. John Vianney Theological Seminary.
Aquino, Conrado *m.sp.s.* '00 (LA) [3] Oxnard, CA Our Lady of Guadalupe Church.
Aquino, James J. '65 (WOR) [11] Worcester, MA Our Lady of Loreto Church.
Aquino, Joe *m.s.* '69 (ORL) [2] Orlando, FL Blessed Trinity Church.
Aquino, Msgr. Oscar '64 (NY) [36] New York, NY St. Francis de Sales Church.
Aquino, Peter M. '69 (NEW) [13] Elizabeth, NJ SS. Peter and Paul's Church.
Aquwa, Jude '78 (NY) Croton Falls, NY St. Joseph Church.
Arabia, Peter K. *s.j.* '99 (BUF) [D] Buffalo, NY Canisius High School; [O] Buffalo, NY Canisius Jesuit Community.
Aracich, Anthony S. *s.j.* '67 (BRK) [105] Brooklyn, NY Shrine of Our Lady of Mount Carmel Church.
Aracil, Javier *s.d.b.* '63 (NY) [DD] New Rochelle, NY Salesian Provincial House.
Arackal, Joseph J. *v.c.* '67 (STP) Vermillion, MN St. John the Baptist Church.
Arackal, Thomas *i.m.s.* '82 (LR) Jacksonville, AR St. Jude the Apostle Church.
Arago, John J. Tobin '95 (BRK) [170] Queens, NY St. Gabriel Church.
Aragon, Ramon '50 (SFE) [9] Albuquerque, NM Our Lady of Guadalupe Church; Retired.
Aragon, Salvador *o.f.m.* '55 (SFE) Los Ojos, NM San Jose Church; Tierra Amarilla, NM Santo Nino Church.
Arambasick, Dennis *o.f.m.* '87 (PRT) [I] Kennebunkport, ME St. Anthony's Friary.
Aramburo, Eugenio '88 (MRY) Greenfield, CA Holy Trinity Church.
Aramburu, Jose A. *m.m.* '84 (NY) [DD] Maryknoll, NY Maryknoll Fathers and Brothers.
Arana, Francisco '64 (SJN) [1] Toa Baja, PR Nuestra Senora de Covadonga Church.
Arango, Fabio '66 (MIA) [G] Miami, FL Mercy Hospital.
Arango, Gilberto '75 (STO) Manteca, CA St. Anthony Church.
Arango, John J. '95 (BRK) [170] Queens, NY St. Gabriel Church.
Arango, Miguel '65 (SAT) Von Ormy, TX St. Peter the Fisherman Church.
Arango, Rafael (BO) [2] Lawrence, MA Asuncion de la Virgen Maria Church.
Aranha, George '75 (SJ) [24] San Jose, CA Church of the Transfiguration; San Jose, CA Presentation High School; [D] San Jose, CA Presentation High School.
Araque, Alvaro U. '72 (STO) [5] Stockton, CA St. Gertrude Church.
Arata, Miguel A. '95 (NEW) On Duty Outside the Archdiocese.
Araujo, Manuel *c.m.* '54 (ARE) [3] Manati, PR Sagrada Familia Church.
Araujo, Robert *s.j.* '93 (NY) [DD] New York, NY Jesuit Community at Fordham University.
Araujo, Robert J. *s.j.* '93 (BO) [W] Boston, MA The Society of Jesus of New England-Provincial Offices.
Araujo, Robert J. *s.j.* '93 (SPK) [C] Spokane, WA Gonzaga University.
Aravindassery, Antony '75 (CHI) [128] Chicago, IL St. Mary, Star of the Sea Church.
Aravindathu, Thadeus (STP) South St. Paul, MN St. John Vianney Church.
Araya-Morales, Reynord '89 (ORL) [4] Lakeland, FL St. Joseph's Church.
Arbanas, Harold P. '48 (GF) Retired.
Arbelaez, Ernesto *s.j.* '56 (SJ) [L] Los Gatos, CA Sacred Heart Jesuit Center.
Arbelaez, Ernesto *s.j.* '56 (STO) Hughson, CA St. Anthony Church.
Arbizu, Juventino '44 (NO) Retired.
Arboleda, Vidal '55 (ORL) [9] Orlando, FL St. John Vianney Church; Retired.
Arcaba, Pablito '83 (STO) [10] Stockton, CA Presentation of B.V.M. Church.
Arcamo, Msgr. Floro B. '65 (SFR) Belmont, CA St. Mark Church.
Arce, Carlos *o.f.m.conv.* '91 (R) Burlington, NC Blessed Sacrament Church; [E] Burlington, NC Conventual Franciscans.
Arce, Robert P. '64 (NY) [162] Bronx, NY St. Margaret Mary Church.
Arceneaux, Chester '92 (LAF) Abbeville, LA St. Therese of the Child Jesus Church.
Arceneaux, Jules M., II '90 (LAF) Rayne, LA St. Joseph Church.
Arceneaux, Louis A. *c.m.* '66 (LAF) [J] Grand Coteau, LA Jesuit Spirituality Center (St. Charles College).
Archambault, Donald (DET) [35] Detroit, MI Immaculate Heart of Mary Church.
Archambault, Donald '70 (DET) [26] Detroit, MI St. Gerard Church; [65] Detroit, MI Presentation-Our Lady of Victory Church.
Archambault, Msgr. Henry N. '59 (NOR) Taftville, CT Sacred Heart Church.
Archambault, James H. '67 (HRT) Retired.
Archambault, Richard *m.afr.* '73 (FgM) Missionaries of Africa Foreign Missions.
Archambault, Richard L. '55 (NOR) [G] Putnam, CT Holy Spirit Provincial House.
Archer, Arthur A. '80 (NOR) Niantic, CT St. Agnes Church.
Archer, R. R. *o.p.* '58 (KNX) Elizabethton, TN St. Elizabeth Church.
Archer, Scott '90 (PEO) Fairbury, IL St. John the Baptist Church.
Archer, W. Donald '48 (CR) Retired.
Archey, Eugene C. '40 (WOR) Retired.
Arciga, Michael '92 (KC) Leave of Absence.
Arcilesi, Leonard '89 (OWN) Rome, KY St. Martin Church.
Arcilia, M. David *o.d.c.* '93 (CHI) Mundelein, IL Santa Maria Del Popolo Church.
Arciszewski, Gilbert G. '59 (MIL) On Leave.
Arcoleo, Douglas '98 (RVC) Smithtown, NY St. Patrick Church.
Arcuri, Carmen J. '61 (COL) [30] Columbus, OH St. Mary Magdalene Church.
Arcuri, Francis A. *s.j.* '56 (MIL) [P] Wauwatosa, WI Jesuit Community at St. Camillus.
Ardagh, Brian '95 (CHI) Orland Hills, IL St. Elizabeth Seton Church.
Ardis, John B. *c.s.p.* '90 (BO) [P] Boston, MA Paulist Center; [W] Boston, MA Paulist Fathers Residence; [BB] Boston, MA Chapel of the Holy Spirit.
Ardoff, Edward J. '64 (NU) Sleepy Eye, MN St. Mary Church.
Ardolf, Paul C. '49 (STP) Norwood, MN Ascension Church.
Ardos, Msgr. George A. '59 (TR) Washington Crossing, NJ St. George Church; Trenton, NJ Mercer County Correction Center.
Arechiga, Dennis '00 (SAT) [1] San Antonio, TX Cathedral of San Fernando.
Arejola, Rodolfo '68 (AGN) Asan, GU Holy Family, Nino Perdido Church.
Arella, Msgr. Gerard J. (BRK) Retired.
Arella, Msgr. Gerard J. '54 (BRK) [79] Brooklyn, NY St. Mark's Church.
Arellano, Edgardo M. (WIL) [K] Dover, DE Secular Institute of the Two Hearts.
Arenas, Msgr. Francisco '47 (SJN) [25] San Juan, PR San Jorge Church.
Arenas, Joseph Victor '70 (NY) [199] Staten Island, NY Blessed Sacrament Church.
Arens, John F. '74 (BO) [E] Needham, MA St. Sebastian's Country Day School, Inc.
Arens, Patrick O. '00 (WIN) [2] Rochester, MN Pax Christi Church.
Arenz, James *s.j.* '65 (LA) [C] Los Angeles, CA Loyola Marymount University.
Ares, Francisco '83 (BRK) [77] Brooklyn, NY St. Malachy's Church.
Aresta, Frank *s.c.j.* '81 (MIL) [P] Hales Corners, WI Sacred Heart Monastery.
Arevalo, Joseph '65 (RVC) Huntington Station, NY St. Hugh of Lincoln Church.
Arflack, Gregory '98 (OWN) [1] Paducah, KY St. Francis de Sales Church; [2] Paducah, KY Rosary Chapel Church.
Argent, Robert W. '55 (STL) [16] St. Louis, MO Resurrection of Our Lord Church.
Argentino, Ralph J. '68 (SP) Brandon, FL Church of the Nativity.
Argue, Patrick *ss.cc.* '62 (LA) [D] Mission Hills, CA Alemany High School; [Q] Mission Hills, CA Congregation of the Sacred Hearts.
Arguelles, I. Anthony '74 (BLX) [1] Biloxi, MS Cathedral of the Nativity of the Blessed Virgin Mary .
Arguinzoniz, Francisco '54 (PCE) On Duty Outside the Diocese.
Argy, Msgr. William J. '40 (OG) [1] Ogdensburg, NY St. Mary's Church; Lisbon, NY SS. Philip and James Church; Retired.
Ariano, Msgr. Joseph W. '51 (OM) Retired.
Arias, Ariel '85 (RNO) Fallon, NV St. Patrick Church.
Arias, Guillermo *s.j.* '72 (MIA) [H] Miami, FL Villa Javier.
Arias, Guillermo *s.j.* '72 (PMB) [A] Boynton Beach, FL St. Vincent de Paul Regional Seminary.
Arias, Guillermo '73 (NEW) [2] Newark, NJ St. Patrick's Pro-Church; [7] Newark, NJ St. Augustine's Church.
Arias, Hernan '85 (PAT) [2] Passaic, NJ St. Anthony of Padua Church; Paterson, NJ Passaic County Jail.
Arias, Jesus '92 (MIA) [4] Miami, FL Epiphany Church.
Arias, Jose *o.a.r.* '60 (NEW) [N] West Orange, NJ Augustinian Recollects.
Arico, Carl '60 (NEW) [5] Bayonne, NJ St. Vincent de Paul Church.
Aridas, Christopher '73 (RVC) Selden, NY St. Margaret of Scotland Church.
Arimond, James C.L. *s.j.* '70 (CHI) [D] Chicago, IL St. Ignatius College Prep; [D] Chicago, IL St. Ignatius Jesuit Community.
Arimond, Vincent '55 (DUL) Retired.
Arinze, Paul Ugochukwu '99 (MAD) Sun Prairie, WI Sacred Hearts of Jesus and Mary Church.

Aririatu, Samuel '79 (LA) [81] Los Angeles, CA St. Mary Magdalen Church.
Arista, Gregorio *o.a.r.* '96 (NY) [FF] Bronx, NY St. Joseph's Center.
Ariza, Campo Emilio '75 (CGS) [14] Caguas, PR Divino Nino Church.
Ariza, Vicente '75 (SJN) [G] Guaynabo, PR Opus Dei.
Arizpe, Samuel '87 (BWN) San Carlos, TX St. Joseph the Worker Church.
Arizti, Fernando *s.j.* '71 (LA) [52] Los Angeles, CA St. Brigid's Church; [BB] Los Angeles, CA Archdiocesan Office for Campus Ministry.
Arkins, Michael *s.s.s.* '73 (CLV) [O] Cleveland, OH Blessed Sacrament Community.
Arkins, Michael J. *s.s.s.* '73 (CLV) Highland Heights, OH St. Paschal Baylon Church.
Arko, Richard '90 (CLV) [4] Barberton, OH St. Mary's Church.
Arle, David '84 (VEN) [1] Fort Myers, FL St. Vincent de Paul Church.
Arledge, Joseph H. '97 (OKL) Sulphur, OK St. Francis Xavier Church.
Arledge, Thaddaeus R. *o.s.b.* '56 (SEA) [L] Lacey, WA St. Martin's Abbey.
Arlotta, Jack '92 (NY) Rye, NY Resurrection Church.
Armada, Leo *c.ss.r.* '90 (NY) [23] New York, NY St. Cecilia Church.
Armaio, Robert J. '95 (BRK) [18] Brooklyn, NY St. Bernadette Church.
Armbrust, Leo F. '77 (PMB) Special Assignment.
Armbruster, Julius *o.s.b.* '42 (SFS) [F] Marvin, SD Blue Cloud Abbey.
Armell, Francisco *o.carm.* '68 (SJN) [59] San Juan, PR Santa Teresita Del Nino Jesus Church.
Armendariz, Antonio *m.sp.s.* (P) [A] Mount Angel, OR Felix Rougier House of Studies.
Armenio, Peter V. '80 (CHI) [W] Chicago, IL Prelature of the Holy Cross and Opus Dei.
Armenta, Benito '87 (LA) South El Monte, CA Epiphany Church.
Armey, Charles R. '80 (WOR) [3] Southbridge, MA Sacred Heart Church.
Arminio, Alfonse M. '61 (NEW) Military Chaplains.
Arminio, Alfonse M. '61 (TR) Little Silver, NJ Fort Monmouth.
Arminio, Thomas '81 (NEW) Retired.
Arminio, Thomas G. '81 (NEW) Woodcliff Lake, NJ Our Lady Mother of the Church.
Armistead, Msgr. John M. '71 (STO) [4] Stockton, CA St. George Church.
Armour, James E. '99 (NSH) [1] Nashville, TN Cathedral of the Incarnation; [B] Nashville, TN Father Ryan High School.
Arms, Michael M. '68 (STP) Inver Grove Heights, MN St. Patrick Church.
Armshaw, Joseph *c.ss.r.* '52 (BLX) [E] Biloxi, MS St. John Neumann Residence.
Armshaw, Msgr. Patrick J. '62 (RVC) Greenlawn, NY St. Francis of Assisi Church; [K] Bethpage, NY Central Council.
Armstrong, Christopher R. '80 (CIN) [52] Cincinnati, OH St. Louis Church; [V] Cincinnati, OH Priests Eucharistic League.
Armstrong, Daniel F. '78 (IND) Retired.
Armstrong, James L. '77 (PIT) Slippery Rock, PA St. Peter Church; [R] Pittsburgh, PA Office for Campus Ministry.
Armstrong, John F. *s.j.* '78 (NO) [C] New Orleans, LA Loyola University New Orleans.
Armstrong, John F. *s.j.* '78 (WDC) [M] Washington, DC Leonard Neale House.
Armstrong, Msgr. Peter G. '54 (SFR) Redwood City, CA St. Pius Church.
Armstrong, Regis J. *o.f.m.cap.* '67 (ROC) [I] Interlaken, NY St. Fidelis Friary.
Armstrong, Msgr. Robert A. '62 (BAL) [1] Baltimore, MD Cathedral of Mary Our Queen.
Armstrong, Rodney J. *s.s.j.* '91 (BEA) [3] Beaumont, TX Blessed Sacrament Church.
Armstrong, Steven A. *s.j.* '87 (OAK) [N] Berkeley, CA Jesuit Community at Jesuit School of Theology at Berkeley.
Armstrong, Steven A. *s.j.* '87 (SFR) [39] San Francisco, CA Our Lady of Fatima Byzantine Catholic Church.
Arnao, Thomas V. '82 (RVC) Wantagh, NY St. Frances de Chantal Church.
Arnaud, Michael (LAF) [2] New Iberia, LA Nativity of Our Lady Church.
Arnberg, Todd '76 (SAG) Coleman, MI St. Philip Neri Church.
Arneson, James E. '67 (IND) Retired.
Arnheiter, Burkard *o.s.b.* '37 (SCL) [I] Collegeville, MN St. John's Abbey, of the Order of St. Benedict.
Arnhols, Msgr. Richard J. '73 (NEW) Bergenfield, NJ St. John the Evangelist Church.
Arnholt, Joseph M. '73 (PH) Ardmore, PA St. Colman Church.
Arnister, Msgr. Edward J. '79 (TR) [4] Trenton, NJ Holy Cross Church.
Arnold, Andrew L. '59 (WH) Retired.
Arnold, Msgr. Daniel K. '75 (E) [14] Erie, PA St. Boniface Church.
Arnold, Edward C. '57 (NSH) Franklin, TN St. Philip Church.
Arnold, Edward R. *m.m.* '63 (NY) [DD] Maryknoll, NY Maryknoll Fathers and Brothers.
Arnold, Erik J. (BAL) Clarksville, MD St. Louis Church.
Arnold, Friedrich *s.m.* '70 (FgM) Marist Foreign Missions.
Arnold, J. Ralph '41 (BEL) Retired.
Arnold, John D. *s.j.* '73 (STL) [F] St. Louis, MO De Smet Jesuit High School; [P] St. Louis, MO De Smet Jesuit High School Community.
Arnold, John P. '98 (TUC) Yuma, AZ Immaculate Conception Church.
Arnold, Robert P. '75 (SCR) [1] Luzerne, PA Holy Family Church.
Arnold, Roger S. *s.v.d.* '61 (CHI) [B] Techny, IL Divine Word Residence; [N] Chicago, IL Divine Word Theologate; [N] Techny, IL Society of the Divine Word, Provincial Headquarter-Chicago Prov.
Arnold, Wayne H. '00 (MEM) [16] Memphis, TN St. Louis Church.
Arnold, William L. '80 (COL) Dover, OH St. Joseph Church.
Arnoldt, David M. '68 (WIN) Military Chaplains.
Arnone, A. '80 (SJ) On Leave of Absence.
Arnone, Harry *c.m.* '98 (BRK) [V] Jamaica, NY Vincentian Residence.
Arnone, John C. '99 (NO) Gretna, LA St. Cletus Church.
Arnone, Leo F. (ALT) [B] Johnstown, PA Bishop McCort High School.
Arnone, Leo F. '93 (ALT) [20] Johnstown, PA St. Andrew's Church.
Arnott, John J. '74 (PIT) Peters Township, PA St. Benedict the Abbot Church.
Arnout, Eric R., Jr. '96 (ALN) [11] Allentown, PA St. Thomas More Church.
Arnsparger, Roger '77 (CHL) Arden, NC St. Barnabas Church.
Arnsparger, Roger '77 (LEX) Special Assignment.
Arnzen, Kenneth '57 (B) Nezperce, ID Holy Trinity Church.
Arocho, Jose Antonio '00 (CGS) Humacao, PR Dulce Nombre de Jesus Church.
Arocho, Marcelino '88 (MGZ) [9] Mayaquez, PR Church of the Resurrection.
Arockiam, Emmanuel *s.j.* '87 (MIL) [P] Milwaukee, WI Jesuit Community at Marquette University.
Arokiasamy, Joseph Xavier (NY) Carmel, NY St. James the Apostle Church.
Arokiasamy, Kulan-Daisamy '71 (DET) [3] Eastpointe, MI St. Veronica Church.
Arold, Richard J. '67 (NY) Retired.
Arona, Francisco '64 (SJN) [E] San Juan, PR Centro Medico de P.R.
Arong, Jose *o.m.i.* '66 (OAK) [N] Oakland, CA Oblate Provincial House & Procure.
Arong, Jose *o.m.i.* '66 (WDC) [M] Washington, DC Missionary Oblates of Mary Immaculate.
Aronica, Paul *s.d.b.* '47 (NO) [D] Marrero, LA Archbishop Shaw High School.
Aronyu, Cuthbert '72 (OAK) [5] Oakland, CA St. Benedict Church.
Arpie, Msgr. Robert A. '47 (NY) Retired.
Arputham, Michael A. '78 (NY) [201] Staten Island, NY St. Christopher Church.
Arraiza, Fray Luis *o.f.m.cap.* (DAL) [N] Dallas, TX The National Cursillo Center and Office of the National Secretariat.
Arraiza, Luis Gerardo *o.f.m.cap.* '88 (DAL) [8] Dallas, TX Our Lady of Lourdes Church.
Arrambide, James C. *c.ss.r.* '73 (GAL) [51] Houston, TX St. Raphael the Archangel Church.
Arrando, Angelo S. '71 (BGP) [1] Danbury, CT St. Gregory Church.
Arregui Moso, Miguel '59 (CGS) Juncos, PR Inmaculada Concepcion Church.
Arriaga, Ernesto *c.s.b.* '01 (GAL) [Q] Sugar Land, TX Basilian Mission Center.
Arriaga, Joaquin S. '97 (FRS) Fowler, CA St. Lucy Church.
Arriaga, Martin (ELP) [15] El Paso, TX Our Lady of Guadalupe Church.
Arribas, Pedro *d.l.p.* (SB) [2] Riverside, CA Our Lady of Perpetual Help Church.
Arribas, Pedro *d.l.p.* '60 (SB) [A] Riverside, CA Blessed Junipero Serra House of Formation.
Arribas, Santiago *c.m.* '58 (ARE) [1] Manati, PR La Candelaria Church.
Arrien, Mariano *c.p.* '32 (ARE) Lares, PR St. Joseph Church.
Arrieta, David '62 (SJN) [13] Carolina, PR Nuestra Senora de Lourdes Church.
Arrilucea, Jesus Maria P. *o.a.r.* '65 (ELP) [8] El Paso, TX Guardian Angel Church.
Arrioyave, Luis (BO) [3] Lynn, MA St. Joseph Church.
Arrizurieta, Candido *c.m.* '54 (NY) [44] New York, NY Holy Agony Church; [DD] New York, NY Vincentian Fathers.
Arroyo, Brigido U. '61 (AGN) Tamuning, GU St. Anthony and St. Victor Church.
Arroyo, Edward B. *s.j.* '75 (FgM) Provinces.
Arroyo, Edward B. *s.j.* '75 (NO) [C] New Orleans, LA Loyola University New Orleans.
Arroyo, Joseph A. *s.j.* '62 (PH) [C] Philadelphia, PA St. Joseph's University; [AA] Philadelphia, PA Jesuit Community at St. Joseph's University.
Arroyo, Mario J. '77 (GAL) [24] Houston, TX St. Cyril of Alexandria Church.
Arroyo, Miguel A. *o.c.d.* '99 (CGS) [2] Caguas, PR San Jose Church.
Arruda, Henry S. '67 (FR) [7] New Bedford, MA Our Lady of Mt. Carmel Church.
Arsenault, Edward J. '91 (MAN) [15] Manchester, NH St. Pius X Church.
Arsenault, James M. '89 (RIC) Blacksburg, VA St. Mary & Newman Community Church.
Arsenault, Joseph B. *m.m.* '59 (NY) [DD] Maryknoll, NY Maryknoll Fathers and Brothers.
Arsenault, Raymond J. *s.m.* '51 (BO) [Y] Framingham, MA The Marist House.
Arseneau, Vernon '72 (JOL) West Chicago, IL St. Mary Church.
Arseneault, David J. (ALT) Huntingdon, PA Most Holy Trinity Church.
Arseneault, David J. '81 (ALT) [H] Hollidaysburg, PA Campus Ministry.
Arter, Ronald L. '61 (COL) Lancaster, OH St. Mark Church.
Arthasseril, Jerome S. '66 (NEW) [1] East Orange, NJ Holy Name of Jesus Church.
Arthur, David J. *c.s.c.* '54 (FR) [A] North Easton, MA Holy Cross Fathers Religious.
Arthur, E. Eugene *s.j.* '66 (COS) [F] Sedalia, CO Sacred Heart Jesuit Community; [H] Sedalia, CO Sacred Heart Jesuit Retreat House.
Arthur, Msgr. E. Robert '38 (WDC) Retired.
Arthur, Francis Quintin '79 (FAR) Cayuga, ND SS. Peter and Paul Church; Cogswell, ND Our Lady of Mercy Church; Forman, ND St. Mary's Church.
Arthur, James (LC) Blair, WI St. Ansgar Church; Whitehall, WI St. John the Apostle Church.
Artim, Michael '63 (VNN) Retired.
Artis, George *s.v.d.* '62 (BLX) [A] Bay St. Louis, MS St. Augustine's.
Artmann, Robert J. '64 (MIL) St. Michael, WI St. Michael Church.
Arts, Paul-Louis '64 (SC) [6] Sioux City, IA Immaculate Conception Church.
Arturi, Bradley K. '62 (NY) [II] New York, NY Prelature of the Holy Cross and Opus Dei.
Artuso, Grazioso '64 (BGP) [19] Bridgeport, CT St. Raphael Church.
Artysiewicz, Chet *glmy.* '73 (LR) Crossett, AR Holy Cross Church; Hamburg, AR Holy Spirit Church; Monticello, AR St. Mark Church.
Artzer, James *s.v.d.* '50 (TR) [M] Bordentown, NJ Society of the Divine Word.
Arude, Aristide Z. '58 (BO) Stoughton, MA Immaculate Conception Church.
Arul, John '70 (MRY) San Luis Obispo, CA San Luis Obispo Church.
Arul, Joseph *s.v.d.* '89 (BIR) [1] Huntsville, AL Good Shepherd Church.
Arulandu, Thaines '82 (FAR) Larimore, ND St. Stephen's Church.
Arvay, Alfred S. '58 (NEW) On Duty Outside the Archdiocese.
Arzola, Roberto *o.p.* '74 (SJN) [16] Bayamon, PR Nuestra Senora del Perpetuo Socorro Church.
Asaf, Paul '93 (OLL) [A] Ann Arbor, MI Maronite Order of Blessed Virgin Mary.
Asante, Appiah (PH) Wayne, PA St. Katharine of Siena Church.
Asare-Dankwah, John '94 (NO) [48] New Orleans, LA St. Monica Church.
Ascencio, Joseph A. '82 (COL) On Duty Outside the Diocese.
Ascheman, Thomas *s.v.d.* '82 (FgM) Society of the Divine Word Foreign Missions.
Aschenbrenner, George A. *s.j.* '65 (ALN) [A] Wernersville, PA Jesuit Center; [A] Wernersville, PA Jesuit Center; [N] Wernersville, PA Jesuit Center for Spiritual Growth.
Aschenbrenner, Ralph L. '61 (SAL) Lincoln, KS St. Patrick's Church.
Ascherl, Vincent '81 (ELP) Retired.
Aschmann, Karl '50 (CHL) Concord, NC St. James Church.
Ascolese, Robert J. '89 (MET) Washington, NJ St. Joseph Church.
Asencio, Enrique (CGS) [B] Aibonito, PR Casa Manresa.
Asencios-Pablo, Maximo *m.ss.a.* '68 (HRT) [2] Waterbury, CT Immaculate Conception Church.
Asencios-Pablo, Maximo *m.s.a.* '68 (NOR) [F] Cromwell, CT Society of the Missionaries of the Holy Apostles.
Asenjo, Jose Maria '65 (GAL) South Houston, TX Our Lady of Grace Church.

Ash, Joseph H. '58 (WOR) Retired; [M] Worcester, MA Vianney House.
Ashbaugh, William '51 (LAN) [O] Lansing, MI Diocesan Service Committee.
Ashbaugh, William A. '93 (LAN) Howell, MI St. Joseph Church.
Ashbeck, David K. '68 (GB) Isaar, WI St. Sebastian Church.
Ashe, Brendan Michael '59 (CC) Vattman, TX Our Lady of Consolation Church.
Ashe, John F. '63 (NOR) Portland, CT St. Mary Church.
Ashe, Joseph C. '76 (NOR) [2] Middletown, CT St. John Church.
Ashe, Kevin P. '63 (NEW) [3] Jersey City, NJ St. Anne's Church; Special Assignment; [S] Union City, NJ Park Performing Arts, Inc.
Ashenbrenner, Ray *o.p.* '48 (MAD) [G] Janesville, WI St. Elizabeth Home.
Ashenbrenner, Robert D. *o.s.f.s.* '54 (PH) [AA] Philadelphia, PA Oblates of St. Francis De Sales.
Ashfeld, Bernard '82 (SFS) [4] Sioux Falls, SD Our Lady of Guadalupe Church; Sioux Falls, SD South Dakota State Penitentiary & Minnehaha County Jail.
Ashkar, Dominic F. '62 (SAM) Washington, DC Our Lady of Lebanon Church.
Ashley, Benedict M. *o.p.* '48 (STL) [P] St. Louis, MO Dominican Community of St. Louis.
Ashman, Robert '86 (NY) [1] Yonkers, NY St. Anthony Church.
Ashman, Robert F. '86 (NY) [190] Bronx, NY St. Theresa of the Infant Jesus Church.
Ashmore, Ron '76 (IND) [5] Terre Haute, IN St. Margaret Mary Church.
Ashton, Msgr. John P. '55 (Y) Campbell, OH St. Lucy's Church.
Ashurst, Peter '92 (OKL) Absent on Leave.
Ashwell, Barry G. '69 (SEA) Unassigned.
Asika, Raphael *m.s.p.* '92 (BEA) Ames, TX Our Mother of Mercy Church; Raywood, TX Sacred Heart Church.
Asip, Msgr. James W. '37 (BRK) [191] Queens, NY St. Luke Church; Retired; [L] Brooklyn, NY Catholic Charities; [L] Brooklyn, NY Catholic Charities.
Asir, Antony '82 (RVC) Lynbrook, NY Our Lady of Peace Church; Rockville Centre, NY Mercy Medical Center.
Asis, Alfonso '75 (AGN) Toto, GU Immaculate Heart of Mary Church.
Asma, Lawrence *c.m.* '83 (STL) St. Louis, MO DePaul Health Center.
Asma, Lawrence F. *c.m.* '83 (STL) [K] Bridgeton, MO SSM De Paul Health Center; [P] St. Louis, MO Vincentian Residence.
Asmar, Maroun '93 (SAM) Somerset, NJ St. Sharbel Church.
Aspinall, Campion W. *c.j.* '61 (LA) Santa Maria, CA St. Louis de Montfort Church.
Aspiras, Jose '47 (SEA) Retired.
Assenheimer, Roy C. *m.m.* '65 (FgM) Maryknoll Foreign Missions.
Assenmacher, Hugh *o.s.b.* '58 (LR) [A] Subiaco, AR Subiaco Monastery.
Assenyoh, Bernard Kwame *s.v.d.* '98 (NO) [51] New Orleans, LA St. Paul the Apostle Church.
Astorino, Robert F. *m.m.* '70 (FgM) Maryknoll Foreign Missions.
Astruc, Rene *s.j.* '54 (FBK) Kotlik, AK St. Joseph Church; Mountain Village, AK St. Lawrence Church; [E] St. Marys, AK Brother Joe Prince Jesuit Community.
Astudillo, Antonio P. '73 (LA) [7] Long Beach, CA Holy Innocents Church.
Asturi, Bruno '76 (PBR) Upper St. Clair, PA St. Gregory Nazianzus Church.
Astuto, Lucian S. '57 (OM) [34] Omaha, NE St. Patrick Church.
Asuah, Joseph '64 (NY) Nyack, NY St. Ann Church.
Asuncion, Leo Alban '79 (OAK) [4] Fremont, CA St. Joseph Church.
Atamian, Antranik '73 (ARM) Philadelphia, PA St. Mark's Armenian Catholic Church.
Atcher, Joseph R. *o.carm.* '76 (NEW) Cresskill, NJ St. Therese of Lisieux Church.
Atchison, Donald W. '57 (KAL) Retired.
Atehortua, Jairo '95 (SP) New Port Richey, FL Our Lady Queen of Peace Church.
Aten, Robert L. '79 (STL) Special Assignment; [P] Centerville, MO Contemplative Heart of Mary Hermitage.
Atencio, Luis *i.v.e.* '93 (SJ) [14] San Jose, CA St. Leo the Great Church.
Atkin, Tim *c.i.c.m.* '74 (FgM) Missionhurst Foreign Missions.
Atkins, Daniel '87 (IND) Bloomington, IN St. Paul Catholic Center Church; [N] Bloomington, IN Indiana University, Bloomington Newman Center.
Atkins, James '72 (RVC) East Northport, NY St. Anthony of Padua Church.
Atkins, James '75 (PRM) Akron, OH St. Michael the Archangel Church.
Atkins, James '81 (SFR) Retired.
Atkins, James P. '75 (ATL) On Duty Outside the Archdiocese.
Atkinson, Anselm *o.s.b.* '82 (WOR) [N] Petersham, MA St. Mary's Monastery.
Atkinson, John V. '61 (MEM) [18] Memphis, TN St. Michael's Church.
Atkinson, Sean '69 (JKS) Leland, MS St. James Church.
Atkinson, William E. *o.s.a.* '74 (PH) [D] Drexel Hill, PA Monsignor Bonner High School.
Ato, Lorenzo (NY) [191] Bronx, NY St. Thomas Aquinas Church.
Atok, George *s.d.b.* '82 (NY) [FF] Stony Point, NY Don Bosco Retreat Center and Marian Shrine; [FF] Stony Point, NY Marian Shrine.
Atomori, Paschal '83 (CHI) [114] Chicago, IL St. Leo The Great Church.
Atonio, Falaniko '92 (SPP) [1] Pago Pago, AS Cathedral of the Holy Family.
Atoyebi, John B. '94 (CHI) [41] Chicago, IL St. Clotilde Church.
Attak, Cyril '64 (PRM) Allen Park, MI St. Stephen Church.
Attanasio, Scott F. '95 (NEW) Kearny, NJ St. Stephen's Church.
Attansey, Matthew '79 (FAR) Dazey, ND St. Mary's Church; Sanborn, ND Sacred Heart Church.
Attard, Joseph (BRK) [119] Brooklyn, NY Most Precious Blood Church.
Attea, Msgr. Antoine '58 (BUF) Jamestown, NY St. James Church.
Attumaly, Anthony '88 (E) Warren, PA St. Joseph Church.
Atuahene-Nsowaah, Jacob '89 (HRT) [I] New Haven, CT Hospital of St. Raphael.
Atunzu, Kevin '79 (LR) Engelberg, AR St. John the Baptist Church; Walnut Ridge, AR Immaculate Heart of Mary Church.
Atwater, John T. '63 (BO) Groton, MA St. James Church; Groton, MA Sacred Heart Church; Senior Priests.
Atwill, Msgr. William H. '44 (LA) Retired.
Atwood, Ray E. (DUB) Riceville, IA Immaculate Conception Church.
Atwood, Ray E. '94 (DUB) Chester, IA St. Stephen's Church; New Haven, IA St. Peter's Church.
Atwood, Ronald E. '84 (OAK) Richmond, CA St. David of Wales Church.
Atwood, Ronald J. '69 (COL) [43] Columbus, OH St. Thomas the Apostle Church.
Atwood, Wilbur J. *s.s.j.* '58 (NO) [P] New Orleans, LA Josephite Fathers and Brothers.
Atzert, Edward P. '37 (TR) Retired; [L] Lawrenceville, NJ Morris Hall-Saint Lawrence, Inc.
Au, Thomas Y. '79 (LIN) Roseland, NE Sacred Heart Church.
Au, William A. '75 (BAL) [82] Baltimore, MD SS. Philip and James Church.
Au Quoc Thanh, Vincent de Paul M. *c.m.c.* (SPC) [E] Carthage, MO Congregation of the Mother Co-Redemptrix, United States Assumption Province.
Aube, Paul L. '70 (MAN) Sabbatical.
Aubespin, Francis Borgia *s.v.d.* '65 (LAF) [4] Lafayette, LA Immaculate Heart of Mary Church.
Aubin, Msgr. Joseph '55 (OG) [5] Plattsburgh, NY St. Peter Church.
Aubin, Joseph '61 (LAN) Durand, MI St. Mary Church.
Aubin, Msgr. Joseph G., 55 (OG) Retired.
Aubin, Pierre *m.s.c.* '58 (OG) Chaumont, NY All Saints Church; [F] Watertown, NY Missionaries of the Sacred Heart; [J] Chaumont, NY Mission Project Service; [J] Watertown, NY Sacred Heart Foundation.
Aubin, Ronald B. '81 (SP) Land O'Lakes, FL Our Lady of the Rosary Church.
Auble, Theodore J. '75 (ROC) Churchville, NY St. Vincent De Paul Church.
Aubrey, Robert J. '71 (DM) Cumming, IA St. John Church; [D] Des Moines, IA Mercy Medical Center.
Aubry, Ronald J. '81 (COL) Millersburg, OH St. Peter Church.
Aubut, Charles E. '41 (BO) Senior Priests.
Auby, John R. '94 (MAD) Clyde, WI St. Malachy Church; Spring Green, WI St. John the Evangelist Church.
Auchter, Msgr. John A. '54 (ALN) Lake Harmony, PA St. Peter the Fisherman Church.
Aucoin, Msgr. Charles '47 (MOB) Retired.
Aucoin, Msgr. Robert H. '70 (OG) [A] Ogdensburg, NY Wadhams Hall.
Auda, Lawrence '60 (SFD) Benld, IL St. Joseph Church; Gillespie, IL SS. Simon and Jude Church.
Audet, Arthur J. '85 (HRT) Forestville, CT St. Matthew Church.
Audet, Dennis J. '78 (MAN) Merrimack, NH Our Lady of Mercy Church.
Audette, Albert D. '93 (BGP) Brookfield, CT St. Marguerite Bourgeoys Church.
Audibert, John L. '67 (PRT) Madawaska, ME St. Thomas Aquinas Church.
Auer, Benedict L. *o.s.b.* '80 (SEA) [L] Lacey, WA St. Martin's Abbey.
Auer, John '79 (COS) [14] Colorado Springs, CO Saint Paul Church.
Auer, John J. '57 (BAL) Millersville, MD Our Lady of the Fields Church.
Auer, Joseph E. '57 (CHI) [4] Oak Lawn, IL St. Linus Church.
Auer, Peter J. *s.o.l.t.* '93 (CC) [H] Robstown, TX Society of Our Lady of the Most Holy Trinity.
Auer, Robert F. '51 (DUB) Retired.
Auerbach, Shay W. *s.j.* '99 (R) [7] Raleigh, NC St. Raphael Church; [E] Raleigh, NC Jesuit Community.
Aufdermauer, Joseph A. '68 (MIL) [57] Milwaukee, WI St. Matthias Church.
Aufieri, Robert J. '74 (NY) [161] Bronx, NY St. Margaret of Cortona Church.
Aufiero, Louis D. '65 (BRK) [V] Jamaica, NY Parsons Manor.
Auger, Gaston E. '32 (PRT) Retired.
Auger, George *c.s.v.* '61 (CHI) [N] Arlington Heights, IL Viatorian Province Center-Clerics of St. Viator.
Auger, Gerald E. '55 (MAN) Retired.
Auger, Raymond D. '56 (PRT) Biddeford, ME St. Joseph's Church; Retired.
Auguste, Jean-Miguel '91 (BRK) [57] Brooklyn, NY Holy Innocents Church.
Augustin, Francois (BRK) [139] Brooklyn, NY St. Therese of Lisieux Church.
Augustine, Kenneth J. '77 (MIL) Franklin, WI St. James Church.
Augustine, M. Selvan *s.j.* '90 (CHI) [C] Chicago, IL Jesuit Community at Loyola University of Chicago.
Augustine, M. Selvan *s.j.* '90 (JOL) Wheaton, IL St. Michael Church.
Augustine, Msgr. Roger J. '59 (SC) Moville, IA Immaculate Conception Church.
Augustine, Russell A. '89 (BGP) [7] Fairfield, CT St. Thomas Aquinas Church.
Augustinowitz, Michael E. '75 (BUR) Hardwick, VT St. Norbert Church.
Augustyn, Andrew M. '47 (GI) Retired.
Augustyn, Boguslaw *c.ss.r.* '93 (MET) Manville, NJ Sacred Heart of Jesus Church.
Augustyn, James M. '63 (BUF) [6] Lackawanna, NY St. Michael the Archangel Church.
Augustyn, Richard H. '76 (BUF) [34] Buffalo, NY Immaculate Heart of Mary Church; Buffalo, NY Buffalo General Hospital.
Auman, Robert '47 (SFE) Retired.
Aumann, Jordan *o.p.* '45 (CHI) [N] River Forest, IL St. Thomas Aquinas Priory.
Aumen, Paul *c.pp.s.* '49 (CIN) [M] Dayton, OH Provincial Office of the Cincinnati Province of the Society of the Precious Blood.
Aurelio, John R. '66 (BUF) Retired.
Aureus, Antonio '77 (DAL) Sherman, TX St. Mary Church.
Aurilia, John *o.f.m.cap.* '66 (NEW) [N] Union City, NJ Capuchin Friars - Province of the Sacred Stigmata of St. Francis.
Aurilia, John C. *o.f.m.cap.* '66 (CHL) Hendersonville, NC Immaculate Conception Church.
Ausenbaugh, Andrew '95 (OWN) Henderson, KY Holy Name of Jesus Church.
Ausperk, Michael '89 (CLV) Absent on Leave.
Ausperk, Michael D. '89 (CLV) [1] Elyria, OH St. Agnes Church.
Austgen, Robert J. *c.s.c.* '58 (FTW) [B] Notre Dame, IN University of Notre Dame Du Lac; [G] Notre Dame, IN University Health Services; [J] Notre Dame, IN Holy Cross Community, Corby Hall, University of Notre Dame.
Austin, C. Gerard *o.p.* '59 (VEN) [B] Arcadia, FL Blessed Edmund Rice School for Pastoral Ministry.
Austin, John J. '97 (PRT) Bangor, ME St. John's Church; Bangor, ME Eastern Maine Medical Center.
Austin, Jonathan G. '97 (DAL) [21] Dallas, TX St. Monica Church.
Austin, Michael Paul '00 (BLX) Long Beach, MS St. Thomas the Apostle Church.
Austin, Stephen E. '84 (TLS) Bartlesville, OK St. John's Church; Dewey, OK Our Lady of Guadalupe Church.
Austin, Walter J. '81 (NO) Chalmette, LA Prince of Peace Church.
Auth, Clifford H. '99 (SY) Johnson City, NY St. James Church.
Auth, James E. '61 (TOL) [13] Toledo, OH Regina Coeli Church.
Auth, William G. *o.s.f.s.* '69 (TOL) [K] Toledo, OH Oblates of St. Francis de Sales.
Auther, John P. *s.j.* '90 (SD) [12] San Diego, CA Our Lady of Guadalupe Church; San Diego, CA George F. Bailey Maximum Security Facility.
Auva'a, Falaniko '91 (SPP) [8] Pago Pago, AS Church of St. Peter and Paul.
Auve, Msgr. Perron Joseph '62 (YAK) Ellensburg, WA St. Andrew's Church.
Avallone, Paul P. *s.d.b.* '50 (PAT) [D] Paterson, NJ Don Bosco Technical High School; [D] Paterson, NJ Don Bosco Technical High School; [N] Haledon, NJ

Institute of the Daughters of Mary Help of Christians.
Avau, Felix A. *c.i.c.m.* '54 (SAT) Poteet, TX St. Philip Benizi Church.
Avella, Alberto '80 (GLP) Show Low, AZ St. Rita Church.
Avella, Robert E. '75 (ARL) [7] Alexandria, VA St. Mary's Church.
Avella, Steven M. '79 (MIL) Special Assignment.
Avella, William '50 (RNO) Retired.
Avello, Vicente Salas *o.de.m.* '66 (PCE) [13] Ponce, PR Santuario San Judas Tadeo Church.
Avendano, Alvaro D. '91 (ATL) [2] Atlanta, GA Holy Cross Church.
Aveni, Paul J. '98 (BO) [2] Revere, MA Immaculate Conception Church.
Averbeck, Ronald J. '61 (CIN) [79] Cincinnati, OH St. Stephen Church.
Aversa, Domenic R. *t.o.r.* '59 (ALT) [F] Hollidaysburg, PA St. Joseph Friary.
Avery, Edward V. '70 (PH) [75] Philadelphia, PA St. Jerome Church; [U] Philadelphia, PA Nazareth Hospital.
Avery, Raymond '44 (MET) Retired; [H] Somerset, NJ Maria Regina Residence.
Avia, Martin '57 (SFR) [K] San Rafael, CA Nazareth House.
Avicolli, Maurice C. *o.praem.* '68 (PH) Paoli, PA St. Norbert Church; [AA] Paoli, PA Daylesford Abbey.
Avila, Carlos Antonio Massieu '89 (MIA) [L] Coral Gables, FL House of the Divine Will, Inc. dba Casa de la Divina Voluntad.
Avila, Daniel C. '87 (FRS) Hanford, CA St. Brigid Church.
Avila, Martin C. '57 (SFR) Retired.
Avila, Sigifredo Misael '98 (STO) Turlock, CA Sacred Heart Church.
Avila, Msgr. Stephen J. '81 (FR) East Freetown, MA St. John Neumann Church.
Aviles, Joe '90 (SAT) [60] San Antonio, TX St. Paul Church.
Aviles, Mario Alberto *c.o.* '98 (BWN) [3] Pharr, TX St. Jude Thaddeus Church; [E] Pharr, TX Oratory of St. Philip Neri, of Pontifical Right.
Avitabile, Camillo *m.s.* '53 (ORL) [2] Orlando, FL Blessed Trinity Church.
Avramenko, Alex '96 (STN) Sacramento, CA St. Andrew the Apostle Church.
Avramenko, Alexander '96 (STN) San Francisco, CA Immaculate Conception Church; Santa Clara, CA St. Vladimir Church.
Awad, Msgr. Assad '57 (SAM) Worcester, MA Our Lady of Mercy Church.
Awalt, Msgr. William J. '47 (WDC) Potomac, MD Our Lady of Mercy Church; Retired.
Award, Richard *c.p.* '81 (FgM) Passionist Foreign Missions.
Axe, Thomas R. '60 (CIN) [29] Cincinnati, OH Good Shepherd Church.
Axe, William J. *o.ss.t.* '74 (BAL) Jessup, MD St. Lawrence Church.
Axen, Ronald J. '40 (DUB) Retired.
Axen, Ronald J. '40 (FWT) [H] Crowley, TX St. Francis Village, Inc.
Ayala, Augustin Mateo '90 (WDC) [1] Washington, DC St. Matthew Church.
Ayala, Jose Ramon '97 (NSH) On Special or Other Diocesan Assignment.
Ayala, Marcus *o.f.m. conv.* '89 (R) Lumberton, NC St. Francis De Sales Church.
Ayamanthil, Matthew '59 (NEW) [N] Caldwell, NJ The Rev. Msgr. James F. Kelley Residence for Retired Priests.
Ayang, John *s.o.l.t.* (CC) Skidmore, TX Immaculate Conception Church.
Ayathupadam, Joseph '61 (CHL) Denver, NC Holy Spirit Church.
Aydt, Raymond A. '46 (BIS) Grenora, ND St. Boniface Church.
Ayem, Alfred *s.v.d.* '83 (IND) [34] Indianapolis, IN St. Rita Church.
Ayers, Dan '99 (COS) [3] Colorado Springs, CO Divine Redeemer Church.
Ayers, J. Cameron *s.j.* '86 (PHX) [B] Phoenix, AZ Brophy College Preparatory.
Ayers, John J. '51 (SPR) Northfield, MA St. Patrick Church.
Ayla, Francisco '84 (LA) [J] Los Angeles, CA St. Vincent Medical Center.
Aylward, Gerard J. *c.s.p.* '53 (CHR) Clemson, SC St. Andrew Church.
Aylward, James W. '64 (SFR) Absent on Leave.
Aylward, Richard A. *m.m.* '53 (FgM) Maryknoll Foreign Missions.
Aymanamkuzhy, Jacob '60 (PMB) Retired.
Ayo, Nicholas *c.s.c.* '59 (FTW) [B] Notre Dame, IN University of Notre Dame Du Lac; [J] Notre Dame, IN Holy Cross Community, Corby Hall, University of Notre Dame.
Ayoob, John '65 (PIT) Moon Township, PA St. Margaret Mary Church.
Ayoub, Fawaz (SLC) Milford, UT St. Bridget Church.
Ayoub, Msgr. S. Paul '53 (BUF) [6] Cheektowaga, NY Mother of Divine Grace Church.
Ayres, William G. '99 (PH) [72] Philadelphia, PA Incarnation of Our Lord Church.
Ayuyu, Isaac M. '86 (CHK) Garapan Village, District 11, MP Kristo Rai Church.
Azadian, Joseph G *s.j.* '52 (SJ) [L] Los Gatos, CA Sacred Heart Jesuit Center.
Azar, Fahed '80 (SAM) Wilkes-Barre, PA St. Anthony/St. George Church.
Azar, John (NTN) Atlanta, GA St. John Church.
Azaro, Stanley *o.p.* '75 (FgM) Dominican - Order of Preachers Foreign Missions.
Azcoiti, Vicente '56 (BWN) [2] Mission, TX Our Lady of the Holy Rosary Church.
Azcoitia, Florentino *s.j.* '52 (MIA) [H] Miami, FL Villa Javier.
Azcona, Eric *o.f.m.cap.* '51 (FWT) [6] Fort Worth, TX Our Lady of Guadalupe Church.
Azcona, Jose Luis *o.c.d.* '85 (DAL) Irving, TX St. Luke Church.
Azcona, Samuel *o.f.m.* '73 (SJN) [51] San Juan, PR Resurreccion del Senor Church.
Azevedo, Ferdinand T. *s.j.* '70 (FgM) Provinces.
Aziz, George *s.j.* '57 (SR).
Azizo, Toma B. '54 (OLD) Farmington Hills, MI St. Toma Church.
Aznar, Manuel *c.m.* '66 (SJN) [60] San Juan, PR San Vicente de Paul Church.
Azoon, Philip '94 (NTN) Scranton, PA St. Joseph Church.
Azpericueta, Lucas '79 (FRS) Arvin, CA St. Thomas Church.
Azpiazu, Jose *o.m.i.* '28 (SAT) [K] San Antonio, TX Oblate Madonna Residence.
Azrak, Albert *c.s.s.* '60 (NY) [4] White Plains, NY Our Lady of Mt. Carmel Church.
Azzarone, Daniel M. '78 (PRO) [5] Cranston, RI St. Mary Church.
Azzarto, Anthony J. *s.j.* '69 (NEW) [C] Jersey City, NJ St. Peter's Preparatory School.

B

Ba Do, Ai '51 (ALN) [3] Bethlehem, PA Holy Ghost Church.
Ba Do, James Cong '61 (BEA) Beaumont, TX Federal Work Camp & U.S. Penitentiary.
Baabuge, Martin Atanga '91 (TUC) [9] Tucson, AZ Our Lady, Queen of All Saints Church.
Babb, James C. *s.j.* '46 (ATL) [L] Atlanta, GA Ignatius House.
Babcock, David J. *o.f.m.* '53 (FgM) Franciscan Foreign Missions.
Babcock, James K. '81 (NTN) Placentia, CA Holy Cross Church.
Babcock, Timothy F. '68 (DET) Rochester, MI St. Andrew Church.
Babeu, Gill C. '87 (BGP) [3] Stamford, CT St. Bridget Church.
Babich, Ronald J. '77 (DET) Fraser, MI Our Lady Queen of All Saints Church.
Babicz, Edmund A. '84 (MAN) Sanbornville, NH St. Anthony Church.
Babiczuk, Fred '86 (FR) [8] Fall River, MA Our Lady of the Angels Church.
Babiczuk, Freddie '86 (FR) [20] Fall River, MA St. Patrick's Church.
Babin, Albert *c.ss.r.* '52 (BLX) [E] Biloxi, MS St. John Neumann Residence.
Babin, Victor '75 (MIA) [15] Miami, FL St. Agatha Church.
Babineau, Alexis A. *a.a.* '45 (WOR) [N] Worcester, MA Assumptionists (Augustinians of the Assumption).
Babineau, William E. '68 (MAN) Franklin, NH St. Paul Church.
Babinski, Donald E. '81 (RVC) Elmont, NY St. Vincent de Paul Church.
Babka, Robert H. '68 (STL) On Medical Leave.
Babonas, Alphonse '62 (DET) [9] Detroit, MI St. Anthony Church.
Babowitch, John F. '96 (PH) [20] Philadelphia, PA St. Barnabas Church.
Babu, Gangolu Bob *s.a.c.* '92 (VEN) [4] Sarasota, FL St. Martha Church.
Bac, Isidore M. Dinh Thanh *c.m.c.* (SPC) [E] Carthage, MO Congregation of the Mother Co-Redemptrix, United States Assumption Province.
Baca, Al S. '89 (ORG) Anaheim, CA St. Anthony Claret Church.
Bacalso, Felipe *s.j.* '90 (BO) [W] Chestnut Hill, MA The Jesuit Community at Boston College.
Baccaro, Gaetano T. '85 (SY) [3] Liverpool, NY St. John Church.
Baccellieri, Joseph A. '66 (P) [2] Portland, OR St. Agatha Church; [34] Portland, OR Sacred Heart Church.
Bacchi, Lee F. '77 (JOL) Chebanse, IL SS. Mary and Joseph's Church; Clifton, IL St. Peter's Church.
Bacchi, Robert '77 (CHI) Brookfield, IL St. Barbara Church.
Bacevice, Joseph A. '77 (CLV) [25] Cleveland, OH St. George Church.
Bacevicius, John J. *o.f.m.* '62 (PRT) [I] Kennebunkport, ME St. Anthony's Friary.
Bach, Msgr. Frank J. '56 (SPK) Retired.
Bach, Gregory J. '99 (COV) Elsmere, KY St. Henry Church; [B] Erlanger, KY St. Henry District High School.
Bach, Ignacio *o.c.d.* '50 (TUC) [24] Tucson, AZ Santa Cruz Church; Tucson, AZ Kino Community Hospital.
Bach, James Nguyen '94 (NO) [6] Metairie, LA St. Christopher the Martyr Church.
Bach, James To Duc '52 (LUB) Retired.
Bach, John A. '71 (LFT) [D] Lafayette, IN St. Anthony Health Care; [F] Lafayette, IN Monastery of the Precious Blood.
Bach, Lester *o.f.m.cap.* '57 (GB) [M] Appleton, WI Monte Alverno Retreat Center.
Bacher, Anthony A. *c.s.sp.* '46 (VEN) [G] Sarasota, FL Congregation of the Holy Ghost.
Bacher, Arthur '54 (CLV) Retired.
Bacher, Arthur A. '54 (CLV) Richfield, OH St. Victor Church.
Bacher, Msgr. Robert E. '48 (CLV) Clinton, OH St. George Church.
Bachkay, John M. '83 (PIT) [74] Pittsburgh, PA Incarnation of the Lord Church.
Bachman, Michael J. '84 (BGP) [17] Bridgeport, CT St. Patrick Church.
Bachmeier, Benjamin '68 (SD) San Diego, CA Scripps Mercy Hospital; [F] San Diego, CA Scripps Mercy Hospital.
Bachmeier, Bernard A. '68 (FAR) On Duty Outside the Diocese.
Bachmeier, Brian '97 (FAR) Walhalla, ND St. Boniface's Church.
Bachmeier, Mark V. '89 (P) [3] Eugene, OR St. Mary Church.
Bachner, James M. '96 (PIT) Aliquippa, PA St. Titus Church.
Bacia, Eliot *o.f.m.* '62 (GB) [I] Pulaski, WI Assumption of B.V.M. Friary.
Bacik, James J. '62 (TOL) [5] Toledo, OH Corpus Christi, University of Toledo Church; [N] Toledo, OH University of Toledo Campus Ministry; [O] Toledo, OH U.T. Newman Foundation for Student Education and Development.
Bacik, Leonard M. '72 (CLV) Middleburg Heights, OH St. Bartholomew Church.
Bacino, Ben '75 (PBL) [13] Pueblo, CO St. Leander Church.
Backes, Hugo G. '36 (BIS) Retired.
Backes, John J. '73 (NY) Garnerville, NY St. Gregory Barbarigo Church.
Backherms, Robert J. *s.m.* '56 (BAL) [S] Baltimore, MD Society of Mary (Marianists).
Backiel, Bernard *m.i.c.* '60 (WDC) [M] Brookeville, MD Marian Monastery-Brookeville.
Backmann, Albert P. '00 (STP) Eagan, MN St. John Neumann Church.
Backous, Timothy *o.s.b.* '86 (SCL) [B] Collegeville, MN St. John's University; [I] Collegeville, MN St. John's Abbey, of the Order of St. Benedict.
Bacleon, Misael '84 (NY) [52] New York, NY Immaculate Conception Church.
Bacon, Roger L. '60 (PRO) [12] Woonsocket, RI Sacred Heart Church.
Bacovin, Ronald J. '66 (TR) Pennington, NJ St. James Church.
Badaoui, Adib '52 (NTN) Retired.
Baddick, Thomas D. '81 (ALN) Whitehall, PA Holy Trinity Church.
Badding, Joseph P. '69 (BUF) Gasport, NY St. Mary Church; Middleport, NY St. Stephen Church.
Badeaux, James '99 (PSC) Wilkes-Barre, PA St. John's Church.
Badeaux, Kevin '84 (BEA) Orange, TX St. Francis of Assisi Church.
Badem, Wendel J. '48 (MIL) Retired.
Baden, Robert D. '77 (RC) Kadoka, SD Our Lady of Victory Church; Wall, SD St. Patrick's Church.
Badenes, Jose Ignacio *s.j.* '93 (LA) [C] Los Angeles, CA Loyola Marymount University.
Bader, Edward '82 (NY) [153] Bronx, NY St. Joan of Arc Church.
Bader, Edward A. *c.s.b.* '63 (GAL) [C] Houston, TX University of St. Thomas; [Q] Houston, TX Residence of the Basilian Fathers of the University of St. Thomas.
Bader, Paul A. '61 (CIN) [85] Cincinnati, OH St. William Church.
Bader, Paul L. '58 (ALN) Coplay, PA St. Peter Church.
Badger, Arthur A. '53 (TOL) Retired.
Badgley, T. Augustine (NY) [165] Bronx, NY St. Mary Star of the Sea Church.
Badgley, T. Augustine '87 (NY) Tuckahoe, NY Immaculate Conception Church; Tuckahoe, NY Assumption Church.
Badia, Leonard F. '60 (BRK) [192] Queens, NY St. Margaret Church.

Badnerosky, Myron M. '56 (PSC) Levittown, PA Our Lady of Perpetual Help Church.
Bado, Walter *s.j.* '59 (LEX) [2] Lexington, KY The Newman Center, Holy Spirit Church; [L] Lexington, KY The Newman Center Holy Spirit Parish University of Kentucky.
Badovsky, Thomas '73 (PEO) Peru, IL St. Valentine's Church.
Badurina, Gabriel *t.o.r.* '62 (PIT) [5] Millvale, PA St. Nicholas Church; [O] Pittsburgh, PA Croatian Commissariate, T.O.R.
Badway, Gavin '00 (PMB) [1] West Palm Beach, FL Holy Name of Jesus Church.
Bae, Costantine K. (DEN) [5] Aurora, CO St. Lawrence Korean Catholic Church.
Baehr, David J. '64 (SY) [1] Oswego, NY St. John the Evangelist Church; [4] Oswego, NY St. Mary Church.
Baenziger, Edward J. *c.s.b.* '76 (GAL) [Q] Houston, TX Residence of the Basilian Fathers of the University of St. Thomas.
Baer, Campion *o.f.m.cap.* '56 (MIL) [B] Mount Calvary, WI St. Lawrence Seminary; [P] Mount Calvary, WI St. Lawrence Friary.
Baer, M. Stuart '92 (LA) [J] Burbank, CA Providence Saint Joseph Medical Center; [J] Burbank, CA Providence Health System.
Baer, M. Stuart '92 (PEO) On Duty Outside the Diocese.
Baer, Robert W. *c.s.p.* '54 (NY) [DD] Jamaica Estates, NY Paulist Fathers Generalate.
Baer, Timothy K. (WDC) Cheverly, MD St. Ambrose Church.
Baer, William J. '96 (STP) [A] St. Paul, MN St. John Vianney Seminary; [C] St. Paul, MN University of St. Thomas.
Baerwald, Jeffrey P. *s.j.* '89 (BAL) [B] Baltimore, MD Loyola College in Maryland; [S] Baltimore, MD Jesuit Community of Loyola College, Inc.
Baeten, David R. '62 (GB) [11] Green Bay, WI St. Matthew Church.
Baeten, Lambert C. *o.praem.* '59 (GB) [I] De Pere, WI St. Norbert Abbey.
Baeza, Manuel *m.c.c.j.* '96 (FgM) Comboni Foreign Missions.
Bafaro, Michael P. '53 (WOR) [13] Worcester, MA Our Lady of Mt. Carmel and St. Ann Church.
Baffa, Robert J. '66 (BUR) North Bennington, VT St. John the Baptist Church.
Bagan, Francis *o.m.i.* '52 (PT) Perry, FL Immaculate Conception Church.
Bagatin, Tarcisio *c.s.* '58 (SY) [21] Syracuse, NY St. Peter Church.
Bagdanavicius, Vytautas *m.i.c.* '36 (CHI) [N] Chicago, IL Congregation of Marian Fathers of the Immaculate Conception.
Bagdonis, Raymond *o.carm.* '94 (NY) Middletown, NY Our Lady of Mt. Carmel Church.
Bagert, Matthew '97 (DAL) Grand Prairie, TX Immaculate Conception Church.
Baggarly, John D. *s.j.* '60 (DET) [P] Clarkston, MI Colombiere Center.
Baggetta, Joseph J. '74 (BO) [27] Boston, MA St. James the Greater Church; Roslindale, MA Judge John J. Connelly Youth Center; Mattapan, MA Metropolitan Youth Service Center.
Baggio, Gianantonio *c.s.* '92 (SD) Imperial, CA St. Anthony of Padua Church.
Bagienski, Ronald A. '69 (BUF) [28] Buffalo, NY Holy Apostles SS. Peter and Paul Church.
Baginskis, Boleslaus *m.i.c.* '42 (CHI) [142] Chicago, IL Our Lady of Aglona Church.
Bagley, Gary J. '72 (BUF) [S] Allegany State Park, NY Camp Turner.
Bagley, John J. '60 (WOR) North Grafton, MA St. Mary's Church.
Bagley, Ronald M. *c.j.m.* '77 (BUF) [1] West Seneca, NY St. Bonaventure Church; [O] West Seneca, NY Eudist Fathers, St. John Eudes Center.
Bagnato, James D. *o.praem.* '69 (WIL) [5] Wilmington, DE St. Elizabeth Church.
Bagnato, James D. *o.praem.* '79 (WIL) [I] Claymont, DE Norbertine Fathers of Delaware, Inc.
Bahash, James J. '99 (SD) Lemon Grove, CA St. John of the Cross Church.
Bahhuth, Albert '96 (LA) Glendale, CA Holy Family Church.
Bahl, Edmund *s.s.c.* '43 (BUF) [M] Silver Creek, NY St. Columbans on the Lake, Home for the Aged.
Bahleda, Aloysius J. '58 (GBG) Retired; [G] Greensburg, PA Neumann House.
Bahlinger, Donald G. *s.j.* '59 (FgM) Provinces.
Bahlinger, Donald G. *s.j.* '59 (NO) [P] New Orleans, LA Jesuit Provincial Office.
Bahning, Frederick C. '45 (DUB) Retired.
Bahr, Joseph E. '60 (DOD) Garden City, KS St. Dominic Church; Ingalls, KS St. Stanislaus Church.
Baiardi, Sereno *o.f.m.* '66 (MIL) [P] Burlington, WI Queen of Peace Friary; [Y] Waterford, WI General Secretariat of the Franciscan Missions, Inc.
Baidoo, Joseph '85 (RVC) Mastic Beach, NY St. Jude Church.
Baidoo, Joseph K. '85 (RVC) Deer Park, NY SS. Cyril and Methodius Church.
Baidoo, Raphael *o.ss.t.* '77 (VIC) Goliad, TX Immaculate Conception Church.
Baier, Donald '75 (VEN) Retired.
Baier, Donald M. '70 (RVC) Malverne, NY Our Lady of Lourdes Church.
Baier, William J. '82 (STL) Bridgeton, MO St. Mary Church.
Bailey, Casey *o.c.s.o.* '83 (P) [L] Lafayette, OR The Cistercian (Trappist) Abbey of Our Lady of Guadalupe.
Bailey, Declan *o.f.m.* '44 (PAT) [M] Ringwood, NJ Holy Name Friary, Inc.
Bailey, Douglas *s.d.s.* '77 (ORL) [E] Melbourne, FL Florida Institute of Technology Campus Ministry.
Bailey, Fred '83 (ORG) Aliso Viejo, CA Corpus Christi Church.
Bailey, Harold (PIT) Allegheny County, PA Mayview State Hospital.
Bailey, Msgr. John L. '41 (WDC) [14] Washington, DC St. Francis Xavier Church; Retired.
Bailey, Justin J. *o.f.m.* '60 (BO) [P] Andover, MA Franciscan Center; [W] Andover, MA St. Francis Friary; [Y] Andover, MA Franciscan Center - Retreat House.
Bailey, Lawrence '86 (SEA) Military Chaplains.
Bailey, Paul F. '58 (BO) [4] Plymouth, MA St. Peter Church.
Bailey, Richard L. *s.j.* '58 (STL) [P] St. Louis, MO De Smet Jesuit High School Community.
Bailey, Robert L. '93 (PRO) Bristol, RI St. Elizabeth Church.
Bailey, Scott *c.ss.r.* '98 (STV) [2] Christiansted, VI Church of the Holy Cross;
Baillargeon, Albert G. '47 (MAN) Retired.
Baillargeon, Anatole '41 (BO) [W] Lowell, MA Missionary Oblates of Mary Immaculate.
Bailleres, Anthony *l.c.* '81 (HRT) [B] Cheshire, CT Novitiate of the Legion of Christ; [V] Orange, CT Legion of Christ, Inc.
Bailon, Abelardo '58 (LA) Huntington Park, CA St. Matthias Church.
Bailon, Cirilo '93 (P) Gresham, OR St. Anne Church.
Baily, Harold '69 (PIT) [3] McKees Rocks, PA St. John of God Church.
Baily, Harold E. '69 (PIT) [R] Pittsburgh, PA Office for Campus Ministry.
Baima, Thomas A. '80 (CHI) [A] Mundelein, IL University of St. Mary of the Lake-Mundelein Seminary.
Bain, Daniel '64 (RIC) Elkton, VA Holy Infant Church; Greene County, VA Shepherd of the Hills Church.
Bain, J.F. Michael '62 (PHX) Williams, AZ St. Joseph's Church.
Bain, John K. '70 (RNO) Zephyr Cove, NV Our Lady of Tahoe Church.
Bain, Ken '90 (SFS) Clark, SD St. Michael Church.
Bain, Richard C. '80 (SFR) Olema, CA Sacred Heart Church; Special Assignment.
Bain, Thomas J. *s.j.* '56 (CLV) [D] Cleveland, OH St. Ignatius High School.
Baird, James R. '93 (DEN) Brush, CO St. Mary Church.
Baird, Joseph A. *o.s.f.s.* '68 (WIL) [I] Childs, MD Oblates of St. Francis De Sales.
Baird, Msgr. Lawrence J. (ORG) [O] Orange, CA Orange Catholic Foundation.
Baird, Msgr. Lawrence J. '69 (ORG) Newport Beach, CA Our Lady Queen of Angels Church.
Baird, Stephen E. *s.j.* '96 (COS) [F] Sedalia, CO Sacred Heart Jesuit Community; [H] Sedalia, CO Sacred Heart Jesuit Retreat House.
Baistra, Jorge '74 (SAT) Special Assignment.
Bajek, Gerald '69 (NEW) Closter, NJ St. Mary Church; Paramus, NJ Bergen Regional Medical Center.
Bajek, Mietek *o.m.i.* '81 (CR) Ogema, MN Most Holy Redeemer Church.
Bajkowski, Dennis W. '71 (CAM) Pine Hill, NJ St. Edward's Church.
Bajorek, James (PH) [133] Philadelphia, PA Our Mother of Sorrows Church.
Bajorek, James R. '80 (PH) [68] Philadelphia, PA St. Ignatius of Loyola Church.
Bajorek, Joseph S. *s.d.b.* '45 (NEW) Mahwah, NJ Immaculate Heart of Mary Church.
Bak, Bernard '88 (BAL) Retired.
Bakatuinamina, Sebastien *c.i.c.m.* '83 (STP) Cedar Lake, MN St. Patrick Church.
Baker, Msgr. Andrew R. '91 (ALN) On Duty Outside the Diocese.
Baker, Andrew R. '91 (PH) [A] Wynnewood, PA Theological Seminary of St. Charles Borromeo, Overbrook.
Baker, Bartley P. '93 (NEW) [20] Jersey City, NJ Our Lady of Mercy Church.
Baker, Brad '00 (JOL) Elmhurst, IL Immaculate Conception Church.
Baker, Bruce *o.carm.* '99 (JOL) [J] Darien, IL Carmelite Provincial Office.
Baker, Donald C. '95 (NY) [141] Bronx, NY St. Frances de Chantal Church.
Baker, Donald H. '66 (WOR) [4] Gardner, MA Sacred Heart of Jesus Church.
Baker, Donald P. '80 (CHL) Absent On Leave.
Baker, Gerald H. '83 (OWN) Hopkinsville, KY SS. Peter and Paul Church.
Baker, Jack H. '93 (DET) Wayne, MI St. Mary Church.
Baker, James E. '63 (DOD) Deerfield, KS Christ the King Church; Garden City, KS St. Mary Church.
Baker, James H. *s.j.* '69 (STL) [C] St. Louis, MO Saint Louis University; [P] St. Louis, MO Jesuit Community Corporation at St. Louis University - Jesuit Hall.
Baker, Jay '92 (HT) Morgan City, LA Holy Cross Church.
Baker, John C. '82 (MIA) [4] Fort Lauderdale, FL St. Anthony Church.
Baker, John C. '82 (PRO) On Duty Outside the Diocese.
Baker, John Sims '94 (NSH) McEwen, TN St. Patrick Church; Tennessee Ridge, TN St. Elizabeth Ann Seton Church.
Baker, John W. '39 (SPC) Retired.
Baker, Joseph M. '85 (TUC) [4] Tucson, AZ Holy Family Church.
Baker, Msgr. Joseph W. '51 (STL) [37] St. Louis, MO St. Hedwig Church.
Baker, Joseph W. '69 (NY) [60] New York, NY St. John the Martyr Church.
Baker, Justin J. '99 (BUR) St. Johnsbury, VT St. John the Evangelist Church.
Baker, Kenneth *s.j.* '62 (PAT) Pequannock, NJ Our Lady of Fatima Chapel (Tridentine) Church.
Baker, Kenneth J. '84 (CHI) [176] Chicago, IL Queen of All Saints Basilica Church.
Baker, Kenneth R. '62 (CIN) [27] Dayton, OH St. Rita Church.
Baker, Michael '74 (LA) Los Angeles, CA L.A. County/University of Southern California Hospital.
Baker, Nicholas J. '63 (LIN) Crete, NE Sacred Heart Church.
Baker, Richard '92 (GAL) Deer Park, TX St. Hyacinth Church.
Baker, Richard M. *m.m.* '71 (FgM) Maryknoll Foreign Missions.
Baker, Robert R. *c.s.c.* '70 (FgM) Holy Cross Foreign Missions.
Baker, Stephen J. *o.s.a.* '90 (NY) [216] Staten Island, NY Our Lady of Good Counsel Church.
Baker, Thomas E. '89 (LA) [26] Los Angeles, CA Our Lady of Guadalupe Church.
Baker, W. Pierre '78 (MAN) Keene, NH St. Bernard Church; West Swanzey, NH St. Anthony Church.
Baker, William F. '77 (FR) Absent on Leave.
Baker, William S. '55 (SY) Clayville, NY St. Patrick Church.
Baker, William T. '82 (ALN) Catasauqua, PA St. Lawrence Church.
Bakewell, Donald V. '66 (DUB) Preston, IA St. Joseph's Church; Sabula, IA St. Peter Church; St. Catherine, IA St. Catherine's Church; St. Donatus, IA St. Donatus Church; Springbrook, IA SS. Peter and Paul Church; [D] Bellevue, IA Marquette High School; [F] Bellevue, IA Bellevue Area Catholic Elementary School.
Bakey, Christopher T. '98 (CAM) Villas, NJ St. Raymond Church.
Bakh, Antoine '88 (OLL) Anaheim, CA St. John Maron Church.
Bakke, Lawrence M. '75 (MAD) [4] Madison, WI Holy Redeemer Church; Madison, WI University Hospitals.
Bakker, Richard T. *s.m.a.* '59 (BO) [2] Malden, MA St. Joseph Church.
Bakle, John L. *s.m.* '67 (CIN) [M] Dayton, OH Marianist Provincialate.
Bakle, John L. *s.m.* '67 (COL) [2] Columbus, OH St. Agatha Church; [39] Columbus, OH Saint Stephen the Martyr Church.
Bakos, Stephen '36 (Y) Retired.
Baky, Isidore '72 (MIA) [8] Fort Lauderdale, FL St. Helen Church.
Bakyil, Alphonsus *s.o.l.t.* '85 (GAL) [52] Houston, TX St. Monica Church.
Bala, Paul W. '69 (SAG) Cass City, MI St. Pancratius Church; Gagetown, MI St. Agatha Church; Wilmot, MI St. Michael Church.
Balaban, Oryst '57 (SJP) Retired.
Balado, Msgr. Armando '49 (MIA) [29] Miami, FL St. Raymond Church.
Balagapo, Victorio '66 (SFR) [12] San Francisco, CA St. Charles Borromeo Church.
Balagat, Arturo '75 (SB) Ontario, CA St. George Church.
Balagtas, Rodel '91 (LA) Canoga Park, CA St. Joseph the Worker Church.
Balance, Harvey '57 (NEW) On Duty Outside the Archdiocese.
Balas, David *o.cist.* '54 (DAL) [B] Irving, TX University of Dallas; [K] Irving, TX Cistercian Abbey of Our Lady of Dallas.
Balasawamy, Gangarapu (ANC) [2] Anchorage, AK St. Anthony Church.
Balash, Michael D. '87 (Y) Ashtabula, OH Our Lady of Mt. Carmel Church.

Balasko, George J. '67 (Y) East Liverpool, OH St. Ann's Church.
Balazs, Richard *c.r.* '65 (CHI) [189] Chicago, IL St. Stanislaus, Bishop and Martyr Church.
Balazy, Edwin W. '62 (DET) [3] Dearborn Heights, MI St. John the Baptist Church.
Balbi, Mario *s.d.b.* (NEW) [S] Orange, NJ Salesians of Don Bosco, S.D.B.
Balcerski, Duane *c.s.c.* '71 (COS) [8] Colorado Springs, CO Sacred Heart Church.
Balchunas, Henry A. '65 (HRT) Wolcott, CT St. Pius X Church.
Balczeniuk, Mark G. '83 (SCR) Dorrance, PA Our Lady Help of Christians Church.
Balczewski, Leslaw *s.j.* '59 (CHI) [N] Chicago, IL Sacred Heart Mission House.
Baldacchino, Peter '96 (NEW) On Duty Outside the Archdiocese.
Balderas, Jose Luis '68 (LAR) La Pryor, TX St. Joseph Church.
Balderas, Msgr. Luis G. '44 (SD) Retired.
Balderrama, George *s.c.j.* '73 (MIL) [K] Milwaukee, WI St. Francis Hospital; [P] Franklin, WI Villa Maria.
Baldonado, Angel (CC) [8] Corpus Christi, TX Our Lady of Perpetual Help Church.
Baldonado, Felipe *o.f.m.* '38 (LA) [Q] Santa Barbara, CA Franciscan Friary, Order of Friars Minor (Old Mission).
Baldonado, Luis *o.f.m.* '52 (PHX) [19] Phoenix, AZ St. Mary's Basilica Church; [23] Phoenix, AZ Sacred Heart Church.
Baldonieri, Thomas F. '90 (CHI) [195] Chicago, IL St. Tarcissus Church.
Baldovin, John *s.j.* '75 (BO) [W] Cambridge, MA Weston Jesuit Community.
Baldrick, Msgr. James F. '63 (PH) Plymouth Meeting, PA Epiphany of Our Lord Church.
Balducelli, Roberto *o.s.f.s.* '36 (WIL) [3] Wilmington, DE St. Anthony of Padua Church.
Balduck, Walter *o.f.m.cap.* '73 (SAG) [9] Saginaw, MI St. Anthony of Padua Church.
Balduf, Raymond J. *s.j.* '51 (NEW) [C] Jersey City, NJ St. Peter's Preparatory School.
Baldus, Leonard *o.m.i.* '42 (BEL) [F] Belleville, IL Shrine of Our Lady of the Snows.
Baldwin, Bradley *t.o.r.* '94 (STP) Brooklyn Park, MN St. Gerard Church.
Baldwin, David E. '77 (CHI) [26] Chicago, IL St. Benedict the African (East) Church.
Baldwin, Msgr. Edward J. '55 (DET) Retired.
Baldwin, John F. '59 (CHI) Retired.
Baldwin, Michael E. '83 (WCH) [20] Wichita, KS St. Vincent de Paul Church.
Baldwin, Paul C. '90 (DUB) [D] Gilbertville, IA Don Bosco High School.
Baldwin, Paul C. '97 (DUB) Jesup, IA St. Athanasius Church; Raymond, IA St. Joseph's Church.
Baldwin, Paul G. '97 (DUB) [D] Waterloo, IA Columbus High School.
Baldyga, William L. '69 (HRT) Suffield, CT St. Joseph's Church.
Balen, Moacir *c.s.* (BO) [2] Somerville, MA St. Anthony Church.
Bales, Robert J. '57 (MIL) Slinger, WI St. Peter Church.
Bales, Msgr. Thomas E. *v.f.* '74 (RCK) Sterling, IL St. Mary Church.
Balestino, Francis P. '60 (ALT) [3] Johnstown, PA Immaculate Conception Church; [12] Johnstown, PA St. Michael's Church.
Balestrieri, Edward '59 (BEL) Sesser, IL St. Mary Church.
Balige, Bonaventura *s.j.* '99 (CHI) [C] Chicago, IL Jesuit Community at Loyola University of Chicago.
Balili, Peter (SB) San Bernardino, CA San Bernardino Community Hospital.
Balili, Peter '89 (SB) [4] Fontana, CA St. Mary Church; Special or Other Diocesan Assignment.
Balinong, Alfredo *s.j.* '64 (NY) [18] New York, NY Blessed Sacrament Church.
Balint, R. James '61 (DAL) Plano, TX Prince of Peace Church.
Balint, Stephen J. '65 (BGP) [3] Norwalk, CT St. Ladislaus Church.
Balio, Paul '72 (SD) [1] San Diego, CA St. Joseph Church; San Diego, CA UCSD Medical Center.
Balistreri, Anthony '93 (SJP) Johnstown, PA St. John the Baptist Church.
Balizan, Daniel M. '89 (SFE) [23] Albuquerque, NM St. Anne Church.
Balkan, Paschal *o.c.s.o.* '55 (ARL) [J] Berryville, VA Cistercian Abbey of Our Lady of the Holy Cross.
Balker, Msgr. Joseph W. '44 (FRS) Retired.
Ball, Edward *m.s.c.* '66 (RCK) [G] Aurora, IL Missionaries of the Sacred Heart Community.
Ball, Harry W. *s.j.* '42 (BO) [W] Weston, MA Campion Health Center, Inc.
Ball, Matthew J. '91 (RVC) Absent on Leave.
Ball, Raymond A. '87 (MAN) [11] Manchester, NH St. John the Baptist Church; [C] Manchester, NH Trinity High School.
Ball, Richard D. '77 (SC) Charter Oak, IA St. Boniface Church; Dow City, IA St. Mary's Church.
Ball, Thomas J. '66 (BUR) [1] Burlington, VT Cathedral of the Immaculate Conception.
Ball, Wayne '89 (RIC) [3] Norfolk, VA Holy Trinity Church.
Ballard, Kevin *s.j.* '85 (SJ) [17] San Jose, CA Most Holy Trinity Church.
Ballard, Mark (BO) [1] Lowell, MA St. Anthony Church.
Ballester, Msgr. Buenaventura '43 (ARE) [2] Arecibo, PR Church of Sagrado Corazon de Jesus.
Ballester, Msgr. Pedro J. '58 (PCE) [6] Ponce, PR San Conrado Church.
Ballesteros, Rodolfo Gonzalez '88 (TR) Mount Holly, NJ Christ the Redeemer Church.
Ballestrazzi, Libero *c.s.j.* '44 (CLV) [O] Avon, OH Congregation of St. Joseph.
Balleza, John '85 (SFR) Absent on Leave.
Ballien, Paul K. '99 (DET) Grosse Pointe Farms, MI St. Paul Catholic Church.
Ballman, Theophane *o.f.m.* (GRY) [J] Cedar Lake, IN San Damiano Friary.
Ballman, Thomas J. '43 (CIN) [4] Dayton, OH St. Anthony of Padua Church; Retired.
Ballor, Milton *c.pp.s.* '55 (CIN) [B] Carthagena, OH St. Charles.
Balluff, John '88 (JOL) Gilman, IL Immaculate Conception Church; Piper City, IL St. Peter Church.
Ballweber, Eugene L. (CHI) Retired.
Ballweg, John M. '56 (NEW) Union, NJ Holy Spirit Church; Retired; [B] South Orange, NJ Seton Hall University.
Ballweg, Msgr. Lawrence F. '40 (RVC) Retired; [M] Uniondale, NY St. Pius X Residence.
Balmeo, Simeon '65 (AGN) Maina, GU Our Lady of the Purification Church.
Balog, Robert A. '72 (RCK) Johnsburg, IL St. John the Baptist Church.
Baloga, Herbert C. *o.f.m.conv.* '38 (SPR) [10] Chicopee, MA St. Stanislaus Basilica Church; [G] Springfield, MA CHE - The Mercy Hospital, Inc.
Balogh, Donald J. '49 (CLV) [5] Parma, OH St. Francis de Sales Church; Retired.
Balsam, John B. *o.p.* '47 (DAL) [K] Irving, TX Dominican Priory of St. Albert the Great.
Balser, Edward '56 (JKS) [5] Jackson, MS Holy Family Church.
Balser, Robert *c.ss.r.* '49 (GR) [3] Grand Rapids, MI St. Alphonsus Church.
Balskus, Charles '65 (CHI) [4] Oak Lawn, IL St. Linus Church.
Balta, Msgr. Raymond A. '69 (PBR) Johnstown, PA St. Mary's Church.
Baltazar, Ayala '43 (SJ) Retired.
Baltes, Gabriel *o.s.b.* '91 (JOL) [J] Lisle, IL St. Procopius Abbey.
Baltes, Timothy '76 (SCL) [8] St. Cloud, MN St. Paul Church.
Balthazar, Msgr. Norman '63 (SP) Zephyrhills, FL St. Joseph Church.
Baltrucki, Leon S. '40 (BRK) Retired.
Baltrusaitis, Gabriel *o.f.m.* '54 (PRT) [I] Kennebunkport, ME St. Anthony's Friary.
Baltrushumas, Anthony P. '37 (BO) Senior Priests.
Baltz, Albert G. '70 (BUR) Brandon, VT St. Mary's Church.
Baltz, David *m.c.c.j.* '67 (FgM) Comboni Foreign Missions.
Baltz, John P., Jr. '43 (NSH) Retired.
Baluyot, Michael '97 (BEA) Nederland, TX St. Charles Borromeo Church.
Balvo, Msgr. Charles D. '76 (NY) On Duty Outside the Archdiocese.
Balwinski, Gerald E. '69 (SAG) [12] Bay City, MI Our Lady of the Visitation Church.
Balys, Thomas I. *o.c.d.* '63 (GRY) [J] Munster, IN Discalced Carmelite Fathers Monastery.
Bambaren, Luis *s.j.* '58 (MIA) [L] Miami, FL Peruvian Mission, Inc.
Bambenek, Oliver *o.f.m.cap.* '65 (MIL) [B] Mount Calvary, WI St. Lawrence Seminary; [B] Mount Calvary, WI St. Felix Friary.
Bamber, William J. *c.m.* '55 (PH) [AA] Philadelphia, PA Congregation of the Mission; [AA] Philadelphia, PA Congregation of the Mission.
Bambera, Msgr. Joseph C. '83 (SCR) Conyngham, PA St. John Bosco Church.
Bamberg, Callistus M. *o.f.m.* '61 (ALB) [B] Loudonville, NY Siena College.
Bambir, Vjekoslav *o.f.m.* '40 (CHI) [N] Chicago, IL Croatian Franciscan Custody of the Holy Family.
Bambol, John *o.f.m.conv.* '41 (BAL) [S] Ellicott City, MD Order of Friars Minor Conventual.
Bambol, John *o.f.m.conv.* '41 (SPR) [5] Holyoke, MA Mater Dolorosa Church.
Bambrick, John P. '91 (TR) Manalapan, NJ St. Thomas More Church.
Bambrick, John W. '70 (ALN) [3] Minersville, PA Our Lady of Mount Carmel Church.
Bambrick, Msgr. Kevin '47 (BLX) [7] Biloxi, MS St. Louis Church; Retired.
Banach, Henry S. '48 (WOR) Retired.
Banach, Michael '88 (WOR) On Special or Other Diocesan Assignment; On Duty Outside the Diocese.
Banach, Walter F. '39 (LIN) Retired.
Banas, James T. *c.s.c.* '57 (FgM) Holy Cross Foreign Missions.
Banas, Leonard N. *c.s.c.* '57 (FTW) [B] Notre Dame, IN University of Notre Dame Du Lac; [J] Notre Dame, IN Holy Cross Community, Corby Hall, University of Notre Dame.
Banazak, Gregory '85 (DET) Special Assignment; [A] Orchard Lake, MI SS. Cyril and Methodius Seminary.
Banden, Joseph W. '69 (STL) [11] Florissant, MO Transfiguration Church.
Bandiera, Colombo F. '52 (WH) Morgantown, WV The New St. Theresa & St. Elizabeth Ann Seton Church; Retired.
Bandle, Ronald J. '68 (MIL) Special Assignment.
Bandres, Antonio *o.f.m.* '75 (FWT) [5] Fort Worth, TX Immaculate Heart of Mary Church.
Bandsuch, Mark R. *s.j.* (DET) [K] Detroit, MI Jesuit Community at the University of Detroit.
Bandurski, Pawel *s.chr.* '92 (SJ) [10] San Jose, CA St. Brother Albert Chmielowski Polish Catholic Pastoral Church.
Bane, Msgr. Raymond T. '51 (NO) Retired.
Banet, Charles H. *c.pp.s.* '49 (GAL) [2] Galveston, TX Holy Rosary Church.
Banet, Paul H. *s.s.j.* '55 (GAL) [2] Galveston, TX Holy Rosary Church.
Banet, Stephen J. '77 (IND) On Duty Outside the Archdiocese.
Banfield, Lawrence E. *o.p.* '41 (P) [18] Portland, OR Holy Rosary Parish & Dominican Priory Church.
Bang, Le Huy *c.ss.r.* '46 (LA) [Q] Baldwin Park, CA Vietnamese Redemptorist Mission.
Baniak, Walter '41 (ALB) Retired.
Banick, Msgr. Thomas V. '63 (SCR) [14] Wilkes-Barre, PA St. Mary's Church of the Immaculate Conception .
Banigan, Herbert '46 (DEN) Retired.
Banken, Robert L. '68 (STL) [61] St. Louis, MO St. Sebastian Church.
Banker, Richard A. '88 (STP) Prior Lake, MN St. Michael Church.
Banks, Charles *o.m.i.* (OAK) [N] Oakland, CA Oblate Provincial House & Procure.
Banks, Charles D. *o.m.i.* '66 (WDC) [M] Washington, DC Missionary Oblates of Mary Immaculate; [M] Washington, DC Oblate College/Center for Mission Studies Community.
Banks, David A. '73 (SP) Homosassa, FL St. Thomas the Apostle Church.
Banks, Edward J. *s.j.* '50 (BO) Dedham, MA St. Mary Church; [W] Boston, MA The Society of Jesus of New England-Provincial Offices; [W] Weston, MA Campion Jesuit Community.
Banks, Evan *o.f.m.* '50 (NEW) Fair Lawn, NJ St. Anne's Church.
Banks, Gary *s.t.* '76 (ARL) [J] Arlington, VA Missionary Servants of the Most Holy Trinity, S.T.
Banks, John P. *s.j.* '51 (FgM) Provinces.
Banks, Michael *o.f.m.cap.* '84 (NY) [DD] White Plains, NY St. Conrad Friary.
Banks, Peter *o.f.m.cap.* '73 (LA) [75] Los Angeles, CA St. Lawrence of Brindisi Church.
Banks, Robert F. *s.j.* '51 (BO) [W] Weston, MA Campion Health Center, Inc.
Bannan, Msgr. Martin '56 (BRK) [115] Brooklyn, NY St. Patrick Church; [V] Brooklyn, NY St. Joseph's Priest Residence.
Bannan, Peter F. '67 (NY) Pelham, NY St. Catharine Church.
Bannantine, Thomas E. *s.j.* '65 (OM) [K] Omaha, NE Jesuit Community at Creighton University.
Banner, Russell J. '67 (CLV) [7] Cleveland, OH Annunciation Church.
Bannin, Eugene T. *s.j.* '50 (NO) [P] New Orleans, LA Ignatius Residence.
Bannon, Anthony *l.c.* '75 (HRT) [V] Orange, CT Legion of Christ, Inc.
Bannon, Anthony *l.c.* '75 (NY) [HH] Rye, NY Catholic Women's Network, Inc.; [HH] Thornwood, NY Consolidated Catholic Administrative Services, Inc.
Banos, Felix '58 (ORL) Lake Wales, FL Holy Spirit Church; Retired.
Bantle, Charles *o.f.m.cap.* '48 (DET) [K] Detroit, MI St. Bonaventure Friary.
Bantle, Charles *o.f.m.cap.* '48 (FgM) Capuchin Foreign Missions.
Bantz, William E. '60 (Y) Maximo, OH St. Joseph Church.
Banuelas, Msgr. Arturo '76 (ELP) [30] El Paso, TX St. Pius X Church.
Banzin, Robert S. '64 (CHI) Riverside, IL St. Mary Church.
Bao, Tran Quoc *c.ss.r.* '90 (LA) [Q] Baldwin Park, CA Vietnamese Redemptorist Mission.
Baptista, Diego '69 (SAC) Ione, CA Sacred Heart Church; Sacramento, CA Mule Creek State Prison.
Baptista, Diego '69 (SR) On Duty Outside the Diocese.

Baptiste, Chuck '96 (PIT) Center Township, PA St. Frances Cabrini Church.

Baptiste, Glen *c.r.* '91 (CHI) [N] Chicago, IL Provincial Office of the Congregation of the Resurrection.

Baraan, Geoffrey '97 (OAK) Pinole, CA St. Joseph's Church.

Barachini, Nello A. *c.m.* '86 (BGP) [2] Bridgeport, CT St. Ambrose Church; Bridgeport, CT Bridgeport Hospital.

Barajas, Abel '96 (MIA) [6] Fort Lauderdale, FL St. Clement Church.

Barajas, Msgr. Ricardo '52 (FRS) Mendota, CA Our Lady of Guadalupe Church.

Barak, Christopher L. '87 (LIN) Palmyra, NE St. Leo's Church.

Baraki, Tesfamariam '75 (WDC) [15] Washington, DC St. Gabriel Church; [25] Washington, DC Kidane-Mehret Ge'ez Rite Catholic Church; [V] Washington, DC Ethiopian and Eritrean Catholic Mission, USA.

Barameda, Arnel (TOL) [1] Lima, OH St. Charles Borromeo Church.

Baran, Blaise R. '88 (MET) Middlesex, NJ Our Lady of Mount Virgin Church.

Baran, Jody '89 (PSC) Swoyersville, PA St. Nicholas Church.

Baran, John P. '84 (BGP) [2] Fairfield, CT Assumption Church.

Baran, Joseph L. '47 (MIL) Retired.

Baran, Zbigniew *s.d.b.* '93 (LA) [C] Rosemead, CA Don Bosco Technical Institute; [D] Rosemead, CA Don Bosco Technical Institute.

Baranek, Raymond '76 (CLV) Absent on Leave.

Baraniak, James T. *o. praem.* '93 (GB) [5] De Pere, WI Our Lady of Lourdes Church; [A] De Pere, WI St. Norbert Abbey; [I] De Pere, WI St. Joseph Priory.

Baraniewicz, Joseph M. *o.s.f.s.* '57 (LAN) Adrian, MI St. Mary of Good Counsel Church.

Baranowski, Arthur R. '68 (DET) Marysville, MI St. Christopher Church; [T] Marysville, MI National Alliance of Parishes Restructuring into Communities.

Baranowski, David J. '73 (HRT) [7] Hamden, CT St. Stephen's Church.

Baranowski, Stanley A. '55 (MIL) Retired.

Baranski, Andrew E. '92 (SY) Phoenix, NY St. Stephen Church.

Baransky, Francis J. '79 (ALN) Jim Thorpe, PA St. Joseph Church.

Barasinski, John B. '81 (GRY) Beverly Shores, IN St. Ann Church.

Barattini, John H. '44 (NO) Retired.

Barbato, Robert *o.f.m.cap* '87 (LA) Solvang, CA Old Mission Santa Ines Church.

Barbella, John J. '87 (MET) Flemington, NJ St. Magdalen de Pazzi Church.

Barber, Bradley A. '94 (CC) [21] Corpus Christi, TX St. Pius X Church; [G] Corpus Christi, TX Bishop Rene H. Gracida Retreat House.

Barber, Eugene J. *s.j.* '63 (BAL) [S] Baltimore, MD Jesuit Fathers and Brothers Maryland Provincial Curia.

Barber, Eugene J. *s.j.* '63 (FgM) Provinces.

Barber, Hal '67 (SFS) Pierre, SD SS. Peter and Paul Church.

Barber, Michael *s.m.* '90 (STL) [P] St. Louis, MO Provincialate of the Society of Mary, Province of St. Louis.

Barber, Michael C. '85 (SFR) Special Assignment; [E] San Francisco, CA St. Ignatius College Preparatory (Coed); [N] San Francisco, CA Jesuit Community at St. Ignatius College Preparatory.

Barber, Michael D. *s.j.* '79 (STL) [C] St. Louis, MO Saint Louis University; [P] St. Louis, MO Leo Brown Jesuit Community.

Barber, Michael L. *s.j.* '75 (PH) [AA] Philadelphia, PA Jesuit Community at St. Joseph's University.

Barber, Stephen *s.j.* '98 (LA) [F] Los Angeles, CA Loyola High School of Los Angeles.

Barbernitz, John P. '50 (BAL) Retired.

Barbero, Mario *i.m.c.* '65 (WDC) [V] Washington, DC Consolata Missionaries House of Studies.

Barbetta, Philip '72 (BRK) Absent on Leave.

Barbian, Leonard M. '65 (MIL) [4] Waukesha, WI St. William Church.

Barbieto, Alex '86 (NEW) Nutley, NJ Holy Family Church.

Barbone, Joseph F. '72 (NEW) [7] Bayonne, NJ Our Lady of the Assumption Church.

Barbour, Claude-Marie (CHI) [B] Chicago, IL The Catholic Theological Union at Chicago.

Barbour, Hugh C. *o.praem* '90 (ORG) [A] Silverado, CA St. Michael's Norbertine Postulancy, Novitiate and Juniorate; [I] Silverado, CA Norbertine Fathers of Orange Inc.

Barcellona, Thomas '95 (CAM) Atco, NJ Assumption Church.

Barch, Howard C., Jr. '93 (PEO) Granville, IL Sacred Heart Of Jesus Church; Hennepin, IL St. Patrick's Church.

Barcio, Robert G. '47 (E) [1] Erie, PA St. Peter Church; Retired.

Barclay, Robert F. '75 (BRK) [170] Queens, NY St. Gabriel Church.

Barclift, Richard L. '66 (PEO) Andalusia, IL St. Patrick's Church.

Barcome, Earl '52 (GB) Retired.

Barczak, Rene *o.f.m.* '64 (PH) [D] Philadelphia, PA Archbishop Ryan High School; [AA] Philadelphia, PA St. Pius X Friary.

Bardes, Msgr. George F. '44 (NY) Mt. Kisco, NY St. Francis of Assisi Church; Retired; [E] White Plains, NY Archbishop Stepinac High School.

Bardino, Jose '62 (MIA) [3] Hialeah, FL St. Benedict Church.

Barerra, Luis A. '95 (ORL) [1] Ocala, FL Blessed Trinity Church.

Barett, Robert '46 (SY) [S] Syracuse, NY St. Pius X Home, Inc.

Barfield, Daniel R. *s.j.* '67 (LSC) Alamogordo, NM St. Jude Church.

Barfknecht, David *o.s.b.* '89 (HON) [G] Waialua, Oahu, HI Benedictine Monastery of Hawaii/Retreat Center.

Barga, Louis J. *c.pp.s.* '54 (CIN) Philothea, OH St. Mary Church.

Bargielski, John C. '45 (GRY) Retired.

Baribeau, Donald G. *m.s.* '75 (R) Swansboro, NC St. Mildred Church.

Barica, Dan *o.f.m.* '99 (LA) [Q] Santa Barbara, CA Franciscan Friary, Order of Friars Minor (Old Mission).

Baril, Gerald M. *m.s.* '59 (MAN) Lebanon, NH Sacred Heart Church.

Barile, Ralph (BRK) [192] Queens, NY St. Margaret Church.

Barille, Nicholas *s.t.* (ORG) [I] Santa Ana, CA Trinitarian Missionaries/Missionary Servants of the Most Holy Trinity.

Barimah-Apay, Michael '82 (BRK) [204] Queens, NY Nativity of the Blessed Virgin Mary Church.

Baris, Bernard *m.s.* '69 (FR) Brewster, MA Our Lady of the Cape Church.

Barita, Joseph '87 (LA) Temple City, CA St. Luke the Evangelist Church.

Barius, Placid *o.f.m.* '43 (PRT) [I] Kennebunkport, ME St. Anthony's Friary.

Barjacoba, Peter '60 (NY) Absent on Leave.

Barkemeyer, John H. '90 (CHI) [34] Chicago, IL St. Cajetan Church.

Barkenquest, Lehr *o.s.f.s.* '64 (LAN) Clarklake, MI St. Rita Church.

Barker, Brian '94 (BEL) Royalton-Zeigler, IL St. Aloysius/Sacred Heart Church; West Frankfort, IL St. John the Baptist Church.

Barker, Jack D. '92 (SB) La Quinta, CA St. Francis of Assisi Church.

Barker, James M. '80 (BAL) [63] Baltimore, MD St. Michael Church; Special Assignment; [W] Baltimore, MD Serra Club Vocation Office.

Barker, John A. '59 (L) [11] Louisville, KY St. Barnabas Church.

Barker, Joseph '53 (ALB) Retired.

Barker, Ronald A. '75 (BO) Stoneham, MA St. Patrick Church.

Barkett, James S. '91 (ARL) Lake Ridge, VA St. Elizabeth Ann Seton Church.

Barkey, Patrick '90 (PIT) Conway, PA Our Lady of Peace Church.

Barkin, Martin F. '77 (PIT) Penn Hills, PA St. Susanna Church.

Barletta, Michael G. '66 (E) [27] Erie, PA St. Patrick/St. Hedwig Church; [M] Erie, PA Holy Family Monastery.

Barley, Tom '91 (SAN) On Special or Other Diocesan Assignment.

Barlow, James P. '73 (SAT) Military Chaplains.

Barman, William '81 (ORG) [4] Santa Ana, CA Our Lady of Lourdes Church.

Barmann, Karl *o.s.b.* '65 (KC) [12] Kansas City, MO St. Gabriel Archangel Church; [J] Conception, MO Conception Abbey.

Barmasse, Gerald R. *c.s.c.* '76 (FgM) Holy Cross Foreign Missions.

Barmasse, Gerald R. *c.s.c.* '76 (FTW) [J] South Bend, IN Congregation of Holy Cross, Indiana Province, Provincial House.

Barnd, Donald *s.c.j.* '78 (MIL) [P] Franklin, WI Villa Maria.

Barnes, Bernard M. *o.s.m.* '48 (CHI) [N] Chicago, IL Order of Friar Servants of Mary (Servites) United States of America Province, Inc.

Barnes, David J. (BO) [3] Beverly, MA St. Mary Star of the Sea Church.

Barnes, Gavin *o.s.b.* '52 (IND) [J] St. Meinrad, IN St. Meinrad Archabbey.

Barnes, Gerard J. '62 (PH) Retired.

Barnes, James H. '69 (LA) [71] Los Angeles, CA St. Joan of Arc Church.

Barnes, John E. '55 (LR) Retired; [H] Little Rock, AR St. John Manor.

Barnes, John G. '52 (DUB) Retired.

Barnes, Joseph A. '57 (ALN) Retired; [J] Bethlehem, PA Holy Family Villa.

Barnes, Msgr. Joseph C. '58 (FRS) Tehachapi, CA St. Malachy Church.

Barnes, Robert W. (NOR) Fishers Island, NY Our Lady of Grace Church.

Barnes, Thomas C. '87 (COV) [5] Covington, KY Holy Cross Church.

Barnett, Daniel '00 (SPK) Pasco, WA St. Patrick Church.

Barnett, Fred J. '52 (JC) Laurie, MO Shrine of St. Patrick Church.

Barnett, James Q. *o.p.* '65 (MIL) [P] Kenosha, WI Order of Preachers, Province of St. Albert the Great.

Barnett, Larry *o.s.b.* '76 (SFS) [F] Marvin, SD Blue Cloud Abbey.

Barnett, Msgr. Steven '70 (SFS) Clear Lake, SD St. Mary Church.

Barnhardt, Bruno *o.s.b.cam.* '66 (MRY) [F] Big Sur, CA New Camaldoli Hermitage.

Barnhart, Victor A. '90 (STL) Pagedale, MO St. Catherine of Siena Church.

Barnhill, Robert K. '85 (LIN) [1] Lincoln, NE Cathedral of the Risen Christ.

Barnufsky, Stephen *o.f.m.* '76 (OAK) [N] Oakland, CA Franciscan Friars Provincial Office, Province of St. Barbara; [N] Oakland, CA Franciscan Friars Provincial Office, Province of St. Barbara.

Barnum, Martin '74 (CHI) On Duty Outside the Archdiocese.

Barnum, Martin '74 (MIL) [B] Hales Corners, WI Sacred Heart School of Theology.

Barnwell, Gerald P. '77 (FR) [2] Fall River, MA Blessed Sacrament Church.

Baron, John B. (NEW) [Q] Newark, NJ Archdiocesan Campus Ministry.

Baron, John B. '73 (NEW) Lodi, NJ St. Francis de Sales Church; [Q] Teaneck, NJ Fairleigh Dickinson Univ.-Teaneck Campus.

Barona, German *m.s.c.* '86 (RCK) [G] Aurora, IL Missionaries of the Sacred Heart Community.

Barona, Jaime '98 (ATL) Cedartown, GA St. Bernadette's Church.

Barone, Michael (TYL) Nacogdoches, TX Sacred Heart Church.

Barone, Robert J. '67 (SCR) [3] Scranton, PA St. Anthony of Padua Church; [A] Dalton, PA Saint Pius X Seminary; [O] Scranton, PA Immaculate Heart of Mary Center, Marywood.

Baroni, Barry J. '79 (ALT) [20] Johnstown, PA St. Andrew's Church.

Baronti, David '73 (SPK) On Duty Outside the Diocese.

Baroody, Sami W. '94 (NTN) West Paterson, NJ St. Ann Church.

Barousse, Raphael *o.s.b.* '55 (NO) Mandeville, LA St. Dymphna Catholic Center and Chapel Church; Mandeville, LA Southeast Louisiana Hospital; [P] St. Benedict, LA St. Joseph Abbey.

Barozzi, Al (BRK) [215] Queens, NY Our Lady of the Miraculous Medal Church.

Barr, Brian '93 (RVC) Huntington, NY St. Patrick's Church.

Barr, Msgr. Eric R. '84 (RCK) Durand, IL St. Mary Church; Special Assignment.

Barr, Frederick *c.s.c.* '54 (P) [B] Portland, OR University of Portland; [L] Portland, OR Holy Cross Fathers & Brothers, C.S.C. - University of Portland.

Barr, Frederick L. (BO) [9] Quincy, MA Star of the Sea Church.

Barr, Joseph F. '78 (BAL) Davidsonville, MD Holy Family Church.

Barr, Liam M. '74 (LAN) [1] Ann Arbor, MI Christ the King Church.

Barr, Liam M. '74 (LIN) On Duty Outside the Diocese.

Barr, Philip R. '48 (PH) Retired.

Barr, Pierre J. '51 (CHI) [143] Chicago, IL Our Lady of Fatima Church; Retired.

Barr, Stanley J. '57 (CAM) Retired.

Barr, Walter M. '59 (BEL) Christopher, IL St. Andrew Church.

Barragan, Juan Carlos '97 (AMA) Borger, TX St. John the Evangelist Church; Bovina, TX St. Ann's Church.

Barranco, Rogelio *s.d.b.* '61 (SJN) [37] San Juan, PR Maria Auxiliadora Church.

Barrand, James '89 (VNN) On Leave.

Barranger, Joseph *o.p.* (BO) [Y] Dover, MA St. Stephen Priory Spiritual Life Center.

Barranger, Joseph *o.p.* '87 (BO) [Y] Dover, MA St. Stephen Priory Spiritual Life Center.

Barranger, Ralph '61 (ELP) [4] El Paso, TX Blessed Sacrament Church.

Barras, Greg '84 (BLX) [1] Biloxi, MS Cathedral of the Nativity of the Blessed Virgin Mary.

Barras, Michael J. '73 (LKC) [2] Lake Charles, LA Immaculate Heart of Mary Church.

Barras, Robert '80 (GAL) Katy, TX St. Edith Stein Church.

Barre, Michael L. *s.s.* '70 (BAL) [A] Baltimore, MD St. Mary's Seminary and University.

Barreda, Giles *o.f.m.* '61 (ALB) [1] Troy, NY St. Anthony of Padua Church.

Barreneche, Franco *o.carm.* '44 (SJN) [59] San Juan, PR Santa Teresita Del Nino Jesus Church.

Barrera, Albino F. *o.p.* '93 (PRO) [P] Providence, RI St. Thomas Aquinas Priory at Providence College.
Barrera, Filiberto '98 (OAK) [2] Hayward, CA St. Bede Church.
Barrera, Gustavo '79 (BWN) [10] Brownsville, TX Saint Mary, Mother of the Church.
Barrera, Jose A. '92 (PCE) Coamo, PR St. Blase Church.
Barres, Msgr. John O. '89 (WIL) [2] Wilmington, DE St. Ann Church.
Barrett, Charles J. *s.m.* '42 (WDC) [M] Washington, DC Marist Center.
Barrett, D. Oliver *c.s.sp.* '48 (PT) [7] Pensacola, FL St. Anne Church.
Barrett, Daniel J. '46 (BO) Senior Priests.
Barrett, David A. '97 (STP) [23] Minneapolis, MN SS. Cyril & Methodius Church.
Barrett, David S. (GB) Gresham, WI St. Francis Solanus Church.
Barrett, David S. '64 (GB) Keshena, WI St. Michael Church; South Branch, WI St. Joseph of the Lake Church.
Barrett, Edward F. '61 (SCR) [10] Scranton, PA Immaculate Conception Church.
Barrett, Edward J. '57 (HBG) On Duty Outside the Diocese.
Barrett, Edward J. '75 (CHI) Palatine, IL St. Theresa Church.
Barrett, Emmett A. *o.f.m.* '55 (PAT) [M] Butler, NJ St. Anthony Friary.
Barrett, Msgr. Francis X. '55 (ALN) Retired.
Barrett, Gerard *o.m.i.* '64 (BWN) San Juan, TX St. John the Baptist Church.
Barrett, Msgr. Harry C. '73 (NY) On Special or Other (Arch)Diocesan Assignment.
Barrett, James L. '56 (KAL) Marshall, MI St. Mary Church.
Barrett, James L. '82 (CHI) Skokie, IL St. Joan of Arc Church.
Barrett, John '59 (JOL) Elmhurst, IL Mary, Queen of Heaven Church.
Barrett, John J. *s.j.* '42 (NY) [DD] New York, NY Murray-Weigel Hall.
Barrett, John J. '78 (RVC) Babylon, NY St. Joseph's Church.
Barrett, John W. '52 (WOR) Retired.
Barrett, Kevin S. '92 (PCE) On Duty Outside the Diocese.
Barrett, Michael *c.ss.r.* (BO) [53] Boston, MA Our Lady of Perpetual Help Church.
Barrett, Michael '85 (GAL) [33] Houston, TX Holy Cross Chapel Church; [P] Houston, TX Opus Dei.
Barrett, Michael G. '76 (MIL) Grafton, WI St. Joseph Church.
Barrett, Michael G. *o.f.m.* '90 (IND) [12] Indianapolis, IN Sacred Heart of Jesus Church.
Barrett, Miles J. '82 (SC) On Duty Outside the Diocese.
Barrett, Patrick H. '57 (MET) [4] Carteret, NJ St. Elizabeth of Hungary Church.
Barrett, Patrick J. '52 (PRT) [1] Portland, ME Cathedral of the Immaculate Conception; Retired.
Barrett, Patrick J. '59 (GAY) Mapleton, MI St. Joseph Church.
Barrett, Robert E. '63 (BO) Permanent Disability.
Barrett, Robert P. '48 (Y) Retired.
Barrett, Thomas '71 (BEL) Bridgeport, IL Immaculate Conception Church; Lawrenceville, IL St. Lawrence Church.
Barrett, Thomas '88 (ORL) [7] Orlando, FL St. Charles Borromeo Church; Special Assignment; [A] Orlando, FL Bishop Moore High School.
Barrett, Thomas '93 (PMB) On Duty Outside the Diocese.
Barrett, Thomas J. *c.ss.r.* '67 (TOL) [2] Lima, OH St. Gerard Church.
Barrett, Thomas M. '71 (BEL) St. Francisville, IL St. Francis Xavier Church.
Barrett, William M. '59 (ROC) Lyons, NY St. Michael Church.
Barretta, Msgr. Anthony J. '47 (BRK) [212] Queens, NY Our Lady of Hope Church; Retired; [Z] Brooklyn, NY Holy Cross.
Barrette, Donat A. '54 (PRO) [M] North Smithfield, RI St. Antoine Residence.
Barrette, Eugene *m.s.* '67 (ATL) Smyrna, GA St. Thomas the Apostle Church.
Barricks, Robert '94 (P) [16] Portland, OR Holy Family Church.
Barrientos, Gustavo (OM) [4] Omaha, NE St. Ann Church; [35] Omaha, NE St. Peter Church.
Barringer, Robert J. *c.s.b.* '74 (GAL) [Q] Sugar Land, TX Basilian Mission Center.
Barrios, Diego *c.m.f.* '42 (LA) [Q] Rancho Dominguez, CA Dominguez Seminary Inc.
Barron, Cecil *c.m.f.* '42 (FRS) [8] Fresno, CA St. Anthony Mary Claret Church; Retired.
Barron, Clemente *c.p.* '70 (SAT) [M] San Antonio, TX Casa Pasionista Guadalupe.
Barron, Dale F. *m.m.* '65 (FgM) Maryknoll Foreign Missions.
Barron, Daniel *o.m.v.* '96 (SFD) [2] Alton, IL Immaculate Conception-St. Mary's Church.
Barron, Edward M. '38 (CHI) Retired.
Barron, Gerald *o.f.m.cap.* '66 (SFR) Burlingame, CA Our Lady of Angels Church.
Barron, John P. *s.j.* '82 (ALN) [A] Wernersville, PA Jesuit Center; [N] Wernersville, PA Jesuit Center for Spiritual Growth.
Barron, Robert E. '86 (CHI) [A] Mundelein, IL University of St. Mary of the Lake-Mundelein Seminary.
Barron, Stanley C. '74 (PAT) Ogdensburg, NJ St. Thomas of Aquin Church.
Barron, Wayne J. *c.m.f.* '58 (SPC) [D] Springfield, MO St. John's Mercy Villa; [E] Springfield, MO Claretians Missionaries' Residence-Villa Claret.
Barrons, Brian *m.m.* '84 (FgM) Maryknoll Foreign Missions.
Barrow, John A. '80 (PMB) Stuart, FL St. Andrew Church.
Barrow, Joseph A. '96 (NEW) Special Assignment.
Barruetabena, Esteban '54 (ARE) Lares, PR St. Joseph Church.
Barruetabena, Felix *c.p.* '52 (SJN) [9] Carolina, PR Santa Gema Galgani Church.
Barry, Bernard J. '39 (SPK) Retired.
Barry, Bernard John *s.j.* '00 (STL) [C] St. Louis, MO Saint Louis University.
Barry, David E. *s.j.* '78 (PH) [AA] Philadelphia, PA Jesuit Community at St. Joseph's University.
Barry, Donald M. *s.j.* '66 (BGP) [E] Fairfield, CT Fairfield College Preparatory School; [P] Fairfield, CT The Fairfield Jesuit Community-Fairfield University.
Barry, Msgr. Edward '73 (NY) Dover Plains, NY St. Charles Borromeo Church.
Barry, Francis '75 (SAV) Retired.
Barry, Garrett J. '66 (BO) [1] Quincy, MA St. Ann Church.
Barry, Gerard D. '50 (BO) [1] Newton, MA St. Bernard Church.
Barry, Gerard S. *s.j.* '63 (BAL) [S] Baltimore, MD Jesuit Fathers and Brothers Maryland Provincial Curia.
Barry, Gerard S. *s.j.* '63 (FgM) Provinces.
Barry, Henry F. '41 (BO) Rockland, MA Holy Family Church; Senior Priests.
Barry, James (CAM) Haddonfield, NJ Christ the King Church.
Barry, James '59 (NEW) [N] Cliffside Park, NJ St. Patrick's Missionary Society.
Barry, James *c.p.* '69 (CHI) [N] Chicago, IL Passionist Community-CTU.
Barry, James D. '61 (NU) Retired.
Barry, James F. '67 (CAM) West Collingswood, NJ Transfiguration Church.
Barry, James J. '69 (BO) [4] Chelsea, MA Our Lady of Grace Church.
Barry, Msgr. John F. '61 (LA) Manhattan Beach, CA American Martyrs Church.
Barry, John G. *c.ss.r.* '48 (ORL) New Smyrna Beach, FL Sacred Heart Church.
Barry, John M. '88 (WDC) [6] Silver Spring, MD St. John the Baptist Church.
Barry, Lawrence E. *s.j.* '58 (STL) [O] St. Louis, MO Fusz Pavilion.
Barry, Leo '51 (WOR) Retired.
Barry, Maurice J. '67 (HRT) Windsor, CT St. Gertrude's Church.
Barry, Michael W. *ss.cc.* '64 (LA) [Q] La Verne, CA Congregation of the Sacred Hearts of Jesus and Mary.
Barry, Msgr. Patrick J. '54 (NY) [5] Mt. Vernon, NY SS. Peter and Paul Church.
Barry, Paul '48 (WDC) Retired.
Barry, Peter J. *m.m.* '65 (FgM) Maryknoll Foreign Missions.
Barry, Raymond *c.s.sp.* (BO) [48] Boston, MA Most Precious Blood Church.
Barry, Raymond J. '65 (HRT) Branford, CT St. Therese Church.
Barry, Robert L. *o.p.* '73 (CHI) [N] Chicago, IL Dominicans (Provincial Office).
Barry, Ronald A. '52 (RVC) Retired.
Barry, Thomas J. '67 (HRT) Newington, CT St. Mary Church.
Barry, Thomas M. '61 (WOR) Spencer, MA Mary, Queen of the Rosary Church; [K] Worcester, MA Providence Extended Care Center.
Barry, Msgr. Thomas P. '39 (DEN) [1] Englewood, CO All Souls Church; Retired.
Barry, William A *s.j.* '62 (BO) [W] Weston, MA Campion Jesuit Community.
Barry, William J. '44 (LA) Retired.
Barsen, Msgr. Herman J. '40 (LAF) Retired.
Barszcz, Jozef A. '88 (SUP) Glenwood City, WI St. John the Baptist Church.
Barszczewski, Msgr. Francis A. '68 (PH) Clifton Heights, PA Sacred Heart Church.
Barta, Ardel H. '63 (DUB) [3] Dubuque, IA St. Columbkille's Church; [4] Dubuque, IA St. Mary's Church; [5] Dubuque, IA St. Patrick's Church.
Barta, Msgr. James O. '55 (DUB) On Special or Other Archdiocesan Assignment; [L] Dubuque, IA St. Joseph's Convent, Mount Carmel.
Barta, Wayne J. '60 (MIL) Ashford, WI St. Martin Church; Retired.
Barta, William (GB) Graduate Studies.
Bartak, James J. '89 (OM) Newcastle, NE St. Peter Church; Ponca, NE St. Joseph Church.
Bartchak, Mark L. '81 (E) [29] Erie, PA St. Stanislaus Church.
Bartek, James F. '53 (OM) Retired.
Bartek, Valerian '82 (LIN) Ulysses, NE Immaculate Conception Church.
Bartek, William C. '61 (OM) Retired.
Bartel, Franklin '70 (PHX) Sun City, AZ St. Elizabeth Seton Church.
Bartel, Leo J. '58 (RCK) Morrison, IL St. Mary Church.
Bartel, Martin R. *o.s.b.* '85 (GBG) [H] Latrobe, PA Saint Vincent Archabbey.
Bartell, Ernest J. *c.s.c.* '61 (FTW) [B] Notre Dame, IN University of Notre Dame Du Lac; [J] Notre Dame, IN Holy Cross Community, Corby Hall, University of Notre Dame.
Bartelme, James P. '82 (SUP) Lac du Flambeau, WI St. Anthony of Padua Catholic Church; Odanah, WI St. Mary Church.
Bartelt, Victor (MIL) [N] Wauwatosa, WI St. Camillus Health Center, Inc.
Barter, Robert J. '61 (PRM) Detroit, MI St. Nicholas Church.
Barth, J. Robert *s.j.* '61 (BO) [W] Chestnut Hill, MA The Jesuit Community at Boston College.
Barth, John C. *m.m.* '91 (FgM) Maryknoll Foreign Missions.
Barth, Michael D. '94 (COV) Carrollton, KY St. John the Evangelist Church.
Barth, Michael K. *s.t.* '79 (CLV) [3] Cleveland, OH St. Agnes - Our Lady of Fatima Church; [O] Cleveland, OH Missionary Servants of the Most Holy Trinity.
Barth, Raymond J. '85 (KAL) Bridgman, MI Our Lady Queen of Peace Church.
Barthel, Charles '82 (STL) [63] St. Louis, MO St. Stephen, Protomartyr Church.
Bartholomew, Carl *s.a.c.* '00 (VEN) [4] Sarasota, FL St. Martha Church.
Bartko, Gerald L. *o.s.f.s.* '66 (BUF) [5] Lockport, NY St. Patrick Church; [D] Niagara Falls, NY Niagara Catholic Junior-Senior High School.
Bartko, Louis *o.f.m.* (PEO) [3] Peoria, IL Sacred Heart Church.
Bartkus, Msgr. Algimantas A. '65 (ALN) On Duty Outside the Diocese.
Bartlett, Albert P. *s.j.* '54 (NY) [145] Bronx, NY St. Helena Church; [DD] New York, NY Jesuit Community at Fordham University.
Bartlett, H. James *s.m.* '69 (CIN) [24] Dayton, OH Queen of Apostles Church; [M] Dayton, OH Marianist Provincialate.
Bartlett, Lee F. '72 (WOR) [16] Worcester, MA Sacred Heart Church.
Bartlett, Richard *c.m.f.* '50 (CHI) [163] Chicago, IL St. Paul Church.
Bartley, David J. '70 (BO) [7] Salem, MA St. Thomas the Apostle Church.
Bartley, Denis *s.s.c.* '51 (OM) [K] St. Columbans, NE St. Columban's Foreign Mission Society.
Bartley, Vincent '69 (NY) [223] Staten Island, NY St. Paul Church.
Bartman, Roch *o.f.m.conv.* '31 (MRY) [F] Arroyo Grande, CA St. Joseph's Cupertino Novitiate.
Bartnik, Harry S. '56 (TLS) Retired.
Bartnik, James T. '75 (BUF) [18] Buffalo, NY St. Casimir Church.
Bartnikowski, Raymond '63 (CLV) Richfield, OH St. Victor Church.
Bartniski, William D. (GAL) [U] Galveston, TX The Bishop's Palace.
Bartniski, William D. '67 (GAL) [5] Galveston, TX St. Peter the Apostle Church.
Bartok, Msgr. Charles '47 (ORL) Retired.
Bartollotta, Victor W., Jr. '90 (ROC) On Duty Outside the Diocese.
Bartolo, Salvador *o.carm.* '52 (FgM) Carmelite Foreign Missions.
Bartolo, Salvador *o.carm.* '52 (JOL) [J] Darien, IL Carmelite Provincial Office.
Bartolotta, Victor '90 (DAL) [C] Dallas, TX Bishop Lynch High School, Inc.
Barton, Michael *m.c.c.j.* '75 (FgM) Comboni Foreign Missions.
Barton, Msgr. Raymond A. '66 (RIC) [10] Virginia Beach, VA St. Nicholas Church.
Bartone, Donald E. '48 (DET) Retired.
Bartos, Andrezej '83 (CHI) [112] Chicago, IL St. Ladislaus Church.
Bartos, Francis J. '54 (PH) Retired.
Bartos, Kris '85 (MIA) Pembroke Pines, FL St. Boniface Church.
Bartosic, Mark '94 (CHI) [5] Chicago, IL St. Agnes of Bohemia Church.
Bartosz, Andrzej (CHI) [181] Chicago, IL St. Richard Church.

Bartoszek, Justin *c.p.* '64 (FgM) Mission Procurators.
Bartoul, William '77 (SAM) On Duty Outside the Diocese.
Bartruff, Louis B. '45 (BRK) Retired; [V] Douglaston, NY Bishop Mugavero Residence.
Bartsch, Edward C. '49 (VIC) Praha, TX St. Mary's Church.
Bartsch, Ken *o.f.m.conv.* '75 (STP) [Q] Prior Lake, MN Franciscan Retreat House.
Bartz, Richard B. '74 (CHI) [J] Chicago, IL Columbus Hospital.
Barusefski, Ronald '89 (PSC) Lansford, PA St. John the Baptist Church.
Barwig, Regis N. '59 (GB) [I] Oshkosh, WI Community of Our Lady.
Barwin, John G. '80 (E) Linesville, PA St. Philip Church; Bradford, PA Federal Correction Institution.
Baryski, Wojciech *s.ch.* '65 (DET) [73] Detroit, MI Sweetest Heart of Mary Church; Hamtramck, MI St. Florian Church.
Barzyk, Andrew A. '94 (CHI) Other Assignments.
Barzyk, Msgr. Robert R. '58 (GAL) Retired.
Basa, Francis J. '71 (CLV) [4] Akron, OH Christ the King Church.
Basarab, John G. '79 (PSC) Annandale, VA Epiphany of Our Lord Church.
Baseford, Paul '57 (SB) Retired.
Basetti-Sani, Giulio *o.f.m.* '35 (NY) [DD] New York, NY Franciscan Friars, Order of Friars Minor, Holy Name Province.
Bash, Cletus '56 (OKL) Special Assignment; [E] Oklahoma City, OK Mercy Health Center.
Bashand, Brian G. (BO) Holliston, MA St. Mary Church.
Bashista, Brian G. '99 (ARL) Fairfax, VA St. Mary of Sorrows Church.
Basil, John E. (NEW) Teaneck, NJ Holy Name Hospital.
Basile, Benjamin *c.pp.s.* '69 (CIN) [M] Dayton, OH Provincial Office of the Cincinnati Province of the Society of the Precious Blood.
Basile, Gioacchino '95 (NEW) On Duty Outside the Archdiocese.
Basile, Gioacchino '95 (PCE) Penuelas, PR St. Joseph Church.
Basile, Nicholas F. '49 (NY) [174] Bronx, NY Our Lady of Mt. Carmel Church; Retired.
Basinow, Leonard '53 (SAM) West Palm Beach, FL Mary Mother of Light Maronite Church.
Baskara Tulus Wardaya, Francis Xavier *s.j.* '92 (MIL) [P] Milwaukee, WI Jesuit Community at Marquette University.
Basler, Msgr. Howard B. '58 (BRK) [169] Queens, NY St. Francis de Sales Church; [L] Brooklyn, NY Catholic Charities; [V] Brooklyn, NY St. Joseph's Priest Residence.
Basols, Jose A. *sch.p.* '68 (PCE) [C] Coto Laurel, PR Colegio Ponceno.
Basquel, Thomas *c.s.sp.* '76 (BRK) [141] Brooklyn, NY St. Thomas Aquinas Church; [141] Brooklyn, NY St. Thomas Aquinas Church.
Bass, Francis E. '48 (DAV) Retired; [M] Davenport, IA St. Vincent Center.
Bass, Michael E. '87 (LR) Benton, AR Our Lady of Fatima Church.
Bass, Msgr. Ricardo E. '74 (DET) [4] St. Clair Shores, MI St. Joan of Arc Church.
Bassano, Michael *m.m.* '75 (FgM) Maryknoll Foreign Missions.
Bassano, Michael '75 (SY) On Duty Outside the Diocese.
Bassett, Frank '00 (NY) Goshen, NY St. John the Evangelist Church.
Bassil, Pierre '98 (OLL) Warren, MI St. Sharbel Church.
Basso, Richard '62 (SEA) Puyallup, WA All Saints Church; [C] Bellevue, WA Eastside Catholic High School.
Bastia, Raymond B. '75 (PRO) [4] Providence, RI St. Ann Church.
Bastiaensen, Jos *c.i.c.m.* '64 (FgM) Missionhurst Foreign Missions.
Bastian, James R. '95 (BUF) Williamsville, NY St. Gregory the Great Church.
Bastian, Robert J. '43 (CIN) Retired.
Bastidas, Alexis '84 (NY) [18] New York, NY Blessed Sacrament Church.
Bastos, Luis '95 (PMB) Wellington, FL St. Rita Church.
Bastos, Luiz C. '85 (ORL) On Duty Outside the Diocese.
Bastress, Msgr. Arthur W. '51 (BAL) [5] Baltimore, MD St. Alphonsus, Shrine of Church.
Basznianin, Richard '84 (TR) Forked River, NJ St. Pius X Church.
Batch, Thomas A. '76 (SAC) Retired and in Senior Ministry.
Batcha, James '85 (PRM) Lorain, OH St. Michael Church; Lorain, OH St. Nicholas Church.
Batcheldor, C. Joseph '57 (L) Bardstown, KY St. Joseph Church; Retired.
Batcho, Michael '73 (PHU) Absent on Leave.
Batcho, Robert '88 (STF) Auburn, NY SS. Peter and Paul Church.
Bateman, John R. '96 (HBG) Hanover, PA St. Joseph Church.
Bates, Donald J. *o.s.a.* '60 (CHI) [N] Olympia Fields, IL Austin Friary.
Bates, James R. '63 (LFT) Noblesville, IN Our Lady of Grace Church.
Bates, Urban M. *o.p.* '53 (ANC) [1] Anchorage, AK Holy Family Church.
Bath, Winston L. '72 (ALB) Hudson, NY Church of St. Mary.
Bathke, Joseph *c.pp.s.* '78 (DAV) Centerville, IA St. Mary's Church; [J] Centerville, IA Mercy Medical Center - Centerville.
Bathula, Babu '96 (OKL) Ponca City, OK Church of St. Mary.
Batista, George L. '83 (NEW) On Duty Outside the Archdiocese.
Batkiewicz, Joseph '71 (LC) Cassel, WI Sacred Heart Church; Halder, WI St. Patrick Church.
Batoon, Robert '72 (HON) Ewa Beach, HI Our Lady of Perpetual Help Church.
Batson, Msgr. John R. '57 (MEM) Retired.
Batt, Dacian *o.f.m.* '58 (PEO) Metamora, IL St. Mary's Church; Washburn, IL St. Elizabeth Church.
Battafarano, Gregory *o. carm.* '81 (NEW) Bogota, NJ St. Joseph's Church.
Battaglia, Ignatius *c.s.* '59 (PRO) [16] Providence, RI Holy Ghost Church.
Batterberry, Michael J. '70 (SEA) [B] Seattle, WA John F. Kennedy Memorial High School.
Battersby, Gerard (DET) [26] Detroit, MI St. Gerard Church; [35] Detroit, MI Immaculate Heart of Mary Church.
Battiato, Ronald A. '61 (OM) Randolph, NE St. Frances de Chantal Church.
Battirossi, Bartholomew *m.c.c.j.* '42 (LA) [12] Los Angeles, CA Holy Cross Church.
Battista, Msgr. Leo '48 (WOR) Retired.
Battisti, Lewis A. '62 (CAM) Margate, NJ Blessed Sacrament Church.
Battle, Lawrence '49 (SB) Retired.
Battocletti, Richard L. '53 (STU) Martins Ferry, OH St. Mary Church; Retired.
Battolini, Ottaviano *o.f.m.* '43 (FgM) Franciscan Foreign Missions.
Batts, Peter *o.p.* '81 (WDC) [11] Washington, DC St. Dominic Church & Priory Church.
Batule, Robert J. '85 (RVC) Mineola, NY Corpus Christi Church.
Batykefer, John '90 (PIT) Pleasant Hills, PA St. Elizabeth Church; [C] Mt. Lebanon, PA Seton-LaSalle Catholic High School.
Bau, Chau Xuan *c.ss.r.* '62 (LA) [Q] Baldwin Park, CA Vietnamese Redemptorist Mission.
Bau, Mark Doan Quang *c.m.c.* '77 (BO) [58] Boston, MA St. Peter Church.
Baudhuin, Robert F. *m.m.* '54 (FgM) Maryknoll Foreign Missions.
Baudone, Louis '59 (GR) Retired.
Bauer, Carl E. '63 (WH) Star City, WV St. Mary's Church.
Bauer, Charles A. '78 (MEM) Humboldt, TN Sacred Heart Church; Milan, TN St. Matthew Church.
Bauer, Daniel *s.v.d.* '74 (FgM) Society of the Divine Word Foreign Missions.
Bauer, Donald J. '48 (SY) [3] Utica, NY Our Lady of Lourdes Church; Retired.
Bauer, Elmer, III *c.m.* '93 (FgM) Vincentian Foreign Missions.
Bauer, Elmer, III *c.m.* '93 (PH) [AA] Philadelphia, PA Congregation of the Mission.
Bauer, Erwin J. '47 (DET) Retired.
Bauer, Msgr. Henry '48 (KC) Retired.
Bauer, Jacob F. '48 (GI) Retired.
Bauer, John F. '65 (E) Punxsutawney, PA SS. Cosmas and Damian Church; Warren, PA Warren State Hospital.
Bauer, John M. '73 (PIT) Carmichaels, PA St. Hugh Church; Nemacolin, PA Our Lady of Consolation Church.
Bauer, John M. '79 (STP) [20] St. Paul, MN St. Gregory the Great (Highland Catholic Community) Church; [23] St. Paul, MN St. Leo (Highland Catholic Community) Church; [33] St. Paul, MN St. Therese (Highland Catholic Community) Church; [W] St. Paul, MN The Highland Catholic Community.
Bauer, Karl A. '67 (NY) [1] Yonkers, NY St. Anthony Church.
Bauer, Lawrence T. *c.s.c.* '35 (FTW) [J] South Bend, IN Congregation of Holy Cross, Indiana Province, Provincial House.
Bauer, Msgr. Leonard A. '37 (BEL) [E] Belleville, IL Meredith Memorial Home; [J] Belleville, IL Serra Club of St. Clair County.
Bauer, Mark F. '86 (GR) Rothbury, MI Our Lady of the Assumption Church; Shelby, MI Our Lady of Fatima Church.
Bauer, Paul '91 (SD) Unassigned.
Bauer, Ralph '47 (LR) Retired.
Bauer, Richard W. '85 (FgM) Maryknoll Foreign Missions.
Bauer, Rick '59 (SLC) On Duty Outside the Diocese.
Bauer, Robert A. '87 (DET) Carleton, MI St. Patrick Church.
Bauer, Robert J. *s.d.b.* '71 (COL) [A] Columbus, OH Pontifical College Josephinum; [H] Columbus, OH Salesian Center.
Bauer, Roy R. '59 (SFD) [9] Quincy, IL St. Peter Church.
Bauer, Scott A. '98 (LC) Cashton, WI Sacred Heart of Jesus Church; Norwalk, WI St. Augustine of Hippo Church; Saint Mary's Ridge, WI Nativity of the Blessed Virgin Mary Church; Summit, WI St. John the Baptist Church.
Bauer, Stephan *o.s.c.* '92 (STP) [N] Shoreview, MN Crosier Community of Shoreview.
Bauer, Stephen F. '77 (STL) Dutzow, MO St. Vincent de Paul Church.
Bauer, Sylvester W. '42 (JC) Jefferson City, MO Missouri Intermediate Reformatory.
Bauer, Sylvester W. '42 (SPC) Retired.
Bauer, William M. '73 (ALB) Greenville, NY St. John the Baptist Church.
Bauerle, Bernhard *o.carm.* '64 (CHI) [N] Mundelein, IL Carmelite Monastery.
Bauernfeind, Thomas J. '63 (BAL) [55] Baltimore, MD Little Flower, Shrine of Church; Retired.
Baugh, David G. '57 (CLV) [6] Euclid, OH St. William Church.
Bauhoff, Msgr. Richard C. '73 (RVC) Roslyn, NY St. Mary's Church.
Bauhs, Eugene J. '48 (MAD) Retired.
Bauler, Msgr. Gary P. '67 (LA) Simi Valley, CA St. Peter Claver Church.
Baum, Boniface *o.f.m.* '46 (CHI) [N] Chicago, IL St. Peter's Friary.
Baum, Terrence A. *s.j.* '81 (CHI) [D] Wilmette, IL Loyola Academy.
Bauman, Dale '82 (FTW) Albion, IN Blessed Sacrament Church; Ligonier, IN St. Patrick Church.
Bauman, John F. '69 (NEW) [26] Jersey City, NJ St. Paul's Church.
Bauman, Richard J. *s.j.* '75 (CHI) [N] Chicago, IL Chicago Province of the Society of Jesus-Provincial Office.
Bauman, Rodger R. '82 (STP) Richfield, MN St. Peter Church.
Bauman, Stephen '92 (ORL) [A] Melbourne, FL Central Catholic High School.
Bauman, William A. '60 (KC) [39] Kansas City, MO St. Thomas More Church.
Baumann, Anthony *o.f.m.* '44 (SFR) [5] San Francisco, CA St. Anthony of Padua Church.
Baumann, Charles R. *s.j.* '80 (MIL) [P] Milwaukee, WI Jesuit Community at Marquette University.
Baumann, Gregory *s.j.* '93 (SD) [4] San Diego, CA Christ the King Church.
Baumann, Hugh *o.s.b.* '41 (NO) [P] St. Benedict, LA St. Joseph Abbey.
Baumann, John A. *s.j.* '69 (OAK) [N] Oakland, CA Murray Residence Community; [S] Oakland, CA Pacific Institute for Community Organization.
Baumann, Lawrence '64 (PHX) Lake Havasu City, AZ Our Lady of the Lake Church.
Baumann, Richard J. *s.j.* '75 (CHI) [N] Chicago, IL Miguel Pro Jesuit Community.
Baumann, Richard J. *s.j.* '75 (CIN) [V] Cincinnati, OH St. Xavier Church Property Corporation.
Baumann, Richard J. *s.j.* '75 (FgM) Provinces.
Baumann, Silas *o.f.m.cap.* '51 (GB) [I] Appleton, WI St. Fidelis Friary.
Baumann, Stephen (ORL) Melbourne, FL Our Lady of Lourdes Church.
Baumann, Msgr. Theodore J. '67 (BEL) Freeburg, IL St. Joseph Church.
Baumberger, Richard '89 (SFS) Kranzburg, SD Holy Rosary Church.
Baumert, Frank J. '78 (OM) Albion, NE St. Michael Church; Petersburg, NE St. John the Baptist Church.
Baumgaertner, Msgr. William L. '46 (STP) Retired; [C] St. Paul, MN University of St. Thomas.
Baumgardner, Michael '95 (SD) [5] San Diego, CA Good Shepherd Church.
Baumgartel, David A. '73 (WIL) Newark, DE St. John the Baptist-Holy Angels Church; Wilmington, DE A.I. du Pont Institute.
Baumgartner, Msgr. A. Thomas '58 (BAL) [93] Baltimore, MD St. Ursula Church.
Baumgartner, Andrew *o.s.b.* '60 (B) [C] Jerome, ID Monastery of the Ascension.
Baumgartner, Bernard *c.ss.r.* '44 (BAL) Annapolis, MD St. Mary Church; [S] Annapolis, MD Saint Mary Rectory.
Baumgartner, David '90 (CR) Ada, MN St. Joseph's Church.
Baumgartner, John H. '63 (MIL) [1] West Allis, WI St. Aloysius Church.
Baumhart, Raymond C. *s.j.* '57 (CHI) [C] Chicago, IL Jesuit Community at Loyola University of Chicago.
Baumiller, Robert C. *s.j.* '65 (CIN) [M] Cincinnati, OH

Jesuit Community at Xavier University.
Baumstein, Paschal M. *o.s.b.* '79 (CHL) [J] Belmont, NC Belmont Abbey.
Baur, Joseph A. *o.f.m.* '52 (PHX) Guadalupe, AZ Our Lady of Guadalupe Church.
Baures, Steven H. '83 (LC) Germantown, WI Our Lady of the Lake Church; New Lisbon, WI St. Paul Church.
Bausch, Michael J. '79 (ROC) Henrietta, NY Church of the Good Shepherd.
Bausch, William J. '55 (TR) Manasquan, NJ St. Denis Church; Retired.
Bauschka, Joseph '55 (GB) Absent on Leave.
Bauta, Krzysztof T. '86 (CC) On Duty Outside the Diocese.
Bautista, Gaspar '75 (FRS) [1] Fresno, CA St. John Church.
Bautista, Jose '91 (ORL) Apopka, FL St. Francis of Assisi Church.
Bautista, Jose A. '99 (LA) Van Nuys, CA St. Elisabeth Church.
Bauwens, Thomas E. '87 (OM) Elgin, NE St. Boniface Church; Raeville, NE St. Bonaventure Church.
Bava, David '73 (WDC) [18] Washington, DC Holy Redeemer Church.
Bavaro, John D. *o.f.m.* '63 (BO) [P] Andover, MA Franciscan Center; [W] Andover, MA St. Francis Friary; [Y] Andover, MA Franciscan Center - Retreat House.
Baver, John J. '91 (PIT) [38] Pittsburgh, PA Sacred Heart Church.
Baver, Msgr. William F. '81 (ALN) [3] Bethlehem, PA Holy Ghost Church.
Bavero, Benvenute *o.f.m.* '44 (LA) [Q] Santa Barbara, CA Franciscan Friary, Order of Friars Minor (Old Mission).
Bavinger, R. Bruce '78 (WDC) [2] Washington, DC St. Aloysius Church.
Bawiec, Edward J. '54 (PEO) Retired.
Bawyn, Anthony '82 (SEA) [14] Seattle, WA St. Mark Church.
Baxa, Henry R. '90 (SAL) Beloit, KS St. John the Baptist Church.
Baxter, Gregory '88 (OM) [2] Omaha, NE St. Adalbert Church.
Baxter, Michael J. *c.s.c.* '85 (FTW) [B] Notre Dame, IN University of Notre Dame Du Lac; [J] Notre Dame, IN Holy Cross Community, Corby Hall, University of Notre Dame.
Baxter, Stephen R. '81 (WCH) Fredonia, KS Sacred Heart Church; Neodesha, KS St. Ignatius Church.
Baxter, Msgr. Thomas F. '76 (MAD) Lancaster, WI St. Clement Church.
Baxter, Thomas-Benedict *o.s.b.* '79 (CHI) [N] Chicago, IL Monastery of the Holy Cross.
Bay, Joseph N. '94 (COL) [8] Columbus, OH St. Catharine Church.
Bayard, Michael S. *s.j.* '98 (SEA) [A] Seattle, WA Seattle University.
Bayard, Nicholas R. '46 (CHR) [11] Charleston, SC Church of the Nativity; Retired.
Baybay, Felicito '74 (ORL) [5] Orlando, FL Holy Family Church.
Bayer, Edward J. '56 (BAL) Randallstown, MD Holy Family Church; [W] Baltimore, MD Cursillo Movement.
Bayer, Lawrence J. '58 (CLV) [2] Parma, OH St. Bridget Church.
Bayer, Leonard '51 (SFE) Retired.
Bayer, Peter '71 (ROC) [43] Rochester, NY St. Margaret Mary Church; Rochester, NY St. Ann's Home/Heritage.
Bayer, Peter T. '71 (ROC) [F] Rochester, NY St. Ann's Home for the Aged; [F] Rochester, NY St. Ann's Nursing Home Co., Inc.
Bayer, Walter C. '42 (STA) Korona, FL St. Mary's Church.
Bayhi, M. Jeffrey '79 (BR) [2] Baton Rouge, LA St. Agnes Church.
Bayhi, Peter *s.j.* '66 (LAF) [J] Grand Coteau, LA Jesuit Spirituality Center (St. Charles College).
Bayless, Louis I. *m.m.* '46 (NY) [DD] Maryknoll, NY Maryknoll Fathers and Brothers.
Baylis, Thomas J. '59 (HRT) [2] Milford, CT St. Ann's Church.
Bayne, David C. *s.j.* (DET) [K] Detroit, MI Jesuit Provincial Office-Detroit Province of the Society of Jesus.
Bayne, Joseph *o.f.m.conv.* '85 (BUF) [J] Buffalo, NY The Franciscan Center, Inc.
Bayne, Robert C. *m.m.* '63 (FgM) Maryknoll Foreign Missions.
Baz, Msgr. Louis '81 (OLL) Detroit, MI St. Maron Church.
Bazan, Msgr. Joaquin '62 (SFE) [3] Albuquerque, NM Community of the Risen Savior Church.
Bazan, Msgr. Joaquin '62 (WDC) On Duty Outside the Archdiocese.
Bazan, Michael J. '84 (ARL) Warrenton, VA St. John the Evangelist Church.
Bazina, Basile (BO) Burlington, MA St. Margaret Church.
Bazton, Jose M. Garcia *m.ss.cc.* '59 (SJN) [10] Bayamon, PR San Juan Bautista de la Salle Church.
Bazzi, Michael J. '64 (EST) El Cajon, CA St. Peter Chaldean Church.
Bazzi, Michael J. '64 (SD) El Cajon, CA St. Peter Church.
Bazzoli, Robert *o.s.f.s.* '88 (PH) [76] Philadelphia, PA St. Joachim Church.
Beach, Msgr. Francis W. '76 (PH) On Special or Other Archdiocesan Assignment.
Beach, Raymond *o.f.m.* '48 (PAT) [K] Totowa, NJ St. Joseph's Home for the Elderly.
Beachamp, Henry *c.ss.r.* '78 (CGS) Fajardo, PR Santiago Apostol Church.
Beachum, Edwin P. '84 (MOB) [2] Mobile, AL St. Catherine of Siena Church.
Beacom, John F. '37 (OM) Retired.
Beacom, Vincent L. '44 (SC) Retired.
Beal, John P. '74 (E) On Duty Outside Diocese.
Beal, John P. '74 (WDC) [C] Washington, DC Catholic University of America, The.
Beale, Kenneth R. '92 (NEW) Military Chaplains.
Beale, Robert P. (BO) Dedham, MA Norfolk County House of Correction.
Bean, Charles S. '62 (CAM) On Sick Leave.
Bean, Donald A. '63 (BUR) Retired.
Beans, Elmer '86 (FBK) Mountain Village, AK St. Lawrence Church.
Beard, Msgr. Raymond '41 (BAK) Retired.
Beardsley, Frederick '60 (RIC) Retired.
Bearss, James M. '97 (GAY) Frankfort, MI St. Ann Church.
Beary, Thomas J. '62 (BUR) Retired; [D] Burlington, VT St. Joseph's Home.
Beasley, Msgr. Thomas J. '53 (BUF) [1] Orchard Park, NY Nativity of Our Lord Church.
Beat, Jerome A. '63 (WCH) [17] Wichita, KS St. Patrick Church.
Beath, James D. '79 (CHI) [2] Cicero, IL St. Frances of Rome Church.
Beaton, Kevin J. '87 (SAM) New Castle, PA St. John the Baptist Church.
Beattie, Msgr. James T. '61 (WDC) [1] Bethesda, MD St. Bartholomew Church.
Beattie, John A. *o.s.f.s.* '65 (VEN) [A] Fort Myers, FL Bishop Verot High School.
Beattie, Joseph A. *o.s.f.s.* '65 (VEN) [A] Fort Myers, FL Bishop Verot High School.
Beattie, Thomas '93 (SEA) Sequim, WA St. Joseph Church.
Beatty, James H. '74 (CLV) Avon Lake, OH Holy Spirit Church.
Beatty, Michael D. '64 (CIN) [78] Cincinnati, OH St. Simon the Apostle Church.
Beaubien, David W. '93 (WDC) [1] Silver Spring, MD St. Andrew Apostle Church.
Beauchamp, E. William *c.s.c.* '82 (FTW) [B] Notre Dame, IN University of Notre Dame Du Lac; [J] South Bend, IN Congregation of Holy Cross, Indiana Province, Provincial House; [J] Notre Dame, IN Holy Cross Community, Corby Hall, University of Notre Dame.
Beauchemin, Ronald *m.s.* '68 (GAL) Friendswood, TX Mary, Queen Church.
Beauclair, Stephen *o.s.b.* '67 (SCL) [I] Collegeville, MN St. John's Abbey, of the Order of St. Benedict.
Beauclair, Stephen G. *o.s.b.* '67 (STP) Hastings, MN St. Elizabeth Ann Seton Church.
Beaudet, Christopher J. '00 (STP) Edina, MN Our Lady of Grace Church.
Beaudet, Eugene J. '53 (OG) Star Lake, NY St. Hubert Church.
Beaudet, George W. '75 (PRT) Special or Other Diocesan Assignment; Sabbatical.
Beaudin, William *o.f.m.* '81 (PRO) [P] Providence, RI St. Francis Friary.
Beaudin, William R. '82 (BUR) Montpelier, VT St. Augustine Church; [H] Burlington, VT University of Vermont-The Catholic Center at UVM.
Beaudoin, Andrew *s.s.s.* '54 (CLV) [O] Cleveland, OH Congregation of the Blessed Sacrament Provincial House.
Beaudoin, Andrew *s.s.s.* '54 (SP) Spring Hill, FL St. Frances Xavier Cabrini Church.
Beaudoin, Hubert N. *o.praem.* '56 (PH) [AA] Philadelphia, PA St. Norbert Priory; [AA] Paoli, PA Daylesford Abbey.
Beaudry, David B. '82 (GB) Northeim, WI St. Thomas the Apostle Church.
Beaulieu, Earl G. '60 (SHP) Retired.
Beaulieu, Peter R. '83 (WOR) [J] Worcester, MA Saint Vincent Hospital, Inc.
Beaulieu, Raymond '42 (PRO) Retired.
Beaulieu, Richard C. '76 (BO) Winchester, MA St. Mary Church.
Beaulieu, Richard M. '71 (FR) Acushnet, MA St. Francis Xavier's Church.
Beaulieu, Robert J. '57 (HEL) Bozeman, MT Holy Rosary Church.
Beaumont, Gregory '96 (FRS) Tipton, CA St. John The Evangelist Church.
Beaumont, Msgr. Joachim '59 (NY) [33] New York, NY St. Emeric Church.
Beaumont, Msgr. Joachim B. '59 (NY) [31] New York, NY St. Elizabeth Church.
Beaumont, Richard '58 (FWT) [9] Fort Worth, TX St. Bartholomew Church.
Beaupre, R. Bradley *c.s.c.* '68 (FR) [A] North Easton, MA Stonehill College; [A] North Easton, MA Holy Cross Fathers Religious.
Beauregard, David N. *o.m.v.* '80 (BO) [B] Boston, MA Our Lady of Grace Seminary; [BB] Boston, MA St. Clement's Archdiocesan Eucharistic Shrine.
Beauregard, Jim '70 (BUR) Newport, VT St. Mary Star of the Sea Church.
Beauregard, Paul *o.m.i.* (BO) [4] Lowell, MA Saint Jeanne d'Arc Church.
Beauregard, Paul *o.m.i.* '61 (BO) [W] Lowell, MA Missionary Oblates of Mary Immaculate.
Beauregard, Thomas J. '51 (TOL) [24] Toledo, OH St. Hyacinth Church; Retired.
Beausoleil, Gerald L. *m.m.* '52 (FgM) Maryknoll Foreign Missions.
Beauvais, David E. '62 (RCK) [6] Rockford, IL St. James Church.
Beaven, Robert W. '68 (CHI) Grayslake, IL St. Gilbert Church.
Beaver, Nelson G. '76 (TOL) Norwalk, OH St. Mary, Mother of the Redeemer Church; Peru, OH St. Alphonsus Liguori Church.
Beaver, Reinard W. '56 (SPK) Retired.
Beaver, William A. *o.s.b.* '85 (GBG) Jeannette, PA Sacred Heart Church.
Beavers, Carl A. '68 (CHY) Jackson, WY Our Lady of the Mountains Church.
Bebak, Brian '86 (WCH) Fort Scott, KS Mary Queen of Angels Church.
Bebedik, Hilarion *o.s.b.m.* '48 (RVC) [M] Glen Cove, NY St. Josaphat's Monastery, Novitiate and Retreat House.
Bebek, Dominic L. '53 (LA) Retired.
Bebel, Alfred J. '58 (SY) [8] Syracuse, NY Our Lady of Solace Church; Syracuse, NY University Hospital; Special Assignment.
Becerra, Robert '59 (PMB) [2] Lake Worth, FL St. Luke Church.
Becerra, Robert L. '89 (NEW) On Duty Outside the Archdiocese.
Bechamps, Vincent *o.ss.t.* '66 (NO) New Orleans, LA University Hospital.
Bechard, Bernard J. *s.s.e.* '49 (BUR) Sheldon Springs, VT St. Anthony Church.
Bechard, Dean P. *s.j.* '91 (NY) [DD] New York, NY Jesuit Community at Fordham University.
Bechard, Gerard V. '80 (DET) [5] Westland, MI SS. Simon and Jude Church.
Becherer, David '48 (MOB) Retired.
Becherer, James R. '54 (CLV) Retired.
Becht, James D. '53 (RC) Bonesteel, SD Immaculate Conception Church; Fairfax, SD St. Anthony's Church.
Bechtel, James C. '71 (ALN) Weatherly, PA St. Nicholas Church.
Bechtold, Paul I. *c.p.* '41 (CHI) [N] Chicago, IL Passionist Community-Immaculate Conception Monastery.
Beck, Aelred J. *o.s.b.* '48 (GBG) [H] Latrobe, PA Saint Vincent Archabbey.
Beck, Msgr. Albert '49 (GAL) Retired.
Beck, Charles L. '45 (MAD) Retired.
Beck, David J. '67 (TOL) Bluffton, OH St. Mary Church; [3] Lima, OH St. John the Evangelist Church.
Beck, Edward *c.p.* '85 (NY) [DD] Bronx, NY Passionist Residence.
Beck, Erwin G. *s.j.* '60 (NEW) [C] Jersey City, NJ St. Peter's Preparatory School.
Beck, Msgr. George A. '41 (GAL) Retired.
Beck, Henry *o.f.m.* '80 (CIN) [M] Cincinnati, OH St. Francis Seraph Friary; [M] Cincinnati, OH St. Francis Seraph Friary.
Beck, Henry *o.f.m.* '80 (FgM) Franciscan Foreign Missions.
Beck, Joseph C. '84 (PIT) [5] Pittsburgh, PA St. Bede Church; Allegheny County, PA Forbes Nursing Center; Allegheny County, PA Kane Regional Center - Glen Hazel; Allegheny County, PA Woodhaven Convalescent Center; Allegheny County, PA Greater Pittsburgh Rehab Hospital; Allegheny County, PA Independent Court of Monroeville; Allegheny County, PA Manorcare Health Services.
Beck, Lawrence J. '88 (LA) On Duty Outside the Archdiocese.
Beck, Richard *o.m.i.* '67 (GAL) [S] Dickinson, TX Christian Renewal Center.
Beck, Richard P. '55 (MIL) Retired.
Beck, Richard W. '74 (SCR) Pleasant Mount, PA St. James Church.
Beck, Robert P. '76 (BEA) Military Chaplains.
Beck, Robert R. '66 (DUB) [C] Dubuque, IA Loras College.

Beck, Steven Thomas '93 (NY) Absent on Leave.
Becka, Robert *s.j.* '60 (FgM) Provinces.
Becker, Anthony J. '47 (RCK) Retired.
Becker, Arthur '73 (ALB) [1] Cohoes, NY Holy Trinity Church.
Becker, Bruno *o.s.b.* '51 (P) [L] St. Benedict, OR Mt. Angel Abbey.
Becker, Charles P. '86 (CHI) Other Assignments.
Becker, Daniel J. '96 (WOR) [28] Worcester, MA St. Stephen's Church; [C] Worcester, MA St. Peter-Marian Central Catholic Junior/Senior High School.
Becker, David R. '66 (ALT) McConnellsburg, PA St. Stephen's Church.
Becker, Dennis E. '62 (NU) Retired.
Becker, Donald W. '67 (BUF) [3] Batavia, NY St. Mary Church.
Becker, Franklyn W. '64 (MIL) On Leave.
Becker, Msgr. Frederick J. '59 (NY) [159] Bronx, NY St. Lucy Church; Bronx, NY Our Lady of Mercy Medical Center; [W] New York, NY Our Lady of Mercy Medical Center.
Becker, John J. '72 (GB) [1] Oshkosh, WI St. Peter Church; [2] Oshkosh, WI St. Mary Church.
Becker, John R. *s.j.* '56 (PHX) [B] Phoenix, AZ Brophy College Preparatory.
Becker, Joseph M. '39 (DET) [P] Clarkston, MI Colombiere Center.
Becker, Joseph P. *o.s.f.s.* (ALN) [B] Center Valley, PA Desales University.
Becker, Joseph P. *o.s.f.s.* '69 (ALN) Allentown, PA Lehigh Valley Hospital at Cedar Crest; [K] Center Valley, PA Oblates of St. Francis de Sales.
Becker, Michael '75 (ALT) Loretto, PA Basilica of St. Michael the Archangel.
Becker, Michael C. '99 (STP) New Brighton, MN St. John the Baptist Church.
Becker, Nicholas J. '38 (SC) Retired.
Becker, Paul D. '73 (BIS) Foxholm, ND St. Mary Church.
Becker, Richard F. '72 (PBL) [12] Pueblo, CO St. Joseph Church; Vineland, CO St. Therese Church.
Becker, Robert '79 (AUS) [9] Austin, TX Sacred Heart Church.
Becker, Robert T. '64 (SFD) [5] Springfield, IL St. Agnes Church.
Becker, Ronald '72 (TR) [13] Trenton, NJ St. Francis of Assisium Church.
Becker, Russell C. *o.f.m.* '72 (NY) [115] New York, NY St. Stephen of Hungary Church.
Becker, Thomas G. '80 (SCL) Glenwood, MN Sacred Heart Church.
Becker, Vincent J. '62 (BUF) [46] Buffalo, NY St. Martin Church.
Becker, William M. '88 (WIN) [B] Winona, MN Saint Mary's University of Minnesota.
Beckfelt, John W. '74 (LC) Big River, WI Nativity of the Blessed Virgin Mary Church.
Beckley, Clarence *s.s.c.* '66 (OM) [K] St. Columbans, NE St. Columban's Foreign Mission Society.
Beckley, John *s.m.* (SP) [K] Tampa, FL St. Joseph's Hospital, Inc.
Beckman, David M. '92 (DUB) Belmond, IA St. Francis Xavier Church; Clarion, IA St. John's Church; Eagle Grove, IA Sacred Heart Church.
Beckman, Gary L. '95 (DAV) Charlotte, IA Assumption and St. Patrick's Church; Sugar Creek, IA Ss. Mary and Joseph Church.
Beckman, John *s.j.* '54 (CIN) [M] Cincinnati, OH Faber Jesuit Community.
Beckman, John J. *s.j.* '54 (CIN) [F] Cincinnati, OH St. Xavier High School.
Beckman, Joseph F. '54 (CIN) Retired; [B] Cincinnati, OH Mt. St. Mary's Seminary of the West.
Beckman, Mark '90 (NSH) Springfield, TN Our Lady of Lourdes Church.
Beckman, Martin A. '58 (STP) Retired.
Beckman, Richard J. '56 (OKL) Newkirk, OK St. Francis of Assisi Church.
Beckman, Robert E. *s.j.* '56 (CHI) [N] Chicago, IL Chicago Province of the Society of Jesus-Provincial Office.
Beckman, Robert E. *s.j.* '56 (FgM) Provinces.
Beckmann, Msgr. Donald M. '70 (RVC) Woodbury, NY Holy Name of Jesus Church.
Becnel, Msgr. Terry B. '64 (NO) Buras, LA Our Lady of Good Harbor Church.
Becquet, Paul L. *c.pp.s.* '56 (JC) Sedalia, MO St. Patrick Church; Sedalia, MO Sacred Heart Church.
Beczak, Mariusz *o.s.j.* '98 (SAC) [A] Loomis, CA Mount St. Joseph Novitiate and Seminary.
Bedard, Andre L. '57 (MAN) [6] Nashua, NH Infant Jesus Church; Retired.
Bedard, J. Raymond '53 (WOR) Retired.
Bedard, Paul *s.d.b.* '65 (NY) [FF] Stony Point, NY Don Bosco Retreat Center and Marian Shrine; [FF] Stony Point, NY Marian Shrine.
Bedenikovic, Steven *o.f.m.* '85 (CHI) [186] Chicago, IL Sacred Heart Church.
Bedessem, Henry W. '59 (GB) Retired.
Bedillion, James R. *j.c.l.* '75 (PIT) O'Hara Township, PA St. Joseph Church.
Bednar, Dwayne '91 (CLV) [3] Parma, OH St. Charles Borromeo Church.
Bednar, Gerald J. '83 (CLV) [A] Wickliffe, OH St. Mary Seminary and Graduate School of Theology.
Bednar, Thomas V. *c.s.c.* '85 (FgM) Holy Cross Foreign Missions.
Bednar, Thomas V. *c.s.c.* '85 (FTW) [B] Notre Dame, IN University of Notre Dame Du Lac.
Bednarik, John *o.f.m.cap.* '68 (FgM) Capuchin Foreign Missions.
Bednark, Walter '47 (SCL) Lake Henry, MN St. Margaret's Church; Retired.
Bednarski, Mitchell J. '44 (LAN) Retired.
Bednartz, Msgr. August C. '52 (BRK) Retired; [Z] Farmingdale, NY St. Charles.
Bednarz, Jan '72 (SLC) Vernal, UT St. James the Greater Church.
Bednarz, Matt A. '42 (CHI) [76] Chicago, IL St. Hilary Church; [198] Chicago, IL St. Thecla Church; Retired.
Bedoya, Carlos '90 (ORL) Melbourne, FL Our Lady of Lourdes Church.
Bedoya, Guillermo L. Corrales '89 (PRO) [6] Providence, RI Assumption of the Blessed Virgin Mary Church.
Bedoya, Hugo *c.m.* '56 (BRK) [194] Queens, NY St. Mary Church.
Bedoya, Ruben D. '91 (TYL) Palestine, TX Sacred Heart Church.
Beebe, Msgr. Charles J. '70 (PEO) [13] Peoria, IL St. Philomena's Church.
Beebe, David E. '61 (CAM) [6] Cherry Hill, NJ Queen of Heaven Church.
Beeching, Roy T. '74 (GRY) [6] Hammond, IN St. Joseph Church.
Beeda, Msgr. Francis J. '61 (SCR) [6] Hazleton, PA St. Joseph's Church.
Beegan, James *m.s.f.* '00 (SAT) [B] San Antonio, TX MSF Formation Community.
Beekman, Carl Edward '00 (RCK) St. Charles, IL St. Patrick Church.
Beeman, James W. '53 (HBG) Retired.
Beemster, John *s.v.d.* '40 (CHI) [B] Techny, IL Divine Word Residence.
Beemsterboer, Francis *s.v.d.* '51 (FgM) Society of the Divine Word Foreign Missions.
Beerman, Andrew J. '96 (WIN) Luverne, MN St. Catherine's Church.
Beerntsen, Harold (GB) Oconto Falls, WI St. Anthony Church; Stiles, WI St. Patrick Church.
Beerntsen, Harold '61 (GB) Retired.
Beers, Ervan *o.f.m.* '55 (FRS) Delano, CA Our Lady of Guadalupe Church.
Beers, John Michael *s.s.l.* '79 (ALN) On Duty Outside the Diocese.
Beeson, Msgr. Lawrence A. '60 (DM) Atlantic, IA SS. Peter and Paul Church.
Beever, Carlton J. '74 (IND) [32] Indianapolis, IN St. Philip Neri Church.
Beez, John E. *s.j.* '61 (COL) [25] Columbus, OH Community of Holy Rosary and St. John Church.
Beezer, Arnold R. *s.j.* '64 (P) [L] Portland, OR Colombiere Community.
Befort, Daryl '95 (WCH) Kingman, KS St. Patrick Church.
Befort, Earl *o.f.m.cap.* (SAL) Hays, KS St. Joseph's Church.
Befort, Earl *o.f.m.cap.* '70 (SAL) [D] Hays, KS St. Joseph's Friary.
Begay, Joseph *s.s.j.* '59 (WDC) [B] Washington, DC St. Joseph's Seminary.
Begay, Joseph N. *s.s.j.* '59 (WDC) [27] Washington, DC St. Luke Church.
Begg, Christopher T. '77 (WDC) [24] Washington, DC St. Joseph on Capitol Hill Church; Special Ministries; [C] Washington, DC Catholic University of America, The.
Beggane, Thomas (LSC) Absent On Sick Leave.
Beggans, Msgr. Joseph A. '43 (NEW) [12] Jersey City, NJ St. John the Baptist Church; Retired.
Beggiani, Seely '61 (SAM) [A] Washington, DC Our Lady of Lebanon Maronite Seminary.
Beggiani, Seely '61 (WDC) [C] Washington, DC Catholic University of America, The.
Beggin, Thomas M. '79 (GF) Retired.
Begin, Daniel L. '75 (CLV) [16] Cleveland, OH St. Cecilia Church; [23] Cleveland, OH Epiphany Church.
Begin, Msgr. Raymond F. '52 (PRT) Retired.
Begin, Robert T. '64 (CLV) [17] Cleveland, OH St. Colman Church; Avon, OH Our Lady of the Wayside.
Begley, James J. '82 (RIC) Mechanicsville, VA Church of the Redeemer.
Begley, John J. *s.j.* '62 (BO) [W] Boston, MA The Society of Jesus of New England-Provincial Offices.
Begley, John J. *s.j.* '62 (SCR) [C] Scranton, PA University of Scranton.
Begley, Paul '55 (OM) [11] Omaha, NE St. Bridget Church; Retired.
Begley, Thomas B. '60 (SPR) Cheshire, MA St. Mary of the Assumption Church.
Begley, Thomas M. '89 (STL) [28] St. Louis, MO St. Boniface Church.
Begly, Mark S. '84 (ALT) New Baltimore, PA St. John the Baptist Church.
Begnaud, Adam *o.s.b.* '96 (NO) [P] St. Benedict, LA St. Joseph Abbey.
Begolly, Michael J. '81 (GBG) [1] Greensburg, PA Blessed Sacrament Church.
Begue, Joseph E. *c.m.* '55 (STL) [P] St. Louis, MO Lazarist Residence; [V] St. Louis, MO The Vincentian Press Religious Supply.
Behan, George P. '56 (PRO) [12] Warwick, RI St. William Church.
Behan, Harry P. '73 (NU) St. Peter, MN St. Peter Church.
Behan, Hugh F. '64 (JC) Absent on Leave.
Behan, Jim *o.s.f.s.* '73 (R) Wilmington, NC Immaculate Conception Church.
Behan, Msgr. Philip A. '70 (SB) Palm Springs, CA St. Theresa Church.
Behan, Thomas W. *o.s.a.* '58 (OAK) Castro Valley, CA Our Lady of Grace Church.
Behen, John *c.pp.s.* '46 (CIN) [M] Dayton, OH Provincial Office of the Cincinnati Province of the Society of the Precious Blood.
Behen, John M. *c.pp.s.* '46 (JC) Sedalia, MO Sacred Heart Church.
Behl, Msgr. Richard A. '66 (MET) [1] Metuchen, NJ Cathedral of St. Francis.
Behler, Donald A. '47 (CIN) [23] Cincinnati, OH St. Dominic Church; Retired.
Behman, Toma A. '54 (DET) [2] Southfield, MI St. Bede Church.
Behnen, Robert *o.f.m.* '60 (STL) Oakville, MO St. Francis of Assisi Church; [P] Oakville, MO St. Francis Friary.
Behnke, John J. *c.s.p.* '76 (STP) [29] Minneapolis, MN St. Lawrence Church; [N] Minneapolis, MN Paulist Fathers; [V] Minneapolis, MN Newman Center at St. Lawrence.
Behnke, Robert C. '73 (CHI) [202] Chicago, IL St. Thomas More Church.
Behrend, Thomas J. '00 (CLV) [4] Lakewood, OH St. James Church.
Behrens, Msgr. A.W. '45 (SC) Retired.
Behrens, James Stephen *o.c.s.o.* '74 (ATL) [J] Conyers, GA The Monastery of the Holy Spirit.
Behringer, William *s.m.* '60 (CLV) [4] Cleveland, OH St. Aloysius - St. Agatha Church.
Behrmann, Msgr. Elmer H. '38 (STL) Retired.
Beichner, Paul E. *c.s.c.* '39 (FTW) [J] South Bend, IN Congregation of Holy Cross, Indiana Province, Provincial House.
Beidelman, Patrick J. '98 (IND) [30] Indianapolis, IN St. Monica Church.
Beierschmitt, Msgr. Leo A. '48 (HBG) [1] Lancaster, PA St. Anne Church.
Beierwaltes, Charles *c.ss.r.* '67 (FgM) Redemptorist Foreign Missions.
Beierwaltes, Charles C. *c.ss.r.* '67 (CHI) [N] Chicago, IL Redemptorist Theology Residence; [N] Glenview, IL The Redemptorists of Glenview, Illinois.
Beighlie, James T. *c.m.* '79 (STL) [P] St. Louis, MO Vincentian Residence.
Beilman, J. Brian '86 (OM) [6] Omaha, NE Assumption, B.V.M. Church.
Beining, Paul R. *s.j.* '55 (SCR) [C] Scranton, PA University of Scranton.
Beirne, Charles J. *s.j.* (SY) [B] Syracuse, NY Le Moyne College; [S] Syracuse, NY Jesuits at LeMoyne, Inc.
Beirne, Charles J. *s.j.* '69 (FgM) Provinces.
Beirne, Gerald E. '62 (PRO) Smithfield, RI St. Philip Church.
Beirne, M. Christen '69 (NEW) Mahwah, NJ Immaculate Conception Church.
Beirne, Robert M. '63 (PRO) On Duty Outside the Diocese.
Beischel, Richard L. *c.pp.s.* '56 (CIN) [M] Dayton, OH Provincial Office of the Cincinnati Province of the Society of the Precious Blood.
Beischel, Thomas *c.pp.s.* '58 (CIN) [3] Dayton, OH St. Albert the Great Church; [M] Dayton, OH Provincial Office of the Cincinnati Province of the Society of the Precious Blood.
Beischel, Thomas J. *c.pp.s.* '58 (CIN) [U] Dayton, OH Community Support Charitable Trust.
Beisel, James D. '80 (PH) [D] Warminster, PA Archbishop Wood Catholic High School; [V] Warminster, PA Regina Coeli Residence for Priests.
Beitansopf, John '73 (IND) [24] Indianapolis, IN St. Lawrence Church.
Beiter, Eugene J. '64 (LAN) Leslie, MI SS. Cornelius and Cyprian Church.
Beiter, Robert G. '64 (BUF) Brocton, NY St. Patrick Church.
Beiting, Msgr. Ralph '49 (LEX) Louisa, KY St. Jude Church.
Beitzinger, George J. '45 (MIL) Retired.
Bejarano, Ramon '98 (STO) [4] Stockton, CA St. George Church.
Bejgrowicz, Joseph S. '70 (NEW) Kenilworth, NJ St. Theresa's Church.

Bek, Viktor '92 (PHU) Carteret, NJ St. Mary's Church; Marlboro, NJ St. Volodymyr's Church.
Beksha, Francis W. '46 (BO) Franklin, MA St. Mary Church; Senior Priests.
Belair, Eugene '53 (SCL) Retired.
Belanger, Gerald R. '75 (MAN) North Conway, NH Our Lady of the Mountains Church.
Belanger, Rene A. *s.s.s.* '50 (CLV) [O] Cleveland, OH Congregation of the Blessed Sacrament Provincial House.
Belanggoy, Plutarco *c.i.c.m.* '96 (BWN) La Joya, TX Our Lady, Queen of Angels Church.
Belanich, Giordano '75 (NEW) Fairview, NJ St. John the Baptist Church.
Belauskas, August J. '68 (CHI) [A] Mundelein, IL University of St. Mary of the Lake-Mundelein Seminary.
Belcher, Francis H. *s.j.* '61 (BO) [Y] Gloucester, MA Eastern Point Retreat House.
Belcher, Paul F. *s.j.* '63 (SAC) [14] Sacramento, CA St. Ignatius of Loyola Church.
Belcher, Sandy Augustine '86 (HRT) [I] New Haven, CT Hospital of St. Raphael.
Belchez, Caesar A. '95 (HBG) Hershey, PA St. Joan of Arc Church.
Belczak, Edward A. '72 (DET) [1] Troy, MI St. Thomas More Church.
Belczak, Thomas A. '80 (DET) [4] Redford, MI St. Valentine Church.
Belda, Leo W. '42 (MIL) Retired.
Belen, Germain *o.f.m.conv.* '50 (SAV) St. Simons Island, GA St. Williams Church.
Belfield, John '58 (STU) Retired.
Belford, Msgr. William J. '74 (NY) Blauvelt, NY St. Catharine Church; [CC] Nyack, NY Catholic Community Services of Rockland, Inc.
Belgarde, George H. *s.j.* '88 (NY) [DD] New York, NY Jesuit Provincial's Office.
Belgarde, George H. *s.j.* '88 (OG) [J] Hogansburg, NY St. Regis Mission.
Belhumeur, Paul *m.s.* '61 (BUR) Windsor, VT St. Francis of Assisi Church.
Belhumeur, Roger E. '61 (PRO) Retired.
Beligotti, Richard '68 (ROC) Auburn, NY Mercy Health and Rehabilitation Center.
Beligotti, Richard J. '68 (ROC) East Bloomfield, NY St. Bridget Church.
Beligotti, Robert L. '68 (ROC) [7] Auburn, NY St. Francis of Assisi Church.
Belinda, Augustine *t.o.r.* '93 (SFS) Wessington Springs, SD St. Joseph Church.
Belinski, Michael *c.s.c.* '89 (FTW) [9] South Bend, IN Holy Cross Church.
Belisch, Carl L. *c.s.b.* '65 (GAL) [F] Houston, TX St. Thomas High School.
Belisle, Peter Damian *o.s.b. cam.* '72 (MRY) [F] Big Sur, CA New Camaldoli Hermitage.
Belisle, Ronald H. '62 (SEA) Camas, WA St. Thomas Aquinas Church.
Belitz, Justin *o.f.m.* '61 (IND) [12] Indianapolis, IN Sacred Heart of Jesus Church.
Belitz, Ronald C. (GB) [4] Green Bay, WI Annunciation of the Blessed Virgin Mary Church.
Belitz, Ronald C. '79 (GB) [8] Green Bay, WI St. Jude Church.
Beliveau, Richard '60 (BRK) Absent on Leave.
Belizaire, Hilaire Ruiz '00 (BRK) [85] Brooklyn, NY St. Matthew's Church.
Belizario, Nelson *o.carm* '68 (TOL) [29] Toledo, OH St. Jude Church.
Bell, Brian (PHX) Luke Air Force Base, AZ Luke Catholic Community.
Bell, Brian T. '70 (TUC) On Duty Outside the Diocese.
Bell, Msgr. Carl F. '66 (LA) Encino, CA St. Cyril Church.
Bell, Edward H. '77 (PH) [77] Philadelphia, PA St. Joan of Arc Church.
Bell, Edward M. '64 (WH) Parkersburg, WV St. Margaret Mary Church.
Bell, Gerald L. '73 (L) Lebanon Junction, KY St. Benedict Church; Shepherdsville, KY St. Aloysius Church.
Bell, Gerard P. *s.j.* '57 (NY) [DD] New York, NY Jesuit Provincial's Office.
Bell, Gerard P. *s.j.* '57 (WDC) [V] Silver Spring, MD Apostleship of Prayer.
Bell, Ira J. '52 (STL) Retired.
Bell, Joseph W. '74 (SPK) [2] Spokane, WA Assumption of the Blessed Virgin Mary Church.
Bell, Michael J. '79 (SAG) Port Austin, MI St. Michael Church.
Bell, Michael T. '61 (MRY) San Luis Obispo, CA California Men's Colony West.
Bell, Milford C. '49 (FTW) Retired.
Bell, Richard A. *m.m.* '36 (SJ) [L] Los Altos, CA Maryknoll.
Bellamah, Timothy F. *o.p.* '98 (PRO) [P] Providence, RI St. Thomas Aquinas Priory at Providence College.
Belland, David '87 (SCL) Special Assignment.
Bellantonio, Albert '69 (BRK) [111] Brooklyn, NY Our Lady of Solace Church.
Bellefeuille, Albert A. '54 (MAN) Colebrook, NH St. Brendan Church.
Bellenoit, George C. '72 (FR) Mansfield, MA St. Mary's Church.
Belleque, Thomas A. '85 (SEA) Sumner, WA St. Andrew Church; Orting, WA U.S. Soldiers' Home.
Beller, Frederic J. *o.s.b.* '43 (JOL) [J] Lisle, IL St. Procopius Abbey.
Bellesorte, Anthony R. *o.c.s.o.* '69 (SAC) [A] Vina, CA Abbey of New Clairvaux, Trappist Seminary; [H] Vina, CA Abbey of New Clairvaux, Trappist.
Bellester, Msgr. Pedro J. '58 (PCE) Special Assignment.
Belletty, Emile '78 (LA) La Mirada, CA Beatitudes of Our Lord Church; La Mirada, CA St. Paul of the Cross Church.
Bellew, Msgr. Francis P. '66 (NY) Wappingers Falls, NY St. Mary Church.
Bellew, Lawrence *c.p.* '53 (BRK) [V] Jamaica, NY Immaculate Conception Monastery.
Bellew, Lawrence *c.p.* '53 (RVC) West Islip, NY Good Samaritan Hospital Medical Center.
Belley, Bernard *o.m.i.* '54 (FgM) Oblates Foreign Missions.
Bellinghausen, David *o.s.b.* '86 (LR) [A] Subiaco, AR Subiaco Monastery.
Bellino, Samuel P. *s.j.* '88 (SFR) [E] San Francisco, CA St. Ignatius College Preparatory (Coed); [N] San Francisco, CA Jesuit Community at St. Ignatius College Preparatory.
Bellisario, Andrew E. '84 (LA) [Q] Montebello, CA Vincentian Fathers and Brothers; [Q] Montebello, CA Vincentian Fathers & Brothers; [W] Montebello, CA DePaul Center.
Bellittiere, David A. '89 (BUF) Snyder, NY Christ the King Church.
Belliveau, Gary J. '85 (MAN) Hudson, NH St. Kathryn Church.
Belliveau, Paul D. *m.m.* '69 (FgM) Maryknoll Foreign Missions.
Bello, David *o.p.* '81 (FgM) Dominican - Order of Preachers Foreign Missions.
Bello, David *o.p.* '81 (OAK) [N] Oakland, CA Western Dominican Province.
Bello, Giles F. *o.f.m.* '55 (PAT) [M] Butler, NJ St. Anthony Friary.
Bellopede, Louis P. '91 (PH) [2] Norristown, PA Holy Saviour Church.
Bellow, Richard '70 (CHL) [5] Charlotte, NC St. Gabriel Church.
Belluomini, Msgr. Ralph (FRS) On Leave.
Belmonte, John *s.j.* '96 (CHI) [D] Chicago, IL St. Ignatius College Prep.
Belmonte, John M. *s.j.* '96 (CHI) [D] Chicago, IL St. Ignatius Jesuit Community.
Belogi, James '81 (ALB) Guilderland, NY St. Madeleine Sophie Church.
Beloin, Robert L. '73 (HRT) [R] New Haven, CT Yale University-St. Thomas More Catholic Center and Chapel.
Belongea, David *o.f.m.cap.* '59 (GB) [I] Appleton, WI St. Fidelis Friary.
Belschner, Wayne '95 (BO) [3] Woburn, MA St. Charles Church.
Belsole, Kurt *o.s.b.* '78 (GBG) [A] Latrobe, PA St. Vincent Seminary.
Belsole, Kurt J. *o.s.b.* '78 (GBG) [H] Latrobe, PA Saint Vincent Archabbey.
Belsome, Garland T. '90 (BR) Belle Rose, LA St. Jules Church; Paincourtville, LA St. Elizabeth Church.
Belt, David D. '90 (OM) Norfolk, NE Sacred Heart Church.
Belt, Stephen M. *s.j.* (STL) [52] St. Louis, MO St. Matthew, Apostle Church.
Belt, Stephen M. *s.j.* '00 (STL) [C] St. Louis, MO Saint Louis University.
Beltrami, Robert *o.f.m.* '62 (P) [6] Portland, OR Ascension Church.
Beltran, Esteban *ss.cc.* '56 (SJN) [1] Guaynabo, PR Corazon de Jesus Church; [9] Guaynabo, PR Sagrados Corazones Church.
Beltran, Jacque (CHI) Winnetka, IL Sacred Heart Church.
Beltran, Justo '69 (BRK) [143] Brooklyn, NY St. Vincent de Paul Church.
Beltzner, Lucian W. *o.carm.* '63 (NY) Middletown, NY Our Lady of Mt. Carmel Church.
Belzer, Msgr. Paul J. '54 (BUF) Pendleton, NY Good Shepherd Church.
Benacchio, Onorio *c.s.* '50 (VEN) Immokalee, FL Our Lady of Guadalupe Church.
Benack, Henry I. '51 (RVC) Glen Cove, NY St. Patrick's Church; Retired.
Benak, Wes E. *o.s.a.* '91 (CHI) [N] Olympia Fields, IL The Augustinians-Provincialate.
Benakovic, Benedict *o.f.m.conv.* '49 (GRY) [12] Gary, IN St. Joseph The Worker Church.
Benas, Rolando T. '85 (SJ) [4] Sunnyvale, CA Church of The Resurrection.
Benavente, James L.G. '94 (AGN) [1] Agana, GU Dulce Nombre de Maria Cathedral - Basilica Church.
Bench, John F. '64 (CHR) Absent On Leave.
Benda, Frank M. '57 (DUB) Retired.
Benda, Frederick J. *s.j.* '72 (COL) [25] Columbus, OH Community of Holy Rosary and St. John Church.
Benda, M. Eugene '60 (DAV) Tipton, IA St. Mary's Church.
Bendel, Eugene '57 (STL) [4] University City, MO St. Patrick Church.
Benden, Stephen *c.ss.r.* '89 (CHI) [133] Chicago, IL St. Michael Church.
Benden, Stephen *c.ss.r.* '89 (DEN) [M] Denver, CO The Redemptorists/Denver Province.
Bender, Arthur C. *s.j.* '78 (NY) [F] New York, NY Regis High School; [DD] New York, NY Xavier Jesuit Community.
Bender, James W. *c.pp.s.* '52 (CIN) [M] Dayton, OH Provincial Office of the Cincinnati Province of the Society of the Precious Blood.
Bender, Lawrence A. *s.s.* '51 (BAL) [O] Baltimore, MD St. Charles Villa; [S] Baltimore, MD St. Charles Villa.
Bender, Lawrence A. *s.s.* '51 (WDC) Retired.
Bender, Philip M. '64 (ALT) State College, PA Good Shepherd Church.
Bender, Reginald G. *o.s.b.* '59 (GBG) [H] Latrobe, PA Saint Vincent Archabbey.
Bender, Msgr. Thomas G. '56 (COL) Bremen, OH St. Mary Church.
Bender, Thomas J. '61 (ALN) Unassigned.
Bendernagel, Cajetan *c.p.* '52 (HRT) [M] West Hartford, CT Holy Family Monastery/Retreat.
Bendik, Msgr. John J. '67 (SCR) [4] Pittston, PA St. John the Evangelist Church.
Bendixen, Arthur '76 (ORL) Sabbatical.
Bendorf, Richard *o.f.m.* '87 (STL) [P] St. Louis, MO Franciscan Friary of St. Anthony of Padua.
Bendyk, Marian '82 (CLV) [2] Garfield Heights, OH SS. Peter and Paul Church.
Bendzella, Sylvester J. '59 (ALT) Clarence, PA St. Michael's Church; Snow Shoe, PA St. Mary's Church.
Bene, Philip J. '94 (STL) Graduate Studies.
Benecki, Stanley '84 (COL) [7] Columbus, OH Sts. Augustine and Gabriel Church.
Benedetti, Edmund *s.j.* '50 (CC) [17] Corpus Christi, TX St. Patrick Church.
Benedic, Danut *o.f.m.conv.* '98 (RNO) [1] Reno, NV St. Thomas Aquinas Church.
Benedict, Francis *o.s.b.* '76 (LA) [W] Valyermo, CA St. Andrew's Abbey Retreat House (All Groups).
Benedict, John *o.carm.* '77 (CHI) [66] Chicago, IL St. Gelasius Church.
Benedict, Joseph M. '97 (SJ) Campbell, CA St. Lucy Church.
Benedicto, Benjamin L. '62 (ORG) Anaheim, CA St. Anthony Claret Church.
Benedik, Hilarion *o.s.b.m.* '48 (STF) [B] Glen Cove, NY Basilian Fathers Novitiate of the Order of St. Basil the Great.
Benefiel, Msgr. Harry E. '60 (LAF) Retired.
Benestad, Msgr. Thomas J. '70 (ALN) On Duty Outside the Diocese.
Benestad, Msgr. Thomas J. '70 (PH) [A] Wynnewood, PA Theological Seminary of St. Charles Borromeo, Overbrook.
Bengco, Jose C. '65 (COL) Chillicothe, OH Veteran's Affairs Medical Center.
Bengford, Ronald J. '94 (PRO) [2] Westerly, RI Immaculate Conception Church.
Benguria, Juan Bautista *c.p.* '57 (SJN) [46] San Juan, PR Nuestra Senora de la Piedad Church.
Benham, Michael '76 (MIL) Elkhorn, WI St. Patrick Church.
Benicewicz, Joseph '88 (BUF) [D] Athol Springs, NY St. Francis High School; [O] Athol Springs, NY St. Francis of Assisi Friary.
Beninati, Francis H. *m.m.* '55 (FgM) Maryknoll Foreign Missions.
Benintende, Joseph '70 (ALB) Ilion, NY Annunciation Church.
Benischeck, Bernard J. '53 (PH) [40] Philadelphia, PA St. Dominic Church.
Benish, William '72 (AUS) Cedar Park, TX St. Margaret Mary Church.
Benitez, Eduardo '66 (ORL) Retired.
Benjamin, Robert '00 (SR) Eureka, CA St. Bernard Church.
Benkert, Gerald *o.s.b.* '34 (FgM) American - Cassinese Congregation Foreign Missions.
Benko, Robert *o.f.m.conv.* '00 (R) Burlington, NC Blessed Sacrament Church; [E] Burlington, NC Conventual Franciscans.
Benkovic, Theodore *o.f.m.* '41 (CHI) [N] Chicago, IL Croatian Franciscan Custody of the Holy Family.
Benkowski, Gregory '84 (OM) Fordyce, NE St. John the Baptist Church; Menominee, NE St. Boniface Church.
Benliro, Fernando C. '58 (OM) [29] Omaha, NE St. Mary Magdalene Church.
Benn, Walter J. '77 (PH) Downingtown, PA St. Joseph Church.
Bennerfield, Herbert, III '99 (LAF) Abbeville, LA St. Therese of the Child Jesus Church.
Bennett, Msgr. Austin P. '49 (BRK) Retired; [N]

Brooklyn, NY St. Mary's Hospital of Brooklyn; [V] Brooklyn, NY Curial Residence; [W] Brooklyn, NY Monastery of the Sisters Adorers of the Precious Blood.
Bennett, Christopher '90 (SJ) [11] San Jose, CA St. Christopher Church.
Bennett, Msgr. Donald T. '67 (RVC) Hicksville, NY St. Ignatius Loyola Church.
Bennett, Gordon D. *s.j.* (BAL) [10] Baltimore, MD St. Anthony of Padua Church; [66] Baltimore, MD Most Precious Blood Church.
Bennett, John E. *s.j.* '53 (PH) [C] Philadelphia, PA St. Joseph's University; [AA] Philadelphia, PA Jesuit Community at St. Joseph's University.
Bennett, Msgr. John F. '71 (RVC) Baldwin, NY St. Christopher Church.
Bennett, Joseph R. '66 (CHI) South Holland, IL Holy Ghost Church.
Bennett, Joseph T. *s.j.* '57 (BO) [E] Boston, MA Boston College High School & Jesuit Community.
Bennett, Melvin J. '69 (LFT) Crawfordsville, IN St. Bernard Church; [H] Crawfordsville, IN Newman Center at Wabash College.
Bennett, Michael X. '71 (HBG) Absent on Leave.
Bennett, Noel I. '59 (MIA) [2] Miami Beach, FL St. Joseph Church.
Bennett, Norman S. *c.ss.r.* '71 (BRK) [107] Brooklyn, NY Our Lady of Perpetual Help Basilica Church.
Bennett, Richard *c.ss.r.* (BO) [53] Boston, MA Our Lady of Perpetual Help Church.
Bennett, Richard '72 (JOL) [1] Naperville, IL Holy Spirit Catholic Community Church.
Bennett, Rolland *o.m.i.* '61 (PMB) Riviera Beach, FL St. Francis of Assisi Church.
Bennett, Thomas F. '68 (HRT) Washington Depot, CT Our Lady of Perpetual Help Church.
Bennett, Msgr. Thomas M. '57 (COL) [22] Columbus, OH Immaculate Conception Church; [C] Columbus, OH St. Charles Preparatory School.
Bennington, Msgr. J. Clement '45 (PH) Abington, PA Our Lady Help of Christians Church; Retired.
Beno, Brian M. '76 (MIL) Special Assignment.
Beno, Joseph '57 (P) Retired.
Benoit, Adrian J. '65 (SPR) [7] Springfield, MA Immaculate Conception Church.
Benoit, Bryan *s.c.j.* '93 (MIL) [P] Hales Corners, WI Priests of the Sacred Heart.
Benoit, Lloyd F. '90 (LAF) Cecilia, LA St. Joseph Church.
Benoit, Louis '79 (RIC) Chincoteague, VA St. Andrew Church.
Benoit, Raymond P. '89 (BO) [39] Boston, MA St. Margaret Church; Boston, MA Boston Medical Center.
Benoit, Ronald H. '55 (BUR) Richmond, VT Our Lady of the Holy Rosary Church.
Benoit, Vincent *o.p.* '84 (P) [D] Eugene, OR Marist High School; [N] McKenzie Bridge, OR St. Benedict Lodge-Dominican Retreat & Conference Center.
Benonis, Richard R. '52 (SAT) San Antonio, TX Audie Murphy VA Hospital.
Benonis, Richard R. '58 (PH) Retired.
Benonis, William J. '52 (PH) Swarthmore, PA Notre Dame de Lourdes Church.
Bensman, Gerald E. '64 (CIN) Sidney, OH Holy Angels Church.
Bensman, John L. '56 (CIN) Chickasaw, OH Most Precious Blood Church; St. Sebastian, OH St. Sebastian Church.
Benson, Gerard *o.carm.* '42 (VEN) [G] Venice, FL Carmel in Venice.
Benson, James A. *s.j.* '56 (BO) [3] Newton, MA St. Ignatius Church.
Benson, Msgr. John D. '47 (WDC) Retired.
Benson, Joseph A. '84 (NO) [28] New Orleans, LA St. Cecilia Church.
Benson, Richard *c.m.* '78 (LA) [A] Camarillo, CA St. John's Seminary; [A] Camarillo, CA St. John's Seminary.
Bentivegna, Salvatore A. *o.s.j.* '63 (SCR) [16] Scranton, PA St. Lucy's Church.
Bentley, David '75 (ALB) Unassigned.
Bentley, David '99 (LSC) Deming, NM Holy Family Church.
Bentley, Michael E. (GB) Florence, WI Immaculate Conception Church.
Benton, James F. '73 (LIN) [6] Lincoln, NE St. John the Apostle Church.
Bentz, John B. '66 (COL) Marysville, OH Our Lady of Lourdes Church; Marysville, OH Ohio Reformatory for Women.
Benwell, Msgr. William '80 (MET) Warren, NJ Our Lady of the Mount Church.
Benya, Edward G. *s.j.* '84 (FgM) Provinces.
Benya, Edward G. *s.j.* '84 (NO) [P] New Orleans, LA Jesuit Provincial Office.
Benz, David H. '75 (PH) Kennett Square, PA St. Patrick Church.
Benz, Gary '99 (BIS) Carson, ND St. Theresa the Child Jesus Church; Flasher, ND St. Lawrence Church; Raleigh, ND St. Gertrude Church.
Benz, James J. '74 (STL) Richmond Heights, MO Little Flower, St. Teresa of the Infant Jesus Church.
Benz, Thomas G. '00 (NY) [F] New York, NY Fordham Preparatory School; [DD] New York, NY Jesuit Community at Fordham University.
Benzinger, Oscar L. *s.j.* '67 (MIL) [P] Milwaukee, WI Jesuit Provincial Office, Wisconsin Province.
Benzmiller, James T. '99 (LC) Pittsville, WI St. Joachim Church; Sigel, WI Holy Rosary Church; Vesper, WI St. James Church.
Benzoni, Martin R. *o.praem.* '81 (ORG) [1] Huntington Beach, CA St. Bonaventure Church; [I] Silverado, CA Norbertine Fathers of Orange Inc.
Beof, Marlon *o.a.r.* '96 (NY) [B] Suffern, NY Tagaste Monastery.
Berard, Aram *s.j.* '66 (ALN) [10] Reading, PA St. Paul Church.
Berard, Aram J. *s.j.* '66 (BO) [W] Boston, MA The Society of Jesus of New England-Provincial Offices.
Berardi, Msgr. Ferdinando D. '77 (NY) [76] New York, NY St. Monica Church; [HH] New York, NY Catholic Medical Mission Board, Inc.; [HH] New York, NY Committee for Mission Responsibility Society, Inc.
Berardi, James J. '59 (CLV) [1] Akron, OH Annunciation Church; Akron, OH Akron City Hospital.
Berardi, Thomas F. '76 (ALB) Cobleskill, NY St. Vincent de Paul Church; [B] Albany, NY Maria College; [R] Cobleskill, NY State University of New York College of Agricultural & Technology at Cobleskill.
Berbena, Christopher '80 (OAK) [2] Walnut Creek, CA St. John Vianney Church.
Berberian, David '74 (ALB) [10] Albany, NY St. Margaret Mary Church; Special Assignment.
Berberich, Thomas E. '59 (HRT) Kent, CT Sacred Heart Church.
Berbig, Steven A. '87 (RVC) Huntington, NY St. Patrick's Church.
Berchmans, Britto *s.d.b.* (CHI) Barrington, IL St. Anne Church.
Berchmanz, Anthony '67 (NEW) Military Chaplains.
Berciano, Jose '64 (MIA) [28] Miami, FL SS. Peter and Paul Church.
Bercier, Barry *a.a.* '85 (WOR) [N] Worcester, MA Assumptionists of Assumption College.
Bercik, G. Michael *o.f.m.* '79 (BO) [1] Marlborough, MA St. Ann Church.
Berding, Richard P. '84 (L) [48] Louisville, KY St. Luke Church.
Berdis, Donald E. '63 (E) [2] Farrell, PA Our Lady of Fatima Church.
Berdugo, Hernan '83 (SJN) [10] Carolina, PR Inmaculada Concepcion Church.
Berean, Christopher H. '87 (NY) Saugerties, NY St. Mary of the Snow Church.
Bereda, Stanislaw J. '65 (GAY) Posen, MI St. Casimir Church.
Berendt, George *p.i.m.e.* '74 (DET) [K] Detroit, MI P.I.M.E. Missionaries of SS. Peter and Paul.
Berendt, Msgr. James M. '55 (COL) Retired.
Berendt, Peter *c.p.* '57 (CHI) [88] Chicago, IL Immaculate Conception Church; [N] Chicago, IL Passionist Community-Immaculate Conception Monastery.
Berens, Cyprian E. *o.f.m.* '51 (MAR) Calumet, MI St. Paul the Apostle Church.
Beres, Kevin J. '00 (ARL) Springfield, VA St. Bernadette's Church.
Beretta, J. Christian *o.s.f.s* '97 (VEN) [A] Fort Myers, FL Bishop Verot High School.
Beretta, John W. *o.s.a.* '45 (CHI) [N] Olympia Fields, IL The Augustinians-Provincialate.
Bereza, Stepan '93 (STF) New Britain, CT St. Josaphat Church.
Berg, Msgr. Arnold J. '33 (NU) Retired.
Berg, Blaise '97 (SAC) Roseville, CA St. Rose of Lima Church.
Berg, Daniel J. '00 (BIS) Mandan, ND Christ the King Church.
Berg, Donald M. '47 (LC) Retired.
Berg, John *f.s.s.p.* '97 (SCR) [M] Elmhurst, PA Priestly Fraternity of St. Peter (F.S.S.P.), North American District Headquarters.
Berg, Paul '48 (DET) Retired.
Berg, Peter M. '71 (OG) Dannemora, NY St. Joseph Church; Dannemora, NY Clinton Correctional Facility.
Berg, Ralph *c.m.f.* '64 (LA) [Q] Los Angeles, CA Missionary Sons of the Immaculate Heart of Mary; [Q] Los Angeles, CA Claretian Retreat Center Community.
Berg, Ramon A. '82 (CHL) Retired.
Berg, Richard F. *c.s.c.* '63 (P) [O] Portland, OR Macdonald Center.
Berg, Richard V. '52 (STP) Retired.
Berg, Msgr. S. Theodore '61 (BUF) [63] Buffalo, NY St. Teresa Church.
Berg, Steven '99 (FWT) Bedford, TX St. Michael Church.
Berg, Timothy '79 (SFE) On Duty Outside the Archdiocese.
Bergamo, Msgr. John A. '65 (SCR) East Stroudsburg, PA St. Matthew's Church; [D] East Stroudsburg, PA Notre Dame Junior/Senior High School.
Bergbower, Daniel J. '88 (SFD) Edgewood, IL St. Anne Church; Effingham, IL Sacred Heart Church.
Bergedick, Charles T. *s.m.* '57 (CIN) [9] Dayton, OH Emmanuel Church; [M] Dayton, OH Marianist Provincialate.
Bergen, William J. *s.j.* '55 (NY) [51] New York, NY St. Ignatius Loyola Church; [DD] New York, NY St. Ignatius Loyola Residence.
Berger, Bernard M. '64 (GI) Burwell, NE Sacred Heart Church.
Berger, John '98 (HON) [1] Honolulu, HI Cathedral of Our Lady of Peace.
Berger, John G. '67 (NU) St. Peter, MN St. Peter Regional Treatment Center; [F] St. Peter, MN St. Peter Regional Treatment Center.
Berger, John Gerald '67 (NU) Nicollet, MN St. Paul Church.
Berger, Lawrence B. '66 (LC) [4] La Crosse, WI Holy Trinity Church.
Berger, Marc H. '70 (FR) [I] Fall River, MA St. John Vianney House.
Berger, Robert F. '62 (HBG) Myerstown, PA Mary, Gate of Heaven Church.
Bergeron, Msgr. Albert G. '62 (HT) Retired.
Bergeron, C. Paul '81 (LAF) Retired.
Bergeron, Marc H. '70 (FR) [13] Fall River, MA St. Anne's Church.
Bergeron, Michael '96 (HT) Chacahoula, LA St. Lawrence Church; Schriever, LA St. Bridget Church.
Bergeron, Robert E. '52 (BO) Senior Priests.
Bergeur, John X. '45 (NEW) Retired.
Bergewisch, Fred F. *s.j.* '55 (CHI) [C] Chicago, IL Jesuit Community at Loyola University of Chicago.
Berggreen, Msgr. Robert H. '64 (BR) [2] Baton Rouge, LA St. Agnes Church.
Berghammer, Robert J. '49 (MIL) Retired.
Berghout, Paul A. '96 (ARL) Falls Church, VA St. Anthony's Church.
Bergin, Msgr. Clifford E. '53 (CHI) Retired.
Bergin, James *s.v.d.* '69 (CHI) [B] Techny, IL Divine Word Residence; [N] Techny, IL Society of the Divine Word, Provincial Headquarter-Chicago Prov.
Bergin, John J. *s.v.d.* '67 (BO) [W] Duxbury, MA Society of the Divine Word.
Bergin, John J. *s.j.* '67 (STL) [P] St. Louis, MO De Smet Jesuit High School Community.
Bergin, Paschal '57 (CC) On Duty Outside the Diocese.
Bergin, Paschal '57 (SAT) Runge, TX St. Anthony's Church.
Bergin, Patrick A. *m.m.* '59 (NY) [DD] Maryknoll, NY Maryknoll Fathers and Brothers.
Bergin, Patrick P. '57 (SAT) Kenedy, TX Our Lady of Peace Church.
Bergin, Msgr. Robert D. '62 (HRT) Special and other Archdiocesan Assignment; [N] West Hartford, CT Mercyknoll, Incorporated.
Bergin, Msgr. Thomas J. '61 (NY) [58] New York, NY St. John the Evangelist Church; [D] New York, NY Department of Education; [E] New York, NY Cathedral High School.
Bergin, Thomas J. '62 (ORL) New Smyrna Beach, FL Our Lady Star of the Sea Church.
Bergkamp, Roger *o.m.i.* '64 (FgM) Oblates Foreign Missions.
Bergman, Charles B. '58 (PIT) Zelienople, PA St. Gregory Church.
Bergman, Richard '55 (DM) Retired.
Bergman, Msgr. Robert '71 (KCK) Shawnee, KS St. Joseph's Church.
Bergner, David *s.d.s.* '76 (WDC) [B] Silver Spring, MD Salvatorian Community.
Bergner, David J. *s.d.s.* '76 (RIC) [K] Richmond, VA Commonwealth Catholic Charities.
Bergquist, Patrick '90 (BAL) Special Assignment.
Bergquist, Patrick D. '90 (FBK) [4] Fairbanks, AK St. Raphael's Church.
Bergs, David J. '76 (LSC) Carrizozo, NM St. Rita Church.
Bergsbaken, Dennis L. (GB) Kimberly, WI Holy Name of Jesus Church; Wrightstown, WI St. Paul Church.
Bergstadt, John (GB) [2] Appleton, WI St. Bernard Church.
Berinti, Ben *c.pp.s.* '85 (ORL) [6] Orlando, FL St. Andrew Church.
Beristain, Juan M. '71 (SJN) [6] Toa Baja, PR Santisima Trinidad Church.
Berkery, Patrick J. '56 (HRT) [3] Ansonia, CT St. Anthony's Church.
Berkhout, Frans J. (ALN) [9] Allentown, PA Sacred Heart of Jesus Church; [C] Allentown, PA Allentown Central Catholic High School.
Berkhout, Frans J. '87 (ALN) [5] Allentown, PA Our Lady Help of Christians Church.
Berko, Matthew '62 (SJP) Apopka, FL St. Mary's Church; St. Petersburg, FL Epiphany of Our Lord Church.
Berland, Mark '74 (SAL) Grainfield, KS St. Agnes Church; Park, KS Sacred Heart Church.
Berling, Alban *o.s.b.* '45 (IND) [J] St. Meinrad, IN St.

Meinrad Archabbey.
Berlo, Benedict *c.p.* '57 (SCR) [M] Scranton, PA Saint Ann's Passionist Monastery.
Bermingham, Msgr. Charles E. '23 (RVC) Williston Park, NY St. Aidan's Church; Retired.
Bermudez, Alberto '86 (NO) [1] Marrero, LA Immaculate Conception Church.
Berna, Frank *o.f.m.* '80 (PH) [AA] Philadelphia, PA St. Pius X Friary.
Bernabe, Humberto '92 (LA) Altadena, CA St. Elizabeth of Hungary Church.
Bernacki, Edward *c.s.sp.* '45 (SB) [E] Hemet, CA Holy Ghost Fathers.
Bernacki, William J. *o.p.* '56 (CHI) [D] Oak Park, IL Fenwick High School; [N] River Forest, IL St. Thomas Aquinas Priory.
Bernadicou, Paul *s.j.* '81 (LA) [C] Los Angeles, CA Loyola Marymount University.
Bernal, Edward '87 (SAT) [49] San Antonio, TX St. Leo Church.
Bernal, Melchor B. *s.v.d.* '78 (LA) Carpinteria, CA St. Joseph Church.
Bernans, Arvids '64 (COL) Retired.
Bernard, Andre '73 (SR) On Leave.
Bernard, Donald *o.m.i.* '64 (LA) San Fernando, CA Santa Rosa Church.
Bernard, George C. *c.s.c.* '49 (P) [B] Portland, OR University of Portland; [L] Portland, OR Holy Cross Fathers & Brothers, C.S.C. - University of Portland.
Bernard, John P. '62 (BUF) Batavia, NY Veterans Hospital; Retired.
Bernard, John P. '62 (CAM) Retired.
Bernardi, Peter J. *s.j.* (NO) [C] New Orleans, LA Loyola University New Orleans.
Bernardi, Peter J. *s.j.* '87 (DET) [K] Detroit, MI Jesuit Provincial Office-Detroit Province of the Society of Jesus.
Bernardin, Paul A. *o.p.* '61 (HRT) [14] New Haven, CT St. Mary's Priory Church.
Bernardy, Patrick '60 (GB) Retired.
Bernas, Casimir *o.c.s.o.* '58 (SLC) [F] Huntsville, UT Abbey of Our Lady of the Holy Trinity of the Order of Cistercians.
Bernas, Elwood S. '84 (STU) Absent on Leave.
Bernas, Eugene '66 (NEW) [28] Newark, NJ Our Lady of Mt. Carmel Church.
Bernas, Thomas A. '94 (CHI) [181] Chicago, IL St. Richard Church; [U] Chicago, IL Catholic League for Religious Assistance to Poland.
Bernasconi, Gino '50 (VIC) Retired.
Bernatonis, John F. '45 (BO) Senior Priests.
Bernauer, Edmund G. '61 (NEW) Short Hills, NJ St. Rose of Lima Church.
Bernauer, James '52 (CR) Retired.
Bernauer, James W. *s.j.* '75 (BO) [W] Chestnut Hill, MA The Jesuit Community at Boston College.
Bernbrock, John *s.j.* '56 (PHX) [2] Scottsdale, AZ Our Lady of Perpetual Help Church.
Berndt, Wayne *o.f.m.cap.* '83 (FgM) Capuchin Foreign Missions.
Bernelli, Matthew '64 (BGP) [13] Bridgeport, CT St. Mary Church.
Berner, Albert J. '68 (NEW) [Q] Upper Montclair, NJ Montclair State University.
Berner, Francis '70 (NO) [64] New Orleans, LA St. Thomas the Apostle Church; New Orleans, LA Delgado College; New Orleans, LA Southern University in New Orleans; New Orleans, LA University of New Orleans.
Berner, Michael '86 (DM) Defiance, IA St. Peter Church; Earling, IA St. Joseph Church.
Bernhardt, Gary *o.f.m.* '99 (STL) Oakville, MO St. Francis of Assisi Church; [P] Oakville, MO St. Francis Friary.
Bernier, Lawrence J. '63 (SPR) East Longmeadow, MA St. Michael's Church.
Bernier, Paul *s.s.s.* (NY) [55] New York, NY St. Jean Baptiste Church.
Bernier, Paul '00 (FR) South Yarmouth, MA St. Pius Tenth Church.
Berning, James *s.d.b.* '93 (NEW) [N] Orange, NJ The Salesian Community; [S] Orange, NJ Salesians of Don Bosco, S.D.B.
Berning, James *s.d.b.* '93 (NO) [D] Marrero, LA Archbishop Shaw High School; [G] Marrero, LA Archbishop Shaw Junior High School.
Berning, James C. '91 (WIN) Madelia, MN St. Mary Church; St. James, MN St. James Church.
Berning, John B. '34 (CIN) Retired.
Bernotas, Robert J. '83 (LFT) Kentland, IN St. Joseph Church.
Bernott, Albert R. '43 (GR) Retired.
Bernott, Ernest J. '43 (GR) [5] Muskegon, MI St. Mary's Church.
Berns, Eric P. '96 (LC) Special Assignment.
Berns, Eric R. '96 (LC) [H] La Crosse, WI Holy Cross (Seminary) Diocesan Center.
Berny, Paul W. '72 (ATL) [3] Marietta, GA St. Joseph Church.
Berran, Donald M. '60 (BRK) [158] Queens, NY Blessed Virgin Mary, Help of Christians Church.
Berret, Anthony J. *s.j.* '71 (PH) [C] Philadelphia, PA St. Joseph's University; [AA] Philadelphia, PA Jesuit Community at St. Joseph's University.
Berrigan, Daniel J. *s.j.* '52 (NY) [DD] New York, NY West Side Jesuit Community.
Berrio, Augusto *s.j.* '63 (SD) [12] San Diego, CA Our Lady of Guadalupe Church.
Berrio, Ignacio (BO) [2] Chelsea, MA St. Rose of Lima Church.
Berrios, George '89 (TR) [1] Trenton, NJ St. Mary Church.
Berrios, Israel '96 (CGS) Aibonito, PR Church of St. Joseph.
Berrios, Raul Morales '88 (CGS) Cidra, PR Nuestra Senora del Carmen Church.
Berruete, Joseph *s.d.b* '62 (PMB) Belle Glade, FL St. Philip Benizi Church.
Berry, Dennis *s.t.* '74 (PAT) [P] Stirling, NJ Father Judge Apostolic Center.
Berry, James A. '75 (HON) Kailua-Kona, HI St. Michael The Archangel Church.
Berry, Thomas *c.p.* '42 (MET) [H] South River, NJ Passionist Provincial Office.
Berry, William F. '66 (WDC) College Park, MD Holy Redeemer Church.
Berryman, Harold '58 (GB) [1] Appleton, WI St. Bernadette Church.
Bersabal, Rey (SAC) [K] Chico, CA Newman Centers.
Bersabal, Rey '91 (SAC) Davis, CA St. James Church.
Berschied, Paul L. '86 (COV) Independence, KY St. Cecilia Church.
Berson, Robert C. *glmy.* '53 (CIN) [M] Cincinnati, OH Headquarters of Glenmary Home Missioners; [U] Fairfield, OH Glenmary Home Missioners Charitable Trust.
Bertand, Conley '59 (LAF) [M] Lafayette, LA Come Lord Jesus.
Bertasius, Msgr. Anthony (PAT) Retired.
Bertasius, Anthony '37 (ELP) Retired.
Bertelli, Ameilio J. '59 (BO) Senior Priests.
Bertels, George '55 (KCK) Beattie, KS St. Malachy's Church; Marysville, KS St. Gregory's Church.
Bertels, Henry J. *s.j.* '62 (NY) [DD] New York, NY Jesuit Provincial's Office.
Bertha, Joseph '80 (PSC) Amherst, NY St. Stephen's Church.
Bertha, Joseph W. '80 (BUF) Amherst, NY Millard Fillmore Suburban Hospital.
Berthelette, Ernest H. '74 (PRO) On Duty Outside the Diocese.
Berther, Patrick *o.f.m.cap.* '34 (GB) [I] Appleton, WI St. Fidelis Friary.
Berthiaume, Eugene F. (WOR) Retired.
Berthiaume, Gary D. '68 (CLV) Released from Diocesan Assignment.
Berthold, George C. '63 (BO) Unassigned.
Bertin, Gerard L. '89 (MAN) Rochester, NH Holy Rosary Church.
Bertini, Angelo '73 (AUS) [7] Waco, TX St. Mary of the Assumption Church.
Bertino, Dominic V. '75 (GRY) Hobart, IN St. Bridget Church.
Bertke, Erwin J. '43 (CIN) [50] Cincinnati, OH St. Lawrence Church; Retired.
Bertocchi, Luigi *o.s.b.* '70 (SCL) [I] Collegeville, MN St. John's Abbey, of the Order of St. Benedict.
Bertogli, John '77 (DM) [3] Council Bluffs, IA St. Patrick Church.
Bertolucci, John P. '65 (ALB) Latham, NY St. Ambrose Church.
Bertone, Thomas C. *c.s.c.* '81 (FR) [A] North Easton, MA Holy Cross Fathers Religious.
Bertoni, Albert *s.m.* '79 (RVC) [D] Uniondale, NY Kellenberg Memorial High School.
Bertoniere, Gabriel *o.c.s.o.* '58 (WOR) [N] Spencer, MA St. Joseph's Abbey.
Bertrand, Aloysius J. '43 (PBL) [E] Grand Junction, CO St. Mary Hospital and Medical Center.
Bertrand, Armand J. '89 (SC) Cherokee, IA Immaculate Conception Church.
Bertrand, C. Conley '59 (LAF) Rynella, LA St. Marcellus Church.
Bertrand, Evarist *o.f.m.cap.* '63 (FgM) Capuchin Foreign Missions.
Bertrand, Joseph *c.ss.r.* '55 (STV) [3] Frederiksted, VI Church of St. Patrick.
Bertrand, Joseph '60 (BEA) Retired.
Bertrand, Richard D. *s.j.* '79 (BO) [W] Boston, MA The Society of Jesus of New England-Provincial Offices.
Bertrand, Richard D. *s.j.* '79 (PRT) Westbrook, ME St. Edmund Church.
Bertrand, Robert E. *o.p.* '58 (FgM) Dominican - Order of Preachers Foreign Missions.
Bertrand, Victor E. '62 (CHI) [N] Arlington Heights, IL Viatorian Province Center-Clerics of St. Viator.
Bertrand, Victor E. *c.s.v.* '62 (LR) Little Rock, AR U.S. Veterans Administration Hospital; North Little Rock, AR U.S. Veterans Administration Hospital.
Bertrand, Vincent E. '87 (SPC) [3] Springfield, MO Immaculate Conception Church.
Bertsche, Conrad J. '45 (BEL) Retired.
Berube, John J. '48 (BO) Senior Priests.
Berube, Louis F. '47 (PRT) Retired; [H] Lewiston, ME St. Mary's Regional Medical Center.
Berube, Paul W. '60 (BO) Chelmsford, MA St. Mary Church.
Berube, Richard N. *s.s.e.* '70 (BUR) [E] Colchester, VT Society of St. Edmund.
Berube, Theodore E. '41 (NOR) Retired.
Besanceney, Paul H. *s.j.* '56 (FgM) Provinces.
Beseau, Steven '95 (KCK) Ottawa, KS Sacred Heart Church.
Besendorfer, Ralph L. *j.c.d.* '59 (STA) Callahan, FL Our Lady of Consolation Church.
Beshara, Msgr. Ronald N. '71 (PMB) [D] West Palm Beach, FL St. Mary's Foundation of Palm Beach County, Inc.
Beshara, Msgr. Ronald N. '71 (SAM) On Duty Outside the Diocese.
Beshoner, Sebastian *o.s.b.* '85 (FWT) Lindsay, TX St. Peter Church.
Besinga, Jon D. '83 (LAV) [8] Las Vegas, NV St. Elizabeth Ann Seton Church.
Besse, Joseph A. '45 (PRO) Retired.
Bessellieu, Mel '97 (FWT) Denton, TX Immaculate Conception Church.
Bessert, James '80 (SAG) Midland, MI St. Brigid Church.
Bessert, James W. '80 (SAG) [I] Midland, MI The James Cardinal Hickey Educational Endowment Fund for St. Brigid Catholic School.
Best, Richard '61 (JOL) Absent on Sick Leave.
Best, Russell W. '86 (BO) [31] Boston, MA St. Joseph Church; [56] Boston, MA St. Patrick Church.
Bester, Robert '79 (CR) On Duty Outside the Diocese.
Bester, Robert '79 (OM) Valley, NE St. John Church.
Bestler, Joseph '57 (GB) Retired.
Bestler, Joseph L. (GB) Dyckesville, WI St. Louis Church.
Beston, William J. *c.s.c.* '48 (FTW) [J] South Bend, IN Congregation of Holy Cross, Indiana Province, Provincial House.
Betancourt, Rigoberto '83 (SHP) [1] Shreveport, LA St. John Berchmans Church.
Betancur, Gonzalo '92 (BRK) [63] Brooklyn, NY Immaculate Conception of the Blessed Virgin Mary Church.
Betancur, Nelson (PAT) [7] Paterson, NJ St. George Church.
Bethancourt, Michael A. '60 (MRY) Soledad, CA Salinas Valley State Prison; Special Assignment.
Betley, Michael E. (GB) Aurora, WI Sacred Heart Church; Niagara, WI St. Anthony Church; Pembine, WI St. Margaret Church.
Betoni, John P. *o.s.a.* '62 (PH) [C] Villanova, PA Villanova University; [AA] Villanova, PA St. Thomas Monastery.
Betowski, E. Paul *s.j.* '49 (BAL) [S] Baltimore, MD Jesuit Fathers and Brothers Maryland Provincial Curia.
Betrand, R. Emmanuel *o.p.* '58 (CIN) [28] Cincinnati, OH St. Gertrude Church.
Betrozoff, Larry '73 (MRY) Tres Pinos, CA Immaculate Conception Church.
Betschart, Joseph '99 (P) Beaverton, OR St. Cecilia Church.
Bettendorf, James '59 (LAN) [M] Flint, MI St. Leo the Great Church.
Bettendorf, James B. '59 (LAN) [8] Flint, MI St. Leo the Great Church.
Betti, Frederick G. *s.j.* '90 (ROC) [C] Rochester, NY McQuaid Jesuit High School.
Betti, Mark J. '96 (R) Roanoke Rapids, NC St. John the Baptist Church.
Bettinger, Eugene *o.carm.* '76 (NEW) Demarest, NJ St. Joseph's Church.
Bettinger, Mark T. '93 (PBL) Delta, CO St. Michael Church.
Bettley, Emil '83 (NY) Nyack, NY St. Ann Church.
Betts, David R. '98 (SCR) [5] Dunmore, PA St. Mary of Mount Carmel Church.
Betts, John C. '68 (P) Albany, OR Our Lady of Perpetual Help Church.
Betz, James F. '71 (CAM) Swedesboro, NJ St. Joseph's Church.
Betz, James S. '89 (WDC) [1] Bowie, MD Ascension Church.
Betz, Kenneth '65 (EVN) Haubstadt, IN St. James Church.
Betz, Robert L. '73 (MIL) [2] South Milwaukee, WI St. John Church; [3] South Milwaukee, WI St. Mary Church.
Betz, Thomas *o.f.m.cap.* '91 (PH) [80] Philadelphia, PA St. John the Evangelist Church.
Betzen, James G. *c.pp.s.* '81 (KC) [29] Kansas City, MO Sacred Heart-Guadalupe Church.
Beunen, Emmanuel *o.f.m.* '70 (CLV) Warrensville Heights, OH St. Jude Church; Cleveland, OH Cleveland House of Correction; [O] Cleveland, OH St. Jude Friary.
Beuth, William J. *c.pp.s.* '59 (CIN) [M] Dayton, OH Provincial Office of the Cincinnati Province of the Society of the Precious Blood.

Beuther, Richard J. '96 (BRK) [199] Queens, NY St. Matthias Church.

Beutner, Edward F. '65 (SUP) Lake Tomahawk, WI St. John Vianney Church; Woodruff, WI Our Lady Queen of the Universe Church.

Beuzer, Vincent *s.j.* (ANC) [G] Anchorage, AK Jesuit House.

Bevan, James J., Jr. '75 (LAV) [9] Las Vegas, NV St. Francis de Sales Church.

Bevan, Norman E. *c.s.sp.* '63 (PIT) [Q] Bethel Park, PA Holy Ghost Animation Center.

Bevan, Thomas R. '63 (BAL) Cumberland, MD St. Patrick Church.

Bevans, Stephen B. *s.v.d.* '71 (CHI) [B] Chicago, IL The Catholic Theological Union at Chicago; [B] Techny, IL Divine Word Residence; [B] Techny, IL Divine Word Residence; [N] Chicago, IL Divine Word Theologate; [N] Techny, IL Society of the Divine Word, Provincial Headquarter-Chicago Prov.

Bevard, Herbert A. '72 (PH) [17] Philadelphia, PA St. Athanasius Church.

Bevenour, Richard F. '57 (DAV) On Duty Outside the Diocese.

Beveridge, John P. '72 (SFD) Collinsville, IL SS. Peter and Paul Church.

Bevilacqua, Carlo *c.s.s.* '45 (BO) [Z] Waltham, MA Stigmatine Fathers and Brothers.

Bevilacqua, Jerome *o.s.a.* '65 (SD) [B] San Diego, CA Austin House; [H] San Diego, CA Augustinian Community.

Bevington, William S. '51 (NSH) Hendersonville, TN Our Lady of the Lake Church; [L] Hendersonville, TN Legion of Mary; [L] Hendersonville, TN Priests Eucharistic League.

Bevins, John J. '58 (HRT) [2] Waterbury, CT Immaculate Conception Church.

Beyer, Emil J. '40 (MAR) Retired; [D] Escanaba, MI Bishop Noa Home for Senior Citizens.

Beyer, Gregory *o.f.m.cap.* '62 (DEN) [3] Denver, CO Annunciation Church; Northglenn, CO Immaculate Heart of Mary Church; [M] Denver, CO Annunciation Friary.

Beyer, Lawrence A. '96 (DAL) Plano, TX Prince of Peace Church.

Beyer, Leroy O. '66 (WH) Retired.

Beyer, Richard '81 (AUS) Temple, TX V.A. Hospital; Waco, TX V.A. Hospital.

Beyer, Richard J. '81 (DAV) On Duty Outside the Diocese.

Beyette, Paul V. '50 (OG) Retired.

Bezunartea, Herman O. '58 (FRS) Bass Lake, CA Our Lady of the Sierra Church.

Bezuszka, Stanley J. *s.j.* '46 (BO) [W] Chestnut Hill, MA The Jesuit Community at Boston College.

Bezzina, Benjamin '77 (GLP) On Duty Outside of Diocese.

Bhia Wea, Raymundus *s.v.d.* '82 (ORG) [G] Fullerton, CA St. Jude Medical Center.

Biabandi, Deogratias '90 (COL) Grove City, OH Our Lady of Perpetual Help Church.

Biagi, Vincent L. *s.j.* '78 (NY) [F] New York, NY Regis High School; [DD] New York, NY St. Ignatius Loyola Residence.

Biain, Jose *o.f.m.* '48 (MIA) [H] Miami, FL Franciscan Fathers' Residence.

Bialkowski, David W. '88 (BUF) [3] Cheektowaga, NY St. John Gualbert Church.

Bialkowski, Henry A. '49 (NOR) Retired.

Bialkowski, Jacek '96 (SCR) Sayre, PA Church of the Epiphany.

Bialoncik, Emmanuel *o.f.m.* '73 (BWN) Elsa, TX Sacred Heart Church.

Bianchi, Paul '64 (DM) Portsmouth, IA St. Mary Church.

Bianchi, Raymond S. '52 (TR) Retired.

Bianco, Anthony M. *c.r.s.p.* '51 (ALN) [K] Bethlehem, PA The Barnabite Fathers Barnabite Spiritual Center.

Biasiatto, Richard P. *o.f.m.* '64 (NEW) Elmwood Park, NJ St. Leo's Church.

Biasio, Mariano *c.s.j.* '54 (LA) Lancaster, CA Blessed Junipero Serra Church.

Biasiol, Virgilio *o.f.m.* '42 (LA) [Q] Santa Barbara, CA Franciscan Friary, Order of Friars Minor (Old Mission).

Bibeault, Norbert P. *c.s.v.* '56 (LAV) [A] Las Vegas, NV Bishop Gorman High School; [D] Las Vegas, NV Clerics of St. Viator Retirement Home.

Biber, J. Morton '85 (RIC) Powhatan, VA St. John Neumann Church; [G] Powhatan, VA St. John Neumann Family Life Center.

Bich, John Tran Gnoc *c.ss.r.* '52 (TUC) [8] Tucson, AZ Our Lady of La Vang Church; [F] Tucson, AZ Regina Cleri Center.

Bich, Tran Ngoc *c.ss.r.* '52 (LA) [Q] Baldwin Park, CA Vietnamese Redemptorist Mission.

Bichl, William M. *s.j.* '67 (CLV) [B] Cleveland, OH John Carroll University; [B] Cleveland, OH John Carroll Jesuit Community.

Bickel, Timothy C. '92 (MIL) Butler, WI St. Agnes Church.

Bickerstaff, Albert *o.s.b.* '67 (SAV) [B] Savannah, GA Benedictine Military School; [F] Savannah, GA The Benedictine Priory.

Bickett, Anthony '83 (OWN) [7] Owensboro, KY SS. Joseph and Paul Church.

Bickle, John *o.f.m.* (NY) Manhattan, NY St. Vincent Hospital.

Bickle, John *o.f.m.conv.* '84 (NY) [B] Staten Island, NY St. Francis Friary.

Bico, Anthony '93 (NEW) [26] Newark, NJ Our Lady of Fatima Church; Newark, NJ Essex County Juvenile Correctional Center; Newark, NJ Cura (Community United to Rehabilitate Addicts).

Bicomong, Sergio (CAM) [3] Vineland, NJ St. Francis of Assisi Church; Fairton, NJ Federal Correctional Institution.

Bicomong, Sergio '79 (TR) On Duty Outside the Diocese.

Bicsko, Stephen C. *c.m.* '70 (BRK) [V] Queens Village, NY DePaul Residence.

Bicz, Marian '88 (RVC) Glen Cove, NY St. Patrick's Church.

Biczak, Arkad '63 (SFE) [28] Albuquerque, NM St. John the Apostle Church.

Bida, John A. '73 (NY) Brewster, NY St. Lawrence O'Toole Church.

Bidawid, Kamal Warda '68 (EST) Turlock, CA St. Thomas Assyrian-Chaldean Church.

Biddle, Ward *c.p.* '51 (FgM) Mission Procurators.

Bidinger, Bruce M. *s.j.* '86 (PH) [AA] Philadelphia, PA Jesuit Community at St. Joseph's University.

Bidlack, Bede *o.s.b.* (WDC) [M] Washington, DC St. Anselm's Abbey.

Bidwill, Joseph E. *o.p.* '55 (STP) [15] Minneapolis, MN St. Albert the Great Church.

Bie, Paul R. '83 (RVC) West Hempstead, NY St. Thomas, the Apostle Church.

Biebel, Msgr. William E. '62 (E) [1] Erie, PA St. Peter Church.

Bieberle, Victor '51 (WCH) Retired.

Biecker, Thomas C. *s.j.* '40 (DET) [P] Clarkston, MI Colombiere Center.

Biedermann, Msgr. Arnold '45 (LA) Ventura, CA Sacred Heart Church; Retired.

Bieganowski, Ronald R. *s.j.* '72 (MIL) [P] Milwaukee, WI Jesuit Community at Marquette University.

Biegler, Steven '93 (RC) McIntosh, SD St. Bonaventure's Church; McLaughlin, SD St. Bernard Church; Standing Rock, SD Standing Rock Reservation Church.

Bielak, Andrew '95 (NY) [133] Bronx, NY St. Benedict Church.

Bielanski, Joseph J. '80 (STU) Absent Without Leave.

Bielawa, Thomas G. *s.d.s.* '72 (PHX) Cashion, AZ St. William Church.

Bielby, Donald J. *c.s.c.* '63 (FTW) [16] South Bend, IN St. Patrick Church.

Bielecki, Michael *o.s.a.* '83 (PH) Villanova, PA St. Thomas of Villanova Church.

Bielek, Robert M. '74 (CLV) [43] Cleveland, OH St. Leo the Great Church.

Bielen, Msgr. Stephen A. '45 (MET) Hackettstown, NJ Assumption of the Blessed Virgin Mary Church, Retired; [H] Somerset, NJ Maria Regina Residence.

Bielewicz, Harry R. '86 (PIT) [5] Butler, PA St. Wendelin Church.

Bielonko, Joseph '59 (WOR) Dudley, MA St. Andrew Bobola Church.

Bielskas, Edward J. '41 (GR) Retired.

Bielski, Francis V. '57 (PH) Willow Grove, PA St. David Church.

Bieluch, Chester A. '48 (HRT) Retired.

Bien, Francis P. '58 (BRK) [186] Queens, NY St. Josaphat Church.

Bien Quang Do, Joseph '64 (SD) [2] El Cajon, CA Our Lady of Grace Church.

Bienia, Michael A. '58 (GBG) Retired; [G] Greensburg, PA Neumann House.

Bieniek, Stanislaus '67 (GAL) Pasadena, TX St. Pius the Fifth Church.

Bienvenu, Kenneth A. '60 (LAF) St. Martinville, LA St. Martin of Tours Church; Retired.

Bienvenu, Paul G. '92 (LAF) [13] Lafayette, LA St. Leo the Great Church.

Bier, Louis C. '76 (PH) [3] Norristown, PA St. Patrick Church.

Biergans, Kent *o.f.m.conv.* '67 (FgM) Conventual Franciscan Foreign Missions.

Biergans, Kent *o.f.m.conv.* '67 (IND) St. Joseph Hill, IN St. Joseph Church; [I] Mount Saint Francis, IN Mount Saint Francis Friary and Retreat Center; [J] Mount Saint Francis, IN Provincial Headquarters for the Conventual Franciscan Province.

Bierman, Earl C. '57 (COV) Leave of Absence; Retired.

Biermann, John G. *s.a.c.* '69 (BAL) [51] Baltimore, MD St. Jude Church.

Biernacki, Jacob S. '67 (SPC) Lamar, MO St. Mary Church.

Biernat, Leon J. '92 (BUF) [5] Depew, NY Our Lady of the Blessed Sacrament Church.

Biersack, Thomas E. '81 (MIL) New Munster, WI St. Alphonsus Church.

Bierschenk, Stephen W. '76 (DAL) [28] Dallas, TX St. Thomas Aquinas Church.

Bierster, Msgr. Leo N. '52 (HBG) Hershey, PA St. Joan of Arc Church.

Biesiada, Msgr. Louis W. (PAT) Retired.

Biesinger, Robert J. '56 (BUF) Absent on Leave; [O] Buffalo, NY Sheehan Residence for Priests.

Bietighofer, Alfred J. '65 (BGP) Weston, CT St. Francis of Assisi Church.

Bietz, Crispin *o.f.m.* '50 (SFE) [J] Santa Fe, NM Discalced Carmelite Monastery.

Biffar, Cornelius *ss.cc.* '51 (FR) [I] Fairhaven, MA Sacred Hearts Provincial House.

Biffar, William *c.ss.r.* '47 (ALB) [L] Saratoga Springs, NY St. John Neumann Residence.

Bigelow, William R. '67 (BUF) [30] Buffalo, NY Holy Family Church.

Biggers, Clarence J. *o.c.s.o.* '50 (ATL) [J] Conyers, GA The Monastery of the Holy Spirit.

Biggs, Anselm G. *o.s.b.* '40 (CHL) [J] Belmont, NC Belmont Abbey.

Bigley, Michael J. *s.d.s.* (MIL) [5] Wauwatosa, WI St. Pius X Church.

Biglin, Martin J. '67 (NY) [5] New Rochelle, NY Holy Name of Jesus Church.

Bignall, Douglas J. '93 (DET) Algonac, MI St. Catherine Church.

Bihr, Msgr. Louis J. '68 (PAT) [3] Wayne, NJ Immaculate Heart of Mary Church.

Bijura, Fortunatus '79 (PEO) [2] Champaign, IL St. John's Catholic Chapel Church; [P] Champaign, IL St. John's Catholic Student Chapel and Newman Foundation, University of Illinois.

Bik, Michael *o.s.b.* '93 (SCL) [I] Collegeville, MN St. John's Abbey, of the Order of St. Benedict.

Bikoma, Msgr. Edward J. '51 (EST) Chicago, IL St. Ephrem's Church; Chicago, IL Mart Mariam Church.

Bilanych, Msgr. John '40 (PHU) Retired.

Bilinsky, William '65 (CHI) [J] Chicago, IL Resurrection Medical Center.

Bilinsky, William M. '65 (STN) Chicago, IL Resurrection and Our Lady of Resurrection.

Biliran, Giovanni D. *s.v.d.* '87 (CHK) Chalan Kanoa Village, MP Cathedral of Our Lady of Mt. Carmel .

Bill, J. Armand '56 (PRT) Retired.

Bill, Msgr. Ronald '57 (SY) Cicero, NY Sacred Heart Church.

Bill, Thomas *c.s.c.* '55 (P) [B] Portland, OR University of Portland; [L] Portland, OR Holy Cross Fathers & Brothers, C.S.C. - University of Portland.

Billac, Christopher A. *s.j.* '65 (GAL) [F] Houston, TX Strake, Jesuit College Preparatory Inc.

Biller, Andrew *s.v.d.* '61 (FgM) Society of the Divine Word Foreign Missions.

Biller, Harold N. '70 (ALT) [9] Johnstown, PA St. Patrick's Church.

Billett, Robert *c.m.f.* '57 (FRS) [8] Fresno, CA St. Anthony Mary Claret Church.

Billian, Michael R. '84 (TOL) [34] Toledo, OH St. Patrick Historic Church.

Billicky, Louis S. '49 (BO) Senior Priests.

Billig, Maynard *o.f.m.* '39 (STL) [P] St. Louis, MO Franciscan Friary of St. Anthony of Padua.

Billing, Jerome D. '71 (STL) Shrewsbury, MO St. Michael Church.

Billinger, James J. '83 (WCH) [12] Wichita, KS St. Elizabeth Ann Seton Church.

Billman, George B. '72 (GAY) [D] Traverse City, MI Infant Jesus of Prague Monastery.

Billotte, Philip J. (ROC) Stanley, NY St. Theresa Church.

Billotte, Philip J. '66 (ROC) Naples, NY Our Lady of the Lakes Catholic Community Church; Penn Yan, NY St. Michael Church.

Billotti, Joseph E. *s.j.* '63 (CHK) Saipan, MP San Jude Church.

Billotti, Joseph E. *s.j.* '63 (FgM) Provinces.

Billy, Dennis *c.ss.r.* '80 (NY) [DD] Esopus, NY Redemptorist Priests and Brothers C.Ss.R. (Province of Baltimore).

Billy, George '48 (PSC) Retired.

Bilodeau, Florent R. '57 (MAN) [4] Concord, NH Immaculate Heart of Mary Church.

Bilodeau, Leopold J. '73 (BUR) Newport, VT St. Mary Star of the Sea Church.

Bilodeau, Roger P. '65 (MAN) Lincoln, NH St. Joseph Church.

Bilot, James D. '92 (DET) Special Assignment.

Bilotte, Phil (ROC) [M] Rochester, NY Diocesan Department of Campus Ministry.

Bilskie, Msgr. Maurilius '43 (EVN) [8] Evansville, IN Holy Rosary Church; Retired.

Bily, Msgr. Edward '51 (SAT) New Braunfels, TX SS. Peter and Paul Church.

Bily, John C. '58 (VIC) Weimar, TX St. Michael Church.

Bily, Lambert S. '63 (SAT) [20] San Antonio, TX Our Lady of Sorrows Church.

Binder, Mark J. '71 (SPC) Houston, MO St. Mark Church.

Bindner, Charles J. '58 (L) [31] Louisville, KY St. Helen Church.
Bingham, John K. *s.j.* '58 (BAL) [S] Baltimore, MD Jesuit Fathers and Brothers Maryland Provincial Curia.
Bingham, John K. *s.j.* '58 (FgM) Provinces.
Binh, John Phan Cong '51 (SHP) Retired.
Binh-Minh, Thomas Duong '90 (OAK) [5] San Leandro, CA Our Lady of Good Counsel Church.
Biniek, Joseph P. '78 (ARL) Middleburg, VA St. Stephen the Martyr Church.
Biniszkiewicz, Msgr. Leonard E. '63 (BUF) [14] Niagara Falls, NY St. Teresa of the Infant Jesus Church.
Binkowski, Msgr. George '72 (STF) Fresh Meadows, NY Annunciation of the B.V.M. Church.
Binkowski, James P. '56 (LC) Retired; [H] La Crosse, WI Holy Cross (Seminary) Diocesan Center.
Binsfeld, Douglas '98 (SFS) Aberdeen, SD St. Mary Church.
Binsfeld, Msgr. Michael A. '67 (RCK) Crystal Lake, IL St. Elizabeth Ann Seton Church.
Binsfeld, Steven '79 (SCL) [1] St. Cloud, MN St. Mary's Cathedral of St. Cloud.
Bionda, Bonaventure *o.f.m.* '59 (ALB) [1] Troy, NY St. Anthony of Padua Church.
Biondi, Lawrence H. *s.j.* '70 (STL) [C] St. Louis, MO Saint Louis University; [P] St. Louis, MO Jesuit Community Corporation at St. Louis University - Jesuit Hall.
Biondolillo, Gabriel *o.m.i.* '56 (BEL) [F] Belleville, IL Shrine of Our Lady of the Snows.
Biosca, Emilio *o.f.m.cap.* '94 (FgM) Capuchin Foreign Missions.
Bir, Stanley *o.f.m.* '52 (CIN) [M] Cincinnati, OH St. Clement Friary.
Birarelli, Carl A. '58 (CIN) Retired.
Birarelli, Carl A. '58 (VEN) [4] Sarasota, FL St. Martha Church.
Birch, Donald G. '67 (PH) Fallsington, PA St. Joseph the Worker Church.
Birch, Keith L. '71 (DUB) Garwin, IA St. Boniface Church; Tama-Toledo, IA St. Patrick's Church.
Birch, Msgr. Thomas J. '59 (ALN) Shillington, PA St. John Baptist de la Salle Church; Retired.
Birchmeyer, Robert J. '73 (SY) Solvay, NY St. Cecilia Church.
Bircumshaw, Colin F. '75 (SLC) [3] Ogden, UT St. Joseph's Church; [C] Ogden, UT St. Joseph Regional School.
Bird, James F. '91 (E) [3] Sharon, PA St. Joseph Church.
Bird, Stephen J. '76 (OKL) [17] Oklahoma City, OK St. Patrick Church; Special Assignment.
Bird, Steven '00 (PEO) On Duty Outside the Diocese.
Birdsall, Anthony J. '60 (GB) Sturgeon Bay, WI Corpus Christi Church.
Birdsall, Hugh *s.d.s.* '62 (MIL) [P] Greendale, WI Salvatorian Formation Community.
Birdsall, Hugh G. *s.d.s.* '62 (MIL) [B] Hales Corners, WI Sacred Heart School of Theology.
Birdsall, John M. '56 (RC) Retired.
Bireley, Robert L. *s.j.* '64 (CHI) [C] Chicago, IL Jesuit Community at Loyola University of Chicago.
Biren, Timothy E. '99 (WIN) Austin, MN St. Edward's Church.
Birge, Msgr. George D. '56 (BGP) Sherman, CT Holy Trinity Church.
Biriruka, Ernest '81 (MIA) [24] Miami, FL St. Kevin Church.
Birk, John '63 (SPK) Pasco, WA St. Patrick Church; Special Ministry; [G] Pasco, WA Lourdes Medical Center.
Birk, John W. '70 (L) [34] Louisville, KY Holy Name Church.
Birkel, John B. '96 (LIN) Alma, NE St. Joseph's Church.
Birkel, Robert C. '49 (L) Retired.
Birkenfeld, Darryl '88 (AMA) Stratford, TX St. Joseph's Church.
Birkenhauer, Henry F. *s.j.* '45 (DET) [P] Clarkston, MI Colombiere Center.
Birket, Dwight J. (WCH) Wichita, KS Sedgwick County Adult Detention Facility.
Birket, Dwight J. '72 (WCH) [2] Wichita, KS All Saints Church.
Birkhead, Henry G. '56 (PH) [34] Philadelphia, PA Christ the King Church; Retired.
Birkle, Walter A. '58 (NY) [172] Bronx, NY Our Lady of Grace Church; [Q] Bronx, NY District Council of the Bronx.
Birkmaier, James E. '68 (GF) [G] Great Falls, MT Benefis Health Care.
Birkmeyer, John R. *c.s.c.* '57 (AUS) [H] Austin, TX Congregation of Holy Cross - Southern Province.
Birmingham, Kevin M. '97 (CHI) Blue Island, IL St. Benedict Church.
Birmingham, Kieran '75 (NY) [HH] New York, NY St. Patrick's International Inc.
Birmingham, Robert F. '93 (HRT) Branford, CT St. Mary Church.
Birney, Timothy P. '98 (DET) Utica, MI St. Lawrence Church.
Biron, Gerald R. *m.s.* (R) Washington, NC Mother of Mercy Church.
Biron, Gerald R. *m.s.* '60 (HRT) [M] Hartford, CT Missionaries of LaSalette, Provincial Secretary.
Biron, Robert G. '74 (MAN) Somersworth, NH St. Martin Church.
Biroschak, Robert V. '93 (LA) Pasadena, CA St. Philip the Apostle Church.
Birringer, Raphael *s.d.s.* '51 (MIL) [P] Milwaukee, WI Salvatorian Provincial Residence.
Birzer, W. L. '39 (DOD) Retired.
Bisaillon, Rene '59 (HON) Waipahu, HI St. Joseph Church.
Bisbee, Burnell B. *s.j.* '75 (OM) [36] Omaha, NE SS. Peter and Paul Church; [K] Omaha, NE Jesuit Community at Creighton University.
Bischof, Donald R. '83 (PIT) Beaver Falls, PA Divine Mercy Church.
Bischof, Simon *o.s.b.* '55 (SCL) [5] St. Cloud, MN St. Augustine Church; [I] Collegeville, MN St. John's Abbey, of the Order of St. Benedict.
Bischoff, Albert J. *s.j.* '56 (CIN) [74] Cincinnati, OH St. Robert Bellarmine Church; [M] Cincinnati, OH Jesuit Community at Xavier University; [Q] Cincinnati, OH Xavier University Campus Ministry.
Bischoff, Msgr. Francis J. (PAT) Retired.
Bisenius, Thomas R. '54 (DUB) Garryowen, IA St. Patrick's Church.
Bisgrove, Charles *s.c.j.* '90 (MIL) [P] Hales Corners, WI Sacred Heart Monastery.
Bishara, Boctor '51 (LA) [J] Lynwood, CA St. Francis Medical Center.
Bisharat, George Said '92 (NTN) El Cajon, CA St. Jacob Church.
Bishop, Clifton E., Jr. '98 (ALN) Hellertown, PA St. Theresa of the Child Jesus Church.
Bishop, E. Louis *s.j.* '64 (PHX) [B] Phoenix, AZ Brophy College Preparatory.
Bishop, Joseph E. '58 (SAC) Yuba City, CA St. Isidore Church; Retired and in Senior Ministry.
Bishop, Patrick A. '74 (ATL) [4] Marietta, GA Church of the Transfiguration.
Bishop, Robert *c.m.f.* '71 (LA) [Q] Rancho Dominguez, CA Dominguez Seminary Inc.
Bishop, Thomas '75 (CHI) Glenview, IL Our Lady of Perpetual Help Church.
Bishop, Thomas G. '70 (Y) [1] Canton, OH All Saints Church; [4] Canton, OH St. Anthony's Church.
Bisignano, Joseph F. '81 (NY) Beacon, NY St. Joachim Church.
Bisignano, Joseph J. '81 (NY) Beacon, NY St. John Evangelist Church.
Bismonte, Honesto '54 (LA) Gardena, CA St. Anthony of Padua Church.
Bisoffi, Joseph L. *o.s.cam.* '72 (MIL) [K] Milwaukee, WI St. Francis Hospital; [P] Wauwatosa, WI St. Camillus Community House.
Bisson, Andrew R. '93 (PRT) [I] Kennebunkport, ME St. Anthony's Friary.
Bisson, Eddy N. '68 (MAN) Farmington, NH St. Peter Church.
Bisson, Joseph *s.v.d.* '63 (FgM) Society of the Divine Word Foreign Missions.
Bisson, Roger *m.afr.* '55 (WDC) [M] Washington, DC Missionaries of Africa.
Bissonette, James '88 (DUL) Proctor, MN St. Rose Catholic Church.
Bissonnette, Bernard (NOR) On Duty Outside the Diocese.
Bissot, Robert H. '57 (GAY) West Branch, MI St. Joseph Church.
Bistany, Msgr. Joseph '37 (SAM) Retired.
Bistricky, Frederick J. '65 (MIL) Retired.
Biszek, Msgr. Robert J. '65 (ALN) [4] Bethlehem, PA Holy Infancy Church.
Bitanga, Msgr. Fred A. '64 (SFR) [42] San Francisco, CA St. Patrick Church.
Bitangjol, Albert P. '56 (SFR) Retired.
Bitchapogu, Anthaiah '92 (KAL) Battle Creek, MI St. Philip Church.
Bitsko, Daniel J. '65 (PSC) Smithtown, NY Resurrection Church; Westbury, NY St. Andrew the Apostle Church.
Bittel, Patrick M. '82 (OWN) Morganfield, KY St. Ann's Church.
Bitterman, John L. *s.s.* '69 (BAL) [S] Baltimore, MD Sulpician Provincial House.
Bittmenn, David J. '94 (SLC) [6] Salt Lake City, UT St. Ambrose Church; Park City, UT St. Mary of the Assumption Church.
Bittner, Wayne W. '64 (MIL) On Leave.
Bittner,, Gregory, J.C.L. '85 (BIR) [5] Birmingham, AL Blessed Sacrament Church.
Bitz, Al '69 (FAR) Buffalo, ND St. Thomas Church; Casselton, ND St. Leo Church.
Biven, Louis Russell '57 (MOB) [17] Mobile, AL Our Savior Church.
Bixenman, Joseph E. '72 (AMA) [10] Amarillo, TX St. Mary's Church.
Bizaca, Mate '73 (LA) [46] Los Angeles, CA St. Anthony Church.
Bizard, Hubert *f.s.s.p.* '98 (SCR) [M] Elmhurst, PA Priestly Fraternity of St. Peter (F.S.S.P.), North American District Headquarters.
Bizzotto, Giovanni *c.s.* '86 (LA) [88] Los Angeles, CA St. Peter Church.
Bjorklund, Brian '66 (DET) Military Chaplains.
Bjorum, James L. '76 (DET) [1] St. Clair Shores, MI St. Germaine Church.
Blacet, Msgr. William J. '46 (KC) [27] Kansas City, MO Our Lady of Good Counsel Church.
Blach, Leo M. '53 (DEN) Retired.
Black, Alvin A. *o.f.m.* '60 (PAT) [M] Butler, NJ St. Anthony Friary.
Black, Frank A. '80 (BRK) [73] Brooklyn, NY St. Laurence Church.
Black, James P. '88 (COL) Chillicothe, OH St. Peter Church; Waverly, OH St. Mary, Queen of the Missions Church.
Black, Joseph '56 (P) Junction City, OR St. Helen Church; Monroe, OR St. Rose Church.
Black, Michael Gerard '00 (RCK) Woodstock, IL St. Mary Church.
Blackall, John C. '51 (HRT) [9] Waterbury, CT St. Cecilia's Church; [T] Waterbury, CT Spanish-Speaking Center.
Blackall, L. Randall '54 (HRT) Glastonbury, CT St. Paul's Church.
Blackburn, Clifford *o.m.i.* '47 (SAT) [K] San Antonio, TX Oblate Madonna Residence.
Blackburn, David *o.c.s.o.* '54 (SPC) [E] Ava, MO Assumption Abbey (Trappist).
Blackburn, Michael *o.f.m.* '86 (LAV) [10] Las Vegas, NV St. James the Apostle Church.
Blackowski, Theodore A. *o.f.m.* '45 (SP) [O] St. Petersburg, FL St. Anthony Friary.
Blackwell, Edward A. '76 (HBG) On Duty Outside the Diocese.
Blackwell, Edward A. '76 (MIA) [B] Opa Locka, FL St. Thomas University.
Blackwell, Maurice J. '74 (BAL) Absent on Leave.
Blackwell, Michael J. '73 (WDC) Landover Hills, MD St. Mary's Catholic Church.
Blackwood, Wallace E. '67 (BO) [2] Peabody, MA St. Ann Church.
Blade, Kevin *m.s.c.* (AUS) Goldthwaite, TX St. Peter's Church.
Blade, Kevin *m.s.c.* '91 (AUS) Lampasas, TX St. Mary's Church; Lometa, TX Good Shepherd Church; [H] Blanco, TX Missionaries of the Sacred Heart, M.S.C.
Bladt, Joel S. *s.t.* '61 (SAV) Bainbridge, GA St. Joseph's Church.
Blaes, James F. *c.s.c.* '55 (FTW) [17] South Bend, IN Faith & Hope & Charity Chapel Church; [J] South Bend, IN Congregation of Holy Cross, Indiana Province, Provincial House.
Blaes, Paul '51 (KC) Retired.
Blaeser, Alfred A. '32 (BRK) Retired.
Blaeser, Don *o.f.m.* '70 (CHI) [N] Countryside, IL St. Gratian Friary, Franciscan Friars.
Blaettler, James *s.j.* '80 (NY) [28] New York, NY Corpus Christi Church.
Blaettler, James R. *s.j.* '80 (SJ) [L] Los Gatos, CA Sacred Heart Jesuit Center.
Blaha, John '75 (GB) Absent on Leave.
Blahner, Joseph H. '58 (BUR) [5] Burlington, VT St. Mark's Church.
Blain, Lionel A. '54 (PRO) [8] Woonsocket, RI St. Joseph Church.
Blaine, James E. '77 (SLC) American Fork, UT St. Peter's Church; Draper, UT State Penitentiary.
Blaine, Michael J. '91 (PH) Absent on Leave.
Blaine, Philip *o.f.m.conv.* '63 (NY) [B] Staten Island, NY St. Francis Friary.
Blair, Guy *s.c.j.* '82 (CHI) [N] Chicago, IL Priests of the Sacred Heart.
Blair, Leonard P. '76 (DET) Grosse Pointe Farms, MI St. Paul Catholic Church.
Blair, Msgr. Raymond O. '60 (MAN) Retired.
Blais, Denis *c.p.m.* '93 (OWN) [F] South Union, KY Fathers of Mercy.
Blais, George '90 (ORG) Laguna Niguel, CA St. Timothy Church.
Blais, Melvin J. '42 (STP) Retired.
Blais, Robert L. '63 (PRO) On Duty Outside the Diocese.
Blais, Robert R. *o.p.* '68 (L) [47] Louisville, KY St. Louis Bertrand Church.
Blais, Roland O. '44 (MAN) [9] Manchester, NH St. George Church; Retired.
Blake, Andrew P. (RVC) Retired.
Blake, Andrew P. '63 (RVC) Sag Harbor, NY St. Andrew's Church.
Blake, Caryle (OAK) [S] Berkeley, CA Maria House.
Blake, David D. *o.f.m.* '95 (BUF) [59] Buffalo, NY SS. Rita & Patrick Church; [C] St. Bonaventure, NY St. Bonaventure University; [O] St. Bonaventure, NY St. Bonaventure Friary.
Blake, Jerry W. '00 (DUB) Dyersville, IA Basilica of St. Francis Xavier.

Blake, John Vincent *o.p.* '51 (DEN) [29] Denver, CO St. Dominic's Church.
Blake, John Vincent *o.p.* '51 (SFE) [31] Albuquerque, NM St. Thomas Aquinas University Church.
Blake, Lawrence R. '99 (STP) Chanhassen, MN St. Hubert Church.
Blake, Peter M. '84 (STL) Union, MO Immaculate Conception Church.
Blake, Philip *s.j.* '61 (PHX) [11] Phoenix, AZ St. Francis Xavier Church.
Blake, Richard *s.j.* '69 (BO) [W] Chestnut Hill, MA The Jesuit Community at Boston College.
Blake, Robert '77 (SR) Cloverdale, CA St. Peter's Church.
Blake, William B. '63 (SCR) Jessup, PA St. James Church.
Blakely, Leonard J. '80 (WIL) Chestertown, MD Sacred Heart Church; Chestertown, MD Washington College; [O] Chestertown, MD Washington College Catholic Campus Ministry; [O] Newark, DE Univ. of Delaware Newman Center.
Blakely, Paige A. '84 (ORL) DeBary, FL St. Ann's Church.
Blaker, John '96 (OAK) El Cerrito, CA St. John the Baptist Church.
Blanch, Jose Maria *s.f.* '51 (SFE) Santa Cruz, NM Holy Cross Church.
Blanchard, David *o.carm.* '87 (WDC) [B] Washington, DC Whitefriars Hall.
Blanchard, Donald V. '69 (BR) [12] Baton Rouge, LA St. Jean Vianney Church.
Blanchard, John L. *s.j.* '48 (DET) [P] Clarkston, MI Colombiere Center.
Blanchard, Kirby '53 (DUL) Retired.
Blanchard, Peter R. *s.m.* '67 (NO) [P] New Orleans, LA Marist Fathers.
Blanchet, Leo '86 (MOB) Whistler, AL St. Bridget Church.
Blanchette, Brian D. '85 (PRT) Calais, ME Immaculate Conception Church.
Blanchette, Melvin C. *s.s.* (BAL) [A] Baltimore, MD St. Mary's Seminary and University.
Blanchette, Michael '84 (JOL) Absent on Leave.
Blanchette, Oliver *a.a.* '44 (BO) [W] Boston, MA Assumptionist Center.
Blanchette, Roger E. *s.j.* '64 (HEL) [5] Missoula, MT St. Francis Xavier Church; [E] Missoula, MT St. Patrick Hospital and Health Sciences Center, Sisters of Providence of Montana Corporation.
Blanchfield, David W. '82 (BGP) [1] Norwalk, CT St. Jerome Church.
Blanchfield, John P. '50 (HRT) Plantsville, CT St. Aloysius Church.
Blanco, Gonzalo *o.s.b.* (FgM) American - Cassinese Congregation Foreign Missions.
Blanco, Gonzalo *o.s.b.* '92 (BIS) [A] Richardton, ND Assumption Abbey.
Blanco, Gonzalo *o.s.b.* '92 (FgM) American - Cassinese Congregation Foreign Missions.
Blanco, Ignacio *c.m.f.* '51 (SAT) [12] San Antonio, TX Immaculate Heart of Mary Church.
Blanco, Ildefonso *o.s.a.* '64 (SJN) [1] Bayamon, PR San Agustin Church.
Blanco, John P. *s.d.b.* '64 (NY) [72] New York, NY Mary Help of Christians Church.
Blanco, Jose '77 (LA) Carpinteria, CA St. Joseph Church.
Blanco, Joseph J. '84 (DEN) Roggen, CO Sacred Heart Church.
Blanco, Telesforo R. *o.s.a.* '60 (BEA) [1] Port Arthur, TX Our Lady of Guadalupe Church.
Bland, Thomas A. '74 (SAC) Jackson, CA St. Patrick's Church.
Blanda, William C. '91 (LAF) Kaplan, LA Our Lady of the Holy Rosary Church.
Blandford, James T. '38 (LEX) Retired.
Blandino, Salvatore '53 (SJ) Retired.
Blaney, Jim *o.m.i.* '65 (JUN) Haines, AK Sacred Heart Church; Skagway, AK St. Therese of the Child Jesus Church.
Blaney, Robert M. '93 (BO) Belmont, MA St. Luke Church.
Blangiardi, B. Jeffrey *s.j.* '86 (BO) [W] Boston, MA The Society of Jesus of New England-Provincial Offices.
Blank, Godfrey *o.f.m.* '45 (GLP) Grants, NM St. Teresa Church.
Blank, Severius '58 (FWT) Burkburnett, TX St. Jude Thaddeus Church.
Blank, William H. '87 (NO) Franklinton, LA Holy Family Church.
Blankenship, John P. '63 (RIC) Petersburg, VA Federal Correctional Institution.
Blankinship, Calvin, Jr. '96 (B) Soda Springs, ID St. Mary's Church.
Blanpied, Robert D. '48 (PBL) Retired.
Blantz, James *c.s.c.* '56 (LA) [O] Chatsworth, CA Rancho San Antonio.
Blantz, Thomas E. *c.s.c.* '60 (FTW) [B] Notre Dame, IN University of Notre Dame Du Lac; [J] Notre Dame, IN Holy Cross Community, Corby Hall, University of Notre Dame.
Blaschko, Harvey *o.p.* '81 (CHI) [84] Chicago, IL Holy Trinity Church.
Blasco, Ignacio '62 (MIA) [21] Miami, FL St. Joachim Church.
Blaser, John R. '64 (TOL) [7] Toledo, OH Good Shepherd Church; [30] Toledo, OH St. Louis Church; [41] Toledo, OH St. Thomas Aquinas Church.
Blasich, Bernard '67 (MIL) [P] Wauwatosa, WI St. Camillus Provincialate.
Blaska, John A. '53 (DET) [2] Troy, MI St. Alan Church; Retired.
Blasko, Joseph A. '99 (GAY) Petoskey, MI St. Francis Xavier Church.
Blastic, Michael *o.f.m.conv.* '75 (BUF) [C] St. Bonaventure, NY St. Bonaventure University; [O] St. Bonaventure, NY St. Bonaventure Friary.
Blaszczak, Gerald R. *s.j.* '79 (NY) [DD] New York, NY Jesuit Community at Fordham University.
Blaszczak, Gerry *s.j.* '79 (NY) [GG] New York, NY University Apostolate.
Blaszczyk, Thaddeus J. '53 (DET) Retired.
Blattner, Joseph H. '58 (STL) On Duty Outside the Archdiocese.
Blau, Thomas J. '99 (RIC) Charlottesville, VA St. Thomas Aquinas Church.
Blaufuss, Tony '58 (KCK) Retired.
Blauvelt, Robert W. '59 (BRK) [218] Queens, NY Our Lady, Queen of Martyrs Church.
Blay, Msgr. Roberto Garcia '86 (PCE) [3] Ponce, PR Church of the Resurrection.
Blazak, Camillus '51 (BIR) Retired.
Blazejewski, Richard J. '74 (BUF) Perry, NY St. Stanislaus Kostka Church.
Blazejewski, Richard W. '74 (BUF) Perry, NY St. Joseph Church.
Blazek, David J. '97 (DET) Harper Woods, MI Our Lady Queen of Peace Church.
Blazek, Eugene E. '76 (HON) Military Chaplains.
Blazek, James F. '79 (CHI) [92] Chicago, IL Immaculate Heart of Mary Church.
Blazek, John *c.s.c.* '58 (CLV) [D] Gates Mills, OH Gilmour Academy.
Blazek, John '98 (CHI) [9] Chicago, IL St. Alphonsus Church.
Blazewicz, William J. '59 (LC) Camp Douglas, WI St. James Church; Indian Creek, WI St. Michael Church.
Blazine, Msgr. James A. '62 (BEL) New Baden, IL St. George Church.
Blazovics, Victor '00 (SPK) [4] Spokane, WA Our Lady of Fatima Church.
Bleaux, Floyd J., Jr. '73 (OG) [1] Plattsburgh, NY Our Lady of Victory Church.
Blecha, Charles A. '40 (LC) Retired.
Blecha, Jordan R. *o.praem.* '39 (GB) [I] De Pere, WI St. Norbert Abbey.
Blee, Edward C. *s.m.* '55 (SFR) [N] San Francisco, CA Marist Center of the West.
Blehl, Vincent F. *s.j.* '52 (NY) [DD] New York, NY Jesuit Provincial's Office.
Bleich, Msgr. Russell M. '60 (DUB) On Special or Other Archdiocesan Assignment.
Bleichner, Howard P. '67 (PIT) On Duty Outside the Diocese.
Bleichner, Howard P. *s.s.* '67 (WDC) [A] Washington, DC Theological College of the Catholic University of America; [C] Washington, DC Catholic University of America, The; [C] Washington, DC Catholic University of America, The.
Bleiler, William C. '82 (CHR) Absent On Leave.
Bleiler, William James '66 (CAM) Cedarville, NJ St. Michael's Church; Leesburg, NJ New Jersey State Medium Security Prison.
Bleilevens, Msgr. Charles A. '50 (BRK) [153] Queens, NY Ascension Church; Retired.
Blenker, Ambrose J. '62 (LC) Plum City, WI St. John the Baptist Church.
Blenkle, Joseph A. '90 (NY) Valhalla, NY Holy Name of Jesus Church.
Blesnuk, Donald J. '85 (BUF) [20] Buffalo, NY Coronation of the Blessed Virgin Mary Church; [53] Buffalo, NY Our Lady of Loretto Church.
Blessin, Thomas C. *s.j.* '63 (NEW) [B] Jersey City, NJ Saint Peter's College; [N] Jersey City, NJ Jesuits of Saint Peter's College, Inc.
Blessing, Howard '76 (LAF) [15] Lafayette, LA St. Patrick Church.
Blessing, Loren *o.f.m.* '81 (FRS) [7] Fresno, CA St. Anthony of Padua Church.
Blessinger, James '64 (EVN) [5] Evansville, IN Corpus Christi Church.
Blessington, Msgr. William H. '43 (DUB) Retired.
Blethen, John *o.s.a.* '49 (SD) [H] San Diego, CA Augustinian Community.
Blewett, John E. *s.j.* '53 (STL) [O] St. Louis, MO Fusz Pavilion.
Blicharski, Michael *o.cist.* '93 (CHI) [N] Willow Springs, IL Cistercian Fathers, Our Lady Mother of the Church.
Blick, Ned J. '92 (WCH) Hutchinson, KS Our Lady of Guadalupe Church; [B] Hutchinson, KS Trinity High School.
Blickhan, Donald '74 (SFD) Military Chaplains.
Blighton, Francis E. '74 (ROC) [12] Rochester, NY St. Charles Borromeo Church.
Blind, Thomas F. '81 (NEW) Summit, NJ St. Teresa's Church.
Bline, G. David '98 (CLV) Lyndhurst, OH St. Clare Church.
Blinn, Mark R. '43 (CLV) [3] Garfield Heights, OH St. Therese Church; Retired.
Blinn, Richard J. *s.j.* '69 (SAC) Davis, CA St. James Church.
Bliss, Dennis '00 (Y) [11] Youngstown, OH St. Christine's Church.
Bliss, Michael '91 (PEO) [J] Peoria, IL St. Francis' Medical Center.
Bliszcz, Michael '87 (SJP) Parma, OH St. Andrew Church.
Bliven, Edmond '50 (P) Retired.
Bliven, Robert J. *o.s.c.* '56 (PHX) [4] Glendale, AZ St. Louis The King Church; [G] Phoenix, AZ Crosier Community of Phoenix (Canons Regular of the Order of the Holy Cross).
Block, John G. '63 (PMB) On Duty Outside the Diocese.
Blocker, James *c.s.b.* '75 (GAL) Rosenberg, TX Our Lady of Guadalupe Church.
Blocklinger, James L. '66 (DUB) [2] Cedar Rapids, IA All Saints Church.
Bloh, John F. '64 (CAM) Retired.
Bloh, Stephen R. '81 (PH) Absent on Sick Leave.
Blomberg, John '59 (STL) [21] St. Louis, MO St. Aloysius Gonzaga Church.
Blondell, Robert H. '66 (DET) Macomb, MI St. Maximilian Kolbe Church.
Blonigen, Aloysius *c.m.m.* '65 (DET) [K] Dearborn Heights, MI Our Lady of Grace Monastery.
Blonski, Joachim '92 (GLP) Aztec, NM St. Joseph Church; Flora Vista, NM Holy Trinity Church.
Blonski, Joe '92 (GLP) [F] Gallup, NM Southwest Indian Foundation.
Blood, Bernard M. *s.m.m.* '50 (RVC) West Islip, NY Good Samaritan Hospital Medical Center; [M] Bay Shore, NY Montfort Missionaries.
Blood, Francis X. '79 (STL) [30] St. Louis, MO St. Cecilia Church.
Bloom, Phillip '71 (SEA) [24] Seattle, WA Holy Family Church.
Bloomer, Matthew '99 (SFR) [S] San Francisco, CA Prelature of the Holy Cross and Opus Dei.
Blotsky, Hugo L. '88 (BIS) Garrison, ND St. Nicholas Church; [A] Richardton, ND Assumption Abbey.
Blottman, William P. (FR) [H] Fall River, MA Catholic Memorial Home Inc.
Blough, E. C. '33 (PEO) Retired.
Blough, E. C. '37 (PEO) [L] Peoria, IL St. Augustine Manor.
Blough, William G. '58 (PIT) Retired.
Blount, James *s.o.l.t.* '99 (CC) Robstown, TX St. Anthony Church.
Blout, Daniel L. '86 (GBG) [3] Greensburg, PA Our Lady of Grace Church; [C] Greensburg, PA Greensburg Central Catholic High School.
Blow, Thomas D. *o.f.m.* '87 (BUF) [C] St. Bonaventure, NY St. Bonaventure University; [C] St. Bonaventure, NY St. Bonaventure University; [O] St. Bonaventure, NY St. Bonaventure Friary.
Blowers, Leslie F. *m.m.* '63 (CIN) [M] Cincinnati, OH The Catholic Foreign Mission Society of America, Inc.; [V] Cincinnati, OH St. Andrew Kim Korean Catholic Community.
Blowey, David *o.f.m.conv.* '87 (BAL) [S] Ellicott City, MD Order of Friars Minor Conventual.
Blowey, David *o.f.m.conv.* '87 (FgM) Conventual Franciscan Foreign Missions.
Blubaugh, Homer D. '69 (COL) Westerville, OH St. Paul the Apostle Church.
Bludnicki, Dennis G. '75 (BGP) [2] Bridgeport, CT St. Ambrose Church.
Blue, Peter W. *o.s.b.* '70 (FgM) American - Cassinese Congregation Foreign Missions.
Blue, Peter W. *o.s.b.* '70 (PAT) [M] Newton, NJ St. Paul's Abbey.
Blue Jacket, David '88 (DEN) Littleton, CO St. Mary Church.
Bluett, Anthony '69 (ORL) Winter Haven, FL St. Joseph's Church.
Bluett, James '67 (OG) Watertown, NY U.S. Army Headquarters Fort Drum.
Bluett, James K. '67 (PT) Military Chaplains.
Bluett, John J. '63 (ORL) Winter Springs, FL St. Stephen Church.
Blum, John '96 (SP) [2] Tampa, FL Christ the King Church.
Blum, Msgr. Orville '62 (AMA) Hereford, TX St. Anthony's Church.
Blum, Stephen J. '76 (TOL) Vermilion, OH St. Mary Church.
Blum, William *c.s.c.* '65 (FgM) Holy Cross Foreign Missions.
Blum, William G. *c.s.c.* '65 (FTW) [J] South Bend, IN Congregation of Holy Cross, Indiana Province, Provincial House.

Bluma, Dacian *o.f.m.* (FTW) [K] Mishawaka, IN Our Lady of the Angels Convent.
Bluma, Dacian '49 (GRY) [J] Cedar Lake, IN Our Lady of Lourdes Friary.
Blume, Michael *s.v.d.* '72 (FgM) Society of the Divine Word Foreign Missions.
Blumenfeld, Donald E. '79 (NEW) [Q] Mahwah, NJ Ramapo College.
Blumeyer, A. James *s.j.* '63 (STL) [C] St. Louis, MO Saint Louis University; [P] St. Louis, MO Jesuit Community Corporation at St. Louis University - Jesuit Hall.
Blumm, John L. *m.s.* '45 (LKC) De Quincy, LA Our Lady of La Salette Church.
Blums, Burton *o.s.b.* '45 (SCL) [I] Collegeville, MN St. John's Abbey, of the Order of St. Benedict.
Blute, Robert H. '56 (BO) [1] Peabody, MA St. Adelaide Church.
Bly, Walter J. '64 (FTW) [7] South Bend, IN Corpus Christi Church; [C] South Bend, IN Saint Joseph's High School.
Blyman, Robert Y. '70 (RVC) [M] Uniondale, NY St. Pius X Residence.
Blyskosz, Joseph J. '95 (FR) West Harwich, MA Holy Trinity Church.
Boachie-Yiadom, Godfred '95 (CIN) [4] Cincinnati, OH St. Aloysius Gonzaga Church.
Boackle, Paul H. '89 (SAM) Retired.
Boadt, Lawrence *c.s.p.* '69 (NEW) [S] Mahwah, NJ Paulist Press.
Boadt, Lawrence E. *c.s.p.* '69 (NY) [41] New York, NY Good Shepherd Church.
Boarman, Leon J. *c.s.c.* '37 (AUS) [H] Austin, TX Congregation of Holy Cross - Southern Province.
Boarman, Leon J. *c.s.c.* '37 (FTW) [J] South Bend, IN Congregation of Holy Cross, Indiana Province, Provincial House.
Boateng-Mensah, Semanhyia '73 (PT) [1] Tallahassee, FL Co-Cathedral of St. Thomas More.
Bobal, Msgr. Joseph K. '63 (E) Ridgway, PA St. Leo the Great Church.
Boban, Dujo *o.f.m.* '69 (SJ) [26] San Jose, CA St. Mary of the Assumption Church.
Bobber, Raymar *o.f.m.* '57 (FWT) [H] Crowley, TX St. Francis Village, Inc.; [I] Crowley, TX St. Maximilian Kolbe Friary.
Bober, Bernard S. '62 (STU) Retired.
Bober, Charles S. '72 (PIT) [54] Pittsburgh, PA St. John Vianney Church.
Bober, Francis J. '69 (WDC) Retired.
Bober, Marjan L. '63 (CAM) Collings Lakes, NJ Our Lady of the Lakes Church.
Bober, Richard J. '57 (CLV) [2] Euclid, OH St. Felicitas Church.
Boberek, Aurelius *o.s.b.* '57 (IND) [J] St. Meinrad, IN St. Meinrad Archabbey.
Bobersky, Michael '35 (STN) Retired.
Bobis, Antonio '79 (AGN) Tamuning, GU St. Anthony and St. Victor Church.
Bobola, Adam *s.ch.* '92 (DET) [8] Sterling Heights, MI Our Lady of Czestochowa Church.
Bobrek, Edwin *o.f.m.* '51 (NY) [DD] New York, NY Franciscan Province of the Immaculate Conception.
Bocad, Deo '74 (NEW) East Orange, NJ East Orange Hospital; Orange, NJ Hospital Center at Orange.
Boccaccio, Michael A. '71 (BGP) [6] Norwalk, CT St. Philip Church.
Boccafola, Msgr. Kenneth '63 (RVC) Priests Released from Diocesan Assignment.
Boccali, Ronald *p.i.m.e.* '60 (COL) [H] Newark, OH P.I.M.E. Mission & Retreat Center.
Boccard, Raymond C. '52 (PIT) Retired.
Boccio, Msgr. Charles P. '61 (BRK) [181] Queens, NY Immaculate Conception Church.
Boccio, Msgr. Charles P. '61 (NY) Bronx, NY Veterans Administration Hospital.
Bochanski, Philip G. '99 (PH) Doylestown, PA Our Lady of Mount Carmel Church.
Bochenek, Joseph G. '71 (BAL) [19] Baltimore, MD St. Brigid Church.
Bochicchio, Paul L. '71 (NEW) [1] Garfield, NJ Our Lady of Mt. Virgin Church.
Bochinski, Mark J. '58 (SCR) Avoca, PA SS. Peter and Paul Church.
Bocian, Msgr. Ronald C. '72 (ALN) [C] Reading, PA Central Catholic High School of Berks County; [L] Reading, PA Sacred Heart Convent.
Bocianowski, Thaddeus Nicholas '71 (BUF) [2] Buffalo, NY St. Adalbert's Basilica Church.
Bock, Lawrence R. '62 (HRT) Newington, CT Holy Spirit Church.
Bockenfeld, Elgar *o.f.m.* '44 (STP) St. Benedict, MN St. Benedict Church; Union Hill, MN St. John the Evangelist Church.
Bocklage, Richard F. *s.j.* '55 (DEN) [M] Denver, CO Xavier Jesuit Center.
Bockskopf, Richard J. '70 (STL) Maryland Heights, MO St. Blaise Church.
Boczek, Zenon *s.d.s.* '96 (GRY) [J] Merrillville, IN Salvatorian Fathers (Society of the Divine Savior).
Bodah, Henry J. '78 (PRO) [20] Providence, RI St. Joseph Church; [S] Providence, RI Brown University.
Bodde, Frederick '53 (DET) Marine City, MI Holy Cross Church.
Bodde, Frederick A. '53 (DET) Retired.
Bodden, Charles J. *o.s.a.* '78 (CHI) [N] Olympia Fields, IL The Augustinians-Provincialate.
Bodden, Charles J. *o.s.a.* '78 (FgM) Foreign Missions.
Bodden, Clarence A. *c.ss.r.* '49 (STL) [P] Liguori, MO St. Clement Health Care Center.
Boddie, James R., Jr. '78 (STA) [20] Jacksonville, FL St. Pius the Fifth Church.
Boddie, John D. '88 (RIC) Mathews, VA Church of Francis de Sales; Middlesex County, VA Church of the Visitation.
Bodenschatz, Ronald *t.o.r.* '49 (ALT) [F] Loretto, PA Mount Assisi Friary.
Bodenstedt, James A. *m.m.* '56 (SJ) [L] Los Altos, CA Maryknoll.
Bodensteiner, Peter C. '45 (DUB) Retired.
Bodero, Fortunato *o.p.* '66 (PCE) Yauco, PR Holy Rossary Church.
Bodnar, Edward W. *s.j.* '52 (WDC) [M] Washington, DC The Jesuit Community at Georgetown University.
Bodo, Murray *o.f.m.* '64 (CIN) [V] Cincinnati, OH Franciscans Network.
Bodo, Murray L. *o.f.m.* '64 (CIN) [M] Cincinnati, OH Pleasant Street Friary.
Bodziak, Charles F. '67 (ALT) Central City, PA Our Lady Queen of Angels Church.
Bodziony, Ralph A. '58 (CLV) [37] Cleveland, OH St. John Cantius Church; Grafton, OH Assumption Church.
Boeckman, Floyd B. *o.m.i.* '55 (BEL) [F] Belleville, IL Shrine of Our Lady of the Snows; [J] Belleville, IL Missionary Association of Mary Immaculate-Missionary Oblates of Mary Immaculate.
Boeckman, John R. '84 (E) [1] Farrell, PA Holy Trinity Church; [3] Farrell, PA St. Adalbert Church.
Boeding, Damian '52 (SPC) Retired.
Boedy, Thomas G. *s.j.* '70 (STP) Delano, MN St. Joseph Church; Delano, MN St. Peter Church; [N] Minneapolis, MN La Storta Jesuit Community.
Boeff, Dismas *o.s.b.* '76 (CLV) Brook Park, OH St. Peter the Apostle Church; Cleveland, OH SouthWest General Hospital; [O] Cleveland, OH Benedictine Order of Cleveland.
Boegel, Joseph L. *c.m.* '49 (PH) [AA] Philadelphia, PA Congregation of the Mission.
Boeglin, John '78 (EVN) Jasper, IN Holy Family Church.
Boehm, Claude L. *c.s.c.* '35 (FTW) [J] South Bend, IN Congregation of Holy Cross, Indiana Province, Provincial House.
Boehm, Msgr. James A. '58 (STU) Retired.
Boehm, Michael '75 (CHI) [4] Waukegan, IL Holy Family Church.
Boehm, Michael P. '94 (STL) Ballwin, MO Holy Infant Church; [V] St. Louis, MO Archdiocesan Stewardship Education Committee.
Boehme, Arnold *o.c.d.* '68 (MIL) [P] Milwaukee, WI Provincial Offices - Discalced Carmelites.
Boehme, Ferdinand '97 (LIN) Curtis, NE St. James Church.
Boehme, Walter E. *s.j.* '70 (OM) [7] Omaha, NE St. Benedict the Moor Church; [K] Omaha, NE Jesuit Community at Creighton University.
Boehmicke, Roger A. '38 (L) Retired; [M] St. Catharine, KY Sansbury Care Center.
Boehning, John A. '62 (NY) [118] New York, NY St. Thomas More Church.
Boeke, Aloysius B. '41 (CIN) Retired; [B] Carthagena, OH St. Charles.
Boeke, Anselm F. '43 (CIN) Piqua, OH St. Mary Church; Retired.
Boekelman, Timothy J. '77 (SC) Dayton, IA Christ the King Church; Duncombe, IA St. Joseph's Church; Moorland, IA Our Lady of Good Counsel Church.
Boel, Joseph H. *s.j.* '59 (CHI) [N] Chicago, IL Chicago Province of the Society of Jesus-Provincial Office.
Boenzi, Joseph *s.d.b.* (OAK) [A] Berkeley, CA Dominican School of Philosophy and Theology.
Boenzi, Joseph *s.d.b.* '79 (OAK) [N] Berkeley, CA Salesian Community.
Boes, Clair L. '65 (SC) Ashton, IA St. Mary's Catholic Church; Sibley, IA St. Andrew's Church.
Boes, Edward *s.a.* (NY) [DD] Garrison, NY Franciscan Friars of the Atonement.
Boes, Marvin J. '62 (SC) Madrid, IA St. Malachy's Church; Woodward, IA St. John of God Church.
Boes, Steven (OM) [O] Winnebago, NE Feathers.
Boes, Steven '85 (OM) Winnebago, NE St. Augustine's Church; [O] Winnebago, NE St. Augustine's Indian Mission.
Boesel, Msgr. James E. '54 (RVC) Hicksville, NY Our Lady of Mercy Church.
Boeshans, Msgr. Francis G. '48 (NO) Retired.
Boessen, Msgr. Bernard H. '50 (JC) Argyle, MO St. Aloysius Church.
Boessen, Msgr. Bernard H. '50 (STL) Retired.
Boettcher, John '91 (SR) On Leave.
Boettner, David A. '94 (KNX) Athens, TN St. Mary Church.
Boever, Richard *c.ss.r.* '73 (STL) [B] St. Louis, MO St. John Neumann House.
Boff, Bernard J. '61 (TOL) [29] Toledo, OH St. Jude Church; [O] Toledo, OH Office of Global Concerns.
Boffa, William L. '75 (FR) [3] Attleboro, MA St. Stephen's Church.
Bofto, Robert C. '63 (GF) Retired.
Bogart, Kenneth C. *s.j.* '56 (FgM) Provinces.
Bogda, Dennis M. '67 (PBR) Lyndora, PA St. John the Baptist Church.
Bogdan, Msgr. Henry S. '48 (TR) [6] Trenton, NJ Incarnation Church; Retired.
Bogdan, Leonard A. '60 (KAL) Retired.
Bogdan, Palka *s.d.s.* '92 (NEW) [N] Verona, NJ The Salvatorian Fathers.
Bogert, James '67 (RVC) Priests Released from Diocesan Assignment.
Bogetto, Clarence J. *c.m.* '45 (STL) [P] Perryville, MO Congregation of The Mission.
Boggs, Msgr. Dennis R. '86 (ALT) Lock Haven, PA Immaculate Conception Church.
Bognanno, Msgr. Frank (DM) On Sabbatical.
Bogniak, Msgr. Casimir A. '57 (E) Meadville, PA St. Mary Church.
Bogolin, Leonard *o.f.m.* '34 (CHI) [N] Lemont, IL The Slovene Franciscan Fathers, Order of Friars Minor, Commissariat of the Holy Cross.
Bogovich, Msgr. Paul P. '41 (GRY) [2] East Chicago, IN Holy Trinity Church.
Bohan, Philip F. *o.f.m.cap.* '67 (BRK) [87] Brooklyn, NY St. Michael's Church; [V] Brooklyn, NY St. Michael's Friary.
Bohdanowycz, Peter (STN) Denver, CO Transfiguration of Our Lord Church.
Bohl, Ronald *o.f.m. conv.* (L) [39] Louisville, KY Incarnation Church; [L] Louisville, KY St. Francis Friary.
Bohlinger, Kenneth '76 (LFT) Leave of Absence.
Bohn, John Joseph '97 (JKS) [3] Jackson, MS St. Richard Church.
Bohn, Raymond G. '43 (BUF) Retired; [O] Buffalo, NY Sheehan Residence for Priests.
Bohner, Allan G. '98 (SR) Ferndale, CA Church of the Assumption.
Bohnert, Edward A. '85 (SFR) [4] Menlo Park, CA St. Raymond Church.
Bohnsack, David *m.c.c.j.* '94 (FgM) Comboni Foreign Missions.
Boholnick, Theodore '53 (PHU) Simpson, PA SS. Peter and Paul Church.
Bohr, Msgr. David A. '71 (SCR) [A] Dalton, PA Saint Pius X Seminary.
Bohr, Gail G. *s.j.* '73 (OM) [K] Omaha, NE Jesuit Community at Creighton University.
Bohr, Luke *o.s.b.* '48 (RCK) [G] Aurora, IL Marmion Abbey-St. Augustine's Abbey.
Bohrer, John '78 (SFR) Half Moon Bay, CA Our Lady of the Pillar Church.
Bohula, Edwin V. '55 (CHI) [4] Lemont, IL St. James at Sag Bridge Church.
Boiko, John G. '87 (AUS) Elgin, TX Sacred Heart Church.
Boileau, David A. '56 (NO) [15] New Orleans, LA Mater Dolorosa Church; [C] New Orleans, LA Loyola University New Orleans.
Boisaubin, Robert D. '69 (STL) Wildwood, MO St. Alban Roe Church; Retired.
Boisselle, Aime A. '59 (MAN) [3] Concord, NH Sacred Heart Church.
Boisvert, Gilbert O. '71 (OG) Altona, NY Holy Angels Church; Sciota, NY St. Louis Church.
Boisvert, Gregory *a.a.* '51 (BO) [W] Boston, MA Assumptionist Center.
Boisvert, Gregory *a.a.* '51 (KNX) Fairfield Glade, TN St. Francis of Assisi Church.
Boisvert, Keith W. '79 (BAL) Frederick, MD St. John the Evangelist Church.
Boisvert, Marc *o.m.i.* '84 (BO) [W] Lowell, MA Missionary Oblates of Mary Immaculate.
Boisvert, Marc *o.m.i.* '84 (FgM) Oblates Foreign Missions.
Boisvert, Marc *o.m.i.* '84 (WDC) [M] Washington, DC Missionary Oblates of Mary Immaculate.
Boisvert, Ralph '99 (PRT) Waterville, ME Parish of the Holy Spirit Church.
Boisvert, Robert G. '58 (MAN) Retired.
Boisvert, Russel L. '64 (NOR) Montville, CT St. John Church.
Boivin, Henry P. '57 (BO) Senior Priests.
Boivin, John '76 (CHI) [1] Chicago, IL Cathedral of the Holy Name.
Boivin, Louis R. '48 (FR) Retired.
Bojczuk, Thaddeus J. '73 (CHI) Summit, IL St. Joseph Church.
Boji, Manuel Y. '68 (EST) Southfield, MI Our Lady of Chaldeans Cathedral, Mother of God Chaldean Church.
Bok, James M. *o.f.m.* '74 (CIN) [M] Cincinnati, OH St.

Francis Seraph Friary; [M] Cincinnati, OH St. Clare Friary.
Bok, John *o.f.m.* '62 (GAL) [4] Galveston, TX St. Patrick Church.
Bokenkotter, Thomas '50 (CIN) [11] Cincinnati, OH Assumption of the Blessed Virgin Mary Church.
Bokinskie, Richard '79 (SAG) Marlette, MI St. Elizabeth Church; Mayville, MI St. Joseph Church.
Bokota, Marek Roman '81 (NEW) Wallington, NJ Most Sacred Heart of Jesus Church.
Boks, Lawrence E. '66 (GAY) Harrisville, MI St. Anne Church; Mikado, MI St. Raphael Church.
Bolan, John *c.pp.s.* '52 (CIN) [M] Dayton, OH Provincial Office of the Cincinnati Province of the Society of the Precious Blood.
Bolan, John E. *c.pp.s.* '53 (CLV) Cleveland, OH Veterans Administration Hospitals, Brecksville V.A.
Boland, Eamonn '69 (DUL) Eveleth, MN Resurrection Church.
Boland, Edward F. '44 (PRO) Retired; [P] Providence, RI St. John Vianney Residence.
Boland, Msgr. Eugene M. '63 (PAT) Totowa Borough, NJ St. James of the Marches Church.
Boland, Jeremiah M. '81 (CHI) Deerfield, IL Holy Cross Church.
Boland, John '75 (GLP) Crownpoint, NM St. Paul Church; Thoreau, NM St. Bonaventure Church.
Boland, Msgr. John P. '55 (PH) North Wales, PA St. Rose of Lima Church.
Boland, Msgr. John V. '65 (PAT) McAfee, NJ St. Francis de Sales Church.
Boland, Michael M. '86 (CHI) [1] Chicago, IL Cathedral of the Holy Name; [G] Chicago, IL Catholic Charities of the Archdiocese of Chicago-Archdiocesan Offices; [G] Chicago, IL Catholic Charities of the Archdiocese of Chicago-Archdiocesan Offices.
Boland, Stephen *m.s.c.* '86 (Y) [A] Youngstown, OH Sacred Heart Retreat House & Renewal Center.
Boland, Steve *m.s.c.* (Y) [N] Youngstown, OH Sacred Heart Retreat and Renewal Center.
Boland, Thomas L. '65 (L) [35] Louisville, KY Holy Spirit Church.
Bolcar, Andrew J. '65 (CAM) Westville, NJ St. Anne's Church.
Bolderson, John D. '81 (STL) On Duty Outside the Archdiocese.
Boldt, William J. '49 (NY) [230] Staten Island, NY St. Teresa Church.
Bolduc, Gerard *o.f.m.* '69 (DET) [A] Detroit, MI Sacred Heart Major Seminary, Inc.
Bolduc, Marcel '39 (BO) [W] Lowell, MA Missionary Oblates of Mary Immaculate.
Bolduc, Paul J. '60 (BO) [9] Boston, MA St. Anne Church; Health Leave.
Bolduc, Richard *o.m.i.* '64 (FgM) Oblates Foreign Missions.
Boldyc, John *s.m.* '70 (BRK) [45] Brooklyn, NY St. Francis of Assisi-St. Blaise Church.
Boleli, Faustin *c.i.c.m.* '99 (BWN) Rio Grande City, TX Immaculate Conception Church.
Boler, Martin *o.s.b.* '60 (ROC) [I] Pine City, NY Mount Saviour Monastery.
Bolerasky, Msgr. Peter E. '55 (PEO) [4] Streator, IL St. Stephen's Church.
Boles, John P. (BO) [23] Boston, MA St. Gregory Church.
Boles, Joseph M. *v.f.* '65 (SCR) Dalton, PA Our Lady of the Abingtons Church.
Bolesta, Michael C. '89 (PH) [U] Meadowbrook, PA Holy Redeemer Hospital and Medical Center; [BB] Huntingdon Valley, PA Sisters of the Holy Redeemer Provincialate.
Boley, Robert *o.carm.* '75 (NEW) Englewood, NJ St. Cecilia's Church.
Bolez, Edward C. '74 (ALN) [5] Bethlehem, PA St. John Capistrano Church.
Bolger, Anthony '69 (HON) Kihei, HI St. Theresa Church.
Bolger, James '74 (NY) Absent on Leave.
Bolger, Msgr. John F. . '50 (SP) [9] St. Petersburg, FL Transfiguration Church; Retired.
Bolger, Michael J. '92 (RCK) Shannon, IL St. Wendelin Church; [B] Freeport, IL Aquin Central Catholic Junior-Senior High School.
Bolger, Richard T. '66 (PH) Willow Grove, PA St. David Church.
Bolger, Msgr. William '53 (SD) Retired.
Bolha, Jeremy J. *o.s.b.* '59 (ALT) Carrolltown, PA St. Benedict's Church.
Bolieau, Henry G. '72 (NOR) Absent on Leave.
Boll, John E. '70 (SAC) Woodland, CA Holy Rosary Church.
Boll, John J. *o.p.* '82 (GAL) [Q] Houston, TX Dominican Fathers and Brothers, St. Mark Priory, Inc.; [T] Houston, TX Catholic Newman Association at the University of Houston Central Campus.
Bollea, Richard C. '62 (HRT) [7] Waterbury, CT Sacred Heart Church; Waterbury, CT Waterbury Hospital.
Boller, Kenneth J. *s.j.* '75 (NY) [5] New York, NY St. Aloysius Church.
Boller, Robert J. '91 (STP) Retired.
Bolling, Joseph M. '91 (MOB) [13] Mobile, AL St. Matthew Church.
Bollman, Richard W. *s.j.* '69 (CIN) [74] Cincinnati, OH St. Robert Bellarmine Church; [D] Cincinnati, OH Xavier University; [M] Cincinnati, OH Jesuit Community at Xavier University.
Bolman, Anthony P. '60 (SFE) Retired.
Bologna, Anthony F. '43 (DET) [24] Detroit, MI St. Gabriel Church; Retired.
Bolser, Charles *c.s.v.* '73 (JOL) Bourbonnais, IL Maternity of the Blessed Virgin Mary Church.
Bolser, Robert *c.s.v.* '95 (LAV) Henderson, NV St. Thomas More Church.
Bolster, M. Thomas '82 (GR) [1] Grand Rapids, MI Cathedral of St. Andrew; On Special Assignment.
Bolte, Richard G. '83 (COV) [1] Newport, KY Holy Spirit Church.
Bolte, Thomas L. '80 (CIN) [36] Cincinnati, OH St. Ignatius Loyola Church.
Bolton, Bill *s.d.b.* '86 (LA) [W] Rosemead, CA St. Joseph's Salesian Youth Renewal Center.
Bolton, Donald *c.ss.r.* '52 (ORL) [F] New Smyrna Beach, FL St. Alphonsus Villa-Redemptorist Fathers and Brothers.
Bolton, Norman B. '83 (SPR) [1] Holyoke, MA Blessed Sacrament Church; [Q] Springfield, MA Newman Apostolates and Campus Ministries.
Bolton, Paul J. '62 (PRO) On Duty Outside the Diocese.
Bolvary, Paul L. '47 (PIT) Retired.
Boly, S.J., Craig '74 (SEA) [11] Seattle, WA St. Joseph Church.
Bomar, Msgr. Fred '60 (AUS) [20] Austin, TX St. Peter the Apostle Church.
Bomba, Paul M. '77 (WOR) Military Chaplains.
Bombardier, Dennis P. '68 (SPR) Millers Falls, MA St. John's Church.
Bombardier, Paul A. '82 (SPR) [6] Pittsfield, MA St. Francis Church; [9] Pittsfield, MA St. Mary the Morning Star Church.
Bombera, Alex *t.o.r.* '46 (SFS) Plankinton, SD St. John Church.
Bomberger, Ray P. *s.s.j.* '71 (NO) [5] New Orleans, LA Corpus Christi Church.
Bommarito, Vincent R. '77 (STL) [23] St. Louis, MO St. Ambrose Church.
Bona, Joseph F. *s.j.* '72 (DEN) [M] Denver, CO Xavier Jesuit Center.
Bonacci, Louis A. *s.j.* '73 (WH) [A] Wheeling, WV Wheeling Jesuit University.
Bonacci, Paul '91 (ROC) Geneva, NY St. Stephen Church.
Bonacci, Thomas *c.p.* '72 (MET) [H] South River, NJ Passionist Provincial Office.
Bonacci, Thomas P. *c.p.* '72 (R) [H] Greenville, NC Catholic Student Center for Students at East Carolina University.
Bonaccorsi, Salvatore S. '55 (PH) [AA] Villanova, PA St. Thomas Monastery.
Bonacum, Thomas '79 (SB) Retired.
Bonadies, Kenneth P. '65 (HRT) [4] Hamden, CT St. Ann's Church.
Bonadio, Joseph J. *s.s.* (BAL) [A] Baltimore, MD St. Mary's Seminary and University.
Bonadio, Joseph J. *s.s.* '64 (BAL) [32] Baltimore, MD St. Francis of Assisi Church; [S] Baltimore, MD Sulpician Provincial House.
Bonafed, Joseph E. '92 (GBG) [2] Leechburg, PA Christ The King Church.
Bonanno, Raphael *o.f.m.* (FgM) Custody of St. Mary of the Angels. Byzantine-Slavonic.
Bonano, Salvatore *c.m.f.* '84 (LA) [Q] Rancho Dominguez, CA Dominguez Seminary Inc.
Bonanti, Thomas A. '85 (PT) [8] Pensacola, FL St. Anthony of Padua Church; [10] Pensacola, FL St. Joseph Church.
Bonar, Clyde A. '84 (ORL) Apopka, FL St. Francis of Assisi Church.
Bonarrigo, David C. *t.o.r.* '78 (ARL) Herndon, VA St. Joseph Church.
Bonavitacola, John M. '88 (PH) Absent on Leave.
Boncilla, Jean Pierre '91 (SFR) [1] San Francisco, CA Cathedral of St. Mary (Assumption).
Bonczewski, Msgr. William D. '76 (OLL) [C] North Jackson, OH National Shrine of Our Lady of Lebanon.
Bond, Daniel '84 (RIC) Hopewell, VA St. James Church.
Bond, Ernest W. '88 (COS) Bailey, CO St. Mary of the Rockies Church.
Bond, Robert '60 (CHL) Andrews, NC Holy Redeemer Church.
Bond, Robert E. *o.p.* '55 (PRO) [P] Providence, RI St. Thomas Aquinas Priory at Providence College.
Bond, Thomas Aquinas *o.c.s.o.* '39 (ROC) [I] Piffard, NY Abbey of the Genesee.
Bond, William D. '99 (OM) [26] Omaha, NE St. Leo Church.
Bonderenko, Thomas S. '80 (BAL) Absent on Leave.
Bondi, Paul '48 (ALB) Retired.
Bondi, Paul '48 (SP) [2] St. Petersburg, FL Blessed Trinity Church.
Bondi, Richard A. '74 (SPR) South Hadley, MA St. Theresa of the Infant Jesus Church; [Q] Springfield, MA Newman Apostolates and Campus Ministries.
Bondi, Steven '86 (JOL) Braidwood, IL Immaculate Conception Church.
Bondy, Alberto P. '86 (DET) [6] Livonia, MI St. Michael Church.
Boneck, Norman D. '62 (LC) Bloomer, WI St. Paul Church; New Auburn, WI St. Jude Church.
Boned, Enrique '57 (MIA) Retired.
Bonelli, Charles *i.m.c.* '69 (MET) [H] Somerset, NJ Consolata Society for Foreign Missions.
Bonelli, Msgr. Theodore V. '61 (NEW) Retired.
Bonello, Joseph *o.f.m.* '85 (FgM) Franciscan Foreign Missions.
Bonetti, Henry *s.d.b.* '73 (FgM) Salesians of Don Bosco Foreign Missions.
Boney, Vincent *c.p.* '57 (SCR) [M] Scranton, PA Saint Ann's Passionist Monastery.
Bonfadini, Leo '74 (PBL) Absent on Leave.
Bonfiglio, David G. '51 (BO) Senior Priests.
Bonfiglio, Gregory R. *s.j.* '94 (SAC) [C] Sacramento, CA Jesuit High School; [H] Carmichael, CA Jesuit High School Community of Sacramento.
Bongard, Joseph '86 (PH) Collegeville, PA St. Eleanor Church.
Bonghanoy, Edgardo C. '80 (HON) Mountain View, HI St. Theresa Church.
Bongiorno, Angelo *s.d.b.* '43 (BO) [E] Boston, MA Savio Preparatory High School.
Bonham, Ray O. '94 (OM) Heun, NE Holy Trinity Church.
Bonian, Stephen *s.j.* '82 (OLL) Tulsa, Maronite Catholic Community Church.
Bonian, Stephen J. *s.j.* '82 (BO) [W] Boston, MA The Society of Jesus of New England-Provincial Offices.
Bonifas, Roger D. '45 (TOL) Retired.
Bonifazi, Flavian *s.a.c.* '43 (BAL) [51] Baltimore, MD St. Jude Church.
Bonifazi, Remo J. *c.s.sp.* '45 (FgM) Holy Ghost Foreign Missions.
Bonikowski, Leon V. *o.s.f.s.* '65 (FgM) Oblates of St. Francis de Sales Foreign Missions.
Bonikowski, Leon V. *o.s.f.s.* '65 (PH) [AA] Philadelphia, PA Oblates of St. Francis De Sales.
Bonilla, Fernando '78 (ORL) [1] Orlando, FL St. James Church.
Bonilla, Luis Angel '00 (ALN) Orefield, PA St. Joseph The Worker Church.
Bonin, David L. '74 (ROC) Odessa, NY St. Benedict Church; Watkins Glen, NY St. Mary of the Lake Church.
Bonin, Harold '65 (CHI) Buffalo Grove, IL St. Mary Church.
Bonin, Harold A. '65 (CHI) [98] Chicago, IL St. Jerome Church.
Bonin, Richard G. '46 (NU) Gaylord, MN St. Michael Church; Winthrop, MN St. Francis de Sales Church.
Bonjean, Jerry *s.d.b.* '67 (SFR) [46] San Francisco, CA SS. Peter and Paul Church.
Bonjean, Richard '76 (MRY) Retired.
Bonk, Carl A. *s.j.* '83 (DET) [61] Detroit, MI SS. Peter and Paul Jesuit Church.
Bonk, Matthew *c.ss.r.* (CHI) [N] Chicago, IL Redemptorist Theology Residence.
Bonke, James R. '70 (IND) [1] Indianapolis, IN SS. Peter and Paul Church.
Bonn, Ferdinand C. '49 (JC) Retired.
Bonnacci, Paul (ROC) Geneva, NY St. Francis de Sales Church.
Bonnar, David J. '88 (PIT) [A] Pittsburgh, PA Saint Paul Seminary.
Bonneau, Normand *o.m.i.* '76 (FgM) Oblates Foreign Missions.
Bonneau, Normand *o.m.i.* '76 (WDC) [M] Washington, DC Missionary Oblates of Mary Immaculate.
Bonneau, Roger *o.carm.* '60 (JOL) [J] Darien, IL Carmelite Community; [M] Darien, IL National Shrine of St. Therese.
Bonnell, Robert A. '49 (CLV) Oberlin, OH Sacred Heart Church; Retired.
Bonnell, Victor G. '60 (SLC) Layton, UT St. Rose of Lima Church.
Bonner, Charles E. '65 (PH) Yeadon, PA St. Louis Church.
Bonner, Dismas *o.f.m.* '58 (STL) [T] Dittmer, MO Il Ritiro-The Little Retreat.
Bonner, Joseph P. '53 (SCR) Retired.
Bonner, Michael J. *s.v.d.* '66 (CHI) [32] Chicago, IL St. Bronislava Church; [B] Techny, IL Divine Word Residence.
Bonner, Patrick J. *o.s.b.* '59 (PAT) [M] Newton, NJ St. Paul's Abbey.
Bonner, William J. *s.v.d.* '67 (LA) [77] Los Angeles, CA St. Malachy Church.
Bonnet, Godfred '88 (BRK) [139] Brooklyn, NY St. Therese of Lisieux Church.
Bonneville, Lionel E. '63 (SPR) [3] Ludlow, MA St. John the Baptist Church; Northampton, MA Veterans Administration Hospital.
Bonnici, John S. '91 (NY) [34] New York, NY Epiphany Church; [D] New York, NY Department of Education.

Bonnici, William '67 (DET) [5] Roseville, MI Sacred Heart Church.
Bonnot, Bernard R. '67 (Y) On Duty Outside the Diocese.
Bonsall, Leo *o.s.b.* '67 (FWT) Cisco, TX Holy Rosary Church; Eastland, TX St. Francis Xavier Church; Ranger, TX St. Rita Church; Strawn, TX St. John Church.
Bonsignore, Dennis '97 (ROC) [30] Rochester, NY St. John Evangelist Church.
Bonsignore, Mark '95 (HRT) [I] Hartford, CT Saint Francis Hospital and Medical Center.
Bonsignore, Mark J. '67 (HRT) Wallingford, CT Resurrection Church.
Bonsor, Jack '74 (SJ) Los Gatos, CA Presentation Center; Special Assignment.
Bonvouloir, Philip *a.a.* (PRO) [6] Pawtucket, RI St. Joseph Church.
Bonvouloir, Philip *a.a.* '57 (PRO) [P] Warwick, RI Augustinians of the Assumption.
Bonvouloir, Philip E. *a.a.* '57 (PRO) Cranston, RI Department of Corrections.
Bonzagni, John J. '80 (SPR) Lenox Dale, MA St. Vincent de Paul's Church.
Book, Msgr. A. Joseph '63 (E) McKean, PA St. Francis Xavier Church.
Boone, Thomas A. '61 (CLV) Brook Park, OH Assumption of Mary Church.
Booth, Earl J. '44 (LR) Retired.
Booth, Earl J. '60 (LR) [H] Little Rock, AR St. John Manor.
Booth, Edward '74 (STA) Switzerland, FL San Juan Del Rio Church.
Booth, John '82 (SY) Binghamton, NY Binghamton Psychiatric Hospital; Binghamton, NY Binghamton Psychiatric Hospital.
Booth, John, Jr. '82 (SY) Windsor, NY Our Lady of Lourdes Church.
Booth, John A. '82 (SY) Deposit, NY St. Joseph Church.
Booth, Mark-Thomas *o.f.m.conv.* '85 (NOR) Stafford Springs, CT St. Edward Church.
Booth, Raymond '57 (ROC) Pittsford, NY St. Louis Church; Retired.
Booth, Stephen R. *m.m.* '86 (NY) [DD] Maryknoll, NY Maryknoll Fathers and Brothers.
Booth, Steve '86 (BLX) Biloxi, MS Keesler Airforce Base.
Bootkoski, Paul G. '71 (NEW) [1] Newark, NJ Cathedral Basilica of the Sacred Heart.
Boquet, Gregory M. *o.s.b.* '88 (NO) [A] St. Benedict, LA St. Joseph's Seminary College; [P] St. Benedict, LA St. Joseph Abbey.
Boquet, Shenan J. '93 (HT) Galliano, LA St. Joseph Church.
Boracco, John B. *p.i.m.e.* '30 (DET) [K] Detroit, MI P.I.M.E. Missionaries of SS. Peter and Paul.
Boras, Kurt D. '86 (CHI) Evergreen Park, IL St. Bernadette Church.
Borawski, Gerald J. '72 (LFT) Frankfort, IN St. Mary Church.
Borba, Joseph (SB) [11] Riverside, CA St. Thomas the Apostle Church.
Borbely, James A. *s.j.* '76 (ALN) [A] Wernersville, PA Jesuit Center; [A] Wernersville, PA Jesuit Center.
Borbridge, David *s.j.* '63 (MOB) [A] Mobile, AL Spring Hill College.
Borbridge, David C. *s.j.* '63 (FgM) Provinces.
Borca, Dennis L. '81 (MAR) Munising, MI Sacred Heart of Jesus Church.
Borchardt, Edgar '96 (SPK) Pullman, WA Sacred Heart Church.
Borcherding, Martin '73 (LAF) [3] Lafayette, LA Holy Cross Church.
Borcic, John J. '76 (STL) Webster Groves, MO Mary, Queen of Peace Church.
Borcz, Casimir Adalbert *o.c.d.* '45 (GRY) [J] Munster, IN Discalced Carmelite Fathers Monastery.
Borda, Peter '42 (SD) National City, CA St. Anthony of Padua Church.
Borda, Peter Paul '42 (SD) Retired.
Bordeaux, Henry *o.c.d.* '62 (LR) [A] Little Rock, AR Marylake - Carmelite Novitiate.
Bordeleau, Normand G. '85 (BRK) Released from Diocesan Assignment.
Bordelon, H. Gerald *v.f.* '56 (ALX) Cloutierville, LA St. John the Baptist Church.
Bordelon, Msgr. Roland '50 (ALX) On Duty Outside the Diocese.
Borden, Wilfred F. *o.m.i.* '63 (LA) [C] Santa Paula, CA Thomas Aquinas College.
Bordenave, Ian G. *o.p.* '00 (NO) [30] New Orleans, LA St. Dominic Church.
Bordenca, Charles '55 (BIR) Retired.
Bordenkircher, Robert A. *o.p.* '54 (GAL) [Q] Houston, TX Dominican Fathers and Brothers, St. Mark Priory, Inc.
Borders, Larry '00 (IND) Columbus, IN St. Bartholomew Church.
Borders, William Donald '40 (BAL) Retired.
Bordignon, Narciso *c.r.s.* '67 (GAL) [11] Houston, TX Assumption Church.
Bordonaro, Joseph C. '89 (PH) Primos, PA St. Eugene Church; [D] Springfield, PA Cardinal O'Hara High School.
Borek, Derek J. '99 (BO) Newburyport, MA Immaculate Conception Church.
Boren, Edward Daniel *o.f.m.* '64 (VIC) Bay City, TX Our Lady of Guadalupe Church.
Borer, Gerard J. *s.j.* '59 (COS) [7] Colorado Springs, CO Our Lady of the Pines-Black Forest Church.
Borer, Robert D. '76 (STU) Cambridge, OH St. Benedict Church.
Boretto, Christopher '87 (SY) Binghamton, NY Our Lady of Lourdes Memorial Hospital.
Borg, Carmel '78 (BRK) [244] Queens, NY St. Teresa of Avila Church.
Borg, Marcellinus *o.f.m.* '59 (MAN) Derry, NH St. Thomas Aquinas Church.
Borg, Ron *c.s.b.* '79 (DET) [43] Detroit, MI St. Louis the King Church.
Borgelt, Daniel E. '93 (TOL) Delphos, OH St. John the Evangelist Church.
Borgen-Reithel, Alfonso *o.f.m.conv.* '98 (LA) Torrance, CA Nativity Church.
Borger, Marvin G. '91 (TOL) Perrysburg, OH St. Rose Church.
Borger, Theodore R. '83 (DAV) Retired.
Borgerding, Terry J. '77 (STL) Mattese, MO Assumption Church.
Borgers, Charles *o.m.i.* '41 (SAT) [K] San Antonio, TX Oblate Madonna Residence.
Borges, Charles *s.j.* '81 (BAL) [B] Baltimore, MD Loyola College in Maryland.
Borges, Jose A. *s.j.* (SJN) [D] Rio Piedras, PR Centro Universitario Catolico.
Borges, Lawrence J. '59 (BO) [18] Boston, MA St. Columbkille Church.
Borges, Mario L. '82 (OAK) Castro Valley, CA Transfiguration Church.
Borgesen, Kenneth *o.ss.t.* '87 (NO) Terrytown, LA Christ the King Church.
Borgia, Anthony A. '84 (TOL) Fort Jennings, OH St. Joseph Church; Ottoville, OH Immaculate Conception Church.
Borgmeyer, Dean G. '81 (WH) Dunbar, WV Christ the King Church; Nitro, WV Holy Trinity Church.
Borgo, John V. *s.j.* '57 (BGP) [P] Fairfield, CT The Fairfield Jesuit Community-Fairfield University.
Borgognoni, Msgr. Charles L. '48 (SY) Retired.
Borgonovo, Mario *s.d.b.* '51 (MGZ) Aguadilla, PR San Jose Obrero Church.
Borho, Charles D. '57 (P) St. Paul, OR St. Paul Church.
Borhorquez, Carlos M. '99 (SFD) [4] Springfield, IL Little Flower Church.
Borino, David J. '86 (HRT) [1] Meriden, CT Our Lady of Mount Carmel Church.
Bork, Vincent P. '95 (ARL) Colonial Beach, VA St. Elizabeth Church.
Borkowski, Aloysius J. '39 (GBG) Retired.
Borkowski, Edward *s.v.d.* '44 (CHI) [B] Techny, IL Divine Word Residence.
Borkowski, Francis '77 (NY) Military Chaplains.
Borkowski, John A. '49 (PRO) Retired.
Borkowski, Mark '96 (DET) Allen Park, MI St. Frances Cabrini Church.
Borkowski, Raymond *o.f.m.conv.* '61 (NOR) Cromwell, CT St. John Church.
Borkowski, Thomas '81 (KC) [39] Kansas City, MO St. Thomas More Church.
Borlang, Stephen M. '86 (SAC) Vallejo, CA St. Basil Church.
Bormann, Charles P. '58 (PHX) Retired.
Bormann, Paul D. '85 (SC) Bancroft, IA St. John the Baptist's Church; Ledyard, IA Sacred Heart Church.
Bornbach, Raymond H. '41 (LC) Retired.
Borntrager, Conrad M *o.s.m.* '60 (ORG) [I] Buena Park, CA Order of Friar Servants of Mary (Servites).
Borntrager, Conrad M. *o.s.m.* '60 (CHI) [14] Chicago, IL Annunciata Church; [N] Chicago, IL Order of Friar Servants of Mary (Servites) United States of America Province, Inc.; [N] Chicago, IL Order of Friar Servants of Mary (Servites) United States of America Province, Inc.
Borodach, John J. '57 (PBR) Donora, PA St. Michael Church.
Borodach, Joseph '60 (PBR) Bradenville, PA St. Mary's Church.
Boronat, Francis *sch.p.* '54 (LA) [Q] Los Angeles, CA Piarist Fathers.
Boronat, Frank *sch.p.* '54 (LA) [76] Los Angeles, CA St. Lucy Church.
Borosh, Carl A. '68 (STU) Retired.
Boroughs, Philip L. *s.j.* '78 (SEA) [A] Seattle, WA Seattle University.
Borowczyk, Martin R. '42 (CHI) [44] Chicago, IL St. Constance Church; [62] Chicago, IL St. Francis Borgia Church; Retired.
Borowiak, David J. '71 (BUF) [3] Depew, NY St. James Church.
Borowiak, Kenneth A. '87 (LIN) Exeter, NE St. Stephen's Church.
Borowik, John '66 (NEW) Harrison, NJ Our Lady of Czestochowa Church.
Borowski, Charles E.J. (WOR) [1] Southbridge, MA St. Hedwig's Church.
Borowski, Ladislaus '48 (DET) Retired.
Borowski, Paul J. *c.ss.r.* '87 (BRK) [C] Whitestone, NY St. Alphonsus Formation Residence.
Borre, Robert J. (CHI) Chicago, IL V.A. Lakeside Medical Center.
Borrelli, Msgr. Anthony '54 (COL) [28] Columbus, OH St. Margaret of Cortona Church.
Borrero, Victor R. *s.e.m.v.* '89 (ARE) Hatillo, PR Our Lady of Guadalupe Church.
Borsari, John Peter *c.r.s.* '94 (GAL) [11] Houston, TX Assumption Church.
Borski, Charles J *o.m.i.* '70 (GAL) [37] Houston, TX Immaculate Conception Church.
Borski, Msgr. Chester L. '67 (GAL) [A] Houston, TX St. Mary's Seminary.
Borski, Jerome *o.s.b.* '92 (PAT) [M] Morristown, NJ St. Mary's Abbey.
Borstelmann, James E. '67 (NY) Croton Falls, NY St. Joseph Church.
Borsuk, Msgr. Alan J. '59 (PSC) Hillsborough Township, NJ St. Mary's Church.
Borsuk, Ronald W. '58 (PBR) Conemaugh, PA Holy Trinity Church.
Bortolazzo, Peter *c.s.* '39 (BO) [64] Boston, MA Sacred Heart Church.
Boruszewski, Msgr. Joseph A. '53 (BUF) Varysburg, NY St. Joseph Church.
Boruta, Alexander *o.f.m.* '60 (GAY) Skidway Lake, MI St. Stephen of Hungary Church.
Borycz, Edmund S. '68 (DET) Military Chaplains.
Borzaga, Rinaldo '47 (BRK) Retired.
Borzaga, Rinaldo *f.s.c.a.* '47 (NY) [DD] New York, NY Brothers of the Christian Schools of Manhattan College, Inc.
Borzuchowski, John W. '68 (NY) [2] Kingston, NY Immaculate Conception Church.
Borzych, Alexander J. '80 (GI) Military Chaplains.
Bosack, Albert J. '43 (BUF) Lyndonville, NY St. Joseph Church; Retired.
Bosch, Stan *s.t.* '86 (LA) Compton, CA Our Lady of Victory Church; Compton, CA Sagrado Corazon, Sacred Heart Church.
Bosch, William J. *s.j.* '60 (SY) [S] Syracuse, NY Jesuits at LeMoyne, Inc.
Boschert, Hubert *s.j.* '68 (WIN) Austin, MN St. Edward's Church; Brownsdale, MN Our Lady of Loretto Church.
Boschert, Joseph N. '60 (COV) California, KY Sts. Peter and Paul Church.
Bosco, John (BO) [2] Chelsea, MA St. Rose of Lima Church.
Bosco, John M. '71 (LAN) Milan, MI Immaculate Conception Church.
Boscoe, John L. *c.s.b.* '72 (GAL) [Q] Sugar Land, TX Basilian Mission Center.
Boscutti, Darrio L. '86 (CHI) [173] Chicago, IL St. Priscilla Church.
Bosken, Robert E. *s.j.* '56 (STL) [P] St. Louis, MO De Smet Jesuit High School Community.
Boslett, Donald E. '59 (ALT) Renovo, PA St. Joseph's Church.
Bosnich, David A. '95 (PBR) Irving, TX St. Basil the Great Church.
Bossa, Barry *s.a.c.* '81 (NY) [13] Yonkers, NY Our Lady of Mt. Carmel Church.
Bosse, Dennis *o.f.m.* '91 (CIN) [C] Cincinnati, OH St. Anthony Shrine, Franciscan Candidacy; [E] Cincinnati, OH Roger Bacon High School.
Bosse, Roger T. *o.f.m.* '83 (CIN) [E] Cincinnati, OH Roger Bacon High School; [M] Cincinnati, OH St. Clement Friary; [U] Cincinnati, OH Roger Bacon High School Endowment.
Bossi, Paul R. '69 (BUF) [14] Buffalo, NY Blessed Sacrament Church.
Bossi, Stephen E. *c.s.p.* '85 (P) [29] Portland, OR St. Philip Neri Church.
Bossi, Stephen E. *c.s.p.* '86 (P) [Q] Portland, OR Paulist Fathers Catholic Center for Evangelization.
Bossie, Robert W. *s.c.j.* '75 (CHI) [N] Chicago, IL Priests of the Sacred Heart.
Bossman, David M. *o.f.m.* '65 (NY) [DD] New York, NY Franciscan Friars, Order of Friars Minor, Holy Name Province.
Bosso, Stephen C. '78 (PMB) [A] Boynton Beach, FL St. Vincent de Paul Regional Seminary.
Bosso, Stephen C. '78 (PT) On Duty Outside the Diocese.
Bostwick, John '69 (RIC) Unassigned.
Bostwick, John *o.praem* '76 (GB) [B] De Pere, WI St. Norbert College; [I] De Pere, WI St. Joseph Priory.
Bostwick, John L. *o.praem.* '76 (GB) [A] De Pere, WI St. Norbert Abbey; [M] De Pere, WI Norbertine Center for Spirituality.
Boszko, Msgr. Antoni '66 (BRK) [94] Brooklyn, NY Our Lady of Czestochowa-St. Casimir Church.
Botean, John Michael '86 (ROM) Canton, OH St. George Church.

Boteju, Bernard '85 (TYL) Mineola, TX St. Peter the Apostle Church.
Boteler, William M. *m.m.* '68 (LA) [Q] Los Angeles, CA Maryknoll Fathers and Brothers.
Botenhagen, Paul *o.f.m.* '82 (LSC) Mescalero, NM St. Joseph Church.
Botheroyd, Thomas '00 (JOL) Lisle, IL St. Joan of Arc Church.
Botkin, Edward A. '73 (DAV) Delmar, IA St. Patrick's Church; Petersville, IA Immaculate Conception Church; Welton, IA St. Anne Church; [B] Davenport, IA St. Ambrose University.
Botsko, Jerome G. '82 (PBR) Brownsville, PA St. Nicholas Church.
Bottazzo, Alex '43 (LAN) Retired.
Botte, Gregory *o.f.m.* '68 (NY) [DD] New York, NY Franciscan Province of the Immaculate Conception.
Botthof, Robert J. *o.p.* '87 (CHI) River Forest, IL St. Vincent Ferrer Church.
Bottino, Msgr. Dominic J. '78 (CAM) Pennsauken, NJ St. Stephen Church.
Bottino, Msgr. Edward J. '52 (BRK) [197] Queens, NY Mary's Nativity Church.
Botton, Msgr. Pierre A. '56 (BGP) Retired.
Botz, Lawrence '40 (SCL) Elrosa, MN SS. Peter and Paul Church; Retired.
Botz, Roger *o.s.b.* '60 (SCL) [G] St. Cloud, MN St. Cloud Hospital; [I] Collegeville, MN St. John's Abbey, of the Order of St. Benedict.
Botzum, William A. *c.s.c.* '43 (FTW) [17] South Bend, IN Faith & Hope & Charity Chapel Church; [J] South Bend, IN Congregation of Holy Cross, Indiana Province, Provincial House.
Bou, Pedro L. *s.v.d.* '74 (TR) Lakewood, NJ St. Anthony Claret Church.
Bou Sallem, George *m.l.m.* '91 (OLL) [A] Houston, TX The Congregation of Maronite Lebanese Missionaries.
Bou-Merhi, Gebran '88 (OLL) Murray, UT Saint Jude Church.
Bou-Merhi, Gebran '88 (SLC) [5] Murray, UT St. Jude Church.
Bou-Msallem, Georges '96 (OLL) El Paso, TX St. Anthony of the Desert Church.
Bouchard, Alfred '56 (MAN) [8] Nashua, NH St. Patrick Church.
Bouchard, Charles E. *o.p.* '79 (STL) [B] St. Louis, MO Aquinas Institute of Theology; [P] St. Louis, MO Dominican Community of St. Louis.
Bouchard, Denis *f.s.s.p.* '00 (SCR) [M] Elmhurst, PA Priestly Fraternity of St. Peter (F.S.S.P.), North American District Headquarters.
Bouchard, Dennis *f.s.s.p.* '00 (PAT) Pequannock, NJ Our Lady of Fatima Chapel (Tridentine) Church.
Bouchard, Louis *c.p.* (HRT) [M] West Hartford, CT Holy Family Monastery/Retreat.
Bouchard, Lucien *o.m.i.* '55 (FgM) Oblates Foreign Missions.
Bouchard, Marcel H. '72 (FR) Sandwich, MA Corpus Christi Church.
Bouchard, Norman '88 (PBL) Absent on Leave.
Bouchard, Paul L. '72 (MAN) [7] Manchester, NH St. Edmund Church.
Bouchard, Robert P. '84 (PRT) Gardiner, ME St. Joseph's Church; South Portland, ME Men's Correctional Center; Thomaston, ME Maine State Prison; Warren, ME Super Maximum Facility & Minimum Facility.
Bouchard, Thomas '53 (DUL) Retired.
Boucher, Clarence R. '40 (BO) Senior Priests.
Boucher, Edward F. '60 (SAG) Retired.
Boucher, Gerard A. '53 (MAN) Meredith, NH St. Charles Church; Retired.
Boucher, Gilmond *o.m.* (BO) [9] Lowell, MA St. Marie Church; [16] Lowell, MA Sacred Heart Church.
Boucher, Kevin J. '91 (FAR) Bottineau, ND St. Mark's Church; [J] Bottineau, ND Minot State University-Bottineau.
Boucher, Maurice U. *s.s.e.* '48 (BUR) Alburg, VT St. Amadeus Church; [I] Isle La Motte, VT St. Anne's Shrine.
Boucher, Richard R. *m.s.* '60 (HRT) [M] Hartford, CT Missionaries of LaSalette, Provincial Secretary.
Boucher, Roger R. '73 (WOR) Military Chaplains.
Boucree, Thaddeus *s.v.d.* '52 (BLX) [A] Bay St. Louis, MS St. Augustine's.
Boudion, Burt '82 (SD) San Marcos, CA St. Mark Church.
Boudreau, C. Paul '83 (NOR) On Duty Outside the Diocese.
Boudreau, George R. *o.p.* '83 (STL) [B] St. Louis, MO Aquinas Institute of Theology; [P] St. Louis, MO St. Dominic Priory.
Boudreau, Paul (SPR) Retired.
Boudreau, Thomas '56 (LA) [10] Los Angeles, CA Divine Saviour Church.
Boudreau, Thomas C. (BO) Abington, MA St. Bridget Church.
Boudreaux, Claude P. *s.j.* '55 (NO) [F] New Orleans, LA Jesuit High School.
Boudreaux, John S. '73 (LAF) On Duty Outside the Diocese.
Boudreaux, John S. '73 (MOB) [3] Mobile, AL Corpus Christi Church.
Bouffard, Msgr. James F. '70 (NEW) Haworth, NJ Sacred Heart Church.
Bouffard, Lionel A. *m.m.* '63 (NY) [DD] Maryknoll, NY Maryknoll Fathers and Brothers.
Bouffier, Robert *s.m.* '74 (BO) [10] Boston, MA St. Anthony Church.
Bouffier, Robert J. *s.m.* '74 (CIN) [M] Dayton, OH Marianist Provincialate.
Boufford, Thomas F. '81 (GR) Lake Odessa, MI St. Edward's Church.
Boughton, Michael *s.j.* '79 (BGP) [E] Fairfield, CT Fairfield College Preparatory School; [P] Fairfield, CT The Fairfield Jesuit Community-Fairfield University.
Bouhall, William '94 (CLV) [3] Euclid, OH Holy Cross Church.
Boulanger, Albert L. '62 (MAN) Retired.
Boulanger, Andre '65 (PHX) Unassigned.
Boulanger, Gerald *m.s.* '73 (NOR) Jewett City, CT St. Mary Church.
Boulanger, Maurice R. '47 (MAN) [H] Rochester, NH St. Charles Children's Home.
Boulanger, Raymond *s.m.* '51 (BO) [Y] Framingham, MA The Marist House.
Boulden, Garry '77 (SPK) Absent on Leave.
Boule, Roland B. '32 (FR) Retired.
Boulet, Marshall '71 (LKC) Elton, LA St. Paul Church.
Boulet, Norman J. '69 (FR) Absent on Leave; [I] Fall River, MA Priests' Hostel.
Boulette, Michael J. '76 (SAT) Kerrville, TX Notre Dame Church.
Bouley, Allan *o.s.b.* '62 (SCL) [I] Collegeville, MN St. John's Abbey, of the Order of St. Benedict.
Boulos, Peter '93 (SAM) Atlanta, GA St. Joseph's Maronite Church.
Boulton, David G. *s.j.* '61 (BO) [W] Weston, MA Campion Jesuit Community; [W] Weston, MA Campion Health Center, Inc.
Boumans, Albert '52 (LAF) Retired.
Boumans, Albert J. '52 (LAF) [2] New Iberia, LA Nativity of Our Lady Church.
Bourassa, Msgr. Stanley '55 (CR) Retired.
Bourbon, Frank C. *s.j.* '65 (WH) [A] Wheeling, WV Wheeling Jesuit University.
Bourcy, Robert Scott '82 (ROC) Macedon, NY St. Patrick Church.
Bourdeau, Leo *s.m.* '42 (BO) [4] Methuen, MA St. Theresa Church.
Bourdon, Norman W. '73 (PRO) [2] Cumberland, RI St. Joan of Arc Church.
Bourek, David F. (LIN) Friend, NE St. Joseph's Church.
Bouressa, Donald J. '61 (PRO) Narragansett, RI St. Mary, Star of the Sea Church.
Bourg, Edwin '48 (LAF) Retired.
Bourg, Rodney P. '78 (NO) [3] Slidell, LA St. Luke the Evangelist Church.
Bourgault, Ronald L. '63 (BO) Wayland, MA St. Zepherin Church.
Bourgea, Roger *s.m.* '70 (BRK) [45] Brooklyn, NY St. Francis of Assisi-St. Blaise Church.
Bourgeois, Bernard '95 (BUR) Waterbury, VT State Hospital.
Bourgeois, Bernard W. '95 (BUR) Waterbury, VT St. Andrew Church.
Bourgeois, Donald E. '85 (SY) Bainbridge, NY St. John the Evangelist Church.
Bourgeois, Francis L. '61 (LAF) Robert's Cove, LA St. Leo IV Church.
Bourgeois, Frank '54 (HON) Ewa, HI Immaculate Conception Church.
Bourgeois, Henry *c.s.c.* '62 (BO) [X] Framingham, MA Fontbonne Hall.
Bourgeois, Msgr. Joseph E. '58 (NO) [3] Metairie, LA St. Ann Church and Church; Metairie, LA St. Ann National Church.
Bourgeois, Msgr. Lloyd V. '57 (SD) [38] San Diego, CA San Rafael Church.
Bourgeois, Louis D. '59 (BO) Hamilton, MA St. Paul Church.
Bourgeois, Richard J. *o.s.b.* '76 (BO) [W] Hingham, MA Glastonbury Abbey.
Bourgeois, Roger *s.s.s.* '57 (CLV) Highland Heights, OH St. Paschal Baylon Church; [O] Cleveland, OH Blessed Sacrament Community.
Bourgeois, Roy L. *m.m.* '72 (NY) [DD] Maryknoll, NY Maryknoll Fathers and Brothers.
Bourget, Laurence *o.c.s.o.* '42 (WOR) [N] Spencer, MA St. Joseph's Abbey.
Bourgoin, Raymond *o.m.i.* '66 (FgM) Oblates Foreign Missions.
Bourke, Charles E. '70 (BO) Winthrop, MA St. John the Evangelist Church.
Bourke, John F. '60 (CAM) Waterford, NJ St. Anthony Church.
Bourke, Martin '74 (SEA) Des Moines, WA St. Philomena Church.
Bourke, Msgr. Myles M. '42 (NY) [28] New York, NY Corpus Christi Church; Retired.
Bourke, Nathaniel J. '59 (GF) Retired.
Bourke, Ulick *s.m.a.* '68 (FgM) Society of African Missions.
Bourke, Ulick *s.m.a.* '68 (NEW) [N] Tenafly, NJ Society of African Missions, Provincialate, S.M.A. Fathers.
Bourke, William D. *s.s.c.* '54 (FgM) St. Columban's Foreign Mission.
Bourne, Peter '61 (B) Salmon, ID St. Charles Church; [C] Lemhi, ID Hermitage of St. Joseph.
Bourque, Msgr. Charles J. '62 (BO) [51] Boston, MA Our Lady of Lourdes Church.
Bourque, John R. '48 (SPR) Retired.
Bourque, Msgr. Joseph A. '55 (LKC) Retired.
Bourque, Real *o.m.i.* '54 (FgM) Oblates Foreign Missions.
Bourque, Thomas *t.o.r.* '82 (WDC) [M] Washington, DC St. Louis Friary.
Bourret, Philip L. *s.j.* '41 (SJ) [L] Los Gatos, CA Sacred Heart Jesuit Center.
Bousquet, Roland '54 (FR) Retired.
Bouterie, Thomas R. '80 (HT) [7] Houma, LA St. Louis Church.
Boutin, Emil (BO) Stoughton, MA Immaculate Conception Church.
Bouton, Thomas F. '83 (BO) Belmont, MA St. Luke Church.
Boutot, Michel *c.s.sp.* '93 (NO) [7] New Orleans, LA Holy Ghost Church.
Boutros, Peter (NTN) On Special Projects.
Bova, Eugene R. '57 (BIS) Retired.
Bova Conti, Michael J. '71 (BO) Sudbury, MA Our Lady of Fatima Church.
Bovard, William R. '64 (PIT) Franklin Park Borough, PA St. John Neumann Church.
Bove, Ralph A. *c.s.* '78 (NY) [64] New York, NY St. Joseph Church.
Bovee, Brian '81 (RCK) [7] Rockford, IL St. Mary Shrine, Institute of Christ the King Sovereign Priest Church.
Bovenzi, Angelo D. *c.s.b.* '67 (ROC) [I] Rochester, NY Basilian Residence.
Bovenzi, Robert *c.p.* '85 (GAL) [Q] Houston, TX Congregation of the Passion, Holy Name Retreat Center; [S] Houston, TX Holy Name Retreat Center.
Bowden, John V. '62 (TR) Brick Town, NJ Epiphany Church.
Bowden, Lloyd '49 (JOL) Retired.
Bowe, John C. *c.r.* '68 (PBL) Pagosa Springs, CO Immaculate Heart of Mary Church.
Bowe, John F. '73 (PH) Sellersville, PA St. Agnes Church.
Bowen, Donald J. '64 (FgM) Society of St. James the Apostle.
Bowen, Donald J. '64 (FR) Special Assignment.
Bowen, Gerard J. '77 (BAL) [13] Baltimore, MD St. Augustine Church.
Bowen, Henry G. '56 (WOR) [21] Worcester, MA St. Charles Borromeo Church.
Bowen, John W. *s.s.* '49 (BAL) [57] Baltimore, MD St. Mark Church; [A] Baltimore, MD St. Mary's Seminary and University; [O] Baltimore, MD St. Charles Villa; [S] Baltimore, MD St. Charles Villa.
Bowen, Joseph D. '57 (PH) Abington, PA Our Lady Help of Christians Church.
Bowen, Robert *s.s.j.* '59 (NO) [P] New Orleans, LA Josephite Fathers and Brothers.
Bowens, Lorin M. '74 (MAD) La Valle, WI Holy Family Church; Lime Ridge, WI St. Boniface Church.
Bower, Alan (STA) [1] St. Augustine, FL Cathedral of St. Augustine.
Bower, Lawrence C. '88 (BAK) Milton Freewater, OR St. Francis of Assisi Church.
Bowering, Gerhard H. *s.j.* '70 (BGP) [P] Fairfield, CT The Fairfield Jesuit Community-Fairfield University.
Bowers, Mark R. '98 (TOL) Fostoria, OH St. Wendelin Church.
Bowers, Phillip T. '64 (LFT) Fishers, IN Holy Spirit Church.
Bowers, Robert J. '87 (BO) [1] Milton, MA St. Agatha Church.
Bowers, Ronald '64 (STP) [A] St. Paul, MN The Saint Paul Seminary; [C] St. Paul, MN University of St. Thomas.
Bowers, Vernon J. '39 (RIC) Retired.
Bowes, Bruce '92 (NY) Absent on Leave.
Bowes, Charles J. '71 (CIN) [66] Cincinnati, OH Our Lady of the Rosary Church.
Bowes, David '46 (KNX) Retired.
Bowes, James J. *s.j.* '66 (NY) [DD] New York, NY Jesuit Provincial's Office.
Bowker, Jeffrey *l.c.* '94 (HRT) [B] Cheshire, CT Novitiate of the Legion of Christ.
Bowlds, Kent '93 (JKS) Clarksdale, MS St. Elizabeth Church; Clarksdale, MS Immaculate Conception Church.
Bowler, James S. *s.j.* '74 (BGP) [P] Fairfield, CT The Fairfield Jesuit Community-Fairfield University.
Bowler, Joseph D. *o.s.f.s.* '49 (PH) [D] Philadelphia, PA Father Judge High School for Boys; [AA] Philadelphia, PA Father Judge Faculty House.
Bowler, Michael '57 (CHI) [205] Chicago, IL St.

Turibius Church.
Bowles, Richard J. '61 (PT) [12] Pensacola, FL St. Michael Church.
Bowles, William H. '91 (NU) Kandiyohi, MN St. Patrick Church; Lake Lillian, MN St. Thomas More Church.
Bowling, Frederick T. '64 (BAL) Retired.
Bowling, George K. '47 (L) Retired.
Bowling, Msgr. Robert A. '54 (RNO) [6] Reno, NV St. Therese Church of the Little Flower.
Bowling, Theodore B. *s.j.* '53 (FgM) Provinces.
Bowling, William S. '97 (L) Shelbyville, KY Annunciation of the Blessed Virgin Mary Church.
Bowman, James C. '65 (RVC) St. James, NY SS. Philip and James Church.
Bowman, John '65 (SEA) Mercer Island, WA St. Monica Church.
Bowman, R. Peter '55 (CHI) [196] Chicago, IL St. Teresa Church.
Bowski, Eugene '77 (GLP) Cuba, NM Immaculate Conception Church.
Boxleitner, Msgr. J. Jerome '56 (STP) Lino Lakes, MN Minnesota Correctional Facility; Retired; [I] Minneapolis, MN St. Joseph's Home for Children.
Boyack, Kenneth G. *c.s.p.* '79 (WDC) [B] Washington, DC St. Paul's College; [V] Washington, DC Paulist National Catholic Evangelization Assoc.
Boyce, Edmund J. *o.s.b.* '62 (MIL) [P] Benet Lake, WI St. Benedict's Abbey.
Boyce, James *o.carm.* '77 (NEW) Leonia, NJ St. John the Evangelist's Church.
Boyce, Thomas '66 (JKS) Batesville, MS St. Mary Church.
Boyd, C. Morris *d.min.* '78 (CHL) Franklin, NC St. Francis of Assisi Church.
Boyd, Daniel A. *m.m.* '82 (FgM) Maryknoll Foreign Missions.
Boyd, Douglas A. '79 (PIT) [54] Pittsburgh, PA St. John Vianney Church.
Boyd, James A. '63 (BRK) Released from Diocesan Assignment.
Boyd, John D. *s.j.* '47 (NY) [DD] New York, NY Murray-Weigel Hall.
Boyd, Joseph '50 (NY) Larchmont, NY SS. John and Paul Church.
Boyd, Norman *s.a.* '65 (NY) [DD] Garrison, NY Franciscan Friars of the Atonement.
Boyd, Richard '79 (CR) Park Rapids, MN St. Peter's Church.
Boyd, Rick '79 (CR) Two Inlets, MN St. Mary's Church.
Boyd, Theophane *o.c.s.o.* '55 (DEN) [M] Snowmass, CO St. Benedict's Monastery.
Boyea, Msgr. Earl (DET) On Duty Outside the Archdiocese.
Boyea, Msgr. Earl '78 (COL) [A] Columbus, OH Pontifical College Josephinum.
Boyea, Earl '78 (DET) [A] Detroit, MI Sacred Heart Major Seminary, Inc.
Boyer, Msgr. Leland J. '49 (LA) La Canada Flintridge, CA St. Bede the Venerable Church; Retired.
Boyer, Mark G. '76 (SPC) Special Assignment.
Boyer, Millard G. '75 (LAF) On Special Assignment.
Boyer, Thomas J. '68 (OKL) [1] Oklahoma City, OK Cathedral of Our Lady of Perpetual Help.
Boyer, Wayne M. '87 (JC) Martinsburg, MO St. Joseph Church; Wellsville, MO Resurrection Church.
Boyhan, J. Patrick *m.s.a.* '77 (NOR) [F] Cromwell, CT Society of the Missionaries of the Holy Apostles.
Boykins, Charles *s.v.d.* '65 (JKS) Vicksburg, MS St. Mary Church.
Boylan, Colman *o.f.m.cap.* '49 (NOR) [4] Middletown, CT St. Pius X Church.
Boylan, Dennis '74 (AMA) Childress, TX Holy Angels Church.
Boylan, John J. '56 (BRK) [176] Queens, NY Holy Child Jesus Church.
Boylan, Martin M. '80 (SCR) Gouldsboro, PA St. Rita Church.
Boyle, Bernard J. *s.j.* '65 (PH) [G] Philadelphia, PA St. Joseph's Preparatory School; [AA] Philadelphia, PA Jesuit Community, Arrupe House.
Boyle, Daniel J. '78 (SPR) [4] Adams, MA Notre Dame des Sept Douleurs and St. Thomas Aquinas Church.
Boyle, Dennis P. '73 (PH) Military Chaplains.
Boyle, Edward F. *s.j.* '69 (BO) [E] Boston, MA Boston College High School & Jesuit Community.
Boyle, Msgr. Eugene '46 (SJ) Retired.
Boyle, Msgr. Francis V. '55 (NY) [199] Staten Island, NY Blessed Sacrament Church.
Boyle, George J. '52 (PH) Brookline, PA Annunciation B.V.M. Church; Manoa, PA Sacred Heart Church; Retired.
Boyle, Gregory *s.j.* '84 (LA) [11] Los Angeles, CA Dolores Church.
Boyle, James '61 (SEA) Buckley, WA Rainier School.
Boyle, James A. (RCK) [H] Aurora, IL Provena McAuley Manor.
Boyle, James A. '49 (FWT) Retired.
Boyle, James E. '66 (ROC) Fairport, NY St. John of Rochester Church.
Boyle, James F. *c.s.c.* '57 (SCR) [4] Wilkes-Barre, PA St. Casimir's Church.
Boyle, James M. '56 (HRT) Retired.
Boyle, John *s.j.* '60 (LA) [BB] Los Angeles, CA Archdiocesan Office for Campus Ministry.
Boyle, John '83 (NY) [226] Staten Island, NY St. Roch Church.
Boyle, John B. '76 (SCR) Pocono Pines, PA Our Lady of the Lake Church.
Boyle, John J. '56 (ALT) Retired.
Boyle, John L. *s.j.* '60 (LA) [C] Los Angeles, CA Loyola Marymount University.
Boyle, John P. '56 (DAV) Special Assignment.
Boyle, John T. '69 (CHI) [55] Chicago, IL St. Felicitas Church.
Boyle, Msgr. Lawrence P. '62 (CAM) Retired.
Boyle, Leo A. '44 (CLV) [M] Cleveland, OH Sts. Mary and Joseph Home for the Aged.
Boyle, Leo A. '44 (KC) Retired.
Boyle, Michael '95 (RVC) Hauppauge, NY St. Thomas More Church.
Boyle, Michael J. *c.m.* '59 (PHX) [26] Phoenix, AZ St. Vincent de Paul Church.
Boyle, Neil *s.s.c.* '43 (FgM) St. Columban's Foreign Mission.
Boyle, Patrick *o.c.s.o.* '67 (SLC) [F] Huntsville, UT Abbey of Our Lady of the Holy Trinity of the Order of Cistercians.
Boyle, Patrick *o.f.m.* '80 (NY) [DD] New York, NY Franciscan Province of the Immaculate Conception.
Boyle, Patrick '94 (NY) [11] Yonkers, NY St. John the Baptist Church.
Boyle, Patrick J. *s.j.* '63 (CHI) [A] Mundelein, IL University of St. Mary of the Lake-Mundelein Seminary.
Boyle, Msgr. Patrick J. '65 (NY) [135] Bronx, NY St. Brendan Church.
Boyle, Patrick M. *o.s.m.* '56 (CHI) [N] Chicago, IL Order of Friar Servants of Mary (Servites) United States of America Province, Inc.
Boyle, Msgr. Raymond J. '56 (PEO) Seneca, IL St. Patrick's Church.
Boyle, Richard *o.s.m.* '84 (CHI) [N] Chicago, IL Order of Friar Servants of Mary (Servites) United States of America Province, Inc.
Boyle, Richard M. *o.s.m.* '84 (ORG) [D] Anaheim, CA Servite High School; Servite High School Development Fund; [I] Anaheim, CA Servite Fathers and Brothers; [I] Buena Park, CA Order of Friar Servants of Mary (Servites).
Boyle, Richard P. *s.j.* '75 (BO) [W] Boston, MA The Society of Jesus of New England-Provincial Offices.
Boyle, Richard P. *s.j.* '75 (TUC) [F] Tucson, AZ Jesuit Community of the Vatican Observatory.
Boyle, Msgr. Robert J. '51 (BO) Senior Priests.
Boyle, Robert J. '63 (PIT) Finleyville, PA St. Francis of Assisi Church.
Boyle, Stephen M. (BO) [1] Malden, MA Immaculate Conception Church.
Boyle, Stephen M. *o.praem.* '90 (ORG) [I] Silverado, CA Norbertine Fathers of Orange Inc.
Boyle, Thomas '56 (PHX) Retired.
Boyle, Thomas S. '41 (CHI) [55] Chicago, IL St. Felicitas Church; Retired.
Boyle, Valentine L. *o.carm.* '46 (PHX) [16] Phoenix, AZ St. Luke Church; [G] Phoenix, AZ Carmelite Community.
Boyle, Victor J. '60 (BRK) Absent on Leave.
Boyle, William M. '56 (ORL) [1] Orlando, FL Mary Queen of the Universe Church.
Boymer, Lloyd J. '43 (CLV) Brecksville, OH St. Basil the Great Church; Macedonia, OH Our Lady of Guadalupe Church; Retired.
Bozada, Mark S. '81 (STL) Apple Creek, MO St. Joseph Church; Biehle, MO St. Maurus Church.
Bozek, Robert J. '78 (WDC) [5] Silver Spring, MD Christ the King Church.
Bozel, Msgr. Robert A. '48 (BAL) Retired; [O] Timonium, MD Stella Maris.
Bozeman, Anthony M. '00 (PH) Penndel, PA Our Lady of Grace Church.
Boznar, Joseph P. '70 (CLV) [77] Cleveland, OH St. Vitus Church.
Bozung, James M. '61 (GR) Belmont, MI Assumption of the Blessed Virgin Mary Church.
Bozza, Nicholas G. (PAT) Netcong, NJ St. Michael's Church.
Bozzelli, Joseph V. '67 (WIL) Bear, DE St. Elizabeth Ann Seton Church.
Bozzelli, Richard J. (BAL) [27] Baltimore, MD Corpus Christi Church.
Bozzo, Kenneth J. '80 (FRS) Chowchilla, CA St. Columba Church.
Braak, Thomas E. '59 (DUB) Blessing, IA Immaculate Conception Church; Eagle Center, IA St. Mary of Mt. Carmel Church; La Porte City, IA Sacred Heart Church.
Braaten, James B. '89 (BIS) Mohall, ND St. Jerome Church.
Braband, James *s.v.d.* '80 (CHI) [B] Techny, IL Divine Word Residence; [N] Techny, IL Society of the Divine Word, Provincial Headquarter-Chicago Prov.
Brabandt, James *o.f.m.* '95 (WDC) [M] Washington, DC Commissariat of the Holy Land, Franciscan Monastery - Mount St. Sepulchre.
Bracco, Theodore *o.f.m.* '66 (SFD) [K] Teutopolis, IL St. Francis Assisi Friary.
Bracht, Donald F. *s.m.* '43 (CIN) [M] Dayton, OH Marianist Provincialate.
Bracikowski, Felix *o.f.m.conv.* '38 (BUF) [O] Athol Springs, NY St. Francis of Assisi Friary.
Bracke, James A. *c.s.c.* '80 (FTW) [20] South Bend, IN St. Therese, Little Flower Church.
Bracken, Jerome *c.p.* '68 (BRK) [V] Jamaica, NY Immaculate Conception Monastery.
Bracken, Msgr. John J. '67 (BRK) [Z] Brooklyn, NY Alive in Hope Foundation of the Diocese of Brooklyn.
Bracken, Joseph A. *s.j.* '62 (CIN) [M] Cincinnati, OH Jesuit Community at Xavier University.
Bracken, W. Jerome *c.p.* '68 (NEW) [A] South Orange, NJ Immaculate Conception Seminary; [B] South Orange, NJ Seton Hall University.
Bracken, Walter *s.v.d.* '71 (CHI) [B] Techny, IL Divine Word Residence; [N] Techny, IL Society of the Divine Word, Provincial Headquarter-Chicago Prov.
Brackenridge, David F. '52 (PH) Retired.
Bracket, Louis P. '47 (MAR) Retired.
Brackett, Anthony H. '59 (BUR) Retired.
Brackett, Christopher *l.c.* '93 (HRT) [B] Cheshire, CT Novitiate of the Legion of Christ.
Brackin, James D. *s.c.j.* '75 (MIL) [B] Hales Corners, WI Sacred Heart School of Theology; [P] Hales Corners, WI Sacred Heart Monastery.
Brackley, J. Dean *s.j.* '76 (FgM) Provinces.
Bracq, Edward E. '50 (MAN) Retired.
Bradbury, Henry M. *c.m.* '59 (BUF) [8] Niagara Falls, NY Our Lady of Lebanon Church.
Braddock, Stephen (MIL) [P] Wauwatosa, WI St. Camillus Provincialate.
Braden, Msgr. Leroy H. '53 (GAL) Retired; [N] Houston, TX St. Dominic Village.
Braden, Michael L. *s.j.* (BAL) [B] Baltimore, MD Loyola College in Maryland.
Braden, Michael L. *s.j.* '79 (BAL) [S] Baltimore, MD Jesuit Community of Loyola College, Inc.
Braden, Patrick O. *c.s.b.* '52 (GAL) [Q] Houston, TX Residence of the Basilian Fathers of the University of St. Thomas.
Bradford, Richard S. '98 (BO) [66] Boston, MA St. Theresa of Avila Church; Special Chaplaincies.
Bradican, Msgr. Francis L. '36 (ARL) Annandale, VA Holy Spirit Church; Retired.
Bradler, Robert C. '62 (ROC) [59] Rochester, NY St. Thomas the Apostle Church; [L] Rochester, NY Holy Childhood Association.
Bradley, Alfred *c.ss.r.* '88 (STV) [2] Christiansted, VI Church of the Holy Cross.
Bradley, Allan P. '72 (SUP) Erin, WI St. Patrick Church; New Richmond, WI Immaculate Conception Church.
Bradley, Allan W. '70 (COV) Ludlow, KY Sts. Boniface and James Church.
Bradley, Bruce '78 (DAL) [7] Dallas, TX Mary Immaculate Church.
Bradley, Daniel P. *m.s.* '93 (ORL) [3] Orlando, FL Good Shepherd Church.
Bradley, Dennis J. '77 (PIT) Midland, PA St. Blaise Church.
Bradley, Edward C. *s.j.* '79 (PH) [AA] Philadelphia, PA Jesuit Community at St. Joseph's University; [AA] Philadelphia, PA Jesuit Community at St. Joseph's University.
Bradley, Edward G. '66 (NEW) [C] West Orange, NJ Seton Hall Preparatory School.
Bradley, Gary J. *s.j.* '75 (FgM) Provinces.
Bradley, H. Cornell *s.j.* '69 (PH) [C] Philadelphia, PA St. Joseph's University; [AA] Philadelphia, PA Jesuit Community at St. Joseph's University.
Bradley, Harold C. *s.j.* '61 (MIL) [P] Milwaukee, WI Jesuit Community at Marquette University.
Bradley, Hugh J. '89 (CAM) Somers Point, NJ St. Joseph's Church.
Bradley, J. Edward '75 (OWN) Henderson, KY Holy Name of Jesus Church.
Bradley, J. Richard '81 (TLS) Muskogee, OK Saint Joseph Church.
Bradley, James *s.j.* '58 (BAL) [D] Baltimore, MD Loyola Blakefield.
Bradley, James *s.d.s.* '61 (LA) Whittier, CA St. Bruno Church.
Bradley, James *o.s.f.s.* '61 (LAN) [B] Jackson, MI Lumen Christi High School.
Bradley, James '73 (BRK) [A] Douglaston, NY Immaculate Conception Center.
Bradley, James F. '43 (PH) Media, PA Nativity of the Blessed Virgin Mary Church; Retired.
Bradley, James P. (NO) [C] New Orleans, LA Loyola University New Orleans.
Bradley, James P. *s.j.* '67 (NO) [P] New Orleans, LA Jesuit Provincial Office.
Bradley, John (PH) [U] Philadelphia, PA St. Agnes Medical Center.
Bradley, John A. '65 (ORG) Capistrano Beach, CA San Felipe de Jesus Church.

Bradley, John J. '63 (PH) [145] Philadelphia, PA Sacred Heart of Jesus Church.
Bradley, John J. '67 (ALB) [3] Albany, NY Blessed Sacrament Church.
Bradley, John Paul '44 (CHL) Absent On Leave.
Bradley, Joseph '91 (SFR) Burlingame, CA St. Catherine of Siena Church; Special Assignment; [D] San Mateo, CA Junipero Serra High School (Boys).
Bradley, Jude C. *o.s.b.* '47 (PAT) [M] Newton, NJ St. Paul's Abbey.
Bradley, Matthew '72 (BO) [Y] Scituate, MA Foyer of Charity.
Bradley, Michael *o.m.i.* '66 (FgM) Oblates Foreign Missions.
Bradley, Michael '91 (TUC) Globe, AZ Holy Angels Church.
Bradley, Michael J. (CHI) Graduate Studies.
Bradley, Msgr. Paul F. '41 (TR) Retired.
Bradley, Paul J. '71 (PIT) Ross Township, PA St. Sebastian Church.
Bradley, Robert (DAL) [B] Irving, TX University of Dallas.
Bradley, Robert *s.j.* '55 (AUS) [9] Austin, TX Sacred Heart Church.
Bradley, Robert '73 (CC) Retired.
Bradley, Robert M. '57 (LA) Retired.
Bradley, Theodore F.X. '58 (SPK) Spokane, Wa U.S. Veterans Hospital; Retired.
Bradley, Thomas J. '93 (CHI) [98] Chicago, IL St. Jerome Church.
Bradley, Msgr. William J. '57 (NY) [1] New Rochelle, NY Blessed Sacrament Church.
Bradlo, Antoni *c.ss.r.* '57 (CHI) [80] Chicago, IL Holy Innocents Church.
Bradower, Theodore J. *t.o.r.* '50 (FWT) [8] Fort Worth, TX St. Andrew Church.
Bradshaw, Alexander H. '85 (ROC) [23] Rochester, NY Holy Ghost Church; [40] Rochester, NY Our Mother of Sorrows Church.
Bradshaw, Jordan *o.p.* '92 (OAK) [4] Berkeley, CA St. Mary Magdalen Church.
Bradshaw, Jordan C. *o.p.* '92 (OAK) [N] Oakland, CA Western Dominican Province.
Bradshaw, Paul F. '70 (FTW) [B] Notre Dame, IN University of Notre Dame Du Lac.
Bradshaw, Terry L. '80 (L) [9] Louisville, KY St. Athanasius Church.
Bradt, Kevin M. *s.j.* '79 (OAK) [N] Berkeley, CA Jesuit Community at Jesuit School of Theology at Berkeley.
Bradtke, Thomas '62 (DEN) Basalt, CO St. Vincent Church.
Bradunas, John J. *o.s.f.s.* '73 (WIL) [I] Childs, MD Oblates of St. Francis De Sales.
Brady, Charles '55 (SAC) [3] Sacramento, CA Holy Spirit Church.
Brady, Coman V. '59 (BRK) [144] Brooklyn, NY St. Vincent Ferrer Church.
Brady, Daniel J. '61 (CHI) [1] Mt. Prospect, IL St. Cecilia Church.
Brady, Daniel O. '84 (RIC) Pocahontas, VA St. Elizabeth Church; Tazewell, VA St. Theresa Church.
Brady, Daniel P. *o.p.* '48 (DAL) [K] Irving, TX Dominican Priory of St. Albert the Great.
Brady, Edmund P. '59 (BRK) [193] Queens, NY St. Margaret Mary Church; [216] Queens, NY Our Lady of Mount Carmel Church.
Brady, Edward E. '90 (PH) [102] Philadelphia, PA Maternity B.V.M. Church.
Brady, Edward J. *s.j.* '59 (BAL) [S] Baltimore, MD Jesuit Fathers and Brothers Maryland Provincial Curia.
Brady, Edward J. *s.j.* '59 (FgM) Provinces.
Brady, Msgr. Frank J. '46 (SC) Retired.
Brady, G. James *c.s.c.* '59 (P) Shaw, OR St. Mary Church.
Brady, Gerald '83 (SPR) [6] Springfield, MA Holy Name Church.
Brady, Msgr. Gerard J. '59 (SR) Napa, CA St. Thomas Aquinas Church.
Brady, James '89 (BAL) [O] Timonium, MD Stella Maris.
Brady, James *s.m.m.* '92 (BRK) [195] Queens, NY St. Mary Gate of Heaven Church; [V] Ozone Park, NY Montfort Missionaries Provincialate (Missionaries of the Company of Mary) - Formation Community.
Brady, James H.T. *s.o.l.t.* '89 (CC) [H] Robstown, TX Society of Our Lady of the Most Holy Trinity.
Brady, James J. '53 (MIL) Retired.
Brady, James J. '57 (ALN) Retired.
Brady, James J. '72 (TR) Brick Town, NJ St. Dominic Church.
Brady, James R. '57 (ALN) Tremont, PA Immaculate Conception Church.
Brady, Jeremiah A. *s.s.j.* '51 (MOB) [10] Mobile, AL St. Joseph Church.
Brady, Jeremiah D. *s.s.j.* '51 (MOB) [18] Mobile, AL Prince of Peace Church.
Brady, John '49 (LA) Van Nuys, CA St. Elisabeth Church.
Brady, John '55 (SFS) Retired.
Brady, Msgr. John B. '55 (WDC) Avenue, MD Holy Angels Church; [V] Pomfret, MD Ministr-O-Media, Inc.
Brady, John F. *s.j.* '48 (DEN) [31] Denver, CO St. Ignatius Loyola Church; [M] Denver, CO Loyola Parish - Jesuit Community.
Brady, Joseph '89 (SD) [22] San Diego, CA St. Catherine Laboure Church.
Brady, Jude W. *o.s.b.* '80 (SAV) [B] Savannah, GA Benedictine Military School; [F] Savannah, GA The Benedictine Priory.
Brady, Jules M. *s.j.* '53 (STL) [O] St. Louis, MO Fusz Pavilion.
Brady, Leo *c.p.* '44 (CHI) [N] Chicago, IL Daneo Hall.
Brady, Martin D. *t.o.r.* '56 (ALT) [F] Newry, PA St. Bernardine Monastery.
Brady, Mel P. *o.f.m.* '50 (DET) [3] Detroit, MI St. Aloysius Church.
Brady, Patrick *o.m.i.* '48 (NY) [FF] Newburgh, NY Our Lady of Hope Center.
Brady, Msgr. Patrick A. '61 (WIL) Retired.
Brady, Patrick J. '64 (CAM) [5] Atlantic City, NJ Our Lady Star of the Sea Church.
Brady, Patrick J. '93 (PH) Graduate Studies.
Brady, Philip W. '43 (BGP) Retired.
Brady, Reginald '93 (WDC) [16] Washington, DC Holy Comforter—St. Cyprian Church.
Brady, Richard J. '59 (BO) [4] Lawrence, MA St. Francis Church.
Brady, Msgr. Roger J. '58 (BO) Belmont, MA St. Luke Church.
Brady, Severin *o.f.m.* '66 (PRO) [P] Providence, RI St. Francis Friary.
Brady, Theodore E.A. *s.j.* '61 (BAL) [M] Baltimore, MD Mercy Health Services Inc.; [S] Baltimore, MD Ferdinand Wheeler Jesuit Community.
Brady, Msgr. Thomas C. '54 (RCK) South Beloit, IL St. Peter Church.
Brady, Thomas E. *s.j.* '47 (NY) [DD] New York, NY Murray-Weigel Hall.
Brady, Msgr. Thomas F. '59 (BRK) [50] Brooklyn, NY Good Shepherd Church.
Brady, Vincent '67 (SAC) Lincoln, CA St. Joseph Church.
Brady, Vincent M. '95 (PSC) Endicott, NY SS. Peter and Paul's Church.
Brady, William J. '80 (SFR) [17] San Francisco, CA St. Emydius Church.
Braganza, Joe (NY) [1] Port Chester, NY Our Lady of Mercy Church.
Braganza, Simon '92 (CHI) [75] Chicago, IL St. Henry Church.
Bragotti, Joseph *m.c.c.j.* '62 (CIN) [M] Cincinnati, OH Comboni Missionaries (Verona Fathers)-Comboni Mission Center.
Bragotti, Joseph *m.c.c.j.* '62 (FgM) Comboni Foreign Missions.
Brahears, Msgr. Bill '82 (AMA) Retired.
Brahill, John *o.s.b.* '82 (FgM) American - Cassinese Congregation Foreign Missions.
Brahill, John *o.s.b.* '82 (RCK) [G] Aurora, IL Marmion Abbey-St. Augustine's Abbey.
Brahm, Harvey W. '51 (MIL) Brookfield, WI St. Luke Church.
Braida, Ernest E. '64 (DAV) Newton, IA Sacred Heart Church.
Brainard, Arthur *s.d.b.* '53 (OAK) [E] Richmond, CA Salesian High School.
Brainard, Ernest B. '45 (OAK) [2] Oakland, CA St. Andrew-St. Joseph Church; Retired.
Brainerd, Winthrop '87 (WDC) [12] Washington, DC Epiphany Church.
Brajkovich, Thomas R. '61 (PEO) Retired.
Brakora, Anthony '35 (LAN) Retired.
Braley, James E. '75 (BO) Graduate Studies.
Braley, James P. '75 (BO) [1] Norwood, MA St. Catherine of Siena Church.
Braman, Dennis J. '96 (ALT) Absent on Leave.
Brambilla, Charles A. '71 (STP) Lindstrom, MN St. Bridget of Sweden Church.
Brambilla, Sigmund *o.f.m.* '55 (NY) [DD] New York, NY Franciscan Province of the Immaculate Conception.
Bramble, Donald *o.p.* '76 (LA) [60] Los Angeles, CA St. Dominic Church.
Bramble, Donald J. *o.p.* '76 (OAK) [N] Oakland, CA Western Dominican Province.
Bramlage, Gregory '96 (IND) Enochsburg, IN St. John the Evangelist Church; Hamburg, IN St. Anne Church; St. Maurice, IN St. Maurice Church.
Bramlage, James A. '64 (CIN) [1] Cincinnati, OH St. Peter in Chains Church.
Bramwell, Bevil '85 (BO) [W] Lowell, MA Missionary Oblates of Mary Immaculate.
Bramwell, Bevil *o.m.i.* '85 (STU) [A] Steubenville, OH Franciscan University of Steubenville; [F] Steubenville, OH Holy Spirit Friary.
Brancaccio, Alberto A. *s.o.l.t.* '93 (CC) [H] Robstown, TX Society of Our Lady of the Most Holy Trinity.
Branch, Edward B. '74 (ATL) [M] Atlanta, GA Campus Ministry.
Branch, Edward B. '74 (L) On Duty Outside the Archdiocese.
Branch, Leslie '71 (WDC) Retired; [D] Washington, DC Archbishop Carroll High School.
Branche, John S. '54 (OG) Retired.
Brancolini, Luca (FR) [N] Fall River, MA Bristol Community College Newman Center.
Brancolini, Luca '99 (FR) [2] Attleboro, MA St. Joseph's Church; [N] Norton, MA Wheaton College Newman Center; [O] Attleboro, MA Priestly Fraternity of the Missionaries of St. Charles Borromeo, Inc.
Branconnier, Gerard '78 (WOR) Absent on Leave.
Brand, Edmund H. *o.c.s.o.* '54 (ATL) [J] Conyers, GA The Monastery of the Holy Spirit.
Brand, William *o.f.m.* '74 (LA) [73] Los Angeles, CA St. Joseph Church.
Brande, Edward W. *s.j.* '63 (NEW) [B] Jersey City, NJ Saint Peter's College; [N] Jersey City, NJ Jesuits of Saint Peter's College, Inc.
Brandenberger, Robert J. *c.m.* '52 (PH) [AA] Philadelphia, PA Congregation of the Mission.
Brandenhoff, Peter B. '70 (WIN) On Duty Outside the Diocese.
Brandes, John F. '51 (NU) Retired.
Brandes, John F. '51 (STP) On Duty Outside the Archdiocese; Retired.
Brandow, Stephen J. '96 (ALX) Pineville, LA Veterans Administration Medical Center.
Brandstrader, Frederick L. '68 (CHI) Wheeling, IL St. Joseph the Worker Church.
Brandt, Daniel J. '99 (CHI) [210] Chicago, IL St. William Church.
Brandt, Joseph D. '83 (PH) Glenside, PA St. Luke the Evangelist Church; [D] Downingtown, PA Bishop Shanahan High School.
Brandt, Msgr. Lawrence E. '69 (E) [17] Erie, PA St. Hedwig/St. Patrick Church.
Brandt, Paul C. '84 (PH) Lafayette Hill, PA St. Philip Neri Church; [D] Philadelphia, PA Roman Catholic High School for Boys.
Brankin, Anthony J. '75 (CHI) [202] Chicago, IL St. Thomas More Church.
Brankin, Patrick M. '79 (CHI) On Duty Outside the Archdiocese.
Brankin, Patrick M. '79 (TLS) Collinsville, OK St. Therese Church.
Brannan, Patrick T. *s.j.* '63 (BAL) [S] Baltimore, MD Jesuit Fathers and Brothers Maryland Provincial Curia.
Brannen, Brett A. '91 (SAV) Macon, GA St. Peter Claver Church.
Brannon, Robert F. '58 (GBG) [G] Greensburg, PA Neumann House.
Branon, Philip J. '51 (BUR) South Hero, VT St. Rose of Lima Church.
Bransfield, Brian J. '94 (PH) Graduate Studies.
Bransfield, Christopher '98 (SJ) Los Gatos, CA St. Mary of the Immaculate Conception Church.
Bransfield, J. Brian '94 (PH) [D] Warminster, PA Archbishop Wood Catholic High School.
Bransfield, Msgr. Michael J. '71 (PH) On Duty Outside the Archdiocese.
Bransfield, Msgr. Michael J. '71 (WDC) [Q] Washington, DC Basilica of the National Shrine of the Immaculate Conception.
Bransfield, Thomas A. '64 (BUR) Orleans, VT St. Theresa of Child Jesus Church.
Branson, Bernard E. '59 (KC) Smithville, MO Church of the Good Shepherd.
Branson, Dale A. '97 (TUC) [12] Tucson, AZ St. Ambrose Church.
Branson, Keith *c.pp.s.* '00 (KC) [7] Kansas City, MO St. Charles Borromeo Church.
Brant, David A. '65 (SEA) [1] Seattle, WA St. James Church.
Brant, Paul W. *s.j.* '77 (R) [E] Raleigh, NC Jesuit Community.
Brantman, Thomas E. '75 (RCK) Hampshire, IL St. Charles Borromeo Church.
Brantome, Oscar '88 (MIA) Miami Lakes, FL Our Lady of the Lakes Church; Absent on Sick Leave.
Brantschen, Bruno *s.j.* '99 (CHI) [C] Chicago, IL Jesuit Community at Loyola University of Chicago.
Braquet, David J. '94 (ALX) Lecompte, LA St. Martin Church.
Braquet, Patrick X. '97 (ALX) [J] Alexandria, LA Louisiana State University at Alexandria; [K] Alexandria, LA St. Joseph House of Formation.
Brasher, C. John '75 (SFE) Springer, NM St. Joseph Church.
Brassard, Leo *a.a.* '69 (BO) [W] Boston, MA Assumptionist Center.
Brassard, Ronald E. '74 (PRO) [3] Cranston, RI Immaculate Conception Church.
Brassil, Msgr. James (RVC) Bayville, NY St. Gertrude's Church.
Brassil, Msgr. James A. (RVC) Retired.
Brassil, Kevin J. '58 (PRO) Portsmouth, RI St. Barnabas Church.
Bratek, Martin *c.r.* '72 (PT) Panama City, FL St. John the Evangelist Church.
Brath, John A. '68 (SPC) Kimberling City, MO Our Lady of the Cove Church.

Bratko, Ken *c.r.* '72 (CHI) [D] Chicago, IL Gordon Tech High School.
Bratko, Kenneth R. *c.r.* '64 (CHI) Schaumburg, IL St. Matthew Church.
Bratkowski, Allen '89 (MIL) [51] Milwaukee, WI St. Margaret Mary Church.
Bratus, Walter N. '56 (GBG) Retired.
Braud, Dominic R. *o.s.b.* '61 (NO) [P] St. Benedict, LA St. Joseph Abbey.
Braud, Ronald '64 (NO) [11] Metairie, LA St. Louis King of France Church.
Braudis, Joseph M. '77 (ALN) Hamburg, PA St. Mary Church.
Brauer, Frank J. '86 (BAL) Edgewater, MD Our Lady of Perpetual Help Church.
Brauer, Mark S. '92 (DET) [16] Detroit, MI St. Christine Church; [25] Detroit, MI St. Gemma Galgani Church; [T] Detroit, MI West Detroit Catholic Schools Alliance.
Braukman, Donald '86 (CR) Greenbush, MN Blessed Sacrament Church.
Brault, Bernard *s.m.m.* '68 (BRK) [195] Queens, NY St. Mary Gate of Heaven Church.
Brault, Gilles '71 (MAR) Champion, MI Sacred Heart Church; Republic, MI St. Augustine Church; Marquette, MI Marquette General Hospital.
Brault, Laurence V. '77 (WOR) Upton, MA Holy Angels Church.
Brault, Y. David '77 (WDC) Poolesville, MD Our Lady of the Presentation Church.
Braun, Brian *o.f.m.cap.* '60 (MIL) [52] Milwaukee, WI St. Martin de Porres Church; [P] Milwaukee, WI St. Conrad Friary.
Braun, Charles F. *s.m.* '67 (WDC) [M] Washington, DC Marist Center.
Braun, David J. '55 (MIL) Lake Geneva, WI St. Francis de Sales Church.
Braun, David L. '81 (BEL) Stringtown, IL St. Joseph Church; Wendelin, IL Holy Cross Church.
Braun, Donald B. '57 (MIL) Retired.
Braun, Edgar F. '40 (MIL) Retired.
Braun, Msgr. Francis '54 (BUF) [45] Buffalo, NY St. Mark Church.
Braun, Gary G. '77 (STL) [U] St. Louis, MO Washington University Newman Centers.
Braun, Gerard E. *s.j.* '46 (NY) [DD] New York, NY St. Ignatius Loyola Residence; [HH] New York, NY Jesuit Seminary and Mission Bureau, Inc.
Braun, H. Gerard '85 (FAR) Valley City, ND St. Catherine's Church.
Braun, John J. *m.afr.* '57 (SP) [O] St. Petersburg, FL Missionaries of Africa.
Braun, John S. '87 (SPC) Buffalo, MO St. William Church; Conway, MO Sacred Heart Church; Conway, MO Ozark Correctional Center.
Braun, Michael C. '61 (LC) Black River Falls, WI St. Joseph Church.
Braun, Msgr. Michael R. '67 (FRS) [2] Bakersfield, CA Our Lady of Perpetual Help Church.
Braun, Robert *o.m.i.* '51 (BEL) [F] Belleville, IL Shrine of Our Lady of the Snows.
Braun, Virgil R. '60 (SCL) Eden Valley, MN The Church of the Assumption.
Braunreuther, Robert J. *s.j.* '65 (BAL) [39] Baltimore, MD St. Ignatius Church; [J] Baltimore, MD St. Ignatius Loyola Academy.
Braunreuther, Robert J. *s.j.* '65 (BO) [W] Boston, MA The Society of Jesus of New England-Provincial Offices.
Bravata, Kevin W. '00 (MEM) [8] Memphis, TN St. Francis of Assisi Church.
Bravo, Enrique *c.s.b.* '62 (GAL) Angleton, TX Most Holy Trinity Church.
Bravo, Gregorio '58 (SJN) [36] San Juan, PR Maria Madre de La Iglesia Church.
Bravo, Joseph A. '77 (SFR) On Duty Outside the Archdiocese.
Bray, Kevin '67 (FRS) Absent on Sick Leave.
Brazaskas, Bob '66 (TUC) Sunsites, AZ St. Jude Thaddeus Church.
Breaker, Donald J. '64 (CIN) On Special and Archdiocesan Assignment.
Bream, James '64 (SFS) Watertown, SD Immaculate Conception Church.
Breau, Paschal *s.a.* '79 (NY) [DD] Garrison, NY Franciscan Friars of the Atonement, Minister General Office.
Breault, Charles *o.m.i.* (SAT) [C] San Antonio, TX Oblate School of Theology.
Breault, Charles *o.m.i.* '52 (BO) [FF] Lowell, MA Oblate Ministry Development Service.
Breault, Charles *o.m.i.* '59 (FgM) Oblates Foreign Missions.
Breault, Charles *o.m.i.* '59 (SAT) [M] San Antonio, TX Missionary Oblates of Mary Immaculate.
Breault, William F. *s.j.* '62 (SAC) [H] Carmichael, CA Jesuit High School Community of Sacramento.
Breaux, Allen '81 (LAF) Breaux Bridge, LA St. Bernard Church.
Breaux, O. Joseph '68 (LAF) Duson, LA St. Theresa of the Child Jesus Church.
Brecheteau, Gabriel *c.p.* '48 (FgM) Mission Procurators.
Brecht, David *o.s.a.* '65 (JOL) New Lenox, IL St. Jude Church.
Brechtl, Joseph A. '44 (MAD) Retired.
Breck, Steven H. '00 (CLV) Strongsville, OH St. John Neumann Church; Strongsville, OH St. John Neumann Church.
Breckensiek, Marne *o.f.m.* '65 (PEO) [3] Peoria, IL Sacred Heart Church.
Breczinski, Paul (BAL) Bradshaw, MD St. Stephen Church.
Bredeck, Martin J. *s.j.* '64 (KC) [B] Kansas City, MO Rockhurst University; [J] Kansas City, MO Rockhurst Jesuit Community.
Bredemann, George '83 (PHX) Unassigned.
Breedlove, Lawrence '56 (FWT) [4] Fort Worth, TX Holy Name of Jesus Church.
Breen, Bernard J. '72 (L) [49] Louisville, KY St. Margaret Mary Church.
Breen, Brendan *c.p.* '50 (BO) [21] Boston, MA St. Gabriel Church; [W] Boston, MA St. Gabriel Passionist Community.
Breen, Damian *o.s.b.* '98 (NEW) [1] Linden, NJ St. Elizabeth's Church.
Breen, Damian B. *o.s.b.* (PAT) [M] Morristown, NJ St. Mary's Abbey.
Breen, Msgr. Edward J. '58 (BRK) [210] Queens, NY Our Lady of Fatima Church.
Breen, Francis J. *m.m.* '70 (BO) [W] East Walpole, MA Maryknoll Mission Promotion Department.
Breen, James '80 (BGP) Wilton, CT Our Lady of Fatima Church.
Breen, John M. *m.m.* '51 (SJ) [L] Los Altos, CA Maryknoll.
Breen, Joseph P. '61 (NSH) [5] Nashville, TN St. Edward's Church.
Breen, Michael *s.s.c.* '47 (BO) [W] Quincy, MA St. Columban's Foreign Mission Society.
Breen, Philip M. '65 (NSH) [2] Nashville, TN St. Ann Church.
Breen, Robert H. '57 (PH) Riegelsville, PA St. Lawrence Church.
Breen, Stephen B. '55 (WIL) Retired.
Breidenbach, John '87 (EVN) [8] Evansville, IN Holy Rosary Church.
Breier, Donald P. '69 (PIT) Castle Shannon, PA St. Anne Church.
Breier, Henry '94 (STL) Special Assignment.
Breig, Gary R. '76 (STL) Military Chaplains.
Breig, Gary R. '78 (FAR) Grand Forks, ND Grand Forks Air Force Base; [J] Grand Forks, ND Air Force Base, Our Lady of the Snows Catholic Community.
Breighner, Joseph (BAL) [9] Baltimore, MD Annunciation Church.
Breighner, Joseph F. '71 (BAL) [1] Baltimore, MD Cathedral of Mary Our Queen; Special Assignment.
Breindel, Charles L. '00 (RIC) [9] Richmond, VA St. Edward The Confessor Church.
Breit, Melvin P. '62 (MIL) [70] Milwaukee, WI St. Philip Neri Church.
Breitbach, Richard C. '61 (MIL) Allenton, WI Resurrection Church.
Brelivet, Alan *o.m.i.* '31 (SAT) [K] San Antonio, TX Oblate Madonna Residence.
Brelsford, William J. '70 (LA) [95] Los Angeles, CA St. Timothy Church.
Brembos, Msgr. George M. '56 (MET) Far Hills, NJ St. Elizabeth Church; [N] Peapack, NJ Msgr. George E. Everitt Academy.
Brenberger, Thomas *c.pp.s.* '66 (CIN) Celina, OH Immaculate Conception of the Blessed Virgin Mary Church; Rockford, OH St. Teresa Church.
Brenberger, Thomas R. *c.pp.s.* '66 (CIN) Egypt, OH St. Joseph Church; [U] Dayton, OH Community Support Charitable Trust.
Brenda, William H. *o.p.* '49 (GAL) [36] Houston, TX Holy Rosary Church; [Q] Houston, TX Dominican Fathers and Brothers, St. Mark Priory, Inc.
Brenk, Frederick E. *s.j.* '63 (MIL) [P] Milwaukee, WI Jesuit Provincial Office, Wisconsin Province.
Brenkert, Edward J. '72 (BRK) [164] Queens, NY St. Clement Pope Church.
Brenkle, Msgr. John J. '58 (SR) Saint Helena, CA St. Helena Church; [O] Santa Rosa, CA Apostolic Endowment Trust.
Brennan, Anthony V. *m.m.* '61 (FgM) Maryknoll Foreign Missions.
Brennan, Bernard '61 (SFR) Special Assignment.
Brennan, Bernard '65 (DUL) [D] Duluth, MN Benedictine Health Center.
Brennan, Brian C. '79 (NY) [1] New York, NY Cathedral of St. Patrick; Mahopac, NY St. John the Evangelist Church.
Brennan, C. John '54 (SC) Retired.
Brennan, Cathal '52 (P) Retired.
Brennan, Charles M. *o.s.m.* '48 (CHI) [N] Chicago, IL Order of Friar Servants of Mary (Servites) United States of America Province, Inc.
Brennan, Msgr. Daniel H. '43 (ORG) Costa Mesa, CA St. John the Baptist Church.
Brennan, Msgr. Dermot R. '56 (NY) Yorktown Heights, NY St. Patrick Church.
Brennan, Donald *o.s.a.* '53 (FWT) Pilot Point, TX St. Thomas Aquinas Church.
Brennan, Edmund J. '82 (ALN) Newtown, PA Sacred Heart Church; Unassigned.
Brennan, Elmer F. '42 (CIN) Retired.
Brennan, Eugene P. '70 (STL) Warrenton, MO Holy Rosary Church.
Brennan, Eugene P. *m.s.* '80 (HRT) [M] Hartford, CT Missionaries of LaSalette, Provincial Secretary.
Brennan, Francis C. *s.j.* '58 (STL) [P] St. Louis, MO Jesuit Community Corporation at St. Louis University - Jesuit Hall.
Brennan, George *m.s.* '75 (FR) [I] Attleboro, MA La Salette Shrine.
Brennan, George '87 (VEN) [6] Sarasota, FL St. Patrick Church.
Brennan, Msgr. George J. '49 (BUF) Retired.
Brennan, George P. '68 (STL) [5] St. Louis, MO Holy Innocents Church.
Brennan, Gerard M. '50 (BO) Senior Priests.
Brennan, J. Gregory *o.f.m.* '79 (BUF) Humphrey, NY St. Pacificus, Mission of St. Bonaventure University Friary Church; [C] St. Bonaventure, NY St. Bonaventure University; [O] St. Bonaventure, NY St. Bonaventure Friary.
Brennan, James '89 (CHR) [E] Moncks Corner, SC Mepkin Abbey.
Brennan, James F. '55 (BO) Senior Priests.
Brennan, James H. *s.s.* '31 (BAL) [O] Baltimore, MD St. Charles Villa; [S] Baltimore, MD St. Charles Villa.
Brennan, James J. '89 (PH) Feasterville, PA Assumption B.V.M. Church; On Duty Outside the Archdiocese.
Brennan, James P. *c.ss.r.* '64 (WDC) [M] Washington, DC Holy Redeemer College.
Brennan, Msgr. John '55 (TYL) [A] Tyler, TX Trinity Mother Frances Health System.
Brennan, John D. '70 (PIT) Penn Hills, PA St. Gerard Majella Church; On Sabbatical.
Brennan, John J. *s.j.* '46 (LA) [6] Los Angeles, CA Blessed Sacrament Church.
Brennan, John J. '78 (SPR) [3] Westfield, MA St. Casimir's Church; [5] Westfield, MA St. Peter's Church.
Brennan, John P. *s.m.a.* '64 (LA) [A] Camarillo, CA St. John's Seminary.
Brennan, John W. *o.s.f.s.* '65 (PH) [131] Philadelphia, PA Our Mother of Consolation Church.
Brennan, Joseph *o.s.c.* '45 (SCL) [I] Onamia, MN Crosier Monastery.
Brennan, Joseph (Dennis) *o.s.b.* '74 (LA) [Q] Valyermo, CA St. Andrew's Abbey.
Brennan, Joseph F. *s.j.* (BO) [Y] Weston, MA Campion Renewal Center.
Brennan, Msgr. Joseph F. (LA) Retired.
Brennan, Joseph F. *s.j.* '56 (BO) [W] Weston, MA Campion Health Center, Inc.
Brennan, Msgr. Joseph F. '56 (LA) Long Beach, CA Veterans Affairs Medical Center.
Brennan, Msgr. Joseph F. '56 (SD) Retired.
Brennan, Joseph F. '59 (LAF) Retired.
Brennan, Joseph L. *c.m.* '43 (LA) [96] Los Angeles, CA St. Vincent De Paul Church.
Brennan, Joseph P. '54 (ROC) Retired.
Brennan, Joseph T. *s.j.* '69 (CHI) [D] Chicago, IL St. Ignatius College Prep; [D] Chicago, IL St. Ignatius Jesuit Community.
Brennan, Joseph T. *o.s.f.s.* '98 (ARL) Reston, VA St. John Neumann Church.
Brennan, Joseph V. '80 (LA) Norwalk, CA St. Linus Church.
Brennan, Keith *s.d.s.* '70 (MIL) [P] Milwaukee, WI Salvatorian Provincial Residence.
Brennan, Keith R. (STA) [F] Jacksonville, FL Casa San Pedro.
Brennan, Keith R. '84 (STA) Special Assignment.
Brennan, Lawrence C. '76 (STL) [A] St. Louis, MO Kenrick-Glennon Seminary.
Brennan, Mark E. '76 (WDC) [42] Washington, DC St. Thomas Apostle Church.
Brennan, Matthew '62 (BIR) Pell City, AL Our Lady of the Lake Church.
Brennan, Michael *c.p.* '50 (SAC) [G] Redding, CA Catholic Healthcare West North State dba Mercy Medical Center Redding.
Brennan, Michael *c.p.* '53 (MET) [H] South River, NJ Passionist Provincial Office.
Brennan, Msgr. Michael J. (BRK) [28] Brooklyn, NY St. Cecilia Church.
Brennan, Patrick *c.p.* '73 (LA) [Q] Pasadena, CA Passionist Community; [W] Sierra Madre, CA Mater Dolorosa Retreat Center.
Brennan, Patrick '77 (P) On Duty Outside the Archdiocese.
Brennan, Patrick A. *o.s.a.* '63 (ORG) Buena Park, CA St. Pius V Church.
Brennan, Patrick J. '73 (CHI) Inverness, IL Holy Family Church.

Brennan, Paul '59 (ROC) [2] Auburn, NY Sacred Heart Church; Retired.
Brennan, Pierce A. *s.j.* '76 (RVC) Oceanside, NY St. Anthony Church.
Brennan, Msgr. Ralph '57 (AUS) Retired.
Brennan, Raymond *c.ss.r.* '59 (FgM) Redemptorist Foreign Missions.
Brennan, Robert E. '45 (SY) Retired.
Brennan, Robert F. '51 (CLV) [65] Cleveland, OH SS. Philip and James Church; Retired.
Brennan, Robert J. '49 (NY) Retired.
Brennan, Robert J. *c.s.c.* '68 (ORL) [F] Cocoa Beach, FL Holy Cross Fathers, Eastern Priests Province.
Brennan, Msgr. Robert J. '89 (RVC) [1] Rockville Centre, NY St. Agnes Church.
Brennan, Robert L. '64 (PH) [141] Philadelphia, PA Resurrection of Our Lord Church.
Brennan, Robert M. '65 (NEW) Upper Montclair, NJ St. Cassian Church.
Brennan, Roderick *o.f.m.cap.* '45 (FgM) Capuchin Foreign Missions.
Brennan, Ronan P. '50 (SAC) Sutter Creek, CA Immaculate Conception Church; Retired and in Senior Ministry.
Brennan, Msgr. Seamus F. '72 (MET) Edison, NJ St. Matthew Church.
Brennan, Terrence M. *s.j.* '76 (MIL) [E] Milwaukee, WI Marquette University High School; [P] Milwaukee, WI Pere Marquette House Jesuit Community.
Brennan, Thomas *s.d.b.* (BO) [11] Cambridge, MA St. Paul Church.
Brennan, Thomas *s.j.* '63 (BO) [W] Chestnut Hill, MA The Jesuit Community at Boston College.
Brennan, Thomas '66 (TR) Bay Head, NJ Sacred Heart Church.
Brennan, Thomas '89 (LAN) Retired.
Brennan, Thomas E. *s.d.b.* '82 (BO) [CC] Cambridge, MA Harvard Catholic Student Center.
Brennan, Thomas J. '74 (PH) [3] Phoenixville, PA St. Mary of the Assumption Church.
Brennan, Thomas J. *s.j.* '96 (BAL) [S] Baltimore, MD Jesuit Fathers and Brothers Maryland Provincial Curia.
Brennan, Thomas N. *s.j.* '67 (MIL) [P] Milwaukee, WI Arrupe House Jesuit Community.
Brennan, Timothy J. *o.s.b.* '78 (PAT) [M] Morristown, NJ St. Mary's Abbey.
Brennan, Walter *s.j.* '60 (FgM) Provinces.
Brennan, Walter M. *o.s.m.* '61 (CHI) Hillside, IL St. Domitilla Church; [N] Chicago, IL Order of Friar Servants of Mary (Servites) United States of America Province, Inc.; [N] Chicago, IL Order of Friar Servants of Mary (Servites) United States of America Province, Inc.; [N] Chicago, IL Order of Friar Servants of Mary (Servites) United States of America Province, Inc.
Brennan, William B. '53 (DET) [8] Dearborn Heights, MI St. Sebastian Church.
Brennan, William J. '42 (SPK) Retired.
Brennan, William J. '49 (L) [49] Louisville, KY St. Margaret Mary Church; Retired.
Brennan, William P. '63 (CAM) [4] Cherry Hill, NJ St. Pius X Church.
Brennell, John J. '78 (STL) Kirkwood, MO St. Peter Church.
Brennen, John E. '00 (TOL) Sandusky, OH SS. Peter and Paul Church.
Brenner, Raymond A. '69 (EVN) [11] Evansville, IN Resurrection Church.
Brenner, Msgr. Thomas R. '61 (HBG) Chambersburg, PA Corpus Christi Church; [K] Harrisburg, PA Catholic Campus Ministry.
Brennick, Stephen '59 (BO) [6] Somerville, MA St. Joseph Church.
Brenninkmeijer, Paul A. *o.s.b.* '67 (CHR) [17] Charleston, SC Christ Our King Church.
Brenny, Kenneth (SCL) Retired.
Brenon, Terence '91 (SAN) [4] San Angelo, TX St. Mary's Church.
Brenon, Terry '91 (SAN) Carlsbad, TX St. Therese of the Child Jesus Church.
Brensinger, Richard C. (ALN) Kelayres, PA Immaculate Conception Church; [3] McAdoo, PA St. Patrick Church.
Brensinger, Richard C. '92 (ALN) [C] Tamaqua, PA Marian Catholic High School.
Brentrup, Bruce *s.d.s.* '59 (MIL) [P] Milwaukee, WI Salvatorian Provincial Residence.
Brenza, William J. '70 (HRT) Naugatuck, CT St. Francis of Assisi Church.
Breski, Martin *o.f.m.conv.* '69 (ALT) Boswell, PA All Saints Church.
Breslawski, William G. '79 (RVC) Nesconset, NY Church of the Holy Cross.
Bresler, C. John '75 (SFE) Cimarron, NM Immaculate Conception Church.
Breslin, Cornelius J. '00 (WIL) Easton, MD SS. Peter and Paul Church.
Breslin, J. Michael '65 (RIC) Cape Charles, VA St. Charles Church.
Breslin, John *s.m.m.* '56 (BRK) [V] Ozone Park, NY Montfort Missionaries Provincialate (Missionaries of the Company of Mary) - Formation Community.
Breslin, John B. *s.j.* '73 (SY) [S] Syracuse, NY Jesuits at LeMoyne, Inc.
Breslin, Msgr. John E. '61 (PH) Doylestown, PA Our Lady of Mount Carmel Church.
Breslin, John S. '85 (CHI) [6] Chicago, IL St. Ailbe Church.
Breslin, Joseph W. '39 (SCR) Retired; [N] Dunmore, PA Villa St. Joseph.
Breslin, Msgr. Lawrence K. '57 (CIN) [7] Dayton, OH St. Charles Borromeo Church.
Breslin, Paul *o.f.m.* '88 (CAM) [2] Camden, NJ St. Anthony of Padua Church.
Breslin, Peter W. *s.j.* '91 (CHI) [D] Wilmette, IL Loyola Academy.
Breslin, William E. '74 (DEN) [1] Aurora, CO Queen of Peace Church.
Bresnahan, James F. *s.j.* '59 (BO) [W] Boston, MA The Society of Jesus of New England-Provincial Offices.
Bresnahan, James F. *s.j.* '59 (CHI) [N] Chicago, IL Chicago Province of the Society of Jesus-Provincial Office.
Bresnahan, John E. *o.s.a.* '36 (PH) [AA] Villanova, PA St. Thomas Monastery.
Bresnahan, John J. *s.j.* '58 (BO) [Y] Gloucester, MA Eastern Point Retreat House.
Bresnahan, John J. '60 (CHI) Schiller Park, IL St. Beatrice Church.
Bresnahan, Richard F. '58 (PEO) Coal Valley, IL St. Maria Goretti Church.
Bresnahan, Thomas J. '40 (DET) Retired; [Q] Troy, MI Gabriel Richard Institute.
Bresnahan, Thomas J. '60 (MAN) Retired.
Bresnahan, Thomas J., (Retired) '60 (MAN) Salem, NH St. Joseph Church.
Bresnehan, Msgr. Paul M. '54 (BUR) Proctor, VT St. Dominic Church.
Brethour, Gary G. '89 (LIN) McCook, NE St. Patrick Church.
Bretl, James J. *s.d.s.* '65 (NSH) McMinnville, TN St. Catherine Church; Smithville, TN St. Gregory Church.
Breton, Albert '54 (SPR) Retired.
Breton, Denis R. '76 (BUR) Morrisville, VT Holy Cross Church.
Breton, Louis *o.s.m.* '49 (P) [L] Portland, OR The Grotto, The National Sanctuary of Our Sorrowful Mother.
Breton, Louis M. *o.s.m.* '49 (CHI) [N] Chicago, IL Order of Friar Servants of Mary (Servites) United States of America Province, Inc.
Bretone, Richard '89 (BRK) [128] Brooklyn, NY Sacred Heart Church.
Brett, Frank X. '59 (KNX) Norris, TN St. Joseph Church.
Brett, James D. '41 (CHI) Retired.
Brett, James G. '44 (JKS) Retired.
Brett, Stephen *s.s.j.* '76 (WDC) [B] Washington, DC St. Joseph's Seminary.
Brett, Stephen F. *s.s.j.* '76 (PH) [A] Wynnewood, PA Theological Seminary of St. Charles Borromeo, Overbrook.
Bretton, Ray (OAK) Graduate Studies.
Bretzke, James T. *s.j.* '81 (OAK) [A] Berkeley, CA The Jesuit School of Theology at Berkeley; [N] Berkeley, CA Jesuit Community at Jesuit School of Theology at Berkeley.
Breu, David L. '73 (NU) Ivanhoe, MN SS. Peter & Paul Church; Wilno, MN St. John Cantius Church.
Breunig, Robert L. '51 (DEN) Retired.
Breunig, Rudy *s.t.* '65 (FgM) Trinity Missions.
Breuning, Walter A. '54 (PEO) Retired.
Brew, Frederick A. *s.j.* '43 (ALN) [A] Wernersville, PA Jesuit Center.
Brewczynski, Jacek '96 (DET) [9] Warren, MI St. Martin de Porres Church.
Brewer, Dexter S. '89 (NSH) Decherd, TN Good Shepherd Church.
Brewer, Gervase '43 (MAR) Retired.
Brewer, James P. '77 (PRT) Westbrook, ME St. Hyacinth Church.
Brewer, Martin L. *s.j.* '54 (LA) [3] Santa Barbara, CA Our Lady of Sorrows Church.
Brewer, Timothy M. '79 (WOR) [5] Leominster, MA Our Lady of the Lake Church.
Brewerton, Peter H. '40 (HT) Retired.
Brey, Christopher '97 (SFD) [M] Charleston, IL Eastern Illinois University Newman Center.
Brey, Lawrence S. '53 (MIL) Retired.
Breza, Paul J. '63 (WIN) Hokah, MN St. Peter's Church.
Brezik, Victor B. *c.s.b.* '40 (GAL) [Q] Houston, TX Residence of the Basilian Fathers of the University of St. Thomas.
Brezinski, Blaine *c.p.* '96 (RVC) [O] Shelter Island Heights, NY St. Gabriel's Youth House.
Brezovec, John F. '66 (ALT) [1] Johnstown, PA St. John Gualbert Church.
Brian, Bertrand J. '50 (L) Retired; [M] St. Catharine, KY Sansbury Care Center.
Brice, Donald '58 (WDC) [4] Washington, DC Annunciation Church.
Brice, Frederick J. '69 (MIA) Lighthouse Point, FL St. Paul the Apostle Church.
Brice, Steven J. '82 (LC) [3] Wausau, WI St. Anne Church.
Briceland, Alan *s.j.* '63 (BRK) Queens, NY Elmhurst General Hospital.
Briceland, W. Alan *s.j.* '65 (NY) [DD] New York, NY West Side Jesuit Community.
Briceno, Joseph '81 (PHX) Unassigned.
Brichetto, James *s.j.* '63 (CIN) [M] Cincinnati, OH Faber Jesuit Community.
Brick, Donald *o.c.d.* '00 (MIL) [P] Holy Hill, WI Discalced Carmelite Monastery.
Brick, Maurice J. *o.f.m.* '45 (PAT) [M] Butler, NJ St. Anthony Friary.
Brick, Paul T. *s.d.s.* '63 (SAV) [4] Columbus, GA St. Benedict the Moor Church.
Bricker, Brian *o.p.* (DEN) [29] Denver, CO St. Dominic's Church.
Brickl, Joseph M. '37 (MAD) Retired.
Brickler, R. Richard '61 (ROC) [9] Rochester, NY St. Boniface Church.
Brickman, Donald P. '81 (CLV) [1] Cleveland, OH Cathedral of St. John the Evangelist.
Brickner, Charles W. '75 (RIC) Woodlawn, VA St. Joseph's Church.
Brickner, Ronald J. '92 (TOL) Awaiting Assignment.
Bride, Msgr. Thomas R. *p.a.* '67 (NOR) Quaker Hill, CT Our Lady of Perpetual Help Church; On Special or Other Diocesan Assignment.
Bridge, George H. *c.ss.r.* '48 (ALB) [L] Saratoga Springs, NY St. John Neumann Residence.
Bridge, George H. *c.ss.r.* '48 (VEN) Wauchula, FL St. Michael Church.
Bridge, Robert E. '72 (CHI) [165] Chicago, IL St. Peter Canisius Church.
Bridges, Clarence S. '88 (ALT) [1] Johnstown, PA St. John Gualbert Church.
Bridges, James P. '62 (SAN) [4] Midland, TX St. Stephen's Church.
Bridgman, Mark '96 (OM) O'Neill, NE St. Patrick Church.
Bried, William *o.f.m.* '79 (NY) [48] New York, NY Holy Name of Jesus Church.
Brieffies, John (RIC) West Point, VA Our Lady of the Blessed Sacrament Church.
Brieffies, John *m.s.f.* '56 (RIC) [L] West Point, VA Missionaries of the Holy Family, General Mission Office—M.S.F., Inc.
Brien, Paul *m.m.* '60 (DET) [K] Detroit, MI Maryknoll Fathers and Brothers.
Brienz, Edward '96 (Y) Absent on Leave.
Bries, Marvin J. '73 (DUB) Britt, IA St. Patrick's Church; Corwith, IA St. Mary's Church; Woden, IA Sacred Heart Church.
Briese, Dominic R. *o.p.* '96 (SFR) [14] San Francisco, CA St. Dominic Church; [N] San Francisco, CA St. Dominic Priory.
Brietske, Msgr. Richard C. '62 (TR) Willingboro, NJ Corpus Christi Church.
Briffa, Philip '60 (DET) [3] Warren, MI St. Cletus Church.
Briffa, Salvino '71 (DET) [4] Roseville, MI Holy Innocents Church.
Brigandi, Msgr. Paul A. '54 (SY) [8] Binghamton, NY St. Mary of the Assumption Church; [W] Oswego, NY St. Peter & St. Paul.
Brigandi, Stephen J., Jr. '97 (RVC) Valley Stream, NY Holy Name of Mary Church.
Briganti, Philip J. '73 (PAT) Military Chaplains.
Briggman, Michael J. '68 (ALN) Bally, PA Most Blessed Sacrament Church; Retired; [J] Bethlehem, PA Holy Family Villa.
Briggs, Everett F. '33 (WH) Retired.
Brigham, Kenneth M. '61 (CHI) [12] Chicago, IL St. Angela Church; [148] Chicago, IL Our Lady Help of Christians Church.
Brighenti, Kenneth D. '88 (MET) Raritan, NJ St. Ann Church.
Brignac, Horace L., Jr. '83 (NO) [56] New Orleans, LA St. Raphael the Archangel Church.
Brillantes, Msgr. Edgar B. '80 (HON) [9] Honolulu, HI St. John the Baptist Church.
Brimley, Wilfred A. *c.s.p.* '62 (NY) [DD] Jamaica Estates, NY Paulist Fathers Generalate.
Brimley, Wilfred A. *c.s.p.* '62 (STP) [29] Minneapolis, MN St. Lawrence Church; [N] Minneapolis, MN Paulist Fathers.
Brindamou, Maurice L. '74 (PRO) [8] Woonsocket, RI St. Joseph Church.
Brindamour, Albert H. '46 (PRO) [11] Woonsocket, RI Precious Blood Church; Retired.
Bringas, Daniel '76 (FRS) Wasco, CA Prison Facility.
Brink, Joseph C. '63 (COV) Alexandria, KY St. Mary of the Assumption Church.
Brinker, Brian J. '88 (RVC) Holbrook, NY Good Shepherd Church.
Brinker, Louis B. '50 (COV) Cynthiana, KY St. Edward Church.

Brinker, Maurice J. '54 (LEX) Retired; [F] Versailles, KY Taylor Manor Nursing Home.
Brinker, Paul J. '36 (COV) Dayton, KY St. Bernard Church; Retired.
Brinker, William *c.s.c.* '46 (CHI) [D] Niles, IL Notre Dame High School.
Brinkman, Barry '91 (SAL) [3] Salina, KS St. Mary's Church.
Brinkman, Charles J. *c.ss.r.* '56 (RIC) [N] Hampton, VA Holy Family Retreat.
Brinkman, Charles J. '77 (PH) [3] Philadelphia, PA St. Agatha-St. James Church; [EE] Philadelphia, PA Newman Center at Drexel University; [EE] Philadelphia, PA Newman Center at Drexel University; [EE] Philadelphia, PA Newman Center at Drexel University.
Brinkman, James J. '81 (SUP) Farmington, WI Assumption of the Blessed Virgin Mary Church; Somerset, WI St. Anne Church.
Brinkman, John T. *m.m.* '71 (NY) [DD] Maryknoll, NY Maryknoll Fathers and Brothers.
Brinkman, Terence *s.t.d.* '73 (GAL) Kingwood, TX St. Martha Church.
Brinkman, Terence P. '73 (GAL) [U] Houston, TX Martha's Kitchen Food Services.
Brinkmann, Frederick C. *c.ss.r.* '75 (NY) [HH] Esopus, NY Holy Shroud Guild.
Brinkmann, Frederick C. *c.ss.r.* '75 (ROC) [K] Canandaigua, NY Notre Dame Retreat House.
Brinkmann, Gerard J. *c.ss.r.* '61 (PH) [25] Philadelphia, PA St. Boniface Church.
Brinkmann, Herman *c.ss.r.* '54 (PH) [136] Philadelphia, PA St. Peter the Apostle Church.
Brinkmoeller, David E. '71 (CIN) [5] Dayton, OH Ascension Church.
Brinn, Adrian '68 (SB) Palm Springs, CA Our Lady of Guadalupe Church.
Brinn, John J. '62 (NY) [2] Poughkeepsie, NY St. Mary Church.
Brinsmade, John F. '81 (HRT) [1] Manchester, CT Assumption Church.
Briody, Hugh J. '63 (SUP) Retired.
Briody, Msgr. Thomas '39 (SD) Retired.
Briones, Jose Maria '94 (TLS) [6] Tulsa, OK St. Francis Xavier Church.
Brioni, Luigi *s.x.* '61 (OAK) [N] Berkeley, CA Salesian Community.
Brioschi, Thomas H. '86 (STP) [29] St. Paul, MN St. Pascal Baylon Church.
Brioso, Luis *c.m.* '93 (PCE) [14] Ponce, PR San Vicente-Cantera Church.
Briscoe, Orville '84 (NSH) Retired.
Briseno, Miguel *o.f.m.conv.* '90 (SAT) [B] San Antonio, TX San Damiano Friary, Prenovitiate House of Formation; [C] San Antonio, TX Our Lady of the Lake University; [M] San Antonio, TX San Damiano Friary.
Briseno, Pedro '81 (BWN) Ranchito, TX St. Ignatius Church; [I] Harlingen, TX KMBH-TV 60/KHID-FM 88.1/KMBH-FM 88.9.
Briske, Larry F. '64 (MIL) On Duty Outside the Archdiocese.
Brislin, Thomas *c.p.* '68 (FgM) Passionist Foreign Missions.
Brisotti, William F. '68 (RVC) Wyandanch, NY Our Lady of the Miraculous Medal Church.
Brissette, Eugene C. *s.j.* '51 (BO) [W] Weston, MA Campion Health Center, Inc.
Brissette, Reginald R. '63 (PRT) Biddeford, ME St. Andre's Church.
Brisson, Robert A. '85 (NY) [II] New York, NY Prelature of the Holy Cross and Opus Dei.
Bristow, David '98 (FWT) Bedford, TX St. Michael Church.
Brito, Cristiano Aparecido *o.s.b.* '91 (GBG) [H] Latrobe, PA Saint Vincent Archabbey.
Brito, Lawrence R. '00 (SFE) [1] Santa Fe, NM The Cathedral of San Francisco de Asis.
Britt, Jerome C. '82 (COV) Burlington, KY Immaculate Heart of Mary Church.
Britt, William J. '53 (STL) Retired.
Brittain, Gerald W. '62 (MIL) West Bend, WI Holy Angels Church.
Britto, Msgr. Federico A. '82 (PH) [39] Philadelphia, PA Saint Cyprian Church.
Britz, Francis '55 (SCL) Mayhew Lake, MN Annunciation Church.
Britz, Gerald F. '48 (DET) Retired.
Brixius, Hilary R. '68 (WIN) Worthington, MN St. Mary's Church.
Brizzolara, Andrew *c.s.* '75 (HRT) [15] New Haven, CT St. Michael's Church.
Broach, Richard '77 (MIL) On Leave.
Broadhurst, T. Paul *c.s.b.* '60 (ROC) [I] Rochester, NY Basilian Residence.
Brobst, James *o.m.i.* '90 (SAT) [B] San Antonio, TX George Sexton House of Studies.
Brobst, Richard A. '65 (Y) Boardman, OH St. Luke Church.
Brocato, Robert (SJ) Graduate Studies.
Broccolo, Gerard T. '65 (CHI) On Duty Outside the Archdiocese.
Brochu, Albert E. *a.a.* '43 (WOR) [N] Worcester, MA Assumptionists (Augustinians of the Assumption).
Brochu, Gerard H. '50 (BUR) Retired.
Brock, Bill (DEN) [32] Denver, CO St. James Church.
Brock, David F. '56 (DET) Retired.
Brock, John '62 (JKS) Grenada, MS St. Peter Church.
Brock, William '91 (DEN) [35] Denver, CO St. Mary Magdalene's Church.
Brocke, George '89 (LC) [D] Stevens Point, WI St. Michael's Hospital of Stevens Point, Inc.
Brockel, Kenneth E. '69 (JC) Perry, MO St. William Church.
Brockett, Norman L. '87 (HRT) Cheshire, CT Church of the Epiphany.
Brockhaus, Msgr. Edward '64 (SD) Lemon Grove, CA St. John of the Cross Church.
Brockhaus, Thomas Aq. *o.s.b.* '39 (P) [L] St. Benedict, OR Mt. Angel Abbey.
Brockland, John '91 (STL) Hazelwood, MO St. Bartholomew Church.
Brockland, Robert J. *c.m.* '74 (STL) [P] Perryville, MO Congregation of The Mission.
Brockman, Blaise '77 (LA) Santa Clarita, CA Blessed Kateri Tekakwitha Church.
Brockman, David D. '90 (R) [6] Raleigh, NC St. Luke the Evangelist Church.
Brockman, Leon *o.c.s.o.* '55 (SPC) [E] Ava, MO Assumption Abbey (Trappist).
Brockman, Norbert *s.m.* '73 (SAT) [M] San Antonio, TX Marianist Woodlawn Community.
Brockman, Norbert C. *s.m.* '73 (CIN) [M] Dayton, OH Marianist Provincialate.
Brockman, Norbert C. *s.m.* '73 (SAT) [C] San Antonio, TX St. Mary's University of San Antonio, Texas.
Brockson, Scott '96 (ARE) Barceloneta, PR Church of Our Lady of Mt. Carmel.
Brockson, Scott D. '96 (PH) On Duty Outside the Archdiocese.
Broderick, Gerald '42 (BAL) [O] Timonium, MD Stella Maris.
Broderick, Msgr. Gerard W. '42 (BAL) Retired.
Broderick, James M. '60 (BO) [8] Haverhill, MA Sacred Hearts Church; Senior Priests.
Broderick, John F. *s.j.* '45 (BO) [W] Weston, MA Campion Jesuit Community; [W] Weston, MA Campion Health Center, Inc.
Broderick, Msgr. Kilian J. '67 (DAL) Coppell, TX St. Ann Church.
Broderick, Leo P. '56 (DET) Retired.
Broderick, Michael '87 (WOR) Whitinsville, MA St. Patrick's Church.
Broderick, Richard '70 (ALB) Albany, NY Albany County Jail.
Broderick, Richard J. '70 (ALB) Special Assignment.
Broderick, William '49 (SAC) Carmichael, CA Our Lady of the Assumption Church; Retired and in Senior Ministry.
Brodersen, Msgr. Charles F. '48 (OM) Retired.
Brodersen, Steven W. '85 (SC) Algona, IA St. Cecelia Church.
Broderson, Donald '68 (OAK) Retired.
Brodeur, Dennis A. '77 (PRO) On Duty Outside the Diocese.
Brodeur, Henry *m.s.* '66 (FR) Brewster, MA Our Lady of the Cape Church.
Brodeur, Scott N. *s.j.* '90 (BO) [W] Boston, MA The Society of Jesus of New England-Provincial Offices.
Brodeur, Theodore J. '66 (MAR) [1] Sault Sainte Marie, MI Holy Name of Mary Church; Sugar Island, MI Sacred Heart Church.
Brodfuehrer, Robert S. '45 (CHI) [45] Chicago, IL St. Cornelius Church; [62] Chicago, IL St. Francis Borgia Church; Retired.
Brodniak, Anthony B. *m.m.* '54 (FgM) Maryknoll Foreign Missions.
Brodnick, Edward J. '76 (COV) Union, KY St. Timothy Church.
Brodnick, Joseph '69 (CLV) Absent on Leave.
Brodnick, Joseph '69 (ROC) Elmira, NY Elmira Correctional Facility, Center and Camp Monterey.
Brodnick, Joseph F. '69 (ROC) [3] Elmira, NY St. Mary Church; Elmira, NY St. Joseph Hospital.
Brody, Donald *o.f.m.cap.* '47 (GB) [I] Appleton, WI St. Fidelis Friary.
Brodzeller, Robert E. *s.j.* '63 (OM) [K] Omaha, NE Jesuit Community at Creighton University.
Broering, Joseph H. '53 (COV) Retired.
Broering, Raymond L. '53 (COV) Retired.
Broering, Victor F. '42 (CIN) Retired.
Brogan, Hugh T. '69 (WDC) Retired.
Brogan, John F. '75 (BRK) [80] Brooklyn, NY St. Martin of Tours-Fourteen Holy Martyrs Church; [Z] Brooklyn, NY Society of the Immaculate Conception of Brooklyn.
Brogan, Leo '67 (PHX) [3] Tempe, AZ Resurrection Church.
Brogan, Malachy *o.f.m.* '57 (CIN) [M] Cincinnati, OH St. Francis Seraph Friary.
Brogan, Malachy *o.f.m.* '57 (FgM) Franciscan Foreign Missions.
Brogan, Neal E. '66 (TLS) Retired.
Brogan, Paul '94 (LA) Woodland Hills, CA St. Bernardine of Siena Church.
Brogan, William '68 (NY) Absent on Leave.
Brogley, Charles F. *s.m.* '44 (WDC) [M] Washington, DC Marist Center.
Broglio, Msgr. Timothy '77 (CLV) Released from Diocesan Assignment.
Brogus, Albert G. '45 (SCR) Retired.
Brohammer, Ronald '60 (MIA) Retired.
Broker, John A. *c.ss.r.* '44 (MIL) [S] Oconomowoc, WI The Redemptorist Retreat Center.
Broker, William *c.ss.r.* '49 (MIL) [S] Oconomowoc, WI The Redemptorist Retreat Center.
Brokman, James P. '97 (DUB) [4] Cedar Rapids, IA St. Jude Church.
Brom, D. Giles (PEO) Retired.
Bromenshenkel, Fintan *o.s.b.* '45 (FgM) American - Cassinese Congregation Foreign Missions.
Bromenshenkel, Fintan *o.s.b.* '45 (SCL) [I] Collegeville, MN St. John's Abbey, of the Order of St. Benedict.
Bromenshenkel, Silvan *o.s.b.* '47 (SCL) [I] Collegeville, MN St. John's Abbey, of the Order of St. Benedict.
Bromley, Vincent M. '65 (SUP) Radisson, WI Sacred Heart Church; Winter, WI St. Peter Church.
Bromschwig, Arthur (STL) [O] St. Louis, MO Mother of Good Counsel Home.
Bromschwig, Arthur F. '50 (STL) Retired.
Bronder, Joseph P. *o.s.b.* '69 (GBG) [H] Latrobe, PA Saint Vincent Archabbey.
Broniak, Leonard *c.ss.r.* '79 (GAL) [34] Houston, TX Holy Ghost Church.
Bronk, Philip *s.t.* '51 (SD) La Mesa, CA Little Flower Haven; [G] La Mesa, CA Little Flower Haven.
Bronkiewicz, Msgr. Laurence R. '73 (BGP) Westport, CT Assumption Church.
Brooker, Richard L. *m.m.* '55 (FgM) Maryknoll Foreign Missions.
Brooks, Armand L. (Bud) '97 (FAR) St. John, ND St. John the Baptist Church.
Brooks, Bryan V. '93 (TLS) Okmulgee, OK St. Anthony's Church.
Brooks, Charles R. '65 (GB) Mackville, WI St. Edward Church.
Brooks, David R. *s.j.* '78 (WDC) [E] Washington, DC Gonzaga College High School.
Brooks, Edwin *s.j.* '39 (NY) [DD] New York, NY Murray-Weigel Hall.
Brooks, Jeddie P. '77 (SPR) Monson, MA St. Patrick's Church.
Brooks, John E. *s.j.* '59 (WOR) [N] Worcester, MA Jesuits of Holy Cross College, Inc.
Brooks, Lawrence V. *s.j.* '74 (FgM) Provinces.
Brooks, Michael J. *ss.cc.* '61 (SB) Cathedral City, CA St. Louis Church.
Brooks, Robert C. '61 (ARL) Leesburg, VA St. John the Apostle Church.
Brooks, Robert E. '95 (SAC) Susanville, CA Sacred Heart Church.
Brooks, Thomas M. '78 (E) [10] Erie, PA Our Lady of Peace Church.
Brooks, William C. '76 (AUS) [2] Austin, TX St. Albert The Great Church.
Broom, Edward *o.m.v.* '86 (LA) Hawaiian Gardens, CA St. Peter Chanel Church.
Brophy, Msgr. Charles D. '39 (GR) Retired.
Brophy, Edward '93 (BRK) [34] Brooklyn, NY St. Edmund's Church.
Brophy, John L. '69 (MIL) On Duty Outside the Archdiocese.
Brophy, Michael *s.j.* '69 (CIN) [M] Cincinnati, OH Jesuit Community at St. Xavier High School.
Brophy, Peter V. *o.f.m.* '85 (NY) [115] New York, NY St. Stephen of Hungary Church; [DD] New York, NY The Franciscan Vocation Ministry of Holy Name Province.
Brophy, R. Michael *s.j.* '69 (CIN) [F] Cincinnati, OH St. Xavier High School.
Brophy, Robert J. '56 (MAD) Retired.
Brosk, Steven J. '90 (NEW) Military Chaplains.
Broski, Mark *o.s.b.* '91 (KCK) [A] Atchison, KS Benedictine College; [H] Atchison, KS St. Benedict's Abbey.
Brosmer, Thomas J. '69 (COL) [32] Columbus, OH St. Michael Church.
Brosnan, Msgr. Dermot N. '57 (SAT) [U] San Antonio, TX The Patrician Movement.
Brosnan, Msgr. John R. '37 (LA) [44] Los Angeles, CA St. Ann Church; Retired.
Brosnan, Msgr. Liam P. '59 (SAT) [63] San Antonio, TX St. Pius X Church.
Brosnan, Thomas F. '81 (BRK) [21] Brooklyn, NY Blessed Sacrament Church.
Brossart, Scott *s.o.l.t.* '00 (CC) [H] Robstown, TX Society of Our Lady of the Most Holy Trinity.
Brost, Frederick '56 (SUP) Stetsonville, WI Sacred Heart of Jesus Church.
Brothersen, Maynard J. '48 (DAV) Retired; [M] Davenport, IA St. Vincent Center.

Brou, Francis R. *s.j.* '61 (BR) [11] Baton Rouge, LA Immaculate Conception Church; [K] Baton Rouge, LA Martin Luther King, Jr. Student Center.
Broudou, Joseph '96 (OM) [8] Sarpy Co., NE St. Bernadette Church.
Brougher, Douglas C. '62 (NO) [38] New Orleans, LA St. James Major Church; New Orleans, LA Touro Infirmary.
Brouillard, Donald *s.s.s.* '50 (NY) [55] New York, NY St. Jean Baptiste Church.
Brouillard, John '56 (P) Retired.
Brouillard, Louis A. (AGN) Retired.
Brouillette, Thomas '96 (LIN) North Platte, NE St. Elizabeth Ann Seton Church.
Brouke, Gabriel Vanden *ss.cc.* '48 (HON) [G] Kaneohe, HI Sacred Hearts Center.
Broussard, A. Rex '66 (LAF) Leroy, LA Our Lady of Perpetual Help Church.
Broussard, Dennis A. '91 (MAN) Keene, NH St. Margaret Mary Church.
Broussard, F. David '93 (LAF) Iota, LA St. Joseph Church.
Broussard, Henry J. '72 (LAF) Judice, LA St. Basil Church.
Broussard, Hubert C. '52 (HT) Retired.
Broussard, John S. *c.s.b.* '48 (GAL) Manvel, TX Sacred Heart of Jesus Church.
Broussard, Kenneth M. '76 (LAF) Absent on Leave.
Broussard, Oris '60 (LKC) Jennings, LA Immaculate Conception Church; [C] Lake Charles, LA Holy City Community.
Broussard, Paul '98 (LAF) [5] Lafayette, LA Our Lady of Fatima Church.
Broussard, Richard Dale '00 (LAF) [11] Lafayette, LA St. Genevieve Church.
Broussard, Ronald *v.g.* '88 (LAF) Duson, LA St. Benedict the Moor Church.
Broussard, Warren J. *s.j.* '88 (LAF) [A] Grand Coteau, LA St. Charles College.
Broussard, Msgr. William L. '56 (AUS) [O] Austin, TX Texas Conference of Catholic Health Facilities.
Broussard, Msgr. William L. '56 (GAL) On Duty Outside the Diocese.
Brouwers, Hans A.L. (PH) [C] Immaculata, PA Immaculata College.
Brovdou, Joseph '96 (OM) [B] Omaha, NE Daniel J. Gross Catholic High School of Omaha.
Brovey, Steven L. '91 (CHR) Taylors, SC Prince of Peace Church.
Brown, Msgr. Anthony M. '49 (HEL) Retired.
Brown, Arnold *o.f.m.* '49 (SP) [O] St. Petersburg, FL St. Anthony Friary.
Brown, Arthur A. '57 (BO) Health Leave.
Brown, Benedict J. '74 (L) Military Chaplains.
Brown, Charles *s.c.j.* '84 (MIL) [B] Hales Corners, WI Sacred Heart School of Theology; [P] Hales Corners, WI Priests of the Sacred Heart; [P] Milwaukee, WI St. Joseph House of Formation.
Brown, Charles '87 (PSC) Retired.
Brown, Charles '89 (NY) On Duty Outside the Archdiocese.
Brown, Charles C. '58 (SFE) Los Alamos, NM Immaculate Heart of Mary Church.
Brown, Charles D. '93 (GR) Weare Twp., MI St. Joseph's Church.
Brown, Charles E. '71 (WDC) Burtonsville, MD Resurrection Church.
Brown, Charles L. '73 (BRK) Absent on Leave.
Brown, Charles L., III '67 (WIL) Bear, DE St. Elizabeth Ann Seton Church.
Brown, David G. *o.s.b.* '75 (CHL) [J] Belmont, NC Belmont Abbey.
Brown, David M. *o.s.m.* '48 (CHI) [17] Chicago, IL Assumption of the Blessed Virgin Mary Church; [N] Chicago, IL Order of Friar Servants of Mary (Servites) United States of America Province, Inc.
Brown, Dennis '89 (RCK) [2] Aurora, IL Holy Angels Church; [M] Aurora, IL Association of the Communications Congregation.
Brown, Dom Lawrence *o.s.b.* '84 (BUR) [F] Westfield, VT Monastery of the Immaculate Heart of Mary.
Brown, Edward J. *m.s.* '81 (RVC) [P] Rockville Centre, NY The Campus Parish of Long Island.
Brown, Eugene M. '60 (NU) Marshall, MN Holy Redeemer Church.
Brown, Everett *s.m.m.* '61 (BRK) [V] Ozone Park, NY Montfort Missionaries Provincialate (Missionaries of the Company of Mary) - Formation Community.
Brown, Francis E. '64 (BO) On Duty Outside the Archdiocese.
Brown, George *o.m.i.* '64 (BO) [W] Lowell, MA Missionary Oblates of Mary Immaculate.
Brown, George *o.m.i.* '64 (MAN) [K] Les Cayes, Haiti Paroisse Ste. Anne.
Brown, Gerald *s.s.* '64 (SAT) [C] San Antonio, TX Oblate School of Theology.
Brown, Gerald J. *c.m.* '57 (SPC) Charleston, MO St. Henry Church.
Brown, Gerald L. '64 (SAT) [A] San Antonio, TX The Assumption-St. John's Seminary.
Brown, Gerard J. '46 (TR) Leave of Absence.
Brown, Harold C. *c.pp.s.* '59 (TOL) Glandorf, OH St. John the Baptist Church.
Brown, Henry P. '51 (IND) Retired.
Brown, Isaac Jogues *o.s.b.* '84 (P) [L] St. Benedict, OR Mt. Angel Abbey.
Brown, James '62 (BWN) [4] Pharr, TX St. Margaret Mary Church.
Brown, James '97 (NEW) New Milford, NJ Ascension Church.
Brown, James E. '72 (TOL) Marblehead, OH St. Joseph Church.
Brown, James J. '62 (L) On Duty Outside the Archdiocese.
Brown, James V. *o.a.r.* '46 (OM) [21] Omaha, NE St. James Church.
Brown, John J. '83 (BRK) [120] Brooklyn, NY Queen of All Saints Church.
Brown, John T. '48 (STP) Retired.
Brown, John T. *glmy.* '84 (TLS) Idabel, OK St. Francis De Sales Church.
Brown, Joseph A. *s.j.* '72 (MIL) [P] Milwaukee, WI Jesuit Provincial Office, Wisconsin Province.
Brown, Joseph E. *s.j.* '56 (STL) [C] St. Louis, MO Saint Louis University; [P] St. Louis, MO Jesuit Community Corporation at St. Louis University - Jesuit Hall.
Brown, Joseph L. *c.pp.s.* '97 (IND) St. Anne, IN St. Anne Church; St. Joseph, IN St. Joseph Church.
Brown, Joseph L. *c.pp.s.* '97 (OAK) [N] San Leandro, CA Society of the Precious Blood.
Brown, Joseph Mary '97 (PEO) [N] Peoria, IL Congregation of St. John; [P] Peoria, IL Newman Foundation at Bradley University & Illinois Central College.
Brown, Justin *o.s.b.* '90 (NO) [P] St. Benedict, LA St. Joseph Abbey.
Brown, Kenneth '77 (STL) [47] St. Louis, MO St. Margaret of Scotland Church.
Brown, Konstantin K. '88 (ROM) Special Assignment or On Duty Outside the Diocese.
Brown, Leonard J. *c.m.f.* '82 (CHI) [N] Chicago, IL Claretian Missionaries, St. Jude League, Inc.; [N] Oak Park, IL Claretian Fathers Headquarters of U.S.A. Eastern Province; [N] Oak Park, IL Claretian Fathers Headquarters of U.S.A. Eastern Province.
Brown, Lewis '67 (ROC) On Duty Outside the Diocese.
Brown, Lewis E. '67 (ROC) Military Chaplains.
Brown, Matthew F. '63 (SY) Vestal, NY Our Lady of Sorrows Church; Vestal, NY Binghamton Nursing Homes; Special Assignment.
Brown, Matthew J. *o.s.b.* '49 (OKL) Konawa, OK Sacred Heart Church; [I] Shawnee, OK St. Gregory's Abbey.
Brown, Michael *o.carm.* '93 (FgM) Carmelite Foreign Missions.
Brown, Michael *o.carm.* '93 (JOL) [J] Darien, IL Carmelite Provincial Office.
Brown, Michael J. '89 (ROC) Mount Morris, NY St. Patrick Church.
Brown, Michael O. '74 (TOL) [3] Toledo, OH Christ the King Church.
Brown, Michael R. '89 (ROC) Corning, NY St. Mary Church; Corning, NY St. Patrick Church; Corning, NY St. Vincent de Paul Church; Nunda, NY Holy Angels Church; Painted Post, NY Immaculate Heart of Mary Church.
Brown, Ned *l.c.* '98 (DET) [T] Bloomfield Hills, MI Logos, Inc. (Michigan).
Brown, Nicholas *s.c.j.* '76 (SAT) San Antonio, TX St. Luke's Baptist Hospital; University Hospital; [B] San Antonio, TX Priests of the Sacred Heart-House of Formation; [M] San Antonio, TX Hospital Ministry House.
Brown, Patrick '66 (PAT) On Duty Outside the Diocese.
Brown, Patrick *o.c.s.o.* '74 (WOR) [N] Spencer, MA St. Joseph's Abbey.
Brown, Msgr. Patrick E. '78 (PAT) Stirling, NJ St. Vincent de Paul Church; Morristown, NJ Morris County Jail.
Brown, Patrick M. *o.f.m.* '59 (PAT) [M] Butler, NJ St. Anthony Friary.
Brown, Phillip '89 (BIS) [5] Dickinson, ND St. Wenceslaus Church.
Brown, Richard '80 (DAL) Absent on Leave.
Brown, Richard H. *s.j.* '58 (SD) [12] San Diego, CA Our Lady of Guadalupe Church.
Brown, Robert '63 (SC) Maple River, IA St. Francis of Assisi Church; Mount Carmel, IA Our Lady of Mt. Carmel Church.
Brown, Robert A. '42 (L) Howardstown, KY St. Ann Church; Retired.
Brown, Robert A. *o.s.f.s.* '67 (ARL) Reston, VA St. John Neumann Church.
Brown, Msgr. Robert L. '69 (NOR) Montville, CT St. John Church; On Special or Other Diocesan Assignment.
Brown, Robert W. '66 (ORL) [10] Orlando, FL St. Joseph Church.
Brown, Roderick M. *o.p.* '79 (BUF) [49] Buffalo, NY St. Martin de Porres Church.
Brown, Roderick M. *o.p.* '79 (CHI) [N] Chicago, IL Dominicans (Provincial Office).
Brown, Shaun '94 (NTN) Military Chaplains.
Brown, Stephen *s.v.d.* (STL) [53] St. Louis, MO St. Nicholas Church.
Brown, Steven P. '77 (SJ) Alviso, CA Our Lady, Star of the Sea Church; Special Assignment.
Brown, Sylvester F. '56 (WIN) Janesville, MN St. Ann's Church.
Brown, Theophile W. *o.s.b.* '50 (RIC) [L] Richmond, VA Mary Mother of the Church Abbey.
Brown, Thomas *o.m.i.* '55 (FgM) Oblates Foreign Missions.
Brown, Thomas E. '78 (E) Corry, PA St. Thomas The Apostle Church; Corry, PA St. Elizabeth Church.
Brown, Thomas J. '99 (GR) [2] Muskegon, MI St. Francis de Sales Church.
Brown, Timothy B. *s.j.* '86 (BAL) [B] Baltimore, MD Loyola College in Maryland; [S] Baltimore, MD Jesuit Community of Loyola College, Inc.
Brown, Timothy T. '88 (ROC) [1] Rochester, NY Sacred Heart Church.
Brown, Victor *o.p.* '63 (NO) [30] New Orleans, LA St. Dominic Church.
Brown, Vincent A. '34 (BRK) Retired.
Brown, Vincent A. '57 (HRT) Branford, CT St. Mary Church.
Brown, W. P. '80 (PT) Bayou George, FL Our Lady of the Rosary Church.
Brown, W.T. St. John '92 (CC) Retired.
Brown, Walter W. '94 (JKS) Woodville, MS St. Joseph Church.
Brown, Warren *o.m.i.* '82 (SAT) [C] San Antonio, TX Oblate School of Theology.
Brown, Wayland Y. '77 (SAV) Unassigned.
Brown, William E. '88 (SFR) Daly City, CA Our Lady of Mercy Church.
Brown, William J. '55 (SY) [S] Syracuse, NY St. Pius X Home, Inc.
Brown, William Joseph '99 (IND) [24] Indianapolis, IN St. Lawrence Church; [C] Indianapolis, IN Bishop Chatard High School.
Brown, William M. *o.m.v.* '94 (BO) [B] Boston, MA Our Lady of Grace Seminary; [B] Boston, MA Oblate Provincialate; [FF] Boston, MA Lanteri Charitable Trust.
Brown, William P. '80 (PT) Fountain, FL Our Lady Queen of Peace Church.
Browne, Denis P. *m.m.* '47 (FgM) Maryknoll Foreign Missions.
Browne, Dennis '79 (SJ) On Leave of Absence.
Browne, Msgr. Edward P. '51 (ARL) [1] Alexandria, VA Blessed Sacrament Church; Retired.
Browne, Francis J. *c.ss.r.* '68 (HRT) [5] Enfield, CT St. Patrick's Church.
Browne, George (DET) [1] Eastpointe, MI St. Barnabas Church.
Browne, George '55 (DET) Marine City, MI Holy Cross Church; Retired.
Browne, George E. *c.m.* '46 (PH) [AA] Philadelphia, PA Congregation of the Mission.
Browne, Gerald '81 (MET) [3] Carteret, NJ Sacred Heart Church.
Browne, Msgr. J. Patrick '67 (SJ) [1] San Jose, CA Cathedral Basilica of St. Joseph.
Browne, John T. *o.s.b.* '56 (NEW) Maplewood, NJ St. Joseph's Church; [N] Newark, NJ Newark Abbey.
Browne, Joseph P. *c.s.c.* '55 (P) [8] Portland, OR St. Birgitta Church; [L] Portland, OR Holy Cross Fathers & Brothers, C.S.C. - University of Portland.
Browne, Joseph T. *s.j.* '56 (NY) [FF] Staten Island, NY Mount Manresa Jesuit Retreat House.
Browne, Michael E. *s.j.* '71 (NEW) [C] Jersey City, NJ St. Peter's Preparatory School.
Browne, Robert M. '61 (BO) Stoneham, MA St. Patrick Church.
Browne, Ronald '91 (DET) Special Assignment; [A] Detroit, MI Sacred Heart Major Seminary, Inc.
Browne, Stanley T. (GB) Lakewood, WI St. Mary of the Lake Church.
Browne, Vincent T. '54 (MAD) Retired.
Brownell, Patrick P. '94 (KNX) Crossville, TN St. Alphonsus Church.
Brownell, Robert A. '69 (RIC) [18] Richmond, VA St. Peter Church.
Brownfield, Frowin '56 (SPC) Retired.
Brownfield, Robert L. '92 (DAV) Retired; [M] Iowa City, IA O'Keefe Hall.
Brownholtz, George J. *o.s.f.s.* '69 (FgM) Oblates of St. Francis de Sales Foreign Missions.
Brownholtz, George J. *o.s.f.s.* '69 (WIL) [I] Childs, MD Oblates of St. Francis De Sales.
Browning, Joseph E. *s.j.* '54 (NO) [P] New Orleans, LA Ignatius Residence.
Browning, Thomas *s.s.c.* '90 (FgM) St. Columban's Foreign Mission.
Browning, William *c.p.* '49 (CHI) [N] Chicago, IL Daneo Hall.
Brownsey, Brian '96 (PEO) Pekin, IL St. Joseph's Church.
Brownstein, Donald '81 (COS) [13] Colorado Springs, CO St. Patrick's Church.
Broxmeyer, Dominic *o.s.b.* '45 (P) [L] St. Benedict, OR Mt. Angel Abbey.

Brozat, Charles *s.a.* '57 (NY) [DD] Garrison, NY Franciscan Friars of the Atonement, Minister General Office.
Brozena, Joseph M. '58 (SCR) [3] Old Forge, PA St. Michael's Church.
Brozonowicz, Gregorsz '96 (NOR) Putnam, CT St. Mary Church.
Brubaker, Claude E. '55 (VEN) [5] Sarasota, FL St. Michael the Archangel Church.
Brubaker, George J. '80 (WIL) Milford, DE St. John the Apostle Church; Wilmington, DE Delaware Air National Guard.
Brubaker, Scott '82 (PHX) [22] Phoenix, AZ Our Lady of the Valley Church.
Bruce, Joseph J. *s.j.* '81 (BO) [43] Boston, MA St. Mary of the Angels Church; [W] Boston, MA Loyola House; [W] Boston, MA The Society of Jesus of New England-Provincial Offices.
Bruce, Robert J. '64 (Y) Retired.
Bruce, Terry '67 (KC) [1] Independence, MO St. Ann's Church.
Bruch, James A. '65 (SC) Milford, IA St. Joseph's Church.
Bruch, Lynn (SC) Fort Dodge, IA Holy Rosary Church.
Bruch, Walter L. '50 (SC) Retired.
Bruck, Donald '68 (DM) Hamburg, IA St. Mary Church; Shenandoah, IA St. Mary Church.
Bruck, Raymond E. '58 (GR) Retired.
Brucker, G. Fredrick '76 (GR) Greenville, MI St. Charles Church; On Special Assignment.
Brucker, George W. '56 (ALB) [16] Schenectady, NY St. Paul the Apostle Church.
Bruckner, Ronald L. '65 (SFE) [1] Albuquerque, NM Annunciation Church.
Brucksch, James L. '69 (GAY) Oscoda, MI Sacred Heart Church.
Brucz, James M. *c.s.p.* '74 (CHR) Clemson, SC St. Andrew Church; [H] Clemson, SC Clemson University, Southern Wesleyan University.
Bruder, John W. *o.c.s.o.* '56 (BUR) Other Residence.
Brudzynski, Peter F. '50 (BO) Senior Priests.
Brudzynski, Peter F. '50 (VEN) [1] Venice, FL Epiphany Church.
Bruecken, Albert *o.s.b.* '77 (KC) [A] Conception, MO Conception Seminary College; [J] Conception, MO Conception Abbey; [N] Conception, MO Conception Benedictine Trust.
Bruemmer, Joseph A. '48 (CIN) Withamsville, OH St. Thomas More Church; Retired.
Bruemmer, Joseph J. *o.s.c.* '47 (PHX) [G] Phoenix, AZ Crosier Community of Phoenix (Canons Regular of the Order of the Holy Cross).
Bruening, Allen '51 (CLV) Retired.
Bruening, Bernard H. '59 (CIN) Miamisburg, OH Our Lady of Good Hope Church.
Bruening, Joseph B. '53 (CIN) Franklin, OH St. Mary Church.
Bruetsch, Joseph J. '70 (LFT) [1] Lafayette, IN St. Mary Church; Retired.
Bruggeman, Donald R. '62 (DUB) [6] Dubuque, IA Church of the Resurrection.
Bruggeman, Gerald H. '49 (COS) Retired; [C] Colorado Springs, CO Penrose-St. Francis Health Services.
Brugger, Craig F. '73 (PH) [55] Philadelphia, PA St. Helena Church.
Brugger, Donald E. *s.j.* '70 (CHI) [C] Chicago, IL Jesuit Community at Loyola University of Chicago.
Brugger, Msgr. Robert L. '68 (E) [21] Erie, PA St. Jude the Apostle Church.
Brugli, Msgr. Angelo F. '47 (BRK) Retired.
Brum, Louis (BWN) [D] San Juan, TX San Juan Nursing Home.
Brum, Louis L. '74 (BWN) Alamo, TX Resurrection Church.
Brumleve, Matthew '88 (KC) [6] St. Joseph, MO St. Patrick's Church; Easton, MO St. Joseph's Church.
Brummel, Mark *c.m.f.* '60 (CHI) [X] Chicago, IL Villa Guadalupe Senior Services Corporation.
Brummel, Mark J. *c.m.f.* '60 (CHI) [N] Chicago, IL Claretian Missionaries, St. Jude League, Inc.; [N] Oak Park, IL Claretian Fathers Headquarters of U.S.A. Eastern Province.
Brummer, Lawrence *o.f.m.* '58 (SAT) [69] San Antonio, TX San Francisco de la Espada Church.
Brundage, John '70 (MET) Highland Park, NJ St. Paul the Apostle Church.
Brundage, Thomas T. '88 (MIL) Special Assignment; [B] Hales Corners, WI Sacred Heart School of Theology; [Y] Milwaukee, WI St. Thomas More Lawyers Society.
Brune, James '48 (EVN) Retired.
Brune, Meinrad *o.s.b.* '61 (IND) [J] St. Meinrad, IN St. Meinrad Archabbey.
Brunelle, J. Ernest *m.m.* '59 (NY) [DD] Maryknoll, NY Maryknoll Fathers and Brothers.
Brunelle, Richard *a.a.* '63 (BO) [W] Boston, MA Assumptionist Center.
Brunet, Msgr. Frederic J. '60 (HT) Chauvin, LA St. Joseph Church.
Brunet, Gerald O. *o.m.i.* '57 (SEA) Forks, WA St. Anne Church; Seattle, WA Callum Bay Correction Center; Seattle, WA Olympic/Clearwater Correction Center.
Brunet, Jules A. '55 (BR) White Castle, LA Our Lady of Prompt Succor Church.
Brunett, John L. *s.j.* '55 (BAL) [B] Baltimore, MD Loyola College in Maryland; [S] Baltimore, MD Jesuit Community of Loyola College, Inc.
Brunette, Bernard M. *o.praem.* '51 (GB) [I] De Pere, WI St. Norbert Abbey.
Brunette, Larry H. '99 (SFD) Collinsville, IL SS. Peter and Paul Church.
Bruney, J. Lawrence '84 (PIT) [23] Pittsburgh, PA St. Louise de Marillac Church.
Brungandt, John B. '98 (WCH) [4] Wichita, KS Christ the King Church.
Brungardt, Aloysius '71 (SAL) Junction City, KS St. Francis Xavier's Church.
Brungardt, John B. '98 (WCH) [B] Wichita, KS Bishop Mark K. Carroll Catholic High School.
Brungs, Robert A. *s.j.* '64 (STL) [C] St. Louis, MO Saint Louis University; [P] St. Louis, MO Jesuit Community Corporation at St. Louis University - Jesuit Hall; [V] St. Louis, MO Institute for Theological Encounter with Science & Technology (ITEST).
Bruni, John E. '76 (CAM) Gibbstown, NJ St. Michael's Church.
Brunick, Charles J. *c.s.p.* '70 (CHI) [122] Chicago, IL Old St. Mary Church.
Bruning, David R. '78 (TOL) [21] Toledo, OH St. Clement Church.
Bruning, William '93 (KCK) Blue Rapids, KS St. Elizabeth Church; Frankfort, KS Annunciation Church; Waterville, KS St. Monica's Church.
Brunkan, Msgr. Walter L. '56 (DUB) Greene, IA St. Mary's Church; Roseville, IA St. Mary Church.
Brunner, Frank J. '55 (WH) Retired.
Brunner, Msgr. James C. '54 (VIC) [5] Victoria, TX St. Mary's Church.
Brunner, John H. '62 (NU) Fairfax, MN St. Andrew Church; Fairfax, MN St. Andrew Church; Franklin, MN Sacred Heart Church.
Brunner, Thomas J. '74 (CIN) Troy, OH St. Patrick Church.
Brunner, William M. *s.s.c.* '62 (SB) Needles, CA St. Ann Church.
Brunnert, Jude *m.s.* '64 (LKC) Oberlin, LA St. Joan of Arc Church.
Brunnert, Theodore J. '54 (STL) Sullivan, MO St. Anthony Church.
Bruno, Anthony J. '68 (HRT) [2] Enfield, CT St. Adalbert's Church.
Bruno, John *r.c.j.* '74 (LA) [Q] North Hills, CA Rogationist Fathers.
Bruno, Robert *o.f.m.* '77 (CIN) [M] Cincinnati, OH St. Francis Seraph Friary.
Bruno, Robert *o.f.m.* '77 (FgM) Franciscan Foreign Missions.
Brunovsky, Michael *o.s.b.* '93 (CLV) [D] Cleveland, OH Benedictine High School; [O] Cleveland, OH Benedictine Order of Cleveland.
Brunovsky, Stephen K. '92 (CLV) Hudson, OH St. Mary Church.
Bruns, Wilbert H. *c.m.* '51 (STL) [P] St. Louis, MO Lazarist Residence.
Brunskill, Richard W. '83 (PEO) Chatsworth, IL SS. Peter and Paul Church; Cullom, IL St. John's Church.
Brunsman, Barry *o.f.m.* '56 (OAK) [P] Danville, CA San Damiano Retreat.
Brunton, Daniel B. '60 (SPR) Lenox, MA St. Ann's Church; Lenox Dale, MA St. Vincent de Paul's Church.
Brusato, Martin '89 (SAC) Absent on Leave.
Brusatti, Louis T. *c.m.* '75 (GAL) [A] Houston, TX St. Mary's Seminary; [C] Houston, TX University of St. Thomas.
Bruse, James C. '84 (ARL) Kilmarnock, VA St. Francis de Sales Church.
Bruso, Robert D. '93 (WOR) [1] Fitchburg, MA St. Anthony of Padua Church.
Brutus, Ferry '80 (MIA) North Miami, FL Holy Family Church.
Bryan, Francis E. '62 (IND) [B] Indianapolis, IN Marian College.
Bryan, Kevin J. '76 (L) On Special Assignment.
Bryan, Paul *c.ss.r.* '59 (HBG) [H] Ephrata, PA St. Clement's Mission House.
Bryant, Curtis *s.j.* '67 (LA) [C] Los Angeles, CA Loyola Marymount University.
Bryant, F. Michael '69 (WDC) [16] Washington, DC Holy Comforter—St. Cyprian Church; [V] Washington, DC District of Columbia Detention Facility.
Bryant, Michael '69 (WDC) Special Ministries; [V] Hyattsville, MD Prison Outreach Ministry.
Bryant, Michael M. '78 (SCR) [C] Dallas, PA College Misericordia.
Bryce, Edward M. '60 (PIT) [5] Pittsburgh, PA St. Bede Church.
Bryce, Vincent *o.p.* '57 (GR) Edmore, MI St. Margaret Mary Church; Stanton, MI St. Bernadette of Lourdes Church; [J] Edmore, MI Montcalm Community College Newman Center.
Bryce, Vincent W. *o.p.* '57 (CHI) [N] Chicago, IL Dominicans (Provincial Office).
Bryda, Ronald J. '66 (CLV) Litchfield, OH Our Lady Help of Christians Church.
Bryerton, Robert R. '74 (TUC) Sierra Vista, AZ Our Lady of the Mountains Church.
Bryk, Daren '00 (GAL) [72] Houston, TX Queen of Peace Church.
Bryk, John J. '53 (CLV) [3] Lakewood, OH St. Hedwig Church.
Bryl, Thaddeus (MIL) [N] Racine, WI St. Monica's Senior Citizens Home, Inc.
Bryl, Thaddeus J. '66 (MIL) Retired.
Brylinski, Bruce C. *glmy.* '83 (COV) Vanceburg, KY Holy Redeemer Church.
Brylinski, Bruce C. *glmy.* '83 (LEX) Grayson, KY Ss. John & Elizabeth Church.
Brylka, Vincent R. '65 (OAK) Martinez, CA St. Catherine of Siena Church.
Brynda, Msgr. Gerald J. '57 (TUC) Apache Junction, AZ St. George Church; Retired.
Brynes, John *o.s.a.* '55 (PH) [112] Philadelphia, PA St. Nicholas of Tolentine Church.
Bryon, Paul J. '46 (R) Retired.
Bryon, Thomas C. '63 (STL) [49] St. Louis, MO St. Mary Magdalen Church.
Bryson, John *s.m.* '53 (DET) [E] Harper Woods, MI Notre Dame High School.
Bryson, John H. (MAN) [J] Jaffrey, NH Good Shepherd Nursing Home.
Bryson, Robert C. '46 (BO) Senior Priests.
Brzek, Jon J. '83 (PIT) Military Chaplains.
Brzezicki, Zbigniew '88 (STF) Hamptonburgh, NY St. Andrew's Church.
Brzezinski, Hilary *o.f.m.* '76 (JKS) Greenwood, MS St. Francis of Assisi Church; Lexington, MS St. Thomas Church; Lexington, MS St. Thomas Church; [H] Goodman, MS Holmes Community College Newman Center.
Brzezinski, Jerome A. '69 (DET) Auburn Hills, MI St. John Fisher Chapel University Church; [S] Auburn Hills, MI St. John Fisher Chapel University Parish.
Brzezniak, Aurelian W. *o.f.m.conv.* '45 (BUF) [O] Athol Springs, NY St. Francis of Assisi Friary.
Brzezowski, Michael '00 (YAK) [1] Yakima, WA St. Paul Church.
Brzoska, David '00 (CHL) Huntersville, NC St. Mark Church.
Brzostowski, Hilary *o.f.m.conv.* '69 (NOR) Cromwell, CT St. John Church.
Brzozowski, Edward J. '44 (CHI) [140] Chicago, IL St. Nicholas of Tolentine Church; Retired.
Brzozowski, Simon *m.s.f.* '64 (STL) [O] St. Louis, MO Little Sisters of the Poor, Home for the Aged.
Buby, Bertrand A. *s.m.* '64 (CIN) [D] Dayton, OH The University of Dayton; [M] Dayton, OH Marianist Provincialate.
Bucaria, James A. '72 (SP) Masaryktown, FL St. Mary, Our Lady of Sorrows Church.
Bucaro, Michael '80 (SB) Chino, CA Southern Conservation Center.
Buccafurni, Ferdinand '58 (PH) [41] Philadelphia, PA St. Donato Church; [113] Philadelphia, PA Our Lady of Angels Church.
Buccellato, Sebastian *o.f.m.* '51 (NY) [DD] New York, NY Padua Friary.
Buccheri, Vincenzo *r.c.j.* '79 (LA) [Q] North Hills, CA Rogationist Fathers.
Bucchino, John *o.f.m.* '73 (NY) [DD] New York, NY Franciscan Province of the Immaculate Conception.
Bucci, Evan *o.f.m. conv.* '57 (TR) Seaside Heights, NJ Our Lady of Perpetual Help Church.
Bucci, Michael J. '62 (GBG) Retired.
Bucci, Richard A. '73 (PRO) [8] West Warwick, RI SS. Peter and Paul Church.
Bucciantini, Charles '72 (JKS) Cleveland, MS Our Lady of Victories Church; Rosedale, MS Sacred Heart Church; [H] Cleveland, MS Delta State University Newman Center.
Bucciarelli, Michael R. '75 (TUC) San Manuel, AZ St. Bartholomew Church.
Bucciarelli, Robert P. '60 (BO) [V] Cambridge, MA Opus Dei, Prelature of the Holy Cross and Opus Dei.
Buccicone, Ananius G. *o.s.b.* '93 (E) St. Marys, PA Sacred Heart of Jesus Church.
Bucciferro, Eugene '63 (JOL) [17] Joliet, IL St. Patrick Church.
Bucciferro, William *s.d.b.* (CHI) [103] Chicago, IL St. John Bosco Church.
Bucek, Timothy P. '76 (GAL) Bellville, TX SS. Peter & Paul Church.
Buchanan, Caleb A. '97 (BRK) [238] Queens, NY Sacred Heart Church.
Buchanan, David '93 (BIR) Florence, AL St. Joseph's Church; [H] Florence, AL University of North Alabama.
Buchanan, David '95 (BIR) [I] Florence, AL Society of St. Vincent de Paul, St. Joseph Conference.
Buchanan, Donald '45 (SD) Retired.
Buchanan, LCDR Donald E., CHC, USN '65 (IND) Retired.

Buchanan, Robert E. '68 (RNO) [2] Reno, NV Our Lady of the Snows Church.
Buchanan, Robert E. '68 (SB) On Duty Outside the Diocese.
Buchanan, Scott J. A. '97 (CHR) Summerton, SC St. Mary's Church.
Buchek, Basil '68 (STN) Tucson, AZ St. Michael Church.
Bucher, Mel *o.f.m.* '61 (SD) [H] Oceanside, CA Mission San Luis Rey; [K] Oceanside, CA Mission San Luis Rey Retreat.
Bucher, Otto N. *o.f.m.cap.* '59 (MIL) [B] Hales Corners, WI Sacred Heart School of Theology; [P] Milwaukee, WI St. Conrad Friary.
Bucher, Msgr. Philip A. '61 (SPC) Branson, MO Our Lady of the Lake Church.
Bucher, Raymond J. *o.f.m.* '64 (OAK) [P] Danville, CA San Damiano Retreat.
Buchette, Anthony J. '57 (BO) Senior Priests.
Buchheit, Edward '63 (BRK) [180] Queens, NY Immaculate Conception Church; [V] Jamaica, NY Immaculate Conception Monastery.
Buchheit, Msgr. Jerome J. '51 (STL) Ballwin, MO Holy Infant Church.
Buchheit, Msgr. Richard A. '63 (STL) [29] St. Louis, MO St. Bridget of Erin Church.
Buchholz, Athanasius *o.s.b.* '54 (P) [L] St. Benedict, OR Mt. Angel Abbey.
Buchignani, Msgr. Peter P. '65 (MEM) [8] Memphis, TN St. Francis of Assisi Church.
Buchignani, Richard G. '62 (NSH) Lawrenceburg, TN Sacred Heart Church.
Buchlein, Neil '98 (WH) Parkersburg, WV St. Margaret Mary Church.
Buchleitner, Donald N. '70 (PIT) [50] Pittsburgh, PA Holy Innocents Church.
Buchman, Joel R. '91 (TOL) Toledo, OH St. Vincent Mercy Medical Center; [H] Toledo, OH St. Vincent Mercy Medical Center.
Buchmeier, Francis X. *s.j.* '73 (FgM) Provinces.
Buchmeier, Robert P. '91 (WDC) Laurel, MD St. Nicholas Church.
Buchmiller, Ronald J. '69 (SD) Military Chaplains.
Bucia, Msgr. Edward H. '62 (CAM) [6] Camden, NJ St. Joseph's Church.
Buck, Daniel P. '71 (CHI) [2] Cicero, IL St. Frances of Rome Church.
Buck, Frank '85 (ORL) Haines City, FL St. Ann Church.
Buckalew, Jack '74 (SEA) Bremerton, WA Holy Trinity Church.
Buckel, John J. '80 (IND) [A] St. Meinrad, IN St. Meinrad Seminary.
Bucki, John P. *s.j.* '79 (NY) [37] New York, NY St. Francis Xavier Church; [DD] New York, NY Xavier Jesuit Community.
Buckius, Walter A. *s.j.* '52 (WH) [A] Wheeling, WV Wheeling Jesuit University.
Buckles, David '88 (LFT) Special Assignment.
Buckles, Luke D. *o.p.* '78 (OAK) [A] Berkeley, CA Dominican School of Philosophy and Theology; [N] Oakland, CA Dominican Order (Western Province), St. Albert's Priory.
Buckley, Brendan *o.f.m.cap.* '81 (MAN) [N] Manchester, NH Campus Ministries; [N] Hanover, NH The Catholic Student Center at Dartmouth, Aquinas House, Aquinas at Dartmouth, Inc.
Buckley, Charles *o.s.b.* '70 (OKL) [I] Shawnee, OK St. Gregory's Abbey.
Buckley, Cornelius M. *s.j.* '62 (LA) [J] Duarte, CA Santa Teresita Hospital.
Buckley, Francis *s.j.* '58 (OAK) [A] Oakland, CA Graduate School of Theology, School of Applied Theology.
Buckley, Francis J. *s.j.* '58 (SFR) [N] San Francisco, CA Jesuit Community at University of San Francisco.
Buckley, Frederick J. '45 (BO) Senior Priests.
Buckley, Gerald A. *o.p.* '57 (P) Ashland, OR Our Lady of the Mountain Church.
Buckley, Gerald J. '57 (SY) Binghamton, NY Binghamton Psychiatric Hospital; Binghamton, NY Binghamton Psychiatric Hospital.
Buckley, Harold P. '53 (RVC) Retired.
Buckley, James '82 (GLP) Absent on Leave.
Buckley, James '90 (OM) Osmond, NE St. Mary of the Seven Dolors Church.
Buckley, James B. *f.s.s.p.* (LIN) [A] Denton, NE Our Lady of Guadalupe Seminary.
Buckley, James B. *f.s.s.p.* '65 (SCR) [M] Elmhurst, PA Priestly Fraternity of St. Peter (F.S.S.P.), North American District Headquarters.
Buckley, James F. '59 (FR) Chatham, MA Holy Redeemer Church.
Buckley, James M. '90 (OM) Plainview, NE St. Paul Church.
Buckley, John *c.m.* (BAL) Emmitsburg, MD St. Joseph Church.
Buckley, John *s.s.c.* '68 (OM) [K] St. Columbans, NE St. Columban's Foreign Mission Society.
Buckley, John A. *s.s.c.* '68 (FgM) St. Columban's Foreign Mission.
Buckley, John E. '59 (BO) Burlington, MA St. Margaret Church.
Buckley, John J. *c.m.* (MOB) Opelika, AL St. Mary of the Church.
Buckley, John K. '47 (BO) Senior Priests.
Buckley, John M. *s.j.* '56 (NEW) [B] Jersey City, NJ Saint Peter's College; [N] Jersey City, NJ Jesuits of Saint Peter's College, Inc.
Buckley, Joseph F. '43 (BRK) Retired; [V] Douglaston, NY Bishop Mugavero Residence.
Buckley, Lawrence J. *c.ss.r.* '49 (BO) [53] Boston, MA Our Lady of Perpetual Help Church.
Buckley, Michael *o.c.d.* '47 (SR) [M] Oakville, CA Carmelite House of Prayer.
Buckley, Michael '55 (LA) Retired.
Buckley, Michael *s.j.* '62 (BO) [W] Chestnut Hill, MA The Jesuit Community at Boston College.
Buckley, Thomas E. *s.j.* '70 (OAK) [A] Berkeley, CA The Jesuit School of Theology at Berkeley.
Buckley, Thomas J. '61 (BO) Amesbury, MA Holy Family Church.
Buckley, Thomas J. *s.j.* '70 (OAK) [N] Berkeley, CA Jesuit Community at Jesuit School of Theology at Berkeley.
Buckley, Thomas J. *s.j.* '74 (WDC) [M] Washington, DC The Jesuit Community at Georgetown University.
Buckley, Thomas R. '76 (ALN) Limeport, PA St. Joseph Church.
Buckley, Thomas W. '55 (BO) Essex, MA St. John the Baptist Church.
Buckman, Franklin J. '63 (BAK) Klamath Falls, OR St. Pius Xth Church.
Buckman, Franklin J. '63 (ORG) On Duty Outside the Diocese.
Buckman, Thomas Joseph, Jr. '00 (OWN) [1] Owensboro, KY St. Stephen Church.
Buckner, Christopher M. '80 (ARL) Herndon, VA St. Veronica Church.
Bucko, Raymond A. *s.j.* '83 (OM) [K] Omaha, NE Jesuit Community at Creighton University.
Buckon, Neal '95 (CLV) Military Chaplains.
Buckson, John R. '92 (OM) [15] Omaha, NE St. Francis Assisi Church; [32] Omaha, NE Our Lady of Guadalupe Church.
Bucolo, Joseph W. '54 (SCR) Pardeesville, PA St. Nazarius Church.
Bucon, Raymond H. '79 (DET) [7] Livonia, MI St. Priscilla Church.
Buczyna, Andrew L. '87 (JOL) [3] Lockport, IL St. John Vianney Church; Joliet, IL Silver Cross Hospital.
Buczynski, Edward '61 (DUL) Hill City, MN St. John Church.
Budai, Frank A. '88 (GLP) Retired.
Budde, John G. '77 (DET) Novi, MI Holy Family Church.
Budden, William A. '68 (RCK) Oregon, IL St. Mary Church.
Buddendorff, Kenneth *s.j.* '61 (LAF) [J] Grand Coteau, LA Our Lady of the Oaks Retreat House.
Budenholzer, Francis *s.v.d.* '72 (FgM) Society of the Divine Word Foreign Missions.
Budka, Dennis G. '84 (MIL) [1] Fond du Lac, WI Holy Family Church.
Budke, Jon *l.c.* '01 (WDC) [M] Potomac, MD Legionaries of Christ.
Budnar, Randy J. '88 (MAD) Blanchardville, WI Immaculate Conception Church; Hollandale, WI St. Patrick Church.
Budney, Msgr. David F. '57 (CAM) [5] Cherry Hill, NJ St. Thomas More Church.
Budnick, Austin J. *o.f.m.* '51 (ROC) [I] Watkins Glen, NY St. Anthony of Padua Residence.
Budovic, Francis X. *s.j.* '38 (DET) [61] Detroit, MI SS. Peter and Paul Jesuit Church.
Budwick, Msgr. John J. '64 (NY) [1] Newburgh, NY St. Patrick Church.
Budzikowski, Kenneth A. '80 (CHI) [198] Chicago, IL St. Thecla Church.
Budzynski, Daniel A. '56 (MIL) Retired.
Buebendorf, Victor J. '64 (NY) [213] Staten Island, NY St. Mary Church.
Bueche, Charles C. *c.ss.r.* '53 (STL) [P] Liguori, MO Liguori Mission House/Redemptorists.
Bueche, Gary '70 (DET) Washington, MI SS. John and Paul Church.
Bueche, Walter *c.ss.r.* '38 (ORL) [F] New Smyrna Beach, FL St. Alphonsus Villa-Redemptorist Fathers and Brothers.
Bueche, William *c.ss.r.* (CHI) [29] Chicago, IL Blessed Sacrament Church.
Buechele, Andrew C. *sch.p.* '69 (WDC) [B] Washington, DC Queen of Pious Schools House of Studies-Piarist Fathers.
Buehler, John A. '74 (SY) [9] Utica, NY St. John Church.
Buehler, Paul A. *c.pp.s.* '44 (CIN) [M] Dayton, OH Provincial Office of the Cincinnati Province of the Society of the Precious Blood.
Buelt, Msgr. Edward (DEN) [4] Englewood, CO Our Lady of Loretto Church; Englewood, CO Our Lady of Loreto Church.
Buenger, Edward A. *c.s.c.* '53 (FTW) [J] South Bend, IN Congregation of Holy Cross, Indiana Province, Provincial House.
Buening, Robert B. '58 (CIN) West Chester, OH St. John Church; Retired.
Buening, Ulric *o.f.m.cap.* '53 (MIL) [27] Milwaukee, WI St. Francis of Assisi Church; [Y] Milwaukee, WI Capuchin Franciscan Tertiary Province of St. Joseph of Wisconsin, Inc.
Buennon, William *s.j.* '51 (MIL) [67] Milwaukee, WI St. Patrick Church.
Buentello, Michael A. *c.s.b.* '95 (DET) [E] Redford, MI Catholic Central High School.
Buenzil, August H. '53 (MAD) Retired.
Buenzli, August H. '53 (MAD) [H] Madison, WI Bishop O'Connor Catholic Pastoral Center.
Buerger, Francis J. '44 (CIN) Retired.
Buermann, Eric R. *o.s.b.* '45 (CGS) Humacao, PR Maria Reina de la Paz Church.
Buersmeyer, David A. '80 (DET) Lincoln Park, MI Christ the Good Shepherd Church.
Buerster, Msgr. James A. '79 (BEL) [1] Belleville, IL Cathedral of St. Peter.
Buescher, David G. '71 (JC) Jefferson City, MO Capital Region Medical Center.
Bueter, Paul '59 (FTW) Milford, IN Our Lady of Guadalupe Church.
Buetow, Harold A. '44 (BRK) Retired; [V] Douglaston, NY Bishop Mugavero Residence.
Buettner, George '52 (BAL) Retired.
Bufalini, Mario *c.pp.s.* '56 (NY) [174] Bronx, NY Our Lady of Mt. Carmel Church.
Buffardi, Joseph G. '76 (PAT) [10] Paterson, NJ St. Mary's Church.
Buffer, Thomas J. '91 (COL) Graduate Studies.
Buffington, Jon '81 (EST) On Assignment Outside the Diocese.
Buffington, Jon '81 (P) [J] Portland, OR Providence Portland Medical Center.
Buga, John '99 (ROM) Unassigned.
Bugarin, Fred '75 (ANC) Kodiak, AK St. Mary's of Kodiak and the Islands Church.
Bugarin, G. Michael '91 (DET) [T] Detroit, MI Pope John Paul II Cultural Foundation, Inc.
Bugarin, Michael '91 (DET) Special Assignment.
Bugay, Stephen R. '84 (GBG) Republic, PA Holy Rosary Church.
Bugayong, Demetrio '70 (LA) Carson, CA St. Philomena Church.
Buggert, Donald W. *o.carm.* '66 (WDC) [B] Washington, DC Whitefriars Hall.
Bugler, Msgr. Henry J. '75 (NO) [58] New Orleans, LA St. Rita Church.
Bugliosi, Mario *o.s.f.s.* '43 (WIL) [3] Wilmington, DE St. Anthony of Padua Church; [G] Wilmington, DE The Antonian.
Bugman, Msgr. John H. '52 (BUF) [1] Lackawanna, NY Basilica of Our Lady of Victory; Retired.
Bugno, Krzysztof '85 (GRY) [J] Merrillville, IN Salvatorian Fathers (Society of the Divine Savior).
Bugno, Krzysztof S. *s.d.s* '85 (GRY) [2] Gary, IN Blessed Sacrament Church.
Buhl, Wilbert L. '60 (GB) Maplewood, WI St. Mary Church.
Buhler, Richard O. *s.j.* '70 (STL) [P] St. Louis, MO White House Retreat Jesuit Community; [T] St. Louis, MO White House Retreat.
Buhman, Leo T. '48 (JC) Retired.
Buholzer, Robert E. '56 (MAD) Retired.
Buhr, Donald L. '66 (STL) [2] Florissant, MO Our Lady of Fatima Church.
Buhr, Eugene '54 (LA) Hawthorne, CA St. Joseph Church.
Buhrfeind, William J. '38 (CHI) [3] Mt. Prospect, IL St. Raymond de Penafort Church; [2] Oak Lawn, IL St. Gerald Church; Retired.
Buhrman, Donald A. '86 (GI) Lexington, NE St. Ann's Church.
Bui, Francis '90 (HT) Amelia, LA Thanh Gia Church.
Bui, Francis T. '75 (LA) [9] Long Beach, CA St. Lucy Church.
Bui, Joseph '85 (WDC) Pastoral Center Special Ministries.
Bui, Marion *o.c.d.* '95 (DAL) [I] Dallas, TX Mount Carmel Center.
Bui, Peter *s.d.b.* '90 (LA) [C] Rosemead, CA Don Bosco Technical Institute.
Bui, Tin Mahn '75 (SFE) [10] Albuquerque, NM Our Lady of Lavang Church.
Bui, Vincent '95 (LAN) On Duty Outside the Diocese.
Bui, Vincent D. *s.s.* '95 (BAL) [S] Baltimore, MD Sulpician Provincial House.
Bui-Tien, Joseph '97 (GAL) [15] Houston, TX Christ, The Incarnate Word Church.
Bui-Trang-Nghiem, Joseph '73 (WDC) [L] Washington, DC Cardinal O'Boyle Residence for Priests.
Buitrago, Alex '67 (DAL) [17] Dallas, TX St. Elizabeth Church.
Buitrago, Tarsicio '64 (ARL) [1] Alexandria, VA Blessed Sacrament Church.
Buitron, Luis S. '00 (CR) [1] Crookston, MN Cathedral

of the Immaculate Conception.
Bujnak, George A. '65 (PSC) Absent on Sick Leave.
Bukala, Casimir R. *s.j.* '66 (CLV) [B] Cleveland, OH John Carroll Jesuit Community.
Bukase, Joseph *c.i.c.m.* '84 (BWN) Hidalgo, TX Sacred Heart Church.
Bukaty, Lawrence J. '76 (ALN) [1] Mahanoy City, PA Assumption B.V.M. Church; [3] Mahanoy City, PA St. Casimir Church; [6] Mahanoy City, PA Sacred Heart Church.
Bukauskas, Anthony '46 (STL) Retired.
Bukofsky, James '71 (BRK) [95] Brooklyn, NY Our Lady of Good Counsel Church.
Bukoski, Joseph, III *ss.cc.* '79 (HON) Lahaina, HI Maria Lanakila Church.
Bulfer, Stephen C. '73 (FRS) Mariposa, CA St. Joseph Church.
Bulgarella, Tony (GR) [18] Grand Rapids, MI Our Lady of Sorrows Church.
Bulger, Albion F. '56 (MAN) [9] Nashua, NH Resurrection Church.
Bulger, John '64 (SEA) Retired.
Bulinda, Ernest (RIC) Williamsburg, VA St. Bede's Church.
Bull, Albert D. '41 (CHI) Retired.
Bullene, Richard S. *c.s.c.* '83 (FTW) [B] Notre Dame, IN University of Notre Dame Du Lac; [J] Notre Dame, IN Holy Cross Community, Corby Hall, University of Notre Dame.
Bullman, Rudolph C. '00 (HEL) [1] Helena, MT Cathedral of St. Helena.
Bullock, Gabriel G. *o.s.b.* '61 (PEO) [A] Peru, IL St. Bede Abbey and Academy.
Bullock, Myron F. '53 (BO) [4] Gloucester, MA Sacred Heart Church.
Bullock, Robert W. '56 (BO) Sharon, MA Our Lady of Sorrows Church.
Bullock, Scott E. '91 (DUB) St. Catherine, IA St. Catherine's Church; St. Donatus, IA St. Donatus Church; [A] Dubuque, IA Seminary of St. Pius X.
Bulman, Msgr. Robert T. '40 (TR) Sea Girt, NJ St. Mark Church; Retired.
Bultman, Robert S. '67 (EVN) Celestine, IN St. Peter Celestine Church.
Bulwith, Richard E. '67 (CHI) [30] Chicago, IL St. Bonaventure Church; [G] Chicago, IL Catholic Charities of the Archdiocese of Chicago-Archdiocesan Offices; [G] Chicago, IL Catholic Charities of the Archdiocese of Chicago-Archdiocesan Offices.
Bumbar, Philip '68 (SJP) Wheeling, WV Our Lady of Perpetual Help Church.
Bumbarger, Bruce *m.ss.cc.* '92 (BIR) Russellville, AL Good Shepherd Church.
Bump, James F. '78 (GBG) Masontown, PA All Saints Church.
Bumpus, Msgr. Harold '63 (SP) Sun City Center, FL Prince of Peace Church.
Bunch, Timothy S. '79 (CIN) [4] Hamilton, OH St. Peter in Chains Church.
Bunchek, Edward P. '65 (PIT) [3] West Mifflin, PA Holy Trinity Church.
Bunda, Roland *s.m.* '78 (MRY) [F] Santa Cruz, CA Society of Mary, Marianists; [I] Monterey, CA Department of Campus Ministry; [I] Monterey, CA Department of Campus Ministry; [I] Monterey, CA Department of Campus Ministry.
Bundz, Michael '81 (STF) Rome, NY St. Michael Church; Utica, NY St. Volodymyr the Great Church.
Bunger, Kevin J. '83 (SY) Sanitaria Springs, NY St. Joseph Church.
Bungo, Samuel '77 (E) Frenchville, PA St. Mary of the Assumption Church.
Buni, Leon '75 (TR) Bayville, NJ St. Barnabas Church.
Bunn, James F. '64 (ALT) Ashville, PA St. Thomas Aquinas Church; Fallentimber, PA St. Mary Magdalen's Church; Fallentimber, PA St. Joan of Arc Church.
Bunnell, Adam E. *o.f.m.conv.* '74 (WDC) [B] Washington, DC St. Bonaventure Friary; [C] Washington, DC Georgetown University.
Bunnell, Thomas J. *s.j.* '74 (YAK) Special Assignment.
Bunny, Msgr. Michael '65 (LA) Newbury Park, CA St. Julie Billiart Church.
Bunofsky, Walter *s.v.d.* '60 (DUB) [B] Epworth, IA Divine Word College.
Bunse, Gerald L. '83 (SFD) Edwardsville, IL St. Mary Church.
Bunsic, Albert *o.c.d.* '67 (SB) [G] Redlands, CA El Carmelo Retreat House.
Buntel, Richard A. '71 (BO) Unassigned.
Bunyk, Vasyl '93 (PHU) Passaic, NJ St. Nicholas Church.
Buonanno, Vito '81 (BRK) [153] Queens, NY Ascension Church.
Buono, Joseph *c.ss.r.* '43 (BRK) [107] Brooklyn, NY Our Lady of Perpetual Help Basilica Church.
Buote, Martin L. '60 (FR) [10] New Bedford, MA St. Anne Church.
Bur, George W. *s.j.* '72 (PH) [I] Philadelphia, PA The Gesu School; [AA] Philadelphia, PA Gesu School Jesuit Community and Outreach Center(S.J.); [CC] Philadelphia, PA Urban House of Prayer.
Bur, George W. *s.j.* '92 (PH) [AA] Philadelphia, PA Jesuit Community, Arrupe House.
Bur, Stanislaus '50 (SAG) Retired.
Bura, Msgr. John '71 (PHU) Millville, NJ St. Nicholas Church; Chester, PA Holy Ghost Church.
Burak, Alex '62 (PHU) Edwardsville, PA St. Vladimir's Church; Wilkes-Barre, PA SS. Peter and Paul Church.
Burak, Paul '72 (CHI) Chicago Ridge, IL Our Lady of the Ridge Church.
Burakowski, Anthony E. '36 (HBG) Retired.
Burakowski, Wieslaw '92 (NSH) Clarksville, TN Immaculate Conception Church.
Buranosky, Dennis M. '72 (PIT) Bellevue, PA Assumption of the Blessed Virgin Mary on the Beautiful River Church.
Burasa, James *c.s.c.* '95 (FTW) [J] South Bend, IN Congregation of Holy Cross, Indiana Province, Provincial House.
Burba, Edward A. '75 (CLV) [11] Akron, OH St. Mary Church.
Burbach, Jude *o.s.b.* '53 (KCK) Blaine, KS St. Columbkille Church; Lillis, KS St. Joseph's Church; Onaga, KS St. Vincent de Paul Church.
Burbach, Richard C. *s.j.* '88 (STP) [6] St. Paul, MN The Immaculate Heart of Mary Church; [25] St. Paul, MN St. Luke Church.
Burbank, F. James *c.s.c.* '57 (FR) [A] North Easton, MA Stonehill College.
Burbank, Foster J. *c.s.c.* '57 (FR) [A] North Easton, MA Holy Cross Fathers Religious.
Burbank, Robert J. '64 (HRT) East Haven, CT St. Vincent de Paul's Church.
Burbank, William '62 (HRT) [17] New Haven, CT St. Rose of Lima Church.
Burbank, William M. '62 (HRT) [9] New Haven, CT St. Francis Church.
Burbidge, Msgr. Michael F. '84 (PH) [A] Wynnewood, PA Theological Seminary of St. Charles Borromeo, Overbrook.
Burch, Francis F. *s.j.* '63 (PH) [C] Philadelphia, PA St. Joseph's University; [AA] Philadelphia, PA Jesuit Community at St. Joseph's University.
Burch, Thaddeus J. *s.j.* '61 (MIL) [P] Milwaukee, WI Jesuit Community at Marquette University.
Burchell, Richard '75 (CLV) [1] Barberton, OH St. Augustine Church.
Burchfield, Michael '93 (FRS) On Special Assignment.
Burchianti, Leo R. '64 (PIT) Retired; [O] Pittsburgh, PA St. John Vianney Manor.
Burchill, John P. *o.p.* '65 (PRO) [29] Providence, RI St. Pius V Church; [P] Providence, RI St. Pius Priory.
Burckhart, William C. '53 (BO) Belmont, MA St. Joseph Church.
Burden, George W. *s.s.j.* '91 (BR) Donaldsonville, LA St. Catherine of Siena Church.
Burden, Lewis E. '97 (SUP) Bruce, WI St. Mary Church; Flambeau, WI St. Francis of Assisi Church; Strickland, WI Assumption of the Blessed Virgin Mary Church; Weyerhaeuser, WI SS. Peter and Paul Church.
Burdess, James J. '88 (ALN) Tower City, PA SS. Peter and Paul Church; Tremont, PA Immaculate Conception Church.
Burdick, Thomas (SB) Redlands, CA Sacred Heart Church.
Burdiek, Fabian F. *o.f.m.* '74 (STP) [10] St. Paul, MN Sacred Heart Church; Maplewood, MN St. John's Hospital.
Bureau, Germain H. '53 (PRT) Retired; [I] Waterville, ME Mt. St. Joseph Priest Retirement Home.
Burek, Frank J. '71 (CHI) [5] Oak Lawn, IL St. Louis De Montfort Church.
Bures, Francis *s.v.d.* '53 (FgM) Society of the Divine Word Foreign Missions.
Burg, Thomas R. '64 (CLV) Absent on Leave.
Burgaleta, Claudio *s.j.* '92 (NY) [DD] New York, NY Jesuit Community at Fordham University.
Burgard, David G. '94 (DET) Anchorville, MI Immaculate Conception Church.
Burgdorf, Joseph *c.p.m.* '52 (OWN) [F] South Union, KY Fathers of Mercy.
Burge, Robert A. '71 (CLV) Brook Park, OH St. Peter the Apostle Church.
Burger, Edward K. *s.j.* '70 (KC) [B] Kansas City, MO Rockhurst University; [J] Kansas City, MO Rockhurst Jesuit Community.
Burger, Frank '69 (KCK) Olathe, KS Prince of Peace Church.
Burger, Frank J. '38 (KAL) Retired.
Burger, John *s.s.c.* (OM) [K] St. Columbans, NE St. Columban's Foreign Mission Society.
Burger, Joseph W. '54 (OKL) Blackwell, OK St. Joseph's Church; Tonkawa, OK St. Joseph's Church; [K] Norman, OK Campus Ministry for the Archdiocese of Oklahoma City.
Burger, Mark J. '80 (CIN) [33] Cincinnati, OH Holy Family Church.
Burger, Matthias *o.s.b.* '47 (P) [L] St. Benedict, OR Mt. Angel Abbey.
Burger, Philip G. *v.f.* '83 (HBG) Coal Township, PA Our Lady of Hope Church; Trevorton, PA St. Patrick Church.
Burger, Raymond '60 (KCK) Lenexa, KS Holy Trinity Church.
Burger, Raymond O. *s.j.* '48 (MIL) [P] Wauwatosa, WI Jesuit Community at St. Camillus.
Burger, Robert '48 (KCK) Lenexa, KS Holy Trinity Church; Retired.
Burget, Joel *o.f.m.conv.* '61 (IND) Terre Haute, IN Regional Hospital/Union Hospital.
Burget, Joel *o.f.m.conv.* '66 (IND) [3] Terre Haute, IN St. Benedict Church.
Burghardt, Walter J. *s.j.* '41 (WDC) [E] Washington, DC Gonzaga College High School; [V] Washington, DC Woodstock Theological Center.
Burghoff, Theodore '55 (STL) Kirkwood, MO St. Peter Church.
Burghoff, Theodore H. '55 (STL) Retired.
Burgoon, Charles E. '64 (STL) [36] St. Louis, MO St. Gabriel the Archangel Church.
Burgos, Adnel '88 (BRK) [26] Brooklyn, NY St. Catharine of Alexandria Church.
Burgos, Jose Casco (ARE) Retired.
Burgos, Juan *o.p.* '89 (SJN) [6] Bayamon, PR Santo Domingo de Guzman Church.
Burgoyne, Sidney C. (PH) Ridley Park, PA St. Madeline Church.
Burgoyne, Sidney C. '54 (PH) Retired.
Burian, Msgr. Edward '65 (SFS) Britton, SD St. John de Britto Church.
Burkard, Msgr. Paul J.E. '69 (BUF) [3] Orchard Park, NY Our Lady of the Sacred Heart Church.
Burkart, Donald R. '58 (GB) Crivitz, WI St. Mary Church.
Burkart, James M. '93 (GAL) Hempstead, TX Mary, Mother of God Church; Prairie View, TX St. Martin de Porres Church; [T] Prairie View, TX Prairie View A & M University Catholic Center.
Burkauskas, Peter M. '79 (PH) [10] Philadelphia, PA St. Andrew Church; [30] Philadelphia, PA St. Casimir Church.
Burke, Adrian *o.s.b.* '97 (IND) [J] St. Meinrad, IN St. Meinrad Archabbey.
Burke, Alfred J. '69 (NEW) Berkeley Heights, NJ Church of the Little Flower.
Burke, Alfred M. *o.s.a.* '57 (CHI) [N] Olympia Fields, IL The Augustinians-Provincialate.
Burke, Alfred M. *o.s.a.* '57 (FgM) Foreign Missions.
Burke, Amadeus *o.f.m.* '35 (PAT) [M] Ringwood, NJ Holy Name Friary, Inc.
Burke, Christopher R. '86 (PBR) Trauger, PA St. Mary's Church.
Burke, Clement J. '61 (DUB) Retired.
Burke, Clement J. '61 (STP) Minneapolis, MN Abbott-Northwestern Hospital.
Burke, David M. '42 (BO) [4] Milton, MA St. Pius Tenth Church.
Burke, Donal *o.f.m.cap.* '75 (FRS) Fresno, CA Community Hospital, Veterans' Hospital & University Medical Center.
Burke, Edmund M. '77 (NY) [4] Kingston, NY St. Mary Church.
Burke, Edward *o.f.m.* '62 (SP) [O] St. Petersburg, FL St. Anthony Friary.
Burke, Edward P. '73 (PH) [5] Philadelphia, PA All Saints Church.
Burke, Edward T., S.J. '56 (SJ) [B] Santa Clara, CA Santa Clara University.
Burke, Msgr. Edwin F. '62 (BGP) [3] Norwalk, CT St. Ladislaus Church.
Burke, Eugene A. *c.s.c.* '53 (PHX) Lake Havasu City, AZ Our Lady of the Lake Church; [G] Phoenix, AZ Holy Cross Congregation/Casa Santa Cruz.
Burke, Francis J. *s.j.* '60 (STP) [N] Minneapolis, MN La Storta Jesuit Community.
Burke, Geoffrey D. '79 (ALB) Latham, NY Our Lady of the Assumption Church; [M] Latham, NY Provincial House of the Sisters of St. Joseph of Carondelet (Albany Province).
Burke, Gilbert J. *o.s.b.* '62 (GBG) [H] Latrobe, PA Saint Vincent Archabbey.
Burke, Gregory *o.c.d.* (WDC) [B] Washington, DC Discalced Carmelite Friars.
Burke, Gregory '51 (HEL) Retired; [E] Butte, MT St. James Healthcare, Sisters of Charity of Leavenworth Healthcare Corporation.
Burke, Harry '63 (NY) [E] New York, NY Cardinal Hayes High School.
Burke, Henry J. '45 (CHR) Retired.
Burke, Herbert '92 (CHL) Winston-Salem, NC St. Leo's Church.
Burke, Herbert '92 (WDC) On Duty Outside the Archdiocese.
Burke, James *o.p.* '49 (DAL) [K] Irving, TX Dominican Priory of St. Albert the Great.
Burke, James *c.s.sp.* '52 (SB) [E] Hemet, CA Holy Ghost Fathers.
Burke, Msgr. James A. '56 (NEW) Retired.
Burke, James C. '64 (ROC) [1] Auburn, NY Holy Family Church.
Burke, James E. '58 (NY) [227] Staten Island, NY

Sacred Heart Church.
Burke, James G. '77 (BO) [4] Brookline, MA Infant Jesus-St. Lawrence Church.
Burke, James J. *c.ss.r.* '56 (VEN) Wauchula, FL St. Michael Church.
Burke, Msgr. James M. '64 (PMB) Port St. Lucie, FL St. Lucie Church.
Burke, Msgr. John F. '46 (MAN) [13] Manchester, NH Our Lady of Perpetual Help Church; Retired.
Burke, John F. '55 (WOR) West Boylston, MA Our Lady of Good Counsel Church.
Burke, John R. '54 (E) On Duty Outside Diocese.
Burke, John R. '72 (L) [20] Louisville, KY Christ the King Church.
Burke, John W. *o p.* '60 (WDC) [B] Washington, DC Dominican House of Studies.
Burke, Joseph A. *s.j.* '51 (WH) [A] Wheeling, WV Wheeling Jesuit University.
Burke, Joseph F. *s.j.* '78 (BUF) [A] East Aurora, NY Christ the King Seminary; [O] Buffalo, NY Canisius Jesuit Community.
Burke, Kevin *s.j.* '86 (BO) [W] Cambridge, MA Weston Jesuit Community.
Burke, Lawrence *o.f.m.* '41 (PAT) [N] Ringwood, NJ Mt. St. Francis.
Burke, Leonard J. '42 (BO) Senior Priests.
Burke, Mark J. *s.j.* '93 (BGP) [P] Fairfield, CT The Fairfield Jesuit Community-Fairfield University.
Burke, Michael '50 (CC) Retired.
Burke, Michael '50 (HRT) [2] Waterbury, CT Immaculate Conception Church.
Burke, Michael *s.c.j.* '63 (MIL) [P] Milwaukee, WI St. Joseph House of Formation.
Burke, Michael A. '76 (PAT) Prospect Park, NJ St. Paul's Church.
Burke, Msgr. Michael J. '62 (PH) Exton, PA SS. Philip and James Church.
Burke, Msgr. Michael L. '74 (MAD) [10] Madison, WI St. Maria Goretti Church.
Burke, Michael M. *o.p.* '68 (R) [E] Raleigh, NC Dominican Community.
Burke, Paul (ATL) [3] Atlanta, GA Holy Spirit Church.
Burke, Paul E. *o.s.f.s.* '54 (WIL) [I] Childs, MD Oblates of St. Francis De Sales.
Burke, Peter D. '65 (PH) East Lansdowne, PA St. Cyril of Alexandria Church.
Burke, Richard *c.p.* '76 (PIT) [O] Pittsburgh, PA St. Paul of the Cross Monastery.
Burke, Robert *s.s c.* '49 (OM) [K] St. Columbans, NE St. Columban's Foreign Mission Society.
Burke, Robert E. '47 (DET) Birmingham, MI Holy Name Church.
Burke, Robert M. *o.s.a.* '55 (BO) [C] North Andover, MA Merrimack College.
Burke, Robert R. *s.j.* '64 (BO) [W] Weston, MA Campion Health Center, Inc.
Burke, Robert R. *s.j.* '64 (KC) [J] Kansas City, MO Rockhurst Jesuit Community.
Burke, Ronald A. '54 (SFR) [34] San Francisco, CA Mission Dolores Basilica Church; Retired.
Burke, Ronald J. '72 (HON) Waipio, HI Resurrection of the Lord Church.
Burke, Sean P. *m.m.* '78 (FgM) Maryknoll Foreign Missions.
Burke, Terence '75 (AMA) [E] Amarillo, TX Catholic Family Service, Inc.
Burke, Thomas J. *o.ss.t.* '78 (BAL) [A] Baltimore, MD St. Mary's Seminary and University; [A] Baltimore, MD St. Mary's Seminary and University; [P] Baltimore, MD Trinitarian Counseling Services, Inc.; [S] Baltimore, MD Holy Trinity Monastery.
Burke, Msgr. Thomas P. '53 (CHL) Retired.
Burke, Vincent *o.s f.s.* '57 (WIL) [I] Childs, MD Oblates of St. Francis De Sales.
Burke, Vincent *s.v.d.* '61 (FgM) Society of the Divine Word Foreign Missions.
Burke, Walter Dev '90 (SAC) Retired and in Senior Ministry.
Burke, Walter E. '47 (DET) Retired.
Burke, Walter J. *o.praem* '44 (PH) Paoli, PA St. Norbert Church.
Burke, Walter J. *o.praem.* '44 (WIL) [I] Claymont, DE Immaculate Conception Priory of the Canons Regular of Premontre.
Burke, William *s.d.b.* '93 (NY) [FF] Stony Point, NY Don Bosco Retreat Center and Marian Shrine; [FF] Stony Point, NY Marian Shrine.
Burke, William A. '65 (CHI) Arlington Heights, IL St. James Church.
Burke, Msgr. William F. '43 (BRK) Retired; [V] Douglaston, NY Bishop Mugavero Residence.
Burke, Msgr. William F. '59 (BAL) [32] Baltimore, MD St. Francis of Assisi Church.
Burke, William F. '75 (MEM) [28] Memphis, TN St. William Church.
Burke, William T. *s.j.* '69 (ANC) [G] Anchorage, AK Holy Spirit Center.
Burkemper, Robert W. '81 (STL) [5] Florissant, MO St. Dismas Church.
Burkert, Gerald F. '61 (IND) Beech Grove, IN Holy Name Church.
Burkert, William C. '71 (MIL) [75] Milwaukee, WI St. Roman Church.
Burkey, Blaine *o.f.m.cap.* '61 (STL) [P] St. Louis, MO St. Crispin's Friary.
Burkhalter, Ross C. '94 (OM) Hartington, NE Holy Family Church of Cedar County.
Burkhard, John *o.f.m.conv.* '67 (WDC) [B] Silver Spring, MD Austin Friars Hall, Order of St. Augustine.
Burkhardt, Alan T. '86 (LC) [3] Stevens Point, WI St. Joseph Church; [L] Stevens Point, WI St. Joseph's Congregation, Stevens Point Endowment Trust.
Burkhardt, Godfrey F. *o.s.b.* '45 (GBG) [H] Latrobe, PA Saint Vincent Archabbey.
Burkhardt, Odilo *o.s.b.* '50 (SFS) [F] Marvin, SD Blue Cloud Abbey.
Burkhart, John L. *o.s.a.* '56 (CHI) [N] Olympia Fields, IL The Augustinians-Provincialate.
Burkholder, Robert '47 (DET) Retired.
Burkle, Raymond A. '90 (DUB) Epworth, IA St. Patrick's Church; Placid, IA St. John's Church.
Burkley, John '70 (CLV) Absent on Leave.
Burks, William P. '86 (L) Pleasure Ridge Park, KY St. Polycarp Church.
Burkus, John '40 (ELP) Retired.
Burla, Frank J. '63 (NEW) Montclair, NJ Immaculate Conception Church.
Burlas, Anthony J. *o.s.b.* '58 (GBG) Forbes Road, PA St. Mary Church; [H] Latrobe, PA Saint Vincent Archabbey.
Burlton, Msgr. Francis H. '54 (BEA) [6] Beaumont, TX Our Lady of the Assumption Church.
Burmester, Edwin J. '40 (STL) [36] St. Louis, MO St. Gabriel the Archangel Church; Retired.
Burn, William C. '56 (CHR) Retired
Burnell, George F. *o.s.a.* '45 (PH) [C] Villanova, PA Villanova University; [AA] Villanova, PA St. Thomas Monastery.
Burnell, Robert J. '70 (CHI) Morton Grove, IL St. Martha Church.
Burnell, Thomas *s.j.* (SPK) Pasco, WA St. Patrick Church; [E] Tri Cities, WA Tri Cities Prep, A Catholic High School.
Burnemann, Tim (DAV) [J] Iowa City, IA Mercy Hospital.
Burnet, Jerome *o.m.i.* '53 (SAN) [2] Midland, TX Our Lady of Guadalupe Church.
Burnett, Eugene David *o.f.m.* '54 (LA) [73] Los Angeles, CA St. Joseph Church.
Burnett, Eugene David *o.f.m.* '54 (ORG) [C] Santa Ana, CA Mater Dei High School.
Burnett, George P. '61 (HRT) [1] Ansonia, CT Assumption Church.
Burnett, James '68 (JOL) [3] Naperville, IL Sts. Peter and Paul Church.
Burnett, James E. (CHI) Chicago, IL Hines V.A. Hospital.
Burnett, John C. '85 (SFD) [2] Springfield, IL Blessed Sacrament Church.
Burnett, Robert E. '55 (SCR) Retired.
Burnett, Timothy J. *o.s.b.* '80 (NO) [P] St. Benedict, LA St. Joseph Abbey.
Burnette, Kurt '89 (VNN) Portland, OR St. Irene Byzantine Catholic Church.
Burnham, Alfred S. '76 (LA) Culver City, CA St. Augustine Church.
Burnia, Scott A. '88 (SD) Jamul, CA St. Pius X Church.
Burnie, James H. *c.s.sp.* '93 (SB) Hemet, CA Our Lady of the Valley Church; [E] Hemet, CA Holy Ghost Fathers.
Burniston, Blase *s a.* '51 (NY) [DD] Garrison, NY Franciscan Friars of the Atonement.
Burns, Msgr. A. Francis '63 (NY) [6] Yonkers, NY Christ the King Church.
Burns, Bernard J. '53 (SAC) Retired and in Senior Ministry.
Burns, Charles *s.v.d.* '62 (SB) [A] Riverside, CA Divine Word Seminary.
Burns, Charles E. '58 (GAL) Retired.
Burns, Charles F. *s.j.* '72 (STP) [6] St. Paul, MN The Immaculate Heart of Mary Church.
Burns, David E. '61 (GAL) Retired.
Burns, Dennis J. '50 (BO) Marblehead, MA Our Lady, Star of the Sea Church.
Burns, Donald W. '50 (STP) Retired.
Burns, Douglas *o.s.f.s.* '99 (ALN) [B] Center Valley, PA Desales University.
Burns, Edward J. '54 (FR) Retired.
Burns, Edward J. '83 (PIT) On Duty Outside the Diocese.
Burns, Ernest '51 (HEL) Retired.
Burns, Eugene P. '55 (CHI) Retired.
Burns, Francis H. '48 (DET) Retired.
Burns, Msgr. G. Thomas '57 (NEW) Livingston, NJ St. Raphael Church.
Burns, Gerald H. '69 (BR) [3] Baton Rouge, LA St. Aloysius Church.
Burns, Gerard '80 (PH) East Lansdowne, PA St. Cyril of Alexandria Church.
Burns, Hugh D. *o.p.* '82 (NEW) [28] Jersey City, NJ Sacred Heart Church.
Burns, James '62 (GLP) Retired.
Burns, John '65 (ALB) Morris, NY Holy Cross Church.
Burns, John '90 (PEO) Kewanee, IL St. Francis of Assisi Church.
Burns, John A '48 (BRK) [83] Brooklyn, NY Mary Queen of Heaven Church; Retired.
Burns, John F. '48 (BO) Senior Priests.
Burns, John M. '82 (STP) [O] Lake Elmo, MN Carmel of Our Lady of Divine Providence; [T] Lake Elmo, MN Hermits of the Most Blessed Virgin Mary of Mount Carmel.
Burns, Joseph '55 (JOL) Steger, IL St. Liborius Church.
Burns, Joseph C. *o.p.* '54 (L) [47] Louisville, KY St. Louis Bertrand Church.
Burns, Joseph H. '60 (CAM) Hammonton, NJ St. Anthony of Padua Church.
Burns, Lawrence (SC) Clare, IA St. Matthew's Church.
Burns, Msgr. Lawrence E. '56 (MAN) Portsmouth, NH St. Catherine of Siena Church.
Burns, Lawrence E. '62 (BUF) Blasdell, NY Our Mother of Good Counsel Church.
Burns, Malcolm J. '85 (RVC) Oyster Bay, NY St. Dominic's Church.
Burns, Michael J. '58 (SJ) Los Altos, CA St. William Church.
Burns, Michael J. '73 (TR) Bordentown, NJ St. Mary Church.
Burns, Norbert C. *s m.* '53 (CIN) [D] Dayton, OH The University of Dayton; [M] Dayton, OH Marianist Provincialate.
Burns, Patrick *s.j.* '63 (RC) Pine Ridge, SD Holy Rosary Church; [B] Pine Ridge, SD Jesuit Community of Holy Rosary Mission.
Burns, Patrick G. '92 (BRK) [80] Brooklyn, NY St. Martin of Tours-Fourteen Holy Martyrs Church.
Burns, Paul D. *c.s.s.* '62 (WOR) Milford, MA Sacred Heart Church.
Burns, Peter *s.j.* '92 (LA) [70] Los Angeles, CA St. Jerome Church.
Burns, Robert A. *o.p.* '61 (TUC) [27] Tucson, AZ St. Thomas More Chapel Church; [I] Tucson, AZ University of Arizona.
Burns, Robert I. *s.j.* '52 (LA) [C] Los Angeles, CA Loyola Marymount University.
Burns, Robert O. *s.j.* '57 (OM) [K] Omaha, NE Jesuit Community at Creighton University.
Burns, T. Lee '56 (PRT) Retired.
Burns, Thomas '44 (SFS) Retired.
Burns, Thomas E. '60 (CAM) Retired.
Burns, Thomas J. '54 (SFR) Retired.
Burns, Thomas J. *m m.* '69 (FgM) Maryknoll Foreign Missions.
Burns, Thomas L. *s.c.j.* '65 (JKS) Booneville, MS St. Francis of Assisi Church; Corinth, MS St. James Church.
Burns, Tom *m.s.c.* '65 (SB) Upland, CA St. Joseph Church.
Burns, Vincent M. *s.j.* '57 (BGP) [P] Fairfield, CT The Fairfield Jesuit Community-Fairfield University.
Burns, Vincent P. '67 (PH) Military Chaplains.
Burns, William A. '33 (ROC) Waverly, NY St. James Church; Retired.
Burns, William W. '53 (BO) Senior Priests.
Burr, Jeremiah R. *m.m.* '67 (FgM) Maryknoll(M.M.).
Burr, Jeremiah R. *m.m.* '67 (NY) [DD] Maryknoll, NY Maryknoll Fathers and Brothers.
Burr, Thomas E. '73 (RCK) McHenry, IL St. Mary Church.
Burr, Thomas W. '61 (ROC) Horseheads, NY St. Mary Our Mother Church.
Burrascano, Anthony P. *o.s.a.* '79 (FgM) Foreign Missions.
Burrascano, Anthony P *o.s.a.* '79 (PH) Bryn Mawr, PA Our Mother of Good Counsel Church; [AA] Villanova, PA Provincial Offices of the Order of St. Augustine, Province of St. Thomas of Villanova.
Burrell, David B. *c.s c.* '59 (FTW) [A] Notre Dame, IN Moreau Seminary; [B] Notre Dame, IN University of Notre Dame Du Lac.
Burrill, Jeffrey D. (LC) [C] Eau Claire, WI Catholic Area Schools of the Eau Claire Deanery (C.A.S.E.).
Burrill, Jeffrey D. '98 (LC) [C] Eau Claire, WI Catholic Area Schools of the Eau Claire Deanery (C.A.S.E.).
Burrows, Michael *o.s b.* '80 (RCK) [G] Aurora, IL Marmion Abbey-St. Augustine's Abbey.
Burshek, James J. *s.j.* '75 (DEN) [D] Aurora, CO Regis Jesuit High School; [M] Aurora, CO Regis Jesuit High School - Jesuit Community.
Burshnick, Francis J. *s.c.j.* '70 (JKS) Southhaven, MS Christ the King Church; Walls, MS Sacred Heart Church; [F] Nesbit, MS St. Michael Community House.
Burson, James *c.j m.* '63 (SD) [3] San Diego, CA Blessed Sacrament Church; San Diego, CA Alvarado, Grossmont and Kaiser Hospitals.
Burt, Donald X. *o.s a.* '55 (PH) [C] Villanova, PA Villanova University; [AA] Villanova, PA St. Thomas Monastery.
Burt, William '85 (MIL) [P] Wauwatosa, WI St. Camillus Provincialate.
Burtchaell, James T. *c.s.c.* '60 (FTW) [J] South Bend,

IN Congregation of Holy Cross, Indiana Province, Provincial House.
Burton, C. Jeffries *s.j.* '67 (CAM) Ventnor, NJ St. James Church; [R] Mays Landing, NJ Atlantic Community College; [R] Pomona, NJ Richard Stockton College of New Jersey.
Burton, Charles '80 (KNX) Kingsport, TN St. Dominic Church.
Burton, John H. '72 (CAM) Villas, NJ St. Raymond Church.
Burton, Msgr. Richard '63 (WDC) [5] Washington, DC St. Anthony Church.
Burton, William *o.f.m.* '89 (SFD) [B] Quincy, IL Quincy University.
Burtschi, J. Richard *s.j.* '71 (STL) [P] St. Louis, MO Jesuit Community Corporation at St. Louis University - Jesuit Hall.
Burus, Douglas C. *o.s.f.s.* '99 (ALN) [K] Center Valley, PA Oblates of St. Francis de Sales.
Burwinkel, Elmer J. '84 (IND) Retired.
Bury, Antonio (CHI) [33] Chicago, IL St. Bruno Church.
Bury, Harold J. '55 (STP) On Duty Outside the Archdiocese.
Buryska, James F. '65 (WIN) On Special or Other Diocesan Assignment; [D] Rochester, MN Saint Marys Hospital.
Burzawa, Janusz (SP) [7] St. Petersburg, FL St. Paul Church.
Burzynski, Michael H. '89 (BUF) Kenmore, NY St. John the Baptist Church; [7] Niagara Falls, NY St. Mary of the Cataract Church.
Bus, Anthony *c.r.* '84 (CHI) [190] Chicago, IL St. Stanislaus Kostka Church.
Busch, Msgr. Aloysius J. (PAT) Retired.
Busch, Msgr. Aloysius J. '52 (PAT) [P] Chester, NJ Nazareth Village.
Busch, August '56 (EVN) Retired.
Busch, Jan H. *o.s.a.* '49 (PH) [C] Villanova, PA Villanova University; [AA] Villanova, PA St. Thomas Monastery.
Busch, John *o.m.i.* '40 (SAT) [K] San Antonio, TX Oblate Madonna Residence.
Busch, Joseph '80 (ALB) [1] Watervliet, NY St. Brigid Church.
Busch, Robert '93 (AMA) [11] Amarillo, TX St. Thomas the Apostle Church; [J] Canyon, TX Catholic Student Center at West Texas A & M University.
Busch, Robert A. '93 (AMA) Umbarger, TX St. Mary's Church.
Busch, Robert A. '93 (SAT) [C] San Antonio, TX Oblate School of Theology.
Busch, Vernon *o.f.m.cap.* '60 (BAL) Cumberland, MD SS. Peter and Paul Church; [S] Cumberland, MD SS. Peter and Paul Friary.
Busch, Vincent J. *s.s.c.* '74 (FgM) St. Columban's Foreign Mission.
Buscher, Adelbert *o.s.b.* '41 (IND) [J] St. Meinrad, IN St. Meinrad Archabbey.
Busco, Msgr. J. John '40 (PH) [2] Norristown, PA Holy Saviour Church.
Busco, Msgr. John J. '40 (PH) Retired.
Buse, Harold J. '77 (OM) [26] Omaha, NE St. Leo Church.
Busemeyer, Louis E. *s.j.* '70 (CHI) [D] Chicago, IL St. Ignatius Jesuit Community.
Bush, Bernard J. *s.j.* '65 (SJ) [K] Los Altos, CA Jesuit Retreat House.
Bush, Edward E. '57 (PEO) Colona, IL St. Patrick's Church.
Bush, Frederick W. '51 (ROC) Penfield, NY Holy Spirit Church.
Bush, John H. '39 (LAN) Retired.
Bush, Robert '69 (SAN) [1] Abilene, TX Sacred Heart Church.
Bush, Scott '92 (HON) Hilo, HI St. Joseph Church.
Bush, Thomas R. '99 (LIN) McCook, NE St. Patrick Church.
Bush, William C. '62 (LEX) Nicholasville, KY St. Luke Church.
Bushee, Richard J. '88 (PRO) Retired.
Bushell, Ralph *c.pp.s.* '49 (KC) [J] Liberty, MO Precious Blood Center; [N] Liberty, MO St. Gaspar Society.
Busher, Robert J. '76 (DAV) Oskaloosa, IA St. Mary's Church.
Bushmaker, Godfrey E. *o.praem.* '00 (ORG) [D] Silverado, CA St. Michael's College Preparatory High School.
Bushy, Timothy F. '83 (CR) Red Lake Falls, MN St. Joseph's Church.
Bussen, Robert J. '71 (SLC) Park City, UT St. Mary of the Assumption Church.
Busteed, Robert T. '69 (SCR) Bastress, PA Immaculate Conception Church.
Butcavage, Leonard M. '72 (SCR) [5] Hazleton, PA Holy Trinity Church.
Butch, Brian T. '93 (TR) Neptune, NJ Holy Innocents Church.
Butera, George J. '68 (BO) [2] Beverly, MA St. John the Evangelist Church.
Butkowski, Alto *o.s.b.* '41 (SCL) [I] Collegeville, MN St. John's Abbey, of the Order of St. Benedict.
Butler, Allan L. '67 (BO) Abington, MA St. Bridget Church.
Butler, Daniel J. '66 (PT) Niceville, FL Holy Name of Jesus Church.
Butler, David A. *o.p.* '57 (NY) [22] New York, NY St. Catherine of Siena Church; Manhattan, NY New York Presbyterian Hospital.
Butler, David Aloysius *o.p.* '57 (NY) [DD] New York, NY St. Catherine of Siena Priory.
Butler, Francis *s.s.j.* '96 (LAF) Church Point, LA Our Mother of Mercy Church.
Butler, James F. '69 (R) Southern Pines, NC St. Anthony of Padua Church.
Butler, James P. '86 (BO) Permanent Disability.
Butler, John '60 (HON) On Duty Outside the Diocese.
Butler, John J. '54 (L) Retired; [M] Louisville, KY Ursuline Motherhouse of the Immaculate Conception.
Butler, John M. '72 (GBG) [2] Connellsville, PA Holy Trinity Church; [3] Connellsville, PA St. John the Evangelist Church.
Butler, John R. '57 (MET) Colonia, NJ St. John Vianney Church.
Butler, John T. *s.j.* '00 (BO) [W] Boston, MA Arrupe House.
Butler, Leo J. '98 (NEW) Belleville, NJ St. Peter's Church.
Butler, Michael A. '85 (R) Kitty Hawk, NC Holy Redeemer Church.
Butler, Norman H. *m.s.* '75 (HRT) [M] Hartford, CT Missionaries of LaSalette, Provincial Secretary.
Butler, Patrick J. '82 (ALB) Guilderland, NY Christ the King Church.
Butler, Paul F. '87 (RVC) Ronkonkoma, NY St. Joseph's Church.
Butler, Rene '73 (STL) [P] St. Louis, MO La Salette Missionaries.
Butler, Richard J. '62 (BO) Stow, MA St. Isidore Church.
Butler, Robert E. *s.j.* '58 (LA) Alhambra, CA St. Thomas More Church.
Butler, Robert J. '62 (BO) Pepperell, MA St. Joseph Church.
Butler, Robert R. *m.s.* '69 (HRT) [M] Hartford, CT Missionaries of LaSalette, Provincial Secretary.
Butler, Thomas '50 (TUC) [A] Tucson, AZ Salpointe Catholic High School; [F] Tucson, AZ Carmelite Priory.
Butler, Thomas W. '82 (LAN) Hillsdale, MI St. Anthony Church.
Butler, Timothy A. '88 (BO) Military & VA Chaplains.
Butler, Victor *s.v.d.* '64 (TR) [M] Bordentown, NJ Society of the Divine Word.
Butler, Vincent E. *s.j.* '63 (NY) [F] New York, NY Xavier High School; [DD] New York, NY Xavier Jesuit Community.
Butler, William L. '61 (BO) [4] Revere, MA St. Mary of the Assumption Church.
Butori, Harry '52 (HEL) [1] Butte, MT Butte Catholic Community North Church; Retired.
Butryn, Msgr. Richard E. '58 (E) Meadville, PA St. Brigid Church; Meadville, PA Crawford Country Home.
Butsch, Matthew *o.s.b.* '43 (P) [L] St. Benedict, OR Mt. Angel Abbey.
Butters, Craig '83 (ORG) Mission Viejo, CA St. Kilian Church.
Butters, Joseph '65 (JOL) On Duty Outside the Diocese.
Butters, Joseph '65 (MRY) Arroyo Grande, CA St. Patrick Church.
Buttimer, Joseph '63 (SB) [E] Morongo Valley, CA St. Michael's of Morongo Valley, Inc.
Buttimer, Joseph '63 (SD) Retired.
Buttinelli, Anthony '38 (NY) Retired.
Buttini, Mario *o.s.j.* '39 (SCR) [B] Pittston, PA St. Joseph's Oblate Seminary.
Buttino, James V. *m.m.* '47 (FgM) Maryknoll Foreign Missions.
Buttner, Michael '75 (BAL) Special Assignment.
Buttner, Michael '78 (CHL) Lenoir, NC St. Francis of Assisi Church.
Buttomer, Jeremiah R. *c.s.c.* '43 (AUS) [H] Austin, TX Congregation of Holy Cross - Southern Province.
Buttomer, Jeremiah R. *c.s.c.* '43 (FTW) [J] South Bend, IN Congregation of Holy Cross, Indiana Province, Provincial House.
Buttrick, Dean T. '63 (SUP) [3] Superior, WI St. Anthony Church; Lake Nebagamon, WI St. Anthony Church.
Butz, Joseph *c.ss.r.* '70 (FgM) Redemptorist Foreign Missions.
Butz, Robert Joseph '00 (MAD) [1] Madison, WI St. Raphael Church.
Buu, Francis X. '74 (NY) [52] New York, NY Immaculate Conception Church.
Buvala, Andrew *o.f.m.* '47 (GAY) Peshabestown, MI Blessed Kateri Tekakwitha Church.
Buvala, Medard *o.f.m.* '43 (JOL) [11] Joliet, IL St. John the Baptist Church; [J] Joliet, IL St. John the Baptist Friary.
Buvens, Edward P. *s.j.* (NO) [C] New Orleans, LA Loyola University New Orleans.
Buvens, Msgr. Norman C. '64 (SHP) Retired; [B] Shreveport, LA Christus Schumpert Health System.
Buxkemper, Msgr. Roland '65 (LUB) Idalou, TX St. Philip Benizi Church.
Buxman, Donald R. '70 (P) Milwaukie, OR Christ the King Church.
Buyansky, Timothy *o.s.b.* '69 (CLV) [D] Cleveland, OH Benedictine High School; [O] Cleveland, OH Benedictine Order of Cleveland.
Buzga, John *glmy.* '59 (TLS) Idabel, OK St. Francis De Sales Church.
Buzzelli, Aaron N. *o.s.b.* '77 (GBG) Trauger, PA Forty Martyrs Church; [H] Latrobe, PA Saint Vincent Archabbey.
Buzzerio, Joseph '77 (NEW) Paramus, NJ Bergen Regional Medical Center; Hackensack, NJ Bergen County Jail.
Bwanal, Peter N. *s.j.* '99 (MIL) [P] Milwaukee, WI Jesuit Community at Marquette University.
Byabato, Deus-Dedit '93 (NOR) On Duty Outside the Diocese.
Byaruhanga, Frederick '89 (LA) [71] Los Angeles, CA St. Joan of Arc Church.
Bydlon, Msgr. Adam J. '46 (PH) [79] Philadelphia, PA St. John Cantius Church; Retired.
Byer, James M. '81 (CHL) Statesville, NC St. Philip the Apostle Church.
Byerley, E. Joseph '93 (CAM) Pine Hill, NJ St. Edward's Church; [A] Haddonfield, NJ Paul VI High School.
Byerley, Timothy '85 (CAM) Somerdale, NJ Our Lady of Grace Church.
Byers, Dohrman W. '74 (CIN) Arnheim, OH St. Mary Church; Sardinia, OH St. Elizabeth Church.
Byers, John '95 (LAN) [4] Lansing, MI Immaculate Heart of Mary Church.
Byington, Edward J. '70 (FR) Somerset, MA St. Thomas More Church.
Bykowski, Norbert H. '56 (CHI) Retired.
Bynon, Msgr. Joseph P. '56 (BRK) [233] Queens, NY Resurrection-Ascension Church.
Byrd, Freddie '88 (OWN) [2] Owensboro, KY Blessed Mother Church.
Byrd, Howard W. *s.s.j.* '75 (NO) [4] New Orleans, LA Blessed Sacrament Church.
Byrne, Albert J. '79 (ALN) Mohnton, PA St. Benedict's Church.
Byrne, Alexius W. *s.j.* '53 (SEA) [A] Seattle, WA Seattle University.
Byrne, Basil *o.c.s.o.* '76 (WOR) [N] Spencer, MA St. Joseph's Abbey.
Byrne, Bernard '82 (ORL) [9] Orlando, FL St. John Vianney Church.
Byrne, Bernard P. *m.m.* '56 (FgM) Maryknoll Foreign Missions.
Byrne, David (WIN) [3] Rochester, MN Resurrection Church.
Byrne, David J. '78 (CHI) Palos Heights, IL Incarnation Church.
Byrne, Edward *c.ss.r.* '44 (BRK) [107] Brooklyn, NY Our Lady of Perpetual Help Basilica Church.
Byrne, Edward G. '64 (NY) Ossining, NY St. Ann Church.
Byrne, Francis A. *c.m.* '62 (STL) [P] Perryville, MO Congregation of The Mission.
Byrne, Frederick *o.s.b.* '82 (ALT) [I] University Park, PA Penn State Catholic Community.
Byrne, George '69 (SD) San Diego, CA Nazareth House; [G] San Diego, CA Nazareth House Retirement Home.
Byrne, Glen F. (BO) [10] Boston, MA St. Anthony Church.
Byrne, Glenn '75 (BAL) Special Assignment.
Byrne, Msgr. Harry J. '46 (NY) Retired.
Byrne, Harry M. *o.p.* '78 (STL) [B] St. Louis, MO Aquinas Institute of Theology; [P] St. Louis, MO Dominican Community of St. Louis.
Byrne, Msgr. Henry L. '37 (STL) Retired.
Byrne, Hugh A. '62 (BRK) [246] Queens, NY St. Thomas More-St. Edmund Church.
Byrne, James A.P. *s.j.* '47 (WDC) [E] North Bethesda, MD Georgetown Preparatory School.
Byrne, James O. '37 (CIN) St. Marys, OH Holy Rosary Church; Retired.
Byrne, James P. *o.s.f.s.* '60 (R) Whiteville, NC Sacred Heart Church.
Byrne, Joel *o.f.m.* '51 (CIN) [M] Cincinnati, OH St. Clement Friary.
Byrne, John F. *s.s.j.* '66 (BAL) [S] Baltimore, MD St. Joseph Society of the Sacred Heart House of Central Administration.
Byrne, Joseph F. '69 (BO) [5] Waltham, MA Our Lady, Comforter of the Afflicted Church.
Byrne, Joseph L. '54 (HEL) Townsend, MT Holy Cross Church.
Byrne, Msgr. Laserian '48 (FRS) Retired; [I] Merced, CA Catholic Professional & Business Breakfast Club of the Fresno Diocese.
Byrne, Laurence *s.d.b.* '53 (OAK) [E] Richmond, CA

Salesian High School.
Byrne, Luke J. *s.j.* '65 (KC) [B] Kansas City, MO Rockhurst University; [J] Kansas City, MO Rockhurst Jesuit Community.
Byrne, Mark *s.o.l.t.* '98 (FAR) Belcourt, ND St. Ann Church; Turtle Mountain Reservation, ND (Chippewa Indians) Church.
Byrne, Patrick J. '55 (COL) Retired.
Byrne, Peter D. *s.j.* '75 (P) [L] Portland, OR Colombiere Community; [N] Portland, OR The Jesuit Spirituality Center.
Byrne, Peter J. '84 (NY) [207] Staten Island, NY Immaculate Conception Church; [208] Staten Island, NY St. John the Baptist de La Salle Church.
Byrne, Raymond J. '57 (NY) Irvington-on-the-Hudson, NY Immaculate Conception Church.
Byrne, Robert H. '75 (SAG) Mount Pleasant, MI Sacred Heart Church.
Byrne, Robert P. '50 (LA) Retired.
Byrne, Thomas '58 (DET) Retired.
Byrne, Thomas H. *s.j.* '53 (SJ) [L] Los Gatos, CA Sacred Heart Jesuit Center.
Byrne, Thomas J. *s.j.* '53 (SJ) San Jose, CA Agnews State Hospital.
Byrne, Tom *c.s.sp.* '64 (GAL) [69] Houston, TX St. Philip Neri Church.
Byrne, W. Gordon '32 (NEW) Retired; [N] Rutherford, NJ St. John Vianney Residence for Priests.
Byrne, William D. '94 (WDC) Special Ministries; [S] Washington, DC Archdiocesan Campus Ministry.
Byrnes, Donald M. '55 (NO) [4] Kenner, LA St. Jerome Church; Retired.
Byrnes, Francis '51 (BRK) [V] Douglaston, NY Bishop Mugavero Residence.
Byrnes, Francis J. '51 (BRK) Retired.
Byrnes, James '86 (NY) [E] New York, NY Cardinal Hayes High School.
Byrnes, James J. '80 (STL) [1] Florissant, MO North American Martyrs Church.
Byrnes, John D. '94 (ALT) [2] Altoona, PA Immaculate Conception Church.
Byrnes, John J. '66 (CAM) Merchantville, NJ St. Peter's Church.
Byrnes, John P. '45 (TR) Retired.
Byrnes, John W. '47 (BRK) [183] Queens, NY SS. Joachim and Anne Church; Retired.
Byrnes, Michael J. '96 (DET) [4] St. Clair Shores, MI St. Joan of Arc Church; Graduate Studies.
Byrnes, Paul A. (BAL) [V] Frostburg, MD St. Michael School Endowment Trust.
Byrnes, Paul A. '62 (BAL) Frostburg, MD St. Michael Church.
Byrnes, Robert R. '67 (GBG) Greensburg, PA Westmoreland Hospital.
Byrnes, Thomas '99 (NY) Warwick, NY St. Stephen Church.
Byrnes, Thomas M. *c.m.* '50 (FgM) Vincentian Foreign Missions.
Byrnes, Timothy '52 (LAN) [3] Lansing, MI Holy Cross Church.
Byrns, Joseph P. '69 (BRK) [127] Brooklyn, NY St. Rose of Lima Church.
Byrolly, Bruce '58 (WIL) Cambridge, MD St. Mary Refuge of Sinners Church.
Byron, J. Michael '89 (STP) Graduate Studies; [A] St. Paul, MN The Saint Paul Seminary.
Byron, Michael '89 (STP) [C] St. Paul, MN University of St. Thomas.
Byron, Patrick J. '58 (YAK) Retired.
Byron, William '62 (YAK) Goldendale, WA Holy Trinity Church.
Byron, William J. *s.j.* '61 (WDC) [20] Washington, DC Holy Trinity Church.
Byrth, Peter *o.carm.* '59 (NEW) Tenafly, NJ Our Lady of Mount Carmel Church.
Bzdyra, Stephen H. '79 (HRT) Union City, CT St. Hedwig Church; [18] Waterbury, CT St. Stanislaus Kostka Church.

C

Caamano, Raphael '78 (BO) [V] Chestnut Hill, MA Opus Dei.
Cabala, Thomas S. '79 (CHI) South Holland, IL St. Jude the Apostle Church.
Caballero, Francisco '53 (TOL) Retired.
Caballero, Lloyd C. '40 (BR) Retired.
Cabanas, R. Jaime '55 (BWN) Retired.
Cabante, Enrique '83 (HON) Hilo, HI St. Joseph Church.
Cabarello, Francisco *o.de.m.* '90 (SB) Rancho Cucamonga, CA Our Lady of Mount Carmel Church.
Cabasino, Philip *c.s.s.r.* (BO) Bedford, MA Veterans Administration Hospital Bedford.
Cabasino, Philip A. *c.ss.r.* '47 (BO) [53] Boston, MA Our Lady of Perpetual Help Church.
Cabazi, Ruta A. '65 (IND) [F] Beech Grove, IN St. Francis Hospital and Health Centers.
Cabell, Barry E. *c.s.c.* '89 (AUS) [H] Austin, TX Congregation of Holy Cross - Southern Province.
Cabezas, Richard E. '99 (NEW) Nutley, NJ Holy Family Church.
Caboboy, Juan '76 (ORG) Laguna Hills, CA St. Nicholas Church.
Cabra, M. Arturo (R) Wilmington, NC St. Mark Church.
Cabral, Clifford J. '79 (PRO) [1] Burrillville, RI St. Joseph Church.
Cabrera, Albert *c.p.* '65 (ALT) [J] Bedford, PA St. Mary's House of Greater Solitude.
Cabrera, Alberto '99 (MRY) Greenfield, CA Holy Trinity Church.
Cabrera, Sergio '73 (MIA) [29] Miami, FL St. Raymond Church.
Cabrerizo, Juan L. *sch.p.* '77 (PCE) [C] Coto Laurel, PR Colegio Ponceno.
Cabrita, Paul *s.m.* '86 (ATL) [C] Atlanta, GA Marist School.
Caccavale, Charles '91 (BRK) Graduate Studies.
Caccavalle, Paschal *o.f.m. cap.* (NEW) [4] Hackensack, NJ Church of St. Francis of Assisi.
Caccavalle, Pius *o.f.m.cap.* '47 (NY) [DD] New York, NY Immaculate Conception Friary.
Cacciapuoti, Antonio '90 (LA) [8] Los Angeles, CA Christ the King Church.
Caceres, Alonso '59 (ORG) [2] Santa Ana, CA Our Lady of Guadalupe Church.
Caceres, Angel Diaz '76 (SJN) [A] Bayamon, PR Bayamon Central University.
Caceres, Blas *c.ss.r.* '88 (NY) [23] New York, NY St. Cecilia Church.
Caceres, Marco A. *c.ss.r.* '67 (MET) [2] New Brunswick, NJ St. John the Baptist Church.
Cach, Mark J. '83 (P) Cornelius, OR St. Alexander Church.
Cachat, Leo P. *s.j.* '66 (FgM) Provinces.
Cadden, Donald R. *s.j.* '58 (SPK) [C] Spokane, WA Gonzaga University.
Cadden, Thomas J. '55 (COL) [G] Columbus, OH St. Rita Home.
Caddy, James L. '64 (CLV) Gates Mills, OH St. Francis of Assisi Church.
Cadei, Adriano *p.i.m.e.* '56 (COL) [H] Newark, OH P.I.M.E. Mission & Retreat Center.
Cadera, James R. '57 (FRS) Coalinga, CA Pleasant Valley State Prison.
Cadera, James R. '57 (MRY) On Duty Outside the Diocese.
Cadigan, Timothy J. *s.j.* '91 (SCR) [C] Scranton, PA University of Scranton.
Cadorette, Curtis R. *m.m.* '77 (NY) [DD] Maryknoll, NY Maryknoll Fathers and Brothers.
Cadran, Raymond G. *m.s.* '78 (ATL) [2] Marietta, GA Church of St. Ann.
Cadri, Diego '95 (PIT) Penn Hills, PA St. Bartholomew Church.
Cadusale, Jose '60 (BRK) Queens, NY Queens Hospital Center—Pastoral Care Office; [V] Jamaica, NY Parsons Manor.
Cadwallader, George B. '92 (PH) [148] Philadelphia, PA Stella Maris Church.
Cady, Frank G. '81 (TUC) Rio Rico, AZ Nativity of Our Lord Jesus Christ Church.
Caesar, Floyd '75 (ALN) Ashland, PA St. Joseph Church; Ashland, PA St. Mauritius Church.
Caesar, Roger *s.s.j.* '77 (GAL) [63] Houston, TX Our Mother of Mercy Church.
Cafarelli, Aquinas F. *o.s.b.* '65 (MAN) [K] Manchester, NH St. Anselm Abbey.
Caffe, John I. '62 (STL) St. Ann, MO St. Gregory Church.
Caffery, James *m.s.* '60 (ATL) Smyrna, GA St. Thomas the Apostle Church.
Caffrey, Benet W. *o.s.b.* '58 (PAT) [M] Morristown, NJ St. Mary's Abbey.
Caffrey, Edward F. '57 (SPK) Clayton, WA St. Joseph Church; Deer Park, WA St. Mary's Presentation Church.
Caffrey, Gerald *c.m.f.* '80 (PHX) Prescott, AZ United States Veterans Hospital (Prescott).
Caffrey, Joseph (PT) Bonifay, FL Blessed Trinity Church.
Caffrey, Joseph P. '63 (PT) De Funiak Springs, FL St. Margaret Church; Freeport, FL Christ the King Church.
Caffrey, William *s.v.d.* '59 (SB) [A] Riverside, CA Divine Word Seminary.
Cafiero, John Paul *o.f.m.* '95 (CHI) [D] Chicago, IL Hales Franciscan High School, Inc.
Cafone, James M. '65 (NEW) [B] South Orange, NJ Seton Hall University.
Caforio, Stephen *o.f.m.* '49 (NY) [DD] New York, NY Padua Friary.
Caggiano, Frank '73 (BRK) [33] Brooklyn, NY St. Dominic Church.
Caggiano, Kyrin *o.carm.* '62 (L) [B] Louisville, KY St. Francis DeSales High School.
Cagney, John M. *o.praem.* '48 (PH) [AA] Philadelphia, PA St. Norbert Priory; [AA] Paoli, PA Daylesford Abbey.
Cahahan, Patrick J. *s.j.* '65 (LA) [C] Los Angeles, CA Loyola Marymount University.
Cahalan, Patrick J. *s.j.* '65 (LA) [C] Los Angeles, CA Loyola Marymount University.
Cahalane, Msgr. Thomas P. '63 (TUC) [10] Tucson, AZ Our Mother of Sorrows Church.
Cahill, Brendan '90 (GAL) [A] Houston, TX St. Mary's Seminary.
Cahill, Clemente *c.ss.r.* '51 (CGS) [1] Caguas, PR Cathedral Dulce Nombre de Jesus Church.
Cahill, Daniel '73 (TR) Keansburg, NJ St. Ann Church.
Cahill, Msgr. Daniel R. '43 (SFR) [43] San Francisco, CA St. Paul Church; Retired.
Cahill, Dennis H. '77 (DUB) Mason City, IA Holy Family Church; [G] Mason City, IA Newman Catholic.
Cahill, Donald C. '67 (CHI) Tinley Park, IL St. George Church.
Cahill, Edward B. '60 (PH) Springfield, PA Holy Cross Church.
Cahill, Frank '68 (MIA) Retired.
Cahill, J. Donald *s.m.* (STL) [P] St. Louis, MO Provincialate of the Society of Mary, Province of St. Louis.
Cahill, J. Donald *s.m.* '61 (STL) [4] Creve Coeur, MO Our Lady of the Pillar Church; [F] Kirkwood, MO St. John Vianney High School.
Cahill, James P. '61 (CHL) Sylva, NC St. Mary Church.
Cahill, John F. '51 (WOR) [M] Worcester, MA Vianney House.
Cahill, John W. '63 (RCK) [2] Freeport, IL St. Joseph Church.
Cahill, John W. '73 (COV) [1] Covington, KY Cathedral, Basilica of the Assumption.
Cahill, Joseph W. '76 (PRT) North Vassalboro, ME St. Bridget's Church; Oakland, ME St. Theresa Church.
Cahill, Neil *s.j.* '56 (MIL) [P] Milwaukee, WI Jesuit Provincial Office, Wisconsin Province.
Cahill, Neil *s.j.* '56 (OM) [K] Omaha, NE Jesuit Community at Creighton University.
Cahill, Patrick G. *c.s.v.* '62 (SFD) Rochester, IL Church of St. Jude.
Cahill, Msgr. Richard '39 (NY) New York, NY National Catholic Community Service.
Cahill, Msgr. Richard M. '58 (BUF) Retired.
Cahill, Thomas *m.j.* '88 (PCE) [7] Ponce, PR Santa Maria Church.
Cahill, William C. '61 (SY) [5] Rome, NY Transfiguration Church; Mohawk, NY Oneida Correctional Facility I.; Special Assignment.
Cahoon, John E. '89 (GAL) [19] Houston, TX St. Charles Borromeo Church.
Cahouet, Ralph Eugene *o.p.* '62 (NY) [DD] New York, NY St. Vincent Ferrer Priory.
Cahoute, Eugene *o.p.* '62 (NY) [185] Bronx, NY St. Raymond Church.
Caiazzo, Nicholas '92 (NOR) On Duty Outside the Diocese.
Caiazzo, Nickolas '92 (RIC) Military Chaplains.
Caicedo, Felix '90 (MRY) [3] Salinas, CA St. Mary of the Nativity Church.
Caimi, Luke A. '58 (WDC) Retired.
Cain, Dennis R. '79 (DUB) Farley, IA St. Joseph's Church.
Cain, Frederick L. '70 (PIT) [2] Bridgeville, PA Holy Child Church.
Cain, Gervase *t.o.r.* '57 (WH) Benwood, WV St. John's Church; McMechen, WV St. James Church.
Cain, Harry J. *s.j.* '63 (BO) [W] Weston, MA Campion Jesuit Community.
Cain, J. C. *o.m.i.* '89 (SAT) [M] San Antonio, TX Oblate Benson Residence (Southwest Area).
Cain, Msgr. James E. '50 (STO) Retired.
Cain, James R. '56 (OM) Springfield, NE St. Joseph Church.
Cain, John C. '58 (CHI) Harwood Heights, IL St. Rosalie Church.
Cain, John F. (SC) Sioux Rapids, IA St. Joseph Church.
Cain, John F. '56 (SC) Retired.
Cain, John N. '47 (NSH) Retired.
Cain, Joseph P. *o.s.c.* '44 (PHX) [G] Phoenix, AZ Crosier Community of Phoenix (Canons Regular of the Order of the Holy Cross).
Cain, Randy '88 (LAR) [14] Laredo, TX St. John Neumann Church.
Cain, Robert K.C. '95 (TLS) On Duty Outside the Diocese.
Cain, Thomas *m.s.c.* (ALN) [A] Center Valley, PA Missionaries of the Sacred Heart.
Cain, Urban *o.f.m.* '48 (PAT) [M] Ringwood, NJ Holy Name Friary, Inc.
Cain, William F. *s.j.* '69 (LA) [C] Los Angeles, CA Loyola Marymount University.
Cain, William P. *s.j.* '76 (NY) [DD] New York, NY Xavier Jesuit Community.
Caine, Msgr. Martin J. '46 (BUF) Retired.
Cairns, James *c.m.* '69 (FRS) Fresno, CA Valley Children's Hospital.
Cairns, John L. '63 (ALB) Clifton Park, NY St. Edward the Confessor Church.
Cairns, Stephen P. '68 (TOL) [10] Toledo, OH Little Flower of Jesus Church.
Cairns, Thomas '63 (BIR) Absent on Leave.

Cairone, A. Robert '64 (CAM) Magnolia, NJ St. Gregory's Church.
Calabrese, Charles L. '72 (FWT) [N] Fort Worth, TX Texas Christian University Catholic Community.
Calabrese, Charles L. '72 (STU) On Duty Outside the Diocese.
Calabrese, Daniel '87 (NY) Absent on Leave.
Calabrese, Peter M. *c.r.s.p.* (ALN) [K] Bethlehem, PA The Barnabite Fathers Barnabite Spiritual Center.
Calabrese, Peter M. *c.r.s.p.* '00 (BUF) [B] Youngstown, NY St. Anthony M. Zaccaria Seminary; [B] Youngstown, NY The National Shrine Basilica of Our Lady of Fatima.
Calabrese, William M. '99 (E) Du Bois, PA St. Catherine Church.
Calabro, John E. '73 (PH) [45] Philadelphia, PA Epiphany of Our Lord Church.
Calabro, Nicholas J. '66 (BGP) [4] Greenwich, CT St. Roch Church.
Calais, Floyd J. '50 (LAF) Retired.
Calamari, Joseph *s.s.j.* '45 (BAL) [S] Baltimore, MD St. Joseph's Manor.
Calamari, Paul '80 (NO) On Duty Outside the Archdiocese.
Calamari, Paul '80 (WIL) Newark, DE Christiana Care Health Services, Inc.
Calamari, Paul D. '80 (WIL) New Castle, DE St. Peter Church.
Caldara, John N. '46 (ALB) Retired.
Caldarella, James J. '71 (WOR) Princeton, MA Prince of Peace Church.
Caldas, Msgr. Constantino R. '51 (BGP) [15] Bridgeport, CT Our Lady of Fatima Church; Retired.
Calder, Kenneth J. '60 (BRK) [91] Brooklyn, NY Our Lady of Angels Church.
Calderon, Francisco '50 (MIA) [16] Miami, FL St. Brendan Church.
Calderon, Vicente, Jr. '63 (ELP) [31] El Paso, TX St. Raphael Church.
Calderon, Wilfredo '91 (SJN) [37] San Juan, PR Maria Auxiliadora Church.
Calderone, Joseph D. *o.s.a.* '73 (CHI) [J] Maywood, IL Foster G. McGaw Hospital of Loyola University of Chicago.
Calderone, Joseph D. *o.s.a.* '73 (PH) [AA] Villanova, PA St. Thomas of Villanova Friary.
Calderone, Philip J. *s.j.* '56 (FgM) Provinces.
Calderwood, Vincent T. '44 (BRK) Retired.
Caldognetto, Dominic *s.x.* '66 (MIL) [B] Franklin, WI Xaverian Missionary Fathers College Seminary.
Caldwell, Msgr. Frank J. '81 (RVC) [1] Rockville Centre, NY St. Agnes Church.
Caldwell, Fred '95 (DAL) Ennis, TX St. John Nepomucene Church.
Caldwell, J. Ripley '54 (SJ) [L] Los Gatos, CA Sacred Heart Jesuit Center.
Caldwell, James '60 (SD) Retired.
Caldwell, James V. '60 (SD) Chula Vista, CA South Bay Detention Facility.
Caldwell, John A. '70 (L) Pewee Valley, KY St. Aloysius Church.
Caldwell, William *s.t.b.* '68 (KC) Excelsior Springs, MO St. Ann Church.
Caldwell, William T. '44 (L) Retired.
Calegari, Leonard J. '63 (SFR) Pacifica, CA St. Peter Church.
Calendine, Caren (COL) [A] Columbus, OH Pontifical College Josephinum.
Calero, Luis F. *s.j.* '83 (SJ) [B] Santa Clara, CA Santa Clara University.
Calero, Nomar J. '91 (MGZ) [1] Mayaquez, PR Cathedral of Our Lady of Purification.
Calgaro, John *o.f.m.conv.* '74 (CHI) [N] Chicago, IL Conventual Franciscans of St. Bonaventure Province.
Calgaro, John *o.f.m.conv.* '74 (FgM) Conventual Franciscan Foreign Missions.
Calhoun, C. John '64 (NY) Absent on Leave.
Calhoun, Gerald '61 (OWN) Madisonville, KY Christ the King Church.
Calhoun, Lawrence E. *c.s.c.* '63 (FTW) [J] South Bend, IN Congregation of Holy Cross, Indiana Province, Provincial House.
Calhoun, Nathan C. '00 (ATL) Duluth, GA Catholic Church Of St. Monica.
Calhoun, Ronald G. (BO) Emergency Response Group.
Calicchio, Isaac J. *o.f.m.* '56 (HRT) [5] Meriden, CT St. Rose of Lima Church.
Calicott, John W. '74 (CHI) [77] Chicago, IL Holy Angels Church.
Caligiuri, Msgr. Angelo M. '58 (BUF) [2] Cheektowaga, NY Infant of Prague Church.
Caligiuri, Msgr. Anthony J. '49 (BUF) Retired; [O] Tonawanda, NY O'Hara Residence.
Calik, Joseph *s.ch.* '60 (SEA) [13] Seattle, WA St. Margaret of Scotland Church.
Calimeri, Anthony F. '47 (ROC) Retired.
Calip, Ben '66 (STV) [1] St. Thomas, VI Cathedral of Sts. Peter and Paul.
Calis, Joseph Anton '99 (WDC) La Plata, MD Sacred Heart Church.
Calise, Joseph P. '80 (BRK) [B] Elmhurst, NY Cathedral Preparatory Seminary of the Immaculate Conception.
Caliwan, Marc '72 (BRK) [215] Queens, NY Our Lady of the Miraculous Medal Church.
Calkins, Msgr. Arthur B. '70 (NO) On Duty Outside the Archdiocese.
Calkins, Gerard M. *o.s.m.* '45 (ORG) [I] Buena Park, CA Order of Friar Servants of Mary (Servites).
Calkins, Msgr. Howard W. '67 (NY) [1] Mt. Vernon, NY Sacred Heart Church; [HH] Bronx, NY Abraham House, Inc.
Calkins, John J. '49 (RCK) Loves Park, IL St. Bridget Church; Retired.
Calkins, Martin J. *s.j.* '94 (DET) [K] Detroit, MI Jesuit Provincial Office-Detroit Province of the Society of Jesus.
Calkins, Martin J. *s.j.* '94 (SJ) [B] Santa Clara, CA Santa Clara University.
Calkins, Raymond J. '46 (SC) Retired.
Calkins, Ronald L. '78 (NO) Mandeville, LA Mary Queen of Peace Church.
Callaghan, Msgr. Aloysius '71 (BAL) [A] Emmitsburg, MD Mount St. Mary's Seminary.
Callaghan, Msgr. Aloysius R. '71 (ALN) On Duty Outside the Diocese.
Callaghan, George J. *o.s.a.* '56 (PH) [AA] Villanova, PA St. Thomas Monastery.
Callaghan, Michael J. *c.m.* '76 (BRK) [V] Jamaica, NY Vincentian Residence.
Callaghan, Michael J. '90 (BAL) Millersville, MD Our Lady of the Fields Church.
Callaghan, Patrick C. *o.f.m.* '46 (NY) [DD] New York, NY Franciscan Friars, Order of Friars Minor, Holy Name Province.
Callaghan, Patrick C. *o.f.m.* '46 (OG) Retired.
Callaghan, Philip P. *s.j.* '60 (SFR) [C] San Francisco, CA University of San Francisco.
Callaham, Richard *m.m.* '64 (NY) [HH] Maryknoll, NY Asian Catholic Church Fund.
Callahan, Msgr. Brian F. '65 (BRK) [141] Brooklyn, NY St. Thomas Aquinas Church.
Callahan, Daniel *s.a.* '87 (NY) [DD] Garrison, NY Franciscan Friars of the Atonement, Minister General Office.
Callahan, Daniel P. *s.a.* '87 (OG) [E] Saranac Lake, NY St. Joseph's Rehabilitation Center, Inc.; [F] Saranac Lake, NY Atonement Friars.
Callahan, David P. '87 (BO) Littleton, MA St. Anne Church.
Callahan, Dennis D. '62 (MIL) Pell Lake, WI St. Mary Church.
Callahan, Edward M. '59 (SPR) [12] Springfield, MA Sacred Heart Church; Springfield, MA Olympus Specialty Hospital.
Callahan, Msgr. Francis J. '72 (SCR) [20] Wilkes-Barre, PA St. Therese's Church.
Callahan, Francis X. '49 (HRT) Woodmont, CT St. Agnes Church.
Callahan, Francis X. '63 (BAL) Bel Air, MD St. Margaret Church.
Callahan, James A. '73 (PH) [34] Philadelphia, PA Christ the King Church.
Callahan, James B. '98 (WOR) Athol, MA Our Lady Immaculate Church.
Callahan, James F. *s.m.a.* '50 (WIN) St. Charles, MN St. Charles Borromeo Church.
Callahan, James P. '74 (STL) [2] St. Charles, MO St. Cletus Church.
Callahan, Jerome *o.carm.* '52 (VEN) [7] Sarasota, FL St. Thomas More Church.
Callahan, John J. *s.j.* '70 (KC) [B] Kansas City, MO Rockhurst University; [J] Kansas City, MO Rockhurst Jesuit Community.
Callahan, Joseph F. *c.s.c.* '70 (FR) [A] North Easton, MA Holy Cross Fathers Religious; [K] North Easton, MA Holy Cross Fathers Retreat House.
Callahan, Joseph H. '86 (CLV) El Salvador, C.A., OH Parroquial de Nuestra Senora de Guadalupe.
Callahan, Joseph W. '66 (PH) [153] Philadelphia, PA St. Timothy Church.
Callahan, Kevin G. '84 (STL) [5] Lemay, MO St. Martin of Tours Church.
Callahan, Michael *m.m.* (LA) Arcadia, CA Annunciation Church.
Callahan, Michael G. *m.m.* '60 (LA) [Q] Los Angeles, CA Maryknoll Fathers and Brothers.
Callahan, Nelson J. '53 (CLV) Bay Village, OH St. Raphael Church.
Callahan, Patrick J. '00 (RVC) Rocky Point, NY St. Anthony of Padua Church.
Callahan, Richard *m.m.* (NY) [HH] Maryknoll, NY The Asian Catholic News Fund.
Callahan, Richard B. *m.m.* '64 (NY) [DD] Maryknoll, NY Maryknoll Fathers and Brothers; [DD] Maryknoll, NY Maryknoll Fathers and Brothers; [DD] Maryknoll, NY M.M.A.F. Charitable Trust; [EE] Maryknoll, NY Maryknoll Sisters Charitable Trust.
Callahan, Msgr. Richard J. '51 (CAM) Haddon Heights, NJ St. Rose's Church.
Callahan, Ronan *c.p.* '51 (HRT) [M] West Hartford, CT Holy Family Monastery/Retreat.
Callahan, Ronan P. *c.p.* '51 (NOR) [A] Cromwell, CT Holy Apostles College and Seminary.
Callahan, Msgr. Steven '87 (SD) [A] San Diego, CA St. Francis Seminary.
Callahan, Vincent '75 (CHI) [N] Chicago, IL St. Peter's Friary.
Callahan, William P. *o.f.m.conv.* '77 (MIL) [47] Milwaukee, WI Basilica of St. Josaphat.
Callahan, Zachary '58 (RVC) Retired; [M] Uniondale, NY St. Pius X Residence.
Callam, Daniel D. *c.s.b.* '64 (GAL) [Q] Houston, TX Residence of the Basilian Fathers of the University of St. Thomas.
Callan, Dennis *s.v.d.* '87 (FgM) Society of the Divine Word Foreign Missions.
Callan, John '82 (MIA) [C] Fort Lauderdale, FL Cardinal Gibbons High School.
Callan, L. James '45 (ROC) Retired.
Callanan, Edward E. *s.j.* '58 (PHX) [11] Phoenix, AZ St. Francis Xavier Church.
Callanan, Jonas *i.c.* '60 (PEO) Pontiac, IL Illinois State Penitentiary.
Callari, William P. '79 (MAR) Vulcan, MI St. Barbara Church.
Calle, Juan de la '54 (PMB) Retired.
Calle-Perez, Sergio M. '98 (ATL) Buford, GA Prince of Peace Church.
Calleja, Msgr. Guido '53 (MOB) Magnolia Springs, AL St. John the Baptist Church.
Callery, Peter J. *s.j.* '72 (SP) [C] Tampa, FL Jesuit High School.
Calles, Msgr. Robert S. '63 (ELP) [13] El Paso, TX Most Holy Trinity Church.
Callipare, Joseph P. '85 (PT) Mary Esther, FL St. Peter Church.
Callis, Elbert '76 (MEM) Dyersburg, TN Holy Angels Church.
Caloca-Rivas, Rigoberto *o.f.m.* (OAK) [S] Berkeley, CA Multicultural Institute.
Caloca-Rivas, Rigoberto *o.f.m.* '82 (OAK) [A] Berkeley, CA Franciscan School of Theology; [N] Oakland, CA Franciscan Friars.
Calovini, Msgr. Gerald E. '73 (STU) Wintersville, OH Blessed Sacrament Church; Wintersville, OH Our Lady of Lourdes Church; [J] Steubenville, OH Campaign for Human Development.
Calter, Arthur M. (BO) [5] Weymouth, MA Sacred Heart Church.
Calter, Arthur M. '56 (BO) Senior Priests.
Caluda, Charles J. '62 (NO) Garyville, LA St. Hubert Church.
Calumba, Faron '79 (HRT) Naugatuck, CT St. Francis of Assisi Church.
Calvert, Roland *o.s.f.s.* '65 (LAN) [J] Adrian, MI Motherhouse of the Sisters of St. Dominic.
Calvo, Gabriel '52 (WDC) [B] Washington, DC Diocesan Laborer Priests, House of Studies.
Calvo, Randolph '77 (SFR) Redwood City, CA Our Lady of Mount Carmel Church.
Calvo Muniain, Jose M. '59 (CGS) Juncos, PR Inmaculada Concepcion Church.
Calzada, Teodoro *c.m.* '53 (MGZ) [8] Mayaquez, PR San Vicente Church.
Camacho, Enrique '81 (YAK) Retired.
Camacho, Henry *o.p.* '60 (NEW) [28] Jersey City, NJ Sacred Heart Church.
Camacho, Jose Fco. Baez '87 (MGZ) [3] Mayaquez, Mayaguez Ascension Church.
Camacho, P. Orlando, Torres '92 (SJN) [F] Dorado, PR Santuario del Espiritu Santo.
Camacho, Robert '79 (RCK) [9] Aurora, IL Sacred Heart Church.
Camacho, Msgr. Zoilo L.G. '54 (AGN) Dededo, GU Santa Barbara Church; Retired.
Camadella, Christian F. *o.f.m.* '56 (NY) [35] New York, NY St. Francis of Assisi Church.
Camara, Michael *o.f.m.* '89 (FR) [7] New Bedford, MA Our Lady of Mt. Carmel Church.
Camarda, Ronald A. '90 (STA) [18] Jacksonville, FL St. Patrick Church.
Cambra, Dan *m.i.c.* '86 (MIL) [10] Kenosha, WI St. Peter Church.
Cambra, Daniel *m.i.c.* '86 (CHI) [N] Chicago, IL Congregation of Marian Fathers of the Immaculate Conception.
Cambra, Raymond '77 (FR) [12] Fall River, MA Sacred Heart Church.
Cameli, Louis J. '70 (CHI) [30] Chicago, IL St. Bonaventure Church.
Camera, Bede G. *o.s.b.* '88 (MAN) [16] Manchester, NH St. Raphael Church; [K] Manchester, NH St. Anselm Abbey.
Cameron, Ben *c.p.m.* '97 (OWN) [F] South Union, KY Fathers of Mercy.
Cameron, Hilary J. '64 (PRT) Berwick, ME Our Lady of Peace Church.
Cameron, Kevin (DM) On Special Assignment.
Cameron, Peter John *o.p.* '86 (NY) [A] Yonkers, NY St. Joseph's Seminary; [DD] New York, NY St. Vincent Ferrer Priory.

Cameron, Robert '59 (KC) Special Assignment.
Camille, Edward J. '58 (CLV) Brecksville, OH St. Basil the Great Church; Retired.
Camilleri, Emanuel *o.p.* '37 (FgM) Dominican - Order of Preachers Foreign Missions.
Camilleri, Emanuel M. *o.p.* '37 (NO) [P] New Orleans, LA Dominican Friars, Southern Dominican Province of St. Martin de Porres.
Camilleri, Joseph M. '74 (BR) Bayou Pigeon, LA St. Joan of Arc Church.
Camilleri, Roberto *o.f.m.* '75 (FgM) Franciscan Foreign Missions.
Camilli, E. Michael *m.s.c.* '60 (ALN) [A] Center Valley, PA Missionaries of the Sacred Heart.
Camire, Bernard J. *s.s.s.* '66 (NY) [55] New York, NY St. Jean Baptiste Church.
Cammayo, Ruben '80 (NY) [131] Bronx, NY St. Augustine Church; Bronx, NY Bronx-Lebanon Hospital Center.
Cammisa, James N. '49 (TR) Retired.
Camora, Tony (AGN) Dededo, GU Santa Barbara Church.
Camorlinga, Angel *m.c.c.j.* '96 (FgM) Comboni Foreign Missions.
Camp, Alfred L. '57 (JKS) Natchez, MS St. Mary Basilica Church.
Camp, Steven '87 (RVC) Seaford, NY St. William, the Abbot Church.
Campagna, Robert M. *o.f.m.* '77 (NY) [DD] New York, NY Franciscan Province of the Immaculate Conception; [HH] Mount Vernon, NY Franciscan Mission Associates; [HH] Mount Vernon, NY St. Dymphna Devotion.
Campagnone, Msgr. Francis '48 (ORL) Retired.
Campagnone, Msgr. Francis A. '48 (BGP) Retired.
Campagnone, Nicholas '65 (ALB) Retired.
Campana, Pedro '56 (SJN) [19] Bayamon, PR Santa Rosa de Lima Church.
Campana, Thomas S. '80 (CHI) [161] Chicago, IL St. Pascal Church.
Campbell, Andrew S. *o.s.b.* '81 (GBG) [H] Latrobe, PA Saint Vincent Archabbey.
Campbell, Bernard '89 (STV) [1] Barrenspot, VI Church St. Ann Church.
Campbell, Bernard J. *c.s.p.* '68 (CHR) Clemson, SC St. Andrew Church.
Campbell, Bernard J. *o.f.m.cap* '68 (MAN) [2] Manchester, NH St. Anne Church.
Campbell, Donald C. *c.s.p.* (NY) [41] New York, NY Good Shepherd Church.
Campbell, Douglas '76 (WCH) [15] Wichita, KS St. Jude Church.
Campbell, Dwight P. '91 (PEO) Philo, IL St. Thomas Church.
Campbell, Edward *o.s.b.* '56 (PMB) [E] West Palm Beach, FL Noreen McKeen Residence for Geriatric Care.
Campbell, Francis *o.m.i.* '42 (BO) [Z] Tewksbury, MA Immaculate Heart of Mary Infirmary.
Campbell, Msgr. Frank '53 (P) North Plains, OR St. Edward Church.
Campbell, Frederick (DAL) [B] Irving, TX University of Dallas.
Campbell, Gerard J. *s.j.* '51 (WDC) [20] Washington, DC Holy Trinity Church.
Campbell, Gerardo *c.ss.r.* '67 (CGS) [1] Caguas, PR Cathedral Dulce Nombre de Jesus Church.
Campbell, Howard W. '88 (PIT) Scott Township, PA Our Lady of Grace Church.
Campbell, Msgr. Hugh P. '61 (PH) Westtown, PA St. Maximilian Kolbe Church.
Campbell, Msgr. J. Michael '71 (STU) Malvern, OH St. Francis Xavier Church.
Campbell, James *m.s.c.* '72 (FgM) Missionaries of the Sacred Heart Foreign Missions.
Campbell, James *m.s.c.* '72 (RCK) [G] Aurora, IL Missionaries of the Sacred Heart Community.
Campbell, James D. *o.p.* '62 (R) [E] Raleigh, NC Dominican Community.
Campbell, Msgr. James F. '57 (PEO) Retired; [O] Peoria, IL Immaculate Conception Convent.
Campbell, Msgr. James F. '64 (BUF) [1] Buffalo, NY St. Joseph's Church.
Campbell, Joel A. *o.f.m.* '50 (BUF) [A] East Aurora, NY Christ the King Seminary; [D] Buffalo, NY Bishop Timon-St. Jude High School.
Campbell, John '50 (SFD) Retired.
Campbell, Msgr. John '55 (ORG) Retired.
Campbell, John D. *s.j.* '76 (MIL) [31] Milwaukee, WI Gesu Church.
Campbell, John J. *s.j.* '50 (DEN) [M] Denver, CO Xavier Jesuit Center.
Campbell, John Joseph '99 (KNX) [6] Knoxville, TN St. John Neumann Church.
Campbell, Msgr. John Michael '71 (STU) Minerva, OH St. Gabriel the Archangel Church.
Campbell, John P. *c.s.p.* '69 (BO) [W] Boston, MA Paulist Fathers Residence.
Campbell, John R. '58 (STL) Retired.
Campbell, Msgr. John S. '66 (ALN) [5] Minersville, PA St. Vincent de Paul Church.
Campbell, Joseph '60 (FAR) Retired.
Campbell, Joseph '60 (SPC) Caruthersville, MO Sacred Heart Church.
Campbell, Louis J. *f.s.s.p.* '61 (SCR) [M] Elmhurst, PA Priestly Fraternity of St. Peter (F.S.S.P.), North American District Headquarters.
Campbell, Msgr. Mark A. '71 (SD) [10] San Diego, CA Mission Basilica San Diego De Alcala Church.
Campbell, Michael '79 (STL) [14] St. Louis, MO Our Lady of Sorrows Church.
Campbell, Michael '93 (ATL) [12] Atlanta, GA Shrine of the Immaculate Conception Church.
Campbell, Norbert J. '60 (PIT) [3] Butler, PA St. Paul Church.
Campbell, Paul B. *s.j.* '88 (SY) [S] Syracuse, NY Jesuits at LeMoyne, Inc.
Campbell, Paul F. '65 (WOR) Dudley, MA St. Anthony's Church.
Campbell, Paul J. *o.s.f.s.* '82 (WIL) Salisbury, MD St. Francis De Sales Church.
Campbell, Peter E. *m.s.c.* '60 (RCK) [G] Aurora, IL Missionaries of the Sacred Heart Community.
Campbell, Robert *o.p.* '56 (CHI) [N] River Forest, IL St. Thomas Aquinas Priory.
Campbell, Robert *m.s.* '58 (MAN) [K] Enfield, NH Shrine of Our Lady of La Salette; [M] Enfield, NH La Salette Shrine and Center of Enfield.
Campbell, Robert B. *s.j.* '57 (FgM) Provinces.
Campbell, Robert I. *o.p.* '56 (CHI) [N] River Forest, IL St. Thomas Aquinas Priory.
Campbell, Stephen *s.j.* '85 (MOB) [A] Mobile, AL Spring Hill College.
Campbell, Theodore C. '72 (STP) Golden Valley, MN Good Shepherd Church.
Campbell, Thomas E. '80 (SAV) Retired.
Campbell, Thomas L. '48 (FR) [A] North Easton, MA Holy Cross Fathers Religious; [I] North Dartmouth, MA Holy Cross Mission House.
Campbell, Msgr. Thomas P. '43 (BRK) [168] Queens, NY St. Francis of Assisi Church; Retired.
Campbell, Wayne '86 (OAK) [3] San Leandro, CA St. Felicitas Church.
Campbell, William D. '58 (SCR) [10] Scranton, PA Immaculate Conception Church.
Campbell, William G. '63 (FR) Marion, MA St. Rita's Church.
Campbell, William R. *s.j.* '98 (BO) [E] Boston, MA Boston College High School & Jesuit Community; [H] Boston, MA Nativity Preparatory School.
Campbell, William W. '52 (BO) Senior Priests.
Campechano, Francisco '94 (STO) [5] Stockton, CA St. Gertrude Church.
Campellone, Joseph G. *o.s.f.s.* '96 (PH) [D] Philadelphia, PA Father Judge High School for Boys; [AA] Philadelphia, PA Father Judge Faculty House.
Campi, Vincent L. '45 (WH) Retired.
Campion, Msgr. John J. '51 (SD) Retired.
Campion, John R. '48 (HBG) Chambersburg, PA Corpus Christi Church; Doylesburg, PA Our Lady of Refuge Church.
Campion, Joseph J. '73 (ALN) [J] Bethlehem, PA Holy Family Villa.
Campion, Joseph J. *s.s.j.* '91 (NO) [2] New Orleans, LA All Saints Church.
Campion, Owen F. '66 (NSH) On Duty Outside the Diocese.
Campion, Thomas B. '52 (HRT) Wethersfield, CT Corpus Christi Church; Wethersfield, CT Sacred Heart Church.
Campion, Thomas F. '57 (MAD) [F] Monroe, WI The Monroe Clinic, Inc.
Campion, William (ALN) [I] Easton, PA Antonian Towers.
Campion, William T. '77 (ALN) [1] Easton, PA St. Anthony of Padua Church.
Campo, Lance J. '93 (NO) [1] Kenner, LA Nativity of Our Lord Church.
Campo, Richard W. '85 (ALN) [2] Easton, PA St. Bernard Church.
Campobello, Mark A. '91 (RCK) Crystal Lake, IL St. Thomas the Apostle Church.
Campoli, John F. '70 (TR) On Duty Outside the Diocese.
Campoli, Timothy J. '74 (SPR) Greenfield, MA Blessed Sacrament Church.
Campos, Miguel '96 (LA) [23] Los Angeles, CA Our Lady Help of Christians (Maria Auxiliadora) Church; [Q] Los Angeles, CA Piarist Fathers.
Campuzano, J. Eduardo '46 (CAM) Retired.
Camuso, Robert '92 (SEA) [3] Seattle, WA St. Anne Church; [13] Seattle, WA St. Margaret of Scotland Church.
Canaan, Timothy G. '93 (OG) [A] Ogdensburg, NY Wadhams Hall.
Canal, Manuel '58 (MRY) [1] Salinas, CA Christ the King Church.
Canary, John F. '69 (CHI) [A] Mundelein, IL University of St. Mary of the Lake-Mundelein Seminary.
Canas, Eugene *o.m.i.* '64 (FgM) Oblates Foreign Missions.
Canas, Eugene *o.m.i.* '64 (GAL) [S] Dickinson, TX Christian Renewal Center.
Canavan, Edward P. *o.s.f.s.* (FgM) Oblates of St. Francis de Sales Foreign Missions.
Canavan, Francis P. *s.j.* '50 (NY) [DD] New York, NY Jesuit Community at Fordham University.
Canavan, Gerald D. '69 (PH) Eddystone, PA St. Rose of Lima Church.
Canavan, John D. '55 (DET) Retired.
Canavan, Joseph T. '70 (BO) [8] Cambridge, MA St. Mary of the Annunciation Church.
Canavan, Mark P. '71 (CHI) [2] Mt. Prospect, IL St. Emily Church.
Canavan, Msgr. Martin '68 (PHU) Absent on Leave.
Canavan, Msgr. Martin A. '68 (PRO) [31] Providence, RI St. Sebastian Church.
Canavera, Lawrence J. '67 (GB) [14] Green Bay, WI St. Philip the Apostle Church.
Canazos, Gilberto *o.f.m.* (CHI) [D] Chicago, IL Hales Franciscan High School, Inc.
Cancro, Francis T. '81 (CHL) Asheville, NC St. Eugene Church.
Cancro, Frank (CHL) [L] Charlotte, NC Diocesan Office of Campus Ministry.
Candanedo, Wilmo *o.p.* '99 (NO) [25] New Orleans, LA St. Anthony of Padua Church.
Candelaria, Ernest *c.s.j.* '58 (LA) Lancaster, CA Blessed Junipero Serra Church.
Candelas, Rafael '59 (SJN) [55] San Juan, PR Sagrado Corazon de Jesus Church.
Candreva, Arthur A. *i.v.dei* '00 (BRK) [212] Queens, NY Our Lady of Hope Church.
Candreva, Msgr. Thomas D. '63 (RVC) East Rockaway, NY St. Raymond's Church.
Cane, Pere '93 (MIL) [Y] Racine, WI Missionary Community of St. Paul the Apostle and Mary, Mother of the Church, Inc.
Canepa, Jorge A. *c.s.c.* '56 (FTW) [J] South Bend, IN Congregation of Holy Cross, Indiana Province, Provincial House.
Canez, Jorge '79 (PHX) [3] Phoenix, AZ Holy Family Church; [10] Phoenix, AZ St. Edward Confessor Church.
Canfield, Francis E. *s.j.* '67 (TOL) [C] Toledo, OH St. John's Jesuit High School.
Cangemi, Dominic *s.t.* '44 (BLX) Pearlington, MS St. Joseph Church.
Caniga, Branislav '96 (JOL) [10] Joliet, IL SS. Cyril and Methodius Church.
Canino, Louis *o.f.m.* '69 (CHL) [J] Greensboro, NC Franciscan Friary.
Canizares, Dwight M. '81 (GAL) Kingwood, TX St. Martha Church.
Canjar, John A. '49 (DEN) Retired.
Cann, Hilarion V. '53 (WH) Retired.
Canna, Joseph '70 (LA) Irwindale, CA Our Lady of Guadalupe Church.
Cannan, Walter F. '68 (SY) Oriskany, NY St. Stephen, Protomartyr Church.
Cannariato, Paul A. '83 (NEW) [3] Bayonne, NJ St. Henry's Church.
Canniff, James B. '60 (BO) [42] Boston, MA St. Mary Church.
Canning, John *o.carm.* '55 (NY) [97] New York, NY Our Lady of the Scapular/St. Stephen Church.
Canning, Wilfred S. *c.s.b.* '55 (GAL) [Q] Houston, TX Dillon House.
Cannizzo, Vito *c.s.s.* '43 (BO) [Z] Waltham, MA Stigmatine Fathers and Brothers.
Cannoles, Antonio *c.ss.r.* '69 (FgM) Redemptorist Foreign Missions.
Cannon, Hugh D. '66 (RVC) Plainview, NY St. Pius X Church.
Cannon, James *c.ss.r.* '48 (ALB) Saratoga Springs, NY St. Clement Church.
Cannon, John A. '48 (PH) [G] Holland, PA Villa Joseph Marie High School for Girls; [Y] Holland, PA St. Joseph Home for the Aged; [BB] Holland, PA Villa Joseph Marie.
Cannon, Kenneth *s.x.* '97 (FgM) Xaverian Foreign Missions.
Cannon, Kenneth *s.x.* '97 (PAT) [M] Wayne, NJ Xaverian Missionary Fathers.
Cannon, Maro *c.f.a.* '85 (KNX) [C] Signal Mountain, TN Alexian Village Health Care Center; [F] Signal Mountain, TN Alexian Brothers.
Cannon, Richard E. '86 (BO) [68] Boston, MA St. Vincent de Paul Church; [BB] South Boston, MA Our Lady of Good Voyage Chapel.
Cannon, Robert R. *j.c.l.* '78 (VEN) [1] Venice, FL Epiphany Church.
Cannon, Msgr. Thomas '55 (CAM) Retired.
Cannon, Msgr. Thomas '55 (ORL) Retired.
Cannuli, John *s.v.d.* '85 (CHI) [B] Techny, IL Divine Word Residence.
Cannuli, Richard G. *o.s.a.* '99 (PH) [C] Villanova, PA Villanova University; [AA] Villanova, PA St. Thomas of Villanova Friary.
Canny, Michael '77 (SAC) Redding, CA Our Lady of Mercy Church.
Canny, Stephen J. '61 (SR) Cotati, CA St. Joseph Church.
Cano, Emilio '37 (PCE) Retired.

Cano, Nicolas *o.s.b.* '97 (BIS) [A] Richardton, ND Assumption Abbey.
Cano, Nicolas '97 (FgM) American - Cassinese Congregation Foreign Missions.
Canonici, Msgr. Paul '57 (JKS) Retired.
Canterbury, Keith '94 (SAC) Weaverville, CA St. Patrick Church.
Canterna, Charles J. '76 (BAL) Baltimore, MD Maryland Correctional Adjustment Center; Special Assignment.
Cantillon, John Joseph '76 (OAK) Retired.
Cantley, Msgr. Michael J. '55 (BRK) [149] Queens, NY St. Anastasia Church.
Cantones, Joel P. '81 (NO) [8] Metairie, LA St. Edward the Confessor Church.
Cantore, John *c.m.* '63 (SPC) [C] Cape Girardeau, MO Saint Francis' Medical Center.
Cantu, Oscar '94 (GAL) On Duty Outside the Diocese.
Cantwell, Edward F. '54 (ALB) Special Assignment.
Cantwell, Edward F. '58 (ALB) Hudson, NY Church of St. Mary; Glens Falls, NY Hudson Correctional Facility.
Cantwell, James *o.f.m.conv.* '61 (L) [7] Louisville, KY St. Anthony Church.
Cantwell, John '69 (SAC) Placerville, CA St. Patrick's Church.
Cantwell, Stephen F. *c.m.* '82 (PH) [AA] Philadelphia, PA Congregation of the Mission.
Cantwell, William J. *c.s.p.* '56 (NY) [DD] Jamaica Estates, NY Paulist Fathers Generalate.
Cantwell, William J. *c.s.p.* '56 (PMB) [H] Vero Beach, FL Paulist Fathers Residence.
Canty, Richard J. '85 (SAV) Special Assignment.
Canuel, Paul E. '66 (FR) Special Assignment; [L] Fall River, MA Special Apostolates.
Canzio, Celestino *o.f.m.* '73 (NY) [DD] New York, NY Franciscan Province of the Immaculate Conception.
Cao, John '89 (HT) On Duty Outside the Diocese.
Cao, Joseph T. '00 (DEN) Littleton, CO St. Mary Church.
Cao, Nghia *c.ss.r.* (CHI) [N] Chicago, IL Redemptorist Theology Residence.
Cao Phuong Ky, Joseph *s.s.* (SPC) [E] Carthage, MO Congregation of the Mother Co-Redemptrix, United States Assumption Province.
Cao Xuan Canh, Joseph M. *c.m.c.* (SPC) [E] Carthage, MO Congregation of the Mother Co-Redemptrix, United States Assumption Province.
Capacetti, Luis O. '87 (SJN) Graduate Studies.
Capacillo, Euben *o.a.r.* '75 (LA) [4] Oxnard, CA Mary Star of the Sea Church.
Capalbo, Kenneth *o.f.m.* '74 (FgM) Franciscan Foreign Missions.
Capalbo, Kenneth *o.f.m.* '74 (STL) [P] St. Louis, MO Franciscan Friary of St. Anthony of Padua.
Capato, Justin *o.s.b.* '80 (PAT) Cedar Knolls, NJ Notre Dame of Mt. Carmel Church; [M] Morristown, NJ St. Mary's Abbey.
Capdepon, Federico (MIA) Sabbatical.
Capdeville, Henri *o.s.b.* '93 (TUC) [F] St. David, AZ Holy Trinity Monastery.
Capella, Joseph *s.a.c.* '90 (CAM) [C] Pennsauken, NJ Bishop Eustace Prep School.
Capelle, John J. *s.j.* '47 (NO) [F] New Orleans, LA Jesuit High School.
Capetola, Nicholas *c.r.m.* '62 (CHR) Goose Creek, SC Immaculate Conception Church.
Capewell, Timothy J. '83 (TR) West Windsor, NJ Church of St. David the King.
Capik, Msgr. William J. '55 (MET) Basking Ridge, NJ St. James Church.
Capillo, John E. '69 (BRK) [64] Brooklyn, NY Immaculate Heart of Mary Church.
Capitani, Msgr. Anthony L. '46 (TR) Retired; [M] Trenton, NJ Villa Vianney.
Capitani, Sylvan P. '64 (HBG) New Freedom, PA St. John the Baptist Church.
Capitolo, Mario L. *s.j.* '59 (SJ) [D] San Jose, CA Bellarmine College Preparatory.
Capitolo, Paul F. *s.j.* '69 (SFR) [E] San Francisco, CA St. Ignatius College Preparatory (Coed); [N] San Francisco, CA Jesuit Community at St. Ignatius College Preparatory.
Capizzi, Simeon *o.f.m.* '53 (SP) [O] St. Petersburg, FL St. Anthony Friary.
Caplice, Richard J. *s.j.* '64 (NEW) [24] Jersey City, NJ Parish of the Resurrection Church.
Caplis, Roger J. '58 (CHI) [109] Chicago, IL St. Juliana Church.
Capo Iriarte, Rafael *sch.p.* '96 (SJN) [57] San Juan, PR Santisimo Salvador Church.
Capone, Albert L. '80 (BO) [10] Lowell, MA St. Michael Church.
Capone, Robert '00 (ORG) [1] Orange, CA Cathedral of the Holy Family.
Caponi, Francis J. *o.s.a.* '89 (WDC) [B] Washington, DC Augustinian College, Order of St. Augustine.
Caponi, Jerome '60 (VIC) Retired.
Caporalli, Paul M. *s.d.b.* '54 (LA) [W] Rosemead, CA St. Joseph's Salesian Youth Renewal Center.
Caporiccio, Louis *c.p.m.* '97 (OWN) [F] South Union, KY Fathers of Mercy.
Capoverdi, James D., Jr. '97 (PRO) Bristol, RI Our Lady of Mount Carmel Church.
Capozzelli, Anthony M. '73 (E) Retired.
Capozzelli, Msgr. Emmanuel M. '49 (NEW) Retired; [N] Caldwell, NJ The Rev. Msgr. James F. Kelley Residence for Retired Priests.
Cappalletti, Joseph '82 (CLV) Shaker Heights, OH St. Dominic Church.
Cappel, Charles H. *m.m.* '44 (FgM) Maryknoll Foreign Missions.
Cappel, Joseph H. *m.m.* '35 (FgM) Maryknoll Foreign Missions.
Cappelletti, Edward *s.d.b.* '50 (NY) [DD] New Rochelle, NY Salesian Provincial House.
Cappelli, Msgr. Angelo J. '48 (STU) Retired.
Cappelloni, David P. '86 (SCR) Muncy, PA Resurrection Church; Muncy, PA Muncy Prison; [G] Muncy, PA Resurrection Early Childhood Center.
Cappelloni, Thomas A. '76 (SCR) Jackson, PA St. Martin of Tours Church.
Cappo, Louis C. '46 (MAR) [1] Marquette, MI St. Peter Church.
Cappucci, Chester *o.m.i.* '63 (STP) [16] St. Paul, MN St. Casimir Church.
Cappuccino, Gregory J. '73 (RVC) Valley Stream, NY Blessed Sacrament Church.
Caprio, Albert Augustine *o.p.* '66 (NY) [DD] New York, NY St. Vincent Ferrer Priory.
Caprio, Robert J. *o.f.m.* '63 (BO) [P] Andover, MA Franciscan Center; [W] Andover, MA St. Francis Friary; [Y] Andover, MA Franciscan Center - Retreat House.
Capriolo, Victor R. '71 (MIL) [1] Fond du Lac, WI Holy Family Church.
Capua, Msgr. Nicholas J. '56 (BRK) [191] Queens, NY St. Luke Church.
Capuano, Vincent J. *s.j.* '98 (BAL) [S] Baltimore, MD Jesuit Fathers and Brothers Maryland Provincial Curia.
Capuano, Vincent J. *s.j.* '98 (FgM) Provinces.
Capuci, John M. (BO) Chelmsford, MA St. John the Evangelist Church.
Capuci, John M. '90 (BO) [D] Braintree, MA Archbishop Williams High School.
Caputo, Ralph '75 (BRK) [19] Brooklyn, NY St. Bernard's Church.
Caputo, Salvatore S. *s.s.c.* '76 (FgM) St. Columban's Foreign Mission.
Caraballo, Antonio '81 (ARE) [3] Camuy, PR Our Lady of Asumption Church.
Carabello, Francis J. '68 (NO) Gretna, LA St. Joseph Church.
Carao, Jorge '93 (AGN) Tamuning, GU St. Anthony and St. Victor Church.
Carapella, Thomas *t.o.r.* '92 (ALT) [F] Loretto, PA Mount Assisi Friary.
Carathers, Patrick '81 (AMA) [7] Amarillo, TX St. Hyacinth's Church; Vega, TX Immaculate Conception Church.
Carbajales, Ignacio '60 (MIA) Retired.
Carberry, John '81 (SFD) [3] Quincy, IL St. Boniface Church.
Carbine, Msgr. Francis A. '62 (PH) [1] Bensalem, PA St. Charles Borromeo Church.
Carbo, Msgr. Eugene J. '62 (PH) Retired.
Carbo, Richard '75 (NY) [42] New York, NY Guardian Angel Church.
Carbonaro, Dennis J. '81 (PH) [A] Wynnewood, PA Theological Seminary of St. Charles Borromeo, Overbrook.
Carbone, Anthony J. '93 (ARL) [5] Alexandria, VA St. Lawrence Church.
Carbone, Joseph M. *o.s.m.* (DEN) [22] Denver, CO Our Lady of Mt. Carmel Church.
Carbone, Joseph M. *o.s.m.* '59 (CHI) [N] Chicago, IL Order of Friar Servants of Mary (Servites) United States of America Province, Inc.
Carbone, Roland *o.s.b.* '54 (KC) Parnell, MO St. Joseph's Church; [A] Conception, MO Conception Seminary College.
Carbone, Vito J. '62 (PH) Downingtown, PA St. Joseph Church.
Carboneau, Dominique '99 (FTW) [C] Fort Wayne, IN Bishop Luers High School.
Carboneau, Dominique Andrew '99 (FTW) [4] Fort Wayne, IN St. Elizabeth Ann Seton Church.
Carbonneau, Robert *c.p.* '78 (CHI) [N] Chicago, IL Passionist Community-CTU.
Carboy, Daniel J. *c.ss.r.* '66 (CHR) Sumter, SC St. Anne's Church.
Carcerano, Michael J. '76 (LA) Simi Valley, CA St. Rose of Lima Church.
Carchidi, Rudolph V. *c.s.c.* '55 (FR) [A] North Easton, MA Stonehill College; [A] North Easton, MA Holy Cross Fathers Religious.
Carcich, G. John '45 (R) Retired.
Cardelli, Daniel E. '57 (OAK) Danville, CA St. Isidore's Church; [S] Oakland, CA Italian Catholic Federation.
Carden, Robert F. '56 (PBL) Vineland, CO St. Therese Church.
Carden, Robert J. '57 (NY) On Duty Outside the Archdiocese.
Carden, Robert J. '57 (PBL) [12] Pueblo, CO St. Joseph Church.
Cardenas, David J. '61 (GAL) [73] Houston, TX Resurrection Church.
Cardenas, Eugenio *m.sp.s.* '82 (LA) [A] Camarillo, CA St. John's Seminary.
Cardenas, Juan Raul '00 (PMB) [2] Lake Worth, FL St. Luke Church.
Cardenas, Mario S. '94 (SAT) [52] San Antonio, TX St. Margaret Mary Church.
Cardente, Edward S. '74 (PRO) [12] Providence, RI St. Edward Church; [1] North Providence, RI St. Anthony Church.
Cardenzana, Philip A. '65 (DAV) Colfax, IA Immaculate Conception Church; Newton, IA Sacred Heart Church.
Cardiff, Msgr. John I. '45 (CHI) [4] Oak Lawn, IL St. Linus Church; Retired.
Cardillo, Clement *s.d.b.* (PAT) [7] Clifton, NJ St. Paul Church.
Cardillo, Clement *s.d.b.* '54 (NEW) [N] Orange, NJ The Salesian Community.
Cardinal, Maurice *m.s.* '50 (HON) Hawi, HI Sacred Heart Church.
Cardinale, Kenneth R. '98 (WOR) [4] Southbridge, MA St. Mary's Church.
Cardinali, Fred '38 (FTW) Retired.
Cardinalli, Angelo *o.f.m.* (MRY) [H] San Juan Bautista, CA St. Francis Retreat Center.
Cardona, Carlos Garcia '92 (LKC) Kinder, LA St. Philip Neri Church.
Cardona, George '53 (MIA) [5] Hialeah, FL St. John the Apostle Church; Retired.
Cardona, Jorge D. '93 (CGS) Humacao Playa, PR Nuestra Senora del Carmen Church.
Cardona-Matta, Jose Miguel '98 (SJN) Dorado, PR San Antonio de Padua Church.
Cardone, Christopher *o.p.* '86 (FgM) Dominican - Order of Preachers Foreign Missions.
Cardone, Joseph P. '87 (TOL) Sylvania, OH St. Joseph Church.
Cardone, Thomas A. *s.m.* '85 (RVC) [D] Uniondale, NY Kellenberg Memorial High School; [M] Mineola, NY Provincial Residence and Novitiate.
Cardoni, Albert A. *s.j.* '60 (BGP) [P] Fairfield, CT The Fairfield Jesuit Community-Fairfield University.
Cardoso, Luis A. '58 (FR) [19] Fall River, MA St. Michael's Church.
Cardoso, Reinaldo M. '60 (PRO) [1] West Warwick, RI St. Anthony Church.
Cardoza, Edward (SB) Retired.
Cardoza, Timothy N. '83 (FRS) Tulare, CA St. Rita Church.
Cardy, William E. *o.f.m.* '72 (FBK) Delta Junction, AK Our Lady of Sorrows Church; Tok, AK Holy Rosary Church.
Cardy, William E. *o.f.m.* '72 (FgM) Franciscan Foreign Missions.
Carek, Peter P. '60 (MIL) [4] Wauwatosa, WI St. Jude the Apostle Church.
Carelli, Msgr. Richard J. '53 (WOR) Retired.
Carew, Alphonso (WDC) [2] Rockville, MD Shrine of St. Jude Church.
Carew, Lawrence F. '66 (BGP) [1] Trumbull, CT Christ the King Church.
Carey, Brian *c.s.sp.* '58 (STA) [3] Jacksonville, FL Christ the King Church.
Carey, David M. '62 (BAL) Special Assignment; [T] Baltimore, MD The School Sisters of Notre Dame in the City of Baltimore (Baltimore Prov.).
Carey, Dennis G. '98 (NOR) Old Saybrook, CT St. John Church.
Carey, Dominic A. '98 (SCR) [M] Shohola, PA Society of Saint John.
Carey, Donald D. '96 (STL) [5] St. Charles, MO St. Peter Church.
Carey, Gerald P. '98 (PH) Upper Gwynedd, PA Corpus Christi Church.
Carey, J. Peter *s.j.* '64 (IND) [D] Indianapolis, IN Brebeuf Jesuit Preparatory School, Inc.
Carey, James H. '66 (SY) [14] Syracuse, NY St. Charles Church.
Carey, John *o.f.m.cap.* '53 (GBG) Export, PA St. Mary Church.
Carey, Msgr. Leo P. '51 (PAT) Retired; [P] Chester, NJ Nazareth Village.
Carey, Michael *o.p.* '77 (OAK) [N] Oakland, CA Dominican Order, Siena House; [N] Moraga, CA Dominican Community.
Carey, Paul J. '42 (PH) New Hope, PA St. Martin of Tours Church; Retired.
Carey, Paul V. '71 (SY) Lee Center, NY St. Joseph Church.
Carey, Raymond '70 (P) Special Assignment.
Carey, Richard '55 (LA) Pico Rivera, CA St. Mariana de Paredes Church.
Carey, Richard T. '65 (WOR) North Brookfield, MA St. Joseph's Church.
Carey, Robert H. *c.s.v.* '58 (CHI) [N] Arlington Heights, IL Viatorian Province Center-Clerics of St. Viator.

Carey, Stephen '62 (CAM) Sea Isle City, NJ St. Joseph's Church.
Carey, Stephen A. '98 (NEW) Roseland, NJ Our Lady of the Blessed Sacrament Church.
Carey, William '59 (SHP) [B] Monroe, LA St. Francis Medical Center.
Carey, William F. '67 (BGP) Military Chaplains.
Carey, William F. '67 (KCK) Fort Leavenworth, KS St. Ignatius Chapel Church.
Carey, William G. '81 (BGP) [4] Greenwich, CT St. Roch Church.
Carey, Msgr. William J. '43 (PRO) Retired.
Carfagna, Msgr. Frank A. '67 (Y) [8] Canton, OH St. Joseph's Church; [Q] Youngstown, OH Catholic Cemeteries of the Diocese of Youngstown.
Carges, Bernard L. '60 (ROC) Dryden, NY Holy Cross Church; Groton, NY St. Anthony Church.
Cargill, Msgr. Eugene '59 (GAL) League City, TX St. Mary Church.
Cargo, Thomas '78 (JOL) Bolingbrook, IL St. Dominic Church.
Caridi, Michael A. '94 (PIT) [3] Charleroi, PA Mary Mother of the Church.
Carie, Giles *o.f.m.conv.* '61 (ELP) [17] El Paso, TX Our Lady of Mt. Carmel Church.
Cariglio, Msgr. Michael J. '70 (Y) [6] Youngstown, OH Our Lady of Mt. Carmel Church.
Carignan, Armand *o.m.i.* '53 (FgM) Oblates Foreign Missions.
Carignan, Raymond P. *s.s.j.* '61 (BLX) [5] Gulfport, MS St. Therese Church.
Carillo, J.M. *m.c.c.j.* '40 (NEW) [N] Montclair, NJ Comboni Missionaries of the Heart of Jesus (Verona Fathers).
Carina, Chester H. '85 (MET) Bernardsville, NJ Our Lady of Perpetual Help Church; [K] Bernardsville, NJ Sacred Heart Chapel.
Carini, James P. '65 (NOR) Tolland, CT St. Matthew Church.
Carkenord, David '62 (FTW) Waterloo, IN St. Michael the Archangel Church.
Carkhuff, Thomas *o.s.c.* '76 (FgM) Crosier Foreign Missions.
Carkhuff, Thomas R. *o.s.c.* '76 (STP) [N] Shoreview, MN Crosier Provincial House Province of St. Odilia.
Carl, Scott M. '00 (STP) Maplewood, MN Presentation of the Blessed Virgin Mary Church.
Carles, Alexander J. '88 (MET) Somerville, NJ Immaculate Conception Church.
Carleton, Robert J. *m.m.* '64 (FgM) Maryknoll Foreign Missions.
Carley, Patrick F. '69 (SLC) [8] West Jordan, UT St. Joseph the Worker Church.
Carlin, Bernard L. *c.ss.r.* '78 (CHI) [N] Chicago, IL Redemptorist Theology Residence.
Carlin, George (NY) Manhattan, NY St. Clare's Hospital & Health Center.
Carlin, George *s.o.l.t.* '84 (CC) [H] Robstown, TX Society of Our Lady of the Most Holy Trinity.
Carlin, George *s.o.l.t.* '87 (NY) [17] New York, NY St. Bernard Church.
Carlin, George P. *o.p.* (NY) Manhattan, NY Rockefeller University.
Carlin, Harry V. *s.j.* '48 (SFR) [E] San Francisco, CA St. Ignatius College Preparatory (Coed); [N] San Francisco, CA Jesuit Community at St. Ignatius College Preparatory.
Carlin, John T. '76 (CLV) [3] Parma, OH St. Charles Borromeo Church.
Carlin, Warren *o.carm.* '58 (JOL) [J] Darien, IL Carmelite Provincial Office.
Carlino, Richard A. '79 (ALB) [13] Schenectady, NY Our Lady of the Assumption Church.
Carlo, Cyprian '73 (LA) Palmdale, CA St. Mary Church.
Carlo, Edgar '97 (MGZ) Lajas, PR De la Merced Church.
Carlo, Joseph C. '63 (BUF) Pavilion, NY St. Mary Church.
Carlo, Raymond J. '87 (CHR) Gaffney, SC Sacred Heart Church; Union, SC St. Augustine's Church; [H] Gaffney, SC Limestone College.
Carlo, Raymond J. '87 (STA) On Duty Outside the Diocese.
Carlone, Carmen A. '69 (CAM) Williamstown, NJ St. Mary's Church.
Carlos, Joseph '75 (STL) [P] St. Louis, MO Franciscan Friary of St. Anthony of Padua.
Carlsen, James F. '00 (MOB) Daphne, AL Christ the King Church.
Carlsen, Jeffrey '72 (BAL) Special Assignment.
Carlson, Edward A. '83 (CHI) [50] Chicago, IL St. Edward Church.
Carlson, Msgr. George F. (BO) [25] Boston, MA Holy Name Church.
Carlson, Gerald J. '97 (GI) Greeley, NE Sacred Heart Church.
Carlson, Gregory I. *s.j.* '74 (OM) [K] Omaha, NE Jesuit Community at Creighton University.
Carlson, James R. '73 (SAG) Birch Run, MI Sacred Heart Church.
Carlson, Kenneth F. '98 (CHI) Chicago Ridge, IL Our Lady of the Ridge Church.
Carlson, Richard D. '69 (NEW) Saddle Brook, NJ St. Philip the Apostle Church.
Carlson, Robert D. '63 (GAL) Galena Park, TX Our Lady of Fatima Church.
Carlson, Robert J. '70 (SFS) [1] Sioux Falls, SD St. Joseph Church.
Carlson, Steven V. '96 (R) On Duty Outside the Diocese.
Carlton, Maurice T. '68 (MET) Highland Park, NJ St. Paul the Apostle Church; [G] Somerset, NJ McCarrick Care Center.
Carlucci, F. Antonio *r.c.j.* '78 (LA) [Q] Camarillo, CA Rogationist Fathers.
Carman, Bernard P. *s.a.c.* '79 (WDC) [B] West Hyattsville, MD Pallottine Seminary at Green Hill.
Carman, Paul '00 (SY) [3] Endicott, NY St. Anthony of Padua Church.
Carmichael, Eugene J. *s.j.* '73 (CIN) [M] Cincinnati, OH Jesuit Community at Xavier University.
Carmichael, John F. '97 (BO) Dracut, MA St. Francis Church.
Carmody, James '63 (RVC) Hicksville, NY St. Ignatius Loyola Church.
Carmody, James F. '70 (WOR) [17] Worcester, MA St. Andrew the Apostle Church.
Carmody, Lawrence W. '90 (COS) Security, CO Holy Family Church.
Carmody, Michael J. '83 (GAL) [17] Houston, TX St. Catherine of Siena Church.
Carmody, Stephen *o.p.* (NY) Manhattan, NY New York Presbyterian Hospital.
Carmody, Stephen Francis *o.p.* '81 (NY) [22] New York, NY St. Catherine of Siena Church.
Carmola, Michael J. '64 (SY) Special Assignment; [U] Syracuse, NY Christ the King Retreat House.
Carmon, Dominic *s.v.d.* '60 (NO) [3] Kenner, LA St. Elizabeth Ann Seton Church.
Carmona, Edwardo '82 (SB) [E] Riverside, CA Operarios Del Reino De Cristo, O.R.C.
Carmona, Henry '78 (B) Rupert, ID St. Nicholas Church.
Carmona, Hugo (PRO) [12] Providence, RI St. Edward Church.
Carmona, Hugo '85 (PRO) [26] Providence, RI Our Lady of Mt. Carmel Church.
Carmone, Anthony F. '47 (PRO) Retired.
Carnago, William J. '88 (DET) Absent on Leave.
Carne, Joseph D. '71 (MAR) Bessemer, MI St. Sebastian Church.
Carneiro, Denis '68 (CHI) Inverness, IL Holy Family Church; [J] Hoffman Estates, IL St. Alexius Medical Center.
Carnevale, John *o.f.m.* '66 (PAT) Pompton Lakes, NJ Our Lady of the Assumption Church.
Carnevale, Thomas J. '61 (PRO) Retired.
Carney, Aloysius S. '60 (NEW) Plainfield, NJ St. Mary Church; Plainfield, NJ Muhlenberg Medical Center.
Carney, Angus N. *o.s.a.* '43 (PH) [AA] Villanova, PA St. Thomas Monastery.
Carney, Christopher M. '71 (BAL) [63] Baltimore, MD St. Michael Church.
Carney, Edward '63 (PEO) Special Residence.
Carney, J. Michael '70 (SY) [3] Utica, NY Our Lady of Lourdes Church.
Carney, James R. *s.j.* '56 (NY) [F] New York, NY Regis High School; [DD] New York, NY St. Ignatius Loyola Residence.
Carney, John '63 (BAL) Retired.
Carney, John F. '91 (SFE) Tijeras, NM Holy Child Church.
Carney, John J. *c.m.* '82 (FgM) Vincentian Foreign Missions.
Carney, Joseph T. '68 (MIA) Miami Springs, FL Blessed Trinity Church.
Carney, Patrick J. '55 (NY) Hartsdale, NY Sacred Heart Church.
Carney, Richard F. '55 (KC) Retired.
Carney, Robert E. '91 (TUC) Douglas, AZ St. Luke Church; Pirtleville, AZ St. Bernard's Church.
Carney, Robert E., Jr. '91 (TUC) [I] Douglas, AZ Cochise Community College.
Carney, Robert V. *s.a.c.* '66 (MIL) [D] Milwaukee, WI Pius XI High School; [P] Milwaukee, WI Pallotti House; [P] Milwaukee, WI St. Vincent Community; [Y] Milwaukee, WI Pallottine Fathers and Brothers, Inc., Disability Trust; [Y] Milwaukee, WI Pallottine Fathers and Brothers, Inc., Educational and Apostolic Ministry Trust.
Carney, Thomas *m.s.c.* '54 (Y) [A] Youngstown, OH Sacred Heart Retreat House & Renewal Center.
Carney, Thomas A. *m.s.c.* '54 (Y) [20] Youngstown, OH St. Rose of Lima Church.
Carnicelli, Xavier *o.f.m.* '57 (NY) [DD] New York, NY Franciscan Province of the Immaculate Conception.
Caro, Robert V. *s.j.* '70 (LA) [C] Los Angeles, CA Loyola Marymount University.
Caro Morales, Jorge L. '89 (MGZ) Sabana Grande, PR Church of San Isidro.
Carol, David *o.p.* '89 (STL) [P] St. Louis, MO St. Dominic Priory.
Carola, Joseph A. *s.j.* '93 (NO) [P] New Orleans, LA Jesuit Provincial Office.
Carolan, Charles *s.s.c.* (LA) [92] Los Angeles, CA St. Teresa of Avila Church.
Carolan, Charles B. (VIC) Cistern, TX SS. Cyril and Methodius Church.
Carolan, Charles B. '55 (VIC) Flatonia, TX Sacred Heart Church.
Carolan, Craig G. '91 (BWN) [2] Harlingen, TX Immaculate Heart of Mary Church.
Carolan, Emmet '62 (SAT) [41] San Antonio, TX St. James the Apostle Church.
Carolan, J. Lawrence '69 (SR) Boyes Hot Springs, CA St. Leo Church.
Carolan, John J. '51 (CHI) [2] Oak Park, IL St. Catherine of Siena-St. Lucy Church; Retired.
Carolan, Thomas *o.f.m.* '58 (CLV) Warrensville Heights, OH St. Jude Church; [O] Cleveland, OH St. Jude Friary.
Carolin, Joeseph C. '66 (HBG) South Mountain, PA Restoration Center.
Carolin, William J. '45 (LAN) Brighton, MI St. Patrick Church; Retired.
Caroluzza, Msgr. Thomas J. '58 (RIC) [4] Virginia Beach, VA Holy Spirit Church.
Caron, Antonin R. '69 (PRT) Retired.
Caron, Eduardo *c.s.sp.* '57 (SJN) [F] Dorado, PR Santuario del Espiritu Santo.
Caron, Gerard *s.m.* '54 (BO) [W] Boston, MA Marist Fathers Lourdes Residence; [BB] Boston, MA Chapel of Our Lady of Lourdes.
Caron, Gerard J. '94 (PRO) [1] Woonsocket, RI St. Agatha Church; [11] Woonsocket, RI Precious Blood Church.
Caron, Marc B. '89 (PRT) [1] Portland, ME Cathedral of the Immaculate Conception; Special or Other Diocesan Assignment.
Caron, Paul A. '83 (FR) Nantucket, MA St. Mary's, Our Lady of the Isle Church.
Caronan, John E. *o.praem.* '94 (ORG) [A] Silverado, CA St. Michael's Norbertine Postulancy, Novitiate and Juniorate; [I] Silverado, CA Norbertine Fathers of Orange Inc.; [O] Silverado, CA Norbertine Association of St. Joseph, Inc.
Carosella, Jerome A. '63 (VEN) Boca Grande, FL Our Lady of Mercy Church.
Carota, Peter '97 (STO) Ceres, CA St. Jude Church.
Carotenuto, Anthony M. '68 (TR) Red Bank, NJ St. Anthony Church.
Carpena, Octavio R. '84 (MET) On Duty Outside the Diocese.
Carpender, John W. '53 (DUB) Retired.
Carpender, Thomas J. '48 (DUB) Retired.
Carpenter, Christopher '95 (PHX) [2] Mesa, AZ Christ the King Church.
Carpenter, Edward C. '95 (ELP) [32] El Paso, TX St. Stephen, Deacon and Martyr Church; San Elizario, TX San Elceario Church.
Carpenter, Edward V. '43 (SC) Retired.
Carpenter, Todd *o.f.m.* '99 (CAM) [2] Camden, NJ St. Anthony of Padua Church.
Carpenter, William L. *c.s.v.* '77 (CHI) [N] Chicago, IL Viatorian Residence.
Carpentier, Normand E. '71 (PRT) Old Orchard Beach, ME St. Margaret's Church.
Carpentier, Robert A. '67 (PRO) Absent on Leave.
Carpine, Eric T. *o.f.m.* '75 (PRO) [P] Providence, RI St. Francis Friary.
Carpinelli, Vincent G. '71 (CAM) Rosenhayn, NJ St. Mary's Church.
Carr, Alton *c.ss.r.* '60 (SAT) [37] San Antonio, TX St. Gerard Majella Church.
Carr, Andrew *c.ss.r.* '55 (BAL) [62] Baltimore, MD St. Michael Church; [78] Baltimore, MD St. Patrick Church.
Carr, Bernard J. '76 (SB) Anza, CA Sacred Heart Church.
Carr, Brandon (BAL) Glen Burnie, MD Holy Trinity Church.
Carr, Cornelius J. *s.j.* '51 (BUF) [50] Buffalo, NY St. Michael Church.
Carr, David W. '80 (PMB) [2] Lake Worth, FL St. Luke Church; [B] West Palm Beach, FL Cardinal Newman High School.
Carr, David W. '80 (WOR) On Duty Outside the Diocese.
Carr, Ephrem *o.s.b.* '67 (IND) [J] St. Meinrad, IN St. Meinrad Archabbey.
Carr, Eugene R. '63 (SCR) Retired.
Carr, Gary M. '82 (SPC) West Plains, MO St. Mary Church.
Carr, George W. *o.f.m.* '45 (P) Rockaway, OR St. Mary by the Sea Church.
Carr, Gerald F. *o.f.m.* '56 (NY) [35] New York, NY St. Francis of Assisi Church.
Carr, Msgr. James A. '55 (CAM) Retired.
Carr, James V. '69 (RIC) Portsmouth, VA Church of the Resurrection.
Carr, John A. *c.s.p.* '40 (NY) [DD] Jamaica Estates, NY Paulist Fathers Generalate.
Carr, John A. *c.s.p.* '40 (SFR) [32] San Francisco, CA Old St. Mary's Church.

Carr, John F. '47 (BO) Senior Priests.
Carr, Mark V. '52 (BO) Senior Priests.
Carr, Martin P. '74 (GB) Special Assignment.
Carr, Matthew A. '99 (ARL) Annandale, VA Holy Spirit Church.
Carr, Michael '68 (CHY) Casper, WY St. Anthony of Padua Church; [B] Casper, WY St. Anthony Manor.
Carr, Paul J. *f.s.s.p.* '92 (SCR) [M] Elmhurst, PA Priestly Fraternity of St. Peter (F.S.S.P.), North American District Headquarters.
Carr, Peter *o.f.m.* '39 (SP) [O] St. Petersburg, FL St. Anthony Friary.
Carr, Robert J. '93 (BO) [2] Chelsea, MA St. Rose of Lima Church.
Carr, Walter F. '92 (AUS) Andice, TX Santa Rosa Church.
Carr, William F. *s.j.* '56 (BGP) [P] Fairfield, CT The Fairfield Jesuit Community-Fairfield University.
Carr, William H. '69 (RIC) Williamsburg, VA St. Bede's Church.
Carr, William M. '59 (WCH) [1] Wichita, KS Cathedral of the Immaculate Conception.
Carranco, Juan *s.m.* '50 (SFR) [N] San Francisco, CA Marist Center of the West.
Carrano, Michael A. (BRK) [12] Brooklyn, NY Assumption of the Blessed Virgin Mary Church.
Carrano, Michael A. '70 (BRK) [E] Brooklyn, NY Office of Religious Education: Evangelization and Catholic Formation.
Carranza, Fernando '95 (NEW) [3] Union City, NJ Sts. Joseph and Michael Church.
Carranza, Riz '80 (LA) Santa Maria, CA St. Mary of the Assumption Church.
Carrara, Christopher C. '94 (OG) Tupper Lake, NY Holy Name of Jesus Church.
Carraro, Francesco '95 (PCE) Penuelas, PR St. Joseph Church.
Carraro, Francesco '97 (NEW) On Duty Outside the Archdiocese.
Carreira, Emmanuel M. *s.j.* '60 (CLV) [B] Cleveland, OH John Carroll Jesuit Community.
Carreiro, Walter (BO) Wilmington, MA St. Thomas of Villanova Church.
Carrella, Eugene J. '84 (NY) [194] Staten Island, NY St. Adalbert Church.
Carreon, Albert S. '51 (GAL) Retired.
Carrero, Angel Dario '95 (SJN) [A] Bayamon, PR Bayamon Central University.
Carrero, Dario *o.f.m.* '95 (SJN) [4] Toa Baja, PR San Jose Obrero Church.
Carrero, Jesse *c.m.f.* '85 (MET) [4] Perth Amboy, NJ Our Lady of Fatima Church.
Carrier, Herve G. '47 (PRT) Retired.
Carrier, J. Victor '69 (SPR) [4] Chicopee, MA St. Anne's Church.
Carrier, Mark F. '99 (ARL) Fairfax, VA St. Leo's Church.
Carrier, Michael J. '95 (WIL) Ogletown, DE Holy Family Church.
Carrier, Paul E. *s.j.* '77 (BGP) [B] Fairfield, CT Fairfield University; [P] Fairfield, CT The Fairfield Jesuit Community-Fairfield University; [W] Fairfield, CT Newman Centers - Campus Ministry.
Carriere, Henry G. '46 (CR) Retired.
Carrieri, Leonard *m.ss.cc.* '36 (CAM) [M] Linwood, NJ Villa Pieta.
Carriero, John P. *s.j.* '63 (ROC) [C] Rochester, NY McQuaid Jesuit High School.
Carrigan, Fred (NY) Manhattan, NY Columbia Presbyterian Medical Center.
Carrigan, Frederick (NY) [109] New York, NY St. Rose of Lima Church.
Carrigan, Fredrick '61 (PRT) On Duty Outside the Diocese.
Carrigan, Thomas C. '60 (SAC) Retired and in Senior Ministry.
Carrigg, George A. '57 (BO) [17] Boston, MA St. Christopher Church.
Carrigg, William J. '56 (BO) On Duty Outside the Archdiocese.
Carrigg, William J. '56 (PRT) Fort Fairfield, ME St. Denis Church; Limestone, ME St. Louis Church.
Carrilllo, Sergio '82 (MIA) Retired.
Carrillo, Arhtur *c.p.* '70 (CHI) [N] Chicago, IL Passionist Provincial Office.
Carrillo, Msgr. Arsenio S. '56 (TUC) [1] Tucson, AZ St. Augustine's Church; Special Assignment.
Carrillo, Ron *s.f.* '74 (SFE) Santa Cruz, NM Holy Cross Church.
Carrillo, Victor '87 (SAT) Floresville, TX Sacred Heart Church.
Carrington, Richard J. '76 (NEW) West New York, NJ St. Joseph of the Palisades Church.
Carrion, Jose A. *o.f.m.cap.* '92 (PCE) [5] Ponce, PR Santa Teresita Church; [E] Ponce, PR Residencia Asis.
Carrion, Jose Antonio '77 (SJN) [1] Toa Alta, PR San Esteban, Protomartir Church.
Carrion, Michael W. (BAL) [42] Baltimore, MD Immaculate Heart of Mary Church.
Carrion, Patrick (BAL) Bel Air, MD St. Margaret Church.
Carrion, Patrick M. '82 (BAL) [24] Baltimore, MD St. Clare Church; Special Assignment.
Carriveau, Ernest J. *m.s.* '64 (FR) [I] Attleboro, MA La Salette Shrine.
Carrola, Rudolph T., Jr. '88 (SAT) Macdona, TX Our Lady Queen of Heaven Church; Von Ormy, TX Sacred Heart Church.
Carroll, Msgr. Aidan M. '63 (LA) Valinda, CA St. Martha Church; [D] La Puente, CA Bishop Amat Memorial High School.
Carroll, Alban *s.a.* '55 (R) Apex, NC St. Andrew the Apostle Church.
Carroll, Brian '62 (JKS) Brandon, MS St. Paul Church.
Carroll, Brian *o.f.m.* '86 (NY) [35] New York, NY St. Francis of Assisi Church.
Carroll, Msgr. Daniel '37 (CHY) Retired.
Carroll, Daniel *s.d.s.* '44 (MIL) [N] Milwaukee, WI St. Mary's Nursing Home.
Carroll, Daniel *o.carm.* '60 (CHI) [D] Chicago, IL Mt. Carmel High School; [N] Chicago, IL Carmelite Priory of St. Cyril.
Carroll, Msgr. Donald M. '34 (CHI) Retired.
Carroll, Eamon *o.carm* '46 (VEN) [G] Nokomis, FL Carmel at Mission Valley.
Carroll, Eamon R. *o.carm.* '46 (CHI) [N] Chicago, IL Brandsma House.
Carroll, Edmund F. *t.o.r.* '57 (FgM) T.O.R. Foreign Missions.
Carroll, Edmund F. *t.o.r.* '57 (PIT) [O] Pittsburgh, PA Third Order Regular of Saint Francis - Province of the Most Sacred Heart of Jesus.
Carroll, Edward E. '50 (MIL) Retired.
Carroll, Edward G. '67 (BO) [2] Woburn, MA St. Barbara Church; Health Leave.
Carroll, Emmett *o.f.m. conv.* '54 (TR) Seaside Heights, NJ Our Lady of Perpetual Help Church.
Carroll, Emmett H. *s.j.* '62 (SEA) [A] Seattle, WA Seattle University.
Carroll, Francis P. *s.s.c.* '62 (FgM) St. Columban's Foreign Mission.
Carroll, Gilbert A. '41 (CHI) [203] Chicago, IL St. Timothy Church; Retired.
Carroll, Howard '54 (SFS) Retired; [I] Sioux Falls, SD The Berakhah House.
Carroll, J. Alfred *s.j.* '59 (SPK) [C] Spokane, WA Gonzaga University.
Carroll, James '49 (JKS) Retired.
Carroll, James *o.f.m.* '79 (PSC) [A] Sybertsville, PA Holy Dormition Friary.
Carroll, Msgr. James J. '45 (COL) Retired.
Carroll, James J. '56 (NEW) Fairview, NJ St. John the Baptist Church.
Carroll, James M. '68 (BO) Georgetown, MA St. Mary Church.
Carroll, John A. *s.s.j.* (WDC) [23] Washington, DC Incarnation Church.
Carroll, John J. *s.j.* '55 (FgM) Provinces.
Carroll, Msgr. John J. '66 (PAT) Kinnelon, NJ Our Lady of the Magnificat Church.
Carroll, John P. '53 (BO) [6] Quincy, MA Most Blessed Sacrament Church.
Carroll, John R. (BO) Boston, MA Beth Israel Deaconess Medical Center.
Carroll, Joseph *s.j.* '42 (OAK) [17] Oakland, CA St. Mary, Immaculate Conception-St. Francis de Sales Church.
Carroll, Joseph '55 (HON) Retired.
Carroll, Msgr. Joseph A. '74 (SD) [35] San Diego, CA St. Rita Church; [J] San Diego, CA St. Vincent de Paul Village; [J] San Diego, CA S.V.D.P. Management Inc.; [M] San Diego, CA Catholic Committee on Scouting.
Carroll, Joseph D. '41 (ALN) Retired; [J] Bethlehem, PA Holy Family Villa.
Carroll, Joseph P. *s.j.* '41 (OAK) [N] Berkeley, CA Jesuit Community at Jesuit School of Theology at Berkeley.
Carroll, Lawrence J. '81 (BGP) Brookfield, CT St. Joseph Church.
Carroll, Michael (GB) Eland, WI St. William Church.
Carroll, Michael '72 (SAC) [7] Sacramento, CA Presentation of the Blessed Virgin Mary Church.
Carroll, Michael A. '85 (RVC) St. James, NY SS. Philip and James Church.
Carroll, Michael J. (LA) Walnut, CA St. Lorenzo Ruiz Church.
Carroll, Msgr. Michael J. '61 (PH) Rydal, PA St. Hilary of Poitiers Church.
Carroll, Michael J. *c.m.* '77 (BRK) [D] Staten Island, NY St. John's University, Staten Island Campus; [D] Jamaica, NY St. John's University; [V] Jamaica, NY Vincentian Residence.
Carroll, Michael R. (GB) Wittenberg, WI Holy Family-St. William Church.
Carroll, Michael R. '70 (GB) Marion, WI St. Mary Church; Tigerton, WI St. Anthony Church.
Carroll, Norman P. '93 (WIL) Ridgely, MD St. Benedict Church.
Carroll, Owen '73 (NTN) Oakland, CA St. John The Theologian Church.
Carroll, Owen '73 (OAK) [A] Berkeley, CA Dominican School of Philosophy and Theology; [B] Moraga, CA St. Mary's College.
Carroll, Patrick *c.s.sp.* '66 (STA) Elkton, FL St. Ambrose Church.
Carroll, Patrick A. '43 (OM) Retired.
Carroll, Patrick C. *s.j.* '66 (YAK) [4] Yakima, WA St. Joseph's Church.
Carroll, Patrick J. '53 (NY) [88] New York, NY Our Lady of Loreto Church.
Carroll, Patrick M. '71 (NY) [E] White Plains, NY Archbishop Stepinac High School.
Carroll, Msgr. Ralph E. '58 (NO) [7] Metairie, LA St. Clement of Rome Church.
Carroll, Msgr. Richard L. '59 (NO) Retired.
Carroll, Robert *o.carm.* (CHI) [D] Mundelein, IL Carmel High School.
Carroll, Robert *o.carm.* '71 (CHI) [N] Mundelein, IL Carmelite Monastery.
Carroll, Msgr. Robert B. '63 (PAT) Highland Lakes, NJ Our Lady of Fatima Church.
Carroll, Robert J. '75 (PH) Flourtown, PA St. Genevieve Church; Wyndmoor, PA Seven Dolors Church.
Carroll, Roger F. '63 (STP) [13] St. Paul, MN St. Andrew Church.
Carroll, Sean O. *s.j.* '00 (OAK) [20] Oakland, CA St. Patrick's Church; [N] Berkeley, CA Jesuit Community at Jesuit School of Theology at Berkeley.
Carroll, Thomas J. *m.s.* '54 (ATL) Snellville, GA St. Oliver Plunkett Church.
Carroll, Thomas J. *s.j.* '84 (BO) [W] Boston, MA Jesuit Urban Center & Immaculate Conception Community; [BB] Boston, MA Immaculate Conception Church.
Carroll, Thomas M. *o.s.m.* '53 (CHI) [N] Chicago, IL Order of Friar Servants of Mary (Servites) United States of America Province, Inc.
Carroll, Thomas R. *sch.p.* '70 (LEX) [B] Martin, KY The Piarist School; [G] Prestonsburg, KY Piarist Fathers.
Carroll, William '50 (B) Retired.
Carroll, William C. *s.j.* '69 (PH) [83] Philadelphia, PA Old St. Joseph's Church.
Carroll, William E. *o.p.* (CHI) [N] Chicago, IL Dominicans (Provincial Office).
Carroll, William R. '70 (BO) [1] Arlington, MA St. Agnes Church.
Carron, Malcolm *s.j.* '51 (DET) [P] Clarkston, MI Colombiere Center.
Carrozza, Andrew P. '90 (NY) Suffern, NY Sacred Heart Church.
Carrozza, Benedict *o.f.m.* '39 (ALB) [A] Catskill, NY St. Anthony Friary.
Carrozzo, Anthony M. *o.f.m.* '66 (NY) [115] New York, NY St. Stephen of Hungary Church.
Carruthers, Michael '91 (MIA) [1] Hialeah, FL Immaculate Conception Church.
Carscallen, Edward C. '47 (TUC) Special Assignment; Retired; [K] Tucson, AZ Holy Hope Cemetery and Mausoleum.
Carson, David (ROC) Bath, NY Soliders' Home and Veterans' Hospital.
Carson, David L. '84 (NY) On Duty Outside the Archdiocese.
Carson, John '64 (NY) [3] Yonkers, NY St. Ann Church.
Carson, Michael '98 (SJ) [12] San Jose, CA St. John Vianney Church.
Carson, Robert E. *o.praem.* '46 (GB) [I] De Pere, WI St. Norbert Abbey; [I] De Pere, WI St. Norbert Abbey.
Carson, Msgr. Stanley B. '79 (ALT) [4] Altoona, PA Sacred Heart Church.
Cartagena, Antonio '85 (CGS) [11] Barrio Bairoa, PR San Juan Apostol y Evangelista Church.
Carten, Thomas F. *c.s.c.* '79 (SCR) [C] Wilkes-Barre, PA Kings College.
Carter, Augustine W. *o.carm.* '51 (LA) [F] Encino, CA Crespi Carmelite High School; [Q] Los Angeles, CA Mount Carmel Priory, Carmelite Fathers and Brothers.
Carter, Daniel E. '79 (SFR) [27] San Francisco, CA St. James Church; San Francisco, CA Youth Guidance Center.
Carter, Edward W. *s.j.* '62 (CIN) [M] Cincinnati, OH Faber Jesuit Community.
Carter, Eli '75 (HON) On Sabbatical.
Carter, Francis T. '86 (HRT) [1] West Hartford, CT St. Brigid's Church.
Carter, Msgr. James A. '66 (CHR) [17] Charleston, SC Christ Our King Church.
Carter, James C. *s.j.* '58 (NO) [C] New Orleans, LA Loyola University New Orleans.
Carter, Msgr. John T. '49 (E) [16] Erie, PA St. George Church.
Carter, John T. '70 (BAL) [41] Baltimore, MD Immaculate Conception Church; Absent on Sick Leave.
Carter, Joseph F. '97 (PRT) On Leave.
Carter, Kevin E. '86 (NEW) [18] Jersey City, NJ St. Nicholas Church.
Carter, Martin J. *s.a.* '75 (BRK) [113] Brooklyn, NY Our Lady of Victory Church; [U] Brooklyn, NY Catholic Migration & Refugee Office, Catholic Migration Services, Inc.
Carter, Raymond J. '49 (COL) Retired.
Carter, Robert E. *s.j.* '63 (NY) [DD] New York, NY West

Side Jesuit Community.
Carter, Stephen *o.f.m.cap.* '82 (WDC) [39] Washington, DC Shrine of the Sacred Heart Church.
Carton, A. Richard '93 (PAT) Sparta, NJ Our Lady of the Lake Church.
Carton, Msgr. William J. '59 (TR) Sea Girt, NJ St. Mark Church.
Cartwright, Christopher *s.j.* '80 (PHX) [B] Phoenix, AZ Brophy College Preparatory.
Carty, John A. *s.j.* '59 (FgM) Provinces.
Carty, John T. '50 (PRO) Retired.
Caruana, Alfred E. *s.j.* '71 (NY) [DD] New York, NY Xavier Jesuit Community; [HH] New York, NY Xavier Society for the Blind.
Carucci, David P. '95 (MOB) [7] Montgomery, AL Our Lady, Queen of Mercy Church; [J] Montgomery, AL Huntington College Newman Center.
Carungay, Jevito '92 (BRK) Brooklyn, NY Wyckoff Heights Hospital.
Carusi, Angelo N. '98 (PRO) [4] Providence, RI St. Ann Church.
Caruso, Carmen A. '66 (JOL) On Duty Outside the Diocese.
Caruso, Carmen A. '66 (VEN) Sanibel, FL St. Isabel Church.
Caruso, Daniel M. '94 (SY) Vestal, NY St. Vincent de Paul Church.
Caruso, Michael P. *s.j.* '82 (SFR) [N] San Francisco, CA Jesuit Community at University of San Francisco.
Caruso, Philip J. '78 (NY) [172] Bronx, NY Our Lady of Grace Church; [3] New Rochelle, NY St. Joseph Church.
Caruso, Robert '80 (PHX) [1] Mesa, AZ All Saints Church.
Caruso, Vincent *o.de.m.* '27 (CLV) [57] Cleveland, OH Our Lady of Mount Carmel Church.
Carvajal, Damian '53 (SJN) [12] San Juan, PR Cristo Redentor Church.
Carvajal, Msgr. Felipe N. '68 (PAT) [1] Passaic, NJ St. Nicholas Church.
Carvajal, Raul H. '65 (MRY) Retired.
Carvalho, Antonio (BO) [1] Everett, MA St. Anthony Church.
Carvalho, David *o.s.b.* '57 (SD) [H] Oceanside, CA Prince of Peace Abbey, Benet Hill.
Carvalho, Gordian J., Jr. '85 (HON) Mililani Town, HI St. John Apostle and Evangelist Church.
Carven, John W. *c.m.* '60 (PH) [B] Philadelphia, PA St. Vincent's Seminary; [AA] Philadelphia, PA Congregation of the Mission.
Carver, Dennis J. '94 (BLX) Pass Christian, MS St. Paul Church.
Carvill, Michael *f.s.c.b.* '90 (FR) [2] Attleboro, MA St. Joseph's Church; [O] Attleboro, MA Priestly Fraternity of the Missionaries of St. Charles Borromeo, Inc.
Carville, John *s.t.d.* '63 (BR) [21] Baton Rouge, LA St. Thomas More Church.
Cary, Liam '92 (P) Medford, OR Sacred Heart of Jesus Church.
Cary, Robert '57 (SJ) [G] San Jose, CA O'Connor Hospital.
Cary, Robert *c.s.p.* '84 (GR) Grand Rapids, MI Chapel of St. Paul-Catholic Information Center.
Cary, William J. '58 (SUP) Retired.
Carzon, Thomas *o.m.v.* '96 (BO) [B] Boston, MA Our Lady of Grace Seminary; [BB] Boston, MA St. Francis Chapel.
Casabon, Luis '61 (MIA) [5] Hialeah, FL St. John the Apostle Church.
Casagram, Michael *o.c.s.o.* '82 (L) [L] Trappist, KY Abbey of Our Lady of Gethsemani, of the Order of Cistercians of the Strict Observance.
Casale, Charles '69 (FRS) Bishop, CA Our Lady of Perpetual Help Church.
Casale, Msgr. Franklyn M. (MIA) [B] Opa Locka, FL St. Thomas University.
Casale, Msgr. Franklyn M. '67 (NEW) On Duty Outside the Archdiocese.
Casaliggi, John R. '36 (GBG) Retired.
Casari, Michael T. '95 (WIL) Absent on Sick Leave.
Casarotto, Secondo *c.s.* '66 (BUF) [9] Buffalo, NY St. Anthony of Padua Church.
Casas, Miguel delas *o.p.* '88 (OAK) [N] Oakland, CA Western Dominican Province.
Casaus, Vicente *sch.p.* '52 (LA) [76] Los Angeles, CA St. Lucy Church.
Casavantes, Carlos S. *f.s.s.p.* '85 (SCR) [M] Elmhurst, PA Priestly Fraternity of St. Peter (F.S.S.P.), North American District Headquarters.
Casavantes, Carlos S. *f.s.s.p.* '86 (SCR) [19] Scranton, PA St. Michael's Church.
Casazza, Msgr. David J. '43 (NEW) River Edge, NJ St. Peter the Apostle Church; Retired.
Cascelli, Msgr. George J. '55 (NY) [34] New York, NY Epiphany Church.
Cascia, Philip J. '77 (HRT) Prospect, CT St. Anthony's Church.
Cascino, Marion *o.f.m.* '49 (FgM) Franciscan Foreign Missions.
Cascino, Marion *o.f.m.* '49 (NY) [1] New York, NY Cathedral of St. Patrick; [DD] New York, NY Franciscan Province of the Immaculate Conception; [DD] New York, NY Padua Friary.
Casciotti, James A. *s.j.* '78 (WDC) [M] Washington, DC Leonard Neale House; [V] Washington, DC Jesuit Conference, Inc.
Case, Francis E. *s.j.* '69 (P) [L] Portland, OR Jesuit Provincial Office (Society of Jesus, Oregon Prov.).
Case, Francis J. '66 (SY) New Berlin, NY St. Theresa of the Infant Jesus Church; Sherburne, NY St. Malachy of Armach Church.
Case, Lowell D. *s.s.j.* '80 (WDC) [32] Washington, DC Our Lady of Perpetual Help Church.
Case, Richard D. *s.j.* (FBK) [C] Fairbanks, AK Jesuit Residence.
Casella, Thomas A. *c.m.* '71 (BRK) [V] Jamaica, NY Vincentian Residence.
Casellas, Ramon Jaime *o.f.m.cap.* '85 (SJN) [18] San Juan, PR San Francisco de Asis Church.
Caserta, Angelo C. '45 (CIN) Piqua, OH St. Boniface Church; Retired.
Caserta, Charles W. '54 (CIN) Retired.
Caserta, Thomas G. '79 (BRK) [B] Douglaston, NY Cathedral Seminary Residence of the Immaculate Conception.
Casey, Anthony C. '58 (BRK) [236] Queens, NY St. Rose of Lima Church.
Casey, Daniel '58 (SAC) Retired and in Senior Ministry.
Casey, David J. *s.j.* '69 (NY) [DD] New York, NY Jesuit Community at Fordham University.
Casey, Denis '57 (TLS) [E] Tulsa, OK Saint Francis Hospital, Inc.
Casey, Diarmuid *c.s.sp.* '69 (SJ) Mountain View, CA St. Athanasius Church.
Casey, Donald A. '65 (SB) Retired.
Casey, Edward J. '79 (PH) [V] Darby, PA Villa Saint Joseph; [V] Ventnor, PA Villa St. Joseph by the Sea; [Y] Darby, PA Little Flower Manor.
Casey, Francis M. '64 (RVC) Seaford, NY Maria Regina Church; Retired.
Casey, Msgr. George T. '37 (SCR) Retired.
Casey, James R. '00 (PH) [78] Philadelphia, PA St. John the Baptist Church.
Casey, John *s.a.c.* '67 (LUB) Seminole, TX St. James Church.
Casey, John D. '55 (HRT) [5] New Haven, CT St. Boniface's Church; [7] New Haven, CT St. Casimir's Church.
Casey, Msgr. John F. '54 (BRK) [182] Queens, NY Incarnation Church.
Casey, Msgr. John H. '57 (CAM) Haddon Township, NJ St. Vincent Pallotti Church.
Casey, John J. '32 (LA) [Q] Montebello, CA Vincentian Fathers & Brothers; [W] Montebello, CA DePaul Center.
Casey, John J. *m.m.* '56 (FgM) Maryknoll Foreign Missions.
Casey, John J. '84 (MET) North Plainfield, NJ St. Joseph Church.
Casey, John P. *m.m.* '56 (NY) [DD] Maryknoll, NY Maryknoll Fathers and Brothers.
Casey, John V. *o.s.a.* '39 (BO) [C] North Andover, MA Merrimack College.
Casey, John W. '45 (SCR) Retired.
Casey, Joseph H. *s.j.* '49 (BO) [W] Weston, MA Campion Jesuit Community.
Casey, Joseph M. '66 (PAT) Morristown, NJ Assumption of the Blessed Virgin Mary Church; Morris Plains, NJ Greystone Park Psychiatric Hospital.
Casey, Kevin *c.p.* '67 (MET) [H] South River, NJ Passionist Provincial Office.
Casey, Kevin M. *c.p.* '56 (MET) Old Bridge, NJ St. Thomas the Apostle Church.
Casey, Liam C. '62 (ALB) On Duty Outside the Diocese.
Casey, Liam C. '93 (HRT) [I] Hartford, CT Saint Francis Hospital and Medical Center.
Casey, M. Joseph *s.j.* '67 (DET) [K] Detroit, MI Jesuit Provincial Office-Detroit Province of the Society of Jesus; [P] Clarkston, MI Colombiere Center.
Casey, Marion G. '34 (NU) Ivanhoe, MN Divine Providence Hospital & Home; Retired; [B] Ivanhoe, MN Divine Providence Health Center; [C] Ivanhoe, MN Divine Prividence Health Center.
Casey, Martin J. *s.j.* '43 (WDC) [M] Washington, DC The Jesuit Community at Georgetown University.
Casey, Matthew *o.m.i.* '47 (WDC) [M] Washington, DC Oblate College/Center for Mission Studies Community.
Casey, Noah *o.s.b.* '76 (IND) [17] Indianapolis, IN St. Bernadette Church; [J] St. Meinrad, IN St. Meinrad Archabbey.
Casey, Patrick '97 (DET) [20] Detroit, MI St. Dominic Church; [60] Detroit, MI St. Patrick Church.
Casey, Patrick L. (NU) Darwin, MN St. John Church.
Casey, Patrick M. *s.j.* '72 (FgM) Provinces.
Casey, Patrick T. *o.m.i.* '80 (CHI) [116] Chicago, IL St. Malachy Church; [171] Chicago, IL Precious Blood Church.
Casey, Paul E. *s.s.c.* '54 (OM) [K] St. Columbans, NE St. Columban's Foreign Mission Society.
Casey, Peter J. '68 (BO) [1] Milton, MA St. Agatha Church.
Casey, Richard L. '65 (BO) Emergency Response Group.
Casey, Msgr. Robert A. '43 (SY) Retired.
Casey, Robert E. (BO) [14] Boston, MA St. Brigid Church.
Casey, Robert G. '94 (CHI) [141] Chicago, IL Notre Dame Church.
Casey, Thomas J. *s.j.* '00 (SFD) [1] Springfield, IL Cathedral of the Immaculate Conception.
Casey, Thomas J. *s.j.* '62 (KC) [B] Kansas City, MO Rockhurst University; [J] Kansas City, MO Rockhurst Jesuit Community.
Casey, Thomas J. *o.s.a.* '69 (BO) [3] Lawrence, MA St. Augustine Church.
Casey, Thomas M. *o.s.a.* '65 (BO) [C] North Andover, MA Merrimack College.
Casey, Walter E. '48 (BO) Senior Priests.
Casey, William '69 (KNX) Retired.
Casey, William P. *c.p.m.* '91 (OWN) [F] South Union, KY Fathers of Mercy.
Cash, Richard '89 (OWN) Cadiz, KY St. Stephen Church.
Cash, Richard L. '89 (OWN) Aurora, KY St. Henry Church.
Cashel, Richard '54 (SFS) Retired.
Cashen, M.E. '91 (TLS) Cushing, OK SS. Peter and Paul Church.
Cashin, Msgr. James '65 (SAT) Brackettville, TX St. Mary Magdalen Church.
Cashioli, Lawrence J. '82 (MET) Retired.
Cashman, Christopher T. '89 (BRK) [147] Queens, NY St. Aloysius Church.
Cashman, James *o.s.c.* '48 (SCL) Foreston, MN St. Louis Bertrand Church; [I] Onamia, MN Crosier Monastery.
Cashman, Jeremiah '55 (LC) Cornell, WI Holy Cross Church; Jim Falls, WI Sacred Heart Church.
Cashman, John *c.p.* '67 (MET) [H] South River, NJ Passionist Provincial Office.
Cashman, John *c.p.* '67 (VEN) [1] Naples, FL St. Ann Church.
Cashman, Joseph C. '60 (WIN) Absent on Leave.
Cashman, Msgr. Michael J. '75 (MET) Woodbridge, NJ St. James Church.
Cashman, Patrick *s.s.c.* '42 (BUF) [M] Silver Creek, NY St. Columbans on the Lake, Home for the Aged.
Casillas, Rafael '72 (LA) [37] Los Angeles, CA Resurrection Church.
Casillas, Richard *s.v.d.* '97 (LA) [28] Los Angeles, CA Our Lady of Loretto Church.
Casimano, Santino (NOR) [B] Uncasville, CT St. Bernard High School; [B] Uncasville, CT St. Bernard High School.
Casimano, Santino '75 (GLP) On Duty Outside of Diocese.
Casio, Efrin (OAK) Pleasanton, CA Federal Correctional Institution.
Caskey, John '82 (SCL) Browerville, MN Christ the King Church.
Caskey, John U. '59 (L) [56] Louisville, KY Most Blessed Sacrament Church.
Caskey, Virgilio *c.ss.r.* '44 (PCE) Guayama, PR St. Anthony of Padua Church.
Caskin, John J. *s.j.* (BO) Dorchester, MA Carney Hospital.
Caskin, John J. *s.j.* '60 (BO) [W] Boston, MA The Society of Jesus of New England-Provincial Offices; [W] Weston, MA Campion Jesuit Community.
Caslin, Msgr. Peter C. '41 (LA) [4] Long Beach, CA St. Bartholomew Church; Retired.
Casper, Kenneth R. *o.f.m.cap.* '80 (MIL) [B] Mount Calvary, WI St. Felix Friary.
Casper, Paul M. *s.c.j.* '57 (JKS) Holly Springs, MS St. Joseph Church.
Caspers, William A. '54 (CHY) Thermopolis, WY St. Francis Church; Retired.
Cassar, Edward A. '69 (BRK) [126] Brooklyn, NY St. Rosalia-Regina Pacis Church.
Cassar, Julian '77 (RVC) Priests Released from Diocesan Assignment.
Cassar, Mario '74 (DET) [3] Eastpointe, MI St. Veronica Church.
Cassato, Msgr. David L. '72 (BRK) [9] Brooklyn, NY Annunciation of the Blessed Virgin Mary Church; [105] Brooklyn, NY Shrine of Our Lady of Mount Carmel Church.
Cassel, Harry A. *o.s.a.* '50 (PH) Bryn Mawr, PA Our Mother of Good Counsel Church.
Cassella, John J. '58 (PIT) [4] Swissvale, PA Madonna del Castello Church.
Cassem, Ned H. *s.j.* '70 (BO) [W] Weston, MA Campion Jesuit Community.
Casserly, Eugene D. '69 (PT) [11] Pensacola, FL St. Mary Church.
Cassese, Anthony '77 (CLV) [36] Cleveland, OH St. Jerome Church.
Cassese, John-Marie *o.f.m.* '50 (NY) [DD] New York, NY Padua Friary.
Cassidy, Bernard F. *s.j.* '63 (HON) [G] Honolulu, HI Jesuit Fathers House.
Cassidy, Msgr. Charles C. (PAT) Retired.

Cassidy, Daniel H. *s.s.j.* '43 (BAL) [S] Baltimore, MD St. Joseph's Manor.
Cassidy, Daniel J. *o.p.* '57 (PRO) [P] Providence, RI St. Thomas Aquinas Priory at Providence College.
Cassidy, Daniel J. '78 (CHI) [76] Chicago, IL St. Hilary Church.
Cassidy, Dominic J. '74 (DAV) On Duty Outside the Diocese.
Cassidy, Felix F. *o.p.* '54 (SFR) [14] San Francisco, CA St. Dominic Church; [N] San Francisco, CA St. Dominic Priory.
Cassidy, Francis '59 (LA) Monrovia, CA Immaculate Conception Church.
Cassidy, Francis P. '57 (CHI) [140] Chicago, IL St. Nicholas of Tolentine Church.
Cassidy, James '78 (STP) Minneapolis, MN Metropolitan Medical Center.
Cassidy, James *o.s.a.* '90 (CHL) [6] Charlotte, NC St. John Neumann Church.
Cassidy, James G. *o.s.b.* '84 (MAN) [K] Manchester, NH St. Anselm Abbey.
Cassidy, James M. '61 (CLV) Ashland, OH St. Edward Church.
Cassidy, Msgr. James P. '51 (NY) [HH] New York, NY Catholic Foundation for the Dominican Republic.
Cassidy, James W. *o.s.a.* '90 (CHL) [D] Charlotte, NC Mecklenburg Area Catholic Schools (M.A.C.S.).
Cassidy, John M. '58 (CHI) [47] Chicago, IL St. Daniel the Prophet Church.
Cassidy, John T. '79 (PT) [15] Pensacola, FL St. Thomas More Church.
Cassidy, John V. '69 (LC) Eastman, WI St. Wenceslaus Church.
Cassidy, Joseph L. '45 (NEW) Retired; [N] Rutherford, NJ St. John Vianney Residence for Priests.
Cassidy, Kevin W. '60 (MAD) Pine Bluff, WI St. Mary of Pine Bluff Church.
Cassidy, Laurence L. *s.j.* '61 (NEW) [B] Jersey City, NJ Saint Peter's College; [N] Jersey City, NJ Jesuits of Saint Peter's College, Inc.
Cassidy, Martin J. '57 (MIA) [1] Pompano Beach, FL Assumption Church.
Cassidy, Matthew J. *s.j.* '99 (NY) [5] New York, NY St. Aloysius Church.
Cassidy, Patrick '47 (RIC) Retired.
Cassidy, Richard '67 (BUF) [A] East Aurora, NY Christ the King Seminary.
Cassidy, Richard '67 (DET) On Duty Outside the Archdiocese.
Cassidy, Robert T. '58 (STP) Edina, MN Our Lady of Grace Church.
Cassidy, Terry A '84 (PEO) [4] Peoria, IL St. Ann Church.
Cassidy, Theodore *s.m.* '68 (CAM) [P] Cape May Point, NJ Marianist Family Retreat Center.
Cassidy, Thomas *s.v.d.* '45 (FgM) Society of the Divine Word Foreign Missions.
Cassidy, Msgr. Thomas J. '57 (ARL) Purcellville, VA St. Francis de Sales Church.
Cassiere, Achilles *o.f.m.cap.* '52 (NEW) [4] Orange, NJ Mt. Carmel Church.
Cassiero, Daniel '68 (NY) Absent on Leave.
Cassin, Msgr. Andrew J. '54 (WDC) Waldorf, MD St. Peter Church; Retired.
Cassista, Fernand *m.s.* '65 (FR) [I] Attleboro, MA La Salette Shrine; [K] Attleboro, MA La Salette Center for Christian Living.
Casstevens, Jennifer (BO) [FF] Cambridge, MA The Youville House, Inc.
Castaldi, Joseph '63 (NOR) New London, CT St. Joseph Church.
Castaldo, John J. '87 (BGP) [12] Stamford, CT St. Maurice Church; [C] Stamford, CT Trinity Catholic High School.
Castaneda, Antonio '99 (YAK) Moses Lake, WA Our Lady of Fatima Church; Warden, WA Queen of All Saints Church.
Castaneda, Brian T. '99 (LA) [42] Los Angeles, CA St. Alphonsus Church.
Castaneda, Heibar '94 (MRY) Seaside, CA St. Francis Xavier Church.
Castaneda, Mario '95 (STO) [1] Stockton, CA Cathedral of the Annunciation.
Castaneda, Oscar '87 (MIA) Opa Locka, FL Our Lady of Perpetual Help Church.
Castaneda, Severiano '71 (LA) [63] Los Angeles, CA San Francisco Church.
Castano-Fernandez, Raphael A. '98 (ATL) [4] Marietta, GA Church of the Transfiguration.
Casteel, Michael J. '84 (SPC) Marshfield, MO Holy Trinity Church.
Casteig, Alfonso *o.f.m.cap.* '56 (DAL) [9] Dallas, TX Our Lady of Perpetual Help Church; [10] Dallas, TX Our Lady of San Juan De Los Lagos and St. Theresa Church.
Castellani, John J. '48 (HRT) Retired.
Castellani, Paul A. '96 (PH) [15] Philadelphia, PA Ascension of Our Lord Church.
Castellano, Msgr. Francis J. *v.f.* '60 (SCR) [5] Williamsport, PA Mater Dolorosa Church.
Castellanos, Ricardo C. '70 (MIA) [3] Pompano Beach, FL San Isidro Church; [L] Coconut Creek, FL Word & Life Catholic Ministry, Inc.; [L] Coconut Creek, FL Ministerio Catolico Verbo y Vida, Inc.
Castellanos Ruiz, Yesid Ricardo '82 (SJN) Rio Grande, PR San Francisco de Asis Church.
Castellino, Albert *c.ss.r.* (DEN) [33] Denver, CO St. Joseph's Church.
Castelow, Ralph '89 (WIL) Wilmington, DE St. Catherine of Siena Church.
Caster, Gary C. '92 (PEO) [P] Normal, IL St. Robert Bellarmine Newman Center, Illinois State University.
Castille, Jorge Jo '89 (SJN) Military Services.
Castillejo-Llusia, Jorge J. '89 (SJN) [4] Carolina, PR Santo Cristo de la Agonia Church.
Castillo, Carlos '83 (SFR) Novato, CA Our Lady of Loretto Church.
Castillo, Carlos C. *c.m.f.* '73 (LA) [Q] Los Angeles, CA Claretian Retreat Center Community.
Castillo, Domingo '91 (AMA) Absent on Leave.
Castillo, Francisco '67 (BWN) [3] Mission, TX Our Lady of St. John of the Fields Church.
Castillo, Jose '80 (SD) San Ysidro, CA Our Lady of Mt. Carmel Church.
Castillo, Miguel (NY) Haverstraw, NY St. Peter Church.
Castillo, Rene '89 (RIC) Wytheville, VA St. Mary's Church.
Castillo, Richard '83 (PT) On Leave of Absence.
Castillo, Rolando '94 (MIA) [A] Miami, FL St. John Vianney College Seminary.
Castillo, Rolo B. '92 (RIC) Rocky Mount, VA Francis of Assisi Church.
Castillo Aguillon, Pedro Alfonso '85 (AUS) Round Rock, TX St. William's Church.
Castle, Nathan *o.p.* '76 (PHX) [I] Phoenix, AZ Office of Youth and Young Adult Ministries.
Castle, Nathan *o.p.* '85 (OAK) [N] Oakland, CA Western Dominican Province.
Castle, Nathan G. *o.p.* '85 (PHX) [G] Tempe, AZ Dominicans (Dominican Community-Jordan House).
Castles, Patrick J. '69 (TR) Allentown, NJ St. John Church.
Castori, Michael T. *s.j.* '98 (OAK) [N] Berkeley, CA Jesuit Community at Jesuit School of Theology at Berkeley.
Castrillo, Jesus *c.m.f.* '49 (LA) El Monte, CA Our Lady of Guadalupe Church.
Castrillo, Jesus Saez *o.de.m.* '69 (CGS) Cayey, PR Nuestra Senora de la Merced Church.
Castro, Antonio '84 (GAL) [54] Houston, TX Notre Dame Church.
Castro, Dominic *o.f.m.conv.* '98 (OAK) San Pablo, CA St. Paul Church.
Castro, John *o.m.i.* (SAN) [E] San Angelo, TX Christ the King Retreat Center.
Castro, Mario Alberto '00 (BWN) [1] McAllen, TX Our Lady of Perpetual Help Church.
Castro, Patrick *o.f.m.cap.* '88 (AGN) Yona, GU San Francisco d'Assisi Church; [F] Agana Heights, GU St. Fidelis Friary.
Castro, Robert '85 (SR) Sonoma, CA St. Francis Solano Church.
Castronovo, Edmund A. '76 (SY) New Hartford, NY St. Thomas Church; Georgetown, NY Camp Georgetown; South Plymouth, NY Camp Pharsalia.
Caswell, Thomas C. '66 (SPK) Cheney, WA St. Rose of Lima Church; [N] Cheney, WA Catholic Newman Center at Eastern Washington University.
Catagnus, James N. '70 (PH) [9] Philadelphia, PA St. Ambrose Church.
Catalana, Mark '91 (SJ) San Jose, CA St. Francis High School; Special Assignment; [D] Mountain View, CA St. Francis High School.
Catalano, James *o.s.j.* '63 (FRS) [1] Bakersfield, CA Our Lady of Guadalupe Church.
Catalano, James A. *s.j.* '95 (NEW) [B] Jersey City, NJ Saint Peter's College; [N] Jersey City, NJ Jesuits of Saint Peter's College, Inc.
Catallo, Sylvester *o.f.m.cap.* '54 (NY) [B] Beacon, NY St. Lawrence of Brindisi Friary.
Catanach, Richard '88 (LSC) Deming, NM St. Ann's Church.
Catanello, Ignatius '66 (BRK) [178] Queens, NY Holy Family Church.
Catania, Thomas M. '73 (BRK) [158] Queens, NY Blessed Virgin Mary, Help of Christians Church; Released from Diocesan Assignment.
Catanise, Joseph '82 (ROC) [M] Rochester, NY Diocesan Department of Campus Ministry.
Catanzaro, Albert *c.p.* '45 (BRK) [V] Jamaica, NY Immaculate Conception Monastery.
Cataudo, Anthony I. *o.p.* '60 (CAM) [M] Camden, NJ Dominican Sisters of the Perpetual Rosary Chaplain's Residence.
Catoir, John T. (PAT) Retired.
Catoir, John T. '60 (PAT) [P] Chester, NJ Nazareth Village; [P] Passaic, NJ St. Jude Media Ministries.
Catucci, Thomas F. '82 (SY) Kirkwood, NY St. Mary Church; Special Assignment.
Catullo, Pasquale R. '63 (PH) Retired.
Catuso, Orville J. *s.j.* '53 (GB) [M] Oshkosh, WI Jesuit Retreat House.
Cauagnaro, John A. '75 (CAM) Merchantville, NJ St. Peter's Church.
Caufield, Msgr. John J. '48 (PH) Retired.
Caufield, Kenneth J. *s.j.* (NY) [F] New York, NY Regis High School.
Caufield, Kenneth J. *s.j.* '67 (NY) [DD] New York, NY St. Ignatius Loyola Residence.
Caul, Robert F. '61 (PRO) [R] Narragansett, RI Our Lady of Peace Spiritual Life Center.
Cauley, Robert W. '42 (CLV) Retired.
Cauley, Thomas F. '81 (PMB) Port St. Lucie, FL Holy Family Church.
Caulfield, John '59 (ORL) [4] Lakeland, FL St. Joseph's Church.
Caulfield, John F. *s.j.* '44 (BO) [W] Chestnut Hill, MA The Jesuit Community at Boston College.
Caulfield, Msgr. John J. '48 (PH) [1] Philadelphia, PA Cathedral Basilica of SS. Peter and Paul; Exton, PA SS. Philip and James Church.
Caulfield, Sean '49 (B) Retired.
Cautela, Mauro J. '74 (PIT) Ellwood City, PA Holy Redeemer Church.
Cauterucci, Francis J. '90 (PH) Chester Heights, PA St. Thomas the Apostle Church.
Cavagnaro, Camillus *o.f.m.* '46 (FgM) Franciscan Foreign Missions.
Cavagnaro, John A. '75 (CAM) Swedesboro, NJ St. Joseph's Church.
Cavagnaro, Mark R. '70 (CAM) Marmora, NJ The Church of the Resurrection.
Cavagnuolo, Salvatore F. '67 (HRT) Yalesville, CT Our Lady of Fatima Church.
Cavalier, Robert C. '72 (NO) On Duty Outside the Archdiocese.
Cavalier, Wayne A. *o.p.* (BO) [25] Boston, MA Holy Name Church.
Cavalier, Wayne A. *o.p.* '93 (NO) [P] New Orleans, LA Dominican Friars, Southern Dominican Province of St. Martin de Porres.
Cavallaro, Msgr. Galliano J. '42 (PRO) Retired.
Cavalli, Victor '21 (SAC) Benicia, CA St. Dominic Church.
Cavallyzz, Kevin P. '93 (BRK) [233] Queens, NY Resurrection-Ascension Church.
Cavanagh, Brian '58 (LA) Covina, CA Sacred Heart Church.
Cavanagh, David '85 (FTW) [I] South Bend, IN Prelature of the Holy Cross and Opus Dei.
Cavanagh, Gerald F. *s.j.* '64 (DET) [K] Detroit, MI Jesuit Community at the University of Detroit.
Cavanagh, Msgr. James M. '52 (BRK) Retired.
Cavanagh, Joseph A. *s.j.* '62 (CI) [C] Kolonia, Pohnpei, FM Jesuit House.
Cavanagh, Joseph A. *s.j.* '62 (FgM) Provinces.
Cavanagh, Michael J. '59 (PBL) Retired.
Cavanaugh, Brian *t.o.r.* '82 (STU) [A] Steubenville, OH Franciscan University of Steubenville; [F] Steubenville, OH Holy Spirit Friary.
Cavanaugh, Daniel J. '66 (PH) Ambler, PA St. Joseph Church.
Cavanaugh, Harry M. *c.pp.s.* '54 (TOL) Alvada, OH St. Peter Church; New Riegel, OH St. Boniface Church.
Cavanaugh, Jack *s.c.j.* '79 (GAL) [48] Houston, TX St. Matthew the Evangelist Church.
Cavanaugh, James '80 (LA) On Sick Leave.
Cavanaugh, James K. '51 (Y) Retired.
Cavanaugh, John *c.ss.r.* '46 (ORL) New Smyrna Beach, FL Sacred Heart Church.
Cavanaugh, John *m.ss.cc.* '71 (NEW) [I] Jersey City, NJ St. Joseph's Home for the Blind.
Cavanaugh, John '90 (FAR) West Fargo, ND Blessed Sacrament Church.
Cavanaugh, John J. *m.ss.cc.* (HBG) Blue Ridge Summit, PA St. Rita Church.
Cavanaugh, John J. *m.ss.cc.* '71 (HBG) Fairfield, PA Immaculate Conception of the Blessed Virgin Mary Church.
Cavanaugh, John L. '51 (NY) Retired.
Cavanaugh, John L. '56 (CIN) Retired.
Cavanaugh, John R. '55 (ROC) [I] Rochester, NY Basilian Residence.
Cavanaugh, Kevin P. '86 (HRT) South Glastonbury, CT St. Augustine Church.
Cavanaugh, Michael T. *o.s.f.s.* '76 (WIL) [I] Wilmington, DE Oblates of St. Francis De Sales.
Cavanaugh, Peter M. '66 (PRO) [1] Westerly, RI St. Clare Church.
Cavazos-Gonzales, Gilberto *o.f.m.* '85 (CHI) [B] Chicago, IL The Catholic Theological Union at Chicago.
Caveglia, Patrick *o.s.b.* '94 (KC) [A] Conception, MO Conception Seminary College; [J] Conception, MO Conception Abbey.
Cavell, Lawrence '89 (HT) Raceland, LA St. Mary's Nativity Church.
Cavellier, Richard '87 (DET) [6] Clinton Twp., MI St. Valerie of Ravenna Church.
Caverly, Msgr. J. Bernard '65 (SP) [8] St. Petersburg, FL St. Raphael Church.
Caverly, Patrick J. '61 (ORL) Altamonte Springs, FL Annunciation Church.

Caverte, Rolando A. '62 (SFR) [2] South San Francisco, CA Mater Dolorosa Church.
Cavey, Donald J. '76 (RIC) [4] Hampton, VA St. Rose of Lima Church; Hampton, VA VA Medical Center.
Caviedes, Victor '99 (VEN) LaBelle, FL Our Lady Queen of Heaven Church.
Caviglia, Caesar '55 (LAV) Retired.
Cavoto, Joseph F. *s.a.* '80 (NY) Harrison, NY St. Vincent Hospital and Medical Center of New York; [DD] New York, NY Atonement Friars.
Cawley, John F. *c.m.* (CHI) [N] Chicago, IL DePaul Vincentian Residence.
Cawley, Martin *o.c.s.o.* '61 (P) [L] Lafayette, OR The Cistercian (Trappist) Abbey of Our Lady of Guadalupe.
Cawley, Patrick '70 (GR) Retired.
Cawley, Thomas *c.m.* '57 (KCK) Nortonville, KS St. Joseph's Church.
Cawley, Msgr. Thomas J. '36 (SCR) Retired; [N] Dunmore, PA Villa St. Joseph.
Cawley, William M. '73 (GF) On Duty Outside of the Diocese.
Cawley, William M. '73 (HBG) [3] York, PA St. Patrick Church; [A] York, PA York Catholic High School.
Cayer, John '96 (PT) [4] Pensacola, FL Nativity of Our Lord Church.
Caylor, Dennis J. '75 (CIN) [2] Springfield, OH St. Joseph Church; [4] Springfield, OH St. Raphael Church.
Cazayoux, Clair M. *s.j.* '62 (SP) [8] Tampa, FL Sacred Heart Church.
Cazenavette, John J. *s.j.* '53 (LAF) [J] Grand Coteau, LA Jesuit Spirituality Center (St. Charles College).
Ceballos, Meliton (Enrique) '90 (P) Cornelius, OR St. Alexander Church.
Cebula, Joseph S. '75 (ALB) Stamford, NY Sacred Heart Church.
Cebula, Richard S. *o.s.b.* '41 (SEA) [L] Lacey, WA St. Martin's Abbey.
Cebula, Thomas '68 (Y) Massillon, OH St. Barbara's Church.
Cebulka, Peter R. *c.o.* '93 (MET) [H] Somerset, NJ The Metuchen Oratory, Congregation of the Oratory of St. Philip Neri.
Cecere, Michael *c.m.f.* '43 (SAT) [12] San Antonio, TX Immaculate Heart of Mary Church.
Cecero, John J. *s.j.* '89 (NY) [DD] New York, NY Xavier Jesuit Community.
Cecil, Bruce *c.s.c.* '92 (SB) Coachella, CA Our Lady of Soledad Church; Thermal, CA San Felipe de Jesus Church.
Cecil, Ivo E. '54 (L) Lebanon Junction, KY St. Benedict Church; Shepherdsville, KY St. Aloysius Church; Retired.
Cecil, Patrick G. '78 (CHI) Wadsworth, IL St. Patrick Church.
Cedolia, Robert J. '78 (PIT) Holiday Park, PA Our Lady of Joy Church.
Cedrone, Laurence C. '48 (BO) Senior Priests.
Cegielka, Francis A. *s.a.c.* '31 (BUF) [O] North Tonawanda, NY Society of the Catholic Apostolate.
Ceja, Miguel '90 (SB) Palm Springs, CA Our Lady of Solitude Church.
Cejudo, Serafin '56 (GAL) [4] Galveston, TX St. Patrick Church.
Celano, Freddy '87 (CGS) Caguas, PR Government Regional Hospital; Caguas, P.R. Hospital Hima.
Celano, Joseph G. '87 (MET) Bridgewater, NJ St. Bernard Church.
Celano, Leo J. *o.praem.* '72 (ORG) [I] Silverado, CA Norbertine Fathers of Orange Inc.
Celano, Leo John *o.praem.* '72 (LA) Camarillo, CA Youth Correctional Facility, California Youth Authority; Camarillo, CA Youth Correctional Facility.
Celeste, Charles R. '80 (ALB) [4] Little Falls, NY Holy Family Church.
Celia, Joseph A. '67 (HBG) Selinsgrove, PA St. Pius X Church; Selinsgrove, PA Selinsgrove Center; [K] Harrisburg, PA Catholic Campus Ministry.
Celiano, Alfred V. '53 (NEW) Retired; [B] South Orange, NJ Seton Hall University.
Celichowski, John *o.f.m.cap.* '93 (MIL) [12] Milwaukee, WI St. Benedict the Moor Church.
Celino, Anthony '97 (ELP) Alpine, TX Our Lady of Peace Church.
Celino, Juventino '82 (ELP) [28] El Paso, TX St. Matthew Church.
Cell, Robert *m.s.c.* '47 (ALN) [A] Center Valley, PA Missionaries of the Sacred Heart.
Cella, John *o.f.m.* '78 (GB) [I] Pulaski, WI Assumption of B.V.M. Friary.
Cella, John *o.f.m.* '78 (MIL) [P] Milwaukee, WI Francis and Clare House.
Cellini, Ronald R. '79 (CHR) Beaufort, SC St. Peter's Church; [H] Beaufort, SC University of South Carolina, Beaufort Extension.
Cellini, Ronald R. '79 (PIT) On Duty Outside the Diocese.
Cellucci, Carl D. '53 (PH) Retired.
Celso, Thomas B. '79 (ROC) On Duty Outside the Diocese.
Cembor, Thomas M. '79 (NEW) [2] Irvington, NJ St. Leo's Church.
Cencula, Leonard T. '63 (STU) [8] Steubenville, OH St. Pius X Church.
Cenefeldt, Harry E. '54 (TR) [M] Trenton, NJ Villa Vianney.
Cenkner, William *o.p.* '58 (WDC) [11] Washington, DC St. Dominic Church & Priory Church; [C] Washington, DC Catholic University of America, The.
Centala, Theodore *o.c.d.* '65 (WDC) [B] Washington, DC Discalced Carmelite Friars.
Centner, David *o.c.d.* '71 (SEA) Stanwood, WA St. Cecilia Church.
Centrella, Msgr. Arthur J. '54 (PH) [2] Norristown, PA Holy Saviour Church.
Centrella, Dismas *o.f.m.* '55 (BO) [38] Boston, MA St. Leonard of Port Maurice Church.
Centurion, Diosnel *s.v.d.* '81 (WDC) [M] Washington, DC Divine Word College.
Cepeda, Abrahan *s.d.b.* (ARE) Orocovis, PR San Juan Bautista Church.
Cepeda, Jose Arturo '96 (SAT) Special Assignment.
Cepeda, Raymond F. '79 (AGN) Dededo, GU Santa Barbara Church.
Ceperley, Eugene F. '55 (SC) Retired.
Ceplecha, Christian W. *o.s.b.* '53 (JOL) [A] Lisle, IL Benedictine University; [J] Lisle, IL St. Procopius Abbey.
Cepress, Adalbert J. '44 (NU) Retired.
Cera, James B. '64 (MIL) Kansasville, WI St. Mary-Dover Church.
Cera, Raymond *c.pp.s.* '46 (CIN) [B] Carthagena, OH St. Charles.
Cerank, Gerald A. '72 (OG) Mooers, NY St. Joseph Church; Mooers Forks, NY St. Ann Church.
Ceranowski, Albert B. '64 (TOL) Oregon, OH St. Ignatius Church.
Ceranowski, Gerald L. '67 (TOL) [26] Toledo, OH St. Joan of Arc Church.
Cerbin, Walter *s.s.j.* '55 (GAL) [63] Houston, TX Our Mother of Mercy Church.
Cerbone, James *s.d.b.* '80 (NY) [GG] New York, NY University Apostolate.
Ceresko, Anthony R. *o.s.f.s.* '70 (TOL) [K] Toledo, OH Oblates of St. Francis de Sales.
Cerezo, Alberto '60 (SEA) [23] Seattle, WA Christ the King Church; Shelton, WA St. Edward Church.
Cerezo, Alberto F. '60 (YAK) On Duty Outside the Diocese.
Cerezo, Alfonso '43 (SB) Retired.
Ceriello, Joseph A. '78 (BRK) Military Chaplains.
Cerio, Frank '86 (ORL) Lake Wales, FL Holy Spirit Church.
Cerkas, John W. '70 (GB) Laona, WI St. Leonard Church; Long Lake, WI St. Norbert Church; Newald, WI St. Hubert Church.
Cernak, Michael *o.mar.* '95 (SAM) [C] Petersham, MA Most Holy Trinity Monastery.
Cernauskas, Daniel '54 (MIA) Tamarac, FL St. Malachy Church.
Cernich, Joseph '83 (SFD) Absent on Leave.
Cerniglia, Francis J. '53 (CHI) Elk Grove Village, IL Queen of the Rosary Church; Retired.
Cerniglia, George J. *s.m.* '69 (BAL) [S] Baltimore, MD Society of Mary (Marianists); [W] Baltimore, MD Marianist Conference.
Cernoch, Gerard '64 (VIC) Shiner, TX SS. Cyril and Methodius Church.
Cerny, George F. '64 (CHI) [22] Chicago, IL St. Bartholomew Church.
Cerpich, Richard J. '61 (MIL) Random Lake, WI Our Lady of the Lakes Church.
Cerreto, Michael *c.s.b.* (LSC) [1] Las Cruces, NM Cathedral of Immaculate Heart of Mary.
Cerretto, Michael *c.s.b.* '69 (LSC) [B] Las Cruces, NM Basilian Fathers.
Cerrito, Msgr. Albert J. '51 (PRO) Retired.
Cerrone, Michael J. '81 (SAV) Military Chaplains.
Cerullo, Fritz J. *o.s.a.* '71 (MAN) Dover, NH St. Mary Church.
Cerulo, Thomas N. *o.ss.t.* '78 (NY) [218] Staten Island, NY Our Lady of Mt. Carmel-St. Benedicta Church.
Cervantes, Fidel (ELP) Retired.
Cervantes, Leo T. '62 (RIC) Emporia, VA St. Richard Church; Lake Gaston, VA St. Peter The Apostle Church.
Cervantes, Lucius F. *s.j.* '46 (STL) [P] St. Louis, MO Jesuit Community Corporation at St. Louis University - Jesuit Hall.
Cervantes, Rhenne A. '92 (NO) [43] New Orleans, LA St. Leo the Great Church.
Cervantes, Timothy '00 (GLP) Farmington, NM St. Mary's Church.
Cervella, Albert T. '79 (ALN) Retired; [J] Bethlehem, PA Holy Family Villa.
Cervenak, Andrew '78 (TR) Retired.
Cervera, Pascual '87 (NY) [149] Bronx, NY Holy Spirit Church.
Cervero, Joseph '89 (BGP) Darien, CT St. John Church.
Cervini, Msgr. John '68 (RVC) Priests Released from Diocesan Assignment.
Cervinski, Paul L. '61 (BIS) [5] Minot, ND St. Theresa, the Little Flower Church.
Cervoni, Stephen F. '67 (CAM) Woodstown, NJ St. Joseph's Church.
Cerwonka, Clarence G. '61 (PBL) Military Chaplains.
Cerwonka, Clarence J. '61 (SY) [8] Binghamton, NY St. Mary of the Assumption Church.
Cerwronka, Francis *c.s.v.* '59 (JOL) [2] Kankakee, IL St. Patrick Church.
Cesa, Dean E. '98 (CHL) [1] Charlotte, NC St. Patrick Church.
Cesanek, Damian *o.f.m.* '69 (IND) Batesville, IN St. Louis Church.
Cesario, Victor *o.f.m.* '39 (NY) [DD] New York, NY Franciscan Province of the Immaculate Conception.
Cesaro, Nicholas J. '54 (HRT) [9] Hartford, CT St. Augustine Church.
Cesarone, Jeffrey T. *o.praem.* '94 (WIL) [B] Claymont, DE Archmere Academy; [I] Claymont, DE Immaculate Conception Priory of the Canons Regular of Premontre; [I] Claymont, DE Norbertine Fathers of Delaware, Inc.
Cessario, Romanus *o.p.* '71 (BO) [A] Boston, MA St. John's Seminary School of Theology; [W] Dover, MA St. Stephen Priory.
Cesta, James M. '74 (SY) [2] Oswego, NY St. Joseph Church.
Cestare, Gerald '95 (RVC) [1] Rockville Centre, NY St. Agnes Church.
Cestaro, Joseph A. '62 (BRK) [34] Brooklyn, NY St. Edmund's Church.
Cestaro, Joseph J. '46 (NEW) Belleville, NJ St. Anthony's Church; Retired; [N] Rutherford, NJ St. John Vianney Residence for Priests.
Cestero, Luis '36 (CGS) [2] Caguas, PR San Jose Church.
Cevasco, Darrell *c.ss.r.* (CHL) Concord, NC St. James Church.
Ch'e, James '54 (AGN) Tamuning, GU St. Anthony and St. Victor Church.
Chaanine, Georges '96 (OLL) Wheeling, WV Our Lady of Lebanon Church.
Chaback, Msgr. Michael J. '70 (ALN) [2] Bethlehem, PA SS. Cyril and Methodius Church.
Chaback, Msgr. Michael J. '70 (ALT) [J] Hollidaysburg, PA Conference of Slovak Clergy.
Chaback, Msgr. Michael J. '70 (PH) [A] Wynnewood, PA Theological Seminary of St. Charles Borromeo, Overbrook.
Chabak, Msgr. Robert M. '72 (NEW) Bloomfield, NJ St. Valentine Church.
Chabala, Brian J. '77 (DET) Farmington Hills, MI St. Fabian Church.
Chabot, Bertrand R. '46 (FR) Retired.
Chabot, Peter L. *m.m.* '65 (CIN) [M] Cincinnati, OH The Catholic Foreign Mission Society of America, Inc.
Chabot, Robert *s.s.s.* '66 (SFE) [25] Albuquerque, NM St. Charles Borromeo Church.
Chabot, Roger P. '65 (PRT) Farmington, ME St. Joseph's Church; [M] Farmington, ME University of Maine at Farmington.
Chachlowski, Marek '82 (NEW) [4] Linden, NJ St. Theresa of the Child Jesus Church.
Chackalackal, Mathews *c.m.i.* '89 (SAN) [5] Odessa, TX St. Mary's Church.
Chacko, Abraham '75 (DAL) [1] Garland, TX Good Shepherd Church; [3] Garland, TX St. Mary Malankara Church.
Chacko, Abraham '88 (NY) [4] Newburgh, NY Sacred Heart Church.
Chacko, Joseph C. '68 (MET) Lyons, NJ U.S. Veterans Medical Center.
Chacko, Joy T. '92 (TR) Delran, NJ Holy Name Church.
Chacko, Sebastian '76 (HON) Waianae, HI Sacred Heart Church.
Chacko, Vincent (AUS) Goldthwaite, TX St. Peter's Church.
Chacko, Vincent V. *i.m.s.* (AUS) San Saba, TX St. Mary's Church.
Chacon, Frank '89 (GLP) Concho, AZ San Rafael Church; St. Johns, AZ St. John the Baptist Church.
Chacon, Gilbert *s.j.* '73 (SD) [12] San Diego, CA Our Lady of Guadalupe Church.
Chacon, Jorge '74 (NEW) [5] Elizabeth, NJ Immaculate Conception Church.
Chacon, William '91 (MIA) [3] Pompano Beach, FL San Isidro Church.
Chadwick, John '95 (NEW) Cedar Grove, NJ St. Catherine of Siena Church.
Chadwick, Lawrence A. '75 (RVC) Dix Hills, NY St. Matthew Church.
Chadwick, Matthew *o.f.m.conv.* '88 (PH) [88] Philadelphia, PA St. Leo Church.
Chaffman, Charles J. '84 (LA) Graduate Studies.
Chaguaceda, Juan Manuel *o.s.a.* '53 (NY) [49] New York, NY Holy Rosary Church.
Chaisson, John C. '66 (BO) [1] Peabody, MA St. Adelaide Church.
Chaisson, Louis '65 (HT) On Leave.
Chakian, Joy '78 (DET) [1] Roseville, MI St. Angela Church.

Chalakal, A. David *c.m.i.* '88 (MET) [I] Flemington, NJ The Carmel of Mary Immaculate and St. Mary Magdalen.
Chalany, Robert '52 (WH) Retired.
Chalhoub, Maximos '39 (NTN) Retired.
Chalifour, Gerald F. '52 (MAN) Retired.
Chalinor, Michael '91 (NY) [7] Yonkers, NY St. Denis Church.
Chalissery, Joy '90 (BIR) Sylacauga, AL St. Jude Church; Talladega, AL St. Francis of Assisi Church.
Chalkey, Andrew G. *o.m.i.* '56 (BEL) [E] Belleville, IL Our Lady of the Snows Apartment Community Retirement Home; [F] Belleville, IL Missionary Oblates of Mary Immaculate - St. Henry's Oblate Residence.
Challancin, James '68 (MAR) Ishpeming, MI St. Joseph Church.
Challman, Stephen G. '96 (NY) [206] Staten Island, NY Holy Rosary Church.
Chalmers, H. Edward '79 (WOR) [2] Fitchburg, MA St. Bernard's Church.
Chaloult, Msgr. Gilman J. '47 (PRT) Caribou, ME Holy Rosary Church; Retired.
Chaloux, Joseph J. '94 (ATL) [12] Atlanta, GA Shrine of the Immaculate Conception Church.
Chalupa, Fred '73 (AUS) On Duty Outside the Diocese.
Chalupka, Anselm *o.s.p.p.e.* '95 (NOR) Rockville, CT St. Joseph Church.
Chamberlain, Charles R. '93 (ARL) [J] Alexandria, VA Oblates of St. Francis de Sales Residence.
Chamberlain, Francis M. *s.j.* '68 (FgM) Provinces.
Chamberlain, Henry T *s.j.* '61 (CHI) [N] Chicago, IL Chicago Province of the Society of Jesus-Provincial Office.
Chamberlain, Robert F. '57 (GI) Retired.
Chamberlain, Msgr. Robert J. '64 (DM) [9] Des Moines, IA St. Joseph's Church.
Chamberlain, Tom '70 (AUS) Taylor, TX Our Lady of Guadalupe Church.
Chamberland, Gary *c.s.c.* (FTW) [B] Notre Dame, IN University of Notre Dame Du Lac.
Chamberland, Gary *c.s.c.* '98 (FTW) [J] Notre Dame, IN Holy Cross Community, Corby Hall, University of Notre Dame.
Chamberlin, Gregory D. *o.s.b.* '65 (EVN) [1] Evansville, IN St. Benedict Church; [2] Evansville, IN Holy Trinity Church.
Chamberlin, Gregory D. *o.s.b.* '65 (IND) [J] St. Meinrad, IN St. Meinrad Archabbey.
Chamberlin, Mark '68 (CC) Portland, TX Our Lady of Mount Carmel Church.
Chambers, Frank E. *o.s.a.* '78 (PH) [C] Villanova, PA Villanova University.
Chambers, Henry G. '65 (BO) Millis, MA St. Thomas the Apostle Church.
Chambers, James E. *s.j.* '55 (CHI) [D] Chicago, IL St. Ignatius Jesuit Community.
Chambers, John E. *s.j.* '64 (FgM) Provinces.
Chambers, Leonard R. '65 (SPC) Retired.
Chambers, Thomas E. *c.s.c.* '61 (NO) [22] New Orleans, LA Sacred Heart of Jesus Church; [C] New Orleans, LA Our Lady of Holy Cross College.
Chamblain, Joseph *o.s.m.* '84 (STL) Affton, MO Seven Holy Founders Church.
Chamblain, Joseph M. *o.s.m.* '84 (CHI) [N] Chicago, IL Order of Friar Servants of Mary (Servites) United States of America Province, Inc.
Champagne, Dennis V. '71 (SEA) Lakewood, WA St. John Bosco Church.
Champagne, Jean-Paul *m.s.* (FR) [I] Attleboro, MA La Salette Shrine.
Champagne, Michael '94 (LAF) On Special Assignment; [M] Lafayette, LA Community of Jesus Crucified.
Champagne, Rene *c.p.* '49 (DET) [K] Detroit, MI St. Paul of the Cross Community, Congregation of the Passion.
Champagne, Robert E. *s.m.* '51 (BO) Framingham, MA Metro West Medical Center; [Y] Framingham, MA The Marist House.
Champigny, Richard *o.carm.* '65 (NY) [DD] Middletown, NY St. Albert's Priory; [DD] Middletown, NY St. Albert's Priory; [FF] Middletown, NY National Shrine of Our Lady of Mount Carmel.
Champigny, Roger G. '60 (PRO) [2] Warwick, RI St. Catherine Church.
Champigny, Thomas R. '81 (SPR) Easthampton, MA Our Lady of Good Counsel Church.
Champion, James D. '76 (WOR) Blackstone, MA St. Paul's Church.
Champlin, Msgr. Joseph M. '56 (SY) [1] Syracuse, NY The Cathedral of the Immaculate Conception.
Champlin, Michael A. *o.p.* '66 (SUP) [I] Webster, WI Thomas More Center for Preaching and Prayer, Inc.
Champlin, William E. '93 (WOR) [8] Worcester, MA Our Lady of the Angels Church.
Champoux, Brian *o.f.m.cap.* (FgM) Capuchin Foreign Missions.
Champoux, Thomas C. '67 (YAK) Richland, WA Christ the King Church.
Chan, Albert *s.j.* '47 (SFR) [K] San Francisco, CA Home for the Aged of the Little Sisters of the Poor; [N] San Francisco, CA Jesuit Community at University of San Francisco; [T] San Francisco, CA The Ricci Institute for Chinese-Western Cultural History at the Center for the Pacific Rim.
Chan, Paul '50 (NY) [HH] New York, NY Chinese Catholic Information Center.
Chan-A-Sue, Andrew '00 (MIA) North Miami, FL Holy Family Church.
Chanappa, Ambrose (TYL) Jacksonville, TX Our Lady of Sorrows Church.
Chancler, Joseph *t.o.r.* '83 (SP) [13] Tampa, FL St. Patrick Church.
Chancy, Richard F. '91 (BO) [CC] Boston, MA University of Massachusetts at Boston Campus Ministry.
Chandler, Anthony L. '89 (L) [12] Louisville, KY St. Bartholomew Church.
Chandler, John *s.j.* '83 (SFR) [2] San Francisco, CA St. Agnes Church.
Chandonnet, A. J. *c.ss.r.* '50 (GAL) [34] Houston, TX Holy Ghost Church.
Chandrankunnel, Mathew '64 (NEW) Dumont, NJ St. Mary's Church; Englewood, NJ Englewood Hospital.
Chane, Lawrence J. '62 (BO) Dracut, MA St. Therese Church.
Chaney, Robert E. '88 (SAV) [6] Savannah, Savannah Resurrection of Our Lord Church.
Chang, Benedict '63 (SFR) [49] San Francisco, CA Star of the Sea Church.
Chang, Cornelius P. *o.s.b.* '62 (GBG) [H] Latrobe, PA Saint Vincent Archabbey.
Chang, Gordon '84 (LA) Montrose, CA Holy Redeemer Church.
Chang, Jeffrey G.L. *s.j.* '99 (BAL) [S] Baltimore, MD Jesuit Fathers and Brothers Maryland Provincial Curia.
Chang, Jeffrey G.L. *s.j.* '99 (FgM) Provinces.
Chang, John O. '00 (TR) Red Bank, NJ St. James Church.
Chang, Joseph *o.s.b.* '57 (JOL) [J] Lisle, IL St. Procopius Abbey.
Chang, Romeo Yu *s.m.* '94 (BO) [W] Boston, MA Marist Fathers of Our Lady of Victories (Boston Prov.).
Chang, Simeon '49 (SFR) [35] San Francisco, CA St. Monica Church; Retired.
Channine, Georges (OLL) Millbrae, CA Our Lady of Lebanon Church.
Chant, William S. '88 (BUR) Retired.
Chantry, Stephen *s.j.* '81 (SPK) [C] Spokane, WA Gonzaga University.
Chao, Joseph '61 (NY) [54] New York, NY St. James Church.
Chap, Robert W. *c.m.* '66 (FgM) Vincentian Foreign Missions.
Chapdelaine, Gerard E. *s.j.* '66 (SEA) [C] Tacoma, WA Bellarmine Preparatory School.
Chapeau, Mary Paul *o.cart.* '45 (BUR) [E] Arlington, VT Carthusian Foundation, Charterhouse of the Transfiguration.
Chapel, Joseph R. '92 (NEW) [A] South Orange, NJ Immaculate Conception Seminary; [B] South Orange, NJ Seton Hall University.
Chapell, Norbert A. '48 (CHI) Hickory Hills, IL St. Patricia Church; Retired.
Chapin, Daniel L. '72 (OG) Gouverneur, NY St. James Church; Gouverneur, NY Gouverneur Correctional Facility.
Chaplin, John G. *c.s.c.* '68 (E) Houtzdale, PA Christ the King Church.
Chapman, Gerard C. (PH) [D] Norristown, PA Kennedy-Kenrick Catholic High School.
Chapman, Gerard C. '91 (PH) Conshohocken, PA St. Matthew Church.
Chapman, Lawrence J. '77 (MIL) [D] Burlington, WI Catholic Central High School.
Chapman, Michael A. '82 (PH) [1] Philadelphia, PA Cathedral Basilica of SS. Peter and Paul; [124] Philadelphia, PA Chapel of Our Lady of the Miraculous Medal (La Milagrosa) Church.
Chapman, Michael L. '69 (OKL) Weatherford, OK St. Eugene's Church; [K] Norman, OK Campus Ministry for the Archdiocese of Oklahoma City.
Chapman, Robert J. '67 (PH) Lansdowne, PA St. Philomena Church.
Chappell, Arthur B. *o.s.a.* (PH) [AA] Villanova, PA Fray de Leon Community.
Chappell, Arthur B. *o.s.a.* '69 (PH) [C] Villanova, PA Villanova University.
Chappell, James T. '67 (DUB) [7] Dubuque, IA Sacred Heart Church; [F] Dubuque, IA Holy Trinity-Sacred Heart Consolidation.
Chappetto, Msgr. Raymond F. '71 (BRK) [220] Queens, NY Our Lady of the Snows Church.
Charankat, Peter '59 (OAK) [3] Walnut Creek, CA St. Mary's Church; Walnut Creek, CA Kaiser-Permanente Medical Center.
Charbonneau, Damian M. *o.s.m.* '50 (CHI) [N] Chicago, IL Order of Friar Servants of Mary (Servites) United States of America Province, Inc.
Charbonneau, Roger L. '71 (BUR) Colchester, VT Holy Cross Church.
Charbonneau, William R. '73 (HRT) On Duty Outside the Archdiocese.
Charest, Antoine *s.m.* (BO) [55] Boston, MA Our Lady of Victories Church.
Charest, Antoine *s.m.* '40 (BO) [W] Boston, MA Marist Fathers and Brothers Provincial House; [W] Boston, MA Marist Fathers of Our Lady of Victories (Boston Prov.).
Charest, Edmund P. '60 (BO) Emergency Response Group.
Charest, Roger M. *s.m.m.* '42 (RVC) [M] Bay Shore, NY Montfort Missionaries.
Charipar, Henry '68 (DUB) [F] Cresco, IA Notre Dame System of Education.
Chariper, Henry W. '68 (DUB) Bluffton, IA St. Bridget Church; Cresco, IA Notre Dame Church.
Charland, George A. '60 (WOR) East Brookfield, MA St. John the Baptist Church.
Charland, Paul A. '71 (PRO) Foster, RI St. Paul the Apostle Church.
Charlebois, Msgr. John J. '54 (GRY) Retired.
Charlebois, Msgr. Robert L. '57 (GRY) On Duty Outside the Diocese.
Charles, Robes C. '99 (MIA) [1] Miami, FL St. Mary's Church.
Charles, Vincent Michael (NY) Millbrook, NY St. Joseph Church.
Charlot, Lucien '61 (BRK) Brooklyn, NY Kings County Hospital Center.
Charlton, Robert *ss.cc.* '88 (FR) Fairhaven, MA St. Mary's Church.
Charlton, Terrence P. *s.j.* '76 (FgM) Provinces.
Charman, Eugene J. '71 (HRT) Cheshire, CT St. Thomas Becket Church; Special and other Archdiocesan Assignment.
Charnley, George '76 (DET) Canton, MI Saint John Neumann Church.
Charnoki, Andrew J. '43 (GBG) Retired; [G] Greensburg, PA St. Anne Home.
Charnoki, John J. '45 (PIT) [35] Pittsburgh, PA St. Raphael Church; Retired.
Charnoki, Msgr. William G. *j.c.l.* '65 (GBG) Indiana, PA St. Bernard Church.
Charpentier, Alfred *o.m.i.* '71 (FgM) Oblates Foreign Missions.
Charpentier, Dale '83 (HT) On Leave.
Charvet, Louis *o.s.b.* '45 (FgM) American - Cassinese Congregation Foreign Missions.
Chase, Charles E. '79 (OG) Retired.
Chase, Kenneth M. '84 (DET) South Lyon, MI St. Joseph Church.
Chase, Lee P. '93 (ROC) [60] Rochester, NY St. Thomas More Church; [M] Rochester, NY Diocesan Department of Campus Ministry.
Chase, Martin *s.j.* '91 (NY) [DD] New York, NY Jesuit Community at Fordham University.
Chase, Martin L. *s.j.* '91 (DET) [K] Detroit, MI Jesuit Provincial Office-Detroit Province of the Society of Jesus.
Chase, Maurice '53 (SD) Retired.
Chase, P. Geoffrey *o.s.b.* '59 (PRO) [P] Portsmouth, RI Abbey of St. Gregory the Great.
Chase, Raymond '78 (BAL) Special Assignment; [L] Timonium, MD Villa Maria Treatment Center.
Chase, Terrence R. '84 (GRY) [2] Merrillville, IN St. Andrew Church.
Chassaniol, Warren F. '65 (HT) Grand Isle, LA Our Lady of the Isle Church.
Chasse, Joseph S. *s.m.* '52 (PRT) Hamlin, ME St. Joseph Church; Van Buren, ME St. Bruno - St. Remi Church.
Chasse, Lucien *s.m.* '43 (BO) [55] Boston, MA Our Lady of Victories Church; [W] Boston, MA Marist Fathers of Our Lady of Victories (Boston Prov.).
Chateau, Paul F. '66 (DET) Oak Park, MI Our Lady of Fatima Church.
Chatigny, Donat W. *m.m.* '34 (NY) [DD] Maryknoll, NY Maryknoll Fathers and Brothers.
Chau, Jospeh Bau *c.ss.r.* (DAL) [24] Dallas, TX St. Peter Vietnamese Catholic Church.
Chau, Peter Do Quang '73 (NSH) On Special or Other Diocesan Assignment.
Chaupetta, Victor W. *m.s.* '70 (BGP) [Q] Wilton, CT School Sisters of Notre Dame Motherhouse (Northeastern Province); [Q] Wilton, CT Lourdes Health Care Center, Inc.
Chauvin, David M. '64 (BR) Vacherie, LA St. Philip Church.
Chavannes, Jacques E. '85 (PRO) [23] Providence, RI St. Michael the Archangel Church.
Chavarin, Jose '79 (SFR) [1] San Francisco, CA Cathedral of St. Mary (Assumption); San Francisco, CA St. Thomas More Society.
Chavarria, Horacio '66 (BWN) [3] Brownsville, TX Church of the Good Shepherd.
Chavarria, Jerome *c.ss.r.* '84 (ATL) Hapeville, GA St. John the Evangelist Church.
Chavarria, Juan *c.m.* '95 (FgM) Vincentian Foreign Missions.
Chavez, Msgr. Adolphus '56 (SB) [5] San Bernardino, CA Our Lady of Guadalupe Church; Loma Linda, CA Jerry Pettis Memorial Hospital.

Chavez, Arturo '91 (SB) Morena Valley, CA Riverside County Regional Medical Center.

Chavez, Carlos '84 (SFE) Clovis, NM Sacred Heart Church.

Chavez, Frank '76 (SAN) [1] Odessa, TX Holy Redeemer Church.

Chavez, Gerald F. '73 (FRS) Corcoran, CA Our Lady of Lourdes Church.

Chavez, Johnny Lee '76 (SFE) [15] Albuquerque, NM Queen of Heaven Church.

Chavez, Jose *c.ss.r.* '84 (SAT) [M] San Antonio, TX Redemptorists of Texas-San Antonio #1.

Chavez, Jose '96 (MRY) Watsonville, CA St. Patrick Church.

Chavez, Jose M. '98 (GI) [1] Grand Island, NE Cathedral of the Nativity of the Blessed Virgin Mary

Chavez, Luis N. '91 (TUC) Douglas, AZ Immaculate Conception Church.

Chavez, Manuel '96 (SR) Windsor, CA Our Lady of Guadalupe Church.

Chavez, Manuel Maya *o.s.m.* '58 (ORG) [I] Buena Park, CA Order of Friar Servants of Mary (Servites).

Chavez, Patrick J. '68 (SFE) El Rito, NM San Juan Nepomuceno Church.

Chavez, Phillip *s.o.l.t.* '93 (CC) [H] Robstown, TX Society of Our Lady of the Most Holy Trinity.

Chavez, Ricardo A. '63 (OAK) Pittsburg, CA St. Peter Martyr of Verona Church.

Chavez, Vincent P. '91 (SFE) Arroyo Seco, NM La Santisima Trinidad Church.

Chavez, W. Scott '97 (OAK) [7] Fremont, CA St.Leonard-Santa Paula Church.

Cheah, Joseph M. *o.s.m.* '92 (CHI) [N] Chicago, IL Order of Friar Servants of Mary (Servites) United States of America Province, Inc.; [N] Chicago, IL Order of Friar Servants of Mary (Servites) United States of America Province, Inc.

Cheatham, Louis W. '45 (GBG) Retired; [G] Greensburg, PA Neumann House.

Checchio, Msgr. James '92 (CAM) [M] Blackwood, NJ Bishop's Residence.

Chechia, Jose *c.ss.r.* '63 (MGZ) [2] Mayaquez, PR Our Lady of Mt. Carmel Church.

Check, Paul N. '97 (BGP) [4] Norwalk, CT St. Mary Church; [9] Stamford, CT St. John the Evangelist Church.

Checon, Amarilho '57 (BRK) [U] Brooklyn, NY Catholic Migration & Refugee Office, Catholic Migration Services, Inc.

Cheerakathil, Augustine *m.s.* '88 (HON) Waipahu, HI St. Joseph Church.

Cheesman, Robert *c.ss.r.* '57 (BRK) [C] Whitestone, NY St. Alphonsus Formation Residence.

Cheetham, William J. '46 (PIT) Retired.

Cheikho, John Hanna '68 (EST) West Bloomfield, MI St. Thomas Chaldean Catholic Church.

Cheimel, Tony '91 (VEN) [5] Fort Myers, FL St. Francis Xavier Church.

Chelena, Thomas '68 (PRM) Absent on Leave.

Chelick, James A. '76 (GR) [23] Grand Rapids, MI St. Thomas the Apostle Church.

Cheline, Paschal *o.s.b.* '64 (P) [L] St. Benedict, OR Mt. Angel Abbey.

Chellaian, Lawrence '92 (TYL) Mount Vernon, TX Sacred Heart Church.

Chemazar, Blase *o.f.m.* '53 (CHI) [N] Lemont, IL The Slovene Franciscan Fathers, Order of Friars Minor, Commissariat of the Holy Cross; [T] Lemont, IL St. Mary's Retreat House.

Chembakassery, Vincent (CHI) Evanston, IL St. Athanasius Church.

Chemino, Stephen Scott '93 (ALX) [2] Alexandria, LA Our Lady of Prompt Succor Church.

Chen, Anthony K. '52 (CHI) Retired.

Chen, Peter '98 (DAL) Richardson, TX Mission of the Sacred Heart of Jesus Church.

Chen, Raphael '52 (AMA) Retired.

Chen, Vincent P. '57 (MET) Phillipsburg, NJ St. Philip & St. James Church; Phillipsburg, NJ Warren Hospital.

Cheney, Edward K. *s.j.* '42 (BO) [W] Weston, MA Campion Health Center, Inc.

Cheney, James '95 (FAR) Aneta, ND Sacred Heart Church; Cooperstown, ND St. George's Church; Jessie, ND St. Lawrence Church.

Cheney, Jesse C. '43 (LR) Retired; [H] Little Rock, AR St. John Manor.

Cheng, Joseph *s.d.b.* '59 (LA) [53] Los Angeles, CA St. Bridget's Chinese Catholic Center Church; [Q] Los Angeles, CA Dominic Savio Salesian Residence.

Chennakadan, Jacob *c.m.* '72 (NO) [61] New Orleans, LA St. Stephen Church.

Chenot, Paul *c.p.* '51 (BRK) Queens, NY Creedmoor Psychiatric Center; [V] Jamaica, NY Immaculate Conception Monastery.

Chenoweth, Robert '63 (JC) Retired.

Cheong, Antonius '54 (ORG) [H] Anaheim, CA St. Thomas Korean Catholic Center.

Cheong, Antonius '64 (ORG) Special Assignment.

Chepaitis, Peter S. *o.f.m.* '72 (NY) [DD] New York, NY Franciscan Friars, Order of Friars Minor, Holy Name Province.

Chepanis, Anthony J. '48 (PMB) Highland Beach, FL St. Lucy Church; Retired.

Cheplic, Msgr. Peter A. '72 (NEW) [2] Jersey City, NJ St. Aloysius Church.

Chepponis, James J. '85 (PIT) [1] Pittsburgh, PA St. Paul Church.

Cheramie, Lonnie '00 (HT) [2] Houma, LA Annunziata Church.

Cheri, Fernand J., III *o.f.m.* '78 (NSH) [13] Nashville, TN St. Vincent de Paul Church; [H] Nashville, TN Franciscan Friars.

Chern, James N. '99 (NEW) West Orange, NJ Our Lady of Lourdes Church.

Cherolikal, John '74 (LUB) Anson, TX St. Michael's Church.

Cherry, Athanasius C. *o.s.b.* '68 (GBG) [2] Latrobe, PA St. Vincent Basilica Church; [H] Latrobe, PA Saint Vincent Archabbey.

Cherry, Richard W. *s.j.* '69 (FgM) Provinces.

Cherubini, Perry A. '85 (CAM) Margate, NJ Blessed Sacrament Church.

Cherukarakunnel, Alexander J. '63 (HRT) North Haven, CT St. Therese Church.

Cherup, Michael '81 (PT) Fort Walton Beach, FL St. Mary Church.

Cheruparambil, Francis '82 (TR) Union Beach, NJ Holy Family Church.

Chervenak, Greg *o.f.m.cap.* (PIT) Allegheny County, PA St. Francis Medical Center.

Chervenak, Gregory *o.f.m.cap.* '79 (PIT) [O] Pittsburgh, PA St. Conrad Friary; [P] Millvale, PA St. Francis Convent.

Chervenak, Stephen M. '60 (PIT) White Oak Boro, PA St. Angela Church.

Chesebrough, Charles S. '67 (IND) Bloomington, IN St. Charles Borromeo Church.

Chesney, Michael E. *s.j.* '91 (SP) [C] Tampa, FL Jesuit High School.

Chester, Thomas '93 (TR) Leave of Absence.

Chethipuzha, Varghese I. '69 (NY) New City, NY St. Augustine Church.

Chetock, James J. '93 (WH) Fort Ashby, WV Annunciation of the Lord Church; Ridgeley, WV St. Anthony Church.

Chetwynde, Clyde H. '80 (BO) Townsend, MA St. John Church.

Chevalier, Martin G. '83 (DM) Lacona, IA Holy Trinity Church of Southeast Warren County.

Chevalier, Thomas H. '80 (ALB) [10] Albany, NY St. Margaret Mary Church.

Chevedden, James *s.j.* '78 (FgM) Provinces.

Chevedden, James N. *s.j.* '78 (SJ) [L] Los Gatos, CA Sacred Heart Jesuit Center.

Cheveney, Anthony *s.s.p.* (DET) [K] Dearborn, MI Society of St. Paul.

Chew, Randolph G. '71 (PRO) [7] Cranston, RI St. Paul Church.

Chewning, Seraphim John '93 (PBR) Pleasant City, OH St. Michael Church.

Chiang, John D. '50 (NY) [116] New York, NY St. Teresa Church; Retired.

Chiang, Msgr. Joseph '59 (NEW) [11] Jersey City, NJ Holy Rosary Church.

Chiara, Msgr. Peter A. '48 (RVC) East Islip, NY St. Mary's Church; Retired.

Chiaramonte, Anthony '65 (ALB) Special Assignment.

Chiaravalle, Dominic M. '65 (PH) [45] Philadelphia, PA Epiphany of Our Lord Church.

Chiarilli, Msgr. Patrick S. '61 (CAM) Blackwood, NJ St. Jude's Church.

Chiasson, Arthur B. *m.afr.* '38 (LR) St. Vincent, AR St. Mary Church.

Chiawa, Francis '96 (SJ) [3] Santa Clara, CA St. Justin Church.

Chichetto, James W. *c.s.c.* '68 (FR) [A] North Easton, MA Stonehill College; [A] North Easton, MA Holy Cross Fathers Religious.

Chidiac, Bakhos '91 (OLL) St. Paul, MN Holy Family Church.

Chidili, Bartholomew *o.s.a.* (BRK) [54] Brooklyn, NY Holy Family Church.

Chidozie, Marcus '93 (DAL) [4] Garland, TX St. Michael the Archangel Church.

Chieffo, Ralph J. '75 (PH) [85] Philadelphia, PA King of Peace Church; Media, PA St. Mary Magdalen Church.

Chiesa, Robert *s.j.* '68 (FgM) Provinces.

Chiezey, Daniel *o.p.* '76 (SEA) [1] Tacoma, WA St. Ann Church; [3] Tacoma, WA St. John of the Woods Church; [12] Tacoma, WA Sacred Heart Church.

Chiffriller, Edward J. *s.s.j.* '74 (BAL) [S] Baltimore, MD St. Joseph Society of the Sacred Heart House of Central Administration.

Chihak, Msgr. John P. '36 (DUB) Retired.

Chikawe, Hugh '71 (SP) [14] Tampa, FL St. Paul Church.

Chikri, Roger *o.m.m.* '93 (OLL) [A] Ann Arbor, MI Maronite Order of Blessed Virgin Mary.

Child, John F. '59 (DET) Retired.

Childs, Guy A. '00 (ALB) [9] Troy, NY Our Lady of Victory Church.

Chilen, Msgr. Michael D. '69 (CC) Military Chaplains.

Chiles, Richard P. *o.praem.* '87 (JKS) [2] Jackson, MS St. Mary Church; [7] Jackson, MS Christ the King Church; [F] Jackson, MS Priory of St. Moses the Black; [H] Jackson, MS Jackson State University Newman Center.

Chillog, Thomas A. '84 (STU) Lore City, OH SS. Peter and Paul Church; Freeport, OH St. Matthias Church.

Chilmark, Richard '60 (NEW) Livingston, NJ St. Barnabas Medical Center.

Chilson, Richard W. *c.s.p.* '72 (P) [29] Portland, OR St. Philip Neri Church; [Q] Portland, OR Paulist Fathers Catholic Center for Evangelization.

Chimera, Angelo M. '69 (BUF) [52] Buffalo, NY The Nativity of the Blessed Virgin Church.

Chimeziri, Casimir E. (MAD) Kieler, WI Immaculate Conception Church.

Chimeziri, Casimir E. '71 (MAD) Sinsinawa, WI St. Joseph Church.

Chimiak, Karl A. '80 (WDC) Issue, MD Holy Ghost Church.

Chin, Bertram *c.p.* '91 (FgM) Passionist Foreign Missions.

Chin, Donald J. *o.f.m.* '67 (FgM) Franciscan Foreign Missions.

Chinchar, Gerald T. *s.m.* '82 (CIN) [D] Dayton, OH The University of Dayton; [M] Dayton, OH Marianist Provincialate.

Chinchilla, Ricardo *c.j.m.* '93 (SD) [L] San Diego, CA Newman Center - SDSU.

Ching, Herbert '47 (HON) Retired.

Chinh, Michael Do Quang *c.m.c.* (BO) [58] Boston, MA St. Peter Church.

Chinh, Peter '50 (ORG) Retired.

Chini, Silvio *o.s.j.* '29 (SCR) Exeter, PA St. Anthony of Padua Church.

Chinnabathini, Ghana Prakasham '95 (CC) Refugio, TX St. James the Apostle Church.

Chinnabathini, Gnana Prakasham '95 (CC) Refugio, TX Our Lady of Refuge Church.

Chinnappan, Rozario (NY) [1] Poughkeepsie, NY St. Peter Church.

Chinnappan, Rozario (RVC) Bay Shore, NY St. Patrick's Church.

Chinnici, Joseph P. *o.f.m.* (OAK) [A] Berkeley, CA Franciscan School of Theology.

Chinnici, Joseph P. *o.f.m.* '72 (OAK) [A] Berkeley, CA Franciscan School of Theology; [N] Oakland, CA Franciscan Friars Provincial Office, Province of St. Barbara.

Chiodini, Msgr. Jasper J. '42 (STL) Retired.

Chiodo, Msgr. Frank E. '76 (DM) [8] Des Moines, IA Basilica of Saint John.

Chiodo, Peter *c.pp.s.* '60 (CIN) Wapakoneta, OH St. Joseph Church.

Chioso, James *s.d.b.* '49 (NY) [FF] Stony Point, NY Marian Shrine.

Chiosso, James *s.d.b.* '49 (NY) [FF] Stony Point, NY Don Bosco Retreat Center and Marian Shrine.

Chirapurathel, Felix *o.praem.* '72 (TYL) Trinity, TX Most Holy Trinity Church.

Chirayath, Chummar *o.s.j.* '78 (FRS) [1] Bakersfield, CA Our Lady of Guadalupe Church.

Chirayath, Joseph Vadake '75 (TLS) Henryetta, OK St. Michael Church.

Chirayath, Koshy George '80 (NY) [101] New York, NY Our Saviour Church.

Chirdon, Howard *c.p.* '50 (ALT) [J] Bedford, PA St. Mary's House of Greater Solitude.

Chiriaco, William J. '86 (PH) Jenkintown, PA Immaculate Conception Church; [D] Wyncote, PA Bishop McDevitt High School.

Chirichiello, Richard *o.s.b.* '95 (WH) [G] Wheeling, WV Wheeling Hospital.

Chirico, Peter F. *s.s.* '56 (SEA) [1] Seattle, WA St. James Church.

Chirovsky, John '90 (SJP) Miami, FL Assumption of B.V.M. Church.

Chisek, Anthony S. '43 (CHI) Retired.

Chisholm, Gregory C. *s.j.* '93 (BO) [W] Boston, MA The Society of Jesus of New England-Provincial Offices.

Chisholm, Gregory C. *s.j.* '93 (LA) [13] Los Angeles, CA Holy Name of Jesus Church.

Chisholm, Thomas *o.s.b.* '89 (JOL) [J] Lisle, IL St. Procopius Abbey.

Chithalan, Vijayakumar Tom *c.m.i.* '75 (PH) [64] Philadelphia, PA Holy Spirit Church.

Chiu, Abraham *o.f.m.* '90 (SD) [H] Oceanside, CA Mission San Luis Rey; [K] Oceanside, CA Mission San Luis Rey Retreat.

Chiusano, Louis *o.f.m.cap.* '57 (FgM) Capuchin Foreign Missions.

Chivico, Peter *s.s.* '56 (SEA) Retired.

Chizmar, Msgr. John G. '75 (ALN) Jim Thorpe, PA Immaculate Conception Church.

Chladek, Melchior *o.cist.* '55 (DAL) [K] Irving, TX Cistercian Abbey of Our Lady of Dallas.

Chlebo, John C. '80 (CLV) Rocky River, OH St. Christopher Church.

Chleborad, Gerald '60 (CHY) Saratoga, WY St. Ann's Church.
Chlopecki, Robert J. '74 (BEL) Leave of Absence.
Chmiel, Bronislaus '69 (CHI) [73] Chicago, IL St. Helen Church.
Chmiel, Gerald J. '70 (TOL) [2] Fremont, OH St. Ann Church.
Chmielewski, Francis J. '73 (BUF) [13] Buffalo, NY St. Bernard Church; Buffalo, NY Veterans Hospital.
Chmielewski, Philip J. *s.j.* '81 (CHI) [N] Chicago, IL Chicago Province of the Society of Jesus-Provincial Office.
Chmil, John J. '95 (SCR) [1] Scranton, PA St. Peter's Church.
Chmura, Gary D. '78 (CLV) [58] Cleveland, OH Our Lady of Peace Church.
Chmura, Julian '64 (DET) [4] Detroit, MI St. Andrew Church.
Chmura, Stanislaus '70 (RIC) Retired.
Chmurski, Marek '95 (FR) Centerville, MA Our Lady of Victory Church.
Cho, MinHyun '99 (NEW) Hohokus, NJ St. Luke's Church.
Cho, Paul Pyung Ki (RIC) [13] Richmond, VA St. Kim Taegon Church.
Cho, Sung hak Laurentius (ANC) [2] Anchorage, AK St. Anthony Church.
Choate, Lawrence *o.s.m.* (CHI) [61] Chicago, IL St. Francis of Assisi/Our Lady of the Angels Church.
Choate, Lawrence M. *o.s.m.* '78 (CHI) [N] Chicago, IL Order of Friar Servants of Mary (Servites) United States of America Province, Inc.
Choate, Norman *c.r.* '63 (SP) Ruskin, FL St. Anne Church.
Choby, David R. '74 (NSH) Gallatin, TN St. John Vianney Church.
Choc, Pedro *o.s.b.* '90 (SFS) [F] Marvin, SD Blue Cloud Abbey.
Chochol, Ronald '64 (STL) [63] St. Louis, MO St. Stephen, Protomartyr Church.
Chodacki, Jeremy *o.f.m.conv.* '29 (SPR) [A] Granby, MA St. Hyacinth College and Seminary.
Chodakowski, Ireneusz *m.i.c.* '78 (PRT) [4] Portland, ME St. Louis Church.
Chodakowski, Ireneusz *m.i.c.* '78 (SPR) [J] Stockbridge, MA Congregation of Marians of The Immaculate Conception of the BVM.
Choi, Francesco '91 (BIR) [11] Birmingham, AL Korean Catholic Community, St. Luke Hwang Church.
Choi, Gregorius Young-Geun '98 (ARL) Fairfax, VA St. Paul Chung Church.
Choi, Mark '94 (LA) Paramount, CA Our Lady of the Rosary Church.
Choi, Youngmin *s.j.* '00 (BO) [W] Cambridge, MA Weston Jesuit Community.
Choiniere, John Marie *o.mar.* '95 (SAM) [C] Petersham, MA Most Holy Trinity Monastery.
Chojnacki, Anthony (MIL) [P] Burlington, WI Queen of Peace Friary.
Chojnacki, Gerald J. *s.j.* '73 (NY) [80] New York, NY Nativity Church.
Cholette, John B. '36 (NY) Retired.
Choma, James A. '86 (NEW) Clark, NJ St. Agnes Church.
Chomko, Stephen '46 (PHU) Berwick, PA SS. Cyril and Methodius Church.
Chomko, Stephen '46 (STF) Retired.
Chong, Damien Mugun *s.j.* '00 (NY) [DD] New York, NY St. Ignatius Loyola Residence.
Chonko, Michael J. '43 (Y) Retired.
Chontos, Joseph '82 (KCK) Special Assignment.
Choo, Thomas *ss.cc.* '69 (HON) [4] Honolulu, HI St. Augustine Church.
Choondassery, Yesudasan '90 (NEW) Lodi, NJ St. Francis de Sales Church.
Choong, Norbert '84 (AMA) Retired.
Choorackunnel, John Vianney '64 (LAF) [13] Lafayette, LA St. Leo the Great Church; On Special Assignment.
Choppesky, John C. *s.j.* '44 (STL) [O] St. Louis, MO Fusz Pavilion.
Choquet, Alexei '83 (CHR) Joanna, SC St. Boniface Church.
Choquet, Alexei H. '83 (CHL) On Duty Outside the Diocese.
Choquet, Alexei R. '83 (CHR) Newberry, SC St. Mark Church; [H] Clinton, SC Presbyterian College; [H] Newberry, SC Newberry College.
Choquette, David '98 (NOR) [1] Norwich, CT St. Patrick Church.
Chorikavunkal, Joseph Augustine '75 (LUB) Muleshoe, TX Immaculate Conception Church.
Chornyak, Joseph I. '53 (PBR) Retired.
Chorpenning, Joseph F. *o.s.f.s.* '79 (PH) [C] Philadelphia, PA St. Joseph's University; [AA] Wyndmoor, PA Villa de Sales Oblate Residence; [AA] Wyndmoor, PA Oblates of St. Francis de Sales (O.S.F.S.).
Chortos, Donald '66 (PIT) Tarentum, PA Holy Martyrs Church.
Chortos, George F. '64 (PIT) Allegheny County, PA Allegheny County Jail.
Chortos, George F. '66 (PIT) [59] Pittsburgh, PA Our Lady of Loreto Church.
Chotin, Msgr. Joseph L. '64 (NO) Mandeville, LA Our Lady of the Lake Church.
Chouinard, Lionel G. '65 (PRT) Lisbon Falls, ME Holy Trinity Church.
Chouinard, Marcel G. '56 (PRT) Skowhegan, ME Notre Dame De Lourdes Church.
Chovanec, Paul R. '72 (GAL) [22] Houston, TX St. Christopher Church.
Chow, Luke L. '54 (PH) Levittown, PA St. Michael the Archangel Church.
Chow, Stephen *s.j.* '94 (BO) [W] Cambridge, MA Faber House; [W] Cambridge, MA Weston Jesuit Community.
Chowning, Daniel *o.c.d.* '88 (MIL) [P] Holy Hill, WI Discalced Carmelite Monastery.
Chowning, Michael *o.f.m.* '68 (LEX) Hazard, KY Mother of Good Counsel Church; Jackson, KY Holy Cross Church; [K] Hazard, KY Father Farrell Spiritual Life Center.
Chrepta, Msgr. Stephen J. '45 (STF) Retired.
Chretien, Richard L. '67 (FR) [7] Fall River, MA Notre Dame de Lourdes Church.
Christ, John P. *o.s.c.* '65 (DET) Royal Oak, MI St. Dennis Church; [K] Riverview, MI Crosier Community of Riverview.
Christ, Raymond J. *o.s.f.s.* '51 (PH) [AA] Wyndmoor, PA Villa de Sales Oblate Residence.
Christancho, Fernando (BAL) Hickory, MD St. Ignatius Church.
Christancho, Jorge '78 (ATL) Gainesville, GA St. Michael's Church.
Christensen, Brian Patrick '99 (RC) [1] Rapid City, SD Cathedral of Our Lady of Perpetual Help.
Christensen, Christian *i.sch.* '71 (CC) [J] Corpus Christi, TX Secular Institute of the Schoenstatt Fathers aka Schoenstatt Fathers.
Christensen, Christian *c.c.* '71 (MIL) [T] Waukesha, WI Secular Institute of Schoenstatt Fathers.
Christensen, Donald L. '59 (SAG) [8] Saginaw, MI St. Andrew Church.
Christensen, Joseph *o.f.m.i.* '97 (FAR) [F] Pisek, ND Franciscan Friars of Mary Immaculate.
Christensen, Michael R. '79 (LIN) [10] Lincoln, NE St. Peter Church.
Christensen, Peter '85 (STP) [8] St. Paul, MN The Nativity of Our Lord Church.
Christensen, William A. *s.m.* '73 (STL) [P] St. Louis, MO Provincialate of the Society of Mary, Province of St. Louis.
Christian, George G. *o.p.* '55 (L) [47] Louisville, KY St. Louis Bertrand Church.
Christian, John S. '84 (TR) Leave of Absence.
Christian, Lawrence J. *c.m.f.* '83 (SAT) Jourdanton, TX St. Matthew's Church.
Christian, Norman H. '67 (STL) On Medical Leave.
Christian, Robert *o.p.* '76 (OAK) [N] Oakland, CA Western Dominican Province.
Christiana, Nicholas M. '78 (ALT) Absent on Leave.
Christiansen, Andrew J. *s.j.* '72 (WDC) [M] Washington, DC Woodstock Jesuit Community; [V] Washington, DC Woodstock Theological Center.
Christie, Frank M. *o.s.m.* '56 (CHI) [N] Chicago, IL Order of Friar Servants of Mary (Servites) United States of America Province, Inc.
Christman, Msgr. Bernard E. '59 (OG) Lyon Mountain, NY St. Bernard Church; Lyon Mountain, NY Lyon Mountain Correctional Facility.
Christman, Ralph F. *m.m.* '56 (SFR) [N] San Francisco, CA Maryknoll Fathers and Brothers, Catholic Foreign Mission Society of America, Inc.
Christman, Robert '79 (MIA) Absent on Leave.
Christof, Francis T. *o.s.f.s.* '82 (WIL) [I] Childs, MD Oblates of St. Francis De Sales.
Christofferson, Kevin (GF) On Duty Outside of the Diocese.
Christofferson, Kevin '97 (HEL) [1] Butte, MT Butte Catholic Community North Church; [4] Butte, MT Immaculate Conception Church; [9] Butte, MT St. Joseph Church; [11] Butte, MT St. Patrick Church.
Christopher, Mark '57 (PMB) Fort Pierce, FL St. Anastasia Church; Retired.
Christopher, Patrick '91 (STL) Washington, MO St. Francis Borgia Church.
Christy, William H. *c.s.sp.* '92 (FgM) Holy Ghost Foreign Missions.
Chriszt, Dennis *c.pp.s.* '82 (CIN) [23] Dayton, OH Precious Blood Church.
Chriszt, Dennis *c.pp.s.* '83 (CIN) [M] Dayton, OH Provincial Office of the Cincinnati Province of the Society of the Precious Blood.
Chrobak, Lyle *o.f.m.* '62 (FgM) Franciscan Foreign Missions.
Chrobak, Lyle *o.f.m.* '62 (GB) [I] Pulaski, WI Assumption of B.V.M. Friary.
Chrobot, Leonard F. '64 (FTW) [8] South Bend, IN St. Hedwig Church.
Chruma, Francis '57 (AUS) [H] Jonestown, TX Hermitage.
Chrusciel, Bogumil '68 (NEW) [35] Newark, NJ St. Stanislaus Church.
Chrysostom, Francis X. '60 (LA) [J] Inglewood, CA Daniel Freeman Memorial Hospital.
Chryst, Robert D. '68 (SY) [12] Syracuse, NY St. Anthony of Padua Church; Special Assignment.
Chrzastek, Brian *o.p.* '92 (CHI) River Forest, IL St. Vincent Ferrer Church.
Chrzastek, Brian *o.p.* '92 (PRO) [P] Providence, RI St. Thomas Aquinas Priory at Providence College.
Chu, Bernard M.C. *s.j.* '60 (OAK) [S] Berkeley, CA Inter-Friendship House Association, Friendship Center.
Chu, Peter '55 (GAL) [N] Houston, TX St. Dominic Village.
Chu, Peter *s.j.* '68 (LA) [Q] Los Angeles, CA Columbiere House.
Chu, Peter Ngoc Thanh (GAL) Retired.
Chu, Quang '91 (ORG) Garden Grove, CA St. Columban Church.
Chua, Freddie '98 (LA) [1] Long Beach, CA St. Anthony Church.
Chubirko, Michael *s.d.b.* '60 (PSC) Elizabeth, NJ SS. Peter and Paul Church.
Chudy, Carl *s.x.* '86 (FgM) Xaverian Foreign Missions.
Chudy, Carl *s.x.* '86 (PAT) [M] Wayne, NJ Xaverian Missionary Fathers.
Chueca, Ubaldo '66 (LA) [41] Los Angeles, CA St. Aloysius Gonzaga Church.
Chukwu, Christopher *c.s.sp.* '93 (ARE) [8] Arecibo, PR Inmaculado Corazon de Maria Church.
Chukwu, Donatus '93 (CHI) [71] Chicago, IL St. Gregory Church.
Chukwuleta, Daniel '91 (FTW) [14] Fort Wayne, IN St. Patrick Church; Fort Wayne, IN St. Joseph Medical Center.
Chun, Francis '63 (P) Milwaukie, OR St. John the Baptist Church.
Chung, Alex '00 (LA) Pico Rivera, CA St. Hilary Church.
Chung, Anthony '83 (SFR) Redwood City, CA St. Pius Church; Special Assignment.
Chung, Brian G. '00 (LA) Paramount, CA Our Lady of the Rosary Church.
Chung, Francis *s.j.* '93 (AUS) Harker Heights, TX St. Paul Chong Hasang Church; Leander, TX St. Andrew Kim Taegon Korean Catholic Church.
Chuong, Joseph Doan Huy '77 (GAL) [Q] New Caney, TX Congregation of the Mother Coredemptrix.
Chuong, Matthias Nguyen H. '81 (SB) [6] San Bernardino, CA St. Anne Church.
Chupela, Msgr. Andrew A. '55 (GBG) [3] Uniontown, PA Nativity of the Blessed Virgin Mary Church.
Chura, Andrew '58 (PBR) Toronto, OH St. Joseph Church.
Church, Msgr. James '58 (SAC) [11] Sacramento, CA St. Charles Borromeo Church.
Church, Timothy A. '95 (DAL) Allen, TX St. Jude Church.
Church, Wenceslaus '59 (CHI) [N] Chicago, IL St. Peter's Friary.
Churchwell, Stephen T. '76 (ATL) [8] Atlanta, GA Sacred Heart of Jesus Church.
Chwalek, John C. '48 (SPR) [2] Adams, MA St. Stanislaus Kostka Church.
Chwalek, Kazimierz *m.i.c.* '87 (SPR) [J] Stockbridge, MA Congregation of Marians of The Immaculate Conception of the BVM.
Chwalinski, Stanley R. '67 (BUF) Attica, NY St. Vincent de Paul Church.
Chwaliszewski, Roman *o.f.m.conv.* '60 (FR) [8] New Bedford, MA Our Lady of Perpetual Help Church.
Chwieroth, Edward J. '50 (PH) Retired.
Chycinski, Gregory A. '71 (MIL) [66] Milwaukee, WI Our Lady of Sorrows Church.
Chylewski, Msgr. Anthony '52 (SD) Retired.
Chylko, Gerard *c.s.s.r.* (BAL) [68] Baltimore, MD Our Lady of Fatima Church.
Chylko, Gerard *c.ss.r.* '79 (BAL) [68] Baltimore, MD Our Lady of Fatima Church.
Ciaiola, Joseph A. '47 (E) [2] Farrell, PA Our Lady of Fatima Church.
Cialone, Donald '75 (NEW) Montclair, NJ Our Lady of Mt. Carmel Church.
Ciambelli, Blase A. '64 (WOR) On Special or Other Diocesan Assignment.
Ciampaglio, Msgr. Joseph A. '62 (PAT) Rockaway Township, NJ St. Clement, Pope and Martyr Church.
Ciampietro, Anthony E. *c.s.b.* '93 (NY) [DD] New York, NY Jesuit Community at Fordham University.
Ciancimino, David S. *s.j.* '88 (NY) [F] New York, NY Xavier High School.
Ciandella, Roch *o.f.m.* '72 (NY) [FF] Wappingers Falls, NY Mt. Alvernia Retreat House.
Ciani, Francis P. '39 (ALB) Retired.
Ciano, Ken '95 (IND) Seelyville, IN Holy Rosary Church.
Ciappi-Azcorra, Angel '98 (SJN) [17] San Juan, PR Francisca Javiera Cabrini Church.
Ciaramitaro, Victor P. '72 (MEM) Paris, TN Holy Cross Church.
Ciaravolo, Ronald '58 (NY) Absent on Leave.

Ciardiello, Bruno *o.f.m.* '45 (BRK) [106] Brooklyn, NY Our Lady of Peace Church.
Ciavaglia, Julio M. *c.r.s.p.* '66 (BUF) [B] Youngstown, NY St. Anthony M. Zaccaria Seminary; [B] Youngstown, NY The National Shrine Basilica of Our Lady of Fatima.
Ciba, Thomas J. '74 (NEW) Nutley, NJ Our Lady of Mount Carmel Church.
Cibangu, Sylvian '95 (COS) [1] Colorado Springs, CO St. Mary's Church.
Cibulskis, Pete *m.i.c.* '53 (MIL) [10] Kenosha, WI St. Peter Church.
Ciccarino, Christopher M. '96 (NEW) Union, NJ St. Michael's Church.
Ciccolini, Samuel R. '69 (CLV) [8] Akron, OH Immaculate Conception Church; [U] Akron, OH Interval Brotherhood Home Alcohol-Drug Rehabilitation Center.
Ciccone, Joseph J. *c.s.p.* '89 (CHI) [122] Chicago, IL Old St. Mary Church.
Ciccone, Mark C. *s.j.* '85 (SJ) [L] Los Gatos, CA Sacred Heart Jesuit Center.
Ciccone, Michael A. *o.p.* '75 (BO) [W] Dover, MA St. Stephen Priory.
Ciccone, Nicholas '84 (BO) [39] Boston, MA St. Margaret Church.
Cicerale, Charles W. '75 (MET) Raritan, NJ St. Joseph Church.
Cichanowicz, Casimir *s.s.e.* '43 (VEN) [G] Englewood, FL Society of St. Edmund Residence.
Cichon, Michael W. '85 (NY) [202] Staten Island, NY St. Clare Church.
Cici, William '59 (E) Retired.
Cicinato, Michael '76 (MRY) San Luis Obispo, CA Nativity of Our Lady Church.
Cicola, Alfred C. '67 (PIT) Canonsburg, PA St. Patrick Church.
Ciemiega, Ernest D. '57 (CHI) Blue Island, IL St. Isidore Church; Retired.
Ciemiega, Ernest D. '58 (CHI) [33] Chicago, IL St. Bruno Church.
Cieri, Domenic L. '81 (BAL) Severn, MD St. Bernadette Church.
Ciesielski, Heinc '46 (PEO) Retired.
Ciesla, Fred *c.r.* '94 (CHI) [D] Chicago, IL Gordon Tech High School.
Ciesla, Marek *s.ch.* '82 (TOL) [15] Toledo, OH St. Adalbert Church.
Ciesla, Walter M. '81 (GRY) [4] Michigan City, IN St. Stanislaus Kostka Church; Westville, IN Westville Correctional Center.
Cieslak, William M. *o.f.m.cap.* '73 (OAK) [A] Berkeley, CA Franciscan School of Theology; [A] Berkeley, CA Franciscan School of Theology; [N] Oakland, CA Franciscan Friars Provincial Office, Province of St. Barbara.
Cieslik, Mark *s.j.* '00 (BO) [W] Cambridge, MA Weston Jesuit Community.
Cieslik, R. Dale '82 (L) [52] Louisville, KY St. Martin de Porres Church.
Cieslik, Robert Dale '82 (L) [59] Louisville, KY Our Lady of Lourdes Church.
Cieslikowski, Thomas J. '88 (HRT) [7] New Britain, CT St. Jerome's Church.
Cieslinski, Robert '43 (P) Retired.
Ciesniewski, Richard P. '57 (DET) Retired.
Ciferni, Andrew D. *o.praem.* '66 (PH) [AA] Paoli, PA Daylesford Abbey.
Cigan, John J. *j.c.b.* '74 (PSC) Binghamton, NY Holy Spirit Church.
Cihak, John '98 (P) Grants Pass, OR St. Anne Church.
Cilia, Francis V. '79 (SJ) Special Assignment.
Cilia, Joseph *o.carm.* '68 (FgM) Carmelite Foreign Missions.
Ciliberti, Francis J. *o.praem.* '44 (WIL) [I] Claymont, DE Immaculate Conception Priory of the Canons Regular of Premontre.
Cilinski, Msgr. John T. '48 (ARL) [2] Arlington, VA St. Agnes Church; Retired.
Cilinski, Julius J. '45 (ARL) Clifton, VA St. Andrew the Apostle Church; Retired.
Cilinski, Robert C. '79 (ARL) Manassas, VA All Saints Church.
Cillo, David '85 (PIT) Pleasant Hills, PA St. Elizabeth Church.
Cilwick, Theodore T. '43 (CHR) Retired.
Cima, Jose '58 (SB) Retired.
Cima, Thomas E. '67 (CHI) Calumet City, IL St. Victor Church.
Cimarrusti, Francis A. '64 (CHI) [57] Chicago, IL St. Fidelis Church; [131] Chicago, IL St. Matthias Church; [G] Chicago, IL Catholic Charities of the Archdiocese of Chicago-Archdiocesan Offices.
Cimbala, Edward G. '88 (PSC) Trenton, NJ St. Mary of the Assumption Church.
Cimerman, Krizolog *o.f.m.* '73 (NY) [30] New York, NY St. Cyril Church.
Cimino, John V. *o.praem.* '61 (WIL) [I] Claymont, DE Immaculate Conception Priory of the Canons Regular of Premontre.
Cimino, Michael '86 (SFE) [11] Albuquerque, NM Our Lady of the Assumption Church.
Cimperman, Victor J. '43 (CLV) [4] Akron, OH Christ the King Church; Retired.
Cimpl, Charles L. '78 (SFS) [8] Sioux Falls, SD St. Therese Church.
Cincinnati, Anthony '87 (WH) Follansbee, WV St. Anthony Church.
Cincoski, Edward E. *s.j.* '50 (DET) [P] Clarkston, MI Colombiere Center.
Cincotta, Anthony '74 (SY) On Duty Outside the Diocese.
Cindric, John R. '74 (GBG) Belle Vernon, PA St. Sebastian Church.
Cinesi, Joseph '80 (MIA) Absent on Leave.
Cingle, Martin A. '73 (ALT) [16] Johnstown, PA St. Francis of Assisi Church.
Cinguegrani, David *c.p.* '96 (HRT) [Q] West Hartford, CT Holy Family Retreat Center.
Cini, Msgr. J. Thomas '68 (WIL) Liftwood, DE Immaculate Heart of Mary Church.
Cini, Robert *m.s.s.p.* '53 (DET) [55] Detroit, MI Our Lady of Mt. Carmel Church.
Cink, James '85 (MOB) Tillman's Corner, AL St. Vincent de Paul Church.
Cinque, Stephen J. '81 (NEW) Maywood, NJ Our Lady Queen of Peace Church.
Cinquegrani, David *c.p.* '96 (HRT) [C] West Hartford, CT Saint Joseph College; [M] West Hartford, CT Holy Family Monastery/Retreat.
Cinquegrani, R. Bruce '79 (MEM) [2] Memphis, TN St. Ann Church.
Cinson, Victor, Jr. '74 (STU) Harriettsville, OH St. Henry Church; Lowell, OH Our Lady of Mercy Church.
Cintron, Angel Luis '91 (CGS) Cidra, PR Nuestra Senora del Carmen Church.
Cintron, Freddy '87 (BRK) [39] Brooklyn, NY St. Fortunata Church; [39] Brooklyn, NY St. Fortunata Church.
Cintron, Segismundo '89 (PCE) Yauco, PR St. Martin de Porres Church; [B] Ponce, PR The Pontifical Catholic University of Puerto Rico.
Cintula, Francis M. '65 (CHL) Retired.
Cio, Robert '74 (NEW) [4] Irvington, NJ St. Paul the Apostle Church.
Cioch, Grzegorz J. (DEN) [24] Denver, CO Church of the Risen Christ.
Cioffi, Alfred '85 (MIA) Higher Studies.
Cioffi, Paul L. *s.j.* '59 (WDC) [M] Washington, DC The Jesuit Community at Georgetown University; [V] Washington, DC Institute for Pastoral Renewal, Inc.
Cioffi, Phillip F. '81 (CHI) Forest Park, IL St. Bernardine Church.
Cioffi, Ronald J. '69 (TR) Keyport, NJ St. Joseph Church.
Ciolek, Msgr. Casimir S. '46 (CLV) [37] Cleveland, OH St. John Cantius Church; [2] Garfield Heights, OH SS. Peter and Paul Church; Cleveland, OH Airport, Cleveland Hopkins International; Retired; [U] Cleveland, OH Society of St. Vincent de Paul, Diocesan Central Council.
Ciolek, Joseph F. '47 (CLV) [K] Cleveland, OH Holy Family Home.
Ciomek, Christopher '98 (CHI) [137] Chicago, IL St. Monica Church.
Ciona, Calin '00 (NEW) Roseland, NJ Our Lady of the Blessed Sacrament Church.
Cioppa, John A. *m.m.* '59 (FgM) Maryknoll Foreign Missions.
Cioppa, Philip M. '83 (ALB) Hoosick Falls, NY Immaculate Conception Church.
Cioppi, Martin T. '81 (PH) Upper Gwynedd, PA Corpus Christi Church; [F] Lansdale, PA Lansdale Catholic High School.
Ciordia, Pedro M. '61 (LA) Retired.
Ciorra, Anthony J. *o.f.m.cap.* '73 (PAT) [B] Morristown, NJ College of Saint Elizabeth; [P] Morristown, NJ College of St. Elizabeth, Center for Theological and Spiritual Development.
Ciosek, Scott A. '00 (FR) [7] New Bedford, MA Our Lady of Mt. Carmel Church.
Ciotola, Msgr. Romano '65 (COL) [35] Columbus, OH Our Lady of Victory Church.
Ciotoli, Vincent J. '76 (ALB) Ravena, NY St. Patrick Church.
Cipar, Daniel *m.s.c.* '61 (Y) East Palestine, OH Our Lady of Lourdes Church; [A] Youngstown, OH Sacred Heart Retreat House & Renewal Center.
Cipolla, Richard G. '84 (BGP) [T] Darien, CT Convent of St. Birgitta.
Cippel, Msgr. John A. '60 (SP) Spring Hill, FL St. Frances Xavier Cabrini Church.
Ciprian, Carl A. '76 (CLV) [3] Barberton, OH Holy Trinity Church.
Cipriano, Joseph F. '59 (SCR) [2] Old Forge, PA St. Mary's Church.
Cipriano, Robert P. '87 (SFR) Fairfax, CA St. Rita Church.
Ciranni, Sal *r.c.j.* '55 (LA) [Q] North Hills, CA Rogationist Fathers.
Cirba, Richard J. '89 (SCR) [26] Scranton, PA St. Vincent de Paul Church.
Ciriaco, Dominic G. '99 (NEW) Clark, NJ St. Agnes Church.
Cirignani, Anthony (MIL) [P] Burlington, WI Queen of Peace Friary.
Cirillo, Nicholas A. '95 (BGP) Huntington, CT St. Lawrence Church.
Ciriza, Jesus M. *m.ss.cc.* (SJN) [10] Bayamon, PR San Juan Bautista de la Salle Church.
Cirone, Theodore *c.m.f.* (CHI) [78] Chicago, IL Holy Cross/Immaculate Heart of Mary Church.
Cirrincione, Msgr. Joseph A. '34 (ROC) Retired.
Cis, James '38 (FTW) Retired.
Ciscar, Tomas *o.carm.* '78 (SJN) [59] San Juan, PR Santa Teresita Del Nino Jesus Church.
Cisco, Bede *o.s.b.* '78 (IND) [A] St. Meinrad, IN St. Meinrad Seminary; [J] St. Meinrad, IN St. Meinrad Archabbey.
Cisek, Herman W. *m.m.* '65 (FgM) Maryknoll Foreign Missions.
Cisetti, Joseph I. '91 (KC) Richmond, MO Immaculate Conception Church.
Cisewski, John '71 (NO) [18] New Orleans, LA Our Lady of Lourdes Church; [46] New Orleans, LA St. Matthias Church.
Cislo, Robert '65 (DET) [4] Taylor, MI St. Paschal Church.
Cisneros, Msgr. Octavio '71 (BRK) [B] Douglaston, NY Cathedral Seminary Residence of the Immaculate Conception.
Cisneros, Msgr. Octavio '71 (NY) [HH] New York, NY Felix Varela Foundation, Inc., The.
Cistone, Msgr. Joseph R. '75 (PH) On Special or Other Archdiocesan Assignment.
Citero, Samuel *o.carm.* '84 (CHI) [20] Chicago, IL St. Barbara Church.
Citero, Samuel *o.carm.* '84 (NEW) Cresskill, NJ St. Therese of Lisieux Church.
Citino, Angelo R. '77 (PH) [110] Philadelphia, PA Mother of Divine Grace Church.
Citro, Anthony M. '94 (GAY) Roscommon, MI St. Michael Church.
Ciuba, Msgr. Edward J. '59 (NEW) North Caldwell, NJ Notre Dame Church.
Ciudice, Anthony *o.f.m.cap.* (NY) [B] Beacon, NY St. Lawrence of Brindisi Friary.
Ciulek, Joseph '43 (ALB) Retired.
Ciullo, Michael J. '75 (MAN) Claremont, NH St. Mary Church.
Ciullo, Salvator L. '60 (ARL) [3] Alexandria, VA Queen of Apostles Church.
Ciungu, John '42 (ROM) Retired.
Ciupek, James D. '97 (BUF) Hamburg, NY SS. Peter and Paul Church.
Ciurej, Richard S. '54 (OM) Retired.
Ciurpita, John '89 (PHU) Cherry Hill, NJ St. Michael's Church.
Civiello, John D. '68 (PRT) [5] Portland, ME St. Patrick's Church.
Civille, John R. '66 (CIN) Middletown, OH Holy Family Church.
Civzelis, Victor *m.i.c.* '64 (CHI) [142] Chicago, IL Our Lady of Aglona Church.
Cizewski, Albert '71 (SFS) Florence, SD Blessed Sacrament Church.
Cizik, Ladis '87 (PIT) On Duty Outside the Diocese.
Cizur, Ignacio *o.f.m.cap.* '72 (DAL) [8] Dallas, TX Our Lady of Lourdes Church.
Claerr, Francis *c.m.m.* '48 (DET) [K] Dearborn Heights, MI Our Lady of Grace Monastery.
Clagett, Msgr. Carl P. '55 (COL) Retired.
Clair, John J. '82 (CHI) Other Assignments.
Clancy, Msgr. Douglas P. '71 (HRT) [4] Manchester, CT St. James Church.
Clancy, Frank *s.c.j.* '74 (BWN) Harlingen, TX Valley Baptist Medical Center; [E] Harlingen, TX Priests of the Sacred Heart.
Clancy, Patrick M.J. *o.p.* '39 (CHI) [N] Chicago, IL Dominicans (Provincial Office).
Clancy, Raphael '74 (AUS) Killeen, TX St. Joseph Church.
Clancy, Rian *c.p.* '53 (CHI) [N] Chicago, IL Passionist Community-Immaculate Conception Monastery.
Clancy, Richard F. '91 (BO) [14] Boston, MA St. Brigid Church.
Clancy, Robert E. '74 (CLV) [16] Akron, OH Sacred Heart of Jesus Church; Akron, OH Akron General Hospital.
Clancy, Thomas *s.j.* '55 (NO) [C] New Orleans, LA Loyola University New Orleans.
Clancy, Msgr. Thomas C. '45 (BRK) [23] Brooklyn, NY St. Brendan's Church; Retired.
Clancy, Timothy R. *s.j.* '89 (SPK) [C] Spokane, WA Gonzaga University.
Clanton, Bruce *s.d.s.* '78 (MIL) [P] Milwaukee, WI Salvatorian Provincial Residence.
Clapham, Bruce R. '95 (CHY) Newcastle, WY Corpus Christi Church.
Clapp, Kenneth A. '90 (MIL) On Duty Outside the Archdiocese.
Clapsaddle, Harlan '77 (RCK) [F] Rockford, IL Provena

Cor Mariae Center.
Clarahan, Michael '58 (CHI) [N] Chicago, IL St. Peter's Friary.
Clark, Andrew '83 (NY) Absent on Leave.
Clark, Anthony '79 (LSC) Lordsburg, NM St. Joseph Church.
Clark, Anthony *s.v.d.* '85 (IND) [34] Indianapolis, IN St. Rita Church.
Clark, Benjamin *o.c.s.o.* '50 (CHR) [E] Moncks Corner, SC Mepkin Abbey.
Clark, Curtis L. '84 (ARL) McLean, VA St. Luke's Church.
Clark, Daniel C. '80 (L) On Special Assignment.
Clark, David '84 (P) On Duty Outside the Archdiocese.
Clark, Msgr. Dennis R. '66 (SD) Rancho Santa Fe, CA Church of the Nativity.
Clark, Douglas K. '76 (SAV) [1] Savannah, GA Cathedral of St. John the Baptist.
Clark, Msgr. Edward Wm. '72 (LA) [A] Camarillo, CA St. John's Seminary College of the Archdiocese of Los Angeles.
Clark, Msgr. Eugene V. '51 (NY) [2] New York, NY St. Agnes Church; [HH] New York, NY Friends of American Art in Religion, Inc.; [HH] New York, NY Patrons of the Arts in the Vatican Museums.
Clark, Francis X. *s.j.* '43 (FgM) Provinces.
Clark, Gerard J. '40 (MIL) Retired.
Clark, Howard T. '57 (WIL) Retired.
Clark, J. Donald *s.j.* '48 (SY) [S] Syracuse, NY Jesuits at LeMoyne, Inc.
Clark, J. Michael '95 (OWN) Clinton, KY St. Jude Church; Fulton, KY St. Edward Church; Hickman, KY Sacred Heart Church.
Clark, James B. (BO) Rockland, MA Holy Family Church.
Clark, James E. '96 (ALB) Wynantskill, NY St. Jude the Apostle Church.
Clark, James M. '72 (TR) Lincroft, NJ St. Leo the Great Church.
Clark, James P. '52 (NY) [140] Bronx, NY St. Francis of Assisi Church.
Clark, James W. '84 (GBG) Mount Pleasant, PA Transfiguration Church; Connellsville, PA Highlands Hospital & Health Center; Mount Pleasant, PA Frick Community Health Center.
Clark, John F. *c.m.* '70 (STL) [A] St. Louis, MO Kenrick-Glennon Seminary; [P] St. Louis, MO Lazarist Residence.
Clark, Msgr. John J. '53 (CAM) Retired.
Clark, John R. '96 (WDC) [8] Silver Spring, MD St. Michael Church.
Clark, John W. *s.j.* '59 (LA) [Q] Los Angeles, CA Columbiere House.
Clark, John W. *s.j.* '59 (SFR) [C] San Francisco, CA University of San Francisco.
Clark, Joseph J. '96 (ARL) Manassas, VA Sacred Heart Church.
Clark, Joseph L. '76 (RIC) Fort Monroe, VA St. Mary Star of the Sea Church.
Clark, Keith *o.f.m.cap.* '65 (MIL) [B] Mount Calvary, WI St. Lawrence Seminary; [P] Mount Calvary, WI St. Lawrence Friary.
Clark, Kevin *o.s.b.* '76 (NO) [P] St. Benedict, LA St. Joseph Abbey.
Clark, Msgr. Laurence E. '54 (LA) Retired.
Clark, Lucian *c.p.* '65 (PH) [AA] Philadelphia, PA St. Michael's Passionist Residence.
Clark, Matthew *o.s.b.* '87 (NO) [J] St. Benedict, LA Abbey Youth Camp, Inc.
Clark, Matthew R. *o.s.b.* '87 (NO) [P] St. Benedict, LA St. Joseph Abbey.
Clark, Patrick S. '61 (SEA) Issaquah, WA St. Joseph Church.
Clark, Peter A. *s.j.* '92 (PH) [AA] Philadelphia, PA Jesuit Community at St. Joseph's University.
Clark, Ray '91 (OWN) Mayfield, KY St. Joseph Church.
Clark, Richard '93 (MRY) Hollister, CA Sacred Heart/St. Benedict Catholic Community Church.
Clark, Richard D. (ALT) [17] Johnstown, PA Visitation of the B.V.M. Church.
Clark, Robert (STP) [12] St. Paul, MN St. Agnes Church.
Clark, Robert *s.s.c.* '65 (OM) [K] St. Columbans, NE St. Columban's Foreign Mission Society.
Clark, Robert J. '99 (CHI) Orland Park, IL St. Michael Church.
Clark, Robert P., Jr. '84 (NU) On Duty Outside the Diocese.
Clark, Steven E. '90 (NY) Peekskill, NY Assumption Church.
Clark, Thomas F. *s.j.* '81 (BO) [19] Boston, MA St. Francis de Sales-St. Philip Church; [W] Boston, MA Loyola House; [W] Boston, MA The Society of Jesus of New England-Provincial Offices.
Clark, Thomas R. '62 (L) [2] Valley Station, KY Our Lady Help of Christians Church; [4] Valley Station, KY St. Timothy Church.
Clark, Timothy *o.c.s.o.* '80 (P) [L] Lafayette, OR The Cistercian (Trappist) Abbey of Our Lady of Guadalupe.
Clark, Vernon F. '80 (CHY) [3] Cheyenne, WY St. Joseph's Church.
Clark, William *o.m.i.* '55 (GAL) [S] Dickinson, TX Christian Renewal Center.
Clark, William *s.j.* '93 (BO) [W] Cambridge, MA Weston Jesuit Community.
Clarke, Daniel '54 (DM) Stuart, IA All Saints Church.
Clarke, David M. *s.j.* '64 (DEN) [B] Denver, CO Regis University; [M] Denver, CO Regis Jesuit Community (The Jesuits at Regis University).
Clarke, Gerard R. *o.s.f.s.* '57 (WIL) [I] Childs, MD Oblates of St. Francis De Sales.
Clarke, Msgr. Hugh '50 (CC) Retired.
Clarke, Msgr. James A. '70 (Y) North Canton, OH St. Paul's Church.
Clarke, Msgr. James T. '38 (SCR) Retired; [N] Dunmore, PA Villa St. Joseph.
Clarke, Jim '80 (LA) Redondo Beach, CA St. James Church.
Clarke, John '45 (DM) Retired.
Clarke, John A. '59 (CAM) Washington Township, NJ SS. Peter and Paul Church.
Clarke, Kevin T. *s.j.* '73 (HEL) [5] Missoula, MT St. Francis Xavier Church.
Clarke, Peter '63 (CHR) Murphy Village, SC St. Edward Church.
Clarke, Thomas E. *s.j.* '50 (NY) [EE] Highland Mills, NY Religious of Jesus and Mary; [FF] Highland Mills, NY Bethany Retreat House.
Clarke, Msgr. Thomas J. '34 (EVN) Retired.
Clarke, W. Norris *s.j.* '45 (NY) [DD] New York, NY Jesuit Community at Fordham University.
Clarke, W. Norris *s.j.* '70 (WH) [A] Wheeling, WV Wheeling Jesuit University.
Clarkin, Herbert '45 (HRT) [K] West Hartford, CT Saint Mary Home.
Clarkson, Theodore J. *s.j.* '44 (SY) [S] Syracuse, NY Jesuits at LeMoyne, Inc.
Claro, Carlos L. *c.s.v.* '98 (CHI) [N] Arlington Heights, IL Viatorian Province Center-Clerics of St. Viator.
Claro, Mario R. '67 (WH) Franklin, WV St. Elizabeth Ann Seton Church; Moorefield, WV Epiphany of the Lord Church; Petersburg, WV St. Mary's Church.
Clary, Brian M. '96 (BO) Braintree, MA St. Clare Church.
Clary, Michael O. '77 (KC) Blue Springs, MO St. John La Lande Church.
Class, Michael D. *s.j.* '90 (MIL) [P] Milwaukee, WI Jesuit Community at Marquette University.
Classick, Bede E. *o.s.b.* '67 (PAT) [M] Newton, NJ St. Paul's Abbey.
Clauder, J. Gibbs '73 (MAD) Leave of Absence.
Claudio, Antonio '75 (SFR) [4] San Francisco, CA St. Anne Church.
Clausen, Kenneth J. '53 (GF) Retired.
Clausen, Msgr. William J. '62 (RCK) Maple Park, IL St. Mary Church.
Clauss, Joseph '56 (EVN) Retired.
Clavenna, Msgr. Charles G. '56 (STL) On Medical Leave.
Clavero, Jose M. *sch.p.* '64 (NY) [12] New York, NY Annunciation Church; [DD] New York, NY Calasanzian Fathers (Piarists).
Clavey, William J. '98 (CHI) Berwyn, IL St. Mary of Celle Church.
Clavin, M. Oliver '70 (SPC) Kelso, MO St. Augustine Church.
Clavin, Nicholas P. '73 (SD) [37] San Diego, CA St. Vincent de Paul Church.
Clay, Christopher '98 (SCR) [D] Hazleton, PA Bishop Hafey Junior/Senior High School.
Clay, Christopher R. '98 (SCR) [M] Mount Pocono, PA Newman House.
Clay, David J. *s.s.c.* '62 (FgM) St. Columban's Foreign Mission.
Clay, John C. '51 (STP) [32] St. Paul, MN St. Stanislaus Church.
Clay, Michael G. '80 (R) Special Assignment; [I] Chapel Hill, NC Vocations Office.
Clayton, Msgr. C. Murray '56 (SHP) [5] Shreveport, LA Sacred Heart of Jesus Church.
Clayton, Daniel J. '68 (DAL) Rowlett, TX Sacred Heart Church.
Cleare, Rudi '83 (ORL) Sabbatical.
Cleary, Christopher *c.p.* '86 (PH) [AA] Philadelphia, PA St. Michael's Passionist Residence.
Cleary, Dennis W. (NY) [DD] New York, NY Maryknoll House.
Cleary, Dennis W. *m.m.* '77 (NY) [DD] Maryknoll, NY Maryknoll Fathers and Brothers.
Cleary, Donald M. '71 (OM) Clarks, NE St. Peter Church; Fullerton, NE St. Peter Church.
Cleary, Donald R. '68 (KC) Retired.
Cleary, Edward '56 (SFR) [4] South San Francisco, CA St. Veronica Church.
Cleary, Edward J. '40 (MEM) Retired.
Cleary, Edward L. *o.p.* '57 (PRO) [P] Providence, RI St. Thomas Aquinas Priory at Providence College.
Cleary, Edward M. '56 (SFR) Retired.
Cleary, Francis X. *s.j.* '63 (STL) [P] St. Louis, MO Jesuit Community Corporation at St. Louis University - Jesuit Hall.
Cleary, Francis X. *s.j.* '66 (STL) [C] St. Louis, MO Saint Louis University.
Cleary, Gerard '61 (BLX) Pascagoula, MS Our Lady of Victories Church.
Cleary, Herbert J. *s.j.* '68 (BO) [U] Boston, MA Marian Manor; [W] Boston, MA Loyola House.
Cleary, James *o.f.m.* (LA) [J] Lynwood, CA St. Francis Medical Center.
Cleary, James *t.o.r.* '41 (ARL) [J] White Post, VA Sacred Heart Friary.
Cleary, James L. *o.f.m.cap.* '70 (LA) [75] Los Angeles, CA St. Lawrence of Brindisi Church.
Cleary, Msgr. Kevin '48 (FRS) Retired.
Cleary, Michael J. '53 (SR) Napa, CA St. Apollinaris Church.
Cleary, Paul '74 (SAT) [34] San Antonio, TX St. Dominic Church.
Cleary, Philip C. '79 (CHI) Missionary Work.
Cleary, Richard *o.s.b.* '55 (WCH) [3] Wichita, KS Blessed Sacrament Church.
Cleary, Richard E. *o.s.f.s.* '59 (R) [2] Durham, NC Holy Infant Church.
Cleary, Richard T. *s.j.* '66 (BO) [W] Chestnut Hill, MA The Jesuit Community at Boston College.
Cleary, William *c.ss.r.* '62 (DEN) [M] Denver, CO The Redemptorists/Denver Province.
Cleary, William D. '55 (IND) Retired.
Cleary, William M. *o.s.a.* '61 (WDC) [B] Silver Spring, MD Austin Friars Hall, Order of St. Augustine.
Cleary, William M. *c.ss.r.* '62 (FgM) Redemptorist Foreign Missions.
Cleaton, C. Thomas '75 (CLV) Avon, OH St. Mary of the Immaculate Conception Church.
Cleator, Gerard B. *o.p.* '65 (CHI) [N] Chicago, IL Dominicans (Provincial Office).
Clegg, Thomas (IND) [3] Indianapolis, IN Good Shepherd Church.
Clegg, Thomas '90 (IND) Indianapolis, IN Indianapolis Fire Department.
Clegg, Timothy '71 (LFT) On Duty Outside the Diocese.
Clemens, Bailey '98 (PEO) Monmouth, IL Immaculate Conception Church; Raritan, IL Church of St. Patrick.
Clemens, John W. '72 (CHI) Other Assignments; [X] Chicago, IL The Aquin Guild.
Clemens, Norbert H. *c.s.b.* '41 (GAL) [Q] Houston, TX Dillon House.
Clement, Frederick *m.ss.cc.* (CAM) [I] Pleasantville, NJ Our Lady's Residence.
Clement, James P. '45 (BR) Retired.
Clement, Richard '85 (ALN) [7] Reading, PA St. Joseph Church.
Clement, Thomas '95 (SFS) Ipswich, SD Holy Cross Church; Leola, SD Our Lady of Perpetual Help Church.
Clemente, Joseph J. '81 (SY) [1] Rome, NY St. John the Baptist Church.
Clemente, Michael '55 (ALB) Retired.
Clemente, Vincent L. '76 (VEN) [4] Sarasota, FL St. Martha Church.
Clementich, LeRoy E. *c.s.c.* '57 (FTW) [J] South Bend, IN Congregation of Holy Cross, Indiana Province, Provincial House.
Clements, Charles '62 (MIA) [2] Miami, FL Christ the King Church; Special Assignment.
Clements, Daniel A. '54 (NSH) Retired.
Clements, George H. '57 (CHI) On Duty Outside the Archdiocese.
Clements, Gerald '70 (CAM) [I] Cherry Hill, NJ St. Mary's Nursing Home; [M] Cherry Hill, NJ Vianney Villa.
Clements, Richard '46 (OWN) Retired.
Clements, Robert '90 (PHX) Chandler, AZ St. Mary's Church.
Clements, Thomas P. '55 (CHL) Retired.
Clemins, Msgr. Francis J. '50 (PH) Trooper, PA Visitation B.V.M. Church; Retired.
Clemo, Ronald M. *s.j.* '67 (SJ) [D] San Jose, CA Bellarmine College Preparatory.
Clemons, Delma '66 (OWN) Fancy Farm, KY St. Jerome Church.
Clenaghan, Gerard *o.m.i.* '47 (SEA) [4] Seattle, WA St. Benedict Church.
Clennon, Raymond *o.carm.* '67 (CHI) Gurnee, IL St. Paul the Apostle Church.
Clerkin, Robert J. '80 (RVC) Patchogue, NY St. Francis de Sales Church.
Clerkin, Thomas J. *c.s.p.* (NY) [41] New York, NY Good Shepherd Church; Manhattan, NY Columbia Presbyterian Medical Center.
Clermont, John *o.f.m.cap.* '53 (FgM) Capuchin Foreign Missions.
Clermont, John *o.f.m.cap.* '53 (NY) [57] New York, NY St. John the Baptist Church.
Clerx, Theodore *c.i.c.m.* '57 (SAT) [K] San Antonio, TX Padua Place.
Cletus, Sales T. (Ranjan) *i.m.s.* '84 (TYL) Crockett, TX St. Francis of the Tejas Church.
Cleu, Paul E. '74 (OAK) [3] Fremont, CA St. James The Apostle Church.
Cleveland, S. Gregory *o.m.v.* '95 (BO) [B] Boston, MA Our Lady of Grace Seminary.

Cleves, Simeon *o.f.m.* '55 (CIN) [M] Cincinnati, OH St. Francis Seraph Friary.
Cleves, William F. '78 (COV) [1] Covington, KY Cathedral, Basilica of the Assumption; [A] Covington, KY Thomas More College.
Click, Patrick R. '71 (LFT) Noblesville, IN Our Lady of Grace Church.
Clifford, Donald G. '61 (BO) Senior Priests.
Clifford, Donald G. *s.j.* '62 (PH) [C] Philadelphia, PA St. Joseph's University; [AA] Philadelphia, PA Jesuit Community at St. Joseph's University.
Clifford, Donald P. '61 (BO) Marshfield, MA Our Lady of the Assumption Church.
Clifford, Francis M. '54 (MAN) Retired.
Clifford, James *o.s.a.* '72 (P) Central Point, OR Shepherd of the Valley Church; [L] Sheridan, OR Augustinian Community.
Clifford, James J. '45 (WOR) Retired.
Clifford, Jerome *s.c.j.* '61 (MIL) [P] Hales Corners, WI Priests of the Sacred Heart.
Clifford, Joseph G. '89 (VEN) Bradenton, FL Sacred Heart Church.
Clifford, Leo *o.f.m.* '45 (NY) [115] New York, NY St. Stephen of Hungary Church.
Clifford, Marc *o.s.f.s.* (SLC) [B] Salt Lake City, UT Judge Memorial Catholic High School.
Clifford, Michael J. '60 (GB) Suring, WI St. Michael Church; Special Assignment.
Clifford, Paul T. '92 (BO) Dracut, MA St. Therese Church.
Clifford, Peter C. '76 (ROC) Newark, NY St. Michael Church.
Clifford, Richard J. *s.j.* '66 (BO) [W] Cambridge, MA Weston Jesuit Community.
Clifford, Richard L. *m.m.* '53 (FgM) Maryknoll Foreign Missions.
Clifford, Thomas A. *o.p.* '60 (GAL) [Q] Houston, TX Dominican Fathers and Brothers, St. Mark Priory, Inc.
Clifford, Thomas F. *s.j.* '81 (PH) [G] Philadelphia, PA St. Joseph's Preparatory School; [AA] Philadelphia, PA Jesuit Community, Arrupe House.
Clift, James C. '57 (OAK) Retired; [M] Oakland, CA Bishop Begin Villa.
Clifton, James F. '88 (OM) [K] Omaha, NE Jesuit Community at Creighton University.
Clinch, Kevin D. '83 (TUC) [I] Casa Grande, AZ Central Arizona College, Holy Family Newman Center.
Clinch, Kevin O. '88 (TUC) Casa Grande, AZ St. Anthony of Padua Church.
Clines, Paul J. '44 (CLV) [1] Barberton, OH St. Augustine Church; Retired.
Clinton, Donald E. '90 (MAN) [1] Concord, NH St. John the Evangelist Church.
Clinton, Kevin I. '74 (STP) Mendota, MN St. Peter Church; [H] Eagan, MN Faithful Shepherd Catholic School.
Clisch, Norman A. '65 (MAR) Iron River, MI St. Agnes Church.
Clody, Msgr. Albert W. '65 (BUF) [5] Buffalo, NY All Saints Church.
Clogan, Paul '99 (PRT) Waterville, ME Parish of the Holy Spirit Church.
Cloherty, Francis J. '62 (BO) [7] Brockton, MA St. Patrick Church.
Cloherty, John J. '60 (SFR) Colma, CA Holy Angels Church.
Cloherty, Thomas '74 (DAL) [2] Dallas, TX All Saints Church.
Clohessy, Kevin P. '85 (JC) Absent on Leave.
Cloney, Michael '68 (SR) Ukiah, CA St. Mary of the Angels Church.
Cloney, Robert D. *s.j.* '60 (NY) [DD] New York, NY Jesuit Community at Fordham University.
Cloonan, Joseph F. '44 (ROC) Retired.
Clooney, David '64 (PHU) [A] Washington, DC St. Josaphat Seminary.
Clooney, Francis X. *s.j.* '78 (BO) [W] Chestnut Hill, MA The Jesuit Community at Boston College.
Cloquet, Victor '50 (SEA) Retired.
Clore, Victor '65 (DET) [17] Detroit, MI Christ the King Church.
Clorra, Anthony J. *o.p.m.cap.* '73 (PAT) Madison, NJ St. Vincent Martyr Church.
Close, James J. '63 (CHI) [H] Chicago, IL Mission of Our Lady of Mercy-Mercy Home for Boys and Girls.
Close, John '82 (ALB) New Lebanon, NY Immaculate Conception Church.
Close, Msgr. John A. '69 (PH) [1] Philadelphia, PA Cathedral Basilica of SS. Peter and Paul.
Close, John L. '82 (ALB) [16] Albany, NY St. Teresa of Avila Church.
Cloud, Charles W. '89 (TUC) Florence, AZ Assumption of the Blessed Virgin Mary Church.
Clough, Wulfstan F. *o.s.b.* '96 (GBG) [H] Latrobe, PA Saint Vincent Archabbey.
Clougherty, Paul L. '60 (BO) Senior Priests.
Cloutier, Edmond '46 (OAK) Retired.
Cloutier, Rolamd C. '66 (NOR) Putnam, CT St. Mary Church.
Cloutier, Roland (NOR) [J] Portland, CT Affirmation Counseling Center.
Cloutier, Ronald F. '72 (GAL) [2] Houston, TX All Saints Church; Houston, TX Harris County Jail.
Cloutier, Ronald G. '72 (GAL) Houston, TX Federal Correctional Center.
Cloutier, Timothy D. '83 (STP) Crystal, MN St. Raphael Church.
Clovis, Stephen '89 (P) [4] Eugene, OR St. Paul Church.
Clubb, Ronald E. (HON) Honaunau, HI St. Benedict Church.
Clubb, Ronald E. '86 (STP) Retired.
Clune, Gerald F. '40 (ALB) Retired.
Clune, Gerald F. '40 (SB) [E] Morongo Valley, CA St. Michael's of Morongo Valley, Inc.
Clune, Malac *o.p.* '60 (SJN) Catano, PR Nuestra Senora del Carmen Church.
Clyde, George A. '42 (NEW) Retired.
Clyne, Msgr. James B. '47 (LA) Retired.
Clyne, Msgr. Vincent F. '45 (NY) [195] Staten Island, NY St. Ann Church; Retired.
Coady, Frank '76 (SAL) [2] Salina, KS St. Elizabeth Ann Seton Church.
Coady, John '59 (GF) Retired.
Coakey, Paul S. '83 (BAL) [A] Emmitsburg, MD Mount St. Mary's Seminary.
Coakley, John P. *s.j.* '70 (CHI) [D] Chicago, IL St. Ignatius Jesuit Community; [J] Maywood, IL Foster G. McGaw Hospital of Loyola University of Chicago.
Coakley, Lawrence '76 (HBG) Lewistown, PA Sacred Heart of Jesus Church.
Coakley, Paul S. '83 (BAL) [A] Emmitsburg, MD Mount St. Mary's Seminary.
Coakley, Richard J. *s.j.* '37 (BO) [W] Weston, MA Campion Health Center, Inc.
Coates, John T. '45 (PH) Center Square, PA St. Helena Church; Retired.
Coates, Rodrick J.D. *s.s.j.* '89 (GAL) McNair, TX Holy Family Church.
Cobb, Gerald T. *s.j.* '81 (SEA) [A] Seattle, WA Seattle University.
Cobb, Richard E. *s.j.* '62 (SJ) [L] Los Gatos, CA Sacred Heart Jesuit Center.
Cobel, Lawrence F. '73 (BUF) [4] Lackawanna, NY St. Barbara Church.
Coble, Scott W. *s.j.* '79 (SPK) [C] Spokane, WA Gonzaga University.
Coburn, Msgr. Vincent P. '41 (NEW) Bloomfield, NJ Church of St. Thomas the Apostle; Retired.
Coburn, Msgr. Vincent P., (Retired) '41 (NEW) Short Hills, NJ St. Rose of Lima Church.
Coby, Thomas W. '73 (RVC) Riverhead, NY St. John the Evangelist Church.
Cocca, Stephen M. '96 (WDC) Absent On Leave.
Coccarelli, August '63 (Y) Struthers, OH St. Nicholas Church.
Coccia, Christopher A. *o.f.m.* (SP) [O] St. Petersburg, FL St. Anthony Friary.
Cochran, George L. *o.p.* '62 (PRO) [P] Providence, RI St. Thomas Aquinas Priory at Providence College.
Cochran, Paul W. '88 (LFT) Alexandria, IN St. Mary Church.
Cocio, Carlos '83 (TUC) Absent on Leave; [F] Tucson, AZ Regina Cleri Center.
Cockayne, John E. '85 (HRT) Thomaston, CT St. Thomas Church.
Coco, Francis J. *s.j.* '51 (LAF) [J] Grand Coteau, LA Our Lady of the Oaks Retreat House.
Cocozza, Dennis E. '75 (NEW) Roselle Park, NJ The Assumption Church.
Cocucci, Joseph M.P.R. '96 (WIL) Fairfax, DE St. Mary Magdalen Church.
Cocuzzi, Bruno *o.c.d.* '55 (BO) [W] Boston, MA Carmelite Monastery.
Cocuzzi, Msgr. George A. '49 (ROC) Fairport, NY Assumption of the Blessed Virgin Mary Church; Retired.
Coda, Joseph F. '63 (NEW) Oradell, NJ St. Joseph's Church; Retired; [N] Rutherford, NJ St. John Vianney Residence for Priests.
Codd, Kevin '79 (SPK) On Duty Outside the Diocese.
Coddaire, Louis *o.s.b.cam.* '52 (SR) [K] Arcata, CA Newman Community, Humboldt State University.
Coddaire, Louis *o.s.b.cam.* '78 (MRY) [F] Big Sur, CA New Camaldoli Hermitage.
Code, Sean A. '93 (ALT) Somerset, PA St. Peter's Church.
Codega, John C. '99 (PRO) North Kingstown, RI St. Francis De Sales Church.
Cody, Aelred *o.s.b.* '57 (IND) [J] St. Meinrad, IN St. Meinrad Archabbey.
Cody, Daniel '62 (STA) [16] Jacksonville, FL St. Joseph's Church.
Cody, Henry P. '58 (HRT) [7] West Hartford, CT St. Timothy's Church.
Cody, Msgr. John K. '73 (COL) [19] Columbus, OH Holy Family Church; Graduate Studies.
Cody, Kevin W. '93 (MAN) Military Chaplains.
Cody, Michael '58 (SEA) Retired.
Cody, Nicholas A. '54 (STP) Retired.
Cody, Thomas '68 (STA) [13] Jacksonville, FL Resurrection Church.
Coelho, Blaise (CHI) Tinley Park, IL St. George Church.
Coelho, Gabriel Prashant *o.f.m.cap.* '78 (DET) [K] Detroit, MI St. Bonaventure Friary.
Coelho, Paul *s.j.* '88 (MIL) [P] Milwaukee, WI Jesuit Community at Marquette University.
Coen, Alphonsus *c.p.* '74 (SCR) [M] Scranton, PA Saint Ann's Passionist Monastery.
Coen, Charles P. '68 (NY) Red Hook, NY St. Christopher Church.
Coen, Mark '90 (DUL) Silver Bay, MN St. Mary's Church; Two Harbors, MN Holy Spirit Church.
Coen, Msgr. William R. '49 (BO) [2] Milton, MA St. Elizabeth Church; Senior Priests.
Coenen, Thomas '77 (DM) Bedford, IA Sacred Heart Church; Clarinda, IA St. Clare Church; Villisca, IA St. Joseph Church.
Coens, Frank *o.f.m.* '73 (MEM) [5] Memphis, TN St. Augustine Church; [I] Memphis, TN Franciscan Friars (Sacred Heart Prov.) of Memphis.
Coerber, Joseph H. '66 (MIL) Johnsburg, WI St. John the Baptist Church; Marytown, WI St. Mary Church.
Coerver, Richard V. '76 (STL) Pacific, MO St. Bridget Church.
Coerver, Robert F. *c.m.* '41 (STL) [P] St. Louis, MO Lazarist Residence.
Cofenas, Robert G. '73 (ALN) Unassigned.
Coffey, Msgr. Andrew V. '47 (SAC) Davis, CA St. James Church; Retired and in Senior Ministry.
Coffey, Edward N. '37 (CHI) Retired.
Coffey, James Brian *m.h.m.* '72 (NY) [DD] Hartsdale, NY Mill Hill Fathers Residence.
Coffey, Msgr. James F. '31 (RVC) Bay Shore, NY St. Patrick's Church; Retired.
Coffey, James H. '45 (BO) Senior Priests.
Coffey, Joseph L. '96 (PH) [84] Philadelphia, PA St. Katherine of Siena Church.
Coffey, Michael J. '91 (CAM) Stratford, NJ St. Luke Church.
Coffey, Peter *s.d.s.* '68 (NSH) Cookeville, TN St. Thomas Aquinas Church.
Coffey, Msgr. Thomas A. '48 (TR) Retired; [M] Trenton, NJ Villa Vianney.
Coffield, Msgr. John V. '41 (ORG) Capistrano Beach, CA San Felipe de Jesus Church; Retired.
Cogan, Patrick *s.a.* '77 (NY) [DD] Garrison, NY Franciscan Friars of the Atonement, Minister General Office.
Cogan, Patrick *s.a.* '77 (WDC) [B] Washington, DC Atonement Seminary-Franciscan Friars of the Atonement.
Cogan, William B. *s.j.* '55 (NY) [DD] New York, NY Murray-Weigel Hall.
Coghill, Elstan *o.f.m.* '48 (GAY) Indian River, MI Cross in the Woods Catholic Church.
Coghlan, Msgr. Brian '63 (ORG) Seal Beach, CA Holy Family Church.
Coghlan, John '74 (MOB) Citronelle, AL St. Thomas Church; Mount Vernon, AL St. Cecilia Church.
Coghlan, John A. '44 (STO) Retired.
Cogo, Joseph A. *c.s.* '58 (NY) [94] New York, NY Our Lady of Pompeii Church.
Cohalan, Msgr. Florence '38 (NY) Retired.
Cohan, Dennis J. '74 (NEW) Glen Rock, NJ St. Catharine Church.
Cohan, Msgr. Robert W. '55 (E) [18] Erie, PA St. James Church.
Cohea, Victor H. '80 (NO) [33] New Orleans, LA St. Francis De Sales Church.
Cohelo, Gabriel *o.f.m.cap.* (DET) Detroit, MI Harper Hospital and Rehabilitation Center.
Cohen, Harold F. *s.j.* '58 (NO) [C] New Orleans, LA Loyola University New Orleans.
Coholan, John F. *m.m.* '46 (FgM) Maryknoll Foreign Missions.
Coine, Robert E. '76 (WIL) Easton, MD SS. Peter and Paul Church.
Coiro, Gregory *o.f.m.cap.* '82 (SFR) Burlingame, CA Our Lady of Angels Church.
Coiro, Mark J. '94 (BO) [4] Weymouth, MA St. Jerome Church.
Cokonougher, Brian K. '99 (DET) [4] St. Clair Shores, MI St. Joan of Arc Church; [R] Detroit, MI C.Y.O. Girls Camp.
Cokonougher, Brian L. '99 (DET) [R] Detroit, MI C.Y.O. Boys Camp.
Cokus, Msgr. Joseph J. '58 (LA) Sierra Madre, CA St. Rita Church.
Colacicco, Frank L. '79 (OAK) Danville, CA St. Isidore's Church.
Colacicco, Frank L. '79 (SAN) Retired.
Colacicco, Msgr. Gerardo J. '82 (NY) [4] Newburgh, NY Sacred Heart Church.
Colacino, John *c.pp.s.* (ROC) [4] Rochester, NY St. Anne Church.
Colacino, John '80 (ROC) [A] Rochester, NY St. Bernard's Institute.
Colacino, John A. *c.pp.s.* '80 (ROC) [I] Rochester, NY Missionaries of the Precious Blood.
Colagreco, Michael A. '77 (PH) Newtown Square, PA St. Anastasia Church.

Colaiacovo, Arthur J. '92 (PAT) Hawthorne, NJ St. Anthony's Church.
Colaj, Rene Otzoy *o.s.b.* '82 (RCK) [G] Aurora, IL Marmion Abbey-St. Augustine's Abbey.
Colamarino, Dennis '73 (PIT) Duquesne, PA St. Joseph Church; Duquesne, PA Christ the Light of the World Church.
Colankin, Dimitrij '76 (AUS) Caldwell, TX St. Mary's Church; Frenstat, TX Holy Rosary Church.
Colapietro, Peter M. '76 (NY) [45] New York, NY Holy Cross Church; New York, NY New York Sanitation Department.
Colaresi, Robert E. *o.carm.* '67 (JOL) [J] Darien, IL Carmelite Community; [L] Darien, IL Carmelite Spiritual Center; [M] Darien, IL Society of the Little Flower.
Colasito, Basil C. '59 (RVC) Hicksville, NY Our Lady of Mercy Church.
Colautti, John *o.s.b.* '55 (DET) [K] Detroit, MI St. Sylvester Monastery.
Colavechio, Francis D. '50 (LR) Fairfield Bay, AR St. Francis Assisi Church.
Colavechio, Xavier G. *o.praem.* '55 (JKS) [F] Jackson, MS Priory of St. Moses the Black.
Colberg, Msgr. James P. '55 (LA) Santa Maria, CA St. Mary of the Assumption Church; Retired.
Colbert, John '96 (BEA) Special Assignment.
Colbert, Richard *s.m.* '64 (SP) [7] Tampa, FL Our Lady of Perpetual Help Church.
Colbert, Richard *c.pp.s.* '69 (JC) Warsaw, MO St. Ann Church.
Colborn, Francis '64 (LA) Pasadena, CA St. Andrew Church.
Colchin, Stephen E. '84 (FTW) Besancon, IN St. Louis Church.
Cole, Barry '82 (CHI) [W] Oak Park, IL Oak Park Study Center.
Cole, Basil B. *o.p.* '66 (OAK) [N] Oakland, CA Dominican Order (Western Province), St. Albert's Priory.
Cole, Basil Burr *o.p.* '66 (WDC) [B] Washington, DC Dominican House of Studies.
Cole, Edwin J. '64 (JC) Columbia, MO Sacred Heart Church; Columbia, MO University Hospital & Clinics; Columbia, MO Veterans' Administration Medical Center.
Cole, James J. '71 (BGP) [Q] Monroe, CT Provincial House, Immaculate Heart of Mary Province, Sisters of the Holy Family of Nazareth, C.S.F.N.
Cole, Raymond L. '72 (MET) East Millstone, NJ St. Joseph Church.
Cole, Robert F. '72 (MAN) Dover, NH St. Joseph Church.
Cole, Robert J. '72 (CLV) Olmsted Falls, OH St. Mary of the Falls Church.
Cole, Russan *o.f.m.conv.* '51 (TOL) Carey, OH Our Lady of Consolation, Basilica-National Church.
Cole, Vincent P. *m.m.* '71 (FgM) Maryknoll Foreign Missions.
Colella, David *o.ss.t* '57 (BAL) [S] Baltimore, MD Holy Trinity Monastery.
Colella, David L. *o.ss.t.* '57 (DAL) [29] Dallas, TX Santa Clara Church.
Coleman, Msgr. Brian P. (GB) [12] Green Bay, WI St. Patrick Church.
Coleman, C. Michael '67 (KC) Special Assignment.
Coleman, Christopher Lee '94 (BRK) [158] Queens, NY Blessed Virgin Mary, Help of Christians Church.
Coleman, Donald E. '74 (SD) Carlsbad, CA St. Elizabeth Seton Church.
Coleman, Ed *o.m.i.* '56 (PHX) Sun City, AZ St. Elizabeth Seton Church.
Coleman, Edward W. '70 (ALN) Nesquehoning, PA Sacred Heart Church.
Coleman, Msgr. George W. '64 (FR) [17] Fall River, MA St. Joseph's Church.
Coleman, Gerald D. *s.s.* '68 (SFR) [A] Menlo Park, CA St. Patrick Seminary; [A] Menlo Park, CA St. Patrick Seminary; [T] Menlo Park, CA Hospital and Health Services Liaison.
Coleman, Gerald J. '78 (TLS) [17] Tulsa, OK St. Thomas More Church.
Coleman, James '46 (SAN) Retired.
Coleman, James '46 (SAT) [K] San Antonio, TX Padua Place.
Coleman, James '73 (FgM) Society of St. James the Apostle.
Coleman, James '73 (P) On Duty Outside the Archdiocese.
Coleman, James *p.i.m.e.* '76 (DET) [K] Detroit, MI P.I.M.E. Missionaries of SS. Peter and Paul.
Coleman, James F. *s.j.* '56 (NY) [DD] New York, NY Murray-Weigel Hall.
Coleman, Msgr. James G. '62 (HRT) Guilford, CT St. George Church.
Coleman, James G. '77 (TUC) Absent on Leave; [F] Tucson, AZ Regina Cleri Center.
Coleman, James Montini '99 (MOB) [7] Mobile, AL St. Ignatius Church.
Coleman, John '50 (SJ) Gilroy, CA St. Mary Church; Retired.
Coleman, John '54 (NY) Absent on Sick leave.
Coleman, John *s.j.* '67 (LA) [C] Los Angeles, CA Loyola Marymount University.
Coleman, John '71 (SFR) On Duty Outside the Archdiocese.
Coleman, John *o.carm.* '78 (LA) [F] Encino, CA Crespi Carmelite High School.
Coleman, John '88 (PHX) Surprise, AZ St. Clare of Assisi Church.
Coleman, John P. '50 (KC) [6] Kansas City, MO St. Catherine of Siena Church; Retired.
Coleman, Joseph K. '81 (BO) [54] Boston, MA Our Lady of the Presentation Church; Brighton, MA St. John of God Hospital; [R] Brighton, MA St. John of God Hospital.
Coleman, Michael *ss.cc.* '58 (FR) [I] Fairhaven, MA Sacred Hearts Provincial House.
Coleman, Michael A. '81 (JC) Moberly, MO St. Pius X Church; Moberly, MO Missouri Training Center For Men.
Coleman, R. Ed '86 (P) Molalla, OR St. James Church.
Coleman, Msgr. Robert F. (NEW) [B] South Orange, NJ Seton Hall University.
Coleman, Msgr. Robert F. '69 (NEW) [B] South Orange, NJ Seton Hall University.
Coleman, Msgr. Robert F. '78 (NEW) [A] South Orange, NJ Immaculate Conception Seminary; [B] South Orange, NJ Seton Hall University.
Coleman, Robert J. '87 (JOL) Beaverville, IL St. Mary Church; Martinton, IL St. Martin Church.
Coleman, Robert P. '78 (CHI) Other Assignments.
Coleman, Thomas '87 (GLP) Aragon, NM Santo Nino Church.
Coleman, W. Philip '59 (BGP) Retired.
Coleman, William J. *m.m.* '39 (NY) [DD] Maryknoll, NY Maryknoll Fathers and Brothers.
Colendrino, J. Rudolpho '94 (CHK) San Antonio Village, District 6, MP San Antonio De Padua Church.
Coless, Gabriel M. *o.s.b.* '57 (PAT) [M] Morristown, NJ St. Mary's Abbey.
Coletta, Carmen J. *o.s.a.* '38 (BO) [C] North Andover, MA Merrimack College.
Coletta, Carmen J. *o.s.a.* '38 (CHI) [N] Olympia Fields, IL The Augustinians-Provincialate.
Coletta, Ralph V. '61 (CLV) [9] Akron, OH St. John the Baptist Church.
Coletta, Msgr. Thomas J. '63 (PAT) [14] Paterson, NJ Our Lady of Victories Church.
Coletti, Arnold F. '62 (BO) Lexington, MA Sacred Heart Church.
Coley, James E. '47 (TR) Retired.
Colfer, Robert *o.m.i.* '40 (PMB) Riviera Beach, FL St. Francis of Assisi Church.
Colgan, Arthur J. *c.s.c.* '73 (BGP) [P] Bridgeport, CT Provincial Offices of the Priests and Brothers of Holy Cross, Eastern Province.
Colgan, Arthur J. *c.s.c.* '73 (FgM) Holy Cross Foreign Missions.
Colgan, John '48 (SP) Retired.
Colgan, Marvin '40 (PEO) Retired.
Colgan, Richard J. *s.j.* '55 (PH) [AA] Philadelphia, PA Jesuit Community at St. Joseph's University.
Colgan, Richard J. *c.s.p.* '79 (BO) [P] Boston, MA Paulist Center; [W] Boston, MA Paulist Fathers Residence; [BB] Boston, MA Chapel of the Holy Spirit.
Colgan, Thomas *s.j.* '75 (SPK) [K] Spokane, WA Regis Community.
Colgan, Thomas A. '75 (SPK) [O] Spokane, WA Kateri Northwest Ministry Institute.
Colgan, Thomas J. '49 (RVC) Northport, NY St. Philip Neri Church; Retired.
Colgan, Tobias *o.s.b.* '82 (IND) [J] St. Meinrad, IN St. Meinrad Archabbey.
Colhour, David *c.p.* '94 (DET) [K] Detroit, MI St. Paul of the Cross Community, Congregation of the Passion; [P] Detroit, MI St. Paul of the Cross Retreat Center.
Colibraro, Daniel '56 (CHY) Casper, WY Our Lady of Fatima Church; Retired.
Colibraro, Philip '57 (CHY) Casper, WY Our Lady of Fatima Church.
Colicchio, Damian *o.f.m.cap.* '62 (NEW) [B] Lodi, NJ Felician College; [O] Lodi, NJ Immaculate Conception Convent.
Colicchio, Ralph M. '67 (HRT) Branford, CT St. Elizabeth Church; East Haven, CT St. Clare Church.
Coll, Eduardo *i.v.e.* '88 (PH) [155] Philadelphia, PA St. Veronica Church.
Coll, Jerome B. *s.j.* '59 (PH) [C] Philadelphia, PA St. Joseph's University; [AA] Philadelphia, PA Jesuit Community at St. Joseph's University.
Coll, John J. *s.j.* '56 (WH) [A] Wheeling, WV Wheeling Jesuit University.
Coll, Msgr. Robert J. '59 (ALN) Retired.
Collard, Bruce W. '80 (MAN) [3] Nashua, NH St. Christopher Church; [N] Manchester, NH Campus Ministries.
Colleary, Patrick '74 (PHX) [2] Scottsdale, AZ Our Lady of Perpetual Help Church.
Collen, Patrick P. '68 (BIR) [14] Birmingham, AL St. Mark the Evangelist Church.
Colleoni, Xavier *m.c.c.j.* '52 (LA) [12] Los Angeles, CA Holy Cross Church.
Coller, Jerome *o.s.b.* '59 (SCL) [I] Collegeville, MN St. John's Abbey, of the Order of St. Benedict.
Colleran, Desmond '56 (ORG) Inactive Leave.
Colleran, James A. '63 (CHI) [125] Chicago, IL St. Mary of the Lake Church.
Colleran, Msgr. Kevin J. '72 (NY) [183] Bronx, NY St. Philip Neri Church.
Collet, John (DAL) [B] Irving, TX University of Dallas.
Collet, John '67 (DAL) [A] Irving, TX Holy Trinity Seminary.
Collette, Msgr. Richard E. '52 (WOR) [5] Fitchburg, MA Immaculate Conception Church.
Colletti, Joseph A. '71 (LFT) Unassigned.
Colletti, Peter '84 (CLV) Absent on Leave.
Colletti, Richard M. '78 (WIN) [3] Mankato, MN St. John the Baptist's Church.
Collier, Joseph Mel '58 (SD) [19] San Diego, CA St. Agnes Church.
Colligan, Flavian *o.f.m.* '39 (PAT) [M] Ringwood, NJ Holy Name Friary, Inc.
Colligan, James P. *m.m.* '55 (LA) [Q] Los Angeles, CA Maryknoll Fathers and Brothers.
Colligan, James P. *m.m.* '55 (NY) [DD] Maryknoll, NY Maryknoll Fathers and Brothers.
Colligan, Msgr. Joseph F. '50 (RVC) Centerport, NY Our Lady Queen of Martyrs Church; Retired.
Collignon, James A. *m.m.* '53 (FgM) Maryknoll Foreign Missions.
Colling, Paul J. '87 (GI) Scottsbluff, NE Our Lady of Guadalupe Church.
Collini, Msgr. Celsus O. '47 (BRK) [231] Queens, NY Queen of Peace Church; Retired.
Collins, Austin I. *c.s.c.* '82 (FTW) [B] Notre Dame, IN University of Notre Dame Du Lac; [J] Notre Dame, IN Holy Cross Community, Corby Hall, University of Notre Dame.
Collins, Msgr. Bernard G. '37 (DUB) Retired.
Collins, Carl '91 (HT) Golden Meadow, LA Our Lady of Prompt Succor Church.
Collins, Charles E. '72 (BO) [7] Cambridge, MA St. John the Evangelist Church.
Collins, Charlie I. '82 (WIN) Byron, MN Christ the King Church; Kasson, MN Holy Family Church.
Collins, Corwin *o.s.b.* '57 (SCL) Albany, MN Seven Dolors Church; [I] Collegeville, MN St. John's Abbey, of the Order of St. Benedict.
Collins, Daniel J. '58 (CHI) [125] Chicago, IL St. Mary of the Lake Church; [J] Evanston, IL Saint Francis Hospital.
Collins, David J. *s.j.* '98 (CHI) [C] Chicago, IL Jesuit Community at Loyola University of Chicago.
Collins, Denis E. *s.j.* '69 (SFR) [N] San Francisco, CA Jesuit Community at University of San Francisco.
Collins, Edward A. '68 (PAT) Pequannock, NJ Holy Spirit Church.
Collins, Edward F. '35 (DAV) Retired.
Collins, Edwin J. '54 (RVC) Malverne, NY Our Lady of Lourdes Church; Retired.
Collins, Msgr. Fachtna P. '50 (LA) Retired.
Collins, Francis *c.ss.r.* '57 (TR) [Q] Long Branch, NJ San Alfonso Retreat House.
Collins, Frederick J. '55 (BO) Senior Priests.
Collins, Msgr. James E. '39 (RVC) Oyster Bay, NY St. Dominic's Church; Retired.
Collins, James J. '64 (PH) [C] Philadelphia, PA Holy Family College.
Collins, James M. *s.j.* '58 (BO) [W] Chestnut Hill, MA The Jesuit Community at Boston College; [W] Cohasset, MA Bellarmine House.
Collins, James M. '95 (CHL) Newton, NC St. Joseph Church.
Collins, James P. '69 (BRK) [19] Brooklyn, NY St. Bernard's Church; [G] Brooklyn, NY Bishop Kearney High School.
Collins, James R. '68 (CIN) [39] Cincinnati, OH St. James of the Valley Church.
Collins, James R. '81 (PRO) [6] Cranston, RI St. Matthew Church.
Collins, John E. *c.s.p.* '74 (NY) [104] New York, NY St. Paul the Apostle Church.
Collins, John J.L. *s.j.* '44 (BO) [W] Weston, MA Campion Health Center, Inc.
Collins, John M. '69 (LA) On Duty Outside the Archdiocese.
Collins, John M. '79 (CHI) [100] Chicago, IL St. Joachim Church.
Collins, John P. '72 (PH) [148] Philadelphia, PA Stella Maris Church.
Collins, John T. '98 (LA) Montebello, CA Our Lady of the Miraculous Medal Church.
Collins, Joseph I. '40 (BO) Senior Priests.
Collins, Kevin '80 (LA) [A] Camarillo, CA St. John's Seminary.
Collins, Kevin *o.m.i.* '82 (SAT) [C] San Antonio, TX Oblate School of Theology; [O] San Antonio, TX Oblate Renewal Center.
Collins, Lawrence E. '77 (CHI) [6] Cicero, IL Our Lady of the Mount Church.
Collins, Leonard J. *c.s.c.* '69 (AUS) [H] Austin, TX

Congregation of Holy Cross - Southern Province.
Collins, Msgr. Michael '43 (ORG) Seal Beach, CA St. Anne's Church; Retired.
Collins, Michael '64 (ORL) Sabbatical.
Collins, Michael G. *m.m.* '59 (FgM) Maryknoll Foreign Missions.
Collins, Michael J. *o.s.b.* '37 (PAT) [M] Morristown, NJ St. Mary's Abbey.
Collins, Michael J. '67 (BR) [15] Baton Rouge, LA Most Blessed Sacrament Church.
Collins, Michael J. '85 (JOL) Absent on Leave.
Collins, Michael T. *o.praem.* '78 (WIL) [B] Claymont, DE Archmere Academy; [I] Claymont, DE Immaculate Conception Priory of the Canons Regular of Premontre.
Collins, Neil J. '58 (NEW) Belleville, NJ St. Anthony's Church.
Collins, Patrick W. '64 (PEO) On Duty Outside the Diocese.
Collins, Raymond *c.ss.r.* '70 (HBG) [H] Ephrata, PA St. Clement's Mission House.
Collins, Raymond F. '59 (PRO) On Duty Outside the Diocese.
Collins, Raymond F. *s.t.d.* '59 (WDC) [C] Washington, DC Catholic University of America, The.
Collins, Raymond F. *c.ss.r.* '70 (HBG) Ephrata, PA Mother of Perpetual Help Church.
Collins, Raymond G. *o.s.f.s.* '59 (ARL) Vienna, VA Our Lady of Good Counsel Church.
Collins, Robert '81 (AUS) Retired.
Collins, Robert C. *s.j.* '67 (NY) [DD] New York, NY "America;" Residence and publication office of the America Press; [HH] New York, NY America Press, Inc.
Collins, Msgr. Russell J. '37 (BO) Senior Priests.
Collins, Seamus *o.p.* '58 (SP) Hudson, FL St. Michael Church.
Collins, Shannon *c.p.m.* '00 (OWN) [F] South Union, KY Fathers of Mercy.
Collins, Stephen L. '80 (E) Delancey, PA St. Adrian Church.
Collins, Stephen L. '83 (E) Anita, PA St. Joseph Church; Walston, PA St. Anthony Church.
Collins, Stephen L., III '83 (E) On Leave of Absence.
Collins, T. Byron *s.j.* '52 (WDC) [M] Washington, DC The Jesuit Community at Georgetown University.
Collins, Terrence '71 (R) Hampstead, NC St. Jude the Apostle Church.
Collins, Thomas *o.p.* '45 (WDC) [11] Washington, DC St. Dominic Church & Priory Church.
Collins, Thomas E. '92 (NY) [E] White Plains, NY Archbishop Stepinac High School.
Collins, Thomas R. '72 (RIC) Richlands, VA St. Mary Church.
Collins, Thomas S. '92 (PT) [1] Tallahassee, FL Co-Cathedral of St. Thomas More.
Collins, Timothy '54 (BAK) Retired.
Collins, Msgr. Timothy '58 (NY) [96] New York, NY Our Lady of the Rosary Church.
Collins, Vincent '72 (ARL) [J] Berryville, VA Cistercian Abbey of Our Lady of the Holy Cross.
Collins, William *c.ss.r.* '49 (TR) [Q] Long Branch, NJ San Alfonso Retreat House.
Collins, William *m.s.c.*. '67 (SAT) [11] San Antonio, TX Immaculate Conception Church.
Collins, William A. '61 (BAL) Randallstown, MD Holy Family Church; Special Assignment.
Collins, William B. '74 (PAT) Hamburg, NJ St. Jude the Apostle Church.
Collins, William F. '65 (CAM) Franklinville, NJ Nativity Church.
Collins, Msgr. William J. '60 (NY) [5] Kingston, NY St. Peter Church.
Collins, William P. '56 (RCK) [8] Rockford, IL St. Patrick Church.
Collins, Wm. Emmett *c.ss.r.* '52 (STL) [B] St. Louis, MO St. John Neumann House.
Collison, Craig A. '78 (SC) Willey, IA St. Mary's Church; [B] Carroll, IA Kuemper Catholic High School.
Collogan, Robert '82 (JOL) Oswego, IL St. Anne Church.
Collopy, Msgr. John C. (BAL) Hydes, MD St. John the Evangelist Church.
Collopy, Msgr. John C. '56 (BAL) Special Assignment; Retired; [O] Timonium, MD Stella Maris.
Colloton, Paul *o.p.* '90 (GR) [H] Grand Rapids, MI Motherhouse of the Dominican Sisters.
Collova, S. Joseph '76 (MIL) On Leave.
Collucci, Bennett '57 (SAL) Hays, KS St. Joseph's Church; [D] Hays, KS St. Joseph's Friary.
Collum, Patrick '92 (NO) [16] New Orleans, LA Our Lady of Good Counsel Church.
Colnaghi, Andrew *o.s.b.cam.* '79 (MRY) [F] Big Sur, CA New Camaldoli Hermitage.
Colnaghi, Andrew '79 (OAK) [S] Berkeley, CA Incarnation Monastery, Camaldolese Benedictines.
Colohan, Edward A. '61 (BGP) [3] Trumbull, CT St. Stephen Church.
Colom, Marti '00 (MIL) [71] Milwaukee, WI Prince of Peace/Principe de Paz Church; [Y] Racine, WI Missionary Community of St. Paul the Apostle and Mary, Mother of the Church, Inc.
Colomb, Jackson '90 (CHI) Mundelein, IL Santa Maria Del Popolo Church.
Colombo, Ronald A. (GB) Denmark, WI All Saints Church; New Denmark, WI Holy Trinity Church.
Colombo, Ronald A. '72 (GB) Cooperstown, WI St. James Church; Kellnersville, WI St. Joseph Church.
Colon, Angel '95 (CGS) Vieques, PR Inmaculada Concepcion Church.
Colon, Jorge *c.ss.r.* '77 (MGZ) [2] Mayaquez, PR Our Lady of Mt. Carmel Church.
Colon, Msgr. Jose '61 (PCE) Retired.
Colon, Jose E. '63 (PCE) On Duty Outside the Diocese.
Colon, Jose E. '63 (SJN) [E] San Juan, PR VA Medical Center.
Colon, Juan Jose '95 (CGS) Barranquitas, PR Church of St. Anthony of Padua.
Colon, Ricardo '00 (SJN) [18] San Juan, PR San Francisco de Asis Church.
Colon, Vincent A. '50 (STP) Retired.
Colonnese, Louis M. '57 (DAV) On Duty Outside the Diocese; [P] Davenport, IA Commitment.
Colopy, James L. '86 (COL) [14] Columbus, OH St. Dominic Church.
Colosimo, Eugene J. '43 (SJ) [L] Los Gatos, CA Sacred Heart Jesuit Center.
Colosimo, Felix R. '65 (SY) New Hartford, NY Our Lady of the Rosary Church.
Colpitts, Albert B. '73 (PRT) York Harbor, ME St. Christopher-by-the-Sea Church.
Colter, Dennis J. '66 (DUB) Fillmore, IA Sacred Heart Church; [C] Dubuque, IA Loras College; [L] Dubuque, IA Mt. St. Francis.
Colton, Bernard '50 (PHX) Retired.
Colton, Bradford '45 (HRT) Wethersfield, CT Corpus Christi Church; Retired.
Colton, Gary '68 (HON) Haiku, HI St. Rita Church; Paia, HI Holy Rosary Church.
Colucci, Gregory (PAT) Retired.
Colunga, John (CC) [B] Robstown, TX St. Anthony School.
Colwell, Michael '93 (AMA) [K] Amarillo, TX Marriage Encounter.
Comandini, Glenn J. '86 (MET) [6] Perth Amboy, NJ Our Lady of the Most Holy Rosary Church.
Comboy, Richard J. *s.j.* '69 (PH) [AA] Philadelphia, PA Jesuit Community at St. Joseph's University.
Combs, Gordon *o.f.m.cap.* '64 (AGN) [F] Agana Heights, GU St. Fidelis Friary.
Combs, Gordon *o.f.m.cap.* '64 (HON) Aiea, HI St. Elizabeth Church; [E] Honolulu, HI St. Francis Healthcare System of Hawaii.
Combs, J. Derran *o.f.m.* '93 (MEM) [I] Memphis, TN Franciscan Friars (Sacred Heart Prov.) of Memphis.
Combs, J. Derran *o.f.m.* '94 (MEM) [K] Memphis, TN Campus Ministry, University of Memphis, Rhodes College, UT - Memphis.
Combs, Regis V. '46 (LA) Retired.
Comeau, Gerard *m.s.* '61 (FR) [I] Attleboro, MA La Salette Provincial House.
Comeau, Ronald R. '71 (LFT) On Duty Outside the Diocese.
Comelo, Gabriel (DET) Detroit, MI Detroit Receiving Hospital; Detroit, MI Hutzel Hospital.
Comer, Michael E. '80 (COV) Dayton, KY St. Bernard Church.
Comerford, Christopher '96 (SFD) Jacksonville, IL Our Saviour Church; [M] Jacksonville, IL Illinois College Newman Center; [M] Jacksonville, IL MacMurray College Newman Center.
Comerford, John J. *o.carm.* '77 (CHI) [N] Mundelein, IL Carmelite Monastery.
Comerford, Patrick '69 (LA) [J] Santa Monica, CA Saint John's Health Center.
Comesanas, Raul E.L. '77 (NEW) [37] Newark, NJ St. Thomas Aquinas Church.
Comeskey, John H. '56 (SY) [O] Utica, NY St. Elizabeth Hospital.
Comey, John M. *s.j.* '44 (PH) [AA] Philadelphia, PA Jesuit Community at St. Joseph's University.
Comiskey, Msgr. James '50 (LUB) Retired.
Comiskey, John *s.s.c.* '68 (FgM) St. Columban's Foreign Mission.
Comiskey, John P. '60 (NY) [E] New York, NY Monsignor Farrell High School.
Comisky, Benedict J. (TYL) Nacogdoches, TX Sacred Heart Church.
Commane, William J. '51 (BO) Senior Priests.
Commons, Patrick M. '51 (IND) Retired.
Commons, Thomas *s.v.d.* '47 (CHI) [B] Techny, IL Divine Word Residence.
Commyn, James E. '86 (DET) Richmond, MI St. Augustine Church.
Como, Denis R. *s.j.* '66 (BO) [W] Boston, MA The Society of Jesus of New England-Provincial Offices; [W] Boston, MA Jesuit Urban Center & Immaculate Conception Community.
Compaired, Fernando '63 (MIA) [9] Miami, FL Mother of Our Redeemer Church.
Compentente, Virgilio '67 (NY) [9] Yonkers, NY Immaculate Conception Church.
Complo, Daniel C. '54 (DET) Retired.
Comstock, Douglas G. '67 (OG) Sackets Harbor, NY St. Andrew Church.
Comstock, Eliot *o.f.m.conv.* '69 (IND) [I] Mount Saint Francis, IN Mount Saint Francis Friary and Retreat Center.
Comtois, Norman *o.m.i.* '73 (BO) [W] Lowell, MA Missionary Oblates of Mary Immaculate.
Comtois, Norman *o.m.i.* '73 (MAN) [K] Les Cayes, Haiti Paroisse Ste. Anne.
Conaboy, Conan *c.p.* '47 (MET) [H] South River, NJ Passionist Provincial Office.
Conaboy, Conan *c.p.* '47 (SCR) [15] Scranton, PA St. Joseph's Church; [M] Scranton, PA Saint Ann's Passionist Monastery.
Conahan, Msgr. John J. '62 (PH) Jenkintown, PA Immaculate Conception Church.
Conan, Constantine J. *c.s.sp.* '48 (PIT) [Q] Bethel Park, PA Holy Ghost Animation Center.
Conard, James A. *m.m.* '56 (FgM) Maryknoll Foreign Missions.
Conard, Raymond J. (GB) Poy Sippi, WI Sacred Heart of Jesus Church.
Conaty, Charles '88 (CAM) National Park, NJ St. Matthew's Church.
Conboy, Joseph T. '53 (SCR) Retired; [N] Dunmore, PA Villa St. Joseph.
Conboy, Michael F. '62 (ROC) East Rochester, NY St. Jerome Church.
Conboy, Michael F. '74 (ROC) Corning, NY St. Mary Church; Corning, NY St. Patrick Church; Corning, NY St. Vincent de Paul Church; Painted Post, NY Immaculate Heart of Mary Church.
Conboy, Richard L. '60 (PIT) Allegheny County, PA Depaul Institution; Allegheny County, PA Kane Regional Center - Scott; [P] Coraopolis, PA Our Lady of the Sacred Heart Convent.
Concagh, John *c.m.* '52 (NY) [GG] New York, NY University Apostolate.
Concagh, Thomas V. *c.m.* '52 (BRK) [V] Jamaica, NY Vincentian Residence.
Concannon, Stephen F. '64 (PRT) Brunswick, ME St. Charles Church; [M] Brunswick, ME Bowdoin College.
Concepcion, Msgr. Francisco '65 (ARE) Vega-Alta, PR Immaculate Conception of Blessed Virgin Mary Church.
Concepcion, Pablo J. '93 (PCE) [G] Alhambra, Ponce, PR Prelature of the Holy Cross and Opus Dei.
Concha, Alfonso J. '76 (PH) Military Chaplains.
Concha, Antonio *s.j.* '63 (ELP) [21] El Paso, TX Sacred Heart Church.
Concha, Augusto '72 (PH) [157] Philadelphia, PA Visitation B.V.M. Church.
Concha, Sergio E. *c.s.c.* '63 (FTW) [J] South Bend, IN Congregation of Holy Cross, Indiana Province, Provincial House.
Concordia, George Lawrence *o.p.* '58 (NY) [22] New York, NY St. Catherine of Siena Church; [DD] New York, NY St. Catherine of Siena Priory; [HH] New York, NY Dominican Shrine of St. Jude, Inc.
Conde, Jose Maria *s.f.* '68 (SFE) Chimayo, NM Holy Family Church.
Conde, Jose Maria *s.f.* '68 (WDC) Takoma Park, MD Our Lady of Sorrows Church.
Conde, Norberto '89 (GAL) [61] Houston, TX Our Lady of Sorrows Church.
Conde, Thomas P. '87 (CHI) Sauk Village, IL St. James Church.
Condon, Daniel '81 (ROC) Graduate Studies.
Condon, Denis '78 (CHI) Schaumburg, IL St. Marcelline Church.
Condon, Edwin A. '61 (BO) Graduate Studies.
Condon, Edwin D. (BO) Westwood, MA St. Denis Church.
Condon, Eugene L. '56 (CHR) Absent On Leave.
Condon, Gerald A. '56 (DUB) Retired.
Condon, Gerald W. '55 (BAK) Heppner, OR St. Patrick's Church; Ione, OR St. William Church.
Condon, Liam '63 (ALB) Cambridge, NY St. Patrick Church; Salem, NY Holy Cross Church.
Condon, Louis M. '48 (PEO) Retired.
Condon, Msgr. Michael J. '41 (LA) [1] Oxnard, CA St. Anthony Church; Retired.
Condon, Msgr. Robert F. '54 (LA) [71] Los Angeles, CA St. Joan of Arc Church; Retired.
Condon, Robert M. '56 (SC) Retired; [A] Sioux City, IA Briar Cliff College.
Condon, Sean '57 (ORG) Newport Beach, CA Our Lady Queen of Angels Church.
Condon, T. Mark (PAT) Special Assignment.
Condon, Thomas M. *o.p.* '88 (MEM) [23] Memphis, TN St. Peter's Church; [I] Memphis, TN Order Of Preachers (Southern Dominican Prov.).
Condon, William *c.s.c.* '61 (FR) [I] North Dartmouth, MA St. Joseph's Hall.
Condon, William F. '54 (RIC) Retired.
Condow, Thomas *o.p.* '88 (NO) [P] New Orleans, LA Dominican Friars, Southern Dominican Province of St. Martin de Porres.

Condren, William '73 (PT) Gulf Breeze, FL St. Ann Church.
Condron, Patrick A. '76 (WH) [7] Wheeling, WV St. Alphonsus Church.
Condron, Robert F. '69 (HRT) [1] Ansonia, CT Assumption Church.
Condry, John T. *s.j.* '49 (LAF) [J] Grand Coteau, LA Our Lady of the Oaks Retreat House.
Conen, Paul F. '57 (DET) [P] Clarkston, MI Colombiere Center.
Conesa, Msgr. Diego '57 (SP) Retired.
Conesa, Msgr. Diego '57 (STA) Retired.
Confer, Bernard T. *o.p.* '73 (HRT) [14] New Haven, CT St. Mary's Priory Church.
Confer, Thomas B. *o.p.* '73 (HRT) [N] North Guilford, CT Monastery of Our Lady of Grace; [N] North Guilford, CT Monastery of Our Lady of Grace.
Confroy, Mark W. *o.s.b.* '42 (PAT) [M] Morristown, NJ St. Mary's Abbey.
Confroy, Thomas J. *o.s.b.* '58 (PAT) [M] Morristown, NJ St. Mary's Abbey.
Cong, Joseph Chu *o.c.s.o.* '48 (WOR) [N] Spencer, MA St. Joseph's Abbey.
Congdon, John '00 (FRS) [13] Fresno, CA St. Therese Church.
Congdon, John '87 (FRS) On Special Assignment.
Congdon, Robert J. '87 (BO) [A] Boston, MA St. John's Seminary School of Theology.
Congdon, Stephen H. '62 (MET) Cranbury, NJ Nativity of Our Lord Church.
Congro, Basil P. '78 (CHR) [3] Charleston, SC St. Patrick's Church; [5] Charleston, SC Our Lady of Mercy Church.
Conheeney, Thomas P. '55 (NEW) [1] Bayonne, NJ St. Mary Star of the Sea Church.
Coning, Jeffrey '79 (COL) Dublin, OH St. Brigid of Kildare Church.
Conkle, Francis J. *s.t.* '78 (SJN) Loiza, PR Santiago Apostol, El Mayor Church.
Conklin, Christopher J. '73 (SAL) Retired.
Conlan, Msgr. F. Allan '54 (SCR) Elmhurst, PA St. Eulalia Church.
Conlan, James S. '53 (NY) Absent on Sick leave.
Conlan, Timothy *o.p.* '67 (FgM) Dominican - Order of Preachers Foreign Missions.
Conlan, Timothy *o.p.* '67 (OAK) [N] Oakland, CA Western Dominican Province.
Conlan, Walter *s.j.* '76 (BO) [W] Chestnut Hill, MA The Jesuit Community at Boston College.
Conley, Charles '74 (MIL) On Leave.
Conley, Charles E. (MIL) [3] West Allis, WI Holy Assumption Church.
Conley, Edward W. *o.p.* '43 (NO) [30] New Orleans, LA St. Dominic Church.
Conley, James '85 (WCH) On Duty Outside the Diocese.
Conley, John E. *c.s.c.* '79 (FTW) [B] Notre Dame, IN University of Notre Dame Du Lac; [J] Notre Dame, IN Holy Cross Community, Corby Hall, University of Notre Dame.
Conley, John J. *s.j.* '83 (NY) [DD] New York, NY Jesuit Community at Fordham University.
Conley, John P. *c.p.* '76 (GAL) [Q] Houston, TX Congregation of the Passion, Holy Name Retreat Center.
Conley, John P. '93 (SFR) [47] San Francisco, CA St. Philip the Apostle Church.
Conley, Lawrence J. '67 (PRT) Gorham, ME St. Anne Church.
Conley, Martin P. '57 (OM) Tekamah, NE St. Patrick Church.
Conley, Martin R. '83 (PIT) West View, PA St. Athanasius Church.
Conley, Msgr. Peter V. (BO) Norfolk, MA St. Jude Church.
Conley, Msgr. Peter V. '64 (BO) [P] Boston, MA Archdiocesan Information Center.
Conley, Msgr. Raymond J. '36 (DM) Retired.
Conley, Rory T. '89 (WDC) Leonardtown, MD St. Aloysius Church; Special Ministries.
Conley, Roy H. '61 (PIT) Pleasant Hills, PA St. Elizabeth Church.
Conley, Seraphin *t.o.r.* '61 (ALT) [7] Altoona, PA Our Lady of Mt. Carmel Church.
Conley, Thomas P. '47 (CHI) [4] Des Plaines, IL St. Zachary Church; Stickney, IL St. Pius X Church; Retired.
Conlin, Bernard J. '40 (WOR) [12] Worcester, MA Our Lady of Lourdes Church; Retired.
Conlin, Daniel C. '90 (STP) Graduate Studies.
Conlin, Edward '42 (NY) Retired.
Conlin, Edwin J. '42 (NY) [52] New York, NY Immaculate Conception Church.
Conlin, John A. *s.j.* '54 (WDC) [2] Washington, DC St. Aloysius Church; [E] Washington, DC Gonzaga College High School.
Conlisk, Frank '89 (CHI) [N] Chicago, IL St. Patrick's Missionary Society.
Conlon, Anthony J. '62 (WH) Vienna, WV St. Michael's Church.
Conlon, Arthur F. '46 (TR) Retired.
Conlon, Christopher W. *s.m.* '66 (CIN) [M] Dayton, OH Marianist Provincialate; [Q] Dayton, OH University of Dayton Campus Ministry.
Conlon, Colm '59 (ORG) Irvine, CA St. John Neumann Church.
Conlon, James '64 (OAK) [B] Oakland, CA Holy Names College.
Conlon, John J. *s.s.j.* '40 (BAL) [S] Baltimore, MD St. Joseph Society of the Sacred Heart House of Central Administration.
Conlon, Matthew T. *o.f.m.* '45 (ALB) [B] Loudonville, NY Siena College.
Conlon, Philip J. '55 (MAD) Retired.
Conlon, R. Daniel '77 (CIN) New Bremen, OH Holy Redeemer Church.
Conlon, Richard '90 (BRK) [157] Queens, NY Blessed Sacrament Church.
Conlon, Timothy *o.s.c.* '79 (PHX) Special Assignment; [G] Phoenix, AZ Crosier Community of Phoenix (Canons Regular of the Order of the Holy Cross).
Conmy, John J. *o.s.f.s.* '36 (WIL) [I] Childs, MD Oblates of St. Francis De Sales.
Conmy, Thomas M. *c.s.c.* '57 (SP) Dunedin, FL Our Lady of Lourdes Church.
Conn, James J. *s.j.* (BAL) [A] Emmitsburg, MD Mount St. Mary's Seminary.
Conn, James J. *s.j.* '74 (BAL) [A] Baltimore, MD St. Mary's Seminary and University.
Connaghan, Daniel H. '90 (HRT) [12] New Britain, CT St. Peter's Church.
Connall, Darrin '92 (SPK) [A] Spokane, WA Bishop White Seminary.
Connaughton, James '50 (MIA) Deerfield Beach, FL St. Ambrose Church; Retired.
Connaughton, Msgr. Lawrence M. '70 (NY) [62] New York, NY St. Joseph Church.
Conneally, J. Philip *s.j.* '44 (LA) [F] Los Angeles, CA Loyola High School of Los Angeles.
Connealy, Gerald A. '87 (OM) Pierce, NE St. Joseph Church; [G] Norfolk, NE Faith Regional Health Services.
Conneely, Sean *s.s.c.* '69 (CHI) [N] Chicago, IL Columban Fathers Mission Center.
Connell, Msgr. Andrew F. (BO) [BB] Boston, MA St. Thomas More Chapel.
Connell, Msgr. Andrew F. '51 (BO) [68] Boston, MA St. Vincent de Paul Church; [FF] Boston, MA Propagation of the Faith and Holy Childhood Association & Society of St. Peter the Apostle.
Connell, James '87 (MIL) [S] Burlington, WI Franciscan Retreat Center, Inc.; [Y] Milwaukee, WI St. Thomas More Lawyers Society.
Connell, James E. '87 (MIL) [1] Sheboygan, WI St. Clement Church; [4] Sheboygan, WI Holy Name Church; Special Assignment.
Connell, John Andrew (PAT) Sparta, NJ Blessed Kateri Tekakwitha Church.
Connell, John F. '62 (WOR) Northbridge, MA St. Peter Church.
Connell, John M. '85 (LR) [13] Little Rock, AR St. Theresa's Church.
Connell, Kevin *s.j.* (P) [F] Portland, OR St. Andrew Nativity School.
Connell, Kevin G. *s.j.* '95 (P) [L] Portland, OR Colombiere Community.
Connell, Loren *o.f.m.* '76 (CIN) [M] Cincinnati, OH St. John the Baptist Friary.
Connell, Mark '55 (NY) [GG] New York, NY University Apostolate.
Connell, Mark '86 (NY) [C] Newburgh, NY Mt. St. Mary College.
Connell, Martin T. *s.j.* '94 (DET) [E] Detroit, MI University of Detroit Jesuit High School and Academy.
Connell, Patrick J. '92 (DET) Berkley, MI Our Lady of La Salette Church.
Connell, Stephen J. '62 (WIL) Greenville, DE St. Joseph on the Brandywine Church.
Connell, Msgr. William J. '76 (Y) Poland, OH Holy Family Church.
Connell, William R. '75 (MAD) [2] Beloit, WI St. Jude Church.
Connellan, Thomas J. *c.s.p.* '56 (PMB) [H] Vero Beach, FL Paulist Fathers Residence.
Connelly, Brennan *o.f.m.* '56 (NEW) [N] Hohokus, NJ St. Anthony of Padua.
Connelly, Christian '96 (ARL) [7] Alexandria, VA St. Mary's Church.
Connelly, Christopher D. '93 (SPR) [12] Springfield, MA Sacred Heart Church.
Connelly, Donald F. '58 (WIN) Plainview, MN St. Joachim's Church.
Connelly, Edward C. '65 (BAL) Crofton, MD St. Elizabeth Ann Seton Church.
Connelly, George R. '45 (TUC) Retired.
Connelly, James *c.s.c.* '64 (P) [B] Portland, OR University of Portland; [L] Portland, OR Holy Cross Fathers & Brothers, C.S.C. - University of Portland.
Connelly, Msgr. James F. '55 (PH) [148] Philadelphia, PA Stella Maris Church.
Connelly, Msgr. James N. '49 (BUF) Retired; [O] Tonawanda, NY O'Hara Residence.
Connelly, John J. '50 (BO) [8] Newton, MA Sacred Heart Church.
Connelly, Laurence D. (GAL) Retired.
Connelly, Mark J. *s.j.* '87 (BGP) [B] Fairfield, CT Fairfield University.
Connelly, Msgr. Michael J. '60 (BRK) [246] Queens, NY St. Thomas More-St. Edmund Church.
Connelly, Norbert '56 (STU) Retired.
Connelly, Msgr. Paul J. '50 (DM) Retired.
Connelly, Peter *o.s.b.* '87 (WOR) [N] Still River, MA Benedictine Monks, St. Benedict Abbey.
Connelly, Robert J. '49 (SAC) Retired and in Senior Ministry.
Connelly, William P. '45 (RIC) Retired.
Connelly, Xavier *o.s.b.* '89 (WOR) [N] Still River, MA Benedictine Monks, St. Benedict Abbey.
Conner, Glenn T. '52 (PIT) Retired; [O] Pittsburgh, PA St. John Vianney Manor.
Conner, Herbert K. *s.j.* '61 (CHR) Simpsonville, SC St. Mary Magdalene Church.
Conner, James *o.c.s.o.* '57 (L) [L] Trappist, KY Abbey of Our Lady of Gethsemani, of the Order of Cistercians of the Strict Observance.
Conner, Michael P. '85 (GAY) Onekama, MI St. Joseph Church.
Conner, Paul M. *o.p.* '67 (PRO) [P] Providence, RI St. Thomas Aquinas Priory at Providence College.
Conner, Robert J. '49 (PH) Lower Makefield, PA St. John the Evangelist Church; Penndel, PA Our Lady of Grace Church; Retired.
Conner, Steven *s.d.v.* '94 (NEW) Ridgefield, NJ St. Matthew's Church.
Conners, Quinn *o.carm.* '71 (WDC) [B] Washington, DC Whitefriars Hall.
Connerton, Barry R.L. '70 (PRO) [7] Providence, RI St. Augustine Church.
Connery, J. Thomas '63 (ALB) Glenville, NY Immaculate Conception Church.
Connery, John P. *o.s.f.s.* '69 (WIL) Elsmere, DE Veteran's Hospital; [B] Wilmington, DE Salesianum School.
Connery, Thomas '83 (ORL) Indialantic, FL Holy Name of Jesus Church.
Conniff, Msgr. John J. '49 (BUF) Retired.
Connole, Marlin (SEA) [6] Seattle, WA St. Bridget Church.
Connolly, Andrew '56 (RVC) Priests Released from Diocesan Assignment.
Connolly, Brian W. '55 (PIT) On Duty Outside the Diocese.
Connolly, Charles B. *s.j.* '74 (BO) [W] Boston, MA Loyola House.
Connolly, Msgr. Clement J. '64 (LA) South Pasadena, CA Holy Family Church.
Connolly, Edward B. '66 (ALN) Mount Carbon, PA St. Francis de Sales Church; [2] Pottsville, PA St. Joseph Church.
Connolly, Edward J. '49 (SB) [4] Riverside, CA Sacred Heart Church.
Connolly, Eugene G. '54 (NY) [1] New York, NY Cathedral of St. Patrick.
Connolly, Fidelis *c.p.* '50 (WOR) [N] Shrewsbury, MA Calvery Retreat Center, Passionist Fathers of Shrewsbury, Inc.
Connolly, Francis T. '59 (CHL) Retired.
Connolly, Gererd M. *t.o.r.* '69 (ALT) [5] Johnstown, PA St. Clare of Assisi Church.
Connolly, James H. '48 (BO) Bellingham, MA St. Blaise Church.
Connolly, James M. '78 (ALN) Military Chaplains.
Connolly, James P. '54 (NY) [58] New York, NY St. John the Evangelist Church.
Connolly, Jerry '69 (GF) Forsyth, MT Immaculate Conception Church.
Connolly, John '64 (ALB) Special Assignment.
Connolly, John *s.d.b.* '81 (NEW) Bloomfield, NJ Church of St. Thomas the Apostle.
Connolly, John G. '63 (BO) Wrentham, MA St. Mary Church.
Connolly, John J. '75 (GAL) Port Bolivar, TX Our Mother of Mercy Church.
Connolly, John J. '94 (BO) Emergency Response Group; Graduate Studies.
Connolly, John P. *o.s.f.s.* '57 (WIL) [I] Wilmington, DE DeSales House.
Connolly, John T. '78 (PAT) [15] Paterson, NJ St. Stephen's Church.
Connolly, Joseph *s.v.d.* '60 (BO) [W] Duxbury, MA Society of the Divine Word.
Connolly, Joseph *t.o.r.* '68 (VEN) [3] Sarasota, FL Our Lady Queen of Martyrs Church.
Connolly, Joseph A. *o.s.f.s.* '52 (CAM) [M] Pittsgrove, NJ Villa St. Joseph.
Connolly, K. Scott '95 (SEA) Longview, WA St. Rose de Viterbo Church.
Connolly, Kevin '85 (WIN) Madison Lake, MN All Saints Church; St. Clair, MN Immaculate Conception Church.
Connolly, Larkin '47 (PMB) [2] Lake Worth, FL St. Luke Church; Retired.

Connolly, Leo L. '81 (COL) [38] Columbus, OH St. Philip The Apostle Church.
Connolly, Leon '58 (DUB) [1] Waterloo, IA St. Joseph's Church.
Connolly, Luke *c.p.* '52 (CHI) [N] Chicago, IL Passionist Provincial Office; [N] Chicago, IL Passionist Community-Immaculate Conception Monastery.
Connolly, Luke *c.p.* '52 (FgM) Mission Procurators.
Connolly, Mark '57 (BGP) [2] Greenwich, CT St. Michael the Archangel Church; [X] Greenwich, CT Clemons Productions, Inc.
Connolly, Mark J. *s.j.* '87 (BGP) [P] Fairfield, CT The Fairfield Jesuit Community-Fairfield University.
Connolly, Matthew J. '53 (ORL) [2] Orlando, FL Blessed Trinity Church; Special Assignment.
Connolly, Maurice V. '62 (BO) Senior Priests.
Connolly, Maurice V. '68 (BO) [3] Salem, MA St. James Church.
Connolly, Michael *o.f.m.cap.* '78 (RVC) East Patchogue, NY St. Joseph the Worker Church.
Connolly, Michael C. *o.s.f.s.* '74 (R) Shallotte, NC St. Brendan the Navigator Church.
Connolly, Michael J. *s.j.* '68 (BO) [W] Boston, MA The Society of Jesus of New England-Provincial Offices.
Connolly, Michael J. *s.j.* '68 (SPK) [C] Spokane, WA Gonzaga University.
Connolly, Msgr. Neil A. '58 (NY) [70] New York, NY St. Mary Church.
Connolly, Patrick *s.j.* '66 (LA) [Q] Los Angeles, CA Columbiere House.
Connolly, Patrick J. '67 (GRY) Schererville, IN St. Michael Church.
Connolly, Paul E. '83 (DAV) Keokuk, IA All Saints Church.
Connolly, Peter *c.ss.r.* '77 (MIL) [S] Oconomowoc, WI The Redemptorist Retreat Center.
Connolly, Robert P. '79 (PIT) Cecil, PA St. Mary Church.
Connolly, Robert V. '45 (LC) Retired.
Connolly, T. Gerard *s.j.* '58 (NY) [DD] New York, NY Jesuit Community at Fordham University.
Connolly, Thomas '00 (SPK) [15] Spokane, WA St. Mary Church.
Connolly, Thomas '52 (SFS) Retired.
Connolly, Thomas *s.j.* '63 (B) DeSmet, ID Sacred Heart Church.
Connolly, Vincent F. *s.j.* '70 (FgM) Provinces.
Connolly, William *s.j.* '46 (BO) [W] Chestnut Hill, MA The Jesuit Community at Boston College.
Connolly, William A. *s.j.* '46 (BO) [W] Weston, MA Campion Health Center, Inc.
Connor, Adrian J. *o.praem.* '95 (ORG) [I] Silverado, CA Norbertine Fathers of Orange Inc.
Connor, Brian P. '89 (LIN) David City, NE St. Francis Church; [C] David City, NE Aquinas/St. Mary's Schools; [M] David City, NE Aquinas High School Endowment Fund.
Connor, Charles P. '90 (SCR) Susquehanna, PA St. John the Evangelist Church.
Connor, Francis J. '40 (STU) Retired.
Connor, Gerald T. '54 (ROC) [1] Rochester, NY Sacred Heart Church; [57] Rochester, NY St. Theodore Church; Retired.
Connor, J. Patrick '61 (NSH) Columbia, TN St. Catherine Church.
Connor, James *s.j.* '59 (WDC) [M] Washington, DC Woodstock Jesuit Community.
Connor, James '78 (HEL) Kalispell, MT Risen Christ Church.
Connor, James E. '60 (PRT) [J] Saco, ME Bay View Community.
Connor, James L. *s.j.* '59 (WDC) [V] Washington, DC Woodstock Theological Center.
Connor, John *l.c.* '01 (WDC) [M] Potomac, MD Legionaries of Christ.
Connor, John *c.p.* '84 (SCR) [M] Scranton, PA Saint Ann's Passionist Monastery.
Connor, John P. '62 (CAM) Bridgeton, NJ Immaculate Conception Church.
Connor, John S. *c.s.c.* '70 (SB) Coachella, CA Our Lady of Soledad Church; Thermal, CA San Felipe de Jesus Church.
Connor, John V. '46 (WDC) Retired.
Connor, Kevin T. '87 (MAN) Absent on Leave.
Connor, Martin P. '64 (BO) [A] Boston, MA St. John's Seminary School of Theology; [FF] Boston, MA League of Catholic Women of the Archdiocese of Boston.
Connor, Patrick *s.v.d.* '57 (TR) [M] Bordentown, NJ Society of the Divine Word.
Connor, Patrick L. '83 (ROC) [1] Elmira, NY Sts. Peter and Paul of Eastside Catholic Church; [4] Elmira, NY St. John the Baptist of Eastside Catholic Church; [6] Elmira, NY St. Cecilia of Eastside Catholic Church.
Connor, Robert M. (BO) Senior Priests.
Connor, Stephen J. *c.s.p.* '89 (NY) [104] New York, NY St. Paul the Apostle Church.
Connor, William *m.s.c.* '57 (OG) Watertown, NY Watertown Correctional Facility; [F] Watertown, NY Missionaries of the Sacred Heart.
Connor, William J. '46 (COL) Retired.
Connor, William J. '66 (LA) [66] Los Angeles, CA St. Gerard Majella Church.
Connors, Albert *c.m.f.* '73 (LA) [Q] Rancho Dominguez, CA Dominguez Seminary Inc.
Connors, Brocard *o.carm.* '57 (NY) [DD] Tappan, NY St. Eliseus Priory.
Connors, Canice *o.f.m.conv.* '61 (ALB) [A] Rensselaer, NY Conventual Franciscan Friars; [L] Rensselaer, NY Provincialate, Immaculate Conception Friary - Order of Friars Minor Conventual.
Connors, Canice *o.f.m.conv.* '61 (FgM) Conventual Franciscan Foreign Missions.
Connors, Cletus *o.s.b.* '72 (SCL) Cold Spring, MN St. Boniface Church; [I] Collegeville, MN St. John's Abbey, of the Order of St. Benedict.
Connors, Edmund P. '66 (NY) [217] Staten Island, NY Our Lady Help of Christians Church; [E] New York, NY Moore Catholic High School.
Connors, Msgr. Edward M. (NY) Scarsdale, NY Immaculate Heart of Mary Church.
Connors, Msgr. Edward M. '47 (NY) Retired; [E] White Plains, NY Archbishop Stepinac High School.
Connors, Francis B. '50 (FR) Retired.
Connors, Francis E. '73 (BUR) Fairfax, VT St. Luke Church.
Connors, J. M. *o.p.* '51 (FgM) Dominican - Order of Preachers Foreign Missions.
Connors, James V. *c.m.* '40 (LA) [W] Montebello, CA DePaul Center.
Connors, John '99 (CAM) Collingswood, NJ St. John's Church.
Connors, Joseph *s.v.d.* (DUB) [B] Epworth, IA Divine Word College.
Connors, Joseph *s.v.d.* '52 (CHI) [B] Techny, IL Divine Word Residence.
Connors, Michael *c.s.c.* '84 (FTW) [B] Notre Dame, IN University of Notre Dame Du Lac.
Connors, Michael E. *c.s.c.* '84 (FTW) [J] Notre Dame, IN Holy Cross Community, Corby Hall, University of Notre Dame.
Connors, Paul *s.v.d.* '63 (TR) [M] Bordentown, NJ Society of the Divine Word.
Connors, Richard P. '79 (PH) Willow Grove, PA St. David Church.
Connors, Robert A. '55 (NEW) Retired.
Connors, Robert L. '71 (BO) Newburyport, MA Immaculate Conception Church.
Connors, Terrence L. '75 (MAD) Jefferson, WI St. John the Baptist Church.
Conole, Robert W. '91 (BO) Unassigned.
Conoscenti, Frederick M. '65 (BUF) On Duty Outside the Diocese.
Conover, James A. '78 (TR) Keyport, NJ St. Joseph Church.
Conover, Sylvan J. *o.f.m.cap.* '49 (NY) [DD] Yonkers, NY St. Clare Friary.
Conrad, Anthony J. '49 (DAV) Retired; [M] Davenport, IA St. Vincent Center.
Conrad, Brian P. '76 (HBG) Millersville, PA St. Philip the Apostle Church.
Conrad, John F. '63 (GB) Clarks Mills, WI Immaculate Conception Church.
Conrad, Raymond J. (GB) Redgranite, WI St. Mark Church.
Conrad, Robert '70 (SY) [1] Rome, NY St. John the Baptist Church.
Conrad, Simon R. *o.f.m.cap.* '46 (STL) [54] St. Louis, MO St. Patrick Church; [P] St. Louis, MO St. Patrick Friary.
Conrad, Stanley '38 (AUS) Retired.
Conrad, Sylvester A. '52 (DAV) Knoxville, IA Veteran's Administration Hospital; Retired.
Conroy, Donald '64 (WDC) [B] Washington, DC St. Joseph's Seminary.
Conroy, Donald B. '64 (GBG) On Duty Outside the Diocese.
Conroy, Donald B. '64 (WDC) [V] Washington, DC National Institute for the Family, Inc.
Conroy, Francis M. '64 (BO) Unassigned.
Conroy, Francis X. '72 (BEA) [8] Beaumont, TX St. Pius X Church.
Conroy, J. Peter *s.j.* '71 (BUF) [O] Buffalo, NY Canisius Jesuit Community.
Conroy, James A. '53 (CLV) Retired.
Conroy, James R. *s.j.* '78 (BAL) [W] Baltimore, MD Ignatian Lay Volunteer Corps.
Conroy, James R. *s.j.* '78 (WDC) [E] Washington, DC Gonzaga College High School.
Conroy, John Jerome *o.p.* '49 (NY) [22] New York, NY St. Catherine of Siena Church; [DD] New York, NY St. Catherine of Siena Priory.
Conroy, Kevin M. '82 (CLV) Loudonville, OH St. Peter Church; [X] Cleveland, OH Office of Newman Campus Ministry.
Conroy, Martin J. *c.s.sp.* '54 (DET) [47] Detroit, MI St. Mary Church.
Conroy, Michael F. *s.p.s.* '65 (CHI) Park Ridge, IL Mary, Seat of Wisdom Church.
Conroy, Patrick J. *s.j.* '83 (WDC) [M] Washington, DC The Jesuit Community at Georgetown University.
Conroy, Philip '64 (BO) [Q] Boston, MA St. Elizabeth's Hospital of Boston.
Conroy, Phillip M. (BO) Boston, MA St. Elizabeth's Medical Center.
Conroy, Thomas J. '48 (STP) Retired; [C] St. Paul, MN University of St. Thomas.
Conry, Austin '65 (MOB) Butler, AL St. John The Evangelist Church.
Conry, James A. '53 (CLV) [3] Parma, OH St. Charles Borromeo Church; Wadsworth, OH Sacred Heart of Jesus Church.
Conry, Roy *o.carm.* '56 (TUC) [F] Tucson, AZ Carmelite Priory.
Consalvi, Mark *ss.cc.* '43 (HON) [5] Honolulu, HI Blessed Sacrament Church; [G] Kaneohe, HI Sacred Hearts Center.
Consani, Robert E. (KAL) Retired.
Conserva, Stephen *o.m.i.* '74 (MIA) Miramar, FL St. Stephen Church.
Considine, Matthew J. *s.m.m.* '77 (BRK) [195] Queens, NY St. Mary Gate of Heaven Church; [V] Ozone Park, NY Montfort Missionaries Provincialate (Missionaries of the Company of Mary) - Formation Community.
Considine, William J. *s.m.m.* '73 (BRK) [V] Ozone Park, NY Montfort Missionaries Provincialate (Missionaries of the Company of Mary) - Formation Community.
Consiglio, Cyprian *o.s.b.cam.* '98 (MRY) [F] Big Sur, CA New Camaldoli Hermitage.
Consla, Federico J. *c.ss.r.* '70 (CGS) San Lorenzo, PR Nuestra Senora de la Mercedes Church.
Constance, Jogues *o.f.m.cap.* '53 (DET) [P] Washington, MI Capuchin Retreat.
Constance, Msgr. Samuel C. '55 (TR) Retired; [M] Trenton, NJ Villa Vianney.
Constant, Van (HT) Houma, LA Terrebonne Parish General Hospital.
Constantine, Bennett '58 (LAN) Eaton Rapids, MI St. Peter Church.
Constantine, Cyprian G. *o.s.b.* '77 (GBG) [H] Latrobe, PA Saint Vincent Archabbey.
Constantino, Joseph S. *s.j.* '87 (RVC) [O] Manhasset, NY St. Ignatius Retreat House, Inisfada.
Contadino, J. Eugene *s.m.* '70 (CIN) [D] Dayton, OH The University of Dayton; [M] Dayton, OH Marianist Provincialate.
Contant, Robert '46 (CIN) [B] Carthagena, OH St. Charles.
Contant, Msgr. Robert '46 (FTW) Retired.
Contardi, Michael *o.de.m.* '60 (CLV) [68] Cleveland, OH St. Rocco Church.
Conte, Denis A. '75 (BO) Unassigned.
Conte, James W. '48 (NY) Retired.
Conte, John P. '58 (ALN) [6] Reading, PA Holy Rosary Church.
Conte, Msgr. John P. '64 (HRT) [2] Hartford, CT Holy Trinity Church; Special and other Archdiocesan Assignment.
Conterno, Austin *s.d.b.* '48 (SFR) [46] San Francisco, CA SS. Peter and Paul Church.
Conti, Cornelius *o.f.m.* '62 (SP) [O] St. Petersburg, FL St. Anthony Friary.
Conti, Hilary *o.s.b.* '74 (PAT) [M] Clifton, NJ Holy Face of Jesus Monastery.
Conti, John P. '46 (NY) Retired.
Conti, Joseph A. '65 (OG) [5] Plattsburgh, NY St. Peter Church; [C] Plattsburgh, NY Seton Catholic Central.
Conti, Msgr. Leo J. '50 (EVN) Retired.
Contie, Charles E. *o.carm.* '70 (BO) [P] Peabody, MA Catholic Information Center.
Continillo, Msgr. Rocco A. '56 (CAM) Carneys Point, NJ Corpus Christi Church.
Contons, Msgr. Albert J. '48 (BO) Senior Priests.
Contreras, David '93 (AMA) Absent on Leave.
Contreras, Eloy Trujillo '89 (SB) [E] Riverside, CA Operarios Del Reino De Cristo, O.R.C.
Conva, Matthias T. '62 (NEW) Union, NJ St. Michael's Church.
Converse, Brian J. '91 (NOR) Wauregan, CT Sacred Heart Church.
Converset, John *m.c.c.j.* '71 (FgM) Comboni Foreign Missions.
Convertino, David I. *o.f.m.* '77 (PRO) [P] Providence, RI St. Francis Friary.
Convery, Paul C. *c.o.* '84 (PH) [48] Philadelphia, PA St. Francis Xavier Church; [AA] Philadelphia, PA The Philadelphia Congregation of The Oratory of St. Philip Neri.
Convery, Thomas L. *s.s.c.* '40 (PRO) [P] Bristol, RI St. Columban's Retirement House.
Convey, Edwin H. *s.j.* '53 (BAL) [B] Baltimore, MD Loyola College in Maryland; [S] Baltimore, MD Jesuit Community of Loyola College, Inc.
Conway, David '52 (WDC) [29] Washington, DC St. Mary, Mother of God Church.
Conway, Dennis *m.c.c.j.* '68 (CIN) [M] Cincinnati, OH Comboni Missionaries (Verona Fathers)-Comboni Mission Center.
Conway, Dennis *m.c.c.j.* '68 (FgM) Comboni Foreign Missions.
Conway, Edward *o.f.m.cap.* '98 (NY) [17] Yonkers, NY Sacred Heart Church.

Conway, Edwin M. '60 (CHI) [G] Chicago, IL Catholic Charities of the Archdiocese of Chicago-Archdiocesan Offices.
Conway, Gerald W. (WIN) Retired.
Conway, James '65 (SAT) Castroville, TX St. Louis Church.
Conway, Msgr. Jeffrey '73 (NY) [221] Staten Island, NY Our Lady Star of the Sea Church.
Conway, John '62 (FAR) Retired.
Conway, John E. *m.m.* '73 (FgM) Maryknoll Foreign Missions.
Conway, Msgr. John L. '56 (GBG) Irwin, PA Immaculate Conception Church.
Conway, John R. '69 (SFE) [29] Albuquerque, NM St. Jude Thaddeus Church.
Conway, John T. '00 (ATL) Cumming, GA Good Shepherd Church.
Conway, John T. '77 (PH) [39] Philadelphia, PA Saint Cyprian Church.
Conway, Laurence '59 (MIA) Retired.
Conway, Malachy '95 (SAC) Absent on Leave.
Conway, Msgr. Michael (PAT) Retired.
Conway, Msgr. Michael '60 (MIA) [6] Fort Lauderdale, FL St. Clement Church.
Conway, Michael *s.d.b.* '92 (SP) [B] St. Petersburg, FL St. Petersburg Catholic High School.
Conway, Michael J. *o.ss.t.* '73 (NY) [20] New York, NY St. Brigid Church.
Conway, Neil '63 (CLV) Retired.
Conway, Pierre H. *o.p.* '41 (WDC) [B] Washington, DC Dominican House of Studies.
Conway, Richard C. '63 (BO) [4] Brockton, MA St. Margaret Church.
Conway, Richard J. '45 (BAK) Retired.
Conway, Robert *c.pp.s.* '53 (CIN) [B] Carthagena, OH St. Charles.
Conway, Thomas '86 (BLX) Hattiesburg, MS St. Thomas Aquinas Church; Hattiesburg, MS University of Southern Mississippi.
Conway, Thomas A. *c.pp.s.* '57 (KC) Kearney, MO Church of the Annunciation; [J] Liberty, MO Precious Blood Center.
Conway, Thomas D. '60 (BO) Reading, MA St. Athanasius Church.
Conway, Tommy '72 (BLX) [G] Hattiesburg, MS University of Southern Mississippi.
Conway, Msgr. Walter J. '48 (PH) Retired.
Conway, William '77 (JOL) Bensenville, IL St. Alexis Church.
Conwill, Giles '73 (SD) On Duty Outside the Diocese.
Conyard, James R. *s.j.* '62 (P) [L] Portland, OR Colombiere Community.
Conyard, Joseph W. *s.j.* '59 (SEA) [L] Seattle, WA Jesuit Community.
Conyers, Richard *c.s.c.* '69 (CHI) [D] Niles, IL Notre Dame High School.
Coogan, Roch *o.f.m.* '54 (SP) [O] Belleair Bluffs, FL St. James Friary.
Coogan, Thomas M. '97 (RVC) Bay Shore, NY St. Patrick's Church.
Cook, Adrian L. '72 (MOB) Brewton, AL St. Maurice Church.
Cook, Blaine '44 (BIS) Retired.
Cook, Damien J. '99 (OM) [1] Omaha, NE St. Cecilia's Church.
Cook, Daniel '90 (GR) On Duty Outside the Diocese.
Cook, Daniel A. '90 (ALX) Campti, LA Nativity of The Blessed Virgin Mary Church.
Cook, Douglas '94 (ORG) Special Assignment; [H] Yorba Linda, CA Polish Center.
Cook, Edward J. '67 (MIL) [32] Milwaukee, WI Congregation of the Great Spirit Church.
Cook, Emil *o.f.m.conv.* '66 (FgM) Conventual Franciscan Foreign Missions.
Cook, John B. '49 (TR) Retired.
Cook, John N. '56 (GI) Retired.
Cook, John P. '45 (HRT) Retired.
Cook, Joseph T. '86 (CHI) Matteson, IL St. Lawrence O'Toole Church.
Cook, Louis G. '58 (WIN) Retired.
Cook, Michael *s.j.* '66 (BO) [W] Chestnut Hill, MA The Jesuit Community at Boston College.
Cook, Michael J. '73 (WIL) Woodcrest, DE St. Matthew Church.
Cook, Michael L. *s.j.* '66 (SPK) [C] Spokane, WA Gonzaga University.
Cook, Millard *o.s.b.* '92 (GBG) [H] Latrobe, PA Saint Vincent Archabbey.
Cook, Msgr. Paul G. '59 (BAL) Cockeysville, MD St. Joseph Church.
Cook, Philip C. *o.s.a.* '97 (TLS) [B] Tulsa, OK Cascia Hall Preparatory School.
Cook, Robert '00 (CHY) Casper, WY St. Anthony of Padua Church.
Cook, Robert J. '65 (LC) [1] La Crosse, WI St. Joseph the Workman Church.
Cook, Steven '97 (KC) [40] Kansas City, MO Visitation of the Blessed Virgin Mary Church.
Cook, Thomas '88 (LA) Burbank, CA St. Finbar Church.
Cook, Thomas E. '97 (WIN) [7] Rochester, MN St. Pius X Church.
Cook, Thomas R. *o.s.a.* '57 (MIA) [H] Miami, FL Casa San Lorenzo.
Cook, Timothy R. '83 (STL) [17] St. Louis, MO Visitation-St. Ann's Church.
Cook, William C. '88 (NEW) Hillside, NJ Christ the King Church.
Cooke, Colman M. '65 (SP) [5] Clearwater, FL St. Michael The Archangel Church.
Cooke, Msgr. John F. '59 (CAM) Pitman, NJ Our Lady Queen of Peace Church.
Cooke, Kevin '78 (BIR) Gadsden, AL St. James Church.
Cooke, Patrick *c.s.sp.* '63 (STA) [1] St. Augustine, FL Cathedral of St. Augustine.
Cooke, Vincent M. *s.j.* '67 (BUF) [C] Buffalo, NY Canisius College; [O] Buffalo, NY Canisius Jesuit Community.
Cookson, Edmund L. *m.m.* '65 (FgM) Maryknoll Foreign Missions.
Cool, Brian '93 (ROC) [M] Rochester, NY Diocesan Department of Campus Ministry.
Cooley, Fred *s.j.* '54 (FgM) Provinces.
Cooley, John E. '48 (LA) Retired.
Cooley, Stephen V. *o.carm.* '67 (GAL) [50] Houston, TX St. Michael Church.
Coolong, Raymond *s.m.* '71 (FgM) Marist Foreign Missions.
Coombs, James R. *s.s.e.* '52 (BUR) Putney, VT Our Lady of Mercy Church; [E] Colchester, VT Society of St. Edmund.
Coomes, J. Eugene *s.j.* '48 (STL) [P] St. Louis, MO Jesuit Community Corporation at St. Louis University - Jesuit Hall.
Coon, David N. '93 (SPC) Scott City, MO St. Joseph Church.
Coonan, James J. '65 (PH) [U] Meadowbrook, PA Holy Redeemer Hospital and Medical Center; [BB] Huntingdon Valley, PA Sisters of the Holy Redeemer Provincialate.
Coonan, Joseph A. '89 (WOR) [25] Worcester, MA St. John's Church.
Coonan, Robert J. '65 (SPR) Hatfield, MA St. Joseph's Church; Hatfield, MA Holy Trinity Church.
Cooney, Arthur *o.f.m.cap.* '76 (SAG) [14] Saginaw, MI St. Joseph Church.
Cooney, Camillus '56 (LR) [A] Subiaco, AR Subiaco Monastery.
Cooney, David *s.d.s.* '67 (PHX) [17] Phoenix, AZ St. Mark Church.
Cooney, Dennis J. '74 (VEN) Lehigh Acres, FL St. Raphael Church.
Cooney, Francis C. *m.s.* '69 (HRT) [5] Hartford, CT Our Lady of Sorrows Church; [M] Hartford, CT Missionaries of LaSalette, Provincial Secretary.
Cooney, Gerald '50 (FWT) Retired.
Cooney, Msgr. James '64 (BRK) [163] Queens, NY St. Clare Church.
Cooney, John M. '62 (HRT) Watertown, CT St. John the Evangelist Church.
Cooney, Michael N. '75 (DET) Mount Clemens, MI St. Peter Church.
Cooney, Patrick *o.s.b.* '91 (IND) [A] St. Meinrad, IN St. Meinrad Seminary; [J] St. Meinrad, IN St. Meinrad Archabbey.
Cooney, Robert F. *c.s.v.* '57 (LAV) [D] Las Vegas, NV Clerics of St. Viator Retirement Home.
Cooney, Msgr. Roger P. '70 (COV) Melbourne, KY St. Philip Church.
Cooney, Romaeus *o.carm.* '58 (ALB) [4] Troy, NY Holy Trinity Church; [5] Troy, NY St. Joseph Church.
Cooney, Sean K. '59 (ORL) Winter Park, FL Saints Peter and Paul Church.
Cooney, Stephen A. '76 (LIN) Holdrege, NE All Saints Church.
Cooney, Theophane *c.p.* '52 (BRK) [180] Queens, NY Immaculate Conception Church; [V] Jamaica, NY Immaculate Conception Monastery.
Cooney, Xavier *s.v.d.* '83 (WH) War, WV Christ the King Church; Welch, WV St. Peter Church.
Cooper, Angus C. *o.f.m.* '61 (LA) [73] Los Angeles, CA St. Joseph Church.
Cooper, Damian L. '86 (RVC) Lindenhurst, NY Our Lady of Perpetual Help Church.
Cooper, David E. '70 (MIL) [57] Milwaukee, WI St. Matthias Church.
Cooper, Donald A. '53 (NEW) Retired.
Cooper, Donald J. '63 (E) Force, PA St. Joseph Church.
Cooper, Harold V. '49 (SC) Retired.
Cooper, Hilary '65 (OAK) Retired.
Cooper, James W. '80 (LIN) Friend, NE St. Joseph's Church.
Cooper, Jeffrey A. *c.s.c.* (COS) [F] Cascade, CO Holy Cross Novitiate.
Cooper, John A. '80 (LIN) Tecumseh, NE St. Andrew's Church.
Cooper, Joseph M. '95 (MAN) [1] Manchester, NH St. Joseph Church.
Cooper, Leo '43 (KCK) Special Assignment.
Cooper, Mark A. *o.s.b.* '76 (MAN) [K] Manchester, NH St. Anselm Abbey.
Cooper, Michael *s.j.* '73 (SP) [A] Saint Leo, FL Saint Leo University, University Ministry.
Cooper, Michael W. *s.j.* '73 (CHI) [N] Chicago, IL Chicago Province of the Society of Jesus-Provincial Office.
Cooper, Patrick E. '91 (CHR) Cheraw, SC St. Peter's Church.
Cooper, Ronald C. '83 (CIN) Greenfield, OH St. Benignus Church; New Vienna, OH St. Michael Church.
Cooper, Thomas T. '55 (STL) Retired.
Cooper, Warren L. *v.f.* '71 (NO) Chalmette, LA Our Lady of Prompt Succor Church.
Coopmans, Joseph R. *o.praem.* (GB) Norman, WI St. Joseph Church; Tisch Mills, WI Nativity of the Blessed Virgin Mary Church.
Coover, Thomas '78 (SAM) On Duty Outside the Diocese.
Copeland, Leonard R. *o.c.d.* '67 (MIL) [26] Milwaukee, WI St. Florian Church.
Copeland, Robert F. '99 (LAN) [4] Jackson, MI Queen of the Miraculous Medal Church.
Copenhaver, John '88 (LIN) Superior, NE St. Joseph's Church.
Copp, Rodney J. '73 (BO) [1] Waltham, MA St. Charles Borromeo Church.
Coppenrath, Msgr. Leonard '53 (BO) Senior Priests.
Copper, Stephen G. '95 (WOR) [23] Worcester, MA St. George Church.
Coppinger, Edmund T. '59 (WIL) Easton, MD SS. Peter and Paul Church.
Coppinger, John W. *s.a.* '72 (NY) Scarsdale, NY Our Lady of Fatima Church.
Coppola, David L. '86 (PAT) Absent on Leave.
Coppola, Paul R. '51 (BUF) Retired.
Cops, Augustine *o.f.m.cap.* '86 (DET) [15] Detroit, MI St. Charles Borromeo Church.
Cops, Peter *s.s.s.* '52 (CLV) [O] Cleveland, OH Congregation of the Blessed Sacrament Provincial House.
Cops, Peter E. *s.s.s.* '52 (LIN) [F] Waverly, NE Our Lady of Good Counsel Retreat House.
Copsey, Robert *s.o.l.t.* '94 (CC) [H] Robstown, TX Society of Our Lady of the Most Holy Trinity.
Copsey, Robert A. '78 (SAC) [16] Sacramento, CA St. Joseph's Church.
Corali, Serafino A. '47 (RVC) Retired; [M] Uniondale, NY St. Pius X Residence.
Corapi, John *s.o.l.t.* '91 (CC) [H] Robstown, TX Society of Our Lady of the Most Holy Trinity.
Corbaton, P. Jose Alcocer *m.ss.cc.* '64 (SJN) [1] Trujillo Alto, PR San Bartolome Church.
Corbelli, Vincent F. *m.m.* '60 (FgM) Maryknoll Foreign Missions.
Corbett, Carlos *c.ss.r.* '53 (CGS) Aguas Buenas, PR Church of Tres Santos Reyes.
Corbett, Eugene J. *s.j.* '62 (SJ) [D] San Jose, CA Bellarmine College Preparatory.
Corbett, John '95 (NEW) Jersey City, NJ Progressive Health Care.
Corbett, John B. '56 (PIT) [50] Pittsburgh, PA Holy Innocents Church.
Corbett, John Dominic *o.p.* '80 (WDC) [B] Washington, DC Dominican House of Studies.
Corbett, John F. '95 (NEW) [26] Jersey City, NJ St. Paul's Church.
Corbett, Michael E. '54 (PBL) Retired.
Corbett, Richard R. '95 (NEW) Westfield, NJ St. Helen Church.
Corbett, Robert '51 (STL) Manchester, MO Christ, Prince of Peace Church.
Corbett, W. Joseph '95 (ATL) Alpharetta, GA St. Brigid Church.
Corbin, Don '70 (TOL) [H] Oregon, OH St. Charles Mercy Hospital.
Corbino, Thomas A. '72 (JOL) Frankfort, IL St. Anthony Church.
Corbo, Alfred P. '56 (CHI) Franklin Park, IL St. Gertrude Church.
Corces, Pedro '88 (MIA) [14] Miami, FL Prince of Peace Church.
Corciulo, Msgr. Cosimo '56 (SB) Norco, CA California Rehabilitation Center.
Corcoran, Brian M. '72 (SD) [1] El Cajon, CA Holy Trinity Church.
Corcoran, Msgr. Clifton J. '54 (AMA) Retired; [D] Panhandle, TX St. Joseph's Home for Retired Priests.
Corcoran, D. Stanley '90 (DAL) Commerce, TX St. Joseph Church; [M] Irving, TX Diocese of Dallas Campus Ministry.
Corcoran, Frank '54 (JKS) Retired.
Corcoran, John J. '55 (RVC) Center Moriches, NY St. John the Evangelist Church.
Corcoran, John J. *m.m.* '63 (FgM) Maryknoll Foreign Missions.
Corcoran, John W. '53 (BO) East Bridgewater, MA St. John Church.
Corcoran, Kevin '88 (SY) [3] Syracuse, NY Blessed Sacrament Church.
Corcoran, Lawrence E. *s.j.* (BO) [Y] Weston, MA Campion Renewal Center.
Corcoran, Lawrence E. *s.j.* '63 (BO) [W] Weston, MA

Campion Jesuit Community.
Corcoran, Msgr. Lawrence J. '43 (COL) [18] Columbus, OH Holy Cross Church; Retired.
Corcoran, Michael P. '88 (NY) [F] New York, NY Fordham Preparatory School; [DD] New York, NY Jesuit Community at Fordham University.
Corcoran, Shawn D. '00 (COL) [9] Columbus, OH St. Cecilia Church.
Corcoran, T. Kevin '99 (PAT) Hawthorne, NJ St. Anthony's Church.
Corcoran, Thomas B. '98 (BO) Swampscott, MA St. John the Evangelist Church.
Corcoran, William D. '86 (BUR) On Duty Outside the Diocese.
Corcoran, William T. '81 (CHI) [118] Chicago, IL St. Margaret Mary Church.
Corcuera, Manuel '76 (CHK) Tanapag Village, District 8, MP Santa Remedios Church; San Roque Village, District 9, MP San Roque Church.
Cordano, Virgil *o.f.m.* '45 (LA) [Q] Santa Barbara, CA Franciscan Friary, Order of Friars Minor (Old Mission).
Cordaro, Frank (DM) On Special Assignment.
Cordeiro, Anthony *o.p.* '67 (OAK) [N] Oakland, CA Western Dominican Province.
Cordero, Carlos *o.s.a.* '99 (SJN) [1] Bayamon, PR San Agustin Church.
Cordero, Faustino '71 (BRK) [125] Brooklyn, NY St. Rocco's Church.
Cordero, Martin '99 (LSC) [5] Las Cruces, NM St. Genevieve Church.
Cordero, Mert '74 (NEW) Ridgewood, NJ Our Lady of Mount Carmel Church; Ridgewood, NJ Valley Hospital; Westwood, NJ Pascack Valley Hospital.
Cordery, Robert J. '80 (BO) Emergency Response Group.
Cordes, Christopher L. '95 (JC) Clarence, MO St. Patrick Church; Shelbina, MO St. Mary Church.
Cordileone, Msgr. Salvatore '82 (SD) On Duty Outside the Diocese.
Cordori, Joseph B. '00 (PIT) Bethel Park, PA St. Thomas More Church.
Coreas, Edwin '92 (GAL) [39] Houston, TX St. Jerome Church.
Corel, Joseph S. '00 (JC) [2] Jefferson City, MO St. Peter Church.
Coric, Christopher *o.f.m.conv.* '71 (BUF) [7] Lackawanna, NY Our Lady of Bistrica Church.
Coric, Doiminik *o.f.m.* '40 (CHI) [N] Chicago, IL Croatian Franciscan Custody of the Holy Family.
Coriden, James A. '57 (GRY) On Duty Outside the Diocese.
Corigliano, Anthony *c.s.s.* '55 (BO) [W] Waltham, MA Stigmatine Fathers & Brothers Provincial House.
Cork, Ronald *c.p.* '65 (SAC) [H] Citrus Heights, CA Christ the King Retreat.
Corkery, Daniel '55 (ALX) Simmesport, LA Christ the King Church.
Corkery, Raymond *o.carm.* '59 (JOL) [4] Joliet, IL Mount Carmel Church.
Corley, Joseph '75 (PH) Darby, PA Blessed Virgin Mary Church.
Corley, Malachy *o.c.s.o.* '55 (ATL) [J] Conyers, GA The Monastery of the Holy Spirit.
Corley, Theodosius *o.f.m.cap.* '74 (PRT) [3] Portland, ME St. Joseph's Church; [J] Portland, ME Motherhouse of the Sisters of Mercy of the Americas; [M] Portland, ME University of New England-Westbrook College.
Corley, Thomas '85 (JOL) Retired; [I] Naperville, IL St. John Vianney Villa.
Cormack, James B. *c.m.* '76 (STL) [66] St. Louis, MO St. Vincent de Paul Church.
Cormack, Michael J. '54 (SAC) Roseville, CA St. Rose of Lima Church; Retired and in Senior Ministry.
Cormer, John P. '64 (STL) Crestwood, MO St. Elizabeth of Hungary Church.
Cormier, Gregory P. '83 (LAF) Parks, LA St. Joseph Church.
Cormier, Julien *m.afr.* '66 (CHI) [121] Chicago, IL St. Martin De Porres Church; [N] Chicago, IL Missionaries of Africa.
Cormier, Leo G. '57 (BO) Senior Priests.
Cormier, Michael Robert '00 (SP) [7] St. Petersburg, FL St. Paul Church.
Cormier, Norman R. '59 (PRT) Retired.
Cormier, Robert '82 (NEW) Newark, NJ Northern State Prison; Newark, NJ Cura (Community United to Rehabilitate Addicts).
Cormier, Roger C. '61 (BO) [4] Everett, MA St. Therese Church; Senior Priests.
Cormier, William N. '71 (WOR) East Douglas, MA St. Denis Church.
Cornea, Sergio '96 (ROM) Chicago, IL Ss. Peter and Paul Church.
Corneille, Cecil '95 (STV) [4] Mt. Pleasant, VI Church of St. Joseph.
Cornejo, Quirino (SAN) Brady, TX St. Patrick's Church.
Cornejo, Quirino H. '91 (SAN) Junction, TX St. Theresa of the Child Jesus Church; Menard, TX Sacred Heart Church.
Cornejo, Vincent C. '56 (MET) Woodbridge, NJ Our Lady of Mount Carmel Church.
Cornelius, John '75 (SEA) Everett, WA Immaculate Conception Church; Everett, WA Our Lady of Perpetual Help Church.
Cornelius, Leonard *o.f.m.* '69 (MAR) [E] Iron Mountain, MI Monastery of the Holy Cross.
Cornelius, Msgr. William R. (STU) Retired.
Cornell, Peter (DET) [P] Detroit, MI St. Paul of the Cross Retreat Center.
Cornell, Richard P. '99 (BO) [5] Weymouth, MA Sacred Heart Church.
Cornell, Robert J. *o.praem.* '44 (GB) [B] De Pere, WI St. Norbert College; [I] De Pere, WI St. Joseph Priory.
Cornelli, Leo *o.s.b.* '35 (DET) [K] Detroit, MI St. Sylvester Monastery.
Cornelli, Neil '37 (LAN) Retired.
Cornelli, Neil '37 (STA) Fernandina Beach, FL St. Michael's Church.
Cornely, Francis J. '48 (PH) Essington, PA St. Margaret Mary Alacoque Church; Retired.
Cornet, Dave *s.v.d.* '87 (WH) Webster Springs, WV St. Anne's Church.
Cornish, Daryl G. *s.j.* '82 (STL) [O] St. Louis, MO Fusz Pavilion.
Cornish, Ronald '68 (KCK) Holton, KS St. Dominic's Church; Mayetta, KS St. Francis Xavier Church.
Cornwell, Malcolm *c.p.* '30 (NY) [FF] New York, NY Cardinal Spellman Retreat House.
Cornwell, Malcolm *c.p.* '69 (NY) [DD] New York, NY Passionist Spiritual Center.
Corominas, John *c.m.f.* '49 (LA) [Q] Rancho Dominguez, CA Dominguez Seminary Inc.
Corona, Andrew J. '93 (GRY) [3] Michigan City, IN Queen of All Saints Church.
Corona, John '71 (RNO) Retired.
Corona, Msgr. Michael J. '68 (MET) Phillipsburg, NJ St. Philip & St. James Church.
Coronado, Genero '51 (LA) Retired.
Coroztieta, Jose Madoz '53 (SJN) Retired.
Corpora, Joseph V. *c.s.c.* '84 (PHX) Goodyear, AZ Saint John Vianney Church; [K] Goodyear, AZ St. John Vianney School Development Fund.
Corr, Msgr. John F. '51 (PAT) Retired; [C] Madison, NJ Bayley-Ellard High School.
Corr, John Raymond *o.p.* '56 (FgM) Dominican - Order of Preachers Foreign Missions.
Corr, John Raymond *o.p.* '56 (NO) [P] New Orleans, LA Dominican Friars, Southern Dominican Province of St. Martin de Porres; [S] Metairie, LA Southern Dominican Foundation.
Corr, John Raymond *o.p.* '56 (SAT) [26] San Antonio, TX St. Ann Church; [B] San Antonio, TX Dominican Priory of San Juan Macias.
Corradi, Frank *s.c.* '85 (LC) [6] Eau Claire, WI St. Olaf Church.
Corrado, Dennis M. *c.o.* '70 (BRK) [22] Brooklyn, NY St. Boniface Church; [V] Brooklyn, NY Oratory of Saint Philip Neri, Congregation Pontifical Rite.
Corral, Jose M. '79 (SFR) [1] Menlo Park, CA St. Anthony Church.
Corral, Roberto *o.p.* '88 (PHX) [5] Phoenix, AZ Most Holy Trinity Church.
Corrales, Alirio '78 (TYL) Diboll, TX Our Lady of Guadalupe Church.
Corrales, Miguel A. '64 (SJN) [18] Carolina, PR Cristo Rey Church.
Corrall, Jose *s.j.* '66 (LA) [13] Los Angeles, CA Holy Name of Jesus Church.
Correa, Gino *o.f.m.* '75 (SFE) [I] Albuquerque, NM San Antonio Provincial Friary.
Corredato, John *c.s.v.* '68 (SFD) Edwardsville, IL St. Boniface Church.
Correia, Edward E. '68 (FR) [15] New Bedford, MA St. James Church.
Correio, Bruce '85 (LA) [82] Los Angeles, CA St. Michael Church.
Correnti, Joseph M. '72 (LR) Springdale, AR St. Raphael's Church; Tontitown, AR St. Joseph's Church.
Correz, Steven '00 (ORG) Dana Point, CA St. Edward Church.
Corriere, Basil *e.c.* '87 (STU) [F] Bloomingdale, OH Holy Family Hermitage.
Corrigan, Allen F. '82 (CLV) Brunswick, OH St. Ambrose Church.
Corrigan, Msgr. Bernard J. '47 (NY) Warwick, NY St. Stephen Church; Retired.
Corrigan, Edward *s.m.* '43 (CLV) [M] Cleveland, OH Sts. Mary and Joseph Home for the Aged.
Corrigan, Edward C. *s.m.* '43 (WDC) [M] Washington, DC Marist Center.
Corrigan, F. J. '38 (SFD) Retired.
Corrigan, Francis J. '38 (SFD) [K] Springfield, IL Priests' Retirement Facility.
Corrigan, Gregory M. '86 (WIL) Claymont, DE Holy Rosary Church; [A] Wilmington, DE St. Mark's High School.
Corrigan, Msgr. Hugh J. '63 (NY) [9] Yonkers, NY Immaculate Conception Church.
Corrigan, J. David *s.j.* '65 (STL) [P] St. Louis, MO Hallahan House.
Corrigan, James B. *s.j.* '49 (MIL) [P] Wauwatosa, WI Jesuit Community at St. Camillus.
Corrigan, James V. *o.s.a.* '66 (CHI) [N] Olympia Fields, IL The Augustinians-Provincialate.
Corrigan, James V. *o.s.a.* '66 (SD) San Diego, CA Sharp Memorial Hospital.
Corrigan, John D. *s.j.* '65 (STL) Affton, MO St. Timothy Church.
Corrigan, Kevin B. *c.s.sp.* '60 (SJ) Mountain View, CA St. Athanasius Church.
Corrigan, Michael T. '75 (CHR) Florence, SC St. Ann Church; [H] Florence, SC Francis Marion University.
Corrigan, Michael T. '75 (GAL) On Duty Outside the Diocese.
Corrigan, Roy *o.f.m.* '55 (FgM) Franciscan Foreign Missions.
Corriveau, Kip (ROC) Hornell, NY St. Ann Church.
Corriveau, Kip '95 (ROC) Rochester, NY Strong Memorial Hospital.
Corriveau, Kip F. (ROC) [J] Rochester, NY Sisters of Mercy of the Americas Regional Community of Rochester.
Corriveau, Raymond *o.p.* '55 (PRT) [G] Lewiston, ME St. Marguerite d'Youville Pavilion; [I] Lewiston, ME SS. Peter and Paul House.
Corriveau, Real *o.m.i.* '61 (FgM) Oblates Foreign Missions.
Corriveau, Roger R. *a.a.* '74 (WOR) [N] Worcester, MA Assumptionists of Assumption College.
Corriveau, Ronald E. '71 (MAN) Epping, NH St. Joseph Church.
Corry, Francis J. '74 (NY) [142] Bronx, NY St. Frances of Rome Church.
Corry, James J. *c.s.sp.* '57 (STA) [19] Jacksonville, FL St. Paul's Church.
Corry, John J. '52 (RC) Retired.
Corso, Charles W. *c.s.c.* '75 (FTW) [J] South Bend, IN Congregation of Holy Cross, Indiana Province, Provincial House.
Cortes, Antonio '96 (MRY) [2] Salinas, CA Sacred Heart Church.
Cortes, Jesse '63 (LAV) [4] Las Vegas, NV Our Lady of Las Vegas Church.
Cortes, Raul '62 (LA) Reseda, CA St. Catherine of Siena Church.
Cortese, Francis X. *o.praem.* '62 (PH) [AA] Paoli, PA Daylesford Abbey.
Cortese, Patrick S. '48 (SCR) Retired.
Cortese, Richard '82 (MEM) [16] Memphis, TN St. Louis Church.
Cortesi, David J. '63 (CHI) [56] Chicago, IL St. Ferdinand Church.
Cortez, Fernando J. '77 (OAK) [11] Oakland, CA St. Lawrence O'Toole Church.
Cortez, Jose '73 (TYL) Fairfield, TX St. Bernard of Clairvaux Church.
Cortez, Ramiro *o.m.i.* '70 (SAT) Del Rio, TX St. Joseph's Church.
Cortez, Ruben Dario *s.x.* (PAT) [1] Paterson, NJ Cathedral of St. John the Baptist.
Cortney, Edward P. '63 (GI) Chadron, NE St. Patrick's Church.
Cortney, Louis M. *o.s.m.* '39 (CHI) [N] Chicago, IL Order of Friar Servants of Mary (Servites) United States of America Province, Inc.
Coruna, Roberto D. '77 (MET) Piscataway, NJ Our Lady of Fatima Church.
Coryer, Francis J. '82 (OG) De Kalb Junction, NY St. Henry Church; Edwards, NY Sacred Heart Church.
Cos, Rafael '82 (MIA) [17] Miami, FL St. Catherine of Siena Church.
Cosby, Msgr. R. Roy '54 (ARL) Woodbridge, VA Our Lady of Angels Church; Retired.
Coschignano, Joseph C. '69 (RVC) Center Moriches, NY St. John the Evangelist Church.
Cosentino, Jack '70 (VEN) [1] Venice, FL Epiphany Church.
Cosentino, Jack A. '70 (FAR) On Duty Outside the Diocese.
Cosentino, Rocco *c.pp.s.* '54 (CIN) [B] Carthagena, OH St. Charles.
Cosgayon, Gerard *o.a.r.* '88 (NY) [154] Bronx, NY St. John's Church.
Cosgrove, Edward C. *c.ss.r.* '55 (BLX) [E] Biloxi, MS St. John Neumann Residence.
Cosgrove, Francis J. '65 (JKS) Madison, MS St. Francis of Assisi Church.
Cosgrove, J. Kelly '43 (LC) Retired.
Cosgrove, J. Kelly '43 (ORL) Retired.
Cosgrove, James '51 (ROC) Retired.
Cosgrove, Jerome P. '63 (SC) Armstrong, IA St. Mary's Church; Estherville, IA St. Patrick's Church.
Cosgrove, Msgr. Joseph '60 (LA) Moorpark, CA Holy Cross Church.
Cosgrove, Joseph J. '92 (BAL) Pasadena, MD St. Jane Frances de Chantal Church.
Cosgrove, Thomas *c.ss.r.* '45 (STL) [P] Liguori, MO Liguori Mission House/Redemptorists.
Cosgrove, William B. '74 (NY) Hopewell Junction, NY St. Denis Church; [HH] Scarsdale, NY Catholic Charismatic Renewal Office.

Cosgrove, William J. '55 (ROC) Shortsville, NY St. Dominic Church.
Cosgrove, William P. '99 (BIS) New England, ND St. Mary Church; Regent, ND St. Henry Church.
Coskren, Thomas M. *o.p.* '54 (PRO) [P] Providence, RI St. Thomas Aquinas Priory at Providence College.
Coslowsky, Marion '42 (SB) Retired.
Cosmic, John J. '90 (OG) Harrisville, NY St. Francis Solanus Church; Retired.
Cosmos, Andrew '94 (PH) [28] Philadelphia, PA St. Callistus Church.
Coss, John *f.m.s.i.* '56 (BO) [B] Framingham, MA Sylva Maria.
Cossavella, Anthony J. '81 (PH) [107] Philadelphia, PA St. Monica Church.
Cossette, Raymond '55 (DUL) Retired.
Costa, Anthony J. '90 (ALN) [A] Northampton, PA Mary Immaculate Center.
Costa, Anthony J. '90 (PH) [A] Wynnewood, PA Theological Seminary of St. Charles Borromeo, Overbrook.
Costa, Caetano F. '64 (RVC) Deer Park, NY SS. Cyril and Methodius Church.
Costa, Carl A. *m.m.* '71 (FgM) Maryknoll Foreign Missions.
Costa, David A. '85 (FR) North Attleboro, MA Sacred Heart Church.
Costa, Eugene *o.de.m.* '74 (BUF) [O] LeRoy, NY Order of the BVM of Mercy/Mercedarian Friars; [O] LeRoy, NY St. Raymond Nonnatus Novitiate.
Costa, Eugene E. '76 (SFD) Athens, IL Holy Family Church; Sherman, IL St. John Vianney Church.
Costa, Gabriel B. '79 (NEW) [B] South Orange, NJ Seton Hall University.
Costa, Joseph M. *s.j.* '54 (SJ) [L] Los Gatos, CA Sacred Heart Jesuit Center.
Costa, Lucas Torrell deAlmeida *o.s.b.* '67 (GBG) [H] Latrobe, PA Saint Vincent Archabbey.
Costa, Mario '53 (RVC) Brookville, NY St. Paul the Apostle Church.
Costa, Thomas C. '78 (RVC) Glen Cove, NY St. Patrick's Church.
Costa-Soler, Manuel '98 (MIA) Coral Springs, FL St. Andrew Church.
Costantino, Msgr. Anthony J. '44 (SAT) Retired; [K] San Antonio, TX Padua Place.
Costanza, Jared J. '99 (PRO) South Kingstown, RI St. Francis of Assisi Church.
Costanzo, John J. '64 (PBL) Center, CO St. Francis Jerome Church; Monte Vista, CO St. Joseph Church.
Costanzo, John J. '68 (PBL) Del Norte, CO Holy Name of Mary Church.
Costello, Andrew *c.ss.r.* '65 (TOL) [2] Lima, OH St. Gerard Church.
Costello, Aquinas *o.p.* '68 (P) [18] Portland, OR Holy Rosary Parish & Dominican Priory Church.
Costello, Bernard B. '63 (PIT) Natrona Heights, PA Our Lady of the Most Blessed Sacrament Church.
Costello, Brian L. '00 (SFR) Novato, CA St. Anthony of Padua Church.
Costello, Charles P. *s.j.* '60 (BAL) [S] Baltimore, MD Ferdinand Wheeler Jesuit Community; [W] Baltimore, MD Ignatian Lay Volunteer Corps.
Costello, Coleman '67 (BRK) [237] Queens, NY Sacred Heart of Jesus Church.
Costello, Daniel F. '98 (CHI) [105] Chicago, IL St. John Fisher Church.
Costello, Edward *o.f.m.conv.* '61 (TR) Point Pleasant Beach, NJ St. Peter's Church.
Costello, Msgr. Francis M. '45 (NY) Retired.
Costello, Frank B. *s.j.* '52 (SPK) [C] Spokane, WA Gonzaga University.
Costello, James *s.j.* '66 (PBL) Trinidad, CO Most Holy Trinity, Trinidad Area Catholic Community (Trinidad Cluster) Church; [G] Trinidad, CO Trinidad Area Catholic Community.
Costello, James P. '60 (CLV) [6] Parma, OH Holy Family Church.
Costello, John F. *s.j.* '83 (CHI) [N] Chicago, IL Chicago Province of the Society of Jesus-Provincial Office; [N] Chicago, IL Chicago Province of the Society of Jesus-Provincial Office.
Costello, John F. '96 (VEN) [4] Naples, FL St. William Church.
Costello, John J. '53 (SY) Sherrill, NY St. Helena Church.
Costello, John J. '89 (BRK) [64] Brooklyn, NY Immaculate Heart of Mary Church; [Z] Brooklyn, NY Pro Sanctity Movement.
Costello, John M. '72 (STL) Washington, MO St. Francis Borgia Church.
Costello, John M. *s.j.* '84 (ROC) [C] Rochester, NY McQuaid Jesuit High School.
Costello, Joseph J. '60 (CLV) Hudson, OH St. Mary Church.
Costello, Mark Joseph *o.f.m.cap.* '91 (CHI) [N] Chicago, IL St. Clare Friary.
Costello, Paul *o.m.i.* '77 (WDC) [M] Washington, DC Oblate College/Center for Mission Studies Community.
Costello, Raymond *m.s.c.* '45 (ALN) [A] Center Valley, PA Missionaries of the Sacred Heart.
Costello, Richard D. *s.j.* '53 (BGP) [P] Fairfield, CT The Fairfield Jesuit Community-Fairfield University.
Costello, Robert B. '53 (BO) Abington, MA St. Nicholas Church.
Costello, Robert T. *s.j.* '63 (FgM) Provinces.
Costello, Ted '85 (SP) [5] Clearwater, FL St. Michael The Archangel Church.
Costello, Thomas J. '54 (SY) Special Assignment; [W] Syracuse, NY David W. Barry Foundation.
Costello, Timon *o.f.m.cap.* '58 (GB) [M] Appleton, WI Monte Alverno Retreat Center.
Costello, Timon W. '58 (MIL) [P] Milwaukee, WI St. Conrad Friary.
Costello, Vincent F. '76 (CHI) Arlington Heights, IL Our Lady of the Wayside Church.
Costello, Msgr. William F. '52 (RVC) Franklin Square, NY St. Catherine of Sienna Church; Garden City, NY St. Anne Church; Retired.
Costello, William J. '64 (CHI) [54] Chicago, IL St. Eugene Church.
Costello, William M. '74 (FR) East Falmouth, MA St. Anthony's Church.
Coster, Henry C. *s.j.* '59 (SCR) [C] Scranton, PA University of Scranton.
Costigan, George (PAT) Retired.
Costigan, P. James '68 (SAV) [3] Augusta, GA St. Mary on the Hill Church.
Costigan, Richard F. *s.j.* '64 (CHI) [C] Chicago, IL Jesuit Community at Loyola University of Chicago.
Costigan, Richard J. '50 (TUC) Retired.
Cotant, Charles *c.ss.r.* '41 (FgM) Redemptorist Foreign Missions.
Cote, David P. '68 (GF) Special Assignment.
Cote, David P. '68 (PRT) Military Chaplains.
Cote, Duaine M. '62 (FAR) Edgeley, ND Transfiguration Church; Nortonville, ND Holy Ghost (Spirit) Church.
Cote, E. Joseph '69 (BAL) [22] Baltimore, MD St. Charles Borromeo Church.
Cote, Gerald M. '56 (TUC) Retired.
Cote, Joseph A. '51 (MAN) Retired.
Cote, Joseph A. *o.p.* '86 (WDC) [11] Washington, DC St. Dominic Church & Priory Church.
Cote, Michael R. '75 (PRT) [1] Old Town, ME Holy Family Church.
Cote, Normand C. '58 (OG) Coopersville, NY St. Joseph Church.
Cote, Paul E. '71 (PRT) Saco, ME Notre Dame de Lourdes Church.
Cote, Richard *o.m.i.* '60 (WDC) [M] Washington, DC Missionary Oblates of Mary Immaculate.
Cote, Richard G. *o.m.i.* '60 (FgM) Oblates Foreign Missions.
Cote, Roland P. '71 (MAN) [1] Nashua, NH St. Aloysius Church.
Cotone, Michael *o.s.c.* '74 (STP) [N] Shoreview, MN Crosier Provincial House Province of St. Odilia.
Cotta, Myron '87 (FRS) On Special Assignment.
Cotter, Charles B. '50 (OG) Retired.
Cotter, David *o.s.b.* '79 (SCL) [I] Collegeville, MN St. John's Abbey, of the Order of St. Benedict.
Cotter, David W. *o.s.b.* '79 (MAN) [K] Manchester, NH St. Anselm Abbey.
Cotter, Eugene J. '56 (NEW) [B] South Orange, NJ Seton Hall University.
Cotter, Francis Xavier *o.c.d.* '89 (MIL) [P] Holy Hill, WI Discalced Carmelite Monastery.
Cotter, George G. *m.m.* '60 (NY) [DD] Maryknoll, NY Maryknoll Fathers and Brothers.
Cotter, John F. '80 (SAG) Beal City, MI St. Joseph the Worker Church.
Cotter, Lawrence E. '52 (OG) Colton, NY St. Patrick Church; Madrid, NY St. John the Baptist Church; Retired.
Cotter, Patrick John '57 (LA) Retired.
Cotter, Pius *o.f.m.cap.* '88 (GB) Brussels, WI St. Francis-St. Mary Church.
Cotter, Raymond C. '86 (GAY) Special Assignment.
Cotter, Raymond C. '86 (MAR) Gladstone, MI Holy Family Church.
Cotter, Robert '47 (OG) West Leyden, NY St. Mary's Nativity Church.
Cotter, Robert L. '47 (OG) Glenfield, NY St. Mary Church; Retired.
Cotter, Vince '83 (OAK) Antioch, CA St. Ignatius Church.
Cottingham, David T. *c.s.sp.* '75 (PIT) [B] Pittsburgh, PA Duquesne University of the Holy Ghost.
Cotton, Charles E. '73 (COL) [30] Columbus, OH St. Mary Magdalene Church.
Cottone, Paul P. '49 (SCR) [16] Scranton, PA St. Lucy's Church.
Cottrell, Msgr. Frank '50 (SJ) Retired.
Cottrell, James '68 (SP) Retired.
Cotugno, Joseph '64 (ALB) [8] Albany, NY St. James Church; Special Assignment.
Coty, Aaron Joseph *o.p.* (WDC) Germantown, MD Mother Seton Church.
Coucelo, Andres '68 (MIA) Retired.
Couch, Edward W. *o.m.i.* (CC) Sarita, TX Our Lady of Guadalupe Church.
Coughlan, Msgr. Michael J. '52 (SD) Retired.
Coughlan, Robert '90 (SFE) Retired.
Coughlin, Bernard J. *s.j.* '55 (SPK) [C] Spokane, WA Gonzaga University.
Coughlin, Conall R. *o.s.b.* '58 (PAT) [M] Morristown, NJ St. Mary's Abbey.
Coughlin, Daniel C. *c.s.c.* '50 (FTW) [18] South Bend, IN St. Stanislaus Church.
Coughlin, Daniel P. '60 (CHI) On Duty Outside the Archdiocese.
Coughlin, Edward J. *s.j.* '74 (NY) [37] New York, NY St. Francis Xavier Church; [DD] New York, NY Xavier Jesuit Community.
Coughlin, Howard L. '53 (CHR) Mauldin, SC St. Elizabeth Ann Seton Church.
Coughlin, James *s.j.* '98 (NY) [F] New York, NY Xavier High School.
Coughlin, John *o.f.m.* '83 (NY) [A] Yonkers, NY St. Joseph's Seminary; [DD] New York, NY Franciscan Friars, Order of Friars Minor, Holy Name Province.
Coughlin, Msgr. Joseph F. '44 (BUF) [5] West Seneca, NY Queen of Heaven Church; Retired.
Coughlin, Kenneth F. '90 (LAN) Pinckney, MI St. Mary Church.
Coughlin, Leo '56 (LAV) [2] Las Vegas, NV Christ the King Church.
Coughlin, Paul E. '66 (PRT) South Portland, ME Church of the Holy Cross; South Portland, ME St. John the Evangelist Church; [M] South Portland, ME Southern Maine Technical College.
Coughlin, Paul F. '91 (BO) [1] Medford, MA St. Francis of Assisi Church.
Coughlin, Richard '53 (ORG) Inactive Leave.
Coughlin, Roger J. '51 (CHI) Retired; [G] Chicago, IL Catholic Charities of the Archdiocese of Chicago-Archdiocesan Offices.
Coughlin, Thomas '77 (HON) On Duty Outside the Diocese.
Coughlin, William D. '66 (BO) Wakefield, MA Most Blessed Sacrament Church.
Coughlin, William E. '50 (GAL) [Q] Houston, TX Dillon House.
Couhig, Michael *c.s.c.* '80 (CHI) [D] Niles, IL Notre Dame High School.
Coulombe, Dale '79 (ORG) Inactive Leave.
Coulter, Gary L. '99 (LIN) [9] Lincoln, NE St. Patrick's Church.
Coulter, Lawrence W. '86 (GI) Farwell, NE St. Anthony of Padua Church.
Coulthardt, Gregory *s.d.s.* '67 (GB) [I] New Holstein, WI Salvatorian Center Residence.
Counce, Paul D. '79 (BR) Special Assignment.
Countie, Charles *o.carm.* '78 (FgM) Carmelite Foreign Missions.
Countie, Charles *o.carm.* '78 (JOL) [J] Darien, IL Carmelite Provincial Office.
Coupar, David A. '80 (LAF) Absent on Leave.
Coupeau, Carlos *s.j.* '96 (BO) [W] Cambridge, MA Weston Jesuit Community.
Cour, Raymond F. *c.s.c.* '41 (FTW) [17] South Bend, IN Faith & Hope & Charity Chapel Church; [B] Notre Dame, IN University of Notre Dame Du Lac; [J] Notre Dame, IN Holy Cross Community, Corby Hall, University of Notre Dame.
Courier, Rick L. '85 (MAR) Escanaba, MI St. Thomas the Apostle Church.
Cournoyer, Michael (ALB) Rotterdam, NY St. Gabriel the Archangel Church.
Cournoyer, Michael '98 (ALB) Albany, NY Albany Medical Center Hospital.
Courteau, Allen *o.m.i.* '76 (FgM) Oblates Foreign Missions.
Courtemanche, Normand L. '65 (PRO) [10] Pawtucket, RI Our Lady of Consolation Church.
Courtney, Edward '55 (HEL) [8] Butte, MT St. John the Evangelist Church.
Courtney, Joseph B. *c.s.b.* '56 (GAL) [Q] Houston, TX Dillon House.
Courtney, Patrick E. '87 (LFT) Unassigned.
Courtney, Scott M. '00 (LIN) [11] Lincoln, NE St. Teresa's Church.
Courtney, Thomas M. '51 (SPR) [17] Springfield, MA St. Patrick's Church.
Courtney, William (Liam) Hugh '99 (PBL) Grand Junction, CO St. Joseph Church.
Courtright, Lawrence P. '61 (TLS) [E] Tulsa, OK St. John Medical Center, Inc.; [F] Tulsa, OK St. John Villas, Inc.
Courtright, Raymond P. '92 (FAR) [4] Grand Forks, ND St. Thomas Aquinas Parish, UND Church; [I] Grand Forks, ND Univ. of North Dakota Newman Center.
Courville, Msgr. J. Douglas '76 (LAF) [12] Lafayette, LA St. Jules Church.
Courville, Robert W. '63 (LAF) Krotz Springs, LA St. Anthony Church.
Coury, Paul *c.ss.r.* '72 (STL) [P] St. Louis, MO St. Alphonsus Rectory of the Redemptorist.
Coury, Philip *c.m.* '71 (PBL) Aguilar, CO St. Anthony Church.
Cousens, Dennis '77 (L) [51] Louisville, KY St. Martin Church.

Cousin, John *o.f.m.cap.* '76 (DEN) [M] Denver, CO Annunciation Friary.
Cousineau, Robert H. *s.j.* '60 (CHY) Guernsey, WY St. Anthony's Church.
Cousins, John P. *o.f.m.cap.* '76 (DEN) [3] Denver, CO Annunciation Church; [7] Denver, CO Cure D'Ars Church.
Coutinho, Absalom (PAT) On Duty Outside the Diocese.
Coutinho, Absalom '72 (VEN) Palmetto, FL Holy Cross Church.
Coutinita, Paul '82 (FTW) [1] Fort Wayne, IN Cathedral of the Immaculate Conception.
Couto, Robert '96 (MAN) Londonderry, NH St. Jude Church.
Coutts, Virendra '79 (OAK) [1] San Leandro, CA Assumption of the Blessed Virgin Mary Church.
Coutu, Joseph '81 (GLP) On Duty Outside of Diocese.
Couture, Bernard G. '50 (BUR) Retired.
Couture, Fern *s.p.* '70 (AMA) Dimmitt, TX Immaculate Conception Church.
Couture, Fernand '43 (STA) Retired.
Couture, Paul E. *s.s.e.* '56 (BUR) [E] Colchester, VT Society of St. Edmund.
Couture, Roger *o.m.i.* '55 (BO) [W] Lowell, MA Missionary Oblates of Mary Immaculate.
Couture, Roland '53 (BO) [W] Lowell, MA Missionary Oblates of Mary Immaculate.
Couturier, Albert '88 (GAY) St. Helen, MI St. Helen Church.
Couturier, David *o.f.m.cap.* '79 (NY) [DD] White Plains, NY St. Conrad Friary.
Couturier, George M. '81 (HRT) Special and other Archdiocesan Assignment; [A] Bloomfield, CT St. Thomas Seminary.
Covarrubias, Raul R. '83 (B) Mountain Home, ID Our Lady of Good Counsel Church.
Covarrubras-Pina, Salomon '91 (YAK) Grandview, WA Blessed Sacrament Church.
Covas, Peter '57 (SB) Alta Loma, CA St. Peter & St. Paul Church.
Coveney, James B. '64 (ALT) [3] Altoona, PA St. Mark's Church; [H] Hollidaysburg, PA Campus Ministry.
Coveny, Richard C. '56 (BUF) Colden, NY Our Lady of the Sacred Heart Church.
Cover, Phil (BAL) Glen Burnie, MD Holy Trinity Church.
Cover, Phillip B. '70 (LFT) On Duty Outside the Diocese.
Coverdale, Gerald D. *o.p.* '54 (BR) Hammond, LA Holy Ghost Church.
Covert, James A. '76 (L) On Special Assignment.
Covert, Kevin A. *o.f.m.cap.* '90 (KAL) Portage, MI St. Catherine of Siena Church.
Covertino, David I. *o.f.m.* '77 (PRO) [N] Providence, RI St. Francis Chapel & City Ministry Center.
Covington, Larry '85 (AUS) [16] Austin, TX St. Louis Church; Austin, TX School for the Blind.
Covley, James (DAL) [B] Irving, TX University of Dallas.
Cowan, Anthony '95 (NY) [DD] New York, NY West Side Jesuit Community.
Cowan, Anthony '95 (SAT) Special Assignment.
Cowan, George R. '65 (BRK) [144] Brooklyn, NY St. Vincent Ferrer Church.
Cowan, Vincent '43 (MRY) Retired.
Coward, Robert *c.p.* '68 (CHI) [N] Chicago, IL Passionist Provincial Office.
Cowart, Conrad '96 (STA) [14] Jacksonville, FL Sacred Heart Church.
Cowden, David A. '82 (OKL) Okeene, OK St. Anthony's Church.
Cowell, Raymond '56 (CHI) Missionary Work.
Cowell, Raymond '56 (FgM) Society of St. James the Apostle.
Cower, D. Craig '54 (RC) Retired; [D] Rapid City, SD Priest Retirement and Aid Association.
Cowhig, Edward D. '45 (BO) [1] Beverly, MA St. Alphonsus Church; Senior Priests.
Cowie, Donald *s.m.* '61 (SAT) [F] San Antonio, TX Central Catholic High School; [M] San Antonio, TX Central Catholic Marianist Community.
Cowles, James '86 (RIC) Bedford, VA Holy Name of Mary Church.
Cox, Alan B. '76 (B) Salmon, ID St. Charles Church.
Cox, Alan B. '76 (LFT) On Duty Outside the Diocese.
Cox, Bernard '91 (IND) Bedford, IN St. Vincent de Paul Church; Mitchell, IN St. Mary/Assumption Church; [O] Indianapolis, IN International Catholic Deaf Association (Chapter No. 38).
Cox, Brian '68 (BAL) Absent on Leave.
Cox, Christopher '99 (PHX) Goodyear, AZ Saint John Vianney Church.
Cox, Msgr. Craig A. '78 (LA) Encino, CA Our Lady of Grace Church.
Cox, David D. '81 (JC) Ewing, MO Queen of Peace Church; [A] Hannibal, MO St. Thomas Aquinas Seminary.
Cox, Francis '50 (WCH) Retired.
Cox, Msgr. Gregory A. '76 (LA) [43] Los Angeles, CA St. Anastasia Church; [Y] Los Angeles, CA Catholic Charities of Los Angeles, Inc.; [Y] Los Angeles, CA Catholic Charities of Los Angeles, Inc.; [CC] Los Angeles, CA Guadalupe Center, Inc.
Cox, Msgr. Gregory A. '76 (SAC) [O] Sacramento, CA Catholic Charities of California, Inc.
Cox, James M. '98 (PH) [61] Philadelphia, PA Holy Innocents Church.
Cox, Jesse *o.p.* '87 (DET) [20] Detroit, MI St. Dominic Church.
Cox, John *o.m.i.* '87 (BO) [BB] Lowell, MA St. Joseph the Worker Shrine.
Cox, Msgr. John F. '36 (PRO) [7] Warwick, RI St. Peter Church; Retired.
Cox, John J. '53 (PH) [36] Philadelphia, PA St. Clement Church.
Cox, Joseph *o.s.b.* '91 (IND) [J] St. Meinrad, IN St. Meinrad Archabbey.
Cox, Joseph C. '46 (MAD) Retired.
Cox, Michael J. *m.s.* '37 (HRT) [M] Hartford, CT Missionaries of LaSalette, Provincial Secretary.
Cox, Noel *c.s.sp.* '55 (STA) High Springs, FL St. Madeleine Sophie Church.
Cox, Paul '54 (ALB) Retired.
Cox, Robert '80 (DAL) Absent on Leave.
Cox, William E. '42 (MIL) Retired.
Cox, William J. '56 (PH) Honey Brook, PA St. Peter Church.
Coxen, Gervis J. *m.m.* '37 (NY) [DD] Maryknoll, NY Maryknoll Fathers and Brothers.
Coy, Richard D. '00 (MEM) [11] Memphis, TN Holy Spirit Church.
Coy, William J. *m.m.* '55 (NY) [DD] Maryknoll, NY Maryknoll Fathers and Brothers.
Coyle, Alcuin *o.f.m.* '54 (NY) [35] New York, NY St. Francis of Assisi Church.
Coyle, Arthur M. '77 (BO) [A] Boston, MA St. John's Seminary School of Theology.
Coyle, Dan '89 (FRS) [3] Bakersfield, CA Sacred Heart Church.
Coyle, Msgr. Edward J. '80 (ALN) Bally, PA Most Blessed Sacrament Church.
Coyle, Eugene P. '54 (BRK) Retired; [V] Douglaston, NY Bishop Mugavero Residence.
Coyle, James '83 (ORL) Sabbatical.
Coyle, Patrick '60 (DUL) Aitkin, MN St. James Church.
Coyle, Patrick J. *s.m.* '45 (SFR) [N] San Francisco, CA Marist Center of the West.
Coyle, Robert '91 (RVC) Priests Released from Diocesan Assignment; Military Chaplains.
Coyle, Thomas J. '70 (MAD) Kieler, WI Immaculate Conception Church; Sinsinawa, WI St. Joseph Church.
Coyne, Christopher J. '86 (BO) [A] Boston, MA St. John's Seminary School of Theology.
Coyne, Edwin J. '62 (BGP) Retired.
Coyne, Emmett A.. '66 (MAN) On Duty Outside the Diocese.
Coyne, Msgr. George R. '59 (STU) Tiltonsville, OH St. Joseph Church.
Coyne, George V. *s.j.* '65 (TUC) [F] Tucson, AZ Jesuit Community of the Vatican Observatory.
Coyne, Gregory '89 (MIL) [O] Brookfield, WI Prelature of the Holy Cross and Opus Dei.
Coyne, Msgr. James F. '56 (NY) Absent on Sick leave.
Coyne, James P. '75 (SEA) Lakewood, WA St. Francis Cabrini Church.
Coyne, John J. *o.s.f.s.* '71 (FgM) Oblates of St. Francis de Sales Foreign Missions.
Coyne, Joseph '72 (HT) On Leave.
Coyne, Joseph C. '69 (HBG) Quarryville, PA St. Catherine of Siena Church.
Coyne, Liam A. '98 (ATL) [1] Marietta, GA Holy Family Church.
Coyne, Martin P. *s.j.* '66 (FgM) Provinces.
Coyne, Msgr. Michael J. '55 (CAM) Retired.
Coyne, Patrick J. '51 (BAL) Retired.
Coyne, Robert F. *m.m.* '83 (FgM) Maryknoll Foreign Missions.
Coyne, Robert R. '76 (PIT) Franklin Park Borough, PA St. John Neumann Church.
Coyne, Ronald D. '73 (BO) [13] Boston, MA St. Brendan Church.
Coyte, Thomas '74 (DEN) [10] Denver, CO Holy Cross Church.
Cozzens, Andrew '97 (STP) [1] Faribault, MN Immaculate Conception Church.
Cozzens, Donald B. '65 (CLV) [A] Wickliffe, OH St. Mary Seminary and Graduate School of Theology.
Cozzini, Robert P. '60 (NEW) Cliffside Park, NJ Epiphany Church.
Cozzubbo, Gregory P. *c.m.* '84 (PH) [70] Philadelphia, PA Immaculate Conception Church.
Crabb, John T. *s.j.* '79 (BO) Methuen, MA Holy Family Hospital, Inc.; [Q] Methuen, MA Holy Family Hospital and Medical Center; [W] Boston, MA Loyola House; [W] Boston, MA The Society of Jesus of New England-Provincial Offices.
Crable, John M. '53 (OG) Retired.
Crafts, George '65 (SAT) [R] San Antonio, TX Opus Dei Prelature of the Holy Cross and Opus Dei.
Crager, Richard *s.d.b.* '85 (BO) [N] Boston, MA Salesian Boys & Girls Club.
Craig, August Bruce *s.d.b.* '74 (SP) [E] Tampa, FL Mary Help of Christians School.
Craig, Christopher A. '93 (IND) Aurora, IN St. Mary of the Immaculate Conception Church.
Craig, Dale *s.o.l.t.* '97 (FAR) Belcourt, ND St. Ann Church; Dunseith, ND St. Louis Church; Turtle Mountain Reservation, ND (Chippewa Indians) Church.
Craig, Donald R. '74 (CHI) [127] Chicago, IL St. Mary of Perpetual Help Church.
Craig, John V. *s.j.* '77 (STL) [P] St. Louis, MO De Smet Jesuit High School Community.
Craig, Lawrence *ss.cc.* '41 (FR) [I] Fairhaven, MA Sacred Hearts Provincial House.
Craig, Lawrence J. '73 (CHI) [19] Chicago, IL Assumption Church; [19] Chicago, IL Assumption Church; [X] Chicago, IL Kolbe House.
Craig, Paul *o.f.m.cap.* '66 (FgM) Capuchin Foreign Missions.
Craig, Richard J. '61 (BO) Chelmsford, MA St. John the Evangelist Church.
Craig, Richard T. '88 (MAR) Leave of Absence.
Craig, Robert *o.f.m.cap.* '67 (PIT) Allegheny County, PA St. Francis Medical Center; [O] Pittsburgh, PA St. Augustine Friary.
Craig, Robert G. '64 (E) Cambridge Springs, PA Cambridge Springs Correction Institution.
Craig, Roderick L. '77 (FRS) Easton, CA St. Jude Church.
Craig, Samuel L. '76 (WDC) [1] Bowie, MD Ascension Church.
Craig, William R. '55 (WIL) [B] Claymont, DE Archmere Academy.
Crain, George L. *s.j.* '51 (SJ) [L] Los Gatos, CA Sacred Heart Jesuit Center.
Cramblitt, Richard E. '72 (BAL) [89] Baltimore, MD Shrine of the Sacred Heart Church.
Cramer, David W. '91 (SCR) Shohola, PA St. Ann's Church.
Cramer, Harry N. '84 (WH) Bridgeport, WV All Saints Church.
Cramer, Joseph '77 (KCK) LaCygne, KS Our Lady of Lourdes Church; Mound City, KS Sacred Heart Shrine to St. Philippine Duchesne Church; Osawatomie, KS St. Philip Neri Church.
Cramer, Terry A. '99 (ARL) Chantilly, VA St. Timothy Church.
Cramer, William N. '77 (PAT) Paterson, NJ St. Joseph Hospital; [J] Paterson, NJ St. Joseph's Hospital and Medical Center.
Crandall, Thom A. '81 (PT) Milton, FL St. Rose of Lima Church.
Crandall, William '48 (ALB) Retired.
Crane, Jeff '89 (SAT) On Leave.
Crane, Msgr. Thomas E. '57 (BUF) [3] North Tonawanda, NY St. Joseph Church.
Crane, William H. *m.s.* '41 (HRT) [M] Hartford, CT Missionaries of LaSalette, Provincial Secretary.
Crangle, Thomas *o.f.m.cap.* '73 (PAT) [12] Paterson, NJ Our Lady of Lourdes Church.
Cranor, Bernard *o.s.b.* '62 (SFE) [I] Abiquiu, NM Monastery of Christ in the Desert.
Crasta, Rudolf '89 (LUB) [3] Lubbock, TX Our Lady of Grace Church.
Craven, Msgr. Thomas P. '56 (PH) West Chester, PA St. Agnes Church.
Crawford, Brian *o.s.j.* '92 (SAC) [A] Loomis, CA Mount St. Joseph Novitiate and Seminary.
Crawford, C. Slade '65 (PT) [1] Tallahassee, FL Co-Cathedral of St. Thomas More.
Crawford, Canice *t.o.r.* '55 (ARL) [J] White Post, VA Sacred Heart Friary.
Crawford, John G. '63 (CLV) South Euclid, OH St. Gregory the Great Church.
Crawford, Larry P. '66 (IND) [19] Indianapolis, IN St. Gabriel the Archangel Church.
Crawford, Richard E. '75 (PEO) Retired.
Crawford, Robert F. *m.m.* '61 (FgM) Maryknoll Foreign Missions.
Cray, David G. *s.s.e.* '72 (NO) [I] New Orleans, LA Bishop Perry Middle School.
Craycroft, Bernard L. '57 (L) Retired.
Craycroft, George P. '58 (L) Retired.
Creagan, Daniel *s.j.* '58 (GAL) [3] Spring, TX St. Ignatius of Loyola Church.
Creagan, Michael S. '97 (STP) Stillwater, MN St. Mary Church; Stillwater, MN St. Michael Church.
Creagan, Robert F. '88 (KAL) Paw Paw, MI St. Mary Church.
Creager, Robert J. '54 (PEO) [4] Ottawa, IL St. Patrick's Church; Retired.
Creagh, Kevin G. '96 (BRK) [V] Jamaica, NY Vincentian Residence.
Creagh, Richard C. '76 (CHI) [82] Chicago, IL Holy Rosary Church.
Creagh, Thomas P. '67 (L) [33] Louisville, KY Holy Family Church.
Crean, Hugh F. '62 (SPR) [2] Westfield, MA Our Lady of the Blessed Sacrament Church.
Creane, Anthony '56 (SPR) Retired.
Creane, Anthony J. '56 (SPR) [2] Westfield, MA Our Lady of the Blessed Sacrament Church.

Creary, J. Edwin '73 (MEM) [22] Memphis, TN Our Lady Of Perpetual Help Church.
Creason, Hubert E. '58 (STL) Catawissa, MO St. James Church.
Creason, Richard H. '67 (STL) [11] St. Louis, MO Most Holy Trinity Church.
Creaven, John J. *c.ss.r.* '49 (HBG) [H] Ephrata, PA St. Clement's Mission House.
Creed, C. Patrick '51 (L) Retired.
Creed, Peter M. '67 (SY) [2] Endicott, NY St. Ambrose Church.
Creed, William E. *s.j.* '71 (CHI) [C] Chicago, IL Jesuit Community at Loyola University of Chicago.
Creeden, Brendan D. *o.s.b.* '78 (CHI) [N] Chicago, IL Monastery of the Holy Cross.
Creedon, Gerard '68 (ARL) [4] Arlington, VA St. Charles Borromeo Church.
Creedon, James *h.s.a.* (CAM) Wildwood Crest, NJ Assumption B.V.M. Church.
Creedon, James J. *m.s.a.* '79 (NOR) [F] Cromwell, CT Society of the Missionaries of the Holy Apostles.
Creedon, Joseph D. '68 (PRO) South Kingstown, RI Christ the King Church; [S] South Kingstown, RI University of Rhode Island Catholic Center.
Creel, Jesse '57 (R) Retired.
Cregan, Francis *o.a.r.* '94 (LA) [Q] Oxnard, CA St. Augustine Priory O.A.R.
Cregan, Francis A. *o.a.r.* '95 (NY) [W] Suffern, NY Good Samaritan Hospital of Suffern.
Cregan, James F. '63 (PT) [2] Tallahassee, FL Blessed Sacrament Church; Lanark Village, FL Sacred Heart of Jesus Church.
Cregan, John C. '87 (ARL) [1] Alexandria, VA Blessed Sacrament Church.
Cregan, John J. '61 (CLV) [52] Cleveland, OH Our Lady of Angels Church.
Cregan, Mark T. *c.s.c.* '83 (FR) [A] North Easton, MA Holy Cross Fathers Religious.
Cregan, Mark T. *c.s.c.* '83 (NY) [188] Bronx, NY Sacred Heart Church.
Cregan, Robert G. *s.j.* '67 (NEW) [C] Jersey City, NJ St. Peter's Preparatory School.
Cregnan, Mark T. *c.s.c.* '83 (FR) [A] North Easton, MA Stonehill College.
Cregon, Frank *o.a.r.* (NY) Suffern, NY Good Samaritan Hospital.
Crehan, Joseph *s.s.c.* '54 (PRO) [P] Bristol, RI St. Columban's Retirement House.
Crehan, Joseph L. *s.s.c.* '54 (BO) [W] Quincy, MA St. Columban's Foreign Mission Society.
Crehan, Lawrence F. '74 (PH) [75] Philadelphia, PA St. Jerome Church.
Crehan, Matthias *o.f.m.* '75 (CIN) [M] Cincinnati, OH St. John the Baptist Friary.
Creider, Philip B. '77 (OKL) Military Chaplains.
Creighton, Bernard R. *o.f.m.* '67 (PAT) [M] Butler, NJ St. Anthony Friary.
Creighton, Msgr. Edward '47 (SD) Retired.
Creighton, Gerard E. '51 (BO) Senior Priests.
Creighton, Henry *ss.cc.* '49 (FR) [I] Fairhaven, MA Sacred Hearts Provincial House.
Creighton, James J. *s.j.* '60 (CHI) [D] Chicago, IL St. Ignatius Jesuit Community; [J] Maywood, IL Foster G. McGaw Hospital of Loyola University of Chicago.
Creighton, Matthew E. *s.j.* '57 (CHI) [C] Chicago, IL Jesuit Community at Loyola University of Chicago.
Cremaldi, Angelo '60 (LAF) [3] Opelousas, LA Our Lady Queen of Angels Church.
Cremer, Matthias P. *s.c.j.* '44 (MIL) [B] Hales Corners, WI Sacred Heart School of Theology.
Cremer, Patrick M. *s.c.j.* '44 (MIL) [P] Franklin, WI Villa Maria; [Q] Milwaukee, WI Ancilla Convent.
Cremin, Michael *o.carm.* '59 (VEN) [2] Fort Myers, FL Church Of The Resurrection Of Our Lord.
Cremins, John '69 (BRK) [214] Queens, NY Our Lady of Mercy Church.
Cremonie, Louis D. '72 (HRT) [4] Manchester, CT St. James Church.
Crenner, William A. '52 (KAL) Retired.
Crepaz, Ilario '56 (NEW) [4] Union City, NJ St. Anthony of Padua Church.
Crescenzi, Rocco *f.d.p.* '43 (BO) [U] Boston, MA Don Orione Nursing Home.
Creson, Michael '87 (KNX) Soddy Daisy, TN Holy Spirit Catholic Church.
Crespin, George E. '62 (OAK) [1] Berkeley, CA St. Ambrose Church; [3] Berkeley, CA St. Joseph The Worker Church; [S] Berkeley, CA Multicultural Institute.
Cressman, Richard *s.d.b.* '80 (COL) [H] Columbus, OH Salesian Center.
Crewe, Ronald O. '63 (MIL) [16] Racine, WI Sacred Heart Church; [W] Milwaukee, WI Milwaukee Archdiocesan Council of Catholic Women.
Crews, Clyde F. '73 (L) [A] Louisville, KY Bellarmine University.
Crews, John S. '71 (SR) [H] Sonoma, CA Hanna Boys Center.
Cribben, Andrew G. *o.praem.* '94 (GB) [A] De Pere, WI St. Norbert Abbey.
Cribben, Msgr. Philip J. '62 (PH) [77] Philadelphia, PA St. Joan of Arc Church.
Cribbin, Austin J. '56 (BAK) Retired.
Cribbin, James '85 (FgM) Society of St. James the Apostle.
Cribbin, James '85 (SD) On Duty Outside the Diocese.
Cribbin, Msgr. Thomas F. '42 (BRK) [12] Brooklyn, NY Assumption of the Blessed Virgin Mary Church; Retired; [L] Brooklyn, NY Catholic Charities; [L] Brooklyn, NY Catholic Charities; [L] Brooklyn, NY Catholic Charities; [V] Brooklyn, NY St. Joseph's Priest Residence.
Cricchio, Santo *o.f.m.conv.* '91 (BAL) [26] Baltimore, MD St. Clement Mary Hofbauer Church.
Crider, Robert E. '53 (KC) Plattsburg, MO St. Ann's Church.
Crifasi, Peter D. '49 (BR) Special Assignment.
Crilly, James *c.s.v.* '56 (LAV) [1] Las Vegas, NV Guardian Angel Church.
Crilly, Marc *o.s.b.* '93 (WOR) [N] Still River, MA Benedictine Monks, St. Benedict Abbey.
Crilly, Patrick *o.s.a.* '50 (ORG) Buena Park, CA St. Pius V Church.
Crimmins, Msgr. Michael C. '70 (NY) [68] New York, NY St. Malachy's Church; [D] New York, NY Department of Education; [GG] New York, NY University Apostolate.
Crino, Patrick '88 (TUC) Yuma, AZ St. Francis of Assisi Church.
Criqui, Kenneth '63 (KC) Carrollton, MO St. Mary's Church.
Criscitelli, Anthony *t.o.r.* '80 (STP) Brooklyn Park, MN St. Gerard Church.
Criscuolo, Salvatore A. '78 (WDC) Fort Washington, MD St. Ignatius Church; Special Ministries.
Crisologo, Aurelio '59 (SD) Retired.
Crisologo, Aurelio P. '59 (SD) [23] San Diego, CA St. Charles Church.
Crisostomo, Abraham *o.f.m.conv.* '96 (CHI) [N] Chicago, IL Conventual Franciscans of St. Bonaventure Province.
Crisostomo, Abraham *o.f.m.conv.* '96 (FgM) Conventual Franciscan Foreign Missions.
Crisostomo, Michael '96 (AGN) Merizo, GU San Dimas and Our Lady of the Rosary Church; Umatac, GU San Dionisio Church.
Crisp, Michael L. '97 (SUP) Manitowish Waters, WI Our Lady Queen of Peace Church; Mercer, WI St. Isaac Jogues and Companions Church.
Crisp, Robert R. '75 (DAL) [1] Garland, TX Good Shepherd Church; [N] Dallas, TX Commission on Ecumenism.
Crispo, John R. '50 (BO) Burlington, MA St. Margaret Church.
Crispo, Roderick A. *o.f.m.* '55 (BRK) [106] Brooklyn, NY Our Lady of Peace Church.
Cristler, Richard (TLS) [10] Tulsa, OK Church of St. Mary.
Cristobal, Adrian F. '89 (AGN) Barrigada, GU San Vicente Ferrer Church.
Cristobal, Daniel *o.f.m.cap.* '59 (AGN) Talofofo, GU San Miguel Church; [F] Agana Heights, GU St. Fidelis Friary; [H] Agana, GU Secular Franciscans.
Critch, Gerard '89 (NY) [11] Yonkers, NY St. John the Baptist Church.
Critch, Gerard F. '89 (VEN) Bradenton, FL Sacred Heart Church.
Critchlow, Donald E. '82 (CC) Retired.
Crivello, Peter A. '93 (MRY) Aptos, CA Resurrection Church.
Crkva, Odilo *o.s.b.* '53 (JOL) [A] Lisle, IL Benedictine University; [J] Lisle, IL St. Procopius Abbey.
Croak, David P. '66 (DEN) [4] Aurora, CO St. Therese Church.
Croak, Thomas *c.m.* '65 (CHI) [N] Chicago, IL Vincentian Community, Congregation of the Mission, Midwest Province.
Croal, James Joseph '96 (ORG) Inactive Leave.
Croal, Thomas '58 (ORG) Retired.
Croce, Albert A. *c.s.c.* '50 (FR) [I] North Dartmouth, MA St. Joseph's Hall.
Croce, Angelus '58 (PAT) Newton, NJ St. Joseph's Church.
Crochet, Barry F. '93 (LAF) Bayou Vista, LA St. Bernadette Church.
Crocker, John R. *s.j.* '61 (CHI) [N] Chicago, IL Chicago Province of the Society of Jesus-Provincial Office.
Croell, J. Benedict *o.p.* '98 (CIN) [28] Cincinnati, OH St. Gertrude Church; [M] Cincinnati, OH St. Gertrude Priory.
Croft, George *o.m.i.* '44 (BO) [BB] Lowell, MA St. Joseph the Worker Shrine.
Crofut, Robert J. '72 (BGP) [3] Bridgeport, CT St. Andrew Church.
Croghan, James P. *s.j.* '85 (CI) [B] Chuuk, FM Xavier High School.
Croghan, James P. *s.j.* '85 (FgM) Provinces.
Croghan, John P. '75 (SY) Clinton, NY St. Mary Church; Special Assignment; [V] Clinton, NY Hamilton College Newman Center.
Croghan, Joseph F. *m.m.* '62 (NY) [DD] Maryknoll, NY Maryknoll Fathers and Brothers.
Croglio, James '80 (BUF) [D] Buffalo, NY St. Joseph's Collegiate Institute.
Crohan, Robert F. *m.m.* '62 (FgM) Maryknoll Foreign Missions.
Croisetiere, David N. '77 (SD) [14] San Diego, CA Our Lady of Refuge Church.
Croke, Alfred M. '63 (NY) Livingston Manor, NY St. Aloysius Church.
Crombie, Francis H. '68 (SPR) [18] Springfield, MA St. Paul Church.
Crommert, Paul van de '88 (NU) Olivia, MN St. Aloysius Church.
Cron, Steven D. '78 (GR) [11] Grand Rapids, MI St. James Church.
Cron, Walter '59 (NEW) [O] Englewood Cliffs, NJ St. Michael Villa.
Cronauer, David W. '73 (ALT) Absent on Leave.
Cronauer, Patrick T. *o.s.b.* '84 (GBG) [H] Latrobe, PA Saint Vincent Archabbey.
Crone, Patrick H. '71 (CIN) [77] Cincinnati, OH St. Saviour Church.
Cronin, Boniface D. *o.s.b.* '40 (PAT) [M] Newton, NJ St. Paul's Abbey.
Cronin, Brian '74 (ALB) [16] Schenectady, NY St. Paul the Apostle Church.
Cronin, Daniel C. '55 (NOR) Columbia, CT St. Columba Church.
Cronin, Daniel F. '46 (BO) Westford, MA St. Catherine of Alexandria Church; Senior Priests.
Cronin, Daniel V. '53 (PMB) [2] Lake Worth, FL St. Luke Church.
Cronin, Edward J. '80 (CHI) Palos Heights, IL St. Alexander Church.
Cronin, Frank C. '58 (STU) Powhatan Point, OH St. John Vianney Church; Shadyside, OH St. Mary Church.
Cronin, Harry C. *c.s.c.* (FTW) [J] South Bend, IN Congregation of Holy Cross, Indiana Province, Provincial House.
Cronin, James (SFE) [B] Santa Fe, NM College of Santa Fe.
Cronin, James *o.s.b.* '54 (ROC) [I] Pine City, NY Mount Saviour Monastery.
Cronin, James D. '76 (JUN) Retired.
Cronin, James E. '47 (SPR) Retired.
Cronin, Msgr. James J. '45 (BAL) [43] Baltimore, MD St. Isaac Jogues Church; Aberdeen, MD St. Joan of Arc Church; Retired.
Cronin, James J. '62 (HRT) [4] Milford, CT St. Mary's Church.
Cronin, John F. '47 (BRK) Retired; [V] Douglaston, NY Bishop Mugavero Residence.
Cronin, John P. '57 (FR) [I] Fall River, MA St. John Vianney House.
Cronin, Joseph R. '98 (HRT) [17] Waterbury, CT SS. Peter and Paul Church.
Cronin, Kevin *o.f.m.* '74 (NEW) [N] Hohokus, NJ St. Anthony of Padua.
Cronin, Michael J. '73 (CHI) Western Springs, IL St. John of the Cross Church; [U] Chicago, IL National Organization for Continuing Education of Roman Catholic Clergy, Inc.
Cronin, Msgr. Patrick '67 (SAT) [21] San Antonio, TX Prince of Peace Church.
Cronin, Msgr. Paul T. '56 (BUF) Retired; [O] Buffalo, NY Sheehan Residence for Priests.
Cronin, Peadar *ss.cc.* '72 (LA) [D] La Verne, CA Damien High School; [Q] La Verne, CA Congregation of the Sacred Hearts of Jesus and Mary.
Cronin, Peter *s.s.c.* '54 (BUF) [M] Silver Creek, NY St. Columbans on the Lake, Home for the Aged; [P] Silver Creek, NY Missionary Sisters of St. Columban, St. Columban's on the Lake.
Cronin, Richard '60 (JC) Retired.
Cronin, Richard J. *o.s.b.* '66 (PAT) [M] Morristown, NJ St. Mary's Abbey.
Cronin, Robert *s.o.l.t.* '83 (CC) [H] Robstown, TX Society of Our Lady of the Most Holy Trinity.
Cronin, Robert '83 (FAR) Belcourt, ND St. Anthony Church.
Cronin, Robert J. *s.o.l.t.* '83 (FAR) Belcourt, ND St. Ann Church; Turtle Mountain Reservation, ND (Chippewa Indians) Church.
Cronin, Robert W. '52 (NOR) Retired.
Cronin, Sylvester J. '88 (MET) Highland Park, NJ St. Paul the Apostle Church.
Cronin, Thomas '69 (KC) On Duty Outside the Diocese.
Cronin, Thomas '69 (RNO) Fernley, NV St. Robert Bellarmine Church.
Cronin, Thomas J. *s.j.* '53 (BR) [J] Convent, LA Manresa House of Retreats.
Cronin, Timothy P. '85 (STL) [5] Florissant, MO St. Dismas Church.
Cronin, W. Vincent '43 (HRT) Retired.
Cronin, William F. *o.s.cam.* (WOR) [R] Whitinsville, MA St. Camillus Institute, Inc.
Cronin, William F. *o.s.cam.* '76 (MIL) [P] Wauwatosa, WI St. Camillus Provincialate.
Cronk, James F. '69 (DET) Novi, MI St. James Church.
Cronkleton, Thomas E., Jr. '86 (CHY) Pine Bluffs, WY St. Paul's Church.

Cronogue, Michael P. *s.s.e.* '77 (BUR) [E] Colchester, VT Society of St. Edmund.
Crook, David G. '81 (BEL) Leave of Absence.
Crooker, Robert W. *c.s.b.* '53 (GAL) [Q] Houston, TX Residence of the Basilian Fathers of the University of St. Thomas.
Crookes, Brian '53 (VIC) St. John, TX St. John the Baptist Church.
Crookston, James F. '71 (ALT) [12] Altoona, PA St. Rose of Lima Church.
Crookston, Michael J. '80 (GBG) Indiana, PA St. Thomas More University Church.
Crosara, Lawrence *s.x.* '58 (MIL) [B] Franklin, WI Xaverian Missionary Fathers College Seminary.
Crosby, Msgr. Charles E. '56 (MAN) [1] Manchester, NH St. Joseph Church.
Crosby, Dan *o.f.m.cap.* '64 (LC) [G] Marathon City, WI St. Anthony Retreat Center; [H] Marathon City, WI St. Anthony Retreat Center.
Crosby, Donald F. *s.j.* '68 (OAK) [N] Berkeley, CA Jesuit Community at Jesuit School of Theology at Berkeley.
Crosby, Donald W. '89 (JC) Absent on Leave.
Crosby, John M. '52 (CHI) Retired.
Crosby, Michael *o.f.m.* (HON) [2] Honolulu, HI Co-Cathedral of St. Theresa of the Child Jesus.
Crosby, Michael *o.f.m.* '64 (STL) [T] Dittmer, MO Il Ritiro-The Little Retreat.
Crosby, Michael *o.f.m.cap.* '66 (MIL) [12] Milwaukee, WI St. Benedict the Moor Church.
Crosby, Neil A. '81 (CLV) Stow, OH Holy Family Church.
Crosby, Theodore A. '00 (OG) [1] Watertown, NY Holy Family Church.
Crosby, Vincent de Paul *o.s.b.* '72 (GBG) [H] Latrobe, PA Saint Vincent Archabbey.
Crosier, Msgr. Raymond '75 (AMA) [8] Amarillo, TX St. Joseph's Church.
Cross, Charles V. '60 (BIR) [5] Birmingham, AL Blessed Sacrament Church.
Cross, Michael L. '62 (MRY) Felton, CA St. John's Church.
Cross, Peter '60 (DAV) Retired.
Cross, Robert A. '52 (CHI) Retired.
Cross, William D. '85 (STU) Mingo Junction, OH St. Agnes Church.
Cross, William H. '74 (CIN) [45] Cincinnati, OH St. John Vianney Church.
Crosse, Charles '53 (SEA) Retired.
Crossen, Jason K. '00 (DAV) [3] Davenport, IA Holy Family Church.
Crosser, Raymond G. '56 (ALT) Retired.
Crossin, John W. *o.s.f.s.* '76 (ARL) [J] Alexandria, VA Oblates of St. Francis de Sales Residence.
Crossman, James '46 (DUL) [1] Duluth, MN Cathedral of Our Lady of the Rosary.
Crossmeyer, Robert *c.p.* '88 (BIR) [7] Birmingham, AL Holy Family Church.
Crossmyer, Robert *c.p.* (BIR) [I] Birmingham, AL Congregation of the Passion: Holy Family Community, Inc.
Crosthwait, Msgr. Joseph H. '41 (GAL) Retired.
Crosthwaite, Alejandro *o.p.* (ANC) [1] Anchorage, AK Holy Family Church.
Croteau, Fernand A. '57 (MAN) Hooksett, NH Holy Rosary Church.
Croteau, Francois A. '42 (HRT) Retired.
Croteau, Roger H. '67 (MAN) Derry, NH Holy Cross Church.
Crotty, Columban *ss.cc.* '58 (FR) [I] Fairhaven, MA Sacred Hearts Provincial House; [I] Fairhaven, MA National Center of the Enthronement.
Crotty, Desmond G. '72 (NO) [32] New Orleans, LA St. Francis of Assisi Church.
Crotty, John C. *s.s.j.* '55 (BAL) [S] Baltimore, MD St. Joseph's Manor.
Crotty, John M. '47 (NY) Retired.
Crotty, Msgr. Matthew M. '44 (BAK) Special Assignment.
Crotty, Thomas M. *o.s.m.* '60 (CHI) [N] Chicago, IL Order of Friar Servants of Mary (Servites) United States of America Province, Inc.
Crotty, Vincent *c.ss.r.* '49 (RVC) Bethpage, NY St. Martin of Tours Church.
Crouse, William S. '59 (ALT) Penns Valley, PA Blessed Kateri Tekakwitha Church; Bellefonte, PA State Correctional Institution.
Crowe, Francis R. *o.p.* '47 (CHI) [N] River Forest, IL St. Thomas Aquinas Priory.
Crowe, George W. '65 (PH) [122] Philadelphia, PA Our Lady of Lourdes Church.
Crowe, Hugh '58 (LA) [44] Los Angeles, CA St. Ann Church.
Crowe, Martin *c.ss.r.* '40 (BRK) [107] Brooklyn, NY Our Lady of Perpetual Help Basilica Church.
Crowe, Raymond *o.m.i.* '54 (MIA) [2] Miami, FL Christ the King Church.
Crowe, Msgr. William A. '47 (PT) Panama City, FL St. Dominic Church.
Crowley, Alan N. *o.carm.* 41 (BO) [P] Peabody, MA Catholic Information Center; [BB] Peabody, MA St. Theresa Carmelite Chapel.
Crowley, Bonaventure *o.f.m.conv.* '47 (LAN) [3] Lansing, MI Holy Cross Church.
Crowley, Cale J. *s.s.* '69 (BAL) [S] Baltimore, MD Sulpician Provincial House.
Crowley, Charles G. *s.j.* '51 (BO) [W] Boston, MA Loyola House.
Crowley, Charles J. '53 (KAL) Retired.
Crowley, Daniel (BO) South Weymouth, MA South Shore Hospital.
Crowley, Daniel J. '68 (BO) Braintree, MA St. Francis of Assisi Church.
Crowley, Dennis J. '89 (PAT) Morristown, NJ Assumption of the Blessed Virgin Mary Church.
Crowley, Edmund G. '70 (MAN) Military Chaplains.
Crowley, Edward T. *c.s.sp.* '50 (LR) Conway, AR St. Joseph's Church.
Crowley, Francis *c.m.* '57 (KC) [J] Kansas City, MO Vincentian Parish Mission Center.
Crowley, Francis J. '53 (BO) Military & VA Chaplains.
Crowley, Francis J. '53 (PRO) Providence, RI Veterans Administration Hospital.
Crowley, J. David '54 (PIT) [49] Pittsburgh, PA Holy Angels Church.
Crowley, James M. *o.m.i.* '86 (CHR) Camden, SC Our Lady of Perpetual Help Church.
Crowley, John A. '61 (PMB) Vero Beach, FL St. John of the Cross Church.
Crowley, Kenan *o.f.m.cap.* '44 (PIT) [30] Pittsburgh, PA Our Lady of the Angels Church.
Crowley, Kevin J. '64 (BO) Absent on Leave; Emergency Response Group.
Crowley, Patrick J. *ss.cc.* '72 (OAK) [3] Alameda, CA St. Joseph Basilica Church.
Crowley, Paul G. *s.j.* '92 (SJ) [B] Santa Clara, CA Santa Clara University.
Crowley, R. Kevin '68 (MET) Edison, NJ Guardian Angels Church.
Crowley, Richard P. '62 (BO) Middleborough, MA Sacred Heart Church.
Crowley, Stephen L. '55 (HRT) Retired.
Crowley, Thomas '87 (DM) [2] Council Bluffs, IA Our Lady, Queen of Apostles Church.
Crowley, Thomas F. '56 (LC) Cadott, WI St. Rose of Lima Church; Drywood, WI St. Anthony Church.
Crowley, Thomas F. '76 (WDC) Greenbelt, MD St. Hugh Church.
Crowley, Thomas J. '51 (BUF) Retired; [O] Buffalo, NY Sheehan Residence for Priests.
Crowley, Timothy '76 (ANC) [6] Anchorage, AK Our Lady of Guadalupe Church.
Crowley, Timothy '76 (LAN) On Duty Outside the Diocese.
Crowley, William '74 (B) Idaho Falls, ID Christ the King Church.
Crowley, William P. *c.s.sp.* '60 (SFR) [9] San Francisco, CA St. Brendan Church.
Cruces, Angel (NY) [45] New York, NY Holy Cross Church.
Crum, Thomas J. '75 (Y) Rootstown, OH St. Peter of the Fields Church.
Crum, William '76 (NEW) [1] Elizabeth, NJ St. Mary of the Assumption Church.
Crumbley, Charles W. '67 (Y) [4] Warren, OH St. James Church.
Crumley, William *c.s.c.* '64 (LAF) Charenton, LA Immaculate Conception Church.
Crumlish, Msgr. Richard C. '45 (BUF) [63] Buffalo, NY St. Teresa Church; Retired.
Crummy, Michael E. '86 (MET) Milford, NJ St. Edward the Confessor Church.
Crunican, James '63 (P) Retired.
Cruz, David R. (LUB) Hale Center, TX St. Theresa's Church.
Cruz, Domingo '73 (HT) Kraemer, LA St. Lawrence the Martyr Church.
Cruz, Faustino *s.m.* '88 (OAK) [A] Berkeley, CA Franciscan School of Theology.
Cruz, Francisco *c.m.* (BO) [1] Malden, MA Immaculate Conception Church.
Cruz, Gilbert '81 (LA) San Pedro, CA Mary, Star of the Sea Church.
Cruz, Gilbert J. '81 (SJN) Retired.
Cruz, Gustavo '74 (LAV) Bunkerville, NV La Virgen de Guadalupe Church.
Cruz, Hector *s.m.* '77 (MRY) Santa Cruz, CA Star of the Sea Church; [F] Santa Cruz, CA Society of Mary, Marists.
Cruz, Jesse '00 (LUB) [5] Lubbock, TX St. Elizabeth University Church.
Cruz, Johnny '91 (ARE) Isabela, PR St. Anthony Church.
Cruz, Johnny '91 (SJN) [6] Guaynabo, PR San Pedro Martir de Verona Church.
Cruz, Jose Antonio '83 (SJN) [4] San Juan, PR San Antonio Church.
Cruz, Luciano '86 (PAT) [2] Paterson, NJ St. Agnes Church.
Cruz, Luis A. '86 (PCE) [2] Ponce, PR Christ the King Church.
Cruz, Manuel '80 (NEW) Newark, NJ St. Michael Medical Center.
Cruz, Msgr. Manuel '93 (NEW) [G] Newark, NJ Saint Michael's Medical Center.
Cruz, Michael *o.f.m.cap.* (AGN) [F] Agana Heights, GU St. Fidelis Friary.
Cruz, Msgr. Remberto '49 (SJN) Retired.
Cruz, Renato B. '81 (NY) [204] Staten Island, NY Holy Child Church.
Cruz, Robert-Joel T. '96 (HT) [1] Thibodaux, LA St. Joseph Co-Church.
Cruz Davila, Carlos D. '80 (SJN) [9] San Juan, PR Santa Catalina Laboure Church.
Cryan, James F. *o.s.f.s.* '65 (TOL) [K] Toledo, OH Oblates of St. Francis de Sales.
Cryan, John '81 (NEW) [21] Jersey City, NJ Church of Our Lady of Sorrows.
Cryan, John J. '81 (NEW) [20] Jersey City, NJ Our Lady of Mercy Church.
Cryans, Andrew W. '75 (MAN) Milford, NH St. Patrick Church.
Crynes, Msgr. J. Peter '67 (SCR) Shavertown, PA St. Therese Church.
Csaszar, James C. '99 (COL) Zanesville, OH St. Nicholas Church; [C] Zanesville, OH Bishop Rosecrans High School.
Cser, Ladislaus *s.j.* '45 (RVC) St. James, NY SS. Philip and James Church; Retired.
Csete, Ivan L. '81 (NY) Forestburgh, NY St. Thomas Aquinas Church.
Csizmar, Richard A. '68 (BUF) Albion, NY St. Mary Assumption Church; Albion, NY St. Joseph Church.
Csorba, Dominic *o.f.m.* '62 (NY) [115] New York, NY St. Stephen of Hungary Church.
Csorba, Dominic L. *o.f.m.* '35 (NY) [HH] New York, NY Hungarian Catholic League of America, Inc.
Cuadrado, Angel *o.de.m.* '14 (SJN) [40] San Juan, PR Nuestra Senora de la Merced Church.
Cuadrado, Hector F. *c.m.f.* '91 (SJN) [9] Bayamon, PR San Jose Church.
Cuadros, Jesus '66 (BRK) [157] Queens, NY Blessed Sacrament Church.
Cuario, Dindo '91 (DAL) [13] Dallas, TX St. Augustine Catholic Church.
Cuccaro, John J. '79 (PBR) McKeesport, PA St. Nicholas Church.
Cuccia, Sal *o.praem.* (GB) [6] De Pere, WI St. Norbert Campus Ministry Church.
Cuddigan, John *s.j.* '62 (SD) [36] San Diego, CA St. Therese Church.
Cuddihy, Msgr. William '56 (SD) Retired.
Cuddy, John '53 (SAV) Macon, GA St. Joseph Church.
Cuddy, William F. '79 (BO) Military & VA Chaplains.
Cudemo, Nicholas V. '63 (PH) Retired.
Cudnik, Chester C. '48 (CLV) [10] Cleveland, OH St. Barbara Church; Retired.
Cuenin, Walter H. '70 (BO) [6] Newton, MA Our Lady Help of Christians Church.
Cuesta, Benedicto '51 (SFE) Retired.
Cuesta-Padilla, Lazaro *s.f.* '69 (SFE) Chimayo, NM Holy Family Church.
Cuevas, Geronimo E. '86 (MRY) [3] Salinas, CA St. Mary of the Nativity Church.
Cuevas, Jose Luis *m.c.c.j.* '74 (CIN) [M] Cincinnati, OH Comboni Missionaries (Verona Fathers)-Comboni Mission Center.
Cuevas, Jose Luis '76 (LA) [Q] Azusa, CA Casa Comboni Mission Seminary.
Cuevas, Randy M. '82 (BR) Donaldsonville, LA Ascension of Our Lord Jesus Christ Church.
Cuevas, Wilson '81 (ELP) [6] El Paso, TX Corpus Christi Church.
Cuff, John P. *m.m.* '69 (FgM) Maryknoll Foreign Missions.
Culhane, Alberic *o.s.b.* '57 (SCL) [B] Collegeville, MN St. John's University; [I] Collegeville, MN St. John's Abbey, of the Order of St. Benedict.
Culhane, Eugene K. *s.j.* '45 (NY) [DD] New York, NY Murray-Weigel Hall.
Culhane, Msgr. Thomas '47 (KCK) [2] Overland Park, KS Holy Cross Church; Retired.
Culkin, Msgr. Francis J. '44 (SY) [2] Rome, NY St. Mary of the Assumption Church; Retired.
Culkin, Harry M. '42 (BRK) Retired; [V] Douglaston, NY Bishop Mugavero Residence.
Culkin, J. Stewart '71 (ARL) Vienna, VA St. Mark's Church.
Culkin, Michael '78 (WDC) On Duty Outside the Archdiocese.
Cull, Msgr. Lawrence W. '69 (NEW) Ramsey, NJ St. Paul Church.
Cull, Paul J. '45 (CHI) [3] Waukegan, IL St. Dismas Church; Retired.
Cullen, Bernard J. *o.c.s.o.* '48 (DUB) [K] Peosta, IA New Melleray Abbey, Order of Cistercians of the Strict Observance.
Cullen, Daniel *s.m.a.* '47 (NEW) [N] Tenafly, NJ Society of African Missions, Provincialate, S.M.A. Fathers.
Cullen, Donald '71 (KCK) Roeland Park, KS St. Agnes Church.
Cullen, Francis J. '54 (LA) Retired.
Cullen, George H. '48 (CHI) Retired.
Cullen, Msgr. J. Peter '67 (BGP) New Canaan, CT St.

Aloysius Church.
Cullen, John F. '41 (PH) Retired.
Cullen, John J. '99 (BUF) Amherst, NY St. Leo the Great Church.
Cullen, Kevin L. *s.j.* (DEN) [31] Denver, CO St. Ignatius Loyola Church.
Cullen, Martin T. '57 (FAR) Retired.
Cullen, Patrick P. '68 (BIR) [1] Birmingham, AL St. Paul's Church.
Cullen, Paul M. *o.s.m.* '65 (CHI) [14] Chicago, IL Annunciata Church; [N] Chicago, IL Order of Friar Servants of Mary (Servites) United States of America Province, Inc.
Cullen, Robert B. *s.j.* '58 (BAL) [D] Baltimore, MD Loyola Blakefield.
Cullen, Thomas F. '53 (CLV) Westlake, OH St. Ladislas Church; Retired.
Cullen, Msgr. Thomas J. '52 (GAL) Texas City, TX St. Mary Church.
Cullen, Msgr. Thomas J. '52 (MOB) On Leave from the Archdiocese.
Cullen, Msgr. Thomas J. '53 (MOB) Retired.
Cullen, William '48 (JOL) Retired.
Cullen, William '83 (JKS) Canton, MS Sacred Heart Church; Canton, MS Holy Child Jesus Church; Carthage, MS St. Anne Church; [I] Jackson, MS Jackson Diocese Educational Services, Inc.
Cullen, William J. *s.j.* '65 (BGP) [P] Fairfield, CT The Fairfield Jesuit Community-Fairfield University.
Cullen, William J. *s.j.* '65 (BO) [W] Boston, MA The Society of Jesus of New England-Provincial Offices.
Culleton, James P. '46 (PEO) Retired.
Culleton, Thomas L. '91 (SLC) Roosevelt, UT St. Helen's Church.
Culley, Brian *c.m.f.* '84 (AUS) San Marcos, TX St. John the Evangelist Church.
Culley, Thomas D. *s.j.* '65 (NO) [P] New Orleans, LA Ignatius Residence.
Culligan, Kevin *o.c.d.* (CHI) [N] Chicago, IL Discalced Carmelite Friars; Edith Stein House of Studies.
Culligan, Martin J. *c.m.* '57 (STL) [P] St. Louis, MO Lazarist Residence.
Culligan, Michael A. '59 (SR) Petaluma, CA St. James Church.
Cullinan, John '46 (PHX) [14] Phoenix, AZ St. Joan of Arc Church.
Cullinan, John F. '46 (PHX) Retired.
Cullinane, Brian *o.f.m.* '71 (PAT) Little Falls, NJ Our Lady of the Holy Angels Church.
Cullinane, Briant *o.f.m. conv.* '58 (R) Burlington, NC Blessed Sacrament Church; [E] Burlington, NC Conventual Franciscans.
Cullinane, Jeremiah J. '59 (DAL) [M] Irving, TX Diocese of Dallas Campus Ministry.
Cullinane, Jeremiah J. '59 (WH) On Duty Outside the Diocese.
Cullinane, John '56 (BRK) [171] Queens, NY St. Genevieve Church.
Cullings, David Ronald '67 (P) [5] Eugene, OR St. Peter Church.
Culloty, John P. '72 (BO) [4] Norwood, MA St. Timothy Church.
Culnane, William R. '60 (SCR) [5] Wilkes-Barre, PA St. Dominic Church.
Culotta, Joachim N. *o.p.* '64 (DET) [2] St. Clair Shores, MI St. Gertrude Church.
Culotta, Joseph '83 (BIR) Decatur, AL St. Ann's Church.
Culotta, Msgr. Salvador J. '53 (BEA) Retired.
Culotta, Thomas C. '61 (HRT) East Berlin, CT Sacred Heart Church.
Culver, Garry '64 (DM) West Des Moines, IA Sacred Heart Church.
Culver, James A. '55 (SY) [4] Rome, NY St. Peter Church.
Culver, Richard J. '85 (OAK) Bay Point, CA Our Lady Queen of the World Church.
Culver, Msgr. T. Joseph '63 (GAL) La Marque, TX Our Lady Queen of Peace Church.
Cumberland, Matthew T. '92 (LA) La Puente, CA St. Joseph Church.
Cumiskey, Thomas M. *o.p.* '55 (DAL) [K] Irving, TX Dominican Priory of St. Albert the Great.
Cummings, Brian J. *s.s.e.* '96 (BUR) [E] Colchester, VT Society of St. Edmund.
Cummings, Carl '75 (BAL) Sabbatical.
Cummings, Charles *o.c.s.o.* '71 (SLC) [F] Huntsville, UT Abbey of Our Lady of the Holy Trinity of the Order of Cistercians.
Cummings, Charles J. '68 (SCR) [2] Williamsport, PA Ascension Church.
Cummings, Gabriel '84 (SAV) [10] Savannah, GA St. Peter the Apostle Church.
Cummings, Msgr. George '43 (SP) Citrus Springs, FL St. Elizabeth Ann Seton Church; Retired.
Cummings, James (OAK) [1] Alameda, CA St. Albert Church.
Cummings, John J. '88 (LFT) Lake Village, IN St. Augusta Church.
Cummings, Juniper *o.f.m.conv.* '50 (FgM) Conventual Franciscan Foreign Missions.
Cummings, Leo B. *m.s.* '66 (ATL) [2] Marietta, GA Church of St. Ann.
Cummings, Leo P. '64 (SCR) [I] Carbondale, PA Marian Community Hospital.
Cummings, Maurice *o.carm.* '71 (SPR) [L] Williamstown, MA Mount Carmel Retreat Center.
Cummings, McLean A. '98 (BAL) Severna Park, MD St. John the Evangelist Church.
Cummings, P. Jose Emilio *c.m.* '72 (SJN) Rio Grande, PR Cristo Rey Church.
Cummings, Patrick '78 (GAL) [9] Houston, TX Annunciation Church; [K] Houston, TX The Catholic Chaplain Corps.
Cummings, Paul '55 (LAN) Retired.
Cummings, Paul J. '55 (LAN) Ovid, MI Holy Family Church.
Cummings, Thomas W. *s.j.* '69 (DEN) [M] Denver, CO Xavier Jesuit Center.
Cummini, Charles J. *o.c.s.o.* (SLC) [A] Huntsville, UT Abbey of Our Lady of the Holy Trinity.
Cummins, Anthony O. '65 (SAT) Boerne, TX St. Peter the Apostle Church.
Cummins, Charles E. '68 (SLC) [3] Ogden, UT St. Joseph's Church.
Cummins, Charles T. '68 (SLC) Huntsville, UT St. Florence Catholic Community Church; [H] Ogden, UT Weber State University, Newman Center.
Cummins, Charles T. '69 (LA) On Duty Outside the Archdiocese.
Cummins, Joseph V. *c.m.* '72 (PH) [156] Philadelphia, PA St. Vincent de Paul Church.
Cummins, Michael '95 (KNX) [1] Knoxville, TN Cathedral of the Sacred Heart of Jesus.
Cummins, Michael J. *c.m.* '77 (BRK) [V] Queens Village, NY DePaul Residence.
Cummins, Robert L. '82 (RIC) [4] Chesapeake, VA St. Therese of Lisieux Church.
Cummins, Timothy '45 (FRS) Retired.
Cuneo, Msgr. J. James '67 (BGP) [1] Stratford, CT Holy Name of Jesus Church.
Cuneo, James J. '63 (DEN) [4] Arvada, CO Spirit of Christ Church.
Cung, Ephrem M. Vu Khiem *c.m.c.* (SPC) [E] Carthage, MO Congregation of the Mother Co-Redemptrix, United States Assumption Province.
Cunha, Egionor (NEW) Military Chaplains.
Cunnane, Jarlath '77 (LA) [94] Los Angeles, CA St. Thomas the Apostle Church.
Cunnane, Michael A. '61 (SD) Santee, CA Guardian Angels Church.
Cunneen, Sean '67 (NEW) New Providence, NJ Our Lady of Peace Church.
Cunney, Henry H. '59 (BO) Nahant, MA St. Thomas Aquinas Church.
Cunniff, Charles *c.s.p.* (GR) Grand Rapids, MI Chapel of St. Paul-Catholic Information Center.
Cunniff, Declan J. *o.s.b.* '68 (NEW) [N] Newark, NJ Newark Abbey.
Cunniff, Hubert F. *s.j.* '38 (BO) [W] Weston, MA Campion Health Center, Inc.
Cunniff, Vincent '53 (P) Retired.
Cunniffe, James A. *s.c.j.* '57 (JKS) Hernando, MS Holy Spirit Church; [F] Nesbit, MS St. Michael Community House.
Cunningham, Ambrose '50 (PEO) [2] Rock Island, IL Sacred Heart Church.
Cunningham, Augustine W. *o.s.b.* '61 (RIC) [L] Richmond, VA Mary Mother of the Church Abbey.
Cunningham, Christopher '90 (LA) Redondo Beach, CA St. Lawrence Martyr Church.
Cunningham, Donald D. '87 (SY) Oxford, NY St. Joseph Church.
Cunningham, Donald M. *s.j.* '64 (STL) [P] St. Louis, MO White House Retreat Jesuit Community; [T] St. Louis, MO White House Retreat.
Cunningham, Douglas (SY) Norwich, NY St. Bartholomew the Apostle Church.
Cunningham, Douglas '87 (SY) Norwich, NY St. Paul Church.
Cunningham, Edward *o.m.i.* '58 (WIN) Minnesota City, MN St. Paul's Church.
Cunningham, Gerard M. '93 (WDC) Military Chaplains.
Cunningham, James *c.s.s.* '50 (BO) [Z] Waltham, MA Stigmatine Fathers and Brothers.
Cunningham, James '95 (BRK) [154] Queens, NY St. Bartholomew's Church.
Cunningham, James B. '89 (BUF) [4] Buffalo, NY St. Agnes Church.
Cunningham, James J. '61 (NY) [164] Bronx, NY St. Mary Church; Bronx, NY Bronx Psychiatric Center.
Cunningham, John E. '51 (DM) Retired.
Cunningham, John F. *o.p.* '53 (PRO) [P] Providence, RI St. Thomas Aquinas Priory at Providence College.
Cunningham, John F. '56 (LA) [71] Los Angeles, CA St. Joan of Arc Church; Retired.
Cunningham, John F. '74 (PHX) [5] Mesa, AZ St. Bridget Church.
Cunningham, John H. '65 (ALX) Retired.
Cunningham, John J. '56 (CHI) [173] Chicago, IL St. Priscilla Church.
Cunningham, John P. '79 (BAL) [92] Baltimore, MD St. Thomas More Church.
Cunningham, Msgr. Joseph C. '71 (PH) Wayne, PA St. Isaac Jogues Church.
Cunningham, Joseph L. '56 (MIL) Retired.
Cunningham, Joseph L. '63 (BRK) [174] Queens, NY St. Gregory the Great Church.
Cunningham, Kieran P. *o.s.b.* '62 (SEA) [G] Olympia, WA Providence St. Peter Hospital; [L] Lacey, WA St. Martin's Abbey.
Cunningham, Leonard A. *o.c.s.o.* '50 (CHR) [E] Moncks Corner, SC Mepkin Abbey.
Cunningham, Lloyd *s.v.d.* '81 (CHI) [B] Techny, IL Divine Word Residence; [N] Chicago, IL Divine Word Theologate; [N] Techny, IL Society of the Divine Word, Provincial Headquarter-Chicago Prov.
Cunningham, Mark '99 (ALB) Herkimer, NY St. Francis de Sales Church.
Cunningham, Michael '86 (OAK) [4] Concord, CA Queen of All Saints Church.
Cunningham, Nicholas J. '79 (TOL) Kelley's Island, OH St. Michael Church; Put-In-Bay, OH Mother of Sorrows Church.
Cunningham, Msgr. Patrick '41 (PT) Retired.
Cunningham, Peter J. '56 (MOB) [12] Mobile, AL St. Mary Church.
Cunningham, Philip *c.s.p.* '56 (SFR) [32] San Francisco, CA Old St. Mary's Church.
Cunningham, Phillip J. *c.s.p.* '56 (NY) [DD] Jamaica Estates, NY Paulist Fathers Generalate.
Cunningham, Msgr. Richard G. '57 (BO) [A] Boston, MA St. John's Seminary School of Theology.
Cunningham, Robert *s.j.* '55 (FgM) Provinces.
Cunningham, Msgr. Robert J. (BUF) [T] Buffalo, NY SS. Columba-Brigid Montessori School.
Cunningham, Msgr. Robert J. '69 (BUF) [O] Buffalo, NY Bishop's Residence.
Cunningham, Sebastian *o.f.m.conv.* '60 (LSC) [D] Mesilla Park, NM Holy Cross Retreat and Friary.
Cunningham, Vianney *t.o.r.* '70 (ORL) [2] Lakeland, FL St. Anthony's Church; [E] Lakeland, FL Florida Southern College Newman Center.
Cunningham, Vincent P. *s.m.m.* '60 (RVC) West Islip, NY Good Samaritan Hospital Medical Center; [M] Bay Shore, NY Montfort Missionaries.
Cunnion, Theodore J. *s.j.* '43 (NY) [DD] New York, NY Murray-Weigel Hall.
Cuny, W. Timothy *o.s.a.* '70 (CHI) [N] Olympia Fields, IL The Augustinians-Provincialate.
Cuomo, Rocco A. '64 (TR) Freehold, NJ St. Rose of Lima Church.
Cupich, Blase '75 (RC) [D] Rapid City, SD Priest Retirement and Aid Association.
Cupp, Edwin '69 (WH) Absent on Sick Leave.
Cupple, Gerard J. '85 (DET) Lincoln Park, MI St. Henry Church.
Curalli, Joseph *c.ss.r.* '78 (KC) [31] Kansas City, MO Our Lady of Perpetual Help Church; [J] Kansas City, MO Redemptorists of Kansas City.
Curci, Richard G. '72 (GBG) Arnold, PA All Saints Church; New Kensington, PA Mt. St. Peter Church.
Curcio, Ralph V. '61 (NY) [1] Port Chester, NY Our Lady of Mercy Church.
Curesky, Mark L. *o.f.m.conv.* '75 (BAL) [S] Ellicott City, MD Order of Friars Minor Conventual.
Curesky, Mark L. *o.f.m.conv.* '75 (FgM) Conventual Franciscan Foreign Missions.
Curiel, James Anthony *o.c.d.* '95 (SAT) [18] San Antonio, TX Basilica of The National Shrine of Our Lady of Mt. Carmel and St. Therese, Discalced Carmelite Fathers; [M] San Antonio, TX Discalced Carmelites (Prov. of St. Therese).
Curley, Augustine J. *o.s.b.* '88 (NEW) [N] Newark, NJ Newark Abbey.
Curley, John R. *s.m.m.* '51 (RVC) [J] Huntington, NY St. Joseph's Guest Home for the Aged, Inc.
Curley, Msgr. Joseph K. '62 (RVC) Centereach, NY Assumption of the Blessed Virgin Mary Church.
Curley, Martin W. '56 (RVC) West Hempstead, NY St. Thomas, the Apostle Church; Retired.
Curley, Patrick J. '70 (JKS) Yazoo City, MS St. Mary Church; Yazoo City, MS St. Francis Church.
Curley, Robert '51 (RVC) Retired.
Curley, Terence P. (CLV) [Z] Cleveland, OH National Catholic Ministry to the Bereaved, Inc.
Curley, Terence P. '72 (BO) Dedham, MA St. Susanna Church.
Curley, Thomas J. '39 (CHI) [202] Chicago, IL St. Thomas More Church; Retired.
Curley, Thomas J. '70 (NY) Chester, NY St. Columba Church.
Curnutte, William G. '82 (SLC) Retired.
Curran, Anthony '72 (ALB) [9] Schenectady, NY St. John the Evangelist Church.
Curran, Anthony T. '67 (ATL) Lawrenceville, GA St. Lawrence Church.
Curran, Charles E. '58 (ROC) On Duty Outside the Diocese.
Curran, David *c.i.c.m.* '71 (SAT) [B] San Antonio, TX Missionhurst Formation Community.

Curran, Francis D. '50 (CLV) Willoughby, OH Immaculate Conception Church.
Curran, Msgr. Francis L. '38 (MAN) Retired.
Curran, Francis T. '69 (GI) Kimball, NE St. Joseph's Church.
Curran, George A. *s.j.* '51 (DET) [P] Clarkston, MI Colombiere Center.
Curran, Gerald X. '48 (Y) Retired.
Curran, Msgr. Hugh D. '54 (NY) Pelham Manor, NY Our Lady of Perpetual Help Church.
Curran, Hugh J. *c.s.b.* '51 (GAL) Missouri City, TX Holy Family Church.
Curran, James *s.d.b.* '51 (PAT) [3] Paterson, NJ St. Anthony's Church.
Curran, James *c.m.f.* '83 (ORG) Placentia, CA St. Joseph Church.
Curran, James P. '00 (RIC) Williamsburg, VA St. Bede's Church.
Curran, James P. '63 (CAM) Glassboro, NJ Our Lady of Lourdes Church.
Curran, John '54 (WCH) Retired.
Curran, John *o.f.m.conv.* '71 (ELP) [17] El Paso, TX Our Lady of Mt. Carmel Church.
Curran, John *l.c.* '96 (MAN) [A] Center Harbor, NH Immaculate Conception Apostolic School.
Curran, John F. '46 (HRT) Retired.
Curran, John J. *s.j.* '59 (FgM) Provinces.
Curran, Joseph L. '76 (BO) Watertown, MA Sacred Heart Church.
Curran, Michael J. '81 (BRK) Released from Diocesan Assignment.
Curran, Oliver '76 (GLP) Pinetop, AZ St. Mary of the Angels Church.
Curran, Patrick J. '55 (HRT) [6] West Hartford, CT St. Thomas the Apostle Church.
Curran, Patrick J. '55 (SLC) On Duty Outside the Diocese.
Curran, Paul E. '59 (BO) Whitman, MA Holy Ghost Church; Senior Priests.
Curran, Msgr. Paul F. '57 (PH) Huntingdon Valley, PA St. Albert the Great Church.
Curran, Peter *o.m.i.* '71 (FgM) Oblates Foreign Missions.
Curran, Richard G. '76 (BO) Hanover, MA St. Mary of the Sacred Heart Church; Emergency Response Group.
Curran, Robert F. *s.j.* '74 (SFR) [C] San Francisco, CA University of San Francisco.
Curran, Robert F. *s.j.* '74 (SJ) [L] Los Gatos, CA Sacred Heart Jesuit Center.
Curran, Thomas B. '84 (WIL) [B] Wilmington, DE Salesianum School.
Curran, Thomas M. '70 (BO) Hudson, MA St. Michael Church.
Curran, Vincent J. '98 (HRT) Woodbridge, CT Church of the Assumption.
Curran, William *m.afr.* '66 (FgM) Missionaries of Africa Foreign Missions.
Curran, William J. '69 (CHI) Berwyn, IL St. Leonard Church.
Currans, Clem W. '74 (SC) Boone, IA Sacred Heart Church.
Current, Maurice H. '80 (LIN) Beaver Crossing, NE Sacred Heart Church.
Currie, Charles (SY) Dewitt, NY Holy Cross Church.
Currie, Charles L. *s.j.* '63 (WDC) [M] Washington, DC Leonard Neale House.
Currie, Donald '79 (SAT) On Leave.
Currie, Joseph A. *s.j.* '68 (NY) [DD] New York, NY Jesuit Community at Fordham University; [GG] New York, NY University Apostolate.
Currie, Robert F. *s.j.* '71 (BAL) [S] Baltimore, MD Jesuit Fathers and Brothers Maryland Provincial Curia.
Currie, Robert F. *s.j.* '71 (FgM) Provinces.
Currie, William J. *s.j.* '67 (BAL) [S] Baltimore, MD Jesuit Fathers and Brothers Maryland Provincial Curia.
Currie, William J. *s.j.* '67 (FgM) Provinces.
Currier, Thomas F. '50 (DUB) Retired.
Currin, John M. '98 (DET) Grosse Pointe, MI Our Lady Star of the Sea Church.
Curry, Edward V. '47 (GBG) Retired; [G] Greensburg, PA Neumann House.
Curry, Frederic F. '49 (TUC) [17] Tucson, AZ St. Joseph Church; Retired.
Curry, James '94 (CHI) Tinley Park, IL Saint Julie Billiart Church.
Curry, James J. *s.j.* '74 (NY) [F] New York, NY Loyola School; [DD] New York, NY St. Ignatius Loyola Residence.
Curry, Robert *s.j.* '64 (R) [E] Raleigh, NC Jesuit Community.
Curry, Robert O. *c.ss.r.* '73 (BR) [H] Baton Rouge, LA Redemptorist Vice Province.
Curry, Robert S. *s.j.* '64 (R) [7] Raleigh, NC St. Raphael Church.
Curry, Stephen M. *o.s.a.* '96 (PH) [G] Malvern, PA Malvern Preparatory School for Boys; [AA] Malvern, PA Augustinian Friars (O.S.A.).
Curry, Terrence M. *s.j.* '94 (DET) [K] Detroit, MI Jesuit Community at the University of Detroit.
Curry, Terrence W. *s.j.* '77 (WOR) [N] Worcester, MA Jesuits of Holy Cross College, Inc.
Curry, Thomas P. '51 (RVC) Retired; [M] Uniondale, NY St. Pius X Residence.
Curtin, Clifford J. '51 (NOR) Retired.
Curtin, Cornelius L. *s.j.* '56 (DET) [P] Clarkston, MI Colombiere Center.
Curtin, Eugene P. '56 (BO) Lexington, MA St. Brigid Church.
Curtin, Gregory F. *s.j.* '65 (NO) [C] New Orleans, LA Loyola University New Orleans.
Curtin, James E. '52 (DET) Retired.
Curtin, James F. '51 (BO) Senior Priests.
Curtin, Jim '69 (JOL) [2] Lockport, IL St. Dennis Church.
Curtin, Martin *o.f.m.cap.* '90 (NY) [83] New York, NY Our Lady Queen of Angels Church.
Curtin, Paul *c.ss.r.* (TUC) [H] Cortaro, AZ Desert House of Prayer.
Curtin, Paul *c.ss.r.* '67 (TUC) [F] Cortaro, AZ Desert House of Prayer.
Curtin, Msgr. Richard B. '42 (NY) Retired.
Curtin, Timothy *s.j.* '52 (BGP) [R] Bridgeport, CT The Society of Our Lady of the Way.
Curtin, Timothy A. *s.j.* '52 (NY) [DD] New York, NY Murray-Weigel Hall.
Curtin, Vincent *s.j.* '68 (WDC) [20] Washington, DC Holy Trinity Church.
Curtis, Howard *o.c.s.o.* '57 (P) [L] Lafayette, OR The Cistercian (Trappist) Abbey of Our Lady of Guadalupe.
Curtis, John C. '84 (LEX) Berea, KY St. Clare Church; Mt. Vernon, KY Our Lady of Mt. Vernon Church; [L] Berea, KY St. Clare Church-Berea College.
Curtis, Joseph C. '69 (CHI) Indian Creek, IL St. Mary of Vernon Church.
Curtis, Martin *o.carm.* '75 (CHI) [66] Chicago, IL St. Gelasius Church.
Curtis, Robert J. '36 (TOL) Retired.
Curtis, Robert P. *c.s.p.* '71 (NY) [DD] Jamaica Estates, NY Paulist Fathers Generalate.
Curtis, William D. '47 (WIN) Retired.
Curtise, Donald J. '71 (ROC) [6] Rochester, NY St. Anthony of Padua Church; [20] Rochester, NY Holy Apostles Church.
Curtiss, Donald '71 (ROC) Corning, NY St. Patrick Church.
Curtiss, Donald J. '71 (ROC) Corning, NY St. Mary Church; Corning, NY St. Vincent de Paul Church; Painted Post, NY Immaculate Heart of Mary Church; [J] Rochester, NY St. Joseph Convent Infirmary.
Curtsinger, George '52 (FWT) Retired.
Curzydio, Miecislaus I. (ROC) Canandaigua, NY Veteran's Hospital.
Curzydlo, Ignatius *s.a.c.* '39 (BUF) [O] North Tonawanda, NY Society of the Catholic Apostolate.
Cusack, Msgr. Andrew T. '60 (BGP) On Duty Outside the Diocese.
Cusack, Msgr. Andrew T. '60 (NEW) [A] South Orange, NJ Immaculate Conception Seminary; [B] South Orange, NJ Seton Hall University; [B] South Orange, NJ Seton Hall University.
Cusack, Francis V. '54 (MOB) [16] Mobile, AL Our Lady of Lourdes Church.
Cusack, Francis W. *c.p.* '58 (L) [L] Louisville, KY Sacred Heart Retreat.
Cusack, James C. '56 (GR) Retired.
Cusack, John '71 (CHY) Cheyenne, WY U.S. Veterans Administration Hospital 1.
Cusack, John J. *c.m.* '45 (PH) [AA] Philadelphia, PA Congregation of the Mission.
Cusack, Msgr. John J. '71 (PAT) Military Chaplains.
Cusack, Paul *c.p.* '59 (MET) [H] South River, NJ Passionist Provincial Office.
Cusack, Thomas *s.s.c.* '62 (LA) [Q] Los Angeles, CA Columban Fathers, Procure House.
Cusatis, Girard J. '63 (PH) [1] Drexel Hill, PA St. Andrew Church.
Cusato, Michael *o.f.m.* '81 (BUF) [C] St. Bonaventure, NY St. Bonaventure University; [O] St. Bonaventure, NY St. Bonaventure Friary.
Cuschieri, Albert '61 (DAL) Grand Prairie, TX Immaculate Conception Church.
Cush, John P. '98 (BRK) [175] Queens, NY St. Helen Church.
Cushing, Alan '57 (SFE) Retired.
Cushing, Charles B. '54 (BRK) Retired.
Cushing, Robert A. '78 (SAV) Special Assignment.
Cushing, Vincent de Paul *o.f.m.* '63 (WDC) [M] Silver Spring, MD Gemelli House.
Cushing, Walter '56 (ROC) Retired.
Cushing, Walter F. '56 (ROC) [11] Rochester, NY St. Cecilia Church.
Cusick, Eugene G. '64 (PH) Holland, PA St. Bede the Venerable Church.
Cusick, John C. '70 (CHI) [162] Chicago, IL St. Patrick Church.
Cusick, Kevin M. '92 (WDC) Military Chaplains.
Cusick, Thomas H. '64 (DET) Belleville, MI St. Anthony Church.
Cusick, Timothy J. '00 (STA) Ponte Vedra Beach, FL Our Lady Star of the Sea Church.
Cusimano, Salvatore J. '49 (BUF) Retired; [O] Tonawanda, NY O'Hara Residence.
Cusma, Joseph S. '53 (NY) Retired.
Cusmano, John '64 (DET) [8] Dearborn Heights, MI St. Sebastian Church.
Custer, Edward O. *m.m.* '72 (FgM) Maryknoll Foreign Missions.
Custer, John S. '83 (PBR) [A] Pittsburgh, PA Byzantine Catholic Seminary of SS. Cyril and Methodius.
Custer, John S. '83 (PSC) On Duty Outside Diocese.
Custer, Michael H. *o.s.b.* '41 (MAN) [K] Manchester, NH St. Anselm Abbey.
Custodio, Rinaldo B. '62 (STP) Savage, MN St. John the Baptist Church.
Cutajar, Alfred *s.j.* '69 (BAL) [M] Cumberland, MD Sacred Heart Hospital of the Western Maryland Health System.
Cutcher, Anthony E. '99 (CIN) [22] Dayton, OH St. Peter Church.
Cutie, Albert '95 (MIA) [4] Miami Beach, FL St. Patrick Church.
Cutrara, Daniel S. *s.j.* '91 (BAL) [S] Baltimore, MD Jesuit Fathers and Brothers Maryland Provincial Curia.
Cutrone, Dominick F. '55 (BRK) [96] Brooklyn, NY Our Lady of Grace Church.
Cvitkovic, Vincent *o.f.m.* '69 (CHI) [N] Chicago, IL Croatian Franciscan Custody of the Holy Family.
Cwiekowski, Bruce '75 (P) [G] Portland, OR Catholic Charities of the Archdiocese of Portland in Oregon.
Cwiekowski, Frederick J. *s.s.* '62 (HRT) On Duty Outside the Archdiocese.
Cwiekowski, Frederick J. *s.s.* '62 (SFR) [A] Menlo Park, CA St. Patrick Seminary.
Cwik, Patrick '88 (LAN) [E] Jackson, MI St. Joseph Home for Children, Inc.
Cwik, Thomas G. *s.j.* '00 (STL) [P] St. Louis, MO The Jesuits of the Missouri Province.
Cwynar, Paul D. '87 (PIT) Oakmont, PA St. Irenaeus Church.
Cycenas, Joel '00 (STP) Mendota, MN St. Peter Church.
Cyktor, Ronald L., Jr. '00 (GBG) Murrysville, PA Mother of Sorrows Church.
Cylwicki, Albert W. *c.s.b.* '60 (ROC) [I] Rochester, NY Basilian Residence.
Cymbor, Msgr. John A. '50 (STU) Flushing, OH St. Paul's Church.
Cymbrowski, Martin *c.m.* '30 (HRT) [M] Manchester, CT DePaul Provincial Residence.
Cymerman, Alex B. *o.f.m.conv.* '65 (PAT) [6] Clifton, NJ St. John Kanty Church.
Cyprys, Ronald '69 (DET) [6] Dearborn Heights, MI Our Lady of Grace Church.
Cyr, Joel R. '71 (PRT) Brewer, ME St. Joseph's Church; Brewer, ME St. Teresa's Church.
Cyr, L. Chanel '53 (PRT) Limestone, ME St. Louis Church; Retired.
Cyr, L. Philip '69 (PRT) Houlton, ME St. Mary's Church.
Cyr, Lawrence S. *c.pp.s.* '44 (SAN) Coleman, TX Sacred Heart Church.
Cyr, Myles *o.m.i.* '44 (PRT) Lincoln, ME St. Mary Church.
Cyr, Richard E. '60 (DET) [6] Sterling Heights, MI St. Matthias Church.
Cyr, Roger '59 (PRT) Lincoln, ME St. Mary Church.
Cyr, Terrence *o.carm.* '75 (JOL) [J] Darien, IL Carmelite Provincial Office.
Cyr, William F. '71 (SPR) Williamstown, MA SS. Patrick and Raphael Church; [Q] Springfield, MA Newman Apostolates and Campus Ministries.
Cyscon, Peter J. '73 (CHI) Berwyn, IL St. Odilo Church.
Cyscon, Philip E. '84 (CHI) [159] Chicago, IL Our Lady of Victory Church.
Cyvas, Matthew '41 (ALB) Retired.
Cyz, Edward T. '54 (SUP) Retired.
Czachor, Christopher '51 (PSC) Absent on Sick Leave.
Czachor, Richard E. '77 (SCR) Tannersville, PA Our Lady of Victory Church.
Czachorowski, Richard S. '65 (NEW) Lyndhurst, NJ St. Michael's Church.
Czahur, John P. '77 (TR) Riverton, NJ Sacred Heart Church.
Czaja, Blaise *c.p.* '64 (SAC) [H] Citrus Heights, CA Christ the King Retreat.
Czaja, Joseph S. '46 (Y) Retired.
Czajka, Norman M. '61 (CHI) [35] Chicago, IL St. Camillus Church; Retired.
Czajkcwski, Richard *m.m.* '61 (FgM) Maryknoll Foreign Missions.
Czajkowski, Andrew A. '74 (LAN) Davison, MI St. John Church.
Czapiewski, Stanislaus *s.j.* '40 (DET) Hamtramck, MI St. Ladislaus Church; [P] Clarkston, MI Colombiere Center.
Czapinski, Richard J. '58 (PIT) [49] Pittsburgh, PA Holy Angels Church.

Czapla, Bruce C. *o.f.m.* (BO) [1] Marlborough, MA St. Ann Church.
Czarcinski, Edward A. '88 (MET) Milltown, NJ Our Lady of Lourdes Church.
Czarkowski, Joseph R. '74 (E) Lucinda, PA St. Joseph Church.
Czarnecki, Andrew '98 (DET) Novi, MI Holy Family Church.
Czarnecki, Msgr. Anthony '66 (WOR) Webster, MA St. Joseph's Basilica Church.
Czarnecki, Edmund S. '64 (ORL) Cocoa, FL Blessed Sacrament Church.
Czarnecki, Edward R. '66 (BUF) Blasdell, NY Our Mother of Good Counsel Church.
Czarnota, Stanley '56 (LAN) [I] Dimondale, MI Dimondale Nursing Center.
Czartorynski, David F. '84 (ALN) Military Chaplains.
Czaster, Herman *o.f.m.conv.* '65 (HRT) Kensington, CT St. Paul's Church.
Czaus, Joseph C. '89 (ALN) Unassigned.
Czech, Edmund *o.f.m.* '44 (MIL) [P] Burlington, WI Queen of Peace Friary.
Czech, Edward M. '73 (CLV) Military Chaplains.
Czechowicz, Bernard J. '54 (BUF) Retired.
Czechowicz, Walter '51 (ALB) [8] Amsterdam, NY St. Stanislaus Church.
Czeck, Thomas *o.f.m.conv.* '98 (MRY) Pismo Beach, CA St. Paul the Apostle Church.
Czekala, Henry *c.m.* '44 (HRT) [4] Ansonia, CT St. Joseph's Church; [M] Manchester, CT DePaul Provincial Residence.
Czelusniak, Donald '78 (ALB) Gloversville, NY St. Mary of Mt. Carmel Church.
Czerkies, Msgr. Joseph '62 (PAT) [6] Passaic, NJ St. Joseph's Church.
Czerwien, Richard *ss.cc.* '83 (BWN) Edinburg, TX Sacred Heart Church.
Czerwinski, James W. *o.f.m.* '77 (NEW) Wood-Ridge, NJ Our Lady of the Assumption Church.
Czok, Robert W. '66 (BRK) [11] Brooklyn, NY St. Anthony of Padua-St. Alphonsus Church.
Czuba, Flavius *o.f.m.* '47 (GAY) Indian River, MI Cross in the Woods Catholic Church.
Czywil, Valerian *o.f.m.conv.* '37 (BO) [6] Lawrence, MA Holy Trinity Church.
Czyzynski, John *s.c.j.* '63 (MIL) [P] Franklin, WI St. Francis Residence; [P] Hales Corners, WI Priests of the Sacred Heart; [P] Hales Corners, WI Priests of the Sacred Heart.

D

D'Abele, Peter *s.m.m.* '75 (BRK) [V] Ozone Park, NY Montfort Missionaries Provincialate (Missionaries of the Company of Mary) - Formation Community.
D'Aco, Joseph '99 (FAR) [3] Grand Forks, ND St. Michael's Church.
D'Addezio, Msgr. Louis A. '61 (PH) [138] Philadelphia, PA St. Philip Neri Church.
D'Agostini, Mario *s.p.* '65 (STL) [P] St. Louis, MO Servants of the Paraclete.
D'Agostino, Angelo *s.j.* '66 (BAL) [S] Baltimore, MD Jesuit Fathers and Brothers Maryland Provincial Curia.
D'Agostino, Angelo *s.j.* '66 (FgM) Provinces.
D'Agostino, Carl L. '59 (CLV) Independence, OH St. Michael Church.
D'Agostino, Joseph '41 (ALB) Retired.
D'Agostino, Rodolfo *r.c.j.* '64 (FRS) Sanger, CA St. Mary Church.
D'Albro, Thomas G. '71 (BRK) Released from Diocesan Assignment.
D'Alessandro, Benedict (NY) Manhattan, NY U.S.V.A. Medical Center.
D'Alessandro, Benedict J. *o.f.m.* '66 (NY) [4] Mt. Vernon, NY Our Lady of Mount Carmel Church; [DD] Mount Vernon, NY St. Bernardine of Siena Friary.
D'Alessandro, Salvatore '39 (SY) Retired.
D'Alonzo, Alfred F. *c.s.c.* '53 (FTW) [A] Notre Dame, IN Moreau Seminary; [B] Notre Dame, IN University of Notre Dame Du Lac.
D'Amato, James J. '49 (BRK) Retired.
D'Ambrosi, Girolamo *s.a.c.* '39 (NY) [91] New York, NY Our Lady of Mt. Carmel Church; [DD] New York, NY Pallottine Fathers.
D'Ambrosia, Peter (PRO) [B] Newport, RI Salve Regina University.
D'Amico, Carducci S. '64 (BGP) [19] Bridgeport, CT St. Raphael Church.
D'Amico, Carmen A. '82 (PIT) [6] Pittsburgh, PA St. Benedict the Moor Church; [R] Pittsburgh, PA Office for Campus Ministry.
D'Amico, Frank '87 (STL) Kirkwood, MO St. Gerard Majella Church.
D'Amico, Joseph '95 (NEW) [4] Hoboken, NJ SS. Peter and Paul's Church.
D'Amico, Michael H. '64 (CAM) [2] Atlantic City, NJ St. Michael's Church.
D'Anca, Msgr. Achille '45 (BRK) Retired.
D'Andrea, Edward R. '73 (RVC) [A] Huntington, NY Diocesan Seminary of the Immaculate Conception.
D'Andrea, Stephen D. '97 (NEW) North Arlington, NJ Queen of Peace Church.
D'Angelico, Anthony J. '74 (PH) [12] Philadelphia, PA Annunciation B.V.M. Church.
D'Angelo, Anthony *s.d.b.* '67 (BIR) [9] Birmingham, AL St. John Bosco Church.
D'Angelo, Donald S. '68 (SFR) [24] San Francisco, CA Holy Name of Jesus Church.
D'Angelo, Joseph J. '68 (RVC) [2] Rockville Centre, NY Campus Parish of Long Island Church; East Meadow, NY Nassau County Police Department; [P] Rockville Centre, NY The Campus Parish of Long Island; [P] Rockville Centre, NY The Campus Parish of Long Island.
D'Angelo, Rocco '56 (SP) Retired.
D'Angelo, Thomas P. '84 (NY) [140] Bronx, NY St. Francis of Assisi Church; Bronx, NY Our Lady of Mercy Medical Center; [W] New York, NY Our Lady of Mercy Medical Center.
d'Anjou, Henry G. '48 (NY) [4] Port Chester, NY Sacred Heart of Jesus Church; Retired; [E] White Plains, NY Archbishop Stepinac High School.
d'Anjou, John R. *s.j.* '72 (BO) [E] Boston, MA Boston College High School & Jesuit Community.
D'Anjou, Lawrence C. '00 (OAK) [7] Fremont, CA St.Leonard-Santa Paula Church.
D'Antonio, Anthony '39 (NY) [174] Bronx, NY Our Lady of Mt. Carmel Church; Retired.
D'Antonio, John *o.praem.* (SP) [4] Largo, FL St. Patrick Church.
D'Antonio, Nicholas *o.f.m.* '42 (NO) Retired.
D'Antonio, Ronald M. '77 (BRK) [167] Queens, NY St. Fidelis Church.
D'Arcy, William '73 (AGN) Retired.
D'Artiaga, Jose '63 (SJN) [52] San Juan, PR Santa Rosa de Lima Church.
d'Auby, Phillip *s.m.* '61 (SFR) [38] San Francisco, CA Notre Dame des Victoires Church.
D'Auriol, Vincent '60 (NY) Retired.
D'Aurizio, Joseph (ROC) Hilton, NY St. Leo Church.
D'Aurizio, Joseph F. '56 (ROC) [30] Rochester, NY St. John Evangelist Church; Retired.
D'Aversa, Robert J. *t.o.r.* '73 (ORL) [D] Winter Park, FL San Pedro Spiritual Development Center; [F] Winter Park, FL San Pedro Center, Third Order Regular of St. Francis; [F] Winter Park, FL Franciscan Friars, T.O.R., Provincial Residence, San Pedro Friary.
D'Cruz, Ferreolus '59 (ALX) Tallulah, LA St. Edward Church.
D'Cruz, Michael *o.f.m.* '57 (NY) [DD] New York, NY Franciscan Province of the Immaculate Conception.
D'Cunha, John '81 (NY) [203] Staten Island, NY St. Clement Church; [215] Staten Island, NY St. Michael Church.
D'Elia, Michael A. '54 (BGP) Bridgeport, CT Bridgeport Health Care.
D'Emma, Gregory J. '70 (NEW) Military Chaplains.
D'Eon, Earl '89 (PHX) Sun City, AZ St. Clement of Rome Church.
d'Escoto, Miguel F. *m.m.* '61 (NY) [DD] Maryknoll, NY Maryknoll Fathers and Brothers.
D'heedene, Walter O. *c.i.c.m.* '67 (SAT) [23] San Antonio, TX Sacred Heart Church.
D'Incecco, Alfred '75 (NY) [E] New York, NY Cardinal Hayes High School.
D'Onofrio, Ernest *o.f.m.* '43 (NY) County, NY Dutchess County Jail; [FF] Wappingers Falls, NY Mt. Alvernia Retreat House.
D'Ostilio, Silvio *c.s.sp.* '54 (SB) Hemet, CA Holy Spirit Church; [E] Hemet, CA Holy Ghost Fathers.
D'Silva, Aloysius J. '61 (CHL) Spruce Pine, NC St. Lucien Church.
D'Silva, Percival L. '64 (WDC) [10] Washington, DC Blessed Sacrament, Shrine of the Most Church.
D'Sousa, Peter '79 (LUB) [6] Lubbock, TX St. John Neumann Church.
D'Souza, Gilbert P. '73 (BGP) [2] Norwalk, CT St. Joseph Church.
D'Souza, Harris J. '93 (CHI) [3] Cicero, IL St. Mary of Czestochowa Church.
D'Souza, Keith *s.j.* '95 (MIL) [P] Milwaukee, WI Jesuit Community at Marquette University.
D'Souza, Robert '73 (FTW) [10] Fort Wayne, IN St. Jude Church; Fort Wayne, IN Parkview Memorial Hospital.
Da Costa, Darrell A. '97 (BRK) [132] Brooklyn, NY St. Saviour Church.
da Cunha, Domingos M. '71 (PRO) [5] Cumberland, RI Our Lady of Fatima Church.
Da Cunha, Edgar *s.d.v.* '82 (NEW) [25] Newark, NJ St. Michael's Church.
da Cunha, Edgar *s.d.v.* '82 (PAT) [I] Florham Park, NJ Vocationist Fathers Retreat Center.
Da Prato, Felix *o.c.d.* '40 (LR) [A] Little Rock, AR Marylake - Carmelite Novitiate.
Da Roza, George *s.s.c.* '85 (OM) [K] St. Columbans, NE St. Columban's Foreign Mission Society.
da Silva, Antonio L. *s.d.v.* '83 (NEW) Palisades Park, NJ St. Nicholas Church.
Da Silva, Gilberto *c.m.v.* '97 (ARE) [7] Arecibo, PR Nuestra Senora de Fatima Church.
da Silva, Jorge '71 (SJ) [L] Cupertino, CA Marianist Provincial Residence.
da Silva, Joseph '72 (B) [5] Boise, ID Risen Christ Catholic Community Church.
Dabaen, Hisham '72 (LA) Pomona, CA St. Joseph Church.
Dabash, G. Adrian *o.p.* '71 (PRO) [P] Providence, RI St. Thomas Aquinas Priory at Providence College.
Dabbene, Bernard *s.d.b.* '66 (SFR) [N] San Francisco, CA Salesian Provincial Residence.
Dabcosky, Edward J. '56 (ALT) [5] Altoona, PA Holy Rosary Church; Altoona, PA Veterans Medical Center.
Dabney, Philip *c.ss.r.* '78 (BRK) [C] Whitestone, NY St. Alphonsus Formation Residence.
Dabovich, Louis '46 (OAK) Pittsburg, CA Good Shepherd Church; Retired.
Dabria, Jerry J. '55 (NO) Retired.
Dabrowski, George J. *c.m.* '58 (HRT) [M] Manchester, CT DePaul Provincial Residence.
Dabrowski, James '84 (CAM) Brigantine, NJ St. Thomas Church.
Dabruzzi, James S. '53 (SUP) Retired.
Dacey, Donald '53 (DET) Retired.
Dachauer, Andrew C. *s.j.* '64 (STO) Mammoth Lakes, CA St. Joseph Church.
Dachille, Arnold V. '59 (DET) [4] Dearborn, MI St. Clement Church.
DaCorte, Allan *o.f.m.* '77 (STL) [P] St. Louis, MO Franciscan Friary of St. Anthony of Padua.
DaCosta, Eriberto '81 (SC) Storm Lake, IA St. Mary's Church.
DaCosta, Lee '73 (BWN) Weslaco, TX St. Joan of Arc Church; Weslaco, TX St. Pius X Church.
Dadalt, Gelso A. *c.s.* (BO) [5] Framingham, MA St. Tarcisius Church.
DaDamio, Paul A. '00 (ALN) [3] Reading, PA St. Catharine of Siena Church.
Dadey, Neil R. '81 (ALT) Lock Haven, PA St. Agnes Church; [H] Hollidaysburg, PA Campus Ministry.
Dadson, Eric '90 (RVC) Port Jefferson, NY Infant Jesus Church; Port Jefferson, NY St. Charles Hospital, Port Jefferson, New York.
Daechen, Mario *o.s.b.m.* (STF) New York, NY St. George Church.
Dafonte, Gregorio '57 (CGS) Cayey, PR Nuestra Senora de la Merced Church.
Dagcuta, Arnold '93 (HON) [1] Honolulu, HI Cathedral of Our Lady of Peace.
Dagelen, Anthony L. *s.j.* '65 (MIL) [P] Wauwatosa, WI Jesuit Community at St. Camillus.
Dagher, George *b.s.o.* '43 (NTN) Retired.
Dagit, Rick A. '86 (DUB) [F] Gilbertville, IA Immaculate Conception-St. Joseph School.
Dagit, Rick D. '86 (DUB) Gilbertville, IA Immaculate Conception Church; Raymond, IA St. Joseph's Church.
Dagle, Harold F. '59 (ALN) [3] Allentown, PA Immaculate Conception Church.
Dagnoli, Albert *ss.cc.* '68 (FR) [I] Fairhaven, MA Sacred Hearts Provincial House.
Dahl, Henry J. (FR) [N] Fall River, MA Diocesan Education Center.
Dahl, Henry J. '96 (FR) [16] New Bedford, MA St. John the Baptist Church.
Dahlberg, Daniel J. '67 (SUP) [1] Superior, WI Cathedral of Christ the King.
Dahlby, Charles G. '77 (SFD) Kincaid, IL St. Rita Church; Pawnee, IL St. Mary Church.
Dahlheimer, Cosmas *o.s.b.* '36 (SCL) [I] Collegeville, MN St. John's Abbey, of the Order of St. Benedict.
Dahlheimer, Ronald W. '59 (STP) Kilkenny, MN St. Canice Church.
Dahlinger, James H. *s.j.* '91 (SY) [S] Syracuse, NY Jesuits at LeMoyne, Inc.
Dahlke, Robert W. *s.j.* '65 (NY) [DD] New York, NY Murray-Weigel Hall.
Dahlquist, Thomas S. '96 (YAK) White Salmon, WA St. Joseph Church.
Dahm, Charles W. *o.p.* '64 (CHI) [84] Chicago, IL Holy Trinity Church; [170] Chicago, IL St. Pius V Church; [N] Chicago, IL Dominican Community.
Dahmen, Vernon '76 (MOB) On Leave from the Archdiocese.
Dahms, Paul G. '58 (RC) Deadwood, SD St. Ambrose Church.
Dahms, William *s.s.s.* '43 (NY) [55] New York, NY St. Jean Baptiste Church.
Dahn, Paul '62 (RVC) West Islip, NY Good Samaritan Hospital Medical Center.
Daiber, Msgr. Sean J. '67 (CAM) On Duty Outside the Diocese.
Daigle, Chris '78 (TLS) Hartshorne, OK Holy Rosary Church.
Daigle, Donald R. '68 (PRT) Whitefield, ME St. Denis Church.
Daigle, Eugene *c.ss.r.* '72 (ORL) New Smyrna Beach, FL Sacred Heart Church.
Daigle, Gregory J. '93 (BR) Gonzales, LA St. Theresa of Avila Church; St. Amant, LA Holy Rosary Church.
Daigle, H.C. Paul '46 (HT) Retired.
Daigle, Karl J. '97 (SHP) Minden, LA St. Paul Church.

Daigle, Robert E. '63 (GAL) Retired.
Daigle, Roland *o.f.m.cap.* '84 (FgM) Capuchin Foreign Missions.
Daigle, Steven '89 (DUL) Chisholm, MN St. Joseph's Church.
Dailey, Gary M. '85 (SPR) Lee, MA St. Mary's Church.
Dailey, John '64 (Y) On Duty Outside the Diocese.
Dailey, Joseph E. '77 (DET) Orion Township, MI Christ the Redeemer Church.
Dailey, Thomas F. *o.s.f.s.* '87 (ALN) [B] Center Valley, PA Desales University; [K] Center Valley, PA Oblates of St. Francis de Sales.
Dailey, Vincent E. '58 (BO) Senior Priests.
Dailey, William G. '59 (RVC) Dix Hills, NY St. Matthew Church.
Daily, Leo J. '44 (HRT) Yalesville, CT Our Lady of Fatima Church; Retired.
Daily, Vincent (BO) [32] Boston, MA St. Joseph Church.
Daily, Vincent E. '90 (BO) Graduate Studies.
Dair, Richard J. '80 (ARL) Retired.
Daka, Lawrence *s.j.* '00 (BO) [W] Cambridge, MA Weston Jesuit Community.
Dakes, John '87 (WDC) [4] Rockville, MD St. Raphael Church.
Dakes, John T. '87 (WDC) Hyattsville, MD St. Mark Church.
Dakin, Kenneth M. '88 (SAT) Uvalde, TX Sacred Heart Church.
Dakora, Alphonsus B. '88 (PH) [120] Philadelphia, PA Our Lady of Hope Church.
Dalbec, Paul *m.s.* '53 (FR) [I] Attleboro, MA La Salette Shrine.
Dalbon, Luis '47 (CGS) [C] Aibonito, PR Casa Salesiana de Retiros.
Dale, Douglas '88 (ORG) Costa Mesa, CA St. Joachim Church.
Dale, George '58 (SC) On Duty Outside the Diocese.
Daleiden, Francis *o.s.b.* '57 (RCK) Amboy, IL St. Patrick Church; [G] Aurora, IL Marmion Abbey-St. Augustine's Abbey.
Daleke, Don '55 (DM) Retired.
Daleo, Joseph P. '71 (BEA) Orange, TX St. Mary Church.
Daleo, Paul *o.f.m.cap.* '77 (NEW) [N] Union City, NJ Capuchin Friars - Province of the Sacred Stigmata of St. Francis.
Dalessandro, Dennis G. '83 (HBG) Berwick, PA St. Joseph's Church.
Daley, Brian *s.j.* '70 (FTW) [B] Notre Dame, IN University of Notre Dame Du Lac.
Daley, Daniel P. '70 (GLP) Blanco, NM St. Rose of Lima Church; Bloomfield, NM St. Mary Church.
Daley, Msgr. Ernest J. '55 (E) [21] Erie, PA St. Jude the Apostle Church.
Daley, Francis E. '63 (BO) [3] Arlington, MA St. James the Apostle Church.
Daley, Frederick D. '74 (SY) [7] Utica, NY St. Francis de Sales Church; Utica, NY Mohawk Valley Psychiatric Center.
Daley, Jacques de Paul *o.s.b.* '71 (GBG) Greensburg, PA Westmoreland Hospital; [H] Latrobe, PA Saint Vincent Archabbey.
Daley, James D. '54 (ALB) Delmar, NY St. Thomas the Apostle Church.
Daley, James J. '93 (BO) Absent on Leave.
Daley, James M. '42 (BUF) Retired.
Daley, John A. '56 (BO) [2] Malden, MA St. Joseph Church.
Daley, John J. '46 (SY) Fulton, NY Holy Family Church; Retired.
Daley, John T. '43 (RVC) Retired.
Daley, Joseph A. '68 (CHY) Cody, WY St. Anthony Church.
Daley, Joseph D. '37 (BO) Senior Priests.
Daley, Neil '55 (ANC) Retired.
Daley, Owen W. *s.j.* '60 (NY) [DD] New York, NY West Side Jesuit Community.
Daley, Raymond *o.p.* '52 (NY) Pleasantville, NY Holy Innocents Church.
Daley, Msgr. Thomas J. '38 (WOR) Retired; [M] Worcester, MA Vianney House.
Daley, Timothy J. '87 (TLS) Special Assignment.
Daley, William F. *m.m.* '56 (FgM) Maryknoll Foreign Missions.
Dall, Msgr. Norbert P. '45 (LC) Retired.
Dalla Villa, Msgr. Anthony '64 (NY) [1] New York, NY Cathedral of St. Patrick.
Dallen, James '69 (SAL) On Duty Outside the Diocese.
Dallmeier, Michael *o.f.m.* '63 (RNO) Dayton, NV St. Ann Church; Virginia City, NV St. Mary in the Mountains Church.
Dally, Peter F. '85 (TLS) Retired.
Dalseth, Gerald (SCL) [H] Pierz, MN St. Mary's Villa Inc.
Dalseth, Gerald '63 (SCL) [E] Pierz, MN Holy Trinity School.
Dalseth, Gerald '64 (SCL) Pierz, MN St. Joseph's Church.
Dalton, Brendan '69 (MIA) [4] Hollywood, FL St. Bernadette Church.
Dalton, Donald T. '60 (STL) Special Assignment.
Dalton, George R. '84 (PIT) [23] Pittsburgh, PA St. Louise de Marillac Church.
Dalton, J. Paul '78 (SEA) Sammamish, WA Mary, Queen of Peace Church.
Dalton, James '68 (SEA) Lynnwood, WA St. Thomas More Church.
Dalton, James *o.s.f.s.* '72 (WIL) [B] Wilmington, DE Salesianum School.
Dalton, James P. '68 (SAV) Albany, GA St. Teresa Church.
Dalton, John (AMA) [A] Amarillo, TX Holy Cross Catholic Academy.
Dalton, John '48 (CLV) Retired.
Dalton, John A. '55 (L) [67] Louisville, KY St. Raphael the Archangel Church; Retired.
Dalton, John Bryan '70 (MIA) Deerfield Beach, FL St. Ambrose Church.
Dalton, John C. '48 (CLV) [28] Cleveland, OH Holy Name Church.
Dalton, Msgr. John W. '58 (DUB) Retired.
Dalton, Michel *o.f.m.cap.* '78 (HON) Aiea, HI St. Elizabeth Church.
Dalton, Michel W. *o.f.m.cap.* '78 (AGN) [F] Agana Heights, GU St. Fidelis Friary.
Dalton, Peadar '70 (MOB) On Leave from the Archdiocese.
Dalton, Robert *glmy.* (LEX) Grayson, KY Ss. John & Elizabeth Church.
Dalton, Robert '62 (NSH) [H] Nashville, TN Glenmary Home Missioners; [L] Nashville, TN Glenmary Department of Pastoral Services.
Dalton, William P. '56 (NY) Katonah, NY St. Mary of the Assumption Church.
Dalupang, Arturo O. '95 (CHR) Florence, SC St. Anthony's All Souls Memorial Church.
Daly, Albert *o.carm.* '33 (NY) Montrose, NY Franklin D. Roosevelt Hospital; [DD] Middletown, NY St. Albert's Priory.
Daly, Anthony C. *s.j.* '72 (STL) [C] St. Louis, MO Saint Louis University; [P] St. Louis, MO Jesuit Community Corporation at St. Louis University - Jesuit Hall.
Daly, Bartholomew *m.h.m.* '62 (NY) [93] New York, NY Our Lady of Peace Church.
Daly, Msgr. Charles W. '51 (HRT) [13] Hartford, CT St. Luke Church; Retired.
Daly, Christopher H. '60 (NY) [2] White Plains, NY St. John the Evangelist Church.
Daly, Claude *s.j.* '43 (FgM) Provinces.
Daly, Denis E. *s.j.* '64 (STL) [C] St. Louis, MO Saint Louis University; [P] St. Louis, MO Jesuit Community Corporation at St. Louis University - Jesuit Hall.
Daly, Desmond '66 (SP) Hudson, FL St. Michael Church.
Daly, Edwin J. *s.j.* '59 (FgM) Provinces.
Daly, Francis J. *s.j.* '72 (CIN) [F] Cincinnati, OH St. Xavier High School; [M] Cincinnati, OH Jesuit Community at St. Xavier High School.
Daly, George '47 (OAK) Retired.
Daly, J. Daniel *s.j.* '92 (BO) [W] Chestnut Hill, MA The Jesuit Community at Boston College.
Daly, James A. *s.j.* '56 (NY) [DD] New York, NY Murray-Weigel Hall.
Daly, James F. *c.s.sp.* '63 (MIA) [10] Fort Lauderdale, FL St. John the Baptist Church.
Daly, James J. '44 (BO) Senior Priests.
Daly, Msgr. James P. '39 (PH) [133] Philadelphia, PA Our Mother of Sorrows Church; Retired.
Daly, Jerome R. '87 (ARL) Annandale, VA St. Michael's Church.
Daly, Msgr. John '36 (NY) Retired.
Daly, John '59 (LA) [15] Los Angeles, CA Holy Trinity Church; Retired.
Daly, John J. '46 (PH) Retired.
Daly, John J. '58 (HRT) North Haven, CT St. Barnabas Church.
Daly, Msgr. John K. '36 (NY) [5] White Plains, NY Our Lady of Sorrows Church.
Daly, John P. *s.j.* '56 (LA) [C] Los Angeles, CA Loyola Marymount University.
Daly, John R. *s.j.* '63 (STL) [P] St. Louis, MO The Jesuits of the Missouri Province.
Daly, John V. *s.j.* '66 (FgM) Provinces.
Daly, Joseph F. '42 (BRK) Retired.
Daly, Joseph V. *c.m.* '60 (BRK) [D] Staten Island, NY St. John's University, Staten Island Campus; [D] Jamaica, NY St. John's University; [V] Jamaica, NY St. Vincent's House.
Daly, Kevin *o.f.m.* '80 (TR) Brant Beach, NJ St. Francis of Assisi Church.
Daly, Lowrie J. *s.j.* '45 (STL) [C] St. Louis, MO Saint Louis University; [K] Creve Coeur, MO St. John's Mercy Medical Center.
Daly, M. Paul (PAT) Unassigned.
Daly, Manus P. '65 (JC) Marceline, MO St. Bonaventure Church.
Daly, Michael '75 (DET) [L] Livonia, MI Provincial House and Novitiate of the Sisters of St. Felix.
Daly, Paul (BO) [5] Newton, MA Mary Immaculate of Lourdes Church.
Daly, Peter J. '86 (WDC) Prince Frederick, MD St. John Vianney Church.
Daly, Richard '58 (BEL) New Athens, IL St. Agatha Church.
Daly, Robert J. *s.j.* '63 (BO) [W] Chestnut Hill, MA The Jesuit Community at Boston College.
Daly, Robert L. '41 (NEW) Retired.
Daly, Shawn T. '95 (HRT) [17] Waterbury, CT SS. Peter and Paul Church.
Daly, Simeon *o.s.b.* '48 (IND) [J] St. Meinrad, IN St. Meinrad Archabbey.
Daly, Terence G. (RVC) [I] Melville, NY Catholic Health Services of Long Island.
Daly, Msgr. Thomas A. '87 (SFR) San Francisco, CA San Francisco Police Department; Special Assignment; [D] Kentfield, CA Marin Catholic College Preparatory (Coed).
Daly, Msgr. Thomas J. '52 (BO) Senior Priests.
Daly, Timothy P. (ORL) [E] Orlando, FL Embry-Riddle Aeronautical University.
Daly, Timothy P. '96 (ORL) Ormond Beach, FL Prince of Peace Church.
Daly, Vincent M. '71 (BRK) [230] Queens, NY Queen of Angels Church.
Daly, Msgr. William J. '46 (NEW) Livingston, NJ St. Philomena Church; West Orange, NJ St. Joseph's Church; Retired.
Dam, LoXuan *m.m.* '00 (FgM) Maryknoll Foreign Missions.
Damazio, Pedro J. (BO) [1] Lowell, MA St. Anthony Church.
Dambrauskas, Stephen '48 (SP) Retired.
Damhorst, Joseph *s.j.* '68 (RC) Kyle, SD Our Lady of Sorrows Church; Wanblee, SD Ignatius Loyola Church; Pine Ridge, SD Holy Rosary Church; [B] Pine Ridge, SD Jesuit Community of Holy Rosary Mission.
Damian, Lawrence P. '71 (BUF) Collins Center, NY St. Frances Cabrini Church; Eden, NY St. Mary of Immaculate Conception Church; Langford, NY St. Martin Church.
Damian, Ronald '77 (WOR) On Duty Outside the Diocese.
Damico, Rodney M. '92 (COL) Marion, OH St. Mary Church.
Damis, Frank J. '84 (NY) [3] Kingston, NY St. Joseph Church.
Damjanov, Zvonimir '37 (SFD) Retired.
Dammay, Edmundante '77 (STO) Modesto, CA St. Stanislaus Church.
Dammeir, James L. '79 (MIL) [71] Milwaukee, WI Prince of Peace/Principe de Paz Church.
Damor, Casmir *s.v.d.* '88 (BO) [W] Boston, MA Divine Word Missionaries.
Damron, Robert '83 (LEX) Corbin, KY Sacred Heart Church; Jellico, KY St. Boniface Church; Williamsburg, KY Our Lady of Perpetual Help Church.
Damroth, William J., III '93 (NY) Crestwood, NY Church of the Annunciation.
Danagher, Edward F. '46 (LA) [Q] Montebello, CA Vincentian Fathers & Brothers.
Danaher, Msgr. Mortimer '53 (STA) Retired.
Danaher, Peter *o.f.m.cap.* '84 (FgM) Capuchin Foreign Missions.
Danaher, Philip '83 (JOL) [4] Naperville, IL St. Raphael Church.
Danaher, Msgr. T. Leo '55 (STA) Retired.
Danaher, Thomas E. *m.m.* '62 (FgM) Maryknoll Foreign Missions.
Danber, Bernard *o.s.a.* '86 (CHI) [D] Chicago, IL St. Francis de Sales High School.
Danczyk, Mark J. '92 (MIL) [7] Kenosha, WI St. Mary Church.
Dandelet, James D. '54 (WIN) Retired.
Dandry, Anthony '89 (MET) Raritan, NJ St. Ann Church.
Dandurand, Douglas E. '82 (SC) On Duty Outside the Diocese.
Dandurand, Douglas E. '82 (STP) [A] St. Paul, MN The Saint Paul Seminary; [C] St. Paul, MN University of St. Thomas.
Dandurand, Michael G. '97 (TOL) [B] Tiffin, OH Calvert High School; [L] Tiffin, OH St. Francis Convent.
Dane, James E. '83 (MOB) Bay Minette, AL St. Agatha Church.
Dane, John '91 (LEX) Ashland, KY Holy Family Church.
Danek, Michael E. *c.r.* '86 (CHI) [192] Chicago, IL St. Stephen, King of Hungary Church; [209] Chicago, IL St. Wenceslaus Church.
Danel, Christopher M. '00 (CHR) On Duty Outside the Diocese.
Danel, Joseph B. *s.j.* '52 (FgM) Provinces.
Danel, Joseph B. *s.j.* '52 (P) [L] Portland, OR Jesuit Provincial Office (Society of Jesus, Oregon Prov.).
Danella, Francis W. *o.s.f.s.* '73 (ARL) Vienna, VA Our Lady of Good Counsel Church.
Danella, Francis W. *o.s.f.s.* '73 (WDC) [C] Washington, DC Catholic University of America, The.
Danen, Lyle '85 (ORL) Sabbatical.

Danforth, Clarence E. '81 (GRY) Retired.
Dang, Chin Van '83 (RIC) Military Chaplains.
Dang, H. Francis '95 (LA) [2] North Hollywood, CA St. Charles Borromeo Church.
Dang, Hai Duc '99 (GAL) The Woodlands, TX Sts. Simon and Jude Church.
Dang, Minh *s.j.* (PHX) [B] Phoenix, AZ Brophy College Preparatory.
Dang, Oanh *s.v.d.* '93 (NY) [168] Bronx, NY St. Nicholas of Tolentine Church.
Dang, Thien *o.s.b.* '93 (P) [L] St. Benedict, OR Mt. Angel Abbey.
Dang, Thomas De-Nguyen '82 (ORG) [2] Orange, CA La Purisima Church.
Dang, Vincent '95 (SCR) [14] Wilkes-Barre, PA St. Mary's Church of the Immaculate Conception.
Dang Ha, Thuy '84 (SLC) [4] Salt Lake City, UT Our Lady of Perpetual Help Church.
Danhauer, Richard T. '57 (OWN) Princeton, KY St. Paul Church.
Daniel, John C. '92 (SFE) Tucumcari, NM St. Anne Church.
Daniel, Michael A. *s.a.* '57 (ARL) Sterling, VA Christ the Redeemer Church.
Daniel, Michael A. *s.a.* '57 (NY) [DD] Garrison, NY Franciscan Friars of the Atonement, Minister General Office.
Daniele, Anthony J. '56 (BO) Senior Priests.
Danielewicz, Noel *o.f.m.conv.* '76 (BIR) Bessemer, AL St. Francis of Assisi Church.
Daniels, Eugene '84 (NY) Milton, NY St. James Church.
Daniels, Joel *o.f.m.cap.* '67 (NY) [DD] White Plains, NY St. Conrad Friary.
Daniels, John W. '36 (GRY) Retired.
Daniels, Joseph E. '90 (PRT) Bar Harbor, ME Holy Redeemer Church; Northeast Harbor, ME St. Ignatius Church.
Daniels, Lawrence *o.c.d.* '65 (MIL) [P] Milwaukee, WI Provincial Offices - Discalced Carmelites.
Daniels, Leo Francis *c.o.* '65 (BWN) [3] Pharr, TX St. Jude Thaddeus Church; [E] Pharr, TX Oratory of St. Philip Neri, of Pontifical Right.
Daniels, Paul A. '57 (MIL) Retired.
Danielsen, Thomas *c.ss.r.* '64 (TUC) [H] Tucson, AZ Redemptorist Picture Rocks Retreat.
Danielson, Charles R. '92 (BUR) Brattleboro, VT St. Michael Church.
Danielson, Daniel E. '63 (OAK) Pleasanton, CA The Catholic Community of Pleasanton Church.
Danielson, Harold *s.d.b.* '66 (MRY) Watsonville, CA Our Lady Help of Christians Church.
Danik, Daniel A. '48 (NEW) Bloomfield, NJ Sacred Heart Church; Retired.
Danilak, John '61 (PSC) Retired.
Daniss, Peter *s.d.b.* '82 (OAK) [N] Berkeley, CA Salesian Community.
Daniszewski, Msgr. Alfred '45 (MAN) [10] Manchester, NH St. Hedwig Church.
Daniszewski, Msgr. John D. '43 (E) Retired.
Danko, Michael S. '52 (LIN) Retired.
Danks, Arthur J. '43 (GB) Retired.
Danna, Msgr. Anthony (BRK) [215] Queens, NY Our Lady of the Miraculous Medal Church.
Danneker, David L. '82 (HBG) Elizabethtown, PA St. Peter Church; [K] Harrisburg, PA Catholic Campus Ministry.
Danneker, Edward A. '64 (ATL) Dahlonega, GA St. Luke Catholic Church; [M] Atlanta, GA Campus Ministry.
Dannenfelser, Lambert R. *o.f.m.* '40 (CIN) [P] Cincinnati, OH Friarhurst Retreat Center.
Danner, Brian J. '95 (SC) [6] Sioux City, IA Immaculate Conception Church.
Danner, James L. '74 (MEM) Military Chaplains.
Danner, Michael A. '65 (GR) On Special Assignment; [A] Grand Rapids, MI Christopher House-College Department of St. Joseph's Seminary.
Danos, Dean F. '80 (HT) Larose, LA Our Lady of the Rosary Church.
Danowski, Alexander J. '59 (PBL) Retired.
Dansak, Thomas E. '73 (PIT) Military Chaplains.
Dant, J. Nicholas '77 (IND) [7] Indianapolis, IN Holy Spirit Church; [33] Indianapolis, IN St. Pius X Church.
Dante, Neal F. '64 (CAM) Westville Grove, NJ Most Holy Redeemer Church.
Danter, Albert F. '43 (STL) [O] St. Charles, MO St. Joseph Carmelite Home.
Dantinne, Gary J. '68 (GB) Little Suamico, WI St. Pius Church; Suamico, WI St. Benedict Church.
Danylo, Bohdan '96 (STF) [A] Stamford, CT St. Basil College.
Danzi, Rocco C. *s.j.* '00 (BRK) [62] Brooklyn, NY St. Ignatius Church.
Danzine, Rolando *s.v.d.* '98 (TR) Lakewood, NJ St. Anthony Claret Church.
Dao, Anthony Chinh Quang *o.p.* '82 (GAL) [57] Houston, TX Our Lady of Lavang Church.
Dao, Ha Nam Thanh '00 (CHI) [118] Chicago, IL St. Margaret Mary Church.
Dao, Ngo Van *c.ss.r.* '86 (LA) [Q] Baldwin Park, CA Vietnamese Redemptorist Mission.
Dao, Nhuong V. '75 (LA) Retired.
Dao, Paul '94 (NY) [64] New York, NY St. Joseph Church.
Daoust, Joseph P. *s.j.* (OAK) [A] Berkeley, CA The Jesuit School of Theology at Berkeley.
Daoust, Joseph P. *s.j.* '69 (DET) [K] Detroit, MI Jesuit Provincial Office-Detroit Province of the Society of Jesus.
Daoust, Joseph P. *s.j.* '69 (OAK) [A] Berkeley, CA The Jesuit School of Theology at Berkeley; [N] Berkeley, CA Jesuit Community at Jesuit School of Theology at Berkeley.
daPonte, Robert '64 (HON) Retired.
Daprile, James M. '76 (Y) [9] Youngstown, OH St. Brendan's Church.
Darbouze, Gerard '55 (MIA) [10] Miami, FL Notre Dame d'Haiti Church.
Darbouze, Msgr. Rollin '69 (BRK) [109] Brooklyn, NY Our Lady of Refuge Church.
Darby, Bernard M. '49 (CAM) Retired.
Darby, Thomas J. '47 (NY) Retired.
Darcy, Brendan *s.m.a.* '67 (NEW) [N] Tenafly, NJ Society of African Missions, Provincialate, S.M.A. Fathers.
Darcy, David M. '94 (SPR) Lee, MA St. Mary's Church; [Q] Springfield, MA Newman Apostolates and Campus Ministries.
Darcy, James F. '66 (BO) [2] Medford, MA St. James Church; Emergency Response Group.
Darcy, John J. '79 (PRO) [1] Providence, RI Cathedral of SS. Peter and Paul.
Darcy, Michael '00 (WIL) [A] Magnolia, DE St. Thomas More Academy.
Darcy, Michael P. '00 (WIL) Dover, DE Holy Cross Church.
Dardis, Hugh A. '49 (NY) Wurtsboro, NY St. Joseph Church.
Dare, Glenn O. '74 (P) On Duty Outside the Archdiocese.
Dare, Glenn O. '74 (SAC) Portola, CA Holy Family Church.
Dargan, Peter S. '61 (HRT) Orange, CT Holy Infant Church.
Dargis, Andre E. *a.a.* '67 (WOR) [N] Worcester, MA Assumptionists (Augustinians of the Assumption).
Daries, Joseph *c.m.f.* '56 (LA) [Q] Rancho Dominguez, CA Dominguez Seminary Inc.
Darilek, Dennis '73 (SAT) [15] San Antonio, TX Our Lady of Good Counsel Church.
Darin, David M. (BEL) Beaver Prairie, IL St. Felicitas Church; Marydale, IL St. Teresa of Avila Church.
Darin, David M. '91 (BEL) Centralia, IL St. Mary Church.
Darkowski, Msgr. Leon S. '43 (PIT) Retired.
Darling, Franklin '58 (SPR) Retired.
Darling, George E. '84 (GR) Grandville, MI St. Pius X Church; On Special Assignment.
Darling, William G. '73 (ROC) [55] Rochester, NY St. Salome Church.
Darnall, Thomas W. '52 (OKL) Retired.
Darnell, Lawrence T. *o.m.v.* '82 (LA) Hawaiian Gardens, CA St. Peter Chanel Church.
Darnieder, Donald A. '55 (MIL) Retired.
Darow, Robert G. '63 (CHI) [76] Chicago, IL St. Hilary Church.
Darragh, John J. '68 (HEL) Hamilton, MT St. Francis Church.
Das Neves, Antonio '61 (SB) Adelanto, CA Christ the Good Shepherd Church.
Dascenzo, Joseph J. '58 (PIT) Baden, PA St. John the Baptist Church.
Daschbach, Edwin G. *s.v.d.* '66 (WH) Glenville, WV Good Shepherd Church.
Daschbach, Richard *s.v.d.* '64 (FgM) Society of the Divine Word Foreign Missions.
Dash, Alan J. '67 (R) [2] Raleigh, NC Catholic Student Center, North Carolina State University Church; [H] Raleigh, NC Doggett Center for Catholic Campus Ministry at Aquinas House.
Dash, George J. *o.f.m.cap.* '92 (NY) State, NY Bayview Correctional Facility; State, NY Sing Sing Correctional Facility; State, NY Taconic Correctional Facility; City, NY Anna M. Kross Center; [DD] White Plains, NY St. Conrad Friary.
DaSilva, Joseph '72 (B) [E] Boise, ID Nazareth.
DaSilva, Mariano *s.v.d.* '97 (WDC) [M] Washington, DC Divine Word College.
daSilva, Paul '98 (MET) Piscataway, NJ Our Lady of Fatima Church.
Dass, Joseph '90 (LA) Carson, CA St. Philomena Church.
Dasseville, Armand *o.f.m.cap.* '49 (NY) [57] New York, NY St. John the Baptist Church; [HH] West Hempstead, NY La Casa Sollievo Della Sofferenza Opera Di Padre Pio.
Datko, James *o.m.i.* (DUL) [3] Duluth, MN Holy Family Church.
Dattilo, Anthony A. '90 (STL) Crystal City, MO Sacred Heart Church.
Dattilo, Anthony M. '84 (CIN) [21] Dayton, OH Our Lady of the Rosary Church; [28] Dayton, OH St. Stephen Church.
Datty, Edward J. *s.a.* '49 (NY) [207] Staten Island, NY Immaculate Conception Church; Staten Island, NY Bayley Seton Hospital.
Datzman, Harold L. *o.s.b.* '65 (PEO) Ladd, IL St. Benedict's Church; [A] Peru, IL St. Bede Abbey and Academy.
Daues, Mark J. *s.j.* '94 (KC) [J] Kansas City, MO Rockhurst Jesuit Community.
Daugherty, Daniel L. '94 (TYL) Whitehouse, TX Prince of Peace Church.
Daugherty, Scott '83 (FRS) Porterville, CA St. Anne Church.
Daum, Msgr. John J. '45 (Y) [6] Canton, OH St. Joan of Arc Church; Retired.
Dauphinais, Louis Marie *o.mar.* '70 (SAM) [C] Petersham, MA Most Holy Trinity Monastery.
Dauses, Jeffrey S. '90 (BAL) Hunt Valley, MD St. Francis Xavier Church.
Dauss, Francis '48 (SP) Retired.
Dautremont, Charles R. '60 (GR) [14] Grand Rapids, MI St. Dominic Church.
Davadilla, Patrick Joel, Jr. '88 (FRS) Firebaugh, CA St. Joseph Church.
Davalos, Carlos '78 (SAT) Pleasanton, TX St. Andrew Church.
Davanzo, Joseph V. '97 (RVC) Huntington Station, NY St. Hugh of Lincoln Church.
Davenport, Bernard '74 (WOR) Webster, MA St. Louis Church.
Davenport, Christopher M. '61 (PRO) [7] Pawtucket, RI St. Leo the Great Church.
Davenport, Clement A. '48 (SFR) Retired.
Davenport, Thomas J. '42 (SFD) Retired; [K] Springfield, IL Priests' Retirement Facility.
Davern, Raymond J. '58 (KCK) [3] Kansas City, KS Christ the King Church.
Davern, Msgr. Robert B. '51 (SY) Syracuse, NY Van Duyn Home & Hospital; Special Assignment; [S] Syracuse, NY St. Pius X Home, Inc.
Davern, Timothy R. '78 (PHX) [2] Tempe, AZ Our Lady of Mt. Carmel Church; [3] Tempe, AZ Resurrection Church.
Daves, Mark J. *s.j.* '94 (KC) [D] Kansas City, MO Rockhurst High School.
Davey, Edward M. (PAT) Retired.
Davey, M. Edward '53 (PAT) [P] Chester, NJ Nazareth Village.
Davey, Philip *o.s.b.* '65 (PEO) [C] Peru, IL St. Bede Academy.
Davey, Philip D. *o.s.b.* '75 (PEO) [A] Peru, IL St. Bede Abbey and Academy.
Davey, Robert W. '62 (SAG) Midland, MI Assumption Blessed Virgin Mary Church.
Davich, George F. '62 (SLC) [11] Salt Lake City, UT St. Vincent de Paul Church.
David, Christopher J. '97 (DAV) Keokuk, IA All Saints Church.
David, Craig '96 (ATL) [8] Atlanta, GA Sacred Heart of Jesus Church.
David, George '71 (ROM) Roebling, NJ St. Mary Church; Trenton, NJ St. Basil Church.
David, Jose A. *s.v.d.* '80 (CHK) Chalan Kanoa Village, MP Cathedral of Our Lady of Mt. Carmel.
David, Jose A., Jr. '80 (CHK) San Vicente Village, District 10, MP San Vicente Church.
David, Joseph '93 (SAM) Uniontown, PA St. George Church.
Davidowich, Glenn M. '89 (PSC) Mont Clare, PA St. Michael Church.
Davids, John J. '76 (PH) Doylestown, PA Our Lady of Mount Carmel Church.
Davidson, Carl (NO) [A] New Orleans, LA Notre Dame Seminary Graduate School of Theology.
Davidson, John '64 (EVN) [14] Evansville, IN St. Anthony Church.
Davies, Brian *o.p.* '82 (NY) [DD] New York, NY Jesuit Community at Fordham University.
Davies, Daniel *o.p.* '58 (NY) Pleasantville, NY Holy Innocents Church.
Davies, Daniel Thaddeus '58 (NY) [121] New York, NY St. Vincent Ferrer Church.
Davies, Julian A. *o.f.m.* '60 (ALB) [B] Loudonville, NY Siena College.
Davies, Robert F. '00 (DUB) [4] Waterloo, IA St. Edward's Church.
Davies, Steven E. '77 (SFR) [3] Menlo Park, CA The Church of the Nativity.
Davignon, Charles P. '56 (BUR) Retired.
Davignon, Philip A. (FR) Osterville, MA Our Lady of the Assumption Church.
Davila, Andres '72 (ARE) [3] Utuado, PR Our Lady of Angels Church.
Davila, Johnny '84 (SAT) On Leave.
Davila, Justo *s.d.b.* '70 (MRY) Watsonville, CA Our Lady Help of Christians Church.
Davila, Rafael R. *m.m.* '58 (GAL) [Q] Houston, TX Maryknoll Fathers and Brothers.

Davila, Raphael *m.m.* '58 (GAL) [A] Houston, TX St. Mary's Seminary.
Davin, Neil *c.p.* '52 (BRK) [V] Jamaica, NY Immaculate Conception Monastery.
Davin, Neil W. *c.p.* '52 (MET) Edison, NJ St. Matthew Church; [H] South River, NJ Passionist Provincial Office.
Davin, William *c.p.* '56 (PIT) [O] Pittsburgh, PA St. Paul of the Cross Monastery.
Davino, Louis *o.f.m.* '72 (SFD) [B] Quincy, IL Quincy University.
Davino, Michael J. '86 (CHR) Absent On Leave.
Davis, Alexander *o.f.m.cap.* '64 (NEW) [4] Orange, NJ Mt. Carmel Church; East Orange, NJ Veterans Administration Hospital.
Davis, Augustine *o.s.b.* '59 (IND) [J] St. Meinrad, IN St. Meinrad Archabbey.
Davis, Charles J. '62 (CAM) Retired; Retired.
Davis, Chris '58 (FWT) Wichita Falls, TX Our Lady Queen of Peace Church.
Davis, Christopher *o.s.b.* '58 (PRO) [P] Portsmouth, RI Abbey of St. Gregory the Great.
Davis, Christopher '98 (CHL) Reidsville, NC Holy Infant Church.
Davis, Clement T. '70 (IND) Columbus, IN St. Bartholomew Church.
Davis, Clyde F. *m.m.* '63 (SJ) [L] Los Altos, CA Maryknoll.
Davis, Cyprian *o.s.b.* '56 (IND) [A] St. Meinrad, IN St. Meinrad Seminary; [J] St. Meinrad, IN St. Meinrad Archabbey.
Davis, Dan *o.p.* '94 (LFT) West Lafayette, IN St. Thomas Aquinas Church.
Davis, Daniel C. *o.p.* '71 (LFT) [H] West Lafayette, IN St. Thomas Aquinas Parish and Foundation for Catholic Students Attending Purdue University.
Davis, David J. '97 (LIN) Sutton, NE St. Mary's Church.
Davis, Dilworth '98 (E) [3] Sharon, PA St. Joseph Church.
Davis, Edward J. '49 (NOR) Retired.
Davis, Edward V. *m.m.* '61 (FgM) Maryknoll Foreign Missions.
Davis, F. Hampton '90 (NO) [A] New Orleans, LA Notre Dame Seminary Graduate School of Theology.
Davis, Francis R. '45 (ROC) Corning, NY St. Mary Church; Retired.
Davis, Gary G. '75 (L) Jeffersontown, KY St. Michael Church.
Davis, Henry J. *s.s.j.* '93 (NO) [6] New Orleans, LA Epiphany Church.
Davis, James J. *o.p.* '53 (PRO) [P] Providence, RI St. Thomas Aquinas Priory at Providence College.
Davis, John E. '69 (FAR) On Duty Outside the Diocese.
Davis, John E. '69 (FgM) Society of St. James the Apostle.
Davis, John P. '63 (PRT) Retired.
Davis, Joseph E. '76 (PRO) [6] Cumberland, RI St. Patrick Church.
Davis, Joseph P. '72 (PAT) Succasunna, NJ St. Therese Church.
Davis, Kenneth *o.f.m.cap.* '86 (IND) [A] St. Meinrad, IN St. Meinrad Seminary; [I] Mount Saint Francis, IN Mount Saint Francis Friary and Retreat Center.
Davis, Mark E. '96 (TOL) Maumee, OH St. Joseph Church.
Davis, Michael '90 (MIA) [6] Miami, FL Good Shepherd Church; [C] Miami, FL Archbishop Coleman Carroll High School.
Davis, Michael J. '87 (PH) Collingdale, PA St. Joseph Church.
Davis, Noel '62 (LAR) [12] Laredo, TX Santo Nino Independent Church.
Davis, Raphael J. *o.praem.* '99 (ORG) [I] Silverado, CA Norbertine Fathers of Orange Inc.
Davis, Raymond '84 (JOL) Bensenville, IL St. Alexis Church; Retired.
Davis, Richard *t.o.r.* '80 (ALT) [F] Loretto, PA Mount Assisi Friary.
Davis, Richard L. *t.o.r.* '80 (ALT) [F] Loretto, PA St. Bonaventure Friary.
Davis, Richard P. '63 (LR) Adona, AR St. Elizabeth's Church; Bigelow, AR St. Boniface's Church.
Davis, Robert '97 (FRS) Orange Cove, CA St. Isidore the Farmer Church.
Davis, Royden B. *s.j.* '59 (SCR) [C] Scranton, PA University of Scranton.
Davis, Scott K. '80 (STL) [C] St. Louis, MO Saint Louis University.
Davis, Terrence '69 (SJ) Retired.
Davis, Msgr. Thomas A. '68 (LAR) [17] Laredo, TX St. Patrick Church.
Davis, Thomas R. (R) Jacksonville, NC Shrine of the Infant of Prague, Church of the Holy Spirit.
Davis, Thomas R. '83 (R) Fayetteville, NC St. Ann Church.
Davis, W. E. *o.s.f.s.* '82 (PH) [AA] Philadelphia, PA Oblates of St. Francis De Sales.
Davis, William *ss.cc.* '44 (FR) [I] Fairhaven, MA Sacred Hearts Provincial House.
Davis, William *o.m.i.* '57 (GAL) [38] Houston, TX Immaculate Heart of Mary Church.
Davis, William E. *o.s.f.s.* '84 (PH) [D] Philadelphia, PA Northeast Catholic High School for Boys.
Davis, Msgr. William F. '56 (MEM) Retired.
Davis, William F. *o.s.f.s.* '61 (WDC) [B] Washington, DC Oblates of St. Francis de Sales.
Davish, William M. *s.j.* '46 (BAL) [B] Baltimore, MD Loyola College in Maryland.
Davish, William M. *s.j.* '46 (PH) [AA] Philadelphia, PA Jesuit Community at St. Joseph's University.
Davison, Ben '92 (SD) Brawley, CA Sacred Heart Church.
Davison, Don *c.p.p.s.* (IND) Bloomington, IN St. Charles Borromeo Church.
Davison, Timothy L. '85 (TLS) [6] Tulsa, OK St. Francis Xavier Church.
Davitt, James P. '55 (CHI) [4] Lemont, IL St. James at Sag Bridge Church; Retired.
Davitti, Michael *s.x.* '70 (CHI) [199] Chicago, IL St. Therese Catholic Chinese Church.
DaVola, F. Robert '67 (BWN) [4] Mission, TX St. Paul Church.
Davoren, Stephen V. '96 (LA) Temple City, CA St. Luke the Evangelist Church.
Daw, Timothy M. '91 (CLV) [33] Cleveland, OH St. Ignatius of Antioch Church.
Dawber, Stephen F. *s.j.* '69 (BO) [E] Boston, MA Boston College High School & Jesuit Community.
Dawis, Ralph '54 (NY) Staten Island, NY St. Vincent's Medical Center of Richmond.
Dawling, Raymond '61 (GB) Retired.
Daws, Dominic '55 (B) Retired.
Dawson, Cletus *c.p.* '43 (BRK) [V] Jamaica, NY Immaculate Conception Monastery.
Dawson, George *c.ss.r.* '50 (LA) Whittier, CA St. Mary of the Assumption Church; [Q] Whittier, CA Redemptorist Fathers Mission House.
Dawson, Ivan *c.ss.r.* '94 (KC) [31] Kansas City, MO Our Lady of Perpetual Help Church; [J] Kansas City, MO Redemptorists of Kansas City.
Dawson, Msgr. James D. '54 (LIN) Cheney, NE St. Michael Church.
Dawson, Msgr. Joseph '51 (STA) Retired.
Dawson, Joseph I. '62 (L) Calvary, KY Holy Name of Mary Church.
Dawson, Richard E. '81 (PT) Cantonment, FL St. Jude Thaddeus Church.
Dawson, William A. *s.j.* '58 (BAL) [S] Baltimore, MD Jesuit Fathers and Brothers Maryland Provincial Curia.
Dawson, William F. '54 (DAV) [B] Davenport, IA St. Ambrose University.
Dawydowych, Ivan '75 (PHU) Retired.
Day, Charles J. '81 (CHR) Greenville, SC Our Lady of the Rosary Church.
Day, Dennis C. '76 (B) Sandpoint, ID St. Joseph's Church.
Day, James R. *o.ss.t.* '72 (PH) Bristol, PA St. Ann Church.
Day, James Richard '96 (NO) La Place, LA St. Joan of Arc Church.
Day, Jeffrey D. '99 (DET) [5] Dearborn, MI Divine Child Church.
Day, Jerome J. *o.s.b.* '95 (MAN) [K] Manchester, NH St. Anselm Abbey.
Day, Msgr. John D. '39 (BO) Senior Priests.
Day, John P. *c.p.* '72 (CHI) [N] Chicago, IL Passionist Provincial Office.
Day, John Patrick *c.p.* '72 (STL) [6] St. Charles, MO St. Robert Bellarmine Church.
Day, Lenox C. *s.j.* '63 (SJ) [L] Los Gatos, CA Sacred Heart Jesuit Center.
Day, Martin *o.f.m.conv.* '91 (IND) [4] Terre Haute, IN St. Joseph Church.
Day, Wilfred E. '67 (IND) New Albany, IN Holy Family Church.
Day, William F. '86 (GLP) Overgaard, AZ Our Lady of Assumption Church.
Daya, John *o.f.m.cap.* '78 (HBG) [2] York, PA St. Joseph Church.
Daz, Rudolph A. '54 (SLC) Bountiful, UT St. Olaf Church.
Ddungu, Josephat '95 (LA) [81] Los Angeles, CA St. Mary Magdalen Church.
De Agostini, Claudio *c.s.j.* '58 (LA) San Pedro, CA St. Peter Church.
de Alba, Ricardo *m.sp.s.* '81 (LA) Huntington Park, CA St. Martha Church.
De Angelis, Mark '88 (BO) [1] Revere, MA St. Anthony of Padua Church.
De Angelis, Sante *o.f.m.* '62 (MIL) [P] Burlington, WI Queen of Peace Friary; [Y] Waterford, WI General Secretariat of the Franciscan Missions, Inc.
de Armas, Alexio Jose *o.c.d.* '58 (PCE) [12] Ponce, PR San Jose Church; [B] Ponce, PR The Pontifical Catholic University of Puerto Rico.
de Azevedo, Antonio Carvalho '62 (BGP) [2] Danbury, CT Immaculate Heart of Mary Church.
De Bellis, John A. '85 (NY) [3] Yonkers, NY St. Ann Church.
De Blas, Alonso *o.f.m.* '64 (PHX) [19] Phoenix, AZ St. Mary's Basilica Church.
De Brito Alves, Joseph '67 (BGP) [15] Bridgeport, CT Our Lady of Fatima Church.
de Bruijn, Johan *o.cart.* '91 (BUR) [E] Arlington, VT Carthusian Foundation, Charterhouse of the Transfiguration.
De Bruin, Edward *s.d.s.* '53 (MIL) [P] Milwaukee, WI Salvatorians - Jordan Hall.
De Caprio, John '49 (ALB) Retired.
de Cardenas, Msgr. Javier Garcia '85 (NY) [II] New York, NY Prelature of the Holy Cross and Opus Dei.
De Celles, John C. '96 (ARL) Clifton, VA St. Andrew the Apostle Church.
De Clercq, Victor *.c.i.c.m.* '37 (FgM) Missionhurst Foreign Missions.
De Clerk, Msgr. Rainer J. '34 (LR) Retired.
De Condorpusa, Alphonse '95 (NEW) Kearny, NJ St. Cecilia's Church.
De Costa, George '64 (HON) Keaukaha, Hilo, HI Malia Puka'O Kalani (Mary Gate of Heaven) Church.
de Cristobal, Fernando '65 (GRY) [12] East Chicago, IN St. Patrick Church.
de Dios, Alfredo *o.a.r.* '60 (ORG) [5] Santa Ana, CA Our Lady of the Pillar Church.
de Dios, Francisco Mendez '60 (ARL) [4] Arlington, VA St. Charles Borromeo Church.
De Dominici, Lorenzo '46 (LA) San Pedro, CA Mary, Star of the Sea Church.
de Duenas, Jesus *l.d.* '97 (PCE) [18] Ponce, PR Church Santisimo Sacramento Church.
De Folco, Joseph A. '85 (SEA) Bellingham, WA Assumption B.V.M. Church; Bellingham, WA Sacred Heart Church.
De Francisco, Joseph '75 (DAV) [B] Davenport, IA St. Ambrose University.
De Franco, Anthony '38 (ALB) Retired.
De Groot, Ambrose *o.f.m.cap.* '45 (GB) [I] Appleton, WI St. Fidelis Friary.
De Heredia, Agnel '80 (SFR) [1] San Francisco, CA Cathedral of St. Mary (Assumption).
de Herrera, Christopher *o.s.* '97 (PCE) [11] Ponce, PR San Jose Obrero Church.
de Jesus, Carmelo *o.c.d.* '47 (PCE) [B] Ponce, PR The Pontifical Catholic University of Puerto Rico.
de Jesus, Hector Bruno '85 (CGS) Cayey, PR San Esteban Protomartir Church.
de Jesus, Msgr. Herminio '69 (PCE) Juana Diaz, PR Nuestra Senora de Lourdes Church; [B] Ponce, PR The Pontifical Catholic University of Puerto Rico.
de Jesus, Orlando '86 (CGS) [F] Caguas, PR Movimiento Juan XXIII.
de Jesus, Rafael Alvarado '94 (PCE) [1] Ponce, PR Cathedral of Our Lady of Guadalupe.
De Jesus Brenes-Chaves, Fabio R. '85 (NEW) [24] Jersey City, NJ Parish of the Resurrection Church.
de Jong, Jan *s.c.j.* '64 (MIL) [B] Hales Corners, WI Sacred Heart School of Theology; [P] Franklin, WI St. Francis Residence; [P] Hales Corners, WI Priests of the Sacred Heart.
de la Calle, Juan '54 (PMB) Indiantown, FL Holy Cross Church.
de la Cruz, Carlos E. *s.j.* '75 (FgM) Provinces.
De La Cruz, Jenaro *o.c.d.* '66 (OKL) [15] Oklahoma City, OK Our Lady of Mount Carmel and St. Therese Little Flower Church.
de la Cruz, Juan '57 (ATL) [1] Marietta, GA Holy Family Church.
de la Cruz, Luis Maria *s.e.m.v.* '81 (ARE) Hatillo, PR Our Lady of Guadalupe Church.
de La Cruz, Vicente '90 (HT) [7] Thibodaux, LA St. Thomas Aquinas Church; Thibodaux, LA Nicholls State University.
De La Fuente, Javier *m.c.m.* '94 (CHI) [184] Chicago, IL St. Roman Church.
De La Garza, Joseph G. '51 (SAT) Stonewall, TX St. Francis Xavier Church.
de la Iglesia, Celestino *c.m.f.* '31 (LA) [Q] Rancho Dominguez, CA Dominguez Seminary Inc.
De La Madrid, James Gil *m.ss.cc.* '97 (SJN) Rio Grande, PR Nuestra Senora del Carmen Church.
De La Pena, Jose M. '00 (NEW) [9] Elizabeth, NJ Our Lady of Most Holy Rosary/St. Michael Church.
De La Pena, Rick (NY) Fishkill, NY Church of St. Mary, Mother of the; [3] Kingston, NY St. Joseph Church.
De La Pinera, Fernando '51 (NO) Retired.
de la Puebla, Tomas *c.m.* '49 (MGZ) [8] Mayaquez, PR San Vicente Church.
De La Riva, John *o.f.m.cap.* '99 (SFR) Burlingame, CA Our Lady of Angels Church.
De La Rosa, Jose Luis '84 (SAT) [68] San Antonio, TX St. Vincent de Paul Church.
De La Rosa, Vincent '55 (SAT) On Leave.
de la Rosa Peguero, Frank '78 (SJN) [21] Carolina, PR San Francisco de Asis Church.
de la Torre, Bartholomew *o.p.* '67 (LA) [C] Santa Paula, CA Thomas Aquinas College.
de la Torre, Jorge Luis *m.s.c.* '97 (FRS) Earlimart, CA St. Jude Thaddeus Church; McFarland, CA St. Elizabeth Church.
de la Torre, Jorge Luis *m.s.c.* '97 (LA) Cudahy, CA Sagrado Corazon y Santa Maria de Guadalupe.

De La Torre, Mario '86 (LA) Baldwin Park, CA St. John the Baptist Church.
de la Vega, Francis J. *o.a.r.* '43 (ORG) Fullerton, CA St. Mary's Church.
de Laire, George F. '97 (MAN) [C] Dover, NH St. Thomas Aquinas High School.
de Laire, Georges F. '97 (MAN) Pittsfield, NH Our Lady of Lourdes Church.
de las Reyes, Joselito (CLV) [30] Cleveland, OH Holy Rosary Church.
De Laura, Felice J. '63 (BRK) [245] Queens, NY St. Thomas Apostle Church.
de Leis, Sean *c.s.sp.* '81 (PMB) Fort Pierce, FL St. Mark Church.
de Leon, Jose A. '81 (CGS) Barranquitas, PR San Andres Apostol Church.
De Leon, Michael '86 (LAR) [4] Laredo, TX Divine Mercy Church.
de Leon, Robert E. *c.s.c.* '85 (SCR) [C] Wilkes-Barre, PA Kings College; [M] Wilkes-Barre, PA Moreau House.
De Leonardis, Gerard *o.f.m.cap.* '49 (NY) [B] Beacon, NY St. Lawrence of Brindisi Friary.
De Lillio, Richard R. *o.s.f.s.* '66 (WIL) [I] Wilmington, DE Oblates of St. Francis De Sales.
De Llano, Domingo (CC) Retired.
de los Reyes, Joel '75 (AGN) Barrigada, GU San Vicente Ferrer Church.
de los Rios, Enrique '00 (LA) Hawthorne, CA St. Joseph Church.
de Loza, Jose '87 (YAK) Mattawa, WA Our Lady of the Desert Church.
de M. Pereira, Luciano J. '54 (FR) Somerset, MA St. John of God Church.
De Man, Thomas *o.p.* (SEA) [O] Seattle, WA Campus Ministry.
De Man, Thomas *o.p.* '62 (SEA) [O] Seattle, WA Campus Ministry.
De Martinis, O. Robert '86 (ALB) [7] Schenectady, NY Immaculate Conception Church.
De Meersman, Clement *c.i.c.m.* '52 (SAT) Devine, TX St. Joseph's Church.
de Mello, Arthur T. '34 (FR) Absent on Sick Leave.
de Mentque, Edouard *f.s.s.p.* '97 (SCR) [M] Elmhurst, PA Priestly Fraternity of St. Peter (F.S.S.P.), North American District Headquarters.
De Morais, Jonas (PH) [72] Philadelphia, PA Incarnation of Our Lord Church.
de Morchoven, Werner Papeians *o.s.b.* '38 (LA) [Q] Valyermo, CA St. Andrew's Abbey.
De Nard, Silvio *s.c.* '79 (PH) [B] Springfield, PA Don Guanella House of Formation.
De Noble, Augustine *o.s.b.* '55 (P) [L] St. Benedict, OR Mt. Angel Abbey.
De Oca, Jose Montes '96 (NEW) Paramus, NJ Our Lady of the Visitation Church.
De Pascale, Daniel '61 (ALB) Retired.
De Peaux, Rowland C. *o.praem.* '51 (GB) [I] De Pere, WI St. Joseph Priory.
De Peralta, Miguel Grave (SAV) [E] Augusta, GA St. Joseph Hospital, Augusta, GA, Inc.
de Porres Schmitt, Martin *o.f.m.cap.* (FgM) Capuchin Foreign Missions.
De Priest, Ellis *s.m.* '53 (PBR) New Orleans, LA St. Nicholas of Myra Church.
de Ramos, Fidel A. '64 (WDC) [8] Silver Spring, MD St. Michael Church.
de Rivera, Crescente *s.v.d.* '81 (CHI) [N] Techny, IL Society of the Divine Word, Provincial Headquarter-Chicago Prov.
De Rosa, Arnold P. '63 (NEW) [B] South Orange, NJ Seton Hall University.
De Rose, Martin '88 (ALB) Stuyvesant Falls, NY St. Mary/Nativity Church.
De Santi, Bruno *c.s.j.* '51 (LA) San Pedro, CA St. Peter Church.
De Santis, Linus *o.f.m.conv.* '71 (ATL) [M] Atlanta, GA Campus Ministry.
de Serpa, Roberto '46 (PRO) Retired.
de Silva, Lionel A. *c.s.p.* '59 (NY) [41] New York, NY Good Shepherd Church.
De Simonc, David A. '87 (NY) Port Jervis, NY Most Sacred Heart Church.
De Souza, Carl '66 (RIC) Franklin, VA St. Jude Church.
de Souza, Owen '70 (LA) Carson, CA St. Philomena Church.
De Tomasi, Gerardo *m.c.c.j.* '63 (LA) [56] Los Angeles, CA St. Cecilia Church.
De Tommaso, Louis *o.f.m.* '54 (NY) [DD] New York, NY Franciscan Province of the Immaculate Conception.
de Verteuil, Jack '89 (FBK) Healy, AK Holy Mary of Guadalupe Church.
de Vianney Guerra, Jesus *o.p.* '57 (NO) [P] New Orleans, LA Dominican Friars, Southern Dominican Province of St. Martin de Porres.
De Vita, James C. '57 (RVC) Retired.
De Vries, James '76 (MET) [F] New Brunswick, NJ St. Peter's University Hospital.
De Vries, Thomas '89 (MIL) On Leave.
de Water, Joseph M. '67 (NO) [12] New Orleans, LA Immaculate Heart Of Mary Church.
De Young, Thomas J. '83 (GR) [2] Grand Rapids, MI Basilica of St. Adalbert.
Deaconson, James (AUS) [M] Waco, TX Catholic Student Center at Baylor University.
DeAdder, James W. '55 (BO) Senior Priests.
DeAguiar, Luiz Antonio '85 (BRK) [227] Queens, NY St. Pius V Church.
DeAguilar, Arturo '97 (CHL) Absent On Leave.
DeAguire, Luiz Antonio (BRK) [229] Queens, NY Presentation of the Blessed Virgin Mary Church.
DeAmato, Norbert *o.f.m.* '48 (BO) [3] Cambridge, MA St. Francis of Assisi Church.
Dean, Alfred A. *s.s.j.* '89 (BAL) [33] Baltimore, MD St. Francis Xavier Church.
Dean, Frederic D. '65 (PRO) Retired; [P] Providence, RI St. John Vianney Residence.
Dean, Harry '96 (AUS) [9] Austin, TX Sacred Heart Church.
Dean, James N. '91 (MOB) Troy, AL St. Martin of Tours Church; [J] Troy, AL Troy State University Newman Center.
Dean, John T. '72 (SPR) [5] Westfield, MA St. Peter's Church; [Q] Springfield, MA Newman Apostolates and Campus Ministries.
Dean, Joseph *glmy.* '45 (CIN) [M] Cincinnati, OH Headquarters of Glenmary Home Missioners.
Dean, Joseph *s.c.j.* '84 (GB) [M] Baileys Harbor, WI St. Joseph Retreat Center.
Dean, Mark *o.m.i.* '83 (STP) [Q] Buffalo, MN Christ the King Retreat Center.
Dean, Walter R. *o.s.f.s.* '49 (WIL) [I] Wilmington, DE Oblates of St. Francis De Sales.
Dean, William E. '76 (PH) [145] Philadelphia, PA Sacred Heart of Jesus Church.
DeAndrea, Msgr. Joseph A. '53 (GBG) On Duty Outside the Diocese.
Deane, Declan '72 (OAK) Moraga, CA St. Monica Church.
Deane, Edwin *o.f.m.* '44 (HT) [4] Houma, LA Our Lady of the Most Holy Rosary Church.
Deane, Msgr. Gregory S. '54 (CC) Port Aransas, TX St. Joseph Church.
Deane, J. Peter *s.j.* (DET) [K] Detroit, MI Jesuit Provincial Office-Detroit Province of the Society of Jesus.
Deane, Joseph '59 (AUS) Buda, TX Santa Cruz Church.
Deane, Pete *s.j.* (TOL) [G] Toledo, OH St. Anthony Villa/Boysville of Michigan, Inc.
DeAngelis, Antonio *c.s.* '81 (SJ) [6] San Jose, CA Holy Cross Church.
DeAngelo, Jude T. *o.f.m.conv.* '84 (CHL) Winston-Salem, NC Our Lady of Mercy Church; [L] Charlotte, NC Diocesan Office of Campus Ministry.
DeAnta, Carlos *o.m.i.* '50 (FgM) Oblates Foreign Missions.
DeAntoniis, Paul J. *o.praem.* '63 (WIL) [B] Claymont, DE Archmere Academy; [I] Claymont, DE Immaculate Conception Priory of the Canons Regular of Premontre.
DeAntonio, Michael R. '71 (CHR) Spartanburg, SC St. Paul the Apostle Church; [H] Spartanburg, SC Converse College, Spartanburg Methodist College.
Dear, John *s.j.* '93 (NY) [DD] New York, NY West Side Jesuit Community.
Deardorff, Joseph F. *c.pp.s.* '82 (CIN) [M] Dayton, OH Provincial Office of the Cincinnati Province of the Society of the Precious Blood.
Dearhammer, John W. '91 (CHI) [65] Chicago, IL St. Gall Church.
Dearing, Arnold *o.f.m.conv.* '51 (IND) Clarksville, IN St. Anthony of Padua Church.
Deary, John F. *o.s.a.* '66 (VEN) Cape Coral, FL Blessed Katharine Drexel Church.
Deas, Msgr. George T. '51 (BRK) Retired; [V] Douglaston, NY Bishop Mugavero Residence.
Dease, Dennis J. '69 (STP) [C] St. Paul, MN University of St. Thomas.
Deasio, August J. '75 (STU) Retired.
Deasy, Jeremiah (BIR) [I] Tuscaloosa, AL The Harrison Family Endowment Trust for the Benefit of Holy Spirit School.
Deasy, Jeremiah *v.f.* '67 (BIR) Tuscaloosa, AL Holy Spirit Church.
Deasy, Ken '87 (LA) [39] Los Angeles, CA St. Agatha Church.
Deasy, Msgr. Timothy '58 (MOB) Daphne, AL Christ the King Church.
Deasy, Wayman P. *m.m.* '59 (NY) [DD] Maryknoll, NY Maryknoll Fathers and Brothers; [DD] Maryknoll, NY Maryknoll Fathers and Brothers.
Deatrick, John D. '66 (L) [50] Louisville, KY St. Martha Church.
Deaver, Stephen F. '59 (GI) Mitchell, NE St. Theresa's Church.
DeAvila, Rafael *m.g.* '73 (SFR) [1] Menlo Park, CA St. Anthony Church.
Debaenst, Emmanuel '34 (SFE) Retired.
Debany, Edgar J. *s.j.* '84 (BAL) [S] Baltimore, MD Jesuit Fathers and Brothers Maryland Provincial Curia.
Debany, Edgar J. *s.j.* '84 (FgM) Provinces.
DeBellis, John A. '85 (NY) [219] Staten Island, NY Our Lady, Queen of Peace Church.
DeBellis, Peter M. '97 (ROC) Newark, NY St. Michael Church.
DeBenedetto, David J. '94 (BR) On Leave.
Debes, Donald *o.f.m.cap.* '70 (FgM) Capuchin Foreign Missions.
DeBiase, William *o.f.m.* '66 (ALB) [B] Loudonville, NY Siena College.
Debicki, John P. '64 (CHI) [123] Chicago, IL St. Mary of the Angels Church.
DeBillis, Peter M. '97 (ROC) [40] Rochester, NY Our Mother of Sorrows Church.
DeBisschop, James P. '88 (PEO) Rapids City, IL St. John the Baptist Church.
Debitetto, Ronald E. '63 (WOR) Retired.
DeBlanc, Msgr. Irving A. '38 (LKC) [8] Lake Charles, LA Our Lady Queen of Heaven Church; Retired; [E] Lake Charles, LA Our Lady Queen of Heaven Manor.
DeBlanc, Jefferson J., Jr. '77 (LAF) [2] Opelousas, LA Our Lady of Mercy Church.
DeBlase, Dominic *s.d.b.* '61 (FgM) Salesians of Don Bosco Foreign Missions.
Deblasio, Dominck A. '40 (PIT) Retired.
DeBlasio, Ernie '88 (MEM) [24] Memphis, TN Church of the Resurrection.
Debo, Peter '89 (PIT) [2] Swissvale, PA Word of God Church.
Debo, William D. '95 (JC) Salisbury, MO St. Joseph Church.
DeBock, Msgr. William A. '49 (MAD) Retired; [H] Madison, WI Bishop O'Connor Catholic Pastoral Center.
DeBoe, Stanley W. *o.ss.t.* '83 (BAL) Jessup, MD St. Lawrence Church.
Debold, Walter A. '42 (NEW) Retired; [B] South Orange, NJ Seton Hall University.
DeBona, Guerric *o.s.b.* '86 (IND) [A] St. Meinrad, IN St. Meinrad Seminary; [J] St. Meinrad, IN St. Meinrad Archabbey.
Debosz, Jerzy '95 (TYL) Nacogdoches, TX Sacred Heart Church.
DeBruycker, James R. '82 (STP) [30] Minneapolis, MN St. Leonard of Port Maurice Church; Minneapolis, MN Hennepin County Medical Center.
Debski, Joseph E. '64 (MIL) Burlington, WI Immaculate Conception Church.
Decaen, Ramon E. '00 (LIN) Nebraska City, NE St. Mary's Church.
Decal, Wilfredo G. '77 (HT) [6] Houma, LA St. Gregory Barbarigo Church.
DeCarlo, Philip J. '55 (PIT) Retired.
DeCarlo, Thomas M. '69 (DM) [E] Johnston, IA Bishop Drumm Retirement Center.
DeCarolis, Joseph R. '59 (HRT) Prospect, CT St. Anthony's Church.
Decell, Stephen '87 (HT) On Leave.
Decewicz, Michael W. '78 (PIT) Monroeville, PA St. Bernadette Church; [R] Pittsburgh, PA Office for Campus Ministry.
Dechant, Leo *c.s.j.* (CLV) [T] Avon, OH St. Leonard Youth Retreat Center.
Dechant, Leo *c.s.j.* '80 (CLV) [O] Avon, OH Congregation of St. Joseph.
Dechant, Paul G. '90 (ARL) Vienna, VA Our Lady of Good Counsel Church.
Dechering, Msgr. Anton '62 (SP) [2] St. Petersburg, FL Blessed Trinity Church.
DeChico, Philip '74 (HBG) Bonneauville, PA St. Joseph Church; [K] Harrisburg, PA Catholic Campus Ministry.
DeCicco, Pascal A. *o.s.a.* '52 (PH) [18] Philadelphia, PA St. Augustine Church.
Deck, Alcuin *o.s.b.* '39 (RCK) [G] Aurora, IL Marmion Abbey-St. Augustine's Abbey.
Deck, Allan F. *s.j.* '76 (ORG) [H] Orange, CA Loyola Institute for Spirituality.
Deck, Marion *t.o.r.* '69 (ARL) [J] White Post, VA Sacred Heart Friary.
Decker, Douglas '78 (OG) Adams, NY St. Cecilia Church.
Decker, James D. '85 (MAN) Military Chaplains.
Decker, Lawrence J. '84 (ALB) [3] Amsterdam, NY St. Joseph-St. Michael-Our Lady of Mount Carmel Church.
Decker, Maurice C. '50 (DET) Retired.
Decker, Neil F. *s.j.* '58 (BO) [W] Chestnut Hill, MA The Jesuit Community at Boston College.
Decker, Raymond G. '58 (SFR) Retired.
Decker, Robert L. '83 (OG) On Duty Outside the Diocese.
Decker, William Jonathan '76 (OLL) Portland, OR Saint Sharbel Church; Portland, OR Saint Sharbel Church.
Deckman, Peter (ROC) Stanley, NY St. Theresa Church.
Deckman, Peter '64 (ROC) Naples, NY Our Lady of the Lakes Catholic Community Church; Penn Yan, NY St. Michael Church; [M] Rochester, NY Diocesan Department of Campus Ministry.
DeClerk, Msgr. Rainer '34 (LR) [H] Little Rock, AR St. John Manor.

DeClippel, Ludo *c.j.* '68 (LA) [1] Santa Barbara, CA Holy Cross Church.
DeCneudt, Msgr. Ferdinand '39 (DET) Retired.
DeCock, Robert *i.sch.* '96 (CC) [J] Corpus Christi, TX Secular Institute of the Schoenstatt Fathers aka Schoenstatt Fathers.
DeCock, Robert *c.c.* '96 (MIL) [T] Waukesha, WI Secular Institute of Schoenstatt Fathers.
DeCola, Vincent P. *s.j.* '88 (WDC) [M] Washington, DC K Street Jesuit Community.
DeConciliis, Anthony *c.s.c.* '66 (WDC) [1] Rockville, MD St. Elizabeth Church.
DeConciliis, Anthony J. *c.s.c.* (MAN) [B] Manchester, NH Notre Dame College.
DeCosta, Joseph F. '90 (NOR) Gales Ferry, CT Our Lady of Lourdes Church.
Decoteau, Joseph A. '40 (LKC) [2] Sulphur, LA Our Lady of LaSalette Church.
Decoteau, Vernon '75 (SPR) Belchertown, MA St. Francis of Assisi Church.
DeCraemer, Willy *s.j.* '57 (BAL) [S] Baltimore, MD Jesuit Fathers and Brothers Maryland Provincial Curia.
DeCrans, Joseph '84 (CR) Frazee, MN Sacred Heart Church.
Dede, James R. '51 (IND) Retired.
Dede, John F. '47 (IND) Retired.
Dede, Paul M. '64 (IND) Spencer, IN St. Jude the Apostle Church.
Dedek, John F. '55 (CHI) Elk Grove Village, IL St. Julian Eymard Church; Retired.
Dedera, Philip '72 (JOL) Naperville, IL Edward Hospital; [I] Naperville, IL St. Patrick's Residence.
DeDomenico, Dominic *o.p.* '66 (SJ) [5] Santa Clara, CA Our Lady of Peace Church.
DeDomenico, Msgr. Francis A. '56 (NEW) Hasbrouck Heights, NJ Corpus Christi Church.
DeDominici, Lorenzo '46 (LA) Retired.
Dee, Dacian '56 (SP) Indian Rocks Beach, FL St. Jerome Church.
Dee, Neal '64 (AMA) Groom, TX Immaculate Heart of Mary Church.
Deegan, James D. *o.m.i.* '70 (STP) [Q] Buffalo, MN Christ the King Retreat Center.
Deegan, John E. *o.s.a.* '61 (FgM) Foreign Missions.
Deegan, John E. *o.s.a.* '61 (PH) [C] Villanova, PA Villanova University; [AA] Villanova, PA Provincial Offices of the Order of St. Augustine, Province of St. Thomas of Villanova; [AA] Villanova, PA St. John Stone Friary.
Deegan, Ronan J. *t.o.r.* '58 (WH) Moundsville, WV St. Francis Xavier's Church.
Deehan, Robert J. '83 (BO) [2] Plymouth, MA St. Bonaventure Church.
Deehr, Anselm *s.t.* '90 (LA) Long Beach, CA Veterans Affairs Medical Center.
Deehr, Anslem *s.t.* '90 (LA) [10] Long Beach, CA St. Maria Goretti Church.
Deeker, Geoffrey J. *c.s.s.* '60 (SPR) [3] Pittsfield, MA Our Lady of Mt. Carmel Church.
Deeley, Kevin J. (BO) Military & VA Chaplains.
Deeley, Msgr. Robert P. '73 (BO) [1] Quincy, MA St. Ann Church.
Deely, John *o.m.i.* '70 (FgM) Oblates Foreign Missions.
Deely, Thomas (Martin) *c.ss.r.* '65 (NY) [150] Bronx, NY Immaculate Conception Church.
Deeney, Charles J. *o.m.i.* '71 (ORL) Altamonte Springs, FL Annunciation Church.
Deeney, John J. *s.j.* '52 (BAL) [S] Baltimore, MD Jesuit Fathers and Brothers Maryland Provincial Curia.
Deeney, John J. *s.j.* '52 (FgM) Provinces.
Deering, Msgr. Mark '53 (AUS) Retired.
Deering, William '56 (EVN) Fort Branch, IN St. Bernard Church; Retired.
Deery, James T. *o.s.a.* '51 (PH) [AA] Villanova, PA St. Thomas Monastery.
Deery, Laurence *o.m.i.* '41 (BO) [Z] Tewksbury, MA Immaculate Heart of Mary Infirmary.
Deeter, Timothy '81 (BEA) On Duty Outside the Diocese.
Deeves, John F. *s.j.* '58 (DAL) [D] Dallas, TX Jesuit College Preparatory School.
Deevy, Edward '62 (ALX) Absent on Leave.
Defavio, Crescenzio '57 (BIR) [10] Birmingham, AL St. Joseph's Church.
Defayette, Jeffrey M. '88 (WDC) Hyattsville, MD St. Mark Church.
DeFazio, Crescenzio (BIR) [24] Birmingham, AL St. Stanislaus Church.
DeFazio, Crescenzio '57 (BIR) Retired.
DeFazio, Vincent G. '92 (SFE) Las Vegas, NM Our Lady of Sorrows Church.
DeFelice, Jonathan P. *o.s.b.* '74 (MAN) [B] Manchester, NH Saint Anselm College; [K] Manchester, NH St. Anselm Abbey.
Deffenbaugh, Joseph T. '79 (Y) On Duty Outside the Diocese.
Deffenbaugh, Terry A. *o.s.a.* '75 (CHI) [N] Olympia Fields, IL Austin Friary.
DeFillippes, Gerardo (NY) Suffern, NY Good Samaritan Hospital.
Defler, Herman J. *m.s.f.* '38 (BWN) Donna, TX St. Joseph Church.
DeForge, Michael W. '79 (BUR) [H] Burlington, VT University of Vermont-The Catholic Center at UVM; [H] Burlington, VT University of Vermont-The Catholic Center at UVM.
DeFour, Reginald *c.s.sp.* (PIT) [B] Pittsburgh, PA Duquesne University of the Holy Ghost.
DeFrancisco, Joseph '75 (BEA) On Duty Outside the Diocese.
DeFranco, Anthony '38 (ALB) [2] Schenectady, NY St. Anthony Church; [9] Schenectady, NY St. John the Evangelist Church.
DeFrange, Jonathan M. *o.s.b.* '78 (NO) Folsom, LA St. John the Baptist Church; [A] St. Benedict, LA St. Joseph's Seminary College; [P] St. Benedict, LA St. Joseph Abbey.
DeFrias, Hadmels R. '99 (NEW) [1] Elizabeth, NJ St. Mary of the Assumption Church.
DeFronzo, Anthony R. '81 (PSC) On Duty Outside Diocese.
DeGaetano, Louis J. '79 (BRK) [169] Queens, NY St. Francis de Sales Church.
Degagne, Richard E. '82 (FR) [2] Taunton, MA Our Lady of the Immaculate Conception Church.
Degan, Bernard P. *c.m.* '43 (NO) [P] New Orleans, LA Vincentian Fathers.
Degan, Siro Dal *o.s.j.* '60 (MRY) Davenport, CA St. Vincent De Paul Church; [F] Santa Cruz, CA Oblates of St. Joseph Provincial House and Shrine.
DeGante, Adalberto '79 (DEN) Fort Morgan, CO St. Helena Church; Greeley, CO Our Lady of Peace Church.
DeGante, Adalberto '79 (GLP) On Duty Outside of Diocese.
Degaris, Herbert P. (NY) Blauvelt, NY St. Catharine Church.
Degen, Jerome A. '59 (SC) Manson, IA St. Thomas Church; Pomeroy, IA St. Mary's Church.
Degenhardt, Gervase *o.f.m.cap.* '58 (PIT) [30] Pittsburgh, PA Our Lady of the Angels Church.
DeGeorge, Salvatore *o.m.i.* '65 (SAT) [M] San Antonio, TX Oblate Benson Residence (Southwest Area).
DeGeorge, Salvatore *o.m.i.* '65 (WDC) [M] Washington, DC Missionary Oblates of Mary Immaculate.
DeGeorge, Salvatore F. *o.m.i.* '65 (SAT) [M] San Antonio, TX Missionary Oblates of Mary Immaculate.
DeGerolami, Michael '74 (SAT) [62] San Antonio, TX St. Philip of Jesus Church.
Degeyter, Edward '70 (LAF) Jeanerette, LA St. John the Evangelist Church.
DeGiorgio, John M. '80 (RIC) [11] Richmond, VA St. Gabriel Church.
DeGiovine, Christopher '77 (ALB) Special Assignment; [B] Albany, NY The College of Saint Rose; [M] Albany, NY Convent of the Sacred Heart.
DeGiralamo, Gerald F. *s.a.* '81 (RVC) Babylon, NY St. Joseph's Church.
Deglaire, Pierre *c.s.sp.* '70 (SB) Colton, CA San Salvador Church.
Degnan, Daniel A. *s.j.* '66 (NEW) [C] Jersey City, NJ St. Peter's Preparatory School.
Degnan, Henry B. '48 (PH) [4] Norristown, PA St. Paul Church; Retired.
Degnan, James F. '55 (BO) Hopkinton, MA St. John the Evangelist Church.
Degnan, John F. '51 (JC) St. Elizabeth, MO St. Lawrence Church.
DeGrand, Robert L. '80 (SFD) Neoga, IL St. Mary of the Assumption Church; Sigel, IL St. Michael the Archangel Church.
DeGrandis, Robert *s.s.j.* '59 (WDC) [B] Washington, DC St. Joseph's Seminary.
DeGrocco, Joseph '88 (RVC) Wantagh, NY St. Frances de Chantal Church.
DeGrood, Donald '97 (STP) [C] St. Paul, MN University of St. Thomas.
DeGrood, Donald E. '97 (STP) [A] St. Paul, MN St. John Vianney Seminary.
DeGroot, Francis J. '93 (MAR) Rudyard, MI St. Joseph Church.
DeGroot, Ignatius *o.f.m.* '64 (SFR) [5] San Francisco, CA St. Anthony of Padua Church.
DeGroot, Kenneth J. *o.praem.* '61 (GB) [17] Green Bay, WI St. Willebrord Church.
DeGuzman, Dennis '91 (OM) Aloys, NE St. Aloysius Church; Monterey, NE St. Boniface Church; St. Charles, NE St. Anthony Church.
DeGuzman, Francis *o.mar.* '95 (SAM) [C] Petersham, MA Most Holy Trinity Monastery.
Dehetre, Mark '93 (LAN) Goodrich, MI St. Mark the Evangelist Church.
Dehler, William A. *s.j.* '44 (DET) [P] Clarkston, MI Colombiere Center.
Dehne, Carl A. *s.j.* '70 (STL) [P] St. Louis, MO The Jesuits of the Missouri Province.
Dehner, Eugene *o.s.b.* '40 (KCK) [A] Atchison, KS Benedictine College; [H] Atchison, KS St. Benedict's Abbey.
Dehner, Philip R. *o.c.s.o.* '53 (ATL) [J] Conyers, GA The Monastery of the Holy Spirit.
DeHondt, Ronald J. '73 (DET) [28] Detroit, MI St. Gregory Church; [45] Detroit, MI Madonna Church.
Deibel, David L. '83 (SR) [M] Napa, CA Provincialate Community.
Deichert, Joseph '84 (BIS) On Duty Outside the Diocese.
Deig, Robert A. '50 (EVN) [17] Evansville, IN St. John the Evangelist Church.
Deikel, Jeff J. '76 (LA) Panorama City, CA St. Genevieve Church.
Deimeke, L. Edward '75 (ALB) Special Assignment.
Deimeke, Louis '75 (ALB) Colonie, NY St. Clare Church.
Deimel, George *c.ss.r.* '37 (ALB) [L] Saratoga Springs, NY St. John Neumann Residence.
Deis, Dennis *o.m.i.* '65 (SFS) Rosholt, SD St. John the Baptist Church.
Deis, Michael S. *o.m.i.* '47 (BEL) [F] Belleville, IL Missionary Oblates of Mary Immaculate - St. Henry's Oblate Residence.
Deisch, Raymond J. '62 (RC) Gregory, SD St. Joseph Church.
Deister, Charles C. '63 (STL) Kimmswick, MO St. Joseph Church.
Deitch, Richard S. '86 (SFR) Sausalito, CA St. Mary Star of the Sea Church.
Deitchman, Carl *o.s.b.* '84 (IND) [A] St. Meinrad, IN St. Meinrad Seminary; [J] St. Meinrad, IN St. Meinrad Archabbey.
Deitelhoff, Bernard H. '57 (MAD) Argyle, WI St. Joseph Church; Yellowstone, WI St. Michael Church.
Deiters, James E. '91 (BEL) O'Fallon, IL St. Clare Church.
Deiters, Robert M. *s.j.* '58 (FgM) Provinces.
Deitzer, Gerald E. *c.m.* '55 (PH) [AA] Philadelphia, PA Congregation of the Mission; [AA] Philadelphia, PA Congregation of the Mission.
DeJardin, Joseph R. *s.j.* '61 (P) [D] Portland, OR Jesuit High School.
DeJulio, David T. '90 (SP) [1] St. Petersburg, FL Cathedral of St. Jude the Apostle.
DeJulio, Robert J. '72 (NY) Brewster, NY St. Lawrence O'Toole Church.
Deka, John S. '58 (CLV) [32] Cleveland, OH St. Hyacinth Church.
Dekat, Carl '53 (KCK) [7] Topeka, KS St. Joseph's Church.
Dekat, Earl M. '66 (KCK) Emmett, KS Holy Cross Church; Rossville, KS St. Stanislaus Church; St. Marys, KS Immaculate Conception Church.
Deken, John C. '72 (STL) Ste. Genevieve, MO Ste. Genevieve Church.
Dekrem, Bruno '92 (RVC) Williston Park, NY St. Aidan's Church.
del Burgo, Lucio *o.c.d.* '73 (MIA) [L] Miami, FL Discalced Carmelite Friars of Miami, Inc.
del Cerro, Helios *c.m.* '61 (LA) [32] Los Angeles, CA Our Lady of the Rosary of Talpa Church.
Del Conte, Eugene A. *o.s.a.* '55 (MIL) [P] Racine, WI Augustinian Novitiate.
Del Giudice, Carl '81 (CHL) Brevard, NC Sacred Heart Church.
Del Marmol, Alfonso *s.j.* '51 (FgM) Provinces.
Del Monaco, Marian *o.s.b.* '66 (P) [L] St. Benedict, OR Mt. Angel Abbey.
Del Monaco, Marion '66 (P) [K] Mount Angel, OR Providence Benedictine Nursing Center.
del Nino Jesus, Rene A. Maria *s.e.m.v.* '83 (ARE) Hatillo, PR Our Lady of Guadalupe Church.
Del Prete, Msgr. Frank G. '77 (NEW) [4] Hoboken, NJ SS. Peter and Paul's Church.
Del Priore, Kenneth '83 (SD) [11] San Diego, CA Our Lady of Angels Church.
del Real, Jorge Roman '81 (SFR) [4] San Mateo, CA St. Timothy Church.
del Riego, Rutilio J. *d.l.p.* '65 (SB) [2] Riverside, CA Our Lady of Perpetual Help Church.
del Riego, Rutilio J. '65 (WDC) [B] Washington, DC Diocesan Laborer Priests, House of Studies.
del Toro, Alfredo *m.c.c.j.* '86 (CHI) [136] Chicago, IL St. Michael the Archangel Church.
Del Toro, Jose L. *t.o.r.* '95 (ALX) [3] Alexandria, LA St. Frances Xavier Cabrini Church.
del Val, Feliciano '36 (GAL) Retired.
Del Val, Jose '96 (FR) [19] New Bedford, MA St. Kilian Church; [O] New Bedford, MA The Institute of the Incarnate Word, Inc.
Del Valle, Tomas '79 (SJN) On Duty Outside the Archdiocese.
Del Vecchio, Joseph *s.s.j.* (BAL) [81] Baltimore, MD St. Peter Claver Church.
deLadurantaye, Paul F. '88 (ARL) [1] Arlington, VA Cathedral of St. Thomas More.
Delaere, Paul *c.i.c.m.* '43 (FgM) Missionhurst Foreign Missions.
Delahanty, Patrick D. '69 (L) [64] Louisville, KY St. Peter Claver Church.
Delahunty, Richard A. '65 (ORG) Yorba Linda, CA St. Martin Church.
Delahunty, Thomas '54 (SEA) Retired.

Delahunty, Thomas P. '55 (SAC) Retired and in Senior Ministry.
DeLand, Robert J. '73 (SAG) [15] Saginaw, MI SS. Peter and Paul Church.
Delaney, Brian '75 (LA) Montebello, CA Our Lady of the Miraculous Medal Church.
Delaney, Charles A. *c.s.c.* '49 (FgM) Holy Cross Foreign Missions.
Delaney, Charles A. *c.s.c.* '49 (FTW) [J] South Bend, IN Congregation of Holy Cross, Indiana Province, Provincial House.
Delaney, David F. '61 (BO) Senior Priests.
Delaney, Msgr. Dennis M. '76 (STL) [A] St. Louis, MO Kenrick-Glennon Seminary.
Delaney, Donald *s.d.b.* '76 (NEW) [3] Elizabeth, NJ St. Anthony's Church.
Delaney, Francis H. '52 (BO) Senior Priests.
Delaney, Msgr. Howard L. '40 (PBL) Retired.
Delaney, James *c.s.sp.* '54 (BRK) [V] Long Island City, NY Holy Ghost Fathers of Ireland; [Z] Long Island City, NY World Compassion Link.
Delaney, James P. *o.m.i.* '36 (SAT) [K] San Antonio, TX Oblate Madonna Residence.
Delaney, Msgr. John '64 (MIA) Sabbatical.
Delaney, John H. '81 (FTW) Goshen, IN St. John the Evangelist Church.
Delaney, John J. '62 (NY) [52] New York, NY Immaculate Conception Church.
Delaney, John W. (BO) North Andover, MA St. Michael Church.
Delaney, Larry '90 (CR) East Grand Forks, MN Sacred Heart Church.
Delaney, Lawrence '67 (LAN) [L] De Witt, MI St. Francis Retreat Center.
Delaney, Matthew S. '51 (LA) Retired.
Delaney, Msgr. Michael J. '85 (SCR) [1] Hazleton, PA St. Gabriel's Church.
DeLaney, Michael M. *c.s.c.* '87 (P) [B] Portland, OR University of Portland; [L] Portland, OR Holy Cross Fathers & Brothers, C.S.C. - University of Portland.
Delaney, Michael V. *s.j.* '85 (DEN) [1] Fort Collins, CO St. Joseph Church.
Delaney, Richard (RVC) Retired.
Delaney, T. Timothy '79 (SCR) Retired.
Delaney, Thomas '57 (JKS) Greenwood, MS Immaculate Heart of Mary Church.
Delaney, Thomas *o.m.i.* '60 (FgM) Oblates Foreign Missions.
Delaney, Thomas P. *s.j.* '61 (LA) [3] Santa Barbara, CA Our Lady of Sorrows Church.
Delaney, Msgr. William '44 (CHY) [2] Cheyenne, WY Holy Trinity Church; Retired.
Delaney, William *c.pp.s.* '63 (LA) [40] Los Angeles, CA St. Agnes Church.
Delaney, William *s.j.* '85 (LA) [CC] Burbank, CA SCRC (Southern California Renewal Communities).
Delaney, Msgr. William B. '42 (NY) [2] White Plains, NY St. John the Evangelist Church; Retired.
Delaney, William I. '61 (RVC) West Hempstead, NY St. Thomas, the Apostle Church; Retired.
Delaney, William J. '54 (NY) [47] New York, NY Holy Innocents Church.
Delaney, William K. *s.j.* '85 (LA) [Q] Los Angeles, CA Columbiere House.
DeLange, Maurice '71 (COV) Leave of Absence.
Delano, Kenneth J. '60 (FR) [11] Fall River, MA Our Lady of the Immaculate Conception Church.
Delargy, Torlach C. '66 (SFR) [S] San Francisco, CA Prelature of the Holy Cross and Opus Dei.
Delarm, Curtis R. '89 (HBG) [2] Harrisburg, PA St. Catherine Laboure Church.
Delarue, Louis '75 (BEA) [6] Port Arthur, TX St. John Church.
Delauney, Herbert C. '75 (LAF) Absent on Sick Leave.
DeLay, Dominic *o.p.* '93 (ORG) [1] Orange, CA Cathedral of the Holy Family.
Delay, Donald R. '83 (BO) Walpole, MA St. Mary Church.
DeLazzer, Dorino (DEN) [2] Boulder, CO Sacred Heart of Mary Church.
Delbel, James A. '81 (OG) Essex, NY St. Joseph Church; Willsboro, NY St. Philip of Jesus Church; Moriah, NY Moriah Shock Incarceration Correctional Facility.
Delclos, John A. '71 (BAL) [17] Baltimore, MD St. Bernardine Church.
DelConte, Eugene *o.s.a.* '55 (MIL) [14] Racine, WI St. Rita Church.
DelDuca, John A. '68 (CAM) Hammonton, NJ St. Martin de Porres Church.
DeLeers, Stephen '84 (MIL) [B] Hales Corners, WI Sacred Heart School of Theology.
DeLeers, Stephen V. '84 (MIL) [A] St. Francis, WI Saint Francis Seminary.
DeLeers, Vincent J. *o.praem.* '46 (SFE) [I] Albuquerque, NM Santa Maria de la Vid Priory.
DeLeeuw, John '44 (LAF) Retired.
Delehanty, Thomas F. '41 (SPR) Retired.
DeLellis, Francis V. '49 (PRO) Retired.
Delelse, Salvatore '66 (CAM) Retired.
Delendick, John '77 (BRK) [86] Brooklyn, NY St. Michael's Church.
DeLeo, Roy James '69 (NEW) [6] Elizabeth, NJ St. Genevieve's Church.
DeLeon, Benedict '80 (SAC) Vacaville, CA St. Mary Church.
DeLeon, Eddie *c.m.f.* '91 (SPC) [E] Springfield, MO Claretians Missionaries' Residence-Villa Claret; [I] Springfield, MO The Nancy McGregor House, Southwest MO State University, Drury College, Ozarks Technical Comm. College.
DeLeon, Juancho G. '94 (NEW) Bloomfield, NJ St. Valentine Church.
DeLeon, Michael *o.s.b.* '86 (CC) [H] Sandia, TX Corpus Christi Abbey.
Delgado, Enrique '96 (MIA) [2] Hollywood, FL Nativity Church.
Delgado, Joseph '95 (SJ) On Leave of Absence.
Delgado, Leo *c.m.f.* '55 (ORG) [2] Orange, CA La Purisima Church.
Delgado, Leslie N. '55 (LA) [27] Los Angeles, CA Our Lady of Guadalupe Sanctuary Church.
Delgado, Rodolfo '82 (SAC) Gridley, CA Sacred Heart Church.
Delgado, Ruben '90 (BWN) Weslaco, TX San Martin de Porres Church.
Delich, David *o.p.* '63 (CHI) River Forest, IL St. Vincent Ferrer Church.
Deliman, Msgr. Edward M. '73 (PH) [157] Philadelphia, PA Visitation B.V.M. Church.
Delis, Robert *s.d.b.* '79 (SFR) [N] San Francisco, CA Salesian Provincial Residence.
Delisi, Anthony *o.c.s.o.* '54 (ATL) [J] Conyers, GA The Monastery of the Holy Spirit.
DeLisle, Henri A. *o.m.i.* '58 (NOR) [F] Willimantic, CT Missionary Oblates of Mary Immaculate; [I] Willimantic, CT Immaculata Retreat House.
Delisle, Richard *m.s.* '59 (MAN) Lebanon, NH Sacred Heart Church.
Dell, Robert *c.o.* '90 (SEA) [P] Seattle, WA Oratorian Community.
Dell, Robert S. *c.o.* '90 (CHR) [E] Rock Hill, SC Oratory of St. Philip Neri, Congregation of the Oratory of Pontifical Rite.
Dell'Anno, Anthony V. '69 (BRK) [147] Queens, NY St. Aloysius Church.
Dell'Oro, Italo *c.r.s.* '82 (GAL) [11] Houston, TX Assumption Church.
Della Neve, Louis '52 (BUF) Retired.
della Picca, Angelo A. '45 (CIN) [D] Cincinnati, OH College of Mount St. Joseph.
della Picca, Msgr. Paul B. '59 (ALN) [9] Bethlehem, PA Our Lady of Pompeii Church.
Della Pietra, Douglas '96 (ROC) [12] Rochester, NY St. Charles Borromeo Church.
DellaBadia, Leonard *c.s.s.* '35 (NY) [4] White Plains, NY Our Lady of Mt. Carmel Church.
DellaPietra, Douglas '96 (ROC) Canandaigua, NY St. Mary Church; East Bloomfield, NY St. Bridget Church.
Delli Carpini, John J. '76 (PH) Yeadon, PA St. Louis Church.
Dello Russo, John F. *o.s.a.* '87 (NY) [168] Bronx, NY St. Nicholas of Tolentine Church.
Dellos, Richard '68 (SY) Greene, NY Immaculate Conception Church.
Delmonte, Albert (ROC) [23] Rochester, NY Holy Ghost Church.
Delmonte, Albert L. '64 (ROC) East Rochester, NY St. Jerome Church.
Delmore, Eugene P. *s.j.* '69 (FBK) Bethel, AK Immaculate Conception Church; [E] St. Marys, AK Brother Joe Prince Jesuit Community.
DeLong, Allen *s.m.* (HON) [G] Honolulu, HI Marianist Communities.
DeLong, James Allen *s.m.* (HON) [C] Honolulu, HI Saint Louis School; [C] Honolulu, HI Saint Louis School.
Delonnay, Lawrence '75 (DET) Waterford, MI Our Lady of the Lakes Church.
DeLora, John P. '94 (NY) [5] New Rochelle, NY Holy Name of Jesus Church.
DeLorenzo, Francis Solanus *o.f.m.* '47 (ALB) [A] Catskill, NY St. Anthony Friary.
DeLorenzo, John R. '76 (SY) [17] Syracuse, NY St. John the Baptist Church.
DeLorenzo, Vincent '65 (LAN) Burton, MI Holy Redeemer Church.
DeLorme, R. Daniel '57 (SY) Homer, NY St. Margaret Church.
Delort, Norbert E. *c.ss.r.* '62 (STL) [P] Liguori, MO St. Clement Health Care Center.
Delos, Bernard M. '45 (ALB) Retired.
DeLuca, Albert J. '57 (NY) [111] New York, NY Sacred Hearts of Jesus and Mary Church.
DeLuca, Anthony '53 (PIT) Retired.
DeLuca, David *m.s.c.* '66 (RCK) [G] Aurora, IL Missionaries of the Sacred Heart Community.
DeLuca, Francis G. '58 (WIL) Retired.
DeLuca, Paul F. '81 (CIN) [10] Dayton, OH St. Helen Church.
DeLuca, Stephen J. '65 (BGP) [5] Greenwich, CT St. Agnes Church.
DeLucia, Gerald M. '78 (Y) Lowellville, OH Our Lady of the Holy Rosary Church.
DeLucia, Vincent G. *o.p.* '94 (PRO) [29] Providence, RI St. Pius V Church; [P] Providence, RI St. Pius Priory.
Deluney, Gerald C. '69 (SB) [1] Corona, CA Corpus Christi Church.
DelVecchio, Msgr. Michael E. '54 (BUF) Retired.
Delzell, David G. '50 (TR) Retired.
Delzingaro, Richard M. *c.r.s.p., m.a.* '96 (ALN) [K] Bethlehem, PA The Barnabite Fathers Barnabite Spiritual Center.
DeMaio, Joseph *o.carm.* '65 (ROC) [C] Rochester, NY McQuaid Jesuit High School; [I] Rochester, NY Whitefriars Priory.
DeMan, Thomas *o.p.* '62 (SEA) [22] Seattle, WA Blessed Sacrament Church.
DeManuele, James *c.p.* '78 (L) [L] Louisville, KY Sacred Heart Retreat.
Demarais, Garvin J. '81 (OG) Keeseville, NY Church of the Immaculate Conception; Keeseville, NY St. John the Baptist Church.
DeMarco, Peter A. '60 (BGP) [2] Trumbull, CT St. Catherine of Siena Church.
deMaria, Lawrence A. '51 (NO) New Orleans, LA Veterans Affairs Medical Center; Retired.
DeMarinis, Msgr. John H. '62 (Y) [8] Youngstown, OH St. Anthony's Church.
DeMartini, Rodney J. '75 (SR) [O] Sebastopol, CA National Catholic AIDS Network.
DeMartinis, Michael G. '97 (E) [10] Erie, PA Our Lady of Peace Church.
DeMartinis, O. Robert '86 (ALB) Glens Falls, NY Glens Falls Hospital.
DeMartino, Robert J. '92 (ARL) Falls Church, VA St. Philip Church.
Demasi, Michael A. '43 (BUR) Retired.
DeMattia, John '68 (PAT) Whippany, NJ Our Lady of Mercy Church.
DeMayo, John B. '61 (PH) Absent on Sick Leave.
Dembow, Leonard '65 (NEW) Clark, NJ St. Agnes Church.
Demeck, Norman *c.p.* '52 (MET) [H] South River, NJ Passionist Provincial Office.
Demeck, Norman *c.p.* '52 (TR) [A] Lakewood, NJ Georgian Court College.
DeMeester, Peter '28 (WH) Retired.
Demek, Martin H. '75 (BAL) [97] Baltimore, MD St. William of York Church.
Demers, Bertrand '48 (KNX) [B] Knoxville, TN St. Mary's Health System, Inc.
Demers, Francis *o.m.i.* '55 (BO) [W] Lowell, MA Missionary Oblates of Mary Immaculate.
Demers, Gerard A. *s.m.* '59 (BO) [10] Lawrence, MA Sacred Heart Church.
Demers, Normand J. '58 (PRO) [4] East Providence, RI St. Martha Church.
Demers, Paul R. *s.c.* '81 (MAN) [B] Nashua, NH Rivier College; [N] Manchester, NH Campus Ministries.
Demers, Raymond A. '55 (MAN) Retired.
Demers, Richard D. '83 (OG) Louisville, NY St. Lawrence Church; Madrid, NY St. John the Baptist Church.
Demers, Thomas *o.p.* '39 (PRT) [I] Lewiston, ME SS. Peter and Paul House.
Demers, Wilfred G. '59 (MAN) [9] Manchester, NH St. George Church; Retired.
Demetzky, Alex D. '53 (CLV) [7] Lorain, OH St. Ladislaus Church; Retired.
DeMeulemeester, Patrick '95 (PEO) Elkhart, IL St. Patrick Church.
DeMeulenaere, Martin *o.s.b.* '73 (KC) [1] Kansas City, MO Cathedral of Immaculate Conception; [9] Kansas City, MO St. Elizabeth's Church; [H] Blue Springs, MO St. Mary's Manor; [J] Conception, MO Conception Abbey.
Deming, Robert N. '58 (KC) Special Assignment.
Demko, Dennis *c.ss.r.* '80 (CGS) San Lorenzo, PR Nuestra Senora de la Mercedes Church.
Demko, James J. '82 (PSC) Beaver Meadows, PA SS. Peter and Paul Church.
Demkovich, Msgr. John J. (PAT) [5] Clifton, NJ SS. Cyril and Methodius Church.
Demkovich, Msgr. John J. '65 (PAT) [3] Passaic, NJ Assumption of the Blessed Virgin Mary Church.
Demkovich, Michael T. *o.p.* '81 (SFE) [31] Albuquerque, NM St. Thomas Aquinas University Church; [M] Albuquerque, NM Dominican Ecclesial Institute.
Demkowicz, Arthur *s.j.* (DAL) [D] Dallas, TX Jesuit College Preparatory School.
Deml, Frank '57 (DEN) [1] Lakewood, CO St. Bernadette Church.
Demmer, Donald '73 (DET) Garden City, MI St. Dunstan Church.
Demo, John M. '88 (OG) Hopkinton, NY Church of the Holy Cross; Saint Regis Falls, NY St. Ann Church; Malone, NY Barehill Correctional Facility.
DeMolen, Richard '98 (RNO) [6] Reno, NV St. Therese Church of the Little Flower.
DeMoraes, Jonas V. '70 (PH) [67] Philadelphia, PA St. Hugh of Cluny Church.

DeMott, Lester *c.m.* '55 (STA) [E] Jacksonville, FL St. Vincent's Medical Center, Inc.
DeMott, Lester T. *c.m.* '49 (PH) [AA] Philadelphia, PA Congregation of the Mission.
DeMott, Stephen T. *m.m.* '76 (FgM) Maryknoll Foreign Missions.
Dempsey, Dennis '80 (STP) [19] St. Paul, MN St. Francis De Sales Church; [21] St. Paul, MN St. James Church.
Dempsey, Edward M. '67 (NOR) Absent on Leave.
Dempsey, James '56 (BEA) Retired.
Dempsey, John G. '64 (STL) [39] St. Louis, MO St. Joan of Arc Church.
Dempsey, Msgr. Michael J. '58 (BRK) [218] Queens, NY Our Lady, Queen of Martyrs Church.
Dempsey, Nicholas '71 (SD) Del Mar, CA St. William of York Church.
Dempsey, Patrick E. '97 (WDC) [4] Washington, DC Annunciation Church.
Dempsey, Richard J. '58 (CHI) Evergreen Park, IL Most Holy Redeemer Church.
Dempsey, Robert J. '80 (CHI) On Duty Outside the Archdiocese.
Dempsey, Terrence E. *s.j.* '85 (STL) [C] St. Louis, MO Saint Louis University; [P] St. Louis, MO Jesuit Community Corporation at St. Louis University - Jesuit Hall.
Dempsey, Thomas J. '61 (RCK) [3] Elgin, IL St. Mary Church.
Dempsey, Msgr. Thomas J. '62 (STL) Mattese, MO Assumption Church.
Dempski, Daniel G. *o.s.b.* '79 (MAN) [K] Manchester, NH St. Anselm Abbey.
Dempster, Douglas W. '62 (WIL) Retired.
Demse, Thomas P. '76 (MIL) Hartland, WI St. Charles Church.
Demski, Msgr. Arthur A. '54 (BRK) Absent on Sick Leave; Retired.
DeMuro, S. Patrick '85 (HRT) Retired.
Demuth, Msgr. George R. '46 (SCR) Retired.
Demuth, Paul E. '68 (GB) [15] Green Bay, WI Resurrection Church.
DeNardi, Charles A. '36 (OWN) Retired.
Denault, Paul *o.carm.* '80 (NY) [DD] Middletown, NY Brandsma Priory.
Denburger, John J. *o.c.s.o.* '63 (ROC) [I] Piffard, NY Abbey of the Genesee.
Dendinger, Robert L. '75 (TOL) New Washington, OH St. Bernard Church; North Auburn, OH Mother of Sorrows Church.
Dendinger, William J. '65 (OM) Military Chaplains.
Dene, Charles J. '58 (ALN) Lost Creek, PA St. Mary Magdalen Church; Minersville, PA FCI-Schuylkill, Federal Correctional Institute.
Dene, Joseph '62 (WH) Retired.
Deneault, Normand J. '45 (PRO) Retired; [P] Providence, RI St. John Vianney Residence.
Denehy, Msgr. John '45 (ORL) Retired.
Denehy, John F. '56 (FR) Retired.
Denemark, Emil J. *s.j.* '81 (FgM) Provinces.
Denesha, J. Everett '50 (OG) Raymondville, NY St. Raymond Church.
Denha, Suleiman '59 (EST) Oak Park, MI Mar Addai Chaldean Church.
Denham, Jim '78 (AUS) [F] Austin, TX Seton Medical Center.
Denig, Philip '85 (DEN) On Duty Outside the Archdiocese.
Denig, Stephen J. *c.m.* '75 (BRK) [V] Jamaica, NY Vincentian Residence.
Deniger, Joseph *c.s.sp.* '58 (LR) Conway, AR St. Joseph's Church.
DeNinno, Dale E. '78 (PIT) [16] Pittsburgh, PA Immaculate Conception Church; [20] Pittsburgh, PA St. Joseph Church.
DeNinno, Louis '76 (PIT) [7] Pittsburgh, PA St. Catherine of Siena Church.
Denison, Frederick J. '73 (IND) Frenchtown, IN St. Bernard Church; St. Joseph, IN St. Joseph Church.
Denman, Donald '42 (P) Retired.
Denn, James J. *c.s.c.* '61 (FTW) [J] South Bend, IN Congregation of Holy Cross, Indiana Province, Provincial House.
Dennehy, John D. '81 (NEW) [Q] Newark, NJ Essex County College, Rutgers University/Newark, NJIT.
Dennehy, Mark M. *o.s.m.* '46 (CHI) [14] Chicago, IL Annunciata Church; [N] Chicago, IL Order of Friar Servants of Mary (Servites) United States of America Province, Inc.
Dennehy, Martin J. '51 (BGP) Retired.
Dennemann, Thomas J. '73 (CIN) [7] Cincinnati, OH St. Ann Church.
Dennerg, John F. *c.s.c.* '87 (FR) [A] North Easton, MA Stonehill College.
Dennerlein, Arno A. '69 (JOL) Lombard, IL Sacred Heart Church.
Dennerlein, John L. '74 (JOL) [3] Joliet, IL Holy Family Church.
Dennett, John A. '62 (GI) Retired.
Dennigan, Patrick J. '62 (BUR) Retired.
Denning, John F. *c.s.c.* '87 (BO) [CC] Bridgewater, MA Bridgewater State College Catholic Center.
Denning, John F. *c.s.c.* '87 (FR) [A] North Easton, MA Holy Cross Fathers Religious.
Denning, Joseph B. '60 (DAV) Camanche, IA Church of the Visitation.
Dennis, George T. *s.j.* '54 (WDC) [M] Washington, DC Leonard Neale House.
Dennis, James J. '42 (BGP) Retired; [P] Stamford, CT The Catherine Dennis Keefe Queen of the Clergy Retired Priests' Residence.
Dennis, John J. *o.s.f.s.* '45 (PH) [D] Philadelphia, PA Father Judge High School for Boys; [AA] Philadelphia, PA Father Judge Faculty House.
Dennis, John M. *s.j.* '86 (BAL) [D] Baltimore, MD Loyola Blakefield.
Dennis, Patrick '78 (B) [3] Boise, ID St. Mary's Church.
Dennis, Peter K. *ss.cc.* '62 (LA) [Q] La Verne, CA Congregation of the Sacred Hearts of Jesus and Mary.
Dennis, Sam *o.s.b.* (SFE) [I] Pecos, NM Our Lady of Guadalupe Abbey.
Dennis, Samuel *o.s.b.* '57 (SFE) [K] Pecos, NM Our Lady of Guadalupe Olivetan Benedictine Abbey.
Dennis, Thom '92 (SFD) [3] Springfield, IL Christ The King Church.
Dennison, Arthur '73 (MIA) Coral Springs, FL St. Andrew Church.
Denniston, John '79 (RVC) Huntington, NY St. Patrick's Church.
Denny, Charles J. '69 (TOL) Bono, OH Our Lady of Mt. Carmel Church; Oregon, OH St. Charles Mercy Hospital; [H] Oregon, OH St. Charles Mercy Hospital.
Denny, David '80 (PBL) [J] Crestone, CO Spiritual Life Institute of America, Inc.
Denny, John T. *o.s.a.* '90 (PH) [D] Drexel Hill, PA Monsignor Bonner High School.
Denny, Joseph P. '67 (PH) [21] Philadelphia, PA St. Bartholomew Church.
Denny, Thomas F. *s.j.* '68 (NY) [DD] New York, NY St. Ignatius Loyola Residence.
Deno, Msgr. Lawrence M. '59 (OG) Cadyville, NY St. James Minor Church.
Denomme, Msgr. George E. '48 (WOR) [3] Leominster, MA St. Cecilia's Church.
Densmore, Robert J. '61 (MAN) [2] Manchester, NH St. Anne Church; Retired.
Dente, Thomas A. '93 (NEW) Hillsdale, NJ St. John the Baptist Church.
Denti, Msgr. Carl J. '42 (SY) Retired.
Dentici, Msgr. Thomas (DEN) Retired.
Dentinger, Roy E. '50 (L) Retired.
Dentinger, Vincent Paul '54 (L) Retired.
Dentzman, Robert D. *o.f.m.* '48 (KAL) [D] Kalamazoo, MI Borgess Medical Center.
Dentzman, Robert F. *o.f.m.* '48 (KAL) [2] Kalamazoo, MI St. Joseph Church.
Denys, Charles *c.i.c.m.* '44 (ARL) [J] Arlington, VA Missionhurst, C.I.C.M.-Central House and Provincialate.
Denzel, F. William *o.m.i.* '55 (BO) [Z] Tewksbury, MA Immaculate Heart of Mary Infirmary.
Denzer, Joseph W. '68 (BRK) [77] Brooklyn, NY St. Malachy's Church; Absent on Sick Leave.
Denzer, Thomas F. *s.j.* '61 (KC) [B] Kansas City, MO Rockhurst University; [J] Kansas City, MO Rockhurst Jesuit Community.
DeOtero, Roberto '77 (HON) Leave of Absence.
DePaoli, Edward M. '70 (PH) Absent on Leave.
DePasquale, Dominic '61 (SB) Retired.
DePasquale, Leonard *i.m.c.* '71 (MET) [H] Somerset, NJ Consolata Society for Foreign Missions; [N] Somerset, NJ Mission International, Inc.
Depatie, Donald L. '78 (PRO) [1] Cumberland, RI St. Aidan Church.
Depcik, Michael *o.s.f.s.* '00 (LAN) [13] Flint, MI St. Pius X Church.
Depeaux, Bernard F. '50 (BUR) Retired.
DePew, Daniel R. '85 (GR) Alpine, MI Holy Trinity Church.
DePietro, Arthur J. '63 (BO) Permanent Disability.
Depinet, Robert L. *m.m.* '61 (FgM) Maryknoll Foreign Missions.
DePinto, Basil '58 (OAK) Piedmont, CA Corpus Christi Church; Oakland, CA Highland Hospital.
Depman, Francis J. '81 (PH) West Grove, PA Assumption B.V.M. Church.
Deponai, Joseph J. '83 (NY) Military Chaplains.
DePorres-Cox, Jesse *o.p.* '87 (DET) Special Assignment.
DePorter, Arnold W. '63 (WDC) Suitland, MD St. Bernardine Church.
DePra, Italo '51 (P) Retired.
DePriest, Ellis L. *s.m.* '53 (NO) New Orleans, LA Byzantine Catholic Church; [P] New Orleans, LA Marist Fathers.
DeProfio, Msgr. Louis A. '56 (BGP) [4] Trumbull, CT St. Theresa Church.
DeProspero, Nicholas '70 (PSC) Pottstown, PA St. John the Baptist Church.
Deptula, Rick *o.f.m.conv.* '83 (BAL) [S] Ellicott City, MD St. Joseph Cupertino Friary, Friars Minor Conventual of St. Francis of Assisi; [S] Ellicott City, MD Friary of St. Joseph Cupertino.
Deptula, Stanley '96 (PEO) [P] Champaign, IL St. John's Catholic Student Chapel and Newman Foundation, University of Illinois.
Deptula, Stanley L. '96 (PEO) [2] Champaign, IL St. John's Catholic Chapel Church.
Derasmo, John M. '81 (RVC) Farmingville, NY Church of the Resurrection.
Derbes, Louis J. *c.m.* '51 (STL) [P] Perryville, MO Congregation of The Mission.
Derbish, Michael *o.f.m.* '62 (PIT) [O] Ben Avon, PA St. Anthony Friary and Mission House.
Derbish, Michael *o.f.m.* '62 (SJP) Aliquippa, PA Ss. Peter and Paul Church.
Derbyshire, Joseph '46 (NEW) [N] Rutherford, NJ St. John Vianney Residence for Priests.
Derbyshire, Joseph V. '46 (NEW) Retired.
DeRea, Philip *m.s.c.* '68 (ALN) [K] Reading, PA Missionaries of the Sacred Heart.
DeRea, Philip *m.s.c.* '68 (WDC) [V] Washington, DC Missionary Vehicle Association, Inc.
DeRego, Frank '87 (HON) Leave of Absence.
Deresienski, Stanley *s.s.e.* (BUR) Brattleboro, VT St. Michael Church.
Derfus, Kenneth J. '56 (MIL) Retired.
Dericks, Msgr. John H. '41 (PAT) Retired.
Derise, Mark '97 (LAF) [3] New Iberia, LA Our Lady of Perpetual Help Church.
DeRitis, Gilbert J. *m.m.* '54 (SJ) [L] Los Altos, CA Maryknoll.
Derivan, Msgr. Thomas B. '72 (NY) [145] Bronx, NY St. Helena Church.
Derivaux, Don '55 (JKS) Mound Bayou, MS St. Gabriel Church.
Derivaux, Donald F. '55 (JKS) Shaw, MS St. Francis of Assisi Church.
Dermody, Michael (SAC) Retired and in Senior Ministry.
Dermody, Thomas '62 (SAC) On Duty Outside the Diocese.
Dermody, Thomas '62 (SD) Brawley, CA Calipatria State Prison.
Dermond, Msgr. John K. '68 (TR) [13] Trenton, NJ St. Francis of Assisium Church; [T] Trenton, NJ The Haitian Community Center.
Dermott, William (ALN) Military Chaplains.
Dernbach, Arthur P. '53 (P) Sublimity, OR St. Boniface Church.
Dernek, Daniel R. '62 (WIN) [5] Winona, MN St. Stanislaus Church.
Dernek, Richard J. '70 (WIN) Blooming Prairie, MN St. Columbanus Church; Hayfield, MN Sacred Heart Church.
DeRoche, Wilfred L. '65 (OG) Rouses Point, NY St. Patrick Church.
DeRoeck, Walter G. '71 (CHI) Other Assignments.
deRosa, Francis M. '94 (ARL) [6] Arlington, VA Our Lady of Lourdes Church.
Derosier, Edmond M. '73 (BO) Shirley, MA St. Anthony Church.
DeRouen, Keith J. '83 (LAF) [1] Lafayette, LA Cathedral of St. John the Evangelist.
DeRouen, Robert R. *s.j.* '54 (DEN) [M] Denver, CO Xavier Jesuit Center.
Derrane, Mark G. (BO) Lynnfield, MA Our Lady of the Assumption Church.
Derrenbacher, James W. '45 (NY) Centerville, NY St. John the Evangelist Church; Retired.
Derrera, A. Ferdinand *s.j.* '61 (GAL) [42] Houston, TX St. Joseph Church.
Derrig, Joseph M. '63 (PH) Broomall, PA St. Pius X Church.
Derry, Daniel '63 (SJ) Gilroy, CA St. Mary Church.
DeRussy, Edward *s.j.* '57 (GAL) [66] Houston, TX St. Paul Church.
Derwinski, Victor A. '44 (LIN) Retired.
Dery, Henry R. '48 (HRT) Retired; [A] Bloomfield, CT St. Thomas Seminary.
Derylo, Walter W. '68 (GAY) Special Assignment.
Derzack, Thomas A. '76 (ALN) Lansford, PA St. Michael Church.
DeSa, Walter *o.s.f.s.* (FgM) Oblates of St. Francis de Sales Foreign Missions.
DeSalvo, Donald D. '69 (RCK) Somonauk, IL St. John the Baptist Church.
DeSalvo, Raphael *o.s.b.* '45 (LR) Shoal Creek, AR St. Scholastica's Church; [K] Shoal Creek, AR Hesychia House of Prayer.
DeSalvo, William '88 (JOL) Elmhurst, IL Visitation Church.
DeSanctis, Albert '80 (SAL) Tipton, KS St. Boniface's Church.
DeSanctis, Peter '79 (BRK) [207] Queens, NY Our Lady of the Blessed Sacrament Church.
DeSandre, John G. '64 (TR) Deal, NJ St. Mary of the Assumption Church.
DeSantis, Joseph A. '75 (ALN) Frackville, PA St. Joseph Church; Maizeville, PA Our Lady of Siluva Church.
DeSantis, Linus *o.f.m.conv.* '71 (ATL) Lithia Springs,

GA St. John Vianney Church; [M] Atlanta, GA Campus Ministry.
DeSanto, Joseph A. '54 (NY) Larchmont, NY St. Augustine Church.
Desaulniers, Richard P. '70 (PRO) Lincoln, RI St. James Church.
Desautels, Alfred R. *s.j.* '50 (WOR) [N] Worcester, MA Jesuits of Holy Cross College, Inc.
Desch, Paul *o.f.m.* '56 (HT) [4] Houma, LA Our Lady of the Most Holy Rosary Church.
Deschamps, Wilfred H. '90 (MAN) Gorham, NH Holy Family Church.
Deshaies, Richard A. *s.j.* '92 (BGP) [B] Fairfield, CT Fairfield University.
Deshaies, Richard J. *s.j.* '92 (BGP) [P] Fairfield, CT The Fairfield Jesuit Community-Fairfield University.
Desharnais, Gary '00 (YAK) [2] Yakima, WA Holy Family Church.
Deshotel, J. Douglas *v.f.* '78 (DAL) Irving, TX St. Luke Church.
DeSiano, Francis P. *c.s.p.* '72 (NY) [DD] Jamaica Estates, NY Paulist Fathers Generalate.
Desiderio, Frank *c.s.p.* (LA) [CC] Pacific Palisades, CA Paulist Productions.
Desilets, Donald A. '52 (SPR) Retired.
Desilets, Viateur '46 (LAF) Retired.
DeSilva, L. Praxid '69 (NY) Briarcliff Manor, NY St. Theresa Church.
DeSimone, Russell J. *o.s.a.* '51 (PH) [AA] Villanova, PA St. Thomas Monastery.
Desjardins, Msgr. Dominique '38 (SFR) Redwood City, CA Our Lady of Mount Carmel Church.
Desjardins, George A. '59 (MAN) [9] Manchester, NH St. George Church.
Desjardins, James M. *s.j.* '77 (BAL) [S] Baltimore, MD Jesuit Fathers and Brothers Maryland Provincial Curia.
Desjardins, James M. *s.j.* '77 (FgM) Provinces.
Desjardins, Raymond S. '42 (MAN) Retired.
Deskevich, Andrew J. '97 (PBR) Gibsonia, PA St. Andrew the Apostle Church.
DeSloover, A. Robert '74 (TOL) Miller City, OH St. Nicholas Church; New Cleveland, OH Holy Family Church.
Desmarais, Gerard R. '75 (MAN) [7] Nashua, NH St. Joseph Church.
Desmarais, Paul E. '79 (PRO) [11] Pawtucket, RI Sacred Heart of Jesus Church.
Desmarais, Rene L. '63 (DET) Port Huron, MI St. Joseph Church; [S] Port Huron, MI John Courtney Murray Newman Center.
Desmond, Barry '59 (MOB) Retired.
Desmond, Donald J. '64 (RVC) East Hampton, NY Most Holy Trinity Church.
Desmond, Hubert E. '58 (BO) [1] Woburn, MA St. Anthony Church.
Desmond, Msgr. Joseph E. '47 (MAN) Hudson, NH St. John the Evangelist Church; Retired.
Desmond, Joseph L. '74 (MET) Monmouth Junction, NJ St. Cecilia Church.
Desmond, Michael Finbar '40 (MOB) [E] Mobile, AL Little Sisters of the Poor, Home For the Aged, Inc.
Desmond, Msgr. Michael J. '71 (NEW) Kearny, NJ St. Stephen's Church.
Desmond, Nicholas R. '84 (CHI) [8] Chicago, IL St. Aloysius Church.
DeSocio, Benedict '67 (PSC) Special or Other Diocesan Assignment.
DeSocio, John A. '78 (ROC) [I] Rochester, NY Becket Hall; [L] Rochester, NY Catholic Committee on Scouting.
Desormeaux, Roland *c.s.* '82 (PMB) [2] Delray Beach, FL Our Lady of Perpetual Help Church.
DesOrmeaux, Scott '91 (LKC) [5] Lake Charles, LA St. Margaret Church; Lake Charles, LA Lake Charles Memorial Hospital.
Desrochers, Msgr. Timothy H. '64 (MAR) [F] Garden, MI Marygrove Retreat Center.
Desrosiers, Alfred R. '61 (PRO) Retired.
DesRosiers, Denis A. '69 (OAK) [4] Walnut Creek, CA St. Stephen Church.
DesRosiers, N. Wilfrid *s.s.j.* '55 (BAL) [S] Baltimore, MD St. Joseph Society of the Sacred Heart House of Central Administration.
Desrosiers, Paul H. '75 (NO) [31] New Orleans, LA St. Frances Xavier Cabrini Church.
DesRosiers, Philip J. '66 (BO) [3] Everett, MA St. Joseph Church.
DesRosiers, Ronald *s.m.* '63 (DET) [K] Livonia, MI Marist Fathers & Brothers Community.
DesRuisseaux, Charles E. '60 (MAN) [3] Manchester, NH St. Anthony of Padua Church.
Desruisseaux, G. Frantz '78 (BGP) [2] Norwalk, CT St. Joseph Church.
Dessert, Msgr. James A. '34 (LA) Retired.
Desso, Leo '79 (ANC) Palmer, AK St. Michael Church.
DeStefano, Msgr. Richard '62 (BEA) Retired.
DeStephano, Mark T. *s.j.* '88 (NEW) [B] Jersey City, NJ Saint Peter's College; [N] Jersey City, NJ Jesuits of Saint Peter's College, Inc.
DeSutter, Gilbert J. '54 (STP) Retired.
DeSutter, Mark A. '82 (PEO) Morton, IL Blessed Sacrament Church.
DeTemple, Michael *o.p.* '81 (COL) Zanesville, OH St. Thomas Aquinas Church.
Determan, Joseph *o.p.* '51 (SAT) [B] San Antonio, TX Dominican Priory of San Juan Macias.
Deters, Frederick J. *s.j.* '67 (IND) [D] Indianapolis, IN Brebeuf Jesuit Preparatory School, Inc.; [F] Beech Grove, IN St. Francis Hospital and Health Centers.
Deters, Gregory J. '87 (DET) Temperance, MI St. Anthony Church.
Detig, Joseph E. *s.v.d.* '62 (LAF) Jeanerette, LA Our Lady of the Rosary Church.
Detisch, John J. '88 (E) Titusville, PA St. Titus Church.
Detisch, Scott P. '87 (E) [B] Erie, PA Gannon University.
DeTommaso, Louis *o.f.m.* '54 (SP) Tarpon Springs, FL St. Ignatius Church.
Detscher, Msgr. Alan F. '71 (BGP) Riverside, CT St. Catherine of Siena Church.
Dettenwanger, Dennis '64 (CIN) [1] Hamilton, OH St. Ann's Church; [2] Hamilton, OH St. Joseph Church.
Dettling, William *o.p.* '59 (COL) [A] Columbus, OH Pontifical College Josephinum.
Dettmer, Alfred J. '56 (GRY) Dyer, IN St. Maria Goretti Church.
Dettmer, David J. '80 (BRK) [18] Brooklyn, NY St. Bernadette Church; [G] Brooklyn, NY Xaverian.
Deutsch, Bernard F. '51 (STL) Retired.
Deutsch, Daniel J. '94 (RCK) Dixon, IL St. Patrick Church.
Deutsch, Marvin F. *m.m.* '57 (NY) [DD] Maryknoll, NY Maryknoll Fathers and Brothers.
Deutsch, Paul *s.j.* '90 (NO) [F] New Orleans, LA Jesuit High School; [P] New Orleans, LA Jesuit Provincial Office.
Deutsch, Timothy '94 (STP) Crystal, MN St. Raphael Church.
Deutschmann, Msgr. Edward '52 (STL) Mattese, MO Mary, Mother of the Church.
Devan, Msgr. Clarence M. (OG) Massena, NY St. Mary Church.
Devan, Msgr. Clarence M. '37 (OG) Retired.
Devane, John F. *s.j.* '52 (BO) [W] Chestnut Hill, MA The Jesuit Community at Boston College.
Devaney, Michael J. *o.m.i.* '57 (COL) West Jefferson, OH SS. Simon and Jude Church; [H] West Jefferson, OH SS. Simon and Jude.
Devaney, Roy J. '52 (WOR) Retired.
Devany, John *c.p.* '45 (DET) [K] Detroit, MI St. Paul of the Cross Community, Congregation of the Passion.
Devaras, Peter '81 (RVC) Ronkonkoma, NY St. Joseph's Church.
Deveau, Adhemar *o.m.i.* (BO) [4] Lowell, MA Saint Jeanne d'Arc Church.
Deveau, Daniel R. '75 (MAN) Groveton, NH St. Francis Xavier Church; North Stratford, NH Sacred Heart Church.
DeVeer, Richard '65 (BO) [2] Chelsea, MA St. Rose of Lima Church.
Develis, Mark *o.c.d.* '99 (MIL) [P] Holy Hill, WI Discalced Carmelite Monastery.
DeVenney, Timothy '93 (DUB) Unassigned.
Dever, Msgr. Daniel J. '52 (HON) Retired; [I] Kaneohe, HI Augustine Educational Foundation.
Dever, Dennis A. '60 (BO) [5] Somerville, MA St. Clement Church.
Dever, James T. *o.s.f.s.* '73 (PH) [131] Philadelphia, PA Our Mother of Consolation Church.
Dever, Msgr. William '65 (MIA) [8] Fort Lauderdale, FL St. Helen Church.
Devereaux, Thomas W. '68 (SR) Healdsburg, CA St. John the Baptist Church.
Devereux, James A. *s.j.* '58 (R) [E] Raleigh, NC Jesuit Community.
Devereux, Peter '99 (ATL) [J] Atlanta, GA Legionaries of Christ; [N] Atlanta, GA Home and Family, Inc.
Devereux, Raymond P. '68 (CHI) [7] Chicago, IL All Saints-St. Anthony Church.
Devereux, Thomas W. *o.s.b.* '59 (GBG) [H] Latrobe, PA Saint Vincent Archabbey.
deVerteuil, Jack '89 (FBK) Nenana, AK St. Theresa Church.
Devery, Thomas P. '77 (NY) [204] Staten Island, NY Holy Child Church.
DeVille, George T. '57 (PIT) Muse, PA Holy Rosary Church; Allegheny County, PA Mayview State Hospital.
DeVille, William H. '62 (COL) [33] Columbus, OH Our Lady of the Miraculous Medal Church.
Devin, John *c.ss.r.* '49 (BO) [53] Boston, MA Our Lady of Perpetual Help Church.
Devina, Edgar '95 (NEW) North Bergen, NJ Our Lady of Fatima Church.
Devine, Charles '65 (SB) Idyllwild, CA Queen of Angels Church.
Devine, Daniel P. '65 (PH) Feasterville, PA Assumption B.V.M. Church.
Devine, Donald G. *s.j.* '65 (PAT) [I] Morristown, NJ Loyola House of Retreats.
Devine, J. Donald *s.s.c.* '54 (OM) [K] St. Columbans, NE St. Columban's Foreign Mission Society.
Devine, J. Frank *s.j.* '54 (BO) [W] Weston, MA Campion Health Center, Inc.
Devine, James T. '60 (BRK) [217] Queens, NY Our Lady of Perpetual Help Church; [219] Queens, NY Our Lady of the Skies Chapel Church.
Devine, Msgr. Joseph A. '49 (HRT) [4] Waterbury, CT Our Lady of Loreto Church.
Devine, Joseph T. '80 (HRT) [12] Hartford, CT St. Lawrence O'Toole Church.
Devine, Kevin A. *c.s.p.* '56 (NY) [41] New York, NY Good Shepherd Church.
Devine, Msgr. Michael F. (SP) [3] Clearwater, FL St. Brendan Church.
Devine, Patrick A. '69 (HBG) Bloomsburg, PA St. Columba Church.
Devine, Patrick T. '61 (LC) Retired.
Devine, Paul '63 (OAK) Retired.
Devine, Richard J. *c.m.* '55 (BRK) [V] Queens Village, NY DePaul Residence.
Devine, Stephen M. '64 (FRS) Huron, CA St. Frances Cabrini Church.
Devine, Terry '85 (OWN) Hardinsburg, KY St. Romuald Church.
Devine, Msgr. Thomas F. '45 (SPR) Longmeadow, MA St. Mary's Church.
Devine, Thomas J. *o.a.r.* '68 (LSC) Anthony, NM St. Anthony's Church.
Devine, Msgr. W. J. '31 (DM) Retired.
Devine, William B. '58 (SC) Retired.
Devine, William G. *s.j.* '57 (BO) [Y] Gloucester, MA Eastern Point Retreat House.
Devine, William J. (CHI) Retired.
Devine, William J. '73 (BO) Military & VA Chaplains.
Devine, Msgr. William P. '50 (NEW) Retired.
Devine, William P. '52 (DUB) Retired.
Deviney, Raymond L. '59 (SCR) Blakeslee, PA Christ the King Church.
Devino, Terrence P. *s.j.* '87 (BO) [W] Chestnut Hill, MA The Jesuit Community at Boston College.
Deviny, Edward *c.p.* '66 (R) Tarboro, NC St. Catherine Church.
DeVita, Thomas F. '78 (KAL) New Buffalo, MI St. Mary of the Lake Church.
Devito, Darius *o.f.m.cap.* '57 (NY) [DD] Yonkers, NY St. Clare Friary.
DeVliegher, Joseph *c.s.c.* '68 (AUS) Bertram, TX Holy Cross Church; Burnet, TX Our Mother of Sorrows Church.
Devlin, Msgr. Charles V. '55 (PH) On Special or Other Archdiocesan Assignment; [A] Wynnewood, PA Theological Seminary of St. Charles Borromeo, Overbrook.
Devlin, Chester J. '71 (WOR) Northboro, MA St. Bernadette Church.
Devlin, David J. *o.s.f.s.* '77 (ALN) Robesonia, PA St. Francis de Sales Church.
Devlin, Francis X. *o.s.a.* '73 (PH) [D] Drexel Hill, PA Monsignor Bonner High School.
Devlin, James E. '72 (BRK) [91] Brooklyn, NY Our Lady of Angels Church.
Devlin, Joseph D. *s.j.* '66 (BO) [W] Boston, MA Loyola House.
Devlin, Joseph F. '48 (PH) Retired.
Devlin, Msgr. Joseph M. '36 (NY) [141] Bronx, NY St. Frances de Chantal Church; Retired.
Devlin, Joseph P. '91 (PH) Brookline, PA Annunciation B.V.M. Church.
Devlin, Msgr. Joseph W. '56 (CAM) [M] Cherry Hill, NJ Vianney Villa.
Devlin, Kevin '54 (OKL) Perry, OK St. Rose of Lima Church.
Devlin, Mark *s.d.b.* '79 (TR) Medford, NJ St. Mary of the Lakes Church.
Devlin, Michael H. '68 (SPR) Haydenville, MA St. Mary's Church.
Devlin, Philip T. *c.s.c.* '56 (FgM) Holy Cross Foreign Missions.
Devlin, Philip T. *c.s.c.* '56 (FTW) [J] South Bend, IN Congregation of Holy Cross, Indiana Province, Provincial House.
Devlin, Raymond A. *s.j.* '55 (SJ) [L] Los Gatos, CA Sacred Heart Jesuit Center.
Devlin, Vianney M. *o.f.m.* '55 (NY) [115] New York, NY St. Stephen of Hungary Church.
Devoe, Richard M. *m.m.* '56 (FgM) Maryknoll Foreign Missions.
Devold, Cyprian '84 (NO) [21] New Orleans, LA The Resurrection Of Our Lord Church.
DeVolder, Philip '80 (FTW) Decatur, IN St. Mary Church.
Devorak, James '72 (NU) Granite Falls, MN St. Andrew Church.
Devorak, James W. '72 (NU) Montevideo, MN St. Joseph Church.
Devore, C. John *m.s.f.s.* (ATL) [J] Lawrenceville, GA The Missionaries of St. Francis De Sales.
DeVore, David G. '88 (CIN) On Special and Archdiocesan Assignment.
Devore, Gerald T. '62 (BGP) [12] Stamford, CT St. Maurice Church.

Devot, Paul *s.j.* '72 (SJ) [2] Santa Clara, CA St. Clare Church.
Devot, Paul D. *s.j.* '72 (SJ) [D] San Jose, CA Bellarmine College Preparatory.
Devoti, Pio *s.x.* '63 (FgM) Xaverian Foreign Missions.
Devoti, Pio *s.x.* '63 (PAT) [M] Wayne, NJ Xaverian Missionary Fathers.
DeVries, Thomas D. '89 (MIL) [69] Milwaukee, WI SS. Peter and Paul Church.
DeVries, William J. '90 (MEM) Covington, TN St. Alphonsus Church.
Dewaele, Joseph *c.i.c.m.* '49 (ARL) [J] Arlington, VA Missionhurst, C.I.C.M.-Central House and Provincialate.
Dewan, Wilfred *c.s.p.* '53 (BRK) [150] Queens, NY St. Andrew Avellino Church.
Dewan, Wilfred *c.s.p.* '53 (NY) [DD] Jamaica Estates, NY Paulist Fathers Generalate.
Dewan, William G. '86 (JOL) Bradley, IL St. Joseph Church.
Dewane, Daniel '71 (GB) Kewaunee, WI Holy Rosary Church.
Dewane, Msgr. Frank J. '88 (GB) On Duty Outside the Diocese.
Dewane, Msgr. John B. '54 (GB) [O] Green Bay, WI Sacred Heart Seminary, Inc.
Dewane, Msgr. John B. '62 (GB) Special Assignment.
deWasseige, Eric *o.p.* '65 (CHI) [N] Chicago, IL Dominicans (Provincial Office).
Dewes, John W. '65 (CHI) Barrington, IL St. Anne Church.
Dewig, Eugene '50 (EVN) [12] Evansville, IN Sacred Heart Church.
DeWitt, David D. '84 (PIT) Chicora, PA Mater Dolorosa Church; North Oakland, PA St. Joseph Church.
DeWolf, Paul *c.i.c.m.* '50 (ARL) [J] Arlington, VA Missionhurst, C.I.C.M.-Central House and Provincialate.
Dewson, Msgr. John H. '47 (WIL) [13] Wilmington, DE St. Thomas Church; Retired.
Deye, Walter C. *s.j.* '75 (CHI) [N] Chicago, IL Chicago Province of the Society of Jesus-Provincial Office.
Deye, Walter C. *s.j.* '75 (WDC) [M] Washington, DC Leonard Neale House.
Deyo, Paul A. (SC) [B] Sioux City, IA Catholic Schools of Sioux City.
Deyo, Paul A. '76 (DAV) On Duty Outside the Diocese.
Deziel, William '97 (STP) Anoka, MN St. Stephen Church; [N] Anoka, MN Crosier Community of Anoka.
Dharmaraj, Anthony *m.s.f.s.* '92 (ALX) Ferriday, LA St. Patrick Church; Vidalia, LA Our Lady of Lourdes Church.
Dhas, Gnana '78 (NY) Wappingers Falls, NY St. Mary Church.
Dhondt, Edward F. '69 (LFT) Anderson, IN St. Ambrose Church.
Di Cerbo, Almerico F. '46 (ALB) Retired.
Di Giovanni, Msgr. Stephen M. '77 (BGP) [9] Stamford, CT St. John the Evangelist Church.
Di Gregorio, Michael F. *o.s.a.* '73 (PH) [143] Philadelphia, PA St. Rita of Cascia Church.
Di Lella, Alexander A. *o.f.m.* '55 (WDC) [C] Washington, DC Catholic University of America, The.
Di Lella, Mario *o.f.m.* '53 (ATL) [M] Atlanta, GA Campus Ministry.
Di Marzio, Vito *r.c.j.* '75 (FRS) Sanger, CA St. Mary Church.
Di Mauro, Joseph *s.a.* '78 (BO) [W] Brockton, MA Chapel of Our Saviour; [BB] Brockton, MA Chapel of Our Saviour.
di Miglio, Isidoro *o.f.m.* '47 (NY) [DD] New York, NY Franciscan Province of the Immaculate Conception.
Di Pasquale, Donald J. '62 (NEW) Cliffside Park, NJ Epiphany Church.
Di Pasquale, Ralph *o.f.m.* '56 (NY) [DD] New York, NY Franciscan Province of the Immaculate Conception.
Diab, Thomas '71 (SAN) Military Chaplains.
Diacetis, Anthony C. '69 (ALB) Ballston Lake, NY Our Lady of Grace Church.
Diachek, Robert M. (PAT) Special Assignment.
Diachek, Msgr. Robert M. '71 (PAT) [P] Madison, NJ Priests Residence.
Diadia, Chester '58 (RVC) Floral Park, NY St. Hedwig's Church.
Diamond, David E. '83 (PH) [A] Wynnewood, PA Theological Seminary of St. Charles Borromeo, Overbrook.
Diamond, Matthew J. '71 (BRK) [150] Queens, NY St. Andrew Avellino Church.
Dianda, Carl F. '59 (WDC) [13] Washington, DC St. Francis de Sales Church.
Dias, Frank *p.v.* '76 (NY) Hawthorne, NY Holy Rosary Church.
Dias, John (TLS) Krebs, OK St. Joseph's Church.
Dias, John F. *c.s.c.* '63 (FR) [I] North Dartmouth, MA Holy Cross Mission House; [I] North Dartmouth, MA St. Joseph's Hall.
Dias, Soccoro John (TLS) McAlester, OK St. John Church.
Diaz, Alberto '85 (ARE) [3] Arecibo, PR Nuestra Senora del Carmen Church.
Diaz, Alvaro '45 (SJN) Retired.
Diaz, Alvaro *o.f.m.* '73 (CAM) [4] Vineland, NJ St. Isidore Church; [P] Vineland, NJ Spanish Catholic Center.
Diaz, Angel '76 (ARE) [2] Vega-Baja, PR N.S. de la Providencia Church.
Diaz, Angel R. '85 (ARE) Lares, PR St. Judas Tadeos Church.
Diaz, Claudio '00 (CHI) Chicago Heights, IL St. Agnes Church.
Diaz, Francisco '81 (FRS) Taft, CA Correctional Institution.
Diaz, Francisco G. '77 (MIA) [14] Miami, FL Prince of Peace Church.
Diaz, German Perez '97 (KAL) Hartford, MI Immaculate Conception Church.
Diaz, Gilbert '94 (KNX) Oak Ridge, TN St. Mary Church.
Diaz, Gonzalo '52 (SJN) [G] Guaynabo, PR Opus Dei.
Diaz, Gonzalo '63 (MGZ) On Special Assignment.
Diaz, Guillermo *c.s.* '93 (LA) [88] Los Angeles, CA St. Peter Church.
Diaz, Gumersindo *s.d.b.* '70 (MIA) [25] Miami, FL St. Kieran Church.
Diaz, Heberto M., Jr. '89 (BWN) [1] Harlingen, TX Our Lady of the Assumption Church.
Diaz, Hernando '71 (SLC) [5] Salt Lake City, UT Sacred Heart Church.
Diaz, Jamie A. *o.p.* '00 (BR) Hammond, LA Holy Ghost Church.
Diaz, Javier '98 (TR) Hightstown, NJ St. Anthony of Padua Church.
Diaz, Msgr. Jesus '54 (ARE) Vega-Alta, PR Santa Ana Church.
Diaz, Jose Matias '89 (NEW) [A] Kearny, NJ Redemptoris Mater.
Diaz, Juan Alexis *c.m.f.* '93 (SJN) [23] Bayamon, PR Santa Maria Church.
Diaz, Kevin Hunt '84 (PHX) Camp Verde, AZ St. Frances Cabrini Church; Prescott Valley, AZ St. Germaine Church; Prescott Valley, AZ St. Germaine Church.
Diaz, Martin *o.p.* '78 (SB) [10] Riverside, CA St. Andrew's Newman Center Church; [E] Riverside, CA St. Vincent Ferrer House.
Diaz, Michael '73 (SD) Military Chaplains.
Diaz, Oscar '94 (SR) Napa, CA St. John the Baptist Church.
Diaz, Raul '97 (FRS) Parlier, CA Our Lady of Sorrows Church.
Diaz, Robert '79 (BWN) Retired.
Diaz, Thomas K. '81 (SFR) [A] Menlo Park, CA St. Patrick Seminary.
Diaz, Thomas K. '81 (SR) On Duty Outside the Diocese.
Diaz Lamus, Luis Antonio '98 (BRK) [71] Brooklyn, NY St. Joseph Patron of the Universal Church.
Diaz Vilar, J. Juan *s.j.* '69 (NEW) [N] Jersey City, NJ Jesuits of Saint Peter's College, Inc.
Diaz-Toree, Emilio *l.c.* (HRT) [V] Orange, CT Racebrook, Inc.
Diaz-Torre, Emilio *l.c.* (NY) [HH] Thornwood, NY Center for Family Life, Inc.
DiBacco, John V., Jr. '67 (WH) Martinsburg, WV St. Joseph's Church.
DiBardino, Anthony '76 (CAM) Pennsauken, NJ St. Cecilia's Church.
Dibb, William C. *s.j.* '60 (SPK) [K] Spokane, WA Regis Community.
Dibble, Michael '60 (OAK) Pleasant Hill, CA Christ the King Church.
Dibble, Michael B. '60 (NY) [105] New York, NY St. Peter Church.
DiBlasi, Msgr. Augustine J. '45 (NY) Retired; [E] White Plains, NY Archbishop Stepinac High School.
Dibuo, Roger F. '89 (WIL) [2] Wilmington, DE St. Ann Church.
DiCesare, Giosue Scotto *s.d.v.* '52 (NEW) [25] Newark, NJ St. Michael's Church.
Dicharry, Harold E. *c.m.* '42 (NO) [61] New Orleans, LA St. Stephen Church.
Dichoso, Anthony (LC) [C] Wausau, WI Wausau Area Catholic Schools.
Dichoso, Anthony '95 (LC) [2] Wausau, WI Holy Name of Jesus Church; [6] Wausau, WI St. Matthew Church.
DiCicco, Mario *o.f.m.* '59 (CHI) [164] Chicago, IL St. Peter's Church.
Dick, Firmus '54 (EVN) Retired.
Dick, Gregory M. *o.praem* '96 (ORG) [A] Silverado, CA St. Michael's Norbertine Postulancy, Novitiate and Juniorate; [I] Silverado, CA Norbertine Fathers of Orange Inc.
Dick, John '96 (DAL) Coppell, TX St. Ann Church.
Dickes, Jerome H. '48 (OM) Retired.
Dickey, Merrell T. '94 (SP) [4] Clearwater, FL St. Cecelia Church.
Dickie, Msgr. John A. '56 (SD) [31] San Diego, CA St. Mary Magdalene Church.
Dickinson, Stephen '58 (FAR) Retired.
Dickinson, William '89 (CLV) [15] Cleveland, OH St. Catherine Church.
Dickinson, William R. '89 (CLV) Brecksville, OH St. Basil the Great Church.
Dickman, John W. '48 (L) Pewee Valley, KY St. Aloysius Church; Retired.
Dickman, Richard C. '93 (LC) Tomah, WI St. Mary (Immaculate Conception) Church; Warrens, WI St. Andrew Church.
Dickmann, Louis H. '59 (COV) Falmouth, KY St. Francis Xavier Church.
Dickrell, Cyril *s.d.s.* '53 (MIL) [P] Milwaukee, WI Salvatorian Provincial Residence.
Dicks, Thomas K. '87 (NY) [138] Bronx, NY St. Dominic Church.
Dickson, Henry E. *s.s.j.* '60 (MOB) Prichard, AL St. James Major Church.
Dickson, Norman *s.j.* '67 (DET) [27] Detroit, MI Gesu Church.
DiCristina, Frank A. '86 (PAT) On Duty Outside the Diocese.
Dicristina, Frank T. '86 (SB) Beaumont, CA San Gorgonio Church.
Didier, Jacques R. *m.e.p.* '53 (SFR) [N] San Francisco, CA Paris Foreign Mission Society Residence.
Didier-Marie, (PEO) [N] Princeville, IL St. Joseph Priory and Novitiate.
DiDone, Matthew *c.s.* '67 (PMB) [3] Delray Beach, FL Our Lady Queen of Peace Church.
Diebel, Thomas (LUB) Retired.
Diebel, Thomas '79 (LUB) Special Assignment.
Dieckhaus, Anthony W. '62 (PH) [153] Philadelphia, PA St. Timothy Church.
Dieckhaus, Joseph C. '74 (PH) [BB] Philadelphia, PA Sister Servants of the Holy Spirit of Perpetual Adoration (S.Sp.S.A.P.).
Dieckman, Leonard E. *s.j.* '62 (FgM) Provinces.
Dieckmann, Michael '74 (STL) Fenton, MO St. Paul Church.
Diederich, Donald '58 (RVC) Setauket, NY St. James Church.
Diederich, Everett A. *s.j.* '52 (STL) [P] St. Louis, MO Jesuit Community Corporation at St. Louis University - Jesuit Hall.
Diedrick, Charles T. '78 (CLV) Northfield, OH St. Barnabas Church.
Diegel, Ron '75 (TYL) Marshall, TX St. Joseph Church.
Diegelman, Robert W. '93 (R) Pinehurst, NC Sacred Heart Church.
Diehl, Dennis P. '74 (BAL) Fulton, MD St. Francis of Assisi Church.
Diehl, Michael C. '55 (TUC) Retired.
Diehl, Thomas J. *s.j.* '50 (CIN) [P] Milford, OH Milford Spiritual Center.
Diekemper, Barnabas *o.f.m.* (CHI) [164] Chicago, IL St. Peter's Church.
DieKemper, Barnabas '65 (CHI) [N] Chicago, IL St. Peter's Friary.
Dieker, James P. '93 (DOD) Greensburg, KS St. Joseph Church; Pratt, KS Sacred Heart Church.
Diekhans, Joseph '65 (GF) Chester, MT St. Mary's Church.
Diekhoff, Bernard *c.pp.s.* '47 (KC) [3] St. Joseph, MO St. Francis Xavier Church.
Diekmann, Godfrey *o.s.b.* '31 (SCL) [I] Collegeville, MN St. John's Abbey, of the Order of St. Benedict.
Diele, Joseph '85 (BRK) [163] Queens, NY St. Clare Church.
Diels, Gaston *ss.cc.* '47 (HON) [G] Kaneohe, HI Sacred Hearts Center.
Diem, Joseph '85 (BO) Hopkinton, MA St. John the Evangelist Church.
Diemand, James E. '68 (SPR) Retired.
Diemer, Joseph *o.s.b.cam.* '49 (MRY) [F] Big Sur, CA New Camaldoli Hermitage.
Diemer, Michael J. *m.j.* '96 (PCE) [7] Ponce, PR Santa Maria Church.
Dienert, Robert T. '62 (LR) Searcy, AR St. James Church.
Diere, Emiliano Auwen (DET) Detroit, MI Henry Ford Hospital.
Dieringer, James J. '58 (P) Retired.
Dierkes, Richard '81 (KC) [1] St. Joseph, MO St. Joseph's Co-Church.
Diermeier, Joseph *o.f.m.cap.* '78 (LC) Marathon City, WI Nativity of the Blessed Virgin Mary Church.
Diersen, William M. '50 (L) Retired.
Diesbourg, Raymond *m.s.c.* '74 (FgM) Missionaries of the Sacred Heart Foreign Missions.
Diesbourg, Raymond *m.s.c.* '74 (RCK) [G] Aurora, IL Missionaries of the Sacred Heart Community.
Dieter, Thomas '83 (JOL) On Duty Outside the Diocese.
Dieter, Thomas '83 (SP) [3] St. Petersburg, FL Holy Cross Church.
Dieter, Xavier L. *o.c.s.o.* '58 (DUB) [K] Peosta, IA New Melleray Abbey, Order of Cistercians of the Strict Observance.
Dietlein, Damian *o.s.b.* '57 (BIS) [A] Richardton, ND Assumption Abbey.
Dietlein, Damian *o.s.b.* '57 (IND) [A] St. Meinrad, IN St. Meinrad Seminary.
Dietlein, Raymond *o.s.b.* '54 (BIS) [A] Richardton, ND

Assumption Abbey.
Dietrich, Christopher *o.f.m.cap.* '59 (NY) [17] Yonkers, NY Sacred Heart Church.
Dietrich, Douglas D. '96 (LIN) Benkelman, NE St. Joseph's Church.
Dietrich, John J. '93 (HRT) Special and other Archdiocesan Assignment; [A] Bloomfield, CT St. Thomas Seminary.
Dietrich, Robert J. *s.j.* '61 (CLV) [D] Cleveland, OH St. Ignatius High School.
Dietrich, Severin *o.f.m.conv.* '53 (MET) [G] North Plainfield, NJ Villa Maria Sanitarium; [I] North Plainfield, NJ Servants of the Holy Child Jesus Regional House.
Dietsch, William '71 (EVN) Poseyville, IN St. Francis Xavier Church.
Dietz, Conrad R. '57 (BRK) [B] Douglaston, NY Cathedral Seminary Residence of the Immaculate Conception.
Dietz, Msgr. Conrad R. '57 (RVC) Oceanside, NY St. Anthony Church.
Dietz, Donald *o.m.i.* '57 (CHI) Volo, IL St. Peter Church.
Dietz, Francis '40 (DET) Retired.
Dietz, Joseph S. '87 (NY) Sleepy Hollow, NY The Magdalene Church.
Dietz, Msgr. Norbert J. '49 (STL) [3] University City, MO Our Lady of Lourdes Church; Retired.
Dietz, Xavier Ortiz '77 (SAT) On Leave.
Dietzel, Msgr. Elmer J. '51 (MAD) Albany, WI St. Patrick Church; Brodhead, WI St. Rose Church.
Dietzen, John J. '54 (PEO) Retired.
Dietzen, Vincent E. '53 (PEO) [3] Bloomington, IL St. Patrick's Church; Retired.
Dietzenbach, John A. '80 (BAL) Libertytown, MD St. Peter Church.
Dietzler, William J. '69 (MIL) [K] Racine, WI St. Mary's Medical Center, Inc.
Diez, Alvaro '68 (YAK) East Wenatchee, WA Holy Apostles Church.
Diez, Msgr. Antonio '59 (SP) Riverview, FL Resurrection Church.
Diez, Antonio Oscar '68 (DAL) Greenville, TX St. William Church.
Diez, Toribio Pascual *o.s.b.* '40 (MGZ) [6] Mayaquez, PR Sacred Heart Church.
Diez Antonanzas, Msgr. Jesus R. '57 (PCE) [B] Ponce, PR The Pontifical Catholic University of Puerto Rico.
DiFede, Thomas V. *o.p.* '59 (COL) Zanesville, OH St. Thomas Aquinas Church.
DiFederico, Gabriel '78 (MEM) [10] Memphis, TN Holy Rosary Church.
Diffenbacher, Brian (ROC) Hornell, NY St. James Mercy Hospital.
Diffley, Francis A. *m.m.* '64 (NY) [DD] Maryknoll, NY Maryknoll Fathers and Brothers.
Diffley, Jerome E. '45 (SP) [4] St. Petersburg, FL Holy Family Church; Retired.
Diffley, Patrick J. '63 (BRK) [11] Brooklyn, NY St. Anthony of Padua-St. Alphonsus Church.
DiFilippo, John V. *o.s.f.s.* '45 (PH) [AA] Philadelphia, PA Oblates of St. Francis De Sales.
DiFiore, John *s.d.b.* '97 (BO) [E] Boston, MA Savio Preparatory High School.
DiFolco, Thomas P. '83 (CIN) [2] Cincinnati, OH St. Agnes Church; [57] Cincinnati, OH St. Martin De Porres Church.
DiFruscio, John A. '69 (BO) Permanent Disability.
Digal, Danilo C. '78 (NO) [1] Harvey, LA Infant Jesus of Prague Church.
DiGeronimo, Michael A. '76 (WOR) Leicester, MA St. Joseph's Church; Leicester, MA St. Pius X Church.
DiGeronimo, Richard '73 (LFT) Unassigned.
DiGiacobbe, Albert C. '66 (PH) [55] Philadelphia, PA St. Helena Church.
DiGiacomo, James J. *s.j.* '56 (NY) [F] New York, NY Regis High School; [DD] New York, NY "America;" Residence and publication office of the America Press.
DiGiovanni, Alfonso '96 (NEW) On Duty Outside the Archdiocese.
DiGiralamo, Gerald *s.a.* '81 (NY) [DD] Garrison, NY Franciscan Friars of the Atonement.
DiGirolamo, Dante '48 (NEW) Retired.
DiGirolamo, Paul A. '83 (PH) Bridgeport, PA Our Mother of Sorrows Church.
DiGiulio, Richard S. '69 (BUF) [24] Buffalo, NY St. Francis of Assisi Church.
Dignan, Eamon '59 (WDC) Waldorf, MD Our Lady Help of Christians Church.
DiGregorio, Joseph L. '66 (PH) Military Chaplains.
DiGuardo, Domenic *s.d.b.* '37 (NY) [FF] Stony Point, NY Don Bosco Retreat Center and Marian Shrine; [FF] Stony Point, NY Marian Shrine.
DiIanni, Albert *s.m.* '60 (BO) [W] Boston, MA Marist Fathers and Brothers Provincial House; [W] Boston, MA Marist Fathers of Our Lady of Victories (Boston Prov.).
DiIenno, Nicholas C. *o.s.f.s.* '43 (CAM) [M] Pittsgrove, NJ Villa St. Joseph.
DiIorio, Michael C. '77 (PH) [116] Philadelphia, PA Our Lady of Consolation Church.
DiIanni, Albert *s.m.* (BO) [55] Boston, MA Our Lady of Victories Church.
DiLella, Msgr. Christopher C. '79 (PAT) Madison, NJ St. Vincent Martyr Church.
DiLeo, Anthony '64 (SB) Retired.
DiLeo, Richard *s.c.j.* '81 (CHI) [N] Chicago, IL Priests of the Sacred Heart.
DiLeonardi, Rocco *o.carm.* '56 (JOL) [J] Joliet, IL St. Elias Carmelites.
Dilettuso, Joseph '72 (BLX) Biloxi, MS V.A. Center; Gulfport, MS V.A. Hospital; Special Assignment.
Dilg, Donald *c.s.c.* '75 (COS) [8] Colorado Springs, CO Sacred Heart Church.
Dilgen, William M. *s.m.m.* '47 (RVC) [M] Bay Shore, NY Montfort Missionaries.
Dilger, Basil *o.s.b.* '61 (FgM) American - Cassinese Congregation Foreign Missions.
Dilger, Basil *o.s.b.* '61 (SFS) [F] Marvin, SD Blue Cloud Abbey.
Dilger, Donald '59 (EVN) Retired.
Diliberto, Peter J. '43 (LA) [Q] Montebello, CA Vincentian Fathers & Brothers; [W] Montebello, CA DePaul Center.
Dilion, Joseph A. '46 (HRT) Retired.
Dilipiy, Basilio '94 (CI) Tunnuk, FM Immaculate Heart of Mary Church; [C] Tunnuk, Chuuk, FM Vicariate Residence.
Dill, Edwin *s.t.* '59 (WDC) [M] Adelphi, MD Missionary Servants of the Most Holy Trinity.
Dilla, Francis E. (CHI) Retired.
Dillabough, Msgr. Daniel '74 (SD) [B] San Diego, CA University of San Diego.
Dillane, Maurice '63 (SAT) On Duty Outside the Archdiocese.
Dillard, Msgr. Russell L. '78 (WDC) [7] Washington, DC St. Augustine Church.
Dillard, Steven C. *s.j.* '86 (P) [A] Portland, OR Jesuit Novitiate of St. Francis Xavier.
Dillard, William '98 (P) Medford, OR Sacred Heart of Jesus Church.
Dillemuth, Frederick J. *s.j.* '54 (NY) [DD] New York, NY Jesuit Community at Fordham University.
Dillenburg, Msgr. James E. (GB) [16] Green Bay, WI St. Elizabeth Ann Seton Church.
Diller, Harold *c.pp.s.* '34 (CIN) [B] Carthagena, OH St. Charles.
Dilley, Gary *f.s.s.p.* '72 (SCR) [M] Elmhurst, PA Priestly Fraternity of St. Peter (F.S.S.P.), North American District Headquarters.
Dilley, Gary *f.s.s.p.* '72 (Y) Vienna, OH Queen of the Holy Rosary Church.
Dilley, Gary D. '72 (CHR) Absent On Leave.
Dillinger, Joseph A. '96 (SC) Carroll, IA St. Lawrence Church.
Dillingham, Charles C. '73 (WIL) [5] Wilmington, DE St. Elizabeth Church.
Dillio, Albert J. *s.j.* '74 (MIL) [P] Milwaukee, WI Jesuit Provincial Office, Wisconsin Province.
Dillman, Alan M. '59 (ATL) Retired.
Dillmann, Alan M. '59 (ATL) Military Chaplains.
Dillon, Arthur J. '45 (CHI) Barrington, IL St. Anne Church; Retired.
Dillon, Charles P. *s.s.* '39 (BAL) [O] Baltimore, MD St. Charles Villa; [S] Baltimore, MD St. Charles Villa.
Dillon, Ciarian *o.m.i.* '54 (OAK) Crockett, CA St. Rose of Lima Church.
Dillon, David *o.carm.* '65 (JOL) Glendale Heights, IL St. Matthew Church.
Dillon, Dennis T. *s.j.* '69 (CLV) [D] Cleveland, OH St. Ignatius High School.
Dillon, Dennis T. *s.j.* '69 (DET) [K] Detroit, MI Jesuit Provincial Office-Detroit Province of the Society of Jesus.
Dillon, Msgr. Desmond P. '41 (YAK) Kennewick, WA St. Joseph's Church; Retired.
Dillon, Msgr. Edward J. (ATL) [N] Atlanta, GA Catholic Foundation of North Georgia, Inc.
Dillon, Edward J. (PAT) Unassigned.
Dillon, Edward J. *o.f.m.* '55 (NY) [35] New York, NY St. Francis of Assisi Church.
Dillon, Edward J. '60 (ROC) Clifton Springs, NY St. Felix / St. Francis Parish Cluster Church.
Dillon, Msgr. Edward J. '67 (ATL) [3] Atlanta, GA Holy Spirit Church.
Dillon, Geoffrey R. *s.j.* '83 (SFR) [N] San Francisco, CA Jesuit Community at University of San Francisco.
Dillon, Gerald F. *c.s.b.* '62 (GAL) [Q] Houston, TX Dillon House.
Dillon, James P. '73 (BRK) Military Chaplains.
Dillon, Jeffry T. '81 (BRK) [162] Queens, NY Christ the King Church.
Dillon, Jerome V. '77 (OM) Military Chaplains.
Dillon, John '59 (ROC) Moravia, NY Cayuga Correctional.
Dillon, John J. (WDC) Hollywood, MD St. John Church.
Dillon, John J. *s.t.b.* '98 (WDC) Hollywood, MD St. John Church.
Dillon, John T. *s.j.* '63 (CHI) [T] Barrington, IL Bellarmine Hall.
Dillon, Kevin M. '00 (HRT) Yalesville, CT Our Lady of Fatima Church.
Dillon, Michael J. '61 (SAC) Rocklin, CA SS. Peter and Paul Church.
Dillon, Michael L. *c.ss.r.* '56 (ORL) New Smyrna Beach, FL Sacred Heart Church.
Dillon, Richard J. '61 (NY) On Duty Outside the Archdiocese.
Dillon, Robert '65 (RIC) Appomattox, VA Our Lady of Peace Church; Buckingham, VA Church of the Nativity.
Dillon, Msgr. Robert E. '36 (SY) Retired; [S] Syracuse, NY St. Pius X Home, Inc.
Dillon, Robert E. '65 (RIC) Hurt, VA St. Victoria Church.
Dillon, Robert W. '97 (NY) [200] Staten Island, NY St. Charles Church.
Dillon, Thomas J. (GI) Retired.
Dillon, William *s.a.* (NOR) New London, CT U.S. Coast Guard Memorial Chapel.
Dillon, William *s.a.* '69 (NY) [DD] Garrison, NY Franciscan Friars of the Atonement, Minister General Office.
DiLorenzo, Francis '68 (HON) [1] Honolulu, HI Cathedral of Our Lady of Peace.
DiLorenzo, Thomas A. '79 (BO) Winthrop, MA Holy Rosary Church.
DiLoreto, Anthony '54 (B) Retired.
DiLuzio, James (STP) [V] Minneapolis, MN Newman Center at St. Lawrence.
DiLuzio, James *c.s.p.* '93 (STP) [29] Minneapolis, MN St. Lawrence Church; [N] Minneapolis, MN Paulist Fathers.
Dilworth, Kevin *s.j.* '84 (PHX) [B] Phoenix, AZ Brophy College Preparatory.
DiMaggio, Joseph F. '55 (ALB) Johnstown, NY Immaculate Conception Church.
Dimapilis, Jose Rizal *o.p.* '67 (NOR) Middletown, CT Connecticut Valley Hospital.
DiMarco, Msgr. Abel A. '56 (PCE) [B] Ponce, PR The Pontifical Catholic University of Puerto Rico.
DiMaria, Peter J. '93 (PH) [13] Philadelphia, PA St. Anselm Church.
DiMarzio, Vito *r.c.j.* '75 (FRS) Del Rey, CA St. Katherine Church.
DiMascola, Charles J. '81 (SPR) Turners Falls, MA Our Lady of Czestochowa Church.
DiMattei, Robert A., Jr. (BAL) [12] Baltimore, MD St. Athanasius Church.
DiMatteo, John *o.ss.t.* '36 (PH) Bristol, PA St. Ann Church.
DiMauro, John C. *o.f.m.* '56 (BO) [P] Andover, MA Franciscan Center; [W] Andover, MA St. Francis Friary; [Y] Andover, MA Franciscan Center - Retreat House.
DiMauro, Joseph *s.a.* '78 (BO) [P] Brockton, MA Chapel of Our Savior-Catholic Pastoral and Information Center.
DiMauro, Joseph A. *o.s.f.s.* '73 (ALN) [K] Center Valley, PA Oblates of St. Francis de Sales.
Dimauro, Joseph F. *o.s.f.s.* '73 (ALN) [B] Center Valley, PA Desales University.
DiMauro, Msgr. Joseph V. '67 (CAM) Blackwood, NJ St. Agnes Church.
Dimengo, Michael '77 (CLV) Absent on Leave.
Dimic, Milan '85 (BGP) [4] Fairfield, CT Holy Cross Church.
Dimke, John '60 (GF) Retired.
Dimler, G. Richard *s.j.* '63 (NY) [DD] New York, NY Jesuit Community at Fordham University.
Dimock, Giles Richard *o.p.* '66 (WDC) [B] Washington, DC Dominican House of Studies.
Dimond, Arthur J. '51 (COL) [29] Columbus, OH St. Mary Church; Retired.
Dinan, Denis M. '92 (NY) Port Jervis, NY Immaculate Conception Church.
Dinan, John '58 (WCH) Retired.
DiNardo, Daniel A. '66 (CAM) Bridgeton, NJ St. Teresa of Avila Church.
DiNardo, Hector *c.r.m.* '56 (NEW) Lodi, NJ St. Joseph's Church.
DiNardo, Lawrence A. *m.ch.a.* '74 (PIT) [73] Pittsburgh, PA Holy Wisdom Church.
DiNardo, Mark A. '58 (CLV) [61] Cleveland, OH St. Patrick Church.
DiNardo, Msgr. Ramon A. '50 (WDC) Retired.
DiNardo, Salvatore M. *d.c.* '54 (SJ) [J] Mountain View, CA Villa Siena.
DiNardo, Salvatore M. *o.p.* '95 (SJ) San Jose, CA Villa Siena.
Dincher, Carl L. *s.j.* '57 (BAL) [S] Baltimore, MD Jesuit Fathers and Brothers Maryland Provincial Curia.
Dincher, Carl L. *s.j.* '57 (FgM) Provinces.
Dinda, John J. '62 (PH) Spring City, PA St. Joseph Church.
Dindorf, Meinrad *o.s.b.* '58 (SCL) [H] St. Cloud, MN St. Benedict's Senior Community; [H] St. Cloud, MN St. Benedict's Senior Community; [I] Collegeville, MN St. John's Abbey, of the Order of St. Benedict.
Dineen, Michael P. '49 (MIL) Retired.

Dineen, William *c.pp.s.* '66 (KC) [A] Liberty, MO Society of the Precious Blood Provincial Offices; [J] Liberty, MO Precious Blood Society Provincial Office; [J] Liberty, MO Precious Blood Center; [N] Liberty, MO St. Gaspar Society.
Dinelli, William J. '56 (SAC) Sacramento, CA University of California, Davis Medical Center.
Dinello, John E. '85 (PIT) Washington, PA Immaculate Conception Church.
Dineros, Santiago A. (RVC) Retired.
Dinga, William '75 (RIC) Retired.
Dinges, Anthony (RIC) Blackstone, VA Immaculate Heart of Mary Church; Crewe, VA St. John the Baptist Church.
Dinges, Anthony '57 (RIC) Retired.
Dinh, Anthony Tien Minh *o.p.* '97 (ARL) [5] Arlington, VA Holy Martyrs of Vietnam Church.
Dinh, Dominic Hai *c.ss.r.* '95 (DAL) [2] Garland, TX Mother of Perpetual Help Church.
Dinh, Hao '93 (SJ) [19] San Jose, CA St. Patrick Church.
Dinh, Joseph Long '00 (CHL) Salisbury, NC Sacred Heart Church.
Dinh, Joseph Truc *s.d.b.* '99 (ORG) [7] Santa Ana, CA St. Barbara's Church.
Dinh, Peter H. '00 (DEN) [3] Lakewood, CO Our Lady of Fatima Church.
Dinh, Quang Duc *s.v.d.* '92 (DUB) [B] Epworth, IA Divine Word College.
Dinh, Thomas Tranh *i.c.m.* '65 (BR) [H] Baton Rouge, LA Incarnatio Consecratio Mission.
Dinh, Tran Thuc '61 (OAK) [3] San Leandro, CA St. Felicitas Church.
Dinh, Tran Truc (OAK) Retired.
Dinh, Tri M. *s.j.* '00 (LA) [C] Los Angeles, CA Loyola Marymount University; [BB] Los Angeles, CA Archdiocesan Office for Campus Ministry.
Dinh Tuan Ngan, Joseph (SPC) [E] Carthage, MO Congregation of the Mother Co-Redemptrix, United States Assumption Province.
Dinh Viet Luan, Felix M. *c.m.c.* (SPC) [E] Carthage, MO Congregation of the Mother Co-Redemptrix, United States Assumption Province.
Dinh Vuong Can, Anselm M. *c.m.c.* (SPC) [E] Carthage, MO Congregation of the Mother Co-Redemptrix, United States Assumption Province.
Dinh-Van-Thiep, Philip '83 (GB) Wautoma, WI St. Joseph Church.
Dininni, Nicholas J. '93 (PH) [1] Coatesville, PA St. Cecilia Church.
Dinio, Miguel *o.p.* '64 (SAN) [5] San Angelo, TX St. Joseph Church; Carlsbad, TX St. Therese of the Child Jesus Church.
Diniz, Msgr. Pedro D. '71 (BGP) [5] Danbury, CT St. Peter Church.
Dink, Nghia '86 (HT) Larose, LA Our Lady of the Rosary Church.
Dinkel, Emil *c.pp.s.* '53 (TOL) [M] Bellevue, OH Sorrowful Mother Shrine.
Dinkel, Harvey P. *o.f.m.cap.* '61 (DEN) [M] Denver, CO St. Francis of Assisi Friary.
Dinkins, Msgr. Jack M. '63 (GAL) Katy, TX Epiphany of the Lord Church.
Dinneen, James J. *s.j.* '60 (NEW) [C] Jersey City, NJ St. Peter's Preparatory School.
Dinneen, John A. *s.j.* '60 (BO) [W] Chestnut Hill, MA The Jesuit Community at Boston College.
Dinnico, Henry P. '58 (GBG) Retired.
Dino, Gerald N. *o.e.s.l.* '65 (PSC) Linden, NJ St. George's Church.
DiNoia, Joseph Augustine *o.p.* '70 (WDC) [B] Washington, DC Dominican House of Studies.
DiNola, Leonard J. '58 (NY) Buchanan, NY St. Christopher Church.
Diogo, Louis M. '46 (PRO) [2] East Providence, RI St. Francis Xavier Church; Retired.
Diomartich, Msgr. Felix S. '37 (LA) [46] Los Angeles, CA St. Anthony Church; Retired.
Dion, Gerard J. '92 (MAN) Absent on Leave.
Dion, Louis F. *a.a.* '40 (WOR) [B] Worcester, MA Assumption College; [N] Worcester, MA Assumptionists (Augustinians of the Assumption).
Dion, Maurice B. '44 (SAL) Retired.
Dion, Richard H. '99 (MAN) Newport, NH St. Patrick Church.
Dionne, Adrian L. *o.p.* '49 (COL) Somerset, OH St. Joseph's Church; Somerset, OH Holy Trinity Church; [H] Somerset, OH St. Joseph's Rectory.
Dionne, Earl J. '58 (MIL) Retired.
Dionne, Francis '81 (SP) New Port Richey, FL St. Thomas Aquinas Church.
Dionne, Nelson *s.c.* '96 (PRO) [P] Burrillville, RI Brothers of the Sacred Heart Provincial House.
Dionne, Rene *m.afr.* '61 (FgM) Missionaries of Africa Foreign Missions.
Dionne, Vincente *c.ss.r.* '80 (PCE) Guayama, PR St. Anthony of Padua Church.
DiOrio, John R. '99 (PH) Morton, PA Our Lady of Perpetual Help Church.
DiOrio, Ralph A. '57 (WOR) On Special or Other Diocesan Assignment.
DiPeentino, John (DEN) [1] Denver, CO Cathedral of the Immaculate Conception.
DiPeri, Joseph B. '56 (NEW) Retired.
DiPerri, James (BO) [FF] Brighton, MA Caritas Christi Retirement Plan and Trust.
DiPerri, James M. '85 (BO) [66] Boston, MA St. Theresa of Avila Church.
Diphe, Juan '76 (HEL) Military Chaplains.
Diphe, Juan '76 (LAV) Military Chaplains.
DiPietro, Leroy A. '70 (PIT) Brentwood, PA St. Sylvester Church.
DiPietro, Rodric J. '76 (COL) [16] Columbus, OH St. Elizabeth Church.
Dippre, Mark '92 (PHX) [2] Tempe, AZ Our Lady of Mt. Carmel Church.
Dipre, Gilio L. '55 (E) [B] Erie, PA Gannon University.
DiRenzo, Michael J. '70 (LA) San Pedro, CA Fort MacArthur Annex.
Direnzo, Michael J. '70 (STU) On Duty Outside the Diocese.
Dirig, Walter F. *c.m.* '39 (PH) [AA] Philadelphia, PA Congregation of the Mission.
Dirkx, Dennis A. '72 (MIL) [6] Milwaukee, WI All Saints Church.
Dirscherl, Denis A. *s.j.* '67 (CHI) [N] Chicago, IL Chicago Province of the Society of Jesus-Provincial Office.
DiRuscio, Romano *s.c.* '51 (PH) [M] Springfield, PA Don Guanella School for Retarded Boys; [N] Rosemont, PA St. Edmond's Home for Children; [AA] Springfield, PA Servants of Charity (S.C.).
DiRusso, Anthony '63 (MAN) Greenville, NH Sacred Heart Church; Wilton, NH Sacred Heart Church.
DiSalvatore, Remo *o.f.m.cap.* '97 (PIT) [O] Pittsburgh, PA St. Conrad Friary.
Disch, Msgr. John H. '39 (LAF) [1] New Iberia, LA St. Peter Church; Retired.
Dischler, Raymond J. '73 (MAD) Poynette, WI St. Thomas Church.
DiSciacca, Joseph V. '73 (HRT) [3] Meriden, CT St. Laurent Church.
DiSenso, Gerald '53 (NY) Retired.
Diskin, Francis X. *c.s.p.* '46 (NY) [104] New York, NY St. Paul the Apostle Church; [DD] Jamaica Estates, NY Paulist Fathers Generalate.
Diskin, John J. *s.j.* '63 (BO) [W] Weston, MA Campion Health Center, Inc.
Diskin, Michael L. '77 (PHX) [24] Phoenix, AZ St. Theresa Church; Special Assignment.
Diskin, Miles Eric '75 (PIT) [38] Pittsburgh, PA Sacred Heart Church.
DiSpigno, Francis *o.f.m.* '96 (TR) Brant Beach, NJ St. Francis of Assisi Church.
DiSpigno, Gennaro J. '81 (RVC) Seaford, NY Maria Regina Church.
Dissek, Jerome M. '69 (BUF) Cuba, NY Our Lady of Angels Church; Friendship, NY Sacred Heart Church.
DiStefano, Msgr. John '52 (BEA) Retired.
DiStefano, Joseph '84 (ORG) Absent on Sick Leave.
Distefano, Simeon *o.f.m.* '63 (NY) [DD] New York, NY Franciscan Province of the Immaculate Conception.
Dister, John E. *s.j.* '62 (DET) [K] Detroit, MI Jesuit Provincial Office-Detroit Province of the Society of Jesus; [K] Detroit, MI Jesuit Community at the University of Detroit.
Ditaddeo, Alessandro '52 (LAR) [15] Laredo, TX St. Joseph Church.
Ditch, Robert G. '56 (STL) Retired.
Ditenhafer, John A. '61 (STL) [2] University City, MO Christ the King Church.
Ditillo, James J. *s.j.* '76 (BAL) [S] Baltimore, MD Jesuit Fathers and Brothers Maryland Provincial Curia.
DiTomasi, Francisco *o.s.m.* '53 (ELP) [24] El Paso, TX St. Ignatius of Loyola Church.
Ditta, Angelo J. '86 (RVC) East Meadow, NY Nassau County Medical Center; [M] Uniondale, NY St. Pius X Residence.
Dittberner, Jerome M. '64 (STP) [A] St. Paul, MN The Saint Paul Seminary; [C] St. Paul, MN University of St. Thomas.
Dittman, Bernard F. '55 (VEN) Retired.
Dittmeier, Charles R. *m.m.* '70 (FgM) Maryknoll Foreign Missions.
Dittmeier, Charles R. '70 (L) On Duty Outside the Archdiocese.
Dittmer, Antoinio (PEO) [B] Champaign, IL High School of St. Thomas More.
Dittmer, Antonio (PEO) Farmer City, IL Sacred Heart Church.
Dittmer, Antonio '97 (PEO) [2] Champaign, IL St. John's Catholic Chapel Church; [P] Champaign, IL St. John's Catholic Student Chapel and Newman Foundation, University of Illinois.
Ditto, Anthony W. '90 (GBG) Mount Pleasant, PA Visitation of the Blessed Virgin Mary Church.
Dittoe, Msgr. John T. '45 (COL) Retired.
Ditton, Edmund Augustine *o.p.* '84 (NY) [DD] New York, NY St. Vincent Ferrer Priory.
Ditty, James '89 (RIC) Retired.
DiTullio, Peter S. *s.c.* '68 (PRO) [6] East Providence, RI Sacred Heart Church.
DiUlio, Albert J. *s.j.* '74 (FgM) Provinces.
Diurczak, Eugene '68 (NEW) [2] Linden, NJ Holy Family Church.
Divan, Anthony L. '65 (PEO) Retired.
Diver, Patrick *s.d.b.* '74 (FgM) Salesians of Don Bosco Foreign Missions.
Diver, Patrick *s.d.b.* '74 (NY) [DD] New Rochelle, NY Salesian Provincial House.
Divine, Finbarr '70 (LA) San Gabriel, CA St. Anthony Church.
Diviney, Andrew *s.j.* '61 (LA) Northridge, CA Our Lady of Lourdes Church.
Diviney, Msgr. Charles E. '31 (BRK) Retired.
Divis, Daniel O. '79 (CLV) [8] Lorain, OH St. Mary Church.
Divis, M. James '76 (LIN) [A] Seward, NE St. Gregory the Great Seminary.
DiVito, John *c.s.* '52 (CHI) [M] Northlake, IL Villa Scalabrini.
Divizia, John *s.d.b.* '35 (NY) [FF] Stony Point, NY Don Bosco Retreat Center and Marian Shrine; [FF] Stony Point, NY Marian Shrine.
Dixey, Edward J. *o.s.a.* '57 (ALB) [2] Troy, NY St. Augustine Church.
Dixon, Alvin *s.v.d.* '69 (GAL) [47] Houston, TX St. Mary of the Purification Church.
Dixon, Daniel B. '56 (PIT) Allegheny County, PA St. Joseph House of Hospitality.
Dixon, David '57 (PIT) Allegheny County, PA Vincentian Regency Home.
Dixon, David C. '57 (PIT) Allegheny County, PA Vincentian Home for the Chronically Ill; [K] Pittsburgh, PA Vincentian Home Inc.; [L] Allison Park, PA Vincentian Regency; [O] Pittsburgh, PA St. John Vianney Manor.
Dixon, Frank *o.carm.* '76 (WDC) [B] Washington, DC Whitefriars Hall.
Dixon, J. Isidore '64 (WDC) Rosaryville, MD Church of the Most Holy Rosary.
Dixon, James M. *s.j.* '73 (CHI) [N] Chicago, IL Chicago Province of the Society of Jesus-Provincial Office.
Dixon, James M. *s.j.* '73 (LR) Jonesboro, AR Blessed Sacrament Church; Weiner, AR St. Anthony's Church; [L] Jonesboro, AR Catholic Hispanic Center.
Dixon, James R. '70 (NO) Military Chaplains.
Dixon, Jerome A. '57 (PIT) [54] Pittsburgh, PA St. John Vianney Church.
DiZella, Alexander *o.f.m.* '55 (NY) [DD] New York, NY Franciscan Friars, Order of Friars Minor, Holy Name Province.
Dlabal, Norbert '72 (JC) Missionary Assignment in Peru.
Dlabal, Norbert F. '72 (SAL) On Duty Outside the Diocese.
Dmoch, Paul '76 (NY) Rosendale, NY St. Peter Church.
Do, Msgr. Dominic Dinh '72 (SJ) [19] San Jose, CA St. Patrick Church; Special Assignment.
Do, Joseph Luc *o.p.* '74 (GAL) [57] Houston, TX Our Lady of Lavang Church.
Do, Vien Van (PEO) [13] Peoria, IL St. Philomena's Church.
Do, Vincent Tuan Anh '00 (CIN) Liberty Township, OH St. Maximilian Kolbe Church.
Do Ba Cong, James (SPC) [E] Carthage, MO Congregation of the Mother Co-Redemptrix, United States Assumption Province.
Do Binh Dinh, Luke M. *c.m.c.* '77 (SB) [E] Corona, CA Congregation of the Mother Coredemptrix.
Do Cao Tung, Francis Xavier M. *c.m.c.* (SPC) [E] Carthage, MO Congregation of the Mother Co-Redemptrix, United States Assumption Province.
Do-Sek, Zachariah Jeong '82 (ORL) [1] Orlando, FL St. James Church.
Doaling, Patrick (MRY) [K] Watsonville, CA Magnificat the Monterey Bay Chapter.
Doan, Joseph '74 (GAL) [K] Houston, TX The Catholic Chaplain Corps.
Doan Quang Dien, Basil M. *c.m.c.* (SPC) [E] Carthage, MO Congregation of the Mother Co-Redemptrix, United States Assumption Province.
Dobbin, Edmund J. *o.s.a.* '62 (PH) [C] Villanova, PA Villanova University; [AA] Villanova, PA St. Thomas Monastery.
Dobbin, Jay D. '64 (GF) On Duty Outside of the Diocese.
Dobbins, Michael J. '99 (ARL) [1] Alexandria, VA Blessed Sacrament Church.
Dobbins, Robert R. *s.j.* '67 (NY) [DD] New York, NY Jesuit Community at Fordham University.
Dober, Edward J. '76 (LA) Paramount, CA Our Lady of the Rosary Church.
Dobes, Msgr. George E. '68 (CHI) Military Chaplains.
Dobihal, Robert F. '50 (STP) Retired.
Dobitz, Roger '85 (SFS) On Leave of Absence.
Dobkowski, Msgr. Paulin J. '54 (BEL) Retired.
Dobnikar, Ivan *o.s.b.* '49 (JOL) [J] Lisle, IL St. Procopius Abbey.
Dobo, Leo '46 (ORL) Lake Wales, FL Holy Spirit Church; Retired.
Dobosiewciz, Leon W. '46 (Y) Retired.
Dobosiewicz, Stephen J. '42 (E) Retired.
Dobosz, Emil J. '49 (WH) Retired.

Doboz, Eugene '85 (GAL) [22] Houston, TX St. Christopher Church.
DoBranski, John V. '89 (BAL) Westminster, MD St. John Church.
Dobrosky, John M. '83 (TR) New Monmouth, NJ St. Mary Church.
Dobrowolski, Thomas '88 (STN) Mishawaka, IN St. Michael Church.
Dobrowolski, Thomas R. '68 (FTW) [5] Mishawaka, IN St. Michael Ukrainian Catholic Church.
Dobrowski, Peter P. '71 (PHX) Bullhead City, AZ St. Margaret Mary Church.
Dobry, Jerome *o.s.b.* '44 (JOL) [J] Lisle, IL St. Procopius Abbey.
Dobrzenski, Francis G. '77 (MAR) On Duty Outside the Diocese.
Dobrzynski, Martin J. '84 (GRY) New Chicago, IN Assumption of the Blessed Virgin Mary Church.
Dobson, Christopher *t.o.r.* '78 (ARL) Herndon, VA St. Joseph Church.
Dobson, Gregory J. '83 (BUF) Olean, NY St. Mary of the Angels Church.
Dochstader, Richard '75 (JOL) Plainfield, IL St. Mary Immaculate Church.
Dockendorf, Ronald (SCL) [H] Pierz, MN St. Mary's Villa Inc.
Dockendorf, Ronald '82 (SCL) Buckman, MN St. Michael's Church.
Dockendorff, Carl J. '45 (LC) Retired.
Dockerill, Walter J. '60 (PMB) Wellington, FL St. Rita Church.
Doctor, John *o.f.m.* '76 (STL) [P] St. Louis, MO Franciscan Friary of St. Anthony of Padua.
Doctor, John L. *o.f.m.* '76 (FgM) Franciscan Foreign Missions.
Doda, Eugene J., Jr. '77 (MIL) [3] Menomonee Falls, WI St. James Church.
Dodaro, Robert J. *o.s.a.* '82 (CHI) [N] Olympia Fields, IL The Augustinians-Provincialate.
Dodd, Michael *o.c.d.* (CHI) [N] Chicago, IL Discalced Carmelite Friars; Edith Stein House of Studies.
Dodds, Michael *o.p.* '77 (OAK) [A] Berkeley, CA Dominican School of Philosophy and Theology; [N] Oakland, CA Dominican Order (Western Province), St. Albert's Priory; [N] Oakland, CA Western Dominican Province.
Dodds, Perry W. '54 (B) Retired.
Dodge, Erwin J. *o.s.a.* '57 (CHI) [J] Chicago, IL Holy Cross Hospital; [N] Olympia Fields, IL The Augustinians-Provincialate.
Dodo, Andrew '83 (NO) Reserve, LA Our Lady of Grace Church.
Doefler, Joseph *o.f.m.cap.* '54 (GB) [I] Appleton, WI St. Fidelis Friary.
Doerfler, Camilus *o.f.m.cap.* '54 (GB) [I] Appleton, WI St. Fidelis Friary.
Doerfler, John F. (GB) Casco, WI Holy Trinity Church.
Doerfler, Msgr. Marvin G. '59 (SAT) Canyon Lake, TX St. Thomas the Apostle Church.
Doerger, Berard *o.f.m.* '61 (GLP) Acoma, NM San Esteban, Acoma Catholic Indian Church; Laguna, NM St. Joseph Church; [A] Gallup, NM Diocesan Diaconate and Lay Ecclesial Ministry Formation Program.
Doerger, Stanley D. '58 (CIN) [15] Cincinnati, OH St. Bernard Church.
Doerhoff, Dennis E. '76 (STL) [49] St. Louis, MO St. Mary Magdalen Church.
Doering, Christopher E. '98 (CHI) Tinley Park, IL St. George Church.
Doerner, David L. *s.a.* '60 (LA) [64] Los Angeles, CA Maryknoll Japanese Catholic Center Church; [Q] Los Angeles, CA Atonement Friars.
Doerr, Brian '98 (LFT) Special Assignment.
Doerr, Brian M. '98 (LFT) [1] Lafayette, IN St. Mary Church.
Doerr, Richard J. '93 (LFT) Carmel, IN Our Lady of Mount Carmel Church.
Doerre, Edmund J. '63 (LC) Chippewa Falls, WI Holy Ghost Church; Springfield, WI St. Bridget Church.
Doersam, Carl G. '45 (NY) Retired.
Doersching, Lawrence *s.m.* '73 (SAT) [C] San Antonio, TX St. Mary's University of San Antonio, Texas; [M] San Antonio, TX Marianist Woodlawn Community.
Dogali, Michael F. '92 (BGP) Huntington, CT St. Lawrence Church.
Dohar, William J. *c.s.c.* '73 (OAK) [N] Berkeley, CA Holy Cross Fathers-Holy Cross Center.
Doheny, Richard '48 (SAC) Fair Oaks, CA St. Mel Church.
Doheny, Thomas R. '58 (MAD) [4] Beloit, WI St. Thomas the Apostle Church.
Doherty, Charles '58 (CC) Retired.
Doherty, D. G. *o.p.* '57 (FgM) Dominican - Order of Preachers Foreign Missions.
Doherty, Daniel C. *s.j.* '76 (BAL) [S] Baltimore, MD Jesuit Fathers and Brothers Maryland Provincial Curia.
Doherty, Daniel J. (BAL) [A] Baltimore, MD St. Mary's Seminary and University.
Doherty, Daniel J. '94 (SCR) On Duty Outside the Diocese.
Doherty, Declan M. *o.s.m.* '60 (CHI) [N] Chicago, IL Order of Friar Servants of Mary (Servites) United States of America Province, Inc.
Doherty, Donald J. *m.m.* '62 (NY) [DD] Maryknoll, NY Maryknoll Fathers and Brothers.
Doherty, Duane *o.f.m.conv.* '63 (DET) Bloomfield Hills, MI St. Regis Church.
Doherty, Duane *o.f.m.conv.* '63 (IND) [J] Mount Saint Francis, IN Provincial Headquarters for the Conventual Franciscan Province.
Doherty, Edward *o.s.a.* '57 (MIA) [H] Miami, FL Casa San Lorenzo.
Doherty, Edward *m.s.a.* '69 (NOR) [F] Cromwell, CT Society of the Missionaries of the Holy Apostles.
Doherty, Edward C. *m.ss.a.* '68 (BGP) [L] Bridgeport, CT Roncalli Apartments.
Doherty, Msgr. Francis E. '41 (MAD) Retired.
Doherty, George E. '50 (NEW) Retired; [N] Rutherford, NJ St. John Vianney Residence for Priests.
Doherty, Glennon C. '78 (STL) Grantwood, MO Our Lady of Providence Church; [A] St. Louis, MO Kenrick-Glennon Seminary.
Doherty, Henry F. '56 (BO) Hanover, MA St. Mary of the Sacred Heart Church.
Doherty, James J. *c.s.c.* '78 (BGP) [P] Bridgeport, CT Provincial Offices of the Priests and Brothers of Holy Cross, Eastern Province.
Doherty, James J. *c.s.c.* '78 (PRT) Saco, ME Most Holy Trinity Church.
Doherty, Msgr. John B. '39 (LA) Retired.
Doherty, John B. '80 (NY) Absent on Leave.
Doherty, John E. *c.ss.r.* '38 (BO) [53] Boston, MA Our Lady of Perpetual Help Church; Boston, MA Dana Farber Cancer Institute.
Doherty, John R. '64 (NEW) [2] Bayonne, NJ St. Andrew's Church.
Doherty, Msgr. John T. '45 (NY) [144] Bronx, NY St. Gabriel Church; Retired; [E] White Plains, NY Archbishop Stepinac High School.
Doherty, Louis *c.p.* '57 (CHI) [N] Chicago, IL Passionist Provincial Office; [N] Chicago, IL Passionist Community-Immaculate Conception Monastery.
Doherty, Michael *o.f.m.* '76 (LA) [W] Malibu, CA Serra Retreat.
Doherty, Neil '69 (MIA) Margate, FL St. Vincent Church.
Doherty, Patrick A. '56 (ORG) Newport Beach, CA Our Lady of Mount Carmel Church.
Doherty, Patrick D. *s.j.* '65 (SJ) [L] Los Gatos, CA Sacred Heart Jesuit Center.
Doherty, Msgr. Patrick G. '45 (FRS) Retired.
Doherty, Msgr. Patrick J. '55 (BWN) [8] Brownsville, TX St. Joseph Church.
Doherty, Patrick J. '59 (MAD) Absent on Sick Leave.
Doherty, Paul J. '95 (WOR) Uxbridge, MA St. Mary's Church.
Doherty, Raymond J. *s.s.e.* '58 (BUR) [4] Burlington, VT St. Joseph's Church; [E] Colchester, VT Society of St. Edmund.
Doherty, Robert G. *s.j.* '60 (BO) [W] Weston, MA Campion Jesuit Community; [Y] Weston, MA Campion Renewal Center.
Doherty, Robert J. '70 (BO) [5] Medford, MA Sacred Heart Church.
Doherty, Terrance *s.m.a.* '70 (FgM) Society of African Missions.
Doherty, Timothy L. '76 (RCK) Byron, IL St. Mary Church.
Doherty, William J. '55 (SPR) [4] Holyoke, MA Immaculate Conception Church; [G] Springfield, MA CHE - The Mercy Hospital, Inc.
Dohle, Benedict *o.s.b.* '54 (OM) [K] Elkhorn, NE Mount Michael Abbey.
Dohman, William *j.c.l.* '73 (B) Retired.
Dohner, Stephen J. '76 (CLV) Cleveland Heights, OH St. Louis Church.
Dohogne, David J. '92 (SPC) Doniphan, MO St. Benedict Church.
Doiron, David E. '69 (WOR) [1] Worcester, MA St. Paul's Church; On Special or Other Diocesan Assignment.
Dokupil, Edward J. '64 (AUS) Bastrop, TX Ascension Church.
Dolan, Bernard M. '66 (BGP) [1] Trumbull, CT Christ the King Church.
Dolan, Charles *c.s.s.* '58 (BO) [W] Waltham, MA Stigmatine Fathers & Brothers Provincial House.
Dolan, Charles F.X. *s.j.* '46 (NEW) [C] Jersey City, NJ St. Peter's Preparatory School.
Dolan, Charles F.X. *s.j.* '46 (TR) Manasquan, NJ St. Denis Church.
Dolan, Daniel *m.m.* '54 (WDC) [B] Washington, DC Maryknoll Fathers and Brothers.
Dolan, Edward *s.s.c.* '58 (OM) [K] St. Columbans, NE St. Columban's Foreign Mission Society.
Dolan, Francis *o.m.i.* '73 (FgM) Oblates Foreign Missions.
Dolan, Frank *o.m.i.* '73 (BO) [U] Lowell, MA D'Youville Manor.
Dolan, Gerald '90 (DUB) Unassigned.
Dolan, Gerald M. *o.f.m.* '56 (NY) [DD] New York, NY Franciscan Friars, Order of Friars Minor, Holy Name Province.
Dolan, Gerard (NY) [EE] Warwick, NY Mt. Alverno Center, Bon Secours Charity Health System.
Dolan, J. L. *o.p.* '60 (FgM) Dominican - Order of Preachers Foreign Missions.
Dolan, James F. '51 (NEW) [B] Jersey City, NJ Saint Peter's College; [N] Jersey City, NJ Jesuits of Saint Peter's College, Inc.
Dolan, James J. '49 (RVC) Retired; [M] Uniondale, NY St. Pius X Residence.
Dolan, James L. *o.p.* '60 (FgM) Dominican - Order of Preachers Foreign Missions.
Dolan, James Linus *o.p.* '60 (NO) [P] New Orleans, LA Dominican Friars, Southern Dominican Province of St. Martin de Porres.
Dolan, James R. *s.j.* '70 (ROC) [C] Rochester, NY McQuaid Jesuit High School.
Dolan, James W. '75 (PIT) [2] Butler, PA St. Michael the Archangel Church.
Dolan, Jarlath '74 (LA) Camarillo, CA Blessed Junipero Serra Church.
Dolan, John P. '89 (SD) [3] Oceanside, CA St. Mary, Star of the Sea Church.
Dolan, John R. *m.s.* '68 (BO) [BB] Ipswich, MA National Shrine of Our Lady of La Salette.
Dolan, John R. *m.s.* '79 (WOR) [6] Fitchburg, MA St. Joseph's Church.
Dolan, Joseph K. '60 (BRK) [18] Brooklyn, NY St. Bernadette Church.
Dolan, Joseph M. '92 (WOR) [4] Leominster, MA St. Leo's Church.
Dolan, Joseph V. *s.j.* '52 (NY) [DD] New York, NY Jesuit Community at Fordham University.
Dolan, Laurence P. *o.f.m.* '65 (ORG) [3] Huntington Beach, CA SS. Simon and Jude Church.
Dolan, Lawrence F. *c.ss.r.* '42 (BRK) [V] Brooklyn, NY Our Lady of Good Counsel Residence.
Dolan, Leo A. '52 (STP) Retired.
Dolan, Msgr. Leo M. '60 (SAT) [39] San Antonio, TX St. Helena Church.
Dolan, Louis F. *c.s.sp.* '50 (VEN) [G] Sarasota, FL Congregation of the Holy Ghost.
Dolan, Luis M. *c.p.* '45 (NY) [33] New York, NY St. Emeric Church.
Dolan, Mark A. '76 (STL) Bissell Hills, MO St. Jerome Church.
Dolan, Michael F. '98 (WDC) Derwood, MD St. Francis of Assisi Church.
Dolan, Michael J. '96 (HRT) Newington, CT St. Mary Church.
Dolan, Msgr. Neal T. '64 (SD) Lakeside, CA Our Lady of Perpetual Help Church.
Dolan, Patrick (DEN) [36] Denver, CO St. Rose of Lima Church.
Dolan, Patrick G. '71 (JC) Boonville, MO SS. Peter and Paul Church.
Dolan, Patrick J. '78 (L) Radcliff, KY St. Christopher Church.
Dolan, Paul A. '84 (RVC) Kings Park, NY St. Joseph's Church.
Dolan, Paul F. '45 (BAL) Taneytown, MD St. Joseph Church; Retired; [O] Timonium, MD Stella Maris.
Dolan, Peter C. '54 (PMB) Port St. Lucie, FL St. Lucie Church; Retired.
Dolan, Raymond '56 (B) On Duty Outside the Diocese.
Dolan, Robert *s.j.* '76 (LA) [11] Los Angeles, CA Dolores Church.
Dolan, Robert L. *s.j.* '73 (FgM) Provinces.
Dolan, Thomas D. '51 (BRK) [166] Queens, NY St. Elizabeth's Church; Retired.
Dolan, Thomas P. '45 (RCK) Harmon, IL St. Flannen Church; Maytown, IL St. Patrick Church; Walton, IL St. Mary Church.
Dolan, Timothy '83 (STP) Long Lake, MN St. George Church.
Dolan, Msgr. Timothy M. '76 (STL) On Duty Outside the Archdiocese.
Dolan, Walter *o.f.m.* '61 (CLV) [D] Parma, OH Padua Franciscan High School; [O] Cleveland, OH Padua Franciscan Friary.
Dolan, William '96 (DM) [2] Council Bluffs, IA Our Lady, Queen of Apostles Church.
Dolan, William S. *s.j.* '82 (SY) [S] Syracuse, NY Jesuits at LeMoyne, Inc.
Dolbec, Jacques *s.o.l.t.* '95 (CC) [H] Robstown, TX Society of Our Lady of the Most Holy Trinity.
Dolbec, Jacques '96 (MAN) [B] Warner, NH Magdalen College.
Dolciamore, John V. '52 (CHI) Retired; [A] Mundelein, IL University of St. Mary of the Lake-Mundelein Seminary.
Dold, John F. '73 (DEN) Absent on Leave.
Dolehide, John R. *o.p.* '47 (CHI) [1] Oak Lawn, IL St. Catherine of Alexandria Church; [N] Chicago, IL Dominicans (Provincial Office).
Dolezal, Richard R. '76 (MIL) Sharon, WI St. Catherine Church; On Duty Outside the Archdiocese.

Dolezal, Thomas H. '70 (KCK) Axtell, KS St. Michael's Church; Summerfield, KS Holy Family Church.
Dolinic, Louis S. '66 (BUF) [5] Depew, NY Our Lady of the Blessed Sacrament Church.
Doll, Donald A. *s.j.* '68 (OM) [K] Omaha, NE Jesuit Community at Creighton University.
Doll, Msgr. William P. '50 (PBL) Holly, CO St. Frances of Rome Church.
Dollar, Robert J. '60 (BEL) Retired.
Dollard, John J. '45 (OAK) Retired.
Dollard, Mark E. '91 (MAN) Henniker, NH St. Theresa Church.
Dollen, Bernard '53 (ROC) Retired.
Dollen, Bernard '56 (ROC) [M] Rochester, NY Diocesan Department of Campus Ministry.
Dollinger, Cletus *o.c.s.o.* '50 (SLC) [F] Huntsville, UT Abbey of Our Lady of the Holy Trinity of the Order of Cistercians.
Dollinger, Msgr. John M. '57 (E) Erie, PA Erie County Prison.
Dollinger, Robert J. '54 (L) Retired.
Dols, Francisco *t.o.r.* '47 (NEW) [14] Elizabeth, NJ Immaculate Heart of Mary Church.
Dolsina, Stanley '46 (DUL) Retired.
Dolski, V. Anthony '59 (GB) [1] De Pere, WI St. Francis Xavier Church.
Domagas, Reynaldo (NY) Manhattan, NY Beth Israel Medical Center.
Domandich, Anthony '58 (SEA) Retired.
Domas, John '50 (SB) Retired.
Domaszewicz, Chester '78 (VEN) LaBelle, FL Our Lady Queen of Heaven Church.
Dombroski, Dean H. (GB) New Franken, WI St. Kilian Church.
Dombroski, Dean H. '64 (GB) Humbolt, WI St. Thomas the Apostle Church.
Dombrowski, Francis J. *o.f.m.cap.* '59 (MIL) [S] Milwaukee, WI The Dwelling Place.
Dombrowski, John *o.f.m.* '84 (STP) [10] St. Paul, MN Sacred Heart Church.
Dombrowski, Robert J. '60 (FTW) Bremen, IN St. Dominic Church.
Dombrowski, Ronald J. '72 (SAG) Port Sanilac, MI St. Mary Church.
Dombrowski, Stanley J. *o.s.f.s.* '83 (VEN) [3] Fort Myers, FL St. Cecilia Church.
Dombrowski, Steven G. '89 (CHI) Lake Villa, IL Prince of Peace Church.
Dombrowski, Timothy '73 (LAN) [H] Ann Arbor, MI St. Joseph Mercy Hospital.
Dome, Thomas *c.r.i.c.* '98 (LA) [Q] Los Angeles, CA Canons Regular of the Immaculate Conception.
Domec, Msgr. Charles C. '56 (GAL) The Woodlands, TX Sts. Simon and Jude Church.
Domeck, Casimiro '73 (ARE) Florida, PR Our Lady of Mercy Church.
Domhoff, Ronald J. '72 (L) [B] Louisville, KY Trinity High School.
Domin, Edward '88 (ALN) [3] Easton, PA St. Jane Frances de Chantal Church.
Domin, John M. '50 (P) Retired; [K] Beaverton, OR Maryville Nursing Home.
Domingo, Albert *c.m.f.* '79 (LA) [31] Los Angeles, CA Our Lady Queen of the Angels Church.
Domingo, Santiago '65 (LAR) [16] Laredo, TX St. Jude Church.
Domingue, Kenneth '91 (LAF) Basile, LA St. Augustine Church.
Dominguez, Gustavo *i.v.e.* '96 (FR) [O] New Bedford, MA The Institute of the Incarnate Word, Inc.
Dominguez, Julio Fernandez *o.m.* '48 (SJN) [16] San Juan, PR Ntra. Sra. de Fatima Church.
Dominguez, M. Marciano *c.s.b.* '90 (GAL) [Q] Sugar Land, TX Basilian Mission Center.
Dominguez, Marciano *c.s.b.* '90 (DET) [6] Detroit, MI Ste. Anne Church.
Dominguez, Patricio *o.m.i.* '60 (LAR) Eagle Pass, TX Our Lady of Refuge Church.
Dominguez, Ramon '00 (FR) [1] Fall River, MA Cathedral of St. Mary of the Assumption; [13] Fall River, MA St. Anne's Church; [I] Fall River, MA St. John Vianney House.
Dominiak, Gerald J. '59 (MIL) Brookfield, WI St. John Vianney Church.
Dominiak, Thomas M. '61 (GAY) Afton, MI St. Monica Church; Onaway, MI St. Paul Church.
Dominic, Abraham B. '87 (NY) [217] Staten Island, NY Our Lady Help of Christians Church.
Dominic, Francis J. '52 (MAD) Retired.
Dominicis, Severino *s.a.c.* '39 (NY) [91] New York, NY Our Lady of Mt. Carmel Church; [DD] New York, NY Pallottine Fathers.
Dominik, Kevin J. '88 (PIT) [A] Pittsburgh, PA Saint Paul Seminary.
Dominik, Stanley '58 (GRY) [2] Whiting, IN Sacred Heart Church.
Dominik, Stanley J. '58 (GRY) [1] Whiting, IN Immaculate Conception Church.
Dominique, Todd M. '94 (TOL) [4] Fremont, OH St. Joseph Church.
Domme, Edward '79 (SFE) Mountainair, NM St. Alice Church.
Dommer, Ian *o.s.b.* '79 (SCL) [I] Collegeville, MN St. John's Abbey, of the Order of St. Benedict.
Domnick, Alphonsus M. *t.o.r.* '44 (SCR) Retired; [N] Dunmore, PA Villa St. Joseph.
Dompke, Ramon *c.ss.r.* '64 (CHI) [150] Chicago, IL Our Lady of Lourdes Church.
Domurat, Thomas '79 (FgM) Society of St. James the Apostle.
Domurat, Thomas S. '79 (BO) Society of St. James the Apostle.
Don, Sextus '79 (FTW) Columbia City, IN St. Paul of the Cross Church.
Dona, Thomas M. '65 (DEN) Byers, CO Our Lady of the Plains Church.
Donadio, Vincent J. '73 (TR) Leave of Absence.
Donaghey, Bernard '29 (SB) Patton, CA Patton State Hospital.
Donaghey, John *s.v.d.* '54 (CHI) [B] Techny, IL Divine Word Residence; [N] Techny, IL Society of the Divine Word, Provincial Headquarter-Chicago Prov.
Donaghey, Patrick H.M. '85 (ATL) Lilburn, GA St. Stephen the Martyr Church.
Donaghy, Harry '67 (ALB) [7] Troy, NY St. Mary Church.
Donaghy, Thomas J. '79 (BAL) Ellicott City, MD St. Paul Church; [V] Ellicott City, MD The St. Paul's Parish Endowment Trust.
Donahoe, James H. *s.j.* '51 (BAL) [S] Baltimore, MD Jesuit Fathers and Brothers Maryland Provincial Curia.
Donahoe, Patrick *t.o.r.* '74 (ALT) [A] Loretto, PA St. Francis College; [F] Loretto, PA St. Francis Friary, Third Order Regular of St. Francis of Penance.
Donahoe, Msgr. Thomas M. '54 (SC) Graettinger, IA Immaculate Conception Church.
Donahue, Aidan *s.t.m., s.t.l.* '86 (HRT) [C] West Hartford, CT Saint Joseph College.
Donahue, Aidan N. '86 (HRT) Bloomfield, CT Sacred Heart Church; [A] Bloomfield, CT St. Thomas Seminary.
Donahue, Anthony *o.f.m.cap.* '51 (SP) [O] Seminole, FL Capuchin Franciscan Residence.
Donahue, Bernard F. *o.s.f.s.* '58 (ALN) [B] Center Valley, PA Desales University; [K] Center Valley, PA Oblates of St. Francis de Sales.
Donahue, Brian G. '83 (FAR) Special Assignment; [A] Fargo, ND Cardinal Muench Seminary.
Donahue, Cecil J. *o.s.b.* '54 (MAN) [K] Manchester, NH St. Anselm Abbey; [N] Manchester, NH Campus Ministries.
Donahue, Daniel J. '58 (BO) Senior Priests.
Donahue, Denis M. '90 (ARL) [8] Alexandria, VA St. Rita's Church.
Donahue, Edward J. '80 (ALN) Unassigned.
Donahue, Eugene L. *s.j.* '70 (DET) [K] Detroit, MI Jesuit Community at the University of Detroit.
Donahue, Eugene L. '70 (STP) [N] Minneapolis, MN La Storta Jesuit Community.
Donahue, John *s.j.* '64 (OAK) [A] Berkeley, CA The Jesuit School of Theology at Berkeley.
Donahue, John '73 (NEW) Belleville, NJ Clara Maass Hospital.
Donahue, John G. '60 (STP) Retired.
Donahue, John J. *c.s.c.* '70 (NY) Manhattan, NY St. Clare's Hospital & Health Center; [W] New York, NY St. Clare's Hospital and Health Center.
Donahue, John R. *s.j.* '64 (OAK) [N] Berkeley, CA Jesuit Community at Jesuit School of Theology at Berkeley.
Donahue, John R. *s.j.* '79 (FgM) Provinces.
Donahue, Joseph '70 (NY) Absent on Leave.
Donahue, Joseph F. *s.v.d.* '42 (BO) [3] Woburn, MA St. Charles Church.
Donahue, Joseph P. '45 (HRT) Retired.
Donahue, L. Scott '82 (CHI) [183] Chicago, IL St. Robert Bellarmine Church; [H] Chicago, IL Mission of Our Lady of Mercy-Mercy Home for Boys and Girls.
Donahue, Martin P. '61 (WOR) [22] Worcester, MA St. Christopher Church.
Donahue, Michael E. *s.j.* '80 (NY) [DD] New York, NY Jesuit Provincial's Office.
Donahue, Paul H. '49 (DAV) Retired; [M] Davenport, IA St. Vincent Center.
Donahue, Richard T. '68 (BO) On Duty Outside the Archdiocese.
Donahue, Stephen '86 (IND) Charlestown, IN St. Michael Church; Henryville, IN St. Francis Xavier Church.
Donahue, Thomas J. '62 (LR) Retired; [H] Little Rock, AR St. John Manor.
Donahue, Timothy C. '00 (SAV) [3] Columbus, GA St. Anne Church.
Donahue, William H. *c.s.c.* '49 (AUS) Copperas Cove, TX Holy Family Church.
Donahue, William P. '70 (GBG) [4] Latrobe, PA St. Rose Church.
Donahugh, Donald E. '62 (BEA) [C] Port Arthur, TX CHRISTUS St. Mary Hospital.
Donahugh, Donald E. '62 (RCK) Active Outside the Diocese.
Donajkowski, Charles G. '91 (GAY) Rogers City, MI St. Ignatius Church.
Donald, John *s.j.* '72 (FgM) Provinces.
Donald, Joseph F. '87 (B) [3] Boise, ID St. Mary's Church.
Donald, Michael L. '72 (STL) Crystal City, MO Sacred Heart Church.
Donaldson, Raymond J. *s.j.* (CHL) [J] Charlotte, NC Jesuit Community.
Donaldson, Richard *o.f.m.cap.* '57 (NY) New Paltz, NY St. Joseph Church; [DD] New Paltz, NY St. Joseph Friary.
Donaldson, Thomas *c.ss.r.* '79 (GR) [3] Grand Rapids, MI St. Alphonsus Church.
Donaldson, Thomas J. '68 (LC) Ellsworth, WI St. Francis of Assisi Church.
Donarski, Richard *o.c.s.o.* '86 (ATL) [J] Conyers, GA The Monastery of the Holy Spirit.
Donat, Robert J. '66 (SB) Montclair, CA Our Lady of Lourdes Church.
Donatelli, Gino *s.j.* '82 (LEX) [6] Lexington, KY St. Paul Church; [7] Lexington, KY St. Peter Church.
Donatelli, Philip J. '67 (PIT) Peters Township, PA St. Benedict the Abbot Church.
Donato, Gaudelio '87 (HON) Kahului, HI Christ the King Church.
Donato, John *c.s.c.* '91 (P) [B] Portland, OR University of Portland; [L] Portland, OR Holy Cross Fathers & Brothers, C.S.C. - University of Portland; [P] Portland, OR University of Portland.
Donavan, William T. '79 (RVC) [A] Huntington, NY Diocesan Seminary of the Immaculate Conception.
Dondanville, Joseph '95 (PEO) East Moline, IL St. Mary's Church.
Dondapati, John N. '88 (PRO) [K] North Providence, RI St. Joseph Health Services of Rhode Island - Our Lady of Fatima Hospital.
Donders, Joseph *m.afr.* (BAL) Ellicott City, MD Resurrection Church.
Donders, Sjef *m.afr.* '57 (WDC) [M] Washington, DC Missionaries of Africa.
Dondzila, Henry J. '56 (GR) Retired.
Donegan, Augustine *t.o.r.* '46 (STU) [A] Steubenville, OH Franciscan University of Steubenville; [F] Steubenville, OH Holy Spirit Friary.
Donegan, Msgr. James F. '35 (BRK) [184] Queens, NY St. Joan of Arc Church; Retired.
Donegan, William *ss.cc.* '65 (FR) [I] Fairhaven, MA Sacred Hearts Provincial House.
Donehue, Ambrose *o.f.m.* '51 (PRO) [P] Providence, RI St. Francis Friary.
Donelin, John M. '40 (BO) Senior Priests.
Donellan, Msgr. Thomas J. (BAL) Hunt Valley, MD St. Francis Xavier Church.
Donellen, Msgr. Thomas J. '56 (BAL) Retired.
Doner, Roy R. '81 (SAC) Chico, CA Our Divine Savior Church.
Dong, Quang Minh '91 (OAK) Pinole, CA St. Joseph's Church.
Donini, Augustin *o.f.m.* '44 (NY) [DD] New York, NY Franciscan Province of the Immaculate Conception.
Donini, Leone '95 (NEW) On Duty Outside the Archdiocese.
Donio, Frank S. *s.a.c.* '94 (BAL) [51] Baltimore, MD St. Jude Church.
Donio, Thomas S. '95 (CAM) Williamstown, NJ St. Mary's Church.
Donish, Peter M. '70 (PSC) Old Forge, PA St. Nicholas Church.
Donlan, Paul A. '62 (OAK) [R] Berkeley, CA Opus Dei.
Donlan, Robert R. '67 (SP) Brooksville, FL St. Anthony Church.
Donlan, Thomas '44 (NY) [HH] New York, NY Catholic Actors Guild of America, Inc., The.
Donlon, Aidan *s.a.c.* '55 (FWT) Wichita Falls, TX State Hospital; [G] Wichita Falls, TX United Regional Health Care System.
Donlon, James I. '75 (ALB) Lake George, NY Sacred Heart Church; [4] Watervliet, NY St. Patrick Church; Special Assignment.
Donlon, James W. '65 (PH) Conshohocken, PA St. Matthew Church.
Donlon, William J. '37 (BO) Senior Priests.
Donnar, Jeffrey '78 (SAG) Rosebush, MI St. Henry Church.
Donnay, Raymond '50 (SCL) Retired.
Donnellan, Francis A. *s.s.e.* '45 (MOB) [G] Selma, AL Edmundite Fathers.
Donnelly, Arthur *c.ss.r.* '34 (SJN) [2] San Juan, PR San Agustin Church.
Donnelly, Brendan '52 (ORL) Retired.
Donnelly, Brendan P. *o.s.b.* '46 (MAN) [K] Manchester, NH St. Anselm Abbey.
Donnelly, Eamonn *s.v.d.* '70 (FgM) Society of the Divine Word Foreign Missions.
Donnelly, Eamonn *s.v.d.* '70 (LA) [Q] Los Angeles, CA Society of the Divine Word Missionaries, Western Province; [Q] Los Angeles, CA Western Province (1964) Province of St. Therese of the Child Jesus.
Donnelly, Msgr. Edward J. '54 (RVC) Hicksville, NY Holy Family Church.
Donnelly, Eugene F. '48 (BRK) [210] Queens, NY Our

Lady of Fatima Church; Retired.
Donnelly, Msgr. Felix G. '45 (SAV) Retired.
Donnelly, Gerard J. *o.s.b.* '46 (MAN) [K] Manchester, NH St. Anselm Abbey.
Donnelly, James J. *s.j.* '59 (FgM) Provinces.
Donnelly, Jerome A. *o.f.m.* '39 (FgM) Franciscan Foreign Missions.
Donnelly, Msgr. John '58 (SPK) [8] Spokane, WA St. Anthony Church.
Donnelly, John P. *s.j.* '65 (MIL) [P] Milwaukee, WI Jesuit Community at Marquette University.
Donnelly, Joseph T. '71 (HRT) [3] Manchester, CT St. Bridget's Church.
Donnelly, Joseph-Benedict *o.c.s.o.* '43 (P) [L] Lafayette, OR The Cistercian (Trappist) Abbey of Our Lady of Guadalupe.
Donnelly, Msgr. Lawrence E. '49 (LA) Retired.
Donnelly, Lucien R. *o.s.b.* '48 (NEW) [N] Newark, NJ Newark Abbey.
Donnelly, Martin '64 (TOL) [32] Toledo, OH St. Mary of the Assumption Church.
Donnelly, Michael *s.s.c.* '63 (OM) [K] St. Columbans, NE St. Columban's Foreign Mission Society.
Donnelly, P. Martin '64 (TOL) [31] Toledo, OH St. Martin de Porres Church.
Donnelly, Paul J. '58 (BIR) Retired.
Donnelly, Paul V. '88 (STA) Williston, FL Holy Family Church.
Donnelly, Richard A. '62 (PRO) [4] Cranston, RI St. Mark Church.
Donnelly, Robert J. '91 (ALB) [5] Albany, NY St. Catherine of Siena Church; [M] Albany, NY Sisters of Mercy of the Americas Albany Regional Community.
Donnelly, Robert W. '57 (TOL) [1] Toledo, OH Queen of the Most Holy Rosary Church.
Donnelly, Robert W. *m.m.* '59 (HON) [G] Honolulu, HI Maryknoll Fathers House (M.M.).
Donnelly, Russell J. '75 (PH) Absent on Leave.
Donnelly, Sean '54 (SPK) Retired.
Donnelly, Sean '82 (CLV) [5] Akron, OH St. Francis de Sales Church.
Donnelly, Stephen H. '97 (RVC) New Hyde Park, NY Notre Dame Church.
Donnelly, Thomas '61 (RNO) [5] Reno, NV St. Rose of Lima Church.
Donnelly, Timothy *o.s.b.* '65 (LR) [A] Subiaco, AR Subiaco Monastery.
Donnelly, Timothy M. *s.v.d.* '88 (TR) [7] Trenton, NJ Our Lady of the Divine Shepherd Church.
Donnelly, William '64 (ROC) [45] Rochester, NY St. Mary Church; [M] Rochester, NY Diocesan Department of Campus Ministry.
Donnelly, William *o.s.a.* '67 (NY) [168] Bronx, NY St. Nicholas of Tolentine Church.
Donnelly, William E. '71 (JOL) [4] Naperville, IL St. Raphael Church.
Donnelly, William F. *s.j.* '63 (SJ) [B] Santa Clara, CA Santa Clara University.
Donnelly, William J. *m.m.* '65 (FgM) Maryknoll Foreign Missions.
Donnelly, William P. '64 (PH) Upper Darby, PA St. Alice Church.
Donner, Jeffrey '78 (SAG) Mount Pleasant, MI St. Mary University Church.
Donner, Randall G. '92 (OM) Absent on Leave.
Donnolly, Robert '88 (ALB) Special Assignment.
Dono, Abram E. *s.t.* '64 (TUC) [2] Tucson, AZ Blessed Kateri Tekakwitha Church; [J] Tucson, AZ St. Nicholas Indian Center.
Donofrio, Michael J. '76 (PH) On Duty Outside the Archdiocese.
Donoghue, Henry A. '64 (WOR) [23] Worcester, MA St. George Church.
Donoghue, Henry Thomas *o.p.* '57 (WDC) [B] Washington, DC Dominican House of Studies.
Donoghue, John F. '54 (B) Retired.
Donoghue, Patrick '82 (P) Special Assignment.
Donoghue, Paul *s.m.* '68 (STL) [P] St. Louis, MO Provincialate of the Society of Mary, Province of St. Louis.
Donoher, Edward W. *c.s.b.* '49 (DET) [E] Redford, MI Catholic Central High School.
Donohie, John M. '65 (PH) [71] Philadelphia, PA Immaculate Heart of Mary Church.
Donohoe, Edward '50 (STO) Retired.
Donohoe, Patrick K. '82 (CC) [2] Beeville, TX Sacred Heart Church; [4] Beeville, TX St. Joseph Church.
Donohoe, Peter '50 (SFD) Retired.
Donohoe, Philip M. '53 (OKL) El Reno, OK Sacred Heart Church.
Donohoe, Robert W. '50 (CLV) Peninsula, OH Mother of Sorrows Church.
Donohoe, Stephen '67 (TUC) Yuma, AZ MCAS Chapel.
Donohoe, Stephen S. '92 (BO) Military & VA Chaplains.
Donohoe, Thomas E. '62 (RVC) Long Beach, NY St. Mary of the Isle Church.
Donohoe, Thomas P. '52 (BO) Carlisle, MA St. Irene Church.
Donohoe, William *c.pp.s.* '48 (CIN) [B] Carthagena, OH St. Charles.
Donohoe,, Richard E., V.F. '84 (BIR) Anniston, AL Sacred Heart of Jesus Church.
Donohoo, Daniel B. '86 (IND) Bloomington, IN St. John the Apostle Church.
Donohoo, Lawrence J. *o.p.* '85 (WDC) [B] Washington, DC Dominican House of Studies.
Donohue, Aidan N. '86 (HRT) Special and other Archdiocesan Assignment.
Donohue, Edward J. *o.f.m.* '56 (NEW) East Rutherford, NJ St. Joseph's Church.
Donohue, James *c.r.* '83 (BAL) [B] Emmitsburg, MD Mount Saint Mary's College.
Donohue, James T. *c.s.c.* '61 (BGP) [P] Bridgeport, CT Provincial Offices of the Priests and Brothers of Holy Cross, Eastern Province.
Donohue, John F. *o.carm.* '48 (JOL) [J] Darien, IL Carmelite Provincial Office.
Donohue, John J. '48 (CHI) [50] Chicago, IL St. Edward Church; Retired.
Donohue, John J. *s.j.* '59 (FgM) Provinces.
Donohue, John J. '73 (NEW) Bloomfield, NJ St. Valentine Church.
Donohue, John W. *s.j.* '50 (NY) [DD] New York, NY "America;" Residence and publication office of the America Press.
Donohue, Michael T. '75 (NOR) East Lyme, CT St. Matthias Church.
Donohue, Patrick W. '75 (NEW) [1] Hackensack, NJ Holy Trinity Church.
Donohue, Paul *m.c.c.j.* '75 (CIN) [M] Cincinnati, OH Comboni Missionaries (Verona Fathers)-Comboni Mission Center.
Donohue, Peter *c.s.c.* '56 (ORL) Retired; [F] Cocoa Beach, FL Holy Cross Fathers, Eastern Priests Province.
Donohue, Peter M. *o.s.a.* (PH) [AA] Villanova, PA Fray de Leon Community.
Donohue, Peter M. *o.s.a.* '79 (PH) [C] Villanova, PA Villanova University.
Donohue, Raymond A.J. '85 (BUF) Mayville, NY St. Mary Church; Sherman, NY St. Isaac Jogues Church.
Donohue, Robert W. '50 (CLV) Retired.
Donohue, Steven *s.p.s.* '59 (SJ) [L] Saratoga, CA St. Patrick's Missionary Society.
Donohue, Thomas E. '41 (L) [1] Valley Station, KY St. Clement Church; Retired.
Donohue, Timothy C. *o.carm.* '51 (NY) [DD] Scarborough, NY Carmelite Fathers, NY Prov. of St. Elias.
Donoso, Fermin J. *c.s.c.* '67 (FTW) [J] South Bend, IN Congregation of Holy Cross, Indiana Province, Provincial House.
Donovan, Brian G. *o.p.* '64 (GAL) [Q] Houston, TX Dominican Fathers and Brothers, St. Mark Priory, Inc.
Donovan, Charles A. *c.s.p.* '40 (NY) [DD] Jamaica Estates, NY Paulist Fathers Generalate.
Donovan, Charles A. *c.s.p.* '40 (SFR) [32] San Francisco, CA Old St. Mary's Church.
Donovan, Daniel E. *c.m.* '42 (PH) [AA] Philadelphia, PA Congregation of the Mission.
Donovan, David I. *s.j.* '68 (BO) [W] Boston, MA The Society of Jesus of New England-Provincial Offices; [W] Boston, MA The Society of Jesus of New England-Provincial Offices.
Donovan, Dennis *s.d.b.* '83 (COL) [H] Columbus, OH Salesian Center.
Donovan, Donald F. *m.m.* '55 (FgM) Maryknoll Foreign Missions.
Donovan, Edmund J. '41 (E) Retired.
Donovan, Edward *c.s.p.* '59 (LA) [87] Los Angeles, CA St. Paul the Apostle Church.
Donovan, Edward R. *c.s.p.* '59 (NY) [DD] Jamaica Estates, NY Paulist Fathers Generalate.
Donovan, J. Michael '65 (SY) Marcellus, NY St. Francis Xavier Church.
Donovan, J. Paul '58 (TLS) Owasso, OK St. Henry Church.
Donovan, James *o.m.i.* '51 (BEL) [F] Belleville, IL Missionary Oblates of Mary Immaculate - St. Henry's Oblate Residence.
Donovan, James *o.p.* '55 (PRT) [I] Lewiston, ME SS. Peter and Paul House.
Donovan, James J. '87 (CHI) Hometown, IL Our Lady of Loretto Church.
Donovan, James W. *c.s.p.* '68 (CHI) [122] Chicago, IL Old St. Mary Church.
Donovan, John L. '53 (BO) Senior Priests.
Donovan, John P. '86 (SY) Special Assignment; [V] Hamilton, NY Catholic Newman Community of Colgate University.
Donovan, Msgr. John T. '44 (MIL) Retired.
Donovan, Joseph D. '40 (ROC) Retired.
Donovan, Joseph F. '53 (BO) Senior Priests.
Donovan, Msgr. Joseph J. '51 (NEW) Bergenfield, NJ St. John the Evangelist Church; Retired.
Donovan, Joseph J. *m.m.* '79 (FgM) Maryknoll Foreign Missions.
Donovan, Kevin G. '88 (HRT) [7] Waterbury, CT Sacred Heart Church.
Donovan, Michael *o.de.m.* (CLV) [O] Cleveland, OH Mercedarians.
Donovan, Michael A. '62 (DET) [3] Roseville, MI St. Donald Church.
Donovan, Michael B. *o.s.f.s.* '67 (WIL) [I] Childs, MD Oblates of St. Francis De Sales; [L] Childs, MD De Sales Centre.
Donovan, Michael J. *o.de.m.* '00 (CLV) [57] Cleveland, OH Our Lady of Mount Carmel Church.
Donovan, Patrick J. *o.s.m.* '55 (ORG) Fullerton, CA St. Juliana Falconieri Church.
Donovan, Patrick J. *m.m.* '57 (NY) [DD] Maryknoll, NY Maryknoll Fathers and Brothers.
Donovan, Patrick J. *o.s.m.* '98 (ORG) [M] Fullerton, CA California State University Fullerton, Newman Center.
Donovan, Patrick M. *o.s.m.* '55 (CHI) [N] Chicago, IL Order of Friar Servants of Mary (Servites) United States of America Province, Inc.
Donovan, Patrick M. *o.s.m.* '55 (ORG) [I] Buena Park, CA Order of Friar Servants of Mary (Servites).
Donovan, Paul A. *s.j.* '56 (BAL) [S] Baltimore, MD Jesuit Fathers and Brothers Maryland Provincial Curia.
Donovan, Richard J. *o.f.m.* '87 (HRT) [6] New Britain, CT St. Francis of Assisi Church; [R] New Britain, CT Central Connecticut State University Newman House.
Donovan, Richard R. '58 (RVC) Garden City, NY St. Anne Church.
Donovan, Robert '53 (ROC) Retired.
Donovan, Robert C. '70 (FR) Pocasset, MA St. John the Evangelist Church.
Donovan, Msgr. Thomas A. '50 (GAL) Retired; [N] Houston, TX St. Dominic Village.
Donovan, Msgr. Thomas F. '57 (BRK) [237] Queens, NY Sacred Heart of Jesus Church.
Donovan, Thomas P. *s.j.* '44 (BO) [W] Weston, MA Campion Health Center, Inc.
Donovan, Victor *c.p.* '36 (HRT) [M] West Hartford, CT Holy Family Monastery/Retreat.
Donovan, Msgr. Walter J. '44 (ATL) [8] Atlanta, GA Sacred Heart of Jesus Church; Retired.
Donovan, Msgr. William (SY) [W] Utica, NY Calvary.
Donovan, William D. '61 (BGP) [5] Fairfield, CT Holy Family Church.
Donovan, William G. '94 (PH) Graduate Studies.
Donovan, Msgr. William L. '43 (SCR) Retired; [N] Dunmore, PA Villa St. Joseph.
Donovon, Michael '00 (CLV) Cleveland, OH Lutheran Medical Center.
Donton, Joseph P. '91 (PEO) [1] Peoria, IL St. Mary's Church.
Doocey, Michael F. '52 (BO) Senior Priests.
Doody, Cyril J. '56 (BRK) [79] Brooklyn, NY St. Mark's Church.
Doody, Michael J. *s.j.* '78 (BO) [W] Boston, MA The Society of Jesus of New England-Provincial Offices.
Doody, Michael J. *s.j.* '78 (STL) [C] St. Louis, MO Saint Louis University; [P] St. Louis, MO Jesuit Community Corporation at St. Louis University - Jesuit Hall.
Doody, Patrick *c.s.sp.* '68 (BRK) [Z] Long Island City, NY World Compassion Link.
Doody, Patrick *c.s.sp.* '88 (BRK) [V] Long Island City, NY Holy Ghost Fathers of Ireland.
Doody, Msgr. Peter J. '71 (PAT) [8] Clifton, NJ St. Philip the Apostle Church.
Doody, Msgr. Timothy F. '42 (GRY) Retired.
Doogan, James A. *s.j.* '98 (SAC) [C] Sacramento, CA Jesuit High School; [H] Carmichael, CA Jesuit High School Community of Sacramento.
Doogan, Msgr. John P. '46 (SEA) [14] Seattle, WA St. Mark Church; Retired.
Doogan, Joseph H. '48 (SEA) [27] Seattle, WA Our Lady of Fatima Church; Retired.
Dooher, John J. '68 (BO) Dedham, MA St. Mary Church.
Doolan, Ailbe *o.c.d.* '53 (SJ) [L] San Jose, CA Carmelite Monastery, Novitiate.
Doolan, John M. *s.j.* '63 (ALB) [N] Auriesville, NY Shrine of Our Lady of Martyrs.
Doolan, Vincent P. '80 (BO) Marshfield, MA St. Christine Church.
Dooley, Bernard J. *s.j.* '55 (BAL) [S] Baltimore, MD Jesuit Fathers and Brothers Maryland Provincial Curia.
Dooley, Daniel M. '61 (PH) Norwood, PA St. Gabriel Church.
Dooley, Harry J. *c.s.p.* '58 (NY) [DD] Jamaica Estates, NY Paulist Fathers Generalate.
Dooley, Msgr. Joseph P. '56 (ALN) Martins Creek, PA St. Rocco Church.
Dooley, Joseph W. '44 (IND) Retired; [O] Indianapolis, IN International Catholic Deaf Association (Chapter No. 38).
Dooley, Kevin F. '84 (MAD) Mazomanie, WI St. Barnabas Church; Mill Creek, WI St. John the Baptist Church.
Dooley, Malachy R. *o.p.* '49 (CHI) [D] Oak Park, IL Fenwick High School; [N] River Forest, IL St. Thomas Aquinas Priory.
Dooley, Michael D. *s.j.* '85 (DAL) [D] Dallas, TX Jesuit College Preparatory School.
Dooley, Peter C. '76 (RVC) Bellmore, NY St. Barnabas

the Apostle Church.
Dooley, Msgr. R. Joseph '69 (WDC) Retired.
Dooley, Thomas V. '91 (DM) Leon, IA St. Brendan Church; Maloy, IA Immaculate Conception Church.
Dooley, William E. *s.j.* '46 (MIL) [P] Wauwatosa, WI Jesuit Community at St. Camillus.
Doolin, William *c.s.sp.* '37 (SFR) Millbrae, CA St. Dunstan Church.
Doolin, Msgr. William A. '45 (PH) [13] Philadelphia, PA St. Anselm Church; Upper Darby, PA St. Alice Church; Retired.
Dooling, J. Stuart *o.s.f.s.* '40 (CAM) [M] Pittsgrove, NJ Villa St. Joseph.
Dooling, Patrick '82 (MRY) Capitola, CA St. Joseph Church.
Doonan, John A. '52 (BO) Senior Priests.
Dooner, William B. '70 (PH) Penndel, PA Our Lady of Grace Church.
Dora, Msgr. Peter A. '72 (ATL) Covington, GA St. Augustine Church.
Dora, Msgr. Peter P. '67 (BGP) [1] Stratford, CT Holy Name of Jesus Church.
Dorais, Gerald A. '55 (WOR) [4] Fitchburg, MA St. Francis of Assisi Church.
Doran, Austin C. '78 (LA) Encino, CA Our Lady of Grace Church.
Doran, Bob *s.j.* (SPK) [G] Spokane, WA Sacred Heart Medical Center.
Doran, Brian '71 (LA) West Hollywood, CA St. Ambrose Church.
Doran, Edward E. *o.s.a.* '61 (PH) [143] Philadelphia, PA St. Rita of Cascia Church.
Doran, Edward P. '84 (BRK) [172] Queens, NY St. Gerard Majella Church.
Doran, James *o.s.b.* '00 (WOR) [N] Still River, MA Benedictine Monks, St. Benedict Abbey.
Doran, John E. '66 (WOR) [4] Leominster, MA St. Leo's Church.
Doran, Msgr. John E. '72 (NEW) South Orange, NJ Our Lady of Sorrows Church.
Doran, Joseph *s.d.b.* '66 (NY) [DD] New Rochelle, NY Salesian Provincial House.
Doran, Msgr. Thomas M. '47 (SY) Retired.
Doran, William J. *s.j.* '55 (OM) [C] Omaha, NE Creighton Preparatory School.
Dorcey, Joseph *c.ss.r.* '74 (FgM) Redemptorist Foreign Missions.
Dorcey, Joseph *c.ss.r.* '79 (DEN) [M] Denver, CO The Redemptorists/Denver Province.
Dorcy, Roger P. '80 (PBL) [7] Pueblo, CO Our Lady of the Meadows Church.
Dore, Bernard M. '82 (PRO) [1] Westerly, RI St. Clare Church.
Dore, Denis M. '44 (BRK) [228] Queens, NY St. Pius X Church; Retired.
Dore, James M. *o.s.m.* '59 (CHI) [N] Chicago, IL Order of Friar Servants of Mary (Servites) United States of America Province, Inc.
Dore, Robert '89 (JKS) Chatawa, MS St. Teresa Church.
Dore, Thomas M. '61 (CHI) [4] Oak Park, IL St. Giles Church.
Dore, Timothy *o.f.m.conv.* '92 (BAL) [S] Ellicott City, MD Order of Friars Minor Conventual.
Dore, Timothy *o.f.m.conv.* '92 (FgM) Conventual Franciscan Foreign Missions.
Dorenbusch, Thomas A. '57 (CIN) Tipp City, OH St. John the Baptist Church.
Dorff, Francis W. *o.praem* '60 (SFE) [I] Albuquerque, NM Santa Maria de la Vid Priory.
Dorff, John J. *c.ss.r.* '69 (HBG) Ephrata, PA Mother of Perpetual Help Church; [H] Ephrata, PA St. Clement's Mission House.
Dorgan, Gerard L. '58 (BO) Danvers, MA St. Mary of the Annunciation Church.
Dorgan, John J. '65 (RIC) [5] Norfolk, VA Basilica of St. Mary.
Dorhauer, C. Robert '63 (STL) [5] Creve Coeur, MO St. Richard Church.
Dorian, Brendan '58 (YAK) Retired.
Dorich, John M. '61 (VNN) Retired.
Dorin, Robert R. *s.j.* '67 (BO) [W] Boston, MA The Society of Jesus of New England-Provincial Offices.
Dorin, Robert R. *s.j.* '67 (SPK) [C] Spokane, WA Gonzaga University.
Doriot, Thomas E. '49 (FTW) Retired.
Doris, Andrew T. '47 (SAV) [1] Augusta, GA Church of the Most Holy Trinity; Retired.
Doris, John A. '75 (SCR) [5] Dunmore, PA St. Mary of Mount Carmel Church.
Dorley, Paul D. '49 (TOL) Retired.
Dormer, David '77 (OG) Watertown, NY U.S. Army Headquarters Fort Drum.
Dormer, David J. '77 (SCR) Military Chaplains.
Dorn, George *c.ss.r.* '50 (ORL) [F] New Smyrna Beach, FL St. Alphonsus Villa-Redemptorist Fathers and Brothers.
Dorn, Jerry *glmy.* '78 (CIN) [M] Cincinnati, OH Headquarters of Glenmary Home Missioners.
Dorn, Jim Van *o.f.m.conv.* '67 (IND) [I] Mount Saint Francis, IN Mount Saint Francis Friary and Retreat Center.
Dorn, John *o.ss.t.* '81 (BAL) [S] Baltimore, MD Holy Trinity Monastery.
Dorn, Louis E. '72 (JC) Osage Bend, MO St. Margaret of Antioch Church; Wardsville, MO St. Stanislaus Church.
Dorn, Rupert *o.f.m.cap* '51 (MAD) [L] Madison, WI San Damiano Friary.
Dornak, Melvin '92 (AUS) [6] Waco, TX St. Louis Church.
Dornbos, William '68 (HEL) Special Assignments.
Dorner, Joseph E. (GB) Amberg, WI St. Agnes Church; Wausaukee, WI St. Augustine Church.
Dorney, Msgr. Dennis C. '67 (TLS) [10] Tulsa, OK Church of St. Mary.
Dorney, Msgr. James (NY) [G] New York, NY Seton Foundation for Learning, Inc.
Dorney, Msgr. James J. '58 (NY) [224] Staten Island, NY St. Peter Church.
Dorniak, Joseph *o.f.m.conv.* '79 (BUF) Athol Springs, NY St. Francis of Assisi Church.
Doro, Michael J. '72 (MAD) [2] Janesville, WI St. John Vianney Church.
Doroin, Elias E. '64 (GAL) [K] Houston, TX The Catholic Chaplain Corps.
Doron, Joseph (NY) Chester, NY St. Columba Church.
Dorr, James *c.m.* '44 (BRK) [V] Jamaica, NY Vincentian Residence.
Dorr, Richard J. '55 (DET) Retired.
Dorrill, James F. '60 (MOB) [1] Mobile, AL Cathedral of the Immaculate Conception; [J] Mobile, AL University of South Alabama Newman Center.
Dorrler, Michael E. *s.j.* '83 (CHI) [N] Chicago, IL Chicago Province of the Society of Jesus-Provincial Office.
Dorrmann, William J. '55 (CIN) Retired.
Dorsch, Henry L. '68 (SPR) [8] Pittsfield, MA St. Mark's Church; [Q] Springfield, MA Newman Apostolates and Campus Ministries.
Dorsch, Larry W. '75 (WH) [1] Wheeling, WV St. Joseph's Church.
Dorsel, John F. '61 (R) Absent on Leave.
Dorsey, Dan *glmy.* '78 (CIN) [M] Cincinnati, OH Headquarters of Glenmary Home Missioners.
Dorsey, Garrett D. '59 (PIT) Allison Park, PA St. Ursula Church.
Dorsey, Joseph A. *c.s.c.* '57 (FgM) Holy Cross Foreign Missions.
Dorsey, Joseph A. *c.s.c.* '57 (FTW) [J] South Bend, IN Congregation of Holy Cross, Indiana Province, Provincial House.
Dorsey, Patrick J. *s.j.* '96 (MIL) [P] Milwaukee, WI Jesuit Community at Marquette University.
Dorson, James E. '77 (RIC) [11] Virginia Beach, VA Star of the Sea Church.
Dorsonville, Mario E. '85 (WDC) [5] Bethesda, MD Our Lady of Lourdes Church.
Dorta, Juan Manuel *s.j.* '55 (MIA) [D] Miami, FL Belen Jesuit Preparatory School; [H] Miami, FL Villa Arrieta; [H] Miami, FL Villa Arrieta.
Dorton, John '70 (DM) [11] Des Moines, IA St. Peter's Church.
Dorwart, William D. *c.s.c.* '80 (FTW) [J] South Bend, IN Congregation of Holy Cross, Indiana Province, Provincial House.
Dory, Michael '76 (GB) Military Chaplains.
Dos Reis, Jose Q. '64 (PRO) Providence, RI Rhode Island Hospital; [C] Warwick, RI Bishop Hendricken High School.
dos Remedios, Francis *o.s.b.* '82 (BIS) Hebron, ND St. Ann Church; [A] Richardton, ND Assumption Abbey.
Dos Santos, Gildasio *s.d.b.* '82 (LAN) [4] Lansing, MI Immaculate Heart of Mary Church; Montrose, MI Good Shepherd Church.
dos Santos, Jose A.F. '53 (FR) [9] Fall River, MA Our Lady of Health Church.
Dosch, Leander *o.c.s.o.* (SLC) [F] Huntsville, UT Abbey of Our Lady of the Holy Trinity of the Order of Cistercians.
Doscher, Joseph *s.c.j.* '73 (SP) [O] Pinellas Park, FL Priests of the Sacred Heart.
Dosen, Anthony *c.m.* (CHI) [N] Chicago, IL DePaul Vincentian Residence.
Doser, A. Ed *c.s.b.* '55 (GAL) [K] Houston, TX The Catholic Chaplain Corps.
Doser, Edward A. *c.s.b.* '55 (GAL) [F] Houston, TX St. Thomas High School.
Dosh, Mark B. '58 (STP) Excelsior, Lake Minnetonka, MN St. John the Baptist Church.
Doskey, Msgr. Clinton J. '54 (NO) [55] New Orleans, LA St. Pius X Church.
Dostie, Benoit *m.s.c.* '40 (OG) [F] Watertown, NY Missionaries of the Sacred Heart.
Dotson, Msgr. Paul T. '68 (LA) Woodland Hills, CA St. Bernardine of Siena Church.
Doty, Craig A. '97 (LIN) Graduate Studies.
Doub, Nicholas *o.s.b.* '87 (SCL) [I] Collegeville, MN St. John's Abbey, of the Order of St. Benedict.
Doucet, Camille *m.s.* '68 (FR) [I] Attleboro, MA La Salette Provincial House.
Doucet, David A. '69 (BO) [3] Somerville, MA St. Benedict Church.
Doucet, Ovila T. '53 (PRO) Retired; [M] Pawtucket, RI Jeanne Jugan Residence.
Doucette, Michael L. '75 (PRT) St. Francis, ME St. Charles Church; St. John, ME St. John Church.
Doudican, James '48 (CHY) [2] Cheyenne, WY Holy Trinity Church; Retired.
Dougherty, C. Peter '61 (LAN) Special Assignment.
Dougherty, Charles '63 (SJ) Saratoga, CA Church of the Ascension; San Jose, CA San Jose State University Catholic Campus; [N] San Jose, CA The Newman Center/Catholic Campus Ministry.
Dougherty, Charles *c.p.* '68 (RVC) Shelter Island, NY Our Lady of the Isle Church.
Dougherty, Damien R. *o.f.m.* '75 (STL) [A] St. Louis, MO Kenrick-Glennon Seminary; [T] Dittmer, MO Il Ritiro-The Little Retreat.
Dougherty, Daniel J. '70 (PH) [4] Drexel Hill, PA St. Dorothy Church.
Dougherty, David *c.pp.s.* '49 (KC) [J] Liberty, MO Precious Blood Center.
Dougherty, Denis *o.s.b.* (SPC) [6] Springfield, MO St. Joseph's Church.
Dougherty, Edward '53 (TR) [M] Trenton, NJ Villa Vianney.
Dougherty, Edward C.A. *s.j.* '72 (BAL) [S] Baltimore, MD Jesuit Fathers and Brothers Maryland Provincial Curia.
Dougherty, Edward C.A. *s.j.* '72 (FgM) Provinces.
Dougherty, Edward J. '53 (TR) Retired.
Dougherty, Edward J. *s.j.* '70 (FgM) Provinces.
Dougherty, Edward J. *s.j.* '70 (NO) [P] New Orleans, LA Jesuit Provincial Office.
Dougherty, Edward M. *m.m.* '79 (FgM) Maryknoll Foreign Missions.
Dougherty, Eugene J. '53 (PIT) [73] Pittsburgh, PA Holy Wisdom Church; Retired.
Dougherty, Francis D. *o.s.f.s.* '38 (FgM) Oblates of St. Francis de Sales Foreign Missions.
Dougherty, George Patrick '67 (GAL) Retired.
Dougherty, Henry E. '41 (PH) Levittown, PA Queen of the Universe Church; Retired.
Dougherty, Hugh J. '69 (PH) South Coventry, PA St. Thomas More Church.
Dougherty, James '67 (JOL) [18] Joliet, IL St. Paul the Apostle Church.
Dougherty, James J. *s.j.* '59 (STL) [P] St. Louis, MO Hallahan House.
Dougherty, James R. '68 (BEL) Trenton, IL St. Mary Church.
Dougherty, John C. '45 (PH) [28] Philadelphia, PA St. Callistus Church; Retired.
Dougherty, John J. *c.s.c.* '94 (PHX) [12] Phoenix, AZ St. Gregory Church.
Dougherty, Joseph D. '48 (PH) Retired; [EE] Philadelphia, PA Newman Center at Drexel University.
Dougherty, Luke *o.s.b.* '55 (SD) [H] Oceanside, CA Prince of Peace Abbey, Benet Hill.
Dougherty, Paul V. '80 (PH) [A] Wynnewood, PA Theological Seminary of St. Charles Borromeo, Overbrook; [S] Philadelphia, PA Catholic Center for the Deaf and Hard of Hearing.
Dougherty, Stephen J. '73 (PH) Narberth, PA St. Margaret Church; [A] Wynnewood, PA Theological Seminary of St. Charles Borromeo, Overbrook.
Dougherty, Terrence *o.c.d.* '63 (BO) [W] Boston, MA Carmelite Monastery.
Dougherty, William *c.pp.s.* '46 (CIN) [B] Carthagena, OH St. Charles.
Dougherty, William J. *o.s.f.s.* '59 (WIL) Elsmere, DE Veteran's Hospital; [I] Wilmington, DE DeSales House.
Dougherty, William J. *c.s.p.* '63 (AUS) Horseshoe Bay, TX St. Paul the Apostle Church.
Dougherty, William J. '69 (PH) Absent on Leave.
Dougherty, William N. *o.s.f.s.* '65 (WDC) [B] Washington, DC Oblates of St. Francis de Sales.
Doughty, Edward F. '95 (BO) [2] Plymouth, MA St. Bonaventure Church.
Doughty, Rees W. '94 (NY) [132] Bronx, NY St. Barnabas Church.
Douglas, David M. '65 (LFT) West Lafayette, IN Blessed Sacrament Church.
Douglas, Gordon '68 (SEA) [B] Seattle, WA Bishop Blanchet High School.
Douglas, Jack *c.p.* '81 (BRK) [V] Jamaica, NY Immaculate Conception Monastery.
Douglas, Louis '58 (ALB) Retired.
Douglas, Marian *o.f.m.* '57 (MAR) Calumet, MI Sacred Heart Church.
Douglas, Norman K. '74 (CLV) [3] Akron, OH St. Bernard Church.
Douglass, Vincent J. *c.ss.r.* '66 (ATL) Hapeville, GA St. John the Evangelist Church.
Doussan, Msgr. Douglas A. '60 (NO) [34] New Orleans, LA St. Gabriel the Archangel Church.
Dove, Thomas J. '61 (NY) [DD] Jamaica Estates, NY Paulist Fathers Generalate.
Dove, Thomas J. *c.s.p.* '61 (SFR) [32] San Francisco, CA Old St. Mary's Church.

Dover, Edward R. '85 (LA) Monterey Park, CA St. Thomas Aquinas Church.
Dovick, Robert E. '53 (CHI) [2] Oak Lawn, IL St. Gerald Church; Retired.
Dovick, Robert E. '54 (CHI) Palos Heights, IL Incarnation Church.
Dowalgo, Mitchell G. *c.s.b.* '82 (LSC) [4] Las Cruces, NM St. Albert the Great Newman Church; [B] Las Cruces, NM Basilian Fathers.
Dowbush, Yaroslaw '86 (STN) Belfield, ND St. John the Baptist Church; Fairfield, ND St. Demetrius Church.
Dowd, Barry '82 (ORL) [1] Orlando, FL Mary Queen of the Universe Church.
Dowd, Barry G. '84 (BUR) On Duty Outside the Diocese.
Dowd, Brian P. '91 (BRK) [185] Queens, NY St. John Vianney Church.
Dowd, James '56 (P) Cottage Grove, OR Our Lady of Perpetual Help Church.
Dowd, John *c.ss.r.* '61 (CHI) [133] Chicago, IL St. Michael Church.
Dowd, John M. *o.s.m.* '69 (CHI) [17] Chicago, IL Assumption of the Blessed Virgin Mary Church; [N] Chicago, IL Order of Friar Servants of Mary (Servites) United States of America Province, Inc.
Dowd, John R. '63 (MAD) [9] Madison, WI Saint Joseph Church.
Dowd, Karl E. '60 (MAN) [7] Nashua, NH St. Joseph Church; Retired.
Dowd, Robert A. *c.s.c* '94 (FTW) [J] South Bend, IN Congregation of Holy Cross, Indiana Province, Provincial House.
Dowd, Robert A. *c.s.c.* '94 (LA) Santa Monica, CA St. Monica Church.
Dowd, Thomas M. '54 (GI) Retired.
Dowd, William J. '67 (NEW) Hohokus, NJ St. Luke's Church.
Dowdel, Lawrence J., Jr. '91 (LA) Ventura, CA Our Lady of the Assumption Church.
Dowdell, Aaron M. *o.ss.t.* '74 (BAL) [S] Baltimore, MD Holy Trinity Monastery.
Dowdell, Aaron M. *o.ss.t.* '74 (NY) [20] New York, NY St. Brigid Church.
Dowdell, Msgr. Joseph M. '63 (BUF) Lakewood, NY Sacred Heart Church.
Dowdell, Thomas '63 (OKL) [K] Norman, OK Campus Ministry for the Archdiocese of Oklahoma City.
Dowdell, Thomas R. '71 (OKL) [8] Oklahoma City, OK St. Francis of Assisi Church.
Dowds, James *c.ss.r.* '85 (WDC) [M] Washington, DC Holy Redeemer College.
Dowdy, James H. '69 (BAL) Absent on Leave.
Dowell, William J. '45 (DET) Retired.
Dower, Douglas '87 (RVC) Elmont, NY St. Boniface Church.
Dowling, Edward T. *s.j.* '69 (NY) [DD] New York, NY Jesuit Community at Fordham University.
Dowling, Finbarr *o.s.b.* '68 (STL) Concord Hill, MO St. Ignatius Church.
Dowling, John C. '51 (NEW) Retired.
Dowling, John J. *o.s.a.* '68 (CHI) [N] Olympia Fields, IL The Augustinians-Provincialate.
Dowling, John J. *o.s.a.* '68 (FgM) Foreign Missions.
Dowling, John R. '83 (KNX) [6] Knoxville, TN St. John Neumann Church.
Dowling, Joseph Kevin '80 (NSH) Centerville, TN Christ the Redeemer Church; Hohenwald, TN Holy Trinity Church; Waynesboro, TN St. Cecilia Church.
Dowling, Jude '54 (HRT) [M] West Hartford, CT Holy Family Monastery/Retreat.
Dowling, Lawrence R. '91 (CHI) [48] Chicago, IL St. Denis Church.
Dowling, Michael J. '56 (NEW) Retired.
Dowling, P. Finbarr *o.s.b.* '68 (STL) [P] St. Louis, MO The Abbey of St. Mary and St. Louis.
Dowling, Patrick '82 (JC) Chamois, MO Most Pure Heart of Mary Church; Morrison, MO Assumption Church.
Dowling, Msgr. Philip J. '56 (PH) [134] Philadelphia, PA St. Patrick Church.
Dowling, Timothy '92 (PAT) Kinnelon, NJ Our Lady of the Magnificat Church.
Dowling, William P. '54 (SAV) Retired.
Downes, Msgr. Stephen N. '66 (LA) [5] Santa Barbara, CA St. Raphael Church.
Downes, Thomas J. '51 (CHI) Retired.
Downey, Alvin T. *o.s.b.* '70 (GBG) [H] Latrobe, PA Saint Vincent Archabbey.
Downey, Donald David (CC) Violet, TX St. Anthony Church.
Downey, James *o.s.b.* '46 (KCK) [H] Atchison, KS St. Benedict's Abbey.
Downey, Joseph F. *s.j.* '48 (CHI) [N] Evanston, IL Canisius House.
Downey, Joseph F. *s.j.* '48 (DET) [K] Detroit, MI Jesuit Provincial Office-Detroit Province of the Society of Jesus.
Downey, Joseph J. '43 (BO) [U] Somerville, MA Jeanne Jugan Residence.
Downey, Joseph J. '45 (BO) Senior Priests.
Downey, Kevin *o.f.m.* '82 (BUF) Allegany, NY St. Bonaventure Church; Vandalia, NY St. John the Baptist Church.
Downey, Michael '73 (SAC) Fairfield, CA Holy Spirit Church.
Downey, Richard E. *m.m.* '44 (FgM) Maryknoll Foreign Missions.
Downey, Robert '54 (SB) Retired.
Downey, Timothy M. '38 (TOL) Retired.
Downie, Arley T. '88 (GLP) Retired.
Downing, Brendan W. '79 (BRK) [173] Queens, NY St. Gertrude Church.
Downing, Charles H. '65 (PRO) [5] West Warwick, RI St. Joseph Church.
Downing, Msgr. Joseph C. '62 (CAM) Bellmawr, NJ Mary, Mother of the Church.
Downs, Gregory T. (LAF) On Sabbatical.
Downs, James A. '70 (PIT) Hillsville, PA Christ the King Church; Lawrence County, PA Lawrence County Jail.
Downs, John L. '55 (OG) Massena, NY St. Joseph Church.
Downs, L. James '66 (WDC) [3] Rockville, MD St. Mary Church.
Downs, Richard J. '45 (ALB) Retired.
Downs, Robert '51 (ROC) Retired.
Downs, Walter *m.s.c.* (ALN) [A] Center Valley, PA Missionaries of the Sacred Heart.
Doyen, Mitchell S. '91 (STL) [A] St. Louis, MO Kenrick-Glennon Seminary.
Doyle, Alan T. *m.m.* '64 (FgM) Maryknoll Foreign Missions.
Doyle, Brendan '63 (JC) [3] Jefferson City, MO Immaculate Conception Church; Russellville, MO St. Michael Church; [B] Jefferson City, MO Helias High School.
Doyle, Brendan '89 (ATL) Lawrenceville, GA St. Marguerite D'Youville Church.
Doyle, Charles E. '53 (GRY) Retired.
Doyle, Dan F. *s.m.* '67 (MIA) Special Assignment.
Doyle, Daniel E. *o.s.a.* '86 (PH) [B] Villanova, PA St. Augustine Friary; [C] Villanova, PA Villanova University.
Doyle, Daniel J. '48 (BO) [2] Salem, MA Immaculate Conception Church; Senior Priests.
Doyle, Dennis J. '65 (STL) [4] St. Charles, MO Sts. Joachim and Ann Church.
Doyle, Dennis M. '92 (STL) [2] St. Charles, MO St. Cletus Church.
Doyle, Dominic W. *s.j.* '50 (SPK) [K] Spokane, WA Regis Community.
Doyle, Donald E. '53 (ALB) Windham, NY St. Theresa of Child Jesus Church.
Doyle, Donald L. *c.m.* '41 (PH) [AA] Philadelphia, PA Congregation of the Mission.
Doyle, Edward A. '64 (JC) Absent on Leave.
Doyle, Eugene '76 (SCL) Sauk Rapids, MN Sacred Heart Church.
Doyle, Francis J. *o.s.a.* '70 (CHL) Maggie Valley, NC St. Margaret Church.
Doyle, Gerald '73 (GLP) Retired.
Doyle, James '49 (ROC) Retired.
Doyle, James '61 (LKC) [6] Lake Charles, LA St. Theodore's Church.
Doyle, Msgr. James F. '59 (NY) Bronxville, NY St. Joseph Church.
Doyle, Msgr. James J. '35 (PAT) Retired.
Doyle, James J. *c.s.c.* '50 (SCR) [C] Wilkes-Barre, PA Kings College.
Doyle, Msgr. James Michael '57 (SFS) Retired.
Doyle, James P. '57 (CHI) Retired.
Doyle, Msgr. Jerald A. '69 (BGP) [4] Stratford, CT Our Lady of Grace Church.
Doyle, John '52 (DUL) Virginia, MN Holy Spirit Church; Virginia, MN Sacred Heart Church.
Doyle, John A. *c.m.* '41 (PH) [AA] Philadelphia, PA Congregation of the Mission.
Doyle, John J. '58 (JOL) [6] Joliet, IL St. Ambrose Church; [7] Joliet, IL St. Anne Church; Joliet, IL Joliet Correctional Depot.
Doyle, John J. '70 (CHI) Evergreen Park, IL Queen of Martyrs Church.
Doyle, John J. *o.f.m.* '75 (PAT) Butler, NJ St. Anthony Church.
Doyle, John L. '52 (BO) [58] Boston, MA St. Peter Church.
Doyle, John T. *o.s.f.s.* '52 (VEN) [3] Fort Myers, FL St. Cecilia Church.
Doyle, John V. '41 (PRO) Retired.
Doyle, Joseph *s.s.j.* '68 (NO) [P] New Orleans, LA Josephite Fathers and Brothers.
Doyle, Joseph *s.j.* '70 (SP) [C] Tampa, FL Jesuit High School.
Doyle, Joseph C. '72 (NEW) Ridgefield Park, NJ St. Francis of Assisi Church.
Doyle, Joseph M. '40 (NEW) Retired.
Doyle, Joseph M. *s.s.j.* '68 (NO) [F] New Orleans, LA St. Augustine High School; [H] New Orleans, LA St. Augustine High School; [S] New Orleans, LA Pierre Toussaint Foundation of New Orleans, Inc.
Doyle, Joshua *o.f.m.* (FgM) Custody of St. Mary of the Angels. Byzantine-Slavonic.
Doyle, Kennth '66 (ALB) [5] Albany, NY St. Catherine of Siena Church.
Doyle, Lawrence J. '45 (BO) Senior Priests.
Doyle, Lawrence Michael *o.s.m.* '65 (CHI) [N] Chicago, IL Order of Friar Servants of Mary (Servites) United States of America Province, Inc.
Doyle, Mark A. '58 (LC) Retired.
Doyle, Martin *s.j.* '91 (NEW) [B] Jersey City, NJ Saint Peter's College; [N] Jersey City, NJ Jesuits of Saint Peter's College, Inc.
Doyle, Mathias F. *o.f.m.* '62 (WDC) [B] Silver Spring, MD Holy Name College.
Doyle, Michael '59 (CAM) [9] Camden, NJ Sacred Heart Church.
Doyle, Michael *o.s.m.* '65 (STL) Affton, MO Seven Holy Founders Church.
Doyle, Michael A. '94 (TYL) Lindale, TX Holy Family Church.
Doyle, Michael J. (BO) Canton, MA St. John the Evangelist Church.
Doyle, Michael M. '89 (NU) Appleton, MN St. John Church; Appleton, MN Prarie Correctional Facility; [F] Appleton, MN Prairie Correctional Facility.
Doyle, Oliver '78 (GF) [1] Great Falls, MT St. Ann's Church; Special Assignment.
Doyle, Patrick '75 (IND) [13] Indianapolis, IN St. Andrew the Apostle Church.
Doyle, Patrick A. '75 (IND) [20] Indianapolis, IN St. Joan of Arc Church.
Doyle, Paul F. *c.s.c.* '77 (FTW) [B] Notre Dame, IN University of Notre Dame Du Lac; [J] Notre Dame, IN Holy Cross Community, Corby Hall, University of Notre Dame.
Doyle, Philip R. '48 (NY) Retired.
Doyle, Richard J. '54 (ALB) Athens, NY St. Patrick Church.
Doyle, Robert A. *s.j.* '62 (STL) [P] St. Louis, MO White House Retreat Jesuit Community; [T] St. Louis, MO White House Retreat.
Doyle, Robert M. '49 (BO) Senior Priests.
Doyle, Seamus '56 (MIA) Miami Shores, FL St. Rose of Lima Church.
Doyle, Stephen *o.f.m.* '62 (BO) [BB] Boston, MA St. Anthony Shrine.
Doyle, Thomas *s.s.* (NSH) Retired.
Doyle, Msgr. Thomas '54 (LA) Retired.
Doyle, Thomas *s.s.* '60 (BAL) [S] Baltimore, MD Sulpician Provincial House.
Doyle, Thomas '62 (DAV) Mechanicsville, IA St. Mary's Church.
Doyle, Thomas '84 (BRK) [84] Brooklyn, NY St. Mary, Star of the Sea Church.
Doyle, Thomas D. '82 (BUF) Oakfield, NY St. Cecilia Church; Wheatville, NY St. Patrick Church; Albion, NY Orleans Correction Facility.
Doyle, Thomas F. '66 (PH) Royersford, PA Sacred Heart Church.
Doyle, Thomas J. *s.j.* '46 (PH) [AA] Philadelphia, PA Jesuit Community at St. Joseph's University.
Doyle, Thomas M. *s.j.* '97 (MIL) [E] Milwaukee, WI Marquette University High School; [P] Milwaukee, WI Pere Marquette House Jesuit Community.
Doyle, Thomas P. *c.s.c.* '98 (FTW) [B] Notre Dame, IN University of Notre Dame Du Lac; [J] Notre Dame, IN Holy Cross Community, Corby Hall, University of Notre Dame.
Doyle, Msgr. Timothy '48 (ORG) Retired.
Doyle, Msgr. Vincent J. '65 (NEW) Union, NJ Holy Spirit Church.
Doyle, Msgr. Walter H. '43 (STO) Retired.
Doyle, William F. *s.j.* '53 (BO) [W] Boston, MA Loyola House.
Doyne, David A. '56 (PH) Lansdale, PA St. Stanislaus Church.
Drab, John P. '46 (RVC) Retired.
Drab, Stephen J. '37 (GBG) Retired.
Drabek, Howard E. '91 (GAL) Richmond, TX Sacred Heart Church.
Drabik, Richard *m.i.c.* '60 (SPR) [J] Stockbridge, MA Congregation of Marians of The Immaculate Conception of the BVM.
Drabiska, Frank J. '76 (PIT) [2] Swissvale, PA Word of God Church.
Drag, Roderick *o.f.m.* '49 (PH) [AA] Philadelphia, PA St. Pius X Friary.
Dragga, Thomas M. '83 (CLV) [A] Wickliffe, OH Borromeo Seminary; [A] Wickliffe, OH St. Mary Seminary and Graduate School of Theology.
Drago, Julio Mirables '72 (MIL) Lake Geneva, WI St. Francis de Sales Church.
Dragon, Joseph W. '78 (PH) East Goshen, PA SS. Peter and Paul Church.
Draim, David *o.s.b.* '73 (CHL) Hamlet, NC St. James Church.
Draim, David *o.s.b.* '73 (SP) [O] St. Leo, FL St. Leo Abbey.
Drake, Roy A. *s.j.* '63 (NY) [DD] New York, NY Murray-Weigel Hall.
Drake, Sebastian *o.f.m.* '45 (SPK) [11] Spokane, WA St. Francis of Assisi, Friars Church.
Drake, Timothy A. '71 (RIC) [9] Virginia Beach, VA St. Matthew Church.

Drance, George W. *s.j.* '95 (NY) [DD] New York, NY Xavier Jesuit Community.
Drapeau, Benoit J. *c.j.m.* '59 (BUF) [1] West Seneca, NY St. Bonaventure Church; [O] West Seneca, NY Eudist Fathers, St. John Eudes Center.
Draper, Andrew *t.o.r.* '88 (CHL) Mocksville, NC St. Francis of Assisi Church.
Drass, Damian P. *t.o.r.* '60 (WH) Philippi, WV St. Elizabeth Parish and Newman Center Church; [P] Philippi, WV Alderson-Broaddus College Newman Center.
Draugialis, Josef '63 (LA) Los Nietos, CA Our Lady of Perpetual Help Church.
Dravecky, Msgr. Michael A. '33 (PIT) Retired.
Draves-Arpaia, Cornelius '79 (PHX) Phoenix, AZ St. Joseph's Hospital; [D] Phoenix, AZ St. Joseph's Hospital and Medical Center.
Dreasen, Msgr. John R. '79 (RVC) Elmont, NY St. Boniface Church.
Dreckman, Philip *s.j.* '62 (STP) [6] St. Paul, MN The Immaculate Heart of Mary Church.
Dreese, Msgr. John J. '59 (COL) Corning, OH St. Bernard Church; Junction City, OH St. Patrick Church; New Lexington, OH St. Rose of Lima Church.
Dreffein, Larry *o.f.m.* '76 (JOL) [I] Oak Brook, IL Mayslake Village.
Dreger, Msgr. Francis X. '51 (PH) [32] Philadelphia, PA St. Cecilia Church.
Dreher, Ernest O. '48 (MIL) Retired.
Dreher, Jacob J. '43 (DOD) Retired.
Dreher, John D. '64 (PRO) Retired.
Dreici, Pascal *c.ss.r.* '44 (DEN) [M] Denver, CO The Redemptorists/Denver Province.
Dreici, Patrick *c.ss.r.* (FRS) Retired.
Dreier, Msgr. Bruce A. '78 (SFR) [18] San Francisco, CA Church of the Epiphany.
Dreiling, Augustine *o.s.b.* '58 (KC) Conception Junction, MO St. Columba Church.
Dreiling, Gerald G. *c.pp.s.* '58 (CIN) [M] Dayton, OH Provincial Office of the Cincinnati Province of the Society of the Precious Blood.
Dreiling, Msgr. Raymond C. '75 (FRS) Clovis, CA Our Lady of Perpetual Help Church.
Dreisbach, Charles V. '59 (BAK) Klamath Falls, OR Sacred Heart Church.
Drennan, Christopher J. *o.s.a.* '83 (LA) [18] Los Angeles, CA Mother of Good Counsel Church.
Drennan, Jimmy D. '96 (SAT) [60] San Antonio, TX St. Paul Church.
Drennan, Lawrence J. '61 (BO) Bridgewater, MA St. Thomas Aquinas Church.
Drennan, Msgr. William A. '55 (STL) [58] St. Louis, MO St. Raphael The Archangel Church.
Drenzek, Peter C. '69 (MIL) [1] Wauwatosa, WI St. Bernard Church.
Dresen, Arthur G. '44 (COS) Retired.
Dressel, Willard J. *s.j.* '54 (OM) [C] Omaha, NE Creighton Preparatory School.
Dressell, Stephen G. *m.s.* '47 (HRT) [M] Hartford, CT Missionaries of LaSalette, Provincial Secretary.
Dressler, Paul *o.f.m.cap.* '99 (PH) [80] Philadelphia, PA St. John the Evangelist Church.
Dressler, Philip J. '61 (CHI) [109] Chicago, IL St. Juliana Church.
Dressler, Robert A. '59 (ALN) Retired; [J] Bethlehem, PA Holy Family Villa.
Dressman, James J. *s.j.* '61 (NOR) Storrs, CT St. Thomas Aquinas Church; [K] Willimantic, CT Campus Ministry.
Dressman, Richard E. '72 (CIN) [49] Cincinnati, OH St. Jude the Apostle Church; [V] Cincinnati, OH Catholic Charismatic Renewal Liaison.
Dressman, Robert C. *s.j.* (CHI) [T] Barrington, IL Bellarmine Hall.
Dreves, Mark '95 (LEX) Special Assignment.
Drew, Andrew *o.f.m.cap.* (NY) [57] New York, NY St. John the Baptist Church; [X] New York, NY St. Rose's Home.
Drew, George W. *c.ss.r.* '50 (BO) [53] Boston, MA Our Lady of Perpetual Help Church.
Drew, James F. '74 (HON) On Duty Outside the Diocese.
Drew, James F. '74 (RVC) Port Washington, NY St. Peter of Alcantara Church.
Drew, John J. *m.m.* '42 (SJ) [L] Los Altos, CA Maryknoll.
Drewelow, David C. '80 (LIN) Wallace, NE St. Mary's Church.
Drewelow, David C. '80 (SPC) On Duty Outside the Diocese.
Drewniak, Stanley S. '78 (CHI) [38] Chicago, IL St. Christina Church.
Drexel, John *o.m.i.* '62 (FgM) Oblates Foreign Missions.
Drexler, George D. '39 (NEW) Retired.
Drexler, Harold J. '55 (DUB) [7] Dubuque, IA Sacred Heart Church; Retired; [I] Dubuque, IA Holy Family Hall Infirmary.
Drezek, Craig (HRT) [D] Waterbury, CT Sacred Heart High School.
Drieci, Pat *c.ss.r.* '44 (FRS) Faculties Only.
Driesch, Albert *t.o.r.* '46 (WH) Moundsville, WV St. Francis Xavier's Church.
Driesch, David A. '82 (PIT) Hopewell Township, PA Our Lady of Fatima Church.
Drilling, Peter J. '67 (BUF) [2] Lackawanna, NY St. Anthony Church; [A] East Aurora, NY Christ the King Seminary.
Drinan, Dan *c.m.f.* '77 (AUS) Martindale, TX Immaculate Heart of Mary Church; Uhland, TX St. Michael's Church.
Drinan, Robert F. *s.j.* '53 (BO) [W] Boston, MA The Society of Jesus of New England-Provincial Offices.
Drinan, Robert F. *s.j.* '53 (WDC) [M] Washington, DC The Jesuit Community at Georgetown University.
Drinane, Gerald A. *s.j.* '62 (FgM) Provinces.
Drinkwater, Warren *c.ss.r.* '62 (BLX) [E] Biloxi, MS St. John Neumann Residence.
Driscoll, Arthur J. '52 (BO) Andover, MA St. Robert Bellarmine Church.
Driscoll, Daniel '76 (HEL) [1] Anaconda, MT Anaconda Catholic Community Church.
Driscoll, Donald D. *s.j.* '65 (OM) [K] Omaha, NE Jesuit Community at Creighton University.
Driscoll, Donald T. (NY) Orangeburg, NY Rockland Psychiatric Center.
Driscoll, Eugene J. '70 (LUB) [2] Lubbock, TX Holy Spirit Church.
Driscoll, George F. *s.j.* '61 (NY) [DD] New York, NY Murray-Weigel Hall.
Driscoll, James A. *o.p.* '54 (PRO) [B] Providence, RI Providence College; [P] Providence, RI St. Thomas Aquinas Priory at Providence College.
Driscoll, James E. '55 (OAK) Danville, CA St. Isidore's Church; Retired.
Driscoll, James J. '43 (NEW) Retired.
Driscoll, Jeremy *o.s.b.* '81 (P) [L] St. Benedict, OR Mt. Angel Abbey.
Driscoll, John '54 (JOL) Romeoville, IL St. Andrew the Apostle Church; Retired.
Driscoll, John M. *o.s.a.* '51 (PH) [C] Villanova, PA Villanova University; [AA] Villanova, PA St. Thomas Monastery.
Driscoll, John P. '47 (FR) [20] New Bedford, MA St. Lawrence Martyr Church.
Driscoll, John P. *s.j.* '52 (NO) [P] New Orleans, LA Ignatius Residence.
Driscoll, Joseph J. '79 (BO) On Duty Outside the Archdiocese.
Driscoll, Joseph J. '79 (MIL) [Y] Milwaukee, WI National Association of Catholic Chaplains.
Driscoll, Msgr. Maurice F. '42 (BEL) Retired.
Driscoll, Michael *o.carm.* '67 (PMB) [5] Boca Raton, FL St. Jude Church.
Driscoll, Michael '76 (FTW) [B] Notre Dame, IN University of Notre Dame Du Lac.
Driscoll, Michael '77 (HEL) On Duty Outside the Diocese.
Driscoll, Michael A. '68 (MET) Belvidere, NJ St. Patrick Church.
Driscoll, Michael J. '92 (PEO) Camp Grove, IL St. Patrick Church; Earlville, IL St. Theresa's Church.
Driscoll, Michael T. *o.carm.* '67 (NY) [DD] Middletown, NY Carmelite Friars (North American Province of St. Elias).
Driscoll, Nicholas J. '57 (BO) Permanent Disability.
Driscoll, Paul G. '64 (RVC) Levittown, NY St. Bernard Church.
Driscoll, Richard *s.d.s.* '65 (PHX) Buckeye, AZ Saint Henry Church.
Driscoll, Richard A. '55 (BO) Senior Priests.
Driscoll, Samuel *o.f.m.cap.* '59 (FgM) Capuchin Foreign Missions.
Driscoll, Thomas F. '60 (OG) Alexandria Bay, NY St. Cyril of Alexandria Church; Redwood, NY St. Francis Xavier Church.
Driscoll, Msgr. Thomas J. *v.g.* '63 (BGP) Easton, CT Notre Dame of Easton Church.
Driscoll, Timothy Paul '99 (FR) [6] New Bedford, MA Our Lady of the Immaculate Conception Church.
Driscoll, Walter L. '57 (BO) Senior Priests.
Driscoll, William D. (NEW) Retired.
Driscoll, William J. *o.mar.* '63 (SAM) [C] Petersham, MA Most Holy Trinity Monastery.
Drobach, William *s.a.* (NY) [DD] Garrison, NY Franciscan Friars of the Atonement, Minister General Office.
Drobin, Paul J. '66 (SY) [V] Utica, NY SUNY Institute of Technology at Utica/Rome Newman Center; [V] Utica, NY Utica College of Syracuse University Newman Center.
Drobinski, Joseph J. '75 (WIL) Newark, DE Parish of the Resurrection Church.
Droessler, Joseph '95 (ORG) Los Alamitos, CA St. Hedwig Church.
Droessler, Wayne J. '69 (DUB) Central City, IA St. Stephen's Church; Coggon, IA St. John the Evangelist Church; Prairieburg, IA St. Joseph's Church.
Drogon, Gregory '82 (PAT) [11] Paterson, NJ St. Michael the Archangel Church.
Drohan, James J. *s.j.* '43 (BO) [W] Weston, MA Campion Health Center, Inc.
Drohan, James J. *s.j.* '43 (WOR) [N] Worcester, MA Jesuits of Holy Cross College, Inc.
Drohan, Joseph W. '56 (ATL) Retired.
Drolet, Roger C. *c.s.v.* '33 (CHI) [N] Arlington Heights, IL Viatorian Province Center-Clerics of St. Viator.
Droll, Msgr. Larry J. '73 (SAN) Wall, TX St. Ambrose Church.
Droll, Louis J. '68 (SAN) Retired.
Drongowski, Stanley *o.p.* '79 (MAD) [3] Madison, WI Blessed Sacrament Church.
Droski, Norman P. '64 (GR) Muskegon Heights, MI Sacred Heart Church.
Drotar, Kent (DEN) Centennial, CO St. Thomas More Church.
Drouin, Marc B. '90 (MAN) Exeter, NH St. Michael Church.
Drouncheck, Anthony M. '89 (ALN) [3] Reading, PA St. Catharine of Siena Church.
Drozd, Henry J. '62 (DAL) On Duty Outside the Diocese.
Drozd, Marian '91 (MET) Bound Brook, NJ St. Mary of Czestochowa Church.
Drozdzal, John S. '74 (SY) [10] Utica, NY St. Joseph and St. Patrick Church.
Drozdzik, Roch T. '96 (R) Edenton, NC St. Anne Church.
Droze, D. Anthony '85 (CHR) Greenville, SC St. Mary's Church.
Drucker, James '78 (PSC) On Duty Outside Diocese.
Druding, John C. '76 (ATL) Roswell, GA St. Andrew Church.
Druggan, Dennis *o.f.m.cap.* '84 (MIL) [B] Mount Calvary, WI St. Lawrence Seminary; [P] Mount Calvary, WI St. Lawrence Friary.
Drum, John *c.ss.r.* '54 (BAL) [87] Baltimore, MD Sacred Heart of Jesus Church.
Drummond, Alexander R. '94 (ARL) Annandale, VA St. Michael's Church.
Drummond, Elsyn J. '54 (NOR) Retired.
Drummy, John A. '71 (SUP) Amery, WI St. Joseph Church.
Drupieski, Stanley R. *o.s.f.s.* '64 (WIL) [B] Wilmington, DE Salesianum School.
Drury, Dennis G. '82 (GB) Rosiere, WI St. Peter and St. Hubert Church.
Drury, George *s.j.* '52 (BO) [W] Cambridge, MA Weston Jesuit Community.
Drury, Michael J. '71 (PAT) Long Valley, NJ St. Luke Church.
Drury, Michael P. *c.o.* '84 (MRY) [F] Monterey, CA Oratorian Community-Congregation of the Oratory of Pontifical Right.
Drury, Robert '79 (OWN) Calvert City, KY St. Pius Tenth Church.
Drutowski, Robert J. '79 (MIL) Mukwonago, WI St. James Church.
Drybka, Christopher *o.s.p.p.e.* '94 (PH) [AA] Doylestown, PA Pauline Fathers Monastery, Shrine of Our Lady of Czestochowa.
Drzaic, Francis *s.v.d.* '62 (CHI) [B] Techny, IL Divine Word Residence.
Drzaic, Frank *s.v.d.* '62 (CHI) [5] Cicero, IL Our Lady of Charity Church.
Drzal, Stanislaw *s.ch.* (ATL) Lawrenceville, GA St. Lawrence Church.
Du Buisson, William *o.m.i.* '55 (SAN) Sonora, TX St. Ann's Church.
Du Preez, Frank V. '86 (GAL) Kingwood, TX St. Martha Church.
Duaime, Jeffrey T. *c.s.sp.* '86 (ARL) [7] Arlington, VA Our Lady, Queen of Peace Church.
Duane, Robert J. '53 (NY) Ardsley, NY Our Lady of Perpetual Help Church; Retired.
Duane, Msgr. Thomas J. '71 (PH) Roslyn, PA St. John of the Cross Church.
Duarte, J. Scott '78 (RIC) Caroline County, VA St. Mary of the Annunciation Church.
Dubay, Thomas E. *s.m.* '50 (WDC) [M] Washington, DC Marist Center.
Dube, Andre R. '85 (BGP) [5] Stamford, CT St. Clement Church.
Dube, Donald V. '61 (SPR) Absent on Leave.
Dube, George *m.s.* '48 (FR) [I] Attleboro, MA La Salette Provincial House.
Dube, Joseph *s.j.* '99 (PHX) [11] Phoenix, AZ St. Francis Xavier Church.
Dube, Stephen D. '78 (WH) Weirton, WV St. Joseph the Worker Church.
Dubel, Edward A. *c.r.* '57 (SB) Rialto, CA St. Thomas More Church.
Dubell, Msgr. James H. '65 (TR) Burlington, NJ St. Paul Church.
Dubert, James W. '98 (DUB) [10] Dubuque, IA Nativity Church.
Dubi, Leonard A. '68 (CHI) Hazel Crest, IL St. Anne Church.
Dubitsky, Roman '65 (PHU) Perth Amboy, NJ Assumption of B.V.M. Church; Toms River, NJ St. Stephen's Church.
Dublinski, Steven L. '85 (SPK) [15] Spokane, WA St. Mary Church; Rockford, WA St. Joseph Church.

DuBois, Andrew '95 (PRT) [3] Lewiston, ME Holy Family Church.
Dubois, Msgr. Charles J. '64 (LKC) [6] Lake Charles, LA St. Theodore's Church.
DuBois, David '80 (GAL) Pattison/Brookshire, TX Sacred Heart Church.
DuBois, Francis J. '70 (ALB) Latham, NY St. Ambrose Church.
Dubois, Raymond J. *s.s.s.* '49 (CLV) [O] Cleveland, OH Blessed Sacrament Community.
DuBois, Msgr. William '48 (SP) Retired.
Dubois, Yvon *a.a.* '53 (BO) [W] Boston, MA Assumptionist Center.
Dubovici, Mihai '94 (STF) [A] Stamford, CT St. Basil College.
Dubovsky, Peter *s.j.* '89 (BO) [W] Cambridge, MA Weston Jesuit Community.
Dubowski, George (MIL) [P] Burlington, WI Queen of Peace Friary.
Dubriske, Edward J. *s.s.e.* '64 (BUR) [E] Colchester, VT Society of St. Edmund.
Dubriske, Edward J. *s.s.e.* '64 (FgM) Edmundite Foreign Missions.
Dubrouillet, James N. '00 (CHR) [H] Anderson, SC Anderson College.
Dubrouillet, James N. '97 (CHR) Anderson, SC St. Joseph's Church.
Duc, Dominic Tran Minh '90 (PH) Pottstown, PA St. Aloysius Church.
Duc Tien, Msgr. Peter '60 (ORG) Special Assignment.
Duc-Minh, Joseph '61 (LA) [A] Camarillo, CA St. John's Seminary College of the Archdiocese of Los Angeles.
Duca, Michael '78 (DAL) [A] Irving, TX Holy Trinity Seminary.
Ducaji, John '54 (JOL) Wheaton, IL St. Mark Church.
Ducate, Richard '67 (KC) Butler, MO St. Patrick's Church.
Ducci, Alex '61 (STA) Retired.
Ducette, Msgr. John I. '62 (BUF) [7] Tonawanda, NY St. Timothy Church.
Ducey, William *ss.cc.* '55 (FR) [I] Fairhaven, MA Sacred Hearts Provincial House.
Duch, Robert G. '64 (PIT) Aspinwall, PA St. Scholastica Church.
Duchaine, Msgr. R. Mark '78 (SC) Holstein, IA Our Lady of Good Counsel Church.
DuCharme, Paul '55 (GB) Retired.
DuChez, Daniel B. *o.s.* '56 (PCE) On Duty Outside the Diocese.
Duchschere, Paul '90 (FAR) [6] Fargo, ND St. Paul Newman Center, N.D.S.U. Church; [I] Fargo, ND St. Paul's Catholic Chapel.
Ducre, Kennon Y. *s.t.l.* '83 (ELP) [2] El Paso, TX All Saints Church.
Ducthuan, Polycarp *c.m.c.* '91 (AMA) [5] Amarillo, TX Our Lady of Vietnam Church.
Duda, Francis '43 (SPR) [I] Holyoke, MA Mont Marie Health Care Center, Inc.
Duda, Robert '84 (JOL) Villa Park, IL St. John the Apostle Church.
Dudak, Msgr. George A. (PAT) Retired.
Dudash, Derrick F. '74 (GRY) Hebron, IN St. Helen Church.
Duddy, Patrick A. '39 (PH) Stowe, PA St. Gabriel of the Sorrowful Mother Church; Retired.
Dudek, Berard *o.f.m.conv.* '54 (BGP) [1] Fairfield, CT St. Anthony of Padua Church.
Dudek, Ladislaus J. '66 (ALN) [8] Allentown, PA SS. Peter and Paul Church.
Dudek, Stanislaw '62 (BUF) Perrysburg, NY St. Joan of Arc Church; South Dayton, NY St. John Fisher Church.
Dudek, Stephen S. '84 (GR) Holland, MI St. Francis de Sales Church; On Special Assignment.
Dudink, Edward *s.v.d.* '46 (BO) [W] Duxbury, MA Society of the Divine Word.
Dudkiewicz, Stanley '52 (SY) [9] Syracuse, NY Sacred Heart Basilica Church.
Dudley, James *m.s.c.* '56 (AUS) [H] Blanco, TX Missionaries of the Sacred Heart, M.S.C.
Dudley, James *m.s.c.* '56 (SAT) [M] San Antonio, TX Missionaries of the Sacred Heart.
Dudziak, Paul M. '69 (WDC) Dunkirk, MD Jesus the Good Shepherd Church.
Dudzik, Dariusz '95 (NOR) On Duty Outside the Diocese.
Dudzinski, Andrew J. '96 (FAR) Rugby, ND St. Therese, Little Flower Church.
Dudzinski, Brian A. '97 (LFT) Muncie, IN St. Mary Church.
Dudzinski, Paul L. '86 (ARL) Clifton, VA St. Claire of Assisi Church.
Due, J. Michael '00 (COV) Florence, KY St. Paul Church; [B] Covington, KY Covington Latin School.
Duell, James S. '82 (CIN) Bradford, OH Immaculate Conception Church; Covington, OH St. Teresa Church.
Duellman, Virgil S. '60 (WIN) Austin, MN Queen of Angels Church.
Duenas, Jaime H. '50 (NY) [167] Bronx, NY Nativity of Our Blessed Lady Church.
Duenas, Jose Luis *o.a.r.* '59 (LSC) San Miguel, NM San Miguel Church; [B] Mesilla, NM Augustinian Recollect Fathers.
Dueppen, David A. '99 (MIA) Plantation, FL St. Gregory Church.
Duerr, Gregory *o.s.b.* '64 (P) [L] St. Benedict, OR Mt. Angel Abbey.
Duesdieker, Robert W. '80 (JC) Bourbon, MO St. Francis Church; Cuba, MO Holy Cross Church; Steelville, MO St. Michael Church.
Duesman, Msgr. Jerome P. '68 (DAL) Irving, TX Holy Family of Nazareth Church.
Duesman, Msgr. Leon '65 (DAL) Frisco, TX St. Francis of Assisi Church.
Duesterhaus, Michael R. '91 (ARL) Annandale, VA St. Michael's Church.
Duet, Wayne J. '75 (LAF) Erath, LA Our Lady of Lourdes Church.
Dueweke, Donald G. '66 (SAG) Croswell, MI St. Patrick Church.
Dueweke, Robert *o.s.a.* '79 (CHI) [N] Olympia Fields, IL The Augustinians-Provincialate.
Dueweke, Robert F. *o.s.a.* '79 (CHI) [182] Chicago, IL St. Rita of Cascia Church.
Dufault, Wilfred J. *a.a.* '34 (WOR) [N] Worcester, MA Assumptionists (Augustinians of the Assumption).
Dufault, Wilfrid J. *a.a.* '34 (WOR) [B] Worcester, MA Assumption College.
Duff, Bill (LAV) [4] Las Vegas, NV Our Lady of Las Vegas Church.
Duff, Gerard M. *o.s.a.* '59 (PH) [V] Flourtown, PA St. Joseph Villa; [AA] Villanova, PA St. Thomas Monastery.
Duff, John J. '77 (NY) Pawling, NY St. John the Evangelist Church.
Duff, Paul J. *c.s.c.* '55 (FR) [A] North Easton, MA Holy Cross Fathers Religious.
Duff, Thomas M. *o.s.m.* '49 (CHI) [N] Chicago, IL Order of Friar Servants of Mary (Servites) United States of America Province, Inc.
Duff, William '63 (LAV) Retired.
Duffe, Stephen J. '96 (NEW) Washington Township, NJ Our Lady of Good Counsel Church.
Duffell, John P. '69 (NY) [14] New York, NY Ascension Church.
Duffey, Joseph A. '52 (PH) Bryn Mawr, PA Our Mother of Good Counsel Church.
Duffey, Thomas '49 (DET) Retired.
Duffey, Thomas J. '49 (DET) [60] Detroit, MI St. Patrick Church.
Duffey, William R. *s.j.* '51 (MIL) [P] Milwaukee, WI Jesuit Provincial Office, Wisconsin Province.
Dufficy, Edward C. '50 (CHI) [3] Oak Park, IL St. Edmund Church; Retired.
Duffin, Stephen (BO) [69] Boston, MA St. William Church.
Duffner, Paul *o.p.* '40 (OAK) [N] Oakland, CA Western Dominican Province.
Duffner, Paul A. *o.p.* '40 (P) [18] Portland, OR Holy Rosary Parish & Dominican Priory Church.
Duffner, Ralph J. '56 (SPC) Chaffee, MO St. Ambrose Church.
Dufford, Robert *s.j.* '73 (GB) [M] Oshkosh, WI Jesuit Retreat House.
Duffy, Aidan *o.f.m.* '56 (BO) [BB] Boston, MA St. Anthony Shrine.
Duffy, David J. *o.s.a.* '57 (PH) [G] Malvern, PA Malvern Preparatory School for Boys; [AA] Malvern, PA Augustinian Friars (O.S.A.).
Duffy, Donald '59 (NO) Destrehan, LA St. Charles Borromeo Church; Retired.
Duffy, Donald J. '43 (CHI) Buffalo Grove, IL St. Mary Church; Retired.
Duffy, Edward V. '52 (NEW) Harrington Park, NJ Our Lady of Victories Church.
Duffy, Edwin J. '61 (HON) Retired.
Duffy, Emmanuel *o.f.m.* '30 (PAT) [M] Butler, NJ St. Anthony Friary.
Duffy, Eugene J. '50 (LA) Retired.
Duffy, Francis C. *o.p.* '60 (PRO) [P] Providence, RI St. Thomas Aquinas Priory at Providence College.
Duffy, Msgr. Francis J. '70 (PAT) Morristown, NJ St. Margaret's Church.
Duffy, Francis L. *s.j.* '58 (BAL) [M] Baltimore, MD Mercy Health Services Inc.
Duffy, Francis R. (PH) [AA] Bensalem, PA Congregation of the Holy Ghost.
Duffy, Francis R. *c.s.sp.* '41 (PH) [AA] Philadelphia, PA Holy Ghost Fathers.
Duffy, Msgr. Francis X. '49 (NY) Retired; [HH] New York, NY St. Paul's Guild, Inc.
Duffy, G. Ralph '65 (WDC) [2] Rockville, MD Shrine of St. Jude Church; Retired.
Duffy, George '63 (MIA) Plantation, FL St. Gregory Church.
Duffy, George A. *s.j.* '55 (BO) [E] Boston, MA Boston College High School & Jesuit Community.
Duffy, Hugh '66 (PMB) Okeechobee, FL Sacred Heart Church.
Duffy, Hugh E. *o.s.f.s.* '60 (WIL) [I] Childs, MD Oblates of St. Francis De Sales.
Duffy, James '55 (JOL) Retired.
Duffy, James D. *s.m.* (ATL) [6] Atlanta, GA Our Lady of the Assumption Church.
Duffy, James H. '56 (MIL) Special Assignment.
Duffy, Msgr. John F. (ROC) [8] Rochester, NY Blessed Sacrament Church.
Duffy, Msgr. John F. '45 (ROC) Retired.
Duffy, John F. *c.s.p.* '75 (WDC) [B] Washington, DC St. Paul's College.
Duffy, John J. '52 (PH) [2] Bensalem, PA St. Elizabeth Ann Seton Church; Retired.
Duffy, Joseph P. *s.j.* '57 (BO) [W] Chestnut Hill, MA The Jesuit Community at Boston College.
Duffy, Jude *o.f.m. cap* '58 (CHL) [3] Charlotte, NC Our Lady of Consolation Church.
Duffy, Jude *o.f.m.cap.* '58 (NEW) [N] Union City, NJ Capuchin Friars - Province of the Sacred Stigmata of St. Francis.
Duffy, Michael A. *o.f.m.* '71 (PH) [W] Philadelphia, PA Order of Friars Minor - Holy Name Province; [AA] Philadelphia, PA Order of Friars Minor of the Province of the Most Holy Name aka Holy Name Province.
Duffy, Michael M. '76 (RIC) Tappahannock, VA St. Timothy Church.
Duffy, Patrick '74 (CIN) McCartyville, OH Sacred Heart of Jesus Church.
Duffy, Patrick S. *o.c.s.o.* '81 (SFE) Anton Chico, NM San Jose Church.
Duffy, Raymond J. '68 (FRS) Riverdale, CA St. Ann Church.
Duffy, Regis A. *o.f.m.* '61 (BUF) [C] St. Bonaventure, NY St. Bonaventure University; [O] St. Bonaventure, NY St. Bonaventure Friary.
Duffy, Msgr. Robert E. '48 (NEW) Retired.
Duffy, Robert M. '42 (CHI) Tinley Park, IL Saint Julie Billiart Church; Retired.
Duffy, Stephen '57 (NO) Unassigned; [C] New Orleans, LA Loyola University New Orleans.
Duffy, Stephen V. *s.j.* '43 (NY) [F] New York, NY Regis High School; [DD] New York, NY St. Ignatius Loyola Residence.
Duffy, Thomas J. '66 (PH) Linfield, PA St. Clare Church.
Duffy, Msgr. Thomas M. '53 (WDC) [10] Washington, DC Blessed Sacrament, Shrine of the Most Church.
Duffy, Msgr. Thomas R. '58 (CHR) Garden City, SC St. Michael Church.
Duffy, Vincent *s.d.b.* '48 (PAT) [3] Paterson, NJ St. Anthony's Church.
Dufner, Andrew J. *s.j.* '67 (P) [N] Pacific City, OR Nestucca Sanctuary.
Dufner, Daniel G. '96 (YAK) Bridgeport, WA St. Anne's Church; Chelan, WA St. Francis de Sales Church.
Dufner, Thomas W. '83 (STP) St. Louis Park, MN Holy Family Church.
Dufour, Clement E. '58 (FR) Retired.
Dufour, David '94 (NO) [7] Metairie, LA St. Clement of Rome Church.
Dufour, George J. '70 (BO) [1] Salem, MA St. Anne Church.
Dufour, Louis C. '58 (BO) Senior Priests.
DuFour, Rene *o.m.i.* '54 (BEL) [F] Belleville, IL Missionary Oblates of Mary Immaculate - St. Henry's Oblate Residence.
Dufresne, Oliver J. '45 (STP) Retired.
Dufresne, Vincent J. '83 (BR) Labadieville, LA St. Philomena Church.
Dugal, James *c.pp.s.* '56 (CIN) [M] Dayton, OH Provincial Office of the Cincinnati Province of the Society of the Precious Blood.
Dugal, James H. *c.pp.s.* '56 (CIN) Montezuma, OH Our Lady of Guadalupe Church.
Dugan, J. Thomas '70 (E) Fairview, PA Holy Cross Church.
Dugan, James L. *s.j.* '73 (NY) [DD] New York, NY Jesuit Provincial's Office; [DD] New York, NY St. Ignatius Loyola Residence.
Dugan, James M. '89 (ALT) [12] Altoona, PA St. Rose of Lima Church.
Dugan, John L. *c.s.b.* '90 (ROC) [2] Rochester, NY St. Ambrose Church; [I] Rochester, NY Basilian Residence.
Dugan, Paul J. *s.j.* '56 (BUF) [O] Buffalo, NY Canisius Jesuit Community.
Dugan, T. Michael '88 (DAL) [17] Dallas, TX St. Elizabeth Church.
Dugan, Thomas P. *c.s.b.* '60 (GAL) [Q] Sugar Land, TX Basilian Mission Center.
Dugan, William M. '49 (SPK) Retired.
Dugandzic, Nicholas *o.p.* '65 (CHI) [28] Chicago, IL Blessed Alojzije Cardinal Stepanic Church; [N] Chicago, IL Croatian Dominican Fathers.
Dugandzic, Peter '95 (RVC) Manhasset, NY St. Mary's Church.
Dugas, Jerome A. '62 (BR) Plaquemine, LA St. Clement of Rome Church; Plaquemine, LA St. John the Evangelist Church.
Dugas, Laurence A. *m.m.* '54 (FgM) Maryknoll Foreign Missions.
Dugas, Scott '77 (HT) [3] Thibodaux, LA Christ The Redeemer Church; [5] Thibodaux, LA St. John The

Evangelist Church.
Dugas, Willard '77 (LAF) Retired.
Dugay, Anthony *s.v.d.* '62 (FgM) Society of the Divine Word Foreign Missions.
Duggan, Charles T. '44 (BO) [4] Medford, MA St. Raphael Church; Senior Priests.
Duggan, Dennis D. '80 (DET) [52] Detroit, MI Our Lady Gate of Heaven Church; [72] Detroit, MI St. Suzanne Church.
Duggan, Eugene F. '46 (SFR) Sausalito, CA St. Mary Star of the Sea Church; Retired.
Duggan, J. Edward '50 (CHI) [22] Chicago, IL St. Bartholomew Church; Retired.
Duggan, John H. *s.j.* '57 (SCR) [C] Scranton, PA University of Scranton.
Duggan, Msgr. John M. '43 (BUF) Retired.
Duggan, Joseph P. '64 (VEN) Retired.
Duggan, Karl J. '98 (ATL) Dunwoody, GA All Saints Catholic Church.
Duggan, Kevin *s.m.* '86 (AUS) [B] Waco, TX Reicher Catholic High School; [H] Waco, TX Marist Community; [M] Waco, TX Catholic Student Center at Baylor University.
Duggan, Kevin F.X. '98 (SEA) Kirkland, WA St. John Mary Vianney Church.
Duggan, Kevin P. '87 (MET) South River, NJ Corpus Christi Church.
Duggan, Michael A. *m.m.* '59 (NY) [DD] Maryknoll, NY Maryknoll Fathers and Brothers.
Duggan, Nicholas '62 (SAC) [18] Sacramento, CA St. Paul Church.
Duggan, Oliver '71 (SEA) [21] Seattle, WA Assumption Church.
Duggan, Paul '48 (SFR) [35] San Francisco, CA St. Monica Church.
Duggan, Paul E. '48 (SFR) Retired.
Duggan, Paul O'Donnell (PAT) [6] Paterson, NJ St. Casimir's Church.
Duggan, Peter '55 (SEA) [19] Seattle, WA St. Peter Church.
Duggan, Robert D. '69 (WDC) Gaithersburg, MD St. Rose of Lima Church.
Duggan, Robert J. *c.s.b.* '64 (DET) [6] Detroit, MI Ste. Anne Church.
Duggan, Sean B. *o.s.b.* '88 (NO) [A] St. Benedict, LA St. Joseph's Seminary College; [P] St. Benedict, LA St. Joseph Abbey.
Duggan, Thomas '47 (JC) Brookfield, MO Immaculate Conception Church.
Duggan, Thomas *c.ss.r.* '53 (STL) [P] Liguori, MO Liguori Mission House/Redemptorists.
Duggan, William E. '53 (SFR) Retired.
Duggins, Dominic *glmy.* '74 (CIN) [M] Cincinnati, OH Headquarters of Glenmary Home Missioners.
Dugue, Nerva W. '93 (NEW) Fort Lee, NJ Holy Trinity Church.
Duhaime, James H. '61 (PRO) Retired.
Duhaime, John N. '58 (WH) Retired.
Duhe, Thomas P. '78 (BR) [5] Baton Rouge, LA St. Charles Borromeo Church.
Duhe', Thomas P. '78 (BR) Greenwell Springs, LA St. Alphonsus Liguori Church.
Duignan, Msgr. Andrew '58 (CAM) Ocean City, NJ Our Lady of Good Counsel Church.
Dukart, George A. '59 (BIS) Menoken, ND St. Hildegard Church.
Dukart, Norman J. '67 (BIS) Crosby, ND St. Patrick Church.
Duke, Msgr. Charles J. '47 (NO) Retired.
Duke, Jerome J. '68 (CLV) [2] Lakewood, OH SS. Cyril and Methodius Church.
Dukehart, Claude H. *s.s.* '43 (BAL) [O] Baltimore, MD St. Charles Villa; [S] Baltimore, MD St. Charles Villa.
Dukeley, Boris '98 (SJP) Spring Hill, FL St. Andrew Church.
Duker, Msgr. Russell A. *s.e.o.d.* '70 (PBR) [1] Pittsburgh, PA Holy Spirit Church.
Dukowski, Jaime *o.m.i.* '67 (FgM) Oblates Foreign Missions.
DuLac, Msgr. Henri '45 (STP) [C] St. Paul, MN University of St. Thomas.
DuLac, Msgr. Henri J. '45 (STP) Retired.
Dulaney, William R. '73 (BRK) [83] Brooklyn, NY Mary Queen of Heaven Church.
Dulanto, Angel *o.s.a.* '51 (NY) [49] New York, NY Holy Rosary Church.
Dulberg, Albert V. '36 (B) Retired.
Dulek, Lawrence V. '73 (MIL) [8] Milwaukee, WI St. Anthony Church; [A] St. Francis, WI Saint Francis Seminary.
Dullahan, Robert J. '57 (ALN) [A] Wernersville, PA Jesuit Center.
Dullea, Charles W. *s.j.* '47 (SFR) [C] San Francisco, CA University of San Francisco.
Dullea, Charles W. *s.j.* '47 (SJ) [L] Los Gatos, CA Sacred Heart Jesuit Center.
Dullea, Denis '61 (ATL) Retired.
Dulock, Vincent *c.s.b.* '69 (GAL) Angleton, TX Most Holy Trinity Church.
Dulzer, Kenan '48 (CHI) [N] Chicago, IL St. Peter's Friary.
Dumais, George J. *s.j.* '71 (HEL) Special Assignments.
Dumais, Steven *s.d.b.* (NEW) [C] Ramsey, NJ Don Bosco Preparatory High School for Boys.
Duman, Charles J. '52 (SFS) Retired.
Duman, Charles J. '53 (SFS) Salem, SD St. Mary Church.
Dumas, Emile E. *m.m.* '67 (FgM) Maryknoll Foreign Missions.
Dumas, Salvador '74 (CHK) San Jose Village, MP San Jose Church.
Dumas, Terrence J. '88 (LAN) [3] Ann Arbor, MI St. Patrick Church.
Duminiak, John J. '60 (ALN) Beaver Meadows, PA St. Mary Church.
Duminuco, Vincent J. *s.j.* '64 (NY) [DD] New York, NY "America;" Residence and publication office of the America Press.
Dumm, Demetrius R. *o.s.b.* '47 (GBG) [H] Latrobe, PA Saint Vincent Archabbey.
Dumm, Wilfred M. *o.s.b.* '45 (SAV) [B] Savannah, GA Benedictine Military School; [F] Savannah, GA The Benedictine Priory.
Dummer, Anthony B. *o.m.i.* '80 (JUN) [2] Juneau, AK St. Paul The Apostle Church.
Dummer, Donald *o.m.i.* '64 (STP) [27] St. Paul, MN St. Mary Church.
Dumont, C. Peter '71 (MAN) Suncook, NH St. John the Baptist Church.
Dumont, Gerald '80 (BRK) [27] Brooklyn, NY St. Catherine of Genoa Church.
Dumoulin, Marcel L. '61 (PRT) Fairfield, ME Immaculate Heart of Mary Church.
Dumphrey, Joseph C. *o.s.f.s.* '64 (BUF) [2] Lockport, NY St. John the Baptist Church; [5] Lockport, NY St. Patrick Church.
Dumphy, Charles J. '55 (WOR) [3] Worcester, MA Blessed Sacrament Church.
Dumpson, Roland J. '83 (NY) Retired.
Dunavan, Thomas '98 (LIN) [12] Lincoln, NE St. Thomas Aquinas Church; [J] Lincoln, NE University of Nebraska, Newman Club.
Dunbar, Francis '55 (ALB) Retired.
Duncan, Andrew '93 (CHY) Douglas, WY St. James Church.
Duncan, Msgr. Arthur L. '47 (CHL) Retired.
Duncan, Msgr. Edward J. '41 (PEO) Retired; [P] Champaign, IL St. John's Catholic Student Chapel and Newman Foundation, University of Illinois.
Duncan, Msgr. John C. '60 (LFT) Carmel, IN Our Lady of Mount Carmel Church; [I] Carmel, IN Our Lady of Mount Carmel Parochial School.
Duncan, Joseph '89 (PH) Manoa, PA Sacred Heart Church.
Duncan, William H. '90 (GR) Holland, MI Our Lady of the Lake Church; On Special Assignment.
Duncanson, Msgr. Richard F. '71 (SD) [4] Chula Vista, CA St. Rose of Lima Church.
Duncklee, Lawrence '80 (RVC) Brentwood, NY St. Luke Church.
Dundon, Robert W. *s.j.* '69 (FgM) Provinces.
Dundon, Robert W. *s.j.* '69 (MIL) [P] Milwaukee, WI Jesuit Provincial Office, Wisconsin Province.
Dunfee, Dirk J. *s.j.* '97 (KC) [J] Kansas City, MO Rockhurst Jesuit Community.
Dunfree, James M. '84 (STU) [8] Steubenville, OH St. Pius X Church.
Dungan, Cormac *o.f.m.* '41 (BO) [Z] Boston, MA Saint Anthony Residence.
Dunghe, Adelmo P. *s.j.* '95 (NY) [DD] New York, NY Jesuit Provincial's Office.
Dunham, Larry C. *o.f.m.* (SFE) [I] Albuquerque, NM San Antonio Provincial Friary.
Dunklee, Lawrence G. '78 (LC) Genoa, WI St. Charles Borromeo Church.
Dunkley, George '70 (SD) San Marcos, CA St. Mark Church.
Dunkley, George '70 (WOR) On Duty Outside the Diocese.
Dunlap, James E. (CHI) [J] Evanston, IL Saint Francis Hospital.
Dunlap, William M. '74 (TR) Brick Town, NJ Visitation Church.
Dunleavy, Francis J. '40 (MIA) Retired.
Dunleavy, Thomas J. *m.m.* '75 (FgM) Maryknoll Foreign Missions.
Dunleavy, Thomas J. '75 (PH) [23] Philadelphia, PA St. Bernard Church.
Dunleavy, Thomas P. '34 (MAR) Retired.
Dunmyer, Raymond A. '76 (BIR) Bessemer, AL St. Aloysius Church; [I] Bessemer, AL St. Aloysius Educational Foundation.
Dunn, Bob '85 (CC) [5] Corpus Christi, TX Most Precious Blood Church.
Dunn, Bradley *s.f.o.* (BEL) [J] Milstadt, IL Secular Franciscan Order.
Dunn, Charles J. *s.j.* '55 (WOR) [N] Worcester, MA Jesuits of Holy Cross College, Inc.
Dunn, Christopher J. *o.f.m.* '82 (FgM) Franciscan Foreign Missions.
Dunn, Didacus Joseph *o.f.m.cap.* '56 (STL) [P] St. Louis, MO St. Crispin's Friary.
Dunn, Donald F. '61 (COS) [1] Colorado Springs, CO St. Mary's Church.
Dunn, Edmond J. '72 (DAV) [A] Davenport, IA St. Ambrose University Seminary; [B] Davenport, IA St. Ambrose University.
Dunn, Msgr. Edward C. '43 (TOL) Tiffin, OH St. Joseph Church; Retired.
Dunn, Edward T. *s.j.* '56 (BUF) [O] Buffalo, NY Canisius Jesuit Community.
Dunn, Gerald R. '57 (MAN) Retired.
Dunn, Harold *m.s.a.* '78 (NOR) [F] Cromwell, CT Society of the Missionaries of the Holy Apostles.
Dunn, Harold F. *m.s.a.* '78 (WH) Hinton, WV St. Patrick Church; Rainelle, WV Sacred Heart Church.
Dunn, Jerome *o.f.m.cap.* '68 (BAL) [S] Cumberland, MD SS. Peter and Paul Friary.
Dunn, John '54 (DET) Retired.
Dunn, John P. '49 (STP) Retired.
Dunn, Larry *m.i.c.* '87 (SPR) [J] Stockbridge, MA Congregation of Marians of The Immaculate Conception of the BVM.
Dunn, Laurence J. '68 (CHI) Northfield, IL St. Philip the Apostle Church.
Dunn, Lawrence E. '61 (DET) Yale, MI Sacred Heart Church.
Dunn, Leo F. *c.ss.r.* '44 (ROC) [K] Canandaigua, NY Notre Dame Retreat House.
Dunn, Msgr. Louis W. '47 (PRO) Retired.
Dunn, Michael L. '94 (BGP) Bethel, CT St. Mary Church.
Dunn, Ralph F. *c.s.c.* '60 (FTW) [J] South Bend, IN Congregation of Holy Cross, Indiana Province, Provincial House.
Dunn, Raymond V. *s.j.* '57 (BO) [W] Boston, MA The Society of Jesus of New England-Provincial Offices.
Dunn, Richard '80 (SY) Military Chaplains.
Dunn, Richard C. '45 (TOL) Retired.
Dunn, Msgr. Richard F. '58 (BRK) [165] Queens, NY Corpus Christi Church.
Dunn, Robert M. '92 (NY) Ossining, NY St. Augustine Church.
Dunn, Robert T. '44 (NY) Retired.
Dunn, Stephen *c.p.* '64 (MET) [H] South River, NJ Passionist Provincial Office.
Dunn, Stephen '71 (SD) Unassigned; [B] San Diego, CA University of San Diego.
Dunn, Steven '98 (MIL) Elm Grove, WI St. Mary Church.
Dunn, Msgr. William A. '65 (COL) [32] Columbus, OH St. Michael Church.
Dunn, William J. '51 (OAK) San Lorenzo, CA St. John the Baptist Church; Retired.
Dunne, Andrew J. *o.s.f.s.* '59 (LAN) Michigan Center, MI Our Lady of Fatima Church.
Dunne, Dennis T. '90 (STP) [N] Bloomington, MN Maryknoll Fathers and Brothers, Catholic Foreign Mission Society of America.
Dunne, Dermot J. '00 (OM) [48] Douglas Co., NE St. Wenceslaus Church.
Dunne, Edward *c.ss.r.* '49 (BRK) [107] Brooklyn, NY Our Lady of Perpetual Help Basilica Church.
Dunne, Gerald M. *o.s.f.s.* '77 (PH) [D] Philadelphia, PA Father Judge High School for Boys; [AA] Philadelphia, PA Father Judge Faculty House.
Dunne, James J. *s.s.c.* '47 (STP) [J] Hastings, MN Regina Medical Center; [M] Hastings, MN Regina Convalescent and Nursing Care and Retirement Center.
Dunne, James M. '61 (BRK) [160] Queens, NY St. Camillus Church.
Dunne, James P. *s.j.* (FgM) Provinces.
Dunne, John S. *c.s.c.* '54 (FTW) [B] Notre Dame, IN University of Notre Dame Du Lac; [J] Notre Dame, IN Holy Cross Community, Corby Hall, University of Notre Dame.
Dunne, Msgr. Joseph A. '42 (NY) Retired.
Dunne, Patrick J. '70 (NY) [5] White Plains, NY Our Lady of Sorrows Church; White Plains, NY Burke Rehabilitation Center.
Dunne, Peter '50 (OM) [M] Omaha, NE Institute of the Apostolic Oblates.
Dunne, Msgr. Peter F. '44 (OM) Boys Town, NE Immaculate Conception B.V.M. Church; Retired.
Dunne, Peter J. '54 (PH) Retired.
Dunne, Raymond A. *s.j.* '50 (CHI) Prospect Heights, IL St. Alphonsus Liguori Church.
Dunnigan, Daniel D. *s.j.* (DET) [P] Bloomfield Hills, MI Manresa Jesuit Retreat House.
Dunning, James P. '63 (ORG) Mission Viejo, CA St. Kilian Church.
Dunnivan, John '53 (KCK) Retired.
Dunphy, James R. *m.s.* '57 (STL) [P] St. Louis, MO La Salette Missionaries.
Dunphy, Larry *o.f.m.* '60 (FRS) [F] Three Rivers, CA St. Anthony's Retreat House.
Dunphy, Richard W. *s.j.* '73 (DEN) [M] Denver, CO Regis Jesuit Community (The Jesuits at Regis University).
Dunphy, Robert J. '65 (CAM) Mount Ephraim, NJ

Sacred Heart Church.
Dunphy, Thomas R. '58 (CLV) Valley City, OH St. Martin of Tours Church.
Dunson, Donald '82 (CLV) [A] Wickliffe, OH Borromeo Seminary; [A] Wickliffe, OH St. Mary Seminary and Graduate School of Theology.
Duoba, Jonas *m.i.c.* '46 (CHI) [N] Chicago, IL Congregation of Marian Fathers of the Immaculate Conception.
Duong, Cu Minh '87 (MOB) [14] Mobile, AL St. Monica Church.
Duong, Duc Quang '00 (BEA) [4] Port Arthur, TX St. Catherine of Siena Church.
Duong, Ignatius '89 (FWT) [15] Fort Worth, TX St. Rita Church.
Duong, Paul '74 (SJ) Saratoga, CA Church of the Ascension.
Duong Phan, Joseph '93 (OAK) Bay Point, CA Our Lady Queen of the World Church.
DuPerry, Irenee *s.m.* '69 (BO) [4] Methuen, MA St. Theresa Church.
Duplessis, Donald M. *o.s.m.* '61 (CHI) [N] Chicago, IL Order of Friar Servants of Mary (Servites) United States of America Province, Inc.
Duplessis, Donald M. *o.s.m.* '61 (ORG) Fullerton, CA St. Juliana Falconieri Church; [I] Buena Park, CA Order of Friar Servants of Mary (Servites).
Duplessis, Omer *o.m.i.* '43 (FgM) Oblates Foreign Missions.
DuPont, Arthur J. '54 (HRT) Plantsville, CT Mary Our Queen Church; [V] Hartford, CT Catholic Cemeteries Association of the Archdiocese of Hartford, Inc.
Dupont, Guy B. *o.p* '68 (WDC) [11] Washington, DC St. Dominic Church & Priory Church.
Dupre, Matthew '98 (BR) [6] Baton Rouge, LA Christ the King Church.
Dupre, Matthew C. '98 (BR) [K] Baton Rouge, LA Christ the King Parish and Catholic Student Center.
Duprey, Msgr. Dennis J. '70 (OG) Chasm Falls, NY St. Helen Church; Malone, NY Notre Dame Church; Malone, NY Upstate Correctional Facility.
Dupuis, George H. '50 (BUR) Arlington, VT St. Margaret Mary Church.
Dupuis, Laurent *o.m.i.* '36 (SAT) [K] San Antonio, TX Oblate Madonna Residence.
Dupuis, Philip (LAN) Retired.
Dupuis, Ronald S. *s.c.* '77 (PRO) [P] Burrillville, RI Brothers of the Sacred Heart Provincial House.
Dupuis, Wayne G. *c.s.v.* '70 (LAV) [15] Las Vegas, NV St. Viator Church.
Duque, Luis A. (BO) [5] Lawrence, MA Holy Rosary Church.
DuQuesnay, Damian *o.s.b.* '46 (SP) [O] St. Leo, FL St. Leo Abbey.
Duquet, Heribert *m.e.p.* '39 (SFR) [11] San Francisco, CA St. Cecilia Church; [N] San Francisco, CA Paris Foreign Mission Society Residence.
Duquette, Don Bosco *o.f.m.cap.* '64 (PRT) [3] Portland, ME St. Joseph's Church; [M] Portland, ME University of New England-Westbrook College.
Duquette, Lucien G. '56 (BUR) Retired.
Duquette, Roy H. '58 (SPR) [1] Northampton, MA Annunciation Church.
Dura, Eduardo '77 (SFR) [4] San Francisco, CA St. Anne Church.
Durack, Jerome F. *s.j.* '60 (FgM) Provinces.
Duraczynski, Msgr. Jerome A. '42 (SFS) Retired.
Duran, Alfonso M. *m.j.* '56 (PCE) On Duty Outside the Diocese.
Duran, Ernesto '42 (BRK) Retired.
Duran, Msgr. George '52 (LA) Maywood, CA St. Rose of Lima Church.
Duran, Jorge '75 (SAT) On Leave.
Duran, Said '94 (TYL) Tyler, TX Our Lady of Guadalupe Church.
Durand, Donald A. '58 (P) [12] Portland, OR St. Clare Church.
Durant, Thomas M. '76 (SY) [14] Utica, NY St. Peter Church.
Durbin, Clarence R. *c.s.c.* '45 (FTW) [B] Notre Dame, IN University of Notre Dame Du Lac; [J] Notre Dame, IN Holy Cross Community, Corby Hall, University of Notre Dame.
Durbin, Clement B. '54 (COL) Retired.
Durbin, John G. '79 (R) Chapel Hill, NC St. Thomas More Church.
Durchholz, Jack '95 (EVN) [15] Evansville, IN St. Boniface Church.
Durette, Mathias D. *o.s.b.* '93 (MAN) [K] Manchester, NH St. Anselm Abbey.
Durham, J. Charles '90 (BUR) Castleton, VT St. John the Baptist Church; [H] Burlington, VT University of Vermont-The Catholic Center at UVM.
Durham, Neil *s.d.s.* (MIL) [N] Milwaukee, WI St. Anne's Home for the Elderly.
Durham, Neil *s.d.s.* '82 (MIL) [P] Milwaukee, WI Salvatorian Provincial Residence.
Durig, D. Kent '93 (WH) Weirton, WV Sacred Heart of Mary Church.
Duris, Lawrence M. '69 (CHI) [154] Chicago, IL Our Lady of Peace Church; [168] Chicago, IL St. Philip Neri Church.
Duritsa, George M. '53 (Y) [15] Youngstown, OH St. Elizabeth's Church; Retired.
Durka, Michael '97 (VNN) Olympia, WA St. George Byzantine Church.
Durkee, David R. '80 (CLV) Green, OH Queen of Heaven Church.
Durken, Daniel *o.s.b.* '56 (SCL) [I] Collegeville, MN St. John's Abbey, of the Order of St. Benedict.
Durkin, Msgr. Charles '55 (SFR) [T] San Francisco, CA Italian Catholic Federation.
Durkin, Msgr. Charles J. '55 (SFR) [49] San Francisco, CA Star of the Sea Church.
Durkin, Charles T. '79 (CHI) [20] Chicago, IL St. Barbara Church.
Durkin, Daniel '73 (FTW) Avilla, IN St. Mary of the Assumption Church.
Durkin, Edward J. *s.j.* '75 (NY) [5] New York, NY St. Aloysius Church.
Durkin, Eugene F. '49 (CHI) [1] Chicago, IL Cathedral of the Holy Name; ; Retired.
Durkin, James J. '68 (CAM) Stratford, NJ St. Luke Church.
Durkin, John (NY) Wassaic, NY Wassaic Development Center.
Durkin, John F., Jr. '99 (ATL) Lilburn, GA St. John Neumann Church.
Durkin, John L. '67 (NY) Amenia, NY Immaculate Conception Church.
Durkin, John R. '42 (DAV) Retired.
Durkin, Joseph T. *s.j.* '33 (WDC) [M] Washington, DC The Jesuit Community at Georgetown University.
Durney, Charles W. '63 (PH) Retired.
Duron, Apolonio *m.n.m.* '68 (ARE) [2] Camuy, PR Our Lady of the Miraculous Medal Church.
Durr, Edmund J. '65 (SY) [4] Syracuse, NY Holy Trinity Church.
Durrie, Robert L. '54 (DEN) Retired.
Durso, Michael H. *s.j.* '66 (STL) [P] St. Louis, MO De Smet Jesuit High School Community.
Duscher, Romuald *o.s.b.cam.* '76 (MRY) [F] Big Sur, CA New Camaldoli Hermitage.
Duschl, Frederick J. '65 (TOL) Blakeslee, OH St. Joseph Church; Montpelier, OH Sacred Heart Church.
Dusecina, Regis '73 (PBR) Greensburg, PA St. Nicholas of Myra Church.
Dushack, Douglas L. '72 (MAD) [8] Madison, WI St. James Church.
Dusheck, Leo *s.v.d.* '61 (TR) [M] Bordentown, NJ Society of the Divine Word.
Dussan, Louis R. *c.m.f.* '49 (LUB) Petersburg, TX Sacred Heart Church.
Duster, Charles *s.s.c.* '61 (FgM) St. Columban's Foreign Mission.
Duster, James J. '59 (DUB) Mount Vernon, IA St. John's the Baptist Church; Springville, IA St. Isidore's Church.
Duston, Allen *o.p.* '78 (OAK) [N] Oakland, CA Western Dominican Province.
Duston, Thomas L. '92 (MAN) Marlborough, NH Sacred Heart Church; Troy, NH Immaculate Conception Church.
Dusza, Donald W. '83 (ALT) Meyersdale, PA SS. Philip and James Church.
Dutchoff, C. Robert '56 (MAD) Absent on Sick Leave.
Dutel, Gilbert J. '70 (LAF) Scott, LA SS. Peter and Paul Church.
Dutkiewicz, Eugene M. *s.j.* '61 (MIL) [P] Milwaukee, WI Jesuit Provincial Office, Wisconsin Province; [P] Wauwatosa, WI Jesuit Community at St. Camillus; [Y] Milwaukee, WI The Jesuit Partnership.
Dutkiewicz, Eugene M. *s.j.* '61 (NO) [P] New Orleans, LA Jesuit Provincial Office.
Dutkiewicz, Thomas A. *o.f.m.cap.* '56 (PIT) [O] Pittsburgh, PA St. Francis Friary.
Dutra, Luis C. '55 (LAF) Retired.
Dutra, Luiz C. '55 (LAF) [H] Lafayette, LA De La Salle Christian Brothers.
Dutram, Charles J. '58 (WOR) Retired.
Duvall, Justin *o.s.b.* '78 (IND) [A] St. Meinrad, IN St. Meinrad Seminary; [J] St. Meinrad, IN St. Meinrad Archabbey.
Duvelius, Dennis *f.s.s.p.* '96 (IND) [6] Indianapolis, IN Holy Rosary Church.
Duvelius, Dennis *f.s.s.p.* '96 (SCR) [M] Elmhurst, PA Priestly Fraternity of St. Peter (F.S.S.P.), North American District Headquarters.
Duvelius, Dennis M. *f.s.s.p.* '96 (IND) [1] Indianapolis, IN SS. Peter and Paul Church.
Duvelsdorf, Peter L. (RVC) Retired.
Duvelsdorf, Peter L. '58 (RVC) [M] Uniondale, NY St. Pius X Residence.
DuWell, Ralph I. '00 (ORL) Deltona, FL Our Lady of the Lakes Church.
Dux, James M. '48 (PH) Retired.
Dux, John H. '73 (STA) On Duty Outside the Diocese.
Duyka, Stephen Joseph '97 (TYL) Mount Pleasant, TX St. Michael Church.
Duyshart, Edwin C. '84 (LA) Altadena, CA St. Elizabeth of Hungary Church.
Duzinski, Paul *o.f.m.conv.* '81 (BAL) [S] Ellicott City, MD Order of Friars Minor Conventual.
Duzinski, Paul *o.f.m.conv.* '81 (CLV) [M] Cleveland, OH Sts. Mary and Joseph Home for the Aged.
Dvorak, Donald T. *o.p.* '63 (NO) [25] New Orleans, LA St. Anthony of Padua Church.
Dvorak, Franklin A. '70 (OM) [48] Douglas Co., NE St. Wenceslaus Church.
Dvorak, Gerald L. '79 (STP) West St. Paul, MN St. Michael Church.
Dvorscak, James '76 (JOL) Lombard, IL Christ the King Church.
Dwomoh, Charles '86 (VIC) Palacios, TX St. Anthony's Church.
Dworak, Joseph J. '65 (ALB) Special Assignment; [H] Amsterdam, NY St. Mary's Hospital.
Dworak, Walter W. (PIT) Crafton, PA St. Philip Church.
Dwornik, Piotr J. '99 (HRT) Newington, CT Holy Spirit Church.
Dwulit, Andrij Taras '90 (STN) Houston, TX Protection of the Mother of God Church.
Dwyer, Msgr. Adrian I. '36 (STL) [59] St. Louis, MO St. Roch Church; Retired.
Dwyer, Arthur J. *m.m.* '49 (NY) [DD] Maryknoll, NY Maryknoll Fathers and Brothers.
Dwyer, Daniel P. *o.f.m.* '88 (ALB) [B] Loudonville, NY Siena College.
Dwyer, David P. *c.s.p.* '00 (DEN) [P] Boulder, CO University of Colorado (Boulder).
Dwyer, Dennis E. '66 (COS) Parker, CO Ave Maria Church.
Dwyer, Dermot '62 (SAC) Colfax, CA St. Dominic Church.
Dwyer, Donald M. '79 (NY) [170] Bronx, NY Our Lady of the Assumption Church.
Dwyer, Eugene F. *s.j.* '59 (CHI) [C] Chicago, IL Jesuit Community at Loyola University of Chicago.
Dwyer, J. Floyd '48 (LC) Retired; [H] La Crosse, WI Holy Cross (Seminary) Diocesan Center.
Dwyer, Jack '92 (TR) Bayville, NJ St. Barnabas Church; Keyport, NJ Jesus the Lord Church.
Dwyer, James D. *s.s.c.* '58 (BRK) [V] Kew Gardens, NY St. Columbans Foreign Mission Society.
Dwyer, John A. '74 (WOR) [8] Fitchburg, MA Sacred Heart of Jesus Church.
Dwyer, John F. '56 (NY) Tappan, NY Our Lady of the Sacred Heart Church.
Dwyer, Msgr. John R. '67 (BRK) [206] Queens, NY Our Lady of the Angelus Church.
Dwyer, Kevin F. *o.s.a.* '62 (BO) [C] North Andover, MA Merrimack College.
Dwyer, Kevin F. *o.s.a.* '62 (PH) [C] Villanova, PA Villanova University.
Dwyer, Msgr. Michael F. '38 (NY) Retired.
Dwyer, Morris '55 (ALB) Retired.
Dwyer, Msgr. Morris L. '38 (OG) [5] Plattsburgh, NY St. Peter Church; Retired.
Dwyer, Robert D. '62 (SY) East Syracuse, NY St. Matthew Church.
Dwyer, Thomas P. *o.s.a.* '53 (FgM) Foreign Missions.
Dwyer, Timothy *s.m.* '68 (STL) [P] St. Louis, MO Provincialate of the Society of Mary, Province of St. Louis.
Dwyer, Vincent *o.c.s.o.* '61 (WOR) [N] Spencer, MA St. Joseph's Abbey.
Dwyer, William M. '38 (SY) Retired.
Dy, Angel '69 (DOD) Great Bend, KS St. Rose of Lima Church.
Dybas, Richard W. '59 (ALB) [6] Cohoes, NY St. Michael Church.
Dybdal, Gerald '68 (OAK) Retired.
Dye, David M. '92 (ATL) Dunwoody, GA All Saints Catholic Church.
Dye, Robert M. '91 (TLS) Muskogee, OK Saint Joseph Church; Special Assignment.
Dyer, Donald L. '57 (STL) [4] Florissant, MO St. Christopher Church.
Dyer, Edward J. '41 (WOR) Retired.
Dyer, Francis X. *o.p.* '69 (CHI) [N] Chicago, IL Dominicans (Provincial Office).
Dyer, Gene J. '85 (CHI) [1] Des Plaines, IL St. Mary Church.
Dyer, George *o.p.* '61 (BIR) Guntersville, AL St. William's Church.
Dyer, George J. '53 (CHI) Wadsworth, IL St. Patrick Church; Retired; [X] Mundelein, IL Civitas Dei Foundation.
Dyer, James '97 (STL) Ellisville, MO St. Clare of Assisi Church.
Dyer, Joseph '74 (JKS) Oxford, MS St. John Church; [H] Oxford, MS University of Mississippi Newman Center.
Dyer, Raymond E. '46 (PRO) Retired.
Dyer, Thomas P. '69 (Y) [6] Canton, OH St. Joan of Arc Church.
Dyer, Msgr. Timothy J. '74 (LA) [20] Los Angeles, CA Nativity Church; [58] Los Angeles, CA St. Columbkille Church.
Dyer, William *m.afr.* '70 (FgM) Missionaries of Africa Foreign Missions.

Dykas, Benjamin '61 (ALT) [6] Johnstown, PA St. Columba's Church.
Dyke, Neil Van '98 (CHI) [24] Chicago, IL St. Bede the Venerable Church.
Dylag, Msgr. Michael R. '65 (GBG) On Duty Outside the Diocese.
Dymcwski, Thomas *o.ss.t.* '85 (BAL) [S] Baltimore, MD Holy Trinity Monastery.
Dymowski, Thomas H. *o.ss.t.* '73 (SAT) [A] San Antonio, TX The Assumption-St. John's Seminary.
Dymski, Daniel J. '60 (E) [11] Erie, PA Sacred Heart Church.
Dymski, J. Daniel '60 (E) Erie, PA Soldiers and Sailors Home.
Dynak, Waldemar '80 (CHI) [205] Chicago, IL St. Turibius Church.
Dyrcz, Michael S. '73 (CLV) [10] Cleveland, OH St. Barbara Church.
Dyrwal, Justin *o.s.b.* '98 (CLV) [D] Cleveland, OH Benedictine High School.
Dysinger, Luke *o.s.b.* '86 (LA) [Q] Valyermo, CA St. Andrew's Abbey.
Dytkowski, Louis M. '60 (BGP) [2] Stratford, CT St. James Church.
Dzankic, Zvonko *o.p.* '00 (CHI) [N] Chicago, IL Croatian Dominican Fathers.
Dzermejko, David F. '74 (PIT) [3] Charleroi, PA Mary Mother of the Church.
Dziadosz, Edward T. '55 (PH) Retired.
Dziedzic, Gerald H. '74 (HRT) Terryville, CT Immaculate Conception Church; Terryville, CT St. Casimir Church.
Dziedziejko, Edwin F. *o.f.m.cap.* '79 (MIL) [B] Mount Calvary, WI St. Lawrence Seminary; [P] Mount Calvary, WI St. Lawrence Friary.
Dzieglewicz, John T. *s.j.* '83 (NY) [DD] New York, NY Jesuit Community at Fordham University.
Dziekan, Wayne H. '94 (GAY) Northport, MI St. Gertrude Church; Suttons Bay, MI St. Michael the Archangel Church.
Dzielak, Msgr. Thomas L. '63 (RCK) Rock Falls, IL St. Andrew Church.
Dzien, Joseph Duc '83 (NO) [13] Metairie, LA St. Philip Neri Church.
Dzienkiewicz, Edwin '64 (PT) Retired.
Dzienkiewicz, Edwin '64 (TR) [L] Lawrenceville, NJ Morris Hall-Saint Lawrence, Inc.
Dzierzek, Zygmunt *o.m.i.* '42 (BEL) [F] Belleville, IL Shrine of Our Lady of the Snows.
Dzieszko, Thaddeus '88 (CHI) [3] Cicero, IL St. Mary of Czestochowa Church; [U] Chicago, IL Catholic League for Religious Assistance to Poland.
Dzikowski, Piotr *s.ch.* '87 (SEA) [7] Tacoma, WA SS. Peter & Paul Church.
Dziob, Msgr. Michael W. '42 (PRO) Retired; [P] Providence, RI St. John Vianney Residence.
Dziordz, Walter *m.i.c.* '84 (SPR) [J] Stockbridge, MA Congregation of Marians of The Immaculate Conception of the BVM; [J] Stockbridge, MA Congregation of Marians of The Immaculate Conception of the BVM.
Dziorek, Anthony *c.r.* '75 (CHI) [189] Chicago, IL St. Stanislaus, Bishop and Martyr Church.
Dzokapor, Vitalis D. (BRK) [181] Queens, NY Immaculate Conception Church.
Dzuban, Giles *o.c.d.* '44 (BO) [W] Boston, MA Carmelite Monastery.

E

Eades, B. G. '73 (DAL) Retired.
Eagan, Joseph *s.j.* '53 (SFR) Larkspur, CA St. Patrick Church.
Eagan, William *s.j.* '75 (PRT) [C] Portland, ME Cheverus High School.
Eagan, William J. '75 (PRT) [I] Portland, ME St. Ignatius Residence.
Eagle, Raphael *t.o.r.* '67 (FWT) [10] Fort Worth, TX St. George Church.
Eagleson, Donald W. '85 (SR) Eureka, CA Sacred Heart Church.
Earl, Marcellus R. *o.c.s.o.* '63 (ROC) [I] Piffard, NY Abbey of the Genesee.
Earl, Patrick F. *s.j.* '74 (BAL) [B] Baltimore, MD Loyola College in Maryland; [B] Baltimore, MD Loyola College in Maryland.
Earl, Patrick F. *s.j.* '74 (OAK) [N] Berkeley, CA Jesuit Community at Jesuit School of Theology at Berkeley.
Earley, Daniel J. *o.s.f.s.* '48 (TOL) [C] Toledo, OH St. Francis de Sales High School; [K] Toledo, OH Oblates of St. Francis de Sales.
Earley, Jerome *o.c.d.* '95 (SAT) [18] San Antonio, TX Basilica of The National Shrine of Our Lady of Mt. Carmel and St. Therese, Discalced Carmelite Fathers; [M] San Antonio, TX Discalced Carmelites (Prov. of St. Therese).
Earley, Kiernan *c.p.* '57 (HRT) [M] West Hartford, CT Holy Family Monastery/Retreat.
Earley, Philip B. '74 (BO) [DD] Boston, MA The Archdiocese of Boston Self-Insurance Group, Inc.
Earls, John Patrick *o.s.b.* '65 (SCL) [I] Collegeville, MN St. John's Abbey, of the Order of St. Benedict.
Early, Francis J. '85 (WDC) Bushwood, MD Sacred Heart Church.
Early, Jerome *o.c.d.* '95 (SAT) [T] San Antonio, TX Basilica of the National Shrine of the Little Flower.
Early, Joseph E. *m.m.* '39 (NY) [DD] Maryknoll, NY Maryknoll Fathers and Brothers.
Early, Philip B. '74 (BO) Wilmington, MA St. Thomas of Villanova Church.
Early, Msgr. Thomas C. '51 (ALX) Retired.
Early, William F. '68 (BRK) Absent on Sick Leave.
Earner, Thomas '62 (SP) Retired.
East, Msgr. Raymond G. '81 (WDC) [30] Washington, DC Nativity Church.
Easterling, William T. '82 (LA) Valinda, CA St. Martha Church.
Eastman, Patrick W. '84 (TLS) [3] Tulsa, OK St. Bernard of Clairvaux Church.
Easton, Msgr. Frederick C. '66 (IND) [19] Indianapolis, IN St. Gabriel the Archangel Church.
Easton, Msgr. William M. '70 (DET) Royal Oak, MI Shrine of the Little Flower Church.
Eaton, John *o.f.m.* '78 (SHP) Grambling, LA St. Benedict the Black Church; West Monroe, LA St. Paschal Church.
Ebach, Al *c.pp.s.* (KC) [19] Kansas City, MO St. James Church.
Ebach, Al *c.pp.s.* '74 (KC) [A] Kansas City, MO Gaspar Mission House.
Ebacher, Jerome *o.c.s.o.* '49 (P) [L] Lafayette, OR The Cistercian (Trappist) Abbey of Our Lady of Guadalupe.
Ebarb, Walter E. '62 (SAT) [59] San Antonio, TX St. Patrick Church.
Ebarb, Walter E. '62 (SHP) On Duty Outside the Diocese.
Ebben, Bertrand '59 (MEM) [23] Memphis, TN St. Peter's Church.
Ebben, Bertrand E. *o.p.* '59 (MEM) [I] Memphis, TN Order Of Preachers (Southern Dominican Prov.).
Ebbesmier, John '78 (PHX) [1] Glendale, AZ Our Lady of Perpetual Help Church; [A] Phoenix, AZ Bourgade Catholic High School.
Ebejer, George '47 (BRK) [125] Brooklyn, NY St. Rocco's Church; Retired.
Ebejer, Lino P. '91 (WH) Thomas, WV St. Thomas Aquinas Church.
Ebel, Stephen P. '70 (DAV) Le Claire-Princeton, IA Our Lady of the River Church; Long Grove, IA St. Ann's Church.
Ebenhoeh, John O. *o.s.f.s.* '64 (TOL) [C] Toledo, OH St. Francis de Sales High School; [K] Toledo, OH Oblates of St. Francis de Sales.
Eberhardy, William '77 (GB) Absent on Leave.
Eberle, Richard *o.s.f.s.* '82 (TOL) [27] Toledo, OH St. John the Baptist Church.
Eberly, Herbert *c.p.* '58 (FgM) Passionist Foreign Missions.
Ebert, Mark S. '76 (STL) [4] Lemay, MO St. Bernadette Church.
Ebey, Carl *c.s.c.* '72 (FTW) [B] Notre Dame, IN University of Notre Dame Du Lac.
Ebey, Carl F. *c.s.c.* '72 (FTW) [J] Notre Dame, IN Holy Cross Community, Corby Hall, University of Notre Dame.
Eble, Jr., James E. *m.m.* '88 (FgM) Maryknoll Foreign Missions.
Eblen, James '64 (SEA) [8] Seattle, WA St. Edward Church; [9] Seattle, WA St. George Church; [18] Seattle, WA St. Paul Church; Special Assignment.
Ebner, Frank '47 (SCL) Retired.
Ebrom, Robert L. '71 (CHI) Elk Grove Village, IL Queen of the Rosary Church.
Ebron, Jose Erlito (NEW) Kenilworth, NJ St. Theresa's Church.
Eburn, Brian '66 (STA) Crescent City, FL St. John the Baptist Church.
Eburuche, Eugene *s.m.m.m.* '95 (FTW) [4] Fort Wayne, IN St. Elizabeth Ann Seton Church; Fort Wayne, IN Lutheran Hospital.
Eccleston, John '55 (SCL) Special Assignment; [J] Little Falls, MN St. Francis Convent.
Echeandia, Jesus *c.p.* '59 (SJN) [46] San Juan, PR Nuestra Senora de la Piedad Church.
Echert, John '87 (STP) [A] St. Paul, MN The Saint Paul Seminary; [C] St. Paul, MN University of St. Thomas.
Echevarria, Jose Miguel *m.ss.cc.* '95 (SJN) Rio Grande, PR Nuestra Senora del Carmen Church.
Echevarria, Pedro Faustino '84 (PCE) Jayuya, PR Our Lady of Monserrate Church.
Echevarria, Roberto Garcia '82 (PCE) Patillas, PR Inmaculado Corazon de Maria Church.
Echevarria, Wilfredo *o.ss.t.* '81 (ARE) Isabela, PR St. Anthony Church.
Echeverria, Miguel *o.a.r.* '61 (LSC) Anthony, NM St. Anthony's Church.
Echevia, Les Suberi '61 (RCK) Virgil, IL SS. Peter and Paul Church.
Echle, Msgr. Harry A. '42 (WDC) [35] Washington, DC Our Lady of Victory Church; Retired.
Eck, Gregory J. *s.j.* '99 (WDC) [E] North Bethesda, MD Georgetown Preparatory School.
Eck, Ivan C. '51 (WCH) Mount Vernon, KS St. Rose Church; Ost, KS St. Joseph Church; Waterloo, KS St. Louis Church.
Eck, John E. *c.s.v.* '63 (CHI) [206] Chicago, IL St. Viator Church.
Eck, Reinhard C. '50 (WCH) Andale, KS St. Joseph Church.
Eckard, John A. '00 (BAL) [49] Baltimore, MD St. Joseph Church.
Eckart, Frank E. '69 (TOL) [8] Toledo, OH Holy Rosary Church.
Eckart, Frank K. '69 (TOL) [14] Toledo, OH Sacred Heart of Jesus Church; [39] Toledo, OH St. Stephen Church.
Eckart, Placidus *o.s.b.* '49 (LR) Scranton, AR St. Ignatius Church.
Eckberg, Joseph A. '00 (WCH) [12] Wichita, KS St. Elizabeth Ann Seton Church.
Eckelkamp, David *o.f.m.* '53 (STL) Oakville, MO St. Francis of Assisi Church; [P] Oakville, MO St. Francis Friary.
Eckenrod, Edward L. '78 (ALT) [11] Altoona, PA Our Lady of Lourdes Church; Altoona, PA Altoona Hospital.
Ecker, Msgr. John A. '58 (YAK) [1] Yakima, WA St. Paul Church.
Ecker, Msgr. Robert J. '51 (BRK) Released from Diocesan Assignment; Retired.
Eckermann, Msgr. Charles H. '56 (SY) Manlius, NY St. Ann Church.
Eckert, Carl E. '54 (LFT) Retired.
Eckert, John C. '72 (PH) Morrisville, PA Holy Trinity Church.
Eckert, Sidney J. '66 (DET) [5] Livonia, MI St. Maurice Church.
Eckert, William F. '64 (CAM) Retired.
Eckert, William F. '64 (SPR) [8] Pittsfield, MA St. Mark's Church; Retired.
Eckhoff, Evan *o.f.m.* '57 (KNX) [F] Mountain City, TN Franciscan Friars.
Eckinger, Ambrose *o.p.* '81 (COL) [36] Columbus, OH St. Patrick Church.
Eckley, Michael P. '91 (OM) Battle Creek, NE St. Patrick's Church.
Eckman, Mark A. '85 (PIT) Brentwood, PA St. Sylvester Church.
Eckrich, James P. '53 (WIL) Nursing Homes.
Eckroth, Leonard A. '58 (BIS) Hague, ND St. Mary Church; Strasburg, ND Sts. Peter and Paul Church.
Eckroth, Richard *o.s.b.* '52 (SCL) [I] Collegeville, MN St. John's Abbey, of the Order of St. Benedict.
Eckstein, Francis '58 (IND) New Marion, IN St. Magdalen Church; Osgood, IN St. John Church; St. Denis, IN St. Denis Church.
Eckstein, Frank '58 (IND) Millhousen, IN Immaculate Conception Church.
Eco, Roy V. '80 (OAK) Union City, CA Our Lady of the Rosary Church; [K] Hayward, CA St. Rose Hospital.
Edamattan, Thomas '66 (RVC) Huntington, NY St. Patrick's Church; Huntington, NY Huntington Hospital.
Edapaddy, Thomas *c.m.i.* '64 (LAF) Coteau Holmes, LA St. Elizabeth Church.
Edassery, Mathew '74 (TYL) Canton, TX St. Therese Church.
Edayadiyil, Jose '73 (SCL) Isanti, MN St. Elizabeth Ann Seton Church.
Eddy, Corbin *s.t.l.* (BAL) [A] Baltimore, MD St. Mary's Seminary and University.
Eddy, William A. '75 (CHI) Chicago Heights, IL St. Kieran Church.
Edelen, Luke A. *o.s.b.* '80 (NEW) [N] Newark, NJ Newark Abbey.
Edelen, Richard D. '75 (LEX) Beattyville, KY Queen of All Saints Church.
Eden, Timothy *s.m.* (HON) [G] Honolulu, HI Marianist Communities.
Eder, Donald '54 (LAN) Retired.
Eder, Donald '60 (LFT) Oxford, IN St. Patrick Church.
Ederer, John '77 (SAG) Vassar, MI St. Frances Xavier Cabrini Church.
Edgerly, Leo J., Jr. '84 (OAK) Piedmont, CA Corpus Christi Church.
Ediza, Manuel '79 (SD) [29] San Diego, CA St. John the Evangelist Church; San Diego, CA Children's Hospital; San Diego, CA Sharp Memorial Hospital.
Edmiston, James *o.f.m.* '98 (SFD) [B] Quincy, IL Quincy University.
Edmonds, Stephen B. *m.m.* '40 (FgM) Maryknoll Foreign Missions.
Edmunds, Garrett *o.f.m.* '82 (PHX) [19] Phoenix, AZ St. Mary's Basilica Church.
Edmunds, John *s.t.* '76 (NEW) [10] Jersey City, NJ Christ, the King Church.
Edogwo, Linus V. '86 (NEW) [23] Newark, NJ St. Mary's Church.
Edomobi, Eustace '75 (NEW) [5] Newark, NJ St. Antoninus Church; Newark, NJ University of Medicine & Dentistry.
Edrich, Paul J. '54 (CIN) [45] Cincinnati, OH St. John Vianney Church.
Eduarte, Edmund '93 (GAL) [1] Houston, TX Sacred

Heart Co-Church.
Eduvala, Andre *o.f.m.cap.* (AGN) [F] Agana Heights, GU St. Fidelis Friary.
Edwards, Bill '85 (OG) Burke, NY St. George Church; Malone, NY Franklin Correctional Facility.
Edwards, Brice '70 (WOR) [N] Shrewsbury, MA Calvery Retreat Center, Passionist Fathers of Shrewsbury, Inc.
Edwards, Byron H. '87 (SPC) Retired.
Edwards, Charles A. '86 (SFD) Camp Point, IL St. Thomas Church; Liberty, IL St. Brigid Church; [D] Quincy, IL Quincy Notre Dame High School.
Edwards, Cyril D. '84 (SCR) [1] Freeland, PA St. Ann's Church.
Edwards, Dale '83 (FWT) Retired.
Edwards, Edward M. *o.s.m.* '83 (CHI) [N] Chicago, IL Order of Friar Servants of Mary (Servites) United States of America Province, Inc.
Edwards, Edward M. *o.s.m.* '83 (MET) [I] Watchung, NJ Mount St. Mary.
Edwards, J. Daniel '94 (LAF) Richard, LA St. Edward Church.
Edwards, James F. '61 (ORL) Retired.
Edwards, James T. '76 (STL) Normandy, MO St. Ann Church.
Edwards, John F. '55 (HRT) Wethersfield, CT Incarnation Church.
Edwards, John H. *s.j.* '54 (NO) [P] New Orleans, LA Ignatius Residence.
Edwards, Michael W. '79 (PMB) Vero Beach, FL St. Helen Church.
Edwards, Paul '83 (MIA) [9] Fort Lauderdale, FL St. Jerome Church.
Edwards, Philip *o.s.b.* '67 (LA) [Q] Valyermo, CA St. Andrew's Abbey; [W] Valyermo, CA St. Andrew's Abbey Retreat House (All Groups).
Edwards, Robert '81 (Y) Lisbon, OH St. George Church.
Edwards, Roy D. '46 (LAF) Retired.
Edwards, Thomas '90 (OAK) [2] Oakland, CA St. Andrew-St. Joseph Church.
Edwards, Thomas L. '58 (ALN) Retired.
Edwards, Tom J. (OAK) [21] Oakland, CA Sacred Heart Church.
Edwin, Rex '95 (CI) Kolonia, FM Our Lady of Mercy Church.
Edyk, Msgr. Eugene '61 (DET) [3] Clinton Twp., MI St. Paul of Tarsus Church.
Edyvean, Msgr. Walter J. '64 (BO) On Duty Outside the Archdiocese.
Eelman, William C. '53 (TR) Retired.
Eftink, Msgr. Edward M. '66 (SPC) Jackson, MO Immaculate Conception Church.
Eftink, Glenn A. '93 (SPC) Glennonville, MO St. Teresa Church; Malden, MO St. Ann Church.
Egan, Anthony *o.f.m.cap.* '65 (PRT) [3] Portland, ME St. Joseph's Church.
Egan, Arthur '57 (CLV) Retired.
Egan, Arthur B. '57 (CLV) Avon, OH St. Mary of the Immaculate Conception Church.
Egan, Bartholomew *c.s.sp.* '59 (BRK) [178] Queens, NY Holy Family Church.
Egan, Brennan *o.f.m.* '65 (NY) [FF] Wappingers Falls, NY Mt. Alvernia Retreat House.
Egan, Brian *v.a.* '50 (BIR) [17] Birmingham, AL Our Lady of Sorrows Church; On Special or Other Diocesan Assignment; [I] Birmingham, AL Catholic Housing of Birmingham, Inc.
Egan, Brian J. '87 (WCH) Hutchinson, KS Holy Cross Church; [L] Wichita, KS Serra Club of Reno County.
Egan, Charles *c.s.s.* '46 (BO) [Z] Waltham, MA Stigmatine Fathers and Brothers.
Egan, Daniel *s.a.* '45 (NY) [HH] Barryville, NY New Hope Manor.
Egan, Msgr. Edward F. '41 (PRO) Retired; [P] Providence, RI St. John Vianney Residence.
Egan, Msgr. Eugene E. '54 (WIN) Retired.
Egan, George A. *m.m.* '55 (NY) [DD] Maryknoll, NY Maryknoll Fathers and Brothers.
Egan, Gerard P. '65 (CHI) Other Assignments.
Egan, Harvey D. *s.j.* '69 (BO) [W] Chestnut Hill, MA The Jesuit Community at Boston College.
Egan, Harvey F. '41 (STP) Retired.
Egan, James A. *s.j.* '65 (FgM) Provinces.
Egan, James A. *s.j.* '65 (MIL) [P] Milwaukee, WI Jesuit Provincial Office, Wisconsin Province.
Egan, Msgr. John J. '43 (CHI) [1] Chicago, IL Cathedral of the Holy Name; Retired.
Egan, John Martin *o.p.* '56 (WDC) [B] Washington, DC Dominican House of Studies.
Egan, Joseph M. '42 (ROC) Retired.
Egan, Patrick '66 (LAN) [O] Ann Arbor, MI Catholic Men's Movement.
Egan, Philip '82 (KC) [22] Kansas City, MO St. Monica Church.
Egan, Richmond J. *s.m.* '67 (ATL) [C] Atlanta, GA Marist School.
Egan, Robert '51 (ROC) Retired.
Egan, Robert J. *s.j.* '62 (SEA) [L] Seattle, WA Jesuit House, Seattle.
Egan, Robert J. *s.j.* '73 (SPK) [C] Spokane, WA Gonzaga University.
Egan, Robert M. '78 (CHI) [N] Chicago, IL Viatorian Residence; [N] Arlington Heights, IL Clerics of St. Viator-Provincial Residence; [N] Arlington Heights, IL Viatorian Mission House.
Egan, Thomas F. '75 (WOR) [2] Leominster, MA Holy Family of Nazareth Church.
Egan, Thomas R. *m.m.* '64 (FgM) Maryknoll Foreign Missions.
Egbeji, Jude '96 (NY) [17] New York, NY St. Bernard Church.
Egbers, James B. '96 (COV) Fort Thomas, KY St. Catherine of Siena Church.
Egbulem, Nwaka Chris *o.p.* '97 (BAL) [W] Baltimore, MD Catholic Community at Relay.
Egegl, Christian Paul '72 (SAC) Citrus Heights, CA Holy Family Church.
Egert, Clifford A. '38 (DAV) Retired; [M] Davenport, IA St. Vincent Center.
Eggerling, Milton '54 (BO) [W] Boston, MA The Society of St. James the Apostle, Inc.; [BB] Boston, MA St. Stephen.
Eggerling, Milton '54 (FgM) Society of St. James the Apostle.
Eggerling, Milton '54 (OAK) Retired.
Eggert, Charles M. '38 (STP) Retired.
Eggert, Francis X. '58 (SFE) [8] Albuquerque, NM Our Lady of Fatima Church.
Egging, Martin L. '93 (GI) Chappell, NE St. Joseph's Church.
Eggleston, Earl '96 (SD) Encinitas, CA St. John the Evangelist Church.
Eggleton, Christopher T. *o.p.* '88 (BR) Hammond, LA Holy Ghost Church.
Egierd, Henry A. '80 (MET) Retired.
Egitto, Philip J. '88 (ORL) Daytona Beach, FL Our Lady of Lourdes Church.
Egloff, Adolph '40 (EVN) Retired.
Eglsaer, Harry S. *s.j.* '51 (OM) [K] Omaha, NE Jesuit Community at Creighton University.
Ego, Anthony M. '85 (PEO) Chillicothe, IL St. Edward's Church.
Eguiguren, Jose' Martin '67 (CGS) [5] Caguas, PR Santisimo Sacramento Church.
Eguino, Desiderio *o.p.* '78 (MIA) [18] Miami, FL St. Dominic Church; [H] Miami, FL Dominican Fathers of Miami, Inc.
Egurrola, Vicente '46 (SJN) [44] San Juan, PR Santos Pedro y Pablo los Apostoles Church; Retired.
Ehalt, William L. '99 (IND) Madison, IN Prince of Peace Church; Vevay, IN Most Sorrowful Mother of God Church; [C] Madison, IN Shawe Memorial Junior-Senior High School; [N] Madison, IN Hanover College Newman Center.
Ehiemere, Michael O. '81 (CHY) Thermopolis, WY St. Francis Church.
Ehmann, Benedict A. '29 (ROC) Retired.
Ehmke, Lyle *o.s.c.* '70 (STP) [N] Anoka, MN Crosier Community of Anoka.
Ehr, Donald J. *s.v.d.* '55 (CHI) [15] Chicago, IL St. Anselm Church.
Ehrens, Richard J. '58 (CHI) Harwood Heights, IL St. Rosalie Church.
Ehrhardt, Joseph B. *o.f.m.* '76 (FgM) Franciscan Foreign Missions.
Ehrhardt, Philip *o.m.i.* '27 (FgM) Oblates Foreign Missions.
Ehrhart, Charles '60 (RVC) Priests Released from Diocesan Assignment.
Ehrich, John T. '00 (PHX) [25] Phoenix, AZ St. Thomas the Apostle Church.
Ehrman, Dale *o.s.c.* '90 (STP) [N] Shoreview, MN Crosier Community of Shoreview.
Ehrman, Terrence P. *c.s.c.* '00 (FTW) [6] South Bend, IN Christ the King Church.
Ehwald, Joseph A. '62 (COL) Reynoldsburg, OH St. Pius X Church.
Eichenberger, Thomas '76 (MIL) [85] Milwaukee, WI St. Veronica Church.
Eichenseer, Msgr. Donald W. '61 (BEL) [8] Belleville, IL St. Teresa of the Child Jesus Church.
Eichhoff, Paul E. '70 (TLS) Claremore, OK St. Cecilia Church.
Eichhorst, Franklin *o.f.m.cap.* '57 (LSC) Lovington, NM St. Thomas Aquinas Church.
Eichner, Philip K. *s.m.* '66 (RVC) [D] Uniondale, NY Kellenberg Memorial High School; [M] Mineola, NY Provincial Residence and Novitiate.
Eichor, Msgr. Edward C. '59 (STL) [A] St. Louis, MO Kenrick-Glennon Seminary.
Eichorn, Harry B. *c.s.c.* '57 (FR) [A] North Easton, MA Stonehill College; [A] North Easton, MA Holy Cross Fathers Religious.
Eickhoff, Jeffrey R. '95 (LIN) Graduate Studies.
Eickhoff, Mathew F. '89 (LIN) Brainard, NE Holy Trinity Church.
Eickholt, Henry C. '44 (SAG) Retired.
Eid, Frederick M. '47 (NEW) [1] Hoboken, NJ Our Lady of Grace Church; Retired.
Eidenschenk, John *o.s.b.* '41 (SCL) [I] Collegeville, MN St. John's Abbey, of the Order of St. Benedict.
Eidt, Joao Ramon *s.j.* '98 (CHI) [N] Chicago, IL Miguel Pro Jesuit Community.
Eifler, John G. '61 (L) [26] Louisville, KY St. Frances of Rome Church.
Eigo, Francis A. *o.s.a.* '64 (PH) [C] Villanova, PA Villanova University; [AA] Villanova, PA St. Thomas Monastery.
Eikens, Leroy F. '62 (WIN) Retired.
Eikhuenelo, Bernadine '96 (PIT) [56] Pittsburgh, PA St. Mary of the Mount Church.
Eikmeier, Msgr. Bernard J. '51 (HON) Retired.
Eilerman, Craig R. '87 (COL) [9] Columbus, OH St. Cecilia Church.
Eilerman, William *c.pp.s.* '51 (CIN) Wapakoneta, OH St. Joseph Church.
Eilers, Joseph B. '49 (STL) Retired.
Eilert, Msgr. Edward J. '64 (NEW) Livingston, NJ St. Philomena Church.
Eimer, Frank J. '58 (L) Jeffersontown, KY St. Edward Church.
Einck, Gregory J. '44 (DUB) Retired.
Eis, Charles '66 (SPK) Retired.
Eisel, Howard P. *s.s.c.* '54 (DUL) Crosby, MN St. Joseph's Church.
Eisele, Francis X. '66 (RVC) West Islip, NY Our Lady of Lourdes Church.
Eisele, James F. '88 (LAN) [1] Flint, MI St. Agnes Church.
Eisele, Paul F. '68 (SC) Bode, IA St. Joseph's Church.
Eisemann, Frederick F. '53 (ROC) [21] Rochester, NY Holy Cross Church.
Eisler, Msgr. Rudolph '63 (NY) Pearl River, NY St. Margaret Church.
Eisweirth, Thomas '74 (Y) [7] Youngstown, OH Sacred Heart of Jesus Church; Salem, OH St. Paul's Church.
Eivers, Msgr. Michael '55 (MIA) Pembroke Pines, FL St. Edward Church.
Ejifor, Pius (NY) Staten Island, NY Staten Island University Hospital South.
Ejimadu, Festus '93 (DET) Romulus, MI St. Aloysius Church.
Ejimofor, Frances '90 (CLV) [3] Akron, OH St. Bernard Church.
Ekanachi, Donatus (LA) [82] Los Angeles, CA St. Michael Church.
Ekanem, Anthony *m.s.p.* '89 (GAL) Barrett Station, TX St. Martin de Porres Church.
Ekdahl, Kenneth W. '91 (TR) Keansburg, NJ St. Ann Church.
Eke, Casimir *c.s.sp.* '74 (CHI) [55] Chicago, IL St. Felicitas Church.
Ekemgba, Fidelis '81 (BRK) [90] Brooklyn, NY St. Nicholas Church.
Ekiert, Iraneusz *o.ss.t.* (WDC) [M] Hyattsville, MD St. John de Matha Monastery, Order of Most Holy Trinity.
Ekpo, Joseph '86 (CHI) Bellwood, IL St. Simeon Church; [D] Oak Park, IL Fenwick High School.
Eksterowicz, Frank C. '85 (BUR) Richford, VT All Saints Church.
El-Bacha, Assaad *m.l.m.* '92 (OLL) Lewisville, TX Our Lady of Lebanon Church; [A] Houston, TX The Congregation of Maronite Lebanese Missionaries.
El-Hayek, Nehmatallah '62 (SAM) Retired.
El-Khalli, Georges '81 (SAM) Williamsville, NY St. John Maron Church.
El-Thom, Gregory *b.c.o.* '93 (NTN) Warren, MI Our Lady of Redemption Church.
Elam, Raymond *o.s.a.* '70 (P) Grand Ronde, OR St. Michael Church; Sheridan, OR Good Shepherd Church; [L] Sheridan, OR Augustinian Community.
Elambassery, Xavier '66 (SJP) Latrobe, PA Assumption of B.V.M. Church.
Elamparayil, Joseph *o.c.d.* '96 (ALN) [3] Easton, PA St. Jane Frances de Chantal Church.
Elanjileth, John M. '45 (ROM) McKeesport, PA St. Mary Church.
Elanjileth, John M. '50 (PIT) Allegheny County, PA McKeesport Hospital.
Elbert, William '73 (MIA) North Miami Beach, FL St. Lawrence Church.
Elder, Jerome C. '57 (LA) [4] Long Beach, CA St. Bartholomew Church.
Elder, John W. *s.j.* '65 (BGP) [B] Fairfield, CT Fairfield University; [P] Fairfield, CT The Fairfield Jesuit Community-Fairfield University.
Elder, Leonard F. *s.c.j.* '96 (GAL) [21] Houston, TX Christ the Redeemer Church.
Elder, William S. '81 (NY) [62] New York, NY St. Joseph Church.
Eldred, Richard '99 (IND) Mooresville, IN St. Thomas More Church.
Eldredge, Richard *t.o.r.* '78 (FWT) Megargel, TX St. Mary Church; Seymour, TX Sacred Heart Church.
Eldridge, Francis *s.a.* '77 (R) Apex, NC St. Andrew the Apostle Church.
Eldridge, Frank *s.a.* '77 (NY) [DD] Garrison, NY Franciscan Friars of the Atonement, Minister General Office.
Eldringhoff, John P. (KC) Retired.
Elejalde, Manuel *c.p.* '49 (SJN) [9] Carolina, PR Santa Gema Galgani Church.

Eles, Joseph '65 (PSC) Retired.
Elewaut, Thomas J. *c.j.* '86 (LA) [B] Santa Maria, CA St. Joseph Seminary (Josephite Fathers' Novitiate); [D] Santa Maria, CA St. Joseph High School.
Elford, Ricardo *c.ss.r.* '64 (DEN) [M] Denver, CO The Redemptorists/Denver Province.
Eli, Jude *o.p.* '76 (OAK) [N] Oakland, CA Dominican Order (Western Province), St. Albert's Priory; [N] Oakland, CA Western Dominican Province.
Elia, Faouzi Y. '77 (OLL) Peoria, IL St. Sharbel Church.
Elia, Victor *c.m.* '57 (NY) [44] New York, NY Holy Agony Church; [DD] New York, NY Vincentian Fathers.
Elias, Woodrow '43 (DM) Retired.
Elias-Haddix, Ralph *o.c.d.* '98 (MIL) [26] Milwaukee, WI St. Florian Church.
Elis, Patrick H. '69 (BUF) Cassadaga, NY Immaculate Conception Church; Sinclairville, NY St. John the Evangelist Church.
Elis, Tomas A. '70 (LA) South El Monte, CA Epiphany Church.
Elizondo, Ernesto '00 (AUS) [26] Austin, TX San Jose Church.
Elizondo, Eusebio *m.sp.s.* '84 (SEA) Bothell, WA St. Elizabeth Ann Seton Church.
Elizondo, Virgil '63 (SAT) [64] San Antonio, TX St. Rose of Lima Church.
Elkin, Fredic F. '77 (SY) Military Chaplains.
Elko, Joseph M. '70 (HRT) [13] New Haven, CT Saint Martin de Porres Church.
Eller, Hugh *o.f.m.* '53 (PRO) [P] Providence, RI St. Francis Friary.
Ellerman, Thomas *s.m.* '61 (NO) [C] New Orleans, LA Our Lady of Holy Cross College.
Ellias, John J. (ALT) Retired.
Ellifritz, Robert Michael '67 (COL) [40] Columbus, OH St. Timothy Church.
Ellinghausen, Jude T. '58 (DET) North Branch, MI SS. Peter and Paul Church.
Elliott, Edward C. '44 (MEM) Retired.
Elliott, James '99 (SEA) [31] Seattle, WA Our Lady of Mount Virgin Church; Renton, WA St. Anthony Church.
Elliott, Joseph *c.ss.r.* '49 (LA) Whittier, CA St. Mary of the Assumption Church; [Q] Whittier, CA Redemptorist Fathers Mission House.
Elliott, Joseph W. '71 (OG) Brownville, NY Immaculate Conception of the B.V.M. Church.
Elliott, Patrick H. '00 (SLC) [1] Salt Lake City, UT Cathedral of the Madeleine.
Elliott, Msgr. Peter J. '73 (WDC) [V] Silver Spring, MD Catholics Committed to Support the Pope.
Elliott, Roger *c.p.* '58 (SCR) [2] Scranton, PA St. Ann's Basilica Church; [M] Scranton, PA Saint Ann's Passionist Monastery.
Elliott, Thomas *c.s.c.* '67 (BGP) [J] Bridgeport, CT St. Vincent's Medical Center.
Elliott, Thomas Allen '99 (LR) [2] Little Rock, AR St. Anne Church; [7] Little Rock, AR Immaculate Conception Church.
Elliott, Thomas F. *c.s.c.* '67 (FTW) [J] South Bend, IN Congregation of Holy Cross, Indiana Province, Provincial House.
Elliott, Timothy P. '82 (STL) Josephville, MO St. Joseph Church.
Elliott, Trumie Culpepper '88 (L) Samuels, KY St. Gregory Church.
Elliott, W. Gregg '00 (TLS) Bartlesville, OK St. John's Church.
Elliott, Msgr. William '60 (SD) Retired.
Elliott, William *o.m.i.* '61 (AUS) [7] Austin, TX Our Lady of Guadalupe Church.
Elliott, William J. *s.j.* '61 (WDC) [E] North Bethesda, MD Georgetown Preparatory School.
Ellis, Alfred J. *o.s.a.* '63 (BO) Andover, MA St. Augustine Church.
Ellis, John H.R. '91 (VEN) Holmes Beach, FL St. Bernard's Church.
Ellis, Kail C. *o.s.a.* '67 (PH) [C] Villanova, PA Villanova University; [AA] Villanova, PA St. John Stone Friary.
Ellis, Matthew '88 (DET) Absent on Leave.
Ellison, Joseph *c.ss.r.* '39 (ALB) [L] Saratoga Springs, NY St. John Neumann Residence.
Ellos, William J. *s.j.* '68 (MIL) [P] Milwaukee, WI Jesuit Provincial Office, Wisconsin Province.
Ellspermann, Camillus *o.s.b.* '50 (EVN) Ferdinand, IN St. Henry Church.
Ellspermann, Camillus *o.s.b.* '50 (IND) [J] St. Meinrad, IN St. Meinrad Archabbey.
Elmer, Msgr. Charles '52 (AUS) On Duty Outside the Diocese.
Elmer, Gregory *o.s.b.* '76 (LA) [Q] Valyermo, CA St. Andrew's Abbey.
Elmer, John *o.f.m. conv.* (L) Pleasure Ridge Park, KY St. Paul Church.
Elmer, Richard J. *c.s.b.* '57 (DET) [E] Redford, MI Catholic Central High School.
Elmer, Timothy '73 (SY) Chittenango, NY St. Patrick Church.
Elmlinger, Msgr. Herbert '42 (FRS) Retired.
Elmo, Francis E. '63 (NY) Absent on Leave.
Elo, Richard *c.pp.s.* '63 (CIN) [B] Carthagena, OH St. Charles.
Elorriaga, Javier *o.ss.t.* '68 (SJN) [13] Bayamon, PR Ascension Del Senor Church.
Elsasser, Thomas G. '88 (CLV) Middleburg Heights, OH St. Bartholomew Church.
Elsbernd, Elmer *s.v.d.* '65 (FgM) Society of the Divine Word Foreign Missions.
Elsbernd, James H. '90 (CIN) On Special and Archdiocesan Assignment.
Elsemann, Frederick F. '53 (ROC) Retired.
Elsen, Vincent *o.f.m.* (FWT) Colleyville, TX Good Shepherd Church.
Elsen, Vincent *o.f.m.* '47 (FWT) [12] Fort Worth, TX St. Mary of the Assumption Church; [I] Crowley, TX St. Maximilian Kolbe Friary.
Elser, William '86 (LR) Barling, AR Sacred Heart of Mary Church; Fort Smith, AR St. Boniface Church.
Elshoff, Matthew *o.f.m.cap.* '82 (LA) [F] La Canada Flintridge, CA St. Francis High School.
Elsinghorst, Francis X. *s.j.* '54 (NY) [DD] New York, NY Murray-Weigel Hall.
Elskamp, Frederick J. '62 (JC) [1] Jefferson City, MO St. Joseph Church.
Elsner, Martin L. *s.j.* '62 (SAT) [17] San Antonio, TX Our Lady of Guadalupe Church.
Elston, Joseph '85 (SCR) Avoca, PA St. Mary's Church.
Elworthy, Joseph *c.ss.r.* '39 (BLX) [E] Biloxi, MS St. John Neumann Residence.
Ely, Peter B. *s.j.* '69 (SEA) [A] Seattle, WA Seattle University.
Elzi, Joseph A. *c.m.* '52 (CHL) [3] Greensboro, NC St. Mary Church.
Emanuel, John '92 (TUC) Willcox, AZ Sacred Heart Church; Willcox, AZ Federal Prison Camp; Fort Grant Rural Station, AZ Fort Grant Training Center.
Emanuel, Steven D. '93 (OM) Columbus, NE St. Isidore Church; [B] Columbus, NE Scotus Central Catholic High School.
Emechete, Innocent '72 (SAC) Vacaville, CA California Medical Facility.
Emeli, Edwin (NY) [125] Bronx, NY St. Ann Church.
Emerick, David *s.c.j.* '86 (MIL) [P] Hales Corners, WI Priests of the Sacred Heart.
Emerick, Hydo *c.m.* '50 (MET) [H] Plainsboro, NJ Vincentian Residence.
Emerick, Stephen J. '58 (CIN) [L] Cincinnati, OH Mercy Franciscan Senior Health and Housing Services Inc. dba Mercy St. Theresa Center.
Emerling, James R. '53 (HRT) Retired.
Emerson, George F. '56 (BO) [4] Framingham, MA St. Stephen Church.
Emerson, Richard A. '78 (GRY) Munster, IN St. Thomas More Church.
Emerson, Robert F. '55 (JOL) [I] Naperville, IL St. John Vianney Villa.
Emery, Robert E. '87 (NEW) Weehawken, NJ St. Lawrence's Church.
Emezie, Charles '83 (SFS) [D] Aberdeen, SD Avera St. Luke's; [D] Aberdeen, SD Avera St. Luke's.
Emge, John P. '50 (EVN) Retired.
Emling, Marion J. *o.s.b.* '78 (GBG) [H] Latrobe, PA Saint Vincent Archabbey.
Emmanuel, Joseph (NY) Tuckahoe, NY Assumption Church.
Emmanuel, Joseph '81 (NY) Tuckahoe, NY Immaculate Conception Church.
Emmons, Rayford E. '74 (PH) [55] Philadelphia, PA St. Helena Church; Graduate Studies.
Emo, Eugene '61 (ROC) Absent on Leave.
Emon, Neil *o.s.c.* '67 (PHX) [G] Phoenix, AZ Crosier Community of Phoenix (Canons Regular of the Order of the Holy Cross).
Emon, Neil J. *o.s.c.* '67 (DET) [K] Riverview, MI Crosier Community of Riverview.
Emperur, James L. *s.j.* '65 (SAT) [1] San Antonio, TX Cathedral of San Fernando.
Emrisek, Gene J. *o.f.m.cap.* '68 (DEN) [3] Denver, CO Annunciation Church; [M] Denver, CO Annunciation Friary.
Emuwen, Victor (NY) [63] New York, NY St. Joseph of the Holy Family Church.
Enciso, Jesus A. '75 (NEW) Lodi, NJ St. Francis de Sales Church.
Endebrock, Msgr. Donald M. '51 (MET) [1] Carteret, NJ St. Joseph Church; Retired.
Endebrock, Msgr. John J. '38 (TR) Avon, NJ St. Elizabeth Church; Retired.
Endejan, John H. '57 (MIL) [1] Milwaukee, WI St. John Church; [Y] Milwaukee, WI Cathedral Preservation Foundation, Inc.
Enderle, Gilbert A. *c.ss.r.* '62 (SAT) [19] San Antonio, TX Our Lady Of Perpetual Help Church; [C] San Antonio, TX Oblate School of Theology; [M] San Antonio, TX Redemptorists of Texas-San Antonio #1.
Enderlin, E. E. '69 (PEO) Raritan, IL Church of St. Patrick.
Enderlin, Joseph J. '46 (LR) Bella Vista, AR St. Bernard Church.
Enderlin, R. E. '69 (PEO) Monmouth, IL Immaculate Conception Church.
Enders, Robert F. '39 (MIL) Retired.
Endres, Gilbert J. '52 (STP) Retired.
Endres, James F. '82 (PH) Warminster, PA Nativity of Our Lord Church; [D] Warminster, PA Archbishop Wood Catholic High School.
Endres, John C. *s.j.* '76 (OAK) [A] Berkeley, CA The Jesuit School of Theology at Berkeley; [N] Berkeley, CA Jesuit Community at Jesuit School of Theology at Berkeley.
Endres, William '82 (ROC) Rochester, NY Rochester General Hospital/Via Health.
Endress, James R. '60 (EVN) Special Assignment.
Enette, Rawlin B. *s.s.j.* '59 (GAL) [68] Houston, TX St. Peter Claver Church.
Engbarth, David R. '76 (RCK) [9] Aurora, IL Sacred Heart Church.
Engbers, Thomas J. '67 (MIA) Miami Shores, FL St. Martha Church.
Engbers, William J. '39 (IND) St. Nicholas, IN St. Nicholas Church; Retired.
Engel, John '54 (P) Retired.
Engel, Paul '55 (ALB) Retired.
Engel, Paul *o.f.m.cap.* '64 (NY) [DD] White Plains, NY St. Conrad Friary.
Engel, Ronald '77 (MIL) [85] Milwaukee, WI St. Veronica Church.
Engelbrecht, Msgr. Henry H. '68 (NO) [36] New Orleans, LA St. Henry Church.
Engelbrecht, Scott S. '00 (PEO) [4] Champaign, IL St. Matthew Church.
Engelen, R. J. '30 (ALX) Retired.
Engelhardt, Charles F. *o.s.f.s.* '77 (PH) [101] Philadelphia, PA Mater Dolorosa Church.
Engelhardt, Msgr. Herbert G. '40 (BUF) Retired.
Engelhart, Henry R. '63 (BEL) Fairfield, IL St. Edward Church; St. Sebastian, IL St. Sebastian Church.
Engelhart, William '70 (JKS) Retired.
Engels, Francis C. '62 (PEO) Absent on Leave.
Engels, Richard J. '60 (WIN) Retired.
Engen, Bruce '89 (DUL) Deer River, MN St. Mary's Church.
Engh, Michael E. *s.j.* '81 (LA) [C] Los Angeles, CA Loyola Marymount University.
England, Barry C. '68 (FTW) [1] Mishawaka, IN St. Bavo Church.
Engle, Richard F. '56 (COL) Retired.
Engler, Clarence A. *m.m.* '59 (FgM) Maryknoll Foreign Missions.
Engler, Ernest J. '51 (DUB) Mount Vernon, IA St. John's the Baptist Church; Retired.
Engler, Simon *t.o.r.* '49 (ALT) [F] Loretto, PA Mount Assisi Friary.
Englert, Anthony A. '87 (CHI) [143] Chicago, IL Our Lady of Fatima Church; [S] Chicago, IL Kolping Center.
Englert, James '78 (SFS) On Leave of Absence.
Englert, Michael *o.f.m.conv.* '89 (BAL) [S] Ellicott City, MD Order of Friars Minor Conventual.
Englert, Wilfred '86 (EVN) Dubois, IN St. Raphael Church.
Englert, William J. '53 (CLV) Fairport Harbor, OH St. Anthony of Padua Church; Retired.
English, James M. *s.j.* '66 (BAL) [S] Baltimore, MD Jesuit Fathers and Brothers Maryland Provincial Curia.
English, Joseph *o.f.m.cap.* '90 (AGN) Mangilao, GU Santa Teresita Church; [F] Agana Heights, GU St. Fidelis Friary.
English, Joseph R. *m.m.* '44 (NY) [DD] Maryknoll, NY Maryknoll Fathers and Brothers.
English, Paul F. '85 (ROC) [I] Rochester, NY Basilian Residence; [M] Rochester, NY Diocesan Department of Campus Ministry.
English, Richard P. *s.j.* '51 (NY) [DD] New York, NY Murray-Weigel Hall.
English, Robert K. '88 (OM) Constance, NE St. Joseph Church; Crofton, NE St. Rose of Lima Church.
English, Msgr. Tobias P. '63 (LA) Pasadena, CA St. Andrew Church; Retired.
English, William J. '60 (BO) [6] Quincy, MA Most Blessed Sacrament Church.
English, Msgr. William J. '69 (WDC) [7] Silver Spring, MD St. John the Evangelist Church.
Engo, David M. *f.p.o.* '97 (FR) [I] New Bedford, MA Franciscans of Primitive Observance.
Enke, Msgr. Paul P. '72 (COL) Granville, OH St. Edward the Confessor Church.
Enlow, Leo J. '75 (SFD) Effingham, IL St. Anthony of Padua Church.
Enman, Frederick *s.j.* '88 (BO) [W] Chestnut Hill, MA The Jesuit Community at Boston College.
Enneking, Marvin '91 (SCL) Becker, MN Immaculate Conception Church; Duelm, MN St. Lawrence's Church; Sauk Rapids, MN St. Patrick Church.
Enneking, Thomas *o.s.c.* '84 (CHI) [N] Chicago, IL Crosier Community of Chicago.
Ennin-Essien, Sylvester '86 (BGP) New Fairfield, CT St. Edward the Confessor Church.
Ennis, James E. '50 (LC) [D] Hillsboro, WI St. Joseph's Memorial Hospital, Inc.

Ennis, William '64 (ORL) [5] Orlando, FL Holy Family Church.
Enojo, Jesus P. '67 (NY) [54] New York, NY St. James Church.
Enright, Edward J. *o.s.a.* '73 (PH) [B] Villanova, PA St. Augustine Friary; [C] Villanova, PA Villanova University.
Enright, Msgr. Frank E. '43 (WIN) Retired; [F] Austin, MN Sacred Heart Care Center, Inc.
Enright, James (ROC) [2] Auburn, NY Sacred Heart Church.
Enright, James C. '69 (BUF) On Duty Outside the Diocese.
Enright, James C. '69 (ROC) [3] Auburn, NY St. Mary Church; Auburn, NY Auburn Correctional Facility.
Enright, John P. '53 (CHI) [52] Chicago, IL Epiphany Church; Retired.
Enright, Michael P. '84 (CHI) [91] Chicago, IL Immaculate Conception of the Blessed Virgin Mary Church.
Enright, Thomas M. '66 (CHI) Wauconda, IL Transfiguration Church.
Enright, Timothy *c.s.sp.* '51 (SFR) San Francisco, CA Laguna Honda Home.
Enright, Msgr. Vincent L. '47 (E) Retired.
Enriquez, Alex '85 (TR) Red Bank, NJ St. James Church.
Enriquez, Juan '80 (LA) Pacoima, CA Guardian Angel Church.
Enriquez, Rean Frederick *m.s.* '93 (HON) Ewa, HI Immaculate Conception Church.
Ensey, Eric S. '95 (SCR) [M] Shohola, PA Society of Saint John.
Enslow, Batholomew *s.s.j.* '49 (BLX) Pass Christian, MS Our Mother of Mercy Church.
Ensman, Raymond E. '66 (TOL) Port Clinton, OH Immaculate Conception Church.
Enyan-Boadu, Peter '84 (ROC) Brockport, NY Nativity of the Blessed Virgin Mary Church.
Enzler, Msgr. John J. '73 (WDC) Potomac, MD Our Lady of Mercy Church.
Enzman, David '83 (CLV) Absent on Leave.
Enzweiler, Donald A. '87 (COV) On Duty Outside the Diocese.
Eppenbrock, Donald J. '60 (SAG) Lexington, MI St. Denis Church.
Epperley, Wayne *c.s.sp.* '83 (SLC) St. George, UT St. George's Church; [H] St. George, UT Dixie College, Newman Center.
Epperly, Wayne *c.s.sp.* '83 (SLC) Kanab, UT St. Christopher's Church.
Epping, Robert L. *c.s.c.* '70 (FTW) [J] South Bend, IN Congregation of Holy Cross, Indiana Province, Provincial House.
Eraly, Matthew '75 (NY) [195] Staten Island, NY St. Ann Church.
Erb, Charles *s.v.d.* '33 (CHI) [B] Techny, IL Divine Word Residence.
Erb, Francis J. '54 (ROC) Retired.
Erb, Vincent I. '50 (CHL) Retired.
Erbacher, Joseph F. '72 (EVN) Cannelburg, IN All Saints Church; Montgomery, IN St. Peter Church.
Erbacher, William J. '87 (ARL) [5] Alexandria, VA St. Lawrence Church.
Erbe, Edward J. '51 (MAD) Middleton, WI St. Bernard Church; Retired.
Erbland, Philip N. *m.m.* '66 (FgM) Maryknoll Foreign Missions.
Ercolano, Anthony S. '73 (BRK) [148] Queens, NY American Martyrs Church; [G] Middle Village, NY Christ the King.
Erdei, Joseph J. *o.s.b.m.* '58 (PSC) [A] Matawan, NJ Basilian Fathers of Mariapoch.
Erdeljac, Frank G. '83 (PIT) [10] New Castle, PA St. Vincent de Paul Church; Lawrence County, PA Jameson Memorial Hospital; Lawrence County, PA St. Francis Hospital; [P] Villa Maria, PA Sisters of the Humility of Mary.
Erdle, Thomas M. '55 (ROC) [44] Rochester, NY St. Mark Church.
Erdlen, Harry J. *o.s.a.* (BO) Andover, MA St. Augustine Church.
Eremito, Anthony '67 (NY) Absent on Leave.
Erhart, Charles M. '60 (RVC) Military Chaplains.
Erhart, Henry J. *s.j.* '55 (ALN) [A] Wernersville, PA Jesuit Center.
Erickson, David '97 (PEO) Westville, IL St. Mary's Church.
Erickson, John '66 (KCK) [6] Topeka, KS Sacred Heart Church.
Erickson, John R. *o.s.b.* '50 (GBG) [H] Latrobe, PA Saint Vincent Archabbey.
Erickson, Philip L. '95 (L) Brandenburg, KY St. John the Apostle Church.
Erickson, Richard M. '85 (BO) Military & VA Chaplains.
Erickson, Robert '58 (SB) Retired.
Erickson, Robert *s.j.* '74 (SPK) Keller, WA St. Rose of Lima Church; Nespelem, WA Sacred Heart Church.
Erickson, Robert E. *c.s.v.* '67 (CHI) [N] Arlington Heights, IL Viatorian Province Center-Clerics of St. Viator.
Erickson, Ryan G. '00 (SUP) Hudson, WI St. Patrick Church.
Erickson, Scott Matthew *o.p.* '90 (NY) [DD] New York, NY St. Catherine of Siena Priory.
Erixson, Jim (ORG) [G] Fullerton, CA St. Jude Medical Center.
Erlander, Michael '68 (STP) St. Paul, MN St. Joseph's Hospital.
Ermer, James R. '78 (FAR) [5] Fargo, ND St. Anthony of Padua Church; [B] Fargo, ND Fargo Catholic Schools Network.
Ermis, Norman '83 (SAT) [A] San Antonio, TX The Assumption-St. John's Seminary.
Ernest, Bryan D. '82 (GI) Alliance, NE Holy Rosary Church.
Ernest, Stephen *s.v.d.* (OAK) [A] Berkeley, CA Dominican School of Philosophy and Theology.
Ernest, Stephen *s.v.d.* '67 (OAK) [6] Oakland, CA St. Bernard's Church.
Erno, Shaun A. '00 (MAR) Ironwood, MI Our Lady of Peace Church.
Ernst, Albert C. '53 (NO) Retired.
Ernst, Anthony '98 (EVN) Jasper, IN St. Joseph Church.
Ernst, Francis P. *s.j.* '57 (BAL) [39] Baltimore, MD St. Ignatius Church; [S] Baltimore, MD Jesuit Fathers and Brothers Maryland Provincial Curia.
Ernst, Frank *s.j.* (BAL) [13] Baltimore, MD St. Augustine Church.
Ernst, Jeff *o.f.m.cap.* '96 (STL) [P] St. Louis, MO St. Crispin's Friary.
Ernst, Norbert A. '72 (STL) House Springs, MO Our Lady, Queen of Peace Church.
Ernst, Stephen *s.t.* '86 (PAT) [M] Stirling, NJ Holy Spirit Missionary Cenacle.
Ernst, William W. '64 (IND) New Albany, IN St. Mary Church.
Ernster, James M. '55 (MIL) Retired.
Ernster, Milo '55 (WIN) Retired.
Ernstmann, Mark C. '51 (SPC) Forsyth, MO Our Lady of the Ozarks Church.
Erondu, Isaac Emeka '93 (BWN) Grulla, TX Holy Family Church.
Erpelding, Edward '66 (FTW) Syracuse, IN St. Martin de Porres Church.
Erpelding, Martin L. '42 (DET) Retired.
Erpelding, Michael (SC) [B] Fort Dodge, IA Fort Dodge Catholic Schools, Inc.
Erpelding, Michael '89 (SC) Fort Dodge, IA Corpus Christi Church.
Erpen, Msgr. B. A. '47 (AMA) Retired.
Erpen, Msgr. B.A. '47 (AMA) [K] Amarillo, TX Monsignor B.A. Erpen Trust Fund.
Erps, James *s.j.* '80 (BO) [W] Chestnut Hill, MA The Jesuit Community at Boston College; [CC] Newton, MA Boston College Campus Ministry.
Errecalde, Javier *o.de.m.* '54 (PCE) [13] Ponce, PR Santuario San Judas Tadeo Church.
Erro, Sabino *o.f.m.* '54 (DAL) [9] Dallas, TX Our Lady of Perpetual Help Church.
Erstad, William '56 (SB) Retired.
Ertle, Thomas *o.p.* '56 (PRO) [B] Providence, RI Providence College.
Ertle, Thomas J. *o.p.* '56 (PRO) [P] Providence, RI St. Thomas Aquinas Priory at Providence College.
Ertzbischoff, Edmond L. '76 (LAN) [2] Ypsilanti, MI St. John Church.
Eruva, Paul '96 (SCR) [1] Wilkes-Barre, PA St. Aloysius Church.
Ervin, Mark '90 (WDC) [1] Bethesda, MD St. Bartholomew Church.
Ervin, Thomas (SFR) On Duty Outside the Archdiocese.
Ervin, Thomas '74 (SFR) Absent on Leave.
Erving, James (BO) [3] Lowell, MA Immaculate Conception Church.
Erwin, Michael J. '98 (MIL) [74] Milwaukee, WI St. Robert Church.
Erwin, Patrick O. '68 (PAT) On Duty Outside the Diocese.
Erwin, Patrick O. '91 (MGZ) [4] Mayaquez, PR Church De El Buen Pastor Church.
Escala, Rafael '57 (MIA) Retired.
Escalante, Agustin M. '88 (SFR) [28] San Francisco, CA St. John the Evangelist Church.
Escalante, Peter '78 (SD) [21] San Diego, CA St. Brigid Church.
Escalante, Ronald S. '95 (ARL) [2] Alexandria, VA Good Shepherd Church.
Esch, Eugene *o.s.b.* '54 (B) Glenns Ferry, ID Our Lady of Limerick Station Church; [C] Jerome, ID Monastery of the Ascension.
Eschbach, Victor J. '72 (PH) Parkesburg, PA Our Lady of Consolation Church.
Eschbacher, Jerome J. '56 (SPC) Retired.
Eschweiler, Edward R. '48 (MIL) Retired.
Escobar, Alonso '69 (NY) [162] Bronx, NY St. Margaret Mary Church.
Escobar, Joseph A. *o.p.* '88 (PRO) [1] Pawtucket, RI St. Anthony Church.
Escobar, Octavio '67 (STO) Ceres, CA St. Jude Church.
Escobedo, Armando '64 (BWN) Mercedes, TX Our Lady of Mercy Church.
Escobedo, Gilberto '00 (ORG) El Toro, CA Santiago de Compostela Church.
Escobedo, Jaime '93 (SD) El Centro, CA Our Lady of Guadalupe Church.
Escribano, Peter E. '88 (MET) On Duty Outside the Diocese.
Escutin, Msgr. Ciriaco E. '80 (LA) Retired.
Esenther, Keith J. *s.j.* '71 (DET) [E] Detroit, MI University of Detroit Jesuit High School and Academy; [K] Detroit, MI Jesuit Provincial Office-Detroit Province of the Society of Jesus.
Eshiowu, Evaristus *f.s.s.p.* '83 (LR) [L] North Little Rock, AR Priestly Fraternity of St. Peter.
Eskind, Jace '87 (LKC) [7] Lake Charles, LA Our Lady of Good Counsel Church; [F] Lake Charles, LA Catholic Student Center.
Esmilla, Efren V. '93 (PH) Wallingford, PA St. John Chrysostom Church.
Esmond, William '55 (ALB) Retired.
Esparza, Javier *ss.cc.* '58 (SJN) [8] Guaynabo, PR Nuestra Senora de la Paz Church.
Espejel, Rene J. *c.s.b.* '87 (GAL) [Q] Sugar Land, TX Basilian Mission Center.
Espelage, Thomas '70 (CIN) [43] Cincinnati, OH St. John the Evangelist Church.
Espeleta, Bonifacio G. '84 (CHK) Garapan Village, District 11, MP Kristo Rai Church.
Espenshade, William T. '68 (CHY) Riverton, WY St. Margaret's Church.
Esper, Abraham L. '85 (SY) Whitesboro, NY St. Paul Church.
Esper, Jerome *c.s.c.* '61 (CHI) [D] Niles, IL Notre Dame High School; [D] Niles, IL Notre Dame High School.
Esper, John C. '83 (DET) [5] St. Clair Shores, MI St. Lucy Church; [T] Eastpointe, MI Detroit Catholic Charismatic Renewal.
Esper, Joseph M. '82 (DET) Lakeport, MI St. Edward's on the Lake Church.
Esper, Thomas '51 (DET) Retired.
Espin, Orlando (SD) [B] San Diego, CA University of San Diego.
Espineda, Cesar Ching *s.v.d.* (NY) [46] New York, NY Holy Family Church.
Espinel, Luis *o.p.* '59 (SJN) [A] Bayamon, PR Bayamon Central University.
Espinel, Marcos '61 (SJN) [8] Bayamon, PR Invencion de la Santa Cruz Church.
Espinosa, Anthony '96 (OM) [32] Omaha, NE Our Lady of Guadalupe Church.
Espinosa, Donald B. *a.a.* '71 (WOR) Fiskdale, MA St. Anne's and St. Patrick's Church.
Espinosa, Jesus *o.a.r.* '64 (LSC) [6] Las Cruces, NM Santa Rosa de Lima Church.
Espinoza, Carlos A. *o.f.m.* '96 (ELP) [B] El Paso, TX St. Anthony's School of Theology.
Espinoza, David '98 (BRK) [208] Queens, NY Our Lady of the Cenacle Church.
Espinoza, Galo *o.a.r.* '92 (NEW) [N] West Orange, NJ Augustinian Recollects.
Espinoza, Walter '99 (MRY) [4] Salinas, CA Madonna Del Sasso Church.
Espinoza, Xavier '67 (DEN) [1] Boulder, CO Sacred Heart of Jesus Church.
Espitia, David '94 (SAN) Colorado City, TX St. Ann's Church.
Esplana, Ramilo '93 (PAT) [2] Passaic, NJ St. Anthony of Padua Church.
Espona, Msgr. Juan '82 (PCE) Special Assignment.
Esposito, Anthony '56 (Y) Retired.
Esposito, Augustine M. *o.s.a.* '79 (PH) [A] Wynnewood, PA Theological Seminary of St. Charles Borromeo, Overbrook; [AA] Villanova, PA St. Thomas Monastery.
Esposito, Charles P. '99 (GBG) New Kensington, PA Mt. St. Peter Church.
Esposito, Ernest T. '67 (BGP) [2] Fairfield, CT Assumption Church; [H] Bridgeport, CT Catholic Charities of Fairfield County.
Esposito, Joseph J. (BRK) Retired.
Esposito, Joseph J. '54 (BRK) Absent on Sick Leave.
Esposito, Lawrence J. '76 (WOR) Auburn, MA St. Joseph's Church.
Esposito, Luigi '64 (BAL) [74] Baltimore, MD Our Lady of Pompei Church.
Esposito, Mario *o.carm.* '77 (ALB) [M] Germantown, NY St. Teresa's Motherhouse.
Esposito, Mario *o.carm.* '77 (NY) [DD] Tappan, NY St. Eliseus Priory.
Esposito, Ralph '67 (LR) Van Buren, AR St. Michael's Church.
Esposito, Samuel J. '78 (PIT) Allegheny County, PA UPMC University of Pittsburgh Medical Center.
Esposito, William C. '58 (SY) Cleveland, NY St. Mary of the Assumption Church.
Esquivel, Carlos *o.s.j.* '83 (FRS) Madera, CA St. Joachim Church.
Esquivel, Msgr. John '68 (FRS) [1] Fresno, CA St. John Church.

Esquivez, Miguel '82 (SAN) On Duty Outside the Diocese.
Ess, Thomas '66 (CHI) [N] Chicago, IL St. Peter's Friary.
Ess, Thomas *o.f.m.* '66 (SFD) Montrose, IL St. Rose of Lima Church; [K] Teutopolis, IL St. Francis Assisi Friary.
Esseff, Msgr. John A. '53 (SCR) [A] Dalton, PA Saint Pius X Seminary.
Esselman, Thomas E. *c.m.* '80 (STL) [B] St. Louis, MO Aquinas Institute of Theology; [P] St. Louis, MO Vincentian Residence.
Esser, James J. *o.f.m.* '67 (GB) Krakow, WI St. Casimir Church.
Esser, Paul M. '57 (MIL) [11] Racine, WI St. Paul the Apostle Church.
Essex, Msgr. Donald S. '73 (WDC) [2] Bethesda, MD St. Jane Frances de Chantal Church.
Essig, Edward '94 (ALN) Boyertown, PA St. Columbkill Church.
Essig, Herbert '74 (JOL) Lombard, IL St. Pius X Church.
Essling, Harold *c.s.c.* (AUS) [13] Austin, TX St. Ignatius Martyr Church.
Essling, Harold W. *c.s.c.* '78 (AUS) [H] Austin, TX Steiner Lodge Retreat.
Essman, Charles P. '56 (COL) Retired.
Essman, Ronald J. '76 (DET) [4] Troy, MI St. Elizabeth Ann Seton Church.
Esswein, Michael J. '98 (STL) Ellisville, MO St. Clare of Assisi Church.
Estabrook, Joseph '69 (ALB) Military Chaplains.
Esteban, Pedro Antonio '85 (LA) Maywood, CA St. Rose of Lima Church.
Estensoro, Jose '60 (ARE) Hatillo, PR Perpetual Help Church.
Estepa, Isaias (CC) [4] Corpus Christi, TX Holy Family Church.
Estephan, Andre '90 (OLL) Houston, TX Our Lady of the Cedars Maronite Church.
Estephan, Andre S. *m.l.m.* '90 (OLL) [A] Houston, TX The Congregation of Maronite Lebanese Missionaries.
Esterka, Peter '63 (ORG) [3] Orange, CA St. Norbert Church.
Estes, Dan *s.o.l.t.* '99 (FAR) Belcourt, ND St. Ann Church.
Estevez, Felipe '70 (MIA) [15] Miami, FL St. Agatha Church.
Estibalez, Inocencio '52 (SP) Retired.
Estilette, Grady J. '63 (LAF) Gueydan, LA St. Peter Church.
Estok, Edward T. '85 (CLV) [1] Cleveland, OH Cathedral of St. John the Evangelist.
Estrada, Enrique '93 (MIA) [13] Miami, FL Our Lady of Lourdes Church.
Estrada, Hector Diaz '82 (SJN) [E] San Juan, PR VA Medical Center.
Estrada, Jose Joaquin (YAK) Wapato, WA St. Peter Claver Church.
Estrada, Lawrence E. '80 (LA) Monterey Park, CA St. Stephen Church.
Estrada, Manuel '86 (SFR) [18] San Francisco, CA Church of the Epiphany.
Estrada, Miguel *c.m.f.* '60 (CHI) [78] Chicago, IL Holy Cross/Immaculate Heart of Mary Church.
Estrada, Sabino '72 (BRK) [240] Queens, NY St. Sebastian Church.
Estrem, John '86 (STP) [1] St. Paul, MN Cathedral of St. Paul.
Esty, Gregory L. '75 (STP) St. Paul Park, MN St. Thomas Aquinas Church; [H] Richfield, MN Blessed Trinity Catholic School of Richfield, Minnesota.
Etchingham, Msgr. Lawrence '56 (CHY) [2] Cheyenne, WY Holy Trinity Church; Retired.
Ethen, Jeff '88 (SCL) Belle River, MN St. Nicholas Church; Parkers Prairie, MN Church of St. William ; Urbank, MN Sacred Heart Church.
Etheredge, F. William (RCK) [B] Aurora, IL Aurora Central Catholic High School.
Ethier, Raymond '85 (ALB) Philmont, NY Sacred Heart Church; West Taghkanic, NY Holy Cross Church.
Ethier, Robert D. '45 (PRO) Retired.
Etienne, Bernard '93 (EVN) Oakland City, IN Blessed Sacrament Church; Princeton, IN St. Joseph Church; Special Assignment.
Etienne, Paul D. '92 (IND) New Albany, IN Our Lady of Perpetual Help Church.
Ettampola, Patrick '90 (NY) [101] New York, NY Our Saviour Church.
Ettel, Dale *o.s.c.* '82 (STP) Dayton, MN St. John the Baptist Church; [N] Anoka, MN Crosier Community of Anoka.
Ettensohn, John *o.m.i.* '89 (BEL) [F] Belleville, IL Missionary Oblates of Mary Immaculate - St. Henry's Oblate Residence.
Etter, Kenneth J. '00 (STL) [39] St. Louis, MO St. Joan of Arc Church.
Ettlinger, Gerard H. *s.j.* '66 (NY) [DD] New York, NY Jesuit Provincial's Office.
Ettner, Wilhelm '93 (ARL) Chantilly, VA St. Timothy Church.
Ettolil, Sebastian *m.c.b.s.* '68 (MAR) Chassell, MI St. Anne Church; South Range, MI Holy Family Church.
Ettorre, George P. '62 (PH) [1] Norristown, PA St. Francis of Assisi Church.
Etuale, Etuale '77 (HON) Pahoa, HI Sacred Heart Church.
Etuale, Viane '90 (SPP) [6] Pago Pago, AS St. Paul Church.
Etzel, George A. '42 (MIL) Retired.
Etzel, Peter J. *s.j.* '94 (STP) [6] St. Paul, MN The Immaculate Heart of Mary Church.
Etzel, Raymond A. '50 (TOL) Retired.
Euk, Vincent '86 (NY) [96] New York, NY Our Lady of the Rosary Church.
Euker, John T. '74 (GBG) Perryopolis, PA St. John the Baptist Church.
Euresti, Jesse '65 (AUS) Luling, TX St. John the Evangelist Church.
Eustace, Alexander F. *o.f.m.* '50 (FgM) Franciscan Foreign Missions.
Euteneuer, Thomas '88 (PMB) Indiantown, FL Holy Cross Church.
Euvard, Scott A. '94 (BO) Graduate Studies.
Evan, John, II (FAR) [D] Fargo, ND Prairie Psychiatric Center.
Evancho, George '64 (PBR) East Pittsburgh, PA St. Mary's Church; Rankin, PA St. John's Church.
Evancho, Robert '79 (PSC) St. Petersburg, FL St. Therese Church.
Evangelisto, Louis Anthony '54 (HRT) [8] New Haven, CT St. Donato's Church; [R] Hamden, CT Catholic Community at Quinnipac College.
Evanick, Michael '60 (PRM) Merrillville, IN St. Michael Church.
Evanish, Robin S. '83 (PIT) Monaca, PA St. John the Baptist Church.
Evanko, Joseph J. '91 (SCR) [5] Dunmore, PA St. Mary of Mount Carmel Church.
Evanofski, Bernard P. '86 (SCR) Larksville, PA St. Anthony of Padua Church.
Evans, Albert *ss.cc.* '48 (FR) [I] Fairhaven, MA Sacred Hearts Provincial House.
Evans, Edward '80 (WDC) Retired.
Evans, Eldridge T. '65 (CAM) Glassboro, NJ Our Lady of Lourdes Church.
Evans, G. William '78 (TR) Eatontown, NJ St. Dorothea Church.
Evans, George *s.s.s.* '57 (CLV) [O] Cleveland, OH Congregation of the Blessed Sacrament Provincial House; [O] Cleveland, OH Blessed Sacrament Community.
Evans, George J. *o.c.s.o.* '61 (ATL) [J] Conyers, GA The Monastery of the Holy Spirit.
Evans, George J. *o.c.s.o.* '61 (SAT) Retired.
Evans, George P. '77 (BO) [A] Boston, MA St. John's Seminary School of Theology.
Evans, James L. '94 (AUS) Dripping Springs, TX St. Martin de Porres Church.
Evans, John, II '80 (FAR) Fargo, ND Prairie Psychiatric Center; Special Assignment.
Evans, Michael A. *s.j.* '83 (DET) [K] Detroit, MI Jesuit Provincial Office-Detroit Province of the Society of Jesus.
Evans, Michael A. *s.j.* '83 (FgM) Provinces.
Evans, Michael J. '92 (LA) Manhattan Beach, CA American Martyrs Church.
Evans, Paul J. '42 (DUB) Retired.
Evans, Richard A. '82 (CLV) [3] Parma, OH St. Charles Borromeo Church.
Evans, Msgr. Robert C. '73 (PRO) East Greenwich, RI Our Lady of Mercy Church.
Evans, Tim *k.h.s.* (MOB) [J] Monroeville, AL Alabama Southern Community College Newman Center.
Evans, Tim I. (DEN) [3] Lakewood, CO Our Lady of Fatima Church.
Evans, Tim J. '93 (DEN) [4] Fort Collins, CO St. Elizabeth Ann Seton Church.
Evans, Timothy '94 (MOB) Camden, AL St. Joseph Church; Monroeville, AL Annunciation Church.
Evans, Timothy G. '73 (PIT) Elizabeth, PA St. Michael Church.
Evans, Wilfred F. '68 (SY) Syracuse, NY Veterans Administration Hospital; Special Assignment.
Evans, William Morris '81 (CHL) Brevard, NC Sacred Heart Church; Franklin, NC St. Francis of Assisi Church.
Evanstock, Philip D. *c.s.sp.* '55 (GAL) [B] Houston, TX Holy Ghost Fathers and Brothers.
Evard, Paul A. '61 (IND) On Duty Outside the Archdiocese.
Evatt, Msgr. Thomas A. '76 (CHR) Aiken, SC St. Mary, Help of Christians Church.
Evenson, Dennis D. '67 (STP) Hazelwood, MN Annunciation of the B.V.M. Church.
Evenson, Robert L. '91 (SEA) Friday Harbor, WA St. Francis Church.
Everding, Richard F. '66 (STL) [2] Lemay, MO Most Precious Blood Church.
Everett, William J. *s.j.* '53 (FgM) Provinces.
Everitt, Edward E. *o.p.* '68 (MEM) [23] Memphis, TN St. Peter's Church; [I] Memphis, TN Order Of Preachers (Southern Dominican Prov.); [I] Memphis, TN The Dominican Friars of Memphis, Inc.
Everling, Robert M. '47 (SCR) Retired; [N] Dunmore, PA Villa St. Joseph.
Evernden, Michael E. *c.s.p.* '74 (NY) [104] New York, NY St. Paul the Apostle Church.
Evers, Gerard A. '40 (CIN) [60] Cincinnati, OH St. Matthias Church; Retired.
Evers, Leonard M. '68 (GB) Cecil, WI St. Martin Church; Shawano, WI Sacred Heart Church.
Evers, Linus J. *c.pp.s.* '71 (KCK) Basehor, KS Holy Angels Church.
Evers, Paul '80 (HON) Military Chaplains.
Evers, Msgr. Paul C. '54 (WIN) Currie, MN Immaculate Heart of Mary Church.
Evers, Paul K. '71 (KC) Leave of Absence.
Evers, Robert B. '60 (GRY) Lake Station, IN St. Francis Xavier Church.
Eversole, Paul M. '92 (WDC) [Q] Washington, DC Basilica of the National Shrine of the Immaculate Conception.
Eversole, Paul M. '95 (ARL) On Duty Outside the Diocese.
Everson, Joseph M. *m.m.* '99 (FgM) Maryknoll Foreign Missions.
Everts, Donald (GB) [2] Green Bay, WI Nativity of Our Lord Church.
Evoy, John J. *s.j.* '43 (SPK) [C] Spokane, WA Gonzaga University.
Evrard, Donald J. '56 (IND) On Duty Outside the Archdiocese.
Ewald, Daniel *m.j.* '86 (PCE) [7] Ponce, PR Santa Maria Church.
Ewen, Kurt '93 (ORL) Sabbatical.
Ewen, Sharbel *o.s.b.* '88 (SD) [H] Oceanside, CA Prince of Peace Abbey, Benet Hill.
Ewers, Paul *m.c.c.j.* '65 (NEW) [N] Montclair, NJ Comboni Missionaries of the Heart of Jesus (Verona Fathers).
Ewert, J. Michael *o.f.m.* '59 (CHI) [X] Chicago, IL S.F.V., Inc.
Ewert, J. Michael *o.f.m.* '59 (FWT) [H] Crowley, TX St. Francis Village, Inc.; [H] Crowley, TX St. Francis Village, Inc.
Ewert, Michael *o.f.m* '59 (FWT) [I] Crowley, TX St. Maximilian Kolbe Friary.
Ewherido, Anthony '86 (RVC) Stony Brook, NY Stony Brook University Hospital.
Ewing, Mathias *o.carm.* '54 (LA) [F] Encino, CA Crespi Carmelite High School.
Ewing, Matt J. *o.carm.* '54 (LA) [Q] Los Angeles, CA Mount Carmel Priory, Carmelite Fathers and Brothers.
Ewing, Richard A. '46 (MET) Retired.
Exley, Thomas G. '46 (NU) Retired.
Extejt, John I. *o.s.f.s.* '85 (TOL) [C] Toledo, OH St. Francis de Sales High School; [K] Toledo, OH Oblates of St. Francis de Sales.
Extejt, Thomas J. '73 (TOL) [20] Toledo, OH St. Charles Borromeo Church.
Eybel, John W. *m.m.* '70 (FgM) Maryknoll Foreign Missions.
Eyerman, Matthew S. '95 (CHI) [43] Chicago, IL St. Columbanus Church.
Eyman, Bryan R. '85 (PRM) Fairport Harbor, OH St. Michael Church; Mentor-on-the-Lake, OH St. Andrew the Apostle Church.
Eyrrick, John (NY) New Hampton, NY MID Hudson Psychiatric Center.
Ezaki, Bernard J. '88 (ALN) [7] Bethlehem, PA Notre Dame of Bethlehem Church; [C] Bethlehem, PA Bethlehem Catholic High School.
Ezama, Natale (CHI) [48] Chicago, IL St. Denis Church.
Eze, Cyprian '88 (LKC) Westlake, LA St. John Bosco Church.
Ezecke, Alphonsus '90 (NEW) Hackensack, NJ Hackensack University Medical Center.
Ezeh, Gabriel '94 (BWN) Raymondville, TX St. Anthony Church.
Ezeh, Raphael *m.s.p.* '96 (NO) [18] New Orleans, LA Our Lady of Lourdes Church.
Ezeibeke, Samuel '79 (FAR) Lomice, ND St. Catherine Church; Michigan, ND St. Lawrence O'Toole Church.
Ezeibeke, Samuel O. '79 (FAR) Bechyne, ND SS. Peter & Paul Church.
Ezerskis, Charles E. '61 (CHI) Other Assignments.
Ezharath, Joseph '66 (WH) Paden City, WV Mater Dolorosa Church; Sistersville, WV Holy Rosary Church.
Ezop, Dwight M. '97 (LAN) De Witt, MI St. Jude Church.

F

Faber, Emmet N. '55 (LC) Retired.
Faber, Msgr. William '36 (FTW) Retired.
Fabian, Andrew C. *o.p.* (WIN) [B] Winona, MN Saint Mary's University of Minnesota.

Fabian, Cyril *o.p.* '56 (WIN) [1] Winona, MN Cathedral of the Sacred Heart.
Fabian, Jack '68 (DET) [T] Detroit, MI Clergy Health Plan; [T] Paradise, MI Companions of Christ the Lamb.
Fabian, John '68 (DET) Special Assignment.
Fabian, John C. *o.p.* '59 (CHI) [N] Chicago, IL Dominicans (Provincial Office).
Fabian, John L. '48 (SCR) Retired; [N] Dunmore, PA Villa St. Joseph.
Fabien, Rony '93 (NEW) [7] Jersey City, NJ Assumption/All Saints Church; [23] Jersey City, NJ St. Patrick's Church.
Fabing, Robert J. *s.j.* '74 (SJ) [K] Los Altos, CA Jesuit Retreat House; [O] Los Altos, CA Jesuit Institute for Family Life.
Fabish, Rapael A. *o.p.* '53 (CHI) [N] Chicago, IL Dominicans (Provincial Office).
Fabish, Raphael '42 (PEO) [K] Rock Island, IL St. Anthony's Continuing Care Center; [O] Rock Island, IL St. Mary of the Angels Convent.
Fabj, Frank T. '84 (GAL) [6] Galveston, TX Sacred Heart Church; [D] Galveston, TX O'Connell Catholic High School.
Fabre, Richard (LAF) Lydia, LA St. Nicholas Church.
Fabre, Shelton J. '89 (BR) Grosse Tete, LA St. Joseph Church; Maringouin, LA Immaculate Heart of Mary Church.
Facci, John *s.a.c.* '71 (ALB) [7] Cohoes, NY St. Rita-Sacred Heart Church.
Fackler, Neil E. '98 (CHI) Park Ridge, IL St. Paul of the Cross Church.
Facura, Joseph C. '68 (RIC) Norton, VA St. Anthony Church.
Fadallan, Elbert '80 (LUB) Plainview, TX Sacred Heart Church.
Fadden, Msgr. Joseph A. '54 (SCR) [11] Scranton, PA St. Clare Church.
Faddish, Alan *o.f.m.* '63 (NY) [DD] New York, NY Franciscan Friars, Order of Friars Minor, Holy Name Province.
Faddish, Alvin *o.f.m.* '63 (CAM) [M] Margate, NJ Franciscan Friary.
Fador, Francis R. '96 (HRT) Madison, CT St. Margaret Church.
Fadrowski, Stanislaus '39 (SCL) Retired.
Fadrowski, Msgr. William J. '87 (NEW) North Arlington, NJ Queen of Peace Church.
Faeh, Linus *o.f.m.cap.* (FgM) American Capuchin Missions (O.F.M.Cap.).
Faesser, Arthur A. '76 (GI) North Platte, NE Holy Spirit Church.
Fafinski, Donald S. '66 (BUF) Jamestown, NY St. John Church.
Fagan, Arthur J. '67 (CHI) Elk Grove Village, IL Queen of the Rosary Church.
Fagan, Edward J. *o.a.r.* '63 (NY) [154] Bronx, NY St. John's Church.
Fagan, Msgr. Emmet (BRK) [L] Brooklyn, NY Catholic Charities.
Fagan, George V., Jr. '69 (COS) [G] Colorado Springs, CO Mount St. Francis.
Fagan, John E. *s.j.* '83 (BO) [43] Boston, MA St. Mary of the Angels Church; [W] Boston, MA Loyola House; [W] Boston, MA The Society of Jesus of New England-Provincial Offices.
Fagan, Msgr. John T. '52 (BRK) Retired; [P] Brooklyn, NY Little Flower Children's Services.
Fagan, Msgr. John T. '52 (RVC) [G] Wading River, NY Little Flower Children's Services of New York.
Fagan, Joseph P. '37 (NEW) Retired.
Fagan, Paul *c.p.* '86 (NY) [DD] New York, NY Passionist Spiritual Center.
Fagan, Paul E. *m.m.* '60 (FgM) Maryknoll Foreign Missions.
Fagan, Paul R. *c.p.* '86 (NY) [FF] New York, NY Cardinal Spellman Retreat House.
Fagan, Msgr. Robert E. '55 (RVC) Mastic Beach, NY St. Jude Church.
Fagan, Robert R. '58 (ALN) [1] Easton, PA St. Anthony of Padua Church.
Faggioni, Ernest '47 (NY) [F] New Rochelle, NY Salesian High School.
Fagin, Gerald M. *s.j.* '69 (NO) [A] New Orleans, LA Notre Dame Seminary Graduate School of Theology; [C] New Orleans, LA Loyola University New Orleans.
Fagone, Benedict *o.f.m.conv.* '67 (SPR) [5] Chicopee, MA St. Anthony's Church.
Fagot, Hacker J. *s.j.* '57 (BR) [J] Convent, LA Manresa House of Retreats.
Faherty, William B. *s.j.* '44 (STL) [P] St. Louis, MO Jesuit Community Corporation at St. Louis University - Jesuit Hall; [P] St. Louis, MO The Jesuits of the Missouri Province; [V] St. Louis, MO The Museum of Western Jesuit Missions.
Fahey, Msgr. Charles J. *(s.y.)* '58 (NY) [DD] New York, NY Jesuit Community at Fordham University.
Fahey, Msgr. Charles J. '59 (BRK) [L] Brooklyn, NY Catholic Charities.
Fahey, Msgr. Charles J. '59 (SY) [19] Syracuse, NY St. Lucy Church; On Duty Outside the Diocese.
Fahey, Edward J. (TR) On Duty Outside the Diocese.
Fahey, Edward J. '86 (WIL) Ocean City, MD St. Luke and St. Andrew Church.
Fahey, Msgr. Gerard '51 (SR) [5] Santa Rosa, CA Star of the Valley Church.
Fahey, James *c.s.c.* '56 (FTW) [2] South Bend, IN St. Adalbert Church.
Fahey, James L. '59 (BO) [4] Beverly, MA St. Margaret Church.
Fahey, James W. '70 (FR) [5] Attleboro, MA St. Theresa of the Child Jesus Church.
Fahey, John *c.ss.r.* '96 (OAK) [N] Oakland, CA Redemptorists.
Fahey, John H. '61 (WH) Lubeck, WV St. Monica's Church; Ravenswood, WV St. Matthew Church.
Fahey, John K. *s.j.* '45 (NY) [DD] New York, NY Murray-Weigel Hall.
Fahey, John M. '54 (TUC) Tombstone, AZ Sacred Heart Church.
Fahey, John P. '84 (LA) Torrance, CA Nativity Church.
Fahey, Joseph *s.j.* '68 (BO) [W] Chestnut Hill, MA The Jesuit Community at Boston College.
Fahey, Joseph R. *s.j.* '68 (BO) [W] Boston, MA The Society of Jesus of New England-Provincial Offices.
Fahey, Kevin '53 (R) Laurinburg, NC St. Mary Church.
Fahey, Michael A. *s.j.* '64 (BO) [W] Boston, MA The Society of Jesus of New England-Provincial Offices.
Fahey, Michael A. *s.j.* '64 (MIL) [P] Milwaukee, WI Arrupe House Jesuit Community; [Y] Milwaukee, WI Theological Studies, Inc.
Fahey, Robert *s.m.* '53 (SP) [7] Tampa, FL Our Lady of Perpetual Help Church.
Fahey, Thomas C. *o.f.m.* '47 (CHY) Retired.
Fahey, Thomas C. '47 (FTW) [K] Huntington, IN Victory Noll—Motherhouse of Our Lady of Victory Missionary Sisters.
Fahnestock, John '71 (SB) Victorville, CA St. Joan of Arc Church.
Fahnlander, William J. '46 (BIS) Retired; [G] Bismarck, ND Emmaus Place.
Fahrbach, Paul A. '84 (TOL) Custar, OH St. Louis Church; Deshler, OH Immaculate Conception Church.
Fahy, Msgr. Francis J. '61 (BRK) [122] Brooklyn, NY Resurrection Church.
Fahy, Joseph A. *c.p.* '56 (ATL) [11] Atlanta, GA St. Paul of the Cross Church.
Fahy, Murty M. *o.s.f.s.* '58 (STO) Lodi, CA St. Anne Church.
Fahy, Thomas *o.s.b.* '57 (WDC) [M] Washington, DC St. Anselm's Abbey.
Faida, Thomas *o.f.m.cap.* '85 (NY) [98] New York, NY Our Lady of Sorrows Church.
Faiella, William W. *c.s.c.* '79 (FTW) [J] South Bend, IN Congregation of Holy Cross, Indiana Province, Provincial House.
Failla, Anthony (BRK) Absent on Sick Leave.
Faiola, Msgr. Samuel J. '49 (BUF) Retired.
Fairbairn, Frank '69 (FgM) Society of St. James the Apostle.
Fairbanks, Gregory J. '90 (PH) Graduate Studies; [EE] Philadelphia, PA Newman Center at Drexel University.
Fairbanks, Patrick *s.j.* '00 (CHI) [D] Chicago, IL St. Ignatius College Prep.
Fairbanks, Patrick A. *s.j.* '00 (CHI) [D] Chicago, IL St. Ignatius Jesuit Community.
Fairchild, Msgr. Edward J. '59 (COL) Westerville, OH St. Paul the Apostle Church.
Fairfield, Jeffry *o.carm.* '46 (JOL) [J] Darien, IL Carmelite Provincial Office.
Fairman, Timothy J. '88 (CHI) Arlington Heights, IL St. James Church.
Faistl, Msgr. Clement F. '37 (COL) [10] Columbus, OH Christ the King Church; Retired.
Fait, Thomas G. '74 (MIL) On Leave.
Faith, Rudolph '41 (DUL) Retired.
Fajella, Francis *m.s.a.* '82 (NOR) [F] Cromwell, CT Society of the Missionaries of the Holy Apostles.
Fala, John G. '65 (PH) [23] Philadelphia, PA St. Bernard Church; Retired.
Falanga, Anthony J. *c.m.* '45 (STL) [P] St. Louis, MO Lazarist Residence.
Falardeau, Ernest *s.s.s.* '56 (SFE) [25] Albuquerque, NM St. Charles Borromeo Church.
Falardeau, Normand R. *s.s.s.* '52 (SFE) [25] Albuquerque, NM St. Charles Borromeo Church.
Falbo, Samuel '60 (SFE) Retired.
Falco, Frank M. *o.s.m.* '67 (CHI) Hillside, IL St. Domitilla Church; [N] Chicago, IL Order of Friar Servants of Mary (Servites) United States of America Province, Inc.
Falco, Ronald G. '81 (WOR) [1] Leominster, MA St. Anna's Church.
Falcone, Emilio '57 (RCK) Retired.
Falcone, Mark *o.praem.* (BAL) [76] Baltimore, MD Our Lady, Queen of Peace Church.
Falcone, Sabastian '51 (ROC) Retired.
Falduti, James *o.f.m.* '94 (ALB) [B] Loudonville, NY Siena College.
Faletoi, Konelio '92 (HON) Ewa Beach, HI Our Lady of Perpetual Help Church.
Faletti, Stephen L. '83 (JC) Absent on Leave.
Faliskie, Edmund J. *c.ss.r.* '91 (FgM) Redemptorist Foreign Missions.
Falk, Msgr. Dennis G. '57 (B) Retired.
Falk, Gerald R. '59 (GB) [8] Appleton, WI St. Thomas More Church.
Falk, Robert *s.d.b.* '63 (FgM) Salesians of Don Bosco Foreign Missions.
Falkenhan, Pierre M. '80 (PIT) Ellsworth, PA Ave Maria Church.
Falkenthal, Thomas W. '75 (CHI) Military Chaplains.
Falla, Gustavo Adolfo '96 (BGP) [7] Bridgeport, CT St. Charles Church.
Faller, Henry E. '47 (KC) Retired.
Falletta, Frank J. '66 (ROC) [41] Rochester, NY St. Lawrence Church.
Falletta, Joseph '72 (ALB) Special Assignment.
Fallon, Daniel R. '76 (CHI) [152] Chicago, IL Our Lady, Mother of the Church.
Fallon, David F. '70 (CLV) [60] Cleveland, OH Sagrada Familia Church; [W] Cleveland, OH Office of Hispanic Ministry.
Fallon, James J. '62 (SY) Johnson City, NY St. James Church; Absent on Sick Leave.
Fallon, Msgr. James L. '43 (PAT) Morris Plains, NJ St. Virgilius Church; Retired; [C] Madison, NJ Bayley-Ellard High School.
Fallon, James P. *s.s.j.* (MOB) Chastang, AL St. Peter the Apostle Church.
Fallon, John '69 (BIR) [22] Birmingham, AL Prince of Peace Church.
Fallon, John '95 (FAR) Pisek, ND St. John Nepomucene Church.
Fallon, John C. '71 (ATL) Atlanta, GA Prison Apostolate.
Fallon, John C.K. (ATL) [3] Atlanta, GA Holy Spirit Church.
Fallon, John F. '58 (BO) Senior Priests.
Fallon, John J. '46 (BO) Senior Priests.
Fallon, John J. '55 (OG) Retired.
Fallon, John P. *o.s.f.s.* '60 (STO) [A] Stockton, CA St. Mary's High School.
Fallon, Joseph P. '96 (NY) Middletown, NY St. Joseph Church.
Fallon, Vincent *ss.cc.* '90 (OAK) [3] Alameda, CA St. Joseph Basilica Church.
Fallon, William J. '64 (CAM) Paulsboro, NJ St. John's Church.
Falls, Msgr. Thomas B. '32 (PH) Manoa, PA Sacred Heart Church; Retired.
Falotico, Ronald S. '69 (CAM) Pleasantville, NJ St. Peter's Church.
Falsetto, Francis J. *s.j.* '48 (P) Oakridge, OR St. Michael Church.
Falsey, James E. '72 (SAG) AuGres, MI St. Mark Church.
Falter, John F. *c.pp.s.* '61 (CIN) [M] Dayton, OH Provincial Office of the Cincinnati Province of the Society of the Precious Blood.
Faluszak, James G. '96 (E) Ridgway, PA St. Leo the Great Church.
Faluszczak, James G. '96 (E) [C] Saint Marys, PA Elk County Christian High School.
Falvella, Richard J. '41 (BUR) Retired.
Falvey, Edmund F. '61 (WOR) Retired.
Falvey, Jeremiah A. *c.s.sp.* '55 (PIT) [Q] Bethel Park, PA Holy Ghost Animation Center.
Falvey, Msgr. Sinon '45 (ORG) Retired.
Falzon, Angelo *o.f.m.* '84 (FgM) Franciscan Foreign Missions.
Fama, Benjamin '83 (ORG) Inactive Leave.
Fama, Lawrence J. '92 (NEW) Westfield, NJ St. Helen Church.
Famania, Edison *c.m.* '94 (FgM) Vincentian Foreign Missions.
Fambrini, Robert A. *s.j.* '79 (LA) [Q] Culver City, CA Ignatius House, The Novitiate of the California Province, Society of Jesus.
Famiglietti, Rocco *o.f.m.* '47 (FgM) Franciscan Foreign Missions.
Famiyeh, Emmanuel (LC) Richland Center, WI St. Mary (Assumption of B.V.M.) Church.
Fanale, James *c.s.v.* '69 (JOL) St. Anne, IL St. Anne Church.
Fane, Kevin R. *o.p.* (CHI) River Forest, IL St. Vincent Ferrer Church.
Fane, Kevin R. *o.p.* '69 (CHI) [J] Chicago, IL St. Joseph Hospital.
Fanelli, Charles V. '71 (CHI) Northlake, IL St. John Vianney, Cure of Ars Church; [X] Northlake, IL Italian Catholic Federation.
Fanelli, James G. '56 (HRT) [3] East Hartford, CT St. Christopher Church.
Faneye, Benedict *o.p.* '94 (WDC) Washington, DC Washington Hospital Center; Washington, DC Children's Medical Center; [V] West Hyattsville, MD Dominican Province of Nigeria.
Fangman, Frederick '63 (DUB) [H] Oelwein, IA Mercy Hospital of Franciscan Sisters.
Fangman, James E. '63 (SC) Kingsley, IA St. Michael's Church.

Fangman, Paul J. '49 (OM) Retired.
Fangman, Robert M. (SC) Carroll, IA St. Lawrence Church.
Fangman, Robert M. '54 (SC) Retired.
Fangman, Thomas M. '92 (OM) [42] Omaha, NE Sacred Heart Church; [F] Omaha, NE Christian Urban Education Service Foundation; [O] Omaha, NE Christian Urban Education Service.
Fangmann, Frederick C. '63 (DUB) Oelwein, IA Sacred Heart Church.
Fangmeyer, Lee J. '89 (WDC) Special Ministries.
Fangmeyer, Leroy J. '89 (WDC) Garrett Park, MD Holy Cross Church; Pastoral Center Special Ministries.
Fanning, John E. '68 (NY) [99] New York, NY Our Lady of Victory Church.
Fanning, Leo M. '54 (ORL) Retired.
Fanning, Leo M. '54 (PAT) Retired.
Fanning, Patrick F. *ss.cc.* '83 (FR) [I] Fairhaven, MA Sacred Hearts Provincial House.
Fannon, Noel '61 (BLX) Waveland, MS St. Clare Church.
Fannon, Msgr. Thomas J. (BAL) Pasadena, MD St. Jane Frances de Chantal Church.
Fannon, Msgr. Thomas J. '41 (BAL) Retired; [O] Timonium, MD Stella Maris.
Fanrak, James M. '71 (LR) Berryville, AR St. Anne Church; Eureka Springs, AR St. Elizabeth of Hungary Church; Eureka Springs, AR St. Elizabeth of Hungary Church.
Fanta, Thomas G. '88 (CLV) Brooklyn, OH St. Thomas More Church.
Fanti, Joseph J. '90 (ALN) On Duty Outside the Diocese.
Fanti, Joseph J. '90 (SCR) Peckville, PA Sacred Heart of Jesus Church.
Fanucci, Santino J. '58 (SCR) Peckville, PA Sacred Heart of Jesus Church.
Faour, George '91 (NEW) [1] Orange, NJ St. John's Church.
Farabaugh, Kenneth '68 (BAL) Hickory, MD St. Ignatius Church.
Farace, Frederick A. '55 (HBG) Retired.
Faraci, Douglas F. '69 (BUF) Buffalo, NY Buffalo General Hospital; Buffalo, NY Roswell Park Memorial Institute.
Faraci, Francis '59 (LAN) [10] Flint, MI St. Mary Church.
Faraj, John *b.s.o.* '78 (NTN) Brooklyn, NY Church of the Virgin Mary.
Farana, Mario P. '71 (SFR) [43] San Francisco, CA St. Paul Church.
Farano, Michael A. '68 (ALB) Loudonville, NY St. Pius X Church; Special Assignment.
Farao, John *o.f.m. conv.* '88 (RNO) [1] Reno, NV St. Thomas Aquinas Church; [2] Reno, NV Our Lady of the Snows Church.
Faraone, David J. '85 (ROC) Sodus, NY Epiphany Church.
Faraone, Emmanuel *o.f.m.* '41 (NY) [DD] New York, NY Padua Friary.
Faraone, Joseph J. '72 (NY) Carmel, NY St. James the Apostle Church.
Fardelone, Emil *s.d.b.* '44 (MIA) [25] Miami, FL St. Kieran Church.
Fares, Lawrence '50 (DET) Retired.
Faretra, Albert M. '86 (BO) Hingham, MA St. Paul Church.
Farge, William J. *s.j.* (NO) [C] New Orleans, LA Loyola University New Orleans.
Faria, Andre H., Jr. '93 (FR) Absent on Leave.
Faria, Carl M.D. '88 (MRY) Marina, CA St. Jude Parish Community Church.
Farias, Joseph '64 (SFE) [27] Albuquerque, NM St. Francis Xavier Church.
Farias, Joseph A. *s.d.b.* '64 (SFE) [20] Albuquerque, NM San Jose Church.
Farias, Joseph G. '75 (PAT) Mount Hope, NJ St. Bernard's Church; [O] Madison, NJ Drew University Catholic Campus Ministry; [O] Madison, NJ Fairleigh Dickinson University.
Faricy, Robert L. *s.j.* '62 (MIL) [P] Milwaukee, WI Jesuit Provincial Office, Wisconsin Province.
Farin, Paul W. '88 (BRK) [47] Brooklyn, NY St. Francis Xavier Church.
Farina, Carlo A. *s.j.* '64 (SJ) [D] San Jose, CA Bellarmine College Preparatory.
Farina, Msgr. Michael diTeccia '54 (WDC) [36] Washington, DC St. Patrick Church; [V] Washington, DC Paul VI Institute for the Arts.
Farina, Msgr. Michael F. '54 (WDC) Retired.
Farkas, Paul *o.f.m.cap.* '51 (PIT) [O] Pittsburgh, PA St. Augustine Friary.
Farke, Rodney '72 (SFS) Yankton, SD St. Benedict Church; [I] Yankton, SD The House of Mary Shrine, Inc.
Farland, David M. '74 (SPR) [1] Springfield, MA St. Michael's Church.
Farland, George A. '68 (SPR) [12] Springfield, MA Sacred Heart Church.
Farland, Norman '66 (ORL) Bartow, FL St. Thomas Aquinas Church.
Farland, Roch *o.f.m.* '54 (DET) [5] Southfield, MI St. Michael Church.
Farleo, Brennan Joseph *o.f.m.conv.* '86 (TR) Seaside Park, NJ St. Catharine of Siena Church.
Farley, Bernard C. '68 (PH) [69] Philadelphia, PA Immaculate Conception Church.
Farley, Daniel H. '98 (LC) Southeastern Portage County, WI St. Maximilian Maria Kolbe Church.
Farley, Jack *s.v.d.* (NEW) [S] Plainfield, NJ RENEW International.
Farley, James V. '65 (PRO) Hopkinton, RI Our Lady of Victory Church; [4] Westerly, RI St. Vincent de Paul Church.
Farley, John *s.v.d.* '60 (NEW) Scotch Plains, NJ Immaculate Heart of Mary Church.
Farley, John B. '93 (PBL) Rocky Ford, CO St. Peter Church.
Farley, Msgr. John J. '62 (NY) [161] Bronx, NY St. Margaret of Cortona Church.
Farley, Leo O. '54 (NEW) Retired; [N] Caldwell, NJ The Rev. Msgr. James F. Kelley Residence for Retired Priests.
Farley, Leslie A. '93 (LR) [8] Little Rock, AR Immaculate Heart of Mary Church.
Farley, Thomas B. '79 (P) McMinnville, OR St. James Church.
Farmer, Bruce L. '81 (TOL) [20] Toledo, OH St. Charles Borromeo Church; Marygrove, OH Immaculate Conception Church; Richfield Center, OH St. Elizabeth of Hungary Church.
Farmer, J. Kevin '93 (BAL) Special Assignment; [R] Sparks, MD Msgr. Clare J. O'Dwyer Retreat House.
Farmer, James '79 (BAL) [91] Baltimore, MD St. Thomas Aquinas Church.
Farmer, Michael L. '95 (MOB) [19] Mobile, AL St. Pius X Church.
Farmer, Regis M. '73 (PIT) Wildwood, PA St. Catherine of Sweden Church.
Farmer, Richard R. *o.p.* '56 (CHI) [N] River Forest, IL St. Thomas Aquinas Priory.
Farnan, Donald '87 (KC) [23] Kansas City, MO St. Louis Church; [37] Kansas City, MO St. Therese Little Flower Church.
Farnan, James B. '00 (PIT) Hopewell Township, PA Our Lady of Fatima Church.
Farnik, John *c.ss.r.* '62 (SAT) [37] San Antonio, TX St. Gerard Majella Church.
Farnum, David '99 (AUS) [11] Austin, TX St. Austin Church; [M] Austin, TX University Catholic Center.
Faroh, Paul *o.f.m.conv.* '85 (FTW) LaGrange, IN St. Joseph Church.
Farrand, John L. *s.j.* '53 (NY) [DD] New York, NY Murray-Weigel Hall.
Farrar, Charles P. '97 (DET) [24] Detroit, MI St. Gabriel Church.
Farre, Ramon *sch.p.* '53 (LA) [23] Los Angeles, CA Our Lady Help of Christians (Maria Auxiliadora) Church.
Farre, Raymond *sch.p.* '53 (LA) [93] Los Angeles, CA Santa Teresita Church.
Farre, Raymond P. '41 (TR) Retired.
Farrel, Patrick J. *o.c.d.* '62 (MIL) [P] Holy Hill, WI Discalced Carmelite Monastery.
Farrell, Anthony '64 (ORL) Eustis, FL St. Mary of the Lakes Church.
Farrell, Anthony G. '64 (DAV) On Duty Outside the Diocese.
Farrell, Bernard '65 (BLX) Ocean Springs, MS St. Alphonsus Church.
Farrell, Daniel J. '78 (YAK) Hartline, WA St. Patrick's Church.
Farrell, David E. *c.s.c.* '68 (FgM) Holy Cross Foreign Missions.
Farrell, Dennis J. '73 (BRK) [58] Brooklyn, NY Holy Name Church.
Farrell, Donald J. '54 (PH) East Lansdowne, PA St. Cyril of Alexandria Church; Retired.
Farrell, Edmund J. '43 (GR) Retired.
Farrell, Edward '56 (DET) Special Assignment.
Farrell, Emmet L. '65 (SD) San Ysidro, CA Our Lady of Mt. Carmel Church.
Farrell, Emmett L. '65 (SC) On Duty Outside the Diocese.
Farrell, Msgr. Francis '55 (BLX) [3] Biloxi, MS Our Lady of Fatima Church.
Farrell, George A. '96 (MET) Edison, NJ St. Matthew Church.
Farrell, Gerald J. *m.m.* '57 (FgM) Maryknoll Foreign Missions.
Farrell, J. Aloysius *c.s.p.* '43 (NY) [DD] Jamaica Estates, NY Paulist Fathers Generalate.
Farrell, James (OAK) [S] Berkeley, CA Maria House.
Farrell, James *s.j.* '46 (CLV) [T] Cleveland, OH Jesuit Retreat House.
Farrell, James '75 (IND) [11] Indianapolis, IN Our Lady of Lourdes Church; [17] Indianapolis, IN St. Bernadette Church.
Farrell, James E. *s.j.* '46 (CLV) [D] Cleveland, OH St. Ignatius High School.
Farrell, Jeremiah '87 (HON) On Duty Outside the Diocese.
Farrell, Jeremiah P. *s.s.* '87 (BAL) [S] Baltimore, MD Sulpician Provincial House.
Farrell, John *c.ss.r.* '48 (BAL) [87] Baltimore, MD Sacred Heart of Jesus Church.
Farrell, John E. '62 (BO) Lynnfield, MA Our Lady of the Assumption Church.
Farrell, John F. '47 (PRO) Retired.
Farrell, Msgr. John J. '34 (CHI) Berwyn, IL St. Leonard Church; Retired.
Farrell, John J. *o.s.a.* '59 (PH) [C] Villanova, PA Villanova University; [AA] Villanova, PA St. Thomas Monastery.
Farrell, Joseph A. *m.m.* (BO) Braintree, MA St. Clare Church.
Farrell, Joseph A. *m.m.* '59 (NY) [DD] Maryknoll, NY Maryknoll Fathers and Brothers.
Farrell, Joseph J. '74 (TR) New Egypt, NJ Assumption Church.
Farrell, Joseph L. *o.s.a.* '91 (BO) [C] North Andover, MA Merrimack College; [CC] North Andover, MA Merrimack College Campus Ministry Center.
Farrell, Joseph L. '95 (PH) Upper Gwynedd, PA Corpus Christi Church.
Farrell, Msgr. Kevin J. '78 (WDC) [4] Washington, DC Annunciation Church; Pastoral Center Special Ministries.
Farrell, Kevin R. '65 (JOL) Wood Dale, IL Holy Ghost Church.
Farrell, Kurt (WIN) Lake Crystal, MN Holy Family Church.
Farrell, Kurt '98 (WIN) [I] Mankato, MN St. Thomas More Newman Center, Minnesota State University.
Farrell, Lawrence *o.p.* '71 (SB) [E] Riverside, CA St. Vincent Ferrer House.
Farrell, Michael A. '70 (ORL) Merritt Island, FL Divine Mercy Church.
Farrell, Michael J. *s.s.j.* '60 (FWT) [7] Fort Worth, TX Our Mother of Mercy Church.
Farrell, Patrick '60 (JKS) [1] Jackson, MS St. Peter Church; [H] Jackson, MS Belhaven College Newman Center; [H] Jackson, MS Millsaps College Newman Center; [H] Jackson, MS University of Mississippi Medical Center - Newman Center.
Farrell, Patrick '61 (VEN) Clewiston, FL St. Margaret Church.
Farrell, Paul *c.ss.r.* '52 (STL) [P] Liguori, MO Liguori Mission House/Redemptorists.
Farrell, Philip N. '93 (PIT) Glenshaw, PA St. Mary of the Assumption Church.
Farrell, Richard *c.m.f.* '52 (CHI) [N] Oak Park, IL Claretian Fathers Headquarters of U.S.A. Eastern Province.
Farrell, Richard *c.m.f.* '52 (PHX) Prescott, AZ Sacred Heart Church.
Farrell, Richard T. '84 (ROC) [3] Elmira, NY St. Mary Church; Pine City, NY Southport Correctional Facility.
Farrell, Robert *s.j.* '64 (BO) [W] Chestnut Hill, MA The Jesuit Community at Boston College.
Farrell, Robert J. '80 (CIN) [13] Cincinnati, OH St. Bartholomew Church.
Farrell, Ronald J. '00 (CHR) Myrtle Beach, SC St. Andrew's Church.
Farrell, Seamus J. '67 (OAK) [2] Hayward, CA St. Bede Church.
Farrell, Thomas (GB) [13] Green Bay, WI SS. Peter and Paul Church.
Farrell, Thomas '82 (LEX) [2] Lexington, KY The Newman Center, Holy Spirit Church; [L] Lexington, KY The Newman Center Holy Spirit Parish University of Kentucky.
Farrell, Thomas F. '43 (HRT) Windsor Locks, CT St. Robert Bellarmine Church.
Farrell, Timothy '89 (GLP) Farmington, NM Sacred Heart Church.
Farrell, Walter L. *s.j.* '47 (DET) [27] Detroit, MI Gesu Church; [K] Detroit, MI Jesuit Provincial Office-Detroit Province of the Society of Jesus.
Farrell, William '78 (CHL) On Duty Outside the Diocese.
Farrell, William J. *s.j.* '52 (NY) [DD] New York, NY Murray-Weigel Hall.
Farrelly, John *o.s.b.* '55 (WDC) [M] Washington, DC St. Anselm's Abbey.
Farrelly, John P. '84 (ATL) Carrollton, GA Church of Our Lady of Perpetual Help; [M] Atlanta, GA Campus Ministry.
Farrelly, Matthew *c.s.sp.* '42 (NY) [2] New York, NY St. Agnes Church.
Farrelly, Msgr. Terence J. '50 (ORL) Rockledge, FL St. Mary's Church; Retired.
Farrely, John P. '84 (ATL) Carrollton, GA Church of Our Lady of Perpetual Help.
Farren, John *o.p.* '64 (HRT) [14] New Haven, CT St. Mary's Priory Church.
Farris, Daniel L. '67 (SFE) [21] Albuquerque, NM Santuario San Martin de Porres Church.
Farris, James M. '76 (ORG) Inactive Leave.
Farris, John V. *c.m.* '49 (STL) [P] St. Louis, MO Vincentian Residence.
Farris, Msgr. Semaan '54 (ORL) Retired.
Farris, William J. *o.f.m.* '77 (IND) Batesville, IN St.

Louis Church; St. Peter, IN St. Peter Church.
Farrow, Raphael G. '85 (FRS) Goshen, CA St. Thomas the Apostle Church; Visalia, CA Holy Family Church.
Farrugia, David J. *o.p.* '34 (SAC) Benicia, CA St. Dominic Church.
Farrugia, Edwin W. '60 (SFR) [16] San Francisco, CA St. Elizabeth Church.
Farry, John A. '65 (CHI) [1] Chicago, IL Cathedral of the Holy Name.
Farry, John J. '67 (PH) [88] Philadelphia, PA St. Leo Church.
Farsaci, Francis A. *o.s.a.* '64 (PH) [AA] Villanova, PA St. Thomas Monastery.
Farwell, Richard B. '81 (CHL) On Duty Outside the Diocese.
Fary, Francis Solanus *o.f.m.cap.* '67 (FgM) Capuchin Foreign Missions.
Fasano, Jerome W. '77 (ARL) Clifton, VA St. Andrew the Apostle Church.
Faschan, Matthew '46 (BR) Retired.
Fasching, Jeffrey A. '97 (WCH) Pittsburg, KS Our Lady of Lourdes Church.
Fasciglione, Max S. '74 (CAM) Cape May Court House, NJ Our Lady of the Angels Church.
Fasline, Anthony '62 (Y) Retired.
Faso, Charles '67 (CHI) [N] Chicago, IL St. Peter's Friary.
Fassbender, Anthony D. *c.m.* '38 (NO) [P] New Orleans, LA Vincentian Fathers.
Fassbinder, Richard W. '53 (CHI) Lake Villa, IL Prince of Peace Church; Retired.
Fassero, Jonathan *o.s.b.* '78 (IND) [A] St. Meinrad, IN St. Meinrad Seminary; [J] St. Meinrad, IN St. Meinrad Archabbey.
Fassett, Edward S. *s.j.* '88 (SFR) [E] San Francisco, CA St. Ignatius College Preparatory (Coed); [N] San Francisco, CA Jesuit Community at St. Ignatius College Preparatory.
Fata, Joseph A. '68 (Y) Boardman, OH St. Luke Church.
Fater, Msgr. Douglas '70 (SAT) [10] San Antonio, TX Holy Trinity Church.
Fath, Howard *m.s.c.* '61 (FgM) Missionaries of the Sacred Heart Foreign Missions.
Fath, Howard *m.s.c.* '61 (RCK) [G] Aurora, IL Missionaries of the Sacred Heart Community.
Fath, Robert *c.m.f.* '79 (CHI) [N] Oak Park, IL Claretian Fathers Headquarters of U.S.A. Eastern Province.
Fatooh, Msgr. Charles '85 (MRY) Hollister, CA Sacred Heart/St. Benedict Catholic Community Church.
Fatooh, Msgr. Charles G. '85 (MRY) Seaside, CA St. Francis Xavier Church; Special Assignment.
Fatora, Joachim R. *o.s.b.* '54 (ALT) Hastings, PA St. Bernard Church.
Faucher, Eugene J. '51 (CHI) Arlington Heights, IL St. Edna Church; Morton Grove, IL St. Martha Church; Retired.
Faucher, Henry '52 (SFR) [K] San Rafael, CA Nazareth House.
Faucher, Henry L. '52 (SR) Retired.
Faucher, W. Thomas '71 (B) On Duty Outside the Diocese.
Faucher, W. Thomas '71 (BAK) Sisters, OR St. Edward Church.
Faugno, Valerian *o.f.m.* '58 (BO) [W] Boston, MA St. Bonaventure Friary, Franciscan Friars.
Faul, Charles '80 (RIC) [1] Virginia Beach, VA Church of the Ascension; [2] Virginia Beach, VA Church of the Holy Apostles.
Faulhaber, Gregory M. '79 (BUF) [A] East Aurora, NY Christ the King Seminary.
Faulkner, Matthew *o.carm.* '89 (NY) [97] New York, NY Our Lady of the Scapular/St. Stephen Church.
Faulstich, Paul J. *s.j.* '68 (CHI) [D] Wilmette, IL Loyola Academy.
Fauser, Arthur W. '50 (DET) Farmington, MI Our Lady of Sorrows Church; Retired.
Faust, Gary J. '78 (STL) Richmond Heights, MO Immacolata Church.
Faust, Louis J. '74 (WDC) Baden, MD St. Michael Church.
Faustina, John M. '47 (PHX) Retired.
Faustner, William J. '76 (COL) Kenton, OH Immaculate Conception Church.
Fausz, Kevin P. *c.m.* '91 (STL) Perryville, MO St. Vincent De Paul Church; Silver Lake, MO St. Rose of Lima Church; [V] Perryville, MO St. Vincent De Paul Educational Foundation.
Favalora, John C. '61 (MIA) [L] Miami Shores, FL Archdiocese of Miami Millennium Appeal, Inc.; [L] Miami Shores, FL Archdiocese of Miami, Inc.
Favara, Joseph F. '41 (SAG) Retired.
Favreau, Bruce T. '80 (OG) Au Sable Forks, NY Holy Name Church; Black Brook, NY St. Matthew Church.
Favret, J. Raymond '48 (CIN) West Chester, OH St. John Church.
Favret, Raymond J. '48 (CIN) Retired.
Fawcett, Brian '97 (RC) Faith, SD St. Joseph Church.
Fawcett, Msgr. Henry F. '64 (SD) [13] San Diego, CA Our Lady of Mt. Carmel Church.
Fawls, Daniel J. '97 (BUF) [2] Depew, NY St. Barnabas Church.
Fay, David E. '64 (CIN) [27] Cincinnati, OH St. Gabriel Church.
Fay, Edmund G. *o.p.* '53 (BIR) Scottsboro, AL St. Jude Church.
Fay, Gregory '76 (STA) [5] Jacksonville, FL Holy Family Church.
Fay, John F. *m.m.* '52 (NY) [DD] Maryknoll, NY Maryknoll Fathers and Brothers.
Fay, Michael Jude '78 (BGP) Darien, CT St. John Church.
Fay, Robert D. '67 (BO) Health Leave.
Fay, William J. '64 (GBG) [A] Latrobe, PA St. Vincent Seminary.
Fay, William J. '64 (PIT) On Duty Outside the Diocese.
Fay, Msgr. William P. '74 (BO) On Duty Outside the Archdiocese.
Fayad, Samuel *c.s.s.* '48 (BO) [Z] Waltham, MA Stigmatine Fathers and Brothers.
Fayle, Vaughn *o.f.m.* (CHI) [B] Chicago, IL The Catholic Theological Union at Chicago.
Fayle, Vaugn *o.m.i.* '87 (CHI) [N] Chicago, IL The Oblate House of Theology.
Fayos, Javier *l.c.* '97 (PRO) [E] South Kingstown, RI Immaculate Conception Academy; [G] Warwick, RI Overbrook Academy at Our Lady of Providence Center.
Fazio, Paul *o.f.m.conv.* '74 (OAK) San Pablo, CA St. Paul Church.
Fazzalaro, Msgr. Francis J. '45 (MIA) [6] Pompano Beach, FL St. Gabriel Church.
Fears, Ernest '99 (VEN) Bonita Springs, FL St. Leo Church.
Fecher, Msgr. Vincent '50 (SAT) Retired; [G] San Antonio, TX St. Anthony's School; [K] San Antonio, TX Casa De Padres.
Fechner, Erich A. '92 (STL) [3] Florissant, MO St. Angela Merici Church.
Fecht, Geoffrey *o.s.b.* '76 (SCL) [I] Collegeville, MN St. John's Abbey, of the Order of St. Benedict.
Fecko, Leonard '89 (CIN) [53] Cincinnati, OH St. Margaret of Cortona Church.
Fecteau, Raymond L. '72 (WDC) Darnestown, MD Our Lady of the Visitation Church.
Fedak, Dennis Z. '98 (PH) East Lansdowne, PA St. Cyril of Alexandria Church.
Fedak, Paul C. '98 (FR) [B] North Dartmouth, MA Bishop Stang High School.
Fedar, Paul Cark '98 (FR) [21] New Bedford, MA St. Mary's Church.
Fedders, William J. '68 (LEX) Morehead, KY Church of Jesus Our Savior; [L] Morehead, KY Catholic Student Center-Morehead State University.
Fedello, Anthony R. *o.f.m.* '66 (NEW) Fair Lawn, NJ St. Anne's Church.
Federici, Martin J. '66 (BGP) Leave of Absence.
Federico, Cesidio J. '57 (WH) Clarksburg, WV Immaculate Conception Church.
Federico, Ralph P. '52 (BUF) Retired.
Federline, Thomas A. '85 (GBG) Brady's Bend, PA St. Patrick Church; Parker, PA St. Mary, Our Lady of the Snows Church.
Feders, Joseph *o.s.b.* '99 (SCL) [I] Collegeville, MN St. John's Abbey, of the Order of St. Benedict.
Federspiel, Conrad *c.p.* (HRT) [M] West Hartford, CT Holy Family Monastery/Retreat.
Fedewa, Eugene F. '36 (DET) Harper Woods, MI Our Lady Queen of Peace Church; Retired.
Fedewa, Matthew J. '58 (LAN) Morrice, MI St. Mary Church.
Fedewa, Msgr. Sylvester L. '54 (LAN) Retired.
Fedigan, James J. *s.j.* '65 (NY) [DD] New York, NY Murray-Weigel Hall.
Fedor, Gregory F. '83 (Y) Orwell, OH St. Mary Church.
Fedor, Lawrence *o.s.b.* '65 (CHY) Riverton, WY St. Margaret's Church.
Fedor, Lawrence M. *o.s.b.* '76 (TUC) [F] St. David, AZ Holy Trinity Monastery.
Fedor, Mark Q. '72 (CLV) [49] Cleveland, OH St. Mel Church.
Fedor, Robert P. '61 (E) Meadville, PA St. Agatha Church.
Fedora, Joseph *m.m.* '84 (FgM) Maryknoll Foreign Missions.
Fedorek, Msgr. Joseph J. '53 (PHU) Elizabeth, NJ St. Vladimir's Church.
Fedorowich, Msgr. Michael '55 (PHU) Shamokin, PA Transfiguration of Our Lord Church.
Fedyk, Msgr. Jaroslaw '52 (SJP) Retired.
Fee, James M. *o.m.i.* '71 (LA) Pacoima, CA Mary Immaculate Church.
Fee, Msgr. John B. '37 (PH) [23] Philadelphia, PA St. Bernard Church; Retired.
Fee, John M. *ss.cc.* '56 (DET) Harper Woods, MI Our Lady Queen of Peace Church.
Fee, Pat '61 (ORG) Absent on Sick Leave.
Fee, Msgr. Paul A. '40 (BEA) Retired.
Feehan, Kenneth *s.v.d.* '59 (FgM) Society of the Divine Word Foreign Missions.
Feehan, Stephen S. '62 (NEW) Berkeley Heights, NJ Church of the Little Flower.
Feehily, John W. '73 (OKL) Moore, OK St. Andrew's Church.
Feela, Paul F. '78 (STP) [A] St. Paul, MN The Saint Paul Seminary; [C] St. Paul, MN University of St. Thomas.
Feeley, Michael J. *s.m.a.* '41 (BO) [W] Dedham, MA African Mission House.
Feeley, Sylvester E. *c.ss.r.* '48 (BRK) [107] Brooklyn, NY Our Lady of Perpetual Help Basilica Church.
Feeley, Thomas M. '55 (FR) [A] North Easton, MA Holy Cross Fathers Religious.
Feely, Msgr. James B. (GB) [6] Oshkosh, WI Sacred Heart Church.
Feely, Thomas H. *s.j.* '75 (NY) [B] Bronx, NY Ciszek Hall.
Feenan, Msgr. J. Francis '53 (PAT) Convent Station, NJ St. Thomas More Church.
Feeney, Bernard (PAT) Retired.
Feeney, Msgr. J. Edward '37 (E) [3] Erie, PA Holy Family/St. Ann/St. Casimir Church; Retired.
Feeney, John J. '54 (PRT) Retired.
Feeney, John J. '55 (LA) Retired.
Feeney, John P. '52 (GB) Retired.
Feeney, Joseph J. *s.j.* '65 (PH) [C] Philadelphia, PA St. Joseph's University; [AA] Philadelphia, PA Jesuit Community at St. Joseph's University.
Feeney, Kevin J. *m.a.s., m.div.* '77 (CHI) [A] Mundelein, IL University of St. Mary of the Lake-Mundelein Seminary.
Feeney, Msgr. Leo (DAV) [3] Davenport, IA Holy Family Church.
Feeney, Msgr. Leo J. '66 (DAV) [M] Davenport, IA St. Vincent Center.
Feeney, Martin E. *s.j.* '72 (NY) [DD] New York, NY Murray-Weigel Hall.
Feeney, Patrick '64 (CHI) [N] Chicago, IL St. Patrick's Missionary Society.
Feeney, Robert T. '86 (PH) [125] Philadelphia, PA Our Lady of Mt. Carmel Church.
Feeney, Thomas M. '48 (PH) Retired.
Feeney, Thomas P. '79 (CC) Sinton, TX Sacred Heart Church.
Feeney, William P. '72 (PIT) Monongahela, PA Transfiguration Church.
Feeny, Michael *o.f.m.* (PAT) [M] Ringwood, NJ Holy Name Friary, Inc.
Feeser, William '77 (SAC) Vacaville, CA St. Mary Church.
Fehlner, Peter Damian Mary '57 (NOR) [F] Griswold, CT Marian Friary of Our Lady of Guadalupe.
Fehn, Jerome W. '78 (STP) Edina, MN Our Lady of Grace Church; Edina, MN Fairview-Southdale Hospital; St. Louis Park, MN Methodist Hospital.
Fehrenbach, Charles '35 (ALB) [L] Saratoga Springs, NY St. John Neumann Residence.
Fehrenbach, James *o.f.m.* '71 (CIN) [M] Cincinnati, OH St. Francis Seraph Friary.
Fehrenbach, James *o.f.m.* '71 (FgM) Franciscan Foreign Missions.
Fehrenbacher, Henry '48 (SCL) Special Assignment.
Fehring, Fabian *o.f.m.cap.* '53 (GF) Hardin, MT St. Joseph's Church.
Feicht, Donald L. '70 (Y) Alliance, OH St. Joseph's Church.
Feierfeil, Gerald '67 (SC) [9] Sioux City, IA Nativity of Our Lord Jesus Christ Church.
Feigh, Conan E. *o.s.b.* '57 (ALT) [I] University Park, PA Penn State Catholic Community.
Feil, Carl *o.s.m.* '61 (SFE) Tome, NM Immaculate Conception Church.
Feil, Carl M. *o.s.m.* '61 (CHI) [N] Chicago, IL Order of Friar Servants of Mary (Servites) United States of America Province, Inc.
Feild, Martin Eugene '59 (BAL) Taneytown, MD St. Joseph Church.
Feiss, Hugh *o.s.b.* '66 (B) [C] Jerome, ID Monastery of the Ascension.
Feit, Matthias '56 (PHX) Sun City, AZ St. Clement of Rome Church; Retired.
Fekete, George J. '65 (GR) Lowell, MI St. Mary's Church; On Special Assignment.
Feketie, Michael J. '57 (NEW) Rahway, NJ St. Mary's Church.
Felago, John F. *m.m.* '68 (FgM) Maryknoll Foreign Missions.
Felczak, Leonard J. '44 (CHI) [195] Chicago, IL St. Tarcissus Church; Retired.
Feld, Norbert F. *s.s.c.* '49 (PRO) [P] Bristol, RI St. Columban's Retirement House.
Feldbrugge, Theo M. *m.h.m.* '54 (LA) [Q] Los Angeles, CA Mill Hill Missionaries Procure.
Feldcamp, Msgr. William J. '65 (SCR) Carbondale, PA St. Rose of Lima Church.
Feldhaus, Msgr. Eugene A. '46 (BRK) [172] Queens, NY St. Gerard Majella Church; Retired.
Feldhaus, Thomas F. '76 (CIN) Ripley, OH St. Michael Church.
Feldkamp, Angelo J. *o.praem.* '68 (GB) [I] De Pere, WI St. Norbert Abbey.
Feldmeier, Peter E. '87 (STP) [A] St. Paul, MN The

Saint Paul Seminary; [C] St. Paul, MN University of St. Thomas.
Feldmeier, Russell J. *m.m.* '80 (FgM) Maryknoll Foreign Missions.
Felice, John M. *o.f.m.* '68 (NY) [35] New York, NY St. Francis of Assisi Church; [DD] New York, NY Franciscan Friars, Order of Friars Minor, Holy Name Province; [HH] New York, NY Shrine of St. Jude, Inc.; [HH] New York, NY Foundation of the Order of Friars Minor Province of the Most Holy Name.
Felice-Pace, Albert *o.p.* '60 (TUC) [27] Tucson, AZ St. Thomas More Chapel Church; [I] Tucson, AZ University of Arizona.
Felices-Sanchez, Msgr. Fernando B. '82 (SJN) [21] San Juan, PR Nuestra Sra. de Guadalupe Church.
Felion, Jerome '47 (BWN) [2] Harlingen, TX Immaculate Heart of Mary Church.
Felion, Jerome '47 (CR) Retired.
Felix, Paul G. '90 (GAL) Navasota, TX Christ Our Light Church.
Felix, William P. '81 (LC) Chippewa Falls, WI St. Charles Borromeo Church; Cooks Valley, WI St. John the Baptist Church; Tilden, WI St. Peter Church; [M] Tilden, WI Institute of St. Joseph.
Feliz, Normando '75 (VEN) [1] Venice, FL Epiphany Church.
Felker, Joseph '73 (SB) [11] Riverside, CA St. Thomas the Apostle Church.
Fell, Gall *o.s.b.* '33 (SCL) [I] Collegeville, MN St. John's Abbey, of the Order of St. Benedict.
Fell, John N. '88 (MET) On Duty Outside the Diocese.
Fell, Timothy J. '99 (BAL) Ellicott City, MD Resurrection Church.
Fellenz, Ralph *o.f.m.cap.* '68 (FgM) Capuchin Foreign Missions.
Feller, Donald J. '46 (GB) Retired.
Feller, Richard J. '53 (CHI) South Holland, IL Holy Ghost Church; Retired.
Fellin, Joseph *c.s.s.* '45 (BO) [Z] Waltham, MA Stigmatine Fathers and Brothers.
Fellner, Msgr. John V. '49 (BEL) Retired.
Fellrath, Frank W. '89 (MET) Old Bridge, NJ St. Ambrose Church.
Felsecker, Henry J. *m.m.* '31 (NY) [DD] Maryknoll, NY Maryknoll Fathers and Brothers.
Felt, James W. *s.j.* '56 (SJ) [B] Santa Clara, CA Santa Clara University.
Felt, Richard '69 (PHX) [3] Scottsdale, AZ St. Bernadette Church; [C] Scottsdale, AZ Pope John XXIII Catholic School Community.
Felten, John N. *s.j.* '52 (CIN) [M] Cincinnati, OH Faber Jesuit Community.
Felter, Francis J. *m.m.* '69 (FgM) Maryknoll Foreign Missions.
Feltis, Jerome '79 (FAR) Absent on Leave.
Feltman, Harold R. '55 (GR) Retired.
Feltman, Philip S. '66 (TOL) Sandusky, OH St. Mary Church.
Felton, Daniel J. '81 (GB) [7] Oshkosh, WI St. Raphael Church.
Feltz, John G. '73 (BUR) [5] Burlington, VT St. Mark's Church.
Feltz, Joseph E. '79 (PIT) Monongahela, PA St. Anthony Church.
Feltz, Thomas F. '85 (LA) Bellflower, CA St. Bernard Church.
Feminelli, John '87 (CC) Retired.
Femminineo, Joseph P. '58 (DET) Retired.
Fenech, Francis X. '50 (PMB) [1] Lake Worth, FL Sacred Heart Church; Retired.
Fenelon, David '70 (DM) Retired.
Fenger, Guy '77 (MIA) Sunrise, FL All Saints Church; [C] Fort Lauderdale, FL St. Thomas Aquinas High School.
Fenili, J. Robert *c.ss.r.* '62 (DEN) [M] Denver, CO The Redemptorists/Denver Province.
Fenlon, John P. '70 (SY) Cortland, NY St. Mary Church; [W] Cortland, NY St. Mary.
Fenlon, Thomas B. '61 (NY) [159] Bronx, NY St. Lucy Church.
Fenlon, Thomas J. '42 (HEL) Retired.
Fennell, Joseph G. *s.j.* '45 (BO) [W] Weston, MA Campion Health Center, Inc.
Fennell, Patrick A. *o.s.b.* '89 (PEO) [A] Peru, IL St. Bede Abbey and Academy; [C] Peru, IL St. Bede Academy.
Fenner, Eric *o.f.m.conv.* '46 (TR) Seaside Park, NJ St. Catharine of Siena Church.
Feneness, Keith G. '84 (NY) [102] New York, NY St. Patrick Old Church.
Fennessy, James J. '68 (ATL) Lilburn, GA St. John Neumann Church.
Fennessy, Joseph H. '56 (HBG) Retired.
Fennessy, Peter J. *s.j.* '70 (BO) [W] Boston, MA The Society of Jesus of New England-Provincial Offices.
Fennessy, Peter J. *s.j.* '70 (CLV) [B] Cleveland, OH John Carroll Jesuit Community.
Fennessy, Peter J. *s.j.* '70 (OAK) [N] Berkeley, CA Jesuit Community at Jesuit School of Theology at Berkeley.
Fenske, Donald J. '58 (CHI) Calumet City, IL Our Lady of Knock Church.
Fenstermaher, James *c.s.c.* '84 (FR) [A] North Easton, MA Holy Cross Fathers Religious.
Fenton, Cornelius *c.pp.s.* '49 (CIN) [B] Carthagena, OH St. Charles.
Fenton, Jerry F. '00 (STP) White Bear Lake, MN St. Pius X Church.
Fenton, Joseph D. *s.m.* '72 (WDC) [M] Washington, DC Marist Center.
Fenton, Norman H. *o.p.* '62 (WDC) [B] Washington, DC Dominican House of Studies.
Fenton, William *o.c.d.* '48 (LA) Alhambra, CA St. Therese Church.
Fenzl, Roderick R. *o.praem.* '55 (GB) [I] De Pere, WI St. Norbert Abbey.
Ferangco, Nicanor S., Jr. '84 (DOD) Ashland, KS Holy Spirit Station Church; Ashland, KS St. Joseph Church.
Ferens, Boniface D. '64 (BUF) Retired.
Ferens, Joseph F. '53 (DET) Retired.
Feret, Msgr. Francis S. '62 (PH) [2] Philadelphia, PA St. Adalbert Church.
Fergus, Kieran *o.p.* '65 (MET) [H] New Brunswick, NJ De Porres House; [M] New Brunswick, NJ Catholic Center at Rutgers University.
Ferguson, Carlos '77 (GAL) Retired.
Ferguson, Gary M. '71 (TOL) Archbold, OH St. Peter Church; Stryker, OH St. John the Evangelist Church.
Ferguson, Ivan '70 (HRT) [A] Bloomfield, CT St. Thomas Seminary.
Ferguson, James A. '85 (ALX) Marksville, LA St. Joseph's Church.
Ferguson, James J. *c.s.c.* '64 (FTW) [J] South Bend, IN Congregation of Holy Cross, Indiana Province, Provincial House.
Ferguson, James J. *c.s.c.* '65 (FgM) Holy Cross Foreign Missions.
Ferguson, John *s.j.* '54 (SLC) [4] Ogden, UT St. Mary's Church.
Ferguson, Peter A. '90 (GAL) Hitchcock, TX Our Lady of Lourdes Church.
Ferguson, Ronald J. *s.j.* '65 (CHI) [C] Chicago, IL Jesuit Community at Loyola University of Chicago.
Ferguson, Thomas P. '94 (ARL) McLean, VA St. Luke's Church.
Ferland, Martin *o.mar.* '95 (SAM) [C] Petersham, MA Most Holy Trinity Monastery.
Ferland, Thomas J. '87 (PRO) Bristol, RI St. Elizabeth Church.
Ferlita, Ernest *s.j.* '62 (NO) [C] New Orleans, LA Loyola University New Orleans.
Fernan, Matthew F. '89 (NY) Scarsdale, NY Immaculate Heart of Mary Church.
Fernandes, Babasino '75 (FTW) Monroeville, IN St. Rose of Lima Church.
Fernandes, David A. '97 (PH) Collingdale, PA St. Joseph Church.
Fernandes, John '77 (OAK) [8] Oakland, CA St. Cyril Church; [19] Oakland, CA St. Paschal Baylon Church.
Fernandes, Jose Manuel '59 (NEW) [15] Elizabeth, NJ Our Lady of Fatima Church.
Fernandes, Lourdino '69 (FTW) New Carlisle, IN St. Stanislaus Kostka Church.
Fernandes, Lucian '67 (RVC) East Islip, NY St. Mary's Church.
Fernandes, Mauro de Souza *o.s.b.* '84 (GBG) [H] Latrobe, PA Saint Vincent Archabbey.
Fernandes, Patrick O. '83 (BUF) Jamestown, NY St. James Church.
Fernandes, Rogue '69 (LA) Azusa, CA St. Frances of Rome Church.
Fernandes, Stephen A. '76 (FR) Hyannis, MA St. Francis Xavier's Church.
Fernandes, Sydney '79 (HON) Kahuku, HI St. Roch Church.
Fernandez, Cesar A. '95 (LA) La Puente, CA St. Louis of France Church.
Fernandez, Daniel '96 (ARE) [A] Arecibo, PR Seminario de Jesus Maestro.
Fernandez, Eduardo C. *s.j.* '92 (OAK) [N] Berkeley, CA Jesuit Community at Jesuit School of Theology at Berkeley.
Fernandez, Edward P. '70 (DAL) Retired.
Fernandez, Elias *o.ss.t.* '69 (ARE) Isabela, PR Our Lady of Mount Carmel Church.
Fernandez, Emmanuel '79 (LAF) Berwick, LA St. Stephen Church.
Fernandez, Epifanio *o.ss.t.* '59 (ARE) Isabela, PR St. Anthony Church.
Fernandez, Fausto '61 (MIA) Absent on Leave.
Fernandez, Felipe *o.s.a.* '71 (SJN) [42] San Juan, PR Ntra. Sra. de la Monserrate Church.
Fernandez, Fernando '90 (NY) [53] New York, NY Incarnation Church.
Fernandez, Fidel *o.m.* '74 (CGS) Cayey, PR Nuestra Senora de la Asuncion Church.
Fernandez, Francis *o.f.m.cap* '58 (FWT) [6] Fort Worth, TX Our Lady of Guadalupe Church.
Fernandez, Frank '79 (PHX) [15] Phoenix, AZ St. Joseph Church.
Fernandez, Gerardo '91 (SD) Calexico, CA Our Lady of Guadalupe Church.
Fernandez, Gustavo *s.j.* '67 (FgM) Provinces.
Fernandez, Joaquin *s.m.* '68 (FgM) Marist Foreign Missions.
Fernandez, Jose *o.p.* '53 (PCE) Yauco, PR Holy Rosary Church.
Fernandez, Jose A. '60 (BGP) Retired.
Fernandez, Jose Luis *o.ss.t.* '69 (PCE) [10] Ponce, PR La Santisima Trinidad Church.
Fernandez, Jose Maria '59 (GAL) [20] Houston, TX Christ the King Church.
Fernandez, Luis J. '71 (NO) On Duty Outside the Archdiocese.
Fernandez, Manual *s.d.b.* '69 (SFE) [20] Albuquerque, NM San Jose Church.
Fernandez, Msgr. Manuel '52 (TR) [1] Trenton, NJ St. Mary Church; [18] Trenton, NJ St. Joseph Church.
Fernandez, Manuel *s.d.b.* '69 (SFE) [27] Albuquerque, NM St. Francis Xavier Church.
Fernandez, Manuel A. '62 (ORL) Eustis, FL St. Mary of the Lakes Church.
Fernandez, Marcellus '68 (B) Emmett, ID Sacred Heart Church.
Fernandez, Marcellus '68 (STA) On Duty Outside the Diocese.
Fernandez, Michael *c.m.f.* '53 (CHI) [147] Chicago, IL Our Lady of Guadalupe Church.
Fernandez, Miguel A. '50 (MIA) Retired.
Fernandez, Nelson '56 (MIA) Retired.
Fernandez, Nobincio *ss.cc.* '65 (HON) [G] Kaneohe, HI Sacred Hearts Center.
Fernandez, P. Ricardo *c.m.* '60 (SJN) [24] San Juan, PR Jesus Maestro Church.
Fernandez, Rafael *o.f.m.* '87 (FgM) Franciscan Foreign Missions.
Fernandez, Romualdo *c.m.f.* '53 (SJN) [9] Bayamon, PR San Jose Church.
Fernandez, Serapio '50 (ARE) [5] Arecibo, PR Church of Christ the King.
Fernandez, Severiano *o.s.a.* '64 (BEA) Vidor, TX Our Lady of Lourdes Church.
Fernandez, Vicente '82 (SJN) [5] Guaynabo, PR Maria Madre de la Misericordia Church.
Fernando, A. Thomas '66 (KAL) [1] Kalamazoo, MI St. Augustine Church.
Fernando, Augustine '64 (RVC) Farmingdale, NY St. Kilian Church.
Fernando, Bernard '65 (NEW) Hackensack, NJ Hackensack University Medical Center.
Fernando, C.A. Quintus '80 (ROC) Dansville, NY St. Mary Church.
Fernando, Christopher '88 (TLS) Holdenville, OK St. Stephen's Church.
Fernando, Cresus '82 (NY) Nyack, NY St. Ann Church.
Fernando, Damian '70 (LA) Tujunga, CA Our Lady of Lourdes Church.
Fernando, Gamini E. '71 (NY) [3] Poughkeepsie, NY Holy Trinity Church.
Fernando, Gamini E. '72 (NY) State, NY Green Haven Correctional Facility.
Fernando, Joachim '62 (BRK) [228] Queens, NY St. Pius X Church.
Fernando, Lionel '87 (TYL) Mineola, TX St. Peter the Apostle Church.
Fernando, Peter '64 (BAK) Enterprise, OR St. Katherine's Church.
Fernando, Simon '60 (RVC) Commack, NY Christ the King Church.
Fernando, Stan '78 (CHI) [J] Elk Grove Village, IL Alexian Brothers Medical Center.
Fernando, Susil '87 (LKC) De Ridder, LA St. Joseph's Church.
Fernando, Venantius M. '61 (NEW) Hillside, NJ Christ the King Church.
Fernando, Walter '73 (LA) Pasadena, CA Assumption of the Blessed Virgin Mary Church.
Fernando, Wellington *s.j.* '89 (BO) [W] Chestnut Hill, MA The Jesuit Community at Boston College.
Fernz, John (BO) Wrentham, MA Wrentham State School.
Ferone, John M. *s.j.* '83 (CIN) [M] Cincinnati, OH Faber Jesuit Community.
Ferracini, Placido *o.m.v.* '86 (BO) [B] Boston, MA Oblate Provincialate.
Ferraioli, Msgr. Frank B. '61 (PAT) Parsippany, NJ St. Christopher Church.
Ferraioli, Joseph *o.m.i.* '77 (NO) [1] New Orleans, LA St. Louis Church; [17] New Orleans, LA Our Lady of Guadalupe /International Shrine of St. Jude Church; New Orleans, LA Shrine of St. Jude Thaddeus Church.
Ferrante, Frank J. *c.m.f.* '70 (LA) [Q] Los Angeles, CA Claretian Retreat Center Community; [W] Los Angeles, CA Claretian Retreat Center (All Groups).
Ferrara, Alberto A. *c.s.b.* '00 (GAL) [Q] Sugar Land, TX Basilian Mission Center.
Ferrara, Angelus *o.s.b.* '90 (SD) [H] Oceanside, CA Prince of Peace Abbey, Benet Hill.
Ferrara, Bede *o.f.m.* '50 (BO) [W] Lynn, MA Franciscan Community (Province of Immaculate Conception).
Ferrara, Charles F. *s.j.* '90 (STL) [P] St. Louis, MO The

Jesuits of the Missouri Province.
Ferrara, John *o.m.v.* '82 (BO) [B] Boston, MA Oblate Provincialate.
Ferrara, Joseph J. '42 (SCR) Retired.
Ferrara, Joseph R. '77 (CAM) Egg Harbor Township, NJ St. Katharine Drexel Church.
Ferrara, Pasquale L. '37 (DAV) Retired; [L] Davenport, IA Kahl Home for the Aged and Infirm.
Ferrarese, Fernando '77 (BRK) [L] Brooklyn, NY Catholic Charities.
Ferrarese, Msgr. Fernando A. *m.div.* '77 (BRK) [13] Brooklyn, NY St. Athanasius Church.
Ferraro, Joseph '67 (OAK) Retired.
Ferraro, Joseph '90 (NEW) Maplewood, NJ St. Joseph's Church.
Ferraro, Michael M. '68 (BO) [4] Lynn, MA St. Mary Church.
Ferraro, Pat '92 (Y) Poland, OH Holy Family Church.
Ferraro, Romano J. '60 (BRK) Absent on Leave; [V] Jamaica, NY Parsons Manor.
Ferraro, Ronald A. '60 (HRT) [5] Waterbury, CT Our Lady of Lourdes Church.
Ferraro, Vincent J. '70 (BUF) Kenmore, NY St. Andrew Church; [K] Kenmore, NY Kenmore Mercy Hospital.
Ferrazoli, Henry R. '61 (NEW) Retired.
Ferre, Antonio '53 (PCE) Retired.
Ferreira, Alfonse *o.f.m.* '72 (BO) [W] Lynn, MA Franciscan Community (Province of Immaculate Conception); [W] Lynn, MA Franciscan Community (Province of Immaculate Conception).
Ferreira, Jose S. '56 (BO) [1] Cambridge, MA St. Anthony Church.
Ferreira, Joseph A. (OAK) [M] Oakland, CA Bishop Begin Villa.
Ferreira, Joseph A. '59 (OAK) Retired.
Ferreira, Manuel P. '60 (FR) [5] Taunton, MA St. Anthony's Church.
Ferrence, John J. *o.s.a.* '52 (PH) [D] Drexel Hill, PA Monsignor Bonner High School.
Ferrer, Anthony P. *t.o.r.* '56 (AUS) [2] Waco, TX St. Francis on the Brazos Church.
Ferrer, Charles M. '64 (CHI) [123] Chicago, IL St. Mary of the Angels Church.
Ferrer, Gonzalo *t.o.r.* '81 (SHP) [B] Shreveport, LA Christus Schumpert Health System; [B] Shreveport, LA Christus Schumpert Health System.
Ferrer, Guillermo Casa *t.c.* '46 (BAL) Odenton, MD St. Joseph Church.
Ferrer, Joaquin *s.v.d.* '87 (CHI) [B] Techny, IL Divine Word Residence.
Ferrer, Melchor M. *s.d.b.* '74 (FR) [I] Fall River, MA St. John Vianney House.
Ferrer, Miguel (SJN) Detention Ministries.
Ferrer, Miguel '67 (SJN) [8] Carolina, PR San Fernando Church.
Ferrer, P. Jorge *s.j.* '77 (SJN) [C] Rio Piedras, PR Jesuit Novitiate.
Ferrer, Peter C. '61 (LA) Retired.
Ferrer, Vincent *p.v.* (LAN) Fowler, MI Most Holy Trinity Church.
Ferrero, Anthony '81 (SB) Perris, CA St. James Church.
Ferrero, Bartholomew '60 (DET) Retired.
Ferrett, Walter L. '66 (SCR) [24] Scranton, PA Sacred Hearts of Jesus and Mary Church.
Ferretti, Samuel J. '74 (SCR) Military Chaplains.
Ferri, Gregory J. '98 (BAL) Clarksville, MD St. Louis Church.
Ferrick, Michael P. '99 (E) [2] Erie, PA Blessed Sacrament Church.
Ferrick, Raymond J. '77 (PRO) Barrington, RI Holy Angels Church.
Ferrie, Francis '65 (NO) [13] New Orleans, LA Incarnate Word Church.
Ferrier, Francis V. *s.j.* '61 (BR) [20] Baton Rouge, LA Sacred Heart of Jesus Church; Special Assignment.
Ferrier, Ronald J. '68 (PH) [BB] Philadelphia, PA Provincial House of the Sisters of the Holy Family of Nazareth.
Ferrigan, Robert E. '61 (CHI) Winnetka, IL Sacred Heart Church.
Ferrigno, Denis P. '50 (HRT) Retired.
Ferring, Msgr. Robert L. '50 (DUB) Retired.
Ferris, Carl A. '55 (GI) Retired.
Ferris, James *c.ss.r.* '35 (ALB) [L] Saratoga Springs, NY St. John Neumann Residence.
Ferris, Msgr. Norman J. '53 (SAM) Fall River, MA St. Anthony of the Desert Church.
Ferris, Thomas B. '63 (PIT) [70] Pittsburgh, PA St. Cyril of Alexandria Church.
Ferrito, Msgr. Joseph L. (PAT) Retired.
Ferro, Ralph '71 (RVC) Roosevelt, NY Queen of the Most Holy Rosary Church; East Meadow, NY Nassau County Correctional Center.
Ferro, Robert A. '73 (BRK) Absent on Leave.
Ferron, Joseph B. '45 (LC) Retired.
Ferruzzi, William A. *s.d.b.* '76 (COL) [H] Columbus, OH Salesian Center.
Ferry, James '84 (FR) [3] Fall River, MA Espirito Santo Church.
Ferry, James T. *m.m.* '56 (FgM) Maryknoll Foreign Missions.
Fertal, Joseph *s.v.d.* '59 (SB) [A] Riverside, CA Divine Word Seminary.
Fesen, Thomas '98 (TR) Brick Town, NJ St. Dominic Church.
Feser, Victor *o.s.b.* '64 (BIS) [A] Richardton, ND Assumption Abbey; [B] Bismarck, ND University of Mary.
Fessard, Gerald B. *j.c.l.* '72 (LA) [R] Monrovia, CA Convent of the Maryknoll Sisters of St. Dominic.
Fest, Donald M. *s.s.j.* '76 (BAL) [94] Baltimore, MD St. Veronica Church.
Festle, Robert H. '55 (CHI) Retired; [X] Wilmette, IL Musica Pacis.
Fetcho, John E. '64 (SY) Lakeland, NY Our Lady of Peace Church.
Fete, Msgr. Joseph N. '74 (COL) On Duty Outside the Diocese.
Fete, Kevin L. '85 (Y) Middlebranch, OH St. Therese Little Flower Church.
Fetscher, James F. '68 (MIA) [26] Miami, FL St. Louis Church.
Fetterer, Raymond A. '35 (MIL) Retired.
Fetters, Donald *c.s.c.* '76 (FgM) Holy Cross Foreign Missions.
Fetters, Donald G. *c.s.c.* '76 (FTW) [J] South Bend, IN Congregation of Holy Cross, Indiana Province, Provincial House.
Feucht, Urban *o.s.p.* '55 (SEA) [G] Tacoma, WA St. Joseph Medical Center.
Feucht, Urban C. '55 (SEA) [L] Lacey, WA St. Martin's Abbey.
Feudjio, Jerome '90 (STV) [1] St. Thomas, VI Cathedral of Sts. Peter and Paul.
Feuerbacher, Edward F. '57 (STL) Retired.
Feusahrens, Frederick J. '72 (RIC) [17] Richmond, VA St. Paul Church.
Fewing, Ross '77 (SEA) Snoqualmie, WA Our Lady of Sorrows Church; Special Assignment.
Fey, Albert J. *c.pp.s.* '46 (KCK) Baileyville, KS Sacred Heart Church.
Fey, Christian *o.f.m.cap.* '45 (SAL) [D] Victoria, KS St. Fidelis Friary.
Fey, George *c.pp.s.* '43 (SAN) [4] San Angelo, TX St. Mary's Church.
Fey, Joseph H. *c.s.c.* '51 (FTW) [J] South Bend, IN Congregation of Holy Cross, Indiana Province, Provincial House.
Fey, Thomas J. '70 (ALX) Military Chaplains.
Fey, William *o.f.m.cap.* '68 (FgM) Capuchin Foreign Missions.
Fiala, John M. *s.o.l.t.* '15 (KC) [N] Kansas City, MO Society of Our Lady of the Most Holy Trinity.
Fiala, John M. '84 (OM) On Duty Outside the Archdiocese; Absent on Leave.
Fiala, Timothy R. '96 (CHI) Westchester, IL Divine Providence Church.
Fiala, Vit *o.f.m.* '98 (Y) [J] Youngstown, OH Mt. Alverna Friary.
Fialkowski, Edward '78 (CHI) Niles, IL St. Isaac Jogues Church.
Fialkowski, Thomas M. '66 (E) Erie, PA Veterans Administration Hospital.
Fiano, Guy *o.carm.* '83 (PMB) [B] Boca Raton, FL Pope John Paul II High School; [H] Boca Raton, FL St. Elias Priory-Order of Carmelites, NY.
Fice, Joseph J. *s.j.* '72 (SJ) [K] Los Altos, CA Jesuit Retreat House.
Ficenec, Leonard C. '57 (OM) Tarnov, NE St. Michael Church; Retired.
Fichler, James *c.i.c.m.* '76 (SAT) Del Rio, TX Sacred Heart Church.
Fichteman, William L. '81 (L) [1] Louisville, KY Cathedral of the Assumption.
Fichtner, Joseph '43 (PHX) [25] Phoenix, AZ St. Thomas the Apostle Church.
Fichtner, Joseph A. *o.s.c.* '43 (PHX) [G] Phoenix, AZ Crosier Community of Phoenix (Canons Regular of the Order of the Holy Cross).
Fichtner, Robert C. '55 (BO) Watertown, MA St. Patrick Church.
Fick, David J. '88 (ALN) West Reading, PA Sacred Heart Church; Reading, PA Reading Hospital.
Fickel, William F. *s.s.s.* '81 (CLV) [O] Cleveland, OH Blessed Sacrament Community.
Fickes, Daniel R. '91 (CLV) Olmsted Falls, OH St. Mary of the Falls Church.
Ficorilli, Chad R. *o.s.b.* '79 (GBG) Whitney, PA St. Cecilia Church; Youngstown, PA Sacred Heart Church.
Fictum, Robert A. '78 (MIL) Ripon, WI St. Wenceslaus Church.
Fidalgo, Federico '63 (CC) Retired.
Fider, William P. '66 (DUL) [14] Duluth, MN St. Michael's Church.
Fiebelkorn, Daniel F. '97 (BUF) Grand Island, NY St. Stephen Church.
Fiedler, Donald J. '59 (DOD) On Duty Outside the Diocese.
Fiedler, Donald J. '59 (TUC) [23] Tucson, AZ Saints Peter and Paul Church.
Fiedler, Msgr. Ernest J. '52 (KC) [1] Kansas City, MO Cathedral of Immaculate Conception; [26] Kansas City, MO Old St. Patrick's Church.
Fiedler, Msgr. Kenneth J. '71 (MAD) [6] Madison, WI Our Lady, Queen of Peace Church.
Fiedler, Lloyd *s.v.d.* '70 (FgM) Society of the Divine Word Foreign Missions.
Fiedorczyk, Henry P. '42 (HRT) [2] New Britain, CT Holy Cross Church; Retired.
Fiedorowicz, Joseph (OAK) [3] San Leandro, CA St. Felicitas Church.
Fiedurek, Jan *s.chr.* '89 (MIA) [2] Pompano Beach, FL Our Lady of Czestochowa Church.
Field, Eugene J. '94 (NEW) Ridgefield Park, NJ St. Francis of Assisi Church.
Field, James A. '90 (BO) [4] Norwood, MA St. Timothy Church.
Field, Michael J. '82 (CAM) [3] Cherry Hill, NJ St. Peter Celestine Church.
Field, Raymund *c.s.v.* '48 (SJ) Saratoga, CA Church of the Ascension; Retired.
Field, Msgr. William N. '40 (NEW) [B] South Orange, NJ Seton Hall University.
Fields, John '86 (PHU) Lansdale, PA Presentation of Our Lord Church; Warrington, PA St. Anne's Church; [D] Philadelphia, PA Ascension Manor, Inc.
Fields, Robert (JC) [C] Jefferson City, MO St. Marys Health Center.
Fields, Robert H. '82 (JC) [2] Jefferson City, MO St. Peter Church.
Fields, Stephen M. *s.j.* '86 (WDC) [M] Washington, DC The Jesuit Community at Georgetown University.
Fields, William '91 (MOB) On Leave from the Archdiocese.
Fierro, Msgr. David G. '76 (ELP) [16] El Paso, TX Our Lady of the Light Church.
Fierros, Rick '78 (FRS) Delano, CA St. Mary's of the Miraculous Medal Church.
Fifagrowicz, Joseph G. '62 (BUF) Lyndonville, NY St. Joseph Church; Medina, NY Sacred Heart Church.
Figge, Glennon E. *c.m.* '55 (STL) [P] St. Louis, MO Lazarist Residence.
Figge, Urban '57 (BEL) [F] Belleville, IL Missionary Oblates of Mary Immaculate - St. Henry's Oblate Residence.
Figler, Michael B. '98 (TR) [1] Toms River, NJ St. Joseph Church.
Figlia, Sidney *s.d.b.* '68 (NO) [2] Harvey, LA St. John Bosco Church.
Figliola, Nicholas J. '64 (RVC) Coram, NY St. Frances Cabrini Church.
Figliozzi, Richard '79 (RVC) Freeport, NY Our Holy Redeemer Church.
Figueiredo, Anthony J. '94 (NEW) [A] South Orange, NJ Immaculate Conception Seminary.
Figueiredo, Anthony Jesus '94 (NEW) On Duty Outside the Archdiocese; Higher Studies.
Figueredo, Sergio *s.j.* '60 (MIA) [5] Miami, FL Gesu Church.
Figueroa, Alberto '90 (SJN) [18] San Juan, PR San Francisco de Asis Church; [H] Rio Piedras, PR The Viceprovince of Saint John the Baptist, Puerto Rico, of the Order Friars Minor Capuchin.
Figueroa, Angel *o.m.i.* '86 (SJN) [24] Bayamon, PR Santa Teresa de Jesus Church.
Figueroa, Edward *o.m.i.* '60 (FgM) Oblates Foreign Missions.
Figueroa, Honecimo '99 (BWN) [6] Brownsville, TX Our Lady of Guadalupe Church.
Figueroa, Marco Antonio *o.f.m.* '93 (OAK) [9] Oakland, CA St. Elizabeth's Church; [15] Oakland, CA Mary Help of Christians Church; [N] Oakland, CA Franciscan Friars.
Figueroa, Oscar '00 (SAC) Vallejo, CA St. Vincent Ferrer Church.
Figueroa, Rubin *o.f.m.* '70 (TYL) Jacksonville, TX Our Lady of Sorrows Church.
Figuerola, Adrian '71 (IND) [H] Indianapolis, IN St. Augustine Home, Little Sisters of the Poor.
Figurelle, Elwood F. '63 (ALT) Mount Union, PA St. Catherine's Church.
Figurelli, Nicholas G. '82 (NEW) [D] Summit, NJ The Oratory Catholic Preparatory School.
Filacchione, Msgr. Marc A. '80 (NY) [74] New York, NY St. Michael Church; New York, NY New York Fire Department.
Filardi, Edward J. '94 (WDC) Kensington, MD Holy Redeemer Church.
Filary, Richard M. '82 (SAG) [3] Bay City, MI St. Hedwig Church.
Filiatreau, Hilary *o.s.b.* '49 (LR) Altus, AR St. Mary Church.
Filice, Francis '79 (SFR) [52] San Francisco, CA St. Thomas the Apostle Church.
Filice, Francis P. '79 (SFR) Retired.
Filice, Peter F. *s.j.* '71 (SJ) [B] Santa Clara, CA Santa Clara University.
Filice, Richard '76 (CC) [12] Corpus Christi, TX Saint Andrew By the Sea Church.
Filip, John T. '44 (ROM) Retired.
Filipich, Nicholas '53 (BLX) Retired.
Filipkowski, Peter '86 (PAT) Newton, NJ St. Joseph's Church.

Filipowicz, Stefan *s.j.* '61 (CHI) [N] Chicago, IL Sacred Heart Mission House; [N] Chicago, IL Sacred Heart Mission House.
Filippelli, John L.M. *s.s.j.* '57 (WDC) [B] Washington, DC St. Joseph's Seminary.
Filippello, Michael A. '00 (PH) Springfield, PA St. Francis of Assisi Church.
Filippine, John E. '58 (CIN) [84] Cincinnati, OH St. Vivian Church.
Filips, Mark D. '89 (OM) O'Neill, NE St. Patrick Church.
Filipski, Raymond R. '75 (NEW) Bergenfield, NJ St. John the Evangelist Church.
Fillion, Normand (BO) [4] Lowell, MA Saint Jeanne d'Arc Church.
Fillion, Normand A. *o.m.i.* '50 (MAN) [3] Manchester, NH St. Anthony of Padua Church.
Fillion, Steven '79 (SAG) Argyle, MI St. Joseph Church.
Fillman, G. Allan '77 (TOL) Paulding, OH St. Joseph Church; Payne, OH St. John the Baptist Church.
Filmanski, Francis E. '53 (RVC) Floral Park, NY St. Hedwig's Church.
Filmyer, Bernard G. *s.j.* '52 (BAL) [S] Baltimore, MD Jesuit Fathers and Brothers Maryland Provincial Curia.
Filut, David C. '68 (MIL) New Berlin, WI Holy Apostles Church.
Fimbel, Duane G. '57 (BUF) [2] North Tonawanda, NY St. Albert the Great Church; North Tonawanda, NY DeGraff Memorial Hospital.
Fimiani, Msgr. Louis F. '60 (NEW) Roseland, NJ Our Lady of the Blessed Sacrament Church.
Fin, Robert G. '43 (E) Retired; [B] Erie, PA Gannon University.
Finamore, Robert A. '70 (WDC) Fort Washington, MD St. Ignatius Church.
Finan, James '59 (WDC) Retired.
Finan, James A. '59 (BAL) [W] Upper Marlboro, MD Knights of Columbus.
Finan, Joseph L. *m.m.* '79 (NY) [DD] Maryknoll, NY Maryknoll Fathers and Brothers.
Finch, G. William '89 (WDC) Cheverly, MD St. Ambrose Church.
Finch, Joseph E. '58 (ALB) [M] Germantown, NY St. Teresa's Motherhouse.
Finch, Joseph E. '58 (OM) Absent on Sick Leave.
Finch, Raymond J. *m.m.* '76 (FgM) Maryknoll(M.M.).
Finch, Raymond J. *m.m.* '76 (NY) [DD] Maryknoll, NY Maryknoll Fathers and Brothers.
Fincutter, John F. *s.v.d.* '50 (MIL) [P] East Troy, WI Divine Word Seminary.
Fincutter, Patrick *s.v.d.* '55 (FgM) Society of the Divine Word Foreign Missions.
Finder, L. James '91 (JC) Owensville, MO Immaculate Conception Church.
Findlan, Msgr. Joseph G. '38 (PIT) Retired; [O] Pittsburgh, PA St. John Vianney Manor.
Findlay, David '67 (E) [11] Erie, PA Sacred Heart Church.
Finegan, Gerard '67 (VEN) [1] Sarasota, FL Incarnation Church.
Finegan, Lawrence '70 (SFR) [4] South San Francisco, CA St. Veronica Church.
Finegan, Paul J. '70 (BO) Randolph, MA St. Bernadette Church.
Finelli, Jay A. '92 (PRO) [2] East Providence, RI St. Francis Xavier Church.
Finelli, Victor F. '89 (ALN) [10] Bethlehem, PA SS. Simon and Jude Church.
Fineran, A. Gerard *s.j.* '50 (FgM) Provinces.
Fineran, A. Gerard *s.j.* '50 (NO) [P] New Orleans, LA Jesuit Provincial Office.
Finerty, D. Bryan '59 (PRO) [6] Woonsocket, RI St. Charles Church.
Finerty, Raymond *o.p.* '71 (P) Ashland, OR Our Lady of the Mountain Church; [P] Portland, OR University of Portland.
Fingerle, Fred G. '63 (BUF) Andover, NY Blessed Sacrament Church; Whitesville, NY St. John of the Cross Church.
Finis, John '40 (EVN) Retired.
Fink, Msgr. Charles R. '76 (RVC) Hewlett, NY St. Joseph's Church.
Fink, Frederick T. '61 (NU) Regal, MN St. Anthony (Mission) Church; Spicer, MN Our Lady of the Lakes Church.
Fink, John '71 (MIA) Special Assignment.
Fink, John F. '69 (IND) Shelbyville, IN St. Joseph Church.
Fink, Joseph '83 (STP) Shakopee, MN St. Mary Church.
Fink, Karel '91 (AUS) Kovar, TX Sts. Peter and Paul Church; Smithville, TX St. Paul the Apostle Church.
Fink, Peter *s.j.* '69 (BO) [W] Cambridge, MA Weston Jesuit Community.
Fink, Philip *o.f.m.cap.* '77 (PIT) [P] Baden, PA St. Joseph Convent.
Fink, Philip *o.f.m.cap.* '77 (PIT) Rochester, PA St. Cecilia Church; [O] Rochester, PA St. Cecilia Friary.
Finken, Basil *o.s.b.* '40 (KCK) [H] Atchison, KS St. Benedict's Abbey.
Finlan, Robert T. (ALN) [1] Shenandoah, PA Annunciation Church.
Finlan, Robert T. '94 (ALN) [C] Ashland, PA Cardinal Brennan Jr./Sr. High School.
Finlay, Joseph F. '57 (STA) Palatka, FL St. Monica's Church; Palatka, FL St. Monica's Church.
Finley, James F. '63 (BRK) Released from Diocesan Assignment.
Finley, James J. *s.j.* '52 (NY) [DD] New York, NY Murray-Weigel Hall.
Finley, Jeffrey *c.pp.s.* '90 (OAK) Newark, CA St. Edward's Church; Fremont, CA Washington Hospital.
Finley, John Thomas '75 (LAF) On Special Assignment.
Finley, Thomas '75 (LAF) [6] Lafayette, LA Our Lady of Wisdom, University of Louisiana Church.
Finley, Thomas M. *c.m.* '54 (PH) [AA] Philadelphia, PA Congregation of the Mission.
Finley, William '81 (ORL) Sabbatical.
Finn, Alfred E. '55 (BO) Senior Priests.
Finn, Daniel J. '72 (BO) [40] Boston, MA St. Mark Church.
Finn, Dominick F. *o.s.f.s.* '56 (PH) [1] Norristown, PA St. Francis of Assisi Church; Norristown, PA Norristown State Hospital.
Finn, Edward S. '52 (SCR) On Special or Other Diocesan Assignment.
Finn, Firmin *o.f.m.conv.* '55 (ALB) [J] Latham, NY Our Lady of Hope Residence.
Finn, Firmin *o.f.m.conv.* '55 (SY) Syracuse, NY St. Joseph's Hospital Health Center.
Finn, Francis J. '39 (NEW) Retired.
Finn, Gregory T. *o.s.j.* '89 (SCR) Exeter, PA St. Anthony of Padua Church; [M] Pittston, PA Eastern Province of the Oblates of St. Joseph.
Finn, John '62 (WIL) Wilmington, DE St. Francis Hospital; [H] Wilmington, DE St. Francis Hospital, Inc.
Finn, John *m.s.c.* '84 (AUS) Blanco, TX St. Ferdinand's Church.
Finn, John A. *o.s.f.s.* '62 (WIL) [I] Wilmington, DE DeSales House.
Finn, John P. '81 (NO) Luling, LA Holy Family Church.
Finn, Joseph P. '98 (LIN) [2] Lincoln, NE Blessed Sacrament Church.
Finn, Michael E. '77 (SCR) Moscow, PA St. Catherine of Siena Church.
Finn, Msgr. Peter G. '65 (NY) [211] Staten Island, NY St. Joseph, St. Thomas Church; [I] New York, NY The Catholic Charities of the Archdiocese of New York.
Finn, Raymond C. *o.p.* '70 (NO) [P] New Orleans, LA Dominican Friars, Southern Dominican Province of St. Martin de Porres.
Finn, Robert E. *s.j.* '91 (CHI) [N] Chicago, IL Chicago Province of the Society of Jesus-Provincial Office.
Finn, Robert W. '79 (STL) Webster Groves, MO Holy Redeemer Church.
Finn, Seamus *o.m.i.* '76 (FgM) American Oblate Missions(O.M.I.).
Finn, Seamus P. *o.m.i.* '76 (WDC) [M] Washington, DC Missionary Oblates of Mary Immaculate; [M] Washington, DC Oblate College/Center for Mission Studies Community.
Finn, William '73 (JUN) On Duty Outside the Diocese.
Finn, William P. '48 (PH) [AA] Philadelphia, PA Congregation of the Mission.
Finnane, Daniel P. '63 (MAD) Westport, WI St. Mary of the Lake Church.
Finnegan, Ambrose *o.f.m.conv.* '26 (STP) [Q] Prior Lake, MN Franciscan Retreat House.
Finnegan, Charles V. (Thomas), O.F.M. '58 (PRO) [P] Providence, RI St. Francis Friary.
Finnegan, Corentine J. *o.c.s.o.* '47 (ATL) [J] Conyers, GA The Monastery of the Holy Spirit.
Finnegan, Gerald F. *s.j.* '67 (BO) [W] Boston, MA The Society of Jesus of New England-Provincial Offices.
Finnegan, Gerald F. *s.j.* '67 (PH) [C] Philadelphia, PA St. Joseph's University; [AA] Philadelphia, PA Jesuit Community at St. Joseph's University.
Finnegan, James P. *o.s.f.s.* '58 (ALN) Colesville, PA Assumption B.V.M. Church; [B] Center Valley, PA Desales University; [K] Center Valley, PA Oblates of St. Francis de Sales.
Finnegan, John P. '54 (CHI) Indian Creek, IL St. Mary of Vernon Church; Retired.
Finnegan, John S. '56 (SY) Camillus, NY St. Joseph Church.
Finnegan, John T. '60 (BO) Senior Priests.
Finnegan, Joseph '65 (HEL) Whitehall, MT St. Teresa Church; Special Assignments.
Finnegan, Kevin '90 (GLP) Absent on Leave.
Finnegan, Kevin '96 (STP) [1] Faribault, MN Immaculate Conception Church.
Finnegan, Michael J. '74 (SP) [1] Largo, FL St. Catherine of Siena Church.
Finnegan, Peter J. '42 (WCH) Retired.
Finnegan, Robert K. *o.praem.* '52 (GB) [I] De Pere, WI St. Norbert Abbey; [O] De Pere, WI Canons Regular of Magnovarad, Ltd.; [O] De Pere, WI Norbertine Generalate, Inc.
Finnegan, Roscoe L. '47 (SCL) Retired.
Finnegan, Msgr. Thomas J. '51 (BO) Senior Priests.
Finnegan, William J. '57 (CHI) Flossmoor, IL Infant Jesus of Prague Church; Orland Park, IL Our Lady of the Woods Church; Retired.
Finnell, John H. '78 (WH) Camden, WV St. Boniface Church.
Finnell, Terrell M. '92 (KC) Lexington, MO Immaculate Conception Church.
Finnerty, Msgr. D. Joseph '63 (BRK) [240] Queens, NY St. Sebastian Church.
Finnerty, Msgr. James J. '55 (NEW) [18] Newark, NJ St. John's Church.
Finnerty, Joseph G. '61 (NOR) [4] Norwich, CT St. Mary Church; [J] Uncasville, CT Emmaus-Diocesan Spiritual Life Center.
Finnerty, Msgr. Joseph L. '57 (SD) Poway, CA St. Michael Church.
Finnerty, Peter F. '71 (CAM) Pomona, NJ Assumption Church.
Finnerty, Vincent H. *c.m.* '79 (CHL) [3] Greensboro, NC St. Mary Church; [O] Charlotte, NC Centro Catolico Hispano.
Finnerty, William A. '55 (KCK) [3] Overland Park, KS Holy Spirit Church.
Finnestad, Jerald L.C. '80 (FAR) [2] Grand Forks, ND St. Mary's Church.
Finney, Donald T. *m.i.c.* '94 (PMB) Port St. Lucie, FL St. Lucie Church.
Finnigan, Francis *c.p.* '68 (MET) [H] South River, NJ Passionist Provincial Office.
Finnigan, Francis *c.p.* '68 (PMB) [H] North Palm Beach, FL Our Lady of Florida Spiritual Center.
Finnigan, John B. '61 (MAN) Newmarket, NH St. Mary Church.
Finnigan, Msgr. John C. '59 (Y) [12] Canton, OH St. Peter's Church.
Finno, James (CHI) Tinley Park, IL St. Stephen, Deacon and Martyr Church.
Finster, Paul V. *s.j.* '45 (FgM) Provinces.
Finsterbach, Thomas P. *s.j.* '76 (SJ) [L] Los Gatos, CA Sacred Heart Jesuit Center.
Finucan, J. Thomas '55 (LC) Retired.
Finucan, Msgr. James P. '47 (LC) Retired; [H] La Crosse, WI Holy Cross (Seminary) Diocesan Center.
Finucane, Gerard '99 (KNX) Johnson City, TN St. Mary Church.
Finucane, Joseph F. '59 (E) [24] Erie, PA St. Mark the Evangelist Church.
Finucane, Robert '54 (B) Genesee, ID St. Mary Station Church.
Fior, Ubaldo M. *c.r.s.p.* '51 (BUF) Youngstown, NY Holy Family Church; [B] Youngstown, NY St. Anthony M. Zaccaria Seminary.
Fiore, Arthur B. '75 (WIL) New Castle, DE St. Peter Church.
Fiore, Benjamin *s.j.* '74 (BUF) [O] Buffalo, NY Canisius Jesuit Community.
Fiore, James '72 (PMB) [1] Delray Beach, FL Emmanuel Church.
Fiore, John J. *c.s.b.* '57 (GRY) [B] Merrillville, IN Andrean High School; [J] Merrillville, IN Basilian Fathers Residence.
Fiore, Joseph A. '68 (BUF) Darien Center, NY Our Lady of Good Counsel Church.
Fiore, Joseph A. '70 (BUF) Bennington Center, NY Sacred Heart of Jesus Church.
Fiore, Peter A. *o.f.m.* '55 (ALB) [B] Loudonville, NY Siena College.
Fiorelli, Lewis S. *o.s.f.s.* '70 (WDC) [B] Washington, DC Deshairs Community-Oblates of St. Francis de Sales Residence.
Fioretti, Jerome '32 (PRO) Retired.
Fiorillo, Antimo '43 (NY) [180] Bronx, NY Santa Maria Church; Retired.
Fiorino, Alfred L. *s.j.* '60 (NY) [DD] Cornwall, NY Jogues Retreat.
Fiorino, Joseph '61 (NEW) Retired.
Firestone, Thomas M. '78 (LAN) [5] Ann Arbor, MI St. Mary Student Church; [M] Ann Arbor, MI St. Mary Student Parish; [O] Ann Arbor, MI Alma Redemptoris Mater.
Firko, Frank A. *s.t.l.* '77 (PBR) Hermitage, PA St. Michael Church.
Firpo, John A. '77 (ROC) [19] Rochester, NY St. Helen Church.
Fisch, Gerald M. '57 (SC) Ida Grove, IA Sacred Heart Church.
Fischer, Adrian *o.f.m.* '75 (SFD) [2] Quincy, IL St. Anthony of Padua Church; [7] Quincy, IL St. Joseph Church; [B] Quincy, IL Quincy University.
Fischer, Andrew C. '82 (PIT) Sharpsburg, PA St. John Cantius Church; Sharpsburg, PA St. Mary Church; Sharpsburg, PA Madonna of Jerusalem Church.
Fischer, Barry J. *c.pp.s.* '73 (CIN) [M] Dayton, OH Provincial Office of the Cincinnati Province of the Society of the Precious Blood.
Fischer, Brian J. '79 (CHI) [A] Mundelein, IL University of St. Mary of the Lake-Mundelein Seminary.
Fischer, Charles G. '50 (OWN) Clarkson, KY St.

Elizabeth of Hungary Church; St. Paul, KY St. Paul Church.
Fischer, Charles H. '71 (KAL) Hastings, MI St. Rose of Lima Church.
Fischer, Charles M. '90 (FAR) [A] Fargo, ND Cardinal Muench Seminary.
Fischer, Charles M., Jr. '90 (FAR) Special Assignment.
Fischer, Msgr. Don L. '67 (DAL) Richardson, TX St. Joseph Church.
Fischer, Emil *o.f.m.cap.* '66 (PIT) [O] Pittsburgh, PA St. Conrad Friary.
Fischer, Emil W. *o.f.m.cap.* '66 (PIT) Clairton, PA St. Clare of Assisi Church.
Fischer, Eugene '65 (SD) Retired.
Fischer, G. William *o.s.f.s.* '69 (E) Special or Diocesan Assignment.
Fischer, Henry J. '71 (BEL) Bartelso, IL St. Cecilia Church.
Fischer, Hilary *m.s.c.* '57 (FgM) Missionaries of the Sacred Heart Foreign Missions.
Fischer, Hilary *m.s.c.* '57 (RCK) [G] Aurora, IL Missionaries of the Sacred Heart Community.
Fischer, James *c.m.* (LR) [J] Fayetteville, AR Catholic Campus Ministries.
Fischer, James *c.m.* '43 (LR) Fayetteville, AR St. Thomas Aquinas University Church.
Fischer, James J. *s.j.* '55 (ROC) [C] Rochester, NY McQuaid Jesuit High School.
Fischer, John '86 (SFS) Yankton, SD Sacred Heart Church.
Fischer, John M. '63 (E) Albion, PA St. Lawrence Church.
Fischer, John P. '76 (CIN) Withamsville, OH St. Thomas More Church.
Fischer, Jonathan *o.s.b* '61 (STP) St. Paul, MN Bethesda Medical Center.
Fischer, Jonathon *o.s.b.* '61 (SCL) [I] Collegeville, MN St. John's Abbey, of the Order of St. Benedict.
Fischer, Kenneth J. '71 (CHI) River Forest, IL St. Luke Church.
Fischer, Louis A. '63 (SLC) Retired.
Fischer, Lowell '54 (JOL) Retired; [K] Frankfort, IL Franciscan Sisters of the Sacred Heart.
Fischer, Mark *f.s.s.p.* '95 (SCR) [M] Elmhurst, PA Priestly Fraternity of St. Peter (F.S.S.P.), North American District Headquarters.
Fischer, Norman A. '00 (LEX) [5] Lexington, KY St. Elizabeth Ann Seton Church; [8] Lexington, KY St. Peter Claver Church.
Fischer, Philip C. *s.j.* '61 (STL) [P] St. Louis, MO Jesuit Community Corporation at St. Louis University - Jesuit Hall.
Fischer, Richard O. '76 (BAK) Burns, OR Holy Family Church.
Fischer, William '69 (E) [C] Erie, PA Cathedral Preparatory School.
Fischer, William J. *o.praem.* '78 (PH) [AA] Paoli, PA Daylesford Abbey.
Fisette, Kevin R. '81 (PRO) [17] Providence, RI Holy Name of Jesus Church.
Fish, Alfred H. '77 (OG) Brushton, NY St. Mary Church.
Fish, Eugene J. '97 (FAR) Bremen, ND St. Joseph Church; Fessenden, ND St. Augustine's Church.
Fish, Michael *c.s.s.r.* '78 (MRY) [F] Big Sur, CA New Camaldoli Hermitage.
Fishel, Gregory *s.d.b.* (BIR) [9] Birmingham, AL St. John Bosco Church.
Fishel, Gregory *s.d.b.* '89 (BIR) [A] Birmingham, AL John Carroll Catholic High School.
Fisher, A. J. '56 (BAK) Retired.
Fisher, Albert '81 (BIR) [5] Huntsville, AL Our Lady Queen of the Universe Church.
Fisher, Andrew J. '98 (ARL) Stafford, VA St. William of York Church.
Fisher, Bernard *s.v.d.* '45 (MIL) [P] East Troy, WI Divine Word Seminary.
Fisher, Clarence L. '61 (HON) Wahiawa, HI Our Lady of Sorrows Church.
Fisher, Craig B. '79 (PH) Absent on Leave.
Fisher, D. Theodore *s.j.* '53 (LA) [C] Los Angeles, CA Loyola Marymount University.
Fisher, David '84 (OLL) Special Assignment.
Fisher, David E. '86 (LAN) Owosso, MI St. Joseph Church.
Fisher, Msgr. David L. '56 (GBG) Penn, PA St. Boniface Church.
Fisher, Donald C. '61 (PIT) [36] Pittsburgh, PA St. Regis Church.
Fisher, Edward '93 (PT) Tallahassee, FL Federal Correctional Institution.
Fisher, Msgr. Edward T. '49 (BUF) [2] North Tonawanda, NY St. Albert the Great Church.
Fisher, Frederick J. '55 (CHI) Retired.
Fisher, Gerald '51 (LC) [H] La Crosse, WI Holy Cross (Seminary) Diocesan Center.
Fisher, Gerald E. '51 (LC) Retired.
Fisher, Harold *o.m.i.* (PMB) [4] West Palm Beach, FL St. John Fisher Church.
Fisher, James F. *c.s.p.* '59 (MEM) [20] Memphis, TN St. Patrick's Church; [I] Memphis, TN Paulist Fathers (New York).
Fisher, James F. *c.s.p.* '59 (NY) [DD] Jamaica Estates, NY Paulist Fathers Generalate.
Fisher, John J. *o.s.f.s.* '88 (WIL) [B] Wilmington, DE Salesianum School.
Fisher, Kyle *c.ss.r.* (DEN) [33] Denver, CO St. Joseph's Church.
Fisher, Mark F. *f.s.s.p.* '95 (ATL) Mableton, GA St. Francis De Sales Church.
Fisher, Martin '51 (GF) Retired; [G] Billings, MT St. Vincent Healthcare.
Fisher, Martin '86 (ALB) Special Assignment; [C] Glens Falls, NY St. Mary-St. Alphonsus Regional Catholic School.
Fisher, Merle J. *s.m.* '50 (STP) [24] St. Paul, MN St. Louis King of France Church.
Fisher, Michael W. '90 (WDC) Gaithersburg, MD St. John Neumann Church.
Fisher, Paul R. *o.praem.* '95 (HBG) Millersburg, PA Queen of Peace Church.
Fisher, Raymond A. '71 (TOL) [I] Green Springs, OH St. Francis Health Care Centre.
Fisher, Robert '80 (TOL) [22] Toledo, OH St. Francis de Sales Church.
Fisher, Robert B. *s.v.d.* (LAF) [8] Lafayette, LA St. Anthony Church.
Fisher, Robert D. '80 (DEN) [21] Denver, CO Our Lady of Lourdes Church.
Fisher, Robert J. '80 (TOL) [33] Toledo, OH St. Michael Church.
Fisher, Robert J. '92 (DET) [1] Roseville, MI St. Angela Church.
Fisher, Terry '85 (FTW) [3] South Bend, IN St. Anthony de Padua Church.
Fisher, William '93 (KCK) Baldwin, KS Annunciation Church; Edgerton, KS Assumption of the Blessed Virgin Mary Church.
Fisher, William F. *o.s.f.s.* '61 (DET) [1] Monroe, MI St. Anne Church; [3] Monroe, MI St. Joseph's Church.
Fisherkeller, William P. *c.s.v.* '60 (SFD) Granite City, IL Holy Family Church.
Fishwick, Joseph '75 (MIA) Special Assignment; [G] Miami, FL Mercy Hospital.
Fiske, Jack J. *c.ss.r.* '80 (ROC) [K] Canandaigua, NY Notre Dame Retreat House.
Fister, Anselm *o.s.b.* '82 (BAK) Dufur, OR St. Alphonsus Church; Wasco, OR St. Mary's Church.
Fister, Anselm *o.s.b.* '82 (SD) [H] Oceanside, CA Prince of Peace Abbey, Benet Hill.
Fitch, David *s.j.* '54 (SJ) [L] Los Gatos, CA Sacred Heart Jesuit Center.
Fitterer, L. Paul *s.j.* '63 (SEA) [L] Seattle, WA Jesuit Community.
Fittin, Edward Seton *o.s.b.* '93 (PAT) [M] Morristown, NJ St. Mary's Abbey.
Fittin, Edward Seton J. *o.s.b.* '93 (PAT) [D] Morristown, NJ Delbarton School.
Fitts, Robert L. *s.j.* '69 (SPK) [K] Spokane, WA Regis Community.
Fitz, James F. *s.m.* '74 (CIN) [D] Dayton, OH The University of Dayton; [M] Dayton, OH Marianist Provincialate; [Q] Dayton, OH University of Dayton Campus Ministry.
Fitz-Henry, Edward '85 (MRY) San Juan Bautista, CA San Juan Bautista Church.
Fitz-Patrick, David M. '79 (WDC) Military Chaplains.
Fitzgerald, Alfred J. '66 (STL) On Medical Leave.
Fitzgerald, Brennan *o.f.m.* '61 (NY) [35] New York, NY St. Francis of Assisi Church.
Fitzgerald, Christopher *i.c.* '58 (SP) Seffner, FL St. Francis of Assisi Church.
Fitzgerald, David *s.a.* '65 (NY) [DD] Garrison, NY Franciscan Friars of the Atonement.
Fitzgerald, David E. *s.a.* '65 (R) Apex, NC St. Andrew the Apostle Church.
Fitzgerald, Donald J. '55 (BUF) Retired.
Fitzgerald, Durkin '49 (GR) [3] Grand Rapids, MI St. Alphonsus Church.
Fitzgerald, Edmund H. '57 (PRO) Retired.
Fitzgerald, Msgr. Edmund J. '68 (FR) Westport, MA St. John the Baptist Church.
Fitzgerald, Edward P. '40 (CHI) Retired.
Fitzgerald, Edward T. '59 (SPR) Ware, MA All Saints Church.
Fitzgerald, Edward W. '94 (CHR) On Duty Outside the Diocese.
Fitzgerald, Garret J. '75 (MET) Hampton, NJ St. Ann Church.
Fitzgerald, Garrett J. *s.j.* '55 (NY) [DD] New York, NY Jesuit Community at Fordham University.
Fitzgerald, Gerald J. '73 (BO) [1] Somerville, MA St. Ann Church.
Fitzgerald, Howard '78 (DM) Harlan, IA St. Michael Church.
Fitzgerald, J. Thomas '68 (MAD) Clinton, WI St. Stephen Church.
Fitzgerald, James '64 (JOL) Mokena, IL St. Mary Church.
Fitzgerald, James E. *s.j.* '61 (MIL) [P] Milwaukee, WI Jesuit Community at Marquette University.
Fitzgerald, James E. '67 (BUF) Brant, NY Our Lady of Mt. Carmel Church.
Fitzgerald, James W. *m.m.* '50 (FgM) Maryknoll Foreign Missions.
Fitzgerald, John *o.s.a.* '41 (CHI) [N] Olympia Fields, IL The Augustinians-Provincialate.
Fitzgerald, John '58 (RVC) Setauket, NY St. James Church; [P] Rockville Centre, NY The Campus Parish of Long Island.
Fitzgerald, John '63 (STO) Twain Harte, CA All Saints Church.
Fitzgerald, John '74 (PIT) Robinson Township, PA Holy Trinity Church.
Fitzgerald, John B. (LA) Retired.
Fitzgerald, John B. *c.m.* '61 (ALN) Bangor, PA Our Lady of Good Counsel Church.
Fitzgerald, John E. '57 (PH) [141] Philadelphia, PA Resurrection of Our Lord Church.
Fitzgerald, John G. '62 (LA) Lompoc, CA Our Lady Queen of Angels Church.
Fitzgerald, John J. *o.s.a.* '41 (PH) [AA] Villanova, PA St. Thomas Monastery.
Fitzgerald, Msgr. John L. '67 (BAL) Sabbatical.
Fitzgerald, John W. '53 (SFE) Retired.
Fitzgerald, Joseph *o.carm.* '86 (LA) [F] Encino, CA Crespi Carmelite High School.
Fitzgerald, Msgr. Joseph M. '58 (BGP) Huntington, CT St. Lawrence Church.
FitzGerald, Kevin T. *s.j.* '88 (CHI) [C] Chicago, IL Jesuit Community at Loyola University of Chicago.
Fitzgerald, Mark J. *c.s.c.* '40 (FTW) [B] Notre Dame, IN University of Notre Dame Du Lac; [J] Notre Dame, IN Holy Cross Community, Corby Hall, University of Notre Dame.
Fitzgerald, Matthew '68 (PMB) Special Assignment.
Fitzgerald, Michael C. '78 (DUB) On Leave of Absence.
Fitzgerald, Michael J. '80 (PH) [12] Philadelphia, PA Annunciation B.V.M. Church.
Fitzgerald, Neil F. '54 (HRT) Retired.
Fitzgerald, P. Timothy '75 (DM) On Special Assignment.
Fitzgerald, Paul J. *s.j.* '92 (SJ) [B] Santa Clara, CA Santa Clara University.
Fitzgerald, R. Martin '89 (R) On Duty Outside the Diocese.
Fitzgerald, Raymond R. *s.j.* '91 (NO) [F] New Orleans, LA Jesuit High School.
Fitzgerald, Richard W. '87 (BO) Wellesley, MA St. Paul Church.
Fitzgerald, Robert H. *s.j.* '66 (ANC) [G] Anchorage, AK Holy Spirit Center.
Fitzgerald, Robert H. *s.j.* '66 (MIL) [P] Milwaukee, WI Jesuit Provincial Office, Wisconsin Province.
Fitzgerald, Thomas '66 (STP) Centerville, MN St. Genevieve Church.
Fitzgerald, Thomas J. '42 (CHI) [200] Chicago, IL St. Thomas Apostle Church; Retired.
Fitzgerald, Thomas J. *s.s.s.* '64 (SAT) [45] San Antonio, TX St. Joseph Church.
Fitzgerald, Thomas J. '75 (PAT) [4] Clifton, NJ St. Clare's Church.
Fitzgerald, Thomas R. *s.j.* '52 (WDC) [M] Washington, DC The Jesuit Community at Georgetown University.
Fitzgerald, Timothy *c.p.* '56 (PIT) [O] Pittsburgh, PA St. Paul of the Cross Monastery; [O] Pittsburgh, PA St. Paul of the Cross Monastery.
Fitzgerald, Timothy J. '90 (SC) Royal, IA St. Louis Church.
Fitzgerald, Vincent *o.m.i.* '50 (BEL) [F] Belleville, IL Missionary Oblates of Mary Immaculate - St. Henry's Oblate Residence.
Fitzgerald, William (BAL) [10] Baltimore, MD St. Anthony of Padua Church; [66] Baltimore, MD Most Precious Blood Church.
Fitzgerald, William *c.ss.r.* '43 (DEN) [M] Denver, CO The Redemptorists/Denver Province.
FitzGerald, William '44 (BAL) Retired.
Fitzgerald, Msgr. William F. '50 (TR) [8] Trenton, NJ Our Lady of Good Counsel Church.
Fitzgerald, William F. '58 (OM) Retired.
Fitzgerald, William J. '57 (KAL) Battle Creek, MI St. Philip Church.
Fitzgerald, William M. *o.praem.* '79 (COL) [A] Columbus, OH Pontifical College Josephinum.
Fitzgerald, Willliam *c.ss.r.* '43 (FgM) Redemptorist Foreign Missions.
Fitzgibbon, Edmond J. '59 (STL) Shrewsbury, MO St. Michael Church.
Fitzgibbons, Al. L. '54 (RCK) Retired.
Fitzgibbons, John A. '68 (PH) Springfield, PA St. Kevin Church.
Fitzgibbons, John P. *s.j.* '85 (OM) [K] Omaha, NE Campion House.
Fitzgibbons, Peter L. '84 (CHL) Statesville, NC St. Philip the Apostle Church; Military Chaplains.
Fitzhenry, John Stephen *o.p.* '58 (BO) [W] Dover, MA St. Stephen Priory.
Fitzhenry, Stephen *o.p.* (BO) [Y] Dover, MA St. Stephen Priory Spiritual Life Center.

Fitzhenry, Stephen *o.p.* '58 (BO) [Y] Dover, MA St. Stephen Priory Spiritual Life Center.
Fitzhugh, David '85 (SAM) [C] Petersham, MA Most Holy Trinity Monastery.
Fitzmaurice, Msgr. Francis J. '48 (PH) Retired.
Fitzmaurice, James *o.f.m.* '84 (BO) [W] Boston, MA Ministry of the Word.
Fitzmaurice, James T. '84 (ALB) Johnstown, NY St. Anthony Church; Johnstown, NY St. Patrick Church.
Fitzmaurice, Terence *o.s.b.* '63 (JOL) [J] Lisle, IL St. Procopius Abbey.
Fitzmaurice, V. Paul '73 (GBG) Harrison City, PA St. Barbara Church.
Fitzmyer, Joseph A. *s.j.* '51 (WDC) [C] Washington, DC Catholic University of America, The; [M] Washington, DC The Jesuit Community at Georgetown University.
Fitzpatrick, Bede *o.f.m.* '55 (FgM) Franciscan Foreign Missions.
Fitzpatrick, Daniel J. *s.j.* '55 (NY) [DD] New York, NY Jesuit Community at Fordham University.
Fitzpatrick, Donnelly J. '63 (PEO) Atkinson, IL St. Anthony's Church.
Fitzpatrick, Edmund J. '47 (CHI) Retired.
Fitzpatrick, Edward '58 (ALB) Retired.
Fitzpatrick, Edward C. '68 (RVC) Uniondale, NY St. Martha Church.
Fitzpatrick, Edward J. '70 (DAV) [H] Iowa City, IA Newman Catholic Student Center; [M] Iowa City, IA O'Keefe Hall.
Fitzpatrick, Edward T. *o.s.f.s.* '74 (WIL) [I] Wilmington, DE Oblates of St. Francis De Sales.
FitzPatrick, Emmett J. '58 (PHX) Sun Lakes, AZ St. Steven Church.
Fitzpatrick, Msgr. Franklin E. '47 (BRK) Retired.
Fitzpatrick, Gerald J. *s.j.* '71 (CAM) [4] Camden, NJ Holy Name Church.
Fitzpatrick, J. Vincent '92 (FAR) Lakota, ND St. Mary's Church.
Fitzpatrick, James '95 (BRK) [170] Queens, NY St. Gabriel Church; [X] Astoria, NY St. Paul Center.
Fitzpatrick, Msgr. James J. '84 (PH) [138] Philadelphia, PA St. Philip Neri Church.
Fitzpatrick, James M. '71 (SAG) Standish, MI Resurrection of the Lord Church.
Fitzpatrick, James M. '84 (FR) North Attleboro, MA St. Mary's Church.
Fitzpatrick, Jerold F. '62 (MAD) Gratiot, WI St. Joseph Church; South Wayne, WI St. John Church.
Fitzpatrick, Msgr. John E. '70 (PAT) Oak Ridge, NJ St. Thomas, the Apostle Church.
Fitzpatrick, John J. '60 (SAV) Tybee Island, GA St. Michael Church.
Fitzpatrick, John P. (BO) Sudbury, MA St. Anselm Church.
Fitzpatrick, John P. '52 (STP) Retired.
Fitzpatrick, Joseph F. *s.j.* '65 (PH) Newtown Square, PA St. Anastasia Church.
Fitzpatrick, Kevin P. '83 (BGP) [4] Trumbull, CT St. Theresa Church.
Fitzpatrick, Mallick J. *s.j.* '60 (NY) [F] New York, NY Fordham Preparatory School; [DD] New York, NY Jesuit Community at Fordham University.
Fitzpatrick, Michael J. *s.j.* '77 (BAK) Pendleton, OR St. Andrew's Indian Church.
Fitzpatrick, Michael J. '83 (PH) [153] Philadelphia, PA St. Timothy Church.
Fitzpatrick, Patrick G. '62 (TR) Union Beach, NJ Holy Family Church.
Fitzpatrick, Paul K. '98 (LA) Santa Monica, CA St. Monica Church.
Fitzpatrick, Peter A. '45 (PH) [134] Philadelphia, PA St. Patrick Church; Retired.
Fitzpatrick, R. Michael *s.t.l.* '71 (OM) [43] Omaha, NE St. Stanislaus Church.
Fitzpatrick, R. Michael '71 (OM) Special Assignment.
Fitzpatrick, Robert *o.m.i.* '71 (FgM) Oblates Foreign Missions.
Fitzpatrick, Robert J. '54 (CHI) Ingleside, IL St. Bede Church; Retired.
Fitzpatrick, Robert J. '73 (STP) Little Canada, MN St. John the Evangelist Church.
Fitzpatrick, Thomas J. *o.s.f.s.* '61 (CHL) Thomasville, NC Our Lady of the Highways Church.
Fitzpatrick, Thomas J. *s.j.* '68 (FgM) Provinces.
Fitzpatrick, Thomas P. '61 (SY) [6] Syracuse, NY Our Lady of Lourdes Church.
Fitzpatrick, Thomas R. *s.j.* '59 (FgM) Provinces.
Fitzpatrick, Vincent *s.t.* '44 (PAT) [M] Stirling, NJ Holy Spirit Missionary Cenacle.
Fitzsimmons, Donald J. *c.s.v.* '60 (CHI) [N] Arlington Heights, IL Viatorian Province Center-Clerics of St. Viator.
Fitzsimmons, Msgr. Eugene J. (CAM) Haddon Township, NJ St. Vincent Pallotti Church.
Fitzsimmons, Francis *m.s.* '68 (LKC) [4] Sulphur, LA St. Theresa Church.
Fitzsimmons, Gerald *s.s.m.* (HRT) [V] Litchfield, CT Lourdes Shrine Guild, Inc.
Fitzsimmons, Gerald J. *s.m.m.* '75 (BRK) [V] Ozone Park, NY Montfort Missionaries Provincialate (Missionaries of the Company of Mary) - Formation Community.
Fitzsimmons, J. Thomas '62 (CIN) Eaton, OH Visitation of the Blessed Virgin Mary Church; New Paris, OH St. John the Evangelist Church.
Fitzsimmons, Philip *o.p.* (NY) Manhattan, NY New York Presbyterian Hospital.
Fitzsimmons, Richard '56 (PEO) Peterstown, IL SS. Peter and Paul Church.
Fitzsimmons, Robert Philip *o.p.* '55 (NY) [22] New York, NY St. Catherine of Siena Church; [DD] New York, NY St. Catherine of Siena Priory.
Fitzsimmons, Thomas B. '62 (CAM) Wildwood, NJ St. Ann's Church.
Fitzsimons, Philip '81 (SEA) [4] Vancouver, WA St. John Church.
Fitzwilliam, Ivan '48 (SB) Retired.
Fives, Carl J. '42 (BAL) [B] Emmitsburg, MD Mount Saint Mary's College.
Fives, Carl J. '42 (SCR) On Duty Outside the Diocese.
Fix, Donald P. '80 (PIT) Military Chaplains.
Fix, Joseph J. '68 (GR) Baldwin, MI St. Ann's Church; Evart, MI Sacred Heart Church; Marion, MI St. Agnes Church.
Fix, Robert H. '53 (CHR) [4] Columbia, SC Our Lady of the Hills Church.
Flaat, Bart A. *c.i.c.m.* '63 (BWN) [4] McAllen, TX St. Joseph the Worker Church.
Flach, Carl J. '58 (P) Redland, OR St. Philip Benizi Church.
Flach, James A. '86 (SFD) Grantfork, IL St. Gertrude Church; Marine, IL St. Elizabeth Church; St. Jacob, IL St. James Church.
Flach, LaVern S. *o.s.a.* '55 (CHI) [N] Olympia Fields, IL Tolentine Monastery at Tolentine Center.
Flach, Msgr. Thomas D. '71 (BEL) Waterloo, IL SS. Peter and Paul Church.
Flack, Robert S. *s.j.* '74 (STL) [C] St. Louis, MO Saint Louis University; [P] St. Louis, MO Jesuit Community Corporation at St. Louis University - Jesuit Hall.
Fladung, Charles J. '83 (DAV) Richland, IA St. Frances Xavier Cabrini Church.
Fladung, Charles J. '92 (DAV) East Pleasant Plain, IA St. Joseph's Church.
Flagg, Robert W. '65 (BO) [A] Boston, MA St. John's Seminary School of Theology; [A] Brighton, MA St. John's Seminary.
Flagg, Wayne N. '88 (VIC) Frelsburg, TX SS. Peter and Paul Church; Mentz, TX St. Roch Church.
Flagherty, Daniel '54 (DEN) Louisville, CO St. Louis Church.
Flagor, David A. '91 (DOD) Claflin, KS Immaculate Conception Church; Ellinwood, KS St. Joseph Church.
Flahavan, Edward J. '57 (STP) St. Paul, MN Ramsey County Correctional Facilities; Retired.
Flaherty, Charles B. *s.s.c.* '50 (BO) [29] Boston, MA St. John Chrysostom Church; [W] Quincy, MA St. Columban's Foreign Mission Society.
Flaherty, Daniel E. '70 (BO) [3] Salem, MA St. James Church.
Flaherty, Daniel J. '54 (DEN) Retired.
Flaherty, Daniel L. *s.j.* '60 (CHI) [N] Chicago, IL Chicago Province of the Society of Jesus-Provincial Office; [N] Evanston, IL Canisius House.
Flaherty, Edward F. *s.j.* '65 (DEN) [M] Denver, CO Xavier Jesuit Center.
Flaherty, Francis T. '62 (WDC) Retired.
Flaherty, Frederick R. *m.s.* '57 (HRT) [M] Hartford, CT Missionaries of LaSalette, Provincial Secretary.
Flaherty, Msgr. J. Francis '55 (CAM) Retired.
Flaherty, Jack R. '90 (DUB) Williams, IA St. Mary's Church.
Flaherty, Msgr. James J. '80 (PT) Santa Rosa Beach, FL St. Rita Church.
Flaherty, James P. *s.j.* '92 (NY) [DD] New York, NY Xavier Jesuit Community.
Flaherty, Jay '85 (KNX) Gatlinburg, TN St. Mary Church.
Flaherty, Jay M. '85 (NSH) On Duty Outside the Diocese.
Flaherty, John J. *o.s.a.* '55 (CHI) [N] Olympia Fields, IL Tolentine Monastery at Tolentine Center.
Flaherty, John R. '90 (DUB) Webster City, IA St. Thomas Aquinas Church.
Flaherty, Kenneth *t.o.r.* '57 (ALT) [F] Loretto, PA Mount Assisi Friary.
Flaherty, Kevin H. *s.j.* '83 (CHI) [N] Chicago, IL Chicago Province of the Society of Jesus-Provincial Office.
Flaherty, Kevin H. *s.j.* '83 (FgM) Provinces.
Flaherty, Leon *c.pp.s.* '61 (GRY) [4] Whiting, IN St. John the Baptist Church.
Flaherty, Malachy *o.c.s.o.* '60 (SLC) [F] Huntsville, UT Abbey of Our Lady of the Holy Trinity of the Order of Cistercians.
Flaherty, Malachy C. *o.f.m.cap.* '42 (RVC) Retired.
Flaherty, Michael T. '73 (CIN) Mount Carmel, OH St. Veronica Church.
Flaherty, Richard C. *o.f.m.* '82 (BUF) [C] St. Bonaventure, NY St. Bonaventure University; [O] St. Bonaventure, NY St. Bonaventure Friary.
Flaherty, Thomas *o.s.b.* '48 (KCK) [H] Atchison, KS St. Benedict's Abbey.
Flaherty, William J. '52 (CHI) Flossmoor, IL Infant Jesus of Prague Church; Winnetka, IL SS. Faith, Hope and Charity Church; Retired.
Flahive, James J. '48 (SPR) [2] Chicopee, MA Holy Name of Jesus Church.
Flak, Mirko *s.d.b.* '49 (LA) [W] Rosemead, CA St. Joseph's Salesian Youth Renewal Center.
Flamm, Paul M. *c.s.sp.* '99 (FgM) Holy Ghost Foreign Missions.
Flammia, Paul '96 (BO) Saugus, MA Blessed Sacrament Church.
Flanagan, Austin E. '66 (SCR) [I] Hazleton, PA Hazleton-Saint Joseph Medical Center.
Flanagan, Bernard A. '82 (ALN) [3] Pottsville, PA Mary Queen of Peace Church.
Flanagan, Brian '63 (PAT) [7] Clifton, NJ St. Paul Church.
Flanagan, Brian M. '98 (PMB) [2] Boca Raton, FL Our Lady of Lourdes Church.
Flanagan, Bruce G. '78 (BO) Danvers, MA St. Richard Church.
Flanagan, Christopher J. '99 (R) Chapel Hill, NC St. Thomas More Church.
Flanagan, Damian '91 (MIA) Coral Gables, FL St. Augustine Church.
Flanagan, David J. '87 (MAD) Cuba City, WI St. Rose of Lima Church.
Flanagan, Edward *o.f.m.* '64 (SP) [O] Belleair Bluffs, FL St. James Friary.
Flanagan, Edward R. '88 (MET) Parlin, NJ St. Bernadette Church.
Flanagan, Msgr. Francis B. '32 (BUR) Retired.
Flanagan, James *s.o.l.t.* '52 (CC) Robstown, TX St. Anthony Church; [H] Robstown, TX Society of Our Lady of the Most Holy Trinity.
Flanagan, James D. '71 (NY) [147] Bronx, NY Holy Family Church.
Flanagan, James W. '61 (DUB) On Duty Outside the Archdiocese.
Flanagan, John '59 (SY) [4] Utica, NY Sacred Heart Church.
Flanagan, John *m.s.f.* '74 (SAT) Kenedy, TX Our Lady of Peace Church; Runge, TX St. Anthony's Church.
Flanagan, John '96 (PH) Swarthmore, PA Notre Dame de Lourdes Church.
Flanagan, John B. '97 (PH) [D] Springfield, PA Cardinal O'Hara High School.
Flanagan, Joseph F. X. *s.j.* '59 (BO) [W] Chestnut Hill, MA The Jesuit Community at Boston College.
Flanagan, Lawrence W. *s.j.* '52 (OM) [K] Omaha, NE Jesuit Community at Creighton University.
Flanagan, Michael '61 (DAL) Retired.
Flanagan, Michael J. *m.s.* '60 (ATL) Snellville, GA St. Oliver Plunkett Church.
Flanagan, Michael T. '65 (JC) Columbia, MO Our Lady of Lourdes Church.
Flanagan, Msgr. P. Kevin '59 (PAT) Chester, NJ St. Lawrence the Martyr Church.
Flanagan, Patrick *c.m.* '92 (CHI) [N] Chicago, IL DePaul Vincentian Residence.
Flanagan, Msgr. Patrick J. '56 (SAT) Converse, TX St. Monica Church.
Flanagan, Patrick S. *c.m.* '88 (PH) [AA] Philadelphia, PA Congregation of the Mission.
Flanagan, Msgr. Sean B. '59 (LA) Reseda, CA St. Catherine of Siena Church.
Flanagan, Msgr. Thomas J. '49 (BRK) Retired.
Flanagan, Thomas J. '74 (SC) On Duty Outside the Diocese.
Flanagan, William '64 (JC) Monroe City, MO Holy Rosary Church.
Flanagan, William '68 (JC) Indian Creek, MO St. Stephen Church.
Flanagan, William J. '28 (SFR) Belmont, CA St. Mark Church.
Flanagan, William J. '46 (SFR) Retired.
Flanery, Joseph-Mary *o.c.d.* '55 (MIL) [P] Holy Hill, WI Discalced Carmelite Monastery.
Flanigan, Edward J. *m.m.* '56 (FgM) Maryknoll Foreign Missions.
Flanigan, Msgr. Gerald A. '51 (DET) Retired.
Flanigan, James *c.s.c.* '62 (FTW) [A] Notre Dame, IN Moreau Seminary.
Flanigan, James F. *c.s.c.* '62 (FTW) [B] Notre Dame, IN University of Notre Dame Du Lac.
Flanigan, Thomas '50 (ALB) Retired.
Flanigan, Msgr. Thomas P. '69 (PH) Upper Gwynedd, PA Corpus Christi Church.
Flannery, Gerald K. '59 (DET) [1] Livonia, MI St. Aidan Church.
Flannery, John *o.p.* '60 (SD) [A] San Diego, CA St. Francis Seminary.
Flannery, Joseph D. '53 (SCR) Retired; [N] Dunmore, PA Villa St. Joseph.
Flannery, Kevin L. *s.j.* '87 (DET) [K] Detroit, MI Jesuit Provincial Office-Detroit Province of the Society of Jesus.

Flannery, Michael '64 (JKS) [1] Jackson, MS St. Peter Church.
Flannery, Michael '97 (ALB) Delmar, NY St. Thomas the Apostle Church.
Flannery, Patrick R. '97 (NEW) Summit, NJ St. Teresa's Church.
Flannery, Robert B. '73 (BEL) Carbondale, IL St. Francis Xavier Church.
Flannigan, John G. *s.j.* '43 (STL) [O] St. Louis, MO Fusz Pavilion.
Flannigan, Patrick *o.f.m.* '90 (WDC) [M] Washington, DC Commissariat of the Holy Land, Franciscan Monastery - Mount St. Sepulchre.
Flaska, John A., Jr. '68 (SFE) [5] Santa Fe, NM St. John the Baptist Church.
Flaska, Michael J. '97 (DEN) Sterling, CO St. Anthony Church.
Flater, Gerald *o.m.i.* '57 (BO) [Z] Tewksbury, MA Immaculate Heart of Mary Infirmary.
Flatley, Brian M. '66 (BO) [1] Arlington, MA St. Agnes Church.
Flatley, Eugene T. '46 (GB) Retired.
Flattery, John J. '55 (PEO) Retired.
Flavin, James A. '87 (BO) [3] Brockton, MA St. Edward Church.
Flavin, James Joseph *o.m.i.* '63 (MIA) [2] Miami, FL Christ the King Church.
Flavin, John E. '61 (CHI) Glenview, IL Our Lady of Perpetual Help Church; [M] Glenview, IL Maryhaven Inc.
Flax, Myron *o.f.m.cap.* '64 (FgM) Capuchin Foreign Missions.
Fleck, David '75 (EVN) Mount Vernon, IN St. Philip's Church.
Fleck, John W. '59 (TOL) Landeck, OH St. John Baptist Church; Spencerville, OH St. Patrick Church.
Fleck, Kenneth J. '76 (CHI) [21] Chicago, IL St. Barnabas Church.
Fleck, Richard A. *o.p.* '55 (BO) [W] Dover, MA St. Stephen Priory.
Flecky, Michael J. *s.j.* '77 (OM) [K] Omaha, NE Jesuit Community at Creighton University.
Flegge, William '60 (SLC) Provo, UT St. Francis of Assisi Church.
Fleischhacker, John J. *o.s.c.* '61 (DUL) McGregor, MN Holy Family Church.
Fleischhacker, John J. *o.s.c.* '61 (SCL) [I] Onamia, MN Crosier Monastery.
Fleischman, Richard J. '68 (MIL) [2] Sheboygan, WI SS. Cyril and Methodius Church; [Y] Sheboygan, WI St. Thomas High School, Inc.
Fleischmann, George R. '56 (MIL) Retired.
Fleiter, Robert V. '61 (STL) Herculaneum, MO Church of the Assumption of B.V.M..
Flek, Msgr. Ladislaus J. (PAT) Retired.
Fleming, Alfred J. *m.m.* '60 (FgM) Maryknoll Foreign Missions.
Fleming, Austin H. '73 (BO) Concord, MA Our Lady Help of Christians Church.
Fleming, Brendan '52 (P) Retired.
Fleming, Daniel J. '96 (ATL) Alpharetta, GA St. Thomas Aquinas Church.
Fleming, David *s.m.* '69 (STL) [P] St. Louis, MO Provincialate of the Society of Mary, Province of St. Louis.
Fleming, David '90 (DM) On Special Assignment.
Fleming, David J. *o.f.m.* '43 (BO) [Z] Boston, MA Saint Anthony Residence.
Fleming, David L. *s.j.* '65 (STL) [P] St. Louis, MO Jesuit Community Corporation at St. Louis University - Jesuit Hall; [P] St. Louis, MO The Jesuits of the Missouri Province; [V] St. Louis, MO Review for Religious.
Fleming, Msgr. Edward J. '44 (NEW) Retired; [B] South Orange, NJ Seton Hall University.
Fleming, Msgr. Francis J. '39 (STP) Retired; [M] St. Paul, MN Franciscan Health Community.
Fleming, George '94 (ALB) Chestertown, NY St. John the Baptist Church; Hague, NY Blessed Sacrament Church; North Creek, NY St. James Church.
Fleming, James *s.j.* '95 (BO) [W] Chestnut Hill, MA The Jesuit Community at Boston College.
Fleming, Jeffrey '92 (HEL) [B] Helena, MT Carroll College.
Fleming, John F. '49 (NY) Retired.
Fleming, John M. '61 (CAM) Hammonton, NJ St. Anthony of Padua Church.
Fleming, John R. '42 (NU) Retired.
Fleming, John R. '42 (STP) [M] St. Paul, MN Franciscan Health Community.
Fleming, John W. '96 (MAN) Salem, NH Mary, Queen of Peace Church.
Fleming, Msgr. Joseph H. '43 (ALT) Retired.
Fleming, Joseph W. '74 (ALT) St. Augustine, PA St. Augustine Church.
Fleming, Martin M.P. '52 (STP) Retired; [M] St. Paul, MN Franciscan Health Community.
Fleming, Patrick J. *c.m.* '43 (PH) [AA] Philadelphia, PA Congregation of the Mission.
Fleming, Msgr. Patrick V. '48 (ALT) Retired.
Fleming, Raymond '82 (ROC) [49] Rochester, NY Roman Catholic Community of the 19th Ward Church.
Fleming, Raymond H. '82 (ROC) [46] Rochester, NY Emmanuel Church of the Deaf of the Diocese of Rochester; [48] Rochester, NY St. Monica Church.
Fleming, Terence K. '67 (ROC) On Duty Outside the Diocese.
Fleming, Terence K. '67 (SP) [K] St. Petersburg, FL St. Anthony's Hospital, Inc.
Fleming, Msgr. Terrance L. '73 (LA) [1] Los Angeles, CA Cathedral Residence Church.
Fleming, Thomas '55 (JOL) Retired; [I] Naperville, IL St. John Vianney Villa.
Fleming, Thomas B. (WOR) [L] Worcester, MA Compassion House.
Fleming, Thomas B. '76 (WOR) [7] Worcester, MA Notre Dame des Canadiens - St. Joseph Church; [H] Worcester, MA Catholic Charities.
Fleming, Thomas F. *s.j.* '42 (BO) [W] Chestnut Hill, MA The Jesuit Community at Boston College.
Fleming, Thomas J. '59 (BO) [3] Gloucester, MA St. Peter Church.
Fleming, Thomas J. '85 (SAG) Ubly, MI St. Columbkille Church; Ubly, MI St. John the Evangelist Church.
Fleming, Msgr. Vincent A. '44 (SR) Retired.
Fleming, Msgr. W. Stanley '52 (COV) Retired.
Flemming, James K. '86 (VEN) Cape Coral, FL St. Andrew Church.
Flens, Daniel A. '89 (CHI) Chicago Heights, IL St. Kieran Church.
Flesey, Msgr. John W. '69 (NEW) [A] South Orange, NJ Immaculate Conception Seminary; [B] South Orange, NJ Seton Hall University.
Fletcher, Patrick '85 (PCE) On Duty Outside the Diocese.
Flickinger, Don D. '64 (FRS) On Duty Outside the Diocese.
Flickinger, Don D. '64 (SJ) [5] San Jose, CA St. Frances Cabrini Church.
Flickinger, Robert E. '75 (KAL) Portage, MI St. Catherine of Siena Church.
Flinn, Msgr. George (ALT) [E] Hollidaysburg, PA Dmitri Manor Priests' Residence.
Flinn, Msgr. George B. '66 (ALT) [1] Johnstown, PA St. John Gualbert Church.
Flint, Edward A. *s.j.* (DET) [K] Detroit, MI Jesuit Provincial Office-Detroit Province of the Society of Jesus.
Flint, Edward A. *s.j.* '69 (COL) [25] Columbus, OH Community of Holy Rosary and St. John Church.
Flint, James *o.s.b.* '83 (JOL) [A] Lisle, IL Benedictine University; [J] Lisle, IL St. Procopius Abbey.
Flint, Kenneth '42 (NOR) Retired.
Flis, Stanislaw '69 (DET) [A] Orchard Lake, MI SS. Cyril and Methodius Seminary.
Flisiak, Stefan '32 (OM) Retired.
Fliss, James W. '75 (BUF) Farnham, NY St. Anthony's Church.
Fliss, Richard L. '66 (LC) On Duty Outside the Diocese.
Floch, W. Roy '77 (SPK) Odessa, WA St. Joseph Church; Wilbur, WA Sacred Heart Church.
Flock, Robert H. '82 (LC) Foreign Missions.
Floeckler, Christopher M.J. '86 (PCE) On Duty Outside the Diocese.
Floersh, Philip M. *c.m.* '62 (STL) [P] St. Louis, MO Vincentian Residence.
Flohr, Gregory J. '64 (GBG) Saltsburg, PA St. Matthew Church.
Flood, Augustine A. '64 (GBG) [H] Latrobe, PA Saint Vincent Archabbey.
Flood, Charles *o.ss.t.* '81 (WDC) [M] Hyattsville, MD St. John de Matha Monastery, Order of Most Holy Trinity.
Flood, David *o.f.m.* '58 (BUF) [C] St. Bonaventure, NY St. Bonaventure University; [O] St. Bonaventure, NY St. Bonaventure Friary.
Flood, Eric *f.s.s.p.* '00 (OM) [34] Omaha, NE St. Patrick Church.
Flood, Eric *f.s.s.p.* '00 (SCR) [M] Elmhurst, PA Priestly Fraternity of St. Peter (F.S.S.P.), North American District Headquarters.
Flood, Francis *o.s.b.* '93 (NEW) [N] Newark, NJ Newark Abbey.
Flood, J. Michael '68 (PH) Glenside, PA St. Luke the Evangelist Church; [EE] Philadelphia, PA Newman Center at Drexel University.
Flood, Msgr. James J. '58 (PH) Narberth, PA St. Margaret Church.
Flood, John F. '62 (CLV) [M] Fairlawn, OH St. Edward Home dba The Village at St. Edward Nursing Care and Assisted Living; [M] Fairlawn, OH St. Edward Home dba The Village at St. Edward Nursing Care and Assisted Living.
Flood, Matthew C. *s.j.* '61 (NY) [F] New York, NY Fordham Preparatory School; [DD] New York, NY Jesuit Community at Fordham University.
Flood, Maurice *o.c.s.o.* '91 (ARL) [J] Berryville, VA Cistercian Abbey of Our Lady of the Holy Cross.
Flood, Maurice *o.c.s.o.* '91 (SR) [N] Whitethorn, CA Our Lady of the Redwoods Abbey.
Flood, Msgr. Patrick '45 (FRS) Retired.
Flood, Paul A. '90 (ATL) Lithonia, GA Christ Our Hope Church.
Flood, Peter J. '69 (TR) Military Chaplains.
Flood, Msgr. William '57 (BRK) [211] Queens, NY Our Lady of Grace Church.
Flora, Carmel *o.f.m.cap.* '53 (DET) [K] Detroit, MI St. Bonaventure Friary.
Flora, Carmel *o.f.m.cap.* '53 (FgM) Capuchin Foreign Missions.
Florczyk, Franciszek '81 (CHI) Argo, IL St. Blase Church.
Florczyk, Walter '62 (SY) Absent on Sick Leave.
Florek, Msgr. Frederick J. '64 (SD) [36] San Diego, CA St. Therese Church.
Florek, Richard *o.f.m.conv.* '72 (BAL) [26] Baltimore, MD St. Clement Mary Hofbauer Church.
Florek, Thomas W. *s.j.* (DET) [T] Detroit, MI Midwest Cultural Institute of Leadership.
Florek, Thomas W. *s.j.* '86 (CHI) [N] Chicago, IL Chicago Province of the Society of Jesus-Provincial Office.
Florek, Thomas W. *s.j.* '86 (DET) [61] Detroit, MI SS. Peter and Paul Jesuit Church.
Flores, Arturo *o.m.i.* '93 (SAT) [F] San Antonio, TX St. Anthony Catholic High School; [M] San Antonio, TX Oblate Benson Residence (Southwest Area).
Flores, Benjamin '93 (ELP) Pecos, TX Santa Rosa Church.
Flores, Msgr. Daniel E. '88 (CC) [1] Corpus Christi, TX Corpus Christi Church.
Flores, Efrain *s.v.d.* '91 (LA) [72] Los Angeles, CA St. John, The Evangelist Church.
Flores, Francisco Q. '00 (B) Nampa, ID St. Paul's Church.
Flores, Gabriel '85 (SFR) [34] San Francisco, CA Mission Dolores Basilica Church.
Flores, Gabriel R. *m.c.c.j.* '85 (SFR) [55] San Francisco, CA Visitacion, Church of the.
Flores, Gerardo *v.d.m.f.* '95 (SFR) [N] Daly City, CA Verbum Dei Missionary Fraternity.
Flores, J. Carmen '91 (OKL) Guymon, OK St. Peter's Church.
Flores, Jesus (ROC) Newark, NY St. Michael Church.
Flores, Jesus E. *m.j.* '91 (GAL) [75] Houston, TX St. Stephen Church.
Flores, Juan '98 (YAK) Cashmere, WA St. Francis Xavier Church; Leavenworth, WA Our Lady of the Snows Church.
Flores, Juan Carlos Diaz *o.p.* (P) [P] Portland, OR University of Portland.
Flores, Lee '85 (GAL) Sweeny, TX Our Lady of Perpetual Help Church.
Flores, Manuel M. *s.j.* '87 (LA) [Q] Los Angeles, CA Columbiere House.
Flores, Manuel M. *m.n.m.* '88 (ARE) [4] Camuy, PR Our Lady of Monserrate Church.
Flores, Miguel '94 (FRS) [5] Fresno, CA Sacred Heart Church; [10] Fresno, CA St. Helen Church.
Flores, Ramiro '95 (OAK) Antioch, CA St. Ignatius Church.
Flores, Richard '84 (FWT) [15] Fort Worth, TX St. Rita Church.
Flores, Roberto *s.v.d.* '96 (OAK) [6] Oakland, CA St. Bernard's Church.
Flores, Virgilio '66 (LSC) Bayard, NM Our Lady of Fatima Church.
Floretta, Edward A. '60 (BRK) [133] Brooklyn, NY SS. Simon and Jude Church.
Florez, Andrew L. (NY) Washingtonville, NY St. Mary Church.
Florez, Jhon Jaime '96 (CGS) Humacao, PR Dulce Nombre de Jesus Church.
Florez, Laurence A. '59 (PHX) Retired.
Florez, Luis '59 (STA) [1] Jacksonville, FL Assumption Church.
Flori, David J. '86 (DAL) Richardson, TX St. Paul the Apostle Church.
Floridi, Nick '00 (PHX) [8] Phoenix, AZ St. Augustine Church.
Florido, Msgr. Raphael A. '45 (BRK) Retired.
Florido, Robert A. '79 (CHI) [204] Chicago, IL Transfiguration of Our Lord Church.
Florio, Anselmo M. *o.cist.* '54 (TR) Mount Laurel, NJ St. John Neumann Church; [M] Mount Laurel, NJ Cistercian Monastery of Our Lady of Fatima.
Florival, Lys *c.s.sp.* '93 (GRY) Highland, IN St. James the Less Church.
Flovival, Lys *c.s.sp.* '93 (CHI) [98] Chicago, IL St. Jerome Church.
Flower, Thomas A. '65 (HRT) Tariffville, CT St. Bernard's Church.
Flowers, Thomas A. '77 (WIL) Middletown, DE St. Joseph Church.
Fluet, Gregoire J. '82 (NOR) Moodus, CT St. Bridget Church.
Fluetsch, John P. '91 (FRS) Wasco, CA St. John the Evangelist Church.
Flusche, Ernest A. '54 (OKL) Norman, OK St. Joseph's Church; Retired; [L] Oklahoma City, OK All Saints Catholic School.

Flusche, Vincent '90 (LR) Atkins, AR Assumption B.V.M. Church.
Flusk, Msgr. Joseph F. '53 (NEW) Retired.
Flynn, Anthony G. '66 (PH) Springfield, PA St. Kevin Church.
Flynn, Arthur C. '52 (BO) Reading, MA St. Agnes Church.
Flynn, Brian V. *o.f.m.* '60 (SPK) [11] Spokane, WA St. Francis of Assisi, Friars Church.
Flynn, Charles '69 (DUL) [8] West Duluth, MN St. James Church.
Flynn, D. Michael *s.j.* '73 (NEW) [C] Jersey City, NJ St. Peter's Preparatory School.
Flynn, Msgr. Daniel V. '48 (NY) Harrison, NY St. Gregory the Great Church.
Flynn, Dennis *s.v.d.* '61 (FgM) Society of the Divine Word Foreign Missions.
Flynn, Edmund *o.c.s.o.* '70 (ARL) [J] Berryville, VA Cistercian Abbey of Our Lady of the Holy Cross.
Flynn, Edward J. '44 (RVC) Retired; [M] Uniondale, NY St. Pius X Residence.
Flynn, Edward R. '54 (SD) On Duty Outside the Diocese.
Flynn, Francis '67 (PMB) Retired.
Flynn, Francis J. '50 (BRK) Retired.
Flynn, Francis J. '53 (BRK) Absent on Sick Leave.
Flynn, Francis J. '69 (OG) Bloomingdale, NY St. Paul Church; Gabriels, NY Gabriel's Correctional Facility.
Flynn, Francis J. *m.m.* '76 (NY) [DD] Maryknoll, NY Maryknoll Fathers and Brothers.
Flynn, George '41 (JOL) Retired.
Flynn, George '56 (FgM) Society of St. James the Apostle.
Flynn, George R. '56 (BO) Society of St. James the Apostle.
Flynn, J. Francis *m.m.* '52 (FgM) Maryknoll Foreign Missions.
Flynn, J. Michael *s.j.* '96 (BO) [W] Chestnut Hill, MA The Jesuit Community at Boston College.
Flynn, Msgr. James B. '48 (SFR) [1] San Francisco, CA Cathedral of St. Mary (Assumption); Retired.
Flynn, James B. '64 (WOR) Southborough, MA St. Matthew Church; [C] Worcester, MA Holy Name Central Catholic Junior/Senior High School.
Flynn, James E. '55 (L) Retired.
Flynn, James E. *s.j.* '73 (PHX) [B] Phoenix, AZ Brophy College Preparatory.
Flynn, James F. '67 (CHI) [81] Chicago, IL Holy Name of Mary Church.
Flynn, James P. '36 (BUF) Retired.
Flynn, James P. '47 (NY) Patterson, NY Sacred Heart Church; Retired.
Flynn, James R. *o.s.a.* '72 (PH) [C] Villanova, PA Villanova University; [G] Malvern, PA Malvern Preparatory School for Boys; [AA] Malvern, PA Augustinian Friars (O.S.A.).
Flynn, John C. '55 (NY) [163] Bronx, NY St. Martin of Tours Church.
Flynn, John H. '55 (BO) Senior Priests.
Flynn, John L. *s.j.* '64 (SJ) [D] San Jose, CA Bellarmine College Preparatory.
Flynn, John R. *o.s.a.* '71 (ORL) Casselberry, FL St. Augustine Church.
Flynn, Joseph *o.f.m.cap.* '66 (NY) [DD] White Plains, NY St. Conrad Friary.
Flynn, Joseph A. '47 (HRT) Retired.
Flynn, Joseph D. '62 (BO) Hingham, MA St. Paul Church.
Flynn, Joseph P. *c.s.p.* '44 (NY) [104] New York, NY St. Paul the Apostle Church; [DD] Jamaica Estates, NY Paulist Fathers Generalate.
Flynn, Lawrence W. *m.m.* '87 (NY) [DD] Maryknoll, NY Maryknoll Fathers and Brothers.
Flynn, Mark F. '72 (HRT) Southbury, CT Sacred Heart Church.
Flynn, Msgr. Martin J. '30 (RVC) Huntington, NY St. Patrick's Church; Retired.
Flynn, Matthew *o.c.s.o.* '58 (WOR) [N] Spencer, MA St. Joseph's Abbey; [P] Spencer, MA St. Joseph Abbey.
Flynn, Michael *o.carm.* '60 (CHI) [139] Chicago, IL Nativity of Our Lord Church.
Flynn, Michael '71 (RVC) Copiague, NY Our Lady of the Assumption Church.
Flynn, Michael E. '77 (CHI) Hickory Hills, IL St. Patricia Church.
Flynn, Michael F. '91 (BGP) [7] Norwalk, CT St. Thomas the Apostle Church.
Flynn, Michael J. '94 (PT) [2] Pensacola, FL Little Flower Church.
Flynn, Patrick *c.ss.r.* (BAL) [68] Baltimore, MD Our Lady of Fatima Church.
Flynn, Patrick *c.ss.r.* (HBG) [2] Lancaster, PA St. Anthony of Padua Church.
Flynn, Robert G. '53 (BO) Senior Priests.
Flynn, Robert J. *s.j.* '50 (FgM) Provinces.
Flynn, Robert V. '56 (Y) Streetsboro, OH St. Joan of Arc Church; Retired.
Flynn, Msgr. Sean P. '75 (TR) [1] Toms River, NJ St. Joseph Church.
Flynn, Stephen '58 (ALN) [J] Bethlehem, PA Holy Family Villa.
Flynn, Stephen F.X. '58 (ALN) Retired.
Flynn, Thomas '61 (HEL) On Duty Outside the Diocese.
Flynn, Thomas A. '49 (SCR) Retired.
Flynn, Thomas A. '57 (SCR) [N] Dunmore, PA Villa St. Joseph.
Flynn, Thomas A. '60 (CLV) North Olmsted, OH St. Clarence Church.
Flynn, Thomas J. *c.s.sp.* '53 (SHP) Rayville, LA Sacred Heart Church.
Flynn, Msgr. Thomas M. '58 (CAM) Oaklyn, NJ St. Aloysius Church.
Flynn, Thomas P. '60 (DET) Retired.
Flynn, Thomas P. '80 (NY) [132] Bronx, NY St. Barnabas Church.
Flynn, William J. *s.s.* '59 (SCR) Montdale, PA Corpus Christi Church.
Flynn, William J. '64 (NOR) Taftville, CT Sacred Heart Church.
Flynt, James M. '85 (MIL) [18] Milwaukee, WI St. Casimir Church; [54] Milwaukee, WI St. Mary of Czestochowa Church; [H] Milwaukee, WI All Saints Catholic East School System, Inc.
Fobare, Scott D. '87 (OG) Carthage, NY St. James Minor Church; Copenhagen, NY St. Mary Church.
Fodor, Nicholas Vitez *sch.p.* '49 (BUF) [O] Lackawanna, NY Piarist Fathers.
Foeckler, Christopher *m.j.* (CHI) [X] Chicago, IL Miles Jesu.
Foelker, James *o.m.i.* '55 (CC) [4] Kingsville, TX St. Martin Church.
Foeller, Msgr. Charles J. '50 (COL) Cardington, OH Sacred Hearts Church.
Foerch, Benjamin J. *o.f.m.* '65 (SCR) [12] Wilkes-Barre, PA St. Joseph Church; Wilkes-Barre, PA Veteran's Administration Hospital; [M] Wilkes-Barre, PA St. Joseph's Friary.
Foerstler, Vincent *o.p.* '57 (PHX) [5] Phoenix, AZ Most Holy Trinity Church.
Fogal, Joseph B. '75 (WIN) Fairmont, MN St. John Vianney Church.
Fogarty, Austin '81 (ATL) McDonough, GA St. James The Apostle Church.
Fogarty, Daniel '49 (NY) Retired.
Fogarty, Declan (Finbarr) *o.s.a.* '59 (ORG) Buena Park, CA St. Pius V Church.
Fogarty, Msgr. George V. '46 (BRK) [189] Queens, NY St. Kevin Church; Retired; [V] Douglaston, NY Bishop Mugavero Residence.
Fogarty, Gerald J. *o.m.i.* '59 (NO) [R] Crown Point, LA Ave Maria Retreat House.
Fogarty, Gerald P. *s.j.* '70 (WDC) [M] Washington, DC The Jesuit Community at Georgetown University.
Fogarty, James '54 (SLC) Retired.
Fogarty, John C. *o.carm.* '50 (VEN) [G] Nokomis, FL Carmel at Mission Valley.
Fogarty, Msgr. Noel '57 (MIA) Plantation, FL St. Gregory Church.
Fogarty, Paul '67 (ATL) [2] Atlanta, GA Holy Cross Church.
Fogarty, Thomas *s.s.p.* '57 (Y) [A] Canfield, OH Society of St. Paul.
Fogerty, Joseph *o.p.* '59 (DET) [2] St. Clair Shores, MI St. Gertrude Church.
Fogle, Bruce '83 (OWN) Axtel, KY St. Anthony Church; McQuady, KY St. Mary-of-the-Woods Church.
Foglio, John '61 (LAN) Retired.
Foisy, Leonard R. '57 (MAN) [11] Manchester, NH St. John the Baptist Church; Retired.
Foix, Evarist V. *o.c.d.* '28 (LR) [A] Little Rock, AR Marylake - Carmelite Novitiate.
Foken, Herman J. '43 (TLS) Muskogee, OK Saint Joseph Church; Retired.
Folbrecht, Robert A. '75 (LA) West Covina, CA St. Christopher Church; Los Angeles, CA L.A. County Fire Dept.
Folchetti, John T. '74 (BRK) Released from Diocesan Assignment.
Folda, John T. '89 (LIN) [A] Seward, NE St. Gregory the Great Seminary.
Foley, Msgr. Andrew E. '54 (SFS) Retired.
Foley, Augustine E. *o.s.b.* '89 (NO) [A] St. Benedict, LA St. Joseph's Seminary College; [P] St. Benedict, LA St. Joseph Abbey.
Foley, Bernard *c.s.c.* '56 (SAT) [M] San Antonio, TX Holy Cross Community.
Foley, Bernard P. *c.s.c.* '56 (FTW) [J] South Bend, IN Congregation of Holy Cross, Indiana Province, Provincial House.
Foley, Brendan P. '55 (HT) Retired.
Foley, Daniel R. '60 (SPR) [11] Holyoke, MA St. Jerome's Church.
Foley, David E. '56 (BIR) [1] Birmingham, AL St. Paul's Church.
Foley, David M. '72 (MEM) [27] Memphis, TN St. Therese of the Infant Jesus Church.
Foley, Dennis *c.ss.r.* '61 (TR) [Q] Long Branch, NJ San Alfonso Retreat House.
Foley, Edward *o.f.m.cap.* '75 (CHI) [B] Chicago, IL The Catholic Theological Union at Chicago.
Foley, Edwin G. *c.ss.r.* '47 (BAL) [87] Baltimore, MD Sacred Heart of Jesus Church.
Foley, Eugene *o.carm* (NY) [E] Goshen, NY John S. Burke Catholic High School.
Foley, Eugene *o.carm.,* '86 (NY) [DD] Middletown, NY Brandsma Priory.
Foley, F. Joseph *s.m.a.* '67 (BO) [W] Dedham, MA African Mission House.
Foley, Francis P. '84 (PH) Military Chaplains.
Foley, George '58 (FWT) Breckenridge, TX Sacred Heart Church; Throckmorton, TX San Patricio Church.
Foley, Gerald J. '55 (BO) Senior Priests.
Foley, Gerald J. '59 (GB) [2] Manitowoc, WI Holy Innocents Church.
Foley, Gerald K. '61 (CR) On Duty Outside the Diocese.
Foley, Gerald K. '61 (STP) St. Paul, MN HealthEast, Inc.
Foley, Gerard M. '56 (ALX) Tioga, LA Immaculate Heart of Mary Church.
Foley, Msgr. James '32 (TR) [L] Lawrenceville, NJ Morris Hall-Saint Lawrence, Inc.
Foley, James D. '60 (BO) [5] Salem, MA St. Joseph Church.
Foley, James F. '49 (BUR) Retired.
Foley, James J. '66 (PH) East Goshen, PA SS. Peter and Paul Church.
Foley, James J. '78 (BO) Health Leave.
Foley, Msgr. James S. '32 (TR) Retired.
Foley, James S. *s.j.* '52 (NEW) [C] Jersey City, NJ St. Peter's Preparatory School.
Foley, Jerome '84 (SFR) San Francisco, CA San Francisco State Univ., Newman Center; Special Assignment.
Foley, Jerome P. '80 (SFR) [R] San Francisco, CA Newman Center, San Francisco State University.
Foley, Jerome P. '84 (SFR) [53] San Francisco, CA St. Thomas More Church.
Foley, John *o.s.f.s.* '59 (STO) Sonora, CA St. Patrick Church.
Foley, John B. *s.j.* '72 (STL) [C] St. Louis, MO Saint Louis University; [P] St. Louis, MO Jesuit Community Corporation at St. Louis University - Jesuit Hall.
Foley, John F. *s.j.* '58 (BO) [W] Boston, MA The Society of Jesus of New England-Provincial Offices; [W] Weston, MA Campion Jesuit Community.
Foley, John Fenton *s.j.* '58 (BO) [U] Framingham, MA St. Patrick's Manor, Inc.
Foley, John I. '41 (BO) Senior Priests.
Foley, John J. *c.s.p., j.c.d.* '67 (PAT) [A] Oak Ridge, NJ Paulist Novitiate; [I] Oak Ridge, NJ Mount Paul Retreat Center.
Foley, John J. '74 (WOR) [4] Worcester, MA Christ the King Church.
Foley, John K. '59 (LA) Montrose, CA Holy Redeemer Church.
Foley, John P. *s.j.* '67 (CHI) [174] Chicago, IL St. Procopius Church; [D] Chicago, IL Cristo Rey Jesuit High School, Inc.; [N] Chicago, IL Miguel Pro Jesuit Community.
Foley, John T. '58 (BO) Senior Priests.
Foley, Joseph *c.m.* (PH) [46] Philadelphia, PA St. Francis of Assisi Church.
Foley, Leo A. *s.m.* '43 (WDC) [M] Washington, DC Marist Center.
Foley, Louis *o.f.m.* '41 (PAT) [M] Ringwood, NJ Holy Name Friary, Inc.
Foley, Marc *o.c.d.* (CHI) [N] Chicago, IL Discalced Carmelite Friars; Edith Stein House of Studies.
Foley, Matthew E. '89 (CHI) [5] Chicago, IL St. Agnes of Bohemia Church.
Foley, Msgr. Matthew F. '56 (BRK) [37] Brooklyn, NY Epiphany Church.
Foley, Msgr. Maurice D. '34 (LFT) Retired.
Foley, Michael '70 (PT) [3] Tallahassee, FL Good Shepherd Church.
Foley, Michael G. '70 (WOR) Milford, MA St. Mary of the Assumption Church.
Foley, Michael G. '86 (CHI) [200] Chicago, IL St. Thomas Apostle Church.
Foley, Msgr. Noel '63 (JKS) [3] Jackson, MS St. Richard Church; Jackson, MS Institute for the Blind, Institute for the Deaf and Speech Impaired.
Foley, Patrick '73 (SD) Unassigned.
Foley, Patrick H. (PT) Marianna, FL St. Anne Church.
Foley, Patrick H. '72 (PT) Chipley, FL St. Joseph the Worker Church.
Foley, Patrick H. '72 (STA) On Duty Outside the Diocese.
Foley, Paul T. '55 (WOR) Retired.
Foley, Peter J. '67 (PH) Maple Glen, PA St. Alphonsus Church.
Foley, Richard L. *o.s.a.* '60 (BO) Andover, MA St. Augustine Church.
Foley, Stephen C. '67 (HRT) [A] Bloomfield, CT St. Thomas Seminary.
Foley, Thomas *c.s.p.* '77 (AUS) [11] Austin, TX St. Austin Church.
Foley, Thomas C. '57 (BO) [3] Milton, MA St. Mary of the Hills Church.
Foley, Thomas F. *m.m.* '48 (SJ) [L] Los Altos, CA Maryknoll.
Foley, Thomas S. '86 (BO) Winchester, MA Immaculate

Conception Church.
Foley, Timothy M. '65 (STL) Ferguson, MO Sts. John and James Church.
Foley, Walter W. '76 (ATL) Retired.
Foley, William A. *s.m.* '48 (ORL) Retired.
Foley, William B. *s.j.* '77 (BO) [W] Boston, MA The Society of Jesus of New England-Provincial Offices.
Foley, William B. '77 (STL) [P] St. Louis, MO Jesuit Community Corporation at St. Louis University - Jesuit Hall.
Foley, William E. '79 (WDC) [35] Washington, DC Our Lady of Victory Church.
Foley, Msgr. William J. '67 (NY) New City, NY St. Augustine Church.
Foley, William P. '74 (BAL) [9] Baltimore, MD Annunciation Church.
Folger, Benedict *ss.cc.* '58 (WDC) Seat Pleasant, MD St. Margaret Church.
Folger, Roland H. '67 (CHI) Antioch, IL St. Peter Church.
Folgeri, Benedict *ss.cc.* '57 (FR) [I] Fairhaven, MA Sacred Hearts Provincial House.
Folinio, Frank *o.f.m.* (CHI) [D] Chicago, IL Hales Franciscan High School, Inc.
Follen, George R. *s.j.* '49 (DET) [61] Detroit, MI SS. Peter and Paul Jesuit Church.
Folliard, Msgr. John '50 (LA) [5] Long Beach, CA St. Cornelius Church.
Folliard, Msgr. John P. '50 (LA) Retired.
Follmann, Roland F. *o.s.a.* '60 (JOL) [C] New Lenox, IL Providence Catholic High School; [J] New Lenox, IL Augustinian Friary.
Follmar, A. Joseph '59 (LC) Greenwood, WI St. Mary Help of Christians Church; Willard, WI Holy Family Church.
Folorunso, Stephen Olutade '00 (RCK) [5] Rockford, IL Holy Family Church.
Folsey, William David *o.p.* '60 (PRO) [P] Providence, RI St. Thomas Aquinas Priory at Providence College.
Folsom, Cassian *o.s.b.* '84 (IND) [J] St. Meinrad, IN St. Meinrad Archabbey.
Folsom, Paul '65 (SCL) Battle Lake, MN Our Lady of the Lake Church; Maine, MN Church of Saint James at Maine.
Folsom, William P., Jr. '91 (MOB) [5] Montgomery, AL St. John the Baptist Church; [J] Montgomery, AL Alabama State University Newman Center; [K] Montgomery, AL St. John's Soup Kitchen, Inc.
Foltyn, Msgr. Emilian '64 (AUS) Dime Box, TX St. Joseph's Church; Lexington, TX Holy Family Church.
Foltz, Michael H. *j.c.l.* '89 (CR) Moorhead, MN St. Joseph's Church.
Folzenlogen, John N. *s.j.* '65 (GAL) [F] Houston, TX Strake, Jesuit College Preparatory Inc.
Folzenlogen, Joseph D. *s.j.* '71 (IND) [D] Indianapolis, IN Brebeuf Jesuit Preparatory School, Inc.
Fonck, Benet *o.f.m.* (STL) Oakville, MO St. Francis of Assisi Church.
Fonck, Benet *o.f.m.* '72 (STL) [P] Oakville, MO St. Francis Friary.
Fondevilla, Perfecto '62 (SJN) [19] San Juan, PR San Francisco de Monte Alvernia Church.
Fones, Michael *o.p.* '92 (P) [6] Eugene, OR St. Thomas More Church; [P] Portland, OR University of Portland.
Fonseca, Erwin A. *c.s.c.* '91 (FTW) [J] South Bend, IN Congregation of Holy Cross, Indiana Province, Provincial House.
Fonseca, Harvey '92 (FRS) Livingston, CA St. Jude Thaddeus Church.
Fonseca, John '50 (BGP) Retired.
Fonseca, Samuel (BO) [1] Everett, MA St. Anthony Church.
Fonseka, Matthew '69 (NEW) Saddle Brook, NJ St. Philip the Apostle Church.
Fontaine, Edouard '43 (LAF) Retired.
Fontaine, John-Paul '52 (WOR) Retired.
Fontana, Alphonso R. '97 (HRT) East Haven, CT St. Vincent de Paul's Church.
Fontana, Charles S. '69 (DET) Trenton, MI St. Timothy Church.
Fontana, Glenn '92 (PEO) [11] Peoria, IL St. Martin de Porres Church.
Fontana, John *o.s.m.* '78 (STL) Affton, MO Seven Holy Founders Church.
Fontana, John M. *o.s.m.* '78 (CHI) [N] Chicago, IL Order of Friar Servants of Mary (Servites) United States of America Province, Inc.
Fontanella, Andrew J. '56 (HBG) Carlisle, PA St. Patrick Church.
Fontanez, Msgr. Rafael '57 (SJN) [26] San Juan, PR San Jose Church.
Fontanini, Christopher '97 (DM) Audubon, IA St. Patrick Church; Exira, IA Holy Trinity Church.
Fonte, Martin M. *f.f.i.* '94 (FR) [I] New Bedford, MA Marian Friary of Our Lady, Queen of the Seraphic Order.
Fontenot, Bryan J. *o.p.* '81 (NO) [25] New Orleans, LA St. Anthony of Padua Church.
Fonti, Joseph G. '92 (BRK) [97] Brooklyn, NY Our Lady of Guadalupe Church.
Foody, Michael *c.s.sp.* (NY) [193] Bronx, NY Visitation Church.
Foote, Job *o.s.b.* '89 (PIT) [81] Pittsburgh, PA St. Peter Church.
Foote, Job V. *o.s.b.* '89 (PIT) [R] Pittsburgh, PA Office for Campus Ministry.
Foradori, V. David '86 (E) Tidioute, PA St. John Church.
Foran, Peter '22 (LA) [6] Long Beach, CA St. Cyprian Church.
Forand, Clarence W. '45 (SPR) Retired.
Forbes, Eric *o.f.m.cap.* '90 (AGN) [F] Agana Heights, GU St. Fidelis Friary.
Forbes, Msgr. Eugene A. '41 (SAG) Fisherville, MI St. Anthony Church.
Forbes, John J. '91 (R) Sanford, NC St. Stephen Church.
Forbes, Richard L. '67 (CAM) North Cape May, NJ St. John of God Church.
Forbes, Wayne A. '61 (P) [21] Portland, OR St. John Fisher Church.
Forbi, Kizito S. *s.j.* '92 (NY) [DD] New York, NY Jesuit Community at Fordham University.
Forbidussi, John E. '94 (PIT) Washington, PA Immaculate Conception Church; [R] Pittsburgh, PA Office for Campus Ministry.
Forcano, Benito *sch.p.* '66 (SJN) [57] San Juan, PR Santisimo Salvador Church.
Forcelle, Joseph (SFS) Wakonda, SD St. Patrick Church.
Forcier, Richard-Jacob *o.f.m.conv.* '86 (NOR) Stafford Springs, CT St. Edward Church.
Ford, Christopher M. '87 (HRT) [11] Hartford, CT St. Justin Church.
Ford, David R. '86 (CHI) [1] Des Plaines, IL St. Mary Church.
Ford, Harold L. '49 (LA) [8] Long Beach, CA St. Joseph Church; Retired.
Ford, J. Joseph '67 (PRT) Wells, ME St. Mary Church.
Ford, James M. '66 (LA) [6] Santa Barbara, CA San Roque Church.
Ford, John *c.s.s.* '56 (BO) [Z] Waltham, MA Stigmatine Fathers and Brothers.
Ford, John E. *s.t.* '74 (BLX) DeLisle, MS The Catholic Church in DeLisle Church.
Ford, John T. *c.s.c.* '59 (FTW) [J] South Bend, IN Congregation of Holy Cross, Indiana Province, Provincial House.
Ford, John T. *c.s.c.* '59 (WDC) [C] Washington, DC Catholic University of America, The.
Ford, Larry *o.f.m.* (FTW) [B] Notre Dame, IN University of Notre Dame Du Lac.
Ford, Lawrence D. *o.f.m.* '96 (NY) [DD] New York, NY Franciscan Friars, Order of Friars Minor, Holy Name Province.
Ford, Mark *c.m.* '92 (GLP) Page, AZ Immaculate Heart of Mary Church.
Ford, Matthew M. *o.s.m.* '48 (CHI) [N] Chicago, IL Order of Friar Servants of Mary (Servites) United States of America Province, Inc.
Ford, Michael F. *s.j.* '75 (WOR) [N] Worcester, MA Jesuits of Holy Cross College, Inc.; [Q] Worcester, MA Campus Ministry.
Ford, Nevin *o.f.m.* '54 (LA) [Q] Santa Barbara, CA Franciscan Friary, Order of Friars Minor (Old Mission); [Q] Santa Barbara, CA St. Anthony's Seminary.
Ford, Patrick J. *s.j.* '74 (SPK) [C] Spokane, WA Gonzaga University.
Ford, Richard J. '60 (ALN) [10] Allentown, PA St. Stephen of Hungary Church.
Ford, William A. '82 (STO) Retired.
Fording, John D. '42 (PIT) Retired; [O] Pittsburgh, PA St. John Vianney Manor.
Forest, Gerald *m.s.* '49 (FR) [I] Attleboro, MA La Salette Shrine.
Forester, Raymond L. '66 (WIL) Rehoboth, DE St. Edmond Church.
Forgach, Carl J. '60 (Y) Retired.
Forgit, Ambrose *ss.cc.* (WDC) [B] Cheverly, MD Damien House.
Forintos, Bradley '91 (DET) Armada, MI St. Mary Mystical Rose Church.
Forish, Andrew '42 (DET) Retired.
Foriska, John M. '70 (GBG) Calumet, PA St. Stanislaus Church; United, PA St. Florian Church.
Forkin, Gerald *o.m.i.* '52 (BO) [Z] Tewksbury, MA Immaculate Heart of Mary Infirmary.
Forliti, John E. '62 (STP) [31] Minneapolis, MN St. Olaf Church.
Forman, Bruce H. '74 (STL) [55] St. Louis, MO Sts. Peter and Paul Church.
Forman, Patrick J. '89 (BUR) Barton, VT Conversion of St. Paul Church.
Formusa, Salvatore '35 (JOL) Retired.
Fornace, Albert J. '98 (ORL) Sanford, FL All Souls Church.
Fornasari, Archimede *m.c.c.j.* '50 (CHI) Blue Island, IL St. Donatus Church; [B] Chicago, IL The Catholic Theological Union at Chicago.
Forner, Craig '75 (SFR) San Francisco, CA Serra Club of San Francisco (Downtown); Special Assignment.
Forni, John V. '77 (ROC) [30] Rochester, NY St. John Evangelist Church; Red Creek, NY St. Thomas the Apostle Church; Wolcott, NY St. Mary Magdalene Church.
Forno, R. Adam '87 (ALB) Rensselaer, NY St. John the Evangelist Church; Rensselaer, NY St. Joseph Church.
Forrest, Thomas *c.ss.r.* '54 (WDC) [M] Washington, DC Holy Redeemer College.
Forrester, Donal F. *c.s.p.* '34 (NY) [104] New York, NY St. Paul the Apostle Church; [DD] Jamaica Estates, NY Paulist Fathers Generalate.
Forrey, William C., Jr. '90 (HBG) Marysville, PA Our Lady of Good Counsel Church; [K] Harrisburg, PA Catholic Campus Ministry.
Forry, Thomas P. '68 (BO) Emergency Response Group.
Forsen, James R. '79 (LA) Baldwin Park, CA St. John the Baptist Church.
Forsmann, Leonard '76 (SPK) Clarkston, WA Holy Family Church.
Forson, Cletus '92 (BRK) [115] Brooklyn, NY St. Patrick Church.
Forst, Aloysius A. '49 (STL) Retired.
Forst, Msgr. Charles '45 (STL) [2] Lemay, MO Most Precious Blood Church.
Forst, Msgr. Charles J. '49 (STL) Retired.
Forst, Msgr. Robert M. '51 (ALN) [7] Allentown, PA St. Paul Church.
Forst, William '54 (JC) Retired.
Forster, Francis P. *o.s.b.* '64 (CHL) [J] Belmont, NC Belmont Abbey.
Forster, Msgr. William J. '54 (BO) [4] Everett, MA St. Therese Church; Senior Priests.
Forsthoefel, Paulinus F. *s.j.* '47 (DET) [K] Detroit, MI Jesuit Community at the University of Detroit.
Forsyth, George W. '46 (BRK) Retired.
Forsyth, Kevin J. '86 (HRT) [11] Waterbury, CT St. Joseph Church.
Forte, Anthony '91 (NEW) [22] Newark, NJ St. Lucy's Church.
Forte, Anthony J. *s.j.* '83 (BO) [W] Boston, MA The Society of Jesus of New England-Provincial Offices.
Forte, John Paul *o.p.* '93 (SJ) Stanford, CA Catholic Community at Stanford Church.
Fortenbaugh, Msgr. Francis W. '47 (BAL) [3] Baltimore, MD St. Agnes Church; Retired.
Fortenberry, Jerome D. *c.m.* '55 (BEL) Cairo, IL St. Patrick Church.
Fortener, Kenneth R. '69 (L) [53] Louisville, KY St. Mary Church.
Fortier, Joel F. '69 (JOL) Bloomingdale, IL St. Isidore Church.
Fortier, Joseph C *s.j.* '90 (SPK) [C] Spokane, WA Gonzaga University.
Fortier, Roger A. '80 (MAN) Absent on Leave.
Fortier, Theodore L. *a.a.* (BO) Quincy, MA Quincy Hospital.
Fortier, Theodore L. *a.a.* '53 (BO) [3] Quincy, MA St. John the Baptist Church; [W] Boston, MA Assumptionist Center.
Fortin, Ernest *a.a.* '49 (BO) [W] Boston, MA Assumptionist Center.
Fortin, John R. *o.s.b.* '76 (MAN) [K] Manchester, NH St. Anselm Abbey.
Fortin, Philip '00 (PT) [3] Tallahassee, FL Good Shepherd Church.
Fortin, Richard A. '62 (WOR) Millbury, MA Assumption Church.
Fortin, Robert *a.a.* '58 (BO) [W] Boston, MA Assumptionist Center; [W] Boston, MA Assumptionist Center.
Fortin, Roger M. '65 (PRO) [5] Warwick, RI St. Gregory the Great Church.
Fortner, Douglas F. '70 (COV) [6] Covington, KY St. John Church.
Fortner, Mark *s.c.j.* '68 (CHI) [N] Chicago, IL Priests of the Sacred Heart.
Fortney, Kenneth E. '79 (HEL) Plains, MT St. James Church; Thompson Falls, MT St. William Church.
Fortuna, George B. '57 (DET) Retired.
Fortuna, Joseph J. '80 (CLV) [8] Cleveland, OH Ascension Church.
Fortuna, Stanley *c.f.r.* (NY) [DD] Bronx, NY Our Lady of the Angels Friary.
Fortunato, Anthony M. *o.de.m.* '67 (SP) [9] St. Petersburg, FL Transfiguration Church.
Fortunato, Vincent (NEW) [N] Union City, NJ Capuchin Friars - Province of the Sacred Stigmata of St. Francis.
Fortunato, Vincent *o.f.m.cap.* '80 (NEW) [N] Union City, NJ Capuchin Friars - Province of the Sacred Stigmata of St. Francis.
Fortunio, Carlo *o.p.* '85 (NEW) West New York, NJ St. Mary Help of Christians Church.
Fosado, Aaron '89 (LR) Fort Smith, AR Immaculate Conception Church.
Foschiatti, Pedro (BO) [8] Cambridge, MA St. Mary of the Annunciation Church.
Foschiatti, Pedro *s.d.b.* (NY) [188] Bronx, NY Sacred Heart Church; Yonkers, NY Yonkers General Hospital.
Foshage, Nathanael *o.s.b.* '68 (OM) [K] Elkhorn, NE Mount Michael Abbey.
Foshage, Nathanael *o.s.b.* '68 (PBL) Ouray, CO St.

Daniel the Prophet Church; Silverton, CO St. Patrick Church; Telluride, CO St. Patrick Church.
Foshage, Ronald *m.s.* '75 (BEA) Jasper, TX St. Michael Church; Kirbyville, TX Our Lady of La Salette Church; Sam Rayburn, TX St. Raymond Church.
Fosnot, James '94 (RIC) Clarksville, VA St. Catherine of Siena Church; South Hill, VA Good Shepherd Church.
Fosselman, Albert '60 (RNO) Retired.
Fosselman, Msgr. John A. '42 (LA) Downey, CA St. Raymond Church; Downey, CA Rancho Los Amigos Medical Center; Retired.
Fosselman, Robert J. '42 (LFT) Retired.
Fossier, Emile '43 (HT) Retired.
Foster, Clyde K. '75 (CLV) Maple Heights, OH St. Wenceslas Church.
Foster, Edward M. '51 (DUL) Pine River, MN Our Lady of Lourdes Church.
Foster, James A. '72 (ALX) Colfax, LA St. Joseph Church.
Foster, James J. '80 (STL) [1] Jennings, MO Corpus Christi Church.
Foster, James K. *c.s.c.* '95 (FTW) [A] Notre Dame, IN Moreau Seminary; [B] Notre Dame, IN University of Notre Dame Du Lac; [J] Notre Dame, IN Holy Cross Community, Corby Hall, University of Notre Dame.
Foster, James M. '85 (ALT) Bellefonte, PA St. John the Evangelist's Church.
Foster, John F. *s.j.* '68 (SEA) [A] Seattle, WA Seattle University.
Foster, John J. '51 (PH) Retired.
Foster, John J.M. '91 (STO) [1] Stockton, CA Cathedral of the Annunciation.
Foster, Jonathan D. *o.f.m.* '60 (JOL) [L] Downers Grove, IL Mayslake Marmion Ministries, Inc.
Foster, Joseph R. '91 (BO) Marblehead, MA Our Lady, Star of the Sea Church.
Foster, Michael S. '80 (BO) [6] Newton, MA Our Lady Help of Christians Church.
Foster, Patrick '56 (EVN) Retired.
Foster, Raymond *o.carm.* '73 (JOL) [J] Joliet, IL St. Elias Carmelites.
Foster, Reginald *o.c.d.* '66 (MIL) [P] Milwaukee, WI Provincial Offices - Discalced Carmelites.
Foster, Thomas '82 (DUL) [12] Duluth, MN St. Margaret Mary Church.
Foster, Thomas W. *s.j.* '72 (SJ) [L] Los Gatos, CA Sacred Heart Jesuit Center.
Fostner, Jay M. *o.praem.* '88 (GB) [B] De Pere, WI St. Norbert College; [F] Green Bay, WI St. Vincent Hospital; [I] De Pere, WI St. Joseph Priory.
Fosu, Dominic '94 (STU) [7] Steubenville, OH St. Peter's Church; [9] Steubenville, OH St. Stanislaus Church.
Fosu, Peter (MAR) Stephenson, MI Precious Blood Church.
Foudy, Msgr. John T. '40 (SFR) [11] San Francisco, CA St. Cecilia Church; Retired.
Foudy, Msgr. Robert E. '43 (SPR) [4] Springfield, MA Holy Cross Church; Retired.
Foudy, Thomas F. '67 (MIA) [4] Pompano Beach, FL St. Coleman Church.
Fountain, Dennis (LSC) Artesia, NM St. Anthony Church.
Fountain, Dennis *o.f.m.* '81 (LSC) Roswell, NM St. Peter Church.
Fountain, Robert J. '55 (BO) [3] Medford, MA St. Joseph Church.
Fournier, Denis *o.s.b.* '60 (BIS) [A] Richardton, ND Assumption Abbey; [B] Bismarck, ND University of Mary.
Fournier, Raymond *s.m.* '49 (BO) [10] Lawrence, MA Sacred Heart Church.
Fournier, Raymond J. *o.c.s.o.* '81 (ROC) [I] Piffard, NY Abbey of the Genesee.
Fournier, W. Donald '53 (SPR) Retired.
Fournier, William '73 (DUL) [11] Duluth, MN St. Lawrence's Church.
Fouser, Otto *o.f.m.conv.* '55 (MET) [I] Watchung, NJ McAuley Hall Inc.
Foutts, Patrick D. *o.praem.* '93 (ORG) [I] Silverado, CA Norbertine Fathers of Orange Inc.
Fowerbaugh, Msgr. F. Raymond '55 (GRY) Retired.
Fowler, Msgr. Eugene A. '48 (NY) Retired.
Fowler, J. Richard (HRT) Bristol, CT Bristol Hospital.
Fowler, John W. '53 (DAL) Retired.
Fowler, Joseph M. '73 (L) [36] Louisville, KY Holy Trinity Church.
Fowler, Richard A. '88 (BUR) Retired.
Fowlkes, Eric L. '89 (NSH) Clarksville, TN Immaculate Conception Church.
Fox, Charles J. *s.j.* '44 (FgM) Provinces.
Fox, Daniel *o.f.m.cap.* '75 (DET) [K] Detroit, MI St. Bonaventure Friary; [K] Detroit, MI St. Bonaventure Friary.
Fox, Daniel *o.f.m.cap.* '75 (FgM) Capuchin Foreign Missions.
Fox, Daniel '82 (LA) Bellflower, CA St. Bernard Church.
Fox, Donal R. *o.s.b.* '66 (NEW) [1] Linden, NJ St. Elizabeth's Church.
Fox, Donal R. *o.s.b.* '66 (PAT) [M] Morristown, NJ St. Mary's Abbey.
Fox, Francis E. '58 (PH) [102] Philadelphia, PA Maternity B.V.M. Church.
Fox, Gabriel '74 (GAY) Manistee, MI St. Mary of Mt. Carmel Church.
Fox, George W. '61 (MAD) Retired.
Fox, James E. (DEN) [2] Aurora, CO St. Michael the Archangel Church.
Fox, James F. *s.j.* '71 (BUF) [D] Buffalo, NY Canisius High School; [O] Buffalo, NY Canisius Jesuit Community.
Fox, James R. '90 (DEN) Westminster, CO St. Mark Church.
Fox, John J. '60 (BUF) Retired.
Fox, Joseph Edward *o.p.* '74 (NY) [DD] New York, NY St. Vincent Ferrer Priory.
Fox, Joseph F. '43 (SCR) Retired.
Fox, Leo '56 (SFS) Retired.
Fox, Leonard '55 (SFS) Retired.
Fox, Martin F. '65 (GB) Seymour, WI St. John Church.
Fox, Melvin E. '63 (GR) Ionia, MI SS. Peter and Paul Church.
Fox, Msgr. Patrick '52 (SD) La Jolla, CA All Hallows Church.
Fox, Richard *o.c.s.o.* '59 (SPC) [E] Ava, MO Assumption Abbey (Trappist).
Fox, Richard '85 (SFS) Mitchell, SD Holy Spirit Church.
Fox, Richard E. '92 (SCR) Blossburg, PA St. Mary's Church.
Fox, Robert J. '55 (SFS) Alexandria, SD St. Mary of Mercy Church; [I] Alexandria, SD Fatima Family Apostolate.
Fox, Robert J. '59 (GF) Retired.
Fox, Sean P. '53 (SEA) Mountlake Terrace, WA St. Pius X Church.
Fox, Thomas *o.f.m.* '62 (IND) [31] Indianapolis, IN St. Patrick Church.
Fox, Thomas E. '59 (BRK) [54] Brooklyn, NY Holy Family Church.
Fox, Thomas E. '60 (LFT) Remington, IN Sacred Heart Church.
Fox, Thomas J. *o.f.m.* '46 (FgM) Franciscan Foreign Missions.
Fox, Thomas P. *m.m.* '56 (FgM) Maryknoll Foreign Missions.
Fox, Tom *o.f.m.* '62 (IND) [12] Indianapolis, IN Sacred Heart of Jesus Church.
Foxen, David *m.s.c.* '67 (FgM) Missionaries of the Sacred Heart Foreign Missions.
Foxen, David *m.s.c.* '67 (RCK) [G] Aurora, IL Missionaries of the Sacred Heart Community.
Foy, Edward J. '45 (ROC) [4] Auburn, NY St. Alphonsus Church; Retired.
Foy, Felican *o.f.m.* '47 (NEW) Fair Lawn, NJ St. Anne's Church.
Foy, Felician A. *o.f.m.* '47 (PAT) [P] Paterson, NJ St. Anthony's Guild.
Foye, Harold J. *c.s.p.* '46 (BO) [W] Boston, MA Paulist Fathers Residence.
Foye, Harold J. *c.s.p.* '46 (NY) [DD] Jamaica Estates, NY Paulist Fathers Generalate.
Foye, Thomas M. '55 (NEW) [2] Bayonne, NJ St. Andrew's Church; Retired.
Foynes, Aiden '33 (SP) [F] Clearwater, FL Little Nazareth Early Childhood Center.
Foynes, Aiden '61 (SP) [4] Clearwater, FL St. Cecelia Church.
Foyo, Alexis *o.s.b.* '83 (SD) [H] Oceanside, CA Prince of Peace Abbey, Benet Hill.
Foys, Msgr. Roger J. '73 (STU) [10] Steubenville, OH Servants of Christ the King Church; Toronto, OH St. Francis of Assisi Church; Toronto, OH St. Joseph's Church; [B] Steubenville, OH Catholic Central High School; [J] Steubenville, OH Charismatic Renewal; [J] Steubenville, OH Diocesan Committee of Administrative Review; [J] Steubenville, OH Lay Employees Pension Plan; [J] Steubenville, OH Synod Committee.
Fraats, Ralph J. '60 (ROC) [59] Rochester, NY St. Thomas the Apostle Church.
Fracaro, Mark '67 (JOL) Minooka, IL St. Mary Church.
Frade, Paulo '97 (NEW) Harrison, NJ Holy Cross Church.
Fraenzle, Wilfred J. '64 (LEX) [5] Lexington, KY St. Elizabeth Ann Seton Church.
Fraga, Bento R. *v.f.* '56 (FR) [9] Taunton, MA St. Paul's Church.
Fragomeni, Richard '75 (ALB) On Duty Outside the Diocese.
Fragomeni, Richard '75 (CHI) [B] Chicago, IL The Catholic Theological Union at Chicago.
Fraher, Joseph P. '50 (CHY) Retired.
Fraher, Kevin *c.ss.r.* '73 (CHI) [N] Glenview, IL The Redemptorists of Glenview, Illinois.
Fraher, Leonard W. '56 (SUP) Retired.
Fraile, Mariano *o.c.d.* '47 (PCE) [12] Ponce, PR San Jose Church.
Fraile, Tomas *c.r.* '63 (DEN) [27] Denver, CO St. Cajetan's Church.
Frambes, John C. *o.f.m.* '79 (ALB) [B] Loudonville, NY Siena College; [B] Loudonville, NY Siena College.
Frana, Clarence L. '51 (DUB) Retired.
Francavilla, Joseph F. '68 (NTN) McLean, VA Holy Transfiguration Church.
France-Kelly, Kenneth A. *o.p.* '81 (WDC) [11] Washington, DC St. Dominic Church & Priory Church; [V] Washington, DC Rosary Shrine of St. Jude.
Franceschini, Mark M. *o.s.m.* '59 (CHI) Hillside, IL St. Domitilla Church; [N] Chicago, IL Order of Friar Servants of Mary (Servites) United States of America Province, Inc.
Franceschini, Msgr. Philip J. '66 (NY) [220] Staten Island, NY Our Lady of Pity Church.
Francesco, Richard G. '87 (NEW) [8] Newark, NJ St. Benedict's Church.
Francez, James *m.c.c.j.* '57 (FgM) Comboni Foreign Missions.
Francik, Gerard '87 (BAL) Special Assignment.
Francis, A. Edwin '45 (CIN) Retired.
Francis, Bernard C. '69 (NO) Hahnville, LA Our Lady of the Holy Rosary Church.
Francis, Cominic (PEO) [N] Princeville, IL St. Joseph Priory and Novitiate.
Francis, Daniel *c.ss.r.* '91 (NY) [150] Bronx, NY Immaculate Conception Church.
Francis, Msgr. Eugene G. '52 (GAL) [40] Houston, TX St. John Neumann Church.
Francis, Isaac O. '97 (GAL) [24] Houston, TX St. Cyril of Alexandria Church.
Francis, John '90 (BRK) [240] Queens, NY St. Sebastian Church.
Francis, Joseph A. *o.p.* '78 (NY) [76] New York, NY St. Monica Church.
Francis, Paul R. '41 (BO) Senior Priests.
Francis, Rashid *o.f.m.* '80 (BO) [W] Boston, MA St. Bonaventure Friary, Franciscan Friars.
Francis, Ray A. '63 (NEW) Belleville, NJ St. Anthony's Church.
Francis, Vyjay Kumar '88 (PH) [95] Philadelphia, PA St. Martin of Tours Church.
Francis, Msgr. William C. '58 (BO) [24] Boston, MA Holy Family Church.
Francisco, Alexander '79 (HT) [5] Houma, LA St. Bernadette Church.
Francisco, Manuel *s.j.* '97 (BO) [W] Cambridge, MA Weston Jesuit Community.
Francisko, Gary '82 (PRM) Absent on Leave.
Franck, James *c.pp.s.* '64 (LA) [40] Los Angeles, CA St. Agnes Church.
Franck, John J. *c.pp.s.* '67 (ORL) Winter Garden, FL Resurrection Church.
Franck, John L. *a.a.* '77 (BO) [W] Boston, MA Assumptionist Center.
Franco, David *o.s.f.s.* '76 (LAN) [6] Ypsilanti, MI Transfiguration Catholic Church.
Franco, Geraldo Ildeo (BO) [2] Marlborough, MA Immaculate Conception Church.
Franco, Msgr. Hilary '55 (NY) Ossining, NY St. Augustine Church.
Franco, Robert J. '82 (CLV) [6] Euclid, OH St. William Church.
Franco, Robert M. '73 (PIT) [7] Pittsburgh, PA St. Catherine of Siena Church.
Franco, Ronald *c.s.p.* '95 (NY) [104] New York, NY St. Paul the Apostle Church.
Franco, Salvator '53 (BRK) Retired.
Franco, Victor *l.c.* '81 (MAN) [A] Center Harbor, NH Immaculate Conception Apostolic School.
Francois, Ducasse *i.v. dei.* '98 (PMB) [1] Lake Worth, FL Sacred Heart Church.
Francois, Theodore V. *s.j.* '70 (NY) [DD] New York, NY Jesuit Provincial's Office; [DD] New York, NY West Side Jesuit Community.
Franczek, J. August '48 (GAY) Hale, MI St. Pius X Church.
Franey, John A. '63 (PH) Collegeville, PA St. Eleanor Church; [EE] Philadelphia, PA Newman Center at Drexel University.
Frank, Chrysostom '85 (VNN) Denver, CO Holy Protection of the Mother of God Church.
Frank, Edward R. '57 (SAV) Moultrie, GA Immaculate Conception Church.
Frank, Eugene G. '57 (BIS) Retired.
Frank, Gerald W. '70 (BWN) [5] McAllen, TX Holy Spirit Church.
Frank, Joseph A. '49 (NEW) Retired; [N] Caldwell, NJ The Rev. Msgr. James F. Kelley Residence for Retired Priests.
Frank, Paul *o.m.i.* '50 (MIA) [2] Miami, FL Christ the King Church; [10] Fort Lauderdale, FL St. John the Baptist Church.
Frank, Richard C. *m.m.* '53 (FgM) Maryknoll Foreign Missions.
Frank, Richard W. '72 (JC) St. Clement, MO St. Clement Church; Bowling Green, MO Northeast Correctional Center.
Frank, Thomas R. *s.s.j.* '78 (NO) [B] New Orleans, LA Josephite House of Studies.
Frank, Tom '70 (AUS) Pflugerville, TX St. Elizabeth Church.

Franken, William F. '88 (BAL) Hydes, MD St. John the Evangelist Church.
Frankenberger, William J. *c.s.b.* '73 (GAL) [Q] Sugar Land, TX Basilian Mission Center.
Frankhauser, William E. *s.j.* '66 (BUF) Cattaraugus, NY St. Mary Church; Little Valley, NY St. Mary Church.
Franklin, Claude W., Jr. '97 (SAM) Scranton, PA St. Ann Church.
Franklin, David W. '85 (BGP) [5] Stamford, CT St. Clement Church; Greenwich, CT Greenwich Hospital; Stamford, CT Stamford Hospital.
Franklin, Edward L. '62 (OG) Retired.
Franklin, George '86 (STV) [1] St. Thomas, VI Cathedral of Sts. Peter and Paul; On Duty Outside the Diocese.
Franklin, Osvaldo *j.c.d.* (NY) [19] Yonkers, NY Our Lady of Fatima Church.
Frankman, Gregory '81 (SFS) Parker, SD St. Christina Church.
Franko, George M. '50 (Y) Retired.
Franko, Jack *o.m.i.* '67 (BWN) Port Isabel, TX Our Lady Star of the Sea Church.
Frankovich, Francis A. '68 (GAL) [72] Houston, TX Queen of Peace Church; [Q] Houston, TX Companions of the Cross (Texas); [U] Houston, TX Catholic Charismatic Center.
Frankovich, Frank '68 (SB) On Duty Outside the Diocese.
Frankowski, Miroslaw '98 (DET) [8] Sterling Heights, MI Our Lady of Czestochowa Church.
Franks, Becket '86 (JOL) [K] Lisle, IL Benedictine Sisters of the Sacred Heart, Sacred Heart Monastery.
Franks, Donald E. '79 (COL) Lancaster, OH St. Mary Church; [L] Lancaster, OH St. Mary of the Assumption Foundation.
Franks, Gabriel '57 (VIC) On Special or Other Diocesan Assignment.
Franks, T. Becket *o.s.b.* '86 (JOL) [J] Lisle, IL St. Procopius Abbey.
Fransco, Peter J. '58 (SC) Retired.
Fransiscus, Thomas *c.ss.r.* '64 (DEN) [M] Denver, CO The Redemptorists/Denver Province.
Fransiscus, Thomas J. '65 (RNO) Stead, NV St. Michael's Church.
Frantz, Henry L. *c.pp.s.* '54 (ORL) Longwood, FL Church of the Nativity.
Franxman, Thomas W. *s.j.* '64 (FgM) Provinces.
Franz, Paul R. '66 (BO) Health Leave.
Franz, S. Michael '69 (CLV) [73] Cleveland, OH St. Stephen Church.
Franzen, Robert B. '53 (SFD) Chatham, IL St. Joseph Church.
Franzinell, Benjamin '50 (LAV) Retired.
Franzman, Thomas R. '70 (CHI) [135] Chicago, IL St. Michael Church.
Frapaul, Sam *o.f.m.cap.* '78 (PAT) [7] Passaic, NJ Our Lady Of Mt. Carmel Church.
Frappier, Msgr. George L. '56 (PRO) Retired.
Fraraccio, Ugo *s.d.v.* '42 (PAT) [M] Florham Park, NJ Father Justin Vocationary.
Frascadore, Henry C. '59 (HRT) Southington, CT St. Dominic Church.
Frascati, Marino *o.de.m.* (CLV) [O] Cleveland, OH Mercedarians.
Frascati, Marino *o.de.m.* '51 (CLV) [57] Cleveland, OH Our Lady of Mount Carmel Church.
Fraser, Bernard F. '00 (DET) Centerline, MI St. Clement Church.
Fraser, Daniel J. '99 (TOL) Mansfield, OH St. Peter Church.
Fraser, Donald D. '74 (B) McCall, ID Our Lady of the Lake Church.
Fraser, Gerald C. '72 (BO) Health Leave; Permanent Disability.
Fraser, Gerald D. '38 (CHI) Retired.
Fraser, James F. '65 (BRK) [179] Queens, NY Holy Trinity Church.
Fraser, Michael B. '75 (NO) [5] Marrero, LA The Visitation of Our Lady Church.
Fratic, Joseph P. '64 (BO) Dover, MA Most Precious Blood Church.
Fratt, Gregory Perkins '98 (HT) Cut-Off, LA Sacred Heart Church.
Fratus, James F. '81 (BO) [2] Chelsea, MA St. Rose of Lima Church.
Fratus, Thomas '52 (CHI) [N] Chicago, IL St. Peter's Friary.
Frausto, Jorge *o.f.m.* '86 (ELP) [15] El Paso, TX Our Lady of Guadalupe Church.
Frawley, Gerald (DET) Allenton, MI St. John the Evangelist Church.
Frawley, Gerard *s.c.a.* (DET) Capac, MI St. Nicholas Church.
Frawley, John P. '44 (CHI) [202] Chicago, IL St. Thomas More Church; Retired.
Frawley, Patrick J. '78 (BRK) [210] Queens, NY Our Lady of Fatima Church.
Frayne, Thomas M. '88 (CHI) [95] Chicago, IL St. James Church.
Frazer, Edward J. *s.s.* '61 (WDC) [A] Washington, DC Theological College of the Catholic University of America.
Frazer, J. Francis '75 (PIT) Bethel Park, PA St. Valentine Church.
Frazer, Joseph '84 (AUS) Franklin, TX St. Francis of Assisi Church.
Frazier, Lawrence K. '71 (BAL) Buckeystown, MD St. Joseph-on-Carrollton Manor Church.
Frazier, Richard W. '95 (COV) Cold Spring, KY St. Joseph Church.
Frazier, Richard W. '96 (COV) [B] Alexandria, KY Bishop Brossart High School.
Frazier, William B. *m.m.* '56 (NY) [DD] Maryknoll, NY Maryknoll Fathers and Brothers.
Frazzita, Barry '59 (BRK) [184] Queens, NY St. Joan of Arc Church.
Frechette, Christopher *s.j.* '99 (BO) [W] Cambridge, MA Faber House; [W] Cambridge, MA Weston Jesuit Community.
Frechette, Leo L. '55 (MAN) Retired.
Frechette, Leonard A. '52 (PRT) Retired.
Frechette, Paul *s.m.* '76 (FgM) Marist Foreign Missions.
Frechette, Paul G. '78 (NTN) Worcester, MA Our Lady of Perpetual Help Church.
Frechette, Richard *c.p.* '79 (FgM) Passionist Foreign Missions.
Frechette, Thomas A. '86 (FR) Dighton, MA St. Peter's Church.
Frecker, Msgr. A. Anthony '72 (COL) Canal Winchester, OH Pope John XXIII Church.
Fredeman, Felix '57 (LR) [A] Subiaco, AR Subiaco Monastery.
Frederick, Curt J. '75 (MIL) Brookfield, WI St. Dominic Church.
Frederick, Joseph B. '56 (MIL) Retired.
Frederick, Lawrence A. '66 (LR) [B] Little Rock, AR Catholic High School.
Frederick, Robert A., Jr. '00 (ATL) [10] Atlanta, GA St. Jude Church.
Fredericks, James '77 (LA) [C] Los Angeles, CA Loyola Marymount University.
Fredericks, James L. '77 (SFR) On Duty Outside the Archdiocese.
Fredericks, Michael '87 (SB) [8] Riverside, CA St. John the Evangelist Church.
Fredette, Joseph *m.s.* '57 (FR) [I] Attleboro, MA La Salette Shrine.
Fredette, Joseph *a.a.* '60 (BO) [W] Boston, MA Assumptionist Center.
Free, Daniel *c.p.* (HRT) [M] West Hartford, CT Holy Family Monastery/Retreat.
Free, Henry *c.p.* '58 (FgM) Passionist Foreign Missions.
Freed, Eric '90 (SR) Cotati, CA St. Joseph Church; [K] Penngrove, CA Newman Hall, Sonoma State University, Intercollegiate Catholic Ministries.
Freed, Robert '83 (ALN) Bally, PA Most Blessed Sacrament Church.
Freed, Robert '83 (WCH) Retired.
Freeh, Vincent T. *m.s.c.* '59 (Y) [A] Youngstown, OH Sacred Heart Retreat House & Renewal Center; [N] Youngstown, OH Sacred Heart Retreat and Renewal Center.
Freel, Francis *c.ss.r.* '46 (ALB) [L] Saratoga Springs, NY St. John Neumann Residence.
Freel, Francis *c.ss.r.* '46 (TR) [Q] Long Branch, NJ San Alfonso Retreat House.
Freeman, George J. '65 (STP) New Prague, MN St. Wenceslaus Church.
Freeman, James '65 (DM) On Duty Outside the Diocese.
Freeman, James A. '65 (TUC) [17] Tucson, AZ St. Joseph Church; [E] Tucson, AZ Carondelet Health Network.
Freeman, John A. '73 (PH) Absent on Leave.
Freeman, Joseph M. *s.j.* '44 (STL) [O] St. Louis, MO Fusz Pavilion.
Freeman, Msgr. Robert E. '57 (CC) Refugio, TX Our Lady of Refuge Church; Refugio, TX St. James the Apostle Church.
Freeman, Roland P. '67 (DEN) [G] Denver, CO Special Religious Education-Pastoral Care of Developmentally Disabled Persons.
Freemesser, Paul J. '59 (ROC) [4] Auburn, NY St. Alphonsus Church; Retired.
Freeswick, William J. '69 (PAT) [K] Denville, NJ St. Francis Residential Community.
Freeze, J. Donald '63 (BAL) [S] Baltimore, MD Jesuit Fathers and Brothers Maryland Provincial Curia.
Fregapane, Msgr. Mercurio A. '51 (HBG) [2] Lebanon, PA St. Benedict the Abbot Church.
Fregault, Roland *o.f.m.* (PAT) [M] Ringwood, NJ Holy Name Friary, Inc.
Frego, Max '63 (SAG) Retired.
Freidel, John J. '86 (SPC) [I] Cape Girardeau, MO Southeast Missouri State University, Newman Center.
Freiermuth, Harry '59 (MRY) Retired.
Freifer, Michel '84 (SAM) Miami, FL Our Lady of Lebanon Church.
Freire, Gerardo *s.j.* '56 (MIA) [H] Miami, FL Villa Arrieta.
Freitag, Patrick W. '96 (SEA) Bremerton, WA Our Lady, Star of the Sea Church.
Freitas, Daniel '47 (ORL) Retired.
Freitas, Daniel L. '49 (FR) Retired.
Freitas, Fernando P. '48 (PRO) Retired.
Freitas, Patrick '65 (HON) [12] Honolulu, HI St. Philomena Church.
Fremgen, Edward G. '92 (LA) [4] Long Beach, CA St. Bartholomew Church.
Fremont-Smith, Peter *s.o.l.t.* '92 (CC) [H] Robstown, TX Society of Our Lady of the Most Holy Trinity.
French, D. James *s.j.* '74 (NY) [DD] New York, NY "America;" Residence and publication office of the America Press; [DD] New York, NY Jesuit Provincial's Office.
French, Donald J. '76 (HRT) [6] New Haven, CT St. Brendan's Church.
French, James R. '78 (STL) Park Hills, MO Immaculate Conception Church.
French, John F. '54 (ALB) Ballston Spa, NY St. Mary Church.
French, Michael D. *s.j.* '75 (BAL) [B] Baltimore, MD Loyola College in Maryland; [S] Baltimore, MD Jesuit Community of Loyola College, Inc.
French, Raymond D. *c.s.sp.* '91 (PIT) [B] Pittsburgh, PA Duquesne University of the Holy Ghost; [R] Pittsburgh, PA Office for Campus Ministry.
French, Robert E. '63 (RIC) [2] Hampton, VA Immaculate Conception Church.
French, Thomas *s.m.* '97 (SFR) [N] San Francisco, CA Marianist Community.
French, Msgr. Thomas A. '49 (SAT) [K] San Antonio, TX Incarnate Word Retirement Community; [N] San Antonio, TX Incarnate Word Retirement Community.
French, Walter V. '65 (NEW) Retired.
Frenier, Steven G. *o.f.m.conv.* '82 (BUF) Athol Springs, NY St. Francis of Assisi Church.
Frenoy, Fortune *s.m.* '55 (ORL) [1] Orlando, FL Mary Queen of the Universe Church.
Freret, Warren Joseph '88 (GAL) Retired.
Frerichs, Glenn K. '00 (WIN) [5] Rochester, MN St. Francis of Assisi Church.
Frerker, Jack W. '63 (BEL) Retired.
Frerkes, James J. '62 (MRY) Nipomo, CA St. Joseph Church.
Frese, Joseph R. *s.j.* '44 (NY) [DD] New York, NY Murray-Weigel Hall.
Fresno, Leonidas *o.s.a.* '64 (SAT) [47] San Antonio, TX St. Jude Church.
Freson, Kenan *o.f.m.* '67 (CIN) [C] Cincinnati, OH St. Anthony Shrine, Franciscan Candidacy; [M] Cincinnati, OH St. Francis Seraph Friary; [U] Cincinnati, OH Community Support Charitable Trust; [U] Cincinnati, OH Friars Club Foundation, Inc.
Freuh, Robert '63 (BRK) [14] Brooklyn, NY St. Augustine Church.
Freund, John B. *c.m.* '65 (BRK) [V] Jamaica, NY St. Vincent's House.
Freund, Joseph *c.ss.r.* '66 (BAL) [87] Baltimore, MD Sacred Heart of Jesus Church.
Freund, Melchior *o.s.b.* '57 (SCL) [I] Collegeville, MN St. John's Abbey, of the Order of St. Benedict.
Frey, Msgr. Andrew F. '48 (BR) Retired.
Frey, Francis '58 (SAN) [5] Odessa, TX St. Mary's Church.
Frey, Jerome V. '50 (LAF) On Special Assignment; [M] Lafayette, LA Community of Jesus Crucified.
Frey, Msgr. John T. '70 (CAM) [4] Vineland, NJ St. Isidore Church.
Frey, Paul T. *o.s.f.s.* '69 (WIL) [I] Wilmington, DE Oblates of St. Francis De Sales.
Freyer, Timothy '89 (ORG) Laguna Beach, CA St. Catherine of Siena Church.
Freymuth, Mike '79 (STL) [33] St. Louis, MO St. Elizabeth, Mother of John the Baptist Church.
Freyne, Barry '60 (SJ) Palo Alto, CA St. Thomas Aquinas Church.
Frias, Msgr. Carlos (ELP) [37] El Paso, TX San Juan Bautista Church.
Frias, Ramon *o.f.m.cap.* '72 (NY) [57] New York, NY St. John the Baptist Church.
Frias, Ray *o.f.m.cap.* '72 (NY) [GG] New York, NY University Apostolate.
Frias, Msgr. Santiago C. '59 (RIC) [3] Norfolk, VA Holy Trinity Church.
Friberg, Daniel W. '62 (STP) Hugo, MN St. John the Baptist Church.
Friday, Robert M. '61 (PIT) On Duty Outside the Diocese.
Friday, Robert M. '61 (WDC) [C] Washington, DC Catholic University of America, The; [C] Washington, DC Catholic University of America, The.
Fride, Edward O. '86 (LAN) [1] Ann Arbor, MI Christ the King Church.
Fridrich, Sylevester W. '51 (CLV) Retired.
Fridrich, Sylvester W. '51 (CLV) Gates Mills, OH St. Francis of Assisi Church.
Friebel, Richard *c.pp.s.* '78 (CIN) [23] Dayton, OH Precious Blood Church.

Fried, Francis L. '68 (STP) Northfield, MN St. Dominic Church.
Friedel, James *o.s.a.* '65 (CHI) [N] Olympia Fields, IL Tolentine Monastery at Tolentine Center.
Friedel, Robert E. '57 (CLV) Twinsburg, OH SS. Cosmas and Damian Church.
Friedell, John C. '54 (DUB) Retired; [C] Dubuque, IA Loras College.
Friedell, Ronald G. '66 (DUB) McGregor, IA St. Mary's Church; Monona, IA St. Patrick's Church.
Friederick, John J. '65 (DUB) Colesburg, IA St. Patrick's Church; Edgewood, IA St. Mark's Church.
Friedl, Erwin J. '71 (CHI) Melrose Park, IL Sacred Heart Church.
Friedl, Msgr. Francis P. '43 (DUB) Retired.
Friedl, Thomas '92 (CR) Lake Park, MN St. Francis Xavier's Church.
Friedman, Cecil H. '50 (SC) Retired.
Friedman, Daniel L. '72 (BEL) Aviston, IL St. Francis of Assisi Church.
Friedman, Robert '89 (Y) Hubbard, OH St. Patrick's Church.
Friedrich, Aloys *c.pp.s.* '36 (CIN) [B] Carthagena, OH St. Charles.
Friedrich, Jim D. '89 (SFS) Herreid, SD St. Michael Church.
Friedrich, Lawrence '47 (SFS) Retired.
Friedrich, Ralph '43 (Y) Retired.
Friedrichs, Paul L. '78 (CIN) On Special and Archdiocesan Assignment.
Friedrichs, Richard M. '70 (PRO) [R] Narragansett, RI Our Lady of Peace Spiritual Life Center.
Friedrichsen, Timothy '84 (WDC) [C] Washington, DC Catholic University of America, The.
Friedrichsen, Timothy A. '84 (SC) On Duty Outside the Diocese.
Friel, Edward M. '89 (CAM) Haddon Heights, NJ St. Rose's Church.
Friel, James E. '52 (PBL) [9] Pueblo, CO St. Anne Church.
Friel, John F. *o.s.f.s.* '70 (TUC) [B] Tucson, AZ Yuma Catholic High School.
Friel, Lee G. *o.f.m.cap.* '56 (FgM) Capuchin Foreign Missions.
Friel, Mark J. '63 (BUF) [K] Lewiston, NY Mount St. Mary's Hospital of Niagara Falls.
Friel, Mark M. '63 (BUF) [7] Niagara Falls, NY St. Mary of the Cataract Church; Niagara Falls, NY Niagara Falls Memorial Medical Centers.
Frient, Lawrence '84 (Y) Andover, OH Our Lady of Victory Church.
Fries, Msgr. Francis A. '35 (HRT) Retired.
Fries, Richard R. *m.m.* '76 (FgM) Maryknoll Foreign Missions.
Frigault, Edward F. '49 (NOR) Willimantic, CT St. Joseph Church; Retired.
Frigo, Martin A. *o.praem.* '49 (WIL) [I] Claymont, DE Immaculate Conception Priory of the Canons Regular of Premontre.
Frigo, William M. *o.f.m.cap.* '63 (CHI) [A] Chicago, IL St. Joseph Seminary.
Frilot, Msgr. Eugene P. '55 (LA) Glendale, CA Church of the Incarnation; Retired.
Frink, John A. '87 (ALN) Whitehall, PA Holy Trinity Church; [C] Allentown, PA Allentown Central Catholic High School.
Frisbie, Kenneth J. '48 (HRT) Retired; [A] Bloomfield, CT St. Thomas Seminary.
Frisch, Joseph C. '45 (WIN) Dakota, MN Holy Cross Church.
Frisch, Kenneth J. '78 (MAD) Highland, WI SS. Anthony and Philip Church; Montfort, WI St. Thomas Church.
Frisch, Michael F. *o.praem* '97 (GB) [B] De Pere, WI St. Norbert College; [I] De Pere, WI St. Norbert Abbey.
Frisch, Ralph *s.t.* '59 (WDC) [M] University Park, MD Holy Trinity Missionary Cenacle.
Frische, Emile *m.h.m.* (NY) [DD] Yonkers, NY Parish Mission Team Residence.
Frische, Emile *m.h.m.* '70 (NY) [DD] Hartsdale, NY Mill Hill Fathers Residence.
Friske, Joseph P. (SAG) Retired.
Friske, Joseph P. '62 (SAG) On Duty Outside the Diocese.
Frisoli, John B. *o.f.m.* '48 (ALB) [A] Catskill, NY St. Anthony Friary.
Frisoli, John Baptist *o.f.m.* '48 (BO) [W] Boston, MA St. Christopher Friary.
Frison, Basil *c.m.f.* '36 (LA) [Q] Rancho Dominguez, CA Dominguez Seminary Inc.
Frison, Ted '72 (P) Salem, OR Youth Correctional Facility; Woodburn, OR MacLaren Youth Correctional Facility.
Frister, Jerome '57 (JUN) Retired.
Fritsch, Albert J. *s.j.* '67 (LEX) [J] Mount Vernon, KY Appalachia Science in the Public Interest.
Fritsch, Michael C. '85 (IND) Greencastle, IN St. Paul the Apostle Church; Putnamville, IN Indiana State Farm; [N] Greencastle, IN DePauw Catholic Campus Ministry.
Fritschen, Thomas *f.s.s.p.* (COS) [1] Colorado Springs, CO St. Mary's Church.
Fritschen, Thomas *f.s.s.p.* '00 (SCR) [M] Elmhurst, PA Priestly Fraternity of St. Peter (F.S.S.P.), North American District Headquarters.
Fritz, Francis E. '45 (CIN) Retired.
Fritz, Germain L. *o.s.b.* '61 (PAT) [M] Morristown, NJ St. Mary's Abbey.
Fritz, Gorden N. *m.m.* '42 (NY) [DD] Maryknoll, NY Maryknoll Fathers and Brothers.
Fritz, Henry H. *o.s.b.* '52 (PEO) Peru, IL St. Joseph's Church; [A] Peru, IL St. Bede Abbey and Academy.
Fritz, John Christopher '00 (RCK) Geneva, IL St. Peter Church.
Fritz, Norbert '42 (P) Retired.
Fritz, Peter *o.f.m.* '50 (FWT) [H] Crowley, TX St. Francis Village, Inc.; [I] Crowley, TX St. Maximilian Kolbe Friary.
Fritz, Richard A. '75 (KAL) Bronson, MI St. Mary's Church.
Fritz, Robert J. '75 (CAM) Pomona, NJ Assumption Church.
Fritzen, James C. (SY) [W] Syracuse, NY St. Mary-St. Agnes.
Frizelle, Msgr. John '51 (AUS) Granger, TX SS. Cyril and Methodius Church.
Frizelle, Msgr. John D. '51 (AUS) Retired.
Frizzell, Edward *s.d.b.* (NY) [2] Port Chester, NY Corpus Christi Church.
Frizzell, Lawrence E. '62 (NEW) [B] South Orange, NJ Seton Hall University.
Froehle, Charles L. '63 (STP) Buffalo, MN St. Francis Xavier Church.
Froehlich, Canice *o.f.m.cap.* '47 (STL) [P] St. Louis, MO St. Patrick Friary.
Froehlich, James *o.f.m.cap.* '82 (HBG) [2] York, PA St. Joseph Church.
Froehlich, Msgr. Mark J. '69 (STU) Bridgeport, OH St. Joseph Church.
Froelich, Canice *o.f.m.cap.* '47 (STL) [54] St. Louis, MO St. Patrick Church.
Froeschl, Msgr. Martin H. '49 (KC) Retired.
Froidurot, Michael '78 (SD) Poway, CA St. Gabriel Church.
Fromholzer, Francis J. '58 (ALN) [7] Allentown, PA St. Paul Church.
Frommelt, Robert M. *s.j.* '38 (MIL) [P] Wauwatosa, WI Jesuit Community at St. Camillus; [Y] Milwaukee, WI The Jesuit Partnership.
Fron, Raymond S. '64 (SAG) [6] Bay City, MI St. Joseph Church.
Fronckewicz, Stephen *o.s.b.* '57 (NOR) [E] Willimantic, CT Holy Family Home and Shelter, Inc.
Fronckowiak, Dennis F. '77 (BUF) [4] North Tonawanda, NY Our Lady of Czestochowa Church.
Fronczak, Dennis A. '75 (BUF) Holland, NY St. Joseph Church.
Fronk, Christopher S. *s.j.* '97 (CLV) [B] Cleveland, OH John Carroll Jesuit Community.
Fronske, Edward *o.f.m.* '67 (GLP) Whiteriver, AZ St. Francis Church.
Frontiero, Msgr. Anthony R. '91 (MAN) On Duty Outside the Diocese.
Frontiero, Msgr. Anthony R. '91 (NY) [76] New York, NY St. Monica Church.
Frost, Arthur *c.ss.r.* '41 (LA) Whittier, CA St. Mary of the Assumption Church; [Q] Whittier, CA Redemptorist Fathers Mission House.
Frost, James '76 (BRK) [165] Queens, NY Corpus Christi Church.
Frost, John M. '87 (DM) Avoca, IA St. Mary, Mediatrix of All Graces Church; Walnut, IA St. Patrick Church.
Frost, Peter J. '70 (BO) Health Leave.
Frost, Stephen '84 (ORG) Inactive Leave.
Frost, Msgr. Stephen A. '77 (FRS) Oildale, CA Christ the King Church.
Frost, Thomas *o.f.m.* '60 (TUC) Topawa, AZ San Solano Missions - Tohono O'odham Indian Reservation Church.
Frost, William P. '58 (CIN) [D] Dayton, OH The University of Dayton.
Frozena, Kenneth R. '60 (GB) Sherwood/St. John, WI St. John-Sacred Heart Church.
Frueh, David *s.s.j.* '71 (BEA) [7] Beaumont, TX Our Mother of Mercy Church.
Frueh, Robert '63 (BRK) Brooklyn, NY Kingsboro Psychiatric Center; [V] Brooklyn, NY St. Joseph's Priest Residence.
Fruge, Msgr. Donald J. '72 (AUS) Special Assignments.
Fruge, Msgr. Donald J. '72 (GAL) On Duty Outside the Diocese.
Frugoli, Francis A. *s.j.* '45 (SJ) [L] Los Gatos, CA Sacred Heart Jesuit Center.
Frundt, Oscar H. '56 (WIL) Retired.
Fruth, Paul '74 (DUL) Brainerd, MN St. Andrew's Church; St. Mathias, MN St. Mathias Church.
Fry, Albert *o.p.* (BRK) [97] Brooklyn, NY Our Lady of Guadalupe Church.
Fry, James Q. '79 (ORG) Military Chaplains.
Fry, Richard C. '58 (SJ) [13] San Jose, CA St. Julie Billiart Church.
Fry, Timothy *o.s.b.* '41 (KCK) [H] Atchison, KS St. Benedict's Abbey.
Fryar, Thomas S. '78 (DEN) [1] Englewood, CO All Souls Church.
Fryda, William *m.m.* '88 (FgM) Maryknoll Foreign Missions.
Frydrych, Jerzy *s.ch.* '85 (GAL) [55] Houston, TX Our Lady of Czestochowa Church.
Fryer, Patrick L. '73 (WH) On Duty Outside the Diocese.
Fu, Bartholomew Paul *o.p.* '46 (NY) [DD] New York, NY St. Catherine of Siena Priory.
Fu, John *s.v.d.* '30 (CHI) [B] Techny, IL Divine Word Residence.
Fu, Joseph, (Retired) '60 (NEW) [11] Jersey City, NJ Holy Rosary Church.
Fu, Paul B. *o.p.* '46 (NY) [22] New York, NY St. Catherine of Siena Church; Manhattan, NY New York Presbyterian Hospital.
Fuccile, Dominic G. '66 (NEW) Maplewood, NJ Immaculate Heart of Mary Church.
Fucheck, Robert '66 (ORL) Lady Lake, FL St. Timothy Church.
Fuchs, Athanase *o.s.b.* '41 (SCL) [I] Collegeville, MN St. John's Abbey, of the Order of St. Benedict.
Fuchs, John D. *s.j.* '75 (SEA) [5] Tacoma, WA St. Leo the Great Church.
Fuchs, Moritz A. '55 (SY) Hannibal, NY Our Lady of the Rosary Church.
Fuchs, Msgr. Robert A. '41 (AUS) Retired.
Fuchs, Msgr. Sylvester '49 (AUS) Retired.
Fuchs, Msgr. Sylvester '49 (GAL) Retired.
Fucinaro, Thomas J. '89 (LIN) On Duty Outside the Diocese.
Fuemmeler, James R. '58 (JC) Camdenton, MO St. Anthony Church.
Fuente, Maximo *o.m.i.* '31 (SAT) [K] San Antonio, TX Oblate Madonna Residence.
Fuentes, Roberto T. *m.m.* '92 (FgM) Maryknoll Foreign Missions.
Fuentes, Rodolfo Godinez '91 (STA) [21] Jacksonville, FL San Jose Church.
Fuentes, Ruben *o.f.m.* '64 (SD) Lemon Grove, CA St. John of the Cross Church.
Fuentes, Theo *c.m.f.* '51 (LA) [31] Los Angeles, CA Our Lady Queen of the Angels Church.
Fuentez, Trinidad '78 (ELP) [20] El Paso, TX Queen of Peace Church.
Fugee, Michael C. '94 (NEW) Wyckoff, NJ St. Elizabeth Church.
Fugini, Francis *o.f.m.cap.* '54 (FgM) Capuchin Foreign Missions.
Fugini, Francis *o.f.m.cap.* '54 (PIT) [O] Pittsburgh, PA St. Augustine Friary.
Fugolo, Joseph *c.s.* '67 (BRK) [V] Jamaica, NY Saint Charles House of Studies.
Fugolo, Joseph *c.s.* '67 (NY) [HH] New York, NY Scalabrini Pastoral Center; [HH] New York, NY Friends of RADIO MARIA, Inc.; [HH] New York, NY American Committee on Italian Immigration, Inc.; [HH] New York, NY Trust for the Center for Migration Studies in New York.
Fuhrman, Nicholas *o.s.b.* '54 (LR) [E] Jonesboro, AR St. Bernard's Regional Medical Center.
Fuhrman, Msgr. Robert J. '81 (NEW) Saddle River Borough, NJ St. Gabriel the Archangel Church.
Fuhrman, Msgr. Robert J. '81 (NY) [HH] New York, NY Catholic Medical Mission Board, Inc.
Fuhrmann, Bruno *o.s.b.* '54 (FgM) American - Cassinese Congregation Foreign Missions.
Fuhrmann, Nicholas '54 (LR) Marked Tree, AR St. Norbert Church.
Fuino, Crispin *o.f.m.conv.* '48 (TR) Point Pleasant Beach, NJ St. Peter's Church.
Fuino, Michael '42 (NEW) [N] Rutherford, NJ St. John Vianney Residence for Priests.
Fuino, Michael A. '42 (NEW) Retired.
Fujihara, Fidelis *s.a.* '65 (NY) [DD] Garrison, NY Franciscan Friars of the Atonement, Minister General Office.
Fukes, Gary M. '88 (SY) [S] Syracuse, NY St. Pius X Home, Inc.
Fukes, James '98 (SY) [5] Binghamton, NY SS. Cyril and Method Church.
Fukuchi, Mikio Conrad *s.j.* '80 (BO) [W] Cambridge, MA Weston Jesuit Community.
Fulcher, John M. '56 (COL) Retired.
Fulco, William J. *s.j.* '66 (LA) [C] Los Angeles, CA Loyola Marymount University.
Fuld, Charles '86 (SD) Escondido, CA Church of the Resurrection.
Fulgenzi, Mario (RIC) [5] Virginia Beach, VA St. Gregory the Great Church.
Fullam, Dominick '94 (BLX) Moss Point, MS St. Joseph Church.
Fullam, Matthew N. *s.j.* '42 (FgM) Provinces.
Fullam, Paul Joseph *c.p.* '53 (BRK) [V] Jamaica, NY Immaculate Conception Monastery.
Fullam, Msgr. Vincent F. *j.d.* '65 (RVC) [A] Huntington, NY Diocesan Seminary of the Immaculate Conception.
Fullen, John N. '95 (BAL) Absent on Sick Leave.

Fuller, Donald '58 (GB) Retired.
Fuller, Gerald *o.m.i.* '55 (SPC) Mansfield, MO Immaculate Heart of Mary Church.
Fuller, Jon D. *s.j.* '90 (BO) [W] Boston, MA Jesuit Urban Center & Immaculate Conception Community.
Fuller, Leigh A. *s.j.* '66 (BAL) [S] Baltimore, MD Jesuit Fathers and Brothers Maryland Provincial Curia.
Fuller, Mark (STL) Webster Groves, MO Annunciation Church.
Fuller, Mark L. '79 (STL) Kirkwood, MO St. Joseph Hospital; [K] Kirkwood, MO SSM St. Joseph Hospital of Kirkwood.
Fuller, Michael J.K. '97 (RCK) Special Assignment.
Fuller, Neil D. *s.v.d.* '69 (SB) Frontera, CA California Institute for Women.
Fuller, Msgr. Robert D. '56 (TUC) [14] Tucson, AZ St. Frances Cabrini Church.
Fuller, Roger J. '84 (DEN) Absent on Leave.
Fuller, Timothy '93 (OKL) Elk City, OK St. Matthew's Church.
Fullerton, Daniel J. '91 (SCR) [M] Shohola, PA Society of Saint John.
Fullmer, Hugh '72 (JOL) Aurora, IL Our Lady of Mercy Church.
Fullum, John J. '67 (BRK) [239] Queens, NY Sacred Heart Church.
Fulmer, Jeffrey '97 (CIN) [E] Cincinnati, OH Moeller High School.
Fulton, David I. '67 (MET) Baptistown, NJ Our Lady of Victories Church.
Fulton, Eugene '67 (NY) [FF] Larchmont, NY Trinity Retreat.
Fulton, Eugene '67 (PSC) On Duty Outside Diocese.
Fulton, Kenneth S. '50 (TLS) Retired.
Fulton, Malachy *o.s.b.* '43 (IND) [J] St. Meinrad, IN St. Meinrad Archabbey.
Fulton, Robert W. (MOB) Gulf Shores, AL Our Lady of the Gulf Church.
Fulton, Robert W. '62 (MOB) Andalusia, AL Christ the King Church; Greenville, AL St. Elizabeth Church.
Fulton, Terry '94 (SAC) Chico, CA St. John the Baptist Church.
Fumo, Harold '55 (ORG) San Juan Capistrano, CA Mission Basilica Church.
Funaro, Msgr. Joseph A. '65 (BRK) [218] Queens, NY Our Lady, Queen of Martyrs Church; [L] Brooklyn, NY Catholic Charities.
Funcheon, Gerald A. '65 (LFT) Retired.
Funes, Jose G. *s.j.* '95 (TUC) [F] Tucson, AZ Jesuit Community of the Vatican Observatory.
Funesti, Peter K. '88 (NEW) Bloomfield, NJ Church of St. Thomas the Apostle.
Funk, C. Alan '91 (LFT) Union City, IN St. Mary Church.
Funk, David J. *o.f.m.cap.* (GB) Hortonville, WI SS. Peter and Paul Church; Shiocton, WI St. Denis Church; Stephensville, WI St. Patrick Church.
Funk, Msgr. David R. '74 (COL) [2] Columbus, OH St. Agatha Church.
Funk, Peter C. '64 (BEA) [F] Beaumont, TX Holy Family Retreat Center.
Funk, Peter C. '64 (PH) On Duty Outside the Archdiocese.
Funk, Virgil C. '63 (RIC) On Duty Outside the Diocese.
Funk, Wayne G. '62 (BAL) Frederick, MD St. John the Evangelist Church.
Funk, Wiatt A. '68 (NSH) Murfreesboro, TN St. Rose of Lima Church.
Funke, Gerald J. '80 (B) Nampa, ID St. Paul's Church.
Funke, Msgr. Richard P. '60 (DUB) On Duty Outside the Archdiocese.
Funke, Ronald R. *s.j.* '68 (SEA) [A] Seattle, WA Seattle University.
Funtila, Aloysius '83 (CHI) [1] Waukegan, IL St. Anastasia Church.
Fuoco, Armando '43 (SHP) Retired.
Furey, J. Barry '71 (BGP) Darien, CT St. Thomas More Church.
Furey, John *c.ss.r.* '60 (BO) [53] Boston, MA Our Lady of Perpetual Help Church.
Furey, Matthew '99 (NY) Graduate Studies.
Furey, Matthew J. '99 (NY) [202] Staten Island, NY St. Clare Church.
Furey, Thomas J. '73 (PH) Delphi, PA St. Mary Church.
Furfaro, Msgr. Francis J. '41 (SY) Oswego, NY Oswego County Jail; Retired.
Furfaro, Virgil '83 (SFE) Bernalillo, NM Our Lady of Sorrows Church.
Furlan, Gerard *s.x.* '54 (BO) [W] Holliston, MA Xaverian Missionaries.
Furlan, Michael J. '75 (CHI) [114] Chicago, IL St. Leo The Great Church.
Furlan, William '48 (SCL) Retired.
Furlong, Aidan M. *a.a.* '53 (WOR) Fiskdale, MA St. Anne's and St. Patrick's Church.
Furlong, J. Daryl '66 (MAD) [3] Janesville, WI St. Patrick Church.
Furlong, Thomas D. '60 (OM) Retired.
Furman, Jozef *s.ch.* '58 (CHI) [85] Chicago, IL Holy Trinity Church.
Furman, Walter L. *s.j.* '50 (MOB) [A] Mobile, AL Spring Hill College.
Furnari, Casper J. '68 (BRK) [120] Brooklyn, NY Queen of All Saints Church.
Furrell, Reynold E. '98 (ORG) Cypress, CA St. Irenaeus Church.
Furrevig, Edward G. '67 (NEW) Union, NJ Holy Spirit Church.
Furtado, Alwyn *c.s.sp.* '65 (SFR) San Carlos, CA St. Charles Church.
Furtado, Jose (SP) [1] Tampa, FL Blessed Sacrament Church.
Furtado, Steven R. '73 (FR) [4] Attleboro, MA Holy Ghost Church.
Fusare, Francis '96 (OWN) [F] South Union, KY Fathers of Mercy.
Fusco, Blaise J. *o.f.m.cap.* '41 (PIT) [O] Pittsburgh, PA St. Conrad Friary.
Fusco, Christopher J. '97 (OG) Graduate Studies.
Fusco, Frederick *o.f.m.* '42 (ALB) [A] Catskill, NY St. Anthony Friary.
Fusco, Thomas M. '85 (RVC) [A] Huntington, NY Diocesan Seminary of the Immaculate Conception.
Fuselier, Karl '94 (LKC) [2] Lake Charles, LA Immaculate Heart of Mary Church.
Fushek, Dale (PHX) Special Assignment.
Fushek, Dale J. '78 (PHX) [6] Mesa, AZ St. Timothy Church.
Fuss, Ed *s.m.* '89 (BR) Convent, LA St. Michael the Archangel Church.
Fussner, Donald T. '60 (NY) [105] New York, NY St. Peter Church.
Futie, Richard F. '82 (BGP) [11] Stamford, CT St. Mary Church.
Futo, Ignatius Y. *s.j.* '81 (STL) [P] St. Louis, MO Jesuit Community Corporation at St. Louis University - Jesuit Hall.
Futrell, John C. *s.j.* '58 (DEN) [M] Denver, CO Xavier Jesuit Center.
Futter, Volker *o.s.b.* '69 (OM) [K] Schuyler, NE Benedictine Mission House.
Fye, Msgr. Lawrence C. '59 (Y) [1] Youngstown, OH Cathedral of St. Columba.
Fynn, Isaac A. '79 (TUC) [17] Tucson, AZ St. Joseph Church; Tucson, AZ St. Joseph's Hospital; [E] Tucson, AZ Carondelet Health Network.

G

Gaa, David *o.f.m.* '98 (TUC) [5] Tucson, AZ Mission San Xavier del Bac Church.
Gaalaas, Patrick J. '72 (TLS) Broken Arrow, OK St. Benedict Church.
Gabalski, Msgr. John R. '48 (BUF) [61] Buffalo, NY St. Stanislaus Church; [T] Buffalo, NY Monsignor Adamski Village, Inc.
Gabel, Garold L. '79 (LIN) [4] Lincoln, NE North American Martyrs Church.
Gabel, Manuel '57 (DEN) [28] Denver, CO St. Catherine of Siena Church.
Gabel, Martin '68 (JOL) Wheaton, IL St. Michael Church.
Gabela, Jose Luis Diez *o.s.a.* '72 (MGZ) Aguada, PR St. Francis of Assisi Church.
Gaber, Francis '51 (DUL) Retired.
Gaberle, Jiri P. '89 (MIL) Awaiting Assignment.
Gabet, George *f.s.s.p.* '97 (SCR) [M] Elmhurst, PA Priestly Fraternity of St. Peter (F.S.S.P.), North American District Headquarters.
Gabet, George G. *f.s.s.p.* '97 (TLS) [13] Tulsa, OK Parish of Saint Peter Church.
Gabian, Dennis (NY) Federal, NY Federal Correctional Institution.
Gabin, John D. '75 (PH) Richboro, PA St. Vincent de Paul Church.
Gaborit, Mauricio *s.j.* '78 (FgM) Provinces.
Gaboury, Victor *s.s.c.* '57 (OM) [K] St. Columbans, NE St. Columban's Foreign Mission Society.
Gabriel, John D. '87 (NEW) Fairfield, NJ St. Thomas More Church.
Gabriel, Michael A. '84 (CHI) Lansing, IL St. Ann Church.
Gabriel, Vicente S. '40 (LA) Retired.
Gabriele, John J. '68 (RVC) Absent on Leave.
Gabrielli, Theodore *s.j.* '98 (LA) [11] Los Angeles, CA Dolores Church.
Gabrus, Alois *o.f.m.* '72 (SUP) Hammond, WI Immaculate Conception Church; Wilson, WI St. Bridget Church.
Gabuzda, Richard J. (OM) [O] Omaha, NE The Institute for Priestly Formation.
Gabuzda, Richard J. '81 (SCR) On Duty Outside the Diocese.
Gacki, Peter *o.f.m.cap.* '51 (CHI) [47] Chicago, IL St. Daniel the Prophet Church.
Gacki, Peter *o.f.m.cap.* '51 (PAT) [M] Oak Ridge-Milton, NJ St. Stanislaus B. M. Friary.
Gadarowski, Msgr. Bronislaw A. '43 (NOR) Retired.
Gaddy, Msgr. James '65 (LKC) Jennings, LA Our Lady Help of Christians Church.
Gaddy, Kenneth *c.ss.r.* '88 (STV) [3] Frederiksted, VI Church of St. Patrick; [B] St. Thomas, VI Miscellaneous Organizations.
Gadenz, Pablo '96 (TR) Lawrenceville, NJ St. Ann Church.
Gadient, Peter '45 (LIN) Dwight, NE Assumption Church.
Gadient, Peter J. '45 (LIN) Retired.
Gadingan, Marcial '84 (GAL) [4] Spring, TX St. James the Apostle Church.
Gadziala, Timothy A. '94 (ATL) Graduate Studies.
Gadzinski, Mark '82 (STU) Absent Without Leave.
Gaebelein, Claude '46 (CLV) [M] Cleveland, OH Sts. Mary and Joseph Home for the Aged.
Gaebelein, Claude J. '46 (CLV) [4] Barberton, OH St. Mary's Church; Retired.
Gaeke, Thomas M. '75 (CIN) Medical Leave of Absence.
Gaelens, Albert R. *c.s.b.* '60 (GAL) [F] Houston, TX St. Thomas High School.
Gaelens, Albert R. *c.s.b.* '60 (SFE) [M] Albuquerque, NM St. Pius X High School Foundation, Inc.
Gaertner, Robert *c.pp.s.* '43 (CIN) [B] Carthagena, OH St. Charles.
Gaesser, Ronald E. '61 (ROC) Ithaca, NY St. Catherine of Siena Church.
Gaeta, Bernard N. '73 (Y) East Liverpool, OH St. Aloysius Church; Wellsville, OH Immaculate Conception Church.
Gaeta, David R. '80 (SLC) On Duty Outside the Diocese.
Gaeta, Francis X. '63 (RVC) Westbury, NY St. Brigid Church.
Gaetano, Francis M. *s.a.c.* '48 (NEW) Fairview, NJ Our Lady of Grace Church.
Gaetano, Msgr. Lewis F. '73 (STU) Absent on Leave.
Gaffey, Eugene F. '69 (PRT) Camden, ME Our Lady of Good Hope Church.
Gaffey, Msgr. James P. '60 (SR) [1] Santa Rosa, CA Cathedral of St. Eugene.
Gaffey, Kevin P. '57 (SFR) Novato, CA St. Anthony of Padua Church.
Gaffigan, Charles A. '62 (ALB) Lake Luzerne, NY Holy Infancy Church.
Gaffigan, William J. '64 (ALB) Canajoharie, NY St. Peter's and Paul's Church.
Gaffney, David F. '00 (PRO) Barrington, RI St. Luke Church.
Gaffney, Edward M. *o.p.* (WDC) [11] Washington, DC St. Dominic Church & Priory Church.
Gaffney, Francis (CAM) Elmer, NJ St. Ann's Church.
Gaffney, J. Michael '73 (OG) Lake Placid, NY St. Agnes Church.
Gaffney, J. Patrick *s.m.m.* '54 (RVC) [M] Bay Shore, NY Montfort Missionaries.
Gaffney, James '52 (MEM) Retired.
Gaffney, James F. *m.a.* '85 (ALN) [4] Pottsville, PA St. Patrick Church.
Gaffney, Msgr. James J. '50 (CAM) Glassboro, NJ Our Lady of Lourdes Church; Retired.
Gaffney, James T. '67 (LA) Retired.
Gaffney, John H. *o.s.a.* '45 (TLS) [B] Tulsa, OK Cascia Hall Preparatory School.
Gaffney, Joseph '67 (LA) Thousand Oaks, CA St. Paschal Baylon Church.
Gaffney, Patrick *c.s.c.* '74 (FTW) [B] Notre Dame, IN University of Notre Dame Du Lac; [J] Notre Dame, IN Holy Cross Community, Corby Hall, University of Notre Dame.
Gaffney, Thomas F. '58 (HRT) [9] New Britain, CT St. Joseph's Church.
Gaffney, Msgr. Thomas J. '50 (NY) [200] Staten Island, NY St. Charles Church.
Gaffney, William *c.ss.r.* '60 (NY) [150] Bronx, NY Immaculate Conception Church.
Gagala, John '58 (DET) [1] Southfield, MI St. Beatrice Church; [H] Southfield, MI Providence Hospital.
Gagan, Charles R. *s.j.* '68 (SFR) [25] San Francisco, CA St. Ignatius Church; [N] San Francisco, CA Jesuit Community at University of San Francisco.
Gagan, Philip R. '79 (STA) [8] Jacksonville, FL Immaculate Conception Church.
Gage, George D. '79 (ROM) Youngstown, OH St. Mary Church; Sharon, PA St. John the Baptist Church.
Gage, Gregory A. '67 (P) Newberg, OR St. Peter Church.
Gage, Philip S. *s.m.* '69 (WDC) [M] Washington, DC Marist Center.
Gaggawala, Paul O. *a.j.* '80 (ALN) [3] Shenandoah, PA St. George Church; [P] Shenandoah, PA Apostles of Jesus.
Gaglia, Fred '63 (PHX) [6] Mesa, AZ St. Timothy Church.
Gaglia, Fred '78 (SB) On Duty Outside the Diocese.
Gagliano, Philip J. '76 (NY) Ardsley, NY Our Lady of Perpetual Help Church.
Gagliardi, Carmelo *o.f.m.cap.* '73 (BRK) [105] Brooklyn, NY Shrine of Our Lady of Mount Carmel Church.
Gagliardi, Richard '62 (OAK) Pinole, CA St. Joseph's Church; Retired.
Gagliardo, Anthony F. '61 (BUF) Retired.

Gaglione, John R. '76 (BUF) Kenmore, NY St. Paul Church.
Gaglione, Joseph *c.s.sp.* '64 (SAT) [M] New Braunfels, TX Congregation of the Holy Ghost.
Gagnard, Louis '52 (ALX) Retired.
Gagne, Marc R. '85 (MAN) [5] Nashua, NH Immaculate Conception Church.
Gagne, Rene E. '51 (PRO) Retired; [P] Providence, RI St. John Vianney Residence.
Gagne, Roger C. '75 (PRO) [7] Warwick, RI St. Peter Church.
Gagne, Ron *m.s.* '71 (ORL) [2] Orlando, FL Blessed Trinity Church.
Gagne, Ronald '66 (DUL) Keewatin, MN St. Mary's Church; Nashwauk, MN St. Cecilia's Church.
Gagne, Walter *s.a.* '71 (NY) [DD] Garrison, NY Franciscan Friars of the Atonement.
Gagnepain, John F. *c.m.* '62 (STL) [P] Perryville, MO Congregation of The Mission.
Gagnier, John F. '78 (ROC) [40] Rochester, NY Our Mother of Sorrows Church; Shortsville, NY St. Dominic Church.
Gagnon, Adelard J. '53 (BO) Senior Priests.
Gagnon, Adelard J. '56 (BO) [49] Boston, MA Our Lady of the Assumption Church.
Gagnon, Andre J. '57 (MAN) [J] Laconia, NH St. Francis Health Care Facility; [L] Manchester, NH St. George Manor.
Gagnon, Daniel *o.m.i.* '87 (FgM) Oblates Foreign Missions.
Gagnon, Donald *s.m.* (PRT) Lewiston, ME St. Mary's Regional Medical Center.
Gagnon, George '55 (ALB) Glens Falls, NY St. Alphonsus Church; Hudson Falls, NY Church of St. Mary's/St. Paul's; [C] Glens Falls, NY St. Mary-St. Alphonsus Regional Catholic School.
Gagnon, Henry J. '64 (BO) Senior Priests.
Gagnon, Herve *o.m.i.* '45 (BO) [W] Lowell, MA Missionary Oblates of Mary Immaculate.
Gagnon, Jean Paul '82 (WOR) Millville, MA St. Augustine's Church.
Gagnon, Joseph A. '61 (DET) Melvindale, MI St. Conrad Church.
Gagnon, Leo G. '72 (MAN) Newton, NH Mary, Mother of the Church.
Gagnon, Mariano *o.f.m.* '58 (FgM) Franciscan Foreign Missions.
Gagnon, Michel *o.f.m.* '57 (SD) [1] Oceanside, CA Mission San Luis Rey Church; [H] Oceanside, CA Mission San Luis Rey.
Gagnon, Raymond E. '72 (MAN) [6] Nashua, NH Infant Jesus Church.
Gagnon, Richard *s.d.s.* '65 (NSH) Smyrna, TN St. Luke Church.
Gagnon, Roland *o.m.i.* '51 (FgM) Oblates Foreign Missions.
Gagnon, Ronald P. '56 (TUC) [6] Tucson, AZ Most Holy Trinity Church.
Gahagan, William H. '70 (KNX) Johnson City, TN St. Mary Church; [J] Johnson City, TN ETSU-Catholic Center; [K] Knoxville, TN Diocesan Council of Catholic Women.
Gahan, James L. '68 (STL) [4] St. Charles, MO Sts. Joachim and Ann Church; [E] St. Charles, MO Duchesne High School.
Gaiardo, Martin J. '70 (SCR) Retired.
Gailiusis, George S. *o.f.m.* '40 (PRT) [I] Kennebunkport, ME St. Anthony's Friary.
Gaines, Msgr. Michael T. '87 (E) [1] Erie, PA St. Peter Church.
Gaitan, Ramon *o.a.r.* (ORG) [3] Santa Ana, CA Our Lady of Guadalupe Church.
Gaiter, Chester E. *s.j.* '76 (STL) [O] St. Louis, MO Fusz Pavilion.
Gaiya, Philip '85 (WDC) [B] Washington, DC St. Joseph's Seminary.
Gaj, Zygmut '41 (GAY) Retired.
Gajdos, Thomas '70 (MIL) Cedarburg, WI Divine Word Church.
Gajdzinski, Norman A. '63 (CLV) [3] Garfield Heights, OH St. Therese Church.
Gajewski, Msgr. Chester A. '50 (SCR) Retired; [N] Dunmore, PA Villa St. Joseph.
Galambos, Stephen L. *o.f.m.* '96 (MET) [6] New Brunswick, NJ St. Ladislaus Church.
Galan, Jose M. '65 (PCE) [15] Ponce, PR Church of the Sacred Heart.
Galan, Juan Cerro '88 (SP) On Duty Outside the Diocese.
Galang, Agerico L. '70 (GAL) Galena Park, TX Our Lady of Fatima Church.
Galang, Jose '78 (SJ) [3] Santa Clara, CA St. Justin Church; Special Assignment.
Galante, Joseph (DAL) [B] Irving, TX University of Dallas.
Galarza, Tomas '86 (CGS) Las Piedras, PR San Juan Bautista Church.
Galas, Daniel D. '57 (OM) Retired.
Galasso, Michael S. '71 (HRT) [16] Hartford, CT St. Peter Church.
Galaz, Jesse C. '81 (LA) [42] Los Angeles, CA St. Alphonsus Church.
Galban, Antonio M. *o.s.b.* '63 (MGZ) [6] Mayaquez, PR Sacred Heart Church.
Galban, Timothy S. '97 (WDC) [2] Rockville, MD Shrine of St. Jude Church.
Galcagnon, Jerome *c.m.* '49 (NO) [P] New Orleans, LA Vincentian Fathers.
Galchus, Robert *o.m.* '49 (STA) [E] Jacksonville, FL St. Vincent's Medical Center, Inc.
Galchus, Robert P. *c.m.* '49 (PH) [AA] Philadelphia, PA Congregation of the Mission.
Galdon, Joseph A. *s.j.* '59 (FgM) Provinces.
Galdon, Peter P. '68 (NEW) [5] Bayonne, NJ St. Vincent de Paul Church.
Gale, Robert V. '68 (BO) Unassigned.
Galea, John '62 (STU) [5] Steubenville, OH Our Lady of North America Martyrs Church.
Galea, John M. '62 (STU) Jewett, OH Our Lady of Perpetual Help Church; Retired.
Galea, Michael A. '80 (BR) Donaldsonville, LA St. Francis of Assisi Church.
Galek, Adams S. '71 (CHI) Niles, IL St. John Brebeuf Church.
Galek, Peter '83 (CHI) [35] Chicago, IL St. Camillus Church.
Galens, Jeffrey '90 (NY) [E] New York, NY Cardinal Hayes High School.
Galeone, Msgr. Victor B. '60 (BAL) [3] Baltimore, MD St. Agnes Church.
Galetto, Paul W. '82 (CAM) [C] Richland, NJ St. Augustine Preparatory School.
Galiardi, Roman *o.s.b.* '57 (JOL) [J] Lisle, IL St. Procopius Abbey.
Galic, Bernard J. '70 (FTW) [10] South Bend, IN Holy Family Church.
Galic, Joseph N. *o.f.m.* '66 (ALN) [6] Bethlehem, PA St. Joseph Church.
Galier, Victor A. '98 (ATL) [3] Atlanta, GA Holy Spirit Church.
Galinac, Robert *o.f.m.* '69 (MIL) [2] West Allis, WI St. Augustine Church.
Galinac, Robert *o.f.m.* '69 (STL) [44] St. Louis, MO St. Joseph Church.
Galinada, Michael *s.m.* '78 (ORG) [6] Santa Ana, CA St. Anne's Church.
Galindo, Msgr. Rodolfo '54 (SAT) [K] San Antonio, TX Padua Place.
Galindo, Msgr. Rudolph '54 (SD) Retired.
Galipeau, Roland J. '64 (SPR) [2] Holyoke, MA Holy Cross Church.
Galivan, James F. '81 (CHI) Other Assignments.
Galko, Joseph '80 (ALN) Unassigned.
Gall, Florian J. '61 (MET) Whitehouse Station, NJ Our Lady of Lourdes Church.
Gall, Jacob M. '62 (FTW) Kendallville, IN Immaculate Conception Church.
Gall, Sylvester '38 (SCL) Retired.
Gall, Thomas S. '92 (OM) Walthill, NE St. Joseph Church; Winnebago, NE St. Augustine's Church; Winnebago, NE Our Lady of Fatima of Macy Church.
Gall, Tom '92 (OM) [O] Winnebago, NE St. Augustine's Indian Mission.
Gallagher, Adrian *o.f.m.conv.* '92 (SPR) [10] Chicopee, MA St. Stanislaus Basilica Church.
Gallagher, Andrew J. '46 (RVC) Point Lookout, NY Our Lady of the Miraculous Medal Church; Retired.
Gallagher, Brian *s.s.c.* '52 (PRO) [P] Bristol, RI St. Columban's Retirement House.
Gallagher, Brian T. '60 (YAK) On Duty Outside the Diocese.
Gallagher, Cathal '74 (SFS) De Smet, SD St. Thomas Aquinas Church.
Gallagher, Cathal '94 (OM) [K] St. Columbans, NE St. Columban's Foreign Mission Society.
Gallagher, Charles '44 (CHI) La Grange, IL St. Cletus Church.
Gallagher, Charles A. *s.j.* '58 (NEW) [B] Jersey City, NJ Saint Peter's College; [N] Jersey City, NJ Jesuits of Saint Peter's College, Inc.
Gallagher, Charles G. '44 (CHI) Retired.
Gallagher, Cornelius F. '42 (STU) Retired.
Gallagher, Cyrus *o.f.m.cap.* '65 (DEN) [3] Denver, CO Annunciation Church; [M] Denver, CO Annunciation Friary.
Gallagher, Daniel '65 (JKS) [1] Jackson, MS St. Peter Church; Jackson, MS University of Mississippi Medical Center; Jackson, MS Veterans Administration Hospital.
Gallagher, Daniel B. '99 (GAY) Cadillac, MI St. Ann Church.
Gallagher, Daniel J. '51 (PH) Doylestown, PA Our Lady of Mount Carmel Church.
Gallagher, David (CHI) [U] Techny, IL S.V.D., Catholic Universities, Inc.; [U] Techny, IL Divine Word Missionaries, Inc., Divine Word Funds, Inc.
Gallagher, David F. *c.s.s.* '59 (BO) [W] Waltham, MA Stigmatine House.
Gallagher, Dennis (WOR) [B] Worcester, MA Assumption College.
Gallagher, Dennis *a.a.* '78 (WOR) [N] Worcester, MA Assumptionists of Assumption College.
Gallagher, Dennis J. *o.s.a.* '65 (PH) [C] Villanova, PA Villanova University; [AA] Villanova, PA St. Thomas Monastery.
Gallagher, E. Henry *o.p.* '36 (BO) [W] Dover, MA St. Stephen Priory.
Gallagher, Edward *s.a.* '71 (NY) Retired; [DD] Garrison, NY Franciscan Friars of the Atonement, Minister General Office.
Gallagher, Edward *c.m.* '78 (FgM) Vincentian Foreign Missions.
Gallagher, Edward F. '46 (SCR) Retired; [N] Dunmore, PA Villa St. Joseph.
Gallagher, Edward L. '53 (BO) Senior Priests.
Gallagher, Msgr. Eugene A. '43 (SFR) Retired.
Gallagher, Eugene P. '38 (NY) Retired.
Gallagher, F. Anthony '61 (TOL) Providence, OH St. Patrick Church.
Gallagher, Francis J. *s.j.* '55 (SJ) [L] Los Gatos, CA Sacred Heart Jesuit Center.
Gallagher, Francis J. '73 (PH) North Wales, PA Mary, Mother of the Redeemer Church.
Gallagher, Francis L. '48 (BO) Billerica, MA St. Andrew Church; Senior Priests.
Gallagher, Francis M. '64 (PH) Croydon, PA St. Thomas Aquinas Church.
Gallagher, Gregory *o.m.i.* '92 (BEL) [F] Belleville, IL Shrine of Our Lady of the Snows.
Gallagher, J. Gerald '57 (CAM) Woodbury, NJ St. Patrick's Church.
Gallagher, J. Peter '92 (IND) [C] Indianapolis, IN Father Thomas Scecina Memorial High School.
Gallagher, Jack *o.s.cam.* '81 (WOR) [K] Whitinsville, MA St. Camillus Nursing Home Inc.
Gallagher, James E. '87 (RIC) Prince George County, VA Church of the Sacred Heart.
Gallagher, James R. '65 (CHI) [J] Evergreen Park, IL Little Company of Mary Hospital and Health Care Centers.
Gallagher, John (GB) Suring, WI St. Michael Church.
Gallagher, John '68 (PIT) [J] Cranberry Township, PA St. Francis Nursing Center Cranberry.
Gallagher, John *o.f.m.cap.* '78 (MAN) [4] Manchester, NH St. Augustin Church.
Gallagher, John *o.s.cam.* '81 (WOR) [N] Whitinsville, MA St. Camillus Community.
Gallagher, John '92 (PMB) Fort Pierce, FL St. Anastasia Church.
Gallagher, Msgr. John A. '55 (NY) [15] Yonkers, NY St. Paul the Apostle Church.
Gallagher, John E. '59 (BO) Senior Priests.
Gallagher, John J. *o.s.a.* '45 (PH) [AA] Villanova, PA St. Thomas Monastery.
Gallagher, John J. *o.s.cam.* '81 (WOR) [K] Whitinsville, MA St. Camillus Hospice, Inc.
Gallagher, John M. '71 (GB) Gillett, WI St. John Church.
Gallagher, John M. *o.f.m.cap.* '78 (MAN) [2] Manchester, NH St. Anne Church.
Gallagher, Msgr. John P. '51 (SCR) Retired.
Gallagher, John P. '57 (PH) Huntingdon Valley, PA St. Albert the Great Church.
Gallagher, John P. '68 (PIT) Cranberry Township, PA St. Ferdinand Church.
Gallagher, John P. *j.c.l.* '80 (DAV) [3] Muscatine, IA SS. Mary and Mathias of Muscatine Church.
Gallagher, John P. *c.ss.r.* '95 (FgM) Redemptorist Foreign Missions.
Gallagher, John R. *v.g.* (WH) [R] Wheeling, WV Mount Calvary.
Gallagher, John R. '55 (DUB) [H] Cedar Rapids, IA Mercy Medical Center-Cedar Rapids.
Gallagher, John R. '93 (WH) [1] Wheeling, WV St. Joseph's Church; [I] Wheeling, WV Welty Home for the Aged, Inc.; [O] Wheeling, WV John S. Thoner Family Charitable Trust; [R] Wheeling, WV Retirement Trust Agreement of the Infirm Priests' Association of the Diocese of Wheeling-Charleston.
Gallagher, Joseph J. '55 (BAL) Retired.
Gallagher, Joseph J. '63 (PH) [142] Philadelphia, PA St. Richard Church.
Gallagher, Joseph P. '73 (PH) Ridley Park, PA St. Madeline Church.
Gallagher, Joseph T. '42 (PRO) Retired.
Gallagher, Joseph W. *c.s.p.* '61 (GR) Grand Rapids, MI Chapel of St. Paul-Catholic Information Center.
Gallagher, Kevin '98 (NY) Stony Point, NY Immaculate Conception Church.
Gallagher, Kevin E. *s.j.* '61 (CHI) [N] Chicago, IL Chicago Province of the Society of Jesus-Provincial Office.
Gallagher, Kevin E. *s.j.* '61 (FgM) Provinces.
Gallagher, Kevin P. '83 (ALN) [1] Saint Clair, PA St. Boniface Church; [4] Saint Clair, PA St. Mary Church; [5] Saint Clair, PA SS. Peter and Paul Church.
Gallagher, Maurice O. '50 (PBL) Avondale, CO Sacred Heart Church.
Gallagher, Michael *s.j.* '84 (ELP) [21] El Paso, TX Sacred Heart Church.
Gallagher, Msgr. Michael J. '66 (SD) [2] El Cajon, CA Our Lady of Grace Church.

Gallagher, Michael J. '69 (WIL) On Duty Outside the Diocese.
Gallagher, Michael S. *s.j.* '84 (NO) [P] New Orleans, LA Jesuit Provincial Office.
Gallagher, Otmar *o.f.m.cap.* '48 (VEN) [D] Port Charlotte, FL Bon Secours-St. Joseph Hospital.
Gallagher, Patrick *o.f.m.conv.* '65 (SY) [2] Syracuse, NY Assumption B.V.M. Church.
Gallagher, Msgr. Patrick J. '66 (LA) San Pedro, CA Mary, Star of the Sea Church; [CC] San Pedro, CA Apostleship of the Sea, Catholic Maritime Ministry.
Gallagher, Patrick J. '70 (MOB) Dothan, AL St. Columba Church; [J] Dothan, AL George C. Wallace Jr. Community College Newman Center.
Gallagher, Paul *o.f.m.* '82 (GAL) [T] Houston, TX Catholic Newman Association at the University of Houston Central Campus.
Gallagher, Paul V. '63 (RIC) Retired.
Gallagher, Peter '92 (IND) [36] Indianapolis, IN St. Simon Church.
Gallagher, Raymond '90 (SAN) Retired.
Gallagher, Richard '36 (SEA) Retired.
Gallagher, Richard '44 (TR) Leave of Absence.
Gallagher, Msgr. Richard J. '49 (STL) [39] St. Louis, MO St. Joan of Arc Church.
Gallagher, Robert A. '77 (STU) On Duty Outside the Diocese.
Gallagher, Robert J. '73 (LA) [2] North Hollywood, CA St. Charles Borromeo Church; [D] Santa Fe Springs, CA St. Paul High School.
Gallagher, Roger P. '54 (WDC) Retired; [L] Washington, DC Cardinal O'Boyle Residence for Priests.
Gallagher, Simeon *o.f.m.cap.* '71 (STL) [54] St. Louis, MO St. Patrick Church; [P] St. Louis, MO St. Patrick Friary.
Gallagher, Simon P. *o.s.b.* (BUR) On Special or Other Diocesan Assignment.
Gallagher, Simon P. *o.s.b.* '73 (BUR) Burlington, VT Fletcher Allen Health Care.
Gallagher, Simon P. *o.s.b.* '73 (PAT) [M] Morristown, NJ St. Mary's Abbey.
Gallagher, Thomas *s.p.s.* '49 (NO) [4] Slidell, LA St. Margaret Mary Church; Slidell, LA Greenbriar Nursing & Convalescent Home; Slidell, LA Guest House of Slidell Nursing Home; Slidell, LA Greenery Neurologic Rehabilitation Center at Slidell.
Gallagher, Thomas '61 (CLV) Cleveland, OH Cleveland Psychiatric.
Gallagher, Thomas B. '56 (OAK) Retired; [M] Oakland, CA Bishop Begin Villa.
Gallagher, Thomas G. '68 (RVC) North Merrick, NY Sacred Heart Church.
Gallagher, Thomas J. '61 (CLV) Retired.
Gallagher, Thomas J. *s.j.* '70 (BO) [W] Boston, MA Jesuit Urban Center & Immaculate Conception Community; [BB] Boston, MA Immaculate Conception Church.
Gallagher, Thomas M. *o.f.m.* '82 (WIL) [10] Wilmington, DE St. Paul's Church.
Gallagher, Thomas P. *o.s.f.s.* '67 (PH) [D] Philadelphia, PA Father Judge High School for Boys; [AA] Philadelphia, PA Father Judge Faculty House.
Gallagher, Msgr. Thomas V. '45 (NY) Retired; [DD] New York, NY Our Lady of Consolation Residence.
Gallagher, Timothy *o.m.v.* '79 (BO) [B] Boston, MA Oblate Provincialate.
Gallagher, Timothy M. *o.m.v.* '79 (BO) [B] Boston, MA Our Lady of Grace Seminary.
Gallagher, William E. '46 (SEA) Retired.
Gallagher, William G. (RVC) Retired.
Gallagher, William J. '47 (WOR) Retired.
Gallagher, Msgr. William J. '69 (BUF) [4] Orchard Park, NY St. John Vianney Church.
Gallagher, William M. '53 (PRO) Retired.
Gallagher, William P. '65 (BUR) Woodstock, VT Our Lady of the Snows Church.
Gallahue, John J. *m.m.* '62 (FgM) Maryknoll Foreign Missions.
Gallant, Alfred F. '62 (NY) Pine Bush, NY The Infant Saviour Church.
Gallant, Andrzej *s.ch.* (STP) [6] Minneapolis, MN Holy Cross Church.
Gallant, John P. '60 (NY) Sloatsburg, NY St. Joan of Arc Church.
Gallant, Jon-Paul '78 (FR) [4] Taunton, MA Sacred Heart Church.
Gallant, Rodrigue J. '47 (MAN) Retired.
Gallardo, Dave '84 (LA) Hacienda Heights, CA St. John Vianney Church.
Gallardo, Joseph J. *o.a.r.* '94 (NY) [B] Suffern, NY Tagaste Monastery.
Gallarelli, George A. *s.j.* '62 (BGP) [E] Fairfield, CT Fairfield College Preparatory School; [P] Fairfield, CT The Fairfield Jesuit Community-Fairfield University.
Gallaro, George D. '72 (NTN) Warren, MI Our Lady of Redemption Church.
Gallas, James R. *s.j.* '52 (LA) [6] Los Angeles, CA Blessed Sacrament Church.
Gallatin, Joseph G. '97 (STP) [15] St. Paul, MN St. Bernard Church.
Gallatin, Paul H. '58 (OKL) [3] Oklahoma City, OK St. Charles Borromeo Church.
Gallego, Jose M. *o.m.* '57 (SJN) [16] San Juan, PR Ntra. Sra. de Fatima Church.
Gallegos, Albert *o.s.m.* '64 (SFE) Peralta, NM Our Lady of Guadalupe Church.
Gallegos, Albert M. *o.s.m.* '64 (CHI) [N] Chicago, IL Order of Friar Servants of Mary (Servites) United States of America Province, Inc.
Gallegos, David *o.s.m.* '66 (SFE) Belen, NM Our Lady of Belen Church.
Gallegos, David M. *o.s.m.* '66 (CHI) [N] Chicago, IL Order of Friar Servants of Mary (Servites) United States of America Province, Inc.
Gallegos, Joseph *c.r.* '69 (PBL) Durango, CO Sacred Heart Church.
Gallegos, Stephen *c.m.* '88 (FgM) Vincentian Foreign Missions.
Gallemore, Timothy A. '92 (FRS) Laton, CA Shrine of Our Lady of Fatima Church.
Gallen, Msgr. Charles V. '47 (PH) [V] Immaculata, PA Camilla Hall Nursing Home.
Gallen, Msgr. F. Thomas '47 (COL) Corning, OH St. Bernard Church; Retired.
Gallen, Francis H. '47 (PH) Bridgeport, PA St. Augustine Church; Retired.
Gallen, John '69 (HT) [3] Thibodaux, LA Christ The Redeemer Church; [5] Thibodaux, LA St. John The Evangelist Church.
Gallen, John J. *s.j.* '63 (NY) [DD] New York, NY "America;" Residence and publication office of the America Press.
Gallenbach, Thomas '58 (SFD) On Duty Outside the Diocese.
Gallenbach, Thomas E. '58 (LAV) [12] Las Vegas, NV St. Joseph, Husband of Mary Church.
Gallenstein, Joseph A. '90 (COV) Leave of Absence.
Gallenstein, Stephen (LEX) Salyersville, KY St. Luke Church.
Gallenstein, Stephen '76 (LEX) Pikeville, KY St. Francis of Assisi Church.
Gallerini, Philip G. '62 (SPR) Retired.
Galles, Msgr. Francis A. '52 (WIN) Retired.
Galli, Clarence '53 (SFE) Retired.
Galli, Clarence F. '53 (SFE) Corrales, NM San Ysidro Church.
Gallia, Andrew R. '62 (SCR) Jessup, PA St. Mary's Assumption Church.
Galligan, Charles (PRO) [C] Pawtucket, RI St. Raphael Academy.
Galligan, Charles H. '87 (PRO) [12] Pawtucket, RI St. Teresa of the Child Jesus Church.
Galligan, Eymard *s.s.e.* '47 (BUR) [E] Colchester, VT Society of St. Edmund.
Galligan, James L. *o.s.a.* '50 (PH) [143] Philadelphia, PA St. Rita of Cascia Church.
Galligan, Richard H. *s.j.* '70 (BUF) [O] Buffalo, NY Canisius Jesuit Community.
Galligan, Richard R. *s.j.* '70 (BUF) [C] Buffalo, NY Canisius College; [R] Alfred, NY Campus Ministry.
Gallina, Leo J. '65 (E) Bradford, PA St. Bernard Church.
Gallinger, Carl J. '89 (CHY) Laramie, WY St. Paul's Newman Center Church.
Gallipoli, Mario *c.p.* '61 (BRK) [V] Jamaica, NY Immaculate Conception Monastery.
Gallivan, Msgr. David M. '66 (BUF) [29] Buffalo, NY Holy Cross Church.
Gallo, David M. *a.a.* '88 (WOR) [N] Worcester, MA Assumptionists of Assumption College.
Gallo, Dennis G. *c.m.f.* '85 (LA) San Gabriel, CA San Gabriel Church; [Q] San Gabriel, CA Claretian Missionaries (Missionary Sons of the Immaculate Heart of Mary).
Gallo, Gerardo '85 (NEW) [25] Jersey City, NJ St. Paul of the Cross Church.
Gallo, Msgr. Louis J. '48 (PAT) Retired.
Gallo, Vincent '60 (BRK) [222] Queens, NY St. Pancras Church.
Gallogly, Francis X. *o.s.a.* '65 (VEN) Cape Coral, FL Blessed Katharine Drexel Church.
Gallus, David *o.s.c.* '66 (STP) Dayton, MN St. John the Baptist Church.
Gallus, David E. *o.s.c.* '66 (FgM) Crosier Foreign Missions.
Gallus, David E. *o.s.c.* '66 (STP) [N] Anoka, MN Crosier Community of Anoka; [W] Shoreview, MN Crosier Missions.
Galluzzo, James '90 (P) Absent on Leave.
Galonek, David B. '96 (WOR) Milford, MA St. Mary of the Assumption Church.
Galos, Artemio '85 (DET) [11] Warren, MI St. Sylvester Church.
Galovich, George '71 (STL) Potosi, MO St. James Church.
Galuszka, Thaddeus *m.s.* '51 (MIL) [P] Twin Lakes, WI La Salette Missionaries Shrine.
Galuszka, Walter '38 (BRK) Retired.
Galuszka, Msgr. Walter C. '38 (RVC) [J] Huntington, NY St. Joseph's Guest Home for the Aged, Inc.
Galvan, Alfred '65 (LSC) Ruidoso, NM St. Eleanor Church.
Galvan, John *s.j.* '99 (LA) Lancaster, CA Immigration and Naturalization Service.
Galvan, Michael '77 (OAK) [19] Oakland, CA St. Paschal Baylon Church.
Galvez, Elias *o.f.m.* '56 (FgM) Franciscan Foreign Missions.
Galvez, Jesus Manuel *o.f.m. conv.* '99 (SB) [3] Riverside, CA Queen of Angels Church.
Galvez, Jose Antonio *o.f.m. conv.* '96 (R) Clinton, NC Immaculate Conception Church.
Galvez, Salvador '87 (NO) [42] New Orleans, LA St. Julian Eymard Church.
Galvin, Aloysius C. *s.j.* '57 (WDC) [E] North Bethesda, MD Georgetown Preparatory School.
Galvin, Edward *s.m.a.* '62 (WDC) [V] Washington, DC S.M.A. Social Concerns Department.
Galvin, Edward J. *s.m.a.* '67 (MEM) Lexington, TN St. Andrew Church.
Galvin, Garrett *o.f.m.* '00 (SD) [1] Oceanside, CA Mission San Luis Rey Church; [H] Oceanside, CA Mission San Luis Rey.
Galvin, Gregory (NOR) [B] Middletown, CT Xavier High School.
Galvin, Gregory '94 (NOR) [F] Middletown, CT Congregation of the Brothers of St. Francis Xavier.
Galvin, James G. '94 (SAT) [71] San Antonio, TX San Juan Capistrano Church.
Galvin, James M. '51 (LA) [Q] Montebello, CA Vincentian Fathers & Brothers; [W] Santa Barbara, CA St. Mary's Seminary Center; [CC] Santa Barbara, CA World Wide Marriage Encounter.
Galvin, John *s.m.* '63 (FgM) Marist Foreign Missions.
Galvin, John P. '68 (BO) On Duty Outside the Archdiocese.
Galvin, John P. '68 (WDC) [C] Washington, DC Catholic University of America, The.
Galvin, Richard *o.s.b.* '48 (P) [L] St. Benedict, OR Mt. Angel Abbey.
Galvin, Thomas J. '82 (PIT) [83] Pittsburgh, PA Risen Lord Church.
Galvin, William *m.m.* '56 (FgM) Maryknoll Foreign Missions.
Galyo, Msgr. John M. '54 (PH) [2] Phoenixville, PA Holy Trinity Church; [4] Phoenixville, PA Sacred Heart Church.
Gamache, Barry J. '81 (PRO) Bristol, RI St. Mary Church; [S] Bristol, RI Roger Williams University.
Gamache, Roland L. '67 (WOR) Winchendon, MA Immaculate Heart of Mary Church.
Gamallo, Edito '75 (NEW) [1] Jersey City, NJ St. Aedan's Church.
Gamarra, Manuel (SJN) Santurce, PR Doctors Community Hospital.
Gamarra, Manuel J. '44 (SJN) [14] San Juan, PR Nuestra Senora de la Esperanza Church.
Gamba, John J. '42 (COL) Retired.
Gamba, Jose '86 (NEW) [26] Jersey City, NJ St. Paul's Church.
Gambatese, Angelus *o.f.m.* '59 (PAT) [5] Paterson, NJ St. Bonaventure Church.
Gamber, Matthew T. *s.j.* '95 (MIL) [P] Milwaukee, WI Jesuit Community at Marquette University.
Gamber, William K. '64 (STP) Special Assignment; Retired.
Gambet, Daniel G. *o.s.f.s.* '57 (ALN) [B] Center Valley, PA Desales University; [K] Center Valley, PA Oblates of St. Francis de Sales.
Gamble, Anthony *c.pp.s.* '42 (CIN) [B] Carthagena, OH St. Charles.
Gamboa, Arthur *o.f.m.conv.* '00 (LA) Hermosa Beach, CA Our Lady of Guadalupe Church.
Gamboa, Damian *o.f.m.* '64 (OAK) [9] Oakland, CA St. Elizabeth's Church.
Gamboa, Damian *o.f.m.* '64 (SFR) [8] San Francisco, CA St. Boniface Church.
Gambon, John A. '49 (STL) Retired.
Gambro, John M. *o.p.* '57 (CHI) [D] Oak Park, IL Fenwick High School; [N] River Forest, IL St. Thomas Aquinas Priory.
Gamel, Robert E. '90 (FRS) Ridgecrest, CA St. Ann Church.
Gameros, L. Ignacio '81 (TUC) Absent on Leave.
Gamm, David B. '72 (COV) Erlanger, KY Mary, Queen of Heaven Church.
Gamm, Joseph *c.m.f.* '45 (PHX) Prescott, AZ Sacred Heart Church.
Gamrot, Jaroslaw *m.i.c.* '91 (BAL) [O] Baltimore, MD St. Joseph's Nursing Home.
Gamrot, Jaroslaw *m.i.c.* '91 (WDC) [M] Brookeville, MD Marian Monastery-Brookeville.
Gana, Stanley M. '70 (PH) [69] Philadelphia, PA Immaculate Conception Church.
Ganahl, James '56 (SB) Retired.
Gancayco, Richard K. '92 (WDC) On Duty Outside the Archdiocese.
Gandara, Jose Roberto *c.ss.r.* '92 (CGS) Fajardo, PR Santiago Apostol Church.
Gandolfi, Louis *c.s.* '63 (CHI) [119] Chicago, IL Santa Maria Addolorata Church.

Gandolfi, Luigi *c.s.* '63 (CHI) [N] Chicago, IL Scalabrini House of Theology.
Gandrau, James '58 (SEA) [2] Seattle, WA St. Alphonsus Church.
Gang, Dennis *t.o.r.* '79 (STU) [A] Steubenville, OH Franciscan University of Steubenville; [F] Steubenville, OH Holy Spirit Friary.
Ganiel, Joseph '83 (CAM) Mullica Hill, NJ Holy Name of Jesus Church.
Ganley, Charles '52 (SAG) Retired.
Ganley, Thomas P. '85 (MET) South Plainfield, NJ Sacred Heart Church.
Ganly, John C. *m.m.* '59 (STL) [P] St. Louis, MO Maryknoll House.
Ganmond, Paul J. (NOR) Essex, CT Our Lady of Sorrows Church.
Gann, Sean '94 (RVC) Commack, NY Christ the King Church.
Gannon, Bernard '71 (CAM) Gloucester, NJ St. Mary's Church.
Gannon, Brian P. '97 (BGP) Brookfield, CT St. Marguerite Bourgeoys Church.
Gannon, Charles E. '43 (DAV) Retired; [M] Davenport, IA St. Vincent Center.
Gannon, Clair F. *o.s.b.* '41 (GBG) [H] Latrobe, PA Saint Vincent Archabbey.
Gannon, Daniel J. *s.j.* '68 (CHY) St. Stephens, WY St. Stephen's Church; [C] St. Stephens, WY St. Stephens Mission - Jesuit Community.
Gannon, Dismas *o.c.s.o.* '50 (P) [L] Lafayette, OR The Cistercian (Trappist) Abbey of Our Lady of Guadalupe.
Gannon, Donald C. *s.j.* '76 (NY) [80] New York, NY Nativity Church.
Gannon, Gerard M. '56 (SCR) Archbald, PA St. Thomas Aquinas Church.
Gannon, James G. *o.f.m.* '87 (GRY) [J] Cedar Lake, IN San Damiano Friary.
Gannon, Msgr. John M. '41 (E) [20] Erie, PA St. Joseph Church; Retired.
Gannon, Joseph T. '75 (STP) Retired.
Gannon, Michael F. '65 (NY) [I] New York, NY The Catholic Charities of the Archdiocese of New York; [R] Nanuet, NY St. Agatha Home of the New York Foundling Hospital.
Gannon, Patrick '76 (NO) Gretna, LA St. Anthony Church.
Gannon, Patrick J. '60 (LA) La Mirada, CA St. Paul of the Cross Church.
Gannon, Robert I. '60 (NY) [219] Staten Island, NY Our Lady, Queen of Peace Church; [E] New York, NY Moore Catholic High School.
Gannon, Roger *c.p.* '47 (BO) [21] Boston, MA St. Gabriel Church; [W] Boston, MA St. Gabriel Passionist Community.
Gannon, Msgr. Rowland E. '41 (STL) Retired.
Gannon, Thomas *s.j.* '67 (CIN) [P] Milford, OH Milford Spiritual Center.
Gannon, Thomas M. *s.j.* '67 (GRY) [J] East Chicago, IN Roque Gonzalez Residence-Jesuit Fathers; [O] Hammond, IN Heartland Center.
Gannon, William Robert *o.p.* '53 (NY) Manhattan, NY Memorial Sloan Kettering Cancer Center; [DD] New York, NY St. Vincent Ferrer Priory.
Ganshert, Msgr. Daniel T. '74 (MAD) [1] Madison, WI St. Raphael Church.
Ganss, Karl P. '68 (RCK) DeKalb, IL St. Mary Church.
Ganssle, Joseph *o.f.m.* '58 (NY) [DD] New York, NY Franciscan Friars, Order of Friars Minor, Holy Name Province.
Gantert, Richard M. '75 (MEM) [21] Memphis, TN St. Paul The Apostle Church.
Gantley, Donald M. *o.s.m.* '59 (CHI) [N] Chicago, IL Order of Friar Servants of Mary (Servites) United States of America Province, Inc.
Gantley, Mark J. '91 (SY) [15] Syracuse, NY St. Daniel Church.
Ganuza, Felix *sch.p.* '20 (NY) [DD] New York, NY Calasanzian Fathers (Piarists).
Ganuza, Felix *sch.p.* '76 (NY) [12] New York, NY Annunciation Church.
Ganz, Richard H. *s.j.* '84 (P) [D] Portland, OR Jesuit High School; [D] Portland, OR Jesuit High School.
Ganzy, Alexander '91 (SJP) On Sick Leave.
Gappa, Herbert T. *m.m.* '68 (FgM) Maryknoll Foreign Missions.
Gaquit, Teodulo '70 (HON) [3] Honolulu, HI St. Anthony Church.
Garamendi, Martin *o.m.* '52 (SJN) [16] San Juan, PR Ntra. Sra. de Fatima Church.
Garanzini, Michael J. *s.j.* '80 (WDC) [M] Washington, DC The Jesuit Community at Georgetown University.
Garatea, Juan Maria '59 (B) Burley, ID St. Theresa Church.
Garavaglia, Henry J. '64 (STL) [10] Florissant, MO St. Thomas the Apostle Church.
Garavel, Andrew J. *s.j.* '92 (BGP) [P] Fairfield, CT The Fairfield Jesuit Community-Fairfield University.
Garaventa, Louis T. *s.j.* '76 (BUF) [D] Buffalo, NY Canisius High School; [O] Buffalo, NY Canisius Jesuit Community.
Garayoa, Jose Luis *o.a.r.* '76 (LSC) [B] Mesilla, NM Augustinian Recollect Fathers.
Garbaciak, Dariusz *s.v.d.* '96 (CHI) [B] Techny, IL Divine Word Residence.
Garbacik, Louis S. '54 (SCR) [10] Hazleton, PA St. Stanislaus Church.
Garbacz, Kazimierz *s.v.d.* '70 (CHI) [N] Techny, IL Society of the Divine Word, Provincial Headquarter-Chicago Prov.
Garbacz, Kazimierz *s.v.d.* '69 (CHI) [B] Techny, IL Divine Word Residence.
Garbarino, Joseph J. '83 (PAT) Montville, NJ St. Pius X Church.
Garber, Andrew V. *o.s.b.* '56 (MIL) Bristol, WI St. Scholastica Church.
Garber, Stephen A. *s.j.* '54 (PH) [G] Philadelphia, PA St. Joseph's Preparatory School; [AA] Philadelphia, PA Jesuit Community at St. Joseph's University.
Garbin, Arthur L. '41 (PIT) Retired; [P] Coraopolis, PA Our Lady of the Sacred Heart Convent.
Garbin, Raymond '63 (JOL) Elmhurst, IL Immaculate Conception Church.
Garbo, Francis Mark Ma. *m.m.h.c.* '90 (SFR) Daly City, CA St. Andrew Church.
Garceau, James G. *c.r.i.c.* '84 (LA) [65] Los Angeles, CA St. Francis of Assisi Church; [B] Los Angeles, CA Canons Regular of the Immaculate Conception-Novitiate; [Q] Los Angeles, CA Canons Regular of the Immaculate Conception.
Garced, Wilberto Reyes '34 (NY) [HH] New York, NY Lumen Dei.
Garces, Francis *o.f.m.cap.* '66 (FWT) [6] Fort Worth, TX Our Lady of Guadalupe Church.
Garces-Henao, Carlos '95 (HRT) [2] Ansonia, CT Holy Rosary Church.
Garcia, Abraham R. *m.g.* '80 (LA) [Q] Los Angeles, CA Guadalupe Missioners Procure.
Garcia, Albert *ss.cc.* '69 (HON) Waialua, HI St. Michael Church.
Garcia, Alfredo *ss.cc.* '63 (BWN) Santa Rosa, TX St. Mary Church.
Garcia, Ana (MIA) [C] Miami, FL Msgr. Edward Pace High School.
Garcia, Angel *m.s.c.* '64 (SB) Upland, CA St. Joseph Church.
Garcia, Antonio (LA) [94] Los Angeles, CA St. Thomas the Apostle Church.
Garcia, Antonio *o.dem.* '67 (CGS) Cayey, PR Nuestra Senora de la Asuncion Church.
Garcia, Antonio '81 (SJN) [14] Carolina, PR Ntra. Sra. Del Carmen Church.
Garcia, Avelino '68 (SP) On Duty Outside the Diocese.
Garcia, Avelino R. (BO) Brockton, MA Veterans Administration Hospital Brockton-West Roxbury.
Garcia, Camilo '00 (STO) [4] Stockton, CA St. George Church.
Garcia, Daniel E. '88 (AUS) [24] Austin, TX St. Vincent de Paul Church.
Garcia, David '75 (SAT) [1] San Antonio, TX Cathedral of San Fernando; [S] San Antonio, TX Historical Centre Foundation.
Garcia, Dennis M. '00 (SFE) [3] Albuquerque, NM Community of the Risen Savior Church.
Garcia, Edgar *o.m.i.* '85 (LA) Pacoima, CA Mary Immaculate Church.
Garcia, Eduardo '93 (PCE) Arroyo, PR Our Lady of Mt. Carmel Church.
Garcia, Eliseo *o.s.a.* '59 (SJN) [1] Bayamon, PR San Agustin Church.
Garcia, Francisco *o.f.m.cap.* '78 (PCE) [5] Ponce, PR Santa Teresita Church; [E] Ponce, PR Residencia Asis; [H] Ponce, PR Albergue La Providencia, Inc.
Garcia, George '73 (MIA) Coconut Grove, FL St. Hugh Church.
Garcia, Gerardo *c.s.* '91 (CHI) [N] Chicago, IL Scalabrini House of Theology.
Garcia, Gerrardo M. *o.s.a.* '69 (CHI) [39] Chicago, IL St. Clare of Montefalco Church.
Garcia, Guillermo *c.s.* (CHI) [16] Chicago, IL St. Anthony Church.
Garcia, Guillermo C. *c.j.* '75 (LA) [4] Santa Barbara, CA Our Lady of Guadalupe Church.
Garcia, Gustavo *m.sp.s.* (P) [A] Mount Angel, OR Felix Rougier House of Studies; [L] Mount Angel, OR Missionaries of the Holy Spirit, M.Sp.S.
Garcia, Hector de Jesus '99 (CGS) Unassigned.
Garcia, Higinio '99 (SD) Carlsbad, CA St. Patrick Church.
Garcia, Isidor *c.m.f.* '54 (LA) [Q] Rancho Dominguez, CA Dominguez Seminary Inc.
Garcia, James L. '70 (SFR) [1] Menlo Park, CA St. Anthony Church.
Garcia, Javier (SAC) Absent on Leave.
Garcia, Jesus A. '94 (SJN) [15] Carolina, PR Ntra. Sra. Reina de la Paz Church.
Garcia, John G. '47 (OAK) Brentwood, CA Immaculate Heart of Mary Church.
Garcia, Jorge '84 (B) Fruitland, ID Corpus Christi Church.
Garcia, Jose '52 (MIA) [24] Miami, FL St. Kevin Church.
Garcia, Jose Isidore *o.m.i.* '64 (GAL) [16] Houston, TX Blessed Sacrament Church.
Garcia, Jose Luis '00 (BWN) Weslaco, TX St. Joan of Arc Church.
Garcia, Jose Luis *o.de.m.* '35 (SJN) [40] San Juan, PR Nuestra Senora de la Merced Church.
Garcia, Jose Ma. *ss.cc.* '63 (SJN) [9] Guaynabo, PR Sagrados Corazones Church.
Garcia, Jose Ricardo *o.p.* '72 (FgM) Dominican - Order of Preachers Foreign Missions.
Garcia, Juan F. *c.r.i.c.* '67 (SPR) [2] Springfield, MA All Souls Church; [3] Springfield, MA Blessed Sacrament Church.
Garcia, Juan F. '96 (SHP) On Leave.
Garcia, Juan L. '70 (WDC) [B] Washington, DC Diocesan Laborer Priests, House of Studies.
Garcia, Lorenzo '97 (SAV) Moultrie, GA Immaculate Conception Church.
Garcia, Louis '93 (STO) [5] Stockton, CA St. Gertrude Church.
Garcia, Luis '50 (LA) Lynwood, CA St. Emydius Church.
Garcia, Luis '97 (MIA) Pembroke Pines, FL St. Maximilian Kolbe Church.
Garcia, Luis J. '76 (BWN) San Juan, TX The Basilica of the National Shrine of Our Lady of San Juan del Valle.
Garcia, Manuel '75 (SJN) Dorado, PR Ntra. Sra. de La Salud Church; [E] San Juan, PR Centro Medico de P.R.
Garcia, Marcelino *s.j.* '70 (MIA) [D] Miami, FL Belen Jesuit Preparatory School; [H] Miami, FL Villa Javier.
Garcia, Mario *o.f.m.cap.* (DAL) [8] Dallas, TX Our Lady of Lourdes Church.
Garcia, Mario '78 (LAV) [5] Las Vegas, NV Prince of Peace Church.
Garcia, Michael A. *o.p.* '81 (CHI) [N] Chicago, IL Dominicans (Provincial Office).
Garcia, Miguel A. *c.ss.r.* '72 (MGZ) [2] Mayaquez, PR Our Lady of Mt. Carmel Church.
Garcia, Millan '62 (SFE) Albuquerque, NM Prison Ministry.
Garcia, Msgr. Otto L. '73 (BRK) [1] Brooklyn, NY The Cathedral-Basilica of St. James.
Garcia, Patrick K.Q. (AGN) [H] Agana, GU Our Lady of the Waters House of Prayer.
Garcia, Patrick Kenny Q. '89 (AGN) Mongmong, GU Nuestra Senora de Las Aquas Church.
Garcia, Paul '93 (ELP) [31] El Paso, TX St. Raphael Church.
Garcia, Pedro '64 (MIA) Naranja, FL St. Ann Church.
Garcia, Pedro '92 (AUS) On Duty Outside the Diocese.
Garcia, Pedro V. '65 (GR) [13] Grand Rapids, MI St. Joseph The Worker Church.
Garcia, Rafael *s.j.* '93 (ELP) [21] El Paso, TX Sacred Heart Church.
Garcia, Rafael *o.f.m.* '97 (LAR) Hebbronville, TX Our Lady of Guadalupe Church.
Garcia, Msgr. Ramon '55 (SAT) [K] San Antonio, TX Casa De Padres.
Garcia, Msgr. Raymond '55 (SAT) Retired.
Garcia, Reynaldo *s.j.* '76 (GAY) Gills Pier, MI St. Wenceslaus Church.
Garcia, Reynaldo A. *s.j.* '76 (DET) [P] Clarkston, MI Colombiere Center.
Garcia, Ricardo '92 (BWN) Graduate Studies.
Garcia, Roberto *o.s.a.* '48 (MGZ) San German, PR St. Rose of Lima Church.
Garcia, Roberto *o.f.m.cap* '59 (FWT) [6] Fort Worth, TX Our Lady of Guadalupe Church.
Garcia, Msgr. Roberto '86 (PCE) [B] Ponce, PR The Pontifical Catholic University of Puerto Rico.
Garcia, Rodolfo '98 (DAL) [16] Dallas, TX St. Edward Church.
Garcia, Rolando '86 (MIA) Leisure City, FL St. Martin de Porres Church.
Garcia, Ruben *o.c.d.* '97 (OKL) [15] Oklahoma City, OK Our Lady of Mount Carmel and St. Therese Little Flower Church.
Garcia, Sergio E. *c.r.i.c.* '94 (LA) [65] Los Angeles, CA St. Francis of Assisi Church; [B] Los Angeles, CA Canons Regular of the Immaculate Conception-Novitiate; [Q] Los Angeles, CA Canons Regular of the Immaculate Conception.
Garcia, Toribio Nicholas *c.m.f.* '92 (CGS) [8] Barrio Rio Canas, PR Inmaculado Corazon de Maria Church.
Garcia-Carreras, Carlos E. *s.j.* '76 (ATL) [4] Atlanta, GA Immaculate Heart of Mary Church.
Garcia-Miro, Sergio '78 (MIA) North Miami Beach, FL St. Lawrence Church.
Garcia-Padron, Julio V. '89 (SJN) [20] San Juan, PR San Francisco Javier Church.
Garcia-Pena, Carlos '66 (DOD) Garden City, KS St. Mary Church.
Garcia-Tunon, Guillermo *s.j.* '00 (MIA) [D] Miami, FL Belen Jesuit Preparatory School; [H] Miami, FL Villa Javier.
Gard, Charles W. '87 (LA) [51] Los Angeles, CA St.

Brendan Church.
Gardella, Robert F. *o.s.a.* '66 (DET) Grosse Pointe Park, MI St. Clare of Montefalco Church; [H] Southfield, MI Providence Hospital.
Gardener, Daniel L. '78 (KCK) Emporia, KS Sacred Heart Church; Emporia, KS St. Catherine Church.
Gardin, Msgr. Vernon E. '71 (STL) Clayton, MO St. Joseph Church; [H] St. Louis, MO Catholic Guidance Center; [H] St. Louis, MO St. Mary's Special Services.
Gardiner, Christopher B. '68 (MAR) Bark River, MI St. Elizabeth Ann Seton Church.
Gardiner, James J. *s.a.* '69 (NY) [DD] New York, NY Atonement Friars.
Gardiner, James K. '69 (GAY) Traverse City, MI St. Francis of Assisi Church.
Gardiner, Richard E. '67 (WDC) Solomons, MD Our Lady Star of the Sea Church.
Garding, William '82 (SCL) Special Assignment.
Gardner, Clarence W. '42 (ROC) [4] Auburn, NY St. Alphonsus Church; Retired.
Gardner, Clement '67 (ALT) Hollidaysburg, PA St. Michael's Church.
Gardner, Msgr. Glenn D. '70 (DAL) Plano, TX St. Mark the Evangelist Church.
Gardner, Jerome J. '79 (CIN) Fayetteville, OH St. Patrick Church.
Gardner, Msgr. Laurence R. '36 (MAN) [1] Manchester, NH St. Joseph Church; Retired.
Gardner, Maurice '52 (KCK) Retired.
Gardner, Royal J. '51 (SPR) [4] Pittsfield, MA Sacred Heart Church.
Gardner, Simeon '54 (SP) Retired.
Gardner, Thomas *o.f.m.* '79 (FgM) Franciscan Foreign Missions.
Gardner, Thomas *o.f.m.* '79 (STL) [P] St. Louis, MO Franciscan Friary of St. Anthony of Padua; [P] St. Louis, MO Franciscan Friary of St. Anthony of Padua.
Gardner, William M. '92 (PEO) Lostant, IL St. John the Baptist's Church; Wenona, IL St. Mary's Church.
Gardner, William P. '62 (TR) [1] Toms River, NJ St. Joseph Church.
Gardocki, Thomas F. '65 (WIL) Retired.
Gardzalla, Leo M. '45 (SCR) [4] Nanticoke, PA St. Joseph's Church.
Gareau, Timothy W. '88 (CLV) Bay Village, OH St. Raphael Church.
Gargani, Francis *c.ss.r.* '71 (NY) [150] Bronx, NY Immaculate Conception Church.
Gargantiel, Isidro T. '68 (GR) Scottville, MI St. Jerome Church.
Gargatiel, Isidro '68 (GR) Custer, MI St. Mary's Church.
Gariboldi, Ronald J. '61 (BO) Rockport, MA St. Joachim Church.
Gariepy, Andre M. '58 (WOR) [1] Gardner, MA Holy Spirit Church.
Gariepy, Robert E. '63 (WOR) Retired.
Gariepy, Thomas P. *c.s.c.* '74 (FR) [A] North Easton, MA Stonehill College.
Garinger, Grant S. *s.j.* '97 (LA) [Q] Los Angeles, CA Columbiere House.
Gariolo, Joseph M. *c.r.s.p.* '50 (BUF) [B] Youngstown, NY St. Anthony M. Zaccaria Seminary.
Garisto, James '77 (NY) [219] Staten Island, NY Our Lady, Queen of Peace Church.
Garisto, James A. (NY) [1] Poughkeepsie, NY St. Peter Church.
Garkowski, John G. '66 (BRK) [217] Queens, NY Our Lady of Perpetual Help Church.
Garland, Reynolds *o.f.m.* '61 (BR) Carville, LA National Hansen's Disease Center.
Garland, Msgr. Robert P. '53 (PIT) Retired.
Garland, William T. *o.s.a.* '62 (FR) [N] Fall River, MA Diocesan Education Center.
Garland, William T. *o.s.a.* '62 (PH) [C] Villanova, PA Villanova University.
Garlick, Thomas B. '84 (WOR) Sterling, MA St. Richard of Chichester Church.
Garneau, F. James '84 (R) On Duty Outside the Diocese.
Garneau, James *ph.d.*, '84 (COL) [A] Columbus, OH Pontifical College Josephinum.
Garner, Cliff '99 (DAL) [26] Dallas, TX St. Pius X Church.
Garner, Joel P. *o.praem.* '65 (SFE) [12] Albuquerque, NM Our Lady of Most Holy Rosary Church; [I] Albuquerque, NM Santa Maria de la Vid Priory; [M] Albuquerque, NM Norbertine Community of New Mexico, Inc.
Garner, Kirby D. '77 (AUS) [26] Austin, TX San Jose Church.
Garofalo, Kenneth *o.f.m.* '55 (BO) [52] Boston, MA Our Lady of Mt. Carmel Church.
Garoffolo, Vincent '41 (NEW) Retired.
Garone, Thomas *o.f.m.* '73 (NY) [FF] Wappingers Falls, NY Mt. Alvernia Retreat House.
Garrahy, Michael '51 (WCH) Retired.
Garramone, Dominic M. *o.s.b.* '92 (PEO) [A] Peru, IL St. Bede Abbey and Academy.
Garred, Msgr. John L. '52 (GBG) Retired; [G] Greensburg, PA St. Anne Home.
Garret, Sean '64 (SAT) On Duty Outside the Archdiocese.
Garrett, Mark A. *o.s.a.* '70 (SAT) Spring Branch, TX St. Joseph Church; [C] San Antonio, TX Oblate School of Theology.
Garrett, Thomas P. *o.s.a.* '39 (SD) [H] San Diego, CA Augustinian Community.
Garrido, Alejandro '92 (CHI) [2] Chicago, IL St. Adalbert Church.
Garrigan, Gerard *o.s.b.* '89 (STL) [1] Creve Coeur, MO St. Anselm Church; [P] St. Louis, MO The Abbey of St. Mary and St. Louis.
Garritty, Bernard R. *m.m.* '47 (NY) [DD] Maryknoll, NY Maryknoll Fathers and Brothers.
Garrity, Charles *o.c.d.* '66 (SB) [G] Redlands, CA El Carmelo Retreat House.
Garrity, Francis D. '56 (BO) Needham, MA St. Bartholomew Church.
Garrity, G. Patrick '76 (KNX) Jefferson City, TN Holy Trinity Catholic Church; Morristown, TN St. Patrick Church.
Garrity, John M. '58 (CLV) Berea, OH St. Mary's Church.
Garrity, Msgr. Paul V. '73 (BO) [4] Lynn, MA St. Mary Church.
Garrity, Robert M. '81 (RCK) Huntley, IL St. Mary Church.
Garrity, Sean *c.s.b.* '88 (LSC) Truth or Consequences, NM Our Lady of Perpetual Help Church.
Garrity, Sean *c.s.b.* '88 (ROC) Naples, NY Our Lady of the Lakes Catholic Community Church.
Garrity, Sean M. '88 (ROC) Penn Yan, NY St. Michael Church; Stanley, NY St. Theresa Church.
Garrity, Stephen M. *s.j.* '70 (WDC) [P] Faulkner, MD Loyola on the Potomac Retreat House.
Garrity, Thomas F. *m.m.* '46 (FgM) Maryknoll Foreign Missions.
Garrote, Sancho E. '76 (NY) [143] Bronx, NY St. Francis Xavier Church.
Garrote, Sancho G. '76 (NY) Bronx, NY Bronx Municipal Hospital Center, Abraham Jacobi Hospital, Nathan B. VanEtten Hospital.
Garrott, William *o.p.* '94 (CIN) [M] Cincinnati, OH St. Gertrude Priory.
Garrow, Mark *m.i.c.* '84 (SPR) [J] Stockbridge, MA Congregation of Marians of The Immaculate Conception of the BVM.
Garry, Brian *s.j.* '82 (SP) [C] Tampa, FL Jesuit High School.
Garry, Gerald *s.v.d.* '59 (CHI) [B] Techny, IL Divine Word Residence.
Garry, Peter J. '68 (RVC) Northport, NY St. Philip Neri Church.
Garry, Ronald '83 (RC) Piedmont-Black Hawk, SD Our Lady of the Black Hills Church.
Garst, Charles C. *o.s.f.s.* '83 (WIL) [3] Wilmington, DE St. Anthony of Padua Church.
Garthwaite, Thomas F. '55 (LC) Retired.
Gartland, Daniel B. '82 (LFT) [4] Lafayette, IN St. Lawrence Church.
Gartland, James G. *s.j.* '93 (CHI) [N] Chicago, IL Miguel Pro Jesuit Community.
Gartland, R. Vincent '81 (TR) Lawrenceville, NJ St. Ann Church.
Gartner, Charles A. '58 (RVC) Hicksville, NY Our Lady of Mercy Church; Retired.
Gartner, Joseph *glmy.* '40 (CIN) [M] Cincinnati, OH Headquarters of Glenmary Home Missioners.
Garvey, Charles J. '47 (COV) Retired.
Garvey, Francis J. *m.m.* '43 (SJ) [L] Los Altos, CA Maryknoll.
Garvey, Francis J. '59 (NU) Manannah, MN Church of Our Lady; Willmar, MN Regional Treatment Center; [F] Willmar, MN Willmar Regional Treatment Center.
Garvey, James W. '76 (PIT) Penn Hills, PA St. Bartholomew Church; [S] Pittsburgh, PA The Catholic Historical Society of Western Pennsylvania.
Garvey, John *glmy.* '57 (CIN) [M] Cincinnati, OH Headquarters of Glenmary Home Missioners.
Garvey, John F. *s.j.* '74 (NY) [F] New York, NY Xavier High School.
Garvey, John J. *s.j.* '50 (BUF) [O] Buffalo, NY Canisius Jesuit Community.
Garvey, John M. *m.s.* '53 (HRT) [M] Hartford, CT Missionaries of LaSalette, Provincial Secretary.
Garvey, John M. *m.s.* '53 (STL) [P] St. Louis, MO La Salette Missionaries.
Garvey, John M. '58 (SFS) Webster, SD Christ the King Church.
Garvey, Michael '71 (Y) Military Chaplains.
Garvey, Roderick J. *c.ss.r.* '49 (DEN) [M] Denver, CO The Redemptorists/Denver Province.
Garvey, Roderick J. *c.ss.r.* '49 (LSC) Jal, NM St. Cecilia Church.
Garvey, Thomas J. '57 (STP) Retired.
Garvin, Msgr. Joseph P. '73 (PH) [35] Philadelphia, PA St. Christopher Church.
Garvin, Thomas R. *s.j.* '58 (P) [L] Portland, OR Colombiere Community.
Garvy, John '83 (ORL) Retired.
Gary, Paul Q. '84 (CHL) [1] Charlotte, NC St. Patrick Church.
Garza, Amador '85 (BWN) Rio Grande City, TX Immaculate Conception Church.
Garza, Carlos '90 (BWN) Los Fresnos, TX St. Cecilia Church; Los Fresnos, TX Bayview Detention Center.
Garza, Jesse P. '79 (CHI) Other Assignments.
Garza, Jesus Aguirre *o.f.m.* '96 (FgM) Franciscan Foreign Missions.
Garza, Raul *c.m.* '86 (DAL) Ferris, TX Corpus Christi Church.
Garza, Roberto '96 (MIA) [3] Miami, FL Corpus Christi Church.
Garzarelli, Santo R. '61 (PH) On Duty Outside the Archdiocese.
Garzon, Fabio H. *s.d.b.* '86 (RCK) Carpentersville, IL St. Monica Church.
Garzon, Ignacio *m.j.* '68 (GAL) [75] Houston, TX St. Stephen Church.
Garzon-Blanco, Armando '95 (TUC) [16] Tucson, AZ St. John the Evangelist Church; Tucson, AZ U.S. Veterans Hospital; Absent on Leave.
Gasbarre, Msgr. Francis E. '41 (CLV) Bedford, OH St. Mary Church; Retired.
Gaska, Henry *s.v.d.* '88 (WDC) [M] Washington, DC Divine Word College.
Gaske, Bartholomew *o.f.m.conv.* '40 (SY) [2] Syracuse, NY Assumption B.V.M. Church.
Gaskin, Matthew L. *o.f.m.* '50 (PAT) [M] Butler, NJ St. Anthony Friary.
Gasnick, Roy *o.f.m.* '60 (SP) [O] St. Petersburg, FL St. Anthony Friary.
Gaspar, Joseph *m.s.c.* '41 (ALN) [A] Center Valley, PA Missionaries of the Sacred Heart.
Gaspar, Mark S. '98 (PH) Chalfont, PA St. Jude Church.
Gasparik, Francis *o.f.m.cap.* '86 (NY) [57] New York, NY St. John the Baptist Church.
Gasparin, Giampietro *c.s.j.*. '79 (CLV) [C] Lorain, OH Lorain Catholic High School; [O] Avon, OH Congregation of St. Joseph.
Gasparin, Giampietro *c.s.j.* '79 (LA) [Q] Los Angeles, CA Congregation of St. Joseph Casa Nazareth.
Gasparro, Anthony *o.s.a.* '41 (PH) [112] Philadelphia, PA St. Nicholas of Tolentine Church.
Gaspeny, Peter J. '83 (SAG) [5] Bay City, MI St. James Church.
Gass, Michael W. '77 (DEN) [4] Lakewood, CO St. Jude Church.
Gass, Robert J. (OM) [L] Omaha, NE Sisters of the Annunciation of the Archdiocese of Omaha.
Gass, Robert J. '53 (OM) Retired.
Gass, Msgr. Sylvester F. '39 (MIL) Retired.
Gassert, Adelbert J. '48 (CLV) Brook Park, OH Assumption of Mary Church; Independence, OH St. Michael Church; Northfield, OH Western Reserve Psychiatric Habilitation Center; Retired.
Gassner, Franz *s.v.d.* '95 (BO) [W] Boston, MA Divine Word Missionaries.
Gastalver, Alfredo '76 (SJN) [G] Guaynabo, PR Opus Dei.
Gaston, James T. '70 (GBG) Lower Burrell, PA St. Margaret Mary Church.
Gaston, Juan Cruz *o.f.m.cap.* '67 (DAL) [9] Dallas, TX Our Lady of Perpetual Help Church; [K] Dallas, TX Capuchin Franciscan Friars, Vice Province of Texas.
Gately, R. Troy '89 (GAL) [1] Houston, TX Sacred Heart Co-Church; On Special or Other Diocesan Assignment.
Gately, Robert '52 (SP) [1] St. Petersburg, FL Cathedral of St. Jude the Apostle.
Gately, Robert E. '52 (COL) Retired.
Gathen, Anthony *c.m.m.* '71 (DET) [K] Dearborn Heights, MI Our Lady of Grace Monastery.
Gatlin, Bernard (HON) Waihee, HI St. Ann Church.
Gatlin, Bernard '68 (LA) [69] Los Angeles, CA Santa Isabel Church.
Gatlin, Jeffrey D. '00 (L) [49] Louisville, KY St. Margaret Mary Church.
Gatlin, Larry B. '67 (OKL) Bison, OK St. Joseph's Church.
Gatman, Ronald P. *o.s.b.* '79 (SAV) [B] Savannah, GA Benedictine Military School; [F] Savannah, GA The Benedictine Priory.
Gatschet, Fred '93 (SAL) [G] Hays, KS Comeau Catholic Campus Center at Fort Hays State University.
Gattari, Valentine A. '54 (DET) Retired.
Gatti, Daniel J. *s.j.* '72 (NY) [F] New York, NY Xavier High School.
Gatto, Dennis J. *s.m.* '81 (CIN) [M] Dayton, OH Marianist Provincialate.
Gatto, Joseph C. '83 (BUF) [A] Buffalo, NY Pope John Paul II Residence; [A] East Aurora, NY Christ the King Seminary.
Gatto, Reynold J. *s.j.* '68 (SAC) [C] Sacramento, CA Jesuit High School; [H] Carmichael, CA Jesuit High School Community of Sacramento.

Gatto, Msgr. Vincent S. '55 (WDC) Garrett Park, MD Holy Cross Church.
Gatzak, John P. '75 (HRT) [1] Hartford, CT Cathedral of St. Joseph; Special and other Archdiocesan Assignment.
Gau, David H. *s.j.* '62 (RC) Mission, SD St. Thomas the Apostle Church; Rosebud, SD St. Bridget Church; St. Francis, SD Rosebud Reservation Church.
Gau, Guy *o.s.b.* '62 (SFS) [F] Marvin, SD Blue Cloud Abbey.
Gaucci, Juan A. *c.ss.r.* '59 (SJN) [2] San Juan, PR San Agustin Church.
Gauchat, Eric *o.f.m.cap.* '92 (CLV) [M] Parma, OH Franciscan Communities - Mount Alverna Home; [O] Cleveland, OH St. Paul Friary.
Gauchet, Eric *o.f.m.cap.* '92 (CLV) [18] Cleveland, OH Conversion of St. Paul Church.
Gauci, Albert *o.f.m.* '71 (FgM) Franciscan Foreign Missions.
Gaudet, Joseph A. '52 (BO) [7] Brockton, MA St. Patrick Church.
Gaudet, Joseph A. '57 (BO) Senior Priests.
Gaudet, Roger B. '89 (IND) Fortville, IN St. Thomas Church.
Gaudette, Edward J. '52 (BO) Senior Priests.
Gaudin, Rene *ss.cc.* '57 (FR) [I] Fairhaven, MA Sacred Hearts Provincial House.
Gaudio, Robert '74 (ROC) Marion, NY St. Gregory Church; Palmyra, NY St. Anne Church.
Gaudreau, Bernard E. '75 (BUR) Stowe, VT Blessed Sacrament Church.
Gaudreau, James E. '69 (BO) [3] Lynn, MA St. Joseph Church.
Gaudreau, Walter *s.m.* '64 (PRT) Brunswick, ME St. John the Baptist Church.
Gaudreault, Lucien *s.v.d.* '88 (MIL) [P] East Troy, WI Divine Word Seminary.
Gaughan, Msgr. Patrick E. '68 (STU) Athens, OH St. Paul's Church.
Gaughan, Paul '52 (RIC) [6] Virginia Beach, VA St. John the Apostle Church; Retired.
Gaughan, Thomas E. *c.s.c.* '87 (FTW) [B] Notre Dame, IN University of Notre Dame Du Lac; [J] Notre Dame, IN Holy Cross Community, Corby Hall, University of Notre Dame.
Gaughran, John '53 (PEO) Retired.
Gaugler, Robert *c.ss.r.* '39 (ALB) [L] Saratoga Springs, NY St. John Neumann Residence.
Gaugler, Robert *c.ss.r.* '39 (SJN) [2] San Juan, PR San Agustin Church.
Gaul, Cornelius '45 (DM) Retired.
Gaul, Richard G. '68 (DUB) Garber, IA St. Michael's Church; Garnavillo, IA St. Joseph's Church.
Gaul, Thomas J. '73 (R) Hope Mills, NC Good Shepherd Church.
Gaulin, Frederick J. *c.m.* '50 (PH) [AA] Philadelphia, PA Congregation of the Mission.
Gaulin, Roger M. '65 (NOR) Absent on Leave.
Gaulrapp, Leo *c.pp.s.* '46 (CIN) [B] Carthagena, OH St. Charles.
Gaumond, Normand R. '73 (WOR) Harvard, MA St. Theresa's Church.
Gaunt, James J. *c.s.b.* '64 (GAL) Manvel, TX Sacred Heart of Jesus Church; [Q] Manvel, TX The Basilian Fathers' Monastery of Citeaux.
Gaunt, Thomas P. *s.j.* '81 (BAL) [S] Baltimore, MD Jesuit Fathers and Brothers Maryland Provincial Curia; [S] Baltimore, MD Ferdinand Wheeler Jesuit Community.
Gaus, Msgr. Arnold L. '59 (ALT) Ebensburg, PA Holy Name Church.
Gauthier, Donald F., Jr. '75 (MAN) Goffstown, NH St. Lawrence Church.
Gauthier, Ernest L. '62 (KC) Holden, MO St. Patrick's Church.
Gauthier, John '65 (PHX) On Leave.
Gauthier, Lawrence T. '55 (MAR) Retired.
Gauthreaux, Msgr. L. Earl '56 (NO) [44] New Orleans, LA St. Maria Goretti Church.
Gautreau, Jr., Henry W. '79 (BR) Vacherie, LA Our Lady of Peace Church.
Gautreaux, Francis *c.ss.r.* '50 (FgM) Redemptorist Foreign Missions.
Gauvin, Leo *o.m.i.* '51 (SAT) [K] San Antonio, TX Oblate Madonna Residence.
Gauvin, Maurice '86 (FR) [C] Taunton, MA Taunton Catholic Middle School.
Gauvin, Maurice O. '86 (FR) [5] Taunton, MA St. Anthony's Church.
Gauvreau, Thomas H. '48 (SPR) Retired.
Gavaler, Campion P. *o.s.b.* '59 (GBG) [H] Latrobe, PA Saint Vincent Archabbey.
Gavigan, P. Patrick '53 (CHL) Retired.
Gavigan, Peter '62 (NY) [178] Bronx, NY Our Lady of Victory Church.
Gavigan, Tomas *c.ss.r.* '60 (CGS) Aguas Buenas, PR Church of Tres Santos Reyes.
Gavin, Carney E. '65 (BO) [18] Boston, MA St. Columbkille Church.
Gavin, Emmett *o.carm.* '87 (WDC) [B] Washington, DC Whitefriars Hall.
Gavin, Francis T. '47 (NEW) Retired; [B] South Orange, NJ Seton Hall University.
Gavin, James *o.f.m.cap.* '65 (NY) [17] Yonkers, NY Sacred Heart Church.
Gavin, John *o.s.a.* '48 (STL) [6] St. Louis, MO Immaculate Conception-St. Henry Church.
Gavin, John '60 (CAM) [M] Pittsgrove, NJ Villa St. Joseph.
Gavin, Kenneth J. *s.j.* '75 (FgM) Provinces.
Gavin, Kenneth J. *s.j.* '75 (NY) [DD] New York, NY Jesuit Provincial's Office; [DD] New York, NY St. Ignatius Loyola Residence.
Gavin, Patrick *o.carm.* '97 (PHX) [6] Phoenix, AZ St. Agnes Church.
Gavin, Robert A. *o.f.m.* '59 (NY) [35] New York, NY St. Francis of Assisi Church.
Gavin, Robert V. *s.s.* '61 (SFR) [A] Menlo Park, CA St. Patrick Seminary.
Gavin, Russell *o.carm.* '47 (JOL) Darien, IL Our Lady of Mount Carmel Church.
Gavin, Thomas M. *s.j.* '75 (BAL) [S] Baltimore, MD Jesuit Fathers and Brothers Maryland Provincial Curia.
Gavin, Thomas M. *s.j.* '75 (FgM) Provinces.
Gavin, William F. *s.j.* '62 (PH) [83] Philadelphia, PA Old St. Joseph's Church.
Gavit, James F. '54 (SAG) [7] Bay City, MI St. Maria Goretti Church.
Gavit, Steven M. '97 (SAG) Palms, MI St. Patrick Church.
Gavit, Steven W. '97 (SAG) Ruth, MI SS. Peter and Paul Church.
Gavitt, J. Duane '84 (SCR) [17] Wilkes-Barre, PA St. Patrick's Church.
Gavotto, Robert W. *o.s.a.* '64 (LA) [18] Los Angeles, CA Mother of Good Counsel Church.
Gawer, Peter J. '84 (PRO) [4] Warren, RI St. Mary of the Bay Church.
Gawienowski, John J. '00 (SPR) Wilbraham, MA St. Cecilia's Church.
Gawlik, Gilbert *s.v.d.* '54 (CHI) [B] Techny, IL Divine Word Residence.
Gawlowski, Paul *o.f.m.conv.* '99 (SFR) [44] San Francisco, CA St. Paul of the Shipwreck Church.
Gawronski, Chester J. '76 (E) [13] Erie, PA St. Ann Church.
Gawronski, Marc '91 (DET) [71] Detroit, MI St. Stephen-Mary Mother of the Church.
Gawronski, Raymond T. *s.j.* '86 (MIL) [P] Milwaukee, WI Jesuit Community at Marquette University.
Gawrylewski, Patrick *o.f.m.* (GB) Hofa Park, WI St. Stanislaus Church; Pulaski, WI Assumption of the Blessed Virgin Mary Church.
Gay, James A. '59 (BGP) Military Chaplains.
Gay, John Curry '56 (HRT) [2] Waterbury, CT Immaculate Conception Church.
Gayarre, Domingo *s.s.s.* '52 (CGS) [5] Caguas, PR Santisimo Sacramento Church.
Gayarre, Eugenio '61 (ARE) Corozal, PR Holy Family Church.
Gaydos, Anthony M. *o.s.m.* '48 (CHI) [N] Chicago, IL Order of Friar Servants of Mary (Servites) United States of America Province, Inc.
Gaydos, Anthony M. *o.s.m.* '48 (SPC) Ironton, MO Ste. Marie Du Lac Church.
Gaydos, Francis A. *c.m.* '47 (FgM) Vincentian Foreign Missions.
Gaydos, Robert M. *c.ss.r.* '44 (STL) [P] Liguori, MO St. Clement Health Care Center.
Gaydosik, David '87 (STU) Woodsfield, OH St. Sylvester Church.
Gaydosik, David L. '87 (STU) Burkhart, OH St. Joseph's Church; Miltonsburg, OH St. John the Baptist Church; Sardis, OH St. John Bosco Church.
Gaynard, Thomas P. '65 (PH) King of Prussia, PA Mother of Divine Providence Church.
Gaynor, James E. *c.pp.s.* '67 (CIN) [M] Dayton, OH Provincial Office of the Cincinnati Province of the Society of the Precious Blood.
Gaynor, Joseph T. '45 (ROC) [4] Auburn, NY St. Alphonsus Church; Retired.
Gayso, Edward V. '50 (IND) Retired.
Gaytan, Alfredo *s.o.l.t.* '82 (CC) [H] Robstown, TX Society of Our Lady of the Most Holy Trinity.
Gaytan, Jose Alfredo *s.o.l.t.* '85 (LAR) [13] Laredo, TX St. Frances Cabrini Church.
Gayton, John J. *m.i.c.* '86 (WIL) Elkton, MD Immaculate Conception Church.
Gaza, J. Patrick '68 (GRY) [16] Gary, IN SS. Monica-St. Luke Church.
Gazin, Mark *c.s.b.* (LSC) [4] Las Cruces, NM St. Albert the Great Newman Church.
Gazin, Mark R. *c.s.b.* '90 (LSC) [B] Las Cruces, NM Basilian Fathers.
Gaztelu, Msgr. Angel '38 (MIA) [22] Miami, FL St. John Bosco Church.
Geaney, James *o.carm.* '59 (FgM) Carmelite Foreign Missions.
Geaney, James *o.carm.* '59 (JOL) [J] Darien, IL Carmelite Provincial Office.
Geaney, John J. *c.s.p.* '64 (WDC) [B] Washington, DC St. Paul's College.
Geany, Nash P. (NY) West Point, NY Stewart Field.
Gearhart, Edwin F. '73 (CIN) [16] Cincinnati, OH St. Bonaventure Church; [51] Cincinnati, OH St. Leo the Great Church.
Gearheard, William (LAF) Washington, LA Holy Trinity Church.
Gearheard, William J., Jr. '94 (LAF) Washington, LA Immaculate Conception Church.
Gearing, Barry T. '00 (CLV) Chesterland, OH St. Anselm Church.
Gearing, Edward P. '44 (GBG) Retired.
Geary, Brian '98 (RCK) [1] Rockford, IL St. Peter Church.
Geary, Edward P. '64 (BO) [3] Beverly, MA St. Mary Star of the Sea Church.
Geary, John C. *s.j.* '47 (SJ) [L] Los Gatos, CA Sacred Heart Jesuit Center.
Geary, Patrick G. '56 (DUB) Retired.
Geary, Patrick G. '58 (DUB) Evansdale, IA St. Nicholas Church.
Gebbia, Gregory *o.f.m.* '86 (PAT) Little Falls, NJ Our Lady of the Holy Angels Church.
Gebelein, Gary '74 (STL) [6] Florissant, MO St. Ferdinand Church.
Gebhard, Robert L. '87 (BUF) [35] Buffalo, NY St. James Church.
Gebhardt, Joseph M. '50 (B) Retired.
Gebhardt, Paul L. '91 (CIN) [84] Cincinnati, OH St. Vivian Church.
Gedeon, Thomas W. *s.j.* '56 (CLV) [T] Cleveland, OH Jesuit Retreat House.
Geders, Joseph C. *c.m.* '84 (CHI) [N] Chicago, IL Vincentian Community, Congregation of the Mission, Midwest Province.
Geditz, Roger '69 (SFS) Redfield, SD St. Bernard Church.
Gedvila, Izidorius '48 (GF) Retired.
Gee, Daniel N. '95 (ARL) Woodbridge, VA Our Lady of Angels Church.
Gee, John F. '53 (WOR) Auburn, MA North American Martyrs Church.
Geelan, Thomas E. '62 (SC) [2] Sioux City, IA Blessed Sacrament Church.
Geenen, Roy J. '68 (GB) Menasha, WI St. Patrick Church.
Geers, Frank *o.f.m.* '58 (CIN) [C] Cincinnati, OH St. Anthony Shrine, Francisan Candidacy.
Geers, Harold *o.f.m.* '60 (CIN) [M] Cincinnati, OH St. Francis Seraph Friary.
Geers, Harold *o.f.m.* '60 (FgM) Franciscan Foreign Missions.
Gefell, Msgr. Gerard J. '41 (OG) Retired.
Gefell, Msgr. Gerard J. '41 (ROC) Retired.
Gefell, Msgr. Joseph G. '41 (OG) Retired.
Gefell, Msgr. Joseph G. '41 (ROC) Retired.
Gegotek, Tadeusz '91 (BEL) Elizabethtown, IL St. Joseph Church; Metropolis, IL St. Rose of Lima Church.
Gehant, Rembert *o.s.b.* '44 (IND) [J] St. Meinrad, IN St. Meinrad Archabbey.
Gehl, James C. '74 (LA) Canoga Park, CA St. Joseph the Worker Church.
Gehl, Walter N. '44 (MIL) Retired.
Gehlen, Elzear *s.v.d.* '44 (CHI) [1] Mt. Prospect, IL St. Cecilia Church; [B] Techny, IL Divine Word Residence.
Gehling, Kenneth B. '62 (DUB) Mason City, IA Holy Family Church; [H] Mason City, IA Mercy Medical Center-North Iowa.
Gehret, Mark *o.f.m.* '62 (FgM) Franciscan Foreign Missions.
Gehring, Robert P. '66 (GRY) [1] Gary, IN Cathedral of Holy Angels.
Gehringer, Andrew N. '00 (ALN) [9] Allentown, PA Sacred Heart of Jesus Church.
Geib, David *o.p.* '67 (SB) [10] Riverside, CA St. Andrew's Newman Center Church; [E] Riverside, CA St. Vincent Ferrer House.
Geib, David *o.p.* '97 (SB) [H] Riverside, CA St. Andrews Newman Center.
Geib, Harry F. *s.j.* '92 (PH) [AA] Philadelphia, PA Jesuit Community at St. Joseph's University.
Geigel, Francis '38 (GB) Retired.
Geiger, Angelo Mary '91 (NOR) [F] Griswold, CT Marian Friary of Our Lady of Guadalupe.
Geiger, Bernard *o.f.m.conv.* '59 (CHI) [N] Chicago, IL Conventual Franciscans of St. Bonaventure Province.
Geiger, Damon *o.ss.t.* '71 (BAL) [S] Baltimore, MD Holy Trinity Monastery.
Geiger, Damon *o.ss.t.* '71 (VIC) [F] Victoria, TX Trinity House.
Geiger, Eugene E. '47 (NEW) Orange, NJ Pope John Paul II Pavilion at St. Mary's; Retired.
Geiger, James (RIC) [2] Chesapeake, VA St. Mary Church; [E] Newport News, VA Mary Immaculate Hospital.
Geiger, Msgr. James A. '50 (COL) Sugar Grove, OH St. Joseph Church.
Geiger, James H. *c.ss.r.* '60 (RIC) [N] Hampton, VA Holy Family Retreat.

Geiger, William *c.ss.r.* '54 (HBG) [H] Ephrata, PA St. Clement's Mission House.
Geiger, William G. *c.ss.r.* '54 (HBG) Ephrata, PA Mother of Perpetual Help Church.
Geinzer, Eugene M. *s.j.* '74 (BAL) [S] Baltimore, MD Jesuit Community of Loyola College, Inc.
Geinzer, John A. (PIT) Military Chaplains.
Geinzer, Patrick *c.p.* '95 (R) Greenville, NC St. Peter's Church.
Geis, John F. '64 (IND) St. Mary-of-the-Knobs, IN St. Mary-of-the-Knobs Church.
Geiselhart, Charles T. '86 (PIT) Forest Hills, PA St. Maurice Church.
Geiser, Allen '90 (GB) Askeaton, WI St. Patrick Church.
Geiser, Xavier *o.f.m.* '55 (FgM) Custody of St. Mary of the Angels. Byzantine-Slavonic.
Geisinger, Robert J. *s.j.* '91 (CHI) [N] Chicago, IL Chicago Province of the Society of Jesus-Provincial Office.
Geisler, Michael '79 (BO) [V] Chestnut Hill, MA Opus Dei.
Geisser, Raymond E. *o.s.a.* '60 (MIA) [H] Miami, FL Casa San Lorenzo.
Geissler, Lloyd F. '42 (LC) Retired.
Geissler, Ralph J. '38 (LC) Retired.
Geissler, Msgr. Robert '47 (NY) Retired.
Geiszel, John I. *s.j.* '57 (LA) [F] Los Angeles, CA Loyola High School of Los Angeles.
Geitner, John E. *m.m.* '53 (FgM) Maryknoll Foreign Missions.
Gelati, Dario '53 (PIT) Retired.
Gelencser, Paul L. *o.praem.* '41 (ORG) [I] Silverado, CA Norbertine Fathers of Orange Inc.
Gelfenbien, Gary Paul '71 (ALB) Chatham, NY St. James Church.
Gelfer, Peter *o.h.* (SB) [D] Apple Valley, CA St. Mary Medical Center.
Gelin, Henry C. *s.j.* '51 (DET) [P] Clarkston, MI Colombiere Center.
Gelineau, Msgr. Edward J. '42 (BUR) Retired; [D] Burlington, VT St. Joseph's Home.
Gelineau, H. Raymond '69 (WOR) Absent on Leave.
Gelis, Mark *m.j.* '94 (PCE) On Duty Outside the Diocese.
Gellel, Lawrence *s.j.* '54 (BRK) [221] Queens, NY Our Lady of Sorrows Church.
Geller, Charles H. '73 (BEL) Special Assignment.
Gelpi, Donald L. *s.j.* '64 (OAK) [A] Berkeley, CA The Jesuit School of Theology at Berkeley; [N] Berkeley, CA Jesuit Community at Jesuit School of Theology at Berkeley.
Gelpi, Donald L.. *s.j.* (OAK) [A] Berkeley, CA The Jesuit School of Theology at Berkeley.
Gelson, James N. *s.j.* '60 (BAL) [S] Baltimore, MD Jesuit Fathers and Brothers Maryland Provincial Curia.
Gelthaus, Harry J. '85 (L) [1] Valley Station, KY St. Clement Church.
Gelthaus, Lawrence J. '88 (L) Albany, KY Emmanuel Catholic Church.
Gelvez, Raul O. '60 (BRK) [221] Queens, NY Our Lady of Sorrows Church.
Gembala, Joseph J. '87 (DET) [5] Sterling Heights, MI St. Malachy Church.
Gemperline, Joachim *c.p.* '53 (L) [L] Louisville, KY Sacred Heart Retreat.
Gemskie, Charles A. '77 (JOL) Carol Stream, IL Corpus Christi Church.
Gemuend, Msgr. David W. '65 (GAY) Absent on Leave.
Gemza, Richard J. '95 (BGP) [1] Greenwich, CT St. Mary Church.
Gendernalik, Leonard *sch.p.* '71 (WDC) [B] Washington, DC Queen of Pious Schools House of Studies-Piarist Fathers.
Gendreau, Claude R. '93 (PRT) Frenchville, ME St. Luce's Church; St. Agatha, ME St. Agatha's Church; Sinclair, ME St. Joseph Church.
Gendreau, Michael P. '90 (PRT) Augusta, ME St. Mary's Church.
Gendreau, Richard R. '69 (FR) [3] Swansea, MA St. Michael's Church.
Gendron, Charles A. *m.s.* '44 (LKC) [3] Sulphur, LA Our Lady of Prompt Succor Church.
Gendron, Michael E. '95 (MAN) Plaistow, NH Holy Angels Church.
Gendusa, Anthony *m.s.c.* '40 (RCK) [G] Aurora, IL Missionaries of the Sacred Heart Community.
Genello, Patrick J. '83 (SCR) [3] Hazleton, PA Holy Rosary Church.
Genereux, Wayne C. *o.de.m.* (PH) [AA] Philadelphia, PA Monastery of Our Lady of Mercy.
Genereux, Wayne C. *o.de.m.* '97 (BUF) [O] LeRoy, NY Order of the BVM of Mercy/Mercedarian Friars.
Generose, Anthony J. '99 (SCR) [1] Plymouth, PA Nativity of the Blessed Virgin Mary Church; [D] Kingston, PA Bishop O'Reilly High School.
Genest, Gilles *m.s.* '62 (MAN) Lebanon, NH Sacred Heart Church.
Genevive, Frank *o.f.m.* '83 (FR) [I] Onset, MA St. Joseph Friary-Franciscan Friars.
Geng, Dennis *o.c.d.* '89 (MIL) [P] Milwaukee, WI Provincial Offices - Discalced Carmelites.
Gengaro, Nicholas S. '81 (NEW) [B] South Orange, NJ Seton Hall University.
Gengras, Joseph C. '49 (HRT) Retired; [A] Bloomfield, CT St. Thomas Seminary.
Geniesse, Joseph '57 (AUS) [F] Austin, TX Seton Medical Center.
Geniesse, Joseph F. '57 (AUS) [H] Austin, TX Congregation of Holy Cross - Southern Province.
Genilo, Eric *s.j.* '97 (BO) [W] Cambridge, MA Weston Jesuit Community.
Genito, Joseph A. *o.s.a.* '75 (PH) [143] Philadelphia, PA St. Rita of Cascia Church.
Gennardo, Vincent *c.s.* '64 (CHI) [134] Chicago, IL St. Michael Archangel Church.
Genovese, Anthony M. *o.s.a.* '73 (PH) Villanova, PA St. Thomas of Villanova Church.
Genovese, Seamus D. '75 (OAK) [18] Oakland, CA Our Lady of Lourdes Church.
Genovesi, Vincent J. *s.j.* '69 (PH) [C] Philadelphia, PA St. Joseph's University; [AA] Philadelphia, PA Jesuit Community at St. Joseph's University.
Genska, Depaul A. *o.f.m.* '58 (NY) [DD] New York, NY Franciscan Friars, Order of Friars Minor, Holy Name Province.
Gensler, Harry J. *s.j.* '74 (CLV) [B] Cleveland, OH John Carroll Jesuit Community.
Gentile, Carl J. '60 (PIT) Churchill Borough, PA St. John Fisher Church.
Gentile, Emile A. *t.o.r.* '64 (ORL) Mount Dora, FL St. Patrick's Church; Special Assignment.
Gentile, Gilbert J. *s.j.* '78 (SD) [4] San Diego, CA Christ the King Church.
Gentile, Henry *c.s.* (NY) [205] Staten Island, NY Holy Family Church.
Gentile, Henry S. *c.s.* '59 (NY) [DD] Staten Island, NY Scalabrinian Missionaries.
Gentile, Thomas E. '73 (L) [31] Louisville, KY St. Helen Church.
Gentili, Joseph P. '87 (ALN) [A] Northampton, PA Mary Immaculate Center.
Gentili, Joseph P. '87 (PH) [A] Wynnewood, PA Theological Seminary of St. Charles Borromeo, Overbrook.
Gentleman, Gerard J., Jr. '97 (RVC) Farmingdale, NY St. Kilian Church.
Gentleman, John W. (BO) Amesbury, MA Holy Family Church.
Genua, Ronald L. '65 (HRT) [2] Ansonia, CT Holy Rosary Church.
Genuardi, Gasper A. '68 (PH) Conshohocken, PA SS. Cosmas and Damian Church.
Genuario, Msgr. William A. '56 (BGP) Riverside, CT St. Catherine of Siena Church.
Genzlinger, Walter L. '49 (NEW) [17] Jersey City, NJ Our Lady of Mt. Carmel Church; Retired.
Geogan, Philip J. '79 (NOR) Stonington, CT St. Mary Church.
Geoghegan, Msgr. Arthur T. '41 (MIA) [7] Pompano Beach, FL St. Henry Church.
Geoghegan, Msgr. Arthur T. '41 (PRO) Retired.
Geoghegan, John F. '45 (STL) Retired.
George, Msgr. Alexander C. (LA) Retired.
George, Alexander C. '65 (LA) Retired.
George, Msgr. David M. '76 (SAM) Waterbury, CT Our Lady of Lebanon Church.
George, Francis M. '87 (LAN) Hartland, MI St. John The Baptist Church.
George, Gary *c.ss.r.* '92 (OLL) Youngstown, OH St. Maron Church.
George, George '86 (BLX) Biloxi, MS Keesler Airforce Base.
George, J. Clark '56 (ALT) Retired.
George, Jose (TYL) Daingerfield, TX Our Lady of Fatima Church.
George, Msgr. Joseph S. '62 (LA) Thousand Oaks, CA St. Paschal Baylon Church.
George, Lloyd *s.j.* '73 (BAL) [D] Baltimore, MD Loyola Blakefield.
George, Mark *s.j.* '98 (DET) [B] Berkley, MI Loyola House.
George, Richard '95 (PMB) [B] West Palm Beach, FL Cardinal Newman High School.
George, Robert J. '76 (PIT) [P] Pittsburgh, PA Convent of Mercy.
George, Robert J. '95 (ALN) [1] Allentown, PA Cathedral of St. Catharine of Siena.
George, Saji '92 (RVC) Valley Stream, NY Holy Name of Mary Church.
George, Saji M. '92 (RVC) Hempstead, NY St. John Chrysostom Malankara Church.
George, Wallis W. *c.ss.r.* '50 (STL) [P] Liguori, MO St. Clement Health Care Center.
George, Walter *c.ss.r.* '50 (CHI) [133] Chicago, IL St. Michael Church.
George, William L. '73 (WDC) [E] North Bethesda, MD Georgetown Preparatory School.
Georgia, John J. '75 (HRT) [3] Bristol, CT St. Gregory's Church.
Gephart, John B. '46 (L) Retired; [L] Louisville, KY Bishop David Apartments.
Gera, Francis '64 (PSC) Ormond Beach, FL Holy Dormition Church.
Geracci, John R. *c.s.c.* '92 (SCR) [C] Wilkes-Barre, PA Kings College; [C] Wilkes-Barre, PA Kings College.
Geraci, Anthony J. '74 (CIN) [19] Dayton, OH Our Lady of the Immaculate Conception Church.
Geraets, Chrysostom *o.p.* '56 (FgM) Dominican - Order of Preachers Foreign Missions.
Geraghty, James '86 (NY) Absent on Leave.
Geraghty, Msgr. Martin T. '64 (BRK) [169] Queens, NY St. Francis de Sales Church.
Gerardi, Joseph A. '00 (DET) Royal Oak, MI Shrine of the Little Flower Church.
Gerathy, Msgr. Kenneth A. '54 (NY) [201] Staten Island, NY St. Christopher Church.
Geraughty, Michael '84 (ORG) Inactive Leave.
Gerber, Francis J., Jr. '84 (DEN) Grand Lake, CO St. Anne Church.
Gerbino, A. Richard '52 (CAM) On Sick Leave; [M] Cherry Hill, NJ Vianney Villa.
Gerbus, Berard *o.f.m.* '38 (CIN) [L] Cincinnati, OH Archbishop Leibold Home for the Aged.
Gerdelmann, Clemens J. '85 (PH) [158] Philadelphia, PA St. William Church.
Gerdes, Harry J. '62 (CIN) [48] Cincinnati, OH St. Joseph Church.
Gerena, Ricardo '85 (SJN) [1] San Juan, PR Catedral De San Juan Bautista Church.
Gerend, Lawrence '76 (GB) Retired.
Gerg, Joseph *o.s.b.* '65 (ALT) Patton, PA Our Lady of Perpetual Help Church; Patton, PA Queen of Peace Church.
Gergel, Stephen J. '62 (ALT) Military Chaplains.
Gergen, Charles L. '48 (LIN) Retired.
Gergen, Michael *s.d.b.* '79 (LA) [C] Rosemead, CA Don Bosco Technical Institute; [D] Rosemead, CA Don Bosco Technical Institute.
Gerhard, J. Peter *o.p.* (L) [47] Louisville, KY St. Louis Bertrand Church.
Gerhard, John J. *s.j.* '49 (NY) [DD] New York, NY Jesuit Provincial's Office.
Gerhardt, Msgr. Bernard C. '53 (WDC) [1] Washington, DC St. Matthew Church; Pastoral Center Special Ministries.
Gering, Kenneth *o.f.m.conv.* '58 (IND) St. Joseph Hill, IN St. Joseph Church.
Gerken, Theodore '57 (ALB) Germantown, NY Resurrection Church; Albany, NY Columbia County Jail.
Gerl, Robert '79 (LAN) On Duty Outside the Diocese.
Gerlach, Dominic B. *c.pp.s.* '50 (LFT) [A] Rensselaer, IN Saint Joseph's College.
Gerlach, John H. *o.p.* '63 (SFD) [L] Springfield, IL Convent of Our Lady of the Sacred Heart.
Gerlach, Matthew J. '96 (TLS) [1] Tulsa, OK Holy Family Church.
Gerlach, Michael '82 (PH) Lower Makefield, PA St. John the Evangelist Church.
Gerlich, Robert S. *s.j.* '73 (NO) [C] New Orleans, LA Loyola University New Orleans.
Gerlock, Stanley J. '60 (SY) Chenango Forks, NY St. Rita Church; Binghamton, NY Broome County Jail.
Gerloff, Charles W. '45 (ARL) Retired.
Germain, Jean M. '47 (SHP) Retired.
Germaine, Kenneth *s.d.b.* '67 (SP) [E] Tampa, FL Mary Help of Christians School.
German, Ambrose *o.f.m.* '53 (JC) Hermann, MO St. George Church.
German, Ambrose *o.f.m.* '53 (STL) [P] St. Louis, MO Franciscan Friary of St. Anthony of Padua.
German, Gary *o.f.m.* '88 (STL) [P] St. Louis, MO Franciscan Friary of St. Anthony of Padua.
German, Kenneth N. '81 (BO) Unassigned.
German, Michael J. '68 (NEW) River Edge, NJ St. Peter the Apostle Church.
German, Timothy J. '73 (ORG) Inactive Leave.
Germann, Daniel V. *s.j.* '63 (SJ) [L] Los Gatos, CA Sacred Heart Jesuit Center.
Germann, Lauren A. '78 (SCL) Staples, MN Sacred Heart Church.
Germovnik, Francis *c.m.* '41 (STL) [P] Perryville, MO Congregation of The Mission.
Gernatt, Msgr. David A. '47 (BUF) Retired.
Gerosa, Giuliano *c.r.s.* '78 (MAN) [H] Allenstown, NH Pine Haven Boys Center.
Gerres, Daniel W. '66 (WIL) [13] Wilmington, DE St. Thomas Church; Wilmington, DE Gander Hill Correctional Center.
Gerrety, James P. '57 (COV) Retired.
Gerritts, John R. '91 (SUP) Rhinelander, WI St. Joseph's Church.
Gerrity, John J. '35 (CLV) Maple Heights, OH St. Martin of Tours Church; Retired.
Gerrity, John J. '58 (CLV) [M] Cleveland, OH Sts. Mary and Joseph Home for the Aged.
Gerrity, Raymond J. '45 (CHI) [143] Chicago, IL Our Lady of Fatima Church; Retired.
Gersbach, Karl A. *o.s.a.* '61 (CHI) [N] Olympia Fields, IL The Augustinians-Provincialate.
Gersbach, Karl A. *o.s.a.* '61 (PH) [AA] Villanova, PA St. Thomas Monastery.

Gerth, John '93 (SP) [2] Clearwater, FL Light of Christ Church.
Gerth, Kenneth *m.c.c.j.* (SP) [K] Tampa, FL St. Joseph's Hospital, Inc.
Gerth, Kenneth *m.c.c.j.* '65 (CIN) [M] Cincinnati, OH Comboni Missionaries (Verona Fathers)-Comboni Mission Center.
Gerum, Jerome G. '50 (LC) Retired.
Gerut, William F. *s.j.* '67 (LC) Prairie du Chien, WI St. Gabriel Church; Prairie du Chien, WI St. John Nepomucene Church.
Gervacio, Adrian R. '67 (HON) Military Chaplains.
Gervacio, Adrian R. '67 (LA) Point Mugu, CA Naval Air Station; Port Hueneme, CA Naval Construction Battalion Center.
Gervais, Bernard *o.s.b.* '44 (PBL) [E] Canon City, CO Centura Health-St. Thomas More Hospital.
Gervais, Bernard P. *o.s.b.* '44 (PBL) [G] Canon City, CO Holy Cross Abbey.
Gese, David '78 (SEA) Elma, WA St. Joseph Church; [13] Tacoma, WA Visitation Church.
Gessler, James *s.m.a.* '63 (FgM) Society of African Missions.
Gessner, Glenn *o.f.m.cap.* '60 (FgM) Capuchin Foreign Missions.
Gesuale, Valentine *o.f.m.* '65 (FgM) Franciscan Foreign Missions.
Gesy, Lawrence '75 (BAL) Brunswick, MD St. Francis of Assisi Church.
Getchel, Richard '76 (GB) [3] Green Bay, WI St. Agnes Church.
Getigan, Bernardito '85 (SAN) St. Lawrence, TX St. Lawrence Church.
Getreu, David E. '94 (COL) Leave of Absence.
Getsinger, Ronald A. '68 (WH) New Cumberland, WV Immaculate Conception Church.
Getsy, John *o.f.m.cap.* '66 (PIT) [30] Pittsburgh, PA Our Lady of the Angels Church.
Gettig, Diego J. *c.pp.s.* '71 (GRY) [5] East Chicago, IN Our Lady of Guadalupe Church.
Gettinger, Robert J. '64 (STL) [27] St. Louis, MO St. Augustine Church.
Getty, Roy G. '39 (PIT) Retired.
Getz, Joseph *o.s.a.* '51 (ALB) Mechanicville, NY Assumption-St. Paul Church.
Getz, Msgr. Robert '61 (LSC) Roswell, NM Assumption of the Blessed Virgin Mary Church.
Geurtz, Gary '81 (FWT) [9] Fort Worth, TX St. Bartholomew Church.
Geusic, Stephen *m.s.c.* '43 (ALN) [A] Center Valley, PA Missionaries of the Sacred Heart.
Geyer, Kenneth A. *o.s.b.* '53 (CHL) [J] Belmont, NC Belmont Abbey.
Geyer, Raymond J. *o.s.b.* '49 (CHL) [J] Belmont, NC Belmont Abbey.
Geyman, Donald R. '96 (GAY) [4] Alpena, MI St. Mary Church.
Geysen, Clement *ss.cc.* '49 (HON) [G] Kaneohe, HI Sacred Hearts Center.
Gfroerer, Gerard J. '51 (RVC) Retired; [M] Uniondale, NY St. Pius X Residence.
Ghaby, Jean '92 (NTN) West Paterson, NJ St. Ann Church.
Ghanoum, Gabriel *b.s.o.* '93 (NTN) Miami, FL St. Jude Church; Delray Beach, FL St. Nicholas Church.
Ghazal, Edmond J. *b.c.o.* '58 (NTN) Plymouth, MI St. Michael Church.
Ghezzi, Giancarlo *p.i.m.e.* '84 (PAT) [M] Wayne, NJ P.I.M.E. Missionaries Residence.
Ghezzi, Luciano *p.i.m.e.* '74 (DET) [K] Detroit, MI P.I.M.E. Missionaries of SS. Peter and Paul.
Ghezzi, Richard G. '86 (SCR) Friendsville, PA St. Joseph's Church.
Ghiloni, Mark V. '83 (COL) Portsmouth, OH Holy Redeemer Church.
Ghio, John J. '80 (STL) [5] St. Charles, MO St. Peter Church.
Ghiorso, David '81 (SFR) Redwood City, CA Our Lady of Mount Carmel Church.
Ghiorso, David A. '81 (SFR) [T] San Rafael, CA Catholic Scouting.
Ghisalberti, Giacomo G. '51 (R) Retired.
Ghouzran, Poles (LA) [5] North Hollywood, CA St. Paul Assyrian-Chaldean Church.
Ghozairan, Poulos (EST) North Hollywood, CA St. Paul Assyrian-Chaldean Catholic Church.
Ghys, Philip *o.s.b.* '53 (RIC) [5] Virginia Beach, VA St. Gregory the Great Church.
Ghyselinck, Mark *c.s.c.* '88 (KAL) [1] Kalamazoo, MI St. Augustine Church.
Ghyselinck, Mark R. *c.s.c.* '88 (FTW) [J] South Bend, IN Congregation of Holy Cross, Indiana Province, Provincial House.
Giachino, Valeriano *s.s.p.* '57 (LA) [Q] Los Angeles, CA Society of St. Paul.
Giacomini, Antonio *o.f.m.cap.* '39 (R) Retired.
Giacomini, Salvatore *s.d.b.* '51 (SFR) [46] San Francisco, CA SS. Peter and Paul Church.
Giacopelli, John A. '59 (KC) Retired.
Giacosa, Charley '62 (NSH) Ashland City, TN St. Martha Church.
Giambrone, Charles S. *c.s.sp.* '60 (PIT) [Q] Bethel Park, PA Holy Ghost Animation Center.
Giammona, Msgr. John J. '59 (GR) Retired.
Giandurco, Joseph R. '87 (NY) [A] Yonkers, NY St. Joseph's Seminary.
Gianelli, Gene E. '70 (HRT) Woodbridge, CT Church of the Assumption.
Giangiacomo, Tosello *c.s.sp.* '48 (ARE) Orocovis, PR Our Lady of Fatima Church.
Giangiacomo, Tosello *c.s.sp.* '48 (PCE) [B] Ponce, PR The Pontifical Catholic University of Puerto Rico.
Giannamore, Anthony '56 (CIN) [L] Centerville, OH The Franciscan at St. Leonard.
Giannamore, Msgr. Anthony J. '56 (CIN) [V] Centerville, OH St. Leonard Faith Community.
Giannamore, Msgr. Anthony J. '56 (STU) Retired.
Giannamore, Peter A. '95 (WH) Salem, WV Sacred Heart Church; West Union, WV St. Patrick's Church.
Gianni, Vincent J. '70 (BO) Emergency Response Group.
Giannini, Stephen W. '93 (IND) [1] Terre Haute, IN Sacred Heart of Jesus Church; [2] Terre Haute, IN St. Ann Church.
Giannitelli, Michael C. '91 (NOR) Colchester, CT St. Andrew Church.
Giannone, Ronald *o.f.m.cap.* '90 (WIL) [F] Wilmington, DE Ministry of Caring, Inc.; [I] Wilmington, DE St. Felix Friary; [J] Wilmington, DE Monastery of St. Veronica Giuliani.
Gianola, William '62 (CHY) Retired.
Gianzmann, Edward J. *o.s.b.* '79 (CHI) [N] Chicago, IL Monastery of the Holy Cross.
Giaquinto, Albert C. '48 (NOR) Retired.
Giaquinto, Albert C. *s.s.* '48 (WDC) [A] Washington, DC Theological College of the Catholic University of America.
Giaramitaro, James *o.f.m. conv.* '88 (CHI) [N] Chicago, IL Conventual Franciscans of St. Bonaventure Province.
Giardina, Robert J. '76 (PRO) [9] West Warwick, RI Sacred Heart Church.
Giardino, Andrew *o.f.m.* '62 (HRT) [15] Hartford, CT St. Patrick-St. Anthony Church.
Giardino, Louis *v.f.* '75 (BIR) [4] Huntsville, AL Holy Spirit Church.
Gibas, Robert G. '62 (Y) Navarre, OH St. Clement's Church.
Gibault, Damian '92 (PSC) [C] Miami, FL Holy Cross Community.
Gibbons, Christopher W. *m.m.* '45 (NY) [DD] Maryknoll, NY Maryknoll Fathers and Brothers.
Gibbons, Donald Patrick '91 (SFD) Jerseyville, IL St. Francis Xavier Church.
Gibbons, Edward '97 (VEN) Cape Coral, FL St. Andrew Church.
Gibbons, Francis X. '83 (ORG) Inactive Leave.
Gibbons, James *o.m.i.* '69 (FgM) Oblates Foreign Missions.
Gibbons, James M. '52 (BO) Senior Priests.
Gibbons, John '56 (DEN) [15] Denver, CO Montbello Catholic Parish-Church of the Ascension ; Retired.
Gibbons, John J. '58 (NEW) [8] Bayonne, NJ St. Michael's Church.
Gibbons, John M. '89 (ALN) [1] Bethlehem, PA St. Anne Church.
Gibbons, Peter D. '89 (NY) [143] Bronx, NY St. Francis Xavier Church.
Gibbons, Robert C. '81 (SP) [7] St. Petersburg, FL St. Paul Church.
Gibbons, Thomas F. *m.m.* '48 (NY) [DD] Maryknoll, NY Maryknoll Fathers and Brothers.
Gibbons, Thomas F. *m.m.* '48 (PH) [60] Philadelphia, PA Holy Family Church.
Gibbons, Thomas J. *s.j.* '60 (BO) [W] Boston, MA The Society of Jesus of New England-Provincial Offices.
Gibbons, William F. '57 (CLV) Independence, OH St. Michael Church; [6] Lorain, OH St. Joseph Church; Retired.
Gibbs, Phillip G. '94 (DUB) [C] Dubuque, IA Loras College.
Gibeault, Gerard *m.s.a.* '58 (NOR) [A] Cromwell, CT Holy Apostles College and Seminary.
Gibino, Joseph R. '81 (BRK) [1] Brooklyn, NY The Cathedral-Basilica of St. James; [E] Brooklyn, NY Office of Religious Education: Evangelization and Catholic Formation.
Gibino, Joseph R. '81 (RVC) [A] Huntington, NY Diocesan Seminary of the Immaculate Conception.
Giblin, C. Homer *s.j.* '58 (NY) [DD] New York, NY Jesuit Community at Fordham University.
Giblin, Msgr. Lawrence E. '44 (SY) Retired.
Giblin, Richard J. '66 (SY) Vestal, NY St. Vincent de Paul Church.
Giblin, William M. '59 (NEW) Retired.
Giblin, William M., (Retired) '59 (NEW) Edgewater, NJ Holy Rosary Church.
Gibney, Robert G. '54 (NEW) Ridgewood, NJ Our Lady of Mount Carmel Church; [N] Caldwell, NJ The Rev. Msgr. James F. Kelley Residence for Retired Priests.
Gibney, Robert G. '69 (NEW) Retired.
Gibowski, Boguslaw T. '69 (PRO) [13] Woonsocket, RI St. Stanislaus Church.
Gibson, Beryl '96 (SAL) Beardsley, KS St. John's Church; Bird City, KS St. Joseph's Church; St. Francis, KS St. Francis Church.
Gibson, Bruno *o.p.* '60 (OAK) [4] Berkeley, CA St. Mary Magdalen Church.
Gibson, Christopher *c.p.* '75 (GAL) [Q] Houston, TX Congregation of the Passion, Holy Name Retreat Center; [S] Houston, TX Holy Name Retreat Center.
Gibson, John W. '45 (PIT) Retired; [O] Pittsburgh, PA St. John Vianney Manor.
Gibson, Msgr. Lawrence J. '55 (LA) San Marino, CA Saints Felicitas and Perpetua Church.
Gibson, Michael P. '48 (STL) Retired.
Gibson, Robert J. '58 (SCR) Unassigned or Leave of Absence.
Gibson, Stephen C. *c.s.c.* '70 (FTW) [L] Notre Dame, IN Holy Cross Mission House; [M] Notre Dame, IN Our Lady of Fatima Retreat Center.
Gibson, Stephen G. '81 (GRY) [11] East Chicago, IN St. Mary Church.
Gicewicz, Edward *c.m.* '38 (HRT) [M] Manchester, CT DePaul Provincial Residence.
Gick, Francois *s.j.* '80 (BO) [W] Boston, MA The Society of Jesus of New England-Provincial Offices.
Gidaro, Joseph C. *o.ss.t.* '87 (BAL) [S] Baltimore, MD Holy Trinity Monastery.
Gidaro, Joseph C. *o.ss.t.* '87 (NY) [20] New York, NY St. Brigid Church.
Gideon, Peter M. '76 (COL) New Boston, OH St. Monica Church; Wheelersburg, OH St. Peter Church.
Gideon, Stephen '97 (NSH) Dickson, TN St. Christopher Church.
Gidley, Lawrence *o.s.b.* '40 (KC) [J] Conception, MO Conception Abbey.
Giebel, Alfred W. '72 (ANC) [3] Anchorage, AK St. Benedict Church.
Giedgaudas, Francis *o.f.m.* '47 (BRK) [V] Brooklyn, NY St. Casimir's Monastery, Printing Plant and Cultural Center.
Giel, John C. '78 (ORL) Leesburg, FL St. Paul's Church.
Gielow, Richard *c.m.* '70 (KC) [J] Kansas City, MO Vincentian Parish Mission Center.
Gier, Gregory A. '67 (TLS) [1] Tulsa, OK Holy Family Church.
Gier, Thomas P. *s.o.l.t.* '62 (CC) [H] Robstown, TX Society of Our Lady of the Most Holy Trinity.
Giermek, Joachin *o.f.m.conv.* '69 (BAL) [S] Ellicott City, MD Order of Friars Minor Conventual.
Gierut, Casimir '49 (SFD) Retired.
Gierut, Joseph A. '32 (DET) Retired.
Gies, Norman J. '49 (BAL) Retired.
Gies, William *m.s.c.* '53 (ALN) [K] Reading, PA Missionaries of the Sacred Heart.
Giese, Samuel C. '85 (WDC) On Duty Outside the Archdiocese.
Giese, Vincent J. '65 (CHI) Retired.
Giesen, Donald '95 (MAR) Vulcan, MI St. Barbara Church.
Giesige, Randy P. '98 (TOL) Findlay, OH St. Michael Church.
Giesing, Msgr. Anthony '55 (SD) Retired.
Gietl, Joseph A. '73 (GAL) [2] Spring, TX St. Edward Church.
Gietzen, Albin J. '56 (GAY) Hannah, MI St. Mary Church.
Gigante, Louis R. '59 (NY) [130] Bronx, NY St. Athanasius Church.
Gigantiello, Jamie J. '95 (BRK) [83] Brooklyn, NY Mary Queen of Heaven Church.
Giganto, Jose A. *o.s.a.* '65 (SAT) [47] San Antonio, TX St. Jude Church.
Giggi, Msgr. J. Robert '53 (BO) Natick, MA St. Linus Church.
Giglio, Msgr. Charles J. '58 (CAM) [1] Camden, NJ Immaculate Conception Church.
Giglio, Michael E. '94 (ORL) Winter Park, FL St. Margaret Mary Church; [E] Winter Park, FL Rollins College Campus Ministry.
Gigliotti, James *t.o.r.* '80 (FWT) [5] Arlington, TX St. Maria Goretti Church.
Gigliotti, Vincent J. '76 (GBG) Brownsville, PA St. Peter Church; Brownsville, PA St. Mary Church.
Gignac, Francis T. *s.j.* '67 (DET) [K] Detroit, MI Jesuit Provincial Office-Detroit Province of the Society of Jesus.
Gignac, Francis T. *s.j.* '67 (WDC) [C] Washington, DC Catholic University of America, The; [M] Washington, DC The Jesuit Community at Georgetown University.
Gikonyo, David K. *i.m.c.* '97 (WDC) [V] Washington, DC Consolata Missionaries House of Studies.
Gil, Fernando '88 (ORL) Poinciana, FL St. Rose of Lima Church.
Gil, Miguel '86 (MIA) [22] Miami, FL St. John Bosco Church.
Gilb, Msgr. Eugene A. '57 (LA) Rancho Palos Verdes, CA St. John Fisher Church; Retired.
Gilbert, Dennis '71 (MRY) Cambria, CA Santa Rosa Church.

Gilbert, Msgr. Donald J. '68 (MAN) Windham, NH St. Matthew Church.
Gilbert, John R. '56 (STP) Marystown, MN St. Mary of the Purification Church; Retired.
Gilbert, Joseph T. '79 (SCR) [18] Wilkes-Barre, PA Sacred Heart-St. John Church.
Gilbert, Maurice L. '66 (WOR) [2] Southbridge, MA Notre Dame Church.
Gilbert, Philip F. *c.pp.s.* '60 (LFT) [A] Rensselaer, IN Saint Joseph's College.
Gilbert, Robert J. '98 (CHI) [168] Chicago, IL St. Philip Neri Church.
Gilbert, Valmont R. '57 (PRT) Retired.
Gilbertson, C. Lee '86 (SPR) South Hadley, MA St. Theresa of the Infant Jesus Church.
Gilbo, Robert *c.s.c.* '67 (FgM) Holy Cross Foreign Missions.
Gilbo, Roberto M. *c.s.c.* '67 (FTW) [J] South Bend, IN Congregation of Holy Cross, Indiana Province, Provincial House.
Gilborges, Tony '89 (CHL) [4] Greensboro, NC St. Paul the Apostle Church.
Gilchrist, Francis J. '45 (ALB) [4] Albany, NY St. Casimir Church; Retired.
Gilchrist, Msgr. John J. '57 (NEW) Harrison, NJ Holy Cross Church.
Gilday, Robert J. '75 (IND) [18] Indianapolis, IN St. Christopher Church.
Gildea, Arthur P. *c.ss.r.* '67 (ALB) [L] Saratoga Springs, NY St. John Neumann Residence.
Gildea, Charles *c.ss.r.* '53 (ALB) [L] Saratoga Springs, NY St. John Neumann Residence.
Gildea, John J. (BRK) [210] Queens, NY Our Lady of Fatima Church.
Gildner, Leo H. '53 (PEO) Retired.
Gile, Honesto DeGuzman, Jr. '87 (SFR) [3] San Rafael, CA St. Raphael Church.
Gile, Joseph M. '88 (WCH) [6] Wichita, KS Church of the Resurrection; [H] Wichita, KS Spiritual Life Center.
Giles, Gabriel *o.f.m.cap* '35 (PIT) [O] Pittsburgh, PA St. Conrad Friary.
Giles, John H., Jr. '87 (LKC) [8] Lake Charles, LA Our Lady Queen of Heaven Church.
Gilfether, Francis *s.m.a.* '60 (NEW) [N] Tenafly, NJ Society of African Missions, Provincialate, S.M.A. Fathers.
Gilfillan, Msgr. James M. '47 (SD) La Jolla, CA Mary, Star of the Sea Church; Retired.
Gilg, James E. '66 (OM) [29] Omaha, NE St. Mary Magdalene Church; [B] Omaha, NE V.J. & Angela Skutt Catholic High School of Omaha.
Gilgun, Bernard E. '54 (WOR) Retired.
Gilhooley, James '55 (NY) Retired.
Gilhooley, Msgr. John P. '57 (BRK) Military Chaplains.
Giliberti, Msgr. Francis A. '70 (PH) Media, PA Nativity of the Blessed Virgin Mary Church.
Gill, David *s.j.* (BO) [43] Boston, MA St. Mary of the Angels Church.
Gill, David H. *s.j.* '67 (BO) [W] Boston, MA The Society of Jesus of New England-Provincial Offices; [W] Chestnut Hill, MA The Jesuit Community at Boston College.
Gill, Desmond '46 (SP) Inverness, FL Our Lady of Fatima Church; Sun City Center, FL Prince of Peace Church; Retired.
Gill, G. Dennis '83 (PH) Graduate Studies.
Gill, James J. *s.j.* (CHI) [B] Chicago, IL The Catholic Theological Union at Chicago.
Gill, James J. *s.j.* '57 (CHI) [N] Chicago, IL Chicago Province of the Society of Jesus-Provincial Office.
Gill, James J. *s.j.* '57 (WDC) [V] Washington, DC The Christian Institute for the Study of Human Sexuality; [V] Washington, DC The Jesuit Educational Center for Human Development.
Gill, Joseph C. *s.j.* '59 (RC) St. Francis, SD St. Charles Church; St. Francis, SD Rosebud Reservation Church.
Gill, Michael J. '66 (NOR) Plainfield, CT St. John the Apostle Church.
Gill, Nicholas *c.p.* (HRT) [M] West Hartford, CT Holy Family Monastery/Retreat.
Gill, Paul '66 (SB) Retired.
Gill, Msgr. Richard '56 (BUF) Retired.
Gill, Richard *l.c.* '91 (WDC) [M] Potomac, MD Legionaries of Christ; [V] Bethesda, MD Alpha Omega, Inc. The Legion of Christ Inc.
Gill, William J. '55 (RVC) Hampton Bays, NY St. Rosalie's Church.
Gillece, Eugene E. '51 (GAL) [N] Houston, TX St. Dominic Village.
Gillece, Eugene J. '51 (GAL) Retired.
Gilleece, Msgr. Thomas E. '68 (NY) Congers, NY St. Paul Church.
Gillelan, Robert M., Jr. '89 (HBG) [1] York, PA Immaculate Conception of the Blessed Virgin Mary Church.
Gillen, C. H. '85 (BAK) Retired.
Gillen, George D. '71 (NEW) Roselle, NJ Church of St. Joseph the Carpenter.
Gillen, Msgr. James G. '52 (WDC) Retired.
Gillen, Msgr. John J. '45 (NY) Retired; [A] Bronx, NY St. John Neumann Seminary Residence.
Gillen, Kevin *s.o.l.t.* '00 (CC) [H] Robstown, TX Society of Our Lady of the Most Holy Trinity.
Gillen, Niles J. *o.carm.* '56 (L) [60] Louisville, KY Our Lady of Mount Carmel Church.
Gillen, Peter D. '78 (BRK) [236] Queens, NY St. Rose of Lima Church.
Gillen, Timothy L. '42 (PRO) [6] Pawtucket, RI St. Joseph Church; Retired.
Giller, Roderic *o.s.b.* '62 (KCK) Seneca, KS SS. Peter and Paul's Church.
Gilles, Charles W. *o.m.i.* '38 (WDC) [M] Washington, DC Oblate College/Center for Mission Studies Community.
Gilles, Eugene *s.a.c.* '58 (FAR) Lidgerwood, ND St. Boniface's Church.
Gilles, Richard W. '94 (LC) Special Assignment; [A] La Crosse, WI Holy Cross Seminary House of Formation; [H] La Crosse, WI Holy Cross (Seminary) Diocesan Center.
Gilles, Robert F. '57 (PEO) Minonk, IL St. Patrick's Church.
Gilles, Thomas C. '67 (CLV) Chardon, OH St. Mary Church.
Gillespie, Anthony '82 (FTW) Plymouth, IN St. Michael Church.
Gillespie, Barnabas *o.s.b.* '80 (IND) Cannelton, IN St. Michael Church; Troy, IN St. Pius Church; [J] St. Meinrad, IN St. Meinrad Archabbey.
Gillespie, C. Kevin *s.j.* '86 (BAL) [B] Baltimore, MD Loyola College in Maryland; [S] Baltimore, MD Jesuit Community of Loyola College, Inc.
Gillespie, Edward F. '57 (RCK) [6] Aurora, IL Our Lady of Good Counsel Church.
Gillespie, Francis J. *s.j.* '72 (CHL) [2] Charlotte, NC Our Lady of the Assumption Church; [J] Charlotte, NC Jesuit Community.
Gillespie, Francis T. '59 (ALN) Catasauqua, PA Annunciation B.V.M. - St. Mary's Church.
Gillespie, Jerome F. '82 (BO) [8] Lynn, MA Sacred Heart Church.
Gillespie, John D. '72 (STA) [4] Gainesville, FL St. Augustine Church; [L] Gainesville, FL University of Florida-St. Augustine Parish and Student Center.
Gillespie, John L. '95 (R) Elizabeth City, NC Holy Family Church.
Gillespie, Joseph '50 (PHX) Retired.
Gillespie, Joseph P. '70 (STP) [1] Minneapolis, MN The Basilica of St. Mary Co-; [15] Minneapolis, MN St. Albert the Great Church.
Gillespie, Martin Joseph '00 (BLX) Ocean Springs, MS St. Alphonsus Church.
Gillespie, Paul G. *o.s.f.s.* '56 (TOL) [C] Toledo, OH St. Francis de Sales High School; [K] Toledo, OH Oblates of St. Francis de Sales.
Gillespie, Robert B. '43 (GR) Retired.
Gillespie, Thomas '61 (SB) Retired.
Gillespie, Thomas *o.s.b.* '64 (SCL) [I] Collegeville, MN St. John's Abbey, of the Order of St. Benedict.
Gillespie, Thomas E. '72 (MAD) Jefferson, WI St. Lawrence Church; [J] Jefferson, WI St. Coletta of Wisconsin, Inc.
Gillespie, Thomas M. '68 (BO) North Reading, MA St. Theresa Church.
Gillespie, Victor *o.s.b.* '56 (LR) Subiaco, AR St. Benedict Church.
Gillette, James R. *c.p.* '71 (NY) [DD] Pelham Manor, NY St. Vincent's Residence.
Gillette, Theodore M. '78 (OG) Black River, NY St. Paul Church; Deferiet, NY St. Rita Church.
Gillgannon, Francis G. '54 (JC) California, MO Annunciation Church.
Gillgannon, Michael '58 (KC) Mission Duty.
Gillick, Lawrence E. *s.j.* '72 (OM) [K] Omaha, NE Campion House.
Gillig, John '57 (FTW) Retired.
Gillig, Russell F. '36 (TOL) Retired.
Gilligan, Adrian *o.s.a.* '68 (PH) Bryn Mawr, PA Our Mother of Good Counsel Church.
Gilligan, James M. *m.m.* '55 (FgM) Maryknoll Foreign Missions.
Gilligan, Michael J. '69 (CHI) Other Assignments.
Gillin, Joseph *o.s.a.* '99 (BO) [CC] North Andover, MA Merrimack College Campus Ministry Center.
Gillin, Joseph F. *o.s.a.* '75 (BO) [C] North Andover, MA Merrimack College.
Gillin, Thomas M. *s.j.* '52 (CHR) Aiken, SC St. Gerard's Church.
Gillin, Thomas P. '74 (PH) Springfield, PA St. Kevin Church; [D] Radnor, PA Archbishop John Carroll High School; [G] Bryn Mawr, PA Country Day School of the Sacred Heart.
Gillis, David C. '79 (ALN) Shillington, PA St. John Baptist de la Salle Church.
Gillis, Edward F. '46 (BO) Senior Priests.
Gillis, Francis B. *s.m.a.* '52 (BO) [W] Dedham, MA African Mission House.
Gillis, James *c.s.c.* '56 (FTW) [B] Notre Dame, IN University of Notre Dame Du Lac.
Gillis, James B. *c.s.c.* '56 (FTW) Notre Dame, IN Sacred Heart Church; [J] Notre Dame, IN Holy Cross Community, Corby Hall, University of Notre Dame.
Gillis, Ralph J. (GB) Wabeno, WI St. Ambrose Church.
Gillis, Ralph J. '59 (GB) Argonne, WI St. Mary Church; Crandon, WI St. Joseph Church.
Gillis, Roger S. *s.j.* '78 (SEA) [A] Seattle, WA Seattle University.
Gillis, Ronald '67 (BAL) [A] Emmitsburg, MD Mount St. Mary's Seminary.
Gillis, Ronald '67 (WDC) [T] Washington, DC Prelature of the Holy Cross and Opus Dei.
Gillispie, Barnabas *o.s.b.* '80 (IND) Tell City, IN St. Paul Church.
Gillo, Thomas (BAL) [22] Baltimore, MD St. Charles Borromeo Church.
Gillon, James A. *s.j.* '74 (BO) [W] Boston, MA Arrupe House.
Gillooly, Patrick J. '53 (WH) Retired.
Gillum, William *o.f.m.cap.* '76 (PIT) Rochester, PA St. Cecilia Church; [O] Rochester, PA St. Cecilia Friary.
Gilman, Leonard *o.carm.* '98 (JOL) [J] Darien, IL Carmelite Provincial Office.
Gilmartin, Daniel J. '46 (BO) Senior Priests.
Gilmartin, Daniel J. '47 (BO) Bellingham, MA Assumption Church.
Gilmartin, John D. '72 (RVC) Garden City, NY St. Anne Church.
Gilmartin, Msgr. John E. '56 (BGP) [5] Stratford, CT Our Lady of Peace Church.
Gilmartin, Paul P. *s.j.* '62 (BO) [W] Weston, MA Campion Health Center, Inc.
Gilmore, Alan *o.c.s.o.* '70 (L) [L] Trappist, KY Abbey of Our Lady of Gethsemani, of the Order of Cistercians of the Strict Observance.
Gilmore, Lawrence *s.d.b.* '84 (FgM) Salesians of Don Bosco Foreign Missions.
Gilmore, Raymond V. '62 (HEL) Bonner, MT St. Ann Church.
Gilmore, Vincent M. *o.praem.* '90 (ORG) Newport Beach, CA Our Lady Queen of Angels Church; [I] Silverado, CA Norbertine Fathers of Orange Inc.
Gilmour, James W. *c.ss.r.* '72 (BAL) [78] Baltimore, MD St. Patrick Church.
Gilmour, James-Santiago W. *c.ss.r.* '72 (BAL) [62] Baltimore, MD St. Michael Church.
Gilmour, Robert G. *c.s.c.* '68 (FgM) Holy Cross Foreign Missions.
Gilroy, Robert G. *s.j.* '97 (BO) [W] Boston, MA The Society of Jesus of New England-Provincial Offices.
Gilroy, Robert G. *s.j.* '97 (RC) St. Francis, SD Rosebud Reservation Church.
Gilsdorf, Daniel C. '60 (GB) [7] Appleton, WI St. Theresa Church.
Gilsdorf, Gordon J. '49 (GB) Special Assignment.
Gilsdorf, Richard W. '56 (GB) Special Assignment.
Gilsenan, Msgr. John P. '56 (WCH) [3] Wichita, KS Blessed Sacrament Church.
Gilsoul, James M. '86 (GB) [F] Appleton, WI St. Elizabeth Hospital.
Gilvary, Paul J. *s.j.* '51 (PH) [AA] Philadelphia, PA Jesuit Community at St. Joseph's University.
Gilvey, John *o.s.f.s.* (NY) [HH] New York, NY Christ House, Inc.
Gilvey, John *o.s.f.s.* (RVC) [B] Patchogue, NY St. Joseph's College.
Gilvey, John A. *o.s.f.s.* '79 (WIL) [I] Wilmington, DE Oblates of St. Francis De Sales.
Gimbrone, Richard J. '85 (BUF) Retired.
Gimeno, Fabian G. '60 (ORL) St. Cloud, FL St. Thomas Aquinas Church.
Gimpl, Carl '55 (P) Salem, OR St. Joseph Church; [P] Portland, OR University of Portland.
Ginart, Arthur J. '66 (NO) [49] New Orleans, LA St. Nicholas of Myra Church.
Ginchereau, Dolor *s.m.* '38 (BO) [Y] Framingham, MA The Marist House.
Ginel, Robert J. '78 (NY) Monticello, NY St. Peter Church; Carmel, NY Putnam Hospital Center.
Ging, Regis B. *m.m.* '66 (FgM) Maryknoll Foreign Missions.
Gingras, Jerome R. '78 (ALB) Clinton Heights, NY St. Mary Church.
Gini, John E. *o.f.m.* '63 (MRY) Jolon, CA San Antonio Church.
Ginn, Roman *o.c.s.o.* '53 (L) [L] Trappist, KY Abbey of Our Lady of Gethsemani, of the Order of Cistercians of the Strict Observance.
Gins, Paul M. *o.s.m.* '75 (CHI) [N] Chicago, IL Order of Friar Servants of Mary (Servites) United States of America Province, Inc.; [N] Chicago, IL Order of Friar Servants of Mary (Servites) United States of America Province, Inc.
Gins, Paul M. *o.s.m.* '75 (ORG) [I] Buena Park, CA Order of Friar Servants of Mary (Servites).
Ginsterblum, John M. *s.j.* '53 (STP) [N] Minneapolis, MN La Storta Jesuit Community.
Ginter, Michael '79 (JOL) Peotone, IL St. Paul the Apostle Church.
Ginther, Benjamin H. '41 (KAL) Retired.
Ginther, Lawrence P. '46 (WIN) Retired.
Ginther, Richard M. '83 (IND) [1] Indianapolis, IN SS. Peter and Paul Church.

Gintoli, Msgr. Blase M. '69 (BGP) [2] Fairfield, CT Assumption Church.
Ginty, Msgr. Thomas M. '85 (HRT) Special and other Archdiocesan Assignment.
Gionet, Urbain J. '51 (WOR) Retired.
Giopatto, Alfonso *o.m.i.* '64 (LAR) Eagle Pass, TX Our Lady of Refuge Church.
Giorda, Adolph *o.f.m.* '46 (NY) [FF] Wappingers Falls, NY Mt. Alvernia Retreat House.
Giordani, Msgr. Mark (PAT) [P] Paterson, NJ The Association of the Marian Apostolate of Mercy, Inc.
Giordani, Msgr. Mark J. '69 (PAT) [1] Paterson, NJ Cathedral of St. John the Baptist; Paterson, NJ Passaic County Jail.
Giordano, John C. '67 (MET) North Plainfield, NJ St. Luke Church.
Giordano, Joseph *c.i.c.m.* '72 (ARL) [J] Arlington, VA Missionhurst, C.I.C.M.-Central House and Provincialate.
Giordano, Pasquale T. *s.j.* '72 (FgM) Provinces.
Giorgi, Daniel *o.ss.t.* '41 (VIC) Cuero, TX Our Lady of Guadalupe Church.
Giorno, Stephen *s.t.* '86 (CHI) [A] Mundelein, IL University of St. Mary of the Lake-Mundelein Seminary.
Gipson, Msgr. Robert W. '62 (LA) La Crescenta, CA St. James the Less Church.
Gira, Stephen M. *c.r.* '77 (STL) Spanish Lake, MO Our Lady of Loretto Church.
Giraldo, Ricardo '85 (SAC) [4] Sacramento, CA Immaculate Conception Church.
Girard, Msgr. Armand '45 (SAL) Retired.
Girard, Charles A. *s.m.* '66 (ATL) [C] Atlanta, GA Marist School.
Girard, Peter Michael *o.p.* '92 (WDC) [B] Washington, DC Dominican House of Studies.
Girard, Steven P. '74 (BAL) [25] Baltimore, MD St. Clement Church.
Girardeau, Robert A. '93 (SAV) [3] Augusta, GA St. Mary on the Hill Church.
Girardin, Peter T. '60 (BO) Military & VA Chaplains.
Girdis, Joseph C. '43 (PIT) [5] Munhall, PA St. Therese of Lisieux Church.
Girdis, Joseph C. '44 (PIT) Retired.
Girnius, Charles F. *m.m.* '44 (NY) [DD] Maryknoll, NY Maryknoll Fathers and Brothers.
Giroir, Msgr. Frank J. '81 (NO) Harahan, LA St. Rita Church.
Girolami, Dante L. *o.s.a.* '41 (PH) [AA] Villanova, PA St. Thomas Monastery.
Girone, Joseph D. '83 (NEW) Belleville, NJ St. Peter's Church.
Girone, Joseph F. *o.s.a.* '81 (NY) [216] Staten Island, NY Our Lady of Good Counsel Church.
Girouard, Robert J. '59 (PRT) Sabbatical.
Giroux, Garry B. '76 (OG) Constable, NY St. Francis of Assisi Church; Trout River, NY St. Bridget Church.
Giroux, Harry E. '76 (OG) West Chazy, NY St. Joseph Church.
Giroux, Joseph W. '00 (OG) Malone, NY Notre Dame Church; Graduate Studies.
Giroux, Peter *f.p.o.* '98 (FR) [I] New Bedford, MA Franciscans of Primitive Observance.
Giroux, Raymond A. '63 (BUR) West Rutland, VT St. Bridget Church.
Giroux, Regis J. '70 (SPR) Sabbatical.
Giroux, Richard M. '69 (MAN) Tilton, NH St. Mary of the Assumption Church.
Giroux, William P. '80 (BUR) Essex Center, VT St. Pius X Church.
Girres, Edward M. '79 (SC) Fort Dodge, IA Sacred Heart Church.
Girse, Milton F. *c.ss.r.* '40 (STL) [P] Liguori, MO St. Clement Health Care Center.
Girzone, Joseph '55 (ALB) Retired.
Gits, Douglas J. '53 (WIN) Retired.
Gitter, Paul R. '93 (LC) [4] Eau Claire, WI Sacred Heart of Jesus-St. Patrick Church; Fall Creek, WI St. Raymond of Penafort Church.
Gittins, Anthony *c.s.sp.* '67 (CHI) [B] Chicago, IL The Catholic Theological Union at Chicago.
Gittins, Gordon '68 (DM) [5] Des Moines, IA St. Anthony's Church.
Gitzen, Patrick *o.m.i.* '75 (FgM) Oblates Foreign Missions.
Giudice, Francis J. '56 (PRO) [1] Providence, RI Cathedral of SS. Peter and Paul.
Giudry, Raymond J. *s.v.d.* '57 (GAL) [K] Houston, TX The Catholic Chaplain Corps.
Giuffre, Frank A. (PH) [D] Norristown, PA Kennedy-Kenrick Catholic High School.
Giuffre, Frank A. '97 (PH) [4] Norristown, PA St. Paul Church.
Giuliani, John B. '60 (BGP) [O] West Redding, CT The Benedictine Grange.
Giuliani, John P. *c.o.* '80 (CHR) Rock Hill, SC St. Anne's Church; [E] Rock Hill, SC Oratory of St. Philip Neri, Congregation of the Oratory of Pontifical Rite.
Giuliano, Anthony J. '84 (NY) Hawthorne, NY Holy Rosary Church.
Giuliano, Louis A. '44 (BRK) Retired.
Giuliano, Steven '80 (WIL) Hockessin, DE St. Mary of the Assumption Church.
Giulietti, Julio *s.j.* '72 (BO) [W] Boston, MA The Society of Jesus of New England-Provincial Offices.
Giulietti, Julio *s.j.* '72 (WDC) [M] Washington, DC The Jesuit Community at Georgetown University.
Giunta, Jose *i.v.e.* '91 (FR) [O] New Bedford, MA The Institute of the Incarnate Word, Inc.
Giunta, Jose G. *i.v.e.* '91 (FR) [19] New Bedford, MA St. Kilian Church.
Giunta, S. C. '54 (JOL) Wilton Center, IL St. Patrick Church.
Giuntini, Robert J. '76 (RVC) St. James, NY SS. Philip and James Church.
Giusani, Augustine H. '47 (HRT) [5] New Britain, CT St. Ann Church; Retired.
Giusta, Frank (ELP) [39] El Paso, TX Santa Lucia Church.
Givey, David W. '71 (PH) Milmont Park, PA Our Lady of Peace Church.
Gjergji, Nue '73 (DET) Beverly Hills, MI Our Lady of Albanians Church.
Glab, Joseph *c.r.* '75 (CHI) [D] Chicago, IL Gordon Tech High School.
Glab, Stephen *c.r.* '82 (CHI) [N] Chicago, IL Provincial Office of the Congregation of the Resurrection.
Glacherty, Malachy C. *o.f.m.cap.* '42 (RVC) [J] Huntington, NY St. Joseph's Guest Home for the Aged, Inc.
Glackin, Thomas J. '68 (VEN) [2] Naples, FL St. John the Evangelist Church.
Glade, Albert G. *o.p.* '72 (STL) [B] St. Louis, MO Aquinas Institute of Theology; [P] St. Louis, MO St. Dominic Priory.
Gladstone, James J. *s.j.* '66 (MIL) [P] Milwaukee, WI Jesuit Community at Marquette University.
Glahn, Carl '52 (OWN) Retired.
Glancy, Christopher *c.s.v.* '93 (CHI) [N] Arlington Heights, IL Viatorian Province Center-Clerics of St. Viator.
Glancy, Joseph '59 (SFS) Dimock, SD SS. Peter and Paul Church.
Glapiak, Edward '61 (WIL) Special or Other Diocesan Assignment.
Glaros, Matthew J. '99 (CLV) Maple Heights, OH St. Martin of Tours Church.
Glaser, Kenneth J. '00 (DUB) Greeley, IA St. Joseph's Church; Manchester, IA St. Mary's Church; Ryan, IA St. Patrick's Church.
Glaser, Lawrence A. *o.c.s.o.* '58 (SAC) [A] Vina, CA Abbey of New Clairvaux, Trappist Seminary; [H] Vina, CA Abbey of New Clairvaux, Trappist.
Glasgavi, Msgr. Thomas Gaspard '69 (NO) [60] New Orleans, LA St. Simon Peter Church.
Glasgow, Dennis T. *s.j.* (DET) [K] Detroit, MI Jesuit Provincial Office-Detroit Province of the Society of Jesus.
Glasgow, Dennis T. *s.j.* '84 (LAN) [5] Ann Arbor, MI St. Mary Student Church.
Glasgow, Mark W. '62 (PIT) [2] Munhall, PA St. Maximilian Kolbe Church; Allegheny County, PA Department of Veterans Affairs Medical Center Oakland; Military Chaplains.
Glasgow, Robert K. '85 (MAN) Military Chaplains.
Glasgow, Msgr. T. Gaspard '69 (NO) [27] New Orleans, LA St. Brigid Church.
Glasnovic, Serafin '45 (ALX) Retired.
Glass, Gerald J. '56 (PHX) Retired.
Glass, Robert H. *c.s.b.* '74 (OAK) [C] Oakland, CA Bishop O'Dowd High School.
Glass, Rolland T. '43 (MIL) Retired.
Glassmire, David R. '94 (BUF) Lancaster, NY St. Mary of the Assumption Church.
Glastetter, Donald A. '65 (STL) Wentzville, MO St. Patrick Church.
Glastetter, Michael *o.f.m.conv.* '99 (MIL) [47] Milwaukee, WI Basilica of St. Josaphat.
Glatt, Eugene '59 (SPK) Oakesdale, WA St. Catherine of Alexandria Church; Rosalia, WA Holy Rosary Church; St. John, WA Our Lady of Perpetual Help Church; Tekoa, WA Sacred Heart Church.
Glatts, Joseph M. (PH) [1] Drexel Hill, PA St. Andrew Church.
Glaub, Eugene *o.m.i.* '55 (BEL) [F] Belleville, IL Shrine of Our Lady of the Snows.
Glaves, John J. '56 (LIN) Retired; [E] Lincoln, NE Bonacum House.
Glavin, Joseph A. *s.j.* '48 (BO) [W] Chestnut Hill, MA The Jesuit Community at Boston College.
Glavin, Leonard *o.f.m.cap.* '54 (NY) [57] New York, NY St. John the Baptist Church.
Glavin, Patrick *o.f.m.cap.* '59 (PRT) [3] Portland, ME St. Joseph's Church; Portland, ME Maine Medical Center.
Glavina, Carmelo '54 (NY) Dobbs Ferry, NY Our Lady of Pompeii Church.
Gleason, Carl *s.d.s.* '56 (FgM) Salvatorian Foreign Missions.
Gleason, Jack A. '95 (TLS) [10] Tulsa, OK Church of St. Mary.
Gleason, James '50 (STL) [P] Liguori, MO Liguori Mission House/Redemptorists.
Gleason, Joseph F. '87 (PH) [A] Wynnewood, PA Theological Seminary of St. Charles Borromeo, Overbrook.
Gleason, Laurence '96 (PH) Horsham, PA St. Catherine of Siena Church.
Gleason, Martin *o.p.* '98 (MIA) [H] Miami, FL Dominican Fathers of Miami, Inc.
Gleason, Msgr. Paul D. '47 (PRT) Retired.
Gleba, Peter W. '53 (SY) [9] Syracuse, NY Sacred Heart Basilica Church; [22] Syracuse, NY St. Stephen Church.
Glebe, Edward *c.ss.r.* '57 (GAL) [34] Houston, TX Holy Ghost Church.
Gleeson, Donald P. '97 (NEW) Montclair, NJ Immaculate Conception Church.
Gleeson, Edward D. '69 (CHI) [18] Chicago, IL Assumption of the B.V.M./St. Catherine of Genoa Church; [166] Chicago, IL SS. Peter and Paul Church.
Gleeson, Martin *o.p.* '98 (MIA) [18] Miami, FL St. Dominic Church.
Gleeson, Michael '75 (LA) San Gabriel, CA St. Anthony Church.
Gleeson, Patrick *o.carm.* '52 (JOL) [J] Darien, IL Carmelite Provincial Office.
Gleeson, Stephen J. '63 (BGP) [3] Trumbull, CT St. Stephen Church.
Gleeson, Thomas F. *s.j.* '68 (WDC) [P] Faulkner, MD Loyola on the Potomac Retreat House.
Gleeson, William T. '66 (PBL) Capulin, CO St. Joseph Church.
Gleissner, Leopold *o.f.m.cap.* (GB) Kaukauna, WI St. Mary of the Annunciation Church.
Gleixner, Joseph *m.s.c.* '65 (FgM) Missionaries of the Sacred Heart Foreign Missions.
Gleixner, Joseph *m.s.c.* '65 (RCK) [G] Aurora, IL Missionaries of the Sacred Heart Community.
Glen, Michael G. '90 (DEN) Aspen, CO St. Mary Church.
Glenn, Nicholas '98 (STN) [A] Eagle Harbor, MI Skete of Holy Transfiguration Monastery.
Glennon, James G. *o.s.a.* '52 (MIA) Dania, FL Church of the Resurrection.
Glennon, Thomas G. *s.s.c.* '79 (CHI) [N] Chicago, IL Columban Fathers Mission Center.
Glennon, Msgr. William P. '54 (PAT) Morristown, NJ Assumption of the Blessed Virgin Mary Church.
Glepko, Robert J. '76 (CLV) [9] Lorain, OH Nativity of the Blessed Virgin Mary Church.
Gliatta, Ronald *o.f.m.* '77 (HRT) [15] Waterbury, CT St. Michael Church.
Glimm, Msgr. Francis X. '35 (RVC) Retired; [J] Huntington, NY St. Joseph's Guest Home for the Aged, Inc.
Glinkowski, Raphael K. *o.s.p.p.e.* '62 (GBG) Kittanning, PA Armstrong County Hospital; [H] Kittanning, PA Pauline Fathers Monastery.
Glisson, Nicholas *ph.d.* (PMB) [A] Boynton Beach, FL St. Vincent de Paul Regional Seminary.
Glisson, Nicholas '79 (OAK) [3] Concord, CA St. Francis of Assisi Church.
Glisson, Nicholas J. '79 (STA) On Duty Outside the Diocese.
Glockner, David '66 (WH) Spencer, WV Holy Redeemer Church.
Glockner, Michael W. *c.s.c.* '70 (FTW) [J] South Bend, IN Congregation of Holy Cross, Indiana Province, Provincial House.
Glogowski, John '71 (SFR) Redwood City, CA St. Matthias Church.
Glogowski, John J. '62 (ROC) Hilton, NY St. Leo Church.
Gloisten, Robert '54 (RIC) [16] Richmond, VA St. Patrick Church.
Gloninger, Hugh M. '56 (PIT) [3] Butler, PA St. Paul Church; Butler County, PA Butler County Jail.
Gloria de la Inmaculada, Alberto Jesus *s.e.m.v.* '94 (ARE) Hatillo, PR Our Lady of Guadalupe Church.
Glorie, Msgr. John W. '60 (MIA) [5] Pompano Beach, FL St. Elizabeth of Hungary Catholic Church.
Glorioso, Charles '95 (SHP) [10] Shreveport, LA St. Pius X Church.
Glosser, William F. '84 (ALN) [2] Mahanoy City, PA St. Canicus Church; [4] Mahanoy City, PA St. Fidelis Church.
Gloudeman, Francis M. *o.praem.* '91 (ORG) [I] Silverado, CA Norbertine Fathers of Orange Inc.
Gloudeman, Robert J. '64 (MIL) Wauwatosa, WI Froedtert Memorial Lutheran Hospital.
Glover, Donald F. *m.m.* '70 (FgM) Maryknoll Foreign Missions.
Glover, Francis N. *s.j.* '58 (FgM) Provinces.
Glover, George *o.s.b.* '88 (RCK) [G] Aurora, IL Marmion Abbey-St. Augustine's Abbey.
Glovik, Karl L. '61 (DUB) [1] Cedar Rapids, IA Immaculate Conception Church; [9] Cedar Rapids, IA St. Wenceslaus Church.
Gluc, Vincent *o.f.m.conv.* (ATL) Jonesboro, GA St. Philip Benizi Church.
Gluc, Vincent *o.f.m.conv.* '79 (BAL) [20] Baltimore, MD St. Casimir Church.
Glueckert, Leopold *o.carm.* '68 (JOL) [J] Joliet, IL St.

Elias Carmelites.
Gluszek, Msgr. Joseph '35 (GF) [2] Great Falls, MT Holy Spirit Church; Retired.
Glynn, Edward *s.j.* '67 (CLV) [B] Cleveland, OH John Carroll Jesuit Community.
Glynn, Edward *s.j.* '75 (CLV) [B] Cleveland, OH John Carroll University.
Glynn, Msgr. Francis J. '37 (NY) [205] Staten Island, NY Holy Family Church; Retired.
Glynn, Francis M. '51 (WIN) Retired.
Glynn, Francis M. '70 (BO) [1] Lowell, MA St. Anthony Church.
Glynn, Msgr. Gerard N. '41 (STL) Retired.
Glynn, John F. *o.s.a.* '39 (LA) [F] Ojai, CA Villanova Preparatory School.
Glynn, John P. '48 (PH) Retired.
Glynn, Joseph *c.s.sp.* '76 (SFR) Millbrae, CA St. Dunstan Church.
Glynn, Martin G. '78 (PAT) Franklin, NJ Immaculate Conception Church.
Glynn, Msgr. Michael '46 (JKS) [3] Jackson, MS St. Richard Church; Retired.
Glynn, Seamus A. '58 (ORG) Anaheim, CA San Antonio Church.
Glynn, Thomas J. '54 (LA) San Pedro, CA Holy Trinity Church.
Glynn, Msgr. William F. '47 (BO) Duxbury, MA Holy Family Church.
Gmerek, Ronald E. '71 (E) [28] Erie, PA St. Paul Church; [B] Erie, PA Gannon University.
Gnall, Julian M. *o.s.b.* '55 (PBR) Retired.
Gnarackatt, Joseph '67 (TR) Medford, NJ St. Mary of the Lakes Church.
Gnat, Zdzislaw '88 (KAL) Battle Creek, MI St. Joseph Church.
Gnidzinski, Marek '85 (BUF) [2] Batavia, NY St. Joseph Church.
Gniewyk, Eugene '90 (NEW) Fairfield, NJ St. Thomas More Church.
Gnirk, Lloyd A. '78 (OM) [38] Omaha, NE St. Pius X Church.
Gobbo, Paolo *s.x.* '94 (FgM) Xaverian Foreign Missions.
Gobbo, Paolo *s.x.* '94 (PAT) [M] Wayne, NJ Xaverian Missionary Fathers.
Gober, Christopher '00 (CHL) Gastonia, NC St. Michael Church.
Gobitas, Msgr. Gerald '75 (ALN) [3] Easton, PA St. Jane Frances de Chantal Church.
Goblirsch, Robert P. '60 (NU) Nassau, MN St. James Church; Ortonville, MN St. John Church; Rosen, MN St. Joseph Church.
Goda, Paul J. *s.j.* '66 (SJ) [B] Santa Clara, CA Santa Clara University.
Godecker, Jeffery H. '69 (IND) [9] Indianapolis, IN Immaculate Heart of Mary Church.
Godenciuc, Iura '94 (STF) Kerhonkson, NY Holy Trinity Church.
Godenciuc, Vasile '81 (STF) Rochester, NY Epiphany of Our Lord Church.
Godfrey, Donal *s.j.* (SFR) [N] San Francisco, CA Jesuit Community at University of San Francisco.
Godfrey, Joseph J. *s.j.* '69 (PH) [C] Philadelphia, PA St. Joseph's University; [AA] Philadelphia, PA Jesuit Community at St. Joseph's University.
Godfrey, Timothy S. *s.j.* '85 (OAK) [20] Oakland, CA St. Patrick's Church; [N] Berkeley, CA Jesuit Community at Jesuit School of Theology at Berkeley.
Godic, Frank G. '73 (CLV) [34] Cleveland, OH Immaculate Conception Church.
Godin, James M. '79 (MIL) Whitewater, WI St. Patrick Church.
Godin, Normand J. '73 (PRO) [3] Providence, RI St. Agnes Church.
Godleski, David A. *s.j.* '98 (CHI) [C] Chicago, IL Jesuit Community at Loyola University of Chicago; [N] Chicago, IL Chicago Province of the Society of Jesus-Provincial Office.
Godlewski, Andrew (CHI) Northlake, IL St. John Vianney, Cure of Ars Church.
Godley, Msgr. James '40 (CHY) Retired.
Godley, Patrick '53 (SEA) Retired.
Goebel, Bernard M. '29 (SAT) Retired; [T] San Antonio, TX Our Lady of Czestochowa.
Goebel, Joseph A. '50 (CLV) [36] Cleveland, OH St. Jerome Church; Cleveland, OH Euclid General Hospital; Retired.
Goebel, Nicholas L. '58 (MIL) Retired; [Q] Campbellsport, WI St. Joseph Convent.
Goebel, Robert '74 (CIN) [60] Cincinnati, OH St. Matthias Church.
Goebel, Robert A. *s.j.* '63 (SPK) [E] Spokane, WA Gonzaga Preparatory School.
Goebel, Robert W. '74 (CIN) On Special and Archdiocesan Assignment.
Goeckner, Jeffrey W. '95 (SFD) [2] Decatur, IL Our Lady of Lourdes Church.
Goedde, Bernard C., Jr. '72 (BEL) Millstadt, IL St. James Church.
Goedert, Robert A. *o.p.* '51 (CHI) [N] Chicago, IL Dominicans (Provincial Office).
Goedert, William O. '55 (CHI) [3] Oak Lawn, IL St. Germaine Church; Retired.
Goedken, James J. '66 (DUB) Key West, IA St. Joseph's Church.
Goehring, Msgr. Raymond '64 (LAN) Bellevue, MI St. Ann Church.
Goeke, James *s.j.* '88 (STL) [P] St. Louis, MO Leo Brown Jesuit Community.
Goeke, John W. '59 (COV) Leave of Absence.
Goekler, Thomas F. *m.m.* '67 (FgM) Maryknoll Foreign Missions.
Goekler, Thomas F. '67 (HRT) On Duty Outside the Archdiocese.
Goellen, Richard '63 (FAR) On Duty Outside the Diocese.
Goellner, Glennon '50 (STL) [6] Florissant, MO St. Ferdinand Church.
Goellner, Glennon J. '50 (STL) Retired.
Goentges, Charles J. '40 (DET) Retired.
Goergen, Donald J. *o.p.* '75 (MIL) [P] Kenosha, WI Order of Preachers, Province of St. Albert the Great.
Goergen, Michael A. '62 (CHI) [183] Chicago, IL St. Robert Bellarmine Church.
Goering, Joseph '00 (FAR) [2] Fargo, ND Holy Spirit Church.
Goerner, Basil S. '93 (MAR) Retired.
Goerner, James E. '93 (PH) [103] Philadelphia, PA St. Matthew Church.
Goertz, Msgr. Alois J. '48 (SAT) Retired; [K] San Antonio, TX Casa De Padres.
Goertz, Bernard C. '52 (AUS) [10] Austin, TX Santa Barbara Church; Special Assignments.
Goertz, Howard '77 (AUS) Kyle, TX St. Anthony Marie De Claret Church; Stony Point, TX Blessed Juan Diego Church.
Goertz, Victor '52 (AUS) Special Assignments.
Goeski, Eugene *c.s.c.* '60 (FTW) [B] Notre Dame, IN University of Notre Dame Du Lac.
Goethals, Gregory M. *s.j.* '88 (SFR) [E] San Francisco, CA St. Ignatius College Preparatory (Coed); [N] San Francisco, CA Jesuit Community at St. Ignatius College Preparatory.
Goettemoeller, Leonard *c.pp.s.* '49 (KC) [J] Liberty, MO Precious Blood Center.
Goetz, Donald R. '68 (L) [17] Louisville, KY St. Brigid Church; [40] Louisville, KY St. James Church.
Goetz, Donatus *o.f.m.cap.* '45 (NY) [DD] Yonkers, NY St. Clare Friary.
Goetz, Gerald E. *s.j.* '73 (STP) [Q] Lake Elmo, MN Jesuit Retreat House.
Goetz, J. Raymond '81 (OWN) [I] Murray, KY Murray State University Newman House.
Goetz, Joseph W. '60 (CIN) Retired.
Goetz, Maris *o.f.m.cap.* '64 (SAL) [D] Victoria, KS St. Fidelis Friary.
Goetz, Ray '81 (OWN) Murray, KY St. Leo Church.
Goff, William *c.m.* '66 (BAL) Emmitsburg, MD St. Joseph Church.
Goff, William P. *c.m.* '66 (BAL) [S] Emmitsburg, MD Vincentian House.
Goggin, Cornelius J. '56 (MAN) Retired.
Goggin, John T. '64 (NU) On Duty Outside the Diocese.
Goggin, Thomas J. '57 (VEN) Fort Myers Beach, FL Ascension Church.
Goggins, James K. (DEN) Wheat Ridge, CO SS. Peter and Paul Church.
Goguen, Francis T. '66 (WOR) [3] Leominster, MA St. Cecilia's Church.
Gohm, Robert S. '75 (SAG) Hemlock, MI St. Mary Church.
Gohmann, Myron *c.p.* '55 (CHI) [N] Chicago, IL Passionist Community-Immaculate Conception Monastery.
Gohring, William '84 (ORL) De Land, FL St. Peter's Church.
Goiburu, Ignacio *c.p.* '43 (ARE) Lares, PR St. Joseph Church.
Goicoechea, Greg *o.f.m.* '45 (FWT) [5] Fort Worth, TX Immaculate Heart of Mary Church.
Goin, James A. '92 (OKL) [5] Oklahoma City, OK Corpus Christi Church.
Goiogana, Joseba I. *c.p.* (SJN) [46] San Juan, PR Nuestra Senora de la Piedad Church.
Gojuk, Peter P. *o.m.v.* '81 (BO) [B] Boston, MA Our Lady of Grace Seminary.
Golas, Eugene S. '55 (GR) Retired.
Golas, John S. '81 (HRT) Unionville, CT St. Mary's Church.
Golasinski, Donald J. '62 (BEA) Groves, TX Immaculate Conception Church.
Golasinski, Msgr. James L. '58 (GAL) [9] Houston, TX Annunciation Church.
Gold, Frank '76 (DEN) [H] Denver, CO St. Joseph Hospital.
Gold, William F. '65 (SD) [2] Oceanside, CA St. Margaret Church.
Goldasich, Mark '81 (KCK) Tonganoxie, KS Sacred Heart Church.
Goldbach, Edmund *o.f.m.conv.* '65 (GR) [4] Grand Rapids, MI St. Anthony of Padua Church.
Goldbach, Peter D. *c.m.* '44 (BRK) [V] Jamaica, NY Vincentian Residence.
Goldberg, James M. '76 (GBG) Lucernemines, PA St. Louis Church.
Golden, Edward '61 (ROC) Fairport, NY Assumption of the Blessed Virgin Mary Church.
Golden, Francis P. '71 (NY) [DD] New York, NY Xavier Jesuit Community.
Golden, George E. '76 (WDC) Forestville, MD Mt. Calvary Church.
Golden, James '48 (DUL) Retired.
Golden, Patrick '96 (RIC) Suffolk, VA St. Mary of the Presentation Church.
Golden, Thomas '63 (GB) Special Assignment.
Golden, Thomas P. *m.m.* '51 (FgM) Maryknoll Foreign Missions.
Goldian, Edward R. *s.j.* '69 (STL) [41] St. Louis, MO St. John the Baptist Church.
Goldikovskis, Msgr. Alexander I. '41 (CLV) Retired.
Golding, Edward '88 (ALB) Summit, NY St. Anna Church; Worcester, NY St. Joseph Church.
Goldman, William *c.ss.r.* '89 (NY) [147] Bronx, NY Holy Family Church.
Goldrick, Timothy J. '72 (FR) Assonet, MA St. Bernard's Church.
Gole, Joseph '43 (MIL) [B] Hales Corners, WI Sacred Heart School of Theology; [P] Hales Corners, WI Sacred Heart Monastery.
Golemba, Msgr. Roman '75 (STF) Fall River, MA St. John-the-Baptist Church; Woonsocket, RI St. Michael Church.
Golias, Msgr. Andrew J. '70 (PH) Valley Forge, PA St. Teresa of Avila Church.
Golik, Stanislaus '39 (OM) [46] Omaha, NE St. Thomas More Church; Retired.
Golini, Ronald '68 (NTN) Leave of Absence.
Golino, Arthur A. '80 (NY) [229] Staten Island, NY St. Sylvester Church.
Golish, Robert *m.m.* '53 (SD) [7] San Diego, CA Holy Spirit Church.
Golish, Robert W. *m.m.* '53 (LA) [Q] Los Angeles, CA Maryknoll Fathers and Brothers.
Golish, W. Robert *m.m.* '53 (NY) [DD] Maryknoll, NY Maryknoll Fathers and Brothers.
Golka, James R. '94 (GI) Alliance, NE Holy Rosary Church.
Gollatz, Ronald J. '72 (CHI) Lake Zurich, IL St. Francis de Sales Church.
Gollinge, Donald '58 (NY) Absent on Leave.
Gollob, Timothy A. '58 (DAL) [5] Dallas, TX Holy Cross Church; Dallas, TX Veterans Administration Hospital.
Golobich, John '48 (DUL) Retired.
Golombek, Msgr. Robert K. '65 (BUF) [3] Tonawanda, NY Blessed Sacrament Church.
Goloran, Mauricio O. '84 (LA) Valinda, CA St. Martha Church.
Goltz, William '50 (DUB) Unassigned.
Golueke, Thomas J. '77 (BAL) [84] Baltimore, MD St. Pius X Church.
Goman, Ralph J. '64 (STP) Hopkins, MN St. John the Evangelist Church.
Gomes, Angelo '94 (P) [30] Portland, OR St. Pius X Church.
Gomes, Benedict '69 (BRK) [58] Brooklyn, NY Holy Name Church.
Gomes, Herman *ss.cc.* '78 (HON) Kaneohe, HI St. Ann Church; [A] Honolulu, HI Chaminade University of Honolulu.
Gomes, Ignatius *s.f.x.* '70 (LR) [E] Little Rock, AR St. Vincent Infirmary Medical Center.
Gomes, John (CHI) [9] Chicago, IL St. Alphonsus Church.
Gomes, John A. '69 (FR) [3] Taunton, MA Our Lady of Lourdes Church.
Gomes, Martin *ss.cc.* '69 (FR) [I] Fairhaven, MA Sacred Hearts Provincial House.
Gomes, Robert '66 (CAM) On Duty Outside the Diocese.
Gomes, Ronald A. '87 (BO) Permanent Disability.
Gomes, Stanley J. '95 (NEW) [12] Jersey City, NJ St. John the Baptist Church.
Gomes, William '69 (RVC) Point Lookout, NY Our Lady of the Miraculous Medal Church.
Gomes-Kelly, John R. '62 (SD) Unassigned.
Gomez, Anthony J. '98 (LA) Culver City, CA St. Augustine Church.
Gomez, Msgr. Antonio '51 (SJN) [13] San Juan, PR Cristo Rey Church.
Gomez, Arturo '80 (FRS) Tranquillity, CA St. Paul Church.
Gomez, Daniel '85 (MET) Bernardsville, NJ Our Lady of Perpetual Help Church.
Gomez, Demetrio J. *o.f.m.* '98 (WDC) [33] Washington, DC Our Lady Queen of the Americas Church.
Gomez, Edmund '93 (SB) Colton, CA Immaculate Conception Church.
Gomez, Edmundo '69 (NY) [145] Bronx, NY St. Helena Church.
Gomez, Emerito *o.f.m.* '82 (FRS) Delano, CA Our Lady of Guadalupe Church.
Gomez, Enrique '77 (CGS) Naranjito, PR San Miguel Arcangel Church.

Gomez, Eusebio *o.c.d.* '70 (MIA) [L] Miami, FL Discalced Carmelite Friars of Miami, Inc.
Gomez, Fernando *s.j.* (SJN) [D] Rio Piedras, PR Centro Universitario Catolico.
Gomez, Fernando *o.a.r.* '97 (NEW) [1] Union City, NJ Holy Family Church.
Gomez, Francisco '50 (SLC) [2] Kearns, UT St. Francis Xavier Church; [C] Kearns, UT St. Francis Xavier Regional School.
Gomez, Francisco *s.t.* '83 (LA) [30] Los Angeles, CA Our Lady of Victory Church.
Gomez, Frank '61 (BWN) Retired.
Gomez, Msgr. Henry '58 (LA) Bell Gardens, CA St. Gertrude Church.
Gomez, Humberto (SAC) Preston, CA School of Industry.
Gomez, Humberto '88 (SAC) Ione, CA Sacred Heart Church.
Gomez, Jorge '90 (FRS) [1] Fresno, CA St. John Church.
Gomez, Jose '78 (GAL) [P] Houston, TX Opus Dei.
Gomez, Jose '81 (AMA) Perryton, TX Immaculate Conception Church.
Gomez, Msgr. Jose A. '58 (ELP) [9] El Paso, TX Holy Family Church.
Gomez, Jose H. '78 (GAL) [U] Houston, TX Asociacion Nacional de Sacerdotes Hispanos.
Gomez, Jose L. *s.d.b.* '61 (ARE) Orocovis, PR San Juan Bautista Church.
Gomez, Jose Leonardo '99 (CHI) [146] Chicago, IL Our Lady of Grace Church.
Gomez, Juan '80 (JUN) [2] Juneau, AK St. Paul The Apostle Church.
Gomez, Msgr. Leo '63 (GLP) Farmington, NM St. Mary's Church.
Gomez, Lorenzo *l.c.* (DET) [T] Oxford, MI Queen of the Family Retreat Center.
Gomez, Lorenzo '73 (DET) [T] Clarkson, MI The Legion of Christ, Inc.; [T] Bloomfield Hills, MI Opdyke, Inc.; [T] Bloomfield Hills, MI Logos, Inc. (Michigan).
Gomez, Lorenzo *s.d.v.* '98 (NEW) [25] Newark, NJ St. Michael's Church.
Gomez, Martin Mejia (NY) [181] Bronx, NY St. Peter and St. Paul Church.
Gomez, Miguel '81 (MIA) Hialeah Gardens, FL Santa Barbara Church.
Gomez, Orlando De Jesus '86 (CGS) [7] Caguas, PR El Salvador Church.
Gomez, Pedro *c.m.* (BRK) [116] Brooklyn, NY St. Peter-St. Paul-Our Lady of Pilar Church.
Gomez, Ramon *o.carm.* (ARE) Morovis, PR Nuestra Senora del Carmen Church.
Gomez, Ramon J. '85 (OAK) Union City, CA St. Anne Church.
Gomez, Raul *s.d.s.* '87 (MIL) [B] Hales Corners, WI Sacred Heart School of Theology.
Gomez, Rene J. '63 (SFR) San Bruno, CA St. Bruno Church.
Gomez, Roberto *c.m.* '92 (LA) [A] Camarillo, CA St. John's Seminary.
Gomez, Silvestre '97 (SJN) Catano, PR Nuestra Senora del Carmen Church.
Gomez, Walter (ARE) On Duty Outside the Diocese.
Gomez, Walter '80 (SJN) [26] San Juan, PR San Jose Church.
Gomez del Valle, Jorge *m.sp.s.* '73 (SEA) Bothell, WA St. Elizabeth Ann Seton Church.
Gomez-Serna, Ontoniel J. '90 (PRO) [1] Central Falls, RI The Holy Spirit Catholic Community Church.
Gomide, Tomaz '71 (RVC) Mineola, NY Corpus Christi Church.
Gomolski, Joseph T. '81 (WIL) On Duty Outside the Diocese.
Gomulka, Eugene T. '74 (ALT) Military Chaplains.
Gomulka, Henry J. '42 (GB) Retired.
Gonda, Andrew '46 (GI) Retired.
Gonda, Gerard *o.s.b.* '80 (CLV) [D] Cleveland, OH Benedictine High School; [O] Cleveland, OH Benedictine Order of Cleveland.
Gondek, Albert J. *o.s.f.s.* '66 (CHL) Lexington, NC Our Lady of the Rosary Church.
Gondek, Joseph A. '37 (MAR) Retired.
Gonderinger, Gerald E. '74 (OM) [44] Omaha, NE St. Stephen the Martyr Church.
Gonet, Charles F. '58 (SPR) [14] Springfield, MA St. Catherine of Siena Church.
Goni, Joachim *o.a.r.* '40 (ORG) [5] Santa Ana, CA Our Lady of the Pillar Church.
Goni, Paul *o.a.r.* '51 (ORG) Fullerton, CA St. Mary's Church.
Gonia, Raymond L. '90 (SUP) Military Chaplains.
Gonnelly, Theophane *o.s.b.* '47 (SFS) [F] Marvin, SD Blue Cloud Abbey.
Gonsalves, Valerian *o.s.b.* '90 (TLS) Durant, OK St. William Church.
Gonser, Richard A. '62 (CLV) North Ridgeville, OH St. Julie Billiart Church.
Gonsorcik, Pat *s.c.j.* '70 (MIL) [P] Hales Corners, WI Priests of the Sacred Heart.
Gonter, Louis J. '49 (BUF) Retired.
Gonter, Louis J. '49 (ORL) Lady Lake, FL St. Timothy Church; Retired.
Gonyo, Lance '93 (ROC) Dansville, NY St. Mary Church.
Gonyo, Lance M. '93 (ROC) Sodus, NY Epiphany Church.
Gonyo, Roland G. '73 (OG) Absent on Leave.
Gonzales, Gabriel '39 (NO) Retired.
Gonzales, Gabriel '84 (LA) [38] Los Angeles, CA Sacred Heart Church.
Gonzales, George '71 (SB) La Quinta, CA St. Francis of Assisi Church.
Gonzales, George '87 (BWN) Weslaco, TX San Martin de Porres Church.
Gonzales, Hily *c.s.* '96 (CHI) [N] Chicago, IL Scalabrini House of Theology.
Gonzales, Juan *s.m.* '82 (DET) [E] Harper Woods, MI Notre Dame High School.
Gonzales, Loren M. *o.s.m.* '89 (CHI) [N] Chicago, IL Order of Friar Servants of Mary (Servites) United States of America Province, Inc.
Gonzales, Msgr. Loreto '78 (LA) Artesia, CA Holy Family Church; [CC] Los Angeles, CA Filipino Pastoral Ministry.
Gonzales, Orestes '86 (WDC) [T] Washington, DC Prelature of the Holy Cross and Opus Dei.
Gonzales, Richard (CC) [1] Beeville, TX Our Lady of Victory Church.
Gonzales, Robert A. '78 (COL) [A] Columbus, OH Pontifical College Josephinum.
Gonzales, Robert A. '78 (TUC) On Duty Outside the Diocese.
Gonzales, Teodulo P. *s.j.* '87 (BAL) [S] Baltimore, MD Jesuit Community of Loyola College, Inc.
Gonzalez, Angel *s.p.* '52 (FRS) Reedley, CA St. Anthony Church.
Gonzalez, Anthony '92 (LA) [62] Los Angeles, CA St. Frances Xavier Cabrini Church.
Gonzalez, Antonio '50 (FRS) Retired.
Gonzalez, Msgr. Antonio '62 (LUB) [3] Lubbock, TX Our Lady of Grace Church.
Gonzalez, Aquilino D. *o.s.a.* '72 (FgM) Foreign Missions.
Gonzalez, Arnold *c.m.f.* '58 (LA) San Gabriel, CA San Gabriel Church.
Gonzalez, Arnold J. *c.m.f.* '58 (LA) [Q] San Gabriel, CA Claretian Missionaries (Missionary Sons of the Immaculate Heart of Mary).
Gonzalez, Arturo *o.s.m.* (ELP) [18] El Paso, TX Our Lady of Sorrows Church.
Gonzalez, Charles G. *s.j.* (CAM) [4] Camden, NJ Holy Name Church.
Gonzalez, Charles S. *s.j.* (CAM) Camden, NJ Camden County Jail.
Gonzalez, Cruz Gil '48 (SJN) Retired.
Gonzalez, Daniel '92 (TYL) Gilmer, TX St. Francis of Assisi Church.
Gonzalez, Domingo '64 (ORL) Bartow, FL St. Thomas Aquinas Church.
Gonzalez, Eduardo *s.d.b.* '81 (DAL) [16] Dallas, TX St. Edward Church.
Gonzalez, Emilio '88 (SEA) Bellevue, WA St. Louise Church.
Gonzalez, Flavio V. '77 (CHI) [67] Chicago, IL St. Genevieve Church.
Gonzalez, Francisco *s.f.* '64 (WDC) [B] Silver Spring, MD Holy Family Seminary.
Gonzalez, George A. '67 (SAV) Americus, GA St. Mary Church.
Gonzalez, George G. '67 (SAT) Military Chaplains.
Gonzalez, Gonzalo *o.s.a.* '49 (SJN) [1] Bayamon, PR San Agustin Church.
Gonzalez, Hugo '89 (PHX) Peoria, AZ St. Charles Borromeo Church.
Gonzalez, Jesus *c.m.v.* '87 (ARE) [7] Arecibo, PR Nuestra Senora de Fatima Church.
Gonzalez, Jorge '79 (SP) Beverly Hills, FL Our Lady of Grace Church.
Gonzalez, Jorge L. *s.d.b.* '89 (SJN) Catano, PR San Francisco de Sales Church.
Gonzalez, Jose '54 (SP) [8] St. Petersburg, FL St. Raphael Church.
Gonzalez, Jose '69 (SR) [4] Santa Rosa, CA Resurrection Church.
Gonzalez, Jose '91 (VEN) Lake Placid, FL Communidad Catolica Hispana Santiago Apostol (Santiago Mission) Church; [I] Lake Placid, FL Campo San Jose.
Gonzalez, Juan *c.pp.s.* '76 (GRY) [5] East Chicago, IN Our Lady of Guadalupe Church.
Gonzalez, Juan Jose (P) [A] Mount Angel, OR Felix Rougier House of Studies.
Gonzalez, Julio *s.f.* '99 (SFE) Santa Cruz, NM Holy Cross Church.
Gonzalez, Lazaro *o.f.m.* (ELP) Presidio, TX Santa Teresa de Jesus Church.
Gonzalez, Luis Francisco '98 (SJN) [4] San Juan, PR San Antonio Church.
Gonzalez, Luis O. '00 (NEW) [1] Newark, NJ Cathedral Basilica of the Sacred Heart.
Gonzalez, Luis P. '94 (NEW) [A] Kearny, NJ Redemptoris Mater.
Gonzalez, Marcos J. '94 (LA) Pasadena, CA St. Andrew Church.
Gonzalez, Mario '55 (VEN) Retired.
Gonzalez, Mario *o.s.a.* '58 (SJN) [18] Bayamon, PR Santa Rita de Casia Church.
Gonzalez, Miguel '98 (ORL) [9] Orlando, FL St. John Vianney Church.
Gonzalez, Rafael J. *c.r.l.* '93 (ARE) Corozal-Palmarito, PR La Milagrosa Church.
Gonzalez, Msgr. Ricardo '57 (NEW) [1] Orange, NJ St. John's Church.
Gonzalez, Romualdo *sch.p.* '71 (LA) [23] Los Angeles, CA Our Lady Help of Christians (Maria Auxiliadora) Church.
Gonzalez, Ruben *c.m.f.* '75 (SJN) [27] San Juan, PR San Jose Obrero Church.
Gonzalez, Rudolph F. '87 (NY) [31] New York, NY St. Elizabeth Church; Spring Valley, NY St. Joseph Church.
Gonzalez, Silvino *o.de.m.* '41 (PCE) [9] Ponce, PR La Merced Church.
Gonzalez, Teodulo P. *s.j.* (BAL) [B] Baltimore, MD Loyola College in Maryland.
Gonzalez-Abreu, Hector '79 (MIA) [34] Miami, FL St. Vincent De Paul Church.
Gonzalez-Chao, Luis '58 (SJN) [3] Toa Baja, PR Espiritu Santo Church.
Gonzalez-Florez, Jose Duvan '96 (ATL) [8] Atlanta, GA Sacred Heart of Jesus Church.
Gonzalez-Montenegro, Julian *o.f.m.cap.* '84 (SFR) [B] San Francisco, CA Capuchin House of Studies.
Good, Clarence P. '46 (STL) Shrewsbury, MO Cure' of Ars Church.
Goode, Francis *o.p.* '80 (OAK) Antioch, CA Holy Rosary Church.
Goode, James E. *o.f.m.* '72 (NY) [DD] New York, NY St. Clare Friary.
Goode, Msgr. Joseph J. '73 (PAT) Absent on Leave.
Goode, Lawrence C. '64 (SFR) [19] San Francisco, CA St. Finn Barr Church; [T] San Francisco, CA Legion of Mary.
Goode, Michael *c.pp.s.* '79 (SAN) Sweetwater, TX Holy Family Church; Sweetwater, TX Immaculate Heart of Mary Church.
Goode, William F. '60 (WDC) Indian Head, MD St. Mary Star of the Sea Church.
Goodill, Msgr. Robert D. '38 (E) [23] Erie, PA St. Luke Church; Retired.
Goodly, Timothy '93 (LKC) [4] Lake Charles, LA St. Henry Church.
Goodman, Fidelis C. *m.m.* '49 (NY) [DD] Maryknoll, NY Maryknoll Fathers and Brothers.
Goodman, Frank '59 (ORL) Retired.
Goodman, Frank '59 (SP) Retired.
Goodman, Julian B., Jr. '66 (RIC) Charlottesville, VA Church of the Holy Comforter.
Goodman, Leo M., III '91 (HBG) [2] Harrisburg, PA St. Catherine Laboure Church.
Goodman, Msgr. Norman D. '60 (PEO) Retired.
Goodrow, David C. '00 (BO) Franklin, MA St. Mary Church.
Goodrow, Robert A. '62 (DET) Retired.
Goodrum, James R. '57 (LFT) Monticello, IN Our Lady of the Lakes Church.
Goodwin, Calvin *f.s.s.p.* '79 (SCR) [M] Elmhurst, PA Priestly Fraternity of St. Peter (F.S.S.P.), North American District Headquarters.
Goodwin, Calvin R. *f.s.s.p.* (LIN) [A] Denton, NE Our Lady of Guadalupe Seminary.
Goodwin, James P. *s.j.* '43 (SPK) [K] Spokane, WA Regis Community.
Goodwin, James S. '97 (FAR) Hankinson, ND St. Philip's Church.
Goodwin, Owen *ss.cc.* '54 (FR) [I] Fairhaven, MA Sacred Hearts Provincial House.
Goodwin, Owen F. *ss.cc.* (PRO) [P] Narragansett, RI Christian Brothers' Center.
Goodwin, Patrick (OAK) [S] Oakland, CA Adventus.
Goodwin, Patrick A. '69 (OAK) Dublin, CA St. Raymond Church.
Goodwin, Raymond M., Jr. '69 (WOR) Hopedale, MA Sacred Heart of Jesus Church.
Goodwin, Robert T. '57 (MAN) Retired.
Goodwine, Msgr. Joseph G. '39 (NY) Retired.
Goodyear, Michael *l.c.* '94 (DET) [T] Bloomfield Hills, MI Logos, Inc. (Michigan).
Goodyear, Robert *s.t.* '75 (JKS) Magee, MS St. Stephen Church; Sanatorium, MS Boswell Retardation Center.
Goolsby, Gregory '93 (ATL) Duluth, GA Catholic Church Of St. Monica.
Goossens, Hippolyte L. *c.j.* '56 (LA) Camarillo, CA Camarillo State Hospital-Development Center.
Gootee, Jason E. '99 (ALX) [1] Alexandria, LA St. Francis Xavier Church.
Gootee, Paul *s.v.d.* '55 (FgM) Society of the Divine Word Foreign Missions.
Gootee, Stanley J. *s.v.d.* '44 (GAL) [47] Houston, TX St. Mary of the Purification Church.
Gopaul, Antonius P. '98 (BRK) [65] Brooklyn, NY St. Jerome's Church.

Goraieb, Charles '91 (PHX) [9] Phoenix, AZ St. Catherine of Siena Church.
Gorak, Stanley C. '38 (GI) Retired.
Gorczyca, Andrzej '74 (BRK) [94] Brooklyn, NY Our Lady of Czestochowa-St. Casimir Church.
Gordinier, William '58 (ROC) Geneseo, NY St. Mary Church.
Gordon, Charles *s.t.* '67 (FgM) Trinity Missions.
Gordon, Charles *c.s.c.* '87 (FTW) [B] Notre Dame, IN University of Notre Dame Du Lac.
Gordon, Charles B. *c.s.c.* '87 (FTW) [A] Notre Dame, IN Old College; [A] Notre Dame, IN Moreau Seminary; [A] Notre Dame, IN Moreau Seminary; [J] Notre Dame, IN Holy Cross Community, Corby Hall, University of Notre Dame.
Gordon, Emmanuel *c.p.* '50 (PMB) [H] North Palm Beach, FL Our Lady of Florida Spiritual Center.
Gordon, Gerald R. *s.j.* '60 (SPK) [C] Spokane, WA Gonzaga University; [G] Spokane, WA Sacred Heart Medical Center.
Gordon, Gerard *t.o.r.* (BAL) [30] Baltimore, MD St. Elizabeth of Hungary Church.
Gordon, Gerard A. '88 (RVC) Hicksville, NY St. Ignatius Loyola Church.
Gordon, Gregory W. '88 (LAV) North Las Vegas, NV St. Christopher Church.
Gordon, James *i.c.* '69 (SP) Seminole, FL Blessed Sacrament Church.
Gordon, James E. '81 (RIC) [3] Chesapeake, VA St. Stephen, Martyr Church.
Gordon, John '85 (FgM) Society of St. James the Apostle.
Gordon, John '88 (NEW) [2] Elizabeth, NJ St. Adalbert's Church.
Gordon, John '88 (PAT) [P] Paterson, NJ The Association of the Marian Apostolate of Mercy, Inc.
Gordon, John B. '85 (MET) [8] Perth Amboy, NJ La Asuncion Church.
Gordon, Joseph A. '71 (SFR) East Palo Alto, CA St. Francis of Assisi Church.
Gordon, Kevin M. '83 (SUP) Rice Lake, WI St. Joseph Church.
Gordon, L. William '65 (OG) Chazy, NY Sacred Heart Church.
Gordon, M. Gerald *t.o.r.* '69 (PH) [AA] Fairless Hills, PA St. Anthony Friary.
Gordon, Robert J. '73 (PAT) [8] Clifton, NJ St. Philip the Apostle Church.
Gore, Robert D. '65 (BEL) [5] Belleville, IL St. Henry Church; [G] Belleville, IL Poor Clare Monastery of Our Lady of Mercy.
Gore, William R. *o.s.f.s.* '69 (WIL) [I] Wilmington, DE Oblates of St. Francis De Sales.
Gorena, Pedro *o.ss.t.* (SJN) [F] Toa Alta, PR Hogar Santisima Trinidad; [F] Bayamon, PR Hogar Del Nino "Elave Maria".
Gorena, Pedro *o.ss.t.* '66 (SJN) [13] Bayamon, PR Ascension Del Senor Church; [14] Bayamon, PR Espiritu Santo Church.
Gorges, Bernard X. '95 (WCH) Oxford, KS St. Mary Church; Winfield, KS Holy Name Church.
Gorges, Peter '68 (JUN) Sitka, AK St. Gregory of Nazianzen Church.
Gorgis, Noel (LA) [5] North Hollywood, CA St. Paul Assyrian-Chaldean Church.
Gorgis, Noel '89 (EST) North Hollywood, CA St. Paul Assyrian-Chaldean Catholic Church; Scottsdale, AZ Mar Auraha Chaldean Catholic Church.
Gorham, Peter P. '53 (PRT) Retired.
Gori, Peter G. *o.s.a.* '79 (BO) [3] Lawrence, MA St. Augustine Church.
Gorinas, Vytautas '70 (RCK) Retired.
Gorka, Thaddeus '88 (PH) [2] Philadelphia, PA St. Adalbert Church.
Gorman, Charles '54 (GF) Columbus, MT St. Mary's Church.
Gorman, Charles L. '54 (GF) Retired.
Gorman, Cyril *o.s.b.* '90 (SCL) [I] Collegeville, MN St. John's Abbey, of the Order of St. Benedict.
Gorman, Edward *o.p.* '92 (FgM) Dominican - Order of Preachers Foreign Missions.
Gorman, Francis A. *o.f.m.* '39 (CHR) Greenville, SC St. Anthony of Padua Church.
Gorman, Francis P. '59 (NY) North Tarrytown, NY Holy Cross Church; Sleepy Hollow, NY St. Teresa of Avila Church.
Gorman, Francis X. *o.m.i.* '58 (BO) [2] Milton, MA St. Elizabeth Church.
Gorman, George F. '36 (PRO) Retired; [P] Providence, RI St. John Vianney Residence.
Gorman, James '81 (STP) Burnsville, MN Church of the Risen Savior.
Gorman, James H. *m.m.* '52 (FgM) Maryknoll Foreign Missions.
Gorman, James P. '73 (PH) [120] Philadelphia, PA Our Lady of Hope Church.
Gorman, Msgr. James T. '57 (NY) Bedford, NY St. Patrick Church; [1] Port Chester, NY Our Lady of Mercy Church.
Gorman, Msgr. John '34 (DM) Retired.
Gorman, John '58 (SB) Retired.
Gorman, John J. '45 (RVC) Babylon, NY St. Joseph's Church; Retired.
Gorman, Joseph F. '55 (HRT) [12] Waterbury, CT St. Leo the Great Church.
Gorman, Kevin D. *o.s.b.* '51 (PEO) Arlington, IL St. Patrick's Church; Cherry, IL Holy Trinity Church; [A] Peru, IL St. Bede Abbey and Academy.
Gorman, Leo J. *c.p.* '57 (NY) [DD] Pelham Manor, NY St. Vincent's Residence; [HH] Pelham, NY Passionist Communications, Inc.
Gorman, Michael J. '80 (LC) Special Assignment; [A] La Crosse, WI Holy Cross Seminary House of Formation; [H] La Crosse, WI Holy Cross (Seminary) Diocesan Center; [J] La Crosse, WI Catholic Charities of the Diocese of La Crosse, Inc.
Gorman, Patrick J. '59 (LA) [49] Los Angeles, CA St. Bernadette Church; Retired.
Gorman, Paul J. '40 (NU) Retired.
Gorman, Richard F. '82 (NY) [E] New York, NY Cardinal Spellman High School; [I] New York, NY The Catholic Charities of the Archdiocese of New York.
Gorman, Robert G. '80 (MET) [7] Perth Amboy, NJ Holy Spirit Church.
Gorman, Rody I. '55 (LA) Huntington Park, CA St. Matthias Church; Retired.
Gorman, Thomas J. '59 (TOL) Delphos, OH St. John the Evangelist Church.
Gorman, William A. '73 (ALB) Fort Ann, NY St. Ann Church; Whitehall, NY Our Lady of Hope Church.
Gorman, William N. '76 (MOB) Dauphin Island, AL St. Edmund-by-the-Sea Church.
Gormley, Charles E. '51 (PH) Bala Cynwyd, PA St. Matthias Church; Retired.
Gormley, Eugene *l.c.* '83 (DAL) [D] Irving, TX The Highlands School; [E] Irving, TX The Highland School; [K] Irving, TX Legionaries of Christ.
Gormley, Gerard '85 (SR) [3] Santa Rosa, CA St. Rose of Lima Church.
Gormley, James J. *s.j.* '54 (PH) [AA] Philadelphia, PA Jesuit Community at St. Joseph's University.
Gormley, James W. '54 (PH) Stowe, PA St. Gabriel of the Sorrowful Mother Church.
Gormley, Kevin '64 (JC) Marshall, MO St. Peter Church; Marshall, MO Marshall State School-Hospital.
Gormley, Michael *s.a.c.* '41 (DET) Allen Park, MI St. Frances Cabrini Church; Detroit, MI Oakwood Hospital.
Gormley, Raymond P. '92 (CAM) [6] Cherry Hill, NJ Queen of Heaven Church; [2] Vineland, NJ Sacred Heart Church.
Gormley, William J. *c.m.* '49 (PH) [AA] Philadelphia, PA Congregation of the Mission.
Gorney, Joseph *c.ss.r.* '51 (CHL) Concord, NC St. James Church.
Gorny, Edward V. *glmy.* '68 (SAV) Sylvania, GA Our Lady of the Assumption Church; [J] Sylvania, GA Catholic Cemetery.
Gorospe, Paterno (NEW) Elizabeth, NJ Trinitas Hospital.
Gorospe, Paterno '66 (NEW) [G] Teaneck, NJ Holy Name Hospital.
Gorowski, Roman *c.m.* '72 (BRK) [134] Brooklyn, NY St. Stanislaus Kostka Church.
Gorr, Benjamin '79 (VEN) Retired.
Gorrell, Paul '91 (PAT) Absent on Leave.
Gorsic, Gregor '97 (JOL) [3] Naperville, IL Sts. Peter and Paul Church.
Gorski, Alex F. '43 (WIL) Retired.
Gorski, Barnabas *o.f.m.* '60 (FgM) Franciscan Foreign Missions.
Gorski, Barnabas *o.f.m.* '60 (GB) [I] Pulaski, WI Assumption of B.V.M. Friary.
Gorski, Donald '59 (FgM) Society of St. James the Apostle.
Gorski, Eugene F. *c.s.c.* '60 (FTW) [J] Notre Dame, IN Holy Cross Community, Corby Hall, University of Notre Dame.
Gorski, Msgr. J. Donald '59 (CHR) On Duty Outside the Diocese.
Gorski, John F. *m.m.* '63 (FgM) Maryknoll Foreign Missions.
Gorski, John J. '64 (CLV) Avon, OH Holy Trinity Church; Retired.
Gorski, Lawrence E. '75 (CHI) [146] Chicago, IL Our Lady of Grace Church.
Gorski, Robert E. '80 (MAN) Merrimack, NH St. John Neumann Church.
Gorski, Terrence *o.f.m.* '75 (BWN) Rio Hondo, TX St. Helen Church.
Gorton, Timothy J. '82 (PRO) [4] Warwick, RI St. Francis of Assisi Church.
Gosche, Msgr. Joseph E. '55 (SPC) Retired.
Gosciniak, Darius '92 (HRT) [2] New Britain, CT Holy Cross Church.
Gosma, Robert D. '59 (MIL) Genesee Depot, WI St. Paul Church.
Gosnell, David H. '65 (GRY) Valparaiso, IN St. Elizabeth Seton Church.
Gosnell, Stephen D. '78 (BAL) Edgewood, MD Prince of Peace Church.
Goss, Francis G. '47 (BO) [5] Brockton, MA Our Lady of Lourdes Church.
Goss, Francis J. '47 (BO) Senior Priests.
Goss, Joseph U. *o.p.* '55 (BR) Donaldsonville, LA Ascension of Our Lord Jesus Christ Church.
Gosselin, Andre *s.m.* '64 (BO) [3] Methuen, MA Our Lady of Mount Carmel Church.
Gosselin, Fernand L. *m.m.* '70 (FgM) Maryknoll Foreign Missions.
Gosselin, Gerard G. '85 (PRT) Bangor, ME St. John's Church.
Gosselin, Homer P. '69 (SPR) [3] Ludlow, MA St. John the Baptist Church.
Gosselin, Joseph *m.s.* '65 (FR) [I] Attleboro, MA La Salette Provincial House.
Gosselin, Larry *o.f.m.* '80 (SFE) Jemez Pueblo, NM San Diego Indian Missions Church.
Gosselin, Lawrence '76 (NTN) Military Chaplains.
Gosselin, Lawrence R. *o.f.m.* '82 (ORG) [3] Huntington Beach, CA SS. Simon and Jude Church.
Gosselin, Michael H. '73 (HRT) [1] Hartford, CT Cathedral of St. Joseph; Retired.
Gosselin, Richard R. '58 (BO) Ayer, MA St. Mary Church.
Gosselin, Robert H. '56 (BO) Senior Priests.
Gossman, John A. '71 (DUB) Marion, IA St. Joseph's Church.
Goswitz, Leonard (LA) Redondo Beach, CA St. Lawrence Martyr Church.
Goth, Dennis J. '84 (LFT) Muncie, IN St. Lawrence Church.
Gothe, Marcus '59 (P) Retired.
Gothie, George J. '67 (PAT) Hopatcong, NJ St. Jude's Church.
Gothing, Donald B. '65 (WOR) On Special or Other Diocesan Assignment.
Gothman, August L. '93 (CR) Argyle, MN St. Rose Church; Stephen, MN St. Stephen's Church.
Gotimer, Msgr. James '53 (BRK) Retired.
Gotimer, Msgr. James E. (BRK) [154] Queens, NY St. Bartholomew's Church.
Gott, Camillus '60 (STP) [Q] Prior Lake, MN Franciscan Retreat House.
Gottemoeller, Mark '76 (IND) Martinsville, IN St. Martin of Tours Church.
Gottemoller, Bartholomew *o.c.s.o.* '42 (SLC) [F] Huntsville, UT Abbey of Our Lady of the Holy Trinity of the Order of Cistercians.
Gottschalk, David *o.f.m.cap.* '69 (DEN) [M] Denver, CO St. Francis of Assisi Friary.
Gottschalk, David *o.f.m.cap.* '69 (FgM) Capuchin Foreign Missions.
Gottschalk, Matthew (MIL) [Y] Whitefish Bay, WI Association of Ladies of Charity of Milwaukee, Wisconsin.
Gottschalk, Matthew *o.f.m.cap.* '53 (MIL) [Y] Milwaukee, WI House of Peace.
Gotwalt, Joseph F. '65 (HBG) Hanover, PA St. Joseph Church.
Goudreau, George W. '48 (PRT) Retired.
Goudreau, Joseph L. '63 (PRT) Military Chaplains.
Goudreau, Paul '60 (SP) Holiday, FL St. Vincent De Paul Church.
Goudreau, Remy A. *o.f.m.* '39 (BO) [Z] Boston, MA Saint Anthony Residence.
Goudreau, William G. *s.j.* '52 (FgM) Provinces.
Gouger, John *c.ss.r.* '65 (FgM) Redemptorist Foreign Missions.
Gough, Joseph E. *s.j.* '43 (STL) [O] St. Louis, MO Fusz Pavilion.
Gouin, Joseph O. '65 (MAR) Kingsford, MI American Martyrs Church.
Gould, Clayton '81 (LR) Mena, AR St. Agnes Church.
Gould, James C. *s.j.* '74 (FgM) Provinces.
Gould, Msgr. James C. *s.j.* '74 (MI) Majuro, MH Cathedral of the Assumption Church; MH Outer Island.
Gould, James R. '81 (ARL) Fairfax Station, VA St. Raymond of Penafort Church.
Gould, Michael A. *m.m.* '54 (FgM) Maryknoll Foreign Missions.
Gould, William R. '65 (B) Post Falls, ID St. George's Church.
Goulding, Laurence *glmy.* '62 (SAV) Waynesboro, GA Sacred Heart Church.
Gouldrick, John W. *c.m.* '69 (PH) [70] Philadelphia, PA Immaculate Conception Church; [B] Philadelphia, PA St. Vincent's Seminary; [AA] Philadelphia, PA Congregation of the Mission.
Goulet, Raymond O. '57 (BO) Senior Priests.
Goulet, Wayne F. '74 (PHX) Special Assignment.
Goupil, Ronald R. '00 (MAN) Salem, NH St. Joseph Church.
Gousse, Paul M. '99 (MAN) [1] Concord, NH St. John the Evangelist Church.
Gouthro, Arthur *s.a.* '69 (NY) [DD] Garrison, NY Franciscan Friars of the Atonement, Minister General Office.
Govak, Wladyslaw '82 (NEW) [7] Elizabeth, NJ St. Hedwig's Church.

Goveas, Benedict *o.f.m.* '53 (NY) [DD] New York, NY Franciscan Province of the Immaculate Conception.
Govern, William H. '34 (RVC) Retired.
Governale, Russell *o.f.m.conv.* '88 (BRK) [61] Brooklyn, NY Most Holy Trinity Church.
Govorchin, Vincent '55 (SLC) On Duty Outside the Diocese.
Gowen, Daniel '89 (TR) Spring Lake, NJ St. Catharine Church.
Gower, James M. '53 (PRT) Retired.
Gower, Peter J. '84 (PRO) [3] Warren, RI St. Jean Baptiste Church.
Gowin, Wladyslaw *s.ch.* '54 (CHI) [85] Chicago, IL Holy Trinity Church.
Gowing, Thomas '69 (SR) Garberville, CA Our Lady of the Redwoods Church.
Goyeneche, Venancio '57 (LA) [32] Los Angeles, CA Our Lady of the Rosary of Talpa Church.
Goyette, Giles '82 (RC) [B] Piedmont, SD Holy Nativity Monastery.
Goyette, Giles R. *o.mar.* '82 (SAM) [C] Petersham, MA Most Holy Trinity Monastery.
Gozaloff, Msgr. Paul J. '56 (WDC) Mechanicsville, MD Immaculate Conception Church.
Graap, Augustine *o.carm.* '66 (NY) State, NY Mid-Orange Correctional Facility; State, NY Otisville Correctional Facility; [DD] Middletown, NY St. Albert's Priory.
Grab, Michael J. '77 (HBG) [6] Lancaster, PA Sacred Heart of Jesus Church.
Grabarz, Casimir F. *c.s.c.* '39 (FTW) [J] South Bend, IN Congregation of Holy Cross, Indiana Province, Provincial House.
Grabert, Colman *o.s.b.* '65 (IND) [J] St. Meinrad, IN St. Meinrad Archabbey.
Grabish, John J. '72 (ALN) [2] Easton, PA St. Bernard Church; [5] Easton, PA St. Michael Church.
Grabner, Donald *o.s.b.* '54 (KC) [A] Conception, MO Conception Seminary College; [J] Conception, MO Conception Abbey.
Grabner, Eugene W. '59 (WCH) Columbus, KS St. Rose Church; Scammon, KS St. Bridget's Church.
Grabner, Kenneth *c.s.c.* '60 (FTW) [J] Notre Dame, IN Congregation of Holy Cross, Midwest Province.
Grabner, Robert '00 (STP) Lakeville, MN All Saints Church.
Grabowski, Dennis '76 (Y) Absent on Leave.
Grabowski, Eugene '89 (R) Wrightsville Beach, NC St. Therese Church.
Grabowski, Francis E. '44 (MET) Piscataway, NJ St. Frances Cabrini Church; Retired; [H] Somerset, NJ Maria Regina Residence.
Grabowski, Walter P. '81 (BUF) Eden, NY Immaculate Conception Church.
Grabowsky, Msgr. Myron '67 (PHU) Bristol, PA St. Mary's Church.
Grabrian, Dennis '70 (COS) On Duty Outside Diocese.
Grabrian, John '70 (DEN) [2] Lakewood, CO Christ on the Mountain Church.
Grabys, Joseph '49 (ALB) Retired.
Grace, Edward D. '67 (CHI) Skokie, IL St. Peter Church.
Grace, Edward G. *o.s.a.* '41 (CHI) [N] Olympia Fields, IL The Augustinians-Provincialate.
Grace, Gerald '65 (PMB) Highland Beach, FL St. Lucy Church.
Grace, Gerard *s.s.e.* '55 (VEN) [G] Englewood, FL Society of St. Edmund Residence.
Grace, Hugh R. '64 (NY) Saugerties, NY St. Mary of the Snow Church.
Grace, James N. '59 (CHI) Retired.
Grace, Msgr. James P. '61 (BRK) [150] Queens, NY St. Andrew Avellino Church.
Grace, John '88 (MAN) [12] Manchester, NH St. Marie Church.
Grace, John A. '79 (RIC) Harrisonburg, VA Blessed Sacrament Church.
Grace, John J. '48 (SAC) South Lake Tahoe, CA St. Theresa Church; Retired and in Senior Ministry.
Grace, John J. '50 (CHI) [195] Chicago, IL St. Tarcissus Church; Retired.
Grace, Joseph W. '53 (LFT) Marion, IN U.S. Veteran's Hospital.
Grace, Patrick J. '49 (ROC) Retired.
Grace, Peter A. *c.p.* '72 (SCR) [M] Scranton, PA Saint Ann's Passionist Monastery; [R] Scranton, PA Saint Ann's Media, Inc.
Grace, Robert S. '55 (WDC) Retired.
Grace, Thomas A. *c.m.* '64 (CHI) [G] Chicago, IL Catholic Charities of the Archdiocese of Chicago-Archdiocesan Offices; [N] Chicago, IL Vincentian Community, Congregation of the Mission, Midwest Province.
Gracey, John '93 (FRS) Boron, CA St. Joseph Church.
Gracias, Urbano '52 (NO) Retired.
Gracz, Msgr. Henry C. '65 (ATL) McDonough, GA St. James The Apostle Church.
Graczyk, Carl *o.f.m.* '73 (PH) [D] Philadelphia, PA Archbishop Ryan High School; [AA] Philadelphia, PA St. Pius X Friary.
Graczyk, Glen G. '81 (MIL) [1] Waukesha, WI St. John Neumann Church; [H] Waukesha, WI Waukesha Catholic School System, Inc.
Graczyk, Randolph *o.f.m.cap.* '68 (GF) Pryor, MT St. Charles Borromeo Church.
Grad, Malcolm S. '58 (CIN) On Special and Archdiocesan Assignment.
Graden, John L. *o.s.f.s.* '76 (TOL) [37] Toledo, OH St. Pius X Church; [K] Toledo, OH Oblates of St. Francis de Sales.
Gradilone, Msgr. Thomas (BRK) Retired.
Gradilone, Msgr. Thomas J. '50 (BRK) [V] Douglaston, NY Bishop Mugavero Residence.
Grady, Bernard C. '68 (DUB) Marshalltown, IA St. Mary's Church.
Grady, Brian D. '00 (RCK) [10] Aurora, IL St. Therese of Jesus Church.
Grady, Brian Donlin '00 (RCK) Batavia, IL Holy Cross Church.
Grady, Charles *c.s.s.* '48 (BO) [Z] Waltham, MA Stigmatine Fathers and Brothers.
Grady, Donald F. *s.j.* '44 (BO) [W] Weston, MA Campion Health Center, Inc.
Grady, Francis J. *s.s.c.* '63 (CHI) Forest Park, IL St. Bernardine Church.
Grady, James P. '77 (STL) Elsberry, MO Sacred Heart Church.
Grady, John P. *m.m.* '55 (FgM) Maryknoll Foreign Missions.
Grady, L. Augustine *s.j.* '46 (NY) [DD] New York, NY Jesuit Community at Fordham University.
Grady, Michael '94 (MIA) [C] Fort Lauderdale, FL St. Thomas Aquinas High School.
Grady, Peter W. '53 (FAR) Retired; [E] Fargo, ND Riverview Place.
Grady, William R. '55 (LFT) Muncie, IN St. Mary Church.
Graeber, Msgr. Richard A. '53 (BUF) Retired.
Graef, Msgr. Franz '57 (SHP) [2] Shreveport, LA Holy Trinity Church.
Graehler, Kenneth '63 (EVN) Sullivan, IN St. Mary Church.
Graf, Gary M. '84 (CHI) [4] Waukegan, IL Holy Family Church.
Graf, Harold '68 (PHX) Sun City West, AZ Our Lady of Lourdes Church.
Graf, Henry C. '49 (PH) Retired.
Graf, Herbert *o.f.m.conv.* '59 (SAV) Hazlehurst, GA Good Shepherd Church.
Graf, James W. '72 (L) Lebanon Junction, KY St. Benedict Church; Shepherdsville, KY St. Aloysius Church; Louisville, KY Central State Hospital.
Graf, Msgr. John W. '74 (PH) West Grove, PA Assumption B.V.M. Church.
Graf, Paul '82 (LFT) [C] Lafayette, IN St. Elizabeth Medical Center.
Graf, William E. '60 (ROC) Fairport, NY Church of the Resurrection; [L] Rochester, NY Archivist (Diocese of Rochester Archives); [L] Rochester, NY Censores Librorum.
Graff, Ed '55 (AMA) Tulia, TX Church of the Holy Spirit
Graff, Edward R. '55 (ALN) Retired.
Graff, Francis C. '65 (PIT) Neshannock, PA St. Camillus Church; Lawrence County, PA Almira Home; Lawrence County, PA Belvedere Residence, Inc.; Lawrence County, PA Golden Hill Nursing, Inc.; Lawrence County, PA Haven Convalescent Home; Lawrence County, PA Highland Hall Care Center; Lawrence County, PA Hill View Manor; Lawrence County, PA Indian Creek Nursing Center; Lawrence County, PA Jack Rees Nursing and Rehabilitation Services; Lawrence County, PA Overlook Nursing Home; Lawrence County, PA Castle Manor; Lawrence County, PA Cedar Manor; Lawrence County, PA Majors Manor; Lawrence County, PA Shenango United Presbyterian Home; Lawrence County, PA Silver Oak Nursing.
Graff, J. Austin '36 (CHI) [202] Chicago, IL St. Thomas More Church; Retired.
Graff, Joseph P. '76 (GAY) [1] Alpena, MI St. Anne Church.
Graff, Robert L. '52 (TUC) Retired.
Graff, Timothy G. '85 (NEW) Livingston, NJ St. Philomena Church.
Graffis, Joseph T. '71 (L) [10] Louisville, KY St. Augustine Church.
Graffius, Peregrine M. *o.s.m.* '59 (CHI) [N] Chicago, IL Order of Friar Servants of Mary (Servites) United States of America Province, Inc.; [N] Chicago, IL Order of Friar Servants of Mary (Servites) United States of America Province, Inc.
Grafsky, George J. '71 (STP) Montgomery, MN Holy Redeemer Church; Shieldsville, MN St. Patrick Church.
Graham, Alfred '60 (MEM) [18] Memphis, TN St. Michael's Church.
Graham, D. Clifford *o.m.v.* '81 (BO) [B] Boston, MA Oblate Provincialate.
Graham, Daniel M. '70 (BO) [4] Quincy, MA St. Joseph Church.
Graham, Edgar *s.j.* (BAL) [42] Baltimore, MD Immaculate Heart of Mary Church.
Graham, Edgar *s.j.* '54 (BAL) [S] Baltimore, MD Jesuit Community of Loyola College, Inc.
Graham, Edgar B. *s.j.* '54 (BAL) [B] Baltimore, MD Loyola College in Maryland; [B] Baltimore, MD Loyola College in Maryland.
Graham, Msgr. George P. '52 (RVC) Levittown, NY St. Bernard Church.
Graham, Gilbert J. *o.p.* '49 (CHI) [N] River Forest, IL St. Thomas Aquinas Priory.
Graham, Gilbert J. *o.p.* '49 (DAL) [19] Dallas, TX St. Jude Chapel and Information Center Church.
Graham, J. David '91 (MEM) [L] Collierville, TN Serra Club of Memphis.
Graham, James G. '66 (PIT) [22] Pittsburgh, PA St. Lawrence O'Toole Church.
Graham, Msgr. James J. '73 (PH) North Wales, PA St. Rose of Lima Church.
Graham, James K. '93 (NTN) San Jose, CA St. Elias Church.
Graham, James P. *c.m.* '37 (STL) [P] Earth City, MO Congregation of the Mission Midwest Province (Vincentians); [P] Perryville, MO Congregation of The Mission.
Graham, Jerry *s.j.* '00 (P) [19] Portland, OR St. Ignatius Church.
Graham, John E. '44 (DAV) Retired.
Graham, John J. '90 (BO) [65] Boston, MA Sacred Heart Church.
Graham, John K. *c.ss.r.* '53 (NY) [23] New York, NY St. Cecilia Church.
Graham, Msgr. John K. '74 (NY) [E] New York, NY Cardinal Hayes High School.
Graham, Joseph B. '63 (PH) [75] Philadelphia, PA St. Jerome Church.
Graham, Michael J. *s.j.* '88 (CIN) [D] Cincinnati, OH Xavier University; [M] Cincinnati, OH Jesuit Community at Xavier University.
Graham, Msgr. Neil '59 (NY) [2] White Plains, NY St. John the Evangelist Church.
Graham, Raymond *s.m.m.* '47 (RVC) [M] Eastport, NY Shrine of Our Lady of the Island.
Graham, Robert *s.m.* '50 (BO) [Y] Framingham, MA The Marist House.
Graham, Thomas '60 (STL) [O] St. Louis, MO Nazareth Living Center.
Graham, Msgr. Thomas A. '62 (BRK) [228] Queens, NY St. Pius X Church.
Graham, Thomas D. '48 (PH) Retired.
Graham, Walter F. '49 (BRK) [V] Jamaica, NY Vincentian Residence.
Graham, William *o.f.m.cap.* '72 (WDC) [B] Washington, DC St. Francis Friary-Capuchin College.
Graham, William C. '76 (DUL) On Duty Outside the Diocese.
Graham, William P. '65 (CAM) Lindenwold, NJ St. Lawrence's Church.
Grahmann, Charles V. (DAL) [N] Dallas, TX Bishop's Education Endowment Fund; [N] Dallas, TX Bishop Charles V. Grahmann Seminary Burse Fund; [N] Dallas, TX Santa Clara Endowment Fund; [N] Dallas, TX Mary Benevides Trust; [N] Dallas, TX Dave Fox Inner City School Fund.
Grainson, David M. *c.ss.r.* '98 (FgM) Redemptorist Foreign Missions.
Grajeda, Miguel '99 (MRY) Hollister, CA Sacred Heart/St. Benedict Catholic Community Church.
Grajek, Lawrence '57 (SB) Retired.
Grala, Paul E. *s.o.l.t.* '95 (CC) [H] Robstown, TX Society of Our Lady of the Most Holy Trinity.
Gralapp, Robert W. '64 (SC) Manilla, IA Sacred Heart Church.
Gralinski, Thomas J. '41 (HBG) [3] Lancaster, PA Assumption of the Blessed Virgin Mary Church.
Gramata, Raymond '70 (E) Erie, PA St. Vincent's Health Center; [G] Erie, PA Saint Vincent Health Center.
Grambow, Arnold J. '69 (MAR) Gladstone, MI All Saints Church.
Gramigna, Francis J. '64 (CAM) Barrington, NJ St. Francis de Sales Church.
Gramkee, David '66 (ROC) Seneca Falls, NY St. Patrick Church; [L] Seneca Falls, NY Patrician Fund Trust.
Grammond, Maurice '50 (P) Retired.
Grams, Douglas L. '87 (NU) [2] New Ulm, MN St. Mary Church.
Gramza, Ronald J. '73 (MIL) [4] South Milwaukee, WI St. Sylvester Church.
Gran, Thomas '50 (PBR) Retired.
Granadino, David F. '81 (LA) Azusa, CA St. Frances of Rome Church.
Granados, Carlos E. '88 (ARE) [13] Arecibo, PR Church of Santa Cecilia.
Granahan, Gerard '66 (ORL) Sabbatical.
Granata, Joseph P. '75 (RVC) Central Islip, NY St. John of God Church.
Granato, Anthony F. '56 (NEW) East Newark, NJ St. Anthony's Church.
Granato, Msgr. Joseph J. '55 (NEW) [22] Newark, NJ St. Lucy's Church.

Granato, Marius *o.c.s.o.* '64 (WOR) [N] Spencer, MA St. Joseph's Abbey.
Granatowski, Jacek *s.j.* '99 (OAK) [N] Berkeley, CA Jesuit Community at Jesuit School of Theology at Berkeley.
Grancini, Steven M. *c.r.s.p.* '57 (SD) [15] San Diego, CA Our Lady of the Rosary Church.
Grande, Bernadine *c.p.* '45 (BO) [W] Boston, MA St. Gabriel Passionist Community.
Grande, Bernardine *c.p.* (BO) [21] Boston, MA St. Gabriel Church.
Grande, Kenneth (RVC) [B] Patchogue, NY St. Joseph's College.
Grande, Kenneth J. '78 (BRK) [220] Queens, NY Our Lady of the Snows Church.
Grandillo, James J. '54 (CLV) [1] Cleveland, OH Cathedral of St. John the Evangelist; [29] Cleveland, OH Holy Redeemer Church; Retired.
Grandpre, Louis E. '61 (DET) [3] Clinton Twp., MI St. Paul of Tarsus Church.
Graner, Thomas M. '94 (FAR) Bisbee, ND Holy Rosary Church; Rolette, ND Sacred Heart Church; Willow City, ND Notre Dame des Victoires Church.
Graney, William F. '71 (WIL) Newark, DE Christiana Care Health Services, Inc.
Granfield, David *o.s.b.* '52 (WDC) [M] Washington, DC St. Anselm's Abbey.
Granfield, Patrick *o.s.b.* '57 (WDC) [C] Washington, DC Catholic University of America, The; [M] Washington, DC St. Anselm's Abbey.
Grange, John '66 (NY) [152] Bronx, NY St. Jerome's Church.
Granich, Msgr. Bernard '44 (STL) [O] Kirkwood, MO St. Agnes Home for the Elderly.
Granillo, Paul '97 (SB) Special or Other Diocesan Assignment.
Granito, Mark E. '98 (SFE) Abiquiu, NM St. Thomas Apostle Church; Albuquerque, NM Lovelace Hospital.
Grankauskas, Paul M. '00 (ARL) Manassas, VA All Saints Church.
Grankowski, Zbigniew '83 (DET) [19] Detroit, MI St. Cunegunda Church; [2] Dearborn, MI St. Barbara Church.
Granstrand, Charles P. '66 (NEW) Park Ridge, NJ Our Lady of Mercy Church.
Grant, Frederick A. '62 (BO) Senior Priests.
Grant, James '56 (SPK) Retired.
Grant, James A. '66 (PH) Warrington, PA St. Joseph Church.
Grant, Jeffery A. '82 (SFD) Casey, IL St. Charles Borromeo Church; Greenup, IL Christ the King Church; Marshall, IL St. Mary Church.
Grant, Matthew (BRK) Retired.
Grant, Matthew M. '65 (BRK) Absent on Sick Leave.
Grant, Peter J. '95 (ALX) Winnfield, LA Our Lady of Lourdes Church.
Grant, Robert '84 (DM) On Duty Outside the Diocese.
Grant, Robert J. '93 (HRT) Windsor, CT St. Gabriel's Church.
Grant, Robert L. '80 (DAV) [B] Davenport, IA St. Ambrose University.
Grant, Robert L. '84 (DAV) [B] Davenport, IA St. Ambrose University.
Grant, W. Douglas '80 (PRO) [1] East Providence, RI St. Brendan Church; Providence, RI Rhode Island Hospital.
Grant, William David '86 (LIN) Fairbury, NE St. Michael's Church.
Grant, Zachary (BO) [56] Boston, MA St. Patrick Church.
Grantz, Leon *c.p.* '46 (CHI) [N] Chicago, IL Passionist Community-Immaculate Conception Monastery.
Granville, Msgr. William A. (BO) Stoughton, MA New England Sinai Hospital.
Granville, Msgr. William A. '43 (BO) Senior Priests.
Granzotto, Peter *s.d.b.* '57 (NY) [2] Port Chester, NY Corpus Christi Church.
Grappoli, Frank B. *s.x.* '63 (FgM) Xaverian Foreign Missions.
Grappoli, Frank B. *s.x.* '63 (PAT) [M] Wayne, NJ Xaverian Missionary Fathers.
Grasha, Donald F. '84 (LA) Temple City, CA St. Luke the Evangelist Church.
Grasher, Albert, Jr. '86 (SPK) Chewelah, WA St. Mary of the Rosary Church; Springdale, WA Sacred Heart Church; Valley, WA Holy Ghost Church.
Grasing, John '88 (WIL) Ogletown, DE Holy Family Church.
Graskow, Paul '43 (STF) Retired.
Grass, Aloysius P. *c.m.* '51 (PH) [AA] Philadelphia, PA Congregation of the Mission.
Grass, Msgr. Don C. '61 (GRY) Crown Point, IN St. Mary Church.
Grass, Kenneth E. *c.m.* '56 (STL) [P] Perryville, MO Congregation of The Mission.
Grasselli, Renato '94 (NEW) [A] Kearny, NJ Redemptoris Mater.
Grassi, Dominic J. '73 (CHI) [106] Chicago, IL St. Josaphat Church.
Grassi, Timothy J. '00 (WH) Clarksburg, WV Immaculate Conception Church.
Grassius, Peregrine M. *o.s.m.* '59 (CHI) [17] Chicago, IL Assumption of the Blessed Virgin Mary Church.
Grassl, Joseph A. '50 (LC) Knowlton, WI St. Francis Xavier Church; Peplin, WI St. John the Baptist Church.
Grasso, Aldo *o.s.j.* '44 (MRY) [F] Santa Cruz, CA Oblates of St. Joseph Provincial House and Shrine.
Grasso, Anthony R. *c.s.c.* '78 (SCR) [C] Wilkes-Barre, PA Kings College; [C] Wilkes-Barre, PA Kings College.
Grasso, Joseph *c.pp.s.* '92 (ROC) [I] Rochester, NY Missionaries of the Precious Blood.
Grasso, Philip A. '43 (MAD) Retired.
Grasso, Richard '63 (PAT) On Duty Outside the Diocese.
Grasso, Richard E. '63 (ORL) Retired.
Grat, Timothy *s.c.j.* '78 (CHI) [N] Chicago, IL Priests of the Sacred Heart.
Grathwohl, John M. '55 (KAL) Portage, MI St. Catherine of Siena Church; Retired.
Gratkowski, Eugene W. '67 (CHI) [102] Chicago, IL St. John Berchmans Church.
Grattan, Bernard V. (ALT) Conemaugh, PA Assumption of B.V.M. Church.
Grattan, Bernard V. '75 (ALT) Johnstown, PA Conemaugh Memorial Medical Center; Johnstown, PA UPMC Lee Hospital; [D] Johnstown, PA Good Samaritan Medical Center.
Grattaroti, Robert A. '62 (WOR) Charlton City, MA St. Joseph's Church.
Gratto, Stephen H. '73 (OG) Morrisonville, NY St. Alexander Church; [3] Plattsburgh, NY St. Joseph Church.
Grauel, Frank B. '84 (L) [35] Louisville, KY Holy Spirit Church; Retired.
Grauls, Paul *s.d.b.* '62 (NY) [117] New York, NY St. Thomas the Apostle Church.
Grave de Peralta, Miguel '97 (NTN) Augusta, GA St. Ignatios of Antioch Church; On Special Projects.
Gravel, Claude *o.ss.t.* '81 (BAL) [S] Baltimore, MD Holy Trinity Monastery.
Gravel, Claude J. *o.s.s.t.* '81 (PH) Bristol, PA St. Ann Church.
Graven, John P. '57 (FAR) On Duty Outside the Diocese.
Graven, Thomas J. '68 (STU) Fairpoint, OH St. Joseph Church; Maynard, OH St. Stanislaus Church.
Graves, Alfred C. '67 (SPR) Absent on Leave.
Graves, C. Edwin, III '92 (LR) Helena, AR St. Mary's Church.
Graves, Clarence Edwin '92 (LR) Marianna, AR St. Andrew Church.
Graves, Joseph A. '56 (PEO) Retired.
Graves, W. Robert *c.s.sp.* '50 (VEN) [G] Sarasota, FL Congregation of the Holy Ghost.
Grawe, Michael *o.f.m.* '70 (FgM) Franciscan Foreign Missions.
Gray, Brian M. '86 (BGP) New Fairfield, CT St. Edward the Confessor Church; Danbury, CT Danbury Hospital.
Gray, Daniel J. '76 (PRO) Portsmouth, RI St. Anthony Church.
Gray, Edward J. *c.ss.r.* '58 (ORL) [F] New Smyrna Beach, FL Redemptorist Fathers of the Vice Province of Richmond.
Gray, Francis Jerome '49 (CHI) [N] Chicago, IL St. Peter's Friary.
Gray, Howard *s.j.* '61 (BO) [W] Chestnut Hill, MA The Jesuit Community at Boston College.
Gray, Howard J. *s.j.* '61 (DET) [K] Detroit, MI Jesuit Provincial Office-Detroit Province of the Society of Jesus.
Gray, James C. (STL) St. Louis, MO Barnes Hospital.
Gray, Jason '97 (PEO) [1] Ottawa, IL St. Columba Church.
Gray, John F. '86 (PT) [6] Pensacola, FL St. Anne's Church.
Gray, John H. *s.j.* '55 (BAL) [B] Baltimore, MD Loyola College in Maryland; [B] Baltimore, MD Loyola College in Maryland.
Gray, John Hugh *s.j.* '55 (SJ) [B] Santa Clara, CA Santa Clara University.
Gray, John W. '58 (PRO) [11] Providence, RI St. Charles Borromeo Church.
Gray, Jude J. *o.s.b.* '68 (MAN) [K] Manchester, NH St. Anselm Abbey.
Gray, Kevin J. '84 (HRT) New Hartford, CT Immaculate Conception Church.
Gray, Paul '85 (DAL) [2] Dallas, TX All Saints Church.
Gray, Msgr. Philip A. '60 (SCR) [5] Scranton, PA St. Francis Church.
Gray, Robert '88 (SJ) [4] San Jose, CA Five Wounds Portuguese National Church; Special Assignment.
Gray, Robert B. '57 (L) [24] Louisville, KY St. Elizabeth of Hungary Church; [72] Louisville, KY St. Therese Church; Retired.
Gray, Ronald *o.carm.* '43 (NEW) Leonia, NJ St. John the Evangelist's Church.
Gray, Sherman W., Jr. '70 (BGP) [7] Stamford, CT Holy Name of Jesus Church.
Gray, Timothy *s.c.j.* '78 (MIL) [P] Hales Corners, WI Priests of the Sacred Heart.
Graziadio, Msgr. Domenick T. '66 (RVC) Deer Park, NY SS. Cyril and Methodius Church.
Graziani, Joseph A. '45 (HRT) Retired.
Graziano, George R. *s.j.* '59 (FgM) Provinces.
Graziano, Gerard J. '61 (NEW) [2] Hackensack, NJ Immaculate Conception Church.
Graziano, J. Damien '67 (JOL) Oakbrook Terrace, IL Ascension of Our Lord Church.
Graziano, Peter N. '63 (FR) Attleboro Falls, MA St. Mark's Church.
Grbes, Jozo *o.f.m.* (CHI) [99] Chicago, IL St. Jerome Church.
Greaney, Francis M. '52 (BO) Senior Priests.
Greaney, John '56 (HBG) Retired.
Greaney, Thomas *o.s.m.* '70 (SFE) Belen, NM Our Lady of Belen Church.
Greaney, Thomas M. *o.s.m.* '70 (CHI) [N] Chicago, IL Order of Friar Servants of Mary (Servites) United States of America Province, Inc.
Greany, Brendan *c.ss.r.* '63 (HBG) [H] Ephrata, PA St. Clement's Mission House.
Greany, Brendan P. *c.ss.r.* '63 (HBG) Ephrata, PA Mother of Perpetual Help Church.
Greatorex, Robert W. (LC) Retired.
Greatorex, Robert W. '57 (LC) [I] Stevens Point, WI St. Joseph Congregational Home.
Greaves, Gerald F. '74 (NEW) Allendale, NJ Guardian Angel Church.
Greaves, John G. '58 (PRO) [1] Cranston, RI St. Ann Church.
Greb, Michael *o.f.m.cap.* '89 (PIT) Cabot, PA St. Joseph Church; [O] Herman, PA St. Mary's Friary.
Grebasch, Richard L. '58 (MIL) Retired.
Grecco, Donald '66 (WIL) Perryville, MD Church of the Good Shepherd.
Grecco, Robert J. '93 (PIT) [1] Pittsburgh, PA St. Paul Church.
Grech, Joseph '52 (MRY) Santa Margarita, CA Santa Margarita de Cortona Church.
Greco, Anthony F. '79 (WIL) Secretary, MD Our Lady of Good Counsel Church.
Greco, Evan J. *o.f.m.* '58 (NY) Yulan, NY St. Anthony of Padua Church.
Greco, Raymond *o.s.b.* '63 (MRY) [F] San Luis Obispo, CA Monastery of the Risen Christ.
Greco, Robert *o.carm.* '55 (NY) Middletown, NY Our Lady of Mt. Carmel Church.
Greeley, Andrew M. '54 (CHI) Retired.
Greeley, Msgr. Joseph F. '74 (LA) Wilmington, CA Holy Family Church.
Green, Austin E. *o.p.* '53 (DAL) [K] Irving, TX Dominican Priory of St. Albert the Great.
Green, Bernard *s.d.s.* '73 (GLP) Cibecue, AZ St. Catherine Church.
Green, Charles C. '95 (WDC) [7] Washington, DC St. Augustine Church.
Green, David E. '88 (PRO) [11] Warwick, RI St. Timothy Church.
Green, Fred *s.j.* '58 (FgM) Provinces.
Green, Msgr. Gerard L. '56 (BUF) Retired.
Green, Gregory A. *c.s.c.* '62 (FTW) [B] Notre Dame, IN University of Notre Dame Du Lac; [J] Notre Dame, IN Holy Cross Community, Corby Hall, University of Notre Dame.
Green, Msgr. James P. '76 (PH) On Duty Outside the Archdiocese.
Green, Michael R. *o.s.b.* '70 (DET) [B] Oxford, MI St. Benedict Monastery.
Green, Romuald *o.f.m.* '55 (WDC) [M] Silver Spring, MD Gemelli House.
Green, Ronald (NY) Manhattan, NY Terence Cardinal Cooke Health Care Center.
Green, Ronald '96 (MRY) Watsonville, CA St. Patrick Church.
Green, Ronald L. *m.m.* '85 (NY) [DD] Maryknoll, NY Maryknoll Fathers and Brothers.
Green, Thomas H. *s.j.* '63 (FgM) Provinces.
Green, Msgr. Thomas J. '63 (BGP) On Duty Outside the Diocese.
Green, Thomas J. '63 (WDC) [C] Washington, DC Catholic University of America, The.
Green, Thomas P. *s.j.* '61 (NY) [5] New York, NY St. Aloysius Church.
Green, William H. '63 (SUP) Cable, WI St. Ann Church; Hayward, WI St. Joseph's Church.
Green, William L. *c.m.* '55 (BUF) [C] Niagara University, NY Niagara University; [O] Niagara University, NY Vincentian Community at Niagara University.
Greenburg, Alcuin E. '55 (GAL) [K] Houston, TX The Catholic Chaplain Corps.
Greene, Daniel P. '58 (YAK) Military Chaplains.
Greene, Francis *o.s.f.s.* '48 (WIL) [I] Childs, MD Oblates of St. Francis De Sales.
Greene, Gordon L. '94 (KAL) Albion, MI St. John the Evangelist Church.
Greene, J. Gerard *m.m.* '43 (NY) [DD] Maryknoll, NY Maryknoll Fathers and Brothers; [DD] Maryknoll, NY Maryknoll Fathers and Brothers.
Greene, James F. '61 (FR) [5] New Bedford, MA Our

Lady of Fatima Church.
Greene, John C. '85 (GAY) Absent on Leave.
Greene, John L. '76 (SFR) [35] San Francisco, CA St. Monica Church; San Francisco, CA San Francisco Fire Department.
Greene, Michael *c.p.* '82 (BRK) [V] Jamaica, NY Immaculate Conception Monastery; [X] Jamaica, NY Bishop Molloy Retreat House for Laymen.
Greene, Michael M. '79 (BRK) [229] Queens, NY Presentation of the Blessed Virgin Mary Church.
Greene, Padraig '76 (OAK) Pleasanton, CA The Catholic Community of Pleasanton Church.
Greene, Richard '65 (LAF) Patterson, LA St. Joseph Church.
Greene, Robert W. *m.m.* '37 (NY) [DD] Maryknoll, NY Maryknoll Fathers and Brothers.
Greene, Thomas S. '55 (SPR) Retired; [I] Springfield, MA St. Michael's Residence.
Greene, Msgr. William L. '50 (BR) Retired.
Greenfield, James J. *o.s.f.s.* '90 (WDC) [B] Washington, DC Oblates of St. Francis de Sales; [S] Washington, DC Archdiocesan Campus Ministry.
Greenhalgh, Donald C. '84 (ARL) Fairfax, VA St. Mary of Sorrows Church.
Greenlaw, Martin '68 (SFR) Retired.
Greenleaf, Daniel P. '95 (PRT) [5] Lewiston, ME St. Patrick's Church; [B] Lewiston, ME St. Dominic Regional High School.
Greenough, Patrick *o.f.m.conv.* '88 (CHI) [N] Libertyville, IL Marytown, Our Lady of Fatima Friary; [Q] Libertyville, IL Marytown, U.S. National Center of the Militia of the Immaculata Movement.
Greenslade, Robert J. '54 (DEN) [11] Denver, CO Holy Family Church; [35] Denver, CO St. Mary Magdalene's Church.
Greenwald, Alfred E. '58 (GAL) Retired.
Greenway, George G. '87 (SPR) Retired.
Greenwell, Charles C. '82 (SAN) [2] San Angelo, TX Holy Angels Church.
Greenwell, Joseph *c.ss.r.* '48 (LAF) Crowley, LA Immaculate Heart of Mary Church.
Greenwell, Michael *o.carm.* '79 (JOL) [J] Darien, IL Carmelite Provincial Office.
Greenwell, Michael *o.carm.* '79 (SFR) [27] San Francisco, CA St. James Church; San Francisco, CA Kaiser Hospital San Francisco; San Francisco, CA St. Mary's Medical Center; [J] San Francisco, CA St. Mary's Medical Center.
Greenwood, Kevin L. '90 (STU) Absent on Leave.
Greer, G. Michael '81 (COV) Erlanger, KY St. Barbara Church.
Greer, Michael '75 (MIA) [6] Miami, FL Good Shepherd Church.
Greff, Francis A. *c.s.sp.* '47 (FgM) Holy Ghost Foreign Missions.
Grega, Bernard F. '62 (ALT) Colver, PA Holy Family Church.
Gregoire, Paul L. '55 (MAN) Dover, NH St. Charles Church.
Gregoire, Wilfrid G. '56 (PRO) [2] Westerly, RI Immaculate Conception Church.
Gregorek, Joseph C. *v.f.* '65 (E) [B] Erie, PA Gannon University.
Gregorek, Stan M. '66 (PIT) Natrona Heights, PA Our Lady of the Most Blessed Sacrament Church.
Gregori, Anthony F. '53 (GF) Retired.
Gregori, Emidio O. '58 (BGP) Retired.
Gregorie, Jocelyn *c.s.sp.* '86 (PIT) [B] Pittsburgh, PA Duquesne University of the Holy Ghost.
Gregorio, Robert J. '68 (CAM) Blue Anchor, NJ St. Lucy's Church.
Gregoris, Nicholas L. '97 (SCR) On Duty Outside the Diocese; [M] Mount Pocono, PA Newman House.
Gregory, James T. '99 (HRT) Southington, CT St. Thomas Church.
Gregory, Kenneth '73 (ALB) Berlin, NY Sacred Heart Church; Grafton, NY St. John Francis Regis Church; Albany, NY Albany Medical Center Hospital; Special Assignment; [G] Watervliet, NY St. Colman's Home; [M] Watervliet, NY St. Colman's Convent.
Gregory, Peter A. '73 (SPR) [5] Pittsfield, MA St. Charles Church.
Gregory, Robert S. '69 (KC) [9] Kansas City, MO St. Elizabeth's Church.
Gregovich, Lawrence B. '72 (SPC) Leave of Absence.
Grehl, Paul F. *o.s.f.s.* '60 (LAN) [B] Jackson, MI Lumen Christi High School.
Grehl, Paul F. *o.s.f.s.* '79 (LAN) Manitou Beach, MI St. Mary on the Lake Church.
Greig, Msgr. Harry D., II '76 (LKC) [1] Lake Charles, LA Immaculate Conception Church.
Greig, Msgr. Kenneth R. '67 (BEA) Groves, TX St. Peter the Apostle Church.
Grein, Blane *o.f.m.* '62 (GLP) Chinle, AZ Our Lady of Fatima Church; [A] Chinle, AZ Native American Lay Ministry and Diaconate Program.
Greiner, James A. '63 (OKL) Mustang, OK Church of the Holy Spirit.
Greiner, Kenneth A. '53 (ALT) Retired.
Greiner, Lawrence (SB) Retired.
Greiner, Lawrence '37 (SAG) Retired.
Greiner, Robert M. '93 (BAK) Nyssa, OR St. Bridget of Kildare Church.
Greisen, Thomas A. '82 (OM) [37] Omaha, NE St. Philip Neri Church.
Greiten, Gregory J. '92 (MIL) [4] Menomonee Falls, WI St. Mary Church.
Greiwe, Edward *o.s.c.* '64 (STP) Anoka, MN St. Stephen Church.
Greiwe, Edward *o.s.c.* '67 (STP) [N] Anoka, MN Crosier Community of Anoka.
Grek, Richard *c.r.* '67 (CHI) [N] Chicago, IL Provincial Office of the Congregation of the Resurrection.
Grek, Richard *c.r.* '67 (RCK) [A] Woodstock, IL Resurrection Center Retreat House.
Greka, David '62 (AMA) On Duty Outside the Diocese.
Greka, David E. '62 (GAY) [2] Alpena, MI St. Bernard Church.
Grelak, Andrew T. '71 (BO) [3] Chelsea, MA St. Stanislaus Church.
Grell, Loras K. '96 (LIN) Dwight, NE Assumption Church.
Grellinger, R. Michael '62 (MIL) [1] Pewaukee, WI Queen of Apostles Church.
Grembla, Joseph P. '57 (CHI) [33] Chicago, IL St. Bruno Church.
Grembocki, Joseph L. (ALN) Slatington, PA Assumption B.V.M. Church.
Gremillion, Rickey J. '98 (ALX) [6] Alexandria, LA St. Rita Church.
Gremmels, John '91 (FWT) Keller, TX St. Elizabeth Ann Seton Church.
Grenache, Claude *a.a.* (BO) [CC] Waltham, MA Bentley College Spiritual Life Center.
Grenache, Claude *a.a.* '66 (BO) [W] Boston, MA Assumptionist Center.
Grendler, Albert O. '59 (SC) Spirit Lake, IA St. Mary's Church.
Grenham, John P. '80 (NO) St. Bernard, LA St. Bernard Church.
Grenham, John Patrick '80 (NO) Florissant, LA San Pedro Pescador Church.
Grenham, Thomas *s.p.s.* (BO) [16] Boston, MA St. Cecilia Church.
Grenier, Louis L. *s.j.* '49 (FgM) Provinces.
Grennan, James P. '51 (SAL) Logan, KS St. John's Church; Stockton, KS St. Thomas Church.
Grennan, Lawrence E. '66 (SAL) Manhattan, KS Seven Dolors Church.
Grennan, Thomas J. '48 (NO) Retired.
Grennon, John *o.c.d.* '97 (MIL) [P] Holy Hill, WI Discalced Carmelite Monastery.
Grenon, Paul R. '78 (PRO) [10] Woonsocket, RI Our Lady, Queen of Martyrs Church.
Gres-Gayer, Jacques '69 (WDC) [C] Washington, DC Catholic University of America, The.
Greskiewicz, Joseph A. '69 (SCR) Plains, PA SS. Peter and Paul Church.
Greskoviak, Neri *o.f.m.* '63 (PEO) Benson, IL St. John Church; Roanoke, IL St. Joseph Church.
Greskowiak, Stephen '89 (VNN) Anchorage, AK Saint Nicholas of Myra Church.
Gresock, Thomas G. '85 (BUF) Absent on Leave.
Gress, Armand E. *o.s.b.* '37 (CLV) [O] Cleveland, OH Benedictine Order of Cleveland.
Gretchko, A. Edward '72 (PBR) Ashtabula, OH St. Nicholas Church.
Gretchko, A. Edward '72 (Y) Massillon, OH St. Mary's Church.
Gretz, James R. (PIT) Castle Shannon, PA St. Anne Church.
Grevatch, William N. '64 (LC) [7] Wausau, WI St. Michael Church.
Grevencamp, Raymond *c.pp.s.* '49 (CIN) [B] Carthagena, OH St. Charles.
Greving, Dan '97 (SC) Livermore, IA Sacred Heart Church.
Greving, Daniel M. '97 (SC) [6] Sioux City, IA Immaculate Conception Church; St. Benedict, IA St. Benedict's Church; Wesley, IA St. Joseph's Church.
Greving, Louis H. '46 (SC) Retired.
Grewe, Michael W. '79 (OM) [21] Omaha, NE St. James Church.
Grey, Michael *c.s.sp.* '79 (PIT) [B] Pittsburgh, PA Duquesne University of the Holy Ghost.
Greytak, William '56 (HEL) Boulder, MT St. Catherine Church; Boulder, MT Boulder River School and Hospital; [A] Helena, MT Carroll College; [B] Helena, MT Carroll College.
Grib, Philip J. *s.j.* '72 (CHI) [54] Chicago, IL St. Eugene Church; [D] Chicago, IL St. Ignatius Jesuit Community.
Grib, Robert *s.j.* '72 (CHI) Northbrook, IL Our Lady of the Brook Church.
Grib, Robert I. *s.j.* '72 (CHI) [T] Barrington, IL Bellarmine Hall.
Gribben, Andrew G. *o.praem.* '94 (CHI) [N] Chicago, IL Premonstratensian Fathers and Brothers (Norbertines).
Gribbin, Msgr. Robert C. '47 (HBG) Abbottstown, PA Immaculate Heart of Mary Church.
Gribble, G. Michael '81 (COL) [1] Columbus, OH St. Joseph Church.
Gribble, Richard E. *c.s.c.* '89 (FR) [A] North Easton, MA Holy Cross Fathers Religious.
Gribbon, John J. '50 (BRK) [149] Queens, NY St. Anastasia Church.
Gribbon, Joseph *c.ss.r.* '56 (ORL) [F] New Smyrna Beach, FL St. Alphonsus Villa-Redemptorist Fathers and Brothers.
Gribbon, Michael C. '81 (BRK) [238] Queens, NY Sacred Heart Church.
Gribik, John '89 (SJP) Jeannette, PA St. Demetrius Church.
Grice, Edward '80 (NO) [4] Kenner, LA St. Jerome Church.
Grieco, Michael S. '83 (LA) Simi Valley, CA St. Rose of Lima Church.
Grieco, Msgr. Nicholas V. '59 (BGP) Weston, CT St. Francis of Assisi Church.
Grieman, Gerald G. '79 (STP) [33] St. Paul, MN St. Therese (Highland Catholic Community) Church; Retired.
Griener, George E. *s.j.* '73 (OAK) [A] Berkeley, CA The Jesuit School of Theology at Berkeley; [A] Berkeley, CA The Jesuit School of Theology at Berkeley; [N] Berkeley, CA Jesuit Community at Jesuit School of Theology at Berkeley.
Grier, Matthew *m.h.m.* '69 (NY) Shrub Oak, NY Saint Elizabeth Ann Seton Church.
Gries, Andrew *o.c.s.o.* '59 (ARL) [J] Berryville, VA Cistercian Abbey of Our Lady of the Holy Cross.
Gries, Eugene *o.praem.* '68 (SFE) [12] Albuquerque, NM Our Lady of Most Holy Rosary Church; [I] Albuquerque, NM Santa Maria de la Vid Priory.
Griesbach, John '76 (FRS) Kerman, CA St. Patrick Church.
Griesedieck, Msgr. Edmund O. '65 (STL) Wildwood, MO St. Alban Roe Church.
Griesemer, Edward *s.c.j.* '57 (MIL) [P] Franklin, WI Villa Maria; [W] Wauwatosa, WI Milwaukee Archdiocesan Holy Name Union.
Griffen-Smolenski, Thomas J. *s.j.* '00 (HON) [G] Honolulu, HI Jesuit Fathers House.
Griffey, Brendan M. '74 (JC) Missionary Assignment in Peru.
Griffin, Barry *s.d.s.* '64 (NSH) McMinnville, TN St. Catherine Church.
Griffin, Charles R. '56 (COL) Chillicothe, OH St. Peter Church; Chillicothe, OH Chillicothe Correctional Institution; Chillicothe, OH Ross Correctional Institution and Honor Camp; Retired.
Griffin, Msgr. Charles T. '58 (BUF) [32] Buffalo, NY Holy Spirit Church.
Griffin, David G. '66 (BUF) [6] Niagara Falls, NY St. Leo Church.
Griffin, David R. *o.s.b.* '76 (GBG) [H] Latrobe, PA Saint Vincent Archabbey.
Griffin, Devin *o.carm.* '75 (JOL) [J] Darien, IL Carmelite Provincial Office.
Griffin, Edward V. *o.s.a.* '49 (PH) [143] Philadelphia, PA St. Rita of Cascia Church.
Griffin, George J. '73 (ARL) [2] Alexandria, VA Good Shepherd Church.
Griffin, James *c.m.f.* '48 (PHX) Prescott, AZ Sacred Heart Church.
Griffin, James '49 (NY) Retired.
Griffin, James '82 (RIC) Blacksburg, VA St. Mary & Newman Community Church.
Griffin, John '72 (SR) Rohnert Park, CA St. Elizabeth Seton Church.
Griffin, John Cullen '77 (MRY) Corralitos, CA Holy Eucharist Church.
Griffin, Joseph '82 (SAG) Oakley, MI St. Michael Church.
Griffin, Joseph J. *o.s.f.s.* '56 (PH) [AA] Philadelphia, PA Oblates of St. Francis De Sales.
Griffin, Joseph M. '82 (SAG) Chesaning, MI Our Lady of Perpetual Help Church.
Griffin, Joseph T. *c.s.p.* '46 (BO) [W] Boston, MA Paulist Fathers Residence.
Griffin, Joseph T. *c.s.p.* '46 (NY) [DD] Jamaica Estates, NY Paulist Fathers Generalate.
Griffin, Michael *o.c.d.* '50 (MIL) [P] Holy Hill, WI Discalced Carmelite Monastery.
Griffin, Michael '90 (SFS) White, SD St. Paul Church; [H] Brookings, SD Diocesan Newman Apostolate; [H] Brookings, SD Pius XII Student Center.
Griffin, Michael J. '49 (MAN) Hampton, NH Our Lady of the Miraculous Medal Church.
Griffin, Noel '64 (LA) On Sick Leave.
Griffin, Patrick E. '67 (STP) [33] Minneapolis, MN St. Stephen Church.
Griffin, Msgr. Patrick J. '45 (COL) Retired.
Griffin, Patrick J. *c.m.* '79 (RVC) [A] Huntington, NY Diocesan Seminary of the Immaculate Conception; [M] Oyster Bay, NY Vincentian Community.
Griffin, Paul D. '95 (BGP) Leave of Absence.
Griffin, Richard J. '42 (PH) Retired.
Griffin, Robert E. *s.j.* (B) [D] Mesa, ID Marymount Hermitage, Inc., Hermit Sisters of Mary.
Griffin, Robert E. *s.j.* '61 (LA) [Q] Los Angeles, CA Columbiere House.

Griffin, Robert F. '49 (MAN) Retired.
Griffin, Thomas *o.s.a.* (CHI) [J] Chicago, IL Holy Cross Hospital.
Griffin, Thomas A. *s.j.* '58 (MIA) [5] Miami, FL Gesu Church.
Griffin-Smolenski, Thomas *s.j.* (HON) [E] Honolulu, HI St. Francis Healthcare System of Hawaii.
Griffith, Darragh '97 (ATL) [2] Atlanta, GA Holy Cross Church.
Griffith, Edwin '64 (LSC) Retired.
Griffith, Gavin *o.f.m.* '65 (STL) [T] Dittmer, MO Il Ritiro-The Little Retreat.
Griffith, Sidney H. *s.t.* '65 (WDC) [C] Washington, DC Catholic University of America, The; [M] Riverdale, MD Holy Spirit Missionary Cenacle.
Griffith, Sydney (BAL) Glen Burnie, MD Holy Trinity Church.
Griffith, Thomas *s.v.d.* '69 (CHI) [B] Techny, IL Divine Word Residence; [N] Techny, IL Society of the Divine Word, Provincial Headquarter-Chicago Prov.; [N] Techny, IL Society of the Divine Word, Provincial Headquarter-Chicago Prov.; [N] Techny, IL Society of the Divine Word, Provincial Headquarter-Chicago Prov.; [X] Techny, IL Blessed Arnold Religious Charitable Trust.
Griffiths, James '56 (SJP) Retired.
Griffiths, John M. '76 (CHI) [177] Chicago, IL Queen of Angels Church.
Griffiths, Thomas *c.p.* '57 (BRK) [V] Jamaica, NY Immaculate Conception Monastery.
Grifone, Fabian *o.f.m.* '54 (NY) [79] New York, NY Most Precious Blood Church.
Grigassy, Daniel P. *o.f.m.* '77 (WDC) [B] Silver Spring, MD Holy Name College.
Grigus, John *o.f.m.conv.* (CHI) [N] Libertyville, IL Marytown, Our Lady of Fatima Friary.
Grigus, Paschal *o.f.m.* '53 (MIL) [P] Burlington, WI Queen of Peace Friary.
Grile, Harry A. *c.ss.r.* '63 (STL) [P] Liguori, MO St. Clement Health Care Center.
Grile, Harry A. *c.ss.r.* '68 (STL) [V] Liguori, MO Redemptorist Fathers dba Liguori Publications.
Grile, Patrick *c.ss.r.* '71 (STP) Brooklyn Center, MN St. Alphonsus Church.
Grill, Msgr. Philip L. '43 (LA) Retired.
Grilliot, Thomas J. '76 (CIN) Piqua, OH St. Mary Church.
Grimaldi, Joseph R. '83 (BRK) [79] Brooklyn, NY St. Mark's Church.
Grimaldi, Robert B. *s.j.* '68 (FgM) Provinces.
Grimalia, Msgr. Vincent J. '68 (SCR) [1] Plymouth, PA Nativity of the Blessed Virgin Mary Church.
Grimes, Donald J. *c.s.c.* '73 (SCR) [C] Wilkes-Barre, PA Kings College; [C] Wilkes-Barre, PA Kings College.
Grimes, Edwin T. *o.s.a.* '36 (PH) [AA] Villanova, PA St. Thomas Monastery.
Grimes, Msgr. J. Colby '78 (COL) New Albany, OH Church of the Resurrection.
Grimes, John '71 (FgM) Society of St. James the Apostle.
Grimes, John C. '00 (MET) Woodbridge, NJ St. James Church.
Grimes, John J. '71 (BO) Society of St. James the Apostle.
Grimes, Jordan K. *c.p.* '49 (ORL) [F] Orlando, FL Bethany House of Beutel.
Grimes, Msgr. Kenneth F. '57 (COL) [34] Columbus, OH Our Lady of Peace Church.
Grimes, Mark E. '64 (BGP) Georgetown, CT Sacred Heart Church.
Grimes, Price D., Jr. '88 (OKL) Absent on Sick Leave.
Grimes, Raymond P. '55 (PBL) Retired.
Grimes, Robert R. *s.j.* (NY) [C] Bronx, NY Fordham University.
Grimes, Robert R. *s.j.* '84 (NY) [DD] New York, NY Jesuit Community at Fordham University.
Grimm, Robert B. *s.j.* '76 (FgM) Provinces.
Grimm, Robert B. *s.j.* '76 (P) [L] Portland, OR Jesuit Provincial Office (Society of Jesus, Oregon Prov.); [L] Portland, OR Colombiere Community.
Grimm, William J. *m.m.* '77 (FgM) Maryknoll Foreign Missions.
Grimme, D. Timothy '77 (ALT) Bellefonte, PA St. John the Evangelist's Church.
Grimmer, James A. '54 (BUF) East Eden, NY St. Mary Church.
Grimmond, Christopher J. '87 (OM) Columbus, NE St. Anthony Church.
Grinena, Agustin '46 (PCE) Penuelas, PR Sacred Heart Church.
Griner, William S. '61 (L) [25] Louisville, KY Epiphany Church.
Grinis, Bruno B. '40 (CHI) [166] Chicago, IL SS. Peter and Paul Church; Retired.
Grinis, Julian G. '39 (CHI) [1] Lemont, IL St. Alphonsus Church; Retired.
Grinko, Frank X. *o.f.m.cap.* '81 (SAL) Victoria, KS St. Fidelis Church; Vincent, KS St. Boniface Church; [C] Victoria, KS St. John's Rest Home; [D] Victoria, KS St. Fidelis Friary.
Grinnell, Horace H. '74 (ARL) Falls Church, VA St. Anthony's Church.
Grinnen, John *t.o.r.* '72 (PH) [AA] Fairless Hills, PA St. Anthony Friary.
Grinsell, John *s.d.b.* '71 (MIA) [25] Miami, FL St. Kieran Church.
Grippe, Louis A. '69 (SCR) [2] Swoyersville, PA Holy Name/St. Mary's Church.
Grippo, Robert F. '72 (NY) [190] Bronx, NY St. Theresa of the Infant Jesus Church.
Gripshover, Ronald J., Jr. '96 (ARL) [1] Arlington, VA Cathedral of St. Thomas More.
Grisaitis, Joseph N. '64 (BRK) [151] Queens, NY St. Ann's Church.
Grise, J. Clifford '45 (BGP) Retired.
Grismer, Raymond J. '33 (CLV) Sheffield, OH St. Teresa of Avila Church; Retired.
Grispino, Frank *s.m.* '56 (DET) [K] Livonia, MI Marist Fathers & Brothers Community.
Griswold, Edward J. '73 (TR) Colts Neck, NJ St. Mary Church.
Grix, Robert *o.f.m.cap.* (NY) [DD] New York, NY Immaculate Conception Friary.
Grizzelle-Reid, Paul *s.c.j.* '72 (MIL) [B] Hales Corners, WI Sacred Heart School of Theology; [P] Hales Corners, WI Sacred Heart Monastery.
Groarke, Francis P. '73 (PH) [42] Philadelphia, PA St. Edmond Church.
Grob, Jeffrey S. '92 (CHI) Graduate Studies.
Grochowski, Bernard J. '63 (WOR) Military Chaplains.
Grochowski, Robert *s.v.d.* '96 (FgM) Society of the Divine Word Foreign Missions.
Grodavent, Msgr. Thomas J. '45 (WDC) Retired.
Grodecki, Henry W. *c.m.* '75 (STL) [P] St. Louis, MO Lazarist Residence.
Groden, Msgr. Michael F. '65 (BO) [16] Boston, MA St. Cecilia Church.
Grodnicki, Robert *o.s.a.* (CHI) [125] Chicago, IL St. Mary of the Lake Church.
Groenewold, Robert E. *s.j.* '62 (NY) [FF] Staten Island, NY Mount Manresa Jesuit Retreat House.
Groenewold, Thomas W. '87 (RVC) Franklin Square, NY St. Catherine of Sienna Church.
Groesch, Edward '51 (SFD) Greenfield, IL St. Michael Church; Hagaman, IL St. Catherine Church.
Groeschel, Benedict J. *c.f.r.* '59 (BRK) [P] Brooklyn, NY St. Francis Home for Boys.
Groeschel, Benedict J. *c.f.r.* '59 (NEW) [K] Hoboken, NJ Good Counsel, Inc. (St. Francis Home); [K] Hoboken, NJ Good Counsel, Inc. (St. Francis Home).
Groeschel, Benedict J. *c.f.r.* '59 (NY) [A] Yonkers, NY St. Joseph's Seminary; [DD] New York, NY St. Crispin Friary; [FF] Larchmont, NY Trinity Retreat; [FF] Larchmont, NY St. Francis Retreat, Inc.
Grogan, Brendan '61 (MIA) Absent on Leave.
Grogan, Francis E. *c.s.c.* '55 (FR) [I] North Dartmouth, MA Holy Cross Mission House.
Grogan, Gerald P. '60 (VEN) Avon Park, FL Our Lady of Grace Church.
Grogan, J. Clyde '68 (BEL) [2] East St. Louis, IL St. John Francis Regis Church.
Grogan, James Clyde '68 (BEL) [4] East St. Louis, IL St. Patrick Church.
Grogan, James M. '95 (STP) Cottage Grove, MN St. Rita Church.
Grogan, Richard P. *s.j.* '73 (NY) [FF] Staten Island, NY Mount Manresa Jesuit Retreat House.
Grogan, Todd '90 (CIN) Englewood, OH St. Paul's Church.
Grogan, Vincent B. *o.f.m.* '63 (NY) [35] New York, NY St. Francis of Assisi Church.
Grogan, William E. '83 (PH) Kimberton, PA St. Basil the Great Church.
Grogan, William P. '76 (CHI) [98] Chicago, IL St. Jerome Church.
Groh, Chris '79 (JOL) [2] Joliet, IL Holy Cross Church.
Groh, Christopher '79 (JOL) [16] Joliet, IL St. Mary Nativity Church.
Grohe, Eugene J. *c.ss.r.* '42 (NY) Port Ewen, NY Presentation of the Virgin Mary Church.
Grohe, Eugene J. *c.ss.r.* '50 (NY) [DD] Esopus, NY Redemptorist Priests and Brothers C.Ss.R. (Province of Baltimore).
Groher, Robert C. '66 (GB) Special Assignment.
Grollig, Anthony J. *s.j.* '55 (FgM) Provinces.
Grollig, Francis X. *s.j.* '53 (DET) [P] Clarkston, MI Colombiere Center.
Grollmes, Eugene E. *s.j.* '64 (STL) [P] St. Louis, MO Jesuit Community Corporation at St. Louis University - Jesuit Hall.
Gromadzki, Stanely G. '89 (MET) South River, NJ St. Mary of Ostrabrama Church.
Groncki, Msgr. Richard '66 (NEW) [1] Newark, NJ Cathedral Basilica of the Sacred Heart.
Groner, Eric *s.v.d.* '96 (JKS) Greenville, MS Sacred Heart Church.
Groner, John W. '71 (JC) Richland, MO St. Jude Church; Waynesville, MO St. Robert Bellarmine Church.
Gronert, Stephen F. '86 (WCH) Marion, KS Holy Family Church.
Gronifilo, Alejandro '74 (TR) Brick Town, NJ St. Dominic Church.
Gronowski, Ronald V. '69 (GAY) Tawas City, MI Holy Family Church.
Gronski, Peter '71 (STF) Yonkers, NY St. Michael Church.
Groody, Daniel *c.s.c.* (SB) Coachella, CA Our Lady of Soledad Church.
Groody, Daniel *c.s.c.* '93 (FTW) [B] Notre Dame, IN University of Notre Dame Du Lac; [J] Notre Dame, IN Holy Cross Community, Corby Hall, University of Notre Dame.
Groody, Daniel G. *c.s.c.* '92 (OAK) [N] Berkeley, CA Holy Cross Fathers-Holy Cross Center.
Groover, Henry B. *o.p.* '92 (MIA) [18] Miami, FL St. Dominic Church; [H] Miami, FL Dominican Fathers of Miami, Inc.
Groover, Henry B. *o.p.* '92 (NO) [P] New Orleans, LA Dominican Friars, Southern Dominican Province of St. Martin de Porres.
Gros, Edwin L. (NO) [C] New Orleans, LA Loyola University New Orleans.
Grosch, Robert D. '74 (GF) Havre, MT St. Jude Thaddeus Church.
Groschen, Ronald *m.s.* '63 (GAL) Friendswood, TX Mary, Queen Church.
Groshek, Msgr. Richard J. '62 (LAN) [13] Flint, MI St. Pius X Church.
Grosko, Joseph P. '59 (PIT) [64] Pittsburgh, PA Resurrection Church.
Gross, Barry '75 (LFT) On Duty Outside the Diocese.
Gross, Barry R. '75 (WDC) [E] Wheaton, MD Good Counsel High School.
Gross, Donald '59 (LFT) Dunnington, IN St. Mary Church.
Gross, Donald L. '59 (LFT) Fowler, IN Sacred Heart of Jesus Church.
Gross, Francis *o.s.f.s.* '52 (BUF) [7] Niagara Falls, NY St. Mary of the Cataract Church.
Gross, Francis J. *o.s.f.s.* (FgM) Oblates of St. Francis de Sales Foreign Missions.
Gross, Gary L. '83 (LIN) Wahoo, NE St. Wenceslaus Church; [C] Wahoo, NE Bishop Neumann Jr.-Sr. High School; [M] Wahoo, NE Bishop Neumann High School Endowment Fund.
Gross, Gerard *o.c.s.o.* '78 (ATL) [J] Conyers, GA The Monastery of the Holy Spirit.
Gross, James '99 (FAR) Devils Lake, ND St. Joseph's Church.
Gross, Joseph T. *o.ss.t* '70 (BAL) [S] Baltimore, MD Holy Trinity Monastery.
Gross, Kenneth A. '71 (DM) [1] Council Bluffs, IA Holy Family Church.
Gross, Lawrence A. '66 (ROC) Honeoye Falls, NY St. Paul of the Cross Church.
Gross, Lawrence C. '53 (HBG) Danville, PA St. Joseph Church; Danville, PA Geisinger Medical Center.
Gross, Lawrence F. (ROC) Lima, NY St. Rose Church.
Gross, Lee W. '87 (ARL) On Duty Outside the Diocese.
Gross, Lee W. '87 (BAL) [A] Emmitsburg, MD Mount St. Mary's Seminary; [A] Emmitsburg, MD Mount St. Mary's Seminary.
Gross, Matthew *o.f.m.cap.* '61 (DEN) [M] Denver, CO Annunciation Friary.
Gross, Ralph C. '70 (MIL) [51] Milwaukee, WI St. Margaret Mary Church.
Gross, Richard C. '62 (NU) Watkins, MN Church of St. Anthony.
Gross, Richard J. '63 (FAR) Special Assignment.
Gross, Richard K. *s.j.* '76 (NOR) Storrs, CT St. Thomas Aquinas Church; [K] Willimantic, CT Campus Ministry.
Gross, Stephen F. '66 (LC) [1] Wausau, WI Church of the Resurrection.
Gross, Thomas L. '75 (HON) Kailua, HI St. John Vianney Church.
Gross, Msgr. Val *v.d.* '63 (FAR) [4] Fargo, ND SS. Anne & Joachim Church.
Grossenburg, John Anthony '99 (RC) Philip, SD Sacred Heart Church.
Grosser, Msgr. Elmer J. '46 (COV) Southgate, KY St. Therese of the Infant Jesus Church; Retired.
Grossi, Anthony J. *o.s.b.* '99 (GBG) [H] Latrobe, PA Saint Vincent Archabbey.
Grosskopf, Albert A. *s.j.* '83 (SFR) [25] San Francisco, CA St. Ignatius Church; [N] San Francisco, CA Jesuit Community at University of San Francisco.
Grossman, John A. '71 (DUB) [D] Cedar Rapids, IA Xavier High School.
Grosso, James D. '79 (BGP) [4] Danbury, CT St. Joseph Church.
Grosso, Lucius *o.f.m.* '64 (PHX) [19] Phoenix, AZ St. Mary's Basilica Church.
Grote, Alan W. '82 (GBG) [1] Latrobe, PA Holy Family Church.
Groth, Msgr. Ronald '69 (LKC) [8] Lake Charles, LA Our Lady Queen of Heaven Church.
Grothjan, James *c.pp.s.* '51 (CIN) [M] Dayton, OH Provincial Office of the Cincinnati Province of the Society of the Precious Blood.
Grotovsky, Ed '94 (JOL) Manteno, IL St. Joseph Church.

Groucutt, George L. '46 (E) Retired.
Grous, Albin J. '87 (PH) [107] Philadelphia, PA St. Monica Church.
Grove, Stanley *m.s.a.* '00 (NOR) New London, CT St. Mary, Star of the Sea Church; [F] Cromwell, CT Society of the Missionaries of the Holy Apostles.
Grovenburg, Gregg H. *s.j.* '88 (BGP) [B] Fairfield, CT Fairfield University; [P] Fairfield, CT The Fairfield Jesuit Community-Fairfield University.
Grover, David A. '83 (CAM) Woodbury Heights, NJ St. Margaret's Church.
Grover, Peter *o.m.v.* '90 (BO) Boston, MA Beth Israel Deaconess Medical Center; [B] Boston, MA Our Lady of Grace Seminary; [BB] Boston, MA St. Clement's Archdiocesan Eucharistic Shrine.
Groves, Edmund '49 (PHX) Retired.
Groves, William '80 (PBL) Absent on Leave.
Growney, Eugene R. *s.j.* '72 (LA) [F] Los Angeles, CA Loyola High School of Los Angeles.
Grozio, Stephen M. *c.m.* '78 (BRK) [V] Brooklyn, NY St. John the Baptist Rectory.
Grozio, Stephen M. *c.m.* '78 (PH) [156] Philadelphia, PA St. Vincent de Paul Church.
Grubb, James E. '55 (DAV) Retired.
Grubba, Dale W. '66 (MAD) Neshkoro, WI St. James Church; Princeton, WI St. John the Baptist Church.
Gruben, John A. *o.a.r.* '74 (NEW) [N] West Orange, NJ Augustinian Recollects.
Gruber, Aloys Conrad '67 (STO) Oakdale, CA St. Mary of the Annunciation Church.
Gruber, Anthony '70 (NOR) Moosup, CT All-Hallows Church.
Gruber, Eric J. '91 (ALN) Schuylkill Haven, PA St. Ambrose Church; [O] Allentown, PA The Newman Center.
Gruber, J. Paul '45 (CIN) Retired.
Gruber, Kevin W. '80 (RVC) North Merrick, NY Sacred Heart Church.
Gruber, Mark F.X. *o.s.b.* '83 (GBG) [H] Latrobe, PA Saint Vincent Archabbey.
Gruber, Robert L. '53 (COV) Retired.
Grubisch, Msgr. Donald W. '53 (WIN) La Crescent, MN The Crucifixion Church.
Grubisic, Jozo *o.f.m.* '66 (CHI) [99] Chicago, IL St. Jerome Church.
Gruchot, Stanley J. '45 (CHI) Retired.
Gruden, William J. '79 (SAG) Munger, MI St. Norbert Church; Reese, MI St. Elizabeth Church.
Grudowski, Msgr. Robert J. '61 (PH) Conshohocken, PA St. Mary Church.
Gruenbauer, Hans H. '76 (CIN) Amelia, OH St. Bernadette's Church.
Gruenes, Bernard '98 (SCL) Grey Eagle, MN St. Joseph's Church; Swanville, MN St. John the Baptist Church.
Gruhn, Raymond C. '66 (BRK) [137] Brooklyn, NY St. Sylvester Church.
Grumm, Thomas J. '75 (PH) [78] Philadelphia, PA St. John the Baptist Church.
Grummer, James E. *s.j.* '82 (FgM) Provinces.
Grummer, James E. *s.j.* '82 (MIL) [31] Milwaukee, WI Gesu Church; [P] Milwaukee, WI Jesuit Provincial Office, Wisconsin Province.
Grumsey, Dennis *o.f.m.conv.* '86 (HBG) [5] Shamokin, PA Mother Cabrini Church.
Grundhaus, Msgr. Roger L. *v.g.* '66 (CR) Fertile, MN St. Joseph Church; Mentor, MN St. Lawrence Church.
Grundman, David '97 (SCL) Flensburg, MN Sacred Heart Church; Sobieski, MN St. Stanislaus Church.
Grundowski, Francis M. '71 (ALN) Brockton, PA St. Bartholomew Church; Tuscarora, PA St. Bertha Church.
Grunebach, Paul '76 (PIT) Glenshaw, PA St. Mary of the Assumption Church.
Grunewald, Bernard *er.o.l.s* '77 (OLL) [D] Philippi, WV Our Lady of Solitude, Inc.
Grunloh, Donatus *o.f.m.* '49 (SHP) West Monroe, LA St. Paschal Church.
Grunow, Stephen E. '97 (CHI) [A] Mundelein, IL University of St. Mary of the Lake-Mundelein Seminary.
Grupczynski, Gerald *s.ch.* '88 (DET) [K] Sterling Heights, MI Society of Christ Provincial Home.
Gruss, Robert D. '94 (DAV) Pella, IA St. Mary's Church.
Gruver, David '85 (ORG) Yorba Linda, CA St. Martin Church.
Grybowski, Robert *o.f.m.conv.* '53 (HBG) [5] Shamokin, PA Mother Cabrini Church.
Gryga, Theodore '64 (SY) Military Chaplains.
Grzechowiak, Francis *c.r.* '46 (CHI) [189] Chicago, IL St. Stanislaus, Bishop and Martyr Church.
Grzela, Andrew S. '91 (CHI) Other Assignments.
Grzela, Marek B. '92 (CHI) Burbank, IL St. Albert the Great Church.
Grzelak, Thaddeus A. '69 (BRK) [29] Brooklyn, NY St. Charles Borromeo Church.
Grzeskowiak, Edward S. '36 (STP) Retired.
Grzymski, Donald *o.f.m.conv.* '80 (BAL) [C] Baltimore, MD Archbishop Curley High School; [S] Baltimore, MD Immaculate Heart of Mary Friary.
Gschwend, James P. *s.j.* '65 (CHI) [N] Chicago, IL Chicago Province of the Society of Jesus-Provincial Office; [N] Chicago, IL Chicago Province of the Society of Jesus-Provincial Office.
Gschwind, Fred H. (LFT) [F] Tipton, IN St. Joseph Center: Sisters of St. Joseph.
Gsell, John W. '36 (PH) [60] Philadelphia, PA Holy Family Church; Retired.
Guadagnoli, Michael *p.v.* (DAL) Duncanville, TX Holy Spirit Church.
Guagliardo, Salvatore J. '59 (RCK) Retired.
Guajardo, Hilario '89 (AUS) Gatesville, TX Our Lady of Lourdes Church.
Gualderon, Msgr. Ernest J. '45 (LA) [1] Long Beach, CA St. Anthony Church; Retired.
Gualtieri, Raymond A. '64 (PIT) Retired.
Guarcello, Russell V. '43 (BO) Senior Priests.
Guarin, Angelo Michael M. *f.f.i.* '99 (FR) [I] New Bedford, MA Marian Friary of Our Lady, Queen of the Seraphic Order.
Guarino, Msgr. Charles A. '67 (RVC) Greenport, NY St. Agnes Church.
Guarino, Michael (BO) [6] Revere, MA St. Theresa Church.
Guarino, R. Michael '68 (BO) [3] Revere, MA St. John Vianney Church.
Guarino, Thomas G. '77 (NEW) [A] South Orange, NJ Immaculate Conception Seminary; [B] South Orange, NJ Seton Hall University.
Guarnieri, Lee '77 (RIC) Gloucester, VA St. Therese, the Little Flower Church.
Guarnieri, Richard '71 (NY) [136] Bronx, NY St. Clare of Assisi Church.
Guarracino, Ralph '54 (BRK) [Z] Middle Village, NY St. John's.
Guarracino, Ralph J. '54 (BRK) Retired.
Guastella, Luke *o.f.m.cap.* '41 (PAT) Passaic, NJ St. Mary Hospital.
Guastella, Msgr. Richard J. '72 (NY) [206] Staten Island, NY Holy Rosary Church.
Guay, Robert '73 (PIT) Conway, PA Our Lady of Peace Church.
Guba, Michael '65 (NEW) [3] Garfield, NJ Church of Our Lady of Sorrows.
Gubanich, Michael T. '47 (PIT) Retired.
Gubbels, Richard E. '65 (DM) Adel, IA St. John Church.
Gubbels, Wayne '71 (DM) Churchville, IA Assumption of the Blessed Virgin Mary Church; Irish Settlement, IA St. Patrick Church; St. Marys, IA Immaculate Conception Church.
Gubbins, John '70 (MIA) Military Chaplains.
Gubbins, William B. '55 (CHI) [102] Chicago, IL St. John Berchmans Church; [162] Chicago, IL St. Patrick Church; Retired.
Gubernat, Michael E. '77 (NEW) [6] Jersey City, NJ St. Anthony of Padua Church.
Gubser, John H. '62 (Y) Niles, OH St. Stephen's Church.
Gubser, Paul '67 (Y) Retired.
Guckert, William T. '66 (SY) Brewerton, NY St. Agnes Church.
Guckin, Matthew W. '99 (PH) [32] Philadelphia, PA St. Cecilia Church.
Gudalefsky, Adam B. *m.m.* '59 (FgM) Maryknoll Foreign Missions.
Gude, Thomas A. '66 (WDC) Lexington Park, MD Immaculate Heart of Mary Church.
Gudelis, Rimantas (CHI) [138] Chicago, IL Nativity of the Blessed Virgin Mary Church.
Gudewicz, John A. '70 (PIT) On Sabbatical.
Gudewicz, John L. '70 (PIT) [1] McKeesport, PA St. Martin de Porres Church.
Gudino, Eduardo '94 (SD) La Jolla, CA Mary, Star of the Sea Church.
Guenette, J. Andre '69 (WOR) [3] Gardner, MA Our Lady of the Holy Rosary Church.
Guenther, Bernard J. *c.ss.r.* '31 (STL) [P] Liguori, MO St. Clement Health Care Center.
Guenther, Daniel C. '82 (SC) Emmetsburg, IA Holy Family Church; Grand Junction, IA St. Brigid's Church.
Guenther, Msgr. Donald E. '62 (NEW) Secaucus, NJ Immaculate Conception Church.
Guenther, George J. *s.j.* '45 (MIL) [P] Wauwatosa, WI Jesuit Community at St. Camillus.
Guenther, Msgr. Thomas A. (CAM) Ocean City, NJ Our Lady of Good Counsel Church.
Guentner, Francis J. *s.j.* '47 (STL) [P] St. Louis, MO Jesuit Community Corporation at St. Louis University - Jesuit Hall.
Guentner, Hugh *o.s.m.* (DEN) [4] Denver, CO Assumption Church.
Guentner, Hugh *o.s.m.* '91 (CHI) [N] Chicago, IL Order of Friar Servants of Mary (Servites) United States of America Province, Inc.
Guerdet, Randy J. '89 (SC) [1] Sioux City, IA Cathedral of the Epiphany.
Guerin, Louis '87 (PMB) [4] Lake Worth, FL St.Therese de Lisieux Church.
Guerin, Peter J. *o.s.b.* '63 (MAN) [K] Manchester, NH St. Anselm Abbey.
Guerin, William A. *o.s.f.s.* '57 (PH) [AA] Wyndmoor, PA Villa de Sales Oblate Residence.
Guerini, Ademir *c.s.* (WDC) [38] Washington, DC Our Lady of Fatima Church.
Guerini, Ademir *c.s.* '87 (WDC) [2] Silver Spring, MD St. Bernadette Church.
Guerra, Alcibiades *c.m.* '90 (FgM) Vincentian Foreign Missions.
Guerra, Aroldo (NY) [53] New York, NY Incarnation Church.
Guerra, Aroldo *sch.p.* '54 (NY) [12] New York, NY Annunciation Church.
Guerra, Jesus *o.p.* '57 (FgM) Dominican - Order of Preachers Foreign Missions.
Guerra, Juan Gabriel *l.c.* '91 (DET) [T] Bloomfield Hills, MI Logos, Inc. (Michigan).
Guerra, Richard *o.m.i.* '78 (LAR) Eagle Pass, TX Sacred Heart Church.
Guerra, Robert '00 (VIC) Port Lavaca, TX Our Lady of the Gulf Church.
Guerra-Mayaudon, Gerardo *o.p.* '69 (AUS) [H] Austin, TX Dominican Friars of Austin.
Guerreiro, Clarence L. *ss.cc.* '70 (HON) Kaneohe, HI St. Ann Church.
Guerreiro, Clyde *ss.cc.* '76 (HON) [G] Kaneohe, HI Congregation of the Sacred Hearts of Jesus and Mary (Hawaii Province SS.CC.); [G] Kaneohe, HI Sacred Hearts Center.
Guerrera, Richard P. *s.j.* '73 (FgM) Provinces.
Guerrera, Vittorio '91 (HRT) Avon, CT St. Ann's Church.
Guerrero, Msgr. Andres '57 (PCE) Coamo, PR St. Blase Church.
Guerrero, Felix Leon *o.f.m.cap.* '86 (AGN) [F] Agana Heights, GU St. Fidelis Friary.
Guerrero, Jose Ma. (ARE) On Duty Outside the Diocese.
Guerrero, Juan Manuel '81 (OKL) Ardmore, OK St. Mary Church.
Guerrero, Lawrence M. '83 (STO) Newman, CA St. Joachim Church.
Guerrero, Robert '92 (HON) On Duty Outside the Diocese.
Guerrero, Robert '92 (SB) Lake Elsinore, CA St. Frances of Rome Church.
Guerrero, Toribio C. '96 (LAR) Asherton, TX Immaculate Conception Church.
Guerrero-Orta, Abel '00 (ATL) Dalton, GA St. Joseph's Church.
Guerrette, William A. '55 (BO) Senior Priests.
Guerrini, Roderic M. '63 (LA) Venice, CA St. Mark Church.
Guertin, Donald F. *c.s.c.* '61 (FTW) [20] South Bend, IN St. Therese, Little Flower Church.
Guesnier, Rene *o.s.b.* '61 (DOD) St. John, KS St. John the Apostle Church; Seward, KS St. Francis Xavier Church.
Guessetto, Robert J. *o.s.a.* '79 (WDC) [B] Washington, DC Augustinian College, Order of St. Augustine.
Guest, Richard M. '94 (ARL) Great Falls, VA St. Catherine of Siena Church.
Guevara, Alfonso M. '77 (BWN) [2] Brownsville, TX Christ the King Church.
Guevara, Msgr. Jose Maria '68 (LAR) Crystal City, TX Sacred Heart Church.
Guevara, Miguel H. '67 (GI) Retired.
Guevin, Benedict M. *o.s.b.* '85 (MAN) [K] Manchester, NH St. Anselm Abbey.
Guffey, David L. '91 (COS) [F] Cascade, CO Holy Cross Novitiate.
Guffey, David L. *c.s.c.* '91 (FTW) [J] South Bend, IN Congregation of Holy Cross, Indiana Province, Provincial House.
Gugino, Msgr. Henry J. (BUF) [T] Buffalo, NY Wheatfield Housing Development Fund Company, Inc.
Gugino, Msgr. Henry J. '68 (BUF) [H] Buffalo, NY The Catholic Charities of the Diocese of Buffalo; [H] Buffalo, NY The Catholic Charities of the Diocese of Buffalo; [H] Buffalo, NY The Catholic Charities of the Diocese of Buffalo; [H] Buffalo, NY The Catholic Charities of the Diocese of Buffalo; [H] Buffalo, NY The Catholic Charities of the Diocese of Buffalo; [H] Buffalo, NY The Catholic Charities of the Diocese of Buffalo; [H] Buffalo, NY The Catholic Charities of the Diocese of Buffalo; [M] Williamsville, NY St. Francis Home of Williamsville; [S] Angola, NY St. Vincent de Paul Camp; [T] Buffalo, NY Good Counsel Apartments; [T] Buffalo, NY Timon Towers Housing Development Fund Company, Inc.; [T] Buffalo, NY Monsignor Kirby Apartments Housing Development Fund Company, Inc.; [T] Buffalo, NY St. Timothy's Park Villa Housing Development Fund Company, Inc.; [T] Buffalo, NY La Casa Del Tainos Housing Development Fund Company, Inc.
Guglielmelli, Michael V. '70 (NEW) [3] Hoboken, NJ St. Francis Church.
Guglielmi, Donald A. '84 (BGP) [2] Stratford, CT St. James Church; [C] Bridgeport, CT Kolbe-Cathedral High School.
Guglielmo, Alan '68 (NEW) Bloomfield, NJ St. Valentine Church; Montclair, NJ Mountainside Hospital.
Guglielmone, Msgr. Robert E. '78 (RVC) Wantagh, NY

St. Frances de Chantal Church.
Gugliemelli, Msgr. Neil O. '54 (SCR) [7] Hazleton, PA Our Lady of Grace Church.
Gugliotta, Francis *s.x.* '52 (FgM) Xaverian Foreign Missions.
Gugliotta, Francis *s.x.* '52 (PAT) [M] Wayne, NJ Xaverian Missionary Fathers.
Gugliotta, Kevin A. '96 (NEW) Short Hills, NJ St. Rose of Lima Church.
Guiao, Raymond *s.j.* (CLV) [D] Cleveland, OH St. Ignatius High School.
Guiao, Raymond P. *s.j.* '99 (DET) [K] Detroit, MI Jesuit Provincial Office-Detroit Province of the Society of Jesus.
Guichard, Alvaro '69 (MIA) [1] Miami Beach, FL St. Francis de Sales Church.
Guida, Amedeo '85 (SY) Fairmount, NY Holy Family Church.
Guida, Gerald J. *s.j.* '45 (STL) [P] St. Louis, MO The Jesuits of the Missouri Province.
Guidera, John F. *s.j.* '56 (BAL) [S] Baltimore, MD Jesuit Fathers and Brothers Maryland Provincial Curia.
Guidera, John F. *s.j.* '56 (FgM) Provinces.
Guido, Msgr. John L. '42 (NY) [190] Bronx, NY St. Theresa of the Infant Jesus Church.
Guido, Joseph J. *o.p.* '81 (PRO) [P] Providence, RI St. Thomas Aquinas Priory at Providence College.
Guido, Paul R. *o.f.m.* '66 (HRT) [6] New Britain, CT St. Francis of Assisi Church.
Guido, Thomas '87 (PT) [3] Tallahassee, FL Good Shepherd Church.
Guido, Thomas J. '87 (PT) Port St. Joe, FL St. Joseph Church.
Guido, Msgr. William F. '44 (NY) Retired.
Guidon, Patrick *o.m.i.* '50 (SAT) [K] San Antonio, TX Oblate Madonna Residence.
Guidon, Patrick *o.m.i.* '62 (SAT) [M] San Antonio, TX Missionary Oblates of Mary Immaculate.
Guidry, Dale '82 (AMA) Absent on Leave; [D] Panhandle, TX St. Joseph's Home for Retired Priests.
Guidry, Joseph I. *s.v.d.* '57 (BR) [18] Baton Rouge, LA St. Paul the Apostle Church.
Guidry, Michael '71 (LAF) [3] New Iberia, LA Our Lady of Perpetual Help Church.
Guidry, Mitchell (LAF) Four Corners, LA St. Peter the Apostle Church.
Guidry, Mitchell G. '97 (LAF) Baldwin, LA Sacred Heart Church.
Guidry, Raymond James *s.v.d.* '53 (GAL) [1] Galveston, TX St. Mary's Cathedral Basilica Church.
Guijarro de Corzo, Msgr. Mario A. '78 (SJN) [6] Guaynabo, PR San Pedro Martir de Verona Church.
Guilbault, Msgr. Oscar A. '31 (PRO) Retired; [M] North Kingstown, RI Scalabrini Villa.
Guilbeau, Aubrey '82 (LKC) [5] Lake Charles, LA St. Margaret Church.
Guilbert, Norman J. '97 (BGP) [10] Stamford, CT St. Leo Church.
Guiliano, Carmen *s.a.* (OG) [E] Saranac Lake, NY St. Joseph's Rehabilitation Center, Inc.
Guiliano, Carmen *s.a.* '61 (OG) [F] Saranac Lake, NY Atonement Friars.
Guillemette, Marc F. '90 (MAN) Merrimack, NH Our Lady of Mercy Church.
Guillen, Fernando E. '90 (NEW) [1] Hoboken, NJ Our Lady of Grace Church.
Guillen, Juan '74 (TUC) Yuma, AZ Immaculate Conception Church.
Guillen, Manuel R. '62 (SB) Retired.
Guillen, Patricio '57 (SB) Retired.
Guillen, Randy '96 (TR) Keyport, NJ Jesus the Lord Church.
Guillen, Randy A. '96 (NEW) On Duty Outside the Archdiocese.
Guillermo, Rodrigo J. '65 (GAL) Retired.
Guillet, Bernard *a.a.* '44 (WOR) [N] Worcester, MA Assumptionists (Augustinians of the Assumption).
Guillot, Msgr. Leo '56 (BR) Albany, LA St. Margaret Queen of Scotland Church.
Guillot, Raymond Joseph '00 (NO) Violet, LA Our Lady of Lourdes Church.
Guilmain, Roland O. *a.a.* '53 (WOR) [N] Worcester, MA Assumptionists (Augustinians of the Assumption); [Q] Worcester, MA Campus Ministry.
Guilmette, Emile *s.m.* '57 (BO) [Y] Framingham, MA The Marist House.
Guiltnane, Justin *s.c.j.* '53 (MIL) [P] Hales Corners, WI Sacred Heart Monastery; [Y] Franklin, WI Congregation of the Priests of the Sacred Heart Support and Maintenance Trust.
Guimon, Michael M. *o.s.m.* '70 (CHI) [N] Chicago, IL Order of Friar Servants of Mary (Servites) United States of America Province, Inc.; [N] Chicago, IL Order of Friar Servants of Mary (Servites) United States of America Province, Inc.
Guinan, Frank '66 (PMB) Juno Beach, FL St. Patrick Church.
Guinan, Michael '53 (GF) Retired.
Guinan, Michael D. *o.f.m.* '63 (OAK) [A] Berkeley, CA Franciscan School of Theology.
Guindon, William G. *s.j.* '50 (BO) [W] Weston, MA Campion Health Center, Inc.
Guiney, John *s.m.a.* '61 (JOL) Roselle, IL St. Walter Church.
Guiniven, John *c.ss.r.* '37 (ALB) [L] Saratoga Springs, NY St. John Neumann Residence.
Guischard, John A. '68 (BUR) Retired.
Guise, Cyril *o.c.d.* '59 (MIL) [P] Holy Hill, WI Discalced Carmelite Monastery.
Guiterrez, Jose '76 (CC) [E] Corpus Christi, TX CHRISTUS Spohn Hospital Shoreline.
Guitierrez, Jeronimo '81 (SJ) Gilroy, CA St. Mary Church.
Guitron, Steven '94 (LA) Camarillo, CA St. Mary Magdalen Church.
Guixa, Jaime '82 (SJN) [G] Guaynabo, PR Opus Dei.
Gula, Richard *s.s.* '73 (OAK) [A] Berkeley, CA Franciscan School of Theology.
Gulas, William E. *o.f.m.* '61 (CLV) [72] Cleveland, OH St. Stanislaus Church; [O] Cleveland, OH St. Stanislaus Friary.
Gulash, George M. '92 (ALT) [14] Johnstown, PA Our Mother of Sorrows Church.
Gulczynski, Msgr. John T. '36 (DAL) Retired.
Gulig, Msgr. Robert (GB) Special Assignment.
Gulig, Msgr. Robert F. (GB) Kellnersville, WI St. Joseph Church.
Gulino, Stephen '97 (NOR) New London, CT St. Joseph Church.
Guljas, Andrew *c.s.c.* '68 (FTW) [L] Notre Dame, IN Holy Cross Mission House.
Gulley, Anthony D. '56 (ALB) [3] Albany, NY Blessed Sacrament Church; Special Assignment; [B] Albany, NY The College of Saint Rose.
Gulley, James '81 (ALB) [7] Amsterdam, NY St. Mary Church.
Gullickson, Msgr. Thomas E. '76 (SFS) On Duty Outside the Diocese.
Gullo, Joseph A. '86 (BUF) Falconer, NY Our Lady of Loreto Church; Frewsburg, NY Our Lady of Victory Church.
Gully, Bernard L. '62 (SAN) Andrews, TX Our Lady of Lourdes Church.
Gumapo, Polycarpo '70 (SAC) [2] Sacramento, CA All Hallows Church.
Gumataotao, Agustin *o.f.m.cap.* (AGN) [F] Agat, GU Capuchin Fraternity.
Gumataotao, Agustin *o.f.m.cap.* '82 (AGN) Santa Rita, GU Our Lady of Guadalupe Church; [F] Agana Heights, GU St. Fidelis Friary.
Gumbert, Kenneth R. *o.p.* '85 (PRO) [P] Providence, RI St. Thomas Aquinas Priory at Providence College.
Guminga, Theodore C. '59 (STP) [25] Minneapolis, MN St. Hedwig Church; Retired.
Gummersbach, James L. '54 (STL) Retired.
Gummersheimer, Gary P. '79 (BEL) Murphysboro, IL St. Andrew Church.
Gumpal, Domingo *m.s.* '80 (SFE) [24] Albuquerque, NM St. Bernadette Church.
Gumprecht, Thomas *s.a.* '68 (NY) [14] Yonkers, NY Our Lady of the Rosary Church.
Gunderman, Richard J. *s.a.c.* '50 (MIL) [D] Milwaukee, WI Pius XI High School; [P] Milwaukee, WI St. Vincent Community; [Y] Milwaukee, WI Pallottine Fathers and Brothers, Inc., Disability Trust; [Y] Milwaukee, WI Pallottine Fathers and Brothers, Inc., Educational and Apostolic Ministry Trust.
Gunderson, Gerald T. '76 (CHI) Riverside, IL St. Mary Church.
Gundrum, Alfredo *o.f.m.cap.* '67 (CHI) [110] Chicago, IL St. Kevin Church.
Gunia, Edward S. '49 (CHI) Retired.
Gunn, Andrew '97 (AUS) [18] Austin, TX St. Patrick Church.
Gunn, Francis *o.f.m.* '81 (NY) [48] New York, NY Holy Name of Jesus Church.
Gunn, James L. '77 (MAD) Waunakee, WI St. John the Baptist Church.
Gunning, Eugene L. '55 (SCR) [13] Scranton, PA St. John the Evangelist Church.
Gunning, Joseph *s.v.d.* '47 (TR) [M] Bordentown, NJ Society of the Divine Word.
Gunnoud, James B. '59 (HRT) Cheshire, CT St. Bridget's Church.
Gunshinan, James P. *c.s.c.* '89 (OAK) [N] Berkeley, CA Holy Cross Fathers-Holy Cross Center.
Gunther, William '60 (MIA) Retired.
Gunti, Charles *o.f.m.* '68 (SAT) [70] San Antonio, TX San Jose y San Miguel Church.
Gunti, Charles E. *o.f.m.* '68 (STL) [P] St. Louis, MO Franciscan Friary of St. Anthony of Padua.
Gunti, Frederick W. '64 (LR) On Duty Outside the Diocese.
Gunti, Frederick W. '64 (MOB) [A] Mobile, AL Spring Hill College.
Guntzelman, Louis J. '57 (CIN) On Special and Archdiocesan Assignment.
Guppenberger, August *glmy.* '61 (CIN) [M] Cincinnati, OH Headquarters of Glenmary Home Missioners.
Gural, Marion A. '56 (BRK) Retired.
Gurath, Guy G. '64 (MIL) Awaiting Assignment.
Gurdak, Joseph *o.f.m.cap.* '70 (NY) [98] New York, NY Our Lady of Sorrows Church.
Guredet, Randy J. '89 (SC) Special Assignment.
Gurgul, Walter *m.i.c.* '60 (SPR) [J] Stockbridge, MA Congregation of Marians of The Immaculate Conception of the BVM.
Gurka, Gerald J. '80 (SCR) [2] Plymouth, PA St. John the Baptist Church.
Gurkis, Albin *m.i.c.* '43 (NOR) [C] Thompson, CT Marianapolis Preparatory School; [F] Thompson, CT Marian Fathers.
Gurnee, William H. '00 (WDC) Laurel, MD St. Mary Church.
Gurnell, Anthony '64 (MRY) Cayucos, CA St. Joseph Church.
Gurnell, Anthony '64 (SAC) Retired and in Senior Ministry.
Gurnick, Michael K. '98 (CLV) [43] Cleveland, OH St. Leo the Great Church.
Gurovich, Daniel '74 (PHU) Bethlehem, PA St. Josaphat's Church.
Gurrieri, John A. '67 (BRK) [67] Brooklyn, NY St. John Cantius Church.
Gurski, John K. '64 (NEW) [3] Garfield, NJ Church of Our Lady of Sorrows.
Gurtler, Gary *s.j.* '79 (BO) [W] Chestnut Hill, MA The Jesuit Community at Boston College.
Gurtner, Mark Allen '96 (FTW) [20] Fort Wayne, IN St. Vincent de Paul Church.
Gurzynski, Msgr. James C. '63 (AMA) Retired.
Guschwan, George M. '72 (CLV) [5] Elyria, OH Sacred Heart of Jesus Church.
Gusiora, Alphonsus '83 (PCE) On Duty Outside the Diocese.
Gusmer, Msgr. Charles W. *v.e.* '66 (NEW) Cedar Grove, NJ St. Catherine of Siena Church.
Gussoni, Lino '44 (NY) Retired.
Gustafson, Christopher M. '95 (CHI) Lake Forest, IL St. Mary Church.
Gustafson, Gilbert J. '77 (STP) Mendota, MN St. Peter Church.
Guste, Placid *s.m.p.* '61 (SPC) [E] Marionville, MO The Society of Our Mother of Peace, Sons of Our Mother of Peace.
Guste, Placid *s.m.p.* '61 (STL) [P] High Ridge, MO Society of Our Mother of Peace; [T] High Ridge, MO Society of Our Mother of Peace-Maria Fonte Solitude.
Guste, Msgr. Robert I. '50 (NO) [2] Kenner, LA Our Lady of Perpetual Help Church.
Gustin, Clement N. *o.s.c.* '55 (SCL) [I] Onamia, MN Crosier Monastery.
Gustin, Theodore F. (BIS) [G] Bismarck, ND Emmaus Place.
Gustin, Theodore F. '57 (BIS) Retired.
Gutauskas, Vaclovas *s.j.* '45 (CHI) [N] Chicago, IL Lithuanian American Jesuits.
Gutekunst, John P. '80 (PH) [35] Philadelphia, PA St. Christopher Church.
Gutgsell, Michael F. '74 (OM) [30] Omaha, NE Mary Our Queen Church.
Gutgsell, Stephen J. '84 (OM) Humphrey, NE St. Francis Church; [O] Humphrey, NE St. Francis Church of Humphrey Cemetery Endowment Trust Fund.
Guth, Edward L. *s.j.* '60 (BUF) [50] Buffalo, NY St. Michael Church.
Guthman, William (KCK) Topeka, KS Kansas Neurological Institute and Kansas Reception and Diagnostic Center.
Guthneck, Peter E. '71 (GF) Big Sandy, MT St. Margaret Mary Church.
Guthridge, Timothy J. *c.pp.s.* '97 (JC) Sedalia, MO St. Patrick Church; Sedalia, MO Sacred Heart Church.
Guthrie, Alfred '55 (BRK) [U] Brooklyn, NY Catholic Migration & Refugee Office, Catholic Migration Services, Inc.
Guthrie, Frederick L. '62 (BO) [1] Gloucester, MA St. Ann Church.
Guthrie, John G. '90 (BIS) Williston, ND St. Joseph Church.
Guthrie, Milton J. '57 (MEM) [9] Memphis, TN Holy Names of Jesus and Mary Church.
Guthrie, Paul *o.f.m.* '53 (PHU) Scranton, PA St. Vladimir's Church.
Guthrie, Raymond (PEO) On Duty Outside the Diocese.
Guthrie, Raymond P. '84 (RCK) St. Charles, IL St. Patrick Church.
Gutierrez, Alvin '61 (PIT) [L] Pittsburgh, PA Little Sisters of the Poor Home for the Aged.
Gutierrez, Alvin P. (PIT) Allegheny County, PA James P. Wall Home for the Aged.
Gutierrez, Celestino '64 (VEN) [4] Sarasota, FL St. Martha Church.
Gutierrez, Dionisio (LSC) [3] Las Cruces, NM Our Lady of Health Church.
Gutierrez, Dionisio *o.a.r.* '63 (NY) [126] Bronx, NY St. Anselm Church.
Gutierrez, Msgr. Fernando '66 (SD) [33] San Diego, CA St. Michael Church.
Gutierrez, Franco '65 (SJN) [3] San Juan, PR Nuestra Senora de la Altagracia Church.

Gutierrez, Fulgencio '00 (BRK) [198] Queens, NY St. Mary Star of the Sea Church.
Gutierrez, Gilberto (PAT) [8] Passaic, NJ Our Lady of Fatima Church.
Gutierrez, Javier *o.de.m.* '71 (PCE) [13] Ponce, PR Santuario San Judas Tadeo Church.
Gutierrez, Javier '83 (JUN) On Duty Outside the Diocese.
Gutierrez, Jose (STP) Golden Valley, MN St. Margaret Mary Church.
Gutierrez, Jose Gregorio '97 (NY) [186] Bronx, NY St. Rita of Cascia Church.
Gutierrez, Jose M. '76 (CC) [11] Corpus Christi, TX Sacred Heart Church.
Gutierrez, Julio '49 (CGS) Retired.
Gutierrez, Luis '98 (JOL) Bloomingdale, IL St. Isidore Church.
Gutierrez, Michael D. '94 (LA) Santa Monica, CA St. Anne Church.
Gutierrez, Oscar '96 (SAC) Vacaville, CA St. Mary Church.
Gutierrez, Rafael '89 (TUC) [20] Tucson, AZ St. Monica Church.
Gutkowski, Michal *s.j.* '00 (OAK) [N] Berkeley, CA Jesuit Community at Jesuit School of Theology at Berkeley.
Gutmann, David '83 (P) [7] Portland, OR Assumption Church; [15] Portland, OR Holy Cross Church; [31] Portland, OR Queen of Peace Church.
Gutmann, Don '91 (P) Reedsport, OR St. John the Apostle Church.
Gutmann, Donald K. '91 (P) Florence, OR St. Mary, Our Lady of the Dunes Church.
Gutowski, Edmund *c.m.* '60 (BRK) [134] Brooklyn, NY St. Stanislaus Kostka Church.
Gutowski, Matthew J. '88 (OM) [L] Omaha, NE Sisters of the Annunciation of the Archdiocese of Omaha.
Gutowski, Matthew J. '88 (STL) [A] St. Louis, MO Kenrick-Glennon Seminary.
Guttendorf, James R. '65 (RIC) Highland Springs, VA St. John Church.
Gutting, James G. '75 (E) [4] Erie, PA Holy Rosary Church.
Gutting, John C. '54 (LA) [2] Long Beach, CA St. Athanasius Church; Retired.
Guyder, Thomas F. '40 (SY) Retired; [S] Syracuse, NY St. Pius X Home, Inc.
Guyer, James B. *s.j.* '72 (DEN) [M] Denver, CO Regis Jesuit Community (The Jesuits at Regis University).
Guyon, Guy E. *o.praem* '40 (GB) [I] De Pere, WI St. Norbert Abbey.
Guyot, Gilmore H. *c.m.* '34 (STL) [P] Perryville, MO Congregation of The Mission.
Guz, Edmund F. '55 (CHI) Burnham, IL Mother of God Church.
Guz, Leonard J. '55 (JOL) Downers Grove, IL Divine Savior Church.
Guzikowski, Msgr. Gerard '43 (GAY) Manistee, MI Guardian Angels Church.
Guzinski, Joseph D. *c.p.* '51 (BRK) [V] Jamaica, NY Immaculate Conception Monastery.
Guzman, Alfonso *o.f.m.* '71 (SJN) [4] Toa Baja, PR San Jose Obrero Church.
Guzman, Alfonso D. *o.f.m.* '71 (FgM) Franciscan Foreign Missions.
Guzman, Alfonso D. *o.f.m.* '71 (NY) [DD] New York, NY Franciscan Friars, Order of Friars Minor, Holy Name Province.
Guzman, Armando '86 (SEA) Unassigned.
Guzman, Julian *s.d.s.* '68 (WDC) [B] Silver Spring, MD Salvatorian Community.
Guzman, Mariano *o.f.m.* '57 (FgM) Franciscan Foreign Missions.
Guzman, Salvador '00 (DAL) [1] Dallas, TX Cathedral-Santuario de Guadalupe Church.
Gwiazda, Francis A. '69 (PH) [87] Philadelphia, PA St. Laurentius Church.
Gwinner, David E. (COL) Zaleski, OH St. Sylvester Church.
Gwozdz, John P. '86 (HRT) Cornwall Bridge, CT St. Bridget Church; Sharon, CT St. Bernard's Church.
Gwozdz, Thomas *o.f.m.conv.* '53 (BAL) [S] Ellicott City, MD Order of Friars Minor Conventual.
Gwozdz, Thomas *o.f.m.conv.* '53 (BGP) [6] Danbury, CT Sacred Heart Church.
Gwozdz, Thomas L. *s.b.d.* '75 (NO) [A] St. Benedict, LA St. Joseph's Seminary College.
Gwudz, John S. '72 (NOR) On Duty Outside the Diocese; Military Chaplains.
Gyamfi-Appiah, Aaron *c.ss.p.* (NY) [137] Bronx, NY Christ the King Church.
Gyan, Eric V. '86 (BR) Brusly, LA St. John the Baptist Church.
Gyhra, Lawrence J. '66 (LIN) Hastings, NE St. Cecilia's Church.
Gyhra, Richard A. '99 (LIN) [4] Lincoln, NE North American Martyrs Church.
Gyure, William '91 (NEW) Nutley, NJ Our Lady of Mount Carmel Church; Montclair, NJ Mountainside Hospital; Elizabeth, NJ Union County Jail.

H

Ha, Alex H. '93 (ORG) Irvine, CA St. Elizabeth Ann Seton Church.
Ha, Hieu Minh '00 (ATL) Kennesaw, GA St. Catherine of Siena Church.
Ha, Vinh Van '93 (CHI) Palatine, IL St. Theresa Church.
Haag, Theodore *o.f.m.* '79 (CLV) [O] Cleveland, OH Padua Franciscan Friary.
Haake, Chris '97 (PEO) [B] Peoria, IL Notre Dame High School.
Haake, Thomas *o.m.v.* '81 (BO) [B] Boston, MA Oblate Provincialate.
Haaland, Byron *s.c.j.* '77 (GB) [M] Baileys Harbor, WI St. Joseph Retreat Center.
Haar, George B. '51 (STL) Retired.
Haas, Dietrich A. '67 (MIL) [T] Waukesha, WI Secular Institute of Schoenstatt Fathers.
Haas, Joseph H. '59 (MIL) Port Washington, WI St. Peter of Alcantara Church.
Haas, Julian '65 (STL) [54] St. Louis, MO St. Patrick Church; [P] St. Louis, MO St. Patrick Friary.
Haas, Lawrence '63 (FAR) Carrington, ND Sacred Heart Church.
Haas, Melvin B. '54 (BEL) Retired.
Haas, Ralph L. '55 (BEL) Chester, IL Chester Mental Health Center; Retired.
Haas, Robert L. '62 (TOL) New London, OH Our Lady of Lourdes Church.
Haas, Roger *o.f.m.conv.* '69 (PAT) [6] Clifton, NJ St. John Kanty Church.
Haas, Theodore A. '44 (COS) [1] Colorado Springs, CO St. Mary's Church.
Haase, Albert *o.f.m.* '83 (FgM) Franciscan Foreign Missions.
Haase, Albert '83 (STL) [P] St. Louis, MO Franciscan Friary of St. Anthony of Padua.
Haase, Howard G. '83 (MIL) Union Grove, WI St. Robert Bellarmine Church.
Haasl, Edgar '58 (OAK) Retired.
Hababag, Jimmy '82 (PMB) [2] West Palm Beach, FL Mary Immaculate Church.
Habe, Robert W. '62 (PIT) Russellton, PA Transfiguration Church.
Haber, Edward '58 (NEW) [1] Elizabeth, NJ St. Mary of the Assumption Church; Elizabeth, NJ Trinitas Hospital.
Haberek, Jerome A. '77 (PRO) On Duty Outside the Diocese.
Haberkern, Thomas A. '93 (STL) On Medical Leave.
Haberkorn, Timothy A. '92 (KCK) Hartford, KS St. Mary's Church; Olpe, KS St. Joseph's Church.
Haberman, C. Robert '75 (PBL) On Duty Outside the Diocese.
Haberman, Clayton J. '50 (WIN) Retired.
Haberman, Lawrence R. '68 (DAL) Retired.
Habiger, Msgr. James '51 (STP) [C] St. Paul, MN University of St. Thomas.
Habiger, Msgr. James D. '51 (WIN) Retired.
Habiger, Matthew *o.s.b.* '68 (KCK) [H] Atchison, KS St. Benedict's Abbey.
Habing, Paul '80 (SFD) On Duty Outside the Diocese.
Habison, Gerhart '76 (LA) [66] Los Angeles, CA St. Gerard Majella Church.
Hablewitz, James A. '67 (GB) [2] Green Bay, WI Nativity of Our Lord Church.
Haby, Gerald *s.m.* '69 (FWT) [12] Fort Worth, TX St. Mary of the Assumption Church.
Hacala, Joseph R. *s.j.* '75 (WDC) [M] Washington, DC K Street Jesuit Community.
Hachey, Paul J. *s.m.* '84 (ATL) Special or Other (Arch)Diocesan Assignment; [C] Atlanta, GA Marist School.
Hack, Michael A. '70 (CHI) Flossmoor, IL Infant Jesus of Prague Church.
Hack, Thomas J. '55 (GR) [6] Muskegon, MI St. Michael's Church.
Hackel, Robert E. *s.m.* '65 (GAL) [Q] Houston, TX Marianist Community.
Hackem, Jack (STL) [K] St. Louis, MO SSM St. Mary's Health Center.
Hackenmueller, Jerome B. '69 (STP) [30] St. Paul, MN St. Patrick Church.
Hacker, Jack *c.ss.r.* '59 (STL) [B] St. Louis, MO St. John Neumann House.
Hacker, Leonard G. *s.j.* '47 (FgM) Provinces.
Hacker, Leonard G. *s.j.* '47 (MI) Majuro, MH Cathedral of the Assumption.
Hackert, Eugene C. '51 (NU) Gibbon, MN St. Willibrord Church.
Hackett, James F. '68 (L) [67] Louisville, KY St. Raphael the Archangel Church.
Hackett, John P. '46 (BUR) Retired.
Hackman, Marvin R. '71 (CIN) [K] Springfield, OH Mercy Health System - Western Ohio; [Q] Springfield, OH Mercy Medical Center.
Hadad, Gerard A. '69 (DET) Retired.
Hadberg, Dennis C. '72 (E) Clearfield, PA St. Francis Church.
Haddad, Msgr. Edmond G. '46 (WOR) Retired; [M] Worcester, MA Vianney House.
Haddad, Msgr. James J. '58 (BO) Needham, MA St. Joseph Church.
Haddad, Norman Alfred *o.p.* '61 (NY) [DD] New York, NY St. Vincent Ferrer Priory; [HH] New York, NY St. Thomas Aquinas Foundation.
Haddad, Norman Alfred *o.p.* '61 (FgM) Dominican - Order of Preachers Foreign Missions.
Haddad, Wayne '97 (MET) Sayreville, NJ Our Lady of Victories Church; [A] South Amboy, NJ St. Mary Regional High School.
Haddad, William *b.s.o.* '42 (NTN) Retired.
Hadden, Msgr. Thomas P. '58 (R) Wilmington, NC St. Mary Church; Retired.
Hadel, Richard E. *s.j.* '65 (STL) [F] St. Louis, MO St. Louis University High School, George H. Backer Memorial; [P] St. Louis, MO St. Louis University High School Jesuit Community.
Haden, Kyle '97 (KCK) Easton, KS St. Lawrence Church; [5] Leavenworth, KS St. Joseph of the Valley Church; Mooney Creek, KS Corpus Christi Church.
Hadgkiss, Joseph '93 (BRK) [152] Queens, NY St. Anthony of Padua Church.
Hadgkiss, Joseph *s.o.l.t.* '93 (CC) [H] Robstown, TX Society of Our Lady of the Most Holy Trinity.
Hadnagy, John Raphael *o.f.m.conv.* '90 (IND) St. Joseph Hill, IN St. Joseph Church.
Hadusek, Paul J. '69 (NU) Cottonwood, MN St. Mary Church; Green Valley, MN St. Clotilde Church.
Hadyka, Richard J. '67 (CAM) Salem, NJ St. Mary's Church.
Haefeli, Joaquin '52 (LA) [2] Oxnard, CA Santa Clara Church.
Haefling, Maurice *o.s.b.* '94 (KCK) [H] Atchison, KS St. Benedict's Abbey.
Haefner, Douglas J. '83 (MET) Somerset, NJ St. Matthias Church.
Haegelin, William M. '76 (KCK) Prairie Village, KS St. Ann's Church.
Haemmerle, Gerald R. '67 (CIN) [A] Cincinnati, OH The Athenaeum of Ohio; [B] Cincinnati, OH Mt. St. Mary's Seminary of the West; [B] Cincinnati, OH Mt. St. Mary's Seminary of the West.
Haener, Robert W. '57 (DET) Retired.
Haenke, Roger '91 (FAR) Absent on Leave.
Haesaert, William F. *c.s.v.* '80 (LAV) [15] Las Vegas, NV St. Viator Church.
Hafeman, Harry G. '76 (GB) Leopolis, WI St. Mary Church.
Hafemann, George T. M. '99 (NY) [3] Poughkeepsie, NY Holy Trinity Church.
Haffey, Thomas P. '69 (HEL) [6] Butte, MT St. Ann Church.
Hafner, M. Gerald (ROC) Hilton, NY St. Leo Church.
Hafner, M. Gerard (ROC) Hamlin, NY St. Elizabeth Ann Seton Church.
Hafner, M. Gerard '61 (ROC) Churchville, NY St. Vincent De Paul Church.
Hafner, M. Gerard '62 (ROC) Spencerport, NY St. John the Evangelist Church.
Hafner, Walter *s.v.d.* '37 (CHI) [B] Techny, IL Divine Word Residence.
Hagan, Aelred *o.c.s.o.* '89 (CHR) [E] Moncks Corner, SC Mepkin Abbey.
Hagan, Barry J. *c.s.c.* '60 (P) [B] Portland, OR University of Portland; [L] Portland, OR Holy Cross Fathers & Brothers, C.S.C. - University of Portland.
Hagan, Charles H. '70 (PH) Hatboro, PA St. John Bosco Church.
Hagan, David I. *o.s.f.s.* '66 (PH) [AA] Philadelphia, PA Inner City House.
Hagan, Harry *o.s.b.* '86 (IND) [A] St. Meinrad, IN St. Meinrad Seminary; [J] St. Meinrad, IN St. Meinrad Archabbey.
Hagan, James '69 (SFR) On Duty Outside the Archdiocese.
Hagan, Martin *s.j.* '50 (STL) [F] St. Louis, MO St. Louis University High School, George H. Backer Memorial; [P] St. Louis, MO Jesuit Community Corporation at St. Louis University - Jesuit Hall.
Hagan, Paul '82 (LFT) Unassigned.
Hagan, Robert A. *s.j.* '72 (PBL) Trinidad, CO Most Holy Trinity, Trinidad Area Catholic Community (Trinidad Cluster) Church; [G] Trinidad, CO Trinidad Area Catholic Community.
Hagan, Thomas C. '61 (PH) [32] Philadelphia, PA St. Cecilia Church.
Hagarman, Vincent A. *s.j.* '54 (CLV) [D] Cuyahoga Falls, OH Walsh Jesuit High School; [T] Akron, OH Loyola of the Lakes Jesuit Retreat House, Inc.
Hage, Simon '39 (NTN) Retired.
Hagedorn, Robert L. '44 (CIN) Retired.
Hagedorn, Thomas J. '71 (CLV) [62] Cleveland, OH St. Patrick Church.
Hagee, Robert J. *s.j.* '61 (CIN) [M] Cincinnati, OH Faber Jesuit Community.
Hagemann, John *o.s.b.* '75 (OM) [C] Elkhorn, NE Mount Michael High School; [K] Elkhorn, NE Mount Michael Abbey.
Hagen, Gerald A. '91 (SUP) Phillips, WI Our Lady of the North Church.
Hagen, John J. *o.s.a.* '57 (PH) [C] Villanova, PA

Villanova University; [AA] Villanova, PA St. Thomas Monastery.
Hagen, Joseph B. *o.f.m.* '46 (SFD) Madison, IL Our Lady of Czestochowa Church.
Hagenbach, George G. '54 (PH) Berwyn, PA St. Monica Church.
Hagendorf, Thomas *o.praem.* (GB) [4] Green Bay, WI Annunciation of the Blessed Virgin Mary Church; [8] Green Bay, WI St. Jude Church.
Hager, G. Carl *c.s.c.* '39 (FTW) [J] South Bend, IN Congregation of Holy Cross, Indiana Province, Provincial House.
Hager, Raymond D. '97 (STL) [3] Creve Coeur, MO St. Monica Church.
Hagerman, James W. '86 (MET) Bloomsbury, NJ Church of the Annunciation.
Hagerty, Msgr. John B. '55 (E) Hermitage, PA Church of Notre Dame.
Haggarty, Msgr. James J. '45 (BRK) Retired.
Haggarty, Msgr. James J. '45 (SFR) Redwood City, CA St. Pius Church.
Haggerty, Colman *c.p.* '46 (BRK) [V] Jamaica, NY Immaculate Conception Monastery.
Haggerty, Donald F. '89 (NY) [A] Yonkers, NY St. Joseph's Seminary.
Haggerty, Edward '57 (CIN) [14] Dayton, OH Holy Family Church; [M] Cincinnati, OH Headquarters of Glenmary Home Missioners.
Haggerty, Msgr. James J. '50 (BRK) Retired.
Haggerty, Thomas J. '79 (RVC) East Meadow, NY St. Raphael Church.
Haggerty, Thomas M. '64 (BRK) [137] Brooklyn, NY St. Sylvester Church.
Haggins, Martin *o.f.m.cap.* '65 (BAK) Bend, OR St. Francis of Assisi Church.
Hagileiram, John S. *s.j.* '85 (CI) Woleai and Neighboring Islands, FM St. Ignatius Church.
Haglof, Anthony *o.c.d.* '71 (BO) [W] Boston, MA Carmelite Monastery.
Hagman, William J. '55 (OWN) Retired.
Hagstrom, Thomas '93 (SFD) Batchtown, IL St. Barbara Church; Belleview, IL St. Agnes Church; Brussels, IL St. Mary Church; Hardin, IL St. Norbert Church; Kampsville, IL St. Anselm Church; Meppen, IL St. Joseph Church; Michael, IL St. Michael Church.
Hahn, Bernardine *o.f.m.* '43 (STL) Oakville, MO St. Francis of Assisi Church; [P] Oakville, MO St. Francis Friary.
Hahn, Dominic D. *o.s.b.* '80 (SEA) Shelton, WA St. Edward Church; [L] Lacey, WA St. Martin's Abbey.
Hahn, Francis *o.m.i.* '72 (FgM) Oblates Foreign Missions.
Hahn, Gerald T. '79 (NEW) Westwood, NJ St. Andrew's Church.
Hahn, James David '61 (SCL) Cambridge, MN Christ the King Church.
Hahn, Raymond W. '74 (E) [14] Erie, PA St. Boniface Church; [C] Erie, PA Cathedral Preparatory School.
Hai, Dinh Minh *c.ss.r.* '96 (LA) [Q] Baldwin Park, CA Vietnamese Redemptorist Mission.
Hai, Nguyen Tat *c.ss.r.* '97 (LA) [Q] Baldwin Park, CA Vietnamese Redemptorist Mission.
Hai-Nguyen, Joseph '67 (RIC) [6] Norfolk, VA Our Lady of Lavang Church.
Haig, Frank R. *s.j.* '60 (BAL) [B] Baltimore, MD Loyola College in Maryland; [S] Baltimore, MD Jesuit Community of Loyola College, Inc.
Haig, Scott *s.s.s.* '98 (CLV) Highland Heights, OH St. Paschal Baylon Church.
Haigerty, Leo J. '57 (LFT) Logansport, IN All Saints Church.
Haigt, Roger *s.j.* '67 (BO) [W] Cambridge, MA Weston Jesuit Community.
Hain, Msgr. Raymond B. '48 (LIN) Retired.
Haines, Jeffrey R. '85 (MIL) West Bend, WI St. Frances Cabrini Church.
Haines, Kevin J. '87 (LFT) Westfield, IN St. Maria Goretti Church.
Haiss, Maurice '56 (MOB) Holy Trinity, AL St. Joseph Church.
Hajduch, Joseph *c.pp.s.* '47 (CIN) [B] Carthagena, OH St. Charles.
Hajduk, Msgr. Edward J. '53 (NEW) [3] Bayonne, NJ St. Henry's Church.
Hajkowski, Stanislaw *s.ch.* '82 (WDC) [10] Silver Spring, MD Our Lady Queen of Poland and Saint Maximilian Kolbe Church; [V] Silver Spring, MD Friends of John Paul II Foundation.
Hakala, Thomas *o.carm.* '78 (JOL) [J] Darien, IL Carmelite Provincial Office.
Hake, Msgr. James E. '60 (SAL) [1] Salina, KS Cathedral of the Sacred Heart.
Hakenewerth, Quentin *s.m.* '60 (STL) [P] St. Louis, MO Provincialate of the Society of Mary, Province of St. Louis.
Halabura, Stephen J. '61 (ALN) Lansford, PA St. Ann Church; Lansford, PA SS. Peter and Paul Church.
Halaburda, Walter A. '59 (HBG) [1] Lebanon, PA Assumption of the Blessed Virgin Mary Church.
Haladus, Jerome Joachim *o.p.* '64 (NY) [DD] New York, NY St. Vincent Ferrer Priory.
Haladus, Victorian *o.f.m.* '61 (CHI) [N] Chicago, IL Chaplains:.
Haladus, Victorian *o.f.m.* '61 (SFD) [K] Sherman, IL Our Lady of Angels Friary.
Halaiko, David J. '67 (CLV) [13] Akron, OH Nativity Of the Lord Jesus Church.
Halbert, John K. *m.m.* '59 (NY) [DD] Maryknoll, NY Maryknoll Fathers and Brothers.
Halbing, William J. '82 (NEW) [5] Newark, NJ St. Antoninus Church.
Halborg, John E. (NY) [HH] New York, NY St. Ansgar Scandinavian Catholic League.
Halborg, John E. '80 (NY) [118] New York, NY St. Thomas More Church.
Haldane, Richard S. '92 (B) Lewiston, ID St. James Church.
Hale, Msgr. Harry L. '52 (BGP) Retired; [P] Stamford, CT The Catherine Dennis Keefe Queen of the Clergy Retired Priests' Residence.
Hale, Robert *o.s.b.cam* '66 (MRY) [F] Big Sur, CA New Camaldoli Hermitage.
Hale, Robert *o.s.b.cam.* '66 (OAK) [S] Berkeley, CA Incarnation Monastery, Camaldolese Benedictines.
Haley, James '87 (ARL) [5] Alexandria, VA St. Lawrence Church.
Haley, James A. *c.s.p.* '68 (KNX) [3] Knoxville, TN Immaculate Conception Church; [K] Knoxville, TN Calvary.
Haley, Joseph V. *c.m.* '54 (SJ) [M] Los Altos Hills, CA Daughters of Charity of St. Vincent de Paul (Laboure Residence), Seton Provincialate.
Haley, Thomas J. '78 (STL) Crestwood, MO St. Elizabeth of Hungary Church.
Haley, William J. '52 (BO) Holliston, MA St. Mary Church.
Halfacre, Philip '91 (PEO) [4] Ottawa, IL St. Patrick's Church.
Halfmann, Msgr. Curtis T. '59 (LUB) [6] Lubbock, TX St. John Neumann Church.
Halfpenny, Patrick '75 (DET) Special Assignment.
Halfpenny, Patrick F. '75 (DET) [A] Detroit, MI Sacred Heart Major Seminary, Inc.
Halka, Frantisek A. '98 (ALT) State College, PA Our Lady of Victory Church.
Halkovic, Thomas M. *c.s.c.* '71 (FR) [A] North Easton, MA Stonehill College; [A] North Easton, MA Holy Cross Fathers Religious.
Hall, Adrian B. '64 (NO) [47] New Orleans, LA St. Maurice Church.
Hall, Alan S. *o.m.v.* '95 (MET) Avenel, NJ St. Andrew Church.
Hall, Bernard '77 (GR) Retired.
Hall, Charles D. '79 (GR) Portland, MI St. Patrick's Church.
Hall, Daniel *c.s.v.* '88 (CHI) [N] Arlington Heights, IL Viatorian Province Center-Clerics of St. Viator.
Hall, Douglas C. '79 (OM) Military Chaplains.
Hall, Eric *o.f.m.cap.* '96 (NY) [151] Bronx, NY Immaculate Conception Church; [DD] New York, NY Immaculate Conception Friary.
Hall, Henry '48 (MRY) Retired.
Hall, Howard *o.f.m.* '53 (LA) [2] Santa Barbara, CA Old Mission Santa Barbara Church; [Q] Santa Barbara, CA Franciscan Friary, Order of Friars Minor (Old Mission).
Hall, Howard B. '62 (BR) Morganza, LA St. Ann Church.
Hall, James W. '70 (ELP) [33] El Paso, TX St. Thomas Aquinas Church.
Hall, Jerome M. *s.j.* '77 (BAL) [S] Baltimore, MD Jesuit Fathers and Brothers Maryland Provincial Curia.
Hall, John '82 (PHX) Special Assignment.
Hall, John F. '55 (DET) Retired.
Hall, John M. '80 (IND) French Lick, IN Our Lady of the Springs Church; Paoli, IN Our Lord Jesus Christ the King Church.
Hall, John R. '80 (CHI) Niles, IL Our Lady of Ransom Church.
Hall, Joseph S. '85 (L) Clementsville, KY St. Bernard Church.
Hall, Martin J. '52 (RVC) Levittown, NY St. Bernard Church; Retired.
Hall, Michael *o.s.b.* '65 (WDC) [M] Washington, DC St. Anselm's Abbey.
Hall, Ralph T. *o.p.* '55 (PRO) [P] Providence, RI St. Thomas Aquinas Priory at Providence College.
Hall, Randall C. *s.j.* '58 (DEN) [M] Denver, CO Loyola Parish - Jesuit Community.
Hall, Randall C. *s.j.* '58 (STL) [P] St. Louis, MO The Jesuits of the Missouri Province.
Hall, Richard *o.m.i.* '93 (LAR) Eagle Pass, TX Sacred Heart Church.
Hall, Robert '85 (HEL) Bozeman, MT Resurrection Church; [H] Bozeman, MT Montana State University.
Hall, Robert C. (ALT) Conemaugh, PA Sacred Heart Church; Conemaugh, PA Assumption of B.V.M. Church.
Hall, Rodney '91 (SAC) Westwood, CA Our Lady of the Snows Church.
Hall, Sidney Peter '57 (SAC) [19] Sacramento, CA St. Peter Church.
Hall, Thomas P. *c.s.p.* '77 (NY) [DD] Jamaica Estates, NY Paulist Fathers Generalate.
Hall, Walter J. '49 (ALN) Heckscherville, PA St. Kieran Church.
Hall, Warren R. '89 (NEW) On Duty Outside the Archdiocese.
Hall, Warren R. '89 (WIL) [5] Wilmington, DE St. Elizabeth Church.
Halladay, Paul A. '00 (MOB) [19] Mobile, AL St. Pius X Church.
Hallahan, Kenneth P. '75 (CAM) [5] Camden, NJ St. Joan of Arc Church.
Hallahan, Timothy J. '57 (SPR) Southwick, MA Our Lady of the Lake Church.
Hallahan, William *o.m.i.* '59 (SEA) [28] Seattle, WA Our Lady of Guadalupe Church.
Hallee, Roger *o.m.i.* '63 (FgM) Oblates Foreign Missions.
Hallemann, John L. '55 (STL) Oakville, MO Queen of All Saints Church.
Haller, James W. '62 (MAN) Auburn, NH St. Peter Church.
Haller, Joseph A. *s.j.* '55 (WDC) [M] Washington, DC The Jesuit Community at Georgetown University.
Halleran, Thomas *s.v.d.* '44 (CHI) [B] Techny, IL Divine Word Residence.
Halleron, James E. '97 (TOL) [4] Fremont, OH St. Joseph Church.
Hallett, Garth L. *s.j.* '59 (STL) [C] St. Louis, MO Saint Louis University; [P] St. Louis, MO Jesuit Community Corporation at St. Louis University - Jesuit Hall.
Halley, Thomas A. *s.j.* '48 (MIL) [P] Milwaukee, WI Jesuit Provincial Office, Wisconsin Province.
Halley, Thomas A. *s.j.* '48 (OM) [K] Omaha, NE Jesuit Community at Creighton University.
Halligan, Damian O. *s.j.* '67 (RVC) [O] Manhasset, NY St. Ignatius Retreat House, Inisfada.
Halligan, James '43 (LIN) Retired.
Halligan, James J. '51 (NY) [105] New York, NY St. Peter Church.
Halligan, John J. *s.j.* '61 (FgM) Provinces.
Halligan, Raymond Ferrer *o.p.* '60 (NY) [DD] New York, NY St. Vincent Ferrer Priory; [HH] New York, NY Dominican Friars' Guilds.
Hallin, Msgr. Albert W. '61 (PEO) [1] Champaign, IL Holy Cross Church.
Hallinan, Edward J. '83 (PH) [94] Philadelphia, PA St. Martin De Porres Church.
Hallinan, Mark C. *s.j.* '95 (NY) [51] New York, NY St. Ignatius Loyola Church; [DD] New York, NY St. Ignatius Loyola Residence.
Hallissey, Msgr. James T. '40 (B) Retired.
Hallissey, LaSalle *o.p.* '73 (OAK) Antioch, CA Holy Rosary Church.
Hallisy, Peter *c.p.* '51 (HRT) [M] West Hartford, CT Holy Family Monastery/Retreat.
Halliwell, Raymond *m.s.a.* '93 (NOR) [A] Cromwell, CT Holy Apostles College and Seminary; [F] Cromwell, CT Society of the Missionaries of the Holy Apostles.
Halliwell, Robert J. '57 (NEW) Northvale, NJ St. Anthony's Church.
Hallock, Addison *m.s.a.* '74 (NOR) [A] Cromwell, CT Holy Apostles College and Seminary; [F] Cromwell, CT Society of the Missionaries of the Holy Apostles.
Halloran, Msgr. Edward D. '35 (BGP) Retired; [P] Stamford, CT The Catherine Dennis Keefe Queen of the Clergy Retired Priests' Residence.
Halloran, Emmett J. (ROC) Canandaigua, NY St. Mary Church; Retired.
Halloran, James '43 (COS) Retired.
Halloran, Jerome D. '54 (WIN) Retired.
Halloran, John '48 (HON) Retired.
Halloran, John C. '62 (PRO) Narragansett, RI St. Thomas More Church.
Halloran, John J. '48 (LA) Retired.
Halloran, John M. '87 (PH) [72] Philadelphia, PA Incarnation of Our Lord Church.
Halloran, Joseph '53 (ALB) [11] Troy, NY St. Paul the Apostle Church; Retired.
Halloran, Joseph H. '47 (COS) Retired.
Halloran, Paul F. '53 (WIN) Retired.
Halloran, Walter H. *s.j.* '54 (SD) La Mesa, CA St. Martin of Tours Church.
Hallsten, Thomas *o.s.b.* '90 (SCL) [I] Collegeville, MN St. John's Abbey, of the Order of St. Benedict.
Halphen, Jude (LAF) [1] New Iberia, LA St. Peter Church.
Halphen, Marshall J. *o.s.a.* '63 (ALB) Waterford, NY St. Mary of the Assumption Church.
Halpin, John P. '54 (RVC) Central Islip, NY St. John of God Church; West Brentwood, NY Pilgrim Psychiatric Center.
Halpin, Joseph '79 (TR) [2] Toms River, NJ St. Justin Church.
Halpin, Joseph W. *m.m.* '52 (FgM) Maryknoll Foreign Missions.
Halpin, Leo F. '42 (NY) Retired.
Halpine, Msgr. James F. '37 (TLS) Retired.

Halpine, Msgr. James F. '52 (TLS) [1] Tulsa, OK Holy Family Church.
Halsema, Douglas '00 (PT) [13] Pensacola, FL St. Paul Church.
Halstead, James R. *o.s.a.* '76 (CHI) Evanston, IL St. Nicholas Church.
Halstead, James R. *o.s.a.* '96 (CHI) [N] Olympia Fields, IL The Augustinians-Provincialate.
Halstead, Philip '62 (PT) Retired.
Halter, Robert *o.s.b.* '60 (OM) [C] Elkhorn, NE Mount Michael High School.
Halton, Thomas P. '50 (WDC) [C] Washington, DC Catholic University of America, The.
Halus, Robert E. '82 (PBR) Perryopolis, PA St. Nicholas Church.
Haluska, Charles A. '51 (COL) Retired.
Halvey, William *s.v.d.* '76 (TR) [M] Bordentown, NJ Society of the Divine Word.
Ham, George E. '67 (MAN) Hampton, NH Our Lady of the Miraculous Medal Church.
Ham, Msgr. Jerome '68 (PEO) [2] Streator, IL St. Anthony of Padua Church; [3] Streator, IL St. Casimir Church.
Hamaday, Ronald A. *o.s.a.* '78 (CAM) [C] Richland, NJ St. Augustine Preparatory School.
Hamak, William '92 (SFS) Armour, SD St. Paul the Apostle Church.
Hambach, Lawrence *s.v.d.* '61 (FgM) Society of the Divine Word Foreign Missions.
Hambrough, Patrick K. '85 (STL) Affton, MO St. Timothy Church.
Hamburger, Msgr. Donald C. '46 (CHR) Retired.
Hamel, Edward L. *o.s.a.* '54 (CHI) [N] Olympia Fields, IL Tolentine Monastery at Tolentine Center.
Hamel, Joseph L. *m.m.* '85 (FgM) Maryknoll Foreign Missions.
Hamel, Philip N. '85 (FR) [3] Swansea, MA St. Michael's Church.
Hamel, Robert F. '83 (STP) Retired.
Hamel, Roland M. *o.m.i.* '53 (MAN) [K] Colebrook, NH Shrine of Our Lady of Grace.
Hamel, Thomas *s.j.* '58 (BO) [W] Cambridge, MA Weston Jesuit Community.
Hamernick, Joseph M. *s.j.* '62 (SCR) [C] Scranton, PA University of Scranton.
Hamernik, Peter P. '56 (WOR) West Warren, MA St. Stanislaus Church.
Hamill, Francis J. *s.j.* '61 (NEW) [C] Jersey City, NJ St. Peter's Preparatory School.
Hamill, Gregory J. '94 (PH) On Duty Outside the Archdiocese.
Hamill, William A. *o.s.a.* '72 (CHI) [N] Olympia Fields, IL The Augustinians-Provincialate.
Hamilton, Daniel E. '72 (ARL) Fredericksburg, VA St. Mary Church.
Hamilton, Msgr. Daniel S. '58 (RVC) Lindenhurst, NY Our Lady of Perpetual Help Church.
Hamilton, Donald Joseph *o.c.s.o.* '46 (SPC) [E] Ava, MO Assumption Abbey (Trappist).
Hamilton, Edward A. '59 (ORL) Retired.
Hamilton, James '58 (CC) Retired.
Hamilton, James J. '53 (PRO) [11] Warwick, RI St. Timothy Church.
Hamilton, John W. '70 (BUR) South Burlington, VT St. John Vianney Church.
Hamilton, Joseph K. '54 (L) Retired.
Hamilton, Ken *s.v.d.* '82 (OAK) [8] Oakland, CA St. Cyril Church.
Hamilton, Kenneth *s.v.d.* '82 (IND) [34] Indianapolis, IN St. Rita Church.
Hamilton, Msgr. Lamont R. '79 (NY) [148] Bronx, NY Holy Rosary Church.
Hamilton, Mark M. '94 (L) Graduate Studies.
Hamilton, Philip A. '44 (DUB) Retired.
Hamilton, Stephen V. '99 (OKL) Edmond, OK St. John the Baptist Church.
Hamilton, Terence J. '73 (CIN) [82] Cincinnati, OH St. Vincent Ferrer Church.
Hamilton, Thomas *o.f.m.conv.* '76 (LA) [J] Torrance, CA Little Company of Mary Hospital.
Hamilton, Thomas M. *s.m.* '88 (OAK) [N] Berkeley, CA Marist Fathers and Brothers.
Hamilton, William J. *s.j.* '63 (BO) [E] Boston, MA Boston College High School & Jesuit Community; [W] Boston, MA The Society of Jesus of New England-Provincial Offices.
Hamilton, William J. *s.j.* '63 (MAN) [7] Manchester, NH St. Edmund Church.
Hamilton, William J. *k.h.s.* '80 (SPR) Easthampton, MA Immaculate Conception Church.
Hamlet, Ralph '62 (RIC) Retired.
Hamlett, Christopher '82 (E) [B] Erie, PA Gannon University.
Hamlin, Raymond '91 (CLV) Absent on Leave.
Hamm, David A. *s.t.* '75 (JKS) Philadelphia, MS Holy Rosary Church.
Hamm, M. Dennis *s.j.* '70 (OM) [K] Omaha, NE Jesuit Community at Creighton University.
Hamm, Robert E. *s.j.* '68 (BAL) [S] Baltimore, MD Jesuit Fathers and Brothers Maryland Provincial Curia.
Hamm, Robert E. *s.j.* '68 (FgM) Provinces.
Hamm, Thomas F., Jr. '00 (STU) Woodsfield, OH St. Sylvester Church.
Hammel, Gerald *s.m.* '78 (SAT) Helotes, TX Our Lady of Guadalupe Church.
Hammelman, William *o.s.b.* '71 (P) [A] St. Benedict, OR Mount Angel Seminary; [L] St. Benedict, OR Mt. Angel Abbey.
Hammer, Msgr. Edmond '42 (NY) Retired.
Hammer, Jack '79 (SAG) Alma, MI St. Mary Church.
Hammer, James *o.f.m.cap.* '65 (NOR) [4] Middletown, CT St. Pius X Church.
Hammer, Jefferson '60 (NY) Manhattan, NY St. Vincent Hospital.
Hammer, John E. '79 (SAG) St. Louis, MI St. Joseph Church.
Hammer, Michael J. '69 (MIL) Special Assignment.
Hammer, William D. '80 (L) [28] Louisville, KY St. Gabriel the Archangel Church.
Hammerl, Msgr. Leo E. '44 (BUF) Retired; [O] Tonawanda, NY O'Hara Residence.
Hammerschmitt, Clemens '73 (PMB) [3] Lake Worth, FL St. Matthew Church.
Hammerschmitt, Clemens '77 (PMB) [K] Palm Beach Gardens, FL Diocesan Council of Catholic Women.
Hammerstein, Harold *o.s.b.* '48 (IND) [J] St. Meinrad, IN St. Meinrad Archabbey.
Hammett, Peter E. *o.s.b.* '72 (NO) [A] St. Benedict, LA St. Joseph's Seminary College; [P] St. Benedict, LA St. Joseph Abbey.
Hammil, William A. *o.s.a.* '72 (TLS) [5] Tulsa, OK Christ the King Church.
Hammond, Charles '76 (SAG) Helena, MI St. Anthony Church; Parisville, MI St. Mary Church.
Hammond, Gerard E. *m.m.* '60 (FgM) Maryknoll Foreign Missions.
Hammond, H. Martin '73 (BAL) [43] Baltimore, MD St. Isaac Jogues Church.
Hammond, John *o.s.b.* '50 (BUR) [E] Weston, VT Priory of Benedictine Monks.
Hammond, Joseph '89 (KNX) Morristown, TN St. Patrick Church.
Hammond, Joseph Mary *c.h.s.* '89 (KNX) Greeneville, TN Notre Dame Church.
Hammond, Mark J. '89 (COL) [29] Columbus, OH St. Mary Church.
Hammond, Robert (FTW) [H] Fort Wayne, IN Saint Anne Home & Retirement Community.
Hammond, Robert '52 (FTW) Retired.
Hampe, Ray '54 (STL) [K] St. Charles, MO SSM St. Joseph Health Center.
Hampe, Msgr. Raymond A. '54 (STL) [5] St. Charles, MO St. Peter Church.
Hampe, Msgr. Raymond H. '54 (STL) St. Charles, MO St. Joseph Health Center.
Hamperzonian, Jerry '70 (PSC) On Duty Outside Diocese.
Hamperzonian, Jerry '70 (SD) [3] San Diego, CA Blessed Sacrament Church; La Jolla, CA Veterans Administration Hospital.
Hampsch, John *c.m.f.* '52 (LA) [Q] Los Angeles, CA Claretian Retreat Center Community.
Hampton, Davis '90 (LAF) On Duty Outside the Diocese.
Hampton, James '88 (MIA) Retired.
Hamrogue, John *c.ss.r.* '63 (BRK) [107] Brooklyn, NY Our Lady of Perpetual Help Basilica Church.
Han, Andrew '48 (LA) Retired.
Han Kim, Andrew Sung '91 (P) [11] Portland, OR Church of Korean Martyrs.
Hanacsek, John '49 (TOL) Retired.
Hanauska, Joseph F. '40 (MIL) Retired.
Hanbury, Kevin M. '72 (NEW) [B] South Orange, NJ Seton Hall University.
Hanchak, Augustine *c.pp.s.* '52 (CIN) [B] Carthagena, OH St. Charles.
Hanchon, Donald F. '74 (DET) [33] Detroit, MI Holy Redeemer Church.
Hancock, Msgr. George H. '47 (OWN) Grand Rivers, KY St. Anthony of Padua Church.
Hancock, Walter '47 (OWN) Retired.
Hand, Chester, Jr. '86 (AUS) Retired.
Hand, Dennis M. '75 (GRY) On Duty Outside the Diocese.
Hand, John D. '98 (PH) [95] Philadelphia, PA St. Martin of Tours Church.
Hand, Kenneth J. '72 (BRK) [237] Queens, NY Sacred Heart of Jesus Church.
Hand, Msgr. Kevin '52 (AMA) White Deer, TX Sacred Heart Church; Retired; [K] Amarillo, TX Monsignor B.A. Erpen Trust Fund.
Hand, Robert T. '97 (SAV) [4] Savannah, GA Most Blessed Sacrament Church.
Hand, Thomas G. *s.j.* '51 (SJ) [L] Los Gatos, CA Sacred Heart Jesuit Center.
Handges, Msgr. William E. '64 (ALN) [7] Bethlehem, PA Notre Dame of Bethlehem Church.
Handrahan, John *s.j.* '58 (MIA) [1] Pompano Beach, FL Assumption Church.
Handrahan, John B. *s.j.* '58 (BO) [W] Boston, MA The Society of Jesus of New England-Provincial Offices.
Hands, Michael '93 (RVC) East Meadow, NY St. Raphael Church.
Handwerker, Valentine '74 (MEM) [C] Memphis, TN Immaculate Conception Cathedral Middle and High School.
Handwerker, Valentine N. '74 (MEM) [1] Memphis, TN Cathedral of the Immaculate Conception.
Hane, Howard S. '67 (BO) Senior Priests.
Hanefeldt, Joseph G. '84 (OM) [13] Omaha, NE St. Elizabeth Ann Church.
Hanel, Charles '83 (MIL) Lake Five, WI St. Columba Church.
Hanel, Charles T. '83 (MIL) Hubertus, WI St. Hubert Church; Richfield, WI St. Mary Church.
Haney, John R. '61 (PIT) Whitehall, PA St. Gabriel of the Sorrowful Virgin Church.
Haney, Michael *o.f.m.* '74 (SHP) West Monroe, LA St. Paschal Church.
Haney, Thomas R. '58 (HBG) New Cumberland, PA St. Theresa of the Infant Jesus Church.
Haney, William *o.f.m.* '84 (SD) [H] Oceanside, CA Mission San Luis Rey; [K] Oceanside, CA Mission San Luis Rey Retreat.
Hanh, Joseph Phan Trong '70 (KC) [16] Kansas City, MO Church of the Holy Martyrs.
Hanhauser, Martin A. *o.f.m.* '42 (SP) [O] St. Petersburg, FL St. Anthony Friary.
Hanic, John D. '83 (CHL) [5] Charlotte, NC St. Gabriel Church.
Hanicak, Msgr. Robert A. '36 (GBG) Retired; [G] Greensburg, PA Neumann House.
Hanifin, Michael P. '87 (ORG) Garden Grove, CA St. Columban Church.
Hankiewicz, Edward '79 (GR) On Special Assignment.
Hankiewicz, Edward A. '79 (GR) [21] Grand Rapids, MI Sacred Heart Church.
Hankinson, Aloysius *t.o.r.* '50 (ALT) [F] Hollidaysburg, PA St. Joseph Friary.
Hankomoone, Cornelius '96 (BAL) [S] Baltimore, MD Sulpician Provincial House.
Hanks, Joseph H. '81 (NOR) Old Saybrook, CT St. John Church.
Hankus, David '84 (JOL) Bolingbrook, IL St. Francis of Assisi Church.
Hanley, Msgr. Andrew W. '40 (SD) Retired.
Hanley, Dennis P. '81 (HRT) Military Chaplains.
Hanley, Foster *o.carm.* '63 (TUC) [A] Tucson, AZ Salpointe Catholic High School; [F] Tucson, AZ Carmelite Priory.
Hanley, Francis *c.s.sp.* (PIT) [B] Pittsburgh, PA Duquesne University of the Holy Ghost.
Hanley, Gerald T. '73 (RNO) Carson City, NV St. Teresa's of Avila Church.
Hanley, James F. *s.j.* '47 (MIL) [P] Milwaukee, WI Jesuit Provincial Office, Wisconsin Province.
Hanley, Msgr. James P. '51 (COL) Retired.
Hanley, James R. *s.j.* '58 (SJ) [K] Los Altos, CA Jesuit Retreat House.
Hanley, James T. '62 (PAT) Retired.
Hanley, John '56 (PHX) [1] Tempe, AZ Holy Spirit Church.
Hanley, John A. *o.s.f.s.* '86 (WDC) [B] Washington, DC Oblates of St. Francis de Sales.
Hanley, John P. '51 (MIL) Retired.
Hanley, John P. '94 (PAT) [8] Paterson, NJ St. Gerard Majella Church.
Hanley, John W. *o.m.i.* (BO) [3] Lowell, MA Immaculate Conception Church.
Hanley, Joseph F. '68 (CHR) [7] Charleston, SC Blessed Sacrament Church.
Hanley, Lawrence F. '52 (CHI) Retired.
Hanley, Thomas E. '65 (WIL) Dover, DE Holy Cross Church.
Hanley, William '45 (SPK) Retired.
Hanley, William '69 (ORL) Melbourne, FL Our Lady of Lourdes Church.
Hanlon, Msgr. Andrew J. '68 (PH) Brookhaven, PA Our Lady of Charity Church.
Hanlon, Berard J. *o.f.m.* '63 (FgM) Franciscan Foreign Missions.
Hanlon, Capistran *o.f.m.* '60 (ALB) [B] Loudonville, NY Siena College.
Hanlon, Edward J. '86 (WOR) Milford, MA Sacred Heart Church.
Hanlon, Francis J. *o.s.f.s.* '76 (CAM) [M] Pittsgrove, NJ Villa St. Joseph.
Hanlon, Francis J. *o.s.f.s.* '76 (WIL) [I] Wilmington, DE Oblates of St. Francis De Sales.
Hanlon, Gavin P. *o.f.m.* '56 (FgM) Franciscan Foreign Missions.
Hanlon, Msgr. James J. '38 (NY) Retired; [Z] New York, NY Kateri Residence.
Hanlon, John R. '55 (BO) Senior Priests.
Hanlon, Kevin J. *m.m.* '89 (FgM) Maryknoll Foreign Missions.
Hanlon, Robert *o.s.f.s.* '57 (WIL) [I] Childs, MD Oblates of St. Francis De Sales.
Hanlon, Robert M. *s.j.* '64 (BO) [W] Boston, MA The Society of Jesus of New England-Provincial Offices.
Hanly, Denis J. *m.m.* '59 (FgM) Maryknoll Foreign Missions.

Hanly, John J. '50 (LA) Retired.
Hanly, Joseph M. *c.s.p.* '53 (NY) [DD] Jamaica Estates, NY Paulist Fathers Generalate.
Hanly, Joseph M. *c.s.p.* '53 (SFR) [32] San Francisco, CA Old St. Mary's Church.
Hanly, Michael A. '67 (NEW) Verona, NJ Our Lady of the Lake Church.
Hanly, Thomas '62 (MIA) [1] Hollywood, FL Little Flower Church; Retired.
Hann, Michael *c.i.c.m.* '73 (FgM) Missionhurst Foreign Missions.
Hanna, Austin B. '36 (ROC) Retired.
Hanna, Don Michael '64 (RIC) Yorktown, VA St. Joan of Arc Church.
Hanna, George *s.d.b.* '66 (NY) [117] New York, NY St. Thomas the Apostle Church; [HH] New York, NY Don Bosco Harlem Association, Inc.
Hanna, Jack H. *c.s.b.* '74 (GAL) [F] Houston, TX St. Thomas High School.
Hannafey, Francis T. '93 (BGP) [B] Fairfield, CT Fairfield University; [P] Fairfield, CT The Fairfield Jesuit Community-Fairfield University.
Hannah, Raymond *s.v.d.* '60 (LAF) Leonville, LA St. Catherine Church.
Hannan, Gabriel *s.t.* '55 (WDC) [M] Adelphi, MD Missionary Servants of the Most Holy Trinity.
Hannan, Msgr. Herbert J. '37 (OG) Retired.
Hannan, James E. *o.s.a.* '44 (SD) [H] San Diego, CA Augustinian Community.
Hannan, James G. '81 (BRK) [103] Brooklyn, NY Our Lady of Miracles Church.
Hannan, John '55 (SAC) [20] Sacramento, CA St. Philomene Church.
Hannan, Msgr. John P. '47 (ARL) Retired.
Hannan, Robert '54 (HON) [1] Honolulu, HI Cathedral of Our Lady of Peace.
Hannappel, Joseph A. '84 (GI) Spalding, NE St. Michael's Church.
Hannaway, Arthur W. '85 (VEN) [6] Sarasota, FL St. Patrick Church.
Hanneke, Richard E. '76 (STL) Ellisville, MO St. Clare of Assisi Church.
Hanneman, Dennis A. '72 (OM) [47] Omaha, NE St. Vincent de Paul Church.
Hannes, David A. '83 (PRM) Flushing, MI St. Michael Church.
Hannick, Anthony S. '58 (OAK) [1] Walnut Creek, CA St. Anne Church; Military Chaplains.
Hannick, Anthony S. '58 (YAK) Retired.
Hannifin, Francis M. '45 (L) Retired.
Hannigan, John T. '76 (CHI) Other Assignments.
Hannigan, John T. '76 (SFD) Morrisonville, IL St. Maurice Church; Raymond, IL St Raymond Church.
Hannigan, Raymond J. '91 (HEL) Libby, MT St. Joseph Church.
Hannigan, Thomas J. '49 (MAN) [6] Manchester, NH St. Catherine Church.
Hannon, Msgr. James J. '45 (BLX) Retired.
Hannon, James J. '57 (RVC) Brentwood, NY St. Anne's Church.
Hannon, James W. '88 (BAL) Westernport, MD St. Peter Church.
Hannon, John M. '60 (BO) Hanson, MA St. Joseph the Worker Church.
Hannon, John P. '76 (HRT) Retired.
Hannon, Ken *o.m.i.* '72 (SAT) [C] San Antonio, TX Oblate School of Theology; [M] San Antonio, TX De Mazenod House.
Hannon, Kevin E. '75 (SY) Mattydale, NY St. Margaret Church.
Hannon, Michael '47 (ORL) Retired.
Hannon, Richard T. '93 (GAY) Elmira, MI St. Thomas Aquinas Church.
Hannon, Robert E. '54 (HON) Retired.
Hannon, Robert J. '79 (Y) Masury, OH St. Bernadette Church.
Hannon, Timothy G. '62 (MIA) [4] Fort Lauderdale, FL St. Anthony Church.
Hannon, W. Patrick *c.s.c.* '69 (CHI) [D] Niles, IL Notre Dame High School.
Hanowsky, Andrew '88 (SJP) Parma, OH St. Josaphat Church.
Hanrahan, Denis G. '59 (OKL) Guthrie, OK St. Mary's Church.
Hanrahan, Edward J. *s.j.* '61 (BO) [W] Chestnut Hill, MA The Jesuit Community at Boston College.
Hanrahan, John A. '66 (RCK) Polo, IL St. Mary's Church.
Hanrahan, John W. '55 (L) Retired.
Hanrahan, William P. '69 (NEW) Military Chaplains.
Hanratty, Brendan '45 (SR) Retired.
Hanratty, Brendan *o.c.s.o.* '58 (SLC) [F] Huntsville, UT Abbey of Our Lady of the Holy Trinity of the Order of Cistercians.
Hansen, Albert M. '65 (BUF) [6] Tonawanda, NY St. Francis of Assisi Church.
Hansen, Howard *o.f.m.conv.* '57 (DUB) Ames, IA St. Cecilia Church.
Hansen, John R. *s.m.p.* '81 (SPC) [E] Marionville, MO The Society of Our Mother of Peace, Sons of Our Mother of Peace.
Hansen, Lawrence H. '68 (NU) On Duty Outside the Diocese.
Hansen, Lawrence H. '68 (PH) [U] Philadelphia, PA Mercy Hospital of Philadelphia; [U] Darby, PA Mercy Catholic Medical Center.
Hansen, Michael '67 (NEW) Emerson, NJ Church of the Assumption.
Hansen, Robert H. '40 (LC) Retired.
Hansen, Thomas J. *s.j.* '96 (OM) [K] Omaha, NE Campion House.
Hanser, David J. '58 (MIL) [K] Milwaukee, WI St. Joseph's Hospital of Franciscan Sisters, Milwaukee, Inc.
Hanser, F. Patrick *c.m.* '70 (DAL) [G] Dallas, TX St. Paul Medical Center.
Hansmann, Joseph D. '62 (BEL) Hecker, IL St. Augustine of Canterbury Church; Paderborn, IL St. Michael Church.
Hanson, Christopher *o.s.b.* '96 (STL) [F] Creve Coeur, MO St. Louis Priory School; [P] St. Louis, MO The Abbey of St. Mary and St. Louis.
Hanson, Donald M. '71 (RVC) Carle Place, NY Church of Our Lady of Hope.
Hanson, Howard *o.f.m.conv.* '57 (DUB) Gilbert, IA SS. Peter and Paul Church.
Hanson, Msgr. James E. '61 (STL) Zell, MO St. Joseph Church.
Hanson, Kirby C. '70 (SFR) [52] San Francisco, CA St. Thomas the Apostle Church.
Hanson, Richard N. '75 (CHL) [11] Charlotte, NC St. Vincent de Paul Church.
Hanson, William A. '72 (RVC) Port Jefferson, NY St. Gerard Majella Church.
Hanudel, Francis *o.f.m.* (NY) [13] New York, NY St. Anthony of Padua Church.
Hanus, Thomas J. '66 (AUS) Cameron, TX St. Monica's Church.
Hanwell, John J. *s.j.* '91 (BO) [E] Boston, MA Boston College High School & Jesuit Community.
Hanzely, Joseph B. *s.j.* '48 (ALN) [A] Wernersville, PA Jesuit Center.
Hanzo, Robert G. '56 (CLV) Painesville, OH St. Mary Church; Retired.
Hapanowicz, Arthur R. '56 (SY) [2] Utica, NY Holy Trinity Church; [W] Utica, NY Holy Trinity.
Hapka, Jerome A. *s.a.c.* '55 (MIL) [P] Milwaukee, WI Pallotti House.
Happe, Lawrence L. '60 (GBG) Coral, PA St. Francis Church.
Happel, Stephen *ph.d.* '59 (WDC) [C] Washington, DC Catholic University of America, The.
Happel, Stephen P. '70 (IND) On Duty Outside the Archdiocese.
Happel, Stephen W. '70 (WDC) [C] Washington, DC Catholic University of America, The.
Harahan, Msgr. Robert E. '74 (NEW) Summit, NJ St. Teresa's Church.
Harak, G. Simon *s.j.* '79 (BO) [W] Boston, MA The Society of Jesus of New England-Provincial Offices.
Harak, G. Simon *s.j.* '79 (NY) [DD] New York, NY West Side Jesuit Community.
Haran, Ignatius '59 (SAC) Folsom, CA St. John the Baptist Church.
Haran, James E. '44 (BUF) Retired.
Harasim, Edward A. '78 (CHI) [75] Chicago, IL St. Henry Church.
Harbaugh, James M. *s.j.* '76 (SEA) [A] Seattle, WA Seattle University.
Harbaugh, Paul E. '74 (BEL) Leave of Absence.
Harbert, William S. '62 (PEO) Absent on Leave.
Harbison, William *c.ss.r.* '66 (BAL) [87] Baltimore, MD Sacred Heart of Jesus Church.
Harbour, Gerald G. '73 (PRO) Providence, RI Rhode Island Hospital.
Harbour, Linn S. '86 (MOB) On Leave from the Archdiocese.
Harcarik, Bernard M. '63 (PIT) [63] Pittsburgh, PA Prince of Peace Church.
Hardebeck, Donald E. '45 (LFT) Retired.
Harder, Ken '96 (TLS) Pryor, OK St. Mark's Church.
Harder, Kenneth '96 (TLS) Wagoner, OK Holy Cross Church.
Harder, William '86 (NY) [214] Staten Island, NY St. Mary of the Assumption Church.
Hardesty, Ernest L. '75 (LR) Russellville, AR St. John's Church; [J] Russellville, AR St. Leo the Great University Parish.
Hardiman, Msgr. James C. '39 (CHI) Retired.
Hardiman, Michael J. '78 (BRK) [A] Douglaston, NY Immaculate Conception Center; [V] Douglaston, NY Institutional Services Residence.
Hardin, Boniface *o.s.b.* '59 (IND) [J] St. Meinrad, IN St. Meinrad Archabbey.
Hardin, John *o.f.m.* '82 (OAK) [N] Oakland, CA Franciscan Friars Provincial Office, Province of St. Barbara.
Hardin, John S. *o.f.m.* '86 (OAK) [N] Oakland, CA Franciscan Friars Provincial Office, Province of St. Barbara.
Hardin, Roy (CAM) [M] Cherry Hill, NJ Vianney Villa.
Hardin, Roy '64 (CAM) On Sick Leave.
Harding, Ignatius *o.f.m.* '65 (FgM) Franciscan Foreign Missions.
Harding, Nicholas J. '99 (GAL) [19] Houston, TX St. Charles Borromeo Church.
Harding, Pius X *o.s.b.* '93 (P) [L] St. Benedict, OR Mt. Angel Abbey.
Hardman, John *s.s.j.* (WDC) [32] Washington, DC Our Lady of Perpetual Help Church.
Hardon, John *s.j.* '47 (WDC) [V] Kensington, MD Inter Mirifica.
Hardon, John A. *s.j.* '47 (DET) [P] Clarkston, MI Colombiere Center.
Hardy, John J. '38 (DET) Retired.
Hare, Robert '70 (NSH) [H] Nashville, TN Glenmary Home Missioners; [L] Nashville, TN Glenmary Department of Pastoral Services.
Haremza, Shawn T. '00 (WIN) [1] Winona, MN Cathedral of the Sacred Heart; [I] Winona, MN St. Thomas Aquinas Newman Center.
Haren, Donald J. *m.m.* '47 (SJ) [L] Los Altos, CA Maryknoll.
Haren, Thomas A. '73 (CLV) [36] Cleveland, OH St. Jerome Church.
Harer, Eric K. '84 (SY) [5] Oswego, NY St. Paul Church.
Harfmann, John G. *s.s.j.* '62 (LA) [52] Los Angeles, CA St. Brigid's Church.
Hargaden, Kevin J. '99 (ATL) [3] Marietta, GA St. Joseph Church.
Hargadon, James E. (L) Retired.
Hargadon, James E. '55 (L) [62] Louisville, KY St. Patrick Church.
Hargesheimer, Thomas J. '68 (WIN) Owatonna, MN St. Joseph's Church.
Hargreaves, Henry G. *s.j.* '47 (FBK) [E] St. Marys, AK Brother Joe Prince Jesuit Community.
Hargrove, Jerry E. '76 (WDC) Retired.
Harguindeguy, Msgr. John '67 (FRS) [7] Fresno, CA St. Anthony of Padua Church.
Harhager, John H. *s.m.* '79 (WDC) [M] Washington, DC Marist Center.
Hari Kustanto, Johannes B. *s.j.* '91 (BGP) [P] Fairfield, CT The Fairfield Jesuit Community-Fairfield University.
Harkabus, Don '57 (JOL) [4] Lockport, IL St. Joseph Church.
Harkabus, Donald W. *o.s.a.* '58 (CHI) [N] Olympia Fields, IL The Augustinians-Provincialate.
Harkin, William C. *o.s.a.* (CHL) Maggie Valley, NC St. Margaret Church.
Harkins, Conrad *o.f.m.* '61 (STU) [A] Steubenville, OH Franciscan University of Steubenville; [F] Steubenville, OH Holy Spirit Friary.
Harkins, John M. '65 (PH) [9] Philadelphia, PA St. Ambrose Church.
Harkins, Kenneth *o.p.* '67 (WDC) [B] Washington, DC Dominican House of Studies.
Harkins, Michael J. '79 (BO) Pembroke, MA St. Thecla Church.
Harkins, Msgr. Thaddeus '55 (JKS) Port Gibson, MS St. Joseph Church.
Harkins, Thomas '71 (CAM) [M] Cherry Hill, NJ Vianney Villa.
Harkrader, Edward O. '69 (PEO) Princeton, IL St. Louis Church.
Harland, Norman E. *s.j.* '67 (CHI) [D] Wilmette, IL Loyola Academy.
Harley, Ronald P. '67 (ROC) Avon, NY St. Agnes Church.
Harlow, Denis '58 (BLX) [5] Biloxi, MS Sacred Heart Church; Biloxi, MS Biloxi Regional Hospital, Gulf Coast Community Hospital.
Harlow, Lance (BUR) On Special or Other Diocesan Assignment.
Harlow, Lance W. '93 (BUR) Essex Junction, VT Holy Family Church; Burlington, VT Fletcher Allen Health Care.
Harlow, Sean *o. carm.* '69 (BRK) [140] Brooklyn, NY St. Thomas Aquinas Church.
Harman, Charles W. '54 (LA) Retired.
Harman, Paul F. *s.j.* '68 (BO) [W] Boston, MA The Society of Jesus of New England-Provincial Offices.
Harman, Paul F. *s.j.* '68 (CHI) [C] Chicago, IL Jesuit Community at Loyola University of Chicago.
Harman, Peter C. '00 (SFD) [1] Springfield, IL Cathedral of the Immaculate Conception.
Harmening, Adrian W. *o.s.b.* '55 (RIC) [12] Richmond, VA St. Joseph Tridentine Chapel Church; [L] Richmond, VA Mary Mother of the Church Abbey.
Harmless, J. William *s.j.* '87 (MOB) [A] Mobile, AL Spring Hill College.
Harmon, Alban *f.n., c.p.* '58 (BAL) [S] Baltimore, MD St. Joseph's Passionist Community.
Harmon, Barry J. '90 (SFD) Carrollton, IL St. John the Evangelist Church; White Hall, IL All Saints Church.
Harmon, John '93 (DM) Logan, IA St. Anne Church.
Harmon, Philip Gregory '76 (STN) Waianae, St. Sophia Byzantine Missions Church.
Harms, Msgr. William C. '65 (NEW) Westfield, NJ St. Helen Church; [B] South Orange, NJ Seton Hall University.

Harnan, James *m.s.c.* '64 (SAT) [M] San Antonio, TX Missionaries of the Sacred Heart.
Harness, H. Robert '82 (DAV) DeWitt, IA St. Joseph's Church.
Harnett, Brendan G. '73 (PRT) Biddeford, ME St. Mary's Church.
Harnett, Edward F. '58 (CHI) Wilmette, IL St. Francis Xavier Church.
Harnett, Msgr. Timothy '56 (SD) Encinitas, CA St. John the Evangelist Church.
Harney, Kenneth '89 (NO) [6] Metairie, LA St. Christopher the Martyr Church.
Harney, Thomas C. '62 (GF) Laurel, MT St. Anthony's Church.
Harnischfeger, William '93 (PHX) Sun City, AZ St. Elizabeth Seton Church.
Harnish, Lionel '54 (GAY) Retired.
Haro, Salvador Cazares '00 (TUC) [16] Tucson, AZ St. John the Evangelist Church.
Harold, Thomas J. '91 (RVC) Valley Stream, NY Holy Name of Mary Church.
Harpe, David '94 (GR) [4] Muskegon, MI St. Joseph's Church.
Harpel, John *s.v.d.* '44 (DUB) [H] New Hampton, IA Mercy Medical Center-New Hampton.
Harper, Henry *s.s.j.* '50 (BAL) [81] Baltimore, MD St. Peter Claver Church.
Harper, John '47 (R) Retired.
Harper, John H. '87 (GB) [2] De Pere, WI St. Mary Church.
Harr, Gerald J. '62 (GI) Gering, NE Christ the King Church.
Harr, Richard *o.m.i.* '52 (FgM) Oblates Foreign Missions.
Harren, Robert C. '66 (SCL) [4] St. Cloud, MN St. Anthony of Padua Church.
Harrer, Frederic J. '45 (RVC) Hicksville, NY St. Ignatius Loyola Church; Retired.
Harrer, Ronald R. *o.m.i.* '70 (STP) Albertville, MN St. Albert Church.
Harrigan, Maurice D. '96 (LA) Lancaster, CA Sacred Heart Church.
Harrigan, Philip K. *s.j.* '56 (BO) [W] Weston, MA Campion Health Center, Inc.
Harriman, Michael '68 (SFR) [Q] San Rafael, CA Catholic Youth Organization of the Archdiocese of San Francisco.
Harriman, Michael D. '68 (SFR) [11] San Francisco, CA St. Cecilia Church.
Harrington, Ashley *o.carm.* '67 (NEW) Tenafly, NJ Our Lady of Mount Carmel Church.
Harrington, Bernard J. '59 (DET) [T] Detroit, MI Pope John Paul II Cultural Foundation, Inc.
Harrington, Brian J. '67 (FR) North Dartmouth, MA St. Julie Billiart Church.
Harrington, Cornelius '41 (SEA) Retired.
Harrington, Daniel J. *s.j.* '71 (BO) [W] Cambridge, MA Weston Jesuit Community.
Harrington, Donald J. *c.m.* '73 (BRK) [D] Staten Island, NY St. John's University, Staten Island Campus; [D] Jamaica, NY St. John's University; [V] Jamaica, NY St. Vincent's House.
Harrington, Donald J. *c.m.* '73 (NY) [C] Staten Island, NY St. John's University Staten Island Campus.
Harrington, Ignatius '82 (NTN) Columbus, OH Holy Resurrection Church; Zanesville, OH Holy Trinity Church.
Harrington, James J. '53 (BO) Manchester by the Sea, MA Sacred Heart Church.
Harrington, Jay *o.p.* '85 (STL) [B] St. Louis, MO Aquinas Institute of Theology.
Harrington, Jay M. *o.p.* '85 (STL) [P] St. Louis, MO Dominican Community of St. Louis.
Harrington, Jeremy *o.f.m.* '59 (CIN) [22] Cincinnati, OH Corpus Christi Church; [U] Cincinnati, OH Community Support Charitable Trust.
Harrington, Msgr. John '45 (NY) Pearl River, NY St. Margaret Church.
Harrington, John D. '56 (BO) [E] Reading, MA Austin Preparatory School.
Harrington, Msgr. John F. '35 (SPR) Retired; [I] Springfield, MA St. Michael's Residence.
Harrington, Msgr. John M. '45 (NY) Retired.
Harrington, John P. '66 (BRK) [234] Queens, NY St. Rita Church.
Harrington, John S. *s.j.* '48 (HEL) [5] Missoula, MT St. Francis Xavier Church.
Harrington, John S. *s.j.* '48 (SPK) [K] Spokane, WA Regis Community.
Harrington, Msgr. Joseph D. '56 (HEL) Retired; [B] Helena, MT Carroll College.
Harrington, Kevin J. (FR) [3] New Bedford, MA Nuestra Senora de Guadalupe Church; [14] New Bedford, MA St. Hedwig Church.
Harrington, Kevin J. '75 (FR) [20] New Bedford, MA St. Lawrence Martyr Church.
Harrington, Mark (SC) Anthon, IA St. Joseph's Church.
Harrington, Mark '79 (SC) Danbury, IA St. Mary's Church.
Harrington, Michael C. (BO) Wellesley, MA St. Paul Church.
Harrington, Richard L. '66 (BO) Randolph, MA St. Mary Church.
Harrington, Msgr. Robert J. '71 (NEW) [1] Elizabeth, NJ St. Mary of the Assumption Church.
Harrington, Msgr. Russell J. (LAF) Mire, LA Assumption of the Blessed Virgin Mary Church.
Harrington, Msgr. Thomas J. '64 (FR) [2] New Bedford, MA Holy Name of the Sacred Heart of Jesus Church.
Harris, Alfred J '94 (WDC) [34] Washington, DC Our Lady Queen of Peace Church.
Harris, Andrew *o.m.i.* '53 (P) Sweet Home, OR St. Helen Church.
Harris, Anton J. *s.j.* '75 (SEA) [A] Seattle, WA Seattle University.
Harris, Daniel E. *c.m.* '74 (LA) [A] Camarillo, CA St. John's Seminary.
Harris, Daniel E. *c.m.* '74 (STL) [P] St. Louis, MO Vincentian Residence.
Harris, David T. '47 (MAR) Retired.
Harris, Edward D. *s.j.* '45 (STL) [O] St. Louis, MO Fusz Pavilion.
Harris, Edwin B. *s.j.* '75 (SAC) [H] Carmichael, CA Jesuit High School Community of Sacramento.
Harris, George '65 (BWN) San Benito, TX Our Lady, Queen of the Universe Church.
Harris, George G. *c.s.v.* '63 (CHI) [D] Arlington Heights, IL St. Viator High School.
Harris, Gerald P. '79 (SUP) River Falls, WI St. Bridget Church.
Harris, Glenn H. (PEO) Marseilles, IL St. Joseph's Church.
Harris, Jack D. '74 (LR) Jonesboro, AR Blessed Sacrament Church; [J] Jonesboro, AR Blessed John Newman University Parish.
Harris, Msgr. James E. (LAR) [H] Laredo, TX San Agustin Historical Preservation & Restoration Society, Inc.
Harris, Msgr. James E. '85 (CC) [J] Laredo, TX San Augustin Historical Preservation & Restoration Society, Inc.
Harris, Msgr. James E. '85 (LAR) [1] Laredo, TX San Agustin Church.
Harris, John E. '84 (PRT) Oquossoc, ME Our Lady of the Lakes Church.
Harris, Julian P. '91 (PMB) Tequesta, FL St. Jude Church.
Harris, Msgr. Martin P. '55 (WDC) Hollywood, MD St. John Church.
Harris, Msgr. Michael '72 (ORG) Inactive Leave.
Harris, Michael B. '89 (SCR) Dushore, PA St. Basil's Church.
Harris, Raymond L. '94 (BAL) Special Assignment.
Harris, Raymond L., Jr. '94 (BAL) [B] Emmitsburg, MD Mount Saint Mary's College.
Harris, Raymond Lee, Jr. '79 (BAL) [41] Baltimore, MD Immaculate Conception Church.
Harris, Richard D. '93 (CHR) Greenwood, SC Our Lady of Lourdes Church; [H] Greenwood, SC Lander College.
Harris, Robert (DM) Missouri Valley, IA St. Patrick Church.
Harris, Msgr. Robert M. '59 (BRK) [P] Brooklyn, NY St. Vincent's Services, Inc.
Harris, Scott T. *m.m.* '78 (FgM) Maryknoll Foreign Missions.
Harris, Steven J. '80 (PH) [151] Philadelphia, PA St. Therese of the Child Jesus Church.
Harris, Msgr. Wallace A. '72 (NY) [24] New York, NY St. Charles Borromeo Church; [Q] New York, NY Society of St. Vincent De Paul, Archdiocesan Central Council of New York.
Harris, Whitney G. '80 (LKC) [3] Lake Charles, LA Sacred Heart of Jesus Church; On Special Assignment.
Harris, William R. '78 (SEA) Anacortes, WA St. Mary Church.
Harris, Xavier J. *o.f.m.* '48 (OAK) [A] Berkeley, CA Franciscan School of Theology.
Harrison, Arthur '56 (SJ) Retired.
Harrison, Brian W. *o.s.* '85 (PCE) [11] Ponce, PR San Jose Obrero Church; [B] Ponce, PR The Pontifical Catholic University of Puerto Rico; [H] Ponce, PR Oblates of Wisdom.
Harrison, Craig F. '87 (FRS) [4] Bakersfield, CA St. Francis Church.
Harrison, Cyprian *o.c.s.o.* (SPC) [A] Ava, MO Assumption Novitiate (Trappists).
Harrison, Frank J. '37 (SY) [S] East Syracuse, NY Vianney House.
Harrison, George E. '68 (FR) Seekonk, MA Our Lady of Mt. Carmel Church.
Harrison, James '55 (ATL) Kennesaw, GA St. Catherine of Siena Church.
Harrison, Jeffrey D. *s.j.* '82 (STL) [52] St. Louis, MO St. Matthew, Apostle Church.
Harrison, Jeffrey D. *s.j.* '87 (STL) [F] St. Louis, MO St. Louis University High School, George H. Backer Memorial; [P] St. Louis, MO St. Matthew Jesuit Community.
Harrison, John *c.ss.r.* '67 (WIL) Seaford, DE Our Lady of Lourdes Church.
Harrison, Michael *s.s.c.* '48 (PRO) [P] Bristol, RI St. Columban's Retirement House.
Harrison, Patrick C. *j.c.l.* '91 (OM) [22] Omaha, NE St. Joan of Arc Church.
Harrison, Robert '64 (NY) [E] New York, NY Cardinal Hayes High School.
Harrison, Timothy '75 (ALB) Leave of Absence.
Harrison, Timothy A. '91 (BO) Belmont, MA St. Joseph Church.
Harrison, Todd W. *s.j.* '96 (MIL) [P] Milwaukee, WI Jesuit Community at Marquette University.
Harrison, William S. '72 (PH) Cheltenham, PA St. Joseph Church; Cheltenham, PA Presentation of Blessed Virgin Mary Church.
Harrity, Msgr. Dennis '60 (DET) Grosse Pointe, MI Our Lady Star of the Sea Church.
Harrity, Francis P. '33 (WOR) Retired.
Harrity, Patrick *c.m.* '68 (EVN) [E] Evansville, IN Seton Residence; [G] Evansville, IN Daughters of Charity of St. Vincent de Paul of Indiana, Inc.
Harrity, Patrick V. *c.m.* '68 (STL) [P] Perryville, MO Congregation of The Mission.
Harrold, John '73 (SY) On Duty Outside the Diocese.
Harrold, John J. '92 (GBG) Donegal, PA St. Raymond of the Mountains Church.
Harrold, Michael '50 (VIC) [1] Victoria, TX Our Lady of Victory Church.
Harry, Alwyn C. *s.j.* '54 (BO) [W] Weston, MA Campion Health Center, Inc.
Harry, William J. '83 (TUC) [F] Tucson, AZ Carmelite Priory.
Harshaw, Albert E. '73 (CAM) [1] Camden, NJ Immaculate Conception Church; Woodbine, NJ St. Casimir's Church.
Hart, Addison H. '99 (RCK) DeKalb, IL Christ the Teacher, University Parish of Northern Illinois University Church; [L] DeKalb, IL Newman Foundation for Catholic Students of Northern Illinois University.
Hart, Brian '63 (SEA) Unassigned.
Hart, Charles *o.f.m.* '79 (DET) [K] Detroit, MI St. Bonaventure Friary.
Hart, Edward J. '55 (BUR) Retired; [D] Burlington, VT St. Joseph's Home.
Hart, Edward James '96 (FWT) [17] Fort Worth, TX St. Thomas More Church.
Hart, Gene *s.o.l.t.* '90 (CC) [H] Robstown, TX Society of Our Lady of the Most Holy Trinity.
Hart, Gregory G. '84 (LR) Harrison, AR Mary, Mother of God Church.
Hart, James '65 (KC) Lee's Summit, MO Our Lady of the Presentation Church.
Hart, James '96 (FWT) [14] Fort Worth, TX St. Peter The Apostle Church.
Hart, John E. '81 (PAT) Rockaway, NJ St. Cecilia's Church; Rockaway, NJ Sacred Heart Church.
Hart, Joseph A. '73 (ROC) [38] Rochester, NY Our Lady Queen of Peace Church; [L] Rochester, NY Censores Librorum.
Hart, Joseph L. *s.s.e.* '55 (VEN) [G] Englewood, FL Society of St. Edmund Residence.
Hart, Kevin T. '74 (WDC) [3] Washington, DC St. Ann Church.
Hart, Paul S. '89 (NO) [24] New Orleans, LA St. Andrew the Apostle Church.
Hart, Msgr. Peter F. '36 (BO) [7] Lynn, MA St. Pius Fifth Church; Senior Priests.
Hart, Philip W. '73 (NY) [DD] Jamaica Estates, NY Paulist Fathers Generalate.
Hart, Richard *o.f.m.cap.* '55 (MIL) [P] Milwaukee, WI St. Conrad Friary.
Hart, Robert '00 (STP) [1] St. Paul, MN Cathedral of St. Paul.
Hart, Robert A. '75 (GR) North Muskegon, MI Prince of Peace Church.
Hart, Robert P. *s.j.* '62 (OM) [K] Omaha, NE Jesuit Community at Creighton University.
Hart, Rolland A. '64 (OG) Indian Lake, NY St. Mary's Church.
Hart, Ronald '71 (JOL) Herscher, IL St. Margaret Mary Church; Irwin, IL St. James The Apostle Church.
Hart, Thomas '80 (NEW) New Providence, NJ Our Lady of Peace Church.
Hart, Thomas B. '44 (PRO) Retired.
Hart, Thomas J. '74 (SC) Remsen, IA St. Mary's Church.
Hart, Thomas M. *o.s.b.* '88 (GBG) [H] Latrobe, PA Saint Vincent Archabbey.
Hart, William '58 (GLP) Retired.
Hart, William C. '58 (CAM) [A] Cherry Hill, NJ Camden Catholic High School.
Hart, William H. '58 (CAM) Retired.
Harte, Msgr. Al F. '64 (RCK) [H] Rockford, IL The Poor Clares of Rockford.
Harte, F. Joseph '61 (ORL) [1] Orlando, FL Mary Queen of the Universe Church.
Hartel, Edward T. '62 (WDC) Retired.
Harten, Dennis J. *o.s.a.* '75 (PH) Villanova, PA St. Thomas of Villanova Church.
Hartenbach, William E. *c.m.* '64 (FgM) Vincentian Foreign Missions.
Hartenbach, William E. *c.m.* '64 (STL) [66] St. Louis,

MO St. Vincent de Paul Church; [P] Earth City, MO Congregation of the Mission Midwest Province (Vincentians).
Harter, Benedict W. '46 (SPC) Joplin, MO Joplin Hospital Ministry; Retired; [C] Joplin, MO St. John's Regional Medical Center; Mercy Lifecare Systems, Inc.
Harter, Leon A. *m.m.* '39 (SJ) [L] Los Altos, CA Maryknoll.
Harter, Michael G. *s.j.* '74 (STP) [B] St. Paul, MN Jesuit Novitiate.
Hartgen, Dennis T. '73 (ALN) [5] Reading, PA Holy Guardian Angels Church; [I] Reading, PA Queen of Angels Apartment.
Hartgen, William E. *s.s.* '76 (BAL) [S] Baltimore, MD Sulpician Provincial House.
Harth, Charles F. '36 (BRK) Retired; [S] Queens Village, NY Queen of Peace Residence.
Harth, John M. '87 (SPC) Neosho, MO St. Canera Church; Seneca, MO St. Mary Church.
Hartigan, Daniel J. *o.s.a.* '45 (CHI) [39] Chicago, IL St. Clare of Montefalco Church.
Hartigan, Dennis P. '80 (TOL) Bluffton, OH St. Mary Church; [4] Lima, OH St. Rose Church; [B] Lima, OH Central Catholic High School.
Hartlage, Albert J. '56 (L) Fairfield, KY St. Michael Church.
Hartlage, William C. '41 (L) Retired; [L] Louisville, KY Bishop David Apartments.
Hartle, Thomas R. *o.f.m.* '79 (PAT) Butler, NJ St. Anthony Church.
Hartlein, Msgr. Jerome D. '58 (BEL) Mascoutah, IL Holy Childhood of Jesus Church.
Hartley, Christopher (NY) [77] New York, NY Most Holy Crucifix Church.
Hartley, Gregory C. *s.j.* '86 (BAL) [S] Baltimore, MD Jesuit Community of Loyola College, Inc.
Hartley, Paul M. '81 (JC) Linn, MO St. George Church.
Hartling, Charles W. '79 (NEW) Rutherford, NJ St. Mary's Church.
Hartlove, Walter J. *o.s.f.s.* '48 (FgM) Oblates of St. Francis de Sales Foreign Missions.
Hartman, Alan *s.f.o.* (CIN) [V] Cincinnati, OH Franciscans Network.
Hartman, Glenn '76 (CAM) Cape May, NJ Our Lady Star of the Sea Church.
Hartman, John B. (SAV) [E] Columbus, GA St. Francis Hospital.
Hartman, Joseph F. *o.s.a.* '47 (DET) Grosse Pointe Park, MI St. Clare of Montefalco Church.
Hartman, Msgr. Joseph W. '52 (WDC) Retired; [L] Washington, DC Cardinal O'Boyle Residence for Priests.
Hartman, Ralph C. '59 (COV) Retired.
Hartman, Raymond S. '68 (COV) Crescent Springs, KY St. Joseph Church.
Hartman, Msgr. Thomas J. '71 (RVC) [C] Hicksville, NY Holy Trinity.
Hartmann, Edward J. '76 (FBK) [1] Fairbanks, AK Sacred Heart Church.
Hartmann, Edward J. '76 (NY) On Duty Outside the Archdiocese.
HartmanN, Msgr. John F. '53 (BRK) Retired.
Hartmann, Paul *j.c.l.* '94 (MIL) [B] Hales Corners, WI Sacred Heart School of Theology.
Hartmann, Richard A. '73 (DET) [18] Detroit, MI St. Christopher Church.
Hartmann, Robert '89 (STL) [C] St. Louis, MO Saint Louis University.
Hartmann, Robert J. '85 (WCH) Coffeyville, KS Holy Name Church.
Hartmayer, Gregory J. *o.f.m.conv.* '79 (ATL) Jonesboro, GA St. Philip Benizi Church.
Hartnett, Daniel F. *s.j.* '74 (CHI) [C] Chicago, IL Jesuit Community at Loyola University of Chicago.
Hartnett, George F. '74 (SY) Solvay, NY St. Cecilia Church.
Hartnett, James '72 (ORG) Westminster, CA Blessed Sacrament Church.
Hartnett, James L. *s.m.* '55 (ATL) [C] Atlanta, GA Marist School.
Hartnett, Msgr. James R. '38 (STL) Retired.
Hartnett, Richard G. *s.j.* '43 (NO) [P] New Orleans, LA Ignatius Residence.
Hartnett, Robert L. '79 (BAL) [72] Baltimore, MD Our Lady of Mount Carmel Church.
Hartnett, Walter J. '45 (PH) Retired.
Hartrich, Kurt *o.f.m.* '66 (SFD) [5] Quincy, IL St. Francis Solanus Church.
Hartshorn, Christopher '94 (DM) Winterset, IA St. Joseph Church.
Hartz, Gerald A. '59 (SC) Special Assignment; [D] Sioux City, IA Holy Spirit Retirement Home.
Hartzer, John '54 (IND) Lawrenceburg, IN St. Lawrence Church.
Hartzler, Joseph *s.m.* (SFR) [N] San Francisco, CA Marianist Community.
Harvey, Arthur S. *c.s.c.* '51 (FTW) [J] South Bend, IN Congregation of Holy Cross, Indiana Province, Provincial House.
Harvey, Charles K. '52 (WCH) Retired.
Harvey, David W. '68 (LAN) Fenton, MI St. John Church.
Harvey, Frederick R., Jr. '00 (BIS) Williston, ND St. Joseph Church.
Harvey, James '86 (ORG) Inactive Leave.
Harvey, James P. *o.s.f.s.* '60 (WIL) [I] Childs, MD Oblates of St. Francis De Sales.
Harvey, James P. '96 (KNX) Greeneville, TN Notre Dame Church.
Harvey, James P., II '96 (KNX) Newport, TN Good Shepherd Church.
Harvey, Jeffery H. '93 (LA) [Q] Montebello, CA Vincentian Fathers and Brothers.
Harvey, Jeffrey H. *c.m.* '93 (LA) [Q] Montebello, CA Vincentian Fathers & Brothers.
Harvey, John A. '66 (PIT) McDonald, PA St. Alphonsus Church.
Harvey, John D. *o.f.m. cap.* '72 (BAL) [45] Baltimore, MD St. Jerome Church; [58] Baltimore, MD St. Martin Church; [80] Baltimore, MD St. Peter the Apostle Church.
Harvey, John F. *o.s.f.s.* (NY) [122] New York, NY St. Vincent de Paul Church.
Harvey, John F. *o.s.f.s.* '44 (ALN) [B] Center Valley, PA Desales University; [K] Center Valley, PA Oblates of St. Francis de Sales.
Harvey, John F. *o.s.f.s.* '44 (NY) [HH] New York, NY Courage.
Harvey, John L. '86 (CHI) [124] Chicago, IL St. Mary of the Assumption Church.
Harvey, L. Warren '88 (LR) [3] Little Rock, AR St. Augustine Church; [9] Little Rock, AR St. Mary Church; [12] Little Rock, AR St. Patrick's Church.
Harvey, Michael K. '99 (BO) Randolph, MA St. Mary Church.
Harvey, Michael L. *o.f.m.* '89 (ORG) [3] Huntington Beach, CA SS. Simon and Jude Church.
Harvey, Peter J. *o.s.f.s.* '60 (FgM) Oblates of St. Francis de Sales Foreign Missions.
Harvey, Richard R. '51 (PRT) Retired.
Harvey, Wilfred *o.m.i.* '63 (BO) [W] Lowell, MA Missionary Oblates of Mary Immaculate.
Harvey, Wilfred *o.m.i.* '63 (MAN) [K] Les Cayes, Haiti Paroisse Ste. Anne.
Harwas, Roman '98 (SJP) McKees Rocks, PA St. John the Baptist Church.
Haryasz, Francis S. '58 (STA) Retired.
Hasbrouck, John-Baptist *o.c.s.o.* '54 (P) [L] Lafayette, OR The Cistercian (Trappist) Abbey of Our Lady of Guadalupe.
Hascall, John S. *o.f.m.cap.* '67 (MAR) Barbeau, MI Holy Family Church; [3] Sault Sainte Marie, MI St. Isaac Jogues Church; Sault Sainte Marie, MI St. Isaac Jogues Church.
Haschka, David J. *s.j.* '75 (MIL) [31] Milwaukee, WI Gesu Church; [P] Milwaukee, WI Jesuit Provincial Office, Wisconsin Province.
Haschka, Jonathan *s.j.* '75 (FgM) Provinces.
Hascinger, Philip S. '72 (LFT) Grissom, IN Grissom Air Force Base, St. Michael's Chapel.
Hasehka, Jonathan *s.j.* '75 (OM) [K] Omaha, NE Jesuit Community at Creighton University.
Haselbauer, Joseph *s.c.j.* '55 (SFS) [B] Chamberlain, SD St. Joseph Indian School.
Haselhorst, Msgr. Vincent '57 (BEL) Retired.
Hasenberg, Aloysius J. '49 (MAR) Watersmeet, MI Immaculate Conception Church; Retired.
Hasenkamp, Robert '63 (KCK) Mission, KS St. Pius X Church.
Hasenoehrl, Daniel *o.s.b.* '60 (P) [L] St. Benedict, OR Mt. Angel Abbey.
Hasiebar, Joseph S. '73 (PH) Coatesville, PA Veterans Administration Medical Center.
Hasieber, Joseph S. '73 (ALX) On Duty Outside the Diocese.
Haskamp, Edward F. '50 (CIN) [35] Cincinnati, OH Holy Trinity Church; Retired.
Haskamp, Gregory '93 (KC) [2] St. Joseph, MO Our Lady of Guadalupe Church.
Haske, Henry B. *s.j.* '57 (R) [E] Raleigh, NC Jesuit Community.
Haskin, Jay C. '67 (BUR) Colchester, VT Our Lady of Grace Church.
Haskins, Robert J. *s.j.* '54 (NY) [DD] New York, NY Murray-Weigel Hall.
Haslach, Stephen *c.p.* '54 (NY) [DD] Pelham Manor, NY St. Vincent's Residence; [HH] Pelham, NY Passionist Communications, Inc.
Hasler, Clifford *m.s.* '71 (ATL) Snellville, GA St. Oliver Plunkett Church.
Haslinger, Philip S. '72 (LFT) Peru, IN St. Charles Borromeo Church.
Haspedis, George '56 (SPK) Retired.
Hasselhoff, Robert W. '59 (CIN) Retired.
Hassett, James F. '75 (BUF) Barker, NY St. Patrick Church; Olcott, NY St. Charles Borromeo Church.
Hassey, Athanase '50 (NTN) Retired.
Hasso, Bede J. *o.s.b.* '57 (GBG) [H] Latrobe, PA Saint Vincent Archabbey.
Hastings, Edward T. *o.s.a.* (PH) [AA] Villanova, PA Fray de Leon Community.
Hastings, James J. *s.s.c.* '72 (FgM) St. Columban's Foreign Mission Society (S.S.C.).
Hastings, James J. *s.s.c.* '72 (OM) [K] St. Columbans, NE St. Columban's Foreign Mission Society.
Hastings, Joel '99 (DUL) [1] Duluth, MN Cathedral of Our Lady of the Rosary.
Hastings, Timothy (SAG) [E] Saginaw, MI St. Mary's Medical Center of Saginaw, Inc.
Hastings, William J. '73 (CHI) [210] Chicago, IL St. William Church.
Hastrich, Msgr. George M. '50 (MAD) Argyle, WI St. Joseph Church; Yellowstone, WI St. Michael Church; [J] Madison, WI Saint Martin House.
Hastrich, George M. '50 (RCK) [M] St. Charles, IL Queen of Americas Guild.
Hatcher, John *s.j.* '74 (RC) [4] Rapid City, SD St. Isaac Jogues Church; [B] Howes, SD Kino Jesuit Community; [D] Howes, SD The Diocese of Rapid City Mahpiya na Maka Okoigna.
Hatcher, Msgr. William C. '71 (NEW) Bloomfield, NJ Church of St. Thomas the Apostle.
Hater, Robert J. '59 (CIN) [20] Cincinnati, OH St. Clare Church; Retired; [D] Dayton, OH The University of Dayton.
Hatfield, Placid W. *o.s.b.* '58 (PEO) Dalzell, IL St. Thomas More Church; [A] Peru, IL St. Bede Abbey and Academy.
Hathaway, Edward C. '91 (ARL) McLean, VA St. John's Church.
Hatrick, Brian M. '79 (BUF) North Evans, NY St. Vincent Church.
Hattie, Eugene F. *s.j.* '53 (FgM) Provinces.
Hatton, Ronald '95 (PSC) Williamsburg, VA Ascension of Our Lord Church.
Hattrick, Edward V. *o.s.a.* '56 (FgM) Foreign Missions.
Hauber, Doug '89 (JOL) Roselle, IL St. Walter Church.
Hauck, Herbert C. '64 (STL) Kirkwood, MO St. Gerard Majella Church.
Hauer, Joseph L. '81 (DUB) Graduate Studies.
Hauer, Maurus *o.f.m. conv.* '45 (LSC) Carlsbad, NM St. Edward Church.
Hauf, Edward *o.m.i.* '66 (PT) Perry, FL Immaculate Conception Church.
Haugen, John S. '81 (DUB) Cedar Falls, IA St. Patrick Church.
Haugen, John S. '84 (DUB) [N] Cedar Falls, IA St. Stephen the Witness Catholic Student Center, University of Northern Iowa.
Haugh, John '61 (DAL) Retired.
Haughey, John C. *s.j.* '61 (CHI) [C] Chicago, IL Jesuit Community at Loyola University of Chicago.
Haughney, Msgr. William J. '47 (MET) Cranbury, NJ Nativity of Our Lord Church; Retired.
Haupt, Lloyd '54 (SCL) Retired.
Haus, Robert A. *s.j.* '55 (BUF) [O] Buffalo, NY Canisius Jesuit Community.
Hausen, William '65 (PIT) Sewickley, PA St. James Church.
Hauser, Albert *o.s.b.* '60 (KCK) [3] Overland Park, KS Holy Spirit Church.
Hauser, Albert J. '81 (OG) [A] Ogdensburg, NY Wadhams Hall.
Hauser, Gerald B. '45 (MIL) Retired.
Hauser, Nathanael *o.s.b.* '83 (SCL) [I] Collegeville, MN St. John's Abbey, of the Order of St. Benedict.
Hauser, Richard J. *s.j.* '68 (OM) [K] Omaha, NE Jesuit Community at Creighton University.
Hausfeld, Bruce *o.f.m.* '62 (LSC) Alamogordo, NM Immaculate Conception Church.
Hausfeld, Bryant *o.f.m.* '65 (LSC) Alamogordo, NM Immaculate Conception Church.
Hausmann, Leo '92 (RC) Colome, SD St. Isidore Church; Winner, SD Immaculate Conception Church; [D] Rapid City, SD Priest Retirement and Aid Association.
Hausmann, William C. *s.j.* '66 (SPK) [C] Spokane, WA Gonzaga University; [K] Spokane, WA Regis Community.
Haut, Msgr. Vincent J. '68 (STA) Orange Park, FL St. Catherine's Church.
Hautz, Roland *glmy.* '53 (RIC) Gate City, VA St. Bernard Church.
Hauver, James '97 (DUL) Hibbing, MN Blessed Sacrament Church.
Havane, James '98 (NY) Hyde Park, NY Regina Coeli Church.
Havel, Elias '95 (RC) [B] Piedmont, SD Holy Nativity Monastery.
Havel, Elias *o.mar.* '95 (SAM) [C] Petersham, MA Most Holy Trinity Monastery.
Havel, Gregory G. '90 (WIN) [4] Rochester, MN St. Bridget's Church; Stewartville, MN St. Bernard's Church.
Havener, J. Riley *o.s.a.* '55 (ALB) Waterford, NY St. Mary of the Assumption Church.
Havens, James '79 (MOB) Grove Hill, AL Sacred Heart Church.
Haviland, William T. '62 (HBG) Sunbury, PA St. Monica Church.
Havron, Daniel *o.f.m.* '77 (DET) Special Assignment.
Hawes, Msgr. Cletus J. '52 (DUB) Festina, IA Our Lady

of Seven Dolors Church; Ossian, IA St. Francis de Sales Church; [E] Calmar, IA Christian Family School.
Hawes, Donald J. '53 (DUB) Calmar, IA St. Aloysius Church; Spillville, IA St. Wenceslaus Church; [F] Calmar, IA Calmar-Festina-Spillville (CFS) Catholic Elementary School.
Hawk, Patrick *c.ss.r.* '69 (TUC) [H] Tucson, AZ Redemptorist Picture Rocks Retreat.
Hawken, Michael '94 (KCK) Burlington, KS St. Francis Xavier's Church; Emerald, KS St. Patrick's Church; Waverly, KS St. Joseph's Church; Westphalia, KS St. Teresa's Church.
Hawker, James '63 (CHL) [4] Charlotte, NC St. Ann Church.
Hawker, James F. '63 (BO) On Duty Outside the Archdiocese.
Hawkes-Teeples, Steven B. *s.j.* '93 (FgM) Provinces.
Hawkins, Allan R.G. '94 (FWT) [1] Arlington, TX Church of St. Mary the Virgin.
Hawkins, Charles '78 (PMB) [1] Boca Raton, FL Ascension Church.
Hawkins, Donald A. *s.j.* '76 (MOB) [A] Mobile, AL Spring Hill College; [J] Mobile, AL Spring Hill College Campus Ministry.
Hawkins, Douglas W. *c.s.c.* '57 (BUR) Bennington, VT Sacred Heart St. Francis de Sales Church; Springfield, VT Maternity of the Blessed Virgin Mary Church; Retired.
Hawkins, John G. *o.s.c.* '66 (DET) Riverview, MI St. Cyprian Church.
Hawkins, Ray '52 (PBL) [F] Pueblo, CO Villa Pueblo.
Hawkins, Robert F. '75 (PRO) [6] Warwick, RI St. Kevin Church.
Hawkins, Msgr. Stephen B. '75 (COL) Grove City, OH Our Lady of Perpetual Help Church.
Hawkins, Thomas '70 (KC) Weston, MO Holy Trinity Church.
Hawley, Benjamin *s.j.* (IND) [D] Indianapolis, IN Brebeuf Jesuit Preparatory School, Inc.; [D] Indianapolis, IN Brebeuf Jesuit Preparatory School, Inc.
Hawley, Gerard L. '92 (SCR) Lords Valley, PA St. John Neumann Church.
Haworth, Marcus A. *s.j.* '46 (STL) [P] St. Louis, MO Jesuit Community Corporation at St. Louis University - Jesuit Hall.
Hawthorne, Patrick J. '82 (WOR) [26] Worcester, MA St. Margaret Mary Church.
Hay, Francis J. '42 (WCH) Retired.
Hay, Theodore H. '55 (MOB) Retired.
Hay, W. Michael '92 (CIN) [49] Cincinnati, OH St. Jude the Apostle Church.
Hayatsu, Ricahrd K. '65 (SEA) Seahurst, WA St. Francis of Assisi Church.
Hayburn, Edmund L. '45 (OAK) Retired; [M] Oakland, CA Bishop Begin Villa.
Haycock, Anthony J. '72 (SEA) [15] Seattle, WA St. Mary Church; [K] Seattle, WA Catholic Seamen's Club.
Haycock, Donald J. *c.s.c.* '58 (ROC) [41] Rochester, NY St. Lawrence Church.
Hayda, Pavlo '92 (STN) [2] Chicago, IL St. Joseph Church.
Hayde, Msgr. Ronald E. '81 (RVC) [1] Rockville Centre, NY St. Agnes Church; Ocean Beach, NY Our Lady of the Magnificat Church.
Hayden, Msgr. Carl T. '45 (GI) Retired.
Hayden, Donald C. '81 (RVC) Sayville, NY St. Lawrence the Martyr Church.
Hayden, Hilary *o.s.b.* '56 (WDC) [M] Washington, DC St. Anselm's Abbey.
Hayden, James P. '91 (GAY) Traverse City, MI Immaculate Conception Church.
Hayden, Johnrose H. '95 (LUB) Rotan, TX St. Joseph Church.
Hayden, Joseph F. '63 (L) On Duty Outside the Archdiocese.
Hayden, Joseph J. *s.j.* '70 (WH) [A] Wheeling, WV Wheeling Jesuit University.
Hayden, Joseph M. '48 (CAM) Retired.
Hayden, Joseph M. '48 (ORL) [2] Lakeland, FL St. Anthony's Church.
Hayden, Joseph Mark '48 (ORL) Retired.
Hayden, Lucian P. '45 (OWN) Retired.
Hayden, Michael M. *o.c.s.o.* '54 (ROC) [I] Piffard, NY Abbey of the Genesee.
Hayden, Michael T. '85 (SUP) Boulder Junction, WI St. Anne Church; Sayner, WI St. Mary Church.
Hayden, Patrick T. '90 (STL) On Duty Outside the Archdiocese.
Hayden, Ralph W. '64 (NU) Retired.
Hayden, Robert L. '70 (RVC) Williston Park, NY St. Aidan's Church.
Hayden, Terence '77 (NO) Crown Point, LA St. Pius X Church.
Hayden, Thomas *s.m.a.* '58 (FgM) Society of African Missions.
Haydinger, Christian '76 (RIC) [1] Chesapeake, VA Prince of Peace Church.
Haydock, Kenneth '80 (SEA) Edmonds, WA Holy Rosary Church.
Hayduk, Michael '77 (PRM) Cleveland, OH St. Nicholas Church.
Hayek, Herbert *o.p.* '71 (COS) Castle Rock, CO St. Francis of Assisi Church.
Hayek, Msgr. Sami '59 (SAM) Easton, PA Our Lady of Lebanon Church.
Hayek, Msgr. Stanley J. '59 (DUB) Charles City, IA Immaculate Conception Church.
Hayer, James '89 (PSC) Wilkes-Barre, PA St. Mary's Church.
Hayes, Bonaventure F. *o.f.m.* '67 (BUF) [A] East Aurora, NY Christ the King Seminary.
Hayes, Brian '92 (SD) [17] San Diego, CA Our Mother of Confidence Church.
Hayes, Charles V. *o.f.m.* '46 (PAT) [M] Butler, NJ St. Anthony Friary.
Hayes, Msgr. Denis A. '37 (PAT) Retired.
Hayes, Dennis J. '76 (SY) South Onondaga, NY Corpus Christi Church.
Hayes, Dennis J., III '86 (NO) [53] New Orleans, LA SS. Peter and Paul Church; [A] New Orleans, LA Notre Dame Seminary Graduate School of Theology.
Hayes, Donald J. *s.j.* '56 (CLV) [D] Cuyahoga Falls, OH Walsh Jesuit High School.
Hayes, Edward A. *m.m.* '59 (FgM) Maryknoll Foreign Missions.
Hayes, Edward J. '41 (NEW) Retired.
Hayes, Edward J. '57 (SY) Chadwicks, NY St. Anthony of Padua Church.
Hayes, Eugene J. *o.praem.* '77 (ORG) [O] Silverado, CA Norbertine Association of St. Joseph, Inc.
Hayes, Finbarr *o.p.* '59 (OAK) [N] Oakland, CA Dominican Order (Western Province), St. Albert's Priory.
Hayes, Gary '85 (OWN) Peonia, KY St. Anthony's Church.
Hayes, Gary '90 (OWN) Grayson Springs, KY St. Augustine Church; Wax, KY St. Benedict Church.
Hayes, Gerard C. '60 (HT) Bayou Black, LA St. Anthony Church.
Hayes, Giles P. *o.s.b.* '65 (PAT) [M] Morristown, NJ St. Mary's Abbey.
Hayes, Msgr. J. Wayne '59 (FRS) Los Banos, CA St. Joseph Church.
Hayes, James '66 (ALB) Guilderland, NY St. Madeleine Sophie Church; Albany, NY New York State Department of Corrections; Special Assignment.
Hayes, James *s.s.s.* '77 (NY) [8] New York, NY St. Andrew Church.
Hayes, James A. *m.s.c.* '50 (CC) Agua Dulce, TX St. Frances of Rome Church.
Hayes, James A. *s.s.j.* '55 (WDC) [B] Washington, DC St. Joseph's Seminary.
Hayes, James C. '65 (SY) Onondaga Hill, NY St. Michael Church; Warners, NY Our Lady of Good Counsel Church; Syracuse, NY Community General Hospital; Special Assignment.
Hayes, James E. '89 (DUB) Ames, IA St. Thomas Aquinas Church (and Catholic Student Center) Church; [N] Ames, IA St. Thomas Aquinas Church and Catholic Student Center (Iowa State University).
Hayes, James L. '38 (DET) Retired.
Hayes, James M. *s.j.* '85 (BO) [W] Boston, MA The Society of Jesus of New England-Provincial Offices; [W] Boston, MA The Society of Jesus of New England-Provincial Offices.
Hayes, James M. *s.j.* '85 (FgM) Provinces.
Hayes, John '60 (CLV) Retired.
Hayes, John H. '87 (ROC) Livonia, NY St. Joseph Church.
Hayes, John J. '60 (CLV) [34] Cleveland, OH Immaculate Conception Church.
Hayes, Msgr. John M. '30 (CHI) [52] Chicago, IL Epiphany Church; Retired.
Hayes, Joseph '79 (MIA) Absent on Leave.
Hayes, Lawrence J. *o.f.m.* '89 (WIL) [10] Wilmington, DE St. Paul's Church.
Hayes, Leo J. '61 (BEL) Ava, IL St. Elizabeth Church; Raddle, IL St. Ann Church; Willisville, IL St. Joseph Church; Menard, IL Menard Correctional Center.
Hayes, Martin E. '84 (OWN) Knottsville, KY St. William Church; Philpot, KY St. Lawrence Church.
Hayes, Maurice *o.f.m.conv.* '69 (L) Pleasure Ridge Park, KY St. Paul Church.
Hayes, Michael T. '60 (DUL) Moose Lake, MN Holy Angels Church; Moose Lake, MN Moose Lake State Hospital.
Hayes, Patrick '71 (BLX) Gautier, MS St. Mary Church.
Hayes, Patrick J. *c.s.v.* '43 (CHI) [N] Arlington Heights, IL Viatorian Province Center-Clerics of St. Viator.
Hayes, Msgr. Paul J. '48 (NEW) New Providence, NJ Our Lady of Peace Church; Retired.
Hayes, Peter F. '38 (CHI) [152] Chicago, IL Our Lady, Mother of the Church; Retired.
Hayes, Robert '71 (SJ) Cupertino, CA St. Joseph of Cupertino Church.
Hayes, Sam W. '83 (CHY) Casper, WY Saint Patrick's Church.
Hayes, Stephen D. *o.p.* '88 (COL) [36] Columbus, OH St. Patrick Church.
Hayes, Terrence M. '72 (STP) [14] Minneapolis, MN Our Lady of Victory Church.
Hayes, Thomas *o.m.i.* (OAK) [21] Oakland, CA Sacred Heart Church.
Hayes, Thomas *o.p.* '59 (OAK) [N] Oakland, CA Western Dominican Province.
Hayes, Thomas *o.p.* '59 (SFR) [N] San Francisco, CA St. Dominic Priory.
Hayes, Msgr. Thomas G. '46 (LA) Retired.
Hayes, Msgr. Thomas J. '35 (SY) New Hartford, NY St. John the Evangelist Church; Retired.
Hayes, Thomas J. *o.p.* '59 (SFR) [14] San Francisco, CA St. Dominic Church.
Hayes, Thomas J. '73 (ALB) Crescent, NY St. Mary Church.
Hayes, Thomas P. '67 (STO) Lodi, CA St. Anne Church.
Hayes, Timothy M. '85 (COL) Newark, OH Church of the Blessed Sacrament.
Hayes, William E. *s.j.* '58 (P) [D] Portland, OR Jesuit High School.
Hayes, William J. '42 (HRT) Retired.
Hayes, William L. *s.j.* '44 (FgM) Provinces.
Hayes, Xavier *c.p.* '59 (BRK) [V] Jamaica, NY Immaculate Conception Monastery; [X] Jamaica, NY Bishop Molloy Retreat House for Laymen.
Hayes, Zachary *o.f.m.* '59 (CHI) [B] Chicago, IL The Catholic Theological Union at Chicago; [N] Chicago, IL St. Joseph Interprovincial Post-Novitiate Formation House.
Hayman, Robert W. '66 (PRO) [31] Providence, RI St. Sebastian Church.
Hayn, Carl H. *s.j.* '47 (SJ) [B] Santa Clara, CA Santa Clara University.
Haynes, Mark J. '85 (PH) Absent on Leave.
Haynes, Stephen S. *c.ss.r.* '88 (TOL) [2] Lima, OH St. Gerard Church.
Hays, Edward '58 (KCK) Special Assignment.
Hays, Henry Bryan *o.s.b.* '62 (SCL) [I] Collegeville, MN St. John's Abbey, of the Order of St. Benedict.
Hays, John '93 (SP) Zephyrhills, FL St. Joseph Church.
Hays, Joseph C. '51 (BEL) Retired.
Hays, Kevin (BO) [W] Boston, MA The Society of St. James the Apostle, Inc.; [BB] Boston, MA St. Stephen.
Hays, Kevin '77 (FgM) Society of St. James the Apostle.
Hays, Kevin W. '77 (CHI) Missionary Work.
Hays, Timothy '96 (SPK) Othello, WA Sacred Heart Church.
Hayward, William *m.i.c.* '89 (JOL) Darien, IL Our Lady of Peace Church.
Hazard, Michael D. '72 (KAL) [2] Kalamazoo, MI St. Joseph Church.
Hazebrouck, Maurice L. '45 (PRO) Retired.
Hazel, Robert '66 (STP) New Hope, MN St. Joseph Church.
Hazel, Terrence J. '75 (Y) Canfield, OH St. Michael's Church.
Hazelton, James '61 (HEL); On Duty Outside the Diocese.
Hazeur, Darren S. *s.s.j.* (WDC) [8] Washington, DC St. Benedict the Moor Church.
Hazeur, Darren S. *s.s.j.* '00 (WDC) [44] Washington, DC St. Vincent De Paul Church.
Hazewski, Eugene J. '59 (NEW) Emerson, NJ Church of the Assumption.
Hazler, George F. '67 (VEN) [2] Naples, FL St. John the Evangelist Church; [G] Naples, FL Voluntas Dei Institute.
Hazuka, Jeremy L. '97 (LIN) Bellwood, NE St. Peter's Church.
Hazzard, William M. '63 (WIL) Woodcrest, DE St. Matthew Church.
Hazzouri, Alex J. '57 (SCR) [N] Dunmore, PA Villa St. Joseph.
Head, Bernard '53 (IND) Retired.
Head, Joseph G. '99 (ALX) Absent on Leave.
Headley, Donald J. '58 (CHI) [151] Chicago, IL Our Lady of Mercy Church.
Headley, William R. *c.s.sp.* '64 (PIT) [B] Pittsburgh, PA Duquesne University of the Holy Ghost.
Heagerty, Kevin *o.f.m.cap.* '61 (FgM) Capuchin Foreign Missions.
Heagle, John L. '65 (LC) On Duty Outside the Diocese.
Healey, Andrew *ss.cc.* '59 (FR) [I] Fairhaven, MA Sacred Hearts Provincial House.
Healey, Augustine *o.c.d.* '49 (FWT) [H] Crowley, TX St. Francis Village, Inc.; [I] Crowley, TX St. Maximilian Kolbe Friary.
Healey, Bernard A. '95 (PRO) [7] Providence, RI St. Augustine Church.
Healey, Charles J. *s.j.* '65 (BO) [A] Weston, MA Pope John XXIII National Seminary; [W] Chestnut Hill, MA The Jesuit Community at Boston College.
Healey, Msgr. Edward F. '43 (COL) Retired.
Healey, Edward J. '87 (FR) [1] Fall River, MA Cathedral of St. Mary of the Assumption.
Healey, Fergus *o.f.m.* '54 (BO) [BB] Boston, MA St. Anthony Shrine.
Healey, John E. '70 (MAN) [8] Nashua, NH St. Patrick Church.
Healey, Joseph G. *m.m.* '66 (FgM) Maryknoll Foreign Missions.
Healey, Kenneth *s.m.* '70 (BO) [E] Reading, MA Austin

Preparatory School.
Healey, Patrick D. '51 (SCR) [17] Scranton, PA St. Mary of the Assumption Church.
Healey, Timothy A. *s.j.* '61 (NY) Manhattan, NY Goldwater Memorial Hospital; [DD] New York, NY St. Ignatius Loyola Residence.
Healey, William B. '55 (SCR) Hawley, PA Blessed Virgin Mary, Queen of Peace Church.
Healy, Clement *o.f.m.* '45 (SP) [O] St. Petersburg, FL St. Anthony Friary.
Healy, Cletus J. *s.j.* '51 (MIL) [P] Wauwatosa, WI Jesuit Community at St. Camillus.
Healy, Gabriel *ss.cc.* '57 (FR) [I] Fairhaven, MA Sacred Hearts Provincial House; [K] Wareham, MA Sacred Hearts Retreat Center.
Healy, George *c.s.sp.* '53 (SB) Hemet, CA Our Lady of the Valley Church.
Healy, Gerald W. *s.j.* '46 (FgM) Provinces.
Healy, Msgr. Gerard M. '61 (MAD) Stoughton, WI St. Ann Church.
Healy, Jack *o.carm.* '70 (ROC) [C] Rochester, NY McQuaid Jesuit High School; [I] Rochester, NY Whitefriars Priory.
Healy, James E. '72 (KC) [3] Independence, MO St. Mark Church.
Healy, James F. '66 (NY) Mamaroneck, NY St. Vito Church.
Healy, James J. *s.s.* '46 (BAL) [O] Baltimore, MD St. Charles Villa; [S] Baltimore, MD St. Charles Villa.
Healy, John '41 (SR) Retired.
Healy, John J. '66 (SAC) [G] Sacramento, CA Mercy General Hospital.
Healy, Joseph '98 (SFR) Belmont, CA Immaculate Heart of Mary Church.
Healy, Kieran J. *o.p.* '61 (FgM) Dominican - Order of Preachers Foreign Missions.
Healy, Kieran J. *o.p.* '61 (OAK) [N] Oakland, CA Western Dominican Province.
Healy, Kilian *o.carm.* '37 (BO) [P] Peabody, MA Catholic Information Center; [BB] Peabody, MA St. Theresa Carmelite Chapel.
Healy, Michael J. '70 (SFR) [47] San Francisco, CA St. Philip the Apostle Church.
Healy, Neal '66 (SFR) San Anselmo, CA St. Anselm Church.
Healy, Patrick F. *o.m.i.* '47 (BO) [Z] Tewksbury, MA Immaculate Heart of Mary Infirmary.
Healy, Patrick J. '66 (E) Mercer, PA State Correctional Facility.
Healy, Patrick S. '76 (NO) [29] New Orleans, LA St. David Church.
Healy, Msgr. Peter C. '53 (LA) Burbank, CA St. Robert Bellarmine Church; Retired.
Healy, Robert *glmy.* '46 (CIN) [M] Cincinnati, OH Headquarters of Glenmary Home Missioners.
Healy, Robert *glmy.* '46 (SAV) Claxton, GA St. Christopher Church.
Healy, Stephen M. '85 (BO) Marshfield, MA St. Ann Church.
Healy, Terence (ALB) Richfield Springs, NY St. Joseph Church.
Healy, Terence P. '62 (ALB) West Winfield, NY St. Joseph Church.
Healy, Thomas '67 (SAV) On Duty Outside the Diocese.
Healy, Thomas C. '95 (BO) Absent on Leave.
Healy, Thomas F. *s.j.* '65 (HEL) [5] Missoula, MT St. Francis Xavier Church.
Healy, Thomas I. '52 (CHI) [153] Chicago, IL Our Lady of Mount Carmel Church.
Healy, Thomas J. '66 (BRK) [221] Queens, NY Our Lady of Sorrows Church.
Healy, William (PHX) Fountain Hills, AZ Ascension Church.
Healy, William *o.c.d.* '46 (MIL) [26] Milwaukee, WI St. Florian Church.
Heaney, John F. '57 (PRO) Charlestown, RI St. Mary Church.
Heaney, John J. *s.j.* '52 (DAL) [27] Dallas, TX St. Rita Church.
Heaney, Msgr. John P. '53 (SFR) San Francisco, CA San Francisco Police Department; Retired.
Heaney, Joseph P. '53 (PRO) [1] Woonsocket, RI St. Agatha Church; Retired.
Heanue, William *c.ss.r.* '47 (ALB) [L] Saratoga Springs, NY St. John Neumann Residence.
Hearn, Philip A. '66 (SY) [4] Rome, NY St. Peter Church.
Heath, Christopher '88 (ORG) San Clemente, CA Our Lady of Fatima Church.
Heath, Mark *o.p.* '47 (WDC) [11] Washington, DC St. Dominic Church & Priory Church.
Heath, T. R. *o.p.* '50 (FgM) Dominican - Order of Preachers Foreign Missions.
Heavey, Edward J. *s.j.* '60 (NEW) [1] East Orange, NJ Holy Name of Jesus Church; [B] Jersey City, NJ Saint Peter's College; [N] Jersey City, NJ Jesuits of Saint Peter's College, Inc.
Hebda, Bernard A. '89 (PIT) On Duty Outside the Diocese.
Hebda, Martin J. '67 (CHI) [J] Chicago, IL Mercy Hospital and Medical Center.
Hebda, Michael J. '96 (SAC) Red Bluff, CA Sacred Heart Church.
Hebden, Scott '99 (CHI) [169] Chicago, IL St. Philomena Church.
Hebekeuser, William '00 (DAL) Richardson, TX St. Joseph Church.
Heberle, Frederick L. '56 (SPR) Sheffield, MA Our Lady of the Valley Church.
Heberlein, Kenneth '71 (GAL) Deer Park, TX St. Hyacinth Church.
Heberlein, Msgr. Louis J. '51 (E) Brandy Camp, PA Holy Cross Church; Brockway, PA St. Tobias Church.
Hebert, Adrien T. *c.s.sp.* '58 (FgM) Holy Ghost Foreign Missions.
Hebert, Albert *s.m.* '54 (BR) Convent, LA St. Michael the Archangel Church.
Hebert, Daniel '79 (ANC) [6] Anchorage, AK Our Lady of Guadalupe Church.
Hebert, Donald J. '68 (SY) Utica, NY St. Luke.
Hebert, Donald J. '81 (SY) [8] Utica, NY St. George Church; [10] Utica, NY St. Joseph and St. Patrick Church.
Hebert, Earl '52 (SPR) [2] Pittsfield, MA Notre Dame Church.
Hebert, Francis '60 (B) Retired.
Hebert, Gerard A. '81 (FR) Westport, MA St. George's Church.
Hebert, Msgr. J. Gaston '60 (LR) [5] Little Rock, AR Christ the King Church.
Hebert, John M. '51 (LIN) Retired.
Hebert, John M. '51 (OM) Retired.
Hebert, Joseph E. *m.afr.* '63 (SP) [O] St. Petersburg, FL Missionaries of Africa.
Hebert, Joseph L. *s.j.* '47 (STL) [P] St. Louis, MO The Jesuits of the Missouri Province.
Hebert, Marvin A. '51 (GAL) Retired.
Hebert, Michael '92 (LAF) Port Barre, LA Sacred Heart of Jesus Church.
Hebert, Oliver J. *t.o.r.* '71 (ALT) [A] Loretto, PA St. Francis College; [F] Loretto, PA St. Francis Friary, Third Order Regular of St. Francis of Penance.
Hebert, Paul L. '59 (NOR) Pomfret, CT Most Holy Trinity Church.
Hebert, Msgr. Ray P. '52 (NO) [1] Marrero, LA Immaculate Conception Church.
Hebert, Roger '49 (PAT) [3] Wayne, NJ Immaculate Heart of Mary Church; Retired.
Hebert, Roland G. '47 (WOR) Retired.
Hebert, Ronald '65 (SD) [18] San Diego, CA Sacred Heart Church.
Hebert, T. J. '49 (LAF) Retired.
Hebl, Msgr. John H. '61 (MAD) Palmyra, WI St. Mary Church; Sullivan, WI St. Mary Help of Christians Church.
Hechenberger, Gerald R. '96 (BEL) Cahokia, IL Holy Family Church; Dupo, IL Sacred Heart of Jesus Church.
Hecht, F. Torrens *s.j.* '46 (DET) [P] Clarkston, MI Colombiere Center.
Heck, Donald '63 (STL) On Medical Leave.
Heck, Quintin '00 (FAR) [5] Fargo, ND St. Anthony of Padua Church.
Heck, Roger C. '51 (MIL) Retired.
Heck, Theodore *o.s.b.* '29 (IND) [J] St. Meinrad, IN St. Meinrad Archabbey.
Heck, Thomas A. '76 (SFS) Brookings, SD St. Thomas More Church.
Heck, Msgr. Thomas W. '57 (NEW) [2] Union City, NJ St. Augustine's Church.
Heckathorne, Brad *o.f.m.conv.* '81 (BAL) [S] Ellicott City, MD Order of Friars Minor Conventual.
Heckel, Guerric Frederick A. '66 (CHR) [E] Moncks Corner, SC Mepkin Abbey.
Heckel, John *o.s.f.s.* '44 (WIL) [I] Childs, MD Oblates of St. Francis De Sales.
Hecker, Msgr. Lawrence A. '58 (NO) Destrehan, LA St. Charles Borromeo Church.
Hedderman, Augustine Mary *m.f.v.a.* '95 (BIR) [E] Birmingham, AL Franciscan Missionaries of the Eternal Word, A Public Association of the Christian Faithful.
Hedderman, Msgr. John J. '60 (SLC) [6] Salt Lake City, UT St. Ambrose Church.
Hederman, James J. *s.j.* '99 (BGP) [E] Fairfield, CT Fairfield College Preparatory School; [P] Fairfield, CT The Fairfield Jesuit Community-Fairfield University.
Hederman, Kevin F. '75 (STL) On Duty Outside the Archdiocese.
Hedges, John P. '87 (DET) [6] Wyandotte, MI St. Stanislaus Kostka Church; Mount Clemens, MI Mount Clemens General Hospital.
Hedges, L. John '43 (ROC) Penfield, NY St. Joseph Church; Retired.
Hedrick, John H. '70 (MAD) Briggsville, WI St. Mary Help of Christians Church; Buffalo, WI St. Andrew Church; Pardeeville, WI St. Mary Church.
Hedrick, Msgr. Kenneth J. '73 (NO) [1] New Orleans, LA St. Louis Church.
Heeg, Lawrence S. '57 (GRY) Chesterton, IN St. Patrick Church.
Heekin, John M. '63 (PAT) Retired.
Heelan, Patrick A. *s.j.* '58 (WDC) [M] Washington, DC The Jesuit Community at Georgetown University.
Heemrood, Jan *o.m.i.* '45 (SAT) [C] San Antonio, TX Oblate School of Theology; [M] San Antonio, TX De Mazenod House.
Heenan, Michael F. (RVC) Retired.
Heenan, Patrick F. '55 (MEM) [13] Memphis, TN St. James Church.
Heeney, Walter *o.s.b.* '43 (KC) [J] Conception, MO Conception Abbey.
Heery, William *o.carm.* '42 (LA) [F] Encino, CA Crespi Carmelite High School.
Heet, Alan *o.f.m.* '46 (CIN) [M] Cincinnati, OH St. Clement Friary.
Heet, Donald J. *o.s.f.s.* '76 (WDC) [B] Washington, DC Deshairs Community-Oblates of St. Francis de Sales Residence; [C] Washington, DC Catholic University of America, The.
Hefferan, John E. '56 (CHI) Ingleside, IL St. Bede Church; Retired.
Heffern, Colman *o.s.b.* '76 (LSC) [E] San Patricio, NM Benedictine Center.
Heffern, Colman *o.s.b.* '76 (SFE) [I] Pecos, NM Our Lady of Guadalupe Abbey; [K] Pecos, NM Our Lady of Guadalupe Olivetan Benedictine Abbey.
Heffernan, A. Joseph '65 (FRS) Hilmar, CA Holy Rosary Church.
Heffernan, Enda *o.f.m.cap.* '57 (SFR) [N] Burlingame, CA Capuchin Provincial House.
Heffernan, Enda *o.f.m.cap.* '73 (MRY) [H] Soquel, CA St. Clare's Retreat House.
Heffernan, Henry G. *s.j.* '62 (WDC) [E] Washington, DC Gonzaga College High School.
Heffernan, James F. '50 (BRK) Released from Diocesan Assignment; Retired.
Heffernan, John J. *o.f.m.* '89 (R) [3] Durham, NC Immaculate Conception Church.
Heffernan, Raymond J. '57 (SEA) Port Townsend, WA St. Mary's, Star of the Sea Church.
Heffernan, Robert G. '63 (HRT) [5] Hamden, CT St. Joan of Arc Church.
Heffernan, Thomas A. '61 (BRK) Released from Diocesan Assignment.
Heffernan, Thomas A. '61 (PAT) Randolph, NJ Resurrection Church.
Heffernan, William P. *m.m.* '55 (FgM) Maryknoll Foreign Missions.
Heffner, Carroll E. '61 (NO) Unassigned.
Heffner, George *s.v.d.* '57 (LAF) Mowata, LA St. Lawrence Church.
Heffron, William *ss.cc.* '68 (FR) Fairhaven, MA St. Joseph's Church.
Heffron, William M. '53 (MIL) Retired.
Hefger, Msgr. Helmut '69 (LA) [A] Camarillo, CA St. John's Seminary.
Heft, James L. *s.m.* '73 (CIN) [D] Dayton, OH The University of Dayton; [D] Dayton, OH The University of Dayton; [M] Dayton, OH Marianist Provincialate.
Hegarty, Daniel P. '63 (BO) [10] Boston, MA St. Anthony Church.
Hegarty, Frederick J. *m.m.* '53 (FgM) Maryknoll Foreign Missions.
Hegarty, John C. *c.s.sp.* '53 (NO) Diamond, LA St. Jude Church.
Hegarty, Michael P. '95 (CAM) Haddon Heights, NJ St. Rose's Church.
Hegarty, William '67 (CHI) [15] Chicago, IL St. Anselm Church.
Hegedus, Gaspar '65 (SAV) [3] Augusta, GA St. Mary on the Hill Church.
Hegenbarth, Robert S. '56 (LC) Bangor, WI St. Mary Church; West Salem, WI St. Leo the Great Church.
Hegener, Wilbert *o.f.m.* '36 (SFD) [K] Sherman, IL Our Lady of Angels Friary.
Hegumen, Juan Jensen '79 (VNN) [A] Ramona, CA Good Shepherd Monastery.
Hegyi, Martin A. *s.j.* '63 (NY) [DD] New York, NY Jesuit Community at Fordham University.
Heher, Michael '78 (ORG) Cypress, CA St. Irenaeus Church.
Hehir, J. Bryan '66 (BAL) Ellicott City, MD Resurrection Church.
Hehir, J. Bryan '66 (BO) [11] Cambridge, MA St. Paul Church; On Duty Outside the Archdiocese.
Hehman, Lawrence W. '65 (LEX) [4] Lexington, KY Pax Christi Catholic Church.
Hehn, Robert E. '63 (DEN) Rifle, CO St. Mary's Church.
Hehr, Horst '67 (DAV) [J] Clinton, IA Mercy Medical Center - Clinton.
Heiar, Donald Joseph, Jr. '00 (MAD) Briggsville, WI St. Mary Help of Christians Church; Buffalo, WI St. Andrew Church; Pardeeville, WI St. Mary Church; Portage, WI St. Mary of the Immaculate Conception Church.
Heiar, James *s.v.d.* (DUB) [B] Epworth, IA Divine Word College.
Heid, Clement J. *o.s.b.* '44 (GBG) [H] Latrobe, PA Saint Vincent Archabbey.

Heid, Richard J. '47 (SCL) Brandon, MN Church of St. Ann; Retired.
Heid, Roland L. *o.s.b.* '41 (GBG) [H] Latrobe, PA Saint Vincent Archabbey.
Heidelberger, Ronald '46 (DET) Retired.
Heidenreich, Robert A. '69 (CHI) [25] Chicago, IL St. Benedict Church.
Heidenrich, Peter J. '77 (CHI) [208] Chicago, IL St. Walter Church.
Heidlage, Benno *o.f.m.* '48 (IND) Batesville, IN St. Louis Church.
Heidt, Charles A. '59 (BIS) [5] Bismarck, ND St. Mary Church.
Heier, Thomas *c.m.m.* '58 (DET) [K] Dearborn Heights, MI Our Lady of Grace Monastery.
Heier, Vergil *c.m.m.* '63 (DET) [K] Dearborn Heights, MI Our Lady of Grace Monastery.
Heigl, John J. *m.afr.* '59 (BUF) Silver Springs, NY St. Mary Church; Warsaw, NY St. Michael Church.
Heikkala, Gregory R. '91 (MAR) Assinins, MI The Most Holy Name of Jesus-Blessed Kateri Tekakwitha Church; L'Anse, MI Sacred Heart Church; Assinins, MI The Most Holy Name of Jesus-Blessed Kateri Tekakwitha Church.
Heil, John P. '74 (STL) Grantwood, MO Our Lady of Providence Church; [A] St. Louis, MO Kenrick-Glennon Seminary.
Heille, Gregory J. *o.p.* '75 (STL) [B] St. Louis, MO Aquinas Institute of Theology; [P] St. Louis, MO St. Dominic Priory.
Heilman, Richard M. '88 (MAD) Montello, WI St. John the Baptist Church; Westfield, WI Good Shepherd Church.
Heim, Edward L. '71 (STL) Augusta, MO Immaculate Conception Church.
Heim, Gerald B. *c.ss.r.* '51 (STL) [P] Liguori, MO St. Clement Health Care Center.
Heim, Howard J. *s.j.* '53 (PH) [C] Philadelphia, PA St. Joseph's University; [AA] Philadelphia, PA Jesuit Community at St. Joseph's University; [BB] Philadelphia, PA Monastery of the Visitation Nuns.
Heim, John P. *s.j.* '65 (CIN) [M] Cincinnati, OH Faber Jesuit Community.
Heim, John S. '51 (PH) Retired; [Y] Philadelphia, PA Sacred Heart Manor.
Heim, Joseph A. *m.m.* '61 (FgM) Maryknoll Foreign Missions.
Heim, Michael J. '82 (PH) [40] Philadelphia, PA St. Dominic Church.
Heiman, Harold *o.s.b.* '39 (LR) Ratcliff, AR St. Anthony Church; [A] Subiaco, AR Subiaco Monastery.
Heiman, Lawrence F. *c.pp.s.* '43 (LFT) [A] Rensselaer, IN Saint Joseph's College.
Heimer, Michael G. '71 (GRY) Fish Lake, IN St. Anthony Church; Rolling Prairie, IN St. John Kanty Church.
Heimerman, Francis D. '44 (DUB) Retired.
Heimos, Robert L. '67 (STL) Washington, MO Our Lady of Lourdes Church.
Heimsoth, Larry '99 (AUS) Temple, TX St. Luke's Church.
Hein, John '63 (RVC) Floral Park, NY Our Lady of Victory Church.
Heina, Steven '82 (SAL) Concordia, KS Our Lady of Perpetual Help Church.
Heindel, Harold J. '66 (RVC) Centerport, NY Our Lady Queen of Martyrs Church.
Heindl, Arthur W. '40 (MAD) Retired.
Heindl, Elmer W. '36 (ROC) [12] Rochester, NY St. Charles Borromeo Church; Retired.
Heine, Michael *o.f.m.conv.* '90 (BAL) [C] Baltimore, MD Archbishop Curley High School; [S] Baltimore, MD Immaculate Heart of Mary Friary.
Heine, Simeon *s.a.* '48 (NY) [DD] Garrison, NY Franciscan Friars of the Atonement.
Heinecke, Gary L. *c.ss.r.* '73 (STL) [P] Liguori, MO St. Clement Health Care Center.
Heineman, Msgr. Donald P. '47 (DUB) Retired.
Heinen, Francis A. '59 (NEW) New Providence, NJ Our Lady of Peace Church.
Heinen, Virgil O. '60 (SUP) Retired.
Heines, Timothy '94 (DAL) Duncanville, TX Holy Spirit Church.
Heiney, Lawrence W. '75 (CHL) Albemarle, NC Our Lady of the Annunciation Church.
Heinl, David A. '57 (CIN) St. Marys, OH Holy Rosary Church.
Heinlein, Anthony J. '65 (RVC) Massapequa Park, NY Our Lady of Lourdes Church.
Heinlein, Msgr. John T. '61 (RVC) Sayville, NY St. Lawrence the Martyr Church.
Heinrich, Harold D. '56 (HRT) [8] New Britain, CT St. John the Evangelist Church.
Heinsch, James *o.f.m.* '67 (FgM) Franciscan Foreign Missions.
Heinsch, James *o.f.m.* '67 (GB) [I] Pulaski, WI Assumption of B.V.M. Friary.
Heinsz, Vernon R. *s.j.* '73 (FgM) Provinces.
Heintz, Daniel '54 (SY) North Syracuse, NY St. Rose of Lima Church.
Heintz, Michael '93 (FTW) [1] South Bend, IN St. Matthew Church; [C] South Bend, IN Saint Joseph's High School.
Heintz, Robert L. '49 (SFD) Retired.
Heintzelman, Edward F. (CAM) Clayton, NJ St. Catherine's Church.
Heintzelman, Gerard '59 (SR) [G] Napa, CA Queen of the Valley Hospital of Napa.
Heinz, David C. '77 (PEO) [1] Bloomington, IL Holy Trinity Church.
Heinz, John *o.f.m. conv.* '93 (SFR) [44] San Francisco, CA St. Paul of the Shipwreck Church.
Heinz, Martin G. '94 (RCK) [2] Aurora, IL Holy Angels Church.
Heinz, Robert P. '80 (CHI) Prospect Heights, IL St. Alphonsus Liguori Church.
Heinz, Walter E. '62 (STU) Pomeroy, OH Sacred Heart Church.
Heinze, Arthur G. '68 (MIL) Hales Corners, WI St. Mary Church.
Heinzel, Thomas R. '75 (HON) Kula, HI Our Lady Queen of the Angels Church.
Heis, Clarence G. '82 (CIN) Mechanicsburg, OH St. Michael's Church; North Lewisburg, OH Immaculate Conception Church.
Heise, Bert *o.f.m.* '57 (HT) [4] Houma, LA Our Lady of the Most Holy Rosary Church; [8] Houma, LA St. Lucy Church.
Heiser, Basil *o.f.m.conv.* '32 (IND) [J] Mount Saint Francis, IN Provincial Headquarters for the Conventual Franciscan Province.
Heiser, W. Charles *s.j.* '53 (STL) [C] St. Louis, MO Saint Louis University; [P] St. Louis, MO Jesuit Community Corporation at St. Louis University - Jesuit Hall.
Heisig, James *s.v.d.* '69 (FgM) Society of the Divine Word Foreign Missions.
Heisig, Kazimierz '78 (HRT) [10] Hartford, CT SS. Cyril and Methodius Church.
Heisler, John F. '99 (ARL) McLean, VA St. John's Church.
Heit, Bruce *o.m.i.* '64 (FgM) Oblates Foreign Missions.
Heithoff, James H. '77 (GI) Valentine, NE St. Nicholas Church.
Heiting, Paul (WIN) On Duty Outside the Diocese.
Heitkamp, Samuel '67 (SAT) Kirby, TX St. Joan of Arc Church.
Heitz, Louis S. '57 (LFT) Winchester, IN St. Joseph Church.
Heitz, Warren *o.s.b.* '66 (IND) [J] St. Meinrad, IN St. Meinrad Archabbey.
Heitzman, Clarence J. '56 (COV) Southgate, KY St. Therese of the Infant Jesus Church.
Heizman, Leo J. '69 (SY) East Syracuse, NY St. Matthew Church.
Hejdak, Andres '84 (PHX) Seligman, AZ St. Francis Church.
Hejna, Lewis E. '81 (SPC) Oran, MO Guardian Angel Church.
Helbing, Brendan *o.s.b.* '65 (OKL) [I] Shawnee, OK St. Gregory's Abbey.
Helduser, Msgr. Frederick J. '60 (PH) [4] Drexel Hill, PA St. Dorothy Church.
Heles, Msgr. Frederic G. '44 (DUB) Retired.
Helfenstein, Maurice R. '27 (SPK) Retired.
Helfrey, Donald '68 (KC) [30] Kansas City, MO Our Lady of Peace Church.
Helfrich, Emil G. *o.m.i.* '49 (SFD) Green Creek, IL St. Mary Help of Christians Church; Lillyville, IL Sacred Heart of Jesus Church.
Helfrich, Frederick '71 (ROC) [57] Rochester, NY St. Theodore Church.
Helfrich, George J. '54 (CHI) Retired.
Helfrich, P. Jeremiah *s.j.* '68 (LA) [3] Santa Barbara, CA Our Lady of Sorrows Church.
Helfrich, Paul D. *c.s.p.* '00 (BO) [CC] Boston, MA The Catholic Center at Boston University.
Helfrich, Peter G. '76 (OG) Absent on Sick Leave.
Helfrich, Thomas J. *o.s.f.s.* '78 (LAN) Adrian, MI St. Mary of Good Counsel Church.
Heliarko, Gregorius *s.j.* '00 (MIL) [P] Milwaukee, WI Jesuit Community at Marquette University.
Hellenberg, Anthony *o.s.b.* '66 (FgM) American - Cassinese Congregation Foreign Missions.
Heller, Christopher J. '79 (RVC) Port Jefferson, NY St. Gerard Majella Church.
Heller, James '68 (SAG) [8] Bay City, MI St. Mary Church.
Hellman, Michael P. '83 (CHY) Green River, WY Immaculate Conception Church.
Hellmann, Msgr. Donald F. '53 (COV) Florence, KY St. Paul Church; Williamstown, KY St. William Church; Retired.
Hellmann, Wayne *o.f.m.conv.* '67 (IND) [J] Mount Saint Francis, IN Provincial Headquarters for the Conventual Franciscan Province.
Hellwig, Lee W. '86 (HRT) Military Chaplains.
Helly, Victor J. *s.j.* '54 (FgM) Provinces.
Helm, John B. '77 (L) [8] Louisville, KY Ascension of Our Lord Church.
Helman, Bradford N. '68 (Y) [10] Canton, OH St. Michael the Archangel Church.
Helmich, George F. *c.s.p.* '57 (NY) [DD] Jamaica Estates, NY Paulist Fathers Generalate.
Helmich, George F. *c.s.p.* '57 (PMB) [H] Vero Beach, FL Paulist Fathers Residence.
Helmick, Raymond G. *s.j.* '63 (BO) [66] Boston, MA St. Theresa of Avila Church; [W] Chestnut Hill, MA The Jesuit Community at Boston College.
Helmick, Msgr. William M. '62 (BO) [66] Boston, MA St. Theresa of Avila Church.
Helmin, Virgil A. '75 (SCL) [3] St. Cloud, MN Holy Spirit Church.
Helms, Michael '90 (DOD) Lakin, KS St. Anthony Church.
Helms, Walter (DAV) [3] Iowa City, IA St. Thomas More Church.
Helms, Walter B. '69 (DAV) Oxford, IA St. Mary's Church.
Helmueller, Lawrence C. *s.j.* '42 (OM) [K] Omaha, NE Jesuit Community at Creighton University.
Heltemes, Alfred J. '54 (SCL) Foley, MN St. John's Church.
Helwig, Alan R. '58 (WDC) [2] Bethesda, MD St. Jane Frances de Chantal Church.
Helwig, Paul C. '74 (HBG) Camp Hill, PA Good Shepherd Church.
Heman, Richard J. '67 (STL) Affton, MO St. Dominic Savio Church.
Hemann, Everett '71 (DUB) Ames, IA St. Thomas Aquinas Church (and Catholic Student Center) Church; [N] Ames, IA St. Thomas Aquinas Church and Catholic Student Center (Iowa State University).
Hemann, John W. '60 (DUB) Ionia, IA St. Boniface's Church; Nashua, IA St. Michael's Church; North Washington, IA Immaculate Conception Church.
Hemann, Maurice *o.m.i.* '50 (FgM) Oblates Foreign Missions.
Hemann, Melvin D. '59 (DUB) Retired.
Hemauer, Gil *o.f.m.cap.* '64 (GF) Miles City, MT Sacred Heart Church.
Hemberger, Kent A. '88 (WCH) [10] Wichita, KS St. Anne Church.
Hemberger, Robert E. '70 (WCH) [G] Wichita, KS Mt. St. Mary Convent, Motherhouse and Novitiate of the Sisters of St. Joseph.
Hembrow, William '60 (SFD) Fieldon, IL St. Mary Church; Jerseyville, IL Holy Ghost Church.
Hemkens, Edward B. '54 (STL) Retired.
Hemler, Edward B. '64 (BAL) Fallston, MD St. Mark Church.
Hemler, Thomas J. '56 (HBG) Waynesboro, PA St. Andrew Church.
Hemm, Thomas *c.pp.s.* '78 (CIN) [M] Dayton, OH Provincial Office of the Cincinnati Province of the Society of the Precious Blood.
Hemm, Thomas *c.pp.s.* '78 (TOL) Ottawa, OH SS. Peter and Paul Church.
Hemmelgarn, Larry J. *c.pp.s.* '84 (CIN) [M] Dayton, OH Provincial Office of the Cincinnati Province of the Society of the Precious Blood.
Hemmer, Joseph *o.f.m.* '54 (FBK) Kaltag, AK St. Teresas Church; Ruby, AK St. Peter-in-Chains Church.
Hemmer, Joseph *o.f.m.* '54 (FgM) Franciscan Foreign Missions.
Hemmerle, R. Joseph '67 (L) [12] Louisville, KY St. Bartholomew Church; [B] Louisville, KY Trinity High School.
Hemmerling, Henry L. '66 (MET) Old Bridge, NJ Most Holy Redeemer Church.
Hemmersbach, Alfred F. '45 (LC) Retired; [H] La Crosse, WI Holy Cross (Seminary) Diocesan Center.
Hemming, Philip M. '67 (P) Keizer, OR St. Edward Church.
Hemp, Lawrence A. '67 (LUB) Slaton, TX Our Lady of Guadalupe Church; Slaton, TX St. Joseph's Church.
Hempel, John L. '54 (ROC) Retired.
Hemphil, Anthony *s.v.d.* '58 (LAF) On Special Assignment.
Hemrick, Eugene '63 (WDC) [24] Washington, DC St. Joseph on Capitol Hill Church.
Hemrick, Eugene F. '63 (JOL) On Duty Outside the Diocese.
Hemsing, John D. '88 (MIL) Wind Lake, WI St. Clare Church.
Henao, Alfonso '79 (NY) [1] Newburgh, NY St. Patrick Church.
Henao, Luis Emilio '74 (NO) [3] New Orleans, LA Annunciation Church.
Henault, James A. *m.s.* '80 (HRT) [M] Hartford, CT Missionaries of LaSalette, Provincial Secretary.
Henault, John *o.m.i.* '63 (FgM) Oblates Foreign Missions.
Henchal, Michael J. '73 (PRT) Cape Elizabeth, ME St. Bartholomew Church.
Henchey, Joseph *c.s.s.* '56 (BO) [W] Waltham, MA Stigmatine Fathers & Brothers Provincial House.
Hencier, John Gregory *c.m.f.* '72 (LA) San Gabriel, CA San Gabriel Church; [Q] San Gabriel, CA Claretian Missionaries (Missionary Sons of the Immaculate Heart of Mary).
Hendel, Lawrence '77 (SJ) [12] San Jose, CA St. John Vianney Church; Military Chaplains.

Hendel, Msgr. Richard P. '48 (RVC) Bay Shore, NY St. Patrick's Church; Retired.
Hendel, Msgr. Thomas W. '45 (BRK) Retired.
Henden, Brian *o.carm.* '93 (TUC) [A] Tucson, AZ Salpointe Catholic High School; [F] Tucson, AZ Carmelite Priory.
Henderson, Christopher *c.p.m.* '98 (OWN) [F] South Union, KY Fathers of Mercy.
Henderson, Christopher J. '94 (SAM) Brockton, MA St. Theresa Church.
Henderson, David (PEO) [1] Champaign, IL Holy Cross Church.
Henderson, James B. *o.c.s.o.* '60 (DUB) [K] Peosta, IA New Melleray Abbey, Order of Cistercians of the Strict Observance.
Henderson, John A. '87 (JC) Jefferson City, MO Jefferson City Correctional Center; Boonville, MO Boonville Correctional Center.
Henderson, John H. '87 (JC) Folk, MO St. Anthony of Padua Church.
Henderson, Paul *c.ss.r.* '50 (BO) [53] Boston, MA Our Lady of Perpetual Help Church.
Henderson, Robert J. '65 (COV) Cold Spring, KY St. Joseph Church.
Hendian, Patrick '98 (PEO) Utica, IL St. Mary Church.
Hendren, Lucien '63 (SFE) Retired.
Hendrick, Msgr. Frank J. '54 (ARL) Retired.
Hendrick, John H. '70 (MAD) Portage, WI St. Mary of the Immaculate Conception Church.
Hendrick, Matthew D. '85 (R) Wilmington, NC St. Mark Church.
Hendricks, Clare '63 (GRY) On Duty Outside the Diocese.
Hendricks, Msgr. Donald W. '55 (NY) Buchanan, NY St. Christopher Church.
Hendricks, Edward S. '77 (BAL) Special Assignment; [U] Baltimore, MD Archdiocesan Office-Newman Center.
Hendricks, James P. '60 (L) [22] Louisville, KY St. Denis Church; [L] Louisville, KY Bishop David Apartments.
Hendricks, John '52 (FgM) Society of St. James the Apostle.
Hendricks, John J. '52 (TR) On Duty Outside the Diocese.
Hendricks, Joseph M. (COL) [L] Columbus, OH Diocesan Retirement Community Corp.
Hendricks, Msgr. Joseph M. '72 (COL) Dublin, OH St. Brigid of Kildare Church; [L] Columbus, OH The Villas at St. Therese Independent Living, Inc.; [L] Columbus, OH The Villas at St. Therese Assisted Living, Inc.
Hendricks, Scott B. '86 (BO) Absent on Leave; Emergency Response Group.
Hendricks, Theodore J. '65 (GB) Francis Creek, WI St. Anne Church; Kossuth, WI St. Augustine Church.
Hendrickson, Daniel S. *s.j.* (OM) [K] Omaha, NE Jesuit Community at Creighton University.
Hendrickson, W. Frederick '56 (L) [A] Louisville, KY Bellarmine University.
Hendriks, Boniface '45 (SFE) Retired.
Hendriks, Joseph *ss.cc.* '48 (HON) Kalaupapa, HI St. Francis Church; [F] Kalaupapa, HI Kalaupapa Settlement.
Hendry, Gerald '85 (SP) [3] St. Petersburg, FL Holy Cross Church.
Hendry, Simon J. *s.j.* '77 (OAK) [N] Berkeley, CA Jesuit Community at Jesuit School of Theology at Berkeley.
Heneghan, James A. '83 (CHI) [30] Chicago, IL St. Bonaventure Church.
Heneghan, Jarlath '55 (SEA) Retired.
Heneghan, John F. '55 (YAK) Retired.
Heneghan, Martin '71 (NY) [II] New York, NY Prelature of the Holy Cross and Opus Dei.
Heneghan, Sean '53 (SEA) Retired.
Heneghan, Msgr. Thomas F. '51 (NY) [174] Bronx, NY Our Lady of Mt. Carmel Church.
Henehan, Patrick (PEO) [B] Ottawa, IL Marquette High School.
Henehan, Thomas P. *m.m.* '65 (FgM) Maryknoll(M.M.).
Henehan, Thomas P. *m.m.* '65 (NY) [DD] Maryknoll, NY Maryknoll Fathers and Brothers.
Henery, Ronald *o.p.* '58 (NO) [25] New Orleans, LA St. Anthony of Padua Church; New Orleans, LA Delgado College.
Henery, Ronald *o.p.* '78 (NY) [DD] New York, NY St. Vincent Ferrer Priory.
Henesy, William P. '51 (RVC) Retired.
Heney, David '78 (LA) [A] Camarillo, CA St. John's Seminary; [A] Camarillo, CA St. John's Seminary College of the Archdiocese of Los Angeles.
Heney, Frederick J. *s.j.* '63 (LA) [Q] Los Angeles, CA Columbiere House.
Hengel, Warren, Jr. '92 (FRS) [3] Fresno, CA Our Lady of Mt. Carmel Church.
Henger, Alcuin *o.m.i.* '55 (DUL) Sandstone, MN St. Luke's Church.
Hengesbach, Julius L. '53 (KAL) Retired.
Hengle, John R. '68 (CLV) Tallmadge, OH Our Lady of Victory Church.
Heninger, Michael B. '00 (ATL) Conyers, GA St. Pius X Catholic Church.
Henk, Jan '83 (CHI) [35] Chicago, IL St. Camillus Church.
Henke, Donald E. '93 (STL) [2] St. Charles, MO St. Cletus Church; [E] St. Charles, MO Duchesne High School.
Henke, Msgr. James '66 (SAT) [35] San Antonio, TX St. Francis of Assisi Church.
Henkel, William A. '55 (CHI) Retired.
Henkel, William M. '55 (CHI) Westchester, IL Divine Infant Church.
Henkels, Edmund *o.s.b.* '59 (WDC) [M] Washington, DC St. Anselm's Abbey.
Henkes, Donald E. '66 (MEM) On Duty Outside the Diocese.
Henkes, Donald E. '66 (SAG) Mount Pleasant, MI Sacred Heart Church.
Henkle, Charles *o.f.m. conv.* '97 (CLV) [1] Lorain, OH St. Anthony of Padua Church.
Henley, Earl *m.s.c.* (SB) Soboba Indian Reservation, CA St. Joseph Church.
Henley, Fred M. *s.j.* '58 (DET) [P] Clarkston, MI Colombiere Center.
Henley, John R. '75 (ATL) Retired.
Henn, Joseph *s.d.s.* '78 (MIL) [P] Milwaukee, WI Salvatorian Provincial Residence.
Henne, Paul '56 (PIT) [2] Swissvale, PA Word of God Church.
Hennelly, Alfred T. *s.j.* '60 (NY) [DD] New York, NY Murray-Weigel Hall.
Hennelly, Michael F. (PH) [69] Philadelphia, PA Immaculate Conception Church.
Hennelly, Michael F. '91 (PH) [D] Philadelphia, PA John W. Hallahan Catholic Girls High School.
Hennen, Joseph *o.s.c* '67 (STP) [N] Shoreview, MN Crosier Provincial House Province of St. Odilia.
Hennesey, James J. *s.j.* '57 (NY) [DD] New York, NY Murray-Weigel Hall.
Hennessey, John E. '67 (CHI) Libertyville, IL St. Joseph Church.
Hennessey, John J. *c.ss.r.* (BO) [53] Boston, MA Our Lady of Perpetual Help Church.
Hennessey, John P. '47 (BUF) Retired.
Hennessey, Joseph F. '91 (BO) [7] Boston, MA St. Ann Church.
Hennessey, Lawrence R. '71 (CHI) [A] Mundelein, IL University of St. Mary of the Lake-Mundelein Seminary.
Hennessey, Robert F. '78 (BO) [47] Boston, MA Most Holy Redeemer Church.
Hennessey, Robert J. *o.p.* '56 (PRO) [B] Providence, RI Providence College.
Hennessey, William *s.s.c.* '35 (FgM) St. Columban's Foreign Mission.
Hennessey, Msgr. William J. '61 (MIA) [B] Opa Locka, FL St. Thomas University; [L] Miami Shores, FL Archdiocese of Miami Millennium Appeal, Inc.; [L] Miami Shores, FL Archdiocese of Miami, Inc.
Hennessy, Augustine Paul *c.p.* (SPR) [I] Holyoke, MA Mont Marie Health Care Center, Inc.
Hennessy, Brian P. '99 (PH) Hatfield, PA St. Maria Goretti Church.
Hennessy, Douglas J. '63 (PEO) Danville, IL St. Paul's Church.
Hennessy, James W. '61 (WIN) [2] Winona, MN St. Casimir's Church.
Hennessy, John '78 (FWT) Burleson, TX St. Ann Church.
Hennessy, John A. *s.j.* '52 (RC) St. Francis, SD Rosebud Reservation Church.
Hennessy, John J. *s.j.* '69 (RC) Martin, SD Our Lady of the Sacred Heart Church.
Hennessy, John P. *o.s.a.* '44 (NY) [216] Staten Island, NY Our Lady of Good Counsel Church.
Hennessy, Joseph I. '63 (PHX) Chandler, AZ St. Andrew the Apostle Church.
Hennessy, Thomas C. *s.j.* '47 (NY) [DD] New York, NY Jesuit Community at Fordham University.
Hennessy, Thomas J. '96 (ATL) Griffin, GA Sacred Heart Church.
Henning, Edward *o.f.m.cap.* (PH) [V] Aston, PA Assisi House.
Henning, Edward *o.f.m.cap.* '96 (WIL) [I] Wilmington, DE Capuchin Franciscan Friars, St. Francis Renewal Center; [L] Wilmington, DE St. Francis Renewal Center.
Henning, James *o.f.m.conv.* '82 (DET) [58] Detroit, MI Our Lady Queen of Angels Church.
Henning, Michael L. '74 (STL) St. Peters, MO All Saints Church; [V] St. Louis, MO Archdiocesan Stewardship Education Committee.
Henning, Phillip D. '93 (SAT) Fredericksburg, TX St. Mary's Church.
Henning, Richard '92 (RVC) Graduate Studies.
Henning, Richard G. '92 (RVC) [A] Huntington, NY Diocesan Seminary of the Immaculate Conception.
Henninger, George (IND) Indianapolis, IN Indiana University Hospital/Riley Hospital for Children.
Henninger, George '85 (VIC) On Duty Outside the Diocese.
Henninger, Mark G. *s.j.* '78 (DET) [K] Detroit, MI Jesuit Community at the University of Detroit.
Hennington, Bruce M. '68 (MAD) Columbus, WI St. Jerome Church.
Henrich, Steven *o.s.c.* '74 (STP) [N] Shoreview, MN Crosier Community of Shoreview.
Henrick, John C. '62 (NSH) Antioch, TN St. Ignatius of Antioch Church.
Henricksen, Francis C. (DAV) Retired.
Henriot, Peter J. *s.j.* '70 (FgM) Provinces.
Henriquez, Genaro '99 (BWN) San Juan, TX The Basilica of the National Shrine of Our Lady of San Juan del Valle; [I] San Juan, TX The Basilica of the National Shrine of Our Lady of San Juan.
Henriquez, Mauricio '92 (WDC) [4] Silver Spring, MD St. Catherine Laboure Church.
Henritzy, Curtis E. *o.p.* '93 (PRO) [P] Providence, RI St. Thomas Aquinas Priory at Providence College.
Henry, Carol Ann *r.s.m.* (TR) [T] Asbury Park, NJ Mercy Center, Inc.
Henry, Charles W. *o.s.b.* '53 (IND) [F] Indianapolis, IN St. Vincent Hospital and Health Care Center, Inc.; [J] Indianapolis, IN St. Maur Priory.
Henry, Charles W. *o.s.b.* '53 (NEW) [N] Newark, NJ Newark Abbey.
Henry, Donald H. '71 (VEN) [2] Naples, FL St. John the Evangelist Church.
Henry, Earl J. *o.s.b.* '64 (GBG) [H] Latrobe, PA Saint Vincent Archabbey.
Henry, James *s.v.d.* '59 (LA) [D] Lakewood, CA Saint Joseph High School.
Henry, James '71 (MRY) Arroyo Grande, CA St. Patrick Church.
Henry, James T. '64 (PH) Southampton, PA Our Lady of Good Counsel Church.
Henry, John F. *s.j.* '55 (BAL) [S] Baltimore, MD Jesuit Fathers and Brothers Maryland Provincial Curia.
Henry, John F. *s.j.* '55 (FgM) Provinces.
Henry, John P. '52 (RVC) Cutchogue, NY Sacred Heart Church; Retired.
Henry, John P. '52 (SP) Tarpon Springs, FL St. Ignatius Church.
Henry, Joseph *s.j.* '60 (ALN) [A] Wernersville, PA Jesuit Center.
Henry, Msgr. Joseph L. '36 (MAD) Retired.
Henry, Joseph P. '58 (PRO) Coventry, RI SS. John and Paul Church.
Henry, Lawrence J. *c.s.c.* '61 (FTW) [J] South Bend, IN Congregation of Holy Cross, Indiana Province, Provincial House.
Henry, Leo G. '55 (PIT) Retired; [O] Pittsburgh, PA St. John Vianney Manor.
Henry, Patrick '81 (CLV) Painesville, OH St. Mary Church.
Henry, Patrick J. '89 (CHI) [38] Chicago, IL St. Christina Church.
Henry, Patrick J. '92 (SAC) Alturas, CA Sacred Heart Church.
Henry, Paul '70 (BAL) Special Assignment.
Henry, Paul J. '68 (ORL) [9] Orlando, FL St. John Vianney Church.
Henry, Perry F. *c.m.* '83 (NO) [41] New Orleans, LA St. Joseph Church; [61] New Orleans, LA St. Stephen Church.
Henry, Peter '68 (ORL) On Duty Outside the Diocese.
Henry, Robert P. '79 (NY) Nyack, NY St. Ann Church.
Henry, Terence *t.o.r.* '75 (STU) [F] Steubenville, OH Holy Spirit Friary.
Henry, Terence *t.o.r.* '76 (STU) [A] Steubenville, OH Franciscan University of Steubenville.
Henry, Terrence *t.o.r.* (ALT) [H] Hollidaysburg, PA Campus Ministry.
Henry, Thomas '44 (RIC) Retired.
Henry, William '84 (JKS) McComb, MS St. Alphonsus Church.
Henseler, Edwin, Jr. '00 (CHI) [3] Mt. Prospect, IL St. Raymond de Penafort Church.
Henseler, J. Thomas '63 (PEO) On Duty Outside the Diocese.
Henseler, Joseph N. '52 (LC) Neillsville, WI St. Mary Church; Retired.
Henseler, Michael *s.d.s.* '77 (MIL) [P] Milwaukee, WI Salvatorian Provincial Residence.
Henseler, Thomas '63 (SFD) Mount Sterling, IL Holy Family Church.
Hensell, Eugene *o.s.b.* '69 (IND) [A] St. Meinrad, IN St. Meinrad Seminary; [J] St. Meinrad, IN St. Meinrad Archabbey.
Henson, Jerome M. '77 (ORG) Costa Mesa, CA St. John the Baptist Church.
Henson, Joel '93 (LA) [A] Camarillo, CA St. John's Seminary College of the Archdiocese of Los Angeles.
Hentschel, Cletus B. '51 (BEL) Retired.
Hentz, Otto H. *s.j.* '68 (WDC) [M] Washington, DC The Jesuit Community at Georgetown University.
Hentzner, John T. '45 (MIL) Retired.
Henz, Kenneth W. '51 (CIN) Retired.
Heon, Charles *o.m.i.* '64 (FgM) Oblates Foreign Missions.
Heon, Paul J. *m.afr.* '41 (SP) [O] St. Petersburg, FL Missionaries of Africa.

Hepburn, Timothy M. '93 (ATL) [N] Atlanta, GA The Catholic Charismatic Renewal in Atlanta.
Hephner, John (GB) Coleman/Klondike, WI Ss. Francis/Wenceslaus Church.
Hephner, John J. (GB) Oconto Falls, WI St. Anthony Church; Stiles, WI St. Patrick Church.
Hepnar, Bede *o.f.m.* '57 (GRY) Shelby, IN St. Theresa Church; [J] Cedar Lake, IN Our Lady of Lourdes Friary.
Hepner, Ernest C. '61 (CLV) Bedford Heights, OH Holy Trinity Church.
Heppe, Patrick E. '77 (MIL) [1] Fond du Lac, WI Holy Family Church.
Heppen, Michael J. *c.s.c.* '63 (DET) Birmingham, MI Our Lady Queen of Martyrs Church.
Heppner, Sylvester *o.f.m.* '59 (IND) Oldenburg, IN Holy Family Church; [K] Oldenburg, IN Motherhouse of the Congregation of the Sisters of the Third Order of St. Francis.
Hept, Wilfrid *o.f.m.* '44 (BO) [BB] Boston, MA St. Anthony Shrine.
Herald, Robert '89 (AUS) Rockdale, TX St. Joseph's Church.
Heramb, James '68 (JOL) Paxton, IL St. Mary Church.
Herard, Msgr. Joseph P. '55 (DUB) Retired.
Heras, Msgr. Michael '84 (CC) [8] Corpus Christi, TX Our Lady of Perpetual Help Church.
Heraty, John T. '67 (RCK) Sandwich, IL St. Paul Church.
Herba, Stanislaw '64 (SLC) [4] Midvale, UT St. Therese of the Child Jesus Church.
Herbe, Donnan *o.f.m.* '45 (SFE) Cerrillos, NM St. Joseph Church.
Herbein, John J. '74 (E) Franklin, PA St. Patrick Church.
Herbek, Msgr. Adrian F. '59 (LIN) David City, NE St. Mary's Church.
Herber, Alvin L. *c.pp.s.* '50 (KC) Cameron, MO St. Munchin Church.
Herber, John '68 (TOL) Kalida, OH St. Michael Church.
Herber, Stanley J. '64 (IND) Connersville, IN St. Gabriel Church; Knightstown, IN St. Rose Church; New Castle, IN St. Anne Church.
Herberger, Edward *s.v.d.* '60 (FgM) Society of the Divine Word Foreign Missions.
Herberger, Roy T. '68 (BUF) [19] Buffalo, NY SS. Columba & Brigid Church; Buffalo, NY Sheehan Memorial Emergency Hospital.
Herbers, Simon *c.p.* '50 (GAL) [Q] Houston, TX Congregation of the Passion, Holy Name Retreat Center.
Herbert, Eugene '81 (LA) Arcadia, CA Annunciation Church.
Herbert, G. Paul '86 (WDC) [1] Washington, DC St. Matthew Church; Pastoral Center Special Ministries.
Herbert, J. Marc *c.s.c.* '50 (FR) [I] North Dartmouth, MA Holy Cross Mission House.
Herbert, John J. '83 (BUR) Rutland, VT St. Peter Church.
Herbert, Leo P. '67 (ATL) Newnan, GA St. George's Church.
Herbert, Lloyd P. '57 (LAF) Retired.
Herbst, Charles T. *c.m.* '50 (STL) [P] Perryville, MO Congregation of The Mission.
Herbst, Justin J. '58 (TR) [J] Lawrenceville, NJ Morris Hall/Saint Lawrence, Inc.; [L] Lawrenceville, NJ Morris Hall-Saint Lawrence, Inc.; [O] Lawrenceville, NJ Our Lady of the Rosary Chapel; [T] Lawrenceville, NJ Morris Hall/St. Lawrence, Inc.
Herbst, Robert M. *o.f.m.conv.* '91 (SB) [11] Riverside, CA St. Thomas the Apostle Church.
Herbst, Thomas *o.f.m.* '92 (OAK) [N] Oakland, CA Franciscan Friars Provincial Office, Province of St. Barbara.
Herbster, Kenneth J. (NEW) [2] Hoboken, NJ St. Joseph's Church.
Herbster, Kenneth J. '63 (NEW) [1] Hoboken, NJ Our Lady of Grace Church; [Q] Hoboken, NJ Stevens Institute of Technology.
Hercek, Joseph R. '72 (MRY) Atascadero, CA St. William's Church.
Hercik, Terry A. '80 (GBG) Ford City, PA St. Mary Church; Ford City, PA St. Francis of Paola Church; Ford City, PA Holy Trinity Church.
Herda, Jerome G. '90 (MIL) [E] Milwaukee, WI Divine Savior Holy Angels High School, Inc.
Herdegen, Msgr. Anthony '46 (FRS) Retired.
Heredia, Juan Victor '91 (BWN) [9] Brownsville, TX St. Luke Church.
Hereford, Thomas D. '56 (JC) On Duty Outside the Diocese.
Herek, Daniel P. '71 (OM) Absent on Leave.
Hereley, Peter J. *o.p.* '63 (CHI) [N] River Forest, IL St. Thomas Aquinas Priory; [N] River Forest, IL St. Thomas Aquinas Priory; [U] River Forest, IL American Friends of the Ecole Biblique.
Hererra, Manuel '94 (NY) [95] New York, NY Our Lady Queen of Martyrs Church.
Hereshko, David M. '00 (HBG) [4] Lancaster, PA St. John Neumann Church.
Herff, Jerome *c.m.* '67 (GLP) Kayenta, AZ Our Lady of Guadalupe Church; [A] Gallup, NM Diocesan Diaconate and Lay Ecclesial Ministry Formation Program.
Hergenrother, John '66 (CHI) [112] Chicago, IL St. Ladislaus Church.
Herhenreader, Peter V. '59 (SCR) Royal, PA St. Pius X Church.
Heria, Fernando '96 (MIA) Coconut Grove, FL St. Hugh Church.
Herian, Kenneth J. *s.j.* '55 (MIL) [31] Milwaukee, WI Gesu Church.
Herk, Charles W.A. '48 (NEW) [N] Rutherford, NJ St. John Vianney Residence for Priests.
Herkowski, Arthur M. '54 (MIL) Retired.
Herkowski, Arthur M. '54 (RNO) Retired.
Herle, Clifford *o.f.m.* '55 (LSC) Tularosa, NM St. Francis de Paula Church.
Herlihy, Daniel J. '67 (MET) South Bound Brook, NJ Our Lady of Mercy Church.
Herlihy, Jude M. *o.s.m.* '56 (CHI) [N] Chicago, IL Order of Friar Servants of Mary (Servites) United States of America Province, Inc.
Herlihy, Jude M. *o.s.m.* '56 (ORG) Fullerton, CA St. Juliana Falconieri Church; [I] Buena Park, CA Order of Friar Servants of Mary (Servites).
Herlong, T.L. '58 (LKC) [6] Lake Charles, LA St. Theodore's Church.
Herlong, Theophilus L. '58 (LKC) Retired.
Herman, Charles A. '97 (FTW) Auburn, IN Immaculate Conception Church.
Herman, Gerard *o.f.m.conv.* '57 (SAV) St. Simons Island, GA St. Williams Church.
Herman, Jerome A. '43 (DET) Retired.
Herman, John *c.s.c.* '95 (FTW) [B] Notre Dame, IN University of Notre Dame Du Lac.
Herman, John A. *c.s.c.* '95 (FTW) [J] South Bend, IN Congregation of Holy Cross, Indiana Province, Provincial House; [J] Notre Dame, IN Holy Cross Community, Corby Hall, University of Notre Dame.
Herman, Michael T. '89 (CHI) [193] Chicago, IL St. Sylvester Church.
Herman, Robert D. '60 (WIN) Medford, MN Christ the King Church.
Herman, William J. '00 (DET) Clawson, MI Guardian Angels Church.
Hermann, Msgr. Carlton P. '35 (SFS) Retired.
Hermann, Robert '63 (STL) [V] St. Louis, MO Archdiocesan Stewardship Education Committee.
Hermann, Robert J. '63 (STL) Chesterfield, MO Incarnate Word Church.
Hermanns, Harold T. '54 (NEW) Retired; [N] Rutherford, NJ St. John Vianney Residence for Priests.
Hermanns, Mel *o.f.m.cap.* '64 (CHI) [144] Chicago, IL Our Lady Gate of Heaven Church.
Hermansen, Douglas U. '79 (TR) Avon, NJ St. Elizabeth Church; Neptune, NJ Jersey Shore Medical Center.
Hermes, Msgr. Daniel J. '69 (RCK) [5] Rockford, IL Holy Family Church.
Hermes, Eustace A. '41 (VIC) Retired.
Hermes, Joseph H. *m.m.* '62 (FgM) Maryknoll Foreign Missions.
Hermes, Michael '91 (KCK) [9] Kansas City, KS SS. Cyril and Methodius Church; [13] Kansas City, KS St. Joseph and St. Benedict Church.
Hermes, Richard T. *s.j.* '98 (NO) [F] New Orleans, LA Jesuit High School.
Hermes, Roger J. '53 (STP) Retired.
Hermes, Thomas W. '82 (KC) Clinton, MO Holy Rosary Church.
Hermoso, Joseph '57 (ELP) [25] El Paso, TX St. Joseph's Church.
Hermoso, Msgr. Seth '67 (GAL) [12] Houston, TX St. Augustine Church.
Hernanco, Henry L. '67 (LA) Terminal Island, CA Federal Correctional Institution.
Hernandez, Alberto *o.f.m.* '70 (ELP) [B] El Paso, TX Roger Bacon College.
Hernandez, Msgr. Alfred '55 (LA) Retired.
Hernandez, Alfred '82 (LA) Torrance, CA Nativity Church.
Hernandez, Alfred Ricardo '66 (SAT) Military Chaplains.
Hernandez, Alfredo '92 (PMB) [5] West Palm Beach, FL St. Juliana Church.
Hernandez, Angelo '93 (PH) [158] Philadelphia, PA St. William Church.
Hernandez, Anthony (BRK) Graduate Studies.
Hernandez, Anthony '00 (VNN) Los Gatos, CA St. Basil the Great Church.
Hernandez, Antonio '92 (SAT) On Leave.
Hernandez, Antonio A. *c.ss.r.* '67 (PCE) Guayama, PR St. Anthony of Padua Church; [B] Ponce, PR The Pontifical Catholic University of Puerto Rico.
Hernandez, Baltazar Nunez '88 (CGS) [F] Naranjito, PR Seminario Pablo VI - Propedeutico.
Hernandez, Bernardo *c.m.* '63 (PCE) [14] Ponce, PR San Vicente-Cantera Church.
Hernandez, Eliseo *o.r.c.* '82 (SB) [5] San Bernardino, CA Our Lady of Guadalupe Church; [E] Riverside, CA Operarios Del Reino De Cristo, O.R.C.
Hernandez, Enrico '96 (SJ) Mountain View, CA St. Joseph Church; San Jose, CA Archbishop Mitty High School; [C] San Jose, CA Archbishop Mitty High School.
Hernandez, Enrique (CHI) [120] Chicago, IL St. Mark Church.
Hernandez, Esteban *m.s.f.* '87 (BWN) Edinburg, TX Holy Family Church.
Hernandez, Felix Nunez '99 (CGS) Unassigned.
Hernandez, Fernando *t.o.r.* '00 (AUS) [2] Waco, TX St. Francis on the Brazos Church.
Hernandez, Fernando A. '90 (NY) [137] Bronx, NY Christ the King Church.
Hernandez, Fidel *o.a.r.* (LA) [Q] Oxnard, CA St. Augustine Priory O.A.R.
Hernandez, Francis G. *s.j.* '63 (SAC) [C] Sacramento, CA Jesuit High School; [H] Carmichael, CA Jesuit High School Community of Sacramento.
Hernandez, Francisco '94 (MIA) [28] Miami, FL SS. Peter and Paul Church.
Hernandez, Francisco J. '90 (YAK) Prosser, WA Sacred Heart Church.
Hernandez, George M. '97 (BRK) [230] Queens, NY Queen of Angels Church.
Hernandez, Msgr. Gonzalo Diaz '63 (MGZ) Hormigueros, PR Shrine of Our Lady of Monserrate Church.
Hernandez, Guillermo '89 (SJN) Graduate Studies.
Hernandez, Isaias '93 (YAK) [1] Yakima, WA St. Paul Church.
Hernandez, Javier '74 (CGS) Fajardo, PR Santisimo Redentor Church.
Hernandez, Jimmy (ARE) Retired.
Hernandez, Jorge *o.f.m.* '98 (SD) [1] Oceanside, CA Mission San Luis Rey Church; [H] Oceanside, CA Mission San Luis Rey.
Hernandez, Jose '60 (SFE) [26] Albuquerque, NM St. Edwin Church.
Hernandez, Jose Luis '00 (SPK) Walla Walla, WA St. Francis of Assisi Church; Walla Walla, WA St. Patrick Church.
Hernandez, Joseph '69 (LA) Fillmore, CA St. Francis of Assisi Church.
Hernandez, Juan Ramon *c.ss.r.* '80 (CGS) San Lorenzo, PR Nuestra Senora de la Mercedes Church.
Hernandez, Lawrence C. *o.ss.t.* '78 (BAL) [S] Baltimore, MD Holy Trinity Monastery.
Hernandez, Lorenzo '85 (ORG) [6] Santa Ana, CA St. Anne's Church.
Hernandez, Luis E. *o.s.a.* '74 (GAL) Baytown, TX Our Lady of Guadalupe Church.
Hernandez, Manuel, Jr. '96 (CC) [6] Corpus Christi, TX Our Lady of Guadalupe Church.
Hernandez, Marco A. *c.s.b.* '87 (GAL) [Q] Sugar Land, TX Basilian Mission Center.
Hernandez, Martin A. '81 (BR) Prairieville, LA St. John the Evangelist Church.
Hernandez, Pedro '89 (ARE) [4] Utuado, PR Nuestra Senora del Monte Carmelo Church.
Hernandez, Rafael '93 (BWN) Mercedes, TX Sacred Heart Church.
Hernandez, Ramon '73 (SP) Dade City, FL St. Rita Church.
Hernandez, Rene J. '95 (MGZ) [1] Mayaquez, PR Cathedral of Our Lady of Purification.
Hernandez, Ricardo F. '00 (RCK) Belvidere, IL St. James Church.
Hernandez, Rodrigo Manrique '90 (SJN) [7] Bayamon, PR Santa Elena Church.
Hernandez, Stephen C. '82 (LA) [26] Los Angeles, CA Our Lady of Guadalupe Church; Retired.
Hernandez, Victor M. *s.j.* '76 (MIA) [D] Miami, FL Belen Jesuit Preparatory School; [H] Miami, FL Villa Javier.
Hernandez-Morales, Ricardo '98 (SJN) [21] San Juan, PR Nuestra Sra. de Guadalupe Church.
Hernando, Henry L. '67 (LA) [17] Los Angeles, CA Immaculate Heart of Mary Church.
Hernando, Jose L. '62 (MIA) Key Biscayne, FL St. Agnes Church.
Herne, Robert G. '47 (CHI) Northbrook, IL Our Lady of the Brook Church; Palos Hills, IL Sacred Heart Church; Retired.
Hernick, Jan *o.f.m.conv.* (BO) Boston, MA New England Medical Center.
Herold, Anthony '79 (DAV) Clinton, IA Jesus Christ, Prince of Peace Church.
Heron, J. Thomas '78 (PH) [52] Philadelphia, PA Good Shepherd Church.
Herondi, Fernandes *s.x.* '76 (CHI) [199] Chicago, IL St. Therese Catholic Chinese Church.
Herp, Joseph T. '73 (L) [46] Louisville, KY St. Leonard Church.
Herpin, Msgr. L. Michael '66 (LAF) Broussard, LA Sacred Heart of Jesus Church.
Herpin, Wayne *s.j.* (DAL) [27] Dallas, TX St. Rita Church.
Herr, Charles W. '48 (NEW) Retired.
Herr, Kenneth '68 (EVN) Special Assignment; [A] Evansville, IN Reitz Memorial High School.
Herrador, Blas P. '52 (GAL) [73] Houston, TX Resurrection Church.

Herradura, Rainer '91 (TR) [2] Toms River, NJ St. Justin Church.
Herrera, Anthony '91 (OAK) Pleasanton, CA The Catholic Community of Pleasanton Church.
Herrera, David '89 (SAN) Fort Stockton, TX St. Joseph's Church; Fort Stockton, TX St. Agnes Church; Sanderson, TX St. James Church.
Herrera, Edward '91 (LSC) Sunland Park, NM St. Martin de Porres Church.
Herrera, Emigdio '77 (LA) Santa Maria, CA St. John Neumann Church.
Herrera, Enrique '96 (MRY) Nipomo, CA St. Joseph Church.
Herrera, Francisco '67 (ELP) Retired.
Herrera, Hernando '98 (FR) Seekonk, MA Our Lady of Mt. Carmel Church; [B] Taunton, MA Coyle and Cassidy High School.
Herrera, Javier Saravia *s.j.* '72 (DET) [61] Detroit, MI SS. Peter and Paul Jesuit Church.
Herrera, Jose (STV) On Duty Outside the Diocese.
Herrera, Jose '88 (BRK) [165] Queens, NY Corpus Christi Church.
Herrera, Jose G. (KC) Special Assignment.
Herrera, Jose G. '89 (KC) [8] Kansas City, MO Christ the King Church.
Herrera, Lawrence *s.j.* '81 (LA) [A] Camarillo, CA St. John's Seminary College of the Archdiocese of Los Angeles.
Herrera, Pedro E. *c.s.v.* '80 (CHI) [N] Arlington Heights, IL Viatorian Province Center-Clerics of St. Viator.
Herrera, Rosendo '96 (AMA) [2] Amarillo, TX St. Laurence Church; [4] Amarillo, TX Our Lady of Guadalupe Church.
Herreras, Jose Maria *s.j.* '57 (MIA) [3] Miami, FL Corpus Christi Church.
Herrero, Jose M. '52 (PCE) [3] Ponce, PR Church of the Resurrection; [B] Ponce, PR The Pontifical Catholic University of Puerto Rico.
Herrero, Msgr. Nicolas '59 (FRS) Exeter, CA Sacred Heart Church.
Herres, Msgr. Joseph W. '72 (LA) [47] Los Angeles, CA San Antonio de Padua Church.
Herrick, Marion L. *o.f.m.* '67 (GBG) Uniontown, PA Uniontown Hospital.
Herrlich, Neale W. *s.j.* '52 (SJ) [L] Los Gatos, CA Sacred Heart Jesuit Center.
Herrman, Gilbert P. '49 (DOD) Syracuse, KS St. Raphael Church.
Herrmann, Austin C. *c.pp.s.* '48 (SAN) Coleman, TX Sacred Heart Church.
Herrmann, Frank R. *s.j.* '74 (BO) [W] Chestnut Hill, MA The Jesuit Community at Boston College.
Herrmann, Jim *o.s.c.* '70 (STP) [N] Anoka, MN Crosier Community of Anoka.
Herrmann, Richard J. '44 (LC) Retired.
Herrmann, Robert W. '58 (PIT) Robinson Township, PA Holy Trinity Church.
Herron, Bernard J. '54 (PH) [20] Philadelphia, PA St. Barnabas Church.
Herron, Msgr. Denis M. '73 (BRK) [243] Queens, NY St. Teresa Church.
Herron, Francis X. '55 (PH) Southampton, PA Our Lady of Good Counsel Church.
Herron, Jack B. '74 (FAR) Military Chaplains.
Herron, Msgr. Joseph P. '62 (CAM) Longport, NJ Epiphany Church; [G] Camden, NJ The Frank J. and Rosina W. Suttill Catholic Foundation.
Herron, Msgr. Thomas J. '73 (PH) Highland Park, PA St. Laurence Church.
Hersey, Bryan '98 (SEA) [5] Vancouver, WA St. Joseph Church.
Hertel, Msgr. Herbert N. '42 (WCH) Retired.
Hertel, James R. '65 (PAT) [4] Wayne, NJ Our Lady of Consolation Church.
Hertel, John *o.carm.* '53 (FgM) Carmelite Foreign Missions.
Hertel, John *o.carm.* '53 (JOL) [J] Darien, IL Carmelite Provincial Office.
Hertel, Joseph M. *o.f.m.* '66 (NY) [35] New York, NY St. Francis of Assisi Church.
Hertel, Joseph M. *o.f.m.* '66 (PAT) [P] Paterson, NJ St. Anthony's Guild.
Herttna, Matthew M. '45 (Y) Retired; [P] Massillon, OH National Shrine of St. Dymphna.
Hertweck, Robert W. *s.m.* '64 (CIN) [M] Dayton, OH Marianist Provincialate.
Heruday, Msgr. Joseph C. '43 (CLV) Maple Heights, OH St. Wenceslas Church; Retired.
Hervey, Paul '95 (SP) [5] Tampa, FL Incarnation Church.
Herzing, Joseph '99 (SCL) Bowlus, MN St. Stanislaus Kostka Church; Elmdale, MN St. Edward's Church; North Prairie, MN Holy Cross Church; Upsala, MN St. Mary Church.
Herzog, John M. '56 (DUB) Retired.
Herzog, Lawrence A. '80 (STL) [59] St. Louis, MO St. Roch Church.
Herzog, Mark J. '79 (TOL) [1] Fremont, OH Sacred Heart Church.
Herzog, Msgr. Ronald P. '68 (BLX) Laurel, MS Immaculate Conception Church; Waynesboro, MS St. Bernadette Church.
Herzstein, Joseph M. *c.s.sp.* '63 (FgM) Holy Ghost Foreign Missions.
Hesburgh, Theodore M. *c.s.c.* '43 (FTW) [B] Notre Dame, IN University of Notre Dame Du Lac; [J] Notre Dame, IN Holy Cross Community, Corby Hall, University of Notre Dame.
Heskamp, Charles *s.v.d.* '58 (BLX) [A] Bay St. Louis, MS St. Augustine's.
Heskamp, Charles *s.v.d.* '58 (LAF) [4] Lafayette, LA Immaculate Heart of Mary Church; On Special Assignment.
Hesketh, John E. *o.s.b.* '94 (PAT) [M] Morristown, NJ St. Mary's Abbey.
Heskin, Thomas M. *o.s.m.* '55 (CHI) [J] Maywood, IL Foster G. McGaw Hospital of Loyola University of Chicago; [N] Chicago, IL Order of Friar Servants of Mary (Servites) United States of America Province, Inc.
Hesko, Daniel C. '84 (TR) Middletown, NJ St. Catherine Church.
Hesler, Raymond F. *s.s.* '35 (BAL) [O] Baltimore, MD St. Charles Villa; [S] Baltimore, MD St. Charles Villa.
Heslin, Msgr. James J. '54 (STA) [7] Jacksonville, FL Holy Spirit Church.
Heslin, Philip J. '57 (SUP) On Special or Other Diocesan Assignment.
Heslin, Sean '67 (ORL) [1] Orlando, FL St. James Church.
Hess, George A. *s.j.* '50 (BAL) [S] Baltimore, MD Jesuit Fathers and Brothers Maryland Provincial Curia.
Hess, George A. *s.j.* '50 (FgM) Provinces.
Hess, James *o.carm.* '76 (PMB) [B] Boca Raton, FL Pope John Paul II High School; [H] Boca Raton, FL St. Elias Priory-Order of Carmelites, NY.
Hess, James W. '53 (MIL) Retired.
Hess, John Paul '83 (STL) [7] Florissant, MO Sacred Heart Church.
Hess, Joseph R. '00 (PH) Yardley, PA St. Ignatius of Antioch Church.
Hess, Larry J. '79 (ALN) Gordon, PA Our Lady of Good Counsel Church.
Hess, Michael N. '71 (DM) West Des Moines, IA Sacred Heart Church.
Hess, Norbert F. *c.s.c.* '56 (FTW) [J] South Bend, IN Congregation of Holy Cross, Indiana Province, Provincial House.
Hess, Richard J. '60 (DUB) [1] Cedar Rapids, IA Immaculate Conception Church; Retired.
Hess, Robert *s.c.j.* '67 (MIL) [P] Hales Corners, WI Priests of the Sacred Heart.
Hess, Stephen M. *s.j.* '75 (SEA) [A] Seattle, WA Seattle University.
Hesse, Paul A '91 (CC) Odem, TX Sacred Heart Church.
Hesse, Paul A. '91 (CC) [2] Kingsville, TX St. Gertrude Church.
Hesse, Peter *o.f.m.cap.* '43 (LC) [H] Marathon City, WI St. Anthony Retreat Center.
Hesse, Robert T. *c.s.c.* '58 (FgM) Holy Cross Foreign Missions.
Hesse, Robert T. *c.s.c.* '58 (FTW) [J] South Bend, IN Congregation of Holy Cross, Indiana Province, Provincial House.
Hesse, Thomas N. '63 (KCK) Flush, KS St. Joseph's Church; Wamego, KS St. Bernard's Church.
Hessel, Gerald J. '67 (MIL) Caledonia, WI St. Louis Church.
Hesseling, Jason Edward '00 (MAD) [7] Madison, WI St. Dennis Church.
Hessian, Msgr. Patrick J. '53 (STP) Retired.
Hessian, Roger J. '61 (STP) Cannon Falls, MN St. Pius V Church.
Hession, Anthony '99 (FAR) Munich, ND St. Mary's Church; Starkweather, ND Assumption of the Blessed Virgin Mary Church.
Hession, Msgr. Edward I. '41 (FTW) [3] Fort Wayne, IN St. Charles Borromeo Church; Retired.
Hession, James J. '59 (BO) Senior Priests.
Hession, Mark R. '84 (FR) Centerville, MA Our Lady of Victory Church.
Hessling, Ambrose B. *o.s.b.* '57 (PEO) [A] Peru, IL St. Bede Abbey and Academy.
Hester, John '59 (SJ) Palo Alto, CA St. Thomas Aquinas Church; Milpitas, CA Stanford Medical Center.
Heter, Bernard P. '74 (NY) Cornwall-on-Hudson, NY St. Thomas of Canterbury Church.
Hetteberg, Marcan *o.f.m.* '54 (CIN) [M] Cincinnati, OH St. Clement Friary.
Hettinger, Msgr. Clarence J. '42 (PEO) [15] Peoria, IL St. Vincent De Paul Church; Special Assignment; Retired.
Hettinger, Paul W. '39 (PEO) Retired.
Hetzler, Leo A. *c.s.b.* '55 (ROC) [I] Rochester, NY Basilian Residence.
Heuberger, Joseph '70 (P) Verboort, OR Visitation B.V.M. Church.
Heugh, John (DAL) Frisco, TX St. Francis of Assisi Church.
Heumann, Carl J. *s.j.* '72 (FgM) Provinces.
Heuring, Msgr. Alvan P. '44 (DUB) Retired.
Heuschkel, Robert R. '50 (Y) [13] Youngstown, OH St. Dominic's Church.
Heusel, Daniel '00 (STU) Mingo Junction, OH St. Agnes Church.
Heuser, Frederick A. '55 (MIL) [5] Kenosha, WI St. James Church.
Heuser, James *s.d.b.* '84 (NEW) [N] Orange, NJ The Salesian Community; [S] Orange, NJ Salesians of Don Bosco, S.D.B.
Heuser, James *s.d.b.* '84 (NY) [72] New York, NY Mary Help of Christians Church.
Heusser, John F. '51 (PAT) [4] Paterson, NJ Blessed Sacrament Church; Paterson, NJ Preakness Hospital.
Hever, John J. '52 (BO) Foxborough, MA St. Mary Church; Medfield, MA Medfield State Hospital.
Hever, Thomas '62 (PHX) [2] Scottsdale, AZ Our Lady of Perpetual Help Church.
Hevern, Vincent W. *s.j.* '76 (SY) [S] Syracuse, NY Jesuits at LeMoyne, Inc.
Hevia, Todd O. '67 (PT) On Leave of Absence.
Hewawasam, Charles '88 (TLS) Sapulpa, OK Sacred Heart Church.
Hewes, James E. '74 (ROC) Clyde, NY St. John the Evangelist Church; Lyons, NY St. Michael Church.
Hewes, Robert S. '78 (RVC) Seaford, NY St. James Church.
Hewett, Alfred J. '56 (CAM) Retired.
Hewitt, Anthony '99 (VEN) Cape Coral, FL St. Andrew Church.
Hewitt, Msgr. Bernard P. '47 (CAM) Retired.
Hewitt, Charles L. '31 (BGP) [L] Trumbull, CT St. Joseph's Manor.
Hewitt, Charles L. '31 (HRT) Retired.
Hewitt, Kenneth R. (PAT) Retired.
Hewitt, William J. '57 (MET) Hampton, NJ St. Ann Church.
Hewson, William J. '40 (BR) Retired.
Heyburn, Kevin (SAN) Retired.
Heyburn, Msgr. Kevin '48 (SAT) [K] San Antonio, TX Padua Place.
Heyburn, Theodore *c.s.s.r.* (BAL) Annapolis, MD St. Mary Church.
Heyburn, Theodore *c.ss.r.* '60 (BAL) [S] Annapolis, MD Saint Mary Rectory.
Heyd, James '89 (CHI) Evanston, IL St. Athanasius Church.
Heyd, Joseph J. *o.s.b.* '56 (PEO) Peru, IL St. Joseph's Church; [A] Peru, IL St. Bede Abbey and Academy.
Heydens, Donald J. '70 (GR) On Special Assignment.
Heying, John Joseph '00 (RC) Custer, SD St. John the Baptist Church; Hill City, SD St. Rose of Lima Church; Hot Springs, SD St. Anthony's Church.
Heyman, George P. '80 (ROC) Red Creek, NY St. Thomas the Apostle Church.
Heyman, George P. '81 (ROC) Ithaca, NY Immaculate Conception Church; Wolcott, NY St. Mary Magdalene Church.
Heyman, Jerome M. *o.s.a.* '61 (KAL) Allegan, MI Blessed Sacrament Church.
Heymen, Richard H. '56 (GB) Whitelaw, WI St. Michael Church.
Heymer, Msgr. Edward D. '45 (MEM) Retired.
Heyndricks, Eugene P. '81 (NEW) Fairview, NJ St. John the Baptist Church.
Hezel, Francis X. *s.j.* '69 (CI) [A] Pohnpei, FM Micronesian Seminar; [C] Kolonia, Pohnpei, FM Jesuit House.
Hezel, Francis X. *s.j.* '69 (FgM) Provinces.
Hezel, Kenneth J. *s.j.* '66 (AGN) [H] Mangilao, GU Campus Ministry, Newman Center, University of Guam.
Hezel, Kenneth J. *s.j.* '66 (FgM) Provinces.
Hibner, Cyprian *o.carm.* '61 (PHX) [5] Glendale, AZ St. Raphael Church.
Hibner, Jerome '64 (BEL) Scheller, IL St. Barbara Church.
Hibner, Jerome H. '64 (BEL) Radom, IL St. Michael Church.
Hicarte, Mateo '53 (LA) [17] Los Angeles, CA Immaculate Heart of Mary Church.
Hickel, Msgr. John J. '55 (STL) St. Paul, MO St. Paul Church.
Hickens, William F. *c.s.c.* '46 (FTW) [J] South Bend, IN Congregation of Holy Cross, Indiana Province, Provincial House.
Hickey, Christopher J. '94 (BO) Dedham, MA St. Mary Church.
Hickey, Daniel J. '59 (BO) [3] Malden, MA Sacred Hearts Church.
Hickey, Dennis W. *c.s.p.* '76 (NY) [104] New York, NY St. Paul the Apostle Church.
Hickey, Msgr. Edward T. '45 (COV) Retired.
Hickey, George J. *i.m.c.* '80 (MET) [H] Somerset, NJ Consolata Society for Foreign Missions.
Hickey, George W. '73 (PRT) Hallowell, ME Sacred Heart Church.
Hickey, Gerald J. '63 (BO) Unassigned.
Hickey, Gregory J. '79 (PH) Center Square, PA St. Helena Church; [D] Norristown, PA Kennedy-Kenrick Catholic High School.
Hickey, James C. *s.m.a.* '46 (NEW) [N] Tenafly, NJ

Society of African Missions, Provincialate, S.M.A. Fathers.
Hickey, James F. '68 (BO) Rockland, MA Holy Family Church.
Hickey, James V. '64 (HRT) [3] West Haven, CT St. Lawrence's Church.
Hickey, Jerome J. *o.c.s.o.* '59 (ATL) [J] Conyers, GA The Monastery of the Holy Spirit.
Hickey, John '96 (AMA) [9] Amarillo, TX St. Martin De Porres Church.
Hickey, John P. '86 (PIT) Bellevue, PA Assumption of the Blessed Virgin Mary on the Beautiful River Church.
Hickey, Joseph '55 (NY) Tarrytown, NY Transfiguration Church.
Hickey, Kieran *o.f.m.cap.* (GB) Kaukauna, WI St. Mary of the Annunciation Church.
Hickey, Meldon *o.f.m.* '51 (GLP) Fort Defiance, AZ Our Lady of Blessed Sacrament Church; St. Michaels, AZ St. Michael Church; [A] Gallup, NM Diocesan Diaconate and Lay Ecclesial Ministry Formation Program.
Hickey, Michael '62 (VEN) Retired.
Hickey, Peter D. *s.j.* '76 (BO) [E] Boston, MA Boston College High School & Jesuit Community.
Hickey, Regis *o.s.b.* '50 (KCK) [H] Atchison, KS St. Benedict's Abbey.
Hickey, Msgr. Robert P. '65 (NY) Ellenville, NY St. Mary and St. Andrew Church.
Hickey, Thomas D. '49 (MIL) Retired.
Hickey, Thomas E. '70 (CHI) [40] Chicago, IL St. Clement Church.
Hickey, Thomas F. *c.ss.r.* '54 (BRK) [107] Brooklyn, NY Our Lady of Perpetual Help Basilica Church.
Hickey, Timothy *c.s.sp.* (PIT) [R] Pittsburgh, PA Office for Campus Ministry.
Hickey, William M. '86 (ATL) Cumming, GA St. Brendan Church.
Hickey, Msgr. William T. '47 (BRK) [206] Queens, NY Our Lady of the Angelus Church; Retired.
Hickie, J. Noel '67 (BAK) On Duty Outside the Diocese.
Hickie, J. Noel '67 (P) [J] Eugene, OR Sacred Heart Medical Center.
Hickin, Michael '97 (COL) [A] Columbus, OH Pontifical College Josephinum.
Hickl, Robert *o.m.i.* '79 (FgM) Oblates Foreign Missions.
Hickman, J. Stephen '82 (RIC) Military Chaplains.
Hicks, Alfred J. *s.j.* '66 (BO) [H] Boston, MA Nativity Preparatory School; [W] Boston, MA The Society of Jesus of New England-Provincial Offices.
Hicks, Francis J. '00 (LA) San Pedro, CA Holy Trinity Church.
Hicks, Ronald A. '94 (CHI) [A] Chicago, IL St. Joseph Seminary.
Hicks, Steven '82 (SAN) Military Chaplains.
Hidaka, Ronald E. *s.j.* '74 (FgM) Provinces.
Hidding, Thomas J. *s.j.* '86 (MIA) [5] Miami, FL Gesu Church.
Hiebl, Charles J. (LC) Poniatowski, WI Holy Family Church.
Hiebl, Charles J. '62 (LC) Athens, WI St. Anthony de Padua Church.
Hien, Joseph '64 (NY) [27] New York, NY St. Columba Church.
Higdon, C. Paul '46 (DET) Retired; [H] Port Huron, MI Mercy Hospital of Port Huron.
Higdon, Francis *m.m.* '67 (PH) [AA] Philadelphia, PA Maryknoll House.
Higdon, Francis *m.m.* '67 (WDC) [B] Washington, DC Maryknoll Fathers and Brothers.
Higginbotham, Matthew P. '94 (LAF) Coteau, LA Our Lady of Prompt Succor Church.
Higginbotham, Robert '75 (BLX) Military Chaplains.
Higgins, Brian J. '99 (ATL) [1] Atlanta, GA Cathedral of Christ the King.
Higgins, Charles J. '75 (BO) [5] Brookline, MA St. Mary of the Assumption Church.
Higgins, Charles J. '88 (BO) [66] Boston, MA St. Theresa of Avila Church.
Higgins, Msgr. Cornelius P. '44 (SAC) [7] Sacramento, CA Presentation of the Blessed Virgin Mary Church; Retired and in Senior Ministry.
Higgins, Donald *c.s.s.* '64 (BO) [W] Waltham, MA Stigmatine House.
Higgins, E. Edward '57 (PEO) Lincoln, IL Holy Family Church.
Higgins, Edward F. '54 (GBG) Retired.
Higgins, Edward J. '76 (PSC) Philadelphia, PA Holy Ghost Church.
Higgins, Francis C. '68 (SAV) [7] Savannah, GA Sacred Heart of Jesus Church.
Higgins, Francis E. '64 (SC) On Duty Outside the Diocese.
Higgins, Msgr. George C. '40 (CHI) Retired.
Higgins, Msgr. George G. '40 (WDC) [C] Washington, DC Catholic University of America, The.
Higgins, Msgr. Grant J. '56 (BUF) Retired.
Higgins, James J. *c.ss.r.* '37 (STL) [P] Liguori, MO Liguori Mission House/Redemptorists.
Higgins, James P. *s.j.* '85 (BUF) [C] Buffalo, NY Canisius College; [D] Buffalo, NY Canisius High School; [O] Buffalo, NY Canisius Jesuit Community.
Higgins, Jerome *o.f.m.cap.* '54 (MIL) [B] Hales Corners, WI Sacred Heart School of Theology; [P] Milwaukee, WI St. Conrad Friary.
Higgins, John *s.j.* '65 (BGP) [B] Fairfield, CT Fairfield University.
Higgins, John '81 (LA) Ventura, CA Sacred Heart Church.
Higgins, John F. *m.s.* '72 (HRT) [M] Hartford, CT Missionaries of LaSalette, Provincial Secretary.
Higgins, John J. '52 (WDC) Retired.
Higgins, John J. *s.j.* '66 (BGP) [P] Fairfield, CT The Fairfield Jesuit Community-Fairfield University.
Higgins, John J. '96 (NY) [148] Bronx, NY Holy Rosary Church.
Higgins, Msgr. Joseph P. '57 (MAD) Middleton, WI St. Bernard Church.
Higgins, Msgr. Laurence E. '53 (SP) [10] Tampa, FL St. Lawrence Church.
Higgins, Leonard H. '82 (TLS) Pawhuska, OK Immaculate Conception Church.
Higgins, Michael *o.carm.* '68 (LA) [3] North Hollywood, CA St. Jane Frances de Chantal Church.
Higgins, Michael *c.p.* '70 (CHI) [N] Chicago, IL Passionist Provincial Office; [N] Chicago, IL Passionist Community-Immaculate Conception Monastery.
Higgins, Michael *c.p.* '70 (FgM) Mission Procurators.
Higgins, Michael *t.o.r.* '85 (ALT) [A] Loretto, PA St. Francis College; [F] Loretto, PA St. Francis Friary, Third Order Regular of St. Francis of Penance.
Higgins, Michael J. '62 (BO) Permanent Disability.
Higgins, Msgr. Patrick '54 (CC) [3] Corpus Christi, TX Holy Cross Church.
Higgins, Patrick O. '47 (SFD) Retired.
Higgins, Peter '56 (VIC) Retired.
Higgins, Phillip (RIC) Retired.
Higgins, Raymond '94 (DM) Perry, IA St. Patrick Church.
Higgins, Richard B. '68 (SAC) Military Chaplains.
Higgins, Robert J. *s.j.* '50 (BO) [W] Weston, MA Campion Health Center, Inc.
Higgins, Thomas C. *m.m.* '50 (NY) [DD] Maryknoll, NY Maryknoll Fathers and Brothers.
Higgins, Thomas M. '85 (PH) [128] Philadelphia, PA Our Lady of the Rosary Church.
Higgins, Thomas P. *s.j.* '64 (LA) [C] Los Angeles, CA Loyola Marymount University; [BB] Los Angeles, CA Archdiocesan Office for Campus Ministry.
Higgs, Donald X. '88 (WH) Morgantown, WV St. John University Parish, Newman Hall Church.
Highberger, Donald E. *s.j.* '81 (SPK) [C] Spokane, WA Gonzaga University.
Highberger, George '61 (PHX) [4] Phoenix, AZ Immaculate Heart of Mary Church; [7] Phoenix, AZ SS. Anthony and Pius X Church.
Highfill, Brian (LAV) [4] Las Vegas, NV Our Lady of Las Vegas Church.
Highfill, H. Brian '74 (NO) On Duty Outside the Archdiocese.
Hight, Michael '82 (RC) [1] Rapid City, SD Cathedral of Our Lady of Perpetual Help.
Hightower, O. Lee. '61 (HEL) Military Chaplains.
Higley, Gregory L. '81 (JC) [3] Jefferson City, MO Immaculate Conception Church.
Higson, John P. '80 (LA) On Sick Leave.
Higuera, Federico '82 (BEL) Cobden, IL St. Joseph Church.
Higuera, Julio '78 (PHX) Gilbert, AZ St. Anne Church.
Higuero, Francisco J. '68 (BRK) Absent on Leave.
Hiland, George '58 (PEO) Retired.
Hiland, Gerard P. '85 (CIN) Owensville, OH St. Louis Church; Stonelick, OH St. Philomena Church.
Hilbert, J. Robert *s.j.* '56 (CHY) St. Stephens, WY St. Stephen's Church; [C] St. Stephens, WY St. Stephens Mission - Jesuit Community.
Hilbert, Joseph C. '52 (HBG) Gettysburg, PA St. Francis Xavier's Church.
Hilbert, Michael P. *s.j.* '83 (NY) [DD] New York, NY Jesuit Provincial's Office.
Hildebrand, Thomas M. '75 (TLS) [15] Tulsa, OK St. Pius X Church.
Hildebrandt, Henry F. '87 (DOD) Liberal, KS St. Anthony Church.
Hilden, Michael J. *o.s.a.* '73 (FgM) Foreign Missions.
Hilderbrand, H. Michael '76 (IND) Jeffersonville, IN Sacred Heart Church; [C] Clarksville, IN Our Lady of Providence Junior & Senior High School.
Hilferty, John G. '78 (ALN) Unassigned.
Hilferty, Msgr. Thomas J. '52 (PH) Ardsley, PA Queen of Peace Church; West Chester, PA St. Agnes Church.
Hilfiker, Robert G. '87 (NY) New Windsor, NY St. Joseph Church.
Hilgartner, Richard B., Jr. '95 (BAL) [1] Baltimore, MD Cathedral of Mary Our Queen; [A] Baltimore, MD St. Mary's Seminary and University.
Hilgeman, Edward J. '52 (STL) [3] Lemay, MO St. Andrew Church.
Hilgeman, James L. *m.m.* '65 (FgM) Maryknoll Foreign Missions.
Hilgendorf, Patrick '97 (DAV) Burlington, IA SS. John & Paul Church; West Burlington, IA SS. Mary and Patrick Church.
Hilgert, E. John *c.p.* '75 (GAL) [Q] Houston, TX Congregation of the Passion, Holy Name Retreat Center.
Hilinski, Joseph T. '76 (CLV) [55] Cleveland, OH Our Lady of Mercy Church.
Hilkert, Robert C. '42 (CLV) Brunswick, OH St. Ambrose Church.
Hill, Allan J. '83 (HRT) Harwinton, CT Immaculate Heart of Mary Church.
Hill, Benet *o.s.b.* '85 (WDC) [M] Washington, DC St. Anselm's Abbey.
Hill, Msgr. Charles '64 (LA) [48] Los Angeles, CA St. Basil's Church.
Hill, Donald '67 (BIS) On Duty Outside the Diocese.
Hill, Donald M. '94 (L) [3] Louisville, KY St. Albert the Great Church.
Hill, Edward T. '60 (BAL) Retired.
Hill, Eric (ATL) Atlanta, GA Cobb County Jail.
Hill, Eric J. '00 (ATL) [4] Marietta, GA Church of the Transfiguration.
Hill, Frederick '67 (RVC) Smithtown, NY St. Patrick Church; Smithtown, NY St. Catherine of Siena Hospital.
Hill, George H. '68 (NY) [185] Bronx, NY St. Raymond Church.
Hill, George H. '68 (WOR) On Duty Outside the Diocese.
Hill, J. Clifton *c.s.sp.* '65 (PIT) [B] Pittsburgh, PA Duquesne University of the Holy Ghost.
Hill, James B. *s.m.a.* '45 (BO) [W] Dedham, MA African Mission House.
Hill, Lawrence B. *s.j.* '46 (NY) [DD] New York, NY Murray-Weigel Hall.
Hill, Lawrence H. *o.s.b.* '65 (GBG) [H] Latrobe, PA Saint Vincent Archabbey.
Hill, Michael W. *o.f.m.* '77 (HON) [2] Honolulu, HI Co-Cathedral of St. Theresa of the Child Jesus .
Hill, Patrick '68 (LA) [50] Los Angeles, CA St. Bernard Church.
Hill, Patrick J. '68 (LA) Graduate Studies.
Hill, Paul J. *m.s.c.* '50 (Y) [A] Youngstown, OH Sacred Heart Retreat House & Renewal Center.
Hill, Msgr. Peter J. '36 (SFE) Retired.
Hill, Msgr. Philip W. '71 (NY) Military Chaplains.
Hill, R. Cary '66 (WDC) Beltsville, MD St. Joseph Church; Pastoral Center Special Ministries.
Hill, Robert '57 (Y) Retired.
Hill, Scott F. *o.m.i.* '79 (MRY) Special Assignment.
Hill, Thomas F. *o.f.m.cap.* '66 (STP) Rosemount, MN St. Joseph Church.
Hill, Timothy '59 (BIR) Retired.
Hill, W. Paul '64 (WDC) [4] Bowie, MD St. Pius X Church.
Hill, William B. *s.j.* '45 (SCR) [C] Scranton, PA University of Scranton.
Hill, William J. *o.p.* '50 (WDC) [B] Washington, DC Dominican House of Studies.
Hillen, Daniel P. '69 (HEL) [B] Helena, MT Carroll College.
Hillenbrand, John T. '70 (CHI) [165] Chicago, IL St. Peter Canisius Church.
Hillenbrand, Thomas '65 (FgM) American - Cassinese Congregation Foreign Missions.
Hiller, Everett J. '54 (RCK) Retired.
Hillesheim, Gerald A. (NU) Ghent, MN St. Eloi Church.
Hillesheim, Gerald A. '68 (NU) Minneota, MN St. Edward Church.
Hilley, Stephen '79 (MIA) Coconut Creek, FL St. Luke Church.
Hilliard, Richard '79 (SJ) On Leave of Absence.
Hilliard, William H. '62 (HRT) Enfield, CT Carl Robinson Correctional Institution.
Hilliard, William J. '62 (HRT) [1] Enfield, CT Holy Family Church.
Hillier, David A. '76 (TR) Bradley Beach, NJ Ascension Church.
Hillier, John '88 (NOR) [A] Cromwell, CT Holy Apostles College and Seminary.
Hillier, John G. '88 (WOR) Brookfield, MA St. Mary's Church.
Hillman, Eugene H. *c.s.sp.* '50 (VEN) [G] Sarasota, FL Congregation of the Holy Ghost.
Hills, Richard L. '32 (CHI) Flossmoor, IL Infant Jesus of Prague Church; Retired.
Hillyard, Matthew J. *o.s.f.s.* '91 (ARL) [D] Alexandria, VA Bishop Ireton High School; [J] Alexandria, VA Oblates of St. Francis de Sales Residence.
Hilmer, Garth L. '00 (GAY) [1] Gaylord, MI St. Mary Church.
Hilmer, Robert E. '86 (DUB) [2] Waterloo, IA St. Mary's Church.
Hils, Damian J. '95 (FAR) Veseleyville, ND St. Luke Church; Warsaw, ND St. Stanislaus Church.
Hilton, Francis G. *s.j.* '92 (BAL) [S] Baltimore, MD Jesuit Community of Loyola College, Inc.
Hilton, Hank *s.j.* '92 (BAL) [B] Baltimore, MD Loyola College in Maryland.
Hilton, John L. (DEN) Westminster, CO Holy Trinity Church.

Hiltz, John T. '59 (ORG) Yorba Linda, CA St. Martin Church.
Hiltz, John T. '59 (TOL) On Duty Outside the Diocese.
Himes, Kenneth R. *o.f.m.* '76 (WDC) [M] Silver Spring, MD Gemelli House.
Himes, Michael J. '72 (BRK) Released from Diocesan Assignment.
Himes, Robert P. (YAK) Grand Coulee, WA St. Henry's Church.
Himes, Robert P. '58 (YAK) Hartline, WA St. Patrick's Church.
Himmelsbach, James R. '77 (STP) Military Chaplains.
Himsworth, Raymond J. '62 (PH) Elkins Park, PA St. James Church; [EE] Philadelphia, PA Newman Center at Drexel University.
Hinch, Msgr. Lawrence E. '59 (BRK) [176] Queens, NY Holy Child Jesus Church.
Hinde, Peter *o.carm.* '52 (JOL) [J] Darien, IL Carmelite Provincial Office.
Hindel, Richard *o.s.b.* (IND) [28] Indianapolis, IN St. Matthew Church.
Hindel, Richard *o.s.b.* '47 (IND) [J] St. Meinrad, IN St. Meinrad Archabbey.
Hindelang, Joseph C. *s.m.* '78 (DET) [D] Pontiac, MI Notre Dame Preparatory High School and Marist Academy.
Hindley, Robert J. *o.s.f.s.* '58 (FgM) Oblates of St. Francis de Sales Foreign Missions.
Hindman, John (SB) Big Bear Lake, CA St. Joseph Church.
Hinds, Edward J. '74 (PAT) Boonton, NJ Our Lady of Mount Carmel Church.
Hinds, William H. '87 (COV) Maysville, KY St. Patrick Church; [B] Maysville, KY St. Patrick High School; [T] Fort Mitchell, KY Mission Share.
Hindsley, Leonard *o.p.* (FR) [7] Fall River, MA Notre Dame de Lourdes Church.
Hines, Bede F. *t.o.r.* '47 (ALT) [A] Loretto, PA St. Francis College; [F] Loretto, PA St. Francis Friary, Third Order Regular of St. Francis of Penance.
Hines, Hugh *o.f.m.* '60 (BO) [BB] Boston, MA St. Anthony Shrine.
Hines, J. William '72 (WDC) Landover Hills, MD St. Mary's Catholic Church.
Hines, William F. '47 (SCR) Retired.
Hinfey, Donald J. *s.j.* '63 (FgM) Provinces.
Hinkle, Ignatius *o.f.m.conv.* '59 (OAK) San Pablo, CA St. Paul Church.
Hinkley, Michael F. X. '91 (HRT) Glastonbury, CT St. Paul's Church.
Hinnebusch, John Frederick *o.p.* '50 (WDC) [B] Washington, DC Dominican House of Studies.
Hinnebusch, Paul G. *o.p.* '44 (DAL) [K] Irving, TX Dominican Priory of St. Albert the Great.
Hinnen, James W. '71 (MAD) Mineral Point, WI Congregation of St. Mary-St. Paul Church.
Hinni, Thomas R. *c.m.* '63 (PBL) [11] Pueblo, CO St. Francis Xavier Church.
Hinojal, Ricardo *o.a.r.* '68 (LSC) [3] Las Cruces, NM Our Lady of Health Church.
Hinojosa, P. Nolasco, Jr. '96 (LAR) [5] Laredo, TX Holy Family Church; Encinal, TX Immaculate Heart of Mary Church.
Hinrichsen, Msgr. Carl D. '55 (NEW) Park Ridge, NJ Our Lady of Mercy Church; Retired.
Hinsvark, John '66 (FBK) Nome, AK St. Joseph Church; Teller, AK St. Ann Church.
Hinton, Frederick '70 (BUF) Kenmore, NY St. Paul Church.
Hinton, John T. '73 (NO) [15] New Orleans, LA Mater Dolorosa Church.
Hintz, David R. '86 (LIN) [9] Lincoln, NE St. Patrick's Church; [M] Lincoln, NE Calvary Cemetery and Mausoleum.
Hippee, Msgr. Michael E. '73 (MAD) [2] Madison, WI St. Bernard Church.
Hipsley, Milton A. '70 (BAL) Cumberland, MD St. Mary Church.
Hipwell, Patrick J. '77 (STP) Minnetonka, MN Immaculate Heart of Mary Church.
Hiramatsu, Joseph *s.a.* '82 (NY) [DD] Garrison, NY Franciscan Friars of the Atonement, Minister General Office.
Hire, Richard '70 (FTW) New Haven, IN St. John the Baptist Church.
Hirniak, Mark '98 (STF) Special Assignment.
Hirsch, Msgr. Clinton F. '45 (EVN) Retired.
Hirsch, Harold L. '53 (MET) Spotswood, NJ Immaculate Conception Church.
Hirsch, Joseph W. '86 (LC) Cashton, WI Sacred Heart of Jesus Church; Norwalk, WI St. Augustine of Hippo Church; Saint Mary's Ridge, WI Nativity of the Blessed Virgin Mary Church; Summit, WI St. John the Baptist Church.
Hirsch, Robert M. '47 (DUB) Retired.
Hirt, Alan *o.f.m.* '77 (CIN) [62] Cincinnati, OH St. Monica-St. George Parish Newman Center Church; [Q] Cincinnati, OH University of Cincinnati Newman Center; [V] Cincinnati, OH Concerned Catholics for Gay/Lesbian Inclusion - Within Archdiocese of Cincinnati.
Hirt, Edwin H. '39 (GBG) Retired; [G] Greensburg, PA St. Anne Home.
Hirten, Timothy '93 (BRK) [237] Queens, NY Sacred Heart of Jesus Church.
Hirtz, Daniel '73 (SPC) Salem, MO Sacred Heart Church.
Hisky, William G. '59 (BAL) Retired.
Hislop, Edward J. '73 (HEL) [2] Helena, MT St. Mary Church.
Hissey, L. Pierre '66 (PHX) [13] Phoenix, AZ St. Jerome Church.
Hissrich, John E. '86 (PIT) [47] Pittsburgh, PA Guardian Angels Church.
Hitch, David F. '68 (DAV) Special Assignment.
Hitchcock, Msgr. James R. '46 (NSH) Joelton, TN St. Lawrence's Church.
Hitchcock, Martin B. '51 (BGP) Retired.
Hitchens, Robert '94 (PHU) Shenandoah, PA St. Michael's Church.
Hitchko, Daniel D. '64 (SCR) Exeter, PA St. Cecilia Church.
Hite, Gregory R. '81 (TOL) [B] Toledo, OH Central Catholic High School.
Hite, James C. '73 (OWN) Retired.
Hite, Jordan *t.o.r.* '70 (SFS) Dante, SD Assumption B.V.M. Church; Wagner, SD St. John the Baptist Church.
Hite, Richard *m.s.a.* '70 (NOR) [F] Cromwell, CT Society of the Missionaries of the Holy Apostles.
Hite, Richard B. *m.s.a.* '70 (WH) [F] Old Fields, WV Holy Spirit Hermitage.
Hitpas, Joseph H. *o.m.i.* '65 (STP) [N] St. Paul, MN Oblate Residence; [W] St. Paul, MN Missionary Oblates of Mary Immaculate.
Hitpas, Joseph H. *o.m.i.* '65 (WDC) [M] Washington, DC Missionary Oblates of Mary Immaculate.
Hitpas, Msgr. William J. '67 (BEL) O'Fallon, IL St. Nicholas Church.
Hitt, Tobin '96 (SFE) [L] Portales, NM University Catholic Center - St. Thomas More Chapel.
Hitt, Tobin E. '96 (SFE) Portales, NM St. Helen Church.
Hitti, Michael '38 (OLL) Retired.
Hitti, Michael '38 (SAM) Retired.
Hix, John L. '54 (KC) [2] Kansas City, MO St. Aloysius Church.
Hladik, Dusan (CHI) [6] Cicero, IL Our Lady of the Mount Church.
Hladky, Sylvester '36 (PBR) Warren, OH SS. Peter and Paul's Church.
Hladni, Mirko '71 (CLV) [63] Cleveland, OH St. Paul Church.
Hlavacek, John F. '55 (LR) Retired; [H] Little Rock, AR St. John Manor.
Hlavaty, Kirby '99 (VIC) [1] Victoria, TX Our Lady of Victory Church.
Hlebs, Milan (SJ) Retired.
Hlond, Waclaw *c.m.* '55 (HRT) [18] New Haven, CT St. Stanislaus Church.
Hlopko, John J. '36 (SCR) Retired.
Hlubik, Joseph G. '93 (ALT) State College, PA Good Shepherd Church; [I] University Park, PA Penn State Catholic Community.
Hmircik, Donald A. '56 (MIL) Retired.
Hnatyshyn, Robert '64 (SJP) McKeesport, PA St. John the Baptist Church.
Ho, Antonius *c.s.j.b.* '95 (BRK) [V] Astoria, NY Congregation of St. John the Baptist of China.
Ho, Joseph Khanh '90 (BEA) Winnie, TX St. Louis Church.
Ho, Matthias '55 (ORG) Stanton, CA St. Polycarp Church; Retired.
Ho, Viet-Peter '00 (ORG) Garden Grove, CA St. Callistus Church.
Hoa Do, Bartholomew Thai *c.m.c.* '94 (DEN) Wheat Ridge, CO Queen of Vietnamese Martyrs Church.
Hoag, Michael R. *s.j.* '71 (NEW) [C] Jersey City, NJ St. Peter's Preparatory School.
Hoag, Timothy '95 (RC) Presho, SD Christ the King Church.
Hoagland, James N. '57 (WCH) Lyons, KS St. Paul Church.
Hoagland, Victor *c.p.* '59 (NEW) [N] Union City, NJ Congregation of the Passion (Passionists)-St. Michael's Residence.
Hoak, Jack W. *o.f.m.* '75 (HRT) New Milford, CT St. Francis Xavier's Church.
Hoan, Basil P. '21 (TYL) Hemphill, TX St. Pius I Church.
Hoan, Joseph Nguyen '73 (FRS) [10] Fresno, CA St. Helen Church.
Hoan, Michael '72 (ORG) Anaheim, CA St. Boniface Church.
Hoang, Binh '96 (P) [1] Portland, OR Cathedral of the Immaculate Conception.
Hoang, Doan *s.j.* '97 (SJ) [17] San Jose, CA Most Holy Trinity Church.
Hoang, Dominic Hung '90 (OKL) [2] Oklahoma City, OK St. Andrew Dung-Lac Church.
Hoang, Joseph '99 (P) Salem, OR St. Joseph Church.
Hoang, Joseph Vien *s.d.b.* '83 (NO) [D] Marrero, LA Archbishop Shaw High School.
Hoang, Joseph Viet '94 (SD) Lakeside, CA Blessed Kateri Tekakwitha Church.
Hoang, Khanh San '94 (COS) [12] Colorado Springs, CO St. Joseph's Church.
Hoang, Louis Trung (DOD) Johnson, KS St. Bernadette Church; Ulysses, KS Mary Queen of Peace Church.
Hoang, Louis Trung Dinh '95 (DOD) Satanta, KS St. Alphonsus Church.
Hoang, Phuong '89 (SEA) Auburn, WA Holy Family Church.
Hoang, Thuan Van '97 (SFR) [11] San Francisco, CA St. Cecilia Church.
Hoang Minh Thu, Anthony (SPC) [E] Carthage, MO Congregation of the Mother Co-Redemptrix, United States Assumption Province.
Hoar, Leo James '66 (SPR) [5] Northampton, MA St. Mary of the Assumption Church; [Q] Springfield, MA Newman Apostolates and Campus Ministries.
Hoar, Richard J. *s.j.* '56 (BUF) [50] Buffalo, NY St. Michael Church.
Hoar, Thomas F.X. *s.s.e.* '78 (NOR) [A] Enders Island, CT St. Edmund's Novitiate; [F] Mystic, CT Society of St. Edmund; [I] Mystic, CT St. Edmund's Retreat.
Hoare, Richard '69 (BRK) [244] Queens, NY St. Teresa of Avila Church.
Hoat, Rochus Vu Dinh '60 (BAL) [59] Baltimore, MD St. Mary of the Assumption Church.
Hoatson, Robert M. '97 (NEW) [1] Hackensack, NJ Holy Trinity Church.
Hoban, Michael *s.s.c.* '70 (FgM) St. Columban's Foreign Mission.
Hoban, Paul T. *o.carm.* '41 (NEW) Cresskill, NJ St. Therese of Lisieux Church.
Hoban, Robert L. '79 (CLV) [5] Parma, OH St. Francis de Sales Church.
Hoban, Msgr. Thomas E. '60 (ALN) Emmaus, PA St. Ann Church.
Hobbes, Thomas F. '56 (SY) Endwell, NY Christ the King Church.
Hobbs, Msgr. James V. '57 (BAL) [2] Baltimore, MD Basilica of the National Shrine of the Assumption of the Blessed Virgin Mary.
Hober, Raymond *s.v.d.* '60 (FgM) Society of the Divine Word Foreign Missions.
Hobert, James M., Jr. '85 (TUC) Pirtleville, AZ St. Bernard's Church.
Hobson, J. Mark '86 (CLV) Solon, OH Resurrection of Our Lord Church.
Hobson, Michael A. '97 (BO) [1] Framingham, MA St. Bridget Church.
Hobt, Phillip '92 (DM) [A] Council Bluffs, IA Council Bluffs Area Catholic Education Systems, Inc.; [C] Council Bluffs, IA Saint Albert Catholic Schools.
Hoch, George B. *s.j.* '44 (NY) [DD] New York, NY Jesuit Community at Fordham University.
Hochheim, William A. '60 (STA) Starke, FL St. Edward's Church.
Hochreiter, Robert S. '68 (SCR) Military Chaplains.
Hochstatter, Theodore '80 (PEO) On Duty Outside the Diocese.
Hochwalt, Richard A. *m.m.* '51 (FgM) Maryknoll Foreign Missions.
Hock, G. Harry *s.j.* '64 (RIC) [5] Richmond, VA Sacred Heart Church.
Hock, William T. '48 (CHI) Retired.
Hocking, Harold J. *s.j.* '52 (ALN) [A] Wernersville, PA Jesuit Center.
Hockman, Richard C. *c.s.c.* '80 (FR) South Easton, MA Holy Cross Church.
Hoctor, Thomas (ROC) Webster, NY Holy Trinity Church.
Hoctor, Thomas '57 (ROC) [4] Rochester, NY St. Anne Church.
Hoctor, Thomas D. '57 (ROC) Retired.
Hodapp, Timothy L. '85 (WIN) Absent on Leave.
Hodde, William G. '52 (FTW) Yoder, IN St. Aloysius Church.
Hoderny, Thomas S. '79 (E) Crown, PA St. Mary Church.
Hodes, Bertrand *o.f.m.conv.* '39 (FgM) Conventual Franciscan Foreign Missions.
Hodge, William A. '74 (CAM) [4] Atlantic City, NJ St. Nicholas of Tolentine Church.
Hodges, Leo '86 (ORL) Palm Bay, FL Our Lady of Grace Church.
Hodges, Robert S. *o.praem.* '74 (ORG) [C] Santa Ana, CA Mater Dei High School; [I] Silverado, CA Norbertine Fathers of Orange Inc.
Hodgson, Bill (SPC) Verona, MO Sacred Heart Church.
Hodgson, William M. '79 (SPC) Special Assignment.
Hodnett, John J. *c.m.* '59 (PH) [AA] Philadelphia, PA Congregation of the Mission.
Hoeberechts, Dwight *o.m.i.* '96 (BO) Tewksbury, MA St. William Church.
Hoebing, Philibert *o.f.m.* '50 (SFD) [B] Quincy, IL Quincy University.
Hoedebeck, Paul '43 (LR) [A] Subiaco, AR Subiaco Monastery.
Hoedl, Daniel J. '98 (FAR) Esmond, ND St. Boniface Church; Maddock, ND St. William Church.

Hoeffner, Robert J. '73 (ORL) Palm Bay, FL St. Joseph Church.
Hoefgen, Francis *o.s.b.* '79 (SCL) [I] Collegeville, MN St. John's Abbey, of the Order of St. Benedict.
Hoefgen, Raymond J. '63 (MAR) Nadeau, MI St. Bruno Church; Stephenson, MI Precious Blood Church.
Hoefler, Alexander *s.v.d.* '50 (SB) [A] Riverside, CA Divine Word Seminary.
Hoefler, Robert A. '85 (DM) [12] Des Moines, IA St. Theresa of the Child Jesus Church.
Hoegerl, Carl W. *c.ss.r.* '50 (BRK) [V] Brooklyn, NY Our Lady of Good Counsel Residence.
Hoehmann, George '92 (NY) Absent on Leave.
Hoelck, Frank L. '59 (GI) [2] Grand Island, NE Blessed Sacrament Church; [A] Grand Island, NE Central Catholic Schools.
Hoelle, Philip C. *s.m.* '42 (CIN) [L] Centerville, OH The Franciscan at St. Leonard; [M] Dayton, OH Marianist Provincialate.
Hoelscher, James '58 (SAT) Pleasanton, TX St. Luke-Loire Church.
Hoelsken, Mark A. *s.j.* '91 (FBK) Chefornak, AK St. Catherine Church; Newtok, AK Holy Family Church; [E] St. Marys, AK Brother Joe Prince Jesuit Community.
Hoene, Robert E. *s.j.* '53 (OM) [K] Omaha, NE Jesuit Community at Creighton University.
Hoenig, Gerald A. '52 (DAV) Montrose, IA St. Joseph's Church; Fort Madison, IA Iowa State Penitentiary.
Hoenisch, Richard '80 (SFR) Absent on Leave.
Hoeper, Robert J. *s.m.* '51 (CIN) [M] Huntsville, OH St. George Chapel of Marianist Community.
Hoeppner, Michael J. '75 (WIN) [1] Winona, MN Cathedral of the Sacred Heart.
Hoerburger, Henry R. '43 (LC) Elk Mound, WI St. Joseph Church.
Hoernig, Alphonse X. *c.m.* '56 (STL) [P] Perryville, MO Congregation of The Mission.
Hoerning, Richard P. '73 (RVC) East Northport, NY St. Anthony of Padua Church.
Hoeser, Jerome G. '63 (LC) Mosinee, WI St. Paul Church.
Hoesing, Kenneth F. '97 (LIN) Davey, NE St. Mary's Church.
Hoevel, Robert J. '42 (FTW) Retired.
Hoewischer, Harry E. *s.j.* '57 (DEN) [M] Denver, CO Xavier Jesuit Center.
Hoey, James F. '65 (WOR) Spencer, MA Mary, Queen of the Rosary Church.
Hoey, Robert F. *s.j.* '54 (BO) [W] Weston, MA Campion Health Center, Inc.
Hoff, Alphonse *o.f.m.* '44 (IND) Batesville, IN St. Louis Church.
Hoff, James E. *s.j.* '65 (CIN) [M] Cincinnati, OH Jesuit Community at Xavier University.
Hoffay, Thomas '74 (NY) Absent on Leave.
Hoffbauer, James A. '00 (CIN) Mason, OH St. Susanna Church.
Hoffenkamp, Robert A. '89 (JOL) Morris, IL Immaculate Conception of the Blessed Virgin Mary Church.
Hoffer, Charles J. '46 (COV) [5] Covington, KY Holy Cross Church; Retired.
Hoffman, Andrew '79 (SC) [B] Le Mars, IA Gehlen Catholic School.
Hoffman, David (GB) [4] Manitowoc, WI Sacred Heart Church.
Hoffman, David '75 (BAL) On Duty Outside the Archdiocese.
Hoffman, Dennis '70 (DUL) Crosslake, MN Immaculate Heart Church.
Hoffman, Dennis L. '90 (DAV) Houghton, IA St. John's Church; St. Paul, IA St. James Church.
Hoffman, Donald J. '54 (STL) Crestwood, MO St. Elizabeth of Hungary Church; Retired.
Hoffman, Edward L. '61 (PIT) Allegheny County, PA West Penn Allegheny Health System-West Penn Hospital; Allegheny County, PA Collins Nursing Center; Allegheny County, PA Heartland Health Care Center; Allegheny County, PA Shadyside Nursing and Rehabilitation Center; Allegheny County, PA Mercy Senior Care; [J] Pittsburgh, PA St. Francis Nursing Center-East.
Hoffman, Emmett G. '53 (GF) Retired.
Hoffman, Frank '71 (RNO) On Duty Outside the Diocese.
Hoffman, Frank '92 (CHI) [W] Chicago, IL Prelature of the Holy Cross and Opus Dei.
Hoffman, Gerard J. '73 (PH) [D] Philadelphia, PA Roman Catholic High School for Boys; [Y] Elverson, PA St. Mary of Providence Center.
Hoffman, James A. *o.f.m.* '67 (CHI) [N] Countryside, IL St. Gratian Friary, Franciscan Friars.
Hoffman, James A. '67 (SUP) Lake Tomahawk, WI St. John Vianney Church; Woodruff, WI Our Lady Queen of the Universe Church.
Hoffman, James R. '57 (TOL) [1] Toledo, OH Queen of the Most Holy Rosary Church.
Hoffman, John R. '75 (CHI) [196] Chicago, IL St. Teresa Church.
Hoffman, Joseph M. '79 (BRK) [154] Queens, NY St. Bartholomew's Church.
Hoffman, Matthias H. '40 (CHI) Flossmoor, IL Infant Jesus of Prague Church; Retired.
Hoffman, Michael *s.d.s.* '82 (MIL) [P] Milwaukee, WI Salvatorian Provincial Residence.
Hoffman, Patrick '68 (AMA) [2] Amarillo, TX St. Laurence Church.
Hoffman, Raniero *o.s.b.cam.* (MRY) [H] Big Sur, CA New Camaldoli Hermitage.
Hoffman, Raniero *o.s.b.cam.* '75 (MRY) [F] Big Sur, CA New Camaldoli Hermitage.
Hoffman, Richard L. '50 (EVN) Retired.
Hoffman, Robert (PEO) Retired.
Hoffman, Robert *c.s.c.* '47 (FTW) [L] Notre Dame, IN Holy Cross Mission House.
Hoffman, Msgr. Robert B. '69 (RCK) St. Charles, IL St. John Neumann Church.
Hoffman, Robert E. *m.m.* '60 (FgM) Maryknoll Foreign Missions.
Hoffman, Robert G. (PAT) Budd Lake, NJ St. Jude Church.
Hoffman, Robert G. '69 (MET) Annandale, NJ Mountainview Youth Correctional Facility.
Hoffman, Thomas '80 (CHI) [210] Chicago, IL St. William Church.
Hoffman, Thomas A. *s.j.* '56 (OM) [K] Omaha, NE Jesuit Community at Creighton University.
Hoffman, William '61 (ATL) [M] Atlanta, GA Campus Ministry.
Hoffman, William G. '61 (ATL) Dalton, GA St. Joseph's Church.
Hoffmann, Andrew W. '74 (SC) Le Mars, IA St. Joseph's Church.
Hoffmann, Charles G. '63 (GB) Antigo, WI St. John Church.
Hoffmann, Christopher A. '87 (ORL) Deltona, FL St. Clare Church; [E] De Land, FL Stetson University Catholic Campus Ministry.
Hoffmann, Edward M. '72 (DEN) [24] Denver, CO Church of the Risen Christ.
Hoffmann, Emmett G. '53 (GF) [K] Ashland, MT St. Labre Indian School Educational Association.
Hoffmann, Francis T. '90 (BGP) Shelton, CT St. Joseph Church.
Hoffmann, Frank '71 (SD) San Diego, CA Scripps Mercy Hospital; [F] San Diego, CA Scripps Mercy Hospital.
Hoffmann, Lawrence R. '71 (DM) [5] Des Moines, IA St. Anthony's Church.
Hoffmann, Philip A. '64 (GB) Special Assignment.
Hoffmann, Msgr. Ralph '37 (GRY) Retired.
Hoffmann, Robert G. '69 (PAT) Morris Plains, NJ Morris County Youth Center; Newton, NJ Sussex County Jail.
Hoffmann, William A. '80 (GB) On Duty Outside the Diocese.
Hoffmaster, Harry '70 (DET) Retired.
Hoffner, Carlos '92 (RCK) South Beloit, IL St. Peter Church.
Hofmann, Arthur '44 (SJ) Retired.
Hofmann, Charles A. *s.j.* '66 (CHI) [N] Chicago, IL Chicago Province of the Society of Jesus-Provincial Office.
Hofmann, Charles A. *s.j.* '66 (SFR) [E] San Francisco, CA St. Ignatius College Preparatory (Coed); [N] San Francisco, CA Jesuit Community at St. Ignatius College Preparatory.
Hofmann, Raymond *c.r.* '56 (L) [L] Louisville, KY Villa Pacis, Resurrectionist Retirement Home.
Hofmann, Stephen *o.s.b.* '41 (P) [L] St. Benedict, OR Mt. Angel Abbey.
Hofmann, Msgr. Thomas X. '77 (CHR) Special Assignment.
Hofschulte, Charles *c.j.* '71 (LA) [4] Santa Barbara, CA Our Lady of Guadalupe Church; [D] Santa Barbara, CA Bishop Garcia Diego High School.
Hofstede, John M. '75 (STP) [5] Minneapolis, MN Christ the King Church.
Hofstetter, Robert J. '54 (KNX) [3] Chattanooga, TN St. Jude Church; [K] Knoxville, TN Diocesan Council of Catholic Women.
Hogan, Benedict *o.carm.* '59 (VEN) Grove City, FL St. Francis of Assisi Church.
Hogan, Daniel M. '53 (STL) O'Fallon, MO St. Barnabas Church.
Hogan, Dennis J. '73 (PAT) Lincoln Park, NJ St. Joseph's Church.
Hogan, Edward P. '46 (BRK) Retired.
Hogan, Francis T. '46 (BUF) Retired.
Hogan, Francis X. *c.m.f.* '49 (LA) [Q] Rancho Dominguez, CA Dominguez Seminary Inc.
Hogan, Gary *c.r.* '86 (CHI) [72] Chicago, IL St. Hedwig Church; [N] Chicago, IL Provincial Office of the Congregation of the Resurrection.
Hogan, George '73 (VEN) [4] Sarasota, FL St. Martha Church.
Hogan, George C. '73 (BO) North Andover, MA St. Michael Church.
Hogan, James J. '61 (HEL) [1] Missoula, MT Christ the King Church; [H] Missoula, MT University of Montana.
Hogan, John (BO) [3] Lowell, MA Immaculate Conception Church.
Hogan, John *s.s.c.* '62 (ORG) Special Assignment; [H] Westminster, CA Korean Catholic Ministry; [I] Westminster, CA Columban Fathers.
Hogan, John A. '57 (GRY) Retired.
Hogan, Msgr. John F. '63 (WDC) [2] Bowie, MD Sacred Heart Church; Retired.
Hogan, John F., Jr. '88 (SY) Lacona, NY St. Frances Xavier Cabrini Church; Pulaski, NY St. John the Evangelist Church.
Hogan, John J. *o.m.i.* '65 (BO) Lowell, MA Saints Memorial Medical Center.
Hogan, John P. (LC) [L] Wisconsin Rapids, WI St. Lawrence Parish, Wisconsin Rapids Endowment Trust.
Hogan, John P. '73 (LC) Rudolph, WI St. Philip Church; [2] Wisconsin Rapids, WI St. Lawrence Church.
Hogan, John P. *o.f.m.* '75 (BO) [BB] Boston, MA St. Anthony Shrine.
Hogan, Joseph F. '88 (MET) Hillsborough, NJ Mary, Mother of God Church.
Hogan, Joseph T. '88 (PEO) Bement, IL St. Michael Church; Monticello, IL St. Philomena Church.
Hogan, LeRoy '57 (GB) Retired.
Hogan, Michael *o.s.a.* (CHI) [J] Chicago, IL Holy Cross Hospital.
Hogan, Michael '65 (ALB) [3] Schenectady, NY Sacred Heart-St. Columba Church; [8] Schenectady, NY St. John the Baptist Church; [10] Schenectady, NY St. Joseph Church; [B] Albany, NY Maria College.
Hogan, Michael C. '51 (ROC) Fairport, NY St. John of Rochester Church; Retired.
Hogan, Peter E. *s.s.j.* '46 (BAL) [S] Baltimore, MD St. Joseph Society of the Sacred Heart House of Central Administration.
Hogan, Phil D. *o.f.m.* '62 (CHI) [D] Chicago, IL Hales Franciscan High School, Inc.
Hogan, Ralph R. '52 (PRO) Retired.
Hogan, Richard '86 (DET) Absent on Leave.
Hogan, Richard M. '81 (STP) [22] St. Paul, MN St. John of St. Paul Church.
Hogan, Robert C. *s.j.* '64 (FgM) Provinces.
Hogan, Robert E. *s.m.* '83 (CIN) [M] Dayton, OH Marianist Provincialate.
Hogan, Robert E. *s.m.* '83 (SAT) [56] San Antonio, TX St. Mary Magdalen Church; [M] San Antonio, TX Casa San Juan Marianist Community; [U] San Antonio, TX Brothers of the Beloved Disciplel.
Hogan, Msgr. Robert G. '59 (DUB) Clear Lake, IA St. Patrick's Church.
Hogan, Sean M. *c.s.sp.* '69 (PIT) [B] Pittsburgh, PA Duquesne University of the Holy Ghost.
Hogan, Terence '80 (MIA) [1] Miami, FL St. Mary's Church.
Hogan, Thomas *s.m.* '46 (LA) [F] Chatsworth, CA Chaminade College Preparatory.
Hogan, Thomas J. *s.j.* '65 (STL) [P] St. Louis, MO Hallahan House.
Hogan, Timothy A. '66 (L) [16] Louisville, KY St. Boniface Church.
Hogan, Timothy D. '82 (DET) Military Chaplains.
Hogan, Timothy J. '82 (SC) [8] Sioux City, IA St. Michael Church.
Hogan, Verne F. '57 (COV) Flemingsburg, KY St. Charles Church; May's Lick, KY St. Rose of Lima Church.
Hogan, Msgr. Vincent (WCH) Retired.
Hogan, William *c.ss.r.* '48 (STL) [P] Liguori, MO Liguori Mission House/Redemptorists.
Hogan, William A. '66 (GF) [7] Billings, MT St. Thomas the Apostle Church.
Hogan, William D. *s.s.j.* '51 (LKC) Welsh, LA St. Joseph Church.
Hogan, William E. '38 (L) Retired.
Hogan, William H. *s.j.* '60 (CHI) [C] Chicago, IL Jesuit Community at Loyola University of Chicago.
Hogan, William T. *s.j.* '54 (NY) [DD] New York, NY Jesuit Community at Fordham University.
Hogarty, Paul '48 (PT) Retired.
Hoge, James *o.s.b.* '43 (SP) Lecanto, FL St. Scholastica Church; [O] St. Leo, FL St. Leo Abbey.
Hogenkamp, Leon J. *s.j.* '70 (ROC) [C] Rochester, NY McQuaid Jesuit High School.
Hohenbrink, Michael G. '74 (TOL) Findlay, OH St. Michael Church.
Hohenstein, Robert '68 (ALB) Albany, NY Albany Medical Center Hospital.
Hohenstein, Robert J. '68 (ALB) [13] Albany, NY Our Lady Help of Christians Church.
Hohenwarter, Norman C., Jr. '96 (HBG) [4] York, PA St. Rose of Lima Church.
Hohl, Alan *o.c.s.o.* (SLC) [F] Huntsville, UT Abbey of Our Lady of the Holy Trinity of the Order of Cistercians.
Hohl, Alan *o.c.s.o.* '63 (SLC) [A] Huntsville, UT Abbey of Our Lady of the Holy Trinity.
Hohlmayer, Louis R. '53 (CIN) Lebanon, OH St. Francis de Sales Church; [S] Cincinnati, OH Archdiocesan Central Council of Cincinnati.
Hohman, Andrew *o.f.m.cap.* '54 (CLV) [18] Cleveland,

OH Conversion of St. Paul Church; [O] Cleveland, OH St. Paul Friary.
Hohman, George R. *s.j.* '58 (CHL) Mars Hill, NC St. Andrew the Apostle Church; [J] Charlotte, NC Jesuit Community; [M] Hot Springs, NC Jesuit House of Prayer.
Hoi, Joseph '84 (JC) Milan, MO St. Mary Church.
Hoisington, Thomas '95 (WCH) On Duty Outside the Diocese.
Hojsik, Ambrose *o.f.m.conv.* '36 (SY) [5] Binghamton, NY SS. Cyril and Method Church.
Hokanson, Richard P. '74 (CHL) Belmont, NC Queen of the Apostles Church.
Hoke, Thomas R. '75 (HBG) [4] York, PA St. Rose of Lima Church.
Holaham, Matthew *o.f.m.* (PEO) Washburn, IL St. Elizabeth Church.
Holahan, Matthew *o.f.m.* '79 (PEO) Metamora, IL St. Mary's Church.
Holahan, Thomas J. *c.s.p.* '77 (DEN) [4] Boulder, CO St. Thomas Aquinas University Church; [P] Boulder, CO University of Colorado (Boulder).
Holberton, William B. '61 (ROC) Retired.
Holbrook, Harold '57 (FgM) Society of St. James the Apostle.
Holbrook, Harold M. '57 (BGP) On Duty Outside the Diocese.
Holbrook, John G. *s.j.* '52 (OM) [K] Omaha, NE Jesuit Community at Creighton University.
Holbrook, William M. '70 (CHI) [56] Chicago, IL St. Ferdinand Church.
Holbrook, William M. '70 (LFT) On Duty Outside the Diocese.
Holbus, Brian T. '81 (MIL) [11] Kenosha, WI St. Therese Church.
Holcomb, Joseph T. '80 (BRK) [38] Brooklyn, NY St. Finbar's Church.
Hold, William '77 (SAC) Retired and in Senior Ministry.
Holden, Edgar *o.f.m.conv.* '45 (NY) [B] Staten Island, NY St. Francis Friary.
Holden, James '62 (MOB) [6] Montgomery, AL St. Jude Church.
Holden, Paul '57 (WDC) Retired.
Holden, Robert A. '62 (TOL) Wauseon, OH St. Caspar Church.
Holder, Thomas '95 (KC) [14] Kansas City, MO Holy Cross Church.
Holderied, Kurt *o.carm.* '59 (NEW) [P] Mahwah, NJ Carmel Retreat House.
Holdren, John C. '71 (RCK) Absent on Leave.
Holguin, Jose R. '75 (LA) Burbank, CA St. Finbar Church.
Holian, John P. '63 (NEW) Summit, NJ Overlook Hospital.
Holick, Robert '69 (NY) [143] Bronx, NY St. Francis Xavier Church; Bronx, NY Bronx Municipal Hospital Center, Abraham Jacobi Hospital, Nathan B. VanEtten Hospital.
Holicky, Gregory '72 (GRY) [F] Hammond, IN St. Margaret Mercy Healthcare Centers - North Campus.
Holihan, Daniel M. '57 (CHI) [G] Chicago, IL Catholic Charities of the Archdiocese of Chicago-Archdiocesan Offices.
Holihan, John W. '49 (NY) Retired.
Holinga, Thomas P. '74 (SFD) Petersburg, IL St. Peter Church.
Holl, James E. '48 (STP) Coon Rapids, MN Church of the Epiphany; Retired.
Holl, Kermit *o.s.c.* '90 (STP) [N] Shoreview, MN Crosier Community of Shoreview.
Holladay, Jerrilyn Szelle (WCH) [H] Wichita, KS Spiritual Life Center.
Holland, Cajetan *c.s.c.* '79 (ORL) Retired; [F] Cocoa Beach, FL Holy Cross Fathers, Eastern Priests Province.
Holland, Daniel F. '65 (ROC) [57] Rochester, NY St. Theodore Church.
Holland, Edward '97 (CLV) [6] Parma, OH Holy Family Church.
Holland, Francis M. '52 (BUR) Retired.
Holland, George G. '55 (WOR) Retired.
Holland, Msgr. George T. '48 (PBL) Retired.
Holland, Msgr. Ian E. '58 (LA) Culver City, CA St. Augustine Church; Retired.
Holland, James P. '98 (PIT) Castle Shannon, PA St. Anne Church.
Holland, Jeremiah *ss.cc.* '67 (OAK) [3] Alameda, CA St. Joseph Basilica Church.
Holland, Jerome *c.ss.r.* '56 (NY) [78] New York, NY Most Holy Redeemer Church.
Holland, Msgr. John P. '48 (STL) Warson Woods, MO Ste. Genevieve Du Bois Church; Retired.
Holland, Joseph I. *s.j.* '41 (BO) [W] Weston, MA Campion Health Center, Inc.
Holland, Kilian '56 (SD) Retired.
Holland, Kirk *o.f.m.conv.* (ALB) [Q] Fonda, NY The National Shrine of Blessed Kateri Tekakwitha and Friary.
Holland, Kirk *o.f.m.conv.* '69 (ALB) Fonda, NY St. Cecilia Church.
Holland, Paul D. *s.j.* '80 (NOR) Storrs, CT St. Thomas Aquinas Church; [K] Willimantic, CT Campus Ministry.
Holland, Stanley *t.o.r.* '96 (STU) [A] Steubenville, OH Franciscan University of Steubenville; [F] Steubenville, OH Holy Spirit Friary.
Holland, Thomas D. '55 (SC) Retired.
Hollas, Eric *o.s.b.* '75 (SCL) [B] Collegeville, MN St. John's University; [I] Collegeville, MN St. John's Abbey, of the Order of St. Benedict.
Holleman, John (MOB) [7] Mobile, AL St. Ignatius Church.
Holleman, John L. (MOB) Andalusia, AL Christ the King Church; Greenville, AL St. Elizabeth Church.
Hollenbach, David *s.j.* '71 (BO) [W] Chestnut Hill, MA The Jesuit Community at Boston College.
Hollenbach, Frank A. '49 (MAR) Retired.
Holler, Martin J. '66 (STU) Athens, OH Christ the King University Church; [I] Athens, OH Christ the King University Parish - Ohio University.
Holleran, Msgr. J. Warren '52 (SFR) Special Assignment; [A] Menlo Park, CA St. Patrick Seminary.
Holleran, Leo C. *m.s.* '78 (ATL) Tyrone, GA St. Matthew's Church.
Holleran, Michael K. '79 (NY) [61] New York, NY St. Joseph Church.
Holley, Martin D. '87 (PT) [2] Pensacola, FL Little Flower Church.
Holley, Walter *o.f.m.* '51 (TUC) [5] Tucson, AZ Mission San Xavier del Bac Church.
Hollfelder, Eugene F. '68 (MAD) Ashton, WI St. Peter's Church.
Hollick, Leonard '61 (PSC) McAdoo, PA St. Michael Church.
Hollis, Mark L. '72 (CLV) Medina, OH St. Francis Xavier Church.
Holloran, Michael J. '82 (CIN) [1] Dayton, OH St. Adalbert Church; [13] Dayton, OH Holy Cross Church.
Holloway, Alvin J. *s.j.* '56 (NO) [C] New Orleans, LA Loyola University New Orleans.
Holloway, David L. '82 (KC) On Duty Outside the Diocese.
Holloway, Gerald '98 (BIR) [4] Huntsville, AL Holy Spirit Church; [A] Huntsville, AL Catholic High School.
Holloway, James P. '70 (WDC) Riverdale, MD St. Bernard Church.
Holloway, Thomas '99 (PEO) Pontiac, IL St. Mary's Church.
Holly, Dennis *glmy.* '64 (OWN) Franklin, KY St. Mary of the Woods Church; Scottsville, KY Christ the King Church.
Holly, John *o.f.m.cap.* '80 (GB) [3] Appleton, WI St. Joseph Church; [I] Appleton, WI St. Joseph Friary.
Hollywood, Patrick J. *o.m.i.* (BO) [11] Lowell, MA Notre Dame de Lourdes Church.
Hollywood, Patrick J. *o.m.i.* '60 (BO) [W] Tewksbury, MA Oblate Fathers-Office of the Provincial Treasurer.
Holm, Greg *s.x.* '87 (FgM) Xaverian Foreign Missions.
Holm, Greg *s.x.* '87 (PAT) [M] Wayne, NJ Xaverian Missionary Fathers.
Holmer, James J. '76 (TOL) Kirby, OH St. Mary Church; Upper Sandusky, OH St. Peter Church.
Holmes, Albert '93 (SCL) Wadena, MN St. Ann's Church.
Holmes, Caedmon '96 (PRO) [P] Portsmouth, RI Abbey of St. Gregory the Great.
Holmes, Del *glmy.* '63 (CIN) [M] Cincinnati, OH Headquarters of Glenmary Home Missioners.
Holmes, Dennis '72 (BAK) Absent on Leave.
Holmes, Emmett P. *s.j.* '59 (CLV) [D] Cuyahoga Falls, OH Walsh Jesuit High School.
Holmes, John '69 (STU) Absent on Leave.
Holmes, Kevin D. '84 (MAD) Dane, WI St. Michael Church; Sauk City, WI St. Aloysius Church.
Holmes, Paul A. '81 (NEW) [B] South Orange, NJ Seton Hall University.
Holmes, Raymond M. '65 (NEW) Hasbrouck Heights, NJ Corpus Christi Church.
Holmes, Msgr. Richard J. '44 (NEW) Glen Rock, NJ St. Catharine Church; Hohokus, NJ St. Luke's Church; Retired.
Holmes, Stephen '00 (ARL) Fairfax, VA St. Mary of Sorrows Church.
Holmes, Thomas '91 (ALB) Middleburgh, NY St. Catherine Church; Schoharie, NY St. Joseph Church.
Holmgren, Raymond O. '53 (RCK) East Dubuque, IL St. Mary Church.
Holohan, Patrick *c.s.sp.* '56 (BRK) [V] Long Island City, NY Holy Ghost Fathers of Ireland.
Holoman, Msgr. Thomas L. '55 (LIN) Denton, NE St. Mary's Church; Denton, NE U.S. Veterans' Hospital.
Holoubek, K. William '97 (LIN) Colon, NE St. Joseph's Church.
Holoubek, Roger '69 (MIA) [12] Fort Lauderdale, FL St. Maurice Church.
Holpp, Lawrence V. '62 (PIT) Bobtown, PA St. Ignatius of Antioch Church.
Holquin, Arthur '74 (ORG) [1] Orange, CA Cathedral of the Holy Family.
Holroyd, Patrick '74 (ARL) Reston, VA St. Thomas a Becket Church.
Holscher, Frank *c.i.c.m.* '56 (ARL) [3] Alexandria, VA Queen of Apostles Church; [J] Arlington, VA Mission-house, C.I.C.M.-Central House and Provincialate.
Holscher, Raymond T. *s.j.* '72 (FgM) Provinces.
Holt, Paul '72 (DM) Des Moines, IA United States Veterans Hospital.
Holt, Paul-Stephen '72 (WDC) On Duty Outside the Archdiocese.
Holt, William *o.p.* '76 (HRT) [14] New Haven, CT St. Mary's Priory Church.
Holtel, Melvin *o.f.m.* '60 (L) [43] Louisville, KY St. Joseph Church.
Holterhoff, Edward G. '70 (PAT) On Duty Outside the Diocese.
Holterhoff, Edward J. '70 (MRY) Morro Bay, CA St. Timothy Church.
Holterman, Herbert J. '51 (SPC) Retired.
Holtey, Gary '84 (SD) Spring Valley, CA Santa Sophia Church.
Holtgrewe, Don *o.f.m.* '63 (CIN) [22] Cincinnati, OH Corpus Christi Church.
Holthaus, Paul '70 (BAL) [93] Baltimore, MD St. Ursula Church.
Holtman, Elmer E. '64 (AUS) [22] Austin, TX St. Thomas More Church.
Holtman, W. Jeffrey *s.f.o.* '85 (SFD) Maryville, IL Mother of Perpetual Help Church.
Holtmann, Christopher F. '00 (STL) Chesterfield, MO Ascension Church.
Holtschneider, Dennis *c.m.* '89 (BRK) [V] Jamaica, NY St. Vincent's House.
Holtschneider, Dennis *c.m.* '89 (BUF) [O] Niagara University, NY Vincentian Community at Niagara University.
Holtschneider, Dennis H. *c.m.* '89 (BUF) [C] Niagara University, NY Niagara University.
Holtz, Albert T. *o.s.b.* '69 (NEW) [N] Newark, NJ Newark Abbey.
Holtz, Arthur *o.s.b.* '54 (GBG) New Derry, PA St. Martin Church.
Holtz, James A. '74 (GAY) Fife Lake, MI St. Aloysius Church; Kalkaska, MI St. Mary of the Woods Church.
Holtz, Louis J. '58 (COV) Retired.
Holtz, Raymond C. '58 (COV) [7] Covington, KY Mother of God Church.
Holtz, Vernon A. *o.s.b.* '62 (GBG) [H] Latrobe, PA Saint Vincent Archabbey.
Holtzinger, Bill '00 (P) Sutherlin, OR St. Francis Xavier Church.
Holtzinger, William '00 (P) Roseburg, OR St. Joseph Church.
Holtzman, Jerome '57 (SFS) Retired.
Holubowicz, Vincent B. '89 (MIL) Lomira, WI St. Mary Church; Theresa, WI St. Theresa Church.
Holup, James '59 (JOL) Ashkum, IL Assumption of the Blessed Virgin Mary Church.
Holup, Joseph M. '60 (MET) [H] Somerset, NJ Maria Regina Residence.
Holwell, Harry '89 (P) Grants Pass, OR St. Anne Church.
Holzhauser, J. Joseph '82 (SFS) Huron, SD Holy Trinity Church.
Holzmann, Michael F. '88 (RVC) Medford, NY St. Sylvester Church.
Homa, Joseph '56 (PSC) Retired.
Homa, Richard M. '73 (CHI) Palos Hills, IL Sacred Heart Church.
Homa, Thomas D. '57 (PH) [4] Bensalem, PA Our Lady of Fatima Church.
Homan, Daniel J. *o.s.b.* '69 (DET) [B] Oxford, MI St. Benedict Monastery.
Homan, Victor (TYL) Nacogdoches, TX Sacred Heart Church.
Homann, Frederick A. *s.j.* '62 (PH) [C] Philadelphia, PA St. Joseph's University; [AA] Philadelphia, PA Jesuit Community at St. Joseph's University.
Homar, Anthony *c.r.* '38 (DEN) [A] Denver, CO St. Andrew's Theatine Religious House.
Hombach, Leo J. *s.j.* '61 (LA) [Q] Culver City, CA Ignatius House, The Novitiate of the California Province, Society of Jesus.
Homco, Edward C. *c.pp.s.* '43 (GRY) [4] Whiting, IN St. John the Baptist Church.
Homer, Lawrence P. '59 (SCR) Unassigned or Leave of Absence.
Homes, Ronald G. '93 (LIN) Prague, NE St. John's Church.
Hometowu, Paul '85 (NY) [135] Bronx, NY St. Brendan Church.
Homets, Frank S. '92 (SCR) [4] Pittston, PA St. John the Evangelist Church; [D] Pittston, PA Seton Catholic High School.
Homick, Joseph '91 (STN) [A] Redwood Valley, CA Holy Transfiguration Monastery.
Hommel, George W. '66 (NY) West Hurley-Woodstock, NY St. John Church.

Hommrich, Thomas A. '64 (L) [23] Louisville, KY St. Elizabeth Ann Seton Church; [53] Louisville, KY St. Mary Church.
Homola, William B. '50 (SFE) Retired.
Homolak, William J. '59 (GBG) Avonmore, PA St. Ambrose Church.
Homrich, Eugene E. *c.s.c.* '55 (FgM) Holy Cross Foreign Missions.
Homsey, Sam *c.p.p.s.* (SAN) Sweetwater, TX Immaculate Heart of Mary Church.
Homsey, Sam *c.pp.s.* '36 (SAN) Sweetwater, TX Holy Family Church.
Honan, Eugene D. '67 (SPR) [5] Northampton, MA St. Mary of the Assumption Church.
Honea, Lonnie '96 (DAL) Absent on Leave.
Honeygosky, Stephen R. *o.s.b.* '75 (GBG) Marguerite, PA St. Benedict Church.
Hong, Seung Sik (STL) Ellisville, MO St. Andrew Kim Korean Catholic Community Church.
Honhart, Mark A. '80 (KC) Savannah, MO St. Rose of Lima Church.
Honma, Kenji *ss.cc.* '89 (FR) [I] Fairhaven, MA Sacred Hearts Provincial House.
Honner, Paschal D. *o.s.b.* '56 (JOL) [J] Lisle, IL St. Procopius Abbey.
Honold, Thomas G. '87 (MIA) [3] Miami Beach, FL St. Mary Magdalen Church.
Honore, Lionel P. *s.j.* '68 (WOR) [N] Worcester, MA Jesuits of Holy Cross College, Inc.
Hont, Leon *o.s.b.* '80 (E) St. Marys, PA Queen of the World Church.
Hood, Carl J. '86 (MEM) Bolivar, TN St. Mary Church; Selmer, TN St. Jude Church.
Hood, Msgr. Mervin J. '54 (SC) Retired.
Hoogterp, John P. '49 (SAG) Retired.
Hool, Fernando *o.s.b.* '98 (SFE) [I] Abiquiu, NM Monastery of Christ in the Desert.
Hoolahan, Michael J. *c.p.* '61 (CHI) [88] Chicago, IL Immaculate Conception Church; [N] Chicago, IL Passionist Community-Immaculate Conception Monastery.
Hooper, J. Leon *s.j.* '75 (WDC) [V] Washington, DC Woodstock Theological Center.
Hooper, Robert K. '70 (PAT) [7] Clifton, NJ St. Paul Church; Passaic, NJ Passiac General Hospital.
Hoorman, Albert F.H. '67 (PHX) [2] Phoenix, AZ Corpus Christi Church.
Hoormann, Harry H. *s.j.* '58 (STL) [P] St. Louis, MO Jesuit Community Corporation at St. Louis University - Jesuit Hall.
Hoover, Brett *c.s.p.* '97 (NY) [104] New York, NY St. Paul the Apostle Church.
Hoover, Conrad '89 (CHL) [4] Charlotte, NC St. Ann Church.
Hoover, Gary *o.s.b.* '83 (CLV) [D] Cleveland, OH Benedictine High School; [O] Cleveland, OH Benedictine Order of Cleveland.
Hoover, James F. '60 (SAL) Oberlin, KS Sacred Heart Church; Selden, KS Sacred Heart Church.
Hoover, John '74 (NOR) [A] Cromwell, CT Holy Apostles College and Seminary.
Hoover, John P. '76 (CHL) Special Assignment.
Hoover, Matthew N. '95 (COL) Gahanna, OH St. Matthew Church.
Hopcus, Daniel R. '64 (ORG) Los Alamitos, CA St. Hedwig Church.
Hope, Abbott J. '54 (CAM) Retired.
Hope, Donald E. '76 (SLC) [2] Ogden, UT St. James Church.
Hopefl, Gregory J. '76 (SUP) New Post, WI St. Ignatius Church; Reserve, WI St. Francis of Solanus Church; Stone Lake, WI St. Philip Church.
Hopf, George S. '49 (MIL) Retired.
Hopka, John '79 (DAL) On Duty Outside the Diocese.
Hopkins, Edward *l.c.* '91 (DAL) [D] Irving, TX The Highlands School; [K] Irving, TX Legionaries of Christ.
Hopkins, John *l.c.* '91 (ATL) [J] Atlanta, GA Legionaries of Christ; [N] Atlanta, GA Home and Family, Inc.
Hopkins, John P. '78 (WIL) Glasgow, DE St. Margaret of Scotland Church.
Hopkins, Michael *c.ss.r* '63 (PH) [136] Philadelphia, PA St. Peter the Apostle Church.
Hopkins, Peter *l.c.* (NY) [HH] Thornwood, NY Legion of Christ, Incorporated.
Hopkins, Richard J. '44 (GF) [1] Billings, MT St. Patrick's Co-Church; Retired.
Hopkins, Robert F. '48 (BAL) Retired.
Hopkins, William J. '90 (FWT) Graford, TX St. Francis of Assisi Church; Mineral Wells, TX Our Lady of Lourdes Church.
Hopmeir, Ronald J. '91 (STL) De Soto, MO St. Rose of Lima Church.
Hopp, Raymond '65 (BAK) Lakeview, OR St. Patrick's Church.
Hopp, Thomas R. '66 (CIN) [25] Dayton, OH Queen of Martyrs Church.
Hoppe, Arthur '47 (SCL) Retired.
Hoppe, Leslie J. *o.f.m.* '71 (CHI) [B] Chicago, IL The Catholic Theological Union at Chicago; [N] Chicago, IL Holy Name Friary.
Hoppe, Msgr. Ronald C. '58 (ALX) [3] Alexandria, LA St. Frances Xavier Cabrini Church; Glenmora, LA St. Louis Church.
Hoppe, Sean *o.s.b.* '82 (IND) Leopold, IN St. Augustine Church; St. Mark, IN St. Mark Church; [J] St. Meinrad, IN St. Meinrad Archabbey.
Hoppe, Sylvester J. '46 (KC) Retired.
Hoppe, William M. '78 (BRK) [245] Queens, NY St. Thomas Apostle Church.
Hoppenjans, Terence E. '55 (LEX) Paintsville, KY St. Michael Catholic Church.
Hopping, John-Paul '85 (ORG) Costa Mesa, CA St. John the Baptist Church.
Hoppough, Gregory J. *c.s.s.* '74 (BO) [W] Waltham, MA Stigmatine Fathers & Brothers Provincial House.
Hopwood, Msgr. Frederick J. '51 (CHR) Retired.
Hopwood, Robert *c.ss.r.* '52 (FgM) Redemptorist Foreign Missions.
Hora, Robert J. '83 (BUF) [31] Buffalo, NY Holy Name of Jesus Church.
Horacek, Mark (GAL) [54] Houston, TX Notre Dame Church.
Horacek, Mark '43 (ALX) Retired.
Horack, Francis *c.p.* '42 (FgM) Mission Procurators.
Horak, Msgr. Donald E. '63 (STU) Athens, OH Christ the King University Church; Athens, OH St. Paul's Church; Retired; [I] Athens, OH Christ the King University Parish - Ohio University.
Horak, Mark F. *s.j.* '94 (BAL) [S] Baltimore, MD Ferdinand Wheeler Jesuit Community.
Horan, Brendan R. *s.j.* '93 (R) [1] Durham, NC Holy Cross Church; [E] Raleigh, NC Jesuit Community; [H] Durham, NC North Carolina Central University.
Horan, Denis F. '48 (MAN) Retired.
Horan, Edward *s.o.l.t.* '87 (CC) [H] Robstown, TX Society of Our Lady of the Most Holy Trinity.
Horan, George '72 (LA) [38] Los Angeles, CA Sacred Heart Church; Los Angeles, CA Los Angeles County Jails in the City of Los Angeles, Adult Facilities.
Horan, Gerald M. *o.s.m.* '82 (CHI) [N] Chicago, IL Order of Friar Servants of Mary (Servites) United States of America Province, Inc.; [N] Chicago, IL Order of Friar Servants of Mary (Servites) United States of America Province, Inc.; [N] Chicago, IL Order of Friar Servants of Mary (Servites) United States of America Province, Inc.
Horan, Gerald M. *o.s.m.* '82 (ORG) [D] Anaheim, CA Servite High School; Servite High School Development Fund; [I] Anaheim, CA Servite Fathers and Brothers; [I] Buena Park, CA Order of Friar Servants of Mary (Servites); [I] Buena Park, CA Order of Friar Servants of Mary (Servites).
Horan, James *s.d.b.* '81 (PAT) [D] Paterson, NJ Don Bosco Technical High School.
Horan, John '46 (SEA) Mercer Island, WA St. Monica Church; Retired.
Horan, John C. '51 (MAN) Hudson, NH St. John the Evangelist Church.
Horan, Michael '80 (SAT) [57] San Antonio, TX St. Matthew's Church; Special Assignment.
Horan, Paul *o.carm.* '97 (WDC) [B] Washington, DC Whitefriars Hall.
Horan, Raymond F. '68 (ATL) [5] Atlanta, GA Most Blessed Sacrament Church.
Horan, Terence J. '68 (SFR) [3] San Mateo, CA St. Matthew Church.
Horan, Thomas A. '62 (ALN) Retired.
Horan, Timothy E. '79 (ROC) [3] Rochester, NY St. Andrew Church; [53] Rochester, NY St. Philip Neri Church.
Horanzy, Joseph M. '59 (SCR) [19] Wilkes-Barre, PA St. Stanislaus Kostka Church.
Horath, George B. '63 (MAD) Fennimore, WI St. Mary Church; Mount Hope, WI St. Lawrence O'Toole Church.
Horath, James R. '73 (SUP) Merrill, WI St. Francis Xavier Church.
Horath, William G. '75 (SUP) Sugar Camp, WI St. Kunegunda Church; Three Lakes, WI St. Theresa Church.
Horejsi, Jeffrey P. '91 (NU) Madison, MN St. Michael Church.
Horgan, D. Brian '98 (PMB) [4] Delray Beach, FL St. Vincent Ferrer Church.
Horgan, John A. '36 (HRT) Retired.
Horgan, John E. '72 (WOR) Millbury, MA St. Brigid Church.
Horgan, Joseph E. '53 (PRO) Retired.
Horgan, Joseph J. *m.s.* '44 (HRT) [M] Hartford, CT Missionaries of LaSalette, Provincial Secretary.
Horgan, Paul J. *s.j.* '68 (FgM) Provinces.
Horgan, Paul L. *s.j.* '68 (CI) [B] Pohnpei, FM PATS (Pohnpei Agriculture and Trade School).
Horgan, Timothy J. '55 (NEW) Retired.
Horgan-Kung, Msgr. John V. '40 (BGP) Retired; [P] Stamford, CT The Catherine Dennis Keefe Queen of the Clergy Retired Priests' Residence.
Horgas, Robert '91 (E) Ridgway, PA St. Leo the Great Church.
Horkan, Msgr. Vincent J. (DET) [4] Dearborn, MI St. Clement Church.
Horkan, Msgr. Vincent J. '41 (DET) Retired; [L] Livonia, MI Provincial House and Novitiate of the Sisters of St. Felix.
Horley, Ray J. '58 (CLV) [49] Cleveland, OH St. Mel Church.
Horn, Augustine S. *o.s.b.* '45 (OKL) [I] Shawnee, OK St. Gregory's Abbey.
Horn, Francis J. *o.s.a.* '75 (WDC) [B] Washington, DC Augustinian College, Order of St. Augustine.
Horn, John P. *s.j.* '85 (OM) [K] Omaha, NE Jesuit Community at Creighton University.
Horn, Joseph K. *o.praem.* '81 (ORG) [I] Silverado, CA Norbertine Fathers of Orange Inc.
Horn, Joseph R. '97 (DET) Royal Oak, MI Shrine of the Little Flower Church.
Horn, Stephen R. '73 (GAL) [45] Houston, TX St. Luke the Evangelist Church.
Hornacek, Joseph F. '66 (MIL) Special Assignment.
Hornat, Stephen W. *s.s.e.* '76 (BUR) [4] Burlington, VT St. Joseph's Church.
Horner, Arnold *c.p.* '34 (BRK) [V] Jamaica, NY Immaculate Conception Monastery.
Horner, Timothy *o.s.b.* '53 (STL) [P] St. Louis, MO The Abbey of St. Mary and St. Louis.
Hornick, J. Michael '69 (ANC) [G] Anchorage, AK Holy Spirit Center.
Hornstein, Eugene *o.s.b.* '46 (BIS) [A] Richardton, ND Assumption Abbey.
Horoshko, Michael '37 (PHU) Retired.
Horrigan, Msgr. Alfred F. '40 (L) Retired.
Horrigan, Kevin D. '53 (STL) [R] Ladue, MO Carmel of St. Joseph.
Horrigan, Kevin P. '70 (BO) Emergency Response Group.
Horrigan, Leo R. '59 (DEN) [18] Denver, CO Notre Dame Church.
Horrigan, Sean P. '98 (GAL) [50] Houston, TX St. Michael Church.
Horst, Bernard L. *s.m.* '45 (CIN) [M] Dayton, OH Marianist Provincialate.
Horst, Kenneth M. '95 (NY) [6] Poughkeepsie, NY St. Martin de Porres Church.
Hortiguela, Fernando *o.f.m.* '75 (SJN) [3] Carolina, PR Santa Clara de Asis Church.
Horton, John C. '66 (PEO) Mahomet, IL Our Lady of the Lake Church.
Horton, W. Peter '79 (PIT) [B] Pittsburgh, PA La Roche College; [R] Pittsburgh, PA Office for Campus Ministry.
Horvat, Francis '58 (KCK) [10] Kansas City, KS St. John the Baptist Church.
Horvat, Matt J. '65 (KCK) [8] Kansas City, KS St. Mary-St. Anthony Church.
Horvath, Andrew B. '42 (GBG) Retired; [G] Greensburg, PA St. Anne Home.
Horvath, Bert '70 (AMA) [7] Amarillo, TX St. Hyacinth's Church; Vega, TX Immaculate Conception Church; [I] Amarillo, TX St. Francis Convent, Novitiate and U.S. Provincial House.
Horvath, Gerlac A. *o.praem.* '46 (ORG) [I] Silverado, CA Norbertine Fathers of Orange Inc.
Horvath, Pius L. *o.s.b.* '53 (SFR) [N] Portola Valley, CA Woodside Priory.
Horvath, Stephen '50 (Y) Retired.
Horvath, Stephen G. '40 (TR) Retired.
Horzen, Bernard A. *o.s.b.* '53 (PEO) [A] Peru, IL St. Bede Abbey and Academy.
Hosak, Peter J. '83 (PSC) Allentown, PA St. Michael Church.
Hose, Samuel '91 (AUS) Round Rock, TX St. John Vianney Church.
Hosey, Keith P. '56 (LFT) [G] Hartford City, IN John XXIII Center.
Hosie, James J. *s.j.* '65 (BO) [E] Boston, MA Boston College High School & Jesuit Community.
Hosie, Stanley W. *s.m.* '46 (WDC) [M] Washington, DC Marist Center.
Hosinski, Thomas *c.s.c.* '73 (P) [B] Portland, OR University of Portland; [L] Portland, OR Holy Cross Fathers & Brothers, C.S.C. - University of Portland.
Hosko, George H. *c.s.b.* '68 (GAL) [Q] Houston, TX Residence of the Basilian Fathers of the University of St. Thomas.
Hospodar, Robert J. *j.c.l.* '78 (PSC) New York, NY St. Mary's Church.
Hossan, Msgr. John B. '53 (BGP) Redding, CT St. Patrick Church.
Host, Dick '74 (GR) [16] Grand Rapids, MI St. Mary's Church.
Hostetter, Larry '87 (OWN) Non-Parochial Assignments; [A] Owensboro, KY Brescia University.
Hostettler, Paul A. '50 (KNX) Copperhill, TN St. Catherine Laboure Church; Retired.
Hostia de la Purisima, Anibal Jesus *s.e.m.v.* '91 (ARE) Hatillo, PR Our Lady of Guadalupe Church.
Hosty, Thomas J. '35 (CHI) Retired.
Hotard, Msgr. Howard H. '55 (NO) [1] Slidell, LA Our Lady of Lourdes Church.
Hotchkin, John F. '60 (CHI) On Duty Outside the Archdiocese.
Hotchkiss, Msgr. Eugene '48 (GB) Retired.

Hotovy, Dennis W. '57 (LIN) Wymore, NE St. Mary's Church.
Hottinger, Paul '75 (JOL) Downers Grove, IL St. Joseph Church.
Hottinger, Theodore *s.j.* '63 (WIN) [1] Mankato, MN SS. Peter and Paul's Church.
Hottle, Maximilian *o.f.m.* '61 (TUC) Topawa, AZ San Solano Missions - Tohono O'odham Indian Reservation Church.
Hottovy, Jamie S. '99 (LIN) [1] Lincoln, NE Cathedral of the Risen Christ.
Hotz, Ernest *c.p.* '45 (BRK) [V] Jamaica, NY Immaculate Conception Monastery.
Hotz, Robert V. *s.j.* '86 (OM) [C] Omaha, NE Creighton Preparatory School.
Hotze, Clement *s.v.d.* '47 (FgM) Society of the Divine Word Foreign Missions.
Hotze, John V. '93 (WCH) [13] Wichita, KS St. Francis of Assisi Church.
Hotze, Leo *s.v.d.* '43 (CHI) [B] Techny, IL Divine Word Residence.
Houck, Gregory *o.carm.* '92 (GAL) [Q] Houston, TX Carmelite Priory.
Houck, Peter '46 (ANC) Retired.
Houck, Richard '65 (SD) Retired.
Houde, Arthur O. '48 (MAN) Retired.
Houde, Daniel *o.ss.t.* '87 (NY) [218] Staten Island, NY Our Lady of Mt. Carmel-St. Benedicta Church.
Houde, Paul C. '96 (BUR) Montpelier, VT St. Augustine Church.
Houdek, Francis J. *s.j.* '65 (DET) [K] Detroit, MI Jesuit Provincial Office-Detroit Province of the Society of Jesus.
Houdek, Francis J. *s.j.* '65 (OAK) Lafayette, CA St. Perpetua Church; [A] Oakland, CA Graduate School of Theology, School of Applied Theology.
Hough, Marianus (CC) [H] Laredo, TX St. John's Priory, (F.J.).
Hough, Marianus (LAR) [E] Laredo, TX St. John Priory, F.J.
Hough, Roger W. '64 (SAL) Osborne, KS St. Aloysius Church.
Houghton, Msgr. Francis J. '51 (NEW) Retired.
Houghton, Timothy '91 (RVC) Absent on Leave.
Houlahan, Richard A. *o.m.i.* '58 (SAT) [K] San Antonio, TX Oblate Madonna Residence; [T] San Antonio, TX Oblate Lourdes Grotto Shrine of the Southwest, Tepeyac de San Antonio; [U] San Antonio, TX Oblate Missions.
Houle, Andre L. *o.m.i.* '52 (PRT) Howland, ME St. Leo Church.
Houle, Carroll B. *m.m.* '62 (FgM) Maryknoll Foreign Missions.
Houle, Carroll B. *m.m.* '62 (NY) [DD] Maryknoll, NY Maryknoll Fathers and Brothers.
Houle, Michael R. '79 (STA) [A] Jacksonville, FL Bishop Kenny High School.
Houle, Norman H. *s.j.* '76 (BO) [W] Boston, MA Loyola House.
Houle, Roger A. '77 (PRO) [2] Woonsocket, RI All Saints Catholic Community Church.
Houle, Thomas *o.f.m.cap.* '78 (NY) [57] New York, NY St. John the Baptist Church; City, NY Correctional Institution for Men; City, NY James A. Thomas Center.
Houle, Wilfred Andre '74 (BUR) Rutland, VT St. Peter Church.
Houlihan, John J. '64 (GF) [1] Billings, MT St. Patrick's Co-Church.
Houlihan, Michael K. '79 (LIN) Hastings, NE St. Michael's Church.
Houlihan, Ralph D. *s.j.* '65 (STL) [F] St. Louis, MO St. Louis University High School, George H. Backer Memorial; [P] St. Louis, MO St. Louis University High School Jesuit Community.
Houlihan, Robert F. *s.j.* '57 (STL) [O] St. Louis, MO Fusz Pavilion.
Houndjame, Felician (DET) [10] Detroit, MI Assumption Grotto Church.
Houran, J. William '52 (MIA) [G] Fort Lauderdale, FL Holy Cross Hospital.
Houran, J. William '52 (SFD) Retired.
Hourigan, Michael '66 (MIA) Sunrise, FL St. Bernard Church.
Hourihan, Msgr. John P. '49 (NEW) Retired.
Hourihan, Raymond B. '87 (CHL) Retired.
Hourihane, Francis '51 (RVC) Retired.
House, Richard M. '92 (YAK) Military Chaplains.
House, Richard Mel '92 (YAK) Ephrata, WA St. Rose of Lima Church.
Householder, Paul C. '73 (PIT) [3] McKees Rocks, PA St. John of God Church.
Houseknecht, Eric '95 (CHL) Shelby, NC St. Mary's Church.
Houser, Samuel E. '76 (HBG) [5] Steelton, PA Prince of Peace Church.
Housey, Walter *c.m.* '56 (LA) [W] Santa Barbara, CA St. Mary's Seminary Center.
Housey, Walter L. '89 (LA) [Q] Montebello, CA Vincentian Fathers & Brothers.
Houston, James A. '68 (WOR) Northboro, MA St. Rose of Lima Church.
Houston, Joseph F. '64 (SCR) [4] Plymouth, PA St. Vincent de Paul Church.
Houston, Michael *c.ss.r.* '98 (STV) [2] Christiansted, VI Church of the Holy Cross; [B] St. Thomas, VI Miscellaneous Organizations; [B] St. Thomas, VI Miscellaneous Organizations.
Hove, Brian Van *s.j.* '82 (COL) [A] Columbus, OH Pontifical College Josephinum.
Hovley, Vincent E. *s.j.* '69 (COS) [F] Sedalia, CO Sacred Heart Jesuit Community; [H] Sedalia, CO Sacred Heart Jesuit Retreat House.
Howaniec, Henry *o.f.m.* '56 (FgM) Franciscan Foreign Missions.
Howaniec, Henry *o.f.m.* '56 (GB) [I] Pulaski, WI Assumption of B.V.M. Friary.
Howard, Anthony '37 (L) Retired.
Howard, Anthony *o.f.m.conv.* '84 (SB) [3] Riverside, CA Queen of Angels Church.
Howard, C. Donald *s.a.* '72 (ARL) Sterling, VA Christ the Redeemer Church.
Howard, Clarence J. '61 (L) New Haven, KY St. Catherine Church; New Hope, KY St. Vincent de Paul Church.
Howard, Dennis '90 (LAN) [K] Flushing, MI Mt. Zion Pastoral Center.
Howard, Donald *c.s.p.* (BO) [4] Malden, MA St. Peter Church.
Howard, Donald E. *c.s.p.* '58 (NY) [DD] Jamaica Estates, NY Paulist Fathers Generalate.
Howard, Edward F. *s.j.* '66 (BO) [W] Boston, MA The Society of Jesus of New England-Provincial Offices.
Howard, Edward F. *s.j.* '66 (SPR) [14] Springfield, MA St. Catherine of Siena Church.
Howard, Evan *o.f.m.* '55 (PHX) [19] Phoenix, AZ St. Mary's Basilica Church.
Howard, Msgr. James J. '52 (PH) Retired.
Howard, John *c.j.m.* '67 (SD) Solana Beach, CA St. James Church.
Howard, John W. *s.j.* '68 (BO) [W] Chestnut Hill, MA The Jesuit Community at Boston College.
Howard, Joseph '89 (ARL) Dale City, VA Holy Family Church.
Howard, Joseph, Jr. '89 (SHP) On Duty Outside the Diocese.
Howard, Kenneth *s.s.j.* '87 (GAL) [31] Houston, TX St. Francis Xavier Church.
Howard, Msgr. Robert E. '62 (LA) [97] Los Angeles, CA Transfiguration Church.
Howard, Theodore J. '65 (RVC) Shoreham, NY St. Mark Church.
Howard, Timothy J. *s.j.* '63 (MIL) [P] Milwaukee, WI Jesuit Provincial Office, Wisconsin Province.
Howard, Timothy J. *s.j.* '63 (TUC) [26] Tucson, AZ St. Thomas the Apostle Church.
Howard, Msgr. Vincent '47 (LAN) Retired.
Howarth, Joseph A. '90 (PRO) [7] Providence, RI St. Augustine Church.
Howarth, Joseph E. '80 (PH) [3] Bensalem, PA Saint Ephrem Church.
Howarth, Theodore J. *o.s.b.* '49 (NEW) [N] Newark, NJ Newark Abbey.
Howe, Christopher *o.s.a.* '86 (CHI) [N] Chicago, IL St. Rita Monastery.
Howe, J. Norbert '56 (TOL) [4] Lima, OH St. Rose Church.
Howe, Robert J. '94 (SAG) Shepherd, MI St. Vincent De Paul Church.
Howe, Timothy A. *s.j.* '98 (CHI) [174] Chicago, IL St. Procopius Church; [N] Chicago, IL Miguel Pro Jesuit Community.
Howell, Charles W. '98 (LEX) [1] Lexington, KY Cathedral of Christ the King.
Howell, David '78 (LAN) Brighton, MI St. Mary Magdalen Church.
Howell, David W. '65 (BGP) [2] Norwalk, CT St. Joseph Church.
Howell, F. Scott *s.j.* '77 (BAL) [S] Baltimore, MD Jesuit Fathers and Brothers Maryland Provincial Curia.
Howell, F. Scott *s.j.* '77 (FgM) Provinces.
Howell, Joseph W. '53 (TLS) [E] Tulsa, OK Saint Francis Hospital, Inc.
Howell, Msgr. Michael '74 (CC) [1] Corpus Christi, TX Corpus Christi Church.
Howell, Michael J. '69 (KAL) [G] Nazareth, MI Motherhouse and Novitiate of the Sisters of St. Joseph.
Howell, Patrick J. *s.j.* '72 (SEA) [A] Seattle, WA Seattle University.
Howell, Stephen H. '74 (SFR) Belmont, CA Immaculate Heart of Mary Church; Special Assignment; [D] San Mateo, CA Junipero Serra High School (Boys).
Hower, William J. '64 (MAD) Edgerton, WI St. Joseph Church.
Howley, Vincent '97 (NY) Carmel, NY St. James the Apostle Church.
Howlin, Carroll '61 (JOL) On Duty Outside the Diocese.
Howlin, Carroll '61 (LEX) Whitley City, KY Good Shepherd Chapel Church.
Howren, John T. '96 (ATL) Covington, GA St. Augustine Church.
Howze, Joseph Lawson '59 (BLX) [H] Biloxi, MS Gabriel Manor II, Inc.
Hoy, Daniel J. '48 (PH) Strafford, PA Our Lady of the Assumption Church; Retired.
Hoye, Msgr. Daniel F. '72 (FR) [1] Attleboro, MA St. John the Evangelist Church.
Hoye, Ronald J. *c.m.* '91 (KC) [J] Kansas City, MO Vincentian Parish Mission Center.
Hoyek, Elias (SAM) Retired.
Hoyer, Michael '80 (MIA) [3] Fort Lauderdale, FL Our Lady Queen of Martyrs Church.
Hoying, David A. *c.pp.s.* '83 (CIN) Carthagena, OH St. Aloysius Church; Cranberry Prairie, OH St. Francis Church.
Hoying, John J. *c.pp.s.* '62 (LFT) Winamac, IN St. Peter Church.
Hoying, Leo A. '56 (CIN) Frenchtown, OH Holy Family Church; Versailles, OH St. Denis Church.
Hoying, Vincent *c.pp.s.* '58 (TOL) Lima, OH St. Rita Hospital and Medical Center; [H] Lima, OH St. Rita's Medical Center.
Hoynes, Richard '88 (LA) Compton, CA St. Albert the Great Church.
Hoyng, William *c.pp.s.* '61 (CIN) Minster, OH St. Augustine Church.
Hoyos, Jose E. '84 (ARL) Falls Church, VA St. Anthony's Church.
Hoyt, Stephen *o.f.m.cap* (CHL) [3] Charlotte, NC Our Lady of Consolation Church.
Hoza, Rudolph *s.s.c.* '42 (PRO) [P] Bristol, RI St. Columban's Retirement House.
Hrdlicka, Lambert A. '50 (STL) Retired.
Hrebic, Alban *o.s.b.* '52 (FgM) American - Cassinese Congregation Foreign Missions.
Hrebic, Alban *o.s.b.* '52 (JOL) [J] Lisle, IL St. Procopius Abbey.
Hreha, James D. '87 (WIL) Rehoboth, DE St. Edmond Church.
Hren, Joseph I. *o.p.* '47 (CHI) [D] Oak Park, IL Fenwick High School; [N] River Forest, IL St. Thomas Aquinas Priory.
Hrezo, Paul '00 (STU) Marietta, OH St. Mary's Church.
Hribsek, Aloysius '49 (VEN) Holmes Beach, FL St. Bernard's Church.
Hribsek, Aloysius J. '49 (BGP) Retired.
Hricko, Michael A. *s.j.* '73 (SCR) [C] Scranton, PA University of Scranton; [E] Scranton, PA Scranton Preparatory School.
Hrisko, Zachary *o.s.b.* '57 (JOL) [J] Lisle, IL St. Procopius Abbey.
Hritsko, William Anthony '98 (COL) Newark, OH St. Francis de Sales Church.
Hritz, Paul '53 (CLV) [A] Wickliffe, OH St. Mary Seminary and Graduate School of Theology.
Hritz, Paul J. '53 (CLV) [44] Cleveland, OH Community of St. Malachi Church; [45] Cleveland, OH St. Malachi Church; Retired.
Hritzko, John '89 (STN) Munster, IN St. Josaphat Church.
Hrubiak, Dennis M. '70 (PRM) Parma, OH Holy Spirit Church.
Hruby, Paul '82 (LA) Glendale, CA Church of the Incarnation.
Hruska, Eugene P. '58 (GF) Fort Shaw, MT St. Ann Church; Retired.
Hruska, Timothy W. '96 (MAR) Engadine, MI Our Lady of Lourdes Church.
Hrynkiw, Wasyl '91 (STF) Lackawanna, NY Our Lady of Perpetual Help Church.
Hrynuck, Stephen '38 (PHU) Olyphant, PA SS. Cyril and Methodius Church.
Hryoziuszko, Michael '95 (DET) Macomb, MI St. Isidore Church.
Hsu, Peter '57 (BEL) Retired.
Hu, Paul '94 (CC) [J] Corpus Christi, TX Our Lady of Corpus Christi Catholic Undergraduate Liberal Arts.
Huan, Joseph Van Tran '73 (RIC) Military Chaplains.
Huar, Ralph F. '81 (STP) Rush City, MN Sacred Heart Church.
Huard, Jeffrey '94 (STP) [C] St. Paul, MN University of St. Thomas.
Huard, Leo *o.carm.* '65 (JOL) [J] Darien, IL Carmelite Provincial Office.
Hubba, David C. '74 (NEW) Nutley, NJ St. Mary's Church.
Hubbard, J. Randall '90 (L) [67] Louisville, KY St. Raphael the Archangel Church.
Hubbard, Lawrence E. '68 (STP) [33] Minneapolis, MN St. Stephen Church; Special Assignment; [W] Minneapolis, MN Sagrado Corazon de Jesus.
Hubbert, Joseph G. *c.m.* '77 (BUF) [C] Niagara University, NY Niagara University; [O] Niagara University, NY Vincentian Community at Niagara University.
Hubble, Karl D. '39 (DET) Retired.
Hubbs, Timothy L. '84 (CAM) Hammonton, NJ St. Martin de Porres Church.
Huber, Clarence '69 (LUB) Retired.
Huber, Msgr. Daniel R. '50 (PBL) Montrose, CO St. Mary Church.
Huber, David W. '86 (RCK) [1] Elgin, IL St. Joseph Church.
Huber, George L. '48 (MIL) Retired.

Huber, J. William '59 (PBL) [16] Pueblo, CO St. Pius X Church.
Huber, John *c.s.b.* '92 (OAK) [C] Oakland, CA Bishop O'Dowd High School.
Huber, Kevin R. '91 (GRY) Highland, IN Our Lady of Grace Church.
Huber, Larry T., Jr. '95 (STL) House Springs, MO Our Lady, Queen of Peace Church.
Huber, Leo R. '67 (STP) Retired; [C] St. Paul, MN University of St. Thomas.
Huber, Mark D. '94 (LIN) [1] Lincoln, NE Cathedral of the Risen Christ.
Huber, Matthew '87 (HEL) [2] Missoula, MT Holy Family Church.
Huber, Paul A. *s.j.* '45 (CIN) [26] Cincinnati, OH St. Francis Xavier Church; [V] Cincinnati, OH Apostleship of Prayer.
Huber, Richard *m.s.c.* '59 (OG) [F] Watertown, NY Missionaries of the Sacred Heart.
Huber, Robert L. '56 (L) [9] Louisville, KY St. Athanasius Church; Retired.
Huber, Vincent J. '64 (STU) Toronto, OH St. Francis of Assisi Church; Toronto, OH St. Joseph's Church.
Huber, Walter *s.m.b.* '46 (DEN) [18] Denver, CO Notre Dame Church.
Hubert, Raymond '58 (PMB) [1] Delray Beach, FL Emmanuel Church.
Hubert, Raymond P. '58 (PMB) Retired.
Hubertus, Msgr. Albert '50 (SAT) Retired; [K] San Antonio, TX Casa De Padres.
Hubertus, Msgr. Gerald '64 (SAT) Seguin, TX St. James Church.
Huberty, Mark A. '96 (STP) [21] Minneapolis, MN St. Charles Borromeo Church.
Huberty, Ronald U. '90 (NU) Clara City, MN St. Clara Church.
Huberty, Ronald V. '90 (NU) Benson, MN St. Francis Church; Clontarf, MN St. Malachy Church; Danvers, MN Church of the Visitation; De Graff, MN St. Bridget Church; Murdock, MN Church of the Sacred Heart.
Hubler, Tony '92 (IND) Navilleton, IN St. Mary Church.
Hubmann, William H. '79 (IND) [F] Indianapolis, IN St. Vincent Hospital and Health Care Center, Inc.
Huck, Joseph '69 (MIA) North Lauderdale, FL Our Lady Queen of Heaven Church.
Hudak, Cyril '53 (MIA) Retired.
Hudak, Msgr. Francis J. '55 (HBG) New Oxford, PA Immaculate Conception of the Blessed Virgin Mary Church.
Hudak, Mark *o.f.m.* '93 (CIN) [E] Cincinnati, OH Roger Bacon High School.
Hudak, Ralph '77 (CLV) [35] Cleveland, OH Immaculate Heart of Mary Church.
Hudak, Richard E. '68 (CLV) South Euclid, OH St. Margaret Mary Church.
Hudak, Thomas R. '73 (SCR) Lake Silkworth, PA Our Lady of Mount Carmel Church.
Hudanish, Jeffrey A. '93 (BGP) Leave of Absence.
Hudelpohl, Al *o.f.m.* '56 (IND) St. Peter, IN St. Peter Church.
Hudepohl, Howard *o.f.m.* '54 (CIN) [M] Cincinnati, OH St. Clement Friary.
Hudert, John P. *m.m.* '62 (NY) [DD] Maryknoll, NY Maryknoll Fathers and Brothers; [DD] Maryknoll, NY Maryknoll Fathers and Brothers.
Hudgin, Christopher J. *o.s.f.s.* (ALN) [B] Center Valley, PA Desales University.
Hudgin, Christopher J. *o.s.f.s.* '81 (ALN) [K] Center Valley, PA Oblates of St. Francis de Sales.
Hudgins, James C. '98 (ARL) [3] Alexandria, VA Queen of Apostles Church.
Hudock, Barry M. '96 (E) Wilcox, PA St. Anne Church.
Hudock, Paul '98 (WH) [1] Charleston, WV Sacred Heart Co-Church.
Hudson, Frank '74 (CAM) Deptford, NJ St. John Vianney Church.
Hudson, Frank X. '74 (CAM) [Q] Blackwood, NJ Family Treatment of Addiction Center.
Hudson, Gerald F. *s.j.* '81 (SFR) [E] San Francisco, CA St. Ignatius College Preparatory (Coed); [N] San Francisco, CA Jesuit Community at St. Ignatius College Preparatory.
Hudson, Richard '96 (AUS) Belton, TX Christ the King Church.
Hudziak, Jerome M. '64 (MIL) [3] Wauwatosa, WI St. Joseph Congregation Church.
Huebner, Donald C. '54 (CIN) [1] Springfield, OH St. Bernard Church.
Huebner, Msgr. Ralph J. (WDC) Pastoral Center Special Ministries.
Huebner, Terrance J. '74 (MIL) [2] Cudahy, WI Nativity of the Lord Church.
Huebsch, Joseph R. '50 (FAR) Retired.
Huegelmeyer, Charles T. *m.m.* '51 (NY) [DD] Maryknoll, NY Maryknoll Fathers and Brothers.
Huehlefeld, Matthew '96 (VIC) Yoakum, TX St. Joseph Church.
Hueller, Francis *s.a.c.* '48 (MIL) [P] Milwaukee, WI St. Vincent Community.
Huels, John M. *o.s.m.* '76 (CHI) [N] Chicago, IL Order of Friar Servants of Mary (Servites) United States of America Province, Inc.
Huelsing, Justin *o.m.i.* '54 (SPC) Mountain Grove, MO Sacred Heart Church.
Huelsman, Richard J. *s.j.* '54 (DET) [P] Clarkston, MI Colombiere Center.
Huerga, Alvaro *o.p.* '50 (PCE) [B] Ponce, PR The Pontifical Catholic University of Puerto Rico.
Huerta, Enrique *s.v.d.* '86 (LA) [77] Los Angeles, CA St. Malachy Church.
Huertas, Ivan L. '93 (SJN) [4] Bayamon, PR Cristo Salvador Church.
Huesca, Omar A. '81 (MIA) [31] Miami, FL St. Robert Bellarmine Church.
Huesing, Paul *c.s.p.* (DEN) [4] Boulder, CO St. Thomas Aquinas University Church.
Huesing, Paul D. *c.s.p.* '82 (DEN) [P] Boulder, CO University of Colorado (Boulder).
Huesman, E. Gerard '41 (BAL) [11] Baltimore, MD Ascension Church.
Huesman, John E. *s.j.* '49 (SJ) [L] Los Gatos, CA Sacred Heart Jesuit Center.
Huete, Francis W. *s.j.* '82 (LAF) [A] Grand Coteau, LA St. Charles College.
Huff, Thomas *f.i.* '90 (SY) [W] Maine, NY Mount St. Francis Hermitage, Inc.
Huffman, David L. '72 (STU) Belpre, OH St. Ambrose Church; [J] Belpre, OH Boy Scouts; [J] Steubenville, OH Ohio Conference Advisory Council.
Huffman, Timothy J. '93 (STU) Absent on Leave.
Huffman, Timothy J. '93 (Y) [8] Canton, OH St. Joseph's Church.
Huffstetter, Stephen *s.c.j.* '89 (MIL) [P] Hales Corners, WI Priests of the Sacred Heart.
Huffstetter, Stephen *s.c.j.* '89 (SAT) [B] San Antonio, TX Priests of the Sacred Heart-House of Formation.
Hug, James E. *s.j.* '72 (WDC) [M] Washington, DC K Street Jesuit Community; [V] Washington, DC Center of Concern.
Huggins, Michael '89 (SD) On Duty Outside the Diocese.
Huggins, William A. '67 (SPC) Leopold, MO St. John Church.
Hughes, Albert C. '57 (BO) [2] Framingham, MA St. George Church; Senior Priests.
Hughes, Brian '81 (SC) [10] Sioux City, IA Sacred Heart Church.
Hughes, Charles *glmy.* '54 (CIN) [M] Cincinnati, OH Headquarters of Glenmary Home Missioners.
Hughes, Charles *glmy.* '54 (SAV) Dublin, GA Immaculate Conception Church.
Hughes, Charles J. '74 (BO) [3] Beverly, MA St. Mary Star of the Sea Church.
Hughes, Christopher '98 (SFS) Aberdeen, SD Sacred Heart Church.
Hughes, Dennis E. '75 (SP) Port Richey, FL St. James the Apostle Church.
Hughes, Derek '86 (MRY) Paso Robles, CA St. Rose Church.
Hughes, Donald R. '52 (BUF) Retired.
Hughes, Edward J. '51 (CHI) Retired.
Hughes, Edward R. '58 (RCK) Sublette, IL Our Lady of Perpetual Help Church; West Brooklyn, IL St. Mary Church.
Hughes, Eugene E. *s.m.* '57 (WDC) [M] Washington, DC Marist Center.
Hughes, F. Rodger '64 (WH) Chester, WV Sacred Heart Church.
Hughes, Francis *s.v.d.* '52 (CHI) [B] Techny, IL Divine Word Residence.
Hughes, Francis J. '80 (BRK) [175] Queens, NY St. Helen Church.
Hughes, Gerald *s.j.* '85 (DAL) [27] Dallas, TX St. Rita Church.
Hughes, James A. '80 (BRK) [88] Brooklyn, NY St. Michael Archangel and St. Edward Church.
Hughes, James F. '52 (PH) Media, PA St. Mary Magdalen Church; Retired.
Hughes, John *m.s.* '53 (WOR) [6] Fitchburg, MA St. Joseph's Church.
Hughes, John '94 (BEA) [9] Beaumont, TX St. Jude Thaddeus Church.
Hughes, Msgr. John C. '49 (LA) Camarillo, CA St. Mary Magdalen Church; Retired.
Hughes, John F. '37 (BRK) Retired; [S] Queens Village, NY Queen of Peace Residence.
Hughes, John J. '54 (ARL) Springfield, VA St. Bernadette's Church.
Hughes, John Jay '54 (STL) [2] University City, MO Christ the King Church.
Hughes, Joseph B. '67 (BAL) Retired.
Hughes, Joseph W. '70 (TR) Rumson, NJ Holy Cross Church.
Hughes, Kenneth *s.j.* '66 (BO) [W] Cambridge, MA Weston Jesuit Community.
Hughes, Kenneth J. *s.j.* '66 (BO) [W] Cambridge, MA Faber House.
Hughes, Lawrence J. '64 (MAN) Retired.
Hughes, Mark '82 (WDC) [15] Washington, DC St. Gabriel Church.
Hughes, Matthew '96 (JOL) Hinsdale, IL St. Isaac Jogues Church.
Hughes, Msgr. Michael '45 (LA) Ventura, CA San Buenaventura Church.
Hughes, Msgr. Michael '45 (ORG) Retired.
Hughes, Michael J. *o.s.a.* '75 (ORL) Casselberry, FL St. Augustine Church.
Hughes, Msgr. Nicholas V. '44 (B) Retired.
Hughes, Patrick M. '56 (LA) Retired.
Hughes, Pete '81 (OWN) [5] Owensboro, KY Precious Blood Church.
Hughes, Peter *c.s.sp.* '61 (FAR) [1] Fargo, ND St. Mary's Church; Argusville, ND St. William Church.
Hughes, Raymond *c.r.* (ORL) Indialantic, FL Holy Name of Jesus Church.
Hughes, Msgr. Richard A. '52 (WDC) Upper Marlboro, MD Saint Mary of the Assumption Church.
Hughes, Robert E. *s.m.* '59 (CIN) [M] Dayton, OH Marianist Provincialate.
Hughes, Robert E. '90 (CAM) Bellmawr, NJ Mary, Mother of the Church.
Hughes, Robert T. '54 (PEO) Retired.
Hughes, Robert W. '68 (MAD) Military Chaplains.
Hughes, Ronald J. '82 (SCR) Towanda, PA SS. Peter and Paul Church.
Hughes, Royce (GAL) Retired.
Hughes, Vincent *o.f.m.* '85 (SD) [H] Oceanside, CA Mission San Luis Rey.
Hughes, William C. '47 (STO) Retired.
Hughson, D. Thomas *s.j.* '71 (MIL) [P] Milwaukee, WI Arrupe House Jesuit Community.
Hughson, Robert S. '79 (BUF) [1] Niagara Falls, NY St. Charles Borromeo Church.
Hugli, Richard *o.s.b.* '95 (SP) [O] St. Leo, FL St. Leo Abbey.
Hugo, William *o.f.m.cap.* '80 (BRK) [V] Brooklyn, NY St. Michael's Friary.
Hugo, William *o.f.m.cap.* '81 (BRK) [87] Brooklyn, NY St. Michael's Church.
Huguley, Vernon '93 (BIR) [19] Birmingham, AL Our Lady Queen of the Universe Church.
Huhmann, Msgr. John F. '50 (KC) Retired.
Huhn, Donald W. '49 (STL) Retired.
Huhn, Thomas J. *m.s.* '69 (TYL) Lufkin, TX St. Patrick Church.
Huitrado, Juan '80 (CHI) Graduate Studies.
Hulko, Joseph D. '64 (ALN) [7] Bethlehem, PA Notre Dame of Bethlehem Church.
Hull, Francis M. *s.s.j.* '57 (WDC) [8] Washington, DC St. Benedict the Moor Church; [44] Washington, DC St. Vincent De Paul Church.
Hull, Michael F. '93 (NY) [A] Yonkers, NY St. Joseph's Seminary.
Hullinger, Jon '99 (KCK) Olathe, KS Prince of Peace Church; [B] Overland Park, KS Saint Thomas Aquinas High School, Inc.
Hullings, Clifford '61 (SPK) Retired.
Hulscher, Alfred J. *o.s.b.* '60 (SEA) [L] Lacey, WA St. Martin's Abbey.
Hulshof, David F. '82 (SPC) [1] Springfield, MO Cathedral of St. Agnes; Aurora, MO Holy Trinity; Verona, MO Sacred Heart Church; Special Assignment.
Hultberg, William J. *o.s.f.s.* '62 (WIL) [I] Wilmington, DE Oblates of St. Francis De Sales.
Hultquist, Thomas H. '76 (WOR) Barre, MA St. Joseph's Church.
Humbert, Robert G. *s.j.* '53 (DET) [P] Clarkston, MI Colombiere Center.
Humbrecht, T. Allen '72 (KNX) [1] Knoxville, TN Cathedral of the Sacred Heart of Jesus.
Hume, Kenneth '63 (P) Retired.
Hume, Robert B. '43 (BRK) [57] Brooklyn, NY Holy Innocents Church; Retired.
Humenay, Robert '69 (E) On Duty Outside Diocese.
Huminski, Gregory J. '80 (BGP) [4] Norwalk, CT St. Mary Church.
Humitz, Msgr. Robert S. '60 (DET) Clarkston, MI St. Daniel Church.
Hummel, Donald K. '78 (NEW) Scotch Plains, NJ St. Bartholomew Church.
Hummel, Kenneth '98 (PEO) [15] Peoria, IL St. Vincent De Paul Church.
Hummell, John F. '65 (PH) Oxford, PA Sacred Heart Church; [EE] Philadelphia, PA Newman Center at Drexel University.
Hummer, Lawrence L. '73 (COL) Chillicothe, OH St. Mary Church.
Humphrey, Arthur Frank '75 (NEW) Little Ferry, NJ St. Margaret of Cortona Church.
Humphrey, Delos A. *m.m.* '54 (FgM) Maryknoll Foreign Missions.
Humphrey, Stephen J. '67 (BEL) Germantown, IL St. Boniface Church.
Humphrys, Richard '57 (SB) Bloomington, CA St. Charles Borromeo Church.
Hund, Francis '82 (KCK) Meriden, KS St. Aloysius Church; Perry, KS St. Theresa's Church.
Hund, William *c.s.c.* '60 (P) [B] Portland, OR University of Portland; [L] Portland, OR Holy Cross Fathers & Brothers, C.S.C. - University of Portland.

Hundt, George F. '81 (PAT) [8] Paterson, NJ St. Gerard Majella Church.
Hundt, Robert P. '61 (LC) [2] La Crosse, WI Blessed Sacrament Church.
Huneger, Richard J. '73 (P) [33] Portland, OR St. Rose of Lima Church.
Huneke, Robert D. '69 (RVC) Absent on Leave.
Hung, Ignatius *s.j.* '97 (BO) [W] Cambridge, MA Weston Jesuit Community.
Hung, Joseph K. '68 (ORG) On Duty Outside the Diocese.
Hung, Joseph Pham '70 (SFR) [2] San Mateo, CA St. Gregory Church.
Hung, Pham Quoc *c.ss.r.* '94 (LA) [Q] Baldwin Park, CA Vietnamese Redemptorist Mission.
Hung, Trinh Peter (CHI) [201] Chicago, IL St. Thomas of Canterbury Church; [V] Chicago, IL Ministry in Higher Education.
Hunke, Norman F. '73 (OM) [1] Omaha, NE St. Cecilia's Church.
Hunkeler, Edward J. '44 (OM) Retired.
Hunkler, Jerome '83 (FAR) McHenry, ND SS. Peter & Paul Church; New Rockford, ND St. John's Church.
Hunko, Gerard A. '91 (GAY) Lake Leelanau, MI St. Mary Church.
Hunstiger, Thomas P. '63 (STP) [20] St. Paul, MN St. Gregory the Great (Highland Catholic Community) Church; [23] St. Paul, MN St. Leo (Highland Catholic Community) Church; [33] St. Paul, MN St. Therese (Highland Catholic Community) Church; [W] St. Paul, MN The Highland Catholic Community.
Hunt, Brendan *o.m.i.* '42 (BO) [Z] Tewksbury, MA Immaculate Heart of Mary Infirmary.
Hunt, Dennis '81 (LIN) Lawrence, NE Sacred Heart Church.
Hunt, Douglas *c.r.* (DEN) [2] Fort Collins, CO Holy Family Church.
Hunt, George *s.j.* '67 (NY) [DD] New York, NY Jesuit Community at Fordham University.
Hunt, James M. '83 (GI) Ainsworth, NE St. Pius X Church.
Hunt, John M. '69 (OG) Canton, NY St. Thomas More Church; Potsdam, NY St. Francis of Assisi Campus Parish (Newman Center) Church.
Hunt, John W. '68 (PRO) [4] Cumberland, RI St. Joseph Church.
Hunt, Kevin *o.c.s.o.* '79 (WOR) [N] Spencer, MA St. Joseph's Abbey.
Hunt, Lawrence J. *s.j.* '57 (CHL) Winston-Salem, NC St. Benedict the Moor Church; [J] Charlotte, NC Jesuit Community.
Hunt, Msgr. Luke '67 (PT) Gulf Breeze, FL St. Ann Church.
Hunt, Mark J. '85 (PH) Southampton, PA Our Lady of Good Counsel Church.
Hunt, Michael *c.s.p.* '67 (NEW) [S] Mahwah, NJ Paulist Press.
Hunt, Michael J. '41 (BRK) [43] Brooklyn, NY St. Frances de Chantal Church.
Hunt, Michael J. *c.s.p.* '67 (NY) [104] New York, NY St. Paul the Apostle Church.
Hunt, Patrick J. '39 (PRO) Retired.
Hunt, Richard D. *s.j.* '71 (BUF) [O] Buffalo, NY Canisius Jesuit Community.
Hunt, Robert *c.pp.s.* '54 (CIN) [M] Dayton, OH Provincial Office of the Cincinnati Province of the Society of the Precious Blood.
Hunt, Thomas *o.f.m.conv.* (BAL) [S] Baltimore, MD Immaculate Heart of Mary Friary.
Hunt, Thomas *s.c.j.* '55 (MIL) [P] Franklin, WI Villa Maria.
Hunter, Alan '77 (SFD) Assumption, IL Assumption B.V.M. Church; Macon, IL St. Stanislaus Church; Moweaqua, IL St. Frances de Sales Church.
Hunter, Alcuin *o.f.m. conv.* '67 (LSC) Artesia, NM Our Lady of Grace Church.
Hunter, Charles T. *s.j.* '45 (FgM) Provinces.
Hunter, Eric '72 (SP) [5] Tampa, FL Incarnation Church.
Hunter, John J. '86 (NY) [2] Poughkeepsie, NY St. Mary Church.
Hunter, William R. '86 (LA) Retired.
Hunthausen, John F. '52 (HEL) Retired; [B] Helena, MT Carroll College.
Hunthausen, John M. *s.j.* '70 (FgM) Provinces.
Huntimer, Donald W. *c.s.v.* '59 (CHI) [N] Arlington Heights, IL Viatorian Province Center-Clerics of St. Viator.
Huntzinger, Msgr. Ralph J. '50 (COL) Retired.
Huon, Phan Phat *c.ss.r.* '53 (LA) [Q] Baldwin Park, CA Vietnamese Redemptorist Mission.
Huot, Leopold J. '45 (PRT) Retired.
Hupp, Msgr. Robert P. '40 (OM) Retired.
Huppenbauer, Walter '57 (CHI) [M] Chicago, IL Little Sisters of the Poor Center for the Aging.
Hurd, R. Scott '00 (WDC) Special Ministries; Pastoral Center Special Ministries.
Hurd, Steven F. *s.j.* '80 (CHI) [D] Wilmette, IL Loyola Academy.
Hurd, Timothy C. '92 (SHP) [1] Monroe, LA Jesus the Good Shepherd Church.
Hurkes, Charles *o.m.i.* '58 (WDC) [M] Washington, DC Missionary Oblates of Mary Immaculate.
Hurlbert, James F. '90 (CHI) [9] Chicago, IL St. Alphonsus Church.
Hurley, Cornelius P. *s.j.* '59 (NY) [DD] New York, NY Murray-Weigel Hall.
Hurley, Daniel A. *o.f.m.* '45 (BUF) [C] St. Bonaventure, NY St. Bonaventure University; [Q] West Clarksville, NY Mount Irenaeus, Franciscan Mountain Retreat & Holy Peace Friary; [R] Alfred, NY Campus Ministry.
Hurley, Msgr. Daniel J. '59 (RVC) Massapequa, NY St. Rose of Lima Church.
Hurley, Msgr. Edward '70 (DM) West Des Moines, IA St. Francis of Assisi Church.
Hurley, Francis J. *c.s.c.* '53 (FR) [A] North Easton, MA Stonehill College; [A] North Easton, MA Holy Cross Fathers Religious.
Hurley, George '55 (JOL) Retired.
Hurley, Gerard '76 (JKS) Columbus, MS Annunciation Church; [H] Columbus, MS Mississippi University for Women Student Center.
Hurley, J. Patrick *s.j.* '57 (SPK) [C] Spokane, WA Gonzaga University.
Hurley, James P. *m.s.* '48 (ATL) [2] Marietta, GA Church of St. Ann.
Hurley, Jerome M. *o.s.m.* '38 (CHI) [N] Chicago, IL Order of Friar Servants of Mary (Servites) United States of America Province, Inc.
Hurley, John '82 (MAN) West Swanzey, NH St. Anthony Church.
Hurley, John E. *c.s.p.* '77 (WDC) [B] Washington, DC St. Paul's College.
Hurley, John J. '56 (CHI) Arlington Heights, IL St. Edna Church.
Hurley, John J. *o.s.f.s.* '68 (FgM) Oblates of St. Francis de Sales Foreign Missions.
Hurley, John J. *o.s.f.s.* '68 (WIL) [I] Wilmington, DE DeSales House.
Hurley, John J. '82 (MAN) Keene, NH St. Bernard Church.
Hurley, John J. '82 (WDC) On Duty Outside the Archdiocese.
Hurley, John W. '74 (CHI) [4] Cicero, IL Mary, Queen of Heaven Church.
Hurley, Joseph T. *c.ss.r.* '54 (CHI) [N] Glenview, IL The Redemptorists of Glenview, Illinois.
Hurley, Msgr. Leonard F. '58 (WDC) Special Ministries; Hospital & Nursing Home Ministries; [L] Washington, DC Cardinal O'Boyle Residence for Priests; [V] Washington, DC Carroll Manor Nursing & Rehabilitation Center.
Hurley, Michael F. '43 (PHX) Cottonwood, AZ Immaculate Conception Church.
Hurley, Patrick M. *o.s.b.* '76 (PAT) [I] Morristown, NJ St. Mary's Abbey Retreat Center; [M] Morristown, NJ St. Mary's Abbey.
Hurley, Paul K. '95 (BO) Military & VA Chaplains.
Hurley, Paul W. '70 (BO) [2] Cambridge, MA Blessed Sacrament Church.
Hurley, Thomas J. '93 (CHI) [A] Chicago, IL St. Joseph Seminary.
Hurley, Msgr. Walter A. '65 (DET) Farmington, MI Our Lady of Sorrows Church; [T] Detroit, MI Pope John Paul II Cultural Foundation, Inc.
Hurst, H. David *o.s.b.* '46 (PRO) [P] Portsmouth, RI Abbey of St. Gregory the Great.
Hurst, Maynard E., Jr. *m.s.n.* '79 (BR) [5] Baton Rouge, LA St. Charles Borromeo Church; [14] Baton Rouge, LA St. Louis, King of France Church.
Hurst, Paul F. '77 (CIN) Germantown, OH St. Augustine Church.
Hurst, Thomas *s.s.* (ALB) On Duty Outside the Diocese.
Hurst, Thomas R. *s.s.* '73 (BAL) [S] Baltimore, MD Sulpician Provincial House.
Hurtado-Badillo, Domingo '93 (CHI) Other Assignments.
Hurteau, Robert A. *m.m.* '89 (FgM) Maryknoll Foreign Missions.
Hurteau, Robert A. *m.m.* '89 (LA) [Q] Los Angeles, CA Maryknoll Fathers and Brothers.
Hurtuk, Joseph C. *s.m.* '74 (WDC) [B] Washington, DC Marist College, The Scholasticate.
Husain, Nicolas '85 (LC) [D] Marshfield, WI Saint Joseph's Hospital of Marshfield, Inc.
Huse, Charles *o.a.r.* '61 (NEW) [N] West Orange, NJ Augustinian Recollects.
Huse, Ralph G. *s.j.* '75 (STL) [P] St. Louis, MO Bellarmine House of Studies.
Huse, Robert *o.a.r.* '58 (LA) [Q] Oxnard, CA St. Augustine Priory O.A.R.
Hushen, Mark A. *o.s.f.s.* '91 (WIL) [3] Wilmington, DE St. Anthony of Padua Church.
Huske, Leonard G. '56 (CHI) Retired.
Hussack, Emil M. '49 (SCR) [24] Scranton, PA Sacred Hearts of Jesus and Mary Church.
Husselbeck, Francis E. '58 (ALB) Retired.
Hussey, Daniel C. '85 (GLP) Winslow, AZ St. Joseph's Church; Winslow, AZ Madre de Dios Church.
Hussey, Dennis R. '45 (HRT) East Haven, CT Our Lady of Pompeii Church.
Hussey, Edmund M. '58 (CIN) Retired.
Hussey, Gerald W. '78 (PRO) Little Compton, RI St. Catherine of Siena Church; [3] Tiverton, RI St. Madeleine Sophie Church.
Hussey, Michael J. *o.m.i.* '60 (CHR) Ridgeland, SC St. Anthony's Church.
Hussey, Patrick *s.j.* '68 (TOL) [C] Toledo, OH St. John's Jesuit High School.
Hussey, Robert *s.j.* (R) [7] Raleigh, NC St. Raphael Church.
Hussey, Robert M. *s.j.* '00 (R) [E] Raleigh, NC Jesuit Community.
Hussey, Thomas F. *s.j.* '43 (BO) [W] Weston, MA Campion Health Center, Inc.
Hussli, Edward J. '67 (MIL) Retired.
Hussmann, John R. '54 (DUB) Retired.
Husted, Richard S. *o.f.m.* '66 (NEW) East Rutherford, NJ St. Joseph's Church.
Hustedde, Edwin H. (BEL) Madonnaville, IL Immaculate Conception Church.
Hustedde, Edwin H. '56 (BEL) Valmeyer, IL Seven Dolors of the B.V.M. Church; [A] Waterloo, IL Gibault Catholic High School.
Huston, Richard '95 (SD) [5] San Diego, CA Good Shepherd Church.
Huszti, Michael J. '76 (PRM) Burton, OH Church of Mariapoch; Solon, OH St. John the Baptist Church; [B] Burton, OH Shrine of Mariapoch.
Hut, Clemens '36 (EVN) Retired.
Hutcherson, Bartholomew *o.p.* '97 (SLC) [8] Salt Lake City, UT St. Catherine of Siena Church; [H] Salt Lake City, UT University of Utah, Newman Center.
Hutchins, James '67 (PH) Broomall, PA St. Pius X Church.
Hutchins, Michael *s.v.d.* '75 (DUB) [B] Epworth, IA Divine Word College.
Hutchinson, Ronald D. '94 (GR) Parnell, MI St. Patrick's Church.
Hutchison, William *s.j.* '66 (STL) [P] St. Louis, MO St. Matthew Jesuit Community.
Hutchison, William J. *s.j.* '66 (STL) [52] St. Louis, MO St. Matthew, Apostle Church; [C] St. Louis, MO Saint Louis University.
Huth, James P. *o.praem.* '88 (SFE) Albuquerque, NM St. Joseph Medical Center; [I] Albuquerque, NM Santa Maria de la Vid Priory.
Hutmacher, Robert '79 (CHI) [N] Chicago, IL St. Peter's Friary.
Hutnik, William J. '44 (PIT) Retired.
Hutsko, Basil J. '79 (PRM) Sterling Heights, MI St. Basil Church.
Hutsko, Joseph (SB) [5] Fontana, CA St. Nicholas Church.
Hutsko, Joseph '79 (DEN) [13] Denver, CO Holy Protection of the Mother of God Church.
Hutsko, Joseph '79 (VNN) Fontana, CA St. Nicholas Church.
Hutsko, Michael '84 (PHU) Middleport, PA Nativity of B.V.M. Church; Minersville, PA St. Nicholas Church.
Hutter, Eugene '88 (PSC) Hazleton, PA St. John the Baptist Church.
Hutter, John S. '92 (PH) [115] Philadelphia, PA Our Lady of Calvary Church.
Hutton, Leon '80 (LA) [A] Camarillo, CA St. John's Seminary; [A] Camarillo, CA St. John's Seminary.
Hutzler, Jim '80 (AMA) Panhandle, TX St. Theresa Church.
Huvane, James H. *m.m.* '70 (CLV) [O] Cleveland, OH Maryknoll Fathers.
Huy Quyen, Nguyen '73 (JOL) Glen Ellyn, IL Queenship of Mary Church; Glen Ellyn, IL St. Petronille Church.
Huyen, Leo Vu Dinh *c.m.c.* (SB) [2] Riverside, CA Our Lady of Perpetual Help Church.
Huyett, Gerald T. *s.j.* '73 (NY) [DD] New York, NY West Side Jesuit Community.
Huynh, Joseph Dinh C. '67 (PH) [152] Philadelphia, PA St. Thomas Aquinas Church.
Huynh, Mark Nguyen Thanh *c.m.c.* '77 (LIN) [3] Lincoln, NE Immaculate Heart of Mary Church.
Huynh, Viet '93 (PT) Gulf Breeze, FL St. Ann Church.
Hvozdovic, Andrew S. '87 (SCR) Jersey Shore, PA St. Luke's Church; [D] Williamsport, PA Bishop Neumann Junior/Senior High School.
Hwang, Bernard *o.s.b.* (P) Retired.
Hwang, Suk-Mo (JOL) Darian, IL Our Lady of Korean Martyrs Church.
Hy, Hilary Tran-Khac '57 (WDC) [6] Bethesda, MD Our Lady of Vietnam Church.
Hyatt, Donald *c.s.b.* (LSC) Truth or Consequences, NM Our Lady of Perpetual Help Church.
Hyatt, J.P. Martin A. *b.s.o.* '84 (NTN) [B] Methuen, MA Basilian Salvatorian Order.
Hyatt, John R. *s.j.* '77 (BRK) [62] Brooklyn, NY St. Ignatius Church.
Hyatt, Robert A. '63 (RVC) Amityville, NY South Oaks Psychiatric Hospital; West Islip, NY Consolation Nursing Home; [J] West Islip, NY Our Lady of Consolation Geriatric Care Center.
Hybner, Joseph '63 (VIC) Ganado, TX Assumption of the B.V.M. Church.

Hyclak, Walter J. '69 (CLV) [T] Cleveland, OH St. Joseph Christian Life Center.
Hyde, Gregory J. *s.j.* (DET) [K] Detroit, MI Jesuit Provincial Office-Detroit Province of the Society of Jesus.
Hyde, Gregory J. *s.j.* '98 (FgM) Provinces.
Hyde, Mark *s.d.b* '81 (BIR) [9] Birmingham, AL St. John Bosco Church; [9] Birmingham, AL St. John Bosco Church.
Hyde, Robert L. *o.praem.* '43 (GB) [I] De Pere, WI St. Norbert Abbey.
Hyde, Robert P. '88 (SY) Whitney Point, NY St. Patrick Church.
Hyden, Michael T. '85 (SUP) Presque Isle, WI St. Rita Church.
Hying, Donald (MIL) [62] Milwaukee, WI Our Lady of Good Hope Church.
Hykavy, Roman *o.s.b.m.* '94 (STN) Warren, MI St. Josaphat Church.
Hyl, Robert J. '63 (BGP) [8] Stamford, CT Holy Spirit Church.
Hyland, Edward F. '67 (HRT) [17] Waterbury, CT SS. Peter and Paul Church.
Hyland, James M. '81 (CHI) [145] Chicago, IL Our Lady of Good Counsel Church.
Hyland, John M. '68 (DAV) Burlington, IA SS. John & Paul Church.
Hyland, Sean J. '84 (MIA) [12] Miami, FL Our Lady of the Holy Rosary Church.
Hyland, Terrance W. *o.s.a.* '71 (CHL) Maggie Valley, NC St. Margaret Church; [N] Maggie Valley, NC Living Waters Catholic Reflection Center.
Hyland, Thomas J. '63 (CLV) North Ridgeville, OH St. Peter Church.
Hyman, David L. *o.f.m.* '60 (CHR) Anderson, SC St. Mary of the Angels Church.
Hyman, Robert A. '61 (TUC) Marana, AZ St. Christopher's Church.
Hymel, Ray '87 (NO) [4] Slidell, LA St. Margaret Mary Church.
Hyndman, Ernest R. '96 (MOB) [6] Mobile, AL Holy Family Church.
Hynes, Aidan '81 (PMB) Hobe Sound, FL St. Christopher Church.
Hynes, Christopher J. '92 (NEW) [B] South Orange, NJ Seton Hall University.
Hynes, Gerald *c.p.* '51 (BAL) [93] Baltimore, MD St. Ursula Church.
Hynes, Gerald *c.p.* '51 (MET) [H] South River, NJ Passionist Provincial Office.
Hynes, James F. *o.f.m.* '80 (HRT) [15] Hartford, CT St. Patrick-St. Anthony Church.
Hynes, James P. '49 (PRO) Retired.
Hynes, John '54 (NY) [205] Staten Island, NY Holy Family Church.
Hynes, John F. '55 (DAV) Retired.
Hynes, John M. '65 (WIL) Wilmington, DE St. Catherine of Siena Church.
Hynes, Joseph P. '55 (PRO) Retired.
Hynes, Michael *s.d.b.* '82 (OAK) [N] Berkeley, CA Salesian Community.
Hynes, Patrick J. '85 (PIT) Turtle Creek, PA St. Colman Church.
Hynes, Richard P. '72 (CHI) Western Springs, IL St. John of the Cross Church.
Hynes, Thomas J. *c.m.* '59 (BIR) Alexander City, AL St. John the Apostle Church.
Hynes, Msgr. William '49 (SR).
Hynous, David M. *o.p.* '59 (CHI) [N] River Forest, IL St. Thomas Aquinas Priory.
Hypolite, Douglas J. *s.j.* '80 (GAL) [F] Houston, TX Strake, Jesuit College Preparatory Inc.

I

Iaconis, Anthony (RVC) Bellmore, NY St. Barnabas the Apostle Church.
Iacono, Leonardo '50 (ALN) Retired.
Iacovacci, Nicholas J. '51 (PRO) [7] Warwick, RI St. Peter Church; Retired.
Iacovone, Angelo *c.p.* '46 (BRK) [V] Jamaica, NY Immaculate Conception Monastery.
Iaia, Paul J. (BAL) Buckeystown, MD St. Joseph-on-Carrollton Manor Church.
Iaia, Paul P. '56 (BAL) Retired.
Ianieri, Stanley A. '89 (WIL) Sherwood Park, DE St. John the Beloved Church.
Iannarella, James M. '96 (PH) Absent on Leave.
Iannone, Raphael *o.f.m.cap.* '64 (BRK) [87] Brooklyn, NY St. Michael's Church; [V] Brooklyn, NY St. Michael's Friary.
Ianotti, Pascal '61 (ALB) Retired.
Iantosca, August J. '77 (BRK) [214] Queens, NY Our Lady of Mercy Church; Queens, NY Creedmoor Psychiatric Center.
Ianucci, Thomas A. '94 (RIC) Bristol, VA St. Anne Church.
Iaquinta, Patsy '70 (WH) Bluefield, WV Sacred Heart Church.
Iaquinto, Richard *o.s.b.* '68 (BUR) [E] Weston, VT Priory of Benedictine Monks.
Iasiello, Louis V. *o.f.m.* '78 (NY) [DD] New York, NY Franciscan Friars, Order of Friars Minor, Holy Name Province.
Iavarone, Armand *o.ss.t.* '43 (BAL) [S] Baltimore, MD Holy Trinity Monastery.
Iavarone, Armand *o.ss.t.* '43 (NY) Spring Valley, NY St. Joseph Church.
Iazzetta, Athanasius *o.f.m.* '54 (FgM) Franciscan Foreign Missions.
Iazzetta, Frank J. '67 (TR) Leave of Absence.
Ibach, Michael J. '73 (YAK) Selah, WA Our Lady of Lourdes Church.
Ibach, William *s.j.* '59 (BO) [W] Cambridge, MA Weston Jesuit Community.
Ibanez, Armando *o.p.* '93 (LA) [R] Los Angeles, CA Monastery of the Angels (Contemplative).
Ibanez, Armando *o.p.* '93 (NO) [P] New Orleans, LA Dominican Friars, Southern Dominican Province of St. Martin de Porres.
Ibanez, Armando *o.p.* '93 (OAK) [N] Oakland, CA Western Dominican Province.
Ibanez, Rodolfo '51 (BR) Retired.
Ibarra, J. Brando '99 (PAT) Morristown, NJ St. Margaret's Church.
Ibarra, Manuel '98 (LSC) [2] Las Cruces, NM Holy Cross Church.
Ibasco, Philip (NY) [183] Bronx, NY St. Philip Neri Church.
Ibe, Sanctus Kodilinye, Jr. '00 (MAD) Waunakee, WI St. John the Baptist Church.
Ibeh, Eliseus *m.s.p.* '89 (GAL) [8] Houston, TX St. Anne de Beaupre Church.
Ibrahim, Ibrahim *b.s.o.* '87 (NTN) Brooklyn, OH St. Elias Church.
Ide, Harold J. '52 (MIL) Retired.
Idler, Peter M. '97 (CAM) Woodbury, NJ St. Patrick's Church.
Idranyi, Edmund M. '54 (VNN) San Luis Obispo, CA Saint Anne Church.
Idyu, Mathias *c.s.sp.* (PIT) [B] Pittsburgh, PA Duquesne University of the Holy Ghost.
Idyu, Matthias *c.s.sp.* (PIT) [R] Pittsburgh, PA Office for Campus Ministry.
Idzik, George '74 (NEW) [5] Jersey City, NJ St. Ann's Church.
Iffert, John C. (BEL) Columbia, IL Immaculate Conception of the B.V.M. Church.
Iffert, Wilbert J. '52 (BEL) Retired.
Ifkovits, Edward M. *s.j.* '86 (CHL) Mars Hill, NC St. Andrew the Apostle Church; [J] Charlotte, NC Jesuit Community.
Igbokwe, Sebastian '81 (MAD) East Bristol, WI St. Joseph Church.
Igelsias, Etelvino *o.a.r.* '60 (LA) [4] Oxnard, CA Mary Star of the Sea Church.
Iglesias, Clement '58 (BEA) Retired.
Iglesias, Fernando '56 (LA) Pico Rivera, CA St. Mariana de Paredes Church.
Iglesias, Jose Esteves *o.de.m.* (SJN) [40] San Juan, PR Nuestra Senora de la Merced Church.
Iglesias, Luis Fernando '53 (CC) Retired.
Ignacio, Alex C. '74 (FRS) Lindsay, CA Sacred Heart Church.
Ignacio, Roberto '74 (TR) [1] Toms River, NJ St. Joseph Church.
Ignaszak, Michael A. '84 (MIL) [35] Milwaukee, WI St. Helen Church.
Ignaszek, Gabriel *o.f.m.conv.* '49 (CHI) [N] Libertyville, IL Marytown, Our Lady of Fatima Friary.
Igo, James P. '54 (OG) Retired.
Igoe, Martin S. '62 (BGP) [6] Greenwich, CT Sacred Heart Church.
Iguabita-Rodriguez, Kelvin E. '99 (BO) [1] Haverhill, MA All Saints Church.
Igwe, Pascal '96 (DET) Walled Lake, MI St. William Church.
Iheaka, Emmanuel '90 (BIR) [17] Birmingham, AL Our Lady of Sorrows Church.
Iheanacho, Anthony '80 (MAD) [1] Madison, WI St. Raphael Church.
Iheanaho, Kenneth '90 (TLS) Tahlequah, OK St. Brigid Church; [H] Tahlequah, OK Northeastern State University Catholic Student Organization.
Iheoha, Bernard '82 (NY) [142] Bronx, NY St. Frances of Rome Church; Bronx, NY Our Lady of Mercy Medical Center; [W] New York, NY Our Lady of Mercy Medical Center.
Ihnatowicz, Janusz '62 (GAL) [Q] Houston, TX Residence of the Basilian Fathers of the University of St. Thomas.
Ihrie, Bernard R., Jr. '55 (WDC) Camp Springs, MD St. Philip the Apostle Church; Retired.
Ijeoma, John Vianney '89 (LKC) Dequincy, LA Phelps Correctional Center.
Ikataere, John *m.s.c.* '72 (CI) [B] Chuuk, FM Saramen Chuuk Academy.
Ikemeh, John Bosco *o.p.* '96 (OAK) [22] Oakland, CA St. Theresa of the Infant Jesus (The Little Flower) Church.
Ikeocha, Ikechukuu "I.K." '00 (LA) Diamond Bar, CA St. Denis Church.
Ikeocha, Ikechukwu "I.K." '00 (LA) Glendora, CA St. Dorothy Church.
Ikpah, Kevin '74 (PHX) [9] Phoenix, AZ St. Catherine of Siena Church.
Ilano, Ven '96 (RIC) Portsmouth, VA Holy Angels Church.
Ililau, John Paul '90 (CI) Ioueldoab, FM St. John Baptist Church; Babeldaob, FM St. Thomas Apostle Church.
Illies, Wilfred '50 (SCL) Retired.
Illig, A. Mark '85 (BUF) [1] Tonawanda, NY St. Amelia Church; [R] Alfred, NY Campus Ministry.
Illikattil, Mathew K. '71 (KAL) Three Rivers, MI Immaculate Conception Church.
Illo, Joseph '91 (STO) Modesto, CA St. Joseph Church.
Ilnicki, Theodosius *o.s.b.m.* '88 (STF) Long Island City, NY Holy Cross Church.
Ilokada, Damian (ROC) [19] Rochester, NY St. Helen Church.
Ilokoba, Damian (ROC) Scottsville, NY St. Mary of the Assumption Church.
Im, Seung-Chul (Thomas Aquinas) '88 (WDC) College Park, MD St. Andrew Kim Church.
Imamshah, Harold '90 (ALX) [H] Pineville, LA Maryhill Renewal Center.
Imbelli, Robert '66 (NY) On Duty Outside the Archdiocese.
Imberi, Anthony '62 (SFS) Brandon, SD Risen Savior Church; Garretson, SD St. Rose of Lima Church.
Imbroll, Gregory E. *o.f.m.* '57 (NY) [DD] New York, NY Franciscan Province of the Immaculate Conception.
Imfeld, Thomas J. '59 (LEX) Corbin, KY Sacred Heart Church; Retired.
Imgrund, Norman P. '64 (ALT) Everett, PA St. John the Evangelist Church.
Imholte, Otto J. *s.s.c.* '63 (PRO) [P] Bristol, RI St. Columban's Retirement House.
Iminga, Wilfredo *m.s.* '92 (SB) Moreno Valley, CA St. Christopher Church.
Immel, Joseph '49 (LAN) Retired.
Immel, William A. '53 (DET) Retired.
Imming, David B. '65 (OKL) Alva, OK Sacred Heart Church; [K] Norman, OK Campus Ministry for the Archdiocese of Oklahoma City.
Imming, Donald '60 (SFS) Vermillion, SD St. Agnes Church.
Imokhai, Charles '68 (NY) [1] New Rochelle, NY Blessed Sacrament Church.
Imperial, Francisco '59 (NY) [177] Bronx, NY Our Lady of Solace Church.
Ince, Michael W. '64 (STP) Elysian, MN St. Andrew, Waterville, MN Church; Waterville, MN Holy Trinity Church.
Ince, Owen F. '00 (NEW) Bloomfield, NJ Church of St. Thomas the Apostle.
India, Stephen J. *c.m.* '49 (ALB) [L] Albany, NY Vincentian Fathers Residence.
Ines, Paul *s.d.b.* '96 (SCR) [3] Williamsport, PA St. Boniface's Church.
Infante, Richard A. '92 (PIT) South Park, PA Nativity Church.
Infiesta, Ramon Alvarez '81 (MGZ) [E] Mayaguez, PR Opus Dei (Prelature of the Holy Cross and Opus Dei).
Infuhr, Frank J. '49 (LA) Retired.
Ingalls, Fred D. '74 (BUF) Alden, NY St. John the Baptist Church.
Ingels, Gregory G. *j.c.d.* '74 (SFR) Special Assignment.
Ingemie, Dominic '67 (ALB) [8] Albany, NY St. James Church.
Ingham, G. Nicholas *o.p.* '81 (PRO) [P] Providence, RI St. Thomas Aquinas Priory at Providence College.
Ingham, Jeffrey A. (R) On Duty Outside the Diocese.
Inghilterra, Vincent J. '72 (TR) Military Chaplains.
Inglot, Mark (LAN) East Lansing, MI St. John the Evangelist, Student Church.
Ingold, Michael (GB) [7] Green Bay, WI St. Joseph Church.
Ingram, Brian '90 (RVC) Bellmore, NY St. Barnabas the Apostle Church.
Inigo, Javier *c.m.* '61 (SJN) [60] San Juan, PR San Vicente de Paul Church.
Inman, Leonard T. '61 (ALT) Retired.
Innes, Ben R. *o.f.m.* '84 (SD) [H] Oceanside, CA Mission San Luis Rey; [K] Oceanside, CA Mission San Luis Rey Retreat.
Innocenti, Mark '99 (SCL) [4] St. Cloud, MN St. Anthony of Padua Church.
Innocenzi, Msgr. James G. '76 (TR) [19] Trenton, NJ St. Michael Church.
Inserra, Ceaser *o.f.m.conv.* '47 (LA) [Q] Torrance, CA Franciscan Friars, St. Bonaventure Friary.
Intranuovo, Ralph J. '83 (GAL) [27] Houston, TX St. Elizabeth Ann Seton Church.
Introini, Msgr. Elso C. '62 (PAT) Hawthorne, NJ St. Anthony's Church.
Introvigne, Raymond D. '64 (NOR) Coventry, CT St. Mary Church.
Inverso, Leon J. '85 (TR) Atlantic Highlands, NJ St. Agnes Church.
Inweregbu, Jude '87 (DET) Garden City, MI St. Raphael the Archangel Church.

Inzeo, Lawrence C. '78 (NY) [1] White Plains, NY St. Anthony Church.
Inzerillo, Peter '70 (WOR) On Duty Outside the Diocese.
Inzina, Joseph Robert '60 (SHP) Bastrop, LA St. Joseph Church.
Iorio, Peter J. '93 (CHI) [A] Mundelein, IL University of St. Mary of the Lake-Mundelein Seminary.
Iott, Martin J. *o.p.* '70 (R) [E] Raleigh, NC Dominican Community.
Iovino, Paul '61 (PAT) Totowa Borough, NJ St. James of the Marches Church.
Ipolito, Pascal D. '70 (BUF) [2] West Seneca, NY St. Catherine of Siena Church.
Ippolito, Robert F. *m.s.* '73 (HRT) [M] Hartford, CT Missionaries of LaSalette, Provincial Secretary.
Irace, Dominic P. '75 (ARL) [1] Arlington, VA Cathedral of St. Thomas More.
Ireland, David R. '83 (CLV) Eastlake, OH St. Justin Martyr Church.
Ireland, Donald '63 (MIA) Retired.
Iriondo, Msgr. Josu '62 (NY) [129] Bronx, NY St. Anthony of Padua Church; [HH] New York, NY Centro Carismatico Catolico Hispano De La Arquidiocesis De Nueva York; [HH] New York, NY Hispanic Catholic Charismatic Center of the Archdiocese of New York.
Irish, Robert '92 (LAN) On Duty Outside the Diocese.
Irizar, Miguel *c.p.* '57 (MIA) [L] Miami, FL Peruvian Mission, Inc.
Irizarry, Elvin '67 (ARE) [4] Arecibo, PR Santa Ana Church.
Irizarry, Rafael (ARE) Retired.
Irizarry, Msgr. Raul '41 (PCE) Retired.
Iroh, Anthony '94 (BRK) [27] Brooklyn, NY St. Catherine of Genoa Church.
Ironuma, Donatus '94 (BWN) La Joya, TX Our Lady, Queen of Angels Church.
Iroz, Anthony *o.a.r.* '36 (LA) [9] Los Angeles, CA Cristo Rey Church.
Irrgang, Kenneth E. '68 (NU) Retired.
Irudayaraj, Y. C. '92 (OKL) Woodward, OK St. Peter's Church.
Irvin, Charles E. '67 (LAN) Manchester, MI St. Mary Church.
Irving, Alfred '58 (PRT) Benedicta, ME St. Benedict's Church; Island Falls, ME St. Agnes Church.
Irving, Peter '83 (LA) Wilmington, CA SS. Peter and Paul's Church.
Irwin, James W. *c.s.c.* '65 (FgM) Holy Cross Foreign Missions.
Irwin, James W. *c.s.c.* '65 (FTW) [J] South Bend, IN Congregation of Holy Cross, Indiana Province, Provincial House.
Irwin, Joseph F. '62 (NY) Mamaroneck, NY Holy Trinity Church.
Irwin, Msgr. Kevin W. '71 (NY) On Duty Outside the Archdiocese.
Irwin, Kevin W. '71 (WDC) [C] Washington, DC Catholic University of America, The.
Irwin, Michael *f.s.s.p.* '64 (KCK) [E] Maple Hill, KS Our Lady of Compassion.
Irwin, Michael T. *f.s.s.p.* '64 (SCR) [M] Elmhurst, PA Priestly Fraternity of St. Peter (F.S.S.P.), North American District Headquarters.
Irwin, Patrick '69 (SP) Valrico, FL St. Stephen Church.
Irwin, Patrick F. '59 (MAN) Retired.
Irwin, Robert C. '95 (BAK) [1] Baker, OR Cathedral of St. Francis De Sales.
Irwin, Robert P. '78 (FAR) Special Assignment.
Isacsson, Alfred J. *o.carm.* '58 (NY) Tarrytown, NY Transfiguration Church.
Isaza, Luis Guillermo Cordoba '00 (ATL) Duluth, GA St. Benedict Church.
Ischay, Matthew A. '75 (CLV) [12] Cleveland, OH Blessed Sacrament Church.
Ischler, Paul *o.m.i.* '39 (STP) [N] St. Paul, MN Oblate Residence.
Isek, Frederick *m.s.p.* '97 (GAL) [67] Houston, TX St. Peter the Apostle Church.
Isenecker, Lawrence E. *s.j.* '57 (DET) [P] Clarkston, MI Colombiere Center.
Isern, Fernando '93 (MIA) Key Biscayne, FL St. Agnes Church.
Iskander, Sabri A. '68 (EST) El Cajon, CA St. Michael Chaldean Catholic Church.
Isla, Elias (NY) [65] New York, NY St. Jude Church.
Isopo, Dominic '80 (ALB) [11] Schenectady, NY St. Luke Church.
Issac, Jose '75 (RNO) Winnemucca, NV St. Paul Church.
Issing, Daniel J. *c.s.c.* (BO) [1] Newton, MA St. Bernard Church.
Istok, Adolph *c.r.* '44 (CHI) [D] Chicago, IL Gordon Tech High School.
Itatiro, Adelwald *o.f.m.cap* (WDC) [B] Washington, DC St. Francis Friary-Capuchin College.
Iten, Werner *o.f.m.conv.* '74 (FgM) Conventual Franciscan Foreign Missions.
Itodo, Pius '90 (LA) [66] Los Angeles, CA St. Gerard Majella Church.
Ittiyappara, Mathew '67 (SR) Yountville, CA St. Joan of Arc Church.
Ittykunju, Michael '74 (BRK) [220] Queens, NY Our Lady of the Snows Church; [U] Brooklyn, NY Catholic Migration & Refugee Office, Catholic Migration Services, Inc.
Iturbe, Rene *s.m.* '74 (MRY) Santa Cruz, CA Star of the Sea Church; [F] Santa Cruz, CA Society of Mary, Marists.
Iturraran, Jose Luis *o.de.m.* '63 (PCE) [9] Ponce, PR La Merced Church.
Itzaina, John *s.d.b.* '74 (LA) [F] Bellflower, CA St. John Bosco High School; [CC] Bellflower, CA St. John Bosco High School Alumni.
Ivan, Nicholas '56 (PRM) Livonia, MI Sacred Heart Church.
Ivans, Joseph *o.c.d.* '53 (GRY) [J] Munster, IN Discalced Carmelite Fathers Monastery.
Ivers, Msgr. Leslie J. '79 (NY) [141] Bronx, NY St. Frances de Chantal Church.
Ivers, Michael T. '74 (CHI) Other Assignments.
Ivers, Victor J. '45 (CHI) Libertyville, IL St. Joseph Church; Retired.
Iverson, Msgr. Stanley J. '49 (NO) Retired.
Ivey, David J. '86 (LA) Lompoc, CA Vandenberg Air Force Base.
Ivory, Msgr. Thomas '64 (NEW) Upper Saddle River, NJ Church of the Presentation.
Iwan, Janusz '76 (DET) Lapeer, MI Immaculate Conception of the Blessed Virgin Mary Church.
Iwaniec, Wieslaw '86 (SAT) Stockdale, TX St. Mary Church.
Iwanowski, Thomas B. '75 (NEW) [19] Jersey City, NJ Our Lady of Czestochowa Church.
Iwasiw, Nestor '93 (PHU) Frackville, PA St. Michael's Church.
Iweh, Emmanuel '84 (SEA) Bellevue, WA St. Madeleine Sophie Church.
Iwuagwu, Nicholas (BRK) [192] Queens, NY St. Margaret Church.
Iwuanyanwu, Linus (NY) [4] New York, NY All Saints Church.
Iwuc, Anthony D. '53 (PRO) [3] Central Falls, RI St. Joseph Church.
Iwuchukwu, Pius '77 (LR) Magnolia, AR Immaculate Heart of Mary Church.
Iwuchukwu, Pius A. '77 (LR) El Dorado, AR Holy Redeemer Church.
Iwuji, Matthew C. '74 (GRY) [7] Hammond, IN St. Margaret Mary Church.
Izac, Andre C. '64 (R) Buxton, NC Our Lady of the Seas Church.
Izac, Andre C. '64 (WDC) On Duty Outside the Archdiocese.
Izczuk, Cyril *o.s.b.m.* (STF) [B] Glen Cove, NY Basilian Fathers Novitiate of the Order of St. Basil the Great.
Izer, Wesley W. *s.d.b.* '77 (VNN) [A] Phoenix, AZ Salesians of Don Bosco.
Izquierdo, William *l.c.* '58 (WDC) [M] Potomac, MD Legionaries of Christ.
Izral, John '56 (BLX) Retired.
Izyk, Andrew '73 (CHI) [44] Chicago, IL St. Constance Church.
Izzo, Brian A. '98 (PH) Southampton, PA Our Lady of Good Counsel Church.
Izzo, David D. *o.p.* '94 (FgM) Dominican - Order of Preachers Foreign Missions.
Izzo, Januarius *o.f.m.* '62 (VNN) Sacramento, CA St. Philip the Apostle Church.
Izzo, John *s.j.* '80 (BO) [W] Chestnut Hill, MA The Jesuit Community at Boston College.

J

Jablinske, Raymond D. '68 (WH) [5] Wheeling, WV Our Lady of Peace Church.
Jablonowski, Anthony *c.m.m.i.* '70 (STU) Churchtown, OH St. John the Baptist Church.
Jablonowski, James N. '68 (MIL) [14] Milwaukee, WI Blessed Sacrament Church.
Jablonski, Edward J. '96 (PH) Absent on Leave.
Jablonski, Joseph *m.s.c.* '76 (RCK) [G] Aurora, IL Missionaries of the Sacred Heart Community.
Jablonski, Msgr. Stanislaus '41 (NY) [192] Bronx, NY St. Valentine Church; Retired.
Jablonski, Msgr. William W. '63 (RVC) East Rockaway, NY St. Raymond's Church.
Jabusch, Willard F. '56 (CHI) [V] Chicago, IL Ministry in Higher Education; [X] Wilmette, IL Musica Pacis.
Jach, Edward M. *s.m.* '64 (CIN) [25] Cincinnati, OH St. Francis de Sales Church.
Jach, Edward M. *s.m.* '64 (STL) [P] St. Louis, MO Provincialate of the Society of Mary, Province of St. Louis.
Jack, Cuthbert A. *o.s.b.* '90 (GBG) [H] Latrobe, PA Saint Vincent Archabbey.
Jack, Duane C. '67 (PEO) Kewanee, IL St. Mary's Catholic Church.
Jack, Edward M. *s.m.* '64 (CIN) [M] Cincinnati, OH De Sales Crossings Marianist Community.
Jack, J. Robert '92 (CIN) [B] Cincinnati, OH Mt. St. Mary's Seminary of the West.
Jackanich, Msgr. Joseph '26 (PSC) Retired.
Jackels, Msgr. Michael O. '81 (LIN) On Duty Outside the Diocese.
Jackiewicz, Frederick W. '71 (TR) West Long Branch, NJ St. Jerome Church; [S] Princeton, NJ Campus Ministry for the Diocese of Trenton.
Jacklin, Richard '84 (JOL) Kankakee, IL Shapiro Development Center.
Jackovic, George V. '46 (PIT) Retired.
Jackson, Charles A. '60 (COL) [A] Columbus, OH Pontifical College Josephinum.
Jackson, David *s.c.j.* '66 (BWN) Lyford, TX Prince of Peace Church.
Jackson, James *f.f.s.p.* (LIN) [A] Denton, NE Our Lady of Guadalupe Seminary.
Jackson, James *f.s.s.p.* '85 (SCR) [M] Elmhurst, PA Priestly Fraternity of St. Peter (F.S.S.P.), North American District Headquarters.
Jackson, James A. *m.m.* '48 (NY) [DD] Maryknoll, NY Maryknoll Fathers and Brothers.
Jackson, James J. '72 (SUP) Butternut, WI Immaculate Conception Church; Fifield, WI St. Francis of Assisi Church; Park Falls, WI St. Anthony Church.
Jackson, James M. '75 (WIL) Absent on Sick Leave.
Jackson, James R. *m.m.* '58 (FgM) Maryknoll Foreign Missions.
Jackson, James W. '60 (STP) Minneapolis, MN Hennepin County Courts; Special Assignment; [K] St. Paul, MN Our Lady of Good Counsel Home.
Jackson, Joseph M. '74 (CHI) Palatine, IL St. Thomas of Villanova Church.
Jackson, Lawrence J. '60 (DET) [7] Sterling Heights, MI St. Michael Church.
Jackson, O. Tom (VEN) Holmes Beach, FL St. Bernard's Church.
Jackson, Pio *o.f.m.* '91 (NSH) [13] Nashville, TN St. Vincent de Paul Church; [H] Nashville, TN Franciscan Friars.
Jackson, Raymond A. *c.s.b.* '58 (VIC) Wharton, TX Our Lady of Mt. Carmel Church.
Jackson, Robert H. '84 (CLV) [17] Akron, OH St. Sebastian Church; [D] Akron, OH St. Vincent-St. Mary High School.
Jackson, William J. *c.s.sp.* '58 (VEN) [G] Sarasota, FL Congregation of the Holy Ghost.
Jacmierski, Jan '60 (NY) [5] Poughkeepsie, NY St. Joseph Church.
Jacob, Anthony J. *o.s.b.* '65 (JOL) [C] Lisle, IL Benet Academy; [J] Lisle, IL St. Procopius Abbey.
Jacob, Jerome '92 (CHI) [3] Mt. Prospect, IL St. Raymond de Penafort Church.
Jacob, Joseph E. '00 (LFT) Kewanna, IN St. Ann Church; Rochester, IN St. Joseph Church.
Jacob, William *c.ss.r.* '46 (NY) [23] New York, NY St. Cecilia Church.
Jacobberger, Joseph '65 (P) [1] Portland, OR Cathedral of the Immaculate Conception.
Jacobi, Arthur '81 (DET) [3] Clinton Twp., MI St. Paul of Tarsus Church.
Jacobi, Joseph A. '91 (OKL) Altus, OK Prince of Peace Church.
Jacobs, Charles E. '86 (HRT) [9] Hartford, CT St. Augustine Church.
Jacobs, David E. '75 (LR) Pocahontas, AR St. Paul the Apostle Church.
Jacobs, Eugene S. '46 (WH) Retired.
Jacobs, Gilbert H. *o.praem.* '55 (GB) [I] De Pere, WI St. Norbert Abbey.
Jacobs, Harry W. '73 (WDC) Retired.
Jacobs, James T. '43 (GB) Retired.
Jacobs, Joseph A. '40 (FTW) Retired.
Jacobs, Pierre P. *s.j.* '44 (SJ) [L] Los Gatos, CA Sacred Heart Jesuit Center.
Jacobs, Richard '75 (ALB) Catskill, NY St. Patrick Church.
Jacobs, Richard *o.s.a.* '76 (PH) [C] Villanova, PA Villanova University.
Jacobs, Richard A. (PAT) Retired.
Jacobs, Richard M. *o.s.a.* '83 (CHI) [N] Olympia Fields, IL The Augustinians-Provincialate.
Jacobs, Timothy *ss.cc.* '35 (HON) [G] Kaneohe, HI Sacred Hearts Center.
Jacobsen, James E. *s.j.* '59 (P) [L] Portland, OR Colombiere Community.
Jacobsmeyer, Gregory H. *s.j.* '46 (STL) [P] St. Louis, MO Hallahan House.
Jacobson, Cliff '96 (CHY) Sheridan, WY Holy Name Church.
Jacobson, Gary '65 (P) Retired.
Jacobson, James *s.j.* '59 (P) Salem, OR Oregon State Penitentiary; Salem, OR Santiam Correctional Institution; Salem, OR Mill Creek Correctional Facility.
Jacoby, Aloysius *o.f.m.conv.* '47 (FgM) Conventual Franciscan Foreign Missions.
Jacquel, John B. '83 (E) Edinboro, PA Our Lady of the Lake Church.
Jacquemin, George '72 (CIN) [20] Cincinnati, OH St. Clare Church.
Jacques, Alfred '60 (PRT) Rumford, ME St. Athanasius-St. John Church.

Jacques, Donald '43 (MAN) Milford, NH St. Patrick Church.
Jacques, Donald W. '53 (PRT) Retired.
Jacques, E. J. *s.j.* '66 (MOB) [9] Mobile, AL St. Joseph Church.
Jacques, Eugene F. '80 (NO) Gretna, LA St. Cletus Church.
Jacques, Kenneth *o.s.b.* (P) Salem, OR Oregon Women's Correction Center.
Jacques, Kenneth *o.s.b.* '67 (P) Gervais, OR Sacred Heart-St. Louis Church; [L] St. Benedict, OR Mt. Angel Abbey.
Jacques, Michael P. *s.s.e.* '82 (NO) [52] New Orleans, LA St. Peter Claver Church.
Jacques, Roger N. '78 (BO) [2] Waltham, MA St. Joseph Church.
Jacunski, Robert D. '56 (NEW) Caldwell, NJ St. Aloysius Church.
Jadaa, John '46 (NTN) Retired.
Jadin, Samuel D. *o.praem.* '55 (GB) [J] Manitowoc, WI Holy Family Convent of Franciscan Sisters of Christian Charity.
Jadwisiak, Edmund '79 (PRM) Retired.
Jae Ik Yoon, Bartholomeo (SFR) [33] San Francisco, CA St. Michael Korean Church.
Jaeb, Maurus P. *o.s.b.* '95 (OKL) Shawnee, OK St. Benedict Church; [I] Shawnee, OK St. Gregory's Abbey.
Jaeger, David '69 (SEA) Special Assignment.
Jaeger, James P. '86 (ROC) Hornell, NY St. Ann Church; Hornell, NY St. Ignatius Loyola Church.
Jaeger, Louis M. '73 (DUB) Haverhill, IA Immaculate Conception Church; Marshalltown, IA St. Henry's Church; [F] Marshalltown, IA Marshalltown Area Consolidated Catholic School.
Jaeger, Robert E. '90 (COS) Monument, CO St. Peter Church.
Jaekle, Lawrence E. '38 (CIN) Retired.
Jaenicke, Alfred J. (HRT) Retired.
Jagdfeld, Lawrence *o.f.m.* '75 (JOL) [J] Joliet, IL St. John the Baptist Friary.
Jagela, Walter M. '94 (WH) Cameron, WV St. Martin Church; Wellsburg, WV St. John The Evangelist Church.
Jagelfeld, Lawrence *o.f.m.* '75 (JOL) [11] Joliet, IL St. John the Baptist Church.
Jagielski, James '77 (DET) Military Chaplains.
Jagodensky, Joe *s.d.s.* '80 (MIL) [N] Milwaukee, WI Alexian Village of Milwaukee, Inc.
Jagodzinski, Charles *ofm conv.* '68 (BUF) [D] Athol Springs, NY St. Francis High School; [O] Athol Springs, NY St. Francis of Assisi Friary.
Jagodzinski, Msgr. John J. '62 (PH) Wayne, PA St. Katharine of Siena Church.
Jagoe, Bede *o.p.* '60 (FgM) Dominican - Order of Preachers Foreign Missions.
Jagoe, Bede R. *o.p.* '60 (CHI) [N] Chicago, IL Dominicans (Provincial Office); [N] River Forest, IL St. Thomas Aquinas Priory.
Jagosz, Mitchell '86 (ORG) Inactive Leave.
Jahner, Anton P. *s.j.* '67 (SPK) [K] Spokane, WA Regis Community.
Jakel, Pat G. '85 (SFD) Nokomis, IL St. Louis Church; Witt, IL St. Barbara Church.
Jakobiak, Arthur '56 (SFE) Santa Fe, NM St. Vincent's Hospital.
Jakopac, George I. (BAL) [42] Baltimore, MD Immaculate Heart of Mary Church.
Jakows, Ronald M. '90 (PH) [59] Philadelphia, PA Holy Cross Church; [D] Philadelphia, PA Roman Catholic High School for Boys.
Jaksina, Edward S. '55 (HRT) Seymour, CT Good Shepherd Church.
Jakubauskas, Richard A. '99 (WOR) [3] Leominster, MA St. Cecilia's Church.
Jakubco, Bernard *m.s.c.* '64 (OG) Evans Mills, NY St. Mary Church; Evans Mills, NY St. Mary Church; [F] Watertown, NY Missionaries of the Sacred Heart.
Jakubek, Eugene J. *s.j.* '54 (OM) [K] Omaha, NE Jesuit Community at Creighton University.
Jakubik, Richard '93 (CHI) Wilmette, IL St. Francis Xavier Church; [A] Chicago, IL Archbishop Quigley Preparatory Seminary.
Jakubowski, Allen F. '75 (LC) Abbotsford, WI St. Bernard Church; Owen, WI Holy Rosary Church.
Jakubowski, Joseph J. '40 (KC) Retired.
Jakubowski, Kenneth J. '91 (CLV) [5] Lakewood, OH St. Luke Church.
Jalbert, Marcel '38 (SB) Retired.
Jalbert, Robert A. *m.m.* '79 (FgM) Maryknoll Foreign Missions.
Jallas, Robert J. '84 (SFD) [1] Quincy, IL All Saints Church.
Jamail, Msgr. James A. '68 (GAL) [78] Houston, TX St. Vincent de Paul Church.
Jamail, Msgr. Michael '60 (BEA) [2] Beaumont, TX St. Anne Church.
James, David J. '91 (SY) Pompey, NY Immaculate Conception Church.
James, David L. '96 (ALN) [1] Allentown, PA Cathedral of St. Catharine of Siena.
James, Jamels (CHI) [95] Chicago, IL St. James Church.
James, John J. '82 (PH) [EE] Philadelphia, PA Newman Center at Drexel University.
James, Msgr. Joseph W. '57 (LUB) [C] Slaton, TX Our Lady of Mercy Retreat Center.
James, Melvin P. *s.v.d.* '75 (LA) [72] Los Angeles, CA St. John, The Evangelist Church; [Q] Los Angeles, CA Western Province (1964) Province of St. Therese of the Child Jesus.
James, Peter Paul *o.f.m.* '51 (CIN) [M] Cincinnati, OH St. Francis Seraph Friary.
James, Msgr. R. Joseph '61 (STA) [9] Jacksonville, FL Mary Queen of Heaven Church.
James, Thomas *s.v.d.* '69 (LAF) [4] New Iberia, LA St. Edward Church.
James, Thomas *s.v.d.* '96 (BLX) [E] Bay St. Louis, MS Southern Province of St. Augustine - Provincial Residence.
James, V. Warwick '80 (SJ) [4] Santa Clara, CA St. Lawrence the Martyr Church.
James, Msgr. William R. '54 (MOB) Robertsdale, AL St. Patrick Church.
Jameson, Msgr. W. Ronald '68 (WDC) [1] Washington, DC St. Matthew Church.
Jamieson, Andrew V. *o.f.m.cap* '88 (TR) Marlton, NJ St. Joan of Arc Church.
Jammes, Jean Marie '43 (LAF) St. Martinville, LA St. Martin of Tours Church; Retired.
Jammo, Sarhad '64 (EST) Troy, MI St. Joseph Chaldean Church.
Jamnicky, John A. '72 (CHI) Chicago, IL Chicago O'Hare International Airport; [X] Chicago, IL Catholic Chaplaincy at O'Hare.
Jamros, Daniel P. *s.j.* '76 (BO) [W] Boston, MA The Society of Jesus of New England-Provincial Offices.
Jamros, Daniel P. *s.j.* '76 (BUF) [O] Buffalo, NY Canisius Jesuit Community.
Jamroz, Sigmund S. *m.m.* '66 (FgM) Maryknoll Foreign Missions.
Jamroz, Waclaw *s.d.s.* '92 (CHI) [156] Chicago, IL Our Lady of the Snows Church.
Janacek, Msgr. Balthasar J. '50 (SAT) [1] San Antonio, TX Cathedral of San Fernando; San Antonio, TX Old Spanish Missions Church; [S] San Antonio, TX National Foundation for Mexican-American Vocations; [U] San Antonio, TX Pillars of San Fernando Cathedral.
Janaczek, Joseph J. '71 (BUF) [1] Dunkirk, NY St. Hedwig Church.
Janaites, Stanley (BAL) Poplar Springs, MD St. Michael Church.
Janaites, Stanley '55 (BAL) Sykesville, MD Springfield Hospital Center; Special Assignment.
Janak, Gary W. *j.c.l.* '88 (VIC) Yoakum, TX St. Joseph Church.
Janas, Camillus W. *o.f.m.* (GB) [1] Manitowoc, WI St. Boniface Church; [5] Manitowoc, WI St. Andrew Church.
Janasik, Basil *o.f.m.* '45 (MIL) [P] Burlington, WI Queen of Peace Friary.
Jancarz, Janusz '83 (VEN) Parrish, FL St. Frances Xavier Cabrini Church.
Jancius, John *m.i.c.* '34 (CHI) [N] Chicago, IL Congregation of Marian Fathers of the Immaculate Conception.
Janda, James A. '72 (SLC) [6] Sandy, UT Blessed Sacrament Church.
Jandaczek, Peter *m.s.* '99 (SPR) [1] Westfield, MA Holy Trinity Church.
Jandernoa, Ronald L. '94 (MET) Iselin, NJ St. Cecelia Church.
Janecek, James (CC) [J] Corpus Christi, TX Cursillo Movement Eastern Vicariate.
Janeck, Thomas More *o.f.m.cap.* '46 (DEN) [M] Denver, CO St. Francis of Assisi Friary; [N] Denver, CO Monastery of Our Lady of Light (Capuchin Poor Clares).
Janeczek, Vladimir '59 (GRY) [3] Hammond, IN St. Casimir Church.
Janelli, Msgr. Anthony '64 (FRS) Dinuba, CA St. Catherine Church.
Janes, David '75 (P) Yamhill, OR St. John Church.
Janes, David '83 (SFS) Bristol, SD St. Anthony Church; Groton, SD St. Elizabeth Ann Seton Church.
Janesko, Francis J. '46 (LR) Retired.
Janesko, John A. '52 (LR) Slovak, AR SS. Cyril and Methodius Church; Stuttgart, AR Holy Rosary Church; [L] Stuttgart, AR Holy Rosary Catholic School "Vision 2000" Educational Trust Fund.
Janette, Paul '63 (MIL) Retired.
Janezic, Larry *o.f.m.* '78 (CHI) [X] Chicago, IL Franciscan Outreach Association.
Janezic, Lawrence *o.f.m.* (CHI) [N] Chicago, IL St. Peter's Friary.
Jang, Theodore '88 (LA) [15] Los Angeles, CA Holy Trinity Church.
Janicki, Carl F. '94 (PH) Flourtown, PA St. Genevieve Church; Wyndmoor, PA Seven Dolors Church; [D] Philadelphia, PA Cardinal Dougherty High School.
Janicki, Joseph A. '64 (MIL) Thiensville, WI St. Cecilia Church.
Janicki, Laurian *o.f.m.* '64 (JOL) Wayne, IL Resurrection Church.
Janiga, Bruce G. '83 (NEW) [C] West Orange, NJ Seton Hall Preparatory School.
Janiga, Joseph '45 (DET) Retired.
Janik, Anthony F. *o.f.m.* '70 (GRY) [F] Crown Point, IN St. Anthony Medical Center of Crown Point; [J] Cedar Lake, IN Our Lady of Lourdes Friary.
Janik, Bruno '66 (CHI) Burbank, IL St. Albert the Great Church.
Janik, Leszek T. '92 (NOR) Occum, CT St. Joseph Church.
Janish, James '69 (SAT) Spring Branch, TX St. Joseph Church.
Janiszeski, Joseph J. *t.o.r.* '78 (PIT) [28] Pittsburgh, PA St. Matthew Church.
Janiunas, Albin F. '48 (BO) Senior Priests.
Jankaitis, Ronald V. (ALN) [I] Saint Clair, PA Neumann Apartments.
Jankaitis, Ronald V. '79 (ALN) [2] Saint Clair, PA St. Casimir Church; [C] Pottsville, PA Nativity B.V.M. High School; [C] Pottsville, PA Nativity B.V.M. High School.
Janko, Jack *s.d.b.* '78 (BO) [E] Boston, MA Savio Preparatory High School; [N] Boston, MA Salesian Boys & Girls Club.
Jankowiak, Patrick '92 (SAG) Gladwin, MI Sacred Heart Church.
Jankowski, Daniel C. '73 (CHI) [27] Chicago, IL St. Benedict the African (West) Church.
Jankowski, James *o.f.m.conv.* '99 (RCK) [2] Rockford, IL St. Anthony of Padua Church.
Jankowski, Marcellus A. '57 (KC) Special Assignment.
Jankowski, Peter '96 (JOL) [18] Joliet, IL St. Paul the Apostle Church.
Jankowski, Richard '92 (SP) Lecanto, FL St. Scholastica Church.
Jankowski, Valentine (LSC) Loving, NM Our Lady of Grace Church.
Jankowski, Valentine *o.f.m. conv.* '61 (LSC) Carlsbad, NM San Jose Church.
Jann, Francis J. '47 (BUF) Rushford, NY St. Mark Church; Retired.
Janning, Timothy J. '82 (CIN) Military Chaplains.
Janoch, Edward J. '00 (CLV) Lyndhurst, OH St. Clare Church.
Janocha, Carl W. '91 (OKL) Frederick, OK St. Helen Church.
Janoski, Steven A. '88 (SFD) Troy, IL St. Jerome Church.
Janovec, James J. '64 (GI) Sutherland, NE Sacred Heart Church.
Janowiak, Paul A. *s.j.* '84 (SEA) [A] Seattle, WA Seattle University.
Janowicz, Barney J. '57 (SAG) Retired.
Janowicz, Richard '80 (STN) Springfield, OR Nativity of the Mother of God Church.
Janowski, Lawrence *o.f.m.* '73 (CHI) [N] Chicago, IL Holy Name Friary.
Janowski, Rock '64 (LA) Simi Valley, CA St. Peter Claver Church.
Janowski, Stanley *o.f.m.* '66 (CHI) [O] Chicago, IL Mother of Good Counsel Provincialate.
Janowski, Wieslaw *c.r.* '93 (CHI) [86] Chicago, IL St. Hyacinth Church.
Jansch, Ronald *o.f.m.cap.* '50 (MIL) [P] Mount Calvary, WI St. Lawrence Friary.
Jansen, James H. '55 (BEL) Fairview Heights, IL Our Lady of the Assumption Church.
Jansen, Raymond L. '99 (LIN) Graduate Studies.
Jansen, William *m.c.c.j.* '66 (CIN) [7] Cincinnati, OH St. Ann Church; [M] Cincinnati, OH Comboni Missionaries (Verona Fathers)-Comboni Mission Center.
Janski, Jerome J. '50 (STP) Retired.
Janson, Christian *s.m.* '73 (SAT) [C] San Antonio, TX St. Mary's University of San Antonio, Texas; [M] San Antonio, TX Casa Maria Marianist Community; [M] San Antonio, TX Marianist Vocation Ministry.
Janson, Eugene '76 (SAT) [K] San Antonio, TX Padua Place.
Janson, Eugene '76 (VIC) Retired.
Janson, Leo F. '45 (GF) Retired.
Janssen, Henry *o.m.i.* '43 (BWN) [3] McAllen, TX Sacred Heart Church.
Janssen, James M. '48 (DAV) Retired; [M] Davenport, IA St. Vincent Center.
Janton, Anthony W. '77 (PH) [95] Philadelphia, PA St. Martin of Tours Church.
Janus, Mark D. *c.s.p.* '79 (COL) [J] Columbus, OH Campus Ministry.
Januszkiewicz, Henry '62 (WDC) Retired.
Janze, John E. '75 (ORG) Irvine, CA St. Thomas More Church.
Jaques, Domingos '47 (OAK) Retired.
Jaramillo, Bud A. *c.r.* '98 (PBL) Conejos, CO Our Lady of Guadalupe Church.
Jaramillo, Fabio E. '81 (NY) [89] New York, NY Our Lady of Lourdes Church.

Jaramillo, Jose E. *m.g.* '80 (STO) Lodi, CA St. Anne Church.
Jaramillo, Luis D. '60 (SFE) [11] Albuquerque, NM Our Lady of the Assumption Church.
Jaramillo, Luis M. '95 (HRT) Wallingford, CT Holy Trinity Church.
Jaramillo, Oscar '90 (B) Homedale, ID St. Hubert Church; Parma, ID Sacred Hearts of Jesus and Mary Church.
Jaramillo, Peter '81 (AMA) Absent on Leave.
Jaramillo, Roberto '93 (SAC) Roseville, CA St. Rose of Lima Church.
Jaranilla, Roberto, Jr. '96 (LA) Downey, CA St. Raymond Church.
Jarboe, J. Bruce '86 (BAL) Special Assignment.
Jarboe, W. Raymond '89 (BAK) Ontario, OR Blessed Sacrament Church.
Jarco, Emil *s.d.s.* '74 (NEW) [N] Verona, NJ The Salvatorian Fathers.
Jardiniano, Rolly P. '84 (LA) Artesia, CA Holy Family Church.
Jarecki, Michael S. '44 (OG) Retired.
Jarecki, Reynold *o.f.m.* '55 (MIL) [P] Burlington, WI Queen of Peace Friary.
Jarema, William *s.m.m.* '83 (COS) [3] Colorado Springs, CO Divine Redeemer Church; [I] Colorado Springs, CO Society of Missionaries of Mary.
Jarka, Thomas H. '59 (CAM) [6] Cherry Hill, NJ Queen of Heaven Church.
Jarmak, Claude *o.f.m.conv.* '54 (SPR) [A] Granby, MA St. Hyacinth College and Seminary.
Jarman, Glenn *c.p.m.* '98 (OWN) Russellville, KY Sacred Heart Church.
Jarmoluk, Msgr. Joseph F. '84 (RCK) Geneva, IL St. Peter Church.
Jarnot, Clement (NOR) [3] Middletown, CT St. Mary of Czestochowa Church.
Jarnot, Clement *o.f.m.conv.* '65 (BAL) [S] Ellicott City, MD Order of Friars Minor Conventual.
Jarnot, Clement *o.f.m.conv.* '65 (NOR) [3] Middletown, CT St. Mary of Czestochowa Church.
Jaros, Joseph P. '56 (TOL) Retired.
Jarosch, Eugene H. *s.a.c.* '51 (MIL) [P] Milwaukee, WI St. Vincent Community.
Jarosewic, Daniel '71 (CHI) [128] Chicago, IL St. Mary, Star of the Sea Church.
Jarosz, Joseph B. '62 (PH) [147] Philadelphia, PA St. Stanislaus Church.
Jarosz, Peter (JOL) Bloomingdale, IL St. Isidore Church.
Jarosz, Stanley '65 (MET) Helmetta, NJ Holy Trinity Church.
Jaroszeski, Paul A. '76 (STP) [17] St. Paul, MN St. Cecilia Church.
Jarrell, Stephen '73 (IND) Greenwood, IN SS. Francis and Clare of Assisi Church.
Jarret, Peter A. *c.s.c.* '92 (FTW) Granger, IN St. Pius X Church; [J] South Bend, IN Congregation of Holy Cross, Indiana Province, Provincial House.
Jarumbo, James J. '66 (MIL) [3] Sheboygan, WI St. Dominic Church.
Jarvais, Msgr. Walter G. '30 (NEW) Retired; [N] Rutherford, NJ St. John Vianney Residence for Priests.
Jarvis, Edward A. *s.j.* '54 (WH) [A] Wheeling, WV Wheeling Jesuit University.
Jarzombek, Casimir '60 (VIC) Bay City, TX Holy Cross Church.
Jarzombek, Dennis A. '79 (SAT) [52] San Antonio, TX St. Margaret Mary Church.
Jarzynski, Edward M. '48 (CHI) Retired.
Jasaitis, Raymond J. '62 (PAT) Retired; [P] Chester, NJ Nazareth Village.
Jasany, Robert J. '79 (CLV) [38] Cleveland, OH St. John Nepomucene Church; Solon, OH St. Rita Church.
Jasinski, Andrew M. '98 (FAR) [1] Fargo, ND St. Mary's Church; Argusville, ND St. William Church.
Jasinski, Msgr. Anthony J. '49 (BUF) [9] Cheektowaga, NY St. Philip the Apostle Church; Retired.
Jasinski, Paul F. *c.s.v.* '46 (JOL) Goodrich, IL Sacred Heart Church.
Jasinski, Raymond J. '54 (CHI) Retired.
Jaskot, Robert J. '98 (BAL) Frederick, MD St. John the Evangelist Church.
Jaskula, Edward J. *c.r.* '55 (CHI) [D] Chicago, IL Gordon Tech High School.
Jaskulski, Bronislaus *o.f.m.* '46 (GRY) [J] Cedar Lake, IN Our Lady of Lourdes Friary.
Jaskulski, George *o.f.m.* '55 (CLV) [O] Cleveland, OH St. Stanislaus Friary; [P] Cleveland, OH Marymount Congregational Home.
Jaskulski, Nathan *o.f.m.* '61 (GB) [10] Green Bay, WI St. Mary of the Angels Church; [I] Green Bay, WI St. Mary of the Angels Friary.
Jasper, Frank *o.f.m.* '73 (IND) [12] Indianapolis, IN Sacred Heart of Jesus Church.
Jasper, John R. (BAK) [1] Baker, OR Cathedral of St. Francis De Sales.
Jasper, Louis H. '51 (COV) Retired.
Jaspers, J. Dennis '66 (CIN) [3] Cincinnati, OH All Saints Church.
Jaspers, Louis *c.i.c.m.* '52 (SAT) [36] San Antonio, TX St. Gabriel Church.
Jasso, Stephen *t.o.r.* '65 (FWT) [2] Fort Worth, TX All Saints Church.
Jastrab, David J. '75 (PIT) Perrysville, PA St. Teresa of Avila Church.
Jastrzebski, Edmund '74 (CHI) [104] Chicago, IL St. John Cantius Church.
Jaszovsky, Joseph '31 (SFR) Retired; [K] San Francisco, CA Home for the Aged of the Little Sisters of the Poor.
Jatsiv, Miroslaw '94 (STF) Ansonia, CT SS. Peter and Paul Church.
Jaume, John *c.r.* '66 (NY) Plattekill, NY Our Lady of Fatima Church.
Jautz, Martin (MIL) [N] Wauwatosa, WI St. Camillus Health Center, Inc.
Jautz, Martin L. '44 (MIL) Retired.
Java, Miguel '73 (LA) Baldwin Park, CA St. John the Baptist Church.
Javier, Nazareno C. '98 (BRK) [167] Queens, NY St. Fidelis Church.
Javier, Senen *c.ss.r.* (NY) [23] New York, NY St. Cecilia Church.
Javor, Egon J. *o.s.b.* '41 (SFR) San Francisco, CA Knights of Malta; [N] Portola Valley, CA Woodside Priory.
Jawidzik, Edward M. '81 (TR) Belmar, NJ St. Rose Church.
Jaworowski, Msgr. Anthony E. '44 (PH) [2] Philadelphia, PA St. Adalbert Church; Swedesburg, PA Sacred Heart Church; Retired.
Jaworowski, Leon E. '43 (PH) Retired.
Jayachandra, Hermanagild '68 (DEN) [3] Boulder, CO St. Martin de Porres Church.
Jayasuriya, Jerome '61 (DAL) Waxahachie, TX St. Joseph Church.
Jazdzewski, Brian J. (LC) [C] Chippewa Falls, WI Chippewa Falls Area Catholic Schools.
Jazdzewski, Brian J. '99 (LC) Chippewa Falls, WI Notre Dame Church.
Jazmin, Romeo '85 (RIC) [4] Virginia Beach, VA Holy Spirit Church.
Jazmines, Vicente F. '79 (OG) Peru, NY St. Augustine Church.
Jazowski, Msgr. John F. '48 (BGP) Retired.
Jazwiecki, John *s.m.* '64 (SP) [7] Tampa, FL Our Lady of Perpetual Help Church.
Jazwiecki, John L. *s.m.* '64 (WDC) [M] Washington, DC Marist Center.
Je, Gabriel Byong-Young *s.j.* (ATL) [10] Atlanta, GA St. Jude Church.
Je, Gabriel Byong-Young *s.j.* '94 (ATL) [N] Doraville, GA Korean Martyrs Pastoral Center.
Jean, Agapit H., Jr. '95 (MAN) Portsmouth, NH St. James Church.
Jean, Antonio '99 (VEN) Port Charlotte, FL St. Charles Borromeo Church.
Jean, Franky '93 (MIA) [2] Fort Lauderdale, FL Divine Mercy Church.
Jean, Lesly '83 (MIA) [10] Miami, FL Notre Dame d'Haiti Church.
Jean, Raymond J. '57 (NOR) Absent on Leave.
Jean, Thony R. '00 (ATL) [1] Atlanta, GA Cathedral of Christ the King.
Jean-Paul, Souvenir *s.m.* '96 (PRT) Hamlin, ME St. Joseph Church; Van Buren, ME St. Bruno - St. Remi Church.
Jeanfreau, James J. '92 (NO) [3] Slidell, LA St. Luke the Evangelist Church.
Jeannot, Msgr. Leandre '70 (BO) [45] Boston, MA St. Matthew Church.
Jebadu, Alex *s.v.d.* (WH) War, WV Christ the King Church.
Jebadu, Alex *s.v.d.* '95 (WH) Welch, WV St. Peter Church.
Jecewiz, Jerome T. '75 (BRK) [60] Brooklyn, NY Holy Spirit Church.
Jedrychowski, Janusz '95 (STF) Elmira Heights, NY St. Nicholas Church.
Jedrzejewski, Richard '61 (BUF) [10] Buffalo, NY Assumption Church.
Jedrzejewski, Richard '74 (BUF) [22] Buffalo, NY St. Elizabeth of Hungary Church.
Jeffers, Brian E. '92 (ROC) Aurora, NY Good Shepherd Catholic Community Church; [M] Rochester, NY Diocesan Department of Campus Ministry.
Jeffers, Robert A. '54 (NY) [162] Bronx, NY St. Margaret Mary Church; Bronx, NY Bronx-Lebanon Hospital Center.
Jeffers, Msgr. Vincent W. '31 (NY) Retired; [DD] New York, NY Our Lady of Consolation Residence.
Jeffrey, Donald P. *m.s.* '64 (MAN) West Lebanon, NH Holy Redeemer Church.
Jeffrey, George A. '65 (SCR) [20] Wilkes-Barre, PA St. Therese's Church.
Jeffrey, James C. '59 (FAR) Retired.
Jeffries, Brian E. '73 (HRT) Seymour, CT St. Augustine's Church.
Jelenek, Matthew M. '96 (NY) Hopewell Junction, NY St. Columba Church.
Jelinek, Anthony J. (CHI) [N] Libertyville, IL Marytown, Our Lady of Fatima Friary.
Jendrek, Michael (BAL) Hagerstown, MD St. Ann Church.
Jendrysik, Mark '85 (JOL) Bolingbrook, IL St. Dominic Church.
Jendzura, John M. '47 (PIT) [Q] Bethel Park, PA Holy Ghost Animation Center.
Jenemann, Albert H. *s.j.* '60 (PH) [C] Philadelphia, PA St. Joseph's University; [AA] Philadelphia, PA Jesuit Community at St. Joseph's University.
Jenik, Msgr. John J. '70 (NY) [176] Bronx, NY Our Lady of Refuge Church.
Jenkins, Alan *s.v.d.* '73 (FgM) Society of the Divine Word Foreign Missions.
Jenkins, Floyd A. *s.j.* '48 (LA) [C] Los Angeles, CA Loyola Marymount University.
Jenkins, J. Michael '79 (SFD) Barry, IL Holy Redeemer Church; Pittsfield, IL Immaculate Conception Church.
Jenkins, John I. *c.s.c.* '83 (FTW) [B] Notre Dame, IN University of Notre Dame Du Lac; [J] Notre Dame, IN Holy Cross Community, Corby Hall, University of Notre Dame.
Jenkins, John M. '60 (CLV) [14] Akron, OH St. Paul Church.
Jenkins, Joseph A. '86 (WDC) Forestville, MD Church of the Holy Spirit.
Jenkins, Kenneth '80 (SB) Yucaipa, CA St. Frances Xavier Cabrini Church.
Jenkins, Ron E. '89 (SAT) [C] San Antonio, TX Oblate School of Theology.
Jenkins, Wayne '72 (L) [11] Louisville, KY St. Barnabas Church.
Jenkins, Wayne *s.c.j.* '77 (MIL) [P] Hales Corners, WI Sacred Heart Monastery.
Jenkinson, William R. '57 (PRO) Barrington, RI St. Luke Church.
Jenko, Aloysius '35 (NY) Retired.
Jenks, Francis C. '70 (CHI) [1] Oak Park, IL Ascension Church.
Jenne, Walter H. '70 (CLV) Brecksville, OH St. Basil the Great Church.
Jenner, James *o.p.* '51 (SEA) [22] Seattle, WA Blessed Sacrament Church.
Jennett, Michael '74 (LA) Ventura, CA Our Lady of the Assumption Church.
Jenniges, Leonard J. '48 (NU) Retired.
Jenniges, Leonard J. '48 (STP) Retired.
Jennings, Bernard J. '41 (LA) Altadena, CA St. Elizabeth of Hungary Church; Retired.
Jennings, Earl *t.o.r.* (BAL) [8] Baltimore, MD St. Ann Church.
Jennings, Earl *t.o.r.* '59 (BAL) [96] Baltimore, MD St. Wenceslaus Church.
Jennings, Francis *c.ss.r.* '48 (ORL) Retired; [F] New Smyrna Beach, FL St. Alphonsus Villa-Redemptorist Fathers and Brothers.
Jennings, Henry J. '62 (BO) [6] Somerville, MA St. Joseph Church.
Jennings, John A. '50 (SEA) Retired; [M] Seattle, WA St. Joseph's Residence.
Jennings, John J. '49 (BO) Senior Priests; [U] Boston, MA St. Joseph Nursing Care Center.
Jennings, John P. '41 (CIN) Retired.
Jennings, Msgr. Joseph '43 (MOB) Retired.
Jennings, Kenneth E. '93 (NEW) [3] Newark, NJ Blessed Sacrament/St. Charles Borromeo Church.
Jennings, Michael T. '69 (KNX) Rogersville, TN St. Henry Church.
Jennings, Mike '69 (KNX) Sneedville, TN St. James the Apostle Church.
Jennings, Oliver '72 (CHI) [101] Chicago, IL St. John de la Salle Church.
Jennings, Paul F., Jr. '74 (WIL) Chester, Kent Island, MD St. Christopher Church.
Jennings, Thomas J. '69 (WIN) [A] Winona, MN Immaculate Heart of Mary Seminary.
Jennings, Tommie '88 (SD) Military Chaplains.
Jennings, William E. '40 (WIL) Retired.
Jenniskens, Thomas J. *s.j.* '56 (LAF) [J] Grand Coteau, LA Jesuit Spirituality Center (St. Charles College).
Jennrich, Michael J. *o.f.m.* '87 (NO) [P] New Orleans, LA Franciscan Fraternity.
Jensen, Benjamin E. '88 (SC) Ruthven, IA Sacred Heart Church.
Jensen, Daniel P. *m.m.* '62 (SJ) [L] Los Altos, CA Maryknoll.
Jensen, John A. *m.m.* '44 (FgM) Maryknoll Foreign Missions.
Jensen, Joseph *o.s.b.* '54 (WDC) [C] Washington, DC Catholic University of America, The; [M] Washington, DC St. Anselm's Abbey; [V] Washington, DC Catholic Biblical Association.
Jensen, Larry '88 (SAM) Danbury, CT St. Anthony Church.
Jenson, Glen T. '95 (STP) Cleveland, MN Church of the Nativity of the Blessed Virgin Mary; Marysburg, MN Immaculate Conception Church.
Jeong, Cheon Bong Benedic (STA) [15] Jacksonville, FL St. Francis Choe Chapel Church.

Jerabeck, Joseph F. '48 (COL) Retired.
Jerek, John M. '88 (Y) Kent, OH Immaculate Heart of Mary Church; [O] Kent, OH Kent State University Newman Center.
Jerge, Joseph W. '51 (E) Retired.
Jerge, Lawrence A. *c.s.c.* '68 (FR) [A] North Easton, MA Holy Cross Fathers Religious.
Jernejcic, Timothy '92 (SB) Norco, CA St. Mel Church.
Jerome, Msgr. Albert '59 (BEL) Okawville, IL St. Barbara Church.
Jerome, Msgr. Harry J. '61 (BEL) Du Quoin, IL Sacred Heart of Jesus Church.
Jerome, Louis '88 (NY) Yorktown Heights, NY St. Patrick Church.
Jerome, Marc-Arthur (RVC) Central Islip, NY St. John of God Church.
Jerome, Patrick '91 (KCK) Shawnee, KS Sacred Heart Church.
Jerse, William M. '80 (CLV) [4] Euclid, OH St. Paul Church.
Jeruzal, Joseph *o.f.m.cap.* (GF) Lame Deer, MT Blessed Sacrament Church.
Jervis, Paul W. '83 (BRK) [225] Queens, NY St. Paul the Apostle Church.
Jeselnick, Stephen E. '77 (E) On Duty Outside Diocese.
Jesiolowski, Sylvester E. '41 (PEO) Retired.
Jesionowski, Richard A. '68 (BUF) [7] Cheektowaga, NY Our Lady Help of Christians Church.
Jeske, Richard M. *o.f.m.* '59 (SFD) Quincy, IL Illinois Veterans' Home; [B] Quincy, IL Quincy University.
Jesselli, Kenneth A. '84 (NY) Croton-on-Hudson, NY Holy Name of Mary Church.
Jesudas, Thaliyam Joseph *c.m.e.* '70 (SFS) Mitchell, SD Holy Family Church.
Jesudasan, V. A. '72 (STO) Modesto, CA St. Joseph Church.
Jesuraja, Paul *s.j.* '70 (WH) [A] Wheeling, WV Wheeling Jesuit University.
Jesus Diaz, Jaime de '55 (PMB) Fellsmere, FL Our Lady of Guadalupe Church; Sebastian, FL St. Sebastian Church.
Jesus Puertos Hernandez, Cristobal de '97 (TYL) Mount Pleasant, TX St. Michael Church.
Jette, Donald J. *s.s.s.* '53 (CLV) Highland Heights, OH St. Paschal Baylon Church; [O] Cleveland, OH Blessed Sacrament Community.
Jette, Mark R. '72 (HRT) [2] Meriden, CT St. Joseph Church; [4] Meriden, CT St. Mary Church.
Jeub, Richard H. '66 (STP) Special Assignment.
Jewison, Harry P. '54 (WIN) Retired.
Jewitt, Bernard C. '59 (TLS) [3] Tulsa, OK St. Bernard of Clairvaux Church.
Jezak, Thomas M. '66 (ALX) Brouillette, LA St. Genevieve Church.
Jezeski, Henry '51 (CLV) Retired.
Jezierski, Zbigniew J. '61 (CAM) Lindenwold, NJ St. Lawrence's Church.
Jezowski, Anthony C. '74 (BO) Health Leave.
Jicha, John '95 (BAL) Cockeysville, MD St. Joseph Church.
Jillisky, William F. '56 (ALB) Menands, NY St. Joan of Arc Church.
Jimenez, Adrian '87 (ARE) [1] Camuy, PR St. Joseph Church.
Jimenez, Alvaro (CGS) Yabucoa, PR Santos Angeles Cutodios Church.
Jimenez, Msgr. Armando '46 (WDC) Retired; [L] Washington, DC Cardinal O'Boyle Residence for Priests.
Jimenez, Carlos '67 (SJN) [25] San Juan, PR San Jorge Church.
Jimenez, David J. '95 (YAK) Cowiche, WA St. Peter's Church.
Jimenez, Edgar A. '84 (FRS) Planada, CA Sacred Heart Church.
Jimenez, Eduardo '82 (MIA) [6] Miami, FL Good Shepherd Church.
Jimenez, Emilio B. '99 (CC) Alice, TX St. Joseph Church.
Jimenez, Felix *sch.p.* '26 (NY) [DD] New York, NY Calasanzian Fathers (Piarists).
Jimenez, Felix *sch.p.* '70 (NY) [12] New York, NY Annunciation Church.
Jimenez, Francisco '65 (SJN) [2] Guaynabo, PR El Buen Pastor Church.
Jimenez, Francisco '88 (ARE) Vega-Alta, PR Perpetuo Socorro Church.
Jimenez, Fredy '93 (PRO) [26] Providence, RI Our Lady of Mt. Carmel Church.
Jimenez, Gabriel A. '78 (SJN) [56] San Juan, PR Santismo Sacramento Church.
Jimenez, Jorge '80 (NY) [110] New York, NY Sacred Heart of Jesus Church.
Jimenez, Jose (BRK) [210] Queens, NY Our Lady of Fatima Church.
Jimenez, Jose Luis '59 (ORG) [5] Santa Ana, CA Our Lady of the Pillar Church.
Jimenez, Jose Pio *c.m.* '68 (FgM) Vincentian Foreign Missions.
Jimenez, Rafael '74 (DET) [71] Detroit, MI St. Stephen-Mary Mother of the Church.
Jimenez-Londono, Fredy '93 (PRO) [5] West Warwick, RI St. Joseph Church.
Jiminez, Juan Bosco *s.d.b.* (CHI) [103] Chicago, IL St. John Bosco Church.
Jindra, Frank E. '84 (OM) Lynch, NE Assumption B.V.M. Church; Spencer, NE St. Mary Church.
Jiru, Richard A. '65 (MAD) Leave of Absence.
Joaquin, M. Joseph '81 (BGP) Georgetown, CT Sacred Heart Church.
Jobst, Frank *o.m.i.* '72 (FgM) Oblates Foreign Missions.
Jocco, Joseph P. *o.s.f.s.* '84 (WIL) [I] Childs, MD Oblates of St. Francis De Sales.
Jocelyn, Yves '62 (MIA) Miramar, FL St. Bartholomew Church.
Jocson, Salvador '57 (SFR) Retired.
Jocys, Leonard (GAY) Retired.
Jocys, Leonard '51 (GAY) Riggsville, MI Sacred Heart Church.
Joda, Robert J. *s.j.* '58 (MIL) [P] Milwaukee, WI Jesuit Community at Marquette University.
Joensen, William '89 (DUB) Graduate Studies.
Joensen, William '89 (WDC) [2] Bethesda, MD St. Jane Frances de Chantal Church.
Joerger, Jacob *o.p.* '48 (RCK) [M] St. Charles, IL Queen of Americas Guild.
Joerger, Jacob *o.p.* '48 (STP) [8] Minneapolis, MN Holy Rosary Church; [15] Minneapolis, MN St. Albert the Great Church.
Joerger, Robert *c.p.* '77 (NY) [DD] Bronx, NY Passionist Residence.
Joffe, William I. '57 (RCK) On Disability Leave.
Johanek, John '43 (GB) Retired.
Johannes, Nicholas A. '70 (GB) Maple Grove, WI St. Patrick Church.
John, Arun *i.m.s.* '92 (BR) [16] Baton Rouge, LA Our Lady of Mercy Church.
John, Francis Reginald '60 (NY) [129] Bronx, NY St. Anthony of Padua Church.
John, Reginald '60 (NY) City, NY Manhattan Detention Center.
John, Richard *o.s.c.* '46 (SCL) Milaca, MN St. Mary's Church.
John, Richard T. *o.s.c.* '41 (SCL) [I] Onamia, MN Crosier Monastery.
Johns, Thomas W. '78 (CLV) Mentor, OH St. John Vianney Church.
Johnson, Andrew *o.c.s.o.* '91 (WOR) [N] Spencer, MA St. Joseph's Abbey.
Johnson, Arte *s.a.* (NY) [HH] Barryville, NY New Hope Manor.
Johnson, Arthur D. *o.s.a.* '63 (NY) [216] Staten Island, NY Our Lady of Good Counsel Church.
Johnson, Arthur M *s.a.* '77 (NY) [DD] Garrison, NY Franciscan Friars of the Atonement, Minister General Office.
Johnson, Bede L. *c.j.* '39 (LA) [B] Santa Maria, CA St. Joseph Seminary (Josephite Fathers' Novitiate).
Johnson, Bernard M. *o.praem.* '81 (ORG) [I] Silverado, CA Norbertine Fathers of Orange Inc.
Johnson, Brian *c.ss.r.* '86 (SEA) [32] Seattle, WA Sacred Heart of Jesus Church.
Johnson, Brian '97 (OWN) Bowling Green, KY Holy Spirit Church.
Johnson, Carl '77 (LEX) Special Assignment.
Johnson, Carl D. '78 (NY) Monroe, NY Sacred Heart Church.
Johnson, Msgr. Charles B. '60 (HRT) [1] West Hartford, CT St. Brigid's Church; Special and other Archdiocesan Assignment.
Johnson, Christopher *o.p.* '60 (NY) [22] New York, NY St. Catherine of Siena Church; [DD] New York, NY St. Catherine of Siena Priory; [HH] New York, NY Dominican Shrine of St. Jude, Inc.
Johnson, Daniel '54 (ORG) [2] Huntington Beach, CA St. Mary's by the Sea Church.
Johnson, Daniel E. '51 (HRT) Wallingford, CT Resurrection Church.
Johnson, Dave '89 (OWN) Leitchfield, KY St. Joseph's Church; Sunfish, KY St. John the Evangelist Church.
Johnson, David *o.f.m.* (FRS) Bakersfield, CA Kern Medical Center, Bakersfield Memorial Hospital & San Joaquin Community Hospital.
Johnson, David *o.f.m.* '84 (SD) [H] Oceanside, CA Mission San Luis Rey.
Johnson, David W. *s.j.* '69 (WDC) [C] Washington, DC Catholic University of America, The; [M] Washington, DC The Jesuit Community at Georgetown University.
Johnson, Donald '55 (NY) Manhattan, NY Columbia Presbyterian Medical Center.
Johnson, Douglas '83 (SFS) On Leave of Absence.
Johnson, Earl *s.j.* '58 (NO) [P] New Orleans, LA Ignatius Residence.
Johnson, Edward A. '55 (PRO) Retired.
Johnson, Edward J. '58 (LA) [67] Los Angeles, CA St. Gregory Nazianzen Church.
Johnson, Msgr. Edwin '42 (DAL) Retired.
Johnson, Edwin *s.m.* '86 (LA) [F] Chatsworth, CA Chaminade College Preparatory.
Johnson, Francis P. '60 (HRT) [2] West Hartford, CT St. Helena Church.
Johnson, Gary *o.f.m.conv.* '00 (SPR) [10] Chicopee, MA St. Stanislaus Basilica Church.
Johnson, Msgr. Gregory '47 (BLX) Retired.
Johnson, H. Thomas '78 (DET) Shelby Twp., MI St. Kieran Church.
Johnson, Harold J. '49 (BO) Senior Priests.
Johnson, Henry J. '57 (LA) Retired.
Johnson, Howard '60 (JKS) On Duty Outside the Diocese.
Johnson, Howard '60 (WDC) [B] Washington, DC St. Joseph's Seminary.
Johnson, Howard J. '54 (MIL) Retired.
Johnson, J. Raymond '65 (NY) [DD] New York, NY Jesuit Community at Fordham University; [DD] New York, NY Jesuit Provincial's Office.
Johnson, Jacob *c.m.* '47 (FgM) Vincentian Foreign Missions.
Johnson, Msgr. James '42 (NEW) Retired.
Johnson, James *o.f.m.cap.* '68 (OAK) [N] Berkeley, CA Capuchin Franciscan Order, House of Studies.
Johnson, Msgr. James, (Retired) '42 (NEW) Ridgefield, NJ St. Matthew's Church.
Johnson, James B. '80 (SP) Inverness, FL Our Lady of Fatima Church; [S] St. Petersburg, FL Our Lady of Good Counsel Camp.
Johnson, James O., Jr. '00 (SEA) [2] Tacoma, WA St. Charles Borromeo Church.
Johnson, James R. *s.p.* '60 (Y) Hubbard, OH St. Patrick's Church.
Johnson, Jef *o.m.i.* '86 (WDC) [M] Washington, DC Oblate College/Center for Mission Studies Community.
Johnson, Jeff G. '92 (MAR) Brimley, MI St. Francis Xavier Church; Bay Mills, MI Blessed Kateri Tekakwitha Church.
Johnson, Jeffrey *s.o.l.t.* '91 (CC) [H] Robstown, TX Society of Our Lady of the Most Holy Trinity.
Johnson, Jerome A. '86 (MET) Iselin, NJ St. Cecelia Church.
Johnson, Msgr. John G. '74 (COL) [37] Columbus, OH St. Peter Church.
Johnson, John J. '48 (SPR) West Springfield, MA Immaculate Conception Church; [H] Springfield, MA Marriage Counseling Service.
Johnson, John J. '66 (STL) [40] St. Louis, MO St. John the Apostle and Evangelist Church.
Johnson, John R. '72 (SAG) Midland, MI Blessed Sacrament Church.
Johnson, Joseph R. '98 (STP) [31] Minneapolis, MN St. Olaf Church.
Johnson, Kevin '87 (PT) Fort Walton Beach, FL St. Mary Church.
Johnson, L. Bede *c.j.* '39 (LA) Santa Maria, CA St. Louis de Montfort Church.
Johnson, Lawrence C. *o.praem.* (ORG) [I] Silverado, CA Norbertine Fathers of Orange Inc.
Johnson, Lawrence C. *o.praem.* '94 (ORG) [D] Silverado, CA St. Michael's College Preparatory High School.
Johnson, Lawrence M. '83 (BAL) Special Assignment; [O] Timonium, MD Stella Maris.
Johnson, Lawrence P. '76 (DUL) On Duty Outside the Diocese.
Johnson, Lawrence R. '75 (STP) Chaska, MN Guardian Angels Church; Rogers, MN St. Martin Church.
Johnson, Lyle M. '76 (LIN) On Duty Outside the Diocese.
Johnson, Malcolm D. *c.s.c.* '59 (FgM) Holy Cross Foreign Missions.
Johnson, Malcolm D. *c.s.c.* '59 (FTW) [J] South Bend, IN Congregation of Holy Cross, Indiana Province, Provincial House.
Johnson, Maxwell E. '78 (FTW) [B] Notre Dame, IN University of Notre Dame Du Lac.
Johnson, O. Kenneth '92 (FgM) Provinces.
Johnson, O. Kenneth *s.j.* '92 (NO) [P] New Orleans, LA Jesuit Provincial Office.
Johnson, Oliver F. '62 (AUS) [12] Austin, TX St. Catherine of Siena Church.
Johnson, Patrick *c.s.p.* '74 (AUS) [11] Austin, TX St. Austin Church; Austin, TX State School.
Johnson, Paul *o.p.* '59 (SB) Redlands, CA Sacred Heart Church.
Johnson, Paul T. '63 (GR) Lakewood Club, MI St. Mary of the Woods Church.
Johnson, Peter '91 (CHY) Greybull, WY Sacred Heart Church; Lovell, WY St. Joseph's Church.
Johnson, Philip L. '64 (FWT) [7] Arlington, TX St. Vincent de Paul Church.
Johnson, Richard *c.p.* '51 (CHI) [N] Chicago, IL Passionist Provincial Office.
Johnson, Msgr. Richard E. '60 (DAL) [22] Dallas, TX St. Patrick Church.
Johnson, Richard G. '47 (BO) [3] Gloucester, MA St. Peter Church; Senior Priests.
Johnson, Msgr. Robert '51 (DAL) Retired.
Johnson, Robert *s.v.d.* '92 (FgM) Society of the Divine Word Foreign Missions.
Johnson, Robert E. '76 (STP) Bloomington, MN Nativity of the Blessed Virgin Mary Church.
Johnson, Robert K. '90 (WOR) [1] Worcester, MA St. Paul's Church.

Johnson, Stephen D. '72 (WOR) Athol, MA Our Lady Immaculate Church.
Johnson, Terrance M. '94 (CHI) [A] Mundelein, IL University of St. Mary of the Lake-Mundelein Seminary.
Johnson, Tim '91 (SC) [B] Granville, IA Spalding Catholic High School.
Johnson, Timothy *o.carm.* '83 (PMB) [5] Boca Raton, FL St. Jude Church.
Johnson, Timothy A. (SC) Sanborn, IA St. Cecilia's Church.
Johnson, Timothy K. '71 (OAK) [12] Oakland, CA St. Leo's Church.
Johnson, Msgr. W. Robert '60 (FWT) [H] Crowley, TX St. Francis Village, Inc.
Johnson, Walter W. '53 (SJ) [L] Los Altos, CA Maryknoll.
Johnson, William '83 (OAK) [4] Concord, CA Queen of All Saints Church; Concord, CA Mount Diablo Hospital, Pastoral Care; Martinez, CA Kaiser-Permanente Medical Center.
Johnson, William J. '50 (CLV) Newbury, OH St. Helen Church; Retired.
Johnson, William T. *s.j.* '91 (MIL) [G] Milwaukee, WI Nativity Jesuit Middle School, Inc.
Johnston, Donald '55 (NY) [95] New York, NY Our Lady Queen of Martyrs Church.
Johnston, German Bartolome Vasquez *o.s.b.* '93 (TUC) Sierra Vista, AZ St. Andrew Church.
Johnston, Henry P. '76 (STO) Angels Camp, CA St. Patrick Church.
Johnston, J. Vann, Jr. *j.c.l.* '90 (KNX) [5] Knoxville, TN Holy Ghost Church.
Johnston, Jeffrey W. '86 (RVC) Seaford, NY St. William, the Abbot Church.
Johnston, John F. '64 (BRK) Released from Diocesan Assignment.
Johnston, John F. '64 (NEW) [D] Summit, NJ The Oratory Catholic Preparatory School.
Johnston, Joseph A. *s.j.* '52 (FgM) Provinces.
Johnston, Kenneth J. '68 (CAM) Runnemede, NJ St. Teresa of the Infant Jesus Church.
Johnston, Michael O. '70 (NSH) [6] Nashville, TN St. Henry Church.
Johnston, Michael P. '91 (P) [38] Portland, OR St. Thomas More Church.
Johnston, Richard A. *s.c.j.* '58 (GAL) Wallis, TX Guardian Angel Church.
Johnston, Robert F. '62 (STL) Grantwood, MO Our Lady of Providence Church.
Johnston, Robert F. '71 (SAT) Retired.
Johnston, Thomas J. *o.p.* '86 (CHI) [N] Chicago, IL Dominicans (Provincial Office); [N] River Forest, IL St. Thomas Aquinas Priory.
Jolic, Roberto *o.f.m.* '94 (NY) [29] New York, NY SS. Cyril and Methodius - St. Raphael Church.
Jollet, Robert *m.s.c.* '49 (OG) Retired; [A] Ogdensburg, NY Wadhams Hall.
Jollett, Robert *m.s.c.* '49 (OG) [F] Watertown, NY Missionaries of the Sacred Heart.
Jolley, Msgr. Edward W. '38 (BRK) Retired; [V] Douglaston, NY Bishop Mugavero Residence.
Joly, Henry L. '58 (ALT) Retired.
Joly, Michael D. '94 (PAT) [1] Clifton, NJ Sacred Heart Church.
Jonaitis, Peter '44 (ALB) Retired.
Jonas, Lawrence A. *s.j.* '59 (SFS) Canton, SD St. Dominic Church.
Joncas, Jan Michael '69 (STP) [C] St. Paul, MN University of St. Thomas.
Jonczyk, Dariusz G. '97 (PRO) [3] Warren, RI St. Jean Baptiste Church; [4] Warren, RI St. Mary of the Bay Church.
Jones, Anthony '89 (OWN) Calhoun, KY St. Sebastian Church.
Jones, Augustine *o.s.b.* '53 (RCK) [G] Aurora, IL Marmion Abbey-St. Augustine's Abbey.
Jones, C. Gregory *c.s.v.* '96 (BEL) [I] Carbondale, IL The Newman Center.
Jones, Carleton Parker *o.p.* '87 (HRT) [14] New Haven, CT St. Mary's Priory Church; [M] New Haven, CT St. Mary Priory.
Jones, Charles '45 (DEN) Retired.
Jones, Charles F. '63 (KC) [4] Independence, MO St. Mary's Church.
Jones, Clarence *c.o.* '94 (SEA) [16] Seattle, WA St. Matthew Church.
Jones, Clarence Edward *c.o.* '94 (CHR) [E] Rock Hill, SC Oratory of St. Philip Neri, Congregation of the Oratory of Pontifical Rite.
Jones, Clarence Edward *c.o.* '94 (SEA) [P] Seattle, WA Oratorian Community.
Jones, Daniel J. '97 (DET) Graduate Studies.
Jones, David A. '89 (CHI) [10] Chicago, IL St. Ambrose Church; [A] Chicago, IL Archbishop Quigley Preparatory Seminary.
Jones, David J. *m.m.* '62 (NY) [DD] Maryknoll, NY Maryknoll Fathers and Brothers.
Jones, Dunstan *o.f.m.cap.* '61 (FgM) Capuchin Foreign Missions.
Jones, Frank W. '67 (GAL) Magnolia, TX St. Matthias the Apostle Church.
Jones, Herbert *o.f.m.* '77 (SAT) [70] San Antonio, TX San Jose y San Miguel Church; [B] San Antonio, TX Franciscan Formation Program in San Jose Friary (Casa Juan Diego).
Jones, Herbert J. *o.carm.* '60 (BO) [BB] Peabody, MA St. Theresa Carmelite Chapel.
Jones, J. Overton '64 (CAM) [1] Atlantic City, NJ Holy Spirit Church; [3] Atlantic City, NJ St. Monica's Church.
Jones, Jack B. '48 (GAL) [N] Houston, TX St. Dominic Village.
Jones, James *o.s.b.* '48 (KC) [A] Conception, MO Conception Seminary College.
Jones, Msgr. James '57 (R) Retired.
Jones, James *o.f.m.* '76 (SP) [O] St. Petersburg, FL St. Anthony Friary.
Jones, James *o.f.m.cap.* '77 (NY) [DD] White Plains, NY St. Conrad Friary.
Jones, Msgr. James R. '51 (R) New Bern, NC St. Paul Church.
Jones, James W. '69 (COL) [10] Columbus, OH Christ the King Church; Retired.
Jones, Jason T. '99 (OG) [1] Ogdensburg, NY St. Mary's Church; Ogdensburg, NY St. Lawrence Psychiatric Center.
Jones, Jim *o.f.m.* '76 (SP) [K] St. Petersburg, FL St. Anthony's Hospital, Inc.
Jones, Msgr. John B. '48 (GAL) Retired.
Jones, John E. '59 (L) Retired.
Jones, John L. '45 (ALB) [16] Albany, NY St. Teresa of Avila Church; Retired.
Jones, Joseph *c.p.* '65 (FgM) Passionist Foreign Missions.
Jones, Joseph *c.p.* '65 (MET) [H] South River, NJ Passionist Provincial Office.
Jones, Kenneth '69 (NEW) Plainfield, NJ St. Mary Church.
Jones, Mark R. '92 (MIL) Kewaskum, WI Holy Trinity Church.
Jones, Martin J.W. '94 (NOR) New London, CT St. Mary, Star of the Sea Church.
Jones, Michael K. '92 (BGP) Graduate Studies.
Jones, Michael T. '85 (WDC) [1] Silver Spring, MD St. Andrew Apostle Church; Special Ministries; [E] Wheaton, MD Good Counsel High School.
Jones, Neil G. *m.s.* '72 (ATL) Canton, GA Our Lady of LaSalette Church.
Jones, Patrick J. '56 (PIT) Retired.
Jones, R. Donald '86 (PIT) Elizabeth, PA St. Michael Church.
Jones, Raymond *s.v.d.* (LAF) [4] Opelousas, LA Holy Ghost Church; Port Barre, LA St. Mary Church.
Jones, Raymond '36 (DET) Retired.
Jones, Raymond *s.v.d.* '67 (LAF) On Special Assignment.
Jones, Msgr. Raymond N. (DEN) [17] Denver, CO Mother of God Church; [Q] Denver, CO Bishop Machebeuf High School, Inc.; [Q] Denver, CO Holy Family High School, Inc.
Jones, Richard S. '88 (PIT) Kennedy Township, PA St. Malachy Church.
Jones, Richard T. *s.j.* '46 (RC) St. Francis, SD Rosebud Reservation Church.
Jones, Rick L. '90 (SPC) Webb City, MO Sacred Heart Church.
Jones, Robert *s.v.d.* '68 (BO) [W] Duxbury, MA Society of the Divine Word.
Jones, Robert *s.j.* '70 (SEA) [L] Seattle, WA Jesuit Community.
Jones, Robert J. *c.m.* '69 (LA) [54] Los Angeles, CA St. Camillus De Lellis Church; Los Angeles, CA L.A. County/University of Southern California Hospital; [Q] Montebello, CA Vincentian Fathers & Brothers; [W] Montebello, CA DePaul Center.
Jones, Robert M. '68 (BO) [Y] Duxbury, MA Miramar Retreat Center.
Jones, Robert W. '92 (RCK) Stockton, IL Holy Cross Church.
Jones, Ronald A. '73 (RCK) [7] Aurora, IL St. Peter Church.
Jones, Thomas *o.f.m.* '59 (NY) Narrowsburg, NY St. Francis Xavier Church.
Jones, Thomas J. *c.s.c.* '72 (FTW) [6] South Bend, IN Christ the King Church.
Jones, Thomas W. *c.s.p.* '82 (NY) [DD] Jamaica Estates, NY Paulist Fathers Generalate.
Jones, Tom *c.s.p.* '82 (LA) [87] Los Angeles, CA St. Paul the Apostle Church.
Jones, Tony '89 (OWN) Brown's Valley, KY St. Anthony Church; Livermore, KY St. Charles Church.
Jones, Msgr. William E. (ALN) [I] Pottsville, PA Queen of Peace Apartments; [P] Orwigsburg, PA Seton Manor, Inc.
Jones, Msgr. William E. '60 (ALN) [4] Pottsville, PA St. Patrick Church.
Jones, Msgr. William H. '47 (DEN) Retired; [I] Denver, CO Little Sisters of the Poor Mullen Home for the Aged.
Jones, William P. '69 (ALN) Retired; [J] Bethlehem, PA Holy Family Villa.
Jones, William R. '67 (SY) [8] Syracuse, NY Our Lady of Solace Church.
Jonientz, Bernard '63 (SEA) Retired.
Jordan, Brian *o.f.m.* '85 (NY) [35] New York, NY St. Francis of Assisi Church.
Jordan, Collins P. '85 (RC) Retired.
Jordan, Daniel J. '99 (BUR) Morrisville, VT Holy Cross Church.
Jordan, Msgr. Edward '62 (AUS) [14] Austin, TX St. John Neumann Church.
Jordan, Francis G. '60 (DOD) Ingalls, KS St. Stanislaus Church.
Jordan, Francis W. '50 (MIL) Retired.
Jordan, Msgr. Harold F. '49 (STA) [1] St. Augustine, FL Cathedral of St. Augustine; [2] St. Augustine, FL Mission of Nombre de Dios and Shrine of Our Lady of La Leche Church.
Jordan, Msgr. Harry J. '61 (CAM) Gloucester, NJ St. Mary's Church.
Jordan, Jesus *m.ss.c.* '94 (SJN) [25] Bayamon, PR Santiago Apostol Church.
Jordan, Msgr. John J. '69 (SCR) On Duty Outside the Diocese.
Jordan, John M. '83 (PIT) Allegheny County, PA West Penn Allegheny Health System-West Penn Hospital.
Jordan, Joseph A. *o.s.a.* '58 (PH) [AA] Villanova, PA St. Thomas Monastery.
Jordan, Maryon *o.s.b.* (LC) [H] La Crosse, WI Holy Cross (Seminary) Diocesan Center.
Jordan, Maryon *o.s.b.* '79 (CC) [H] Sandia, TX Corpus Christi Abbey.
Jordan, Michael *s.o.l.t.* '83 (CC) [H] Robstown, TX Society of Our Lady of the Most Holy Trinity.
Jordan, Milton '72 (PH) [134] Philadelphia, PA St. Patrick Church.
Jordan, Milton '72 (WDC) On Duty Outside the Archdiocese.
Jordan, Phelim *s.v.d.* '81 (WDC) Washington, DC Providence Hospital; [K] Washington, DC Providence Hospital; [M] Washington, DC Divine Word College.
Jordan, Regis *o.c.d.* '64 (WH) [M] Hinton, WV Monastery of Christ on the Mountain.
Jordan, Salvador *s.j.* (WDC) Chapel Point, MD St. Ignatius Church.
Jordan, Thomas *o.carm.* '70 (FgM) Carmelite Foreign Missions.
Jordan, Thomas *o.carm.* '70 (JOL) [J] Darien, IL Carmelite Provincial Office.
Jorden, James A. '83 (PT) Retired.
Jorgenson, James '69 (DET) [A] Detroit, MI Sacred Heart Major Seminary, Inc.
Joseph, Augustine *s.d.b.* (OAK) Danville, CA St. Isidore's Church.
Joseph, Benedict *o.p.* '49 (COL) [I] Columbus, OH St. Mary of the Springs.
Joseph, Dominic '93 (SJ) [5] San Jose, CA St. Frances Cabrini Church.
Joseph, Eappen '77 (LKC) Raymond, LA St. Lawrence Church.
Joseph, George '94 (NEW) Belleville, NJ Clara Maass Hospital.
Joseph, George, Jr. '99 (AUS) [26] Austin, TX San Jose Church.
Joseph, Jacob *c.m.i.* '83 (NY) Irvington-on-the-Hudson, NY Immaculate Conception Church.
Joseph, John K. *c.m.i.* '77 (TOL) Leipsic, OH St. Mary Church.
Joseph, Msgr. Joseph D. '47 (BUF) Retired.
Joseph, Msgr. Joseph D. '47 (SAM) Retired.
Joseph, Louis '55 (CC) Retired.
Joseph, Msgr. Milam '64 (DAL) [B] Irving, TX University of Dallas.
Joseph, Msgr. Milam '64 (TYL) Special Assignment.
Joseph, Moussa '83 (SAM) On Duty Outside the Diocese.
Joseph, Rayappan Arul '87 (NY) Mahopac, NY St. John the Evangelist Church.
Joseph, Simon (BRK) [131] Brooklyn, NY Sacred Hearts of Jesus and Mary and St. Stephen Church.
Joseph, Varkey V. *s.a.c.* '79 (LC) Elmwood, WI Sacred Heart Church.
Joseph, Vincent E. (WH) Williamson, WV Sacred Heart Church.
Joseph, William '62 (PT) Retired.
Joseph, William T. '66 (PH) Retired.
Joslin, James R. '74 (ALB) [9] Schenectady, NY St. John the Evangelist Church; Albany, NY Capital District Psychiatric Center; Special Assignment.
Joslyn, James W. '73 (CHI) Military Chaplains.
Josoma, Stephen S. '81 (BO) [13] Boston, MA St. Brendan Church.
Josson, Marcel *c.i.c.m.* '36 (FgM) Missionhurst Foreign Missions.
Jost, Al *o.f.m.* (IND) [31] Indianapolis, IN St. Patrick Church.
Jost, Al *o.f.m* '80 (IND) [12] Indianapolis, IN Sacred Heart of Jesus Church.
Jost, C. Thomas '68 (DEN) [31] Denver, CO St. Ignatius Loyola Church; [M] Denver, CO Loyola Parish - Jesuit Community.
Jost, Edward F., Jr. '96 (BUF) [1] Lackawanna, NY

Basilica of Our Lady of Victory.
Josten, Paul '87 (SFS) Platte, SD St. Peter the Apostle Church.
Jovanovic, Msgr. Robert P. '61 (STL) Oakville, MO Queen of All Saints Church.
Jowdy, Albert W. '84 (ATL) Alpharetta, GA St. Thomas Aquinas Church.
Joy, Msgr. James B. '61 (WDC) Retired.
Joy, Laurence '60 (LA) On Duty Outside the Archdiocese.
Joy, William '72 (BO) [6] Boston, MA St. Angela Church.
Joyal, Rene J. '52 (BO) Senior Priests.
Joyce, Brian T. '63 (OAK) Pleasant Hill, CA Christ the King Church.
Joyce, David J. '68 (SPR) [8] Springfield, MA Our Lady of Hope Church.
Joyce, Donald J. *o.m.i.* '58 (SAT) [C] San Antonio, TX Oblate School of Theology; [M] San Antonio, TX De Mazenod House.
Joyce, Edmund P. *c.s.c.* '49 (FTW) [B] Notre Dame, IN University of Notre Dame Du Lac; [J] Notre Dame, IN Holy Cross Community, Corby Hall, University of Notre Dame.
Joyce, Edward *c.pp.s.* '56 (CIN) [M] Dayton, OH Provincial Office of the Cincinnati Province of the Society of the Precious Blood.
Joyce, Edwin '58 (JOL) Absent on Sick Leave.
Joyce, Fabian *o.f.m.* (PAT) [M] Ringwood, NJ Holy Name Friary, Inc.
Joyce, George V. '43 (SPR) [8] Springfield, MA Our Lady of Hope Church.
Joyce, George V. '43 (WDC) Retired.
Joyce, Gerald P. '61 (CHI) Westchester, IL Divine Infant Church.
Joyce, Jack *o.m.i.* '61 (FgM) Oblates Foreign Missions.
Joyce, James '48 (SFS) Retired.
Joyce, James F. *s.j.* '75 (BUF) [7] Buffalo, NY St. Ann Church.
Joyce, James K. '72 (SPR) [4] Pittsfield, MA Sacred Heart Church.
Joyce, John J. '89 (BEL) Evansville, IL St. Boniface Church; Walsh, IL St. Pius Church.
Joyce, John M. '54 (ORG) [3] Orange, CA St. Norbert Church.
Joyce, Joseph *o.carm.* '71 (SAC) Fairfield, CA Our Lady of Mount Carmel, Church.
Joyce, Kevin '80 (SJ) [15] San Jose, CA St. Maria Goretti Church.
Joyce, Michael '63 (OAK) Retired.
Joyce, Michael *o.f.m.* '66 (BO) [BB] Boston, MA St. Anthony Shrine.
Joyce, Michael *o.f.m.cap.* '84 (CLV) [O] Cleveland, OH St. Paul Friary.
Joyce, Michael *o.f.m.cap.* '85 (CLV) [18] Cleveland, OH Conversion of St. Paul Church.
Joyce, Michael P. *c.m.* '76 (STL) [34] St. Louis, MO St. Francis de Sales Church; [P] St. Louis, MO Vincentian Community; [V] St. Louis, MO Hispanic Ministry of the Archdiocese of St. Louis.
Joyce, Peter '83 (WOR) [4] Southbridge, MA St. Mary's Church.
Joyce, Randal *c.p.* '50 (DET) [K] Detroit, MI St. Paul of the Cross Community, Congregation of the Passion.
Joyce, Stephen G. '78 (STL) Normandy, MO Ascension-St. Paul Church.
Joyce, Thomas *c.m.f.* '59 (CHI) [78] Chicago, IL Holy Cross/Immaculate Heart of Mary Church.
Joyce, Thomas *c.p.* '69 (BRK) [180] Queens, NY Immaculate Conception Church; [V] Jamaica, NY Immaculate Conception Monastery.
Joyce, Thomas J. '91 (NY) [2] White Plains, NY St. John the Evangelist Church.
Joyce, Timothy J. '59 (BO) [W] Hingham, MA Glastonbury Abbey.
Joyce, William F. '60 (BO) [9] Boston, MA St. Anne Church.
Joynes, Msgr. Joseph P. '64 (CAM) Brigantine, NJ St. Thomas Church.
Jozefiak, Gregory '92 (PEO) Oglesby, IL Holy Family Church.
Jozefiak, Matthew *c.pp.s.* '87 (CIN) St. Wendelin, OH St. Wendelin Church; Sharpsburg, OH St. Paul Church.
Jozefiak, Matthew W. *c.pp.s.* '87 (CIN) Burkettsville, OH St. Bernard Church.
Jozwiak, Lawrence '87 (GAL) On Special or Other Diocesan Assignment.
Jozwiak, Richard E. '59 (SAG) Carrollton, MI St. Josaphat Church.
Jozwiak, Richard M. '48 (CHI) [3] Lemont, IL SS. Cyril and Methodius Church; Retired.
Jozwiak, Ronald J. '79 (DET) [39] Detroit, MI St. Josaphat Church; Special Assignment.
Jozwiak, Stanislaus J. '45 (PIT) Retired.
Juan, Dennis Ramesh '98 (ATL) [1] Marietta, GA Holy Family Church.
Juan, Francisco *s.d.b.* '63 (ARE) Orocovis, PR San Juan Bautista Church.
Juan, Marcial '66 (LA) Panorama City, CA St. Genevieve Church.
Juan, Saturnino *o.s.a.* '64 (SJN) [15] Bayamon, PR Ntra. Sra. de la Monserrate Church.
Juango, Jose Maria *o.a.r.* '61 (NEW) [1] Union City, NJ Holy Family Church.
Juantorena, Rafael '96 (BR) [16] Baton Rouge, LA Our Lady of Mercy Church.
Juarez, Alejandro *o.f.m.* '88 (ELP) [B] El Paso, TX St. Anthony's School of Theology.
Juarez, Jaime Molina *m.n.m.* '88 (ATL) Smyrna, GA St. Thomas the Apostle Church.
Juarez, Jose Roberto (Beto) (AUS) [O] Austin, TX Texas Catholic Historical Society.
Juarez, Rene *o.f.m.* '69 (SJ) [18] San Jose, CA Our Lady of Guadalupe Church.
Juarez, Robert '80 (LA) [25] Los Angeles, CA Our Lady of Guadalupe Church.
Juarez, Rudolph T. '80 (DAV) [7] Davenport, IA St. Mary's Church.
Juarez, Thomas L. *s.d.b.* '66 (SFR) [13] San Francisco, CA Corpus Christi Church.
Juchcinski, Clarence J. '48 (CHI) Harvey, IL St. John the Baptist Church; Retired.
Juchniewicz, Leon (SAC) [L] Marysville, CA Grand Council, Catholic Ladies Relief Society of the Diocese of Sacramento.
Juchniewicz, Leon '80 (SAC) Marysville, CA St. Joseph Church.
Juchnowski, Msgr. Francis B. '56 (BUF) [13] Buffalo, NY St. Bernard Church.
Juda, Stephen *c.r.* '42 (CHI) [D] Chicago, IL Gordon Tech High School.
Judd, P. Augustine *o.p.* '96 (PRO) [P] Providence, RI St. Thomas Aquinas Priory at Providence College; [P] Providence, RI St. Thomas Aquinas Priory at Providence College.
Judd, Stephen P. *m.m.* '78 (FgM) Maryknoll Foreign Missions.
Judd, Timothy '56 (LUB) Retired.
Judd, Timothy E. '56 (LUB) Petersburg, TX Sacred Heart Church.
Jude, Anthony *c.ss.r.* '79 (OAK) [N] Oakland, CA Redemptorists.
Jude, Robert J. '49 (STP) Retired.
Jude, Msgr. Walter F. '45 (GR) Retired.
Judge, James G. '72 (BUF) North Collins, NY Holy Spirit Church.
Judge, John G. '69 (NEW) Upper Montclair, NJ St. Cassian Church.
Judge, Michael *o.f.m.* '61 (NY) [35] New York, NY St. Francis of Assisi Church.
Judge, Philip G. *s.j.* '93 (ROC) [C] Rochester, NY McQuaid Jesuit High School.
Judge, Robert *s.j.* '65 (RIC) Radford, VA St. Jude Church.
Judge, Russell R. '78 (JC) Macon, MO Immaculate Conception Church.
Judge, Timothy M. '79 (PH) [U] Meadowbrook, PA Holy Redeemer Hospital and Medical Center; [BB] Huntingdon Valley, PA Sisters of the Holy Redeemer Provincialate.
Judie, John T. '87 (L) [57] Louisville, KY Mother of Good Counsel Church.
Judy, Albert G. *o.p.* '62 (CHI) [N] River Forest, IL St. Thomas Aquinas Priory.
Judy, Albert P. *o.p.* '62 (CHI) [173] Chicago, IL St. Priscilla Church.
Judy, Edward *o.f.m.cap.* '68 (DEN) [3] Denver, CO Annunciation Church; [M] Denver, CO Annunciation Friary.
Judy, Myron *o.carm.* '63 (JOL) [J] Darien, IL Carmelite Provincial Office.
Juelfs, Daniel '73 (RC) New Underwood, SD St. John the Evangelist Church.
Juenker, Msgr. Paul R. '45 (BUF) Retired; [O] Tonawanda, NY O'Hara Residence.
Juergens, William H. *o.s.f.s.* '57 (WIL) [I] Wilmington, DE DeSales House.
Juettner, Mark R. '79 (STP) Crystal, MN St. Raphael Church.
Jugan, Joseph '58 (PBR) Canonsburg, PA St. Michael Church.
Jugenheimer, James R. '87 (PH) Ambler, PA St. Joseph Church; [D] Wyncote, PA Bishop McDevitt High School.
Juhas, John S. '75 (CLV) Brooklyn, OH St. Thomas More Church.
Juhasz, Ladislaus F. *s.j.* '54 (BUF) [O] Buffalo, NY Canisius Jesuit Community.
Juhl, Dennis D. '73 (DUB) [6] Waterloo, IA Blessed Sacrament Church.
Juknialis, Joseph J. '69 (MIL) [69] Milwaukee, WI SS. Peter and Paul Church; [A] St. Francis, WI Saint Francis Seminary; [A] St. Francis, WI Saint Francis Seminary.
Juleen, Stuart '77 (SAT) [42] San Antonio, TX St. John, The Evangelist Church.
Julian, Arent *o.f.m.* '48 (GB) [I] Pulaski, WI Assumption of B.V.M. Friary.
Julian, Mario F. *o.f.m.* '81 (HRT) New Milford, CT St. Francis Xavier's Church.
Julien, Jean Ridly '96 (BGP) [X] Stamford, CT Haitian American Catholic Center of Greater Stamford.
Julien, Roland M. (STA) [K] Gainesville, FL Spirit Radio of North Florida, Inc.
Julien, Roland M. '65 (STA) [1] Gainesville, FL St. Patrick's Church.
Julius, James '65 (BLX) Gulfport, MS U.S. Naval Home.
Julius, James A. '65 (STL) Retired.
Julius, Joseph W. '45 (KNX) Alcoa, TN Our Lady of Fatima Church; Townsend, TN St. Francis of Assisi Church.
Julius, Joseph W. '45 (NSH) Retired.
Jung, Dennet *o.f.m.* '63 (CIN) [62] Cincinnati, OH St. Monica-St. George Parish Newman Center Church; [M] Cincinnati, OH St. Ann Friary; [Q] Cincinnati, OH University of Cincinnati Newman Center.
Jung, Dominic *c.pp.s.* (ROC) [4] Rochester, NY St. Anne Church.
Jung, Dominic *c.pp.s.* '95 (BUF) [2] Tonawanda, NY St. Andrew Kim Church.
Jung, Eugene *m.s.c.* '50 (ALN) [K] Reading, PA Missionaries of the Sacred Heart.
Jung, Jay *c.m.* '77 (COS) Limon, CO Our Lady of Victory(1925) Church.
Jung, Jerome '93 (PEO) [Q] Urbana, IL Opus Dei.
Jung, Joseph B. '56 (PH) Retired.
Jung, Michael *o.s.b.* '63 (BR) [20] Baton Rouge, LA Sacred Heart of Jesus Church; Baton Rouge, LA Baton Rouge General Medical Center.
Jung, Michael *o.s.b.* '63 (NO) [P] St. Benedict, LA St. Joseph Abbey.
Jung, Pius-Bio '89 (ALB) [11] Albany, NY St. Mary Church; Special Assignment.
Jung, Tae Woo '95 (PIT) [60] Pittsburgh, PA St. Pamphilus Church.
Junge, Heiko '96 (P) St. Helens, OR St. Frederic Church; Vernonia, OR St. Mary Church.
Jungwirth, Alphonse *c.pp.s.* '43 (CIN) [B] Carthagena, OH St. Charles.
Juniet, Paul *o.f.m.* '66 (SFE) [14] Albuquerque, NM Queen of Angels Native American Center and Archdiocesan Shrine to Kateri Tekakwitha Church.
Junio, Joven *m.s.* '86 (HON) Waipahu, HI St. Joseph Church.
Junius, Richard *o.m.i.* '56 (FgM) Oblates Foreign Missions.
Junod, Louis J. '65 (KNX) Retired; [D] Signal Mountain, TN Alexian Village of Tennessee.
Jupin, Alan D. '62 (ALB) [14] Schenectady, NY Our Lady of Fatima Church.
Juracek, Joseph *o.f.m.* '83 (NY) [35] New York, NY St. Francis of Assisi Church.
Juran, Michael P. '76 (BUF) Belfast, NY St. Patrick Church; Fillmore, NY St. Patrick Church.
Juras, Callistus *o.f.m.conv.* '54 (BAL) [S] Baltimore, MD Immaculate Heart of Mary Friary.
Jurasko, Joseph J. *o.p.* '40 (WDC) [11] Washington, DC St. Dominic Church & Priory Church.
Jurcak, Lawrence '81 (CLV) [1] Cleveland, OH Cathedral of St. John the Evangelist.
Jurcik, Peter '93 (ALN) [2] Allentown, PA St. Francis of Assisi Church; On Duty Outside the Diocese.
Jurek, Daniel J. '73 (BEL) Mount Vernon, IL St. Mary Church.
Jurewicz, Francis Z. '59 (PIT) Richeyville, PA St. Agnes Church.
Jurgelonis, Joseph J. '73 (WOR) Ashburnham, MA St. Denis Church; South Ashburnham, MA St. Anne Church.
Jurgensen, John W. '51 (BRK) [155] Queens, NY St. Benedict Joseph Labre Church; Retired.
Jurgensmeier, Charles L. *s.j.* '88 (OM) Papillion, NE St. Columbkille Church; [K] Omaha, NE Jesuit Community at Creighton University.
Juric, Jakov '00 (GLP) Winslow, AZ St. Joseph's Church.
Jurich, James P. *s.j.* '67 (NY) [DD] New York, NY Murray-Weigel Hall.
Jurisich, Melvin A. *o.f.m.* '70 (OAK) [N] Oakland, CA Franciscan Friars Provincial Office, Province of St. Barbara; [N] Oakland, CA Franciscan Friars Provincial Office, Province of St. Barbara.
Jurkiewicz, Benedict '83 (STA) [J] Bunnell, FL Discalced Carmelite Fathers of Florida.
Jurkowski, Joseph V. '58 (CAM) [4] Atlantic City, NJ St. Nicholas of Tolentine Church.
Jurkus, Alan F. '70 (MIL) Whitefish Bay, WI St. Monica Church.
Jurus, Stanislaw *s.j.* '36 (CHI) [N] Chicago, IL Sacred Heart Mission House.
Jussaume, Andre P. '52 (FR) Retired.
Jussaume, Lucien '41 (FR) Retired.
Jusseaume, John E. '46 (BO) Senior Priests.
Jusseaume, John J. '46 (BO) Newburyport, MA Immaculate Conception Church.
Just, Felix *s.j.* '91 (LA) [C] Los Angeles, CA Loyola Marymount University.
Justavino, Teodoro *c.m.* '90 (FgM) Vincentian Foreign Missions.
Justen, Bernard *s.d.b.* '48 (SP) [E] Tampa, FL Mary Help of Christians School.

Justi, Marvin *o.f.m.cap.* '58 (BAL) Cresaptown, MD St. Ambrose Church; [S] Cumberland, MD SS. Peter and Paul Friary.
Justice, Joseph '75 (ORG) Anaheim, CA St. Boniface Church.
Justice, William J. '68 (SFR) [1] South San Francisco, CA All Souls Church.
Juszczak, Walter *c.ss.r.* '88 (CHI) [56] Chicago, IL St. Ferdinand Church.
Jutt, Anthony J. '51 (SPR) Housatonic, MA Corpus Christi Church; Housatonic, MA All Saints Church.
Jutt, Julius A. '51 (SPR) South Deerfield, MA St. James Church.
Jutton, David J. '66 (SY) Cicero, NY Sacred Heart Church.
Juya, Filemon '81 (CHR) Special Assignment.
Juza, Philip J. '95 (SUP) Gilman, WI SS. Peter and Paul Church; Jump River, WI St. Michael Church; Lublin, WI St. Stanislaus Church; Sheldon, WI St. John the Apostle Church.
Juzix, Richard '75 (FRS) [F] Three Rivers, CA St. Anthony's Retreat House.

K

Kabat, Daniel *o.f.m.cap.* '60 (LA) Solvang, CA Old Mission Santa Ines Church.
Kabat, Robert J. (GB) Wrightstown, WI St. Paul Church.
Kabat, Robert J. '79 (GB) Greenleaf, WI St. Mary Church.
Kaberia, Joseph (STL) [57] St. Louis, MO St. Pius the Fifth Church.
Kabura, Paschal '87 (E) [19] Erie, PA St. John the Baptist Church.
Kacarzak, Stan '85 (ROC) [L] Rochester, NY Catholic Charismatic Renewal.
Kacena, T. Edward '97 (LFT) Fishers, IN Holy Spirit Church.
Kacerguis, Edward '71 (ALB) Special Assignment; [R] Troy, NY Rensselaer Polytechnic Institute.
Kachel, C. Leon '57 (PRO) [K] Providence, RI St. Joseph Health Services of Rhode Island - St. Joseph Hospital for Specialty Care.
Kachel, Steven J. '95 (LC) Viroqua, WI Annunciation of the Blessed Virgin Mary Church.
Kachmar, Msgr. Walter '43 (SJP) Retired.
Kachuba, John S. '74 (PRM) Euclid, OH St. Stephen Church.
Kachurka, Edward M. '89 (BRK) [79] Brooklyn, NY St. Mark's Church.
Kacirk, Raymond J. *s.m.* '59 (CIN) [M] Dayton, OH Marianist Provincialate.
Kacprowicz, Joseph A. '36 (E) Retired.
Kacprzak, Stanley G. '85 (ROC) [35] Rochester, NY Our Lady of Mercy Church.
Kaczkowski, Conrad J. *s.m.* '68 (SAT) [C] San Antonio, TX St. Mary's University of San Antonio, Texas; [M] San Antonio, TX Chaminade Community House.
Kaczmarek, Msgr. James A. '69 (MAR) Iron Mountain, MI Immaculate Conception of the Blessed Virgin Mary Church.
Kaczmarek, Peter '69 (RVC) Bayville, NY St. Gertrude's Church.
Kaczmarek, Thaddeus J. '71 (GBG) North Huntingdon, PA St. Agnes Church.
Kaczorek, Placid *o.f.m.conv.* '64 (FgM) Conventual Franciscan Foreign Missions.
Kaczorek, Placid *o.f.m.conv.* '64 (SPR) [10] Chicopee, MA St. Stanislaus Basilica Church.
Kaczorek, Placido *o.f.m.conv.* '64 (FgM) Conventual Franciscan Foreign Missions.
Kaczorowski, Edward J. '58 (WIL) [12] Wilmington, DE St. Stanislaus Kostka Church.
Kaczorowski, James T. '73 (CHI) [149] Chicago, IL Our Lady of Lourdes Church.
Kaczynski, Krzysztof '93 (NY) [99] New York, NY Our Lady of Victory Church.
Kadera, Thomas '87 (CHY) Gillette, WY St. Matthew's Church.
Kadlec, Jared C. '97 (FAR) Rolla, ND St. Joachim's Church.
Kadlec, Josef *s.j.* '77 (WDC) [M] Washington, DC The Jesuit Community at Georgetown University.
Kadrmas, Christopher J. '00 (BIS) [5] Dickinson, ND St. Wenceslaus Church.
Kadzielawski, Edwin J. *c.s.c.* '49 (AUS) [H] Austin, TX Steiner Lodge Retreat.
Kaeding, Robert F. '73 (TR) Wayside, NJ St. Anselm Church; Wayside, NJ Monmouth County Jail.
Kaelin, Dennis (NEW) [D] East Orange, NJ Bishop Francis Catholic High School.
Kaelin, Walter *c.p.* '42 (CHI) [N] Chicago, IL Passionist Provincial Office.
Kaelin, Walter *c.p.* '42 (FgM) Mission Procurators.
Kaelin, Walter *c.p.* '42 (L) [L] Louisville, KY Sacred Heart Retreat.
Kafara, Andrew '85 (SAT) Pearsall, TX Immaculate Heart of Mary Church.
Kafka, Matthew '65 (FTW) Arcola, IN St. Patrick Church.
Kagan, Msgr. David D. '75 (RCK) Special Assignment.
Kahan, Paul *s.v.d.* '69 (GAL) [47] Houston, TX St. Mary of the Purification Church.
Kahle, George G. *c.s.c.* '53 (FTW) [J] South Bend, IN Congregation of Holy Cross, Indiana Province, Provincial House.
Kahlhamer, Bernard '59 (SCL) Sauk Centre, MN Our Lady of the Angels Church.
Kahlich, Daniel P. '66 (VIC) Columbus, TX St. Anthony's Church.
Kahn, Eric *o.f.m.* '55 (SPC) [G] Republic, MO Cordis House.
Kahn, Eric *o.f.m.* '55 (STL) [P] St. Louis, MO Franciscan Friary of St. Anthony of Padua.
Kahrs, Lee J. (GB) Stark, WI St. Mary Church.
Kaicher, Bud '80 (SD) San Diego, CA Rainbow Work Camp.
Kaicher, Edward '80 (SD) Fallbrook, CA St. Peter Church.
Kaifer, William J. *s.j.* '53 (WDC) [M] Washington, DC The Jesuit Community at Georgetown University.
Kaija, Peter '80 (FTW) [15] South Bend, IN Our Lady of Hungary Church.
Kail, Michael J. '74 (OLL) Columbus, OH Maronite Catholic Community Church; Fairlawn, OH Our Lady of the Cedars of Mt. Lebanon Church.
Kaimann, Gerald J. '70 (JC) Jonesburg, MO St. Patrick Church; Montgomery City, MO Immaculate Conception Church.
Kain, Msgr. Peter V. '65 (BRK) [36] Brooklyn, NY St. Ephrem's Church.
Kain, Stephen *o.f.m.* '74 (SFR) [8] San Francisco, CA St. Boniface Church.
Kaiser, Msgr. Charles '32 (EVN) Retired.
Kaiser, Joseph A. '71 (BAL) Retired; [O] Timonium, MD Stella Maris.
Kaiser, Joseph W. '55 (RCK) Richmond, IL St. Joseph Church.
Kaiser, Lawrence B. '73 (DEN) Fort Morgan, CO St. Helena Church.
Kaiser, Lawrence H. '64 (DET) [8] Dearborn, MI Sacred Heart Church.
Kaiser, Leonard G. '58 (LC) Independence, WI SS. Peter and Paul Church; North Creek, WI St. Michael Church.
Kaiser, Ralph L. '54 (KC) Buckner, MO Church of the Santa Fe.
Kaiser, Roman F. '58 (LC) Loyal, WI St. Anthony of Padua Church.
Kaiser, Thomas J. '49 (SLC) [11] Salt Lake City, UT St. Vincent de Paul Church; Salt Lake City, UT Decker Lake Youth Center; Retired.
Kaithackal, Sebastian D. *c.m.i.* '81 (MET) Woodbridge, NJ St. James Church; Perth Amboy, NJ Raritan Bay Medical Center.
Kaithamatton, Sebastian *c.m.i.* '80 (STA) Palm Coast, FL St. Elizabeth Ann Seton Church.
Kakalec, Joseph M. *s.j.* '67 (PH) [C] Philadelphia, PA St. Joseph's University.
Kakalec, Joseph M. *s.j.* '67 (SCR) [C] Scranton, PA University of Scranton.
Kakaniyil, Chacko D. '73 (MAR) Wakefield, MI Immaculate Conception of the Blessed Virgin Mary Church.
Kakareka, Joseph R. '72 (SCR) [6] Nanticoke, PA St. Stanislaus Church.
Kakascik, Msgr. Edward '55 (STU) Marietta, OH St. Mary's Church; [I] Marietta, OH Marietta College.
Kalabat, Frank Y. '95 (EST) Southfield, MI Our Lady of Chaldeans Cathedral, Mother of God Chaldean Church.
Kalafsky, Andrew J. '43 (ROC) Bradford, NY St. Stanislaus Church; Retired.
Kalamaja, Theodore M. *s.j.* '67 (NO) New Orleans, LA Orleans Parish Correctional Center; [C] New Orleans, LA Loyola University New Orleans.
Kalappura, George *c.m.i.* '60 (BEA) Cheek, TX St. Martin de Porres Church; Fannett, TX St. Mary Church.
Kalarickal, Luke '88 (TYL) Center, TX St. Therese Church.
Kalarickal, Thomas *c.m.i.* '55 (NY) [2] White Plains, NY St. John the Evangelist Church.
Kalariparampil, Joseph '53 (MIA) [8] Fort Lauderdale, FL St. Helen Church.
Kalas, Ronald N. '59 (CHI) Park Ridge, IL Mary, Seat of Wisdom Church.
Kalata, Dominik P. '65 (ALN) Frackville, PA St. Ann Church; Frackville, PA Annunciation B.V.M. Church.
Kalb, Bertram J. '44 (DUB) Retired.
Kalb, Howard E. *s.j.* '54 (OM) [K] Omaha, NE Jesuit Community at Creighton University.
Kalchik, Paul J. '99 (CHI) [135] Chicago, IL St. Michael Church.
Kalchthaler, James C. *m.m.* '56 (FgM) Maryknoll Foreign Missions.
Kalcic, Dismas B. *o.s.b.* '61 (JOL) [J] Lisle, IL St. Procopius Abbey.
Kalcic, Dismas B. *o.s.b.* '61 (SUP) Catawba, WI St. Paul the Apostle Church; Prentice, WI St. John the Baptist Church.
Kalck, Michael V. '74 (CHI) [6] Cicero, IL Our Lady of the Mount Church.
Kaleikoa, Charles '81 (HON) Leave of Absence.
Kalema, Josephat Kato *o.c.s.o.* '85 (NEW) [32] Newark, NJ St. Rocco's Church.
Kaler, Adolph *o.m.i.* '57 (GAL) Alvin, TX St. John the Baptist Church.
Kalert, David *o.m.i.* '64 (FgM) Oblates Foreign Missions.
Kalert, David A. *o.m.i.* '64 (STP) [W] St. Paul, MN Oblate Media and Communication Corporation.
Kalert, David A. *o.m.i.* '64 (WDC) [M] Washington, DC Missionary Oblates of Mary Immaculate; [M] Washington, DC Oblate College/Center for Mission Studies Community.
Kaley, Richard *o.f.m.conv.* '75 (IND) [I] Mount Saint Francis, IN Mount Saint Francis Friary and Retreat Center; [J] Mount Saint Francis, IN Provincial Headquarters for the Conventual Franciscan Province.
Kalich, Patrick J. '94 (GRY) Crown Point, IN St. Mary Church.
Kalick, Quentin F. *s.s.c.* '42 (FgM) St. Columban's Foreign Mission.
Kalicky, John E. *c.pp.s.* '61 (GRY) [4] Whiting, IN St. John the Baptist Church.
Kalil, Gordon '94 (SR) Saint Helena, CA St. Helena Church.
Kalin, Msgr. Leonard I. '56 (LIN) Retired.
Kalin, William '59 (BAK) Hermiston, OR Our Lady of Angels Church.
Kalin, William A. '59 (LIN) On Duty Outside the Diocese.
Kalina, Isaac *o.s.b.* '89 (LA) [Q] Valyermo, CA St. Andrew's Abbey.
Kalinowski, Dariusz '99 (FR) Mansfield, MA St. Mary's Church.
Kalinowski, Loren M. '75 (SAG) [13] Saginaw, MI St. John Vianney Church.
Kalinowski, Ryszard '74 (JKS) [6] Jackson, MS Holy Ghost Church; [H] Jackson, MS Tougaloo College Newman Center.
Kalinowski, Stainslaus J. '45 (SCR) Retired.
Kalinski, Eugene E. '60 (GB) [I] Oshkosh, WI Community of Our Lady.
Kalita, Thomas M. '74 (WDC) Olney, MD St. Peter Church.
Kaliyadan, William *m.s.* '94 (FR) Brewster, MA Our Lady of the Cape Church.
Kalkman, Richard '56 (SCL) On Duty Outside the Diocese.
Kall, Anthony *o.f.m.conv.* '71 (TR) [5] Trenton, NJ Immaculate Conception Church.
Kallabat, Stephen '66 (EST) Oak Park, MI Mar Addai Chaldean Church.
Kalladan, Joseph K. '69 (GAL) New Waverly, TX St. Joseph Church.
Kallaher, Timothy S. '72 (CIN) [41] Cincinnati, OH St. John the Baptist Church.
Kallampally, George '80 (BAL) [15] Baltimore, MD St. Benedict Church.
Kallarackal, George J. *m.c.b.s.* '81 (MAR) Assinins, MI The Most Holy Name of Jesus-Blessed Kateri Tekakwitha Church; Baraga, MI St. Ann Church; Assinins, MI The Most Holy Name of Jesus-Blessed Kateri Tekakwitha Church.
Kallarackal, Sebastian *c.m.i.* '77 (SHP) [B] Monroe, LA St. Francis Medical Center.
Kallock, Michael J. *c.s.p.* '73 (NY) [DD] Jamaica Estates, NY Paulist Fathers Generalate.
Kallookalam, Joseph *c.m.i.* '71 (TYL) Gun Barrel City, TX St. Jude Church.
Kallumady, Thomas '73 (NY) [227] Staten Island, NY Sacred Heart Church; Beacon, NY St. John Evangelist Church.
Kallumkalkudiyil, George *c.m.i.* '76 (ALX) Moreauville, LA Our Lady of Sorrows Church.
Kalonga, Simon '84 (DEN) [3] Englewood, CO St. Louis Church.
Kalousieh, George '81 (ARM) Paterson, NJ Sacred Heart Church.
Kalscheuer, Henry N. '59 (MAD) Dodgeville, WI St. Joseph Church.
Kalscheuer, Roger '80 (OM) [14] Omaha, NE St. Frances Cabrini Church.
Kaltenbach, Victor J. '62 (SFD) Greenville, IL St. Lawrence Church.
Kaltreider, Carl E. '79 (CHL) Absent On Leave.
Kalu, Martin-Ralph '89 (ATL) Kennesaw, GA St. Catherine of Siena Church.
Kalwak, Marek '97 (SB) [A] Riverside, CA Divine Word Seminary.
Kamanda, Joseph '85 (WDC) [B] Washington, DC St. Joseph's Seminary.
Kamas, John *s.s.s.* '75 (NY) [55] New York, NY St. Jean Baptiste Church.
Kamau, Francis Ngumi *f.m.h.* (SHP) [3] Shreveport, LA Our Lady of the Blessed Sacrament Church.
Kamber, Kenneth L. '53 (L) Jeffersontown, KY St. Michael Church; Retired.
Kambitsch, Lawrence J. '69 (MRY) King City, CA St. John the Baptist Church.

Kamenski, Thomas *o.f.m.* '82 (LAF) On Special Assignment; [F] Lafayette, LA Our Lady of Lourdes Regional Medical Center, Inc.
Kamide, Paul T. '63 (ORL) Port Orange, FL Epiphany Church.
Kamienski, Luciano *s.d.b.* '66 (LA) Inglewood, CA St. John Chrysostom Church.
Kamiensky, Joseph J. *s.j.* '77 (BUF) [D] Buffalo, NY Canisius High School; [O] Buffalo, NY Canisius Jesuit Community.
Kaminski, Dariusz '91 (PAT) [6] Passaic, NJ St. Joseph's Church.
Kaminski, Edward J. *c.s.c.* '75 (MRY) [1] Monterey, CA Cathedral of San Carlos Borromeo; [F] Monterey, CA Congregation of the Holy Cross.
Kaminski, Frank *s.j.* (CAM) Camden, NJ Riverfront Prison.
Kaminski, Frank T. *s.j.* '76 (WDC) [P] Faulkner, MD Loyola on the Potomac Retreat House.
Kaminski, Joseph M. '51 (GF) Retired.
Kaminski, Kevin A. '78 (MET) Raritan, NJ St. Joseph Church.
Kaminski, Ladislaus J. '54 (HRT) Retired.
Kaminski, Louis T. '77 (SCR) Mansfield, PA Holy Child Church.
Kaminski, Martin *s.d.s.* '95 (SAT) St. Hedwig, TX Annunciation of the Blessed Virgin Mary Church.
Kaminski, Neal *o.f.m.* '56 (CHI) [N] Chicago, IL St. Joseph Interprovincial Post-Novitiate Formation House.
Kaminski, Stephen '91 (CLV) Medina, OH St. Francis Xavier Church.
Kaminski, Sy '53 (Y) [10] Youngstown, OH St. Casimir's Church.
Kaminski, Thomas J. '66 (CHI) [74] Chicago, IL St. Helena Church.
Kaminsky, Joseph T. '61 (HRT) Oakville, CT St. Mary Magdalen Church.
Kamla, Jerome J. '42 (LC) Retired.
Kamlage, Herman '57 (COV) Retired.
Kammer, Fred *s.j.* '76 (WDC) [M] Washington, DC K Street Jesuit Community.
Kammerer, James '97 (SAT) On Leave.
Kammerer, Joseph J. '98 (LA) San Pedro, CA Holy Trinity Church.
Kammerer, Raymond '64 (CIN) Waynesville, OH St. Augustine Church.
Kammerer, Richard F. '80 (RVC) Lindenhurst, NY Our Lady of Perpetual Help Church.
Kamp, Francis J. *s.v.d.* '47 (CHI) [B] Techny, IL Divine Word Residence; [N] Techny, IL Society of the Divine Word, Provincial Headquarter-Chicago Prov.
Kampa, Dennis C. '68 (STP) Kenyon, MN St. Michael Church; Pine Island, MN St. Michael Church.
Kampfer, Gerald D. '67 (ALB) Special Assignment.
Kampschneider, Daniel J. '79 (OM) [37] Omaha, NE St. Philip Neri Church.
Kan, Moses *s.j.* '87 (OAK) [N] Berkeley, CA Jesuit Community at Jesuit School of Theology at Berkeley.
Kana, Steven '95 (AUS) Bryan, TX St. Anthony's Church.
Kanai, Charles '94 (CIN) [14] Dayton, OH Holy Family Church.
Kanar, Richard '94 (PSC) Absent on Sick Leave.
Kanat, Joseph Kurian '58 (LAF) [1] Lafayette, LA Cathedral of St. John the Evangelist; On Special Assignment.
Kanda, Francis P. *c.s.sp.* '53 (PRO) [1] Tiverton, RI St. Christopher Church.
Kanda, John R. *c.s.sp.* '42 (PIT) [Q] Bethel Park, PA Holy Ghost Animation Center.
Kandathikudy, Jos '71 (NY) Nanuet, NY St. Anthony Church.
Kandathiparampil, Joseph '63 (WIL) Salisbury, MD St. Francis De Sales Church.
Kandel, Timothy '81 (ORL) On Duty Outside the Diocese.
Kandrac, Antone *o.f.m.conv.* '57 (ALB) Nassau, NY St. Mary Church; [L] Rensselaer, NY Franciscan Mission House.
Kandt, Gregory '90 (RIC) West Point, VA Our Lady of the Blessed Sacrament Church.
Kane, Aloysius T. '38 (PH) Retired.
Kane, Brian P. '00 (LIN) [6] Lincoln, NE St. John the Apostle Church.
Kane, Cornelius T. *o.p.* '52 (WDC) [11] Washington, DC St. Dominic Church & Priory Church.
Kane, Edward *c.ss.r.* '47 (KC) [31] Kansas City, MO Our Lady of Perpetual Help Church; [J] Kansas City, MO Redemptorists of Kansas City.
Kane, Edward R. '78 (BRK) [55] Brooklyn, NY Holy Family Church.
Kane, Eugene '54 (PEO) Urbana, IL St. Patrick's Church; Retired.
Kane, Farrell J. *o.carm.* '65 (CHI) Gurnee, IL St. Paul the Apostle Church.
Kane, Francis J. '53 (PRT) Retired.
Kane, Francis J. '69 (CHI) Wilmette, IL St. Joseph Church.
Kane, George J. '51 (CHI) Schaumburg, IL Church of the Holy Spirit; Retired.
Kane, Herbert T. *s.j.* '52 (NY) [DD] Cornwall, NY Jogues Retreat.
Kane, Ignatius B. *o.s.b.* '61 (BIR) [E] Cullman, AL St. Bernard Abbey.
Kane, Msgr. James D. '58 (SY) Johnson City, NY Blessed Sacrament Church.
Kane, James E. '51 (DEN) Retired.
Kane, James J. '71 (ALB) [5] Schenectady, NY St. Helen Church; Special Assignment.
Kane, John E. *c.m.* '70 (FgM) Vincentian Foreign Missions.
Kane, Msgr. John T. '63 (LA) Hacienda Heights, CA St. John Vianney Church.
Kane, John W. *c.ss.r.* '44 (TUC) [H] Cortaro, AZ Desert House of Prayer.
Kane, Joseph E. '67 (EVN) Jasper, IN Precious Blood Church.
Kane, Joseph F. '46 (SY) [S] Syracuse, NY St. Pius X Home, Inc.
Kane, Joseph M. '70 (BO) [U] Boston, MA Marian Manor.
Kane, Joseph P. *s.j.* '68 (NY) City, NY George M. Motchan Detention Center; City, NY George Vierno Center; City, NY Rose M. Singer Center; [DD] New York, NY Murray-Weigel Hall; [DD] New York, NY Jesuit Provincial's Office.
Kane, Msgr. Joseph T. '62 (PH) Warrington, PA St. Robert Bellarmine Church.
Kane, Justin '44 (DUB) [3] Waterloo, IA Sacred Heart Church; Retired.
Kane, Michael A. *s.j.* (NO) [C] New Orleans, LA Loyola University New Orleans.
Kane, Michael N. '80 (PSC) Coconut Creek, FL Our Lady of the Sign Church.
Kane, Paul '96 (MIA) [33] Miami, FL St. Timothy Church.
Kane, Philip M. '88 (JC) Glasgow, MO St. Mary Church; Slater, MO St. Joseph Church.
Kane, Terence '66 (ATL) Hartwell, GA Sacred Heart of Jesus Church.
Kane, Thomas '69 (WOR) Absent on Leave.
Kane, Msgr. Thomas A. '44 (PH) Bala Cynwyd, PA St. Matthias Church; Retired.
Kane, Msgr. Thomas A. '52 (WDC) Norbeck, MD St. Patrick Church.
Kane, Thomas A. *c.s.p.* '75 (NY) [DD] Jamaica Estates, NY Paulist Fathers Generalate.
Kane, Thomas C. *o.p.* '52 (WDC) [C] Washington, DC Catholic University of America, The.
Kane, Msgr. Thomas S. '67 (RVC) Franklin Square, NY St. Catherine of Sienna Church.
Kane, Timothy '82 (DET) [67] Detroit, MI St. Rita Church.
Kane, William *s.v.d.* '47 (BO) [W] Duxbury, MA Society of the Divine Word.
Kane, William J. *s.j.* '48 (STL) [O] St. Louis, MO Fusz Pavilion.
Kane, Msgr. William J. '60 (WDC) [3] Bethesda, MD Little Flower Church.
Kanfush, Philip M. *o.s.b.* '00 (GBG) [2] Latrobe, PA St. Vincent Basilica Church.
Kanfush, Philip Michael *o.s.b.* '00 (GBG) [H] Latrobe, PA Saint Vincent Archabbey.
Kang, John '59 (HON) [16] Honolulu, HI St. Pius X Church.
Kang, Lawrence '75 (PHX) [5] Scottsdale, AZ St. Daniel the Prophet Church.
Kang, Paul '91 (NY) On Duty Outside the Archdiocese.
Kangley, Bernard *o.carm.* '44 (LA) [Q] Los Angeles, CA Mount Carmel Priory, Carmelite Fathers and Brothers.
Kania, Wojciech M. *s.chr.* '41 (LA) [24] Los Angeles, CA Our Lady of the Bright Mount Church.
Kanicki, Philip A. '85 (RIC) Military Chaplains.
Kaniseli, Tuikolongahau '86 (SAC) Auburn, CA St. Joseph Church.
Kanjiramkuzhy, John '64 (LAF) Franklin, LA St. Jules Church.
Kanka, Robert '56 (ROC) Hornell, NY St. Ann Church; Retired.
Kannampalackal, Abraham *c.m.i.* '94 (NY) Irvington-on-the-Hudson, NY Immaculate Conception Church.
Kannampuzha, Jose '92 (TYL) Longview, TX St. Mary Church.
Kanonik, Stephen F. '82 (CHI) [112] Chicago, IL St. Ladislaus Church.
Kantanka, Michael (KCK) [4] Topeka, KS Most Pure Heart of Mary Church.
Kantner, William R. '75 (MEM) [12] Memphis, TN Incarnation Church.
Kantor, Msgr. Adolph A. '43 (SY) Retired.
Kantor, Robert '98 (VEN) Bradenton, FL SS. Peter and Paul the Apostles Church.
Kanzic, Gerald B. '92 (PAT) Ringwood, NJ St. Catherine of Bologna Church.
Kao, Paulus '59 (LSC) Bayard, NM Our Lady of Fatima Church.
Kapa, Benedict E. '00 (WH) Weirton, WV St. Joseph the Worker Church.
Kapalczynski, Msgr. Eugene J. '40 (MIL) Retired.
Kapfer, Lee *s.j.* '53 (SEA) [11] Seattle, WA St. Joseph Church.
Kapinus, Augustine *o.f.m.conv.* '58 (ALB) Fonda, NY St. Cecilia Church; Tribes Hill, NY Sacred Heart Church; [Q] Fonda, NY The National Shrine of Blessed Kateri Tekakwitha and Friary.
Kapitan, John *o.f.m.* '95 (PRM) Indianapolis, IN St. Athanasius Church.
Kapitz, Donald '73 (SFE) Retired.
Kaplan, Jan F. '67 (CHI) [3] Lemont, IL SS. Cyril and Methodius Church.
Kaplinski, Peter '72 (VIC) Schulenburg, TX St. Rose of Lima Church.
Kapoun, Robert E. '64 (STP) Special Assignment; Retired.
Kappalumakkel, Mathew '89 (HRT) Orange, CT Holy Infant Church.
Kappe, John H. '71 (GAL) [23] Houston, TX St. Clare of Assisi Church.
Kappes, Joseph B. *s.j.* '77 (TOL) [6] Toledo, OH Gesu Church.
Kapphahn, Leo W. *o.s.c.* '39 (PHX) [G] Phoenix, AZ Crosier Community of Phoenix (Canons Regular of the Order of the Holy Cross).
Kappler, Stephan '84 (OAK) [13] Oakland, CA St. Louis Bertrand Church.
Kapral, Richard J. '70 (SY) Waterville, NY St. Bernard Church.
Kapron, Alan '94 (PSC) On Duty Outside Diocese.
Kapushion, Msgr. Marvin J. '56 (PBL) [3] Pueblo, CO Holy Family Church.
Kapusnak, Joseph '66 (PBR) Leisenring, PA St. Stephen Church.
Kapustka, Gerald *o.m.i.* '65 (FgM) Oblates Foreign Missions.
Karabin, Joseph D. '74 (PIT) Braddock, PA Good Shepherd Church; Allegheny County, PA UPMC Braddock.
Karachira, Thomas '90 (WH) Harrisville, WV Christ Our Hope Church; St. Marys, WV St. John Church.
Karaffa, James G. *c.s.c.* '80 (FTW) [9] South Bend, IN Holy Cross Church.
Karal, John W. '53 (DUB) Retired.
Karalus, Peter J. '97 (BUF) Blossom, NY St. Gabriel Church.
Karamitis, Dennis R. *s.j.* '75 (CHI) [C] Chicago, IL Jesuit Community at Loyola University of Chicago.
Karamitis, Dennis R. *s.j.* '75 (STP) [N] Minneapolis, MN La Storta Jesuit Community.
Karas, Blase *o.f.m.* '59 (FgM) Franciscan Foreign Missions.
Karas, Stephen C. '65 (Y) Struthers, OH Holy Trinity Church.
Karasek, Edward '87 (AUS) West, TX Assumption Church.
Karaszewski, Piotr *s.a.c.* '98 (BRK) [43] Brooklyn, NY St. Frances de Chantal Church.
Karath, William E. '71 (P) Bandon, OR Holy Trinity Church.
Karava, Norbert *o.f.m.cap.* '80 (PAT) [M] Oak Ridge-Milton, NJ St. Stanislaus B. M. Friary.
Karava, Norbert M *o.f.m.cap.* '80 (MET) [4] New Brunswick, NJ St. Joseph Church.
Karban, Roger R. '64 (BEL) Renault, IL Our Lady of Good Counsel Church; [A] Waterloo, IL Gibault Catholic High School.
Karcher, Jerome T. '83 (ORG) [4] Huntington Beach, CA St. Vincent de Paul Church.
Karcsinski, George M. '63 (BGP) [6] Bridgeport, CT Blessed Sacrament Church.
Karcsinski, Joseph J. '79 (BGP) Monroe, CT St. Jude Church.
Karczewski, Julian '74 (CAM) Westville Grove, NJ Most Holy Redeemer Church.
Kardas, Thaddeus '70 (WOR) Absent on Leave.
Kardian, Richard S. *m.m.* '56 (CLV) [O] Cleveland, OH Maryknoll Fathers.
Kardong, Terrence *o.s.b.* '63 (BIS) [A] Richardton, ND Assumption Abbey.
Kardos, Blase B. *o.f.m.conv.* '43 (NY) Staten Island, NY Seaview Hospital and Home; [B] Staten Island, NY St. Francis Friary.
Kardzis, Christopher '84 (TOL) On Duty Outside the Diocese; [O] Toledo, OH Office of Global Concerns.
Karegeye, Jean-Pierre *s.j.* '99 (OAK) [N] Berkeley, CA Jesuit Community at Jesuit School of Theology at Berkeley.
Karekatt, Raphael *m.s.f.s.* '86 (ALX) Echo, LA St. Francis de Sales Church.
Karels, Agdus S. '44 (NU) Retired.
Karels, Agdus S. '44 (STP) Retired.
Karels, Ambrose G. '59 (KC) [32] Kansas City, MO Our Lady of Sorrows Church; Retired.
Karem, Peter '88 (OLL) Special Assignment.
Karempelis, Daniel *m.s.a.* '87 (NOR) [F] Cromwell, CT Society of the Missionaries of the Holy Apostles.
Karenbauer, Richard P. '70 (GBG) New Kensington, PA St. Mary of Czestochowa Church.
Karepin, James M. *o.p.* '90 (CHI) [N] Chicago, IL Dominicans (Provincial Office).
Karepin, James M. *o.p.* '90 (SY) Onondaga Hill, NY St.

Michael Church.
Kareta, Gregory *o.f.m. con.* '56 (FRS) Avenal, CA St. Joseph Church.
Karg, Msgr. Andrew H. '64 (E) Greenville, PA St. Michael Church.
Karg, Msgr. William C. '57 (E) [3] Sharon, PA St. Joseph Church.
Karg, William D. '64 (CLV) [17] Akron, OH St. Sebastian Church.
Kari, Arnold A. '77 (RC) Belle Fourche, SD St. Paul Church.
Karieakatt, Paul *o.s.b.* '52 (PAT) [M] Clifton, NJ Holy Face of Jesus Monastery.
Karikilate, Thomas M. '75 (NY) [212] Staten Island, NY St. Margaret Mary Church.
Karimi, Samuel (BRK) [106] Brooklyn, NY Our Lady of Peace Church.
Kariuki, Alphonsus Mwariri *i.m.c.* '86 (MET) [H] Somerset, NJ Consolata Society for Foreign Missions.
Karl, Charles '43 (PEO) Wyoming, IL St. Dominic's Church.
Karl, Charles E. '57 (PEO) Retired.
Karl, Msgr. Edward B. '57 (BGP) Bethel, CT St. Mary Church.
Karl, Kevin '69 (OWN) Absent on Leave.
Karl, Ralph J. *o.m.i.* '57 (COL) West Jefferson, OH SS. Simon and Jude Church; [H] West Jefferson, OH SS. Simon and Jude.
Karl, Robert J. '57 (PBR) Portage, PA SS. Peter and Paul Church; South Fork, PA St. Michael's Church.
Karle, William J. '72 (SCR) Sayre, PA Church of the Epiphany.
Karlen, Donald H. '64 (SY) [3] Utica, NY Our Lady of Lourdes Church; [W] Whitesboro, NY Mount Olivet.
Karlin, Paulinus I. *o.f.m.cap.* '43 (SAL) Hays, KS St. Joseph's Church; [D] Hays, KS St. Joseph's Friary.
Karlowicz, Edwin *c.r.* '48 (CHI) [104] Chicago, IL St. John Cantius Church.
Karls, Victor *c.ss.r.* '70 (STL) [P] Liguori, MO Liguori Mission House/Redemptorists.
Karmanocky, Bernard *o.f.m.* '73 (ALT) [18] Johnstown, PA St. Therese of the Child Jesus Church.
Karnik, George W. '58 (DUB) Evansdale, IA St. Nicholas Church; [5] Waterloo, IA St. John's Church.
Karnish, Robert A. '66 (GI) Gordon, NE St. Leo's Church.
Karnogora, Philipus Pito *s.v.d.* '95 (LAF) Broussard, LA St. Joseph Church.
Karns, David W. '74 (ALN) [1] Easton, PA St. Anthony of Padua Church.
Karoblis, Andrew K. '54 (LC) [4] Wisconsin Rapids, WI SS. Peter and Paul Church.
Karoor, Isaac '69 (BAL) Ellicott City, MD Our Lady of Perpetual Help Church.
Karottekunnel, Paul P. *m.s.t.* '97 (MAR) Escanaba, MI St. Joseph & St. Patrick Church.
Karpiey, Daniel J. '59 (HRT) Wallingford, CT SS. Peter and Paul Church.
Karpil, Luke '56 (BRK) Brooklyn, NY Veterans Administration Medical Center.
Karpinski, Robert D. (BGP) Weston, CT St. Francis of Assisi Church; Westport, CT Assumption Church.
Karpinski, Robert D. '93 (BGP) [C] Trumbull, CT St. Joseph High School.
Karpyn, Gregory '87 (ALN) [7] Bethlehem, PA Notre Dame of Bethlehem Church.
Karr, Raymond E. '59 (ALT) Absent on Leave.
Karrer, Walter *c.ss.r.* '47 (WCH) [14] Wichita, KS St. Joseph Church; [F] Wichita, KS Redemptorist Mission House.
Karris, Robert *o.f.m.* '65 (BUF) [C] St. Bonaventure, NY St. Bonaventure University; [O] St. Bonaventure, NY St. Bonaventure Friary.
Karris, Robert *o.f.m.* '65 (CHI) [N] Chicago, IL St. Peter's Friary.
Karssen, John H. *c.m.* '46 (DEN) [26] Denver, CO St. Anthony of Padua Church; [M] Denver, CO Congregation of the Mission Midwest Province: De Paul House.
Karuhn, Robert J. (GB) [6] Appleton, WI Sacred Heart Church.
Karuthi, Cyrus *i.m.c.* '98 (WDC) [V] Washington, DC Consolata Missionaries House of Studies.
Karuvelli, George *s.j.* '89 (BO) [W] Chestnut Hill, MA The Jesuit Community at Boston College.
Karvelis, Msgr. Bryan J. '56 (BRK) [142] Brooklyn, NY Transfiguration Church.
Karvelis, Francis V. (HRT) Retired.
Karwacki, Bart *o.f.m.conv.* '75 (BAL) [S] Ellicott City, MD St. Joseph Cupertino Friary, Friars Minor Conventual of St. Francis of Assisi; [S] Ellicott City, MD Friary of St. Joseph Cupertino.
Karwacki, Francis J. '83 (HBG) Lykens, PA Our Lady Help of Christians Church; Williamstown, PA Sacred Heart of Jesus Church.
Karwacki, Marion T. '36 (ORL) Retired.
Karwel, Henry *o.f.m.conv.* '57 (BAL) [S] Ellicott City, MD Order of Friars Minor Conventual.
Karwel, Henry *o.f.m.conv.* '57 (SPR) Ware, MA St. Mary's Church.
Karwin, John J. *s.j.* '67 (BO) [W] Boston, MA The Society of Jesus of New England-Provincial Offices.
Karwin, John J. *s.j.* '67 (WH) [A] Wheeling, WV Wheeling Jesuit University.
Karwowski, Edmund K '87 (HRT) Plainville, CT Our Lady of Mercy Church.
Karwowski, Ephrem *o.f.m.cap.* '88 (NY) [DD] White Plains, NY St. Conrad Friary.
Kasarda, John '61 (PBR) Newton Falls, OH St. Michael Church.
Kaschenbach, Msgr. Arthur J. '51 (SCR) Mount Pocono, PA St. Mary of the Mount Church.
Kasel, Joseph M. '48 (NU) Retired.
Kaserow, John M. *m.m.* '69 (NY) [DD] Maryknoll, NY Maryknoll Fathers and Brothers.
Kaseta, Peter *o.f.m.cap.* '67 (FgM) Capuchin Foreign Missions.
Kaseta, Peter *o.f.m.cap.* '67 (NY) [57] New York, NY St. John the Baptist Church.
Kash, Robert J. '52 (CHI) Retired.
Kashmer, George B. '58 (GRY) Retired.
Kasinski, James J. '66 (BUF) [12] Niagara Falls, NY Sacred Heart Church.
Kaska, E. William '69 (DAV) [2] Davenport, IA Our Lady of Victory Church.
Kaskie, Brian '92 (JKS) [5] Jackson, MS Holy Family Church; Madison, MS St. Francis of Assisi Church.
Kaslyn, Robert J. '85 (WOR) [N] Worcester, MA Jesuits of Holy Cross College, Inc.
Kasparek, John A. *s.c.j.* '69 (PMB) [1] Palm Beach, FL Cathedral of St. Ignatius Loyola.
Kasper, John *o.s.f.s.* '79 (OAK) Lafayette, CA St. Perpetua Church.
Kasper, Larry '97 (TUC) Hayden, AZ St. Joseph's Church.
Kasperek, David D. '63 (GB) Flintville, WI SS. Edward and Isidore Church.
Kasprick, Roger *o.s.b.* '59 (SCL) [I] Collegeville, MN St. John's Abbey, of the Order of St. Benedict.
Kasprzak, John F. '75 (BUF) Woodlawn, NY Our Lady of Grace Church.
Kasprzak, Roman A. *m.m.* '51 (NY) [DD] Maryknoll, NY Maryknoll Fathers and Brothers.
Kasprzyk, James H. '65 (BUF) Retired.
Kasprzyk, Leon J. '61 (MET) Lambertville, NJ St. John the Evangelist Church.
Kasputis, Thomas R. '76 (CHI) [179] Chicago, IL St. Rene Goupil Church.
Kass, George P. '43 (LA) Retired.
Kass, Thomas G. *c.s.v.* '77 (CHI) [N] Arlington Heights, IL Viatorian Province Center-Clerics of St. Viator.
Kass-Hanna Saissa, Boutros Sleiman '88 (SAM) Fall River, MA St. Anthony of the Desert Church.
Kassian, Jeffrey '96 (STN) On Duty Outside the Diocese.
Kassian, Jeffrey A. '96 (KAL) Paw Paw, MI St. Mary Church.
Kassis, Daniel '81 (GLP) Absent on Leave.
Kassis, Daniel '91 (SR) [1] Santa Rosa, CA Cathedral of St. Eugene.
Kasteel, Ben *v.g.* '64 (LUB) [1] Lubbock, TX Cathedral Christ the King Church.
Kasten, Edward F. '54 (MIL) Retired.
Kastenholz, John *o.praem.* (GB) Stephensville, WI St. Patrick Church.
Kastenholz, John P. *o.praem.* '65 (GB) [B] De Pere, WI St. Norbert College; [I] De Pere, WI St. Norbert Abbey.
Kaster, Alfred D. '60 (DUL) On Duty Outside the Diocese.
Kaster, Alfred D. '60 (SAC) Grass Valley, CA St. Patrick Church.
Kastigar, James J. (CHI) [A] Chicago, IL St. Joseph Seminary.
Kastigar, James J. '82 (CHI) [1] Cicero, IL St. Anthony Church.
Kastigar, John J. '52 (CHI) Retired.
Kastner, Edwin H. '51 (BEL) Retired.
Kastner, James A. '59 (OKL) [4] Oklahoma City, OK Christ the King Church.
Kastner, Juan Patron '77 (SJN) [6] Carolina, PR Epifania Del Senor Church.
Kasuboski, Walter *o.f.m.cap.* '74 (FgM) Capuchin Foreign Missions.
Kasun, Stanley L. '94 (OM) Madison, NE St. Leonard Church.
Kasza, John '93 (DET) Special Assignment.
Kaszczak, Ivan '85 (STF) [A] Stamford, CT St. Basil College.
Kasznel, Richard C. '65 (STL) St. Mary, MO Immaculate Conception Church.
Kaszynski, Robert S. '60 (FR) [22] Fall River, MA St. Stanislaus Church.
Katcher, Eugene '92 (DET) White Lake, MI St. Patrick Church.
Kathol, Quentin *o.s.b.* '63 (KC) [A] Conception, MO Conception Seminary College; [J] Conception, MO Conception Abbey.
Kato, Stephen M. '48 (PIT) Retired.
Katorski, Robert '63 (MIL) [9] West Allis, WI St. Rita Church.
Katoski, Eugene *o.f.m.* '45 (CLV) [62] Cleveland, OH St. Patrick Church; [P] Cleveland, OH Monastery of the Poor Clares.
Katren, Scott E. '92 (E) [24] Erie, PA St. Mark the Evangelist Church.
Katricak, Kenneth *o.s.b.* (CLV) [E] Cleveland, OH Incarnate Word Academy.
Katricak, Kenneth *o.s.b.* '83 (CLV) [P] Cleveland, OH Sisters of the Incarnate Word and Blessed Sacrament.
Katricak, Kenneth J. *o.s.b.* '83 (CLV) [O] Cleveland, OH Benedictine Order of Cleveland.
Katsouros, Stephen *s.j.* '98 (NEW) [C] Jersey City, NJ St. Peter's Preparatory School.
Katsuno, Peter *s.a.* '40 (NY) [DD] Garrison, NY Franciscan Friars of the Atonement, Minister General Office.
Kattackal, Joseph Varkey (CHI) [J] Blue Island, IL St. Francis Hospital and Health Center.
Kattady, Augustine '71 (TUC) Superior, AZ St. Francis of Assisi Church.
Katz, Jerome A. '71 (SY) Cortland, NY St. Anthony Church.
Katz, Roger L. '89 (DUB) Retired.
Katzenberger, Scott R. *c.ss.r.* '97 (GAL) [34] Houston, TX Holy Ghost Church.
Katziner, Stephen F. '74 (PH) Warminster, PA Nativity of Our Lord Church.
Kauchak, Justin R. *o.p.* '66 (BR) Ponchatoula, LA St. Joseph Church.
Kaucheck, Kenneth R. '76 (DET) [3] Troy, MI St. Anastasia Church.
Kaucky, Francis '59 (CHI) Oak Forest, IL St. Damian Church.
Kauffman, John G. '75 (DEN) Kremmling, CO St. Peter Church.
Kauffman, Niles J. *o.f.m.cap.* '58 (MIL) [A] St. Francis, WI Saint Francis Seminary; [P] Milwaukee, WI St. Conrad Friary.
Kauffman, William B. '90 (WIL) [1] Wilmington, DE Cathedral of St. Peter; Apostleship of the Sea.
Kauffmann, James '76 (RIC) [7] Richmond, VA St. Benedict Church.
Kaufman, Kent R. '93 (TOL) Fostoria, OH St. Wendelin Church.
Kaufman, Philip *o.s.b.* '45 (SCL) [I] Collegeville, MN St. John's Abbey, of the Order of St. Benedict.
Kaufman, William C. '74 (PH) [141] Philadelphia, PA Resurrection of Our Lord Church.
Kaukus, Edwin J. '57 (BUF) Retired.
Kaul, John '75 (DET) Military Chaplains.
Kaunas, Bronius *o.s.j.* '42 (MRY) [F] Santa Cruz, CA Oblates of St. Joseph Provincial House and Shrine.
Kaut, Msgr. Bernd (WDC) [4] Bethesda, MD Nativity of the Blessed Virgin (German Mission) Church; [V] Washington, DC Archdiocese of Washington.
Kauta, John B. '67 (NY) Bedford, NY St. Patrick Church.
Kauth, Matthew '00 (CHL) [8] Charlotte, NC St. Matthew Church.
Kauzlarich, John '55 (CHI) Retired.
Kavanagh, Aelred *o.s.b.* '94 (NO) [A] St. Benedict, LA St. Joseph's Seminary College; [P] St. Benedict, LA St. Joseph Abbey.
Kavanagh, Aidan *o.s.b.* '57 (IND) [J] St. Meinrad, IN St. Meinrad Archabbey.
Kavanagh, Charles J. *s.j.* '44 (SJ) [L] Los Gatos, CA Sacred Heart Jesuit Center.
Kavanagh, Msgr. Charles M. '63 (NY) [185] Bronx, NY St. Raymond Church; [HH] New York, NY Alfred E. Smith Memorial Foundation, Inc., The; [HH] New York, NY Partnership for Quality Education, Inc.
Kavanagh, Dermon *c.s.sp.* '60 (SFR) Millbrae, CA St. Dunstan Church.
Kavanagh, Donald '72 (BRK) [213] Queens, NY Our Lady of Lourdes Church.
Kavanagh, Msgr. Edward J. '48 (SAC) [22] Sacramento, CA St. Rose Church; [E] Sacramento, CA St. Patrick Children's Home, Inc.
Kavanagh, Francis X. *o.c.s.o.* '38 (ATL) [J] Conyers, GA The Monastery of the Holy Spirit.
Kavanagh, Henry *c.p.* '75 (BRK) [V] Jamaica, NY Immaculate Conception Monastery.
Kavanagh, James F. '64 (LA) [70] Los Angeles, CA St. Jerome Church.
Kavanagh, Msgr. John C. '42 (PH) Wynnewood, PA Presentation B.V.M. Church.
Kavanagh, Kevin J. '83 (COL) Delaware, OH St. Mary Church.
Kavanagh, Msgr. Richard T. '36 (IND) Retired.
Kavanaugh, John '48 (SFR) [35] San Francisco, CA St. Monica Church.
Kavanaugh, Msgr. John C. '42 (PH) Retired.
Kavanaugh, John F. *s.j.* '71 (STL) [P] St. Louis, MO Jesuit Community Corporation at St. Louis University - Jesuit Hall.
Kavanaugh, John J. '57 (WIL) Sherwood Park, DE St. John the Beloved Church.
Kavanaugh, John J. *s.j.* '71 (STL) [C] St. Louis, MO Saint Louis University.
Kavanaugh, John P. '48 (SFR) San Francisco, CA

Knights of Malta; Retired.
Kavanaugh, Kieran *o.c.d.* '55 (WDC) [B] Washington, DC Discalced Carmelite Friars; [V] Washington, DC Institute of Carmelite Studies and ICS Publications.
Kavanaugh, Michael J. '85 (SAV) Port Wentworth, GA Our Lady of Lourdes Church.
Kavanaugh, Philip M. '73 (LA) [35] Los Angeles, CA Precious Blood Church.
Kavanaugh, Thomas *c.m.* '41 (SAT) Losoya, TX El Carmen Catholic Church; Retired.
Kavaney, C. R. '85 (BIS) New Town, ND St. Anthony Church.
Kavcik, John P. *m.s.c.* '73 (ALN) Nazareth, PA Holy Family Church.
Kaveney, Thomas J. '47 (CHI) Berwyn, IL St. Odilo Church; Retired.
Kavin, Msgr. Edward F. '56 (NEW) [N] Rutherford, NJ St. John Vianney Residence for Priests.
Kavookjian, Perry '87 (FRS) [12] Fresno, CA St. Paul Church; [G] Fresno, CA St. Paul Newman Center.
Kavumkal, Sebastian *m.s.t.* '79 (MAR) [1] Sault Sainte Marie, MI Holy Name of Mary Church.
Kawa, Edward *s.d.s.* '64 (GRY) [J] Merrillville, IN Salvatorian Fathers (Society of the Divine Savior).
Kawa, Msgr. Robert J. '69 (STU) Beverly, OH St. Bernard Church; [J] Beverly, OH Marriage Encounter.
Kawamata, Louis *ss.cc.* '74 (FR) [I] Fairhaven, MA Sacred Hearts Provincial House.
Kawamura, Peter *o.s.b.* '88 (SCL) [I] Collegeville, MN St. John's Abbey, of the Order of St. Benedict.
Kawczynski, Ronald '90 (FAR) Military Chaplains.
Kawecki, Andrew M. '80 (GBG) Leckrone, PA Our Lady of Perpetual Help (St. Mary) Church.
Kawka, Frederick J. '64 (SAG) Frankenmuth, MI Blessed Trinity Church.
Kay, Joseph *m.afr.* '48 (SP) [O] St. Petersburg, FL Missionaries of Africa.
Kayatta, Francis P. '80 (PRO) [33] Providence, RI St. Thomas Church.
Kaylor, Lee '81 (SFR) Absent on Leave.
Kaylor, Robert W. '62 (Y) [C] Canton, OH Central Catholic High.
Kaylor, Robert W. '70 (Y) Brewster, OH St. Therese Church.
Kayrouz, Victor '64 (OLL) Hillside, IL Our Lady of Lebanon Church; Hillside, IL Our Lady of Lebanon Church.
Kayser, DeWayne '98 (SFS) Yankton, SD Sacred Heart Church.
Kayser, Leonard '59 (SFS) Mayfield, SD St. Columba Church; Sigel, SD St. Agnes Church; Yankton, SD State Hospital.
Kayser, Robert '52 (RVC) Dix Hills, NY St. Matthew Church; Retired.
Kaza, Msgr. Charles A. '72 (E) Brockway, PA St. Tobias Church.
Kazanchy, Cordius P. *o.f.m.* '60 (PAT) [M] Butler, NJ St. Anthony Friary.
Kazanecki, Thaddeus J. '77 (BRK) [197] Queens, NY Mary's Nativity Church.
Kazarnowicz, Anthony S. '75 (WOR) [9] Worcester, MA Our Lady of Czestochowa Church.
Kazer, Michael '80 (DET) [1] Warren, MI St. Anne's Church.
Kazhuvidayil, Joseph (NY) Spring Valley, NY St. Joseph Church.
Kazista, Francis G. '66 (WDC) [6] Silver Spring, MD St. John the Baptist Church.
Kazmekcziak, Eugene '51 (FTW) Retired.
Kazmierczak, Carl M. '55 (MIL) [46] Milwaukee, WI St. John Kanty Church.
Kazmierczak, Msgr. Edward L. '51 (BUF) Retired.
Kaznowski, Valentine J. '41 (DET) Retired.
Kcira, Anton '67 (DET) [10] Warren, MI St. Paul Albanian Catholic Community Church.
Keahi, Christopher *ss.cc.* '65 (HON) Kalaheo, HI Holy Cross Church.
Kealey, Edward J. '89 (RVC) Medford, NY St. Sylvester Church.
Kealy, Francis de Paul *o.f.m.* '50 (NY) [35] New York, NY St. Francis of Assisi Church.
Kealy, Hubert J. '64 (GAL) Pasadena, TX St. Pius the Fifth Church.
Kealy, Robert L. '72 (CHI) Highland Park, IL Immaculate Conception Church; [X] Chicago, IL Court of Appeals-Province of Chicago.
Kealy, Sean *c.s.sp.* '65 (PIT) [B] Pittsburgh, PA Duquesne University of the Holy Ghost.
Kealy, Stephen *s.s.c.* '48 (PRO) [P] Bristol, RI St. Columban's Retirement House.
Kean, James '97 (DET) Waterford, MI Our Lady of the Lakes Church.
Kean, Joseph H. '64 (ALN) Unassigned.
Keane, Alfred V. *m.m.* '58 (NY) [DD] Maryknoll, NY Maryknoll Fathers and Brothers.
Keane, Aquinas *o.c.s.o.* '73 (WOR) [N] Spencer, MA St. Joseph's Abbey.
Keane, Brendan '50 (SFD) Retired.
Keane, Denis J. '63 (GF) Fort Benton, MT Immaculate Conception Church.
Keane, Msgr. Dennis P. '71 (NY) [85] New York, NY Our Lady of Good Counsel Church.
Keane, Edward M. '39 (BRK) [178] Queens, NY Holy Family Church; Retired.
Keane, Eugene '55 (NY) Highland, NY St. Augustine Church.
Keane, James '47 (OAK) Retired.
Keane, Msgr. James P. '45 (SFR) Retired.
Keane, James T. '55 (LFT) Muncie, IN St. Mary Church.
Keane, John *s.a.* '62 (NY) [DD] Garrison, NY Franciscan Friars of the Atonement, Minister General Office.
Keane, John F. '65 (BO) Emergency Response Group; Health Leave.
Keane, John J. '62 (HRT) [10] New Haven, CT St. John the Baptist Church.
Keane, John J. '62 (PIT) [7] McKeesport, PA St. Pius V Church.
Keane, John J. *s.a.* '62 (SAC) [10] Sacramento, CA St. Anthony Church.
Keane, Joseph P. '49 (BRK) Retired.
Keane, Martin T. '43 (HRT) Retired.
Keane, Michael '90 (NY) [E] Poughkeepsie, NY Our Lady of Lourdes High School.
Keane, Michael J. '57 (SFR) [2] San Rafael, CA St. Isabella Church.
Keane, Patrick J. '51 (SFR) Retired.
Keane, Patrick J. *o.s.a.* '52 (LA) Ojai, CA St. Thomas Aquinas Church.
Keane, Philip S. *s.s.* '67 (BAL) [A] Baltimore, MD St. Mary's Seminary and University.
Keane, Philip S. *s.s.* '67 (SY) [14] Syracuse, NY St. Charles Church; On Duty Outside the Diocese.
Keane, Robert E. '78 (STP) Retired.
Keane, Robert L. *s.j.* '78 (BO) [W] Boston, MA The Society of Jesus of New England-Provincial Offices.
Keane, Thomas F. '56 (BO) Senior Priests.
Keane, Thomas S. *m.m.* '56 (NY) [DD] Maryknoll, NY Maryknoll Fathers and Brothers.
Keane, Msgr. Vincent A. '58 (BRK) [207] Queens, NY Our Lady of the Blessed Sacrament Church.
Keane, Vincent E. '83 (TR) Retired; [M] Trenton, NJ Villa Vianney.
Keane, William F. *s.d.b.* '74 (SP) [4] Tampa, FL Good Shepherd Church; [E] Tampa, FL Mary Help of Christians School.
Keaney, Denis P. '61 (SAC) Retired and in Senior Ministry.
Keaney, Francis *s.s.c.* '65 (PRO) [P] Bristol, RI St. Columban's Retirement House.
Keaney, James P. '54 (R) Retired.
Keaney, John B. *m.m.* '55 (FgM) Maryknoll Foreign Missions.
Kearney, A. Damian *o.s.b.* '56 (PRO) [P] Portsmouth, RI Abbey of St. Gregory the Great.
Kearney, Brendan *s.j.* '68 (LA) Redondo Beach, CA St. James Church.
Kearney, Christopher *o.f.m.cap.* '68 (LA) [B] Santa Ynez, CA San Lorenzo Novitiate and Seminary.
Kearney, Daniel S. '87 (NY) [95] New York, NY Our Lady Queen of Martyrs Church.
Kearney, Edward J. '51 (NEW) [23] Jersey City, NJ St. Patrick's Church; Retired.
Kearney, George W. '53 (DEN) Retired.
Kearney, John T. '83 (NY) Lake Katrine, NY St. Catherine Laboure Church.
Kearney, Joseph A. '67 (SCR) [2] Wilkes-Barre, PA Blessed Sacrament Church; Wilkes-Barre, PA Geisinger Wyoming Valley Hospital.
Kearney, Msgr. Joseph V. '46 (LA) Carpinteria, CA St. Joseph Church; Retired.
Kearney, Michael J. '82 (BO) [2] Quincy, MA St. Boniface Church.
Kearney, Myles J. '71 (BR) [17] Baton Rouge, LA St. Patrick Church.
Kearney, Msgr. Patrick J. '53 (SD) Retired.
Kearney, Timothy '96 (BO) [4] Lynn, MA St. Mary Church.
Kearney, Msgr. Vincent L. '43 (KC) Retired.
Kearney, William (SP) Citrus Springs, FL St. Elizabeth Ann Seton Church.
Kearney, William '83 (SP) Retired.
Kearns, Adam '54 (TR) Retired; [M] Trenton, NJ Villa Vianney.
Kearns, Daniel J. '86 (PH) Glenside, PA St. Luke the Evangelist Church.
Kearns, Daniel P. *c.m.* '69 (STL) [P] St. Louis, MO Vincentian Community.
Kearns, David *o.carm.* '61 (NY) [189] Bronx, NY St. Simon Stock Church.
Kearns, Edward A. '63 (MET) Retired.
Kearns, Edward T. '77 (PH) Newtown, PA St. Andrew Church.
Kearns, Harold M. '61 (HRT) Thomaston, CT St. Thomas Church.
Kearns, John P. '88 (BO) Absent on Leave.
Kearns, Joseph J. '48 (SAG) St. Charles, MI Immaculate Conception Church.
Kearns, Owen *l.c.* '83 (HRT) [B] Cheshire, CT Novitiate of the Legion of Christ.
Kearns, Paul R. '71 (PRT) Bradley, ME St. Ann Church.
Kearns, Robert M. *s.s.j.* '63 (BAL) [S] Baltimore, MD St. Joseph Society of the Sacred Heart House of Central Administration.
Kearns, Thomas '60 (KCK) Paola, KS Holy Trinity Church.
Keating, Msgr. Bernard A. '47 (BAK) Retired.
Keating, C. Patrick '69 (SY) [6] Binghamton, NY St. John the Evangelist Church.
Keating, Carroll *s.j.* '61 (SAC) Fair Oaks, CA St. Mel Church.
Keating, David '54 (SFS) Retired.
Keating, Douglas '61 (MRY) Retired.
Keating, Earl *c.p.* '58 (HRT) [M] West Hartford, CT Holy Family Monastery/Retreat; [Q] West Hartford, CT Holy Family Retreat Center.
Keating, Edward C. *o.f.m.* '58 (SP) [10] Tampa, FL St. Lawrence Church.
Keating, Edward J. '94 (HBG) Carlisle, PA St. Patrick Church.
Keating, Edward J., Jr. '94 (HBG) [K] Harrisburg, PA Catholic Campus Ministry.
Keating, George M. '54 (NEW) Kenilworth, NJ St. Theresa's Church; Union, NJ Union Hospital; [S] Union, NJ The Association of St. Philomena's Helpers to the Suffering & Poor.
Keating, James P. '51 (CHI) [63] Chicago, IL St. Francis de Sales Church; Retired.
Keating, James R. *o.s.a.* '84 (ORL) Casselberry, FL St. Augustine Church.
Keating, Msgr. James V. '43 (NY) [3] Kingston, NY St. Joseph Church; Retired.
Keating, James W. '34 (CHI) Lyons, IL St. Hugh Church; Retired.
Keating, John R. *s.j.* '61 (NY) [DD] New York, NY Jesuit Community at Fordham University.
Keating, Joseph H. (HRT) Retired.
Keating, Joseph H. '77 (HRT) [3] Bristol, CT St. Gregory's Church.
Keating, Joseph R. '57 (LC) Retired.
Keating, Michael P. '97 (OM) Bellevue, NE St. Mary Church.
Keating, Pius F. *s.a.* '46 (NY) [DD] Garrison, NY Franciscan Friars of the Atonement, Minister General Office.
Keating, Thomas *o.c.s.o.* '49 (DEN) [M] Snowmass, CO St. Benedict's Monastery.
Keating, Thomas F. '66 (SY) Maine, NY Most Holy Rosary Church.
Keating, Timothy *c.ss.r.* '66 (NY) [DD] Esopus, NY Redemptorist Priests and Brothers C.Ss.R. (Province of Baltimore); [FF] Esopus, NY Mount St. Alphonsus Redemptorist Retreat Center.
Keating, Timothy G. *s.m.* '85 (WDC) [M] Washington, DC Marist Center.
Keaveney, George J. *c.ss.r.* '66 (BRK) [V] Brooklyn, NY Our Lady of Good Counsel Residence.
Keaveney, George J. *c.ss.r.* '66 (FgM) Redemptorist Foreign Missions.
Keaveney, John J. (NY) Washingtonville, NY St. Mary Church.
Keblesh, John W. '93 (PRM) Brunswick, OH St. Emilian Church.
Keck, Barnabas *o.f.m.cap.* '51 (NY) New Paltz, NY St. Joseph Church; [DD] New Paltz, NY St. Joseph Friary.
Keck, Edward L. '73 (COL) Newcomerstown, OH St. Francis de Sales Church.
Keck, Robert J. *s.j.* '60 (NY) [DD] New York, NY West Side Jesuit Community.
Kedzierski, Casimir '60 (PIT) Glassport, PA Queen of the Rosary Church.
Kedziora, Gerald *o.f.m.conv.* '41 (HBG) [5] Shamokin, PA Mother Cabrini Church.
Kee, James S. '95 (MOB) Auburn, AL St. Michael Church.
Keebler, Paul J. '66 (SY) [2] Binghamton, NY St. Ann Church; Binghamton, NY Broome Developmental Center.
Keebler, William (PEO) Thomasboro, IL St. Elizabeth's Church.
Keebler, William C., Jr. '91 (PEO) Penfield, IL St. Lawrence's Church.
Keech, William J. *o.s.f.s.* '57 (WIL) [I] Wilmington, DE DeSales House.
Keefe, Bernard A. '63 (BGP) [12] Stamford, CT St. Maurice Church.
Keefe, Charles R. '76 (MIL) [N] Milwaukee, WI Milwaukee Catholic Home.
Keefe, Danel T. '54 (OG) [4] Plattsburgh, NY St. Mary of the Lake Church.
Keefe, Daniel G. '83 (HRT) [3] Hamden, CT Our Lady of Mt. Carmel Church.
Keefe, Dennis A. '89 (BO) Unassigned.
Keefe, Donald J. *s.j., s.t.d.* '62 (NY) [A] Yonkers, NY St. Joseph's Seminary.
Keefe, Francis J. '58 (PRO) Scituate, RI St. Joseph Church.
Keefe, Francis L. *c.s.s.* '55 (BO) [W] Waltham, MA Stigmatine House.
Keefe, Gerald E. '47 (STP) Hopkins, MN St. Joseph's

Church; Retired.
Keefe, James *ss.cc.* '42 (FR) [I] Fairhaven, MA Sacred Hearts Provincial House.
Keefe, Jeffrey *o.f.m.conv.* '52 (SY) [2] Syracuse, NY Assumption B.V.M. Church.
Keefe, John *c.s.c.* '59 (RNO) Battle Mountain, NV St. John Bosco Church.
Keefe, John A. '49 (ALB) [5] Albany, NY St. Catherine of Siena Church; Retired.
Keefe, John J. '68 (LIN) Aurora, NE St. Mary's Church.
Keefe, John P. *c.s.c.* '59 (FTW) [J] South Bend, IN Congregation of Holy Cross, Indiana Province, Provincial House.
Keefe, Joseph L. '71 (WIN) [4] Winona, MN St. Mary's Church; [A] Winona, MN Immaculate Heart of Mary Seminary; [J] Winona, MN St. Mary's Parish of Winona Endowment Fund, Inc.
Keefe, Thomas H. *m.m.* '55 (NY) [DD] Maryknoll, NY Maryknoll Fathers and Brothers; [DD] Maryknoll, NY Maryknoll Fathers and Brothers.
Keefer, Hugh *o.s.b.* '67 (KCK) [H] Atchison, KS St. Benedict's Abbey.
Keefer, John *o.p.* '56 (SAT) [Q] San Antonio, TX Catholic Campus Ministry.
Keefer, John E. *o.p.* '56 (SAT) [B] San Antonio, TX Dominican Priory of San Juan Macias.
Keeffe, Anthony J. '63 (SY) Parish, NY St. Ann Church.
Keegan, Fintan *s.s.c.* '33 (PRO) [P] Bristol, RI St. Columban's Retirement House.
Keegan, James M. *s.j.* '71 (BO) [W] Boston, MA The Society of Jesus of New England-Provincial Offices.
Keegan, John E. *m.m.* '60 (NY) [DD] Maryknoll, NY Maryknoll Fathers and Brothers.
Keegan, John W. *s.j.* '69 (BO) [W] Boston, MA The Society of Jesus of New England-Provincial Offices.
Keegan, John W. *s.j.* '69 (PRT) [9] Portland, ME St. Pius X Church; [C] Portland, ME Cheverus High School; [C] Portland, ME Cheverus High School.
Keegan, Martin P. *m.m.* '65 (NY) [DD] Maryknoll, NY Maryknoll Fathers and Brothers.
Keegan, Terence *o.p.* '68 (PRO) [B] Providence, RI Providence College; [P] Providence, RI St. Thomas Aquinas Priory at Providence College.
Keegan, William F. *c.s.c.* '56 (FTW) [J] South Bend, IN Congregation of Holy Cross, Indiana Province, Provincial House.
Keegstra, Garrett *o.f.m.cap.* '86 (MAD) [F] Madison, WI St. Marys Hospital Medical Center; [L] Madison, WI San Damiano Friary.
Keehan, Msgr. Daniel J. '54 (NY) [205] Staten Island, NY Holy Family Church.
Keehan, Edward J. '57 (NY) [16] Yonkers, NY St. Peter Church.
Keehan, John J. '67 (CHI) [13] Chicago, IL St. Ann Church.
Keehan, Terence M. '86 (CHI) [131] Chicago, IL St. Matthias Church.
Keehner, John (Y) [1] Youngstown, OH Cathedral of St. Columba.
Keel, Edwin L. *s.m.* '70 (NO) [P] New Orleans, LA Marist Fathers.
Keelen, Kevin *o.s.a.* '91 (TR) Rumson, NJ Holy Cross Church.
Keeler, Robert Gregory *o.p.* '82 (NY) [22] New York, NY St. Catherine of Siena Church.
Keeley, Isaac '92 (WOR) [A] Spencer, MA St. Joseph's Abbey School of Theology and Institute of Monastic Studies; [N] Spencer, MA St. Joseph's Abbey.
Keeley, Patrick J. *c.m.* '58 (STL) Sappington, MO St. Catherine Laboure Church.
Keeley, Patrick P. '54 (NY) Military Chaplains.
Keeling, Paul M. *c.r.s.p.* '75 (BUF) [B] Youngstown, NY St. Anthony M. Zaccaria Seminary; [B] Youngstown, NY The National Shrine Basilica of Our Lady of Fatima.
Keena, James *c.ss.r.* '57 (DEN) [M] Denver, CO The Redemptorists/Denver Province.
Keenan, Alexander J. '76 (BO) [22] Boston, MA Gate of Heaven Church.
Keenan, Basil *o.s.b.* '67 (OKL) Seminole, OK Immaculate Conception Church; [I] Shawnee, OK St. Gregory's Abbey.
Keenan, Msgr. Charles J. '42 (LIN) Retired; [E] Lincoln, NE Bonacum House.
Keenan, Christopher *o.f.m.* '71 (NY) [35] New York, NY St. Francis of Assisi Church.
Keenan, Eugene '71 (TR) Leave of Absence.
Keenan, Francis X. *c.p.* '61 (CHI) [N] Chicago, IL Passionist Community-Immaculate Conception Monastery.
Keenan, James *s.j.* '82 (BO) [W] Cambridge, MA Weston Jesuit Community.
Keenan, James F. *s.j.* '69 (NEW) [C] Jersey City, NJ St. Peter's Preparatory School.
Keenan, James O. *o.s.f.s.* '49 (WIL) [I] Childs, MD Oblates of St. Francis De Sales.
Keenan, James R. '99 (RCK) [4] Rockford, IL St. Edward Church.
Keenan, John *s.s.s.* '69 (CHI) [U] Chicago, IL Trinity House.
Keenan, John *s.s.s.* '69 (CLV) [O] Cleveland, OH Congregation of the Blessed Sacrament Provincial House.
Keenan, Msgr. John C. '51 (ORG) Retired.
Keenan, John J. '43 (SD) Retired.
Keenan, John J. *s.j.* '55 (ALN) [A] Wernersville, PA Jesuit Center.
Keenan, Joseph A. *c.ss.r.* '47 (BRK) [107] Brooklyn, NY Our Lady of Perpetual Help Basilica Church.
Keenan, Joseph F. '84 (PIT) Monroeville, PA St. Bernadette Church.
Keenan, Msgr. Patrick J. '69 (NY) Cortlandt Manor, NY St. Columbanus Church.
Keenan, Paul *s.t.* '50 (WDC) [M] Adelphi, MD Missionary Servants of the Most Holy Trinity.
Keenan, Paul A. '77 (NY) [93] New York, NY Our Lady of Peace Church.
Keenan, Terence '65 (FR) South Dartmouth, MA St. Mary's Church.
Keenan, Thomas E. '55 (MAN) Retired.
Keenan, Thomas L. '63 (PRO) [3] East Providence, RI St. Margaret Church.
Keenan, Vincent *s.s.j.* '52 (NO) [P] New Orleans, LA Josephite Fathers and Brothers.
Keenan, William R. *o.f.m.* '56 (FgM) Franciscan Foreign Missions.
Keene, David A. '97 (BO) [2] Methuen, MA St. Monica Church.
Keene, James H. *s.j.* '73 (LA) [C] Los Angeles, CA Loyola Marymount University.
Keene, Kenneth R. '95 (PIT) [6] Ambridge, PA Good Samaritan Church.
Keene, Mark A. '84 (COV) [2] Covington, KY St. Agnes Church.
Keene, Michael *o.s.b.* '37 (IND) [J] St. Meinrad, IN St. Meinrad Archabbey.
Keene, Warren '81 (STA) [8] Jacksonville, FL Immaculate Conception Church.
Keener, Mark P. (BAL) [Q] Baltimore, MD Associated Catholic Charities, Inc. (Catholic Charities).
Keener, Michael '92 (MIA) Absent on Leave.
Keener, Robert J. '95 (CHI) Hazel Crest, IL St. Anne Church.
Keeney, Charles '77 (NY) City, NY Anna M. Kross Center.
Keeney, Charles P. '78 (BRK) [G] Astoria, NY St. John Preparatory School.
Keeney, Edward *ss.cc.* '61 (FR) [I] Fairhaven, MA Sacred Hearts Provincial House.
Keeney, Timothy '96 (RIC) Newport News, VA Our Lady of Mount Carmel Church.
Keenoy, John A. '87 (STL) [1] St. Charles, MO St. Charles Borromeo Church.
Keensy, Charles P. '78 (BRK) [168] Queens, NY St. Francis of Assisi Church.
Keese, John '74 (LA) Sepulveda, CA Our Lady of Peace Church.
Keesler, Robert L. '36 (WDC) Laurel, MD St. Mary Church; Retired.
Keferl, Francis J. '73 (CIN) Vandalia, OH St. Christopher Church.
Keffer, Joseph D. *o.s.a.* '47 (ALB) [2] Troy, NY St. Augustine Church.
Keffer, Robert *o.cist.* '97 (LC) [H] Sparta, WI Our Lady of Spring Bank, Cistercian Abbey.
Keffer, Robert F. '68 (WDC) Burtonsville, MD Resurrection Church.
Keffer, Thomas '77 (SR) Retired.
Keffler, Leopold *o.f.m.conv.* '63 (IND) [B] Indianapolis, IN Marian College; [J] Mount Saint Francis, IN Provincial Headquarters for the Conventual Franciscan Province.
Kegel, William M. *s.j.* '42 (OAK) [1] Walnut Creek, CA St. Anne Church; [N] Berkeley, CA Jesuit Community at Jesuit School of Theology at Berkeley.
Kegley, Jeffrey J. '96 (TR) New Monmouth, NJ St. Mary Church.
Kehew, Donal R. '63 (PRO) New Shoreham, RI St. Andrew Church.
Kehoe, Charles B. '73 (BRK) [189] Queens, NY St. Kevin Church.
Kehoe, Daniel J. '39 (PH) Sharon Hill, PA Holy Spirit Church; Retired.
Kehoe, James P. '70 (CHI) [139] Chicago, IL Nativity of Our Lord Church.
Kehoe, Joel *o.s.b.* '78 (B) [C] Jerome, ID Monastery of the Ascension.
Kehoe, Joseph F. '66 (SY) Durhamville, NY St. Francis Church; Morrisville, NY St. Joan of Arc Church; New London, NY Holy Cross Church.
Kehoe, Mark E. '99 (MET) Fords, NJ Our Lady of Peace Church.
Kehoe, Richard J. *c.m.* '49 (PH) [AA] Philadelphia, PA Congregation of the Mission.
Kehoe, Richard J. *c.m.* '57 (GR) [I] Spring Lake, MI St. Lazare Retreat House.
Kehoe, Thomas F. '75 (WDC) [3] Bowie, MD St. Edward Church.
Kehres, Franklin P. '68 (TOL) Norwalk, OH St. Paul Church.
Kehres, John C. *s.j.* '50 (DET) [27] Detroit, MI Gesu Church.
Kehres, Paul S. *s.j.* '51 (FgM) Provinces.
Keigher, Bernard '74 (TR) Lakehurst, NJ St. John Church.
Keilbasa, Richard A. '59 (SC) Rockwell City, IA Calhoun County State Reformatory, Minimum Security for Men.
Keilty, Msgr. John P. '41 (BO) Senior Priests.
Keine, Joachim *o.f.m.conv.* (IND) Indianapolis, IN Veterans' Administration Hospital.
Keiser, Jerome F. '71 (STP) [26] St. Paul, MN St. Mark Church.
Keiser, Ray W. '70 (BIR) Gardendale, AL St. Elizabeth Ann Seton Church.
Keith, Christopher R. '89 (GI) Bridgeport, NE All Souls Church.
Keith, John C. '56 (SD) Retired.
Keitz, Bernard Lawrence *o.p.* '54 (NY) [DD] New York, NY St. Vincent Ferrer Priory.
Kekeisen, William '58 (SFD) Retired.
Kelash, David '94 (PHX) El Mirage, AZ Santa Teresita Church.
Kelbel, Joseph '80 (BAK) The Dalles, OR St. Peter's Church.
Kelchak, Joseph '50 (GRY) [F] Hobart, IN St. Mary Medical Center.
Kelchak, Joseph M. '50 (SUP) Retired.
Keleher, Msgr. J. Patrick '68 (BUF) [R] Alfred, NY Campus Ministry.
Keliher, Michael *c.s.v.* '76 (LAV) Henderson, NV St. Thomas More Church.
Kelleher, Cornelius '56 (DUL) Beroun, MN St. Joseph's Church; Hinckley, MN St. Patrick's Church.
Kelleher, Cyril *o.f.m.cap.* '46 (LA) Solvang, CA Old Mission Santa Ines Church.
Kelleher, Dennis *s.d.b.* (NEW) [S] South Orange, NJ Salesians of Don Bosco.
Kelleher, James L. '54 (PRO) [1] Johnston, RI St. Brigid Church.
Kelleher, James R. *s.o.l.t.* '96 (CC) [H] Robstown, TX Society of Our Lady of the Most Holy Trinity; [J] Corpus Christi, TX Our Lady of Corpus Christi Catholic Undergraduate Liberal Arts.
Kelleher, John *o.f.m.* '89 (NEW) [N] Hohokus, NJ St. Anthony of Padua.
Kelleher, Joseph '53 (CHL) Retired.
Kelleher, Lawrence A. '93 (GAY) Black River, MI St. Gabriel Church; Ossineke, MI St. Catherine Church.
Kelleher, Mark A. '96 (WIL) Newark, DE St. John the Baptist-Holy Angels Church.
Kelleher, Matthew H. *m.m.* '67 (FgM) Maryknoll Foreign Missions.
Kelleher, Michael '65 (BLX) Pascagoula, MS Sacred Heart Church.
Kelleher, Robert N. '59 (BO) Emergency Response Group.
Kelleher, Timothy J. '71 (BO) Walpole, MA Blessed Sacrament Church.
Kelleher, Walter T. *m.m.* '56 (NY) [DD] Maryknoll, NY Maryknoll Fathers and Brothers.
Kelleher, William A. '91 (NY) Bronxville, NY St. Joseph Church; Retired.
Kellen, Elmer W. '50 (WIN) Retired.
Keller, Bernard C. *s.v.d.* '55 (LR) Pine Bluff, AR St. Peter's Church.
Keller, Brendan '60 (MOB) Retired.
Keller, Brian M. (BRK) [222] Queens, NY St. Pancras Church.
Keller, Daniel E. '82 (OM) Columbus, NE St. Bonaventure Church.
Keller, David S. '98 (HBG) [5] Harrisburg, PA Holy Name of Jesus Church.
Keller, Gary W. '71 (HEL) Ronan, MT Sacred Heart Church.
Keller, Gerald J. '65 (CLV) Berea, OH St. Adalbert Church.
Keller, Harvey M. '45 (TOL) Norwalk, OH St. Paul Church; Retired.
Keller, Herbert B. *s.j.* '81 (SCR) [C] Scranton, PA University of Scranton; [E] Scranton, PA Scranton Preparatory School.
Keller, J. Rod '54 (ORG) Retired.
Keller, John '74 (GAL) [71] Houston, TX Prince of Peace Church.
Keller, John D. *o.s.a.* '64 (SD) [B] San Diego, CA University of San Diego; [H] San Diego, CA Augustinian Community.
Keller, Ken '69 (AMA) [10] Amarillo, TX St. Mary's Church.
Keller, Lawrence E. '47 (STP) Retired.
Keller, Lawrence W. '53 (COV) Retired.
Keller, Neil J. '55 (CIN) Retired.
Keller, Robb '84 (B) Twin Falls, ID St. Edward The Confessor Church.
Keller, Robert *o.p.* '83 (SFE) [L] Albuquerque, NM St. Thomas Aquinas (Newman Center) University Parish.
Keller, Robert J. '74 (DET) Harper Woods, MI St. Peter the Apostle Church.
Keller, Robert J. *o.p.* '83 (SFE) [31] Albuquerque, NM St. Thomas Aquinas University Church.

Keller, Robert L. '67 (CIN) [73] Cincinnati, OH Resurrection of Our Lord Church.
Keller, Theodore '46 (LEX) [7] Lexington, KY St. Peter Church; Retired.
Keller, Thomas G. '97 (STL) Mehlville, MO St. Margaret Mary Alacoque Church.
Keller, Thomas J. *m.s.c.* '55 (ORG) Los Alamitos, CA St. Hedwig Church.
Keller, Thomas W. '58 (LR) Jacksonville, AR St. Jude the Apostle Church.
Kellerman, Raymond C. '73 (CIN) [35] Cincinnati, OH Holy Trinity Church.
Kellermann, Leonard P. *s.m.* '46 (WDC) [M] Washington, DC Marist Center.
Kellett, William K. *s.j.* '65 (STL) [P] St. Louis, MO Hallahan House.
Kelley, Aloysius P. *s.j.* '62 (BGP) [B] Fairfield, CT Fairfield University; [E] Fairfield, CT Fairfield College Preparatory School; [P] Fairfield, CT The Fairfield Jesuit Community-Fairfield University.
Kelley, Arnold E. '56 (BO) Unassigned.
Kelley, Charles F. *s.j.* '84 (BO) [E] Boston, MA Boston College High School & Jesuit Community.
Kelley, Clark T. *o.s.f.s.* '64 (STO) [A] Stockton, CA St. Mary's High School.
Kelley, Danny '95 (FWT) Clifton, TX Holy Angels Church; Morgan, TX Our Lady of Guadalupe Church.
Kelley, David *o.s.a.* '73 (ALB) Mechanicville, NY Assumption-St. Paul Church.
Kelley, David F. (WIL) Bethany Beach, DE St. Ann Church.
Kelley, David J. '74 (CIN) [K] Cincinnati, OH Mercy Hospital Anderson.
Kelley, Donald *s.s.c.* '62 (OM) [K] St. Columbans, NE St. Columban's Foreign Mission Society.
Kelley, Edward J. '66 (MAN) Portsmouth, NH Immaculate Conception Church.
Kelley, Edward J. '68 (PRO) On Duty Outside the Diocese.
Kelley, Msgr. Francis H. '68 (BO) [65] Boston, MA Sacred Heart Church.
Kelley, J. Ralph '34 (NOR) Retired.
Kelley, James F. '61 (ANC) Dillingham, AK Holy Rosary Church.
Kelley, John E. '61 (WOR) Baldwinville, MA St. Vincent De Paul Church; Otter River, MA Walter E. Fernald State School.
Kelley, John J. '45 (SCR) Retired.
Kelley, John J. *s.m.* '53 (CIN) [M] Dayton, OH Marianist Provincialate.
Kelley, John W. '59 (STP) [8] St. Paul, MN The Nativity of Our Lord Church.
Kelley, Joseph '46 (SPK) Retired.
Kelley, Joseph '87 (PH) Horsham, PA St. Catherine of Siena Church.
Kelley, Laurence E. '60 (BO) Health Leave.
Kelley, Michael A. '00 (PRO) [1] East Providence, RI St. Brendan Church.
Kelley, Michael H. '85 (IND) Starlight, IN St. John the Baptist Church.
Kelley, Michael J. '75 (WDC) [28] Washington, DC St. Martin of Tours Church.
Kelley, Omer C. '49 (GB) White Lake, WI Ss. James & Stanislaus Church; Retired; [F] Antigo, WI Langlade Memorial Hospital.
Kelley, Paul G. '49 (BO) Winchester, MA St. Mary Church; Senior Priests.
Kelley, Raymond H. *m.m.* '58 (FgM) Maryknoll Foreign Missions.
Kelley, Richard J. '72 (MAN) Jaffrey, NH St. Patrick Church; [3] Nashua, NH St. Christopher Church; [10] Nashua, NH St. Stanislaus Church.
Kelley, Robert E. '79 (WOR) Millbury, MA St. Brigid Church.
Kelley, Thomas '67 (E) On Duty Outside Diocese.
Kelley, Thomas '67 (SAN) [3] Midland, TX Our Lady of San Juan de Los Lagos Church.
Kelley, Thomas J. '51 (PH) [103] Philadelphia, PA St. Matthew Church; Retired.
Kelley, Thomas L. '88 (MAD) Darlington, WI Holy Rosary Church.
Kelley, Thomas W. *o.s.f.s.* '50 (CAM) [M] Pittsgrove, NJ Villa St. Joseph.
Kelley, William *s.v.d.* '67 (BLX) [A] Bay St. Louis, MS St. Augustine's; [A] Bay St. Louis, MS St. Augustine's; [E] Bay St. Louis, MS Southern Province of St. Augustine - Provincial Residence.
Kelley, William H. *c.s.c.* '70 (BUR) Bennington, VT Sacred Heart St. Francis de Sales Church.
Kelley, William J. '54 (MAN) Peterborough, NH St. Peter Church.
Kelley, William J. *s.j.* '85 (CHL) Mooresville, NC St. Therese Church; [J] Charlotte, NC Jesuit Community.
Kellick, John W. '52 (GAL) Retired.
Kelligar, Msgr. William L. '53 (OM) Retired.
Kelliher, Alexander *s.a.* '77 (NY) [DD] Garrison, NY Franciscan Friars of the Atonement.
Kelliher, Daniel *o.c.s.o.* '48 (DEN) [M] Snowmass, CO St. Benedict's Monastery.
Kelliher, Msgr. John J. '58 (WOR) [14] Worcester, MA Our Lady of the Rosary Church.
Kelliher, Michael M. *s.j.* '67 (SEA) [A] Seattle, WA Seattle University.
Kellner, Winfried M. '63 (ROC) [39] Rochester, NY Our Lady of Victory-St. Joseph Church.
Kelly, William A. '59 (STA) Jacksonville Beach, FL St. Paul's Church.
Kelly, Albert P. '72 (MOB) Millbrook, AL St. Elizabeth Ann Seton Church.
Kelly, Andrew E. '70 (DAV) Iowa City, IA Veteran's Administration Hospital; [J] Iowa City, IA Mercy Hospital.
Kelly, Anthony *s.a.c.* '59 (NY) [91] New York, NY Our Lady of Mt. Carmel Church.
Kelly, Anthony *s.c.j.* '73 (SFS) Chamberlain, SD St. James Church.
Kelly, Arnold E. '56 (BO) Dracut, MA St. Mary of the Assumption Church.
Kelly, Augustine G. *o.s.b.* '88 (MAN) [K] Manchester, NH St. Anselm Abbey.
Kelly, Bernard *c.h.s.* '73 (NY) [DD] New York, NY Apostolic Society of the Crusade of the Holy Spirit.
Kelly, Bernard R. '61 (FR) Woods Hole, MA St. Joseph's Church.
Kelly, Bernard T. '41 (LC) Retired.
Kelly, Brian F. '77 (SCR) Military Chaplains.
Kelly, C. Richard '70 (DET) Canton, MI St. Thomas a Becket Church.
Kelly, Charles *s.c.j.* '71 (GAL) [35] Houston, TX Holy Name Church.
Kelly, Charles '99 (SAC) South Lake Tahoe, CA St. Theresa Church.
Kelly, Msgr. Charles A. '67 (RIC) [1] Richmond, VA Cathedral of the Sacred Heart.
Kelly, Charles F. '48 (CHI) [47] Chicago, IL St. Daniel the Prophet Church; Retired; [X] Chicago, IL Apostolate of the Handicapped.
Kelly, Charles F. '64 (MET) Old Bridge, NJ St. Ambrose Church.
Kelly, Msgr. Charles S. '69 (NY) Haverstraw, NY St. Peter Church.
Kelly, Columba *o.s.b.* '58 (IND) [A] St. Meinrad, IN St. Meinrad Seminary; [J] St. Meinrad, IN St. Meinrad Archabbey.
Kelly, Cornelius F. *o.f.m.* '39 (BO) [Z] Boston, MA Saint Anthony Residence.
Kelly, Daniel '72 (RIC) Amherst, VA St. Francis of Assisi Church; Lovingston, VA St. Mary Church; Scottsville, VA St. George Church.
Kelly, Daniel A. '67 (PAT) [3] Wayne, NJ Immaculate Heart of Mary Church.
Kelly, Daniel J. '56 (LC) Retired.
Kelly, Daniel J. '59 (DAV) Retired.
Kelly, David (DET) [T] Detroit, MI Co-Chairpersons:.
Kelly, David A. *c.pp.s.* '82 (CHI) [19] Chicago, IL Assumption Church; [X] Chicago, IL Kolbe House.
Kelly, David C. *m.m.* '57 (FgM) Maryknoll Foreign Missions.
Kelly, David F. '66 (WOR) On Duty Outside the Diocese.
Kelly, Donald '63 (ALB) Green Island, NY St. Joseph Church.
Kelly, E. Francis '67 (SCR) [8] Wilkes-Barre, PA Holy Saviour Church.
Kelly, Edgar M. '43 (MEM) Retired.
Kelly, Edward '65 (MEM) On Duty Outside the Diocese.
Kelly, Edward '80 (SAT) Selma, TX Our Lady of Perpetual Help Church.
Kelly, Edward C. '90 (PH) [102] Philadelphia, PA Maternity B.V.M. Church.
Kelly, Edward J. '68 (PH) Lafayette Hill, PA St. Philip Neri Church.
Kelly, Edward M. '68 (MIA) Coral Springs, FL St. Elizabeth Ann Seton Church.
Kelly, Emmett '54 (HEL) [E] Missoula, MT St. Patrick Hospital and Health Sciences Center, Sisters of Providence of Montana Corporation.
Kelly, Emmett '55 (HEL) Retired.
Kelly, Ernest *o.p.* '43 (Y) [13] Youngstown, OH St. Dominic's Church.
Kelly, Eugene A. '38 (OG) Rosiere, NY St. Vincent de Paul Church; Retired.
Kelly, Eugene D. *s.j.* '53 (STL) [O] St. Louis, MO Fusz Pavilion.
Kelly, Eugene L. *o.s.f.s.* '65 (PH) [D] Philadelphia, PA Father Judge High School for Boys; [AA] Philadelphia, PA Father Judge Faculty House.
Kelly, Evangelist *o.f.m.cap.* '46 (LA) [B] Santa Ynez, CA San Lorenzo Novitiate and Seminary.
Kelly, Francis '57 (LA) West Los Angeles, CA Veterans Administration Wadsworth Hospital Center; Military and VA Chaplains.
Kelly, Francis *o.f.m.* '89 (PH) [D] Philadelphia, PA Archbishop Ryan High School.
Kelly, Msgr. Francis D. '63 (BO) [A] Weston, MA Pope John XXIII National Seminary.
Kelly, Msgr. Francis D. '80 (WOR) On Duty Outside the Diocese.
Kelly, Francis E. '55 (PH) Pottstown, PA St. Aloysius Church; Valley Forge, PA St. Teresa of Avila Church.
Kelly, Francis Joseph *f.p.o.* '98 (FR) [I] New Bedford, MA Franciscans of Primitive Observance.
Kelly, Francis X. *o.f.m.* '88 (PH) [AA] Philadelphia, PA St. Pius X Friary.
Kelly, Frank F. '77 (GF) Retired.
Kelly, George *c.ss.r.* '59 (NEW) [2] East Orange, NJ Holy Spirit-Our Lady Help of Christians Church.
Kelly, George *c.ss.r.* '59 (ORL) [F] New Smyrna Beach, FL Redemptorist Fathers of the Vice Province of Richmond.
Kelly, Msgr. George A. '42 (NY) [58] New York, NY St. John the Evangelist Church; Retired.
Kelly, George F. *c.ss.r.* '59 (MET) Lyons, NJ U.S. Veterans Medical Center.
Kelly, Gerald E. *m.m.* '67 (BO) [W] East Walpole, MA Maryknoll Mission Promotion Department.
Kelly, Gerald G. '34 (ROC) Retired.
Kelly, Gerard D. '49 (PIT) Retired; [O] Pittsburgh, PA St. John Vianney Manor.
Kelly, Gerard P. *c.m.* '82 (CHI) [G] Chicago, IL Catholic Charities of the Archdiocese of Chicago-Archdiocesan Offices; [N] Chicago, IL Vincentian Community, Congregation of the Mission, Midwest Province.
Kelly, Gregory '82 (DAL) McKinney, TX St. Gabriel the Archangel Church.
Kelly, J. Patrick *o.f.m.* '71 (NY) [DD] New York, NY Franciscan Friars, Order of Friars Minor, Holy Name Province.
Kelly, James '44 (DOD) Retired.
Kelly, James *glmy.* '48 (CIN) [M] Cincinnati, OH Headquarters of Glenmary Home Missioners.
Kelly, James *c.m.* '53 (BRK) [V] Jamaica, NY Vincentian Residence.
Kelly, James '57 (ALB) Retired.
Kelly, James *c.s.c.* '58 (FgM) Holy Cross Foreign Missions.
Kelly, James *o.s.b.* '58 (ROC) [I] Pine City, NY Mount Saviour Monastery.
Kelly, James '60 (PHX) Camp Verde, AZ St. Frances Cabrini Church.
Kelly, James *o.f.m.* '78 (STL) [P] St. Louis, MO Franciscan Friary of St. Anthony of Padua.
Kelly, Msgr. James A. '82 (NY) [II] New York, NY Prelature of the Holy Cross and Opus Dei.
Kelly, James E. *c.s.c.* '58 (FTW) [J] South Bend, IN Congregation of Holy Cross, Indiana Province, Provincial House.
Kelly, Msgr. James G. '62 (BUF) [44] Buffalo, NY St. Margaret Church.
Kelly, James J. '50 (PH) Brookhaven, PA Our Lady of Charity Church; Plymouth Meeting, PA Epiphany of Our Lord Church; Retired.
Kelly, Msgr. James J. '60 (BRK) [24] Brooklyn, NY St. Brigid Church.
Kelly, James J. '83 (LA) Diamond Bar, CA St. Denis Church.
Kelly, James Joseph '50 (PH) Retired.
Kelly, James M. '53 (BRK) [S] Bayside, NY Ozanam Hall of Queens Nursing Home, Inc.
Kelly, Msgr. James P. '62 (RVC) [1] Rockville Centre, NY St. Agnes Church.
Kelly, James Patrick '63 (CAM) [M] Pittsgrove, NJ Villa St. Joseph.
Kelly, James T. '92 (BO) [8] Haverhill, MA Sacred Hearts Church.
Kelly, Joel *o.s.b.* '66 (SCL) St. Cloud, MN Minnesota State Reformatory for Men; [I] Collegeville, MN St. John's Abbey, of the Order of St. Benedict.
Kelly, John D. '86 (ARL) Fairfax, VA St. Leo's Church.
Kelly, John E. '73 (BO) Stoughton, MA St. James Church.
Kelly, John E. '87 (BUF) Amherst, NY St. Leo the Great Church.
Kelly, John F. '84 (PT) Crestview, FL Our Lady of Victory Church.
Kelly, John J. *o.s.a.* '42 (MIA) [H] Miami, FL Casa San Lorenzo.
Kelly, John J. '64 (BLX) Clermont Harbor, MS St. Ann Church.
Kelly, John J. *o.s.f.s.* '71 (CHL) High Point, NC Immaculate Heart of Mary Church.
Kelly, John J. '87 (PH) Huntingdon Valley, PA St. Albert the Great Church.
Kelly, John L. (BAL) [V] Glen Burnie, MD The Church of the Good Shepherd Parish Endowment Trust.
Kelly, John L. '54 (BAL) Glen Burnie, MD Church of the Good Shepherd.
Kelly, John P. '45 (BO) [6] Somerville, MA St. Joseph Church; Senior Priests.
Kelly, John R. '68 (NY) Military Chaplains.
Kelly, John R. '68 (R) Fayetteville, NC St. Patrick Church.
Kelly, John T. '61 (ALB) Albany, NY Memorial Hospital; Special Assignment.
Kelly, John T. *s.j.* '74 (BAL) [S] Baltimore, MD Jesuit Fathers and Brothers Maryland Provincial Curia.
Kelly, John W. '44 (LIN) Retired; [E] Lincoln, NE Bonacum House.
Kelly, John W. *c.ss.r.* '51 (HBG) [H] Ephrata, PA St. Clement's Mission House.
Kelly, John W. '59 (STP) Retired.

Kelly, Joseph A. *s.j.* '63 (NEW) [B] Jersey City, NJ Saint Peter's College.
Kelly, Joseph A. *s.j.* '63 (NY) [68] New York, NY St. Malachy's Church.
Kelly, Joseph J. '78 (NY) [127] Bronx, NY St. Anthony Church.
Kelly, Joseph L. *c.s.sp.* '50 (FgM) Holy Ghost Foreign Missions.
Kelly, Msgr. Joseph P. '66 (SCR) [20] Scranton, PA Nativity of Our Lord Church; [Q] Tunkhannock, PA Camp St. Andrew.
Kelly, Justin *s.j.* (DET) [23] Detroit, MI St. Francis de Sales Church.
Kelly, Justin J. *s.j.* (DET) [E] Detroit, MI Loyola High School.
Kelly, Kenneth W. '79 (KCK) Wea, KS Queen of the Holy Rosary Church.
Kelly, Lawrence D. *s.j.* '46 (MIL) [P] Milwaukee, WI Arrupe House Jesuit Community.
Kelly, Leonard *o.f.m.* '43 (PAT) [M] Ringwood, NJ Holy Name Friary, Inc.
Kelly, Msgr. Martin '47 (NEW) [2] Jersey City, NJ St. Aloysius Church.
Kelly, Martin C. '48 (PHX) Retired.
Kelly, Martin T. '89 (MAN) [8] Nashua, NH St. Patrick Church.
Kelly, Msgr. Matthew H. '42 (LA) Retired.
Kelly, Maurus *o.f.m.* '56 (LA) [Q] Santa Barbara, CA Franciscan Friary, Order of Friars Minor (Old Mission).
Kelly, Michael *ss.cc.* '65 (FR) [I] Fairhaven, MA Sacred Hearts Provincial House.
Kelly, Michael '76 (SFS) [C] Sioux Falls, SD Sioux Falls Catholic School System.
Kelly, Michael C. '95 (ARL) Annandale, VA St. Ambrose Church.
Kelly, Michael D. '71 (MOB) Foley, AL St. Margaret Church.
Kelly, Michael D. '76 (SFS) Hartford, SD St. George Church.
Kelly, Msgr. Michael E. '66 (NEW) [C] West Orange, NJ Seton Hall Preparatory School.
Kelly, Michael E. '73 (STO) San Andreas, CA St. Andrew Church.
Kelly, Michael J. '53 (OM) Retired.
Kelly, Michael J. '82 (PH) [120] Philadelphia, PA Our Lady of Hope Church.
Kelly, Michael M. '81 (SR) Arcata, CA St. Mary's Church.
Kelly, Michael T. *s.j.* '77 (MIL) [P] Milwaukee, WI Jesuit Community at Marquette University.
Kelly, Neil '91 (NY) [159] Bronx, NY St. Lucy Church.
Kelly, Pat '58 (IND) [13] Indianapolis, IN St. Andrew the Apostle Church.
Kelly, Patrick J. (BO) [3] Woburn, MA St. Charles Church.
Kelly, Patrick J. '48 (BO) Senior Priests.
Kelly, Patrick J. '58 (IND) [D] Indianapolis, IN Cathedral High School (Cathedral Trustees, Inc.).
Kelly, Patrick M. *s.j.* '99 (DET) [K] Detroit, MI Jesuit Provincial Office-Detroit Province of the Society of Jesus.
Kelly, Paul *s.c.j.* '77 (MIL) [B] Hales Corners, WI Sacred Heart School of Theology; [P] Milwaukee, WI St. Joseph House of Formation.
Kelly, Paul J. '74 (OG) Lake Pleasant, NY St. James Major Church; Wells, NY St. Ann Church.
Kelly, Paul J. '83 (SC) [1] Sioux City, IA Cathedral of the Epiphany.
Kelly, Paul M. '47 (LA) Retired.
Kelly, Philip J. '93 (NY) [63] New York, NY St. Joseph of the Holy Family Church.
Kelly, Randy J. '94 (SAG) Maple Grove, MI St. Michael Church.
Kelly, Raymond J. '61 (BRK) [77] Brooklyn, NY St. Malachy's Church; [L] Brooklyn, NY Catholic Charities.
Kelly, Raymond M. '49 (PRO) [28] Providence, RI St. Patrick Church.
Kelly, Richard J. '88 (NEW) Kearny, NJ St. Stephen's Church.
Kelly, Robert '68 (WOR) Absent on Leave.
Kelly, Robert *s.v.d.* '86 (BLX) [A] Bay St. Louis, MS St. Augustine's; [E] Bay St. Louis, MS Southern Province of St. Augustine - Provincial Residence.
Kelly, Robert D. '00 (PRM) Euclid, OH St. Stephen Church.
Kelly, Robert F. *o.praem.* '53 (WIL) [B] Claymont, DE Archmere Academy; [I] Claymont, DE Immaculate Conception Priory of the Canons Regular of Premontre; [I] Claymont, DE Norbertine Fathers of Delaware, Inc.
Kelly, Robert G. *s.j.* '57 (NY) [A] Yonkers, NY St. Joseph's Seminary; [DD] New York, NY Jesuit Community at Fordham University.
Kelly, Robert J. *s.j.* '52 (FgM) Provinces.
Kelly, Msgr. Robert J. '53 (CHR) [11] Charleston, SC Church of the Nativity; [A] Charleston, SC Bishop England High School.
Kelly, Robert J. '74 (ALT) Philipsburg, PA SS. Peter and Paul Church.
Kelly, Robert L. '77 (SY) [1] Utica, NY Blessed Sacrament Church.
Kelly, Robert M. *o.p.* '89 (CHI) [23] Chicago, IL St. Basil/Visitation Church; [D] Oak Park, IL Fenwick High School.
Kelly, Stephen M. *s.j.* '90 (SJ) [L] Los Gatos, CA Sacred Heart Jesuit Center.
Kelly, Thomas *o.f.m.* '62 (NEW) Wood-Ridge, NJ Our Lady of the Assumption Church.
Kelly, Thomas '86 (HRT) Lakeville, CT St. Mary's Church.
Kelly, Thomas D. '77 (DEN) On Duty Outside the Archdiocese.
Kelly, Thomas E.J. *s.j.* '79 (STL) [C] St. Louis, MO Saint Louis University; [P] St. Louis, MO Leo Brown Jesuit Community.
Kelly, Thomas F. '41 (BRK) [91] Brooklyn, NY Our Lady of Angels Church; Retired.
Kelly, Msgr. Thomas F. '47 (Y) Retired.
Kelly, Thomas F. '56 (PEO) Retired.
Kelly, Thomas J. '43 (PH) Maple Glen, PA St. Alphonsus Church; Retired.
Kelly, Thomas J. '68 (ALB) [10] Troy, NY St. Patrick Church.
Kelly, Thomas J. C. *s.j.* '48 (BO) [W] Weston, MA Campion Health Center, Inc.
Kelly, Thomas M. '90 (BIR) Guntersville, AL St. William's Church.
Kelly, Thomas P. '70 (BO) Watertown, MA St. Patrick Church.
Kelly, Thomas R. '67 (NY) [144] Bronx, NY St. Gabriel Church.
Kelly, Timothy *o.s.b.* '61 (SCL) [I] Collegeville, MN St. John's Abbey, of the Order of St. Benedict.
Kelly, Timothy J. '99 (TYL) [1] Tyler, TX Cathedral of the Immaculate Conception.
Kelly, Tony *s.a.c.* '55 (NY) [DD] New York, NY Pallottine Fathers.
Kelly, Msgr. Vincent (MIA) [L] Miami Shores, FL Catholic Community Foundation, Inc.
Kelly, Vincent J. *c.ss.r.* '39 (BO) [53] Boston, MA Our Lady of Perpetual Help Church.
Kelly, Vincent J. '57 (SY) Oriskany Falls, NY St. Joseph Church.
Kelly, Msgr. Vincent T. '56 (MIA) [10] Fort Lauderdale, FL St. John the Baptist Church; [C] Fort Lauderdale, FL St. Thomas Aquinas High School.
Kelly, William E. '40 (NY) Retired; [DD] New York, NY Our Lady of Consolation Residence.
Kelly, William J. '48 (CHI) Retired.
Kelly, William J. *s.j.* '54 (MIL) [P] Milwaukee, WI Jesuit Community at Marquette University.
Kelly, Msgr. William M. '47 (SY) [3] Rome, NY St. Paul Church.
Kelly, William M. *s.d.s.* '79 (BIR) [2] Huntsville, AL St. Mary of the Visitation Church.
Kelly, William T. '78 (CIN) On Duty Outside the Archdiocese.
Kelly, William T. '88 (BO) [A] Boston, MA St. John's Seminary School of Theology.
Kelmartin, John J. '49 (BAL) Retired.
Kelpinski, Donald *o.m.v.* '89 (BO) [B] Boston, MA Oblate Provincialate.
Kelpsas, Anthony *m.i.c.* '53 (JOL) Darien, IL Our Lady of Peace Church.
Kelpsas, Jaunius '94 (CHI) [89] Chicago, IL Immaculate Conception Church.
Kelso, Francis E. '61 (MAN) Rochester, NH St. Mary Church.
Kelso, Ronald *s.s.c.* '73 (FgM) St. Columban's Foreign Mission.
Keltos, Adam *o.f.m.conv.* '62 (SY) [V] Syracuse, NY Syracuse University, St. Thomas More Foundation, Inc.
Kelty, Edward *o.s.* '89 (PCE) On Duty Outside the Diocese.
Kelty, Msgr. Leo A. '60 (TR) Howell Township, NJ St. William the Abbot Church.
Kelty, Matthew *o.c.s.o.* '46 (L) [L] Trappist, KY Abbey of Our Lady of Gethsemani, of the Order of Cistercians of the Strict Observance.
Kemeter, Robert '72 (PSC) Pittston, PA St. Michael Church.
Kemme, Allen '91 (SFD) Tuscola, IL Forty Martyrs Church.
Kemme, Carl A. '86 (SFD) [1] Decatur, IL Holy Family Church.
Kemme, Joseph A. *s.j.* '64 (STL) [P] St. Louis, MO Jesuit Community Corporation at St. Louis University - Jesuit Hall.
Kemme, Joseph A. *s.j.* '64 (WDC) [P] Faulkner, MD Loyola on the Potomac Retreat House.
Kemmer, Victor A. '43 (MIL) St. Kilian, WI St. Kilian Church; Retired.
Kemmery, Robert J. '54 (MAN) Retired.
Kemner, Gregory *o.f.m.* '55 (FgM) Franciscan Foreign Missions.
Kemner, Kieran *o.f.m.* '53 (CHI) [N] Countryside, IL St. Gratian Friary, Franciscan Friars.
Kemo, Msgr. Kurt H. '83 (STU) Toronto, OH St. Francis of Assisi Church; Toronto, OH St. Joseph's Church; [J] Steubenville, OH RCIA.
Kemp, Dennis '73 (SEA) [14] Seattle, WA St. Mark Church.
Kemp, Patrick W. '55 (WDC) Retired.
Kemp, Raymond B. '67 (WDC) [40] Washington, DC St. Stephen Martyr Church; Special Ministries; [V] Washington, DC Woodstock Theological Center.
Kemp, Thomas L. '52 (BUF) East Bethany, NY Immaculate Conception Church.
Kempa, Stanislaus '73 (BO) [2] Lowell, MA Holy Trinity Church.
Kempczynski, Msgr. John '57 (BUF) [7] Tonawanda, NY St. Timothy Church; Retired.
Kemper, Gerald B. *o.praem.* '51 (GB) [I] De Pere, WI St. Norbert Abbey.
Kemper, Jeffrey M. '79 (CIN) [B] Cincinnati, OH Mt. St. Mary's Seminary of the West.
Kemper, John *s.s.* '83 (SAT) [A] San Antonio, TX The Assumption-St. John's Seminary; [C] San Antonio, TX Oblate School of Theology.
Kemper, John C. *s.s.* '83 (HBG) On Duty Outside the Diocese.
Kempf, Joseph G. '80 (STL) O'Fallon, MO Assumption Church.
Kempf, William (STL) [U] St. Louis, MO University of Missouri, St. Louis, Newman House.
Kempfer, James T. '69 (JOL) Addison, IL St. Joseph Church.
Kempfirl, Fred '65 (NY) Milton, NY St. James Church.
Kemphues, Carl *o.f.m.* '56 (CIN) [M] Cincinnati, OH St. Francis Seraph Friary.
Kemphues, Carl *o.f.m.* '56 (FgM) Franciscan Foreign Missions.
Kempkes, Lambert *c.m.m.* '50 (CHI) [J] Evergreen Park, IL Little Company of Mary Hospital and Health Care Centers.
Kempkes, Lambert *c.m.m.* '50 (DET) [K] Dearborn Heights, MI Our Lady of Grace Monastery.
Kempski, Leonard J. '66 (WIL) [4] Wilmington, DE Christ Our King Church; Perryville, MD Church of the Good Shepherd.
Kenaston, Perry '99 (JUN) Yakutat, AK St. Ann Church.
Kencik, Marian M. '62 (KAL) Niles, MI St. Mary Church.
Kendall, Jeffrey A. '97 (CHR) [4] Charleston, SC Sacred Heart Church; [16] Charleston, SC Christ the Divine Teacher Church; [H] Charleston, SC The Citadel.
Kendall, Michael *s.d.s.* '61 (MIL) [P] Milwaukee, WI Salvatorian Provincial Residence.
Kendall, Philip *c.s.v.* '62 (KCK) [1] Kansas City, KS Cathedral of St. Peter the Apostle ; [I] Kansas City, KS Convent of the Sisters, Servants of Mary.
Kendall, R. Daniel *s.j.* '70 (SFR) [N] San Francisco, CA Jesuit Community at University of San Francisco.
Kendzierski, James *o.f.m.* '81 (MIL) Sturtevant, WI St. Sebastian Church.
Kendzierski, Norbert V. '64 (DET) Farmington, MI St. Colman Church.
Kenealy, John J. *s.j.* '58 (FgM) Provinces.
Kenealy, Thomas L. *s.j.* '58 (CHI) [N] Evanston, IL Canisius House.
Kenefick, Paul F. '56 (HRT) [12] Hartford, CT St. Lawrence O'Toole Church.
Kenehan, David A. *o.s.f.s.* '74 (TOL) [K] Toledo, OH Oblates of St. Francis de Sales.
Kenkel, Benedict J. '53 (DM) Guthrie Center, IA St. Mary Church.
Kenkel, Leonard A. '60 (DM) Creston, IA Holy Spirit Church.
Kenlon, Knute *o.f.m. cap.* '58 (BRK) [87] Brooklyn, NY St. Michael's Church.
Kenna, Daniel *o.f.m.* '73 (R) [4] Raleigh, NC St. Francis of Assisi Church.
Kenna, Donald J. '64 (BRK) [4] Brooklyn, NY All Saints Church.
Kenna, John A. '39 (DET) Retired.
Kenna, Joseph J. '67 (YAK) On Duty Outside the Diocese.
Kenna, Joseph R. '99 (ARL) Manassas, VA All Saints Church.
Kenna, Richard A. *s.j.* '57 (BAL) [S] Baltimore, MD Jesuit Fathers and Brothers Maryland Provincial Curia.
Kenna, Richard A. *s.j.* '57 (FgM) Provinces.
Kenna, Thomas J. '63 (NEW) Lyndhurst, NJ Our Lady of Mount Carmel Church.
Kennard, George V. *s.j.* '50 (STL) [P] St. Louis, MO Jesuit Community Corporation at St. Louis University - Jesuit Hall.
Kenneally, John A. '69 (SAV) [9] Savannah, GA St. James Church.
Kenneally, William F. '52 (BO) [1] Milton, MA St. Agatha Church.
Kenneally, William F. '53 (BO) Senior Priests.
Kenneally, William G. '61 (CHI) [69] Chicago, IL St. Gertrude Church.
Kennealy, Thomas P. *s.j.* '62 (CIN) [D] Cincinnati, OH Xavier University; [M] Cincinnati, OH Jesuit Community at Xavier University.

Kennebeck, Brian A. '00 (STL) Cottleville, MO St. Joseph Church.
Kennedy, Alan '52 (P) Retired.
Kennedy, Alex '90 (TLS) Grove, OK St. Elizabeth Church; Langley, OK St. Frances of Rome Church; Vinita, OK Holy Ghost Church.
Kennedy, Andrew '63 (BIR) [16] Birmingham, AL Our Lady of Lourdes Church.
Kennedy, Arthur L. (BO) [A] Brighton, MA St. John's Seminary.
Kennedy, Arthur L. '66 (BO) On Duty Outside the Archdiocese.
Kennedy, Arthur L. '67 (BO) [A] Boston, MA St. John's Seminary School of Theology.
Kennedy, Arthur L. '67 (STP) [C] St. Paul, MN University of St. Thomas.
Kennedy, Bernard *o.f.m.* '88 (CHI) [J] Oak Park, IL Oak Park Hospital.
Kennedy, Brian *c.s.s.r* '75 (RNO) Elko, NV St. Joseph's Church.
Kennedy, Charles J. '66 (PH) Bridgeport, PA St. Augustine Church.
Kennedy, Msgr. Christopher J. '44 (LA) [3] Long Beach, CA St. Barnabas Church; Retired.
Kennedy, David G. '55 (BUR) Retired.
Kennedy, Msgr. David W. '53 (GAL) Conroe, TX Sacred Heart Church.
Kennedy, David William '97 (OWN) Oak Grove, KY St. Michael the Archangel Church.
Kennedy, Donal P. '60 (YAK) [3] Yakima, WA Holy Redeemer Church.
Kennedy, Edward '68 (PH) Darby, PA Blessed Virgin Mary Church.
Kennedy, Edward F.X. *s.j.* '52 (NY) [DD] New York, NY Jesuit Community at Fordham University.
Kennedy, Msgr. Edward J. '59 (CAM) Retired.
Kennedy, Edward J. '68 (PH) [X] Darby, PA St. Francis Country House.
Kennedy, Edward J. '93 (GRY) Cedar Lake, IN Holy Name Church.
Kennedy, Edward M. '59 (SPR) [I] Holyoke, MA Providence Place, Inc.; [K] Holyoke, MA Sisters of Providence.
Kennedy, Msgr. Edwin J. '32 (SFR) Retired; [K] San Francisco, CA Home for the Aged of the Little Sisters of the Poor.
Kennedy, Ernest E. '56 (CHR) Special Assignment.
Kennedy, Msgr. Francis B. '39 (CIN) [85] Cincinnati, OH St. William Church; Retired.
Kennedy, Francis M. '64 (SPR) [7] Chicopee, MA St. Mary's Church.
Kennedy, Gary L. '68 (PBL) Alamosa, CO Sacred Heart Church.
Kennedy, Glenn '00 (RVC) Massapequa, NY St. Rose of Lima Church.
Kennedy, Hugh A. *s.j.* '48 (BAL) [S] Baltimore, MD Jesuit Fathers and Brothers Maryland Provincial Curia.
Kennedy, Msgr. J. Nevin '58 (MET) Somerville, NJ Immaculate Conception Church.
Kennedy, James M. '54 (SY) North Syracuse, NY St. Rose of Lima Church.
Kennedy, Jerome *o.p.* '60 (WDC) [11] Washington, DC St. Dominic Church & Priory Church.
Kennedy, Jerrold F. '66 (OAK) [17] Oakland, CA St. Mary, Immaculate Conception-St. Francis de Sales Church.
Kennedy, Msgr. John '50 (MRY) Retired.
Kennedy, John '56 (SFD) Retired.
Kennedy, John A. '50 (LA) Retired.
Kennedy, John D. '93 (SHP) [B] Monroe, LA St. Francis Medical Center.
Kennedy, John F. *m.m.* '55 (FgM) Maryknoll Foreign Missions.
Kennedy, John F. '63 (NEW) Scotch Plains, NJ Immaculate Heart of Mary Church.
Kennedy, Msgr. John J. '49 (STL) Retired.
Kennedy, John V. *c.m.* '49 (PH) [AA] Philadelphia, PA Congregation of the Mission.
Kennedy, Joseph J. '48 (PH) Media, PA Nativity of the Blessed Virgin Mary Church; Retired.
Kennedy, Joseph M. *s.j.* '55 (BAL) [B] Baltimore, MD Loyola College in Maryland; [S] Baltimore, MD Jesuit Community of Loyola College, Inc.; [W] Baltimore, MD Jesuit Mission Bureau, Maryland Province, Inc.; [W] Baltimore, MD Jesuit Jamshedpur Mission Society, Inc.; [W] Baltimore, MD Jesuit Seminary Guild, Maryland Province, Inc.
Kennedy, Joseph P. '73 (WDC) [1] Silver Spring, MD St. Andrew Apostle Church.
Kennedy, Kevin '99 (SFR) [2] San Mateo, CA St. Gregory Church.
Kennedy, Kevin C. '95 (WDC) Gaithersburg, MD St. Martin Church.
Kennedy, Laurence W. '57 (SY) [13] Syracuse, NY St. Brigid and St. Joseph Church.
Kennedy, Leo *o.f.m.conv.* '90 (L) [7] Louisville, KY St. Anthony Church.
Kennedy, Leo R. *m.m.* '59 (NY) [DD] Maryknoll, NY Maryknoll Fathers and Brothers.
Kennedy, Louis J.P '57 (CHR) Greer, SC Blessed Trinity Church.
Kennedy, Louis J.P. '57 (CHR) Greenville, SC St. Mary's Church.
Kennedy, Malcolm M. (NY) [II] New York, NY Prelature of the Holy Cross and Opus Dei.
Kennedy, Michael E. *s.j.* '77 (LA) [11] Los Angeles, CA Dolores Church.
Kennedy, Michael J. *c.m.* '51 (BAL) [S] Emmitsburg, MD Vincentian House.
Kennedy, Michael J. *c.m.* '67 (BAL) Emmitsburg, MD St. Joseph Church.
Kennedy, Michael J. '67 (STP) Cedar, MN St. Patrick Church.
Kennedy, Oliver *s.s.c.* '47 (OM) [K] St. Columbans, NE St. Columban's Foreign Mission Society.
Kennedy, Patrick (SP) [16] Tampa, FL St. Timothy Church.
Kennedy, Patrick '53 (DEN) [19] Denver, CO Our Lady of Grace Church.
Kennedy, Patrick A. '77 (STP) Fridley, MN St. William Church.
Kennedy, Patrick J. R. '70 (NO) Luling, LA St. Anthony of Padua Church; Retired.
Kennedy, Paul M. '77 (PH) Rydal, PA St. Hilary of Poitiers Church; [D] Philadelphia, PA Cardinal Dougherty High School.
Kennedy, Richard *m.s.c.* '67 (FgM) Missionaries of the Sacred Heart Foreign Missions.
Kennedy, Richard *m.s.c.* '67 (RCK) [G] Aurora, IL Missionaries of the Sacred Heart Community.
Kennedy, Richard C. '73 (ORG) [7] Santa Ana, CA St. Barbara's Church.
Kennedy, Robert (ROC) Rush, NY St. Joseph Church.
Kennedy, Robert *o.f.m.* '90 (NY) [35] New York, NY St. Francis of Assisi Church.
Kennedy, Robert E. *s.j.* '65 (NEW) [B] Jersey City, NJ Saint Peter's College; [N] Jersey City, NJ Jesuits of Saint Peter's College, Inc.
Kennedy, Robert J. '74 (ROC) [8] Rochester, NY Blessed Sacrament Church.
Kennedy, Robert R. '66 (BO) [44] Boston, MA St. Mary, Star of the Sea Church.
Kennedy, Robert T. '59 (NY) On Duty Outside the Archdiocese.
Kennedy, Robert T. '59 (WDC) [C] Washington, DC Catholic University of America, The.
Kennedy, Russell '75 (NOR) [4] Norwich, CT St. Mary Church.
Kennedy, Stanley T. *m.s.* '70 (HRT) [M] Hartford, CT Missionaries of LaSalette, Provincial Secretary.
Kennedy, T. Frank *s.j.* '76 (BO) [W] Chestnut Hill, MA The Jesuit Community at Boston College.
Kennedy, Thaddeus J. *o.c.s.o.* '58 (DUB) [K] Peosta, IA New Melleray Abbey, Order of Cistercians of the Strict Observance.
Kennedy, Msgr. Thomas I. '41 (SFR) Retired; [K] San Rafael, CA Nazareth House.
Kennedy, Thomas R. *c.m.* '64 (PH) [AA] Philadelphia, PA Congregation of the Mission.
Kennedy, Victor P. '77 (NEW) [3] Jersey City, NJ St. Anne's Church.
Kennedy, William H. '65 (ALB) Stottville, NY Holy Family Church.
Kennedy, William J. *s.j.* '65 (BGP) [2] Greenwich, CT St. Michael the Archangel Church; [P] Fairfield, CT The Fairfield Jesuit Community-Fairfield University.
Kennedy, William J. *s.j.* '65 (BO) [W] Boston, MA The Society of Jesus of New England-Provincial Offices.
Kennedy, William J. '69 (NY) Retired.
Kennedy, William M. '71 (BO) Military & VA Chaplains.
Kennedy, William M. '71 (CIN) [12] Cincinnati, OH Assumption Church.
Kennedy, Msgr. William P. '33 (STO) Retired.
Kennehan, John P. '62 (OG) Potsdam, NY St. Mary Church.
Kennelley, James J. '70 (E) Mercer, PA Immaculate Heart Church.
Kennelly, Daniel '77 (BGP) [J] Bridgeport, CT St. Vincent's Medical Center.
Kennelly, Michael F. *s.j.* '46 (SP) [C] Tampa, FL Jesuit High School.
Kennelly, Stephen '69 (SAN) Miles, TX St. Thomas Church; Olfen, TX St. Boniface Church; Rowena, TX St. Joseph's Church.
Kennerk, T. Daniel *c.s.c.* '53 (FgM) Holy Cross Foreign Missions.
Kennerley, David *s.m.* '82 (DET) [D] Pontiac, MI Notre Dame Preparatory High School and Marist Academy.
Kenney, Albert A. '94 (PRO) [A] Providence, RI Seminary of Our Lady of Providence; [E] Providence, RI La Salle Academy.
Kenney, C. Douglas '99 (BAL) Bel Air, MD St. Margaret Church.
Kenney, Daniel J. *s.j.* '63 (FgM) Provinces.
Kenney, Daniel J. *s.j.* '63 (MIL) [P] Milwaukee, WI Jesuit Provincial Office, Wisconsin Province.
Kenney, Francis J. *s.m.* '49 (CIN) [9] Dayton, OH Emmanuel Church; [M] Dayton, OH Marianist Provincialate.
Kenney, Francis P. '87 (WIL) Brandywood, DE Church of the Holy Child.
Kenney, Gerard J. '97 (LUB) Plainview, TX Our Lady of Guadalupe Church.
Kenney, Henry *s.j.* '52 (LEX) [7] Lexington, KY St. Peter Church; Special Assignment.
Kenney, James J. *s.j.* '57 (FgM) Provinces.
Kenney, Msgr. Jeremiah E. '72 (BAL) [W] Baltimore, MD Holy Name Society (Union).
Kenney, Msgr. Jeremiah F. '72 (BAL) [41] Baltimore, MD Immaculate Conception Church; Special Assignment.
Kenney, John B. '57 (BUR) Retired.
Kenney, Joseph *m.s.a.* '79 (NOR) [F] Cromwell, CT Society of the Missionaries of the Holy Apostles.
Kenney, Joseph A. '43 (BAL) [25] Baltimore, MD St. Clement Church; Retired; [O] Timonium, MD Stella Maris.
Kenney, Kevin T. '94 (STP) [12] Minneapolis, MN Our Lady of Peace Church.
Kenney, Mark G. *s.m.* '79 (WDC) [B] Washington, DC Marist College, The Scholasticate.
Kenney, Paul C. *s.j.* '72 (BO) [W] Boston, MA The Society of Jesus of New England-Provincial Offices.
Kenney, Paul C. *s.j.* '72 (WDC) [M] Washington, DC Leonard Neale House.
Kenney, Peter J. *s.s.j.* '46 (BAL) [S] Baltimore, MD St. Joseph Society of the Sacred Heart House of Central Administration.
Kenney, Msgr. Philip J. '39 (MAN) Retired.
Kenney, Robert D. *o.s.f.s.* '52 (WIL) [B] Wilmington, DE Salesianum School.
Kenney, Sean W. '91 (MET) Somerville, NJ Immaculate Conception Church.
Kenney, Msgr. Timothy '58 (Y) Kent, OH St. Patrick's Church.
Kenney, Timothy M. *s.m.* '82 (SFR) [D] San Francisco, CA Archbishop Riordan High School (Boys); [N] San Francisco, CA Marianist Community.
Kenney, William J. *c.s.p.* '51 (NY) [DD] Jamaica Estates, NY Paulist Fathers Generalate.
Kenney, William J. '56 (STP) [11] Minneapolis, MN Our Lady of Mount Carmel Church; Retired.
Kenney, William T. *c.s.p.* '51 (LA) [87] Los Angeles, CA St. Paul the Apostle Church.
Kenning, Herman H. '43 (CIN) Retired; [N] Cincinnati, OH St. Clare Convent, Franciscan Sisters of the Poor.
Kennington, John *c.ss.r.* '59 (NY) [DD] Esopus, NY Redemptorist Priests and Brothers C.Ss.R. (Province of Baltimore); [HH] Esopus, NY Holy Shroud Guild.
Kenny, Albert N. '54 (BRK) Retired.
Kenny, Donald '66 (JOL) [6] Naperville, IL St. Thomas the Apostle Church.
Kenny, Msgr. Donald A. '84 (ATL) On Duty Outside the Archdiocese.
Kenny, Eugene '53 (DOD) Retired.
Kenny, Gregory D. *c.m.f.* '59 (ATL) Stone Mountain, GA Corpus Christi Church; [M] Atlanta, GA Campus Ministry.
Kenny, James E. '49 (OM) Retired.
Kenny, Msgr. James T. '45 (SLC) Retired.
Kenny, John *c.s.p.* (GR) Grand Rapids, MI Chapel of St. Paul-Catholic Information Center.
Kenny, John '51 (OAK) Retired.
Kenny, Msgr. John J. '29 (SFR) Retired.
Kenny, John R. '51 (OAK) [M] Oakland, CA Bishop Begin Villa.
Kenny, Joseph H. *o.p.* '50 (FgM) Dominican - Order of Preachers Foreign Missions.
Kenny, Joseph P. *o.p.* '63 (CHI) [N] Chicago, IL Dominicans (Provincial Office).
Kenny, Kevin *o.f.m.conv.* '66 (ALB) Fonda, NY St. Cecilia Church; [N] Fonda, NY Blessed Kateri Guest House; [Q] Fonda, NY The National Shrine of Blessed Kateri Tekakwitha and Friary.
Kenny, Michael '73 (SAT) On Duty Outside the Archdiocese.
Kenny, P. Edward, Jr. '74 (BAL) [18] Baltimore, MD Blessed Sacrament Church; [59] Baltimore, MD St. Mary of the Assumption Church.
Kenny, Patrick J. *o.s.a.* '35 (PH) [AA] Villanova, PA St. Thomas Monastery.
Kenny, Pierce *c.ss.r.* '69 (BRK) [107] Brooklyn, NY Our Lady of Perpetual Help Basilica Church.
Kenny, Raymond G. '63 (SJ) [23] San Jose, CA Santa Teresa Church.
Kenny, Stephen K. '91 (MEM) Camden, TN St. Mary Church.
Kenny, Msgr. Thomas '65 (ATL) [1] Atlanta, GA Cathedral of Christ the King.
Kenny, Thomas A. '46 (NEW) Retired.
Kenny, Thomas C. *o.s.a.* '56 (BO) [C] North Andover, MA Merrimack College.
Kenny, Msgr. Walter F. '54 (NY) Larchmont, NY St. Augustine Church.
Kenny, William J.M. '71 (LAV) [2] Las Vegas, NV Christ the King Church.
Kenshol, Joseph W. '73 (GR) Sand Lake, MI Mary Queen of Apostles Church.
Kent, Daniel '63 (MIA) [B] Opa Locka, FL St. Thomas University.

Kent, James *o.f.m.conv.* '91 (IND) [J] Mount Saint Francis, IN Provincial Headquarters for the Conventual Franciscan Province.
Kent, James *o.f.m.conv.* '91 (L) Pleasure Ridge Park, KY St. Paul Church.
Keogh, James *s.j.* '52 (CHL) Mooresville, NC St. Therese Church; [J] Charlotte, NC Jesuit Community.
Keogh, Simeon *o.f.m.cap.* '49 (MIL) [B] Mount Calvary, WI St. Felix Friary.
Keogh, Stephen *s.a.c.* '53 (DET) [K] Wyandotte, MI Pallottine Fathers.
Keogh, Thomas '45 (SR) Retired.
Keogh, Msgr. Thomas J. '33 (NY) Retired.
Keogh, William '78 (JC) Absent on Leave.
Keohan, Edward M. '59 (BO) [6] Salem, MA St. Mary Church; Salem, MA North Shore Medical Center.
Keohane, Daniel T. '78 (SFR) [1] San Mateo, CA St. Bartholomew Church.
Keohane, Donal '68 (LA) [79] Los Angeles, CA St. Martin of Tours Church.
Keohane, Donal '68 (SAV) On Duty Outside the Diocese.
Keolker, Richard F. '63 (YAK) On Duty Outside the Diocese.
Keon, James J. *c.s.b.* '52 (GAL) [Q] Houston, TX Residence of the Basilian Fathers of the University of St. Thomas.
Keough, Joseph F. '96 (HRT) Middlebury, CT St. John of the Cross Church.
Keppel, Timothy F. *c.r.* '77 (SB) Lake Arrowhead, CA Our Lady of the Lake Church; Running Springs, CA St. Anne in the Mountains Church.
Keppeler, Richard J. '54 (BUF) Bergen, NY St. Brigid Church; South Byron, NY St. Michael Church.
Keppens, Gustaaf M. *s.j.* '61 (WDC) [K] Washington, DC Georgetown University Hospital; [M] Washington, DC The Jesuit Community at Georgetown University.
Kepple, Robert '74 (LR) Retired.
Keppler, Daniel J. '58 (DUB) Retired.
Keppler, Msgr. John F. '60 (BRK) [148] Queens, NY American Martyrs Church.
Kerbawy, Kevin '76 (SAG) [1] Bay City, MI Holy Trinity Church.
Kerber, John V. '58 (STL) Festus, MO Our Lady Church.
Kerber, Joseph P. '88 (SFD) Alexander, IL Visitation B.V.M. Church; Franklin, IL Sacred Heart of Jesus Church; New Berlin, IL Sacred Heart of Mary Church.
Kerber, Justin *c.p.* '72 (R) Greenville, NC St. Peter's Church.
Kerby, Robert L. '70 (NTN) South Bend, IN St. John of Damascus Church.
Kerdiejus, John B. *s.j.* '58 (BO) [Y] Gloucester, MA Eastern Point Retreat House.
Kerestes, Michael '89 (PSC) Beltsville, MD St. Gregory of Nyssa Church.
Kerestus, Thomas J. '69 (ALN) Unassigned; [J] Bethlehem, PA Holy Family Villa.
Kereszty, Rochus *o.cist.* '60 (DAL) [K] Irving, TX Cistercian Abbey of Our Lady of Dallas.
Kerin, Msgr. Joseph A. '57 (CHL) Huntersville, NC St. Mark Church.
Kerin, Michael *glmy.* '88 (BIR) Winfield, AL Holy Spirit Church.
Kerin, Mike '88 (WDC) [M] Washington, DC Glenmary House of Studies.
Kerketta, Sylverius '97 (STL) [P] St. Louis, MO Provincialate of the Society of Mary, Province of St. Louis.
Kerkof, Loren *o.f.m.* '60 (P) [6] Portland, OR Ascension Church.
Kern, Charles P. '77 (NEW) Retired.
Kern, Msgr. Crosby W. '65 (NO) [2] Metairie, LA St. Angela Merici Church.
Kern, Jerome C. '66 (STP) Forest Lake, MN St. Peter Church.
Kern, John R. '68 (MIL) [13] Racine, WI St. Richard of Chichester Church.
Kern, Joseph R. '57 (IND) Montezuma, IN Immaculate Conception Church; Rockville, IN St. Joseph Church.
Kern, Martin F. '94 (ALN) [8] Bethlehem, PA Our Lady of Perpetual Help Church.
Kern, Msgr. Walter O. '58 (BUF) Bowmansville, NY Sacred Heart Church.
Kernan, Msgr. Eugene J. '49 (CAM) Retired.
Kernan, James *o.m.i.* '59 (SD) Calipatria, CA St. Patrick Church.
Kernan, Michael H. '54 (PIT) Retired.
Kernan, Timothy J. '65 (STP) [11] St. Paul, MN St. Adalbert Church.
Kernan, William A. '93 (SD) Valley Center, CA St. Stephen Church.
Kerner, Terrence D. '72 (DET) [2] Monroe, MI St. John The Baptist Church.
Kerner, Timothy J. *c.ss.r.* '81 (BR) [F] Baton Rouge, LA Our Lady of the Lake Regional Medical Center.
Kerns, John '85 (P) [3] Portland, OR All Saints Church.
Kerns, Paul R. '71 (PRT) [4] Old Town, ME St. Ann Church, Indian Island Church.
Kerper, Michael '85 (MAN) Candia, NH St. Paul Church.
Kerr, Charles L. *s.j.* '50 (WIN) [1] Mankato, MN SS. Peter and Paul's Church.
Kerr, Cherubin *o.s.a.* '44 (CAM) [C] Richland, NJ St. Augustine Preparatory School.
Kerr, John W. '98 (LR) De Queen, AR St. Barbara's Church.
Kerr, Robert '95 (KC) Hamilton, MO Sacred Heart Church; Hamilton, MO Sacred Heart Church.
Kerr, Robert T. '64 (LAN) [3] Ypsilanti, MI St. Joseph Church.
Kerr, Msgr. William A. '66 (PIT) [B] Pittsburgh, PA La Roche College.
Kerr, Msgr. William A. '66 (PT) On Duty Outside the Diocese.
Kerrigan, Bernard A. '48 (WIN) Retired.
Kerrigan, James P. '70 (WOR) Rutland, MA St. Patrick's Church.
Kerrigan, Joseph J. '90 (MET) East Brunswick, NJ St. Bartholomew Church.
Kerrigan, Michael F. '64 (DEN) Idaho Springs, CO St. Paul's Church.
Kerrigan, Michael P. *c.s.p.* '87 (NY) [DD] Jamaica Estates, NY Paulist Fathers Generalate.
Kerrigan, Neal *o.f.m.cap.* '52 (NY) Yonkers, NY St. John Hospital; [DD] Yonkers, NY St. Clare Friary.
Kerschen, Leo A. '62 (WCH) Eureka, KS Sacred Heart Church; Hamilton, KS St. John Church; Madison, KS St. Teresa of Avila Church.
Kerschen, Leon J. '62 (WCH) Iola, KS St. John Church; Yates Center, KS St. Joseph Church.
Kerscher, Charles J. '79 (ATL) Conyers, GA St. Pius X Catholic Church; Retired.
Kerscher, Francis '55 (GB) Retired.
Kersey, Walter L. '81 (BR) Retired.
Kersgieter, Paul J. '45 (STL) Retired.
Kershner, Joseph J. *sch.p.* '64 (MIA) [C] Fort Lauderdale, FL Cardinal Gibbons High School.
Kerst, Pat '90 (SPK) Brewster, WA Sacred Heart Church; Twisp, WA St. Genevieve Church.
Kersten, Edward J. *o.s.a.* '56 (CHI) [182] Chicago, IL St. Rita of Cascia Church.
Kersten, Jay Joseph '98 (LAN) [2] Ann Arbor, MI St. Francis of Assisi Church.
Kersten, John *s.v.d.* '40 (BLX) [A] Bay St. Louis, MS St. Augustine's.
Kersten, Kevin *s.j.* '72 (BO) [W] Chestnut Hill, MA The Jesuit Community at Boston College.
Kertz, Leo *o.m.i.* '63 (FgM) Oblates Foreign Missions.
Kertz, Msgr. Raymond N. '67 (MAD) [1] Janesville, WI Nativity of St. Mary Church.
Kerwan, Francis T. '43 (HRT) [1] Enfield, CT Holy Family Church.
Kerwin, Msgr. Eugene H. '52 (OM) Retired.
Kerze, William F. '69 (LA) Malibu, CA Our Lady of Malibu Church.
Kesicki, Michael '88 (E) [B] Erie, PA Gannon University.
Kesicki, Michael T. '88 (E) [A] Erie, PA St. Mark's Seminary.
Kesicki, Timothy *s.j.* (CLV) [D] Cleveland, OH St. Ignatius High School.
Kesicki, Timothy J. *s.j.* (DET) [K] Detroit, MI Jesuit Provincial Office-Detroit Province of the Society of Jesus.
Kessel, Gerald *o.f.m.cap.* '82 (DET) [P] Washington, MI Capuchin Retreat.
Kessing, Bernadine C. *o.f.m.* '60 (NEW) Fair Lawn, NJ St. Anne's Church.
Kessinger, David R. *o.s.b.* '58 (CHL) [J] Belmont, NC Belmont Abbey.
Kessler, Edward L. '48 (COL) Lancaster, OH Southeastern Correctional Institution; Retired.
Kessler, Matthew *c.ss.r.* '91 (CHI) [133] Chicago, IL St. Michael Church.
Kessler, Peter *o.s.b.* '74 (STL) [P] St. Louis, MO The Abbey of St. Mary and St. Louis.
Kessler, T. Peter *o.s.b.* '74 (STL) [F] Creve Coeur, MO St. Louis Priory School.
Kessler, Thomas '75 (EVN) Loogootee, IN St. Martin's Church; St. Joseph, IN St. Joseph's Church.
Kessler, Thomas J. '84 (ALN) On Duty Outside the Diocese.
Kessler, Thomas J. '84 (CHL) Lincolnton, NC St. Dorothy Church.
Kessler, Thomas Peter *o.s.b.* '74 (COL) On Duty Outside the Diocese.
Kessler, William '99 (SFD) [2] Springfield, IL Blessed Sacrament Church.
Kester, William J. '70 (STL) [6] Lemay, MO St. Matthias Church.
Kestermeier, Charles T. *s.j.* '75 (OM) [K] Omaha, NE Jesuit Community at Creighton University.
Kesting, Philip A. '41 (CIN) Retired.
Kestler, Theodore E. *s.j.* '75 (FBK) St. Marys, AK Church of the Nativity; [E] St. Marys, AK Native Ministry Training Program; [E] St. Marys, AK Brother Joe Prince Jesuit Community.
Ketcham, Gregory K. '94 (PEO) Nauvoo, IL SS. Peter and Paul's Church.
Ketchersid, Corbin W. '47 (R) Retired.
Kettelberger, John A. *c.m.* '78 (BUF) [C] Niagara University, NY Niagara University; [O] Niagara University, NY Vincentian Community at Niagara University; [R] Alfred, NY Campus Ministry.
Ketteler, Ronald M. '61 (COV) Crescent Springs, KY St. Joseph Church.
Kettler, Msgr. Donald '70 (SFS) [2] Sioux Falls, SD Christ the King Church.
Kettner, Joseph F. *m.s.* '50 (HRT) [M] Hartford, CT Missionaries of LaSalette, Provincial Secretary.
Kettron, W. Michael '57 (LFT) Cicero, IN Sacred Heart Church.
Keul, Msgr. Francis X. '48 (PH) Retired.
Keulman, Kenneth P. '69 (NO) [C] New Orleans, LA Loyola University New Orleans.
Keulman, Kenneth P. '69 (SJ) On Duty Outside the Diocese.
Keusal, Eugene L. '61 (CHI) On Duty Outside the Archdiocese.
Keusal, Eugene L. '61 (HON) Waikane, HI Our Lady of Mt. Carmel Church.
Keuter, Alfons *o.m.i.* (CHI) [X] Chicago, IL Oblates for International Pastoral.
Keutzer, Walter J. '56 (STL) Retired.
Keveney, William '56 (DET) Retired.
Keville, Joseph '96 (BO) [2] Beverly, MA St. John the Evangelist Church.
Kew, Larry J. '66 (GRY) [4] Hammond, IN St. Catherine of Siena Church.
Key, Oren W. *s.j.* '53 (FWT) Crowell, TX St. Joseph Church; Quanah, TX St. Mary Church; Vernon, TX Holy Family Church.
Key, William W. '75 (MIL) Beaver Dam, WI St. Michael Church; Beaver Dam, WI St. Patrick Church; Beaver Dam, WI St. Peter Church; [W] Racine, WI Cursillos in Christianity.
Keyes, Jeffrey R. *c.pp.s.* '91 (OAK) [2] Alameda, CA St. Barnabas Church; [N] San Leandro, CA Society of the Precious Blood.
Keyes, Patrick *c.ss.r.* '89 (DEN) [M] Denver, CO The Redemptorists/Denver Province.
Keyes, Paul T. '63 (BO) North Andover, MA St. Michael Church.
Keyes, Raphael '64 (JC) Missionary Assignment in Peru.
Keyes, Thomas '73 (FgM) Society of St. James the Apostle.
Keyes, Thomas E. (BO) [5] Revere, MA Our Lady of Lourdes Church.
Keymont, Walter F. '80 (BO) [7] Boston, MA St. Ann Church.
Keyrouze, Joseph '50 (ALB) Retired.
Keys, Gordon L. *s.j.* '55 (SPK) [K] Spokane, WA Regis Community.
Keys, Msgr. Thomas J. '70 (SR) [5] Santa Rosa, CA Star of the Valley Church; [F] Rohnert Park, CA Society of St. Vincent de Paul, District Council of Sonoma County.
Kezmarsky, Kenneth E. '86 (PIT) Monroeville, PA St. Bernadette Church.
Khachan, Bernard C. '60 (OLL) Cleveland, OH St. Maron Church.
Khai Vu, Joseph '96 (NEW) [2] Newark, NJ St. Patrick's Pro-Church; Kearny, NJ West Hudson Hospital.
Khalil, Naim *b.s.o.* '89 (NTN) [B] Methuen, MA Basilian Salvatorian Order.
Khanh, Hilary *c.m.c.* '94 (FWT) [19] Fort Worth, TX Christ the King Church.
Kharuk, Wasyl '92 (PHU) Nanticoke, PA Transfiguration of Our Lord Church; Plymouth, PA SS. Peter and Paul Church.
Khien Mai Luu, John *s.v.d.* '92 (FgM) Society of the Divine Word Foreign Missions.
Khoa, Nguyen *o.f.m.* '95 (WDC) [B] Silver Spring, MD Holy Name College.
Khoi, Jim N. *c.m.c.* '91 (STP) [28] Minneapolis, MN St. Joseph Hien Church.
Khoueiry, Joseph '00 (SAM) Easton, PA Our Lady of Lebanon Church.
Khoury, Ghattas '90 (OLL) Louisville, KY Maronite Catholic Community of Louisville Church; Cincinnati, OH St. Anthony of Padua Church.
Khoury, Msgr. James T. '75 (SAM) Lawrence, MA St. Anthony Church.
Khue, Thomas L.T. '91 (SPK) [17] Spokane, WA St. Patrick Church.
Kiarie, James K. '94 (ROC) [I] Rochester, NY Basilian Residence.
Kibby, J. Patrick '84 (NSH) [1] Nashville, TN Cathedral of the Incarnation.
Kibby, Patrick J. '84 (NSH) [L] Nashville, TN Growing in Faith for Tomorrow Capital Campaign Trust, Inc.
Kibler, Gary R. '71 (BUF) [4] Lockport, NY St. Mary Church.
Kibuka, Matthias W. '58 (BUF) Retired.
Kichak, Joseph A. '43 (MAR) Retired.
Kickham, Robert T. '97 (BO) [40] Boston, MA St. Mark Church.

Kicmal, Casimir C. *c.s.v.* '57 (CHI) [N] Arlington Heights, IL Viatorian Province Center-Clerics of St. Viator.
Kiczuk, Casimir *c.m.* '34 (HRT) [M] Manchester, CT DePaul Provincial Residence.
Kidd, Colin *o.f.m.* '48 (ORL) Merritt Island, FL Divine Mercy Church; Retired.
Kidd, Michael C. '54 (WDC) Mitchellville, MD Holy Family Church.
Kidd, Wayne R. '73 (LC) Hillsboro, WI St. Aloysius Church; Richland Center, WI St. Mary (Assumption of B.V.M.) Church; Wonewoc, WI St. Jerome Church.
Kidd, William J. *s.j.* '63 (MIL) [P] Milwaukee, WI Jesuit Community at Marquette University.
Kidder, Msgr. James C. '67 (SAC) El Dorado Hills, CA Holy Trinity Church.
Kiddy, Curtis '92 (MIA) Absent on Leave.
Kidner, M. Paul *o.s.b.* '58 (STL) [F] Creve Coeur, MO St. Louis Priory School; [P] St. Louis, MO The Abbey of St. Mary and St. Louis.
Kidney, Msgr. Liam J. '68 (LA) Pacific Palisades, CA Corpus Christi Church.
Kidney, Timothy '71 (SJ) [2] Sunnyvale, CA St. Cyprian Church.
Kidwell, William *s.j.* '55 (MIA) [5] Miami, FL Gesu Church.
Kiedinger, Daniel J. '91 (LC) Cazenovia, WI St. Anthony de Padua Church; Keyesville, WI Nativity of the Blessed Virgin Mary Church; Lone Rock, WI Sacred Heart Church.
Kiefer, John D. '70 (LFT) Muncie, IN St. Francis of Assisi Church.
Kiefer, R. David '62 (GB) Mattoon, WI Holy Family Church; Neopit, WI St. Anthony Church; Phlox, WI St. Joseph Church.
Kiefer, Robert '91 (SJ) [5] San Jose, CA St. Frances Cabrini Church.
Kiefer, Msgr. Thomas '46 (LA) [2] North Hollywood, CA St. Charles Borromeo Church.
Kiefer, Msgr. Thomas A. '37 (LA) Retired.
Kiefer, Thomas P. '81 (SPC) [1] Springfield, MO Cathedral of St. Agnes.
Kiefer, William J. '58 (SB) Trona, CA St. Madeleine Sophie Barat Church; Retired.
Kieferle, Norbert '66 (AMA) Retired.
Kieffer, Charles G. '80 (PHX) [24] Phoenix, AZ St. Theresa Church.
Kieffer, Henry '40 (SAL) [C] Concordia, KS Mount Joseph Senior Community.
Kieffer, John L. *s.j.* '68 (DET) [K] Detroit, MI Jesuit Provincial Office-Detroit Province of the Society of Jesus.
Kieffer, John L. *s.j.* '68 (LEX) Monticello, KY St. Peter Church; [J] Mount Vernon, KY Appalachia Science in the Public Interest.
Kieffer, Kenneth *o.f.m.* '55 (STL) [P] St. Louis, MO Franciscan Friary of St. Anthony of Padua.
Kieffer, Lawrence J. '50 (MAD) Retired.
Kieffer, Merlin (SAL) Washington, KS St. Augustine's Church.
Kieffer, Merlin '60 (SAL) Clay Center, KS SS. Peter and Paul Church.
Kieffer, Robert '69 (SCL) Fergus Falls, MN Our Lady of Victory Church.
Kieffer, Thomas A. *c.o.* '65 (MRY) [F] Monterey, CA Oratorian Community-Congregation of the Oratory of Pontifical Right; [K] Monterey, CA Newman Institute for Historical and Religious Studies.
Kiel, William J. '93 (GBG) [1] Uniontown, PA St. John The Evangelist Church.
Kielb, John T. '75 (TR) Monmouth Beach, NJ Church of the Precious Blood.
Kielbasa, Richard '59 (SC) Rockwell City, IA St. Francis of Assisi Church.
Kieliszewski, Jan M. '73 (MIL) Burlington, WI St. Charles Church.
Kielkowski, Andrzej *s.d.s.* '81 (BRK) [187] Queens, NY St. Joseph Church.
Kielkowski, Andrzej *s.d.s.* '81 (NEW) [N] Verona, NJ The Salvatorian Fathers.
Kieltyka, Robert '58 (MOB) On Leave from the Archdiocese.
Kiely, Benedict *o.f.m.* '94 (BUR) Winooski, VT St. Stephen Church; [H] Burlington, VT University of Vermont-The Catholic Center at UVM.
Kiely, Brian P. '78 (BO) Dracut, MA St. Francis Church.
Kiely, Cornelius '67 (BAK) On Duty Outside the Diocese.
Kiely, Cornelius '67 (FgM) Society of St. James the Apostle.
Kiely, Thomas P. (NY) Cortlandt Manor, NY Holy Spirit Church.
Kiem, Anthony '46 (PT) Retired.
Kiemen, Mathias *o.f.m.* '43 (FWT) [H] Crowley, TX St. Francis Village, Inc.
Kiemen, Mathias *o.f.m* '43 (SFD) [K] Sherman, IL Our Lady of Angels Friary.
Kiener, Hugolinus *o.f.m.* '37 (SFD) [K] Sherman, IL Our Lady of Angels Friary.
Kienzle, Jerome C. '72 (MIL) Military Chaplains.
Kiepura, Kenneth '69 (CHI) Mundelein, IL St. Mary Church.
Kiepura, Kenneth G. '69 (CHI) Arlington Heights, IL St. James Church.
Kieran, Edward '59 (AMA) Retired.
Kieran, John C. '67 (ATL) Conyers, GA St. Pius X Catholic Church.
Kieran, Richard A. '65 (ATL) On Sick Leave.
Kierce, J. Joseph '45 (BO) [4] Boston, MA St. Ambrose Church; Senior Priests.
Kiernan, Msgr. Donald '49 (ATL) [N] Doraville, GA Korean Martyrs Pastoral Center.
Kiernan, Msgr. Donald R. '49 (ATL) Special or Other (Arch)Diocesan Assignment.
Kiernan, Edward J. '54 (BRK) [30] Brooklyn, NY St. Columba Church.
Kiernan, James F. *c.m.* '70 (BRK) [D] Staten Island, NY St. John's University, Staten Island Campus; [D] Jamaica, NY St. John's University; [V] Jamaica, NY St. Vincent's House.
Kiernan, James F. *c.m.* '70 (NY) [C] Staten Island, NY St. John's University Staten Island Campus.
Kiernan, James O. *c.m.* (BAL) Emmitsburg, MD St. Joseph Church.
Kiernan, James O. *c.m.* '70 (BAL) [S] Emmitsburg, MD Vincentian House.
Kiernan, James W. '62 (DM) [1] Des Moines, IA St. Ambrose Church.
Kiernan, John G. '55 (PBL) Retired.
Kiernan, John L. '48 (BRK) Retired; [V] Jamaica, NY Parsons Manor.
Kiernan, Joseph *o.f.m.* '69 (SP) [O] St. Petersburg, FL St. Anthony Friary.
Kiernan, Michael F. '73 (SAC) Anderson, CA Sacred Heart Church.
Kiernan, Msgr. R. Donald '49 (ATL) Dunwoody, GA All Saints Catholic Church.
Kiernan, Robert J. *o.s.b.* '60 (BUR) [E] Weston, VT Priory of Benedictine Monks.
Kiernan, Thomas '48 (SY) Retired.
Kierney, Bede *o.s.b.* '83 (WOR) [N] Petersham, MA St. Mary's Monastery.
Kies, Emil '44 (P) Retired.
Kiesel, James P. '95 (BAL) Columbia, MD St. John the Evangelist Church.
Kiesel, Leo C. '63 (EVN) Loogootee, IN St. John Church; [I] Loogootee, IN American-Innsbruck Alumni Association.
Kieselbach, Joseph '61 (CR) Barnesville, MN Assumption Church.
Kiesling, John *s.a.* '68 (NY) [DD] Garrison, NY Franciscan Friars of the Atonement, Minister General Office.
Kieton, Dennis J. '85 (PRO) [5] Cumberland, RI Our Lady of Fatima Church.
Kiewicz, Dariusz Andrzej (BRK) [241] Queens, NY St. Stanislaus Bishop and Martyr Church.
Kiff, Herbert J., Jr. '95 (NO) Covington, LA St. Peter Church.
Kiffmeyer, James G. '85 (CIN) [E] Cincinnati, OH Elder High School.
Kiggins, Roy '64 (ROC) Geneva, NY St. Stephen Church.
Kiggins, Roy '67 (ROC) Geneva, NY St. Francis de Sales Church; [M] Rochester, NY Diocesan Department of Campus Ministry.
Kigozi, Denis S. '91 (COL) Lancaster, OH St. Mary Church.
Kihm, Frederick C. '93 (STU) Wintersville, OH Blessed Sacrament Church; Wintersville, OH Our Lady of Lourdes Church.
Kihm, Peter J. (NY) [4] Poughkeepsie, NY St. John the Baptist Church.
Kihm, Peter J. '81 (NY) [7] Poughkeepsie, NY Our Lady of Mt. Carmel Church.
Kihneman, Msgr. Louis F. '77 (CC) Rockport, TX Sacred Heart Church.
Kijauskas, Gediminas *s.j.* '60 (CLV) [59] Cleveland, OH Our Lady of Perpetual Help Church.
Kilarecki, George W. '46 (PIT) Retired.
Kilas, Joseph F. '54 (JOL) Joliet, IL Joliet Correctional Depot.
Kilbride, Eugene M. '59 (HRT) [2] West Hartford, CT St. Helena Church.
Kilbridge, Robert *o.p.* '47 (CHI) River Forest, IL St. Vincent Ferrer Church.
Kilburn, Clayton F. *c.m.* '79 (GLP) Keams Canyon, AZ St. Joseph's Indian Church.
Kilcarr, Stephen M. '56 (NEW) [C] West Orange, NJ Seton Hall Preparatory School.
Kilcline, Francis I. '81 (LFT) Kokomo, IN St. Patrick Church.
Kilcourse, George A. '76 (L) [A] Louisville, KY Bellarmine University.
Kilcoyne, John '45 (CLV) Retired.
Kilcoyne, Patrick (SJ) Absent on Sick Leave.
Kilcoyne, Terence T. '76 (WOR) Westminster, MA St. Edward the Confessor Church.
Kilcrann, John *c.s.sp.* '76 (CHI) [34] Chicago, IL St. Cajetan Church.
Kiley, Francis *o.f.m.conv.* '54 (CHI) [N] Chicago, IL Conventual Franciscans of St. Bonaventure Province.
Kiley, J. Cletus '74 (CHI) On Duty Outside the Archdiocese.
Kiley, John A. '66 (PRO) [7] Pawtucket, RI St. Leo the Great Church.
Kiley, John G. '70 (BO) Lincoln, MA St. Joseph Church.
Kiley, Philip S. *s.j.* '71 (BO) [W] Boston, MA The Society of Jesus of New England-Provincial Offices; [W] Weston, MA Campion Jesuit Community.
Kiley, Philip S. *s.j.* '71 (NOR) [A] Cromwell, CT Holy Apostles College and Seminary.
Kiley, Phillip C. '78 (CHI) [180] Chicago, IL Resurrection Church.
Kiley, Raymond P. '96 (BO) Canton, MA St. John the Evangelist Church.
Kilfoil, Msgr. Patrick '37 (EVN) Retired.
Kilgallen, John J. *s.j.* '65 (CHI) [C] Chicago, IL Jesuit Community at Loyola University of Chicago.
Kilgallon, John J. '69 (PH) Roslyn, PA St. John of the Cross Church.
Kilian, Bill '53 (SAL) Damar, KS St. Joseph's Church.
Kilian, John '68 (BUF) Attica, NY Attica Correctional Facility.
Kilian, Sabbas J. *o.f.m.* '43 (NY) [6] Mt. Vernon, NY St. Ursula Church.
Kilian, Waldemar '87 (CHI) River Grove, IL St. Cyprian Church.
Kilian, William T. '53 (SAL) Retired.
Kilianski, Edward *s.c.j.* '83 (MIL) [P] Franklin, WI St. Francis Residence.
Kilianski, Edward *s.j.c.* '83 (SR) Special Assignment.
Kilidjian, Vincent *m.s.a.* '68 (NOR) [F] Cromwell, CT Society of the Missionaries of the Holy Apostles.
Kilkelly, Timothy *m.m.* '90 (FgM) Maryknoll Foreign Missions.
Kill, Donald *s.s.c.* '72 (FgM) St. Columban's Foreign Mission.
Kill, Robert J. '71 (TOL) Hamler, OH St. Paul Church; Holgate, OH St. Mary Church.
Killackey, Cyprian *o.c.d.* '52 (TUC) [24] Tucson, AZ Santa Cruz Church.
Killackey, Edward R. *m.m.* '57 (NY) [DD] Maryknoll, NY Maryknoll Fathers and Brothers.
Killackey, Thomas B. *m.m.* '56 (HON) Mililani Town, HI St. John Apostle and Evangelist Church; [G] Honolulu, HI Maryknoll Fathers House (M.M.).
Killeen, Bernard D. '49 (HRT) Orange, CT Holy Infant Church.
Killeen, John C. '59 (CAM) [1] Cherry Hill, NJ St. Mary's Church.
Killeen, John F. *s.j.* '56 (LA) [C] Los Angeles, CA Loyola Marymount University.
Killeen, John P. '57 (CC) George West, TX St. George Church; George West, TX St. George Church.
Killeen, Joseph P. '62 (DET) Holly, MI St. Rita Church.
Killeen, Msgr. Michael F. '59 (LA) Rowland Heights, CA St. Elizabeth Ann Seton Church.
Killeen, Thomas M. *o.m.i.* '58 (COS) Leadville, CO Catholic Community of Leadville, Annunciation (1879) & St. Joseph (1899) Church.
Killeen, Thomas M. *o.m.i.* '58 (WDC) [M] Washington, DC Missionary Oblates of Mary Immaculate.
Killeen, William E. '75 (CHI) Midlothian, IL St. Christopher Church.
Killeen, William J. '59 (HRT) Derby, CT St. Jude Church.
Killey, Steven S. '98 (SAG) [9] Bay City, MI St. Stanislaus Church.
Killian, Wayne E. (ALN) [C] Easton, PA Notre Dame High School.
Killian, Wayne E. '84 (ALN) [C] Pottsville, PA Nativity B.V.M. High School; [O] Allentown, PA The Newman Center.
Killilea, Patrick *ss.cc.* '69 (FR) Fairhaven, MA St. Mary's Church.
Killion, Dennis W. *o.s.f.s.* '80 (PH) [D] Philadelphia, PA Father Judge High School for Boys; [AA] Philadelphia, PA Father Judge Faculty House.
Killion, Robert L. '53 (WOR) Bolton, MA St. Francis Xavier Church.
Killop, John *o.f.m.* (SAG) [6] Bay City, MI St. Joseph Church.
Killoren, John J. '45 (STL) [P] St. Louis, MO Jesuit Community Corporation at St. Louis University - Jesuit Hall.
Kilmartin, John *f.d.p.* (BO) [34] Boston, MA St. Joseph-St. Lazarus Church.
Kilmartin, John *f.d.p.* '86 (BO) Shirley, MA MCI-Shirley; [BB] Boston, MA Madonna Queen Shrine.
Kilmurray, Fintan J. '77 (BLX) [1] Gulfport, MS St. Ann Church.
Kilpatrick, Andrew W. '96 (SCR) On Duty Outside the Diocese.
Kilpatrick, John J. '61 (SCR) [8] Scranton, PA Holy Name Church.
Kilroy, Brendan K. *s.p.s.* '62 (NEW) [C] Ramsey, NJ Don Bosco Preparatory High School for Boys; [N] Cliffside Park, NJ St. Patrick's Missionary Society.
Kilroy, C. A. *o.p.* '61 (STP) [15] Minneapolis, MN St. Albert the Great Church.
Kilroy, Paul E. '70 (BO) [8] Boston, MA St. Ann Church; [6] Newton, MA Our Lady Help of Christians Church;

[CC] Boston, MA St. Ann's University Parish.
Kilroy, Robert F. *o.m.i.* '40 (BO) [Z] Tewksbury, MA Immaculate Heart of Mary Infirmary.
Kilsdonk, Edward '37 (GB) Retired.
Kilty, Cornelius F. *o.s.f.s.* '69 (PH) [AA] Philadelphia, PA Oblates of St. Francis De Sales.
Kilzer, James *o.s.b.* '98 (BIS) [A] Richardton, ND Assumption Abbey.
Kim, Alapaki *c.s.p.* '82 (HON) Nanakuli, HI St. Rita Church.
Kim, Albert K.H. *c.s.p.* '82 (NY) [DD] Jamaica Estates, NY Paulist Fathers Generalate.
Kim, Alex K. '91 (ORG) Rancho Santa Margarita, CA San Francisco Solano Church.
Kim, Alfonso *m.m.* '97 (FgM) Maryknoll Foreign Missions.
Kim, Anselmus Hak-rok '86 (SAC) [15] Sacramento, CA St. Jeong-Hae Elizabeth Church.
Kim, Anthony (RVC) New Hyde Park, NY Notre Dame Church.
Kim, Augustine Doo Wan '82 (IND) [24] Indianapolis, IN St. Lawrence Church.
Kim, Carlos C. '91 (BO) Franklin, MA St. Mary Church.
Kim, Chrysostom *o.s.b.* '60 (SCL) [I] Collegeville, MN St. John's Abbey, of the Order of St. Benedict.
Kim, David H. '92 (SAT) Boerne, TX Korean Martyrs Catholic Church.
Kim, Denis Woo-Seon *s.j.* '00 (OAK) [N] Berkeley, CA Jesuit Community at Jesuit School of Theology at Berkeley.
Kim, Dong Chun John '91 (STP) [14] St. Paul, MN St. Andrew Kim Church.
Kim, Francis *o.f.m.* '96 (NY) [35] New York, NY St. Francis of Assisi Church; [HH] New York, NY Franciscan Missionary Charities, Inc.
Kim, Il Yung (Peter) '93 (BRK) [226] Queens, NY St. Paul Chong Ha-Sang Roman Catholic Chapel Church.
Kim, Insung (John Vianney) '72 (BRK) [226] Queens, NY St. Paul Chong Ha-Sang Roman Catholic Chapel Church.
Kim, Joseph (NY) [146] Bronx, NY Holy Cross Church.
Kim, Joseph S. (LAN) Burton, MI Blessed Sacrament Church.
Kim, Joseph Y. '74 (BAL) [37] Baltimore, MD Holy Korean Martyrs Church.
Kim, Luis '61 (NEW) [6] Orange, NJ St. Andrew Kim Church.
Kim, Martin S. '84 (PH) [57] Philadelphia, PA Holy Angels Church.
Kim, Mary Joseph *o.cart* '92 (BUR) [E] Arlington, VT Carthusian Foundation, Charterhouse of the Transfiguration.
Kim, Myung-Hwan '90 (NO) [1] New Orleans, LA Korean Catholic Chapel and Community Center Church.
Kim, Paul *c.p.* '00 (DET) [K] Detroit, MI St. Paul of the Cross Community, Congregation of the Passion.
Kim, Peter *s.j.* '80 (LA) [40] Los Angeles, CA St. Agnes Church.
Kim, Roy '35 (ORG) [H] Anaheim, CA St. Thomas Korean Catholic Center.
Kim, Simon '98 (ORG) Cypress, CA St. Irenaeus Church.
Kim, Tu-Jin Paul *c.p.* '00 (DET) [P] Detroit, MI St. Paul of the Cross Retreat Center.
Kim Han Ki, Simon '83 (RVC) Great Neck, NY St. Aloysius Church.
Kim Thien, Joseph Tran '81 (PH) Upper Darby, PA St. Alice Church.
Kim-Yong-Hwa, Paul '89 (OAK) [N] Berkeley, CA Salesian Community.
Kimbrough, Conrad '78 (CHL) Retired.
Kime, Dave W. '97 (GRY) Hobart, IN St. Bridget Church.
Kimecz, Aloysius *o.cist.* '53 (DAL) [K] Irving, TX Cistercian Abbey of Our Lady of Dallas.
Kimla, James '76 (MIL) [72] Milwaukee, WI St. Rafael the Archangel Church.
Kimm, Gregory '87 (SJ) Palo Alto, CA St. Thomas Aquinas Church.
Kimminau, Bernard F. '94 (LIN) Morse Bluff, NE St. George Church.
Kimminau, Irenaeus *o.f.m.* '49 (SFD) [2] Quincy, IL St. Anthony of Padua Church; [7] Quincy, IL St. Joseph Church; [B] Quincy, IL Quincy University.
Kimpel, Edward J. *o.praem.* '49 (PH) [AA] Paoli, PA Daylesford Abbey.
Kin, Bohdan '77 (PHU) Absent on Leave.
Kinane, Gerard P. '73 (NO) [3] Slidell, LA St. Luke the Evangelist Church.
Kinane, Joseph J. '52 (CHI) Park Ridge, IL St. Paul of the Cross Church; Retired.
Kinane, William P. '57 (SAC) Vallejo, CA St. Catherine of Siena Church.
Kinast, Robert L. '68 (ATL) On Duty Outside the Archdiocese.
Kinast, Timothy J. '90 (CC) Tivoli, TX Our Lady of Guadalupe Church.
Kinch, Edwin M. *o.s.b.* '45 (CHI) [N] Chicago, IL Order of Friar Servants of Mary (Servites) United States of America Province, Inc.
Kincl, Robert L. '67 (ARL) [A] Front Royal, VA Christendom College.
Kincl, Robert L. '67 (AUS) On Duty Outside the Diocese.
Kindall, John J. *s.j.* '57 (P) [A] Portland, OR Jesuit Novitiate of St. Francis Xavier.
Kindon, Frederick '67 (PH) [78] Philadelphia, PA St. John the Baptist Church.
Kinerk, Edward *s.j.* '72 (KC) [B] Kansas City, MO Rockhurst University; [B] Kansas City, MO Rockhurst University; [J] Kansas City, MO Rockhurst Jesuit Community.
Kines, G. Jerome *o.s.a.* '62 (CHI) [N] Olympia Fields, IL Austin Friary.
King, Andrew R. '96 (NY) [A] Yonkers, NY St. Joseph's Seminary; [E] New York, NY Monsignor Farrell High School.
King, Anthony S. '59 (YAK) Retired.
King, Arthur J. *o.m.i.* '59 (BO) [Z] Tewksbury, MA Immaculate Heart of Mary Infirmary.
King, Brian '00 (PMB) [5] West Palm Beach, FL St. Juliana Church.
King, Brian Madison '97 (LKC) [B] Lake Charles, LA CHRISTUS St. Patrick Hospital of Lake Charles.
King, Msgr. Charles '56 (FWT) Denton, TX Immaculate Conception Church.
King, David G. *s.j.* '49 (P) [L] Portland, OR Colombiere Community.
King, Donald E. '74 (Y) [1] Warren, OH Blessed Sacrament Church.
King, Donald J. '37 (PRO) Retired; [P] Providence, RI St. John Vianney Residence.
King, Edward L. '42 (BO) [3] Haverhill, MA St. James Church.
King, Edward L. '55 (BO) Senior Priests.
King, Francis *o.c.s.o.* '58 (P) [L] Lafayette, OR The Cistercian (Trappist) Abbey of Our Lady of Guadalupe.
King, Frederick Bruce *i.c.* '85 (PEO) Abingdon, IL Sacred Heart Church; Galesburg, IL St. Patrick's Church.
King, George L. '53 (B) Kamiah, ID St. Catherine's of Siena Church; Orofino, ID St. Theresa's Church.
King, Gerald J. *t.o.r.* '71 (FgM) T.O.R. Foreign Missions.
King, Gregory C. '76 (LA) [4] North Hollywood, CA St. Patrick Church.
King, Howard J. '63 (E) Bradford, PA St. Francis of Assisi Church; Lewis Run, PA Our Mother of Perpetual Help Church.
King, Hugh *o.f.m.* '44 (PAT) [M] Ringwood, NJ Holy Name Friary, Inc.
King, James *c.s.c.* '88 (FTW) [B] Notre Dame, IN University of Notre Dame Du Lac.
King, James B. *c.s.c.* '88 (FTW) [A] Notre Dame, IN Moreau Seminary.
King, James E. '71 (NTN) Retired.
King, James E. '71 (PBL) Canon City, CO St. Michael Church.
King, James E. '92 (PEO) Creve Coeur, IL Sacre Coeur Church.
King, James J. *s.j.* '63 (CLV) [D] Cuyahoga Falls, OH Walsh Jesuit High School.
King, Msgr. James P. '46 (BRK) Retired; [V] Douglaston, NY Bishop Mugavero Residence.
King, James W. '91 (BRK) [19] Brooklyn, NY St. Bernard's Church.
King, Jeffrey '87 (GLP) Chichiltah, NM St. Patrick Church; Pinehaven, NM Good Shepherd Catholic Church; Tinaja, NM San Lorenzo Church.
King, Jeremy *o.s.b.* '75 (IND) Fulda, IN St. Boniface Church; St. Meinrad, IN St. Meinrad Church; Siberia, IN St. Martin of Tours Church; [J] St. Meinrad, IN St. Meinrad Archabbey.
King, Jim B. *c.s.c.* '88 (FTW) [J] Notre Dame, IN Holy Cross Community, Corby Hall, University of Notre Dame.
King, John '48 (PEO) Retired.
King, John *o.m.i.* '54 (MAN) [K] Les Cayes, Haiti Paroisse Ste. Anne.
King, John *o.m.i.* '54 (NY) [FF] Newburgh, NY Our Lady of Hope Center.
King, John D. '88 (CLV) El Salvador, C.A., OH Casa Parroquial San Pedro Teotepeque.
King, John F. *c.m.* '42 (PH) [AA] Philadelphia, PA Congregation of the Mission.
King, John J. *s.j.* '53 (NY) [FF] Staten Island, NY Mount Manresa Jesuit Retreat House.
King, John R. *m.m.* '53 (NY) [DD] Maryknoll, NY Maryknoll Fathers and Brothers.
King, Kenneth A. '57 (TLS) Grove, OK St. Elizabeth Church; Retired.
King, Larry '89 (GR) [12] Grand Rapids, MI St. John Vianney Church.
King, Leo *ss.cc.* '45 (FR) [I] Fairhaven, MA Sacred Hearts Provincial House.
King, Martin '96 (P) On Duty Outside the Archdiocese.
King, Michael J. '77 (WDC) Largo, MD St. Joseph Church.
King, Nicholas '66 (ORL) Rockledge, FL St. Mary's Church.
King, Norbert E. '33 (LC) Retired.
King, Norm '88 (RNO) Sparks, NV Immaculate Conception Church.
King, Philip J. '49 (BO) Senior Priests.
King, Stephen *o.f.m.conv.* '96 (TR) Riverside, NJ St. Casimir Church.
King, Thomas *o.f.m.* (OAK) [N] Oakland, CA Franciscan Friars Provincial Office, Province of St. Barbara.
King, Thomas *c.s.c.* '69 (FTW) Lakeville, IN Sacred Heart Church.
King, Thomas F. '64 (LA) [49] Los Angeles, CA St. Bernadette Church.
King, Thomas J. '60 (ALN) Miller Heights, PA Sacred Heart of Jesus Church.
King, Thomas M. *s.j.* '64 (WDC) [M] Washington, DC The Jesuit Community at Georgetown University.
King, Thomas M. '73 (CIN) [81] Cincinnati, OH St. Therese, The Little Flower Church.
King, Thomas P. *c.s.c.* '69 (FTW) [B] Notre Dame, IN University of Notre Dame Du Lac; [J] Notre Dame, IN Holy Cross Community, Corby Hall, University of Notre Dame.
King, Tommy *o.f.m.* '93 (OAK) [9] Oakland, CA St. Elizabeth's Church.
King, William F. *s.j.* '57 (CIN) [M] Cincinnati, OH Jesuit Community at Xavier University.
King, William F. *s.j.* '57 (DET) [K] Detroit, MI Jesuit Provincial Office-Detroit Province of the Society of Jesus.
King, William J. (HBG) Camp Hill, PA Good Shepherd Church.
King, William M. *s.j.* '60 (SFE) [6] Albuquerque, NM Immaculate Conception Church.
Kingery, Patrick J. '93 (ATL) Woodstock, GA St. Michael the Archangel Church.
Kingery, Victor *o.f.m.* '49 (SFD) [B] Quincy, IL Quincy University.
Kingsbury, John G. *c.ss.r.* '80 (NY) [DD] Esopus, NY Redemptorist Priests and Brothers C.Ss.R. (Province of Baltimore); [FF] Esopus, NY Mount St. Alphonsus Redemptorist Retreat Center.
Kingsley, Richard '83 (TUC) [3] Tucson, AZ Corpus Christi Church.
Kiniry, Msgr. Joseph R. '50 (ALT) [23] Johnstown, PA St. Benedict's Church.
Kiniry, Lawrence R. '65 (GBG) [3] Greensburg, PA Our Lady of Grace Church.
Kinkead, Cormac *c.p.* '51 (HRT) [M] West Hartford, CT Holy Family Monastery/Retreat.
Kinkead, James A. '55 (BR) French Settlement, LA St. Joseph Church.
Kinkel, Robert J. '70 (DEN) [4] Arvada, CO Spirit of Christ Church.
Kinkopf, John J. '57 (CLV) Chagrin Falls, OH St. Joan of Arc Church; Kirtland, OH Divine Word Church; Retired.
Kinn, James W. '57 (CHI) Mundelein, IL Santa Maria Del Popolo Church.
Kinnaman, Leroy G. '73 (LFT) Tipton, IN St. John the Baptist Church.
Kinnane, James F. '63 (HRT) Newington, CT Holy Spirit Church; Special and other Archdiocesan Assignment.
Kinney, Francis L. *c.pp.s.* '47 (STU) Pine Grove, OH St. Mary Church.
Kinney, George R. '63 (STP) Corcoran, MN St. Thomas the Apostle Church.
Kinney, James J. '98 (SUP) Pelican Lake, WI St. John Church; Rhinelander, WI Immaculate Conception Church.
Kinney, John M. '76 (LFT) Military Chaplains.
Kinney, Leo '92 (FAR) Anamoose, ND St. Francis Xavier Church.
Kinney, M. Eugene '84 (MIL) Horicon, WI St. Malachy Church; Juneau, WI Immaculate Conception Church; [W] Horicon, WI Legion of Mary.
Kinney, Thomas '77 (NO) [9] Metairie, LA St. Francis Xavier Church.
Kinney, William G. '96 (CHR) Yonges Island, SC St. Mary Church.
Kinney, William J. *m.s.* '42 (HRT) [M] Hartford, CT Missionaries of LaSalette, Provincial Secretary.
Kinsella, Arthur L. *o.p.* '46 (STL) [P] St. Louis, MO St. Dominic Priory.
Kinsella, Charles R. '65 (BO) Permanent Disability.
Kinsky, Richard *c.s.b.* (ROC) Rush, NY St. Joseph Church.
Kinsky, Richard C. *c.s.b* '59 (ROC) [I] Rochester, NY Basilian Residence.
Kinter, John P. '67 (WDC) [43] Washington, DC St. Thomas More Church; Hospital & Nursing Home Ministries.
Kintiba, George *s.v.d.* '69 (CHI) [51] Chicago, IL St. Elizabeth Church.
Kinzer, Gary '70 (ORG) Absent on Sick Leave.
Kinzer, Victor (SCL) Retired.
Kinzler, Dale '74 (FAR) [3] Fargo, ND Nativity Church; [B] Fargo, ND Shanley High School.
Kipfer, David '88 (PEO) [1] Ottawa, IL St. Columba Church.
Kirby, Daniel '94 (DM) Neola, IA St. Patrick Church;

Weston, IA St. Columbanus Church.
Kirby, Donald J. *s.j.* '72 (SY) [S] Syracuse, NY Jesuits at LeMoyne, Inc.
Kirby, Edward A. '61 (PT) Retired.
Kirby, Gerald S. '84 (NOR) On Duty Outside the Diocese.
Kirby, Jim '96 (DM) [C] West Des Moines, IA Dowling High School.
Kirby, Jon *s.v.d.* '71 (FgM) Society of the Divine Word Foreign Missions.
Kirby, Louis M. *o.s.b.* '48 (PBL) Westcliffe, CO Our Lady of the Assumption Church; [G] Canon City, CO Holy Cross Abbey.
Kirby, Marc Daniel *o.cist.* '86 (NOR) [A] Cromwell, CT Holy Apostles College and Seminary.
Kirby, Mark Daniel *o.cist.* '86 (NOR) Portland, CT St. Mary Church.
Kirby, Martin F. '67 (BRK) [B] Douglaston, NY Cathedral Seminary Residence of the Immaculate Conception.
Kirby, Martin F. '67 (RVC) Oceanside, NY St. Anthony Church.
Kirby, Robert F. '59 (FR) Retired.
Kirby, Thomas (PIT) Washington County, PA West Penn Allegheny Health System-Canonsburg Hospital.
Kirby, Thomas M. '57 (PIT) Blawnox, PA St. Edward Church; Washington County, PA Canon House; Washington County, PA Charles House Home for the Aged; Washington County, PA Greenery Nursing Home; Washington County, PA Horizon Senior Care; Washington County, PA Pine Lawn Home; Washington County, PA Rest Haven Personal Care Home I; Washington County, PA Rest Haven Personal Care Home II; Washington County, PA Rest Haven Personal Care Home V; Washington County, PA Beverly South Hills; Washington County, PA The Bradley Center.
Kircher, Edward '57 (CC) Retired.
Kirchgessner, Christopher A. *o.s.b.* '80 (CHL) [J] Belmont, NC Belmont Abbey.
Kirchhoefer, Tom '98 (STL) Maryland Heights, MO St. Blaise Church.
Kirchmeyer, Robert W. '52 (BO) [1] Beverly, MA St. Alphonsus Church.
Kirchner, Donnell *c.ss.r.* '66 (FgM) Redemptorist Foreign Missions.
Kirchner, James '63 (SAV) Waycross, GA St. Joseph's Church.
Kirchner, James A. '63 (NEW) On Duty Outside the Archdiocese.
Kirchner, Peter K., Jr. '93 (SCL) BlueGrass, MN St. Hubert's Church; Verndale, MN St. Frederick's Church.
Kireilis, Fabian P. '39 (CHI) Retired.
Kirila, Michael '87 (ROM) Detroit, MI St. John the Baptist Church.
Kirk, Albert E. '68 (MEM) [11] Memphis, TN Holy Spirit Church.
Kirk, Allan F. *s.j.* '65 (CHI) [C] Chicago, IL Jesuit Community at Loyola University of Chicago; [J] Maywood, IL Foster G. McGaw Hospital of Loyola University of Chicago.
Kirk, Daniel *o.s.b.* '49 (WDC) [M] Washington, DC St. Anselm's Abbey.
Kirk, David '64 (NTN) Leave of Absence.
Kirk, David R. '83 (TOL) Military Chaplains.
Kirk, James T., Jr. '86 (WIL) Brandywood, DE Church of the Holy Child.
Kirk, John L. '70 (NSH) Tullahoma, TN St. Paul the Apostle Church.
Kirk, Msgr. Raymond '59 (SD) [21] San Diego, CA St. Brigid Church.
Kirk, Thomas '69 (MEM) Savannah, TN St. Mary's Church.
Kirk, William J. *o.s.b.* '46 (PEO) [A] Peru, IL St. Bede Abbey and Academy.
Kirk, William S. '72 (PH) Secane, PA Our Lady of Fatima Church.
Kirke, Eugene K. '62 (BO) Society of St. James the Apostle.
Kirke, Eugene K. '62 (FgM) Society of St. James the Apostle.
Kirkendoll, Tom *glmy.* (OWN) [F] Hartford, KY Glenmary House.
Kirkhoff, Gerald J. '69 (IND) [23] Indianapolis, IN St. Jude Church.
Kirkilas, Michael '36 (CHI) Retired.
Kirkness, Michael D. '77 (GF) On Duty Outside of the Diocese.
Kirkness, Michael D. '77 (LA) Lompoc, CA Lompoc Federal Correctional Institution; Lompoc, CA US Penitentiary.
Kirkpatrick, Cletus '56 (BAK) [A] Ontario, OR The Dominican Sisters of Ontario, Inc. dba Holy Rosary Medical Center.
Kirlin, Bernard '71 (MIA) Coral Gables, FL St. Augustine Church.
Kirouac, Richard '85 (STN) [1] Chicago, IL St. Nicholas Ukrainian Catholic Church.
Kirrane, James A. '45 (RVC) Hicksville, NY Holy Family Church.
Kirrane, James A. '46 (BRK) Retired.
Kirsch, Edmund D. '88 (CHL) Retired.
Kirsch, Gerard D. *o.s.b.* '70 (SEA) [L] Lacey, WA St. Martin's Abbey.
Kirsch, Gregory A. '81 (E) Morrisdale, PA St. Agnes Church.
Kirsch, Gregory G. '88 (STL) St. Louis, MO Saint Louis University Hospital; [C] St. Louis, MO Saint Louis University.
Kirsch, John B. '69 (HEL) Retired.
Kirsch, Myron M. *o.s.b.* '73 (GBG) [H] Latrobe, PA Saint Vincent Archabbey.
Kirsch, Patrick V. '81 (SB) Phelan, CA Blessed Junipero Serra Church; Wrightwood, CA Our Lady of the Snows Church.
Kirschner, Anthony *c.m.m.* '37 (DET) [K] Dearborn Heights, MI Our Lady of Grace Monastery.
Kirtland, Robert B. '55 (TOL) Retired.
Kirtz, Raymond R. *o.m.i.* '58 (STP) [Q] Buffalo, MN Christ the King Retreat Center.
Kirwan, Christopher J., Jr. '92 (BO) Graduate Studies.
Kirwan, Thomas P. '69 (DET) Garden City, MI St. Raphael the Archangel Church.
Kirwen, Michael C. *m.m.* '63 (FgM) Maryknoll Foreign Missions.
Kirwin, Arthur R. *o.p.* '84 (R) [E] Raleigh, NC Dominican Community.
Kirwin, Christopher J., Jr. (BO) [4] Brookline, MA Infant Jesus-St. Lawrence Church.
Kirwin, George *o.m.i.* '58 (BUF) [27] Buffalo, NY Holy Angels Church.
Kirwin, John '66 (ALB) [2] Albany, NY St. John-St. Ann Church.
Kirwin, Michael J. '76 (SCR) [1] Old Forge, PA St. Lawrence O'Toole Church.
Kirwin, Peter *o.f.m.* '81 (PHX) [H] Scottsdale, AZ Franciscan Renewal Center, Inc. (Casa de Paz Y Bien).
Kirwin, Msgr. Robert J. '45 (RVC) Williston Park, NY St. Aidan's Church; Retired.
Kis-Horvath, Pascal *o.cist.* '57 (DAL) [K] Irving, TX Cistercian Abbey of Our Lady of Dallas.
Kisala, Robert *s.v.d.* '85 (FgM) Society of the Divine Word Foreign Missions.
Kiselica, John *s.m.* '84 (DET) [K] Livonia, MI Marist Fathers & Brothers Community.
Kiser, Karl *s.j.* '97 (DET) [B] Berkley, MI Loyola House.
Kish, Carl '62 (Y) Cortland, OH St. Robert Bellarmine Church.
Kish, Jerome '98 (JOL) Downers Grove, IL St. Joseph Church.
Kish, Leslie P. '97 (B) Lewiston, ID Our Lady of Lourdes Church.
Kish, Matthew J. '43 (GRY) Retired.
Kish, Michael A. '65 (MIA) [26] Miami, FL St. Louis Church.
Kisluk, Aloysius J. '57 (NOR) [3] Middletown, CT St. Mary of Czestochowa Church.
Kiss, Barnabas G. *o.f.m.* '78 (DET) [31] Detroit, MI Holy Cross Church.
Kiss, Gabriel *s.j.* '55 (NY) [12] Yonkers, NY St. Margaret of Hungary Church.
Kiss, Matthew *o.f.m.* '55 (NY) [DD] New York, NY Franciscan Province of the Immaculate Conception.
Kissane, James M. '92 (RVC) East Northport, NY St. Anthony of Padua Church.
Kissane, Maurice J. '64 (CHI) Brookfield, IL St. Barbara Church.
Kissane, Michael *o.carm.* '86 (NY) [189] Bronx, NY St. Simon Stock Church; [DD] Middletown, NY Carmelite Friars (North American Province of St. Elias).
Kissane, Richard *c.s.sp.* '45 (SB) [E] Hemet, CA Holy Ghost Fathers.
Kissel, Anthony '73 (EVN) On Duty Outside the Diocese.
Kissel, Anthony '73 (SP) [A] Saint Leo, FL Saint Leo University, University Ministry.
Kissel, Francis J. *s.m.* '71 (ATL) [C] Atlanta, GA Marist School.
Kissel, Ignatius M. *o.s.m.* '65 (CHI) [N] Chicago, IL Order of Friar Servants of Mary (Servites) United States of America Province, Inc.
Kissel, Ignatius M. *o.s.m.* '65 (ORG) Fullerton, CA St. Philip Benizi Church; [I] Buena Park, CA Order of Friar Servants of Mary (Servites); [I] Buena Park, CA Order of Friar Servants of Mary (Servites).
Kissell, Terrence (DEN) Commerce City, CO Our Lady Mother of the Church.
Kissell, Wilbur '51 (MOB) [2] Montgomery, AL St. Andrew Church.
Kissinger, Rodney T. *s.j.* '53 (SP) [C] Tampa, FL Jesuit High School.
Kissling, John M. '53 (DUB) Retired.
Kist, Harold W. '74 (CIN) Russells Point, OH St. Mary of the Woods Church.
Kisting, Thomas '73 (DUL) Absent on Sick Leave.
Kistler, Leonard A. *c.pp.s.* '61 (TOL) Alvada, OH St. Peter Church; New Riegel, OH St. Boniface Church.
Kistner, Hilarion H. *o.f.m.* '55 (CIN) [P] Cincinnati, OH Friarhurst Retreat Center.
Kita, August *s.d.b.* '60 (NY) [FF] Stony Point, NY Don Bosco Retreat Center and Marian Shrine; [FF] Stony Point, NY Marian Shrine.
Kita, John M. '98 (SCR) [1] Williamsport, PA Annunciation Church.
Kitchin, George '70 (BLX) Ocean Springs, MS St. Elizabeth Ann Seton Church.
Kitenge, Denis (SP) Dunedin, FL Our Lady of Lourdes Church.
Kitira, Gabriel *c.s.sp.* '83 (GAL) [13] Houston, TX St. Benedict the Abbot Church.
Kitko, Joseph F. (BAL) Laurel, MD Resurrection of Our Lord Church.
Kitko, Joseph F. '55 (BAL) Retired.
Kitt, Liam J. '43 (CLV) Elyria Township, OH St. Vincent de Paul Church.
Kitt, William J. '43 (CLV) Retired.
Kitten, Marvin C. *s.j.* '65 (NO) [C] New Orleans, LA Loyola University New Orleans.
Kittock, Francis R. '55 (STP) Retired.
Kitz, Raphael *o.c.d.* '59 (LR) [A] Little Rock, AR Marylake - Carmelite Novitiate.
Kitzke, Timothy L. '89 (MIL) [84] Milwaukee, WI Three Holy Women Church.
Kivel, Joseph G. '61 (STP) [17] Minneapolis, MN St. Anthony of Padua Church.
Kiwanuke, Deo Gratias '91 (PIT) [66] Pittsburgh, PA St. Wendelin Church.
Kiyaka, Isaac *s.j.* '98 (CHI) [C] Chicago, IL Jesuit Community at Loyola University of Chicago.
Kizhakkedath, Cyriac *c.m.i.* '64 (ALX) Dupont, LA Immaculate Conception Church.
Kizis, Kenneth G. '59 (SCR) Olyphant, PA St. Michael the Archangel Church.
Klaas, Gregory '67 (SR) [H] Sonoma, CA Hanna Boys Center.
Klaas, Msgr. Raymond E. '50 (MAD) Marshall, WI St. Mary's of the Nativity Church.
Klaers, Marvin J. '50 (STP) Miesville, MN St. Joseph Church; New Trier, MN St. Mary Church.
Klaiber, Jeffrey L. *s.j.* '74 (CHI) [N] Chicago, IL Chicago Province of the Society of Jesus-Provincial Office.
Klaiber, Jeffrey L. *s.j.* '74 (FgM) Provinces.
Klajbor, Richard J. '79 (CHI) [80] Chicago, IL Holy Innocents Church.
Klak, Jan '79 (SAT) [27] San Antonio, TX St. Anthony Mary Claret Church.
Klak, Jan Piotr '79 (SAT) [C] San Antonio, TX Oblate School of Theology.
Klamet, Francis X. '78 (CLV) Released from Diocesan Assignment.
Klamut, Charles '99 (PEO) [13] Peoria, IL St. Philomena's Church.
Klapp, John S. '45 (PH) Retired.
Klapperich, Giles R. *o.p.* '53 (MIL) [P] Kenosha, WI Order of Preachers, Province of St. Albert the Great.
Klapps, William J. '58 (WIL) Woodcrest, DE St. Matthew Church; Retired.
Klarer, Michael E. '79 (MAD) Military Chaplains.
Klasek, Stephen A. '83 (NSH) [7] Nashville, TN Holy Rosary Church.
Klasinski, George '51 (KCK) Retired.
Klasinski, Stanley J. '61 (CLV) Lyndhurst, OH St. Clare Church.
Klassen, John *o.s.b.* '77 (SCL) [B] Collegeville, MN St. John's University.
Klassen, Roger *o.s.b.* '66 (SCL) Freeport, MN Sacred Heart Church; New Munich, MN Immaculate Conception Church; St. Rosa, MN St. Rose of Lima Church; [I] Collegeville, MN St. John's Abbey, of the Order of St. Benedict.
Klatka, Joseph S. '67 (MAN) Littleton, NH St. Rose of Lima Church.
Klauck, Michael '94 (BIR) On Duty Outside the Diocese.
Klauck, Msgr. Peter '55 (GB) Retired.
Klauck, Stanley B. '46 (MIL) Retired.
Klauder, Francis *s.d.b.* '47 (NEW) [N] Orange, NJ The Salesian Community; [S] Orange, NJ Salesians of Don Bosco, S.D.B.
Klauer, Gary *o.f.m.conv.* '75 (LA) Hermosa Beach, CA Our Lady of Guadalupe Church; [Q] Torrance, CA Franciscan Friars, St. Bonaventure Friary.
Klaus, John Mark *t.o.r.* '99 (ALT) [A] Loretto, PA St. Francis College; [F] Loretto, PA St. Francis Friary, Third Order Regular of St. Francis of Penance; [H] Hollidaysburg, PA Campus Ministry.
Klaus, Joseph J. '54 (R) Absent on Leave.
Kleas, Msgr. Milam E. '51 (GAL) Dickinson, TX Shrine of the True Cross Church.
Kleber, Cecil *o.f.m.* '50 (SFE) [J] Rio Rancho, NM Felician Sisters.
Klecha, Joseph A. *m.m.* '69 (SJ) [L] Los Altos, CA Maryknoll.
Kleczewski, Kieran '78 (PHX) Litchfield Park, AZ St. Thomas Aquinas Church.
Klee, Robert A. '49 (COL) Retired.
Klees, Raymond F. '73 (CHI) La Grange, IL St. Cletus Church.
Kleffman, James (DM) Imogene, IA St. Patrick Church.

Kleffman, James F. '60 (DM) Red Oak, IA St. Mary Church.
Kleiber, Kenneth R. '68 (CHI) Retired.
Klein, Albert J. '36 (Y) Retired.
Klein, Bernard C. '49 (STP) Retired.
Klein, Charles (BAL) Baltimore, MD Harbor Hospital.
Klein, Msgr. Charles R. '54 (NY) [DD] New York, NY Our Lady of Consolation Residence.
Klein, Charles R. '59 (BAL) Retired.
Klein, David *s.j.* '71 (SAC) Rancho Cordova, CA St. John Vianney Church.
Klein, David F. *s.j.* '71 (SAC) [C] Sacramento, CA Jesuit High School; [H] Carmichael, CA Jesuit High School Community of Sacramento.
Klein, David J. '90 (CAM) [2] Vineland, NJ Sacred Heart Church.
Klein, Dennis D. '66 (BRK) [B] Douglaston, NY Cathedral Seminary Residence of the Immaculate Conception.
Klein, Donald L. '65 (DUB) [8] Cedar Rapids, IA St. Pius X Church; [F] Cedar Rapids, IA Regis Middle School.
Klein, Douglas M. '96 (SC) Storm Lake, IA St. Mary's Church.
Klein, Msgr. Edward '43 (WIN) Retired.
Klein, Eugene J. '45 (DM) Retired.
Klein, Msgr. Frank W. '45 (WIN) Retired.
Klein, George W. '54 (CIN) Trenton, OH Holy Name Church.
Klein, George W. '59 (CHI) Wilmette, IL St. Francis Xavier Church.
Klein, Gregory *o.carm.* '75 (JOL) [J] Darien, IL Carmelite Provincial Office.
Klein, Gregory L. *o.carm.* '75 (BUF) [C] Niagara University, NY Niagara University.
Klein, J. Leo *s.j.* '64 (CIN) [D] Cincinnati, OH Xavier University; [M] Cincinnati, OH Jesuit Community at Xavier University.
Klein, James T. '78 (CLV) Westlake, OH St. Bernadette Church.
Klein, John J. '70 (PAT) [7] Paterson, NJ St. George Church.
Klein, John P. '78 (LAN) [7] Lansing, MI St. Gerard Church.
Klein, John Paul *o.m.v.* '89 (SFD) [2] Alton, IL Immaculate Conception-St. Mary's Church.
Klein, Larry '84 (BWN) [5] Brownsville, TX Our Lady of Good Counsel Church.
Klein, Louis S. '81 (BUF) [K] Buffalo, NY Sisters of Charity Hospital of Buffalo, NY.
Klein, Martin L. '91 (RVC) Babylon, NY St. Joseph's Church.
Klein, Pascal L. '87 (DOD) Hoisington, KS St. John the Evangelist Church; Odin, KS Holy Family Church.
Klein, Peter J. '74 (WIN) Owatonna, MN Sacred Heart Church.
Klein, Pius *o.s.b.* '74 (EVN) Huntingburg, IN Visitation of the Blessed Virgin Mary Church.
Klein, Pius *o.s.b.* '74 (IND) [J] St. Meinrad, IN St. Meinrad Archabbey.
Klein, Robert P. '53 (COV) Retired.
Klein, Msgr. Stanley H. '44 (BUF) Retired.
Klein, Terrance W. '84 (COL) On Duty Outside the Diocese.
Klein, Terrence W. '84 (BRK) [14] Brooklyn, NY St. Augustine Church.
Klein, Theodore J. '69 (NOR) Retired.
Kleiner, James (DEN) [1] Denver, CO Cathedral of the Immaculate Conception.
Kleiner, James E. '67 (DEN) [2] Arvada, CO St. Joan of Arc Church.
Kleiner, Robert *m.c.c.j.* '71 (CHI) Blue Island, IL St. Donatus Church.
Kleinfehn, Walter J. '60 (DUB) Norway, IA St. Michael's Church; Watkins, IA St. Patrick's Church.
Kleinhans, Msgr. Thomas G. '67 (FRS) Visalia, CA St. Mary Church.
Kleinheinz, Joseph L. '54 (SUP) Retired.
Kleinhenz, John H. *s.j.* '52 (CLV) [D] Cleveland, OH St. Ignatius High School.
Kleinmann, Dennis W. '93 (ARL) [7] Alexandria, VA St. Mary's Church.
Kleinschmidt, Sylvester '50 (SCL) Retired.
Kleinstuber, Joseph J. '64 (WDC) Barnesville, MD St. Mary Church and Shrine of Our Lady of Fatima Church.
Kleinwachter, John '77 (CR) Akeley, MN St. John's Church.
Kleinweber, Dennis J. '78 (CLV) East Cleveland, OH St. Philomena Church.
Kleinworth, Robert (ELP) Absent on Leave.
Kleissler, Msgr. Thomas A. '57 (NEW) Special Assignment; [S] Plainfield, NJ RENEW International.
Klem, Daniel N. '83 (RIC) [8] Virginia Beach, VA St. Mark Church.
Klem, Robert J. *c.s.b.* '56 (GAL) [Q] Sugar Land, TX Basilian Mission Center.
Klementowicz, Chester '46 (ALB) Retired.
Klemme, Dennis C. '57 (MIL) Retired; [Q] Pewaukee, WI Carmel of the Mother of God.
Klemme, Robert '91 (LFT) [1] Lafayette, IN St. Mary Church.
Klemmer, Marvin J. '66 (BIS) [2] Bismarck, ND Ascension Church.
Klepac, Msgr. Kenneth J. '58 (MOB) [8] Mobile, AL St. Joan of Arc Church.
Klepacki, Michael S. '78 (CHL) Military Chaplains.
Klepec, George F. '71 (JOL) [12] Joliet, IL St. Joseph Church.
Kleppner, Joseph J. '71 (PIT) Center Township, PA St. Frances Cabrini Church.
Klettner, Frederick J. '65 (DET) Farmington Hills, MI St. Clare of Assisi Church.
Kletzel, Thomas P. '83 (PH) [128] Philadelphia, PA Our Lady of the Rosary Church; [130] Philadelphia, PA Our Lady of Victory Church.
Kleve, Arthur W. '57 (DUB) Retired.
Klevence, John P. '85 (WIL) Ocean City, MD St. Mary, Star of the Sea Church.
Klieber, Kenneth '68 (PHX) Phoenix, AZ United States Veterans Affairs Medical Center.
Klikunas, Bruce J. *o.s.m.* '72 (OAK) [K] Hayward, CA St. Rose Hospital; [N] Berkeley, CA Servite Community, Sarpi Priory.
Klikunas, Bruce M. *o.s.m.* '72 (CHI) [N] Chicago, IL Order of Friar Servants of Mary (Servites) United States of America Province, Inc.
Klima, James A. '76 (COL) Marion, OH St. Mary Church.
Klimanskis, Adolfo '53 (NOR) On Duty Outside the Diocese.
Klimanskis, Adolph '53 (PRO) [10] Providence, RI St. Casimir Church.
Klimas, George H. '51 (SAG) Retired.
Klimchuk, Walter '66 (STN) On Duty Outside the Diocese.
Klimczyk, John '81 (FTW) [3] Fort Wayne, IN St. Charles Borromeo Church.
Klimczyk, Leon F. *s.j.* '79 (STP) [31] Minneapolis, MN St. Olaf Church; [N] Minneapolis, MN La Storta Jesuit Community.
Klimek, Edmund J. '53 (LC) [2] Eau Claire, WI Newman Community Church; [D] Eau Claire, WI Sacred Heart Hospital; [K] Eau Claire, WI Newman Parish.
Klimek, Jan '56 (FAR) Mooreton, ND St. Anthony's Church.
Klimek, Jan '71 (FAR) Mantador, ND SS. Peter and Paul's Church.
Klimowicz, Sigmund M. *o.f.m.cap.* '45 (PAT) [M] Oak Ridge-Milton, NJ St. Stanislaus B. M. Friary.
Kline, Charles '62 (LFT) Attica, IN St. Francis Xavier Church; Covington, IN St. Joseph Church.
Kline, Donald '95 (PHX) [1] Phoenix, AZ SS. Simon and Jude Church; Special Assignment.
Kline, John J. '47 (CLV) [8] Lorain, OH St. Mary Church; Retired.
Kline, Omer U. *o.s.b.* '49 (GBG) [H] Latrobe, PA Saint Vincent Archabbey.
Kline, Robert W. '48 (CLV) Mentor, OH St. John Vianney Church; Retired; [A] Wickliffe, OH Borromeo Seminary.
Kline, Msgr. Roy F. '51 (ALT) Duncansville, PA St. Catherine of Siena Church.
Klingeisen, Richard '72 (GB) [F] Manitowoc, WI Holy Family Memorial, Inc.
Klingeisen, Richard H. '72 (GB) [F] Manitowoc, WI Holy Family Memorial, Inc.
Klinger, Attilio *s.d.b.* '54 (NY) [DD] New Rochelle, NY Salesian Provincial House.
Klinger, Charles F. '83 (COL) Zanesville, OH St. Nicholas Church.
Klinger, Msgr. Nevin J. *j.c.l.* '82 (ALN) Birdsboro, PA Immaculate Conception Church.
Klingler, Donald P. '61 (KAL) Otsego, MI St. Margaret Church.
Klingler, John *s.c.j.* '67 (MIL) [P] Hales Corners, WI Priests of the Sacred Heart; [P] Milwaukee, WI St. Joseph House of Formation.
Klingler, Ronald M. '65 (Y) [7] Canton, OH St. John the Baptist Church.
Klink, Anthony G. '58 (MIL) Retired.
Klink, Delbert D. '60 (MAD) [4] Janesville, WI St. William Church.
Klink, Eugene A. '63 (LC) [1] Eau Claire, WI Immaculate Conception Church.
Klink, Kenneth J. '66 (MAD) Belleville, WI St. Mary of Lourdes Church; Dayton, WI St. James Church.
Klink, Peter J. *s.j.* '81 (RC) Pine Ridge, SD Holy Rosary Church; [B] Pine Ridge, SD Jesuit Community of Holy Rosary Mission.
Klintworth, William P. *s.j.* '61 (FgM) Provinces.
Klinzing, Msgr. Thomas '71 (PMB) Special Assignment.
Klister, Msgr. Roy (GB) [1] Green Bay, WI St. Francis Xavier Church.
Klister, Msgr. Roy M. (GB) [6] Green Bay, WI St. John Church.
Klizek, Duane R. '82 (BUF) [9] Niagara Falls, NY Our Lady of Mount Carmel Church.
Kloak, David G. '78 (CHI) Military Chaplains.
Klobuka, John *s.m.* '78 (SAT) Helotes, TX Our Lady of Guadalupe Church.
Klobuka, John J. *s.m.* '78 (CIN) [M] Dayton, OH Marianist Provincialate.
Kloc, Thaddeus '70 (VEN) Bonita Springs, FL St. Leo Church.
Klockeman, John A. '00 (STP) [31] Minneapolis, MN St. Olaf Church.
Klocker, Harry R. *s.j.* '51 (STL) [O] St. Louis, MO Fusz Pavilion.
Klocker, Msgr. Henry '43 (CIN) Retired.
Klocker, John G. '58 (STL) Webster Groves, MO Annunciation Church.
Kloda, Marshall J. '89 (PH) [95] Philadelphia, PA St. Martin of Tours Church.
Kloeckner, William '43 (SCL) Retired.
Kloepfer, John S. '53 (JOL) Retired.
Kloepfer, John S. '53 (RIC) Retired.
Kloppenborg, Thomas *c.m.* '91 (COS) Cheyenne Wells, CO Sacred Heart Church.
Klores, Stanley (NO) [A] New Orleans, LA Notre Dame Seminary Graduate School of Theology.
Klores, Stanley P. '82 (NO) [50] New Orleans, LA St. Patrick Church.
Klos, Joseph '80 (BUF) On Duty Outside the Diocese.
Klos, Michael E. '00 (LC) [4] Stevens Point, WI St. Peter Church; [C] Stevens Point, WI Stevens Point Area Catholic Schools; [C] Stevens Point, WI Stevens Point Area Catholic Schools.
Klos, Walter '40 (BUF) Retired.
Kloskowski, Msgr. Stanley E. '58 (CAM) Bridgeton, NJ St. Teresa of Avila Church.
Kloss, Anthony *o.s.b.* '91 (WOR) [N] Still River, MA Benedictine Monks, St. Benedict Abbey.
Kloster, Carl G. *s.j.* '48 (DEN) [M] Denver, CO Xavier Jesuit Center.
Kloster, George M. '68 (CHL) Murphy, NC St. William Church.
Kloton, Michael J. '87 (SCR) Tobyhanna, PA St. Ann Church.
Klotter, Frederick W. (L) Holy Cross, KY Holy Cross Church.
Klotter, Frederick W. '96 (L) Lebanon, KY St. Augustine Church; Raywick, KY St. Francis Xavier Church; St. Francis, KY St. Francis of Assisi Church.
Klotz, Claude *s.d.s.* '43 (MIL) [P] Milwaukee, WI Salvatorians - Jordan Hall.
Kluba, Zbigniew '73 (PAT) Convent Station, NJ St. Thomas More Church; Morristown, NJ Morristown Memorial Hospital.
Klubertanz, Kenneth E. '66 (MAD) Lodi, WI St. Patrick Church.
Klucinec, Benedict *m.s.a.* '87 (NOR) [A] Cromwell, CT Holy Apostles College and Seminary; [F] Cromwell, CT Society of the Missionaries of the Holy Apostles.
Kluckman, Anthony *s.c.j.* (RC) [B] Eagle Butte, SD Sacred Heart Community House.
Kluckman, Anthony *s.c.j.* '73 (RC) Eagle Butte, SD All Saints Church; Eagle Butte, SD Cheyenne River Reservation Church.
Kluczynski, Campion '59 (GB) [I] Green Bay, WI St. Mary of the Angels Friary.
Klug, Jerome G. '49 (CHI) Bartlett, IL St. Peter Damian Church; Retired.
Klug, Richard L. '51 (CIN) [8] Cincinnati, OH Annunciation of the Blessed Virgin Mary Church.
Klump, Gregory S. '98 (STL) Dardenne, MO Immaculate Conception Church.
Kluonius, Joseph V. '47 (GAY) Retired.
Kmech, John '61 (STN) Retired.
Kmiec, Roman *c.m.* '86 (HRT) [18] New Haven, CT St. Stanislaus Church.
Knapek, John A. *s.j.* '57 (CLV) [B] Cleveland, OH John Carroll Jesuit Community.
Knapik, Andrew '78 (CLV) [35] Cleveland, OH Immaculate Heart of Mary Church.
Knapik, Andrew G. '57 (ALT) Retired.
Knapp, Charles D. '63 (TUC) [10] Tucson, AZ Our Mother of Sorrows Church.
Knapp, Gerard J. *c.ss.r.* '75 (BRK) [V] Brooklyn, NY Our Lady of Good Counsel Residence.
Knapp, James G. *s.j.* '81 (STL) [F] St. Louis, MO St. Louis University High School, George H. Backer Memorial; [P] St. Louis, MO St. Louis University High School Jesuit Community.
Knapp, John M. '86 (NY) [177] Bronx, NY Our Lady of Solace Church.
Knapp, Joseph G. *o.c.s.o.* '48 (DUB) [K] Peosta, IA New Melleray Abbey, Order of Cistercians of the Strict Observance.
Knapp, Msgr. Kenneth R. '63 (EVN) [4] Evansville, IN Christ the King Church; Special Assignment.
Knapp, Msgr. Richard '55 (SFR) Novato, CA Our Lady of Loretto Church; Retired; [T] San Rafael, CA Third Order of St. Dominic Support and Charitable Trust Fund.
Knapp, Roger A. '85 (DET) Gibraltar, MI St. Victor Church.
Knapp, William L. '48 (SFR) [2] San Rafael, CA St. Isabella Church; Retired.
Knappik, Richard *c.ss.r.* '58 (ALB) [L] Saratoga Springs, NY St. John Neumann Residence.

Knauer, Msgr. Paul F. '64 (PAT) Sparta, NJ Our Lady of the Lake Church.
Knauf, Edwin L. '33 (LC) Retired.
Knaup, Alan J. '77 (STL) Mehlville, MO St. Margaret Mary Alacoque Church; Retired.
Kneafsey, Msgr. Cornelius T. '58 (BRK) [208] Queens, NY Our Lady of the Cenacle Church.
Kneal, Msgr. Ellsworth '44 (STP) Retired; [C] St. Paul, MN University of St. Thomas.
Kneemiller, William C. '99 (DAV) [8] Davenport, IA St. Paul the Apostle Church.
Kneifl, Rodney V. '85 (OM) Platte Center, NE St. Joseph Church.
Kneip, Paschal *o.s.b.* '51 (RIC) [5] Virginia Beach, VA St. Gregory the Great Church.
Kneipp, August J. '41 (CIN) Retired.
Knepper, Daniel J. '70 (DUB) [2] Dubuque, IA St. Anthony's Church.
Knerr, Joseph '80 (ORG) Fountain Valley, CA Holy Spirit Church.
Knestout, Msgr. Barry '89 (WDC) Pastoral Center Special Ministries.
Knestout, Mark David '98 (WDC) Potomac, MD Our Lady of Mercy Church.
Kniepp, August J. '41 (CIN) [L] Cincinnati, OH Archbishop Leibold Home for the Aged.
Knier, Aloysius M. '42 (GB) Retired.
Knies, G. Jerome *o.s.a.* '62 (CHI) [N] Olympia Fields, IL The Augustinians-Provincialate.
Knight, David B. '61 (MEM) [25] Memphis, TN Sacred Heart Church.
Knight, Dennis D. '77 (LEX) Somerset, KY St. Mildred Church.
Knight, Jeffrey N. '88 (STL) O'Fallon, MO Assumption Church.
Knighton, Marv (PHX) [A] Phoenix, AZ St. Mary's High School.
Knighton, Marvin T. '75 (MIL) On Duty Outside the Archdiocese.
Knipe, Michael J. '88 (TLS) [16] Tulsa, OK Resurrection Church.
Knipe, William T. *m.m.* '58 (FgM) Maryknoll Foreign Missions.
Knippel, Kenneth P. '76 (MIL) Fox Point, WI St. Eugene Church.
Knippenberg, Robert '00 (VIC) Hallettsville, TX Sacred Heart Church.
Knipper, Daniel J. '67 (DUB) Lansing, IA Immaculate Conception Church; Lycurgus, IA St. Mary's Church; New Albin, IA St. Joseph's Church; [E] Lansing, IA Lansing School of Religion.
Knittel, Kilian M. '60 (CHI) [42] Chicago, IL St. Columba Church.
Knoblach, Thomas '87 (SCL) Bertha, MN St. Joseph's Church; Henning, MN Church of St. Edward of Henning.
Knoebel, Thomas L. '69 (MIL) Special Assignment; [B] Hales Corners, WI Sacred Heart School of Theology.
Knoernschild, John *o.carm.* '70 (LA) [F] Encino, CA Crespi Carmelite High School.
Knoerschild, John *o.carm.* '70 (CHI) [N] Chicago, IL Carmelite Priory of St. Cyril.
Knoke, Kenneth F. '55 (FAR) Reynolds, ND Our Lady of Perpetual Help Church.
Knoll, Charles *o.f.m.cap.* '54 (GBG) Export, PA St. Mary Church.
Knoll, Jerome E. *c.s.c.* '60 (FTW) [B] Notre Dame, IN University of Notre Dame Du Lac; [J] Notre Dame, IN Holy Cross Community, Corby Hall, University of Notre Dame.
Knoll, Lester *o.f.m.cap.* '64 (PIT) Herman, PA St. Mary of the Assumption Church; [O] Herman, PA St. Mary's Friary.
Knoll, Mark *c.ss.r.* '36 (ALB) [L] Saratoga Springs, NY St. John Neumann Residence.
Knoll, Mark *c.ss.r.* '36 (ORL) Retired.
Knoll, Urban H. '69 (STL) Retired.
Knop, Andrew *o.m.i.* '89 (DUL) [3] Duluth, MN Holy Family Church.
Knopik, Andrew J. '83 (BEL) [4] Belleville, IL St. Augustine of Canterbury Church.
Knopp, Benjamin *o.f.m.conv.* '55 (TOL) Carey, OH Our Lady of Consolation, Basilica-National Church.
Knopp, John '78 (ELP) Absent on Leave.
Knotek, John T. '38 (MIL) Retired.
Knotek, Michael P. '96 (CHI) [40] Chicago, IL St. Clement Church.
Knoth, Bernard P. *s.j.* '77 (NO) [C] New Orleans, LA Loyola University New Orleans.
Knott, Edward J. '45 (MAN) Retired.
Knott, Francis X. *s.j.* '45 (PH) [AA] Philadelphia, PA Jesuit Community at St. Joseph's University.
Knott, William P. '59 (RCK) Retired.
Knox, James '51 (PRT) Retired.
Knox, Stephen J. '89 (RCK) DeKalb, IL Christ the Teacher, University Parish of Northern Illinois University Church; [L] DeKalb, IL Newman Foundation for Catholic Students of Northern Illinois University.
Knudsen, Ronald '72 (SEA) Mountlake Terrace, WA St. Pius X Church.
Knueven, Gerald E. '68 (TOL) [7] Toledo, OH Good Shepherd Church; [18] Toledo, OH St. Anthony Church; [38] Toledo, OH St. Stanislaus Church.
Knueven, Harold L. '58 (IND) Greenwood, IN Our Lady of the Greenwood Church.
Knuffman, Donald '65 (SFD) [4] Quincy, IL St. Dominic Church.
Knuge, Richard K. *s.m.* '56 (CIN) [M] Dayton, OH Marianist Provincialate.
Knurek, Dennis A. '77 (BGP) Retired.
Knusel, Frank '73 (P) Absent on Leave.
Kobak, Cantius J. *o.f.m.* (MIL) [N] Milwaukee, WI St. Ann Rest Home.
Kobasuk, Maxim *o.s.b.m.* '77 (STF) Hempstead, NY St. Vladimir Church.
Kobayashi, Augustine *ss.cc.* '64 (FR) [I] Fairhaven, MA Sacred Hearts Provincial House.
Kobbeman, Gerald P. '66 (RCK) [10] Rockford, IL St. Rita Church.
Kobe, Robert S. '79 (ELP) [5] El Paso, TX Christ The Savior Church.
Kobel, Stanley *o.f.m.cap.* '96 (CHL) [10] Charlotte, NC St. Thomas Aquinas Church.
Kobia, Vincent F. '80 (MIL) [87] Milwaukee, WI St. Vincent de Paul Church.
Kobida, Vincent '80 (MIL) [63] Milwaukee, WI Our Lady of Guadalupe Church.
Kobler, John F. *c.p.* '54 (CHI) [N] Chicago, IL Passionist Community-Immaculate Conception Monastery.
Kobos, Martin *o.f.m.conv.* '76 (BAL) [S] Ellicott City, MD Order of Friars Minor Conventual.
Kobti, Labib '99 (SFR) [29] San Francisco, CA St. John of God Church; [R] San Francisco, CA Newman Center, University of California Medical Center.
Kobus, Boguslaw '92 (PAT) [2] Clifton, NJ St. Andrew the Apostle Church.
Kobus, Damian M. *o.s.m.* '49 (CHI) [N] Chicago, IL Order of Friar Servants of Mary (Servites) United States of America Province, Inc.
Kobus, Damian M. *o.s.m.* '49 (P) [32] Portland, OR St. Rita Church; [L] Portland, OR The Grotto, The National Sanctuary of Our Sorrowful Mother.
Kobus, John '77 (CHI) [J] Chicago, IL St. Mary of Nazareth Hospital Center.
Kobuszewski, Thomas P. '64 (SY) [25] Syracuse, NY Transfiguration Church.
Kobza, John *m.i.c.* '54 (WDC) [M] Brookeville, MD Marian Monastery-Brookeville.
Koch, Andrew *o.s.b.* '97 (WOR) [N] Still River, MA Benedictine Monks, St. Benedict Abbey.
Koch, Msgr. Charles J. '63 (EVN) Special Assignment.
Koch, David J. '69 (GB) Neenah, WI St. Margaret Mary Church.
Koch, Eugene R. '59 (DM) Granger, IA Assumption of the Blessed Virgin Mary Church; Woodward, IA St. Ann Church.
Koch, George J. *s.j.* '59 (SJ) [L] Los Gatos, CA Sacred Heart Jesuit Center.
Koch, Ivor '84 (FWT) Wichita Falls, TX Sacred Heart Church.
Koch, Kevin A. '85 (CHY) Torrington, WY St. Rose Church.
Koch, Marius Casmir *c.f.r.* '31 (NY) [DD] Yonkers, NY St. Leopold's Friary.
Koch, Michael R. '53 (GB) Special Assignment; [J] Oshkosh, WI SSM Franciscan Courts.
Koch, Patrick H. *s.j.* '57 (DAL) [27] Dallas, TX St. Rita Church.
Koch, Paul M. '61 (DM) On Duty Outside the Diocese.
Koch, Paul M. '61 (FgM) Society of St. James the Apostle.
Koch, Terrence E. *s.j.* '60 (SJ) [L] Los Gatos, CA Sacred Heart Jesuit Center.
Kocher, Aloisius *o.r.c.* (DET) [10] Detroit, MI Assumption Grotto Church.
Kocherry, Varghese '62 (RVC) Hicksville, NY Holy Family Church.
Kochery, Peter '70 (TR) Howell Township, NJ St. Veronica Church.
Kochu, Paul '74 (SP) Gulfport, FL Most Holy Name of Jesus Church.
Kochupurkal, Sebastian (HRT) Plainville, CT Our Lady of Mercy Church.
Kocik, Franc W. '76 (CAM) On Duty Outside the Diocese.
Kocik, Thomas M. '97 (FR) Hyannis, MA St. Francis Xavier's Church.
Kociolek, Charles J. *c.s.c.* '79 (SCR) [C] Wilkes-Barre, PA Kings College.
Kociolek, Henry *s.ch.* '88 (P) [35] Portland, OR St. Stanislaus Church.
Kocour, Robert F. '43 (WCH) Retired.
Koebel, Joseph A. '54 (VIC) Nada, TX Nativity of the Blessed Virgin Mary Church.
Koehl, Keith '97 (AUS) [22] Austin, TX St. Thomas More Church.
Koehler, Frederick C. *s.j.* '51 (PH) [AA] Philadelphia, PA Jesuit Community at St. Joseph's University.
Koehler, John '65 (SEA) Retired.
Koehler, Jon C. '74 (BR) [19] Baton Rouge, LA St. Pius X Church.
Koehler, Kenneth '72 (DEN) [16] Denver, CO Most Precious Blood Church.
Koehler, Paul L. '38 (FAR) Retired; [E] Hankinson, ND St. Gerard Community Nursing Home.
Koehler, Ralph *o.s.b.* (KCK) Kelly, KS St. Bede's Church.
Koehler, Steven C. '82 (DET) Madison Heights, MI St. Vincent Ferrer Church.
Koehler, Theodore A. *s.m.* '41 (CIN) [D] Dayton, OH The University of Dayton; [M] Dayton, OH Marianist Provincialate.
Koehne, David '49 (GB) Retired.
Koehr, Louis A. '87 (BEL) Albers, IL St. Bernard Church; Damiansville, IL St. Damian Church.
Koelker, Harry '68 (DUB) [5] Cedar Rapids, IA St. Ludmila's Church; [F] Cedar Rapids, IA Holy Family Catholic Consolidated School.
Koelsch, John W. '56 (B) [6] Boise, ID Sacred Heart Church.
Koen, Stephen A. '58 (BO) [5] Newton, MA Mary Immaculate of Lourdes Church.
Koenig, Bernard '56 (HEL) Retired.
Koenig, Msgr. Harry C. '32 (CHI) Retired.
Koenig, Msgr. John H. '42 (NEW) Summit, NJ St. Teresa's Church; Union, NJ Holy Spirit Church; Retired.
Koenig, Paul *o.f.m.cap.* '93 (MIL) [27] Milwaukee, WI St. Francis of Assisi Church.
Koenig, Paul *o.c.d.* '93 (SEA) Stanwood, WA St. Cecilia Church.
Koenig, Msgr. William A. '32 (PH) [T] Philadelphia, PA St. Vincent's Day Care Center.
Koenig, William E. '83 (RVC) Seaford, NY St. William, the Abbot Church.
Koenigsfeld, James F. '68 (PBL) Crested Butte, CO Queen of All Saints Church; Gunnison, CO St. Peter Church.
Koenigsknecht, William J. '68 (LAN) [5] Lansing, MI Resurrection Church; Retired.
Koeninger, Frances F. '79 (STL) Cottleville, MO St. Joseph Church.
Koeplin, John P. *s.j.* '91 (SFR) [N] San Francisco, CA Jesuit Community at University of San Francisco.
Koerber, George M. '60 (TOL) Retired.
Koerner, Frederick C. '59 (NEW) Retired; [N] Rutherford, NJ St. John Vianney Residence for Priests.
Koerner, Robert H. '66 (GF) [G] Billings, MT St. Vincent Healthcare.
Koesel, Douglas H. '78 (CLV) [46] Cleveland, OH St. Mark Church.
Koester, Timothy J. '83 (BUF) Military Chaplains.
Koesterer, David W. *s.j.* '64 (STL) [P] St. Louis, MO White House Retreat Jesuit Community; [T] St. Louis, MO White House Retreat.
Koetter, Paul D. '77 (IND) [30] Indianapolis, IN St. Monica Church.
Koeune, August '84 (CHY) Worland, WY St. Mary Magdalen Church.
Koeune, George '95 (CHI) [176] Chicago, IL Queen of All Saints Basilica Church.
Kofski, James W. *m.m.* '91 (FgM) Maryknoll Foreign Missions.
Koharchik, George D. '74 (ALT) Shade Gap, PA St. Mary's Church; Huntingdon, PA State Correctional Institution.
Kohler, Edward '77 (HEL) Browning, MT Church of the Little Flower.
Kohler, Girard J. *c.s.sp.* '63 (PIT) [O] Bethel Park, PA Holy Ghost Fathers and Brothers Provincialate; [Q] Bethel Park, PA Holy Ghost Animation Center.
Kohler, Joseph M. '54 (STL) [V] St. Louis, MO Dismas House of St. Louis.
Kohler, Lawrence A. *m.s.* '61 (LKC) [2] Sulphur, LA Our Lady of LaSalette Church.
Kohler, Peter D. '68 (STL) Maplewood, MO Immaculate Conception Church; [P] St. Louis, MO La Salette Missionaries.
Kohler, Russell E. '73 (DET) [50] Detroit, MI Most Holy Trinity Church; [Q] Detroit, MI Pope John XXIII Hospitality House; [Q] Onsted, MI St. Patrick's Retreat.
Kohler, Thomas M. '68 (PH) Absent on Sick Leave.
Kohler, William (Guillo) *c.ss.r.* '83 (TUC) [17] Tucson, AZ St. Joseph Church; Tucson, AZ Tucson Medical Center.
Kohler, William E. (MIL) Special Assignment.
Kohler, William F. '55 (PIT) [4] Bridgeville, PA St. Barbara Church.
Kohlerman, Charles W. *c.s.c.* '63 (FTW) [A] Notre Dame, IN Moreau Seminary.
Kohli, Charles F. '61 (RVC) Stony Brook, NY L.I. State Veterans' Home.
Kohlmann, Vernon *s.d.v.* '98 (NEW) Palisades Park, NJ St. Nicholas Church.
Kohls, Msgr. Eugene C. '57 (STA) [1] Jacksonville, FL Assumption Church.
Kohmescher, Matthew F. *s.m.* '48 (CIN) [D] Dayton, OH The University of Dayton; [M] Dayton, OH Marianist Provincialate.
Kohmetscher, James *o.m.i.* '55 (FgM) Oblates Foreign Missions.
Kohner, David W. '90 (STP) [4] Faribault, MN Sacred

Heart - St. Lawrence of Faribault Church; [A] St. Paul, MN The Saint Paul Seminary; [C] St. Paul, MN University of St. Thomas.
Kohrman, Glenn '92 (FTW) [14] Fort Wayne, IN St. Patrick Church; [15] Fort Wayne, IN St. Paul Church.
Kohuch, Robert Andrew '66 (PIT) Elrama, PA St. Isaac Jogues Church; Allegheny County, PA Jefferson Hospital.
Kohut, Msgr. Joseph J. '62 (BGP) Darien, CT St. John Church.
Koilparampil, Augustine '64 (OAK) Livermore, CA St. Michael Church; Livermore, CA Veterans Administration Hospital; Military Chaplains.
Koilparampil, Joseph '53 (BRK) [47] Brooklyn, NY St. Francis Xavier Church.
Kok, Bede *o.c.s.o.* '41 (L) [L] Trappist, KY Abbey of Our Lady of Gethsemani, of the Order of Cistercians of the Strict Observance.
Kokeram, Joseph (NEW) Paramus, NJ Bergen Regional Medical Center.
Kokjohn, Joseph E. '54 (DAV) Retired; [B] Davenport, IA St. Ambrose University.
Kokocinski, Bernard A. '66 (TOL) Columbus Grove, OH St. Anthony of Padua Church.
Kolaczek, John Baptista *o.c.d.* '45 (GRY) [J] Munster, IN Discalced Carmelite Fathers Monastery.
Kolakowski, Marcel *o.f.m.* '49 (PH) [93] Philadelphia, PA Saint Martha Church.
Kolanda, George A. '45 (MIL) Retired; [N] Wauwatosa, WI St. Camillus Health Center, Inc.
Kolanko, John R. '40 (MIL) [62] Milwaukee, WI Our Lady of Good Hope Church; Retired.
Kolar, Thomas F. '60 (STP) Retired.
Kolarec, William T. *s.j.* '69 (OM) [K] Omaha, NE Jesuit Community at Creighton University.
Kolasa, Stanley *ss.cc.* '70 (FR) [I] Fairhaven, MA Sacred Hearts Provincial House.
Kolasinski, Daniel '57 (P) Retired.
Kolath, George '72 (STP) North St. Paul, MN St. Peter Church.
Kolb, James *c.s.p.* (STP) Lake St. Croix Beach, MN St. Francis Of Assisi Church.
Kolb, James *c.s.p.* '76 (NY) [DD] Jamaica Estates, NY Paulist Fathers Generalate.
Kolb, Joseph '53 (OKL) Elgin, OK St. Ann Church.
Kolb, Joseph E. *s.j.* '63 (WH) [A] Wheeling, WV Wheeling Jesuit University.
Kolb, Michael R. *s.j.* '82 (MIL) [E] Milwaukee, WI Marquette University High School; [P] Milwaukee, WI Arrupe House Jesuit Community.
Kolbasz, Stanley '55 (GB) Retired.
Kolberg, Lawrence R. '68 (ORG) Absent on Sick Leave.
Kolcun, Stephen '46 (PBR) Beaverdale, PA St. Mary's Church.
Kolczaski, Richard '55 (PEO) Peru, IL St. Mary's Church.
Kolda, Donald *s.j.* '55 (ORG) Laguna Niguel, CA St. Timothy Church.
Kolde, Steven J. '00 (CIN) [65] Cincinnati, OH Our Lady of Lourdes Church.
Kole, Eugene R. *ofm.conv.* '75 (SFD) [B] Quincy, IL Quincy University.
Kolenkiewicz, Louis J. '93 (PH) Hatboro, PA St. John Bosco Church.
Kolenski, Robert D. '62 (LAN) Owosso, MI St. Paul Church.
Kolesar, Msgr. John C. '64 (STU) Adena, OH St. Casimir's Church; Dillonvale, OH St. Adalbert Church.
Kolf, Gerald '95 (GAL) [P] Houston, TX Opus Dei.
Kolibas, Kenneth R. '94 (MET) Raritan, NJ St. Ann Church.
Kolinovsky, Sebastian *c.p.* '51 (FgM) Mission Procurators.
Kolinovsky, Sebastian *c.p.* '51 (NEW) [N] Union City, NJ Congregation of the Passion (Passionists)-St. Michael's Residence.
Kolio, Paulino '90 (SPP) [10] Pago Pago, AS Church of the Immaculate Conception.
Kollar, Anton *o.carm.* '51 (JOL) [J] Darien, IL Carmelite Provincial Office.
Kollar, Edmund '46 (ARL) Retired.
Kollar, Rene M. *o.s.b.* '74 (GBG) [H] Latrobe, PA Saint Vincent Archabbey.
Kollasch, Eugene C. *s.j.* '59 (GB) [M] Oshkosh, WI Jesuit Retreat House.
Kollasch, Eugene C. *s.j.* '59 (MIL) [P] Milwaukee, WI Jesuit Community at Marquette University.
Kollasch, Eugene C. *s.j.* '59 (STL) [P] St. Louis, MO Jesuit Community Corporation at St. Louis University - Jesuit Hall.
Kollasch, Louis '58 (SC) Retired.
Kollasch, Merle (SC) Rolfe, IA St. Margaret's Church.
Kollasch, Merle F. '64 (SC) Pocahontas, IA Church of the Resurrection; [F] Pocahontas, IA Opus Spiritus Sancti.
Kollath, Robert '97 (GB) Special Assignment; [N] Green Bay, WI Ecumenical Center-UWGB.
Koller, Gerold *c.pp.s.* '49 (CIN) [B] Carthagena, OH St. Charles.
Kolling, James L. '65 (LA) [CC] Los Angeles, CA Rosary Hour Inc., The.
Kollithanath, Philip '84 (CHL) High Point, NC Christ the King Church.
Kollman, Paul V. *c.s.c.* '91 (FTW) [A] Notre Dame, IN Moreau Seminary; [J] South Bend, IN Congregation of Holy Cross, Indiana Province, Provincial House.
Kollross, Dennis D. '81 (SFD) [5] Decatur, IL St. Thomas the Apostle Church; [M] Decatur, IL Millikin University Newman Catholic Community.
Kolmaga, Bogdan *o.s.p.* '92 (NY) [113] New York, NY St. Stanislaus Church.
Kolmaga, Jan *o.s.p.p.e.* '82 (PH) [AA] Doylestown, PA Pauline Fathers Monastery, Shrine of Our Lady of Czestochowa.
Kolo, Vincent F. '95 (PIT) Penn Hills, PA St. Bartholomew Church.
Kolodziej, John A. *o.s.f.s.* '99 (WIL) [B] Wilmington, DE Salesianum School.
Kolodziej, Maynard *o.f.m.* '53 (GB) [10] Green Bay, WI St. Mary of the Angels Church; [I] Green Bay, WI St. Mary of the Angels Friary.
Kolodziej, Michael *o.f.m.conv.* '70 (SPR) [10] Chicopee, MA St. Stanislaus Basilica Church.
Kolodziej, Ryszard '96 (R) Castle Hayne, NC St. Stanislaus Kostka Church.
Kolodziejczyk, Sebastian J. '99 (LC) Foreign Missions.
Kolodziejski, Karl *o.f.m.conv.* '78 (BUF) [21] Buffalo, NY Corpus Christi Church.
Kolp, Msgr. James '50 (Y) Retired.
Kolp, James R. '50 (Y) Massillon, OH St. Mary's Church.
Kolson, Lawrence F. '74 (BAL) Bradshaw, MD St. Stephen Church.
Kolton, Stanislaus J. '46 (CAM) Retired.
Koltuniak, Michael P. '39 (DET) Retired.
Koltzenburg, Otto '81 (SPK) Walla Walla, WA Assumption of the Blessed Virgin Mary Church.
Kolumber, Denis *m.s.* '67 (ATL) Canton, GA Our Lady of LaSalette Church.
Kolzow, Andrew K. *o.p.* '58 (DAL) [K] Irving, TX Dominican Priory of St. Albert the Great.
Koma, Joseph W. *c.s.c.* '61 (KAL) Niles, MI St. Mark Church.
Komar, John E. '64 (NEW) Ridgefield, NJ St. Matthew's Church; Englewood, NJ Englewood Hospital.
Komar, Msgr. Michael A. '36 (NEW) [2] Linden, NJ Holy Family Church; Retired.
Komaska, James R. '54 (STL) Retired.
Komatz, David M. '75 (GB) [A] De Pere, WI St. Norbert Abbey; [B] De Pere, WI St. Norbert College; [I] De Pere, WI St. Norbert Abbey; [O] De Pere, WI NORBERT & CO.
Kombarakaran, Francis Anthony *s.d.b.* '90 (COL) [H] Columbus, OH Salesian Center.
Kombo, Honore (BO) [7] Newton, MA St. Philip Neri Church.
Komechak, Michael E. *o.s.b.* '59 (JOL) [A] Lisle, IL Benedictine University; [J] Lisle, IL St. Procopius Abbey.
Kommer, Jason *o.f.m.* '43 (JOL) [J] Joliet, IL St. John the Baptist Friary.
Kommer, Venard *o.f.m.* '46 (JOL) Clarendon Hills, IL Notre Dame Church; [J] Joliet, IL St. John the Baptist Friary.
Kommers, Thomas M. '80 (STP) Eagan, MN St. Thomas Becket Church.
Komonchak, Joseph A. '64 (NY) On Duty Outside the Archdiocese.
Komonchak, Joseph A. '64 (WDC) [C] Washington, DC Catholic University of America, The.
Komorowski, Louis A. *o.s.f.s.* '56 (LAN) Adrian, MI St. Mary of Good Counsel Church.
Konarzewski, Bogdah *c.m.* (MAN) [2] Concord, NH St. Peter Church.
Konath, Jacob '95 (BIS) Glenburn, ND St. Philomena Church.
Koncik, Michael *c.ss.r.* '82 (VEN) Wauchula, FL St. Michael Church.
Konda, Bernard A. '67 (TUC) Clifton, AZ Sacred Heart Church.
Kondeja, Stanley '62 (RVC) Southampton, NY Our Lady of Poland Church.
Konderla, David A. '95 (AUS) College Station, TX St. Mary's Church; [M] College Station, TX St. Mary's Catholic Center.
Kondik, Curtis L. '00 (CLV) Fairview Park, OH St. Angela Merici Church; Fairview Park, OH St. Angela Merici Church.
Kondik, David M. *o.s.m.* '48 (CHI) [N] Chicago, IL Order of Friar Servants of Mary (Servites) United States of America Province, Inc.
Kondik, David M. *o.s.m.* '48 (ORG) Fullerton, CA St. Juliana Falconieri Church; [I] Buena Park, CA Order of Friar Servants of Mary (Servites).
Kondrath, James A. '50 (SFD) Retired.
Kondzielski, Thaddeus T. '67 (E) Crossingsville, PA St. Philip Church.
Kondziolka, Ron '76 (GRY) [F] Dyer, IN St. Margaret Mercy Healthcare Centers, South Campus.
Kondziolka, Ronald L. '76 (CHI) [82] Chicago, IL Holy Rosary Church; [J] Chicago Heights, IL St. James Hospital and Health Centers.
Konechne, Louis '83 (GLP) Retired.
Konen, Lyle *c.ss. r.* '61 (SEA) [7] Seattle, WA St. Catherine Church; Monroe, WA Washington State Reformatory; Monroe, WA Monroe Correctional Complex.
Konerman, Gregory J. '93 (CIN) [23] Cincinnati, OH St. Dominic Church.
Konicek, John *s.j.* '93 (BO) [W] Chestnut Hill, MA The Jesuit Community at Boston College.
Konieczka, Edward J. '63 (SAG) [4] Bay City, MI St. Hyacinth Church.
Konieczny, Anthony M. *o.f.m.conv.* '43 (BUF) [21] Buffalo, NY Corpus Christi Church.
Koninkx, Msgr. William '46 (HT) Retired.
Konisky, Edward '38 (ALB) Retired.
Konkel, Eugene J. *s.s.* '57 (MIL) On Duty Outside the Archdiocese.
Konkel, Eugene J. *s.s.* '57 (SFR) [T] Menlo Park, CA Vatican II Institute for Clergy Formation.
Konkel, Joseph D. *o.p.* '70 (GAL) [36] Houston, TX Holy Rosary Church; [Q] Houston, TX Dominican Fathers and Brothers, St. Mark Priory, Inc.
Konkler, Paul Jerome *o.c.s.o.* '68 (SAC) [A] Vina, CA Abbey of New Clairvaux, Trappist Seminary; [H] Vina, CA Abbey of New Clairvaux, Trappist.
Konkol, Robert *o.f.m.* '94 (MIL) [P] Burlington, WI Queen of Peace Friary.
Konnully, Berchmans '59 (BIS) Bowbells, ND St. Joseph Church.
Konobrocki, Marian '91 (VEN) [5] Fort Myers, FL St. Francis Xavier Church.
Konold, Lon *o.m.i.* (NOR) [F] Willimantic, CT Missionary Oblates of Mary Immaculate.
Konopa, Brian D. '98 (LC) Marshfield, WI St. John the Baptist Church; [C] Marshfield, WI Holy Family Middle School.
Konopa, Robert *o.f.m.* '91 (SAG) [18] Saginaw, MI St. Thomas Aquinas Church.
Konopacky, Joseph R. '82 (LC) On Leave of Absence.
Konopka, Edward F. '45 (DET) Retired.
Konopka, Edward M. '60 (NOR) Higganum, CT St. Peter Church.
Konopka, Thomas E. '90 (ALB) Cambridge, NY St. Patrick Church; Greenwich, NY St. Joseph Church; Special Assignment.
Konowalek, Zenon '89 (CC) Three Rivers, TX Sacred Heart Church.
Konrad, Erwin '89 (JC) Retired.
Konrad, Msgr. Joseph G. '43 (BRK) [199] Queens, NY St. Matthias Church; Retired.
Konz, Gregory N.P. *s.j.* '90 (CLV) [B] Cleveland, OH John Carroll Jesuit Community.
Konzen, Joel M. *s.m.* '79 (ATL) [C] Atlanta, GA Marist School.
Koo, Mark Chung-Mo *s.j.* '95 (OAK) [N] Berkeley, CA Jesuit Community at Jesuit School of Theology at Berkeley.
Koo, Matthew '88 (SJ) [14] San Jose, CA St. Leo the Great Church; [1] Santa Clara, CA Chinese Catholic Community Church.
Koob, Edward H. '45 (PH) Retired.
Kookoothe, Neil P. '95 (CLV) Fairview Park, OH St. Angela Merici Church.
Koons, Thomas P. '97 (ALN) Emmaus, PA St. Ann Church.
Koonz, John A. '63 (SPR) Dalton, MA St. Agnes Church.
Koop, Cecil *o.f.m.* '45 (SFD) [K] Sherman, IL Our Lady of Angels Friary.
Koopman, Dennis *o.f.m.* '70 (CHI) [N] Countryside, IL St. Gratian Friary, Franciscan Friars.
Koopmann, Robert *o.s.b.* '81 (SCL) [I] Collegeville, MN St. John's Abbey, of the Order of St. Benedict.
Koos, Gerald J. '66 (E) [13] Erie, PA St. Ann Church; Erie, PA Hamot Medical Center.
Kopacek, Jerry '88 (DUB) [4] Waterloo, IA St. Edward's Church.
Kopacz, Joseph R. '77 (SCR) [A] Dalton, PA Saint Pius X Seminary.
Kopacz, K. S. '95 (FAR) Fingal, ND Holy Trinity Church; Oriska, ND St. Bernard's Church.
Kopacz, Mark '92 (WIL) Newark, DE St. Thomas More Oratory Church.
Kopacz, Msgr. Matthew S. '63 (BUF) [18] Buffalo, NY St. Casimir Church.
Kopacz, Stephen A. '72 (NEW) Livingston, NJ St. Philomena Church.
Kopaczynski, Germain *o.f.m. conv.* '74 (BO) [50] Boston, MA Our Lady of Czestochowa Church; [FF] Brighton/Boston, MA National Catholic Bioethics Center.
Kopczewski, Linus E. *o.f.m.* '65 (PH) [AA] Philadelphia, PA St. Pius X Friary.
Kopczewski, Linus E. *o.f.m.* '65 (TR) Trenton, NJ St. Francis Medical Center.
Kopczynski, Sean *c.p.m.* '00 (OWN) Hopkinsville, KY SS. Peter and Paul Church.
Kopec, Chester *o.p.* '63 (SB) Chino, CA California Institute for Men.
Kopec, Edward S. '92 (PEO) [4] Spring Valley, IL SS. Peter and Paul's Church.

Kopec, Jerome E. '79 (BUF) [4] Niagara Falls, NY St. John de La Salle Church.
Kopec, Rajmund '92 (NEW) Military Chaplains.
Kopecky, Joseph A. '45 (PIT) Retired.
Kopel, Jerry '77 (SFS) Tyndall, SD St. Leo Church.
Koper, Msgr. Francis B. '71 (DET) [A] Orchard Lake, MI SS. Cyril and Methodius Seminary; [C] Orchard Lake, MI Saint Mary's College.
Koper, Msgr. Francis B. '71 (WIL) On Duty Outside the Diocese.
Koper, Ryszard '78 (BRK) [177] Queens, NY Holy Cross Church.
Kopfensteiner, Thomas R. '81 (NY) [45] New York, NY Holy Cross Church.
Kopfensteiner, Thomas R. '81 (STL) On Duty Outside the Archdiocese.
Kopff, Herbert C. '38 (BEL) Retired.
Kopinski, Richard '64 (RVC) Glen Head, NY St. Hyacinth Church.
Koplik, Msgr. William J. '62 (NEW) Northvale, NJ St. Anthony's Church.
Koplinka, Steven '79 (PRM) Cleveland, OH St. Mary Church.
Kopp, Anthony Mary J. *o.praem.* '93 (ORG) [I] Silverado, CA Norbertine Fathers of Orange Inc.
Kopp, Richard M. '69 (SY) Baldwinsville, NY St. Mary Church.
Kopp, Thomas A. '72 (BO) [8] Brockton, MA Sacred Heart Church.
Koppert, Elias *o.f.m.* '41 (IND) [12] Indianapolis, IN Sacred Heart of Jesus Church.
Koppes, Albert P. *o.carm.* '59 (JOL) [J] Darien, IL Carmelite Provincial Office.
Koppes, Albert P. *o.carm.* '59 (LA) [C] Los Angeles, CA Loyola Marymount University.
Koprowski, Mitchell J. '41 (GI) Retired.
Kopystynski, Rafael *c.m.* '88 (BRK) [32] Brooklyn, NY SS. Cyril and Methodius Church.
Korabik, Joseph *c.r.* '38 (CHI) [D] Chicago, IL Gordon Tech High School.
Korba, Msgr. Frank '66 (PRM) Munster, IN Saint Nicholas Church.
Korban, Janusz '97 (RC) Colome, SD St. Isidore Church; Winner, SD Immaculate Conception Church.
Korbelak, John J. '74 (NEW) North Bergen, NJ Our Lady of Fatima Church.
Korbic, Benno *o.f.m.* '40 (CHI) [N] Lemont, IL The Slovene Franciscan Fathers, Order of Friars Minor, Commissariat of the Holy Cross.
Korcsmar, John S. *c.s.c.* '74 (AUS) [8] Austin, TX Nuestra Senora De Dolores Church; [H] Austin, TX Congregation of Holy Cross - Southern Province.
Korda, Msgr. Edward L. (CAM) Retired.
Korda, Msgr. Edward L. '49 (CAM) Magnolia, NJ St. Gregory's Church.
Korda, J. James '79 (Y) [16] Youngstown, OH St. Joseph Church.
Kordas, Edward J. '68 (CLV) South Amherst, OH Nativity of Blessed Virgin Mary Church; [X] Cleveland, OH Office of Newman Campus Ministry.
Kordek, Frank *o.f.m.* '72 (GAY) Harbor Springs, MI Holy Childhood of Jesus Church.
Kordsmeier, Msgr. John '49 (LR) Retired; [H] Little Rock, AR St. John Manor.
Korecki, Maximilian *o.f.m. conv.* '62 (IND) [I] Mount Saint Francis, IN Mount Saint Francis Friary and Retreat Center.
Korecki, Maximilian *o.f.m.conv.* '62 (L) [K] Louisville, KY St. Joseph Home for the Aged.
Koren, Henry J. *c.s.sp.* '37 (PIT) [O] Bethel Park, PA Holy Ghost Fathers and Brothers Provincialate; [Q] Bethel Park, PA Holy Ghost Animation Center.
Korenek, Gregory E. '93 (VIC) [2] Victoria, TX Holy Family of Joseph, Mary & Jesus Church.
Koressel, James '69 (EVN) Boonville, IN St. Clement Church.
Korf, Joseph '74 (SCL) Elk River, MN The Church of St. Andrew.
Korinchock, Joseph '85 (PHU) Absent on Leave.
Kornacki, Matthew J. '73 (PH) [A] Wynnewood, PA Theological Seminary of St. Charles Borromeo, Overbrook.
Kornacki, Thomas J. *o.f.m.* '88 (FgM) Franciscan Foreign Missions.
Kornath, Edwin M. '84 (MIL) Waterford, WI St. Thomas Aquinas Church.
Kornely, Benno G. *s.j.* '59 (DET) [P] Bloomfield Hills, MI Manresa Jesuit Retreat House.
Kornmeyer, Thomas E. '90 (OG) Long Lake, NY St. Henry Church; Newcomb, NY St. Therese Church.
Koros, John J. '45 (OM) Retired.
Koros, John J. '45 (VEN) Lake Placid, FL St. James Church.
Korte, Ed '62 (BIS) Underwood, ND St. Bonaventure Church.
Korte, Harry G. *c.ss.r.* '46 (STL) [P] Liguori, MO St. Clement Health Care Center.
Korte, Owen W. '81 (OM) Fremont, NE St. Patrick Church.
Korte, William L. '83 (JC) Fulton, MO St. Peter Church; Fulton, MO Missouri School for the Deaf.
Kortendick, Steven J. '85 (MAD) [1] Madison, WI St. Raphael Church; [12] Madison, WI St. Paul University Church; [L] Madison, WI University of Wisconsin - Madison Roman Catholic Foundation Inc.
Korth, David M. '92 (OM) Duncan, NE St. Stanislaus Church; Silver Creek, NE St. Lawrence Church; [B] Columbus, NE Scotus Central Catholic High School.
Korycki, Walter R. '49 (RVC) Retired.
Korzinek, Richard *o.s.cam.* '53 (MIL) [P] Wauwatosa, WI St. Camillus Community House.
Kos, Donald *o.f.m.conv.* '61 (BAL) [S] Ellicott City, MD Order of Friars Minor Conventual.
Kos, Stanislaus '96 (RCK) [3] Elgin, IL St. Mary Church.
Kosak, Msgr. Michael F. '70 (STV) [1] Barrenspot, VI Church St. Ann Church; [1] Barrenspot, VI Church St. Ann Church; [B] St. Thomas, VI Miscellaneous Organizations; [B] St. Thomas, VI Miscellaneous Organizations; [B] St. Thomas, VI Miscellaneous Organizations.
Kosaka, Paulo R. *o.f.m.cap.* '83 (AGN) Agana Heights, GU Our Lady of the Blessed Sacrament Church; [F] Agana Heights, GU St. Fidelis Friary.
Kosanke, Charles '85 (DET) Special Assignment; [A] Detroit, MI Sacred Heart Major Seminary, Inc.; [T] Detroit, MI American Friends of the Vatican Library.
Kosanke, Charles G. '85 (DET) [14] Detroit, MI St. Cecilia Church.
Kosatka, Leonard *c.p.* '59 (FgM) Mission Procurators.
Kosch, Leo D. '93 (LIN) Bellwood, NE Presentation Church.
Kosco, Arnold J. '60 (DET) West Bloomfield, MI Prince of Peace Church.
Kosco, William '00 (PHX) [2] Mesa, AZ Christ the King Church.
Kose, Robert *o.f.m.cap.* '92 (MIL) [27] Milwaukee, WI St. Francis of Assisi Church.
Kosem, Frank P. '70 (CLV) [3] Elyria, OH St. Jude Church.
Koser, Albert C. '59 (PIT) Boyers, PA St. Alphonsus Church.
Koser, Rudolph J., Jr. '74 (GBG) Military Chaplains.
Koshko, Dennis '75 (HON) Kailua, HI St. Anthony Church.
Kosicki, Bohdan W. '50 (DET) Retired.
Kosicki, George *c.s.b.* '54 (ROC) [I] Rochester, NY Basilian Residence.
Kosinski, Pawel *s.j.* '92 (CHI) [N] Chicago, IL Sacred Heart Mission House.
Kosinski, Stephen D. '81 (GRY) [7] Gary, IN St. Ann Church.
Kosisko, Richard J. '85 (GBG) North Huntingdon, PA St. Elizabeth Ann Seton Church.
Kosler, Timothy '71 (VIC) Ammannsville, TX St. John The Baptist Church; High Hill, TX Nativity of the Blessed Virgin Mary Church; Schulenburg, TX St. Rose of Lima Church.
Kosmicki, Raymond M. '68 (GI) Wood River, NE St. Mary's Church.
Kosmoski, David B. *o.m.v.* '81 (MET) Avenel, NJ St. Andrew Church.
Kosmowski, Gary J. '90 (MAN) Laconia, NH St. Joseph Church.
Kosnac, Benjamin '93 (DET) [2] Sterling Heights, MI SS. Cyril and Methodius Church.
Kosnik, Anthony '55 (DET) Retired.
Kosnik, Eugene A. '60 (NY) Gardiner, NY St. Charles Borromeo Church.
Kosowicz, Wojciech '65 (LAR) [18] Laredo, TX St. Peter The Apostle Church.
Kossak, Michael J. *s.j.* '87 (BO) [W] Boston, MA Loyola House.
Kosse, Gerald C. '76 (WIN) Adrian, MN St. Adrian Church; Lismore, MN St. Anthony's Church.
Kosse, Theodore C. '71 (CIN) Peebles, OH St. Mary Queen of Heaven Church; West Union, OH Holy Trinity Church.
Kossel, Clifford *s.j.* '48 (SPK) [C] Spokane, WA Gonzaga University.
Kostek, John '73 (ALB) On Duty Outside the Diocese.
Kostek, John S. '73 (NY) [99] New York, NY Our Lady of Victory Church.
Kostelnick, Albert T. '54 (PH) Feasterville, PA Assumption B.V.M. Church.
Kostelnik, Msgr. Kevin J. '82 (LA) [1] Los Angeles, CA Cathedral Residence Church.
Kostelz, Richard F. '52 (JOL) Cabery, IL St. Joseph Church.
Koster, Dale F. '54 (SC) Retired.
Koster, John *s.v.d.* '44 (CHI) [B] Techny, IL Divine Word Residence.
Koster, Kenneth '76 (SFS) Tea, SD St. Nicholas Church.
Koster, Theodore *o.c.s.o.* (SPC) [G] Ava, MO Assumption Abbey.
Koster, Theodore *o.c.s.o.* '59 (SPC) [E] Ava, MO Assumption Abbey (Trappist).
Kosterman, Richard A. '93 (GAY) Copemish, MI St. Raphael Church.
Kostic, Andrew (PAT) Permanent Deacons.
Kostiuk, Nick '80 (PHU) Retired.
Kostka, Leonard J. *c.pp.s.* '40 (LFT) Rensselaer, IN St. Augustine Church; [A] Rensselaer, IN Saint Joseph's College.
Kostrzomb, Stanley '77 (NEW) [10] Newark, NJ St. Casimir's Church.
Kosty, Robert J. '74 (WDC) Medley's Neck, MD Our Lady's Church.
Kostyk, Jaroslaw '97 (STF) Pittsfield, MA St. John the Baptist Church; Hudson, NY St. Nicholas Church.
Kostyk, Marian '90 (STF) Amsterdam, NY St. Nicholas Church; Little Falls, NY St. Nicholas Church.
Kostyk, Oleska (STF) Glen Spey, NY St. Volodymyr Church.
Koszarek, Msgr. Paul P. '54 (GB) Antigo, WI St. Hyacinth Church.
Koszarek, Robert J. '74 (SUP) Eagle River, WI St. Peter the Fisherman Church; Land-O'-Lakes, WI St. Albert Church; Phelps, WI St. Mary Church.
Koszarek, Thaddeus J. '39 (GB) Retired; [H] Green Bay, WI The McCormick Memorial Home for the Aged.
Koszyk, Seweryn J. *s.a.c* '59 (BUF) [2] Niagara Falls, NY St. George Church; [O] North Tonawanda, NY Society of the Catholic Apostolate.
Kot, Christian *s.d.b.* '94 (FgM) Salesians of Don Bosco Foreign Missions.
Kot, Luke C. *o.c.s.o.* '48 (ATL) [J] Conyers, GA The Monastery of the Holy Spirit.
Kotara, James '76 (SAT) [5] San Antonio, TX Holy Family Church.
Kotecki, Ronald E. '72 (MIL) [42] Milwaukee, WI St. Hyacinth Church.
Koterski, Joseph W. *s.j.* '92 (NY) [DD] New York, NY Jesuit Community at Fordham University.
Koth, Arthur R. '57 (MAD) Retired.
Kotiaram, Matthew '78 (RVC) Setauket, NY St. James Church.
Kotlanger, Michael J. *s.j.* '78 (SFR) [E] San Francisco, CA St. Ignatius College Preparatory (Coed); [N] San Francisco, CA Jesuit Community at St. Ignatius College Preparatory.
Kotlarczyk, Mark E. '88 (SB) Victorville, CA Holy Innocents Church.
Kotlarz, Robert '69 (DET) [44] Detroit, MI St. Luke Church.
Kotlinski, Bede *o.s.b.* '84 (CLV) [D] Cleveland, OH Benedictine High School; [O] Cleveland, OH Benedictine Order of Cleveland.
Kotnis, Gregory M. '56 (PHX) Retired.
Kottar, Michael T. '94 (CHL) North Wilkesboro, NC St. John Baptist de LaSalle Church.
Kottar, Michael T. '94 (MET) On Duty Outside the Diocese.
Kottas, Charles '70 (DM) [4] Council Bluffs, IA St. Peter Church.
Kottayil, Joseph '79 (MIA) [17] Miami, FL St. Catherine of Siena Church.
Kottenstette, William P. '73 (JC) Kirksville, MO Mary Immaculate Church; Memphis, MO St. John Church; [F] Kirksville, MO Catholic Newman Center, Truman State University.
Kottiry, Alphonsus '59 (DUL) On Duty Outside the Diocese.
Kottoor, Thomas '72 (NY) [133] Bronx, NY St. Benedict Church.
Kotyuk, Stephen '47 (E) Retired.
Kotz, Anthony A. '50 (LIN) Retired.
Kouba, Charles J. '51 (CHI) [188] Chicago, IL St. Simon the Apostle Church; Retired.
Koury, James '92 (NTN) Leave of Absence.
Koury, Msgr. Joseph A. '50 (JKS) Retired.
Koury, Joseph J. '77 (PRT) Orono, ME St. Mary's Church; Orono, ME Our Lady of Wisdom Personal Campus Church; [M] Orono, ME University of Maine.
Koutnik, Jerome P. '99 (RCK) Cary, IL SS. Peter & Paul Church.
Kovach, Blaise '55 (PBR) Braddock, PA SS. Peter and Paul Church.
Kovach, John '65 (PRM) Burton, OH Church of Mariapoch; [B] Burton, OH Shrine of Mariapoch.
Kovach, John '65 (VNN) On Special Assignment.
Kovach, Raymond J. '69 (NY) Absent on Leave.
Kovach, William J. '55 (ALT) Revloc, PA Most Holy Redeemer Church.
Kovacic, Msgr. Anthony '47 (CHL) Retired.
Kovacik, Josef '98 (ALT) [1] Altoona, PA Cathedral of the Blessed Sacrament.
Kovacs, Louis D. '44 (PH) East Goshen, PA SS. Peter and Paul Church; Retired.
Kovacs, Matthew *o.cist.* '57 (DAL) [K] Irving, TX Cistercian Abbey of Our Lady of Dallas.
Kovacsik, Clement *s.t.* '44 (MOB) Holy Trinity, AL St. Joseph Church.
Kovalcin, John A. '81 (B) Mountain Home Air Force Base, ID St. Mary's Church.
Kovalcin, John A. '81 (STL) Military Chaplains.
Kovalik, George J. '47 (STP) [2] Minneapolis, MN All Saints Church.
Kovanis, Joel M. '94 (SP) [1] St. Petersburg, FL Cathedral of St. Jude the Apostle.
Kovarik, James *o.s.cam.* '66 (MIL) Wood, WI Veterans

Administration Medical Center.
Kovarik, James *o.s.cam.* '90 (MIL) [P] Wauwatosa, WI St. Camillus Community House; [Y] Wauwatosa, WI St. Camillus Health System, Inc.
Kovarik, Peter '91 (RC) Timber Lake, SD Holy Cross Church.
Kowal, John P. '57 (DOD) Retired.
Kowalczyk, Joseph *m.m.* '61 (GAL) [Q] Houston, TX Maryknoll Fathers and Brothers.
Kowalczyk, Mirek *f.d.p.* (BO) [34] Boston, MA St. Joseph-St. Lazarus Church.
Kowalczyk, Sigismund C. '56 (DET) Retired.
Kowalczyk, Thomas M. '67 (SAG) Linwood, MI St. Anne Church.
Kowaleski, Msgr. Edward '53 (Y) Rock Creek, OH Sacred Heart Church.
Kowalewski, Francis P. '59 (BUF) Darien Center, NY Our Lady of Good Counsel Church; Retired.
Kowalewski, John A. *o.s.f.s.* '77 (WIL) [B] Wilmington, DE Salesianum School.
Kowalozyk, Adolph M. '88 (BUF) [3] Buffalo, NY St. Agatha Church.
Kowalske, Kevin '85 (MIL) Mequon, WI St. James Church.
Kowalski, Al, (Retired) (NEW) Kenilworth, NJ St. Theresa's Church.
Kowalski, Alfred J. '51 (NEW) Retired.
Kowalski, Eric '93 (CHL) [1] Greensboro, NC Our Lady of Grace Church.
Kowalski, Erich '93 (NEW) On Duty Outside the Archdiocese.
Kowalski, George '56 (DET) Retired.
Kowalski, Isidore *o.f.m.conv.* '43 (FR) [8] New Bedford, MA Our Lady of Perpetual Help Church.
Kowalski, James C. '68 (GR) Ada, MI St. Robert Church.
Kowalski, John '89 (LC) [5] La Crosse, WI St. James the Less Church.
Kowalski, Kasimierz A. '91 (NY) [2] New York, NY St. Agnes Church.
Kowalski, Lawrence T. '69 (OKL) Enid, OK St. Gregory the Great Church.
Kowalski, Leo S. '39 (MIL) Retired.
Kowalski, Matthew '87 (SFS) [F] Marvin, SD Blue Cloud Abbey.
Kowalski, Ralph E. '42 (DET) Retired.
Kowalski, Ronald C. '81 (MIL) Twin Lakes, WI St. John Church.
Kowalski, Wladyslaw J. '51 (LC) Peplin, WI St. John the Baptist Church.
Kowalski, Wladyslaw J. '51 (SUP) Retired.
Kowatch, Thomas P. '85 (CLV) [4] Lakewood, OH St. James Church; Cleveland, OH Lakewood Hospital.
Kownacki, Francis J. *s.j.* '60 (SCR) [C] Scranton, PA University of Scranton.
Kownacki, Raymond F. '60 (BEL) Leave of Absence.
Kownacki, Robert '63 (CHI) [J] Chicago, IL Resurrection Medical Center.
Kownacki, Robert '63 (SAT) On Duty Outside the Archdiocese.
Kowrach, Edward '38 (SPK) Retired.
Koychick, George J. (HBG) McSherrystown, PA Annunciation of the Blessed Virgin Mary Church.
Koys, Thomas R. '85 (CHI) [89] Chicago, IL Immaculate Conception Church.
Koza, John J., III '77 (PBR) Warren, OH SS. Peter and Paul's Church.
Kozak, David J. '83 (ALN) [4] Bethlehem, PA Holy Infancy Church.
Kozak, Eligius *o.f.m.conv.* '42 (BUF) [O] Athol Springs, NY Father Justin Rosary Hour Radio Apostolate.
Kozak, Remigius A. '54 (BLX) Retired.
Kozak, Richard J. '67 (CHI) Homewood, IL St. Joseph Church.
Kozanecki, Charles *o.f.m.conv.* '53 (MRY) Pismo Beach, CA St. Paul the Apostle Church.
Kozanko, Andrzej Jacek '00 (FR) Sandwich, MA Corpus Christi Church.
Kozar, John E. '71 (PIT) Aleppo Township, PA St. Mary Church.
Kozar, Joseph F. *s.m.* '77 (CIN) [D] Dayton, OH The University of Dayton; [M] Dayton, OH Marianist Provincialate.
Kozel, Msgr. Robert F. '61 (ALN) [1] Bethlehem, PA St. Anne Church.
Kozen, Bert S. '82 (SCR) Canton, PA St. Michael Church.
Koziczuk, Andrzej A. '79 (SAC) Quincy, CA St. John Church.
Koziel, Piotr A. '97 (CC) [1] Kingsville, TX Our Lady of Good Counsel Church; [5] Kingsville, TX St. Thomas Aquinas, University Catholic Center Church.
Kozien, Casimir J. '50 (CHI) [22] Chicago, IL St. Bartholomew Church; Retired.
Kozikowski, Thad '75 (GF) Glasgow, MT St. Raphael's Church.
Kozina, Mark *o.f.m.* '59 (CHI) [186] Chicago, IL Sacred Heart Church; [N] Chicago, IL Croatian Franciscan Custody of the Holy Family.
Kozina, Vladimir '45 (OAK) Retired.
Koziol, Stanley N. '58 (BGP) [3] Stratford, CT St. Mark Church.
Kozlak, Stanley '74 (STP) Annandale, MN St. Ignatius Church.
Kozlowski, Daniel E. '72 (LC) Mill Creek, WI St. Bartholomew Church; [6] Stevens Point, WI St. Stephen Church.
Kozlowski, Edward A. '38 (NY) Bronx, NY Veterans Administration Hospital.
Kozlowski, Joseph F. '73 (BUF) Holley, NY St. Mary Church; Kendall, NY St. Mark Church.
Kozlowski, Joseph P. '49 (RVC) Glen Head, NY St. Hyacinth Church; Retired.
Kozlowski, Louis '38 (E) Retired.
Kozlowski, Theodore '58 (GR) [18] Grand Rapids, MI Our Lady of Sorrows Church.
Kozma, Raymond M. '70 (BRK) Absent on Leave.
Kozminski, Msgr. Max M. '60 (BUF) Retired.
Kozoil, Micah E. '76 (GBG) Clymer, PA Church of the Resurrection.
Kozon, John A. '32 (NOR) Retired.
Kozub, Tomasz *s.ch.* '92 (BAL) [38] Baltimore, MD Holy Rosary Church.
Kozub, Tomasz *s.c.* '93 (CC) [21] Corpus Christi, TX St. Pius X Church.
Kozuch, John L. *s.d.s.* '58 (NEW) [N] Verona, NJ The Salvatorian Fathers.
Kozyra, Oscar Z. *o.dem.* '73 (SP) [9] St. Petersburg, FL Transfiguration Church.
Krach, Joseph W. '57 (BAL) Retired.
Kraeger, David *t.o.r.* '68 (FWT) Scotland, TX St. Boniface Church; Windthorst, TX St. Mary Church.
Kraemer, Bartholomew *o.s.b.* '64 (DET) [K] Detroit, MI St. Sylvester Monastery.
Kraemer, Edwin '55 (SCL) Retired.
Kraemer, John A. '57 (RCK) Retired.
Kraeszig, Charles J. '52 (IND) Retired.
Krafchak, John S. '56 (SCR) [5] Nanticoke, PA St. Mary of Czestochowa Church.
Krafcik, Andrew W. '59 (ARL) Retired.
Krafcik, Andrew W.P. '59 (ARL) Dale City, VA Holy Family Church.
Krafinski, Thomas S. *c.m.* '68 (BRK) [66] Brooklyn, NY St. John the Baptist Church; [V] Brooklyn, NY St. John the Baptist Rectory.
Kraft, Niles E. *o.f.m.* '55 (GLP) Navajo, NM St. Berard Church.
Kraft, Philip '62 (SFD) Special or Other Diocesan Assignment.
Kraft, Thomas *o.p.* '86 (FgM) Dominican - Order of Preachers Foreign Missions.
Kraft, Thomas *o.p.* '86 (OAK) [N] Oakland, CA Western Dominican Province.
Kraft, Thomas K. *o.p.* '86 (FgM) Dominican - Order of Preachers Foreign Missions.
Kraft, William '86 (STO) Sonora, CA St. Patrick Church.
Kraft, Msgr. William A. '51 (SD) Retired.
Krah, James B. '71 (PIT) Darlington, PA St. Rose of Lima Church.
Krah, Joseph E. '63 (SB) [3] San Bernardino, CA Our Lady of the Assumption Church.
Krahel, David H. '86 (BGP) [14] Stamford, CT Our Lady Star of the Sea Church.
Krahenbuhl, Gary L. '84 (MAD) [1] Beloit, WI Our Lady of the Assumption Church.
Krahman, Phil '72 (STL) [5] Creve Coeur, MO St. Richard Church.
Krahman, Philip G. (STL) St. Louis, MO St. John's Mercy Medical Center.
Krahman, Philip G. '72 (STL) [K] Creve Coeur, MO St. John's Mercy Medical Center.
Kraig, Robert J. '72 (CLV) Strongsville, OH St. John Neumann Church.
Krajci, Anthony *s.v.d.* '45 (CHI) [B] Techny, IL Divine Word Residence.
Krajcovic, Bernard '56 (STU) Yorkville, OH St. Lucy's Church.
Krajewski, Henry T. *o.f.m.cap.* '58 (PAT) [M] Oak Ridge-Milton, NJ St. Stanislaus B. M. Friary.
Krajewski, Henry T. *o.f.m.cap.* '58 (TR) [4] Trenton, NJ Holy Cross Church.
Krajewski, Joseph A. '73 (MET) South Amboy, NJ Sacred Heart Church.
Krajewski, Paul A. (PAT) Retired.
Krajewski, Robert J. '98 (SUP) [1] Superior, WI Cathedral of Christ the King; [G] Superior, WI Superior-UW.
Krajicek, Robert P. '53 (OM) Retired.
Krajnak, Jozef '91 (NY) [59] New York, NY St. John Nepomucene Church.
Krajnik, Paul '50 (CLV) [2] Lorain, OH SS. Cyril and Methodius Church.
Kraker, James J. '65 (SUP) On Leave.
Kraker, Joseph H. '64 (CLV) [18] Akron, OH St. Vincent Church.
Kralik, Emil *s.v.d.* '97 (CHI) [B] Techny, IL Divine Word Residence; [N] Chicago, IL Divine Word Theologate.
Kraljic, John R. '69 (NY) [E] New York, NY Cardinal Spellman High School.
Krall, Jack '63 (P) [22] Portland, OR Church of St. Joseph the Worker.
Krall, Kenneth R. *s.j.* '71 (SPK) [C] Spokane, WA Gonzaga University.
Kralovich, Louis W. '60 (TR) [3] Toms River, NJ St. Luke Church.
Kram, Thomas '49 (PIT) [P] Pittsburgh, PA Sisters of St. Francis of the Providence of God.
Kramberg, Donald F. '74 (OG) Tupper Lake, NY St. Alphonsus Church.
Kramer, Anthony *o.mar.* '95 (SAM) [C] Petersham, MA Most Holy Trinity Monastery.
Kramer, Carl '52 (SAL) Retired.
Kramer, Daniel J. *c.m.* '47 (PH) [AA] Philadelphia, PA Congregation of the Mission.
Kramer, Gary J. '93 (PH) Ridley Park, PA St. Madeline Church.
Kramer, George C. '53 (BO) Senior Priests.
Kramer, George J. '62 (JC) Bonnots Mill, MO St. Louis Church; Frankenstein, MO Our Lady of Help Church.
Kramer, James F. '68 (CLV) Westlake, OH St. Bernadette Church.
Kramer, Msgr. James G. '48 (MAD) Retired; [H] Madison, WI Bishop O'Connor Catholic Pastoral Center.
Kramer, Lawrence A. '60 (FTW) Bluffton, IN St. Joseph Church; [C] Fort Wayne, IN Bishop Luers High School.
Kramer, Noel R. *o.f.m.conv.* '58 (LSC) Carlsbad, NM St. Edward Church.
Kramer, Pete A. '79 (BIS) [G] Bismarck, ND Emmaus Place.
Kramer, Richard R. '66 (RCK) Harvard, IL St. Joseph Church.
Kramer, Robert L. *c.s.c.* '64 (PHX) [G] Phoenix, AZ Holy Cross Congregation/Casa Santa Cruz.
Kramer, Scott *c.pp.s.* '90 (TOL) Cuba, OH St. Isidore Church; Kalida, OH St. Michael Church.
Kramer, Scott T. *c.pp.s.* '90 (CIN) [U] Dayton, OH Community Support Charitable Trust.
Kramer, Thomas E. '58 (BIS) [1] Bismarck, ND Cathedral of the Holy Spirit.
Kramer, Thomas J. '77 (DET) [1] Sterling Heights, MI St. Blase Church.
Kramer, William *c.pp.s.* '44 (CIN) [B] Carthagena, OH St. Charles.
Kramer, William J. '73 (CIN) Beavercreek, OH St. Luke Church.
Kramis, Joseph '57 (SEA) Retired.
Kramlich, Lloyd P. *s.d.s.* '58 (PHX) [4] Mesa, AZ Queen of Peace Church.
Kramper, James P. *s.j.* '44 (OM) [K] Omaha, NE Jesuit Community at Creighton University.
Kramper, James V. '73 (OM) Emerson, NE Sacred Heart Church; Pender, NE St. John Church.
Kranch, Peter V. '51 (ALB) Retired.
Krank, Michael T. '52 (BIS) Retired.
Krantz, Ernest *c.pp.s.* '76 (GRY) [A] Whiting, IN Calumet College of St. Joseph.
Krantz, Robert V. '78 (SFS) Parkston, SD Sacred Heart Church.
Kranyc, Andrew G. '87 (WH) [3] Huntington, WV Sacred Heart Church; [4] Huntington, WV St. Peter Claver Church.
Kranz, Stephen *o.s.b.* '55 (BIS) Mandaree, ND St. Anthony Church; [A] Richardton, ND Assumption Abbey.
Krapfl, Daniel A. '58 (DUB) [E] Cascade, IA Aquin Religious Education Center; [F] Cascade, IA Aquin Elementary School.
Krapfl, Daniel J. '58 (DUB) Cascade, IA St. Matthias Church.
Krapfl, Gary '72 (DUB) Decorah, IA St. Benedict's Church.
Krasauskas, Rapolas (NOR) [G] Putnam, CT Matulaitis Nursing Home Inc.
Krasen, John W. '60 (CLV) Westlake, OH St. Bernadette Church.
Krasevac, Edward *o.p.* '77 (OAK) [A] Berkeley, CA Dominican School of Philosophy and Theology.
Krasman, James *o.f.m.* '86 (GAY) Whittemore, MI St. James Church.
Krason, Edward J. '58 (FTW) Retired.
Krastel, Francis W. '54 (WDC) St. Mary's City, MD St. Cecilia Church; [S] Washington, DC Archdiocesan Campus Ministry.
Krastel, Joseph F. *c.ss.r.* '64 (FgM) Redemptorist Foreign Missions.
Krasulski, Andrew '98 (SJP) St. Petersburg, FL Epiphany of Our Lord Church.
Kraszewski, Thomas J. '97 (Y) Kent, OH St. Patrick's Church.
Kratz, Alex *o.f.m.* '99 (DET) [5] Southfield, MI St. Michael Church.
Kratz, Conrad J. *o. praem.* '73 (GB) [5] De Pere, WI Our Lady of Lourdes Church; [I] De Pere, WI St. Joseph Priory.
Kraus, Charles A. '58 (BRK) [29] Brooklyn, NY St. Charles Borromeo Church.
Kraus, Conrad L. '67 (E) Girard, PA St. John the Evangelist Church.
Kraus, David *o.m.i.* '57 (BEL) [H] Belleville, IL King's

House Retreat and Renewal Center.
Kraus, David H. (DOD) Dighton, KS St. Theresa Church; Scott City, KS St. Joseph Church.
Kraus, Msgr. Donald W. *s.t.d.* '54 (PIT) [73] Pittsburgh, PA Holy Wisdom Church.
Kraus, Leonard E. *s.j.* '72 (STL) [35] St. Louis, MO St. Francis Xavier Church; [P] St. Louis, MO Jesuit Community Corporation at St. Louis University - Jesuit Hall.
Kraus, Philip D. *s.j.* '75 (LA) [Q] Los Angeles, CA Columbiere House.
Kraus, Philip D. *s.j.* '75 (STL) [O] St. Louis, MO Fusz Pavilion.
Kraus, Robert J. '42 (STL) Retired.
Kraus, Stephen '75 (ROC) Cohocton, NY Holy Family Catholic Community Church; Dansville, NY St. Mary Church.
Kraus, Msgr. Theodore W. '63 (OAK) Point Richmond, CA Our Lady of Mercy Church.
Kraus, William *o.f.m.cap.* (FgM) Capuchin Foreign Missions.
Krause, Bruce J. *c.m.* '82 (BIR) Alexander City, AL St. John the Apostle Church.
Krause, Edward C. *c.s.c.* '66 (FTW) [J] South Bend, IN Congregation of Holy Cross, Indiana Province, Provincial House.
Krause, Edward C. *c.s.c.* '70 (E) [6] Erie, PA Immaculate Conception Church; [B] Erie, PA Gannon University.
Krause, Joseph A. '68 (TUC) Payson, AZ Saint Philip the Apostle Church.
Krauser, Karl *c.ss.r.* '85 (NY) [23] New York, NY St. Cecilia Church.
Krauth, Lothar '73 (GF) [7] Great Falls, MT Our Lady of Lourdes Church.
Krautkremer, Leo D. '66 (STP) Golden Valley, MN North Memorial Hospital.
Krautsack, Blaise P. *o.praem.* '74 (WIL) [B] Claymont, DE Archmere Academy; [I] Claymont, DE Immaculate Conception Priory of the Canons Regular of Premontre.
Krauzowicz, Krzysztof *s.d.b* (PRO) [3] Central Falls, RI St. Joseph Church.
Krawchuk, Thaddeus *c.ss.r.* '60 (PHU) Washington, DC Ukrainian Catholic National Shrine of the Holy Family Church.
Krawczyk, Henry R. '78 (PIT) [2] Munhall, PA St. Maximilian Kolbe Church.
Krawinkel, Msgr. Robert M. '58 (STL) Ladue, MO Church of the Annunziata.
Krawontka, Stephen A. '77 (SCR) [6] Hazleton, PA St. Joseph's Church.
Kraynak, Nicholas '59 (PSC) Old Forge, PA St. Nicholas Church.
Kraynak, William B. '81 (Y) Louisville, OH Sacred Heart of Mary Church; [I] Louisville, OH Emmaus House.
Kraynyak, Basil William '66 (PSC) New Port Richey, FL St. Anne's Church.
Krebs, Bruce '78 (BIS) Hazelton, ND St. Paul Church; Linton, ND St. Anthony Church.
Krebs, Donald '55 (MIL) [B] Hales Corners, WI Sacred Heart School of Theology.
Krebs, Msgr. Donald H. '55 (CR) Retired.
Krebs, Gerard H. '63 (E) [20] Erie, PA St. Joseph Church.
Krebs, Msgr. Henry L. '60 (E) Du Bois, PA St. Michael Church.
Krebs, John F. '57 (CHI) Ingleside, IL St. Bede Church.
Krebs, John G. *s.j.* '65 (FgM) Provinces.
Krebs, Paul F. '57 (COV) Retired.
Krebs, Peter *s.t.* '69 (PAT) [M] Stirling, NJ Holy Spirit Missionary Cenacle; [M] Stirling, NJ Shrine of St. Joseph.
Kreckel, Robert G. '54 (ROC) Ontario, NY St. Mary of the Lake Church.
Kredel, Thomas E. '72 (PIT) [23] Pittsburgh, PA St. Louise de Marillac Church.
Kreder, Michael J. '85 (NEW) Rutherford, NJ St. Mary's Church.
Kreft, Henry S. '45 (DET) Retired.
Kreher, Albert E. '65 (BEL) Prairie du Rocher, IL St. Joseph Church.
Kreidler, Thomas W. '77 (CIN) Twenty Mile Stand, OH St. Margaret of York Church.
Kreikemeier, Leo A. '43 (OM) Retired.
Kreilein, Philip '74 (EVN) Jasper, IN St. Joseph Church.
Kreimer, Richard *glmy.* '79 (CIN) [M] Cincinnati, OH Headquarters of Glenmary Home Missioners.
Kreimes, Paul '72 (DET) Special Assignment; [A] Detroit, MI Sacred Heart Major Seminary, Inc.
Kreis, Peter '86 (CHI) [112] Chicago, IL St. Ladislaus Church.
Kreiser, Thomas L. '94 (NY) Graduate Studies.
Kreitinger, Todd '00 (MOB) Auburn, AL St. Michael Church.
Kreitinger, Todd, . (MOB) [J] Auburn, AL Auburn University Newman Center.
Krejci, Msgr. Albert L. '41 (OM) [8] Sarpy Co., NE St. Bernadette Church; Retired.
Krejci, Michael G. '78 (MIL) Eagle, WI St. Theresa Church.
Krekelberg, Richard '73 (LA) [1] Long Beach, CA St. Anthony Church.
Krekelberg, William '70 (ORG) Irvine, CA St. Thomas More Church.
Krelovich, Michael '95 (SB) Rancho Cucamonga, CA Sacred Heart Church.
Kremeier, James '55 (GI) Retired.
Kremen, Justin M. *o.s.m.* '61 (ORG) [I] Buena Park, CA Order of Friar Servants of Mary (Servites).
Kremen, Timothy *o.s.m.* '61 (ORG) Fullerton, CA St. Philip Benizi Church.
Kremen, Timothy M. *o.s.m.* '61 (CHI) [N] Chicago, IL Order of Friar Servants of Mary (Servites) United States of America Province, Inc.
Kremer, Barry *o.carm.* '46 (JOL) [J] Darien, IL Carmelite Provincial Office.
Kremer, John R. '59 (DUB) Delhi, IA St. John's Church; Hopkinton, IA St. Luke's Church.
Kremer, Leroy '68 (SCL) Belle Prairie, MN Holy Family Church.
Kremer, Leroy M. '68 (SCL) Little Falls, MN Our Lady of Lourdes Church.
Kremer, Philip *o.s.b.* '57 (RCK) [G] Aurora, IL Marmion Abbey-St. Augustine's Abbey.
Kremmell, William T. '66 (BO) [1] Plymouth, MA Blessed Kateri Tekakwitha Church.
Kremp, Bruno *o.f.m.* '65 (CIN) [22] Cincinnati, OH Corpus Christi Church.
Krempa, Adam J. (BUR) [H] Burlington, VT University of Vermont-The Catholic Center at UVM.
Krempa, Adam J. '90 (BUR) Middletown Springs, VT St. Anne Church; Poultney, VT St. Raphael Church.
Krempa, Stanley J. '70 (ARL) Winchester, VA Sacred Heart of Jesus Church.
Krempel, Matthew *o.f.m.* '74 (BWN) Progreso, TX Holy Spirit Church.
Krenik, Michael J. '84 (STP) White Bear Lake, MN St. Pius X Church.
Krenik, Robert L. '84 (RIC) Abingdon, VA Christ the King Church; Marion, VA St. John the Evangelist Church.
Krenik, Thomas '77 (STP) Richfield, MN St. Richard Church.
Krenzke, John '57 (COS) Retired.
Krenzke, John '57 (DEN) [6] Denver, CO Christ the King Church.
Krepp, Theodore '82 (PSC) Kingston, PA St. Mary's Church.
Kreps, Anthony L. '38 (CLV) Amherst, OH St. Joseph Church; Retired.
Kresinski, Daniel J. '70 (E) [1] Sharon, PA Sacred Heart Church.
Kress, Dennis '99 (KNX) Kingsport, TN St. Dominic Church.
Kress, Robert '58 (EVN) On Duty Outside the Diocese.
Kret, John A. *o.s.a.* '61 (CHI) [N] Olympia Fields, IL Austin Friary.
Kretowicz, Antoni (CHI) [6] Waukegan, IL Immaculate Conception B.V.M. Church.
Kretschmer, Albert *s.v.d.* '47 (CHI) [B] Techny, IL Divine Word Residence.
Krettek, Daniel '77 (DM) [D] Des Moines, IA Mercy Medical Center; [H] Des Moines, IA Emmaus House.
Krettek, G. Thomas *s.j.* '82 (MIL) [P] Milwaukee, WI Jesuit Community at Marquette University.
Kretz, Edward J. '56 (GBG) [G] Greensburg, PA St. Anne Home.
Kretz, James C. '91 (PEO) Rutland, IL Sacred Heart Church; Toluca, IL St. Ann's Church.
Kreutz, William H. *s.j.* '69 (FgM) Provinces.
Kreutzer, Dan (OWN) Henshaw, KY St. Ambrose Church.
Kreutzer, Dan '97 (OWN) Sturgis, KY St. Francis Borgia Church.
Kreutzer, I. Daniel '97 (OWN) Marion, KY St. William Church.
Kreuzer, Eugene T. '52 (MIL) Retired.
Kreuzer, Msgr. Gerald J. '38 (BUF) Angola, NY Most Precious Blood Church; Retired.
Krewer, Edward M. '43 (PEO) Retired.
Kribs, Charles R. '51 (BEL) Retired.
Kribs, Don R. '61 (LA) [35] Los Angeles, CA Precious Blood Church; Los Angeles, CA Martin Luther King, Jr., Drew Medical Center.
Kricek, Henry C. '80 (CHI) Skokie, IL St. Peter Church.
Krick, Howard K. '58 (PH) Retired.
Krieg, Charles F. *c.m.* '63 (MET) [H] Plainsboro, NJ Vincentian Residence.
Krieg, Gerald '53 (ROC) Retired.
Krieg, Msgr. Gerard C. '53 (ROC) Geneva, NY St. Stephen Church; Pittsford, NY St. Louis Church.
Krieg, Jerome L. '38 (DET) Retired; [I] Waterford, MI Lourdes Nursing Home.
Krieg, Michael '82 (SPK) [5] Spokane, WA Sacred Heart Church.
Krieg, Peter *o.f.m.* (OAK) [9] Oakland, CA St. Elizabeth's Church.
Krieg, Peter *o.f.m.* '43 (OAK) [N] Oakland, CA Franciscan Friars.
Krieg, Robert A. *c.s.c.* '73 (BGP) [P] Bridgeport, CT Provincial Offices of the Priests and Brothers of Holy Cross, Eastern Province.
Krieg, Thomas J. '92 (LC) [2] Eau Claire, WI Newman Community Church; [I] Eau Claire, WI St. Bede Monastery; [K] Eau Claire, WI Newman Parish; [K] Menomonie, WI The Ministry to the University of Wisconsin-Stout.
Krieger, Msgr. Wilfred L. '46 (STL) Retired.
Kriegshauser, J. Laurence *o.s.b.* '69 (STL) [F] Creve Coeur, MO St. Louis Priory School; [P] St. Louis, MO The Abbey of St. Mary and St. Louis.
Kriegsmann, William A. '44 (RCK) Retired.
Krier, John P. '69 (GF) On Duty Outside of the Diocese.
Krier, John P. '69 (SPK) Medical Lake, WA St. Anne Church.
Krijnen, Joseph G. '46 (PHX) [3] Tempe, AZ Resurrection Church; Retired.
Krile, George F. '41 (FAR) Retired.
Krile, Stephen L. '83 (COL) Circleville, OH St. Joseph's Church.
Kriley, Victor *o.f.m.cap.* '64 (HBG) [2] York, PA St. Joseph Church.
Krill, Jude Michael *o.f.m.conv.* '83 (PH) [C] Aston, PA Neumann College.
Krill, Jude Michael *o.f.m.conv.* '83 (TR) Riverside, NJ St. Casimir Church.
Krimes, John Paul (OLL) Special Assignment.
Kringe, Charles J. '64 (SCR) Unassigned or Leave of Absence.
Krings, James A. '71 (STL) [31] St. Louis, MO St. Cronan Church; St. Louis, MO St. Mary's Health Center; [K] Kirkwood, MO SSM St. Joseph Hospital of Kirkwood.
Krinzner, William R. '79 (CLV) [C] Parma Heights, OH Holy Name High School.
Krisak, Anthony F. *s.s.* '75 (TR) On Duty Outside the Diocese.
Krisanda, Stephen *m.s.* '60 (SPR) [4] Holyoke, MA Immaculate Conception Church.
Krische, Francis '57 (KCK) [4] Topeka, KS Most Pure Heart of Mary Church.
Krische, James J. '91 (BRK) [50] Brooklyn, NY Good Shepherd Church.
Krische, Vincent E. '64 (KCK) [J] Lawrence, KS St. Lawrence Catholic Campus Center at the University of Kansas and Residence.
Krisciunevicius, Victor '49 (DET) Retired.
Kriski, Frank *c.ss.r.* '63 (KC) [31] Kansas City, MO Our Lady of Perpetual Help Church; [J] Kansas City, MO Redemptorists of Kansas City.
Krisman, Ronald (LUB) On Duty Outside the Diocese.
Kriss, Aaron J. '91 (PIT) Natrona Heights, PA Our Lady of the Most Blessed Sacrament Church.
Kriss, David J. '79 (PIT) [4] Donora, PA Our Lady of the Valley Church.
Kriss, Zigford J. '58 (HRT) [2] West Hartford, CT St. Helena Church; Special and other Archdiocesan Assignment.
Kristancic, Dennis J. '83 (CLV) Mentor, OH St. John Vianney Church.
Kristofak, Terence *c.p.* '69 (FgM) Passionist Foreign Missions.
Kristofak, Terence *c.p.* '69 (MET) [H] South River, NJ Passionist Provincial Office.
Kristy, Mark *o.c.d.* '85 (SR) [M] Oakville, CA Carmelite House of Prayer.
Krivak, John A. '82 (ALN) [O] Allentown, PA The Newman Center; [O] Allentown, PA The Newman Center; [O] Allentown, PA The Newman Center.
Krivanek, George E. *s.j.* '59 (SJ) [L] Los Gatos, CA Sacred Heart Jesuit Center.
Kriz, Dennis *o.s.m.* '99 (CHI) [N] Chicago, IL Order of Friar Servants of Mary (Servites) United States of America Province, Inc.
Kriz, Mark G. *s.j.* '95 (BUF) [D] Buffalo, NY Canisius High School; [O] Buffalo, NY Canisius Jesuit Community.
Krizner, William R. '79 (CLV) [2] Parma, OH St. Bridget Church.
Krlis, William '68 (BRK) [190] Queens, NY St. Leo Church.
Kroeger, Gerald C. *o.p.* '58 (CHI) Summit, IL St. Joseph Church; [N] Chicago, IL Dominicans (Provincial Office).
Kroeger, James H. *m.m.* '75 (FgM) Maryknoll Foreign Missions.
Kroeger, John '72 (CIN) Monroe, OH Our Lady of Sorrows Church.
Kroeger, Robert S. '94 (MIL) [1] Menomonee Falls, WI St. Anthony Church.
Kroeger, Timothy D. '90 (LFT) Fishers, IN St. Louis de Montfort Church.
Kroes, Ralph S. *m.m.* '58 (FgM) Maryknoll Foreign Missions.
Kroger, Daniel *o.f.m.* '73 (CIN) [M] Cincinnati, OH St. Francis Seraph Friary.
Kroger, Daniel *o.f.m.* '73 (FgM) Franciscan Foreign Missions.
Kroger, John H. '55 (COV) Bellevue, KY St. Anthony Church.

Krogman, David '81 (SFS) [6] Sioux Falls, SD St. Mary Church.
Krogman, Philip J. '60 (MAD) Green Lake, WI Our Lady of the Lake Church.
Krogol, Jude *o.s.b.* '65 (SP) [O] St. Leo, FL St. Leo Abbey.
Krol, Boleslaus '61 (DET) [12] Detroit, MI St. Bartholomew Church; [43] Detroit, MI St. Louis the King Church.
Krol, Miroslaw K. '99 (NEW) Wyckoff, NJ St. Elizabeth Church.
Krolczyk, David B. '72 (CHI) Posen, IL St. Stanislaus Bishop and Martyr Church.
Krolikowski, Lucian *o.f.m.conv.* '46 (SPR) [10] Chicopee, MA St. Stanislaus Basilica Church.
Krolikowski, Walter P. *s.j.* '57 (CHI) [C] Chicago, IL Jesuit Community at Loyola University of Chicago.
Kroll, Anthony '61 (SCL) Kent, MN St. Thomas Church; [G] Breckenridge, MN St. Francis Medical Center; [H] Breckenridge, MN St. Francis Home.
Kroll, Lawrence W. '86 (KAL) [4] Kalamazoo, MI St. Monica Church.
Kroll, Robert '72 (GB) [I] Pulaski, WI Assumption of B.V.M. Friary.
Kroll, Robert J. *s.j.* '99 (MIL) [E] Milwaukee, WI Marquette University High School; [P] Milwaukee, WI Pere Marquette House Jesuit Community.
Kromenaker, Joseph (CHI) [56] Chicago, IL St. Ferdinand Church.
Kromholtz, Bryan *o.p.* (ANC) [1] Anchorage, AK Holy Family Church.
Kronewitter, Frank '62 (FTW) [H] Fort Wayne, IN Saint Anne Home & Retirement Community.
Kronkowski, Leonard J. '55 (GRY) Retired.
Kropac, Robert J. '82 (CLV) [26] Cleveland, OH St. Henry Church.
Kropf, Richard '58 (GAY) [H] Johannesburg, MI Stella Maris Hermitage.
Kropf, Richard '58 (LAN) On Duty Outside the Diocese.
Kropiwnicki, Henry K. '58 (FR) [12] New Bedford, MA St. Casimir Church.
Krosfield, George '70 (ALX) Moreauville, LA Sacred Heart Church.
Krosnicki, Thomas A. *s.v.d.* '66 (CHI) [B] Techny, IL Divine Word Residence; [N] Techny, IL Society of the Divine Word, Provincial Headquarter-Chicago Prov.; [U] Techny, IL S.V.D., Catholic Universities, Inc.; [U] Techny, IL Divine Word Missionaries, Inc., Divine Word Funds, Inc.
Krosnicki, Thomas A. *s.v.d.* '66 (FgM) Society of the Divine Word Foreign Missions.
Krotec, Ivan '70 (STN) [3] Chicago, IL SS. Volodymyr and Olha Church.
Krotkiewicz, Luke '83 (DET) Detroit, MI Bi-County Osteopathic.
Krough, Jack L. '76 (WIN) [7] Rochester, MN St. Pius X Church; [G] Rochester, MN Congregational Center of the Third Order Regular of St. Francis of the Congregation of Our Lady of Lourde.
Krouse, Dennis '68 (SD) [B] San Diego, CA University of San Diego.
Krozser, John J. *c.m.* '56 (NEW) On Duty Outside the Archdiocese.
Kruc, James '89 (RIC) Retired.
Krudwig, William C. '61 (SPC) El Dorado Springs, MO St. Elizabeth Church.
Krueger, Robert W. '56 (P) [4] Portland, OR St. Andrew Church.
Krugel, Stephen A. (HRT) Cheshire, CT Connecticut Correctional Institution.
Krugel, Stephen A. '88 (HRT) [1] Milford, CT Christ the Redeemer Church; Enfield, CT Community Correctional Institution.
Kruger, Brent Allan *c.s.c.* '97 (FTW) On Duty Outside the Diocese.
Kruger, Brent Allan *c.s.c.* '97 (PHX) [K] Phoenix, AZ Andre House of Arizona.
Krukowski, Francis V. '58 (HRT) South Windsor, CT St. Margaret Mary Church.
Krul, Valentine C. '77 (SY) New York Mills, NY St. Mary Church.
Krulak, Michael '95 (PSC) Hazleton, PA St. Mary's Church.
Krull, Michael G. '86 (MET) Port Reading, NJ St. Anthony of Padua Church.
Krumm, Gus *o.f.m.* '82 (P) [6] Portland, OR Ascension Church.
Krumm, John E. '76 (CIN) [14] Dayton, OH Holy Family Church; [18] Dayton, OH St. Mary's Church.
Krupa, Sandor *o.f.m.* '31 (Y) [J] Youngstown, OH Mt. Alverna Friary.
Krupa, Stephen T. *s.j.* '86 (CLV) [B] Cleveland, OH John Carroll Jesuit Community.
Krupa, Thomas J. '71 (ALB) Castleton-on-Hudson, NY Sacred Heart Church.
Krupa, William J. *o.s.a.* (PH) [18] Philadelphia, PA St. Augustine Church.
Krupich, Thomas J. '88 (FAR) Tappen, ND St. Paul's Church.
Krupka, Michael '77 (SJP) Akron, OH Holy Ghost Church.
Krupp, Joseph J. '98 (LAN) East Lansing, MI St. Thomas Aquinas Church.
Kruse, Clarence '57 (DUB) Retired.
Kruse, Msgr. Clement '41 (SAL) Retired.
Kruse, David (BAL) [88] Baltimore, MD Sacred Heart of Mary Church.
Kruse, James '96 (PEO) Pekin, IL St. Joseph's Church.
Kruse, Jay L. '91 (OM) Ewing, NE St. Peter de Alcantara Church; St. John, NE St. John Church.
Kruse, Philip '81 (DUB) [3] Dubuque, IA St. Columbkille's Church.
Kruse, Robert J. *c.s.c.* '58 (FR) [A] North Easton, MA Stonehill College; [A] North Easton, MA Holy Cross Fathers Religious.
Krusinski, Andrew J. '45 (SCR) [4] Williamsport, PA Holy Rosary Church.
Kruszynski, Joseph *o.f.m.conv.* '68 (CHI) [N] Chicago, IL Conventual Franciscans of St. Bonaventure Province.
Krutcik, Stanley F. '80 (WOR) Manchaug, MA St. Anne's Church.
Krutewicz, Jan '00 (CHI) Bridgeview, IL St. Fabian Church.
Krutzik, Norman '57 (GB) Special Assignment.
Kruzel, Leonard M. '83 (CHI) [5] Cicero, IL Our Lady of Charity Church.
Krylowicz, Mark J. '91 (CHI) [158] Chicago, IL Our Lady of Tepeyac Church.
Krymski, Christopher M. *o.s.m.* '83 (CHI) Hillside, IL St. Domitilla Church; [N] Chicago, IL Order of Friar Servants of Mary (Servites) United States of America Province, Inc.; [N] Chicago, IL Order of Friar Servants of Mary (Servites) United States of America Province, Inc.; [N] Chicago, IL Order of Friar Servants of Mary (Servites) United States of America Province, Inc.
Krymski, Christopher M. *o.s.m.* '83 (ORG) [I] Buena Park, CA Order of Friar Servants of Mary (Servites).
Krynski, Leo J. '52 (SUP) Retired.
Krysa, Czeslaw M. '80 (BUF) On Duty Outside the Diocese.
Krysa, Czeslaw M. '80 (DET) [A] Orchard Lake, MI SS. Cyril and Methodius Seminary.
Kryston, Edward '74 (PIT) Baldwin Boro, PA St. Albert the Great Church.
Krystosek, Robert H. '56 (GI) Retired.
Krystosek, Robert H. '56 (NU) Retired.
Kryszak, Marian '56 (SAG) Retired.
Krysztofik, Msgr. Joseph M. '50 (MET) Retired; [H] Somerset, NJ Maria Regina Residence.
Kryvokulsky, Oleh '99 (STN) [3] Chicago, IL SS. Volodymyr and Olha Church.
Krzewinski, Edwin *o.m.i.* '52 (FgM) Oblates Foreign Missions.
Krzysiak, Casimir J. '50 (SY) [15] Utica, NY St. Stanislaus Church.
Krzyston, Stanley '54 (TR) [24] Trenton, NJ St. Vincent de Paul Church.
Krzywda, Leonard *c.r.* (SB) [1] Fontana, CA Church of the Resurrection.
Krzywicki, Lance P. '83 (PT) Military Chaplains.
Krzyzaniak, Timothy D. '91 (LAN) St. Johns, MI St. Joseph Church.
Krzyzanowski, Casimir *m.i.c.* '56 (SPR) [J] Stockbridge, MA Congregation of Marians of The Immaculate Conception of the BVM.
Krzyzanski, John P. *o.f.m.conv.* '82 (ATL) Jonesboro, GA St. Philip Benizi Church.
Krzyzopolski, Al '50 (SFS) Retired.
Kselman, John J. *s.s.* '67 (BAL) [S] Baltimore, MD Sulpician Provincial House.
Kselman, John J. *s.s.* '67 (BO) [W] Cambridge, MA Weston Jesuit Community.
Kselman, John J. *s.s.* '67 (TR) On Duty Outside the Diocese.
Ku, John Baptist *o.p.* '99 (PRO) [29] Providence, RI St. Pius V Church; [P] Providence, RI St. Pius Priory.
Kub, Francis Q. '65 (CHI) [188] Chicago, IL St. Simon the Apostle Church.
Kuba, William M. '62 (E) East Brady, PA St. Eusebius Church.
Kubacki, William J. '78 (TOL) [L] Toledo, OH Notre Dame Provincialate.
Kubajak, James '77 (PRM) Northwood, OH St. Michael the Archangel Church.
Kubala, Daniel I. '76 (MIA) [32] Miami, FL St. Thomas the Apostle Church.
Kubat, Alphonse M. '42 (STP) Retired.
Kubat, Christopher K. '99 (LIN) Hastings, NE St. Cecilia's Church.
Kubeck, John C. '65 (MIL) [O] Brookfield, WI Prelature of the Holy Cross and Opus Dei.
Kubiak, Edward J. '34 (GR) Retired.
Kubiak, Joseph M. *o.f.m.cap.* '74 (MET) [4] New Brunswick, NJ St. Joseph Church; New Brunswick, NJ Robert Wood Johnson University Hospital.
Kubiak, Joseph M. *o.f.m.cap.* '74 (PAT) [M] Oak Ridge-Milton, NJ St. Stanislaus B. M. Friary.
Kubicki, James M. *s.j.* '83 (STP) [Q] Lake Elmo, MN Jesuit Retreat House.
Kubik, John M. '49 (DET) [62] Detroit, MI SS. Peter and Paul Church; Retired.
Kubik, Thomas *c.r.* '72 (CHI) [D] Chicago, IL Gordon Tech High School.
Kubina, Eugene *t.o.r.* '53 (ALT) [F] Newry, PA St. Bernardine Monastery; [F] Newry, PA St. Bernardine Monastery.
Kubinski, Scott '84 (ROC) Lansing, NY All Saints Church.
Kubinski, Scott M. '84 (ROC) [M] Rochester, NY Diocesan Department of Campus Ministry.
Kubinyi, Julius '51 (PBR) Erie, PA SS. Peter and Paul Church.
Kucaj, Wolodymyr (STF) Brooklyn, NY St. Nicholas Church; Staten Island, NY Holy Trinity Church.
Kucan, Jerome *o.f.m.* '51 (CHI) [N] Chicago, IL Croatian Franciscan Custody of the Holy Family.
Kucera, David G. '98 (DUB) Mason City, IA St. Joseph's Church.
Kucera, Edward *o.s.b.* '53 (DEN) Aurora, CO Fitzsimons Army Medical Center.
Kucera, Edward *o.s.b.* '53 (JOL) [J] Lisle, IL St. Procopius Abbey.
Kucera, Edward C, Jr. '73 (GAL) Plantersville, TX St. Mary Church.
Kucera, Robert M. *o.s.m.* '53 (CHI) [N] Chicago, IL Order of Friar Servants of Mary (Servites) United States of America Province, Inc.
Kuchar, Bryan M. '93 (STL) [1] St. Louis, MO Cathedral Basilica of Saint Louis.
Kuchar, Michael W. '80 (LAN) [8] Lansing, MI St. Therese Church.
Kucharczyk, Dennis '80 (SAG) Caseville, MI St. Roch Church; Pinnebog, MI St. Felix Church.
Kucharczyk, Jaroslaw '95 (MET) [2] Perth Amboy, NJ St. Stephen Church.
Kucharczyk, John J. '99 (BAL) Severna Park, MD St. John the Evangelist Church.
Kucharski, Steven M. '77 (MAN) Rollinsford, NH St. Mary Church; Somersworth, NH Holy Trinity Church.
Kucharski, Zbigniew '84 (LC) Coon Valley, WI St. Mary Church.
Kuchera, Michael J. *s.j.* '87 (BAL) [S] Baltimore, MD Jesuit Fathers and Brothers Maryland Provincial Curia.
Kuchinsky, William J. (WH) Marlinton, WV St. John Neumann Church.
Kuchta, Waldemar J. '89 (PRM) Dayton, OH St. Barbara Church.
Kucingis, Msgr. John A. '37 (LA) [55] Los Angeles, CA St. Casimir Church; Retired.
Kucyk, Msgr. Herman W. '57 (DET) [5] Dearborn, MI Divine Child Church.
Kuczaik, Stanislaw *s.ch.* '57 (DET) [K] Sterling Heights, MI Society of Christ Provincial Home.
Kuczborski, Joseph '82 (PMB) Special Assignment.
Kuczmanski, Gregory M. '75 (BWN) Edcouch, TX St. Theresa of the Infant Jesus Church.
Kuczynski, Edward P. '77 (PH) Pottstown, PA St. Peter Church.
Kuczynski, Edwin R. *o.s.a.* '47 (CHI) [N] Olympia Fields, IL Tolentine Monastery at Tolentine Center.
Kuczynski, Francis I. '43 (PIT) Retired.
Kuczynski, James H. *m.s.* '73 (HRT) [M] Hartford, CT Missionaries of LaSalette, Provincial Secretary.
Kuczynski, John *c.m.* '44 (HRT) Derby, CT St. Michael Church.
Kuczynski, Kazimierz '76 (NEW) [6] Bayonne, NJ Mt. Carmel Church.
Kuder, Donald E. *c.s.b.* '63 (GAL) [K] Houston, TX The Catholic Chaplain Corps.
Kuder, Stephen R. *s.j.* '73 (SPK) [C] Spokane, WA Gonzaga University.
Kudilil, Jim '63 (FRS) [2] Bakersfield, CA Our Lady of Perpetual Help Church.
Kudleychuk, Bohdan '97 (PHU) Centralia, PA Assumption of B.V.M. Church; Mount Carmel, PA SS. Peter and Paul Church.
Kudlo, Frank '88 (MIA) Absent on Leave.
Kudrick, John M. '75 (PBR) Munhall, PA St. John the Baptist Church.
Kueber, Michael '00 (P) On Duty Outside the Archdiocese.
Kueber, Michael I. '00 (STP) Little Canada, MN St. John the Evangelist Church.
Kuebler, A.M. Seamus *o.s.a.* '75 (PRT) [I] Peaks Island, ME Mother of the Good Shepherd Monastery by the Sea.
Kuebler, A.M. Seamus '75 (WDC) On Duty Outside the Archdiocese.
Kuehler, Msgr. Norbert '55 (AMA) Borger, TX St. John the Evangelist Church.
Kuehnemund, H. Thomas '93 (DET) Waterford, MI St. Benedict Church.
Kuehner, Joseph (SB) [6] Riverside, CA St. Catherine of Alexandria Church.
Kuehner, Msgr. Ralph J. (WDC) Derwood, MD St. Francis of Assisi Church.
Kuenzig, Aloysius A. '43 (PIT) Retired.
Kuenzig, Peter A. '46 (PIT) Retired.
Kueter, David *o.m.v.* '84 (BO) [W] Milton, MA Oblate Residence (St. Joseph House).

Kuffel, Thomas '89 (LIN) Valparaiso, NE Sts. Mary and Joseph's Church.
Kugi, Gordon '95 (BRK) Brooklyn, NY Brooklyn Development Center; Brooklyn, NY Bernard Fineson Development Center.
Kugler, Michael '89 (GLP) Aztec, NM St. Joseph Church; Flora Vista, NM Holy Trinity Church.
Kuhl, Charles E. '54 (CAM) Retired.
Kuhl, Msgr. Urban B. '45 (BEL) Retired; [J] Belleville, IL Catholic War Veterans.
Kuhlman, Steve *o.p.* '92 (LFT) West Lafayette, IN St. Thomas Aquinas Church.
Kuhlmann, John L. '68 (BUF) Bemus Point, NY Our Lady of Lourdes Church; Jamestown, NY Jamestown Women's Christian Association Hospital.
Kuhlmann, Steven *o.p.* '93 (LFT) [H] West Lafayette, IN St. Thomas Aquinas Parish and Foundation for Catholic Students Attending Purdue University.
Kuhlmann, Steven F. *o.p.* '92 (CHI) [N] Chicago, IL Dominicans (Provincial Office).
Kuhn, Christopher (RCK) [B] Rockford, IL Boylan Central Catholic High School.
Kuhn, Christopher A. *c.s.c.* '77 (CHI) [D] Niles, IL Notre Dame High School.
Kuhn, Christopher J. '97 (RCK) Elizabeth, IL St. Mary Church; Hanover, IL St. John the Evangelist Church.
Kuhn, Dennis R. '82 (CHL) Absent On Leave.
Kuhn, George J. '64 (NY) Rhinebeck, NY The Good Shepherd Church; [S] Rhinebeck, NY Astor Home for Children, The.
Kuhn, James G. '71 (MAD) Fort Atkinson, WI St. Joseph Church.
Kuhn, James J. *m.m.* '51 (FgM) Maryknoll Foreign Missions.
Kuhn, John G. '58 (WDC) Special Ministries.
Kuhn, John H. '43 (BIS) Retired; [G] Bismarck, ND Emmaus Place.
Kuhn, Michael '97 (FR) [1] Fall River, MA Cathedral of St. Mary of the Assumption.
Kuhn, Michael F. (FR) [O] Fall River, MA Youth Apostles.
Kuhn, Michael F. '97 (FR) [B] Attleboro, MA Bishop Feehan High School.
Kuhn, Richard '53 (DUB) [F] Farley, IA Seton Catholic Elementary School.
Kuhn, Richard *s.m.* '58 (R) [E] Surf City, NC Marianist Community.
Kuhn, Richard W. '53 (DUB) New Melleray, IA Holy Family Church; Peosta, IA St. John the Baptist Church.
Kuhn, Thomas A. '67 (CIN) Centerville, OH Incarnation Church.
Kuhn, Thomas W. '57 (TOL) Retired.
Kuhns, Clement *c.pp.s.* '48 (CIN) [B] Carthagena, OH St. Charles.
Kuhns, James '61 (SPK) [4] Spokane, WA Our Lady of Fatima Church.
Kuhr, William M. (GB) Algoma, WI St. Mary Church.
Kuizon, Antonio '77 (NEW) Scotch Plains, NJ St. Bartholomew Church.
Kujovsky, Msgr. Thomas J. '57 (HBG) Elizabethtown, PA St. Peter Church; Retired.
Kukla, Gerald F. '67 (SAG) Harbor Beach, MI Our Lady of Lake Huron Church.
Kuklich, Stepan '96 (STF) Kenmore, NY St. John the Baptist Church.
Kukucka, Joseph G. '65 (PBL) Retired.
Kukulka, Janusz '85 (DET) [A] Orchard Lake, MI SS. Cyril and Methodius Seminary.
Kukulski, Stanislaus C. '55 (DET) Detroit, MI Northville State Hospital; Retired.
Kukura, Joseph W. '67 (NEW) On Duty Outside the Archdiocese.
Kula, Francis *m.s.* '54 (MIL) [68] Milwaukee, WI St. Paul Church; [P] Milwaukee, WI La Salette Fathers.
Kula, Joseph '55 (BIR) Retired.
Kulak, Joseph F. '66 (RCK) [2] Elgin, IL St. Laurence Church.
Kulandai, Peter '69 (NY) Red Hook, NY St. Christopher Church.
Kulandairajan, S. '78 (NY) Shrub Oak, NY Saint Elizabeth Ann Seton Church.
Kulas, John *o.s.b.* '57 (SCL) [I] Collegeville, MN St. John's Abbey, of the Order of St. Benedict.
Kulas, Robert A. '54 (WIN) Retired.
Kulas, William J. '74 (WIN) Rushford, MN St. Joseph's Church.
Kulathinal, Jose *c.m.i.* '92 (STA) Orange Park, FL St. Catherine's Church.
Kulathinal, Joseph *o.s.b.* '70 (PAT) [M] Clifton, NJ Holy Face of Jesus Monastery.
Kulavich, John J. '83 (SCR) Great Bend, PA St. Lawrence's Church.
Kulbicki, Timothy (BAL) Bel Air, MD St. Margaret Church.
Kulbicki, Timothy *o.f.m.conv.* '86 (BAL) [20] Baltimore, MD St. Casimir Church; [A] Baltimore, MD St. Mary's Seminary and University.
Kulbis, Augustine M. *o.s.m.* '58 (CHI) [N] Chicago, IL Order of Friar Servants of Mary (Servites) United States of America Province, Inc.
Kulbis, Lawrence E. *o.s.m.* '58 (DEN) [22] Denver, CO Our Lady of Mt. Carmel Church.
Kulczynski, A. Jason '89 (PH) Lansdowne, PA St. Philomena Church.
Kulczynski, Jason '89 (PH) [D] Drexel Hill, PA Archbishop Prendergast High School.
Kulesa, Daniel J. '62 (Y) McDonald, OH Our Lady of Perpetual Help Church.
Kulhawik, Frank '40 (CR) Retired.
Kulick, Larry J. '92 (GBG) Kent, PA Church of the Good Shepherd.
Kulig, Anthony J. '61 (NEW) [6] Bayonne, NJ Mt. Carmel Church.
Kulig, Francis G. '74 (SCR) [L] Dallas, PA Mercy Center Nursing Unit, Inc.
Kuligowski, Peter J. '97 (ALT) [23] Johnstown, PA St. Benedict's Church.
Kulik, Msgr. Alexander T. '54 (SCR) [15] Wilkes-Barre, PA Maternity of the Blessed Virgin Mary Church.
Kulik, Francis J. '69 (SCR) Unassigned or Leave of Absence.
Kulinski, Kenneth E. '72 (OKL) [9] Oklahoma City, OK St. Paul, Apostle Church.
Kull, John J. *o.f.m.* '66 (PAT) [M] Butler, NJ St. Anthony Friary.
Kull, Martin R. '76 (BRK) [10] Brooklyn, NY St. Anselm's Church.
Kulleck, Msgr. Donald '54 (SD) Retired.
Kulleck, Donald R. '52 (SD) [3] Chula Vista, CA St. Pius X Church.
Kulleck, Tom '74 (BWN) [10] Brownsville, TX Saint Mary, Mother of the Church.
Kuller, Thomas J. *s.j.* '79 (ALN) [A] Wernersville, PA Jesuit Center.
Kullmann, Charles *c.s.p.* '78 (NY) [104] New York, NY St. Paul the Apostle Church.
Kulovits, Fred A. '59 (LC) Retired.
Kulwiec, Richard *o.m.i.* '81 (NY) State, NY Beacon Correctional Facility; [FF] Newburgh, NY Our Lady of Hope Center.
Kumai, Felix (NY) Spring Valley, NY St. Joseph Church.
Kuman, Henry '84 (STL) [P] St. Louis, MO La Salette Missionaries.
Kumbalaparampil, Xavier '66 (SAV) [6] Savannah, Savannah Resurrection of Our Lord Church.
Kumblumkal, Jose G. '90 (TYL) Sulphur Springs, TX St. James Church.
Kumle, Peter *c.p.* '52 (CHI) [N] Chicago, IL Passionist Community-Immaculate Conception Monastery.
Kummer, John R. '72 (CIN) [12] Cincinnati, OH Assumption Church.
Kummer, William '75 (FTW) [7] Fort Wayne, IN St. John Baptist Church.
Kummerer, Timothy M. '83 (TOL) Defiance, OH St. Mary Church.
Kumontis, Msgr. Francis M. '73 (HBG) Hershey, PA St. Joan of Arc Church.
Kumplam, Chacko K. '80 (HRT) [3] West Haven, CT St. Lawrence's Church; [I] New Haven, CT Hospital of St. Raphael.
Kumse, John M. '79 (CLV) [47] Cleveland, OH St. Mary Church; [Z] Cleveland, OH Cleveland Slovenian Community Center.
Kuna, Lech '74 (HRT) [5] Bristol, CT St. Stanislaus Church.
Kunco, Edward J. '69 (PIT) [16] Pittsburgh, PA Immaculate Conception Church; [20] Pittsburgh, PA St. Joseph Church.
Kunda, Brendan J. '65 (SUP) Retired.
Kundrat, Michael J. '41 (DET) Retired.
Kunert, Kenneth M. *s.j.* '57 (DET) [P] Clarkston, MI Colombiere Center.
Kunes, James F. *s.m.* '60 (CIN) [M] Dayton, OH Marianist Provincialate.
Kunigonis, Mark S. '00 (PH) [71] Philadelphia, PA Immaculate Heart of Mary Church.
Kunisch, Robert *c.pp.s.* '56 (TOL) [M] Bellevue, OH Sorrowful Mother Shrine.
Kunkel, A. Henry, III '70 (BAL) Pylesville, MD St. Mary Church.
Kunkel, Albert A. '57 (CLV) [5] Barberton, OH Sacred Heart Church.
Kunkel, Charles *o.s.c.* '67 (SCL) [I] Onamia, MN Crosier Monastery.
Kunkel, George C. '77 (CIN) [56] Cincinnati, OH St. Martin of Tours Church.
Kunkel, James '73 (PIT) [6] Ambridge, PA Good Samaritan Church.
Kunkel, Ronald T. '00 (CHI) Graduate Studies.
Kunnakkattu, Abraham (LAF) Four Corners, LA St. Peter the Apostle Church.
Kunnakkattuthara, Zacharias S. '75 (TYL) Palestine, TX Sacred Heart Church; Palestine, TX Sacred Heart Church.
Kunnalakatt, Peter (CHI) Melrose Park, IL Sacred Heart Church.
Kunnath, George *m.c.b.s.* (CC) Taft, TX Holy Family Church.
Kunnath, Matthew '60 (NEW) Nutley, NJ St. Mary's Church.
Kunnath, Sebastian '73 (NEW) Paramus, NJ Our Lady of the Visitation Church.
Kunnath, Thomas '85 (TR) Brick Town, NJ Epiphany Church.
Kunnel, Lawrence '60 (TR) Neptune, NJ Holy Innocents Church.
Kunnumpuram, Paul *m.s.f.s.* '76 (ALX) Ferriday, LA St. Patrick Church; Vidalia, LA Our Lady of Lourdes Church.
Kunst, Richard '98 (DUL) Floodwood, MN St. Louis Church.
Kuntz, Donald B. '41 (DET) Retired.
Kuntz, Ildephonse *ss.cc.* '46 (HON) [G] Kaneohe, HI Sacred Hearts Center.
Kuntz, James F. *s.j.* '77 (SAC) [C] Sacramento, CA Jesuit High School; [H] Carmichael, CA Jesuit High School Community of Sacramento.
Kuntz, Kenneth E. '77 (DAV) [1] Iowa City, IA St. Mary Church.
Kunz, David C. '80 (LC) On Duty Outside the Diocese.
Kunz, David C. '80 (WIN) [A] Winona, MN Immaculate Heart of Mary Seminary.
Kunz, Francis P. '49 (WIN) Retired.
Kunz, James H. '73 (WIN) On Special or Other Diocesan Assignment; [D] Rochester, MN Saint Marys Hospital.
Kunz, John M. '76 (WIN) Waseca, MN Sacred Heart Church.
Kunze, Robert W. '74 (CAM) Gibbsboro, NJ St. Andrew the Apostle Church.
Kunze, Robert W. '74 (NEW) On Duty Outside the Archdiocese.
Kunzman, Richard T. '63 (CAM) On Duty Outside the Diocese.
Kuolt, Benedict J. '47 (NY) [3] White Plains, NY St. Bernard Church; White Plains, NY White Plains Hospital; Retired.
Kuper, Raymond L '64 (EVN) [8] Evansville, IN Holy Rosary Church.
Kupisz, Julian '74 (FAR) La Moure, ND Holy Rosary Church.
Kupke, Msgr. Raymond J. '73 (PAT) Florham Park, NJ Holy Family Church.
Kuppayil, George J. *m.s.t.* '91 (MAR) Channing, MI St. Rose Church.
Kuppe, Paul *o.f.m.cap.* '70 (FgM) Capuchin Foreign Missions.
Kuppe, Paul *o.f.m.cap.* '70 (PIT) [O] Pittsburgh, PA St. Augustine Friary.
Kuras, Alexander A. '69 (DET) [3] Westland, MI Church of the Divine Savior.
Kuras, Hippolite *o.f.m.conv.* '35 (RCK) [11] Rockford, IL St. Stanislaus Kostka Church.
Kurash, Stanley J. '71 (SCR) [2] Old Forge, PA St. Mary's Church.
Kurber, Robert '60 (ORL) [4] Orlando, FL Holy Cross Church.
Kurdziel, Dennis M. '75 (ALT) [11] Altoona, PA Our Lady of Lourdes Church.
Kure, Josef *s.j.* '88 (WDC) [M] Washington, DC The Jesuit Community at Georgetown University.
Kurek, Gerard '51 (BAL) [87] Baltimore, MD Sacred Heart of Jesus Church.
Kurera, Pius '80 (FRS) [C] Fresno, CA Nazareth House.
Kurgan, Charles *o.carm.* '65 (JOL) [J] Darien, IL Carmelite Provincial Office.
Kuriakose, Francis V. *s.j.* '83 (CHI) [C] Chicago, IL Jesuit Community at Loyola University of Chicago.
Kurian, Joseph *c.m.i.* '83 (TYL) Jefferson, TX Immaculate Conception Church.
Kuriapilly, Augustine '70 (RVC) Roslyn, NY St. Francis Hospital.
Kuriappilly, Johnson (BIS) Tioga, ND St. Thomas Church.
Kurilec, Robert '68 (SB) On Duty Outside the Diocese.
Kurimay, Michael D. *s.j.* '73 (CLV) [B] Cleveland, OH John Carroll Jesuit Community.
Kurimsky, Frank M. '86 (PIT) Monaca, PA St. John the Baptist Church.
Kurkiewicz, Raymond J. '42 (MIL) Retired.
Kurkowski, Innocent *o.f.m.conv.* '56 (BGP) [1] Fairfield, CT St. Anthony of Padua Church.
Kurnath, Joseph G.M. '91 (HRT) [2] Bristol, CT St. Anthony's Church.
Kurovsky, Andrew '85 (SCR) [6] Williamsport, PA St. Ann's Church; [D] Williamsport, PA Bishop Neumann Junior/Senior High School.
Kurowski, Andrzej *s.a.c.* '76 (BRK) [43] Brooklyn, NY St. Frances de Chantal Church.
Kurowski, Andrzej *s.a.c.* '76 (BUF) [O] North Tonawanda, NY Society of the Catholic Apostolate.
Kurowski, Clement *o.f.m.* '53 (PH) [107] Philadelphia, PA St. Monica Church.
Kurpel, Yaroslav '93 (PHU) [8] Philadelphia, PA Christ the King Church.
Kurps, Jack *s.c.j.* '77 (MIL) [P] Hales Corners, WI Priests of the Sacred Heart; [P] Milwaukee, WI St. Joseph House of Formation.
Kurt, Allan J. '55 (DUB) Retired.
Kurt, David L. '77 (PEO) Bushnell, IL St. Bernard Church; St. Augustine, IL St. Augustine Church.

Kurt, Msgr. Edgar J. '41 (DUB) Retired.
Kurtenbach, Harold R. '60 (GI) Retired.
Kurth, Earl J. *s.j.* '49 (RC) Pine Ridge, SD Holy Rosary Church; [B] Pine Ridge, SD Jesuit Community of Holy Rosary Mission.
Kurty, Msgr. John '42 (PRM) Allen Park, MI St. Stephen Church; Retired.
Kurtyka, Msgr. Edward J. '71 (PAT) Prospect Park, NJ St. Paul's Church.
Kurtz, James *o.f.m.cap.* '72 (PIT) Clairton, PA St. Clare of Assisi Church.
Kurtz, Jeffrey A. '90 (MAR) Leave of Absence.
Kurtz, R. James *s.j.* '77 (DET) [E] Detroit, MI University of Detroit Jesuit High School and Academy.
Kurtzke, John *c.s.c.* '85 (P) [B] Portland, OR University of Portland; [L] Portland, OR Holy Cross Fathers & Brothers, C.S.C. - University of Portland.
Kurucz, Frank A. '98 (CHI) Palos Heights, IL St. Alexander Church.
Kurutz, Gregory *o.f.m.* '54 (GAY) Lewiston, MI St. Francis of Assisi Church.
Kurutz, Joseph V. '59 (PIT) [35] Pittsburgh, PA St. Raphael Church.
Kuruvila, Prince *s.j.* '92 (CC) [17] Corpus Christi, TX St. Patrick Church.
Kuruvilla, George *c.m.i.* (STA) Lake City, FL Epiphany Church.
Kurwicki, Robert A. '85 (JC) Westphalia, MO St. Joseph Church.
Kurylo, Michael '34 (STN) San Diego, CA Our Lady of Perpetual Help Church; Retired.
Kurylowicz, Martin '79 (GR) On Duty Outside the Diocese.
Kurz, Michael '75 (RCK) [10] Rockford, IL St. Rita Church.
Kurz, William S. *s.j.* '70 (MIL) [P] Milwaukee, WI Jesuit Community at Marquette University.
Kurzaj, Msgr. Franciszek '76 (SAT) [6] San Antonio, TX Holy Name Church.
Kurzak, John '75 (SC) On Duty Outside the Diocese.
Kurzawa, Ronald W. '64 (DET) [6] St. Clair Shores, MI St. Margaret of Scotland Church.
Kurzawski, Casimir J. '58 (WOR) Retired.
Kurzendoerfer, Mark '81 (EVN) Haubstadt, IN SS. Peter and Paul Church.
Kurzyna, Andrew E. '74 (NY) Verplanck, NY St. Patrick Church.
Kus, Robert J. (R) Wake Forest, NC St. Catherine of Siena Church.
Kus, Sebastian *o.f.m.* '57 (NEW) [O] Lodi, NJ Immaculate Conception Convent.
Kuse, Michael '67 (SFD) [8] Quincy, IL St. Mary Church.
Kusevich, Nicholas C. '69 (PSC) Lake Worth, FL Holy Apostles Church.
Kusevich, Nicholas C. '69 (ROM) Special Assignment or On Duty Outside the Diocese.
Kusi, David (CHI) [77] Chicago, IL Holy Angels Church.
Kusibab, Justin G. *o.f.m.conv.* '87 (CHI) Arlington Heights, IL Our Lady of the Wayside Church.
Kusmirek, Mark '77 (TYL) Kilgore, TX Christ the King Church.
Kusnadi, Rony '99 (BAL) [S] Baltimore, MD Jesuit Community of Loyola College, Inc.
Kuss, Allen R. '84 (BIS) On Duty Outside the Diocese.
Kustanto, Johannes B. Hari *s.j.* '91 (HRT) [5] New Haven, CT St. Boniface's Church.
Kusunoki, Peter *ss.cc.* '79 (FR) [I] Fairhaven, MA Sacred Hearts Provincial House.
Kusy, George '86 (CLV) [72] Cleveland, OH St. Stanislaus Church.
Kuta, Frank J. '53 (CLV) Rittman, OH St. Anne Church; Retired.
Kutch, Joseph P. '88 (SCR) Elkland, PA St. Thomas the Apostle Church.
Kutch, Peter P. *o.f.m.cap.* '66 (MIL) Mount Calvary, WI Holy Cross Church; St. Cloud, WI St. Cloud Church; St. Joe, WI St. Joseph Church.
Kutil, Dale '73 (RC) Fort Pierre, SD St. John Church; [D] Rapid City, SD Priest Retirement and Aid Association.
Kutiuk, Casimir '57 (GB) Retired.
Kutner, Msgr. Raymond W. '64 (BRK) [157] Queens, NY Blessed Sacrament Church.
Kutsch, Eugene C. '51 (DUB) Retired.
Kuttikattukunnel, Francis *s.v.d.* '88 (DUB) [B] Epworth, IA Divine Word College.
Kutulas, Nicholas *s.m.* '55 (SFR) [N] San Francisco, CA Marist Center of the West.
Kutys, Daniel J. '80 (PH) On Duty Outside the Archdiocese.
Kutz, Lawrence A. '65 (WDC) [T] Washington, DC Prelature of the Holy Cross and Opus Dei.
Kutzner, Roger '90 (JOL) Steger, IL St. Liborius Church.
Kuubetersuur, Sylvester (BO) [4] Brookline, MA Infant Jesus-St. Lawrence Church.
Kuupuo, Severo '91 (PIT) [66] Pittsburgh, PA St. Wendelin Church.
Kuveikis, Rufin *o.f.m.cap.* '48 (BGP) [15] Stamford, CT Sacred Heart Church; Norwalk, CT Norwalk Hospital.
Kuykendall, Andy '78 (WCH) Haysville, KS St. Cecilia Church.
Kuykendall, Henry '86 (EVN) [9] Evansville, IN Holy Spirit Church; [10] Evansville, IN Nativity Church.
Kuykendall, Thomas '94 (YAK) Wenatchee, WA St. Joseph's Church.
Kuzara, George *c.pp.s.* '78 (CIN) St. Joseph, OH St. Joseph Church.
Kuzara, George *c.pp.s.* '78 (PHU) Northampton, PA St. John the Baptist Church.
Kuzdal, Anthony P. '56 (NOR) Retired.
Kuzia, Anthony F *c.m.* '76 (HRT) [M] Manchester, CT DePaul Provincial Residence.
Kuziemski, Ignatius H. '60 (MET) Great Meadows, NJ SS. Peter and Paul Church.
Kuzihappallil, George (PAT) Parsippany, NJ St. Christopher Church.
Kuzilla, John A. '55 (E) Kersey, PA St. Boniface Church.
Kuzinskas, John A. '52 (CHI) [138] Chicago, IL Nativity of the Blessed Virgin Mary Church; Retired.
Kuzma, Mykhailo '81 (STN) Palatine, IL Immaculate Conception Church.
Kuzmann, Robert J. '85 (ALN) Girardville, PA St. Joseph Church.
Kuzmeski, Charles H. '75 (SPR) Ware, MA St. Mary's Church.
Kuzmich, John M. '65 (FTW) [20] Fort Wayne, IN St. Vincent de Paul Church.
Kuzniewski, Anthony J. *s.j.* '79 (WOR) [N] Worcester, MA Jesuits of Holy Cross College, Inc.
Kuznik, Robert '98 (RVC) Baldwin, NY St. Christopher Church.
Kvedas, Leonard J. '61 (HRT) Beacon Falls, CT St. Michael's Church.
Kwak, Peter Kilou '67 (CLV) [6] Cleveland, OH St. Andrew Kim Church.
Kwak, Thaddeus '59 (FTW) [15] South Bend, IN Our Lady of Hungary Church.
Kwapisz, Gregory *o.f.m.conv.* '60 (BUF) [21] Buffalo, NY Corpus Christi Church.
Kwatera, Michael *o.s.b.* '77 (SCL) Farming, MN St. Catherine's Church; St. Martin, MN St. Martin's Church; [I] Collegeville, MN St. John's Abbey, of the Order of St. Benedict.
Kweder, Joseph J. '85 (ALN) Whitehall, PA St. Elizabeth Church.
Kwiatkowski, Augustine '89 (STA) [J] Bunnell, FL Discalced Carmelite Fathers of Florida.
Kwiatkowski, Constantine '47 (BUF) Retired.
Kwiatkowski, Michael '78 (SPK) Colbert, WA St. Joseph Church.
Kwiatkowski, Paul M. '64 (TOL) [9] Toledo, OH Immaculate Conception Church; [25] Toledo, OH St. James Church.
Kwiatkowski, Richard P. '72 (NEW) Bloomfield, NJ Sacred Heart Church.
Kwiatkowski, Robert M. '83 (HRT) Woodbury, CT St. Teresa's Church.
Kwiecien, Jan '80 (MET) Manville, NJ Sacred Heart of Jesus Church.
Kwiecien, John S. '76 (BUF) Springville, NY St. Aloysius Church.
Kwiecien, Michael *o.carm.* '80 (PHX) [6] Phoenix, AZ St. Agnes Church; [J] Phoenix, AZ Kino Institute.
Kwiecien, Wojciech '79 (CHI) [96] Chicago, IL St. James Church.
Kwoka, Edward '78 (TR) Lakewood, NJ St. Mary of the Lake Church.
Kwolek, Joseph '45 (BUF) Retired; [O] Buffalo, NY Sheehan Residence for Priests.
Kwon, O'myun *s.j.* '00 (BO) [W] Chestnut Hill, MA The Jesuit Community at Boston College.
Kyebasuuta, John M. '98 (LA) Encino, CA Our Lady of Grace Church.
Kyfes, Robert J. '77 (CHI) [31] Chicago, IL St. Bride Church.
Kyle, Eric *o.f.m.* '52 (NY) [Z] Staten Island, NY Carmel Richmond Nursing Home, Inc.
Kyle, John M. '36 (CHI) Streamwood, IL St. John the Evangelist Church; Retired.
Kyne, John J. '50 (SAC) Dixon, CA St. Peter Church; Retired and in Senior Ministry.
Kyomya, Romanus (WDC) [13] Washington, DC St. Francis de Sales Church.
Kyranon, Emil *o.f.m.* '43 (LA) [73] Los Angeles, CA St. Joseph Church.
Kyrie, James *o.f.m.* '67 (FRS) Delano, CA St. Mary's of the Miraculous Medal Church.
Kyrpczak, James A. (MET) [A] Edison, NJ Bishop Ahr High School.
Kyrpczak, James A. '96 (MET) Dunellen, NJ St. John the Evangelist Church.
Kyte, Michael G. *o.p.* '87 (DEN) [29] Denver, CO St. Dominic's Church; [A] Denver, CO St. Dominic Priory.

L

L'Arche, Jeffrey '75 (ALB) [Q] Altamont, NY La Salette Shrine.
L'Heureux, Ernest L. '62 (PRT) Retired.
L'Heureux, William D. '91 (OM) Hooper, NE St. Rose of Lima Church.
La Belle, Joseph T. *o.m.i.* '92 (SAT) [B] San Antonio, TX George Sexton House of Studies; [C] San Antonio, TX Oblate School of Theology.
La Belle, Ralph W. '78 (NY) Patterson, NY Sacred Heart Church.
La Bonte, Adelard *s.d.b.* '90 (PAT) [D] Paterson, NJ Don Bosco Technical High School.
La Brake, John R. *s.s.e.* '57 (MOB) Belle Fontaine, AL St. Philip Neri Church.
La Casa, Vicente Paz en '66 (PBL) [17] Pueblo, CO Shrine of St. Therese Church.
La charite, Roger J. *s.s.e.* '55 (MOB) [K] Selma, AL Edmundite Guild.
La Count, Daniel '89 (SFD) Absent on Leave.
La France, Val *o.p.* '58 (NEW) [28] Jersey City, NJ Sacred Heart Church.
La Fratta, William E. '63 (RIC) Charlottesville, VA Church of the Incarnation.
La Goe, John P. '61 (GR) Retired.
La Pan, Kenneth *t.o.r.* '52 (ALT) [F] Newry, PA St. Bernardine Monastery.
La Patka, Gerald '56 (DUL) Retired.
La Paz, Gabriel '78 (NY) [53] New York, NY Incarnation Church.
La Plante, Philip *s.m.* '48 (BO) [BB] South Boston, MA Our Lady of Good Voyage Chapel.
La Pointe, Jacques *o.f.m.* (WDC) [3] Silver Spring, MD St. Camillus Church.
La Porta, Gerald '57 (BAL) Retired.
La Porta, Ross A. '51 (BAL) Retired.
La Rocca, Chrostopher *o.c.d.* '97 (SJ) [L] San Jose, CA Carmelite Monastery, Novitiate.
La Rocca, Jack '88 (SJ) [4] San Jose, CA Five Wounds Portuguese National Church.
La Rocca, Vincent '49 (BRK) [131] Brooklyn, NY Sacred Hearts of Jesus and Mary and St. Stephen Church.
La Rosa, Stephen J. *o.s.a.* '65 (CAM) [C] Richland, NJ St. Augustine Preparatory School.
La Rosa-Lopez, Manuel '96 (GAL) Conroe, TX Sacred Heart Church.
La Torre, Anthony P. '97 (SFR) [19] San Francisco, CA St. Finn Barr Church.
La Valley, Terry R. '88 (OG) Heuvelton, NY St. Raphael's Church.
Laba, Gerald *c.p.* '73 (FgM) Passionist Foreign Missions.
Laba, Gerald *c.p.* '73 (MET) [H] South River, NJ Passionist Provincial Office.
LaBaff, Arthur J. '66 (OG) [4] Watertown, NY St. Patrick Church.
LaBaire, Steven M. '87 (WOR) Westborough, MA St. Luke the Evangelist Church.
Labak, Joseph L. '77 (CLV) Wadsworth, OH Sacred Heart of Jesus Church.
Labarda, Nathaniel C. '93 (HRT) [1] Waterbury, CT Blessed Sacrament Church.
LaBarge, Charles F. '46 (DUB) Retired.
LaBarge, Christopher '85 (WIL) Marydel, MD Immaculate Conception Church.
Labarre, Renald D. '60 (PRT) Biddeford, ME St. Joseph's Church.
Labat, Dennis C. '74 (NU) Springfield, MN St. Raphael Church; On Special or Other Diocesan Assignment.
LaBau, Anthony F. *s.j.* '46 (NY) [DD] New York, NY St. Ignatius Loyola Residence; [HH] New York, NY Jesuit Seminary and Mission Bureau, Inc.
LaBauve, J. Joel '70 (BR) Gonzales, LA St. Mark Church; Angola, LA Louisiana State Penitentiary.
LaBauve, John N. *s.v.d.* '51 (GAL) [1] Galveston, TX St. Mary's Cathedral Basilica Church.
Labbe, Clifton *s.v.d.* '69 (FgM) Society of the Divine Word Foreign Missions.
Labbe, Clifton *s.v.d.* '96 (BLX) [E] Bay St. Louis, MS Southern Province of St. Augustine - Provincial Residence.
Labbe, Donavan (LAF) Ville Platte, LA Sacred Heart of Jesus Church.
Labbe, Emil J. *c.pp.s.* '68 (CIN) Maria Stein, OH St. John the Baptist Church.
Labbe, Joseph P. '75 (CLV) Chagrin Falls, OH Holy Angels Church.
Labbe, Wilfred '99 (PRT) [M] Lewiston, ME Bates College.
Labbe, Wilfred P. '99 (PRT) [2] Lewiston, ME Holy Cross Church.
Labedis, Anthony *o.f.m.conv.* '60 (CHI) [N] Chicago, IL Conventual Franciscans of St. Bonaventure Province.
Labedis, Anthony *o.f.m.conv.* '60 (FgM) Conventual Franciscan Foreign Missions.
Labella, Robert '54 (CLV) [2] Akron, OH St. Anthony of Padua Church.
LaBelle, Patrick *o.p.* '65 (OAK) [N] Oakland, CA Western Dominican Province.
LaBelle, Patrick *o.p.* '65 (SJ) Stanford, CA Catholic Community at Stanford Church.
Labinski, Jacek '83 (TR) Burlington, NJ All Saints Church.

Labinsky, Paul '81 (PHU) Manville, NJ St. Michael's Church; New Brunswick, NJ Nativity of B.V.M. Church.
Labita, Francis J. '49 (BRK) [211] Queens, NY Our Lady of Grace Church; Retired.
LaBo, Timothy P. '86 (ORL) Sabbatical.
Laboe, Timothy A. '99 (DET) Pontiac, MI St. Joseph Church; Pontiac, MI St. Michael Church; Pontiac, MI St. Vincent de Paul Church.
Labonte, Jess '85 (LA) [J] Burbank, CA Providence Saint Joseph Medical Center; [J] Burbank, CA Providence Health System.
Labonte, L. Roger '66 (MET) Edison, NJ St. Helena Church.
Labonte, Richard H. '70 (WOR) Blackstone, MA St. Theresa Church.
Labonte, Roger '94 (LA) South Pasadena, CA Holy Family Church.
LaBonte, Roger A. *m.afr.* '62 (FgM) Missionaries of Africa Foreign Missions.
Laboon, Joseph D. '57 (NO) New Orleans, LA Veterans Affairs Medical Center.
Laboon, Joseph D. '57 (PIT) Military Chaplains.
Labor, Jesus '83 (SFR) [24] San Francisco, CA Holy Name of Jesus Church.
Labosky, James M. '79 (R) Wilmington, NC St. Mary Church.
Laboton, Jose *o.f.m.* '74 (WDC) [3] Silver Spring, MD St. Camillus Church.
LaBove, M. Keith '81 (LAF) Milton, LA St. Joseph Church.
LaBran, Joseph J. *s.j.* '47 (WOR) [N] Worcester, MA Jesuits of Holy Cross College, Inc.; [Q] Worcester, MA Campus Ministry.
LaBranche, Raymond (AGN) [A] Agana, GU Redemptoris Mater Seminary.
Labranche, Raymond '94 (NEW) On Duty Outside the Archdiocese.
LaBrecque, Frederick '67 (CHR) Conway, SC St. James Church.
Labrie, Jean Paul '82 (PRT) Hampden, ME St. Matthew Church; Winterport, ME St. Gabriel Church.
LaBrie, Joseph *s.j.* '97 (LA) [C] Los Angeles, CA Loyola Marymount University.
LaBrie, Robert G. '64 (BO) Canton, MA St. John the Evangelist Church.
LaBrie, Robert G. '94 (BO) Norwood, MA Caritas Norwood Hospital.
Labrun, Raymond A. *o.m.i.* '68 (NO) [17] New Orleans, LA Our Lady of Guadalupe /International Shrine of St. Jude Church.
LaBuda, David E. *m.m.* '71 (FgM) Maryknoll Foreign Missions.
LaBurt, Brian *glmy.* '86 (SAV) Claxton, GA St. Christopher Church.
Lacasse, Aime F. *m.afr.* '38 (SP) [O] St. Petersburg, FL Missionaries of Africa.
LaCasse, Andre Joseph *o.p.* '92 (COL) [36] Columbus, OH St. Patrick Church.
Lacasse, Eugene *o.c.s.o.* '54 (WOR) [N] Spencer, MA St. Joseph's Abbey.
Lacasse, J.A. Roger '54 (PRO) [2] Woonsocket, RI All Saints Catholic Community Church.
LaCasse, John P. '74 (DET) Ida, MI St. Joseph Church.
Lacasse, Raymond *o.m.i.* '58 (FgM) Oblates Foreign Missions.
Lacasse, Roger '53 (PRO) Retired.
Lacasse, Roland (BO) [10] Lawrence, MA Sacred Heart Church.
Lacasse, Roland *s.m.* '60 (BO) [3] Methuen, MA Our Lady of Mount Carmel Church.
LaCaze, Msgr. J. Carson '57 (SHP) [4] Shreveport, LA Our Lady of the Holy Rosary Church.
Lacerna, Rodolfo '68 (ELP) [31] El Paso, TX St. Raphael Church.
Lacerte, Henry W. *o.s.b.* '54 (PBL) [G] Canon City, CO Holy Cross Abbey.
Lacey, Msgr. Francis A. *p.a.* '51 (SFR) Tiburon, CA St. Hilary Church; Retired.
Lacey, George F. '45 (STO) [7] Stockton, CA St. Luke Church; Retired.
Lacey, James *c.ss.r.* '43 (ALB) [L] Saratoga Springs, NY St. John Neumann Residence.
Lacey, Joseph P. *s.j.* '71 (BAL) Woodstock, MD St. Alphonsus Rodriguez Church.
Lacey, Mark W. (ATL) Released from Archdiocesan Assignment.
Lacey, Michael '78 (OAK) Dublin, CA St. Raymond Church.
Lacey, Thomas *c.ss.r.* (TOL) [2] Lima, OH St. Gerard Church.
Lachaine, Robert *c.s.v.* (CHI) [206] Chicago, IL St. Viator Church.
LaChance, Charles P. '84 (CHI) Other Assignments.
Lachance, Marcel G. '56 (NOR) Putnam, CT St. Mary Church.
Lachance, Pierre E. *o.p.* '42 (FR) [13] Fall River, MA St. Anne's Church; [I] Fall River, MA St. John Vianney House; [I] Fall River, MA Dominican House.
LaChance, Roger '67 (B) Coeur D'Alene, ID St. Pius X Church; [F] Coeur D'Alene, ID North Idaho College.
Lachapelle, Alphonsus *s.o.cist.* '82 (ALN) [K] New Ringgold, PA Cistercian Conventual Priory, St. Mary's Priory.
LaChapelle, Hector O. *m.s.* '68 (NY) Phoenicia, NY St. Francis de Sales Church.
LaCharite, Roger J. *s.s.e.* '55 (MOB) [G] Selma, AL Edmundite Fathers.
Lachendro, Vincent *o.f.m.conv.* '63 (BAL) [S] Ellicott City, MD Order of Friars Minor Conventual.
Lachendro, Vincent *o.f.m.conv.* '63 (FgM) Conventual Franciscan Foreign Missions.
Lachowicz, Francis B. '60 (PIT) [4] McKeesport, PA St. Mary Czestochowa Church.
Lachowitzer, Charles V. '90 (STP) Maplewood, MN Presentation of the Blessed Virgin Mary Church.
Lachowski, Joseph *c.m.* '54 (BRK) [134] Brooklyn, NY St. Stanislaus Kostka Church.
Lachowsky, Clement *c.s.sp.* '47 (SB) Hemet, CA Our Lady of the Valley Church; [E] Hemet, CA Holy Ghost Fathers.
Lacienski, Michael (MIL) [P] Burlington, WI Queen of Peace Friary.
Lack, Christopher '90 (CIN) Leave of Absence.
Lackenmier, James *c.s.c.* '64 (BGP) [P] Bridgeport, CT Provincial Offices of the Priests and Brothers of Holy Cross, Eastern Province.
Lackenmier, James *c.s.c.* '64 (P) [B] Portland, OR University of Portland; [L] Portland, OR Holy Cross Fathers & Brothers, C.S.C. - University of Portland.
Lackie, Dan *o.f.m.* (OAK) [A] Berkeley, CA Brother Giles Franciscan Formation Community.
Lackie, Dan *o.f.m.* '96 (SFR) [T] San Francisco, CA St. Anthony Foundation.
Lackner, Bede *o.cist.* '52 (DAL) [K] Irving, TX Cistercian Abbey of Our Lady of Dallas.
Lackner, Francis J. X. '44 (PIT) Retired; [O] Pittsburgh, PA St. John Vianney Manor.
Lackner, Joseph H. *s.m.* '72 (CIN) [M] Dayton, OH Marianist Provincialate; [M] Dayton, OH Marianist Provincialate; [M] Dayton, OH Marianist Provincialate.
Lackner, Msgr. Paul M. '42 (PIT) Retired.
Lackovic, Msgr. Stephen F. '39 (BUF) Retired.
Lacomara, Aelred *c.p.* '57 (FgM) Passionist Foreign Missions.
Lacombe, Robert E. '91 (PRO) Smithfield, RI St. Philip Church.
LaCombe, Terrence (GB) Stangelville, WI St. Therese de Lisieux Church.
LaCorte, Richard P. '87 (FAR) On Duty Outside the Diocese.
LaCosse, Norbert R. '52 (MAR) Retired.
LaCoste, James P. *m.m.* '56 (FgM) Maryknoll Foreign Missions.
Lacovic, Lawrence L. (ALT) [4] Northern Cambria, PA Prince of Peace Church.
Lacroix, Daniel W. '88 (FR) Mansfield, MA St. Mary's Church.
Lacroix, Maurice R. '53 (MAN) Retired.
LaCroix, Robert A., Jr. '98 (DET) Lincoln Park, MI Christ the Good Shepherd Church.
LaCroix, Wilfred L. *s.j.* '69 (KC) [B] Kansas City, MO Rockhurst University; [J] Kansas City, MO Rockhurst Jesuit Community.
LaCrosse, James *s.m.* '67 (WH) [11] Wheeling, WV St. Vincent de Paul's Church.
Lacruz, Alfredo Alvarez '86 (PCE) [A] Ponce, PR Diocesan Seminary; [B] Ponce, PR The Pontifical Catholic University of Puerto Rico.
Lacruz, Cecilio *sch.p.* '59 (SJN) [57] San Juan, PR Santisimo Salvador Church.
Lacy, Aidan '93 (PMB) [1] West Palm Beach, FL Holy Name of Jesus Church.
Laczko, Msgr. T. Ansgar '60 (WDC) [6] Washington, DC Assumption Church.
Ladamus, Robert G. '70 (HRT) Retired.
Ladd, John O. '79 (GAY) Prudenville, MI Our Lady of the Lake Church.
Ladden, Timothy M. '53 (OG) Retired.
Ladewski, Roman *c.s.c.* '40 (FTW) [L] Notre Dame, IN Holy Cross Mission House.
Ladish, Robert W. '53 (HRT) [1] Torrington, CT St. Francis of Assisi Church; [3] Torrington, CT St. Mary's Church.
Ladkau, William D. '84 (CHR) [6] Columbia, SC Good Shepherd Church.
Ladra, Jose '82 (NO) Terrytown, LA Christ the King Church.
Ladzinski, Msgr. Casmir H. '62 (TR) Belmar, NJ St. Rose Church.
Laenen, Henry *o.m.i.* '52 (SAN) Ozona, TX Our Lady of Perpetual Help Church.
Laenen, Joseph C. *o.praem.* '51 (PH) [U] Darby, PA Mercy Catholic Medical Center; [AA] Paoli, PA Daylesford Abbey.
Laesch, Dennis C. '96 (DET) [1] Taylor, MI St. Alfred Church.
LaFache, Anthony '68 (SY) [6] Utica, NY St. Anthony of Padua Church.
LaFavia, Louis M. *c.pp.s.* '47 (WDC) [C] Washington, DC Catholic University of America, The.
LaFay, Michael *o.carm.* '60 (FgM) Carmelite Foreign Missions.
Laferrera, John J. '73 (NEW) Caldwell, NJ St. Aloysius Church.
Laferrera, Robert G. '88 (NEW) Dumont, NJ St. Mary's Church.
Laferriere, Raymond H. '60 (MAN) [3] Manchester, NH St. Anthony of Padua Church; Retired.
Laferty, Charles P. *o.s.a.* '53 (PH) [C] Villanova, PA Villanova University; [AA] Villanova, PA St. Thomas Monastery.
Lafey, Kevin *o.carm.* '72 (FgM) Carmelite Foreign Missions.
Lafey, Kevin *o.carm.* '72 (JOL) [J] Darien, IL Carmelite Provincial Office.
Lafferty, Charles L. '55 (BAL) [O] Timonium, MD Stella Maris.
Lafferty, David M. '85 (OKL) Chandler, OK Our Lady of Sorrows Church.
Lafferty, Msgr. James K. '54 (SC) Ogden, IA St. John's Church.
Lafferty, Msgr. John J. '53 (ALT) Retired.
Lafferty, Owen J. '66 (NY) [61] New York, NY St. Joseph Church.
Laffey, Matthew T. *o.s.b.* '00 (E) St. Marys, PA Queen of the World Church.
LaFlamme, Julien J. '58 (BUR) East Dorset, VT St. Jerome Church; Manchester Center, VT Conversion of St. Paul Church.
Laflamme, Paul C., II '98 (SPR) [6] Springfield, MA Holy Name Church.
LaFleur, Alfred *o.s.a.* '44 (FWT) Hillsboro, TX Our Lady of Mercy Church.
LaFleur, Gerard A. '53 (SPR) [1] Chicopee, MA Assumption Church.
LaFleur, Paul J. '85 (LAF) Carencro, LA Our Lady of the Assumption Church.
Lafond, Donald E. '62 (MAN) [9] Manchester, NH St. George Church.
Lafontaine, James F. *s.j.* '77 (WDC) [M] Washington, DC Leonard Neale House.
Lafontaine, James F. *s.j.* '87 (BO) [W] Boston, MA The Society of Jesus of New England-Provincial Offices.
LaFontaine, Paul A. '72 (STP) [18] St. Paul, MN St. Columba Church; [21] Minneapolis, MN St. Charles Borromeo Church.
LaFontant, Roland '69 (NY) [169] Bronx, NY Our Lady of Angels Church; Bronx, NY U.S.V.A. Medical Center.
LaForest, Conrad V. '72 (MAN) Absent on Sick Leave.
LaForge, Joseph M. (TR) On Duty Outside the Diocese.
LaForge, Joseph M. '66 (WIL) Bellefonte, DE St. Helena Church.
LaForge, Paul *s.v.d.* '58 (FgM) Society of the Divine Word Foreign Missions.
LaFosse, William D. *m.s.* '68 (SPR) [1] Westfield, MA Holy Trinity Church.
Laframboise, Ronald *o.m.i.* '67 (FgM) Oblates Foreign Missions.
Lafrenz, James '54 (ELP) Retired.
Lafrenz, James '54 (LSC) Retired.
Lagace, Raymond R. *o.f.m.* (PRT) Togus, ME Dept. of Veteran Affairs.
Lagan, Hugh '54 (SP) Retired.
Lagana, Msgr. Frank A. '39 (GAL) Retired; [N] Houston, TX St. Dominic Village; [U] Houston, TX St. Mary's Children's Relief Fund.
Lagasse, C. Brian '93 (PRO) [12] Providence, RI St. Edward Church; [1] North Providence, RI St. Anthony Church.
Lagasse, Ronald J. (OAK) Military Chaplains.
Lager, John *o.f.m.cap.* '79 (DEN) [M] Denver, CO St. Francis of Assisi Friary.
Lager, John *o.f.m.cap.* '79 (FgM) Capuchin Foreign Missions.
Lagges, Patrick R. '77 (CHI) [151] Chicago, IL Our Lady of Mercy Church.
Lagiovane, John '92 (NY) [E] New York, NY Monsignor Farrell High School.
Lago, Danilo *s.x.* '77 (FgM) Xaverian Foreign Missions.
Lago, Danilo *s.x.* '77 (PAT) [M] Wayne, NJ Xaverian Missionary Fathers.
Lago, William J.P. '99 (TR) [21] Trenton, NJ St. Raphael Church.
Lagoa, Raul M. '79 (FR) Somerset, MA St. John of God Church.
Lagodinski, Dale '72 (FAR) Wahpeton, ND St. John's Church; [I] Wahpeton, ND State College of Science Newman Student Parish.
Lagomarsino, John *s.s.c.* '70 (SAC) Carmichael, CA St. John the Evangelist Church.
Lagomarsino, Vincent J. *s.j.* '56 (WH) [A] Wheeling, WV Wheeling Jesuit University.
Lagonegro, Msgr. Dominick J. '69 (NY) Hopewell Junction, NY St. Columba Church.
Lagor, Joseph J. '54 (BUR) Retired.
Lagueux, Maurice (MAN) [J] Manchester, NH Mt. Carmel Nursing Home.
Laguna-Vargas, Enrique *o.carm.* '90 (JOL) [J] Darien, IL Carmelite Provincial Office.
Lagututta, Nunzio J. '78 (SJ) On Leave of Absence.

Lah, Peter *s.j.* '95 (CHI) [C] Chicago, IL Jesuit Community at Loyola University of Chicago.
Lahart, Daniel K. *s.j.* '94 (BAL) [W] Baltimore, MD Jesuit Educational Association of Maryland, Inc.
Lahart, Daniel K. *s.j.* '94 (WDC) [E] Washington, DC Gonzaga College High School.
LaHart, Msgr. Richard '52 (PH) West Chester, PA SS. Simon and Jude Church.
LaHart, Msgr. Richard T. '52 (PH) Retired.
Lahens, Albert '95 (MIA) [23] Miami, FL St. John Neumann Church; [1] Hollywood, FL Little Flower Church.
Laheta, Andrew P. '43 (CLV) [55] Cleveland, OH Our Lady of Mercy Church; Retired.
Lahey, John '67 (SAL) Retired.
Lahey, John *c.s.c.* '70 (FTW) [B] Notre Dame, IN University of Notre Dame Du Lac; [J] Notre Dame, IN Holy Cross Community, Corby Hall, University of Notre Dame.
Lahey, Msgr. Maurice '50 (FRS) Retired.
Lahey, Piers M. '82 (SFR) Pacifica, CA Good Shepherd Church.
LaHood, Thomas G. '00 (WDC) Olney, MD St. Peter Church.
Lahoud, Msgr. Joseph F. '59 (SAM) Jamaica Plain, MA Our Lady of the Cedars of Lebanon Church.
Lahout, Francis M. '53 (HBG) [5] Harrisburg, PA Holy Name of Jesus Church.
Lahrs, Carey T. *s.d.s.* '72 (MIL) [59] Milwaukee, WI Mother of Good Counsel Church.
Lai, Doan Van '73 (SD) [7] San Diego, CA Holy Spirit Church.
Laible, Jeffrey G. '88 (PEO) Rantoul, IL St. Malachy's Church.
Laicha, Michael '89 (HBG) [8] Harrisburg, PA Our Lady of the Blessed Sacrament Church.
Laing, Vincent Thu (SAL) Washington, KS St. Augustine's Church.
Laini, Valerian '69 (CHI) Evanston, IL St. Mary Church.
Lair, Gerard P. *o.s.b.* '60 (PAT) Flanders, NJ St. Elizabeth Ann Seton Church; [M] Morristown, NJ St. Mary's Abbey.
Laird, Kenneth W. '75 (BR) Zachary, LA St. John the Baptist Church.
Laird, Martin *o.s.a.* '81 (PH) [C] Villanova, PA Villanova University.
Laird, Martin S. *o.s.a.* '90 (PH) [AA] Villanova, PA St. Thomas Monastery.
Laird, Martin S. *o.s.a.* '91 (CHI) [N] Olympia Fields, IL The Augustinians-Provincialate.
Laird, Peter '97 (STP) [C] St. Paul, MN University of St. Thomas.
Laird, William '75 (ROC) [2] Auburn, NY Sacred Heart Church.
Laird, William F. '75 (ROC) Churchville, NY St. Vincent De Paul Church; [L] Rochester, NY Censores Librorum.
Lajack, Edward F. '68 (CLV) [2] Barberton, OH SS. Cyril and Methodius Church.
Lajack, Jerome M. '66 (CLV) [78] Cleveland, OH St. Wendelin Church.
Lajo, Saturnino *o.m.i.* '63 (SAT) [U] San Antonio, TX Oblate Missions.
Lajoie, David *s.m.* '48 (PRT) Hamlin, ME St. Joseph Church; Van Buren, ME St. Bruno - St. Remi Church.
Lajoie, Marcel *s.m.* '56 (BO) [W] Boston, MA Marist Fathers Lourdes Residence; [BB] Boston, MA Chapel of Our Lady of Lourdes.
Lajoie, Roland *s.m.* '74 (FgM) Marist Foreign Missions.
Lajoie, Roland L. '88 (WOR) Warren, MA St. Paul's Church; West Warren, MA St. Thomas Aquinas Church.
Lakers, John J. *o.f.m.* '58 (SFD) [B] Quincy, IL Quincy University.
Lal, Joseph '95 (SD) [30] San Diego, CA St. Jude Church.
Laliberte, George G. (HRT) Retired.
Laliberte, Robert L. '73 (FAR) Special Assignment; [A] Fargo, ND Cardinal Muench Seminary.
Laliberte, Stephen *o.f.m.cap.* '80 (PAT) [M] Oak Ridge-Milton, NJ St. Stanislaus B. M. Friary.
Laliberte, William F. '43 (BUR) Retired.
Lalic, Paul '58 (BGP) [V] Stamford, CT Villa Maria Retreat.
Lalli, Tony *s.x.* '66 (BO) [W] Holliston, MA Xaverian Missionaries; [BB] Holliston, MA Our Lady of Fatima Shrine.
Lally, Brendan G. *s.j.* '77 (SCR) [C] Scranton, PA University of Scranton; [C] Scranton, PA University of Scranton; [E] Scranton, PA Scranton Preparatory School.
Lally, Campion *o.f.m.* '53 (FgM) Franciscan Foreign Missions.
Lally, Msgr. Dennis '65 (GB) Lebanon Township, WI St. Patrick Church.
Lally, Joachim *c.s.p.* '65 (NY) [DD] Jamaica Estates, NY Paulist Fathers Generalate.
Lally, Martin '78 (DEN) Northglenn, CO Immaculate Heart of Mary Church.
Lally, Owen *c.p.* '59 (BRK) [V] Jamaica, NY Immaculate Conception Monastery.
Lally, Owen *c.p.* '59 (NY) [HH] Jamaica, NY The Fellowship of the Beloved Disciple.
LaLonde, Emile G. '41 (OG) Retired.
Lalonde, Venant *o.f.m.* '54 (NY) [DD] New York, NY Franciscan Friars, Order of Friars Minor, Holy Name Province.
Lalor, Thomas '66 (JKS) [4] Jackson, MS St. Therese Church.
Lam, John *s.d.b.* '71 (SFR) [46] San Francisco, CA SS. Peter and Paul Church.
Lama, Michael '84 (SB) Banning, CA Precious Blood Church.
Lamanna, Alfred '49 (ALB) Retired.
Lamanna, Thomas *s.j.* '97 (SPK) [E] Spokane, WA Gonzaga Preparatory School.
Lamantia, A. Robert '48 (TOL) Retired.
LaMar, Joseph P. *m.m.* '83 (NY) [DD] Maryknoll, NY Maryknoll Fathers and Brothers; [DD] Maryknoll, NY Maryknoll Fathers and Brothers.
LaMarre, Theodore E. '45 (SAG) Retired.
LaMartina, Liborio J. *s.j.* '67 (BAL) [S] Baltimore, MD Jesuit Fathers and Brothers Maryland Provincial Curia.
Lamas, Rodolfo '80 (SJN) [7] Guaynabo, PR Divino Nino Jesus Church.
Lamaute, Serges *s.d.b.* (CHI) [103] Chicago, IL St. John Bosco Church.
LaMazza, Carmen G. *m.m.* '55 (FgM) Maryknoll Foreign Missions.
Lamb, Bruce '89 (SR) Willits, CA St. Anthony Church.
Lamb, Gary E. '83 (MEM) Military Chaplains.
Lamb, Louis J. '61 (OKL) Ardmore, OK St. Mary Church.
Lamb, Matthew L. '62 (MIL) On Duty Outside the Archdiocese.
Lamb, Patrick H. (ALN) [C] Easton, PA Notre Dame High School.
Lamb, Patrick H. '83 (ALN) Miller Heights, PA Sacred Heart of Jesus Church.
Lamb, Thomas J. '71 (NEW) [M] South Orange, NJ Opus Dei.
Lamb, Thomas J. '71 (PRO) [O] Providence, RI Prelature of the Holy Cross and Opus Dei.
Lamb, Weston J. *o.ss.t.* '81 (BAL) [S] Baltimore, MD Holy Trinity Monastery.
Lamb, Weston J. *o.ss.t.* '81 (SAV) Jesup, GA St. Joseph Church.
Lambeck, Robert W. *s.j.* '49 (MIL) [P] Milwaukee, WI Jesuit Community at Marquette University.
Lamberson, Bryan T. '00 (L) [1] Louisville, KY Cathedral of the Assumption.
Lambert, Cornelius '83 (CAM) [4] Vineland, NJ St. Isidore Church.
Lambert, Curtis '74 (CHI) [149] Chicago, IL Our Lady of Lourdes Church.
Lambert, James J. '80 (PT) Panama City, FL St. Dominic Church.
Lambert, James L. *s.j.* '66 (NO) [P] New Orleans, LA Jesuit Provincial Office.
Lambert, James L. *s.j.* '66 (SAT) [17] San Antonio, TX Our Lady of Guadalupe Church.
Lambert, John C. '69 (BWN) Retired.
Lambert, John C. '84 (SCR) Dallas, PA Gate of Heaven Church.
Lambert, Leo M. '45 (MIL) Retired.
Lambert, Louis J. *s.j.* '66 (SFE) [6] Albuquerque, NM Immaculate Conception Church.
Lambert, Peter '72 (MIA) [6] Fort Lauderdale, FL St. Clement Church.
Lambert, Peter '79 (DUL) Military Chaplains.
Lambert, Peter S. '79 (BIS) [1] Minot, ND Minot Air Force Base Chapel Church.
Lambert, Raymond P. '55 (BO) Senior Priests.
Lambert, Richard '75 (PBR) [4] Pittsburgh, PA St. John Chrysostom Church.
Lambert, Richard D. '80 (CR) Mahnomen, MN St. Michael's Church.
Lambert, Richard T. *s.j.* '67 (FgM) Provinces.
Lambert, Rollins E. '49 (CHI) Retired.
Lambert, Theodore '76 (STO) Manteca, CA St. Anthony Church; Stockton, CA Karl Holton School.
Lambert, William '55 (RC) Retired.
Lamberty, Darrell '79 (SFS) Arlington, SD St. John the Evangelist Church; Ramona, SD St. William of Vercelli Church.
Lamberty, Philip J. *o.p.* '59 (STL) [P] St. Louis, MO St. Dominic Priory.
Lambertz, Wilfrid *o.s.b.* '58 (SFS) [F] Marvin, SD Blue Cloud Abbey.
Lambeth, K. Michael '94 (TR) [14] Trenton, NJ St. Gregory the Great Church.
Lambour, Stephen *c.s.c.* '55 (ORL) Retired; [F] Cocoa Beach, FL Holy Cross Fathers, Eastern Priests Province.
Lamby, Robert J. '75 (CLV) Mentor, OH St. Mary of the Assumption Church.
Lamela, Juan *c.m.* '62 (PCE) [8] Ponce, PR La Milagrosa Church.
Lamendola, Salvatore R. '90 (BAL) [A] Emmitsburg, MD Mount St. Mary's Seminary; [A] Emmitsburg, MD Mount St. Mary's Seminary.
Lamica, Alan J. '78 (OG) Keene, NY St. Brendan Church.
Lamitie, James F. '53 (OG) Retired.
Lamitie, Robert O. '57 (OG) Ray Brook, NY Adirondack Correctional Facility.
Lamm, Timothy J. *o.s.b.* '54 (SEA) [L] Lacey, WA St. Martin's Abbey.
Lamm, William F. *s.j.* '57 (BAL) [S] Baltimore, MD Jesuit Fathers and Brothers Maryland Provincial Curia.
Lammeier, Francis G. '55 (CIN) Retired.
Lammers, Donald W. '66 (JC) [2] Jefferson City, MO St. Peter Church.
Lammers, Ralph A. '63 (OM) Absent on Sick Leave.
Lammert, Edward H. *o.f.m.* '58 (LEX) Cumberland, KY St. Stephen Church; Harlan, KY Holy Trinity Church; Lynch, KY Church of the Resurrection .
LaMoine, Gary W. '81 (CR) Fosston, MN St. Mary's Church.
Lamonde, Joseph R. '74 (PIT) Military Chaplains.
Lamonde, Msgr. Joseph R. '74 (STA) [3] Jacksonville, FL Christ the King Church.
LaMontagne, Bernard L. '63 (PRO) On Duty Outside the Diocese.
Lamonthe, Daniel '69 (MAN) [E] Salem, NH St. Joseph Regional School.
Lamore, Victor E. '80 (OG) Absent on Sick Leave.
Lamoreaux, Roger *o.m.i.* '70 (BO) [9] Lowell, MA St. Marie Church; [16] Lowell, MA Sacred Heart Church.
LaMorte, Joseph P. '81 (NY) [3] Poughkeepsie, NY Holy Trinity Church.
Lamothe, C. Romero '48 (WOR) Retired.
Lamothe, Daniel O. '62 (MAN) Salem, NH St. Joseph Church.
Lamothe, Donat R. *a.a.* '62 (WOR) [N] Worcester, MA Assumptionists of Assumption College.
Lamothe, Miller *s.j.* '97 (BAL) [S] Baltimore, MD Ferdinand Wheeler Jesuit Community.
LaMothe, Philip R. '55 (BUR) Shelburne, VT St. Catherine of Siena Church.
LaMountain, Michael V. '76 (PRO) Absent on Leave.
Lamoureux, Roger '62 (SR) [2] Santa Rosa, CA Holy Spirit Church.
Lamoureux, Roger J. *o.m.i.* '59 (BO) [W] Lowell, MA Missionary Oblates of Mary Immaculate.
Lamoureux, Roger J. *o.m.i.* '59 (NOR) Willimantic, CT St. Mary Church.
Lamp, Edward '82 (SP) [15] Tampa, FL St. Peter Claver Church.
Lampe, Msgr. Irvin F. '43 (WCH) Retired.
Lampe, Stephen '82 (MIL) On Leave.
Lampert, Robert E. '65 (STL) On Duty Outside the Archdiocese.
Lampert, Vincent '91 (IND) [37] Indianapolis, IN St. Therese of the Infant Jesus (Little Flower) Church.
Lamping, Thomas E. '84 (CHI) [177] Chicago, IL Queen of Angels Church.
Lamprea, Gefford C. '00 (SPC) [1] Cape Girardeau, MO Cathedral of St. Mary.
Lamprich, Mark *m.i.c.* '90 (CHL) [1] Greensboro, NC Our Lady of Grace Church.
Lampron, Alfred J. '75 (PAT) Pequannock, NJ Holy Spirit Church.
Lampron, Maurice W. '63 (MAN) Retired.
Lamy, Raymond J. '81 (MAN) Military Chaplains.
Lamy, Robert E. *c.m.* '51 (NO) [P] New Orleans, LA Vincentian Fathers.
Lanahan, Daniel *o.f.m.* '62 (NEW) [N] Hohokus, NJ St. Anthony of Padua.
Lancaster, Leo '54 (WOR) Shrewsbury, MA St. Mary's Church.
Lancaster, Robert '99 (SFE) Dixon, NM St. Anthony Church; Penasco, NM San Antonio de Padua Church.
Lancellotti, Vincent A. '68 (NY) Elmsford, NY Our Lady of Mt. Carmel Church.
Landa, Salvador '94 (ORG) [7] Santa Ana, CA St. Barbara's Church.
Landauer, Joseph '78 (PIT) [N] Pittsburgh, PA Opus Dei.
Lander, Mark '00 (SB) Barstow, CA St. Joseph Church.
Landewe, Robert A. '59 (SPC) Mount Vernon, MO St. Susanne Church.
Landeza, Jayson '87 (OAK) [7] Oakland, CA St. Columba's Church.
Landgraff, Thomas A. *o.s.f.s.* '64 (TOL) [37] Toledo, OH St. Pius X Church.
Landherr, Clayton R. '91 (DUB) Andrew, IA St. John Church; La Motte, IA Holy Rosary Church; Otter Creek, IA St. Lawrence Church; St. Theresa, IA St. Theresa's Church; Sylvia, IA Assumption Church.
Landi, L. Joseph '90 (SFR) [T] San Francisco, CA Charismatic Movement.
Landi, Lodovico Joseph '90 (SFR) [11] San Francisco, CA St. Cecilia Church.
Landini, Laurence C. *o.s.m.* '61 (COL) [A] Columbus, OH Pontifical College Josephinum.
Landini, Lawrence *o.f.m.* '61 (CIN) [M] Cincinnati, OH St. Francis Seraph Friary.

Landini, Lawrence *o.f.m.* '61 (FgM) Franciscan Foreign Missions.
Lando, Camillo *c.s.* '66 (BO) [1] Everett, MA St. Anthony Church.
Landrau, Jose Antonio '90 (SJN) [35] San Juan, PR San Luis Rey Church.
Landreau, Edward J. '57 (LA) Retired.
Landreville, Norbert B. '58 (MAR) Retired.
Landry, Alduce '80 (HT) Permanent Deacons.
Landry, Charles R. '83 (BR) St. Francisville, LA Our Lady of Mount Carmel Church.
Landry, David J. '87 (FR) Absent on Sick Leave.
Landry, Francis *c.p.* (CHI) [B] Chicago, IL The Catholic Theological Union at Chicago.
Landry, Francis *c.p.* '76 (CHI) [N] Chicago, IL Passionist Community-CTU.
Landry, Gary S. *c.m.* '73 (LA) [A] Camarillo, CA St. John's Seminary College of the Archdiocese of Los Angeles; [Q] Montebello, CA Vincentian Fathers & Brothers.
Landry, George *s.m.a.* '54 (NEW) [N] Tenafly, NJ Society of African Missions, Provincialate, S.M.A. Fathers.
Landry, Msgr. George A. '43 (HT) Retired.
Landry, Leroy *o.m.i.* (NOR) [F] Willimantic, CT Missionary Oblates of Mary Immaculate.
Landry, Leroy *o.m.i.* '61 (FgM) Oblates Foreign Missions.
Landry, Maurice A. *s.m.m.* '41 (RVC) [M] Bay Shore, NY Montfort Missionaries.
Landry, Msgr. Michael '48 (NO) Retired.
Landry, Oneil Anthony '47 (LAF) Centerville, LA St. Joseph Church; Retired.
Landry, Philip G. '88 (NO) Arabi, LA St. Louise De Marillac Church.
Landry, Ralph James '62 (LAF) Retired.
Landry, Richard *m.s.* '69 (FR) [I] Attleboro, MA La Salette Shrine; [K] Attleboro, MA La Salette Center for Christian Living.
Landry, Roger J. (FR) [B] Fall River, MA Bishop Connolly High School.
Landry, Roger J. '99 (FR) [3] Fall River, MA Espirito Santo Church.
Landry, Thomas '83 (WOR) [3] Worcester, MA Blessed Sacrament Church; Worcester, MA Memorial Hospital.
Landsberger, Nicholas '61 (SCL) Little Falls, MN St. Mary Church.
Landsberger, Robert '57 (SCL) Motley, MN St. Michael's Church.
Landwerlen, Paul '54 (IND) St. Vincent de Paul, IN St. Vincent de Paul Church.
Landwermeyer, Bart '56 (FWT) Valley View, TX St. John Church; Retired; [H] Crowley, TX St. Francis Village, Inc.
Landwermeyer, Francis M. *s.j.* '66 (SAT) [32] San Antonio, TX St. Cecilia Church.
Landy, Joseph V. *s.j.* '54 (NY) [DD] New York, NY Murray-Weigel Hall.
Lane, Bernard J. '60 (BO) Senior Priests.
Lane, Brian '89 (RC) [3] Rapid City, SD St. Therese the Little Flower Church; [D] Rapid City, SD Priest Retirement and Aid Association.
Lane, Edmund C. *s.s.p.* '64 (NY) [B] New York, NY Society of St. Paul.
Lane, Msgr. Frank P. '67 (COL) [A] Columbus, OH Pontifical College Josephinum.
Lane, George A. *s.j.* '67 (CHI) [N] Chicago, IL Chicago Province of the Society of Jesus-Provincial Office; [X] Chicago, IL Loyola Press.
Lane, James H. '62 (BO) [11] Boston, MA St. Augustine Church; [46] Boston, MA St. Monica Church.
Lane, John Thomas *s.s.s.* '92 (GAL) [25] Houston, TX Corpus Christi Church.
Lane, Mark '74 (RIC) On Special or Other Diocesan Assignment.
Lane, Mark J. *c.o.* '83 (BRK) [22] Brooklyn, NY St. Boniface Church; [V] Brooklyn, NY Oratory of Saint Philip Neri, Congregation Pontifical Rite.
Lane, Michael '74 (JOL) Elmhurst, IL Visitation Church.
Lane, Robert C. '69 (STL) St. Peters, MO All Saints Church.
Lane, Thomas V. '64 (YAK) Moxee City, WA Holy Rosary Church.
Lane, Timothy R. *c.j.* '95 (LA) [B] Santa Maria, CA St. Joseph Seminary (Josephite Fathers' Novitiate); [D] Santa Maria, CA St. Joseph High School.
Lane, William '50 (SEA) Retired.
Lanergan, James F. '61 (BO) [3] Plymouth, MA St. Mary Church; Bridgewater, MA Bridgewater State Hospital & Treatment Center.
Lanese, John R. '73 (ALB) Clifton Park, NY St. Edward the Confessor Church.
Lanese, Pasquale *o.m.i.* '53 (BWN) [1] Brownsville, TX Immaculate Conception Church.
Lang, B. Benedict *o.s.b.* '53 (PRO) [P] Portsmouth, RI Abbey of St. Gregory the Great.
Lang, Brian E. '98 (SY) [1] Endicott, NY Our Lady of Good Counsel Church.
Lang, Charles '75 (CIN) Fairborn, OH Mary Help of Christians Church.
Lang, Charles E. '65 (DUB) Anamosa, IA St. Patrick's Church; Belle Plaine, IA St. Michael Church; [2] Cedar Rapids, IA All Saints Church; Chelsea, IA St. Joseph's Church; [D] Cedar Rapids, IA Xavier High School Foundation.
Lang, Msgr. Cordell J. '79 (MOB) [12] Mobile, AL St. Mary Church.
Lang, Frederick *c.pp.s.* '54 (CIN) [M] Dayton, OH Provincial Office of the Cincinnati Province of the Society of the Precious Blood.
Lang, Henry A. '46 (BRK) [235] Queens, NY St. Robert Bellarmine Church; Retired.
Lang, Hugh J. '56 (PIT) [5] Munhall, PA St. Therese of Lisieux Church.
Lang, James P. (SY) [16] Syracuse, NY St. James Church.
Lang, James Paul '75 (SY) Special Assignment.
Lang, James Paul '75 (Y) Windham, OH St. Michael's Church.
Lang, Joseph J. '65 (CLV) Released from Diocesan Assignment.
Lang, Joseph R. *m.m.* '52 (NY) [DD] Maryknoll, NY Maryknoll Fathers and Brothers.
Lang, Jovian *o.f.m* '46 (FWT) [I] Crowley, TX St. Maximilian Kolbe Friary.
Lang, Julius '42 (FAR) Retired.
Lang, Julius '42 (VEN) [1] Naples, FL St. Ann Church.
Lang, Leonard P. '75 (TR) Asbury Park, NJ Holy Spirit Church.
Lang, Maurice *o.m.i.* '90 (MAN) [K] Les Cayes, Haiti Paroisse Ste. Anne.
Lang, Michael '83 (TR) New Lisbon, NJ New Jersey State Colony.
Lang, Michael P. '92 (TR) Tabernacle, NJ Holy Eucharist Church.
Lang, Raymond '43 (SCL) Retired.
Langan, James J. '57 (SCR) Retired.
Langan, John P. *s.j.* '72 (DET) [K] Detroit, MI Jesuit Provincial Office-Detroit Province of the Society of Jesus.
Langan, John P. *s.j.* '72 (WDC) [M] Washington, DC The Jesuit Community at Georgetown University.
Langan, Patrick *l.c.* '91 (LA) [Q] Pasadena, CA Legionaries of Christ.
Langan, Thomas F. '59 (HBG) Abbottstown, PA Immaculate Heart of Mary Church.
Langan, Vincent F. '60 (SCR) South Waverly, PA St. John the Evangelist Church.
Langan, William J.P. '77 (SCR) [3] Nanticoke, PA St. Francis of Assisi Church.
Langdon, Robert H. '56 (NEW) Retired; [N] Rutherford, NJ St. John Vianney Residence for Priests.
Lange, Donald F. '70 (MAD) Barneveld, WI Immaculate Conception Church; Ridgeway, WI St. Bridget Church.
Lange, George O. '57 (WOR) Westborough, MA St. Luke the Evangelist Church.
Lange, John J. *m.m.* '58 (FgM) Maryknoll Foreign Missions.
Lange, John W. *s.j.* '61 (SCR) [C] Scranton, PA University of Scranton.
Lange, L. Joseph '59 (PRT) Mexico, ME St. Theresa Church.
Lange, Lawrence P. '63 (TLS) Retired.
Lange, Maurice *o.m.i.* '90 (SFD) [1] Alton, IL SS. Peter and Paul Church.
Lange, Milton R. '52 (LR) Retired.
Lange, Raymond L. '50 (WOR) Retired.
Lange, Robert A. '86 (ARL) Woodbridge, VA Our Lady of Angels Church.
Lange, Ronald *s.v.d.* '71 (FgM) Society of the Divine Word Foreign Missions.
Lange, Timothy J. '61 (OM) Stanton, NE St. Peter Church; [G] Norfolk, NE Faith Regional Health Services.
Lange, William B. '92 (PH) West Chester, PA St. Agnes Church.
Langelier, Msgr. Gerald J. '61 (BRK) [214] Queens, NY Our Lady of Mercy Church.
Langell, Michael '68 (NSH) [L] Nashville, TN Glenmary Department of Pastoral Services.
Langenbrunner, Norman '70 (CIN) Fairfield, OH Sacred Heart of Jesus Church.
Langenderfer, Carl J. *o.f.m.* '71 (CIN) [21] Cincinnati, OH St. Clement Church; [M] Cincinnati, OH St. Clement Friary.
Langenderfer, Norman *s.j.* '54 (FgM) Provinces.
Langenfeld, Thomas G. *c.s.v.* '60 (LAV) [1] Las Vegas, NV Guardian Angel Church.
Langer, Thomas E. '56 (LC) Gays Mills, WI St. Mary Church; Rolling Ground, WI St. Philip Church.
Langerholz, Callistus *o.f.m.* '35 (CHI) [N] Lemont, IL The Slovene Franciscan Fathers, Order of Friars Minor, Commissariat of the Holy Cross.
Langevin, Fernand *m.s.* '48 (FR) [I] Attleboro, MA La Salette Provincial House.
Langford, Terry L. '96 (L) [61] Louisville, KY Our Mother of Sorrows Church.
Langhals, Henry *c.pp.s.* '37 (CIN) [B] Carthagena, OH St. Charles.
Langhans, Victor E. '84 (HEL) Kalispell, MT St. Matthew Church.
Langheim, Albert *o.f.m.* '55 (GAY) Harbor Springs, MI Holy Childhood of Jesus Church.
Langhorst, Randall L. '92 (LIN) Weston, NE St. John Nepomucene Church.
Langille, Justin '80 (SD) Unassigned.
Langley, Barry J. *o.f.m.* '94 (WIL) [7] Wilmington, DE St. Joseph's R.C. Church of Wilmington, Inc.; [10] Wilmington, DE St. Paul's Church; [N] Wilmington, DE The Franciscan Center.
Langley, Terence *s.c.j.* '79 (BO) Carlisle, MA St. Irene Church.
Langley, Terence *s.c.j.* '79 (MIL) [P] Hales Corners, WI Priests of the Sacred Heart.
Langlinais, J. Willis *s.m.* '52 (SAT) [C] San Antonio, TX St. Mary's University of San Antonio, Texas; [M] San Antonio, TX Marianist Residence.
Langlois, Charles (LAF) [1] New Iberia, LA St. Peter Church.
Langlois, Frederick M. '91 (HRT) [4] Milford, CT St. Mary's Church.
Langlois, John A. *o.p.* '91 (PRO) [P] Providence, RI St. Thomas Aquinas Priory at Providence College.
Langlois, William A. '74 (GR) Grand Haven, MI St. Patrick's Church.
Langsch, Gerold *i.sch.* '72 (CC) [J] Corpus Christi, TX Secular Institute of the Schoenstatt Fathers aka Schoenstatt Fathers.
Langsch, Gerold M. *c.c.* '72 (MIL) [T] Waukesha, WI Secular Institute of Schoenstatt Fathers.
Langsdorf, Karl '72 (CHI) [N] Chicago, IL St. Patrick's Missionary Society.
Langsfeld, Msgr. Paul J. '77 (BAL) [A] Emmitsburg, MD Mount St. Mary's Seminary; [A] Emmitsburg, MD Mount St. Mary's Seminary.
Langsfeld, Msgr. Paul J. '77 (WDC) On Duty Outside the Archdiocese.
Langston, Micheas *o.s.b.* '65 (IND) [J] St. Meinrad, IN St. Meinrad Archabbey.
Langton, Bernard F. *o.p.* '69 (PRO) [P] Providence, RI St. Thomas Aquinas Priory at Providence College.
Langweld, John *o.f.m.cap.* '46 (NY) [DD] Yonkers, NY St. Clare Friary.
LaNier, Michael L. '83 (LA) On Sick Leave.
Lanigan, Leo *c.ss.r.* '44 (ORL) [F] New Smyrna Beach, FL St. Alphonsus Villa-Redemptorist Fathers and Brothers.
Lanigan, Patrick J. '51 (SAC) Retired and in Senior Ministry.
Lankford, Michael G. '92 (TR) West Long Branch, NJ St. Jerome Church.
Lannan, Paul A. '66 (LA) [87] Los Angeles, CA St. Paul the Apostle Church.
Lanning, Michael J. '78 (CLV) [4] Parma, OH St. Columbkille Church.
Lannon, Timothy R. *s.j.* '86 (MIL) [P] Milwaukee, WI Jesuit Community at Marquette University.
LaNoue, Bertrand *o.s.b.* '52 (KCK) Atchison, KS St. Joseph's Church; St. Patrick, KS St. Patrick's Church.
Lanphear, William *o.s.f.s.* '63 (LAN) [H] Ann Arbor, MI St. Joseph Mercy Hospital.
Lansang, Ferdinand *o.carm.* '96 (LA) [3] North Hollywood, CA St. Jane Frances de Chantal Church.
Lanser, Jerome E. '58 (MIL) Retired.
Lanser, Wilbert *o.f.m.cap.* '59 (FgM) Capuchin Foreign Missions.
Lantry, Jerome *o.c.d.* '46 (LA) Alhambra, CA St. Therese Church.
Lantry, Stephen C. *s.j.* '81 (P) [L] Portland, OR Jesuit Provincial Office (Society of Jesus, Oregon Prov.).
Lantsberger, James *o.m.i.* '57 (SR) Imola, CA Napa State Hospital.
Lantsberger, John '76 (SFS) Watertown, SD Holy Name Church.
Lantz, David S. '78 (SFD) [3] Springfield, IL Christ The King Church; [C] Springfield, IL Springfield College in Illinois.
Lanuevo, Tarcisio D. '56 (OAK) Retired.
Lanuevo, Victor '75 (HON) Military Chaplains.
Lanz, Mathias F. '94 (FAR) Leeds, ND St. Vincent de Paul Church.
Lanz, Placid *o.a.r.* (LA) [Q] Oxnard, CA St. Augustine Priory O.A.R.
Lanza, Daniel A. *m.m.* '59 (NY) [DD] Maryknoll, NY Maryknoll Fathers and Brothers.
Lanza, Steven M. '81 (CHI) [141] Chicago, IL Notre Dame Church.
Lanzaderas, Francisco H. '82 (NY) [211] Staten Island, NY St. Joseph, St. Thomas Church.
Lanzalaco, Richard C. *c.s.b.* '87 (ROC) [I] Rochester, NY Basilian Residence.
Lanzrath, Curt C. *o.f.m.* '54 (AUS) [H] Brenham, TX Order of Friars Minor; [I] Brenham, TX Monastery of St. Clare.
Lanzrath, John *o.f.m.* '56 (LSC) Roswell, NM St. Peter Church.
Lanzrath, John P. (WCH) [4] Wichita, KS Christ the King Church.
Lao, Jonathan (WDC) [15] Washington, DC St. Gabriel Church.

LaPalme, Paul M. '97 (ALX) On Duty Outside the Diocese.
LaPalme, Paul M. '97 (WOR) Webster, MA St. Joseph's Basilica Church.
Lapan, Robert '60 (BUR) Retired.
LaPastina, Cyprian P. '97 (BGP) [4] Danbury, CT St. Joseph Church.
LaPata, Richard C. *o.p.* '59 (CHI) [D] Oak Park, IL Fenwick High School; [N] River Forest, IL St. Thomas Aquinas Priory.
Lape, Lydell T '90 (OM) Butte, NE SS. Peter and Paul Church.
Lape, Steve W. '99 (ROC) Henrietta, NY Church of the Good Shepherd.
Lapensky, John G. '77 (STP) Veseli, MN Most Holy Trinity Church.
LaPenta, Charles A. *o.s.f.s.* '54 (TOL) [K] Toledo, OH Oblates of St. Francis de Sales.
Lapera, John M. '84 (SCR) [15] Scranton, PA St. Joseph's Church.
Laperle, Theodore R. '54 (WOR) [2] Fitchburg, MA St. Bernard's Church; Retired.
LaPierre, David *o.f.m.cap.* '69 (FRS) Fresno, CA Community Hospital, Veterans' Hospital & University Medical Center.
Lapierre, Yves '61 (PMB) Palm Beach, FL St. Edward Church.
Lapinski, Daniel A. '79 (BUF) [10] Cheektowaga, NY Queen of Martyrs Church.
LaPlante, David W. '78 (OM) Bancroft, NE Holy Cross Church; Lyons, NE St. Joseph Church.
Laplante, Eugene V. *a.a.* '58 (WOR) [N] Worcester, MA Assumptionists of Assumption College.
Laplante, Jean-Paul '50 (BUR) Retired.
LaPlante, Joseph A. '54 (WIN) Retired; [A] Winona, MN Immaculate Heart of Mary Seminary.
Laplante, Laurent R. '57 (PRT) Kennebunk, ME St. Martha's Church.
LaPlante, Lawrence *s.v.d.* '67 (FgM) Society of the Divine Word Foreign Missions.
Laplante, Philip *s.m.* '48 (BO) [55] Boston, MA Our Lady of Victories Church; [W] Boston, MA Marist Fathers of Our Lady of Victories (Boston Prov.).
LaPlante, Robert J. '95 (CR) Roseau, MN Sacred Heart Church.
LaPlante, Roland M. '62 (HRT) South Meriden, CT Holy Angels Church.
Lapointe, J. Donald '67 (SPR) [8] Chicopee, MA St. Patrick's Church.
LaPointe, John G. '72 (PRO) [3] Johnston, RI St. Robert Bellarmine Church.
LaPointe, Laurence A.M. '70 (NOR) [K] Willimantic, CT Campus Ministry; [K] Willimantic, CT Campus Ministry.
Lapointe, Leo *s.m.* '51 (BO) [Y] Framingham, MA The Marist House.
Lapomarda, Vincent A. *s.j.* '64 (WOR) [N] Worcester, MA Jesuits of Holy Cross College, Inc.
LaPore, Arthur '76 (JOL) [8] Joliet, IL St. Anthony Church.
Laporta, Ross A. '51 (BAL) [57] Baltimore, MD St. Mark Church.
LaPorte, Gerard B. *c.ss.r.* '83 (NO) [23] New Orleans, LA St. Alphonsus Church; [6] New Orleans, LA St. Mary's Assumption Church; [7] New Orleans, LA St. Mary's Chapel Church.
Laporte, Paul J. '65 (PRO) Coventry, RI St. Vincent de Paul Church.
Lappe, Derek '00 (SEA) Aberdeen, WA St. Mary Church; Aberdeen, WA SS. Peter and Paul Church; Hoquiam, WA Our Lady of Good Help Church; Ocean Shores, WA St. Jerome Church.
LaPrad, Steve '95 (KNX) Lenoir City, TN St. Thomas the Apostle Church.
Laptuta, Demetrius *c.ss.r.* '45 (STF) Niagara Falls, NY Protection of B.V.M. Church.
Lara, Delfino '69 (LA) Santa Maria, CA St. John Neumann Church.
Lara, Gustavo (LA) [54] Los Angeles, CA St. Camillus De Lellis Church.
Lara, Gustavo '59 (LA) [26] Los Angeles, CA Our Lady of Guadalupe Church; Los Angeles, CA L.A. County/ University of Southern California Hospital.
Lara, Msgr. Jaime C. '57 (SP) Retired.
Lara, Msgr. James C. '57 (SP) Brandon, FL Church of the Nativity.
Lara, Santiago G. '72 (LA) [Q] Los Angeles, CA Guadalupe Missioners Procure.
LaRaia, Joseph P. '46 (BO) Senior Priests.
Larche, James M. '91 (OG) Absent on Leave.
Lardner, Gerald V. *s.s.* '67 (BAL) [S] Baltimore, MD Sulpician Provincial House.
Laredo, Leopoldo *sch.p.* '40 (SJN) [57] San Juan, PR Santisimo Salvador Church.
Larena, Ismael '47 (PCE) Santa Isabel, PR St. James Church.
Large, John J. '75 (PH) Norwood, PA St. Gabriel Church.
Largent, Jeffery '84 (FTW) Culver, IN St. Mary of the Lake Church.
Largente, Laurent '59 (SJ) Retired.
Larger, Raymond E. '77 (CIN) [38] Cincinnati, OH St. James the Greater Church.
Larignan, Ronald *o.m.i.* '59 (FgM) Oblates Foreign Missions.
Lariviere, Robert D. '78 (PRT) [5] Lewiston, ME St. Patrick's Church; [6] Lewiston, ME SS. Peter and Paul Church.
Larkin, Msgr. Alexander C. '67 (SJ) Saratoga, CA Sacred Heart Church.
Larkin, Bartholomew *o.carm.* '58 (VEN) Grove City, FL St. Francis of Assisi Church.
Larkin, Donald L. *s.j.* '66 (FgM) Provinces.
Larkin, Edward A. *s.j.* '54 (OM) [K] Omaha, NE Jesuit Community at Creighton University.
Larkin, Ernest *o.carm.* '46 (PHX) [6] Phoenix, AZ St. Agnes Church.
Larkin, James *m.s.a.* '90 (NOR) [F] Cromwell, CT Society of the Missionaries of the Holy Apostles.
Larkin, James *m.ss.a.* '90 (NY) White Plains, NY St. Agnes Hospital.
Larkin, John P. '44 (NY) Retired.
Larkin, John R. *o.carm.* '51 (PHX) [G] Phoenix, AZ Carmelite Community.
Larkin, Joseph M. '57 (SY) Minetto, NY Our Lady of Perpetual Help Church.
Larkin, Kevin J. '59 (LA) Sherman Oaks, CA St. Francis de Sales Church.
Larkin, Michael J. '59 (STA) [12] Jacksonville, FL Prince of Peace Church.
Larkin, Michael T. '68 (SC) Special Assignment.
Larkin, Patrick '57 (WCH) Retired.
Larkin, Richard '47 (STP) Retired.
Larkin, Msgr. Robert W. '73 (NY) [193] Bronx, NY Visitation Church.
Larkin, Ronald *m.s.c.* '61 (SB) Special or Other Diocesan Assignment.
Larkin, William J. *s.j.* '52 (BO) [W] Weston, MA Campion Health Center, Inc.
Larko, Ronald P. '82 (PBR) McKees Rocks, PA Holy Ghost Church.
Larmann, Marian E. *o.s.b.* '47 (NO) St. Benedict, LA St. Benedict Church; [P] St. Benedict, LA St. Joseph Abbey.
Larmore, Donald E. '63 (GI) [2] Grand Island, NE Blessed Sacrament Church.
Larner, James M. '57 (BO) [23] Boston, MA St. Gregory Church.
LaRocca, Frank *s.j.* '98 (NY) [DD] New York, NY "America;" Residence and publication office of the America Press.
LaRocca, Jack '88 (SJ) San Jose, CA Detention Ministry for Juveniles.
LaRocca, John J. *s.j.* '75 (CIN) [M] Cincinnati, OH Jesuit Community at Xavier University.
LaRocca, Msgr. Vincent (BRK) Retired.
LaRocca, Msgr. Vincent R. '49 (BRK) Released from Diocesan Assignment.
Laroche, Christopher J. '95 (PRT) On Leave.
Laroche, Leonidas B. '61 (BUR) St. Albans, VT Immaculate Conception Church.
Larochelle, Alphonse *m.s.* '59 (HON) Kekaha, HI St. Theresa Church.
Larochelle, Maurice R. '87 (MAN) Londonderry, NH St. Mark the Evangelist Church.
LaRocque, Benedict J. *o.s.b.* '42 (KCK) [H] Atchison, KS St. Benedict's Abbey.
LaRocque, Benedict J. *o.s.b.* '42 (OM) Retired.
LaRocque, Leonard *a.a.* '56 (WOR) [N] Worcester, MA Assumptionists (Augustinians of the Assumption).
Larocque, Paul M. '45 (TUC) Retired.
LaRocque, Msgr. Richard P. '63 (NOR) Old Lyme, CT Christ the King Church.
LaRosa, John J. '81 (PH) [153] Philadelphia, PA St. Timothy Church.
LaRose, Edward M. '66 (HRT) [2] New Britain, CT Holy Cross Church; Retired.
LaRose, Etienne *o.m.i.* '41 (WDC) [M] Washington, DC Missionary Oblates of Mary Immaculate.
LaRousse, William J. *m.m.* '80 (FgM) Maryknoll Foreign Missions.
Larran, Francisco *o.s.a.* '50 (MGZ) San German, PR St. Rose of Lima Church.
Larrea, Hector '94 (NEW) On Duty Outside the Archdiocese.
Larrea, Hector '94 (TR) Keyport, NJ Jesus the Lord Church; [B] Holmdel, NJ St. John Vianney High School.
Larrea, Luis Eduardo *m.f.e.* '77 (TYL) [2] Tyler, TX St. Peter Claver Church.
Larreategui, Jose Luis *sch.p.* '53 (PCE) Jayuya, PR Our Lady of Monserrate Church; [B] Ponce, PR The Pontifical Catholic University of Puerto Rico.
Larrivee, Leo J. *s.s.* '77 (BAL) [67] Baltimore, MD Our Lady of the Angels Catholic Community Church.
Larrivee, Leo J. *s.s.* '77 (SEA) On Duty Outside the Archdiocese.
Larroque, Msgr. H. Alexandre '55 (LAF) [I] Lafayette, LA Discalced Carmelites.
Larry, Anthony J. *o.s.f.s.* '67 (CHL) [4] Greensboro, NC St. Paul the Apostle Church.
Larsen, Kevin J. '93 (ARL) Burke, VA Church of the Nativity.
Larson, James *l.c.* '98 (CHI) [N] Lemont, IL Legion of Christ.
Larson, James F. '57 (RCK) Retired.
Larson, Jan '56 (SEA) Snoqualmie, WA Our Lady of Sorrows Church.
Larson, Lawrence A. '77 (BGP) Newtown, CT St. Rose of Lima Church.
Larson, Paul '79 (DUL) [4] Duluth, MN Our Lady of Mercy Church; [13] Duluth, MN St. Mary Star of the Sea Church; [15] Duluth, MN St. Peter's Church.
Larue, Charles '93 (SAN) Retired.
Larue, Charles '93 (SAT) [K] San Antonio, TX Padua Place.
LaRusch, Msgr. Alton J. '41 (BUF) Retired.
Larussa, Raymond '74 (COL) [21] Columbus, OH Holy Spirit Church.
Las, Stefan '88 (PAT) [4] Passaic, NJ Holy Rosary Church.
Las, Wlodzimierz R. *s.d.s.* '86 (BRK) [93] Brooklyn, NY Our Lady of Consolation Church.
Las, Wlodzimierz R. *s.d.s.* '86 (NEW) [N] Verona, NJ The Salvatorian Fathers.
Lasalle, Donald *s.m.m.* '83 (HRT) [M] Litchfield, CT Montfort Missionaries; [M] Litchfield, CT Montfort Missionaries.
Lascelle, Roger L. '77 (DEN) Craig, CO St. Michael Church; Meeker, CO Holy Family Church; Rangely, CO St. Ignatius Church; [P] Rangely, CO Colorado Northwestern Community College (Rangely).
Lasch, Msgr. Kenneth E. '62 (PAT) Mendham, NJ St. Joseph's Church.
Laschenski, Sigmund J. *s.j.* '55 (BAL) [S] Baltimore, MD Jesuit Fathers and Brothers Maryland Provincial Curia.
Laschenski, Sigmund J. *s.j.* '55 (FgM) Provinces.
Lasecki, Daniel J. '64 (MIL) Elkhart Lake, WI St. George Church; Glenbeulah, WI St. Fridolin Church.
Lasheras, Antonio *o.a.r.* '62 (NEW) [1] Union City, NJ Holy Family Church; [N] Union City, NJ Augustinian Recollects.
Lasic, Miron *o.f.m.* '40 (CHI) [N] Chicago, IL Croatian Franciscan Custody of the Holy Family.
Laska, William M. '88 (E) New Bethlehem, PA St. Charles Church.
Laske, Kenneth S. '58 (CHI) Berwyn, IL St. Leonard Church.
Lasko, Stephen J. *c.s.sp.* '47 (VEN) [G] Sarasota, FL Congregation of the Holy Ghost.
Laskowski, Norbert '71 (NEW) Kearny, NJ St. Cecilia's Church.
Lasky, Msgr. Joseph J. '55 (SCR) Kingston, PA St. Mary's Annunciation Church.
Lasky, Michael *ofm conv.* '00 (BUF) [D] Athol Springs, NY St. Francis High School; [O] Athol Springs, NY St. Francis of Assisi Friary.
Laslavich, Luke S. *o.praem.* '94 (ORG) [C] Santa Ana, CA Mater Dei High School; [I] Silverado, CA Norbertine Fathers of Orange Inc.
Lasrado, Maxim *o.c.d.* '92 (CHI) [56] Chicago, IL St. Ferdinand Church.
Lasseigne, John *o.m.i.* '99 (GAL) [38] Houston, TX Immaculate Heart of Mary Church.
Last, Carl A. '69 (MIL) [1] Milwaukee, WI St. John Church.
Lastiri, Jean-Michael '85 (FRS) Merced, CA Our Lady of Mercy/St. Patrick's Church.
Laszewski, Richard G. *m.m.* '51 (FgM) Maryknoll Foreign Missions.
Latella, Joseph A. *s.j.* '58 (NY) [DD] New York, NY St. Ignatius Loyola Residence; [HH] New York, NY Xavier Society for the Blind.
Lathem, Msgr. E. Christopher '65 (CHR) Summerville, SC St. John the Beloved Church.
LaThiez, Alphonse O. '55 (PRO) [3] West Warwick, RI St. James Church.
Latimer, Msgr. Edward H. '39 (E) Retired.
Latino, Msgr. Joseph N. '63 (HT) [1] Houma, LA Cathedral of St. Francis De Sales.
Latona, Marcello J. '70 (BRK) [179] Queens, NY Holy Trinity Church.
LaTorre, Abraham '51 (SAT) [20] San Antonio, TX Our Lady of Sorrows Church.
Latosynski, Roger '84 (PT) Apalachicola, FL St. Patrick Church.
Latronico, P. '86 (NEW) [S] Rutherford, NJ The Community of God's Love.
Latsko, Andrew J. '92 (CHL) Swannanoa, NC St. Margaret Mary Church.
Lattis, Herbert L. '64 (L) Goshen, KY Transfiguration of Our Lord Church.
Lattus, Herman J. '99 (MEM) Jackson, TN St. Mary's Church.
Latus, Charles J. '68 (ROC) Webster, NY St. Rita Church.
Latzko, Frank '84 (CHI) [105] Chicago, IL St. John Fisher Church.
Lau, Ignatius '58 (ORG) [1] Santa Ana, CA Immaculate Heart of Mary Church.
Lau, Michael '61 (P) Retired.

Lau, Vincent '52 (FRS) [9] Fresno, CA St. Genevieve Church.
Lau, William '79 (SP) Absent on Leave.
Laubach, Barnabas *o.s.b.* '52 (SB) San Bernardino, CA San Bernardino Medical Center; [D] San Bernardino, CA St. Bernardine Medical Center.
Laubach, Barnabas *o.s.b.* '52 (SCL) [I] Collegeville, MN St. John's Abbey, of the Order of St. Benedict.
Laubacher, Carroll *s.j.* '56 (LA) [K] Ojai, CA St. Joseph's Health and Retirement Center.
Laubacker, Jerome *o.de.m.* (SP) [O] St. Petersburg, FL St. Peter Nolasco Residence.
Laubacker, Jerome P. *o.de.m.* '74 (SP) [1] St. Petersburg, FL Cathedral of St. Jude the Apostle.
Laubenthal, Allan R. '61 (CLV) North Olmsted, OH St. Clarence Church.
Lauck, Anthony J. *c.s.c.* '46 (FTW) [J] South Bend, IN Congregation of Holy Cross, Indiana Province, Provincial House.
Lauder, Robert E. '60 (BRK) Released from Diocesan Assignment; [B] Douglaston, NY Cathedral Seminary Residence of the Immaculate Conception.
Laudick, John R. '64 (TOL) [22] Toledo, OH St. Francis de Sales Church; [42] Toledo, OH St. Vincent de Paul Church.
Laudwein, James R. *s.j.* '62 (P) [L] Portland, OR Colombiere Community.
Laudwein, Joseph *s.j.* '62 (FBK) Tanana, AK St. Aloysius Church; [C] Fairbanks, AK Jesuit Residence.
Lauenstein, Gary *c.ss.r.* '71 (STL) [B] St. Louis, MO St. John Neumann House.
Lauer, Albert '74 (CIN) [58] Cincinnati, OH Old St. Mary Church.
Lauer, Douglas J. '94 (COV) [4] Covington, KY St. Benedict Church.
Lauer, Eugene (CHI) [B] Chicago, IL The Catholic Theological Union at Chicago.
Lauer, Eugene A. *o.s.b.* '43 (PEO) [A] Peru, IL St. Bede Abbey and Academy.
Lauer, Eugene F. '61 (PIT) On Duty Outside the Diocese.
Lauerman, James P. '70 (FAR) Napoleon, ND St. Philip Neri Church.
Laughery, Kevin Michael '83 (SFD) Auburn, IL St. Benedict Church; Divernon, IL Sacred Heart Church; Waverly, IL St. Sebastian Church.
Laughlin, James J. '91 (BO) Graduate Studies.
Laughlin, Joseph R. *s.j.* '57 (BO) [E] Boston, MA Boston College High School & Jesuit Community.
Laughlin, Martin T. '52 (DUB) Retired.
Launderville, Dale *o.s.b.* '79 (SCL) [I] Collegeville, MN St. John's Abbey, of the Order of St. Benedict.
Launtrie, Francis *c.s.b.* (GAL) Rosenberg, TX Our Lady of Guadalupe Church.
Launtrie, Francis J. *c.s.b.* '56 (GAL) [Q] Sugar Land, TX Basilian Mission Center.
Laurance, John D. *s.j.* '70 (MIL) [P] Milwaukee, WI Jesuit Community at Marquette University.
Laurano, Anthony J. '50 (BO) Senior Priests.
Laurello, Msgr. Bartholomew J. '46 (BGP) Retired.
Laurent, Edward *o.f.m.cap.* '64 (PIT) [O] Pittsburgh, PA St. Francis Friary.
Laurenzo, James M. '69 (DM) Carlisle, IA St. Elizabeth Seton Church; [A] West Des Moines, IA St. Joseph Educational Center.
Lauretti, George F. '56 (HRT) Southington, CT St. Thomas Church.
Laurick, Richard A. *c.s.c.* '54 (FTW) [16] South Bend, IN St. Patrick Church.
Laurinaitis, Saulius P. '48 (COL) Retired.
Lauriola, Guglielmo *o.f.m.* '53 (OAK) [S] Oakland, CA Missionaries of the Kingship of Christ.
Lauriola, Guglielmo *o.f.m.* '53 (SFR) [5] San Francisco, CA St. Anthony of Padua Church.
Lause, James *o.f.m.* '98 (STL) [P] St. Louis, MO Franciscan Friary of St. Anthony of Padua.
Lause, James A. *o.f.m.* (STL) [25] St. Louis, MO St. Anthony of Padua Church.
Lause, Richard L. *c.m.* '77 (STL) [P] St. Louis, MO Lazarist Residence.
Lautermilch, David J. '62 (TOL) Awaiting Assignment.
Lautz, Boniface *o.s.b.* '60 (B) [C] Jerome, ID Monastery of the Ascension.
Laux, Donald '48 (GB) Retired.
Lauze, Michael *o.m.i.* '75 (BO) [W] Lowell, MA Missionary Oblates of Mary Immaculate.
Lauze, Michael *o.m.i.* '75 (MAN) [K] Les Cayes, Haiti Paroisse Ste. Anne.
Lauzon, Kris C. '78 (OG) Bombay, NY St. Joseph Church.
Lauzon, Kris C. '91 (OG) Fort Covington, NY St. Mary Church; Hogansburg, NY St. Patrick Church.
Lauzon, Paul *s.d.s.* (LC) [C] Marshfield, WI Columbus High School.
Lauzon, Paul *s.d.s.* '71 (LC) [C] Marshfield, WI Holy Family Middle School.
Lauzon, Raymond J. '55 (PRT) Retired.
Lavagetto, Xavier *o.p.* (SFR) [N] San Francisco, CA St. Dominic Priory.
Lavagetto, Xavier M. *o.p.* '96 (SFR) [14] San Francisco, CA St. Dominic Church.
Lavaie, Richard *m.s.* '64 (FR) [I] Attleboro, MA La Salette Shrine.
LaVallee, Pierre A. '61 (BUR) Bristol, VT St. Ambrose Church.
Lavalley, Richard G. '64 (BUR) Winooski, VT St. Francis Xavier Church; Winooski, VT St. Stephen Church; [H] Burlington, VT University of Vermont-The Catholic Center at UVM.
LaVan, Kenneth G. '58 (STP) Retired.
Lavastida, Jose I. '87 (NO) [A] New Orleans, LA Notre Dame Seminary Graduate School of Theology.
Lavelle, Donald *c.m.f.* '46 (CHI) [N] Oak Park, IL Claretian Fathers Headquarters of U.S.A. Eastern Province.
Lavelle, Donald *c.m.f.* '46 (LA) [Q] Rancho Dominguez, CA Dominguez Seminary Inc.
Lavelle, Edward R. '63 (HBG) [G] Harrisburg, PA Villa Teresa Nursing Home.
Lavelle, Francis P. (SPR) [Q] Springfield, MA Newman Apostolates and Campus Ministries.
Lavelle, Francis P. '70 (SPR) [Q] Springfield, MA Newman Apostolates and Campus Ministries.
Lavelle, John-Michael '00 (Y) Massillon, OH St. Mary's Church.
Lavelle, Raymond E. '57 (COL) Westerville, OH St. Paul the Apostle Church; Retired.
Lavelle, Thomas E. *m.m.* '55 (FgM) Maryknoll Foreign Missions.
Lavely, Charles J. *c.s.c.* '65 (FTW) [16] South Bend, IN St. Patrick Church.
LaVerde, Calogero N. '68 (CAM) Woodbury Heights, NJ St. Margaret's Church.
LaVerde, Charles *c.s.* '65 (CHI) [16] Chicago, IL St. Anthony Church.
LaVerdiere, Eugene *s.s.s.* '64 (NY) [55] New York, NY St. Jean Baptiste Church.
Lavere, Philip *o.f.m.* '47 (BO) [BB] Boston, MA St. Anthony Shrine.
LaVerghetta, Richard D. '86 (TR) [14] Trenton, NJ St. Gregory the Great Church.
Laverone, Kenneth J. *o.f.m.* '79 (MRY) Special Assignment.
Laverty, Joseph F. *o.s.a.* '48 (PH) [AA] Villanova, PA St. Thomas Monastery.
Laverty, Seamus '68 (SEA) [6] Tacoma, WA St. Patrick Church.
Lavery, Bruce '67 (ORG) Laguna Niguel, CA St. Timothy Church.
Laviano, Vincent A. *o.f.m.* '74 (NY) [35] New York, NY St. Francis of Assisi Church.
Lavich, David *o.c.s.o.* '73 (WOR) [N] Spencer, MA St. Joseph's Abbey.
Lavigne, Lionel *s.s.s.* '41 (NY) [8] New York, NY St. Andrew Church.
Lavigne, Maurice D. '68 (MAN) Rye Beach, NH St. Theresa Church.
Lavigne, Richard R. '66 (SPR) Absent on Leave.
Lavin, Bernard C. '79 (PRO) Lincoln, RI St. Jude Church.
Lavin, Msgr. James M. '45 (STP) Retired; [C] St. Paul, MN University of St. Thomas.
Lavin, John *c.ss.r.* (BAL) Annapolis, MD St. Mary Church.
Lavin, John (PRO) [B] Newport, RI Salve Regina University.
Lavin, John *c.ss.r.* '66 (BAL) [S] Annapolis, MD Saint Mary Rectory.
Lavin, Msgr. John B. '64 (BRK) [235] Queens, NY St. Robert Bellarmine Church.
Lavin, John J. '64 (PRO) [3] Newport, RI St. Joseph Church.
Lavin, Martin '67 (RIC) Martinsville, VA St. Joseph Church.
Lavin, Paul E. '69 (WDC) [24] Washington, DC St. Joseph on Capitol Hill Church.
Lavin, Msgr. Robert F. '56 (SY) East Syracuse, NY St. Matthew Church; Retired.
Lavin, Thomas *s.v.d.* '41 (MIL) [P] East Troy, WI Divine Word Seminary.
Lavin, Thomas *o.f.m.conv.* '87 (HRT) Kensington, CT St. Paul's Church.
Lavin, Wayne Patrick '71 (CAM) [3] Camden, NJ St. Bartholomew's Church.
LaViolette, Msgr. Matt H. '34 (MAR) Retired.
Lavoie, Alfred *o.m.i.* '40 (SAT) [K] San Antonio, TX Oblate Madonna Residence.
LaVoie, Joseph '64 (SFE) Retired.
Lavoie, Merle L. '68 (SPR) [3] Northampton, MA Sacred Heart Church; [4] Northampton, MA St. John Cantius Church.
Lavoie, Michel J. *m.afr.* '70 (FgM) Missionaries of Africa Foreign Missions.
LaVoie, Raymond J. '00 (HBG) Graduate Studies.
Lavoie, Rene G. '51 (PRT) Retired.
Lavoie, Msgr. Robert G. '53 (PRT) Gray, ME St. Gregory Church.
Lavoie, Victor C. '71 (BO) Winchester, MA St. Eulalia Church.
Lavorin, Anthony F. *o.f.m.* (MRY) Jolon, CA San Antonio Church.
Lavoy, Elwood '53 (LAV) Retired.
Lavrih, John '39 (DOD) Retired.
Law, Charles A. *s.j.* '64 (FgM) Provinces.
Law, Msgr. Joseph A. '49 (SCR) Retired.
Lawie, Richard J. '69 (GR) Jenison, MI Holy Redeemer Church.
Lawler, Bruce '80 (SC) [10] Sioux City, IA Sacred Heart Church.
Lawler, Daniel F. *s.j.* '48 (HBG) Chambersburg, PA Corpus Christi Church.
Lawler, David '62 (IND) Indianapolis, IN Methodist Hospital.
Lawler, Msgr. John F. '45 (BO) Senior Priests.
Lawler, Msgr. Joseph A. '61 (BEL) McLeansboro, IL St. Clement Church; Piopolis, IL St. John the Baptist Church.
Lawler, Msgr. Richard C. '59 (IND) [26] Indianapolis, IN St. Mark the Evangelist Church.
Lawler, Msgr. Robert L. '56 (OG) Waddington, NY St. Mary Church.
Lawler, Ronald *o.f.m.cap.* '51 (PIT) [O] Pittsburgh, PA St. Francis Friary.
Lawler, Terrance M. '74 (MET) Sayreville, NJ Our Lady of Victories Church.
Lawler, Thomas *s.j.* '99 (RC) [B] Howes, SD Kino Jesuit Community.
Lawler, Thomas A. *s.j.* '99 (RC) [D] Howes, SD The Diocese of Rapid City Mahpiya na Maka Okoigna.
Lawler, William J. '72 (WIL) Centreville, MD Our Mother of Sorrows Church.
Lawless, Brendan '64 (JC) Kahoka, MO St. Michael the Archangel Church.
Lawless, Joseph *m.s.f.* '71 (CC) [15] Corpus Christi, TX St. Joseph Church.
Lawless, Timothy J. *s.j.* '61 (DEN) [M] Denver, CO Xavier Jesuit Center.
Lawlor, Brendan W. '44 (BUR) Retired.
Lawlor, David T. *o.praem.* '71 (PH) [AA] Paoli, PA Daylesford Abbey.
Lawlor, Edward J. *s.s.j.* '40 (NO) [N] New Orleans, LA Chateau de Notre Dame.
Lawlor, F. James '63 (ROC) Mendon, NY St. Catherine of Siena Church.
Lawlor, Francis *o.s.a.* '45 (STL) [6] St. Louis, MO Immaculate Conception-St. Henry Church.
Lawlor, Francis '69 (SAC) [22] Sacramento, CA St. Rose Church.
Lawlor, J. Michael '73 (BO) Lynnfield, MA St. Maria Goretti Church.
Lawlor, John J. *c.m.* '44 (PH) [AA] Philadelphia, PA Congregation of the Mission.
Lawlor, John L. *c.m.* '44 (CHR) Gloverville, SC Our Lady of the Valley Church.
Lawlor, Msgr. Joseph (RVC) [J] Huntington, NY St. Joseph's Guest Home for the Aged, Inc.
Lawlor, Joseph '62 (JC) Missionary Assignment in Peru.
Lawlor, Msgr. Joseph A. '61 (BEL) Dahlgren, IL St. John Nepomucene Church.
Lawlor, Msgr. Joseph F. '35 (RVC) Baldwin, NY St. Christopher Church; Retired.
Lawlor, Mark '95 (CHL) Jefferson, NC St. Francis of Assisi Church.
Lawlor, Msgr. Timothy '43 (SB) Ontario, CA St. George Church; Retired.
Lawrence, Andrew F. '00 (DUB) [8] Cedar Rapids, IA St. Pius X Church.
Lawrence, Christopher '84 (LA) San Pedro, CA Mary, Star of the Sea Church.
Lawrence, David *s.j.* '74 (OAK) [2] Concord, CA St. Bonaventure Church.
Lawrence, David '97 (JOL) Woodridge, IL St. Scholastica Church.
Lawrence, Denis (P) [P] Portland, OR University of Portland.
Lawrence, Francis '45 (JOL) [J] Lisle, IL St. Procopius Abbey.
Lawrence, James A. '70 (BUR) Chittenden, VT St. Robert Church; Rutland, VT Immaculate Heart of Mary Church.
Lawrence, James T. '61 (DAV) Retired; [M] Davenport, IA St. Vincent Center.
Lawrence, Jeffrey C. '96 (PEO) [4] Streator, IL St. Stephen's Church.
Lawrence, John M. '76 (SAC) Fort Jones, CA Sacred Heart Church.
Lawrence, Kenneth F. '60 (HBG) Columbia, PA Holy Trinity Church.
Lawrence, Kevin C. '87 (PH) [94] Philadelphia, PA St. Martin De Porres Church; [S] Philadelphia, PA St. John's Hospice for Men.
Lawrence, Michael S. '73 (ALN) [7] Allentown, PA St. Paul Church; [L] Coopersburg, PA Carmelite Monastery.
Lawrence, Neal Henry *o.s.b.* '60 (FgM) American - Cassinese Congregation Foreign Missions.
Lawrence, Neal Henry *o.s.b.* '60 (SCL) [I] Collegeville, MN St. John's Abbey, of the Order of St. Benedict.
Lawrence, Ralph J. '53 (CIN) Retired.
Lawrence, Richard T. '68 (BAL) [95] Baltimore, MD St. Vincent de Paul Church.

Lawrence, Msgr. Robert E. (SB) Special or Other Diocesan Assignment.
Lawrence, Msgr. Robert E. '66 (HBG) New Cumberland, PA St. Theresa of the Infant Jesus Church.
Lawrence, Walter L. '73 (WDC) Kensington, MD Holy Redeemer Church.
Lawryniuk, Lawrence *o.s.b.m.* '64 (STF) New York, NY St. George Church.
Lawsine, Robert '81 (BRK) [132] Brooklyn, NY St. Saviour Church.
Lawson, Harold F. (BO) Senior Priests.
Lawson, J. Douglas '62 (R) Riegelwood, NC Christ the King Church; Southport, NC Sacred Heart Church.
Lawson, Meinrad J. *o.s.b.* '67 (SAV) [B] Savannah, GA Benedictine Military School; [F] Savannah, GA The Benedictine Priory.
Lawson, Robert T. '62 (R) Retired.
Lawson, Theodore *c.ss.r.* '89 (DEN) [M] Denver, CO The Redemptorists/Denver Province.
Lawson, Theodore *c.ss.r.* '89 (OAK) [1] Hayward, CA All Saints Church.
Lawson, Willaim T. '86 (SD) National City, CA St. Anthony of Padua Church.
Lawton, Robert B. *s.j.* '81 (LA) [C] Los Angeles, CA Loyola Marymount University; [C] Los Angeles, CA Loyola Marymount University.
Lawton, Thomas E. *c.s.c.* '52 (FR) North Easton, MA Immaculate Conception Church; [A] North Easton, MA Holy Cross Fathers Religious.
Lawyer, Jerome R. *c.s.c.* '39 (BGP) [P] Bridgeport, CT Provincial Offices of the Priests and Brothers of Holy Cross, Eastern Province.
Lawyer, Jerome R. *c.s.c.* '39 (FTW) [J] South Bend, IN Congregation of Holy Cross, Indiana Province, Provincial House.
Lay, Thomas N. *s.j.* '66 (STL) [P] St. Louis, MO Jesuit Community Corporation at St. Louis University - Jesuit Hall.
Layton, Richard *o.c.s.o.* '82 (P) [L] Lafayette, OR The Cistercian (Trappist) Abbey of Our Lady of Guadalupe.
Laz, Medard P '69 (CHI) [X] LaGrange Park, IL Joyful Again.
Laz, Medard P. '69 (CHI) Other Assignments.
Lazar, Francis M. '60 (GRY) Highland, IN St. James the Less Church.
Lazar, John '42 (STN) Dearborn Heights, MI Our Lady of Perpetual Help Church.
Lazar, John E. '80 (BRK) Absent on Leave.
Lazaro, Felix *sch.p.* '61 (PCE) Jayuya, PR Our Lady of Monserrate Church; [B] Ponce, PR The Pontifical Catholic University of Puerto Rico; [B] Ponce, PR The Pontifical Catholic University of Puerto Rico.
Lazaro, Lesmes Bernabe *o.s.a.* '49 (MGZ) Aguada, PR St. Francis of Assisi Church.
Lazarski, Marvin I. '62 (MIL) Special Assignment.
Lazor, Bernard A. *o.s.a.* '51 (PH) [C] Villanova, PA Villanova University; [AA] Villanova, PA St. Thomas Monastery.
Lazor, Joseph '90 (STF) Manchester, NH Protection of B.V.M. Church.
Le, Benjamin '98 (LA) Alhambra, CA All Souls Church.
Le, Hoang V. '99 (BO) Graduate Studies.
Le, Hoang Viet '61 (TLS) [8] Tulsa, OK St. Joseph Church.
Le, James Vinh '87 (KAL) Dorr, MI St. Stanislaus Church.
Le, Joseph Ahn *s.d.b.* '95 (LA) [F] Bellflower, CA St. John Bosco High School.
Le, Paul Vung *s.v.d.* '85 (SB) [7] San Bernardino, CA St. Anthony Church.
Le, Tuan Quoc *s.j.* '99 (STL) [P] St. Louis, MO The Jesuits of the Missouri Province.
Le Beau, Philip (PAT) [4] Wayne, NJ Our Lady of Consolation Church.
Le Fevre, Francis J. '71 (BAL) Absent on Leave.
Le Frois, Christian G. *o.s.b.* '46 (GBG) [H] Latrobe, PA Saint Vincent Archabbey.
Le Jacq, Peter M. *m.m.* '87 (NY) [DD] Maryknoll, NY Maryknoll Fathers and Brothers; [DD] Maryknoll, NY Maryknoll Fathers and Brothers.
Le Mieux, Thomas A. '59 (MIL) Retired.
Le Quang, Hein Joachim '74 (SPK) [10] Spokane, WA St. Charles Church.
Leach, Gregory '80 (DM) Ankeny, IA Our Lady's Immaculate Heart Church.
Leach, Jerome '76 (SFR) Absent on Leave.
Leach, Phillip M. '85 (R) Chapel Hill, NC Newman Catholic Student Center, University of North Carolina Church; [H] Chapel Hill, NC Newman Catholic Student Center.
Leach, Thomas F. '73 (BRK) [103] Brooklyn, NY Our Lady of Miracles Church.
Leach, William J. '58 (STL) Gildehaus, MO St. John the Baptist Church.
Leack, Lawrence J. '50 (MIL) Retired; [V] Milwaukee, WI Our Blessed Lady of Victory Mission, Inc.
Leahey, Patrick R. '77 (ALT) Dudley, PA Immaculate Conception Church.
Leahy, Anthony '55 (SB) Retired.
Leahy, Clement '50 (CHI) [N] Chicago, IL St. Peter's Friary.
Leahy, Edwin D. *o.s.b.* '72 (NEW) [C] Newark, NJ St. Benedict's Preparatory School; [N] Newark, NJ Newark Abbey.
Leahy, John A. '57 (CLV) Middleburg Heights, OH St. Bartholomew Church; Retired.
Leahy, Juvenal F. *o.f.m.* '58 (FgM) Franciscan Foreign Missions.
Leahy, Liam '72 (TUC) [15] Tucson, AZ St. Francis de Sales Church.
Leahy, Msgr. Patrick J. '38 (DOD) Retired.
Leahy, Robert T. '60 (NEW) On Duty Outside the Archdiocese.
Leahy, Robert T. '60 (TR) [3] Toms River, NJ St. Luke Church.
Leahy, William J. '66 (SAV) St. Marys, GA Our Lady Star of the Sea Church.
Leahy, William P. *s.j.* '78 (BO) [C] Chestnut Hill, MA Boston College; [W] Chestnut Hill, MA The Jesuit Community at Boston College.
Leake, Jerome I. '68 (RCK) [3] Aurora, IL St. Joseph Church.
Leake, Stephen '00 (NY) [F] New Rochelle, NY Salesian High School.
Leakei, Stephen *s.d.b.* '00 (NY) [DD] New Rochelle, NY Salesian Provincial House.
Leannah, Scott R. '93 (MIL) [57] Milwaukee, WI St. Matthias Church.
Leano, Msgr. Oscar (NEW) Kenilworth, NJ St. Theresa's Church.
Leary, Albert R. '54 (BIS) Mandan, ND Christ the King Church; Mandan, ND Christ the King Church; [G] Bismarck, ND Emmaus Place.
Leary, Daniel Paul '97 (WDC) Piscataway, MD St. Mary Church.
Leary, Donald G. '51 (WIN) Retired.
Leary, Edward *s.s.e.* '53 (VEN) [G] Englewood, FL Society of St. Edmund Residence.
Leary, James *o.f.m.cap.* '70 (LC) Sparta, WI St. Patrick Church.
Leary, James F. '68 (HRT) [4] Bristol, CT St. Joseph Church.
Leary, James V. '56 (PH) [4] Phoenixville, PA Sacred Heart Church; Retired.
Leary, Msgr. Patrick R. '76 (LAV) [14] Las Vegas, NV St. Paul Jung-Ha-Sang Church; [16] Las Vegas, NV Shrine of the Most Holy Redeemer Church.
Leary, Richard *c.p.* '46 (FgM) Passionist Foreign Missions.
Leatham, Gerald '65 (LUB) Snyder, TX St. Elizabeth's Church.
Leavens, Joseph *c.i.c.m.* '65 (FgM) Missionhurst Foreign Missions.
Leavey, Msgr. Thomas G. (RVC) Retired.
Leavey, Msgr. Thomas G. '51 (RVC) Seaford, NY St. William, the Abbot Church.
Leavins, Brice *o.f.m.* '69 (BO) [BB] Boston, MA St. Anthony Shrine.
Leavitt, Robert F. *s.s.* '68 (BAL) [A] Baltimore, MD St. Mary's Seminary and University; [A] Baltimore, MD St. Mary's Seminary and University.
Leavitt, Robert F. *s.s.* '68 (HRT) On Duty Outside the Archdiocese.
Lebanowski, Gerald *m.s.* (MIL) [P] Twin Lakes, WI La Salette Missionaries Shrine.
Lebar, Ivan M. *t.o.r.* '58 (WH) Keyser, WV Assumption Church.
LeBar, James J. '62 (NY) Hyde Park, NY Regina Coeli Church; Poughkeepsie, NY Hudson River Psychiatric Center.
Lebdowicz, Jan Christopher '80 (NEW) [4] Linden, NJ St. Theresa of the Child Jesus Church.
LeBeau, Cyril A. '48 (WOR) Retired; [M] Worcester, MA Vianney House.
LeBeau, Joseph *s.v.d.* '49 (CHI) [B] Techny, IL Divine Word Residence.
Lebel, Charles E. *m.afr.* '39 (SP) [O] St. Petersburg, FL Missionaries of Africa.
Lebel, Maurice T. '67 (PRT) Norway, ME St. Catherine of Sienna Church.
Lebiedz, Bernard *o.s.b.* '59 (SFE) [I] Pecos, NM Our Lady of Guadalupe Abbey; [K] Pecos, NM Our Lady of Guadalupe Olivetan Benedictine Abbey.
LeBlanc, Alvin J. '82 (HRT) [8] Waterbury, CT St. Anne Church; Special and other Archdiocesan Assignment; [A] Bloomfield, CT St. Thomas Seminary.
LeBlanc, Charles R. '79 (NOR) East Hampton, CT St. Patrick Church.
LeBlanc, Clyde *s.j.* '75 (NO) [C] New Orleans, LA Loyola University New Orleans.
LeBlanc, Clyde H. *s.j.* '75 (OAK) [N] Berkeley, CA Jesuit Community at Jesuit School of Theology at Berkeley.
LeBlanc, David E. '61 (GR) Caledonia, MI Holy Family Church.
LeBlanc, Gregory S. '94 (DOD) Ness City, KS Sacred Heart Church; Ransom, KS St. Aloysius Church.
LeBlanc, Harold E. '61 (BO) [4] Woburn, MA St. Joseph Church.
LeBlanc, James L. '96 (CHR) [9] Charleston, SC Divine Redeemer Church.
LeBlanc, Keith '96 (BO) [2] Everett, MA Immaculate Conception Church.
LeBlanc, Kenneth A. (BO) Medway, MA St. Joseph Church.
LeBlanc, Kenneth A. '76 (BO) Emergency Response Group.
LeBlanc, Leo *o.m.i.* '67 (SFD) [A] Godfrey, IL Immaculate Heart of Mary Novitiate.
LeBlanc, Leo A. '74 (MAN) [11] Manchester, NH St. John the Baptist Church.
LeBlanc, Leo-Paul J. '79 (WOR) [2] Southbridge, MA Notre Dame Church.
LeBlanc, Omer *c.j.m.* '61 (SD) [2] El Cajon, CA Our Lady of Grace Church.
LeBlanc, Paul '69 (NY) On Duty Outside the Archdiocese.
LeBlanc, Steven C. '77 (LAF) [5] New Iberia, LA Sacred Heart of Jesus Church.
LeBleu, V. Wayne '95 (LKC) Bell City, LA St. John Vianney Church.
LeBoeuf, Gerard '93 (DET) [4] Sterling Heights, MI St. Jane Frances de Chantal Church.
Leboroni-Pierozzi, Gilberto (BAL) [74] Baltimore, MD Our Lady of Pompei Church.
LeBourgeois, Msgr. Louis P. '61 (NO) Jefferson, LA St. Agnes Church.
LeBrun, Paul *c.s.c.* '83 (GRY) Michigan City, IN Indiana State Prison.
Lebrun, Raymond A. *o.m.i.* '68 (NO) [1] New Orleans, LA St. Louis Church.
Lec, John J. '70 (TR) [8] Trenton, NJ Our Lady of Good Counsel Church.
Lech, Ferdinand F. '48 (PIT) Retired.
Lech, George T. '56 (PIT) Retired.
Lech, Waclaw L. *o.c.d.* '74 (GRY) [J] Munster, IN Discalced Carmelite Fathers Monastery.
Lecheler, Anton L. '46 (LC) Rock Falls, WI St. Joseph Church.
Lechiara, Francis J. '59 (PMB) Palm Beach, FL St. Edward Church; [K] Palm Beach Gardens, FL Diocesan Health Plan Trust; [K] Palm Beach Gardens, FL Diocesan Pension Plan Trust.
Lechnar, William J. '97 (GBG) [1] Greensburg, PA Blessed Sacrament Church.
Lechner, Peter *s.p.* '30 (STL) [T] Dittmer, MO Vianney Renewal Center.
Lechner, Peter *s.p.* '68 (SFE) [I] Jemez Springs, NM Our Lady of Lourdes Novitiate; [M] Jemez Springs, NM Fitzgerald Charitable Trust.
Lechner, Msgr. Roger A. '66 (SD) [7] San Diego, CA Holy Spirit Church.
Lechtenberg, Msgr. Edward W. '51 (DUB) Retired.
Leckie, Michael J. '76 (PRO) Hopkinton, RI St. Joseph Church.
LeClair, Lawrence J. '53 (HRT) Retired.
LeClair, Richard J. *c.s.sp.* '51 (FgM) Holy Ghost Foreign Missions.
LeClaire, Fred *c.m.f.* '87 (PHX) Prescott, AZ Sacred Heart Church.
LeClaire, Karl *s.d.s.* '87 (PHX) [4] Mesa, AZ Queen of Peace Church.
Leclerc, Gerard P. '60 (BUR) Enosburg Falls, VT St. John the Baptist Church.
Leclerc, Msgr. Leo A. '61 (SPR) [9] Chicopee, MA St. Rose de Lima Church.
Leclercq, M. Duane '64 (PEO) [4] La Salle, IL St. Patrick's Church.
LeCompte, Glenn D. '86 (NO) [A] New Orleans, LA Notre Dame Seminary Graduate School of Theology.
LeCours, Sylva P. '47 (NOR) Ballouville, CT St. Anne Church.
Lecuivre, Joel A. '72 (PRO) [5] Pawtucket, RI St. John the Baptist Church.
Lecumberri, Rufino '54 (NY) [158] Bronx, NY St. Joseph Church.
Leddy, John J. *o.m.i.* '51 (WDC) [M] Washington, DC Oblate College/Center for Mission Studies Community; [Q] Washington, DC Basilica of the National Shrine of the Immaculate Conception.
Leddy, Leonard '59 (AUS) Retired.
Leddy, Seamus *s.s.c.* '42 (LA) [Q] Los Angeles, CA Columban Fathers, Procure House.
Leder, Dennis M. *s.j.* '76 (FgM) Provinces.
Ledermann, Paul F. '63 (OG) On Duty Outside the Diocese.
Ledermann, Paul F. '63 (SR) Yountville, CA Veterans Administration Home.
Ledesma, Alberto '97 (LA) [5] Santa Barbara, CA St. Raphael Church.
Ledet, Msgr. Donald L. '63 (HT) Raceland, LA St. Mary's Nativity Church.
Ledford, John S. '75 (WH) Berkeley Springs, WV St. Vincent de Paul Church.
Ledoux, Albert H. '71 (ALT) On Duty Outside the Diocese.
Ledoux, Albert H. '87 (BAL) [A] Emmitsburg, MD Mount St. Mary's Seminary.
LeDoux, Jerome *s.v.d.* '57 (NO) [26] New Orleans, LA St. Augustine Church.
Ledoux, John C. '50 (BUR) Retired.

Ledoux, Louis Vernon '52 (LAF) Retired.
Ledoux, Mark Patrick '99 (LAF) Kaplan, LA Our Lady of the Holy Rosary Church.
Ledoux, Michael D. *o.f.m.* '86 (NY) [DD] New York, NY Franciscan Province of the Immaculate Conception.
Ledoux, William J. '93 (PRO) [6] Cranston, RI St. Matthew Church.
LeDuc, Roger D. '60 (FR) [2] Swansea, MA St. Louis de France Church.
Leduff-Gutierrez, Larry *s.s.j.* '85 (BEA) [3] Port Arthur, TX Sacred Heart Church.
Ledwidge, Brendan K. '55 (LAN) Retired.
Ledwith, Harry '74 (TUC) [22] Tucson, AZ St. Pius X Church.
Ledwon, Jacob C. '72 (BUF) [40] Buffalo, NY St. Joseph Church; [R] Alfred, NY Campus Ministry.
Ledwon, Josaphat *o.f.m.* '56 (GB) [I] Pulaski, WI Assumption of B.V.M. Friary.
Lee, Anthony '41 (SFR) Retired; [K] San Francisco, CA Home for the Aged of the Little Sisters of the Poor.
Lee, Anthony '93 (PEO) [B] Danville, IL Schlarman High School.
Lee, Anthony Sangwook '97 (LA) Claremont, CA Our Lady of the Assumption Church.
Lee, Archimandrite Jospeh '72 (PHU) [A] Washington, DC St. Josaphat Seminary.
Lee, Berchmans Yong-Woo *s.j.* '92 (COS) [9] Colorado Springs, CO St. Andrew Kim Quasi Church.
Lee, Bernard J. *s.m.* '67 (NO) [C] New Orleans, LA Loyola University New Orleans.
Lee, Blase '76 (DET) Northville, MI St. Andrew Kim Korean Catholic Church.
Lee, Clemens (CAM) Pleasantville, NJ St. Peter's Church.
Lee, Msgr. David M. '68 (BUF) [6] Buffalo, NY St. Ambrose Church; [R] Alfred, NY Campus Ministry.
Lee, Dominic Savio '94 (SFR) [4] San Francisco, CA St. Anne Church.
Lee, Gabriel '97 (BRK) [232] Queens, NY St. Raphael Church.
Lee, Henry H. '54 (LC) Retired.
Lee, Msgr. Howard T. '54 (FRS) Retired.
Lee, James '75 (SEA) Olympia, WA St. Michael Church.
Lee, Jeffrey E. '92 (TR) [17] Trenton, NJ St. Joachim Church.
Lee, John Edward '99 (NOR) Willimantic, CT St. Joseph Church.
Lee, John M. *c.p.* '72 (MET) [H] South River, NJ Passionist Provincial Office; [H] South River, NJ Passionist Provincial Office.
Lee, John R. *c.s.b.* '56 (ROC) [I] Rochester, NY Basilian Residence.
Lee, Jong-Hyun '94 (COL) [44] Columbus, OH Korean Catholic Community Church.
Lee, Joseph '55 (CHI) [96] Chicago, IL St. James Church; Retired.
Lee, Joseph (Richard) '72 (PHU) [E] Washington, DC Monastery of the Holy Cross.
Lee, Joseph C. '91 (DAL) [11] Dallas, TX St. Andrew Kim Church.
Lee, Joseph P. '57 (LA) On Sick Leave.
Lee, Joshua Peter '89 (LA) Pico Rivera, CA St. Hilary Church.
Lee, Keun-Soo '95 (BR) Whitehall, LA St. Stephen the Martyr Church.
Lee, Lawrence '49 (GAL) Retired; [N] Houston, TX St. Dominic Village.
Lee, Mathias '84 (JOL) Itasca, IL St. Andrew Kim Church.
Lee, Matthew (J.T.) '93 (WDC) Military Chaplains.
Lee, Michael (TR) Eatontown, NJ Immaculate Conception Church.
Lee, Michael C. *s.j.* '96 (NY) [DD] New York, NY Xavier Jesuit Community.
Lee, Michael G. '64 (WH) Absent on Sick Leave.
Lee, Michael J. *o.praem.* '70 (PH) [49] Philadelphia, PA St. Gabriel Church; [AA] Philadelphia, PA St. Norbert Priory; [AA] Paoli, PA Daylesford Abbey.
Lee, Patrick '68 (SAC) Absent on Leave.
Lee, Patrick J. '76 (CHI) [90] Chicago, IL Immaculate Conception of the Blessed Virgin Mary Church.
Lee, Patrick J. *s.j.* '78 (P) [A] Portland, OR Jesuit Novitiate of St. Francis Xavier.
Lee, Paul *o.f.m.* '90 (SD) [H] Oceanside, CA Mission San Luis Rey.
Lee, Paul D. '83 (WDC) Pastoral Center Special Ministries.
Lee, Peter '51 (LA) Retired.
Lee, Pius '84 (CHI) [2] Des Plaines, IL St. Paul Chong Hasang Church.
Lee, R. Anthony '93 (PEO) Hoopeston, IL St. Anthony's Church.
Lee, Robert E. *o.carm.* '55 (JOL) [J] Darien, IL Carmelite Community; [M] Darien, IL Provincial Office of Lay Carmelites and Scapular Confraternity.
Lee, Robert E. '55 (PRT) [1] Portland, ME Cathedral of the Immaculate Conception; Portland, ME St. Joseph's Manor; Retired.
Lee, Robert E. '59 (PEO) Moline, IL Sacred Heart Church.
Lee, Roy A. '86 (MIL) Graduate Studies.
Lee, S. David '98 (NEW) Ramsey, NJ St. Paul Church.
Lee, Sebastian *s.f.* '97 (WDC) [B] Silver Spring, MD Holy Family Seminary.
Lee, Simon *s.j.* '77 (HRT) [3] West Haven, CT St. Lawrence's Church.
Lee, Terence J. *m.h.m.* '57 (NY) [DD] Hartsdale, NY Mill Hill Fathers Residence.
Lee, Msgr. Thaddeus (PAT) Retired.
Lee, Thomas M. '53 (PRT) Lyman, ME St. Philip Church.
Lee, William '62 (HON) On Duty Outside the Diocese.
Lee, William J. *s.s.* '46 (BAL) Edgewood, MD Prince of Peace Church; [O] Baltimore, MD St. Charles Villa; [S] Baltimore, MD St. Charles Villa.
Leeber, Victor F. *s.j.* '53 (BGP) [P] Fairfield, CT The Fairfield Jesuit Community-Fairfield University.
Leedale, Walter F. *s.j.* '59 (SPK) [C] Spokane, WA Gonzaga University.
Leehy, Stephen G. '73 (OG) On Duty Outside the Diocese.
Leek, Michael *o.s.b.* '93 (SFE) [I] Pecos, NM Our Lady of Guadalupe Abbey; [K] Pecos, NM Our Lady of Guadalupe Olivetan Benedictine Abbey.
Leeuw, Daniel '57 (FTW) Fort Wayne, IN Veterans Administration Hospital; [H] Avilla, IN Provena Sacred Heart Home; [H] Avilla, IN Provena LaVerna Terrace.
Lefebure, Leo D. '78 (CHI) Other Assignments.
Lefebure, Leo D. '78 (NY) [6] Yonkers, NY Christ the King Church.
Lefebvre, Bruce A. '73 (SC) Mallard, IA St. Mary's Church; West Bend, IA SS. Peter and Paul Church.
Lefebvre, Msgr. Gerald M. '56 (BR) Retired.
Lefebvre, James '59 (ALB) [11] Albany, NY St. Mary Church.
Lefebvre, Leo P. '55 (MAN) Retired.
Lefebvre, Robert R. *m.m.* '57 (NY) [DD] Maryknoll, NY Maryknoll Fathers and Brothers.
Lefebvre, Simon *c.s.v.* '56 (SD) Borrego Springs, CA St. Richard Church.
LeFevre, Msgr. Michael C. '82 (DET) [1] Sterling Heights, MI St. Blase Church.
LeFevre, Robert J. '66 (ALB) Saratoga Springs, NY St. Peter Church.
Leffler, Richard J. '78 (MAD) Tennyson-Potosi, WI SS. Andrew and Thomas Church.
Lefko, John *c.pp.s.* '38 (CIN) [B] Carthagena, OH St. Charles.
Lefler, John '57 (EVN) Retired.
LeFleur, R. Keith '61 (SAG) Sandusky, MI St. Joseph Church.
Lefor, Jason '99 (FAR) [I] Grand Forks, ND Univ. of North Dakota Newman Center.
Lefor, Jason V. '99 (FAR) [4] Grand Forks, ND St. Thomas Aquinas Parish, UND Church.
LeFort, David '98 (ALB) Latham, NY Our Lady of the Assumption Church.
LeFrois, Christian *o.s.b* '46 (SAV) Lakeland, GA Queen of Peace Church.
LeFrois, Msgr. Marvin J. '49 (SAV) Retired.
Leftwich, David *o.s.b.* '66 (NO) [P] St. Benedict, LA St. Joseph Abbey.
Legarra, Francisco *o.a.r.* '74 (NY) [DD] New York, NY Augustinian Recollects Provincial Residence, Province of St. Nicholas of Tolentine.
Legarra, Francisco J. *o.a.r.* '74 (NY) [126] Bronx, NY St. Anselm Church.
Legarski, Anthony (TR) Colts Neck, NJ Naval Weapons Station Earle.
Legarski, Anthony J. '83 (ALT) Beaverdale, PA Holy Spirit Church.
Legaspi, Alex L. '76 (SFR) Daly City, CA St. Andrew Church.
Legault, Michel *m.s.a.* '71 (NOR) [A] Cromwell, CT Holy Apostles College and Seminary.
Legendre, Msgr. Francis J. '61 (HT) Cut-Off, LA Sacred Heart Church.
Leger, Donald '68 (LAF) Breaux Bridge, LA St. Bernard Church.
Leger, G. Robert '71 (SJ) Milpitas, CA St. John the Baptist Church.
Leger, Jeffrey P. '94 (L) Campbellsville, KY Our Lady of Perpetual Help Church; Finley, KY Our Lady of the Hills Church; Greensburg, KY Holy Redeemer Church.
Leger, Laurie *m.s.* '54 (WOR) [3] Gardner, MA Our Lady of the Holy Rosary Church.
Leger, P. Austin '62 (LAF) St. Martinville, LA St. Martin of Tours Church.
Legere, Germain *c.p.* '42 (L) [K] Louisville, KY Nazareth Home; [L] Louisville, KY Sacred Heart Retreat.
Legerski, John (B) On Duty Outside the Diocese.
Legge, Gregory *o.s.b.* '00 (PBL) [G] Canon City, CO Holy Cross Abbey.
Lego, William E. *o.s.a.* '83 (CHI) [182] Chicago, IL St. Rita of Cascia Church.
Lehane, Brian *s.j.* '97 (TOL) [C] Toledo, OH St. John's Jesuit High School.
Lehane, Joseph *c.s.c.* '57 (FgM) Holy Cross Foreign Missions.
Lehane, Joseph '77 (CLV) Absent on Leave.
Leheny, Msgr. Bernard M. '66 (LA) Norwalk, CA St. John of God Church.
Lehman, Joseph *t.o.r.* '96 (STU) [A] Steubenville, OH Franciscan University of Steubenville.
Lehman, Joseph P. '80 (RIC) Roanoke, VA Our Lady of Nazareth Church.
Lehman, Mark A. '88 (PHX) Unassigned.
Lehman, Paul J. '54 (NEW) Retired.
Lehmann, Anthony *s.j.* '56 (SPK) [C] Spokane, WA Gonzaga University.
Lehmkuhl, Gerhardt B. *s.j.* '74 (STL) [P] St. Louis, MO Jesuit Community Corporation at St. Louis University - Jesuit Hall.
Lehmkuhl, John J. '45 (TOL) Retired.
Lehner, John *o.s.f.s.* '70 (DET) Inkster, MI Holy Family Church; Inkster, MI SS. Kevin and Norbert Church.
Lehnerd, Frank M. '58 (Y) [14] Youngstown, OH St. Edward's Church.
Lehnert, Brian '00 (PMB) Vero Beach, FL St. Helen Church.
Lehning, Thomas J. '70 (ARL) Manassas, VA Sacred Heart Church.
Lehocky, Msgr. Leigh A. '68 (CHR) [1] Columbia, SC St. Peter's Church.
Lehr, James W. *m.m.* '53 (NY) [DD] Maryknoll, NY Maryknoll Fathers and Brothers.
Lehr, Theodore F. *o.f.m.* '56 (NEW) Elmwood Park, NJ St. Leo's Church.
Lehrberger, James *o.cist.* '76 (DAL) [B] Irving, TX University of Dallas; [K] Irving, TX Cistercian Abbey of Our Lady of Dallas.
Leibenguth, Gerald T. *o.s.b.* '72 (BO) [W] Hingham, MA Glastonbury Abbey.
Leibham, David '87 (AUS) [6] Waco, TX St. Louis Church.
Leibold, Alcuin *o.s.b.* '56 (IND) [J] St. Meinrad, IN St. Meinrad Archabbey.
Leibold, James C. '80 (BRK) Military Chaplains.
Leibrecht, Robert G. '58 (STL) Port Hudson, MO Holy Family Church.
Leicht, Gerard *ss.cc.* '45 (HON) [G] Kaneohe, HI Sacred Hearts Center.
Leidich, Kevin A. *s.j.* '82 (LA) [F] Los Angeles, CA Loyola High School of Los Angeles.
Leies, John A. *s.m.* '56 (SAT) [C] San Antonio, TX St. Mary's University of San Antonio, Texas; [M] San Antonio, TX Marianist Residence.
Leif, Gregory P. '78 (WIN) Adams, MN Sacred Heart Church; [A] Winona, MN Immaculate Heart of Mary Seminary.
Leifeld, Msgr. Antony J. '38 (NU) [1] New Ulm, MN Cathedral of The Holy Trinity; Retired.
Leigh, David J. *s.j.* '68 (SEA) [A] Seattle, WA Seattle University.
Leigh, Peter (STN) On Duty Outside the Diocese.
Leigh, Peter (WCH) [D] Wichita, KS Via Christi Regional Medical Center, Inc.
Leighton, Donald E. '62 (PH) Gladwyne, PA St. John Baptist Vianney Church; Penn Valley, PA St. Justin Martyr Church.
Leign, Peter '99 (WCH) [B] Wichita, KS Kapaun Mt. Carmel Catholic High School.
Leiker, Perry D. '76 (LA) Hawthorne, CA St. Joseph Church.
Leikhim, Joel J. *o.s.b.* '61 (PAT) [M] Morristown, NJ St. Mary's Abbey.
Leil, Samir Abu (NTN) Phoenix, AZ St. John of the Desert Church.
Leinen, Ronald *m.s.c.* '57 (RCK) [G] Aurora, IL Missionaries of the Sacred Heart Community.
Leininger, Charles A. *s.j.* '53 (DAL) [D] Dallas, TX Jesuit College Preparatory School.
Leininger, Donald '58 (SP) Retired.
Leininger, Joseph B. *s.j.* '53 (GAL) [F] Houston, TX Strake, Jesuit College Preparatory Inc.
Leininger, William '56 (SJ) Retired.
Leipert, Jack J. '75 (SAG) Bad Axe, MI Sacred Heart Church.
Leiphon, Donald A. '68 (FAR) Fairmount, ND St. Anthony's Church; [G] Wahpeton, ND Carmel of Mary.
Leise, Gerald A. '74 (OM) Schuyler, NE St. Mary Church.
Leise, Leo V. *s.j.* '94 (FgM) Provinces.
Leise, Leo V. *s.j.* '94 (NO) [P] New Orleans, LA Jesuit Provincial Office.
Leisen, Leo '54 (SCL) Lake Henry, MN St. Margaret's Church; Roscoe, MN St. Agnes Church; Spring Hill, MN St. Michael's Church.
Leisen, Richard '56 (SCL) Paynesville, MN St. Louis Church.
Leising, Edmund *o.m.i.* '46 (FgM) Oblates Foreign Missions.
Leising, Msgr. Frederick D. '71 (BUF) Lancaster, NY St. Mary of the Assumption Church.
Leising, John J. '69 (BUF) Newfane, NY St. Bridget Church; Wilson, NY Our Lady of the Rosary Church.
Leising, Robert *o.m.i.* '90 (NY) [FF] Newburgh, NY Our Lady of Hope Center.
Leisle, Charles E. '58 (LC) Retired.
Leissa, Eric B. '95 (CLV) Willoughby, OH Immaculate Conception Church.

Leissler, Joseph L. '32 (SB) Retired.
Leisy, Christian *o.s.b.* '88 (SFE) [I] Abiquiu, NM Monastery of Christ in the Desert.
Leitem, Leon *o.f.m.cap.* '57 (PIT) Freedom, PA St. Felix Church; [O] Rochester, PA St. Cecilia Friary.
Leith, James A. '81 (FAR) West Fargo, ND Holy Cross Church.
Leitheiser, Douglas '49 (FRS) Retired.
Leiting, Robert L. '67 (SC) Retired.
Leitner, John E. '55 (KC) [2] Independence, MO St. Joseph the Worker Church.
Leitner, Thomas Aquinas *o.s.b.* '92 (OM) [K] Schuyler, NE Benedictine Mission House.
Leiton, Rafael '92 (NY) Middletown, NY St. Joseph Church.
Leiweke, Robert W. *s.j.* '58 (MIL) [P] Milwaukee, WI Jesuit Community at Marquette University.
LeJeune, Ronald J. '71 (TOL) [4] Fremont, OH St. Joseph Church.
Leke, Charles (SP) Inverness, FL Our Lady of Fatima Church.
Leketas, Peter J. '43 (LC) Retired.
Leland, Thomas H. '99 (WCH) [19] Wichita, KS St. Thomas Aquinas Church.
Leland, Tom (WCH) [B] Wichita, KS Kapaun Mt. Carmel Catholic High School.
Leliaert, Richard M. *o.s.c.* '67 (DET) Riverview, MI St. Cyprian Church; [K] Riverview, MI Crosier Community of Riverview.
Lelii, Raymond M. *s.j.* '61 (WDC) [E] Washington, DC Gonzaga College High School.
Lelo-Luemba, Albert *c.i.c.m.* '96 (BWN) Alton, TX San Martin de Porres Church.
Leloczky, Julius *o.cist.* '61 (DAL) [K] Irving, TX Cistercian Abbey of Our Lady of Dallas.
LeLonde, Venant *o.f.m.* '54 (NY) [2] New York, NY St. Agnes Church.
Lelonis, Richard '71 (PIT) [P] Bellevue, PA Mount Assisi Convent.
Lemaine, Calonge '89 (BRK) [238] Queens, NY Sacred Heart Church.
Lemanski, William E. *s.a.c.* '74 (MIL) [P] Milwaukee, WI Pallotti House.
Lemaster, Scott '85 (DAV) Georgetown, IA St. Patrick's Church; Lovilia, IA St. Peter's Church; Melrose, IA St. Patrick's Church.
LeMay, Donald *o.s.b.* '57 (SCL) [I] Collegeville, MN St. John's Abbey, of the Order of St. Benedict.
Lemay, Donald H. '89 (RIC) [9] Richmond, VA St. Edward The Confessor Church.
Lemay, Jean '75 (MAN) [18] Manchester, NH St. Theresa Church.
LeMay, John M. *o.s.m.* '84 (CHI) [N] Chicago, IL Order of Friar Servants of Mary (Servites) United States of America Province, Inc.
Lemay, Larry '99 (BEL) [1] Belleville, IL Cathedral of St. Peter.
Lembo, Richard A. '75 (PRT) Lubec, ME Sacred Heart Church.
Lemen, William F. '36 (CR) Bemidji, MN St. Philip's Church; Retired.
LeMere, Cletus *s.d.s.* (GB) Kiel, WI SS. Peter and Paul Church.
Lemire, Paul W. '89 (WOR) Leicester, MA St. Joseph's Church; Leicester, MA St. Pius X Church.
Lemke, Norbert J. *s.j.* '44 (MIL) [P] Wauwatosa, WI Jesuit Community at St. Camillus.
Lemkuhl, David A. '79 (CIN) On Duty Outside the Archdiocese.
Lemkuhl, David A. '79 (FgM) Maryknoll Foreign Missions.
Lemlin, Timothy J. '78 (PRO) [2] Burrillville, RI Our Lady of Good Help Church.
Lemm, Eugene '57 (SCL) Brandon, MN Church of St. Ann; Millerville, MN Seven Dolors Church.
Lemme, Christopher *t.o.r.* '98 (ARL) Luray, VA Our Lady of the Valley Church.
Lemmert, Ronald D. '51 (NY) [HH] Peekskill, NY My Father's House, Inc.
Lemmert, Ronald J. '79 (NY) State, NY Sing Sing Correctional Facility.
Lemming, Patrick W. '81 (MOB) On Leave from the Archdiocese.
Lemoi, Paul R. '75 (PRO) [7] West Warwick, RI Our Lady of Good Counsel Church.
Lemoine, Daniel P. '79 (BR) On Leave.
Lemoine, Msgr. J. Guy '56 (LAF) [1] New Iberia, LA St. Peter Church.
Lemoine, Russell J. '70 (ALX) Mansura, LA St. Paul the Apostle Church.
Lemoine, Msgr. Vincent P. '51 (SAL) Retired.
Lemon, Msgr. Clement P. '64 (WIL) Liftwood, DE Immaculate Heart of Mary Church.
Lemos, Thomas F. *c.s.c.* '74 (FTW) [5] South Bend, IN St. Casimir Church; [19] South Bend, IN St. Stephen Church.
Lemoyne, William '49 (ALB) Retired.
Lemp, Joseph R. '56 (PIT) Koppel, PA Queen of Heaven Church.
Lempart, Ignatius *o.s.c.* '43 (STP) Anoka, MN St. Stephen Church; [N] Anoka, MN Crosier Community of Anoka.
Lemrise, Arthur A. *c.s.v.* '44 (CHI) [N] Arlington Heights, IL Viatorian Province Center-Clerics of St. Viator.
Lemrise, John *c.m.f.* '52 (CHI) [N] Oak Park, IL Claretian Fathers Headquarters of U.S.A. Eastern Province.
Lemus, Francisco *s.j.* '62 (MIA) [H] Miami, FL Villa Javier.
Lemus, Francisco Arrivillaga *o.s.b.* '95 (SFS) [F] Marvin, SD Blue Cloud Abbey.
Lemus, Ovidio Ortega '83 (SJN) [41] San Juan, PR Ntra. Sra. de la Medalla Milagrosa Church.
Lenaghan, James J. *o.p.* '95 (FgM) Dominican - Order of Preachers Foreign Missions.
Lenahan, John B. '49 (L) Retired.
Lenane, Msgr. William '50 (SJ) Palo Alto, CA St. Thomas Aquinas Church; Retired.
Lenarz, Richard J. '56 (MAD) Retired; [H] Madison, WI Bishop O'Connor Catholic Pastoral Center.
Lencewicz, Leonard *o.f.m.* '63 (NY) [DD] New York, NY Franciscan Friars, Order of Friars Minor, Holy Name Province.
Lenczycki, Frederick '92 (STL) [K] Bridgeton, MO SSM De Paul Health Center.
Lendacky, Francis G. '61 (PH) [4] Philadelphia, PA St. Agnes-St. John Nepomucene Church.
Lendvai, John B. '94 (PIT) [63] Pittsburgh, PA Prince of Peace Church.
Lenehan, Claude *o.f.m.* '55 (PAT) [M] Paterson, NJ St. Benedict the Moor Friary.
Lenehan, Vincent '54 (SAC) Retired and in Senior Ministry.
Lengerich, Msgr. Vincent L. '48 (GRY) Retired.
Lengwin, Ronald P. '66 (PIT) [27] Pittsburgh, PA St. Mary of Mercy Church.
Lenihan, Daniel F. *o.c.s.o.* '55 (DUB) [K] Peosta, IA New Melleray Abbey, Order of Cistercians of the Strict Observance.
Lenihan, Msgr. John J. '53 (STA) Retired.
Lenihan, John P. '69 (ORG) Dana Point, CA St. Edward Church.
Lenihan, Michael '27 (CC) Aransas Pass, TX St. Mary, Star of the Sea Church.
Lenihan, Msgr. Michael '52 (LA) Redondo Beach, CA St. Lawrence Martyr Church.
Lenk, Msgr. Charles '52 (WOR) Retired.
Lenk, Dominic *o.s.b.* '98 (STL) [F] Creve Coeur, MO St. Louis Priory School; [P] St. Louis, MO The Abbey of St. Mary and St. Louis.
Lennon, Charles '80 (RVC) Absent on Leave.
Lennon, Francis P. '40 (PH) Collegeville, PA St. Eleanor Church; Retired.
Lennon, James M. '58 (JOL) [17] Joliet, IL St. Patrick Church.
Lennon, John W. '55 (NY) [11] Yonkers, NY St. John the Baptist Church; New York, NY New York Postal Service; New York, NY New York Sanitation Department; Yonkers, NY Yonkers Police Department; Yonkers, NY Yonkers Fire Department.
Lennon, Joseph L. *o.p.* '47 (PRO) [P] Providence, RI St. Thomas Aquinas Priory at Providence College.
Lennon, Peter F. '55 (NEW) Retired; [B] South Orange, NJ Seton Hall University.
Lennon, Raymond *s.v.d.* '64 (BLX) [A] Bay St. Louis, MS St. Augustine's; [A] Bay St. Louis, MS St. Augustine's.
Lennon, Msgr. Richard G. '73 (BO) [A] Boston, MA St. John's Seminary School of Theology.
Lennon, Robert *c.ss.r.* (BO) [53] Boston, MA Our Lady of Perpetual Help Church.
Lennon, Msgr. Robert T. '50 (NEW) Livingston, NJ St. Philomena Church; Retired.
Lenoch, Francis J. '44 (DAV) Retired.
Lenoci, Dominick J. '95 (NEW) Glen Rock, NJ St. Catharine Church.
Lenoir, Jean '85 (SB) Palm Desert, CA Sacred Heart Church.
Lenox, Peter F. '00 (BGP) [3] Bridgeport, CT St. Andrew Church.
Lens, Fred '71 (STL) Maryland Heights, MO St. Blaise Church; St. Louis, MO DePaul Health Center.
Lenti, Arthur *s.d.b.* '50 (OAK) [A] Berkeley, CA Dominican School of Philosophy and Theology; [N] Berkeley, CA Salesian Community.
Lentine, Peter S. '50 (DET) [63] Detroit, MI St. Philomena Church.
Lentz, Gerald J. *s.j.* '60 (SJ) [D] San Jose, CA Bellarmine College Preparatory.
Lentz, Lawrence D. *c.s.v.* '81 (CHI) [206] Chicago, IL St. Viator Church.
Lentz, Robert F. '64 (BAL) [28] Baltimore, MD St. Dominic Church.
Lenz, Daniel *o.s.b.* '85 (OM) [C] Elkhorn, NE Mount Michael High School; [K] Elkhorn, NE Mount Michael Abbey.
Lenz, David *o.f.m. conv.* (IND) Clarksville, IN St. Anthony of Padua Church.
Lenz, Frank B. '94 (VIC) Yorktown, TX Holy Cross Church.
Lenz, Frank M. '69 (MAR) Marquette, MI Marquette General Hospital.
Lenz, Henry *m.s.* '41 (LKC) [3] Sulphur, LA Our Lady of Prompt Succor Church.
Lenz, Henry J. *m.s.* '41 (TYL) Retired.
Lenz, Michael *o.f.m.* '76 (CIN) [L] Cincinnati, OH Archbishop Leibold Home for the Aged; [M] Cincinnati, OH St. John the Baptist Friary.
Lenz, Msgr. Paul A. '49 (ALT) On Duty Outside the Diocese.
Lenzini, Donald J. '51 (BEL) Retired.
Lenzner, George G. '57 (GB) Oneida, WI St. Joseph Church.
Leo, Arthur R. '85 (NY) Peekskill, NY Assumption Church.
Leon, Antonio '57 (STA) [8] Jacksonville, FL Immaculate Conception Church.
Leon, Bartholomew *o.s.b.* '81 (CC) [H] Sandia, TX Corpus Christi Abbey.
Leon, Bartholomew *o.s.b.* '85 (SAM) Dover, NH St. George Church.
Leon, Hector '91 (BGP) [3] Danbury, CT Our Lady of Guadalupe Church.
Leon, J. Francisco *o.s.a.* '78 (GAL) Pasadena, TX Blessed Juan Diego Church.
Leon, Jose M. '81 (OAK) Union City, CA Our Lady of the Rosary Church.
Leon, Mario Rodriguez *o.p.* (SJN) [A] Bayamon, PR Bayamon Central University.
Leon Guerrero, Felixberto C. *o.f.m.cap.* '86 (AGN) Chalan Pago, GU Nuestra Senora de la Paz y Buen Viaje Church.
Leonard, Albert P. '89 (SCR) Conyngham, PA St. John Bosco Church.
Leonard, Clyde A. '64 (BO) Senior Priests.
Leonard, Edmond J. *c.s.sp.* '37 (SB) [E] Hemet, CA Holy Ghost Fathers.
Leonard, Edward '53 (COS) Retired.
Leonard, Edwin M. '84 (CLV) [6] Parma, OH Holy Family Church.
Leonard, Eugene A. '66 (CHR) Spartanburg, SC Jesus Our Risen Savior Church.
Leonard, Francis B. (BO) Chelmsford, MA St. John the Evangelist Church.
Leonard, Francis B. '50 (BO) Senior Priests.
Leonard, Gerald *s.v.d.* '80 (SB) [6] San Bernardino, CA St. Anne Church.
Leonard, John '48 (JKS) Retired.
Leonard, John *o.f.m.* '96 (PAT) Little Falls, NJ Our Lady of the Holy Angels Church.
Leonard, John E. '65 (RIC) [15] Richmond, VA St. Michael Church.
Leonard, John F. '55 (BO) West Newbury, MA St. Ann Church.
Leonard, John J. *s.j.* '50 (NY) [F] New York, NY Fordham Preparatory School; [DD] New York, NY Jesuit Community at Fordham University.
Leonard, Joseph '45 (MRY) Retired.
Leonard, Matthew '98 (CHL) [5] Charlotte, NC St. Gabriel Church.
Leonard, Patrick F. *o.s.a.* '96 (CHL) [6] Charlotte, NC St. John Neumann Church.
Leonard, Patrick J. '63 (NEW) Mountainside, NJ Our Lady of Lourdes Church.
Leonard, Msgr. Paul F. '89 (SCR) [21] Scranton, PA St. Patrick's Church.
Leonard, Peter J. *o.s.f.s.* '86 (ALN) [B] Center Valley, PA Desales University; [K] Center Valley, PA Oblates of St. Francis de Sales.
Leonard, Raymond '90 (MET) [5] New Brunswick, NJ Sacred Heart Church.
Leonard, Robert *s.j.* '49 (LA) [J] Duarte, CA Santa Teresita Hospital.
Leonard, Saysiri '88 (HRT) [2] Waterbury, CT Immaculate Conception Church.
Leonard, Sebastian *o.s.b.* '57 (HRT) [E] New Milford, CT Canterbury School.
Leonard, Sebastian *o.s.b.* '57 (IND) [J] St. Meinrad, IN St. Meinrad Archabbey.
Leonard, Msgr. Thomas P. '56 (NY) [50] New York, NY Holy Trinity Church.
Leonard, William F. '70 (CHR) [14] Charleston, SC St. Thomas The Apostle Church; [H] Charleston, SC Charleston Southern University.
Leonard, Msgr. William P. '43 (DUB) Retired.
Leonard, William T. (BO) Belmont, MA Fernald Developmental Center.
Leonardis, Charles F. '54 (ALT) [5] Windber, PA Holy Child Jesus Church.
Leonards, Martin C. '66 (LAF) Maurice, LA St. Alphonsus Church.
Leone, Arthur '56 (NY) [85] New York, NY Our Lady of Good Counsel Church.
Leone, James M. '60 (BRK) Military Chaplains.
Leone, Kenneth '67 (DEN) Littleton, CO St. Frances Cabrini Church.
Leone, Richard D. *o.s.f.s.* '59 (WIL) [I] Wilmington, DE DeSales House.
Leone, William B. '74 (ROC) Cato, NY St. Patrick Church; Weedsport, NY St. John Church; Weedsport, NY St. Joseph Church.

Leong, Francis J. *m.m.* '87 (NY) [DD] Maryknoll, NY Maryknoll Fathers and Brothers.
Leong, Herman '91 (OAK) [2] Concord, CA St. Bonaventure Church.
Leonhardt, Douglas J. *s.j.* '69 (MIL) [E] Milwaukee, WI Marquette University High School; [P] Milwaukee, WI Pere Marquette House Jesuit Community.
Leonhardt, Louis J. '56 (DAV) Hills, IA St. Joseph's Church; Lone Tree, IA St. Mary's Church; Nichols, IA St. Mary's Church; Iowa City, IA Veteran's Administration Hospital.
Leonhardt, Robert A. *o.f.m.* '59 (SHP) Hodge, LA St. Lucy Church.
Leopold, David C. '82 (BGP) Westport, CT Assumption Church.
Leotilo, Rocco *c.s.s.* '53 (BO) [Z] Waltham, MA Stigmatine Fathers and Brothers.
Lepak, Roy (STP) [C] St. Paul, MN University of St. Thomas.
Lepak, Roy C. '62 (STP) Special Assignment.
LePine, Clement J. '46 (MAR) Retired.
Lepire, Roland M. '75 (PRO) Absent on Leave.
Lepleiter, Robert P. '63 (PH) Chalfont, PA St. Jude Church; Retired.
Lepping, George M. *s.m.* '38 (WDC) [M] Washington, DC Marist Center.
LeQuang, Peter '97 (LR) Fort Smith, AR Christ the King Church.
Lequin, Thomas '77 (PRT) Mars Hill, ME St. Joseph Church; Presque Isle, ME Nativity of B.V.M. Church.
Leraux, Roger *m.s.* '52 (FR) [I] Attleboro, MA La Salette Shrine.
Lerch, Joseph *s.j.* '49 (BAL) [M] Towson, MD St. Joseph Medical Center, Inc.
Lerch, Joseph R. *s.j.* '56 (BAL) [S] Baltimore, MD Jesuit Fathers and Brothers Maryland Provincial Curia.
Leroux, Edward N. '56 (ALB) Fort Edward, NY St. Joseph Church; Retired.
LeRoux, William F. *s.j.* '53 (SEA) [A] Seattle, WA Seattle University.
Lery, Bruce *s.m.* '87 (HON) Kapaa, HI St. Catherine Church.
Lesak, William P. '75 (NEW) Military Chaplains.
Lesch, Howard *c.pp.s.* '44 (CIN) [M] Dayton, OH Provincial Office of the Cincinnati Province of the Society of the Precious Blood.
Lescher, Raymond C. '63 (JOL) [5] Joliet, IL Sacred Heart Church.
Lesczynski, James J. '64 (LC) Necedah, WI St. Francis of Assisi Church.
Leser, Msgr. William J. *c.b.* '63 (LA) Westlake Village, CA St. Jude Church.
Leshney, Michael F. '73 (CIN) [29] Cincinnati, OH Good Shepherd Church.
LeSieur, Msgr. David '76 (LR) [11] Little Rock, AR Our Lady of the Holy Souls Church.
Leskovar, Richard J. '68 (ALB) Special Assignment.
Leslie, Larry B. (STO) On Special or Other Diocesan Assignment.
Leslie, Larry B. '80 (COV) Military Chaplains.
Leslie, Patrick J. '69 (SAC) On Duty Outside the Diocese.
Leslie, Patrick J. '69 (SR) [5] Santa Rosa, CA Star of the Valley Church; Eldridge, CA Sonoma Developmental Center.
Lesniak, David '91 (DET) Port Huron, MI St. Stephen Church.
Lesniak, Marian J. '50 (LAN) [2] Jackson, MI St. Joseph Church.
Lesniak, Richard D. '66 (MAD) Kingston, WI St. Mary Church; Markesan, WI St. Joseph Church.
Lesnick, John F. '78 (BAL) Special Assignment.
Lesnick, Richard '67 (SEA) Unassigned.
Lesniewski, Stephen F. '93 (CHI) [167] Chicago, IL SS. Peter and Paul Church.
Lesniowski, Francis A. '63 (GBG) [4] Connellsville, PA St. Rita Church.
Lesniowski, Stanley '70 (PAT) [4] Passaic, NJ Holy Rosary Church.
Lesousky, John *c.r.* '56 (L) [L] Louisville, KY Villa Pacis, Resurrectionist Retirement Home.
Lessard, Eugene R. '59 (PRO) [1] Central Falls, RI The Holy Spirit Catholic Community Church.
Lessard, Gerard Arthur *o.p.* '84 (L) [4] Springfield, KY St. Rose Church.
Lessard, Joseph M. '80 (PHX) On Duty Outside the Diocese.
Lessard, Joseph M. '80 (RCK) [4] Aurora, IL St. Mary Church; [D] Aurora, IL Provena Mercy Center.
Lessard, Joseph P. '52 (STL) Retired.
Lessard, Leo '60 (GB) Retired.
Lessard, Raymond (PMB) [A] Boynton Beach, FL St. Vincent de Paul Regional Seminary.
Lesseps, Roland J. *s.j.* '65 (FgM) Provinces.
Lesseps, Roland J. *s.j.* '65 (NO) [P] New Orleans, LA Jesuit Provincial Office.
Lester, Msgr. J. William '45 (FTW) [1] Fort Wayne, IN Cathedral of the Immaculate Conception; Retired.
Lester, John E. '59 (TOL) Retired.
Lester, John J. '62 (NEW) Scotch Plains, NJ St. Bartholomew Church.
Lester, Thomas '57 (OAK) Retired.
Lester, William F. *s.j.* '54 (SJ) [L] Los Gatos, CA Sacred Heart Jesuit Center.
LeStrange, Gregory C. '82 (SY) Fayetteville, NY Immaculate Conception Church.
Letendre, Theodore *f.i.c.* '97 (PRT) [I] Alfred, ME Notre Dame Institute; [I] Alfred, ME Notre Dame Institute.
Lethiez, Alphonse O. '55 (PRO) [4] West Warwick, RI St. John the Baptist Church.
Leto, Nelo A. '54 (DM) Retired.
Letoile, Kenneth R. *o.p.* '74 (CIN) [28] Cincinnati, OH St. Gertrude Church; [M] Cincinnati, OH St. Gertrude Priory.
Letourneau, Larry '00 (SAL) [1] Salina, KS Cathedral of the Sacred Heart.
Letourneau, Msgr. Paul R. '54 (BUF) Retired; [O] Tonawanda, NY O'Hara Residence; [T] Buffalo, NY Kolping Catholic Young Men's Association of Buffalo, NY dba Kolping Society of Buffalo.
Lettau, David '53 (Y) Retired.
Letteer, Michael C. '96 (HBG) New Cumberland, PA St. Theresa of the Infant Jesus Church.
Lettic, Edward P. '73 (WOR) Lancaster, MA Immaculate Conception Church.
Lettre, Raymond A. '88 (SP) Citrus Springs, FL St. Elizabeth Ann Seton Church.
LeTure, Theodore J. '49 (RVC) Valley Stream, NY Holy Name of Mary Church; Retired.
Leu, James E. '71 (DAV) Absent on Leave.
Leuer, Msgr. Anthony (LA) [C] Rancho Palos Verdes, CA Marymount College, Palos Verdes, California.
Leurck, Raymond J. '67 (CIN) Military Chaplains.
Leute, Charles J. *o.p.* '69 (FAR) Fort Totten, ND Seven Dolors Church; Tokio, ND Christ the King Church; Fort Totten Reservation, ND (Sioux Indians) Church; Fort Totten Reservation, ND (Sioux Indians) Church.
Leva, Stephen F. '88 (ARL) Dale City, VA Holy Family Church.
Levan, Donald E. '89 (BUF) [P] Buffalo, NY Immaculate Heart of Mary Provincial House and Convent.
Levandusky, Edward '65 (PHU) Palmerton, PA St. Vladimir's Church.
Levario, Gilbert *o.c.d.* '83 (TUC) [18] Tucson, AZ St. Margaret's Church; [F] Tucson, AZ Discalced Carmelite Friars of St. Margaret's.
LeVasseur, Angelo B. '83 (PRT) Sabattus, ME Our Lady of the Rosary Church.
LeVasseur, Giles *o.s.b.* '84 (WDC) [M] Washington, DC St. Anselm's Abbey.
LeVasseur, Lawrence A. *c.s.c.* '51 (SAT) [B] San Antonio, TX Congregation of Holy Cross - Formation Community; [M] San Antonio, TX Holy Cross Community.
LeVay, R. Joseph '50 (SPR) Hinsdale, MA St. Patrick's Church.
LeVecke, John *s.j.* '80 (SFR) [T] Hollywood, CA Christian Life Communities.
LeVecke, John *s.j.* '84 (LA) [6] Los Angeles, CA Blessed Sacrament Church.
Leveille, Andre E. *c.s.c.* '78 (FTW) [J] South Bend, IN Congregation of Holy Cross, Indiana Province, Provincial House.
Leveille, Rudolph J. '57 (PRT) Retired.
Leveillee, Roger L. (SPC) [1] Cape Girardeau, MO Cathedral of St. Mary.
Leven, Marvin '59 (OKL) Special Assignment.
Levenhagen, Robert J. '57 (DUB) Retired.
Levens, Robert J. *s.j.* '81 (BO) [W] Boston, MA The Society of Jesus of New England-Provincial Offices; [W] Boston, MA The Society of Jesus of New England-Provincial Offices.
Levens, Robert J. *s.j.* '81 (FgM) Provinces.
Lever, Msgr. Tony (LA) [BB] Los Angeles, CA Archdiocesan Office for Campus Ministry.
Levernier, Donald *glmy.* '61 (CIN) [M] Cincinnati, OH Headquarters of Glenmary Home Missioners.
Levesque, Msgr. Edmond R. '55 (FR) [11] New Bedford, MA St. Anthony of Padua's Church.
Levesque, Gerald A. '64 (PRT) Auburn, ME St. Louis Church; Auburn, ME St. Philip's Church; Auburn, ME Sacred Heart Church.
Levesque, Joseph L. *c.m.* '67 (BUF) [C] Niagara University, NY Niagara University; [O] Niagara University, NY Vincentian Community at Niagara University.
Levesque, Louis *c.j.m.* '50 (SD) [3] San Diego, CA Blessed Sacrament Church.
Levesque, Paul '89 (ORG) Inactive Leave.
Levesque, Robert G. *o.m.i.* '60 (MAN) [K] Colebrook, NH Shrine of Our Lady of Grace.
Levesque, Roger J. '59 (FR) [18] New Bedford, MA St. Joseph-St. Therese Church.
Levesque, Sylvio E. '46 (SPR) Three Rivers, MA St. Anne's Church.
Levesque, Sylvio J. '55 (PRT) Winthrop, ME St. Francis Xavier Church.
Levi, Anthony W. '93 (LFT) Carmel, IN St. Elizabeth Ann Seton Church.
Levis, Robert J. '48 (E) Retired; [B] Erie, PA Gannon University.
Levitre, J. Albert, Jr. '80 (FBK) North Pole, AK St. Nicholas Church.
Levitt, Donald L. '79 (PEO) Moline, IL Christ the King Church.
Levko, John J. *s.j.* '78 (SCR) [C] Scranton, PA University of Scranton; [C] Scranton, PA University of Scranton.
Levkulic, Msgr. William '55 (PBR) Duquesne, PA SS. Peter and Paul Church.
LeVoir, John M. '81 (STP) South St. Paul, MN Holy Trinity Church; South St. Paul, MN St. Augustine Church.
LeVoy, Joseph T. '54 (CHI) [6] Cicero, IL Our Lady of the Mount Church; Retired.
Levri, Fideles *glmy.* '67 (OWN) Beaver Dam, KY Holy Redeemer Church; Morgantown, KY Holy Trinity Church.
Levy, Cyril '53 (GLP) McNary, AZ St. Anthony Church.
Levy, Michael *o.m.i.* '57 (SAT) [55] San Antonio, TX St. Mary Church.
Lewandowski, Andrew *o.f.m.* '76 (STL) [P] St. Louis, MO Franciscan Friary of St. Anthony of Padua; [R] St. Louis, MO Franciscan Sisters of Mary Administration.
Lewandowski, Andrzej *c.r.* '89 (CHI) [86] Chicago, IL St. Hyacinth Church.
Lewandowski, Bruce *c.ss.r.* '94 (NY) [150] Bronx, NY Immaculate Conception Church.
Lewandowski, David J. '55 (HRT) Southington, CT Immaculate Conception Church.
Lewandowski, Dennis '85 (JOL) Woodridge, IL Christ The Servant Church.
Lewandowski, Donald *o.s.a.* '69 (JOL) [5] Lockport, IL Our Mother of Good Counsel Church; [C] New Lenox, IL Providence Catholic High School.
Lewandowski, Glen *o.s.c.* '74 (FgM) Crosier Foreign Missions.
Lewandowski, John '96 (FAR) Zeeland, ND St. Andrew's Church.
Lewandowski, Leonard A. '77 (PH) Swedesburg, PA Sacred Heart Church.
Lewandowski, Michael *o.f.m.conv.* '75 (ALT) Davidsville, PA St. Anne Church.
Lewandowski, Raymond H. '85 (DET) [5] Wyandotte, MI St. Patrick Church.
Lewandowski, Richard P. '74 (WOR) [3] Fitchburg, MA St. Camillus de Lellis Church; [Q] Worcester, MA Campus Ministry.
Lewandowski, Robert M. *s.m.* '64 (FWT) Denton, TX St. Mark Church; [N] Denton, TX University of North Texas and Texas Woman's University.
Lewandowski, Ronald C. '95 (CHI) Barrington, IL St. Anne Church.
Lewandowski, Theodore V. '98 (RCK) Menominee, IL Nativity of the Blessed Virgin Mary Church.
Lewandowski, Thomas J. '00 (PIT) [43] Pittsburgh, PA St. Basil Church.
Lewanski, Gary J. '82 (CHI) [159] Chicago, IL Our Lady of Victory Church.
Lewczak, Thomas J. '65 (NEW) [7] Elizabeth, NJ St. Hedwig's Church.
Lewett, George *o.f.m.* '88 (FgM) Custody of St. Mary of the Angels. Byzantine-Slavonic.
Lewicki, Roman B. *s.j.* '65 (FgM) Provinces.
Lewinski, Cassian *o.p.* '69 (SD) [L] San Diego, CA University of California at San Diego (Campus Ministry).
Lewinski, Ronald J. '72 (CHI) Mundelein, IL St. Mary Church.
Lewis, Alaric *o.s.b.* '93 (IND) [J] St. Meinrad, IN St. Meinrad Archabbey.
Lewis, Alexander J. *o.f.m.conv.* '85 (LA) [Q] Torrance, CA Franciscan Friars, St. Bonaventure Friary.
Lewis, Alexander J. *o.f.m.conv.* '85 (OAK) [N] San Pablo, CA Franciscans, Conventual of California.
Lewis, Clyde A. '64 (OG) [1] Watertown, NY Holy Family Church.
Lewis, Daniel C. *s.j.* '62 (BO) [E] Boston, MA Boston College High School & Jesuit Community.
Lewis, David '90 (CI) Uman, FM Holy Cross Church; Tolowas, FM St. Anthony's Church; [C] Tunnuk, Chuuk, FM Vicariate Residence.
Lewis, David J. (GB) New London, WI Most Precious Blood Church.
Lewis, Dennis J. '75 (MIL) [58] Milwaukee, WI St. Michael Church; [76] Milwaukee, WI St. Rose Church.
Lewis, Edward J. '84 (SAC) Vallejo, CA St. Vincent Ferrer Church.
Lewis, Edward J. '92 (GBG) Ford City, PA St. Mary Church; Ford City, PA St. Francis of Paola Church; Ford City, PA Holy Trinity Church.
Lewis, Eric A. '69 (LA) La Puente, CA St. Joseph Church; [J] West Covina, CA Citrus Valley Health Partners, Queen of the Valley Campus.
Lewis, Francis C. '68 (PH) Bristol, PA St. Mark Church.
Lewis, Francis W. *s.j.* '60 (BGP) [B] Fairfield, CT Fairfield University; [P] Fairfield, CT The Fairfield Jesuit Community-Fairfield University.
Lewis, Gerald *s.v.d.* '52 (GAL) [K] Houston, TX The Catholic Chaplain Corps.
Lewis, Gerald *s.v.d.* '57 (GAL) [1] Galveston, TX St.

Mary's Cathedral Basilica Church.
Lewis, Gerald '61 (R) Special Assignment.
Lewis, Gerald F. '88 (PAT) Hainesville, NJ St. Thomas the Apostle Church; Montague, NJ St. James the Greater Church.
Lewis, Gerard *o.f.m.* '85 (PAT) [M] Ringwood, NJ Holy Name Friary, Inc.
Lewis, Harry J. '50 (SCR) Retired; [N] Dunmore, PA Villa St. Joseph.
Lewis, James *o.carm.* '83 (JOL) [J] Darien, IL Carmelite Provincial Office.
Lewis, James V. *s.j.* '69 (CLV) [D] Cleveland, OH St. Ignatius High School.
Lewis, Kenneth W. '91 (TLS) Fairfax, OK Sacred Heart Church.
Lewis, Lawrence J. *m.m.* '75 (FgM) Maryknoll Foreign Missions.
Lewis, Leo T. '60 (STL) Retired.
Lewis, Mark *s.j.* '91 (NO) [P] New Orleans, LA Jesuit Provincial Office.
Lewis, Ryan '99 (OM) [9] Omaha, NE St. Bernard Church; [B] Omaha, NE Roncalli Catholic High School of Omaha.
Lewis, Sebastian C. *o.s.b.* '51 (CHI) [107] Chicago, IL St. Joseph Church.
Lewis, Sebastian C. *o.s.b.* '51 (PEO) [A] Peru, IL St. Bede Abbey and Academy.
Lewis, Walter G. '79 (RIC) [14] Richmond, VA St. Mary Church.
Lewkiewicz, Richard '68 (BRK) [91] Brooklyn, NY Our Lady of Angels Church.
Lex, Henry V. '57 (BUF) Retired; [O] Buffalo, NY Sheehan Residence for Priests.
Lex, James '50 (EVN) [14] Evansville, IN St. Anthony Church; Retired.
Lexa, Robert '70 (GB) Retired.
Ley, Richard J. '71 (ARL) Annandale, VA St. Ambrose Church.
Ley, Theodore C. *s.m.* '71 (LA) Gardena, CA Maria Regina Church.
Leykam, John J. '72 (STL) St. Ann, MO St. Kevin Church.
Leykam, Lambert *o.f.m.* '56 (FWT) [H] Crowley, TX St. Francis Village, Inc.
Leyland, Thomas J. '65 (TOL) Perrysburg, OH St. Rose Church.
Leyrita, Norbert L. '63 (GR) Saranac, MI St. Anthony Church.
Lezama, Lester '96 (SFR) [3] San Mateo, CA St. Matthew Church.
Lezochowski, Walter '59 (DET) Detroit, MI Crittendon Hospital.
Li, Vincent *o.p.* (WDC) [B] Washington, DC Dominican House of Studies.
Liable, Adrian *o.s.b.* '58 (OM) [K] Elkhorn, NE Mount Michael Abbey.
Liagas, Carlos *s.j.* (CHI) [149] Chicago, IL Our Lady of Lourdes Church.
Libaire, Nathan *o.s.b.* '81 (SCL) [I] Collegeville, MN St. John's Abbey, of the Order of St. Benedict.
Libaire, Nathan *o.s.b.* '81 (SFE) [7] Albuquerque, NM Nativity of the Blessed Virgin Mary Church.
Libanati, Ciro '93 (SB) San Jacinto, CA St. Anthony Church.
Libasci, Peter '78 (RVC) Montauk, NY St. Therese of Lisieux Church.
Libbey, Fouis *s.j.* '91 (SFR) [N] San Francisco, CA Jesuit Community at University of San Francisco.
Libby, Richard '99 (CC) [21] Corpus Christi, TX St. Pius X Church.
Libens, John F. *s.j.* '70 (DET) [E] Detroit, MI University of Detroit Jesuit High School and Academy; [K] Detroit, MI Jesuit Provincial Office-Detroit Province of the Society of Jesus.
Libens, John F. *s.j.* '70 (FgM) Provinces.
Libera, Angelo '57 (SY) Retired.
Libera, Thomas A. '69 (CHI) Evanston, IL St. Athanasius Church.
Liberatore, Albert M. '89 (SCR) Duryea, PA Sacred Heart of Jesus Church; [A] Dalton, PA Saint Pius X Seminary.
Liberatore, David D. '60 (CLV) Parma Heights, OH St. John Bosco Church.
Liberty, Donald *c.ss.r.* '61 (LA) Whittier, CA St. Mary of the Assumption Church; [Q] Whittier, CA Redemptorist Fathers Mission House.
Libone, John (DAL) [22] Dallas, TX St. Patrick Church.
Liboroni-Pierozzi, Gilberto '63 (BAL) [M] Towson, MD St. Joseph Medical Center, Inc.
Librandi, Michael A. '78 (RCK) Lena, IL St. Joseph Church; Scales Mound, IL Holy Trinity Church.
Librea, Ralph '56 (OM) [16] Omaha, NE Holy Cross Church.
Licari, Jonathan *o.s.b.* '76 (SCL) Collegeville, MN St. John the Baptist Church; [I] Collegeville, MN St. John's Abbey, of the Order of St. Benedict.
Licastro, Antonio '55 (HRT) [3] New Haven, CT St. Anthony's Church.
Licata, Donald B. '59 (NY) State, NY Downstate Correction Facility; State, NY Fishkill Correctional Facility.
Licciardi, Frederick T. *c.pp.s.* '82 (CIN) [M] Dayton, OH Provincial Office of the Cincinnati Province of the Society of the Precious Blood.
Lichtefeld, James J. '59 (L) [71] Louisville, KY St. Stephen, Martyr Church.
Lichtenberger, Doug '88 (SFD) Absent on Leave.
Lichtenthal, Msgr. James J. '63 (BUF) Snyder, NY Christ the King Church.
Lichter, Mark '92 (SFS) [5] Sioux Falls, SD St. Lambert Church.
Lickman, Peter '68 (PSC) Miami, FL St. Basil's Church.
Lickteig, Anthony '54 (KCK) Louisburg, KS Immaculate Conception Church.
Lickteig, Bernard *o.carm.* '46 (KCK) Scipio, KS St. Boniface Church.
Lickteig, Fergus *o.carm.* '55 (KCK) [1] Leavenworth, KS Immaculate Conception Church; [4] Leavenworth, KS St. Joseph's Church.
Lickteig, Norbert '61 (KCK) [2] Topeka, KS Christ the King Church.
Licznerski, Henryk *c.r.* '92 (MOB) [8] Montgomery, AL Resurrection Catholic Church.
Liddy, Msgr. Richard M. '63 (NEW) [B] South Orange, NJ Seton Hall University.
Lidebach, Daniel P. *s.j.* '78 (STL) [P] St. Louis, MO Jesuit Community Corporation at St. Louis University - Jesuit Hall.
Liderbach, Daniel P. *s.j.* '73 (BUF) [O] Buffalo, NY Canisius Jesuit Community.
Liderbach, Daniel P. *s.j.* '73 (DET) [K] Detroit, MI Jesuit Provincial Office-Detroit Province of the Society of Jesus.
Lieb, Germain L. *o.s.b.* '45 (GBG) [H] Latrobe, PA Saint Vincent Archabbey.
Lieb, Joel R. *o.s.b.* '46 (GBG) [H] Latrobe, PA Saint Vincent Archabbey.
Lieb, Marianus D. *t.o.r.* '44 (ALT) [F] Loretto, PA Mount Assisi Friary.
Liebert, William *s.v.d.* '57 (FgM) Society of the Divine Word Foreign Missions.
Lieberth, Joseph J. '68 (CLV) Stow, OH Holy Family Church.
Liebhardt, Kevin M. '74 (CLV) Eastlake, OH St. Justin Martyr Church.
Liebl, Harold J. *s.a.c.* '48 (MIL) [P] Milwaukee, WI St. Vincent Community.
Liebl, Michael *o.s.b.* '77 (OM) [C] Elkhorn, NE Mount Michael High School; [K] Elkhorn, NE Mount Michael Abbey.
Liebler, Thomas '81 (SFD) Granite City, IL St. Elizabeth Church.
Liebner, David C. '80 (ALN) [1] Minersville, PA St. Barbara Church; [2] Minersville, PA St. Francis of Assisi Church.
Liebner, David M. '60 (ALN) Girardville, PA St. Vincent de Paul Church.
Liebner, James *s.v.d.* '85 (FgM) Society of the Divine Word Foreign Missions.
Liebscher, Arthur F. *s.j.* '84 (SJ) [B] Santa Clara, CA Santa Clara University.
Liekens, Ernest *o.m.i.* '61 (FgM) Oblates Foreign Missions.
Liem, Joseph Than Van *c.m.c.* '89 (SPC) Neosho, MO St. Canera Church; Seneca, MO St. Mary Church.
Lienert, Charles J. '68 (P) [14] Portland, OR St. Francis of Assisi Church; Gresham, OR St. Henry Church.
Lienhard, Joseph T. *s.j.* '71 (NY) [A] Yonkers, NY St. Joseph's Seminary; [DD] New York, NY Jesuit Community at Fordham University.
Liermann, Raymond B. '53 (STL) Retired.
Lies, Eric *o.s.b.* '45 (IND) [J] St. Meinrad, IN St. Meinrad Archabbey.
Lies, James M. *c.s.c.* '97 (FTW) [J] South Bend, IN Congregation of Holy Cross, Indiana Province, Provincial House.
Lies, William M. *c.s.c.* '94 (FTW) [J] South Bend, IN Congregation of Holy Cross, Indiana Province, Provincial House.
Lieser, Gregory '63 (SCL) [9] St. Cloud, MN St. Peter Church.
Lieser, Vincent '67 (SCL) Melrose, MN St. Mary's Church.
Liew, Richard (NY) White Plains, NY New York Hospital - Cornell Medical Center.
Liewer, David F. '74 (OM) South Sioux City, NE St. Michael Church.
Lifrak, Richard *ss.cc.* '95 (FR) [4] New Bedford, MA Our Lady of the Assumption Church.
Ligato, Anthony '95 (ALB) Glenville, NY Immaculate Conception Church.
Ligeti, Angelus *o.f.m.* '79 (DET) [31] Detroit, MI Holy Cross Church.
Ligeza, Stanislaw (DEN) Louisville, CO St. Louis Church.
Liggio, John R. *o.s.a.* '75 (PH) [G] Malvern, PA Malvern Preparatory School for Boys; [AA] Malvern, PA Augustinian Friars (O.S.A.).
Lightner, Bede C. *o.s.b.* '41 (CHL) [J] Belmont, NC Belmont Abbey.
Ligory, Joseph '83 (NY) [145] Bronx, NY St. Helena Church.
Ligos, George A. '53 (NEW) Retired.
Liguori, Henry A. '66 (TR) Military Chaplains.
Lih, Dominic A. (PIT) [3] Millvale, PA Holy Spirit Church.
Lihvar, Francis P. *s.j.* '61 (CLV) [B] Cleveland, OH John Carroll Jesuit Community.
Liistro, Frank J. '74 (WOR) [7] Fitchburg, MA Madonna of the Holy Rosary Church.
Lijewski, Thomas F. '70 (MIL) [6] Racine, WI St. John Nepomuk Church.
Lijewski, Timothy M. '93 (CHR) [H] Columbia, SC University of South Carolina, St. Thomas More Center.
Lileart, Richard (DET) Detroit, MI Oakwood Hospital.
Lill, Kenneth J. '91 (TOL) [35] Toledo, OH St. Patrick of Heatherdowns Church.
Lilly, Msgr. E. C. '29 (SC) Retired.
Lilly, Robert A. *m.m.* '62 (NY) [DD] Maryknoll, NY Maryknoll Fathers and Brothers.
Lilly, Robert M. *m.m.* '60 (FgM) Maryknoll Foreign Missions.
Lim, Candido O. *s.j.* '69 (SJ) [25] San Jose, CA St. Victor Church; [L] Los Gatos, CA Sacred Heart Jesuit Center.
Lima, John H. '63 (LAV) Pahrump, NV Our Lady of the Valley Church.
Lima, Joseph *c.pp.s.* '44 (CIN) [B] Carthagena, OH St. Charles.
Lima, Rene '73 (NEW) [8] Newark, NJ St. Benedict's Church.
Lima, Vivian B. '85 (LA) Graduate Studies.
Limanni, Joseph A. '87 (GAL) [29] Houston, TX St. Francis de Sales Church.
Limanowski, Stanley C. '42 (CHI) Retired.
Limbani, George '94 (SEA) [2] Seattle, WA St. Alphonsus Church.
Limbert, William G. '51 (KAL) Retired.
Limmer, George A. '64 (BAL) Hagerstown, MD St. Mary Church.
Limon, Lidio *c.o.* '92 (MRY) [F] Monterey, CA Oratorian Community-Congregation of the Oratory of Pontifical Right.
Linakis, William *s.a.* '77 (NY) [DD] Garrison, NY Franciscan Friars of the Atonement, Minister General Office.
Linan, Jesse S. (GAL) Retired.
Linares, Jose R. '86 (MGZ) Cabo Rojo, PR St. Michael Church.
Lincoln, Daniel L. '84 (L) Jamestown, KY Holy Spirit Church.
Lincoln, Howard A. '93 (SB) Rialto, CA St. Catherine of Siena Church.
Lincon, J. Bruce '89 (SJN) [16] Carolina, PR Ntra. Sra. Reina de los Angeles Church.
Lind, Msgr. Joseph G. '65 (BO) Wellesley, MA St. Paul Church.
Lind, Thomas *s.c.j.* '58 (JKS) [F] Nesbit, MS St. Michael Community House.
Lindauer, Msgr. Clarence '37 (EVN) Retired; [E] Evansville, IN St. John's Home for the Aged.
Lindauer, Prosper *o.s.b.* '50 (IND) [J] St. Meinrad, IN St. Meinrad Archabbey.
Lindblad, Karl-Albert '87 (NY) Military Chaplains.
Lindemann, Gene E. '83 (BIS) [2] Minot, ND Our Lady of Grace Church.
Linden, Emmet '51 (L) [L] Louisville, KY Sacred Heart Retreat.
Linden, Michael D. *s.j.* '80 (FgM) Provinces.
Lindenfelser, Timothy M. '94 (STA) [1] St. Augustine, FL Cathedral of St. Augustine.
Lindenmeyer, James '48 (GLP) Retired.
Linder, Michael '85 (KNX) [J] Chattanooga, TN Newman Foundation of Chattanooga, Inc.
Linder, Msgr. William J. '63 (NEW) [33] Newark, NJ St. Rose of Lima Church.
Lindkugel, William *o.m.i.* '45 (FgM) Oblates Foreign Missions.
Lindle, Lawrence H. '59 (L) Culvertown, KY Immaculate Conception Church; [Q] Louisville, KY Perpetual Eucharistic Adoration; [Q] New Haven, KY World Apostolate of Fatima (Blue Army); [Q] New Haven, KY World Apostolate of Fatima (Blue Army); [Q] New Haven, KY Archdiocesan Marian Committee.
Lindley, Philip '83 (AMA) Absent on Leave.
Lindner, Jerrold W. *s.j.* '76 (SJ) [K] Los Altos, CA Jesuit Retreat House.
Lindner, Thomas F. '95 (LC) [1] Stevens Point, WI Newman University Church; [K] Stevens Point, WI Newman University Parish.
Lindsay, John A. *o.s.f.s.* '70 (STO) [A] Stockton, CA St. Mary's High School.
Lindsay, Michael P. '87 (LSC) Santa Clara, NM Santa Clara Church.
Lindsay, Robert E. *s.j.* '60 (BO) [W] Weston, MA Campion Health Center, Inc.
Lindsay, Stewart *o.s.f.s.* '74 (BUF) [D] Niagara Falls, NY Niagara Catholic Junior-Senior High School.
Lindstrom, Michael *s.v.d.* '82 (FgM) Society of the Divine Word Foreign Missions.
Linebach, Martin A. '87 (L) On Special Assignment.
Linehan, Brian *o.f.m.* (NEW) [N] East Rutherford, NJ

Sacred Heart Friary.
Linehan, Cornelius '43 (P) Retired.
Linehan, David '56 (SEA) Retired.
Linehan, Dennis *s.j.* '72 (NY) [DD] New York, NY "America;" Residence and publication office of the America Press.
Linehan, Eugene J. *s.j.* '53 (WDC) [E] North Bethesda, MD Georgetown Preparatory School.
Linehan, Jeremiah '48 (P) Retired.
Linehan, Maurice *m.s.* '52 (WOR) [6] Fitchburg, MA St. Joseph's Church.
Linehan, Stephen J. (BO) Military & VA Chaplains.
Linehan, Timothy E. (BO) [13] Boston, MA St. Brendan Church.
Lingan, Joseph *s.j.* '90 (BAL) [D] Baltimore, MD Loyola Blakefield.
Lingan, Joseph E. *s.j.* '90 (BAL) [S] Baltimore, MD Jesuit Fathers and Brothers Maryland Provincial Curia.
Linh Uy, Atanasio M. *c.m.c.* '81 (FWT) Wichita Falls, TX Sacred Heart Church.
Lininger, Paul *o.f.m.conv.* '81 (ALB) [A] Rensselaer, NY Conventual Franciscan Friars; [L] Rensselaer, NY Provincialate, Immaculate Conception Friary - Order of Friars Minor Conventual; [S] Rensselaer, NY Order of Friars Minor Conventual Immaculate Conception Province Charitable Trust.
Link, David '91 (OAK) San Lorenzo, CA St. John the Baptist Church.
Link, Fred *o.f.m.* '70 (CIN) [M] Cincinnati, OH St. Francis Seraph Friary.
Link, Frederick G. '69 (CAM) Millville, NJ St. Mary Magdalen's Church.
Link, Mark *s.j.* '60 (DAL) Plano, TX St. Mark the Evangelist Church.
Link, Paul *c.pp.s.* '61 (CIN) [B] Carthagena, OH St. Charles.
Linkchorst, William J. '73 (ALN) Tamaqua, PA SS. Peter and Paul Church.
Linn, Matthew L. *s.j.* '73 (STP) [B] St. Paul, MN Jesuit Novitiate.
Linnan, John E. *c.s.v.* '61 (CHI) [B] Chicago, IL The Catholic Theological Union at Chicago; [N] Chicago, IL Viatorian Residence.
Linnan, Roger '62 (SC) Spencer, IA Sacred Heart Church.
Linnane, Brian F. *s.j.* '86 (WOR) [N] Worcester, MA Jesuits of Holy Cross College, Inc.
Linnebur, David W. '82 (WCH) Caldwell, KS St. Martin of Tours Church; Conway Springs, KS St. Joseph Church.
Linnebur, Leroy '61 (WCH) Clonmel, KS St. John Church.
Linnebur, Vincent '60 (JC) Absent on Leave.
Linnemann, Eugene C. '80 (BEL) Leave of Absence.
Linnenbrink, Harry H. '57 (DAV) Retired.
Linowski, Eugene R. '57 (PRM) Columbus, OH St. John Chrysostom Church; Dayton, OH St. Barbara Church.
Lins, James R. '64 (MAD) Elk Grove, WI St. Peter Church; Seymour, WI Our Lady of Hope Church; Shullsburg, WI St. Matthew Church.
Linse, Henry *c.s.s.* '48 (BO) [Z] Waltham, MA Stigmatine Fathers and Brothers.
Linsky, Gary S. '93 (CHR) Military Chaplains.
Linsler, Christopher E. (ROC) [5] Elmira, NY St. Casimir Church.
Linsler, Christopher E. '78 (ROC) Elmira Heights, NY St. Charles Borromeo Church.
Linster, Joseph B. '69 (RCK) St. Charles, IL St. Patrick Church.
Linton, Edward *o.s.b.* '91 (IND) [J] St. Meinrad, IN St. Meinrad Archabbey.
Lintz, Charles *s.s.c.* '70 (FgM) St. Columban's Foreign Mission.
Lintz, Christoph '94 (NEW) River Edge, NJ St. Peter the Apostle Church.
Lintzenich, Stephen P. '74 (EVN) [16] Evansville, IN St. John the Apostle Church; [20] Evansville, IN St. Mary Church.
Linzmaier, Eric G. (LC) [C] Chippewa Falls, WI Chippewa Falls Area Catholic Schools.
Linzmaier, Eric G. '00 (LC) Chippewa Falls, WI St. Charles Borromeo Church; Cooks Valley, WI St. John the Baptist Church; Tilden, WI St. Peter Church.
Lioi, Frank E. '67 (ROC) [4] Rochester, NY St. Anne Church.
Lion, William J. '58 (CHI) [1] Oak Lawn, IL St. Catherine of Alexandria Church.
Liona, Kenneth J. '78 (BRK) Absent on Leave.
Lionelli, Anthony J. '72 (NEW) [21] Newark, NJ Immaculate Conception Church.
Lipareli, Michael '80 (NY) [125] Bronx, NY St. Ann Church.
Lipari, Anthony R. '89 (NEW) Nutley, NJ Holy Family Church.
Lipczewski, Boleslaus '58 (DET) [10] Detroit, MI Assumption Grotto Church; Retired.
Lipiec, Bartholomew W. '83 (BUF) [8] Buffalo, NY Annunciation Church.
Lipinski, Alberic *o.cist.* '83 (CHI) [N] Willow Springs, IL Cistercian Fathers, Our Lady Mother of the Church.
Lipinski, Andrew Alberic *s.o.cist* '83 (AUS) Rosebud, TX St. Ann's Church.
Lipinski, Edward J. '71 (CAM) Runnemede, NJ St. Maria Goretti Church.
Lipinski, Paul M. '73 (RCK) Hartland, IL St. Patrick Church; [B] Woodstock, IL Marian Central Catholic High School.
Lipnicki, Thomas '78 (NEW) Oakland, NJ Our Lady of Perpetual Help Church.
Lipp, John F. *o.s.a.* '54 (PH) [AA] Villanova, PA St. Thomas Monastery.
Lippert, Donald *o.f.m.cap.* '85 (CLV) [A] Wickliffe, OH Borromeo Seminary.
Lippert, Paul R. '61 (MIL) Retired.
Lippold, John L. '57 (BAL) Linthicum Heights, MD St. Philip Neri Church.
Lipps, Msgr. Frank J. '68 (NO) Violet, LA Our Lady of Lourdes Church.
Lippstock, Paul E. '78 (DUB) [2] Waterloo, IA St. Mary's Church.
Lipscomb, N. Alan '94 (RIC) Lexington, VA St. Patrick Church.
Lipscomb, William W. '97 (GAY) Traverse City, MI St. Francis of Assisi Church.
Liptak, Msgr. David Q. '53 (HRT) Broad Brook, CT St. Catherine's Church; Special and other Archdiocesan Assignment.
Liptak, David Q. '53 (NOR) [A] Cromwell, CT Holy Apostles College and Seminary.
Liptak, Edward *s.d.b.* '59 (FgM) Salesians of Don Bosco Foreign Missions.
LiPuma, David G. '87 (BUF) [O] Buffalo, NY Bishop's Residence.
Lirette, Albert *o.m.i.* '45 (BO) [W] Lowell, MA Missionary Oblates of Mary Immaculate.
Lirette, Albert *o.m.i.* '45 (FgM) Oblates Foreign Missions.
Lirette, Msgr. Arthur J. '49 (LA) Glendale, CA Holy Family Church; Retired.
Liriano, Benito (NY) [163] Bronx, NY St. Martin of Tours Church.
Lis, Albert *o.f.m.* '86 (GB) [10] Green Bay, WI St. Mary of the Angels Church; [I] Green Bay, WI St. Mary of the Angels Friary.
Lis, John S. '73 (SPR) [1] Northampton, MA Annunciation Church.
Lisante, Msgr. James P. '81 (RVC) West Hempstead, NY St. Thomas, the Apostle Church.
Lisbeth, Michael L. *s.m.* '80 (CIN) [M] Cincinnati, OH Marianist Community.
Lischaa, Msgr. Sharbel '61 (SAM) Philadelphia, PA St. Maron Church.
Lischwe, Bruno V. *c.ss.r.* '52 (STL) [P] Liguori, MO St. Clement Health Care Center.
Lisik, Paul A. '81 (GBG) Monessen, PA The Epiphany of Our Lord Church.
Liska, Richard A. '70 (MIL) [80] Milwaukee, WI St. Stephen Church.
Lisowski, Brian '81 (CHI) [24] Chicago, IL St. Bede the Venerable Church.
Lisowski, Edward E. '64 (CHI) North Chicago, IL Veterans Affairs Medical Center.
Lisowski, Edward E. '64 (MIL) Wood, WI Veterans Administration Medical Center.
Lisowski, Jan '39 (SC) Retired.
Lisowski, Lawrence M. '84 (CHI) La Grange, IL St. Francis Xavier Church.
Lisowski, William J. '50 (CHI) [112] Chicago, IL St. Ladislaus Church; Retired.
Liss, Robert C. '62 (STL) Richwoods, MO St. Stephen's Church.
Lisson, Edwin *s.j.* '69 (STL) [C] St. Louis, MO Saint Louis University; [P] St. Louis, MO Jesuit Community Corporation at St. Louis University - Jesuit Hall.
List, John E. '85 (LEX) Georgetown, KY St. John's Church.
Liston, Daniel P. '85 (SPR) [2] Northampton, MA Blessed Sacrament Church.
Liston, Paul F. '58 (WDC) [36] Washington, DC St. Patrick Church.
Liszewski, Francis A. '69 (NOR) Absent on Leave; Retired.
Liszewski, Peter B. '76 (NOR) Lebanon, CT St. Francis of Assisi Church.
Litavec, Edward S. '60 (PIT) Fredericktown, PA St. Oliver Plunkett Church.
Litcheck, Michael P. '71 (SCR) [21] Scranton, PA St. Patrick's Church.
Literski, Msgr. Roy E. '53 (WIN) Retired.
Litot, Msgr. Edward F. '47 (GRY) Retired.
Littelmann, Edward J. '69 (TOL) Huron, OH St. Peter Church.
Little, Msgr. Anthony B. '82 (ALT) [13] Altoona, PA St. Therese of the Child Jesus Church.
Little, Gregory (NY) Bronx, NY U.S.V.A. Medical Center.
Little, John '87 (OWN) Absent on Leave.
Little, Msgr. John J. '77 (ALT) Nanty-Glo, PA St. Mary's Church.
Little, John J. L. '88 (ALN) Northampton, PA Our Lady of Hungary Church.
Little, Msgr. Richard (BO) [FF] Brighton, MA Caritas Christi Retirement Plan and Trust.
Little, Msgr. Richard P. '62 (BO) Health Leave.
Littlefield, Philaret '87 (NTN) Milwaukee, WI St. George Church.
Littleton, Gregory J. '90 (CHL) Tryon, NC St. John the Baptist Church.
Littleton, Gregory J. '90 (MET) On Duty Outside the Diocese.
Litwack, Joshua E. '00 (TLS) [5] Tulsa, OK Christ the King Church.
Litwin, Paul *j.c.l.* '79 (BUF) [A] East Aurora, NY Christ the King Seminary.
Litwin, Paul A. '79 (BUF) [O] Buffalo, NY Bishop's Residence.
Liu, Peter T. '60 (RVC) Ronkonkoma, NY St. Joseph's Church.
Liu, Pius *o.f.m.* '53 (NY) [DD] New York, NY Franciscan Friars, Order of Friars Minor, Holy Name Province.
Liu, Vincent '54 (RVC) Smithtown, NY St. Patrick Church; Retired.
Liuima, Francis *s.j.* '45 (BO) [W] Chestnut Hill, MA The Jesuit Community at Boston College.
Liuzzi, Kenneth (DEN) [5] Denver, CO Blessed Sacrament Church; [Q] Denver, CO Blessed Sacrament Catholic Educational Foundation.
Liuzzi, Peter J. *o.carm.* '65 (LA) [B] Arleta, CA Carmel West Community.
Liuzzo, Vincent *o.f.m.cap.* '49 (PAT) Passaic, NJ St. Mary Hospital; [J] Passaic, NJ St. Mary's Hospital.
Lively, Joseph A. '57 (BUR) St. Johnsbury, VT St. John the Evangelist Church.
Livigni, Salvatore J. '61 (BAL) [9] Baltimore, MD Annunciation Church; Baltimore, MD Johns Hopkins Medical Institutions; Special Assignment; [W] Baltimore, MD Johns Hopkins Hospital Apostolate.
Livingston, James G. '91 (DET) [5] Dearborn Heights, MI St. Mel Church.
Livingston, James T. '90 (STP) Delano, MN St. Mary of Czestochowa Church; St. Bonifacius, MN St. Boniface Church.
Livingston, Msgr. Robert C. '45 (PEO) Kickapoo, IL St. Mary of Kickapoo Church; Retired.
Livojevich, Ronald '70 (KCK) [4] Overland Park, KS Queen of the Holy Rosary Church.
Livolsi, Silvester J. '48 (PAT) [I] Branchville, NJ Sanctuary of Mary-Our Lady of the Holy Spirit.
Livolsi, Sylvester J. '48 (NEW) On Duty Outside the Archdiocese.
Lizarralde, Jose *c.p.* (MGZ) San Sebastian, PR San Sebastian Martir Church.
Lizarralde, Luis *o.f.m.* '51 (SJN) [4] Toa Baja, PR San Jose Obrero Church.
Lizcano, Otoniel '99 (BGP) [4] Norwalk, CT St. Mary Church; [5] Norwalk, CT St. Matthew Church.
Lizio, John R. '57 (BO) [4] Marlborough, MA St. Matthias Church.
Lizor, Joseph S., Jr. '58 (BAL) [56] Baltimore, MD St. Luke Church.
Llagas, Carlos *s.j.* '89 (CHI) [C] Chicago, IL Jesuit Community at Loyola University of Chicago.
Llamas, Rodolfo DCL *v.d.c.* '93 (SAC) Woodland, CA Holy Rosary Church.
Llambias, Martin '73 (SJN) [G] Guaynabo, PR Opus Dei.
Llano, Isidoro '51 (GLP) On Duty Outside of Diocese.
Llanos, Christopher '96 (BO) [W] Cambridge, MA Weston Jesuit Community.
Llanos, Philip S. '78 (LA) Military and VA Chaplains.
Llanos, Philip S. '78 (TUC) Tucson, AZ Christ the King Chapel.
Llanos, Robert (BAL) Laurel, MD Resurrection of Our Lord Church.
Llaria, Vincent '59 (VEN) Lake Placid, FL St. James Church.
Lleo, Pedro '76 (MIA) [4] Pompano Beach, FL St. Coleman Church.
Llewellyn, Anselm *o.s.b.* '41 (KCK) [H] Atchison, KS St. Benedict's Abbey.
Llorente, Amando *s.j.* '48 (MIA) [J] Miami, FL John Paul II Retreat House.
Lloyd, James B. *c.s.p.* '48 (NY) [104] New York, NY St. Paul the Apostle Church; [A] Yonkers, NY St. Joseph's Seminary; [DD] Jamaica Estates, NY Paulist Fathers Generalate.
LLoyd, Patrick J. *s.c.j.* '69 (JKS) Southhaven, MS Christ the King Church; [F] Nesbit, MS St. Michael Community House.
Lloyd, Msgr. Paul A. '37 (PRO) Retired; [M] Pawtucket, RI Jeanne Jugan Residence.
Lloyd, Robert J. *m.m.* '62 (FgM) Maryknoll Foreign Missions.
Lluch, Santiago *c.m.* '42 (NY) [44] New York, NY Holy Agony Church; [DD] New York, NY Vincentian Fathers.
Lluria, Carmel *o.f.m.* '55 (NY) [DD] New York, NY Franciscan Friars, Order of Friars Minor, Holy Name Province.
Lo Sasso, John *o.f.m.cap.* '89 (NY) [151] Bronx, NY Immaculate Conception Church.

Lo Schiavo, John J. *s.j.* '55 (SFR) [N] San Francisco, CA Jesuit Community at University of San Francisco.
Lobacz, James E. '79 (MIL) [C] Milwaukee, WI Cardinal Stritch University.
Lobato, Nicanor '61 (VEN) Palmetto, FL Holy Cross Church.
Lobert, Richard C. '75 (BAL) Special Assignment.
LoBianco, Msgr. Francis R. '54 (NEW) Retired.
LoBianco, Paschal *s.v.d.* '50 (CHI) [B] Techny, IL Divine Word Residence.
LoBianco, Richard J. '79 (CHI) [2] Oak Lawn, IL St. Gerald Church.
LoBiondo, Gasper F. *s.j.* '68 (WDC) [M] Washington, DC Woodstock Jesuit Community; [V] Washington, DC Woodstock Theological Center.
Lobo, Anthony F. *s.s.* '70 (SAT) [A] San Antonio, TX The Assumption-St. John's Seminary.
Lobo, Benjamin R. '63 (GF) Plentywood, MT St. Joseph's Church.
Lobo, Raul Venust '62 (NO) [24] New Orleans, LA St. Andrew the Apostle Church.
Lobo, Stanley '65 (NEW) Fort Lee, NJ Madonna Church.
Lobo, Theodore '57 (TUC) Parker, AZ Sacred Heart Church.
Loc, Timothy Mai Vinh *c.m.c.* '77 (SPC) Carthage, MO St. Ann Church.
Locatelli, Paul L. *s.j.* '74 (SJ) [B] Santa Clara, CA Santa Clara University; [B] Santa Clara, CA Santa Clara University.
Loch, Richard J. '79 (SCR) [17] Scranton, PA St. Mary of the Assumption Church.
Lochner, Robert J. *c.s.c.* '46 (FTW) [J] South Bend, IN Congregation of Holy Cross, Indiana Province, Provincial House.
Lochner, Robert J. *c.s.c.* '46 (ORL) Retired; [F] Cocoa Beach, FL Holy Cross Fathers, Eastern Priests Province.
Lochs, Matthew *ss.cc.* '36 (HON) [G] Kaneohe, HI Sacred Hearts Center.
Lock, Bertram *ss.cc.* '89 (HON) Kaneohe, HI St. Ann Church.
Lockard, Christopher *s.j.* (NO) [C] New Orleans, LA Loyola University New Orleans.
Lockard, Msgr. David (ALT) Johnstown, PA UPMC Lee Hospital.
Locke, James E. '61 (PH) Chadds Ford, PA St. Cornelius Church.
Locke, John K. *s.j.* '64 (FgM) Provinces.
Lockman, V. James '67 (WDC) Laurel, MD St. Mary Church.
Lockulu, Jean-Paulin '95 (JUN) Craig, AK St. John by the Sea Church.
Lockwood, Gregory '88 (STL) On Duty Outside the Archdiocese.
Lockwood, Gregory J. '99 (CIN) [83] Cincinnati, OH St. Vincent de Paul Church.
Loda, Mauro *s.x.* '99 (FgM) Xaverian Foreign Missions.
Loda, Mauro *s.x.* '99 (PAT) [M] Wayne, NJ Xaverian Missionary Fathers.
Lodge, John G. '73 (CHI) [A] Mundelein, IL University of St. Mary of the Lake-Mundelein Seminary.
Lodge, Richard J. '69 (CAM) West Collingswood, NJ Transfiguration Church.
Lodi, George C. '74 (NY) [6] Yonkers, NY Christ the King Church.
Lody, John R. '62 (Y) Canal Fulton, OH SS. Philip and James Church.
Loeb, Karl E. '95 (BUF) [1] Orchard Park, NY Nativity of Our Lord Church.
Loebl, Jeffrey R. *s.j.* '82 (MIL) [P] Wauwatosa, WI Jesuit Community at St. Camillus.
Loecke, Douglas J. '89 (DUB) Graduate Studies.
Loecker, Craig '92 (OM) Neligh, NE St. Francis Church.
Loeffer, Earl A. '51 (TOL) [5] Toledo, OH Corpus Christi, University of Toledo Church; Retired.
Loegering, Leonard '73 (FAR) [1] Grand Forks, ND Holy Family Church.
Loehr, Charles D. '47 (MIL) Retired.
Loehr, James P. '67 (MIL) Delafield, WI St. Joan of Arc Church.
Loehrlein, Richard A. *s.m.* '61 (CIN) [M] Dayton, OH Marianist Provincialate.
Loehrlein, Sylvester '56 (EVN) Red Brush, IN St. Rupert Church.
Loeper, David J. '83 (ALN) [1] Pottsville, PA St. John the Baptist Church.
Loeper, Msgr. Richard J. '50 (ALN) Retired.
Loew, James H. *o.s.b.* '97 (GBG) Jeannette, PA Sacred Heart Church.
Lofgren, Eric D. '93 (SAC) Burney, CA St. Francis of Assisi Church.
LoFranco, Sofronio '60 (BRK) [B] Elmhurst, NY Cathedral Preparatory Seminary of the Immaculate Conception.
Loftin, Don '94 (AUS) [3] Waco, TX St. Jerome Church.
Lofton, Msgr. Edward D. '82 (CHR) Summerville, SC St. Theresa the Little Flower Church.
Lofton, James J. '61 (ALN) Retired.
Loftus, Conrad W. *o.f.m.* '54 (NY) [DD] New York, NY Franciscan Friars, Order of Friars Minor, Holy Name Province.
Loftus, J. Allan *s.j.* '74 (BAL) [S] Baltimore, MD Jesuit Fathers and Brothers Maryland Provincial Curia.
Loftus, John (BGP) [5] Norwalk, CT St. Matthew Church.
Loftus, Joseph J. '56 (ARL) [6] Arlington, VA Our Lady of Lourdes Church; Retired.
Loftus, Kenneth *s.j.* (BO) [3] Newton, MA St. Ignatius Church.
Loftus, Mel M. *o.s.m.* '62 (CHI) [N] Chicago, IL Order of Friar Servants of Mary (Servites) United States of America Province, Inc.
Loftus, Msgr. Padraic '62 (LA) Woodland Hills, CA St. Mel Church.
Loftus, Robert A. '91 (BGP) On Duty Outside the Diocese.
Loftus, Robert A. '91 (WOR) Shrewsbury, MA St. Anne's Church.
Loftus, Thomas B. *c.ss.r.* '57 (BAL) [87] Baltimore, MD Sacred Heart of Jesus Church.
Lofy, Guy *o.c.d.* '48 (MIL) [P] Milwaukee, WI Provincial Offices - Discalced Carmelites.
Logan, Aidan *o.c.s.o.* '85 (WOR) [N] Spencer, MA St. Joseph's Abbey.
Logan, Msgr. Daniel B. '63 (STA) Ponte Vedra Beach, FL Our Lady Star of the Sea Church.
Logan, David '79 (VNN) Spokane, WA SS. Cyril & Methodius Church.
Logan, Francis A. *s.j.* '33 (SEA) [A] Seattle, WA Seattle University.
Logan, Gary '93 (SR) On Leave.
Logan, J. M. '79 (PEO) Silvis, IL Our Lady of Guadalupe Church.
Logan, James J. '59 (LC) Marshfield, WI Our Lady of Peace Church.
Logan, James P. '86 (BAK) Prineville, OR St. Joseph's Church.
Logan, Msgr. James T. '54 (FRS) [2] Fresno, CA Holy Spirit Church.
Logan, John *o.carm.* '64 (NY) [97] New York, NY Our Lady of the Scapular/St. Stephen Church; Manhattan, NY Bellevue Hospital.
Logan, John D. *o.p.* '57 (GAL) [Q] Houston, TX Dominican Fathers and Brothers, St. Mark Priory, Inc.
Logan, John D. *o.p.* '57 (TYL) [D] Nacogdoches, TX Stephen F. Austin University Catholic Student Center.
Logan, John M. *o.praem.* '60 (WIL) [I] Claymont, DE Immaculate Conception Priory of the Canons Regular of Premontre.
Logan, John W. *o.p.* '57 (TYL) Nacogdoches, TX Sacred Heart Church.
Logan, Joseph P. *s.j.* '54 (PH) [83] Philadelphia, PA Old St. Joseph's Church.
Logan, Michael *c.ss.r.* '57 (SEA) [32] Seattle, WA Sacred Heart of Jesus Church.
Logan, William R. '69 (RVC) Long Beach, NY St. Ignatius Martyr Church.
LoGatto, Joseph J. '57 (PAT) Retired.
LoGrasso, Pasquale '57 (DET) [2] Clinton Twp., MI St. Louis Church.
Logrip, Joseph L. '72 (PH) Levittown, PA Immaculate Conception B.V.M. Church.
Logsdon, L. Peter *c.s.c.* '68 (FgM) Holy Cross Foreign Missions.
Logsdon, Wilfrid *o.f.m.conv.* '59 (SAV) Brunswick, GA St. Francis Xavier Church.
Logue, Charles D. '48 (BO) Halifax, MA Our Lady of the Lake Church; Senior Priests.
Logue, Dennis *s.v.d.* '83 (PBR) Girard, PA SS. Cyril and Methodius Church.
Logue, Mark '73 (BAL) Owensville, MD Our Lady of Sorrows Church.
Lohan, James '73 (NO) On Leave.
Lohan, Louis '71 (BLX) Long Beach, MS St. Thomas the Apostle Church.
Lohkamp, Nickolas *o.f.m.* (Y) [K] Canton, OH Sancta Clara Monastery.
Lohr, Charles H. *s.j.* '61 (NY) [DD] New York, NY Jesuit Provincial's Office.
Lohrmeyer, Kenneth '70 (SAL) Delphos, KS St. Paul's Church; Minneapolis, KS Immaculate Conception of the Blessed Virgin Mary Church.
Lohse, Edward M. '89 (E) [A] Erie, PA St. Mark's Seminary.
Lohse, Walter H. '40 (E) Retired.
Loi, Nguyen '66 (OM) [4] Omaha, NE St. Ann Church.
Loiacono, James A. *o.m.i.* '71 (BO) [12] Lowell, MA Nuestra Senora del Carmen Church.
Loiselle, Joseph G. '57 (WOR) Retired.
Loiselle, Lucien H. '49 (BO) Dracut, MA St. Mary of the Assumption Church.
Lokoba, Damian I. '86 (ROC) Rochester, NY Monroe Community Hospital.
Lolio, John W. '70 (PRO) East Greenwich, RI Our Lady of Mercy Church.
Lomasiewicz, Donald E. '62 (GR) [10] Grand Rapids, MI St. Isidore's Church.
Lomasney, John P. *m.m.* '43 (FgM) Maryknoll Foreign Missions.
Lomax, Mark '80 (NO) Chalmette, LA St. Mark Church.
Lombard, Richard J. '53 (SHP) [8] Shreveport, LA St. Joseph Church.
Lombard, Roy A. '47 (WH) Retired.
Lombardi, Albert U. '47 (DET) Retired.
Lombardi, Gary '69 (SR) Petaluma, CA St. Vincent de Paul Church.
Lombardi, John Carl *m.s.f.* '00 (STL) [67] St. Louis, MO St. Wenceslaus Church.
Lombardi, John J. '88 (BAL) Randallstown, MD Holy Family Church.
Lombardi, Joseph L. *s.j.* '75 (PH) [C] Philadelphia, PA St. Joseph's University; [AA] Philadelphia, PA Jesuit Community at St. Joseph's University.
Lombardi, Nicholas D. *s.j.* '72 (NY) [DD] New York, NY Jesuit Community at Fordham University.
Lombardi, Thomas '75 (FTW) Garrett, IN St. Joseph Church.
Lombardo, Msgr. Angelo J. '55 (BEL) Retired.
Lombardo, Francis *o.f.m.conv.* '71 (BAL) [S] Ellicott City, MD St. Joseph Cupertino Friary, Friars Minor Conventual of St. Francis of Assisi; [S] Ellicott City, MD Friary of St. Joseph Cupertino.
Lombardo, Gerard M. '86 (NEW) Ridgewood, NJ Our Lady of Mount Carmel Church.
Lombardo, Gregory J. *c.s.c.* '45 (FTW) [J] South Bend, IN Congregation of Holy Cross, Indiana Province, Provincial House.
Lombardo, Joseph A. '85 (TUC) Green Valley, AZ Our Lady of the Valley Church.
Lombardo, Michael J. '78 (PAT) Pompton Plains, NJ Our Lady of Good Counsel Church; Pompton Plains, NJ Chilton Memorial Hospital; Wayne, NJ Wayne General Hospital.
Lombardo, Robert *c.f.r.* '90 (NY) [DD] New York, NY St. Crispin Friary.
Lombardo, Msgr. Samuel F. '39 (BUF) [O] Buffalo, NY Sheehan Residence for Priests.
Lombardo, Msgr. Samuel L. '39 (BUF) Lancaster, NY Our Lady of Pompeii Church; Retired.
Lombo, German *o.s.a.* '53 (MGZ) Aguada, PR St. Francis of Assisi Church.
Lomello, Lucian B. *s.d.b.* '48 (LA) [80] Los Angeles, CA St. Mary Church; [Q] Los Angeles, CA Dominic Savio Salesian Residence.
Lommel, George D. '46 (FAR) Retired.
Lonakutty, Francis E. *i.m.s.* '84 (BR) [13] Baton Rouge, LA St. Jude the Apostle Church.
Lonardo, Alfred C. '63 (PRO) [5] Cranston, RI St. Mary Church.
Loncar, Sebastian '37 (VEN) Retired.
Loncar, Stephen *o.f.m.conv.* '88 (GRY) [12] Gary, IN St. Joseph The Worker Church.
Loncaric, Msgr. Stanley '36 (KCK) Retired; [G] Olathe, KS Villa St. Francis, Inc.
Lonchyna, Taras R. '77 (PHU) Silver Spring, MD Holy Trinity Church; Manassas, VA Annunciation of the Blessed Virgin Mary Church; Richmond, VA St. John the Baptist Church.
London, Lawrence '53 (RCK) Retired.
London, Orlando '77 (SJN) [26] Bayamon, PR Santo Domingo De Guzman Church.
Londono, Edison Santiago '86 (RVC) Glen Cove, NY St. Patrick's Church.
Londono, Heriberto '84 (SJN) [21] Bayamon, PR Nuestra Sra. del Rosario Church.
Londono, Hugo (ORL) Sanford, FL All Souls Church.
Londono, Hugo '62 (ORL) Mount Dora, FL St. Patrick's Church.
Londono, Saul '88 (RVC) Brentwood, NY St. Luke Church.
Lonek, Stephen C. '76 (NY) On Duty Outside the Archdiocese.
Lonek, Stephen C. '76 (WIL) Fairfax, DE St. Mary Magdalen Church.
Lonergan, David W. '61 (HRT) Wethersfield, CT Corpus Christi Church; Wethersfield, CT Sacred Heart Church.
Lonergan, James B. '66 (ALB) Hudson Falls, NY Church of St. Mary's/St. Paul's.
Lonergan, Michael J. '93 (PH) [2] Bensalem, PA St. Elizabeth Ann Seton Church.
Long, Anthony Vu Khac '92 (RCK) DeKalb, IL St. Mary Church.
Long, Daniel *l.c.* '94 (CHI) [N] Lemont, IL Legion of Christ.
Long, Francis C. '47 (PHX) Retired.
Long, Galen '91 (SAL) Colby, KS Sacred Heart Church.
Long, Garrett J. *s.m.* '66 (RVC) [D] Mineola, NY Chaminade High School (Boys).
Long, Garrett J. *s.m.* '76 (RVC) [M] Mineola, NY Provincial Residence and Novitiate.
Long, Gordon (NU) [F] St. Peter, MN St. Peter Regional Treatment Center.
Long, J. William '89 (R) Henderson, NC St. James the Greater Church.
Long, James T. '63 (BEL) Fairview Heights, IL St. Albert the Great Church.

Long, John '61 (JC) Retired.
Long, John *o.carm.* '87 (GAL) [Q] Houston, TX Carmelite Priory.
Long, John F. *s.j.* '56 (NY) [DD] New York, NY "America;" Residence and publication office of the America Press.
Long, John M. '78 (STP) Hopkins, MN St. Joseph's Church.
Long, John Paul '68 (BGP) [2] Bridgeport, CT St. Ambrose Church.
Long, John R. '89 (SUP) Chelsea, WI Assumption of the Blessed Virgin Mary Church; Rib Lake, WI St. John the Baptist Church; Westboro, WI St. Theresa Church; Whittlesey, WI Our Lady of Perpetual Help Church.
Long, Joseph J. *c.s.c.* '59 (SCR) [C] Wilkes-Barre, PA Kings College.
Long, Loran (SD) [F] San Diego, CA Scripps Mercy Hospital.
Long, Melvin T. '66 (SAL) Manhattan, KS St. Thomas More Church.
Long, Richard E. '90 (BRK) [13] Brooklyn, NY St. Athanasius Church.
Long, Tran Phuc '48 (ORG) Costa Mesa, CA St. John the Baptist Church; Retired.
Long, Vincent P. '69 (SY) Hinckley, NY St. Ann Church; Holland Patent, NY St. Leo Church.
Long, W. Thomas (GB) Brillion, WI St. Mary Church; Reedsville/Maple Grove, WI St. Mary-St. Patrick Church.
Longbucco, John L. '90 (MAR) Ontonagon, MI Holy Family Church; Rockland, MI St. Mary Church.
Longchamps, Adrien R. '75 (MAN) Laconia, NH Sacred Heart Church.
Longo, Paul *m.c.c.j.* '42 (CHI) [N] La Grange Park, IL Comboni Mission Center.
Longobucco, Robert '98 (ALB) Oneonta, NY St. Mary Church; [R] Oneonta, NY New York State University at Oneonta and Hartwick College.
Longoria Gomez, Jose de la Cruz *m.n.m.* (SAT) Del Rio, TX Our Lady of Guadalupe Church.
Longres, Joaquin S. '62 (BRK) [191] Queens, NY St. Luke Church.
Longtin, Lucien F. *s.j.* '65 (WDC) [E] Washington, DC Gonzaga College High School.
Longua, Msgr. Paul '62 (PAT) Sparta, NJ Our Lady of the Lake Church.
Longwill, Cathal (DEN) On Duty Outside the Archdiocese.
Lonsdale, Richard G. '66 (PRT) [J] Waterville, ME Blessed Sacrament Convent.
Lonteen, Daniel '94 (CLV) Absent on Leave.
Looby, John J. '66 (OG) Dannemora, NY St. Joseph Church.
Loomie, Albert J. *s.j.* '52 (NY) [DD] New York, NY Jesuit Community at Fordham University.
Loomis, Dennis J. *m.s.* '77 (FR) [I] Attleboro, MA La Salette Provincial House; [I] Attleboro, MA La Salette Missionary Association; [I] Attleboro, MA La Salette Shrine.
Loomis, Msgr. Richard '76 (LA) [2] North Hollywood, CA St. Charles Borromeo Church.
Loomis, Richard P. '52 (WIN) Fairmont, MN St. John Vianney Church.
Loomis, Thomas A. '92 (WIN) Chatfield, MN St. Mary's Church; Preston, MN St. Columban Church.
Looney, Daniel A. '71 (SAC) Davis, CA St. James Church.
Looney, Joseph E. '67 (HRT) [14] Waterbury, CT St. Margaret's Church.
Looney, Mathew D. '58 (NEW) Retired.
Looney, Thomas P. *c.s.c.* '87 (SCR) [C] Wilkes-Barre, PA Kings College; [M] Wilkes-Barre, PA Moreau House.
Loos, Francis *c.i.c.m.* '47 (SAT) [M] San Antonio, TX Missionhurst Community Residence.
Loos, Frederick C. '63 (SAG) On Duty Outside the Diocese.
Loosbrock, Donald L. '51 (WIN) Retired.
Lopardo, Vito R. '55 (BEL) Retired.
Lopatesky, Msgr. Raymond M. '75 (PAT) [P] Chester, NJ Nazareth Village.
Lopera, Rafael I. *c.s.b.* '94 (GAL) [Q] Sugar Land, TX Basilian Mission Center.
Lopes, Richard *o.f.m.cap.* '82 (SFR) [N] Burlingame, CA Capuchin Provincial House.
Lopes, Thomas C. '65 (FR) North Easton, MA Immaculate Conception Church.
Lopez, Abel '56 (SJ) [22] San Jose, CA Sacred Heart of Jesus Church.
Lopez, Adolfo '87 (GLP) Absent on Leave.
Lopez, Agustin *sch.p.* '57 (SJN) [57] San Juan, PR Santisimo Salvador Church.
Lopez, Alberto '87 (SJN) [2] Trujillo Alto, PR San Pio X Church.
Lopez, Alvaro '86 (STO) Riverbank, CA St. Frances of Rome Church.
Lopez, Amador *o.m.i.* '58 (SD) Calipatria, CA St. Patrick Church.
Lopez, Angel *o.f.m.* '94 (FTW) [14] Fort Wayne, IN St. Patrick Church.
Lopez, Antonio *f.s.c.b.* (BO) [1] Somerville, MA St. Ann Church.
Lopez, Armando *o.f.m.* '88 (LA) [73] Los Angeles, CA St. Joseph Church.
Lopez, Bruce '88 (PEO) [3] Spring Valley, IL St. Anthony's Church.
Lopez, Bruce D. '88 (PEO) Woodhull, IL St. John's Church.
Lopez, Camilo '93 (NEW) [5] Bayonne, NJ St. Vincent de Paul Church.
Lopez, Msgr. Daniel '63 (FRS) Selma, CA St. Joseph Church.
Lopez, Edgardo '83 (MGZ) Cabo Rojo, PR St. Michael Church.
Lopez, Edilberto '97 (ELP) Clint, TX San Lorenzo Church.
Lopez, Eugene '90 (PEO) Galva, IL St. John's Church.
Lopez, Eugenio '86 (SAC) Red Bluff, CA Sacred Heart Church.
Lopez, Fabian '99 (NY) [169] Bronx, NY Our Lady of Angels Church.
Lopez, Fausto '60 (SJ) Retired.
Lopez, Felipe '59 (NEW) [2] Union City, NJ St. Augustine's Church.
Lopez, Felix *c.r.* (DEN) [20] Denver, CO Our Lady of Guadalupe Church.
Lopez, Fernando *s.j.* '54 (MIA) [5] Miami, FL Gesu Church.
Lopez, Msgr. Francis R. '57 (MGZ) San German, PR San German de Auxerre Church.
Lopez, Francisco J. *sch.p.* '78 (PCE) [4] Ponce, PR Our Lady of Mt. Carmel Church.
Lopez, Frank '93 (ELP) [22] El Paso, TX St. Frances Xavier Cabrini Church.
Lopez, G. Edgardo *c.m.* '99 (FgM) Vincentian Foreign Missions.
Lopez, Gerard M. '91 (SB) Special or Other Diocesan Assignment.
Lopez, Humberto '86 (MGZ) San German, PR San German de Auxerre Church.
Lopez, Jaime E. '89 (TUC) Nogales, AZ San Felipe de Jesus Church.
Lopez, Jairo '94 (AUS) Marble Falls, TX St. John the Evangelist Church.
Lopez, Jesus Francisco (CC) Taft, TX Immaculate Conception Church.
Lopez, Jose (BRK) [33] Brooklyn, NY St. Dominic Church.
Lopez, Jose '91 (JKS) On Duty Outside the Diocese.
Lopez, Jose '91 (MIA) Homestead, FL Sacred Heart Church.
Lopez, Jose A. '71 (SAT) [C] San Antonio, TX Oblate School of Theology.
Lopez, Jose Maria '54 (SJN) [F] Rio Piedras, PR Hogar Santa Teresa Jornet for the Aged.
Lopez, Jose R. Montanez *c.p.* '95 (MGZ) San Sebastian, PR San Sebastian Martir Church.
Lopez, Joseph '59 (KCK) [1] Overland Park, KS Church of the Ascension.
Lopez, Juan J. '89 (ARE) On Duty Outside the Diocese.
Lopez, Juan J. '89 (SAV) Tifton, GA Our Divine Saviour Church.
Lopez, Juan M. '62 (MIA) [28] Miami, FL SS. Peter and Paul Church.
Lopez, Kharlosg '77 (CGS) Humacao, PR Maria Reina de la Paz Church.
Lopez, Lionel '96 (BWN) [2] McAllen, TX Our Lady of Sorrows Church; [C] Brownsville, TX Jail Ministry.
Lopez, Luis A. *c.p.* (ARE) Lares, PR St. Joseph Church.
Lopez, Luis E. *c.s.v.* '95 (CHI) [N] Arlington Heights, IL Viatorian Province Center-Clerics of St. Viator.
Lopez, Mario *o.carm.* '76 (BO) [BB] Peabody, MA St. Theresa Carmelite Chapel.
Lopez, Mauricio A. '92 (SAT) [13] San Antonio, TX Our Lady of the Angels Church.
Lopez, Pedro J. '81 (LA) El Monte, CA Nativity Church.
Lopez, Pedro Nel '97 (LA) Sun Valley, CA Our Lady of the Holy Rosary Church.
Lopez, Richard '73 (ATL) [I] Atlanta, GA Our Lady of Perpetual Help Home.
Lopez, Sergio '98 (OAK) Livermore, CA St. Michael Church.
Lopez, Severino *c.m.f.* '44 (ATL) Stone Mountain, GA Corpus Christi Church.
Lopez, Uriel '00 (RCK) Sterling, IL St. Mary Church.
Lopez, Vicente O. *o.carm.* '68 (LA) [89] Los Angeles, CA St. Raphael Church.
Lopez, Victor Bruno '00 (PCE) Coamo, PR St. Blase Church.
Lopez, Vincent *o.p.* '56 (L) Bardstown, KY St. Joseph Church.
Lopez Aponte, Nelson '91 (CGS) Vieques, PR Inmaculada Concepcion Church.
Lopez Mairal, Jose Ma. '54 (SJN) [10] San Juan, PR Santa Cecilia Church.
Lopez Vega, Jose Antonio '92 (PCE) [17] Ponce, PR Our Lady of Mt. Carmel Church.
LoPinto, Alfred P. '70 (BRK) [139] Brooklyn, NY St. Therese of Lisieux Church.
LoPresti, Carl '97 (PEO) Chenoa, IL St. Joseph's Church.
Lorance, Douglas '84 (SJP) Lyndora, PA St. Michael Church.
Lord, Gary F. '92 (MAN) Absent on Sick Leave.
Lord, John *o.carm.* '81 (NEW) Leonia, NJ St. John the Evangelist's Church; Leonia, NJ St. John the Evangelist's Church.
Lord, Laurence J. '64 (SY) [9] Binghamton, NY St. Patrick Church.
Lordemann, Francis W. '72 (OM) Bellevue, NE St. Mary Church.
Loredo, Miguel A. *o.f.m.* '64 (NEW) [37] Newark, NJ St. Thomas Aquinas Church.
Loredo, Miguel A. *o.f.m.* '64 (NY) [35] New York, NY St. Francis of Assisi Church.
Lorenc, Henry '84 (TYL) Jefferson, TX Immaculate Conception Church.
Lorenz, Bernard A. '85 (LIN) Harvard, NE St. Joseph's Church.
Lorenz, John F. '54 (DM) Retired; [G] Des Moines, IA Institute of the Heart of Jesus.
Lorenz, Matthais E. '69 (CHI) On Duty Outside the Archdiocese.
Lorenz, Richard J. *s.a.c.* '60 (MIL) [P] Milwaukee, WI St. Vincent Community.
Lorenz, Vincent E. '53 (SD) Retired.
Lorenz, William A. '63 (SY) Oneida, NY St. Joseph Church.
Lorenzana, Elias *o.de.m.* '82 (CGS) Cayey, PR Nuestra Senora de la Merced Church.
Lorenzetti, Msgr. Dino J. '53 (BUF) Retired; [O] Tonawanda, NY O'Hara Residence.
Lorenzo, Avelino *s.d.b.* '60 (LA) [80] Los Angeles, CA St. Mary Church; [Q] Los Angeles, CA Dominic Savio Salesian Residence.
Lorenzo, Eduardo '66 (LAN) [6] Flint, MI Our Lady of Guadalupe Church.
Lorenzo, Elias R. *o.s.b.* '89 (PAT) [M] Morristown, NJ St. Mary's Abbey.
Lorenzo, John (MIA) Permanent Deacons.
Lorenzo, Joseph F. *o.f.m.* '76 (MAN) Derry, NH St. Thomas Aquinas Church.
Lorenzoni, Larry *s.d.b.* '51 (SFR) [N] San Francisco, CA Salesian Provincial Residence.
Loresco, Alfredo '64 (HT) Retired.
Lorfanfant, Ernest P. *s.m.* '68 (RVC) [M] Mineola, NY Provincial Residence and Novitiate.
Lorge, Felix P. '50 (SPK) Colfax, WA St. Patrick Church; Lacrosse, WA St. Joseph Church.
Lorig, Douglas E. '84 (PHX) Gilbert, AZ St. Anne Church.
Lorilla, Wilfredo '68 (AGN) Piti, GU Assumption of Our Lady Church.
Lorio, Msgr. Joseph O. '54 (NO) [11] Metairie, LA St. Louis King of France Church.
Lorio, Lloyd *s.j.* '56 (FgM) Provinces.
Lorkowski, Robert A. '77 (CLV) Northfield, OH St. Barnabas Church.
Lorrain, Matthew P. '86 (BR) Lakeland, LA Immaculate Conception Church.
Losarcos, Javier '51 (NEW) [4] Newark, NJ St. Aloysius Church.
LoSasso, John *o.f.m.cap.* '89 (NEW) [N] Union City, NJ Capuchin Friars - Province of the Sacred Stigmata of St. Francis.
Losbanes, Hermes G. '86 (AGN) Tumon Bay, GU Blessed Diego Luis de San Vitores Church.
LoSchiavo, John J. *s.j.* '55 (SFR) [C] San Francisco, CA University of San Francisco.
Loscocco, Angelo P. '53 (BO) [1] Methuen, MA St. Lucy Church.
Loseke, Jeffery S. '00 (OM) Graduate Studies.
Losh, Joseph F. '64 (COL) La Rue, OH St. Joseph's Church.
Loshe, Norbert *c.pp.s.* '40 (CIN) Fort Recovery, OH Mary Help of Christians Church.
Losiewicz, George H. '74 (TOL) Retired.
Losito, Msgr. Felix A. '58 (ALN) [6] Reading, PA Holy Rosary Church.
Loskarn, George '65 (BAL) [28] Baltimore, MD St. Dominic Church.
Loskot, Donald *s.d.s.* '76 (MIL) [P] Greendale, WI Salvatorian Formation Community.
Losoya, Jose Encarnacion *c.o.* '91 (BWN) [3] Pharr, TX St. Jude Thaddeus Church; [E] Pharr, TX Oratory of St. Philip Neri, of Pontifical Right.
Lossing, Larry '84 (ORL) [10] Orlando, FL St. Joseph Church; Special Assignment.
Lostritto, Paul '96 (PH) [AA] Philadelphia, PA Order of Friars Minor of the Province of the Most Holy Name aka Holy Name Province.
Loth, Alan J. '68 (OKL) Harrah, OK St. Teresa of Avila Church.
Lotito, Floyd *o.f.m.* '60 (SFR) [T] San Francisco, CA St. Anthony Foundation.
Lotito, Floyd A. *o.f.m.* '60 (SFR) [5] San Francisco, CA St. Anthony of Padua Church; [T] San Francisco, CA Franciscan Friars of California, Provincial Office of Communications.
Lott, Franklin '69 (SEA) Battle Ground, WA Sacred Heart Church.

Lott, Lawrence '90 (MOB) On Leave from the Archdiocese.
Lott, Robert V. '65 (NY) [36] New York, NY St. Francis de Sales Church; [67] New York, NY St. Lucy Church.
Lott, Roger R.S. *o.s.b.* '54 (BIR) [E] Cullman, AL St. Bernard Abbey.
Lotz, Ezekiel *o.s.b.* '00 (P) [L] St. Benedict, OR Mt. Angel Abbey.
Lotz, Robert J. '73 (MIL) [X] Milwaukee, WI Milwaukee Archdiocesan Campus Ministry.
Louapre, Albert C. *s.j.* '60 (LAF) [J] Grand Coteau, LA Jesuit Spirituality Center (St. Charles College).
Loucks, Thomas '77 (B) Grangeville, ID SS. Peter and Paul Church.
Lougen, Louis R. *o.m.i.* '79 (BUF) [27] Buffalo, NY Holy Angels Church.
Loughery, Robert J. *c.s.c.* '89 (OAK) [N] Berkeley, CA Holy Cross Fathers-Holy Cross Center.
Loughlin, Msgr. William J. '69 (BGP) [7] Fairfield, CT St. Thomas Aquinas Church.
Loughman, Kenneth M. '58 (NY) Walden, NY Most Precious Blood Church.
Loughnane, Msgr. James J. '61 (LA) Diamond Bar, CA St. Denis Church.
Loughnane, John B., Jr. '88 (BUR) Canaan, VT Assumption of the Blessed Virgin Mary Church.
Loughnane, John B., Jr. '88 (MAN) West Stewartstown, NH St. Albert Church.
Loughran, Francis J. '56 (PH) Upper Gwynedd, PA Corpus Christi Church; Retired.
Loughran, James *s.a.* '89 (NY) [DD] New York, NY Atonement Friars.
Loughran, James N. *s.j.* '70 (NEW) [B] Jersey City, NJ Saint Peter's College; [B] Jersey City, NJ Saint Peter's College; [N] Jersey City, NJ Jesuits of Saint Peter's College, Inc.
Loughran, John *o.s.f.s.* '80 (LAN) Deerfield, MI St. Alphonsus Church.
Loughran, Peter '48 (SPR) Retired.
Loughran, Peter G. '48 (SPR) [I] Springfield, MA St. Michael's Residence.
Loughrey, Thomas F. '45 (PH) [19] Philadelphia, PA St. Barbara Church; Retired.
Louis, A. Joseph *s.d.b.* '44 (NY) [FF] Stony Point, NY Don Bosco Retreat Center and Marian Shrine; [FF] Stony Point, NY Marian Shrine.
Louis, Anthony *s.d.b.* '49 (NY) West Haverstraw, NY Helen Hayes Hospital.
Louis, Conrad *o.s.b.* '40 (IND) [J] St. Meinrad, IN St. Meinrad Archabbey.
Louis, Jean Woady '91 (VEN) Immokalee, FL Our Lady of Guadalupe Church.
Louis, Msgr. John H. '62 (SCR) Clarks Green, PA St. Gregory Church; [F] Clarks Green, PA Saint Gregory Early Childhood Center.
Louis, Kevin C. '89 (COL) [A] Columbus, OH Pontifical College Josephinum.
Louis, Kevin C. '89 (LC) On Duty Outside the Diocese.
Louis, M. Maria *s.j.* '63 (WDC) [M] Washington, DC Woodstock Jesuit Community.
Louwagie, Herman *c.i.c.m.* '58 (FgM) Missionhurst Foreign Missions.
Louzon, Bede *o.f.m.cap.* '85 (DET) Hazel Park, MI St. Mary Magdalen Church.
Lovas, Donald J. '63 (WIN) Wabasha, MN St. Felix Church.
Lovat, Rene *s.x.* '57 (FgM) Xaverian Foreign Missions.
Lovat, Rene *s.x.* '57 (PAT) [M] Wayne, NJ Xaverian Missionary Fathers.
Lovato, Charles '60 (PAT) Denville, NJ St. Clare Hospital; [J] Denville, NJ Saint Clare's Hospital, Inc.
Love, John W. '90 (LA) Graduate Studies.
Love, Lester E. *s.j.* '91 (CHI) [N] Chicago, IL Chicago Province of the Society of Jesus-Provincial Office.
Love, Lester E. *s.j.* '91 (OAK) [N] Berkeley, CA Jesuit Community at Jesuit School of Theology at Berkeley.
Loveless, William J. '75 (Y) [7] Warren, OH St. Pius X Church.
Lover, Lawrence E. *c.ss.r.* '51 (BRK) [V] Brooklyn, NY Our Lady of Good Counsel Residence.
Lovett, Gerald F. '59 (SEA) Redmond, WA St. Jude Church.
Lovisa, Eugene L. '49 (TOL) Retired.
Lovrencic, Athanasius *o.f.m.* '48 (CHI) [N] Lemont, IL The Slovene Franciscan Fathers, Order of Friars Minor, Commissariat of the Holy Cross.
Lowe, Frank '85 (SB) On Duty Outside the Diocese.
Lowe, Philip J. '82 (PH) Bala Cynwyd, PA St. Matthias Church; [D] Pottstown, PA St. Pius X High School.
Lowe, Russell '92 (CLV) Absent on Leave.
Lower, Richard T. *v.f.* '71 (MAN) New London, NH Our Lady of Fatima Church; [N] New London, NH Colby-Sawyer College Newman Center.
Lowery, Daniel L. *c.ss.r.* '55 (STL) [P] Liguori, MO Liguori Mission House/Redemptorists.
Lowery, James T. *m.s.* '55 (HRT) [M] Hartford, CT Missionaries of LaSalette, Provincial Secretary.
Lowery, Martin J. *m.m.* '68 (NY) [DD] Maryknoll, NY Maryknoll Fathers and Brothers.
Lowery, Msgr. Philip A. '76 (TR) Red Bank, NJ St. James Church.
Lowery, Wil *c.ss.r.* (STP) Brooklyn Center, MN St. Alphonsus Church.
Lowisz, Myron *o.f.m.* '95 (GRY) [H] Crown Point, IN Franciscan Homes & Community Services, Inc.; [J] Cedar Lake, IN Our Lady of Lourdes Friary.
Lowney, Edward *o.m.i.* '40 (BO) Tewksbury, MA St. William Church; Tewksbury, MA Tewksbury Hospital.
Lowney, Jeremiah '88 (HEL) [B] Helena, MT Carroll College.
Lowrey, Robert *o.m.v.* '78 (BO) [W] Milton, MA Oblate Residence (St. Joseph House); [BB] Boston, MA St. Francis Chapel.
Lowry, Joseph K. '66 (BUF) Retired.
Loya, Daniel '66 (PBR) Windber, PA St. Mary (Dormition) Church.
Loya, John F. '74 (CLV) [A] Wickliffe, OH Borromeo Seminary; [A] Wickliffe, OH St. Mary Seminary and Graduate School of Theology.
Loya, Joseph *o.s.a.* '79 (PH) [C] Villanova, PA Villanova University.
Loya, Mario *o.carm.* (TUC) [F] Tucson, AZ Carmelite Priory.
Loya, Thomas J. '82 (PRM) Lockport, IL Annunciation Byzantine Catholic Church.
Loyacono, Charles '57 (JKS) Retired.
Loyd, Frederick A. '70 (COL) [33] Columbus, OH Our Lady of the Miraculous Medal Church.
Loyens, William J. *s.j.* '58 (FgM) Provinces.
Loyens, William L. *s.j.* '58 (P) [L] Portland, OR Jesuit Provincial Office (Society of Jesus, Oregon Prov.).
Loyson, Michael '92 (DET) [5] St. Clair Shores, MI St. Lucy Church; Absent on Leave.
Lozano, Arturo *s.j.* '67 (LAF) On Special Assignment; [J] Grand Coteau, LA Jesuit Spirituality Center (St. Charles College).
Lozano, Freddy '85 (RVC) Freeport, NY Our Holy Redeemer Church.
Lozano, Msgr. Jose '65 (PCE) Juana Diaz, PR St. Raymond Nonato Church.
Lozano, Roland *c.m.f.* '75 (LA) [Q] Los Angeles, CA Missionary Sons of the Immaculate Heart of Mary; [Q] Los Angeles, CA Claretian Retreat Center Community; [Q] Los Angeles, CA Claretian Retreat Center Community; [W] Los Angeles, CA Claretian Retreat Center (All Groups).
Lozier, Donald G. *o.m.i.* '60 (BO) [4] Lowell, MA Saint Jeanne d'Arc Church.
Lozier, Timothy R. '88 (STA) [4] Gainesville, FL St. Augustine Church; [L] Gainesville, FL University of Florida-St. Augustine Parish and Student Center.
Lozinski, Eugene L. '72 (NU) Glencoe, MN St. Pius X Church.
Lozinski, Robert W. *c.s.c.* '73 (PSC) Scranton, PA St. John the Baptist Church.
Lu, Matthias '42 (OAK) Retired.
Luan, Nguyen Truong '98 (LA) [Q] Baldwin Park, CA Vietnamese Redemptorist Mission.
Lubanski, Armand *o.f.m.* '47 (SFD) [K] Sherman, IL Our Lady of Angels Friary.
Lubas, Feliks F. '57 (FAR) Minto, ND Sacred Heart Church.
Lubbers, John W. *c.s.c.* '57 (FTW) [J] South Bend, IN Congregation of Holy Cross, Indiana Province, Provincial House.
Lubbers, John W. *c.s.c.* '57 (SAT) [M] San Antonio, TX Holy Cross Community.
Lubbers, Leland E. *s.j.* '59 (OM) [K] Omaha, NE Jesuit Community at Creighton University.
Lubeley, Msgr. Richard J. '49 (STL) Webster Groves, MO Mary, Queen of Peace Church; Retired.
Luberti, Richard A. *c.ss.r.* '79 (BR) [7] Baton Rouge, LA St. Francis De Sales Church.
Luberti, Richard A. *c.ss.r.* '79 (LAF) On Special Assignment.
Lubic, Robert T. '96 (GBG) Harrison City, PA St. Barbara Church.
Lubicky, Msgr. John R. '48 (CAM) Blackwood, NJ St. Agnes Church; Retired.
Lubinsky, Michael C. '78 (SAV) Warner Robins, GA Sacred Heart Church.
Lubrano, Joseph *s.d.s.* '74 (MIL) [P] Milwaukee, WI Salvatorian Provincial Residence.
Lubrano, Robert '85 (RVC) West Babylon, NY Our Lady of Grace Church.
Luca, Edward J. '54 (CLV) Sheffield, OH St. Teresa of Avila Church.
Luca, Msgr. Joseph L. '70 (BAL) Clarksville, MD St. Louis Church.
Lucal, John A. *s.j.* '61 (DET) [K] Detroit, MI Jesuit Provincial Office-Detroit Province of the Society of Jesus.
Lucarelli, Gabriel M. *c.r.m.* '36 (NEW) Lodi, NJ St. Joseph's Church.
Lucas, Christopher D. *o.f.m.conv.* (PH) [D] Philadelphia, PA St. Hubert's Catholic High School for Girls.
Lucas, David '64 (CIN) [54] Cincinnati, OH St. Margaret Mary Church.
Lucas, Edward '61 (PBR) Weirton, WV St. Mary's Church.
Lucas, George *c.s.c.* '72 (FgM) Holy Cross Foreign Missions.
Lucas, George J. *c.s.c.* '72 (FTW) [J] South Bend, IN Congregation of Holy Cross, Indiana Province, Provincial House.
Lucas, James '00 (GB) Kaukauna, WI Holy Cross Church.
Lucas, Jeffrey J. '81 (E) [4] Erie, PA Holy Rosary Church.
Lucas, Msgr. John L. '65 (E) Warren, PA Holy Redeemer Church.
Lucas, John P. '69 (CHI) [3] Oak Park, IL St. Edmund Church; [X] Chicago, IL Court of Appeals-Province of Chicago.
Lucas, Lawrence E. '59 (NY) [89] New York, NY Our Lady of Lourdes Church; City, NY North Infirmary Command; City, NY Otis Bantum Correctional Center; Manhattan, NY North General Hospital.
Lucas, Neal C. '67 (TOL) Awaiting Assignment.
Lucas, Robert *c.m.* '74 (CHI) [J] Chicago, IL St. Anthony Hospital; [N] Chicago, IL Vincentian Community, Congregation of the Mission, Midwest Province.
Lucas, Theodore '84 (CLV) Willowick, OH St. Mary Magdalene Church.
Lucas, Thomas M. *s.j.* '85 (SFR) [N] San Francisco, CA Jesuit Community at University of San Francisco.
Lucas, William '90 (BIR) Jacksonville, AL St. Charles Church; [H] Jacksonville, AL Jacksonville State University.
Lucasinsky, Raymond *c.m.m.* '62 (DET) [K] Dearborn Heights, MI Our Lady of Grace Monastery.
Lucatero, Heliodoro '86 (SPK) On Duty Outside the Diocese.
Lucavei, Januario *o.s.b.m.* (STF) [B] Glen Cove, NY Basilian Fathers Novitiate of the Order of St. Basil the Great.
Lucavei, Januario *o.s.b.m.* '88 (RVC) [M] Glen Cove, NY St. Josaphat's Monastery, Novitiate and Retreat House.
Lucavei, Tarcisio *o.s.b.m.* '91 (STN) Hamtramck, MI Immaculate Conception of B.V.M. Church.
Lucca, Augustine *s.d.s.* '51 (NSH) Smyrna, TN St. Luke Church.
Lucchesi, Joseph *o.carm.* '84 (FgM) Carmelite Foreign Missions.
Lucchesi, Joseph *o.carm.* '84 (JOL) [J] Darien, IL Carmelite Provincial Office.
Lucero, Augusto (BRK) [111] Brooklyn, NY Our Lady of Solace Church.
Lucero, Msgr. Leo '60 (SFE) [18] Albuquerque, NM San Felipe de Neri Church.
Lucero, Lorenzo '56 (ELP) [38] El Paso, TX San Judas Tadeo Church; Horizon City, TX Holy Spirit Church; Retired.
Lucev, John '65 (SD) Retired.
Lucey, Beatus T. *o.s.b.* '59 (PAT) [M] Morristown, NJ St. Mary's Abbey.
Lucey, Gregory *s.j.* '64 (MOB) [A] Mobile, AL Spring Hill College.
Lucey, J. Roger '58 (MIL) [P] Milwaukee, WI Jesuit Provincial Office, Wisconsin Province.
Lucey, J. Roger *s.j.* '58 (OAK) Orinda, CA Santa Maria Church; [N] Berkeley, CA Jesuit Community at Jesuit School of Theology at Berkeley.
Lucey, John P. '32 (SPR) Retired.
Lucey, Paul T. *s.j.* '48 (BO) [W] Boston, MA Loyola House.
Lucey, Walter D. '98 (NEW) North Arlington, NJ Queen of Peace Church.
Lucey, William F. '52 (BO) [2] Norwood, MA St. George Church; Senior Priests.
Luchi, Robert J. *s.j.* '93 (FgM) Provinces.
Luciana, Msgr. Lawrence '68 (WH) [B] Huntington, WV St. Joseph Central Catholic High School.
Luciana, Msgr. Lawrence J. '63 (WH) [1] Huntington, WV St. Joseph's Church.
Luciani, Pompeo *s.a.c.* '36 (NEW) Fairview, NJ Our Lady of Grace Church.
Luciano, William J. '83 (NY) [166] Bronx, NY St. Michael Church.
Lucid, Msgr. Michael '54 (OAK) [1] San Leandro, CA Assumption of the Blessed Virgin Mary Church.
Lucid, Philip J. *s.j.* '55 (SEA) [A] Seattle, WA Seattle University.
Lucid, Vincent F. '43 (BO) Senior Priests.
Lucido, John '73 (ELP) Kermit, TX St. Thomas & St. Joseph Church; Monahans, TX St. John the Apostle and Evangelist Church.
Lucio, Justin '72 (DAL) Special Assignment.
Luck, Robert O. '62 (LA) Retired.
Lucking, Aloysius '50 (MIA) Retired.
Lucking, Aloysius A. '50 (SB) [E] Morongo Valley, CA St. Michael's of Morongo Valley, Inc.
Lucree, Lawrence A. '60 (SAV) [2] Columbus, GA Our Lady of Lourdes Church.
LucThePhan, Peter '90 (SJ) [15] San Jose, CA St. Maria Goretti Church.
Luczak, Andrew E. '70 (CHI) Skokie, IL St. Lambert Church.
Luczak, Jay R. '92 (TUC) Miami, AZ Our Lady of the

Blessed Sacrament Church.
Luczak, Thomas *o.f.m.* '70 (FgM) Franciscan Foreign Missions.
Luczak, Thomas *o.f.m.* '70 (GB) [I] Pulaski, WI Assumption of B.V.M. Friary.
Luczycki, Msgr. Matthew C. '45 (SY) Oneida, NY St. Joseph Church; Retired.
Ludden, John J. '97 (VEN) [1] Sarasota, FL Incarnation Church.
Ludeman, Edward J. '95 (SFR) Absent on Leave.
Ludescher, Kenneth F. '61 (STP) Maplewood, MN St. Jerome Church.
Ludvik, John J. '71 (SEA) [2] Vancouver, WA Our Lady of Lourdes Church.
Ludwig, Alexander P. '58 (SCL) Alexandria, MN St. Mary's Church.
Ludwig, Augustine W. *o.s.b.* '86 (RIC) [L] Richmond, VA Mary Mother of the Church Abbey.
Ludwig, Eugene *o.f.m.cap.* '71 (SFR) Burlingame, CA Our Lady of Angels Church.
Ludwig, Eugene M. *o.f.m.cap.* '71 (NTN) Oakland, CA St. John The Theologian Church.
Ludwig, Eugene M. *o.f.m.cap.* '71 (OAK) [A] Berkeley, CA Dominican School of Philosophy and Theology; [A] Berkeley, CA Dominican School of Philosophy and Theology.
Ludwig, John '74 (DM) [7] Des Moines, IA St. Catherine of Siena Catholic Student Center Church; [I] Des Moines, IA St. Catherine of Siena Catholic Student Center.
Ludwig, Ray A. '57 (DUB) Retired.
Ludwig, Thomas K. '87 (KC) [5] St. Joseph, MO St. Mary's Church; [C] St. Joseph, MO Bishop LeBlond High School.
Ludwikoski, James E. '73 (KCK) Military Chaplains.
Luebke, Martial *o.f.m.* '39 (FgM) Custody of St. Mary of the Angels. Byzantine-Slavonic.
Luebke, Martial *o.f.m.* '39 (LA) [73] Los Angeles, CA St. Joseph Church.
Luebking, Msgr. Thomas A. '71 (TR) Spring Lake, NJ St. Catharine Church.
Lueckenotte, Daniel I. J. '90 (JC) Palmyra, MO St. Joseph Church.
Lueckenotto, Arthur A. *m.s.* '63 (STL) [P] St. Louis, MO La Salette Missionaries.
Luehrmann, Stanley E. '53 (CIN) Hillsboro, OH St. Mary Church.
Lueras, Charles R. *c.r.i.c.* '81 (LA) [65] Los Angeles, CA St. Francis of Assisi Church; [B] Los Angeles, CA Canons Regular of the Immaculate Conception-Novitiate; [Q] Los Angeles, CA Canons Regular of the Immaculate Conception.
Luerman, John H. '56 (IND) Cambridge City, IN St. Elizabeth of Hungary Church.
Luetkemeyer, Alexander *o.s.b.* '53 (KC) [I] Savannah, MO La Verna Village Apartments; [J] Conception, MO Conception Abbey; [K] Savannah, MO La Verna Heights Provincial House.
Luft, Raymond P. '68 (PRO) [26] Providence, RI Our Lady of Mt. Carmel Church.
Luger, Paul P. *s.j.* '42 (SPK) [K] Spokane, WA Regis Community.
Lugger, William '89 (LAN) [2] Lansing, MI St. Casimir Church.
Lugo, Camillo '70 (RVC) Copiague, NY Our Lady of the Assumption Church.
Lugo, Fidelo '89 (SAN) [2] Odessa, TX St. Anthony Church; [4] Odessa, TX St. Joseph Church.
Lugo, Joseph W. '62 (PAT) Retired.
Lugo, Victor *m.n.m.* '81 (ARE) [4] Camuy, PR Our Lady of Monserrate Church.
Lui, Gabriel '79 (LA) Monterey Park, CA St. Thomas Aquinas Church.
Lui, Pius *o.f.m.* '53 (FgM) Franciscan Foreign Missions.
Lui, Stephen *c.s.j.b.* '76 (BRK) [V] Astoria, NY Congregation of St. John the Baptist of China.
Lui, Tovia '83 (LA) Torrance, CA St. Catherine Laboure Church.
Luis, Anthony F. '50 (BRK) Retired; [V] Douglaston, NY Bishop Mugavero Residence.
Luisi, Joseph G. '83 (PIT) [64] Pittsburgh, PA Resurrection Church.
Luisini, Msgr. Anthony J. '56 (MET) Alpha, NJ St. Mary Church.
Luistro, Abelardo R. '50 (LA) Retired.
Luiten, Gary '92 (FAR) Ellendale, ND St. Helena's Church.
Luiz, Gary M. *c.pp.s.* '77 (OAK) [N] Berkeley, CA Society of the Precious Blood.
Luiz, Lester A. *s.j.* '44 (DET) [P] Clarkston, MI Colombiere Center.
Luka, Ronald *c.m.f.* '63 (CHI) [N] Oak Park, IL Claretian Fathers Headquarters of U.S.A. Eastern Province.
Lukac, Thomas M. '63 (GBG) [3] Latrobe, PA St. John the Evangelist Church.
Lukachinsky, Jerome A. '88 (CLV) [2] Parma, OH St. Bridget Church.
Lukacs, Janos '98 (BO) [W] Cambridge, MA Weston Jesuit Community.
Lukas, Andrew F. '58 (WH) Retired.
Lukas, Joseph S. '46 (BO) Senior Priests.
Lukas, Martin C. *o.s.f.s.* '80 (TOL) [K] Toledo, OH Oblates of St. Francis de Sales.
Lukaschek, Ernest C. *m.m.* '64 (FgM) Maryknoll Foreign Missions.
Lukaszczyk, Josef '80 (STL) [P] Eureka, MO Our Lady of the Angels Monastery.
Lukaszewicz, John C. '55 (MIL) Retired.
Lukaszewsk, Stanley P. '79 (TR) Manasquan, NJ St. Denis Church.
Lukaszewski, Jerome *o.f.m.conv.* '43 (BAL) [S] Ellicott City, MD Order of Friars Minor Conventual.
Lukaszewski, Jerome *o.f.m.conv.* '48 (FgM) Conventual Franciscan Foreign Missions.
Lukaszewski, Leonard '54 (GRY) Retired.
Luke, Eugene *o.s.b.* '61 (LR) Booneville, AR Church of Our Lady of the Assumption; [A] Subiaco, AR Subiaco Monastery.
Lukefahr, Oscar *c.m.* '66 (STL) [P] Perryville, MO Congregation of The Mission; [V] Perryville, MO Catholic Home Study Service.
Lukehart, Frederick '63 (Y) [2] Warren, OH Christ Our King Church.
Lukenda, Raymond T. '56 (NEW) Secaucus, NJ Immaculate Conception Church.
Lukianiuk, Andrzej '86 (BRK) [52] Brooklyn, NY Guardian Angel Church.
Lukie, Bohdan *c.ss.r.* '67 (PHU) Newark, NJ St. John the Baptist Church.
Lukomski, Ryszard *s.a.c.* '93 (BUF) [O] North Tonawanda, NY Society of the Catholic Apostolate.
Lukoskie, Raymond M. '58 (PEO) Warsaw, IL Sacred Heart Church.
Lulf, Ken '99 (SFS) Gettysburg, SD Sacred Heart Church.
Luljak, Louis '61 (MIL) East Troy, WI St. Peter Church.
Lulko, Leo T. '65 (DET) Highland, MI Church of the Holy Spirit.
Lum, William '69 (ROC) Graduate Studies.
Luminais, Msgr. J. Anthony '54 (NO) Bridge City, LA Holy Guardian Angels Church.
Lumpkin, Thomas '64 (DET) Detroit, MI Southwest Detroit Hospital.
Lumsden, Patrick '96 (DAV) Dodgeville, IA St. Mary's Church.
Lumsden, Patrick L. '96 (DAV) Columbus Junction, IA St. Joseph Church; Wapello, IA St. Mary's Church.
Luna, Ezequiel Bas *o.s.b.* '84 (SFE) [I] Abiquiu, NM Monastery of Christ in the Desert.
Luna, Ignacio '65 (BWN) San Benito, TX St. Benedict Church.
Luna, Lambert Joseph '78 (SFE) [3] Santa Fe, NM Cristo Rey Church.
Luna, Luis *m.s.a.* '87 (NOR) [A] Cromwell, CT Holy Apostles College and Seminary.
Luna, Miguel (ELP) [4] El Paso, TX Blessed Sacrament Church.
Luna, Roger *s.d.b.* '55 (OAK) [E] Richmond, CA Salesian High School.
Lund, Donald F. *c.s.v.* '46 (JOL) Bourbonnais, IL Maternity of the Blessed Virgin Mary Church.
Lund, Donald J. '69 (CHI) [70] Chicago, IL Good Shepherd Church.
Lundberg, Jan *o.c.d.* '93 (SJ) [L] San Jose, CA Carmelite Monastery, Novitiate.
Lundberg, John W. '60 (TLS) Retired.
Lundergan, Barnabas *o.s.b.* '45 (RCK) [G] Aurora, IL Marmion Abbey-St. Augustine's Abbey.
Lundgren, Richard '96 (JOL) [6] Naperville, IL St. Thomas the Apostle Church.
Lundgren, Stephen A. '79 (DUB) [H] Dubuque, IA Mercy Medical Center-Dubuque.
Lundy, George F. *s.j.* '78 (DET) [K] Detroit, MI Jesuit Community at the University of Detroit.
Lundy, George F. *s.j.* '78 (WH) [A] Wheeling, WV Wheeling Jesuit University.
Lungay, Jose Roel '84 (NO) Chalmette, LA Our Lady of Prompt Succor Church.
Luniw, Paul '82 (STF) Glastonbury, CT St. John The Baptist Church; Hartford, CT St. Michael Church.
Lunney, Msgr. John A. '56 (ANC) Retired.
Lunney, William '94 (SPR) Agawam, MA St. John the Evangelist Church.
Lunnon, William '82 (DET) Special Assignment; [M] Detroit, MI St. Mary's Residence.
Lunsford, Keith '92 (KCK) Horton, KS St. Leo's Church; Purcell, KS St. Mary's Church.
Lunsford, Msgr. Robert D. '60 (LAN) [1] Lansing, MI St. Mary Church.
Lunzer, Matthew *s.v.d.* '45 (FgM) Society of the Divine Word Foreign Missions.
Luo, Matteo *o.f.m.conv.* '59 (BAL) [S] Ellicott City, MD Order of Friars Minor Conventual.
Luong, Dominic *s.s.s.* '67 (SAT) [45] San Antonio, TX St. Joseph Church; [74] San Antonio, TX Vietnamese Martyrs Catholic Center Church.
Luong, Msgr. Dominic Mai Thanh '66 (NO) [14] New Orleans, LA Mary, Queen of Vietnam Church; [9] New Orleans, LA Chapel of the Vietnamese Martyrs Church.
Luong, James M. Vu Dai *c.m.c.* (SPC) [E] Carthage, MO Congregation of the Mother Co-Redemptrix, United States Assumption Province.
Luong, Tri (HBG) [G] Danville, PA Maria Joseph Manor.
Luong Minh Tuat, Francis M. *c.m.c.* (SPC) [E] Springfield, MO Congregation of Mother Co-Redemptrix, Our Lady of the Rosary House.
Luongo, Anthony V. *s.d.b.* (BO) [25] Boston, MA Holy Name Church.
Luongo, John '78 (ORG) Absent on Sick Leave.
Lupa, Gerard '77 (SY) Absent on Leave.
Lupa, Gerard F. '77 (SCR) [22] Scranton, PA St. Paul's Church; [O] Scranton, PA Marian Convent, Marywood.
Lupico, Samuel (BAL) [29] Baltimore, MD St. Edward Church.
Lupo, David *ss.cc.* '91 (FR) [I] Fairhaven, MA Sacred Hearts Provincial House; [K] Wareham, MA Sacred Hearts Retreat Center.
Lupo, Joseph F. *o.ss.t.* '45 (NY) [218] Staten Island, NY Our Lady of Mt. Carmel-St. Benedicta Church.
Lupo, William L. '65 (CHI) Bartlett, IL St. Peter Damian Church.
Luque, Msgr. Peter '63 (SB) [2] Corona, CA St. Edward Church.
Lusch, Daniel J. *s.j.* '62 (BO) [W] Boston, MA The Society of Jesus of New England-Provincial Offices; [W] Chestnut Hill, MA The Jesuit Community at Boston College.
Lusch, Daniel J. *s.j.* '62 (BUF) [O] Buffalo, NY Canisius Jesuit Community.
Luschen, Timothy D. '88 (OKL) [19] Oklahoma City, OK Sacred Heart Church.
Lusik, William A. '97 (NEW) Little Ferry, NJ St. Margaret of Cortona Church.
Lusoski, Thomas J. '57 (CLV) South Euclid, OH St. Margaret Mary Church; Retired.
Lussier, Andre '55 (FR) [I] Attleboro, MA La Salette Provincial House.
Lussier, Bonaventure *o.c.d.* '75 (WH) [M] Hinton, WV Monastery of Christ on the Mountain.
Lussier, Louis *o.s.cam.* (MAD) Durward's Glen, WI St. Camillus Church; Merrimac, WI St. Mary, Health of the Sick Church.
Lussier, Louis *o.s.cam.* '90 (MAD) [A] Baraboo, WI St. Camillus Monastery and Retreat Center.
Lussier, Louis *o.s.cam.* '90 (MIL) [N] Wauwatosa, WI St. Camillus Health Center, Inc.; [N] Wauwatosa, WI San Camillo, Inc.; [P] St. Francis, WI St. Camillus Formation Community; [Y] Wauwatosa, WI St. Camillus Health System, Inc.; [Y] Wauwatosa, WI St. Camillus Communities, Inc.; [Y] Wauwatosa, WI St. Camillus Ministries, Inc.
Lussier, Marc *m.s.a.* '66 (VEN) Cape Coral, FL St. Andrew Church.
Lussier, Robert *s.s.s.* '56 (GB) Menasha, WI St. Mary Church.
Lussier, Robert *o.s.b.* '92 (SFE) [1] Santa Fe, NM The Cathedral of San Francisco de Asis; [I] Pecos, NM Our Lady of Guadalupe Abbey; [K] Pecos, NM Our Lady of Guadalupe Olivetan Benedictine Abbey.
Lussier, Ronald P. '52 (SPR) [6] Chicopee, MA St. George's Church.
Lusson, David R. '80 (SUP) Frederic, WI St. Dominic Church; Grantsburg, WI Immaculate Conception Church.
Luteri, Evaristo '30 (PIT) Retired; [O] Pittsburgh, PA St. John Vianney Manor.
Lutgen, Richard (SAL) [1] Salina, KS Cathedral of the Sacred Heart.
Lutgen, Richard E. '62 (SAL) Chapman, KS St. Michael's Church.
Luther, Benjamin F. '64 (OWN) [3] Paducah, KY St. John the Evangelist Church.
Luther, Philip L. '87 (LIN) Trenton, NE St. James Church.
Lutjen, George J. '68 (BRK) [149] Queens, NY St. Anastasia Church.
Lutkenhof, Bernard '71 (LEX) Retired.
Lutkenhoff, Bernard '71 (LEX) Barbourville, KY St. Gregory Church; [L] Barbourville, KY St. Gregory Church-Union College.
Lutkenhoff, Bernard '71 (LFT) Unassigned.
Lutmer, Joseph H. '46 (CIN) Retired.
Lutostanski, Anthony '58 (BUF) [39] Buffalo, NY St. John Kanty Church.
Luttenberger, Gerard H. *c.m.* '65 (RVC) [A] Huntington, NY Diocesan Seminary of the Immaculate Conception; [M] Oyster Bay, NY Vincentian Community.
Lutz, Bernard '63 (EVN) Fort Branch, IN St. Bernard Church.
Lutz, Bernard A. '63 (EVN) Fort Branch, IN Holy Cross Church.
Lutz, Donald J. '70 (BUF) [13] Buffalo, NY St. Bernard Church.
Lutz, Frederick J. '73 (SPC) Advance, MO St. Joseph Church.
Lutz, George '62 (NEW) [17] Newark, NJ St. James Church.
Lutz, Gerald J. '56 (PIT) Retired.

Lutz, Herman '58 (IND) North Vernon, IN St. Mary/ Nativity of the Blessed Virgin Mary Church.
Lutz, Msgr. James M. (SY) Retired.
Lutz, Joseph L. '87 (RCK) [3] Freeport, IL St. Mary Church.
Lutz, Kevin F. '78 (COL) [19] Columbus, OH Holy Family Church.
Lutz, Robert J. '50 (CHI) Northbrook, IL St. Norbert Church; Retired.
Lutz, Thomas '93 (NY) Highland, NY St. Augustine Church.
Luu, John Khien *s.v.d.* '92 (FgM) Society of the Divine Word Foreign Missions.
Luu, Joseph '66 (HT) Retired.
Lux, Joachim *o.f.m.* '61 (L) [43] Louisville, KY St. Joseph Church.
Lux, Joseph W. *s.j.* '71 (NEW) [B] Jersey City, NJ Saint Peter's College; [N] Jersey City, NJ Jesuits of Saint Peter's College, Inc.
Lux, Thomas J. '85 (LIN) Bruno, NE St. Anthony Church; [C] David City, NE Aquinas/St. Mary's Schools.
Luyet, Gregory T. *j.c.l.* '95 (LR) [10] Little Rock, AR Our Lady of Good Counsel Church.
Luzbetak, Louis *s.v.d.* '45 (CHI) [B] Techny, IL Divine Word Residence.
Luzetsky, Stephen '50 (PSC) Retired.
Luznicky, George *o.s.m.* '55 (CHI) [14] Chicago, IL Annunciata Church.
Luznicky, George M. *o.s.m.* '55 (CHI) [N] Chicago, IL Order of Friar Servants of Mary (Servites) United States of America Province, Inc.
Luzzi, Anthony *s.d.b.* '49 (NY) [FF] Stony Point, NY Don Bosco Retreat Center and Marian Shrine; [FF] Stony Point, NY Marian Shrine.
Ly, Hilary Tran Cong *c.m.c.* '77 (FWT) [2] Arlington, TX Church of the Vietnamese Martyrs.
Lybarger, Curtis F. '77 (STP) Brooklyn Park, MN St. Vincent de Paul Church.
Lyddy, Daniel F. '34 (OG) Retired.
Lyden, Dennis P. '63 (STU) Retired.
Lydon, John E. *o.p.* '99 (MIA) [18] Miami, FL St. Dominic Church; [B] Miami, FL Barry University; [H] Miami, FL Dominican Fathers of Miami, Inc.
Lydon, John J. *o.s.a.* '84 (FgM) Foreign Missions.
Lydon, Leo B. '50 (WH) Retired.
Lydon, Michael '74 (SP) New Port Richey, FL St. Thomas Aquinas Church; [F] New Port Richey, FL St. Thomas Aquinas Early Childhood Center.
Lydon, Michael J. '84 (STL) [57] St. Louis, MO St. Pius the Fifth Church.
Lyle, Dennis J. '91 (CHI) [A] Mundelein, IL University of St. Mary of the Lake-Mundelein Seminary.
Lyle, John W. *o.s.f.s.* '85 (WIL) [I] Wilmington, DE Oblates of St. Francis De Sales.
Lyman, Edward P. '67 (SCR) Archbald, PA St. Thomas Aquinas Church.
Lynam, Gerald J. '50 (HEL) Retired.
Lynam, Michael John '00 (PIT) [8] Pittsburgh, PA St. Charles Lwanga Church.
Lynam, Robert G. '84 (MET) Kendall Park, NJ St. Augustine of Canterbury Church.
Lynaugh, Msgr. Joseph E. '36 (PH) Ardsley, PA Queen of Peace Church; Retired.
Lynch, Antone J. '81 (BLX) [4] Gulfport, MS St. Joseph Catholic Church.
Lynch, Charles E. *c.s.b.* '58 (GAL) [7] Houston, TX St. Anne Church.
Lynch, Cletus J. '30 (CHI) La Grange Park, IL St. Louise de Marillac Church; Retired.
Lynch, Conall P. *o.f.m.* '51 (GLP) [F] Gallup, NM Southwest Indian Foundation.
Lynch, Cornelius B. '54 (PRO) Retired.
Lynch, Damion '91 (CHL) Absent On Leave.
Lynch, Daniel *s.m.a.* '73 (WDC) [M] Takoma Park, MD Society of African Missions (S.M.A.).
Lynch, Daniel C. '48 (SC) Retired.
Lynch, Daniel F. *o.carm.* '54 (NY) Montrose, NY Franklin D. Roosevelt Hospital.
Lynch, Daniel G. '51 (BO) Senior Priests.
Lynch, Denis '57 (GAL) Retired.
Lynch, Dennis J. '68 (LC) [1] Wisconsin Rapids, WI Our Lady, Queen of Heaven Church.
Lynch, Donald *o'carm.* (NY) Castle Point, NY Veterans Administration Medical Center.
Lynch, Donald D. *s.j.* '59 (BGP) [P] Fairfield, CT The Fairfield Jesuit Community-Fairfield University.
Lynch, E. Patrick *c.s.s.r.* (BAL) Annapolis, MD St. Mary Church.
Lynch, Edward *c.ss.r.* '69 (BAL) [S] Annapolis, MD Saint Mary Rectory.
Lynch, Edward C. *s.j.* '64 (BUF) [O] Buffalo, NY Canisius Jesuit Community.
Lynch, Msgr. Edward J. '57 (BAL) [41] Baltimore, MD Immaculate Conception Church; [O] Timonium, MD Stella Maris; [V] Towson, MD The Immaculate Conception Elementary School Endowment Trust.
Lynch, Eugene *s.m.m.* '54 (HRT) [M] Litchfield, CT Montfort Missionaries; [M] Litchfield, CT Montfort Missionaries.
Lynch, Francis A. *c.m.* '50 (MOB) Tallassee, AL St. Vincent De Paul Church.
Lynch, Frank '57 (BRK) [216] Queens, NY Our Lady of Mount Carmel Church.
Lynch, Gerald P. '73 (SLC) [9] Salt Lake City, UT St. Patrick's Church.
Lynch, Gerard F. *o.ss.t.* '74 (TR) Asbury Park, NJ Our Lady of Mt. Carmel Church.
Lynch, Ibar '52 (SEA) Retired.
Lynch, James *m.m.* '74 (FgM) Maryknoll Foreign Missions.
Lynch, John *m.afr.* '62 (WDC) [M] Washington, DC Missionaries of Africa.
Lynch, John '96 (NY) Monticello, NY St. Peter Church.
Lynch, John A. '60 (ROC) [28] Rochester, NY St. James Church.
Lynch, John E. *c.s.p.* '51 (WDC) [B] Washington, DC St. Paul's College; [C] Washington, DC Catholic University of America, The.
Lynch, John J. *s.j.* '66 (OM) [K] Omaha, NE Jesuit Community at Creighton University.
Lynch, John J. '96 (NY) Woodbourne, NY Immaculate Conception Church.
Lynch, John K. '56 (HRT) Cheshire, CT St. Bridget's Church.
Lynch, John R. '67 (CHI) [69] Chicago, IL St. Gertrude Church.
Lynch, John S. '63 (E) Sharpsville, PA St. Bartholomew Church.
Lynch, Joseph P. '53 (CHI) Burbank, IL St. Albert the Great Church; Retired.
Lynch, Kenny *c.p.* '37 (CHI) [N] Chicago, IL Daneo Hall.
Lynch, Kevin A. *c.s.p.* '53 (NEW) [S] Mahwah, NJ Paulist Press.
Lynch, Kevin A. *c.s.p.* '53 (NY) [104] New York, NY St. Paul the Apostle Church.
Lynch, Kevin A. *m.m.* '61 (FgM) Maryknoll Foreign Missions.
Lynch, Leo A. '93 (ALT) [4] Altoona, PA Sacred Heart Church; [B] Altoona, PA Bishop Guilfoyle High School.
Lynch, Leo X. '56 (BO) [1] Woburn, MA St. Anthony Church.
Lynch, M. Kevin '74 (PRO) [3] Pawtucket, RI St. Edward Church.
Lynch, Maurice J. '65 (DUB) On Leave of Absence.
Lynch, Michael '89 (MIA) Margate, FL St. Vincent Church.
Lynch, Michael J. '71 (LC) Wausau, WI Wausau Hospital Center.
Lynch, Michael J. '82 (TR) Beverly, NJ St. Joseph Church.
Lynch, Michael J. '88 (BRK) [108] Brooklyn, NY Our Lady of the Presentation Church.
Lynch, Michael J. *s.j.* '93 (NY) [80] New York, NY Nativity Church.
Lynch, Michael J.. '88 (BRK) [99] Brooklyn, NY Our Lady of Loreto Church.
Lynch, Myles M. *o.s.m.* '58 (CHI) [N] Chicago, IL Order of Friar Servants of Mary (Servites) United States of America Province, Inc.
Lynch, Noel T. '62 (SAC) Auburn, CA St. Joseph Church.
Lynch, Patrick '59 (DAL) Retired.
Lynch, Patrick J. '46 (ALB) Retired.
Lynch, Msgr. Patrick J. '50 (MEM) Retired.
Lynch, Patrick J. *s.j.* '72 (BUF) [O] Buffalo, NY Canisius Jesuit Community.
Lynch, Peter J. '99 (BGP) [2] Trumbull, CT St. Catherine of Siena Church; [C] Trumbull, CT St. Joseph High School.
Lynch, Ralph *o.s.b.* '46 (IND) [H] Beech Grove, IN St. Paul Hermitage; [J] St. Meinrad, IN St. Meinrad Archabbey.
Lynch, Raymond J. *o.f.m.* '51 (SCR) [12] Wilkes-Barre, PA St. Joseph Church; [M] Wilkes-Barre, PA St. Joseph's Friary.
Lynch, Msgr. Richard '46 (LSC) Retired.
Lynch, Robert B. *o.f.m.* '43 (BO) [Z] Boston, MA Saint Anthony Residence.
Lynch, Robert B. '60 (NOR) [4] Norwich, CT St. Mary Church.
Lynch, Robert G. *s.j.* '56 (CHY) Pinedale, WY Our Lady of Peace Church.
Lynch, Stephen *o.f.m.* '55 (PRO) [P] Providence, RI St. Francis Friary.
Lynch, Stephen '77 (BRK) [229] Queens, NY Presentation of the Blessed Virgin Mary Church.
Lynch, T. Patrick '61 (NEW) [B] Jersey City, NJ Saint Peter's College; [N] Jersey City, NJ Jesuits of Saint Peter's College, Inc.
Lynch, Thomas *o.p.* '86 (FgM) Dominican - Order of Preachers Foreign Missions.
Lynch, Thomas '92 (NY) [110] New York, NY Sacred Heart of Jesus Church; [A] Yonkers, NY St. Joseph's Seminary.
Lynch, Thomas F. '48 (NEW) Retired.
Lynch, Thomas F. '71 (BGP) [2] Stratford, CT St. James Church.
Lynch, Thomas P. *o.p.* '86 (CHI) [N] Chicago, IL Dominicans (Provincial Office).
Lynch, Timothy J. '71 (PMB) [2] West Palm Beach, FL Mary Immaculate Church.
Lynch, William F. '57 (HRT) [4] Manchester, CT St. James Church.
Lynch, William J. *s.j.* '48 (CHL) Mooresville, NC St. Therese Church; [J] Charlotte, NC Jesuit Community.
Lynes, James F. '79 (GAL) Clute, TX St. Jerome Church.
Lynes, John '87 (MOB) Chickasaw, AL St. Thomas the Apostle Church.
Lyness, Stephen J. '98 (ATL) Newnan, GA St. George's Church.
Lynette, C. Franklyn *s.j.* '47 (NO) [C] New Orleans, LA Loyola University New Orleans.
Lyng, Msgr. Eamonn F. '58 (SD) La Jolla, CA Mary, Star of the Sea Church.
Lyng, Matthew '57 (CC) Robstown, TX St. Thomas the Apostle Church.
Lynn, William D. *s.j.* '54 (COL) [A] Columbus, OH Pontifical College Josephinum.
Lynn, Msgr. William J. '76 (PH) Ardsley, PA Queen of Peace Church.
Lyon, George *o.s.b.* '50 (SFS) [F] Marvin, SD Blue Cloud Abbey.
Lyon, Msgr. Gerald F. '49 (SC) Le Mars, IA St. Joseph's Church; Retired.
Lyon, Joseph A. (L) Retired.
Lyons, Adrian *s.j.* '74 (WDC) [M] Washington, DC Woodstock Jesuit Community.
Lyons, Denis '58 (ORG) Dana Point, CA St. Edward Church.
Lyons, Edward D. '62 (CAM) Cape May Court House, NJ Our Lady of the Angels Church.
Lyons, Edward J. *c.s.p.* '53 (NY) [DD] Jamaica Estates, NY Paulist Fathers Generalate.
Lyons, Msgr. Eugene F. '42 (CHI) Winnetka, IL SS. Faith, Hope and Charity Church; Retired.
Lyons, Francis '59 (MIA) Retired.
Lyons, Msgr. Frederick J. '52 (ALX) Retired.
Lyons, James *o.m.i.* (FgM) Oblates Foreign Missions.
Lyons, James A. '94 (PH) [13] Philadelphia, PA St. Anselm Church.
Lyons, James D. '60 (BO) Rowley, MA St. Mary Church.
Lyons, James F. '43 (FR) Retired.
Lyons, James H.C. '96 (CR) Bemidji, MN St. Philip's Church; [F] Bemidji, MN Holy Spirit Newman Center.
Lyons, James M. *v.g.* '88 (HBG) [2] Harrisburg, PA St. Catherine Laboure Church.
Lyons, James P. '45 (KC) Retired.
Lyons, James W. '51 (CHI) Retired.
Lyons, John '42 (BO) [Z] Tewksbury, MA Immaculate Heart of Mary Infirmary.
Lyons, John '80 (SAV) [2] Augusta, GA St. Joseph Church.
Lyons, John *o.m.v.* '83 (LA) Hawaiian Gardens, CA St. Peter Chanel Church.
Lyons, John F. '46 (Y) Retired.
Lyons, John F. '73 (CLV) Released from Diocesan Assignment.
Lyons, John P. '55 (BO) Rochester, MA St. Rose of Lima Church.
Lyons, John P. '88 (TUC) [23] Tucson, AZ Saints Peter and Paul Church; Special Assignment.
Lyons, John T. '74 (PH) Boothwyn, PA St. John Fisher Church.
Lyons, Joseph *o.m.i.* '29 (SAT) [K] San Antonio, TX Oblate Madonna Residence.
Lyons, Lawrence '54 (MIA) Retired.
Lyons, Leo J. (CHI) Retired.
Lyons, Mark (MIL) [N] Wauwatosa, WI St. Camillus Health Center, Inc.
Lyons, Mark J. '38 (MIL) Retired.
Lyons, Michael '96 (VIC) Vanderbilt, TX St. John Bosco Church.
Lyons, Michael J. '70 (DUL) Pine City, MN Immaculate Conception Church.
Lyons, Michael P. '96 (BGP) Brookfield, CT St. Joseph Church.
Lyons, Patrick J. '45 (LIN) Retired; [E] Lincoln, NE Bonacum House.
Lyons, Patrick M. '70 (CHI) Calumet City, IL Our Lady of Knock Church.
Lyons, Peter A. *t.o.r.* '66 (BAL) [8] Baltimore, MD St. Ann Church; [96] Baltimore, MD St. Wenceslaus Church.
Lyons, Richard J. '74 (MET) Dunellen, NJ St. John the Evangelist Church.
Lyons, Robert *s.j.* '77 (SPK) [C] Spokane, WA Gonzaga University.
Lyons, Thomas J. '52 (BRK) [141] Brooklyn, NY St. Thomas Aquinas Church; Retired.
Lyons, Timothy V. *c.m.* '86 (PH) [70] Philadelphia, PA Immaculate Conception Church.
Lyons, Vincent '48 (SAC) Retired and in Senior Ministry.
Lyons, William J. '56 (CHI) Alsip, IL St. Terrence Church.
Lyons, Msgr. William J. '56 (STL) [A] St. Louis, MO Kenrick-Glennon Seminary; [A] St. Louis, MO

Kenrick-Glennon Seminary; [U] St. Louis, MO Washington University Newman Centers.
Lyons, William P. '51 (CLV) [12] Akron, OH St. Matthew Church; Retired.
Lysogorski, John '75 (ALB) [3] Troy, NY St. Francis de Sales Church; Special Assignment; [S] Albany, NY Diocesan HIV/AIDS Services.
Lytle, Gerald A. '60 (HBG) [1] Lancaster, PA St. Anne Church.
Lyttle, Eugene '93 (CR) Laporte, MN St. Theodore Church.
Lyttle, Eugene '93 (DUL) Cass Lake, MN St. Charles Church.
Lyttle, Paul (WDC) [4] Bowie, MD St. Pius X Church.

M

Ma, Didacus W. '52 (SFR) [35] San Francisco, CA St. Monica Church; Retired.
Ma, Peter '55 (NY) [70] New York, NY St. Mary Church; Manhattan, NY Beekman Downtown - New York Infirmary.
Maaq, Ronald E. '78 (BAK) Hood River, OR Immaculate Conception Church.
Maassen, Jeffrey A. (STL) [4] St. Charles, MO Sts. Joachim and Ann Church.
Maat, William A. *o.s.b.* '33 (P) Rockaway, OR St. Mary by the Sea Church.
Maat, William A. *o.s.b.* '33 (SEA) [L] Lacey, WA St. Martin's Abbey.
Mabango, Ashiono Anthony '95 (PAT) Unassigned.
Mabarak, John R. *o.s.a.* '60 (CHI) [N] Olympia Fields, IL Tolentine Monastery at Tolentine Center.
Mabon, Msgr. Thomas K. '57 (ALT) [14] Johnstown, PA Our Mother of Sorrows Church.
Mac Peck, Francis D. *s.j.* '67 (SJ) [L] Los Gatos, CA Sacred Heart Jesuit Center.
MacAdam, Austin *m.afr.* '58 (WDC) [M] Washington, DC Missionaries of Africa.
Macalintal, Dionisio '63 (SD) National City, CA St. Mary Church.
Macaranas, Rafael R. '64 (BRK) [206] Queens, NY Our Lady of the Angelus Church.
Macaranas, Rafael R. '64 (NY) Manhattan, NY Cabrini Medical Center.
MacArthur, Bruce '53 (SFS) Retired.
Macatangay, Francis M. '99 (GAL) [76] Houston, TX St. Theresa Church.
MacAulay, Gerard '59 (OKL) Retired.
Macaulay, Neil *o.m.i.* '63 (SJN) [7] San Juan, PR Ntr. Sra. de la Caridad del Cobre Church.
MacAuley, Stephen A. '51 (TLS) Retired; [F] Tulsa, OK St. John Villas, Inc.
Macaya, Miguel '65 (LSC) Dona Ana, NM Our Lady of the Purification Church.
MacCandless, William J. *o.s.b.* '58 (NO) Abita Springs, LA St. Jane de Chantal Church; [P] St. Benedict, LA St. Joseph Abbey.
MacCarthy, John P. *o.praem.* '69 (GB) [I] De Pere, WI St. Norbert Abbey.
MacCarthy, Joseph T. '97 (BO) [5] Brookline, MA St. Mary of the Assumption Church.
MacCarthy, Justin H. '64 (ORG) La Habra, CA Our Lady of Guadalupe Church.
MacCarthy, Liam '68 (SAC) Sutter Creek, CA Immaculate Conception Church.
MacCarthy, Timothy '60 (ORG) Tustin, CA St. Cecilia Church.
Macchi, William V. '64 (OAK) [3] Concord, CA St. Francis of Assisi Church.
Macchietto, Robert G. '71 (NY) [E] New York, NY Monsignor Farrell High School.
MacDonald, Adam *s.v.d.* '00 (FgM) Society of the Divine Word Foreign Missions.
MacDonald, Msgr. Arthur F. '52 (GLP) Alpine, AZ St. Helena Church.
MacDonald, Charles J. '67 (HRT) Wallingford, CT Holy Trinity Church.
MacDonald, Colin '81 (SAC) Antelope, CA St. Clare Church.
MacDonald, Msgr. Colin A. '45 (MAN) [1] Manchester, NH St. Joseph Church; Retired.
MacDonald, David W. *s.j.* '61 (SAC) [14] Sacramento, CA St. Ignatius of Loyola Church.
MacDonald, Fabian '77 (SEA) [26] Seattle, WA Immaculate Conception Church.
MacDonald, Hugh J. '64 (HRT) North Haven, CT St. Barnabas Church.
MacDonald, James *s.a.c.* '59 (CAM) [C] Pennsauken, NJ Bishop Eustace Prep School.
MacDonald, James H. '67 (SFR) Belmont, CA Immaculate Heart of Mary Church.
MacDonald, Kevin *c.ss.r.* (BO) [53] Boston, MA Our Lady of Perpetual Help Church.
MacDonald, Paul V. '59 (BO) Scituate, MA St. Frances Xavier Cabrini Church.
MacDonald, Richard *s.c.j.* '65 (BWN) Lyford, TX Prince of Peace Church.
MacDonald, Richard J. *s.c.j.* '65 (BWN) Raymondville, TX Our Lady of Guadalupe Church.
MacDonald, Rupert A. *s.s.j.* '40 (BAL) [S] Baltimore, MD St. Joseph's Manor.
MacDonald, Sebastian *c.p.* '58 (DET) [K] Detroit, MI St. Paul of the Cross Community, Congregation of the Passion.
MacDonald, Stirling B. '88 (BO) Senior Priests.
MacDonald, Timothy '00 (LAN) [7] Lansing, MI St. Gerard Church.
MacDonald, Timothy *s.a.* '67 (NY) [DD] Garrison, NY Franciscan Friars of the Atonement, Minister General Office.
MacDonnell, John J. *s.j.* '58 (WOR) [N] Worcester, MA Jesuits of Holy Cross College, Inc.
MacDonnell, Joseph F. *s.j.* '61 (BGP) [B] Fairfield, CT Fairfield University; [P] Fairfield, CT The Fairfield Jesuit Community-Fairfield University.
MacDonnell, Martin *s.j.* '66 (BO) [W] Chestnut Hill, MA The Jesuit Community at Boston College.
MacDonough, Richard *s.s.* '60 (LA) [A] Camarillo, CA St. John's Seminary College of the Archdiocese of Los Angeles.
MacDougall, James L. *o.s.a.* '59 (MIA) [B] Opa Locka, FL St. Thomas University; [H] Miami, FL Casa San Lorenzo.
Mace, John D. *s.j.* '68 (FgM) Provinces.
Mace, John D. *s.j.* '68 (MIL) [P] Milwaukee, WI Jesuit Provincial Office, Wisconsin Province.
MacEachen, Bede *s.a.* '42 (NY) [DD] Garrison, NY Franciscan Friars of the Atonement, Minister General Office.
Maceda, Thomas *c.ss.r.* '63 (BRK) [107] Brooklyn, NY Our Lady of Perpetual Help Basilica Church.
Macedo, Charles '48 (SJ) Palo Alto, CA St. Thomas Aquinas Church; Retired.
Macedo, Stephen A. '93 (HON) Naalehu, HI Sacred Heart Church; Pahala, HI Holy Rosary Church.
Maceli, Anthony J. '48 (BRK) Retired.
MacEntee, Francis J. *s.j.* '54 (SCR) [C] Scranton, PA University of Scranton.
Macey, Richard '75 (DET) Woodhaven, MI Our Lady of the Woods Church; [A] Detroit, MI Sacred Heart Major Seminary, Inc.
MacFarlane, John F. '66 (WDC) [1] Rockville, MD St. Elizabeth Church.
MacGabhann, Kevin '63 (PMB) Lantana, FL Holy Spirit Church.
MacGee, James B. *o.m.i.* '57 (PT) Medart, FL St. Elizabeth Ann Seton Church.
MacGillivray, John J. *c.m.* '76 (FgM) Vincentian Foreign Missions.
Macgregor, Donald '67 (HON) Makawao, HI St. Joseph Church.
Mach, Bernard M. '64 (BUF) Retired.
Machado, Domingos *o.a.r.* '95 (NY) [FF] Bronx, NY St. Joseph's Center.
Machado, Domingos A. *o.a.r.* '95 (LA) [9] Los Angeles, CA Cristo Rey Church.
Machado, Jose '93 (WCH) [9] Wichita, KS Our Lady of Perpetual Help Church.
Machado, Manuel '64 (NY) [109] New York, NY St. Rose of Lima Church.
Machain, David '52 (PH) [23] Philadelphia, PA St. Bernard Church.
Machain, David B. '52 (PH) Retired.
Machalski, Thomas '85 (BRK) [186] Queens, NY St. Josaphat Church.
Machar, Jerome J. *o.c.s.o.* '75 (ROC) [I] Piffard, NY Abbey of the Genesee.
Machcinski, Anthony J. '50 (GAY) Retired.
Machesky, Peter '50 (MIL) [P] Burlington, WI Queen of Peace Friary.
Machlik, Jerome J. '71 (DET) Shelby Twp., MI St. John Vianney Church.
Machnik, Theodore F. '91 (COL) Portsmouth, OH St. Mary Church.
Macho, George S. '53 (NEW) Retired.
Macho, Tomas *s.j.* '46 (MIA) [H] Miami, FL Villa Arrieta.
Macias, Francisco A. '94 (SAT) Gonzales, TX St. James Church.
Macias, Jorge *c.ss.r.* (SJN) [A] Bayamon, PR Bayamon Central University.
Macias, Salvador '82 (OAK) [10] Oakland, CA St. Jarlath's Church.
Maciej, David '80 (SCL) Rice, MN Immaculate Conception Church.
Maciejewski, Norbert '69 (DET) [2] Warren, MI Ascension Church; [6] Warren, MI St. Leonard of Port Maurice Church.
Maciejewski, Tadeusz *c.m.* '88 (BRK) [134] Brooklyn, NY St. Stanislaus Kostka Church.
MacInnis, John E. (BO) [3] Peabody, MA St. John the Baptist Church.
MacInnis, Michael A. *o.f.m.* (BO) [6] Waltham, MA Sacred Heart Church.
MacIntyre, Frederick H. '92 (WDC) Newport, MD St. Mary Church.
Macior, Lazarus *o.f.m.* '56 (CLV) [O] Cleveland, OH St. Stanislaus Friary.
Macior, Lazarus *o.f.m.* '56 (GB) [I] Pulaski, WI Assumption of B.V.M. Friary.
MacIssac, Charles S. *o.s.* '83 (PCE) On Duty Outside the Diocese.
Maciukiewicz, David J. '81 (E) [5] Erie, PA Holy Trinity Church.
Mack, Henry J. '49 (SFD) Retired.
Mack, John P. '85 (BUF) [2] Batavia, NY St. Joseph Church; Lancaster, NY Our Lady of Pompeii Church.
Mack, Joseph W. '89 (CHL) Asheboro, NC St. Joseph Church.
Mack, Mike '69 (GLP) [F] Gallup, NM Catholic Peoples' Initiatives, Inc.
Mack, Robert '57 (BUF) [L] Buffalo, NY St. Francis Geriatric and Healthcare Services, Inc.
Mack, Msgr. Robert A. '57 (BUF) [42] Buffalo, NY St. Louis Church.
Mack, Thomas E. '78 (PEO) Pontiac, IL St. Mary's Church.
Macke, Paul *s.j.* '73 (ANC) [I] Anchorage, AK Holy Spirit Center.
Macke, Paul B. *s.j.* '73 (ANC) [G] Anchorage, AK Jesuit House.
Macke, Richard J. '54 (SC) Retired.
Macken, Forrest *c.p.* '47 (L) [L] Louisville, KY Sacred Heart Retreat.
MacKenzie, John B. '00 (MAN) Hampton, NH Our Lady of the Miraculous Medal Church.
MacKenzie, William M. '66 (BO) [7] Quincy, MA Our Lady of Good Counsel Church.
Mackert, Albert J. '61 (CLV) [34] Cleveland, OH Immaculate Conception Church; Retired.
Mackesy, Robert L. *m.m.* '47 (NY) [DD] Maryknoll, NY Maryknoll Fathers and Brothers.
Mackey, Alan C. '00 (BIR) Madison, AL St. John the Baptist Church; [A] Huntsville, AL Catholic High School.
Mackey, James M. '61 (ALB) [8] Troy, NY St. Michael the Archangel Church; Troy, NY Van Rensselaer Manor.
Mackiewicz, Richard E. (GBG) Lower Burrell, PA St. Margaret Mary Church; New Kensington, PA St. Mary of Czestochowa Church; New Kensington, PA St. Joseph Church.
Mackin, Eamon *c.h.s.* '70 (ORG) [2] Huntington Beach, CA St. Mary's by the Sea Church.
Mackin, Francis C. *s.j.* '54 (BO) [W] Chestnut Hill, MA The Jesuit Community at Boston College.
Mackin, John J. '38 (CHI) Arlington Heights, IL Our Lady of the Wayside Church; Hometown, IL Our Lady of Loretto Church; Retired.
Mackin, Kevin E. '64 (ALB) [B] Loudonville, NY Siena College; [B] Loudonville, NY Siena College.
Mackin, William H. '38 (MIL) Retired.
MacKinnon, William H., III *s.o.l.t.* '97 (STN) St. Joseph, MO St. Joseph's Church; Lincoln, NE St. George's Church; Omaha, NE Assumption of B.V.M. Church.
MacKinson, Donald (OAK) [S] Berkeley, CA Maria House.
Mackle, Daniel E. '80 (PH) [1] Philadelphia, PA Cathedral Basilica of SS. Peter and Paul; [A] Wynnewood, PA Theological Seminary of St. Charles Borromeo, Overbrook.
Mackle, Liam M. *o.s.m.* '58 (CHI) [N] Chicago, IL Order of Friar Servants of Mary (Servites) United States of America Province, Inc.
Macklin, Eckley *s.o.l.t.* (CC) [22] Corpus Christi, TX St. Theresa Church.
Macklin, Eckley *s.o.l.t.* '94 (CC) [H] Robstown, TX Society of Our Lady of the Most Holy Trinity.
Macko, Msgr. John '41 (PBR) Retired.
Mackowski, Richard M. *s.j.* '61 (DET) [K] Detroit, MI Jesuit Provincial Office-Detroit Province of the Society of Jesus.
MacLellan, Iain G. *o.s.b.* '87 (MAN) [K] Manchester, NH St. Anselm Abbey.
MacLennan, Donald '67 (DET) Absent on Sick Leave.
MacLeod, Thomas E. '56 (BO) Senior Priests.
MacLoughlin, James '63 (ORL) Belleview, FL St. Theresa Church.
MacMahon, Craig *o.m.v.* '90 (BO) [B] Boston, MA Oblate Provincialate.
MacMahon, Msgr. Eamon '47 (MRY) Retired.
MacMahon, Michael '66 (BIR) [18] Birmingham, AL Our Lady of the Valley Church.
MacMahon, Patrick '69 (SPK) Colton, WA St. Gall Church; Uniontown, WA St. Boniface Church.
MacMaster, Thomas A. *o.c.s.o.* '57 (DUB) [K] Peosta, IA New Melleray Abbey, Order of Cistercians of the Strict Observance.
MacMillan, Donald A. *s.j.* '72 (BO) [W] Chestnut Hill, MA The Jesuit Community at Boston College.
MacMillan, Leonard '91 (B) [2] Boise, ID St. Mark's Church.
MacNamara, Robert C. '51 (ROC) Horseheads, NY St. Mary Our Mother Church; Retired.
MacNevin, Stanley F. *c.s.p.* '60 (BO) [W] Boston, MA Paulist Fathers Residence.
MacNevin, Stanley F. *c.s.p.* '60 (NY) [DD] Jamaica Estates, NY Paulist Fathers Generalate.
MacNew, James J. *o.s.f.s.* '80 (WIL) [I] Wilmington, DE Oblates of St. Francis De Sales.
Maco, Stephen L. '76 (ALN) [1] Bethlehem, PA St. Anne Church; [C] Bethlehem, PA Bethlehem Catholic High School.

Macora, Athanasius *o.f.m.* '92 (FgM) Custody of St. Mary of the Angels. Byzantine-Slavonic.
Macoskie, Melvin H. '55 (MIL) Retired.
MacPeck, Francis *s.j.* '67 (SFR) [45] San Francisco, CA St. Peter Church.
MacPhaidin, Bartley *c.s.c.* '63 (FR) [A] North Easton, MA Stonehill College.
MacPherson, Albert P. *o.s.a.* '74 (BO) [C] North Andover, MA Merrimack College.
MacPherson, Damian *s.a.* '78 (NY) [DD] Garrison, NY Franciscan Friars of the Atonement, Minister General Office.
MacPherson, Stephen '86 (SR) McKinleyville, CA Christ the King Church.
MacPherson, Walter E. '55 (BEL) Retired.
Macpherson, Walter J. '86 (CIN) [15] Dayton, OH Holy Trinity Church.
MacQuarrie, John D. '78 (CIN) West Milton, OH Transfiguration Church.
MacRae, Gordon J. '82 (MAN) Absent on Leave.
MacRory, Camillus *o.f.m.cap.* '51 (SFR) [N] Burlingame, CA Capuchin Provincial House.
Macunas, Theodore S. '64 (ALN) [10] Reading, PA St. Paul Church.
MacVeigh, Donal T. *s.j.* '72 (NEW) [B] Jersey City, NJ Saint Peter's College; [N] Jersey City, NJ Jesuits of Saint Peter's College, Inc.
MacVeigh, Michael C. '56 (PIT) Overbrook, PA St. Norbert Church; [O] Pittsburgh, PA St. John Vianney Manor.
MacWade, Joseph A. *s.j.* '61 (FgM) Provinces.
Madathiparampil, George '68 (WDC) [36] Washington, DC St. Patrick Church.
Maday, Norbert J. '64 (CHI) Other Assignments.
Maddalena, Joseph P. '86 (GBG) Ligonier, PA Holy Trinity Church.
Maddan, Declan *o.f.m.* '47 (NY) [DD] New York, NY Franciscan Friars, Order of Friars Minor, Holy Name Province.
Maddela, Prasad Rao (KCK) [4] Topeka, KS Most Pure Heart of Mary Church.
Madden, Benjamin *o.f.m.cap.* '58 (FgM) Capuchin Foreign Missions.
Madden, Msgr. Brendan P. '51 (PAT) [4] Clifton, NJ St. Clare's Church.
Madden, Daniel P. *o.p.* '60 (MIA) [B] Miami, FL Barry University; [H] Bal Harbour, FL Dominican Friars Residence.
Madden, Declan A. *o.f.m.* '47 (DEN) [I] Denver, CO Francis Heights, Inc.; [K] Denver, CO Clare Gardens, Inc.
Madden, Denis (NY) [HH] New York, NY Catholic Near East Welfare Association (CNEWA).
Madden, Msgr. Denis J. '67 (BAL) Special Assignment.
Madden, Edward T. '52 (DEN) [1] Boulder, CO Sacred Heart of Jesus Church.
Madden, Henry L. *o.f.m.* '46 (ALB) [B] Loudonville, NY Siena College.
Madden, J. Thomas '53 (SFR) [M] Menlo Park, CA Vallombrosa Center.
Madden, Msgr. James J. '55 (GAL) Retired; [N] Houston, TX St. Dominic Village.
Madden, James J. *m.m.* '60 (FgM) Maryknoll Foreign Missions.
Madden, James P. *c.s.c.* '57 (BGP) [P] Bridgeport, CT Provincial Offices of the Priests and Brothers of Holy Cross, Eastern Province.
Madden, John '62 (NEW) [N] Rutherford, NJ St. John Vianney Residence for Priests.
Madden, John F. '84 (WOR) Clinton, MA Our Lady of Jasna Gora Church.
Madden, John J. '62 (NEW) Retired.
Madden, John J. *s.j.* '69 (FgM) Provinces.
Madden, John P. '86 (Y) Newton Falls, OH St. Joseph Church; Newton Falls, OH St. Mary Church.
Madden, Msgr. John R. '59 (SY) Hamilton, NY St. Mary Church; Munnsville, NY St. Therese of the Infant Jesus Church.
Madden, John R. '70 (SAV) [3] Columbus, GA St. Anne Church.
Madden, Joseph *o.f.m.conv.* '62 (CHL) Winston-Salem, NC Our Lady of Mercy Church.
Madden, Lawrence '64 (BO) [W] Cambridge, MA Weston Jesuit Community.
Madden, Lawrence J. *s.j.* '64 (WDC) [M] Washington, DC The Jesuit Community at Georgetown University.
Madden, Michael '75 (EVN) Mount Vernon, IN St. Matthew Church.
Madden, Michael G. '62 (TOL) [35] Toledo, OH St. Patrick of Heatherdowns Church; Retired.
Madden, Michael J. '95 (BGP) [5] Danbury, CT St. Peter Church.
Madden, Patrick '83 (MOB) Bayou LaBatre, AL St. Margaret Church; Heron Bay, AL St. Michael the Archangel Church.
Madden, Patrick J. '74 (SHP) [3] Monroe, LA Our Lady of Fatima Church; [G] Monroe, LA Catholic Campus Ministry at the University of Louisana at Monroe.
Madden, Msgr. Patrick M. '53 (STA) [14] Jacksonville, FL Sacred Heart Church.
Madden, Paul '70 (FgM) Society of St. James the Apostle.
Madden, Paul '70 (JKS) On Duty Outside the Diocese.
Madden, Stephen (BO) Needham, MA St. Joseph Church.
Madden, Thomas '53 (SFR) Special Assignment.
Madden, Msgr. Thomas E. '32 (ALT) [1] Altoona, PA Cathedral of the Blessed Sacrament; Retired.
Madden, Thomas F. '76 (NY) [A] Bronx, NY St. John Neumann Seminary Residence; [HH] New York, NY The Center for Spirituality and Justice.
Madden, Msgr. Thomas G. '55 (NEW) North Arlington, NJ Queen of Peace Church; Retired; [N] Rutherford, NJ St. John Vianney Residence for Priests.
Madden, Thomas J. *s.j.* '57 (MIA) [5] Miami, FL Gesu Church.
Madden, Thomas L. '81 (SP) Dunedin, FL Our Lady of Lourdes Church.
Madden, William O. *s.j.* '57 (CHI) Chicago, IL Cook County Hospital; [D] Chicago, IL St. Ignatius Jesuit Community; [N] Chicago, IL Chicago Province of the Society of Jesus-Provincial Office.
Madden, William T. *m.m.* '58 (NY) [DD] Maryknoll, NY Maryknoll Fathers and Brothers; [DD] Maryknoll, NY Maryknoll Fathers and Brothers; [HH] Maryknoll, NY Friends of St. Maria Goretti, U.S.A., Inc.
Maddock, Andrew L. *s.j.* '85 (B) DeSmet, ID Sacred Heart Church.
Maddock, George *o.f.m.cap.* '64 (AGN) [F] Agana Heights, GU St. Fidelis Friary.
Maddock, George *o.f.m.cap.* '64 (FgM) Capuchin Foreign Missions.
Maddock, Jay T. '75 (FR) East Taunton, MA Holy Family Church; [M] East Taunton, MA Diocesean Catholic Youth Organization.
Maddock, Laurence F. '56 (CHI) [94] Chicago, IL Saint Ita Church.
Maddox, Edward '96 (AUS) Retired.
Maddux, Jack, Jr. '99 (AUS) Llano, TX Holy Trinity Church; Mason, TX St. Joseph's Church.
Madej, Paul D. '90 (SY) Military Chaplains.
Mader, George L. '59 (NEW) Retired; [N] Caldwell, NJ The Rev. Msgr. James F. Kelley Residence for Retired Priests.
Mader, Joseph '67 (IND) On Disability Leave.
Mader, Stan P. '92 (STP) Mound, MN Our Lady of the Lake Church.
Madera, Luis M. (BO) [7] Lawrence, MA St. Mary Immaculate Conception Church.
Madey, Louis '68 (LAN) [5] Ypsilanti, MI Holy Trinity Student Chapel Church; [M] Ypsilanti, MI Holy Trinity Student Chapel.
Madigan, Arthur R. *s.j.* '77 (BO) [W] Chestnut Hill, MA The Jesuit Community at Boston College.
Madigan, Daniel '64 (SAC) Clarksburg, CA St. Joseph Church.
Madigan, Daniel '80 (SEA) Redmond, WA St. Jude Church.
Madigan, Henry *o.f.m.conv.* '56 (TR) Riverside, NJ St. Peter Church.
Madigan, John *o.m.i.* '77 (MIA) Opa Locka, FL St. Philip Church.
Madigan, John A. *o.p.* (RVC) [B] Rockville Centre, NY Molloy College.
Madigan, John C. '74 (SEA) Renton, WA St. Stephen the Martyr Church.
Madigan, Msgr. John J. '54 (WDC) [9] Silver Spring, MD Our Lady of Grace Church.
Madigan, Patrick S. *s.j.* '83 (FgM) Provinces.
Madigan, Patrick S. *s.j.* '83 (NO) [P] New Orleans, LA Jesuit Provincial Office.
Madison, Martin *s.a.* '62 (BRK) [113] Brooklyn, NY Our Lady of Victory Church.
Madley, Jeffrey (RVC) Riverhead, NY St. John the Evangelist Church.
Madley, Jeffrey J. '76 (RVC) Southampton, NY Sacred Hearts of Jesus and Mary Church.
Madrazo, Higinio *c.m.* '44 (SJN) [47] San Juan, PR Nuestra Senora del Pilar Church; [F] Rio Piedras, PR Asylum For Orphan Girls.
Madrid, Jaime '68 (ELP) Absent on Leave.
Madrid, Marvin Boes '62 (SC) Woodward, IA Woodward State Hospital and School.
Madrigal, Hector '87 (AMA) On Duty Outside the Diocese.
Madrigal, Idelfonso '57 (LA) Paramount, CA Our Lady of the Rosary Church.
Madsen, Msgr. Cletus P. '31 (DAV) Retired; [L] Davenport, IA Kahl Home for the Aged and Infirm.
Madsen, Msgr. John W. '66 (BUF) [2] Depew, NY St. Barnabas Church.
Madu, Cletus '78 (FAR) Hope, ND St. Agatha's Church.
Madu, Emmanuel '78 (BEA) [7] Beaumont, TX Our Mother of Mercy Church.
Madubuko, Michael N. *s.j.* '85 (CHI) [N] Chicago, IL Chicago Province of the Society of Jesus-Provincial Office.
Maduri, John '87 (BRK) [211] Queens, NY Our Lady of Grace Church.
Maduro, Gabriel '59 (ARE) [1] Arecibo, PR Cathedral of San Felipe Apostol.
Madus, Msgr. Peter P. '68 (SCR) [14] Scranton, PA St. Joseph's Church.
Maduzia, Norbert J., Jr. '82 (GAL) [28] Houston, TX St. Frances Cabrini Church.
Maechler, Edmund F. '49 (LA) Retired.
Maechler, Gerald T. '55 (LA) Retired.
Maechler, Robert '62 (LA) La Crescenta, CA St. James the Less Church.
Maekawa, Steven *o.p.* '98 (SFR) [14] San Francisco, CA St. Dominic Church; [N] San Francisco, CA St. Dominic Priory.
Maes, Allen *o.m.i.* '68 (BEL) [F] Belleville, IL Shrine of Our Lady of the Snows.
Maes, Allen *o.m.i.* '68 (WDC) [M] Washington, DC Missionary Oblates of Mary Immaculate.
Maes, Clarence '87 (SFE) [4] Santa Fe, NM St. Anne's Church.
Maes, Clark M. '95 (STL) Chesterfield, MO Incarnate Word Church.
Maes, John J. '67 (DOD) Wright, KS St. Andrew Church.
Maestri, William '77 (NO) [55] New Orleans, LA St. Pius X Church; On Duty Outside the Archdiocese.
Maestri, William F. '77 (NO) [A] New Orleans, LA Notre Dame Seminary Graduate School of Theology.
Maestrini, Nicholas *p.i.m.e.* '30 (PMB) [H] Tequesta, FL P.I.M.E. Missionaries.
Maffei, Vincent R. '64 (BO) Randolph, MA St. Mary Church.
Maffeo, Michael '91 (RVC) Rocky Point, NY St. Anthony of Padua Church.
Magaldi, Philip '60 (FWT) Retired.
Magallanes, Alejandro *o.f.m.cap.* '69 (FRS) Fresno, CA Community Hospital, Veterans' Hospital & University Medical Center.
Magallanes, Manuel *o.s.b.* '76 (OKL) [I] Shawnee, OK St. Gregory's Abbey.
Magallanes, Manuel J. *o.s.b.* (LA) El Segundo, CA St. Anthony Church.
Magana, Jose '98 (LA) Sepulveda, CA Our Lady of Peace Church.
Magary, Thomas A. '66 (STU) Martins Ferry, OH St. Mary Church.
Magbanua, Msgr. Mario '66 (DAL) [15] Dallas, TX St. Cecilia Church.
Magdaleno, Ricardo '89 (FRS) Kingsburg, CA Holy Family Church.
Magdaraog, Vincente '96 (TR) Barnegat, NJ St. Mary Church.
Magee, Andrew T. '45 (NY) Maybrook, NY Assumption Church; Retired.
Magee, Michael K. '91 (PH) On Duty Outside the Archdiocese.
Magee, Patrick F. '70 (TR) Point Pleasant, NJ St. Martha Church.
Magee, Paul L. '94 (STP) On Duty Outside the Archdiocese.
Magee, Robert L. '70 (PMB) Jensen Beach, FL St. Martin de Porres Church.
Magel, John E. '60 (L) Retired; [L] Louisville, KY Bishop David Apartments.
Mager, Martin J. *o.s.b.* '63 (SFR) [N] Portola Valley, CA Woodside Priory.
Maggio, J. Mark '90 (BR) On Leave.
Maggs, William C. *c.ss.r.* '60 (PH) [136] Philadelphia, PA St. Peter the Apostle Church.
Maginnis, Andrew F. *s.j.* '52 (SFR) [E] San Francisco, CA St. Ignatius College Preparatory (Coed).
Maginnis, Edward L. *s.j.* '53 (DEN) [M] Denver, CO Regis Jesuit Community (The Jesuits at Regis University).
Maginnis, Robert P. '61 (PH) Ardmore, PA St. Colman Church.
Maginot, Michael L. '83 (GRY) [5] Merrillville, IN St. Stephen, Martyr Church.
Maginot, Richard J. '50 (CHI) Prospect Heights, IL St. Alphonsus Liguori Church; Retired.
Maglione, Joseph J. '42 (BGP) Retired; [P] Stamford, CT The Catherine Dennis Keefe Queen of the Clergy Retired Priests' Residence.
Magnan, Oscar G. '63 (NEW) [B] Jersey City, NJ Saint Peter's College; [N] Jersey City, NJ Jesuits of Saint Peter's College, Inc.
Magnano, Paul '67 (SEA) [7] Seattle, WA St. Catherine Church; [16] Seattle, WA St. Matthew Church; [20] Seattle, WA St. Therese Church; [23] Seattle, WA Christ the King Church; Aberdeen, WA St. Mary Church; Aberdeen, WA SS. Peter and Paul Church; Hoquiam, WA Our Lady of Good Help Church; Ocean Shores, WA St. Jerome Church; Special Assignment.
Magnaye, Carlo Benjamin (AUS) Mexia, TX St. Mary's Church; Mexia, TX State School.
Magni, Daniel M. '78 (BO) [15] Lowell, MA St. Rita Church.
Magni, Raffaele *p.i.m.e.* '56 (DET) [K] Detroit, MI P.I.M.E. Missionaries of SS. Peter and Paul.
Magoon, R. Dale '60 (GAY) Mancelona, MI St. Anthony Church.
Magpayo, Teodoro '89 (HON) Kihei, HI St. Theresa Church.

Magraw, Daniel E. '75 (E) [2] Erie, PA Blessed Sacrament Church.
Magro, Emanuel '79 (WDC) [35] Washington, DC Our Lady of Victory Church.
Magro, Patrick '00 (BO) [W] Cambridge, MA Weston Jesuit Community.
Maguire, Alban *o.f.m.* (PAT) [M] Ringwood, NJ Holy Name Friary, Inc.
Maguire, Anthony (SFR) On Duty Outside the Archdiocese.
Maguire, Brian '80 (CHI) [N] Chicago, IL St. Patrick's Missionary Society.
Maguire, Connell J. '45 (PH) Retired.
Maguire, Daniel J. '69 (SFR) [45] San Francisco, CA St. Peter Church.
Maguire, Enda J. '59 (STO) Lockeford, CA St. Joachim Church.
Maguire, Eugene '47 (PHX) Retired; [H] Phoenix, AZ Mt. Claret Center.
Maguire, Felix H. '50 (HRT) Retired.
Maguire, Francis *c.m.* '51 (FgM) Vincentian Foreign Missions.
Maguire, Francis *o.p.* '57 (DET) [20] Detroit, MI St. Dominic Church.
Maguire, Francis X. *c.m.* '78 (PH) [AA] Philadelphia, PA Congregation of the Mission.
Maguire, Hugh '57 (MOB) Grand Bay, AL St. John Baptist Church.
Maguire, James F. *s.j.* '35 (DET) [P] Clarkston, MI Colombiere Center.
Maguire, Msgr. John R. '50 (STL) Shrewsbury, MO Cure' of Ars Church.
Maguire, Joseph D. '70 (FR) Retired.
Maguire, Paul J. '48 (CAM) Retired.
Maguire, Robert *o.cist.* '76 (DAL) [B] Irving, TX University of Dallas; [K] Irving, TX Cistercian Abbey of Our Lady of Dallas.
Maguire, Seamus J. '53 (WH) Retired.
Maguire, Thomas '69 (SAC) Folsom, CA St. John the Baptist Church; Folsom, CA Folsom State Prison.
Maguire, Thomas H. '76 (BO) [3] Framingham, MA St. Jeremiah Church.
Maguire, Msgr. William E. '50 (TR) Retired.
Mahalic, Philip A. '83 (LFT) Wheatfield, IN Sorrowful Mother Church.
Mahan, Daniel J. '88 (IND) [25] Indianapolis, IN St. Luke Church.
Mahan, George S. *s.j.* '40 (BO) [W] Weston, MA Campion Health Center, Inc.
Mahan, Terrance L. *s.j.* '54 (LA) [C] Los Angeles, CA Loyola Marymount University; [C] Los Angeles, CA Loyola Marymount University.
Mahaney, Hilary F. '69 (CHI) [123] Chicago, IL St. Mary of the Angels Church.
Mahar, Raymond '58 (BUF) [K] Lackawanna, NY Our Lady of Victory Hospital.
Mahedy, Brian *c.p.* '33 (CHI) [N] Chicago, IL Daneo Hall.
Maher, Arthur '54 (JOL) Retired.
Maher, Byron G. '50 (CHI) Wauconda, IL Transfiguration Church; Retired.
Maher, Charles E. '60 (PRO) [9] Providence, RI Blessed Sacrament Church.
Maher, Daniel J. '62 (ALB) [7] Albany, NY Church of the Holy Cross.
Maher, Daniel J. '91 (ARL) [1] Arlington, VA Cathedral of St. Thomas More.
Maher, Edmund J. '88 (PH) [158] Philadelphia, PA St. William Church; Retired.
Maher, Edward A. *c.s.p.* '49 (NY) [DD] Jamaica Estates, NY Paulist Fathers Generalate.
Maher, Edward A. *c.s.p.* '49 (SFR) [32] San Francisco, CA Old St. Mary's Church.
Maher, Edward J. '81 (CAM) Mays Landing, NJ St. Vincent de Paul Church.
Maher, J. David '71 (JC) Taos, MO St. Francis Xavier Church.
Maher, Msgr. James '43 (SJ) Retired.
Maher, James J. *c.m.* '90 (BRK) [L] Brooklyn, NY Catholic Charities; [V] Jamaica, NY St. Vincent's House.
Maher, James J. '92 (LA) Sherman Oaks, CA St. Francis de Sales Church; [Z] Los Angeles, CA Scouting and Camp Fire Ministry/Catholic Youth Camps.
Maher, Jerry '94 (MRY) San Luis Obispo, CA San Luis Obispo Church.
Maher, John J. '39 (NY) Retired.
Maher, John L. *s.j.* '74 (FgM) Provinces.
Maher, John T. *c.m.* '81 (MET) [H] Plainsboro, NJ Vincentian Residence.
Maher, Michael *s.j.* '86 (STL) [C] St. Louis, MO Saint Louis University.
Maher, Michael L. '48 (SAG) Retired.
Maher, Michael N. *ss.cc.* '63 (SB) Chino Hills, CA St. Paul the Apostle Church; [E] Chino Hills, CA Congregation of the Sacred Hearts, SS.CC.
Maher, Michael W. *s.j.* '86 (STL) [P] St. Louis, MO Jesuit Community Corporation at St. Louis University - Jesuit Hall.
Maher, Patrick '53 (MOB) Orange Beach, AL St. Thomas by the Sea Church.
Maher, Patrick '98 (LUB) Littlefield, TX Sacred Heart Church.
Maher, Msgr. Patrick K. '47 (STU) Retired.
Maher, Paul J. *s.j.* '64 (FgM) Provinces.
Maher, Paul P. *o.m.i.* '58 (P) Lebanon, OR St. Edward Church.
Maher, Raymond '44 (SJ) Retired.
Maher, Raymond *o.carm.* '97 (PMB) [5] Boca Raton, FL St. Jude Church.
Maher, Robert *o.f.m.cap.* '74 (HON) Aiea, HI St. Elizabeth Church.
Maher, Robert E. '71 (BWN) Edinburg, TX St. Joseph Church.
Maher, Robert G. '57 (WIN) Retired.
Maher, Ryan J. *s.j.* '97 (WDC) [E] Washington, DC Gonzaga College High School.
Maher, Thomas *o.m.i.* '57 (FgM) Oblates Foreign Missions.
Maher, Thomas *l.c.* '94 (LA) [Q] Pasadena, CA Legionaries of Christ.
Maher, Thomas F. '47 (CHI) [67] Chicago, IL St. Genevieve Church; [129] Chicago, IL St. Mary of the Woods Church; Retired.
Maher, William *o.m.i.* '66 (FgM) Oblates Foreign Missions.
Maher, William F.X. *s.j.* '57 (NEW) [B] Jersey City, NJ Saint Peter's College; [N] Jersey City, NJ Jesuits of Saint Peter's College, Inc.
Mahfoud, Peter '55 (SAM) Retired.
Mahle, Jan (BUF) [R] Alfred, NY Campus Ministry.
Mahler, Clyde '99 (HT) [4] Thibodaux, LA St. Genevieve Church.
Mahler, Msgr. Frank E. '56 (ARL) Falls Church, VA St. James Church.
Mahler, Michael '73 (ROC) [M] Rochester, NY Diocesan Department of Campus Ministry; [M] Rochester, NY Diocesan Department of Campus Ministry.
Mahlmann, Raymond '85 (GLP) Farmington, NM Sacred Heart Church; Farmington, NM Farmington Area Hospitals.
Mahnke, Ronald *o.s.b.* '62 (CLV) [O] Cleveland, OH Benedictine Order of Cleveland.
Mahon, Ambrose J. '58 (STP) Retired.
Mahon, Msgr. Dennis J. (NEW) [G] Newark, NJ Catholic Community Services (C.C.S.) Mt. Carmel Guild Hospital.
Mahon, Francis *s.v.d.* '40 (TR) [M] Bordentown, NJ Society of the Divine Word.
Mahon, Msgr. Gerald A. '71 (WIN) [6] Rochester, MN St. John's Church.
Mahon, Joseph F. *c.s.p.* '56 (NY) [104] New York, NY St. Paul the Apostle Church.
Mahon, Leo T. '51 (CHI) [129] Chicago, IL St. Mary of the Woods Church; Retired.
Mahon, Matthew Shawn '88 (BAL) Absent on Leave.
Mahon, Ronald *c.pp.s* (CHI) Hometown, IL Our Lady of Loretto Church.
Mahon, William A. '92 (NEW) [3] East Orange, NJ St. Joseph's Church.
Mahone, Casey B. '89 (WH) [2] Fairmont, WV Immaculate Conception Church.
Mahone, Michael Q. '80 (RNO) Incline Village, NV St. Francis of Assisi Church.
Mahoney, Arthur J. *c.ss.r.* '51 (HBG) [H] Ephrata, PA St. Clement's Mission House.
Mahoney, Bernard '53 (AUS) On Duty Outside the Diocese.
Mahoney, Brian E. (BO) Medway, MA St. Joseph Church.
Mahoney, Cornelius H. '78 (BRK) [A] Douglaston, NY Immaculate Conception Center; [B] Douglaston, NY Cathedral Seminary Residence of the Immaculate Conception.
Mahoney, Daniel C. '70 (GBG) [4] Greensburg, PA St. Paul Church.
Mahoney, Daniel F. '46 (NEW) Retired.
Mahoney, Daniel J. '52 (HBG) [5] Harrisburg, PA Holy Name of Jesus Church.
Mahoney, Daniel J. '56 (BO) [20] Boston, MA St. Francis de Sales Church.
Mahoney, Edward P. '86 (R) Chapel Hill, NC Newman Catholic Student Center, University of North Carolina Church; Special Assignment; [H] Chapel Hill, NC Newman Catholic Student Center.
Mahoney, Francis L. '60 (FR) [5] Fall River, MA Holy Name Church.
Mahoney, Gerard J. *o.s.f.s.* '71 (PH) [D] Philadelphia, PA Father Judge High School for Boys; [AA] Philadelphia, PA Father Judge Faculty House.
Mahoney, Gordon '56 (JOL) [3] Naperville, IL Sts. Peter and Paul Church.
Mahoney, Msgr. James '73 (PAT) Chatham Township, NJ Corpus Christi Church.
Mahoney, James F. '45 (BO) Senior Priests.
Mahoney, John *o.m.i.* '54 (FgM) Oblates Foreign Missions.
Mahoney, John *o.f.m.cap.* '64 (NY) [DD] White Plains, NY St. Conrad Friary.
Mahoney, John A. '56 (PEO) Geneseo, IL St. Malachy's Church; Retired.
Mahoney, Msgr. John E. '72 (BRK) [141] Brooklyn, NY St. Thomas Aquinas Church.
Mahoney, John J., Jr. '90 (MAN) [4] Manchester, NH St. Augustin Church.
Mahoney, John L. *s.j.* '51 (BO) [W] Weston, MA Campion Health Center, Inc.
Mahoney, John P. '48 (BO) Senior Priests.
Mahoney, Joseph P. '57 (WOR) [1] Worcester, MA St. Paul's Church; [25] Worcester, MA St. John's Church.
Mahoney, Kevin J. '81 (STL) [3] St. Charles, MO St. Elizabeth Ann Seton Church.
Mahoney, Mark A. '86 (BO) [25] Boston, MA Holy Name Church.
Mahoney, Maurice J. *o.s.a.* '60 (FgM) Foreign Missions.
Mahoney, Michael T. '75 (CIN) On Special and Archdiocesan Assignment.
Mahoney, Msgr. Neil J. '70 (NEW) [2] Newark, NJ St. Patrick's Pro-Church; [7] Newark, NJ St. Augustine's Church.
Mahoney, Peter (BRK) [12] Brooklyn, NY Assumption of the Blessed Virgin Mary Church.
Mahoney, Peter '61 (BRK) [L] Brooklyn, NY Catholic Charities.
Mahoney, Richard J. '58 (STP) Retired.
Mahoney, Robert '59 (AUS) Manor, TX St. Joseph's Church.
Mahoney, Robert J. '55 (KC) Special Assignment; [B] Kansas City, MO Rockhurst University.
Mahoney, Shaun L. '91 (PH) [A] Wynnewood, PA Theological Seminary of St. Charles Borromeo, Overbrook.
Mahoney, Thomas A. '98 (BO) Middleborough, MA Sacred Heart Church.
Mahoney, Thomas D. '65 (CLV) [62] Cleveland, OH St. Patrick Church.
Mahoney, Thomas E. '68 (WOR) Mendon, MA St. Michael's Church.
Mahoney, Thomas M. *o.s.a.* '45 (PH) [AA] Villanova, PA St. Thomas Monastery.
Mahony, James M. '92 (BO) [5] Brockton, MA Our Lady of Lourdes Church.
Mahony, John '58 (SP) Retired.
Mahony, Thomas J. *o.s.a.* '54 (PH) [C] Villanova, PA Villanova University; [AA] Villanova, PA St. Thomas Monastery.
Mahowald, Paul *s.j.* '68 (DM) Cumberland, IA St. Timothy Church; Griswold, IA Our Lady Of Grace Church.
Mahowald, Paul A. *s.j.* '68 (OM) [K] Omaha, NE Jesuit Community at Creighton University.
Mai, Dai *i.c.* '90 (STA) Jacksonville Beach, FL St. Paul's Church.
Mai Chi Thanh, Joseph M. '58 (PEO) Pesotum, IL St. Mary Church; Pesotum, IL St. Joseph Church.
Mai Minh Luan, Dominic (SPC) [E] Carthage, MO Congregation of the Mother Co-Redemptrix, United States Assumption Province.
Maibusch, Henry B. *o.s.a.* '54 (MIL) [9] Kenosha, WI Our Lady of the Holy Rosary Church.
Maichen, Richard F. '54 (DUB) Retired.
Maida, Thaddeus S. '58 (PIT) Perrysville, PA St. Teresa of Avila Church.
Maier, John '90 (DM) Creston, IA Holy Spirit Church.
Maier, John C. '90 (DM) Audubon, IA St. Patrick Church.
Maier, Joseph *c.ss.r.* '65 (FgM) Redemptorist Foreign Missions.
Maier, Paul '70 (RIC) Lebanon, VA Good Shepherd Church; St. Paul, VA St. Therese Church.
Maierle, John P. '55 (DET) Retired.
Maiers, Brennan *o.s.b.* '63 (SCL) [I] Collegeville, MN St. John's Abbey, of the Order of St. Benedict.
Maikowski, Thomas R. '76 (GLP) Special Assignment; [C] Gallup, NM St. Francis of Assisi School.
Mailadiyil, Augustine J. '75 (TYL) Pittsburg, TX Holy Cross Church.
Mailloux, Normand F. *m.s.* '55 (SPR) Bondsville, MA St. Adalbert's Church.
Mailloux, Thomas B. *c.s.b.* '50 (GAL) [7] Houston, TX St. Anne Church.
Maina, Wilson '95 (NY) [50] New York, NY Holy Trinity Church.
Mainardi, Donald G. (ORL) Dunnellon, FL St. John the Baptist Church.
Mainzer, James S. '87 (WCH) Mulvane, KS St. Michael the Archangel Church.
Maio, Anthony V. '49 (SAC) Retired and in Senior Ministry.
Maione, Anthony '85 (ALB) Troy, NY Samaritan Hospital.
Maione, Anthony J. '85 (ALB) Special Assignment.
Maione, Francis T. '65 (NEW) East Newark, NJ St. Anthony's Church.
Mair, Henry *s.a.* '62 (LA) [84] Los Angeles, CA St. Odilia Church.
Mair, Robert G. '65 (CHI) Glenview, IL St. Catherine Laboure Church.
Mairal, Jose Ma. Lopez '54 (SJN) Resident Chaplains.
Maisano, Richard J. '69 (PH) New Garden Township, PA St. Gabriel of the Sorrowful Mother Church.
Maiser, Raymond *c.ss.r.* '64 (CHI) [N] Glenview, IL The Redemptorists of Glenview, Illinois; [T] Glenview, IL

Villa Redeemer.
Maiser, Raymond *c.ss.r.* '64 (TUC) [J] Tucson, AZ Redemptorist Community Support Charity Trust.
Maisog, Alberic *o.c.s.o.* '00 (SPC) [A] Ava, MO Assumption Novitiate (Trappists); [E] Ava, MO Assumption Abbey (Trappist).
Maison, Gabriel *j.c.d.* '78 (VIC) Moulton, TX St. Joseph's Church.
Maisonneuve, Joseph *o.carm.* '86 (JOL) [I] Joliet, IL Our Lady of Angels Retirement Home; [J] Joliet, IL St. Elias Carmelites.
Maivelett, Bruce A. *s.j.* '88 (SY) [A] Syracuse, NY Saint Andrew Hall.
Maiza, Felix A. *s.j.* '52 (LA) [Q] Los Angeles, CA Columbiere House.
Maiza, Jesus Maria *s.s.s.* '67 (CGS) [5] Caguas, PR Santisimo Sacramento Church.
Maj, George C. *s.a.c.* '58 (BUF) [O] North Tonawanda, NY Society of the Catholic Apostolate.
Maj, Jerzy *o.s.p.* (NY) [5] Yonkers, NY St. Casimir Church.
Majarucon, Jon F. '84 (LA) Venice, CA St. Mark Church.
Majchrowski, Anthony P. '44 (LAN) [2] Flint, MI All Saints Church.
Majchrzak, Colman '51 (MIL) [P] Burlington, WI Queen of Peace Friary.
Majda, Francis A. '39 (PIT) Retired.
Majdanik, Albin J. '42 (SY) Retired.
MaJerus, Daniel '57 (SCL) Retired.
Majewicz, Frank *c.r.* '74 (CHI) [D] Chicago, IL Gordon Tech High School.
Majewski, Edmund W. *s.j.* '83 (NEW) [B] Jersey City, NJ Saint Peter's College; [N] Jersey City, NJ Jesuits of Saint Peter's College, Inc.
Majewski, Eugene *c.r.* '74 (CHI) [N] Chicago, IL Provincial Office of the Congregation of the Resurrection.
Majewski, Francis *o.f.m.cap.* '64 (PAT) [M] Oak Ridge-Milton, NJ St. Stanislaus B. M. Friary.
Majewski, Gene *c.r.* '74 (RCK) [A] Woodstock, IL Resurrection Center Retreat House.
Majewski, Joseph B. '66 (RIC) Newport News, VA St. Jerome Church.
Majewski, Joseph J. *c.ss.r.* '67 (RIC) [3] Hampton, VA St. Joseph Church.
Majewski, Stephen *o.f.m.conv.* '34 (BO) [50] Boston, MA Our Lady of Czestochowa Church.
Majic, Milenko '88 (LA) [46] Los Angeles, CA St. Anthony Church.
Majic, Timothy *o.f.m.* '39 (CHI) [N] Chicago, IL Croatian Franciscan Custody of the Holy Family.
Majikas, David J. '97 (CLV) Chagrin Falls, OH St. Joan of Arc Church.
Majka, Frank A. *s.j.* '74 (MIL) [P] Milwaukee, WI Jesuit Community at Marquette University.
Majka, George '72 (MAN) Whitefield, NH St. Matthew Church.
Majka, Philip S. '65 (ARL) Fredericksburg, VA St. Patrick's Church.
Major, Charles M. '59 (SY) [4] Liverpool, NY St. Joseph the Worker Church.
Major, Steven P. '59 (LIN) On Duty Outside the Diocese.
Major, Thomas J. '91 (SCR) [1] Wilkes-Barre, PA St. Aloysius Church.
Majoros, George A. '79 (PH) [33] Philadelphia, PA St. Charles Borromeo Church.
Majoros, Stephen '57 (TOL) [28] Toledo, OH St. Joseph Church.
Makacinas, Stanley *o.carm.* '70 (PHX) Special Assignment; [J] Phoenix, AZ Kino Institute.
Makala, Peter '86 (P) Lake Oswego, OR Our Lady of the Lake Church.
Makara, Michael A. '98 (MET) Old Bridge, NJ St. Thomas the Apostle Church.
Makarewicz, Sylvester E. *o.f.m.* '48 (GB) [I] Pulaski, WI Assumption of B.V.M. Friary.
Makerewicz, Marion J. '87 (JC) [A] Hannibal, MO St. Thomas Aquinas Seminary.
Maki, George S. '88 (MAR) Newberry, MI St. Gregory Church.
Makothakat, John M. '62 (SAT) [66] San Antonio, TX St. Thomas More Church; [C] San Antonio, TX Oblate School of Theology.
Makowski, Douglas T '66 (CLV) [5] Parma, OH St. Francis de Sales Church.
Makowski, Lee J. *o.s.a.* '80 (PH) [C] Villanova, PA Villanova University; [AA] Villanova, PA St. Thomas Monastery.
Makowski, Tomasz '93 (PMB) Lantana, FL Holy Spirit Church.
Makranyi, Steven F. '69 (LAN) Flushing, MI St. Robert Church.
Maksimovich, Victor *o.f.m.* '54 (E) [4] Sharon, PA St. Stanislaus Kostka Church.
Maksvytis, Jerome J. '74 (MAD) Berlin, WI St. Joseph Church; Berlin, WI St. Michael Church; Berlin, WI St. Stanislaus Church.
Maksymowicz, Msgr. John H. '70 (BRK) Released from Diocesan Assignment.
Makuch, Thaddeus J. '53 (CHI) Retired.
Makuru, Simon *s.j.* '93 (BO) [W] Chestnut Hill, MA The Jesuit Community at Boston College.
Malabad, Antonio R. '53 (RIC) Williamsburg, VA St. Bede's Church.
Malacaman, Pericles P. '72 (WH) Beckley, WV St. Francis De Sales Church.
Malacari, Carmelo *o.f.m.conv.* '93 (SY) [1] Syracuse, NY The Cathedral of the Immaculate Conception.
Malachowski, Christopher *o.s.* '58 (PCE) On Duty Outside the Diocese.
Malagon, Eduardo '00 (GRY) Chesterton, IN St. Patrick Church.
Malagreca, Msgr. Joseph P. '76 (BRK) [183] Queens, NY SS. Joachim and Anne Church.
Malain, Dan '66 (BEA) Nederland, TX St. Charles Borromeo Church; [G] Beaumont, TX Rev. Herman Vincent Scholarship Fund.
Malanga, Salvatore T. '57 (NEW) Belleville, NJ St. Anthony's Church.
Malanowski, Msgr. Thaddeus F. '47 (NOR) Retired.
Malanyaon, Jovan '73 (TOL) [J] Oregon, OH Sacred Heart Home.
Malarz, Andrew '92 (GRY) [3] Hammond, IN St. Casimir Church.
Malatesta, Christopher A. '93 (SPR) Easthampton, MA Our Lady of Good Counsel Church; [P] Goshen, MA Holy Cross Camp Grounds.
Malatesta, Vincent R. *s.j.* '61 (ATL) [L] Atlanta, GA Ignatius House.
Malave, Gervasio '87 (CGS) [9] Barrio Rio Canas, PR San Pablo Apostol Church.
Malave, Jason A. '97 (CHI) [25] Chicago, IL St. Benedict Church.
Malawy, Michael D. '81 (DET) Maybee, MI St. Joseph Church.
Malayampuram, Joseph *c.m.i.* '68 (BEA) Cleveland, TX St. Mary Church.
Malcolm, Dennis E. '73 (NY) On Duty Outside the Archdiocese.
Malcolm, Lawrence J. '70 (CHI) [47] Chicago, IL St. Daniel the Prophet Church.
Malczyk, Joseph *c.r.* '69 (CHI) [D] Chicago, IL Gordon Tech High School.
Maldari, Donald C. *s.j.* '85 (SY) [S] Syracuse, NY Jesuits at LeMoyne, Inc.
Maldonada, Fernando '99 (SPK) Pomeroy, WA Holy Rosary Church.
Maldonado, Cesar *s.j.* '92 (WDC) [M] Washington, DC The Jesuit Community at Georgetown University.
Maldonado, Edward '83 (SJN) [4] San Juan, PR San Antonio Church.
Maldonado, Fernando '99 (SPK) Dayton, WA St. Joseph Church; Waitsburg, WA St. Mark Church.
Maldonado, Francisco '90 (TUC) [1] Tucson, AZ St. Augustine's Church.
Maldonado, Leonardo '64 (RCK) Special Assignment.
Maldonado, P. Jose A. Rivera '84 (CGS) Naguabo, PR Nuestra Senora del Rosario Church.
Malec, Raymond S. '54 (BEL) Retired.
Malecki, John '48 (ALB) Special Assignment; Retired; [J] Albany, NY Teresian House.
Malene, Robert '72 (E) On Duty Outside Diocese.
Malesic, Edward C. (HBG) Mechanicsburg, PA St. Elizabeth Ann Seton Church.
Maletta, Sammie L. '80 (GRY) [3] Merrillville, IN St. Joan of Arc Church.
Maletz, Leo J. '73 (ALN) Branchdale, PA St. Mary Star of the Sea Church; [4] Minersville, PA St. Stanislaus Kostka Church.
Mali, Joseph F. '88 (BRK) [132] Brooklyn, NY St. Saviour Church.
Malia, Thomas R. '84 (BAL) [36] Baltimore, MD Holy Cross Church; [60] Baltimore, MD St. Mary, Star of the Sea Church.
Maliekal, Cyriac '71 (HRT) [2] New Haven, CT St. Aedan's Church.
Malik, John E. '53 (LC) Colby, WI St. Mary Help of Christians Church.
Malin, Delbert J. '58 (LC) Holmen, WI St. Elizabeth Ann Seton Church.
Malin, Gary J. '86 (CLV) [4] Elyria, OH St. Mary Church.
Malin, George '46 (SP) Retired.
Malinowski, Francis *c.s.sp.* '50 (HBG) [I] Danville, PA Villa Sacred Heart.
Malinowski, Francis X. (HBG) [G] Danville, PA Maria Hall.
Malinowski, Hilary L. '56 (SCR) Simpson, PA St. Michael's Church.
Malinowski, Msgr. John C. '63 (AUS) College Station, TX St. Thomas Aquinas Church; [F] Bryan, TX St. Joseph Regional Health Center.
Malinowski, Stanley J. '54 (PEO) Rantoul, IL St. Malachy's Church; Retired.
Malinsky, Gregory J. '74 (PIT) Military Chaplains.
Maliszewski, Edward C. '45 (PIT) Retired.
Maliszewski, Francis '46 (PAT) [15] Paterson, NJ St. Stephen's Church; Retired.
Maliszewski, Francis S. '41 (DET) Retired.
Malitz, George M. '97 (PSC) Trumbull, CT St. John the Baptist Church.
Maliyekal, John *v.c.* '60 (SFS) Scotland, SD St. George Church.
Malkiewicz, Edward S. '71 (NEW) [2] Jersey City, NJ St. Aloysius Church.
Malkiewicz, Stephen *o.f.m.* '69 (MIL) [P] Milwaukee, WI Francis and Clare House.
Malkiewicz, Stephen E. *o.f.m.* '69 (MIL) [A] St. Francis, WI Saint Francis Seminary.
Malkov, Leonid *c.ss.r.* '90 (PHU) Newark, NJ St. John the Baptist Church.
Mallaghan, Thomas P. *c.m.* '60 (BUF) [C] Niagara University, NY Niagara University; [O] Niagara University, NY Vincentian Community at Niagara University.
Mallahan, James '52 (SEA) Retired.
Mallak, Mark S. '88 (NU) Litchfield, MN St. Philip Church.
Mallavarapu, Kasparaj (ANC) Wasilla, AK Sacred Heart Church.
Malleck, Joseph L. '56 (BRK) Retired.
Mallen, Charles *c.ss.r.* '44 (VEN) [G] Venice, FL St. Alphonsus Residence; [I] Venice, FL Our Lady of Perpetual Help Retreat and Spirituality Center.
Mallen, Santiago *c.ss.r.* '47 (CGS) San Lorenzo, PR Nuestra Senora de la Mercedes Church.
Mallet, Msgr. Charles J. '55 (LAF) Retired.
Mallet, W. Curtis '92 (LAF) [6] Lafayette, LA Our Lady of Wisdom, University of Louisiana Church; [L] Lafayette, LA Our Lady of Wisdom Catholic Student Center.
Mallett, James K. '66 (NSH) [4] Nashville, TN Church of Christ the King.
Mallette, Daniel J. '57 (CHI) [117] Chicago, IL St. Margaret of Scotland Church.
Malley, James '56 (NY) [209] Staten Island, NY St. John Neumann Church.
Malley, James B. *s.j.* '64 (BO) [W] Chestnut Hill, MA The Jesuit Community at Boston College.
Malley, John *o.carm.* '56 (FgM) Carmelite Foreign Missions.
Malley, John *o.carm.* '56 (JOL) [M] Darien, IL Carmelite Mission Office.
Malley, John *o.carm.* '56 (TUC) [A] Tucson, AZ Salpointe Catholic High School; [F] Tucson, AZ Carmelite Priory.
Malley, Kenneth '97 (SP) Indian Rocks Beach, FL St. Jerome Church.
Malley, Michael A. '34 (HRT) Retired.
Malley, Raymond E. *s.m.* '68 (HON) Wailuku, HI St. Anthony Church; [G] Honolulu, HI Marianist Communities.
Malley, Vernon *o.carm.* '59 (TUC) [F] Tucson, AZ Carmelite Priory.
Malley, William J. *s.j.* '64 (FgM) Provinces.
Mallia, Joseph S. '92 (DET) Plymouth, MI St. Kenneth Church.
Mallick, Andrew '83 (ORL) [1] Lakeland, FL Church of the Resurrection.
Mallinson, Arthur D. '81 (DAL) Lancaster, TX St. Francis of Assisi Church.
Mallo, Walter D. *i.v.e.* '90 (NY) [103] New York, NY St. Paul Church.
Mallon, Elias D. *s.a.* '71 (NY) [DD] New York, NY Atonement Friars; [DD] Garrison, NY Franciscan Friars of the Atonement.
Mallon, John J. '50 (OAK) [3] Walnut Creek, CA St. Mary's Church.
Mallonee, Robert *s.v.d.* '67 (BO) [W] Duxbury, MA Society of the Divine Word.
Malloy, Brendan *o.f.m.cap.* '54 (PIT) [O] Pittsburgh, PA St. Augustine Friary.
Malloy, Msgr. David J. '83 (MIL) On Duty Outside the Archdiocese.
Malloy, Edward A. *c.s.c.* '70 (FTW) [B] Notre Dame, IN University of Notre Dame Du Lac; [J] Notre Dame, IN Holy Cross Community, Corby Hall, University of Notre Dame.
Malloy, Francis X. '85 (MIL) Ashford, WI St. Martin Church; Campbellsport, WI St. Matthew Church; St. Kilian, WI St. Kilian Church.
Malloy, Joseph J. '70 (BGP) [4] Bridgeport, CT St. Ann Church.
Malloy, Michael B. '76 (OM) Verdigre, NE St. Wenceslaus Church.
Malloy, Peter *s.d.b.* '74 (NY) [DD] New Rochelle, NY Salesian Provincial House.
Malloy, Richard G. *s.j.* '88 (CAM) [4] Camden, NJ Holy Name Church.
Malloy, Robert *o.f.m.cap.* (WDC) [B] Washington, DC St. Francis Friary-Capuchin College.
Malloy, Stephen J. '96 (BO) Absent on Leave.
Malloy, Thomas F. *o.s.f.s.* '67 (WIL) [I] Childs, MD Oblates of St. Francis De Sales.
Malloy, William E. '73 (CHI) [3] Oak Lawn, IL St. Germaine Church.
Mally, Edward J. *s.j.* '61 (NY) [DD] New York, NY Jesuit Provincial's Office.
Mallya, Sabas *a.l.c.p.* '91 (LA) [5] Santa Barbara, CA St. Raphael Church.

Malm, Raymond B. '76 (PRO) [23] Providence, RI St. Michael the Archangel Church.
Malnar, Stan '72 (HEL) Special Assignments.
Malner, Msgr. Matthew '66 (AMA) Retired.
Malo, John B. *c.s.b.* '78 (OAK) [C] Oakland, CA Bishop O'Dowd High School.
Malo, Richard C. '87 (PRT) East Millinocket, ME St. Peter's Church; Millinocket, ME St. Martin of Tours Church.
Malonda, Anselme *c.i.c.m.* '92 (SAT) [B] San Antonio, TX Missionhurst Formation Community.
Malone, Alan '59 (PHX) Special Assignment.
Malone, Bernard G. '50 (LR) [8] Little Rock, AR Immaculate Heart of Mary Church.
Malone, Donald '60 (NY) Absent on Leave.
Malone, Edward F. *m.m.* '52 (FgM) Maryknoll Foreign Missions.
Malone, Edward T. (BO) Reading, MA St. Agnes Church.
Malone, Edward T. '72 (BO) Health Leave.
Malone, Msgr. Francis I. '77 (LR) [2] Little Rock, AR St. Anne Church; [7] Little Rock, AR Immaculate Conception Church.
Malone, Francis T. '65 (NEW) [K] Kearny, NJ New Jersey Boystown.
Malone, H. Patrick '69 (WCH) [7] Wichita, KS Holy Savior Church.
Malone, John M. '67 (STP) [2] St. Paul, MN Assumption Church; [C] St. Paul, MN University of St. Thomas.
Malone, John S. *c.s.c.* '55 (RVC) Northport, NY Veteran's Administration Hospital.
Malone, Michael T. *c.s.sp.* '65 (PRO) [B] Newport, RI Salve Regina University.
Malone, Msgr. Quintin J. '38 (WCH) Retired.
Malone, Msgr. Richard '62 (PH) [A] Wynnewood, PA Theological Seminary of St. Charles Borromeo, Overbrook.
Malone, Richard T. (BO) Whitman, MA Holy Ghost Church.
Maloney, Andrew P. '34 (SCR) Retired.
Maloney, Bernard *o.f.m.cap.* '69 (ROC) Interlaken, NY St. Francis Solanus Church; Ovid, NY Holy Cross Church; [I] Interlaken, NY St. Fidelis Friary.
Maloney, Charles F. '57 (TUC) Absent on Leave.
Maloney, Msgr. Christopher '66 (NY) [82] New York, NY Notre Dame Church; [GG] New York, NY University Apostolate.
Maloney, Daniel *o.s.b.* '68 (BIS) [A] Richardton, ND Assumption Abbey; [B] Bismarck, ND University of Mary; [H] Bismarck, ND Annunciation Monastery.
Maloney, Edward F. '55 (NY) [DD] New York, NY Jesuit Community at Fordham University.
Maloney, Edward J. '55 (CHI) Palatine, IL Mission Juan Diego Church; Retired.
Maloney, Francis E. '59 (PMB) Retired.
Maloney, Francis G. '60 (R) Retired.
Maloney, George A. *s.j.* '57 (MIL) [P] Milwaukee, WI Jesuit Provincial Office, Wisconsin Province.
Maloney, James F. *c.m.f.* '60 (CHI) [147] Chicago, IL Our Lady of Guadalupe Church; [N] Oak Park, IL Claretian Fathers Headquarters of U.S.A. Eastern Province.
Maloney, James G. '71 (CLV) Norton, OH St. Andrew the Apostle Church.
Maloney, John '75 (BRK) [196] Queens, NY St. Mary Magdalene Church.
Maloney, John '87 (MAR) Retired.
Maloney, John P. '64 (PIT) Glade Mills, PA Holy Sepulcher Church.
Maloney, John P. '66 (BRK) [189] Queens, NY St. Kevin Church.
Maloney, John W. '75 (BRK) [223] Queens, NY St. Pascal Baylon Church; [G] Brooklyn, NY Catherine McAuley.
Maloney, Joseph *o.f.m.cap.* '58 (DET) [K] Detroit, MI St. Bonaventure Friary.
Maloney, Joseph L. '91 (PH) [A] Wynnewood, PA Theological Seminary of St. Charles Borromeo, Overbrook.
Maloney, Malcolm *o.f.m.cap.* '55 (SAG) [G] Saginaw, MI Queen of Angels Friary and Retreat House.
Maloney, Patrick H. *c.s.c.* '54 (FTW) [B] Notre Dame, IN University of Notre Dame Du Lac; [J] Notre Dame, IN Holy Cross Community, Corby Hall, University of Notre Dame.
Maloney, Richard *s.d.s.* '69 (WDC) [B] Silver Spring, MD Salvatorian Community.
Maloney, Richard E. '50 (DET) Retired.
Maloney, Robert L. *s.j.* '61 (SJ) [L] Los Gatos, CA Sacred Heart Jesuit Center.
Maloney, Robert P. *c.m.* '66 (FgM) Vincentian Foreign Missions.
Maloney, Robert P. *c.m.* '66 (PH) [AA] Philadelphia, PA Congregation of the Mission.
Maloney, Robert S. *s.x.* '57 (BO) [W] Holliston, MA Xaverian Missionaries.
Maloney, Rufino *o.f.m.conv.* '59 (ALB) [12] Albany, NY Our Lady of Angels Church.
Maloney, Msgr. Thomas F. '68 (BUF) [1] Tonawanda, NY St. Amelia Church.
Maloney, Thomas J. '65 (SCR) Hughestown, PA Blessed Sacrament Church.
Maloney, Thomas P. '70 (RVC) Babylon, NY St. Joseph's Church.
Maloney, Timothy *o.s.b.* '50 (OKL) [I] Shawnee, OK St. Gregory's Abbey.
Maloney, Msgr. Tom '67 (PEO) Normal, IL Epiphany Church.
Maloney, Walter '47 (JKS) Retired.
Maloney, Wilfred F. '55 (PH) [61] Philadelphia, PA Holy Innocents Church; Maple Glen, PA St. Alphonsus Church.
Maloney, William J. '48 (E) Retired.
Maloney, William P. '76 (CHI) Other Assignments.
Malooly, Msgr. Francis W. '70 (BAL) [92] Baltimore, MD St. Thomas More Church; Special Assignment.
Malorzo, Luigi *c.p.* '52 (MET) [H] South River, NJ Passionist Provincial Office.
Malovetz, Gregory E. S. '83 (MET) Skillman, NJ St. Charles Borromeo Church.
Maloy, Dale R. '54 (PEO) [1] La Salle, IL Queen of the Holy Rosary Church.
Maltese, James L. '65 (RVC) Valley Stream, NY Holy Name of Mary Church.
Malthaner, John P. '93 (E) [C] Oil City, PA Venango Christian High School.
Maluafiti, Soke *o.f.m.cap.* (AGN) [F] Agana Heights, GU St. Fidelis Friary.
Malvey, James '86 (PMB) Retired.
Malvey, Killian *o.s.b.* '73 (SEA) [L] Lacey, WA St. Martin's Abbey.
Malvey, Sean R. *o.s.b.* '89 (SEA) [L] Lacey, WA St. Martin's Abbey.
Mampara, Mathew '60 (PHX) Sun City, AZ St. Clement of Rome Church.
Man Tran, Joseph '95 (NO) [3] Metairie, LA St. Ann Church and Church.
Mana-Ay, Eusebio (NY) [109] New York, NY St. Rose of Lima Church.
Manahan, Msgr. Emmanuel G. '84 (LA) Granada Hills, CA St. John Baptist de la Salle Church.
Manahan, John J. *s.m.* '68 (SAT) [8] San Antonio, TX Holy Rosary Church; [M] San Antonio, TX Holy Rosary Marianist Community.
Manahan, Martin J. '52 (WOR) Retired.
Manahan, Thomas C. *s.j.* '95 (MAD) [5] Madison, WI Immaculate Heart of Mary Church.
Manahan, Thomas C. *s.j.* '95 (OM) [K] Omaha, NE Jesuit Community at Creighton University.
Manalel, Matthew (NY) [Z] New York, NY Mary Manning Walsh Home.
Manalili, Feliciano *o.c.s.o.* '62 (CHR) [E] Moncks Corner, SC Mepkin Abbey.
Manalis, Msgr. Edward W. '77 (BAL) Hagerstown, MD St. Ann Church.
Manalo, Pantaleon O. '63 (RIC) [E] Portsmouth, VA Maryview Medical Center.
Manalo, Ricky *c.s.p.* '00 (P) [29] Portland, OR St. Philip Neri Church; [Q] Portland, OR Paulist Fathers Catholic Center for Evangelization.
Manapuram, Joseph '69 (GAL) [3] Houston, TX St. Albert of Trapani Church.
Manarchuck, Joseph J. '78 (SCR) Meshoppen, PA St. Joachim's Church.
Manase, Michael *o.c.d.* '77 (ALX) Powhatan, LA St. Francis of Assisi Church.
Mancha, George '88 (SJ) [9] San Jose, CA St. Anthony Church.
Manchapilly, George *c.m.i.* '71 (BEA) [1] Beaumont, TX St. Anthony Church.
Manchas, Lawrence L. '79 (GBG) Herminie, PA St. Edward Church.
Manching, Romulo S. (CHI) [J] Evanston, IL Saint Francis Hospital.
Mancilla, Pedro M. '58 (FRS) Riverdale, CA St. Ann Church.
Mancini, Anthony '78 (PRO) [15] Providence, RI Holy Cross Church.
Mancini, Domenic '76 (PIT) Imperial, PA St. Columbkille Church.
Mancini, James E. '58 (LR) Cherokee Village, AR St. Michael's Church.
Mancini, John *o.s.f.s.* '80 (SAG) Shields, MI Holy Spirit Church.
Mancini, John S. *o.s.f.s.* '80 (SAG) [4] Saginaw, MI SS. Simon and Jude Church.
Mancini, Marc '92 (PAT) Prospect Park, NJ St. Paul's Church.
Mancini, Nicholas (ALT) On Duty Outside the Diocese.
Mancini, Nicholas J. (Y) [11] Canton, OH St. Paul's Church.
Mancini, Robert A. *o.s.f.s.* '77 (WIL) [I] Wilmington, DE Oblates of St. Francis De Sales.
Mancuso, Anthony '83 (SJ) Cupertino, CA St. Joseph of Cupertino Church.
Mancuso, Dennis J. '96 (BUF) [3] West Seneca, NY Fourteen Holy Helpers Church.
Mancuso, Henry '75 (LKC) [3] Lake Charles, LA Sacred Heart of Jesus Church.
Mancuso, Joseph A. '64 (KC) Gladstone, MO St. Andrew the Apostle Church; [N] Kansas City, MO Diocesan Council of Catholic Women.
Mancuso, Joseph A. '70 (ALB) [15] Schenectady, NY Our Lady of Mt. Carmel Church.
Mancuso, Luke *o.s.b.* '83 (SCL) [I] Collegeville, MN St. John's Abbey, of the Order of St. Benedict.
Mandala, Michael J. *s.j.* '77 (LA) [6] Los Angeles, CA Blessed Sacrament Church.
Mandarino, Constantino *o.m.* '65 (LA) [Q] Los Angeles, CA Minim Fathers.
Mandato, Kieran '87 (NY) Military Chaplains.
Mandato, Pio *f.m.h.j.* '85 (SCR) [M] Laceyville, PA Franciscan Missionary Hermits of St. Joseph.
Mandel, Brian L. '94 (NU) Tracy, MN St. Mary Church; Walnut Grove, MN St. Paul Church.
Manderfield, Geraldo R.P. '60 (MAR) Retired.
Mandfield, Scott D. '00 (SFE) Rio Rancho, NM St. Thomas Aquinas Church.
Mandile, John J. *s.j.* '57 (BO) [W] Weston, MA Campion Jesuit Community.
Manding, Benito O. '64 (SJ) [3] Sunnyvale, CA St. Martin Church.
Mandock, Patrick H. '72 (GBG) Military Chaplains.
Mandock, Patrick H. '72 (TUC) Fort Huchuca, AZ Fort Huchuca Army Post.
Mandoli, Richard *o.c.d.* '92 (SJ) [L] San Jose, CA Carmelite Monastery, Novitiate.
Mandry, Stephen A. *s.t.d.* '66 (GAL) Baytown, TX St. Joseph Church.
Mandziuk, Paul *m.s.* '80 (GAL) Friendswood, TX Mary, Queen Church.
Manente, Vladimiro *o.m.i.* '46 (LAR) [8] Laredo, TX San Francisco Javier Independent Church.
Manero, Ismael '37 (GLP) Retired.
Manerowski, Joseph '95 (ALB) Delhi, NY St. Peter Church; [R] Delhi, NY State University of New York College of Agricultural & Technology at Delhi.
Maney, Robert L. '51 (MIL) Retired.
Maney, Thomas J. *m.m.* '56 (NY) [DD] Maryknoll, NY Maryknoll Fathers and Brothers.
Manfred, Donald J. '67 (OG) Massena, NY Sacred Heart Church.
Mangahas, Rene '83 (WIL) Chester, Kent Island, MD St. Christopher Church.
Mangalath, Augustine (HRT) [5] West Haven, CT St. Paul's Church.
Mangalath, Augustine '79 (HRT) [I] New Haven, CT Hospital of St. Raphael.
Mangalath, Jaison G. *s.v.d.* '99 (LAF) [4] Lafayette, LA Immaculate Heart of Mary Church.
Mangampo, Gil '91 (GLP) Milan, NM St. Vivian Church; San Mateo, NM San Mateo Church; San Rafael, NM San Rafael Church.
Mangan, Charles M. '89 (SFS) On Duty Outside the Diocese.
Mangan, James '69 (SPK) Otis Orchards, WA St. Joseph Church.
Mangan, Martin '57 (SFD) [4] Decatur, IL St. James Church.
Mangan, Timothy *s.s.s.* '59 (ALB) Broadalbin, NY St. Joseph Church.
Manganello, Salvatore '82 (BUF) [14] Buffalo, NY Blessed Sacrament Church.
Mangano, Charles N. '90 (RVC) Bohemia, NY St. John Nepomucene Church.
Mangen, Daniel J. *c.pp.s.* '80 (CIN) [M] Dayton, OH Provincial Office of the Cincinnati Province of the Society of the Precious Blood.
Manger, Daniel *o.s.b. cam.* '85 (MRY) [F] Big Sur, CA New Camaldoli Hermitage.
Manger, William '62 (BEA) [2] Beaumont, TX St. Anne Church.
Mangesho, Paulinus M. *a.l.c.p.* '91 (SFR) [48] San Francisco, CA Sacred Heart Church.
Mangiafico, Paul '70 (HRT) [13] Waterbury, CT St. Lucy's Church.
Mangiaracina, Cayet *o.p.* '64 (SAT) [26] San Antonio, TX St. Ann Church; [B] San Antonio, TX Dominican Priory of San Juan Macias.
Mangiaracina, George *o.c.d* '93 (MIL) [P] Milwaukee, WI Provincial Offices - Discalced Carmelites.
Mangini, Richard A. '67 (OAK) [2] Concord, CA St. Bonaventure Church.
Manglaviti, Leo M. *s.j.* '99 (BO) [A] Weston, MA Pope John XXIII National Seminary; [W] Boston, MA The Society of Jesus of New England-Provincial Offices.
Mangulabnan, Jose, Jr. (DOD) Syracuse, KS St. Raphael Church.
Mangulabnan, Jun '86 (DOD) Tribune, KS St. Joseph Church.
Mangum, Peter B. '90 (SHP) [8] Shreveport, LA St. Joseph Church.
Manhard, Edward P. *s.j.* '32 (STL) [O] St. Louis, MO Fusz Pavilion.
Manhart, Paul *s.j.* '58 (RC) Kyle, SD Our Lady of Sorrows Church; Pine Ridge, SD Holy Rosary Church; [B] Pine Ridge, SD Jesuit Community of Holy Rosary Mission.
Mani, David L. '64 (RVC) Plainview, NY St. Pius X Church.
Mania, Edwin '92 (BRK) [201] Queens, NY St. Michael Church.
Maniamkerry, Matthew *o.ss.t.* '84 (BAL) [S] Baltimore,

MD Holy Trinity Monastery.
Maniampra, Mathew *c.m.i.* (BRK) [160] Queens, NY St. Camillus Church.
Maniangat, Joseph '64 (STA) Chiefland, FL St. John the Evangelist Church.
Manieri, Msgr. Francis '60 (STU) Bridgeport, OH St. Anthony of Padua Church; [J] Bridgeport, OH Cursillo Moderator.
Manikowski, Msgr. Stanislaus J. '38 (HT) Raceland, LA St. Mary's Nativity Church; Retired.
Maniola, Francis N. '38 (CHI) [194] Chicago, IL St. Symphorosa and Seven Sons Church; Retired.
Manion, Kevin (AUS) [16] Austin, TX St. Louis Church.
Manion, Thomas F. '57 (PIT) Retired.
Maniscalco, Msgr. Francis '71 (RVC) Priests Released from Diocesan Assignment.
Maniscalco, Paul *s.d.b.* '69 (SFR) [46] San Francisco, CA SS. Peter and Paul Church.
Manista, Clemens D. '74 (WIL) Claymont, DE Holy Rosary Church.
Maniyangat, Jose '75 (STA) Macclenny, FL St. Mary's Church.
Maniyangatt, Joseph *c.s.t.* (NY) [150] Bronx, NY Immaculate Conception Church.
Mank, Virgil '65 (SFD) Godfrey, IL St. Ambrose Church.
Mankel, F. Xavier '61 (KNX) [5] Knoxville, TN Holy Ghost Church; [K] Knoxville, TN Diocesan Council of Catholic Women; [K] Knoxville, TN Diocesan Council of Catholic Women; [K] Knoxville, TN Ladies of Charity.
Manko, Andriy *c.ss.r.* '95 (PHU) Newark, NJ St. John the Baptist Church.
Mankowski, Edmund A. '46 (BRK) Retired.
Mankowski, Marcin *o.p.* (LC) Rosholt, WI St. Adalbert Church.
Mankowski, Paul V. *s.j.* '65 (CHI) [N] Chicago, IL Chicago Province of the Society of Jesus-Provincial Office.
Mankowski, Slawek M. '92 (CHI) [198] Chicago, IL St. Thecla Church.
Manley, Bernard A. '87 (CHL) Retired.
Manly, Msgr. Alex F. '57 (RVC) Kings Park, NY St. Joseph's Church.
Mann, Francis '79 (BRK) [34] Brooklyn, NY St. Edmund's Church.
Mann, Gordon '92 (EVN) [22] Evansville, IN St. Wendel Church.
Mann, Lawrence *s.m.* '53 (LA) [F] Chatsworth, CA Chaminade College Preparatory.
Mann, Peter '67 (RVC) Absent on Leave.
Mann, Raymond *o.f.m.* '59 (BO) [BB] Boston, MA St. Anthony Shrine.
Mann, Robert G. '59 (PEO) [J] Danville, IL Provena United Samaritans Medical Center.
Manna, Louis (IND) Corydon, IN St. Joseph Church.
Manna, Louis '73 (IND) New Middletown, IN Most Precious Blood Church; St. Peter, IN St. Peter Church.
Mannara, Frederick R. '63 (SY) [5] Syracuse, NY Most Holy Rosary Church.
Mannebach, Thomas M. '99 (CIN) Coldwater, OH Holy Trinity Church.
Mannetta, Andrew *o.f.m.cap.* '83 (AGN) [F] Agana Heights, GU St. Fidelis Friary.
Mannetta, Andrew *o.f.m.cap.* '83 (HON) Pearl City, HI Our Lady of Good Counsel Church.
Mannhardt, Daniel C. '57 (DAV) [2] Davenport, IA Our Lady of Victory Church.
Mannikarott, Msgr. Geevarchese (CHI) Chicago, IL Syro-Malankara Catholic Mission of the Archdiocese of Chicago Church.
Manning, Aedan *s.t.* '63 (JKS) Crystal Springs, MS St. John Church.
Manning, Brian F. '74 (BO) [4] Somerville, MA St. Catherine of Genoa Church.
Manning, C. Robert '97 (STL) Wildwood, MO St. Alban Roe Church.
Manning, Charles T. '75 (ROC) [24] Rochester, NY Holy Name of Jesus Church.
Manning, Daniel '91 (SFS) Kimball, SD St. Margaret Church.
Manning, Francis J. '51 (SPR) [4] Ludlow, MA St. Mary Church.
Manning, Msgr. J. Leroy '40 (SAT) Retired; [K] San Antonio, TX Casa De Padres.
Manning, J. Patrick '78 (Y) Alliance, OH Regina Coeli Church.
Manning, James *s.m.m.* '58 (RVC) [M] Bay Shore, NY Montfort Missionaries.
Manning, James J. '75 (CIN) [3] Dayton, OH St. Albert the Great Church.
Manning, James T. *m.m.* '48 (FgM) Maryknoll Foreign Missions.
Manning, John '55 (OAK) Retired.
Manning, John E. '72 (CLV) [76] Cleveland, OH St. Vincent de Paul Church.
Manning, Joseph H. '61 (BO) [5] Brockton, MA Our Lady of Lourdes Church.
Manning, Justinian *c.p.* '54 (BO) [21] Boston, MA St. Gabriel Church; [W] Boston, MA St. Gabriel Passionist Community.
Manning, Martin B. '43 (DAV) Retired.
Manning, Michael '69 (SB) [A] Riverside, CA Divine Word Seminary; [I] Riverside, CA Wordnet, Inc.
Manning, Michael T. '97 (TR) Point Pleasant, NJ St. Martha Church.
Manning, Paul F. '65 (BO) Unassigned.
Manning, Paul R. '59 (NEW) [D] Summit, NJ The Oratory Catholic Preparatory School.
Manning, Paul S. '85 (PAT) Rockaway, NJ St. Cecilia's Church; [C] Denville, NJ Morris Catholic High School.
Manning, Robert E. *s.j.* '67 (BO) [B] Cambridge, MA Weston Jesuit School of Theology; [W] Cambridge, MA Weston Jesuit Community.
Manning, Robert T. '54 (COL) Retired.
Manning, Roger M. *o.s.m.* '45 (CHI) [N] Chicago, IL Order of Friar Servants of Mary (Servites) United States of America Province, Inc.
Manning, Thomas J. '65 (SY) Retired.
Manning, Thomas V. '84 (PIT) Monroeville, PA North American Martyrs Church; Allegheny County, PA Beverly Manor of Monroeville; Allegheny County, PA Presbyterian Seniorcare Westminister Place; Allegheny County, PA St. Margaret Senca Place; Allegheny County, PA Hamilton Hills Personal Care; Allegheny County, PA Ladies of the Grand Army Republic (LGAR).
Mannion, Bernard J. '50 (STO) Oakdale, CA St. Mary of the Annunciation Church.
Mannion, Edward C. *c.m.* '39 (PH) [AA] Philadelphia, PA Congregation of the Mission.
Mannion, Msgr. Francis '73 (CHI) [A] Mundelein, IL University of St. Mary of the Lake-Mundelein Seminary.
Mannion, Frank *s.s.c.* '52 (LA) Whittier, CA St. Bruno Church.
Mannion, James '81 (RVC) Wantagh, NY St. Frances de Chantal Church.
Mannion, John H. '68 (IND) [F] Beech Grove, IN St. Francis Hospital and Health Centers.
Mannion, John H. '68 (LFT) On Duty Outside the Diocese.
Mannion, Mark S. '95 (STL) [Q] Kirkwood, MO Prelature of the Holy Cross and Opus Dei.
Mannion, Martin '66 (TUC) Yuma, AZ Immaculate Conception Church.
Mannion, Msgr. Martin J. '62 (CAM) Collingswood, NJ St. John's Church.
Mannion, Martin K. '66 (STL) On Duty Outside the Archdiocese.
Mannion, Michael T. '71 (CAM) [1] Camden, NJ Immaculate Conception Church; [R] Camden, NJ Rutgers University - Camden Campus.
Mannion, P. John '66 (SAT) [4] San Antonio, TX Divine Providence Church.
Mannion, Thomas F. '46 (BRK) Retired.
Mannion, Thomas F. '46 (P) Brookings, OR Star of the Sea Church.
Mannion, Thomas Ignatius '65 (HBG) Roaring Creek, PA Our Lady of Mercy Church; Danville, PA State Hospital.
Mannion, Thomas J. (LC) Retired.
Mannion, William '89 (BAL) Absent on Leave.
Mannion, William D. '63 (CHI) Rosemont-Des Plaines, IL Our Lady of Hope Church.
Manno, John K. '68 (SCR) [1] Williamsport, PA Annunciation Church.
Manny, Howard '44 (ALB) Retired.
Manny, Howard F. '44 (ALB) [11] Schenectady, NY St. Luke Church; Retired.
Manos, James M. '96 (NEW) Union, NJ Holy Spirit Church.
Manrique, Wilfredo (SJ) Graduate Studies.
Manriquez, Raymundo '00 (LUB) [1] Lubbock, TX Cathedral Christ the King Church.
Mans, Leo (ROC) Retired.
Mansell, C. Kirk *s.j.* '84 (SP) [T] Tampa, FL University of Tampa.
Mansfield, John L. '53 (BO) Senior Priests.
Manship, James C. '98 (HRT) [4] Bristol, CT St. Joseph Church.
Manship, Joseph '76 (PRT) Westbrook, ME St. Mary's Church.
Manship, Paul E. (SPR) [2] Springfield, MA All Souls Church.
Manship, Paul E. '88 (SPR) [5] Springfield, MA Holy Family Church; [N] Springfield, MA Catholic Latino Ministry.
Mansilla, Joaquin '56 (SJN) [6] San Juan, PR Nuestra Senora de Belen Church.
Mansini, Guy *o.s.b.* '77 (IND) [A] St. Meinrad, IN St. Meinrad Seminary; [J] St. Meinrad, IN St. Meinrad Archabbey.
Manson, Sean '99 (NEW) [1] Newark, NJ Cathedral Basilica of the Sacred Heart; Plainfield, NJ St. Mary Church.
Mansour, Gregory J. '82 (OLL) Los Angeles, CA Our Lady of Mt. Lebanon-St. Peter Church; [F] Los Angeles, CA Eparchial Endowments; [F] Los Angeles, CA Bishop's Retirement Trust Fund.
Mansueto, Felix *o.f.m.* '55 (FgM) Franciscan Foreign Missions.
Manternach, Msgr. Albert V. '52 (DUB) Retired.
Manternach, Carl J. '55 (DUB) Anamosa, IA St. Patrick's Church; Retired.
Manternach, Neil J. '85 (DUB) Hiawatha, IA St. Elizabeth Ann Seton Church.
Mantia, Armand '85 (NEW) Roselle Park, NJ The Assumption Church.
Mantica, A. Donald '60 (STU) Piney Fork, OH St. Therese Church; Smithfield, OH Our Lady, Queen of Peace Church.
Manton, Joseph E. *c.ss.r.* '29 (BO) [53] Boston, MA Our Lady of Perpetual Help Church.
Mantoovrni, Firmo *c.s.* (KC) [17] Kansas City, MO Holy Rosary Church.
Manuel, Albert William '87 (MIL) [P] Milwaukee, WI Jesuit Community at Marquette University.
Manuel, Armand J. *s.s.j.* '85 (BAL) [S] Baltimore, MD St. Joseph Society of the Sacred Heart House of Central Administration.
Manuel, Gerdenio M. *s.j.* '84 (SJ) [B] Santa Clara, CA Santa Clara University.
Manuel, Vincent *s.a.c.*, *v.f.* '81 (ALX) [4] Alexandria, LA St. James Memorial Church; [5] Alexandria, LA St. Juliana Church.
Manuppella, Anthony J. '76 (CAM) Merchantville, NJ St. Peter's Church.
Manville, Alex *o.f.m.* (LA) [W] Malibu, CA Serra Retreat.
Manz, Msgr. Joseph C. '40 (NEW) [18] Jersey City, NJ St. Nicholas Church; Woodcliff Lake, NJ Our Lady Mother of the Church; Retired.
Manz, Michael '79 (GAL) [P] Houston, TX Opus Dei.
Manzano, Paul '60 (STO) [8] Stockton, CA St. Mary of the Assumption Church; Stockton, CA DeWitt Nelson Training Center; Stockton, CA O.H. Close School.
Manzelli, Msgr. Michael '57 (RVC) Freeport, NY Our Holy Redeemer Church.
Manzi, Arcangelo *o.de.m.* '64 (BUF) [O] LeRoy, NY Order of the BVM of Mercy/Mercedarian Friars; [Q] LeRoy, NY St. Peter Nolasco Spiritual Center.
Manzo, Fernando L. '83 (TUC) [20] Tucson, AZ St. Monica Church.
Manzo, Msgr. Francis J. '62 (BRK) Absent on Leave.
Manzo, Louis *c.s.c.* (NOR) [K] Willimantic, CT Campus Ministry.
Manzo, Louis A. *c.s.c.* '65 (FR) [A] North Easton, MA Stonehill College; [A] North Easton, MA Holy Cross Fathers Religious.
Maples, Frederic A. *s.j.* '72 (BO) [W] Boston, MA The Society of Jesus of New England-Provincial Offices.
Maples, Frederic A. *s.j.* '72 (MIL) [P] Milwaukee, WI Jesuit Provincial Office, Wisconsin Province.
Maples, Frederic A. *s.j.* '72 (STP) [Q] St. Paul, MN Loyola.
Mappilamattel, Jose '85 (RVC) Port Jefferson, NY St. Charles Hospital, Port Jefferson, New York.
Mappilamattela, Jose (NY) State, NY Eastern Correctional Facility; State, NY Ulster Correctional Facility.
Marable, Gerald C. '88 (CAM) [5] Camden, NJ St. Joan of Arc Church.
Maraczewski, Edward S. '45 (CHI) [1] Waukegan, IL St. Anastasia Church; Retired.
Maraist, Martin '80 (LAF) Retired.
Maraldo, Angelo F. *o.s.f.s.* '86 (VEN) [7] Fort Myers, FL Our Lady of Light Church.
Maramkulan, Mathew (SAC) Carmichael, CA Our Lady of the Assumption Church.
Maramot, Faustino '74 (MEM) Memphis, TN Federal Correctional Institute at Memphis.
Marandu, Nicolaus '52 (P) [20] Portland, OR Immaculate Heart of Mary Church.
Marangone, Mark *s.x.* '84 (FgM) Xaverian Foreign Missions.
Marangone, Mark *s.x.* '84 (PAT) [M] Wayne, NJ Xaverian Missionary Fathers.
Marani, Philip *o.carm.* '65 (NY) [97] New York, NY Our Lady of the Scapular/St. Stephen Church; Manhattan, NY Bellevue Hospital.
Maranki, James J. '99 (ALN) [5] Reading, PA Holy Guardian Angels Church.
Marano, Fred '91 (BRK) [B] Elmhurst, NY Cathedral Preparatory Seminary of the Immaculate Conception.
Maranowski, Michael J. '87 (PIT) [10] New Castle, PA St. Vincent de Paul Church.
Maranto, Charles L. *c.s.v.* '50 (CHI) [N] Arlington Heights, IL Viatorian Province Center-Clerics of St. Viator.
Maranto, Samuel *c.ss.r.* '72 (BR) [10] Baton Rouge, LA St. Gerard Majella Church.
Marasciulo, Msgr. John '45 (YAK) Retired.
Maravi, Raul *o.carm.* '97 (JOL) [J] Darien, IL Carmelite Provincial Office.
Maravilla, Juan A. *f.m.m.* '93 (AUS) Giddings, TX St. Margaret Church.
Maravilla, Primitivo (MOB) Fairhope, AL St. Lawrence Church.
Maraya, Felipe '62 (ELP) Absent on Leave.

Marbach, Msgr. Joseph '43 (NY) Retired.
Marbach, Lawrence J. '52 (SFS) Retired.
Marbaugh, Meinrad '39 (LR) [A] Subiaco, AR Subiaco Monastery.
Marbury, Cabell B. '64 (ALB) Special Assignment; [C] Albany, NY Bishop Maginn High School.
Marcaccio, Anthony J. '91 (CHL) [5] Greensboro, NC St. Pius X Church.
Marcaida, Epifanio '83 (NY) [141] Bronx, NY St. Frances de Chantal Church.
Marcantonio, Clement '59 (PBL) Retired.
Marceau, Emmet L. '67 (SAG) [12] Saginaw, MI St. Helen Church.
Marceau, Timothy R. *o.s.b.* '52 (ALX) Belledeau, LA St. Martin of Tours Church.
Marceau, Timothy R. *o.s.b.* '52 (JOL) [J] Lisle, IL St. Procopius Abbey.
Marceaux, Msgr. Sidney J. '70 (BEA) Military Chaplains.
Marcell, Robert G. '56 (BR) Retired.
Marcellus, Gordon E. *o.s.a.* '59 (PH) [C] Villanova, PA Villanova University.
March, Ralph *o.cist.* '45 (DAL) [K] Irving, TX Cistercian Abbey of Our Lady of Dallas.
Marchand, Gerald A. '54 (NEW) Retired.
Marchand, Robert A. '52 (MAN) Retired.
Marchesani, Gino *f.d.p.* '56 (BO) [B] Haverhill, MA Sons of Divine Providence School for Exceptional Boys; [U] Boston, MA Don Orione Nursing Home; [Y] Haverhill, MA Don Orione Center.
Marchese, Dominic A. *s.s.j.* '40 (BAL) [S] Baltimore, MD St. Joseph Society of the Sacred Heart House of Central Administration.
Marchese, Dominic A. *s.s.j.* '40 (TR) Bay Head, NJ Sacred Heart Church.
Marchese, Joseph P. '69 (SPR) On Duty Outside the Diocese.
Marchese, Msgr. Richard E.. '70 (BRK) [41] Brooklyn, NY St. Frances Cabrini Church.
Marchesin, Ivan *s.x.* '66 (FgM) Xaverian Foreign Missions.
Marchesin, Ivan *s.x.* '66 (PAT) [M] Wayne, NJ Xaverian Missionary Fathers.
Marchessault, Edward T. *c.s.sp.* '64 (FgM) Holy Ghost Foreign Missions.
Marchetti, Carlo M. *o.s.m.* '59 (CHI) [N] Chicago, IL Order of Friar Servants of Mary (Servites) United States of America Province, Inc.
Marchetti, Michael H. '82 (SCR) White Mills, PA St. Joseph's Church.
Marchetti, Peter E. *s.j.* '77 (FgM) Provinces.
Marchewka, Jacek '00 (NEW) Bergenfield, NJ St. John the Evangelist Church.
Marchino, Msgr. Louis H. '39 (IND) Retired.
Marchionda, James *o.p.* '73 (CHI) [N] Oak Park, IL Dominican Community of St. Martin de Porres.
Marchitelli, Msgr. Anthony D. '76 (NY) [E] Somers, NY John F. Kennedy High School; [P] New York, NY Catholic Youth Organization of the Archdiocese of New York Inc.
Marchlewski, Michael A. *s.j.* '67 (STL) [P] St. Louis, MO De Smet Jesuit High School Community.
Marchulones, Kenneth L. '65 (PEO) East Peoria, IL St. Monica's Church.
Marchuronis, Francis V. '52 (PIT) Retired.
Marciano, Charles A. '72 (ALN) [11] Reading, PA St. Peter Church.
Marciano, Robert L. '83 (PRO) [10] Warwick, RI Ss. Rose & Clement Church.
Marcil, Michel *s.j.* '74 (LA) [Q] Culver City, CA Ignatius House, The Novitiate of the California Province, Society of Jesus.
Marciniak, Bartlomiej *o.s.p.p.e.* '93 (PH) [AA] Doylestown, PA Pauline Fathers Monastery, Shrine of Our Lady of Czestochowa.
Marciniak, Felix R. '79 (NEW) Wallington, NJ Most Sacred Heart of Jesus Church.
Marciniak, Henry P. '61 (NEW) [7] Elizabeth, NJ St. Hedwig's Church.
Marciniak, John '56 (NOR) Retired.
Marciniak, Thomas R. *s.j.* '76 (SY) [S] Syracuse, NY Jesuits at LeMoyne, Inc.
Marco, Alfredo '60 (LKC) [3] Lake Charles, LA Sacred Heart of Jesus Church.
Marco, Michael J. *s.j.* '96 (OM) [C] Omaha, NE Creighton Preparatory School.
Marcone, Eugene (NEW) Garwood, NJ Church of St. Anne.
Marconi, John E. '87 (LR) Paragould, AR St. Mary's Church.
Marconi, Paul *c.r.s.p.* '58 (SD) Pala, CA Mission San Antonio de Pala Church.
Marconi, Theodore B. '84 (E) Mount Jewett, PA St. Joseph Church; Smethport, PA St. Elizabeth Church.
Marconyak, Albert J. '43 (PIT) Retired.
Marcotte, David P. *s.j.* '92 (NY) [DD] New York, NY Xavier Jesuit Community.
Marcotte, Joseph A. '69 (WOR) Webster, MA St. Louis Church.
Marcotte, Wayne E. '66 (MAR) Hancock, MI Resurrection Church.
Marcotte, William '60 (SB) Fontana, CA Kaiser Permanente Hospital.
Marcouiller, Douglas *s.j.* '86 (BO) [W] Chestnut Hill, MA The Jesuit Community at Boston College.
Marcoux, A. Stephen, III '93 (MAN) Hanover, NH St. Denis Church.
Marcoux, John *m.s.a.* '87 (NOR) [F] Cromwell, CT Society of the Missionaries of the Holy Apostles.
Marcucci, John A. '68 (PIT) Glenshaw, PA St. Mary of the Assumption Church.
Marczewski, Robert '95 (PH) [2] Philadelphia, PA St. Adalbert Church.
Marczewski, Ronald J. (NEW) [10] Elizabeth, NJ St. Patrick's Church.
Marczewski, Ronald J. '74 (NEW) [2] Elizabeth, NJ St. Adalbert's Church.
Marczuk, Msgr. Scott L. *j.c.l.* '81 (LR) [1] Little Rock, AR Cathedral of St. Andrew.
Marczynski, Wladyslaw '90 (GAY) [1] Alpena, MI St. Anne Church.
Mardian, Pius '44 (SFS) Retired.
Marecki, Ronald (ROC) Bath, NY Soliders' Home and Veterans' Hospital.
Marecki, Ronald '83 (SP) [5] Clearwater, FL St. Michael The Archangel Church.
Marek, Dean V. '65 (MIL) On Duty Outside the Archdiocese.
Marek, Dean V. '65 (WIN) On Special or Other Diocesan Assignment.
Marek, Ray John *o.m.i.* '89 (SAT) [M] San Antonio, TX De Mazenod House.
Marek, Walter '46 (GAY) Retired.
Mares, Philip W. *m.m.* '86 (NY) [DD] Maryknoll, NY Maryknoll Fathers and Brothers.
Maresca, Msgr. Ralph '78 (BRK) Special Assignment.
Maresh, Mark A. '94 (GI) Anselmo, NE St. Anselm's Church.
Marflak, Albert *o.s.b.* '75 (CLV) [O] Cleveland, OH Benedictine Order of Cleveland.
Marflak, Albert *o.s.b.* '75 (ROM) Chesterland, OH Most Holy Trinity Church.
Marfori, Antonio '78 (SCL) Zimmerman, MN St. Pius X Church.
Margason, Msgr. James E. '71 (BEL) [6] Belleville, IL St. Luke Church; [9] Belleville, IL Chapel of St. John Children's Home Church; Lebanon, IL St. Joseph Church; [C] Belleville, IL St. John Children's Home; [J] Belleville, IL The Catholic Diocese of Belleville Deposit and Loan Fund; [J] Belleville, IL The Catholic Diocese of Belleville Custodial Fund; [J] Belleville, IL The Catholic Diocese of Belleville Group Health Insurance Fund; [J] Belleville, IL The Catholic Diocese of Belleville Property Insurance Fund; [J] Belleville, IL The Catholic Diocese of Belleville Ministry Formation Fund.
Margevicius, Thomas S. '99 (STP) [8] St. Paul, MN The Nativity of Our Lord Church.
Marggraf, Brian *ss.cc.* '55 (FR) [I] Fairhaven, MA Sacred Hearts Provincial House.
Margherio, Ronald L. *o.s.b.* '78 (PEO) [A] Peru, IL St. Bede Abbey and Academy.
Margola, Joseph F. '84 (PCE) On Duty Outside the Diocese.
Marhafer, Maury *o.f.m.conv.* '54 (FgM) Conventual Franciscan Foreign Missions.
Maria Alabanza de la Trin, David A. *s.e.m.v.* '95 (ARE) Hatillo, PR Our Lady of Guadalupe Church.
Mariados, Lipton '87 (SFS) Pierre, SD SS. Peter and Paul Church.
Marian, Anthony S. '58 (NY) Poughkeepsie, NY Vassar Brothers Hospital.
Marian, Francis Susai '83 (NY) [10] Yonkers, NY St. Joseph Church.
Mariani, J. Guilbert *s.o.l.t.* '97 (CC) [H] Robstown, TX Society of Our Lady of the Most Holy Trinity.
Mariano, Angelo *s.j.* '92 (SJ) [L] Los Gatos, CA Sacred Heart Jesuit Center.
Mariano, John M. '58 (BRK) Released from Diocesan Assignment.
Marick, Thomas D. '97 (STN) Honolulu, Byzantine Missions Church.
Marickovic, Thomas C. '81 (HBG) Lewistown, PA Sacred Heart of Jesus Church; Mifflintown, PA St. Jude Church.
Marie, Adrien Ste. *c.s.c.* '50 (P) [B] Portland, OR University of Portland.
Marie, Louis '70 (RC) [B] Piedmont, SD Holy Nativity Monastery.
Marien, Roy C. '85 (PT) Destin, FL Church of the Resurrection.
Marier, Edward '88 (SPK) Cusick, WA Our Lady of Sorrows Church; Ione, WA St. Bernard Church; Metaline Falls, WA St. Joseph Church; Newport, WA St. Anthony Church; Usk, WA St. Jude Church.
Marier, Euclid A. '72 (OG) Potsdam, NY St. Mary Church; Retired.
Marin, John L. '83 (MET) On Duty Outside the Diocese.
Marin, Jose '93 (TYL) Kilgore, TX Christ the King Church.
Marin, Miguel '78 (ELP) Absent on Leave.
Marin, Moises '95 (CHI) Palatine, IL Mission Juan Diego Church.
Marin, Tomas M. '89 (MIA) [1] Miami, FL St. Mary's Church; [L] Miami Shores, FL Archdiocese of Miami Millennium Appeal, Inc.; [L] Miami Shores, FL Archdiocese of Miami, Inc.
Marinacci, Msgr. Nicholas '38 (NY) [102] New York, NY St. Patrick Old Church; Retired.
Marinak, Andrew P. '56 (HBG) Cornwall, PA Sacred Heart of Jesus Church.
Marincel, Frank '58 (DUL) Retired.
Marine, Msgr. John C. '76 (PH) On Special or Other Archdiocesan Assignment.
Maring, William J. *s.j.* '45 (SJ) [L] Los Gatos, CA Sacred Heart Jesuit Center.
Marini, Francis J. *j.d.*, *j.c.o.d.* '95 (SAM) Brooklyn, NY Cathedral of Our Lady of Lebanon.
Marini, John L. *c.s.sp.* '92 (CHI) [126] Chicago, IL St. Mary Magdalene Church.
Marini, Joseph J. '52 (SFR) San Bruno, CA St. Robert Church; Retired.
Marini, Michael A. '72 (MRY) Santa Cruz, CA Holy Cross Church.
Marinko, John S. '55 (SCR) Retired; [N] Dunmore, PA Villa St. Joseph.
Marino, Christopher '93 (MIA) [C] Miami, FL Archbishop Curley-Notre Dame High School.
Marino, Edward J. *c.s.* '57 (PRO) [M] North Kingstown, RI Scalabrini Villa.
Marino, Francis J. *s.m.* '57 (MET) [L] Phillipsburg, NJ The Anawim Community.
Marino, John J. *o.f.m.* '88 (BO) [BB] Boston, MA St. Anthony Shrine.
Marino, Msgr. Joseph '79 (BIR) On Duty Outside the Diocese.
Marino, Msgr. Joseph T. '75 (PH) Havertown, PA St. Denis Church.
Marino, Msgr. Ronald T. '73 (BRK) [126] Brooklyn, NY St. Rosalia-Regina Pacis Church; [U] Brooklyn, NY Catholic Migration & Refugee Office, Catholic Migration Services, Inc.; [U] Brooklyn, NY Catholic Migration & Refugee Office, Catholic Migration Services, Inc.; [U] Brooklyn, NY Catholic Migration & Refugee Office, Catholic Migration Services, Inc.; [U] Brooklyn, NY Catholic Migration & Refugee Office, Catholic Migration Services, Inc.; [U] Brooklyn, NY Catholic Migration & Refugee Office, Catholic Migration Services, Inc.; [U] Brooklyn, NY Catholic Migration & Refugee Office, Catholic Migration Services, Inc.
Marino, Umberto J. '54 (NY) On Duty Outside the Archdiocese.
Marinucci, Steven J. (PH) [36] Philadelphia, PA St. Clement Church.
Maristany, Edward G. '80 (CHI) [W] Chicago, IL Prelature of the Holy Cross and Opus Dei.
Maristela, Victor T. '87 (SD) [3] Chula Vista, CA St. Pius X Church.
Marjanczyk, Msgr. Joseph A. '45 (NEW) [6] Bayonne, NJ Mt. Carmel Church; Retired.
Markalonis, Joseph A. *t.o.r.* '66 (PIT) [O] Pittsburgh, PA Franciscan Friars, T.O.R.; [O] Pittsburgh, PA Third Order Regular of Saint Francis - Province of the Most Sacred Heart of Jesus.
Markell, John W. '84 (PIT) Mt. Lebanon, PA St. Bernard Church.
Markelz, Carl *o.carm.* '91 (CHI) [N] Chicago, IL Carmelite Priory of St. Cyril.
Markelz, Carl J. *o.carm.* '91 (CHI) [D] Chicago, IL Mt. Carmel High School.
Markert, Leo F. '62 (ALB) Rotterdam, NY St. Gabriel the Archangel Church.
Market, John C. *o.f.m.* '45 (DET) [5] Southfield, MI St. Michael Church.
Markewuch, Uriy '65 (PHU) Whippany, NJ St. John the Baptist Church.
Markey, Earle L. *s.j.* '63 (WOR) [N] Worcester, MA Jesuits of Holy Cross College, Inc.
Markey, Gerard A. *s.s.c.* '71 (BRK) [V] Kew Gardens, NY St. Columbans Foreign Mission Society.
Markey, Greg J. '99 (BGP) [18] Bridgeport, CT St. Peter Church.
Markey, John *o.p.* '61 (NO) [P] New Orleans, LA Dominican Friars, Southern Dominican Province of St. Martin de Porres; [S] Metairie, LA Southern Dominican Foundation.
Markey, John *o.p.* '93 (MIA) [B] Miami, FL Barry University.
Markey, John J. *o.p.* '93 (NO) [25] New Orleans, LA St. Anthony of Padua Church.
Markey, John J. *o.p.* '93 (OAK) [N] Oakland, CA Order of Preachers (Southern Province).
Markey, Thomas J. '51 (WOR) [3] Worcester, MA Blessed Sacrament Church.
Markham, Msgr. James J. '51 (MAN) [11] Manchester, NH St. John the Baptist Church; Retired.
Markham, John W. '54 (DET) [21] Detroit, MI St. Elizabeth Church; Retired.
Markiewicz, Stanley T. *o.s.b.* '61 (GBG) [2] Latrobe, PA St. Vincent Basilica Church; [H] Latrobe, PA Saint Vincent Archabbey.
Markley, Edward P. *o.s.b.* '66 (BIR) [E] Cullman, AL St. Bernard Abbey.

Markley, Edward P. *o.s.b.* '66 (MOB) Lillian, AL St. Joseph Church.
Marko, Andrew '98 (SJP) Austintown, OH St. Anne Church.
Markowski, Clement A. '53 (SCR) Retired; [N] Dunmore, PA Villa St. Joseph.
Marks, Mark (SFR) Absent on Leave.
Marks, Teodoro Gray '49 (SJN) Retired.
Marks, Thomas C. '79 (LR) Forrest City, AR St. Francis of Assisi Church; Wynne, AR St. Peter's Church.
Marks, William '92 (IND) Bright, IN St. Teresa Benedicta of the Cross Church.
Markunas, Robert '76 (ORL) [8] Orlando, FL St. Isaac Jogues Church; Special Assignment.
Markus, Anthony L. '80 (CHI) Evergreen Park, IL Most Holy Redeemer Church.
Markwell, Benjamin *o.f.m.cap.* '66 (FgM) Capuchin Foreign Missions.
Markwell, George *m.afr.* '65 (WDC) [M] Washington, DC Missionaries of Africa.
Marley, Edward G. *c.s.sp.* '44 (LR) Center Ridge, AR St. Joseph's Church.
Marley, Msgr. Michael F. '40 (PH) [95] Philadelphia, PA St. Martin of Tours Church; Retired.
Marley, Thomas J. *c.s.p.* '49 (NY) [DD] Jamaica Estates, NY Paulist Fathers Generalate.
Marley, Thomas J. *c.s.p.* '49 (PMB) [H] Vero Beach, FL Paulist Fathers Residence.
Marley, William F. *m.m.* '52 (FgM) Maryknoll Foreign Missions.
Marmol, Richard '97 (SJN) [1] San Juan, PR Catedral De San Juan Bautista Church.
Marneni, Ignatius '69 (PH) [3] Norristown, PA St. Patrick Church.
Marneni, M. Julian '67 (WH) [1] Huntington, WV St. Joseph's Church; Wayne, WV Nativity of Our Lord Church.
Maro, Wayne *c.p.p.s.* '86 (LA) [BB] Los Angeles, CA Archdiocesan Office for Campus Ministry.
Marohn, Donald '62 (SFS) On Leave of Absence.
Maroney, Frank (DEN) Minturn, CO St. Patrick's Church.
Maroney, Maurice J. '67 (HRT) [3] Milford, CT St. Gabriel Church.
Maroon, Donald M. '67 (COL) Wellston, OH SS. Peter and Paul Church.
Maroon, Msgr. William J. '67 (COL) Hilliard, OH St. Brendan Church.
Maroor, Joseph '63 (MIA) Pembroke Pines, FL St. Maximilian Kolbe Church.
Marot, Roger L. '50 (PRO) Retired; [N] Woonsocket, RI Fr. Marot CYO Center.
Marotta, Robert G. '63 (NEW) Retired.
Maroun, George F. '74 (OG) [A] Ogdensburg, NY Wadhams Hall.
Maroun, Sharbel G. '89 (OLL) Minneapolis, MN St. Maron Church.
Marpes, Thomas M. '50 (PIT) [62] Pittsburgh, PA St. Pius X Church.
Marquard, Elmer E. '66 (CLV) North Olmsted, OH St. Richard Church.
Marquardt, Donald '51 (GB) Retired.
Marquardt, John J. '44 (TLS) Antlers, OK St. Agnes Church.
Marquart, Ernest J. '70 (SPC) Mountain View, MO St. John Vianney Church.
Marquart, Joseph M. '57 (SEA) Everett, WA St. Mary Magdalen Church.
Marquez, Celso *m.sp.s.* '97 (LA) Huntington Park, CA St. Martha Church.
Marquez, Esteban '95 (LA) Wilmington, CA Holy Family Church.
Marquez, Jose E. '99 (NEW) Bergenfield, NJ St. John the Evangelist Church.
Marquis, Clif *s.t.* (ORG) (SFS) [I] Santa Ana, CA Trinitarian Missionaries/Missionary Servants of the Most Holy Trinity.
Marquis, J. Alphee '39 (PRT) Retired.
Marquis, Paul R. '86 (PRT) Brewer, ME St. Teresa's Church; [H] Bangor, ME St. Joseph Hospital.
Marquis, Raymond *o.m.i.* '74 (FgM) Oblates Foreign Missions.
Marquis, William P. *o.p.* '83 (PRO) [P] Providence, RI St. Thomas Aquinas Priory at Providence College.
Marr, James G. '60 (STU) Retired.
Marr, Thomas P. '70 (MAD) Watertown, WI St. Bernard Church.
Marra, Msgr. Anthony C. '51 (SCR) [3] Dunmore, PA St. Anthony of Padua Church.
Marra, James *s.d.b.* '83 (NY) [2] Port Chester, NY Corpus Christi Church.
Marrapese, Casto *p.i.m.e.* '44 (COL) [H] Newark, OH P.I.M.E. Mission & Retreat Center.
Marreddy, Allam '86 (NY) [143] Bronx, NY St. Francis Xavier Church.
Marrell, Dennis '78 (LA) Covina, CA St. Louise de Marillac Church.
Marrell, Dennis P. '78 (LA) Military and VA Chaplains.
Marren, Hugh M. '76 (ATL) Duluth, GA St. Benedict Church.
Marren, Martin T. '84 (CHI) [2] Oak Lawn, IL St. Gerald Church.
Marrero, Adan *s.d.b.* '97 (SJN) Catano, PR San Francisco de Sales Church.
Marrion, Malachy *o.c.s.o.* '54 (ARL) [J] Berryville, VA Cistercian Abbey of Our Lady of the Holy Cross.
Marro, Nicholas A. *c.s.* '63 (CHI) [115] Chicago, IL Santa Lucia-Santa Maria Incoronata Church.
Marro, Simeon D. *o.carm.* '55 (GBG) [H] Boliver, PA Mount Carmel Hermitage.
Marrodan, Francisco J. *c.m.* '54 (ARE) [3] Manati, PR Sagrada Familia Church.
Marrokal, Donald *c.r.* '58 (Y) Retired.
Marron, Msgr. James '43 (MRY) Retired.
Marron, James F. '62 (BRK) [228] Queens, NY St. Pius X Church.
Marron, Joseph *c.ss.r.* '48 (BRK) [107] Brooklyn, NY Our Lady of Perpetual Help Basilica Church.
Marron, Leonard J. *m.m.* '57 (FgM) Maryknoll Foreign Missions.
Marron, Patrick L. '67 (SAT) Leon Springs, TX St. Elizabeth Ann Seton Church.
Marrone, Robert J. '73 (CLV) [64] Cleveland, OH St. Peter Church.
Marroquin, Luis Antonio '86 (WDC) [5] Silver Spring, MD Christ the King Church.
Marrow, Stanley B. *s.j.* '61 (BO) [W] Boston, MA The Society of Jesus of New England-Provincial Offices; [W] Cambridge, MA Weston Jesuit Community.
Marrufo, Ramon R. '76 (SD) Vista, CA St. Francis of Assisi Church.
Marschner, Msgr. Aloysius J. '36 (STL) Retired.
Marse, John J. '81 (NO) Norco, LA Sacred Heart of Jesus Church.
Marsh, Ivan C. *o.carm* '80 (GAL) [A] Houston, TX St. Mary's Seminary.
Marsh, Robert R. *s.j.* '96 (OAK) [N] Berkeley, CA Jesuit Community at Jesuit School of Theology at Berkeley.
Marshall, David C. *c.s.sp.* '46 (VEN) [G] Sarasota, FL Congregation of the Holy Ghost.
Marshall, Eugene C. *o.s.b.* '50 (OKL) McLoud, OK St. Vincent de Paul Church; [I] Shawnee, OK St. Gregory's Abbey.
Marshall, Hugh *s.t.* '56 (WDC) [M] Adelphi, MD Missionary Servants of the Most Holy Trinity.
Marshall, Msgr. James C. '57 (STU) [3] Steubenville, OH Holy Rosary Church.
Marshall, James C. '59 (STL) Glasgow Village, MO St. Pius X Church.
Marshall, John J. '59 (ALT) [4] Johnstown, PA SS. Casmir & Emerich Church.
Marshall, Joseph M. *s.m.* '90 (BAL) Sykesville, MD St. Joseph Church.
Marshall, Oswald J. *s.j.* '46 (DET) [P] Clarkston, MI Colombiere Center.
Marshall, Patrick M. '79 (CHI) [V] Chicago, IL Ministry in Higher Education.
Marshall, Paul M. *s.m.* '76 (CIN) [M] Dayton, OH Marianist Provincialate.
Marshall, Robert A. '61 (STL) Manchester, MO St. Joseph Church.
Marshall, Robert W. '00 (MEM) [12] Memphis, TN Incarnation Church.
Marshall, Thomas R. *c.s.p.* '59 (NY) [DD] Jamaica Estates, NY Paulist Fathers Generalate.
Marshall, William '63 (OAK) Retired.
Marsicek, Robert *s.d.s.* '68 (MIL) [P] Milwaukee, WI Salvatorian Provincial Residence.
Marsick, James J. '72 (CLV) Cuyahoga Falls, OH St. Joseph Church.
Marszal, Theodore '68 (CLV) [2] Garfield Heights, OH SS. Peter and Paul Church.
Marszalek, Paul B. '52 (CHI) Retired.
Marta, Raul '72 (FRS) Tulare, CA St. Aloysius Church.
Marteka, Anthony T. '61 (WOR) Grafton, MA St. Philip's Church.
Martel, C. James '70 (PRT) Pittsfield, ME St. Agnes Church.
Martel, Leo E. '63 (BO) Chelmsford, MA St. Mary Church.
Martel, Luc *a.a.* '73 (BO) [W] Boston, MA Assumptionist Center.
Martel, Marcel I. '79 (MAN) [4] Nashua, NH St. Francis Xavier Church.
Martel, Robert T. '49 (PRT) Retired; [I] Waterville, ME Mt. St. Joseph Priest Retirement Home.
Martell, James '88 (MEM) [26] Memphis, TN Our Lady of Sorrows Church.
Martelli, Jose M. *c.s.c.* '73 (FTW) On Duty Outside the Diocese; [B] Notre Dame, IN University of Notre Dame Du Lac; [J] South Bend, IN Congregation of Holy Cross, Indiana Province, Provincial House.
Martelli, Jose M. *c.s.c.* '73 (SB) Coachella, CA Our Lady of Soledad Church.
Martello, Ernest *o.s.c.* '70 (FgM) Crosier Foreign Missions.
Martello, Lawrence N. '74 (CLV) Amherst, OH St. Joseph Church.
Martens, L. Gene *s.j.* '63 (STL) [P] St. Louis, MO Hallahan House; [P] St. Louis, MO The Jesuits of the Missouri Province; [V] St. Louis, MO The Jesuits of the Missouri Province.
Martensen, Carsten *s.j.* '77 (RVC) Oceanside, NY St. Anthony Church.
Marterior, Raul A. *o.p.* '94 (GAL) [22] Houston, TX St. Christopher Church.
Marth, Msgr. Loydell J. '56 (FRS) Buttonwillow, CA St. Mary Church; Taft, CA St. Mary Church.
Marthaler, Andrew '90 (SCL) Elbow Lake, MN St. Olaf Church; Tintah, MN St. Gall's Church.
Marthaler, Berard L. *o.f.m.conv.* '52 (WDC) [5] Washington, DC St. Anthony Church; [B] Washington, DC St. Bonaventure Friary; [C] Washington, DC Catholic University of America, The.
Marti, Julio *l.c.* '97 (HRT) [B] Cheshire, CT Novitiate of the Legion of Christ.
Marti, Ramon *sch.p.* '55 (LA) Arcadia, CA Annunciation Church; Duarte, CA City of Hope Medical Center.
Marti, Thomas J. *m.m.* '65 (NY) [DD] Maryknoll, NY Maryknoll Fathers and Brothers.
Marti, Tony '96 (LA) [F] La Canada Flintridge, CA St. Francis High School.
Martignetti, Richard *o.f.m.* '97 (NY) [DD] New York, NY Franciscan Province of the Immaculate Conception.
Martignon, John E. '84 (MAR) Cooks, MI St. Mary Magdalene Church; Garden, MI St. John the Baptist Church; Nahma, MI St. Andrew Church.
Martin, Andrew E. '67 (CAM) [7] Camden, NJ St. Joseph's Pro-Church; [A] Cherry Hill, NJ Camden Catholic High School.
Martin, Anselm *o.f.m.cap.* '45 (PH) [80] Philadelphia, PA St. John the Evangelist Church.
Martin, Benjamin '75 (DOD) LaCrosse, KS St. Michael Church; Liebenthal, KS St. Joseph Church.
Martin, C. Lou '76 (BAL) [10] Baltimore, MD St. Anthony of Padua Church; [66] Baltimore, MD Most Precious Blood Church.
Martin, Charles A. *c.s.p.* (BO) [BB] Boston, MA Chapel of the Holy Spirit.
Martin, Charles A. *c.s.p.* '65 (BO) [P] Boston, MA Paulist Center.
Martin, Charles A. *c.s.p.* '65 (STP) [V] Minneapolis, MN Newman Center at St. Lawrence.
Martin, Clarence A. *s.j.* '46 (ALN) [A] Wernersville, PA Jesuit Center.
Martin, Clifford A. '76 (SFR) [4] San Mateo, CA St. Timothy Church.
Martin, Cristobal *m.id.* '96 (NY) [180] Bronx, NY Santa Maria Church.
Martin, Msgr. Daniel J. '43 (E) Retired.
Martin, David A. '76 (EVN) Washington, IN St. Simon Church.
Martin, David L. '73 (ARL) Gordonsville, VA St. Mark's Church; Orange, VA St. John's Church.
Martin, Dean J. '88 (BR) Plaquemine, LA St. Clement of Rome Church; Plaquemine, LA St. John the Evangelist Church.
Martin, Dennis A. '75 (E) Erie, PA St. Vincent's Health Center; [G] Erie, PA Saint Vincent Health Center.
Martin, Dennis C. '67 (DAV) Washington, IA St. James Church.
Martin, Diodado '66 (LA) Retired.
Martin, Donald *s.j.* (NO) [A] New Orleans, LA Notre Dame Seminary Graduate School of Theology.
Martin, Emilio '52 (MIA) [5] Hialeah, FL St. John the Apostle Church.
Martin, Francis '56 (WDC) Special Ministries.
Martin, Francis T. '39 (LAN) Retired.
Martin, Msgr. Gerald F. '54 (DET) Retired.
Martin, Gerard R. '73 (BR) [21] Baton Rouge, LA St. Thomas More Church.
Martin, Gilmer J. '74 (NO) [8] Metairie, LA St. Edward the Confessor Church.
Martin, Harry '66 (SAT) San Antonio, TX Audie Murphy VA Hospital.
Martin, Hilary *o.p.* '55 (OAK) [4] Berkeley, CA St. Mary Magdalen Church.
Martin, Msgr. Ignatius '41 (LAF) Retired.
Martin, J. Dennis *c.m.* '62 (STL) [P] St. Louis, MO Lazarist Residence; [R] Normandy, MO Marillac Provincial House.
Martin, James (SAG) [E] Saginaw, MI St. Mary's Medical Center of Saginaw, Inc.
Martin, James A. *s.j.* '34 (WDC) [M] Washington, DC The Jesuit Community at Georgetown University.
Martin, James J. '63 (PH) [60] Philadelphia, PA Holy Family Church.
Martin, James J. '68 (CHI) [49] Chicago, IL St. Dorothy Church.
Martin, James J. *s.j.* '99 (BO) [W] Boston, MA The Society of Jesus of New England-Provincial Offices.
Martin, James J. *s.j.* '99 (NY) [DD] New York, NY "America;" Residence and publication office of the America Press.
Martin, Joel W. *o.s.b.* '91 (BIR) [B] Cullman, AL St. Bernard Preparatory School Educational Foundation; [E] Cullman, AL St. Bernard Abbey.
Martin, John *a.a.* '57 (BO) [W] Boston, MA Assumptionist Center.
Martin, John '65 (NEW) [24] Jersey City, NJ Parish of the Resurrection Church.
Martin, John B. '56 (NEW) [34] Newark, NJ Sacred

Heart Church.
Martin, John F. *s.j.* '74 (WDC) [M] Washington, DC The Jesuit Community at Georgetown University.
Martin, John Hilary *o.p.* '55 (OAK) [A] Berkeley, CA Dominican School of Philosophy and Theology.
Martin, John J. '65 (SR) Mendocino, CA St. Anthony Church.
Martin, Msgr. John J. '72 (ALN) Colesville, PA Assumption B.V.M. Church.
Martin, Msgr. John P. '61 (RVC) New Hyde Park, NY Holy Spirit Church.
Martin, John P. *m.m.* '66 (FgM) Maryknoll Foreign Missions.
Martin, Jon C. '65 (BO) Middleton, MA St. Agnes Church; Middleton, MA Essex County Correctional Facility.
Martin, Jose *o.p.* '62 (PCE) Yauco, PR Holy Rossary Church.
Martin, Msgr. Joseph A. '67 (NY) Fishkill, NY Church of St. Mary, Mother of the.
Martin, Joseph C. *s.s.* '48 (BAL) Special Assignment; [S] Baltimore, MD Sulpician Provincial House.
Martin, Joseph I. '56 (BO) Society of St. James the Apostle.
Martin, Joseph I. '56 (FgM) Society of St. James the Apostle.
Martin, Joseph P. '64 (Y) [7] Youngstown, OH Sacred Heart of Jesus Church.
Martin, Kenneth '77 (NEW) Newark, NJ St. James Hospital; Newark, NJ St. Michael Medical Center; [G] Newark, NJ St. James Hospital.
Martin, Kenneth J. '89 (WIL) On Duty Outside the Diocese.
Martin, Msgr. Kieran J. '50 (BRK) [141] Brooklyn, NY St. Thomas Aquinas Church; Retired.
Martin, Larok Obwona '80 (OKL) [13] Oklahoma City, OK St. Joseph Church.
Martin, Leon J. *s.a.c.* '75 (MIL) [P] Milwaukee, WI Pallotti House.
Martin, Leonard A. *s.j.* '73 (SCR) [C] Scranton, PA University of Scranton; [E] Scranton, PA Scranton Preparatory School.
Martin, Luis '55 (ELP) [35] El Paso, TX San Antonio Church.
Martin, Malcolm *s.a.* '62 (BO) [P] Brockton, MA Chapel of Our Savior-Catholic Pastoral and Information Center; [W] Brockton, MA Chapel of Our Saviour; [BB] Brockton, MA Chapel of Our Saviour.
Martin, Marciano G. *c.pp.s.* (SP) Spring Hill, FL Saint Joan of Arc Church.
Martin, Michael *o.f.m.conv.* '89 (BAL) [C] Baltimore, MD Archbishop Curley High School; [S] Baltimore, MD Immaculate Heart of Mary Friary.
Martin, Michael J. *c.s.p.* '77 (WDC) [B] Washington, DC St. Paul's College.
Martin, Norman F. *s.j.* '47 (SJ) [B] Santa Clara, CA Santa Clara University.
Martin, Normand *s.m.* '59 (DET) [E] Harper Woods, MI Notre Dame High School.
Martin, Patrick (PRT) Biddeford, ME St. Joseph's Church.
Martin, Msgr. Paul M. '58 (ORG) San Juan Capistrano, CA Mission Basilica Church.
Martin, Ralph L. '65 (WIL) Smyrna, DE St. Polycarp Church; Smyrna, MD Delaware Home & Hospital for the Chronically Ill.
Martin, Raymond D. (BAL) [69] Baltimore, MD Our Lady of Good Counsel Church.
Martin, Reginald *o.p.* '74 (SEA) [22] Seattle, WA Blessed Sacrament Church.
Martin, Richard B. '66 (ARL) Burke, VA Church of the Nativity.
Martin, Richard J. '63 (CHI) Evergreen Park, IL Most Holy Redeemer Church.
Martin, Robert *c.ss.r.* '50 (FgM) Redemptorist Foreign Missions.
Martin, Robert A. '83 (BUF) Elba, NY Our Lady of Fatima Church; [D] Batavia, NY Notre Dame High School of Batavia.
Martin, Roger '51 (OG) Retired.
Martin, Roosevelt '88 (GAL) [46] Fort Bend Co., TX St. Mark the Evangelist Church.
Martin, Samuel (LC) [C] Wisconsin Rapids, WI Wisconsin Rapids Area Catholic Schools; [C] Wisconsin Rapids, WI Wisconsin Rapids Area Catholic Schools.
Martin, Sean (DAL) [B] Irving, TX University of Dallas.
Martin, Sean Charles '81 (DAL) [4] Dallas, TX Christ the King Church.
Martin, Stephen E. '98 (MOB) On Leave from the Archdiocese.
Martin, Thomas *o.c.d.* '61 (MIL) [P] Milwaukee, WI Provincial Offices - Discalced Carmelites.
Martin, Thomas '70 (OAK) [3] Berkeley, CA St. Joseph The Worker Church.
Martin, Thomas A. '79 (KAL) Mendon, MI St. Edward Church.
Martin, Thomas F. '56 (CLV) [24] Cleveland, OH St. Francis Church; [W] Cleveland, OH Office of Hispanic Ministry.
Martin, Thomas F. *o.s.a.* '69 (CHI) [N] Olympia Fields, IL The Augustinians-Provincialate.
Martin, Thomas F. *o.s.a.* '69 (PH) [B] Villanova, PA St. Augustine Friary; [C] Villanova, PA Villanova University.
Martin, Thomas P. *s.j.* '66 (BAL) [S] Baltimore, MD Jesuit Fathers and Brothers Maryland Provincial Curia.
Martin, Vicente '75 (VEN) Punta Gorda, FL Sacred Heart Church.
Martin, Victor T. '80 (BGP) [7] Fairfield, CT St. Thomas Aquinas Church.
Martin, Warren S. *s.j.* '32 (NO) [P] New Orleans, LA Ignatius Residence.
Martin, William *o.m.i.* '61 (PMB) [4] West Palm Beach, FL St. John Fisher Church; [C] West Palm Beach, FL Rosarian Academy.
Martin, William '63 (NY) On Special or Other (Arch)Diocesan Assignment.
Martin, Msgr. William F. '56 (GRY) Retired.
Martin, William F. '63 (NY) On Duty Outside the Archdiocese.
Martin, William F. '78 (STP) Oakdale, MN Guardian Angels Church.
Martin, William J. '50 (TOL) Marysdale, OH Immaculate Conception Church; The Bend, OH St. Stephen Church.
Martin, William J. '55 (CHI) Berwyn, IL St. Leonard Church; Retired.
Martin, William J. '71 (L) [69] Louisville, KY St. Rita Church.
Martin, Zenaido '91 (ARE) [2] Camuy, PR Our Lady of the Miraculous Medal Church.
Martin-Calama, Florian '95 (DEN) [A] Denver, CO Redemptoris Mater House of Formation; [A] Denver, CO St. John Vianney Theological Seminary; [Q] Denver, CO Family of Nazareth, Inc.
Martin-Rono, Antonio Isidro '79 (SJ) [15] San Jose, CA St. Maria Goretti Church.
Martina, Joseph, Jr. '89 (SHP) Bossier City, LA Christ the King Church.
Martine, Michael '97 (NY) Monroe, NY Sacred Heart Church.
Martineau, Albert P. *o.m.i.* '59 (BO) [BB] Lowell, MA St. Joseph the Worker Shrine.
Martineau, Laurier J. '59 (BO) [3] Marlborough, MA St. Mary Church.
Martineau, Maurice J. '63 (LKC) Lake Arthur, LA Our Lady of the Lake Church.
Martinek, John B. '73 (FBK) Kotzebue, AK St. Francis Xavier Church.
Martinez, Adam '85 (AUS) Lockhart, TX St. Mary's Church.
Martinez, Alfredo (CGS) Retired.
Martinez, Anthony L. '89 (SFE) Moriarty, NM Estancia Valley Catholic Church.
Martinez, Antonio *o.a.r* '48 (LSC) [B] Mesilla, NM Augustinian Recollect Fathers.
Martinez, Benjamin *c.m.f.* '58 (MET) [4] Perth Amboy, NJ Our Lady of Fatima Church.
Martinez, Carlos '89 (ORG) Inactive Leave.
Martinez, Celso '52 (SJN) [5] Carolina, PR Santo Cristo de los Milagros Church.
Martinez, Charlie *o.f.m.* '80 (DEN) [1] Denver, CO Cathedral of the Immaculate Conception.
Martinez, Felipe A. '96 (TUC) Somerton, AZ Immaculate Heart of Mary Church.
Martinez, Felipe J. *c.m.* '55 (STL) Brewer, MO Christ the Savior Church.
Martinez, Francisco (ARE) Retired.
Martinez, Francisco Xavier *s.t.l.* (CC) [4] Corpus Christi, TX Holy Family Church; [B] Corpus Christi, TX Holy Family School.
Martinez, Frank Perez *o.s.b.* '97 (MGZ) [6] Mayaquez, PR Sacred Heart Church.
Martinez, Frank R. '82 (DAV) Special Assignment; [M] Davenport, IA St. Vincent Center.
Martinez, German *o.s.b.* '67 (BGP) [1] Greenwich, CT St. Mary Church.
Martinez, Gil *s.j.* (CIN) [M] Cincinnati, OH Jesuit Community at St. Xavier High School.
Martinez, Gilbert *c.s.p.* '95 (LA) [90] Los Angeles, CA St. Sebastian Church.
Martinez, Gilberto *s.s.p.* '75 (LA) [Q] Los Angeles, CA Society of St. Paul.
Martinez, Ignacio '93 (MRY) Paso Robles, CA St. Rose Church.
Martinez, James E. *o.s.a.* '57 (PH) Bryn Mawr, PA Our Mother of Good Counsel Church; [AA] Bryn Mawr, PA Augustinians Friars (O.S.A.).
Martinez, Joachim *s.j.* '55 (BO) [3] Somerville, MA St. Benedict Church.
Martinez, John J. *s.j.* '62 (RIC) VA St. John Church.
Martinez, Jonas Rivera *c.s.sp.* '98 (SJN) [F] Dorado, PR Santuario del Espiritu Santo.
Martinez, Jose Florencio '95 (PCE) Jayuya, PR Our Lady of Monserrate Church.
Martinez, Jose Luis *o.a.r.* '64 (LA) [Q] Oxnard, CA St. Augustine Priory O.A.R.
Martinez, Juan *s.d.b.* '73 (SJN) [28] San Juan, PR San Juan Bosco Church.
Martinez, Leo '63 (SAT) Special Assignment; On Duty Outside the Archdiocese.
Martinez, Leonel *o.s.a.* '34 (GAL) Pasadena, TX Blessed Juan Diego Church.
Martinez, Lucian C. *s.j.* '99 (CHL) [9] Charlotte, NC St. Peter Church; [J] Charlotte, NC Jesuit Community.
Martinez, Luis '96 (SR) On Leave.
Martinez, Manuel '66 (SAT) On Duty Outside the Archdiocese.
Martinez, Marco T. *s.j.* '96 (OAK) [N] Berkeley, CA Jesuit Community at Jesuit School of Theology at Berkeley.
Martinez, Marcos '52 (CC) [9] Corpus Christi, TX Our Lady of the Pillar Church.
Martinez, Mariano '52 (LAR) Rio Bravo, TX Santa Rita de Casia Independent Church.
Martinez, Mark M. '96 (LA) Norwalk, CA St. Linus Church.
Martinez, Martin S. '93 (TUC) Apache Junction, AZ St. George Church; Eloy, AZ St. Helen Church.
Martinez, Michael '89 (TUC) [25] Tucson, AZ St. Elizabeth Ann Seton Church.
Martinez, Milton *o.s.b.* '97 (BIS) [A] Richardton, ND Assumption Abbey.
Martinez, Milton '97 (FgM) American - Cassinese Congregation Foreign Missions.
Martinez, Otto *s.j.* '63 (MIA) [H] Miami, FL Villa Arrieta.
Martinez, Pastor *o.s.a.* '78 (LAR) [19] Laredo, TX St. Vincent de Paul Church.
Martinez, Raul '95 (CHI) [65] Chicago, IL St. Gall Church.
Martinez, Raymond *c.m.f.* '41 (LA) [Q] Rancho Dominguez, CA Dominguez Seminary Inc.
Martinez, Roberto *o.f.m.cap.* '96 (PCE) [5] Ponce, PR Santa Teresita Church; [E] Ponce, PR Residencia Asis.
Martinez, Roy *o.f.m.cap.* '84 (ARE) [1] Utuado, PR San Miquel Church.
Martinez, Ruben *o.m.i.* '68 (OAK) [N] Oakland, CA Oblate Provincial House & Procure.
Martinez, Tim '90 (SFE) Ranchos De Taos, NM San Francisco de Asis Church.
Martinez, Tomas *s.s.p.* '75 (LA) [Q] Los Angeles, CA Society of St. Paul.
Martinez, Vidal '70 (SFE) Albuquerque, NM University Hospital.
Martinez, Vidal *o.s.m.* '75 (CHI) [N] Chicago, IL Order of Friar Servants of Mary (Servites) United States of America Province, Inc.
Martinez, Vidal *o.s.m.* '75 (ORL) Kissimmee, FL St. Catherine of Siena Church.
Martinez, Vidal M. '70 (SFE) [8] Albuquerque, NM Our Lady of Fatima Church.
Martinez, Virgilio '65 (SJN) [34] San Juan, PR San Luis Gonzaga Church.
Martinez Tobon, Jose Dario '87 (SJN) [2] Toa Baja, PR Ntra. Sra. de la Candelaria Church.
Martinez y Alire, Jerome '76 (SFE) [1] Santa Fe, NM The Cathedral of San Francisco de Asis.
Martinez y Alire, Jerome J. '76 (SFE) [M] Albuquerque, NM Fraternidad Piadosa de Nuestro Padre Jesus Nazareno.
Martinez-Gomez, Hernando A. '66 (ARE) [3] Vega-Baja, PR The Blessed Trinity Church.
Martinez-Mari, Joaquin *s.j.* '55 (BO) [E] Boston, MA Boston College High School & Jesuit Community.
Martini, Ivo '84 (SFS) Retired.
Martini, Richard M. '80 (LA) Pacific Palisades, CA Corpus Christi Church.
Martinka, Stanley V. '61 (NU) On Duty Outside the Diocese.
Martinkovic, Joseph '54 (ALN) [2] McAdoo, PA St. Mary Church.
Martino, Cristobal *m.id.* '96 (NY) [DD] Bronx, NY Idente Missionaries - Santa Maria Residence.
Martino, Joseph F. '70 (PH) [A] Wynnewood, PA Theological Seminary of St. Charles Borromeo, Overbrook.
Martino, Nicholas '82 (PH) Jenkintown, PA Immaculate Conception Church.
Martino, Nicholas J. '82 (PH) Absent on Leave.
Martinosky, Joseph A. '57 (STU) Retired.
Martins, John C. '55 (FR) [14] Fall River, MA St. Anthony of Padua Church.
Martinson, George G. *s.j.* '73 (FgM) Provinces.
Martinson, Kieth Barry *s.j.* '75 (FgM) Provinces.
Martiny, Leon M. *o.p.* '98 (FgM) Dominican - Order of Preachers Foreign Missions.
Martis, Douglas '89 (JOL) Graduate Studies.
Martlock, Loville N. '63 (BUF) Retired.
Marto, Lawrence T. '88 (GB) [1] Marinette, WI Holy Family Church.
Martocchio, Msgr. Peter T. '57 (BO) [3] Weymouth, MA Immaculate Conception Church.
Marton, Bernard *o.cist.* '67 (DAL) [K] Irving, TX Cistercian Abbey of Our Lady of Dallas.
Marton, Henry *o.cist.* '49 (DAL) [K] Irving, TX Cistercian Abbey of Our Lady of Dallas.
Martorano, Nicholas *o.s.a.* '77 (PH) [112] Philadelphia, PA St. Nicholas of Tolentine Church; [AA] Philadelphia, PA Augustinian Community (O.S.A.).

Martusciello, Msgr. Joseph A. '54 (BRK) Retired; [V] Douglaston, NY Bishop Mugavero Residence.
Martyn, George W. *o.s.f.s.* '71 (WIL) [I] Childs, MD Oblates of St. Francis De Sales.
Martyniuk, Pawlo '92 (STF) Willimantic, CT Protection of B.V.M. Church.
Maruca, Dominic W. *s.j.* '58 (BAL) [A] Baltimore, MD St. Mary's Seminary and University.
Marucci, Msgr. Carl J. '83 (CAM) Somerdale, NJ Our Lady of Grace Church.
Marucci, Msgr. Carl J. '83 (NY) [2] New York, NY St. Agnes Church.
Marucci, Louis A. '87 (CAM) [O] Blackwood, NJ St. Pius X Retreat House.
Marullo, Lawrence *v.f.* '75 (OG) Inlet, NY St. Anthony of Padua Church; Old Forge, NY St. Bartholomew Church; Raquette Lake, NY St. William Church.
Marum, Jose *c.s.* '92 (PMB) [3] Delray Beach, FL Our Lady Queen of Peace Church.
Marus, Andrew G. '71 (BGP) [17] Bridgeport, CT St. Patrick Church.
Marusceac, Vladimir '88 (STF) Cohoes, NY SS. Peter and Paul Church; Troy, NY Protection of B.V.M. Church.
Marut, Thomas '74 (STU) Carrollton, OH Our Lady of Mercy Church; Morges, OH St. Mary Church.
Marva, Robert *o.f.m.cap.* '97 (CLV) [18] Cleveland, OH Conversion of St. Paul Church; [31] Cleveland, OH Holy Trinity - St. Edward Church; [O] Cleveland, OH St. Paul Friary.
Marvin, James J. '48 (ROC) Retired.
Marx, John '60 (ANC) Retired.
Marx, Lambert M. '44 (MAD) Retired.
Marx, Louis '66 (SB) Guasti, CA San Secondo d'Asti Church.
Marx, Paul *o.s.b.* '47 (SCL) [I] Collegeville, MN St. John's Abbey, of the Order of St. Benedict.
Marx, Paul *o.m.i.* '65 (FgM) Oblates Foreign Missions.
Marx, Robert '88 (SJ) On Leave of Absence.
Maryanski, Fabian J. '71 (BUF) [9] Cheektowaga, NY St. Philip the Apostle Church.
Maryland, Joseph A. '40 (E) Retired.
Marzen, Msgr. Francis A. '51 (HON) Retired.
Marzilli, Raphael '42 (GBG) Retired.
Marzluf, George J. '46 (COL) Retired.
Marzocchi, Mario *s.s.s.* (NY) [55] New York, NY St. Jean Baptiste Church.
Marzocchi, Mario *s.s.s.* '84 (NY) [HH] New York, NY Nocturnal Adoration Society of the United States.
Marzolf, John G. *s.j.* '66 (ALB) [N] Auriesville, NY Shrine of Our Lady of Martyrs.
Marzullo, Robert *o.p.* '78 (SB) San Bernardino, CA Arrowhead Regional Medical Center; [E] Riverside, CA St. Vincent Ferrer House.
Masabakhwa, Raphael '95 (DM) [3] Council Bluffs, IA St. Patrick Church.
Masad, Frederick F. '60 (CHR) [5] Columbia, SC St. John Neumann Church.
Masakowski, Edward M. '57 (SCR) Inkerman, PA St. Mark's Church.
Masakowski, Msgr. John C. '49 (SCR) Retired.
Masar, Joseph G. '89 (SD) [3] Chula Vista, CA St. Pius X Church.
Mascardo, Editho '83 (STO) [8] Stockton, CA St. Mary of the Assumption Church.
Mascarenhas, Oswald A. *s.j.* '66 (DET) [K] Detroit, MI Jesuit Community at the University of Detroit.
Mascareno, Jose Ramon *o.s.b.* '81 (BIR) [E] Cullman, AL St. Bernard Abbey.
Mascari, Michael *o.p.* '87 (STL) [B] St. Louis, MO Aquinas Institute of Theology.
Mascari, Michael A. *o.p.* '87 (STL) [P] St. Louis, MO St. Dominic Priory.
Mascari, Peter '52 (SFD) Retired.
Mascherino, Alphonse T. '76 (ALT) Absent on Leave.
Maschmann, Elvan *o.f.m.* '46 (STL) [P] St. Louis, MO Franciscan Friary of St. Anthony of Padua.
Masciarelli, Rudolph '49 (BO) Senior Priests.
Masciocchi, Robert *c.s.s.* '54 (BO) [Y] Waltham, MA Espousal Retreat House and Conference Center.
Mascioli, Joseph M. '57 (WH) Retired.
Mascolino, Charles E. '54 (STU) Retired.
Mascolino, Robert A. '45 (STU) Retired.
Masculino, Ramon '83 (WDC) [8] Silver Spring, MD St. Michael Church.
Masek, James J. '74 (CLV) [54] Cleveland, OH Our Lady of Lourdes Church.
Masello, David W. '78 (PRO) [1] Warren, RI St. Alexander Church.
Mash, Wesley M. '90 (HBG) [7] Harrisburg, PA St. Margaret Mary Alacoque Church.
Masiar, Paul E. '69 (ALN) [3] Saint Clair, PA Immaculate Conception Church.
Masich, Michael P. *o.f.m.cap.* '98 (PIT) [30] Pittsburgh, PA Our Lady of the Angels Church.
Masiello, John *s.d.b.* (NEW) Mahwah, NJ Immaculate Heart of Mary Church.
Masiello, Msgr. Joseph P. '69 (NEW) Westfield, NJ Holy Trinity Church.
Masin, Richard H. *p.p.* (CC) On Duty Outside the Diocese.
Maskell, A. Joseph '65 (BAL) Absent on Leave.
Maskell, Stephen J. *m.m.* '48 (NY) [DD] Maryknoll, NY Maryknoll Fathers and Brothers.
Maslach, Paul *o.f.m.* '62 (MIL) [77] Milwaukee, WI Sacred Heart Church.
Maslak, Gregory '72 (PHU) Hazleton, PA St. Michael's Church; McAdoo, PA St. Mary's Church.
Maslanka, Andrew '80 (FBK) Galena, AK St. John Berchman Church; Koyukuk, AK St. Patrick Church; Nulato, AK Our Lady of the Snows Church.
Maslar, William J. '56 (ALN) Retired.
Maslejak, Andrzej *s.ch.* '79 (DET) [K] Sterling Heights, MI Society of Christ Provincial Home.
Maslowski, Krzysztof '88 (NEW) Cranford, NJ St. Michael's Church.
Maslowski, Stanley '63 (STP) Oakdale, MN Guardian Angels Church.
Maslowsky, Michael '86 (P) [5] Portland, OR St. Anthony Church.
Masluk, Alexander '79 (PH) [23] Philadelphia, PA St. Bernard Church; [133] Philadelphia, PA Our Mother of Sorrows Church.
Masnicki, Marek '92 (NOR) Oakdale, CT Our Lady of the Lakes Church.
Maso, Dario *s.x.* '82 (FgM) Xaverian Foreign Missions.
Maso, Dario *s.x.* '82 (PAT) [M] Wayne, NJ Xaverian Missionary Fathers.
Mason, Albert M. '48 (BO) Senior Priests.
Mason, Brian G. '93 (MIL) [3] Waukesha, WI St. Mary Church.
Mason, Carl Louis *o.p.* '64 (L) [47] Louisville, KY St. Louis Bertrand Church.
Mason, Charlon O. '79 (GR) Pewamo, MI St. Joseph's Church.
Mason, Dennis *o.f.m.conv.* '78 (TR) Riverside, NJ St. Casimir Church.
Mason, Edward J. '87 (BRK) Absent on Leave.
Mason, James E. '67 (LC) On Duty Outside the Diocese.
Mason, Mark E. '75 (OKL) Hennessey, OK St. Joseph's Church.
Mason, Robert E. '56 (RVC) Massapequa Park, NY Our Lady of Lourdes Church.
Mason, William *o.m.i.* '71 (BEL) [J] Belleville, IL Oblate Preaching Team.
Mason, William *o.m.i.* '71 (STP) [N] St. Paul, MN Oblate Residence.
Mass, Ronald J. '70 (CHI) Palos Heights, IL Incarnation Church.
Massa, James '86 (BO) [A] Weston, MA Pope John XXIII National Seminary.
Massa, Mark S. *s.j.* '80 (DET) [K] Detroit, MI Jesuit Provincial Office-Detroit Province of the Society of Jesus.
Massa, Mark S. *s.j.* '80 (NY) [DD] New York, NY Jesuit Community at Fordham University.
Massacavalo, Bruno '77 (JOL) Absent on Sick Leave.
Massar, Richard A. '69 (BUF) [2] Cheektowaga, NY Infant of Prague Church.
Massarella, Francis A. '46 (CIN) Retired; [L] Dayton, OH Mercy Siena Woods.
Massaro, Gabriel *o.f.m.cap.* '66 (MAN) [5] Manchester, NH Blessed Sacrament Church.
Massaro, John *c.s.c.* '81 (PMB) Vero Beach, FL Holy Cross Church.
Massaro, Joseph *c.s.s.* '48 (SPR) [9] Springfield, MA Our Lady of Mt. Carmel Church.
Massaro, Michael A. *c.s.c.* '81 (BGP) [P] Bridgeport, CT Provincial Offices of the Priests and Brothers of Holy Cross, Eastern Province.
Massaro, Thomas *s.j.* '93 (BO) [W] Cambridge, MA Weston Jesuit Community.
Massart, James '66 (GB) Absent on Leave.
Masschelein, Patrick *c.i.c.m.* '73 (FgM) Missionhurst Foreign Missions.
Massengill, Peter Damian *o.f.m.conv.* '76 (TOL) Carey, OH Our Lady of Consolation, Basilica-National Church; Salem Twp., OH St. Joseph Church.
Massett, Msgr. Robert D. '66 (NO) [12] Metairie, LA St. Mary Magdalen Church.
Massetti, Philip *o.s.j.* '76 (MRY) Santa Cruz, CA Shrine of St. Joseph Guardian of the Redeemer Church; [F] Santa Cruz, CA Oblates of St. Joseph Provincial House and Shrine.
Massey, Robert E. '73 (MIL) [1] West Allis, WI St. Aloysius Church.
Massey, Sharon (NEW) [14] Newark, NJ Queen of Angels Church.
Massi, Anthony '84 (MIA) [13] Miami, FL Our Lady of Lourdes Church.
Massicotte, Bernard *o.s.b.cam.* '57 (MRY) [F] Big Sur, CA New Camaldoli Hermitage.
Massie, Daniel J. '80 (MIL) Beaver Dam, WI St. Michael Church; Beaver Dam, WI St. Patrick Church; Beaver Dam, WI St. Peter Church.
Massie, Guy '83 (BRK) [7] Brooklyn, NY St. Andrew the Apostle Church.
Massie, Guy A. '83 (BRK) [E] Brooklyn, NY Office of Religious Education: Evangelization and Catholic Formation.
Massimino, Jerome *o.f.m.* '77 (NY) [48] New York, NY Holy Name of Jesus Church.
Massingale, Bryan N. '83 (MIL) [A] St. Francis, WI Saint Francis Seminary.
Massmann, Albert *o.s.b.* '54 (OM) [K] Elkhorn, NE Mount Michael Abbey.
Massucci, Joseph D. '70 (CIN) [D] Dayton, OH The University of Dayton.
Massucci, Joseph D. '70 (STU) On Duty Outside the Diocese.
Massung, Francis G. '40 (PIT) Retired; [O] Pittsburgh, PA St. John Vianney Manor.
Mast, Paul G. '72 (WIL) Hockessin, DE St. Mary of the Assumption Church.
Mastalir, Peter '92 (GB) Absent on Leave.
Masters, Andrew *s.v.d.* '34 (CHI) [B] Techny, IL Divine Word Residence.
Masters, Gerard G. '66 (HRT) [2] Torrington, CT Sacred Heart Church; [4] Torrington, CT St. Peter's Church.
Masterson, Clyde '85 (CC) On Duty Outside the Diocese.
Masterson, Frank D. *s.j.* '53 (SPK) [C] Spokane, WA Gonzaga University; [K] Spokane, WA Regis Community.
Masterson, Thomas D. *s.j.* '64 (SCR) [C] Scranton, PA University of Scranton; [C] Scranton, PA University of Scranton.
Mastey, Gregory '95 (SCL) Bowlus, MN St. Stanislaus Kostka Church; Elmdale, MN St. Edward's Church; North Prairie, MN Holy Cross Church; Upsala, MN St. Mary Church.
Mastolia, Arthur '87 (NY) [DD] Yonkers, NY Bishop Ford Residence.
Mastrain, Mark J. '87 (E) Sykesville, PA Assumption of Blessed Virgin Mary Church.
Mastrangelo, David F. *s.j.* '87 (DET) [E] Detroit, MI Loyola High School.
Mastrangelo, Joseph A. '40 (PIT) Retired.
Mastrangelo, Mario *o.f.m.cap.* '58 (FgM) Capuchin Foreign Missions.
Mastrangelo, Mario *o.f.m.cap.* '58 (PCE) [5] Ponce, PR Santa Teresita Church.
Mastrangelo, Nicholas '64 (PIT) [5] Munhall, PA St. Therese of Lisieux Church.
Mastria, Angelo *o.carm.* '58 (TUC) [D] Tucson, AZ Social Service Agencies: Pima County; [F] Tucson, AZ Carmelite Priory.
Mastrian, Mark J. '87 (E) Polk, PA Polk Center.
Mastriola, Arthur '87 (NY) [DD] Yonkers, NY Cathedral Preparatory Seminary Residence.
Mastrobuono, Peter *s.c.j.* '66 (GAL) [56] Houston, TX Our Lady of Guadalupe Church.
Mastroeni, Anthony J. '72 (ARL) [A] Front Royal, VA Christendom College.
Mastroeni, Anthony J. '72 (PAT) On Duty Outside the Diocese.
Mastrolia, Arthur '87 (NY) [A] New York, NY Cathedral Preparatory Seminary; [A] New York, NY Cathedral Preparatory Seminary.
Mastrongelo, David *s.j.* (DET) [23] Detroit, MI St. Francis de Sales Church.
Mastrovito, Francis *t.o.r.* '51 (OWN) Central City, KY St. Joseph Church.
Masuda, Masashi '97 (BO) [W] Cambridge, MA Weston Jesuit Community.
Maszkiewicz, Msgr. Mark '36 (TLS) Retired.
Mata, Antonio *o.c.d.* '46 (CGS) [2] Caguas, PR San Jose Church.
Matanic, George M. *o.p.* '70 (OAK) [4] Berkeley, CA St. Mary Magdalen Church; [N] Oakland, CA Western Dominican Province.
Matano, Msgr. Salvatore R. '71 (PRO) [7] Providence, RI St. Augustine Church; On Duty Outside the Diocese.
Matar, Ghassan *m.l.m.* '96 (OLL) Phoenix, AZ St. Joseph Church; [A] Houston, TX The Congregation of Maronite Lebanese Missionaries.
Matarazzo, Msgr. Francis '67 (PAT) [3] Clifton, NJ St. Brendan Church; Passaic, NJ Passiac General Hospital.
Matas, Msgr. Juan '65 (LA) Montebello, CA Our Lady of the Miraculous Medal Church.
Matash, Msgr. Edward M. '56 (NEW) [4] Bayonne, NJ St. Joseph's Church.
Mateo, Arturo *m.s.c.* '76 (SJ) San Jose, CA Columbia Regional Hospital.
Mateo, Jose *sch.p.* '49 (PCE) [4] Ponce, PR Our Lady of Mt. Carmel Church.
Mateo, Mateo *ss.cc.* '47 (SJN) [9] Guaynabo, PR Sagrados Corazones Church.
Mateo, Miguel *s.f.* '81 (WDC) [B] Silver Spring, MD Holy Family Seminary.
Mateo, P. Rafael *c.ss.r.* '89 (CGS) Yabucoa, PR Santos Angeles Cutodios Church.
Mateos, Francisco *c.m.* '58 (LA) [32] Los Angeles, CA Our Lady of the Rosary of Talpa Church.
Mateos, Tomas '45 (BWN) Retired; [I] McAllen, TX Secular Franciscan Order, Fraternity of Our Lady of Guadalupe.
Matera, Frank J. '68 (HRT) On Duty Outside the Archdiocese.
Matera, Frank J. '68 (WDC) [C] Washington, DC

Catholic University of America, The.
Matera, Philip T. '51 (TR) Retired.
Maternoski, Robert '62 (JOL) Kinsman, IL Sacred Heart Church; South Wilmington, IL St. Lawrence Church.
Mateu, Gregorio *t.o.r.* '64 (NEW) [20] Newark, NJ Immaculate Heart of Mary Church.
Mateus, Norberto (ATL) Lilburn, GA St. John Neumann Church.
Mathai, John '98 (BIS) Hettinger, ND Holy Trinity Church.
Mathaner, John P. '93 (E) [2] Oil City, PA Our Lady Help of Christians Church.
Matheis, Joseph W. *m.m.* '56 (NY) [DD] Maryknoll, NY Maryknoll Fathers and Brothers.
Matheny, William K., Jr. '96 (WH) Morgantown, WV St. John University Parish, Newman Hall Church.
Mathers, Douglas J. '85 (NY) [101] New York, NY Our Saviour Church.
Mathesius, William P. '76 (WIL) [1] Wilmington, DE Cathedral of St. Peter; Smyrna, MD Delaware State Correctional Center.
Mathew, Abraham P. '97 (BRK) [235] Queens, NY St. Robert Bellarmine Church.
Mathew, Armand *o.m.i.* '49 (WDC) [M] Washington, DC Missionary Oblates of Mary Immaculate; [M] Washington, DC Oblate College/Center for Mission Studies Community.
Mathews, J. Ronald '75 (ALX) Pineville, LA Central Louisiana State Hospital.
Mathews, James D. '62 (SY) [19] Syracuse, NY St. Lucy Church.
Mathews, Kenneth M. '78 (ALX) Absent on Leave.
Mathews, Michael C. *c.s.c.* '98 (FTW) [12] South Bend, IN St. Joseph Church.
Mathewson, Dean '73 (COL) Newark, OH St. Francis de Sales Church.
Mathewson, Robert B. *s.j.* '62 (SJ) [D] San Jose, CA Bellarmine College Preparatory.
Mathias, Edwin J. '67 (TR) Browns Mills, NJ St. Ann Church.
Mathias, Gregory A. '91 (FR) Mashpee, MA Christ The King Church.
Mathie, D. Edward *s.j.* '68 (FgM) Provinces.
Mathie, D. Edward *s.j.* '68 (MIL) [31] Milwaukee, WI Gesu Church; [P] Milwaukee, WI Jesuit Provincial Office, Wisconsin Province.
Mathieu, Rene T. '77 (PRT) [2] Lewiston, ME Holy Cross Church.
Mathieu, Robert E. '76 (GLP) Quemado, NM Sacred Heart Church; Springerville, AZ St. Peter Church.
Mathis, Christian '00 (KNX) [1] Knoxville, TN Cathedral of the Sacred Heart of Jesus.
Mathis, George *glmy.* '55 (CIN) [M] Cincinnati, OH Headquarters of Glenmary Home Missioners.
Mathis, R. Paul '72 (SY) [2] Rome, NY St. Mary of the Assumption Church.
Mathy, Francis H. *s.j.* '58 (FgM) Provinces.
Matienzo, Msgr. Rafael '68 (SJN) [23] San Juan, PR Inmaculado Corazon de Maria Church; Military Services.
Matinez, Vidal *o.s.m.* '75 (CHI) [N] Chicago, IL Order of Friar Servants of Mary (Servites) United States of America Province, Inc.
Matocha, Msgr. Edward C. '45 (AUS) [1] Austin, TX St. Mary's Church; Special Assignments.
Matocha, Msgr. John L. '47 (SAT) Retired.
Matondo, Thomas *c.i.c.m.* '82 (FgM) Missionhurst Foreign Missions.
Matonti, Charles J. '60 (BRK) [30] Brooklyn, NY St. Columba Church.
Matos, Angel '97 (WOR) [4] Fitchburg, MA St. Francis of Assisi Church; [1] Gardner, MA Holy Spirit Church.
Matos, David Diaz '79 (CGS) Humacao, PR Dulce Nombre de Jesus Church.
Matos, Juan A. (SJN) Catano, PR Nuestra Senora del Carmen Church.
Matro, Justin M. *o.s.b.* '89 (GBG) [A] Latrobe, PA St. Vincent Seminary; [H] Latrobe, PA Saint Vincent Archabbey.
Matsumoto, Yukinori F.X. *s.m.* '87 (CIN) [M] Dayton, OH Marianist Provincialate.
Matt, Erwin H. '56 (MIL) Retired.
Matt, J. Wilson '45 (LAF) Retired.
Matt, Joseph H. '74 (KC) Belton, MO St. Sabina's Church.
Matt, Thomas S. '86 (OM) [16] Omaha, NE Holy Cross Church.
Matta, Pablo (ELP) [1] El Paso, TX St. Patrick's Church.
Mattaliano, James *s.j.* '90 (BO) [3] Newton, MA St. Ignatius Church; [W] Chestnut Hill, MA The Jesuit Community at Boston College.
Mattas, Louis '60 (SAL) Retired.
Mattath, Joseph *c.m.i.* '64 (SY) [2] Endicott, NY St. Ambrose Church.
Matte, Richard O. '64 (BO) Unassigned.
Matteo, James P. '72 (PH) Ardsley, PA Queen of Peace Church.
Matter, Robert *o.c.s.o.* (SPC) [A] Ava, MO Assumption Novitiate (Trappists).
Mattern, Joseph A. '59 (GB) Omro, WI St. Mary Church.
Matteucig, Joseph *s.x.* '84 (FgM) Xaverian Foreign Missions.
Matteucig, Joseph *s.x.* '84 (PAT) [M] Wayne, NJ Xaverian Missionary Fathers.
Mattey, Joseph J. '65 (SCR) [1] Freeland, PA St. Ann's Church.
Matthew, Thomas '80 (SFR) San Bruno, CA St. Bruno Church.
Matthews, Andre '84 (ROM) Cleveland, OH St. Helena Church; Lorain, OH St. Basil Church.
Matthews, Donald C. *s.j.* '63 (NY) [DD] New York, NY Jesuit Community at Fordham University.
Matthews, James '74 (OAK) [5] Oakland, CA St. Benedict Church.
Matthews, Robert '64 (OAK) [4] Hayward, CA St. Joachim Church.
Matthiesen, Msgr. Monroe J. '43 (AMA) [D] Panhandle, TX St. Ann's Nursing Home; [D] Panhandle, TX St. Joseph's Home for Retired Priests.
Matthys, Donald R. *s.j.* '68 (MIL) [P] Milwaukee, WI Jesuit Community at Marquette University.
Mattice, George F. '64 (SY) Special Assignment.
Mattiello, Lucian C. '45 (ALT) Retired.
Mattimoe, Edward J. *s.j.* '65 (DET) [K] Detroit, MI Jesuit Provincial Office-Detroit Province of the Society of Jesus.
Mattimore, John J. *s.j.* '88 (BUF) [D] Buffalo, NY Canisius High School; [O] Buffalo, NY Canisius Jesuit Community.
Mattimore, William F. '51 (HON) Waimanalo, HI St. George Church.
Mattimore, William F. '51 (WOR) On Duty Outside the Diocese.
Mattingly, Allen J. *o.s.b.* '57 (PEO) [A] Peru, IL St. Bede Abbey and Academy.
Mattingly, Basil *o.s.b.* '46 (SD) [H] Oceanside, CA Prince of Peace Abbey, Benet Hill.
Mattingly, Jerry Alan '95 (JKS) Greenville, MS St. Joseph Church.
Mattingly, John F. *s.s.* '48 (BAL) [O] Baltimore, MD St. Charles Villa; [S] Baltimore, MD St. Charles Villa.
Mattingly, John S. '72 (WDC) Newtowne, MD St. Francis Xavier Church.
Mattingly, Lawrence *o.f.m.conv.* '64 (AUS) [3] Austin, TX Cristo Rey Church.
Mattingly, Martin '50 (OWN) Dawson Springs, KY Resurrection Church; Earlington, KY Immaculate Conception Church.
Mattingly, Robert '68 (VEN) Murdock, FL St. Maximilian Kolbe Church.
Mattingly, Robert W. *s.j.* '00 (PH) [G] Philadelphia, PA St. Joseph's Preparatory School; [AA] Philadelphia, PA Jesuit Community, Arrupe House.
Mattingly, Thomas '97 (RIC) Roanoke, VA St. Gerard Church; Salem, VA Salem VA Medical Center.
Mattioni, George *o.a.r.* '53 (NY) Suffern, NY Good Samaritan Hospital; [B] Suffern, NY Tagaste Monastery; [W] Suffern, NY Good Samaritan Hospital of Suffern.
Mattison, James H. '78 (BUR) Island Pond, VT St. James the Greater Church.
Mattison, Thomas V. '73 (BUR) Rutland, VT Christ the King Church.
Mattler, Albert A. '56 (STL) Flint Hill, MO St. Theodore Church.
Mattscheck, John J. '53 (CIN) Retired.
Mattucci, James J. '46 (MAD) Retired; [H] Madison, WI Bishop O'Connor Catholic Pastoral Center.
Mattulke, Arthur E. '97 (BUF) [44] Buffalo, NY St. Margaret Church.
Matty, Richard A. '83 (ELP) [1] El Paso, TX St. Patrick's Church.
Matula, Lawrence '62 (VIC) El Campo, TX St. Robert Bellarmine Church.
Matula, Stanley '59 (SY) [9] Syracuse, NY Sacred Heart Basilica Church.
Matulewicz, Ronald '59 (ALB) Hagaman, NY St. Stephen Church.
Maturi, John A. Gregory *o.p.* (HRT) [14] New Haven, CT St. Mary's Priory Church.
Maturi, John Gregory *o.p.* '94 (NY) [GG] New York, NY University Apostolate.
Matus, Walter J. '71 (AUS) Cyclone, TX St. Joseph's Church.
Matusak, Michael W. '75 (GBG) Mount Pleasant, PA St. Pius X Church; Mount Pleasant, PA Transfiguration Church.
Matusz, Michael A. '89 (CLV) [10] Akron, OH St. Martha Church; [1] Garfield Heights, OH St. Monica Church.
Matuszak, Edward S. '55 (LFT) Retired.
Matuszak, Walter L. '58 (BUF) [11] Cheektowaga, NY Resurrection Church.
Matuszewski, Ramon '57 (SAG) Pinconning, MI St. Michael Church.
Matveenko, Michael J. '82 (CAM) Marmora, NJ The Church of the Resurrection.
Maty, Robert J. '57 (BGP) [10] Bridgeport, CT Holy Rosary Church.
Matya, Robert A. '95 (LIN) [12] Lincoln, NE St. Thomas Aquinas Church; [J] Lincoln, NE University of Nebraska, Newman Club.
Matyas, Francis B. '42 (STL) Retired.
Matyas, William T. *o.s.b.* '53 (CLV) [O] Cleveland, OH Benedictine Order of Cleveland.
Matysik, Robert T. '84 (CAM) Somers Point, NJ St. Joseph's Church.
Matz, David *c.pp.s.* '94 (KC) [A] Kansas City, MO Gaspar Mission House.
Matz, George A. '66 (KCK) Garnett, KS Holy Angels Church; Greeley, KS St. John the Baptist's Church.
Matz, Joseph A. '64 (SCR) Jessup, PA St. James Church.
Matz, Leo '61 (MRY) Retired.
Matz, Michael J. '84 (PH) Bryn Mawr, PA St. John Neumann Church.
Matzek, William J. '63 (LC) Onalaska, WI St. Patrick Church.
Matzinger, Robert J. *c.s.b.* '57 (GAL) Sugar Land, TX St. Theresa Church.
Matzko, David G. *s.j.* '79 (CHY) St. Stephens, WY St. Stephen's Church; [C] St. Stephens, WY St. Stephens Mission - Jesuit Community; [F] St. Stephens, WY St. Stephens Indian Mission Foundation.
Mau, Joseph '39 (LAF) Retired.
Mau, Nguyen Duc *c.ss.r.* '70 (LA) [Q] Baldwin Park, CA Vietnamese Redemptorist Mission.
Mauck, George A. '77 (BEL) Carlyle, IL St. Mary Church; Centralia, IL Centralia Correctional Center.
Maudlin, Stanislaus *o.s.b.* '42 (SFS) [F] Marvin, SD Blue Cloud Abbey.
Mauel, James E. *s.j.* '57 (MIL) [P] Milwaukee, WI Jesuit Provincial Office, Wisconsin Province; [Q] Milwaukee, WI St. Joseph Convent, General Motherhouse of the School Sisters of St. Francis.
Mauel, John N. '50 (LC) Retired.
Mauer, Elmar *o.m.i* '62 (BEL) [F] Belleville, IL Missionary Oblates of Mary Immaculate - St. Henry's Oblate Residence.
Maufort, Msgr. Richard A. '54 (GB) Special Assignment.
Maughan, Michael *s.m.a.* '43 (BEL) Retired.
Maughan, Richard N. '72 (NO) [10] Metairie, LA St. Lawrence the Martyr Church.
Maul, William R. '55 (SFD) Retired.
Maullon, Alberto A., Jr. '82 (GAL) Katy, TX St. Bartholomew the Apostle Church.
Maung, Chrysostom Ah (WCH) Council Grove, KS St. Rose Church; Strong City, KS St. Anthony of Padua Church.
Mauntel, Robert J. '49 (CIN) Retired.
Maurer, Daniel J. '97 (PIT) [1] Pittsburgh, PA St. Paul Church.
Maurer, Edward L. '69 (BRK) [188] Queens, NY St. Joseph Church.
Maurer, Russell J. '60 (PIT) Blawnox, PA St. Edward Church.
Maurer, Thomas *s.d.s.* '64 (NSH) Dover, TN St. Francis of Assisi Church.
Mauricci, Bruno R. '90 (LAV) North Las Vegas, NV St. Christopher Church.
Mauricio, Francisco S. *c.s.b.* '97 (GAL) [Q] Sugar Land, TX Basilian Mission Center.
Mauriello, Matthew R. '88 (BGP) [11] Stamford, CT St. Mary Church.
Mauritzen, Joseph H. '96 (FR) Falmouth, MA St. Patrick's Church.
Maus, Christopher P. '93 (DET) [30] Detroit, MI St. Hedwig Church.
Maus, Jasper *o.f.m.* '39 (SAT) Retired.
Maus, Le Roy '66 (SCL) [1] St. Cloud, MN St. Mary's Cathedral of St. Cloud; Retired.
Maus, Mark '91 (STP) Brooklyn Park, MN St. Vincent de Paul Church.
Maus, Omer *o.s.b.* '45 (SCL) [I] Collegeville, MN St. John's Abbey, of the Order of St. Benedict.
Maus, Msgr. Rudolph E. '39 (LR) Retired.
Mausolf, James H. '50 (GAY) Retired.
Mauss, Jasper *o.f.m.* (SAT) [K] San Antonio, TX St. Francis Nursing Home.
Mauthe, Richard '58 (GB) Retired.
Mavsar, Msgr. Joseph '44 (HEL) Retired.
Mawhinney, John J. *s.j.* '65 (PH) [AA] Philadelphia, PA Jesuit Community at St. Joseph's University.
Mawicke, Joseph '63 (SB) Thousand Palms, CA St. Philip the Apostle Church.
Mawn, Francis X. '85 (BO) [3] Haverhill, MA St. James Church.
Maxcy, Walter J. *m.m.* '47 (FgM) Maryknoll Foreign Missions.
Maxfield, Leo *m.s.* '55 (MAN) [K] Enfield, NH Shrine of Our Lady of La Salette; [M] Enfield, NH La Salette Shrine and Center of Enfield.
Maxim, Craig '91 (KCK) Leawood, KS Church of the Nativity.
Maxwell, Bruce C. *o.s.c.* '75 (DET) [K] Riverview, MI Crosier Community of Riverview.
Maxwell, Herbert (CHI) [J] Evanston, IL Saint Francis Hospital.
Maxwell, John '59 (OAK) El Cerrito, CA St. John the

Baptist Church.
Maxwell, Palmer '88 (SAT) San Antonio, TX Santa Rosa Hospital System; [H] San Antonio, TX Christus Santa Rosa Health Care Corporation.
May, Anthony C. '75 (SD) [31] San Diego, CA St. Mary Magdalene Church.
May, Darrin M. '99 (WCH) [13] Wichita, KS St. Francis of Assisi Church.
May, Douglas E. *m.m.* '86 (FgM) Maryknoll Foreign Missions.
May, Gregory *c.ss.r.* '88 (CHI) [133] Chicago, IL St. Michael Church.
May, Herbert '75 (LKC) Welsh, LA Our Lady of the Seven Dolors Church.
May, James M. '98 (STA) Jacksonville Beach, FL St. Paul's Church.
May, Michael K. *s.j.* '93 (STL) [C] St. Louis, MO Saint Louis University; [P] St. Louis, MO Jesuit Community Corporation at St. Louis University - Jesuit Hall.
May, Raymond '93 (KCK) [5] Topeka, KS Our Lady of Guadalupe Church.
May, Ronald P. '86 (HRT) Collinsville, CT St. Patrick's Church.
May, Thomas P. '83 (CHI) Niles, IL St. John Brebeuf Church.
May, William L. *c.s.b.* '00 (GAL) Rosenberg, TX Our Lady of Guadalupe Church.
Maya, Manuel *o.s.m.* '58 (ORG) Fullerton, CA St. Philip Benizi Church.
Maya, Tulio '56 (LA) Compton, CA St. Albert the Great Church.
Maya-Chavez, Manuel *o.s.m.* '58 (CHI) [N] Chicago, IL Order of Friar Servants of Mary (Servites) United States of America Province, Inc.
Mayall, Daniel G. '77 (CHI) [62] Chicago, IL St. Francis Borgia Church.
Mayefske, Thomas J. '62 (GB) On Duty Outside the Diocese.
Mayefske, Thomas J. '62 (SFE) [5] Albuquerque, NM Holy Ghost Church.
Mayer, David *s.v.d.* '66 (FgM) Society of the Divine Word Foreign Missions.
Mayer, Douglas J. '86 (GRY) Valparaiso, IN Our Lady of Sorrows Church.
Mayer, Francis X. *s.j.* '50 (FgM) Provinces.
Mayer, James W. *o.de.m.* (PH) [AA] Philadelphia, PA Monastery of Our Lady of Mercy.
Mayer, John L. '64 (STL) Millwood, MO St. Alphonsus Church.
Mayer, Jules A. '64 (LA) [78] Los Angeles, CA St. Marcellinus Church.
Mayer, Kenneth H. *o.s.b.* '42 (PAT) [M] Morristown, NJ St. Mary's Abbey.
Mayer, Laurence A. *o.praem.* '65 (GB) [I] De Pere, WI St. Norbert Abbey.
Mayer, Laurence A. '65 (SFE) [I] Albuquerque, NM Santa Maria de la Vid Priory.
Mayer, Michael '98 (ROC) [52] Rochester, NY St. Pius Tenth Church.
Mayer, Msgr. Richard G. '61 (E) [16] Erie, PA St. George Church.
Mayer, Robert *o.m.i.* '67 (FgM) Oblates Foreign Missions.
Mayer, Walter W. '59 (OAK) Livermore, CA St. Michael Church; Retired.
Mayer, William C. *c.s.v.* '56 (CHI) [N] Arlington Heights, IL Viatorian Province Center-Clerics of St. Viator.
Mayfield, Olin W. '96 (LA) Arcadia, CA Holy Angels Church.
Mayhew, John A. *c.j.* '65 (LA) Santa Maria, CA St. Louis de Montfort Church.
Mayhew, John A. *c.j.* '66 (LA) [B] Santa Maria, CA St. Joseph Seminary (Josephite Fathers' Novitiate).
Maynard, George C. *s.j.* '61 (DET) [K] Detroit, MI Jesuit Provincial Office-Detroit Province of the Society of Jesus.
Maynard, George C. *s.j.* '61 (LEX) Lexington, KY Veterans' Administration Hospital.
Maynard, Jack G. '78 (COL) Heath, OH St. Leonard Church.
Maynard, Joseph V. *m.m.* '48 (FgM) Maryknoll Foreign Missions.
Maynard, Leo E. '47 (HRT) Retired.
Maynard, Leon C. '54 (PRO) Retired; [P] Providence, RI St. John Vianney Residence.
Maynard, Lewis H. '69 (BRK) [2] Brooklyn, NY St. Agatha's Church.
Maynard, Richard C. '56 (PRO) [6] Pawtucket, RI St. Joseph Church; Retired.
Maynard, Robert J. '48 (PRO) [7] Cranston, RI St. Paul Church; Retired.
Mayne, Kenneth M. '94 (LAF) Evangeline, LA St. Joseph Church.
Mayo, J. Aidan '76 (P) Sandy, OR St. Michael the Archangel Church.
Mayo, James M. '79 (SAV) Hinesville, GA St. Stephen, First Martyr Church.
Mayo, Joseph M. '73 (SLC) [1] Salt Lake City, UT Cathedral of the Madeleine.
Mayo, Reid C. '63 (BUR) Rutland, VT Christ the King Church.
Mayorga, Fulgencio *s.j.* '98 (MIA) [D] Miami, FL Belen Jesuit Preparatory School; [H] Miami, FL Villa Javier.
Mayotte, Allan J. '60 (MAR) Retired.
Mayovsky, David '97 (SEA) Federal Way, WA St. Vincent De Paul Church.
Mayovsky, Frederick P. *s.j.* '75 (SEA) [C] Tacoma, WA Bellarmine Preparatory School.
Mayovsky, Gerald L. '59 (SEA) [30] Seattle, WA Our Lady of Lourdes Church; Tukwila, WA St. Thomas Church.
Mayworm, James A. '66 (DET) Auburn Hills, MI Sacred Heart Church.
Mayzik, James J. *s.j.* '85 (BGP) [B] Fairfield, CT Fairfield University; [P] Fairfield, CT The Fairfield Jesuit Community-Fairfield University.
Maza, Edward J. '59 (CHI) [89] Chicago, IL Immaculate Conception Church.
Mazabel, Hector '77 (NY) [102] New York, NY St. Patrick Old Church.
Mazaika, Joseph J. '53 (TLS) Retired.
Mazanec, James F. '81 (CLV) Maple Heights, OH St. Martin of Tours Church.
Mazewski, Dariusz *m.i.c.* '94 (SPR) [J] Stockbridge, MA Congregation of Marians of The Immaculate Conception of the BVM.
Mazon, Diego *o.f.m.* '60 (GLP) [2] Gallup, NM St. Francis of Assisi Church.
Mazouch, Charles '73 (DOD) Leoti, KS St. Anthony of Padua Church; Marienthal, KS St. Mary Church.
Mazuchowski, Hyacinth '63 (BEL) Flora, IL St. Stephen Church.
Mazuelas, Paulino *o.s.b.* '54 (MGZ) [6] Mayaquez, PR Sacred Heart Church; [6] Mayaquez, PR Sacred Heart Church.
Mazur, Clarence *o.f.m.* '42 (GRY) [J] Cedar Lake, IN Our Lady of Lourdes Friary.
Mazur, Francis X. '76 (BUF) [26] Buffalo, NY St. Gerard Church.
Mazur, Robert C. '76 (ALT) [1] Altoona, PA Cathedral of the Blessed Sacrament.
Mazur, Timothy P. '95 (DET) [3] St. Clair Shores, MI St. Isaac Jogues Church.
Mazurchuk, Michael T. *c.m.* '86 (FgM) Vincentian Foreign Missions.
Mazurek, James K. '73 (DET) [A] Orchard Lake, MI SS. Cyril and Methodius Seminary; [C] Orchard Lake, MI Saint Mary's College.
Mazurek, James K. '73 (PIT) On Duty Outside the Diocese.
Mazurkiewicz, Msgr. Ben J. '55 (AUS) Hostyn Hill, TX St. Mary's Church.
Mazurkiewicz, Msgr. Benedict J. '55 (AUS) Fayetteville, TX St. John's Church.
Mazurkiewicz, Msgr. Harry C. '51 (AUS) La Grange, TX Sacred Heart of Jesus Church.
Mazurkiewicz, Joseph '84 (ALT) Absent on Leave.
Mazyryk, Ivan '95 (STF) Johnson City, NY Sacred Heart Ukrainian Catholic Church.
Mazza, Louis J. '53 (NY) Sleepy Hollow, NY Immaculate Conception Church.
Mazza, Mark G. '80 (GRY) North Judson, IN Ss. Cyril and Methodius Church.
Mazza, Victor J. '70 (PAT) [7] Clifton, NJ St. Paul Church.
Mazzarella, Cadmus D. '85 (CAM) [R] Glassboro, NJ Rowan University.
Mazzarella, Frederick *o.f.m.* '61 (NY) [DD] New York, NY Franciscan Province of the Immaculate Conception.
Mazzarello, Cadmus D. (CAM) [O] Blackwood, NJ St. Pius X Retreat House.
Mazzei, John C. '92 (MAN) Lancaster, NH All Saints Church.
Mazziotta, Msgr. Robert R. '41 (NY) [220] Staten Island, NY Our Lady of Pity Church; Retired.
Mazzitello, John A. *s.j.* '69 (MIL) [P] Milwaukee, WI Jesuit Provincial Office, Wisconsin Province.
Mazzola, Robert E. '63 (IND) [28] Indianapolis, IN St. Matthew Church; On Special or Other Archdiocesan Assignment.
Mazzone, James S. '99 (WOR) [4] Worcester, MA Christ the King Church.
Mazzotta, George J. '66 (PH) Ridley Park, PA St. Madeline Church.
Mazzuchelli, Matthew C. *o.s.b.* '58 (PEO) [A] Peru, IL St. Bede Abbey and Academy.
Mbanisi, Victor '93 (BRK) [200] Queens, NY St. Mel Church.
Mbogo, Lawrence '93 (SY) Vestal, NY Our Lady of Sorrows Church.
Mbogu, Christopher '83 (PIT) [3] McKees Rocks, PA St. John of God Church.
Mbombo, Jean-Marie *c.i.c.m.* '91 (FgM) Missionhurst Foreign Missions.
Mc Menemie, Msgr. James '53 (NEW) Lyndhurst, NJ St. Michael's Church.
McAfee, Franklyn M. '71 (ARL) Great Falls, VA St. Catherine of Siena Church.
McAlear, Richard *o.m.i.* '70 (BO) [W] Lowell, MA Missionary Oblates of Mary Immaculate.
McAlear, Richard *o.m.i.* '70 (WDC) [M] Washington, DC Oblate College/Center for Mission Studies Community.
McAleer, Robert T. '71 (DAV) Bettendorf, IA St. John Vianney Church.
McAlinden, Terence O. '67 (TR) Tuckerton, NJ St. Teresa Church.
McAlister, Msgr. Lawrence J. '44 (BRK) [150] Queens, NY St. Andrew Avellino Church; Retired.
McAlister, Richard A. *o.p.* '61 (PRO) [P] Providence, RI St. Thomas Aquinas Priory at Providence College.
McAllister, Alex '86 (SR) Retired.
McAllister, Donald '71 (PRT) Portland, ME Mercy Hospital; [H] Portland, ME Mercy Hospital.
McAllister, Leo '54 (SAC) Carmichael, CA Our Lady of the Assumption Church.
McAllister, Robert J. *s.j.* '51 (ALN) [A] Wernersville, PA Jesuit Center.
McAloon, Francis X. *s.j.* '92 (OAK) [N] Berkeley, CA Jesuit Community at Jesuit School of Theology at Berkeley.
McAlpin, James C. '64 (SC) Manning, IA Sacred Heart Church.
McAlpin, Leonard '69 (GBG) Fayette City, PA Holy Spirit Church.
McAlpine, Harry D. (SC) Varina, IA St. Columbkille's Church.
McAlpine, Harry D. '87 (SC) Fonda, IA Our Lady of Good Counsel Church.
McAndrew, David T. '63 (HBG) [1] Lebanon, PA Assumption of the Blessed Virgin Mary Church.
McAndrew, James F. *s.j.* '62 (CHL) [J] Charlotte, NC Jesuit Community.
McAndrew, John '86 (ORG) Brea, CA St. Angela Merici Church.
McAndrew, John P. *c.s.sp.* '67 (PIT) [Q] Bethel Park, PA Holy Ghost Animation Center.
McAndrew, Michael *c.ss.r.* '73 (DEN) [33] Denver, CO St. Joseph's Church.
McAndrew, P. Joseph (NY) Greenwood Lake, NY Holy Rosary Church.
McAndrew, Thomas F. '61 (DUB) Manly, IA Sacred Heart Church; Plymouth, IA St. Michael Church.
McAndrews, Msgr. Donald A. '54 (SCR) [1] Wilkes-Barre, PA St. Aloysius Church.
McAndrews, James F. *s.j.* '62 (CHL) Mooresville, NC St. Therese Church.
McAndrews, Richard J. '67 (PH) [111] Philadelphia, PA Nativity of the Blessed Virgin Mary Church.
McAnerney, Brendan *o.p.* '88 (P) Ashland, OR Our Lady of the Mountain Church.
McAnulty, John D. *s.j.* '57 (LA) [Q] Los Angeles, CA Columbiere House.
McArdle, John F. '51 (MAR) Retired.
McArdle, Kevin *o.c.d.* '43 (TUC) [18] Tucson, AZ St. Margaret's Church; [F] Tucson, AZ Discalced Carmelite Friars of St. Margaret's.
McAree, Msgr. Francis J. '75 (NY) [A] Yonkers, NY St. Joseph's Seminary.
McArthur, John B. '74 (MEM) [16] Memphis, TN St. Louis Church.
McArtney, Robert J. '60 (BUF) [K] Lackawanna, NY Our Lady of Victory Hospital.
McAskill, Kenneth F. '50 (BO) [3] Arlington, MA St. James the Apostle Church; Senior Priests.
McAtavey, John J. '54 (PMB) Tequesta, FL St. Jude Church; Retired.
McAtee, John F. '66 (PH) [AA] Villanova, PA St. Thomas Monastery.
McAteer, James *i.c.* (SP) Spring Hill, FL St. Theresa Church.
McAteer, Msgr. Kenneth P. '73 (PH) [120] Philadelphia, PA Our Lady of Hope Church.
McAteer, Patrick J. *s.j.* '73 (CHI) [N] Chicago, IL Chicago Province of the Society of Jesus-Provincial Office.
McAuley, James D. *m.m.* '80 (FgM) Maryknoll Foreign Missions.
McAuley, John J. *m.m.* '81 (NY) [DD] Maryknoll, NY Maryknoll Fathers and Brothers.
McAuliff, R. Richard *s.j.* '92 (MI) Majuro, MH Cathedral of the Assumption.
McAuliff, Richard R. *s.j.* '92 (FgM) Provinces.
McAuliffe, Dennis (BRK) [92] Brooklyn, NY Our Lady of Charity Church.
McAuliffe, Dennis '73 (BRK) [E] Brooklyn, NY Office of Religious Education: Evangelization and Catholic Formation.
McAuliffe, Kevin W. *j.c.l.* '90 (LAV) [8] Las Vegas, NV St. Elizabeth Ann Seton Church.
McAuliffe, Robert F. '57 (BO) [3] Arlington, MA St. James the Apostle Church; Senior Priests.
McAuliffe, Roger D. *s.j.* '49 (SJ) [L] Los Gatos, CA Sacred Heart Jesuit Center.
McAvey, James R. *o.p.* '39 (PRO) [P] Providence, RI St. Thomas Aquinas Priory at Providence College.
McAvoy, Msgr. Ambrose A. '39 (DUB) Retired.
McAvoy, Msgr. C. John '63 (OG) Malone, NY St. Joseph's Church.

McBrady, Lawrence J. '71 (CHI) [90] Chicago, IL Immaculate Conception of the Blessed Virgin Mary Church.
McBrearity, Gerald D. *s.s.* (ATL) On Duty Outside the Archdiocese.
McBrearity, Gerald D. *s.s.* '73 (BAL) [S] Baltimore, MD Sulpician Provincial House.
McBrearity, Gerald D. *s.s.* '73 (WDC) [A] Washington, DC Theological College of the Catholic University of America.
McBrearty, John J. *s.s.j.* '68 (ARL) [4] Alexandria, VA St. Joseph's Church.
McBriar, David J. *o.f.m.* '64 (R) [3] Durham, NC Immaculate Conception Church.
McBride, Alfred *o.praem.* '53 (BO) [A] Weston, MA Pope John XXIII National Seminary.
McBride, Alfred A. '53 (GB) [I] De Pere, WI St. Norbert Abbey.
McBride, Brendan '75 (SFR) [47] San Francisco, CA St. Philip the Apostle Church.
McBride, Daniel '51 (CLV) Northfield, OH St. Barnabas Church.
McBride, Daniel '95 (PHX) Tolleson, AZ Blessed Sacrament Church.
McBride, Eugene J. *o.s.f.s.* '89 (PH) [75] Philadelphia, PA St. Jerome Church; [AA] Philadelphia, PA Father Judge Faculty House.
McBride, Gerald E. '91 (TR) Manalapan, NJ St. Thomas More Church.
McBride, Harold E. *s.m.m.* '47 (RVC) Bay Shore, NY Southside Hospital; [M] Bay Shore, NY Montfort Missionaries.
McBride, Henry '61 (CAM) Somerdale, NJ Our Lady of Grace Church.
McBride, Msgr. James P. '56 (PH) [84] Philadelphia, PA St. Katherine of Siena Church.
McBride, John *s.j.* '61 (P) [L] Portland, OR Colombiere Community.
McBride, John F. '62 (PH) Hilltown, PA Our Lady of the Sacred Heart Church.
McBride, Larry '87 (OWN) [1] Paducah, KY St. Francis de Sales Church; [2] Paducah, KY Rosary Chapel Church.
McBride, Malachy R. *o.f.m.cap.* '62 (DEN) [1] Aurora, CO Queen of Peace Church; [M] Denver, CO St. Francis of Assisi Friary.
McBride, Patrick *c.ss.r.* '85 (FgM) Redemptorist Foreign Missions.
McBride, Msgr. Peter A. (PAT) Retired.
McBride, Msgr. Peter A. '60 (PAT) [P] Chester, NJ Nazareth Village.
McBride, Robert G. '72 (NEW) Saddle Brook, NJ St. Philip the Apostle Church.
McBrien, Kevin *o.carm.* '70 (LA) [F] Encino, CA Crespi Carmelite High School.
McBrien, Kevin F. '86 (BRK) [174] Queens, NY St. Gregory the Great Church.
McBrien, Richard P. '62 (FTW) [B] Notre Dame, IN University of Notre Dame Du Lac.
McBrien, Richard P. '62 (HRT) On Duty Outside the Archdiocese.
McBurney, James D. *o.s.a.* '84 (PH) [B] Villanova, PA St. Augustine Friary; [G] Malvern, PA Malvern Preparatory School for Boys.
McCaa, Msgr. Francis B. '48 (ALT) Retired.
McCabe, Charles J. '92 (MOB) Ozark, AL St. John Church.
McCabe, Edward D. '68 (BO) Military & VA Chaplains.
McCabe, George V. '45 (SPK) Retired.
McCabe, James F. *c.s.p.* '57 (NY) [DD] Jamaica Estates, NY Paulist Fathers Generalate.
McCabe, James F. *c.pp.s.* '58 (TOL) [K] Bellevue, OH Mary Lay Center; [M] Bellevue, OH Sorrowful Mother Shrine.
McCabe, James T. '71 (PH) Malvern, PA St. Patrick Church.
McCabe, John H. '55 (RVC) Retired; [C] Hicksville, NY Holy Trinity.
McCabe, John J. *m.m.* '45 (NY) [DD] Maryknoll, NY Maryknoll Fathers and Brothers.
McCabe, Joseph V. *m.m.* '77 (FgM) Maryknoll Foreign Missions.
McCabe, Louis J. *s.j.* '71 (COS) [F] Sedalia, CO Sacred Heart Jesuit Community; [H] Sedalia, CO Sacred Heart Jesuit Retreat House.
McCabe, Michael G. '89 (LIN) Nebraska City, NE St. Mary's Church; [C] Nebraska City, NE Lourdes Central Catholic Schools; [M] Nebraska City, NE Lourdes Central High School Endowment Fund.
McCabe, Msgr. Patrick A. '61 (CAM) Ocean City, NJ St. Frances Cabrini Church.
McCabe, Ramon J. *m.m.* '56 (FgM) Maryknoll Foreign Missions.
McCabe, Raymond M. *o.p.* '47 (CAM) [M] Camden, NJ Dominican Sisters of the Perpetual Rosary Chaplain's Residence; [N] Camden, NJ Monastery of the Dominican Nuns of the Perpetual Rosary.
McCabe, Msgr. Richard '58 (AUS) [4] Austin, TX Emmaus Catholic Church.
McCabe, Msgr. Robert J. (NY) Haverstraw, NY St. Mary Church.
McCabe, Robert J. '95 (DET) Grosse Pointe Farms, MI St. Paul Catholic Church.
McCabe, Thomas '92 (STP) Belle Plaine, MN Our Lady of the Prairie Church.
McCabe, Msgr. Vincent '46 (LA) Retired.
McCafferty, David L. '64 (CLV) Wickliffe, OH Our Lady of Mount Carmel Church.
McCafferty, James B. *s.m.* '70 (WH) Buckhannon, WV Holy Rosary Church; [P] Buckhannon, WV West Virginia Wesleyan College Newman Center.
McCafferty, Joseph F. '61 (PH) [Y] Lansdale, PA St. Mary Manor.
McCafferty, Michael F. '87 (CHR) Hilton Head Island, SC St. Francis By the Sea Church.
McCafferty, Richard *s.j.* '62 (OAK) Livermore, CA St. Charles Borromeo Church.
McCafferty, Richard B. *s.j.* '62 (BO) [W] Boston, MA The Society of Jesus of New England-Provincial Offices.
McCaffrey, Daniel '58 (OKL) Special Assignment.
McCaffrey, Edmund *o.carm.* '53 (NY) New York, NY New York City Veterans Administration Hospital; Manhattan, NY U.S.V.A. Medical Center.
McCaffrey, Edmund M. '59 (CHR) Hilton Head Island, SC Holy Family Church.
McCaffrey, Gerald T. *o.f.m.* '58 (BO) [BB] Boston, MA St. Anthony Shrine.
McCaffrey, James Leo '58 (STO) Retired.
McCaffrey, James P. *s.j.* '52 (BO) [W] Weston, MA Campion Health Center, Inc.
McCaffrey, John A. '76 (AUS) Bryan, TX St. Joseph's Church; [N] Bryan, TX St. Joseph Memorial Endowment Fund.
McCaffrey, Joseph '77 (ROC) Auburn, NY Auburn Correctional Facility; Red Creek, NY Butler Correctional Facility.
McCaffrey, Joseph C. '99 (PH) Havertown, PA St. Denis Church.
McCaffrey, Joseph J. '77 (ROC) [7] Elmira, NY St. Anthony Church.
McCaffrey, Joseph P. *c.m.* '54 (PH) [AA] Philadelphia, PA Congregation of the Mission.
McCaffrey, Joseph P. '77 (ROC) [2] Elmira, NY St. Patrick Church.
McCaffrey, Joseph R. '87 (PIT) New Bedford, PA St. James Church; Lawrence County, PA Youth Development Center.
McCaffrey, Kevin Palmer *o.p.* '93 (NY) [DD] New York, NY St. Vincent Ferrer Priory.
McCaffrey, Lawrence X. *s.j.* '51 (NY) Harriman, NY St. Anastasia Church; [EE] Harriman, NY St. Patrick's Villa.
McCaffrey, Richard L. *s.j.* '73 (FBK) [2] Fairbanks, AK Immaculate Conception Church; [C] Fairbanks, AK Jesuit Residence.
McCaffrey, Msgr. William J. '72 (PRO) [20] Providence, RI St. Joseph Church.
McCahill, Msgr. Patrick P. '68 (NY) [32] New York, NY St. Elizabeth of Hungary Church; [O] New York, NY New York Catholic Deaf Center.
McCahill, Robert T. *m.m.* '64 (FgM) Maryknoll Foreign Missions.
McCahon, Joseph F.S. '75 (SP) Military Chaplains.
McCaig, John J. '58 (CHI) [5] Lemont, IL St. Patrick Church; Retired.
McCain, William '86 (SFR) Novato, CA Our Lady of Loretto Church.
McCall, James T. '60 (CAM) Delair, NJ St. Veronica's Church.
McCall, Msgr. John '58 (SP) Indian Rocks Beach, FL St. Jerome Church; Retired.
McCall, Peter *o.f.m.cap.* '62 (NY) [17] Yonkers, NY Sacred Heart Church; [HH] New York, NY House of Peace, Inc.
McCall, Stephen P. '79 (SD) Carlsbad, CA St. Patrick Church.
McCallister, Charles '71 (WH) Retired.
McCallister, Richard '91 (SEA) Lynden, WA St. Joseph Church.
McCallum, Dougald J. '97 (HEL) Frenchtown, MT St. John the Baptist Church.
McCallum, Gregory P. '97 (GAY) Higgins Lake, MI St. Hubert Church; Houghton Lake, MI St. James Church.
McCallum, Msgr. John V. '43 (DAL) Retired.
McCallum, Paul F. '62 (AUS) [19] Austin, TX St. Paul's Church.
McCamley, Martin Dugan '62 (ALT) State College, PA Our Lady of Victory Church.
McCandless, William T. *o.s.f.s.* '94 (PH) [D] Philadelphia, PA Northeast Catholic High School for Boys; [AA] Philadelphia, PA Oblates of St. Francis De Sales.
McCann, Arthur '62 (DM) Des Moines, IA City Chaplaincy Program; [J] Des Moines, IA City Hospital Chaplaincy Service.
McCann, Charles '69 (WDC) Camp Springs, MD St. Philip the Apostle Church.
McCann, J. Dennis (BGP) [J] Bridgeport, CT St. Vincent's Medical Center.
McCann, Joachim *o.s.b.* '91 (P) [L] St. Benedict, OR Mt. Angel Abbey.
McCann, Msgr. John B. '85 (ALN) [3] Allentown, PA Immaculate Conception Church.
McCann, John H. *s.m.m.* '55 (HRT) Bantam, CT Our Lady of Grace Church.
McCann, Msgr. John J. '65 (RVC) Manhasset, NY St. Mary's Church.
McCann, Joseph H. '57 (HRT) [2] New Haven, CT St. Aedan's Church.
McCann, Luke W. (NY) [C] Poughkeepsie, NY Marist College.
McCann, Luke W. '79 (NY) [38] New York, NY St. Frances Xavier Cabrini Church.
McCann, Robert J. '81 (OAK) [1] Hayward, CA All Saints Church.
McCann, Stephen *o.s.b.* '98 (KCK) [H] Atchison, KS St. Benedict's Abbey.
McCann, Stephen *o.s.b.* '99 (KCK) [A] Atchison, KS Benedictine College.
McCann, Thomas *c.p.* '66 (R) Greenville, NC St. Gabriel Church.
McCann, Thomas E. '59 (SCR) Harding, PA Church of the Holy Redeemer.
McCann, Thomas M. '98 (NO) Mandeville, LA Our Lady of the Lake Church.
McCann, Thomas W. '68 (CLV) Cuyahoga Falls, OH Immaculate Heart of Mary Church.
McCann, Vincent *o.f.m.* '41 (SP) [O] St. Petersburg, FL St. Anthony Friary.
McCann, Vincent '46 (NY) Retired.
McCann, Vincent, M.H.H. '46 (PRT) [1] Portland, ME Cathedral of the Immaculate Conception.
McCann, William '94 (LSC) Hatch, NM Our Lord of Mercy Church.
McCarren, Charles K. '45 (RCK) Retired.
McCarren, Msgr. Edgar P. '43 (OAK) [B] Moraga, CA St. Mary's College.
McCarren, Msgr. Edgar P. '43 (RVC) Retired.
McCarren, Msgr. Edgar P. '43 (SJ) [5] Santa Clara, CA Our Lady of Peace Church; Retired.
McCarren, Gerald H. '91 (NEW) [B] South Orange, NJ Seton Hall University.
McCarren, Gerard H. '91 (NEW) [A] South Orange, NJ Immaculate Conception Seminary.
McCarren, Msgr. John C. '46 (PIT) Allison Park, PA St. Ursula Church; Retired.
McCarren, Paul '74 (BO) [W] Cambridge, MA Weston Jesuit Community.
McCarren, Msgr. Stephen A. '55 (GBG) Retired.
McCarren, William J. '47 (BRK) Retired.
McCarron, Gerald J. '70 (TR) Normandy Beach, NJ Our Lady of Peace Church.
McCarron, Msgr. Michael D. '77 (RIC) Newport News, VA Our Lady of Mount Carmel Church.
McCarthy, Anthony T. '71 (MIL) Monches, WI St. John Church; North Lake, WI St. Clare Church.
McCarthy, Bernard '47 (HEL) Retired.
McCarthy, Brian P. '75 (NY) [4] Yonkers, NY St. Bartholomew Church.
McCarthy, Brien R. '81 (WDC) [4] Washington, DC Annunciation Church; Special Ministries; [S] Washington, DC Archdiocesan Campus Ministry.
McCarthy, Carl '95 (OWN) Hawesville, KY Immaculate Conception Church; Lewisport, KY St. Columba Church.
McCarthy, Charles A. *c.s.sp.* '51 (PEO) Eagle Township, IL Annunciation of Blessed Virgin Mary Church; Leonore, IL SS. Peter and Paul's Church.
McCarthy, Cornelius Scott '74 (MRY) Carmel Valley, CA Our Lady of Mt. Carmel Church.
McCarthy, D. Joseph '78 (SAC) Absent on Leave.
McCarthy, Daniel *c.s.sp.* '66 (NY) [69] New York, NY St. Mark the Evangelist Church.
McCarthy, Daniel J. *ss.cc.* '42 (FR) [I] Fairhaven, MA Sacred Hearts Provincial House.
McCarthy, Daniel P. '67 (CHI) [195] Chicago, IL St. Tarcissus Church.
McCarthy, David J. '60 (CLV) Doylestown, OH SS. Peter and Paul Church.
McCarthy, Donal *ss.cc.* '65 (LA) [D] La Verne, CA Damien High School; [Q] La Verne, CA Congregation of the Sacred Hearts of Jesus and Mary.
McCarthy, Donald E. *c.s.b.* '58 (ROC) Webster, NY St. Rita Church; [I] Rochester, NY Basilian Residence.
McCarthy, Donald G. '54 (CIN) [10] Cincinnati, OH St. Antoninus Church.
McCarthy, Donald P. '59 (SAL) Hill City, KS Immaculate Heart of Mary Church.
McCarthy, Edward A. '43 (MIA) Retired.
McCarthy, Edward J. '71 (ORL) Deltona, FL Our Lady of the Lakes Church.
McCarthy, Edward P. *c.pp.s.* '40 (LFT) [A] Rensselaer, IN Saint Joseph's College.
McCarthy, Emmanuel Charles '81 (NTN) [A] Brookline, MA Seminary of St. Gregory the Theologian.
McCarthy, Msgr. Emmett '43 (ORG) Brea, CA St. Angela Merici Church; Retired.
McCarthy, Eugene J. '60 (VEN) Marco Island, FL San Marco Church.
McCarthy, Francis *c.pp.s.* '42 (CIN) [M] Dayton, OH

Provincial Office of the Cincinnati Province of the Society of the Precious Blood.
McCarthy, Francis *o.carm.* '51 (TUC) [B] Nogales, AZ Lourdes Catholic School.
McCarthy, Francis E. *o.carm* '51 (VEN) [G] Nokomis, FL Carmel at Mission Valley.
McCarthy, Francis X. '54 (MIA) [9] Fort Lauderdale, FL St. Jerome Church; Retired.
McCarthy, George B. '56 (PRO) [4] Newport, RI St. Mary Church.
McCarthy, Gerald A. '57 (FAR) Bisbee, ND Holy Rosary Church; Retired.
McCarthy, J. Joseph '66 (FgM) Society of St. James the Apostle.
McCarthy, James '45 (FR) Retired.
McCarthy, Msgr. James '68 (NY) [1] New York, NY Cathedral of St. Patrick.
McCarthy, James C. '62 (HEL) On Leave of Absence.
McCarthy, James F. '68 (NY) Shrub Oak, NY Saint Elizabeth Ann Seton Church.
McCarthy, James H. '55 (CHI) Other Assignments.
McCarthy, James J. '63 (BO) Braintree, MA St. Thomas More Church.
McCarthy, Jeremiah *m.s.c.* '50 (SAN) Big Spring, TX Immaculate Heart of Mary Church.
McCarthy, Jeremiah J. '66 (BO) Society of St. James the Apostle.
McCarthy, Msgr. Jeremiah J. '72 (LA) [A] Camarillo, CA St. John's Seminary.
McCarthy, Jeremiah J. '72 (TUC) On Duty Outside the Diocese.
McCarthy, Jeremiah J. '78 (SAV) [4] Savannah, GA Most Blessed Sacrament Church.
McCarthy, Jerry '45 (TLS) Retired.
McCarthy, John *c.ss.r.* '62 (FgM) Redemptorist Foreign Missions.
McCarthy, John E. *c.s.c.* '58 (FR) [A] North Easton, MA Stonehill College; [A] North Easton, MA Holy Cross Fathers Religious.
McCarthy, Msgr. John F. '55 (HEL) On Duty Outside the Diocese.
McCarthy, John J. *m.s.* '69 (HRT) [M] Hartford, CT Missionaries of LaSalette, Provincial Secretary.
McCarthy, Msgr. John J. '84 (HRT) Wallingford, CT Resurrection Church.
McCarthy, John L. *s.j.* '62 (STL) [P] St. Louis, MO Jesuit Community Corporation at St. Louis University - Jesuit Hall.
McCarthy, Msgr. John M. '54 (NY) [222] Staten Island, NY St. Patrick Church.
McCarthy, John M. *m.s.* '69 (STL) [P] St. Louis, MO La Salette Missionaries.
McCarthy, John R. '55 (CLV) East Cleveland, OH St. Philomena Church.
McCarthy, John R. '55 (STU) On Duty Outside the Diocese.
McCarthy, Jose *o.f.m.cap.* '60 (ARE) [1] Utuado, PR San Miquel Church.
McCarthy, Jose *o.f.m.cap.* '60 (FgM) Capuchin Foreign Missions.
McCarthy, Jose *o.f.m.cap.* '60 (NY) [DD] White Plains, NY St. Conrad Friary.
McCarthy, Joseph '48 (BUR) Retired.
McCarthy, Joseph F. '48 (SFD) Retired.
McCarthy, Joseph J. *o.carm.* '60 (GAL) [14] Houston, TX St. Bernadette Soubirous Church.
McCarthy, Joseph L. '69 (CHL) Retired.
McCarthy, Joseph S. '96 (BO) [14] Boston, MA St. Brigid Church.
McCarthy, Kevin P. '89 (GRY) [N] Valparaiso, IN Newman Apostolate-Valparaiso University.
McCarthy, Leo *o.carm.* '62 (FgM) Carmelite Foreign Missions.
McCarthy, Leo *o.carm.* '62 (JOL) [J] Darien, IL Carmelite Community; [J] Darien, IL Carmelite Provincial Office.
McCarthy, Leo F. *m.m.* '47 (NY) [DD] Maryknoll, NY Maryknoll Fathers and Brothers.
McCarthy, Msgr. Leo F. '59 (BUF) [2] Batavia, NY St. Joseph Church.
McCarthy, Martin F. *s.j.* '54 (BO) [W] Weston, MA Campion Health Center, Inc.
McCarthy, Michael J. *c.s.sp.* '48 (BRK) [V] Long Island City, NY Holy Ghost Fathers of Ireland; [Z] Long Island City, NY World Compassion Link.
McCarthy, Michael J. '58 (BGP) [Q] Ridgefield, CT Provincial House, Congregation de Notre Dame.
McCarthy, Michael J. '65 (PH) Absent on Sick Leave.
McCarthy, Patrick '78 (STL) [P] St. Louis, MO La Salette Missionaries.
McCarthy, Patrick P. '44 (SFR) Retired.
McCarthy, Paul '84 (FTW) [14] South Bend, IN St. Mary of the Assumption Church.
McCarthy, Paul E. '80 (BO) [42] Boston, MA St. Mary Church.
McCarthy, Paul J. *s.j.* '57 (BUF) [O] Buffalo, NY Canisius Jesuit Community.
McCarthy, Richard C. '69 (PRT) Retired.
McCarthy, Richard J. *c.m.* '58 (SAT) Losoya, TX El Carmen Catholic Church.
McCarthy, Msgr. Robert '58 (STL) Des Peres, MO St. Clement Church.
McCarthy, Msgr. Robert J. '46 (OG) Retired.
McCarthy, Sean M. '91 (BO) Acton, MA St. Elizabeth of Hungary Church.
McCarthy, Terrence A. '74 (CHI) [1] Waukegan, IL St. Anastasia Church.
McCarthy, Thomas (RVC) Retired.
McCarthy, Thomas *s.j.* '62 (P) Sherwood, OR St. Francis Church.
McCarthy, Thomas *o.s.a.* '94 (CHI) [N] Chicago, IL St. Rita Monastery.
McCarthy, Msgr. Thomas A. '59 (NEW) Washington Township, NJ Our Lady of Good Counsel Church.
McCarthy, Thomas E. '49 (HRT) Avon, CT St. Ann's Church.
McCarthy, Thomas H. '43 (KC) Retired.
McCarthy, Thomas J. '51 (SPR) Retired.
McCarthy, Thomas J. '61 (Y) Mantua, OH St. Joseph's Church.
McCarthy, Thomas J. '80 (BUF) West Valley, NY St. John the Baptist Church.
McCarthy, Thomas P. *c.s.v.* '52 (CHI) [N] Arlington Heights, IL Viatorian Province Center-Clerics of St. Viator.
McCarthy, Vincent *s.s.c.* '79 (OM) [K] St. Columbans, NE St. Columban's Foreign Mission Society.
McCarthy, Warren J. '52 (CHI) Schaumburg, IL St. Marcelline Church; Retired.
McCarthy, William *m.s.a.* '59 (NOR) [F] Cromwell, CT Society of the Missionaries of the Holy Apostles.
McCarthy, Msgr. William '63 (PAT) East Hanover, NJ St. Rose of Lima Church.
McCarthy, William D. *m.m.* '56 (NY) [B] Maryknoll, NY Center for Mission Research and Study at Maryknoll; [DD] Maryknoll, NY Maryknoll Fathers and Brothers.
McCarthy, William E. *m.m.* '58 (NY) [DD] Maryknoll, NY Maryknoll Fathers and Brothers.
McCarthy, William E. '58 (RVC) Shoreham, NY St. Mark Church.
McCarthy, William R. '52 (BO) [3] Quincy, MA St. John the Baptist Church; Senior Priests.
McCartin, Francis P. *o.m.i.* '38 (BO) [Z] Tewksbury, MA Immaculate Heart of Mary Infirmary.
McCartney, James '84 (LUB) Plainview, TX St. Alice Church.
McCartney, James J. *o.s.a.* '70 (PH) [C] Villanova, PA Villanova University.
McCartney, John J. '99 (RVC) Center Moriches, NY St. John the Evangelist Church.
McCartney, Louis R. *o.s.f.s.* '52 (WIL) [I] Childs, MD Oblates of St. Francis De Sales.
McCarty, Bruce '89 (OWN) Cloverport, KY St. Rose Church; Irvington, KY Holy Guardian Angels Church.
McCarty, Kieran *o.f.m.* '49 (LA) [Q] Santa Barbara, CA Franciscan Friary, Order of Friars Minor (Old Mission).
McCarty, Lawrence L. '63 (SC) Auburn, IA St. Mary's Church; Sac City, IA St. Mary's Church.
McCarty, Paul T. *s.j.* '67 (BO) [W] Weston, MA Campion Health Center, Inc.
McCarty, Robert E. *s.j.* '67 (NEW) [B] Jersey City, NJ Saint Peter's College; [N] Jersey City, NJ Jesuits of Saint Peter's College, Inc.
McCarty, Shaun *s.t.* '56 (WDC) [M] Adelphi, MD Missionary Servants of the Most Holy Trinity.
McCarty, Thomas J. *o.c.s.o.* '56 (DUB) [K] Peosta, IA New Melleray Abbey, Order of Cistercians of the Strict Observance.
McCarver, Jim '91 (MEM) Union City, TN Immaculate Conception Church.
McCarville, John J. '65 (CHI) Bellwood, IL St. Simeon Church.
McCasland, Howard '44 (OG) Churubusco, NY Immaculate Heart of Mary Church; Retired.
McCaslin, James J. *s.s.c.* '54 (FgM) St. Columban's Foreign Mission.
McCaslin, John O. '55 (OM) Retired.
McCaslin, John T. *s.j.* '66 (ALN) [A] Wernersville, PA Jesuit Center.
McCaslin, R. Patrick '61 (OM) [24] Omaha, NE St. John Vianney Church.
McCaslin, Richard F. *s.j.* '65 (GB) [M] Oshkosh, WI Jesuit Retreat House.
McCaughley, Sean (NY) [14] New York, NY Ascension Church.
McCauley, Daniel *o.c.d.* '55 (MIL) [P] Milwaukee, WI Provincial Offices - Discalced Carmelites.
McCauley, David '63 (FAR) On Duty Outside the Diocese.
McCauley, David F. '63 (STP) [S] St. Paul, MN Minnesota Catholic Conference.
McCauley, George C. *s.j.* '61 (NY) [DD] New York, NY Jesuit Community at Fordham University.
McCauley, James P. *s.j.* '56 (LAV) Tonopah, NV St. Patrick Church.
McCauley, James P. *s.j.* '56 (SJ) [L] Los Gatos, CA Sacred Heart Jesuit Center.
McCauley, James R. *c.s.p.* '74 (TUC) [13] Tucson, AZ St. Cyril of Alexandria Church.
McCauley, James R. *c.s.p.* '74 (WDC) [B] Washington, DC St. Paul's College.
McCauley, Walter C. *s.j.* '56 (FWT) [K] Lake Dallas, TX Montserrat Jesuit Retreat House.
McCaulley, Cornelius W. '66 (PIT) [41] Pittsburgh, PA St. Stephen Church.
McCausland, Joseph E. '50 (CLV) Military Chaplains.
McCawley, Scott '93 (JOL) Mokena, IL St. Mary Church.
McCawley, William J. '60 (SCR) Brodheadsville, PA Our Lady Queen of Peace Church.
McChesney, Robert W. '81 (LA) Los Angeles, CA Immigration and Naturalization Service; [C] Los Angeles, CA Loyola Marymount University.
McClain, J. Thomas *s.j.* '77 (DET) [K] Detroit, MI Jesuit Provincial Office-Detroit Province of the Society of Jesus.
McClain, J. Thomas *s.j.* '77 (NY) [F] New York, NY Regis High School; [DD] New York, NY St. Ignatius Loyola Residence.
McClain, Joseph P. *c.m.* '49 (MET) [H] Plainsboro, NJ Vincentian Residence.
McClanahan, Robert P., Jr. '84 (BLX) Gulfport, MS Naval Const. Bn. Center.
McClanahan, Robert P., Jr. '84 (PT) Military Chaplains.
McClean, Msgr. John R. '57 (DUB) Guttenberg, IA St. Mary's Church; North Buena Vista, IA Immaculate Conception Church; [F] Guttenberg, IA Guttenberg-North Buena Vista Consolidated School.
McCleane, Michael J. '81 (PH) [15] Philadelphia, PA Ascension of Our Lord Church.
McClear, J. Edmund *m.m.* '42 (NY) [DD] Maryknoll, NY Maryknoll Fathers and Brothers.
McCleary, Michael L. '78 (PBL) Durango, CO St. Columba Church; [E] Durango, CO Centura Health-Mercy Medical Center.
McClellan, Keith J. *o.s.b.* '79 (IND) [J] St. Meinrad, IN St. Meinrad Archabbey.
McClellan, Robert J. '81 (RCK) [3] Rockford, IL St. Bernadette Church.
McClintock, James '86 (BEA) Bridge City, TX St. Henry Church.
McClory, Bernard J. '53 (COL) Retired.
McClory, Robert '99 (DET) Macomb, MI St. Isidore Church.
McClory, Robert J. (DET) Graduate Studies.
McCloskey, C. John '81 (WDC) [T] Washington, DC Prelature of the Holy Cross and Opus Dei.
McCloskey, C. John, III *s.t.d.* '82 (WDC) [V] Washington, DC Catholic Information Center.
McCloskey, Daniel J. '83 (WIL) Georgetown, DE St. Michael the Archangel Church.
McCloskey, Francis '63 (ALB) Special Assignment.
McCloskey, Msgr. James A. '46 (SY) Fayetteville, NY Immaculate Conception Church; Retired.
McCloskey, James P. *c.s.sp.* (PH) [G] Bensalem, PA Holy Ghost Preparatory School.
McCloskey, James P. *c.s.sp.* '80 (PH) [AA] Bensalem, PA Congregation of the Holy Ghost.
McCloskey, John *o.f.m.cap.* '98 (HBG) [2] York, PA St. Joseph Church.
McCloskey, Joseph (PH) [U] Philadelphia, PA St. Agnes Medical Center.
McCloskey, Joseph M. *s.j.* '63 (WDC) [E] Washington, DC Gonzaga College High School.
McCloskey, Joseph W. '61 (PH) [152] Philadelphia, PA St. Thomas Aquinas Church.
McCloskey, Lester '64 (SEA) Port Orchard, WA St. Gabriel Church; Port Orchard, WA Washington Veterans Home Hospital.
McCloskey, Patrick *o.f.m.* '75 (CIN) [E] Cincinnati, OH Roger Bacon High School; [M] Cincinnati, OH St. Clare Friary.
McCloskey, Terrence *c.ss.r.* (OAK) [P] Oakland, CA Holy Redeemer Center, Redemptorist Retreat Center.
McCloskey, Terrence *c.ss.r.* '66 (OAK) [N] Oakland, CA Redemptorists.
McClosky, Msgr. Adam S. '67 (GAL) [2] Houston, TX All Saints Church.
McClure, Jack *c.pp.s.* '76 (DM) West Des Moines, IA Sacred Heart Church.
McClure, John A. '62 (TOL) [L] Sylvania, OH Sisters of St. Francis of the Congregation of Our Lady of Lourdes.
McCluskey, James F. '68 (OM) Wayne, NE St. Mary Church.
McCluskey, John D. *s.j.* '57 (SPK) [K] Spokane, WA Regis Community.
McCluskey, Raymond E. *s.j.* '45 (BO) [W] Weston, MA Campion Health Center, Inc.
McCoart, Charles C. '90 (ARL) [4] Arlington, VA St. Charles Borromeo Church.
McCole, John F. '58 (PH) Pottstown, PA St. Aloysius Church; Pottstown, PA Holy Trinity Church.
McColl, Scott J. '80 (SD) [2] San Diego, CA Ascension Church.
McColligan, Raymond A. '43 (PIT) Retired.
McCollum, Paul '98 (RNO) Yerington, NV Holy Family Church.
McComiskey, Joseph C. '70 (RVC) Syosset, NY St. Edward Confessor Church.

McConaghy, R. Thomas '81 (NOR) [2] Norwich, CT Sacred Heart Church.
McConaghy, Robert J. '75 (ALN) On Duty Outside the Diocese.
McConnell, Bernard J. '49 (PH) [AA] Philadelphia, PA Jesuit Community at St. Joseph's University.
McConnell, James J. '54 (TR) Retired; [M] Trenton, NJ Villa Vianney.
McConnell, James J. *s.m.a.* '72 (NEW) [14] Newark, NJ Queen of Angels Church; [N] Tenafly, NJ Society of African Missions, Provincialate, S.M.A. Fathers.
McConnell, John *s.j.* '55 (NY) [DD] New York, NY Murray-Weigel Hall.
McConnell, William J. (BO) [20] Boston, MA St. Francis de Sales Church.
McConnell, William J. '53 (BO) Senior Priests.
McConnin, Robert J. '73 (BRK) [205] Queens, NY St. Nicholas of Tolentine Church.
McConvey, Michael '79 (GLP) Absent on Leave.
McConville, James '90 (STP) North St. Paul, MN St. Peter Church.
McConville, Philip G. '43 (BO) Senior Priests.
McConville, William E. *o.f.m.* '73 (ALB) [B] Loudonville, NY Siena College.
McConway, Sean J. *o.p.* '87 (NY) Pleasantville, NY Holy Innocents Church.
McCoog, Thomas M. *s.j.* '71 (BAL) [S] Baltimore, MD Jesuit Fathers and Brothers Maryland Provincial Curia.
McCool, Gerald A. *s.j.* '52 (NY) [DD] New York, NY Jesuit Community at Fordham University.
McCool, Malachy '71 (HT) On Leave.
McCool, Patrick *o.s.b.* '63 (OKL) [I] Shawnee, OK St. Gregory's Abbey.
McCord, Kent G. '81 (MET) On Duty Outside the Diocese.
McCorkell, Patrick M. *s.j.* '74 (RC) [4] Rapid City, SD St. Isaac Jogues Church; [B] Howes, SD Kino Jesuit Community.
McCorkle, Msgr. Louis W. '53 (JC) [A] Hannibal, MO St. Thomas Aquinas Seminary.
McCormac, Michael P. '80 (PH) Glenolden, PA St. George Church.
McCormack, Andrew G. *s.m.* '57 (WDC) [M] Washington, DC Marist Center.
McCormack, Brendan '60 (WDC) Retired.
McCormack, Daniel J. '94 (CHI) [4] Chicago, IL St. Agatha Church.
McCormack, Douglas '69 (LFT) Zionsville, IN St. Alphonsus Church.
McCormack, Gerald *o.m.i.* '47 (BO) [Z] Tewksbury, MA Immaculate Heart of Mary Infirmary.
McCormack, John (KC) [I] Kansas City, MO Jeanne Jugan Center.
McCormack, John '61 (KC) Retired.
McCormack, Keith J. '76 (TOL) Mansfield, OH St. Mary Church.
McCormack, Martin L. *o.f.m.* '48 (BO) [Z] Boston, MA Saint Anthony Residence.
McCormack, Michael *o.p.* '87 (RIC) Charlottesville, VA St. Thomas Aquinas Church.
McCormack, Richard J. '61 (BRK) [143] Brooklyn, NY St. Vincent de Paul Church.
McCormack, Msgr. Robert '47 (NY) Retired.
McCormick, Andrew '82 (PH) Holland, PA St. Bede the Venerable Church.
McCormick, Brian '66 (TR) [T] Trenton, NJ Martin House.
McCormick, Daniel J. '57 (ATL) Dunwoody, GA All Saints Catholic Church.
McCormick, Frank '68 (HEL) [3] Missoula, MT Pope John XXIII Church.
McCormick, Gregory *s.p.* '49 (SB) [G] Cherry Valley, CA Servants of the Paraclete Guadalupe Retreat Center.
McCormick, Howard W. '57 (SPR) Agawam, MA St. John the Evangelist Church.
McCormick, James '63 (SFS) On Leave of Absence.
McCormick, James '82 (E) [18] Erie, PA St. James Church; [C] Erie, PA Cathedral Preparatory School.
McCormick, James D. '62 (SC) Carroll, IA Holy Spirit Church.
McCormick, Jeffrey '96 (MIA) Coral Springs, FL St. Andrew Church.
McCormick, Jerry '73 (MRY) Pacific Grove, CA St. Angela Church.
McCormick, John '75 (ORL) Kissimmee, FL Holy Redeemer Church.
McCormick, John '99 (SR) Napa, CA St. Apollinaris Church.
McCormick, John D. '75 (DEN) [1] Arvada, CO Shrine of St. Anne Church.
McCormick, John J. '56 (BO) Billerica, MA St. Theresa of Lisieux Church.
McCormick, Joseph E. *s.j.* '54 (BO) [W] Weston, MA Campion Health Center, Inc.
McCormick, Joseph E. *o.s.a.* '77 (DET) Grosse Pointe Park, MI St. Clare of Montefalco Church.
McCormick, Justin J. *c.s.p.* '61 (NY) [DD] Jamaica Estates, NY Paulist Fathers Generalate.
McCormick, Kieran D. '64 (SFR) San Carlos, CA St. Charles Church.
McCormick, Louis M. *o.f.m.* '65 (BUF) [C] St. Bonaventure, NY St. Bonaventure University; [Q] West Clarksville, NY Mount Irenaeus, Franciscan Mountain Retreat & Holy Peace Friary.
McCormick, Mark '91 (RC) Custer, SD St. John the Baptist Church; Hill City, SD St. Rose of Lima Church; Hot Springs, SD St. Anthony's Church.
McCormick, Martin F. *o.p.* '61 (DET) [L] Farmington Hills, MI Monastery of the Blessed Sacrament.
McCormick, Msgr. Maurice M. '58 (SFR) [34] San Francisco, CA Mission Dolores Basilica Church; [T] Pacifica, CA Cursillo.
McCormick, Michael '85 (WH) Absent on Sick Leave.
McCormick, Myron *o.f.m.* '52 (BO) [BB] Boston, MA St. Anthony Shrine.
McCormick, Patrick G. '96 (PH) [1] Bensalem, PA St. Charles Borromeo Church.
McCormick, Patrick J. '57 (ATL) Military Chaplains.
McCormick, Patrick Joseph '75 (FRS) [11] Fresno, CA St. Mary Church.
McCormick, Paul *o.cist.* '97 (DAL) [K] Irving, TX Cistercian Abbey of Our Lady of Dallas.
McCormick, Richard J. *s.d.b.* '70 (SP) [B] St. Petersburg, FL St. Petersburg Catholic High School.
McCormick, Robert J. '42 (MIL) Retired.
McCormick, Thomas G. '81 (RVC) Levittown, NY St. Bernard Church.
McCormley, Hugh J. '62 (PIT) Harmarville, PA St. Francis of Assisi Church.
McCorry, Msgr. Edward J. '56 (NY) Hastings-on-Hudson, NY St. Matthew Church; Hastings-on-Hudson, NY St. Stanislaus Kostka Church.
McCotter, Daniel E. *c.s.p.* '81 (SFR) [23] San Francisco, CA Holy Family Chinese Church; [32] San Francisco, CA Old St. Mary's Church.
McCouch, Richard S. *s.j.* '93 (CI) [C] Koror, Palau, PW Manresa Jesuit House.
McCouch, Richard S. *s.j.* '93 (FgM) Provinces.
McCough, Richard S. *s.j.* '93 (FgM) Provinces.
McCourt, Gerald P. *s.j.* '72 (SJ) [K] Los Altos, CA Jesuit Retreat House.
McCourt, Msgr. Robert R. '61 (BRK) [223] Queens, NY St. Pascal Baylon Church.
McCown, Robert M. *s.j.* '54 (MOB) Daphne, AL Shrine of the Holy Cross Church.
McCoy, Alan *o.f.m.* '38 (LA) [73] Los Angeles, CA St. Joseph Church.
McCoy, Alfred E. '54 (SC) [A] Sioux City, IA Briar Cliff College; [B] Sioux City, IA Catholic Schools of Sioux City.
McCoy, Bernard *o.cist.* '95 (LC) [H] Sparta, WI Our Lady of Spring Bank, Cistercian Abbey.
McCoy, Charles J. '61 (BO) [7] Newton, MA St. Philip Neri Church.
McCoy, Daniel F. *s.j.* '45 (FgM) Provinces.
McCoy, Floyd (SJN) On Duty Outside the Archdiocese.
McCoy, James B. '63 (PH) [EE] Philadelphia, PA Newman Center at Drexel University.
McCoy, Msgr. James P. '63 (PH) Chalfont, PA St. Jude Church.
McCoy, John '93 (STU) [3] Steubenville, OH Holy Rosary Church; [E] Steubenville, OH Trinity Health System; [E] Steubenville, OH Trinity Health System.
McCoy, Msgr. Kevin C. '81 (SC) On Duty Outside the Diocese.
McCoy, P. Floyd '84 (MGZ) Lajas, PR Our Lady of the Purification Church.
McCoy, Msgr. Patrick '60 (SR) [1] Santa Rosa, CA Cathedral of St. Eugene; [5] Santa Rosa, CA Star of the Valley Church; [G] Santa Rosa, CA Santa Rosa Memorial Hospital.
McCoy, Perry *o.s.m.* (P) Sheridan, OR Federal Correctional Institution.
McCoy, Perry *o.s.m.* '95 (P) [L] Portland, OR The Grotto, The National Sanctuary of Our Sorrowful Mother.
McCoy, Perry M. *o.s.m.* '93 (CHI) [N] Chicago, IL Order of Friar Servants of Mary (Servites) United States of America Province, Inc.
McCracken, John E. '79 (GAY) [1] Gaylord, MI St. Mary Church; Vanderbilt, MI Holy Redeemer Church.
McCracken, Msgr. John T. '44 (OAK) [1] Walnut Creek, CA St. Anne Church.
McCracken, Kevin *c.m.* '82 (LA) [A] Camarillo, CA St. John's Seminary.
McCrane, Gerard T. *m.m.* '59 (FgM) Maryknoll Foreign Missions.
McCrann, Peter J. *s.m.m.* '58 (RVC) Bay Shore, NY Southside Hospital; [M] Bay Shore, NY Montfort Missionaries.
McCrate, D. Stephen '89 (BEA) [7] Port Arthur, TX St. Joseph Church.
McCray, Trinette '81 (MIL) [C] Milwaukee, WI Cardinal Stritch University.
McCready, Daniel A. '47 (PHX) Retired.
McCready, James *s.j.* '63 (SPK) [K] Spokane, WA Regis Community.
McCreanor, James '78 (MIA) Homestead, FL Sacred Heart Church.
McCreary, Glenn E. '95 (SCR) [10] Scranton, PA Immaculate Conception Church.
McCreary, Robert E. *o.f.m.cap.* '64 (HBG) [2] York, PA St. Joseph Church.
McCreedy, Harry E. '72 (PH) [4] Norristown, PA St. Paul Church.
McCreedy, Justin D. *o.s.b.* '70 (SEA) [L] Lacey, WA St. Martin's Abbey.
McCreedy, Justin D. *o.s.b.* '70 (YAK) [D] Yakima, WA Providence Yakima Medical Center.
McCreesh, Eugene P. *s.j.* '54 (CHL) [9] Charlotte, NC St. Peter Church; [J] Charlotte, NC Jesuit Community.
McCreesh, Thomas P. *o.p.* '72 (WDC) [B] Washington, DC Dominican House of Studies.
McCreight, James H. '68 (CLV) [50] Cleveland, OH St. Michael Church; [60] Cleveland, OH Sagrada Familia Church.
McCrillis, Philip (SJ) Absent on Sick Leave.
McCrone, John M. '82 (NEW) Paramus, NJ Annunciation Church.
McCue, Michael J. *o.s.f.s.* '90 (PH) [131] Philadelphia, PA Our Mother of Consolation Church.
McCue, Richard T. '58 (CHL) Retired.
McCue, Will *s.c.* (BR) [H] Baton Rouge, LA Brothers of the Sacred Heart.
McCue, Will *s.c.* '74 (BR) Special Assignment; [M] Baton Rouge, LA Baton Rouge Chancery Office.
McCulken, Msgr. Michael T. '76 (PH) Brookline, PA Annunciation B.V.M. Church.
McCullagh, Msgr. John P. '55 (BRK) [143] Brooklyn, NY St. Vincent de Paul Church.
McCullen, John L. '44 (MIA) Deerfield Beach, FL St. Ambrose Church.
McCullen, John L. '44 (TOL) Retired.
McCulloch, Lawrence F. *m.m.* '70 (NY) [DD] Maryknoll, NY Maryknoll Fathers and Brothers.
McCullough, Brian *s.c.j.* '73 (MIL) [B] Hales Corners, WI Sacred Heart School of Theology; [P] Hales Corners, WI Sacred Heart Monastery.
McCullough, Hugh J. '79 (FR) Wareham, MA St. Patrick's Church.
McCullough, J. Edward '67 (GBG) Dunbar, PA St. Aloysius Church.
McCullough, James '57 (E) [B] Erie, PA Gannon University.
McCullough, Michael . '73 (LA) [97] Los Angeles, CA Transfiguration Church.
McCullough, Michael P. '73 (LA) Los Angeles, CA L.A. Police Department.
McCumber, William W. '83 (STL) [1] Lemay, MO Mary, Queen of the Universe Church.
McCurdy, Richard L. *s.j.* '67 (SAC) [C] Sacramento, CA Jesuit High School; [H] Carmichael, CA Jesuit High School Community of Sacramento.
McCurdy, William J. *s.j.* '61 (ROC) [C] Rochester, NY McQuaid Jesuit High School.
McCurry, James E. *o.f.m.conv.* '77 (SPR) [A] Granby, MA St. Hyacinth College and Seminary; [R] Granby, MA Knights of the Immaculata Movement (Militia Immaculatae, M.I.).
McCusker, William C. *s.j.* '51 (ROC) [C] Rochester, NY McQuaid Jesuit High School.
McDade, Robert *m.ss.cc.* '76 (CAM) [M] Linwood, NJ Villa Pieta.
McDade, Msgr. Thomas J. '74 (NEW) Franklin Lakes, NJ Most Blessed Sacrament Church.
McDaid, Msgr. Edward J. '47 (CAM) Retired.
McDaid, Henry '63 (BIR) Jasper, AL St. Cecilia Church.
McDaid, J. Anthony '75 (DEN) On Duty Outside the Archdiocese.
McDaniel, George '70 (DAV) [B] Davenport, IA St. Ambrose University.
McDaniel, Isaac *o.s.b.* '82 (IND) [J] St. Meinrad, IN St. Meinrad Archabbey.
McDaniel, Isaac *o.s.b.* '82 (L) Fairdale, KY St. Jerome Church.
McDaniel, John W. *s.j.* '71 (PH) [AA] Philadelphia, PA Jesuit Community at St. Joseph's University.
McDaniel, Rodney '58 (CIN) [L] Cincinnati, OH St. Margaret Hall.
McDarby, J. Patrick *o.s.b.* '53 (SCL) [I] Collegeville, MN St. John's Abbey, of the Order of St. Benedict.
McDermott, Brian O. *s.j.* '68 (WDC) [M] Washington, DC The Jesuit Community at Georgetown University.
McDermott, Charles B. '63 (PRO) [6] Pawtucket, RI St. Joseph Church.
McDermott, Charles B. '73 (NEW) Union, NJ St. Michael's Church.
McDermott, Charles S. '60 (SAC) [22] Sacramento, CA St. Rose Church.
McDermott, Christopher H. *c.s.sp.* '81 (PH) [AA] Bensalem, PA Congregation of the Holy Ghost.
McDermott, Edwin J. *s.j.* '49 (SFR) [N] San Francisco, CA Jesuit Community at University of San Francisco.
McDermott, H. Thomas *c.s.c.* '79 (FgM) Holy Cross Foreign Missions.
McDermott, H. Thomas '79 (FTW) [J] South Bend, IN Congregation of Holy Cross, Indiana Province, Provincial House.
McDermott, Msgr. Ignatius D. '36 (CHI) Retired.

McDermott, John '89 (BUR) [H] Burlington, VT University of Vermont-The Catholic Center at UVM.
McDermott, Msgr. John F. '57 (NEW) [S] Plainfield, NJ RENEW International.
McDermott, John J. '86 (DUB) On Leave of Absence.
McDermott, John J. '89 (BUR) Middlebury, VT Assumption of the Blessed Virgin Mary Church.
McDermott, John Michael *s.j.* '71 (COL) [A] Columbus, OH Pontifical College Josephinum.
McDermott, Joseph *s.v.d.* '52 (DUB) [B] Epworth, IA Divine Word College.
McDermott, Joseph M. '95 (PH) Warrington, PA St. Robert Bellarmine Church.
McDermott, Joseph P. '62 (BO) Stoughton, MA Immaculate Conception Church.
McDermott, Martin F. *s.j.* '64 (FgM) Provinces.
McDermott, Michael '66 (PIT) Allegheny County, PA UPMC University of Pittsburgh Medical Center; Allegheny County, PA UPMC Shadyside Hospital.
McDermott, Michael '75 (WIL) Hockessin, DE St. Mary of the Assumption Church.
McDermott, Michael F. '79 (GI) St. Paul, NE SS. Peter and Paul Church.
McDermott, Michael J. '65 (SEA) [2] Tacoma, WA St. Charles Borromeo Church.
McDermott, Neal *o.p.* '61 (NO) [30] New Orleans, LA St. Dominic Church.
McDermott, Patrick '67 (SEA) Aberdeen, WA St. Mary Church; Aberdeen, WA SS. Peter and Paul Church; Hoquiam, WA Our Lady of Good Help Church; Ocean Shores, WA St. Jerome Church.
McDermott, Patrick M. '64 (BLX) [5] Biloxi, MS Sacred Heart Church.
McDermott, Robert '81 (LIN) Shelby, NE Sacred Heart Church.
McDermott, Robert B. '90 (PH) Buckingham, PA Our Lady of Guadalupe Church.
McDermott, Robert J., Jr. '81 (STA) [3] Jacksonville, FL Christ the King Church.
McDermott, Msgr. Robert T. '69 (CAM) [7] Camden, NJ St. Joseph's Pro-Church.
McDermott, Robert T. '81 (MIL) On Duty Outside the Archdiocese.
McDermott, Thomas F. *s.j.* '38 (BO) [W] Weston, MA Campion Health Center, Inc.
McDermott, Msgr. Thomas J. '55 (SD) Retired.
McDermott, Thomas J. '56 (SCR) Carbondale, PA St. Rose of Lima Church.
McDermott, Thomas J. '97 (DUB) Maquoketa, IA Sacred Heart Church.
McDermott, Thomas K. *o.p.* '83 (CHI) [N] Chicago, IL Dominicans (Provincial Office).
McDermott, Thomas K. *o.p.* '83 (FgM) Dominican - Order of Preachers Foreign Missions.
McDermott, William F. '98 (FAR) [3] Grand Forks, ND St. Michael's Church.
McDevitt, Msgr. Anthony J. '49 (MOB) Retired.
McDevitt, Edward P. *c.o.* '71 (CHR) York, SC Divine Saviour Church; [E] Rock Hill, SC Oratory of St. Philip Neri, Congregation of the Oratory of Pontifical Rite; [E] Rock Hill, SC Oratory of St. Philip Neri, Congregation of the Oratory of Pontifical Rite.
McDevitt, Francis N. '41 (PH) Malvern, PA St. Patrick Church; Retired.
McDevitt, James '97 (ALB) Ballston Spa, NY St. Mary Church; Special Assignment.
McDevitt, James A. '90 (BGP) On Duty Outside the Diocese.
McDevitt, James J. '35 (PBL) Retired.
McDevitt, Michael '71 (SPC) Poplar Bluff, MO Poplar Bluff Hospital Ministry.
McDevitt, Michael V. '71 (SPC) Poplar Bluff, MO Sacred Heart Church.
McDevitt, Patrick J. *c.m.* '86 (STL) [P] St. Louis, MO Vincentian Residence.
McDevitt, Robert *s.j.* '60 (SFR) [25] San Francisco, CA St. Ignatius Church.
McDevitt, Robert L. *s.j.* '60 (SFR) [N] San Francisco, CA Jesuit Community at University of San Francisco.
McDevitt, Thomas (LAN) Retired.
McDevitt, Thomas '58 (LAN) [L] De Witt, MI St. Francis Retreat Center.
McDonagh, Andrew J. '42 (CHI) [129] Chicago, IL St. Mary of the Woods Church; Retired.
McDonagh, Edward C. '62 (BO) West Bridgewater, MA St. Ann Church.
McDonagh, John '81 (NY) [2] Mt. Vernon, NY Our Lady of Victory Church.
McDonagh, John P. *p.v.* (NY) Cornwall-on-Hudson, NY St. Thomas of Canterbury Church.
McDonagh, John P. '82 (SPR) [1] Springfield, MA St. Michael's Church.
McDonald, A. John '56 (BR) Retired.
McDonald, Alexander F. *s.j.* '47 (SEA) [L] Seattle, WA Jesuit House, Seattle.
McDonald, Allan J. '80 (SAV) [1] Augusta, GA Church of the Most Holy Trinity; [J] Augusta, GA Catholic Cemetery.
McDonald, Bernard (NY) Port Jervis, NY Mercy Community Hospital.
McDonald, Bill '89 (STO) Modesto, CA St. Stanislaus Church.
McDonald, C. Alexander '91 (CHR) North Augusta, SC Our Lady of Peace Church.
McDonald, Charles *c.ss.r.* '71 (PH) [25] Philadelphia, PA St. Boniface Church.
McDonald, Charles J. '65 (LEX) Lawrenceburg, KY St. Lawrence Church.
McDonald, Daniel C. *s.j.* '81 (MIL) [C] Milwaukee, WI Marquette University; [P] Milwaukee, WI Arrupe House Jesuit Community.
McDonald, David M. '55 (HRT) [2] Hamden, CT Blessed Sacrament Church.
McDonald, Edward J. *c.s.p.* '41 (BO) [W] Boston, MA Paulist Fathers Residence.
McDonald, Edward J. *c.s.p.* '41 (NY) [DD] Jamaica Estates, NY Paulist Fathers Generalate.
McDonald, Elmer J. '49 (ROC) Retired.
McDonald, Elmer J. '49 (SP) St. Pete Beach, FL St. John Church.
McDonald, Eustace *c.p.* '45 (BAL) [S] Baltimore, MD St. Joseph's Passionist Community.
McDonald, Finian *o.s.b.* '62 (SCL) [I] Collegeville, MN St. John's Abbey, of the Order of St. Benedict.
McDonald, Francis B. '60 (JOL) Roselle, IL St. Walter Church.
McDonald, G. Malcolm (PIT) Coraopolis, PA St. Joseph Church.
McDonald, Gerard R. *o.f.m.* '45 (PAT) [M] Butler, NJ St. Anthony Friary.
McDonald, James E. *c.s.c.* '84 (FTW) [J] Notre Dame, IN Holy Cross Community, Corby Hall, University of Notre Dame.
McDonald, Msgr. James M. '67 (RVC) Dix Hills, NY St. Matthew Church.
McDonald, John F. (HRT) Retired.
McDonald, John F. '47 (HRT) [A] Bloomfield, CT St. Thomas Seminary.
McDonald, John J. *s.j.* '57 (NY) [DD] New York, NY Murray-Weigel Hall.
McDonald, Joseph F. '87 (B) [1] Boise, ID Cathedral of St. John the Evangelist.
McDonald, Joseph S. *s.m.* '61 (CIN) [M] Dayton, OH Marianist Provincialate.
McDonald, Kenneth (LAN) Retired.
McDonald, Mark *m.s.c.* '68 (RCK) [G] Aurora, IL Missionaries of the Sacred Heart Community.
McDonald, Martin (MRY) Carmel, CA San Carlos Borromeo Basilica Church.
McDonald, Matthew D. '40 (CHI) Retired.
McDonald, Michael '85 (GI) [D] Kearney, NE University of Nebraska at Kearney Newman Apostolate.
McDonald, Michael D. '85 (GI) Kearney, NE Prince of Peace Church; Kearney, NE Youth Development Center.
McDonald, Paul F. '51 (DUB) Retired.
McDonald, Perry *o.f.m.cap.* '67 (DET) [K] Detroit, MI St. Bonaventure Friary; [K] Detroit, MI St. Bonaventure Friary.
McDonald, Peter '59 (SFR) San Anselmo, CA St. Anselm Church.
McDonald, Richard '99 (KCK) Shawnee, KS St. Joseph's Church.
McDonald, Robert *s.m.* '50 (PRT) Hamlin, ME St. Joseph Church; Van Buren, ME St. Bruno - St. Remi Church.
McDonald, Thomas A. '52 (NY) [W] Poughkeepsie, NY St. Francis Hospital.
McDonald, Thomas F. '52 (NY) Nanuet, NY St. Anthony Church.
McDonald, Thomas M. '56 (NY) On Duty Outside the Archdiocese.
McDonnell, Anthony '70 (LA) On Sick Leave.
McDonnell, David '72 (PAT) Randolph, NJ St. Matthew the Apostle Church.
McDonnell, Donald C. '47 (SFR) Retired.
McDonnell, Francis '60 (SD) Retired.
McDonnell, Francis P. '58 (HRT) Windsor Locks, CT St. Mary Church.
McDonnell, Francis R. *o.s.a.* '42 (DET) Grosse Pointe Park, MI St. Clare of Montefalco Church.
McDonnell, John *c.m.* '43 (BRK) [V] Jamaica, NY Vincentian Residence.
McDonnell, John H. '56 (WH) [3] Charleston, WV St. Agnes Church.
McDonnell, Msgr. John J. '44 (YAK) [2] Yakima, WA Holy Family Church.
McDonnell, John J. '73 (CHI) [1] Chicago, IL Cathedral of the Holy Name; [37] Chicago, IL Christ the Redeemer Byzantine Bielarusian Church.
McDonnell, Msgr. Joseph '67 (DM) Urbandale, IA St. Pius X Church.
McDonnell, Joseph F. '55 (CHI) Western Springs, IL St. John of the Cross Church; Retired.
McDonnell, Joseph M. '30 (ROC) Retired.
McDonnell, Kilian *o.s.b.* '51 (SCL) [I] Collegeville, MN St. John's Abbey, of the Order of St. Benedict.
McDonnell, Lawrence *c.s.p.* (NY) [4] New Rochelle, NY Holy Family Church.
McDonnell, Msgr. Martin '68 (PAT) Parsippany, NJ St. Ann Church.
McDonnell, Michael *o.f.m.* '65 (NY) [35] New York, NY St. Francis of Assisi Church.
McDonnell, Msgr. P. William '64 (RCK) [4] Freeport, IL St. Thomas Aquinas Church.
McDonnell, Msgr. Patrick '57 (MIA) [14] Fort Lauderdale, FL St. Sebastian Church.
McDonnell, Patrick J. '73 (TR) Hightstown, NJ St. Anthony of Padua Church.
McDonnell, Paul A. *o.s.j.* '91 (SCR) [1] Pittston, PA Our Lady of Mt. Carmel Church; [M] Pittston, PA Eastern Province of the Oblates of St. Joseph.
McDonnell, Sean '88 (PAT) Parsippany, NJ St. Christopher Church.
McDonnell, Stephen '89 (RVC) Absent on Leave.
McDonnell, Thomas *s.j.* '68 (RIC) [4] Richmond, VA Our Lady of Lourdes Church.
McDonnell, Msgr. Thomas J. '60 (BO) [11] Boston, MA St. Augustine Church; [46] Boston, MA St. Monica Church.
McDonnell, Thomas P. *m.m.* '65 (NY) [DD] Maryknoll, NY Maryknoll Fathers and Brothers; [DD] Maryknoll, NY Maryknoll Fathers and Brothers.
McDonnell, Msgr. Timothy A. '63 (NY) Chappaqua, NY St. John and St. Mary Church.
McDonnell, Vincent '84 (MOB) Retired.
McDonnell, Msgr. William J. '54 (BUF) Amherst, NY St. Leo the Great Church.
McDonough, Donat Michael '74 (SP) On Duty Outside the Diocese.
McDonough, Edward *c.ss.r.* '48 (BO) [53] Boston, MA Our Lady of Perpetual Help Church.
McDonough, James '42 (AGN) Dededo, GU Santa Barbara Church.
McDonough, James '84 (PIT) [11] Pittsburgh, PA Epiphany Church.
McDonough, James A. *s.j.* '42 (FgM) Provinces.
McDonough, James A. *o.p.* '62 (AUS) [H] Austin, TX Dominican Friars of Austin.
McDonough, James A. *o.p.* '62 (NO) [P] New Orleans, LA Dominican Friars, Southern Dominican Province of St. Martin de Porres; [P] New Orleans, LA Dominican Friars, Southern Dominican Province of St. Martin de Porres; [S] Metairie, LA Southern Dominican Foundation.
McDonough, James E. *ss.cc.* '68 (FR) [I] Fairhaven, MA Sacred Hearts Provincial House.
McDonough, James M. *s.j.* '61 (SPK) [C] Spokane, WA Gonzaga University.
McDonough, Msgr. James T. '57 (PH) Strafford, PA Our Lady of the Assumption Church; [FF] Philadelphia, PA Ladies of Charity.
McDonough, John '00 (PHX) [14] Phoenix, AZ St. Joan of Arc Church.
McDonough, John *o.p.* '89 (OAK) [N] Moraga, CA Dominican Community.
McDonough, Msgr. John P. '52 (BO) Graduate Studies.
McDonough, John P. '95 (WH) Elkview, WV Our Lady of the Hills Church.
McDonough, John T. '50 (CLV) [17] Akron, OH St. Sebastian Church; Hinckley, OH Our Lady of Grace Church; Retired.
McDonough, Joseph (BAL) Glen Burnie, MD Holy Trinity Church.
McDonough, Kevin M. '80 (STP) [31] St. Paul, MN St. Peter Claver Church.
McDonough, Patrick M. '68 (WH) St. Albans, WV St. Francis of Assisi Church.
McDonough, Ray *c.p.* (BIR) [7] Birmingham, AL Holy Family Church.
McDonough, Roger '76 (PMB) [3] Boca Raton, FL St. Joan of Arc Church.
McDonough, Roger F. '76 (BGP) On Duty Outside the Diocese.
McDonough, Msgr. T. Joseph '46 (MAN) [8] Nashua, NH St. Patrick Church; Retired.
McDonough, Thomas R. '89 (STP) [3] St. Paul, MN Blessed Sacrament Church.
McDonough, Timothy T. *c.s.sp.* '56 (VEN) [G] Sarasota, FL Congregation of the Holy Ghost.
McDonough, Vincent *s.j.* '62 (ROC) [C] Elmira, NY Notre Dame High School.
McDougal, Jon '79 (LR) Batesville, AR St. Mary's Church; Newport, AR St. Cecilia's Church.
McDougall, James G. '75 (LAN) [2] Ann Arbor, MI St. Francis of Assisi Church.
McDougall, Russell *c.s.c.* '91 (FgM) Holy Cross Foreign Missions.
McDougall, Russell K. *c.s.c.* '91 (FTW) [J] South Bend, IN Congregation of Holy Cross, Indiana Province, Provincial House.
McDowell, John *o.f.m.* (ATL) Athens, GA St. Joseph's Church; [M] Atlanta, GA Campus Ministry.
McDowell, Leo '94 (GF) Circle, MT St. Francis Xavier Church.
McDowell, Msgr. Patrick '54 (DUL) [4] Duluth, MN Our Lady of Mercy Church; [13] Duluth, MN St. Mary Star of the Sea Church.
McDowell, Patrick D. '68 (SCR) Weston, PA Sacred Heart Church.
McDuffie, Paul A. '95 (BR) Independence, LA Mater Dolorosa Church.

McDuffie, Paul A. '95 (CHR) On Duty Outside the Diocese.

McDyre, Cajetan *s.t.* '45 (PAT) [M] Stirling, NJ Holy Spirit Missionary Cenacle.

McEachern, Bernard *c.p.* '64 (FgM) Passionist Foreign Missions.

McEachin, Cornelius '48 (SAG) Retired.

McEachin, Donald J. *c.s.sp.* '81 (PIT) [O] Bethel Park, PA Holy Ghost Fathers and Brothers Provincialate; [S] Bethel Park, PA Spiritan Support Trust.

McElduff, Edward W. '53 (ALN) Berlinsville, PA St. Nicholas Church.

McEleney, Neil J. *c.s.p.* '53 (NY) [DD] Jamaica Estates, NY Paulist Fathers Generalate.

McEleney, Neil J. *c.s.p.* '53 (WDC) [B] Washington, DC St. Paul's College.

McEleney, Robert J. '58 (RIC) Retired.

McElhinney, Thomas *glmy.* '62 (NSH) Fayetteville, TN St. Anthony Church; Pulaski, TN Immaculate Conception Church.

McElhinny, Michael *s.m.* '80 (BO) Boston, MA Massachusetts General Hospital.

McElligott, Thomas J. '69 (OAK) [3] Berkeley, CA St. Joseph The Worker Church.

McElligott, Thomas J. '69 (SFR) Retired.

McElligott, Tom (OAK) [Q] Moraga, CA St. Mary's College Campus Ministry.

McElroy, Charles J. '64 (PH) Delphi, PA St. Mary Church.

McElroy, Damian '88 (TR) [14] Trenton, NJ St. Gregory the Great Church.

McElroy, Herbert '34 (BRK) Retired.

McElroy, James E. '56 (LA) [15] Los Angeles, CA Holy Trinity Church.

McElroy, John J. '45 (PRO) [6] Pawtucket, RI St. Joseph Church; Retired.

McElroy, John W. '56 (BO) Senior Priests.

McElroy, Msgr. Robert W. '80 (SFR) [2] San Mateo, CA St. Gregory Church.

McElroy, Thomas *ss.cc.* '67 (FR) [K] Wareham, MA Sacred Hearts Retreat Center.

McElwee, Michael A. *s.j.* '95 (BAL) [S] Baltimore, MD Jesuit Fathers and Brothers Maryland Provincial Curia.

McElwee, Michael A. *s.j.* '95 (PH) [C] Philadelphia, PA St. Joseph's University.

McElwee, Robert W. '83 (WCH) Frontenac, KS Sacred Heart Church; [J] Pittsburg, KS St. Pius X Center (Pittsburg State University).

McEneaney, Msgr. John P.A. '43 (SFS) Retired.

McEnery, James G. '53 (MAD) Retired.

McEnhill, Gerald A. '72 (DET) Farmington, MI St. Gerald Church.

McEnhill, John E. *s.m.* '56 (OAK) [S] Oakland, CA Marianist Commmunity.

McEniry, Robert F. *s.j.* '51 (OM) [K] Omaha, NE Jesuit Community at Creighton University.

McEnnis, Thomas '45 (SEA) Retired.

McEntee, John B. '61 (STL) Luebbering, MO St. Francis of Assisi Church.

McEvilly, John W. '64 (BEL) [3] Belleville, IL Our Lady Queen of Peace Church.

McEvoy, David *o.carm.* '88 (KCK) [1] Leavenworth, KS Immaculate Conception Church; [4] Leavenworth, KS St. Joseph's Church.

McEvoy, John '75 (SP) Hudson, FL St. Michael Church.

McEvoy, William '87 (KCK) [2] Kansas City, KS Blessed Sacrament Church.

McEwen, Theophane *c.p.* '54 (ALT) [J] Bedford, PA St. Mary's House of Greater Solitude.

McFadden, Brian '88 (NEW) [3] Linden, NJ St. John the Apostle Church.

McFadden, Edward J. *s.j.* '54 (SJ) [D] San Jose, CA Bellarmine College Preparatory.

McFadden, George B. '52 (SC) Retired.

McFadden, J. Michael (HBG) [1] Harrisburg, PA Cathedral Parish of St. Patrick Church.

McFadden, James J. *m.m.* '61 (HON) [G] Honolulu, HI Maryknoll Fathers House (M.M.).

McFadden, Jim *m.m.* '61 (HON) [9] Honolulu, HI St. John the Baptist Church.

McFadden, John R. '62 (PH) Cheltenham, PA Presentation of Blessed Virgin Mary Church.

McFadden, Msgr. Joseph P. '81 (PH) Morton, PA Our Lady of Perpetual Help Church; [D] Springfield, PA Cardinal O'Hara High School.

McFadden, Msgr. Leo E. '53 (RNO) Retired.

McFadden, Michael J. *o.s.a.* '67 (LA) Ojai, CA St. Thomas Aquinas Church.

McFadden, William C. *s.j.* '59 (WDC) [M] Washington, DC The Jesuit Community at Georgetown University.

McFadin, Marcus '92 (ELP) [32] El Paso, TX St. Stephen, Deacon and Martyr Church.

McFalls, Dean '95 (STO) Modesto, CA Our Lady of Fatima Church.

McFarland, Msgr. Edward J. '55 (COL) Retired.

McFarland, Eugene H. '43 (ROC) Geneseo, NY St. Mary Church; Retired.

McFarland, Msgr. Francis T. '57 (BO) [3] Medford, MA St. Joseph Church.

McFarland, Francis X. *s.j.* '50 (NEW) [C] Jersey City, NJ St. Peter's Preparatory School.

McFarland, James W. '47 (NEW) Retired.

McFarland, Michael C. (WOR) [B] Worcester, MA College of the Holy Cross, Inc.

McFarland, Timothy D. *c.pp.s.* '83 (LFT) [A] Rensselaer, IN Saint Joseph's College.

McGaffin, Joseph '96 (PHX) [21] Phoenix, AZ St. Paul Church.

McGagh, Martin A. '54 (FRS) Porterville, CA St. Anne Church; Retired.

McGahagan, James E. '68 (SCR) Buttonwood, PA Exaltation of the Holy Cross Church.

McGahee, Thomas *s.d.b.* '77 (PAT) [D] Paterson, NJ Don Bosco Technical High School.

McGahey, Charles R. '59 (BO) Health Leave.

McGahren, Joseph *m.m.* '51 (STA) [H] Jacksonville, FL Maryknoll Fathers & Brothers.

McGahren, Joseph J. *m.m.* '98 (DEN) [M] Denver, CO Maryknoll Fathers, Catholic Foreign Mission Society of America (Legal Title).

McGann, Diarmuid F. '64 (RVC) Blue Point, NY Our Lady of the Snow Church.

McGann, Msgr. Francis J. '48 (BO) Needham, MA St. Joseph Church.

McGann, Msgr. Francis J. '49 (BO) Senior Priests.

McGann, Gerard J. '48 (BO) Senior Priests.

McGann, Joseph F. '44 (NY) Retired.

McGann, L. Philip '71 (WIL) Retired.

McGann, Richard P. '70 (HRT) Plainville, CT Our Lady of Mercy Church.

McGann, Thomas *c.m.f.* '76 (CHI) [147] Chicago, IL Our Lady of Guadalupe Church.

McGann, Thomas A. '76 (PH) On Duty Outside the Archdiocese.

McGannon, J. Barry *s.j.* '55 (STL) [C] St. Louis, MO Saint Louis University; [C] St. Louis, MO Saint Louis University; [P] St. Louis, MO Jesuit Community Corporation at St. Louis University - Jesuit Hall.

McGarr, Joseph M. '86 (ALN) Retired.

McGarrigle, Michael '49 (PRT) Retired.

McGarrill, Colman *t.o.r.* '54 (SP) [13] Tampa, FL St. Patrick Church.

McGarrity, Neil '89 (PHX) [6] Mesa, AZ St. Timothy Church.

McGarrity, Patrick . *c.ss.r.* '61 (HBG) [2] Lancaster, PA St. Anthony of Padua Church.

McGarrity, Richard A. *s.j.* '70 (MIL) [P] Milwaukee, WI Jesuit Provincial Office, Wisconsin Province; [P] Milwaukee, WI Jesuit Community at Marquette University; [Y] Milwaukee, WI The Jesuit Partnership.

McGarry, Msgr. James J. '70 (SCR) Clarks Summit, PA Our Lady of the Snows Church.

McGarry, John P. *s.j.* '93 (SAC) [C] Sacramento, CA Jesuit High School; [H] Carmichael, CA Jesuit High School Community of Sacramento.

McGarry, Joseph P. '55 (HRT) [5] West Hartford, CT St. Peter Claver Church.

McGarry, Peter *o.carm.* '69 (NEW) Teaneck, NJ St. Anastasia's Church.

McGarry, Msgr. Thomas (NY) Bronx, NY St. Barnabas Hospital.

McGarry, William C. '59 (BUF) [11] Niagara Falls, NY Prince of Peace Church.

McGarry, William J. *s.j.* '58 (CI) [C] Kolonia, Pohnpei, FM Jesuit House.

McGarry, William J. *s.j.* '58 (FgM) Provinces.

McGarty, Bernard O. '49 (LC) Retired.

McGarvey, Joseph F. '50 (CAM) Retired.

McGaugh, Philip E. '78 (BO) [32] Boston, MA St. Joseph Church; Boston, MA Massachusetts General Hospital.

McGauley, Francis H. *s.j.* '55 (BAL) [39] Baltimore, MD St. Ignatius Church.

McGeady, Ignatius J. *o.f.m.* '48 (FgM) Franciscan Foreign Missions.

McGee, Dominic E. *o.f.m.conv.* '67 (SY) Minoa, NY St. Mary Church.

McGee, Francis J. '45 (BRK) [236] Queens, NY St. Rose of Lima Church; Retired.

McGee, Msgr. H. Desmond '71 (E) Houtzdale, PA Christ the King Church.

McGee, James J. *s.s.* '85 (SCR) Unassigned or Leave of Absence.

McGee, John E. *o.s.f.s.* '82 (R) [2] Durham, NC Holy Infant Church.

McGee, Leo J. '57 (PH) [118] Philadelphia, PA Our Lady Help of Christians Church.

McGee, Michael J. '77 (BRK) [150] Queens, NY St. Andrew Avellino Church.

McGee, Peter J. '53 (LA) Retired.

McGee, Richard F. *c.r.* '74 (SB) [3] Fontana, CA St. Joseph Church.

McGee, Thomas J. *o.s.f.s.* '71 (VEN) [A] Fort Myers, FL Bishop Verot High School.

McGee, Timothy H. '87 (CR) East Grand Forks, MN Sacred Heart Church.

McGeean, John T. '86 (JOL) [16] Joliet, IL St. Mary Nativity Church.

McGeory, Peter '76 (NY) Military Chaplains.

McGeough, Jude P. '58 (PRO) [4] East Providence, RI St. Martha Church.

McGeough, Martin *c.m.* '76 (BIR) Lanett, AL Holy Family Church.

McGeown, Joseph P. '65 (PH) Wallingford, PA St. John Chrysostom Church.

McGeown, William F. '70 (PH) [127] Philadelphia, PA Our Lady of Ransom Church.

McGerity, Francis '84 (SPR) [J] Stockbridge, MA Congregation of Marians of The Immaculate Conception of the BVM.

McGerity, Francis X. '84 (CC) On Duty Outside the Diocese.

McGettigan, Msgr. D. James '67 (PH) [1] Drexel Hill, PA St. Andrew Church.

McGettigan, Neil J. *o.s.a.* '53 (PH) [C] Villanova, PA Villanova University; [AA] Villanova, PA St. Thomas Monastery.

McGettrick, Msgr. Thomas P. '56 (CC) [20] Corpus Christi, TX St. Philip The Apostle Church.

McGhee, James E. '95 (AMA) Dalhart, TX St. Anthony's Church.

McGhee, Msgr. William (BEL) Carterville, IL Church of the Holy Spirit.

McGhee, Msgr. William P. (BEL) Grand Chain, IL St. Catherine Church; Ullin, IL Our Lady of Fatima Church.

McGhee, Msgr. William P. '82 (BEL) Johnston City, IL St. Paul Church; Mound City, IL Church of the Immaculate Conception-St. Mary.

McGill, Joseph F. '56 (NY) Absent on Leave.

McGill, Joseph P. *s.j.* '60 (LAF) [J] Grand Coteau, LA Our Lady of the Oaks Retreat House.

McGill, Malachy *c.p.* '46 (ALT) [J] Bedford, PA St. Mary's House of Greater Solitude.

McGilley, Michael J. '65 (CAM) Audubon, NJ Church of the Holy Maternity.

McGillicuddy, Sean J. *c.ss.r.* '86 (PH) [25] Philadelphia, PA St. Boniface Church.

McGilvary, A. Robert *o.s.f.s.* '62 (ALN) [B] Center Valley, PA Desales University; [K] Center Valley, PA Oblates of St. Francis de Sales.

McGing, Thomas '71 (JKS) Vicksburg, MS St. Paul Church.

McGinley, Anthony J. '45 (HBG) Retired.

McGinley, Bernard P. *m.a.* '61 (HBG) [4] Harrisburg, PA Holy Family Church.

McGinley, Jeremiah V. *o.f.m.* '55 (NEW) Fair Lawn, NJ St. Anne's Church.

McGinley, John F. *o.s.f.s.* '68 (ALN) [B] Center Valley, PA Desales University; [K] Center Valley, PA Oblates of St. Francis de Sales.

McGinley, Peter *m.c.c.j.* '60 (LA) [12] Los Angeles, CA Holy Cross Church; [56] Los Angeles, CA St. Cecilia Church.

McGinn, Anthony F. *s.j.* '79 (NO) [F] New Orleans, LA Jesuit High School; [H] New Orleans, LA Jesuit High School.

McGinn, Charles (KCK) On Leave of Absence.

McGinn, Dan '53 (LA) [Q] Los Angeles, CA Columban Fathers, Procure House.

McGinn, Finian *o.f.m.prov.* '60 (LA) [CC] Los Angeles, CA St. Francis Center.

McGinn, Finian *o.f.m.* '60 (OAK) [N] Oakland, CA Franciscan Friars Provincial Office, Province of St. Barbara.

McGinn, Finian *o.f.m.* '60 (SFR) [5] San Francisco, CA St. Anthony of Padua Church.

McGinn, John J. '52 (DEN) Centennial, CO St. Thomas More Church.

McGinn, Sylvester P. '56 (NY) [195] Staten Island, NY St. Ann Church.

McGinness, Matthew C. '89 (WCH) [18] Wichita, KS St. Paul Church; [J] Wichita, KS Wichita State University.

McGinnis, Albin C. '77 (PIT) Waynesburg, PA St. Ann Church; Greene County, PA Greene County Memorial; Green County, PA State Correctional Institution at Waynesburg (Women's Facility); Green County, PA Waynesburg County Jail; [R] Pittsburgh, PA Office for Campus Ministry.

McGinnis, J. Donald *m.m.* '53 (FgM) Maryknoll Foreign Missions.

McGinnis, Jack P. '63 (GAL) On Duty Outside the Diocese.

McGinnis, Jack P. '63 (SB) Palm Desert, CA Christ of the Desert Church; [H] Palm Desert, CA Christ of the Desert Newman Center.

McGinnis, James J. '78 (PH) [21] Philadelphia, PA St. Bartholomew Church.

McGinnis, Jay W. '76 (BUF) Lancaster, NY Our Lady of Pompeii Church.

McGinnis, Msgr. Joseph R. '46 (WIN) Retired; [D] Wabasha, MN St. Elizabeth's Hospital of Wabasha, Inc.; [F] Wabasha, MN St. Elizabeth's Health Care Center; [F] Wabasha, MN St. Elizabeth's Health Care Center.

McGinnis, N. Charles '41 (LR) Retired.

McGinnity, John C. '75 (CHR) Myrtle Beach, SC St. Andrew's Church.

McGinnity, John C. '75 (WH) Retired.
McGinnity, Joseph P. '56 (CHI) [4] Des Plaines, IL St. Zachary Church; Retired.
McGinnity, P. J. '91 (KNX) [4] Chattanooga, TN St. Stephen Church.
McGinnity, Robert F. '55 (CHI) Palos Hills, IL Sacred Heart Church; Retired.
McGinty, John P. *s.j.* '58 (PH) [AA] Philadelphia, PA Jesuit Community at St. Joseph's University.
McGinty, John P. '83 (BO) Winchester, MA St. Eulalia Church.
McGivern, John W. '91 (CHI) Western Springs, IL St. John of the Cross Church.
McGivney, Thomas, Jr. '90 (JOL) [4] Lockport, IL St. Joseph Church.
McGlade, Desmond *c.s.sp.* '41 (SJ) Mountain View, CA St. Athanasius Church.
McGlade, Thomas F. '43 (RVC) Setauket, NY St. James Church; Retired.
McGlauchlin, Michael J. '86 (STP) Maple Lake, MN St. Timothy Church.
McGlinchey, James J. '56 (TLS) Retired.
McGlinchy, Edward H. *s.j.* '49 (NY) [DD] New York, NY Murray-Weigel Hall.
McGlinn, Charles '67 (KCK) Leawood, KS Cure of Ars Church.
McGlinn, Robert J. '55 (CHI) Other Assignments.
McGlinn, Robert J. '55 (MIL) [2] Racine, WI Cristo Rey Church.
McGloin, James P. *s.j.* '74 (FgM) Provinces.
McGloin, Peter M. '56 (TUC) [7] Tucson, AZ Our Lady of Fatima Church.
McGloin, Richard D. *s.j.* '45 (OM) [K] Omaha, NE Jesuit Community at Creighton University.
McGlone, Gerard J. *s.j.* '87 (BAL) [S] Baltimore, MD Jesuit Fathers and Brothers Maryland Provincial Curia.
McGlone, Gerard M. '84 (NY) [DD] New York, NY Passionist Spiritual Center.
McGlone, Gerard M. '84 (SCR) On Duty Outside the Diocese; Unassigned or Leave of Absence.
McGlone, Joseph F. '52 (BO) [2] Newton, MA Corpus Christi Church.
McGlothlin, Eugene J. *o.s.b.* '60 (SCL) [I] Collegeville, MN St. John's Abbey, of the Order of St. Benedict.
McGlothlin, Eugene J. *o.s.b.* '60 (STP) Hastings, MN St. Elizabeth Ann Seton Church.
McGlynn, Daniel J. '82 (WIL) Elkton, MD Immaculate Conception Church.
McGlynn, Francis '54 (KC) Retired.
McGlynn, Francis '54 (PRM) Sugar Creek, MO St. Luke, Byzantine Catholic Church.
McGlynn, Philip M. *o.s.m.* '65 (CHI) [N] Chicago, IL Order of Friar Servants of Mary (Servites) United States of America Province, Inc.; [N] Chicago, IL Order of Friar Servants of Mary (Servites) United States of America Province, Inc.; [N] Chicago, IL Order of Friar Servants of Mary (Servites) United States of America Province, Inc.
McGlynn, Thomas E. '84 (FR) [1] Fall River, MA Cathedral of St. Mary of the Assumption.
McGoldrick, Albert W. *j.c.l.* '78 (BGP) [3] Greenwich, CT St. Paul Church.
McGoldrick, James F. *s.m.* '67 (ATL) [6] Atlanta, GA Our Lady of the Assumption Church; [M] Atlanta, GA Campus Ministry.
McGoldrick, John T. '38 (B) Retired.
McGoldrick, William J. '43 (DET) Grosse Pointe, MI Our Lady Star of the Sea Church; Retired.
McGonagle, Douglas '00 (SPR) West Springfield, MA St. Thomas the Apostle Church.
McGonagle, James *c.ss.r.* '44 (ORL) [F] New Smyrna Beach, FL St. Alphonsus Villa-Redemptorist Fathers and Brothers.
McGonegal, James R. '71 (CLV) [33] Cleveland, OH St. Ignatius of Antioch Church.
McGonigle, Thomas D. *o.p.* '68 (PRO) [P] Providence, RI St. Thomas Aquinas Priory at Providence College.
McGough, Msgr. James P. '57 (BLX) [2] Gulfport, MS St. James Church.
McGough, Msgr. Stephen D. '68 (SCR) [3] Williamsport, PA St. Boniface's Church.
McGough, Timothy *o.c.d.* '49 (MIL) [26] Milwaukee, WI St. Florian Church.
McGough, William J. '57 (NO) Covington, LA St. Peter Church.
McGourn, Francis T. *m.m.* '64 (FgM) Maryknoll Foreign Missions.
McGourty, Thomas P. *c.m.* '53 (BUF) [C] Niagara University, NY Niagara University; [O] Niagara University, NY Vincentian Community at Niagara University.
McGovern, Arthur F. *s.j.* '62 (DET) [K] Detroit, MI Jesuit Community at the University of Detroit.
McGovern, Brian J. '69 (SEA) [H] Seattle, WA Providence Mount St. Vincent; [J] Seattle, WA Providence Mount St. Vincent.
McGovern, Msgr. Damian E. (HBG) Retired.
McGovern, Donan *o.f.m.* '55 (BO) [BB] Boston, MA St. Anthony Shrine.
McGovern, Edward J. '51 (PRO) Retired; [P] Providence, RI St. John Vianney Residence.
McGovern, Eugene F. (BRK) Retired.
McGovern, Gerald T. *o.m.i.* '57 (CHI) [171] Chicago, IL Precious Blood Church.
McGovern, Harold *o.s.f.s.* '70 (PH) [76] Philadelphia, PA St. Joachim Church.
McGovern, Msgr. James J. '58 (TR) Moorestown, NJ Our Lady of Good Counsel Church.
McGovern, James O. '67 (BAL) Ellicott City, MD Resurrection Church.
McGovern, John J. *m.m.* '54 (FgM) Maryknoll Foreign Missions.
McGovern, John P. '65 (NEW) New Milford, NJ Ascension Church.
McGovern, John Patrick *o.p.* '58 (WDC) [B] Washington, DC Dominican House of Studies.
McGovern, Joseph J. *s.j.* '48 (CHL) Mars Hill, NC St. Andrew the Apostle Church; [J] Charlotte, NC Jesuit Community; [M] Hot Springs, NC Jesuit House of Prayer.
McGovern, Lawrence *s.t.l.* '67 (STO) [10] Stockton, CA Presentation of B.V.M. Church.
McGovern, Mark J. '67 (DUB) Iowa Falls, IA St. Mark's Church.
McGovern, Mark J. '86 (DUB) Eldora, IA St. Mary's Church.
McGovern, Michael '94 (CHI) [40] Chicago, IL St. Clement Church.
McGovern, Robert *m.afr.* '63 (FgM) Missionaries of Africa Foreign Missions.
McGovern, Msgr. Thomas '46 (LA) Retired.
McGovern, Thomas A. '58 (CLV) [12] Akron, OH St. Matthew Church.
McGovern, Walter J. '64 (BAL) Randallstown, MD Holy Family Church; Retired.
McGovern, William W. '55 (WOR) Retired; [M] Worcester, MA Vianney House.
McGowan, Msgr. Andrew J. '49 (SCR) On Special or Other Diocesan Assignment.
McGowan, Msgr. Anthony '41 (ORG) San Clemente, CA Our Lady of Fatima Church; Retired.
McGowan, Denis *c.p.* '55 (FgM) Mission Procurators.
McGowan, Dennis M. *o.s.a.* '83 (CHL) Waynesville, NC St. John the Evangelist Church.
McGowan, Frederick R. '49 (BO) Senior Priests.
McGowan, James J. '62 (BO) Belmont, MA Our Lady of Mercy Church.
McGowan, Jeffrey A. '89 (STA) [3] Gainesville, FL Queen of Peace Church.
McGowan, John *c.ss.r.* '73 (TR) [Q] Long Branch, NJ San Alfonso Retreat House.
McGowan, John J. '52 (RCK) Retired.
McGowan, Joseph F. *o.carm.* '62 (TUC) [11] Tucson, AZ Sacred Heart Church.
McGowan, Joseph O. *s.j.* '74 (SEA) [A] Seattle, WA Seattle University.
McGowan, Kenan *o.f.m.conv.* '52 (SY) [5] Binghamton, NY SS. Cyril and Method Church.
McGowan, Msgr. Myles '37 (BAL) [93] Baltimore, MD St. Ursula Church; Retired.
McGowan, Myles P. '45 (NU) Retired.
McGowan, Richard A. *s.j.* '83 (BO) [W] Chestnut Hill, MA The Jesuit Community at Boston College.
McGowan, Richard W. *s.j.* '60 (SFE) [6] Albuquerque, NM Immaculate Conception Church.
McGowan, Seamus '57 (CC) Retired.
McGowan, Wallace A. '62 (MIA) [26] Miami, FL St. Louis Church.
McGowan, William J. *s.j.* '62 (NY) [F] New York, NY Xavier High School.
McGrade, Kevin M. '85 (BO) Permanent Disability.
McGrail, Charles A. '80 (NOR) Mystic, CT St. Patrick Church.
McGrail, John A. *s.j.* '57 (DET) [P] Bloomfield Hills, MI Manresa Jesuit Retreat House.
McGrane, Camillus M. *o.s.m.* '83 (CHI) [N] Chicago, IL Order of Friar Servants of Mary (Servites) United States of America Province, Inc.
McGrann, John E. '67 (P) [1] Eugene, OR St. Jude Church.
McGrann, John E. '67 (SPK) On Duty Outside the Diocese.
McGrath, Andre *o.f.m.* '67 (SHP) [3] Shreveport, LA Our Lady of the Blessed Sacrament Church.
McGrath, Msgr. Andrew '38 (LA) Lompoc, CA La Purisima Concepcion Church; Retired.
McGrath, Brian '92 (SPR) Orange, MA St. Mary Church.
McGrath, Conor '74 (SAT) Selma, TX Our Lady of Perpetual Help Church.
McGrath, Daniel F. '63 (NOR) Retired.
McGrath, E. Joseph '85 (LKC) Creole, LA Sacred Heart of Jesus Church.
McGrath, Msgr. Edmund G. '37 (YAK) Moxee City, WA Holy Rosary Church; Retired.
McGrath, Edward F. '80 (WIN) Rollingstone, MN Holy Trinity Church; [A] Winona, MN Immaculate Heart of Mary Seminary; [J] Winona, MN Catholic Cemeteries of Winona.
McGrath, Edward H. *s.j.* '53 (BAL) [S] Baltimore, MD Jesuit Fathers and Brothers Maryland Provincial Curia.
McGrath, Edward H. *s.j.* '53 (FgM) Provinces.
McGrath, Felix P. *o.f.m.* '61 (NY) [35] New York, NY St. Francis of Assisi Church.
McGrath, Francis '78 (TR) Leave of Absence.
McGrath, Frank C. '70 (BGP) [5] Stratford, CT Our Lady of Peace Church.
McGrath, Gerald F. '58 (MIA) Key West, FL St. Mary, Star of the Sea Church.
McGrath, Msgr. James '43 (PH) Manoa, PA Sacred Heart Church; Retired.
McGrath, James J. *c.s.c.* '59 (FTW) [B] Notre Dame, IN University of Notre Dame Du Lac; [J] Notre Dame, IN Holy Cross Community, Corby Hall, University of Notre Dame.
McGrath, James R. '54 (BUF) Retired.
McGrath, Jeremiah '80 (BEA) [1] Beaumont, TX St. Anthony Church.
McGrath, John '44 (CHI) [202] Chicago, IL St. Thomas More Church.
McGrath, John *o.m.i.* '53 (LAR) Eagle Pass, TX St. Joseph Church.
McGrath, John *o.m.i.* '66 (SAT) [K] San Antonio, TX Oblate Madonna Residence.
McGrath, John A. *s.m.* '66 (CIN) [D] Dayton, OH The University of Dayton; [M] Dayton, OH Marianist Provincialate.
McGrath, John D. '59 (MIA) Tavernier, FL San Pedro Church.
McGrath, John F. (CHI) Retired.
McGrath, John J. *s.j.* '51 (BO) [W] Weston, MA Campion Jesuit Community.
McGrath, John R. '82 (BLX) Vancleave, MS Holy Spirit Catholic Church.
McGrath, Jordan A. *o.p.* '59 (CHI) [N] River Forest, IL St. Thomas Aquinas Priory.
McGrath, Kevin Anthony *o.p.* '96 (NY) [121] New York, NY St. Vincent Ferrer Church; [DD] New York, NY St. Vincent Ferrer Priory.
McGrath, Kevin D. *o.s.b.* '74 (BIR) Cullman, AL Sacred Heart Church; [E] Cullman, AL St. Bernard Abbey.
McGrath, Msgr. Laurence W. '57 (BO) [A] Boston, MA St. John's Seminary School of Theology.
McGrath, Mark G. *c.s.c.* '49 (FTW) [J] Notre Dame, IN Holy Cross Community, Corby Hall, University of Notre Dame.
McGrath, Michael S. '75 (STL) On Medical Leave.
McGrath, Noel '80 (PMB) [1] Lake Worth, FL Sacred Heart Church.
McGrath, Patrick '65 (SAC) On Duty Outside the Diocese.
McGrath, Peter R. *s.j.* '88 (BO) [W] Boston, MA The Society of Jesus of New England-Provincial Offices.
McGrath, Peter R. *s.j.* '88 (OAK) [17] Oakland, CA St. Mary, Immaculate Conception-St. Francis de Sales Church; [N] Berkeley, CA Jesuit Community at Jesuit School of Theology at Berkeley.
McGrath, Philip J. '54 (LA) Bellflower, CA St. Bernard Church; Retired.
McGrath, Richard H. '50 (COV) Wilder, KY St. John Church; Retired; [N] Fort Thomas, KY Sisters of the Good Shepherd.
McGrath, Richard J. *o.s.a.* '73 (JOL) [C] New Lenox, IL Providence Catholic High School; [J] New Lenox, IL Augustinian Friary.
McGrath, Robert *o.m.i.* '55 (CC) [I] Corpus Christi, TX Incarnate Word Convent.
McGrath, Robert B. '71 (DET) Highland Park, MI St. Benedict Church.
McGrath, Robert D. '43 (HRT) Retired.
McGrath, Sean (DEN) [9] Denver, CO Guardian Angels Church.
McGrath, Sean John *s.s.c.* '54 (LA) [57] Los Angeles, CA St. Columban Church.
McGrath, Thomas '94 (WDC) [4] Bowie, MD St. Pius X Church.
McGrath, Thomas B. *s.j.* '64 (AGN) [1] Agana, GU Dulce Nombre de Maria Cathedral - Basilica Church.
McGrath, Thomas B. *s.j.* '64 (FgM) Provinces.
McGrath, Thomas E. '77 (JC) Absent on Leave.
McGrath, Thomas J. '59 (SY) Skaneateles, NY St. Mary of the Lake Church.
McGrath, Thomas M. (PAT) Special Assignment.
McGrath, W. Aedan *s.s.c.* '29 (OM) [K] St. Columbans, NE St. Columban's Foreign Mission Society.
McGrath, William E. '47 (HRT) [3] East Hartford, CT St. Christopher Church; Retired.
McGrath, William F., Jr. '00 (ROC) [12] Rochester, NY St. Charles Borromeo Church.
McGrath, William J. *s.j.* '59 (SCR) [C] Scranton, PA University of Scranton; [E] Scranton, PA Scranton Preparatory School.
McGratty, John J. '71 (RVC) Manorville, NY St. Peter & Paul Church.
McGraw, John T. '56 (SY) [7] Syracuse, NY Our Lady of Pompei Church; Syracuse, NY Hutchings Psychiatric Center.
McGraw, Msgr. Michael D. '75 (E) [B] Erie, PA Gannon University.
McGraw, Rene *o.s.b.* '62 (SCL) [I] Collegeville, MN St.

John's Abbey, of the Order of St. Benedict.
McGraw, Robert H. '76 (LAN) Grand Ledge, MI St. Michael Church.
McGraw, W. Howard *o.s.a.* '62 (PH) [18] Philadelphia, PA St. Augustine Church.
McGray, James '67 (SD) [B] San Diego, CA University of San Diego.
McGread, Msgr. Thomas '53 (WCH) [L] Wichita, KS Serra Club of Wichita - Metro.
McGready, Oliver '62 (WDC) [2] Rockville, MD Shrine of St. Jude Church.
McGreal, James '48 (SEA) Retired.
McGreevy, James V. '64 (SPK) Lind, WA St. Ambrose Church; Ritzville, WA St. Agnes Church; Sprague, WA Mary Queen of Heaven Church; Washtunca, WA Holy Trinity Church.
McGreevy, John G. *o.p.* '64 (DET) [2] St. Clair Shores, MI St. Gertrude Church.
McGreevy, Thomas More *o.p.* '64 (P) [6] Eugene, OR St. Thomas More Church.
McGregor, John F. *s.m.* '57 (HON) [15] Honolulu, HI Star of the Sea Church.
McGregor, Mark D. *s.j.* '96 (LA) [Q] Culver City, CA Ignatius House, The Novitiate of the California Province, Society of Jesus.
McGrenra, Cornelius D. '51 (TUC) Retired.
McGroarty, Msgr. Charles E. '62 (PH) [103] Philadelphia, PA St. Matthew Church.
McGroarty, Hugh H. '45 (SCR) [4] Pittston, PA St. John the Evangelist Church.
McGroarty, Joseph *o.p.* '46 (TR) Holmdel, NJ St. Catharine Church.
McGroarty, William K. *s.j.* '55 (BAL) [B] Baltimore, MD Loyola College in Maryland; [S] Baltimore, MD Jesuit Community of Loyola College, Inc.
McGrogan, James P. (GRY) [5] Michigan City, IN Sacred Heart Church.
McGrogan, James P. '64 (GRY) [1] Michigan City, IN St. Mary of the Immaculate Conception Church.
McGuffy, James W. '95 (MET) Spotswood, NJ Immaculate Conception Church.
McGuigan, Hugh *o.s.f.s.* '97 (VEN) [A] Fort Myers, FL Bishop Verot High School.
McGuigan, Hugh J. *o.s.f.s.* (VEN) [K] Fort Myers, FL The Bishop Verot High School Foundation.
McGuigan, John J. '68 (PAT) Hopatcong, NJ St. Jude's Church.
McGuigan, Patrick *o.carm.* '79 (NY) Middletown, NY Our Lady of Mt. Carmel Church; [DD] Middletown, NY St. Albert's Priory.
McGuigan, Robert '78 (WDC) Retired.
McGuigan, Steven F.C. '90 (SPR) Stockbridge, MA St. Joseph's Church; West Stockbridge, MA St. Patrick's Church.
McGuill, Martin '64 (ARL) McLean, VA St. Luke's Church.
McGuine, Peter M. '90 (SD) [4] Oceanside, CA St. Thomas More Church.
McGuiness, David '73 (MOB) On Leave from the Archdiocese.
McGuiness, Edward '61 (SB) Desert Hot Springs, CA St. Elizabeth of Hungary Church.
McGuinn, James J. '88 (PH) Downingtown, PA St. Joseph Church.
McGuinness, Fergal '86 (SR) Graduate Studies.
McGuinness, Gerard J. '60 (SB) Sun City, CA St. Vincent Ferrer Church.
McGuinness, J. Roger '65 (OG) [6] Plattsburgh, NY Newman Parish, John XXIII College Community Church.
McGuinness, Msgr. Joseph P. '52 (PBL) Cortez, CO St. Margaret Mary Church; Mancos, CO St. Rita Church; Retired.
McGuinness, Lester A. '49 (NEW) Caldwell, NJ St. Aloysius Church; Retired.
McGuinness, Msgr. Michael '52 (MOB) Retired.
McGuinness, Msgr. Richard M. '51 (NEW) [3] Linden, NJ St. John the Apostle Church.
McGuire, Aidan '54 (LUB) Shallowater, TX St. Phillip Benizi Church.
McGuire, Anthony *o.f.m.* '52 (PAT) [M] Butler, NJ St. Anthony Friary.
McGuire, Msgr. Anthony W. '57 (PH) [102] Philadelphia, PA Maternity B.V.M. Church.
McGuire, Augustus S. *c.s.p.* '59 (CHR) Clemson, SC St. Andrew Church.
McGuire, Bonaventure Maria Pio '99 (NOR) [F] Griswold, CT Marian Friary of Our Lady of Guadalupe.
McGuire, Brendan P. '00 (SJ) [4] Santa Clara, CA St. Lawrence the Martyr Church.
McGuire, David V. '88 (RIC) Danville, VA Sacred Heart Church.
McGuire, Donald J. *s.j.* '61 (CHI) [N] Evanston, IL Canisius House.
McGuire, Edward *o.f.m.* '40 (PAT) [M] Ringwood, NJ Holy Name Friary, Inc.
McGuire, Francis X. *o.s.a.* '35 (PH) [AA] Villanova, PA St. Thomas Monastery.
McGuire, Frederick J. '81 (CIN) On Duty Outside the Archdiocese.
McGuire, J. Frederick '81 (SP) [2] St. Petersburg, FL Blessed Trinity Church.
McGuire, James D. *o.a.r.* '54 (LA) Montebello, CA St. Benedict Church.
McGuire, James E. '70 (PH) [3] Bensalem, PA Saint Ephrem Church.
McGuire, James J. *o.s.f.s.* '50 (WIL) [I] Childs, MD Oblates of St. Francis De Sales.
McGuire, John *c.ss.r.* '44 (ALB) [L] Saratoga Springs, NY St. John Neumann Residence.
McGuire, John *c.ss.r.* '44 (BRK) [107] Brooklyn, NY Our Lady of Perpetual Help Basilica Church.
McGuire, Msgr. John A. '50 (RVC) Sound Beach, NY St. Louis de Montfort Church; Retired.
McGuire, John C. '79 (NY) East Kingston, NY St. Colman Church; [GG] New York, NY University Apostolate.
McGuire, John F. '76 (P) Coquille, OR Holy Name Church.
McGuire, John J. '60 (COV) Retired; [T] Fort Mitchell, KY Mission Share.
McGuire, John Patrick *o.p.* '73 (NY) [DD] New York, NY St. Vincent Ferrer Priory.
McGuire, John R. *m.m.* '43 (FgM) Maryknoll Foreign Missions.
McGuire, Joseph E. '65 (DUB) Dysart, IA St. Joseph Church; Vinton, IA St. Mary's Church.
McGuire, Ken '68 (ALB) [L] Lake George, NY St. Mary of the Lake.
McGuire, Kenneth H. *c.s.p.* '68 (NY) [DD] Jamaica Estates, NY Paulist Fathers Generalate.
McGuire, Paul J. *s.c.j.* '68 (MIL) [P] Franklin, WI Dehon Study Center; [P] Franklin, WI St. Francis Residence; [P] Hales Corners, WI Priests of the Sacred Heart.
McGuire, Richard '67 (SCL) Osakis, MN Immaculate Conception Church.
McGuire, Richard *o.s.c.* '73 (STP) Shoreview, MN St. Odilia Church; [N] Shoreview, MN Crosier Community of Shoreview.
McGuire, Richard G. *o.c.s.o.* '57 (CHR) [E] Moncks Corner, SC Mepkin Abbey.
McGuire, Msgr. Richard J. '60 (E) [22] Erie, PA St. Julia Church.
McGuire, Robert '99 (FTW) [10] South Bend, IN Holy Family Church.
McGuire, Robert A. *s.j.* '58 (RVC) Plainview, NY St. Pius X Church.
McGuire, Thaddeus '90 (PHX) [2] Phoenix, AZ Corpus Christi Church.
McGuire, Thomas D. '81 (LIN) Osceola, NE St. Vincent Ferrer Church.
McGuire, Timothy P. '84 (STU) [B] Steubenville, OH Catholic Central High School.
McGuire, William A. *o.s.a.* '65 (PH) [C] Villanova, PA Villanova University.
McGuirk, Alan '56 (STL) [P] St. Louis, MO La Salette Missionaries.
McGuirk, John '70 (SC) Sheldon, IA St. Patrick's Church.
McGuirk, Raymond A. '47 (BRK) Retired.
McGuirk, William C. '82 (GBG) Delmont, PA St. John Baptist de La Salle Church.
McGuirl, Msgr. John A. '72 (BRK) [184] Queens, NY St. Joan of Arc Church.
McGurk, Patrick '58 (HEL) Deer Lodge, MT Immaculate Conception Church.
McGurn, Richard H. *s.j.* '75 (CHI) [N] Chicago, IL Chicago Province of the Society of Jesus-Provincial Office; [N] Chicago, IL Chicago Province of the Society of Jesus-Provincial Office.
McHale, Anthony I. *s.j.* '53 (WDC) [E] Washington, DC Gonzaga College High School.
McHale, Charles P. '50 (NY) Retired.
McHale, Damian *c.p.* '61 (LA) [Q] Pasadena, CA Passionist Community.
McHenry, John *s.v.d.* '55 (SB) [3] Corona, CA St. Mary Magdalene Church; [A] Riverside, CA Divine Word Seminary.
McHenry, Raymond '00 (DM) West Des Moines, IA St. Francis of Assisi Church.
McHenry, Stephen P. '73 (PH) Ambler, PA St. Anthony of Padua Church; [A] Wynnewood, PA Theological Seminary of St. Charles Borromeo, Overbrook.
McHenry, Vincent *o.p.* (NY) Manhattan, NY New York Presbyterian Hospital.
McHenry, Vincent Ferrer *o.p.* '49 (NY) [22] New York, NY St. Catherine of Siena Church; [DD] New York, NY St. Catherine of Siena Priory.
McHugh, Alphonsus *ss.cc.* '69 (BWN) [3] Harlingen, TX Queen of Peace Church.
McHugh, Brian J. '66 (BO) [63] Boston, MA Sacred Heart Church.
McHugh, Conall C. *o.f.m. conv.* '56 (R) Siler City, NC St. Julia Church.
McHugh, Connell A. '72 (SCR) West Hazleton, PA St. Francis of Assisi Church.
McHugh, Dennis (PAT) Retired.
McHugh, Donald '57 (P) Retired.
McHugh, Edward T. *o.m.i.* '37 (SEA) [4] Seattle, WA St. Benedict Church.
McHugh, Francis '97 (SAT) [63] San Antonio, TX St. Pius X Church.
McHugh, Francis M. *o.f.m.* '76 (SCR) [12] Wilkes-Barre, PA St. Joseph Church; [M] Wilkes-Barre, PA St. Joseph's Friary.
McHugh, James *c.p.* '61 (SCR) [M] Scranton, PA Saint Ann's Passionist Monastery.
McHugh, James L. '60 (COV) Retired.
McHugh, James P. *o.s.f.s.* '66 (SLC) [B] Salt Lake City, UT Judge Memorial Catholic High School.
McHugh, James P. *o.s.f.s.* '77 (SLC) [F] Salt Lake City, UT Oblate House.
McHugh, Jerome *o.f.m.cap.* '60 (NY) [DD] White Plains, NY St. Conrad Friary.
McHugh, John (LC) [C] La Crosse, WI Coulee Catholic Schools.
McHugh, John *s.o.l.t.* '52 (CC) Robstown, TX St. Anthony Church; [H] Robstown, TX Society of Our Lady of the Most Holy Trinity.
McHugh, John '54 (LA) Santa Fe Springs, CA St. Pius X Church.
McHugh, John M *o.m.i.* '73 (BO) [Z] Tewksbury, MA Immaculate Heart of Mary Infirmary.
McHugh, John P. *o.f.m.cap.* '69 (MAN) [N] Manchester, NH Campus Ministries; [N] Hanover, NH The Catholic Student Center at Dartmouth, Aquinas House, Aquinas at Dartmouth, Inc.
McHugh, John T. '93 (LC) Special Assignment; [A] La Crosse, WI Holy Cross Seminary House of Formation; [H] La Crosse, WI Holy Cross (Seminary) Diocesan Center.
McHugh, John W. '76 (HRT) Simsbury, CT St. Mary's Church.
McHugh, Joseph B. *s.j.* '58 (BO) [Y] Gloucester, MA Eastern Point Retreat House.
McHugh, Joseph F. '73 (TR) Leave of Absence.
McHugh, Joseph F. *s.j.* '83 (FgM) Provinces.
McHugh, Kieran A. '70 (PAT) [C] Sparta, NJ Pope John XXIII High School.
McHugh, Michael *s.j.* '51 (HEL) Browning, MT Church of the Little Flower.
McHugh, Michael J. '80 (BRK) [203] Queens, NY Most Precious Blood Church.
McHugh, Owen '50 (COS) Retired.
McHugh, Patrick J. '50 (LA) Torrance, CA Nativity Church; Retired.
McHugh, Paul F. '53 (MAN) Retired.
McHugh, Msgr. Peter J. '65 (PAT) [2] Clifton, NJ St. Andrew the Apostle Church.
McHugh, Richard P. *s.j.* (BAL) Woodstock, MD St. Alphonsus Rodriguez Church.
McHugh, Thomas J. '49 (CHI) [131] Chicago, IL St. Matthias Church; Retired.
McHugh, William *o.m.i.* '52 (P) Shady Cove, OR Our Lady of Fatima Church.
McIlhenny, Bernard R. *s.j.* '56 (SCR) [C] Scranton, PA University of Scranton.
McIlhon, Msgr. John J. '48 (DM) Retired.
McIlhone, James P. '74 (CHI) [A] Mundelein, IL University of St. Mary of the Lake-Mundelein Seminary.
McIlvane, Donald W. '52 (PIT) Retired.
McIlwain, Michael A. *o.s.b.* '94 (GBG) Latrobe, PA Latrobe Area Hospital; [H] Latrobe, PA Saint Vincent Archabbey; [I] Latrobe, PA Discalced Carmelite Nuns.
McInerney, Blaise *o.carm.* '54 (JOL) [J] Darien, IL Carmelite Provincial Office.
McInerney, Henry '77 (BLX) Kiln, MS Annunciation Church.
McInerney, Kieran *o.s.b.* '52 (FgM) American - Cassinese Congregation Foreign Missions.
McInerney, Maurice '59 (DEN) Absent on Leave.
McInerney, Walter L. *c.s.c.* '36 (FTW) [J] South Bend, IN Congregation of Holy Cross, Indiana Province, Provincial House.
McInerny, Msgr. Lawrence B. '79 (CHR) [10] Charleston, SC Stella Maris Church.
McInnes, Val A. *o.p.* '61 (NO) [30] New Orleans, LA St. Dominic Church; [S] New Orleans, LA The Patrons of the Vatican Museums in the South, Inc.
McInnes, William C. *s.j.* '57 (BO) [W] Boston, MA The Society of Jesus of New England-Provincial Offices; [W] Chestnut Hill, MA The Jesuit Community at Boston College.
McInnis, Francis L. '56 (GF) Retired.
McInnis, Gary '98 (LAN) [9] Flint, MI St. Luke Church.
McInnis, John Kevin *s.c.j.* (SP) [O] Pinellas Park, FL Priests of the Sacred Heart.
McInnis, Richard W. '69 (PRT) Retired.
McInnis, Thomas J. '57 (LC) Ettrick, WI St. Bridget Church; Melrose, WI St. Kevin Church.
McIntire, William J. *m.m.* '67 (FgM) Maryknoll Foreign Missions.
McIntosh, Alan *o.s.b.* '61 (SFD) Ste. Marie, IL St. Mary of the Assumption Church.
McIntosh, Alan R. *o.s.b.* '61 (IND) [J] St. Meinrad, IN St. Meinrad Archabbey.
McIntosh, Robert K. *s.j.* '72 (FgM) Provinces.
McIntosh, Thomas *c.ss.r.* '66 (FgM) Redemptorist Foreign Missions.
McIntyre, Allen J. '56 (STP) Retired.

McIntyre, Gerald J. *s.j.* '74 (FgM) Provinces.
McIntyre, James *o.f.m.cap.* '53 (NY) [DD] Yonkers, NY St. Clare Friary.
McIntyre, Msgr. James P. '38 (CLV) [33] Cleveland, OH St. Ignatius of Antioch Church; Rocky River, OH St. Christopher Church; Retired.
McIntyre, Msgr. James P. '71 (CAM) Washington Township, NJ Holy Family Church.
McIntyre, John J. '92 (PH) On Special or Other Archdiocesan Assignment; [BB] Merion, PA Sisters of Mercy of the Americas, Merion Regional Community, Convent.
McIntyre, John P. *s.j.* '63 (BO) [W] Chestnut Hill, MA The Jesuit Community at Boston College.
McIntyre, Justin '81 (SR) Retired.
McIntyre, Louis *t.o.r.* '53 (VEN) [3] Sarasota, FL Our Lady Queen of Martyrs Church.
McIntyre, Raymond T. '52 (RIC) Retired.
McIntyre, Thomas J. *c.m.* '50 (LA) [Q] Montebello, CA Vincentian Fathers & Brothers; [W] Montebello, CA DePaul Center.
McIntyre, Thomas J. *c.m.* '50 (ORG) Laguna Beach, CA St. Catherine of Siena Church.
McIntyre, Msgr. Thomas J. '66 (CAM) [3] Cherry Hill, NJ St. Peter Celestine Church; [G] Camden, NJ The Tuition Assistance Fund, Inc.
McIsaac, Edward F. '48 (FR) Retired.
McKamy, Eldon J. '63 (OM) On Duty Outside the Archdiocese.
McKamy, Eldon J. '63 (P) [J] Portland, OR Providence St. Vincent Medical Center.
McKane, Paul *o.s.b.* '88 (WDC) [M] Washington, DC St. Anselm's Abbey.
McKarns, James '62 (Y) Retired.
McKarns, James E. '62 (Y) North Canton, OH St. Paul's Church.
McKay, Alistair J. *c.ss.r.* '75 (CHR) Sumter, SC St. Anne's Church.
McKay, Anthony *c.s.sp.* '60 (LR) Conway, AR St. Joseph's Church.
McKay, Douglas M. '82 (PH) [Y] Philadelphia, PA Holy Family Home.
McKay, Frank '54 (NY) Absent on Sick leave.
McKay, Msgr. James '56 (SFR) [3] San Mateo, CA St. Matthew Church; San Mateo, CA Serra Club of San Mateo.
McKay, James R. *s.m.* '44 (CIN) [M] Dayton, OH Marianist Provincialate.
McKay, John F. '73 (WDC) Riverdale, MD St. Bernard Church.
McKay, Joseph '84 (ALB) Schuylerville, NY Notre Dame-Visitation Church.
McKay, Michael *o.s.b.* '86 (BAL) [15] Baltimore, MD St. Benedict Church.
McKay, Michael *o.s.b.* '86 (GBG) [H] Latrobe, PA Saint Vincent Archabbey.
McKay, Robert '70 (SJ) Los Altos, CA St. William Church.
McKay, Robert J. '51 (SY) Retired; [S] Syracuse, NY St. Pius X Home, Inc.
McKay, William E. '49 (PHX) Retired.
McKean, Benedict B. *o.s.b.* '59 (PEO) [A] Peru, IL St. Bede Abbey and Academy.
McKean, Dan J. '87 (LAN) Brighton, MI St. Patrick Church.
McKean, Louis '47 (P) Retired.
McKeaney, James J. '69 (PH) West Conshohocken, PA St. Gertrude Church.
McKearney, James L. '97 (SFR) [A] Menlo Park, CA St. Patrick Seminary; [A] Menlo Park, CA St. Patrick Seminary.
McKee, Francis X. '66 (PH) [60] Philadelphia, PA Holy Family Church.
McKee, Henry J. '72 (PH) Manoa, PA Sacred Heart Church.
McKee, James C. *s.j.* '69 (E) Curwensville, PA St. Timothy Church.
McKee, John '46 (FRS) Retired.
McKee, Roderick D. '66 (WDC) Beltsville, MD St. Joseph Church.
McKee, William *c.ss.r.* '48 (STL) [P] Liguori, MO Liguori Mission House/Redemptorists.
McKee, William A. '83 (SEA) [10] Seattle, WA St. John Church.
McKeefry, Brendan '67 (SAC) Paradise, CA St. Thomas More Church.
McKeever, Frederick *o.f.m.* '54 (PAT) [M] Butler, NJ St. Anthony Friary.
McKeever, Henry *c.ss.r.* '48 (STL) [P] Liguori, MO Liguori Mission House/Redemptorists.
McKeever, Msgr. William F. '45 (MIA) [22] Miami, FL St. John Bosco Church; Retired.
McKeirnan, Michael J. *m.m.* '41 (FgM) Maryknoll Foreign Missions.
McKelvey, James P. '93 (PH) Collegeville, PA St. Eleanor Church.
McKelvey, Thomas P. '62 (PH) Linwood, PA Holy Saviour Church.
McKendrick, Norman G. *s.j.* '61 (DET) [K] Detroit, MI Jesuit Community at the University of Detroit.
McKenna, Brian *o.f.m.cap.* '65 (BAK) Bend, OR St. Francis of Assisi Church.
McKenna, Colin J. '99 (BGP) Shelton, CT St. Joseph Church.
McKenna, Daniel *o.m.i.* '58 (GAL) Alvin, TX St. John the Baptist Church.
McKenna, Dennis R. '47 (NEW) [2] Irvington, NJ St. Leo's Church; Retired.
McKenna, Edward J. '65 (CHI) Other Assignments.
McKenna, Msgr. Enda '64 (SAT) [49] San Antonio, TX St. Leo Church.
McKenna, Eugene F. *m.s.* '53 (LKC) Hackberry, LA St. Peter Apostle Church.
McKenna, Eugene J. *s.s.j.* '47 (BAL) [S] Baltimore, MD St. Joseph's Manor.
McKenna, Eugene J. '63 (PRO) Middletown, RI St. Lucy Church.
McKenna, F. Charles '60 (ALN) Retired; [J] Bethlehem, PA Holy Family Villa.
McKenna, Frank W. '94 (NOR) Canterbury, CT St. Augustine Church.
McKenna, George P. '44 (CHI) [1] Oak Lawn, IL St. Catherine of Alexandria Church; Retired.
McKenna, James *s.d.s.* '52 (MIL) [P] Milwaukee, WI Salvatorians - Jordan Hall.
McKenna, James *s.d.b.* '80 (PMB) Belle Glade, FL St. Philip Benizi Church.
McKenna, James George '61 (DAL) [5] Dallas, TX Holy Cross Church; On Duty Outside the Diocese.
McKenna, Msgr. James J. '42 (BRK) [198] Queens, NY St. Mary Star of the Sea Church; Retired.
McKenna, James T. '64 (NEW) Closter, NJ St. Mary Church.
McKenna, John *c.m.* '64 (BRK) [V] Jamaica, NY St. Vincent's House.
McKenna, John *c.ss.r.* '77 (NY) [150] Bronx, NY Immaculate Conception Church.
McKenna, John J. '45 (WOR) Retired.
McKenna, John J. '47 (NY) Retired.
McKenna, John L. (PIT) Allegheny County, PA Mercy Health System of Pittsburgh-Pittsburgh Mercy Hospital.
McKenna, John L. '88 (PIT) [54] Pittsburgh, PA St. John Vianney Church.
McKenna, Joseph C. *s.j.* '49 (NY) [DD] New York, NY Murray-Weigel Hall.
McKenna, Joseph J. *o.s.f.s.* '57 (WIL) Wilmington, DE St. Francis Hospital; [B] Wilmington, DE Salesianum School; [H] Wilmington, DE St. Francis Hospital, Inc.; [I] Wilmington, DE DeSales House.
McKenna, Joseph R. '57 (PRT) Retired.
McKenna, Kenneth N. *o.s.f.s.* '85 (LAN) [L] Brooklyn, MI Lake Vineyard Camps, Inc., (De Sales Center).
McKenna, Kenneth N. *o.s.f.s.* '85 (TOL) [K] Toledo, OH Oblates of St. Francis de Sales.
McKenna, Kevin E. '77 (ROC) [11] Rochester, NY St. Cecilia Church; [19] Rochester, NY St. Helen Church; Scottsville, NY St. Mary of the Assumption Church.
McKenna, Michael G. '73 (GR) Big Rapids, MI St. Mary's Church.
McKenna, Peter '57 (SAT) La Vernia, TX St. Ann Church.
McKenna, Philip (FgM) Society of St. James the Apostle.
McKenna, Philip '62 (MOB) Prattville, AL St. Joseph Church.
McKenna, Thomas F. *c.m.* '67 (FgM) Vincentian Foreign Missions.
McKenna, Thomas F. *c.m.* '70 (PH) [B] Philadelphia, PA St. Vincent's Seminary; [B] Philadelphia, PA DePaul Novitiate; [AA] Philadelphia, PA Congregation of the Mission.
McKenna, Thomas J. '72 (PIT) [40] Pittsburgh, PA St. Patrick-St. Stanislaus Kostka Church; Allegheny County, PA Allegheny General.
McKenna, Timothy J. '79 (SEA) Military Chaplains.
McKenna, William *s.s.j.* '64 (MOB) [15] Mobile, AL Most Pure Heart of Mary Church.
McKenna, William A. *s.j.* '68 (NEW) [B] Jersey City, NJ Saint Peter's College; [N] Jersey City, NJ Jesuits of Saint Peter's College, Inc.
McKenney, Charles R. *s.j.* '44 (WOR) [N] Worcester, MA Jesuits of Holy Cross College, Inc.
McKenzie, John Harold *o.s.b.* '82 (CC) [H] Sandia, TX Corpus Christi Abbey.
McKenzie, John J. *o.s.a.* '65 (PH) [C] Villanova, PA Villanova University; [AA] Villanova, PA St. Thomas Monastery.
McKeon, Brian A. '77 (RVC) East Meadow, NY Nassau County Medical Center; [M] Uniondale, NY St. Pius X Residence.
McKeon, Gerard R. *s.j.* '86 (WOR) [N] Worcester, MA Jesuits of Holy Cross College, Inc.; [Q] Worcester, MA Campus Ministry.
McKeon, John Aedan *o.p.* '56 (NY) [DD] New York, NY St. Vincent Ferrer Priory.
McKeon, Michael '65 (SAC) Roseville, CA St. Rose of Lima Church.
McKeon, Raymond T. '63 (NEW) [17] Newark, NJ St. James Church.
McKeon, Robert '59 (LAN) Gaines, MI St. Joseph Church; Retired.
McKeon, Robert '90 (NY) [A] New York, NY Cathedral Preparatory Seminary; [A] Yonkers, NY St. Joseph's Seminary; [DD] Yonkers, NY Bishop Ford Residence.
McKeon, Thomas *s.s.s.* '50 (NY) [8] New York, NY St. Andrew Church; Manhattan, NY Beekman Downtown - New York Infirmary.
McKeon, William E. *c.m.* '49 (PH) [AA] Philadelphia, PA Congregation of the Mission.
McKeone, William '72 (TR) On Duty Outside the Diocese.
McKeough, Brendan J. *o.praem.* '53 (GB) [I] De Pere, WI St. Joseph Priory.
McKeough, James A. *s.j.* '54 (FgM) Provinces.
McKeown, Peter *m.s.* (R) Havelock, NC Annunciation Church.
McKeown, Peter '67 (NY) [11] Yonkers, NY St. John the Baptist Church.
McKeown, Timothy P. '97 (SAV) Macon, GA St. Joseph Church.
McKercher, Mark J. '97 (OM) West Point, NE Assumption B.V.M. Church.
McKernan, John P. *m.m.* '52 (FgM) Maryknoll Foreign Missions.
McKernan, Kenneth B. *c.s.b.* '66 (DET) [E] Redford, MI Catholic Central High School.
McKernan, Leo '83 (SPK) [A] Spokane, WA Bishop White Seminary.
McKernan, Leo J. (SCR) On Duty Outside the Diocese.
McKernan, Louis F. *c.s.p.* '54 (NY) [DD] Jamaica Estates, NY Paulist Fathers Generalate.
McKevitt, Gerald L. *s.j.* '75 (SJ) [B] Santa Clara, CA Santa Clara University.
McKiernan, Joseph W. '51 (WOR) Sutton, MA St. Mark Church.
McKiernan, Raymond '56 (BRK) [58] Brooklyn, NY Holy Name Church.
McKiernan, Thomas M. '51 (CHI) Retired.
McKiernan, Vincent W. *c.s.p.* '57 (COL) [J] Columbus, OH Campus Ministry.
McKillin, David '76 (LR) [A] Subiaco, AR Subiaco Monastery.
McKillip, Dennis *s.v.d.* '47 (FgM) Society of the Divine Word Foreign Missions.
McKillop, Michael J. *m.m.* '35 (NY) [DD] Maryknoll, NY Maryknoll Fathers and Brothers.
McKinley, Joseph *s.s.j.* (LAF) Rayne, LA Shrine of Our Mother of Mercy Church.
McKinley, Joseph *s.s.j.* '85 (NO) [P] New Orleans, LA Josephite Fathers and Brothers.
McKinley, Michael J. '85 (LFT) [2] Lafayette, IN St. Ann Church.
McKinley, Steve *o.f.m.conv.* '94 (PEO) [2] Peoria, IL Holy Family Church.
McKinney, Floyd E. (WCH) Newton, KS Our Lady of Guadalupe Church; Hutchinson, KS Kansas State Industrial Reformatory.
McKinney, Francis *t.o.r.* '34 (ARL) [J] White Post, VA Sacred Heart Friary.
McKinney, James F. (FAR) Alice, ND St. Henry (of Alice) Church.
McKinney, James F. '96 (FAR) Enderlin, ND St. Patrick's Church.
McKinney, Michael A. '93 (LFT) Muncie, IN St. Francis of Assisi Church; [H] Muncie, IN St. Francis of Assisi University Church.
McKinney, Ronald H. *s.j.* '83 (SCR) [C] Scranton, PA University of Scranton.
McKinney, Thomas A. '61 (GR) Retired.
McKinnon, Eymard *o.f.m.cap.* '54 (AGN) [F] Agana Heights, GU St. Fidelis Friary.
McKinnon, Eymard *o.f.m.cap* '54 (HON) Pearl City, HI Our Lady of Good Counsel Church.
McKinstra, William M. '62 (RCK) [6] Rockford, IL St. James Church; Retired.
McKitrick, James V. '58 (RCK) Retired.
McKnight, James '59 (SAC) Nevada City, CA St. Canice Church.
McKnight, Kevin F. '94 (PIT) Cranberry Township, PA St. Ferdinand Church.
McKnight, Robert J. '73 (BUR) Orwell, VT St. Paul Church.
McKnight, W. Shawn '94 (WCH) St. Mark's, KS St. Mark Church; On Duty Outside the Diocese.
McKnight, William '48 (GR) Retired.
McLachlan, Frederick E. *s.s.e.* '64 (BUR) Putney, VT Our Lady of Mercy Church.
McLain, John J. *s.j.* '98 (R) [E] Raleigh, NC Jesuit Community.
McLaughlin, Adrian T. *o.s.b.* '41 (PAT) [M] Morristown, NJ St. Mary's Abbey.
McLaughlin, Andrew '87 (DET) Absent on Leave.
McLaughlin, Anthony '97 (TYL) Texarkana, TX Sacred Heart Church.
McLaughlin, Bernard P. '59 (BO) Canton, MA St. Gerard Majella Church.
McLaughlin, Charles '62 (BRK) [10] Brooklyn, NY St. Anselm's Church.
McLaughlin, Charles J. '48 (CHI) Retired.
McLaughlin, Daniel *o.s.a.* '83 (PH) [D] Drexel Hill, PA Monsignor Bonner High School.

McLaughlin, Daniel F. '61 (FgM) Maryknoll Foreign Missions.
McLaughlin, Daniel P. *s.t.* '63 (TUC) [2] Tucson, AZ Blessed Kateri Tekakwitha Church; [J] Tucson, AZ St. Nicholas Indian Center.
McLaughlin, David S. '96 (NEW) Guttenberg, NJ St. John Nepomucene Church; North Bergen, NJ Palisades General Hospital.
McLaughlin, Don E. '81 (JOL) Bensenville, IL St. Charles Borromeo Church.
McLaughlin, Donald '67 (NEW) Dumont, NJ St. Mary's Church.
McLaughlin, Edward J. '52 (BO) Bridgewater, MA St. Thomas Aquinas Church.
McLaughlin, Edward J. '59 (CHI) Orland Park, IL St. Michael Church.
McLaughlin, Eugene L. '85 (STU) Absent Without Leave.
McLaughlin, Ferrell '71 (PRO) [4] West Warwick, RI St. John the Baptist Church.
McLaughlin, Ferrell E. '71 (PRO) [3] West Warwick, RI St. James Church.
McLaughlin, Gerald L. *s.j.* '59 (FgM) Provinces.
McLaughlin, Gregory A. '85 (AUS) [21] Austin, TX St. Theresa Church.
McLaughlin, Hugh J. '63 (HBG) Spring Grove, PA Sacred Heart Church.
McLaughlin, James '73 (SB) [9] Riverside, CA St. Patrick Church.
McLaughlin, James '96 (MET) [1] New Brunswick, NJ St. Peter Apostle Church.
McLaughlin, James J. '70 (PH) [103] Philadelphia, PA St. Matthew Church.
McLaughlin, John '56 (GB) Retired.
McLaughlin, John '61 (SEA) Retired.
McLaughlin, John '71 (NEW) [N] Cliffside Park, NJ St. Patrick's Missionary Society.
McLaughlin, John E. '62 (BO) [3] Somerville, MA St. Benedict Church.
McLaughlin, John P. '66 (MIA) [1] Fort Lauderdale, FL Blessed Sacrament Church.
McLaughlin, John R. '95 (BO) Foxborough, MA St. Mary Church.
McLaughlin, Joseph J. '66 (PH) Richboro, PA St. Vincent de Paul Church.
McLaughlin, Joseph J. *s.m.* '72 (FgM) Marist Foreign Missions.
McLaughlin, Joseph M. *s.s.e.* '70 (BUR) [E] Colchester, VT Society of St. Edmund.
McLaughlin, Joseph P. *o.praem.* '70 (PH) [AA] Paoli, PA Daylesford Abbey.
McLaughlin, Michael '82 (DM) Ankeny, IA Our Lady's Immaculate Heart Church.
McLaughlin, Neil P. *s.j.* '59 (SCR) [C] Scranton, PA University of Scranton.
McLaughlin, Owen F. '41 (MIL) Retired.
McLaughlin, Patrick J. '61 (BO) [3] Medford, MA St. Joseph Church.
McLaughlin, Patrick J. '74 (SCR) [4] Hazleton, PA Holy Trinity Church.
McLaughlin, Paul E. '71 (VEN) Military Chaplains.
McLaughlin, Paul J. '55 (BO) [2] Marlborough, MA Immaculate Conception Church.
McLaughlin, Peter A. '78 (CAM) Glassboro, NJ St. Bridget's Church.
McLaughlin, Richard '74 (PRT) [1] Lewiston, ME St. Joseph's Church.
McLaughlin, Robert A. '73 (PH) Kimberton, PA St. Basil the Great Church.
McLaughlin, Robert E. '66 (CHI) [1] Chicago, IL Cathedral of the Holy Name.
McLaughlin, Thomas *o.s.b.* '83 (RCK) [G] Aurora, IL Marmion Abbey-St. Augustine's Abbey.
McLaughlin, Msgr. Thomas C. (VIC) On Special or Other Diocesan Assignment.
McLaughlin, Thomas D. '76 (SCR) Stroudsburg, PA St. Luke's Church.
McLaughlin, Thomas R. '81 (NEW) Newark, NJ Beth Israel Hospital.
McLaughlin, Thomas W. '49 (LA) [92] Los Angeles, CA St. Teresa of Avila Church; Retired.
McLaughlin, Msgr. William '58 (ORG) Newport Beach, CA Our Lady Queen of Angels Church.
McLaughlin, William A. '92 (BRK) [3] Brooklyn, NY St. Agnes Church; [11] Brooklyn, NY St. Anthony of Padua-St. Alphonsus Church.
McLaughlin, William H. '68 (BO) [33] Boston, MA St. Joseph Church.
McLaughlin, William J. '70 (TR) [T] Trenton, NJ Martin House.
McLaverty, Albert J. '00 (CAM) Washington Township, NJ St. Charles Borromeo Church.
McLean, Barry *o.f.m.* '90 (SAN) Big Lake, TX St. Margaret of Cortona Church; Crane, TX Good Shepherd Church.
McLean, Barry L. '90 (SAN) McCamey, TX Sacred Heart Church.
McLean, Edward J. '52 (HRT) [1] West Hartford, CT St. Brigid's Church; Special and other Archdiocesan Assignment.
McLean, George F. *o.m.i.* '55 (WDC) [M] Washington, DC Oblate College/Center for Mission Studies Community; [V] Washington, DC Council for Research in Values and Philosophy.
McLean, James F. *c.s.p.* '41 (NY) [DD] Jamaica Estates, NY Paulist Fathers Generalate.
McLean, William '69 (LA) [2] Long Beach, CA St. Athanasius Church.
McLearen, Daniel J. '92 (HRT) [9] New Haven, CT St. Francis Church.
McLellan, Alan J. *c.m.* '65 (FgM) Vincentian Foreign Missions.
McLellan, Daniel *o.f.m.* '76 (WDC) [B] Washington, DC Washington Theological Union; [M] Silver Spring, MD Gemelli House.
McLellan, James '70 (FR) North Dighton, MA St. Joseph's Church.
McLellan, Michael F. '76 (BO) [12] Boston, MA Blessed Sacrament Church; [51] Boston, MA Our Lady of Lourdes Church.
McLelland, James R. '00 (SHP) Bossier City, LA St. Jude Church.
McLeod, Daniel '42 (OAK) Retired.
McLeod, David (PAT) On Duty Outside the Diocese.
McLeod, Donald J. *c.s.b.* '78 (OAK) [C] Oakland, CA Bishop O'Dowd High School.
McLeod, Frederick G. *s.j.* '62 (BO) [W] Boston, MA The Society of Jesus of New England-Provincial Offices.
McLeod, Frederick G. *s.j.* '62 (STL) [C] St. Louis, MO Saint Louis University; [P] St. Louis, MO Jesuit Community Corporation at St. Louis University - Jesuit Hall.
McLeod, Malcolm C. *m.ss.cc.* '87 (CAM) Linwood, NJ Our Lady of Sorrows Church.
McLeod, Paul *ss.cc.* '84 (HON) Lihue, HI Immaculate Conception Church.
McLernan, Richard L. *o.s.f.s.* '57 (LAN) [B] Jackson, MI Lumen Christi High School.
McLernon, Thomas M. '57 (HBG) On Duty Outside the Diocese.
McLernon, Thomas Michael '57 (MIL) [B] Hales Corners, WI Sacred Heart School of Theology.
McLeroy, Jacob (SFE) Springer, NM St. Joseph Church.
McLinden, James *s.s.j.* '69 (WDC) [B] Washington, DC St. Joseph's Seminary.
McLinden, James E. *s.s.j.* '62 (WDC) [B] Washington, DC Josephite Pastoral Center.
McLinden, James E. *s.s.j.* '71 (WDC) [27] Washington, DC St. Luke Church.
McLoone, Joseph C. '88 (PH) [1] Philadelphia, PA Cathedral Basilica of SS. Peter and Paul.
McLoud, Steven J. '94 (SC) Churdan, IA St. Columbkille's Church; Scranton, IA St. Paul's Church.
McLoughlin, Brendan (PAT) Sabbatical.
McLoughlin, Brendan '70 (PAT) Randolph, NJ Resurrection Church.
McLoughlin, James W. '65 (RCK) Woodstock, IL St. Mary Church.
McLoughlin, John Francis *c.p.* '54 (HRT) [M] West Hartford, CT Holy Family Monastery/Retreat.
McLoughlin, John T. '73 (NY) [6] Mt. Vernon, NY St. Ursula Church.
McLoughlin, Luke '66 (STA) [17] Jacksonville, FL St. Matthew's Church.
McLoughlin, Michael P. '81 (NY) Highland Falls, NY Sacred Heart of Jesus Church; Highland Falls, NY Sacred Heart of Jesus Church.
McLoughlin, Nicholas '66 (VEN) Port Charlotte, FL St. Charles Borromeo Church.
McLoughlin, Paul J. '71 (SPC) Ozark, MO St. Joseph the Worker Church.
McLoughlin, Richard J. '69 (PH) Absent on Leave.
McLucas, James '79 (NY) Absent on Leave.
McMackin, Thomas P. '63 (ORL) Ormond Beach, FL Prince of Peace Church.
McMahon, Albert *o.f.m.* '60 (NY) [DD] New York, NY Franciscan Province of the Immaculate Conception.
McMahon, Bartholomew *o.f.m.* '62 (FgM) Franciscan Foreign Missions.
McMahon, Brian F. '85 (BO) Bellingham, MA Assumption Church.
McMahon, Desmond '60 (SEA) Retired.
McMahon, Edward J. *s.j.* '60 (NY) [DD] New York, NY Xavier Jesuit Community.
McMahon, Edward M. '70 (BO) Billerica, MA St. Mary Church; Senior Priests.
McMahon, Francis X. *s.s.e.* '54 (NOR) Groton, CT Sacred Heart Church.
McMahon, George J. *s.j.* '53 (NY) [DD] New York, NY Jesuit Community at Fordham University.
McMahon, Gerald J. '59 (ROC) Retired.
McMahon, Gerald J. *s.j.* '62 (BUF) [50] Buffalo, NY St. Michael Church.
McMahon, Gerard J. '59 (ROC) Penfield, NY Holy Spirit Church.
McMahon, Gerard T. '61 (BO) On Duty Outside the Archdiocese.
McMahon, Msgr. James B. '53 (BRK) Retired; [V] Douglaston, NY Bishop Mugavero Residence.
McMahon, Msgr. John '66 (PMB) [3] Boca Raton, FL St. Joan of Arc Church.
McMahon, John A. *o.p.* '68 (WDC) [11] Washington, DC St. Dominic Church & Priory Church; [M] Washington, DC Center for Assisted Living.
McMahon, John F. '76 (CLV) Retired.
McMahon, Msgr. John J. (PHX) [H] Phoenix, AZ Mt. Claret Center.
McMahon, John J. '38 (CHI) Skokie, IL St. Joan of Arc Church; Retired.
McMahon, Msgr. John J. '48 (PHX) Special Assignment; [H] Phoenix, AZ Mt. Claret Center; [K] Phoenix, AZ St. Vincent De Paul Society.
McMahon, Joseph '56 (CLV) Kirtland, OH Divine Word Church.
McMahon, Joseph M. '43 (P) Retired.
McMahon, Joseph R. '71 (WIL) [2] Wilmington, DE St. Ann Church.
McMahon, Joseph S. '68 (P) Lake Oswego, OR Our Lady of the Lake Church; [P] Portland, OR University of Portland.
McMahon, Joseph V. '84 (NSH) [6] Nashville, TN St. Henry Church; [B] Nashville, TN Father Ryan High School.
McMahon, Joseph W. '56 (CLV) Retired.
McMahon, Kevin T. '75 (PH) [A] Wynnewood, PA Theological Seminary of St. Charles Borromeo, Overbrook.
McMahon, Kevin T. '75 (WIL) On Duty Outside the Diocese.
McMahon, Kieran F. *o.f.m.* '47 (PAT) [M] Ringwood, NJ Holy Name Friary, Inc.
McMahon, Kieran M. '65 (SAC) [21] Sacramento, CA St. Robert Church.
McMahon, Msgr. Lawrence J. '55 (BGP) [3] Stratford, CT St. Mark Church.
McMahon, Martin J. *o.m.i.* '56 (BUF) [27] Buffalo, NY Holy Angels Church.
McMahon, Michael F. '88 (CHI) River Forest, IL St. Luke Church.
McMahon, Patrick *o.carm.* '76 (WDC) [B] Washington, DC Whitefriars Hall; [B] Washington, DC Whitefriars Hall.
McMahon, Sean '62 (ALB) Cairo, NY Sacred Heart Church.
McMahon, Thomas F. *c.s.v.* '54 (CHI) [N] Arlington Heights, IL Viatorian Province Center-Clerics of St. Viator.
McMahon, Timothy M. *s.j.* '87 (KC) [11] Kansas City, MO St. Francis Xavier Church; [B] Kansas City, MO Rockhurst University; [J] Kansas City, MO Rockhurst Jesuit Community.
McMahon, Walter M. '73 (SJ) [20] San Jose, CA St. Thomas of Canterbury Church.
McMahon, Msgr. William J. '45 (NY) Cortlandt Manor, NY Holy Spirit Church; Retired.
McMain, Msgr. Robert O. '49 (WDC) Retired.
McManamin, Francis G. *s.j.* '61 (BAL) [B] Baltimore, MD Loyola College in Maryland; [S] Baltimore, MD Jesuit Community of Loyola College, Inc.
McManamon, James *o.f.m.* '49 (CLV) [6] Parma, OH Holy Family Church; [O] Cleveland, OH Padua Franciscan Friary.
McManamon, John *s.j.* '80 (LA) [C] Los Angeles, CA Loyola Marymount University.
McManamon, John M. *s.j.* '80 (DET) [K] Detroit, MI Jesuit Provincial Office-Detroit Province of the Society of Jesus.
McManus, Msgr. Charles J. '42 (NY) [144] Bronx, NY St. Gabriel Church; [4] Yonkers, NY St. Bartholomew Church; Retired.
McManus, Denis *c.s.sp.* '58 (SFR) San Quentin, CA California State Prison.
McManus, Dennis *c.s.sp.* '58 (SFR) San Anselmo, CA St. Anselm Church.
McManus, Eamon '54 (WDC) Retired.
McManus, Eugene J. '51 (RVC) [M] Uniondale, NY St. Pius X Residence.
McManus, Eugene J. '57 (RVC) Retired.
McManus, Eugene P. *s.s.j.* '49 (BAL) [S] Baltimore, MD St. Joseph Society of the Sacred Heart House of Central Administration.
McManus, Francis J. *s.j.* '73 (BGP) [P] Fairfield, CT The Fairfield Jesuit Community-Fairfield University.
McManus, Francis J. *s.j.* '73 (BO) [W] Boston, MA The Society of Jesus of New England-Provincial Offices.
McManus, Francis J. *s.j.* '73 (FR) [15] New Bedford, MA St. James Church.
McManus, Msgr. Frederick R. '42 (BO) Senior Priests.
McManus, Gerald D. '79 (PH) Military Chaplains.
McManus, Msgr. Hugh F. '61 (NY) Scarsdale, NY Our Lady of Fatima Church.
McManus, Msgr. J. Fleming '47 (CHR) Retired.
McManus, John H. *o.m.i.* '56 (SCL) [M] St. Cloud, MN St. Therese Center for Special Ministry.
McManus, John H. *o.m.i.* '56 (STP) [Q] Buffalo, MN Christ the King Retreat Center.
McManus, Joseph '56 (BAL) Retired.
McManus, Joseph *s.o.l.t.* '97 (CC) [H] Robstown, TX Society of Our Lady of the Most Holy Trinity.
McManus, Joseph L. '56 (BAL) [42] Baltimore, MD Immaculate Heart of Mary Church.
McManus, Michael '48 (SAT) [41] San Antonio, TX St. James the Apostle Church.

McManus, Michael K. '85 (FR) Raynham, MA St. Ann Church.
McManus, Patrick S. '99 (PH) [141] Philadelphia, PA Resurrection of Our Lord Church.
McManus, Paul C. '65 (DUB) [H] Waterloo, IA Covenant Medical Center, Inc.
McManus, Paul G. (BO) [2] Lawrence, MA Asuncion de la Virgen Maria Church.
McManus, Msgr. Paul J. '42 (BO) Senior Priests.
McManus, Richard *o.f.m.* '83 (MRY) [H] San Juan Bautista, CA St. Francis Retreat Center.
McManus, Msgr. Robert T. '52 (PH) Downingtown, PA St. Joseph Church.
McManus, Thomas *o.s.a.* '70 (ORG) Buena Park, CA St. Pius V Church.
McManus, Thomas F. *s.j.* '98 (NEW) [C] Jersey City, NJ St. Peter's Preparatory School.
McManus, Thomas J. '68 (PH) [A] Wynnewood, PA Theological Seminary of St. Charles Borromeo, Overbrook.
McManus, Thomas J. '69 (PH) Narberth, PA St. Margaret Church.
McMenamin, John J. *o.s.f.s.* '59 (TOL) [C] Toledo, OH St. Francis de Sales High School; [K] Toledo, OH Oblates of St. Francis de Sales.
McMenamy, Alvin *s.m.* '67 (STL) [P] St. Louis, MO Provincialate of the Society of Mary, Province of St. Louis.
McMillan, Cliff J. '90 (DEN) Glenwood Springs, CO St. Stephen Church.
McMillan, John F. *c.p.* '56 (PIT) [O] Pittsburgh, PA St. Paul of the Cross Monastery.
McMillan, Keith P. *s.j.* '93 (FgM) Provinces.
McMillan, Robert G. *s.j.* '62 (BO) [19] Boston, MA St. Francis de Sales-St. Philip Church; [W] Boston, MA Loyola House; [W] Boston, MA The Society of Jesus of New England-Provincial Offices.
McMillen, Michael *s.c.j.* '67 (CHI) [N] Chicago, IL Priests of the Sacred Heart.
McMorrow, Kevin *s.a.* '58 (NY) [A] Yonkers, NY St. Joseph's Seminary; [DD] Garrison, NY Franciscan Friars of the Atonement.
McMullan, John E. '61 (SEA) [29] Seattle, WA Our Lady of the Lake Church.
McMullen, Aidan C. '47 (NEW) [B] Jersey City, NJ Saint Peter's College; [N] Jersey City, NJ Jesuits of Saint Peter's College, Inc.
McMullen, Brendan J. *o.p.* '43 (STP) [15] Minneapolis, MN St. Albert the Great Church.
McMullen, Francis R. '51 (RVC) Priests Released from Diocesan Assignment.
McMullen, John *o.s.b.* '66 (SFS) Wilmot, SD St. Mary Church; [F] Marvin, SD Blue Cloud Abbey; [I] Marvin, SD Blue Cloud Abbey Retirement Trust.
McMullen, Roger '67 (SHP) Retired.
McMullin, Daniel '81 (ROC) [14] Rochester, NY Corpus Christi Church.
McMullin, Ernan '49 (FTW) [B] Notre Dame, IN University of Notre Dame Du Lac.
McMullin, Finian *o.f.m.* '46 (SFD) [H] Granite City, IL St. Elizabeth Medical Center.
McMurrer, Roberto *c.ss.r.* '61 (CGS) Aguas Buenas, PR Church of Tres Santos Reyes.
McMurry, John E. *s.s.* '56 (BAL) [R] Baltimore, MD St. Mary's Spiritual Center.
McMurry, John E. *s.s.* '56 (NSH) On Duty Outside the Diocese.
McMurry, Vincent deP. *s.s.* '49 (BAL) [O] Baltimore, MD St. Charles Villa; [S] Baltimore, MD St. Charles Villa.
McMurry, Vincent deP. *s.s.* '49 (NSH) On Duty Outside the Diocese.
McMurtrie, Msgr. James W. '62 (ARL) Ashburn, VA St. Theresa Church.
McNair, Andrew *l.c.* '97 (PRO) [U] Smithfield, RI Domus Mariae Formation Center ("Mater Ecclesiae").
McNalis, John P. '76 (CHI) [64] Chicago, IL St. Gabriel Church.
McNally, Dennis E. *s.j.* '74 (PH) [C] Philadelphia, PA St. Joseph's University; [AA] Philadelphia, PA Jesuit Community at St. Joseph's University.
McNally, Donald *o.m.i.* (GAL) Richmond, TX Jester I, II, III, IV Unit.
McNally, Edward F. '95 (SY) [V] Oswego, NY Newman Foundation, Inc., State University of New York.
McNally, Joseph '58 (IND) [16] Indianapolis, IN St. Barnabas Church.
McNally, Lawrence R. '77 (CHI) [178] Chicago, IL Queen of the Universe Church.
McNally, Michael J. '73 (PH) [A] Wynnewood, PA Theological Seminary of St. Charles Borromeo, Overbrook.
McNally, Michael J. '73 (PMB) On Duty Outside the Diocese.
McNally, Michael R. (SB) Retired.
McNally, Nathan *o.f.m.* '57 (STL) [T] Dittmer, MO Il Ritiro-The Little Retreat.
McNally, Richard *ss.cc.* '75 (FR) [I] Fairhaven, MA Sacred Hearts Provincial House.
McNally, Stephen '86 (RIC) On Duty Outside the Diocese.
McNally, Theodore A. *o.f.m.* '55 (PAT) [M] Butler, NJ St. Anthony Friary.
McNally, Thomas *c.s.c.* '61 (OAK) [3] Hayward, CA St. Clement Church.
McNally, Vincent '84 (MIL) [B] Hales Corners, WI Sacred Heart School of Theology.
McNally, Vincent M. *s.j.* '48 (BUF) [O] Buffalo, NY Canisius Jesuit Community; [R] Alfred, NY Campus Ministry.
McNamara, Anthony *o.carm.* '69 (JOL) [J] Darien, IL Carmelite Provincial Office.
McNamara, Brian J. '84 (RVC) Garden City, NY St. Joseph's Church.
McNamara, Daniel J. *s.j.* '80 (FgM) Provinces.
McNamara, Dennis L. *s.j.* '76 (WDC) [M] Washington, DC The Jesuit Community at Georgetown University.
McNamara, Donald P. '61 (FgM) Maryknoll Foreign Missions.
McNamara, Donald P. '61 (PH) On Duty Outside the Archdiocese.
McNamara, Elmer A. '33 (ROC) Retired.
McNamara, Msgr. Eugene P. '53 (BO) Scituate, MA St. Mary of the Nativity Church.
McNamara, Francis J. *s.j.* '54 (ROC) [C] Rochester, NY McQuaid Jesuit High School.
McNamara, Msgr. James '71 (RVC) West Babylon, NY Our Lady of Grace Church.
McNamara, John '32 (ALB) Retired.
McNamara, John J. '53 (ALN) Port Carbon, PA St. Stephen Church.
McNamara, John P. '56 (CHI) Palatine, IL St. Theresa Church.
McNamara, John R. '52 (BO) Senior Priests.
McNamara, Joseph '39 (SY) [S] Syracuse, NY St. Pius X Home, Inc.
McNamara, Joseph *s.p.* '56 (STL) [P] St. Louis, MO Servants of the Paraclete.
McNamara, Joseph M. '39 (ROC) Retired.
McNamara, Michael (BO) Natick, MA St. Patrick Church.
McNamara, Patrick M. *o.s.m.* '49 (CHI) [N] Chicago, IL Order of Friar Servants of Mary (Servites) United States of America Province, Inc.
McNamara, Patrick M. *o.s.m.* '49 (P) [L] Portland, OR The Grotto, The National Sanctuary of Our Sorrowful Mother.
McNamara, Patrick V. '60 (NY) [2] New Rochelle, NY St. Gabriel Church.
McNamara, Peter J. '64 (CC) Freer, TX St. Mary Church.
McNamara, Philip *s.a.c.* '58 (FWT) Stephenville, TX St. Brendan Church.
McNamara, Philip D. '56 (WOR) Retired.
McNamara, Robert F. '36 (ROC) [59] Rochester, NY St. Thomas the Apostle Church; Retired; [L] Rochester, NY Archivist (Diocese of Rochester Archives).
McNamara, Robert J. '69 (LA) Chatsworth, CA St. John Eudes Church.
McNamara, Stephen E. '67 (VEN) [2] Fort Myers, FL Church Of The Resurrection Of Our Lord.
Mcnamara, Thomas '47 (STL) [P] St. Louis, MO La Salette Missionaries.
McNamara, Thomas J. '82 (SAG) Essexville, MI St. John the Evangelist Church.
McNamara, Vincent P. '60 (NY) City, NY Bronx House of Detention.
McNamara, William *o.c.d.* '51 (MIL) [P] Milwaukee, WI Provincial Offices - Discalced Carmelites.
McNamara, William '65 (SAT) Elmendorf, TX St. Anthony Church.
McNamee, Msgr. Charles W. '50 (RCK) Retired.
McNamee, Francis G. '95 (ATL) Roswell, GA St. Peter Chanel Church.
McNamee, James P. '73 (LC) Elroy, WI St. Patrick Church; Kendall, WI St. Joseph Church; Wilton, WI St. John the Baptist Church.
McNamee, John P. '59 (PH) [92] Philadelphia, PA St. Malachy Church.
McNamee, Maurice *s.j.* '40 (STL) [C] St. Louis, MO Saint Louis University.
McNamee, Maurice B. *s.j.* '40 (STL) [P] St. Louis, MO Jesuit Community Corporation at St. Louis University - Jesuit Hall.
McNamee, Patrick '70 (P) Salem, OR St. Vincent de Paul Church.
McNea, Mark C. '89 (WIN) Slayton, MN St. Ann's Church.
McNearney, John *glmy.* '62 (CIN) [M] Cincinnati, OH Headquarters of Glenmary Home Missioners.
McNeely, Maurice '58 (HON) [6] Honolulu, HI Holy Family Church.
McNeese, Robert '98 (SPK) Kettle Falls, WA Sacred Heart of Jesus Church; Northport, WA Pure Heart of Mary Church.
McNeese, Robert J. '98 (SPK) Colville, WA Immaculate Conception Church.
McNeff, Thomas C. '77 (CHI) Schiller Park, IL St. Maria Goretti Church.
McNeice, Charles E. *s.s.e.* '62 (MOB) Tuskegee Institute, AL St. Joseph Church; [J] Tuskegee Institute, AL Tuskegee University Newman Center.
McNeil, Aubrey *o.f.m.* '85 (NY) [146] Bronx, NY Holy Cross Church.
McNeil, Dennis '75 (CLV) [Z] Euclid, OH St. Robert's Holy Name Society Boosters.
McNeil, Dennis M. '75 (CLV) [5] Euclid, OH St. Robert Bellarmine Church.
McNeil, Frank J. '71 (SFS) On Leave of Absence.
McNeil, Joel D. '87 (AUS) Round Rock, TX St. William's Church.
McNeil, John R. '61 (BO) On Duty Outside the Archdiocese.
McNeil, Lawrence J. '73 (HBG) Conewago Township, PA Basilica of the Sacred Heart of Jesus.
McNeill, Donald P. *c.s.c.* '65 (FTW) [B] Notre Dame, IN University of Notre Dame Du Lac; [J] Notre Dame, IN Holy Cross Community, Corby Hall, University of Notre Dame.
McNeill, Douglas '70 (GLP) Absent on Leave.
McNeill, John A. '46 (BRK) [213] Queens, NY Our Lady of Lourdes Church; Retired.
McNeill, Malachy '44 (B) Retired.
McNeilly, Dennis P. *s.j.* '85 (OM) [K] Omaha, NE Jesuit Community at Creighton University.
McNelis, Francis J. '65 (ALN) Sinking Spring, PA St. Ignatius Loyola Church.
McNelis, Paul D. *s.j.* '77 (WDC) [M] Washington, DC The Jesuit Community at Georgetown University.
McNellis, Paul *s.j.* '87 (BO) [W] Chestnut Hill, MA The Jesuit Community at Boston College.
McNerney, James '81 (ALB) [11] Troy, NY St. Paul the Apostle Church; [12] Troy, NY St. Peter Church.
McNew, Dwayne A. '95 (COL) Pickerington, OH Seton Church.
McNichol, Daniel '87 (HON) On Sabbatical.
McNichol, Fabian *t.o.r.* '55 (ARL) [J] White Post, VA Sacred Heart Friary.
McNicholas, Edward J. '54 (BRK) Released from Diocesan Assignment; Retired; [V] Douglaston, NY Bishop Mugavero Residence.
McNicholas, Raymond J. *s.s.c.* '49 (BUF) [2] Orchard Park, NY St. Bernadette Church.
McNicholas, Stephen '53 (ORL) Retired.
McNicholas, Stephen '61 (ORL) Sanford, FL All Souls Church.
McNicholl, Michael P. '66 (BUF) Strykersville, NY St. Mary, Queen of the Rosary Church.
McNiff, Msgr. James '36 (SFE) Retired.
McNiff, William T. *o.s.c.* '43 (SCL) Onamia, MN The Church of the Holy Cross of Onamia; [I] Onamia, MN Crosier Monastery.
McNulty, Charles L. '37 (ALN) [3] Pottsville, PA Mary Queen of Peace Church; Retired.
McNulty, Edward P. '93 (SD) [8] San Diego, CA Immaculata Church.
McNulty, Edwin J. '44 (COL) Retired.
McNulty, Francis J. '52 (NEW) Retired.
McNulty, Frank '52 (NEW) Summit, NJ St. Teresa's Church.
McNulty, Gerard J. '67 (LA) Military and VA Chaplains.
McNulty, J. Brendan '74 (CLV) [65] Cleveland, OH SS. Philip and James Church.
McNulty, James '53 (LA) [87] Los Angeles, CA St. Paul the Apostle Church.
McNulty, James D. *c.s.p.* '53 (NY) [DD] Jamaica Estates, NY Paulist Fathers Generalate.
McNulty, Jerry (LAV) Military Chaplains.
McNulty, Msgr. John '43 (SP) Retired.
McNulty, John '74 (PRO) [1] Newport, RI St. Augustin Church.
McNulty, John P. '73 (CLV) [3] Euclid, OH Holy Cross Church.
McNulty, Joseph D. '69 (CLV) [9] Cleveland, OH St. Augustine Church.
McNulty, Joseph P. '43 (BO) Senior Priests.
McNulty, Msgr. Patrick '53 (LA) [50] Los Angeles, CA St. Bernard Church; Retired.
McNulty, Patrick J. '60 (FTW) On Special Assignment.
McNulty, Robert E. '56 (NOR) Retired.
McNulty, Theodore '66 (CHI) [202] Chicago, IL St. Thomas More Church.
McNulty, William J. '61 (CHI) Lake Forest, IL St. Patrick Church.
McNulty, William J. '64 (NOR) Dayville, CT St. Joseph Church; Rogers, CT St. Ignatius Church.
McOwen, James F. '41 (LA) [Q] Montebello, CA Vincentian Fathers & Brothers; [W] Santa Barbara, CA St. Mary's Seminary Center.
McPadden, Charles J. *m.m.* '69 (NY) [DD] Maryknoll, NY Maryknoll Fathers and Brothers.
McPadden, Malachy M. *o.s.b.* '57 (NEW) [N] Newark, NJ Newark Abbey.
McPartland, Paul G. '57 (BO) Halifax, MA Our Lady of the Lake Church.
McPhail, J. Stuart *o.p.* '69 (PRO) [B] Providence, RI Providence College; [P] Providence, RI St. Thomas Aquinas Priory at Providence College.
McPhee, John *c.ss.r.* '46 (DEN) [M] Denver, CO The

Redemptorists/Denver Province.
McPhee, Msgr. Marvin '65 (SFS) Gettysburg, SD Sacred Heart Church; Retired.
McPhillips, James G. '83 (CLV) Newbury, OH St. Helen Church.
McPhillips, Thomas J. '44 (SFS) Retired; [D] Mitchell, SD Avera Queen of Peace.
McPolin, James '62 (BO) [W] Cambridge, MA Weston Jesuit Community.
McPolin, Patrick *c.m.f.* '43 (LA) [Q] Rancho Dominguez, CA Dominguez Seminary Inc.
McQuade, Brian '94 (RVC) Baldwin, NY St. Christopher Church.
McQuade, Donald P. *m.m.* '65 (FgM) Maryknoll Foreign Missions.
McQuade, James F. *c.s.p.* '56 (NY) [104] New York, NY St. Paul the Apostle Church; Manhattan, NY St. Luke's-Roosevelt Hospital Center.
McQuade, Richard E. '57 (BO) Emergency Response Group.
McQuaid, Msgr. Eugene (PAT) Retired.
McQuaid, Thomas W. '79 (CHI) [A] Mundelein, IL University of St. Mary of the Lake-Mundelein Seminary.
McQueeney, Robert *m.s.a.* '82 (NOR) [F] Cromwell, CT Society of the Missionaries of the Holy Apostles.
McQueeny, Thomas F. *s.j.* '56 (STL) [P] St. Louis, MO De Smet Jesuit High School Community.
McQuesten, Mark A. '87 (MAR) Norway, MI St. Mary Church.
McQuillan, Cornelius T. *c.s.sp.* '75 (ARE) [8] Arecibo, PR Inmaculado Corazon de Maria Church.
McQuillan, Edward *c.m.* '44 (STA) [E] Jacksonville, FL St. Vincent's Medical Center, Inc.
McQuillan, Edward F. *c.m.* '44 (PH) [AA] Philadelphia, PA Congregation of the Mission.
McQuillen, Paul G. *s.s.e.* '77 (NO) [4] Marrero, LA St. Joseph the Worker Church.
McQuillen, Thomas J. '94 (TOL) On Duty Outside the Diocese.
McQuinn, Maurice '39 (KC) Retired.
McQuinn, Peter B. '91 (CHI) [52] Chicago, IL Epiphany Church.
McRae, Msgr. Cornelius M. (BO) [1] Norwood, MA St. Catherine of Siena Church.
McReavy, Thomas J. *c.s.b.* '59 (GAL) [7] Houston, TX St. Anne Church.
McReynolds, Eugene *o.s.b.* '70 (OM) Boys Town, NE Immaculate Conception B.V.M. Church; [I] Boys Town, NE Father Flanagan's Boys' Home; [K] Elkhorn, NE Mount Michael Abbey.
McShane, James J. '66 (BUR) Rutland, VT Immaculate Heart of Mary Church.
McShane, John '74 (LAV) [G] Las Vegas, NV Catholic Charities of Southern Nevada.
McShane, John A. '57 (BRK) [55] Brooklyn, NY Holy Family Church.
McShane, Joseph M. *s.j.* '77 (SCR) [C] Scranton, PA University of Scranton; [C] Scranton, PA University of Scranton.
McShane, Patrick E. '79 (CLV) Retired.
McShane, Thomas S. *s.j.* '60 (OM) [K] Omaha, NE Jesuit Community at Creighton University.
McSheffery, Daniel F. '56 (HRT) North Branford, CT St. Augustine Church.
McSherry, John *s.v.d.* '61 (FgM) Society of the Divine Word Foreign Missions.
McSherry, John G. *s.j.* '72 (NY) [DD] New York, NY West Side Jesuit Community.
McSherry, Patrick *o.f.m.cap.* '78 (DET) [K] Detroit, MI St. Bonaventure Friary.
McSherry, Thomas '71 (OKL) Special Assignment.
McSorley, Aidan *o.s.b.* '69 (KC) [A] Conception, MO Conception Seminary College; [J] Conception, MO Conception Abbey.
McSorley, Gerald '64 (LA) [50] Los Angeles, CA St. Bernard Church.
McSorley, James P. *o.m.i.* '46 (OAK) [N] Oakland, CA Oblate Provincial House & Procure.
McSorley, Matthew T. *o.s.b.* '49 (CHL) [J] Belmont, NC Belmont Abbey.
McSorley, Richard T. *s.j.* '46 (WDC) [M] Washington, DC The Jesuit Community at Georgetown University.
McSpiritt, John P. *s.t.* '59 (JKS) Camden, MS Immaculate Conception Church.
McStravog, Patrick B. *o.s.a.* (PH) [AA] Villanova, PA Fray de Leon Community.
McStravog, Patrick B. *o.s.a.* '89 (PH) [AA] Villanova, PA Provincial Offices of the Order of St. Augustine, Province of St. Thomas of Villanova.
McSweeney, Brian T. '88 (NY) [74] New York, NY St. Michael Church.
McSweeney, Edward F. '52 (PIT) Retired.
McSweeney, James '74 (SR) Sonoma, CA St. Francis Solano Church.
McSweeney, Jeremiah F. '72 (WH) Cheat Lake, WV St. Luke Church.
McSweeney, John '48 (MRY) Retired.
McSweeney, Msgr. John J. '74 (CHL) [8] Charlotte, NC St. Matthew Church.
McSweeney, John R. *o.c.d.* '52 (SR) [M] Oakville, CA Carmelite House of Prayer.
McSweeney, Msgr. John R. '61 (BUR) Retired.
McSweeney, John Reginald *o.c.d.* '52 (SR) [L] Oakville, CA Carmelite House of Prayer.
McSweeney, Joseph *s.s.c.* '58 (PRO) [P] Bristol, RI St. Columban's Retirement House.
McSweeney, Liam P. '69 (SAC) Sacramento, CA California Youth Authority.
McSweeney, Msgr. Thomas J. '71 (E) [19] Erie, PA St. John the Baptist Church.
McSweeney, William P. *o.m.i.* '52 (PMB) Riviera Beach, FL St. Francis of Assisi Church.
McSweeney, William P. '69 (SAC) [2] Sacramento, CA All Hallows Church.
McSweeny, Joseph *s.s.c.* '90 (FgM) St. Columban's Foreign Mission.
McSwigan, Gerardo *c.ss.r.* '55 (CGS) Fajardo, PR Santiago Apostol Church.
McSwiggan, Thomas '67 (SAT) [59] San Antonio, TX St. Patrick Church.
McTaggart, Msgr. Edward P. '55 (SFR) [2] San Mateo, CA St. Gregory Church; San Francisco, CA Young Ladies' Institute; San Francisco, CA Serra Club of San Francisco (Golden Gate); Retired.
McTague, Charles, (Retired) (NEW) Harrison, NJ Holy Cross Church.
McTague, Charles H. '47 (NEW) Retired.
McTague, Thomas '57 (GF) Retired.
McTavey, Lawrence G. '55 (ALB) [3] Cohoes, NY St. Bernard Church.
McTeigue, Robert J. *s.j.* '97 (SCR) [C] Scranton, PA University of Scranton.
McTighe, Edward P. *s.j.* '61 (P) [D] Portland, OR Jesuit High School; [J] Portland, OR Providence St. Vincent Medical Center.
McTighe, Simon *o.s.b.* '53 (IND) [J] St. Meinrad, IN St. Meinrad Archabbey.
McTigue, Norman P. '70 (BUF) [1] Tonawanda, NY St. Amelia Church; Buffalo, NY Buffalo Psychiatric Center.
McTommoney, Brian *o.f.m.* '53 (FgM) Custody of St. Mary of the Angels. Byzantine-Slavonic.
McTommoney, Brian *o.f.m.* '53 (WDC) [M] Washington, DC Commissariat of the Holy Land, Franciscan Monastery - Mount St. Sepulchre.
McVean, John J. *o.f.m.* '67 (NY) [35] New York, NY St. Francis of Assisi Church.
McVeigh, James E. (PH) Collingdale, PA St. Joseph Church.
McVeigh, John J. '58 (LAV) Retired.
McVernon, John J. '58 (BRK) Released from Diocesan Assignment.
McVey, T. C. *o.p.* '60 (FgM) Dominican - Order of Preachers Foreign Missions.
McWeeney, Brian E. '73 (NY) [6] Poughkeepsie, NY St. Martin de Porres Church.
McWhorter, Michael L. '92 (ATL) Milledgeville, GA Sacred Heart of Jesus Church; [M] Atlanta, GA Campus Ministry.
McWilliam, James J. '49 (CIN) Retired.
Mead, Brian E. '69 (BUR) Bellows Falls, VT St. Charles Church.
Mead, Gary '97 (NY) [4] New Rochelle, NY Holy Family Church.
Mead, James Herbert *s.j.* '62 (NO) [11] New Orleans, LA Immaculate Conception Church.
Mead, Leland C. '68 (NU) On Duty Outside the Diocese.
Meade, Christopher '98 (HRT) [3] Bristol, CT St. Gregory's Church.
Meade, Denis *o.s.b.* '55 (KCK) [A] Atchison, KS Benedictine College; [H] Atchison, KS St. Benedict's Abbey.
Meade, Emilian *o.f.m.cap.* '46 (SFR) Burlingame, CA Our Lady of Angels Church.
Meade, Henry J. '51 (BO) Senior Priests.
Meade, James '52 (BRK) [S] Queens Village, NY Queen of Peace Residence.
Meade, James '86 (GRY) [1] Michigan City, IN St. Mary of the Immaculate Conception Church.
Meade, James C. '52 (RVC) Retired.
Meade, James W. '81 (CIN) West Chester, OH St. John Church.
Meade, John *s.m.* (BO) [55] Boston, MA Our Lady of Victories Church.
Meade, John *s.m.* '53 (BO) [3] Methuen, MA Our Lady of Mount Carmel Church; [W] Boston, MA Marist Fathers of Our Lady of Victories (Boston Prov.).
Meade, John F. '43 (NY) Retired.
Meade, John F. '43 (RVC) Malverne, NY Our Lady of Lourdes Church.
Meade, Maurice P. '48 (BO) Senior Priests.
Meaden, Paul *o.s.b.* '84 (SFE) [I] Pecos, NM Our Lady of Guadalupe Abbey; [K] Pecos, NM Our Lady of Guadalupe Olivetan Benedictine Abbey.
Meagher, Msgr. Frank J. '60 (COL) Buckeye Lake, OH Our Lady of Mt. Carmel Church.
Meagher, John (NOR) [A] Enders Island, CT St. Edmund's Novitiate.
Meagher, John J. *s.s.e.* '66 (NOR) Groton, CT Sacred Heart Church.
Meagher, Joseph A. '92 (NEW) [3] Linden, NJ St. John the Apostle Church.
Meagher, Michael T. '65 (SY) [1] Binghamton, NY St. Andrew Church.
Meagher, Msgr. Thomas '40 (SB) Retired.
Meagher, Thomas L. '64 (DET) White Lake, MI St. Patrick Church.
Mealey, Mark S. *o.s.f.s.* '78 (ARL) Vienna, VA Our Lady of Good Counsel Church.
Meaney, Brendan J. '65 (CAM) Washington Township, NJ SS. Peter and Paul Church.
Meaney, John J. *m.m.* '59 (NY) [DD] Maryknoll, NY Maryknoll Fathers and Brothers.
Meaney, Patrick '87 (CC) [H] Hebbronville, TX Catholic Solitudes.
Meaney, Peter J. *o.s.b.* '51 (PAT) [M] Morristown, NJ St. Mary's Abbey.
Means, David '81 (ANC) On Duty Outside Archdiocese.
Means, David A. '81 (STL) On Duty Outside the Archdiocese.
Meany, John J. *o.p.* '82 (CHI) [N] Chicago, IL Dominicans (Provincial Office).
Meany, John J. *o.p.* '87 (CHI) [N] Chicago, IL Dominicans (Provincial Office); [N] River Forest, IL St. Thomas Aquinas Priory.
Meany, Michael G. '80 (CHI) Oak Forest, IL St. Damian Church.
Meany, Neill R. *s.j.* '54 (YAK) [4] Yakima, WA St. Joseph's Church.
Measer, Donald L. '63 (BUF) [1] Tonawanda, NY St. Amelia Church; Retired.
Meaux, Glenn *s.o.l.t.* '80 (CC) [H] Robstown, TX Society of Our Lady of the Most Holy Trinity.
Meaux, Glenn '80 (LAF) On Duty Outside the Diocese.
Mecca, Gregg D. '96 (BGP) [5] Danbury, CT St. Peter Church.
Mecca, Msgr. Mark A. '36 (SCR) Retired.
Meccia, Francis S. *m.m.* '66 (NY) [DD] Maryknoll, NY Maryknoll Fathers and Brothers.
Mech, John J. '95 (DET) [3] Redford, MI Our Lady of Loretto Church.
Mecir, Joseph S. '80 (CLV) [70] Cleveland, OH Sacred Heart of Jesus Church.
Mecwel, Pawel J. '90 (MAR) [4] Sault Sainte Marie, MI St. Joseph Church.
Medairos, Anthony J. '73 (BO) Carver, MA Our Lady of Lourdes Church.
Medas, Michael B. (BO) Concord, MA St. Bernard Church; [FF] Newton, MA KOLBE Association, Inc.
Medayil, Joseph *c.m.i.* '76 (GAL) [K] Houston, TX The Catholic Chaplain Corps.
Medayil, Thomas Joseph '76 (GAL) [77] Houston, TX St. Thomas More Church.
Medeiros, Antonio S. '54 (BO) Senior Priests.
Medeiros, Arnold R. '75 (FR) Wareham, MA St. Patrick's Church.
Medeiros, Benjamin *t.o.r.* '77 (FWT) [8] Fort Worth, TX St. Andrew Church.
Medeiros, Paul *o.m.i.* '64 (FgM) Oblates Foreign Missions.
Meder, Stephen A. *s.j.* '43 (DET) [P] Clarkston, MI Colombiere Center.
Medina, Fabio '83 (SFR) Half Moon Bay, CA Our Lady of the Pillar Church.
Medina, Francisco '89 (SJN) [11] Bayamon, PR San Miguel Arcangel Church.
Medina, George '87 (PCE) On Duty Outside the Diocese.
Medina, George A. '97 (TR) [20] Trenton, NJ SS. Peter and Paul Church.
Medina, Hector '84 (FWT) Wichita Falls, TX Our Lady of Guadalupe Church.
Medina, Ignazio '77 (JC) Rosati, MO St. Anthony Church; St. James, MO Immaculate Conception Church.
Medina, Ignazio C. '77 (JC) Rolla, MO St. Patrick Church.
Medina, Jose Antonio *c.ss.r.* '82 (LA) Pico Rivera, CA St. Francis Xavier Church.
Medina, Jose Antonio *m.g.* '82 (SJ) [19] San Jose, CA St. Patrick Church; Palo Alto, CA St. Thomas Aquinas Church.
Medina, Jose Felix *l.c.* '81 (HRT) [B] Cheshire, CT Novitiate of the Legion of Christ.
Medina, Juan B. '69 (CGS) [4] Caguas, PR Nuestra Senora de la Providencia Church.
Medina, Julian '73 (SAC) Rio Vista, CA St. Joseph Church.
Medina, Mauricio '64 (B) Blackfoot, ID St. Bernard's Church.
Medina, Miguel Angel *sch.p.* '55 (SJN) [57] San Juan, PR Santisimo Salvador Church.
Medina, Rolando '71 (MIA) Hialeah Gardens, FL Santa Barbara Church.
Medina, Tito *m.s.c.* '92 (RCK) [G] Aurora, IL Missionaries of the Sacred Heart Community.
Medina-Cruz, D. Jamie '99 (ALX) Marksville, LA Holy Ghost Church; Marksville, LA St. Joseph's Church.
Medio, Joseph Paul *f.p.o.* '99 (FR) [I] New Bedford, MA Franciscans of Primitive Observance.
Medley, Robert W. '90 (MET) Warren, NJ Our Lady of

the Mount Church.
Medley, William F. '82 (L) Bardstown, KY St. Joseph Church.
Medlock, Scott '96 (ANC) [4] Anchorage, AK St. Elizabeth Ann Seton Church.
Medrano, Marcus '86 (DEN) [25] Denver, CO Sacred Heart Church.
Medve, A.A. (ALN) Military Chaplains.
Medwid, John M. '90 (ALB) [2] Schenectady, NY St. Anthony Church.
Medynski, Msgr. Francis J. '48 (BGP) Retired.
Mee, Michael *o.s.b.* '78 (P) [L] St. Benedict, OR Mt. Angel Abbey.
Meegan, William H. '50 (BUF) Retired.
Meehan, Andrew M. (MAN) Manchester, NH Elliott Hospital.
Meehan, Andrew M. '93 (MAN) Bedford, NH St. Elizabeth Seton Church.
Meehan, Barry C. *s.j.* '86 (NOR) [5] Norwich, CT SS. Peter and Paul Church.
Meehan, Barry M. '78 (PRO) [3] West Warwick, RI St. James Church; [4] West Warwick, RI St. John the Baptist Church.
Meehan, Daniel *o.m.i.* '61 (FgM) Oblates Foreign Missions.
Meehan, Francis X. '61 (PH) West Chester, PA SS. Simon and Jude Church.
Meehan, Gabriel '59 (CHL) Forest City, NC Immaculate Conception Church.
Meehan, Gery G. *o.praem.* '60 (GB) [6] De Pere, WI St. Norbert Campus Ministry Church; [B] De Pere, WI St. Norbert College; [I] De Pere, WI St. Joseph Priory.
Meehan, James *s.j.* '59 (HEL) [5] Missoula, MT St. Francis Xavier Church.
Meehan, Msgr. James H. '50 (PH) Bryn Mawr, PA St. John Neumann Church.
Meehan, James L. '41 (OG) Redwood, NY St. Francis Xavier Church.
Meehan, James L. '51 (OG) Retired.
Meehan, James T. *s.j.* '63 (FgM) Provinces.
Meehan, John T. '64 (NY) [3] Mt. Vernon, NY St. Mary Church.
Meehan, Joseph '66 (STA) Atlantic Beach, FL St. John the Baptist Church.
Meehan, Joseph F. *s.j.* '49 (SJ) [L] Los Gatos, CA Sacred Heart Jesuit Center.
Meehan, Joseph J. '61 (PH) Primos, PA St. Eugene Church.
Meehan, Msgr. Joseph P. '54 (NY) Suffern, NY Sacred Heart Church.
Meehan, Kenneth E. *s.j.* '71 (WDC) [E] Washington, DC Gonzaga College High School.
Meehan, Peter '68 (NY) [96] New York, NY Our Lady of the Rosary Church.
Meehan, Richard (SPR) [K] Holyoke, MA Sisters of Providence.
Meehan, Richard F. '69 (SPR) Absent on Leave; [I] Holyoke, MA Providence Place, Inc.
Meehan, Terence A. '67 (CIN) [6] Cincinnati, OH St. Andrew Church; [34] Cincinnati, OH Holy Name Church.
Meehan, Thomas J. '72 (ATL) [9] Atlanta, GA St. Anthony of Padua Church.
Meehan, Thomas J. *o.s.a.* '80 (CHL) [6] Charlotte, NC St. John Neumann Church.
Meehan, Timothy A. '59 (HRT) North Haven, CT St. Therese Church.
Meehling, Donald J. '58 (SFD) [6] Springfield, IL St. Aloysius Church.
Meeks, Delphyn J. '83 (BEA) Mauriceville, TX St. Maurice Church.
Meemken, Eugene A. '59 (SCL) Clarissa, MN St. Joseph Church; Moran, MN St. Isidore Church.
Meenan, Francis P. *c.s.sp.* '44 (PIT) Emsworth, PA Sacred Heart Church.
Meenihan, Regis (E) [P] Erie, PA Newman Centers and Campus Ministry.
Meenihan, Regis J. '92 (E) Meadville, PA St. Brigid Church.
Meersman, Jerome *c.i.c.m.* '49 (ARL) [J] Arlington, VA Missionhurst, C.I.C.M.-Central House and Provincialate.
Meffan, Robert V. '53 (BO) Senior Priests.
Meger, Msgr. Thomas '62 (RNO) Absent on Sick Leave.
Megge, Paul '98 (GAY) Traverse City, MI Immaculate Conception Church.
Mehan, Joseph A., Jr. '96 (DAL) Forney, TX St. Martin Church; Kaufman, TX St. Ann Church.
Mehm, Richard J. (BO) [1] Malden, MA Immaculate Conception Church.
Mehok, Charles J. *s.j.* '48 (MIL) [P] Milwaukee, WI Jesuit Community at Marquette University.
Mehok, William J. *s.j.* '43 (FAR) Retired; [E] Fargo, ND Riverview Place.
Mehrkens, Msgr. William '50 (CR) Kelliher, MN St. Patrick Church; Red Lake, MN St. Mary's Church; Retired.
Mehu, Charles J. *c.s.c.* '93 (TR) [13] Trenton, NJ St. Francis of Assisium Church.
Meidl, Gerald S. '74 (NU) Marshall, MN Holy Redeemer Church.
Meier, Msgr. Allen J. '51 (COV) Retired; [C] Covington, KY Academy of Notre Dame.
Meier, Alphonse H. *o.s.b.* '48 (GBG) [H] Latrobe, PA Saint Vincent Archabbey.
Meier, Cyprian T. '69 (BIS) Mandan, ND Spirit of Life Church.
Meier, Denis '63 (SFS) Beresford, SD St. Teresa of Avila Church.
Meier, Emeric *o.f.m.* '68 (BO) [BB] Boston, MA St. Anthony Shrine.
Meier, Gary M. '98 (STL) [36] St. Louis, MO St. Gabriel the Archangel Church.
Meier, Gerald A. '66 (STL) Webster Groves, MO Mary, Queen of Peace Church.
Meier, John P. (FTW) [B] Notre Dame, IN University of Notre Dame Du Lac.
Meier, Msgr. John P. '67 (NY) On Duty Outside the Archdiocese.
Meier, Msgr. Joseph F. '39 (SCR) Retired; [N] Dunmore, PA Villa St. Joseph.
Meier, Laverne G. '58 (MAD) Roxbury, WI St. Norbert Church.
Meier, Msgr. Raymond '36 (E) [K] Hermitage, PA John XXIII Home.
Meier, Msgr. Raymond O. '36 (E) Retired.
Meier, Timothy J. *s.j.* '91 (CIN) [M] Cincinnati, OH Jesuit Community at Xavier University.
Meier, Timothy J. *s.j.* '91 (DET) [K] Detroit, MI Jesuit Provincial Office-Detroit Province of the Society of Jesus.
Meiergerd, Godfrey A. '42 (OM) Retired.
Meighan, Joseph F. '68 (SCR) [L] Scranton, PA Home for Aged of the Little Sisters of the Poor, Holy Family Residence; [N] Dunmore, PA Villa St. Joseph.
Meighan, Thomas A. '63 (WDC) [7] Silver Spring, MD St. John the Evangelist Church.
Meik, Thomas J. *c.m.* '48 (CHI) [N] Chicago, IL DePaul Vincentian Residence.
Meiklejohn, Norman *a.a.* '54 (BO) [W] Boston, MA Assumptionist Center.
Meiklejohn, Norman A. *a.a.* '54 (MAN) [3] Nashua, NH St. Christopher Church; [10] Nashua, NH St. Stanislaus Church.
Meilak, Peter Paul *o.f.m.* '49 (FgM) Franciscan Foreign Missions.
Meiluta, George J. *s.m.* '40 (WDC) [M] Washington, DC Marist Center.
Meiman, Louis J. '87 (L) [38] Louisville, KY Immaculate Heart of Mary Church.
Meinen, Dennis W. '87 (SC) Special Assignment.
Meiners, Andrew *c.ss.r.* '69 (WCH) [14] Wichita, KS St. Joseph Church; [F] Wichita, KS Redemptorist Mission House.
Meinhart, C. Joseph '91 (OKL) Norman, OK St. Thomas More University Church; [K] Norman, OK Campus Ministry for the Archdiocese of Oklahoma City; [K] Norman, OK Campus Ministry for the Archdiocese of Oklahoma City.
Meinholz, David J. '94 (MIL) [19] Milwaukee, WI St. Catherine Church; [78] Milwaukee, WI St. Sebastian Church.
Meinholz, John M. '77 (MAD) [5] Madison, WI Immaculate Heart of Mary Church.
Meiring, Arnold *c.pp.s.* '40 (CIN) [B] Carthagena, OH St. Charles.
Meiring, Bernard *c.pp.s.* '55 (TOL) Ottawa, OH SS. Peter and Paul Church.
Meirose, Harold R. *s.j.* '62 (DET) [P] Clarkston, MI Colombiere Center.
Meis, J. Anthony (STL) [K] St. Louis, MO St. Anthony's Medical Center.
Meis, J. Anthony '72 (JOL) On Duty Outside the Diocese.
Meis, Peter *o.f.m.cap.* '67 (FgM) Capuchin Foreign Missions.
Meisburger, Joseph C. '66 (KC) Retired.
Meisel, Msgr. Charles '50 (BAL) [O] Timonium, MD Stella Maris.
Meisel, Msgr. Charles F. (BAL) Hydes, MD St. John the Evangelist Church.
Meisel, Msgr. Charles F. '50 (BAL) Retired.
Meisel, Gerald '61 (LA) [11] Long Beach, CA St. Matthew Church.
Meismer, Paul J. '69 (PEO) [1] Spring Valley, IL Immaculate Conception Church.
Meissner, Robert J. '69 (SAG) [10] Bay City, MI St. Vincent de Paul Church.
Meissner, William W. *s.j.* '61 (BO) [W] Chestnut Hill, MA The Jesuit Community at Boston College.
Meister, Msgr. Andrew H. '44 (OM) Retired.
Meitl, Roger (SAL) Hoxie, KS St. Frances Xavier Cabrini Church.
Meitl, Roger K. '59 (SAL) Grinnell, KS Immaculate Conception Church; Oakley, KS St. Joseph's Church.
Mejak, Msgr. Heliodore '35 (KCK) [4] Kansas City, KS Holy Family Church.
Mejia, Jose (LA) [J] Marina Del Rey, CA Daniel Freeman Marina Hospital.
Mejia, Manuel J. *m.m.* '63 (SFR) [N] San Francisco, CA Maryknoll Fathers and Brothers, Catholic Foreign Mission Society of America, Inc.
Mejia, Miguel '00 (SPK) Pasco, WA St. Patrick Church.
Mejia, Ricardo '76 (SD) On Duty Outside the Diocese.
Mejias, Carlos Ortiz '97 (SJN) Graduate Studies.
Mejias, Roy *d.c.d.* '91 (BRK) [207] Queens, NY Our Lady of the Blessed Sacrament Church.
Melaba, Daniel '91 (OAK) [12] Oakland, CA St. Leo's Church.
Melancon, Aaron '97 (LAF) Loreauville, LA St. Joseph Church; Loreauville, LA Our Lady of Victory Church.
Melancon, Bill (LAF) Carencro, LA St. Peter Church.
Melancon, Leo F. *m.m.* '32 (NY) [DD] Maryknoll, NY Maryknoll Fathers and Brothers.
Melancon, Msgr. Louis J. '63 (LAF) Grand Prairie, LA St. Peter Church; [K] Opelousas, LA Cursillo Center.
Melancon, Msgr. Louis J. '63 (LKC) On Duty Outside the Diocese.
Melancon, Robert '62 (HT) On Leave.
Melancon, Thomas '74 (BO) [W] Cambridge, MA Weston Jesuit Community.
Melaniuk, J. Maciej '86 (MET) South River, NJ St. Stephen Protomartyr Church.
Melcher, Francis L. *o.s.a.* '53 (PH) [AA] Villanova, PA St. Thomas Monastery.
Melcher, Michael '92 (LUB) Stamford, TX St. Ann Church.
Melchior, Frank '59 (GB) Retired.
Melchior, Gerald P. (OM) [O] Omaha, NE St. Cecilia Schola Cantorum, Inc.
Melchior, Gerald P. '90 (OM) [40] Omaha, NE St. Robert Bellarmine Church.
Melchior, Thomas '65 (KCK) Absent on Sick Leave.
Mele, Rudolph '77 (NO) Retired.
Mele, Thomas '77 (SPK) [N] Pullman, WA Washington State University - St. Thomas More Catholic Newman Center.
Mele, Vincent *o.f.m.* '40 (NY) [Z] New York, NY Kateri Residence; [DD] New York, NY Franciscan Province of the Immaculate Conception.
Melel, Andrew *o.i.c.* '51 (TYL) Gun Barrel City, TX St. Jude Church.
Melendez, Hector '80 (PAT) [8] Passaic, NJ Our Lady of Fatima Church.
Melendez, Jeronimo *o.s.m.* '72 (ELP) [24] El Paso, TX St. Ignatius of Loyola Church.
Melendez, Michael '89 (BRK) [201] Queens, NY St. Michael Church.
Melepuram, John '78 (DAL) [5] Garland, TX St. Thomas the Apostle Church.
Melevage, Msgr. F. J. '42 (GRY) Retired.
Melicor, Celedonio '56 (DET) [H] Livonia, MI St. Mary Hospital.
Melillo, William J. '66 (NEW) [C] West Orange, NJ Seton Hall Preparatory School.
Melito, August A. '64 (DAL) [14] Dallas, TX St. Bernard of Clairvaux Church.
Melito, Ignatius M. *c.m.* '51 (STL) Sappington, MO St. Catherine Laboure Church.
Melito, Joseph '75 (ORG) Inactive Leave.
Melka, John *o.c.d.* '64 (SR) [M] Oakville, CA Carmelite House of Prayer.
Melki, Pierre '65 (OLD) Laval, St. Ephrem Church.
Melle, James J. '72 (PH) [D] Downingtown, PA Bishop Shanahan High School.
Melley, James J. '77 (MIA) Retired.
Mellitt, John *o.f.m.cap.* '75 (NY) [98] New York, NY Our Lady of Sorrows Church.
Mello, Lawrence D. '73 (BEA) Beaumont, TX Larry Gist State Jail.
Mello, Matthew '87 (ORL) [1] Lakeland, FL Church of the Resurrection.
Melloh, John A. *s.m.* '73 (FTW) [B] Notre Dame, IN University of Notre Dame Du Lac.
Mellone, Michael J. '76 (WDC) Gaithersburg, MD St. Martin Church.
Mellone, Vincent P. '65 (BO) [2] Woburn, MA St. Barbara Church.
Mellott, David *s.s.* '92 (BAL) [S] Baltimore, MD Sulpician Provincial House.
Mellott, David '92 (STU) On Duty Outside the Diocese.
Mellott, Robert '63 (PIT) [J] Pittsburgh, PA Mercy Providence Hospital.
Melmer, John H. '91 (ARL) Colonial Beach, VA St. Elizabeth Church.
Melnic, Msgr. James '78 (PHU) [4] Philadelphia, PA Annunciation of the B.V.M. Church; [D] Philadelphia, PA Ascension Manor, Inc.
Melnick, John E. '86 (SCR) [1] Hazleton, PA St. Gabriel's Church.
Melnick, John P. '00 (HRT) Guilford, CT St. George Church.
Melnick, William D. '75 (WIL) Liftwood, DE Immaculate Heart of Mary Church.
Melo, Fidel '99 (CHL) Albemarle, NC Our Lady of the Annunciation Church.
Melo, Nicholas P. '83 (HRT) [2] Bristol, CT St. Anthony's Church.
Meloch, Msgr. Chester A. '43 (BUF) Retired.
Melody, William P. *c.s.c.* '59 (FTW) [J] South Bend, IN Congregation of Holy Cross, Indiana Province, Provincial House.

Melone, Mark E. '78 (NTN) Sacramento, CA St. George Church.
Melton, John J. *o.s.a.* '55 (PH) [AA] Villanova, PA St. Thomas Monastery.
Melton, Thomas K. '59 (TLS) Bixby, OK St. Clement's Church.
Meluskey, Andre J. '59 (HBG) Carlisle, PA St. Patrick Church.
Melvin, James M. '54 (CAM) Retired.
Memenas, Vytas '57 (JOL) Retired.
Memolo, Rocco C. '76 (MAN) Absent on Leave.
Mena, Antonio '81 (ELP) Fabens, TX Our Lady of Guadalupe Church.
Mena, Francisco De Carlo '50 (SJN) Retired.
Mena, Jesus M. *o.a.r.* '86 (NY) [157] Bronx, NY St. John Vianney, Cure of Ars Church.
Mena, Jose '61 (ORL) Retired.
Mena, Jose '63 (STA) [8] Jacksonville, FL Immaculate Conception Church.
Menapace, James L. '63 (MAR) Retired.
Menard, Clarence C. *o.m.i.* '58 (NO) [A] New Orleans, LA Notre Dame Seminary Graduate School of Theology.
Menard, Francis A. '54 (OG) Retired.
Menard, Gerard E. *s.j.* '99 (KC) [D] Kansas City, MO Rockhurst High School; [J] Kansas City, MO Rockhurst Jesuit Community.
Menard, Gilbert B. '55 (OG) Retired.
Menard, J. Godden *c.m.* '55 (GLP) Tuba City, AZ St. Jude Church.
Menard, James R. *s.j.* '54 (SJ) [L] Los Gatos, CA Sacred Heart Jesuit Center.
Menard, Msgr. Raymond '39 (SAL) [1] Salina, KS Cathedral of the Sacred Heart.
Menard, Robert *o.f.m.* '72 (ARL) Triangle, VA St. Francis of Assisi Church.
Menard, Roland V. '64 (OG) Absent on Sick Leave.
Menard, Wilred A. *c.s.c.* '59 (COS) [F] Cascade, CO Holy Cross Novitiate.
Menasco, Edward J. '90 (OKL) Norman, OK St. Joseph's Church; Special Assignment.
Menchaca, Luis Gerardo '95 (SJ) [1] San Jose, CA Cathedral Basilica of St. Joseph; Special Assignment.
Mencsik, John C. *c.pp.s.* '74 (FTW) [12] Fort Wayne, IN Most Precious Blood Church.
Mende, Dennis W. '83 (BUF) Jamestown, NY St. Peter and Paul Church.
Mendez, Angel '90 (MGZ) Aguadilla, PR St. Charles Borromeo Church.
Mendez, David Perez '87 (MGZ) Moca, PR Our Lady of Monserrate Church.
Mendez, Enrique *s.d.b.* '52 (SJN) [28] San Juan, PR San Juan Bosco Church.
Mendez, Jose R. Ferendez '59 (SJN) Retired.
Mendez, Juan '73 (SFE) [7] Albuquerque, NM Nativity of the Blessed Virgin Mary Church.
Mendez, Manuel '87 (YAK) Kennewick, WA St. Joseph's Church.
Mendez, Oscar *s.j.* '64 (MIA) [A] Miami, FL St. John Vianney College Seminary.
Mendez, Rafael '93 (MGZ) Lajas, PR Our Lady of the Purification Church.
Mendez, Rafael '94 (ARE) Hatillo, PR Our Lady of Mt. Carmel Church.
Mendez, Rafael '94 (PH) On Duty Outside the Archdiocese.
Mendicoa, John J. '67 (BO) [65] Boston, MA Sacred Heart Church.
Mendis, Nimal '82 (NY) Beacon, NY St. John Evangelist Church; [DD] New York, NY Apostolic Society of the Crusade of the Holy Spirit.
Mendiveloso, Joselyn '94 (SAT) Kerrville, TX Notre Dame Church.
Mendl, Michael *s.d.b.* (PAT) [D] Paterson, NJ Don Bosco Technical High School.
Mendnkar, John *c.m.i.* '68 (BRK) [V] Brooklyn, NY Carmelites of Mary Immaculate, Inc.
Mendonca, John '79 (BRK) [172] Queens, NY St. Gerard Majella Church.
Mendonca, John '83 (BO) [5] Peabody, MA Our Lady of Fatima Church.
Mendonca, Robert A. '00 (OAK) [4] San Leandro, CA St. Leander Church.
Mendonsa, August F. '42 (PRO) Retired.
Mendoza, A. Alberto *c.m.* '96 (FgM) Vincentian Foreign Missions.
Mendoza, Andres '95 (LUB) Denver City, TX St. William Church.
Mendoza, Fernando *o.f.m.* '74 (ELP) [B] El Paso, TX St. Anthony's School of Theology.
Mendoza, Gerardo '88 (SB) Victorville, CA St. Joan of Arc Church.
Mendoza, Jose Eduardo '84 (SFR) [45] San Francisco, CA St. Peter Church.
Mendoza, Msgr. Miguel A. '70 (CGS) Barranquitas, PR Church of St. Anthony of Padua.
Mendoza, Ralph Anthony '99 (LAR) [10] Laredo, TX San Martin de Porres Church.
Mendoza, Victor *o.s.j.* '98 (FRS) [1] Bakersfield, CA Our Lady of Guadalupe Church.
Mendrick, Paul P. '47 (PBL) Retired.
Mendyuk, Yaroslav '97 (STN) [3] Chicago, IL SS. Volodymyr and Olha Church.
Menegatto, Gaetano *c.s.j.* '42 (CLV) [O] Avon, OH Congregation of St. Joseph.
Menegay, David C. '88 (PIT) Conway, PA Our Lady of Peace Church; [C] Baden, PA Quigley Catholic High School.
Menegay, Greg '98 (PHX) [13] Phoenix, AZ St. Jerome Church.
Meneghello, Serafino '49 (GRY) Retired.
Menei, Francis T. '67 (PH) On Duty Outside the Archdiocese.
Menendez, Adolph *s.x.* '68 (FgM) Xaverian Foreign Missions.
Menendez, Adolph *s.x.* '68 (PAT) [M] Wayne, NJ Xaverian Missionary Fathers.
Menendez, Jose L. '77 (MIA) [3] Miami, FL Corpus Christi Church.
Meneses, Miguel (ELP) Canutillo, TX St. Patrick Church.
Menezes, Mark '59 (JOL) Monee, IL St. Boniface Church.
Menezes, Wade *c.p.m.* '00 (OWN) [F] South Union, KY Fathers of Mercy.
Meng, David P. '89 (ARL) Spotsylvania, VA St. Matthew Church.
Meng, Robert A. '45 (ROC) Retired.
Menge, James P. '62 (SPR) [3] Holyoke, MA Holy Family Church; Retired.
Mengel, Mark *s.s.c.* '71 (CHI) [N] Chicago, IL Columban Fathers Theologate.
Menghini, Peter D. '80 (SCR) [7] Wilkes-Barre, PA Holy Rosary Church.
Mengon, Albert *s.d.b.* '66 (FgM) Salesians of Don Bosco Foreign Missions.
Menig, Walter F. *c.m.* '47 (BAL) Emmitsburg, MD St. Joseph Church.
Menig, Walter J. *c.m.* '47 (BAL) [S] Emmitsburg, MD Vincentian House.
Menihane, Daniel J. *o.s.a.* '57 (ALB) Waterford, NY St. Anne Church.
Meninger, William *o.c.s.o.* '58 (DEN) [M] Snowmass, CO St. Benedict's Monastery.
Menjivar, Natividad '92 (ARL) Sterling, VA Christ the Redeemer Church.
Menke, Andrew V. '99 (LIN) [7] Lincoln, NE St. Joseph Church.
Menke, George R. *s.j.* '75 (IND) [D] Indianapolis, IN Brebeuf Jesuit Preparatory School, Inc.
Menke, Paul F. '66 (LA) Alhambra, CA St. Thomas More Church.
Menke, Msgr. S. G. '38 (DAV) Retired.
Menke, Msgr. Sebastian J. '38 (DAV) [M] Davenport, IA St. Vincent Center.
Menker, Joseph *o.m.i.* '53 (STP) [27] St. Paul, MN St. Mary Church; St. Paul, MN St. Paul-Ramsey Hospital; St. Paul, MN Gillette Children's Hospital.
Menkhus, James *o.f.m.cap.* '73 (PH) [80] Philadelphia, PA St. John the Evangelist Church.
Menna, F. Dominic '58 (BO) [1] Revere, MA St. Anthony of Padua Church.
Menna, Msgr. Francis A. (PH) [V] Ventnor, PA Villa St. Joseph by the Sea.
Menna, Msgr. Francis A. '64 (PH) [V] Darby, PA Villa Saint Joseph.
Menna, Michael J. '99 (PRO) Coventry, RI SS. John and Paul Church.
Mennella, Luke *o.ss.t.* '56 (BAL) [S] Baltimore, MD Holy Trinity Monastery.
Menner, John H. *c.s.b.* '58 (DET) [E] Redford, MI Catholic Central High School.
Menner, Michael L. '93 (PEO) Alexis, IL St. Theresa's Church; [R] Moline, IL The Order of the Legion of Little Souls of the Merciful Heart of Jesus.
Menner, Robert J. '68 (STL) On Duty Outside the Archdiocese.
Mennis, Msgr. James F. '62 (SAC) Retired and in Senior Ministry.
Menniti, Daniel J. '53 (HBG) Carlisle, PA St. Patrick Church.
Menonkari, John *c.m.i.* '68 (BRK) [56] Brooklyn, NY Holy Family Church.
Mens, Theodore J. '67 (GRY) Griffith, IN St. Mary Church.
Mensah, Gabriel '83 (VIC) On Duty Outside the Diocese.
Mensah, Isaac '81 (RVC) Manhasset, NY North Shore Univ. Hospital.
Mensah, Lawrence '85 (SY) Mattydale, NY St. Margaret Church.
Mensinger, Gary '97 (PSC) Mahanoy City, PA St. Mary's Church.
Menster, William J. '38 (DUB) Retired.
Mentel, Joseph C. '40 (FAR) Retired.
Mentrup, Charles E. '88 (CIN) Centerville, OH Incarnation Church; [E] Middletown, OH Bishop Fenwick High School.
Menty, Ronald A. '69 (ALB) Scotia, NY St. Joseph Church.
Menuba, Elias (ROC) Canisteo, NY St. Joachim Church; Hornell, NY St. Ann Church; Rexville, NY St. Mary Church.
Meny, Hilary G. '40 (IND) Retired.
Menz, Anthony *o.c.s.o.* '68 (SPC) [E] Ava, MO Assumption Abbey (Trappist).
Menzel, Mark *s.s.c.* (CHI) [J] Chicago, IL Holy Cross Hospital.
Menzel, William G. '67 (LC) [3] Wisconsin Rapids, WI St. Vincent de Paul Church.
Menzies, Scott '85 (VEN) Graduate Studies.
Meograssi, Romuald *o.f.m.conv.* '68 (BAL) [S] Ellicott City, MD St. Joseph Cupertino Friary, Friars Minor Conventual of St. Francis of Assisi; [S] Ellicott City, MD Friary of St. Joseph Cupertino.
Meoska, John '82 (PBL) [J] Crestone, CO Spiritual Life Institute of America, Inc.
Mercado, Edwin '87 (ARE) [11] Arecibo, PR Church of San Martin de Porres.
Mercado, Marco A. '98 (CHI) [1] Cicero, IL St. Anthony Church.
Mercado, Miguel '83 (ARE) Quebradillas, PR San Raphael Church.
Merced Reyes, R. Miguel A. '00 (CGS) Barranquitas, PR Church of St. Anthony of Padua.
Mercer, David '87 (SJ) [16] San Jose, CA St. Martin of Tours Church.
Mercer, James *f.s.s.p.* '97 (SCR) [M] Elmhurst, PA Priestly Fraternity of St. Peter (F.S.S.P.), North American District Headquarters.
Mercer, James G. '97 (ARL) On Duty Outside the Diocese.
Mercer, John E. '70 (NY) [220] Staten Island, NY Our Lady of Pity Church.
Mercer, Robert *s.a.* '82 (NY) [DD] Garrison, NY Franciscan Friars of the Atonement, Minister General Office.
Merchant, David M. *o.s.f.s.* '73 (PH) [D] Philadelphia, PA Father Judge High School for Boys; [AA] Philadelphia, PA Father Judge Faculty House.
Mercieca, Anthony '62 (MIA) Miami Springs, FL Blessed Trinity Church.
Mercieca, Cyprian *t.o.r.* '61 (STP) [20] Minneapolis, MN St. Bridget Church.
Mercier, Msgr. Joseph '55 (BLX) Retired.
Mercier, Ronald A. *s.j.* '87 (BO) [W] Boston, MA The Society of Jesus of New England-Provincial Offices.
Mercure, Gary '74 (ALB) [13] Troy, NY Sacred Heart Church; [14] Troy, NY St. Williams Church.
Mercure, Jerome '79 (BUR) Troy, VT Sacred Heart of Jesus Church.
Mercurio, Gregory J. '80 (BO) [1] Lynn, MA Holy Family Church.
Mercurio, Roger *c.p.* '44 (CHI) [N] Chicago, IL Passionist Community-Immaculate Conception Monastery.
Mercy, Richard R. *s.j.* '71 (SPK) [E] Spokane, WA Gonzaga Preparatory School; [O] Spokane, WA Kateri Northwest Ministry Institute.
Merdian, Mark J. '93 (PEO) [12] Peoria, IL St. Peter's Church.
Merdinger, Philip E. '64 (NEW) On Duty Outside the Archdiocese.
Meredith, John R. '80 (OWN) [4] Owensboro, KY Our Lady of Lourdes Church; [J] Owensboro, KY Gideon Productions, Inc.
Meredith, Philip S. '74 (DEN) [1] Fort Collins, CO St. Joseph Church.
Meredith, Richard '78 (OWN) [6] Owensboro, KY St. Pius Tenth Church.
Merek, John Ray *o.m.i.* '89 (SAT) [C] San Antonio, TX Oblate School of Theology.
Merfeld, Vincent C. '44 (DUB) Retired.
Mergenhagen, John J. '54 (BUF) Retired.
Mericantante, John J. '75 (PMB) Pahokee, FL St. Mary Church.
Meridier, Wilfred F. '69 (NO) [58] New Orleans, LA St. Rita Church; Jefferson, LA Ochsner Foundation Hospital.
Merino, Msgr. Baudilio '48 (SJN) [48] San Juan, PR Nuestra Senora de la Providencia Church.
Merino, Mario (LA) [Q] Azusa, CA Casa Comboni Mission Seminary.
Merino, Santiago '46 (LA) Retired.
Meriwether, Stephen A. '83 (SFR) [3] Menlo Park, CA The Church of the Nativity.
Merkatoris, Ralph C. '58 (GB) Pine Grove, WI Holy Trinity Church.
Merkel, James '73 (SP) Pinellas Park, FL Sacred Heart Church.
Merkel, Mark K '92 (OM) Beemer, NE Holy Cross Church.
Merkel, Thomas *s.j.* '97 (RC) Pine Ridge, SD Holy Rosary Church.
Merkel, Tom *s.j.* '97 (RC) [B] Pine Ridge, SD Jesuit Community of Holy Rosary Mission.
Merkelis, John *o.s.a.* (JOL) New Lenox, IL St. Jude Church.
Merkelis, John D. *o.s.a.* '85 (CHI) [N] Olympia Fields, IL The Augustinians-Provincialate.
Merkle, Charles W., III '88 (ARL) Stafford, VA St. William of York Church.
Merkovsky, Paul (PIT) Greene County, PA Greene

County Memorial; Green County, PA State Correctional Institution at Waynesburg (Women's Facility); Green County, PA Waynesburg County Jail.
Merkovsky, Paul '90 (PIT) Nemacolin, PA Our Lady of Consolation Church.
Merkovsky, Paul F. (PIT) Carmichaels, PA St. Hugh Church.
Merkovsky, Paul W. '90 (PIT) [R] Pittsburgh, PA Office for Campus Ministry.
Merkt, Joseph T. '66 (L) [27] Louisville, KY St. Francis of Assisi Church; [K] Louisville, KY Marian Home.
Merkt, Michael F. '81 (MIL) [6] West Allis, WI Mary, Queen of Heaven Church.
Merlino, Darrin *c.m.f.* '00 (PHX) Prescott, AZ Sacred Heart Church.
Merlino, James *o.f.m.* '87 (HRT) Canaan, CT St. Joseph's Church.
Merman, Msgr. Raymond F. '60 (ALN) Hellertown, PA St. Theresa of the Child Jesus Church.
Merold, James E. '71 (CHI) North Chicago, IL Queen of Peace Church.
Meronek, Andrew '43 (GRY) [J] Cedar Lake, IN Our Lady of Lourdes Friary.
Merren, John Benedict M. *o.c.d.* '00 (GRY) [J] Munster, IN Discalced Carmelite Fathers Monastery.
Merrero, Adan *s.d.b.* '97 (SJN) [C] Catano, PR Prenoviciado Salesiano.
Merrifield, Donald P. *s.j.* '65 (LA) [C] Los Angeles, CA Loyola Marymount University; [C] Los Angeles, CA Loyola Marymount University.
Merrill, Paul *c.s.s.* '61 (BO) [Z] Waltham, MA Stigmatine Fathers and Brothers.
Merrill, Thomas *o.f.m.conv.* '79 (STP) Bloomington, MN St. Bonaventure Church.
Merris, Christopher '82 (SD) Military Chaplains.
Merry, Christopher C. '92 (E) Bradford, PA St. Bernard Church.
Merry, Paul F. '71 (BGP) [6] Bridgeport, CT Blessed Sacrament Church.
Mersinger, Arthur '42 (JC) Retired.
Mersinger, Arthur J. '42 (STL) Retired.
Mersinger, Norbert A. '55 (STL) [5] Lemay, MO St. Martin of Tours Church; Retired.
Merson, Msgr. Thomas S. '83 (SFR) [4] San Francisco, CA St. Anne Church; Special Assignment.
Mertens, Msgr. Arthur '49 (SPK) Retired.
Mertens, Michael G. '45 (LC) Retired; [H] La Crosse, WI Holy Cross (Seminary) Diocesan Center.
Mertensotto, Leon J. *c.s.c.* '56 (FTW) [B] Notre Dame, IN University of Notre Dame Du Lac; [J] Notre Dame, IN Holy Cross Community, Corby Hall, University of Notre Dame.
Mertes, Mark '87 (KCK) [2] Overland Park, KS Holy Cross Church.
Mertes, Robert *s.v.d.* '78 (WDC) [L] Hyattsville, MD Sacred Heart Home Inc.; [M] Washington, DC Divine Word College.
Mertes, William H. '59 (COV) Retired.
Merth, Robert J. '44 (NU) Retired.
Mertz, Frederick A. '49 (STP) Retired.
Mertz, William H. '47 (STP) Retired.
Merwald, Melvin '71 (OM) [27] Omaha, NE St. Margaret Mary Church.
Merz, Albert *o.f.m.* '66 (NSH) [H] Nashville, TN Franciscan Friars.
Merz, Daniel '98 (JC) [1] Jefferson City, MO St. Joseph Church.
Merz, Eugene F. *s.j.* '61 (MIL) [P] Milwaukee, WI Arrupe House Jesuit Community.
Merzena, Carl J. '41 (NEW) Retired; [N] Rutherford, NJ St. John Vianney Residence for Priests.
Merzweiler, David W. '77 (Y) Lake Milton, OH St. Catherine Church; North Jackson, OH St. James Parish Family Church.
Mesa, Msgr. Arturo '88 (AMA) [H] Amarillo, TX Bishop DeFalco Retreat Center.
Mesa, Jose *s.j.* (NY) [63] New York, NY St. Joseph of the Holy Family Church.
Mesa, Jose A. *s.j.* '92 (NY) [DD] New York, NY Xavier Jesuit Community.
Mesa, Manuel *o.m.i.* (OAK) [N] Oakland, CA Oblate Provincial House & Procure.
Mesa, Mario *o.f.m.cap.* '64 (SJN) [29] San Juan, PR San Juan de La Cruz Church.
Mescall, Msgr. John '52 (NY) [4] New Rochelle, NY Holy Family Church.
Mescall, John R. *c.p.* '59 (BRK) [V] Jamaica, NY Immaculate Conception Monastery.
Mescher, Michael '83 (DUB) [3] Waterloo, IA Sacred Heart Church.
Mescher, Mike '83 (DUB) [D] Waterloo, IA Columbus High School.
Mesi, Vincent *o.f.m.* '72 (LA) [2] Santa Barbara, CA Old Mission Santa Barbara Church; [Q] Santa Barbara, CA Franciscan Friary, Order of Friars Minor (Old Mission).
Mesias, Edilberto '94 (AUS) [16] Austin, TX St. Louis Church.
Mesiona, Erwin '95 (SAC) Vallejo, CA St. Vincent Ferrer Church.
Meskell, David B. '55 (BO) Health Leave.
Meskenas, Vincent A. '49 (BEL) Retired.
Meskill, David B. '55 (BO) Senior Priests.
Meskill, Patrick A. '53 (LA) Retired.
Mesko, Louis G. *sch.p.* '36 (PH) [G] Devon, PA Devon Preparatory School; [AA] Devon, PA Piarist Fathers (Order of the Pious Schools).
Mesley, Jerry '73 (GLP) Absent on Leave.
Mesmer, William A. '68 (SY) Oneida, NY St. Patrick Church.
Messaro, Michael A. *m.ss.cc.* '68 (HBG) Blue Ridge Summit, PA St. Rita Church; Fairfield, PA Immaculate Conception of the Blessed Virgin Mary Church.
Messaros, Msgr. Michael F. '36 (ALN) Retired.
Messenger, William '77 (LA) [34] Los Angeles, CA Our Saviour Catholic Center Church; [BB] Los Angeles, CA Archdiocesan Office for Campus Ministry.
Messer, Joseph V. '61 (BAL) Glen Burnie, MD Church of the Good Shepherd; Retired.
Messer, Paul A. *s.j.* '67 (BO) [W] Chestnut Hill, MA The Jesuit Community at Boston College.
Messer, Terry *c.f.r.* '94 (NY) [DD] New York, NY St. Crispin Friary.
Messerich, Valerius U. *o.f.m.* '46 (STP) Hampton, MN St. Mathias Church.
Messick, Severin *o.s.b.* '82 (IND) Greenfield, IN St. Michael Church; [J] St. Meinrad, IN St. Meinrad Archabbey.
Messier, Gerard *a.a.* (NY) [122] New York, NY St. Vincent de Paul Church.
Messier, Gerard *a.a.* '58 (BO) [W] Boston, MA Assumptionist Center.
Messier, Raymond P. '68 (WOR) Athol, MA St. Francis Church; Petersham, MA St. Peter Church.
Messina, Angelo '68 (ALX) Leesville, LA St. Michael Church.
Messina, John '96 (BAL) Absent on Leave.
Messina, Joseph M. '72 (CAM) [O] Blackwood, NJ St. Pius X Retreat House.
Messina, Richard C. '65 (BO) Winchester, MA St. Mary Church.
Messina, Samuel '65 (JKS) Belzoni, MS All Saints Church.
Messina, Victor G. '74 (BR) [16] Baton Rouge, LA Our Lady of Mercy Church.
Messing, Francis '59 (MOB) Grove Hill, AL Sacred Heart Church.
Messman, Gerald C. '31 (LIN) Retired.
Messner, Michael E. '98 (HBG) Gettysburg, PA St. Francis Xavier's Church.
Messner, Thomas *o.f.m.* '67 (MRY) [F] San Miguel, CA Franciscan Friars, O.F.M.; [F] San Miguel, CA Novitiate House for the Franciscan Friars, O.F.M.
Mestas, Leonard '81 (SB) Loma Linda, CA Loma Linda Community Hospital; Loma Linda, CA Loma Linda University Medical Center.
Mestas, Leonard J. '81 (BWN) On Assignment Outside the Diocese.
Mestriparampil, Thomas '89 (NY) City, NY George M. Motchan Detention Center; City, NY Otis Bantum Correctional Center.
Mesure, Gerard C. '84 (PH) [96] Philadelphia, PA Old St. Mary's Church; Graduate Studies.
Meszaros, James J. '69 (BRK) [241] Queens, NY St. Stanislaus Bishop and Martyr Church.
Metcalf, Andrew '86 (SR) Calistoga, CA Our Lady of Perpetual Help Church.
Metcko, Leo E. '43 (WCH) Retired.
Methe, Msgr. Normand A. '58 (BGP) Retired; [P] Stamford, CT The Catherine Dennis Keefe Queen of the Clergy Retired Priests' Residence.
Method, Fred '66 (DUL) Duluth, MN Indian Missions Church.
Method, Frederick '66 (DUL) Walker, MN St. Agnes Church.
Metrejean, Msgr. Paul (LAF) Leonville, LA St. Leo the Great Church.
Metrejean, Msgr. Paul '63 (LAF) Mermentau, LA St. John the Evangelist Church.
Metro, LeRoy '63 (SAL) Clyde, KS St. John the Baptist's Church.
Metsy, Msgr. Norman G. '47 (PRO) Retired.
Metts, Ralph E. *s.j.* '73 (WDC) [M] Washington, DC The Jesuit Community at Georgetown University; [V] Washington, DC Jesuit Secondary Education Association.
Metz, David '97 (SAL) Hays, KS Immaculate Heart of Mary Church.
Metz, Earl O. '58 (CIN) Georgetown, OH St. George Church; Mount Orab, OH St. Michael Church.
Metz, Kenneth J. '65 (MIL) [6] Kenosha, WI St. Mark Church.
Metzbower, Francis X. *s.j.* '63 (BAL) [S] Baltimore, MD Jesuit Fathers and Brothers Maryland Provincial Curia.
Metzdorf, Bill '73 (SD) [J] San Diego, CA St. Vincent de Paul Village.
Metzdorf, William C. '73 (WDC) On Duty Outside the Archdiocese.
Metzer, Msgr. Samuel '59 (TYL) Fairfield, TX Boyd Unit, Texas Department of Criminal Justice.
Metzger, Alvin *o.s.a.* '54 (MIL) [14] Racine, WI St. Rita Church.
Metzger, Alvin P. *o.s.a.* '54 (MIL) [P] Racine, WI Augustinian Novitiate.
Metzger, Andrew *o.s.b.* '56 (SP) [O] St. Leo, FL St. Leo Abbey.
Metzger, Clem *s.j.* '65 (CLV) [T] Cleveland, OH Jesuit Retreat House.
Metzger, Dennis M. '74 (TOL) [35] Toledo, OH St. Patrick of Heatherdowns Church.
Metzger, Edward C. *o.f.m.* '59 (NY) [DD] New York, NY Franciscan Friars, Order of Friars Minor, Holy Name Province.
Metzger, Edwin '55 (ROC) Retired.
Metzger, Edwin B. '55 (SAT) Fredericksburg, TX St. Mary's Church.
Metzger, John L. '67 (COL) Retired.
Metzger, Joseph H., III '91 (RIC) [1] Norfolk, VA Blessed Sacrament Church.
Metzger, Msgr. Paul E. '43 (STU) Retired.
Metzger, Richard L. '67 (COL) Johnstown, OH Church of the Ascension.
Metzger, Msgr. Robert E. '60 (COL) Jackson, OH Holy Trinity Church.
Metzger, Msgr. Samuel '59 (TYL) Fairfield, TX St. Bernard of Clairvaux Church.
Metzger, Stephen A. '70 (COL) Utica, OH Church of the Nativity.
Metzger, Thomas H. '82 (LFT) Lebanon, IN St. Joseph Church.
Metzger, William A. '78 (COL) [24] Columbus, OH St. John the Baptist Church.
Metzger, William J. '62 (COL) Dresden, OH St. Ann's Church.
Metzger, William J. *o.s.f.s.* '71 (ARL) Vienna, VA Our Lady of Good Counsel Church.
Metzinger, John '82 (OKL) Norman, OK Church of St. Mark the Evangelist.
Metzler, Warren W. '64 (PIT) Wilkinsburg, PA St. James Church.
Metzler, William R. '72 (HRT) Simsbury, CT St. Mary's Church.
Meulemans, Carl P. *m.m.* '60 (CHI) [N] Chicago, IL Maryknoll Fathers & Brothers.
Meulemans, Dennis T. '61 (SUP) Medford, WI Our Lady of the Holy Rosary Church.
Meulemans, Edward G. '60 (SUP) Retired.
Meulemans, Thomas O. *o.praem.* '59 (GB) [I] De Pere, WI St. Norbert Abbey; [I] De Pere, WI St. Joseph Priory.
Meuree, James *c.i.c.m.* '47 (SAT) [K] San Antonio, TX Padua Place.
Meurer, Msgr. David '51 (SAT) [K] San Antonio, TX Casa De Padres.
Meuret, Donald '84 (WH) Absent on Leave.
Meyer, Albert *o.s.b.* '56 (MRY) [F] San Luis Obispo, CA Monastery of the Risen Christ.
Meyer, Arthur D. '61 (PEO) Canton, IL St. Mary's Church.
Meyer, Benedict *o.s.b.* '54 (IND) [J] St. Meinrad, IN St. Meinrad Archabbey.
Meyer, Benedict *o.s.b.* '54 (LR) Brinkley, AR St. John the Baptist Church.
Meyer, Bernard *s.m.* '51 (SAT) [8] San Antonio, TX Holy Rosary Church; [M] San Antonio, TX Marianist Residence.
Meyer, Bernard A. '59 (SFD) On Duty Outside the Diocese.
Meyer, Charles R. '45 (CHI) Retired; [A] Mundelein, IL University of St. Mary of the Lake-Mundelein Seminary.
Meyer, Clay '66 (SEA) [3] Vancouver, WA St. James Church.
Meyer, Daniel J. '82 (CIN) Centerville, OH Incarnation Church; [V] Centerville, OH Catholic Alumni Club (Dayton Chapter).
Meyer, Dennis '70 (STL) [P] St. Louis, MO La Salette Missionaries.
Meyer, Dennis J. *m.s.* '70 (STL) [P] St. Louis, MO La Salette Missionaries; [P] St. Louis, MO La Salette Missionaries; [P] St. Louis, MO La Salette Missionaries.
Meyer, Earl R. *o.f.m.cap.* '60 (STL) Arnold, MO Immaculate Conception Church; [P] Arnold, MO Immaculate Conception Friary.
Meyer, Elmer J. *m.m.* '54 (FgM) Maryknoll Foreign Missions.
Meyer, Emmett F. '64 (OM) [22] Omaha, NE St. Joan of Arc Church.
Meyer, Eric *c.p.* '66 (CHI) [88] Chicago, IL Immaculate Conception Church; [N] Chicago, IL Passionist Community-Immaculate Conception Monastery.
Meyer, Fred A. '65 (STL) [6] St. Charles, MO St. Robert Bellarmine Church.
Meyer, Frederick C. '56 (STP) St. Henry, MN Church of St. Henry.
Meyer, Fredrick *ss.cc.* (BWN) Edinburg, TX Sacred Heart Church.
Meyer, George R. '46 (SFR) [1] San Mateo, CA St. Bartholomew Church; Retired.
Meyer, Gerald J. '96 (PEO) [2] Ottawa, IL St. Francis of

Assisi Church.
Meyer, Msgr. Gilbert '42 (FRS) Retired.
Meyer, Harold K. *o.c.s.o.* '62 (SAC) [A] Vina, CA Abbey of New Clairvaux, Trappist Seminary; [H] Vina, CA Abbey of New Clairvaux, Trappist.
Meyer, Harry J. '64 (CIN) Mason, OH St. Susanna Church.
Meyer, James '94 (FAR) Kindred, ND St. Maurice Church.
Meyer, James A. '94 (FAR) Wyndmere, ND St. John the Baptist Church; [B] Fargo, ND Shanley High School.
Meyer, John A. '82 (IND) Madison, IN Prince of Peace Church; Vevay, IN Most Sorrowful Mother of God Church; [N] Madison, IN Hanover College Newman Center.
Meyer, John R. '89 (SFR) [S] San Francisco, CA Prelature of the Holy Cross and Opus Dei.
Meyer, Joseph H. *s.j.* '46 (FgM) Provinces.
Meyer, Msgr. Joseph J. '45 (PAT) Retired.
Meyer, Leo A. '65 (NO) [38] New Orleans, LA St. James Major Church.
Meyer, Msgr. Louis F. '44 (STL) Retired; [V] St. Louis, MO Missionaries of the Kingship of Christ.
Meyer, Mark '97 (CIN) [5] Dayton, OH Ascension Church.
Meyer, Michael W. '93 (LA) [8] Long Beach, CA St. Joseph Church.
Meyer, Nicholas W. *o.f.m.* '52 (STP) [10] St. Paul, MN Sacred Heart Church.
Meyer, Msgr. Omer F. '49 (EVN) [12] Evansville, IN Sacred Heart Church; Special Assignment.
Meyer, P. Wayne '49 (COL) Mount Vernon, OH Mount Vernon State Institute.
Meyer, Paul Wayne '49 (COL) Retired.
Meyer, Robert G. '74 (WIN) Mazeppa, MN SS. Peter and Paul Church.
Meyer, Robert J. '64 (PIT) [43] Pittsburgh, PA St. Basil Church.
Meyer, Robert L. (SFD) Beltrees, IL St. Michael Church; Grafton, IL St. Patrick Church.
Meyer, Robert S. '88 (NEW) [B] South Orange, NJ Seton Hall University; [B] South Orange, NJ Seton Hall University.
Meyer, Ronald J. *o.m.i.* '71 (CR) Waubun, MN St. Ann Church.
Meyer, Sebastian *o.carm.* '62 (SAC) Fairfield, CA Our Lady of Mount Carmel, Church.
Meyer, Stephen *c.ss.r.* '76 (DEN) [M] Denver, CO The Redemptorists/Denver Province.
Meyer, Stephen *c.ss.r.* '76 (TUC) [J] Tucson, AZ Redemptorist Community Support Charity Trust.
Meyer, Stephen L. '79 (DUB) Bellevue, IA St. Joseph's Church.
Meyer, Steven J. '90 (FAR) Wimbledon, ND St. Boniface's Church.
Meyer, Thomas *o.m.i.* (DUL) International Falls, MN St. Thomas Aquinas Church.
Meyer, Thomas '55 (SCL) Retired.
Meyer, Thomas C. '98 (SFD) Effingham, IL St. Anthony of Padua Church.
Meyer, Thomas E. '70 (CIN) [12] Dayton, OH Holy Angels Church.
Meyer, Vernon '79 (PHX) On Leave.
Meyer, William *s.m.* '79 (SAT) [C] San Antonio, TX St. Mary's University of San Antonio, Texas.
Meyer, William O. '49 (DAV) [M] Davenport, IA St. Vincent Center.
Meyers, Frederick *ss.cc.* '71 (FR) Fairhaven, MA St. Joseph's Church.
Meyers, James P. '70 (WDC) [5] Bethesda, MD Our Lady of Lourdes Church.
Meyers, John F. '56 (DAL) [21] Dallas, TX St. Monica Church.
Meyers, John F. '83 (PH) [1] Bensalem, PA St. Charles Borromeo Church.
Meyers, Joseph L. *c.s.b.* '43 (GAL) [Q] Houston, TX Residence of the Basilian Fathers of the University of St. Thomas.
Meyers, Louis E. *s.j.* '62 (NO) New Orleans, LA Delgado Community College, School of Nursing; New Orleans, LA Louisiana State University Medical Center; [F] New Orleans, LA Jesuit High School.
Meyers, Msgr. Michael '77 (LA) Glendora, CA St. Dorothy Church.
Meyers, Robert V. '87 (MET) Kendall Park, NJ St. Augustine of Canterbury Church.
Meyett, Irving C. '53 (SUP) Retired.
Meyr, Herbert J. '60 (CHI) Maywood, IL St. James Church.
Meysenberg, James J. '89 (LIN) Doniphan, NE St. Ann's Church; [M] Hastings, NE St. Cecilia High School Endowment Fund.
Meysenburg, James (LIN) Kenesaw, NE Sacred Heart Church.
Meysenburg, James J. '89 (LIN) Hastings, NE St. Cecilia's Church; [C] Hastings, NE St. Cecilia's Middle School/High School.
Meystrik, Gregory C. '90 (JC) Loose Creek, MO Immaculate Conception Church.
Meza, Msgr. Arturo '88 (AMA) [2] Amarillo, TX St. Laurence Church.
Meza, Fernando '95 (SAC) [11] Sacramento, CA St. Charles Borromeo Church.
Meznar, Joseph A. '58 (DEN) [14] Denver, CO Holy Rosary Church.
Meznar, Robert P. '60 (DEN) [28] Denver, CO St. Catherine of Siena Church.
Mezquida, Ramon '58 (PCE) On Duty Outside the Diocese.
Mezydlo, James A. '77 (CHI) [59] Chicago, IL St. Florian Church.
Mezydlo, Leonard T. '50 (CHI) [3] Des Plaines, IL St. Stephen Protomartyr Church; Retired.
Mezyk, Wladek *o.f.m.conv.* '95 (BUF) [O] Athol Springs, NY Father Justin Rosary Hour Radio Apostolate.
Mezzanote, Joseph *o.f.m.cap.* '39 (NEW) [5] Hoboken, NJ St. Ann's Church.
Mezzono, Charles A. '71 (ROM) Alliance, OH St. Theodore Church; Canton, OH St. George Church.
Mgalama, Erasto C. *i.m.c.* '00 (WDC) [V] Washington, DC Consolata Missionaries House of Studies.
Mghanga, Anthony N. '82 (PIT) Braddock, PA Good Shepherd Church.
Miah, Gabriel '77 (RVC) Roslyn, NY St. Francis Hospital.
Miani, Titian A. '55 (STO) [7] Stockton, CA St. Luke Church; Retired.
Mibach, Everett J. *s.j.* '51 (SJ) [L] Los Gatos, CA Sacred Heart Jesuit Center.
Micarelli, Edmond C. '59 (PRO) Retired.
Micca, Louis *s.a.c.* '66 (CAM) Hammonton, NJ St. Joseph's Church.
Micek, Joseph S. '42 (OM) Retired.
Micek, Sylvester *o.f.m.* '51 (GAY) Burt Lake, MI Assumption of St. Mary Church; Pellston, MI St. Clement Church.
Miceli, James A. '75 (ATL) Rome, GA St. Mary's Church; [M] Atlanta, GA Campus Ministry.
Miceli, John P. '94 (CLV) Strongsville, OH St. Joseph Church.
Miceli, Matthew M. *c.s.c.* '52 (FTW) [B] Notre Dame, IN University of Notre Dame Du Lac; [J] Notre Dame, IN Holy Cross Community, Corby Hall, University of Notre Dame.
Miceli, Michael A. '97 (BR) Denham Springs, LA Immaculate Conception Church.
Miceli, Paul W. '72 (BO) [13] Cambridge, MA Sacred Heart of Jesus Church.
Miceli, Vincent F. '91 (BRK) [203] Queens, NY Most Precious Blood Church.
Mich, Kenneth A. '70 (MIL) [2] Menomonee Falls, WI Good Shepherd Church.
Mich, Mario *s.d.b.* '48 (LA) [F] Bellflower, CA St. John Bosco High School.
Michael, Msgr. Chester P. '42 (RIC) Retired.
Michael, David C. '86 (BO) [4] Waltham, MA St. Mary Church; [CC] Waltham, MA Brandeis University Campus Ministry.
Michael, David F. '96 (SAM) Carnegie, PA Our Lady of Victory Church.
Michael, Msgr. Kenneth A. '65 (OLL) Warren, MI St. Sharbel Church.
Michael, Lawrence P. '75 (SAM) Torrington, CT St. Maron Church.
Michael, Leo *s.d.b.* '92 (LR) Huntsville, AR St. John's Church; [E] Rogers, AR St. Mary-Rogers Memorial Hospital.
Michael, Matthew '73 (PH) [U] Philadelphia, PA Mercy Hospital of Philadelphia.
Michael, Peter *s.v.d.* '40 (FgM) Society of the Divine Word Foreign Missions.
Michaels, Dana '82 (OAK) El Sobrante, CA St. Callistus Church.
Michaels, Emmett T. '38 (ALT) Retired.
Michaels, John L. '39 (PIT) Retired; [O] Pittsburgh, PA St. John Vianney Manor.
Michaels, Patrick T. '82 (SFR) [4] Menlo Park, CA St. Raymond Church.
Michalak, Jaromir '91 (CAM) Wildwood, NJ St. Ann's Church.
Michalak, John *o.s.p.* '81 (NY) [5] Yonkers, NY St. Casimir Church.
Michalczak, John T. '70 (NEW) Midland Park, NJ Nativity Church; Ridgewood, NJ Valley Hospital.
Michalek, Henry J. '43 (CHI) [210] Chicago, IL St. William Church; Retired.
Michalek, Stanislaw *s.ch.* '88 (DAL) [23] Dallas, TX St. Peter Church.
Michalenko, Alexei '68 (VNN) On Special Assignment.
Michalenko, S. Seraphim *m.i.c.* '56 (SPR) [J] Stockbridge, MA Congregation of Marians of The Immaculate Conception of the BVM; [J] Stockbridge, MA Congregation of Marians of The Immaculate Conception of the BVM.
Michaletz, James E. *c.s.v.* '60 (CHI) [N] Arlington Heights, IL Viatorian Province Center-Clerics of St. Viator.
Michalicka, John J. '59 (OKL) Ponca City, OK Church of St. Mary; [H] Ponca City, OK St. Mary's Housing Foundation.
Michalik, Gary '80 (DET) [6] Westland, MI St. Theodore of Canterbury Church.
Michalisin, Gregory '92 (PBR) North Huntingdon, PA St. Stephen's Church.
Michalka, Msgr. Arthur '51 (AUS) Jarrell, TX Holy Trinity Church.
Michalowski, John W. *s.j.* (BO) [Y] Weston, MA Campion Renewal Center.
Michalowski, John W. *s.j.* '81 (BO) [W] Weston, MA Campion Jesuit Community.
Michalski, James L. *s.j.* '72 (OM) [F] Omaha, NE The Jesuit Middle School of Omaha; [K] Omaha, NE Jesuit Community at Creighton University.
Michalski, Melvin E. '70 (MIL) [A] St. Francis, WI Saint Francis Seminary.
Michalski, Michael F. '76 (MIL) [2] Waukesha, WI St. Joseph Church.
Michalski, Thaddeus C. '43 (CLV) Retired.
Michalski, Thomas (SAT) [U] San Antonio, TX Polish American Priest Association (P.A.P.A.).
Michatek, William C. '66 (ROC) Spencerport, NY St. John the Evangelist Church.
Michaud, Leo James '77 (PRT) Ellsworth, ME St. Joseph's Church.
Michel, Delix '88 (SFD) East Alton, IL St. Kevin Church; Venice, IL St. Mark Church.
Michel, Engelbert G. '66 (PH) Secane, PA Our Lady of Fatima Church; [L] Philadelphia, PA St. Vincent's Orphanage Tacony; [FF] Philadelphia, PA Catholic Kolping Society.
Michel, Eugene *o.f.m.* (CHI) [108] Chicago, IL St. Joseph Church; [N] Chicago, IL St. Peter's Friary.
Michel, Richard B. *o.s.b.* '86 (GBG) [A] Latrobe, PA St. Vincent Seminary; [H] Latrobe, PA Saint Vincent Archabbey.
Michele, Robert *c.s.p.* '55 (AUS) [11] Austin, TX St. Austin Church; Austin, TX St. David's Hospital.
Michele, Robert P. *c.s.p.* '55 (NY) [DD] Jamaica Estates, NY Paulist Fathers Generalate.
Michelini, Michael S. '71 (CHI) [2] Chicago, IL St. Adalbert Church.
Michell, George J. '64 (RVC) Southold, NY St. Patrick's Church.
Michell, Timothy *o.c.s.o.* '65 (P) [L] Lafayette, OR The Cistercian (Trappist) Abbey of Our Lady of Guadalupe.
Michels, Aloysius *o.s.b.* '39 (FgM) American - Cassinese Congregation Foreign Missions.
Michels, Aloysius *o.s.b.* '39 (SCL) [I] Collegeville, MN St. John's Abbey, of the Order of St. Benedict.
Michels, Andrew J. '85 (NU) Hutchinson, MN Church of St. Anastasia.
Michelson, Chris '80 (KNX) [2] Knoxville, TN All Saints Catholic Church.
Michet, John M. '78 (CHI) [T] Mundelein, IL Cardinal Stritch Retreat House.
Michiels, Kenneth J. '91 (ALX) [B] Marksville, LA Holy Ghost Catholic School.
Michiels, Philip F. '69 (SHP) Mansfield, LA St. Joseph Church; Shreveport, LA Overton Brooks Veteran's Administration Medical Center.
Michini, F. Joseph *s.j.* '80 (BAL) [D] Baltimore, MD Loyola Blakefield.
Michini, Joseph '80 (BO) [W] Cambridge, MA Weston Jesuit Community.
Michler, James R. '75 (STL) Affton, MO St. Dominic Savio Church.
Michlik, Michael '63 (PHU) Baltimore, MD St. Michael's Church.
Michlik, Valerian '00 (SJP) Parma, OH St. Josaphat Church.
Michniewicz, Martin E. '86 (CHI) Calumet City, IL St. Andrew the Apostle Church.
Michota, Piotr '85 (NEW) Mountainside, NJ Our Lady of Lourdes Church.
Michulik, Walter *c.s.c.* '56 (FTW) [L] Notre Dame, IN Holy Cross Mission House.
Mick, Lawrence '49 (CIN) [10] Cincinnati, OH St. Antoninus Church; Retired.
Mick, Lawrence E. '72 (CIN) On Special and Archdiocesan Assignment.
Mick, Robert '49 (CIN) [56] Cincinnati, OH St. Martin of Tours Church; Retired.
Micka, Alphonse *m.i.c.* '49 (JOL) Darien, IL Our Lady of Peace Church.
Micka, Ermin *o.f.m.* '38 (STL) Oakville, MO St. Francis of Assisi Church; [P] Oakville, MO St. Francis Friary.
Mickells, Msgr. Anthony B. '43 (OM) Retired.
Mickelson, Michael T. (NEW) Palisades Park, NJ St. Michael's Church.
Micketti, Gerald F. '83 (GAY) Traverse City, MI St. Patrick Church.
Mickey, Richard L. '88 (MEM) [4] Memphis, TN Church of the Ascension.
Mickiewicz, David '62 (ALB) Special Assignment.
Mickiewicz, David '84 (ALB) Albany, NY Albany Medical Center Hospital.
Mickiewicz, David William '84 (ALB) Delanson, NY Our Lady of Fatima Church.
Mickiewicz, David William '84 (SAM) Troy, NY St. Ann Church.
Mickiewicz, J. William '62 (MET) Califon, NJ St. John Neumann Church.

Mickler, Jeffrey *s.s.p.* '74 (Y) [A] Canfield, OH Society of St. Paul.
Mickus, James J. '72 (OKL) Enid, OK St. Francis Xavier Church.
Miclot, Brian *ph.d.* '74 (DAV) [B] Davenport, IA St. Ambrose University.
Middendorf, Cyril G. *s.m.* '53 (CIN) [M] Dayton, OH Marianist Provincialate.
Middendorf, Eugene *o.f.m.* '45 (SFD) [5] Quincy, IL St. Francis Solanus Church; [K] Quincy, IL St. Francis Solanus Friary.
Middendorf, Raymar *o.f.m.* '50 (IND) Oldenburg, IN Holy Family Church; [K] Oldenburg, IN Motherhouse of the Congregation of the Sisters of the Third Order of St. Francis.
Middendorf, Raymond D. *s.m.* '57 (PCE) Villalba, PR Our Lady Mother of Divine Providence Church.
Middlecamp, Eric *s.d.s.* '52 (FgM) Salvatorian Foreign Missions.
Middlecamp, Eric *s.d.s.* '52 (MIL) [P] Milwaukee, WI Salvatorians - Jordan Hall.
Middleton, Charles '51 (WCH) Baxter Springs, KS St. Joseph Church; Galena, KS St. Patrick Church.
Midile, Theodore *t.o.r.* '60 (WH) [E] Kearneysville, WV Priest Field Pastoral Center.
Midile, Theodore *t.o.r.* '62 (ARL) [J] White Post, VA Sacred Heart Friary.
Midor, Adam '91 (TR) [10] Trenton, NJ Our Lady of Sorrows Church.
Midowski, Leonard '51 (NEW) [N] Rutherford, NJ St. John Vianney Residence for Priests.
Midura, Msgr. Francis S. '70 (RVC) Ronkonkoma, NY St. Joseph's Church.
Midzak, Ihor '90 (STF) New Haven, CT St. Michael Church; [A] Stamford, CT St. Basil College.
Miechielsen, Albert *ss.cc.* '46 (HON) [G] Kaneohe, HI Sacred Hearts Center.
Mieczkowski, Msgr. Chester J. (BAL) [38] Baltimore, MD Holy Rosary Church.
Mieczkowski, Msgr. Chester J. '45 (BAL) Retired.
Miekina, Stanislaw *c.m.* '59 (BRK) [134] Brooklyn, NY St. Stanislaus Kostka Church.
Miele, Joseph J. '56 (TR) Retired.
Mierenfeld, Lawrence E. '73 (CIN) [11] Dayton, OH St. Henry Church.
Mierzwa, Ronald B. '76 (BUF) Ellicottville, NY Holy Name of Mary Church.
Mierzwiak, Ligouri *o.f.m.* '59 (SAG) Bridgeport, MI Assumption of the Blessed Virgin Mary Church.
Mietelski, Joseph *c.m.* '59 (BRK) [32] Brooklyn, NY SS. Cyril and Methodius Church.
Mifsud, Carmelo '59 (OAK) Retired.
Mifsud, James *s.m.* '65 (SJ) [L] Cupertino, CA Marianist Provincial Residence.
Mifsud, James J. *s.m.* '65 (SJ) [21] San Jose, CA Queen of Apostles Church.
Migliazzo, Felix '49 (MRY) Retired; [E] Monterey, CA Ave Maria Convalescent Hospital; [G] Monterey, CA Ave Maria Convent.
Migliore, Angelus *t.o.r.* '64 (SP) [13] Tampa, FL St. Patrick Church.
Mignot, Msgr. John W. '54 (E) Reynoldsville, PA St. Mary Church.
Miguel, Eutiquiano *o.f.m.cap.* '51 (NO) [62] New Orleans, LA St. Theresa of Avila Church; New Orleans, LA Charity Hospital.
Miguelez, Valeriano '66 (SJN) [15] San Juan, PR Espiritu Santo Church.
Mihalak, James J. '76 (ALN) [J] Bethlehem, PA Holy Family Villa.
Mihalco, John J. '83 (PBR) Houston, TX St. John Chrysostom Church.
Mihalec, Peter M. '76 (CLV) Fairport Harbor, OH St. Anthony of Padua Church.
Mihalic, Francis *s.v.d.* '44 (SB) [A] Riverside, CA Divine Word Seminary.
Mihalik, Msgr. Alexis E. '64 (PBR) Boardman, OH Infant Jesus of Prague Church.
Mihan, Msgr. John A. '59 (LA) Retired.
Mihayli, Gilbert *o.praem.* '43 (GB) [I] De Pere, WI St. Joseph Priory.
Mihelich, Leopold '32 (DEN) Retired.
Mihovilovich, John B. '52 (SFR) Retired.
Mijas, Paul J. '85 (RVC) Centereach, NY Assumption of the Blessed Virgin Mary Church.
Mijatovic, Slaven H. *o.f.m.* '91 (NY) [29] New York, NY SS. Cyril and Methodius - St. Raphael Church.
Mika, John M. '72 (LIN) On Sick Leave.
Mika, Joseph *o.f.m.* (CHI) [M] Justice, IL Rosary Hill Home.
Mikalajunas, John '69 (SY) Binghamton, NY Binghamton General Hospital.
Mikalajunas, John E. '69 (SY) [7] Binghamton, NY St. Joseph Church; [11] Binghamton, NY St. Stanislaus Kostka Church.
Mikalofsky, Hilarion A. '75 (MIL) Military Chaplains.
Mikasauskas, Ronald *m.ss.a.* '77 (HRT) [6] Waterbury, CT Our Lady of Mt. Carmel Church.
Mikasauskas, Ronald *m.s.a.* '77 (NOR) [F] Cromwell, CT Society of the Missionaries of the Holy Apostles.
Mikes, Pavel '90 (FAR) On Duty Outside the Diocese.
Mikesch, Gregory R. '75 (STL) Ferguson, MO Good Shepherd Church.
Mikhael, Elie Hares '95 (SAM) Lawrence, MA St. Anthony Church.
Mikkelson, Scott '82 (AUS) Calvert, TX St. Mary Church; Hearne, TX St. Mary's Church.
Miklas, Sebastian F. *o.f.m.cap.* '39 (WDC) [B] Washington, DC St. Francis Friary-Capuchin College.
Miklaszewski, Albin *o.f.m.* '46 (MIL) [P] Burlington, WI Queen of Peace Friary.
Mikolaitis, Vito E. '43 (CHI) [138] Chicago, IL Nativity of the Blessed Virgin Mary Church; Retired.
Mikolajczyk, Bruno '88 (CC) [18] Corpus Christi, TX St. Paul the Apostle Church.
Mikolajczyk, Edward M. '73 (CHI) Evergreen Park, IL Queen of Martyrs Church.
Mikolajczyk, George M. *m.m.* '55 (NY) [DD] Maryknoll, NY Maryknoll Fathers and Brothers.
Mikonis, Gerald S. '74 (PIT) Port Vue, PA St. Mark Church.
Miksch, Joseph A. '66 (OM) Columbus, NE St. Isidore Church.
Mikschl, Luke *s.t.* '53 (SAV) Blakely, GA Holy Family Church.
Mikstay, Michael '59 (Y) Military Chaplains.
Mikula, John J. *o.f.m.conv.* '56 (RCK) [11] Rockford, IL St. Stanislaus Kostka Church.
Mikulanis, Msgr. Dennis '77 (SD) [23] San Diego, CA St. Charles Church.
Mikulcik, Ken '98 (OWN) LaCenter, KY St. Mary Church; [4] Paducah, KY St. Thomas More Church.
Mikulik, Kenneth E. '52 (GAL) Dickinson, TX Shrine of the True Cross Church.
Mikulski, Isadore J. '50 (GAY) Retired.
Mikus, Elemir '57 (DET) Retired.
Mikus, Elemir Joseph '57 (DET) [2] Sterling Heights, MI SS. Cyril and Methodius Church.
Milambo, Gaudence *a.l.c.p.* '97 (SFR) [9] San Francisco, CA St. Brendan Church.
Milanese, John M. '74 (BUR) Randolph, VT SS. Donatian and Rogatian Church; [H] Burlington, VT University of Vermont-The Catholic Center at UVM.
Milani, Fernando *p.i.m.e.* '79 (DET) [K] Detroit, MI P.I.M.E. College Community.
Milani, Msgr. Joseph J. '50 (SJ) Cupertino, CA St. Joseph of Cupertino Church; Retired.
Milani, Vasco J. *s.x.* '67 (MIL) [B] Franklin, WI Xaverian Missionary Fathers College Seminary.
Milano, Cleo J. '83 (BR) Denham Springs, LA Immaculate Conception Church.
Milano, Msgr. James '40 (LSC) Retired.
Milanowski, Paul A. '65 (GR) On Special Assignment.
Milazzo, Nicholas F. '52 (NY) [128] Bronx, NY St. Anthony Church.
Milbauer, Robert '66 (LA) Granada Hills, CA St. John Baptist de la Salle Church.
Milby, Lawrence M. '65 (BUF) Gowanda, NY St. Joseph Church.
Milde, Robert F. '48 (BRK) Retired; [V] Douglaston, NY Bishop Mugavero Residence.
Milek, Richard '83 (CHI) Other Assignments.
Miles, Andrew *o.s.b.* '60 (SFE) [I] Pecos, NM Our Lady of Guadalupe Abbey; [K] Pecos, NM Our Lady of Guadalupe Olivetan Benedictine Abbey.
Miles, Cassian *o.f.m.* '61 (NY) [35] New York, NY St. Francis of Assisi Church.
Miles, Cassian A. *o.f.m.* '61 (PAT) [P] Paterson, NJ St. Anthony's Guild.
Miles, Craig Thomas '99 (CHR) [2] Columbia, SC St. Joseph Church.
Miles, Francis J. *s.j.* '60 (WDC) [P] Faulkner, MD Loyola on the Potomac Retreat House.
Miles, James (BAL) [15] Baltimore, MD St. Benedict Church.
Miles, James '78 (LKC) On Duty Outside the Diocese.
Miles, James C. '77 (BAL) [55] Baltimore, MD Little Flower, Shrine of Church.
Miles, John *c.r.* '51 (L) [L] Louisville, KY Villa Pacis, Resurrectionist Retirement Home.
Miles, Michael '70 (BAK) On Duty Outside the Diocese.
Miles, Richard M. '84 (NO) [2] Kenner, LA Our Lady of Perpetual Help Church.
Miles, Taras (STN) [1] Chicago, IL St. Nicholas Ukrainian Catholic Church.
Milewski, Casmir '68 (TR) Moorestown, NJ Our Lady of Good Counsel Church.
Milewski, Douglas J. '89 (NEW) [B] South Orange, NJ Seton Hall University.
Milewski, John *k.h.s.* '93 (KNX) Dayton, TN St. Bridget Church.
Milewski, Richard R. '83 (TR) Freehold, NJ St. Rose of Lima Church.
Milewski, Robert '80 (E) On Duty Outside Diocese.
Milewski, Msgr. Stanley E. '55 (DET) [A] Orchard Lake, MI SS. Cyril and Methodius Seminary; [C] Orchard Lake, MI Saint Mary's College.
Milewski, Stanley J. '44 (GRY) [3] Gary, IN Holy Family Church.
Miley, Edward *p.i.m.e.* '67 (DET) [K] Detroit, MI P.I.M.E. Missionaries of SS. Peter and Paul.
Milhalak, James J. '76 (ALN) Unassigned.
Mili, Jude J. *o.f.m.* '59 (WH) [F] Morgantown, WV Our Lady of Good Counsel Franciscan Friary.
Milia, Msgr. Anthony A. '50 (OG) [3] Watertown, NY St. Anthony Church.
Milienewicz, Frank J. '76 (NTN) Birmingham, AL St. George Church; [D] Birmingham, AL National Shrine of St. George.
Militello, Benedict P., (Retired) '57 (NEW) Northvale, NJ St. Anthony's Church.
Militello, Cosmo F. '60 (CHI) Melrose Park, IL Sacred Heart Church.
Millan, Jose Luis '00 (SPK) [19] Spokane, WA St. Thomas More Church.
Millane, Thomas J. '63 (TUC) [25] Tucson, AZ St. Elizabeth Ann Seton Church.
Millar, Andrew (RVC) Retired.
Millea, Thomas V. (CHI) Retired.
Millea, Msgr. William V. '80 (BGP) On Duty Outside the Diocese.
Millen, Edwin F. '56 (RCK) Retired.
Miller, Abraham '79 (CHI) [J] Chicago, IL St. Mary of Nazareth Hospital Center.
Miller, Abraham '79 (STN) [4] Chicago, IL St. Michael's Church; Chicago, IL St. Mary of Nazareth Hospital Center.
Miller, Alfred J. '64 (DET) Temperance, MI Our Lady of Mt. Carmel Church.
Miller, Arnold J., Jr. '00 (B) Caldwell, ID St. Mary Church.
Miller, Bernard *m.s.c.* '59 (FgM) Missionaries of the Sacred Heart Foreign Missions.
Miller, Bernard *m.s.c.* '59 (RCK) [G] Aurora, IL Missionaries of the Sacred Heart Community.
Miller, Bert '91 (FAR) Grafton, ND St. John the Evangelist's Church; Grafton, ND Grafton State School.
Miller, Bertin *o.f.m.* '64 (STL) [T] Dittmer, MO Il Ritiro-The Little Retreat.
Miller, Brendan '83 (LR) [A] Subiaco, AR Subiaco Monastery.
Miller, Brian J. *t.o.r.* '53 (SP) [6] St. Petersburg, FL St. Mary Our Lady of Grace Church.
Miller, Byron J. *c.ss.r.* '90 (NO) [23] New Orleans, LA St. Alphonsus Church; [2] New Orleans, LA National Shrine of Blessed Francis Xavier Seelos Church.
Miller, C. Anthony '80 (HBG) [3] York, PA St. Patrick Church.
Miller, Casper J. *s.j.* '64 (FgM) Provinces.
Miller, Charles *o.f.m.* (NY) [146] Bronx, NY Holy Cross Church.
Miller, Charles *s.m.* (STL) [P] St. Louis, MO Provincialate of the Society of Mary, Province of St. Louis.
Miller, Charles *o.f.m.* '38 (CIN) [L] Cincinnati, OH Archbishop Leibold Home for the Aged.
Miller, Charles E. *c.m.* '56 (LA) [A] Camarillo, CA St. John's Seminary.
Miller, Charles E. '91 (SB) Hesperia, CA Holy Family Church.
Miller, Charles H. *s.m.* '64 (SAT) [C] San Antonio, TX St. Mary's University of San Antonio, Texas; [M] San Antonio, TX Chaminade Community House.
Miller, Charles J. *o.f.m.* '66 (NY) [DD] New York, NY Franciscan Friars, Order of Friars Minor, Holy Name Province.
Miller, Charles J. '72 (NEW) Lyndhurst, NJ Sacred Heart Church.
Miller, Cletus *o.s.b.* '44 (FgM) American - Cassinese Congregation Foreign Missions.
Miller, Cletus *o.s.b.* '44 (SFS) [F] Marvin, SD Blue Cloud Abbey.
Miller, Conrad *o.f.m.conv.* '38 (BAL) [O] Timonium, MD Stella Maris.
Miller, David L. '81 (SPC) Cassville, MO St. Edward Church; Shell Knob, MO Holy Family Church.
Miller, Donald A. *o.f.m.* '72 (Y) [B] North Canton, OH Walsh University.
Miller, Donald S. '42 (KC) Maryville, MO St. Gregory Barbarigo Church; Retired.
Miller, Edward M. '71 (BAL) [17] Baltimore, MD St. Bernardine Church.
Miller, Elden J. '54 (FTW) [4] Mishawaka, IN Queen of Peace Church.
Miller, Ferdinand B. '46 (NEW) Retired.
Miller, Francis *o.c.d.* '49 (WDC) [B] Washington, DC Discalced Carmelite Friars.
Miller, Francis J. '50 (CIN) Retired.
Miller, Francis X. *s.j.* '59 (WOR) [N] Worcester, MA Jesuits of Holy Cross College, Inc.
Miller, Msgr. Frank '54 (AUS) Retired.
Miller, Frank P. '54 (COL) Retired.
Miller, Franklin '89 (FAR) Special Assignment.
Miller, Frederick J. '41 (NY) Retired.
Miller, Frederick L. '72 (NEW) On Duty Outside the Archdiocese.
Miller, Frederick L. '72 (NY) [A] Yonkers, NY St. Joseph's Seminary.
Miller, Frederick L. '72 (PH) [A] Wynnewood, PA Theological Seminary of St. Charles Borromeo, Overbrook.
Miller, Gary A. '70 (COV) [N] Erlanger, KY Monastery of the Sacred Passion.

Miller, Gary M. '72 (CHI) [161] Chicago, IL St. Pascal Church.
Miller, Gary R. '83 (TOL) [21] Toledo, OH St. Clement Church.
Miller, George '78 (DET) Special Assignment.
Miller, George '79 (DET) [4] Dearborn Heights, MI St. Linus Church.
Miller, George M. '63 (LA) Retired.
Miller, Gregory *o.s.b.* '73 (SCL) St. Joseph, MN St. Joseph's Church; [I] Collegeville, MN St. John's Abbey, of the Order of St. Benedict.
Miller, Gregory L. *s.j.* '85 (SFR) [E] San Francisco, CA St. Ignatius College Preparatory (Coed).
Miller, Gregory L. *s.j.* '85 (STL) [P] St. Louis, MO Jesuit Community Corporation at St. Louis University - Jesuit Hall.
Miller, Harry *s.j.* '54 (FgM) Provinces.
Miller, Henry *o.s.c.* '43 (SCL) [I] Onamia, MN Crosier Monastery.
Miller, J. Michael *c.s.b.* '75 (GAL) [C] Houston, TX University of St. Thomas; [Q] Houston, TX Residence of the Basilian Fathers of the University of St. Thomas.
Miller, James '54 (CIN) [B] Carthagena, OH St. Charles.
Miller, James *o.m.i.* '57 (GAL) [37] Houston, TX Immaculate Conception Church.
Miller, James '68 (FWT) [4] Arlington, TX St. Joseph's Church.
MIller, James '83 (RVC) Absent on Leave.
Miller, James C. '83 (RVC) Garden City, NY St. Anne Church.
Miller, James H. '68 (LC) Norwalk, WI St. Augustine of Hippo Church; Retired.
Miller, James L. '76 (DUB) Ackley, IA St. Mary's Church; Hampton, IA St. Patrick's Church; Waverly, IA St. Mary's Church.
Miller, James Norman '59 (NSH) [9] Nashville, TN St. Mary's of the Seven Sorrows Church.
Miller, James W. '67 (CHI) [158] Chicago, IL Our Lady of Tepeyac Church.
Miller, John '58 (SCL) St. Stephen, MN St. Stephen's Church.
Miller, John '82 (WCH) Cunningham, KS Sacred Heart Church; St. Leo, KS St. Leo the Great Church.
Miller, John C. '95 (BRK) [97] Brooklyn, NY Our Lady of Guadalupe Church.
Miller, John H. *c.s.c.* '51 (STL) [V] St. Louis, MO Central Bureau of the CCUA.
Miller, Msgr. John J. '64 (PH) Fairless Hills, PA St. Frances Cabrini Church.
Miller, John P. '78 (HEL) [4] Missoula, MT St. Anthony Church.
Miller, John P. '82 (WCH) Willowdale, KS St. Peter's Church; Zenda, KS St. John Church.
Miller, Joseph '36 (SFD) Retired.
Miller, Joseph *s.v.d.* '68 (ORG) [G] Fullerton, CA St. Jude Medical Center.
Miller, Joseph *c.pp.s.* '77 (DAV) Centerville, IA St. Mary's Church.
Miller, Joseph A. *c.s.b.* '54 (DET) [E] Redford, MI Catholic Central High School.
Miller, Joseph A. '89 (BRK) Absent on Leave.
Miller, Joseph B. '36 (TR) Retired.
Miller, Joseph C. '49 (OWN) Retired.
Miller, Joseph K. '57 (SAG) Nine Mile, MI St. Mary Church.
Miller, Joseph N. '48 (SUP) Minocqua, WI St. Patrick Church.
Miller, Joseph W. '59 (PIT) Retired.
Miller, Kenneth E. '77 (Y) Louisville, OH St. Louis Church.
Miller, Lawrence J. '69 (NEW) [1] Bayonne, NJ St. Mary Star of the Sea Church.
Miller, Leo *o.m.i.* '52 (BEL) [F] Belleville, IL Shrine of Our Lady of the Snows.
Miller, Leo M. *o.m.i.* '52 (LA) Long Beach, CA Veterans Affairs Medical Center.
Miller, Loran *o.f.m.cap.* '64 (GB) [I] Appleton, WI St. Fidelis Friary.
Miller, Louis '56 (L) [N] Louisville, KY Sacred Heart Village, Inc.
Miller, Mardean E. '94 (PH) [111] Philadelphia, PA Nativity of the Blessed Virgin Mary Church; Philadelphia, PA Philadelphia Prison System.
Miller, Mark (ROC) [60] Rochester, NY St. Thomas More Church; Corning, NY St. Mary Church.
Miller, Mark '69 (ROC) Corning, NY St. Patrick Church.
Miller, Mark *c.pp.s.* '71 (KC) [A] Liberty, MO Society of the Precious Blood Provincial Offices; [J] Liberty, MO Precious Blood Society Provincial Office.
Miller, Mark A. '69 (ROC) Corning, NY St. Vincent de Paul Church; Painted Post, NY Immaculate Heart of Mary Church.
Miller, Martin J. '94 (PIT) [N] Pittsburgh, PA Opus Dei.
Miller, Maurice R. '49 (LFT) [2] Lafayette, IN St. Ann Church.
Miller, Meinrad *o.s.b.* '94 (KCK) [A] Atchison, KS Benedictine College; [H] Atchison, KS St. Benedict's Abbey.
Miller, Michael *o.f.m.conv.* '00 (BUF) [D] Athol Springs, NY St. Francis High School; [O] Athol Springs, NY St. Francis of Assisi Friary.
Miller, Michael *m.s.c.* '85 (FgM) Missionaries of the Sacred Heart Foreign Missions.
Miller, Michael *m.s.c.* '85 (RCK) [G] Aurora, IL Missionaries of the Sacred Heart Community.
Miller, Michael '87 (ALB) Comstock, NY Great Meadows Correctional Institution; Special Assignment.
Miller, Michael J. '72 (MRY) [2] Salinas, CA Sacred Heart Church.
Miller, Michael J. '96 (STP) West St. Paul, MN St. Joseph Church.
Miller, Neil '61 (ROC) [37] Rochester, NY Our Lady of Perpetual Help Church.
Miller, Oscar J. *c.m.* '39 (SAT) Losoya, TX El Carmen Catholic Church.
Miller, Paul '56 (HBG) Retired.
Miller, Paul A. *c.ss.r.* '33 (NY) Port Ewen, NY Presentation of the Virgin Mary Church.
Miller, Paul A. *c.ss.r.* '62 (ROC) [K] Canandaigua, NY Notre Dame Retreat House.
Miller, Paul D. '44 (FTW) Retired.
Miller, Paul E. '67 (SCR) [21] Scranton, PA St. Patrick's Church.
Miller, Paul W. '44 (KCK) Eudora, KS Holy Family Church.
Miller, Peter (MIL) [N] Wauwatosa, WI St. Camillus Health Center, Inc.
Miller, Peter *s.c.j.* '45 (MIL) [P] Franklin, WI Villa Maria.
Miller, Philip '77 (Y) Ashtabula, OH St. Joseph's Church.
Miller, Randall J. '89 (LAN) Grand Blanc, MI Holy Family Church.
Miller, Richard E. '76 (LFT) Reynolds, IN St. Joseph Church; Special Assignment.
Miller, Richard G. '50 (TOL) Retired; [J] Oregon, OH Sacred Heart Home.
Miller, Robert *o.p.* '56 (CHI) [J] Des Plaines, IL Holy Family Medical Center.
Miller, Robert '70 (SB) [1] San Bernardino, CA Our Lady of the Rosary Church.
Miller, Robert J. *o.p.* '56 (CHI) [N] River Forest, IL St. Thomas Aquinas Priory.
Miller, Robert J. '76 (CHI) [77] Chicago, IL Holy Angels Church.
Miller, Robert J. '80 (PIT) Neshannock, PA St. Camillus Church; [R] Pittsburgh, PA Office for Campus Ministry.
Miller, Robert M. '92 (PIT) Bethel Park, PA St. Valentine Church.
Miller, Roger F. '42 (KC) Retired.
Miller, S. Bruce '77 (ALX) [6] Alexandria, LA St. Rita Church.
Miller, Theodore J. '75 (TOL) Gibsonburg, OH St. Michael Church; Kansas, OH St. James Church; Millersville, OH St. Mary Church.
Miller, Thomas C. '93 (STL) [7] Florissant, MO Sacred Heart Church.
Miller, Msgr. Thomas G. '71 (RIC) [8] Richmond, VA St. Bridget Church.
Miller, Thomas M. *c.s.b.* '45 (ROC) [I] Rochester, NY Basilian Residence.
Miller, Thomas R. '77 (PIT) Clarksville, PA St. Thomas Church.
Miller, Msgr. Thomas R. '79 (PEO) [15] Peoria, IL St. Vincent De Paul Church.
Miller, Msgr. Thomas W. '77 (BEL) Anna, IL St. Mary Church; Anna, IL Anna State Hospital; Vienna, IL Vienna Correctional Center; Vienna, IL Dixon Springs Work Camp; Vienna, IL Shawnee Correctional Center.
Miller, Vernon *o.s.b.* '48 (SCL) [I] Collegeville, MN St. John's Abbey, of the Order of St. Benedict.
Miller, Vincent P. '98 (CR) Moorhead, MN St. Joseph's Church; [F] Moorhead, MN St. Thomas Aquinas Newman Center.
Miller, Walter *s.v.d.* '69 (LA) [28] Los Angeles, CA Our Lady of Loretto Church.
Miller, Walter D. '61 (BUR) On Special or Other Diocesan Assignment.
Miller, Whitney '80 (LKC) [1] Lake Charles, LA Immaculate Conception Church.
Miller, William '61 (L) [59] Louisville, KY Our Lady of Lourdes Church.
Miller, William *c.pp.s.* '63 (DM) Chariton, IA Sacred Heart Church.
Miller, William *s.j.* '72 (P) [A] St. Benedict, OR Mount Angel Seminary.
Miller, William '91 (LKC) Iowa, LA St. Raphael Church.
Miller, William C. '83 (E) Youngsville, PA St. Luke Church.
Miller, William J. '56 (PIT) Retired.
Miller, William M. '56 (PIT) [O] Pittsburgh, PA St. John Vianney Manor.
Miller, William T. *s.j.* '55 (DEN) [M] Denver, CO Xavier Jesuit Center.
Miller, William T. *s.j.* '72 (P) [L] Portland, OR Colombiere Community.
Miller, William T. *i.c.* '84 (PEO) [A] Peoria, IL Rosminian Novitiate.
Millerd, William H. *s.j.* '68 (WDC) [M] Washington, DC The Jesuit Community at Georgetown University.
Millican, Ronald C. '81 (P) [30] Portland, OR St. Pius X Church.
Milligan, John '64 (ROC) [54] Rochester, NY Most Precious Blood Church.
Milligan, Richard A. '60 (PHX) [16] Phoenix, AZ St. Luke Church.
Milligan, Ronald '72 (DET) [3] Sterling Heights, MI St. Ephrem Church.
Milliken, Damian *o.s.b.* '58 (FgM) American - Cassinese Congregation Foreign Missions.
Milliken, Damian J. *o.s.b.* '58 (PAT) [M] Newton, NJ St. Paul's Abbey.
Milliken, David '77 (NEW) Bloomfield, NJ Sacred Heart Church.
Millis, Karl '99 (CHY) Gillette, WY St. Matthew's Church.
Millisor, Daniel J. '86 (COL) Ada, OH Our Lady of Lourdes Church.
Millot, Andre '69 (WDC) [26] Washington, DC Church of St. Louis.
Millott, Thirburse F. '75 (WOR) Southborough, MA St. Anne Church.
Mills, Alexander '80 (TUC) Tucson, AZ Villa Maria.
Mills, Alexander *o.s.b.* '90 (TUC) [F] St. David, AZ Holy Trinity Monastery.
Mills, Alexander M. *o.s.b.* '90 (TUC) [15] Tucson, AZ St. Francis de Sales Church.
Mills, Brindley '64 (DAL) [21] Dallas, TX St. Monica Church.
Mills, Donald J. '82 (PH) Absent on Sick Leave.
Mills, Henry '88 (NY) Absent on Leave.
Mills, Joseph '53 (OWN) [G] Maple Mount, KY Mount St. Joseph.
Mills, Joseph M. '53 (OWN) Non-Parochial Assignments.
Mills, Robert N. '55 (L) Flaherty, KY St. Martin of Tours Church; Retired.
Milon, Augustin *o.f.m.* '28 (CHI) [I] Chicago, IL Port Ministries.
Milosz, Bogdan '80 (DET) Hamtramck, MI Our Lady Queen of Apostles Church.
Milota, Thomas '92 (JOL) Graduate Studies.
Milsted, Gordon '63 (MOB) Fairhope, AL St. Lawrence Church.
Milton, Hilary *o.carm.* '63 (NEW) Teaneck, NJ St. Anastasia's Church.
Milton, Kevin *c.ss.r.* (BO) [53] Boston, MA Our Lady of Perpetual Help Church.
Mimms, Wolfgang *o.ss.t.* '70 (VIC) [4] Victoria, TX Our Lady of Sorrows Church.
Mimnagh, Msgr. Peter F. '48 (SD) Retired.
Min, Andrew Kyeng-Kuk '90 (SJ) [1] Sunnyvale, CA Sts. Andrew and Paul Korean Catholic Mission of San Jose Church.
Mina, John L. '89 (PBR) Clairton, PA Ascension of Our Lord Church.
Minaberry, Martin '64 (LA) [48] Los Angeles, CA St. Basil's Church.
Minarevic, Daniel Miho '84 (FAR) Velva, ND St. Cecilia's Church.
Minassian, Raphael '73 (ARM) Los Angeles, CA Our Lady Queen of Martyrs Church; Glendale, CA St. Gregory Church.
Minassian, Raphael *p.i.a.* '73 (LA) [33] Los Angeles, CA Our Lady Queen of Martyrs Church.
Minch, Richard '69 (SAV) Military Chaplains.
Minchak, Paul *o.f.m.cap.* '69 (AGN) [F] Agana Heights, GU St. Fidelis Friary.
Minchak, Paul *o.f.m.cap.* '69 (HON) Pearl City, HI Our Lady of Good Counsel Church.
Minchiatti, Francis *c.s.* '45 (PRO) [8] Providence, RI St. Bartholomew Church.
Minder, Kevin '89 (YAK) Special Assignment.
Minder, Lawrence *o.s.b.* '89 (P) [L] St. Benedict, OR Mt. Angel Abbey.
Minder, Lawrence *o.s.b.* '89 (SEA) Burlington, WA St. Charles Church; LaConner, WA Sacred Heart Church; LaConner, WA St. Paul Church; Mount Vernon, WA Immaculate Conception Church; Sedro Woolley, WA Immaculate Heart of Mary Church; [P] Mount Vernon, WA Skagit Valley Regional Ministry.
Mindling, J. Daniel *o.f.m.cap.* '80 (BAL) [A] Emmitsburg, MD Mount St. Mary's Seminary; [A] Emmitsburg, MD Mount St. Mary's Seminary.
Mindling, J. Daniel *o.f.m.cap.* '80 (WDC) [B] Washington, DC St. Francis Friary-Capuchin College.
Mindling, Joseph *o.f.m.cap.* '67 (WDC) [39] Washington, DC Shrine of the Sacred Heart Church.
Mindrup, Mark F. *o.f.m.conv.* '39 (STP) [Q] Prior Lake, MN Franciscan Retreat House.
Minehan, Michael P. '80 (SY) Lafayette, NY St. Joseph Church; Special Assignment; [H] Syracuse, NY Bishop Joseph T. O'Keefe, Inc.; [W] Syracuse, NY David W. Barry Foundation.
Minelli, Peter A. '63 (MAR) Manistique, MI St. Francis de Sales Church.
Minette, James '41 (SCL) Retired.

Minh, Peter M. Ngo Chau *c.m.c.* (SPC) [E] Carthage, MO Congregation of the Mother Co-Redemptrix, United States Assumption Province.
Minh, Vincent Cao dang *c.ss.r.* '68 (DEN) [M] Denver, CO The Redemptorists/Denver Province.
Minh, Vu Duc '80 (TLS) On Duty Outside the Diocese.
Minh Thanh Tran, Matthew '53 (COS) [15] Colorado Springs, CO The Vietnamese Holy Martyrs Quasi-Church.
Minh Vu Nguyen, Joseph *s.v.d.* '96 (FgM) Society of the Divine Word Foreign Missions.
Minhoto, Msgr. Walter F. '64 (FRS) [1] Fresno, CA St. John Church; Retired.
Minic, John F. '71 (CIN) Retired.
Minichello, Arthur G. '73 (BRK) [167] Queens, NY St. Fidelis Church.
Minielli, Anthony '45 (BRK) [14] Brooklyn, NY St. Augustine Church.
Minielli, Anthony '45 (NY) Retired.
Minihan, Paul (OAK) [4] Oakland, CA St. Augustine's Church; Graduate Studies.
Miniscalco, Donald *c.ss.r.* '68 (PH) [136] Philadelphia, PA St. Peter the Apostle Church.
Minj, William '95 (BR) [1] Baton Rouge, LA St. Joseph Church.
Mink, John J. '85 (WIL) Wilmington Manor, DE Our Lady of Fatima Church; Wilmington, DE Delaware Army National Guard.
Minkiel, Stephen J. *c.m.* '57 (BRK) [32] Brooklyn, NY SS. Cyril and Methodius Church.
Minkler, John '72 (ALB) Albany, NY Veterans' Administration Hospital; Special Assignment; Military Chaplains.
Minnich, John F. '51 (GRY) Retired.
Minniti, Anthony L. '70 (CAM) Paulsboro, NJ St. John's Church.
Minniti, David V. '72 (CAM) Millville, NJ St. Mary Magdalen's Church.
Minnoggio, Ferrando '47 (CLV) Retired.
Minogue, John P. *c.m.* '72 (CHI) [C] Chicago, IL De Paul University; [N] Chicago, IL DePaul Vincentian Residence.
Minogue, Liam A. '68 (MET) Hillsborough, NJ Mary, Mother of God Church.
Minogue, Michael '81 (PHX) Sun City West, AZ Our Lady of Lourdes Church.
Minson, Bartholomew *o.f.m.cap.* '64 (FgM) Capuchin Foreign Missions.
Minsterman, Joseph '61 (GBG) East Vandergrift, PA Our Lady, Queen of Peace Church.
Minta, John J. '50 (IND) Milan, IN St. Charles Borromeo Church; Retired.
Mintegui, Marc A. '68 (CHR) Absent On Leave.
Mintjal, Frank '59 (Y) Retired.
Minturn, Joseph (RVC) Retired.
Miodek, Piotr R. *o.f.m.conv.* '87 (BUF) [O] Athol Springs, NY Father Justin Rosary Hour Radio Apostolate.
Miodowski, Leonard A. '51 (NEW) Retired.
Miola, Luigi C. '77 (CLV) Madison, OH Immaculate Conception Church.
Miorin, Albert C. '64 (TOL) Retired.
Miotke, Carmel *o.f.m.* '60 (BO) [BB] Boston, MA St. Anthony Shrine.
Miqueli, Peter A. '91 (NY) [229] Staten Island, NY St. Sylvester Church.
Mirabelli, Daniel J. *c.s.v.* '60 (PEO) [B] Rock Island, IL Alleman High School.
Miracky, James J. *s.j.* '88 (WOR) [N] Worcester, MA Jesuits of Holy Cross College, Inc.
Miraglia, Salvatore J. '75 (RVC) Priests Released from Diocesan Assignment.
Miramontes, Francisco '91 (SJ) Morgan Hill, CA St. Catherine of Alexandria Church.
Miranda, Donald '99 (BO) [W] Cambridge, MA Weston Jesuit Community.
Miranda, Msgr. Juan '51 (SJN) [21] San Juan, PR Nuestra Sra. de Guadalupe Church.
Miranda, Lorenzo '91 (LA) La Puente, CA St. Louis of France Church.
Miranda, Luis *o.carm.* '84 (ARE) Ciales, PR Holy Rosary Church.
Miranda, Luke '55 (FWT) Retired.
Miranda, R. Dario '92 (LA) [19] Los Angeles, CA Mother of Sorrows Church.
Miranda, Msgr. Rafael '56 (ELP) [38] El Paso, TX San Judas Tadeo Church.
Miranda, Victor (CHI) Arlington Heights, IL St. Edna Church.
Miranne, Paul *o.s.b.* '47 (NO) [P] St. Benedict, LA St. Joseph Abbey.
Mirecki, Msgr. John '55 (RVC) Riverhead, NY St. Isidore's Church.
Miriani, Gerald C. '62 (BEL) Retired.
Mirro, Joseph A. '76 (RVC) Mastic Beach, NY St. Jude Church.
Mirsberger, Richard E. '66 (MIL) [9] West Allis, WI St. Rita Church.
Mirto, Gregorio L. '65 (DEN) Fort Lupton, CO St. William Church.
Misakabo, Faustin *o.praem.* (GB) Plainfield, WI St. Paul Church.
Misbrener, David M. '95 (Y) Ravenna, OH Immaculate Conception Church.
Miscamble, Wilson D. *c.s.c.* '88 (FTW) [A] Notre Dame, IN Moreau Seminary; [A] Notre Dame, IN Moreau Seminary; [B] Notre Dame, IN University of Notre Dame Du Lac; [J] South Bend, IN Congregation of Holy Cross, Indiana Province, Provincial House.
Mischke, Bernard *o.s.c.* '51 (SCL) [I] Onamia, MN Crosier Monastery.
Mischke, Gerald '64 (SCL) Holdingford, MN St. Hedwig's Church; Holdingford, MN St. Mary's Church; Opole, MN Our Lady of Mt. Carmel Church; St. Anna, MN Immaculate Conception Church; St. Wendel, MN St. Columbkille's Church.
Mischke, Walter *c.m.f.* '43 (CHI) [N] Oak Park, IL Claretian Fathers Headquarters of U.S.A. Eastern Province.
Mischkowiuski, Henry B. '65 (LR) Lake Village, AR Our Lady of the Lake Church.
Mischler, Thomas E. '81 (GRY) [15] Gary, IN St. Mary of the Lake Church.
Misenko, John A. '78 (CLV) Avon, OH Holy Trinity Church.
Misercola, Chester A. '64 (SY) [S] Syracuse, NY St. Pius X Home, Inc.
Misey, Leonard S. '63 (JC) Brunswick, MO St. Boniface Church; Indian Grove, MO St. Raphael Church.
Mish, Roy L. '60 (LC) Eau Galle, WI St. Henry Church.
Misho, Lloyd P. '58 (BEL) Retired.
Misiewicz, Chester J. '73 (WOR) Gilbertville, MA St. Aloysius Church.
Misiolek, Frederick '65 (DET) Flat Rock, MI St. Roch Church.
Miskella, Richard '65 (LA) On Duty Outside the Archdiocese.
Miskella, Richard '65 (MRY) Atascadero, CA Atascadero State Hospital.
Miskiewicz, Paul *o.f.m.conv.* '82 (BRK) [146] Queens, NY St. Adalbert Church.
Miskolczy, Kalman *sch.p.* '45 (BUF) [3] Lackawanna, NY Assumption Church; [O] Lackawanna, NY Piarist Fathers.
Misna, Todd A. '98 (LC) Marshfield, WI St. John the Baptist Church.
Misolich, Msgr. Raymond M. *j.c.l.* '56 (PSC) Retired.
Missa, Msgr. John B. '32 (BO) [6] Brockton, MA Our Lady of Ostrobrama Church.
Missimi, Msgr. Anthony N. '62 (COL) [22] Columbus, OH Immaculate Conception Church.
Missinne, William *c.i.c.m.* '54 (FgM) Missionhurst Foreign Missions.
Missler, John C. '78 (TOL) Bethlehem, OH Sacred Heart of Jesus Church; Shelby, OH Most Pure Heart of Mary Church.
Mistretta, Msgr. Vito F. '42 (SAC) Citrus Heights, CA Holy Family Church; Retired and in Senior Ministry.
Misurda, Matthew '77 (ALT) [2] Windber, PA SS. Cyril and Methodius Church.
Miszkel, Ivot *o.f.m.cap.* '80 (PAT) [M] Oak Ridge-Milton, NJ St. Stanislaus B. M. Friary.
Mitas, Matthew M. '79 (STL) Ste. Genevieve, MO Ste. Genevieve Church.
Mitchell, Charles I. '84 (ORL) Altamonte Springs, FL St. Mary Magdalen Church.
Mitchell, Conan *o.f.m.* '43 (SUP) Ashland, WI Our Lady of the Lake Catholic Community Church.
Mitchell, Darell J. '98 (YAK) Richland, WA Christ the King Church.
Mitchell, Eugene *b.s.o.* '92 (NTN) Manchester, NH Our Lady of the Cedars Church; [B] Methuen, MA Basilian Salvatorian Order.
Mitchell, Francis *o.m.i.* '44 (FgM) Oblates Foreign Missions.
Mitchell, John C. '55 (BGP) On Duty Outside the Diocese.
Mitchell, John E. '54 (STP) Retired.
Mitchell, Msgr. John J. '63 (RCK) Loves Park, IL St. Bridget Church.
Mitchell, John J. '96 (STP) Jordan, MN St. John the Baptist Church.
Mitchell, Joseph O. *c.p.* '81 (SAC) [H] Citrus Heights, CA Christ the King Retreat; [J] Citrus Heights, CA Christ the King Retreat Center.
Mitchell, Joseph P. '79 (SEA) [1] Vancouver, WA Holy Redeemer Church.
Mitchell, Kenneth *s.c.j.* '48 (SP) [O] Pinellas Park, FL Priests of the Sacred Heart.
Mitchell, Lester *o.f.m.* '55 (PHX) [19] Phoenix, AZ St. Mary's Basilica Church.
Mitchell, Mark E. '76 (GR) On Special Assignment.
Mitchell, Msgr. Michael J. (SJ) Saratoga, CA Sacred Heart Church.
Mitchell, Msgr. Michael J. '65 (SJ) Special Assignment; [O] Santa Clara, CA St. Joseph Seminary Corporation; [O] Santa Clara, CA The Roman Catholic Welfare Corporation of San Jose.
Mitchell, Peter '78 (ORL) Port Orange, FL Epiphany Church.
Mitchell, Peter G. '51 (HRT) Derby, CT St. Mary's Church.
Mitchell, Peter M. '99 (LIN) [10] Lincoln, NE St. Peter Church.
Mitchell, Robert '73 (ORL) Rockledge, FL St. Mary's Church.
Mitchell, Robert A. *s.j.* '56 (NY) [DD] New York, NY "America;" Residence and publication office of the America Press.
Mitchell, Robert J. '85 (PAT) Budd Lake, NJ St. Jude Church.
Mitchell, Royce '74 (NO) Retired.
Mitchell, Msgr. Salvatore P. '42 (E) Retired.
Mitchell, Thomas R. '79 (HRT) [6] East Hartford, CT St. Rose's Church.
Mitchell, Tomas *o.s.b.* '61 (SFE) [I] Abiquiu, NM Monastery of Christ in the Desert.
Mitchell, Walter '91 (MIA) Retired.
Mitchell, Walter A. '61 (BRK) [78] Brooklyn, NY St. Margaret Mary Church.
Mitchell, William *ss.cc.* '50 (FR) [I] Fairhaven, MA Sacred Hearts Provincial House.
Mitchell, William J. '49 (PHX) Retired.
Mitchko, James '77 (PSC) North Fort Myers, FL All Saints Byzantine Catholic Church.
Mitka, John J. '66 (BUF) Silver Creek, NY Our Lady of Mt. Carmel Church.
Mitko, Joseph K. *o.ss.t.* '80 (TR) Asbury Park, NJ Our Lady of Mt. Carmel Church.
Mitolo, Frank A. '68 (PIT) [83] Pittsburgh, PA Risen Lord Church; Allegheny County, PA Allegheny General.
Mitolo, Msgr. Nicholas A. '54 (GBG) Jeannette, PA Ascension Church.
Mitoraj, Chester *c.r.* '48 (CHI) [86] Chicago, IL St. Hyacinth Church.
Mitrano, Joseph *c.s.b.* '41 (AUS) Kingsland, TX St. Charles Borromeo Church.
Mitros, Joseph *s.j.* '47 (NY) [DD] New York, NY Jesuit Community at Fordham University.
Mittelstadt, John *o.f.m.* '62 (GLP) Tohatchi, NM St. Mary Church.
Mitten, Stephen F. *s.j.* '95 (RC) [B] Howes, SD Kino Jesuit Community; [D] Howes, SD The Diocese of Rapid City Mahpiya na Maka Okoigna.
Mitty, Msgr. Edward J. *p.a.* '50 (NY) [99] New York, NY Our Lady of Victory Church.
Mitulski, James M. '72 (STL) St. Peters, MO All Saints Church.
Mitzel, Daniel C. '81 (HBG) [3] Harrisburg, PA St. Francis of Assisi Church.
Mixtacki, Eugene *o.f.m.cap.* '77 (CAM) [N] Cherry Hill, NJ Little Servant Sisters of the Immaculate Conception.
Miyares, Carlos '81 (MIA) [30] Miami, FL St. Richard Church.
Miyares, Gustavo J. '73 (MIA) [1] Hialeah, FL Immaculate Conception Church; [C] Miami, FL Msgr. Edward Pace High School.
Mizener, Paul '64 (SP) Beverly Hills, FL Our Lady of Grace Church.
Mizeur, Thomas '73 (PEO) [4] Rock Island, IL St. Pius X Church.
Mizicko, Carroll *o.f.m.* '68 (SHP) [2] Monroe, LA Little Flower of Jesus Church; Monroe, LA Swanson Correctional Center for Youth.
Mkamwa, Thadeus F. (ROC) [5] Elmira, NY St. Casimir Church.
Mlsna, Todd A. '98 (LC) Spencer, WI Christ the King Church; [D] Marshfield, WI Saint Joseph's Hospital of Marshfield, Inc.
Mngomezulu, Sibusiso *o.s.m.* '88 (CHI) [N] Chicago, IL Order of Friar Servants of Mary (Servites) United States of America Province, Inc.
Moala, Saimone '83 (SFR) [4] San Mateo, CA St. Timothy Church.
Moan, Francis X. *s.j.* '57 (CAM) [4] Camden, NJ Holy Name Church.
Moccia, Bonaventure *c.p.* '52 (WOR) [N] Shrewsbury, MA Calvery Retreat Center, Passionist Fathers of Shrewsbury, Inc.
Mocco, Charles W. (GB) Institute, WI SS. Peter and Paul Church; Sturgeon Bay, WI St. Joseph Church.
Mocio, Stephen J. '76 (DAL) [25] Dallas, TX St. Philip Church.
Mociun, Casimir T. '42 (SFS) Retired.
Mock, Robert M. '84 (BUF) Canaseraga, NY St. Mary Church; Portageville, NY Assumption B.V.M. Church.
Mock, Timothy *c.m.m.* '52 (DET) [K] Dearborn Heights, MI Our Lady of Grace Monastery.
Mockel, George E. '75 (OAK) [1] Concord, CA St. Agnes Church.
Mockevicius, Charles L. '47 (ROC) [17] Rochester, NY St. George Church; Retired; [I] Rochester, NY St. George's Rectory.
Mockevicius, Charles L. '47 (RVC) Retired.
Mockevicius, Dominic F. '48 (ROC) [17] Rochester, NY St. George Church; Retired; [I] Rochester, NY St. George's Rectory.
Mockler, Patrick J. '79 (BLX) Wiggins, MS St. Francis Xavier Church.
Mockler, Peter F. '73 (BLX) [3] Biloxi, MS Our Lady of Fatima Church.

Moczarny, Chester B. '47 (LC) Retired; [H] La Crosse, WI Holy Cross (Seminary) Diocesan Center.
Moczydlowski, Msgr. Chester M. '73 (CHR) [1] Charleston, SC Cathedral of St. John the Baptist; [2] Charleston, SC St. Mary's Church.
Modde, Bradley E. '97 (STL) [14] St. Louis, MO Our Lady of Sorrows Church.
Mode, Daniel L. '92 (ARL) Falls Church, VA St. James Church; [D] Arlington, VA Bishop Denis J. O'Connell High School.
Modeen, James '81 (TUC) [E] Tucson, AZ Carondelet Health Network; [F] Tucson, AZ Regina Cleri Center.
Moder, John *s.m.* '79 (STL) [P] St. Louis, MO Provincialate of the Society of Mary, Province of St. Louis.
Modi, Francis Abel *m.c.c.j.* '71 (LA) [56] Los Angeles, CA St. Cecilia Church.
Modica, B. John '45 (COV) [N] Melbourne, KY Holy Family Home.
Modica, John B. '45 (COV) Retired.
Modino, Roman '86 (TR) [3] Long Branch, NJ St. John the Baptist Church.
Modlin, William F. '96 (PRT) Jackman, ME St. Anthony Church.
Modrys, Walter F. *s.j.* '78 (NY) [51] New York, NY St. Ignatius Loyola Church; [DD] New York, NY St. Ignatius Loyola Residence.
Modugno, Msgr. Thomas A. '66 (NY) [76] New York, NY St. Monica Church.
Moeder, August L. '53 (SAL) Retired.
Moeder, John A. '57 (SAL) Belleville, KS St. Edward's Church.
Moeglein, James *o.s.c.* '70 (SCL) [I] Onamia, MN Crosier Monastery.
Moell, Carl J. *s.j.* '53 (CIN) [26] Cincinnati, OH St. Francis Xavier Church.
Moellenberndt, Msgr. Duane R. '76 (MAD) Sun Prairie, WI Sacred Hearts of Jesus and Mary Church.
Moeller, Msgr. George B. '62 (BAL) [49] Baltimore, MD St. Joseph Church.
Moelter, Joel *o.carm.* '51 (FgM) Carmelite Foreign Missions.
Moelter, Joel *o.carm.* '51 (JOL) [J] Darien, IL Carmelite Provincial Office.
Moenkedrick, Leo '86 (SCL) Breckenridge, MN St. Mary of the Presentation Church.
Moerman, Stephen A. '94 (PH) [3] Drexel Hill, PA St. Charles Borromeo Church.
Moeschler, William H. *m.m.* '44 (NY) [DD] Maryknoll, NY Maryknoll Fathers and Brothers.
Moeslein, Francis R. '58 (R) Morehead City, NC St. Egbert Church; Retired.
Mofan, Feliciano T. '79 (SFR) Mill Valley, CA Our Lady of Mt. Carmel Church.
Moffat, Curtis *o.m.i.* (FgM) Oblates Foreign Missions.
Moffat, Gerald '56 (SEA) Langley, WA St. Hubert Church.
Moffatt, Joseph *c.s.b.* '61 (VEN) [1] Naples, FL St. Ann Church.
Moffatt, Timothy *t.o.r.* '66 (SP) [2] Tampa, FL Christ the King Church.
Moffitt, Joseph M. *s.j.* '44 (WDC) [M] Washington, DC The Jesuit Community at Georgetown University.
Moffo, Joseph G. *c.s.* '59 (HRT) [3] New Haven, CT St. Anthony's Church.
Moga, Michael D. *s.j.* '64 (FgM) Provinces.
Mogilka, Erwin E. '49 (MIL) Retired.
Mohahan, Kieran *o.f.m.* '65 (ALB) [A] Catskill, NY St. Anthony Friary.
Mohan, Bernard N. '61 (NEW) West Orange, NJ St. Joseph's Church.
Mohan, Oliver *o.m.i.* '48 (PHX) [25] Phoenix, AZ St. Thomas the Apostle Church.
Mohan, Msgr. Robert Paul '46 (WDC) Retired; [C] Washington, DC Catholic University of America, The.
Mohan, Msgr. Thomas J. '35 (CHI) [67] Chicago, IL St. Genevieve Church; Retired.
Mohl, Andrew (BAL) Westminster, MD St. John Church.
Mohnickey, Ronald J. *t.o.r.* (ARL) Herndon, VA St. Joseph Church.
Mohr, J. Patrick *s.j.* '75 (SCR) [C] Scranton, PA University of Scranton.
Mohr, Richard G. '67 (BEL) Marion, IL St. Joseph Church.
Mohr, Simon *o.f.m.conv.* '57 (ALB) [L] Rensselaer, NY Franciscan Mission House.
Mohrbacher, Austin '57 (PSC) Philadelphia, PA Holy Trinity Church.
Mohrman, J. Gregory *o.s.b.* '86 (STL) [F] Creve Coeur, MO St. Louis Priory School; [G] Creve Coeur, MO St. Louis Priory School; [P] St. Louis, MO The Abbey of St. Mary and St. Louis.
Moineau, John A. '87 (GBG) Murrysville, PA Mother of Sorrows Church.
Moisin, Michael '88 (ROM) Boston, IN Romanian Catholic Mission of Boston Church.
Mojica, Luis Efrain '51 (MIA) [1] Miami Beach, FL St. Francis de Sales Church.
Mokarzel, Galeb *o.m.i.* '51 (SAT) [M] San Antonio, TX Missionary Oblates of Mary Immaculate.
Mokluk, John M. *o.s.f.s.* '70 (WIL) [B] Wilmington, DE Salesianum School.
Mokris, Michael '61 (PBR) Retired.
Mokris, Michael '61 (PHU) Nanticoke, PA St. Nicholas Church.
Mokrzycki, M. Joseph '65 (TR) [1] Long Branch, NJ Our Lady Star of the Sea Church.
Mol, Joseph C. '77 (CHI) Hickory Hills, IL St. Patricia Church; [A] Mundelein, IL University of St. Mary of the Lake-Mundelein Seminary.
Molan, Colman J. *s.t.* '86 (B) Post Falls, ID St. George's Church.
Molan, Msgr. John E. '53 (MAN) Auburn, NH St. Peter Church; Retired.
Molano, Ernesto '56 (MIA) Retired.
Moleski, Martin X. *s.j.* '81 (BUF) [O] Buffalo, NY Canisius Jesuit Community.
Moleski, Pawel '86 (NEW) [27] Newark, NJ Our Lady of Good Counsel Church.
Moletteire, Tom (LA) Norwalk, CA California Youth Authority.
Molewski, Andrew '82 (WIL) [6] Wilmington, DE St. Hedwig Church.
Moley, Kevin *c.ss.r.* '68 (BRK) [107] Brooklyn, NY Our Lady of Perpetual Help Basilica Church.
Molina, Angel '88 (DEN) [A] Denver, CO Redemptoris Mater House of Formation.
Molina, Angel '94 (CGS) [6] Caguas, PR Nuestra Senora del Perpetuo Socorro Church.
Molina, Arturo '83 (LEX) Lexington, KY Federal Medical Center.
Molina, Francisco J. '98 (WDC) [B] Washington, DC Diocesan Laborer Priests, House of Studies.
Molina, Joe '95 (ELP) [40] El Paso, TX Santo Nino De Atocha Church.
Molina, Juan *o.ss.t.* '99 (NY) Mahopac, NY St. John the Evangelist Church.
Molina, Seraphim *s.t.* '97 (WDC) [M] Riverdale, MD Holy Spirit Missionary Cenacle.
Molina-Restrepo, Fernando '99 (ATL) Peachtree City, GA Holy Trinity Catholic Church.
Molinari, Todd '95 (P) Roy, OR St. Francis of Assisi Church.
Molinaro, Kenneth *c.s.c.* '76 (CHI) [D] Niles, IL Notre Dame High School.
Molinaro, Kenneth M. *c.s.c.* '76 (FTW) [J] South Bend, IN Congregation of Holy Cross, Indiana Province, Provincial House.
Molinaro, Matthew J. '49 (LC) Arkansaw, WI St. Joseph Church.
Molinelli, Louis J. *s.d.b.* '90 (SP) [B] St. Petersburg, FL St. Petersburg Catholic High School.
Molini, Thomas M. '85 (STL) [A] St. Louis, MO Kenrick-Glennon Seminary.
Moliski, Wendel *o.f.m.cap.* '50 (PIT) [O] Herman, PA St. Mary's Friary.
Molitor, Donald '63 (STL) [1] University City, MO All Saints Church.
Molka, Victor J., Jr. '78 (PIT) [1] New Castle, PA Mary, Mother of Hope Church.
Moll, Walter J., Jr. '85 (ALT) [1] Portage, PA St. Joseph's Church.
Mollan, Paul '54 (OKL) [1] Oklahoma City, OK Cathedral of Our Lady of Perpetual Help.
Mollan, Paul F. '54 (OKL) Special Assignment.
Mollan, Ralph R. '43 (CHI) [4] Mt. Prospect, IL St. Thomas a Becket Church; Retired.
Molling, Mark L. '80 (MIL) Wales, WI Ethan Allen School for Boys.
Mollohan, J. Lester '51 (CHI) [22] Chicago, IL St. Bartholomew Church.
Mollohan, James L. '51 (CHI) Retired.
Molloy, Msgr. Cronan T. '44 (STU) Minerva, OH St. Gabriel the Archangel Church; Retired.
Molloy, Francis P. *s.j.* '50 (BO) [W] Weston, MA Campion Health Center, Inc.
Molloy, Msgr. James E. '72 (PH) Sellersville, PA St. Agnes Church.
Molloy, John J. *c.p.m.* '46 (L) Glasgow, KY St. Helen Church.
Molloy, Joseph '83 (SFD) Newton, IL St. Thomas Church.
Molloy, Msgr. Patrick J. '40 (STL) Retired.
Molloy, Msgr. Thomas E. *j.c.d.* '70 (RVC) Roosevelt, NY Queen of the Most Holy Rosary Church.
Molnar, Anthony '34 (FTW) Retired.
Molnar, John J. *o.s.a.* '66 (MIL) [9] Kenosha, WI Our Lady of the Holy Rosary Church.
Molnar, Jude *t.o.r.* '65 (WH) [P] Fairmont, WV Fairmont State College Newman Center.
Molnar, Michael '76 (DET) On Duty Outside the Archdiocese.
Molodowitz, Augustine '59 (PHU) Perth Amboy, NJ Assumption of B.V.M. Church.
Molokie, Jerome M. *o.praem.* '95 (ORG) [I] Silverado, CA Norbertine Fathers of Orange Inc.
Moloney, Msgr. Alphonsus '63 (SD) [9] San Diego, CA Immaculate Conception Church.
Moloney, Msgr. James A. '56 (DET) [2] Dearborn Heights, MI St. Anselm Church.
Moloney, John '72 (LA) Downey, CA Our Lady of Perpetual Help Church.
Moloney, John C. '91 (PH) Levittown, PA Queen of the Universe Church.
Moloney, Patrick W. '77 (NTN) Leave of Absence.
Moloney, Sean '58 (SAC) Retired and in Senior Ministry.
Moloney, Msgr. Stephan J. '82 (COL) [39] Columbus, OH Saint Stephen the Martyr Church; Gahanna, OH St. Matthew Church.
Moloney, Thomas J. *s.c.a.* '73 (DET) [3] Wyandotte, MI St. Joseph Church.
Molony, Francis J. '42 (NY) Retired; [DD] New York, NY Our Lady of Consolation Residence.
Molter, Richard J. '64 (MIL) [4] Racine, WI St. Edward Church.
Moltesz, Joseph E. *s.j.* '57 (NY) [FF] Staten Island, NY Mount Manresa Jesuit Retreat House.
Molumby, Donald '56 (SFS) Retired.
Molumby, Edward *s.t.* '61 (SB) [8] San Bernardino, CA St. Bernardine Church.
Molumby, Edward J. *s.t.* '93 (SB) [4] San Bernardino, CA Our Lady of Fatima Church.
Molumby, John '77 (SAC) Absent on Leave.
Molumeli, Felix T. *o.m.i.* '86 (CIN) Beavercreek, OH St. Luke Church.
Molyn, John '81 (ALB) Valatie, NY St. John the Baptist Church.
Molyneux, John *c.m.f.* '97 (ATL) Stone Mountain, GA Corpus Christi Church.
Mompoint, Jean-Claude (PH) [72] Philadelphia, PA Incarnation of Our Lord Church.
Monacell, Cornelius J. *s.j.* '59 (SJ) [L] Los Gatos, CA Sacred Heart Jesuit Center.
Monaco, David *c.p.* '90 (CHI) [N] Chicago, IL Passionist Community-CTU.
Monaco, James M. '85 (BUF) [6] Tonawanda, NY St. Francis of Assisi Church.
Monaco, Samuel '88 (NEW) Saddle River Borough, NJ St. Gabriel the Archangel Church.
Monaghan, Msgr. Charles J. '41 (PH) Retired.
Monaghan, Msgr. George '41 (SFR) [K] San Rafael, CA Nazareth House.
Monaghan, George '80 (DAL) Allen, TX St. Jude Church.
Monaghan, Msgr. George D. '41 (SR) Retired.
Monaghan, J. Fergus '72 (SPC) [5] Springfield, MO St. Elizabeth Ann Seton Church.
Monaghan, James *s.j.* '46 (SJ) [L] Los Gatos, CA Sacred Heart Jesuit Center.
Monaghan, John Joe *l.c.* '75 (SAC) [5] Sacramento, CA Our Lady of Guadalupe Church.
Monaghan, John T. '63 (NY) [E] New York, NY Cardinal Spellman High School.
Monaghan, Joseph F. *s.j.* '52 (BAL) [S] Baltimore, MD Jesuit Fathers and Brothers Maryland Provincial Curia.
Monaghan, Justin D. '66 (SPC) Joplin, MO St. Mary Church.
Monaghan, Robert '62 (STP) [9] Minneapolis, MN Incarnation Church.
Monaghan, Thomas J. '70 (MAD) Reedsburg, WI Sacred Heart Church.
Monagle, Robert J. '91 (BO) [4] Quincy, MA St. Joseph Church.
Monahan, David F. '53 (OKL) Pauls Valley, OK St. Catherine of Siena Church.
Monahan, George J. '97 (PH) [115] Philadelphia, PA Our Lady of Calvary Church.
Monahan, Hugh F. '68 (KC) Leave of Absence.
Monahan, John C. *s.j.* '99 (NOR) [5] Norwich, CT SS. Peter and Paul Church.
Monahan, Joseph *t.o.r.* (PIT) Allegheny County, PA Mercy Health System of Pittsburgh-Pittsburgh Mercy Hospital.
Monahan, Joseph *t.o.r.* '90 (PIT) [O] Pittsburgh, PA Third Order Regular of Saint Francis - Province of the Most Sacred Heart of Jesus.
Monahan, Joseph E. '77 (DEN) Golden, CO St. Joseph Church.
Monahan, Joseph R. '62 (STL) Ballwin, MO Holy Infant Church.
Monahan, Kieran *o.f.m.* '65 (ALB) Palenville, NY Sacred Heart Church.
Monahan, Paul '60 (DM) Glenwood, IA Our Lady of the Holy Rosary Church.
Monahan, Richard J. '59 (BGP) Retired.
Monahan, Thomas J. '58 (RCK) Retired.
Monan, J. Donald *s.j.* '55 (BO) [W] Chestnut Hill, MA The Jesuit Community at Boston College.
Moncada, Fabio '81 (SJN) [1] Canovanas, PR Nuestra Senora del Pilar Church.
Moncher, Raymond F. '58 (MAR) Wakefield, MI Immaculate Conception of the Blessed Virgin Mary Church; Retired.
Monclova, Michael '97 (PEO) Havana, IL St. Patrick's Church.
Mondello, Donald J. '60 (GBG) [1] Latrobe, PA Holy Family Church.
Mondik, Michael '73 (PSC) Minersville, PA SS. Peter and Paul Church.
Mondor, Christian *o.f.m.* '51 (ORG) [3] Huntington Beach, CA SS. Simon and Jude Church.
Mondragon, Antonio '63 (SFE) [13] Albuquerque, NM

Prince of Peace Catholic Community Church.
Mondragon, Ezequiel '62 (DET) Imlay City, MI Sacred Heart Church.
Mondzelewski, Dominic *o.s.b.* '69 (CLV) [42] Cleveland, OH St. Lawrence Church; [D] Cleveland, OH Benedictine High School; [O] Cleveland, OH Benedictine Order of Cleveland.
Moneck, George J. '89 (PIT) Roscoe, PA St. Joseph Church; Green County, PA State Correctional Institute at Green.
Monestero, John '75 (ORG) Anaheim, CA St. Justin Martyr Church; Absent on Sick Leave.
Monestime, Perard C. *s.j.* '85 (BO) [E] Boston, MA Boston College High School & Jesuit Community.
Monet, Zachary *o.carm.* '60 (NEW) Paramus, NJ Carmelite Chapel of St. Therese Church.
Moneta, Msgr. Robert G. '51 (PSC) Newark, NJ St. George Church.
Monette, Michael '99 (MAN) [2] Berlin, NH Good Shepherd Church.
Moneypenny, John W. '98 (ORG) La Habra, CA Our Lady of Guadalupe Church.
Monforton, Jeffrey M. '94 (DET) Special Assignment.
Mongelluzzo, Msgr. James A. (WOR) On Duty Outside the Diocese.
Mongeon, Peter M. '83 (NO) On Medical Leave of Absence.
Mongiello, Anthony P. '80 (ALN) Tamaqua, PA St. Jerome Church.
Mongiello, Robert '87 (VEN) Punta Gorda, FL Sacred Heart Church.
Moni, Fozar David (RVC) Northport, NY Veteran's Administration Hospital.
Moniuk, Evhen '92 (PHU) [5] Philadelphia, PA St. Nicholas Church.
Moniz, Hyacinth '40 (PRO) Retired.
Moniz, Joseph V. '64 (LA) Pasadena, CA St. Philip the Apostle Church.
Monnens, Merle W. '56 (NU) Retired.
Monnerat, Brian W. '88 (HRT) Forestville, CT St. Matthew Church.
Monnig, Francis R. '60 (CIN) Camden, OH St. Mary's Church.
Monnin, Robert J. '55 (CIN) Retired.
Monogue, Michael G. '85 (STP) [16] Minneapolis, MN St. Anne Church.
Monohan, Duncan W. '77 (SD) Winterhaven, CA St. Thomas Church.
Monostori, Benedict *o.cist.* '44 (DAL) [K] Irving, TX Cistercian Abbey of Our Lady of Dallas.
Monreal, Jesus *o.carm.* '69 (ARE) Morovis, PR Nuestra Senora del Carmen Church.
Monroe, Charles F. '75 (WOR) [8] Worcester, MA Our Lady of the Angels Church.
Monroe, Clement J. *c.ss.r.* '53 (BR) [F] Baton Rouge, LA Our Lady of the Lake Regional Medical Center.
Monroe, Edward *c.ss.r.* '61 (MIL) [S] Oconomowoc, WI The Redemptorist Retreat Center.
Monroe, Edward F. *c.ss.r.* (MIL) [1] Sheboygan, WI St. Clement Church.
Monsalve, Alfred (BO) [8] Cambridge, MA St. Mary of the Annunciation Church.
Monsalve, German Barona *m.s.c.* '86 (FgM) Missionaries of the Sacred Heart Foreign Missions.
Monshau, Michael *o.p.* (OAK) [A] Berkeley, CA Dominican School of Philosophy and Theology.
Monshau, Michael *o.p.* '88 (DET) [A] Orchard Lake, MI SS. Cyril and Methodius Seminary.
Monsour, Raymond G. '63 (STP) Le Center, MN St. Mary Church.
Montag, Bernard J. '32 (SC) Retired.
Montag, John *s.j.* '93 (BO) [W] Chestnut Hill, MA The Jesuit Community at Boston College.
Montague, George *s.m.* '51 (STL) [P] St. Louis, MO Provincialate of the Society of Mary, Province of St. Louis.
Montague, George *s.m.* '58 (SAT) [C] San Antonio, TX St. Mary's University of San Antonio, Texas; [U] San Antonio, TX Brothers of the Beloved Disciplel.
Montague, George T. *s.m.* '58 (SAT) [M] San Antonio, TX Casa San Juan Marianist Community.
Montague, Hugh *s.o.cist.* '82 (ALN) [K] New Ringgold, PA Cistercian Conventual Priory, St. Mary's Priory.
Montalbano, Frank *o.m.i.* '47 (NO) [1] New Orleans, LA St. Louis Church; [A] New Orleans, LA Notre Dame Seminary Graduate School of Theology.
Montalbano, Joseph E. '55 (ALX) Retired.
Montanaro, Guido G. '69 (BGP) [10] Bridgeport, CT Holy Rosary Church.
Montanaro, James *o.m.v.* '83 (BO) [W] Milton, MA Oblate Residence (St. Joseph House).
Montano, Angel '92 (CC) Alice, TX St. Joseph Church.
Montano, Msgr. Edward J. '45 (NY) Retired.
Montavon, Thomas G. '61 (CLV) Brunswick, OH St. Colette Church.
Montcalm, Msgr. Rosario L.U. '36 (SPR) Retired.
Montecaldo, Carlo '73 (BEL) [J] Scott AFB, IL Scott Air Force Base.
Montecalvo, Carlo F. '73 (PRO) On Duty Outside the Diocese.
Montecino, Henry R. *s.j.* '47 (LAF) [J] Grand Coteau, LA Jesuit Spirituality Center (St. Charles College).
Monteiro, Alfredo '73 (NY) [116] New York, NY St. Teresa Church.
Monteiro, Galdino *s.f.x.* (P) Independence, OR St. Patrick Church; [P] Portland, OR University of Portland.
Monteiro, Ralph *o.s.a.* '66 (SR) Hoopa, CA Mission of Blessed Kateri Tekakwitha Church.
Montejano, John (LA) Norwalk, CA St. Linus Church.
Montelaro, Thomas (LAF) Plaisance, LA St. Joseph Church.
Montelaro, Thomas '75 (LAF) Chataignier, LA Our Lady of Mount Carmel Church; Absent on Sick Leave.
Monteleone, Jacob '75 (SP) [2] Clearwater, FL Light of Christ Church.
Monteleone, Pascal A. '72 (PH) Wayne, PA St. Katharine of Siena Church.
Montella, Alban V. *o.f.m.* '55 (NY) [DD] Mount Vernon, NY St. Bernardine of Siena Friary.
Montemayor, Ted *s.d.b.* '83 (LA) [Q] Los Angeles, CA Dominic Savio Salesian Residence.
Montenegro, Blas *o.a.r.* '49 (NY) [157] Bronx, NY St. John Vianney, Cure of Ars Church.
Montenegro, Mercurio *m.s.c.* '71 (GAL) [41] Houston, TX St. John Vianney Church.
Montero, Basilio '77 (NY) [C] New Rochelle, NY College of New Rochelle.
Montero, Eduardo G. '73 (PH) [L] Philadelphia, PA St. Vincent's Orphanage Tacony; [FF] Philadelphia, PA St. Vincent's Orphan Asylum-St. Vincent's Comprehensive Emergency Shelter Program.
Montero, Eduardo G. '83 (PH) [12] Philadelphia, PA Annunciation B.V.M. Church; [Y] Philadelphia, PA Sacred Heart Manor.
Montero, Hugo L. '91 (STP) [9] St. Paul, MN Our Lady of Guadalupe Church.
Monterosa, Juan Francisco Molina '98 (WDC) Mount Rainier, MD St. James Church.
Montes, Jesse *s.d.b.* (OAK) [E] Richmond, CA Salesian High School.
Montesanti, Steven G. (MAN) Manchester, NH Hillsborough County Jail.
Montesanti, Steven G. '99 (MAN) [12] Manchester, NH St. Marie Church; [17] Manchester, NH Sacred Heart of Jesus Church.
Montesi, Eugene *s.x.* '62 (BO) [W] Holliston, MA Xaverian Missionaries.
Montesino, Efrain '85 (ARE) [5] Vega-Baja, PR Parroquia de San Martin de Porres Church.
Montez, Paul J. *o.s.b.* '97 (PBL) [G] Canon City, CO Holy Cross Abbey.
Montfort, Raul '96 (PH) [155] Philadelphia, PA St. Veronica Church.
Montgomery, Matthias *o.c.d.* '62 (MIL) [P] Holy Hill, WI Discalced Carmelite Monastery.
Montgomery, William L. '79 (WDC) Special Ministries; [D] Washington, DC Archbishop Carroll High School.
Monti, Dominic V. *o.f.m.* '71 (WDC) [M] Silver Spring, MD Gemelli House; [U] West Bethesda, MD Missionaries of the Kingship of Christ.
Monti, Robert '61 (MIA) [G] Fort Lauderdale, FL Holy Cross Hospital.
Monti, Robert M. '61 (LC) On Duty Outside the Diocese.
Monticello, Msgr. Robert V. '51 (DET) Retired.
Montiel, Jose (FRS) Mariposa, CA Mt. Bullion Conservation Camp.
Montiel, Jose M. '57 (FRS) Merced, CA Sacred Heart Church.
Montminy, Marc R. '77 (MAN) [12] Manchester, NH St. Marie Church; [17] Manchester, NH Sacred Heart of Jesus Church.
Montminy, Paul D. '78 (MAN) Gonic, NH St. Leo Church; Rochester, NH Holy Rosary Church.
Montondon, Walter '57 (BEA) Retired.
Montoya, Ernest '89 (LA) [12] Long Beach, CA Our Lady of Refuge Church.
Montoya, Ernest '89 (SFE) Retired.
Montoya, Francisco '00 (SAL) [1] Salina, KS Cathedral of the Sacred Heart.
Montoya, Jesus '63 (SLC) Brigham City, UT St. Henry Church.
Montoya, Jose J. '57 (PBL) Retired.
Montoya, Jose J. '86 (MRY) [3] Salinas, CA St. Mary of the Nativity Church.
Montoya, Juan *o.f.m.* '81 (LSC) Roswell, NM St. John the Baptist Church.
Montoya, Juan '89 (MIA) Absent on Sick Leave.
Montoya, Msgr. Paul M. '73 (LA) Santa Clarita, CA Our Lady of Perpetual Help Church.
Montplaisir, Roland A. '40 (MAN) Retired.
Montville, Edmund J. *s.j.* '45 (DET) [P] Clarkston, MI Colombiere Center.
Monzillo, Oneil '53 (NO) Retired.
Monzillo, Oneil A. '77 (LAV) [12] Las Vegas, NV St. Joseph, Husband of Mary Church.
Monzon-Tapia, Luis *m.c.c.j.* '95 (FgM) Comboni Foreign Missions.
Moodie, Michael R. *s.j.* '79 (SFR) [E] San Francisco, CA St. Ignatius College Preparatory (Coed); [N] San Francisco, CA Jesuit Community at St. Ignatius College Preparatory.
Moody, Jerome *c.ss.r.* '73 (FgM) Redemptorist Foreign Missions.
Moody, Kenneth J. *m.m.* '70 (NY) [DD] Maryknoll, NY Maryknoll Fathers and Brothers.
Moody, Michael *s.v.d.* '64 (LAF) Plaisance, LA St. Joseph Church.
Moody, Quentin '85 (NO) [63] New Orleans, LA St. Theresa of the Child Jesus Church.
Moody, Thomas A. '67 (OG) Malone, NY St. John Bosco Church.
Moody, William '78 (BAL) Retired.
Moody, William J. (BAL) Frostburg, MD St. Michael Church.
Mooney, Alphonse M. *o.s.m.* '58 (CHI) [N] Chicago, IL Order of Friar Servants of Mary (Servites) United States of America Province, Inc.
Mooney, Dennis M. '77 (PH) [67] Philadelphia, PA St. Hugh of Cluny Church.
Mooney, Msgr. George A. '48 (BRK) Retired.
Mooney, Michael P. '63 (PT) [4] Pensacola, FL Nativity of Our Lord Church.
Mooney, Patrick J. '66 (BGP) Ridgefield, CT St. Mary Church.
Mooney, Richard T. '79 (RIC) Farmville, VA St. Theresa Church.
Mooney, Terence J. *c.m.* '48 (PH) [AA] Philadelphia, PA Congregation of the Mission.
Mooney, Thomas J. '47 (BO) Lakeville, MA Saints Martha and Mary Church; Senior Priests.
Mooney, William '55 (SD) Poway, CA St. Michael Church.
Mooney, William C. '68 (STA) St. Augustine Shores, FL Corpus Christi Church.
Mooney, William J. '68 (PAT) Florham Park, NJ Holy Family Church.
Moons, Joseph *c.p.* '77 (CHI) [N] Chicago, IL Passionist Provincial Office.
Moons, Joseph *c.p.* '77 (FgM) Mission Procurators.
Mooradd, Paul '84 (SAM) Newtown Square, PA St. Sharbel Church.
Moorby, William A. '82 (ROC) Newark Valley, NY St. John the Evangelist Church; Owego, NY St. Patrick Church.
Moore, Andrew '97 (BEA) [2] Beaumont, TX St. Anne Church.
Moore, Anthony F. *o.f.m.* '51 (HRT) Winsted, CT St. Joseph's Church.
Moore, Augustine J. '60 (SFE) Espanola, NM Sacred Heart Church.
Moore, Brian R. '83 (COL) [A] Columbus, OH Pontifical College Josephinum.
Moore, Brian R. '83 (DOD) On Duty Outside the Diocese.
Moore, Christian *o.f.m. conv.* (L) [L] Louisville, KY St. Francis Friary.
Moore, Christian *o.f.m.conv.* '65 (CLV) [1] Lorain, OH St. Anthony of Padua Church.
Moore, Christopher P. '77 (BAL) Hagerstown, MD St. Joseph Church.
Moore, Clarke W. '64 (TUC) Tubac, AZ St. Ann Church.
Moore, Donald C. '65 (OKL) [17] Oklahoma City, OK St. Patrick Church; Special Assignment; [F] Oklahoma City, OK St. Ann's Home Inc.
Moore, Donald J. *s.j.* '60 (NY) [DD] New York, NY West Side Jesuit Community.
Moore, Msgr. Edmund J. '59 (SHP) [1] Monroe, LA Jesus the Good Shepherd Church; Retired.
Moore, Edmund R. *o.f.m.* '45 (L) [L] Louisville, KY Bishop David Apartments.
Moore, Edward F. '59 (BUR) Retired.
Moore, Frederick B. '80 (DET) [H] Pontiac, MI St. Joseph Mercy - Oakland.
Moore, Frederick Thomas '75 (STA) On Duty Outside the Diocese.
Moore, George B. '66 (PH) [22] Philadelphia, PA St. Benedict Church.
Moore, Gerald T. '39 (SEA) Retired.
Moore, Gregory *o.f.m.conv.* '82 (BAL) [S] Ellicott City, MD Order of Friars Minor Conventual; [S] Ellicott City, MD St. Joseph Cupertino Friary, Friars Minor Conventual of St. Francis of Assisi; [S] Ellicott City, MD Friary of St. Joseph Cupertino.
Moore, Gregory J. *o.p.* '55 (MAD) [3] Madison, WI Blessed Sacrament Church.
Moore, Harold W. '50 (WH) Oak Hill, WV SS. Peter and Paul Church.
Moore, J. Pat '89 (P) Aloha, OR St. Elizabeth Ann Seton Church.
Moore, Msgr. J. Raymond '56 (SD) Retired.
Moore, James (SB) Twentynine Palms, CA Blessed Sacrament Church.
Moore, James '88 (SFE) [16] Albuquerque, NM Sacred Heart Church.
Moore, Msgr. James R. '67 (NY) Crestwood, NY Church of the Annunciation.
Moore, James T. '84 (GAL) [62] Houston, TX Our Lady of Walsingham Church.
Moore, James W. *s.j.* '59 (PH) [C] Philadelphia, PA St. Joseph's University; [AA] Philadelphia, PA Jesuit

Community at St. Joseph's University.
Moore, John '45 (FAR) [E] Fargo, ND Riverview Place.
Moore, John Charles '78 (BAL) Middletown, MD Holy Family Catholic Community Church.
Moore, John E. '45 (FAR) Retired.
Moore, Msgr. John F. '60 (FR) North Falmouth, MA St. Elizabeth Seton Church.
Moore, John J. '57 (FRS) Corcoran, CA Calif. State Prison.
Moore, John J. '57 (GF) Retired.
Moore, John P. *c.p.* '47 (BRK) [V] Jamaica, NY Immaculate Conception Monastery.
Moore, John P. '55 (NY) [52] New York, NY Immaculate Conception Church.
Moore, John R. '64 (RVC) East Islip, NY St. Mary's Church.
Moore, Jon H. '81 (WIN) On Duty Outside the Diocese.
Moore, Joseph P. '71 (BGP) Leave of Absence.
Moore, Lawrence *s.j.* '77 (NO) [C] New Orleans, LA Loyola University New Orleans.
Moore, Manning C. *o.s.f.s.* '67 (WIL) [I] Childs, MD Oblates of St. Francis De Sales.
Moore, Matthias *c.s.sp.* '52 (NO) [40] New Orleans, LA St. John the Baptist Church.
Moore, Michael *o.s.f.s.* (FgM) Oblates of St. Francis de Sales Foreign Missions.
Moore, Michael *s.p.s.* '84 (SJ) [L] Saratoga, CA St. Patrick's Missionary Society.
Moore, Michael '97 (FRS) [6] Bakersfield, CA St. Philip the Apostle Church; [G] Bakersfield, CA Bakersfield College Newman Center.
Moore, Neil '60 (P) Retired.
Moore, Raymond H. '81 (WDC) St. Inigoes, MD St. Peter Claver Church.
Moore, Robert A. '46 (BRK) [36] Brooklyn, NY St. Ephrem's Church; Retired.
Moore, Robert J. *o.c.s.o.* '49 (ROC) [I] Piffard, NY Abbey of the Genesee.
Moore, Robert J. '83 (NY) [165] Bronx, NY St. Mary Star of the Sea Church.
Moore, Steven C. '76 (ANC) [8] Anchorage, AK St. Patrick Church.
Moore, Terence M. '67 (SLC) Draper, UT St. John the Baptist Church.
Moore, Thomas M. *o.s.f.s.* '66 (SAG) [4] Saginaw, MI SS. Simon and Jude Church.
Moore, Timothy *o.carm.* '35 (JOL) [J] Darien, IL Carmelite Provincial Office.
Moore, Timothy *o.carm.* '35 (NEW) Englewood, NJ St. Cecilia's Church.
Moore, Ward P. '72 (NEW) Westwood, NJ St. Andrew's Church.
Moore, Wilbur E. '57 (OKL) Nicoma Park, OK Our Lady of Fatima Church.
Moore, William *ss.cc.* '75 (SB) Chino Hills, CA St. Paul the Apostle Church.
Moore, William C. '68 (STO) [2] Stockton, CA St. Bernadette Church.
Moore, William F. '69 (CAM) Pennsville, NJ Queen of the Apostles Church.
Moorman, Dennis *m.m.* '98 (FgM) Maryknoll Foreign Missions.
Moorman, Raymond J. '46 (STP) Retired.
Moorman, William J. *o.ss.t.* '79 (BAL) [S] Baltimore, MD Holy Trinity Monastery.
Moorman, William J. *o.ss.t.* '79 (WDC) [A] Washington, DC Theological College of the Catholic University of America.
Moors, Clif *s.m.* (BO) Burlington, MA Lahey Hitchcock Medical Center.
Moors, Clifton W. *s.m.* '56 (BO) [10] Lawrence, MA Sacred Heart Church.
Moorse, Dustan *o.s.b.* '78 (SCL) [I] Collegeville, MN St. John's Abbey, of the Order of St. Benedict.
Moortgat, Luke *c.i.c.m.* '65 (FgM) Missionhurst Foreign Missions.
Moosbrugger, Robert *o.m.i.* (CHI) [X] Chicago, IL Oblates for International Pastoral.
Moosbrugger, Robert *o.m.i.* (WDC) [V] Washington, DC Archdiocese of Cotabato.
Moosbrugger, Robert *o.m.i.* '70 (WDC) [M] Washington, DC Missionary Oblates of Mary Immaculate; [M] Washington, DC Oblate College/Center for Mission Studies Community.
Moozhikuzhy, Antony *c.m.i.* '66 (BEA) [9] Port Arthur, TX St. Therese the Little Flower of Jesus Church.
Moquin, Raymond *m.s.* '54 (FR) [H] North Attleboro, MA Madonna Manor Inc.; [I] Attleboro, MA La Salette Shrine.
Mora, Jose Sequeira '00 (CHI) [160] Chicago, IL St. Pancratius Church.
Mora, Juan R. '92 (ARE) Corozal-Padilla, PR Our Lady of the Seven Sorrows Church.
Mora, Pablo *s.j.* (CHI) [J] Chicago, IL Holy Cross Hospital.
Mora, Santiago A. *t.o.r.* (CHR) Spartanburg, SC St. Paul the Apostle Church.
Mora, Tito Medina *m.s.c.* '92 (FgM) Missionaries of the Sacred Heart Foreign Missions.
Moraczewski, Albert *o.p.* '54 (GAL) [36] Houston, TX Holy Rosary Church.
Moraczewski, Albert S. *o.p.* '54 (BO) [FF] Brighton/Boston, MA National Catholic Bioethics Center.
Moraczewski, Albert S. *o.p.* '54 (GAL) [Q] Houston, TX Dominican Fathers and Brothers, St. Mark Priory, Inc.
Moraes, Claudio *o.s.b.* '84 (GBG) [H] Latrobe, PA Saint Vincent Archabbey.
Moraga, Cecilio T. '84 (SD) Holtville, CA St. Joseph Church.
Moraghan, Vincent '65 (CLV) Cleveland, OH Cleveland Clinic Foundation.
Moraghan, Vincent J. '65 (CLV) [77] Cleveland, OH St. Vitus Church.
Moragne, Msgr. James C. '75 (NO) Paradis, LA St. John the Baptist Church.
Moral, Alejandro *o.c.d.* '60 (CGS) [2] Caguas, PR San Jose Church.
Morales, Angel L. '83 (ARE) On Duty Outside the Diocese.
Morales, Angel Luis '83 (SJN) Dorado, PR San Antonio de Padua Church.
Morales, Anibal '93 (MIA) [5] Hialeah, FL St. John the Apostle Church.
Morales, Antonio '96 (NY) [186] Bronx, NY St. Rita of Cascia Church.
Morales, Carlos R. *o.s.a.* '88 (SJN) [15] Bayamon, PR Ntra. Sra. de la Monserrate Church.
Morales, Dan '90 (VIC) Port Lavaca, TX Our Lady of the Gulf Church.
Morales, Eduardo D. '96 (SAT) Comfort, TX Sacred Heart Church.
Morales, Msgr. Elias '91 (PCE) [16] Ponce, PR Church of the Good Shepherd; [B] Ponce, PR The Pontifical Catholic University of Puerto Rico.
Morales, Eusebio Ramos '83 (CGS) Humacao, PR Dulce Nombre de Jesus Church.
Morales, Gonzalo '85 (FWT) Bridgeport, TX St. John the Baptizer Church; Decatur, TX Assumption of the Blessed Virgin Mary Church; Jacksboro, TX St. Mary Church.
Morales, Guillermo '88 (AMA) Canadian, TX Sacred Heart Church.
Morales, Msgr. John F. '60 (GRY) Retired.
Morales, Juan Bautista '83 (MGZ) Moca, PR Our Lady of Monserrate Church.
Morales, Manuel (MET) Martinsville, NJ Blessed Sacrament Church.
Morales, Orlando (BO) [2] Lawrence, MA Asuncion de la Virgen Maria Church.
Morales, Oscar *o.p.* '89 (SJN) Catano, PR Nuestra Senora del Carmen Church.
Morales, Raul '75 (PHX) Retired.
Morales, Raymond '81 (LA) Van Nuys, CA St. Bridget of Sweden Church.
Morales, Robert P. '66 (BRK) [63] Brooklyn, NY Immaculate Conception of the Blessed Virgin Mary Church.
Morales, Romain G. *c.m.* '64 (STL) [34] St. Louis, MO St. Francis de Sales Church.
Morales, Romain G. *c.m.* '73 (STL) [P] St. Louis, MO Vincentian Community.
Morales, Salomon de Jesus '63 (ARE) Quebradillas, PR San Raphael Church.
Moran, Msgr. Bernard J. '53 (OAK) [22] Oakland, CA St. Theresa of the Infant Jesus (The Little Flower) Church.
Moran, Charles *o.m.i.* '54 (SAT) Del Rio, TX St. Joseph's Church.
Moran, Charles '67 (STU) Absent Without Leave.
Moran, Daniel F. '47 (BO) Middleborough, MA Sacred Heart Church; Senior Priests.
Moran, Edward C. '89 (RIC) Military Chaplains.
Moran, Edward J. '62 (WOR) Shrewsbury, MA St. Anne's Church.
Moran, Edward M. '76 (HRT) [6] West Hartford, CT St. Thomas the Apostle Church.
Moran, Edwin *c.p.* '61 (PIT) [O] Pittsburgh, PA St. Paul of the Cross Monastery; [O] Pittsburgh, PA St. Paul of the Cross Monastery.
Moran, Faustinus *c.p.* '42 (CHI) [N] Chicago, IL Passionist Provincial Office.
Moran, Francis '59 (ORG) Laguna Hills, CA St. Nicholas Church.
Moran, Gerard K. '71 (OAK) [2] Fremont, CA Holy Spirit Church.
Moran, Msgr. J. Thomas '57 (BUF) Youngstown, NY St. Bernard's Church.
Moran, James *c.o.* '89 (ALX) Mansura, LA Our Lady of Prompt Succor Church.
Moran, James *c.o.* '89 (CHR) [E] Rock Hill, SC Oratory of St. Philip Neri, Congregation of the Oratory of Pontifical Rite.
Moran, James E. '59 (NU) Lafayette, MN St. Gregory the Great Church; West Newton Township, MN St. George Church.
Moran, James F. '71 (BO) On Duty Outside the Archdiocese.
Moran, James F. '71 (WDC) Washington, DC National Rehabilitation Hospital.
Moran, James M. '74 (HRT) Wethersfield, CT Incarnation Church.
Moran, Msgr. James P. '45 (GR) [21] Grand Rapids, MI Sacred Heart Church; Retired.
Moran, Msgr. James P. '72 (MET) Three Bridges, NJ St. Elizabeth Ann Seton Church.
Moran, Jim *c.s.p.* '64 (LA) [BB] Los Angeles, CA Archdiocesan Office for Campus Ministry.
Moran, John F. *s.j.* '57 (FgM) Provinces.
Moran, John J. *m.m.* '66 (NY) [DD] Maryknoll, NY Maryknoll Fathers and Brothers.
Moran, John P. *s.s.c.* '50 (FgM) St. Columban's Foreign Mission.
Moran, John V. '53 (MAN) Retired.
Moran, John W. '51 (DUB) Retired.
Moran, Joseph P. '56 (VEN) Retired.
Moran, Joseph P. '71 (HEL) Columbia Falls, MT St. Richard Church.
Moran, Kevin '65 (SEA) Federal Way, WA St. Theresa Church.
Moran, Lawrence J. '52 (IND) [6] Terre Haute, IN St. Patrick Church.
Moran, Leonard J. *s.m.* '45 (WDC) [M] Washington, DC Marist Center.
Moran, Martin O., III '88 (HBG) [K] Harrisburg, PA Catholic Campus Ministry.
Moran, Michael '63 (VNN) Van Nuys, CA Cathedral of St. Mary.
Moran, Michael *s.m.a.* '81 (FgM) Society of African Missions.
Moran, Michael F. '82 (MIL) Brandon, WI St. Brendan Church; Springvale, WI St. Mary Church; Waupun, WI St. Joseph Church.
Moran, Michael J. '58 (NEW) Hillsdale, NJ St. John the Baptist Church.
Moran, Owen '91 (PAT) Chatham, NJ St. Patrick's Church.
Moran, Patrick '43 (JOL) [I] Naperville, IL St. John Vianney Villa.
Moran, Patrick A. '43 (GF) Retired.
Moran, Patrick J. '58 (DUL) [7] Gary-New Duluth, MN St. Elizabeth's Church; [12] Duluth, MN St. Margaret Mary Church.
Moran, Pedro Lopez *c.m.f.* (CGS) [8] Barrio Rio Canas, PR Inmaculado Corazon de Maria Church.
Moran, Msgr. Peter C. '65 (LA) Northridge, CA Our Lady of Lourdes Church.
Moran, Richard S. '98 (BO) [1] Newton, MA St. Bernard Church.
Moran, Robert B. '64 (SJ) Mountain View, CA St. Joseph Church.
Moran, Robert E. '69 (LFT) Hartford City, IN St. John the Evangelist Church; Montpelier, IN St. Margaret of Scotland Church.
Moran, Salvador N. '72 (BR) On Leave.
Moran, Stephen P. '92 (CLV) [3] Parma, OH St. Charles Borromeo Church.
Moran, Terence J. '90 (BO) [1] Boston, MA Cathedral of the Holy Cross; [56] Boston, MA St. Patrick Church.
Moran, Terrance *c.ss.r.* '82 (NY) [78] New York, NY Most Holy Redeemer Church.
Moran, Terrence *c.ss.r.* '82 (NY) [150] Bronx, NY Immaculate Conception Church.
Moran, Thomas *c.m.f.* '55 (CHI) [147] Chicago, IL Our Lady of Guadalupe Church.
Moran, Thomas A. '71 (CHI) Lyons, IL St. Hugh Church.
Moran, Thomas J. '48 (NY) Retired.
Moran, Msgr. Timothy J. '76 (BO) Medway, MA St. Joseph Church.
Moran, Tom '88 (SFR) [1] San Mateo, CA St. Bartholomew Church.
Moran, W. Lawrence *c.s.b.* '46 (GAL) [Q] Sugar Land, TX Basilian Mission Center.
Moran, William L. *c.s.b.* '38 (GAL) [Q] Houston, TX Dillon House.
Morand, Robert '57 (DET) [56] Detroit, MI Our Lady of the Rosary Church.
Moras, Leo '89 (LUB) Snyder, TX Our Lady of Guadalupe Church.
Moratelli, Ronald J. '69 (HBG) [5] Mount Carmel, PA Our Lady of Mount Carmel Church.
Moratiel, Felix *o.s.a.* '62 (SJN) [42] San Juan, PR Ntra. Sra. de la Monserrate Church.
Moraus, Govie '82 (SHP) Retired.
Morawski, Stefan *o.f.m.conv.* '68 (BGP) [14] Bridgeport, CT St. Michael The Archangel Church.
Morbeck, George H. '52 (SPK) Curlew, WA St. Patrick Church; Republic, WA Immaculate Conception Church.
Morbita, Angelo L. '56 (SY) [25] Syracuse, NY Transfiguration Church.
Morciniec, Peter J. '70 (SPC) Pierce City, MO St. Mary Church; Sarcoxie, MO St. Agnes Church.
Mordino, Robert F. '63 (WDC) Special Ministries; [P] Upper Marlboro, MD Our Lady of Mattaponi Youth Retreat and Conference Center.
Moreau, Charles *o.m.i.* '44 (MAN) [K] Colebrook, NH Shrine of Our Lady of Grace.
Moreau, George '51 (ORL) Retired.
Moreau, Maurice *o.f.m.cap.* '98 (NY) New Paltz, NY St. Joseph Church; [DD] New Paltz, NY St. Joseph Friary.
Moreau, Randall '87 (LAF) Ville Platte, LA Our Lady

Queen of All Saints Church.
Moreau, Raymond J. '85 (OG) North Bangor, NY St. Augustine Church.
Moreci, Francis A. '33 (OM) Retired.
Moreeuw, Leroy *c.pp.s.* '68 (CLV) [53] Cleveland, OH Our Lady of Good Counsel Church.
Moreira, Nelson *s.s.j.* '72 (WIL) [L] Clayton, DE St. Joseph's Center for Prayer.
Moreira, Nelson A. *s.s.j.* '72 (BAL) [S] Baltimore, MD St. Joseph Society of the Sacred Heart House of Central Administration.
Morel, Felipe *c.s.c.* '97 (FTW) [B] Notre Dame, IN University of Notre Dame Du Lac; [J] South Bend, IN Congregation of Holy Cross, Indiana Province, Provincial House; [J] Notre Dame, IN Holy Cross Community, Corby Hall, University of Notre Dame.
Morel, John F. *c.i.c.m.* '39 (ARL) Madison, VA Our Lady of the Blue Ridge Church.
Morel, John J. '55 (NEW) Retired.
Morel, Paul A. '78 (WDC) Retired.
Moreland, J. Gordon *s.j.* '64 (ORG) Special Assignment; [L] Orange, CA House of Prayer for Priests.
Morell, Fernando '87 (ARE) Hatillo, PR Our Lady of Mt. Carmel Church.
Morell, J. William *o.m.i.* '70 (SAT) [C] San Antonio, TX Oblate School of Theology; [C] San Antonio, TX The United Colleges of San Antonio.
Morell, William *o.m.i.* '70 (SAT) [M] San Antonio, TX Missionary Oblates of Mary Immaculate.
Morelle, Edmund J. '53 (SY) Verona, NY Our Lady of Good Counsel Church.
Morelli, Attilio '98 (NEW) [3] Union City, NJ Sts. Joseph and Michael Church.
Morelli, Gary '74 (SEA) Kirkland, WA Holy Family Church.
Morelli, Gary '81 (DET) [3] Taylor, MI St. Cyril of Jerusalem Church.
Morello, Carl '83 (CHI) Park Ridge, IL St. Paul of the Cross Church.
Morello, Peter '78 (GLP) On Duty Outside of Diocese.
Morello, Peter '78 (PHX) Phoenix, AZ United States Veterans Affairs Medical Center.
Morello, Sam Anthony *o.c.d.* '62 (DAL) [I] Dallas, TX Mount Carmel Center.
Morelock, George L. '65 (SFD) Hillsboro, IL Graham Correctional Center.
Morency, Raymond P. '87 (PRT) Dexter, ME St. Anne's Church.
Moreno, Antonio *m.g.* '82 (LA) [86] Los Angeles, CA St. Paul Church.
Moreno, David *s.d.b.* '79 (NEW) Mahwah, NJ Immaculate Heart of Mary Church.
Moreno, Hector '92 (RCK) [1] Elgin, IL St. Joseph Church.
Moreno, James '76 (DEN) [11] Denver, CO Holy Family Church.
Moreno, Joaquin *o.f.m.* '81 (SFR) [8] San Francisco, CA St. Boniface Church.
Moreno, Jorge '63 (SD) Brawley, CA Our Lady of Perpetual Help Church.
Moreno, Jose *s.j.* '89 (MIL) [P] Milwaukee, WI Jesuit Community at Marquette University.
Moreno, Joseph F. '86 (BUF) [5] Buffalo, NY All Saints Church.
Moreno, Juan '60 (LSC) [5] Las Cruces, NM St. Genevieve Church.
Moreno, Robert '93 (BUF) Alden, NY Erie County Correctional Facility.
Moreno, Robert '93 (STF) Lancaster, NY St. Basil Church.
Moreno, Msgr. Wilfredo Pena '74 (SJN) [2] Carolina, PR Santa Bernardita Soubirous Church.
Moreshead, Harold D. '55 (PRT) [1] Portland, ME Cathedral of the Immaculate Conception; Retired.
Moreton, Msgr. John '64 (FRS) [4] Fresno, CA Our Lady of Victory Church.
Moretta, Msgr. John T. '68 (LA) [37] Los Angeles, CA Resurrection Church.
Moretti, Msgr. August '54 (LA) Pasadena, CA Assumption of the Blessed Virgin Mary Church.
Moretti, Edward D. '60 (VEN) Bradenton, FL SS. Peter and Paul the Apostles Church.
Moretti, Mark E. '95 (ARL) [8] Alexandria, VA St. Rita's Church.
Morey, Charles W. '80 (SPC) Special Assignment.
Morey, Daniel *o.f.m.* (NY) [13] New York, NY St. Anthony of Padua Church.
Morey, Robert (BAL) Hagerstown, MD St. Mary Church.
Morfeld, Msgr. Frank G. '51 (DEN) [30] Denver, CO St. Francis de Sales Church.
Morfin, Francois J. *c.s.b.* '77 (GAL) [Q] Sugar Land, TX Basilian Mission Center.
Morfin, John N. '67 (GAL) [41] Houston, TX St. John Vianney Church.
Morgan, Arthur '59 (LSC) Special Assignment.
Morgan, Brendan P. '64 (NO) Retired.
Morgan, Charles J. '79 (ALX) Winnsboro, LA St. Mary Church.
Morgan, D. Terrence '76 (STA) [1] St. Augustine, FL Cathedral of St. Augustine; [L] St. Augustine, FL Flagler College Newman Center.
Morgan, Dare J. *s.j.* '53 (SJ) [K] Los Altos, CA Jesuit Retreat House.
Morgan, Drew P. *c.o.* '85 (PIT) [O] Pittsburgh, PA Congregation of the Oratory of St. Philip Neri; [R] Pittsburgh, PA Office for Campus Ministry; [R] Pittsburgh, PA Office for Campus Ministry; [R] Pittsburgh, PA Office for Campus Ministry.
Morgan, Edward J. '37 (CHI) Retired.
Morgan, Edward Thomas *c.ss.r.* '64 (WCH) [F] Wichita, KS Redemptorist Community; [H] Wichita, KS Spiritual Life Center.
Morgan, Francis C. *ss.cc.* (NY) Manhattan, NY U.S.V.A. Medical Center.
Morgan, George *c.m.r.* '88 (MET) [4] Perth Amboy, NJ Our Lady of Fatima Church.
Morgan, George R. *o.s.a.* '66 (BO) Andover, MA St. Augustine Church; [C] North Andover, MA Merrimack College.
Morgan, Guy *o.f.m.* '54 (SP) [O] St. Petersburg, FL St. Anthony Friary.
Morgan, J. P. '91 (ORL) [7] Orlando, FL St. Charles Borromeo Church.
Morgan, James '60 (ALN) [G] Pottsville, PA Good Samaritan Regional Medical Center.
Morgan, James F. *s.j.* '54 (BO) [3] Newton, MA St. Ignatius Church; [W] Chestnut Hill, MA The Jesuit Community at Boston College.
Morgan, Jerome '62 (SAL) Dorrance, KS St. Joseph's Church; Wilson, KS St. Wenceslaus Church.
Morgan, John '58 (OAK) Retired.
Morgan, John A. '40 (ROC) Retired.
Morgan, John W. '58 (B) Hailey, ID St. Charles Borromeo Church; Sun Valley, ID Our Lady of the Snows Church.
Morgan, Joseph A. '81 (OG) [2] Ogdensburg, NY Notre Dame Church; Ogdensburg, NY Riverview Correctional Facility.
Morgan, Jude *ss.cc.* '50 (FR) [I] Fairhaven, MA Sacred Hearts Provincial House.
Morgan, Julian *c.p.* '53 (HRT) [M] West Hartford, CT Holy Family Monastery/Retreat.
Morgan, Leo *o.f.m.cap.* '44 (FgM) Capuchin Foreign Missions.
Morgan, Lynn (BUF) [A] East Aurora, NY Christ the King Seminary.
Morgan, Maron *o.mar.* '95 (SAM) [C] Petersham, MA Most Holy Trinity Monastery.
Morgan, Martin '70 (TLS) Sand Springs, OK St. Patrick's Church.
Morgan, Matthew A. '51 (PMB) [1] Boca Raton, FL Ascension Church.
Morgan, Raymond J. '42 (BRK) Retired; [V] Douglaston, NY Bishop Mugavero Residence.
Morgan, Thomas (SP) Safety Harbor, FL Espiritu Santo Church.
Morgan, Msgr. Thomas '39 (MRY) Retired.
Morgan, Thomas B. '55 (BO) Salisbury, MA Star of the Sea Church.
Morgan, Msgr. Thomas J. '65 (CAM) Haddonfield, NJ Christ the King Church.
Morgan, Walter N. '44 (MIL) Retired.
Morgan, William P. '57 (BUR) Retired.
Morgen, Paul '62 (SFS) Retired.
Morgenthaler, John N. *o.p.* '41 (NO) [25] New Orleans, LA St. Anthony of Padua Church.
Morgera, Michael A. '85 (MEM) [7] Memphis, TN Blessed Sacrament Church; [L] Memphis, TN Society of St. Vincent DePaul.
Morgia, Robustiano D. '76 (NO) Jefferson, LA St. Agnes Church.
Morhous, Robert *o.c.s.o.* '59 (WOR) [N] Spencer, MA St. Joseph's Abbey.
Moriarity, Daniel J. '64 (PH) [111] Philadelphia, PA Nativity of the Blessed Virgin Mary Church; Absent on Sick Leave.
Moriarity, William J. '66 (CHI) [1] Chicago, IL Cathedral of the Holy Name.
Moriarty, Francis *s.s.e.* '45 (VEN) [G] Englewood, FL Society of St. Edmund Residence.
Moriarty, Frederick L. *s.j.* '44 (BO) [W] Chestnut Hill, MA The Jesuit Community at Boston College.
Moriarty, James F. '51 (CHI) Skokie, IL St. Joan of Arc Church; Stickney, IL St. Pius X Church; Retired.
Moriarty, James J. '48 (NY) Pawling, NY St. John the Evangelist Church; Retired.
Moriarty, John (LEX) Salyersville, KY St. Luke Church.
Moriarty, John '62 (JOL) On Duty Outside the Diocese.
Moriarty, John J. '62 (FgM) Society of St. James the Apostle.
Moriarty, John J. *s.j.* '78 (BO) [W] Boston, MA The Society of Jesus of New England-Provincial Offices; [W] Weston, MA Campion Jesuit Community.
Moriarty, John P. '91 (LEX) Prestonsburg, KY St. Martha Church.
Moriarty, Joseph '93 (IND) [11] Indianapolis, IN Our Lady of Lourdes Church.
Moriarty, Mark D. '99 (STP) South St. Paul, MN Holy Trinity Church; South St. Paul, MN St. Augustine Church.
Moriarty, Philip M. '80 (JC) Wien, MO St. Mary of the Angels Church.
Moriarty, Quentin E. *o.p.* '59 (CHI) [N] River Forest, IL St. Thomas Aquinas Priory.
Moriarty, Robert '92 (SLC) [7] Salt Lake City, UT St. Ann Church.
Moriarty, Thomas '92 (RVC) Floral Park, NY Our Lady of Victory Church.
Moriarty, Thomas W. '42 (BO) Senior Priests.
Moriarty, W. Barry *c.m.* '67 (FgM) Vincentian Foreign Missions.
Morillo, Jose '49 (VEN) Absent on Sick Leave.
Morin, Benjamin R. *s.j.* '56 (DET) [P] Clarkston, MI Colombiere Center.
Morin, Eddy J. '99 (PRT) Greenville, ME Holy Family Church.
Morin, Francis P. '73 (PRT) Indian Township, ME St. Ann Church; Perry, ME St. Ann Church.
Morin, Francis P. '75 (PRT) Baileyville, ME St. James the Greater Church.
Morin, George E. '70 (BO) Saugus, MA St. Margaret Church.
Morin, Henri D. '44 (PRO) [11] Woonsocket, RI Precious Blood Church; Retired.
Morin, John *o.m.i.* '51 (BO) [6] Boston, MA St. Angela Church.
Morin, Joseph *c.ss.r.* '64 (LA) Whittier, CA St. Mary of the Assumption Church; [Q] Whittier, CA Redemptorist Fathers Mission House.
Morin, Marius *m.s.a.* '71 (NOR) [F] Cromwell, CT Society of the Missionaries of the Holy Apostles.
Morin, Maurice N. '64 (PRT) Bingham, ME St. Peter's Church.
Morin, Michael J. '88 (LIN) Cortland, NE St. James Church; [C] Lincoln, NE Pius X Central High School; [M] Lincoln, NE Pius X Foundation and Pius X Endowment Fund.
Morin, Robert *o.m.i.* '69 (BEL) [F] Belleville, IL Missionary Oblates of Mary Immaculate - St. Henry's Oblate Residence; [J] Belleville, IL Oblate Preaching Team.
Morin, Msgr. Roger P. '71 (NO) [13] New Orleans, LA Incarnate Word Church.
Morin, Timothy '77 (STP) Lino Lakes, MN St. Joseph Church.
Morin, William L. '38 (GAL) [Q] Houston, TX Dillon House.
Moriones, Francis *o.a.r.* '34 (NY) [B] Suffern, NY Tagaste Monastery.
Morisco, Cyril *o.f.m.* '45 (NY) [DD] New York, NY Franciscan Province of the Immaculate Conception.
Morisette, Alfred *s.j.* '61 (SPK) [C] Spokane, WA Gonzaga University.
Morisette, Richard P. '61 (SY) Vernon, NY Holy Family Church.
Moritz, Msgr. Paul L. '41 (BO) [7] Brockton, MA St. Patrick Church; Senior Priests.
Morlan, Lawrence A. '95 (PEO) [3] Rock Island, IL St. Joseph's Church.
Morley, Edward T. *o.c.s.o.* '83 (ATL) [J] Conyers, GA The Monastery of the Holy Spirit.
Morley, John F. '62 (NEW) [B] South Orange, NJ Seton Hall University; [B] South Orange, NJ Seton Hall University.
Morley, John J. '32 (PH) [142] Philadelphia, PA St. Richard Church; Retired.
Morlino, Paschal A. *o.s.b.* '66 (BAL) [15] Baltimore, MD St. Benedict Church.
Morman, David G. '89 (BIS) Beach, ND St. John the Baptist Church; [F] Sentinel Butte, ND Home On The Range; [J] Sentinel Butte, ND Home On The Range Foundation.
Morman, James '92 (STU) [A] Steubenville, OH Franciscan University of Steubenville; [F] Steubenville, OH Holy Spirit Friary.
Morman, James *t.o.r.* '92 (WDC) [M] Washington, DC St. Louis Friary.
Morman, Kenneth G. '73 (TOL) [8] Toledo, OH Holy Rosary Church; [14] Toledo, OH Sacred Heart of Jesus Church; [39] Toledo, OH St. Stephen Church.
Morman, Wilbert *s.v.d.* '46 (CHI) [B] Techny, IL Divine Word Residence.
Mormando, Franco *s.j.* '93 (BO) [W] Chestnut Hill, MA The Jesuit Community at Boston College.
Moroney, James P. '80 (WOR) On Duty Outside the Diocese.
Moroney, Joseph E. '54 (CHY) [1] Cheyenne, WY St. Mary's Church; Retired.
Moroney, Martin J. '67 (SAC) Rancho Cordova, CA St. John Vianney Church.
Moroney, Michael J. '71 (BR) [16] Baton Rouge, LA Our Lady of Mercy Church.
Moroney, William *m.afr.* '61 (FgM) Missionaries of Africa Foreign Missions.
Morosini, Louis *s.m.* '56 (FgM) Marist Foreign Missions.
Morquillas, Fructuoso (SB) Retired.
Morras, Ignacio '49 (MIA) [5] Hialeah, FL St. John the Apostle Church; Retired.
Morras, Msgr. Xavier '50 (MIA) Coral Gables, FL Little Flower Church.
Morreale, Matthew *o.f.m.* '85 (NY) [175] Bronx, NY Our Lady of Pity Church.

Morrier, David *t.o.r.* '97 (ALT) [A] Loretto, PA St. Francis College; [F] Loretto, PA St. Francis Friary, Third Order Regular of St. Francis of Penance; [H] Hollidaysburg, PA Campus Ministry.
Morrill, Bruce *s.j.* '92 (BO) [W] Chestnut Hill, MA The Jesuit Community at Boston College.
Morrill, Giles '50 (ALB) Retired.
Morris, Alan E. '92 (PIT) Whitehall, PA St. Gabriel of the Sorrowful Virgin Church.
Morris, Alexis P. *o.f.m.* '56 (SP) [O] St. Petersburg, FL St. Anthony Friary.
Morris, Anthony *c.ss.r.* '94 (RIC) [3] Hampton, VA St. Joseph Church.
Morris, C. Eugene '96 (STL) Graduate Studies.
Morris, Charles M. '83 (DET) [1] Wyandotte, MI St. Elizabeth Church; [T] Roseville, MI Cursillos in Christianity Movement of the Archdiocese of Detroit.
Morris, George O. *s.j.* '68 (SPK) [C] Spokane, WA Gonzaga University.
Morris, Gerald R. '70 (MIA) Marathon, FL San Pablo Church.
Morris, James '93 (STF) Salem, MA St. John the Baptist Church.
Morris, James A. '94 (KAL) St. Joseph, MI St. Joseph Church.
Morris, James H. '66 (SFR) San Bruno, CA St. Robert Church.
Morris, James J. '89 (BRK) Absent on Leave.
Morris, John *o.p.* '66 (OAK) [B] Moraga, CA St. Mary's College; [N] Oakland, CA Western Dominican Province.
Morris, Msgr. John E. (PAT) Retired.
Morris, John J. '44 (CHI) Retired.
Morris, John J. *s.j.* '50 (FgM) Provinces.
Morris, John J. '60 (NEW) Military Chaplains.
Morris, John J. *s.j.* '62 (P) [L] Portland, OR Jesuit Provincial Office (Society of Jesus, Oregon Prov.).
Morris, John S. '62 (BO) Permanent Disability.
Morris, Joseph A. *c.m.* '80 (MET) [H] Plainsboro, NJ Vincentian Residence.
Morris, Joseph E. '96 (ATL) Peachtree City, GA Holy Trinity Catholic Church.
Morris, Joseph W. *s.j.* '59 (SLC) East Carbon, UT Good Shepherd Church.
Morris, Ken *c.s.v.* '54 (LAV) Henderson, NV St. Thomas More Church.
Morris, Kenan *o.f.m.* '50 (BO) [Z] Boston, MA Saint Anthony Residence.
Morris, Kevin '97 (IND) Plainfield, IN St. Susanna Church.
Morris, Lester G. '91 (NOR) Middlefield, CT St. Colman Church.
Morris, Loyd '95 (DAL) Wylie, TX St. Anthony Church.
Morris, Michael *o.p.* (OAK) [N] Oakland, CA Dominican Order, Siena House.
Morris, Michael '76 (NEW) [N] Cliffside Park, NJ St. Patrick's Missionary Society.
Morris, Michael '89 (NY) Larchmont, NY St. Augustine Church.
Morris, Michael P. '89 (NY) [140] Bronx, NY St. Francis of Assisi Church.
Morris, Michael T. *o.p.* '77 (OAK) [A] Berkeley, CA Dominican School of Philosophy and Theology; [N] Moraga, CA Dominican Community.
Morris, Msgr. Philip D. *s.t.d.* '63 (NEW) Hillsdale, NJ St. John the Baptist Church.
Morris, Robert '49 (SFD) Retired.
Morris, Robert '91 (SP) [12] Tampa, FL St. Mary Church.
Morris, Robert A. *o.p.* '50 (PRO) [P] Providence, RI St. Thomas Aquinas Priory at Providence College.
Morris, Robert F. '66 (PT) Destin, FL Corpus Christi Church.
Morris, Stephen P. '79 (ALB) Hancock, NY St. Paul the Apostle Church.
Morris, Thomas *o.ss.t.* '67 (BAL) [R] Baltimore, MD Holy Trinity Spiritual Center.
Morris, Thomas A. *o.ss.t.* '81 (BAL) [S] Baltimore, MD Holy Trinity Monastery.
Morris, William S. *s.s.* '31 (BAL) [O] Baltimore, MD St. Charles Villa; [S] Baltimore, MD St. Charles Villa.
Morris, William T. '69 (MET) [B] Watchung, NJ Mount St. Mary Academy.
Morris, William T. '69 (NEW) Rahway, NJ St. Mark's Church.
Morrison, Anselm *a.a.* '48 (BO) [W] Boston, MA Assumptionist Center.
Morrison, Anselm Harry *a.a.* '48 (SP) Dade City, FL St. Rita Church.
Morrison, Carl T. '69 (MIA) Miami Shores, FL St. Martha Church; [G] Miami, FL Mercy Hospital.
Morrison, Craig *o.carm.* '87 (JOL) [J] Darien, IL Carmelite Provincial Office.
Morrison, Craig *o.carm.* '87 (WDC) [B] Washington, DC Whitefriars Hall.
Morrison, Msgr. David J. '54 (ALN) [8] Bethlehem, PA Our Lady of Perpetual Help Church; Retired.
Morrison, Douglas A. '59 (HRT) On Duty Outside the Archdiocese.
Morrison, Francis X. '55 (PH) Retired.
Morrison, James J. '74 (PRT) Scarborough, ME St. Maximilian Kolbe Church.
Morrison, James R. '87 (HT) [2] Houma, LA Annunziata Church.
Morrison, John '92 (SAM) Fayetteville, NC St. Michael the Archangel Church.
Morrison, John A. *s.j.* '36 (NY) [DD] New York, NY Murray-Weigel Hall.
Morrison, Joseph A. *c.m.* '80 (MET) [J] Plainsboro, NJ Vincentian Renewal Center.
Morrison, Larry '79 (RNO) Sun Valley, NV St. Peter Canisius Church.
Morrison, Michael G. *s.j.* '68 (OM) [K] Omaha, NE Jesuit Community at Creighton University.
Morrison, Robert A. '49 (PH) Retired.
Morrison, Thomas A. *o.p.* '55 (CHI) [J] Chicago, IL Holy Cross Hospital; [N] Chicago, IL Dominicans (Provincial Office).
Morrison, Thomas F. '76 (CHR) Chester, SC St. Joseph's Church; Lancaster, SC St. Catherine's Church.
Morrissette, Dominic '45 (JOL) Retired.
Morrissette, Joseph H. '53 (NOR) Retired.
Morrissette, Robert H. '75 (BO) Absent on Leave.
Morrissey, Daniel W. *o.p.* '62 (CHI) [N] Chicago, IL Dominicans (Provincial Office).
Morrissey, Dunstan R. *o.s.b.* '53 (PEO) [A] Peru, IL St. Bede Abbey and Academy.
Morrissey, J. Michael '78 (P) Gresham, OR St. Anne Church.
Morrissey, Msgr. James L. '55 (PEO) Retired.
Morrissey, Jerome V. '47 (PEO) Wenona, IL St. Mary's Church; Retired.
Morrissey, John '63 (PMB) Sebastian, FL St. Sebastian Church.
Morrissey, John J. '37 (DAV) Retired; [M] Davenport, IA St. Vincent Center.
Morrissey, Joseph G. *o.s.f.s.* '77 (WIL) [I] Wilmington, DE Oblates of St. Francis De Sales.
Morrissey, Lawrence P. '57 (PEO) El Paso, IL St. Mary's Church.
Morrissey, Msgr. Michael (DAV) [3] Davenport, IA Holy Family Church.
Morrissey, Michael *s.s.c.* '51 (ORG) Special Assignment; [H] Westminster, CA Korean Catholic Ministry; [I] Westminster, CA Columban Fathers.
Morrissey, Paul F. *s.m.* '75 (STP) [24] St. Paul, MN St. Louis King of France Church.
Morrissey, Philip T. '46 (BGP) Retired.
Morrissey, Robert O. '83 (RVC) New Hyde Park, NY Holy Spirit Church; Ocean Beach, NY Our Lady of the Magnificat Church.
Morrissey, Robert P. '76 (BGP) Ridgefield, CT St. Mary Church.
Morrissey, Thomas E. '61 (FR) [6] Taunton, MA St. James Church.
Morrissy, Patrick *c.ss.r.* '55 (FgM) Redemptorist Foreign Missions.
Morrone, Louis S. *o.p.* '92 (CHI) River Forest, IL St. Vincent Ferrer Church; [N] Chicago, IL Dominicans (Provincial Office).
Morrow, Brian '80 (DEN) Longmont, CO St. John the Baptist Church.
Morrow, Dennis '75 (GR) [20] Grand Rapids, MI SS. Peter and Paul Church; On Special Assignment.
Morrow, Michael J. '86 (NY) [135] Bronx, NY St. Brendan Church.
Morrow, Richard B. '55 (ATL) [1] Atlanta, GA Cathedral of Christ the King; Retired.
Morrow, Thomas G. '82 (WDC) [4] Silver Spring, MD St. Catherine Laboure Church.
Morrow, Thomas O. '71 (BRK) Absent on Leave.
Morry, Matthew F. *o.p.* '50 (PRO) [P] Providence, RI St. Thomas Aquinas Priory at Providence College.
Morse, Frederick H. '95 (PRT) [7] Portland, ME Sacred Heart/St. Dominic Church; [8] Portland, ME St. Christopher's Church; [M] Portland, ME University of Southern Maine.
Morse, James E. *s.j.* '50 (SJ) [D] San Jose, CA Bellarmine College Preparatory.
Morse, James H. '67 (FR) Centerville, MA Our Lady of Victory Church.
Morse, John *s.j.* '61 (YAK) Moses Lake, WA Our Lady of Fatima Church; Warden, WA Queen of All Saints Church.
Morse, John A. '52 (STL) Retired.
Morse, Jonathan '88 (STF) Special Assignment; [F] Stamford, CT Missionary Sisters of Mother of God.
Morse, Michael '84 (STA) Branford, FL San Juan Church; Lake City, FL Epiphany Church.
Morse, Richard E. *o.s.f.s.* '69 (STO) Manteca, CA St. Anthony Church.
Mort, Ernest C. *c.s.p.* '59 (NY) [DD] Jamaica Estates, NY Paulist Fathers Generalate.
Mortell, Anthony *s.s.c.* '60 (LA) [Q] Los Angeles, CA Columban Fathers, Procure House.
Mortimer, Msgr. James E. '52 (PH) [158] Philadelphia, PA St. William Church.
Morton, Jake *s.j.* '75 (SPK) Ford, WA St. Philip Benizi Church; Inchelium, WA St. Michael's Church; Wellpinit, WA Sacred Heart Church; Westend, WA Our Lady of Lourdes Church.
Morton, John *c.ss.r.* '52 (OM) [19] Omaha, NE Holy Name Church.
Morton, Vincent R. '86 (SP) Crystal River, FL St. Benedict Church.
Morton, William *s.s.c.* '85 (OM) [K] St. Columbans, NE St. Columban's Foreign Mission Society.
Morvant, Kenneth '61 (OLL) Lafayette, LA Maronite Catholic Community Church.
Morvant, Kenneth R. '61 (LAF) On Special Assignment.
Morvay, Andrew '60 (RC) Buffalo, SD St. Anthony Church; Retired.
Mosbrucker, Jacob A. (P) [37] Portland, OR St. Therese of the Child Jesus Church.
Moscardo, Juan *o.f.m.* (NY) [134] Bronx, NY Blessed Sacrament Church.
Moscaritolo, Mario '64 (KC) Special Assignment.
Moschini, Christopher H. *o.p.* '52 (P) [18] Portland, OR Holy Rosary Parish & Dominican Priory Church.
Mosele, Victor *s.x.* '60 (FgM) Xaverian Foreign Missions.
Mosele, Victor *s.x.* '60 (PAT) [M] Wayne, NJ Xaverian Missionary Fathers.
Moseley, Stan *o.s.b.* '53 (NO) [P] St. Benedict, LA St. Joseph Abbey.
Moseley, Stanley *o.s.b.* '53 (NY) [118] New York, NY St. Thomas More Church.
Moser, Albert *c.s.p.* '60 (OAK) [2] Berkeley, CA Holy Spirit Parish/Newman Hall Church.
Moser, Charles J. *s.m.a.* '32 (ORL) Retired.
Moser, Claudio *o.f.m.* '63 (NY) [DD] New York, NY Franciscan Province of the Immaculate Conception.
Moser, John A. '86 (DUB) Fort Atkinson, IA St. John Nepomucene's Church; Little Turkey, IA Assumption of the B. V. M. Church; Protivin, IA Holy Trinity Church.
Moser, Thomas W. '94 (KNX) Dunlap, TN Shepherd of the Valley Church; South Pittsburg, TN Our Lady of Lourdes Church.
Moser, Victor G. '46 (KC) Retired.
Moses, Robert '99 (ORL) [4] Lakeland, FL St. Joseph's Church.
Mosey, Douglas L. *c.s.b.* '74 (NOR) [A] Cromwell, CT Holy Apostles College and Seminary; [L] Cromwell, CT Basilian Fathers of Connecticut, Inc.
Mosher, Mark '88 (SAC) Absent on Leave.
Mosher, Robert E. *s.s.c.* '82 (FgM) St. Columban's Foreign Mission.
Mosher, Thomas L. '81 (BUR) Essex Junction, VT Holy Family Church.
Mosimann, John P. '97 (ARL) Manassas, VA All Saints Church.
Moskal, Joseph E. '65 (SY) Camden, NY St. John Church; Florence, NY St. Mary Church.
Mosko, Msgr. Leon A. '56 (STF) Special Assignment.
Moskus, John T. '63 (HRT) [1] Milford, CT Christ the Redeemer Church.
Moslener, Robert E. '76 (GBG) Sagamore, PA Sacred Heart Church; Yatesboro, PA St. Mary Church.
Mosley, Charles A. '85 (GRY) Griffith, IN St. Mary Church.
Mosley, Daniel E. '77 (STL) Berger, MO St. Paul Church; New Haven, MO Assumption Church.
Mosley, Msgr. Godfrey '79 (WDC) Oxon Hill, MD St. Columba Church.
Moss, Msgr. Charles T. '58 (ALN) West Bangor, PA St. Roch Church.
Moss, Darius G.C. '97 (HBG) [1] Mount Carmel, PA Divine Redeemer Church.
Moss, Donald G. '86 (AUS) Military Chaplains.
Moss, James '82 (STA) [21] Jacksonville, FL San Jose Church.
Moss, James T. (PAT) On Duty Outside the Diocese.
Moss, Ray '86 (CHY) Laramie, WY St. Laurence O'Toole Church.
Moss, Robert D. '69 (BUF) Sloan, NY St. Andrew Church.
Moss, Robert H. *c.s.c.* '74 (FTW) [B] Notre Dame, IN University of Notre Dame Du Lac; [J] Notre Dame, IN Holy Cross Community, Corby Hall, University of Notre Dame.
Mossett, Robert C. *o.s.f.s.* '65 (DET) [1] Monroe, MI St. Anne Church.
Mossi, John P. *s.j.* '73 (SPK) [C] Spokane, WA Gonzaga University.
Mossing, Msgr. Lawrence A. '40 (TOL) Retired.
Mosskolder, Francis *p.i.m.e.* '88 (DET) [K] Detroit, MI P.I.M.E. College Community; [K] Detroit, MI P.I.M.E. Missionaries of SS. Peter and Paul.
Mostardi, Joseph S. *o.s.a.* (PH) [AA] Villanova, PA Fray de Leon Community.
Moster, Humbert *o.f.m.* '57 (CIN) [M] Cincinnati, OH St. Francis Seraph Friary.
Moster, Humbert *o.f.m.* '57 (FgM) Franciscan Foreign Missions.
Moster, James *o.f.m.cap.* '76 (KCK) [H] Lawrence, KS St. Conrad's Friary.
Moszur, Edward J. '71 (GRY) Highland, IN Our Lady of Grace Church.
Motherway, Thomas F. '69 (BO) Permanent Disability.
Motl, James R. *o.p.* '62 (STP) [15] Minneapolis, MN St. Albert the Great Church; [A] St. Paul, MN The Saint

Paul Seminary; [C] St. Paul, MN University of St. Thomas.
Motolinia, Arturo *o.s.a.* '82 (NY) [40] New York, NY St. Gregory Church.
Motsay, Joseph R. '78 (SCR) Military Chaplains.
Motsay, Russell E. '72 (SCR) Carbondale, PA Our Lady of Mt. Carmel Church.
Motsett, Msgr. C. Bourke '34 (PEO) Retired.
Mott, James O. *o.s.a.* '65 (SD) [H] San Diego, CA Augustinian Community.
Motta, Anthony '63 (ALB) Haines Falls, NY Immaculate Conception Church.
Motta, Msgr. Michael J. '72 (HRT) Wethersfield, CT Incarnation Church; Special and other Archdiocesan Assignment.
Mottau, Robert S. '58 (BO) Senior Priests.
Mottet, Marvin A. '56 (DAV) [1] Davenport, IA Sacred Heart Church; [K] Davenport, IA Thomas Merton House, Inc.; [K] Davenport, IA Interfaith Housing, Ltd.; [K] Davenport, IA East Davenport Development Corporation.
Mottin, Msgr. Charles A. '49 (STL) [S] St. Louis, MO Father Jim's Home; [S] St. Louis, MO Father Dempsey's Hotel, Inc.
Mouannes, Nabil '84 (OLL) San Diego, CA Saint Ephrem Church.
Mouawad, Paul '69 (SAM) Pawtucket, RI Holy Trinity-St. George Church.
Mouch, Msgr. Frank (SP) [H] St. Petersburg, FL St. Petersburg Diocesan Library.
Mouch, Msgr. Frank M. '58 (VEN) Retired.
Moudry, Paul G. '87 (STP) Columbia Heights, MN Immaculate Conception Church.
Moudry, Richard P. '50 (STP) Retired.
Mould, Christopher J. '88 (ARL) Fredericksburg, VA St. Mary Church.
Moulder, John '90 (CHI) [1] Oak Park, IL Ascension Church.
Mountain, Edward C. '47 (WIN) Retired.
Mountain, Harold B. '42 (WIN) Retired.
Mountain, Joseph W. '52 (WIN) Mapleton, MN St. Teresa's Church; Retired.
Mounteer, Louis A. *s.j.* '56 (NY) [DD] New York, NY Murray-Weigel Hall.
Mousbrugger, Edwin A. *s.j.* '36 (DET) [P] Clarkston, MI Colombiere Center.
Mouser, J. Irvin '65 (L) St. Thomas, KY St. Thomas Church; [M] Nerinx, KY Motherhouse and Novitiate of the Sisters of Loretto at the Foot of the Cross.
Moussier, Howard R. *o.s.b.* '65 (BIR) [E] Cullman, AL St. Bernard Abbey.
Moussier, Howard R. *o.s.b.* '65 (MOB) Elberta, AL St. Bartholomew Church.
Moutenot, Charles L. *s.j.* '84 (OAK) [N] Berkeley, CA Jesuit Community at Jesuit School of Theology at Berkeley.
Mouton, Msgr. Charles Burton '49 (LAF) Retired.
Mouton, Msgr. Richard von Phul '55 (LAF) [16] Lafayette, LA St. Pius X Church.
Mouton, Thomas Jason '92 (LAF) [7] Lafayette, LA Our Lady Queen of Peace Church.
Mowatt, John J. '57 (BO) Senior Priests.
Mower, Scott '97 (PRT) Ashland, ME St. Mark's Church.
Mowrer, Patrick '97 (PHX) [1] Phoenix, AZ SS. Simon and Jude Church.
Mowry, Raymond G. '44 (SFS) Retired.
Moy, Francis J. *s.j.* '69 (BGP) [4] Stamford, CT St. Cecilia Church; [P] Fairfield, CT The Fairfield Jesuit Community-Fairfield University.
Moy, Francis J. *s.j.* '69 (BO) [W] Boston, MA The Society of Jesus of New England-Provincial Offices.
Moya, Peter O. '85 (MET) On Duty Outside the Diocese.
Moyano, Felipe '48 (CAM) Pleasantville, NJ St. Peter's Church.
Moyer, Joseph M. *c.s.c.* '94 (NO) [22] New Orleans, LA Sacred Heart of Jesus Church.
Moyer, Msgr. Richard (PHX) [K] Phoenix, AZ The Catholic Tuition Organization of the Diocese of Phoenix.
Moyer, Msgr. Richard W. '64 (PHX) Carefree, AZ Our Lady of Joy Church; Special Assignment.
Moyher, Francis *t.o.r.* '65 (ALT) [F] Loretto, PA Mount Assisi Friary.
Moylan, Thomas (NY) [U] Thornwood, NY Catholic World Mission, Inc.
Moylan, Thomas *l.c.* '69 (MAD) [H] Edgerton, WI Legion of Christ, Inc.
Moyna, James *o.p.* (BRK) [158] Queens, NY Blessed Virgin Mary, Help of Christians Church.
Moyna, James Moneta *o.p.* '70 (NY) [DD] New York, NY St. Vincent Ferrer Priory.
Moyna, John L. '73 (ALB) Coxsackie, NY St. Mary Church; Coxsackie, NY Regional Medical Unit.
Moynihan, Eugene R. *s.s.j.* '57 (GAL) [64] Houston, TX Our Lady Star of the Sea Church.
Moynihan, George F. '74 (CHR) North Myrtle Beach, SC Our Lady Star of the Sea Church.
Moynihan, James M. '57 (SY) Special Assignment; [W] Syracuse, NY David W. Barry Foundation.
Moynihan, Jerimiah P. '74 (ROC) [8] Elmira, NY Our Lady of Lourdes Church.
Moynihan, John C. *m.m.* '67 (CHI) [N] Chicago, IL Maryknoll Fathers & Brothers.
Moynihan, Michael '79 (NY) [GG] New York, NY University Apostolate.
Moynihan, Michael Robert '79 (BGP) [2] Greenwich, CT St. Michael the Archangel Church.
Moynihan, Noel *c.s.s.p.* '77 (BRK) [243] Queens, NY St. Teresa Church.
Moynihan, T. Joseph '57 (BO) Westwood, MA St. Margaret Mary Church.
Moynihan, Timothy '32 (SEA) Retired.
Moyo, Mpumelo *s.j.* '99 (BO) [W] Chestnut Hill, MA The Jesuit Community at Boston College.
Moys, Gregory '64 (P) Grants Pass, OR St. Anne Church.
Mozer, Joseph F. '97 (BO) Duxbury, MA Holy Family Church.
Mozeris, Msgr. Damasus A. '39 (CHI) Retired.
Mozos, Sebastian *o.m.i.* '33 (SAT) [K] San Antonio, TX Oblate Madonna Residence.
MPanda, Appolinaire 'Apo' Tshipamba *c.j.* '88 (DAV) [2] Davenport, IA Our Lady of Victory Church.
Mraz, John S. '75 (ALN) [11] Allentown, PA St. Thomas More Church.
Mraz, Louis *o.s.c.* '59 (PHX) [2] Glendale, AZ St. Helen Church.
Mraz, Louis R. *o.s.c.* '59 (PHX) [G] Phoenix, AZ Crosier Community of Phoenix (Canons Regular of the Order of the Holy Cross).
Mraz, Robert J. '74 (NU) Silver Lake, MN Church of the Holy Family.
Mroczkowski, Msgr. Joseph '42 (CHI) [205] Chicago, IL St. Turibius Church.
Mroczkowski, Joseph A. '45 (LIN) Retired.
Mroczkowski, Msgr. Joseph J. '42 (CHI) Retired.
Mroczkowski, Leonard A. '46 (CAM) Retired.
Mroczynski, Edward *s.chr.* '57 (LA) [24] Los Angeles, CA Our Lady of the Bright Mount Church.
Mrowinski, Charles *c.r.* '55 (CHI) [D] Chicago, IL Gordon Tech High School; [M] Chicago, IL St. Joseph Home of Chicago, Inc.
Mrowka, Chester R. *c.m.* '59 (HRT) [M] Manchester, CT DePaul Provincial Residence.
Mroz, Richard J. '92 (NEW) Oradell, NJ St. Joseph's Church.
Mroziewski, Witold '91 (BRK) [94] Brooklyn, NY Our Lady of Czestochowa-St. Casimir Church.
Mruk, Walter Leon *o.f.m.conv.* '49 (HRT) [M] New Britain, CT Conventual Franciscans; [N] New Britain, CT Motherhouse of Daughters of Mary of the Immaculate Conception.
Msemwa, Severine '75 (ROC) [M] Rochester, NY Diocesan Department of Campus Ministry.
Msemwa, Severine S. (ROC) [5] Elmira, NY St. Casimir Church.
Msongore, Josaphat *c.s.sp.* '63 (FgM) Holy Ghost Foreign Missions.
Mthembu, Mafanisa *o.s.m.* '58 (CHI) [N] Chicago, IL Order of Friar Servants of Mary (Servites) United States of America Province, Inc.
Muc, John *o.cist.* '90 (CHI) [N] Willow Springs, IL Cistercian Fathers, Our Lady Mother of the Church.
Mucci, Flavian *o.f.m.* '63 (FgM) Franciscan Foreign Missions.
Muccilli, Sebastian L. '57 (MET) On Duty Outside the Diocese.
Muccino, Keith F. *s.j.* '96 (WDC) [M] Washington, DC The Jesuit Community at Georgetown University.
Muccitelli, Mario *s.d.v.* '48 (PAT) [M] Florham Park, NJ Father Justin Vocationary.
Mucha, Jan '54 (DEN) [34] Denver, CO St. Joseph's Church.
Mucha, John '53 (STU) [I] Nelsonville, OH Hocking Technical College.
Mucha, John '81 (STU) Glouster, OH Holy Cross Church; Nelsonville, OH St. Mary of the Hills Church.
Mucharski, Francis *o.f.m.cap.* '33 (PAT) [M] Oak Ridge-Milton, NJ St. Stanislaus B. M. Friary.
Muchla, Andrzej *s.d.s.* '95 (GRY) [J] Merrillville, IN Salvatorian Fathers (Society of the Divine Savior).
Muckenhaupt, Gregory F. *s.j.* '88 (CI) [B] Pohnpei, FM PATS (Pohnpei Agriculture and Trade School).
Muckenhaupt, Gregory F. *s.j.* '88 (FgM) Provinces.
Muckerman, Norman J. *c.ss.r.* '42 (STL) [P] Liguori, MO Liguori Mission House/Redemptorists.
Mucowski, Richard *o.f.m.* (KCK) [A] Leavenworth, KS Saint Mary College.
Mucowski, Richard *o.f.m.* '71 (NY) [DD] New York, NY Franciscan Friars, Order of Friars Minor, Holy Name Province.
Mudd, David A. '80 (WDC) Military Chaplains.
Mudd, Earl '60 (BEA) Retired.
Mudd, Gerald R. *o.f.m.* '66 (BO) [BB] Boston, MA St. Anthony Shrine.
Mudd, James T. '64 (L) Hodgenville, KY Our Lady of Mercy Church; Howardstown, KY St. Ann Church.
Mudd, Joachim *o.f.m.i.* '97 (FAR) [F] Pisek, ND Franciscan Friars of Mary Immaculate.
Mudd, John '69 (WDC) Special Ministries; [D] Washington, DC Archbishop Carroll High School.
Mudrak, Lloyd '62 (DUL) Coleraine, MN Mary Immaculate Church; Marble, MN St. Mary's Church.
Mudry, Lubomyr '51 (STF) [A] Stamford, CT St. Basil College.
Mueggenborg, Daniel H. '89 (TLS) [9] Tulsa, OK Church of the Madalene; [H] Tulsa, OK St. Philip Neri Newman Center at The University of Tulsa.
Muehlberger, Howard J. *s.s.e.* '71 (BUR) [4] Burlington, VT St. Joseph's Church.
Muelemans, Thomas O. *o.praem.* '59 (GB) [A] De Pere, WI St. Norbert Abbey.
Mueller, Anthony E. '36 (BRK) Retired; [S] Queens Village, NY Queen of Peace Residence.
Mueller, Charles L. '57 (NO) [6] Metairie, LA St. Christopher the Martyr Church; Metairie, LA East Jefferson General Hospital.
Mueller, Donald R. '61 (TOL) Retired.
Mueller, Eugene J. '56 (CIN) Retired.
Mueller, Gary A. *c.m.* '95 (DEN) [P] Denver, CO Auraria Campus.
Mueller, Gary A. *c.m.* '95 (FgM) Vincentian Foreign Missions.
Mueller, Glenn R. *s.j.* '73 (KC) [13] Kansas City, MO Guardian Angels Church; [J] Kansas City, MO Rockhurst Jesuit Community.
Mueller, James *s.m.* '67 (FWT) [B] Fort Worth, TX Nolan Catholic High School.
Mueller, James *o.carm.* '69 (NEW) Bogota, NJ St. Joseph's Church.
Mueller, James J. '66 (BRK) [152] Queens, NY St. Anthony of Padua Church.
Mueller, John F. *s.m.* '41 (CIN) [M] Huntsville, OH St. George Chapel of Marianist Community.
Mueller, John J. '59 (CLV) Wooster, OH St. Mary of the Immaculate Conception Church.
Mueller, John J. *s.j.* '75 (STL) [C] St. Louis, MO Saint Louis University; [P] St. Louis, MO Jesuit Community Corporation at St. Louis University - Jesuit Hall.
Mueller, Joseph G. *s.j.* '93 (DET) [K] Detroit, MI Jesuit Provincial Office-Detroit Province of the Society of Jesus.
Mueller, Joseph G. *s.j.* '93 (MIL) [P] Milwaukee, WI Jesuit Community at Marquette University.
Mueller, Joseph J. '44 (MIL) Retired.
Mueller, Kevin '92 (BAL) [72] Baltimore, MD Our Lady of Mount Carmel Church.
Mueller, Matthias R. *o.p.* '49 (CHI) [170] Chicago, IL St. Pius V Church; [N] Chicago, IL Dominican Community.
Mueller, Michael '85 (ORL) On Duty Outside the Diocese.
Mueller, Noel *o.s.b.* '68 (IND) [A] St. Meinrad, IN St. Meinrad Seminary; [J] St. Meinrad, IN St. Meinrad Archabbey.
Mueller, Paul R. *s.j.* '93 (CHI) [N] Chicago, IL Miguel Pro Jesuit Community.
Mueller, Richard J. '44 (IND) Retired.
Mueller, Richard J. '63 (CHI) Northbrook, IL St. Norbert Church.
Mueller, Richard J. '66 (PIT) On Duty Outside the Diocese.
Mueller, Richard J. '66 (VEN) [3] Naples, FL St. Peter the Apostle Church.
Mueller, Robert F. '46 (MIL) [8] Milwaukee, WI St. Anthony Church; Retired.
Mueller, Roman *s.d.s.* '74 (BIR) [3] Huntsville, AL St. Joseph's Church.
Muellerleile, Ernest H. '44 (ANC) [5] Anchorage, AK Holy Cross Church.
Muench, Joseph '81 (LEX) Harrodsburg, KY St. Andrew Church.
Muench, R. Francis '81 (RIC) [7] Norfolk, VA St. Pius X Church.
Muench, William G. '59 (OG) Crown Point, NY Sacred Heart Church; Ticonderoga, NY St. Mary Church.
Muerder, Edward E. '58 (BUF) Bliss, NY St. Joseph Church; Java Center, NY St. Patrick Church; North Java, NY St. Nicholas Church.
Muesenfechter, Msgr. Robert J. '51 (STL) Fenton, MO St. Paul Church; Retired.
Muessiggang, Emmanuel *o.f.m.* '33 (OAK) [P] Danville, CA San Damiano Retreat.
Mugabowakigeri, Bernardin '86 (SAC) [7] Sacramento, CA Presentation of the Blessed Virgin Mary Church.
Mugan, William L. *s.j.* '55 (STL) [P] St. Louis, MO Jesuit Community Corporation at St. Louis University - Jesuit Hall; [P] St. Louis, MO The Jesuits of the Missouri Province.
Mugavero, Anthony P. '81 (ROC) [10] Rochester, NY St. Bridget Church.
Muggli, Boniface *o.s.b.* '90 (BIS) [A] Richardton, ND Assumption Abbey; [B] Bismarck, ND University of Mary.
Muggli, Florian *o.s.b.* '51 (SCL) Jacob's Prairie, MN St. James Church; [I] Collegeville, MN St. John's Abbey, of the Order of St. Benedict.
Muggli, Odo *o.s.b.* '66 (BIS) [A] Richardton, ND Assumption Abbey.

Mugo, Simon K. '89 (SY) [3] Endicott, NY St. Anthony of Padua Church; [W] Canastota, NY Catholic Diocese of Nakuru Mission Office, Inc.
Mugonya, Alex '65 (GAY) Manistee, MI St. Joseph Church.
Muguerza, Octavio A. '92 (GAL) [18] Houston, TX St. Cecilia Church; Sealy, TX Immaculate Conception Church.
Muha, Edward J. '45 (HRT) Retired.
Muha, Joseph '60 (B) Chubbuck, ID St. Paul's Church; Pocatello, ID St. Joseph's Church; Pocatello, ID St. Anthony's Church.
Muha, Peter J. '88 (GRY) Lowell, IN St. Edward Church; Shelby, IN St. Theresa Church.
Muheim, Martin de Porres J. *o.s.b.* '88 (PBL) [G] Canon City, CO Holy Cross Abbey.
Muhich, Peter '89 (DUL) Hibbing, MN Blessed Sacrament Church.
Muhlbaier, Howard E. '65 (CAM) Washington Township, NJ SS. Peter and Paul Church.
Muhlen, Micah *o.f.m.* '91 (PHX) [H] Scottsdale, AZ Franciscan Renewal Center, Inc. (Casa de Paz Y Bien).
Muhm, William M. '95 (NY) Military Chaplains.
Muhr, Michael '83 (SP) [2] Tampa, FL Christ the King Church.
Muhs, Edward J. '51 (RVC) Bellmore, NY St. Barnabas the Apostle Church; Retired.
Muir, Edmund D. '49 (DET) Retired.
Muir, Gavin W. '65 (PH) [73] Philadelphia, PA Saint Irenaeus Church.
Muka, John R. *c.s.sp.* '39 (PH) [AA] Bensalem, PA Congregation of the Holy Ghost.
Mukalel, Joseph V. '58 (NEW) Retired.
Mukamba, Benoit *c.s.sp.* (GAL) [13] Houston, TX St. Benedict the Abbot Church.
Mukasa, Michael '96 (OM) [27] Omaha, NE St. Margaret Mary Church.
Mulanjanany, Augustine '69 (LKC) Fenton, LA St. Charles Borromeo Church.
Mulcahey, Andrew *l.c.* '96 (LA) [Q] Pasadena, CA Legionaries of Christ; [BB] Los Angeles, CA Archdiocesan Office for Campus Ministry.
Mulcahey, Timothy *l.c.* '97 (ATL) [J] Atlanta, GA Legionaries of Christ; [N] Atlanta, GA Home and Family, Inc.
Mulcahy, Brian *o.p.* '90 (Y) [13] Youngstown, OH St. Dominic's Church.
Mulcahy, Daniel R., Jr. '79 (WOR) Linwood, MA Good Shepherd Church.
Mulcahy, Msgr. Donal '51 (LA) Retired.
Mulcahy, Gerald F. '62 (CHI) Hickory Hills, IL St. Patricia Church.
Mulcahy, Howard J. '44 (ALB) Retired.
Mulcahy, Msgr. James R. '37 (LA) La Puente, CA St. Louis of France Church; Retired.
Mulcahy, John M. *c.s.c.* '65 (FTW) [J] South Bend, IN Congregation of Holy Cross, Indiana Province, Provincial House.
Mulcahy, Louis *o.s.b.* '89 (IND) [J] St. Meinrad, IN St. Meinrad Archabbey.
Mulcahy, Patrick J. '95 (SD) Vista, CA St. Francis of Assisi Church.
Mulcahy, Richard *s.j.* '46 (SJ) [L] Los Gatos, CA Sacred Heart Jesuit Center.
Mulcahy, Sean '62 (MIA) Hallandale, FL St. Charles Borromeo Church.
Mulcair, William W. *m.s.* '65 (HRT) [M] Hartford, CT Missionaries of LaSalette, Provincial Secretary.
Mulcrone, Charles P. '53 (SFD) Retired; [K] Springfield, IL Priests' Retirement Facility.
Mulcrone, Joseph A. '71 (CHI) [62] Chicago, IL St. Francis Borgia Church; [X] Chicago, IL Catholic Office of the Deaf.
Mulcrone, Thomas A. '77 (CHI) [L] Chicago, IL St. Mary of Providence.
Mulderry, Anthony J. '67 (MIA) Sunrise, FL All Saints Church.
Muldoon, Brendan '64 (SP) Indian Rocks Beach, FL St. Jerome Church; [F] Largo, FL St. Jerome Early Childhood Center.
Muldoon, P. Christopher '71 (PAT) Lake Hopatcong, NJ Our Lady Star of the Sea Church.
Muldowney, James D. '52 (ARL) Retired.
Mulenga, Faustin Misakabo *o.praem.* '80 (GB) [I] De Pere, WI St. Norbert Abbey.
Mulewski, Patrick M. '61 (NEW) Old Tappan, NJ St. Pius X Church.
Mulgrew, John E. '56 (PH) Media, PA St. Mary Magdalen Church.
Mulhall, Msgr. Francis X. '47 (BRK) Retired; [V] Douglaston, NY Bishop Mugavero Residence.
Mulhall, J. Gregory '37 (ALB) Retired.
Mulhall, Michael *o.carm.* (CHI) [66] Chicago, IL St. Gelasius Church.
Mulhauser, Daniel J. *s.j.* (AGN) [F] Yigo, GU St. Ignatius of Loyola House of Studies.
Mulhauser, Daniel J. *s.j.* '60 (FgM) Provinces.
Mulhearn, Michael *c.m.* '68 (KC) [J] Kansas City, MO Vincentian Parish Mission Center.
Mulhern, James P. *o.f.m.* '44 (SP) [O] St. Petersburg, FL St. Anthony Friary.
Mulhern, Joseph Hugh *o.p.* '54 (NY) [DD] New York, NY St. Vincent Ferrer Priory.
Mulhern, Kevin P. '76 (SCR) Honesdale, PA St. John the Evangelist Church.
Mulhern, Patrick J. '64 (ATL) On Sick Leave.
Mulhern, Raymond F. '52 (COV) Retired.
Mulholland, Charles H. '56 (R) Retired.
Mulholland, John '65 (PH) Levittown, PA Immaculate Conception B.V.M. Church.
Mulica, James '67 (CLV) Retired.
Mulka, Arthur C. '51 (GAY) Retired.
Mulka, Raymond C. '49 (GAY) Retired.
Mulkerin, Terrence J. '61 (BRK) Military Chaplains.
Mulkern, Daniel *t.o.r.* '66 (ALT) [F] Loretto, PA Mount Assisi Friary.
Mulkern, John F. '43 (BO) Senior Priests.
Mulkern, Stephen M. '49 (PRT) Retired.
Mull, Thomas P. '76 (ROC) [1] Rochester, NY Sacred Heart Church; Canandaigua, NY St. Mary Church; [L] Rochester, NY Apostleship of Prayer.
Mullady, Brian T. *o.p.* '72 (NOR) [A] Cromwell, CT Holy Apostles College and Seminary.
Mullady, Brian T. *o.p.* '72 (SFR) [14] San Francisco, CA St. Dominic Church; [N] San Francisco, CA St. Dominic Priory.
Mullakkara, Joseph *m.s.f.s.* '75 (ATL) Lawrenceville, GA St. Lawrence Church.
Mullally, Gerald F. '76 (SCR) Milford, PA St. Patrick's Church.
Mullally, Thomas A. *s.v.d.* '70 (LAF) St. Martinville, LA Notre Dame de Perpetuel Secours Church.
Mullaly, Conor *o.f.m.* '53 (PAT) [M] Ringwood, NJ Holy Name Friary, Inc.
Mullan, Glen (CC) [B] Corpus Christi, TX Bishop Garriga Middle School.
Mullan, Patrick '67 (PAT) Retired; [P] Chester, NJ Nazareth Village.
Mullan, Raymund A. '62 (FWT) Graham, TX St. Mary Church; Olney, TX St. Theresa of the Infant Jesus Church.
Mullan, William F. *m.m.* '62 (FgM) Maryknoll Foreign Missions.
Mullane, Bernard J. '56 (RCK) Belvidere, IL St. James Church.
Mullane, Thomas '68 (MIA) Big Pine Key, FL St. Peter Church.
Mullaney, Aidan *t.o.r.* '52 (ARL) [J] White Post, VA Sacred Heart Friary.
Mullaney, Msgr. Bernard '58 (SAT) [K] San Antonio, TX Padua Place.
Mullaney, Cornelius J. '71 (BO) [7] Lynn, MA St. Pius Fifth Church.
Mullaney, Edward John *o.c.s.o.* '73 (WOR) [A] Spencer, MA St. Joseph's Abbey School of Theology and Institute of Monastic Studies; [N] Spencer, MA St. Joseph's Abbey.
Mullaney, Gregory C. '90 (NOR) Gales Ferry, CT Our Lady of Lourdes Church.
Mullaney, Leonard M. '62 (FR) Mattapoisett, MA St. Anthony's Church.
Mullany, Lawrence J. '88 (RIC) Tabb, VA Blessed Kateri Tekawitha Church.
Mullarkey, John T. (GB) Hollandtown, WI St. Francis Church.
Mullarkey, John T. '64 (GB) Kaukauna, WI Holy Cross Church.
Mullarkey, Msgr. Patrick J. '64 (SD) [25] San Diego, CA St. Columba Church.
Mullelly, Thomas J. '80 (TR) [S] Princeton, NJ Campus Ministry for the Diocese of Trenton.
Mullen, Austin M. '65 (SP) [11] Tampa, FL St. Mark the Evangelist Church.
Mullen, Bernard *c.pp.s.* '48 (KC) [J] Liberty, MO Precious Blood Center.
Mullen, Bernard J. '61 (DET) Lake Orion, MI St. Joseph Church.
Mullen, Charles F. *s.j.* '43 (OM) [K] Omaha, NE Jesuit Community at Creighton University.
Mullen, Charles F. *c.pp.s.* '64 (FTW) Rome City, IN St. Gaspar del Bufalo Church.
Mullen, David J. '82 (BO) Bellingham, MA St. Brendan Church.
Mullen, Dennis M. '70 (SUP) Almena, WI Sacred Heart of Jesus Church; Cumberland, WI St. Anthony Abbot Church.
Mullen, Msgr. Edward F. '54 (CAM) Ocean City, NJ St. Augustine's Church.
Mullen, Edward F. '58 (CHR) Retired.
Mullen, Glen '94 (CC) [J] Corpus Christi, TX Search Retreats.
Mullen, Godfrey *o.s.b.* '94 (IND) [J] St. Meinrad, IN St. Meinrad Archabbey.
Mullen, John '52 (WCH) Retired.
Mullen, John J. *s.j.* '62 (BO) [W] Boston, MA The Society of Jesus of New England-Provincial Offices; [W] Weston, MA Campion Jesuit Community.
Mullen, Joseph *o.f.m.cap.* '47 (NY) [B] Beacon, NY St. Lawrence of Brindisi Friary.
Mullen, Joseph A. '48 (BRK) Retired.
Mullen, Joseph E. *s.j.* '50 (BO) [W] Boston, MA The Society of Jesus of New England-Provincial Offices.
Mullen, Joseph E. *s.j.* '50 (SD) Carlsbad, CA St. Patrick Church.
Mullen, Kevin J. *o.f.m.* '80 (NEW) Elmwood Park, NJ St. Leo's Church.
Mullen, Michael '62 (KCK) [14] Kansas City, KS St. Patrick's Church.
Mullen, Michael F. *c.m.* '41 (BRK) [V] Jamaica, NY Vincentian Residence.
Mullen, Owen J. '64 (WIL) Military Chaplains.
Mullen, Patrick '85 (LA) [A] Camarillo, CA St. John's Seminary.
Mullen, Paul M. '73 (SCR) Mountaintop, PA St. Jude's Church.
Mullen, Richard '55 (PEO) Retired.
Mullen, Richard G. *o.s.a.* '81 (FgM) Foreign Missions.
Mullen, Thomas '56 (LKC) On Duty Outside the Diocese.
Mullen, Thomas J. *ss.cc.* '75 (LA) San Dimas, CA Holy Name of Mary Church.
Mullen, Timothy F. *o.praem.* '73 (WIL) [B] Claymont, DE Archmere Academy; [I] Claymont, DE Immaculate Conception Priory of the Canons Regular of Premontre.
Mullen, William *o.m.v.* '92 (BO) [W] Milton, MA Oblate Residence (St. Joseph House); [BB] Boston, MA St. Francis Chapel.
Mullen, William E. '76 (ALT) Cresson, PA St. Aloysius Church.
Mullen, Msgr. William J. '47 (OAK) Retired; Retired.
Mullen, Msgr. William J. '51 (HRT) [4] West Hartford, CT St. Mark the Evangelist Church.
Mullenkuzhy, Abraham *m.s.f.s.* '63 (ATL) Norcross, GA Saint Patrick's Church.
Muller, Anthony '68 (CIN) [70] Cincinnati, OH Our Lord, Christ the King Church.
Muller, Francis J. *o.f.m.* '42 (NY) [35] New York, NY St. Francis of Assisi Church.
Muller, Herman J. *s.j.* '41 (DET) [K] Detroit, MI Jesuit Community at the University of Detroit.
Muller, Joseph *m.s.c.* '58 (RCK) [G] Aurora, IL Missionaries of the Sacred Heart Community.
Muller, Joseph T. *m.s.c.* '58 (RCK) [10] Aurora, IL St. Therese of Jesus Church.
Muller, Kennard '66 (BAL) Retired.
Muller, Martin M. '57 (BIR) [17] Birmingham, AL Our Lady of Sorrows Church.
Muller, Myles '48 (BAL) Retired; [O] Timonium, MD Stella Maris.
Muller, Peter D. *o.praem.* '93 (ORG) [I] Silverado, CA Norbertine Fathers of Orange Inc.
Muller, William H. *s.j.* '73 (SJ) [D] San Jose, CA Bellarmine College Preparatory.
Mullet, John '56 (SAG) On Duty Outside the Diocese.
Mullet, John '91 (MIA) [G] Fort Lauderdale, FL Holy Cross Hospital.
Mullet, John '91 (PMB) [D] West Palm Beach, FL St. Mary's Foundation of Palm Beach County, Inc.
Mullett, Msgr. Gene W. '76 (STU) Bellaire, OH St. John Church; Bellaire, OH St. Michael's Church.
Mulligan, Bede J.K. *o.carm.* '58 (GBG) [H] Boliver, PA Mount Carmel Hermitage.
Mulligan, Bernard *c.ss.r.* '42 (SEA) [32] Seattle, WA Sacred Heart of Jesus Church.
Mulligan, Bertram *o.f.m.cap.* '49 (SFR) [N] Burlingame, CA Capuchin Provincial House.
Mulligan, Charles '64 (ROC) Absent on Leave.
Mulligan, Colm *m.s.c.* '58 (SAT) [M] San Antonio, TX Missionaries of the Sacred Heart.
Mulligan, Msgr. Edward '56 (SP) Retired.
Mulligan, Emmett *o.f.m.* '52 (PMB) [D] West Palm Beach, FL St. Mary's Foundation of Palm Beach County, Inc.
Mulligan, George B. *c.s.c.* '82 (FR) [A] North Easton, MA Stonehill College; [A] North Easton, MA Holy Cross Fathers Religious.
Mulligan, Msgr. James J. '61 (ALN) Northampton, PA Our Lady of Hungary Church.
Mulligan, James J. '66 (PH) [40] Philadelphia, PA St. Dominic Church.
Mulligan, John D. *s.m.* '57 (CIN) [M] Dayton, OH Marianist Provincialate.
Mulligan, Joseph '43 (SPR) [I] Holyoke, MA Sisters of Providence Care Centers, Inc.
Mulligan, Joseph E. *s.j.* '73 (DET) [K] Detroit, MI Jesuit Provincial Office-Detroit Province of the Society of Jesus.
Mulligan, Joseph E. *s.j.* '73 (FgM) Provinces.
Mulligan, Joseph V. '75 (CHL) [7] Charlotte, NC St Luke Church.
Mulligan, Louis J. '61 (DAV) Retired.
Mulligan, Paul F. '57 (BO) Ashland, MA St. Cecilia Church.
Mulligan, Robert *m.a.* '90 (PH) [D] Philadelphia, PA Roman Catholic High School for Boys.
Mulligan, Robert G. *o.s.f.s.* '85 (PH) [D] Philadelphia, PA Father Judge High School for Boys; [AA] Philadelphia, PA Father Judge Faculty House.
Mulligan, Robert H. '90 (PH) Royersford, PA Sacred Heart Church.

Mulligan, Robert W. *s.j.* '49 (CHI) [C] Chicago, IL Jesuit Community at Loyola University of Chicago.
Mulligan, William J. *s.j.* (BO) Cambridge, MA Youville Lifecare, Inc.
Mulligan, William L. *s.j.* '65 (BO) [W] Boston, MA Loyola House; [FF] Cambridge, MA The Youville House, Inc.
Mulligan, William R. '45 (BUR) Retired.
Mullin, Douglas *o.s.b.* (SCL) [I] Collegeville, MN St. John's Abbey, of the Order of St. Benedict.
Mullin, Edward J. *c.m.* '54 (STL) [P] Perryville, MO Congregation of The Mission.
Mullin, Francis R. *o.p.* '71 (HBG) [I] Lancaster, PA Monastery of the Dominican Nuns of the Perpetual Rosary.
Mullin, Henry *c.s.sp.* '59 (MIA) [6] Fort Lauderdale, FL St. Clement Church.
Mullin, Hugh J. '46 (KC) Retired.
Mullin, John *s.j.* (MAN) Lebanon, NH Mary Hitchock Memorial Hospital, Dartmouth-Hitchock Medical Center.
Mullin, John A. *s.j.* '75 (NY) [DD] New York, NY Xavier Jesuit Community; [GG] New York, NY University Apostolate.
Mullin, John F. *s.j.* '65 (BO) [W] Boston, MA The Society of Jesus of New England-Provincial Offices; [W] Chestnut Hill, MA The Jesuit Community at Boston College.
Mullin, John F. *s.j.* '65 (MAN) Lebanon, NH Sacred Heart Church.
Mullin, Joseph P. *s.m.* '54 (NO) [P] New Orleans, LA Marist Fathers.
Mullin, Patrick J. '75 (LA) [Q] Montebello, CA Vincentian Fathers & Brothers; [W] Montebello, CA DePaul Center.
Mullin, Thomas '65 (BRK) Brooklyn, NY Veterans Administration Medical Center.
Mullin, Thomas '65 (NY) Military Chaplains.
Mullin, Msgr. Thomas M. '75 (PH) Upper Uwchlan, PA Saint Elizabeth Church.
Mullin, William H. '65 (BO) [3] Quincy, MA St. John the Baptist Church.
Mullins, Carlos '55 (NY) [183] Bronx, NY St. Philip Neri Church.
Mullins, Charles R. '50 (HRT) Retired.
Mullins, Kevin C. *o.s.a.* '90 (OAK) Castro Valley, CA Our Lady of Grace Church.
Mullins, Raymond '52 (PT) [1] Pensacola, FL Cathedral of the Sacred Heart.
Mullins, Richard A. '95 (ARL) Ashburn, VA St. Theresa Church.
Mullins, Robert J. '45 (FAR) Retired.
Mullowney, Edward J. *s.s.j.* '55 (BAL) [S] Baltimore, MD St. Joseph's Manor.
Mullowney, Thomas E. '55 (GI) Retired.
Mulloy, Francis *c.s.sp.* '52 (SFR) Millbrae, CA St. Dunstan Church.
Mulloy, James *s.d.b.* '85 (NY) [F] New Rochelle, NY Salesian High School; [DD] New Rochelle, NY Salesian Provincial House.
Mulloy, John F. '70 (BO) Saugus, MA Blessed Sacrament Church.
Mulloy, Michel '79 (RC) [2] Rapid City, SD Blessed Sacrament Church.
Mulloy, Sylvester '38 (JOL) Retired.
Mulloy, William '54 (NY) Absent on Leave.
Mulnix, John Gabriel R. *c.p.* '68 (CHI) [N] Chicago, IL Passionist Provincial Office.
Mulqueen, John D. '62 (Y) Niles, OH Our Lady of Mt. Carmel Church.
Mulqueen, Msgr. Joseph C. '57 (BRK) [235] Queens, NY St. Robert Bellarmine Church.
Mulqueen, Martin B. '74 (PMB) Palm City, FL Holy Redeemer Church.
Mulranen, Francis J. '82 (PH) Highland Park, PA St. Laurence Church.
Mulranen, John J. '50 (SY) Retired.
Mulrenan, Alexius J. *o.f.m.* '60 (PAT) [M] Butler, NJ St. Anthony Friary.
Mulrenan, Donald P. *s.v.d.* '60 (BO) [W] Boston, MA Divine Word Missionaries.
Mulroney, Joseph G. *j.c.l.* '93 (R) Smithfield, NC St. Ann Church.
Mulrooney, Charles F. '42 (SCR) Retired; [N] Dunmore, PA Villa St. Joseph.
Mulrooney, Conan P. *o.praem.* '67 (GB) [I] De Pere, WI St. Norbert Abbey.
Mulrooney, F. Harold '37 (SCR) Retired.
Mulroy, Richard D. *o.praem.* '40 (GB) [I] De Pere, WI St. Norbert Abbey.
Mulsoff, Donald J. '69 (CHI) Elmwood Park, IL St. Celestine Church.
Mulvanerty, Thomas F. '79 (RVC) Ronkonkoma, NY St. Joseph's Church.
Mulvanerty, Thomas M. '65 (NY) [76] New York, NY St. Monica Church.
Mulvaney, Andrew R. '68 (OG) Military Chaplains.
Mulvaney, James '53 (ORL) Lady Lake, FL St. Timothy Church; Retired.
Mulvaney, James J. '53 (BIR) Retired.
Mulvanity, Francis C. '59 (CLV) [4] Euclid, OH St. Paul Church.
Mulvany, Michael '88 (KCK) Lapeer, KS St. Francis Church; Osage City, KS St. Patrick's Church; Scranton, KS St. Patrick's Church.
Mulvehill, John R. '57 (BO) Cohasset, MA St. Anthony Church.
Mulvehill, Louis J. '53 (ALT) South Fork, PA Most Holy Trinity Church.
Mulvey, Gerard *o.f.m.cap.* '91 (NY) [57] New York, NY St. John the Baptist Church.
Mulvey, Wm. Michael '75 (AUS) Georgetown, TX St. Helen's Church.
Mulvihill, Daniel R. '53 (WCH) Retired.
Mulvihill, David J. '72 (CHI) Zion-Beach Park, IL Our Lady of Humility Church.
Mulvihill, John E. '64 (CHI) Highwood, IL St. James Church; [X] Chicago, IL Court of Appeals-Province of Chicago.
Mulvihill, Martin J. '83 (STL) Hazelwood, MO St. Martin de Porres Church.
Munari, Mario '50 (SR) Retired.
Mundadan, Joseph (LAN) [4] Lansing, MI Immaculate Heart of Mary Church.
Mundakal, Joseph *c.m.i.* '83 (NSH) Loretto, TN Sacred Heart Church; Saint Joseph, TN St. Joseph Church; [K] Liberty, TN Carmel Center of Spirituality.
Mundanmani, Paulson '91 (OAK) [2] Fremont, CA Holy Spirit Church.
Mundell, Msgr. J. Joshua '47 (WDC) [22] Washington, DC Immaculate Conception Church.
Mundwiller, Edmund *o.f.m.* '81 (STL) [P] St. Louis, MO Franciscan Friary of St. Anthony of Padua.
Mundy, Patrick W. '66 (OG) On Duty Outside the Diocese.
Munez, Jose *c.m.* '90 (SJN) [27] San Juan, PR San Jose Obrero Church.
Mung'aho, Matei Alex (CHI) [149] Chicago, IL Our Lady of Lourdes Church.
Munguia, Jorge *s.j.* '67 (MIA) [D] Miami, FL Belen Jesuit Preparatory School; [H] Miami, FL Villa Arrieta.
Muniz, Alberto '77 (PCE) On Duty Outside the Diocese.
Muniz, Orlando Rosas '97 (MGZ) Moca, PR Our Lady of Monserrate Church.
Muniz, William '94 (MIA) [8] Fort Lauderdale, FL St. Helen Church; [G] Fort Lauderdale, FL Holy Cross Hospital.
Munn, Daniel '82 (NTN) Augusta, GA St. Ignatios of Antioch Church.
Munn, Daniel M. '82 (SAV) [1] Augusta, GA Church of the Most Holy Trinity.
Munn, Thomas '51 (SC) [C] Carroll, IA St. Anthony Regional Hospital; [D] Carroll, IA St. Anthony Nursing Home.
Munn, Thomas J. '51 (SC) Carroll, IA St. Anthony Regional Hospital; Retired.
Munoz, Antonio '60 (CGS) [10] Barrio Rio Canas, PR San Pedro Apostol Church.
Munoz, Arcadio '76 (NEW) New Milford, NJ Ascension Church.
Munoz, Ariel '97 (LA) [16] Los Angeles, CA Immaculate Conception Church.
Munoz, Enrique *o.f.m.* '91 (ELP) [B] El Paso, TX St. Anthony's School of Theology.
Munoz, Msgr. Ernesto '55 (ARE) Quebradillas, PR San Raphael Church.
Munoz, Eusiquio '64 (WOR) Milford, MA St. Mary of the Assumption Church.
Munoz, Jose '96 (ORL) Daytona Beach, FL St. Paul's Church.
Munoz, Jose Manuel '86 (TUC) Douglas, AZ Immaculate Conception Church.
Munoz, Juan Francisco *s.d.b.* '73 (LAR) [9] Laredo, TX San Luis Rey Church.
Munoz, Manuel '98 (ELP) Pecos, TX Santa Rosa Church.
Munoz, Rafael '60 (PCE) On Duty Outside the Diocese.
Munoz, Raul Saez '82 (SJN) [1] San Juan, PR Catedral De San Juan Bautista Church.
Munoz, Tomas G. '85 (TUC) Yuma, AZ Immaculate Conception Church.
Munro, Donald R. '87 (PMB) [4] Delray Beach, FL St. Vincent Ferrer Church.
Munroe, Msgr. Henry T. *p.a.* '53 (FR) Retired.
Munsch, Nathan J. *o.s.b.* '91 (GBG) [H] Latrobe, PA Saint Vincent Archabbey.
Munsell, Richard F. '79 (GF) Military Chaplains.
Munshower, William G. '58 (IND) [38] Indianapolis, IN St. Thomas Aquinas Church.
Munson, Thomas N. '54 (PBL) Cortez, CO St. Margaret Mary Church; Retired.
Munson, Tom '54 (PBL) Mancos, CO St. Rita Church.
Munster, Thomas P. *c.m.* '48 (CHI) [N] Chicago, IL DePaul Vincentian Residence.
Munton, J. Walter *c.j.* '66 (LA) [1] Santa Barbara, CA Holy Cross Church.
Muntone, Msgr. Anthony D. '64 (ALN) Whitehall, PA St. Elizabeth Church.
Munz, Theodore G. *s.j.* '83 (CHI) [D] Wilmette, IL Loyola Academy.
Munzing, Joel *o.f.m.* '47 (PAT) [M] Butler, NJ St. Anthony Friary.
Muodiaju, Samuel *c.s.sp.* '85 (MIA) [15] Miami, FL St. Agatha Church.
Muoneke, Romanus O. '94 (GAL) [78] Houston, TX St. Vincent de Paul Church.
Murasso, Jeremiah N. '79 (HRT) Naugatuck, CT St. Vincent Ferrer Church.
Murawski, Edward J. *s.j.* '66 (BO) [W] Boston, MA Loyola House.
Murd, Francis A. '76 (TOL) Tiffin, OH St. Mary Church.
Murd, Frank A. '79 (TOL) Sycamore, OH St. Pius X Church.
Murdick, Msgr. Olin J. '45 (SAG) Retired.
Murdock, Paul J. '75 (NOR) Windham, CT Sagrado Corazon de Jesus Church.
Murhammer, Francis J. '88 (PIT) Monroeville, PA North American Martyrs Church.
Murimi, Michael (ROC) [11] Rochester, NY St. Cecilia Church.
Murnan, Sean *o.f.m.* '73 (GLP) Zuni, NM St. Anthony, Our Lady of Guadalupe Church.
Murnane, Patrick J. '60 (MIA) [2] Hollywood, FL Nativity Church.
Murnane, Theodore *s.v.d.* '59 (FgM) Society of the Divine Word Foreign Missions.
Murnane, Thomas *o.s.a.* '61 (PH) [C] Villanova, PA Villanova University.
Murnane, Thomas M. *o.s.a.* '65 (PH) [AA] Villanova, PA St. Thomas Monastery.
Murnion, Msgr. Philip J. '63 (NY) [88] New York, NY Our Lady of Loreto Church; On Duty Outside the Archdiocese.
Muro, Msgr. Victor '66 (CAM) [O] Vineland, NJ Pope John Paul II Retreat Center.
Muro, Msgr. Victor S. '66 (CAM) [3] Vineland, NJ St. Francis of Assisi Church; [P] Vineland, NJ Spanish Catholic Center.
Murphy, Alfred E. *o.s.a.* '56 (PH) [AA] Villanova, PA St. Thomas Monastery.
Murphy, Arthur J. '55 (HRT) [6] West Hartford, CT St. Thomas the Apostle Church.
Murphy, Bartholomew J. *s.j.* '72 (FgM) Provinces.
Murphy, Bartholomew J. *s.j.* '72 (P) [L] Portland, OR Jesuit Provincial Office (Society of Jesus, Oregon Prov.).
Murphy, Bernard *c.f.r.* '98 (NY) [DD] Bronx, NY Our Lady of the Angels Friary.
Murphy, Brendan *s.v.d.* (LAF) Pine Prairie, LA St. Peter Church.
Murphy, Brendan *o.p.* '00 (CIN) [28] Cincinnati, OH St. Gertrude Church; [M] Cincinnati, OH St. Gertrude Priory.
Murphy, Brian *o.carm.* '58 (ROC) [C] Rochester, NY McQuaid Jesuit High School; [I] Rochester, NY Whitefriars Priory.
Murphy, Campion *s.t.* '56 (PAT) [M] Stirling, NJ Holy Spirit Missionary Cenacle.
Murphy, Charles *s.a.* '61 (NY) [DD] Garrison, NY Franciscan Friars of the Atonement.
Murphy, Charles C. *s.j.* (MIL) [P] Milwaukee, WI Jesuit Community at Marquette University.
Murphy, Charles J. '60 (BO) [2] Weymouth, MA St. Francis Xavier Church.
Murphy, Msgr. Charles M. '61 (PRT) Falmouth, ME Holy Martyrs Church.
Murphy, Charles R. '91 (OKL) [18] Oklahoma City, OK St. Philip Neri Church.
Murphy, Christopher D. '96 (ARL) Warrenton, VA St. John the Evangelist Church.
Murphy, Clarence '47 (FR) Retired.
Murphy, Columba *o.f.m.* '41 (SP) [O] St. Petersburg, FL St. Anthony Friary.
Murphy, Msgr. D. Declan '49 (MRY) Carmel, CA San Carlos Borromeo Basilica Church.
Murphy, Daniel J. '56 (DET) Retired.
Murphy, Daniel S. '70 (BRK) [176] Queens, NY Holy Child Jesus Church.
Murphy, Daniel T. '62 (MIL) [N] Greenfield, WI Clement Manor Health Center.
Murphy, Daniel W. '73 (PAT) Sparta, NJ Blessed Kateri Tekakwitha Church.
Murphy, David (BO) Brockton, MA Brockton Hospital.
Murphy, David *o.carm.* '42 (CHI) [N] Chicago, IL St. Joseph's Priory.
Murphy, David C. '63 (BO) [5] Brockton, MA Our Lady of Lourdes Church.
Murphy, David F. '87 (WIL) Claymont, DE Holy Rosary Church; Wilmington, DE Delaware Army National Guard.
Murphy, David M. '53 (ROC) Retired.
Murphy, Denis J. '53 (LA) Retired.
Murphy, Dennis '74 (PRO) Providence, RI Veterans Administration Hospital.
Murphy, Dennis '74 (RIC) On Duty Outside the Diocese.
Murphy, Dennis '75 (ALB) Rotterdam Junction, NY St. Margaret of Cortona Church.
Murphy, Donald J. *s.j.* '61 (FgM) Provinces.
Murphy, Edward *s.j.* '43 (FgM) Provinces.
Murphy, Edward A. '98 (FR) [5] Fall River, MA Holy Name Church.
Murphy, Edward F. *c.m.* '79 (STL) [P] St. Louis, MO Vincentian Residence.

Murphy, Edward J. *s.j.* '68 (NY) [DD] New York, NY Murray-Weigel Hall.
Murphy, Edward W. '93 (STA) [1] Jacksonville, FL Assumption Church.
Murphy, Emmet *o.f.m.* '86 (NEW) [N] Hohokus, NJ St. Anthony of Padua.
Murphy, Eoin '64 (LAN) Montrose, MI Good Shepherd Church; Otisville, MI St. Francis Xavier Church.
Murphy, Msgr. Eugene '34 (MAN) Retired.
Murphy, Msgr. Eugene F. '52 (RVC) Mineola, NY Corpus Christi Church; Mineola, NY Winthrop Hospital.
Murphy, F. Kevin '81 (NEW) [D] Summit, NJ The Oratory Catholic Preparatory School.
Murphy, Msgr. Francis '46 (MOB) Retired.
Murphy, Francis *c.s.c.* '86 (FgM) Holy Cross Foreign Missions.
Murphy, Msgr. Francis A. '57 (ANC) Retired.
Murphy, Msgr. Francis C. '46 (MOB) [4] Mobile, AL St. Dominic Church.
Murphy, Francis J. '51 (LIN) Retired.
Murphy, Francis J. *s.j.* '56 (KC) [J] Kansas City, MO Rockhurst Jesuit Community.
Murphy, Francis J. '58 (RNO) [2] Reno, NV Our Lady of the Snows Church.
Murphy, Francis J. '58 (WDC) On Duty Outside the Archdiocese.
Murphy, Francis J. '66 (GAY) Cadillac, MI St. Ann Church; Harrietta, MI St. Edward Church.
Murphy, Francis J. *c.s.c.* '86 (FTW) [J] South Bend, IN Congregation of Holy Cross, Indiana Province, Provincial House.
Murphy, Francis X. *c.ss.r.* '40 (BAL) Annapolis, MD St. Mary Church; [S] Annapolis, MD Saint Mary Rectory.
Murphy, Frank '58 (RNO) [3] Reno, NV Our Lady of Wisdom Church; [F] Reno, NV University of Nevada, Newman Community.
Murphy, Msgr. Frederick J. '57 (BO) [1] Boston, MA Cathedral of the Holy Cross.
Murphy, G. Ronald *s.j.* '69 (WDC) [M] Washington, DC The Jesuit Community at Georgetown University.
Murphy, George '66 (BLX) Hattiesburg, MS Sacred Heart Church.
Murphy, George R. *s.j.* '71 (BO) [W] Boston, MA The Society of Jesus of New England-Provincial Offices.
Murphy, George R. *s.j.* '71 (OAK) [A] Berkeley, CA The Jesuit School of Theology at Berkeley; [N] Berkeley, CA Jesuit Community at Jesuit School of Theology at Berkeley.
Murphy, Gerard '79 (SP) Ridge Manor, FL St. Anne Church.
Murphy, Gerasimos *b.s.o.* '67 (NTN) [A] Methuen, MA Seminary of St. Basil the Great.
Murphy, Gordon A. *o.f.m.* '55 (BO) [Z] Boston, MA Saint Anthony Residence.
Murphy, H. Joseph '61 (BO) Wakefield, MA St. Florence Church.
Murphy, Harold B. '68 (CHI) [203] Chicago, IL St. Timothy Church.
Murphy, Harry J. '40 (GBG) Retired.
Murphy, Henry *m.m.* '58 (STA) [H] Jacksonville, FL Maryknoll Fathers & Brothers.
Murphy, Henry J. *s.j.* '57 (BO) [W] Weston, MA Campion Health Center, Inc.
Murphy, Hugh J. '59 (NOR) Retired.
Murphy, Msgr. J. Emmett '38 (ROC) Retired.
Murphy, J. Patrick *c.m.* '76 (CHI) [N] Chicago, IL Vincentian Community, Congregation of the Mission, Midwest Province.
Murphy, James *c.s.c.* '58 (PRT) [J] Biddeford, ME Marie Joseph Spiritual Center; [M] Biddeford, ME University of New England.
Murphy, James '68 (SAC) [1] Sacramento, CA Cathedral of the Blessed Sacrament.
Murphy, James '70 (MIA) Miami Lakes, FL Our Lady of the Lakes Church.
Murphy, James '78 (JOL) Elmhurst, IL Immaculate Conception Church.
Murphy, James A. '39 (PH) Stowe, PA St. Gabriel of the Sorrowful Mother Church; Retired.
Murphy, James D. *o.s.b.* '46 (OKL) [I] Shawnee, OK St. Gregory's Abbey.
Murphy, James E. '52 (STL) Retired.
Murphy, James E. '55 (GI) Retired.
Murphy, James F. *c.s.c.* '58 (PRT) Saco, ME Most Holy Trinity Church; [L] Biddeford, ME Marie Joseph Spiritual Center.
Murphy, James F. '70 (PIT) [1] Butler, PA St. Fidelis of Sigmaringen Church.
Murphy, James H. '81 (MAD) Platteville, WI St. Augustine University Church.
Murphy, James J. '45 (PH) Retired.
Murphy, James J. '52 (RCK) [4] Rockford, IL St. Edward Church.
Murphy, James J. '54 (WH) Weston, WV St. Patrick's Church.
Murphy, James L. '52 (RCK) Retired.
Murphy, James P. '65 (CHI) Glenview, IL St. Catherine Laboure Church.
Murphy, James W. '48 (MEM) Retired.
Murphy, James Wayne '65 (L) [73] Louisville, KY St. Thomas More Church.
Murphy, Jeremiah *m.s.c.* '46 (SAT) [N] San Antonio, TX Cordi-Marian Missionary Sisters.
Murphy, Msgr. Jeremiah '63 (LA) West Hollywood, CA St. Victor Church.
Murphy, Jerome *c.ss.r.* '51 (ORL) [F] New Smyrna Beach, FL St. Alphonsus Villa-Redemptorist Fathers and Brothers.
Murphy, John (ATL) Roswell, GA St. Andrew Church.
Murphy, John *s.d.b.* (NY) [3] Port Chester, NY Our Lady of the Rosary Church.
Murphy, John *o.f.m.* '54 (HRT) [15] Hartford, CT St. Patrick-St. Anthony Church.
Murphy, John *f.m.s.i.* '72 (BO) [B] Framingham, MA Sylva Maria.
Murphy, John '79 (MRY) Retired; [G] Soquel, CA St. Clare's Retreat.
Murphy, John C. '65 (SP) St. Pete Beach, FL St. John Church.
Murphy, John D. *s.j.* '77 (LA) [F] Los Angeles, CA Loyola High School of Los Angeles.
Murphy, John D. '79 (MET) Colonia, NJ St. John Vianney Church; Edison, NJ John F. Kennedy Medical Center.
Murphy, Msgr. John F. '47 (COV) Retired.
Murphy, Msgr. John F. '47 (MIL) Retired.
Murphy, John F. '59 (CLV) [1] Cleveland, OH Cathedral of St. John the Evangelist.
Murphy, John J. (DEN) Lafayette, CO Immaculate Conception Church.
Murphy, John J. '39 (FR) Retired.
Murphy, John J. *c.s.c.* '49 (FR) [A] North Easton, MA Holy Cross Fathers Religious; [A] North Easton, MA Holy Cross Fathers Religious.
Murphy, John J. '57 (ALB) Catskill, NY St. Patrick Church.
Murphy, John M. '45 (MIL) Retired.
Murphy, John M. '51 (NU) Retired.
Murphy, John M. '65 (CHI) [50] Chicago, IL St. Edward Church.
Murphy, John P. *o.s.a.* '57 (JOL) New Lenox, IL St. Jude Church.
Murphy, Msgr. John P. '64 (ALN) [11] Allentown, PA St. Thomas More Church.
Murphy, John P. *s.j.* '69 (CHI) [C] Chicago, IL Jesuit Community at Loyola University of Chicago.
Murphy, John Thaddeus *o.p.* '54 (NY) [22] New York, NY St. Catherine of Siena Church; [DD] New York, NY St. Catherine of Siena Priory.
Murphy, John V. *s.j.* '52 (P) [L] Portland, OR Colombiere Community.
Murphy, Joseph *o.m.i.* '27 (BO) [Z] Tewksbury, MA Immaculate Heart of Mary Infirmary.
Murphy, Joseph '60 (SFS) Retired.
Murphy, Joseph A. *s.j.* '73 (COL) [A] Columbus, OH Pontifical College Josephinum.
Murphy, Joseph E. (PAT) Retired.
Murphy, Joseph E. '60 (COL) [8] Columbus, OH St. Catharine Church.
Murphy, Joseph E. '61 (PAT) [P] Chester, NJ Nazareth Village.
Murphy, Joseph F. '49 (PRO) Retired; [P] Providence, RI St. John Vianney Residence.
Murphy, Joseph G. '44 (HRT) Retired.
Murphy, Joseph H. '61 (NEW) Retired.
Murphy, Msgr. Joseph P. '54 (NY) [202] Staten Island, NY St. Clare Church; [HH] Staten Island, NY Emmaus Ministries, Ltd.
Murphy, Joseph R. *s.s.j.* '43 (BAL) [S] Baltimore, MD St. Joseph Society of the Sacred Heart House of Central Administration.
Murphy, Joseph T. '47 (PH) Glenside, PA St. Luke the Evangelist Church; Retired.
Murphy, Joseph V. '67 (GRY) Winfield Township, IN Holy Spirit Church.
Murphy, Jude *o.f.m.* (PAT) Pompton Lakes, NJ Our Lady of the Assumption Church.
Murphy, Kenneth *o.carm.* '81 (NY) [97] New York, NY Our Lady of the Scapular/St. Stephen Church; Manhattan, NY Bellevue Hospital; [DD] Middletown, NY Carmelite Friars (North American Province of St. Elias).
Murphy, Kenneth R. '86 (MET) Sayreville, NJ St. Stanislaus Kostka Church.
Murphy, Kevin J. *o.s.b.* '62 (MIL) [P] Benet Lake, WI St. Benedict's Abbey.
Murphy, Kevin P. '68 (ROC) Penfield, NY St. Joseph Church.
Murphy, Laurence T. *m.m.* '54 (NY) [DD] Maryknoll, NY Maryknoll Fathers and Brothers.
Murphy, Lawrence *s.j.* (LA) [J] Marina Del Rey, CA Daniel Freeman Marina Hospital.
Murphy, Lawrence B. *s.j.* '64 (LA) [F] Los Angeles, CA Loyola High School of Los Angeles.
Murphy, Lawrence F. '56 (BO) Senior Priests.
Murphy, Lawrence V. '58 (ROC) [26] Rochester, NY Holy Rosary Church; [54] Rochester, NY Most Precious Blood Church.
Murphy, Louis E. *s.t.* '60 (FgM) Trinity Missions.
Murphy, Msgr. Michael D. '66 (LAN) [1] Lansing, MI St. Mary Church.
Murphy, Michael D. '77 (PH) [4] Drexel Hill, PA St. Dorothy Church.
Murphy, Michael F. '83 (SD) Coronado, CA Sacred Heart Church.
Murphy, Michael G. '87 (STL) Imperial, MO St. John Lateran Church.
Murphy, Michael J. *c.s.c.* '49 (FTW) [B] Notre Dame, IN University of Notre Dame Du Lac; [J] Notre Dame, IN Holy Cross Community, Corby Hall, University of Notre Dame.
Murphy, Michael P. '89 (JC) Argyle, MO St. Aloysius Church; Freeburg, MO Holy Family Church.
Murphy, Myles P. '90 (NY) [144] Bronx, NY St. Gabriel Church.
Murphy, Owen *s.a.* '52 (NY) [DD] Garrison, NY Franciscan Friars of the Atonement.
Murphy, Msgr. Patrick '50 (SHP) [D] Monroe, LA Christus St. Joseph Home.
Murphy, Patrick '67 (LIN) [D] Lincoln, NE St. Elizabeth Regional Medical Center.
Murphy, Patrick *c.s.* '80 (CHI) [N] Oak Park, IL Missionaries of Saint Charles.
Murphy, Patrick *l.c.* '92 (ATL) [N] Atlanta, GA Home and Family, Inc.
Murphy, Patrick *l.c.* '97 (ATL) [J] Atlanta, GA Legionaries of Christ.
Murphy, Patrick '97 (SD) [A] San Diego, CA St. Francis Seminary.
Murphy, Patrick E. *o.s.a.* '76 (CHI) [N] Olympia Fields, IL The Augustinians-Provincialate.
Murphy, Patrick E. '85 (MAR) On Duty Outside the Diocese.
Murphy, Msgr. Patrick J. '50 (ALX) Retired.
Murphy, Paul G. '94 (BGP) Westport, CT St. Luke Church.
Murphy, Paul M. *c.m.* '60 (PH) [AA] Philadelphia, PA Congregation of the Mission.
Murphy, Paul P. '78 (MRY) [1] Monterey, CA Cathedral of San Carlos Borromeo.
Murphy, Peter J. (BO) Concord, MA St. Bernard Church; Concord, MA MCI-Concord.
Murphy, Peter P. '68 (PIT) Wexford, PA St. Alphonsus Church.
Murphy, Philip *ss.cc.* '70 (FR) [I] Fairhaven, MA Sacred Hearts Provincial House.
Murphy, Ralph *s.d.b.* '56 (SFR) [N] San Francisco, CA Salesian Provincial Residence.
Murphy, Richard '57 (PMB) Fort Pierce, FL St. Mark Church.
Murphy, Richard '65 (PMB) Vero Beach, FL Holy Cross Church; [K] Palm Beach Gardens, FL Diocesan Property & Liability Insurance Committee.
Murphy, Richard '65 (ROC) Seneca Falls, NY St. Patrick Church; [M] Rochester, NY Diocesan Department of Campus Ministry.
Murphy, Richard '80 (Y) Mineral Ridge, OH St. Mary's Church.
Murphy, Richard Daniel '96 (BGP) [7] Norwalk, CT St. Thomas the Apostle Church.
Murphy, Richard J. *s.j.* '64 (TUC) [F] Tucson, AZ Jesuit Community of the Vatican Observatory.
Murphy, Richard J. '73 (BAL) Walkersville, MD St. Timothy Church.
Murphy, Robert (VEN) Fort Myers Beach, FL Ascension Church.
Murphy, Robert '74 (KC) Grandview, MO Coronation of Our Lady Church.
Murphy, Robert *m.ss.a.* '93 (NOR) Chester, CT St. Joseph Church; [F] Cromwell, CT Society of the Missionaries of the Holy Apostles.
Murphy, Msgr. Robert E. '42 (BUF) [1] Lackawanna, NY Basilica of Our Lady of Victory; Retired.
Murphy, Robert J. *s.j.* '54 (LEX) [1] Lexington, KY Cathedral of Christ the King.
Murphy, Roland *o.carm.* '42 (WDC) [B] Washington, DC Whitefriars Hall.
Murphy, Romeo J. *o.m.i.* (BO) Lowell, MA Saints Memorial Medical Center.
Murphy, Ronan B. '00 (CAM) Gloucester, NJ St. Mary's Church.
Murphy, Rory '88 (SJ) San Jose, CA O'Connor Hospital; [G] San Jose, CA O'Connor Hospital.
Murphy, Msgr. Terrance J. '46 (STP) Retired.
Murphy, Msgr. Terrence J. '46 (STP) [C] St. Paul, MN University of St. Thomas.
Murphy, Theodore *s.m.m.* '58 (RVC) [M] Bay Shore, NY Montfort Missionaries.
Murphy, Thomas *o.f.m.cap.* (NY) Yonkers, NY St. Joseph Hospital.
Murphy, Thomas '36 (PIT) [K] Pittsburgh, PA Vincentian de Marillac.
Murphy, Thomas '43 (RVC) Mineola, NY Winthrop Hospital.
Murphy, Thomas '51 (VEN) Retired.
Murphy, Thomas '51 (Y) Retired.
Murphy, Thomas *s.j.* '57 (NY) [161] Bronx, NY St. Margaret of Cortona Church.
Murphy, Msgr. Thomas '66 (SAT) [61] San Antonio, TX St. Peter Prince of the Apostles Church.
Murphy, Thomas *o.f.m.cap.* '71 (NY) [17] Yonkers, NY Sacred Heart Church; [W] Yonkers, NY St. Joseph's

Medical Center.
Murphy, Thomas '85 (IND) [21] Indianapolis, IN St. John the Evangelist Church.
Murphy, Thomas E. '73 (WDC) [B] Washington, DC Diocesan Laborer Priests, House of Studies.
Murphy, Thomas E. *o.s.f.s.* '76 (VEN) [3] Fort Myers, FL St. Cecilia Church.
Murphy, Thomas F. '70 (RVC) Mineola, NY Corpus Christi Church.
Murphy, Thomas J. '87 (SAV) Thomasville, GA St. Augustine Church.
Murphy, Thomas K. *o.f.m.* '58 (SP) [O] St. Petersburg, FL St. Anthony Friary.
Murphy, Thomas M. '79 (PRT) Portland, ME Maine Medical Center.
Murphy, Thomas P. *c.s.p.* '62 (NY) [DD] Jamaica Estates, NY Paulist Fathers Generalate; [DD] Jamaica Estates, NY Paulist Fathers Generalate.
Murphy, Thomas R. '36 (PIT) Retired.
Murphy, Thomas R. E. *s.j.* '99 (BO) [W] Boston, MA The Society of Jesus of New England-Provincial Offices.
Murphy, Thomas R.E. *s.j.* '99 (SEA) [A] Seattle, WA Seattle University.
Murphy, Msgr. Timothy (SAN) Stanton, TX St. Joseph's Church.
Murphy, Timothy '60 (VEN) Retired.
Murphy, Timothy *o.ss.t.* '67 (BAL) [S] Baltimore, MD Holy Trinity Monastery.
Murphy, Timothy '67 (P) [2] Portland, OR St. Agatha Church; [C] Portland, OR Central Catholic High School.
Murphy, Timothy *glmy.* '93 (JKS) Aberdeen, MS St. Francis of Assisi Church.
Murphy, Msgr. Timothy J. '62 (SAN) [1] Midland, TX St. Ann's Church.
Murphy, Timothy J. '63 (BO) [2] Salem, MA Immaculate Conception Church.
Murphy, Timothy J. '74 (SPR) Hampden, MA St. Mary's Church.
Murphy, Ultan P. '53 (DOD) Olmitz, KS St. Ann Church; Timken, KS Holy Trinity Church.
Murphy, Venard *o.f.m.* '61 (SP) [O] St. Petersburg, FL St. Anthony Friary.
Murphy, Msgr. Walter '58 (BRK) [128] Brooklyn, NY Sacred Heart Church.
Murphy, Warren *t.o.r.* '60 (FWT) [8] Fort Worth, TX St. Andrew Church.
Murphy, Warren L. *t.o.r.* (FWT) [O] Fort Worth, TX Ministry to Gay & Lesbians.
Murphy, William *c.p.* (BAL) [50] Baltimore, MD St. Joseph Passionist Monastery Church.
Murphy, William *s.a.* '40 (NY) [DD] Garrison, NY Franciscan Friars of the Atonement.
Murphy, William *c.p.* '73 (BAL) [S] Baltimore, MD St. Joseph's Passionist Community.
Murphy, William '90 (ARE) Barceloneta, PR Church of Our Lady of Mt. Carmel.
Murphy, William F. (BO) [A] Brighton, MA St. John's Seminary.
Murphy, William F. '56 (PRO) Retired; [P] Providence, RI St. John Vianney Residence.
Murphy, William F. '65 (BO) [DD] Boston, MA Chancery Office.
Murphy, William F. '88 (BO) [A] Boston, MA St. John's Seminary School of Theology.
Murphy, William F. '90 (BO) Graduate Studies.
Murphy, William J. '57 (DET) Orchard Lake, MI Our Lady of Refuge Church.
Murphy, William J. '96 (SUP) Crescent Lake, WI Sacred Hearts of Jesus and Mary Church; Danbury, WI Our Lady of Perpetual Help Church; Webster, WI St. John the Baptist Church.
Murphy, William P. '43 (CHI) Evergreen Park, IL Queen of Martyrs Church; Retired.
Murphy, William P. '65 (DEN) [2] Englewood, CO Holy Name Church.
Murphy, William P. '86 (SPR) Hadley, MA Most Holy Redeemer Church.
Murphy, William S. '90 (PH) On Duty Outside the Archdiocese.
Murphy, William T. '50 (RVC) Retired.
Murphy Phan, Paul-Cuong Q. '99 (SJ) Cupertino, CA St. Joseph of Cupertino Church.
Murr, Charles '77 (NY) [87] New York, NY Our Lady of Guadalupe Church.
Murray, Adrian '51 (OAK) Retired.
Murray, Msgr. Andrew '73 (BLX) [3] Gulfport, MS St. John the Evangelist Church.
Murray, Arthur *o.f.m.* '49 (SP) [O] St. Petersburg, FL St. Anthony Friary.
Murray, Bernard *o.c.s.o.* '50 (L) [L] Trappist, KY Abbey of Our Lady of Gethsemani, of the Order of Cistercians of the Strict Observance.
Murray, Bradley *s.j.* '54 (BAL) [S] Baltimore, MD Jesuit Fathers and Brothers Maryland Provincial Curia.
Murray, Brendan J. '68 (PAT) Rockaway, NJ St. Cecilia's Church.
Murray, Celestine '55 (CC) Woodsboro, TX St. Therese, The Little Flower Church.
Murray, Charles A. *m.m.* '51 (FgM) Maryknoll Foreign Missions.
Murray, Cornelius J. '63 (CLV) North Olmsted, OH St. Brendan Church.
Murray, Cyprian *o.f.m.cap.* '64 (NOR) [4] Middletown, CT St. Pius X Church.
Murray, D. Bradley *s.j.* '54 (BAL) [D] Baltimore, MD Loyola Blakefield.
Murray, Msgr. Daniel A. '64 (PH) [3] Drexel Hill, PA St. Charles Borromeo Church.
Murray, Msgr. Daniel J. '73 (ORG) Newport Beach, CA Our Lady of Mount Carmel Church.
Murray, Donald J. '61 (MAD) [14] Madison, WI St. Thomas Aquinas Church.
Murray, Donnan P. *o.f.m.* '56 (FgM) Franciscan Foreign Missions.
Murray, Edward *o.m.i.* '37 (SAT) [K] San Antonio, TX Oblate Madonna Residence.
Murray, Edward G. '69 (SC) Denison, IA St. Rose of Lima Church.
Murray, Edward K. '62 (SFR) [51] San Francisco, CA St. Teresa Church; San Francisco, CA St. Mary's Medical Center; Special Assignment; [J] San Francisco, CA St. Mary's Medical Center.
Murray, Eugene '65 (SC) Rock Valley, IA St. Mary's Church.
Murray, Eugene M. *m.m.* '58 (FgM) Maryknoll Foreign Missions.
Murray, Msgr. Francis '49 (SAG) Retired.
Murray, Francis '53 (SFR) Special Assignment; Retired.
Murray, Francis J. '51 (LAN) Retired.
Murray, Frank '53 (SFR) Burlingame, CA St. Catherine of Siena Church.
Murray, Frank J. '81 (PRT) Bangor, ME St. Mary's Church.
Murray, Frederick J. '53 (BO) Senior Priests.
Murray, George B. *s.j.* '65 (BO) [W] Weston, MA Campion Jesuit Community.
Murray, George B. *s.j.* '65 (DET) [K] Detroit, MI Jesuit Provincial Office-Detroit Province of the Society of Jesus.
Murray, Gerald '84 (NY) [HH] New York, NY Legion of Mary, Office.
Murray, Gerald E. '84 (NY) [122] New York, NY St. Vincent de Paul Church.
Murray, Msgr. Harold A. '49 (NEW) Retired.
Murray, Msgr. Harrold '29 (TR) Manasquan, NJ St. Denis Church.
Murray, Msgr. Ignatius L. '57 (PH) Brookline, PA Annunciation B.V.M. Church.
Murray, J. Glenn *s.j.* '79 (CLV) [26] Cleveland, OH St. Henry Church.
Murray, James B. '57 (MEM) [21] Memphis, TN St. Paul The Apostle Church.
Murray, James B. '57 (NSH) Retired.
Murray, Msgr. James H. '56 (PAT) Denville, NJ St. Mary's Church.
Murray, Msgr. James J. '56 (NY) [I] New York, NY The Catholic Charities of the Archdiocese of New York; [I] New York, NY The Catholic Charities of the Archdiocese of New York; [Z] New York, NY Mary Manning Walsh Home; [HH] New York, NY The Housing Fund of the Archdiocese of New York; [HH] New York, NY Incarnation Children's Center Fund, Inc.
Murray, James M. *o.s.b.* '93 (PEO) [A] Peru, IL St. Bede Abbey and Academy.
Murray, James Stephen *o.p.* (L) [4] Springfield, KY St. Rose Church.
Murray, Msgr. Jerome E. '49 (LIN) Retired; [E] Lincoln, NE Bonacum House.
Murray, John '54 (Y) Retired.
Murray, John '62 (LA) Burbank, CA St. Francis Xavier Church.
Murray, John *c.s.b.* '67 (ROC) [L] Rochester, NY Marriage Encounter Apostolate.
Murray, John '67 (RVC) New Hyde Park, NY Notre Dame Church.
Murray, John *c.ss.r.* '73 (BRK) [107] Brooklyn, NY Our Lady of Perpetual Help Basilica Church.
Murray, John A. '54 (Y) Hubbard, OH St. Patrick's Church.
Murray, John A. '62 (BO) Concord, MA St. Bernard Church.
Murray, John B. *c.m.* '42 (BRK) [V] Jamaica, NY Vincentian Residence.
Murray, John C. *c.s.b.* '57 (ROC) [I] Rochester, NY Basilian Residence.
Murray, John D. '53 (LA) Saugus, CA Pitchess Detention Center.
Murray, John E. '60 (CHY) Kemmerer, WY St. Patrick's Church.
Murray, John E. '63 (HEL) [1] Anaconda, MT Anaconda Catholic Community Church.
Murray, John E. '67 (RVC) Retired.
Murray, John Francis *s.m.a.* '57 (NEW) [N] Tenafly, NJ Society of African Missions, Provincialate, S.M.A. Fathers.
Murray, John I. '55 (SFS) Retired.
Murray, John J. '47 (PH) Retired.
Murray, John J. '65 (BRK) [148] Queens, NY American Martyrs Church.
Murray, John L. '47 (E) Retired.
Murray, John M. '98 (FR) Sandwich, MA Corpus Christi Church.
Murray, John P. (RVC) Retired.
Murray, John P. *c.m.* '48 (BRK) [V] Jamaica, NY Vincentian Residence.
Murray, John P. *s.j.* '87 (BO) [W] Boston, MA The Society of Jesus of New England-Provincial Offices; [W] Boston, MA The Society of Jesus of New England-Provincial Offices.
Murray, John S. '69 (ORL) Titusville, FL St. Teresa Church.
Murray, John W. '68 (CHI) [2] Oak Park, IL St. Catherine of Siena-St. Lucy Church.
Murray, Joseph '55 (NEW) [5] Bayonne, NJ St. Vincent de Paul Church.
Murray, Msgr. Joseph '56 (RVC) Westhampton Beach, NY Immaculate Conception Church.
Murray, Msgr. Joseph W. '61 (PH) Lansdale, PA St. Stanislaus Church.
Murray, Kevin P. '77 (PH) [2] Chester, PA Saint Katharine Drexel Church.
Murray, Kevin R. *c.ss.r.* '86 (PH) [25] Philadelphia, PA St. Boniface Church.
Murray, Leo A. *s.j.* '62 (PH) [83] Philadelphia, PA Old St. Joseph's Church.
Murray, Maurice M. *s.j.* '66 (FgM) Provinces.
Murray, Michael *o.s.b.* '81 (PBL) Florence, CO St. Benedict Church.
Murray, Michael *o.s.f.s.* '86 (WDC) [B] Washington, DC Oblates of St. Francis de Sales.
Murray, Michael D. *o.s.b.* '56 (PBL) [G] Canon City, CO Holy Cross Abbey.
Murray, Michael J. '76 (WDC) Pastoral Center Special Ministries; [N] Kensington, MD St. John Vianney House.
Murray, Michael S. *o.s.f.s.* '86 (WDC) [B] Washington, DC Deshairs Community-Oblates of St. Francis de Sales Residence.
Murray, Nicholas *s.s.c.* '62 (FgM) St. Columban's Foreign Mission Society (S.S.C.).
Murray, Patrick F. *s.j.* '45 (PH) [AA] Philadelphia, PA Jesuit Community at St. Joseph's University.
Murray, Paul *o.p.* (CHI) [A] Mundelein, IL University of St. Mary of the Lake-Mundelein Seminary.
Murray, Paul '75 (WDC) On Duty Outside the Archdiocese.
Murray, Peter *s.j.* '72 (NY) Manhattan, NY Bird S. Coler Memorial Hospital and Home; [DD] New York, NY West Side Jesuit Community.
Murray, Pius C.W. *c.s.s.* '92 (BO) [W] Waltham, MA Stigmatine Fathers & Brothers Provincial House; [W] Waltham, MA Stigmatine House.
Murray, Msgr. Richard H. '43 (LA) Woodland Hills, CA St. Bernardine of Siena Church; Retired.
Murray, Robert J. *o.s.a.* '83 (PH) [C] Villanova, PA Villanova University; [AA] Villanova, PA St. Thomas Monastery.
Murray, Robert W. '88 (BO) [A] Boston, MA St. John's Seminary School of Theology.
Murray, Russel *o.f.m.* '98 (NY) [DD] New York, NY Franciscan Friars, Order of Friars Minor, Holy Name Province.
Murray, Msgr. Sean '52 (SD) [21] San Diego, CA St. Brigid Church; Retired.
Murray, Sean M. '00 (OG) [1] Ogdensburg, NY St. Mary's Church.
Murray, Steven J. '00 (PBL) Grand Junction, CO Immaculate Heart of Mary Church.
Murray, Steven M. '88 (OG) Hammond, NY St. Peter Church.
Murray, Thomas '44 (SJ) Los Altos, CA St. Simon Church; Retired.
Murray, Msgr. Thomas A. '68 (PH) Trooper, PA Visitation B.V.M. Church.
Murray, Thomas F. '57 (BO) Senior Priests.
Murray, Thomas P. '81 (RVC) Sound Beach, NY St. Louis de Montfort Church.
Murray, Timothy J. '77 (DET) [3] Livonia, MI St. Edith Church.
Murray, Msgr. William F. '45 (PRO) Retired.
Murray, William F. '54 (MIL) Retired.
Murray, William J. *o.s.a.* '47 (PH) [AA] Villanova, PA St. Thomas Monastery.
Murrin, Donald *s.v.d.* '60 (LR) [4] Little Rock, AR St. Bartholomew's Church.
Murrin, Joseph *s.s.c.* '44 (PRO) [P] Bristol, RI St. Columban's Retirement House.
Murrin, Raymond J. '61 (BIR) [20] Birmingham, AL St. Patrick's Church.
Murrman, Jonathan J. *o.s.b.* '65 (GBG) [H] Latrobe, PA Saint Vincent Archabbey.
Murrman, Warren D. *o.s.b.* '65 (GBG) [H] Latrobe, PA Saint Vincent Archabbey.
Murtagh, George O. '50 (BUR) Retired.
Murtagh, James '66 (PMB) [3] West Palm Beach, FL St. Ann Church.
Murtagh, John J. '69 (YAK) [2] Yakima, WA Holy Family Church.

Murtagh, Lawrence '53 (WIN) On Duty Outside the Diocese.
Murtagh, Thomas '81 (BRK) [96] Brooklyn, NY Our Lady of Grace Church.
Murtaugh, Lewis C. *s.j.* '69 (CHI) [N] Chicago, IL Chicago Province of the Society of Jesus-Provincial Office.
Murtaugh, William '72 (STP) New Brighton, MN St. John the Baptist Church.
Murtha, Chester '93 (SFS) Dell Rapids, SD St. Mary's Church.
Murtha, John F. *o.s.b.* '57 (GBG) [H] Latrobe, PA Saint Vincent Archabbey.
Murtha, Michael G. '93 (PH) [1] Phoenixville, PA St. Ann Church.
Murugarren, Jesus *o.s.a.* '55 (SAT) [58] San Antonio, TX St. Michael Church.
Murungi, David J. '79 (ARL) [2] Arlington, VA St. Agnes Church.
Murzyn, John A. '59 (GRY) Absent on Sick Leave.
Muscalino, Daniel C. '78 (SY) [17] Syracuse, NY St. John the Baptist Church; Truxton, NY St. Patrick Church; Special Assignment.
Muscat, John '51 (NY) [2] New Rochelle, NY St. Gabriel Church; New Rochelle, NY South Shore Medical Center.
Muscat, John C. '84 (CAM) Blackwood, NJ St. Jude's Church.
Muschette, Emilian *o.s.b.* '58 (NEW) [N] Newark, NJ Newark Abbey.
Muscolino, Frank J. '68 (BIR) [25] Birmingham, AL St. Stephen the Martyr Church; [H] Birmingham, AL St. Stephen the Martyr Catholic Church and Catholic Campus Center.
Mushalla, Walter '98 (SAT) Falls City, TX Holy Trinity Church.
Mushi, Evaristus '84 (PIT) [62] Pittsburgh, PA St. Pius X Church.
Mushi, Peter *a.j.* (NY) [124] Bronx, NY St. Angela Merici Church.
Mushinsky, John E. (PAT) Retired.
Musial, Msgr. Edward S. '46 (PH) [3] Bensalem, PA Saint Ephrem Church; Conshohocken, PA St. Mary Church; Retired.
Musial, George '67 (CHI) [N] Chicago, IL St. Peter's Friary.
Musico, Edwin '85 (AGN) Tamuning, GU St. Anthony and St. Victor Church.
Musinski, Donald T. '62 (MIL) Retired.
Musinsky, John *s.v.d.* '44 (FgM) Society of the Divine Word Foreign Missions.
Musiol, Jozef *s.d.s.* '72 (AUS) String Prairie, TX St. Mary's of the Assumption Church.
Musiol, Jozel *s.d.s.* '72 (AUS) Rockne, TX Sacred Heart Church.
Musko, Andrew '34 (PSC) Retired.
Musngi, Efren *m.s.* '61 (SB) Moreno Valley, CA St. Christopher Church.
Musso, David *s.m.* (MRY) [F] Santa Cruz, CA Society of Mary, Marists.
Musso, David *s.m.* '98 (MRY) [I] Monterey, CA Department of Campus Ministry;
Mustaciuolo, Msgr. Gregory '90 (NY) [1] New York, NY Cathedral of St. Patrick.
Musteikis, Leonard '38 (OM) Retired.
Mustos, Stephen *sch.p.* '58 (PH) [AA] Devon, PA Piarist Fathers (Order of the Pious Schools).
Mustos, Stephen N. *sch.p.* '58 (PAT) [9] Passaic, NJ St. Stephen's Church.
Musumbu, Gilbert Malu *m.s.p.* '88 (TUC) [1] Tucson, AZ St. Augustine's Church.
Musumeci, James S. '76 (BRK) [200] Queens, NY St. Mel Church.
Mutefunya, Deo Gratias R. '63 (PEO) [1] Streator, IL Immaculate Conception Church.
Muteru, Gabriel '87 (NY) Mamaroneck, NY Holy Trinity Church.
Muth, Joseph L. '74 (BAL) [61] Baltimore, MD St. Matthew Church.
Muth, Stephen (PRM) Barberton, OH St. Nicholas Church.
Muthukattil, Thomas '66 (BRK) [152] Queens, NY St. Anthony of Padua Church.
Muthuplakel, James '67 (HBG) Lancaster, PA Lancaster General Hospital and Lancaster Community Hospital.
Mutsko, Frank J. '00 (ORL) [1] Orlando, FL St. James Church.
Muwonge, Expedito '89 (FTW) Plymouth, IN St. Michael Church.
Muzic, Anthony J. '63 (CLV) [46] Cleveland, OH St. Mark Church; Retired.
Muzzin, Victor *f.d.p.* '72 (NY) [11] New York, NY St. Ann Church.
Mychajlenko, Jaroslaw '78 (SJP) Solon, OH Protection B.V.M. Church.
Mycue, Gordon E. '49 (STP) Retired.
Myer, Blase '68 (PHX) [6] Scottsdale, AZ St. Maria Goretti Church.
Myers, Albert J. '51 (CLV) Retired.
Myers, Christopher *s.o.l.t.* '90 (CC) [H] Robstown, TX Society of Our Lady of the Most Holy Trinity.
Myers, David A. *s.j.* '70 (P) [L] Portland, OR Jesuit Provincial Office (Society of Jesus, Oregon Prov.).
Myers, Edward T. *o.p.* '65 (PRO) [P] Providence, RI St. Thomas Aquinas Priory at Providence College.
Myers, Gabriel *o.s.b.* '99 (WDC) [M] Washington, DC St. Anselm's Abbey.
Myers, J. Edward '55 (NEW) Retired.
Myers, James E. '80 (PEO) On Duty Outside the Diocese.
Myers, James E. *s.s.* '80 (SFR) [28] San Francisco, CA St. John the Evangelist Church.
Myers, Jeremy '84 (DAL) Sherman, TX St. Mary Church.
Myers, John *o.f.m.cap.* '54 (DET) [K] Detroit, MI St. Bonaventure Friary.
Myers, John *o.f.m.cap.* '54 (FgM) Capuchin Foreign Missions.
Myers, Kenneth '80 (PIT) Beaver County, PA The Medical Center Beaver.
Myers, Kenneth C. '68 (CLV) Released from Diocesan Assignment; [Z] Cleveland, OH COAR Peace Mission, Inc.
Myers, Kenneth C. '68 (SAT) [U] San Antonio, TX Missionaries of Pastoral Charity Society.
Myers, Kenneth E. '80 (PIT) Beaver, PA SS. Peter and Paul Church; Beaver County, PA Beaver Valley Geriatric Center.
Myers, Rawley '49 (COS) Retired.
Myers, Regis F. '54 (ALT) Retired.
Myers, Robert *s.v.d.* '49 (CHI) [B] Techny, IL Divine Word Residence.
Myers, William F. '56 (RCK) Active Outside the Diocese.
Myers, Msgr. William R. '69 (STU) Gallipolis, OH St. Louis Church; [I] Rio Grande, OH Rio Grande University.
Myers, William S. '88 (SFR) [54] San Francisco, CA St. Vincent de Paul Church.
Myett, Robert D. *o.p.* '60 (PRO) [P] Providence, RI St. Thomas Aquinas Priory at Providence College.
Myhalyk, Richard M. *s.s.e.* '71 (BUR) [E] Colchester, VT Society of St. Edmund.
Myhalyk, Richard M. *s.s.e.* '71 (FgM) Edmundite Foreign Missions.
Mykhayliuk, Orest '94 (PHU) Jenkintown, PA St. Michael the Archangel Church.
Mykyta, Andrew '48 (STN) Retired.
Mykyta, Myron '97 (SD) San Diego, CA Our Lady of Perpetual Help Church.
Mykyta, Myron '97 (STN) San Diego, CA Our Lady of Perpetual Help Church.
Myladil, Thomas *o.c.d.* '76 (MET) Edison, NJ St. Matthew Church.
Myladil, Thomas *o.c.d.* '78 (NY) [165] Bronx, NY St. Mary Star of the Sea Church.
Myladiyil, Sebastian *s.v.d.* '99 (LAF) [4] New Iberia, LA St. Edward Church.
Mylchreest, William F. '80 (MIA) [14] Fort Lauderdale, FL St. Sebastian Church.
Myler, John T. '82 (BEL) [7] Belleville, IL St. Mary Church; [J] Belleville, IL World Apostolate of Fatima, The Blue Army, U.S.A.
Myles, John '64 (SAC) Maxwell, CA Sacred Heart Church.
Mylet, James J. *m.m.* '75 (FgM) Maryknoll Foreign Missions.
Mynaugh, Msgr. Charles B. '42 (PH) Retired.
Myshchuk, Mikhail '94 (STF) Watervliet, NY St. Nicholas Church.
Myslinski, John F. '80 (WDC) [3] Rockville, MD St. Mary Church.
Mysliwiec, Haldane '70 (CHI) [3] Des Plaines, IL St. Stephen Protomartyr Church; [J] Des Plaines, IL Holy Family Medical Center.
Mysliwiec, Jan J. *s.d.s.* '62 (NEW) [N] Verona, NJ The Salvatorian Fathers.
Mysliwiec, Jordan *s.d.s.* '62 (NEW) [3] Irvington, NJ Sacred Heart of Jesus Church.
Myszel, George G. '53 (MIL) Retired.
Myszka, Msgr. Daniel J. '58 (BUF) Retired.

N

N'go, Anthony Chinh '94 (L) [42] Louisville, KY St. John Vianney Church; Fairdale, KY St. Jerome Church.
N'Zilamba, Norbert *o.praem.* '87 (JKS) [F] Jackson, MS Priory of St. Moses the Black.
Naaeke, Anthony '91 (PIT) [1] McKeesport, PA St. Martin de Porres Church.
Naas, Stephen E. '78 (KAL) [3] Kalamazoo, MI St. Mary Church.
Nabbefeld, Grant '95 (SJ) On Leave of Absence.
Naber, Herman J. '59 (L) [24] Louisville, KY St. Elizabeth of Hungary Church; [72] Louisville, KY St. Therese Church.
Naber, John T. '45 (BUF) Retired.
Nabozny, Peter '54 (ALB) Retired.
Nacarino, Raymond L. '85 (MET) [3] New Brunswick, NJ Our Lady of Mt. Carmel Church.
Nacca, John J. '41 (ROC) Retired.
Naccarato, Francis A. '79 (NY) [199] Staten Island, NY Blessed Sacrament Church.
Naccarato, Frank '79 (NY) State, NY Arthur Kill Correctional Facility.
Nacciarone, Ugo R. *s.j.* '64 (FgM) Provinces.
Nace, Msgr. Arthur J. '57 (PH) Absent on Sick Leave.
Nachajski, Richard E. '71 (ALN) [2] Reading, PA St. Anthony of Padua Church.
Nachtigal, Fred '58 (Y) Retired.
Nacional, Perfecto '62 (SR) Ukiah, CA St. Mary of the Angels Church.
Nacius, Michael A. '89 (CHI) Matteson, IL St. Lawrence O'Toole Church.
Nacke, Xavier *o.s.b.* '63 (KC) [A] Conception, MO Conception Seminary College; [J] Conception, MO Conception Abbey.
Nacu, Jose R. *m.s.* '57 (HON) [10] Honolulu, HI Our Lady of the Mount Church.
Nadackal, Zacharias *c.m.i.* '64 (NY) Rye, NY Resurrection Church.
Nadal, Bart *c.r.* '47 (DEN) [A] Denver, CO St. Andrew's Theatine Religious House.
Naddeo, Henry M. '56 (NEW) [1] Jersey City, NJ St. Aedan's Church.
Nadeau, James L. '88 (PRT) [1] Portland, ME Cathedral of the Immaculate Conception.
Nadeau, Lance P. *m.m.* '90 (FgM) Maryknoll Foreign Missions.
Nadeau, Real J. '62 (PRT) Kittery, ME St. Raphael's Church.
Nadeau, Richard A. '80 (PRT) Limerick, ME St. Matthew Church.
Nadeau, Roland '69 (STL) [P] St. Louis, MO La Salette Missionaries.
Nadeau, Roland P. '00 (PRT) [5] Lewiston, ME St. Patrick's Church; [6] Lewiston, ME SS. Peter and Paul Church.
Nadeau, Timothy J. '91 (PRT) Sanford, ME Holy Family Church; Sanford, ME St. Ignatius Martyr Church.
Nadeau, William *o.m.i.* '68 (RNO) Gardnerville, NV St. Gall Church.
Nader, John *c.s.sp.* (PIT) [3] Millvale, PA Holy Spirit Church.
Nadicksbernd, Elmer *s.v.d.* '64 (WH) Gassaway, WV St. Thomas Church; Maysel, WV Risen Lord Church.
Nadine, Jerome E. '58 (BRK) Released from Diocesan Assignment.
Nadine, Jerome E. '58 (LAV) [8] Las Vegas, NV St. Elizabeth Ann Seton Church.
Nadolny, Edmund S. '59 (HRT) [6] Meriden, CT St. Stanislaus Church.
Nadolny, Paul *s.v.d.* '89 (FgM) Society of the Divine Word Foreign Missions.
Nadolny, Stanley '68 (TUC) Bisbee, AZ St. Patrick Church.
Nadolski, Kevin '97 (ARL) [J] Alexandria, VA Oblates of St. Francis de Sales Residence.
Nadolski, Kevin M. *o.s.f.s.* '97 (ARL) [D] Alexandria, VA Bishop Ireton High School.
Naduvilekoot, Augustine '71 (NOR) Durham, CT Notre Dame Church.
Nadzam, John B. '50 (STU) Retired.
Naegele, Gary P. '79 (WH) [3] Fairmont, WV St. Anthony Church.
Naegele, Zacchaeus Maria *o.s.b.cam.* '98 (MRY) [F] Big Sur, CA New Camaldoli Hermitage.
Naessuns, Philip *o.f.m.cap.* '86 (DET) [K] Detroit, MI St. Bonaventure Friary.
Naffate, Lenin E. '00 (SAT) Gonzales, TX St. James Church.
Nagai, Alan '58 (HON) [14] Honolulu, HI St. Stephen Church.
Nagaroor, Joseph '66 (MAR) Escanaba, MI St. Joseph & St. Patrick Church.
Nagel, Austin *ss.cc.* '54 (FR) [I] Fairhaven, MA Sacred Hearts Provincial House.
Nagel, Kurt '97 (SEA) Port Angeles, WA Queen of Angels Church.
Nagele, John M. *c.pp.s.* '53 (TOL) Bismark, OH St. Sebastian Church; Marywood, OH St. Michael's Church; Reed, OH Assumption Church.
Nagengast, Maynard G. *o.s.b.* '62 (NEW) [N] Newark, NJ Newark Abbey.
Nagle, Alexis *t.o.r.* '74 (ALT) [F] Newry, PA St. Bernardine Monastery; [F] Newry, PA St. Bernardine Monastery.
Nagle, Edmund W. *s.j.* '63 (PAT) [I] Morristown, NJ Loyola House of Retreats.
Nagle, James B. *m.m.* '52 (NY) [DD] Maryknoll, NY Maryknoll Fathers and Brothers.
Nagle, Msgr. Joseph P. '71 (BRK) [132] Brooklyn, NY St. Saviour Church.
Nagle, Michael R. '72 (FR) Edgartown, MA St. Elizabeth Church; Oak Bluffs, MA Sacred Heart Church; Vineyard Haven, MA St. Augustine Church.
Nagle, Richard *o.carm.* '37 (NY) [DD] Middletown, NY St. Albert's Priory.
Nagle, Vincent *f.s.c.b.* '92 (FR) [2] Attleboro, MA St.

Joseph's Church; [O] Attleboro, MA Priestly Fraternity of the Missionaries of St. Charles Borromeo, Inc.
Nagle, Walter M. '99 (NOR) Moosup, CT All-Hallows Church.
Nagle, Msgr. William A. '49 (BGP) Retired; [P] Stamford, CT The Catherine Dennis Keefe Queen of the Clergy Retired Priests' Residence.
Naglich, Robert '91 (MIL) [P] Hales Corners, WI Priests of the Sacred Heart.
Naglich, Robert T. *s.c.j.* '91 (GRY) Portage, IN Nativity of Our Savior Church.
Naguszewski, Edward B. '30 (BO) Senior Priests.
Nagy, Joseph '40 (LA) Retired.
Nahn, William J. '76 (ALN) [4] Pottsville, PA St. Patrick Church.
Nahoe, Francisco *o.f.m.conv.* '94 (LA) [Q] Torrance, CA Franciscan Friars, St. Bonaventure Friary.
Naill, Joseph P. '97 (RCK) Special Assignment.
Nairn, Thomas *o.f.m.* '75 (CHI) [B] Chicago, IL The Catholic Theological Union at Chicago; [D] Chicago, IL Hales Franciscan High School, Inc.
Najdowski, John A. '51 (GR) On Special Assignment.
Najjar, Samuel A. '84 (SAM) Waterville, ME St. Joseph Church.
Nakagawa, Francis *s.m.* (HON) [G] Honolulu, HI Marianist Communities.
Nakagawa, Francis *s.m.* '57 (SJ) [L] Cupertino, CA Marianist Provincial Residence.
Nakowicz, Stanley T. '67 (PRO) [5] East Providence, RI Our Lady of Loreto Church.
Nalepa, Damien '70 (BAL) [35] Baltimore, MD St. Gregory the Great Church; Baltimore, MD Baltimore City Jail.
Nalepa, Richard *c.p.* '70 (SCR) [M] Scranton, PA Saint Ann's Passionist Monastery.
Nall, Brent C. '93 (SAC) Tulelake, CA Holy Cross Church.
Nallen, James F. '66 (CHI) [53] Chicago, IL St. Ethelreda Church.
Nallen, Michael J. '58 (CHI) Markham, IL St. Gerard Majella Church.
Nalley, Robert W. '75 (GAY) Grayling, MI St. Mary Church.
Nally, J. Brendan '56 (WOR) Clinton, MA Our Lady of the Rosary Church.
Nally, John J. *m.s.* '54 (WOR) [6] Fitchburg, MA St. Joseph's Church.
Nally, Joseph M. '72 (WOR) [24] Worcester, MA St. Joan of Arc Church.
Nalty, Christopher '99 (NO) [3] Kenner, LA St. Elizabeth Ann Seton Church.
Nalugon, Nilo '94 (SAN) [3] Abilene, TX St. Francis of Assisi Church; [4] Abilene, TX St. Vincent Pallotti Church.
Nalysnk, Yaroslov '90 (BO) Boston, MA St. Elizabeth's Medical Center; [Q] Boston, MA St. Elizabeth's Hospital of Boston.
Nalysnyk, Bogdan (STN) [1] Chicago, IL St. Nicholas Ukrainian Catholic Church.
Nalysnyk, Jaroslaw '91 (STF) Boston, MA Christ the King Church.
Nam, Heebong '97 (BRK) [226] Queens, NY St. Paul Chong Ha-Sang Roman Catholic Chapel Church.
Nam, Joseph M. Phan *c.m.c.* '89 (NO) [B] Metairie, LA Congregation of the Mother Coredemptrix Formation House.
Nam, Simon '52 (NY) [156] Bronx, NY St John Nam Church.
Namie, Msgr. James B. '54 (STP) On Duty Outside the Archdiocese; Retired.
Namiotka, Edward F. '87 (CAM) [5] Vineland, NJ St. Mary's Church; [B] Vineland, NJ Sacred Heart High School.
Nance, Michael '87 (BLX) Columbia, MS Industrial and Training School.
Nance, Michael '97 (BLX) Columbia, MS Most Holy Trinity Church.
Nangachiveettil, George Joseph (CHI) Bellwood, IL St. Simeon Church.
Nangle, Joseph J. *o.f.m.* '58 (WDC) [B] Washington, DC Franciscan Mission Service of North America.
Nangle, Thomas R. '70 (CHI) Other Assignments.
Nano, Efren '87 (TYL) Jacksonville, TX Our Lady of Sorrows Church.
Nanz, Jack '71 (PIT) [4] Butler, PA St. Peter Church.
Napier, Robert L. '90 (STA) Fernandina Beach, FL St. Michael's Church.
Napoli, Carlo *t.o.r.* '58 (WDC) Washington, DC Providence Hospital; [K] Washington, DC Providence Hospital; [M] Washington, DC St. Louis Friary.
Napoli, Peter *o.f.m.cap.* (NY) [151] Bronx, NY Immaculate Conception Church.
Napolitano, Joseph V. '76 (HRT) [11] New Britain, CT St. Maurice Church.
Nappo, Michael *o.f.m.* '90 (BO) [38] Boston, MA St. Leonard of Port Maurice Church.
Naquin, Roch '62 (HT) Retired.
Naranjo, Francisco '95 (STO) [7] Stockton, CA St. Luke Church.
Narcowich, Edward '53 (FTW) Geneva, IN St. Mary of the Presentation Church.
Nard, Raymond *o.f.m.cap.* (NY) [DD] Yonkers, NY St. Clare Friary.
Nardo, Anthony J. '87 (NEW) Springfield, NJ St. James Church.
Nardoianni, Antonio *o.f.m.* '74 (NY) [DD] New York, NY Franciscan Province of the Immaculate Conception.
Nardone, Amadeo *o.f.m.* '68 (NY) [DD] New York, NY Franciscan Province of the Immaculate Conception.
Nardone, Richard M. '54 (NEW) Retired; [B] South Orange, NJ Seton Hall University.
Narewski, Peter J. '47 (PRO) Retired; [P] Providence, RI St. John Vianney Residence.
Narez, Juan '93 (ELP) [11] El Paso, TX La Purisima Church.
Nargaj, Andrew *o.f.m.* (NY) [171] Bronx, NY Our Lady of Good Counsel Church.
Narimattam, Joseph J. '64 (WIL) Wilmington Manor, DE Our Lady of Fatima Church.
Narita, Michael *ss.cc.* '68 (FR) [I] Fairhaven, MA Sacred Hearts Provincial House.
Narivelil, Victor Z. *c.m.i.* '64 (STA) [14] Jacksonville, FL Sacred Heart Church.
Narkun, Msgr. Peter P. '45 (NY) Retired; [E] New York, NY Cardinal Hayes High School.
Narlaly, Jose T. *o.ss.t.* '81 (BAL) [S] Baltimore, MD Holy Trinity Monastery.
Naro, Carl J. '52 (RIC) Retired.
Narro, Luis *s.j.* '69 (GAL) [A] Houston, TX St. Mary's Seminary.
Nartey, Emmanuel '95 (NY) [62] New York, NY St. Joseph Church.
Nartker, Michael F. *s.m.* '96 (CIN) [M] Dayton, OH Marianist Provincialate.
Nasar, Ayub '85 (GR) [E] Grand Rapids, MI St. Mary's Health Services.
Nascimento, Daniel '98 (SFR) Burlingame, CA St. Catherine of Siena Church.
Naseman, Alfred *c.pp.s.* '67 (CIN) [B] Carthagena, OH St. Charles; [M] Dayton, OH Provincial Office of the Cincinnati Province of the Society of the Precious Blood.
Nash, Denis P. '54 (GR) Retired.
Nash, Edward H. *s.j.* '46 (BAL) [S] Baltimore, MD Jesuit Fathers and Brothers Maryland Provincial Curia.
Nash, Edward H. *s.j.* '46 (FgM) Provinces.
Nash, Francis J. *s.j.* '69 (BAL) [B] Baltimore, MD Loyola College in Maryland; [S] Baltimore, MD Jesuit Community of Loyola College, Inc.
Nash, Howard J. '61 (HRT) [4] New Haven, CT St. Bernadette's Church.
Nash, Msgr. James F. '34 (ORG) Anaheim, CA St. Anthony Claret Church; Retired.
Nash, James R. '89 (SCR) Montrose, PA Holy Name of Mary Church.
Nash, John C. '75 (NOR) Groton, CT St. Mary Church.
Nash, Michael '80 (JUN) [1] Juneau, AK Cathedral of the Nativity of The Blessed Virgin Mary.
Nash, Paul A. *s.j.* '52 (BO) [W] Chestnut Hill, MA The Jesuit Community at Boston College.
Nash, Robert C. '48 (WH) Retired.
Nash, Stephen F. '97 (WDC) [2] Bowie, MD Sacred Heart Church.
Nasini, Gino *s.x.* '65 (FgM) Xaverian Foreign Missions.
Nasini, Gino *s.x.* '65 (PAT) [M] Wayne, NJ Xaverian Missionary Fathers.
Nason, Dennis T. '66 (BO) [1] Haverhill, MA All Saints Church.
Nasr, Toufic '97 (OLL) Las Vegas, NV St. Sharbel Church.
Nasri, Youssef Bochra '85 (BRK) [86] Brooklyn, NY St. Michael's Church; [123] Brooklyn, NY Resurrection Catholic Coptic Chapel Church.
Nassal, Joseph *c.p.p.s.* (BEL) [G] Ruma, IL Province Center, Adorers of the Blood of Christ, United States Province.
Nassaney, Daniel *o.m.i.* '74 (NOR) [F] Willimantic, CT Missionary Oblates of Mary Immaculate; [I] Willimantic, CT Immaculata Retreat House.
Nasser, Joseph M. *s.j.* '75 (GAL) [3] Spring, TX St. Ignatius of Loyola Church.
Nassetta, Peter W. '89 (ARL) Special Assignment; [M] Fairfax, VA George Mason University, Catholic Campus Ministry House; [M] Fairfax, VA George Mason University, Catholic Campus Ministry House.
Nassr, Martin B. '67 (TOL) Sandusky, OH SS. Peter and Paul Church.
Nastold, Donald O. *s.j.* '58 (CIN) [26] Cincinnati, OH St. Francis Xavier Church.
Natale, Samuel '79 (RIC) On Duty Outside the Diocese.
Natalizia, Louis T. '80 (PRO) [4] North Providence, RI Presentation of the Blessed Virgin Mary Church.
Natho, Clifton J. '60 (GAL) Retired.
Nations, David G. *c.m.* '97 (STL) [34] St. Louis, MO St. Francis de Sales Church; [P] St. Louis, MO Vincentian Community.
Nativo, Joseph S. '56 (NEW) [22] Newark, NJ St. Lucy's Church.
Natsuhara, Bruce K. '78 (OKL) [13] Oklahoma City, OK St. Joseph Church.
Nau, Dale '78 (DUL) [F] Duluth, MN University of MN-Duluth; [G] Duluth, MN The Human Life and Development Fund of the Diocese of Duluth; [G] Duluth, MN Calvary Cemetery.
Nau, Thomas R. '78 (STU) Chesapeake, OH St. Ann Church; Ironton, OH St. Joseph Church; Ironton, OH St. Lawrence Church; [I] Ironton, OH Ohio University - Ironton Branch.
Naucke, Alfred E. *s.j.* '65 (SJ) [L] Los Gatos, CA California Province of the Society of Jesus, Jesuit Provincial Office.
Naughton, James *s.d.b.* '67 (BIR) Leeds, AL St. Theresa's Church.
Naughton, Msgr. John T. '49 (LA) Woodland Hills, CA St. Mel Church; Retired.
Naughton, Msgr. Louis '71 (ATL) [1] Atlanta, GA Cathedral of Christ the King; Special or Other (Arch)Diocesan Assignment.
Naughton, Michael *o.s.b.* '66 (SCL) [I] Collegeville, MN St. John's Abbey, of the Order of St. Benedict.
Naughton, Patrick J. '91 (COL) On Duty Outside the Diocese.
Naughton, Patrick J. '91 (MIA) Davie, FL St. David Church.
Naughton, Thomas J. '61 (BO) Lakeville, MA Saints Martha and Mary Church.
Naughton, Msgr. William M. '72 (PAT) Randolph, NJ Resurrection Church.
Naumann, Joseph F. '75 (STL) Richmond Heights, MO Immacolata Church.
Naumann, Paul S. *s.j.* '63 (SY) [S] Syracuse, NY Jesuits at LeMoyne, Inc.
Naumes, Matthew '63 (SEA) Retired.
Naus, John E. *s.j.* '55 (MIL) [P] Milwaukee, WI Jesuit Community at Marquette University.
Nava, Rufino '99 (LA) San Fernando, CA Santa Rosa Church.
Navarra, Peter '81 (SD) Escondido, CA St. Mary Church.
Navarre, Robert G. '45 (SAG) Retired.
Navarrette, Jesus '87 (ARL) [2] Alexandria, VA Good Shepherd Church.
Navarro, Marcelo *i.v.e.* '94 (BRK) [48] Brooklyn, NY St. Gabriel The Archangel Church.
Navarro, Modesto Martinez *t.c.* '37 (BAL) Odenton, MD St. Joseph Church.
Navarro, Nicolas (SJN) [B] Cantera, PR Colegio San Juan Bosco.
Navarro, Nicolas '69 (SJN) [37] San Juan, PR Maria Auxiliadora Church.
Navarro, Msgr. Pablo A. '78 (MIA) [33] Miami, FL St. Timothy Church; [C] Miami, FL Archbishop Coleman Carroll High School.
Navarro, Pedro '63 (NEW) [2] Union City, NJ St. Augustine's Church.
Navarroli, Frederick '43 (RVC) Retired.
Navascues, Moises *sch.p.* '54 (PCE) Santa Isabel, PR St. James Church; [B] Ponce, PR The Pontifical Catholic University of Puerto Rico.
Nave, Francis A. '92 (ALN) Whitehall, PA St. Elizabeth Church.
Nave, Francis R. '60 (ALN) Retired; [J] Bethlehem, PA Holy Family Villa.
Navin, Msgr. Cyril '45 (LA) Encino, CA St. Cyril Church; Retired.
Navin, Timothy M. '79 (VEN) [3] Naples, FL St. Peter the Apostle Church.
Navins, Robert J. '50 (NY) [212] Staten Island, NY St. Margaret Mary Church.
Navit, Zachary W. '94 (PH) Trooper, PA Visitation B.V.M. Church.
Navone, John J. *s.j.* '62 (P) [L] Portland, OR Jesuit Provincial Office (Society of Jesus, Oregon Prov.).
Navoy, Ronald E. '71 (CHI) River Grove, IL St. Cyprian Church.
Nawarskas, Msgr. Frederick '67 (SAN) [2] Abilene, TX Holy Family Church.
Nawrocki, Norman D. '82 (DET) Bloomfield Hills, MI St. Regis Church.
Nawrocki, Robert W. '61 (MIL) [5] Milwaukee, WI St. Alexander Church.
Nawrocki, Xavier *o.f.m.conv.* '57 (ROC) [6] Auburn, NY St. Hyacinth Church.
Nawrocki, Zdzislaw *s.chr.* '73 (PAT) Boonton, NJ SS. Cyril and Methodius Church.
Nayak, Christudas '68 (ALX) [C] Alexandria, LA Christus Health Central Louisiana dba St. Frances Cabrini Hospital.
Nayak, Subal *ss.cc.* '00 (FR) [I] Fairhaven, MA Sacred Hearts Provincial House.
Naylor, David W. '00 (L) Bardstown, KY St. Joseph Church.
Naylor, Ronald J. '60 (RIC) Retired.
Nazabal, Isidro '63 (CGS) Cidra, PR Nuestra Senora de Fatima Church.
Nazar, David *s.j.* '83 (FgM) Jesuit Foreign Missions.
Nazareth, Longinus (NY) [1] Port Chester, NY Our Lady of Mercy Church.
Nazareth, Menino George A. '59 (P) Tillamook, OR Sacred Heart Church.
Nazareth, Valerian '77 (BR) [3] Baton Rouge, LA St. Aloysius Church.

Nazario, Heber *o.s.a.* '65 (SJN) [18] Bayamon, PR Santa Rita de Casia Church.
Nazarro, John *s.d.b.* '83 (NY) [DD] New Rochelle, NY Salesian Provincial House.
Nazhianpara, Jose *c.m.* '91 (CHI) [N] Chicago, IL DePaul Vincentian Residence.
Nazimek, David '93 (GBG) Fairchance, PA SS. Cyril and Methodius Church.
Nazimek, Francis A. '48 (PIT) Fredericktown, PA St. Oliver Plunkett Church; Retired.
Nazzani, Ermete *c.s.* '62 (LA) [P] Sun Valley, CA Villa Scalabrini.
Nazzaro, John *s.d.b.* '83 (NY) [F] New Rochelle, NY Salesian High School.
Nazzaro, Stanley J. '48 (HRT) Retired.
Ndagizimana, Isidore '85 (AUS) [5] Austin, TX Holy Cross Church.
Ndeukoya, Msgr. Augustine '61 (SP) [9] Tampa, FL St. Joseph Church.
Ndeyekiyo, Benedict *a.l.c.p.* (PIT) [78] Pittsburgh, PA Most Holy Name of Jesus Church.
Ndrevashay, Primus P. '61 (DET) Beverly Hills, MI Our Lady of Albanians Church; Retired.
Ndugbu, Polycarp '73 (SAC) Jackson, CA St. Patrick's Church.
Nealon, Msgr. Joseph A. '61 (STU) Retired.
Nealon, Joseph W. '40 (NEW) Haworth, NJ Sacred Heart Church; Retired.
Nealy, Francis Dominic *o.p.* '39 (WDC) [11] Washington, DC St. Dominic Church & Priory Church.
Neary, Anthony *c.p.* '54 (PIT) [O] Pittsburgh, PA St. Paul of the Cross Monastery.
Neary, Mark (SJ) Absent on Sick Leave.
Neary, Pat *c.s.c.* '91 (FTW) [B] Notre Dame, IN University of Notre Dame Du Lac.
Neary, Patrick *c.s.c.* '91 (FTW) [A] Notre Dame, IN Moreau Seminary.
Neary, Patrick M. *c.s.c.* '91 (FTW) [A] Notre Dame, IN Moreau Seminary.
Neary, Thomas E. '54 (SY) Retired.
Neautl, Armand R. '52 (PRT) Retired.
Nebel, Msgr. Charles A. '38 (BEL) Retired.
Nebus, Vincent (ORL) Retired.
Nebus, Vincent J. '51 (MET) Retired.
Nedder, Edward T. '87 (SAM) Springfield, MA St. Anthony Church.
Nediakala, Kuriakose *m.c.b.s.* '78 (BIS) Mott, ND St. Vincent de Paul Church.
Nedimyer, Raymond *t.o.r.* '97 (FWT) [5] Arlington, TX St. Maria Goretti Church.
Nedungatt, John *s.d.b.* '86 (NY) [3] Port Chester, NY Our Lady of the Rosary Church.
Nee, Eugene O. '64 (SAT) Military Chaplains.
Nee, Kenneth T. '53 (RVC) Manorhaven, NY Our Lady of Fatima Church.
Nee, Robert (BO) [5] Brookline, MA St. Mary of the Assumption Church.
Nee, Robert F. *o.f.m.* '62 (NY) Jeffersonville, NY St. George Church.
Nee, Thomas B. '66 (RIC) Retired.
Nee, Thomas M. '39 (PIT) Retired; [O] Pittsburgh, PA St. John Vianney Manor.
Needham, Elliot *o.s.b.* '90 (RIC) [L] Richmond, VA Mary Mother of the Church Abbey.
Needham, James *s.s.c.* '61 (OM) [K] St. Columbans, NE St. Columban's Foreign Mission Society.
Needham, Msgr. Thomas J. '61 (WOR) [6] Worcester, MA Immaculate Conception Church.
Neeley, Peter G. *s.j.* '81 (LA) Los Angeles, CA Immigration and Naturalization Service; San Pedro, CA Immigration and Naturalization Service.
Neely, Harry M. *o.s.a.* '53 (SD) [H] San Diego, CA Augustinian Community.
Neenan, Benedict *o.s.b.* '88 (KC) [A] Conception, MO Conception Seminary College; [J] Conception, MO Conception Abbey.
Neenan, Robert P. *s.j.* '51 (STP) [N] Minneapolis, MN La Storta Jesuit Community.
Neenan, William B. *s.j.* '61 (BO) [W] Chestnut Hill, MA The Jesuit Community at Boston College.
Neff, Eugene J. '71 (BEL) Lebanon, IL St. Joseph Church.
Neff, John '86 (E) [1] Oil City, PA Assumption of the Blessed Virgin Mary Church.
Neff, Msgr. John F. '60 (SP) [14] Tampa, FL St. Paul Church; [F] Tampa, FL St. Paul Preschool.
Neff, John R. '86 (E) Du Bois, PA Du Bois Regional Hospital.
Neffy, Arthur '47 (DET) Retired.
Negherbon, Vincent R. '46 (ALT) [F] Loretto, PA Mount Assisi Friary.
Negrete, Wayne *s.j.* '91 (LA) [C] Los Angeles, CA Loyola Marymount University.
Negrillos, Ferdinand *sch.p.* '41 (PH) [G] Devon, PA Devon Preparatory School; [AA] Devon, PA Piarist Fathers (Order of the Pious Schools).
Negron, Juan Luis '89 (CGS) [F] Naranjito, PR Seminario Pablo VI - Propedeutico.
Nehrig, Robert V. *m.m.* '54 (FgM) Maryknoll Foreign Missions.
Neidhart, William J. *c.s.c.* '56 (FTW) Granger, IN St. Pius X Church.
Neiheisel, Stanley H. '61 (CIN) [32] Cincinnati, OH Holy Cross-Immaculata Church.
Neilson, Joseph *o.c.d.* '62 (DAL) [I] Dallas, TX Mount Carmel Center.
Neilson, Kieran A. *o.s.b.* '60 (CHL) [J] Belmont, NC Belmont Abbey; [L] Charlotte, NC Diocesan Office of Campus Ministry.
Neilson, Richard J. '83 (NY) Retired.
Neiman, John '86 (LA) [1] Oxnard, CA St. Anthony Church.
Neis, Thomas A. '52 (GAY) Charlevoix, MI St. Mary Church.
Neis, William P. (LC) On Duty Outside the Diocese.
Neitzke, Ron P. '89 (JOL) [15] Joliet, IL St. Mary Magdalene Church.
Nekic, Simon J. '43 (CLV) [12] Lorain, OH St. Vitus Church.
Nekoliczak, Ted A. '59 (GI) Sidney, NE St. Patrick's Church.
Nelan, Francis *m.s.c.* '53 (SAT) [K] San Antonio, TX Padua Place.
Nelan, Kevin J. '77 (NY) [16] New York, NY St. Benedict the Moor Church; [110] New York, NY Sacred Heart of Jesus Church.
Nelipowitz, Charles *o.f.m.conv.* '54 (SY) [2] Syracuse, NY Assumption B.V.M. Church.
Nelke, Richard '51 (STL) Chesterfield, MO Ascension Church.
Nelligan, Paul J. *s.j.* '54 (WOR) [N] Worcester, MA Jesuits of Holy Cross College, Inc.
Nellikunnell, James *c.m.i.* '79 (ALX) Evergreen, LA Little Flower Church.
Nellis, Thomas F. '66 (ROC) Webster, NY Holy Trinity Church.
Nellissery, Joy '88 (ATL) Athens, GA St. Joseph's Church.
Nelson, Andrew L. '57 (MIL) [A] St. Francis, WI Saint Francis Seminary.
Nelson, Bertram A. *c.s.c.* (FgM) Holy Cross Foreign Missions.
Nelson, Caye A. '88 (BR) Napoleonville, LA St. Anne Church; Plattenville, LA Assumption of the Blessed Virgin Mary Church.
Nelson, Charles T. '87 (SFD) Bluffs, IL St. Patrick Church; Murrayville, IL St. Bartholomew Church; Winchester, IL St. Mark Church.
Nelson, Daniel C. *o.f.m.* '77 (ALB) [B] Loudonville, NY Siena College.
Nelson, Francis J. '66 (SAV) [8] Savannah, GA St. Frances Xavier Cabrini Church.
Nelson, Francis P. *c.ss.r.* '64 (BRK) [V] Brooklyn, NY Our Lady of Good Counsel Residence.
Nelson, Francis X. '89 (BRK) [84] Brooklyn, NY St. Mary, Star of the Sea Church.
Nelson, Frank M. '88 (RVC) Valley Stream, NY Blessed Sacrament Church.
Nelson, Glenn L. '93 (RCK) Special Assignment.
Nelson, Gregory E. '97 (PEO) [1] Bloomington, IL Holy Trinity Church.
Nelson, James '43 (GAL) [N] Houston, TX St. Dominic Village.
Nelson, Joseph *o.f.m.* '64 (CIN) [V] Cincinnati, OH Hispanic Ministries at St. Charles, Archdiocese of Cincinnati.
Nelson, Kevin '00 (PMB) Stuart, FL St. Joseph Church.
Nelson, Linden '81 (LC) [D] Marshfield, WI Saint Joseph's Hospital of Marshfield, Inc.
Nelson, Martin Lester '97 (BEA) Sour Lake, TX Our Lady of Victory Church; [A] Beaumont, TX Monsignor Kelly Catholic High School.
Nelson, Paul E. '61 (WIN) Austin, MN St. Augustine's Church.
Nelson, Robert W. '77 (LC) Boyd, WI Sacred Heart of Jesus-St. Joseph Church; Stanley, WI Holy Family Church.
Nelson, Thomas *o.praem.* '81 (CHI) [X] Chicago, IL The Institute on Religious Life.
Nelson, Thomas J. *c.m.* '75 (DEN) [M] Denver, CO Congregation of the Mission Midwest Province: De Paul House.
Nelson, Thomas J. '93 (WDC) On Duty Outside the Archdiocese.
Nelson, Thomas W. *o.praem.* '81 (ORG) [A] Silverado, CA St. Michael's Norbertine Postulancy, Novitiate and Juniorate; [I] Silverado, CA Norbertine Fathers of Orange Inc.
Nelson, Timothy '00 (LAN) Burton, MI Holy Redeemer Church.
Nelson, William R. '82 (PBL) Center, CO St. Francis Jerome Church; Del Norte, CO Holy Name of Mary Church; Monte Vista, CO St. Joseph Church.
Nemec, Joseph J. '84 (LIN) [11] Lincoln, NE St. Teresa's Church; [H] Lincoln, NE Adoration Convent and Church of Christ the King.
Nemecek, M. Cyril '60 (CHI) North Riverside, IL Mater Christi Church.
Nemeck, Francis Kelly *o.m.i.* '61 (CC) [G] Sarita, TX Lebh Shomea House of Prayer.
Nemeck, Francis Kelly *o.m.i.* '61 (SAT) [C] San Antonio, TX Oblate School of Theology.
Nemer, Lawrence *s.v.d.* '60 (FgM) Society of the Divine Word Foreign Missions.
Nemergut, Robert S. '77 (EVN) [3] Vincennes, IN St. John the Baptist Church; Special Assignment.
Nemeth, Edward M. *s.j.* '65 (CLV) University Heights, OH Gesu Church.
Nemeth, Maurus B. *o.s.b.* '72 (SFR) [N] Portola Valley, CA Woodside Priory.
Nemmers, Francis J. '57 (SC) Onawa, IA St. John Church.
Nemmers, Mark R. '66 (DUB) [9] Dubuque, IA Holy Trinity Church.
Neneman, John '00 (ORG) Anaheim, CA St. Justin Martyr Church.
Nenneau, Thomas D. '81 (LAN) [4] Jackson, MI Queen of the Miraculous Medal Church.
Nentwick, John '65 (Y) [2] Canton, OH Our Lady of Peace Church.
Neri, Gegorio '92 (NY) Ossining, NY St. Ann Church.
Nerino, Joseph C. *m.m.* '50 (FgM) Maryknoll Foreign Missions.
Neroda, Edward J. '57 (Y) [21] Youngstown, OH St. Stanislaus Kostka's Church.
Nesbit, Walter G. *s.j.* '59 (STL) [P] St. Louis, MO Hallahan House; [P] St. Louis, MO The Jesuits of the Missouri Province.
Nesbitt, John B. '62 (SD) Retired.
Neske, Mark I. '83 (MOB) [11] Mobile, AL Little Flower Church.
Nespolo, Umberto *o.m.i.* (OAK) [N] Oakland, CA Oblate Provincial House & Procure.
Nesrsta, Steven '95 (AUS) Temple, TX St. Mary's Church.
Ness, Bernardine *o.s.b.* '64 (FgM) American - Cassinese Congregation Foreign Missions.
Ness, Bernardine *o.s.b.* '64 (SFS) [F] Marvin, SD Blue Cloud Abbey.
Ness, Scott C. *o.s.a.* '90 (BO) [C] North Andover, MA Merrimack College.
Nessel, William J. *o.s.f.s.* '56 (HBG) Lewisburg, PA Sacred Heart of Jesus Church.
Nester, Edward J. '46 (MET) Baptistown, NJ Our Lady of Victories Church; Retired; [H] Somerset, NJ Maria Regina Residence.
Nesti, Donald *c.s.sp.* (GAL) [C] Houston, TX University of St. Thomas.
Nesti, Donald S. *c.s.sp.* '63 (GAL) [Q] Houston, TX Western Province of the Congregation of the Holy Ghost.
Nestler, W. David *o.f.m.cap.* '89 (PIT) [O] Pittsburgh, PA St. Conrad Friary.
Nestor, Msgr. Michael '65 (SJP) Retired.
Nestor, Robert P. '70 (NEW) [B] South Orange, NJ Seton Hall University.
Nestor, Thomas F. '80 (BO) [A] Brighton, MA St. John's Seminary.
Nestor, Thomas F. '81 (BO) [A] Boston, MA St. John's Seminary School of Theology.
Nesvadba, Msgr. Reginald '66 (GAL) Pearland, TX St. Helen Church.
Netta, John G. '57 (NEW) [6] Elizabeth, NJ St. Genevieve's Church.
Nettekoven, Joseph '75 (ORG) Anaheim, CA St. Justin Martyr Church.
Netzer, Angelus *o.f.m.conv.* '51 (ALB) [L] Rensselaer, NY Franciscan Mission House.
Neu, Msgr. Hubert '51 (FWT) [1] Fort Worth, TX St. Patrick Church.
Neu, Msgr. Leon M. '52 (BUF) Randolph, NY St. Patrick Church.
Neuberger, Michael T. '62 (MIL) On Leave.
Neubert, Germar *o.s.b.* (OM) [O] Schuyler, NE St. Benedict Center Endowment Fund.
Neubert, Germar '65 (OM) [K] Schuyler, NE Benedictine Mission House.
Neufelder, Jerome '55 (IND) [A] St. Meinrad, IN St. Meinrad Seminary.
Neufelder, Msgr. Jerome M. '55 (EVN) On Duty Outside the Diocese.
Neugebauer, Robert G. '73 (ALT) [2] Altoona, PA Immaculate Conception Church.
Neugebaur, John '55 (ALT) [3] Altoona, PA St. Mark's Church.
Neuhaus, Richard J. '91 (NY) [52] New York, NY Immaculate Conception Church.
Neuhaus, William B. '83 (COV) Fort Thomas, KY St. Thomas Church.
Neuman, Eugene (MIL) Sheboygan Falls, WI St. Mary Church.
Neuman, James L. '71 (SFD) Wood River, IL St. Bernard Church.
Neuman, Matthias *o.s.b.* '67 (EVN) [G] Ferdinand, IN Sisters of St. Benedict of Ferdinand, IN, Inc., Monastery Immaculate Conception.
Neuman, Matthias *o.s.b.* '67 (IND) [A] St. Meinrad, IN St. Meinrad Seminary; [J] St. Meinrad, IN St. Meinrad Archabbey.
Neuman, Peter *i.c.* '80 (NO) [14] New Orleans, LA Mary, Queen of Vietnam Church.
Neumann, Aloysius J. '60 (RCK) Genoa, IL St. Catherine of Genoa Church.

Neumann, Don A. '72 (GAL) [K] Houston, TX The Catholic Chaplain Corps.
Neumann, Paul *s.m.* '59 (STL) [P] St. Louis, MO Provincialate of the Society of Mary, Province of St. Louis.
Neumann, Richard J. '65 (HRT) Windsor, CT St. Gabriel's Church.
Neumann, William J. '75 (ORL) [2] Ocala, FL Our Lady of the Springs Church.
Neumeier, Larry '95 (LA) Thousand Oaks, CA St. Paschal Baylon Church.
Neuner, Donald L. '56 (STL) [3] St. Charles, MO St. Elizabeth Ann Seton Church.
Neurohr, Gilbert N. '54 (MAR) Retired; [D] Escanaba, MI Bishop Noa Home for Senior Citizens.
Neuser, John C. '62 (GB) Mishicot, WI Holy Cross Church.
Neuville, Joseph '46 (P) Retired.
Neuzil, Greg '67 (KNX) LaFollette, TN Our Lady of Perpetual Help Church; Tazewell, TN Christ the King Church.
Neva, Roman G. '35 (FAR) Wahpeton, ND St. John's Church; Retired.
Nevans, Robert V. '49 (DEN) Retired.
Nevares, Eduardo *m.s.* '81 (TYL) Lufkin, TX St. Patrick Church.
Nevels, Thomas A. '99 (CIN) [36] Cincinnati, OH St. Ignatius Loyola Church.
Neville, Franklin A. '86 (WH) Farmington, WV St. Peter's Church; Mannington, WV St. Patrick's Church.
Neville, Gary J. *o.praem.* '78 (GB) [A] De Pere, WI St. Norbert Abbey; [I] De Pere, WI St. Norbert Abbey; [O] De Pere, WI NORBERT & CO.
Neville, James J. *s.j.* '56 (PH) [AA] Philadelphia, PA Jesuit Community at St. Joseph's University.
Neville, James J. *s.j.* '56 (WH) Monongah, WV Holy Spirit Church.
Neville, John *o.s.c.* '61 (CHI) [N] Chicago, IL Crosier Community of Chicago.
Neville, John J. *o.s.c.* (CHI) [B] Chicago, IL The Catholic Theological Union at Chicago.
Neville, Joseph B. *s.j.* '60 (SY) [S] Syracuse, NY Jesuits at LeMoyne, Inc.
Neville, Thomas W. '52 (RCK) Retired.
Nevin, Msgr. Emmet R. '77 (NY) [E] New York, NY Monsignor Farrell High School.
Nevins, Donald J. '75 (CHI) [60] Chicago, IL St. Francis of Assisi Church.
Nevins, Eugene J. *s.j.* '80 (CIN) [K] Cincinnati, OH Good Samaritan Hospital; [M] Cincinnati, OH Jesuit Community at St. Xavier High School.
Nevins, John J. '57 (PH) Essington, PA St. Margaret Mary Alacoque Church.
Nevins, Troy '96 (GR) Belding, MI St. Joseph's Church; Miriam, MI St. Mary's Church.
Nevlud, Gregory '82 (SAT) [9] San Antonio, TX Holy Spirit Church.
New, Gary *s.d.s.* '91 (GB) Charlesburg, WI St. Charles Borromeo Church; Charlestown, WI St. Martin Church; Chilton, WI St. Augustine Church; Chilton, WI St. Mary Church; Jericho, WI Holy Trinity Church; Kloten, WI St. Elizabeth Church.
Newbold, Msgr. Robert '45 (PRO) [P] Providence, RI St. John Vianney Residence.
Newbold, Msgr. Robert C. '45 (PRO) Retired.
Newbold, Ronan *c.p.* '69 (SAC) [H] Citrus Heights, CA Christ the King Retreat; [J] Citrus Heights, CA Christ the King Retreat Center.
Newbold, Thomas M. *c.p.* '42 (CHI) [N] Chicago, IL Passionist Provincial Office.
Newbold, Thomas More *c.p.* '42 (SAC) [H] Citrus Heights, CA Christ the King Retreat.
Newburn, Charles *sch.p.* '79 (MIA) [C] Fort Lauderdale, FL Cardinal Gibbons High School.
Newcomer, Joseph '71 (B) [B] Nampa, ID Mercy Medical Center.
Newell, John J. '58 (BRK) Absent on Sick Leave.
Newell, Joseph A. *s.j.* '66 (ALN) [A] Wernersville, PA Jesuit Center.
Newell, Joseph P. '45 (PIT) Cranberry Township, PA St. Ferdinand Church.
Newell, Matthias '87 (RIC) Brookneal, VA St. Elizabeth of Hungary Church; Retired.
Newfield, Msgr. John L. '48 (HT) Retired.
Newhouse, Paul M. *c.i.c.m.* '54 (SAT) Somerset, TX St. Mary's Church.
Newland, Ronald A. '67 (NEW) Military Chaplains.
Newman, Aloysius T. '54 (WDC) Retired.
Newman, Brian *o.f.m.cap.* '61 (FgM) Capuchin Foreign Missions.
Newman, Charles *o.f.m.* '85 (PH) [D] Philadelphia, PA Archbishop Ryan High School; [AA] Philadelphia, PA St. Pius X Friary.
Newman, Earle A. *s.s.j.* '53 (BAL) [S] Baltimore, MD St. Joseph Society of the Sacred Heart House of Central Administration.
Newman, J. Scott '93 (CHR) On Duty Outside the Diocese.
Newman, Jay Scott *s.j.* '93 (COL) [A] Columbus, OH Pontifical College Josephinum.
Newman, Louis '58 (SD) [25] San Diego, CA St. Columba Church.
Newman, Louis I. '58 (RVC) Priests Released from Diocesan Assignment.
Newman, Mark L. *c.j.* '60 (LA) Santa Maria, CA St. Louis de Montfort Church.
Newman, Matthias *o.s.b.* (IND) [K] Beech Grove, IN Our Lady of Grace Monastery.
Newman, Michael J. *s.d.s.* '67 (SAC) [K] Chico, CA Newman Centers.
Newman, Michael T. '69 (MIL) [7] Kenosha, WI St. Mary Church.
Newman, Nelson A. '54 (OM) Central City, NE St. Michael Church.
Newman, Robert V. *s.c.* '81 (HRT) [1] New Haven, CT Sacred Heart Church.
Newman, William '54 (BAL) [W] Linthicum, MD Catholic Daughters of the Americas.
Newman, William *o.p.* '57 (WDC) [11] Washington, DC St. Dominic Church & Priory Church.
Newmeyer, George C. '68 (PIT) Glenshaw, PA St. Bonaventure Church.
Newns, John J. '74 (PH) [1] Phoenixville, PA St. Ann Church.
Newton, David J. '88 (LFT) Gas City, IN Holy Family Church.
Newton, John G. '53 (CAM) Retired.
Newton, Stephen P. *c.s.c.* '89 (FTW) [J] South Bend, IN Congregation of Holy Cross, Indiana Province, Provincial House.
Newton, Thomas A. '88 (CAM) Blackwood, NJ St. Agnes Church.
Ney, Charles '74 (NSH) On Duty Outside the Diocese.
Neyland, Malcolm '73 (LUB) Post, TX Holy Cross Church.
Neyland, Quintin A. *o.f.m.* '46 (NY) [35] New York, NY St. Francis of Assisi Church.
Neylon, Bruce M. '75 (FR) Seekonk, MA St. Mary's Church.
Neyra, Hugo R. '84 (LA) [42] Los Angeles, CA St. Alphonsus Church.
Neyrey, Jerome H. *s.j.* '70 (FTW) [B] Notre Dame, IN University of Notre Dame Du Lac; [N] Granger, IN Jesuit Community.
Ng, Andrew '97 (HON) [15] Honolulu, HI Star of the Sea Church.
Ng, Thomas '61 (OAK) [12] Oakland, CA St. Leo's Church.
Nghiem, Peter '72 (GR) Wyoming, MI Our Lady of LaVang Church.
Nghiem, Peter Hoan-Xuan '72 (GR) On Special Assignment.
Nghiem, Vu Minh *c.ss.r.* '51 (LA) [Q] Baldwin Park, CA Vietnamese Redemptorist Mission; [CC] Baldwin Park, CA The Redemptorist Vietnamese Mission Corporation.
Ngirwa, Apolinari (NY) [76] New York, NY St. Monica Church.
Ngirwa, Apolinari J. (NY) Manhattan, NY Mount Sinai Medical Center.
Ngo, Anthony '94 (RIC) [19] Richmond, VA Church of the Vietnamese Martyrs.
Ngo, Francis Huan '89 (GAL) [32] Houston, TX St. Gregory the Great Church.
Ngo, Lan *s.j.* (PHX) [B] Phoenix, AZ Brophy College Preparatory.
Ngo Duc Vuong, John D.M. *c.m.c.* (SPC) [E] Carthage, MO Congregation of the Mother Co-Redemptrix, United States Assumption Province.
Ngoc Diep, Joseph M. Tran *c.m.c.* '82 (SPC) [A] Carthage, MO Congregation of the Mother Co-Redemptrix.
Ngodcho, Timothy *s.j.* '87 (BO) [W] Chestnut Hill, MA The Jesuit Community at Boston College.
Ngugi, Njoroge '80 (BRK) [127] Brooklyn, NY St. Rose of Lima Church.
Nguyen, Andrew Cuu (NY) Manhattan, NY Manhattan Psychiatric Center.
Nguyen, Andrew Tu Minh '69 (ARL) Annandale, VA Holy Spirit Church.
Nguyen, Anthony (BO) [2] Chelsea, MA St. Rose of Lima Church.
Nguyen, Anthony (OAK) [S] Berkeley, CA Maria House.
Nguyen, Anthony '00 (SJ) [7] San Jose, CA Holy Family Church.
Nguyen, Anthony Giang '66 (BO) [13] Lowell, MA St. Patrick Church.
Nguyen, Augustine '70 (DOD) [1] Dodge City, KS Cathedral of the Sacred Heart.
Nguyen, Bieu Van '00 (MOB) [3] Montgomery, AL St. Bede Church.
Nguyen, Binh *c.m.* '82 (LA) San Gabriel, CA San Gabriel Church; [A] Camarillo, CA St. John's Seminary.
Nguyen, Binh Van A. '82 (LA) [Q] Montebello, CA Vincentian Fathers & Brothers.
Nguyen, Charles '92 (SAC) Absent on Leave.
Nguyen, Chau '86 (ORL) Palm Bay, FL St. Joseph Church.
Nguyen, Chinh '94 (SR) [H] Sonoma, CA Hanna Boys Center.
Nguyen, Cuong H. *m.m.* '98 (FgM) Maryknoll Foreign Missions.
Nguyen, Cuong Hung *s.v.d.* '00 (FgM) Society of the Divine Word Foreign Missions.
Nguyen, Dam '93 (PIT) [2] Swissvale, PA Word of God Church.
Nguyen, Dau '84 (NO) [A] New Orleans, LA Notre Dame Seminary Graduate School of Theology.
Nguyen, Doa Kim '93 (GAL) [45] Houston, TX St. Luke the Evangelist Church.
Nguyen, Dominic *s.j.* '92 (SEA) [5] Tacoma, WA St. Leo the Great Church; [C] Tacoma, WA Bellarmine Preparatory School.
Nguyen, Dominic '95 (B) Twin Falls, ID St. Edward The Confessor Church.
Nguyen, Dominic *s.v.d.* '98 (DUB) [B] Epworth, IA Divine Word College.
Nguyen, Dominic Hoan *c.m.* '99 (LA) [28] Los Angeles, CA Our Lady of Loretto Church.
Nguyen, Dominic Huyen Duc '64 (NO) [14] New Orleans, LA Mary, Queen of Vietnam Church.
Nguyen, Dominic Hoa '95 (ORG) Inactive Leave.
Nguyen, Dovan '93 (TLS) Broken Arrow, OK St. Anne Church.
Nguyen, Francis Khoi '90 (DOD) Elkhart, KS St. Joan of Arc Church; Hugoton, KS St. Helen Church; Scott City, KS St. Joseph Church.
Nguyen, Gan Minh Peter *c.ss.r.* '98 (GAL) [34] Houston, TX Holy Ghost Church.
Nguyen, Gregory V. '98 (LA) El Segundo, CA St. Anthony Church.
Nguyen, Hien Minh '57 (SJ) Special Assignment.
Nguyen, Hien Minh '85 (SJ) Milpitas, CA St. Elizabeth Church.
Nguyen, Hien Paul (WCH) [5] Wichita, KS Church of the Magdalen.
Nguyen, Hieu '69 (SC) [1] Sioux City, IA Cathedral of the Epiphany.
Nguyen, Hoa '95 (OKL) Graduate Studies.
Nguyen, Hoa '98 (FWT) Grapevine, TX St. Francis of Assisi Church.
Nguyen, Hoan N. '99 (LA) [Q] Montebello, CA Vincentian Fathers & Brothers.
Nguyen, Huan Tien '66 (CIN) On Special and Archdiocesan Assignment; [V] Cincinnati, OH Vietnamese Catholic Community of Our Lady of Lavang.
Nguyen, Hung '94 (SEA) Poulsbo, WA St. Olaf Church.
Nguyen, Hung '95 (STO) Modesto, CA Our Lady of Fatima Church.
Nguyen, Hung *o.f.m.cap.* '99 (SFR) Burlingame, CA Our Lady of Angels Church.
Nguyen, Hung Viet *i.c.m.* '69 (BR) [4] Baton Rouge, LA St. Anthony of Padua Church; [H] Baton Rouge, LA Incarnatio Consecratio Mission; [L] Baton Rouge, LA St. Michael's Home.
Nguyen, Huy '95 (LA) Canoga Park, CA St. Joseph the Worker Church.
Nguyen, Hy K. *s.t.b.* '97 (WDC) [A] Washington, DC Theological College of the Catholic University of America.
Nguyen, J. Kim-Dang '93 (LA) Torrance, CA St. Catherine Laboure Church.
Nguyen, Joachim Thanh '67 (PRT) Caribou, ME Sacred Heart Church; Stockholm, ME St. Therese Church.
Nguyen, Joe Van Anh '88 (AUS) [6] Austin, TX Holy Vietnamese Martyrs Church.
Nguyen, John C. '99 (PH) Lansdale, PA St. Stanislaus Church.
Nguyen, John Hoa '72 (LA) Burbank, CA St. Finbar Church.
Nguyen, John Luat *o.f.m.* '94 (SFR) [8] San Francisco, CA St. Boniface Church.
Nguyen, John Trung '95 (MOB) Bayou LaBatre, AL St. Margaret Church.
Nguyen, John Baptist Vuong Due *o.p.* '00 (ARL) [5] Arlington, VA Holy Martyrs of Vietnam Church.
Nguyen, Joseph '73 (FRS) [1] Fresno, CA St. John Church.
Nguyen, Joseph An '92 (CAM) Woodlynne, NJ Immaculate Heart of Mary Church.
Nguyen, Joseph Chinh (BO) [69] Boston, MA St. William Church.
Nguyen, Joseph Chuan '78 (ORG) Inactive Leave.
Nguyen, Joseph D. '90 (NOR) Ashford, CT St. Philip Church.
Nguyen, Joseph Dau Van '84 (NO) [4] Metairie, LA St. Benilde Church.
Nguyen, Joseph Hai '67 (RIC) [5] Hampton, VA Our Lady of Vietnam Chapel Church.
Nguyen, Joseph Hoa '76 (HBG) [8] Harrisburg, PA Our Lady of the Blessed Sacrament Church.
Nguyen, Joseph Huong (SAC) Knights Landing, CA St. Paul Church.
Nguyen, Joseph Kahn V. '63 (DAV) [M] Davenport, IA St. Vincent Center.
Nguyen, Joseph Khan V. '63 (DAV) [9] Davenport, IA Vietnamese Catholic Community of the Quad Cities Church.
Nguyen, Joseph Liem '99 (ATL) Gainesville, GA St. Michael's Church.
Nguyen, Joseph Luan '90 (ORG) Fountain Valley, CA

Holy Spirit Church.
Nguyen, Joseph Ngoc Tu *o.p.* '64 (GAL) [Q] Houston, TX Dominican Fathers and Brothers, St. Mark Priory, Inc.
Nguyen, Joseph Phiet The '73 (GAL) [29] Houston, TX St. Francis de Sales Church.
Nguyen, Joseph Son (OAK) [3] Oakland, CA St. Anthony's Church.
Nguyen, Joseph Son '82 (DAL) Carrollton, TX Sacred Heart of Jesus Christ Church.
Nguyen, Joseph Thai '95 (CHI) [153] Chicago, IL Our Lady of Mount Carmel Church.
Nguyen, Joseph Thai-Doan '88 (BR) Livonia, LA St. Frances Xavier Cabrini Church.
Nguyen, Joseph Thinh Duc '93 (MEM) [2] Memphis, TN St. Ann Church.
Nguyen, Joseph Thuan *o.p.* '93 (PHX) [5] Phoenix, AZ Most Holy Trinity Church.
Nguyen, Joseph Trong *s.v.d.* '91 (FgM) Society of the Divine Word Foreign Missions.
Nguyen, Jude Ban *c.m.c.* '73 (SAC) [23] Sacramento, CA Vietnamese Catholic Martyrs Church.
Nguyen, Kai Minh (NEW) Plainfield, NJ Muhlenberg Medical Center.
Nguyen, Khanh Pham (COS) Parker, CO Ave Maria Church.
Nguyen, Khiet T. '96 (TLS) Poteau, OK Immaculate Conception Church.
Nguyen, Kim Son '87 (SAV) [11] Savannah, GA Sts. Peter and Paul Church.
Nguyen, Lich Van '84 (NO) Arabi, LA St. Robert Bellarmine Church.
Nguyen, Liem *o.s.b.* '94 (P) [A] St. Benedict, OR Mount Angel Seminary; [L] St. Benedict, OR Mt. Angel Abbey.
Nguyen, Linh '97 (LEX) [3] Lexington, KY Mary, Queen of the Holy Rosary Church.
Nguyen, Linh T. '00 (BO) [3] Weymouth, MA Immaculate Conception Church.
Nguyen, Martin Lam *c.s.c.* '89 (FTW) [B] Notre Dame, IN University of Notre Dame Du Lac.
Nguyen, Martin Lan *c.s.c.* '89 (FTW) [A] Notre Dame, IN Moreau Seminary.
Nguyen, Martin Thanh *i.c.m.* '97 (BR) [H] Baton Rouge, LA Incarnatio Consecratio Mission.
Nguyen, Michael J. '90 (NO) [A] New Orleans, LA Notre Dame Seminary Graduate School of Theology.
Nguyen, Michael M. *c.m.* '95 (CHL) [3] Greensboro, NC St. Mary Church.
Nguyen, Michael Nam Hoang '93 (NO) [14] New Orleans, LA Mary, Queen of Vietnam Church.
Nguyen, Minh Hai '92 (NEW) Plainfield, NJ St. Bernard's Church; West New York, NJ St. Joseph of the Palisades Church.
Nguyen, Nghiem Van '89 (NO) River Ridge, LA St. Matthew the Apostle Church.
Nguyen, Nhuan D. *m.m.* '93 (FgM) Maryknoll Foreign Missions.
Nguyen, Nick Hien *s.v.d.* '00 (FgM) Society of the Divine Word Foreign Missions.
Nguyen, Odon *o.s.b.* '65 (SFE) [I] Abiquiu, NM Monastery of Christ in the Desert.
Nguyen, Pascal B. '94 (ORG) Garden Grove, CA St. Columban Church; [I] Silverado, CA Norbertine Fathers of Orange Inc.
Nguyen, Paul Choung *s.d.b.* '88 (NY) [FF] Stony Point, NY Marian Shrine.
Nguyen, Paul Chung '00 (PMB) Port St. Lucie, FL St. Lucie Church.
Nguyen, Paul Chuong *s.d.b.* '88 (NY) [FF] Stony Point, NY Don Bosco Retreat Center and Marian Shrine.
Nguyen, Paul Van Tung '79 (NO) Waggaman, LA Our Lady of the Angels Church.
Nguyen, Peter '61 (SD) Vista, CA St. Francis of Assisi Church; Retired.
Nguyen, Peter Duc Hung '97 (SC) Carroll, IA Holy Spirit Church.
Nguyen, Peter Phong '46 (DAL) Grand Prairie, TX St. Joseph Vietnamese Catholic Community Church.
Nguyen, Peter Quang '90 (DEN) Greeley, CO St. Mary Church.
Nguyen, Peter Sam *s.v.d.* '86 (OAK) [6] Oakland, CA St. Bernard's Church.
Nguyen, Peter Sam Cao *s.v.d.* '86 (FgM) Society of the Divine Word Foreign Missions.
Nguyen, Peter Vinh Q. '86 (NEW) Livingston, NJ St. Barnabas Medical Center.
Nguyen, Phi Thanh '00 (GAL) [78] Houston, TX St. Vincent de Paul Church.
Nguyen, Phien T. '92 (CHI) Berwyn, IL St. Mary of Celle Church.
Nguyen, Phillip D. '87 (GR) On Special Assignment; On Duty Outside the Diocese.
Nguyen, Quang Dang '44 (CC) Rockport, TX St. Peter Indo-Chinese Church.
Nguyen, Raphael Xuan '96 (ORG) Costa Mesa, CA St. John the Baptist Church.
Nguyen, Scott C. '97 (WCH) [16] Wichita, KS St. Margaret Mary Church.
Nguyen, Sieu Cao '00 (BO) [W] Cambridge, MA Weston Jesuit Community.
Nguyen, Stephen Tan *o.f.m.* '59 (SFR) [8] San Francisco, CA St. Boniface Church.
Nguyen, Steve '99 (HON) [13] Honolulu, HI Sacred Heart Church; [16] Honolulu, HI St. Pius X Church.
Nguyen, Sy Uy '91 (ORG) Westminster, CA Blessed Sacrament Church.
Nguyen, Tam '82 (TLS) [5] Tulsa, OK Christ the King Church.
Nguyen, Te Van '86 (SFR) Special Assignment.
Nguyen, Thanh N. '94 (R) [5] Raleigh, NC St. Joseph Church.
Nguyen, Thanh T. '91 (STA) [3] Jacksonville, FL Christ the King Church.
Nguyen, Thanh Van '00 (OKL) [1] Oklahoma City, OK Cathedral of Our Lady of Perpetual Help.
Nguyen, Thanh Van *s.v.d.* '97 (DUB) [B] Epworth, IA Divine Word College.
Nguyen, Thien '89 (WIN) Geneva, MN St. Mary Church.
Nguyen, Thien Chi *s.o.l.t.* '91 (CC) [H] Robstown, TX Society of Our Lady of the Most Holy Trinity.
Nguyen, Thien Van '89 (WIN) New Richland, MN All Saints Church.
Nguyen, Thinh *s.d.b.* '99 (SP) [E] Tampa, FL Mary Help of Christians School.
Nguyen, Thomas Thanh '69 (LAF) Louisa, LA St. Helena Church.
Nguyen, Thong *c.ss.r.* '56 (DAL) [2] Garland, TX Mother of Perpetual Help Church.
Nguyen, Thu Van '92 (VIC) El Campo, TX St. Philip the Apostle Church.
Nguyen, Thuc '98 (BEA) [5] Beaumont, TX St. Joseph Church.
Nguyen, Thuong Hoai '91 (OAK) [3] Oakland, CA St. Anthony's Church.
Nguyen, Thuy Quang '98 (GAL) [74] Houston, TX St. Rose of Lima Church.
Nguyen, Tien-Tri '98 (SFE) Mora, NM St. Gertrude Church.
Nguyen, Tinh Van '98 (BO) Wakefield, MA Most Blessed Sacrament Church.
Nguyen, Toan X. '96 (SFR) [16] San Francisco, CA St. Elizabeth Church.
Nguyen, Truc '00 (LA) Pasadena, CA St. Andrew Church.
Nguyen, Trung '94 (GAL) [1] Houston, TX Sacred Heart Co-Church; On Special or Other Diocesan Assignment; On Duty Outside the Diocese.
Nguyen, Tuan *s.d.b.* '88 (STO) [7] Stockton, CA St. Luke Church.
Nguyen, Tuan '92 (SEA) Centralia, WA St. Mary Church; Chehalis, WA St. Joseph Church; Pe Ell, WA St. Joseph Church; Toledo, WA St. Francis Xavier Church; Chehalis, WA Green Hill School.
Nguyen, Tuan John '95 (ORG) [1] Huntington Beach, CA St. Bonaventure Church.
Nguyen, Tuan Van '86 (JOL) Villa Park, IL St. Alexander Church.
Nguyen, Tuyen (ORG) [H] Orange, CA St. Vincent de Paul Society.
Nguyen, Tuyen '87 (ORG) Tustin, CA St. Cecilia Church.
Nguyen, Van Hiep *s.v.d.* '99 (FgM) Society of the Divine Word Foreign Missions.
Nguyen, Vandennis '90 (PEO) [2] Streator, IL St. Anthony of Padua Church.
Nguyen, Vien The '89 (NO) [19] New Orleans, LA Our Lady of The Rosary Church; [A] New Orleans, LA Notre Dame Seminary Graduate School of Theology.
Nguyen, Vincent '89 (HON) [15] Honolulu, HI Star of the Sea Church.
Nguyen, Vincent The *s.d.d.* (STP) [11] St. Paul, MN St. Adalbert Church.
Nguyen, Vincent-Vuong '99 (GAL) [28] Houston, TX St. Frances Cabrini Church.
Nguyen Chau Dien, Raymond M. *c.m.c.* (SPC) [E] Carthage, MO Congregation of the Mother Co-Redemptrix, United States Assumption Province.
Nguyen Dan, Pius M. *c.m.c.* '83 (SB) [E] Corona, CA Congregation of the Mother Coredemptrix.
Nguyen Duc Hau, Joseph *s.e.* '69 (P) [25] Portland, OR Our Lady of Lavang Church.
Nguyen Huy Chuong, Matthias M. *c.m.c.* '81 (SB) [E] Corona, CA Congregation of the Mother Coredemptrix.
Nguyen Mang Cach, Paul M. *c.m.c.* (SPC) [E] Carthage, MO Congregation of the Mother Co-Redemptrix, United States Assumption Province.
Nguyen Ngoc Tu, Joseph *o.p.* '64 (GAL) [36] Houston, TX Holy Rosary Church.
Nguyen Thanh Hue, Augustine '64 (PT) [5] Pensacola, FL Our Lady Queen of Martyrs, Church.
Nguyen Thanh Lam, Jerome *o.s.b.* (SPC) [E] Carthage, MO Congregation of the Mother Co-Redemptrix, United States Assumption Province.
Nguyen Trong Thuong, Bernard M. *c.m.c.* (SPC) [E] Carthage, MO Congregation of the Mother Co-Redemptrix, United States Assumption Province.
Nguyen-Thanh-Long, Peter '65 (WDC) [6] Bethesda, MD Our Lady of Vietnam Church.
Nguyen-Thinh-Phuoc, Joseph *s.d.b.* '95 (OAK) [N] Berkeley, CA Salesian Community.
Nguyen-Van-Am, Joseph *s.d.b.* '94 (OAK) [N] Berkeley, CA Salesian Community.
Nhan Tran, Michael Van *s.v.d.* '00 (FgM) Society of the Divine Word Foreign Missions.
Nhi, Tren Dinh '71 (ARL) Dale City, VA Holy Family Church.
Nhien, Louis '95 (ROC) [6] Rochester, NY St. Anthony of Padua Church.
Nhien, Louis Minh *c.m.c.* '92 (FWT) [2] Arlington, TX Church of the Vietnamese Martyrs.
Nho, Do Duy '66 (LR) [12] Little Rock, AR St. Patrick's Church.
Nibler, James *o.m.v.* '87 (BO) [W] Milton, MA Oblate Residence (St. Joseph House); [BB] Boston, MA St. Francis Chapel.
Niblick, Charles W. '74 (GRY) [5] Whiting, IN Sts. Peter and Paul Church.
Nicastro, Thomas D. '90 (BGP) [15] Stamford, CT Sacred Heart Church.
Nicastro, Thomas More *o.f.m.* '42 (NY) [FF] Wappingers Falls, NY Mt. Alvernia Retreat House.
Niccolls, Edward D. '74 (WOR) Lunenburg, MA St. Boniface Church.
Nicewicz, Edward '62 (WOR) Absent on Leave.
Nicgorski, David J. *o.m.v.* '91 (MET) Avenel, NJ St. Andrew Church.
Nichol, Msgr. Rex '67 (AMA) [4] Amarillo, TX Our Lady of Guadalupe Church.
Nicholas, Gerald A. *o.s.a.* '66 (JOL) [C] New Lenox, IL Providence Catholic High School; [J] New Lenox, IL Augustinian Friary.
Nicholas-Gingras, Dennis C. '90 (HRT) [1] Bristol, CT St. Ann Church.
Nicholls, Trevor '90 (NY) Goshen, NY St. John the Evangelist Church.
Nichols, Aquinas *o.s.b.* (DM) [8] Des Moines, IA Basilica of Saint John; [J] Des Moines, IA St. Gabriel Benedictine Priory.
Nichols, Aquinas *o.s.b.* '80 (SD) [H] Oceanside, CA Prince of Peace Abbey, Benet Hill.
Nichols, Charles P. '48 (BRK) [131] Brooklyn, NY Sacred Hearts of Jesus and Mary and St. Stephen Church; Retired.
Nichols, Earl W. '46 (OG) Retired.
Nichols, Earl W. '47 (OG) Brasher Falls, NY St. Patrick Church.
Nichols, Edward P. '75 (SPC) Springfield, MO Diocesan Hospital Ministry; Special Assignment.
Nichols, Harry E. '73 (PIT) Green Tree, PA St. Margaret Church.
Nichols, Henry P. '70 (BO) Brockton, MA Veterans Administration Hospital Brockton-West Roxbury; Military & VA Chaplains.
Nichols, Herbert T. '75 (FR) [15] New Bedford, MA St. James Church.
Nichols, John J. '62 (BO) [1] Weymouth, MA St. Albert the Great Church.
Nichols, Joseph E. '62 (NOR) Retired.
Nichols, Louis J. '60 (SR) Clearlake, CA Our Lady, Queen of Peace Church.
Nichols, Louis J. '60 (SY) On Duty Outside the Diocese.
Nichols, Rodrick '89 (LSC) Silver City, NM St. Vincent de Paul Church.
Nichols, Stephen J. (BUR) [H] Burlington, VT University of Vermont-The Catholic Center at UVM.
Nichols, Stephen J. '86 (BUR) Lyndonville, VT St. Elizabeth Church.
Nichols, Timothy '73 (LA) Redondo Beach, CA St. James Church.
Nichols, William H. *s.j.* '60 (DET) [P] Clarkston, MI Colombiere Center.
Nicholson, David *o.s.b.* '49 (P) [L] St. Benedict, OR Mt. Angel Abbey.
Nicholson, Francis J. *s.j.* '53 (BO) [W] Chestnut Hill, MA The Jesuit Community at Boston College.
Nicholson, John A. *s.j.* '46 (NY) [DD] New York, NY Murray-Weigel Hall.
Nicholson, Patrick '69 (MOB) On Leave from the Archdiocese.
Nickas, John P. '66 (NEW) Montclair, NJ St. Peter Claver Church.
Nickel, Leander F. '47 (GB) Stockbridge, WI St. Mary Church.
Nickels, Larry *o.f.m.* '86 (STL) [P] St. Louis, MO Franciscan Friary of St. Anthony of Padua.
Nickels, Lawrence M. *o.f.m.* (BEL) Marydale, IL St. Teresa of Avila Church.
Nickels, Peter *o.f.m. conv.* '60 (GR) [4] Grand Rapids, MI St. Anthony of Padua Church.
Nickerson, Oliver E. *s.j.* '54 (FgM) Provinces.
Nickle, Frederick *o.f.m.cap.* '65 (NOR) [4] Middletown, CT St. Pius X Church.
Nickless, Msgr. R. Walker '73 (DEN) [3] Lakewood, CO Our Lady of Fatima Church.
Nicknair, Bernard L. '54 (PRT) Retired.
Nicknair, Harold '61 (PRT) Retired.
Nicknair, Leopold G. '58 (PRT) Caribou, ME Holy Rosary Church.
Nickol, G. Eugene '73 (BAL) Glen Burnie, MD Holy Trinity Church.

Nickolai, Arthur A. '43 (MIL) Retired.
Nickse, Jose P. '73 (MIA) [16] Miami, FL St. Brendan Church; [C] Miami, FL St. Brendan High School; [L] Key Largo, FL 1-800-Mass-Times Trust.
Nicola, John J. '55 (CHI) Retired.
Nicolas, Jeffrey S. '93 (L) Military Chaplains.
Nicolau, Bernardo *t.o.r.* '65 (FWT) [2] Fort Worth, TX All Saints Church.
Nicolau, Juan '60 (BWN) San Juan, TX The Basilica of the National Shrine of Our Lady of San Juan del Valle; [I] San Juan, TX The Basilica of the National Shrine of Our Lady of San Juan; [I] Mission, TX Cursillos.
Nicoletti, Maurizio *o.cist* '65 (TR) Mount Laurel, NJ St. John Neumann Church; [M] Mount Laurel, NJ Cistercian Monastery of Our Lady of Fatima.
Nicoletti, Robert *m.j.* '92 (PCE) On Duty Outside the Diocese.
Nicoll, Leo A. *s.j.* '61 (NO) [C] New Orleans, LA Loyola University New Orleans.
Nicolo, Joseph J. '74 (PH) Center Square, PA St. Helena Church.
Nicolosi, Joseph P. '97 (RCK) [2] Aurora, IL Holy Angels Church.
Nicolosi, Mark Ronald *o.s.b.* '67 (BUR) [E] Weston, VT Priory of Benedictine Monks.
Nicosia, Peter *o.f.m.cap.* '59 (SP) [6] Tampa, FL Most Holy Redeemer Church.
Nicosia, Vincent A. *s.o.l.t.* '92 (CC) [H] Robstown, TX Society of Our Lady of the Most Holy Trinity.
Nicosia, Vincent A. *s.o.l.t.* '92 (SFE) La Joya, NM Our Lady of Sorrows Church.
Nieberding, Richard *c.pp.s.* '80 (COL) [23] Columbus, OH St. James-the-Less Church.
Nieberding, Robert H. '56 (LEX) [3] Lexington, KY Mary, Queen of the Holy Rosary Church.
Nieblas, James *s.d.b.* '86 (LA) [80] Los Angeles, CA St. Mary Church; [Q] Los Angeles, CA Dominic Savio Salesian Residence.
Niebrugge, Herman J. '56 (SFD) Mattoon, IL Immaculate Conception Church.
Niebrzydowski, Msgr. Walter J. '59 (NY) [34] New York, NY Epiphany Church.
Nieckarz, James P. *m.m.* '66 (NY) [DD] Maryknoll, NY Maryknoll Fathers and Brothers.
Niedergeses, W. Bernard '50 (NSH) [3] Nashville, TN Assumption Church; [12] Nashville, TN St. Pius X Church.
Niedermier, Jerome G. '52 (TOL) Retired.
Niedzwicki, Thomas C. '53 (GR) Irons, MI St. Bernard's Church.
Niedzwiecki, Thomas C. '53 (GR) Free Soil, MI St. John Cantius Church.
Niehaus, Charles W. '74 (CHI) [174] Chicago, IL St. Procopius Church; [N] Chicago, IL Miguel Pro Jesuit Community.
Niehaus, Francis H. '55 (CIN) Retired.
Niehaus, Jonathan J. '94 (MIL) [T] Waukesha, WI Secular Institute of Schoenstatt Fathers.
Niehaus, Theodore *o.f.m.cap.* '65 (FgM) Capuchin Foreign Missions.
Niehoff, Edmund A. '64 (SHP) [9] Shreveport, LA St. Mary of the Pines Church.
Niehoff, Kevin W. *o.p.* (SFE) [31] Albuquerque, NM St. Thomas Aquinas University Church.
Niehoff, Robert L. *s.j.* '82 (SFR) [N] San Francisco, CA Jesuit Community at University of San Francisco.
Nieli, Bruce *c.s.p.* '73 (MEM) [20] Memphis, TN St. Patrick's Church; [I] Memphis, TN Paulist Fathers (New York).
Nielsen, Eric '95 (MAD) Waunakee, WI St. John the Baptist Church.
Nielsen, Eric H. '95 (MAD) Evansville, WI St. Paul Church; Footville, WI St. Augustine Church.
Nielsen, Kenneth M. '80 (BUF) On Duty Outside the Diocese.
Nielsen, Philip W. *o.f.m.* '48 (PAT) [N] Parsippany, NJ St. Francis of Assisi Novitiate-Franciscan Sisters of St. Elizabeth.
Nielson, James P. *o.praem.* '93 (GB) [I] De Pere, WI St. Norbert Abbey.
Nielson, Karl *o.s.b.* '99 (P) [A] St. Benedict, OR Mount Angel Seminary; [L] St. Benedict, OR Mt. Angel Abbey.
Nielson, Thomas A. (NY) [HH] New York, NY St. Ansgar Scandinavian Catholic League.
Nielson, Msgr. Thomas A. '59 (NY) [1] New York, NY Cathedral of St. Patrick.
Nieman, Raymond L. '54 (COV) Retired.
Niemann, Mark E. *s.j.* '50 (OM) [C] Omaha, NE Creighton Preparatory School.
Niemann, Paul '80 (PRM) St. Louis, MO St. Louis Church.
Niemann, Paul J. '80 (STL) [1] St. Louis, MO Cathedral Basilica of Saint Louis.
Niemczyk, Stefan J. '87 (SPR) Three Rivers, MA SS. Peter and Paul Church.
Niemeier, Dennis '73 (CIN) Military Chaplains.
Niemeyer, James J. '74 (JC) Missionary Assignment in Peru.
Niemeyer, John '55 (PEO) Retired.
Niemeyer, Roger *o.f.m.* '40 (SFD) [K] Sherman, IL Our Lady of Angels Friary.
Niemier, Roch *o.f.m.* '65 (MIL) [P] Milwaukee, WI Francis and Clare House; [Y] Milwaukee, WI Franciscan Pilgrimage Programs, Inc.
Niemira, Thomas '65 (JKS) On Duty Outside the Diocese.
Niemira, Thomas J. '53 (AUS) Waco, TX V.A. Hospital.
Nienaber, Msgr. Leonard B. '34 (LEX) Retired.
Nienaber, Paul J. *s.j.* '99 (CHI) [N] Chicago, IL Chicago Province of the Society of Jesus-Provincial Office.
Nienaber, Robert H. '63 (OM) Genoa, NE St. Rose of Lima Church; Krakow, NE SS. Peter and Paul Church.
Nienhaus, Bernard '65 (STL) Hawk Point, MO St. Mary Church.
Nienhaus, Gerald T. '62 (STL) Spanish Lake, MO St. Aloysius Church.
Nienhaus, Ivan R. '89 (DUB) Masonville, IA Immaculate Conception Church; Monti, IA St. Patrick's Church; Winthrop, IA St. Patrick's Church.
Nierengarten, Andrew '66 (RVC) Port Jefferson, NY Infant Jesus Church.
Niese, Larry P. '95 (ATL) LaGrange, GA St. Peter's Church.
Niese, Lawrence P. (ATL) [M] Atlanta, GA Campus Ministry.
Nieset, Frank E. '56 (TOL) Retired.
Niessen, John *s.v.d.* '51 (SB) Perris, CA St. James Church.
Nietfeld, Fred J. '46 (TOL) Retired.
Nietlong, Joseph '86 (TUC) San Manuel, AZ St. Bartholomew Church.
Nieto, Jose *c.m.f.* '66 (SJN) [9] Bayamon, PR San Jose Church.
Nieto-Ruiz, Jose de Jesus (OAK) Richmond, CA St. Mark's Church.
Nieva, Constantino '55 (RVC) Bellport, NY Mary Immaculate Church.
Nieves, Encarnacion '83 (CGS) Aguas Buenas, PR Espiritu Santo Church.
Nieves, Jose Javier (PAT) [5] Clifton, NJ SS. Cyril and Methodius Church.
Niewczas, Taddeus (RVC) Retired.
Niewiadomski, Arthur J. '94 (TOL) Bascom, OH St. Patrick Church; Liberty, OH St. Andrew Church.
Niezgoda, Joseph R. '62 (GRY) [8] East Chicago, IN St. John Cantius Church.
Niggeman, Richard D. (MIL) Permanent Deacons.
Nigli, Francis A. '97 (OM) [47] Omaha, NE St. Vincent de Paul Church.
Niglis, Msgr. Joseph C. '37 (MAD) Retired; [H] Madison, WI Bishop O'Connor Catholic Pastoral Center.
Nigro, Armand M. *s.j.* '56 (SEA) [L] Seattle, WA Jesuit House, Seattle.
Nijem, Fred J. '68 (SAV) Warner Robins, GA Sacred Heart Church.
Niklas, Gerald R. '59 (CIN) [K] Cincinnati, OH Good Samaritan Hospital.
Nikliborc, Robert D. '55 (SD) [20] San Diego, CA St. Anne Church.
Nikodem, Martin J. '67 (BGP) [16] Bridgeport, CT Our Lady of Good Counsel Church.
Nikodem, Ronald J. *s.m.* '94 (ATL) [C] Atlanta, GA Marist School.
Niland, John *o.f.m.cap* '76 (HON) Pearl City, HI Our Lady of Good Counsel Church.
Nilema, Nicholas *a.l.c.p.* '88 (P) Seaside, OR Our Lady of Victory Church.
Nilges, Harold L. '53 (RCK) Genoa, IL St. Catherine of Genoa Church; Retired.
Nilles, Msgr. Allan F. (FAR) Retired.
Nilles, Roger G. '59 (MAD) [13] Madison, WI St. Peter Church.
Nilsson, Richard '71 (RVC) Inwood, NY Our Lady of Good Counsel Church.
Nimerichter, Dean '92 (DM) Greenfield, IA St. John Church.
Nimocks, Michael F. '96 (COL) Bolivar, OH Holy Trinity Church.
Ninedorf, Robert W. '89 (CHR) Edgefield, SC St. Mary's Church; Ward, SC St. William's Church.
Ninemire, Kerry '75 (SAL) [3] Salina, KS St. Mary's Church.
Nino, Andres G. *o.s.a.* '62 (BO) [8] Cambridge, MA St. Mary of the Annunciation Church.
Nir, Roman '64 (DET) [A] Orchard Lake, MI SS. Cyril and Methodius Seminary.
Nirappel, Anthony '63 (GAL) Missouri City, TX Holy Family Church.
Nirschl, Nicholas E. *o.praem.* '56 (SFE) Isleta, NM St. Augustine Church; [I] Albuquerque, NM Santa Maria de la Vid Priory.
Nisari, Joseph Sadiq '68 (AUS) Granger, TX SS. Cyril and Methodius Church.
Nisbet, Jim '69 (MRY) Spreckels, CA St. Joseph Church.
Nischan, James R. '83 (PCE) On Duty Outside the Diocese.
Nishigaya, Raymond J. '64 (HON) Retired.
Nishimura, Bryce T. *m.m.* '56 (FgM) Maryknoll Foreign Missions.
Nishimuta, James K. *m.m.* '54 (FgM) Maryknoll Foreign Missions.
Niskanen, Steven *c.m.f.* '90 (SAT) [B] San Antonio, TX St. Anthony Mary Claret Formation House.
Nissel, John J. *s.j.* '56 (BAL) [S] Baltimore, MD Jesuit Fathers and Brothers Maryland Provincial Curia.
Nissel, John J. *s.j.* '56 (FgM) Provinces.
Nist, Arthur '40 (Y) Retired.
Nistal, Alejandro '66 (ARE) Isabela, PR St. Anthony Church.
Nistler, Edward '54 (CR) Bemidji, MN St. Philip's Church; Retired.
Nitschke, Richard C. *o.c.d.* '89 (GRY) [J] Munster, IN Discalced Carmelite Fathers Monastery.
Nitz, Eliot *s.d.s.* '68 (WDC) [B] Silver Spring, MD Salvatorian Community; [K] Silver Spring, MD Holy Cross Hospital of Silver Spring, Inc.
Nitzki, John *s.c.j.* '56 (MIL) Franklin, WI St. Martin of Tours Church; [P] Franklin, WI St. Francis Residence.
Niven, Timothy L. '98 (ROC) Newark Valley, NY St. John the Evangelist Church; Owego, NY St. Patrick Church.
Nix, Albert '73 (PAT) Stirling, NJ St. Vincent de Paul Church.
Nix, Julian *o.s.b.* '87 (BIS) [A] Richardton, ND Assumption Abbey.
Nixon, Edmond J. *c.ss.r.* '71 (NY) [34] New York, NY Epiphany Church.
Nixon, Joseph J. '85 (RVC) [C] Hicksville, NY Holy Trinity.
Njeim, Elias '58 (OG) Retired.
Njoku, Hyacinth '86 (NY) [183] Bronx, NY St. Philip Neri Church.
Njoku, Peter '74 (STP) Bellechester, MN St. Mary Church; Zumbrota, MN St. Paul Church.
Nkachukwu, Michael C. '80 (DET) [7] Detroit, MI Annunciation Church; [8] Detroit, MI St. Anthony Church.
Nkedife, Peter '76 (LKC) Jennings, LA Our Lady of Perpetual Help Church.
Nlandu, Theo *c.i.c.m.* '98 (BWN) [2] Brownsville, TX Christ the King Church.
Nnabuaku, Nicholas E. *c.s.sp.* '87 (SCR) [1] Williamsport, PA Annunciation Church.
Nnamani, Godwin (NY) Carmel, NY St. James the Apostle Church.
Noah, Daniel '50 (CR) Retired.
Noah, Timothy T. '47 (CR) Hallock, MN St. Patrick's Church.
Nobile, Angelo '53 (MEM) On Duty Outside the Diocese.
Nobiletti, Raymond J. *m.m.* '69 (NY) [119] New York, NY Transfiguration Church; [DD] Maryknoll, NY Maryknoll Fathers and Brothers.
Noble, Bruce H. '87 (GAL) [K] Houston, TX The Catholic Chaplain Corps.
Noble, David H. '87 (GAL) [K] Houston, TX The Catholic Chaplain Corps.
Noble, Jeffrey J. '86 (E) [4] Oil City, PA St. Stephen Church.
Noble, Paul A. '81 (COL) Gahanna, OH St. Matthew Church.
Noble, Wayne '93 (LA) Pomona, CA Sacred Heart Church.
Noboa, Origines '80 (VEN) Absent on Sick Leave.
Nocero, Pascal F. '48 (LA) Retired.
Nochelski, Paul W. *s.j.* '71 (BUF) [O] Buffalo, NY Canisius Jesuit Community.
Nock, James J. '64 (HRT) [2] East Hartford, CT Our Lady of Peace Church.
Nockunas, Anthony N. *m.i.c.* '57 (WOR) [19] Worcester, MA St. Casimir's Church.
Noda, Jorge '84 (MIA) Opa Locka, FL Our Lady of Perpetual Help Church.
Noe, John P. '74 (LEX) Ashland, KY Holy Family Church; Ashland, KY Federal Correctional Institution; [D] Ashland, KY Our Lady of Bellefonte Hospital, Inc.
Noecker, Ronald J. '85 (OM) Fort Calhoun, NE St. John the Baptist Church.
Noel, Damian L. *t.o.r.* '53 (ALT) [F] Loretto, PA Mount Assisi Friary.
Noel, Donald C. *o.praem.* '59 (GB) [I] De Pere, WI St. Norbert Abbey.
Noel, Guyma (ATL) Winder, GA St. Matthew Church.
Noel, Marc A. '98 (ALX) [2] Alexandria, LA Our Lady of Prompt Succor Church.
Noelke, Dennis *c.s.b.* '81 (DET) [33] Detroit, MI Holy Redeemer Church.
Noesen, Gerald '50 (CR) Retired.
Noesen, Robert H. '93 (JOL) Addison, IL St. Philip The Apostle Church.
Noeson, Thomas *o.p.* '76 (DEN) [35] Denver, CO St. Mary Magdalene's Church.
Noetzel, Kenneth J. *s.j.* '51 (DET) [27] Detroit, MI Gesu Church; Detroit, MI Sinai Hospital.
Nofi, Michael *m.s.a.* '74 (NOR) [F] Cromwell, CT Society of the Missionaries of the Holy Apostles.

Noga, Edward P. '76 (Y) [18] Youngstown, OH St. Patrick's Church.
Noga, Gregory J. '79 (PSC) Bethlehem, PA SS. Peter and Paul Church.
Noga, Henry *s.v.d.* '96 (SB) [A] Riverside, CA Divine Word Seminary.
Noga, John T. '99 (CHI) Libertyville, IL St. Joseph Church.
Nogaro, Paul M. '71 (BUF) Grand Island, NY St. Stephen Church.
Nogosek, Robert *c.s.c.* '56 (SB) Special or Other Diocesan Assignment.
Noguera, Dagoberto '85 (BRK) [182] Queens, NY Incarnation Church.
Noguera, Ronald '81 (MIA) [27] Miami, FL St. Michael the Archangel Church.
Nohilly, Thomas '81 (BRK) [53] Brooklyn, NY Holy Cross Church.
Nohs, Joseph E. '93 (RVC) Seaford, NY Maria Regina Church.
Noia, Leonel C. '73 (SJ) [4] San Jose, CA Five Wounds Portuguese National Church.
Noiseux, Donald A. '84 (SPR) Huntington, MA St. Thomas Church.
Nojek, Mark J. '90 (KAL) St. Joseph, MI St. Joseph Church.
Nolan, Brian J. '91 (MET) Watchung, NJ St. Mary-Stony Hill Church.
Nolan, Dan *c.s.v.* '83 (LAV) Henderson, NV St. Thomas More Church.
Nolan, Daniel '66 (SPR) [2] North Adams, MA Notre Dame Church; [4] North Adams, MA Our Lady of Mercy Church; [5] North Adams, MA Our Lady of Mercy Church; [7] North Adams, MA St. Francis Church.
Nolan, David E. '95 (NY) [21] New York, NY St. Catherine of Genoa Church.
Nolan, Msgr. Edward J. '48 (BRK) [182] Queens, NY Incarnation Church; Retired.
Nolan, Emmet J. *c.m.* '92 (FgM) Vincentian Foreign Missions.
Nolan, Eugene A. *s.j.* '71 (WDC) [E] Washington, DC Gonzaga College High School.
Nolan, George W. *s.j.* '54 (BO) [W] Weston, MA Campion Jesuit Community; [W] Weston, MA Campion Health Center, Inc.
Nolan, James L. *o.s.a.* '46 (PH) [AA] Villanova, PA St. Thomas Monastery.
Nolan, Jerome M. '74 (TR) Fair Haven, NJ Nativity Church.
Nolan, John '77 (SFD) Military Chaplains.
Nolan, Joseph A. '60 (ORL) Melbourne Beach, FL Immaculate Conception Church.
Nolan, Joseph J. *m.s.* '48 (ATL) [2] Marietta, GA Church of St. Ann.
Nolan, Joseph M. '47 (BRK) [238] Queens, NY Sacred Heart Church; Retired.
Nolan, Joseph T '53 (WCH) On Duty Outside the Diocese.
Nolan, Justin *o.s.b.* '55 (GBG) [H] Latrobe, PA Saint Vincent Archabbey.
Nolan, Kevin '90 (LA) Van Nuys, CA St. Elisabeth Church.
Nolan, Kieran *o.s.b.* '59 (FgM) American - Cassinese Congregation Foreign Missions.
Nolan, Kieran *o.s.b.* '59 (SCL) [I] Collegeville, MN St. John's Abbey, of the Order of St. Benedict.
Nolan, Larry '58 (COL) [G] Columbus, OH St. Raphael Home for the Aged, Inc.
Nolan, Michael E. '84 (WCH) El Dorado, KS St. John Church; Wichita, KS El Dorado Correctional Facility.
Nolan, Michael F. '87 (KNX) [2] Chattanooga, TN Our Lady of Perpetual Help Church.
Nolan, Michael L. (BO) [A] Boston, MA St. John's Seminary School of Theology.
Nolan, Michael L. '00 (BO) Bedford, MA St. Michael Church.
Nolan, Niall '80 (GAL) [41] Houston, TX St. John Vianney Church.
Nolan, Norbert L. '51 (ROC) Retired.
Nolan, Pat '82 (BRK) [85] Brooklyn, NY St. Matthew's Church.
Nolan, Msgr. Patrick M. '50 (SAC) [20] Sacramento, CA St. Philomene Church; Retired and in Senior Ministry.
Nolan, Paul '57 (NEW) Newark, NJ Northern State Prison.
Nolan, Paul J. '57 (NEW) [2] Union City, NJ St. Augustine's Church; Caldwell, NJ Essex County Jail Annex; South Kearny, NJ Talbot Hall Assessment Center.
Nolan, Peter P. *c.s.sp.* '59 (BO) [48] Boston, MA Most Precious Blood Church.
Nolan, Robert *s.a.c.* '70 (CAM) Hammonton, NJ St. Joseph's Church.
Nolan, Shawn *o.f.m.conv.* '55 (NY) [B] Staten Island, NY St. Francis Friary.
Nolan, Msgr. Terence '66 (SAT) [K] San Antonio, TX Casa De Padres.
Nolan, Timothy '92 (PEO) [13] Peoria, IL St. Philomena's Church; Pekin, IL St. Joseph's Church.
Nolan, Timothy F. '67 (STP) Ham Lake, MN Saint Paul Church.
Nolan, Todd (BO) [16] Boston, MA St. Cecilia Church.
Nolan, Msgr. Walter E. '69 (TR) Princeton, NJ St. Paul Church.
Nolan, William A. '85 (MAD) Cambridge, WI St. Pius X Church.
Nolan, William J. '69 (TR) [2] Toms River, NJ St. Justin Church.
Nolan, William N '57 (NSH) Retired.
Nold, Joseph K. '45 (SY) Retired.
Nolen, Joseph *c.ss.r.* '76 (DEN) [M] Denver, CO The Redemptorists/Denver Province.
Nolette, Mark P. '87 (PRT) Special or Other Diocesan Assignment.
Nolette, Roger '69 (BO) [W] Hingham, MA Glastonbury Abbey.
Nolin, John W. '60 (MAN) Retired.
Nolin, Joseph A. '49 (ORL) Retired.
Nolker, Thomas C. '72 (CIN) [30] Cincinnati, OH Guardian Angels Church.
Noll, Daniel '76 (LEX) [6] Lexington, KY St. Paul Church; [7] Lexington, KY St. Peter Church.
Nollette, Louis A. '75 (GI) Pleasanton, NE St. Mary's Church.
Nollette, Neal P. '80 (GI) Elm Creek, NE Immaculate Conception Church.
Nolte, William '63 (RIC) Colonial Heights, VA St. Ann Church.
Nolte, William J., Jr. '67 (WH) Retired.
Nombrado, Benjamin A. '79 (SFR) [54] San Francisco, CA St. Vincent de Paul Church.
Nomellini, Paul J. '77 (MAR) Kingsford, MI St. Mary Queen of Peace Church.
Nondorf, Aloysius J. '57 (GRY) Military Chaplains.
Nondorf, Timothy '99 (SAC) Elk Grove, CA St. Joseph Church.
Nonis, P. Kingsley '93 (TYL) Sulphur Springs, TX St. James Church.
Noon, Msgr. Robert L. '51 (COL) Lancaster, OH St. Mark Church; Retired.
Noonan, Brad '99 (COS) [4] Colorado Springs, CO Holy Apostles Church.
Noonan, James P. *m.m.* '60 (FgM) Maryknoll Foreign Missions.
Noonan, John '83 (MIA) [A] Miami, FL St. John Vianney College Seminary.
Noonan, Joseph T. '95 (CHI) [62] Chicago, IL St. Francis Borgia Church.
Noonan, Mark L. '59 (BO) [A] Boston, MA St. John's Seminary School of Theology; [A] Brighton, MA St. John's Seminary.
Noonan, Patrick '63 (JKS) Brookhaven, MS St. Francis Church; [H] Brookhaven, MS Lincoln Junior College Newman Center.
Noonan, Robert C. '64 (HEL) Choteau, MT St. Joseph Church; Fairfield, MT St. John Church.
Noonan, Msgr. Thomas F. (BRK) Retired.
Noonan, Msgr. Thomas F. '55 (BRK) [34] Brooklyn, NY St. Edmund's Church.
Noonan, William J. '39 (BO) Senior Priests.
Noone, Charles J. '67 (PH) Absent on Sick Leave.
Noone, David E. '66 (ALB) Loudonville, NY St. Francis de Sales Church.
Noone, John '67 (BLX) Picayune, MS St. Charles Borromeo Church.
Noone, Msgr. Kevin B. '70 (BRK) [97] Brooklyn, NY Our Lady of Guadalupe Church.
Noone, Sean '52 (CC) Retired.
Nooney, P. Joseph '52 (SC) Fort Dodge, IA Trinity Regional Hospital.
Nooney, Patrick J. '52 (SC) Retired.
Norbeck, Ernest '84 (JOL) [2] Naperville, IL St. Elizabeth Seton Church.
Norcavage, Albert R. '50 (ALT) Absent on Leave.
Nord, Clarence C. '43 (L) Retired.
Norden, Emmett M. '62 (MAR) Perkins, MI St. Joseph Church.
Nordenbrock, William A. *c.pp.s.* '83 (CIN) [M] Dayton, OH Provincial Office of the Cincinnati Province of the Society of the Precious Blood.
Norder, John '66 (MAD) Cassville, WI St. Charles Borromeo Church; Glen Haven, WI St. Mary Help of Christians Church.
Nordhaus, Jeffrey J. '72 (TOL) Clyde, OH St. Mary Church.
Nordick, Benedict *o.s.b.* '78 (SCL) [I] Collegeville, MN St. John's Abbey, of the Order of St. Benedict.
Nordick, Jerome '83 (SCL) Dent, MN Sacred Heart Church; Rush Lake, MN St. Lawrence Church.
Nordick, John A. '90 (NU) Graceville, MN Holy Rosary Church.
Nordmeyer, Emeric *o.f.m.* '56 (GLP) Grants, NM St. Teresa Church.
Nordquist, Theodore A. '80 (GRY) La Porte, IN St. Joseph Church.
Noreika, Michael P. *s.s.s.* '70 (SLC) [7] Taylorsville, UT St. Martin de Porres Church.
Noriega, Arnoldo '75 (TUC) Absent on Leave.
Norkett, Edward J. '36 (CHI) Highland Park, IL Immaculate Conception Church; Retired.
Norkett, Michael '68 (OAK) [19] Oakland, CA St. Paschal Baylon Church.
Norkunas, Msgr. Anthony J. '44 (SCR) Retired.
Norman, Charles *o.s.f.s.* '65 (ALN) [O] Allentown, PA The Newman Center; [O] Allentown, PA The Newman Center.
Norman, Clifford A. '60 (PBL) On Duty Outside the Diocese.
Norman, Gary '94 (GF) Special Assignment.
Norman, Gary '94 (YAK) On Duty Outside the Diocese.
Norman, Gary R. '94 (GF) Scobey, MT St. Philip Bonitus Church.
Norman, Gregory *o.cist.* '53 (LC) [H] Sparta, WI Our Lady of Spring Bank, Cistercian Abbey; [O] Genoa, WI The Hermitage of St. Mary, Inc.
Norman, John '71 (SLC) [B] Salt Lake City, UT Judge Memorial Catholic High School.
Norman, John E. '79 (SLC) [3] Salt Lake City, UT Our Lady of Lourdes Church.
Norman, Richard W. *s.j.* '58 (ALN) [A] Wernersville, PA Jesuit Center.
Normanly, Thomas *s.s.c.* '52 (OM) [K] St. Columbans, NE St. Columban's Foreign Mission Society.
Normantowicz, Edmund *m.s.* (WOR) [6] Fitchburg, MA St. Joseph's Church.
Norrell, Msgr. Albert V. '88 (PH) Retired.
Norris, David J. '74 (FRS) [10] Fresno, CA St. Helen Church.
Norris, John P. '46 (ROC) Mendon, NY St. Catherine of Siena Church; Retired.
Norris, Patrick F. *o.p.* '89 (SFE) [31] Albuquerque, NM St. Thomas Aquinas University Church.
Norris, Robert J. '80 (NY) [159] Bronx, NY St. Lucy Church.
Norris, Thomas P. *o.s.f.s.* '73 (R) Goldsboro, NC St. Mary Church.
Norris, Walter J. '41 (WDC) Damascus, MD St. Paul Church; Retired.
Norsworthy, Richard '85 (SHP) [3] Monroe, LA Our Lady of Fatima Church.
North, Robert G. *s.j.* '44 (MIL) [P] Wauwatosa, WI Jesuit Community at St. Camillus.
Northrop, James '97 (SEA) Enumclaw, WA Sacred Heart of Jesus Church.
Northrop, John B. *m.m.* '74 (FgM) Maryknoll Foreign Missions.
Norton, Claude B. '43 (DUB) Retired.
Norton, Daniel J. '65 (CAM) On Duty Outside the Diocese.
Norton, Edward *s.v.d.* '45 (CHI) [B] Techny, IL Divine Word Residence.
Norton, Emmet J. *s.j.* '48 (PAT) [I] Morristown, NJ Loyola House of Retreats.
Norton, George '83 (ROC) [8] Rochester, NY Blessed Sacrament Church; Rochester, NY Genesee Hospital Via Health.
Norton, John *o.p.* '56 (CHY) Sheridan, WY U.S. Veterans Administration Hospital.
Norton, Joseph E. '57 (WDC) Retired.
Norton, Michael *c.pp.s.* '70 (SAT) San Antonio, TX Santa Rosa Hospital System; [H] San Antonio, TX Christus Santa Rosa Health Care Corporation.
Norton, Robert A. '72 (PIT) West View, PA St. Athanasius Church.
Norton, Robert J. *o.f.m.* '74 (NEW) Elmwood Park, NJ St. Leo's Church.
Norton, Thomas '63 (NEW) Northvale, NJ St. Anthony's Church; Westwood, NJ Pascack Valley Hospital.
Norton, William '67 (FR) [I] Fall River, MA Priests' Hostel.
Nortz, Alfred E. '55 (SY) [24] Syracuse, NY St. Vincent de Paul Church.
Norusis, Nicholas M. *o.s.m.* '44 (CHI) [N] Chicago, IL Order of Friar Servants of Mary (Servites) United States of America Province, Inc.
Norwick, Daniel J. (DEN) [26] Denver, CO St. Anthony of Padua Church.
Nosbush, Peter C. '70 (NU) North Mankato, MN Holy Rosary Church.
Noser, J. Homer '43 (STL) Retired.
Nosser, Msgr. Charles J. '53 (RVC) Floral Park, NY Our Lady of Victory Church.
Nosser, Msgr. John C. '64 (RVC) Bay Shore, NY St. Patrick's Church.
Notabartolo, Charles '77 (PMB) Jupiter, FL St. Peter Church.
Notaro, Carlo *o.s.cam.* '88 (MIL) [N] Wauwatosa, WI St. Camillus Health Center, Inc.; [N] Wauwatosa, WI San Camillo, Inc.; [P] Wauwatosa, WI St. Camillus Community House.
Notarpole, Joseph '49 (STA) [11] Jacksonville, FL Our Lady of the Angels Church.
Notebaart, James C. '71 (STP) Special Assignment.
Nott, David L. '93 (RIC) Covington, VA Sacred Heart Church; Hot Springs, VA The Shrine of the Sacred Heart Church.
Notter, Richard E. '63 (TOL) [36] Toledo, OH SS. Peter and Paul Church.
Nourie, Paul *o.m.i.* '64 (LA) San Fernando, CA St. Ferdinand Church.

Nouws, Jacques J. '46 (LA) [Q] Montebello, CA Vincentian Fathers & Brothers.
Nouws, James J. *c.m.* '46 (LA) [W] Montebello, CA DePaul Center.
Nouza, Frank M. *o.p.* '58 (CHI) [N] Chicago, IL Dominicans (Provincial Office).
Novack, Kevin '81 (PBL) Mancos, CO St. Rita Church.
Novak, Alfred *c.ss.r.* (DEN) [M] Denver, CO The Redemptorists/Denver Province.
Novak, David A. '77 (STL) [3] University City, MO Our Lady of Lourdes Church.
Novak, David A. '79 (CLV) [3] Lorain, OH Holy Trinity Church.
Novak, Francis G. *c.ss.r.* '49 (STL) [P] Liguori, MO St. Clement Health Care Center.
Novak, Henry *c.ss.r.* '50 (CHI) [N] Glenview, IL The Redemptorists of Glenview, Illinois.
Novak, James '57 (LAN) Retired.
Novak, John '42 (JOL) Retired.
Novak, Joseph A. *s.j.* '57 (NEW) [B] Jersey City, NJ Saint Peter's College; [N] Jersey City, NJ Jesuits of Saint Peter's College, Inc.
Novak, Kevin '81 (PBL) Cortez, CO St. Margaret Mary Church.
Novak, Msgr. Leonard J. '56 (SCR) [24] Scranton, PA Sacred Hearts of Jesus and Mary Church.
Novak, Mark (E) [F] Fairview, PA Camp Notre Dame.
Novak, Norbert *o.s.b.* '64 (B) [C] Jerome, ID Monastery of the Ascension.
Novak, Paul M. *o.s.m.* '90 (CHI) [17] Chicago, IL Assumption of the Blessed Virgin Mary Church; [N] Chicago, IL Order of Friar Servants of Mary (Servites) United States of America Province, Inc.
Novak, Robert J. '42 (CHI) Retired.
Novak, Thomas *s.d.s.* '59 (MIL) [P] Milwaukee, WI Salvatorian Provincial Residence.
Novak, Vincent M. *s.j.* '55 (NY) [C] Bronx, NY Fordham University; [DD] New York, NY Jesuit Community at Fordham University.
Novak, William '91 (OKL) Special Assignment.
Novak, William '97 (OKL) [B] Oklahoma City, OK Bishop McGuinness High School.
Novak, William L. '97 (OKL) [3] Oklahoma City, OK St. Charles Borromeo Church.
Novakowski, James E. '95 (GI) Stapleton, NE St. John the Evangelist Church.
Novello, Lawrence E. '84 (BO) Absent on Leave.
Novelly, Duane R. '79 (DET) [49] Detroit, MI St. Matthew Church.
Novicky, Msgr. William N. '46 (CLV) South Euclid, OH St. Gregory the Great Church.
Novielli, John J. *o.praem.* '74 (PH) [B] Paoli, PA Daylesford Abbey; [AA] Paoli, PA Daylesford Abbey.
Noviello, Anthony A. '43 (SCR) Retired.
Novoa, Marino *c.m.f.* (CHI) [163] Chicago, IL St. Paul Church.
Novokowsky, Robert *f.s.s.p.* '00 (SCR) [M] Elmhurst, PA Priestly Fraternity of St. Peter (F.S.S.P.), North American District Headquarters.
Novotney, Jerome *o.m.i.* '68 (FgM) Oblates Foreign Missions.
Novotny, Allen P. *s.j.* '82 (WDC) [E] Washington, DC Gonzaga College High School.
Novotny, James F. '64 (OM) Lindsay, NE Holy Family Church; St. Edward, NE St. Edward Church.
Novotny, Richard '81 (RC) On Duty Outside the Diocese.
Novotny, Robert J. '50 (MIL) Retired.
Nowacki, Jerome A. '93 (MAR) DeTour, MI Sacred Heart Church; Goetzville, MI St. Stanislaus Kostka Church.
Nowacki, Piotr *s.chr.* '95 (CHI) [85] Chicago, IL Holy Trinity Church.
Nowak, Bernard J. '52 (LC) Retired.
Nowak, Bernard U. '74 (BUF) Angola, NY Most Precious Blood Church.
Nowak, Christopher W. *o.s.a.* '97 (CHL) Waynesville, NC St. John the Evangelist Church.
Nowak, Daniel *o.f.m.* '59 (SAG) Harrison, MI St. Athanasius Church.
Nowak, Edward C. *c.s.p.* '89 (LA) Goleta, CA St. Mark University Church; [BB] Los Angeles, CA Archdiocesan Office for Campus Ministry.
Nowak, Eugene J. '70 (CHI) Hoffman Estates, IL St. Hubert Church.
Nowak, Francis T. '58 (BUF) Retired.
Nowak, James A. '67 (JOL) Westmont, IL Holy Trinity Church.
Nowak, John H. *c.r.* '71 (CHI) [N] Chicago, IL Provincial Office of the Congregation of the Resurrection.
Nowak, Joseph G. '42 (CHI) [135] Chicago, IL St. Michael Church; Retired.
Nowak, Mark A. '75 (E) McKean, PA St. Francis Xavier Church; Meadville, PA St. Agatha Church; [P] Erie, PA Newman Centers and Campus Ministry.
Nowak, Michael E. '97 (MIL) [2] Wauwatosa, WI Christ King Church.
Nowak, Randolph *o.f.m.cap.* '52 (AGN) [F] Agana Heights, GU St. Fidelis Friary; [F] Agat, GU Capuchin Fraternity.
Nowak, Randolph *o.f.m.cap.* '52 (FgM) Capuchin Foreign Missions.
Nowak, Stanley F. '58 (BUF) [4] Depew, NY SS. Peter and Paul Church.
Nowak, Vincent A. '36 (ALB) Retired.
Nowakowski, Edward S. '48 (GB) Armstrong Creek, WI St. Stanislaus Kostka Church; Goodman, WI St. Joan of Arc Church.
Nowakowski, Jerome F. '63 (TOL) [7] Toledo, OH Good Shepherd Church; [30] Toledo, OH St. Louis Church; [41] Toledo, OH St. Thomas Aquinas Church.
Nowakowski, Rudy *o.m.i.* '60 (SFD) [A] Godfrey, IL Immaculate Heart of Mary Novitiate.
Nowel, Mark D. *o.p.* '86 (PRO) [P] Providence, RI St. Thomas Aquinas Priory at Providence College.
Nowel, Mark S. *o.p.* '86 (PRO) [B] Providence, RI Providence College.
Nowery, C. Richard *c.s.c.* '68 (NO) [22] New Orleans, LA Sacred Heart of Jesus Church.
Nowicki, Chester *s.v.d.* '46 (CHI) [B] Techny, IL Divine Word Residence; [N] Techny, IL Society of the Divine Word, Provincial Headquarter-Chicago Prov.; [N] Techny, IL Society of the Divine Word, Provincial Headquarter-Chicago Prov.
Nowicki, Gary D. '96 (MIL) Hales Corners, WI St. Mary Church.
Nowinski, Dennis '73 (DET) Memphis, MI All Saints Church.
Nowlan, Edward H. *s.j.* '41 (BO) [W] Weston, MA Campion Health Center, Inc.
Nowlan, John T. '66 (DET) Redford Township, MI St. Hilary Church.
Nsibu Tona, Rigobert '00 (BO) [W] Cambridge, MA Weston Jesuit Community.
Nsionu, Patrick N. '85 (NY) [205] Staten Island, NY Holy Family Church.
Nthawie, Joachim *s.j.* '98 (BAL) [S] Baltimore, MD Ferdinand Wheeler Jesuit Community.
Ntsele, Thulani *o.s.m.* '99 (CHI) [N] Chicago, IL Order of Friar Servants of Mary (Servites) United States of America Province, Inc.
Ntsiful-Amissah, Kofi '79 (ALB) Special Assignment.
Nuagbaracha, John *d.s.* (BUR) Burlington, VT Fletcher Allen Health Care; On Special or Other Diocesan Assignment.
Nuanez, Anthony '79 (LA) On Sick Leave.
Nuelle, John R. *m.s.* '64 (HRT) [M] Hartford, CT Missionaries of LaSalette, Provincial Secretary; [M] Hartford, CT Missionaries of LaSalette, Provincial Secretary; [V] Hartford, CT North American La Salette Mission Center, Inc.
Nugent, Anthony A. '72 (JOL) Plainfield, IL St. Mary Immaculate Church.
Nugent, Msgr. Arthur W. '47 (PH) Retired.
Nugent, Frank *s.d.b.* '56 (NEW) [N] Orange, NJ The Salesian Community; [S] Orange, NJ Salesians of Don Bosco, S.D.B.
Nugent, Msgr. Irvine '54 (PMB) Vero Beach, FL St. Helen Church; Retired.
Nugent, James *c.ss.r.* '50 (CHI) [133] Chicago, IL St. Michael Church.
Nugent, James *i.c.* '69 (PEO) [A] Peoria, IL Rosminian Novitiate.
Nugent, Msgr. James B. '56 (STU) Retired.
Nugent, John G. *c.m.* '49 (MET) [H] Plainsboro, NJ Vincentian Residence.
Nugent, Msgr. Joseph '71 (BRK) [68] Brooklyn, NY St. John the Evangelist Church.
Nugent, Kevin *s.t.* '51 (FgM) Trinity Missions.
Nugent, Msgr. Michael A. '43 (COL) Retired.
Nugent, Msgr. Peter D. '62 (LA) [2] Oxnard, CA Santa Clara Church.
Nugent, Raymond H. '58 (RVC) East Islip, NY St. Mary's Church.
Nugent, Msgr. Richard T. '49 (BUF) [2] Orchard Park, NY St. Bernadette Church.
Nugent, Robert *s.d.s.* (BAL) [S] Baltimore, MD Society of Mary (Marianists).
Nugent, Robert '65 (ALB) South Glens Falls, NY St. Michael the Archangel Church.
Nugent, Robert *s.d.s.* '65 (WDC) [B] Silver Spring, MD Salvatorian Community.
Nugent, Vincent J. *c.m.* '42 (PH) [AA] Philadelphia, PA Congregation of the Mission.
Nuin, Jeronimo Sola '35 (SJN) Retired.
Nunan, Jeremiah '63 (ALB) Cairo, NY Sacred Heart Church.
Nunes, James (RVC) Williston Park, NY St. Aidan's Church.
Nunes, Mario '61 (NEW) [26] Newark, NJ Our Lady of Fatima Church.
Nunez, Albert G. '64 (LAF) Lyons Point, LA St. John the Baptist Church.
Nunez, Alberto Vargas *s.j.* '67 (DET) [61] Detroit, MI SS. Peter and Paul Jesuit Church.
Nunez, Msgr. Edward H. '76 (PBL) Fruita, CO Sacred Heart Church; Grand Junction, CO St. Joseph Church.
Nunez, Mario '79 (SAC) Isleton, CA St. Therese's Church.
Nunez, Pedro F. '77 (NO) [35] New Orleans, LA St. Gerard Church; [66] New Orleans, LA St. Vincent De Paul Church.
Nunez, Philip, III '88 (ARE) On Duty Outside the Diocese.
Nunez, Phillip, III '88 (ORL) [8] Orlando, FL St. Isaac Jogues Church.
Nunning, David H. '69 (EVN) [13] Evansville, IN St. Agnes Church.
Nuno, Rafael '69 (ARE) [2] Utuado, PR San Pedro y San Pablo Church.
Nurre, Henry V. *o.s.b.* '56 (MIL) [P] Benet Lake, WI St. Benedict's Abbey.
Nusbaum, Daniel C. (BAL) [A] Emmitsburg, MD Mount St. Mary's Seminary.
Nusbaum, Daniel C. '61 (ALB) On Duty Outside the Diocese.
Nusbaum, Daniel C. '61 (BAL) [B] Emmitsburg, MD Mount Saint Mary's College.
Nuss, David '93 (WDC) [36] Washington, DC St. Patrick Church.
Nuss, David W. '93 (TOL) Graduate Studies.
Nuss, Francis B. '61 (RVC) Dix Hills, NY St. Matthew Church; Sayville, NY Good Samaritan Nursing Home.
Nutt, Maurice *c.ss.r.* '89 (STL) [22] St. Louis, MO St. Alphonsus Liguori Church; [P] St. Louis, MO St. Alphonsus Rectory of the Redemptorist.
Nuttall, J. *o.p.* '69 (FgM) Dominican - Order of Preachers Foreign Missions.
Nutter, N. John '89 (BR) Amite, LA St. Helena Church.
Nuttman, Joseph *c.ss.r.* (SEA) [32] Seattle, WA Sacred Heart of Jesus Church.
Nuwer, Herold M. '61 (BUF) Ransomville, NY Immaculate Conception Church.
Nuyen, Te Van '86 (SFR) [24] San Francisco, CA Holy Name of Jesus Church.
Nuytten, Ralph *c.i.c.m.* '49 (SAT) [M] San Antonio, TX Missionhurst Community Residence.
Nuzzi, Ronald '84 (Y) On Duty Outside the Diocese.
Nwabuzo, Cletus *o.p.* (STL) [30] St. Louis, MO St. Cecilia Church.
Nwachukwu, Oliver '82 (CHI) [118] Chicago, IL St. Margaret Mary Church.
Nwachukwu, Peter '86 (PIT) Unity, PA St. John the Baptist Church.
Nwachukwu, Raphael '74 (NY) Rosendale, NY St. Peter Church.
Nwachukwu, Sabinus '91 (TR) Hainesport, NJ Our Lady Queen of Peace Church.
Nwachukwu-Udaku, Anthony *s.s.j.* '93 (BR) New Roads, LA St. Augustine Church.
Nwadei, Hilary '82 (LA) Santa Monica, CA St. Clement Church.
Nwadgu, Sylvester (ATL) [3] Marietta, GA St. Joseph Church.
Nwagbaraicga, John D.S. (LAF) Kaplan, LA Our Lady of the Holy Rosary Church.
Nwalo, Msgr. Theophilus '65 (NY) [133] Bronx, NY St. Benedict Church.
Nwamadi, Chima '82 (CLV) [17] Akron, OH St. Sebastian Church.
Nwankwo, Nnamdi '89 (CLV) Wickliffe, OH Our Lady of Mount Carmel Church.
Nwanze, John *o.p.* '75 (SEA) [1] Tacoma, WA St. Ann Church; [3] Tacoma, WA St. John of the Woods Church; [12] Tacoma, WA Sacred Heart Church.
Nwaorgu, Anselm '92 (NEW) [4] Elizabeth, NJ Blessed Sacrament Church.
Nwaozor, Finnian '91 (LIN) Beatrice, NE St. Joseph's Church.
Nwaru, Romanus '94 (MIL) Hartland, WI St. Charles Church.
Nwauzor, Reginald U. '81 (PIT) [63] Pittsburgh, PA Prince of Peace Church.
Nwoga, Laserian I. '95 (CAM) Berlin, NJ Our Lady of Mt. Carmel Church.
Nwogwugwu, Emmanuel '86 (NY) [204] Staten Island, NY Holy Child Church.
Nwosu, Augustine Nnamdi *c.s.sp.* '95 (SJN) [F] Dorado, PR Santuario del Espiritu Santo.
Nwosu, Emmanuel '72 (NO) [57] New Orleans, LA St. Raymond Church.
Nyaga, John Peter *i.m.c.* '89 (MET) [H] Somerset, NJ Consolata Society for Foreign Missions.
Nyambo, Callist N. '69 (SP) [5] St. Petersburg, FL St. Joseph Church; [F] St. Petersburg, FL Immaculate Conception Early Childhood Center.
Nyardy, Jeffrey S. *o.s.b.* '90 (SAV) [B] Savannah, GA Benedictine Military School; [F] Savannah, GA The Benedictine Priory.
Nycz, Mieczyslaw F. '94 (BUF) [3] Orchard Park, NY Our Lady of the Sacred Heart Church.
Nydegger, Thomas P. '92 (NEW) [A] South Orange, NJ Immaculate Conception Seminary; [B] South Orange, NJ Seton Hall University.
Nyein, Isidore Usit *s.o.l.t.* '73 (CC) Robstown, TX St. Anthony Church.
Nygaard, Robert C. '64 (STP) Roseville, MN Corpus Christi Church.
Nygren, David *c.m.* '77 (CHI) [N] Chicago, IL Vincentian Community, Congregation of the Mission, Midwest Province.

Nyhan, James '73 (BO) [D] Cambridge, MA Matignon High School.
Nyhan, W. James '74 (BO) Billerica, MA St. Mary Church.
Nylund, Matthew *o.s.b.* (WDC) [M] Washington, DC St. Anselm's Abbey.
Nyman, Vincent R. '99 (STL) [3] St. Charles, MO St. Elizabeth Ann Seton Church.
Nyong, Emmaneul '88 (ROC) [5] Rochester, NY Church of the Annunciation.
Nyquist, Raymond J. '54 (GF) Black Eagle, MT Most Blessed Sacrament Church.
Nys, Loren G. *s.d.s.* '67 (GB) Kiel, WI SS. Peter and Paul Church.
Nyssen, Jacques *s.v.d.* '59 (TR) [M] Bordentown, NJ Society of the Divine Word.
Nzekwe, Anselm '87 (CLV) South Euclid, OH St. Margaret Mary Church.

O

O' Connell, William '66 (VEN) Retired.
O'Bell, John C. '91 (SCR) Bentley Creek, PA St. Ann's Church.
O'Blaney, James *c.ss.r.* '58 (ALB) Saratoga Springs, NY St. Clement Church.
O'Boyle, Leo *c.p.* '00 (BRK) [180] Queens, NY Immaculate Conception Church; [V] Jamaica, NY Immaculate Conception Monastery.
O'Brian, William J., III (BAL) Havre de Grace, MD St. Patrick's Church.
O'Brien, Anthony *ss.cc.* '34 (HON) [G] Kaneohe, HI Sacred Hearts Center.
O'Brien, Anthony '88 (MIA) Coral Gables, FL Little Flower Church.
O'Brien, Arthur '83 (HON) Retired.
O'Brien, Bartholomew J. '40 (ROC) Retired.
O'Brien, Msgr. Bartholomew J. '65 (PH) [71] Philadelphia, PA Immaculate Heart of Mary Church.
O'Brien, Charles H. *o.p.* '54 (L) [47] Louisville, KY St. Louis Bertrand Church.
O'Brien, Christian T. *o.praem.* '62 (SFE) Albuquerque, NM St. Joseph Medical Center; [I] Albuquerque, NM Santa Maria de la Vid Priory.
O'Brien, Christopher '54 (EVN) Retired.
O'Brien, Cornelius '55 (ARL) Falls Church, VA St. James Church.
O'Brien, Msgr. Daniel '39 (SY) [S] Syracuse, NY St. Pius X Home, Inc.
O'Brien, Daniel '75 (SAT) [K] San Antonio, TX Padua Place.
O'Brien, Daniel '75 (VIC) Retired.
O'Brien, Msgr. Daniel B. '39 (SY) Retired.
O'Brien, Daniel J. *s.j.* '59 (NY) [DD] New York, NY Jesuit Community at Fordham University.
O'Brien, Daniel P. '85 (HBG) [5] Steelton, PA Prince of Peace Church.
O'Brien, David *o.m.i.* '59 (FgM) Oblates Foreign Missions.
O'Brien, David G. '62 (BRK) Absent on Sick Leave.
O'Brien, David W. *c.s.p.* '56 (COL) [J] Columbus, OH Campus Ministry.
O'Brien, Denis *m.m.* '53 (DAL) [26] Dallas, TX St. Pius X Church.
O'Brien, Denis E. *m.m.* '53 (NY) [DD] Maryknoll, NY Maryknoll Fathers and Brothers.
O'Brien, Denis J. '44 (RVC) Retired.
O'Brien, Dennis '81 (PT) Quincy, FL St. Thomas the Apostle Church.
O'Brien, Dennis J. '77 (WOR) Shrewsbury, MA St. Mary's Church.
O'Brien, Donald *o.m.i.* '65 (BO) [Z] Tewksbury, MA Immaculate Heart of Mary Infirmary.
O'Brien, Donald J. '61 (GI) Cozad, NE Christ the King Church.
O'Brien, Donald J. '93 (TR) Howell Township, NJ St. Veronica Church.
O'Brien, Donald V. *s.j.* '55 (NY) [2] White Plains, NY St. John the Evangelist Church.
O'Brien, Eamonn '72 (SJ) [5] San Jose, CA St. Frances Cabrini Church.
O'Brien, Edmund M. '57 (HRT) [2] Enfield, CT St. Adalbert's Church.
O'Brien, Edward C. *s.j.* '61 (STL) [P] St. Louis, MO Jesuit Community Corporation at St. Louis University - Jesuit Hall.
O'Brien, Elias *o.carm.* '85 (PBR) Aliquippa, PA St. George the Great Martyr Church.
O'Brien, Eugene C. '57 (MIL) Retired.
O'Brien, Eugene J. *s.j.* '56 (NY) [DD] New York, NY "America;" Residence and publication office of the America Press; [HH] New York, NY Gregorian University Foundation, The.
O'Brien, Francis E. '66 (BO) [2] Framingham, MA St. George Church.
O'Brien, Frederick J. *s.j.* '62 (NY) [DD] New York, NY "America;" Residence and publication office of the America Press; [DD] New York, NY Jesuit Provincial's Office.
O'Brien, Frederick W. '50 (BO) Senior Priests.
O'Brien, George '57 (LA) Beverly Hills, CA Good Shepherd Church.
O'Brien, George L. '58 (WOR) East Templeton, MA Holy Cross Church.
O'Brien, Gerard '95 (LA) Lomita, CA St. Margaret Mary Alacoque Church.
O'Brien, Gerard C. *s.j.* '59 (BO) [W] Chestnut Hill, MA The Jesuit Community at Boston College.
O'Brien, Howard E. *m.m.* '55 (FgM) Maryknoll Foreign Missions.
O'Brien, J. Paul *s.j.* '68 (IND) [D] Indianapolis, IN Brebeuf Jesuit Preparatory School, Inc.
O'Brien, James '56 (BO) [W] Quincy, MA St. Columban's Foreign Mission Society.
O'Brien, James A. *s.j.* '60 (WH) [A] Wheeling, WV Wheeling Jesuit University.
O'Brien, James C. *s.j.* '61 (BO) [W] Chestnut Hill, MA The Jesuit Community at Boston College.
O'Brien, James E. '60 (Y) Retired.
O'Brien, James F. *s.j.* '67 (NY) [HH] New York, NY Jesuit Seminary and Mission Bureau, Inc.; [HH] New York, NY Xavier Society for the Blind.
O'Brien, James F. *s.j.* '75 (NY) [DD] New York, NY Xavier Jesuit Community.
O'Brien, Msgr. James J. '40 (NOR) Retired.
O'Brien, James J. '60 (CHI) [54] Chicago, IL St. Eugene Church.
O'Brien, James M. *m.m.* '49 (FgM) Maryknoll Foreign Missions.
O'Brien, James R. '66 (HBG) Mechanicsburg, PA Saint Katharine Drexel Church.
O'Brien, James T. '63 (BRK) [122] Brooklyn, NY Resurrection Church.
O'Brien, James T. '70 (SY) [3] Syracuse, NY Blessed Sacrament Church.
O'Brien, John *c.p.* (BO) [21] Boston, MA St. Gabriel Church.
O'Brien, John *o.s.b.* '34 (IND) Liberty, IN St. Bridget Church.
O'Brien, John '45 (BLX) Retired.
O'Brien, John '47 (SY) [S] Syracuse, NY St. Pius X Home, Inc.
O'Brien, John '55 (GB) Retired.
O'Brien, John *s.d.b.* '62 (SFR) [13] San Francisco, CA Corpus Christi Church.
O'Brien, John '64 (MIL) On Leave.
O'Brien, John *c.p.* '69 (BO) [W] Boston, MA St. Gabriel Passionist Community.
O'Brien, John '69 (SAV) Valdosta, GA St. John the Evangelist Church.
O'Brien, John '75 (PIT) Retired.
O'Brien, John A. '64 (MIL) North Fond du Lac, WI Presentation of the Blessed Virgin Church.
O'Brien, John E. '46 (NEW) Livingston, NJ St. Raphael Church; Retired.
O'Brien, John E. '50 (CHI) Highland Park, IL Immaculate Conception Church; Retired.
O'Brien, John E. '87 (BAL) Special Assignment; [D] Baltimore, MD Calvert Hall.
O'Brien, Msgr. John F. '61 (PH) [140] Philadelphia, PA St. Raymond of Penafort Church.
O'Brien, John F. '62 (WIL) Fairfax, DE St. Mary Magdalen Church.
O'Brien, Msgr. John H. '62 (BRK) [155] Queens, NY St. Benedict Joseph Labre Church.
O'Brien, John J. '40 (NEW) [B] Jersey City, NJ Saint Peter's College; [N] Jersey City, NJ Jesuits of Saint Peter's College, Inc.
O'Brien, Msgr. John J. '42 (SCR) Retired; [N] Dunmore, PA Villa St. Joseph.
O'Brien, John J. *s.j.* '49 (NEW) Saddle River Borough, NJ St. Gabriel the Archangel Church.
O'Brien, John J. *m.m.* '52 (NY) [DD] Maryknoll, NY Maryknoll Fathers and Brothers.
O'Brien, John M. *o.c.s.o.* '81 (ATL) [J] Conyers, GA The Monastery of the Holy Spirit.
O'Brien, John P. (NY) Scarsdale, NY St. Pius X Church.
O'Brien, John P. '49 (SPK) Retired.
O'Brien, John R. *c.p.m.* '52 (OWN) [F] South Union, KY Fathers of Mercy.
O'Brien, John T. '45 (BLX) Bay St. Louis, MS Our Lady of the Gulf Church.
O'Brien, John W. '67 (BO) [8] Quincy, MA Sacred Heart Church.
O'Brien, Jon J. *s.j.* '63 (WDC) [A] Washington, DC Theological College of the Catholic University of America; [M] Washington, DC The Jesuit Community at Georgetown University.
O'Brien, Joseph (BO) Roxbury, MA New England Baptist Hospital.
O'Brien, Joseph *o.carm.* '63 (JOL) [J] Darien, IL Carmelite Provincial Office.
O'Brien, Joseph *o.p.* '78 (LAV) [G] Henderson, NV Saint Therese Center.
O'Brien, Joseph '91 (ALB) Lake George, NY Sacred Heart Church; Warrensburg, NY St. Cecilia Church.
O'Brien, Joseph C. '84 (BO) Absent on Leave.
O'Brien, Joseph E. '51 (PH) [88] Philadelphia, PA St. Leo Church.
O'Brien, Joseph F. *s.j.* '44 (FgM) Provinces.
O'Brien, Joseph J. *o.m.i.* '54 (BWN) Port Isabel, TX Our Lady Star of the Sea Church.
O'Brien, Joseph J. '60 (CHI) Retired.
O'Brien, Joseph L. '55 (TOL) Retired.
O'Brien, Msgr. Joseph M. '57 (STL) Special Assignment.
O'Brien, Msgr. Joseph T. '46 (STL) Retired.
O'Brien, Joseph V. '57 (DUB) [1] Dubuque, IA St. Raphael's Church; [4] Dubuque, IA St. Mary's Church; [5] Dubuque, IA St. Patrick's Church; Balltown, IA St. Francis of Assisi Church; Sherrill, IA SS. Peter and Paul Church.
O'Brien, Msgr. Kenneth R. '40 (LA) Retired.
O'Brien, Kevin '54 (DET) Retired.
O'Brien, Kevin J. '79 (RIC) Lynchburg, VA St. Thomas More Church.
O'Brien, Kevin J. '81 (OG) [2] Plattsburgh, NY St. John the Baptist Church.
O'Brien, Msgr. Kevin P. '73 (NY) [10] New York, NY St. Ann's Roman Catholic Church; [52] New York, NY Immaculate Conception Church.
O'Brien, Leo P. '56 (ALB) [17] Albany, NY St. Vincent de Paul Church; Special Assignment.
O'Brien, Mark J. '84 (PH) Absent on Leave.
O'Brien, Martin F. '52 (NEW) [A] South Orange, NJ Seton Hall University College Seminary; [B] South Orange, NJ Seton Hall University.
O'Brien, Maurice '68 (SAC) Dixon, CA St. Peter Church.
O'Brien, Michael '72 (JKS) Natchez, MS Assumption of the B.V.M. Church; Natchez, MS St. Mary Basilica Church.
O'Brien, Michael '79 (SP) [2] Largo, FL St. Justin Martyr Church.
O'Brien, Michael C. '65 (SEA) Monroe, WA St. Mary of the Valley Church.
O'Brien, Michael G. *c.s.c.* '42 (FTW) [J] South Bend, IN Congregation of Holy Cross, Indiana Province, Provincial House.
O'Brien, Michael J. '00 (DEN) [18] Denver, CO Notre Dame Church.
O'Brien, Michael J. *c.s.v.* '48 (CHI) [N] Arlington Heights, IL Viatorian Province Center-Clerics of St. Viator.
O'Brien, Michael J. '63 (NEW) Kearny, NJ Our Lady of Sorrows Church.
O'Brien, Nicholas J. '83 (ORL) Leesburg, FL St. Paul's Church.
O'Brien, Patrick (PIT) [B] Pittsburgh, PA La Roche College.
O'Brien, Patrick *c.ss.r.* '64 (OAK) [N] Oakland, CA Redemptorists.
O'Brien, Patrick *c.ss.r.* '64 (TUC) [J] Tucson, AZ Redemptorist Community Support Charity Trust; [J] Tucson, AZ Retorno (Marriage Retorno).
O'Brien, Patrick '69 (SAV) [10] Savannah, GA St. Peter the Apostle Church.
O'Brien, Patrick '74 (HT) [5] Houma, LA St. Bernadette Church.
O'Brien, Msgr. Patrick J. '56 (LA) Ventura, CA San Buenaventura Church.
O'Brien, Patrick K. '46 (SEA) Fife, WA St. Martin of Tours Church.
O'Brien, Paul (BO) [8] Lawrence, MA St. Patrick Church.
O'Brien, Paul *s.j.* '38 (FgM) Provinces.
O'Brien, Paul A. *m.m.* '59 (FgM) Maryknoll Foreign Missions.
O'Brien, Paul B. '91 (BO) [27] Boston, MA St. James the Greater Church.
O'Brien, Peter F. *s.j.* '71 (NEW) [C] Jersey City, NJ St. Peter's Preparatory School.
O'Brien, Raymond C. '75 (WDC) Special Ministries; [C] Washington, DC Catholic University of America, The.
O'Brien, Richard *c.m.* '61 (KC) [J] Kansas City, MO Vincentian Parish Mission Center.
O'Brien, Richard M. '92 (BO) On Duty Outside the Archdiocese.
O'Brien, Richard M. '92 (PRT) Bangor, ME St. John's Church; Brewer, ME St. Teresa's Church.
O'Brien, Robert E. *s.j.* '54 (NY) [DD] New York, NY St. Ignatius Loyola Residence.
O'Brien, Roger '61 (SEA) [12] Seattle, WA St. Luke Church.
O'Brien, Msgr. Roger E. '42 (DUB) Retired.
O'Brien, Scott *o.p.* '92 (MIA) [18] Miami, FL St. Dominic Church; [H] Miami, FL Dominican Fathers of Miami, Inc.
O'Brien, Sean *o.f.m.* '98 (PAT) Pompton Lakes, NJ Our Lady of the Assumption Church.
O'Brien, Sean Patrick '93 (SY) Forestport, NY St. Patrick Church.
O'Brien, Steven '86 (DUB) [6] Cedar Rapids, IA St. Matthew's Church.
O'Brien, Steven G. '86 (DUB) Belle Plaine, IA St. Michael Church; Chelsea, IA St. Joseph's Church; [D] Cedar Rapids, IA Xavier High School.
O'Brien, Terrance (PEO) Absent on Leave.
O'Brien, Thomas '52 (BRK) Retired.
O'Brien, Thomas *o.m.i.* '55 (FgM) Oblates Foreign Missions.
O'Brien, Thomas *o.s.c.* '74 (STP) [N] Shoreview, MN Crosier Community of Shoreview.
O'Brien, Thomas F. '55 (OM) [47] Omaha, NE St.

Vincent de Paul Church.
O'Brien, Thomas F. '56 (WOR) Retired.
O'Brien, Thomas G. *c.s.v.* '47 (CHI) [N] Arlington Heights, IL Viatorian Province Center-Clerics of St. Viator.
O'Brien, Msgr. Thomas J. '50 (KC) Retired.
O'Brien, Thomas J. '55 (SAT) Martinez, TX St. Jerome Church.
O'Brien, Thomas J. *m.m.* '74 (FgM) Maryknoll Foreign Missions.
O'Brien, Msgr. Thomas M. '52 (BRK) [205] Queens, NY St. Nicholas of Tolentine Church.
O'Brien, Timothy A. '94 (HRT) [2] West Haven, CT St. John Vianney Church.
O'Brien, Timothy J. '69 (MIL) Special Assignment.
O'Brien, Msgr. Tom (KC) [H] Blue Springs, MO St. Mary's Manor.
O'Brien, Vincent J. *o.p.* (WDC) Bethesda, MD National Institutes of Health, Clinical Center.
O'Brien, Vincent M. *s.j.* '55 (WDC) [E] North Bethesda, MD Georgetown Preparatory School.
O'Brien, Walter *o.f.m.cap.* '37 (NOR) [4] Middletown, CT St. Pius X Church.
O'Brien, William (GB) [3] Two Rivers, WI Holy Redeemer - Sacred Heart Church.
O'Brien, William *m.s.* '49 (LKC) [3] Sulphur, LA Our Lady of Prompt Succor Church.
O'Brien, William '61 (NEW) Rochelle Park, NJ Sacred Heart Church.
O'Brien, William '88 (VNN) Seattle, WA St. John Chrysostom Church.
O'Brien, Msgr. William B. '51 (NY) On Duty Outside the Archdiocese.
O'Brien, William D. '50 (DUB) Retired.
O'Brien, William G. '51 (WOR) Retired.
O'Brien, William J. *c.m.* '67 (BUF) [T] Niagara University, NY Our Lady of Angels Association.
O'Brien, William J. *c.m.* '67 (PH) [70] Philadelphia, PA Immaculate Conception Church; [B] Philadelphia, PA St. Vincent's Seminary; [FF] Philadelphia, PA The Central Association of the Miraculous Medal.
O'Brien, William J. '73 (CHI) [177] Chicago, IL Queen of Angels Church.
O'Brien, William J. '80 (E) Franklin, PA St. Patrick Church.
O'Brien, William P. *m.s.* '49 (LKC) Sulphur, LA West Clacasieu Cameron Hospital.
O'Brien, William S. '69 (RIC) Waynesboro, VA St. John the Evangelist Church.
O'Bryan, Henry '41 (OWN) Retired.
O'Bryan, Msgr. J. A. '35 (L) Retired.
O'Byrne, Charles J.. *s.j.* '97 (NY) [82] New York, NY Notre Dame Church.
O'Byrne, John '61 (LA) Torrance, CA St. Catherine Laboure Church.
O'Byrne, Liam '41 (SFR) [K] San Francisco, CA Home for the Aged of the Little Sisters of the Poor.
O'Byrne, Patrick J. '60 (LIN) Plattsmouth, NE Church of the Holy Spirit.
O'Byrne, Msgr. Sylvester '51 (LA) Montecito, CA Our Lady of Mount Carmel Church; Retired.
O'Callaghan, Dominic *o.c.d.* '44 (SB) [G] Redlands, CA El Carmelo Retreat House.
O'Callaghan, Msgr. Eugene '55 (SAT) New Braunfels, TX SS. Peter and Paul Church.
O'Callaghan, Msgr. James A. '43 (LA) Hacienda Heights, CA St. John Vianney Church; Retired.
O'Callaghan, John '65 (ORG) Inactive Leave.
O'Callaghan, John F. '59 (DET) Retired.
O'Callaghan, John J. *s.j.* '62 (CHI) [C] Chicago, IL Jesuit Community at Loyola University of Chicago.
O'Callaghan, Matthias J. '62 (SAC) Willows, CA St. Monica Church.
O'Callaghan, Patrick '55 (SAT) Retired.
O'Callaghan, Msgr. Peter '52 (SAT) [24] San Antonio, TX St. Agnes Church.
O'Callaghan, Thomas '54 (SEA) Retired.
O'Callaghan, Tiernan *o.carm.* '56 (PHX) [6] Phoenix, AZ St. Agnes Church.
O'Campo, Arturo M. *o.f.m.* '85 (SAT) [25] San Antonio, TX St. Alphonsus Church.
O'Carroll, Msgr. Donal A. '56 (STU) Retired.
O'Carroll, Eugene '62 (PHX) [21] Phoenix, AZ St. Paul Church.
O'Carroll, Fergus *l.c.* '78 (MAD) [H] Edgerton, WI Legion of Christ, Inc.; [L] Edgerton, WI Oaklawn Incorporated.
O'Carroll, Patrick J. '54 (ORL) Barefoot Bay, FL St. Luke Church.
O'Carroll, Philip A. '58 (SB) [2] Fontana, CA St. George Church.
O'Cinnsealaigh, Benedict (CIN) Mount Carmel, OH St. Veronica Church.
O'Conell, William *s.m.* '56 (HON) [G] Honolulu, HI Marianist Communities.
O'Connell, Anthony M. *o.s.m.* '67 (CHI) [17] Chicago, IL Assumption of the Blessed Virgin Mary Church; [A] Mundelein, IL University of St. Mary of the Lake-Mundelein Seminary; [N] Chicago, IL Order of Friar Servants of Mary (Servites) United States of America Province, Inc.
O'Connell, Brendan M. *m.m.* '63 (FgM) Maryknoll Foreign Missions.
O'Connell, Cuthbert '86 (BLX) Bassfield, MS St. Peter Church.
O'Connell, Damian *s.j.* '75 (NY) [GG] New York, NY University Apostolate.
O'Connell, Daniel '71 (SAV) Douglas, GA St. Paul's Church.
O'Connell, Daniel C. *s.j.* '58 (CHI) [C] Chicago, IL Jesuit Community at Loyola University of Chicago.
O'Connell, Daniel C. '83 (BO) [1] Newton, MA St. Bernard Church.
O'Connell, Daniel P. '71 (SAV) [J] Willacoochee, GA Catholic Cemetery.
O'Connell, David '79 (LA) [4] Los Angeles, CA Ascension Church; [62] Los Angeles, CA St. Frances Xavier Cabrini Church.
O'Connell, David M. *c.m.* '75 (PH) [AA] Philadelphia, PA Congregation of the Mission.
O'Connell, David M. *c.m.* '82 (WDC) [C] Washington, DC Catholic University of America, The.
O'Connell, George *o.m.i.* '41 (SAT) [K] San Antonio, TX Oblate Madonna Residence.
O'Connell, George M. *o.s.m.* '37 (CHI) [N] Chicago, IL Order of Friar Servants of Mary (Servites) United States of America Province, Inc.
O'Connell, James (NY) Manhattan, NY St. Vincent Hospital.
O'Connell, Msgr. James P. '53 (STL) Retired.
O'Connell, James R. *o.f.m.* '83 (NY) [35] New York, NY St. Francis of Assisi Church.
O'Connell, John '59 (SFD) Taylorville, IL St. Mary Church.
O'Connell, John B. '40 (HRT) [4] Enfield, CT St. Martha's Church.
O'Connell, John G. *o.p.* '44 (STP) [15] Minneapolis, MN St. Albert the Great Church.
O'Connell, John Q. *c.m.* '53 (DEN) [M] Denver, CO Congregation of the Mission Midwest Province: De Paul House; [Q] Denver, CO Kateri Catholic Indian Community of Colorado.
O'Connell, John R. '73 (NEW) Midland Park, NJ Nativity Church.
O'Connell, Joseph '51 (SFR) Mill Valley, CA Our Lady of Mt. Carmel Church.
O'Connell, Joseph *s.o.l.t.* '91 (CC) [H] Robstown, TX Society of Our Lady of the Most Holy Trinity.
O'Connell, Msgr. Joseph F. '64 (CAM) Washington Township, NJ St. Charles Borromeo Church.
O'Connell, Joseph F. *s.j.* '73 (WDC) [M] Washington, DC The Jesuit Community at Georgetown University; [V] Washington, DC Jesuit Secondary Education Association.
O'Connell, Joseph P. *s.j.* '52 (SEA) [L] Seattle, WA Jesuit House, Seattle.
O'Connell, Kevin G. *s.j.* '69 (FgM) Provinces.
O'Connell, Luke A. *o.f.m.* '55 (ALB) [B] Loudonville, NY Siena College.
O'Connell, Mark '90 (BO) Graduate Studies.
O'Connell, Mark A. '79 (NEW) Belleville, NJ St. Peter's Church.
O'Connell, Marvin R. '56 (FTW) [B] Notre Dame, IN University of Notre Dame Du Lac.
O'Connell, Marvin R. '56 (STP) On Duty Outside the Archdiocese.
O'Connell, Maurice V. '72 (WDC) Ridge, MD St. Michael Church.
O'Connell, Michael '67 (STP) [1] Minneapolis, MN The Basilica of St. Mary Co-; [4] Minneapolis, MN Ascension Church.
O'Connell, Michael W. '83 (CHI) Orland Park, IL Our Lady of the Woods Church.
O'Connell, Neil J. *o.f.m.* '64 (NY) [115] New York, NY St. Stephen of Hungary Church; [HH] New York, NY Shrine of St. Jude, Inc.
O'Connell, Paul T. '60 (WOR) Shrewsbury, MA St. Mary's Church.
O'Connell, Richard '51 (ROC) [49] Rochester, NY Roman Catholic Community of the 19th Ward Church.
O'Connell, Richard C. '51 (ROC) [48] Rochester, NY St. Monica Church; Retired.
O'Connell, Robert E. '71 (SUP) Hurley, WI St. Mary of the Seven Dolors Church; Montreal, WI Sacred Heart of Jesus Church; Pence, WI Holy Redeemer Church; Saxon, WI St. Ann's Church.
O'Connell, Robert J. *s.s.j.* '41 (BAL) [S] Baltimore, MD St. Joseph's Manor.
O'Connell, Robert J. '70 (RVC) Patchogue, NY Our Lady of Mt. Carmel Church.
O'Connell, Msgr. Robert M. '51 (NY) [105] New York, NY St. Peter Church.
O'Connell, Terrence E. *o.m.i.* (BO) [12] Lowell, MA Nuestra Senora del Carmen Church.
O'Connell, Terry J. '92 (P) Coos Bay, OR St. Monica Church.
O'Connell, Thomas C. '46 (PIT) Retired.
O'Connell, Thomas P. '63 (KNX) Seymour, TN Holy Family Church.
O'Connell, Msgr. Timothy '63 (LA) [98] Los Angeles, CA Visitation Church.
O'Connell, Vincent O. *c.s.sp.* '59 (BRK) [V] Long Island City, NY Holy Ghost Fathers of Ireland.
O'Connell, Walter T. *o.p.* '58 (CHI) [N] River Forest, IL St. Thomas Aquinas Priory.
O'Connell, William *s.m.* (HON) [I] Honolulu, HI Our Lady the Mystical Rose Chapel.
O'Connell, William *s.m.* '56 (HON) [C] Honolulu, HI Saint Louis School.
O'Connell, Msgr. William '57 (RC) McIntosh, SD St. Bonaventure's Church; McLaughlin, SD St. Bernard Church.
O'Connell, William A. '55 (SFR) Retired.
O'Connell, Msgr. William J. '57 (RC) Standing Rock, SD Standing Rock Reservation Church.
O'Conner, Kevin *o.m.i.* '58 (P) Scio, OR St. Bernard Church.
O'Connor, Adrian J. *o.praem.* '95 (ORG) [D] Silverado, CA St. Michael's College Preparatory High School.
O'Connor, Msgr. Albert G. '67 (SAC) Elk Grove, CA St. Joseph Church.
O'Connor, Msgr. Aloysius E. '40 (WDC) Avenue, MD Holy Angels Church; Retired.
O'Connor, Andrew J. '87 (STL) St. Ann, MO St. Kevin Church.
O'Connor, Andrew M. '96 (NY) New City, NY St. Augustine Church.
O'Connor, Bernard *c.m.f.* '50 (LA) Santa Monica, CA St. Monica Church.
O'Connor, Bernard F. *o.s.f.s.* '73 (ALN) [B] Center Valley, PA Desales University; [K] Center Valley, PA Oblates of St. Francis de Sales.
O'Connor, Charles '50 (NEW) [N] Rutherford, NJ St. John Vianney Residence for Priests.
O'Connor, Charles *o.f.m., s.t.d.* '73 (BUF) [A] East Aurora, NY Christ the King Seminary.
O'Connor, Charles J. *c.m.* '34 (PH) [AA] Philadelphia, PA Congregation of the Mission.
O'Connor, Charles P. '50 (NEW) Retired.
O'Connor, Charles T. '83 (MET) Bound Brook, NJ St. Joseph Church.
O'Connor, Christopher '99 (BRK) [155] Queens, NY St. Benedict Joseph Labre Church.
O'Connor, Christopher K. '98 (BO) Chelmsford, MA St. Mary Church.
O'Connor, Msgr. Daniel J. '61 (ATL) [10] Atlanta, GA St. Jude Church.
O'Connor, Daniel P. '90 (ALX) Natchitoches, LA Holy Cross Church; [J] Natchitoches, LA Northwestern State University.
O'Connor, David *s.t.* '55 (WDC) [M] University Park, MD Holy Trinity Missionary Cenacle.
O'Connor, David '64 (JKS) [A] Madison, MS St. Joseph Catholic School.
O'Connor, David H. '86 (DUB) [A] Dubuque, IA Seminary of St. Pius X; [C] Dubuque, IA Loras College.
O'Connor, Dennis J. '98 (SD) [23] San Diego, CA St. Charles Church.
O'Connor, Desmond *s.p.s.* '50 (PAT) Mount Arlington, NJ Our Lady of the Lake Church.
O'Connor, Msgr. Desmond '80 (NY) Warwick, NY St. Stephen Church.
O'Connor, Donal '55 (LA) West Covina, CA St. Christopher Church.
O'Connor, Donald *s.v.d.* '64 (FgM) Society of the Divine Word Foreign Missions.
O'Connor, Donald *s.v.d.* '64 (JOL) Coal City, IL Assumption Church.
O'Connor, Edward '60 (ATL) Thomson, GA Queen of Angels Church.
O'Connor, Edward D. *c.s.c.* '48 (FTW) [B] Notre Dame, IN University of Notre Dame Du Lac; [J] Notre Dame, IN Holy Cross Community, Corby Hall, University of Notre Dame.
O'Connor, Msgr. Edward J. '39 (CAM) Retired.
O'Connor, Edward J. '81 (ALN) Lost Creek, PA St. Mary Magdalen Church; [1] Shenandoah, PA Annunciation Church.
O'Connor, Edward T. '44 (BRK) [64] Brooklyn, NY Immaculate Heart of Mary Church; Retired.
O'Connor, Francis A. '62 (ALB) [4] Albany, NY St. Casimir Church; [14] Albany, NY St. Patrick Church.
O'Connor, Francis J. '53 (MAN) Retired.
O'Connor, Francis M. *s.j.* '58 (BAL) [S] Baltimore, MD Jesuit Fathers and Brothers Maryland Provincial Curia.
O'Connor, Francis M. *s.j.* '69 (FgM) Provinces.
O'Connor, Msgr. Fred P. '52 (GAL) Crosby, TX Sacred Heart Church.
O'Connor, Gerald P. *m.m.* '69 (FgM) Maryknoll Foreign Missions.
O'Connor, Gerald T. '66 (ROC) Addison, NY St. Catherine of Siena Church; Bradford, NY St. Stanislaus Church.
O'Connor, Gerald V. *s.j.* '76 (WDC) [E] Washington, DC Gonzaga College High School.
O'Connor, Gerard (FR) Graduate Studies.
O'Connor, Glenn L. '80 (IND) [14] Indianapolis, IN St. Ann Church; [22] Indianapolis, IN St. Joseph Church; Indianapolis, IN Indianapolis International Airport.
O'Connor, Msgr. Hugh '39 (ORG) Anaheim, CA St. Justin Martyr Church; Retired.

O'Connor, J. Kieran '45 (MAN) [J] Manchester, NH St. Teresa's Manor.
O'Connor, J. Paul *s.j.* '53 (STL) [O] St. Louis, MO Fusz Pavilion.
O'Connor, James '69 (AUS) On Leave.
O'Connor, James '70 (LUB) [4] Lubbock, TX Our Lady of Guadalupe Church.
O'Connor, James C. '71 (BUF) Williamsville, NY SS. Peter and Paul Church.
O'Connor, James E. *o.c.s.o.* '57 (DUB) [K] Peosta, IA New Melleray Abbey, Order of Cistercians of the Strict Observance.
O'Connor, James E. '82 (WH) Madison, WV St. Mary, Queen of Heaven Church.
O'Connor, James J. '43 (FTW) Retired.
O'Connor, James J. '54 (CIN) Retired.
O'Connor, James M. '52 (LIN) Minden, NE St. John's Church.
O'Connor, James T. '54 (CHI) Retired.
O'Connor, James T. '66 (NY) Millbrook, NY St. Joseph Church.
O'Connor, Jay '74 (BAL) Annapolis, MD St. Andrew by the Bay Church.
O'Connor, John C. '61 (LA) Lynwood, CA St. Emydius Church.
O'Connor, John F. '44 (PEO) Retired.
O'Connor, John F. *s.t.b.* '64 (NEW) [21] Newark, NJ Immaculate Conception Church.
O'Connor, John F. *o.f.m.* '73 (ARL) Triangle, VA St. Francis of Assisi Church.
O'Connor, Msgr. John F. '73 (R) [3] Raleigh, NC Our Lady of Lourdes Church.
O'Connor, John H. '62 (PAT) Dover, NJ St. Mary's Church.
O'Connor, John J. '42 (BUF) Retired.
O'Connor, John J. '58 (DUB) New Vienna, IA St. Boniface's Church; Petersburg, IA SS. Peter and Paul Church.
O'Connor, Msgr. John J. '60 (SFR) [1] San Francisco, CA Cathedral of St. Mary (Assumption).
O'Connor, John J. '68 (DUB) [F] New Vienna, IA Archbishop Hennessy Catholic School.
O'Connor, John L. '63 (ROC) [34] Rochester, NY Our Lady of Lourdes Church.
O'Connor, John P. '45 (PH) [84] Philadelphia, PA St. Katherine of Siena Church; Retired.
O'Connor, Msgr. John Philip '61 (NEW) Garwood, NJ Church of St. Anne.
O'Connor, John T. '46 (HRT) Southington, CT St. Dominic Church; Retired.
O'Connor, John T. '52 (MIL) [B] Hales Corners, WI Sacred Heart School of Theology; [P] Hales Corners, WI Sacred Heart Monastery.
O'Connor, Msgr. Joseph A. '47 (TR) Retired; [M] Trenton, NJ Villa Vianney.
O'Connor, Joseph X. *o.s.a.* '53 (BO) [C] North Andover, MA Merrimack College.
O'Connor, Mark *s.a.* '84 (NY) [DD] Garrison, NY Franciscan Friars of the Atonement.
O'Connor, Matthew '71 (MOB) [19] Mobile, AL St. Pius X Church.
O'Connor, Matthew J. '56 (SPR) Retired.
O'Connor, Maurice '52 (NY) Absent on Sick leave.
O'Connor, Maurice J. '53 (BO) Stoughton, MA Our Lady of the Rosary Church.
O'Connor, Michael (CHI) [167] Chicago, IL SS. Peter and Paul Church.
O'Connor, Msgr. Michael '47 (FRS) Retired.
O'Connor, Michael F. '44 (NU) Retired.
O'Connor, Michael F. '44 (STP) Miesville, MN St. Joseph Church.
O'Connor, Msgr. Michael J. '34 (LA) Woodland Hills, CA St. Mel Church; Retired.
O'Connor, Michael J. '65 (SJ) [4] Sunnyvale, CA Church of The Resurrection.
O'Connor, Michael J. *o.s.a.* '71 (CHI) [D] Chicago, IL St. Rita High School.
O'Connor, Michael J. '72 (TR) Delran, NJ Holy Name Church.
O'Connor, Neil D. '69 (CLV) [4] Parma, OH St. Columbkille Church.
O'Connor, Norman J. *c.s.p.* '48 (NY) [DD] Jamaica Estates, NY Paulist Fathers Generalate.
O'Connor, Oliver J. *o.f.m.cap.* '42 (ROC) [I] Interlaken, NY St. Fidelis Friary.
O'Connor, Patrick *m.s.c.* '52 (CC) Bishop, TX St. James Church.
O'Connor, Patrick '55 (KC) Retired.
O'Connor, Patrick C. '78 (SAG) [17] Saginaw, MI St. Stephen Church.
O'Connor, Patrick J. '58 (SAC) Tahoe City, CA Corpus Christi Church.
O'Connor, Patrick J. '64 (GBG) [4] Uniontown, PA St. Therese, the Little Flower of Jesus Church.
O'Connor, Patrick J. '85 (CLV) [3] Elyria, OH St. Jude Church.
O'Connor, Patrick T. *o.s.f.s.* '97 (ARL) Reston, VA St. John Neumann Church.
O'Connor, Msgr. Paul '45 (CAM) Retired.
O'Connor, Paul *a.a.* '78 (BO) [W] Boston, MA Assumptionist Center.
O'Connor, Paul A. *a.a.* (ARM) Boston, MA Holy Cross Church.
O'Connor, Paul F. *c.s.b.* '70 (GAL) [Q] Houston, TX Dillon House.
O'Connor, Raymond '64 (SPC) [I] Joplin, MO Newman Club, Missouri Southern State College.
O'Connor, Raymond E. *c.m.f.* '65 (SPC) Joplin, MO St. Peter Church.
O'Connor, Robert B. '56 (NY) [18] New York, NY Blessed Sacrament Church.
O'Connor, Robert C. *s.j.* '64 (CIN) [26] Cincinnati, OH St. Francis Xavier Church.
O'Connor, Robert D. '55 (PEO) East Moline, IL St. Anne Church.
O'Connor, Robert F. *s.j.* '79 (OM) [K] Omaha, NE Jesuit Community at Creighton University.
O'Connor, Robert W. '48 (PEO) Lewistown, IL St. Mary's Church.
O'Connor, Samuel *o.f.m.* '56 (BO) [BB] Boston, MA St. Anthony Shrine.
O'Connor, Shaun *m.i.c.* '82 (WDC) [B] Washington, DC Marian Fathers Scholasticate.
O'Connor, Shaw *c.f.r.* (NY) [DD] Bronx, NY Our Lady of the Angels Friary.
O'Connor, Steven J. '77 (PT) Tiger Point, FL St. Sylvester Church; [H] Navarre, FL Casa Stella Maris.
O'Connor, Thomas *c.ss.r.* '50 (GR) [3] Grand Rapids, MI St. Alphonsus Church.
O'Connor, Thomas *o.s.b.* '56 (BIR) Retired.
O'Connor, Thomas A. *s.j.* '62 (BUF) [O] Buffalo, NY Canisius Jesuit Community; [R] Alfred, NY Campus Ministry.
O'Connor, Thomas J. '55 (TR) Freehold, NJ St. Robert Bellarmine Church.
O'Connor, Thomas J. *o.s.b.* '56 (BIR) [E] Cullman, AL St. Bernard Abbey.
O'Connor, Thomas J. '93 (BO) [W] Hingham, MA Glastonbury Abbey.
O'Connor, Thomas P. '56 (FTW) [11] Fort Wayne, IN St. Mary Church.
O'Connor, Thomas V. *s.j.* '63 (NEW) [C] Jersey City, NJ St. Peter's Preparatory School.
O'Connor, Timothy J. '75 (CLV) Avon Lake, OH St. Joseph's Church.
O'Connor, Vincent M. '48 (SPR) Leeds, MA St. Catherine's Church.
O'Connor, William (BO) Stoughton, MA New England Sinai Hospital.
O'Connor, William '49 (SJ) Retired.
O'Connor, William B. '47 (BO) Senior Priests.
O'connor, William D. *o.m.i.* '43 (SAT) [K] San Antonio, TX Oblate Madonna Residence.
O'Connor, William F. *s.j.* '48 (BO) [W] Weston, MA Campion Health Center, Inc.
O'Connor, William J. '58 (BO) Senior Priests.
O'Connor, William T. '68 (CHI) Chicago Heights, IL St. Paul Church.
O'Connor,, Eugene, V.F. '54 (BIR) [3] Birmingham, AL St. Barnabas Church.
O'Conor, Kevin *o.m.i.* '58 (P) Jordan, OR Our Lady of Lourdes Church.
O'Day, Msgr. Martin J. '47 (CHI) Oak Forest, IL St. Damian Church; Retired.
O'Day, Michael '38 (SB) Sun City, CA St. Vincent Ferrer Church; Retired.
O'Dea, Msgr. Joseph J. '42 (PEO) Retired; [L] Peoria, IL St. Joseph's Home of Peoria.
O'Dea, Loren F. '93 (DET) Farmington, MI Our Lady of Sorrows Church; Retired.
O'Dea, Thomas '58 (PHX) Fountain Hills, AZ Ascension Church.
O'Dea, Vincent P. '36 (CLV) Hudson, OH St. Mary Church; Retired.
O'Dea, William '56 (PMB) Lantana, FL Holy Spirit Church; Retired.
O'Dell, W. Paul '93 (SFR) [21] San Francisco, CA St. Gabriel Church.
O'Doherty, Gerard *s.v.d.* '74 (LA) [28] Los Angeles, CA Our Lady of Loretto Church; [Q] Los Angeles, CA Society of the Divine Word Missionaries, Western Province; [Q] Los Angeles, CA Western Province (1964) Province of St. Therese of the Child Jesus.
O'Doherty, John *s.s.c.* '39 (PRO) [P] Bristol, RI St. Columban's Retirement House.
O'Doherty, Msgr. Jude '65 (MIA) [4] Miami, FL Epiphany Church.
O'Doherty, Liam '65 (OG) Absent on Sick Leave.
O'Doherty, Patrick J. '70 (ORL) [3] Ocala, FL Queen of Peace Church.
O'Donnell, Brian P. *s.j.* '86 (DET) [K] Detroit, MI Jesuit Community at the University of Detroit.
O'Donnell, Cornelius '55 (SAC) Walnut Grove, CA St. Anthony Church; Retired and in Senior Ministry.
O'Donnell, David P. (BO) [2] Brockton, MA St. Colman of Cloyne Church.
O'Donnell, Dennis '74 (PH) West Chester, PA SS. Simon and Jude Church.
O'Donnell, Dennis '83 (GR) Ludington, MI St. Stanislaus Church.
O'Donnell, Dennis J.W. '74 (PH) [CC] Malvern, PA St. Joseph's-in-the-Hills.
O'Donnell, Edmond G. '64 (SB) Upland, CA St. Anthony Church.
O'Donnell, Msgr. Edward C. '41 (OM) Retired.
O'Donnell, Edward T. *s.j.* '74 (CIN) [M] Cincinnati, OH Jesuit Community at Xavier University.
O'Donnell, Eugene P. '73 (SJ) Morgan Hill, CA St. Catherine of Alexandria Church.
O'Donnell, Francis P. *s.j.* '69 (CHI) [N] Chicago, IL Chicago Province of the Society of Jesus-Provincial Office.
O'Donnell, Francis T. *m.m.* '55 (FgM) Maryknoll Foreign Missions.
O'Donnell, Harold F. *s.j.* '64 (NY) [DD] New York, NY Xavier Jesuit Community.
O'Donnell, Harold F.X. *s.j.* (NY) Manhattan, NY Bird S. Coler Memorial Hospital and Home.
O'Donnell, Hugh '58 (SFR) [2] South San Francisco, CA Mater Dolorosa Church.
O'Donnell, Msgr. Hugh A. '54 (NEW) [6] Elizabeth, NJ St. Genevieve's Church.
O'Donnell, Hugh F. *c.m.* '61 (FgM) Vincentian Foreign Missions.
O'Donnell, James *o.s.b.* '42 (PAT) [M] Morristown, NJ St. Mary's Abbey.
O'Donnell, James '56 (CLV) Cleveland, OH Northeast Pre Release Center.
O'Donnell, James *s.j.* '61 (FgM) Provinces.
O'Donnell, James P. '56 (CLV) Cleveland, OH Cuyahoga County Detention Home.
O'Donnell, John '72 (DUL) Virginia, MN Holy Spirit Church; Virginia, MN Sacred Heart Church.
O'Donnell, John *o.s.b.* '98 (BIR) Cullman, AL Sacred Heart Church; On Special or Other Diocesan Assignment; [E] Cullman, AL St. Bernard Abbey.
O'Donnell, Msgr. John F. '54 (LR) Fort Smith, AR Immaculate Conception Church.
O'Donnell, John F. '63 (BO) [23] Boston, MA St. Gregory Church.
O'Donnell, John J. *s.j.* '74 (BAL) [S] Baltimore, MD Jesuit Fathers and Brothers Maryland Provincial Curia.
O'Donnell, Joseph '48 (CIN) [M] Cincinnati, OH Headquarters of Glenmary Home Missioners.
O'Donnell, Joseph '76 (CLV) [I] Cleveland, OH Marymount Hospital, Inc.
O'Donnell, Joseph A. *glmy.* '48 (OWN) Knottsville, KY St. William Church.
O'Donnell, Joseph F. *c.s.c.* '60 (PHX) [G] Phoenix, AZ Holy Cross Congregation/Casa Santa Cruz.
O'Donnell, Joseph M. *c.m.* '43 (BRK) [V] Jamaica, NY Vincentian Residence.
O'Donnell, Luke N. *o.s.b.* '41 (SEA) [L] Lacey, WA St. Martin's Abbey.
O'Donnell, Mark D. '85 (NOR) Montville, CT St. John Church.
O'Donnell, Matthew '95 (STO) Lodi, CA St. Anne Church.
O'Donnell, Patrick *glmy.* '49 (CIN) [M] Cincinnati, OH Headquarters of Glenmary Home Missioners.
O'Donnell, Paul *m.c.c.j.* '93 (LA) [12] Los Angeles, CA Holy Cross Church.
O'Donnell, Msgr. Peter C. '58 (NY) [84] New York, NY Our Lady of Esperanza Church.
O'Donnell, Philip '58 (LAV) [11] Las Vegas, NV St. Joan of Arc Church.
O'Donnell, Ralph B. '97 (OM) [30] Omaha, NE Mary Our Queen Church.
O'Donnell, Raymond G. '72 (SD) [5] El Cajon, CA St. Luke Church.
O'Donnell, Richard A. (PRT) Retired.
O'Donnell, Richard J. '35 (CHI) [145] Chicago, IL Our Lady of Good Counsel Church; Retired.
O'Donnell, Robert *c.s.p.* (CHI) [V] Chicago, IL Ministry in Higher Education.
O'Donnell, Robert A. *c.s.p.* '51 (NY) [104] New York, NY St. Paul the Apostle Church; [DD] Jamaica Estates, NY Paulist Fathers Generalate.
O'Donnell, Robert J. *c.s.p.* '74 (CHI) [122] Chicago, IL Old St. Mary Church.
O'Donnell, Robert Patrick '49 (TYL) Retired.
O'Donnell, Simon *o.s.b.* '68 (LA) [Q] Valyermo, CA St. Andrew's Abbey.
O'Donnell, Terrence *s.d.b.* '70 (NY) [DD] New Rochelle, NY Salesian Provincial House.
O'Donnell, Thomas (RVC) Retired.
O'Donnell, Thomas '60 (PIT) [2] Munhall, PA St. Maximilian Kolbe Church.
O'Donnell, Thomas D. *s.m.* '44 (ATL) [C] Atlanta, GA Marist School.
O'Donnell, Thomas M. '61 (HEL) East Helena, MT SS. Cyril and Methodius Church.
O'Donnell, Thomas P. '56 (RVC) Long Beach, NY St. Ignatius Martyr Church.
O'Donnell, Thomas V. '67 (CLV) [28] Cleveland, OH Holy Name Church.
O'Donnell, Timothy R. '86 (MAN) Portsmouth, NH Immaculate Conception Church; Retired.
O'Donnell, Walter *s.t.* '55 (SAV) Blakely, GA Holy Family Church.
O'Donnell, William *o.m.i.* '70 (BO) Tewksbury, MA St.

William Church; [W] Tewksbury, MA Oblate World/Missionary Association of Mary Immaculate.
O'Donnell, William *c.pp.s.* '77 (CIN) [23] Dayton, OH Precious Blood Church.
O'Donnell, William A. *c.pp.s.* '77 (CIN) [M] Dayton, OH Provincial Office of the Cincinnati Province of the Society of the Precious Blood.
O'Donnell, Msgr. William F. '62 (WDC) [42] Washington, DC St. Thomas Apostle Church; Special Ministries; [V] Washington, DC The Catholic Cemeteries of the Archdiocese of Washington, Inc.
O'Donnell, William J. '52 (ALN) Retired; [J] Bethlehem, PA Holy Family Villa.
O'Donnell, William J. '52 (PH) Warminster, PA Nativity of Our Lord Church.
O'Donnell, William J. '56 (OAK) [3] Berkeley, CA St. Joseph The Worker Church.
O'Donnell, William J. '58 (NY) Montrose, NY Franklin D. Roosevelt Hospital; On Duty Outside the Archdiocese.
O'Donnell, William J. '66 (NO) Lacombe, LA Sacred Heart Church.
O'Donoghue, Brendon W. '50 (WOR) Retired.
O'Donoghue, Msgr. James P. '43 (SD) Retired.
O'Donoghue, John '64 (SAT) [2] San Antonio, TX Blessed Sacrament Church; [A] San Antonio, TX Diaconate Program.
O'Donoghue, Kevin J. '58 (BRK) [28] Brooklyn, NY St. Cecilia Church.
O'Donoghue, Neil X. '00 (NEW) Maywood, NJ Our Lady Queen of Peace Church.
O'Donoghue, Patrick '61 (BIR) Trussville, AL Holy Infant of Prague Church.
O'Donoghue, Patrick F. *m.m.* '50 (FgM) Maryknoll Foreign Missions.
O'Donohoe, James A. '47 (BO) Senior Priests; [X] Lexington, MA Grey Nuns Provincial Offices.
O'Donohue, John M. '00 (ARL) Annandale, VA Holy Spirit Church.
O'Donovan, Aidan *m.s.c.* '80 (DAL) Irving, TX Holy Family of Nazareth Church.
O'Donovan, Dennis '69 (P) [24] Portland, OR Church of St. Michael, the Archangel; [Q] Portland, OR Oregon Catholic Conference.
O'Donovan, Donal '50 (WH) Retired.
O'Donovan, John '55 (SP) [1] Largo, FL St. Catherine of Siena Church.
O'Donovan, Leo J. *s.j.* '66 (WDC) [C] Washington, DC Georgetown University; [M] Washington, DC The Jesuit Community at Georgetown University.
O'Donovan, Martin E. '78 (CHI) [38] Chicago, IL St. Christina Church.
O'Donovan, Patrick G. '72 (PAT) New Vernon, NJ Christ the King Church.
O'Donovan, Timothy John '49 (B) Retired.
O'Donovan, Tom P. '35 (CC) [3] Beeville, TX St. James Church.
O'Dowd, Bernard J. *o.s.a.* '58 (PH) [AA] Villanova, PA St. Thomas Monastery.
O'Dowd, Brendan '49 (SAC) Retired and in Senior Ministry.
O'Dowd, Msgr. John '42 (VEN) Cape Coral, FL St. Andrew Church; Retired.
O'Driscoll, James J. (BO) [5] Somerville, MA St. Clement Church.
O'Driscoll, James J. '79 (BO) [1] Gloucester, MA St. Ann Church.
O'Driscoll, John C. '87 (PH) [A] Wynnewood, PA Theological Seminary of St. Charles Borromeo, Overbrook.
O'Dwyer, Dominick '66 (MIA) Tamarac, FL St. Malachy Church.
O'Dwyer, James '65 (STO) Retired.
O'Dwyer, Michael *s.a.c.* '61 (LUB) [7] Lubbock, TX St. Joseph's Church.
O'Dwyer, Patrick '72 (LA) Whittier, CA St. Bruno Church.
O'Dwyer, Thomas '70 (MIA) [1] Hollywood, FL Little Flower Church.
O'Farrell, Donal *s.s.c.* '53 (OM) [K] St. Columbans, NE St. Columban's Foreign Mission Society.
O'Flaherty, Edward M. *s.j.* '65 (BO) [W] Chestnut Hill, MA The Jesuit Community at Boston College.
O'Flaherty, John '61 (STA) Flagler Beach, FL Santa Maria Del Mar Church; Korona, FL St. Mary's Church.
O'Flaherty, Michael '75 (PMB) [4] Boca Raton, FL St. John the Evangelist Church.
O'Flaherty, Thomas '48 (PT) [6] Pensacola, FL St. Anne's Church.
O'Flanagan, Thomas '95 (PMB) On Duty Outside the Diocese.
O'Flannigan, Thomas L. '55 (TUC) Retired.
O'Flynn, John '61 (PBL) Florence, CO Federal Correctional Institute at Florence.
O'Flynn, Seamus '59 (STA) [3] St. Augustine, FL St. Anastasia Church.
O'Friel, Msgr. John '45 (FRS) Retired.
O'Friel, LaSalle *o.f.m.* '54 (PAT) [M] Butler, NJ St. Anthony Friary.
O'Friel, Zachary *o.f.m.* '47 (PAT) [M] Ringwood, NJ Holy Name Friary, Inc.
O'Gara, James *c.s.p.* '61 (CHI) [122] Chicago, IL Old St. Mary Church.
O'Gara, Stephen R. '71 (STP) [34] Minneapolis, MN St. Thomas the Apostle Church.
O'Gorman, Msgr. Charles F. '49 (LA) [2] Oxnard, CA Santa Clara Church.
O'Gorman, Eamon T. '67 (ORG) Laguna Beach, CA St. Catherine of Siena Church.
O'Gorman, Msgr. Michael B. '64 (SAT) [38] San Antonio, TX St. Gregory's Church.
O'Gorman, Richard '57 (NY) Bangall, NY Immaculate Conception Church.
O'Gorman, Thomas H. *s.j.* '63 (FgM) Provinces.
O'Grady, Columkille *c.p.* (HRT) [M] West Hartford, CT Holy Family Monastery/Retreat.
O'Grady, Dennis R. '61 (CLV) [50] Cleveland, OH St. Michael Church; [W] Cleveland, OH Office of Hispanic Ministry.
O'Grady, Edward F. '46 (LAN) Retired.
O'Grady, Frank (PAT) Military Chaplains.
O'Grady, James '50 (KCK) Retired.
O'Grady, James F. '53 (LA) Retired.
O'Grady, James F. '54 (LA) El Segundo, CA St. Anthony Church.
O'Grady, James F. '58 (LA) [98] Los Angeles, CA Visitation Church.
O'Grady, John F. '66 (ALB) On Duty Outside the Diocese.
O'Grady, John F. '66 (MIA) [B] Miami, FL Barry University.
O'Grady, John G. '35 (ALB) Windham, NY St. Theresa of Child Jesus Church.
O'Grady, Michael '56 (NEW) [2] Bayonne, NJ St. Andrew's Church.
O'Grady, Michael '58 (PHX) [1] Phoenix, AZ SS. Simon and Jude Church.
O'Grady, Peter '63 (NO) Jefferson, LA St. Agnes Church.
O'Grady, Robert A. '72 (HRT) Windsor Locks, CT St. Mary Church.
O'Grady, Robert M. '78 (BO) Watertown, MA Sacred Heart Church; [P] Boston, MA Archdiocesan Information Center.
O'Guinn, Jon '93 (BEL) Kinmundy, IL St. Elizabeth Ann Seton Church; Salem, IL St. Theresa of Avila Church.
O'Hagan, James P. '47 (DET) Retired.
O'Hagan, Patrick *ss.cc.* '65 (LA) Sepulveda, CA Veterans Administration Medical Center.
O'Haire, John A. '56 (SCR) Retired; [N] Dunmore, PA Villa St. Joseph.
O'Hala, Stephen '88 (MIA) On Duty Outside the Archdiocese.
O'Hala, Steven '88 (PMB) [A] Boynton Beach, FL St. Vincent de Paul Regional Seminary.
O'Hallaran, John E. *s.s.j.* '85 (NO) [57] New Orleans, LA St. Raymond Church.
O'Halloran, Edward P. '78 (NY) [7] Yonkers, NY St. Denis Church.
O'Halloran, Martin J. '47 (PH) Retired.
O'Halloran, Richard '51 (MRY) Retired.
O'Halloran, Richard '59 (MRY) [G] Salinas, CA Sisters of St. Joseph Carondolet.
O'Halloran, Thomas '75 (CHI) [109] Chicago, IL St. Juliana Church.
O'Halloran, William J. *s.j.* '58 (WOR) [N] Worcester, MA Jesuits of Holy Cross College, Inc.
O'Hanlon, James J. '57 (SY) [2] Endicott, NY St. Ambrose Church; Retired.
O'Hanlon, Michael A. '57 (GF) Retired.
O'Hanlon, Thomas '83 (LA) Downey, CA St. Raymond Church.
O'Hanlon, Msgr. William '49 (SHP) Retired.
O'Hara, Charles R. '70 (PH) [V] Downingtown, PA St. John Vianney Center.
O'Hara, Daniel J. '87 (SY) [16] Syracuse, NY St. James Church.
O'Hara, Edward '60 (SAC) Retired and in Senior Ministry.
O'Hara, Eugene (NY) Bronx, NY U.S.V.A. Medical Center.
O'Hara, Eugene *o.f.m. cap.* '61 (ROC) Trumansburg, NY St. James the Apostle Church; [I] Interlaken, NY St. Fidelis Friary.
O'Hara, Eugene P. '45 (NY) [DD] New York, NY Our Lady of Consolation Residence.
O'Hara, Eugene R. '45 (NY) Retired.
O'Hara, Francis A. '56 (BO) Senior Priests.
O'Hara, Francis W. '59 (PRO) [6] Warwick, RI St. Kevin Church.
O'Hara, Frank J. '41 (SFD) [11] Springfield, IL SS. Peter and Paul Church.
O'Hara, James T. '66 (E) [3] Erie, PA Holy Family/St. Ann/St. Casimir Church; [13] Erie, PA St. Ann Church; [15] Erie, PA St. Casimir Church.
O'Hara, John '69 (STP) [20] Minneapolis, MN St. Bridget Church.
O'Hara, John F. '71 (PRT) Bucksport, ME St. Vincent de Paul Church; Stonington, ME St. Mary Star of the Sea Church; [M] Castine, ME Maine Maritime Academy.
O'Hara, John J. '84 (NY) [230] Staten Island, NY St. Teresa Church.
O'Hara, John T. '80 (ARL) Dominican Republic, VA San Francisco de Asis, Banica Church; Dominican Republic, VA San Jose, Pedro Santana Church.
O'Hara, John T. '92 (ARL) On Duty Outside the Diocese.
O'Hara, Martin '41 (SFD) Stonington, IL Holy Trinity Church.
O'Hara, Martin F. '41 (PH) [75] Philadelphia, PA St. Jerome Church; Retired.
O'Hara, Michael *o.m.i.* (NY) Federal, NY Metropolitan Correctional Center.
O'Hara, Michael '67 (SAC) [8] Sacramento, CA Sacred Heart of Jesus Church.
O'Hara, Michael *o.m.i.* '76 (MAN) [K] Les Cayes, Haiti Paroisse Ste. Anne.
O'Hara, Michael *o.m.i.* '76 (NY) [FF] Newburgh, NY Our Lady of Hope Center.
O'Hara, Michael D. '60 (BUF) Franklinville, NY St. Philomena Church.
O'Hara, Peter J. '59 (BO) [3] Weymouth, MA Immaculate Conception Church.
O'Hara, Robert E. *m.s.f.* '65 (SAT) [M] San Antonio, TX MSF Center & Provincialate.
O'Hara, Thomas J. *c.s.c.* '78 (SCR) [C] Wilkes-Barre, PA Kings College; [C] Wilkes-Barre, PA Kings College.
O'Hare, Daniel G. *s.j.* '79 (NY) [DD] New York, NY St. Ignatius Loyola Residence.
O'Hare, Daniel J. '62 (SPR) [6] North Adams, MA St. Anthony of Padua Church.
O'Hare, Daniel M. '65 (NY) Maybrook, NY Assumption Church.
O'Hare, Dennis P. *c.s.c.* '73 (P) [B] Portland, OR University of Portland; [L] Portland, OR Holy Cross Fathers & Brothers, C.S.C. - University of Portland.
O'Hare, Donald J. '54 (WCH) Retired.
O'Hare, Francis C. '51 (BO) Andover, MA St. Robert Bellarmine Church; Senior Priests.
O'Hare, John B. '53 (PMB) Vero Beach, FL Holy Cross Church; Retired.
O'Hare, Joseph A. *s.j.* '61 (NY) [C] Bronx, NY Fordham University; [DD] New York, NY Jesuit Community at Fordham University.
O'Hare, Joseph P. '65 (STO) Modesto, CA St. Joseph Church.
O'Hare, Robert V. *s.j.* '95 (NY) [F] New York, NY Xavier High School.
O'Hearn, Michael '95 (FR) West Harwich, MA Holy Trinity Church.
O'Hearn, Paul V. '60 (BO) Senior Priests.
O'Hern, Edward P. *c.s.p.* '32 (NY) [DD] Jamaica Estates, NY Paulist Fathers Generalate.
O'Hern, Edward Philip *c.s.p.* '32 (AUS) [11] Austin, TX St. Austin Church.
O'Hern, Thomas G. *c.m.* '77 (FgM) Vincentian Foreign Missions.
O'Holohan, John T. *s.j.* '55 (CHR) Simpsonville, SC St. Mary Magdalene Church.
O'Hotto, Kenneth L. '80 (STP) Le Sueur, MN St. Anne Church.
O'Kane, James D. '65 (GI) Scottsbluff, NE St. Agnes Church.
O'Kane, Patrick J. '77 (SC) Early, IA Sacred Heart Church.
O'Keefe, Daniel Paul *o.s.b.* '93 (GBG) [H] Latrobe, PA Saint Vincent Archabbey.
O'Keefe, George L. *o.carm.* '48 (CHI) [D] Chicago, IL Mt. Carmel High School; [N] Chicago, IL Carmelite Priory of St. Cyril.
O'Keefe, J. Kevin '95 (ARL) Falls Church, VA St. James Church.
O'Keefe, John *c.s.c.* '59 (RNO) Carlin, NV Sacred Heart Church; Eureka, NV St. Brendan's Church.
O'Keefe, Msgr. John J. '72 (NY) [E] White Plains, NY Archbishop Stepinac High School.
O'Keefe, Joseph M. *s.j.* '86 (BO) [W] Chestnut Hill, MA The Jesuit Community at Boston College.
O'Keefe, Lawrence '70 (GLP) Holbrook, AZ Our Lady of Guadalupe Church; [A] Gallup, NM Diocesan Diaconate and Lay Ecclesial Ministry Formation Program.
O'Keefe, Mark *o.s.b.* '83 (IND) [A] St. Meinrad, IN St. Meinrad Seminary; [J] St. Meinrad, IN St. Meinrad Archabbey.
O'Keefe, Martin D. *s.j.* '66 (STL) [P] St. Louis, MO Jesuit Community Corporation at St. Louis University - Jesuit Hall.
O'Keefe, Maurice L. '57 (NEW) [N] Rutherford, NJ St. John Vianney Residence for Priests.
O'Keefe, Michael A. '56 (JOL) Glen Ellyn, IL St. Petronille Church.
O'Keefe, Millard '65 (CHI) Other Assignments.
O'Keefe, Millard '65 (JOL) Romeoville, IL St. Andrew the Apostle Church.
O'Keefe, Patrick T. '96 (BUF) Eggertsville, NY St. Benedict Church.
O'Keefe, Thomas E. '48 (NY) Retired; [E] White Plains, NY Archbishop Stepinac High School.
O'Keefe, Vincent T. *s.j.* '50 (NY) [DD] New York, NY

"America;" Residence and publication office of the America Press; [DD] New York, NY Murray-Weigel Hall; [HH] New York, NY John LaFarge Institute, The.
O'Keefe, William F. '60 (HRT) [3] Enfield, CT St. Bernard's Church.
O'Keeffe, Dennis J. '84 (LFT) Kokomo, IN St. Joan of Arc Church.
O'Keeffe, L. Joseph '66 (ALB) Military Chaplains.
O'Keeffe, Michael '68 (SAV) Americus, GA St. Mary Church.
O'Keeffe, Patrick '59 (SB) Retired.
O'Keeffe, Msgr. Richard W. '59 (TUC) Yuma, AZ Immaculate Conception Church; Yuma, AZ Immaculate Conception Church.
O'Keeffe, Msgr. William J. '59 (LA) [12] Long Beach, CA Our Lady of Refuge Church.
O'Keeffe, William T. *s.s.* '45 (BAL) [O] Baltimore, MD St. Charles Villa; [S] Baltimore, MD St. Charles Villa.
O'Kelly, Colm '64 (SAC) Woodland, CA Holy Rosary Church.
O'Kelly, Fritz *o.f.m.conv.* '56 (FgM) Conventual Franciscan Foreign Missions.
O'Kennedy, Philip N. '71 (BIR) [1] Huntsville, AL Good Shepherd Church.
O'Kere, Edmund (NY) Manhattan, NY Beth Israel Medical Center.
O'Kielty, James P. (PAT) Retired.
O'Kielty, James P. '54 (PAT) [P] Chester, NJ Nazareth Village.
O'Konsky, Stanley J. *s.j.* '72 (NY) [F] New York, NY Fordham Preparatory School; [DD] New York, NY Jesuit Community at Fordham University.
O'Kruta, Francis A. '94 (WH) Princeton, WV Sacred Heart Church; [P] Athens, WV Concord College Newman Center.
O'Laughlin, Patrick J. '67 (STL) Wentzville, MO St. Patrick Church.
O'Leary, Adrian P. '47 (BO) Senior Priests.
O'Leary, Arthur P. '75 (BO) Senior Priests.
O'Leary, Bartholomew J. '70 (HON) Retired.
O'Leary, Bernard C. *s.j.* '48 (WDC) La Plata, MD Sacred Heart Church.
O'Leary, Msgr. Cornelius '48 (SB) Retired.
O'Leary, Cornelius F. '56 (WOR) Otter River, MA St. Martin's Church.
O'Leary, Daniel F. *o.m.i.* '50 (BUF) [27] Buffalo, NY Holy Angels Church; [O] Niagara University, NY Vincentian Community at Niagara University.
O'Leary, David A. '45 (WCH) Retired.
O'Leary, David M. '85 (BO) [4] Medford, MA St. Raphael Church; [CC] Medford, MA Tufts University Catholic Center.
O'Leary, Donald J. '37 (HRT) Plantsville, CT St. Aloysius Church; Retired.
O'Leary, Harold V. *c.s.b.* '49 (GAL) [Q] Houston, TX Residence of the Basilian Fathers of the University of St. Thomas.
O'Leary, Hilary *o.s.b.* '68 (PAT) [M] Morristown, NJ St. Mary's Abbey.
O'Leary, J. J. *s.j.* (SD) [B] San Diego, CA University of San Diego.
O'Leary, James E. '68 (BO) [2] Arlington, MA St. Camillus Church.
O'Leary, James J. '56 (DET) Harrison Twp., MI St. Hubert Church.
O'Leary, James J. *s.j.* '65 (MIL) [P] Milwaukee, WI Jesuit Provincial Office, Wisconsin Province.
O'Leary, James M. *s.j.* '91 (CHI) [N] Chicago, IL Chicago Province of the Society of Jesus-Provincial Office.
O'Leary, James M. *s.j.* '91 (FgM) Provinces.
O'Leary, James S. '61 (KAL) Battle Creek, MI St. Joseph Church.
O'Leary, Jerome A. *o.p.* '57 (CHI) [N] River Forest, IL St. Thomas Aquinas Priory.
O'Leary, John (BIS) [G] Bismarck, ND Emmaus Place.
O'Leary, John (OAK) Berkeley, CA Alta Bates Hospital.
O'Leary, John '67 (FgM) Society of St. James the Apostle.
O'Leary, John '67 (MIA) On Duty Outside the Archdiocese.
O'Leary, John '78 (CAM) Atco, NJ Assumption Church.
O'Leary, John J. *s.j.* '60 (FgM) Provinces.
O'Leary, John J. *s.j.* '60 (SEA) Oak Harbor, WA St. Augustine Church.
O'Leary, John P. '54 (BIS) Retired.
O'Leary, Kevin J. (BO) Scituate, MA St. Mary of the Nativity Church.
O'Leary, Msgr. Lawrence '53 (LA) [79] Los Angeles, CA St. Martin of Tours Church.
O'Leary, Lawrence J. '56 (RVC) West Brentwood, NY Pilgrim Psychiatric Center.
O'Leary, Malcolm *s.v.d.* '61 (LAF) [4] Opelousas, LA Holy Ghost Church.
O'Leary, Mark *o.p.* '85 (OAK) [4] Berkeley, CA St. Mary Magdalen Church.
O'Leary, Mark G. *o.p.* '84 (SR) [G] Santa Rosa, CA Santa Rosa Memorial Hospital.
O'Leary, Michael G. '43 (DET) Grosse Pointe Farms, MI St. Paul Catholic Church; Retired.
O'Leary, Michael J. '93 (NY) Valhalla, NY Holy Name of Jesus Church.
O'Leary, Neil F. '60 (LA) Retired.
O'Leary, Niall '60 (LA) South Pasadena, CA Holy Family Church.
O'Leary, Patrick B. *s.j.* '61 (SEA) [A] Seattle, WA Seattle University.
O'Leary, Patrick C. '76 (SY) Absent on Leave.
O'Leary, Patrick D. '51 (Y) Retired.
O'Leary, Raymond J. '62 (ORL) Port Orange, FL Our Lady of Hope Church.
O'Leary, Richard *o.s.a.* '65 (PH) [C] Villanova, PA Villanova University.
O'Leary, Richard T. *o.s.a.* (PH) [AA] Villanova, PA Fray de Leon Community.
O'Leary, Robert A. '53 (NEW) Retired.
O'Leary, Sean *o.carm.* '55 (VEN) [G] Nokomis, FL Carmel at Mission Valley.
O'Leary, Sean '61 (SAC) Yreka, CA St. Joseph Church.
O'Leary, Msgr. Thomas M. '57 (NEW) Wyckoff, NJ St. Elizabeth Church.
O'Leary, Todd '58 (TUC) [26] Tucson, AZ St. Thomas the Apostle Church.
O'Leary, William F. *s.j.* '62 (OM) [C] Omaha, NE Creighton Preparatory School.
O'Leary, William R. *s.j.* '73 (PAT) [I] Morristown, NJ Loyola House of Retreats.
O'Leary, William T. *m.m.* '61 (FgM) Maryknoll Foreign Missions.
O'Lenny, Patrick J. '56 (LC) On Duty Outside the Diocese.
O'Loghlen, Martin P. *ss.cc.* '61 (LA) [Q] La Verne, CA Congregation of the Sacred Hearts of Jesus and Mary.
O'Looney, Martin J. *c.s.p.* '46 (NY) [DD] Jamaica Estates, NY Paulist Fathers Generalate.
O'Looney, Michael *c.s.sp.* (NY) Yorktown Heights, NY St. Patrick Church.
O'Loughlin, Msgr. Eugene E. '44 (BUF) [64] Buffalo, NY St. Thomas Aquinas Church; Retired.
O'Loughlin, Eugene P. '43 (WH) Retired.
O'Loughlin, Francis A. '80 (PRO) [2] Newport, RI Jesus Saviour Church; Newport, RI Newport Hospital.
O'Loughlin, Frank '65 (PMB) Boynton Beach, FL St. Thomas More Church.
O'Loughlin, Michael *s.s.c.* '60 (FgM) St. Columban's Foreign Mission.
O'Loughlin, Padhraic *s.s.c.* '57 (FgM) St. Columban's Foreign Mission.
O'Loughlin, Patrick James '99 (MIL) [33] Milwaukee, WI St. Gregory The Great Church.
O'Mahony, Finbar P. *o.s.b.* '43 (MAN) [K] Manchester, NH St. Anselm Abbey.
O'Mahony, James '70 (HON) Leave of Absence.
O'Mahony, Jerome *m.s.c.* '50 (LA) Sherman Oaks, CA St. Francis de Sales Church.
O'Mahony, Maurice '67 (LA) Montecito, CA Our Lady of Mount Carmel Church.
O'Malley, Bartholomew J. *c.m.* '40 (PH) [AA] Philadelphia, PA Congregation of the Mission.
O'Malley, Dennis O. '90 (WOR) Auburn, MA St. Joseph's Church.
O'Malley, Edward J. '60 (JOL) Manhattan, IL St. Joseph Church.
O'Malley, Francis P. '73 (NY) [193] Bronx, NY Visitation Church; On Special or Other (Arch)Diocesan Assignment.
O'Malley, James '56 (CHI) Highwood, IL St. James Church.
O'Malley, James E. '46 (SFR) Novato, CA St. Anthony of Padua Church; Retired.
O'Malley, James J. '46 (SPK) Retired.
O'Malley, John A. '55 (BWN) Retired.
O'Malley, John J. *o.p.* '59 (CHI) River Forest, IL St. Vincent Ferrer Church.
O'Malley, John J. '65 (PIT) Wilmerding, PA St. Jude the Apostle Church.
O'Malley, John L. *s.j.* '63 (FgM) Provinces.
O'Malley, John W. *s.j.* '59 (BO) [W] Cambridge, MA Weston Jesuit Community.
O'Malley, John W. *s.j.* '59 (DET) [K] Detroit, MI Jesuit Provincial Office-Detroit Province of the Society of Jesus.
O'Malley, Joseph M. '50 (DEN) Retired.
O'Malley, Joseph T. (GAL) Retired.
O'Malley, Joseph T. '54 (GAL) [N] Houston, TX St. Dominic Village.
O'Malley, Kenneth *c.p.* '64 (CHI) [B] Chicago, IL The Catholic Theological Union at Chicago; [N] Chicago, IL Passionist Community-CTU.
O'Malley, Leonard F. '74 (BO) Burlington, MA St. Malachy Church.
O'Malley, Mark Francis '95 (NEW) Caldwell, NJ St. Aloysius Church.
O'Malley, Martin *s.j.* '99 (BO) [W] Chestnut Hill, MA The Jesuit Community at Boston College.
O'Malley, Michael P. '92 (PH) Valley Forge, PA St. Teresa of Avila Church.
O'Malley, Michael W. '52 (WCH) Retired.
O'Malley, Patrick '57 (CHI) [A] Mundelein, IL University of St. Mary of the Lake-Mundelein Seminary.
O'Malley, Paul *s.s.c.* '57 (BO) [W] Quincy, MA St. Columban's Foreign Mission Society.
O'Malley, Paul *s.s.c.* '59 (OM) [K] St. Columbans, NE St. Columban's Foreign Mission Society.
O'Malley, Terrence *s.c.j.* '60 (OAK) [1] Hayward, CA All Saints Church.
O'Malley, Thomas J. '66 (SCR) Ashley, PA St. Leo's Church.
O'Malley, Thomas P. *s.j.* '61 (BO) [W] Boston, MA The Society of Jesus of New England-Provincial Offices; [W] Chestnut Hill, MA The Jesuit Community at Boston College.
O'Malley, Timothy J. '97 (CHI) [5] Chicago, IL St. Agnes of Bohemia Church.
O'Malley, Vincent J. *c.m.* '73 (BUF) [C] Niagara University, NY Niagara University; [O] Niagara University, NY Vincentian Community at Niagara University.
O'Malley, William *o.carm.* '65 (NEW) Demarest, NJ St. Joseph's Church.
O'Malley, William J. *s.j.* '51 (NY) [DD] New York, NY Jesuit Community at Fordham University.
O'Malley, William J. *s.j.* '63 (NY) [F] New York, NY Fordham Preparatory School.
O'Malley, William M. *s.j.* '62 (SPK) [C] Spokane, WA Gonzaga University.
O'Malley, William P. '74 (PIT) [O] Pittsburgh, PA St. John Vianney Manor.
O'Mara, Michael E. '88 (IND) [27] Indianapolis, IN St. Mary/Immaculate Conception Church.
O'Mara, William T. '58 (CHI) Orland Hills, IL St. Elizabeth Seton Church.
O'Meara, Gerard '76 (FgM) Society of St. James the Apostle.
O'Meara, Gerard J. '56 (BO) Society of St. James the Apostle.
O'Meara, Joseph '53 (NY) [96] New York, NY Our Lady of the Rosary Church.
O'Meara, Joseph M. '67 (BAL) [86] Baltimore, MD St. Rose of Lima Church.
O'Meara, Joseph P. '53 (NY) [155] Bronx, NY St. John Chrysostom's Church.
O'Meara, Noel P. *c.s.sp.* '65 (BRK) [V] Long Island City, NY Holy Ghost Fathers of Ireland; [Z] Long Island City, NY World Compassion Link.
O'Meara, Thomas *o.p.* '62 (FTW) [B] Notre Dame, IN University of Notre Dame Du Lac.
O'Meara, Thomas Aquinas *o.p.* '62 (CHI) [N] River Forest, IL St. Thomas Aquinas Priory.
O'Mearain, Msgr. Ciaran P. '60 (CAM) Gibbsboro, NJ St. Andrew the Apostle Church.
O'Melia, Edward A. '77 (DAV) West Branch, IA St. Bernadette Church; West Liberty, IA St. Joseph's Church.
O'Neal, James E. '80 (STA) Interlachen, FL St. John's Church.
O'Neal, Norman B. *s.j.* '59 (NO) [F] New Orleans, LA Jesuit High School.
O'Neal, Patrick K. '90 (PEO) [3] Ottawa, IL St. Mary's Church.
O'Neal, Shawn '00 (CHL) Boone, NC St. Elizabeth Church.
O'Neil, Blane *o.f.m.* '51 (SAT) [46] San Antonio, TX St. Joseph Church.
O'Neil, Msgr. Dennis '66 (LA) Lynwood, CA St. Emydius Church.
O'Neil, Edward '63 (NY) Mamaroneck, NY St. Vito Church.
O'Neil, Flann *o.f.m.* '52 (GLP) Ganado, AZ All Saints Church.
O'Neil, James '85 (GF) Malta, MT St. Mary's Church; [K] Malta, MT St. Mary's Catholic Education Trust.
O'Neil, James W. *s.j.* '57 (BO) [E] Boston, MA Boston College High School & Jesuit Community.
O'Neil, Joseph M. *m.s.* '93 (HRT) [5] Hartford, CT Our Lady of Sorrows Church; [M] Hartford, CT Missionaries of LaSalette, Provincial Secretary.
O'Neil, Kevin *c.ss.r.* '81 (WDC) [M] Washington, DC Holy Redeemer College.
O'Neil, Lee '56 (MOB) Gulf Shores, AL Our Lady of the Gulf Church.
O'Neil, Lee E. '56 (TLS) Retired.
O'Neil, Leo J. (WOR) [21] Worcester, MA St. Charles Borromeo Church.
O'Neil, Leo J. '56 (WOR) Boylston, MA Worcester County Sanitarium.
O'Neil, Michael '59 (SEA) Retired.
O'Neil, Msgr. Philip E. '54 (RCK) Marengo, IL Sacred Heart Church.
O'Neil, Robert J. *m.h.m.* '65 (NY) [70] New York, NY St. Mary Church.
O'Neil, Thomas D. '69 (PIT) Washington, PA St. Hilary Church.
O'Neil, W. Laurence *s.j.* '61 (BGP) [B] Fairfield, CT Fairfield University; [P] Fairfield, CT The Fairfield Jesuit Community-Fairfield University.
O'Neill, Brian E. '68 (CAM) [4] Cherry Hill, NJ St. Pius X Church.
O'Neill, Charles E. *s.j.* '57 (NO) [C] New Orleans, LA Loyola University New Orleans.

O'Neill, Charles F. '46 (DET) [6] Dearborn Heights, MI Our Lady of Grace Church; Retired.
O'Neill, Daniel *o.carm.* '69 (CHI) [N] Chicago, IL St. Joseph's Priory.
O'Neill, Daniel *o.carm.* '69 (JOL) [J] Darien, IL Carmelite Provincial Office.
O'Neill, Daniel J. '76 (ALT) [21] Johnstown, PA St. Gregory's Church; [22] Johnstown, PA St. Barnabas Church.
O'Neill, Dennis B. '73 (CHI) [25] Chicago, IL St. Benedict Church.
O'Neill, Desmond '59 (ROC) Leicester, NY St. Thomas Aquinas Church.
O'Neill, Edward M. '71 (MET) Colonia, NJ St. John Vianney Church.
O'Neill, Francis J. *s.j.* '50 (BO) [E] Boston, MA Boston College High School & Jesuit Community.
O'Neill, George F. '97 (BGP) [4] Bridgeport, CT St. Ann Church.
O'Neill, Hugh '77 (GLP) Gallup, NM Gallup Area Hospitals & Nursing Homes.
O'Neill, Msgr. James '54 (CHY) Casper, WY Saint Patrick's Church; Retired.
O'Neill, James '57 (ALB) Stillwater, NY St. Peter the Apostle Church.
O'Neill, James R. '40 (NEW) Ramsey, NJ St. Paul Church; Retired.
O'Neill, James W. *m.m.* '55 (FgM) Maryknoll Foreign Missions.
O'Neill, James W. *o.s.f.s.* '67 (CHL) [4] Greensboro, NC St. Paul the Apostle Church.
O'Neill, Jeremiah '59 (LA) Alhambra, CA St. Thomas More Church; Retired.
O'Neill, Msgr. Jeremiah P. '57 (NY) [101] New York, NY Our Saviour Church.
O'Neill, John '00 (BRK) [165] Queens, NY Corpus Christi Church.
O'Neill, John *o.s.f.s.* '59 (TOL) [C] Toledo, OH St. Francis de Sales High School.
O'Neill, John B. Charles '99 (KNX) [3] Chattanooga, TN St. Jude Church.
O'Neill, John D. *s.j.* '60 (DET) [K] Detroit, MI Jesuit Community at the University of Detroit.
O'Neill, John J. *m.s.* '62 (HRT) [M] Hartford, CT Missionaries of LaSalette, Provincial Secretary.
O'Neill, John J. *m.s.* '62 (NOR) Danielson, CT St. James Church.
O'Neill, John M. *o.s.f.s.* '73 (ARL) Vienna, VA Our Lady of Good Counsel Church.
O'Neill, John P. '00 (NEW) [B] Lodi, NJ Felician College.
O'Neill, John P. *o.s.f.s.* '59 (TOL) [K] Toledo, OH Oblates of St. Francis de Sales.
O'Neill, Joseph J. *m.m.* '49 (NY) [DD] Maryknoll, NY Maryknoll Fathers and Brothers.
O'Neill, Joseph J. *m.m.* '49 (SJ) [L] Los Altos, CA Maryknoll.
O'Neill, Joseph P. *s.j.* '54 (BO) [E] Boston, MA Boston College High School & Jesuit Community.
O'Neill, Msgr. Kevin P. '77 (SCR) East Stroudsburg, PA St. John Church.
O'Neill, Kevin S. '77 (HEL) [1] Helena, MT Cathedral of St. Helena.
O'Neill, Msgr. Kevin T. '61 (BUF) East Aurora, NY Immaculate Conception Church.
O'Neill, Michael F. '76 (NO) Military Chaplains.
O'Neill, Msgr. Patrick '45 (SD) La Mesa, CA St. Martin of Tours Church.
O'Neill, Patrick '53 (SEA) Retired.
O'Neill, Patrick H. '67 (MIA) Special Assignment.
O'Neill, Msgr. Patrick J. '45 (SD) Retired.
O'Neill, Msgr. Patrick J. '47 (SAC) Retired and in Senior Ministry.
O'Neill, Patrick J. '83 (WIL) Absent on Sick Leave.
O'Neill, Patrick J. '90 (CHI) Alsip, IL St. Terrence Church.
O'Neill, Raymond '66 (SP) Gulfport, FL Most Holy Name of Jesus Church.
O'Neill, Richard V. '54 (SY) [12] Utica, NY St. Mary Church; Marcy, NY Central New York Psychiatric Center.
O'Neill, Robert F. '62 (ROC) North Chili, NY St. Christopher Church.
O'Neill, Rory '55 (DOD) Retired.
O'Neill, Thomas '62 (FRS) Shafter, CA St. Therese Church.
O'Neill, Thomas D. '68 (PRO) On Duty Outside the Diocese.
O'Neill, Thomas H. *s.j.* '90 (NY) [DD] New York, NY Xavier Jesuit Community.
O'Neill, Thomas M. '78 (LC) [B] La Crosse, WI Viterbo University.
O'Neill, Thomas P. *o.s.f.s.* '57 (TOL) [C] Toledo, OH St. Francis de Sales High School; [K] Toledo, OH Oblates of St. Francis de Sales.
O'Neill, Timothy H. '67 (Y) Hubbard, OH St. Patrick's Church.
O'Neill, Virgil *o.s.b.* '46 (SCL) [I] Collegeville, MN St. John's Abbey, of the Order of St. Benedict.
O'Neill, William *c.pp.s.* '52 (CIN) [M] Dayton, OH Provincial Office of the Cincinnati Province of the Society of the Precious Blood.
O'Neill, William *c.pp.s.* '52 (STP) [C] St. Paul, MN University of St. Thomas.
O'Neill, William J. '65 (PRO) Jamestown, RI St. Mark Church.
O'Neill, William O. '67 (SAV) [1] Savannah, GA Cathedral of St. John the Baptist.
O'Neill, William P. '61 (CLV) Hinckley, OH Our Lady of Grace Church.
O'Neill, William R. *s.j.* '81 (OAK) [20] Oakland, CA St. Patrick's Church; [A] Berkeley, CA The Jesuit School of Theology at Berkeley; [N] Berkeley, CA Jesuit Community at Jesuit School of Theology at Berkeley.
O'Rafferty, Patrick '51 (SAC) Retired and in Senior Ministry.
O'Regan, Denis '61 (STA) [2] Jacksonville, FL Blessed Trinity Church.
O'Regan, Hugh H. '57 (BO) [26] Boston, MA Holy Trinity Church; [27] Boston, MA St. James the Greater Church.
O'Reilly, Aidan '60 (SAC) Mount Shasta, CA St. Anthony Church.
O'Reilly, Msgr. Alvin J. '51 (NO) [5] New Orleans, LA St. Mary Church; New Orleans, LA Shrine of St. Lazarus of Jerusalem Church; Retired.
O'Reilly, Andrew *c.pp.s.* '73 (ORL) Haines City, FL St. Ann Church.
O'Reilly, Msgr. Bernard '45 (LA) Paramount, CA Our Lady of the Rosary Church; Retired.
O'Reilly, Bernard M. '69 (PRO) [3] Burrillville, RI St. Patrick Church.
O'Reilly, Edward M. '68 (NY) Military Chaplains.
O'Reilly, Francis J. '45 (PHX) Retired.
O'Reilly, Gabriel '67 (MIA) Davie, FL St. David Church.
O'Reilly, Gerald K. '85 (CHI) [113] Chicago, IL St. Laurence Church.
O'Reilly, James E. *s.j.* '57 (DET) [23] Detroit, MI St. Francis de Sales Church.
O'Reilly, James P. *m.s.* '37 (HRT) [M] Hartford, CT Missionaries of LaSalette, Provincial Secretary.
O'Reilly, Joseph '49 (SFD) Retired.
O'Reilly, Joseph F. '56 (WH) White Sulphur Springs, WV St. Charles Borromeo Church.
O'Reilly, Joseph P. '39 (SFR) [50] San Francisco, CA St. Stephen Church; Retired.
O'Reilly, Kevin '84 (WDC) Great Mills, MD Holy Face Church.
O'Reilly, Michael (SAC) McCloud, CA St. Joseph Church.
O'Reilly, Michael '96 (SAC) Weed, CA Holy Family Church.
O'Reilly, Michael P. '61 (WH) Parkersburg, WV St. Francis Xavier's Church.
O'Reilly, P. J. '53 (ORL) Retired.
O'Reilly, Patrick J. '44 (GF) Retired.
O'Reilly, Patrick J. '65 (OG) [E] Lake Placid, NY Uihlein Mercy Center.
O'Reilly, Msgr. Peter A. '61 (LA) Westlake Village, CA St. Maximilian Kolbe Church.
O'Reilly, Vincent '62 (SAC) Vacaville, CA St. Joseph Church.
O'Reily, Ed '68 (BEA) Beaumont, TX Federal Correctional Complex-Penitentiary.
O'Riley, Aidan '60 (SAC) Dunsmuir, CA St. John the Evangelist Church.
O'Riley, Dennis H. '59 (PEO) Tolono, IL St. Patrick's Church.
O'Riley, James K. '67 (IND) Retired.
O'Riley, Robert F. *o.p.* '58 (CHI) [N] River Forest, IL St. Thomas Aquinas Priory.
O'Riordan, James '64 (JKS) Vicksburg, MS St. Michael Church.
O'Riordan, Jeremiah (PAT) Retired.
O'Riordan, Jeremiah C. '67 (PAT) Rockaway, NJ Sacred Heart Church; Dover, NJ Dover General Hospital.
O'Riordan, William '85 (NO) [3] Harvey, LA St. Martha Church.
O'Rorke, Msgr. James H. '61 (PAT) [5] Wayne, NJ Our Lady of the Valley Church.
O'Rourke, Bryan A. '66 (STP) Plymouth, MN St. Mary of the Lake Church.
O'Rourke, Charles L. *s.s.c.* '57 (LA) [Q] Los Angeles, CA Columban Fathers, Procure House.
O'Rourke, Charles M. '58 (PH) Milmont Park, PA Our Lady of Peace Church.
O'Rourke, Colin *o.f.m.* '61 (BO) [BB] Boston, MA St. Anthony Shrine.
O'Rourke, Daniel '88 (GF) Lewistown, MT St. Leo's Church; [K] Lewistown, MT St. Leo's Catholic Education Trust.
O'Rourke, David *o.p.* '62 (OAK) [N] Oakland, CA Dominican Order, Siena House.
O'Rourke, Dennis J. '80 (PHX) Chandler, AZ St. Benedict Church; [I] Phoenix, AZ Office of Youth and Young Adult Ministries.
O'Rourke, Edmund F. *o.s.f.s.* (FgM) Oblates of St. Francis de Sales Foreign Missions.
O'Rourke, Edmund F. *o.s.f.s.* '56 (CAM) [M] Pittsgrove, NJ Villa St. Joseph.
O'Rourke, Francis J. '75 (CHL) Clemmons, NC Holy Family Church.
O'Rourke, Gabriel A. '45 (SC) Retired.
O'Rourke, Hugh *s.s.c.* '52 (PRO) [P] Bristol, RI St. Columban's Retirement House.
O'Rourke, James J. '58 (BO) [18] Boston, MA St. Columbkille Church.
O'Rourke, John *s.s.j.* '66 (GAL) [64] Houston, TX Our Lady Star of the Sea Church.
O'Rourke, John F. *o.s.a.* '61 (PH) [18] Philadelphia, PA St. Augustine Church.
O'Rourke, John G., V '48 (DAL) Retired.
O'Rourke, John J. *s.s.j.* '66 (LAF) On Special Assignment.
O'Rourke, Kevin *o.p.* (CHI) River Forest, IL St. Vincent Ferrer Church.
O'Rourke, Matthew J. *s.s.j.* '47 (BAL) [S] Baltimore, MD St. Joseph's Manor.
O'Rourke, Michael *o.p.* '96 (NO) [P] New Orleans, LA Dominican Friars, Southern Dominican Province of St. Martin de Porres.
O'Rourke, Michael K. '69 (GB) [4] Appleton, WI St. Mary Church.
O'Rourke, P. Gerard '50 (SFR) [21] San Francisco, CA St. Gabriel Church; Special Assignment.
O'Rourke, Paul J. *s.s.c.* '61 (PRO) [P] Bristol, RI St. Columban's Retirement House.
O'Rourke, Peter J. '99 (SCR) [16] Wilkes-Barre, PA St. Nicholas Church.
O'Rourke, Richard *m.s.c.* '65 (AUS) Harker Heights, TX St. Paul Chong Hasang Church; [H] Blanco, TX Missionaries of the Sacred Heart, M.S.C.
O'Rourke, Robert *s.s.c.* '58 (OM) [K] St. Columbans, NE St. Columban's Foreign Mission Society.
O'Rourke, Terence *o.s.a.* '64 (NY) [195] Staten Island, NY St. Ann Church.
O'Rourke, Thomas J. '64 (HRT) [1] Hamden, CT Ascension Church.
O'Rourke, William '58 (RVC) West Babylon, NY Our Lady of Grace Church.
O'Rourke, William J. '56 (NOR) Quinebaug, CT St. Stephen Church.
O'Ryan, Colm '55 (LA) Beverly Hills, CA Good Shepherd Church.
O'Shaughnessy, Donald *s.j.* '55 (CIN) [M] Cincinnati, OH Faber Jesuit Community.
O'Shaughnessy, James J. '68 (NY) [E] New York, NY Cardinal Spellman High School.
O'Shaughnessy, Michael A. '50 (VIC) Edna, TX St. Agnes Church.
O'Shaughnessy, Patrick '68 (BLX) [9] Biloxi, MS St. Michael Church.
O'Shaughnessy, Richard *s.m.* (STL) [P] St. Louis, MO Provincialate of the Society of Mary, Province of St. Louis.
O'Shaughnessy, Thomas J. *s.j.* '44 (FgM) Provinces.
O'Shea, Daniel *s.a.* '64 (NY) [DD] Garrison, NY Franciscan Friars of the Atonement, Minister General Office; [DD] Garrison, NY Franciscan Friars of the Atonement, Minister General Office.
O'Shea, David T. '61 (PT) Panama City Beach, FL St. Bernadette Church.
O'Shea, Howard '58 (NY) [DD] New York, NY Franciscan Friars, Order of Friars Minor, Holy Name Province.
O'Shea, James *c.p.* '89 (BRK) [76] Brooklyn, NY St. Lucy-St. Patrick Church; [104] Brooklyn, NY Our Lady of Monserrate-St. Ambrose Church.
O'Shea, James (Jim) *c.p.* '89 (MET) [H] South River, NJ Passionist Provincial Office.
O'Shea, James B. '65 (WOR) [12] Worcester, MA Our Lady of Lourdes Church.
O'Shea, James D. '64 (SFD) Bethany, IL St. Isidore Church; Mt. Zion, IL Our Lady of the Holy Spirit Church.
O'Shea, James R. '56 (WCH) Halstead, KS Sacred Heart of Jesus Church.
O'Shea, Jeremiah T. '64 (PIT) Mt. Lebanon, PA St. Winifred Church.
O'Shea, John G. '60 (YAK) Kennewick, WA Holy Spirit Church.
O'Shea, John L. '81 (PIT) Meadowlands, PA Our Lady of the Miraculous Medal Church.
O'Shea, John T. '54 (BUF) Retired.
O'Shea, Msgr. Joseph H. '47 (PMB) [2] Boca Raton, FL Our Lady of Lourdes Church; Retired.
O'Shea, Joseph J. '42 (NY) [145] Bronx, NY St. Helena Church; Retired.
O'Shea, Joseph P. '61 (SEA) Woodland, WA St. Philip Church.
O'Shea, Lawrence '56 (DUL) [17] Duluth, MN St. Raphael's Church.
O'Shea, Michael '52 (LA) Retired.
O'Shea, Michael *o.f.m.cap.* '54 (OAK) [N] Berkeley, CA Capuchin Franciscan Order, House of Studies.
O'Shea, Michael '72 (NY) State, NY Bedford Hills Correctional Facility.
O'Shea, Patrick '61 (LA) On Duty Outside the Archdiocese.
O'Shea, Patrick '61 (MIA) [1] Hollywood, FL Little Flower Church.
O'Shea, Patrick *m.s.c.* '73 (SAT) [28] San Antonio, TX St. Anthony of Padua Church.

O'Shea, Msgr. Patrick J. '58 (SFR) Absent on Leave.
O'Shea, Philip *o.f.m.* '75 (BO) [W] Boston, MA Ministry of the Word.
O'Shea, Philip A. '54 (WDC) Retired.
O'Shea, Robert J. '63 (BEL) Retired.
O'Shea, Vincent M. *o.s.m.* '38 (CHI) [N] Chicago, IL Order of Friar Servants of Mary (Servites) United States of America Province, Inc.
O'Shea, William D. '62 (PMB) North Palm Beach, FL St. Clare Church.
O'Shea, William J. '63 (JOL) [5] Naperville, IL St. Margaret Mary Church.
O'Sullivan, Andrew C. *o.s.b.* '43 (PAT) [M] Newton, NJ St. Paul's Abbey.
O'Sullivan, Barry (BO) [5] Newton, MA Mary Immaculate of Lourdes Church.
O'Sullivan, Brendan '54 (SB) Retired.
O'Sullivan, Brendan *s.s.c.* '70 (FgM) St. Columban's Foreign Mission Society (S.S.C.).
O'Sullivan, Carrol '51 (LA) Montecito, CA Our Lady of Mount Carmel Church.
O'Sullivan, Cyril '80 (SFR) [2] San Rafael, CA St. Isabella Church.
O'Sullivan, Daniel '60 (DET) Detroit, MI Detroit Psychiatric Institute; Retired.
O'Sullivan, Daniel '63 (LA) Ventura, CA Sacred Heart Church.
O'Sullivan, Daniel J. '62 (CHI) Park Forest, IL St. Irenaeus Church.
O'Sullivan, Denis A. '72 (SR) [3] Santa Rosa, CA St. Rose of Lima Church.
O'Sullivan, Eugene M. '60 (BO) Senior Priests.
O'Sullivan, Msgr. Francis G. '47 (BO) [3] Peabody, MA St. John the Baptist Church; Senior Priests.
O'Sullivan, James J. '60 (JC) Eldon, MO Sacred Heart Church.
O'Sullivan, Msgr. Jeremiah '58 (SD) Coronado, CA Sacred Heart Church; Retired.
O'Sullivan, John '50 (B) Retired.
O'Sullivan, John C. '45 (PBL) Retired.
O'Sullivan, John V. '68 (PT) [2] Tallahassee, FL Blessed Sacrament Church.
O'Sullivan, Leo *o.s.a.* '49 (SAC) [3] Sacramento, CA Holy Spirit Church.
O'Sullivan, Martin '53 (BRK) Retired.
O'Sullivan, Michael '48 (MRY) Retired.
O'Sullivan, Michael '55 (SAT) On Leave.
O'Sullivan, Michael J. '55 (WDC) [37] Washington, DC St. Peter Church.
O'Sullivan, Msgr. Peter '34 (LA) Granada Hills, CA St. John Baptist de la Salle Church; Retired.
O'Sullivan, Peter '83 (KCK) On Sabbatical.
O'Sullivan, Raymond '68 (FgM) Society of St. James the Apostle.
O'Sullivan, Raymond S. '68 (BO) Society of St. James the Apostle.
O'Sullivan, Robert '43 (BIR) Retired.
O'Sullivan, Sarsfield '51 (HEL) Retired.
O'Sullivan, Sean *i.c.* '47 (SP) Indian Rocks Beach, FL St. Jerome Church.
O'Sullivan, Sean '64 (MIA) Coral Gables, FL Little Flower Church; Retired.
O'Sullivan, Sean A. *s.j.* '99 (CHI) [C] Chicago, IL Jesuit Community at Loyola University of Chicago.
O'Sullivan, T. Brendan '56 (SAC) [10] Sacramento, CA St. Anthony Church.
O'Sullivan, Thomas C. '51 (LA) Retired.
O'Sullivan, Thomas P. '71 (SR) Point Arena, CA St. Aloysius Church.
O'Sullivan, Timothy *o.f.m.cap.* '36 (LA) Solvang, CA Old Mission Santa Ines Church.
O'Sullivan, Timothy F. '94 (PH) [40] Philadelphia, PA St. Dominic Church.
O'Sullivan, Timothy J. '52 (WDC) [2] Rockville, MD Shrine of St. Jude Church; [V] Rockville, MD Irish Apostolate USA, Inc.
O'Sullivan, Timothy J. '71 (SR) Napa, CA St. John the Baptist Church.
O'Sullivan, Tracy *o.carm.* '62 (LA) [89] Los Angeles, CA St. Raphael Church.
O'Toole, Msgr. Anthony J. '44 (ALT) Retired.
O'Toole, Brian P. '86 (WOR) Sutton, MA St. Mark Church.
O'Toole, Coleman P. '61 (PRT) [5] Portland, ME St. Patrick's Church.
O'Toole, Msgr. Fursey '60 (BRK) [115] Brooklyn, NY St. Patrick Church.
O'Toole, Henry *c.ss.r.* '44 (ORL) [F] New Smyrna Beach, FL St. Alphonsus Villa-Redemptorist Fathers and Brothers.
O'Toole, James '64 (FWT) Bedford, TX St. Michael Church.
O'Toole, John (PH) [136] Philadelphia, PA St. Peter the Apostle Church.
O'Toole, John J. '52 (PEO) Retired.
O'Toole, John M. '67 (PIT) [27] Pittsburgh, PA St. Mary of Mercy Church; [R] Pittsburgh, PA Office for Campus Ministry.
O'Toole, Msgr. Joseph M. '39 (ALT) Retired.
O'Toole, Kenneth E. '44 (NY) Chappaqua, NY St. John and St. Mary Church; Retired.
O'Toole, Lawrence J. *s.j.* '58 (BO) [W] Weston, MA Campion Jesuit Community.
O'Toole, Lawrence J. *s.j.* '88 (BO) [W] Boston, MA The Society of Jesus of New England-Provincial Offices.
O'Toole, Matthew L. '95 (STL) [58] St. Louis, MO St. Raphael The Archangel Church.
O'Toole, Robert F. *s.j.* '67 (FgM) Provinces.
O'Toole, Thomas '69 (OKL) Woodward, OK St. Peter's Church.
O'Toole, Thomas F. *c.ss.r.* '51 (ALB) [L] Saratoga Springs, NY St. John Neumann Residence.
O'Toole, Timothy '89 (PMB) [1] Palm Beach, FL Cathedral of St. Ignatius Loyola.
O'Toole, Timothy L. '89 (B) On Duty Outside the Diocese.
O'Toole, William F. '96 (GRY) Munster, IN St. Thomas More Church.
O'Toole, Msgr. William P. '61 (LA) Alhambra, CA All Souls Church.
Oakes, Alan *c.s.p.* '98 (AUS) [11] Austin, TX St. Austin Church.
Oakes, Edward T. *s.j.* '79 (DEN) [M] Denver, CO Regis Jesuit Community (The Jesuits at Regis University).
Oakham, Ronald *o.carm.* '77 (GAL) [59] Houston, TX Our Lady of Mt. Carmel Church.
Oakshott, Ward '77 (SEA) [23] Seattle, WA Christ the King Church.
Oates, Eugene *c.ss.r.* '44 (KC) [31] Kansas City, MO Our Lady of Perpetual Help Church; [J] Kansas City, MO Redemptorists of Kansas City.
Oates, Thomas '63 (FgM) Society of St. James the Apostle.
Oates, Thomas F. '63 (BO) Society of St. James the Apostle.
Obama, Joseph Marie '86 (PIT) [47] Pittsburgh, PA Guardian Angels Church.
Obaza, Theodore L. '61 (SCR) [9] Wilkes-Barre, PA Holy Trinity Church.
Obba, Thaddeus '87 (NY) Beacon, NY St. Joachim Church.
Obee, Gregory *o.s.b.* '56 (RCK) [G] Aurora, IL Marmion Abbey-St. Augustine's Abbey.
Obele, Oliver *m.s.p.* '95 (BEA) [8] Port Arthur, TX St. Mary Church.
Obeng, Simon (STV) On Duty Outside the Diocese.
Ober, Lawrence M. *s.j.* '77 (CLV) [D] Cleveland, OH St. Ignatius High School.
Oberch, Msgr. Rick J. '85 (PEO) [O] East Peoria, IL Mt. Alverno Novitiate.
Oberg, Paul *s.s.j.* '85 (BIR) [15] Birmingham, AL Our Lady of Fatima Church.
Oberhausen, James *o.f.m.conv.* '82 (SAT) [B] San Antonio, TX San Damiano Friary, Prenovitiate House of Formation; [M] San Antonio, TX San Damiano Friary.
Oberkirch, Msgr. James W. '62 (MOB) [1] Mobile, AL Cathedral of the Immaculate Conception.
Oberle, James P. *s.s.* '87 (SFR) [A] Menlo Park, CA St. Patrick Seminary; [A] Menlo Park, CA St. Patrick Seminary.
Oberle, James P. *s.s.* '87 (WDC) On Duty Outside the Archdiocese.
Oberle, Joseph *c.ss.r.* '37 (ALB) [L] Saratoga Springs, NY St. John Neumann Residence.
Obermeyer, Robert A. '61 (CIN) [70] Cincinnati, OH Our Lord, Christ the King Church.
Obermiller, Edwin *c.s.c.* '96 (P) [B] Portland, OR University of Portland; [L] Portland, OR Holy Cross Fathers & Brothers, C.S.C. - University of Portland; [P] Portland, OR University of Portland.
Oberstar, Richard *m.s.f.* '65 (SAT) New Braunfels, TX Our Lady of Perpetual Help Church.
Obersteiner, Ernest '77 (GLP) Absent on Leave.
Obert, Martin '56 (SP) Retired.
Oberto, Msgr. Peter '78 (MAR) Ishpeming, MI St. John the Evangelist Church.
Oberts, David P. '69 (SUP) Birchwood, WI St. John Evangelist Church; Dobie, WI Our Lady of Lourdes Church; Haugen, WI Holy Trinity Church.
Oberwinder, Robert J. '35 (LC) Retired.
Obi, Celestine (ROC) [M] Rochester, NY Diocesan Department of Campus Ministry.
Obi, Celestine '66 (ROC) [57] Rochester, NY St. Theodore Church; Rochester, NY Unity Health System; Rochester, NY Park Ridge Hospital/Unity Health System.
Obi, Evaristus (PIT) Washington, PA Immaculate Conception Church.
Obi, Obioma Desmond '84 (SAN) Winters, TX Our Lady of Mt. Carmel Church.
Obiajunwa, Chukwudi '82 (PAT) Sparta, NJ Our Lady of the Lake Church.
Obiechina, Jude M. '83 (LAF) Lawtell, LA Holy Family Church; Mallet, LA St. Ann Church.
Obijiski, Herbert *o.f.m.conv.* '65 (HRT) Kensington, CT St. Paul's Church.
Obin, Arthur *o.m.i.* '64 (BO) [W] Lowell, MA Missionary Oblates of Mary Immaculate; [W] Lowell, MA Missionary Oblates of Mary Immaculate.
Obin, Arthur *o.m.i.* '64 (FgM) Oblates Foreign Missions.
Obin, Arthur T. *o.m.i.* '64 (WDC) [M] Washington, DC Missionary Oblates of Mary Immaculate.
Obin, Gilbert *c.i.c.m.* '67 (SAT) [54] San Antonio, TX St. Martin de Porres Church.
Obinabu, Patrick '86 (MIA) [20] Miami, FL St. James Church.
Obioha, Livinus '84 (BAK) Arlington, OR St. Francis Church; Condon, OR St. John's Church.
Obiorah, Edwin S. '85 (ROC) [40] Rochester, NY Our Mother of Sorrows Church.
Oblinger, Joseph B. '46 (HEL) West Yellowstone, MT Our Lady of the Pines Church; Retired.
Obloj, Stanley '93 (DET) [4] St. Clair Shores, MI St. Joan of Arc Church.
Obloy, Leonard G. '77 (CLV) Gates Mills, OH St. Francis of Assisi Church.
Oborny, Paul J. '63 (WCH) Lindsborg, KS St. Bridget of Sweden Church; McPherson, KS St. Joseph Church.
Oborny, Rudolf F. '71 (LIN) Wahoo, NE St. Wenceslaus Church.
Obregon, Miguel *o.f.m.* '81 (SJ) [18] San Jose, CA Our Lady of Guadalupe Church; San Jose, CA Santa Clara County Jail.
Obrimski, Paul G. '70 (BAL) On Duty Outside the Archdiocese.
Obrimski, Paul G. '70 (PH) [89] Philadelphia, PA St. Lucy Church.
Ocampo, Ramon Conde *o.de.m.* '59 (PCE) [9] Ponce, PR La Merced Church.
Occhiuto, Joseph L. '79 (MRY) [1] Monterey, CA Cathedral of San Carlos Borromeo.
Ochej, Tomasz '00 (VEN) Punta Gorda, FL Sacred Heart Church.
Ochieze, Oliver '88 (LR) [3] Little Rock, AR St. Augustine Church; [9] Little Rock, AR St. Mary Church; [12] Little Rock, AR St. Patrick's Church.
Ochiltree, Richard '53 (OAK) [N] Oakland, CA Redemptorists.
Ochoa, Adrian *o.de.m.* '97 (SB) Ontario, CA Our Lady of Guadalupe Church.
Ochoa, David '72 (LA) Lynwood, CA St. Emydius Church.
Ochoa, Einer R. '85 (SAT) Sabinal, TX St. Patrick's Church.
Ochoa, Jose Luis *m.g.* '66 (LA) Santa Fe Springs, CA St. Pius X Church.
Ochoa, Rafael '78 (LA) [16] Los Angeles, CA Immaculate Conception Church.
Ochoa, Stephen *o.s.a.* '83 (SD) [H] San Diego, CA Augustinian Community.
Ochoa, Steven M. *o.s.a.* '65 (SD) [B] San Diego, CA Austin House.
Ochoa, Xavier '69 (SR) Sonoma, CA St. Francis Solano Church.
Ochs, Daniel L. '76 (COL) Reynoldsburg, OH St. Pius X Church.
Ochs, Robert J. *s.j.* '61 (CHI) [N] Chicago, IL Chicago Province of the Society of Jesus-Provincial Office.
Ochs, Robert J. *s.j.* '61 (OAK) [N] Berkeley, CA Jesuit Community at Jesuit School of Theology at Berkeley.
Ochu, Austin Charles *s.m.a.* '92 (WDC) [M] Takoma Park, MD Society of African Missions (S.M.A.).
Ochylski, Ronald S. '87 (SFR) On Duty Outside the Archdiocese.
Ocilka, John A. '94 (CLV) Parma Heights, OH St. John Bosco Church.
Odbert, Jerome K. *s.j.* '69 (DET) [27] Detroit, MI Gesu Church; [K] Detroit, MI Jesuit Provincial Office-Detroit Province of the Society of Jesus.
Odenbrett, Stephen *o.s.b.* '46 (MRY) [F] San Luis Obispo, CA Monastery of the Risen Christ.
Odermann, John *o.s.b.* '55 (BIS) [A] Richardton, ND Assumption Abbey.
Odermann, John *o.s.b.* '55 (FAR) [G] Valley City, ND Sisters of Mary of the Presentation.
Odermann, Valerian *o.s.b.* '73 (BIS) [A] Richardton, ND Assumption Abbey; [B] Bismarck, ND University of Mary.
Odeyemi, John S. '94 (NY) Suffern, NY Sacred Heart Church.
Odien, Terry M. '73 (CAM) Westmont, NJ Holy Saviour Church.
Odilo, Augustine C. *c.s.sp.* '91 (MIA) [3] Pompano Beach, FL San Isidro Church.
Odoemela, Richard U. '92 (NEW) Glen Rock, NJ St. Catharine Church; Paramus, NJ Bergen Regional Medical Center.
Odor, Emeka L. *j.c.l.* (LAN) Ann Arbor, MI Veterans' Hospital.
Odorizzi, Thomas A. *c.o.* '92 (MET) East Brunswick, NJ St. Bartholomew Church; [H] Somerset, NJ The Metuchen Oratory, Congregation of the Oratory of St. Philip Neri.
Odozi, Anthony '97 (FAR) Cavalier, ND St. Bridget's Church; Neche, ND SS. Nereus and Achilleus Church.
Odozor, Paulinus *c.s.sp.* '84 (FTW) [4] South Bend, IN St. Augustine Church.
Odufuye, Francis '79 (RVC) Elmont, NY St. Boniface Church; Valley Stream, NY Franklin Medical Center Hospital.
Oduro, Charles '89 (NY) [227] Staten Island, NY

Sacred Heart Church.
Oedy, Thomas E. '71 (TOL) Edgerton, OH St. Mary Church; Hicksville, OH St. Michael Church.
Oehmler, Gary W. '83 (PIT) [66] Pittsburgh, PA St. Wendelin Church.
Oehrlein, Felix G. '65 (MAD) Wisconsin Dells, WI St. Cecilia Church.
Oelerich, Robert M. *c.ss.r.* '49 (STL) [P] Liguori, MO St. Clement Health Care Center.
Oelrich, Anthony '92 (SCL) Holdingford, MN St. Hedwig's Church; Holdingford, MN St. Mary's Church; Opole, MN Our Lady of Mt. Carmel Church; St. Anna, MN Immaculate Conception Church; St. Wendel, MN St. Columbkille's Church.
Oen, Edward J. *c.pp.s.* '64 (SAL) Greenleaf, KS Sacred Heart Church; Hanover, KS St. John the Baptist Church.
Oesterle, John G. '67 (PIT) East McKeesport, PA St. Robert Bellarmine Church.
Oestreich, Brian W. '93 (NU) Leavenworth, MN Church of the Japanese Martyrs.
Oestreich, Emil C. '45 (PH) [97] Philadelphia, PA St. Mary of the Assumption Church; Retired.
Oetgen, John A. *o.s.b.* '51 (CHL) [J] Belmont, NC Belmont Abbey.
Offerman, Paul '57 (SFS) Bridgewater, SD St. Stephen Church.
Offor, Christopher '91 (LA) Claremont, CA Our Lady of the Assumption Church.
Offutt, Bradley S. '86 (KC) Harrisonville, MO Our Lady of Lourdes Church.
Offutt, J. James '62 (JC) Centralia, MO Holy Spirit Church.
Ofoha, Paul N. *m.s.p.* '88 (GAL) [67] Houston, TX St. Peter the Apostle Church; [Q] Barrett Station, TX Missionary Society of St. Paul, Inc. - U.S. Region.
Ofray, Antonio *s.e.m.v.* '00 (ARE) Hatillo, PR Our Lady of Guadalupe Church.
Ogbemure, Raymond '74 (OAK) El Cerrito, CA St. John the Baptist Church.
Ogboe, Parker '79 (DAV) Iowa City, IA State University of Iowa Hospital.
Ogbonna, Edmund '78 (FAR) Cando, ND Sacred Heart Church.
Ogbonna, Stanislaus *c.s.sp.* '73 (NY) Monticello, NY St. Peter Church; State, NY Sullivan Correctional Facility.
Ogbuji, Vincent '98 (LR) Texarkana, AR St. Edward's Church.
Ogden, Louis P. '85 (HBG) Middletown, PA Seven Sorrows of the Blessed Virgin Mary Church; [K] Harrisburg, PA Catholic Campus Ministry.
Oge, Raymond J. '67 (STL) Bloomsdale, MO St. Agnes Church; Lawrenceton, MO St. Lawrence Church.
Ogg, Thomas '68 (CHY) Powell, WY St. Barbara Church; [E] Powell, WY NorthWest College.
Oggero, Roy J. *c.s.b.* '61 (GAL) [Q] Sugar Land, TX Basilian Mission Center.
Ogle, Sean G. '77 (BRK) [198] Queens, NY St. Mary Star of the Sea Church.
Oglesby, J. Leonard '48 (MEM) Retired.
Ognibene, Joseph F. '52 (CHI) [152] Chicago, IL Our Lady, Mother of the Church; Rolling Meadows, IL St. Colette Church; Retired.
Ogorzaly, Adam '85 (ROC) [56] Rochester, NY St. Stanislaus Church.
Ogrodowski, Msgr. William M. '75 (PIT) Beaver, PA SS. Peter and Paul Church.
Ogu, Cletus (NY) Spring Valley, NY St. Joseph Church.
Oguie, Augustin Ohua (NY) [122] New York, NY St. Vincent de Paul Church.
Ogumere, Augustine *c.s.s.p.* (CHI) [74] Chicago, IL St. Helena Church.
Ogumoro, Isidor T. '89 (CHK) San Jose Village, District 7, MP San Jose Church.
Ogurchock, John J. *m.m.* '54 (FgM) Maryknoll Foreign Missions.
Oh, Sae Wan '83 (NEW) [6] Orange, NJ St. Andrew Kim Church.
Oha, Alphonsus (WDC) [13] Washington, DC St. Francis de Sales Church.
Ohankwere, Desmond *m.s.p.* '92 (SAV) [3] Savannah, GA St. Benedict the Moor Church.
Ohirko, Peter '58 (STF) Retired.
Ohlemacher, Richard N. *o.s.c.* '55 (PHX) [G] Phoenix, AZ Crosier Community of Phoenix (Canons Regular of the Order of the Holy Cross).
Ohlig, John '95 (LUB) Floydada, TX St. Mary Magdalen Church.
Ohlinger, Vincent *s.v.d.* '68 (FgM) Society of the Divine Word Foreign Missions.
Ohm, Edward (PEO) On Duty Outside the Diocese.
Ohmann, Daniel F. *m.m.* '55 (FgM) Maryknoll Foreign Missions.
Ohner, John *o.s.a.* (FWT) Muenster, TX Sacred Heart Church.
Ohno, Ignatius F. *s.j.* '92 (FgM) Provinces.
Ohno, Ignatius F. *s.j.* '92 (P) [L] Portland, OR Jesuit Provincial Office (Society of Jesus, Oregon Prov.); [L] Portland, OR Colombiere Community; [Q] Portland, OR Jesuit Development & Communications Office.
Ojeda, Filemon G. '46 (SFR) Retired.
Ojeda, Gonzalo (OM) [32] Omaha, NE Our Lady of Guadalupe Church.
Ojimba, Felix (BO) Boston, MA Massachusetts General Hospital.
Okafor, Bernard E. (CHI) [101] Chicago, IL St. John de la Salle Church.
Okafor, Patrick '90 (NY) [6] Mt. Vernon, NY St. Ursula Church.
Okagbue, Bartholomew '88 (BRK) [60] Brooklyn, NY Holy Spirit Church.
Okere, Edmund '89 (NY) [131] Bronx, NY St. Augustine Church.
Okere, Michael '91 (LIN) Lawrence, NE Sacred Heart Church.
Okere, Nicholas (MAD) [H] Madison, WI Bishop O'Connor Catholic Pastoral Center.
Okere, Remigius *c.s.sp.* '94 (DM) [9] Des Moines, IA St. Joseph's Church.
Okochi, Cornelius '88 (PIT) [8] Pittsburgh, PA St. Charles Lwanga Church.
Okogba, Joseph '80 (FAR) Windsor, ND St. Mathias Church.
Okogie, Pachomius *o.s.b.* '96 (PIT) Forest Hills, PA St. Maurice Church.
Okolie, Maxwell '88 (RNO) [B] Reno, NV St. Mary's Regional Medical Center.
Okon, Alan J., Jr. '98 (PH) Yardley, PA St. Ignatius of Antioch Church.
Okonkwo, Benedict (DAV) [J] Iowa City, IA Mercy Hospital.
Okonkwo, Benedict '84 (DAV) Lone Tree, IA St. Mary's Church; Nichols, IA St. Mary's Church.
Okonmah, Emmanuel '97 (FAR) Wales, ND St. Michael's Church.
Okonski, Joseph F. '90 (PH) [111] Philadelphia, PA Nativity of the Blessed Virgin Mary Church.
Okopinski, Louis S. '51 (MIL) Retired.
Okorie, Onyema '99 (FRS) Merced, CA Our Lady of Mercy/St. Patrick's Church.
Okorn, Dusan A. '47 (HEL) Swan Valley, MT Swan Valley Catholic Community Church; Retired; [G] Swan Lake, MT The Sycamore Tree Contemplative Prayer Center.
Okoro, Alexander '86 (LIN) Lawrence, NE Sacred Heart Church.
Okoro, Joseph E. *c.m.f.* '90 (NO) [4] New Orleans, LA Blessed Sacrament Church; New Orleans, LA Memorial Medical Center.
Okorobia, Gregory '79 (BAK) Boardman, OR Our Lady of Guadalupe Church.
Okorochukwu, Wilfred C. '75 (LR) Camden, AR St. Louis Church.
Okoth, George (ROC) [60] Rochester, NY St. Thomas More Church.
Okoth, George '59 (ROC) [M] Rochester, NY Diocesan Department of Campus Ministry.
Okoth, George N. '89 (ROC) Leicester, NY St. Thomas Aquinas Church.
Okoye, Clement (PIT) [56] Pittsburgh, PA St. Mary of the Mount Church.
Okoye, James C. *c.s.sp.* '70 (CHI) [B] Chicago, IL The Catholic Theological Union at Chicago.
Okoye, Michael (FTW) [4] Mishawaka, IN Queen of Peace Church.
Okpara, Benson C. '91 (CLV) Bedford, OH St. Pius X Church.
Okpogba, Desmond '89 (TLS) [2] Tulsa, OK St. Augustine's Church; [11] Tulsa, OK St. Monica's Church.
Okroy, Francis *s.ch.* '48 (BAL) [38] Baltimore, MD Holy Rosary Church.
Okumu, Richard U. '81 (DAV) Brooklyn, IA St. Patrick Church; Victor, IA St. Bridget's Church.
Okumu, Victor (BO) [1] Cambridge, MA St. Anthony Church.
Okuroski, Michael *o.c.d.* '44 (SAT) [18] San Antonio, TX Basilica of The National Shrine of Our Lady of Mt. Carmel and St. Therese, Discalced Carmelite Fathers; [M] San Antonio, TX Discalced Carmelites (Prov. of St. Therese).
Okwara, Hyacinth '85 (BAK) Pendleton, OR St. Mary's Church.
Ola'aiga, Vitaliano '91 (P) [A] St. Benedict, OR Mount Angel Seminary.
Olczak, Joseph M. *o.s.p.p.e.* '65 (NOR) Rockville, CT St. Joseph Church; [A] Cromwell, CT Holy Apostles College and Seminary.
Oldani, Louis J. *s.j.* '64 (KC) [B] Kansas City, MO Rockhurst University; [J] Kansas City, MO Rockhurst Jesuit Community.
Oldenski, Kenneth E. '66 (PIT) Richland Township, PA Saint Richard Church.
Oldershaw, Robert H. '62 (CHI) Evanston, IL St. Nicholas Church.
Oldfield, Albert E. '59 (SCR) [18] Scranton, PA St. Mary's Church.
Olds, Daryl *c.m.f.* '92 (AUS) San Marcos, TX St. John the Evangelist Church; [M] San Marcos, TX Catholic Student Center.
Olds, Steven '88 (ORL) On Duty Outside the Diocese.
Olds, Steven '88 (PMB) [A] Boynton Beach, FL St. Vincent de Paul Regional Seminary.
Olejniczak, Henry A. '51 (CHI) [42] Chicago, IL St. Columba Church; Retired.
Olek, Ralph F. *s.m.* '74 (ATL) [C] Atlanta, GA Marist School.
Oleksiak, Donald P. '89 (CLV) [1] Garfield Heights, OH St. Monica Church.
Oleksy, Stanislaw *s.d.s.* '82 (SAT) Bandera, TX St. Stanislaus Church.
Olendzki, Joaquim J. '58 (NY) Pine Island, NY St. Stanislaus Church.
Olenowski, Mark '85 (PAT) [5] Passaic, NJ Holy Trinity Church.
Olesik, William J. '72 (NOR) Bolton, CT St. Maurice Church.
Olges, H. Anthony '70 (L) [1] Louisville, KY Cathedral of the Assumption.
Olguin, Jacinto '74 (VIC) Bloomington, TX St. Patrick Church.
Olguin, Luis '92 (SY) [9] Utica, NY St. John Church; [13] Utica, NY St. Mary of Mt. Carmel Church; Rome, NY Walsh Facility; Special Assignment.
Oligschlaeger, P. Gregory '93 (JC) [A] Hannibal, MO St. Thomas Aquinas Seminary.
Olivares, Jesus *c.s.* '97 (LA) [A] Camarillo, CA St. John's Seminary College of the Archdiocese of Los Angeles.
Olivares, Romeo D. *c.i.c.m.* '74 (SAT) Lytle, TX St. Andrew Church.
Olivas, William *o.s.a.* '97 (LA) [R] Ventura, CA Sisters of the Holy Cross.
Olivas, William V. *o.s.a.* '97 (LA) Ojai, CA St. Thomas Aquinas Church.
Olive, Alphonsus *c.ss.r.* (BAL) Annapolis, MD St. Mary Church.
Olive, Rodney J. *c.ss.r.* '86 (FgM) Redemptorist Foreign Missions.
Oliveira, Albano '55 (OAK) [S] Oakland, CA The Roman Catholic Cemeteries of the Diocese of Oakland.
Oliveira, Aventino *i.m.c.* '57 (MET) [H] Somerset, NJ Consolata Society for Foreign Missions.
Oliveira, Gastao A. '72 (FR) [24] Fall River, MA Santo Christo Church.
Oliveira, Humbert M. '77 (MAN) [1] Manchester, NH St. Joseph Church.
Oliveira, Msgr. John J. *p.a.* '67 (FR) [21] New Bedford, MA St. Mary's Church.
Oliveira, John J. '77 (FR) [16] New Bedford, MA St. John the Baptist Church.
Oliveira, Robert A. '77 (FR) Norton, MA St. Mary's Church.
Oliveira, Vitor '73 (SPR) [2] Ludlow, MA Our Lady of Fatima Church.
Oliveira e.Costa, Virgilio *s.j.* '95 (BO) [W] Chestnut Hill, MA The Jesuit Community at Boston College.
Olivencia, Ramon '97 (ARE) Vega-Alta, PR Immaculate Conception of Blessed Virgin Mary Church.
Oliver, Harry T. *s.j.* '57 (PHX) [B] Phoenix, AZ Brophy College Preparatory.
Oliver, Homer G. '43 (Y) Louisville, OH St. Louis Church; Retired.
Oliver, James M. '88 (PH) [A] Wynnewood, PA Theological Seminary of St. Charles Borromeo, Overbrook.
Oliver, Msgr. John A. '52 (TUC) Retired.
Oliver, John H. *s.s.* '47 (BAL) [O] Baltimore, MD St. Charles Villa; [S] Baltimore, MD St. Charles Villa.
Oliver, Mark (NY) [GG] New York, NY University Apostolate.
Oliver, William A. '77 (GAL) Baytown, TX St. John the Evangelist Church.
Oliveras, Evaristo *c.m.* (SJN) Santurce, PR Hospital Pavia-Santurce.
Oliveras, Evaristo *c.m.* '88 (SJN) [60] San Juan, PR San Vicente de Paul Church.
Oliveras, Jose *o.carm.* '95 (ARE) Morovis, PR Nuestra Senora del Carmen Church.
Oliveras Villanueva, Felix '82 (CGS) [3] Caguas, PR Sagrado Corazon de Jesus Church.
Olivere, Michael S. '94 (PH) [42] Philadelphia, PA St. Edmond Church; [D] Philadelphia, PA St. John Neumann High School.
Oliveri, Armand *s.d.b.* '50 (SFR) [13] San Francisco, CA Corpus Christi Church.
Oliveri, Richard H. '66 (PAT) Dover, NJ St. Mary's Church.
Oliverio, Msgr. Francis E. '56 (NY) Tuckahoe, NY Immaculate Conception Church; Tuckahoe, NY Assumption Church.
Oliverira, Pedro de *o.f.m. conv.* '00 (BRK) [61] Brooklyn, NY Most Holy Trinity Church.
Olivero, Michael A. '74 (CHI) [3] Des Plaines, IL St. Stephen Protomartyr Church.
Oliveros, Renato T. *s.j.* '96 (PH) [AA] Philadelphia, PA Jesuit Community, Arrupe House.
Olivier, David S. *s.j.* '62 (P) [D] Portland, OR Jesuit High School.
Olivier, John H. *s.s.* '47 (MAR) Retired.
Olivier, Robert '57 (JKS) [D] Jackson, MS St. Dominic-Jackson Memorial Hospital.
Oliviera, Joel D. '54 (BO) Senior Priests.
Olivo, Leobardo Heredia *o.f.m.* '90 (AMA) Hereford, TX

San Jose Church.
Olivo, Stephen G. *s.j.* '69 (SJ) [L] Los Gatos, CA Sacred Heart Jesuit Center.
Olkovikas, Msgr. Albert W. '53 (MAN) [L] Manchester, NH Monastery of the Precious Blood.
Ollivier, John J. '50 (TOL) Retired.
Olmer, Vernon J. *o.f.m.* '62 (SUP) Ashland, WI Our Lady of the Lake Catholic Community Church.
Olmo, Luis S. *o.f.m.* '85 (SJN) [3] Carolina, PR Santa Clara de Asis Church.
Olmstead, Daryl '75 (SAL) Goodland, KS Our Lady of Perpetual Help Church.
Olnhausen, James R. '70 (PT) [15] Pensacola, FL St. Thomas More Church.
Olnhausen, James Robert '70 (AUS) On Leave.
Olona, Richard '70 (SFE) [3] Albuquerque, NM Community of the Risen Savior Church.
Olookaran, Joy '60 (NEW) Plainfield, NJ Muhlenberg Medical Center.
Olowin, Msgr. Jan C. '68 (E) Bradford, PA St. Bernard Church.
Ols, James R. '75 (CLV) Elyria Township, OH St. Vincent de Paul Church.
Olsaukas, Msgr. Algirdas '52 (LA) [55] Los Angeles, CA St. Casimir Church.
Olsavsky, John R. '62 (CLV) Chagrin Falls, OH St. Joan of Arc Church.
Olsem, Andrew D. '67 (WIN) Windom, MN St. Francis Xavier's Church.
Olsen, Arthur J. '99 (CHI) Niles, IL St. John Brebeuf Church.
Olsen, Charles R. *s.j.* '68 (SAC) [C] Sacramento, CA Jesuit High School; [H] Carmichael, CA Jesuit High School Community of Sacramento.
Olsen, Ken '73 (P) [J] Eugene, OR Sacred Heart Medical Center.
Olson, David (LC) [C] Wausau, WI Wausau Area Catholic Schools.
Olson, Eric E. '84 (MAR) Hubbell, MI St. Cecilia Church; Lake Linden, MI St. Joseph Church.
Olson, Hans '83 (SEA) [5] Vancouver, WA St. Joseph Church.
Olson, James '91 (PH) [D] Philadelphia, PA St. Maria Goretti High School.
Olson, James P. '88 (PH) [142] Philadelphia, PA St. Richard Church.
Olson, Michael '93 (FWT) On Duty Outside the Diocese.
Olson, Michael P. '94 (GR) [1] Muskegon, MI Our Lady of Grace Church.
Olson, Richard F. *s.j.* '59 (BO) [W] Weston, MA Campion Health Center, Inc.
Olson, Robert *o.m.i.* '66 (BEL) [F] Belleville, IL Shrine of Our Lady of the Snows.
Olson, Ronald *o.f.m.conv.* '75 (SUP) [2] Superior, WI Holy Assumption of the B.V.M. Church; [9] Superior, WI St. William Church.
Olson, Theodore '72 (ORG) Brea, CA St. Angela Merici Church.
Olson, Theodore E. *j.v.* '79 (WIL) Elsmere, DE Corpus Christi Church.
Olson, Thomas F. '53 (NEW) Retired.
Olson, Thomas F. '73 (SCL) Brennyville, MN St. Elizabeth Church; Morrill, MN St. Joseph's Church.
Olsovsky, George J. '56 (GAL) Huffman, TX St. Philip the Apostle Church.
Olszamowski, Leon M. *s.m.* '76 (DET) [D] Pontiac, MI Notre Dame Preparatory High School and Marist Academy.
Olszewski, Bernard *o.f.m.conv.* '79 (BUF) [C] Hamburg, NY Hilbert College; [O] Athol Springs, NY St. Francis of Assisi Friary; [R] Alfred, NY Campus Ministry.
Olszewski, Clarence A. '57 (HBG) York Haven, PA Holy Infant Church.
Olszewski, Daniel D. '51 (SCR) Retired.
Olszewski, Edward '66 (MIA) Key Largo, FL St. Justin Martyr Church.
Olszewski, John S. '47 (NEW) Retired.
Olszewski, John S., (Retired) '47 (NEW) Rahway, NJ St. Mark's Church.
Olszewski, Laurence M. *c.s.c.* '64 (BUR) Bennington, VT Sacred Heart St. Francis de Sales Church.
Olszewski, Paul A. '93 (CAM) Mantua, NJ Incarnation Church.
Olszewski, Ronald W. *o.s.f.s.* '74 (TOL) [C] Toledo, OH St. Francis de Sales High School; [K] Toledo, OH Oblates of St. Francis de Sales; [K] Toledo, OH Oblates of St. Francis de Sales.
Olszyk, Thomas P. '71 (MIL) Military Chaplains.
Oluoha, Godwin '82 (DAL) [12] Dallas, TX St. Anthony Church; Plano, TX St. Mark the Evangelist Church.
Olvida, Victor A. '82 (SEA) Raymond, WA St. Lawrence Church; Seaview, WA St. Mary Church.
Olzacki, Tadeusz *o.s.p.p.e.* '93 (PH) [AA] Doylestown, PA Pauline Fathers Monastery, Shrine of Our Lady of Czestochowa.
Oman, Frank *i.c.* (SP) Spring Hill, FL St. Theresa Church.
Ombao, Manuel '70 (AGN) Inarajan, GU St. Joseph Church.
Omernick, Kenneth E. '74 (MIL) [33] Milwaukee, WI St. Gregory The Great Church.
Onaindia, Bernardo *c.p.* '46 (MGZ) San Sebastian, PR San Sebastian Martir Church.
Onate-Melendez, Jose Refugio '00 (ATL) [4] Atlanta, GA Immaculate Heart of Mary Church.
Onderko, John M. '62 (PEO) [3] La Salle, IL Resurrection Church.
Ondic, John '65 (ALN) [J] Bethlehem, PA Holy Family Villa.
Ondic, John L. '65 (ALN) Retired.
Ondo, Michael A. '54 (LFT) Carmel, IN Our Lady of Mount Carmel Church.
Ondrako, Edward J. *o.f.m.conv.* '72 (ROC) [M] Rochester, NY Diocesan Department of Campus Ministry.
Ondreyka, Richard J. *m.s.* '54 (CLV) [2] Lakewood, OH SS. Cyril and Methodius Church; Retired.
Ong, Walter J. *s.j.* '46 (STL) [O] St. Louis, MO Fusz Pavilion.
Ongaro, Mario *m.c.c.j.* '51 (CIN) [M] Cincinnati, OH Comboni Missionaries (Verona Fathers)-Comboni Mission Center.
Onida, George *s.m.* '86 (PCE) Villalba, PR Our Lady Mother of Divine Providence Church.
Oniskiewicz, Mieczyslaw '92 (SAG) Kinde, MI St. Mary-St. Edward Church.
Oniskiewicz, Mieczyslaw T. (MAR) On Duty Outside the Diocese.
Onofrey, Robert *c.pp.s.* (CHI) [92] Chicago, IL Immaculate Heart of Mary Church.
Onofrey, Robert *c.pp.s.* '63 (CIN) [M] Dayton, OH Provincial Office of the Cincinnati Province of the Society of the Precious Blood.
Ontiveros, Roy *o.carm.* '78 (JOL) [I] Darien, IL Carmelite Carefree Retirement Village; [J] Darien, IL Carmelite Community.
Onubogu, Charles '88 (SFR) [34] San Francisco, CA Mission Dolores Basilica Church.
Onufer, Paul P. '59 (CAM) [5] Vineland, NJ St. Mary's Church.
Onuh, William I. '79 (ROC) Sonyea, NY Groveland Correctional Facility; Sonyea, NY Livingston Correctional Facility and Seneca Correctional Facility.
Onunwa, Paschal U. '74 (PH) Wayne, PA St. Isaac Jogues Church.
Onuoha, Anselm E. '83 (BRK) [21] Brooklyn, NY Blessed Sacrament Church.
Onuoha, Joseph '80 (WDC) [B] Washington, DC St. Joseph's Seminary.
Onuora, Felix *c.s.sp.* '79 (DM) [1] Des Moines, IA St. Ambrose Church; [D] Des Moines, IA Mercy Medical Center.
Onushco, William J. '76 (ALN) Unassigned.
Onyango, Charles *s.j.* '99 (BO) [W] Chestnut Hill, MA The Jesuit Community at Boston College.
Onyeabor, Ukachukwu Sebastian '90 (OM) [1] Omaha, NE St. Cecilia's Church.
Onyebuchi, Martin (NY) [183] Bronx, NY St. Philip Neri Church.
Onyeihe, Cyprian I. '82 (NY) [132] Bronx, NY St. Barnabas Church.
Onyekuru, Michael '00 (ATL) Decatur, GA Sts. Peter and Paul Church.
Onyekwere, Michael (STV) On Duty Outside the Diocese.
Onyenobi, Chris '83 (LA) [J] Torrance, CA Little Company of Mary Hospital.
Onyia, Basil '96 (BWN) [2] Harlingen, TX Immaculate Heart of Mary Church.
Onze, Robert E. '64 (BGP) Retired.
Oosdyke, Raymond *o.f.m.conv.* '37 (GR) [4] Grand Rapids, MI St. Anthony of Padua Church.
Opalewski, Walter '85 (GLP) [4] Gallup, NM St. John Vianney Church.
Opara, Ben M. '85 (ARL) Falls Church, VA St. Anthony's Church.
Opara, Isaac '88 (LAF) [6] Lafayette, LA Our Lady of Wisdom, University of Louisiana Church.
Opat, Kenneth *o.s.c.* '69 (STP) Anoka, MN St. Stephen Church; [N] Anoka, MN Crosier Community of Anoka.
Opeil, Cyril *s.j.* '94 (BO) [W] Chestnut Hill, MA The Jesuit Community at Boston College.
Opem, Anthony '68 (SFS) Dakota Dunes, SD Mother Teresa Catholic Community Church.
Ophals, Donald J. '61 (ALB) [3] Troy, NY St. Francis de Sales Church.
Opira, Simon Peter '93 (STV) [3] Estate Tutu, VI Holy Family Church; [B] St. Thomas, VI Miscellaneous Organizations.
Opoka, Lloyd E. '68 (KC) Blue Springs, MO St. Robert Bellarmine Church.
Opoku, John Paul (NY) [162] Bronx, NY St. Margaret Mary Church.
Opoku-Sarkodie, Samuel '84 (KCK) [14] Kansas City, KS St. Patrick's Church.
Opondo, Protas *s.j.* '95 (BO) [W] Chestnut Hill, MA The Jesuit Community at Boston College.
Oppenheim, Frank M. *s.j.* '55 (CIN) [P] Milford, OH Milford Spiritual Center.
Oppenheimer, Daniel '91 (SCR) [M] Elmhurst, PA Priestly Fraternity of St. Peter (F.S.S.P.), North American District Headquarters.
Oppido, Harold J. *s.j.* '55 (NEW) [C] Jersey City, NJ St. Peter's Preparatory School.
Oppitz, Joseph *c.ss.r.* '43 (BAL) [S] Annapolis, MD Saint Mary Rectory.
Opps, Francis J. '58 (ALN) Coplay, PA St. Peter Church.
Opris, Gheorghe '71 (ROM) East Chicago, IN St. Nicholas Church.
Oranczak, Ronald '78 (ALN) [J] Bethlehem, PA Holy Family Villa.
Oranczak, Ronald J. '78 (ALN) Retired.
Orandi, Nazareno '61 (NEW) Lyndhurst, NJ Our Lady of Mount Carmel Church.
Oravec, Christian R. *t.o.r.* '64 (ALT) [A] Loretto, PA St. Francis College; [F] Loretto, PA St. Francis Friary, Third Order Regular of St. Francis of Penance.
Oravetz, Robert F. '97 (PBR) Tarentum, PA Sts. Peter and Paul Church.
Orbanek, Msgr. Gerald L. '66 (E) [B] Erie, PA Gannon University; [M] Erie, PA Villa Maria.
Orchik, Michael J. '73 (BAL) [55] Baltimore, MD Little Flower, Shrine of Church.
Ordax, Msgr. Emiliano '48 (MIA) [4] Hialeah, FL St. Cecilia Church.
Ordenes, Guillermo *o.f.m.* '85 (ELP) [B] El Paso, TX Roger Bacon College.
Ordonez, Francisco (GAL) [12] Houston, TX St. Augustine Church.
Orel, Paul '84 (PHX) [6] Mesa, AZ St. Timothy Church; Special Assignment.
Orellana, Samuel '68 (LA) Gardena, CA St. Anthony of Padua Church.
Orengo, Juan Rodriguez '79 (PCE) [2] Ponce, PR Christ the King Church.
Oreshoski, Gary '88 (RC) Sturgis, SD St. Francis of Assisi Church.
Orf, Msgr. Raymond V. '55 (SPC) Lebanon, MO St. Francis De Sales Church.
Organ, Patrick C. '71 (VEN) North Port, FL San Pedro Church.
Ori, Kevin '84 (GB) [F] Oshkosh, WI Mercy Medical Center.
Oria, Enrique *o.carm.* '58 (ARE) Morovis, PR Nuestra Senora del Carmen Church.
Oria, Enrique *o.carm.* '58 (SJN) [59] San Juan, PR Santa Teresita Del Nino Jesus Church; [A] Bayamon, PR Bayamon Central University.
Orians, David '85 (RC) [2] Rapid City, SD Blessed Sacrament Church.
Orians, Thomas *s.a.* '92 (FgM) Franciscan Friars Of The Atonement(S.A.).
Orians, Thomas *s.a.* '92 (NY) [DD] Garrison, NY Franciscan Friars of the Atonement.
Orimaco, Domingo '72 (SFR) Half Moon Bay, CA Our Lady of the Pillar Church.
Oriole, Phillip M. '70 (E) [11] Erie, PA Sacred Heart Church.
Orique, David *o.p.* (OAK) [N] Oakland, CA Dominican Order (Western Province), St. Albert's Priory.
Oris, Fabian G. '42 (GBG) Retired.
Orlafsky, Janis (NEW) [K] Kearny, NJ New Jersey Boystown.
Orlandi, Joseph J. '73 (PAT) [11] Paterson, NJ St. Michael the Archangel Church.
Orlando, Gerard A. *c.p.* '46 (MET) [H] South River, NJ Passionist Provincial Office.
Orlando, Gerard A. *c.p.* '46 (NY) [Z] Bronx, NY St. Patrick's Home for the Aged and Infirm.
Orlando, John V. '51 (ALT) Retired.
Orlando, Richard J. '47 (ROC) [60] Rochester, NY St. Thomas More Church; Retired.
Orlando, Samuel '91 (CHL) Absent On Leave.
Orlando, Vincent A. *s.j.* '74 (SP) [C] Tampa, FL Jesuit High School.
Orlett, Raymond *glmy.* '53 (CIN) [M] Cincinnati, OH Headquarters of Glenmary Home Missioners.
Orlik, Dale A. '67 (SAG) [2] Bay City, MI St. Boniface Church.
Orlikiewicz, Stanley '53 (JOL) [1] Joliet, IL The Cathedral of St. Raymond.
Orlinski, Richard '73 (GRY) [5] Hammond, IN St. John Bosco Church.
Orloski, Joseph F. '94 (SCR) [2] Nanticoke, PA Holy Trinity Church.
Orloski, Raymond J. '62 (HBG) Kulpmont, PA Holy Angels Church.
Orlosky, Anselm *o.s.b.* '53 (PBR) Wall, PA Holy Trinity Church; [C] Butler, PA Holy Trinity Monastery.
Orlowski, Robert J. '97 (BUF) [32] Buffalo, NY Holy Spirit Church.
Orlowski, Walter C. '79 (BGP) [5] Norwalk, CT St. Matthew Church.
Orlowsky, Michael T. '93 (ARL) [3] Arlington, VA St. Ann Church.
Ormaza, Antonio Liberman *s.c.s.* '95 (DAL) [29] Dallas, TX Santa Clara Church.
Ormechea, John Baptist *c.p.* '65 (L) [2] Louisville, KY St. Agnes Church; [L] Louisville, KY Sacred Heart Retreat.
Ormond, Henry *o.carm.* (OAK) [B] Oakland, CA Holy

Names College.
Ormond, Henry *o.carm.* '77 (JOL) [J] Darien, IL Carmelite Provincial Office.
Orndorff, Christopher '97 (TUC) [21] Tucson, AZ Saint Odilia Church.
Ornowski, Gerald *m.i.c.* '62 (FBK) [3] Fairbanks, AK St. Mark University Church.
Ornowski, Gerald *m.i.c.* '62 (SPR) [J] Stockbridge, MA Congregation of Marians of The Immaculate Conception of the BVM.
Orobiourritia, Juan J. *o.a.r.* '43 (LA) [9] Los Angeles, CA Cristo Rey Church.
Orosco, James '81 (DAL) [A] Irving, TX Holy Trinity Seminary.
Orozco, Argemiro '92 (YAK) Toppenish, WA St. Aloysius Church.
Orozco, Benjamin *o.f.m.* '64 (LAR) Hebbronville, TX Our Lady of Guadalupe Church.
Orozco, Edicson '99 (BGP) [11] Stamford, CT St. Mary Church.
Orozco, Ramon '96 (FRS) Goshen, CA St. Thomas the Apostle Church; Visalia, CA Holy Family Church.
Orozco, Raphael '50 (CHI) Palatine, IL Mission Juan Diego Church.
Orozco, Raphael R. '50 (CHI) Retired.
Orozco, Rodolfo '48 (FRS) Retired.
Orr, Garrett D. *s.j.* '83 (WDC) [E] North Bethesda, MD Georgetown Preparatory School.
Orr, James R. '79 (PIT) New Brighton, PA Holy Family Church.
Orr, Joseph T. '82 (ALT) Tyrone, PA St. Matthew's Church.
Orr, Sherman '91 (WCH) [6] Wichita, KS Church of the Resurrection.
Orr, Msgr. Stephen '74 (DM) [J] Des Moines, IA Roman Catholic Pastoral Center Foundation.
Orr, Msgr. Stephen '90 (DM) On Special Assignment.
Orrico, Msgr. Caesar G. '43 (NEW) Emerson, NJ Church of the Assumption; Retired.
Orrigo, Mario J. '96 (BO) [10] Lowell, MA St. Michael Church.
Orru, Bruno *s.x.* '63 (FgM) Xaverian Foreign Missions.
Orru, Bruno *s.x.* '63 (PAT) [M] Wayne, NJ Xaverian Missionary Fathers.
Orsini, James '74 (HON) Kaunakakai, HI Molokai Catholic Community Church.
Orsini, Joseph E. '64 (CAM) Retired.
Orsino, Gordon *o.m.i.* '84 (MIA) [19] Miami, FL St. Francis Xavier Church.
Orsino, Jerry *o.m.i.* '66 (WDC) [M] Washington, DC Oblate College/Center for Mission Studies Community.
Orsino, Jerry *o.m.i.* '66 (WOR) [1] Fitchburg, MA St. Anthony of Padua Church.
Orso, Claire Antonio *c.s.* '91 (CHI) Melrose Park, IL St. Charles Borromeo Church.
Orsolin, Vilmar *c.s.* '80 (MIA) [3] Hollywood, FL Our Lady Aparecida Church.
Orsolits, Norbert F. '65 (BUF) [41] Buffalo, NY St. Lawrence Church; Buffalo, NY Buffalo General Hospital; Buffalo, NY Hospice of Buffalo.
Orsulak, Thomas J. '90 (ALN) [11] Reading, PA St. Peter Church; [C] Reading, PA Holy Name High School.
Orsy, Ladislas *s.j.* '51 (NY) [DD] New York, NY Jesuit Community at Fordham University.
Orsy, Ladislas *s.j.* '51 (WDC) [M] Washington, DC The Jesuit Community at Georgetown University.
Orszulak, Henry A. '67 (BUF) [5] Lackawanna, NY St. Hyacinth Church.
Ortega, Carlos '99 (SR) Saint Helena, CA St. Helena Church.
Ortega, Eduardo '77 (SFE) Absent on Leave.
Ortega, Eduardo '95 (BWN) Graduate Studies.
Ortega, Efren '72 (DAL) [18] Dallas, TX St. James Church.
Ortega, Jose *m.sp.s.* '66 (P) Hillsboro, OR St. Matthew Church.
Ortega, Jose Luis '88 (DAL) [A] Irving, TX Holy Trinity Seminary.
Ortega, Ovidio '83 (SJN) Resident Chaplains; [F] Puerta De Tierra, PR Asylum For The Aged and Infirm.
Ortega, Rodrigo (NY) [65] New York, NY St. Jude Church.
Ortega, Russell *o.s.a.* '86 (NY) [168] Bronx, NY St. Nicholas of Tolentine Church.
Ortega, Santos '96 (SB) Murrieta, CA St. Martha Church.
Ortega y Ortiz, Adam Lee '76 (SFE) [7] Santa Fe, NM Santa Maria de la Paz Catholic Community Church.
Orteneau, Eugene F. *s.j.* '82 (BO) [W] Boston, MA The Society of Jesus of New England-Provincial Offices.
Ortez, Sofonias '96 (VEN) Clewiston, FL St. Margaret Church.
Orth, Anthony F. '75 (PH) [3] Bensalem, PA Saint Ephrem Church.
Orthel, Joseph A. '89 (SPC) Special Assignment.
Orthmann, James *o.c.s.o.* '94 (ARL) [J] Berryville, VA Cistercian Abbey of Our Lady of the Holy Cross.
Ortiz, Alexander F. *c.ss.r.* '76 (PH) [25] Philadelphia, PA St. Boniface Church.
Ortiz, Angel '87 (MGZ) Cabo Rojo, PR St. Michael Church.
Ortiz, Arnold *o.s.j.* '72 (SAC) [17] Sacramento, CA St. Mary Church.
Ortiz, Benedicto '57 (BWN) Retired.
Ortiz, Emerito '96 (WOR) [24] Worcester, MA St. Joan of Arc Church.
Ortiz, Francisco *o.carm.* '70 (MGZ) Anasco, PR St. Anthony Abbot Church.
Ortiz, Gary P. '98 (SFE) Ribera, NM San Miguel Del Vado Church; Villanueva, NM Our Lady of Guadalupe Church.
Ortiz, Msgr. Hector '33 (MGZ) Moca, PR Our Lady of Monserrate Church.
Ortiz, J.C. '91 (PHX) Sedona, AZ St. John Vianney Church.
Ortiz, Jose A. '66 (LA) Baldwin Park, CA St. John the Baptist Church.
Ortiz, Jose Angel '00 (CC) [4] Corpus Christi, TX Holy Family Church.
Ortiz, Jose Antonio '85 (CGS) Cayey, PR San Esteban Protomartir Church.
Ortiz, Jose L. (CGS) Barranquitas, PR San Andres Apostol Church.
Ortiz, Juan J. (ARE) [2] Camuy, PR Our Lady of the Miraculous Medal Church.
Ortiz, Leo W. '00 (SFE) Rio Rancho, NM St. Thomas Aquinas Church.
Ortiz, Marco A. '00 (LA) [2] Oxnard, CA Santa Clara Church.
Ortiz, Marianito '82 (TR) Red Bank, NJ St. James Church.
Ortiz, Maximo J. *o.s.a.* '74 (WDC) Washington, DC St. Elizabeth's Hospital (Government Operated); [B] Silver Spring, MD Austin Friars Hall, Order of St. Augustine.
Ortiz, Miguel Angel *o.f.m.cap.* '86 (SFR) [N] Burlingame, CA Capuchin Provincial House.
Ortiz, Mike '56 (SD) [6] San Diego, CA Holy Family Church.
Ortiz, Pedro '82 (CGS) [4] Caguas, PR Nuestra Senora de la Providencia Church.
Ortiz, R. Alfredo (ORL) De Land, FL St. Peter's Church.
Ortiz, Rodolfo (NY) [EE] Sparkill, NY Dominican Convent of Our Lady of the Rosary.
Ortiz, Rodrigo *o.f.m.* '73 (OAK) [N] Oakland, CA Franciscan Friars Provincial Office, Province of St. Barbara.
Ortiz, Salvador '70 (OKL) [19] Oklahoma City, OK Sacred Heart Church.
Ortiz, Msgr. Tomas Maisonet '45 (SJN) Retired.
Ortman, Doc '82 (DET) Plymouth, MI Our Lady of Good Counsel Church.
Ortmann, William (SD) [26] San Diego, CA St. Didacus Church.
Ortmann, William '57 (SD) Retired.
Ortmeier, Paul '72 (OM) Howells, NE SS. Peter and Paul Church; Howells, NE St. John Nepomucene Church.
Ortmeier, Richard J. '56 (SFS) Retired.
Ortner, Paul A. *s.s.j.* '45 (BAL) [S] Baltimore, MD St. Joseph Society of the Sacred Heart House of Central Administration.
Ortner, Paul A. *s.s.j.* '45 (VEN) [D] Port Charlotte, FL Bon Secours-St. Joseph Hospital.
Orumpakkatt, James *c.m.i.* '64 (STA) [1] St. Augustine, FL Cathedral of St. Augustine.
Orzech, Eric S. '93 (CLV) [4] Parma, OH St. Columbkille Church.
Orzechowski, Walter B. '49 (MIL) Retired.
Orzel, David J. '79 (SY) Boonville, NY St. Joseph Church.
Osbahr, Theodore W. '67 (NEW) [4] Irvington, NJ St. Paul the Apostle Church.
Osborn, Bruce J. '81 (SD) [28] San Diego, CA St. Jerome Church.
Osborn, Douglas '68 (LAN) [7] Flint, MI St. John Vianney Church.
Osborn, Michael A. '92 (KAL) Gull Lake, MI St. Ann Church.
Osborn, William '66 (SFS) Tabor, SD St. Wenceslaus Church.
Osborne, Msgr. Francis M. '38 (LA) Encino, CA Our Lady of Grace Church; Retired.
Osborne, Kenan B. *o.f.m.* '55 (OAK) [A] Berkeley, CA Franciscan School of Theology; [S] Berkeley, CA Multicultural Institute.
Osborne, Martin J. '50 (RVC) Southold, NY St. Patrick's Church; Retired.
Osborne, Paul *o.f.m.* '64 (BUF) [59] Buffalo, NY SS. Rita & Patrick Church.
Osborne, Robert *s.m.* (STL) [P] St. Louis, MO Provincialate of the Society of Mary, Province of St. Louis.
Osborne, Robert E. '54 (L) Retired.
Osborne, Ronald J. '83 (HRT) [1] West Haven, CT Our Lady of Victory Church.
Osborne, Stanley L. '59 (L) Cecilia, KY St. Ambrose Church; St. John, KY St. John the Baptist Church.
Osborne, Thomas *o.s.a.* '66 (JOL) [5] Lockport, IL Our Mother of Good Counsel Church.
Osburg, Frank C. '60 (LEX) Versailles, KY St. Leo Church.
Osburg, Gregory E. '77 (COV) Kenton, KY St. Matthew Church.
Osebold, Richard A. '60 (DET) [2] Redford, MI St. John Bosco Church.
Osendorf, James *c.m.* '80 (STO) Patterson, CA Sacred Heart Church.
Oser, Donald '53 (Y) Retired.
Oser, Donald J. '53 (Y) North Canton, OH St. Paul's Church.
Oser, Ronald '92 (ORL) De Land, FL St. Peter's Church.
Osiander, Alfons M. '73 (BUF) Sardinia, NY St. Jude Church.
Osias, Max '94 (NEW) [9] Elizabeth, NJ Our Lady of Most Holy Rosary/St. Michael Church.
Osinski, Ronald V. '72 (ALT) [5] Portage, PA Our Lady of the Sacred Heart Church.
Osorio, Celimo '87 (ELP) [34] El Paso, TX Sts. Peter and Paul Church; San Elizario, TX San Felipe de Jesus Church.
Osorio, Jose Benito *o.de.m.* '35 (SJN) [40] San Juan, PR Nuestra Senora de la Merced Church.
Osorio, Luis '00 (CHL) Monroe, NC Our Lady of Lourdes Church.
Osorio, Rudolfo B. '55 (NEW) Retired.
Osowski, Chester J. '49 (LC) Retired.
Ossa, Pedro Nel '63 (BRK) [128] Brooklyn, NY Sacred Heart Church.
Ossino, Angelo '57 (DEN) [3] Aurora, CO St. Pius X Church.
Ossola, John R. '64 (SFD) [1] Springfield, IL Cathedral of the Immaculate Conception.
Ostaszewski, Andrzej '84 (NEW) [6] Jersey City, NJ St. Anthony of Padua Church.
Ostaszewski, George '58 (PH) Retired.
Ostatek, Albert P. *o.s.p.p.e.* '45 (PH) [AA] Doylestown, PA Pauline Fathers Monastery, Shrine of Our Lady of Czestochowa.
Ostdick, Rupert *o.s.b.* '48 (IND) [J] St. Meinrad, IN St. Meinrad Archabbey.
Ostdiek, Gil *o.f.m.* '60 (CHI) [N] Chicago, IL St. Joseph Interprovincial Post-Novitiate Formation House.
Ostdiek, Gilbert *o.f.m.* '78 (CHI) [B] Chicago, IL The Catholic Theological Union at Chicago.
Ostdiek, Harold *o.p.* '60 (CHI) [D] Oak Park, IL Fenwick High School.
Ostdiek, John *o.f.m.* '49 (SFD) [K] Sherman, IL Our Lady of Angels Friary; [L] Springfield, IL St. Francis Convent.
Ostendorf, Mark '81 (SCL) [7] St. Cloud, MN St. Michael Church.
Osterhage, Louis *c.pp.s.* '58 (CIN) [17] Dayton, OH St. Joseph Church.
Osterhaus, Mark '85 (DUB) [6] Cedar Rapids, IA St. Matthew's Church.
Osterhout, Conrad *c.f.r.* '83 (NY) [DD] New York, NY St. Joseph's Friary.
Osterle, Paul V. *s.j.* '59 (SP) [8] Tampa, FL Sacred Heart Church.
Osterman, Gerald J. '67 (BO) [30] Boston, MA St. John-St. Hugh Church.
Osterman, Richard D. '69 (GF) Red Lodge, MT St. Agnes Church.
Ostertag, Robert C. *s.j.* '49 (MIL) [P] Wauwatosa, WI Jesuit Community at St. Camillus.
Ostidek, Harold D. *o.p.* '60 (CHI) River Forest, IL St. Vincent Ferrer Church.
Ostini, Anthony H. *s.j.* '72 (BR) [J] Convent, LA Manresa House of Retreats.
Ostrander, Gary L. '71 (OM) Ralston, NE St. Gerald Church.
Ostrowski, David T. *o.s.b.* '89 (STP) [6] Minneapolis, MN Holy Cross Church.
Ostrowski, Eugene S. '77 (WH) [3] Wheeling, WV Corpus Christi Church.
Ostrowski, John T. '98 (CLV) Painesville, OH St. Mary Church.
Ostrowski, Joseph C. '52 (SCR) [L] Elmhurst, PA St. Mary's Villa Nursing Home; [L] Elmhurst, PA St. Mary's Villa Nursing Home.
Ostrowski, Theodore L. '81 (CHI) [3] Chicago, IL St. Adrian Church.
Ostrowski, Walter *s.v.d.* '65 (PIT) [O] Pittsburgh, PA Society of The Divine Word.
Osuagwn, Denis A. '89 (LAF) Lawtell, LA Holy Family Church; Mallet, LA St. Ann Church.
Osuagwu, Evaristus '80 (BRK) [181] Queens, NY Immaculate Conception Church.
Osuagwu, Peter Chidi '89 (BRK) [153] Queens, NY Ascension Church.
Osuch, Michael *c.r.* '80 (CHI) [86] Chicago, IL St. Hyacinth Church.
Osuigwe, Basil C. (MAD) Dane, WI St. Michael Church; Sauk City, WI St. Aloysius Church.
Osuji, Martin '96 (LR) [10] Little Rock, AR Our Lady of Good Counsel Church.
Osuji, Ngozi '81 (NY) [82] New York, NY Notre Dame Church.

Osuna, E. Donald '63 (OAK) El Cerrito, CA St. Jerome's Church.
Oswald, John '61 (LR) Retired; [H] Little Rock, AR St. John Manor.
Oswald, Leo P. '78 (PH) [59] Philadelphia, PA Holy Cross Church; [91] Philadelphia, PA St. Madeleine Sophie Church; Fairless Hills, PA St. Frances Cabrini Church.
Oswald, Norman R. '72 (MIL) Wood, WI Veterans Administration Medical Center.
Oswald, Randy *o.m.i.* '97 (SFS) Sisseton, SD St. Catherine Church; Sisseton, SD St. Peter Church.
Oswald, Msgr. Richard S. '65 (LR) Rogers, AR St. Vincent de Paul Church.
Oswald, Ted '84 (SR) Lakeport, CA St. Mary Church.
Oswalt, M. Price '96 (OKL) Anadarko, OK St. Patrick's Church.
Otellini, Msgr. Steven D. '78 (SFR) San Francisco, CA Knights of Malta; Special Assignment; [D] Kentfield, CA Marin Catholic College Preparatory (Coed).
Oterino, Francis L. '87 (MET) On Duty Outside the Diocese.
Otero, Msgr. Henry '62 (WDC) Waldorf, MD St. Peter Church.
Otero, Jose (NY) [103] New York, NY St. Paul Church.
Otillio, Peter *o.p.* '57 (CHI) [N] Chicago, IL Dominicans (Provincial Office).
Otillio, Peter *o.p.* '57 (FgM) Dominican - Order of Preachers Foreign Missions.
Otor, Patrick *m.s.p.* '92 (BEA) Orange, TX St. Therese Church.
Ott, Msgr. Alfred R. '60 (ALN) [1] Allentown, PA Cathedral of St. Catharine of Siena.
Ott, Carlton A. '36 (TOL) Retired.
Ott, Vincent *o.m.i.* '56 (DUL) Garrison, MN Our Lady of Fatima Church; Hillman, MN Holy Family Church.
Ott, W. Richard *s.j.* '72 (BO) [W] Weston, MA Campion Jesuit Community.
Otten, Lammert B. *s.j.* '65 (SEA) [A] Seattle, WA Seattle University.
Ottenweller, Albert H. '43 (TOL) [1] Toledo, OH Queen of the Most Holy Rosary Church.
Otterbacher, John *glmy.* '56 (CIN) [M] Cincinnati, OH Headquarters of Glenmary Home Missioners.
Otting, Loras C. '62 (DUB) Retired.
Otting, Paul J. '66 (DUB) [8] Dubuque, IA Holy Ghost Church.
Ottman, Timothy *o.s.b.* '78 (HON) [G] Waialua, Oahu, HI Benedictine Monastery of Hawaii/Retreat Center.
Otto, David C. '77 (KAL) Edwardsburg, MI Our Lady of the Lake Church.
Otto, James C. *s.j.* '97 (PH) [52] Philadelphia, PA Good Shepherd Church; [D] Philadelphia, PA St. John Neumann High School.
Otto, John A. '39 (DAV) On Duty Outside the Diocese.
Otto, Leo '56 (SCL) Retired.
Otto, Peter '77 (AMA) Happy, TX Holy Name of Jesus Church; Nazareth, TX Holy Family Church.
Otto, Ray *o.s.b.* '82 (SFS) Revillo, SD Annunciation Church; [D] Milbank, SD St. Bernard Providence Hospital; [E] Milbank, SD St. William Home for the Aged.
Otto, Raymond *o.s.b.* '82 (SFS) Big Stone City, SD St. Charles Church; [F] Marvin, SD Blue Cloud Abbey.
Otto, Thomas '73 (PMB) North Palm Beach, FL St. Paul of the Cross Church.
Oubre, Carroll L. '91 (ARL) Dale City, VA Holy Family Church.
Oubre, Louis T. '86 (BR) St. James, LA St. James Church.
Oubre, Sinclair '86 (BEA) [5] Port Arthur, TX St. James Church.
Ouderkirk, Lloyd P. '59 (DUB) Clermont, IA St. Peter's Church; Postville, IA St. Bridget's Church.
Ouelette, Francis *o.m.i.* (BO) [3] Lowell, MA Immaculate Conception Church.
Ouellet, Maurice F. *s.s.e.* '52 (VEN) [G] Englewood, FL Society of St. Edmund Residence.
Ouellette, Donald C. '89 (WOR) [C] Fitchburg, MA St. Bernard's Central Catholic High School.
Ouellette, Donald C. '90 (WOR) Lunenburg, MA St. Boniface Church.
Ouellette, Lionel P. '57 (BO) Senior Priests.
Ouellette, Paul *o.m.i.* '67 (MAN) [K] Les Cayes, Haiti Paroisse Ste. Anne.
Ouellette, Paul M. *o.m.i.* '67 (MIA) Miramar, FL St. Stephen Church.
Ouellette, Raymond *s.m.* '52 (DET) [E] Harper Woods, MI Notre Dame High School.
Ouellette, Richard R. '75 (PRT) Grand Isle, ME St. Gerard-Mt. Carmel Church; Madawaska, ME St. David's Church.
Ouellette, Richard T. *m.m.* '36 (SJ) [L] Los Altos, CA Maryknoll.
Ouellette, Robert *o.f.m.conv* (SFR) [T] San Francisco, CA Shrine of St. Francis of Assisi.
Ouellette, Roger J. '42 (PRT) Retired; [I] Waterville, ME Mt. St. Joseph Priest Retirement Home.
Ouillette, Arthur A. '55 (WOR) Retired.
Ouimet, J. Lawrence '74 (NOR) Coventry, CT St. Mary Church.
Oulds, John V. '68 (PH) [3] Coatesville, PA St. Joseph Church; [4] Coatesville, PA St. Stanislaus Kostka Church.
Ouletta, James F. '60 (CHI) Retired.
Oulvey, William T. *s.j.* '85 (STL) [P] St. Louis, MO Bellarmine House of Studies; [P] St. Louis, MO The Jesuits of the Missouri Province.
Ouper, John '84 (JOL) Frankfort, IL St. Anthony Church.
Ours, Donald *c.m.* '94 (CHI) [207] Chicago, IL St. Vincent de Paul Church; [N] Chicago, IL DePaul Vincentian Residence.
Ours, Robert A. '80 (SY) [9] Binghamton, NY St. Patrick Church; Special Assignment; [C] Binghamton, NY Seton Catholic Central High School of Broome County.
Outlaw, S. Keith '89 (NY) [131] Bronx, NY St. Augustine Church.
Ovalle, Tom *o.m.i.* '77 (SAT) [72] San Antonio, TX San Juan De Los Lagos Church.
Overbaugh, Msgr. Hugh A. '61 (HBG) [2] Harrisburg, PA St. Catherine Laboure Church.
Overbaugh, Msgr. Lawrence R. '55 (HBG) [5] Mount Carmel, PA Our Lady of Mount Carmel Church.
Overbeck, Jerome T. *s.j.* '74 (CHI) [C] Chicago, IL Jesuit Community at Loyola University of Chicago.
Overbeck, Kenneth C. (BO) Chelmsford, MA St. John the Evangelist Church.
Overend, James '77 (ORG) [4] Huntington Beach, CA St. Vincent de Paul Church.
Overman, Msgr. Robert F. '45 (STL) Retired.
Overmann, William J. '62 (SFD) North Arm, IL St. Aloysius Church; Paris, IL St. Mary Church.
Overmyer, John '97 (FTW) Elkhart, IN St. Vincent de Paul Church.
Overstreet, Raymond J. '97 (PH) Warrington, PA St. Joseph Church.
Ovian, Leo *m.s.a.* '66 (NOR) [F] Cromwell, CT Society of the Missionaries of the Holy Apostles.
Ovian, Leo J. *m.s.a.* '66 (WDC) [Q] Washington, DC Basilica of the National Shrine of the Immaculate Conception.
Oviedo, Francisco *o.a.r.* '25 (NY) [187] Bronx, NY St. Roch Church.
Ovsak, William (FAR) [J] Drayton, ND Friends of the International Seminary John Paul II.
Ovsak, William T. '99 (FAR) Drayton, ND St. Edward's Church.
Owambo, Cyril '74 (NY) Crestwood, NY Church of the Annunciation.
Owen, John J. '48 (BIR) Retired.
Owens, Benjamin *c.ss.r.* '75 (OAK) [C] Oakland, CA Bishop O'Dowd High School.
Owens, Bernard C. *c.s.b.* '67 (GAL) [Q] Sugar Land, TX Basilian Mission Center.
Owens, Bernard J. *s.j.* '72 (DET) [P] Bloomfield Hills, MI Manresa Jesuit Retreat House.
Owens, Edward *o.ss.t.* '80 (LA) [A] Camarillo, CA St. John's Seminary.
Owens, J. Edward *o.ss.t.* '80 (BAL) [S] Baltimore, MD Holy Trinity Monastery.
Owens, John '48 (BIR) Trussville, AL Holy Infant of Prague Church.
Owens, John J. '49 (BIS) Retired.
Owens, Joseph P. *s.j.* '48 (CLV) Cleveland, OH Cleveland Clinic Foundation.
Owens, Joseph P. *s.j.* '48 (DET) [P] Clarkston, MI Colombiere Center.
Owens, Joseph V. *s.j.* '71 (FgM) Provinces.
Owens, Leroy E. '64 (BO) Medfield, MA St. Edward the Confessor Church.
Owens, Michael '84 (HON) Lanai City, HI Sacred Hearts Church.
Owens, Robert *o.carm.* '97 (BRK) [140] Brooklyn, NY St. Thomas Aquinas Church.
Owens, S. Brian '95 (WH) Charles Town, WV St. James Church.
Owens, Thomas J. '74 (PH) [A] Wynnewood, PA Theological Seminary of St. Charles Borromeo, Overbrook.
Owens-Howard, Robert J. '74 (CHR) Retired.
Owino, Felix *a.j.* '92 (PIT) [5] Pittsburgh, PA St. Bede Church.
Owusu-Boateng, Johnson '85 (VIC) Cuero, TX St. Michael Church.
Oyabu, Charles '70 (HON) Wailuku, HI St. Anthony Church; [G] Honolulu, HI Marianist Communities.
Oyarbide, Pedro '62 (CGS) Aibonito, PR Church of St. Joseph.
Oyeyipo, Anthony '92 (WDC) [B] Washington, DC St. Joseph's Seminary.
Oyler, George F. '57 (L) Retired.
Ozanne, Thomas *c.pp.s.* '74 (KC) [3] St. Joseph, MO St. Francis Xavier Church.
Ozbun, John W. '84 (WIN) Blue Earth, MN SS. Peter and Paul's Church; Guckeen, MN Our Lady of Mercy Church.
Ozimek, Adam Z. '94 (ATL) Lookout Mountain, GA Our Lady of the Mount Church.
Ozimek, Anthony J. *o.s.b.* '68 (CLV) [O] Cleveland, OH Benedictine Order of Cleveland.
Ozimek, Anthony J. *o.s.b.* '68 (GF) [G] Billings, MT St. Vincent Healthcare.
Ozimek, Eugene F. '45 (SPR) Retired; [I] Holyoke, MA Sisters of Providence Care Centers, Inc.
Ozminkowski, Clyde *o.carm.* '54 (VEN) [G] Venice, FL Carmel in Venice.
Ozodor, Paulinus *c.s.sp.* '84 (FTW) [2] South Bend, IN St. Adalbert Church.
Ozug, John C. '77 (FR) Edgartown, MA St. Elizabeth Church; Oak Bluffs, MA Sacred Heart Church; Vineyard Haven, MA St. Augustine Church.

P

P., Gerard, Dunne *s.s.c.* '69 (LA) [Q] Los Angeles, CA Columban Fathers, Procure House.
Paa, Donald R. '47 (KC) Retired.
Paa, Joseph F. '41 (BUF) Retired.
Paa, Msgr. Raymond F. '55 (BUF) Harris Hill, NY Nativity of the Blessed Virgin Mary Church.
Paala, Jonathan '75 (SFR) Foster City, CA St. Luke Church.
Pabin, Chester J. '92 (STU) Lafferty, OH St. Mary Church.
Pable, Marty *o.f.m. cap.* '58 (LC) [H] Marathon City, WI St. Anthony Retreat Center.
Pablo, Calixto (HON) Kalaheo, HI Holy Cross Church.
Pabst, Peter *s.j.* '86 (SJ) [22] San Jose, CA Sacred Heart of Jesus Church.
Pace, Paul J. '66 (HRT) [10] Waterbury, CT St. Francis Xavier's Church.
Pace, William J. '51 (SCR) Retired; [N] Dunmore, PA Villa St. Joseph.
Pachana, Robert A. '98 (NEW) [6] Bayonne, NJ Mt. Carmel Church.
Pacharoni, Victor *s.j.* '96 (WDC) [M] Washington, DC The Jesuit Community at Georgetown University.
Pacheco, Agostinho S. '60 (BWN) [2] McAllen, TX Our Lady of Sorrows Church.
Pacheco, Alexandre '67 (STO) Manteca, CA St. Anthony Church.
Pacheco, Mario '76 (LA) Covina, CA Sacred Heart Church.
Pacheco, Norbert A. *m.m.* '79 (FgM) Maryknoll Foreign Missions.
Pachence, Ron (SD) [B] San Diego, CA University of San Diego; [B] San Diego, CA University of San Diego.
Pachence, Ronald A. '74 (SAV) On Duty Outside the Diocese.
Pachla, Stanley L., Jr. '83 (DET) [3] Eastpointe, MI St. Veronica Church.
Pacho, Jesus '51 (PCE) Retired.
Pacho, Jesus '65 (PCE) [B] Ponce, PR The Pontifical Catholic University of Puerto Rico.
Pacholczyk, Tedeusz '99 (FR) Falmouth, MA St. Patrick's Church.
Pacholec, Daniel S. '96 (SPR) East Longmeadow, MA St. Michael's Church.
Pacini, Mario *s.a.c.* '66 (ALB) [S] Cohoes, NY Apostolate for the Suffering.
Paciorek, Joseph C. *c.m.* '35 (HRT) [M] Manchester, CT DePaul Provincial Residence.
Pacitti, Gary '89 (PH) Holland, PA St. Bede the Venerable Church.
Packard, Nathan '87 (SCL) Chokio, MN St. Mary's Church; Herman, MN St. Charles Church.
Packard, Walter E. '71 (E) Warren, PA St. Joseph Church.
Pacocha, Edwin D. '62 (CHI) [45] Chicago, IL St. Cornelius Church.
Pacquina, Joseph '83 (SJ) [16] San Jose, CA St. Martin of Tours Church.
Pacudan, Roland '83 (HON) Makakilo, HI St. Jude Church.
Pacwa, Mitchell *s.j.* (DAL) [B] Irving, TX University of Dallas.
Pacwa, Mitchell *s.j.* '76 (DAL) [D] Dallas, TX Jesuit College Preparatory School.
Paczek, Valerian '34 (FAR) Retired.
Paczesny, John R. '61 (MIL) Whitefish Bay, WI St. Monica Church; [K] Milwaukee, WI St. Mary's Hospital of Milwaukee; [K] Mequon, WI St. Mary's Hospital Ozaukee, Inc.
Paczkowski, Vincent '86 (NEW) [3] Elizabeth, NJ St. Anthony's Church.
Padathuruthy, Charles '81 (SCL) Pearl Lake, MN Holy Cross Church; St. Nicholas, MN St. Nicholas Church.
Padavick, William B. '63 (CLV) Oberlin, OH Sacred Heart Church.
Padazinski, C. Michael '88 (SFR) [2] South San Francisco, CA Mater Dolorosa Church; Special Assignment.
Padberg, John W. *s.j.* '57 (STL) [P] St. Louis, MO Jesuit Community Corporation at St. Louis University - Jesuit Hall; [V] St. Louis, MO Institute of Jesuit Sources; [V] St. Louis, MO Seminar on Jesuit Spirituality.
Paddack, John N. '84 (NY) [53] New York, NY Incarnation Church; [F] New York, NY St. Joseph by the Sea, High School.

Padden, Neil *o.f.m.* '55 (PAT) [M] Butler, NJ St. Anthony Friary.
Paddock, Richard W. '59 (RCK) Elburn, IL St. Gall Church.
Padelli, Emilio P. '62 (HRT) [4] East Hartford, CT St. Isaac Jogues Church.
Padgett, Gary T. '99 (L) [35] Louisville, KY Holy Spirit Church.
Padilla, Aquino D. '60 (SFR) Daly City, CA Our Lady of Perpetual Help Church.
Padilla, Glibert '55 (TUC) Retired.
Padilla, Manuel G. '99 (CHI) [130] Chicago, IL Maternity of the Blessed Virgin Mary Church.
Padin, Jose *m.m.* '97 (FgM) Maryknoll Foreign Missions.
Padinjarepeedika, Jose L.F. *c.m.i.* '72 (LAF) Melville, LA St. John the Evangelist Church.
Pado, Thomas '75 (ORG) Irvine, CA St. Elizabeth Ann Seton Church.
Padovani, Martin *s.v.d.* '60 (TR) [M] Bordentown, NJ Society of the Divine Word.
Padrez, Mark *o.p.* '95 (SD) [L] San Diego, CA University of California at San Diego (Campus Ministry).
Padrnos, David *s.s.c.* '71 (FgM) St. Columban's Foreign Mission.
Paduch, Frank '89 (BEA) Liberty, TX Immaculate Conception Church.
Padula, Armand *o.f.m.* '56 (NY) [FF] Wappingers Falls, NY Mt. Alvernia Retreat House.
Pafchik, Lawrence F. *o.f.m.* '42 (PAT) [M] Ringwood, NJ Holy Name Friary, Inc.
Pagan, Alberto *o.p.* '87 (SJN) [3] Bayamon, PR Catalina de Siena Church.
Pagan, Angel M. '80 (ARE) [6] Arecibo, PR Our Lady of Hope Church.
Pagano, Bernard T. '58 (WIL) On Duty Outside the Diocese.
Pagano, Peter E. '52 (SPR) Retired.
Page, Anthony J. '69 (LA) La Mirada, CA Beatitudes of Our Lord Church.
Page, Charles T. '91 (KAL) Buchanan, MI St. Anthony Church.
Page, David '58 (ORL) Indialantic, FL Holy Name of Jesus Church.
Page, Hugh H. '80 (FTW) [B] Notre Dame, IN University of Notre Dame Du Lac.
Page, Leon J. '56 (DET) Retired.
Page, Stephen C. '87 (DAV) Fairfield, IA St. Mary's Church.
Page, Thomas P. '79 (GR) Rockford, MI Our Lady of Consolation Church; On Special Assignment.
Pagel, John M. '80 (CHL) Asheville, NC St. Joan of Arc Church.
Pageot, Roger *s.s.s.* '53 (CLV) [O] Cleveland, OH Blessed Sacrament Community.
Pageot, Roger *s.s.s.* '53 (NY) [8] New York, NY St. Andrew Church.
Pagliara, Alfonso D. *o.f.m.cap.* '81 (SP) [6] Tampa, FL Most Holy Redeemer Church.
Pagliari, Robert *c.ss.r.* (NY) [I] New York, NY The Catholic Charities of the Archdiocese of New York.
Pagliari, Robert M. *c.ss.r.* '75 (ORL) [F] New Smyrna Beach, FL Redemptorist Fathers of the Vice Province of Richmond.
Pagliuca, Joseph P. '43 (BUR) Retired.
Pagnotta, James V. '69 (NEW) [13] Jersey City, NJ St. Joseph's Church.
Pagones, Peter '68 (ALB) [16] Schenectady, NY St. Paul the Apostle Church.
Paguaga, Juan Carlos '00 (MIA) Miami Lakes, FL Our Lady of the Lakes Church.
Pahamtang, Leonardo '77 (LUB) Ralls, TX St. Michael Church.
Pahl, Norman *o.m.i.* '58 (DUL) Willow River, MN St. Mary's Church; Willow River, MN Youth Conservation Camp.
Pahler, Robert E. '57 (CLV) Cuyahoga Falls, OH Immaculate Heart of Mary Church; Green, OH Queen of Heaven Church; Retired.
Pai, Simon '52 (RVC) Retired.
Paider, Paul (GB) Black Creek, WI St. Mary Church; Navarino, WI St. Lawrence Church.
Paik, Francis M. '54 (CLV) [1] Euclid, OH St. Christine Church; Retired.
Paillacho, Jose (MOB) [7] Montgomery, AL Our Lady, Queen of Mercy Church.
Painter, E. B. *s.j.* '75 (P) [23] Portland, OR St. Mary Magdalene Church.
Painter, George F. *m.m.* '44 (FgM) Maryknoll Foreign Missions.
Paisley, James J. '85 (SCR) Laflin, PA St. Maria Goretti Church.
Paisley, John C. '62 (DUB) Hazleton, IA St. Mary's Church; Lamont, IA St. Mary's Church; Strawberry Point, IA St. Mary's Church.
Paithottiyil, Thomas *c.m.i.* '93 (ALX) Marksville, LA Holy Ghost Church.
Paiva, Antonio M. '49 (PRO) [27] Providence, RI Our Lady of the Rosary Church.
Paiz, Bill '79 (SB) [1] San Bernardino, CA Our Lady of the Rosary Church.
Pajk, Thomas J. '87 (CLV) North Ridgeville, OH St. Peter Church.
Pak, Phillip '78 (LA) [48] Los Angeles, CA St. Basil's Church.
Pak, Pyong Gwan *s.j.* '99 (BO) [W] Chestnut Hill, MA The Jesuit Community at Boston College.
Pakenham, Daniel J. '65 (MIL) Elm Grove, WI St. Mary Church.
Pakianather, Aloysius P. '78 (RVC) Valley Stream, NY Blessed Sacrament Church.
Pakiz, Rudolph '46 (DUL) Tower, MN St. Martin's Church.
Pakosta, Francis J. '52 (SUP) Retired.
Pakula, Michael G. '73 (PEO) Geneseo, IL St. Malachy's Church.
Pakutka, Msgr. William J. '43 (SCR) Retired; [N] Dunmore, PA Villa St. Joseph.
Pala, Francis *sch.p.* '55 (MIA) [C] Fort Lauderdale, FL Cardinal Gibbons High School.
Pala, Manuel Soler *m.ss.cc.* '70 (SJN) [A] Bayamon, PR Bayamon Central University.
Palacino, Joseph '82 (BGP) [1] Norwalk, CT St. Jerome Church.
Palacio, Jorge *o.s.m.* '79 (ELP) [18] El Paso, TX Our Lady of Sorrows Church.
Palacios, Joseph M. *s.j.* '87 (LA) On Duty Outside the Archdiocese.
Palacios, Joseph M. *s.j.* '87 (OAK) [N] Oakland, CA Murray Residence Community.
Palackal, Joseph *c.m.i.* '79 (BRK) [242] Queens, NY St. Stanislaus Kostka Church.
Palad, Pio '47 (KNX) [3] Chattanooga, TN St. Jude Church.
Paladino, John '91 (NEW) Scotch Plains, NJ St. Bartholomew Church.
Palafox, Lorenzo J. *s.j.* '67 (SAC) [C] Sacramento, CA Jesuit High School; [H] Carmichael, CA Jesuit High School Community of Sacramento.
Palakovich, Michael G. '87 (DEN) Loveland, CO St. John the Evangelist Church.
Palamattathil, George '86 (OAK) [3] Walnut Creek, CA St. Mary's Church.
Palang, Mansueto "Chito" P. '77 (BR) Darrow, LA St. Anthony of Padua Church; Sorrento, LA St. Anne Church.
Palardy, William B. '85 (BO) [A] Boston, MA St. John's Seminary School of Theology.
Palaroan, Moises '78 (STA) Keystone Heights, FL St. William Church.
Palasits, John A. '58 (NEW) South Orange, NJ Our Lady of Sorrows Church.
Palathingal, Joseph M. (BIR) [21] Birmingham, AL St. Peter the Apostle Church.
Palathingal, Simon '72 (LKC) [8] Lake Charles, LA Our Lady Queen of Heaven Church.
Palazzo, Michael L. '87 (NY) Hyde Park, NY Regina Coeli Church.
Palazzolo, Anthony P. '93 (STA) [21] Jacksonville, FL San Jose Church.
Palcheck, Gerald F. '67 (SD) Descanso, CA Our Lady of Light Church.
Palcisko, Raymond (CR) Retired.
Palen, Robert L. '41 (DUB) Retired.
Paleologos, Gregory (HRT) [S] Hartford, CT Catholic Charities-Catholic Family Services (Archdiocese of Hartford).
Palermo, Albert '63 (AUS) Retired.
Palermo, Albert A. '63 (MIL) Retired.
Palermo, Angelo *s.a.c.* '60 (NY) [221] Staten Island, NY Our Lady Star of the Sea Church.
Palermo, Frank C. '55 (SPC) [2] Springfield, MO Holy Trinity Church; Retired.
Palermo, Joseph S., Jr. '94 (NO) [31] New Orleans, LA St. Frances Xavier Cabrini Church.
Palica, Jacek *o.c.d.* '96 (GRY) [J] Munster, IN Discalced Carmelite Fathers Monastery.
Palick, George '58 (PIT) [1] Butler, PA St. Fidelis of Sigmaringen Church.
Paliokas, Algirdas *s.j.* '73 (CHI) [2] Lemont, IL Blessed Jurgis Matulaitis Church; [N] Chicago, IL Lithuanian American Jesuits.
Palis, Theo '45 (OAK) Bay Point, CA Our Lady Queen of the World Church; Retired.
Palisoc, Fidel '82 (SFR) [4] San Francisco, CA St. Anne Church.
Paliwoda, Steven '94 (SJP) Pittsburgh, PA St. George Church.
Palka, Bernard *s.a.* '72 (NY) [AA] Garrison, NY St. Christopher's Inn; [DD] Garrison, NY Franciscan Friars of the Atonement, Minister General Office; [DD] Garrison, NY Franciscan Friars of the Atonement.
Palka, Bogdan *s.d.s.* '92 (WDC) [B] Silver Spring, MD Salvatorian Community.
Palka, Bogdan *s.d.s.* '93 (BAL) [85] Baltimore, MD St. Rita Church.
Palka, Edwin '96 (SP) Dunedin, FL Our Lady of Lourdes Church.
Palko, John A. '54 (PIT) [1] McKeesport, PA St. Martin de Porres Church; Retired.
Palko, John J. '67 (ALT) Hollidaysburg, PA St. Mary's Church.
Palko, Thomas J. *o.s.f.s.* '59 (VEN) [4] Fort Myers, FL St. Columbkille Church.
Palkowski, Jan '76 (PH) [79] Philadelphia, PA St. John Cantius Church; Clifton Heights, PA Sacred Heart Church.
Palladino, Msgr. Alfonso G. '43 (BO) Melrose, MA St. Mary of the Annunciation Church; Senior Priests.
Palladino, Robert J. '58 (P) Estacada, OR St. Aloysius Church.
Pallard, John *o.m.i.* '72 (PMB) [1] Palm Beach, FL Cathedral of St. Ignatius Loyola.
Pallardy, James G. '60 (PEO) [5] Peoria, IL St. Bernard's Church.
Palliparambil, Jose Simon '62 (RVC) Plainview, NY St. Pius X Church; Plainview, NY North Shore Hospital at Plainview.
Pallivathuckal, Abraham Joseph '73 (MIA) [2] Hollywood, FL Nativity Church.
Pallivathukkall, Jacob M. '65 (PT) Chattahoochee, FL Holy Cross Church.
Pallo, Joseph L. '61 (LR) Blytheville, AR Immaculate Conception Church; Osceola, AR St. Matthew's Church; [L] Blytheville, AR Immaculate Conception Trust Fund.
Palluck, M. Charles '66 (SEA) Black Diamond, WA St. Barbara Church.
Palm, John B. *s.j.* '41 (FgM) Provinces.
Palma, Raul *sch.p.* '58 (LA) [Q] Los Angeles, CA Piarist Fathers.
Palmatier, David *o.s.b.* '57 (RCK) [G] Aurora, IL Marmion Abbey-St. Augustine's Abbey.
Palmeno, Alberto *o.s.a.* '68 (LAR) [19] Laredo, TX St. Vincent de Paul Church.
Palmer, Frank S. '62 (DM) Indianola, IA St. Thomas Aquinas Church.
Palmer, Herbert *o.s.b.* '39 (SD) [H] Oceanside, CA Prince of Peace Abbey, Benet Hill.
Palmer, John *c.s.v.* '71 (JOL) [A] Lisle, IL Benedictine University.
Palmer, Michael C. '63 (BGP) Wilton, CT Our Lady of Fatima Church.
Palmer, Michael J. '70 (STL) On Medical Leave.
Palmer, Msgr. Patrick '48 (SAT) Retired; [K] San Antonio, TX Casa De Padres.
Palmer, Richard *o.s.a.* '87 (FgM) Foreign Missions.
Palmer, Richard D. *o.s.a.* '87 (CHI) [N] Olympia Fields, IL The Augustinians-Provincialate.
Palmer, Ronald L. '80 (PEO) Bartonville, IL St. Anthony Church.
Palmer, Samuel '57 (DM) Urbandale, IA St. Pius X Church.
Palmer, Msgr. Thomas M. '58 (SAT) LaCoste, TX Our Lady of Grace Church.
Palmese, Anthony '76 (ORL) [4] Ocala, FL St. Jude's Catholic Community Church.
Palmieri, Msgr. Alexander J. *j.c.l.* (PH) [FF] Philadelphia, PA Catholic Heritage Center.
Palmieri, Msgr. Alexander J. '76 (PH) Conshohocken, PA SS. Cosmas and Damian Church; [A] Wynnewood, PA Theological Seminary of St. Charles Borromeo, Overbrook.
Palmieri, Armando *s.d.v.* '98 (NEW) Palisades Park, NJ St. Nicholas Church.
Palmieri, Armando *s.d.v.* '98 (PAT) [M] Florham Park, NJ Father Justin Vocationary.
Palmieri, Frank *c.r.m.* '62 (CHR) Goose Creek, SC Immaculate Conception Church.
Palmieri, Louis R. '93 (BO) Holbrook, MA St. Joseph Church.
Palmieri, Luigi '67 (ALN) [7] Allentown, PA St. Paul Church.
Palmieri, Luigi '67 (JC) On Duty Outside the Diocese.
Palmieri, Thaddeus *o.f.m.* '48 (NY) [DD] New York, NY Franciscan Province of the Immaculate Conception.
Palmigiano, James *o.c.s.o.* '88 (WOR) [N] Spencer, MA St. Joseph's Abbey.
Palmiotto, Paul C. '82 (BRK) [156] Queens, NY St. Benedict, the Moor Church; [159] Queens, NY St. Bonaventure's Church.
Palmisano, Peter J. '93 (NEW) Franklin Lakes, NJ Most Blessed Sacrament Church.
Palmitessa, Paul '56 (SD) Retired.
Palo, Anthony *o.carm.* '64 (NEW) Englewood, NJ St. Cecilia's Church.
Paloma, Victor E. '70 (NEW) [22] Jersey City, NJ Our Lady of Victories Church.
Palomera, Ramona G. (LA) Wilmington, CA Holy Family Church.
Palomino, Esviardo '49 (NY) [67] New York, NY St. Lucy Church.
Palomino, Ignacio '85 (HBG) [3] Lancaster, PA Assumption of the Blessed Virgin Mary Church; [J] Lancaster, PA Iglesia de San Juan Bautista.
Palomino, Jesus *s.j.* (PHX) [B] Phoenix, AZ Brophy College Preparatory.
Palomo, Benigno *o.s.a.* '66 (SJN) [18] Bayamon, PR Santa Rita de Casia Church.
Palos, Anthony Z. *o.a.r.* '60 (LA) Montebello, CA St. Benedict Church.

Palpale, Marisi *ss.cc.* '86 (WDC) [B] Cheverly, MD Damien House.
Palsa, Steven M. '79 (PIT) Bethel Park, PA St. Thomas More Church.
Palubeski, Joseph *c.r.* '66 (L) [30] Louisville, KY Guardian Angels Church; [E] Louisville, KY Thomas Merton Academy.
Palubinskas, Vytautas A. '54 (BRK) Retired.
Paluck, Casimir A. '61 (BIS) Fort Yates, ND St. Peter - Catholic Indian Church; Selfridge, ND St. Philomena Church.
Palumbo, Richard '93 (MET) [1] New Brunswick, NJ St. Peter Apostle Church.
Palumbo, Richard W. '93 (MET) [L] Phillipsburg, NJ The Anawim Community.
Palumbos, Edward L. '72 (ROC) [12] Rochester, NY St. Charles Borromeo Church.
Paluse, Richard V. '42 (PIT) Retired.
Palys, Daniel J. '69 (BUF) Blossom, NY St. Gabriel Church.
Pambello, Louis '81 (NEW) Montclair, NJ Montclair Hospital; West Orange, NJ Kessler Institute for Rehabilitation.
Pambello, Louis M. '81 (NEW) Montclair, NJ Immaculate Conception Church.
Pamisetty, Marayya '77 (SPC) Poplar Bluff, MO Sacred Heart Church; Poplar Bluff, MO Poplar Bluff Hospital Ministry.
Pamment, Duaine H. '64 (LAN) Laingsburg, MI St. Isidore Church.
Pamment, Gary W. '63 (KAL) Wayland, MI St. Therese Church.
Pamplaniyil, Matthew '76 (FAR) Sykeston, ND St. Elizabeth's Church.
Panagia, Sal J. '73 (PAT) [13] Paterson, NJ Our Lady of Pompei Church.
Panagoplos, Christopher *t.o.r.* '76 (ORL) Mount Dora, FL St. Patrick's Church.
Panakal, John Bosco '70 (JOL) Winfield, IL St. John the Baptist Church.
Panakal, Thomson '60 (JOL) [2] Lockport, IL St. Dennis Church.
Panaligan, Vicente '77 (BR) Prairieville, LA St. John the Evangelist Church.
Panares, Auxentius V. '62 (WDC) Norbeck, MD St. Patrick Church.
Panaretos, Paul D. *s.j.* '84 (CLV) [D] Cuyahoga Falls, OH Walsh Jesuit High School; [T] Akron, OH Loyola of the Lakes Jesuit Retreat House, Inc.
Panaretos, Paul D. *s.j.* '84 (DET) [K] Detroit, MI Jesuit Provincial Office-Detroit Province of the Society of Jesus.
Panato, Pasquino *m.c.c.j.* '64 (NEW) [N] Montclair, NJ Comboni Missionaries of the Heart of Jesus (Verona Fathers).
Pancheco-Sanchez, Luis '99 (MIL) [2] Milwaukee, WI St. Adalbert Church; [55] Milwaukee, WI St. Mary Magdalen Church.
Panchot, Daniel A. *c.s.c.* '65 (FgM) Holy Cross Foreign Missions.
Panchuk, Myron '82 (STN) [3] Chicago, IL SS. Volodymyr and Olha Church.
Pancorbo, Msgr. Marcos A. '58 (PCE) [1] Ponce, PR Cathedral of Our Lady of Guadalupe; [1] Ponce, PR Church Our Lady of Miraculous Medal Church; [H] Penuelas, PR Training School for the Lay Apostolate (Hermanos Cheos).
Pandarathikudiyil, Sebastian *v.c.* '88 (NY) Highland Mills, NY St. Patrick Church.
Pandolfo, Anthony '60 (STU) Retired.
Pandolfo, Lawrence *o.p.* '39 (NO) Jefferson, LA Elmwood Partners.
Pane, Andrew '87 (NY) Retired.
Panek, Edward B. '91 (CHI) [20] Chicago, IL St. Barbara Church.
Panek, Robert M. '70 (NY) Military Chaplains.
Panepinto, Vincent (ROC) Romulus, NY Five Points Correctional Facility.
Panepinto, Vincent '67 (ROC) Willard, NY Drug Treatment Center.
Panes, Romeo '86 (NEW) [1] Jersey City, NJ St. Aedan's Church.
Panful, Michael (BRK) [146] Queens, NY St. Adalbert Church.
Pangratz, Clement H. *o.s.b.* '47 (SEA) [L] Lacey, WA St. Martin's Abbey.
Paniagua, Carlos *s.v.d.* (TR) Neptune, NJ Our Lady of Providence Church.
Paniagua, Edwin *o.f.m.* '00 (NY) [DD] New York, NY Franciscan Province of the Immaculate Conception.
Paniagua, Jose L. '62 (MIA) [3] Hialeah, FL St. Benedict Church.
Paniagua, Pablo '49 (SAT) [K] San Antonio, TX Casa De Padres.
Paniagua, Pablo '59 (SAT) Retired.
Panickaruparampil, Thomas *t.o.r.* '62 (FWT) Carrollton, TX St. Catherine of Siena Church.
Paninski, John *m.s.* '61 (PEO) Georgetown, IL St. Isaac Jogues Church; [M] Georgetown, IL LaSalette Missionaries.
Pank, Julian F. '40 (L) Retired.
Panke, Robert J. '96 (WDC) [40] Washington, DC St. Stephen Martyr Church; Special Ministries.
Pankratz, Richard L. *s.s.c.* '74 (FgM) St. Columban's Foreign Mission.
Panos, Msgr. Patrick G. '68 (PAT) Ringwood, NJ St. Catherine of Bologna Church.
Panossian, Antoine '66 (ARM) Los Angeles, CA Our Lady Queen of Martyrs Church.
Panossian, Antoine *p.i.a.* '66 (LA) [33] Los Angeles, CA Our Lady Queen of Martyrs Church.
Pansini, Francis David '42 (LA) [Q] Montebello, CA Vincentian Fathers and Brothers; [Q] Montebello, CA Vincentian Fathers & Brothers.
Pansza, Gilbert '00 (FWT) [11] Fort Worth, TX St. John the Apostle Church.
Pantaleo, Daniel C. (PH) [C] Philadelphia, PA LaSalle University.
Pantano, Salvatore *o.f.m.conv.* '51 (ALB) [12] Albany, NY Our Lady of Angels Church.
Panthackal, Joseph '68 (TR) [12] Trenton, NJ St. Anthony Church.
Panthalani, Thomas '64 (LKC) De Ridder, LA St. Joseph's Church.
Pantle, G. Donald *s.j.* '60 (SCR) [C] Scranton, PA University of Scranton.
Pantyra, Anthony '78 (RCK) Tampico, IL St. Mary Church.
Panula, Arne A. '73 (NY) [II] New York, NY Prelature of the Holy Cross and Opus Dei.
Panuska, Joseph A. *s.j.* '60 (ALN) [A] Wernersville, PA Jesuit Center; [A] Wernersville, PA Jesuit Center.
Panza, Msgr. Paul D. '54 (ALT) Retired.
Panza, Robert S. '83 (HBG) Dallastown, PA St. Joseph Church.
Panzer, Joel S. '94 (LIN) Wilber, NE St. Wenceslaus Church.
Paoli, Livius *o.s.b.* '37 (DET) [70] Detroit, MI St. Scholastica Church; [K] Detroit, MI St. Sylvester Monastery.
Paolicelli, Lawrence '84 (NY) Katonah, NY St. Mary of the Assumption Church.
Paolo, Francis de Sales *o.f.m.* '58 (BO) [52] Boston, MA Our Lady of Mt. Carmel Church.
Paolozzi, Joseph L. '61 (MEM) Martin, TN St. Jude's Church; [K] Martin, TN Cooperative Ministries Interfaith Center.
Paone, Ernest C. '57 (PIT) On Duty Outside the Diocese.
Paonessa, Ralph *o.f.m.* '63 (NY) [DD] New York, NY Franciscan Province of the Immaculate Conception.
Papa, Charles E. '67 (RVC) Sound Beach, NY St. Louis de Montfort Church.
Papa, Christopher J. '89 (PH) Norwood, PA St. Gabriel Church; West Chester, PA St. Agnes Church.
Papa, Dominic *c.p.* '60 (FgM) Passionist Foreign Missions.
Papa, Dominic *c.p.* '60 (MET) [H] South River, NJ Passionist Provincial Office.
Papa, Frank *s.o.l.t.* '89 (CC) [H] Robstown, TX Society of Our Lady of the Most Holy Trinity.
Papa, Frank E. *s.o.l.t.* '89 (HRT) [5] East Hartford, CT St. Mary's Church.
Papaj, Joseph J. *s.j.* '70 (NY) [F] New York, NY Loyola School; [DD] New York, NY St. Ignatius Loyola Residence.
Papalia, Pasquale '74 (TR) Holmdel, NJ St. Benedict Church.
Papalia, Pasquale A. '74 (NEW) On Duty Outside the Archdiocese.
Pape, William (ALB) [S] Albany, NY The Cathedral Restoration Corp.
Pape, William H. '70 (ALB) [1] Albany, NY Cathedral of the Immaculate Conception.
Papen, Gerald T. *c.s.c.* '63 (FgM) Holy Cross Foreign Missions.
Papen, Gerald T. *c.s.c.* '63 (FTW) [J] South Bend, IN Congregation of Holy Cross, Indiana Province, Provincial House.
Papera, Lewis V. '67 (NEW) Rochelle Park, NJ Sacred Heart Church.
Paperini, Richard '77 (P) [2] Portland, OR St. Agatha Church; [A] St. Benedict, OR Mount Angel Seminary; [A] St. Benedict, OR Mount Angel Seminary.
Papes, Joseph T. '59 (GF) Retired.
Papes, Louis M. '88 (CLV) Released from Diocesan Assignment.
Papes, Rudy *c.ss.r.* '65 (GR) [3] Grand Rapids, MI St. Alphonsus Church.
Papesh, Michael L. '83 (STP) [5] St. Paul, MN Holy Spirit Church.
Papiernik, Roman J. '40 (LC) Retired.
Papineau, Andre *s.d.s.* '65 (MIL) [B] Hales Corners, WI Sacred Heart School of Theology.
Papineau, Daniel *m.i.c.* '98 (SPR) [J] Stockbridge, MA Congregation of Marians of The Immaculate Conception of the BVM; [J] Stockbridge, MA Congregation of Marians of The Immaculate Conception of the BVM.
Papka, Ihor '92 (STF) Colchester, CT St. Mary Dormition Church.
Papp, Edward E. '60 (OG) Potsdam, NY St. Mary Church.
Pappalliyil, Xavier *o.c.d.* '80 (FRS) Hanford, CA St. Brigid Church.
Pappu, Xavier '81 (TYL) Union Grove-Gladewater, TX St. Theresa of the Infant Jesus Church.
Paprocki, Thomas J. '78 (CHI) [58] Chicago, IL Five Holy Martyrs Church.
Paqueite, Francis '58 (DUL) Silver Bay, MN St. Mary's Church.
Paquet, Fernand *m.m.* '56 (FgM) Maryknoll Foreign Missions.
Paquet, Hubert J. '55 (PRT) Retired.
Paquet, Joseph A. *s.j.* '59 (BO) [W] Weston, MA Campion Health Center, Inc.
Paquet, Michael *o.s.c.* '78 (STP) Anoka, MN St. Stephen Church; [N] Anoka, MN Crosier Community of Anoka.
Paquet, Robert J. *s.j.* '45 (CHL) [9] Charlotte, NC St. Peter Church; [J] Charlotte, NC Jesuit Community.
Paquette, Francis (DUL) Retired.
Paquette, Joseph '78 (PRO) [12] Pawtucket, RI St. Teresa of the Child Jesus Church.
Paquette, Neil *o.c.s.o.* '94 (DUB) [K] Peosta, IA New Melleray Abbey, Order of Cistercians of the Strict Observance.
Paquin, Ronald (BO) Cambridge, MA Youville Lifecare, Inc.; [R] Cambridge, MA Youville Hospital & Rehabilitation Center, Inc.
Paquin, Ronald A. '73 (BO) Unassigned.
Paraday, Mark *o.p.* '83 (FgM) Dominican - Order of Preachers Foreign Missions.
Paraday, Mark R. *o.p.* '83 (CHI) [N] Chicago, IL Dominicans (Provincial Office).
Paradela, Michael R. '82 (NY) [199] Staten Island, NY Blessed Sacrament Church.
Parades, Edmundo '85 (DAL) [N] Dallas, TX Nuestra Senora del Pilar Land & Development Trust.
Paradis, Donald *m.s.* '58 (FR) [I] Attleboro, MA La Salette Shrine.
Paradis, Robert '37 (BO) [Z] Tewksbury, MA Immaculate Heart of Mary Infirmary.
Paradis, Roger *o.m.i.* '48 (FgM) Oblates Foreign Missions.
Paradis, Msgr. Wilfrid H. '49 (MAN) [11] Manchester, NH St. John the Baptist Church; Retired.
Paraguya, Felipe '68 (SAC) Fairfield, CA Holy Spirit Church.
Parambi, Thomas Seraphin *c.s.t.* '60 (NY) [177] Bronx, NY Our Lady of Solace Church.
Paramo, Raymond *c.s.b.* '66 (DET) [E] Redford, MI Catholic Central High School.
Paramo, Thomas *c.m.f.* '56 (CHI) [N] Oak Park, IL Claretian Fathers Headquarters of U.S.A. Eastern Province.
Parampath, Joseph K. '53 (BGP) Weston, CT St. Francis of Assisi Church.
Paraniuk, Michael '81 (CIN) [14] Cincinnati, OH St. Bernard Church; [K] Cincinnati, OH Mercy Health Plaza dba Mercy Franciscan Hospital-Mt. Airy.
Parappally, James '59 (MIA) [6] Pompano Beach, FL St. Gabriel Church; [L] Pompano Beach, FL Indian Catholic Association of Florida, Inc.
Paras, Virgil (AGN) Dededo, GU Santa Barbara Church.
Parayno, Martin *o.s.b.* '94 (SAT) [73] San Antonio, TX Santo Nino de Cebu Church.
Parchem, Peter *o.f.m.conv.* '51 (MRY) Pismo Beach, CA St. Paul the Apostle Church.
Parcheski, Anthony *c.s.s.* '48 (BO) [Z] Waltham, MA Stigmatine Fathers and Brothers.
Parcon, Jose M. '89 (NEW) [3] Jersey City, NJ St. Anne's Church.
Pardee, Charles D. '84 (JC) Columbia, MO St. Thomas More Newman Center, University of Missouri Church; [F] Columbia, MO University of Missouri-Columbia, Campus Ministry.
Pardon, Marek *s.v.d.* '91 (WH) Gary, WV Our Lady of Victory Church; Powhatan, WV Sacred Heart Church.
Pardue, John '88 (SHP) Many, LA St. John the Baptist Church.
Pare, Arthur H. *s.j.* '60 (BO) [W] Boston, MA The Society of Jesus of New England-Provincial Offices.
Pare, Arthur H. *s.j.* '60 (PRT) [9] Portland, ME St. Pius X Church.
Pare, Paul *o.f.m.* '00 (STP) [10] St. Paul, MN Sacred Heart Church.
Pare, Paul M. '53 (PRT) Retired.
Pare, Paul U. '52 (PRT) Retired.
Paredes, Edmundo '85 (DAL) [15] Dallas, TX St. Cecilia Church.
Paredes, Jorge '95 (ARE) [1] Arecibo, PR Cathedral of San Felipe Apostol.
Paredes, Miguel '94 (AUS) [25] Austin, TX San Francisco Church.
Pareja, Rene L. '81 (CHI) [204] Chicago, IL Transfiguration of Our Lord Church.
Parekkat, Winson *c.m.i.* '72 (PH) [158] Philadelphia, PA St. William Church.
Parekkatt, Joseph *s.d.b.* '74 (OAK) [3] Walnut Creek, CA St. Mary's Church.
Parel, Joseph '57 (HRT) Northford, CT St. Monica's Church.
Parella, Francis *s.s.p.* '47 (BUF) Eden, NY Immaculate

Conception Church.
Parella, Francis J. *s.s.p.* '47 (Y) [A] Canfield, OH Society of St. Paul.
Parello, Joseph J. '74 (SJN) On Duty Outside the Archdiocese.
Parent, Basil R. '86 (NTN) Danbury, CT St. Ann Church.
Parent, J. Wilfrid (WDC) [29] Washington, DC St. Mary, Mother of God Church.
Parent, J. Wilfrid '91 (WDC) Pastoral Center Special Ministries.
Parent, Lawrence *o.f.m.* '98 (NY) [DD] New York, NY Franciscan Province of the Immaculate Conception.
Parent, Norman *o.m.i.* (BO) [16] Lowell, MA Sacred Heart Church.
Parent, Philip *s.m.* '81 (BUR) Bradford, VT Our Lady of Perpetual Help Church.
Parent, Rene L. *m.s.* '76 (NOR) Jewett City, CT St. Mary Church.
Parent, Royal J. '56 (PRT) Retired.
Parente, Lino S. *o.cist.* '65 (TR) Mount Laurel, NJ St. John Neumann Church; [M] Mount Laurel, NJ Cistercian Monastery of Our Lady of Fatima.
Parente, Michael *s.a.c.* '47 (CAM) Hammonton, NJ St. Joseph's Church.
Parenteau, William J. '70 (TUC) Yuma, AZ St. John Neumann Church.
Parenti, Thomas M. '74 (SFR) [9] San Francisco, CA St. Brendan Church.
Parenza, John Anthony *c.p.* '50 (L) [L] Louisville, KY Sacred Heart Retreat.
Paret, John J. *s.j.* '51 (ALB) [N] Auriesville, NY Shrine of Our Lady of Martyrs.
Paretsky, Albert *o.p.* '81 (WDC) [B] Washington, DC Dominican House of Studies.
Parham, William J. '76 (MEM) Brownsville, TN St. John Church; Jackson, TN St. Mary's Church.
Pariante, Gregory J. '82 (PH) [62] Philadelphia, PA Holy Name of Jesus Church.
Parillo, Emery *o.f.m.* '55 (ALB) [3] Watervliet, NY Our Lady of Mt. Carmel Church.
Paris, Basil '98 (STN) [A] Eagle Harbor, MI Skete of Holy Transfiguration Monastery.
Paris, Benedetto '95 (MAR) Special Assignment.
Paris, Charles W. '55 (WIL) Retired.
Paris, John *s.j.* '69 (BO) [W] Chestnut Hill, MA The Jesuit Community at Boston College.
Paris, John U. '50 (BO) [4] Malden, MA St. Peter Church; [E] Needham, MA St. Sebastian's Country Day School, Inc.
Paris, Thomas *m.s.* '46 (FR) [I] Attleboro, MA La Salette Shrine.
Parise, Michael J. '79 (BO) Billerica, MA St. Andrew Church.
Parish, John G. '84 (R) [4] Durham, NC St. Matthew Church.
Parisi, Enrique *o.f.m.* '60 (LA) [73] Los Angeles, CA St. Joseph Church.
Parisi, Frank J. '85 (RVC) Smithtown, NY St. Patrick Church.
Parisi, Joseph L. '74 (STL) West Overland, MO St. Jude Church.
Parisi, Michael (PAT) Military Chaplains.
Parisi, Michael '55 (BRK) [189] Queens, NY St. Kevin Church.
Parisi, Michael R. (BRK) Retired.
Parisi, Salvador *o.f.m.* '54 (SFR) [5] San Francisco, CA St. Anthony of Padua Church.
Parizek, Msgr. James F. '72 (DAV) [M] Davenport, IA St. Vincent Center; [P] Davenport, IA Quad Cities Catholic Deaf Ministry.
Park, Msgr. Augustin C. '61 (NEW) [6] Orange, NJ St. Andrew Kim Church.
Park, Augustin Chang D. (NEW) [S] Orange, NJ Mee Joo Catholic Digest, Inc.
Park, Austin *s.j.* '55 (LKC) Kinder, LA St. Philip Neri Church.
Park, Benedict (KCK) Special Assignment.
Park, John Hee Dong '82 (NEW) Saddle Brook, NJ Korean Martyrs Church.
Park, Jung-Woo *s.j.* '91 (NY) [DD] New York, NY Jesuit Community at Fordham University.
Park, Morton '52 (P) [36] Portland, OR St. Stephen Church.
Park, Paul (BO) [7] Newton, MA St. Philip Neri Church.
Park, Robert G. '57 (WH) [1] Wheeling, WV St. Joseph's Church.
Park, Thaddeus '82 (NEW) [6] Orange, NJ St. Andrew Kim Church.
Park, Thomas R. *o.s.b.* '65 (SEA) Seattle, WA Veterans Administration Medical Center; [L] Lacey, WA St. Martin's Abbey.
Parke, Frederick '75 (STA) Bunnell, FL St. Stephen Church; Palm Coast, FL St. Elizabeth Ann Seton Church.
Parke, James E. '65 (RIC) [1] Virginia Beach, VA Church of the Ascension.
Parker, Adam '00 (BAL) Graduate Studies.
Parker, Carroll *o.m.i.* '61 (FgM) Oblates Foreign Missions.
Parker, Charles '71 (PHX) Special Assignment.
Parker, Edmond L '56 (BO) Acton, MA St. Elizabeth of Hungary Church.
Parker, Frank J. *s.j.* '73 (BO) [W] Chestnut Hill, MA The Jesuit Community at Boston College.
Parker, George H. '83 (NOR) Retired.
Parker, Glenn D. *c.ss.r.* '85 (STA) [6] Jacksonville, FL Holy Rosary Church.
Parker, James '82 (CHR) [15] Charleston, SC Church of the Holy Spirit.
Parker, John W. '70 (CHI) [11] Chicago, IL St. Andrew Church.
Parker, Kenneth '65 (R) Retired.
Parker, Larry (WCH) Erie, KS St. Ambrose Church; St. Paul, KS St. Francis Church.
Parker, Larry '84 (WCH) Chetopa, KS Sacred Heart Church; Oswego, KS Mother of God Church.
Parker, Michael '83 (BUF) [3] Dunkirk, NY St. Hyacinth Church.
Parker, Paul M. '82 (BO) [15] Boston, MA St. Catherine of Siena Church.
Parker, Rick '77 (OKL) Absent on Sick Leave.
Parker, Theodore K. *o.s.c.* '72 (NY) [4] New York, NY All Saints Church; [DD] New York, NY Crosier (Canons Regular of the Order of the Holy Cross).
Parker, Thomas Patrick '47 (BRK) [V] Kew Gardens, NY St. Columbans Foreign Mission Society.
Parker, William *c.ss.r.* '73 (OM) [19] Omaha, NE Holy Name Church.
Parker, William C. '64 (TOL) Walbridge, OH St. Jerome Church.
Parkerson, Paul M. '98 (R) Dunn, NC Sacred Heart Church.
Parkes, Bernard *s.d.b.* '74 (OAK) [N] Berkeley, CA Salesian Community.
Parkes, Gregory (ORL) [5] Orlando, FL Holy Family Church.
Parkes, Joseph P. *s.j.* '76 (NY) [F] New York, NY Fordham Preparatory School; [DD] New York, NY Jesuit Community at Fordham University.
Parkes, Stephen D. '98 (ORL) Altamonte Springs, FL Annunciation Church.
Parkinson, Todd '94 (RVC) Absent on Leave.
Parkos, John F. '64 (STP) North Branch, MN St. Gregory Church.
Parks, Jonathan *s.d.b.* '78 (NO) [4] Harvey, LA St. Rosalie Church.
Parks, Msgr. Joseph K. '39 (BRK) [115] Brooklyn, NY St. Patrick Church; Retired.
Parks, Richard *c.p.* '70 (CHI) [N] Chicago, IL Passionist Provincial Office.
Parks, Msgr. Richard E. '59 (BAL) [88] Baltimore, MD Sacred Heart of Mary Church.
Parks, Richard L. *c.p.* '70 (L) [L] Louisville, KY Sacred Heart Retreat.
Parle, Richard '56 (SEA) Lacey, WA Sacred Heart of Jesus Church.
Parlet, Stephen J. '97 (COS) [2] Colorado Springs, CO Corpus Christi Church.
Parlette, Thomas L. '89 (DAV) [3] Fort Madison, IA SS. Mary & Joseph Church.
Parme, George J. '48 (PIT) Retired.
Parmisano, Fabian *o.p.* '53 (OAK) [N] Oakland, CA Dominican Order (Western Province), St. Albert's Priory.
Parnassus, Msgr. George J. '53 (LA) West Hollywood, CA St. Victor Church.
Parnell, Dennis R. *s.j.* '93 (SJ) [B] Santa Clara, CA Santa Clara University.
Parnis, Emmanuel *m.s.s.p.* '85 (DET) [24] Detroit, MI St. Gabriel Church.
Paron, William J. '69 (STP) Carver, MN St. Nicholas Church.
Parr, Charles J. '73 (PAT) [2] Wayne, NJ Holy Cross Church.
Parr, John L. '78 (LC) [2] Wausau, WI Holy Name of Jesus Church; [6] Wausau, WI St. Matthew Church.
Parr, Norman B. '50 (OM) [36] Omaha, NE SS. Peter and Paul Church.
Parr, Raymond A. '39 (MIL) Retired.
Parra, Pedro *c.s.c.* '99 (FTW) [J] South Bend, IN Congregation of Holy Cross, Indiana Province, Provincial House.
Parrales, Napoleon J. '57 (SD) On Duty Outside the Diocese.
Parrinello, Frank P. '00 (OM) Norfolk, NE Sacred Heart Church.
Parrini, Warren '53 (RVC) Retired.
Parrish, Byran K. (BO) [3] Plymouth, MA St. Mary Church.
Parrish, Francis J. *s.j.* '42 (LA) [Q] Los Angeles, CA Columbiere House.
Parrotta, Arthur J. '50 (MAR) Retired.
Parry, Charles J. '81 (WDC) [2] Bowie, MD Sacred Heart Church; Pastoral Center Special Ministries.
Parsch, David L. '80 (SAG) Shields, MI Holy Spirit Church.
Parsieniczyk, Stanley '68 (BO) [4] Salem, MA St. John the Baptist Church.
Parson, Donald J. '90 (BAL) Oakland, MD St. Peter the Apostle Church.
Parsons, Harold J. '29 (NY) Retired.
Parsons, Harry E. '56 (PIT) Retired; [O] Pittsburgh, PA St. John Vianney Manor.
Parsons, LaSalle *o.f.m.cap.* '57 (FgM) Capuchin Foreign Missions.
Parsons, Neil J. *c.p.* '37 (SAC) [H] Citrus Heights, CA Christ the King Retreat.
Parsons, Samuel R. *o.p.* '57 (SFR) [14] San Francisco, CA St. Dominic Church; [N] San Francisco, CA St. Dominic Priory.
Partee, Chrysostom *o.f.m.* '50 (SFE) Jemez Pueblo, NM San Diego Indian Missions Church.
Partensky, Leonard J. '42 (DET) Retired.
Parthie, Ralph R. *o.f.m.* '75 (NO) [P] New Orleans, LA Franciscan Fraternity.
Partida, Rafael A. '86 (SB) Indio, CA Our Lady of Perpetual Help Church.
Partika, Richard (DUL) Retired.
Partridge, Bede *o.s.b.* '58 (P) [L] St. Benedict, OR Mt. Angel Abbey.
Partridge, Donald '90 (NY) [62] New York, NY St. Joseph Church.
Partridge, Francis C. '60 (GAY) Boyne City, MI St. Matthew Church; Boyne Falls, MI St. Augustine Church.
Partusch, Frank A. '72 (OM) [2] Omaha, NE St. Adalbert Church; [33] Omaha, NE Our Lady of Lourdes Church.
Parvensky, Msgr. Andrew D. '50 (PBR) Monessen, PA Assumption of the Blessed Virgin Church.
Parzymies, Joseph K. '77 (HRT) [6] Meriden, CT St. Stanislaus Church.
Pasadilla, Nicholas '72 (GAL) [54] Houston, TX Notre Dame Church.
Pasala, Anthony '96 (CHR) Garden City, SC St. Michael Church.
Pasalic, Nikola *o.f.m.* (CHI) [186] Chicago, IL Sacred Heart Church.
Pascale, Anthony '58 (HON) Retired.
Pascazi, Louis F. '80 (PIT) Coylesville, PA St. John Church.
Paschak, Patrick *o.s.b.m.* '47 (STF) New York, NY St. George Church.
Pasche, Fred *o.f.m.conv.* '64 (FTW) Angola, IN St. Anthony Church.
Pasciak, Marcel J. '74 (CHI) [194] Chicago, IL St. Symphorosa and Seven Sons Church.
Pasciuto, Joseph D. '91 (BRK) [23] Brooklyn, NY St. Brendan's Church.
Pascoe, Louis B. *s.j.* '64 (NY) [DD] New York, NY Jesuit Community at Fordham University.
Pascual, Antonio S. '60 (RVC) East Rockaway, NY St. Raymond's Church.
Pascual, Celestino V. (BO) [20] Boston, MA St. Francis de Sales Church.
Pascual, Celestino Vasquez (BO) Cambridge, MA Mount Auburn Hospital.
Pascual, Elias '51 (ARE) Ciales, PR Holy Rosary Church.
Pascual, Lope D. '82 (MET) [B] Raritan, NJ Shoreless Lake School; [H] New Village, NJ Society of Jesus Christ the Priest; [H] Raritan, NJ Clairvaux House.
Pascual, Manuel '46 (FRS) Retired.
Pascucci, Philip *s.d.b.* '51 (NY) [DD] New Rochelle, NY Salesian Provincial House.
Pasek, Timothy *o.f.m.conv.* '75 (BRK) [146] Queens, NY St. Adalbert Church.
Pash, Joseph '48 (SPK) Retired.
Pashak, Lawrence M. '63 (SAG) Freeland, MI St. Agnes Church.
Pashby, John J. '60 (BO) Society of St. James the Apostle.
Pashby, John J. '60 (FgM) Society of St. James the Apostle.
Pashley, Msgr. Wilfred J. '63 (PH) [19] Philadelphia, PA St. Barbara Church; [144] Philadelphia, PA St. Rose of Lima Church.
Pasieczny, Roman '80 (DET) [9] Warren, MI St. Martin de Porres Church.
Pasik, Mark A. '76 (SY) [5] Rome, NY Transfiguration Church.
Pasion, Lamberto *o.p.* '54 (WDC) [K] Silver Spring, MD Holy Cross Hospital of Silver Spring, Inc.
Paskert, Leonard *o.f.m.* '36 (STL) [T] Dittmer, MO Il Ritiro-The Little Retreat.
Paskey, Robert V. *s.j.* '66 (ANC) [G] Anchorage, AK Jesuit House.
Paskey, Robert V. *s.j.* '66 (BO) [W] Boston, MA The Society of Jesus of New England-Provincial Offices.
Paskowicz, Marian '54 (ALN) Retired.
Pasley, Robert '82 (CAM) [A] Haddonfield, NJ Paul VI High School.
Pasqualetto, Vicente *s.t.* '70 (SJN) [4] Canovanas, PR Santa Maria Madre de Dios Church.
Pasquinelli, Msgr. Frederick A. '52 (STU) Retired.
Pasquini, John J. '98 (PMB) North Palm Beach, FL St. Clare Church.
Passalacqua, Robert '83 (SJ) Campbell, CA St. Lucy Church; Retired.
Passamonte, Philip B. '67 (RVC) Absent on Leave.
Passamonti, Paul G. '95 (WDC) Military Chaplains.

Passant, Paul '98 (NEW) [1] Bayonne, NJ St. Mary Star of the Sea Church.
Passarella, Msgr. Anthony F. '42 (BRK) [11] Brooklyn, NY St. Anthony of Padua-St. Alphonsus Church; Retired.
Passarelli, Msgr. Robert S. '52 (BAL) Hagerstown, MD St. Mary Church; Retired.
Passauer, Gregory P. '86 (E) Curwensville, PA St. Timothy Church; Grampian, PA St. Bonaventure Church.
Passenant, Francis J. '79 (BRK) [78] Brooklyn, NY St. Margaret Mary Church; Released from Diocesan Assignment.
Passenant, Frank '79 (BRK) Brooklyn, NY Brooklyn House of Detention.
Passenant, Frank '79 (NY) City, NY West Facility.
Passeri, Richard *o.f.m.* '47 (FR) [I] Onset, MA St. Joseph Friary-Franciscan Friars.
Passero, Ernest F. *s.j.* (NOR) [5] Norwich, CT SS. Peter and Paul Church.
Pastick, Joseph A. (CHI) Retired.
Pastick, Joseph A. (SP) New Port Richey, FL Our Lady Queen of Peace Church.
Pastirik, Joachim *o.s.b.* '69 (CLV) [D] Cleveland, OH Benedictine High School; [O] Cleveland, OH Benedictine Order of Cleveland.
Pastizzo, Michael H. *s.j.* '70 (BUF) [O] Buffalo, NY Canisius Jesuit Community.
Pastor, Eduardo '50 (MIA) [27] Miami, FL St. Michael the Archangel Church.
Pastore, Peter J. '63 (CAM) Retired.
Pastors, Jerome (GB) [5] Green Bay, WI St. Bernard Church.
Pastro, Vincent '78 (SEA) [1] Tacoma, WA St. Ann Church; [3] Tacoma, WA St. John of the Woods Church; [12] Tacoma, WA Sacred Heart Church.
Paszko, John M. '74 (MIA) [3] Hialeah, FL St. Benedict Church.
Patala, William S. '56 (STU) Retired.
Patalano, Anthony M. *o.p.* '86 (LA) [60] Los Angeles, CA St. Dominic Church.
Patalinghug, Leo (BAL) [72] Baltimore, MD Our Lady of Mount Carmel Church.
Patat, St. John E. '42 (CHR) Retired.
Patella, Michael *o.s.b.* '90 (SCL) [I] Collegeville, MN St. John's Abbey, of the Order of St. Benedict.
Patenaude, Gilbert A. '46 (PRT) Retired.
Pater, Aurel '90 (ROM) Aurora, IL St. Michael Church.
Pater, Daniel R. '79 (CIN) On Duty Outside the Archdiocese.
Pater, Giles H. '58 (CIN) [44] Cincinnati, OH St. John Fisher Church.
Pater, Thomas G. '42 (CIN) Retired.
Pateraude, Andre A. *m.s.* '69 (FR) [I] Attleboro, MA La Salette Shrine.
Paterno, Salvatore (NY) Chester, NY St. Columba Church.
Paterno, Salvatore D. '64 (BRK) Released from Diocesan Assignment.
Paternoster, Alejandro M. '57 (LFT) Kokomo, IN St. Joan of Arc Church.
Pates, Msgr. Richard E. '68 (STP) Woodbury, MN Saint Ambrose of Woodbury Church.
Pathe, Eugene W. '56 (PT) Niceville, FL Holy Name of Jesus Church.
Pathikattil, Peter '74 (SP) [2] Clearwater, FL Light of Christ Church.
Pathiyamoola, Paul '70 (SFS) Eden, SD Sacred Heart Church.
Pathmarajah, Pius (ROC) Penfield, NY St. Joseph Church.
Patil, Gabriel M. *c.r.s.p.* '72 (ALN) [K] Bethlehem, PA The Barnabite Fathers Barnabite Spiritual Center.
Patillo, Bennie J. '67 (BEA) Port Neches, TX St. Elizabeth Church.
Patin, Lawrence *c.ss.r.* '63 (FgM) Redemptorist Foreign Missions.
Patin, Paul *s.j.* '73 (NO) [8] New Orleans, LA Holy Name of Jesus Church.
Patino, Bernardo Fuentes '94 (RCK) [5] Aurora, IL St. Nicholas Church.
Patino, Ruben *c.s.p.* '79 (AUS) [11] Austin, TX St. Austin Church; [M] Austin, TX University Catholic Center.
Patnode, Msgr. Michael '72 (CR) Bemidji, MN St. Philip's Church; [F] Bemidji, MN Holy Spirit Newman Center.
Patnode, Ronald J. '61 (YAK) Cle Elum, WA St. John the Baptist Church; Roslyn, WA Immaculate Conception Church.
Patout, Rivers A. '67 (GAL) [4] Houston, TX St. Alphonsus Church; Galena Park, TX Our Lady of Fatima Church.
Patras, Adam *o.s.b.* '94 (OM) [K] Schuyler, NE Benedictine Mission House.
Patricius, J. M. '57 (NEW) [8] Bayonne, NJ St. Michael's Church; Bayonne, NJ Bayonne Hospital.
Patrick, John E. '67 (MAR) [5] Marquette, MI St. Michael Church.
Patrick, Michael T. '83 (P) [27] Portland, OR St. Patrick Church.
Patrick, Richard Martin *o.p.* '65 (GAL) [Q] Houston, TX Dominican Fathers and Brothers, St. Mark Priory, Inc.
Patrick, William '57 (ORG) [G] Fullerton, CA St. Jude Medical Center.
Patrick, William J. '58 (CLV) Released from Diocesan Assignment.
Patriquin, Garry D. '84 (PIT) Absent on Sick Leave.
Patrizi, Vincent M. '52 (CC) [10] Corpus Christi, TX Our Lady Star of the Sea Church.
Patrizio, Anthony *m.ss.cc.* '66 (CAM) [M] Linwood, NJ Villa Pieta.
Patron, Charles '62 (SB) Barstow, CA St. Joseph Church.
Patron, Juan '73 (SJN) [E] San Juan, PR Centro Medico de P.R.
Patrylak, T. Frank '62 (PHU) [2] Philadelphia, PA Protection of Blessed Virgin Mary Church; Clifton Heights, PA SS. Peter and Paul Church.
Patte, Steven W. '69 (CHI) Indian Creek, IL St. Mary of Vernon Church.
Pattee, Daniel *t.o.r* '87 (STU) [A] Steubenville, OH Franciscan University of Steubenville; [F] Steubenville, OH Holy Spirit Friary.
Patten, Patrick A. *c.s.sp.* '78 (FgM) Holy Ghost Foreign Missions.
Patterson, Alfred *o.s.b.* '90 (E) St. Marys, PA St. Mary Church.
Patterson, Bernardin *o.s.b.* '53 (IND) [J] Indianapolis, IN St. Maur Priory.
Patterson, Bernardin J. *o.s.b.* '53 (NEW) [N] Newark, NJ Newark Abbey.
Patterson, Bruce '86 (ORG) [1] Huntington Beach, CA St. Bonaventure Church.
Patterson, Bryan '99 (BRK) [13] Brooklyn, NY St. Athanasius Church.
Patterson, Msgr. Charles '51 (JC) [D] Jefferson City, MO St. Joseph's Home.
Patterson, David L. '68 (ATL) On Duty Outside the Archdiocese.
Patterson, Frank '67 (SAV) [1] Columbus, GA Holy Family Church.
Patterson, James *c.ss.r.* '54 (STL) [P] Liguori, MO Liguori Mission House/Redemptorists.
Patterson, Patrick *c.pp.s.* '65 (COL) [23] Columbus, OH St. James-the-Less Church.
Patterson, Randall P. '70 (ALB) [9] Troy, NY Our Lady of Victory Church.
Patterson, Robert '58 (NEW) Scotch Plains, NJ Immaculate Heart of Mary Church.
Patterson, Robert A. '71 (STP) Hamel, MN St. Anne Church; Minneapolis, MN Minneapolis Children's Medical Center.
Patterson, Ronald '64 (LIN) Manley, NE St. Patrick's Church.
Patterson, Terrence R. '66 (OG) Retired.
Patterson, William C. '51 (COL) [I] Portsmouth, OH St. Joseph Adoration Monastery, Poor Clares of Perpetual Adoration.
Patti, Angelo J. '82 (ALT) Cresson, PA St. Francis Xavier Church.
Pattison, Msgr. Francis '58 (SD) [35] San Diego, CA St. Rita Church.
Patton, James J. '65 (CLV) Perry, OH St. Cyprian Church.
Patton, John (RVC) Bethpage, NY New Island Hospital.
Patton, John *c.ss.r.* '99 (RVC) Bethpage, NY St. Martin of Tours Church.
Patton, Mel *o.s.b.* '56 (IND) [J] St. Meinrad, IN St. Meinrad Archabbey.
Patton, Mel *o.s.b.* '56 (SFS) [G] Yankton, SD Sacred Heart Monastery.
Patton, Patrick G. '78 (HEL) Military Chaplains.
Paturzo, Louis S. '73 (HRT) [8] Hartford, CT St. Anne-Immaculate Conception Church; Suffield, CT Macdougall Correctional Institute.
Paul, Alexis *c.p.* (HRT) [M] West Hartford, CT Holy Family Monastery/Retreat.
Paul, Alexis *c.p.* '63 (HRT) [Q] West Hartford, CT Holy Family Retreat Center.
Paul, Bededict '78 (NY) [182] Bronx, NY SS. Philip and James Church.
Paul, David *s.m.* '70 (STL) [P] St. Louis, MO Provincialate of the Society of Mary, Province of St. Louis.
Paul, Dennis '93 (JOL) [16] Joliet, IL St. Mary Nativity Church.
Paul, Divya '91 (NY) Hartsdale, NY Sacred Heart Church.
Paul, Gerald *m.s.c.* '60 (FgM) Missionaries of the Sacred Heart Foreign Missions.
Paul, Gerald *m.s.c.* '60 (RCK) [G] Aurora, IL Missionaries of the Sacred Heart Community.
Paul, Gregory *c.p.* (NY) [FF] New York, NY Cardinal Spellman Retreat House.
Paul, Gregory '58 (NY) [DD] New York, NY Passionist Spiritual Center.
Paul, John *s.j.* '92 (ELP) [21] El Paso, TX Sacred Heart Church.
Paul, John J. *m.s.c.* '58 (ALN) [K] Reading, PA Missionaries of the Sacred Heart.
Paul, John M. *s.j.* '80 (STP) [B] St. Paul, MN Jesuit Novitiate.
Paul, John P. '72 (PH) [115] Philadelphia, PA Our Lady of Calvary Church; [D] Warminster, PA Archbishop Wood Catholic High School.
Paul, OH Young-min '75 (OAK) [8] Oakland, CA St. Cyril Church.
Paul, Raphael '87 (SFD) Brighton, IL St. Alphonsus Church; Medora, IL St. John the Evangelist Church.
Paul, Raymond F. '55 (HRT) [2] Ansonia, CT Holy Rosary Church; Retired.
Paul, Raymond L. '62 (Y) Massillon, OH St. Joseph's Church.
Paul, Thomas '77 (JOL) Downers Grove, IL St. Mary of Gostyn Church.
Paul, Msgr. William J. '63 (PH) Lower Makefield, PA St. John the Evangelist Church.
Paulicek, Louis '71 (AUS) Rogers, TX St. Matthew Church.
Paulin, George A. '70 (BUR) North Troy, VT St. Vincent de Paul Church.
Paulish, W. Jeffrey '88 (SCR) Friendsville, PA St. Francis Xavier's Church.
Paulissen, Richard E. *m.m.* '63 (GAL) [Q] Houston, TX Maryknoll Fathers and Brothers.
Paulissen, Richard E. *m.m.* '63 (NY) [DD] Maryknoll, NY Maryknoll Fathers and Brothers.
Paulits, Walter J. '72 (BAL) Pasadena, MD Our Lady of the Chesapeake Church; Retired.
Paulli, Kenneth *o.f.m.* '90 (ALB) [B] Loudonville, NY Siena College.
Paulose, Antony *c.m.i.* '97 (BEA) [1] Beaumont, TX St. Anthony Church.
Paulsen, Harold P. (TYL) Tennessee Colony, TX Michael Unit, Texas Department of Corrections.
Paulsen, Timothy *o.m.i.* '97 (BWN) [1] Mission, TX Our Lady of Guadalupe Church.
Paulshock, Emil '65 (PSC) Special or Other Diocesan Assignment.
Paulson, Brian G. *s.j.* '92 (CHI) [D] Chicago, IL St. Ignatius College Prep; [D] Chicago, IL St. Ignatius Jesuit Community.
Paulson, Jerry E. '61 (NU) Arlington, MN St. Mary Church.
Paulus, Donard *o.f.m.* '48 (GAY) Indian River, MI Cross in the Woods Catholic Church.
Pauly, William *s.j.* '79 (RC) Pine Ridge, SD Holy Rosary Church; [B] Pine Ridge, SD Jesuit Community of Holy Rosary Mission.
Paur, Roman *o.s.b.* '66 (SCL) [B] Collegeville, MN St. John's University; [I] Collegeville, MN St. John's Abbey, of the Order of St. Benedict.
Paurazas, Peter P. '55 (CHI) [179] Chicago, IL St. Rene Goupil Church; Retired.
Pausche, Frederick F. '57 (CLV) Concord Twp., OH St. Gabriel Church.
Pauselli, Francis L. '75 (SCR) South Williamsport, PA St. Lawrence's Church.
Pautler, Mark '74 (SPK) [14] Spokane, WA St. Joseph Church.
Pavela, Wayne S. '79 (OM) Humphrey, NE St. Francis Church.
Pavelis, Harold '51 (SCL) Retired.
Pavese, Paul J. *o.s.j.* '42 (SCR) [B] Pittston, PA St. Joseph's Oblate Seminary.
Pavia, Nicholas S. '00 (BGP) [3] Trumbull, CT St. Stephen Church.
Pavignano, Steven J. *o.f.m.* '78 (CHR) [3] Columbia, SC Saint Martin de Porres Church.
Pavis, Msgr. Victor C. '42 (NY) Retired; [E] New York, NY Cardinal Hayes High School.
Pavlac, Andrew *o.p.* (LFT) [H] West Lafayette, IN St. Thomas Aquinas Parish and Foundation for Catholic Students Attending Purdue University.
Pavlak, Andrew *o.p.* '00 (LFT) West Lafayette, IN St. Thomas Aquinas Church.
Pavlicek, Edward A., Jr. '83 (SAT) [29] San Antonio, TX St. Benedict Church.
Pavlicek, Louis '71 (AUS) Temple, TX St. Luke's Church.
Pavlick, Michael *s.m.* '53 (BO) [W] Boston, MA Marist Fathers Lourdes Residence; [BB] Boston, MA Chapel of Our Lady of Lourdes.
Pavlick, Raymond A. '71 (PAT) On Duty Outside the Diocese.
Pavlik, Albert *o.carm.* '61 (ALB) [5] Troy, NY St. Joseph Church.
Pavlik, David P. '78 (CHI) [184] Chicago, IL St. Roman Church.
Pavlik, James J. '63 (STL) Sullivan, MO Church of the Holy Martyrs of Japan.
Pavlik, John *o.f.m.cap.* '78 (PIT) [O] Pittsburgh, PA St. Augustine Friary.
Pavlik, Paul R. *t.o.r.* '59 (FgM) T.O.R. Foreign Missions.
Pavlina, Mark S. '75 (GRY) Dyer, IN St. Joseph Church.
Pavlock, Martin L. '66 (BUF) [2] Dunkirk, NY Holy Trinity Church.
Pavlosky, John J. '71 (ALN) Coaldale, PA SS. Cyril and Methodius Church; Coaldale, PA St. John the Baptist

Church; Coaldale, PA St. Mary of the Assumption Church.
Pavlovsky, Wencil C. *c.s.b.* '91 (GAL) Richmond, TX St. John Fisher Church.
Pavone, Frank A. '88 (NY) [HH] Staten Island, NY Priests for Life.
Pavur, Claude N. *s.j.* '84 (STL) [C] St. Louis, MO Saint Louis University; [P] St. Louis, MO Jesuit Community Corporation at St. Louis University - Jesuit Hall.
Pawelk, Steven P. *glmy.* '89 (JKS) New Albany, MS St. Francis of Assisi Church.
Pawell, Robert '66 (CHI) [N] Chicago, IL Holy Evangelists Friary.
Pawelski, John '50 (GB) Absent on Leave.
Pawlak, Ed '68 (AMA) Retired.
Pawlak, Edwin F. '68 (ORL) Retired.
Pawlicki, James *s.v.d.* '73 (BLX) [A] Bay St. Louis, MS St. Augustine's; [A] Bay St. Louis, MS St. Augustine's; [E] Bay St. Louis, MS Media Production Center "In A Word".
Pawlik, Walter M. *s.d.s.* '58 (GRY) [J] Merrillville, IN Salvatorian Fathers (Society of the Divine Savior).
Pawlikowski, John M. *o.s.m.* '67 (CHI) [17] Chicago, IL Assumption of the Blessed Virgin Mary Church; [B] Chicago, IL The Catholic Theological Union at Chicago; [N] Chicago, IL Order of Friar Servants of Mary (Servites) United States of America Province, Inc.
Pawlikowski, Matthew '97 (NEW) Military Chaplains.
Pawlos, John D. *s.m.* '59 (CIN) [M] Dayton, OH Marianist Provincialate.
Pawloski, Gregory P. '74 (LIN) Imperial, NE St. Patrick's Church.
Pawlowski, Dariusz '87 (TYL) Henderson, TX St. Jude Church.
Pawlowski, Joseph M. '73 (GRY) Valparaiso, IN St. Paul Church.
Pawson, Msgr. Robert J. '66 (BRK) [213] Queens, NY Our Lady of Lourdes Church.
Pax, Bart *o.f.m.* '68 (CIN) [U] Cincinnati, OH Community Support Charitable Trust.
Pax, Bart *o.f.m.* '68 (NO) [45] New Orleans, LA St. Mary of the Angels Church.
Pax, Joseph *c.pp.s.* '47 (CIN) [M] Dayton, OH Provincial Office of the Cincinnati Province of the Society of the Precious Blood; [N] Dayton, OH Sisters of the Precious Blood, Salem Heights Convent.
Pax, Maurus *o.f.m.* '50 (GLP) Grants, NM St. Teresa Church.
Pax, Raymond *m.c.c.j.* '65 (FgM) Comboni Foreign Missions.
Pax, Ulric *o.f.m.* '59 (GLP) [2] Gallup, NM St. Francis of Assisi Church.
Paxton, Philip *c.p.* '95 (BIR) [7] Birmingham, AL Holy Family Church.
Payant, Remi J. '38 (STP) Retired.
Payant, Romain *o.c.s.o.* '53 (P) [L] Lafayette, OR The Cistercian (Trappist) Abbey of Our Lady of Guadalupe.
Payea, Gerald *o.carm.* '69 (JOL) [J] Darien, IL Carmelite Provincial Office.
Payea, Gerald *o.carm.* '70 (FgM) Carmelite Foreign Missions.
Payer, Emil S. '71 (GBG) Kittanning, PA St. Mary, Our Lady of Guadalupe Church.
Payikat, Zacharias *c.m.i.* '70 (NSH) Lafayette, TN Holy Family Church; Lebanon, TN St. Frances Cabrini Church.
Payikat, Zachary *c.m.i.* '70 (NSH) [K] Liberty, TN Carmel Center of Spirituality.
Payne, Charles E. *o.f.m.* (CHI) [D] Chicago, IL Hales Franciscan High School, Inc.
Payne, Gary '85 (OWN) Absent on Leave.
Payne, John F. *o.s.a.* '89 (WDC) [B] Washington, DC Augustinian College, Order of St. Augustine.
Payne, John Michael *o.c.d.* '70 (OKL) [15] Oklahoma City, OK Our Lady of Mount Carmel and St. Therese Little Flower Church.
Payne, John T. *c.s.c.* '46 (AUS) [13] Austin, TX St. Ignatius Martyr Church.
Payne, Joseph *o.p.* '63 (NY) Pleasantville, NY Holy Innocents Church.
Payne, Mark *o.praem.* '94 (MIL) [4] Waukesha, WI St. William Church.
Payne, Mark M. *o.s.b.* '81 (NEW) [N] Newark, NJ Newark Abbey.
Payne, Stephen *o.c.d.* '82 (MIL) [P] Milwaukee, WI Provincial Offices - Discalced Carmelites.
Payne, Stephen J. '71 (GAL) Huntsville, TX St. Thomas the Apostle Church.
Payne, Thomas H. '50 (SAV) Retired.
Paynter, Clement *c.p.* '52 (FgM) Mission Procurators.
Payo, Reuben '84 (DEN) Conifer, CO Our Lady of The Pines Church.
Paysse, Wayne C. '87 (NO) [2] Slidell, LA St. Genevieve Church.
Payyappilli, Philip *c.m.i.* '59 (BEA) [5] Port Arthur, TX St. James Church.
Paz, Jose M. '52 (MIA) [27] Miami, FL St. Michael the Archangel Church.
Paz, Lorenzo (SB) Ontario, CA St. George Church.
Pazhayakari, Phillip *c.m.i.* '62 (SHP) Minden, LA St. Paul Church.
Pazmany, Geza *sch.p.* '61 (PH) [G] Devon, PA Devon Preparatory School; [AA] Devon, PA Piarist Fathers (Order of the Pious Schools).
Pazo, John T. '55 (RVC) Retired.
Peace, John '36 (SJ) Retired.
Peacha, Thomas '59 (LA) [15] Los Angeles, CA Holy Trinity Church.
Peacock, Francis A. '53 (PHX) [1] Phoenix, AZ SS. Simon and Jude Church; [7] Phoenix, AZ SS. Anthony and Pius X Church.
Peake, Msgr. Daniel A. '49 (NY) [A] Bronx, NY St. John Neumann Seminary Residence.
Pearce, Donald *s.j.* '59 (NO) [8] New Orleans, LA Holy Name of Jesus Church.
Pearce, John S. *c.m.* '57 (PH) [AA] Philadelphia, PA Congregation of the Mission.
Pearce, Joseph Francis *c.o.* '99 (CHR) [E] Rock Hill, SC Oratory of St. Philip Neri, Congregation of the Oratory of Pontifical Rite.
Pearsall, Ernest P. '37 (BO) Senior Priests.
Pearsall, William '53 (FgM) Society of St. James the Apostle.
Pearsall, William T. '37 (BO) Senior Priests.
Pearson, Everett '91 (WDC) [17] Washington, DC Holy Name Church.
Pearson, John A. '66 (NU) Lake Benton, MN St. Genevieve Church; Tyler, MN St. Dionysius Church.
Pearson, John H. *c.s.c.* '73 (FTW) [B] Notre Dame, IN University of Notre Dame Du Lac; [J] Notre Dame, IN Holy Cross Community, Corby Hall, University of Notre Dame.
Pearson, Msgr. Robert A. '65 (SPK) [9] Spokane, WA St. Augustine Church.
Pearson, Robert L. *o.c.s.o.* '60 (ATL) [J] Conyers, GA The Monastery of the Holy Spirit.
Pease, Joseph M. '61 (HBG) [1] Mount Carmel, PA Divine Redeemer Church.
Pease, Raymond A. *s.j.* '68 (FgM) Provinces.
Peatee, Gregory L. '92 (TOL) [3] Toledo, OH Christ the King Church.
Pecaric, Alfred F. '82 (BGP) [15] Stamford, CT Sacred Heart Church.
Pecchie, Paul '95 (SP) Valrico, FL St. Stephen Church.
Pecci, Ronald J. *o.f.m.* '83 (NEW) Fair Lawn, NJ St. Anne's Church.
Pecevich, Conrad S. '77 (WOR) [10] Worcester, MA Our Lady of Fatima Church; [Q] Worcester, MA Campus Ministry.
Pecharich, Michael '73 (ORG) Rancho Santa Margarita, CA San Francisco Solano Church.
Pecharroman, Ovidio '87 (ARL) Falls Church, VA St. Philip Church.
Pecht, Gerard J. *c.ss.r.* '50 (WCH) [F] Wichita, KS Redemptorist Community; [H] Wichita, KS Spiritual Life Center.
Pechulis, John B. *c.p.* '47 (CHI) [N] Chicago, IL Daneo Hall.
Pecinovsky, Albert '65 (KCK) Absent on Sick Leave.
Peck, David A. '94 (RCK) Rochelle, IL St. Patrick Church.
Peck, John D. *o.s.b.* '89 (HBG) Annville, PA St. Paul the Apostle Church; [K] Harrisburg, PA Catholic Campus Ministry.
Peck, Msgr. Leon J. '42 (PH) Warrington, PA St. Joseph Church; Retired.
Pecklers, Keith F. *s.j.* '91 (NY) [DD] New York, NY Jesuit Provincial's Office.
Peckman, R. William '97 (JC) Baring, MO St. Aloysius Church; Edina, MO St. Joseph Church.
Pecoraro, James A. '53 (KC) Retired.
Pecovnik, Karel '44 (SCL) Retired.
Pedata, Msgr. Armand A. '58 (TR) Marlton, NJ St. Joan of Arc Church.
Peddicord, Richard A. *o.p.* '86 (STL) [B] St. Louis, MO Aquinas Institute of Theology; [P] St. Louis, MO St. Dominic Priory.
Pedelesky, Nestor '67 (STN) Retired.
Pedi, Mario *o.s.b.* '57 (RCK) [1] Aurora, IL Annunciation of the Blessed Virgin Mary Church; [G] Aurora, IL Marmion Abbey-St. Augustine's Abbey.
Pedigo, Jon '91 (SJ) [1] San Jose, CA Cathedral Basilica of St. Joseph; [12] San Jose, CA St. John Vianney Church.
Pednekar, Joseph C. *m.s.f.s.* '62 (CLV) [62] Cleveland, OH St. Patrick Church.
Pedone, F. Stephen '78 (WOR) [23] Worcester, MA St. George Church.
Pedrano, Stephanos *o.s.b.* '91 (SD) [H] Oceanside, CA Prince of Peace Abbey, Benet Hill.
Pedretti, Raymond J. '56 (LC) Retired.
Pedretti, Robert F. '64 (LC) Amherst, WI St. James Church; Fancher, WI St. Mary of Mount Carmel Church.
Pedrizetti, Raymond *o.s.b.* '58 (SCL) [I] Collegeville, MN St. John's Abbey, of the Order of St. Benedict.
Pedrosa, Agustin *s.m.* '59 (NEW) West New York, NJ St. Joseph of the Palisades Church.
Pedrosa, Ramon, Jr. *o.s.a.* '78 (SB) Indio, CA Our Lady of Perpetual Help Church.
Pedroso, Rafael '64 (MIA) Retired.
Pedrotti, Frank L. *s.j.* '70 (STL) [P] St. Louis, MO Jesuit Community Corporation at St. Louis University - Jesuit Hall.
Pedroza, Salvador '81 (LAR) Carrizo Springs, TX Our Lady of Guadalupe Church.
Pedulla, John '93 (NY) [E] New York, NY Monsignor Farrell High School.
Peduti, Douglas F. *s.j.* '96 (WH) [A] Wheeling, WV Wheeling Jesuit University.
Pedzich, Henry J. '72 (SY) Onondaga Hill, NY St. Michael Church.
Pedzik, Vitalis B. '61 (RVC) Lindenhurst, NY Our Lady of Perpetual Help Church.
Peek, Kevin T. '98 (ATL) Peachtree City, GA Holy Trinity Catholic Church.
Peet, Msgr. Arthur V. '41 (STL) Retired.
Peeters, Ambrose J. *o.praem.* '53 (GB) [I] De Pere, WI St. Norbert Abbey.
Peeters, John N. *c.s.v.* '83 (JOL) Bourbonnais, IL Maternity of the Blessed Virgin Mary Church.
Peeters, R. Thomas '42 (GB) Retired.
Peffley, Francis J. '90 (ARL) Fredericksburg, VA St. Mary Church.
Pegnam, William '67 (SJ) [11] San Jose, CA St. Christopher Church.
Pegoraro, Germano *s.c.* '52 (LAN) [O] Grass Lake, MI The Pious Union of St. Joseph.
Peguero, Msgr. Lawrence '47 (GAL) Retired; [N] Houston, TX St. Dominic Village.
Pehl, Jeffrey '95 (SAT) Hondo, TX St. John the Evangelist Church.
Pehler, Gerald *o.f.m.cap.* '88 (DET) [P] Washington, MI Capuchin Retreat.
Pehrsson, Alfred R. *c.m.* '58 (ALB) [L] Albany, NY Vincentian Fathers Residence.
Peifer, Claude J. *o.s.b.* '52 (PEO) [A] Peru, IL St. Bede Abbey and Academy.
Peiffer, James E. '67 (TOL) Genoa, OH Our Lady of Lourdes Church; Oak Harbor, OH St. Boniface Church.
Peil, William '49 (FTW) Retired.
Peil, William L. '49 (GRY) Retired.
Peinado, Louis A. *s.j.* '60 (LA) [F] Los Angeles, CA Loyola High School of Los Angeles.
Peiris, Richard (OAK) Fremont, CA Washington Hospital.
Peixotto, Joseph S. *c.s.c.* '61 (FgM) Holy Cross Foreign Missions.
Peji, Rodel (CHI) [176] Chicago, IL Queen of All Saints Basilica Church.
Peji, Rodel '94 (RCK) Algonquin, IL St. Margaret Mary Church.
Pejza, John P. *o.s.a.* '61 (LA) [F] Ojai, CA Villanova Preparatory School.
Pekar, Athanasius B. *o.s.b.m.* '46 (RVC) [M] Glen Cove, NY St. Josaphat's Monastery, Novitiate and Retreat House.
Pekar, Athanasius B. *o.s.b.m.* '46 (STF) [B] Glen Cove, NY Basilian Fathers Novitiate of the Order of St. Basil the Great.
Pekar, Florian *c.p.* '40 (HRT) [M] West Hartford, CT Holy Family Monastery/Retreat.
Pekar, Msgr. Joseph W. '57 (BGP) [8] Bridgeport, CT SS. Cyril and Methodius Church.
Pekarsken, Daniel *s.d.s.* '90 (FgM) Salvatorian Foreign Missions.
Peklo, Edward *s.v.d.* '69 (CHI) [B] Techny, IL Divine Word Residence; [N] Chicago, IL Divine Word Theologate; [N] Techny, IL Society of the Divine Word, Provincial Headquarter-Chicago Prov.
Pekola, David J. '86 (MET) Hackettstown, NJ Assumption of the Blessed Virgin Mary Church.
Pelc, Timothy R. '74 (DET) Grosse Pointe Park, MI St. Ambrose Church.
Pelczar, Edward A. '62 (PH) [82] Philadelphia, PA St. Josaphat Church.
Pelczynski, Walter *m.i.c.* '42 (SPR) [J] Stockbridge, MA Congregation of Marians of The Immaculate Conception of the BVM.
Pelensky, Ihor '43 (STF) Retired.
Peles, David S. '84 (ALT) [23] Johnstown, PA St. Benedict's Church.
Pellegrini, Frederick J. '84 (SY) [A] Syracuse, NY Saint Andrew Hall.
Pellegrino, Francis B. '51 (SLC) [9] West Valley City, UT SS. Peter and Paul Church.
Pellegrino, Gerard *s.d.b.* '74 (SP) [E] Tampa, FL Mary Help of Christians School.
Pellegrino, Joseph A. *v.f.* '77 (SP) Tarpon Springs, FL St. Ignatius Church; [F] Tarpon Springs, FL St. Ignatius Early Childhood Center.
Pellerin, Keith A. '98 (LKC) Vinton, LA St. Joseph Church.
Pelleteri, Manuel J. *c.m.* '53 (CHI) [N] Chicago, IL DePaul Vincentian Residence.
Pelletier, Adrien O. *s.m.* '56 (BUR) White River Junction, VT St. Anthony Church; White River Junction, VT Veterans Administration Hospital.
Pelletier, Clement L. *s.j.* '62 (BO) [E] Boston, MA

Boston College High School & Jesuit Community.
Pelletier, Edgar A. '47 (WOR) Retired.
Pelletier, Emile "Bud" '94 (PHX) Cottonwood, AZ Immaculate Conception Church.
Pelletier, Eugene J. '53 (MAN) Retired.
Pelletier, George C. '79 (PRT) Richmond, ME St. Ambrose Church.
Pelletier, Gerard *s.m.* (HRT) Hartford, CT Hartford Hospital.
Pelletier, Gerard G. *s.m.* '51 (BRK) [45] Brooklyn, NY St. Francis of Assisi-St. Blaise Church.
Pelletier, Leonard E. '69 (BO) [7] Lowell, MA St. Louis de France Church.
Pelletier, Rosaire *o.p.* '50 (PRT) [I] Lewiston, ME SS. Peter and Paul House.
Pelletier, Walter R. *s.j.* '60 (BGP) [E] Fairfield, CT Fairfield College Preparatory School; [P] Fairfield, CT The Fairfield Jesuit Community-Fairfield University.
Pelletieri, Joseph *c.ss.r.* '65 (BR) [H] Baton Rouge, LA The Redemptorist Education and Formation.
Pellettieri, Joseph F. *c.ss.r.* '65 (ALX) Deville, LA St. John the Baptist Church.
Pellicane, Albert *c.p.* '56 (BRK) [V] Jamaica, NY Immaculate Conception Monastery.
Pellicane, Albert *c.p.* '56 (NY) [DD] New York, NY Pope Paul VI Residence.
Pellini, Robert R. *m.m.* '59 (FgM) Maryknoll Foreign Missions.
Peloso, Alex *c.s.* '39 (CHI) [119] Chicago, IL Santa Maria Addolorata Church.
Peloso, John '96 (MIA) [26] Miami, FL St. Louis Church.
Pelotte, Dana G. *s.s.s.* (GB) Menasha, WI St. Mary Church.
Pelous, Donald '98 (LAF) Catahoula, LA St. Rita Church.
Pelton, Robert S. *c.s.c.* '49 (FTW) [B] Notre Dame, IN University of Notre Dame Du Lac; [J] South Bend, IN Congregation of Holy Cross, Indiana Province, Provincial House.
Pelton, Robert S. *c.s.c.* '73 (FTW) [J] Notre Dame, IN Holy Cross Community, Corby Hall, University of Notre Dame.
Pelton, Thomas '66 (CHI) [130] Chicago, IL Maternity of the Blessed Virgin Mary Church.
Peltz, Carl F. '77 (KAL) Parchment, MI St. Ambrose Church.
Peltz, Carl F. '77 (STU) Absent on Leave.
Peltzer, Michael '80 (WCH) Harper, KS St. Joan of Arc Church.
Peluse, Dominic A. *s.c.j.* '74 (GAL) [21] Houston, TX Christ the Redeemer Church.
Peluso, Francis E. *o.a.r.* '61 (NY) [154] Bronx, NY St. John's Church; [FF] Bronx, NY St. Joseph's Center; [HH] Bronx, NY St. Joseph's Center.
Peluso, Michael J. '58 (NY) Absent on Leave.
Pemberton, Joseph '77 (FWT) [3] Fort Worth, TX Holy Family Church.
Pena, Juan Pablo '00 (GAL) [5] Houston, TX St. Ambrose Church.
Pena, Raymundo J. '57 (BWN) [C] Brownsville, TX Catholic Charities; [D] San Juan, TX San Juan Nursing Home.
Pena, Richard '92 (SAT) [3] San Antonio, TX Christ the King Church; [U] San Antonio, TX Archdiocesan Union of Holy Name Societies.
Pena, Roberto *o.m.i.* '55 (GAL) [16] Houston, TX Blessed Sacrament Church.
Pena, Vincente M. *o.p.* '36 (SAT) [26] San Antonio, TX St. Ann Church; [B] San Antonio, TX Dominican Priory of San Juan Macias.
Penafiel, Fausto '83 (PHX) [1] Glendale, AZ Our Lady of Perpetual Help Church.
Penalba, Vicente *c.m.f.* '69 (SJN) [23] Bayamon, PR Santa Maria Church.
Penaloza, Jorge '60 (LA) Pico Rivera, CA St. Francis Xavier Church.
Penaloza, Luis '99 (SR) Petaluma, CA St. Vincent de Paul Church.
Penchi, Edward J. '56 (LC) Retired.
Pendergast, Richard J. *s.j.* '63 (NY) [DD] New York, NY Murray-Weigel Hall.
Penderghest, William *ss.cc.* '67 (FR) Fairhaven, MA St. Joseph's Church.
Pendergraft, W. Michael '81 (STA) Live Oak, FL St. Francis Xavier Church.
Pendleton, Arthur J. *o.s.b.* '64 (CHL) [J] Belmont, NC Belmont Abbey.
Pendolphi, Richard J. '76 (COL) Logan, OH St. John Church.
Pendzick, John S. '97 (ALN) [5] Reading, PA Holy Guardian Angels Church; [O] Allentown, PA The Newman Center.
Penebsky, John P. '65 (SFR) Foster City, CA St. Luke Church; [T] San Francisco, CA Catholics for Truth & Justice.
Peng, John B. (CHI) Retired.
Penhallurick, Robert '96 (COL) [37] Columbus, OH St. Peter Church.
Penkala, Msgr. Edmund S. '45 (SCR) Retired; [N] Dunmore, PA Villa St. Joseph.
Penko, Francis G. '60 (SD) [3] El Cajon, CA St. Kieran Church.
Penn, Michael A. '54 (SCR) [3] Scranton, PA St. Anthony of Padua Church.
Penn, William '97 (VEN) Port Charlotte, FL St. Charles Borromeo Church.
Penn, William J. '97 (VEN) [3] Naples, FL St. Peter the Apostle Church.
Penna, Anthony *c.s.s.* '75 (BO) [W] Waltham, MA Stigmatine House.
Penna, Msgr. Joseph P. '67 (NY) Pearl River, NY St. Aedan Church.
Penna, Michael Della *o.f.m.* '99 (NY) [DD] New York, NY Franciscan Province of the Immaculate Conception.
Pennett, Frederick J. '71 (MAN) Hampstead, NH St. Anne Church.
Pennington, John F. *s.j.* '70 (CHI) Chicago, IL Cook County Hospital; [N] Chicago, IL Chicago Province of the Society of Jesus-Provincial Office.
Pennington, John R. '79 (WDC) Waldorf, MD St. Peter Church.
Pennington, M. Basil *o.c.s.o.* '57 (WOR) [R] Spencer, MA Cistercian Publications, Inc.
Pennington, Matthew '88 (MRY) Scotts Valley, CA San Agustin Church.
Pennisi, Celestine *o.f.m.* '52 (NY) [DD] New York, NY Franciscan Province of the Immaculate Conception.
Pennisi, Ignatius F. *s.j.* '43 (BO) [E] Boston, MA Boston College High School & Jesuit Community.
Pennock, Michael '95 (JOL) Addison, IL St. Joseph Church; Bolingbrook, IL St. Francis of Assisi Church.
Penonzek, Edward M. *o.s.m.* '58 (CHI) [N] Chicago, IL Order of Friar Servants of Mary (Servites) United States of America Province, Inc.
Penonzek, Edward M. *o.s.m.* '58 (ORG) [D] Anaheim, CA Servite High School; Servite High School Development Fund; [I] Anaheim, CA Servite Fathers and Brothers; [I] Buena Park, CA Order of Friar Servants of Mary (Servites).
Penta, Leo J. '78 (BRK) Released from Diocesan Assignment.
Pentareddy, Ghana R. '96 (ROC) Ithaca, NY Immaculate Conception Church.
Pentecost, Denver B. '69 (NO) [1] Marrero, LA Immaculate Conception Church; Marrero, LA West Jefferson General Hospital; Marrero, LA Wynhoven Health Care Center.
Pentello, Richard J. '79 (Y) Garrettsville, OH St. Ambrose Church.
Pentis, William F. *c.o.* '66 (CHR) Rock Hill, SC St. Anne's Church; [E] Rock Hill, SC Oratory of St. Philip Neri, Congregation of the Oratory of Pontifical Rite.
Pentony, Liam '55 (JKS) Retired.
Penunuri, Umberto '72 (SAC) Fairfield, CA Holy Spirit Church.
Penzes, Lawrence M. '78 (RVC) Lynbrook, NY Our Lady of Peace Church.
Peoples, J. Eugene '66 (HEL) [B] Helena, MT Carroll College.
Pepe, Msgr. Joseph A. '70 (PH) On Duty Outside the Archdiocese.
Pepe, Mario P. '56 (HRT) Marlborough, CT St. John Fisher Church.
Pepe, Robert F. '50 (WCH) Retired.
Pepel, Clement '82 (MET) On Duty Outside the Diocese.
Pepin, Darryl J. '78 (MAR) Ironwood, MI Our Lady of Peace Church.
Pepin, Normand A. *s.j.* '63 (BO) [W] Boston, MA The Society of Jesus of New England-Provincial Offices.
Pepin, Normand A. *s.j.* '63 (FBK) [A] Fairbanks, AK Monroe Catholic Junior-Senior High School; [C] Fairbanks, AK Jesuit Residence; [E] Fairbanks, AK House of Prayer.
Pepka, Edward *a.a.* '77 (BO) [W] Boston, MA Assumptionist Center.
Pepka, Edward '78 (SAC) Colusa, CA Our Lady of Lourdes Church.
Peplansky, Joseph *c.m.f.* '60 (SPC) [4] Springfield, MO Sacred Heart Church; [E] Springfield, MO Claretians Missionaries' Residence-Villa Claret.
Pepowski, Bert '61 (GRY) [J] Cedar Lake, IN Our Lady of Lourdes Friary.
Peppard, Patrick F. *s.j.* '73 (CLV) [D] Cuyahoga Falls, OH Walsh Jesuit High School.
Pepper, David J. '58 (DUB) Retired.
Pera, Sylvano *o.f.m.* '52 (LR) McGehee, AR St. Mary Church.
Perales, Jorge I. '78 (MIA) [22] Miami, FL St. John Bosco Church.
Perata, Stephen F. '58 (SJ) [25] San Jose, CA St. Victor Church.
Percic, Janez *s.j.* '94 (WDC) [M] Washington, DC The Jesuit Community at Georgetown University.
Percy, Anthony G. '90 (ARL) McLean, VA St. John's Church.
Perdue, John *m.ss.cc.* '90 (CAM) Linwood, NJ Our Lady of Sorrows Church.
Perea, Don '98 (SEA) Olympia, WA St. Michael Church.
Perea, Michael U. *o.praem.* '90 (LA) [C] Santa Paula, CA Thomas Aquinas College.
Perea, Michael U. *o.praem.* '90 (ORG) [I] Silverado, CA Norbertine Fathers of Orange Inc.
Pereda, James *c.r.c.* (BRK) [W] Queens Village, NY St. Ann's Novitiate, Little Sisters of the Poor.
Pereira, Albert F. '40 (RIC) Retired.
Pereira, Alexander (RIC) [1] Richmond, VA Cathedral of the Sacred Heart.
Pereira, Anthony '82 (SJ) [3] Sunnyvale, CA St. Martin Church.
Pereira, Cyril F. '54 (ALB) [10] Troy, NY St. Patrick Church; Special Assignment.
Pereira, Luciano J. '54 (FR) Retired.
Pereira, Manuel *m.s.* '95 (FR) [I] Attleboro, MA La Salette Shrine.
Pereira, Robert J. '62 (STO) On Special or Other Diocesan Assignment.
Perera, D. Stanislaus '91 (TYL) Carthage, TX St. William of Vercelli Church.
Perera, Denzil M. '58 (NO) [19] New Orleans, LA Our Lady of The Rosary Church; Retired.
Perera, Don Felix '66 (PHX) Grand Canyon, AZ El Cristo Rey Church.
Perera, F.N. Gamini *s.j.* '88 (CHI) [N] Chicago, IL Chicago Province of the Society of Jesus-Provincial Office.
Perera, John Bosco '69 (FTW) [1] Fort Wayne, IN Cathedral of the Immaculate Conception.
Perera, Milroy (NOR) Stonington, CT St. Mary Church.
Perera, Paul (ELP) Retired.
Perera, S. Nicholas '85 (TYL) Madisonville, TX St. Elizabeth Ann Seton Church.
Peres, Mark R. *c.pp.s.* '85 (LFT) Rensselaer, IN St. Augustine Church.
Peretti, Peter L. '73 (GBG) Leisenring, PA St. Vincent de Paul Church.
Perez, Anthony R. *s.s.* (BAL) [A] Emmitsburg, MD Mount St. Mary's Seminary.
Perez, Anthony R. *s.s.* '77 (BAL) [A] Baltimore, MD St. Mary's Seminary and University.
Perez, Antonio '77 (AGN) On Duty Outside the Archdiocese.
Perez, Armando '62 (MIA) [3] Fort Lauderdale, FL Our Lady Queen of Martyrs Church.
Perez, Arturo (CHI) [J] Chicago, IL Holy Cross Hospital.
Perez, Aurelio '86 (MIL) [2] Waukesha, WI St. Joseph Church.
Perez, Boris Espinoza '78 (CGS) Las Piedras, PR Inmaculada Concepcion Church.
Perez, Carlos (NY) [31] New York, NY St. Elizabeth Church.
Perez, Carlos '60 (MIA) [2] Hialeah, FL San Lazaro Church.
Perez, Carlos A. '92 (B) Aberdeen, ID Presentation of the Lord Church.
Perez, Daniel G. (LA) Valinda, CA St. Martha Church.
Perez, Eduardo '95 (STO) Modesto, CA St. Stanislaus Church.
Perez, Eleazar (MIL) [8] Milwaukee, WI St. Anthony Church.
Perez, Enrique '61 (SAC) [4] Sacramento, CA Immaculate Conception Church.
Perez, Enrique A. '71 (ARE) [14] Arecibo, PR Santisimo Sacramento Church.
Perez, Ernesto '71 (CC) [8] Corpus Christi, TX Our Lady of Perpetual Help Church.
Perez, Francisco '00 (AMA) Pampa, TX St. Vincent de Paul Church.
Perez, Gabino '51 (ORG) [5] Santa Ana, CA Our Lady of the Pillar Church.
Perez, Hector R.G. '81 (PT) [14] Pensacola, FL St. Stephen Church.
Perez, Henry '73 (ORG) Inactive Leave.
Perez, Isidro '81 (MIA) [4] Hialeah, FL St. Cecilia Church.
Perez, Javier H. '93 (TUC) Somerton, AZ Immaculate Heart of Mary Church.
Perez, Jesse L. '74 (PBL) [3] Pueblo, CO Holy Family Church.
Perez, John Mary *s.o.l.t.* '00 (CC) Robstown, TX St. Anthony Church; [H] Robstown, TX Society of Our Lady of the Most Holy Trinity.
Perez, Jose '64 (COL) [13] Columbus, OH Santa Cruz Church.
Perez, Jose M. '99 (BRK) [184] Queens, NY St. Joan of Arc Church.
Perez, Joseph '69 (GAL) On Duty Outside the Diocese.
Perez, Juan '98 (SAC) Colusa, CA Our Lady of Lourdes Church; Marysville, CA St. Joseph Church.
Perez, Juan Antonio *o.ss.t.* (CC) [2] Corpus Christi, TX Christ the King Church.
Perez, Leon '60 (ARE) Barceloneta, PR Our Lady of Victory Church.
Perez, Leopoldo G. *o.m.i.* '84 (SAT) [C] San Antonio, TX Oblate School of Theology; [M] San Antonio, TX De Mazenod House.
Perez, Luis '95 (MIA) [12] Miami, FL Our Lady of the Holy Rosary Church.

Perez, Modesto '84 (LA) [5] Los Angeles, CA Assumption Church.
Perez, Moises *c.s.c.* '98 (FTW) [J] South Bend, IN Congregation of Holy Cross, Indiana Province, Provincial House.
Perez, Msgr. Nelson J. (PH) [95] Philadelphia, PA St. Martin of Tours Church.
Perez, Nicholas *o.f.m.* '49 (AMA) Hereford, TX San Jose Church.
Perez, Ovidio Perez '00 (ARE) Corozal, PR Holy Family Church.
Perez, Pedro Luis '52 (MIA) [2] Hialeah, FL San Lazaro Church.
Perez, Rafael *o.s.b.* '79 (CGS) [C] Humacao, PR San Antonio Abad Abbey of the Order of St. Benedict.
Perez, Raul '86 (SAV) Cordele, GA St. Theresa Church.
Perez, Raymond '88 (LA) Hawthorne, CA St. Joseph Church.
Perez, Raymond L. *o.praem.* '88 (ORG) [I] Silverado, CA Norbertine Fathers of Orange Inc.
Perez, Restituto *o.p.* '60 (MIA) [18] Miami, FL St. Dominic Church; [H] Miami, FL Dominican Fathers of Miami, Inc.
Perez, Robert R. '86 (CHI) [175] Chicago, IL Providence of God Church.
Perez, Sacramento *o.de.m.* '72 (SB) Ontario, CA Our Lady of Guadalupe Church.
Perez, Salvador '61 (FWT) Retired.
Perez, Santos *o.f.m.* (ELP) [B] El Paso, TX St. Anthony's School of Theology.
Perez, Urian '97 (MGZ) Aguadilla, PR St. Charles Borromeo Church.
Perez, Victor *o.p.* '59 (SJN) [3] Bayamon, PR Catalina de Siena Church.
Perez, Victor '75 (P) [3] Eugene, OR St. Mary Church.
Perez, Viktor *o.f.m.conv.* '89 (RNO) [1] Reno, NV St. Thomas Aquinas Church.
Perez, William A. *o.s.a.* '62 (TLS) [B] Tulsa, OK Cascia Hall Preparatory School.
Perez Gonzalez, Osualdo *c.s.sp.* (SJN) [C] Bayamon, PR Seminario Misionero del Espiritu Santo.
Perez Munoz, Jaime *o.f.m.cap.* '85 (SJN) [D] Rio Piedras, PR Centro Capuchino.
Perez-Lerena, Francisco *s.j.* '58 (MIA) [D] Miami, FL Belen Jesuit Preparatory School; [H] Miami, FL Villa Javier.
Perez-Pupo, Joaquin '76 (MIA) [8] Miami, FL Mother of Christ Church.
Perez-Recio, Jesus *o.a.r.* '68 (LSC) La Mesa, NM San Jose Church.
Perez-Vasquez, Juan De La Cruz '96 (SJN) [6] Toa Alta, PR San Judas Tadeo Church.
Perfetto, Richard A. '66 (DET) Canton, MI Resurrection Church.
Pergher, Domingos *c.s.* (BO) [2] Somerville, MA St. Anthony Church.
Pergjini, Nikolin '99 (NY) [174] Bronx, NY Our Lady of Mt. Carmel Church.
Pergl, James F. *c.s.sp.* '44 (PIT) [Q] Bethel Park, PA Holy Ghost Animation Center.
Perham, Arnold E. *c.s.v.* '56 (CHI) [D] Arlington Heights, IL St. Viator High School.
Peri, Paul '71 (P) Wilsonville, OR St. Cyril Church.
Pericone, Nicholas P. '96 (NO) Chalmette, LA St. Mark Church.
Peridans, Dominique *f.j.* (LAR) [G] Laredo, TX Holy Spirit Retreat and Conference Center.
Peridans, Dominique F. *f.j.* '96 (CC) [G] Laredo, TX Holy Spirit Retreat and Conference Center; [H] Laredo, TX St. John's Priory, (F.J.).
Peridans, Dominique F., F.J. (LAR) [E] Laredo, TX St. John Priory, F.J.
Peries, Angelito *c.ss.r.* '74 (SR) Windsor, CA Our Lady of Guadalupe Church.
Peries, Ignatius *c.h.s.* '79 (NY) [DD] New York, NY Apostolic Society of the Crusade of the Holy Spirit.
Perillo, Christopher G. '97 (BO) Absent on Leave.
Perin, Glen W. '53 (CIN) Retired.
Perin, Isidro *m.s.* '67 (STL) [P] St. Louis, MO La Salette Missionaries.
Perini, Msgr. Armando J. '56 (MET) Edison, NJ St. Helena Church.
Perino, John M. '79 (NO) Ama, LA St. Mark Church.
Perjak, Edmond J. '67 (BEL) Retired.
Perkin, David R. '78 (NSH) [1] Nashville, TN Cathedral of the Incarnation; On Special or Other Diocesan Assignment; [L] Nashville, TN Diocesan Council of Catholic Women; [L] Nashville, TN Diocesan Properties, Inc. dba Marina Manor East Apartments.
Perkins, Bernard *o.c.d.* '82 (TUC) [18] Tucson, AZ St. Margaret's Church; [F] Tucson, AZ Discalced Carmelite Friars of St. Margaret's.
Perkins, Charles J. '78 (HT) Amelia, LA St. Andrew Church.
Perkins, Dennis M. '95 (NOR) Pawcatuck, CT St. Michael Church.
Perkins, Joseph F. '68 (WDC) [7] Silver Spring, MD St. John the Evangelist Church.
Perkins, Msgr. Robert M. '71 (RIC) Colonial Heights, VA St. Ann Church.
Perkins, Russell H. '58 (WIL) Retired.
Perkinton, John J. '85 (LIN) [F] Waverly, NE Our Lady of Good Counsel Retreat House; [I] Lincoln, NE Villa Marie School and Home for the Educable Mentally Handicapped.
Perkl, James '84 (STP) [C] St. Paul, MN University of St. Thomas.
Perkl, James M. '84 (STP) [A] St. Paul, MN St. John Vianney Seminary.
Perko, F. Michael *s.j.* '75 (CHI) [N] Evanston, IL Canisius House.
Perkovic, Anton '46 (NO) Retired.
Perkovich, Frank '54 (DUL) Biwabik, MN St. John's Church; Gilbert, MN St. Joseph's Church.
Perl, Richard D. *s.j.* '78 (FgM) Provinces.
Perlinski, Daniel A. '57 (TLS) Retired.
Perlite, John J. *s.j.* '49 (PHX) [B] Phoenix, AZ Brophy College Preparatory.
Perlite, Paul A. '46 (SFR) Fairfax, CA St. Rita Church; Retired.
Perluzzi, James *o.f.m.* '65 (FgM) Franciscan Foreign Missions.
Perluzzi, James *o.f.m.* '65 (STL) [P] St. Louis, MO Franciscan Friary of St. Anthony of Padua.
Pernia, Msgr. John R. '58 (SFR) Daly City, CA Our Lady of Perpetual Help Church.
Perno, Gerald D. (BO) [67] Boston, MA St. Thomas Aquinas Church.
Perozich, Richard L. '92 (SD) [16] San Diego, CA Our Lady of the Sacred Heart Church.
Perras, Delfin '83 (RVC) Melville, NY St. Elizabeth Church.
Perreault, Joseph A. '75 (CAM) Brigantine, NJ St. Thomas Church; [A] Absecon, NJ Holy Spirit High School.
Perreault, Leonard J. '54 (SPR) Retired.
Perret, Gary *m.s.f.* '76 (SAT) [M] San Antonio, TX MSF Center & Provincialate.
Perretta, Andrew T. '75 (PAT) [1] Clifton, NJ Sacred Heart Church.
Perricone, Charles A. '74 (PAT) Sussex, NJ St. Monica Church.
Perricone, John A. '75 (NY) [2] New York, NY St. Agnes Church.
Perricone, John A. '76 (NEW) On Duty Outside the Archdiocese.
Perriello, Robert A. '76 (WH) Clarksburg, WV St. James Church.
Perrier, Martin '88 (RNO) Leave of Absence.
Perrier, Monroe *c.ss.r.* '58 (SAT) [37] San Antonio, TX St. Gerard Majella Church; [B] San Antonio, TX Redemptorist Formation Program.
Perrier, Thomas E. *o.s.b.* '80 (NO) [P] St. Benedict, LA St. Joseph Abbey; [R] St. Benedict, LA Abbey Christian Life Center.
Perrin, Thomas *s.d.s.* '97 (NSH) Cookeville, TN St. Thomas Aquinas Church.
Perrins, Samuel T. '86 (SCR) Carbondale, PA St. Rose of Lima Church.
Perron, Gary *a.a.* '66 (BO) [W] Boston, MA Assumptionist Center.
Perron, Richard J. '46 (BO) Senior Priests.
Perron, Robert P. '81 (PRO) [1] Central Falls, RI The Holy Spirit Catholic Community Church.
Perrone, Eduard '78 (DET) [10] Detroit, MI Assumption Grotto Church.
Perry, Carmen J. '77 (SCR) Stroudsburg, PA St. Luke's Church.
Perry, Drew '98 (R) Burgaw, NC St. Joseph Church.
Perry, Francis J. '50 (DUB) Retired.
Perry, Msgr. John A. '63 (FR) Falmouth, MA St. Patrick's Church.
Perry, John J. '83 (FR) [17] Fall River, MA St. Joseph's Church.
Perry, Joseph N. (CHI) [168] Chicago, IL St. Philip Neri Church.
Perry, Killian *t.o.r.* '74 (ORL) [2] Lakeland, FL St. Anthony's Church.
Perry, Michael (BRK) [109] Brooklyn, NY Our Lady of Refuge Church.
Perry, Michael E. *o.de.m.* (SP) [O] St. Petersburg, FL St. Peter Nolasco Residence.
Perry, Paul E. '67 (SFR) Greenbrae, CA St. Sebastian Church.
Perry, Richard D. *s.j.* '70 (SEA) [L] Seattle, WA Jesuit Community.
Perry, Robert U. *o.p.* '59 (BR) Hammond, LA Holy Ghost Church; Tickfaw, LA Our Lady of Pompeii Church.
Perry, Ronald V. *s.j.* '76 (BGP) [E] Fairfield, CT Fairfield College Preparatory School; [P] Fairfield, CT The Fairfield Jesuit Community-Fairfield University.
Perryman, John E. '45 (CIN) Retired.
Persac, Louis A. '47 (NO) Gretna, LA St. Anthony Church; Retired.
Persha, Gerald J. *m.m.* '70 (FgM) Maryknoll Foreign Missions.
Pershe, Joseph N. *s.j.* (STP) Minneapolis, MN University of Minnesota Hospitals.
Pershe, Joseph N. *s.j.* '66 (STP) [N] Minneapolis, MN La Storta Jesuit Community.
Persia, William *c.s.c.* '62 (FgM) Holy Cross Foreign Missions.
Persich, Nicholas E. *c.m.* '46 (STL) [P] Perryville, MO Congregation of The Mission.
Persich, Roy A. '60 (LA) [Q] Montebello, CA Vincentian Fathers & Brothers; [W] Santa Barbara, CA St. Mary's Seminary Center.
Persico, Lawrence T. '77 (GBG) New Alexandria, PA St. James Church.
Persico, Pasquale *p.i.m.e.* '44 (PMB) [H] Tequesta, FL P.I.M.E. Missionaries.
Persico, Philip T. '99 (NY) [204] Staten Island, NY Holy Child Church.
Persing, Charles L. '88 (HBG) Coal Township, PA Our Lady of Hope Church; Trevorton, PA St. Patrick Church.
Persinger, Patrick '87 (FRS) Wofford Heights, CA St. Jude Church.
Perumbilly, Sebastian *o.s.j.* '97 (NOR) [5] Middletown, CT St. Sebastian Church.
Perumpil, Matthew *o.s.c.* '94 (BO) Boston, MA St. Elizabeth's Medical Center; [Q] Boston, MA St. Elizabeth's Hospital of Boston.
Perunilam, Thomas V. '64 (MET) Milltown, NJ Our Lady of Lourdes Church.
Perzan, Stephan B. '73 (PH) [157] Philadelphia, PA Visitation B.V.M. Church.
Pesanka, Nicholas A. '75 (PIT) Bethel Park, PA St. Germaine Church.
Pesarchick, Robert A. '91 (PH) [A] Wynnewood, PA Theological Seminary of St. Charles Borromeo, Overbrook.
Pesaresi, Thomas E. *m.m.* '85 (FgM) Maryknoll Foreign Missions.
Pescatello, Joseph A. '89 (PRO) [10] Woonsocket, RI Our Lady, Queen of Martyrs Church; [S] Smithfield, RI Bryant College.
Pescatore, Terence *o.f.m. conv.* '62 (R) Burlington, NC Blessed Sacrament Church; [E] Burlington, NC Conventual Franciscans.
Pesce, John Baptist *c.p.* '51 (HRT) [M] West Hartford, CT Holy Family Monastery/Retreat.
Pesch, Elroy *o.f.m.cap.* '63 (MIL) [B] Mount Calvary, WI St. Lawrence Seminary; [P] Mount Calvary, WI St. Lawrence Friary.
Peschel, Roland A. '60 (OM) Fremont, NE St. Patrick Church.
Pesci, Thomas A. *s.j.* '79 (KC) [D] Kansas City, MO Rockhurst High School; [J] Kansas City, MO Rockhurst Jesuit Community.
Pesek, Anthony '65 (SAT) [9] San Antonio, TX Holy Spirit Church.
Pesek, Fred C. '89 (CHI) Streamwood, IL St. John the Evangelist Church.
Pesola, Joseph '97 (IND) [16] Indianapolis, IN St. Barnabas Church.
Pesola, Joseph G. '97 (IND) [O] Indianapolis, IN International Catholic Deaf Association (Chapter No. 38).
Pestin, Arturo *o.p.* (SAN) Stanton, TX St. Joseph's Church.
Pestin, Arturo P. *o.p.* '83 (SAN) [1] Midland, TX St. Ann's Church.
Pestun, Aloysius *s.d.b.* '59 (SFR) [13] San Francisco, CA Corpus Christi Church.
Peszkowski, Msgr. Zdzislaw '54 (DET) [A] Orchard Lake, MI SS. Cyril and Methodius Seminary.
Petcavage, Paschal *o.s.b.* '81 (CLV) [D] Cleveland, OH Benedictine High School; [O] Cleveland, OH Benedictine Order of Cleveland.
Pete, Joseph P. '76 (WIN) Lake Crystal, MN Holy Family Church; [4] Mankato, MN St. Joseph the Worker Church.
Petekiewicz, Robert P. (LAV) [4] Las Vegas, NV Our Lady of Las Vegas Church.
Peter, Arul Rajan '85 (NY) [132] Bronx, NY St. Barnabas Church.
Peter, David J. '66 (BUF) [10] Niagara Falls, NY Our Lady of the Rosary Church.
Peter, Martin A. '67 (IND) [33] Indianapolis, IN St. Pius X Church.
Peter, Patrick N. '75 (BEL) Breese, IL St. Dominic Church.
Peter, Valentine J. '59 (OM) Boys Town, NE Immaculate Conception B.V.M. Church; [C] Boys Town, NE Father Flanagan's Boys' Home; [E] Boys Town, NE Father Flanagan's Boys' Home; [I] Boys Town, NE Father Flanagan's Boys' Home.
Petering, Michael '99 (VIC) El Campo, TX St. Philip the Apostle Church.
Peterka, Dale C. '68 (CIN) On Special and Archdiocesan Assignment.
Peterka, Sylvester *c.m.* '76 (BAL) [21] Baltimore, MD St. Cecilia Church; [40] Baltimore, MD Immaculate Conception Church.
Peterlini, Luciano *s.x.* '63 (FgM) Xaverian Foreign Missions.
Peterlini, Luciano *s.x.* '63 (PAT) [M] Wayne, NJ Xaverian Missionary Fathers.
Peterman, Charles '58 (MIA) [16] Miami, FL St. Brendan Church.

Peterman, Thomas J. '57 (WIL) Galena, MD St. Dennis Church.
Petermeier, Virgil *o.s.c.* '77 (FgM) Crosier Foreign Missions.
Peters, Aaron *o.s.b.* '77 (KCK) [I] Paola, KS Our Lady of Lourdes Convent.
Peters, Ambrose J. *o.praem.* '53 (GB) [A] De Pere, WI St. Norbert Abbey.
Peters, Daniel E. '89 (RCK) Prophetstown, IL St. Catherine Church.
Peters, David L. '58 (SFD) Highland, IL St. Paul Church.
Peters, Donald R. '50 (MIL) Retired.
Peters, Eric '80 (SP) [11] Tampa, FL St. Mark the Evangelist Church.
Peters, Fred *s.d.s.* '56 (PHX) [17] Phoenix, AZ St. Mark Church; Phoenix, AZ Maricopa Medical Center.
Peters, Herman B. '41 (CLV) [16] Cleveland, OH St. Cecilia Church; Retired.
Peters, Msgr. John '60 (ELP) [26] El Paso, TX St. Luke Church.
Peters, John B. *c.i.c.m.* '53 (FgM) Missionhurst Foreign Missions.
Peters, John C. *v.f.* '74 (VIC) Hallettsville, TX Sacred Heart Church; Hallettsville, TX St. Mary Church.
Peters, Jude *o.c.d.* '89 (MIL) [26] Milwaukee, WI St. Florian Church; [P] Milwaukee, WI Provincial Offices - Discalced Carmelites; [P] Holy Hill, WI Discalced Carmelite Monastery.
Peters, Julian *o.s.b.* '88 (IND) [A] St. Meinrad, IN St. Meinrad Seminary; [J] St. Meinrad, IN St. Meinrad Archabbey.
Peters, Kenan *c.p.* '60 (BRK) [V] Jamaica, NY Immaculate Conception Monastery.
Peters, Kevin '90 (Y) Ashtabula, OH Mother of Sorrows Church.
Peters, Lyle '96 (DM) [12] Des Moines, IA St. Theresa of the Child Jesus Church.
Peters, Mark *o.s.b.* '80 (GBG) [H] Latrobe, PA Saint Vincent Archabbey.
Peters, Michael G. '88 (DM) Panama, IA St. Mary of the Assumption Church; Westphalia, IA St. Boniface Church.
Peters, Paul R. '62 (DUB) Elkader, IA St. Joseph's Church; Volga, IA Sacred Heart Church.
Peters, Msgr. Roy V. '48 (HON) [17] Honolulu, HI Saints Peter and Paul Church.
Peters, Msgr. Roy V. '48 (SAC) Retired and in Senior Ministry.
Peters, Stephen '67 (ELP) [4] El Paso, TX Blessed Sacrament Church.
Petersen, Msgr. E. James '59 (FRS) [13] Fresno, CA St. Therese Church.
Petersen, Michael '92 (MIL) West Bend, WI St. Frances Cabrini Church.
Petersen, Todd J. '99 (NU) [1] New Ulm, MN Cathedral of The Holy Trinity.
Petersen, Vincent *o.f.m.conv.* '85 (LSC) Artesia, NM Our Lady of Grace Church.
Peterson, Bradley *o.carm.* '92 (TUC) [11] Tucson, AZ Sacred Heart Church.
Peterson, Bruce '57 (STP) Belle Creek, MN St. Columbkill Church.
Peterson, C. Vincent '74 (SEA) [17] Seattle, WA St. Patrick Church.
Peterson, Casimir M. '47 (BAL) Retired; [W] Baltimore, MD Ladies of Charity; [W] Pasadena, MD Reparation Society of the Immaculate Heart of Mary, Inc.
Peterson, Charles *s.j.* '74 (SPK) Omak, WA St. Mary Church; Omak, WA St. Joseph Church.
Peterson, Cyril P. '41 (DM) Retired.
Peterson, Cyril P. '41 (WIN) Retired.
Peterson, Dennis L. '73 (GAL) [76] Houston, TX St. Theresa Church.
Peterson, Francis '60 (HON) Retired.
Peterson, Francis A. '46 (B) Retired.
Peterson, Frederick *o.s.b.* '95 (RCK) [G] Aurora, IL Marmion Abbey-St. Augustine's Abbey.
Peterson, Frederick *o.s.b.* '95 (ROM) Aurora, IL St. George Church.
Peterson, G. Paul *s.j.* '61 (IND) [D] Indianapolis, IN Brebeuf Jesuit Preparatory School, Inc.
Peterson, Gerald *glmy.* '56 (BIR) [G] Fayette, AL Christian Center of Concern.
Peterson, Harry *s.d.b.* '61 (FgM) Salesians of Don Bosco Foreign Missions.
Peterson, Msgr. James W. '47 (E) [O] Erie, PA Special Ministries.
Peterson, John '63 (FgM) Franciscan Foreign Missions.
Peterson, John P. '89 (ARL) Spotsylvania, VA St. Matthew Church; [M] Fredericksburg, VA Mary-Washington College.
Peterson, John S. *o.p.* '62 (PRO) [P] Providence, RI St. Thomas Aquinas Priory at Providence College.
Peterson, Joseph L. '75 (WH) [2] Huntington, WV Our Lady of Fatima Church.
Peterson, Leonard N. '67 (PH) Hatfield, PA St. Maria Goretti Church; [EE] Philadelphia, PA Newman Center at Drexel University.
Peterson, Louis P. '74 (BEL) Leave of Absence.
Peterson, Maurice F. '87 (YAK) East Wenatchee, WA Holy Apostles Church.
Peterson, Stephen J. '94 (WIN) Harmony, MN The Nativity of the Blessed Virgin Church.
Peterson, Steven J. '73 (RVC) East Islip, NY St. Mary's Church.
Peterson, William A. *c.ss.r.* '67 (DEN) [M] Denver, CO The Redemptorists/Denver Province.
Peterson, William A. *c.ss.r.* '67 (FgM) Redemptorist Foreign Missions.
Peterson, William F. '59 (RCK) Retired.
Petilla, Antonio '61 (SFR) [31] San Francisco, CA St. Kevin Church.
Petinge, Roland V. *o.f.m.* '61 (PRT) [6] Portland, ME St. Peter's Church.
Petit, Edmund P. '46 (RCK) Retired.
Petit, Eliades (SJN) [5] Guaynabo, PR Maria Madre de la Misericordia Church.
Petit, Leo *m.s.c.* '51 (RCK) [G] Aurora, IL Missionaries of the Sacred Heart Community.
Petit-Monsieur, Lamartine (BO) [4] Lynn, MA St. Mary Church.
Petkash, Donald J. *s.j.* '71 (CLV) [D] Cuyahoga Falls, OH Walsh Jesuit High School.
Petosa, Joseph '55 (SEA) Retired.
Petracca, Anthony '85 (ALT) Absent on Leave.
Petraitis, Donald S. *m.i.c.* '64 (CHI) [N] Chicago, IL Congregation of Marian Fathers of the Immaculate Conception.
Petrarulo, John D. '53 (PIT) [4] New Castle, PA St. Vitus Church.
Petras, David M. '67 (PBR) [A] Pittsburgh, PA Byzantine Catholic Seminary of SS. Cyril and Methodius.
Petras, David M. '67 (PRM) On Duty Outside the Diocese.
Petrasic, Martin J. '43 (OM) Retired.
Petrauskas, John C. *m.i.c.* '43 (WOR) [19] Worcester, MA St. Casimir's Church.
Petrella, Robert '64 (WDC) Retired.
Petri, Gregg D. *o.f.m.* '61 (LSC) Alamogordo, NM Immaculate Conception Church.
Petri, John C. '45 (TR) Retired.
Petrich, John C. '83 (DUL) Duluth, MN St. Luke's Hospital; Saginaw, MN Northeast Regional Correctional Institution.
Petrie, Harry F. '45 (PIT) Wexford, PA St. Alexis Church; Retired.
Petrie, Michael J. '87 (MIL) Hartford, WI St. Kilian Church.
Petrie, William *ss.cc.* '69 (FR) [I] Fairhaven, MA Sacred Hearts Provincial House.
Petrik, Clement J. *s.j.* '63 (BAL) [S] Baltimore, MD Jesuit Fathers and Brothers Maryland Provincial Curia.
Petrikovic, John J. *o.f.m.cap.* '81 (PIT) [O] Pittsburgh, PA St. Augustine Friary.
Petrillo, Joseph A. '77 (NEW) West Orange, NJ Our Lady of Lourdes Church.
Petrillo, Thomas J. '59 (NEW) Montclair, NJ Our Lady of Mt. Carmel Church.
Petrimoulx, Leo *o.f.m.cap.* '66 (MAD) [F] Madison, WI St. Marys Hospital Medical Center; [L] Madison, WI San Damiano Friary.
Petringa, Gerard '88 (BO) [3] Quincy, MA St. John the Baptist Church.
Petriv, Vasil '92 (SJP) Parma, OH Pokrova Ukrainian Catholic Church.
Petriv, Volodymyr '89 (STN) Sacramento, CA St. Andrew the Apostle Church; Detroit, MI St. John the Baptist Church; Flint, MI St. Vladimir's Church.
Petro, John G. '68 (PBR) Beaver, PA Saint Nicholas Chapel Church; [A] Pittsburgh, PA Byzantine Catholic Seminary of SS. Cyril and Methodius.
Petro, Thomas J. '00 (SCR) Kingston, PA St. Ignatius Church.
Petro, William J. '68 (WH) [P] Huntington, WV Marshall Newman Center.
Petrocelli, John '71 (PRO) [K] North Providence, RI St. Joseph Health Services of Rhode Island - Our Lady of Fatima Hospital.
Petron, William G. '57 (DET) Retired.
Petronek, Msgr. Thomas C. '65 (STU) Absent on Leave.
Petronio, Rolando '78 (CHK) Songsong Village, MP San Francisco de Borja Church.
Petroske, Peter '84 (DET) Southgate, MI St. Pius X Church.
Petroski, Michael A. '00 (LAN) [1] Lansing, MI St. Mary Church.
Petrosky, Arnold *t.o.r.* (SFS) Epiphany, SD Church of the Epiphany.
Petrosky, Christopher *t.o.r.* '55 (ARL) [J] White Post, VA Sacred Heart Friary.
Petrovsky, Felix *o.f.m.cap.* '55 (SAL) [D] Victoria, KS St. Fidelis Friary.
Petrovsky, James F. '68 (GBG) Maxwell, PA St. James Church.
Petroy, Dominic J. *o.s.b.* '86 (GBG) Jeannette, PA Sacred Heart Church; Jeannette, PA Jeannette District Memorial Hospital; Jeannette, PA Monsour Medical Center; [F] Jeannette, PA Jeannette District Memorial Hospital.
Petru, Augustine *o.m.i.* '53 (FgM) Oblates Foreign Missions.
Petru, Msgr. Julius A. '37 (VIC) New Taiton, TX St. John Nepomucene Church.
Petru, Msgr. Stanley J. '48 (VIC) Hostyn, TX Holy Rosary Church; Plum, TX SS. Peter and Paul Church.
Petrucci, Dominic '82 (SFS) Retired.
Petrucci, Peter J. *m.m.* '49 (FgM) Maryknoll Foreign Missions.
Petrucci, Raymond K. '73 (BGP) [1] Bridgeport, CT St. Augustine Church; Shelton, CT St. Margaret Mary Church.
Petruha, Louis *o.f.m.cap.* (PIT) [O] Pittsburgh, PA St. Augustine Friary.
Petrunak, William '59 (Y) [C] Warren, OH John F. Kennedy High School.
Petrusic, Anthony A. '57 (OM) Retired.
Petruska, Christopher '59 (PSC) Somerset, NJ SS. Peter and Paul Church.
Petruska, William M. '73 (SCR) Military Chaplains.
Petry, Thomas G. '78 (COL) Special Assignment; Graduate Studies.
Petsch, Msgr. Joseph '50 (SAT) Retired; [K] San Antonio, TX Casa De Padres.
Petsche, Daniel *o.s.b.* '67 (KC) Stanberry, MO St. Peter's Church; [A] Conception, MO Conception Seminary College; [J] Conception, MO Conception Abbey.
Petta, Gerard *m.s.a.* '84 (NOR) [F] Cromwell, CT Society of the Missionaries of the Holy Apostles.
Pettei, Thomas G. '86 (BRK) [232] Queens, NY St. Raphael Church.
Petter, Henry V. '76 (DAL) Plano, TX St. Elizabeth Ann Seton Church.
Pettingill, David M. '62 (SFR) [17] San Francisco, CA St. Emydius Church; Special Assignment.
Pettit, Edward G. '51 (PBL) [5] Pueblo, CO Our Lady of the Assumption Church; [14] Pueblo, CO St. Mary Church; [15] Pueblo, CO St. Patrick Church; [K] Pueblo, CO Historic Southside Catholic Community.
Pettit, Joseph H. '56 (HRT) Retired.
Pettit, Joseph J. '55 (GR) Retired.
Pettit, William '54 (DET) [1] Redford, MI St. Agatha Church.
Pettit, William J. '54 (DET) Retired.
Pettke, Lawrence A. '81 (DET) [2] Southfield, MI St. Bede Church.
Petty, Ed '77 (DUB) [D] Dyersville, IA Beckman High School.
Petty, Edward C. '77 (DUB) Dyersville, IA Basilica of St. Francis Xavier.
Petuskey, John A. '66 (OKL) Edmond, OK St. John the Baptist Church.
Peverada, Augustine J. *c.s.c.* '45 (FTW) [J] South Bend, IN Congregation of Holy Cross, Indiana Province, Provincial House.
Peyton, Msgr. John T. '61 (BRK) [124] Brooklyn, NY St. Rita's Church.
Peyton, Mark J. '77 (CLV) [67] Cleveland, OH St. Procop Church.
Peyton, Thomas '86 (BRK) Absent on Leave.
Peyton, Thomas A. *m.m.* '58 (FgM) Maryknoll Foreign Missions.
Peyton, Thomas J. '74 (SAV) [4] Augusta, GA St. Teresa of Avila Church.
Pezzotti, Mario *s.x.* '59 (FgM) Xaverian Foreign Missions.
Pezzotti, Mario *s.x.* '59 (PAT) [M] Wayne, NJ Xaverian Missionary Fathers.
Pezzullo, Angelo B. '62 (BRK) [204] Queens, NY Nativity of the Blessed Virgin Mary Church.
Pezzulo, Neil *glmy.* '99 (LR) Hamburg, AR Holy Spirit Church.
Pfab, Cletus H. *s.j.* '69 (MIL) [P] Milwaukee, WI Jesuit Provincial Office, Wisconsin Province.
Pfaff, Aaron (PH) [48] Philadelphia, PA St. Francis Xavier Church.
Pfaff, Aaron J. '96 (MAN) On Duty Outside the Diocese.
Pfaff, Aaron J. '96 (PH) [AA] Philadelphia, PA The Philadelphia Congregation of The Oratory of St. Philip Neri.
Pfaff, Joseph A. '75 (BRK) [179] Queens, NY Holy Trinity Church.
Pfalzer, Juvenal *o.f.m.* '42 (CIN) [M] Cincinnati, OH St. Clement Friary.
Pfalzer, Miles *o.f.m.* '47 (MAR) Ahmeek, MI Our Lady of Peace Church.
Pfalzer, Roman *o.f.m.* '47 (CIN) [M] Cincinnati, OH St. Clement Friary.
Pfannenstiel, Donald F. '75 (SAL) WaKeeney, KS Christ the King Church.
Pfannenstiel, John *o.f.m.cap.* '82 (BAL) [6] Baltimore, MD St. Ambrose Church.
Pfau, Bernard A. '65 (FAR) Jamestown, ND The Basilica of St. James; [J] Jamestown, ND Jamestown College.
Pfeffer, Charles J. '77 (PH) [3] Philadelphia, PA St. Agatha-St. James Church; [EE] Philadelphia, PA Newman Center at Drexel University.
Pfeffer, Msgr. Edward B. (DM) Retired.

Pfeffer, Thomas '60 (DM) [13] Des Moines, IA Visitation Church.
Pfeifer, Francis *o.m.i.* (FgM) Oblates Foreign Missions.
Pfeifer, Frederick A. '93 (NEW) [15] Newark, NJ St. Francis Xavier Church.
Pfeifer, James *o.m.i.* '51 (BWN) [3] McAllen, TX Sacred Heart Church.
Pfeifer, John M. '65 (BIS) Watford City, ND Epiphany Church.
Pfeiffer, Carl *o.ss.t.* '87 (BAL) [S] Baltimore, MD Holy Trinity Monastery.
Pfeiffer, David L. *m.m.* '66 (FgM) Maryknoll Foreign Missions.
Pfeiffer, Msgr. Joseph C. '58 (BRK) [175] Queens, NY St. Helen Church.
Pfeiffer, Mark S. '82 (LIN) Grafton, NE St. Helena's Church; McCool Junction, NE St. Patrick's Church.
Pfeiffer, Robert F. '61 (CLV) Medina, OH Holy Martyrs Church.
Pfiester, Emeric J. *o.s.b.* '48 (GBG) [H] Latrobe, PA Saint Vincent Archabbey.
Pfister, Carl *o.carm.* '49 (NEW) Englewood, NJ St. Cecilia's Church.
Pfister, John F. '66 (FTW) [17] Fort Wayne, IN Queen of Angels Church.
Pfister, Neal A. (DEN) [8] Denver, CO Church of the Good Shepherd.
Pfisterer, Robert *o.f.m.* '51 (SFR) [5] San Francisco, CA St. Anthony of Padua Church.
Pfleger, Michael L. '75 (CHI) [185] Chicago, IL St. Sabina Church.
Pfleger, Phillip C. '79 (TR) Evesham Township, NJ St. Isaac Jogues Church.
Pflomm, Msgr. Peter '70 (RVC) New Hyde Park, NY Notre Dame Church.
Pflumm, Robert '60 (KCK) Lenexa, KS Holy Trinity Church; Retired.
Pfnausch, Edward G. '68 (HRT) Wallingford, CT Holy Trinity Church.
Pfotenhauer, Frederick W. '57 (FTW) [B] Notre Dame, IN University of Notre Dame Du Lac.
Pfundstein, George A. '63 (BRK) [151] Queens, NY St. Ann's Church.
Phalen, John L. '59 (DET) Lake Orion, MI St. Joseph Church.
Phalen, John P. *c.s.c.* '74 (ALB) [S] Albany, NY Family Rosary Albany Office.
Pham, Ai *s.j.* '93 (BO) [W] Chestnut Hill, MA The Jesuit Community at Boston College.
Pham, Anthony '98 (FWT) [19] Fort Worth, TX Christ the King Church.
Pham, Chau *s.v.d.* '95 (STL) [65] St. Louis, MO St. Thomas of Aquin Church.
Pham, Doan T. '98 (LA) Panorama City, CA St. Genevieve Church.
Pham, Dominic '98 (ALN) Bath, PA Sacred Heart Church.
Pham, Dominic Chinh Van *c.ss.r.* '95 (GAL) [43] Houston, TX St. Justin Martyr Church.
Pham, Francis *c.ss.r.* '93 (SAT) [37] San Antonio, TX St. Gerard Majella Church; [B] San Antonio, TX Redemptorist Formation Program.
Pham, Hanh Van '93 (CC) [23] Corpus Christi, TX Collegiate Parish of St. Thomas More Church.
Pham, Hien *s.v.d.* '99 (STL) [65] St. Louis, MO St. Thomas of Aquin Church.
Pham, Hung Q. '89 (WCH) [11] Wichita, KS St. Anthony Church.
Pham, Huy Phi '97 (ORG) Inactive Leave.
Pham, John-Peter (PEO) On Duty Outside the Diocese.
Pham, Joseph '70 (BRK) [216] Queens, NY Our Lady of Mount Carmel Church.
Pham, Joseph Luong '98 (CAM) [5] Atlantic City, NJ Our Lady Star of the Sea Church.
Pham, Joseph Than Xuan '85 (RIC) [19] Richmond, VA Church of the Vietnamese Martyrs.
Pham, Joseph The *c.ss.r.* '98 (STP) Brooklyn Center, MN St. Alphonsus Church.
Pham, Joseph Tuan '88 (ORG) Garden Grove, CA St. Callistus Church.
Pham, Khoi '94 (STO) Turlock, CA Sacred Heart Church.
Pham, Lac *c.pp.s.* '89 (KC) [A] Kansas City, MO Gaspar Mission House.
Pham, Le-Minh '93 (AUS) Cedar Park, TX St. Margaret Mary Church.
Pham, Liem Thanh '95 (BO) [W] Cambridge, MA Weston Jesuit Community.
Pham, Louis Ha *c.m.c.* '94 (BEA) [2] Port Arthur, TX Queen of Vietnam Church.
Pham, Michael M. '99 (SD) [3] Oceanside, CA St. Mary, Star of the Sea Church.
Pham, Min-Uoc '90 (BO) [W] Cambridge, MA Weston Jesuit Community.
Pham, Minh J. *c.m.* '90 (STO) Patterson, CA Sacred Heart Church.
Pham, Peter *s.o.l.t.* '99 (CC) Robstown, TX St. Anthony Church.
Pham, Phong '91 (CHI) [A] Mundelein, IL University of St. Mary of the Lake-Mundelein Seminary.
Pham, Phong Q. '91 (GR) On Duty Outside the Diocese.
Pham, Pierre '71 (SPR) On Duty Outside the Diocese.
Pham, Tan *s.o.l.t.* '91 (CC) [H] Robstown, TX Society of Our Lady of the Most Holy Trinity.
Pham, Tin Cosmas Kim '95 (GAL) Brazoria, TX St. Joseph on the Brazos Church.
Pham, Tuan *c.ss.r.* '99 (LA) Whittier, CA St. Mary of the Assumption Church; [Q] Whittier, CA Redemptorist Fathers Mission House.
Pham, Tuan Anh '99 (NO) [1] Marrero, LA Immaculate Conception Church.
Pham, Tuan Joseph '94 (ORG) Laguna Hills, CA St. Nicholas Church.
Pham, Vincent Hung '97 (ORG) Stanton, CA St. Polycarp Church.
Pham An Su, Bartholomew M. *c.m.c.* (SPC) [E] Carthage, MO Congregation of the Mother Co-Redemptrix, United States Assumption Province.
Pham duc Trin, Joseph '70 (VIC) Palacios, TX St. Anthony's Church.
Pham Minh Van, Bartholomew *c.m.c.* (SPC) [E] Carthage, MO Congregation of the Mother Co-Redemptrix, United States Assumption Province.
Pham Ngoc Bich, James M. *c.m.c.* (SPC) [E] Carthage, MO Congregation of the Mother Co-Redemptrix, United States Assumption Province.
Pham Tien Duc, John Bosco M. *c.m.c.* (SPC) [E] Carthage, MO Congregation of the Mother Co-Redemptrix, United States Assumption Province.
Pham Van Lan, Augustine '63 (CLV) [13] Cleveland, OH St. Boniface Church.
Pham Van Tue, Joseph '73 (NO) [2] Marrero, LA St. Agnes Le Thi Thanh Church.
Pham-Van-Ninh, James *s.e.* '67 (P) [25] Portland, OR Our Lady of Lavang Church.
Phan, Cho Dink Peter '72 (DAL) On Duty Outside the Diocese.
Phan, Dominic '70 (BLX) [2] Biloxi, MS Church of the Vietnamese Martyrs; [9] Biloxi, MS St. Michael Church.
Phan, Minh Cong '97 (NO) Harahan, LA St. Rita Church.
Phan, Nguyen Van *c.ss.r.* '93 (LA) [Q] Baldwin Park, CA Vietnamese Redemptorist Mission.
Phan, Peter C. '72 (WDC) [C] Washington, DC Catholic University of America, The.
Phan, Philip '85 (NY) [42] New York, NY Guardian Angel Church.
Phan, Phu T. '92 (AMA) Canyon, TX St. Ann's Church.
Phan, Vincent Huo '95 (MOB) On Leave from the Archdiocese.
Phan Cong Binh, John M. (SPC) [E] Carthage, MO Congregation of the Mother Co-Redemptrix, United States Assumption Province.
Phan Lam, Anthony '62 (OAK) [8] Oakland, CA St. Cyril Church.
Pharr, Msgr. William N. '60 (CHL) [11] Charlotte, NC St. Vincent de Paul Church.
Phat, Peter Tran Van '67 (NY) Otisville, NY Holy Name Church.
Phelan, Cornelius '59 (LA) Newbury Park, CA St. Julie Billiart Church.
Phelan, Edward '63 (SFR) [16] San Francisco, CA St. Elizabeth Church.
Phelan, Gerald J. '62 (SJ) [L] Los Gatos, CA Sacred Heart Jesuit Center.
Phelan, John E. '74 (SY) Jordan, NY St. Patrick Church.
Phelan, John J. *s.j.* '58 (FgM) Provinces.
Phelan, Julian *o.f.m.cap.* '46 (ROC) [I] Interlaken, NY St. Fidelis Friary.
Phelan, Murray *o.carm.* '47 (CHI) [N] Mundelein, IL Carmelite Monastery.
Phelan, Nicholas '52 (SAC) Grass Valley, CA St. Patrick Church; Retired and in Senior Ministry.
Phelan, Thomas '51 (ALB) Special Assignment; [R] Troy, NY Rensselaer Polytechnic Institute.
Phelan, Thomas '53 (SEA) Retired.
Phelan, Thomas E. '76 (BEA) Dayton, TX St. Joseph the Worker Church; Eastgate, TX St. Anne Church.
Phelan, Walter M. '49 (GI) Grand Island, NE U.S. Veterans' Hospital; Retired.
Phelps, John *c.ss.r.* '66 (CHI) [29] Chicago, IL Blessed Sacrament Church.
Phelps, Lawrence J. *o.s.b.* '63 (NO) Bogalusa, LA Annunciation B.V.M. Church; [P] St. Benedict, LA St. Joseph Abbey.
Phelps, Robert *o.f.m.cap.* '66 (AGN) [F] Agana Heights, GU St. Fidelis Friary.
Phelps, Robert *o.f.m.cap.* '66 (RVC) East Patchogue, NY St. Joseph the Worker Church.
Phen Van Pham, Joseph '78 (SD) [16] San Diego, CA Our Lady of the Sacred Heart Church.
Philbin, Msgr. John J. '44 (BO) Senior Priests.
Philbin, Patrick B. *s.m.* '72 (ORG) [L] Orange, CA House of Prayer for Priests; [M] Irvine, CA U.C.I. Interfaith Center.
Philbin, William '37 (RC) Retired.
Philen, Michael '99 (ORG) [2] Orange, CA La Purisima Church.
Philibert, Paul J. *o.p.* '63 (STL) [P] St. Louis, MO St. Dominic Priory.
Philion, Richard *o.m.i.* '61 (CC) [3] Kingsville, TX St. Joseph Church.
Philippe, Jean-Rony '99 (BGP) [7] Bridgeport, CT St. Charles Church.
Philipsen, Todd K. (GI) Broken Bow, NE St. Joseph's Church.
Phillip, Alan *c.p.* '67 (LA) [Q] Pasadena, CA Passionist Community.
Phillipino, Lucio B. '60 (FR) Retired.
Phillippino, Michael L. '90 (NOR) Killingworth, CT St. Lawrence Church.
Phillips, Benet C. *o.s.b.* '92 (MAN) [K] Manchester, NH St. Anselm Abbey.
Phillips, C. Frank *c.r.* '77 (CHI) [104] Chicago, IL St. John Cantius Church.
Phillips, Christopher G. '83 (SAT) [14] San Antonio, TX Our Lady of the Atonement Catholic Church.
Phillips, Clyde *m.m.* '78 (CHI) [N] Chicago, IL Maryknoll Fathers & Brothers.
Phillips, Edward J. *m.m.* '74 (FgM) Maryknoll Foreign Missions.
Phillips, Eric C. '98 (ROC) Penfield, NY St. Joseph Church.
Phillips, Gene D. *s.j.* '65 (CHI) [C] Chicago, IL Jesuit Community at Loyola University of Chicago.
Phillips, George '45 (ALB) Latham, NY St. Ambrose Church; Retired.
Phillips, George *c.ss.r.* '52 (STA) [6] Jacksonville, FL Holy Rosary Church.
Phillips, Msgr. George M. '40 (OG) Retired.
Phillips, Glenn *o.f.m.* '66 (SUP) Bayfield, WI Holy Family Church; Cornucopia, WI St. Ann Church; LaPointe, WI St. Joseph Church; Red Cliff, WI St. Francis Church.
Phillips, Msgr. Hugh J. '35 (BAL) Retired; [B] Emmitsburg, MD Mount Saint Mary's College.
Phillips, John '53 (ALB) Retired.
Phillips, John '55 (ROC) Retired.
Phillips, John J. '55 (ROC) Fairport, NY St. John of Rochester Church.
Phillips, John M. '87 (STA) [4] Gainesville, FL St. Augustine Church; [L] Gainesville, FL University of Florida-St. Augustine Parish and Student Center.
Phillips, Joseph H. '68 (SY) [11] Syracuse, NY St. Ann Church; Special Assignment; [N] Syracuse, NY Family Life Education.
Phillips, Kenneth '91 (BIS) [2] Dickinson, ND St. Joseph Church.
Phillips, Louis J. (PRT) Auburn, ME St. Louis Church; Auburn, ME St. Philip's Church; Auburn, ME Sacred Heart Church.
Phillips, Msgr. Michael J. '60 (BRK) [10] Brooklyn, NY St. Anselm's Church.
Phillips, Michael T. '69 (DAV) [4] Iowa City, IA St. Wenceslaus Church.
Phillips, Paschal *o.c.s.o.* '57 (L) [L] Trappist, KY Abbey of Our Lady of Gethsemani, of the Order of Cistercians of the Strict Observance.
Phillips, Randall R. '83 (DET) [4] Dearborn Heights, MI St. Linus Church.
Phillips, Randy '97 (SFS) Faulkton, SD St. Thomas the Apostle Church.
Phillips, Rene F. *o.f.m.* '56 (NY) [DD] New York, NY Franciscan Friars, Order of Friars Minor, Holy Name Province.
Phillips, Robert L. *s.j.* '72 (STL) [C] St. Louis, MO Saint Louis University; [P] St. Louis, MO Jesuit Community Corporation at St. Louis University - Jesuit Hall.
Phillips, Thomas L. '71 (BAL) [34] Baltimore, MD St. Gabriel Church.
Phillips, Walter W. '55 (GI) Retired.
Philominraj, Peter G. *s.d.b.* '95 (NY) [99] New York, NY Our Lady of Victory Church.
Philominsamy, Michaelraj '91 (SR) Fort Bragg, CA Our Lady of Good Counsel Church.
Phinn, Gilbert S. '53 (BO) [2] Milton, MA St. Elizabeth Church.
Phinn, Paul A. '57 (BO) [29] Boston, MA St. John Chrysostom Church.
Phipps, Charles T. *s.j.* '59 (SJ) [B] Santa Clara, CA Santa Clara University.
Phuc, Anthony *c.ss.r.* '56 (MRY) Pacific Grove, CA St. Angela Church.
Phuc, Msgr. John *i.v.f.* '83 (NO) Destrehan, LA St. Charles Borromeo Church.
Phuc, Tran Dinh *c.ss.r.* '56 (LA) [Q] Baldwin Park, CA Vietnamese Redemptorist Mission.
Phukuta, Charles *c.i.c.m.* '99 (BWN) La Joya, TX Our Lady, Queen of Angels Church.
Phung, Chi Peter '90 (TLS) [14] Tulsa, OK SS. Peter and Paul Church.
Phung, Le Quang *c.ss.r.* '69 (LA) [Q] Baldwin Park, CA Vietnamese Redemptorist Mission.
Physician, Thomas R. '58 (DET) New Haven, MI St. Francis of Assisi Church; Pontiac, MI St. Joseph Church; Clinton Township, MI State Prisons; [T] Clinton Township, MI St. Mary Magdalen Catholic Community.
Piacentini, David '71 (PRO) [2] North Providence, RI St. Lawrence Church.

Piacitelli, Henry '45 (KC) [39] Kansas City, MO St. Thomas More Church.
Piano, Timothy '77 (MIA) Absent on Leave.
Piansay, Victor V. '64 (FRS) Hanford, CA Immaculate Heart Church.
Piasecki, Timothy '73 (RCK) [9] Rockford, IL SS. Peter and Paul Church.
Piatek, Ignatius M. *o.f.m.conv.* '61 (BAL) [C] Baltimore, MD Archbishop Curley High School; [S] Baltimore, MD Immaculate Heart of Mary Friary.
Piatek, Joseph '69 (ORL) [10] Orlando, FL St. Joseph Church.
Piatkowski, Robert J. '53 (NEW) Springfield, NJ St. James Church.
Piazza, Msgr. Benjamin A. '49 (NEW) Caldwell, NJ St. Aloysius Church; Retired.
Piazza, Salvatore J. '48 (BUF) Ransomville, NY Immaculate Conception Church; Retired.
Picado, Rodrigo '71 (NO) On Duty Outside the Archdiocese.
Picard, Benoit *o.f.f.* '91 (LR) [F] Hot Springs National Park, AR Monastery of Our Lady of Charity of Refuge (Good Shepherd); [I] Hot Springs, AR Monastery of Our Lady of Charity of Refuge (Good Shepherd).
Picard, Daniel '79 (LAF) Lawtell, LA St. Bridget Church.
Picard, Howard *c.i.c.m.* '56 (ARL) [J] Arlington, VA Missionhurst, C.I.C.M.-Central House and Provincialate.
Picard, Michael C. '66 (PH) Newtown, PA St. Andrew Church.
Picard, Raymond '65 (PRT) Boothbay Harbor, ME Our Lady, Queen of Peace Church; Newcastle, ME St. Patrick Church.
Picardi, Aubert Marie *o.f.m.* '62 (BO) [52] Boston, MA Our Lady of Mt. Carmel Church.
Picardi, John M. '83 (BO) On Duty Outside the Archdiocese.
Picardi, John M. '83 (PHX) [6] Scottsdale, AZ St. Maria Goretti Church.
Picariello, Anthony R. *s.j.* '80 (BO) [W] Weston, MA Campion Jesuit Community.
Picavella, Dale (BAL) Glen Burnie, MD Crucifixion, Church of the.
Picciano, Msgr. Daniel A. '71 (RVC) Port Washington, NY St. Peter of Alcantara Church.
Piccinini, Claudio *c.p.* '72 (BRK) [V] Jamaica, NY Immaculate Conception Monastery.
Piccinino, Corey V. '86 (BGP) [5] Danbury, CT St. Peter Church; [C] Danbury, CT Immaculate High School.
Piccione, John T. *o.f.m.* '95 (PAT) [5] Paterson, NJ St. Bonaventure Church.
Piccola, Michael J. '78 (SCR) West Pittston, PA Immaculate Conception Church.
Piccoli, Gino L. *o.f.m.* '65 (TUC) San Carlos, AZ San Carlos Catholic Church.
Piccolo, Bruno *p.i.m.e.* '65 (DET) [K] Detroit, MI P.I.M.E. Missionaries of SS. Peter and Paul; [T] Detroit, MI Foster Parents Mission Club.
Piccolomini, Rocco '85 (WOR) [13] Worcester, MA Our Lady of Mt. Carmel and St. Ann Church.
Pichard, Msgr. Larry '73 (DAL) [26] Dallas, TX St. Pius X Church.
Piche, Lee A. '84 (STP) West St. Paul, MN St. Joseph Church.
Piche, Marc A. '68 (BO) [8] Haverhill, MA Sacred Hearts Church.
Pichette, David '67 (SY) Absent on Leave.
Pichette, Msgr. Fernand L. '58 (MAN) Retired.
Pick, Anthony '67 (SC) Coon Rapids, IA Annunciation Church; Dedham, IA St. Joseph's Church.
Pick, Edward '60 (VEN) Longboat Key, FL St. Mary Star of the Sea Church.
Pick, Philip E. *s.j.* '50 (FgM) Provinces.
Pick, Philip E. *s.j.* '50 (MIL) [P] Milwaukee, WI Jesuit Provincial Office, Wisconsin Province.
Pickard, William B. '76 (SCR) [J] Scranton, PA St. Joseph's Center.
Pickarts, Bernard J. '55 (MAD) Retired.
Pickert, Cecil *o.carm.* '58 (L) [60] Louisville, KY Our Lady of Mount Carmel Church.
Pickett, James B. '61 (OAK) [4] Alameda, CA St. Philip Neri Church.
Pickett, Robert T. '55 (TLS) Retired.
Pico, Fernando *s.j.* '71 (SJN) [H] Hato Rey, PR Jesuit Community - Casa Claver.
Pico, Jaime *c.m.* '42 (BRK) [116] Brooklyn, NY St. Peter-St. Paul-Our Lady of Pilar Church.
Picone, Alfonso '00 (NEW) [1] Garfield, NJ Our Lady of Mt. Virgin Church.
Picornell, Antonio *m.ss.cc.* '42 (SJN) [25] Bayamon, PR Santiago Apostol Church.
Picton, James '75 (SEA) [26] Seattle, WA Immaculate Conception Church; [31] Seattle, WA Our Lady of Mount Virgin Church; Special Assignment.
Picton, James D. '75 (SEA) Bellevue, WA St. Madeleine Sophie Church.
Picton, Thomas D. *c.ss.r.* '71 (BR) [H] Baton Rouge, LA Redemptorist Vice Province.
Piderit, John J. *s.j.* '71 (CHI) [C] Chicago, IL Loyola University-Chicago; [C] Chicago, IL Jesuit Community at Loyola University of Chicago.
Pidgeon, John (PH) [D] Philadelphia, PA West Philadelphia Catholic High School.
Pidgeon, John '87 (PH) [47] Philadelphia, PA St. Francis de Sales Church.
Pieber, Carl L. *c.m.* '80 (PH) [AA] Philadelphia, PA Congregation of the Mission.
Piechocki, Bruce '84 (FTW) [17] Fort Wayne, IN Queen of Angels Church; Pierceton, IN St. Francis Xavier Church; On Special Assignment.
Piechocki, Raymond S. '47 (ALB) Retired; [J] Amsterdam, NY Mt. Loretto Nursing Home.
Piechowski, Leonard E. '51 (MIL) Retired.
Pieczka, Walenty *c.m.* '43 (HRT) Derby, CT St. Michael Church.
Pied, Wilfrid L. '51 (BO) Senior Priests.
Piedra, Ruskin *c.ss.r.* '60 (BRK) [107] Brooklyn, NY Our Lady of Perpetual Help Basilica Church.
Piedrahita, Alberto '98 (CHI) [63] Chicago, IL St. Francis de Sales Church; [68] Chicago, IL St. George Church.
Piedrahita, Gabriel *m.x.y.* '86 (NY) [DD] Bronx, NY Yarumal Mission Society, Inc.
Piedrahita, Guillermo '84 (SJN) [3] Canovanas, PR Sagrado Corazon de Jesus Church.
Piedrahita, Jose Gabriel *m.x.y.* '86 (NY) [179] Bronx, NY Our Saviour Church.
Piegl, Fred '70 (CHI) [W] Oak Park, IL Oak Park Study Center.
Piekarczyk, Marian *s.d.s.* '80 (SAT) [20] San Antonio, TX Our Lady of Sorrows Church; San Antonio, TX Methodist Hospital.
Piekarski, Joseph J. '86 (WIL) Ocean City, MD St. Luke and St. Andrew Church.
Pienciak, Daniel B. '87 (TR) Leave of Absence.
Pienta, Bob '99 (LAN) Brighton, MI St. Patrick Church.
Pientek, Placid *o.s.b.* '44 (CLV) [O] Cleveland, OH Benedictine Order of Cleveland.
Pieper, Herbert *s.m.* '38 (STL) [P] St. Louis, MO Marianist Community; [T] Eureka, MO Marianist Retreat & Conference Center.
Pieper, Msgr. James E. '57 (STL) Des Peres, MO St. Clement Church.
Pieper, Theodore X. '62 (STL) Old Mines, MO St. Joachim Church; Tiff, MO St. Joseph Church.
Piepmeyer, Ronald J. '97 (CIN) [56] Cincinnati, OH St. Martin of Tours Church.
Pier, Andrew *o.s.b.* '37 (CLV) [O] Cleveland, OH Benedictine Order of Cleveland.
Pier, Msgr. Joseph '38 (ALT) Retired.
Pierce, Blaine F. '46 (Y) Retired.
Pierce, Bradley *m.s.a.* '83 (NOR) [A] Cromwell, CT Holy Apostles College and Seminary; [F] Cromwell, CT Society of the Missionaries of the Holy Apostles.
Pierce, Brian J. *o.p.* '83 (FgM) Dominican - Order of Preachers Foreign Missions.
Pierce, Brian J. *o.p.* '88 (NO) [P] New Orleans, LA Dominican Friars, Southern Dominican Province of St. Martin de Porres.
Pierce, Edward J. '72 (SFS) Mitchell, SD Holy Family Church.
Pierce, James L. *s.j.* '77 (BUF) [7] Buffalo, NY St. Ann Church.
Pierce, John *o.f.m.* '63 (NY) Warwick, NY St. Anthony Community Hospital; [Z] Warwick, NY Villa Frances at the Knolls.
Pierce, John J. *o.f.m.* '63 (PAT) [M] Butler, NJ St. Anthony Friary.
Pierce, Joseph B. '92 (WDC) [3] Washington, DC St. Ann Church.
Pierce, Larry E. '58 (SAL) Retired.
Pierce, Mark '81 (WIN) [A] Winona, MN Immaculate Heart of Mary Seminary.
Pierce, Mark R. '81 (LC) [10] La Crosse, WI Roncalli Newman Church; [K] La Crosse, WI Roncalli Newman Parish.
Pierce, Msgr. Robert T. '54 (LA) Covina, CA St. Louise de Marillac Church.
Pierce, William C. (CAM) Millville, NJ St. John Bosco Church.
Pierceall, Patrick L. '69 (JC) Holts Summit, MO St. Andrew Church.
Pierick, Bernard E. '47 (MAD) Retired.
Pierick, Bernard J. '47 (MAD) [H] Madison, WI Bishop O'Connor Catholic Pastoral Center.
Pierini, Pascal *o.c.d.* '48 (SJ) [L] San Jose, CA Carmelite Monastery, Novitiate.
Pierini, Raymond G. *m.m.* '87 (NY) Manhattan, NY Cabrini Medical Center; [DD] Maryknoll, NY Maryknoll Fathers and Brothers.
Pieris, Timothy '46 (NO) Retired.
Pierjok, Harry A '88 (PEO) [9] Peoria, IL St. Jude's Church.
Piermarini, Msgr. Louis R. '69 (WOR) Oxford, MA St. Roch's Church.
Pierog, Stanislaus '76 (VEN) [5] Fort Myers, FL St. Francis Xavier Church.
Pieroni, Christopher J. (SFE) Vaughn, NM St. Mary Church.
Pieroni, Edward L. '85 (PRO) [30] Providence, RI St. Raymond Church; Providence, RI Miriam Hospital.
Pierre, Andre *o.f.m.cap.* (WDC) [39] Washington, DC Shrine of the Sacred Heart Church.
Pierre, Jean '88 (MIA) [20] Miami, FL St. James Church.
Pierre, Kenneth J. '63 (STP) [3] Minneapolis, MN Annunciation Church.
Pierre, Roger P. '63 (STP) White Bear Lake, MN St. Mary of the Lake Church.
Pierre-Louis, Jean Marx '87 (BO) [8] Brockton, MA Sacred Heart Church.
Pierro, Sebastian C. '82 (BUF) Lewiston, NY St. Peter Church.
Pierse, Msgr. James J. '44 (ORG) Seal Beach, CA Holy Family Church; Retired.
Pierson, Robert *o.s.b.* '84 (FgM) American - Cassinese Congregation Foreign Missions.
Pierson, Robert *o.s.b.* '84 (SCL) [I] Collegeville, MN St. John's Abbey, of the Order of St. Benedict.
Pietramale, John L. '92 (OM) [12] Omaha, NE Christ the King Church.
Pietrantonio, Thomas *o.f.m.cap.* '49 (WIL) [I] Wilmington, DE Capuchin Franciscan Friars, St. Francis Renewal Center; [L] Wilmington, DE St. Francis Renewal Center.
Pietras, Robert E. '62 (JOL) Downers Grove, IL Divine Savior Church.
Pietropaoli, David '84 (BAL) Absent on Leave.
Pietropinto, Joseph P. '70 (NEW) Maywood, NJ Our Lady Queen of Peace Church.
Pietrowski, Stephen '92 (RVC) Williston Park, NY St. Aidan's Church.
Pietrucha, Edward S. *c.s.p.* '57 (TUC) [13] Tucson, AZ St. Cyril of Alexandria Church.
Pietrus, Henryk '70 (FAR) Absent on Leave.
Pietrzak, Bernard J. '81 (CHI) [3] Mt. Prospect, IL St. Raymond de Penafort Church.
Pietrzak, Daniel *o.f.m.conv.* '64 (BAL) [S] Ellicott City, MD Order of Friars Minor Conventual.
Pifher, Cletus *o.f.m.conv.* '64 (SAV) Brunswick, GA St. Francis Xavier Church.
Pifher, William A. *c.s.c.* '94 (TOL) Norwalk, OH St. Paul Church.
Pighini, Richard *c.s.v.* '85 (JOL) [2] Kankakee, IL St. Patrick Church.
Pignato, Salvatore A. '68 (PSC) Orlando, FL St. Nicholas of Myra Church.
Pigott, Edward L. *s.j.* '68 (CIN) [F] Cincinnati, OH St. Xavier High School; [M] Cincinnati, OH Jesuit Community at St. Xavier High School.
Pijoan, L. Adrian M. Figuerola '71 (NO) Retired.
Pikturna, Vytautas '45 (BRK) Retired.
Pikula, Zygmunt '55 (NEW) [16] Newark, NJ Holy Trinity Church.
Pikulski, John F. '60 (BGP) [4] Danbury, CT St. Joseph Church; Danbury, CT Danbury Hospital.
Pikus, Karl *f.s.s.p.* '94 (SCR) [M] Elmhurst, PA Priestly Fraternity of St. Peter (F.S.S.P.), North American District Headquarters.
Pikus, Karl A. '92 (LIN) [M] Lincoln, NE St. Francis of Assisi Church.
Pilaczynski, John E. *o.m.i.* '58 (STP) [N] St. Paul, MN Oblate Residence.
Pilarski, Bernard '56 (DET) Detroit, MI Annapolis; Detroit, MI Garden City Osteopathic Hospital.
Pilarski, Chester J. '50 (SAG) Kawkawlin, MI Sacred Heart Church.
Pilarski, Peter R. '59 (PIT) Plum, PA St. Januarius Church.
Pilarski, Raymond J. '55 (GAY) Retired.
Pilarz, Scott R. *s.j.* '92 (WDC) [M] Washington, DC The Jesuit Community at Georgetown University.
Pilato, Sabato '92 (LA) Torrance, CA St. Catherine Laboure Church; [D] Gardena, CA Junipero Serra High School.
Pilatowski, Augustine *o.f.m.conv.* '59 (HRT) [M] New Britain, CT Conventual Franciscans.
Pilatowski, Eugene '60 (NOR) [3] Norwich, CT St. Joseph Church.
Pilcher, Gregory *o.s.b.* '78 (LR) [I] Jonesboro, AR Holy Angels Convent-Motherhouse.
Pilcher, John '99 (KCK) [J] Lawrence, KS St. Lawrence Catholic Campus Center at the University of Kansas and Residence.
Pilecki, Walter J. '43 (KC) Sugar Creek, MO St. Cyril Church.
Pileggi, Anthony J. '81 (KC) Nevada, MO St. Mary's Church.
Pileggi, Francis J. *o.s.f.s.* '61 (PH) [AA] Philadelphia, PA Oblates of St. Francis De Sales.
Piletic, William *c.m.* '77 (LA) [A] Camarillo, CA St. John's Seminary College of the Archdiocese of Los Angeles.
Pilger, G. Richard *i.c.* '79 (SP) Seminole, FL Blessed Sacrament Church.
Pilger, Joseph J. '55 (LEX) Retired.
Pilgram, Paul C. *s.j.* '79 (STL) [P] St. Louis, MO White House Retreat Jesuit Community; [T] St. Louis, MO White House Retreat.
Pili, Ignacio *c.m.v.* '84 (ARE) [7] Arecibo, PR Nuestra Senora de Fatima Church.

Pilipie, John P. '82 (PAT) Whippany, NJ Our Lady of Mercy Church.
Pilla, P. Carl '54 (SY) Retired; [S] Syracuse, NY St. Pius X Home, Inc.
Pillar, Conrad *o.s.b.* '47 (KCK) [H] Atchison, KS St. Benedict's Abbey.
Pillar, James *o.m.i.* '54 (STP) [W] St. Paul, MN Missionary Oblates of Mary Immaculate.
Pilliod, Francis B. '39 (CIN) [22] Dayton, OH St. Peter Church; Retired; [L] Centerville, OH The Franciscan at St. Leonard.
Pillon, Gordon '79 (PEO) Clinton, IL St. John the Baptist's Church; Wapella, IL St. Patrick's Church.
Pilola, Joseph '87 (HT) Grand Caillou, LA Holy Family Church; Theriot, LA St. Eloi Church.
Pilon, Daniel J. '76 (FAR) Wild Rice, ND St. Benedict's Church.
Pilon, James F. '67 (HRT) Farmington, CT St. Patrick's Church.
Pilon, Jerome R. '89 (PEO) Moline, IL St. Mary's Church.
Pilon, Mark A. (BAL) [A] Emmitsburg, MD Mount St. Mary's Seminary.
Pilon, Mark A. '75 (ARL) On Duty Outside the Diocese.
Pilon, Peter '00 (PEO) Mendota, IL Holy Cross Church.
Pilones, Loji *r.c.j.* '75 (LA) [Q] Camarillo, CA Rogationist Fathers.
Pilsner, Peter R. '89 (NY) [E] New York, NY Cardinal Spellman High School.
Pimental, Jose *o.p.* (SD) [B] San Diego, CA University of San Diego.
Pinard, Paul *s.s.e.* '59 (NOR) [A] Enders Island, CT St. Edmund's Novitiate; [F] Mystic, CT Society of St. Edmund.
Pincelli, Thomas L. '70 (BWN) [4] Harlingen, TX St. Anthony Church.
Pinchock, Joseph '72 (ORL) Winter Haven, FL St. Joseph's Church.
Pinciaro, Albert G., III '84 (BGP) [6] Norwalk, CT St. Philip Church.
Pincince, Gerald P. '65 (PRO) On Duty Outside the Diocese.
Pinczewski, Phillip A. '87 (E) Kane, PA St. Callistus Church.
Pineda, Serafin *o.a.r.* (NY) [126] Bronx, NY St. Anselm Church.
Pinero, Geraldo J. '91 (PH) Aston, PA St. Joseph Church.
Pinette, Stuart H. '95 (HRT) [14] Hartford, CT St. Michael Church.
Pingatore, Thomas '44 (STP) [22] St. Paul, MN St. John of St. Paul Church.
Pingatore, Thomas J. '44 (STP) Retired.
Pinillos, Javier Bautista *m.s.c.* '95 (FgM) Missionaries of the Sacred Heart Foreign Missions.
Pinizzotto, Anthony J. *o.s.f.s.* '78 (ARL) Stafford, VA St. William of York Church.
Pinizzotto, Anthony J. *o.s.f.s.* '78 (WIL) [I] Wilmington, DE Oblates of St. Francis De Sales.
Pinkerton, Samuel J. '95 (WCH) Augusta, KS St. James Church.
Pinkston, Robert L. *c.s.p.* '69 (SFR) [32] San Francisco, CA Old St. Mary's Church.
Pinne, Christopher P. *s.j.* '87 (KC) [J] Kansas City, MO Rockhurst Jesuit Community.
Pinon, Gilberto *o.m.i.* '71 (FgM) Oblates Foreign Missions.
Pins, Herbert J. '71 (HEL) Drummond, MT St. Michael Church; Philipsburg, MT St. Philip Church; Deer Lodge, MT Montana State Prison; Warm Springs, MT Warm Springs State Hospital.
Pins, Herbert J. '71 (SEA) On Duty Outside the Archdiocese.
Pins, Msgr. Joseph '70 (STL) Chesterfield, MO Ascension Church.
Pintabone, John A. *k.h.s.* '79 (NY) [197] Staten Island, NY Assumption Church.
Pintacura, Michael '93 (STO) Absent on Leave.
Pinti, Domenico C. '85 (TUC) Safford, AZ St. Rose of Lima Church; [I] Thatcher, AZ Eastern Arizona Junior College.
Pinto, Angelo '71 (BRK) [14] Brooklyn, NY St. Augustine Church.
Pinto, Danny '63 (FTW) Churubusco, IN St. John Bosco Church; Ege, IN Immaculate Conception Church.
Pinto, Fernando *o.c.d.* '98 (TUC) [24] Tucson, AZ Santa Cruz Church.
Pinto, Peter J. '56 (HRT) [4] West Haven, CT St. Louis Church.
Pinto, Santan *s.o.l.t.* '77 (CC) [H] Robstown, TX Society of Our Lady of the Most Holy Trinity.
Pintye, Louis M. *o.f.m.* '90 (BGP) [3] Fairfield, CT St. Emery Church.
Pinyan, Charles '92 (NEW) Berkeley Heights, NJ Church of the Little Flower.
Pinzon, Alvaro '91 (MIA) [1] Miami, FL St. Mary's Church.
Pinzon, Eduardo *s.j.* '60 (CHI) [22] Chicago, IL St. Bartholomew Church; [C] Chicago, IL Jesuit Community at Loyola University of Chicago.
Piombini, Msgr. Mario G. '43 (BRK) Retired.
Piontkowski, Richard L., Jr. '82 (GI) North Platte, NE St. Patrick Church.
Piorkowski, Robert '76 (STN) Madison, IL St. Mary's Church; St. Louis, MO Assumption B.V.M. Church.
Piorkowski, Msgr. Stanley W. '51 (SCR) Dickson City, PA Visitation of the Blessed Virgin Mary Church.
Piotrowski, Adrian *o.s.c.* '64 (STP) Anoka, MN St. Stephen Church; [N] Anoka, MN Crosier Community of Anoka.
Piotrowski, Leonard '93 (SP) [14] Tampa, FL St. Paul Church.
Piovan, Benjamin '64 (NO) La Place, LA Ascension of Our Lord Church.
Pipala, Edward A. '66 (NY) Absent on Leave.
Pipp, Thomas J. *s.j.* '92 (TOL) [C] Toledo, OH St. John's Jesuit High School.
Pipta, Robert M. '94 (VNN) Las Vegas, NV St. Gabriel the Archangel Church.
Piquado, Thomas G. *s.j.* '72 (SFR) [25] San Francisco, CA St. Ignatius Church; [N] San Francisco, CA Jesuit Community at University of San Francisco.
Piran, Louis *c.s.* '71 (GAL) [44] Houston, TX St. Leo the Great Church.
Piraro, Don '67 (LKC) [C] Moss Bluff, LA St. Charles Center.
Pires, Francisco '84 (SLC) Monroe, UT St. Elizabeth's Church; Gunnison, UT State Penitentiary; [H] Ephraim, UT St. Jude Catholic Center.
Piro, Francis '54 (PH) [104] Philadelphia, PA St. Michael Church.
Piro, Frank R. '62 (SFR) Retired.
Piro, Gerald J. '79 (BRK) Absent on Leave.
Pirrera, Aaron *o.s.b.* '85 (LR) [A] Subiaco, AR Subiaco Monastery.
Pirrone, Roberto '88 (LA) Wilmington, CA SS. Peter and Paul's Church.
Pirrung, George '54 (PHX) Retired.
Pisano, Andrew '42 (LA) Retired.
Pisarcik, John G. '70 (PAT) Absent on Leave.
Pisciotta, Justin *o.s.m.* '64 (ORG) Fullerton, CA St. Philip Benizi Church.
Pisciotta, Justin M. *o.s.m.* '64 (CHI) [N] Chicago, IL Order of Friar Servants of Mary (Servites) United States of America Province, Inc.
Piscitelli, Vincent J. '37 (BO) Senior Priests.
Piscitello, Primo *o.f.m.* '60 (NY) [DD] New York, NY Franciscan Province of the Immaculate Conception.
Pisegna, Cedric *c.p.* '91 (SAC) [H] Citrus Heights, CA Christ the King Retreat.
Piselli, Costanzo J. '69 (PRT) Belfast, ME St. Francis of Assisi Church.
Pisfil, Luis Carlos '92 (BRK) [57] Brooklyn, NY Holy Innocents Church.
Pisik, Timothy E. '74 (CAM) On Sick Leave.
Piskula, Louis '75 (OWN) Non-Parochial Assignments; [G] Whitesville, KY St. Joseph's Monastery.
Piskura, Joseph '54 (CLV) Retired.
Piso, Volodymyr '73 (STF) Rochester, NY St. Josaphat Church.
Pisoni, Otto B. '41 (E) Retired.
Pisors, John A. *c.s.v.* '66 (CHI) [N] Arlington Heights, IL Viatorian Province Center-Clerics of St. Viator.
Pispeky, Steve '88 (GLP) Retired.
Pistacchio, Gene B. *o.f.m.* '89 (ARL) Triangle, VA St. Francis of Assisi Church.
Pistone, Bernardo '73 (HBG) [3] Lancaster, PA Assumption of the Blessed Virgin Mary Church; [J] Lancaster, PA Iglesia de San Juan Bautista.
Pistone, Dominic J., Jr. '78 (GAL) [66] Houston, TX St. Paul Church.
Pistorius, Francis X. *s.j.* '72 (GAL) [3] Spring, TX St. Ignatius of Loyola Church.
Pistulka, Celestine C. '56 (NU) Marshall, MN Holy Redeemer Church; Milroy, MN St. Michael Church.
Piszczatowski, Maurice *o.f.m.conv.* '53 (BGP) [6] Danbury, CT Sacred Heart Church.
Piszker, James '91 (E) [B] Erie, PA Mercyhurst College; [P] Erie, PA Newman Centers and Campus Ministry.
Pitcavage, William *s.c.j.* '76 (SFS) [B] Chamberlain, SD St. Joseph Indian School.
Pitol, Marco Antonio Basulto '00 (TUC) Douglas, AZ St. Luke Church.
Pitoyo, Sugiyo *s.j.* '95 (BO) [W] Chestnut Hill, MA The Jesuit Community at Boston College.
Pitre, Eric '81 (GAL) La Porte, TX St. Mary of the Immaculate Conception Church.
Pitt, Msgr. William L. '61 (RIC) [A] Virginia Beach, VA Catholic High School.
Pittapilly, Thomas '61 (GF) Special Assignment.
Pittappilly, Thomas '61 (GF) Culbertson, MT St. Anthony's Church.
Pittard, Wayne M. '83 (GF) Sabbatical.
Pitti, Rigoberto *c.m.* '98 (FgM) Vincentian Foreign Missions.
Pittman, Robert S. *s.s.s.* '58 (CLV) [O] Cleveland, OH Congregation of the Blessed Sacrament Provincial House.
Pittman, Robert S. *s.s.s.* '58 (WDC) [V] Washington, DC Black Leadership and Christ's Kingdom Society; [V] Waldorf, MD Body of Christ Farm Community, Inc.
Pitts, Joseph *o.m.i.* '59 (BEL) [F] Belleville, IL Shrine of Our Lady of the Snows.
Pitts, William L. '70 (R) Pinehurst, NC Sacred Heart Church.
Pittstick, Rory '94 (SPK) Okanogan-Omak, WA Our Lady of the Valley Church.
Pitula, Zygmunt J. '39 (TOL) Retired.
Pitzen, John J. '45 (DUB) Retired.
Pitzer, John M. *o.p.* '99 (NO) [30] New Orleans, LA St. Dominic Church.
Pivarnik, Gabriel *o.p.* '97 (PRO) [29] Providence, RI St. Pius V Church; [P] Providence, RI St. Pius Priory.
Pivonka, David *t.o.r.* '96 (STU) [A] Steubenville, OH Franciscan University of Steubenville; [F] Steubenville, OH Holy Spirit Friary.
Pivonka, Leonard '77 (CC) Alice, TX St. Elizabeth Church.
Piwowar, Stanley J. '51 (MAN) Claremont, NH St. Joseph Church.
Piwowarczyk, Darius *s.v.d.* '90 (WDC) [M] Washington, DC Divine Word College.
Pizmoht, Loius A. '66 (CLV) South Euclid, OH St. Margaret Mary Church.
Pizzamiglio, Ernest E. '66 (PEO) Galesburg, IL Immaculate Heart of Mary Church.
Pizzarelli, Francis *s.m.m.* '79 (RVC) Davis Park, NY Most Precious Blood Church; [M] Bay Shore, NY Montfort Missionaries.
Pizzarelli, Frank *s.m.m.* '80 (RVC) [B] Patchogue, NY St. Joseph's College.
Pizzo, Anthony B. *o.s.a.* '84 (CHI) [39] Chicago, IL St. Clare of Montefalco Church.
Pizzo, Philip '77 (BRK) [138] Brooklyn, NY St. Teresa of Avila Church.
Pizzuto, Alfred R. '55 (NY) Marlboro, NY St. Mary Church.
Placa, Msgr. Alan J. (RVC) [I] Melville, NY Catholic Health Services of Long Island; [I] Melville, NY Catholic Health Services of Long Island.
Placa, Msgr. Alan J. '70 (RVC) Great Neck, NY St. Aloysius Church.
Placa, Stephen '95 (BRK) [174] Queens, NY St. Gregory the Great Church.
Place, Michael D. *s.t.d.* '70 (CHI) On Duty Outside the Archdiocese.
Place, Michael D. *s.t.d.* '70 (STL) [V] St. Louis, MO The Catholic Health Association of the United States.
Place, Terry E. '72 (FTW) [11] South Bend, IN St. John the Baptist Church.
Placencia, Franco '94 (DEN) [A] Denver, CO St. Andrew's Theatine Religious House.
Plagens, James A. '65 (SAN) Big Spring, TX Sacred Heart Church; Big Spring, TX St. Thomas Church.
Plagge, Robert J. '43 (CIN) Retired; [V] Cincinnati, OH Marian Center of Cincinnati.
Plaisted, Eugene D. *o.s.c.* '61 (STP) Anoka, MN St. Stephen Church; [N] Anoka, MN Crosier Community of Anoka.
Plakut, Peter *o.c.s.o.* '58 (P) [L] Lafayette, OR The Cistercian (Trappist) Abbey of Our Lady of Guadalupe.
Plamondon, Donald J. '72 (DUB) Holy Cross, IA Holy Cross Church; Luxemburg, IA Holy Trinity Church; [F] Holy Cross, IA Rickardsville-Holy Cross-Luxemburg (RHCL) Catholic School.
Planas, Salvador '54 (MIA) Retired.
Planea, John '82 (NO) On Duty Outside the Archdiocese.
Planinsek, Henry *c.s.sp.* (SLC) St. George, UT St. George's Church.
Plank, Stephen J. *o.s.b.* '94 (OM) [C] Elkhorn, NE Mount Michael High School; [K] Elkhorn, NE Mount Michael Abbey.
Planning, Stephen W. *s.j.* '99 (BAL) [S] Baltimore, MD Jesuit Fathers and Brothers Maryland Provincial Curia.
Planning, Stephen W. *s.j.* '99 (CHI) [N] Chicago, IL Miguel Pro Jesuit Community.
Plans, John *s.f.* '67 (SFE) [30] Albuquerque, NM St. Therese of the Infant Jesus of the Little Flower Church.
Plante, Georges J. '53 (PRT) Madison, ME St. Sebastian Church.
Plante, Msgr. Jacques L. '82 (PRO) [21] Providence, RI St. Maron Church; [9] Pawtucket, RI St. Mary of the Immaculate Conception Church; [T] Pawtucket, RI Opus Spiritus Sancti-East Coast USA Region; [U] Providence, RI Miscellaneous Listings for the Diocese of Providence.
Plante, Paul A. '71 (PRT) Winslow, ME St. John the Baptist Church.
Plante, Pierre J. '78 (PRO) [1] Warwick, RI St. Benedict Church.
Plante, Richard A. '53 (RC) Retired.
Plantes, Francis P. '45 (PIT) Retired; [O] Pittsburgh, PA St. John Vianney Manor.
Planty, Donald J. '93 (ARL) On Duty Outside the Diocese.
Plascencia, Miguel '53 (LA) [10] Los Angeles, CA Divine Saviour Church.
Plasker, Alexander *o.s.b.* '62 (P) [L] St. Benedict, OR Mt. Angel Abbey; [N] St. Benedict, OR Mount Angel

Abbey Retreat House.
Plasker, Robert *c.s.c.* '57 (FgM) Holy Cross Foreign Missions.
Plasker, Robert L. *c.s.c.* '57 (FTW) [J] South Bend, IN Congregation of Holy Cross, Indiana Province, Provincial House.
Plasse, Eugene J. '72 (SPR) Bondsville, MA St. Bartholomew's Church; Palmer, MA St. Thomas the Apostle Church.
Plassenthal, Vincent A. *s.m.* '44 (PCE) Villalba, PR Our Lady Mother of Divine Providence Church.
Plaster, George F. '80 (IND) [F] Indianapolis, IN St. Vincent Hospital and Health Care Center, Inc.
Plaster, George F. '80 (LFT) On Duty Outside the Diocese.
Plastino, James L. '94 (MRY) [2] Salinas, CA Sacred Heart Church.
Plata, Gregory *o.f.m.* '85 (GB) [I] Pulaski, WI Assumption of B.V.M. Friary.
Plate, Brian G. '96 (NEW) Military Chaplains.
Plathanam, Ignatius J. *c.m.i.* '72 (STA) [2] Gainesville, FL Holy Faith Church.
Plathe, Anthony H. '63 (NU) Retired.
Plathottam, Matthew '67 (PHX) Gilbert, AZ St. Anne Church.
Plathottam, Thomas *c.s.t.* '74 (NOR) Ellington, CT St. Luke Church.
Platt, Stewart '51 (Y) Retired.
Platt, William F. '88 (BGP) Riverside, CT St. Catherine of Siena Church; Greenwich, CT Greenwich Hospital.
Plaushin, Mark *o.s.f.s.* '89 (PH) [76] Philadelphia, PA St. Joachim Church.
Plavac, Timothy '86 (CLV) [A] Wickliffe, OH Borromeo Seminary.
Plavcan, Jon J. '94 (GRY) Highland, IN Our Lady of Grace Church.
Plavunikunnathil, Chrysostom *c.m.i.* '66 (BEA) [1] Beaumont, TX St. Anthony Church; Port Arthur, TX Convalescent Home Ministry.
Plawecki, Joseph '83 (DET) Erie, MI St. Joseph Church.
Plawny, Thaddeus *m.s.* '51 (PEO) [M] Georgetown, IL LaSalette Missionaries.
Playoust, Alfred G. *s.j.* '46 (SJ) [L] Los Gatos, CA Sacred Heart Jesuit Center.
Pleban, Alexander L. '57 (GBG) [2] Uniontown, PA St. Joseph Church.
Pleban, Leo '60 (Y) Retired.
Plechta, Sabin *o.f.m.* '43 (WDC) [M] Washington, DC Commissariat of the Holy Land, Franciscan Monastery - Mount St. Sepulchre.
Pleho, Anthony J. '79 (NY) [18] Yonkers, NY Most Holy Trinity Church.
Plei, Stephen A. *c.ss.r.* '56 (STL) [P] Liguori, MO St. Clement Health Care Center.
Pleier, David (GB) [5] Green Bay, WI St. Bernard Church.
Pleiman, Kenneth F. *c.pp.s.* '70 (CLV) [2] Cleveland, OH St. Adalbert Church.
Pleiness, Gregg A. '81 (LAN) Howell, MI St. Augustine Church.
Plesa, Andrew J. '56 (RCK) Spring Grove, IL St. Peter Church.
Pleskac, Msgr. Myron J. '60 (LIN) [7] Lincoln, NE St. Joseph Church.
Pleus, Adrian C.H. '99 (ATL) Kennesaw, GA St. Catherine of Siena Church.
Pleva, Gerald *s.m.* '77 (SAT) Helotes, TX Our Lady of Guadalupe Church.
Plevyak, Valentine R. '44 (SCR) Retired; [N] Dunmore, PA Villa St. Joseph.
Plewka, Msgr. Mark A. '76 (PBL) [4] Pueblo, CO Holy Rosary Church.
Pliaplis, Christopher '87 (NY) Nanuet, NY St. Anthony Church.
Pliauplis, Christopher '87 (STU) On Duty Outside the Diocese.
Plo, Msgr. John '61 (NY) [10] Yonkers, NY St. Joseph Church.
Ploch, Robert '92 (SAT) Karnes City, TX St. Cornelius Church.
Ploch, Robert '96 (SAT) Panna Maria, TX Immaculate Conception of the Blessed Virgin Mary Church.
Ploch, Timothy C. *s.d.b.* '76 (NY) [3] Port Chester, NY Our Lady of the Rosary Church.
Plocharczyk, Msgr. Daniel J. '74 (HRT) [1] Hartford, CT Cathedral of St. Joseph.
Plociennik, Robert *o.f.m.conv.* '60 (HBG) Manheim, PA St. Richard Church.
Plock, Charles T. *c.m.* '73 (PH) [70] Philadelphia, PA Immaculate Conception Church.
Plocke, Donald J. *s.j.* '84 (BO) [W] Chestnut Hill, MA The Jesuit Community at Boston College.
Plokhooy, Christopher H. '59 (WIL) Retired; [G] Wilmington, DE Vianney House.
Plominski, Walter J. '68 (ROC) Caledonia, NY St. Columba Church.
Ploof, Gerald J. '75 (LAN) Clio, MI SS. Charles and Helena Church.
Ploof, Msgr. Thomas M. '45 (WIN) Retired.
Ploplis, Theodore '77 (CHI) [J] Chicago, IL St. Anthony Hospital; [J] Chicago, IL Columbus Hospital; [J] Chicago, IL St. Joseph Hospital.
Plotka, Frank W. '68 (CHI) [6] Waukegan, IL Immaculate Conception B.V.M. Church.
Plotkowski, John S. '74 (CHI) Buffalo Grove, IL St. Mary Church.
Ploude, Thomas E. '64 (CAM) Brooklawn, NJ St. Maurice's Church.
Plouffe, Paul I. *s.s.e.* '45 (MOB) [G] Selma, AL Edmundite Fathers.
Plough, James H. '58 (PBL) Grand Junction, CO Immaculate Heart of Mary Church.
Plourde, Carroll W. *s.s.e.* '87 (MOB) Orrville, AL Immaculate Conception Church; Selma, AL Our Lady Queen of Peace Church; [G] Selma, AL Edmundite Fathers; [J] Selma, AL Marion Institute Newman Center.
Plourde, James S. '81 (PRT) Fort Kent, ME St. Louis Church.
Plourde, James S. '82 (PRT) [L] Frenchville, ME Christian Life Center.
Plourde, Peter A. '83 (SP) Temple Terrace, FL Corpus Christi Church.
Pluck, Charles T. *c.m.* '73 (BRK) [66] Brooklyn, NY St. John the Baptist Church.
Plummer, J. Bruce '40 (HEL) Retired.
Plummer, James '58 (CAM) Retired.
Plunkett, Gregory J. '88 (PEO) Aledo, IL St. Catherine's Church.
Plunkett, Msgr. Joseph P. '60 (NEW) [27] Newark, NJ Our Lady of Good Counsel Church.
Pluth, Paul *o.s.b.* '96 (LA) [Q] Valyermo, CA St. Andrew's Abbey.
Plutz, Stanley *s.v.d.* '53 (FgM) Society of the Divine Word Foreign Missions.
Poage, Godfrey *c.p.* '46 (LA) [Q] Pasadena, CA Passionist Community.
Poandl, Robert F. *glmy.* '68 (TLS) Hugo, OK Immaculate Conception Church.
Poblocki, Richard M. '83 (BUF) [58] Buffalo, NY Queen of Peace Church.
Pocernich, Eugene '74 (MIL) [K] Milwaukee, WI St. Mary's Hospital of Milwaukee.
Pocetto, Alexander T. *o.s.f.s.* '55 (ALN) [B] Center Valley, PA Desales University; [K] Center Valley, PA Oblates of St. Francis de Sales.
Poche, Daniel M. '78 (HT) Gheens, LA Community of St. Anthony Church; Raceland, LA St. Hilary of Poitiers Church.
Poche, Msgr. Gerard W. '48 (NO) Retired.
Poche, Louis A. *s.j.* '55 (BR) Gramercy, LA Most Sacred Heart of Jesus Church.
Pock, Donald P. '58 (JOL) Itasca, IL St. Peter the Apostle Church.
Pocus, Msgr. Dominick A. '45 (NEW) Kearny, NJ Our Lady of Sorrows Church; Retired.
Poczworowski, Luke *o.f.m.conv.* '64 (RCK) [2] Rockford, IL St. Anthony of Padua Church.
Podesta, Msgr. John F. '35 (JOL) Retired.
Podgorny, Msgr. John (PAT) Retired.
Podgorski, Francis '37 (RVC) Glen Head, NY St. Hyacinth Church.
Podlesny, James F. *o.s.b.* '80 (HBG) Palmyra, PA Holy Spirit Church.
Podolak, William S. '50 (MIL) Retired.
Podraza, Timothy M. '97 (OM) [44] Omaha, NE St. Stephen the Martyr Church.
Podrosky, Alfred '52 (SCL) Retired.
Podsiadlo, John J. *s.j.* '72 (NY) [80] New York, NY Nativity Church; [HH] New York, NY Nativity Mission Center, Inc.
Podson, Theodore E. *sch.p.* '76 (AMA) [6] Amarillo, TX St. Francis Church.
Podson, Theodore E. *sch.p.* '76 (WDC) [B] Washington, DC Queen of Pious Schools House of Studies-Piarist Fathers.
Podvin, Albert J. '62 (SFE) [22] Albuquerque, NM Sangre de Cristo Church.
Podymniak, Miroslaw *o.f.m.cap.* (BO) [50] Boston, MA Our Lady of Czestochowa Church.
Poecking, David '96 (PIT) Unity, PA St. John the Baptist Church.
Poehlmann, Edward J. '67 (DEN) Edwards, CO St. Clare of Assisi Church.
Poelker, Msgr. Gerard L. '42 (JC) Retired.
Poerio, John A. '59 (LKC) Big Lake, LA St. Mary of the Lake Church.
Poettgen, Edward '80 (ORG) Stanton, CA St. Polycarp Church.
Poetz, Lawrence *s.v.d.* '44 (CHI) [B] Techny, IL Divine Word Residence.
Poetzel, Richard K. *c.ss.r.* '63 (BAL) [68] Baltimore, MD Our Lady of Fatima Church.
Poff, Edward '57 (JOL) [G] Kankakee, IL Provena St. Mary's Hospital.
Poff, Pius *o.f.m.conv.* '61 (LAN) [3] Lansing, MI Holy Cross Church.
Poggemeyer, Joseph T. '97 (TOL) Sandusky, OH St. Mary Church.
Pogorelc, Anthony *s.m.* '88 (LFT) [4] Lafayette, IN St. Lawrence Church.
Pogorelc, Anthony *s.m.* '88 (STL) [P] St. Louis, MO Provincialate of the Society of Mary, Province of St. Louis.
Pogorzelski, Eugeniusz '35 (GRY) Retired.
Pohak, Msgr. Nicholas I. '57 (PSC) Freeland, PA St. Mary's Church.
Pohl, Msgr. Daniel J. '53 (LIN) Indianola, NE St. Catherine's Church.
Pohl, Jerome H. '67 (PH) [2] Philadelphia, PA St. Adalbert Church.
Pohl, Leon H. '56 (KAL) Sturgis, MI Holy Angels Church.
Pohl, Stephen A. '85 (L) Bardstown, KY St. Monica Church; St. Thomas, KY St. Thomas Church.
Pohley, Robert G. '75 (BGP) [15] Stamford, CT Sacred Heart Church; [X] Shelton, CT Fr. McKenna St. Vincent de Paul Shoppe; [X] Stamford, CT Stamford Catholic Library.
Pohlman, Stephen J. '84 (SFD) Glen Carbon, IL St. Cecilia Church.
Pohlmeier, Erik T. '98 (LR) [5] Little Rock, AR Christ the King Church.
Pohlmeier, Loren '00 (GI) Crawford, NE St. John the Baptist Church.
Pohorlak, Joseph '61 (PRM) Whiting, IN Assumption of the Blessed Virgin Church.
Pohto, J. Thomas *o.s.a.* '67 (VEN) Bokeelia, FL Our Lady of the Miraculous Medal Church.
Pointek, Msgr. Francis J. '40 (FRS) Retired.
Poirer, Robert *s.j.* '77 (STL) [C] St. Louis, MO Saint Louis University.
Poirier, David *s.a.* '77 (NY) [DD] Garrison, NY Franciscan Friars of the Atonement, Minister General Office.
Poirier, John R. '71 (MAN) Dover, NH St. Joseph Church.
Poirier, Joseph *s.c.j.* '73 (SP) [O] Pinellas Park, FL Priests of the Sacred Heart.
Poirier, Ralph *c.s.sp.* '63 (SD) [2] El Cajon, CA Our Lady of Grace Church.
Poirier, Robert *s.j.* '77 (WDC) [20] Washington, DC Holy Trinity Church.
Poirier, Ronald (SP) [F] Palm Harbor, FL St. Luke Early Childhood Center.
Poirier, Ronald J. (SP) Palm Harbor, FL St. Luke the Evangelist Church.
Poirier, Vincent H. '85 (BO) [2] Newton, MA Corpus Christi Church; [CC] Framingham, MA Framingham State College Campus Ministry; [CC] Wellesley, MA Wellesley College Campus Ministry.
Poissant, Msgr. Leeward J. '63 (OG) Morristown, NY St. John the Evangelist Church; [A] Ogdensburg, NY Wadhams Hall.
Poisson, Joseph *f.s.s.p.* '96 (SCR) [M] Elmhurst, PA Priestly Fraternity of St. Peter (F.S.S.P.), North American District Headquarters.
Poisson, Thomas L. '78 (MAR) Houghton, MI St. Ignatius Loyola Church.
Poitras, Steven '93 (BO) [1] Somerville, MA St. Ann Church.
Pokornowski, Daniel A. '54 (BUF) [3] Cheektowaga, NY St. John Gualbert Church.
Pokorsky, Jerry J. '90 (ARL) Culpeper, VA Precious Blood Church.
Pokrzewinski, Justus *o.p.* '60 (FgM) Dominican - Order of Preachers Foreign Missions.
Pokrzewinski, Justus M. *o.p.* '60 (CHI) [N] Chicago, IL Dominicans (Provincial Office).
Pokusa, Msgr. Joseph W. '70 (CAM) Magnolia, NJ St. Gregory's Church; [G] Camden, NJ Francis, Elizabeth and Edward Roger Welsh Scholarship Trust.
Pol, Dom Te '70 (HT) Retired.
Polak, Michael J. '58 (PIT) [1] West Mifflin, PA St. Agnes Church.
Polakowski, Joseph '59 (MAR) Retired.
Polanco, Dennis *s.a.* '74 (NY) [DD] Garrison, NY Franciscan Friars of the Atonement, Minister General Office.
Poland, Sean '94 (PMB) Boynton Beach, FL St. Mark Church; Special Assignment.
Polando, Msgr. Peter M. *j.c.l.* '80 (Y) [17] Youngstown, OH St. Matthias Church.
Polasek, Jeffrey S. '91 (TLS) Sallisaw, OK St. Francis Xavier Church.
Polc, Msgr. Jaroslav '55 (GB) On Duty Outside the Diocese.
Polcyn, Robert F. *o.f.m.cap.* '68 (LC) Pine Creek, WI Most Sacred Heart Church; [D] Arcadia, WI Franciscan Skemp Healthcare, Mayo Health System, Arcadia Campus Hospital; [F] Arcadia, WI Franciscan Skemp Healthcare, Mayo Health System, Arcadia Campus Nursing Home.
Polczyk, Stanislaus T. '82 (TR) Union Beach, NJ Holy Family Church.
Polednak, John V. '76 (SCR) Nicholson, PA St. Patrick's Church.
Polek, David *c.ss.r.* '62 (STL) [B] St. Louis, MO St. John Neumann House.
Polentarutti, John *i.m.c.* '57 (CAM) Egg Harbor City, NJ St. Nicholas Church.

Polenz, Gordon '82 (ALB) Sidney, NY Sacred Heart Church.
Poletunow, Mark *o.f.m.cap.* '86 (WDC) [B] Washington, DC St. Francis Friary-Capuchin College; [V] Washington, DC Spanish Catholic Center.
Polewczak, Michael J. '73 (ALB) On Duty Outside the Diocese.
Polewczak, Michael J. '73 (CHR) Orangeburg, SC Holy Trinity Church.
Polgar, Capistran L. *o.f.m.* '67 (MET) [6] New Brunswick, NJ St. Ladislaus Church.
Poliafico, David A. '95 (COL) [1] Columbus, OH St. Joseph Church.
Policetti, Prasad (CHI) [137] Chicago, IL St. Monica Church.
Policetti, Sleeva R. '87 (CHI) [195] Chicago, IL St. Tarcissus Church.
Polich, David '76 (DM) [13] Des Moines, IA Visitation Church.
Polich, James '72 (KC) [A] Conception, MO Conception Seminary College.
Polich, James C. (DM) [6] Des Moines, IA St. Augustin's Church.
Polichnowski, Nicholas *t.o.r.* '77 (ALT) [F] Loretto, PA Mount Assisi Friary.
Policicchio, Luke *o.s.b.* '88 (GBG) Crabtree, PA St. Bartholomew Church.
Polidano, Carmel F. '81 (CAM) [2] Vineland, NJ Sacred Heart Church; [I] Vineland, NJ Bishop McCarthy Residence.
Polifka, Charles *o.f.m.cap.* '71 (KCK) Lawrence, KS St. John the Evangelist Church; [H] Lawrence, KS St. Conrad's Friary.
Polimera, Jaya Rao '92 (KAL) Battle Creek, MI St. Philip Church.
Polimine, Alan *t.o.r.* '59 (ALT) [F] Newry, PA St. Bernardine Monastery.
Polinski, Casimir V. *c.r.* '44 (CHI) [72] Chicago, IL St. Hedwig Church.
Polinsky, John R. '60 (BGP) Retired; [P] Stamford, CT The Catherine Dennis Keefe Queen of the Clergy Retired Priests' Residence.
Polito, Martin F. '76 (CLV) [29] Cleveland, OH Holy Redeemer Church.
Polito, Victor V.J. '54 (MAN) On Duty Outside the Diocese.
Polizzi, Daniel '69 (SD) Unassigned.
Polizzi, Msgr. Salvatore E. '56 (STL) [59] St. Louis, MO St. Roch Church.
Poljicak, Vlatko '65 (LA) Pomona, CA St. Joseph Church.
Polk, Thomas '67 (BAL) Urbana, MD St. Ignatius Loyola Church.
Pollack, Anthony J. '55 (ALT) [6] Altoona, PA Our Lady of Fatima Church.
Pollak, Claude W. *o.s.b.* '57 (ALT) Nicktown, PA St. Nicholas Church.
Pollard, Christopher J. '98 (ARL) Vienna, VA St. Mark's Church.
Pollard, John E. '74 (CHI) Wilmette, IL St. Joseph Church.
Pollard, John L. '83 (STA) Absent on Sick Leave.
Pollard, Marcus A. '90 (ARL) Herndon, VA St. Veronica Church.
Pollard, Patrick J. '72 (CHI) [36] Chicago, IL Christ the King Church; [Y] Chicago, IL Central Office.
Pollard, Msgr. Raymond J. '50 (NEW) Mountainside, NJ Our Lady of Lourdes Church; Retired.
Pollard, Roy F. '66 (WIL) Hockessin, DE St. Mary of the Assumption Church.
Pollard, Thomas W. '66 (WDC) Clinton, MD Church of St. John the Evangelist.
Pollauf, Robert A. *s.j.* '46 (DET) [P] Clarkston, MI Colombiere Center.
Pollie, A. Frank '67 (DET) Rochester, MI St. Irenaeus Church.
Pollis, Robert G. '57 (BO) Senior Priests.
Pollock, Paul *s.j.* '73 (FgM) Provinces.
Pollock, Msgr. Robert C. '48 (SLC) Retired.
Polmounter, Richard J. '78 (SCR) [6] Pittston, PA St. Mary, Help of Christians Church.
Polo, Antonio *s.d.b.* '56 (SJN) [37] San Juan, PR Maria Auxiliadora Church.
Poloche-Rodriguez, Pedro '98 (ATL) [10] Atlanta, GA St. Jude Church.
Polosky, Michael '91 (SJP) Ambridge, PA Ss. Peter and Paul Church.
Poloway, Michael '54 (SJP) Pittsburgh, PA St. John the Baptist Church.
Polselli, Leo *c.s.c.* '70 (FR) [A] North Easton, MA Holy Cross Fathers Religious.
Polt, Albert *o.a.r.* '54 (LA) [Q] Oxnard, CA St. Augustine Priory O.A.R.
Poltorak, George *s.a.c.* '90 (BUF) East Aurora, NY Immaculate Conception Church; [O] North Tonawanda, NY Society of the Catholic Apostolate.
Poltorak, Stanley '82 (SAC) Truckee, CA Assumption of the Blessed Virgin Mary Church.
Poluikis, John A. *c.s.b.* '51 (ROC) [I] Rochester, NY Basilian Residence.
Polyak, Anthony V. *m.m.* '62 (FgM) Maryknoll Foreign Missions.
Polyak, John V. '69 (MET) North Brunswick, NJ Our Lady of Peace Church.
Polycarpe, Pierre G. '99 (RCK) [3] Aurora, IL St. Joseph Church.
Polzer, Daniel *l.c.* (DEN) [Q] Englewood, CO Legionaries of Christ, Pastoral Services, Inc.
Polzer, Daniel *l.c.* '94 (LIN) [F] Waverly, NE Our Lady of Good Counsel Retreat House.
Pomaville, Raymond *o.m.i.* '55 (SAT) [K] San Antonio, TX Oblate Madonna Residence.
Pomerleau, Claude *c.s.c.* '65 (P) [B] Portland, OR University of Portland; [L] Portland, OR Holy Cross Fathers & Brothers, C.S.C. - University of Portland.
Pomerleau, William A. '79 (SPR) Indian Orchard, MA St. Jude Church.
Pomeroy, Joseph B. *s.j.* '62 (WOR) [N] Worcester, MA Jesuits of Holy Cross College, Inc.
Pomeroy, Thomas (GB) Darboy, WI Holy Angels Church.
Pomilio, Matthew '62 (BRK) Special Assignment.
Pommier, Richard *o.m.i.* '66 (FgM) Oblates Foreign Missions.
Pompei, Francis *o.f.m.* '74 (PH) [AA] Philadelphia, PA Order of Friars Minor of the Province of the Most Holy Name aka Holy Name Province.
Pompei, Frederick A. '66 (SY) [7] Syracuse, NY Our Lady of Pompei Church; Special Assignment.
Ponce, Francisco '67 (NEW) [13] Jersey City, NJ St. Joseph's Church.
Ponce, Juan Manuel '00 (SAC) Auburn, CA St. Joseph Church.
Poncelet, Frank '87 (SCL) Retired.
Ponciroli, Robert '69 (OAK) Retired.
Pondo, Stanley '98 (IND) Richmond, IN Holy Family Church; Richmond, IN St. Andrew Church; Richmond, IN St. Mary Church.
Ponessa, Joseph '74 (GF) Glendive, MT Sacred Heart Church.
Ponmelil, Thomas '64 (GAL) Pearland, TX St. Helen Church.
Ponnet, Christopher D. '83 (LA) [54] Los Angeles, CA St. Camillus De Lellis Church; Los Angeles, CA L.A. County/University of Southern California Hospital.
Pons, Miguel '53 (SJN) [6] Trujillo Alto, PR San Judas Tadeo Church.
Pons, Ramon *o.a.r.* '88 (SR) Petaluma, CA St. Vincent de Paul Church.
Ponso, Andres *o.s.m.* '50 (ELP) [18] El Paso, TX Our Lady of Sorrows Church.
Pontarelli, Michael M. *o.s.m.* '82 (CHI) [N] Chicago, IL Order of Friar Servants of Mary (Servites) United States of America Province, Inc.
Pontarelli, Michael M. *o.s.m.* '82 (ORG) [D] Anaheim, CA Servite High School; Servite High School Development Fund; [I] Anaheim, CA Servite Fathers and Brothers; [I] Buena Park, CA Order of Friar Servants of Mary (Servites).
Ponticello, Robert D. '81 (MEM) [19] Memphis, TN Church Of The Nativity.
Ponzini, Thomas V. '96 (GAL) [71] Houston, TX Prince of Peace Church.
Pookkattu, George *c.m.i.* '72 (ALX) Jena, LA St. Mary Church.
Pool, Jefferson *s.v.d.* '92 (TR) [M] Bordentown, NJ Society of the Divine Word.
Pool, Robert '55 (KCK) Retired.
Poole, James E. *s.j.* '53 (SEA) [C] Tacoma, WA Bellarmine Preparatory School; [G] Tacoma, WA St. Joseph Medical Center.
Poole, Michael P. '98 (HEL) Harlowton, MT St. Joseph Church; White Sulphur Springs, MT St. Bartholomew Church.
Poole, Richard '94 (SPK) Connell, WA St. Vincent Church; Eltopia, WA St. Paul Church.
Poole, Stafford '56 (LA) [Q] Montebello, CA Vincentian Fathers and Brothers; [Q] Montebello, CA Vincentian Fathers & Brothers.
Poole, Steven F. '96 (BEL) Beckemeyer, IL St. Anthony Church; Breese, IL St. Augustine Church.
Poole, William G. '63 (LEX) Ravenna, KY St. Elizabeth Church.
Pooler, Alfred *c.p.* '60 (LA) [Q] Pasadena, CA Passionist Community; [W] Sierra Madre, CA Mater Dolorosa Retreat Center.
Poon, Stanislaus '62 (OAK) Retired.
Poore, Charles '89 (Y) Girard, OH St. Rose Church.
Poorman, James E. '71 (SJP) Ramey, PA Annunciation B.V.M. Church.
Poorman, Mark L. *c.s.c.* '82 (FTW) [B] Notre Dame, IN University of Notre Dame Du Lac; [J] Notre Dame, IN Holy Cross Community, Corby Hall, University of Notre Dame.
Poorten, William P. *s.j.* '63 (PAT) [I] Morristown, NJ Loyola House of Retreats.
Poovakulam, Antony P. '63 (TR) Whiting, NJ St. Elizabeth Ann Seton Church.
Poovannal, Thomas '76 (WDC) Landover Hills, MD St. Mary's Catholic Church; Landover Hills, MD Syro-Malankara Church; Washington, DC General Hospital.
Pop, Carlos Antonio *o.s.b.* '99 (SFS) [F] Marvin, SD Blue Cloud Abbey.
Popadick, Msgr. Peter J. '70 (BUF) [1] Cheektowaga, NY St. Aloysius Gonzaga Church.
Popadiuk, Mauricio *o.s.b.m.* (STF) [E] New York, NY Provincialate of Basilian Fathers.
Popadiuk, Mauricio *o.s.b.m.* '84 (STF) Bronx, NY St. Mary Protectress Church.
Pope, Benedict *o.f.m.cap.* '54 (PIT) [O] Pittsburgh, PA St. Augustine Friary.
Pope, Charles E. '89 (WDC) [43] Washington, DC St. Thomas More Church; [V] Silver Spring, MD Archdiocese of Washington Division, The Blue Army.
Pope, George F. *c.s.c.* '58 (FgM) Holy Cross Foreign Missions.
Pope, L. Michael *s.j.* '81 (YAK) Toppenish, WA St. Aloysius Church.
Pope, Nicholas F. *s.j.* '72 (MIL) [P] Milwaukee, WI Jesuit Provincial Office, Wisconsin Province.
Popeleski, Frank '79 (BLX) Biloxi, MS V.A. Center; Gulfport, MS V.A. Hospital.
Popelka, Joseph '92 (SAL) Plainville, KS Sacred Heart Church; Zurich, KS St. Ann's Church.
Popesh, Msgr. Bernard '49 (DUL) Retired.
Popish, Edward *ss.cc.* '90 (HON) [G] Kaneohe, HI Sacred Hearts Center.
Popivchak, Msgr. Ronald P. '67 (PHU) Bridgeport, PA SS. Peter and Paul Church; Phoenixville, PA SS. Peter and Paul Church.
Poplawski, John F. '74 (SCR) [2] Dunmore, PA Christ the King Church.
Popochock, James L. '68 (GBG) Footedale, PA St. Thomas Church; New Salem, PA St. Procopius Church.
Popovich, George '51 (Y) [5] Warren, OH St. Joseph Church; [G] Warren, OH St. Joseph Health Center.
Popovich, Ovian '98 (STF) West Islip, NY Holy Family Church.
Popovich, Peter '85 (NY) [171] Bronx, NY Our Lady of Good Counsel Church; Greenburgh, NY Church of Our Lady of Shkodra.
Popovich, Stephen '81 (Y) [4] Youngstown, OH Immaculate Heart of Mary Church.
Popowski, Stanley '83 (HEL) Cut Bank, MT St. Margaret Church; Valier, MT St. Francis Church.
Popp, Kenneth J. '83 (SCL) Greenwald, MN St. Andrew's Church; Meire Grove, MN St. John's Church.
Poppa, Chester *o.f.m.cap.* '53 (GF) Broadus, MT St. David's Church.
Popson, Michael George '87 (PSC) Danbury, CT St. Nicholas Church.
Porada, Casey *o.s.* '89 (LIN) David City, NE St. Mary's Church.
Porada, Casey *o.s.* '89 (PCE) On Duty Outside the Diocese.
Porada, Charles *o.f.m.conv.* '43 (FR) [8] New Bedford, MA Our Lady of Perpetual Help Church.
Porazzo, Francis J. '44 (TR) Retired.
Porcari, Ernest M. '59 (DET) Northville, MI Our Lady of Victory Church.
Pori, Victor (NY) [181] Bronx, NY St. Peter and St. Paul Church.
Pornchoi, Phillip *c.s.s.* (NY) [4] White Plains, NY Our Lady of Mt. Carmel Church.
Porpiglia, Joseph D. '86 (BUF) Salamanca, NY Holy Cross Church; Salamanca, NY St. Patrick Church.
Porpora, Robert '90 (NY) Middletown, NY Holy Cross Church.
Porsch, Ernest *o.f.m.* '49 (CIN) [M] Cincinnati, OH St. John the Baptist Friary.
Port, Dennis R. '74 (STL) Overland, MO Our Lady of the Presentation Church.
Portalatin, Antonio '91 (ARE) Special Assignment.
Portalatin, Antonio '91 (SJN) [C] Rio Piedras, PR Seminario Mayor Regional San Juan Bautista.
Portella, Mario '99 (SCR) [M] Elmhurst, PA Priestly Fraternity of St. Peter (F.S.S.P.), North American District Headquarters.
Porter, Daniel '75 (LSC) Hurley, NM Infant Jesus Church.
Porter, Jack W. '75 (IND) On Special or Other Archdiocesan Assignment; Retired.
Porter, John '56 (CIN) Liberty Township, OH St. Maximilian Kolbe Church.
Porter, John '57 (GR) On Special Assignment.
Porter, John Baptist *o.c.s.o.* '90 (SAC) [H] Vina, CA Abbey of New Clairvaux, Trappist.
Porter, John E. '56 (CIN) [V] Cincinnati, OH St. Andrew Kim Korean Catholic Community.
Porter, John F. '57 (GR) Conklin, MI St. Francis Xavier Church; Ravenna, MI St. Catherine Church.
Porter, Lawrence B. '74 (NEW) [A] South Orange, NJ Immaculate Conception Seminary; [B] South Orange, NJ Seton Hall University.
Porter, Richard L. *s.j.* '47 (MIL) [P] Wauwatosa, WI Jesuit Community at St. Camillus.
Porter, Robert A. '81 (SFD) On Duty Outside the Diocese.
Porter, Robert G. '81 (HEL) Dillon, MT St. Rose of

Lima Church; [H] Dillon, MT Western Montana College.
Porter, Robert N. '64 (SFD) Bunker Hill, IL St. Mary Church; Shipman, IL St. Denis Church; Wilsonville, IL Holy Cross Church.
Porter, Rocco S. '97 (DEN) [1] Aurora, CO Queen of Peace Church.
Porter, Stephen C. '81 (SB) Rancho Cucamonga, CA Sacred Heart Church.
Porter, William '80 (KCK) Leawood, KS St. Michael the Archangel Church.
Porter, William J. '75 (WIL) Ocean City, MD St. Luke and St. Andrew Church.
Porterfield, David J. *c.s.c.* '79 (FTW) [18] South Bend, IN St. Stanislaus Church.
Porterfield, Mark A. '94 (JC) Belle, MO St. Alexander Church; Rich Fountain, MO Sacred Heart Church; On Duty Outside the Diocese.
Portland, Paul *s.d.s.* '76 (NSH) Lewisburg, TN St. John the Evangelist Church.
Portland, Paul *s.d.s.* '76 (PHX) [4] Mesa, AZ Queen of Peace Church.
Portland, Paul J. *s.d.s.* '76 (NSH) Shelbyville, TN St. William Church.
Portman, Msgr. John R. '56 (SD) Coronado, CA Sacred Heart Church; Retired.
Portmann, Frederick '79 (PHX) Retired.
Porto, George *o.s.b.* (WDC) [M] Washington, DC St. Anselm's Abbey.
Portrey, Msgr. Lawrence A. '39 (GI) Retired.
Portucheck, Joseph J. '49 (STL) Retired.
Portula, Ramel *c.i.c.m.* '99 (BWN) [4] McAllen, TX St. Joseph the Worker Church.
Portz, Bernard (MIL) [N] Wauwatosa, WI St. Camillus Health Center, Inc.
Portz, Bernard J. *s.j.* '52 (MIL) [P] Wauwatosa, WI Jesuit Community at St. Camillus.
Portzer, Joseph *f.s.s.p.* '99 (LR) [L] North Little Rock, AR Priestly Fraternity of St. Peter.
Portzer, Joseph *f.s.s.p.* '99 (SCR) [M] Elmhurst, PA Priestly Fraternity of St. Peter (F.S.S.P.), North American District Headquarters.
Posadas, Antonio *o.f.m.* '95 (SAT) [46] San Antonio, TX St. Joseph Church.
Posanski, James B. '65 (MIL) Byron, WI Sons of Zebedee: Saints James and John Church.
Posch, Christopher J. *o.f.m.* '95 (WIL) [10] Wilmington, DE St. Paul's Church.
Poschen, Msgr. Ed '53 (FRS) Retired.
Poser, Gregory *o.s.c.* '75 (FgM) Crosier Foreign Missions.
Posey, Patrick L. '91 (ARL) Dominican Republic, VA San Francisco de Asis, Banica Church; Dominican Republic, VA San Jose, Pedro Santana Church; On Duty Outside the Diocese.
Posey, Thadeus J. *o.f.m.cap.* '71 (STP) [C] St. Paul, MN University of St. Thomas.
Posiewala, John *s.a.c.* '76 (BUF) [23] Buffalo, NY St. Florian Church.
Posiewala, John *s.a.c.* '78 (BUF) [O] North Tonawanda, NY Society of the Catholic Apostolate.
Poslusney, Venard *o.carm.* '42 (JOL) [J] Darien, IL Carmelite Provincial Office.
Posluszny, Francis '62 (BGP) On Duty Outside the Diocese.
Pospishil, Msgr. Victor J. '40 (PHU) Retired.
Post, Robert J. '82 (BGP) Darien, CT St. Thomas More Church.
Postell, Philip S. *s.j.* '70 (DAL) [D] Dallas, TX Jesuit College Preparatory School.
Poster, Richard J. '92 (DAV) Lost Nation, IA Sacred Heart Church; Toronto, IA St. James Church.
Poster, Richard J. '92 (DUB) Oxford Junction, IA Sacred Heart Church.
Postrano, Anastacio '84 (HON) Honokaa, HI Our Lady of Lourdes Church.
Potaczek, John A. '99 (LC) [2] La Crosse, WI Blessed Sacrament Church.
Potemski, Boleskew *c.m.* '73 (HRT) [18] New Haven, CT St. Stanislaus Church.
Poterucha, Michael '85 (SFD) Absent on Leave.
Potes, Javier *a.a.* (NY) [188] Bronx, NY Sacred Heart Church.
Poth, Thomas *s.m.m.* '83 (HRT) [M] Litchfield, CT Montfort Missionaries; [M] Litchfield, CT Montfort Missionaries.
Pothier, Glen '95 (PMB) Boynton Beach, FL St. Mark Church.
Potocek, Msgr. Cyril J. '36 (NY) North Tarrytown, NY Holy Cross Church; Retired.
Potter, Gerald '54 (FAR) Retired.
Potter, Msgr. Joseph D. '54 (BGP) Retired.
Potter, Ronald J. *m.m.* '61 (FgM) Maryknoll Foreign Missions.
Potter, Stephen K. '78 (RCK) McHenry, IL St. Patrick Church.
Potthast, Richard L. *c.s.c.* '67 (FgM) Holy Cross Foreign Missions.
Potthast, Richard L. *c.s.c.* '67 (FTW) [J] South Bend, IN Congregation of Holy Cross, Indiana Province, Provincial House.
Potthoff, Donald W. '49 (LA) Diamond Bar, CA St. Denis Church; Retired.
Potthoff, Msgr. Fred E. '44 (LFT) Retired.
Pottorff, Lisle J. '49 (DOD) Retired.
Potts, Donald G. '60 (KAL) Cassopolis, MI St. Ann Church.
Potts, Richard *c.ss.r.* '91 (STL) [22] St. Louis, MO St. Alphonsus Liguori Church; [P] St. Louis, MO St. Alphonsus Rectory of the Redemptorist.
Potts, Robert J. '64 (ALN) [3] Shenandoah, PA St. George Church; [5] Shenandoah, PA Our Lady of Mt. Carmel Church.
Potts, Ronald A. '89 (WDC) Germantown, MD Mother Seton Church.
Potts, Thomas *s.v.d.* (STL) [53] St. Louis, MO St. Nicholas Church.
Potvin, Leo F. '64 (ALB) Dolgeville, NY St. Joseph Church; Newport, NY St. John the Baptist Church.
Potvin, Raymond H. '48 (SPR) On Duty Outside the Diocese.
Potvin, Raymond H. '58 (WDC) [C] Washington, DC Catholic University of America, The.
Potvin, Raymond J. '80 (MAN) Hinsdale, NH St. Joseph Church; Winchester, NH St. Stanislaus Church.
Potvin, Thomas R. *o.p.* '62 (PRT) [I] Lewiston, ME SS. Peter and Paul House.
Poulin, Arthur *o.s.b.cam.* '81 (MRY) [F] Big Sur, CA New Camaldoli Hermitage.
Poulin, Arthur *o.s.b.cam.* '81 (OAK) [S] Berkeley, CA Incarnation Monastery, Camaldolese Benedictines.
Poulin, Calvin H. *s.j.* '62 (FgM) Provinces.
Poulin, Edward '54 (NOR) Willimantic, CT St. Mary Church.
Poulin, Edward C. '54 (NOR) Retired.
Poulin, Neil C. *s.j.* '66 (CI) Gagil-Tomil, FM St. Joseph Church.
Poulin, Neil C. *s.j.* '66 (FgM) Provinces.
Pouliot, Eugene A. '70 (STP) Farmington, MN St. Michael Church.
Pouliot, Francis A. '58 (STP) [35] Minneapolis, MN Visitation Church.
Poulsen, James N. '68 (SD) [27] San Diego, CA St. Gregory The Great Church.
Poulsen, Thomas R. *o.p.* '67 (STP) [15] Minneapolis, MN St. Albert the Great Church.
Poulson, David (E) [P] Erie, PA Newman Centers and Campus Ministry.
Poulson, David L. '79 (E) Fryburg, PA St. Michael Church.
Poupore, J. Gareth *c.s.b.* '53 (ROC) [I] Rochester, NY Basilian Residence.
Poupore, Norman E. '50 (OG) Retired.
Poussard, Bertrand R. '67 (PRT) [5] Lewiston, ME St. Patrick's Church.
Pousson, Donald '66 (LAF) Morse, LA Immaculate Conception Church.
Poux, Francis A. *c.ss.r.* '62 (BAL) [68] Baltimore, MD Our Lady of Fatima Church.
Poveromo, Robert J. '72 (NY) [54] New York, NY St. James Church; [122] New York, NY St. Vincent de Paul Church; [E] New York, NY Cathedral High School.
Povish, Robert W. '90 (PH) [118] Philadelphia, PA Our Lady Help of Christians Church; [D] Philadelphia, PA Little Flower Catholic High School for Girls.
Powderly, James J. '58 (WDC) Retired; [L] Washington, DC Cardinal O'Boyle Residence for Priests.
Powell, Bernard '58 (PMB) Retired.
Powell, Bernard F. '58 (PMB) Palm City, FL Holy Redeemer Church.
Powell, Daniel F.X. '92 (HBG) [K] Harrisburg, PA Catholic Campus Ministry; [K] Harrisburg, PA Catholic Campus Ministry.
Powell, Edward F. '54 (SUP) Retired.
Powell, Msgr. Eric S '90 (PEO) Kickapoo, IL St. Mary of Kickapoo Church.
Powell, Harold W. '77 (KC) Retired.
Powell, John J. *s.j.* '56 (CHI) [C] Chicago, IL Jesuit Community at Loyola University of Chicago.
Powell, Leon A. '71 (LC) Special Assignment; [H] La Crosse, WI Holy Cross (Seminary) Diocesan Center.
Powell, Matthew D. *o.p.* '75 (PRO) [P] Providence, RI St. Thomas Aquinas Priory at Providence College.
Powell, Michael (JOL) Momence, IL St. Patrick Church.
Powell, Paul P. '48 (OWN) Providence, KY Holy Cross Church; Sebree, KY St. Michael Church.
Powell, Ralph A. *o.p.* '51 (STL) [P] St. Louis, MO Dominican Community of St. Louis.
Powell, Robert J. '74 (PH) Jamison, PA St. Cyril of Jerusalem Church.
Powell, Robert J. *o.s.b.cam.* '76 (FR) North Dartmouth, MA St. Julie Billiart Church.
Powell, Robert John *o.s.b.cam.* '76 (MRY) [F] Big Sur, CA New Camaldoli Hermitage.
Power, Bernard *c.ss.r.* '43 (ALB) [L] Saratoga Springs, NY St. John Neumann Residence.
Power, Bernard *c.ss.r.* '43 (TR) [Q] Long Branch, NJ San Alfonso Retreat House.
Power, David N. *o.m.i.* '56 (WDC) [C] Washington, DC Catholic University of America, The; [M] Washington, DC Oblate College/Center for Mission Studies Community.
Power, Eugene J. *s.j.* '51 (ALN) [A] Wernersville, PA Jesuit Center.
Power, Gerard *o.carm.* '99 (NEW) Cresskill, NJ St. Therese of Lisieux Church.
Power, J. Timothy '66 (STP) Eden Prairie, MN Pax Christi Church.
Power, James F. '62 (BO) Wellesley, MA St. James the Great Church.
Power, Joseph *o.s.f.s.* '62 (BUF) [T] Stella Niagara, NY DeSales Resource Center.
Power, Patrick *c.ss.r.* '66 (KC) [31] Kansas City, MO Our Lady of Perpetual Help Church; [J] Kansas City, MO Redemptorists of Kansas City.
Power, Patrick A. '55 (LA) Santa Clarita, CA Our Lady of Perpetual Help Church; Retired.
Power, Robert E. *c.s.b.* '66 (LSC) [1] Las Cruces, NM Cathedral of Immaculate Heart of Mary; [B] Las Cruces, NM Basilian Fathers.
Power, Virgil '39 (ORL) Retired.
Power, Virgil '39 (RVC) Retired.
Power, William J. *s.j.* '41 (BO) [W] Weston, MA Campion Health Center, Inc.
Powers, Alfred J. '43 (CIN) Retired.
Powers, Aloysius '48 (OWN) Curdsville, KY St. Elizabeth Church.
Powers, Anthony F. '42 (BRK) Retired.
Powers, Msgr. Bernard '52 (OWN) Reed, KY St. Augustine Church; [H] Maple Mount, KY Mount St. Joseph Conference and Retreat Center, Inc.
Powers, Bruce J. '73 (RVC) Melville, NY St. Elizabeth Church.
Powers, Msgr. Charles F. '48 (PAT) Dover, NJ Sacred Heart Church; Retired.
Powers, Charles J. '97 (MIA) Higher Studies.
Powers, Daniel *s.j.* '68 (HEL) Heart Butte, MT St. Anne Church.
Powers, David *sch.p.* (PH) [AA] Devon, PA Piarist Fathers (Order of the Pious Schools).
Powers, David B. *sch.p.* '85 (WDC) [B] Washington, DC Queen of Pious Schools House of Studies-Piarist Fathers.
Powers, Edward R. *s.j.* '45 (SCR) [C] Scranton, PA University of Scranton.
Powers, Gerard E. '69 (SP) New Port Richey, FL Our Lady Queen of Peace Church.
Powers, Glenn E. '87 (MIL) [5] Sheboygan, WI Immaculate Conception Church.
Powers, Harold J. *c.s.p.* '48 (LA) [87] Los Angeles, CA St. Paul the Apostle Church.
Powers, Harold J. *c.s.p.* '48 (NY) [DD] Jamaica Estates, NY Paulist Fathers Generalate.
Powers, Isaias *c.p.* '61 (BRK) [V] Jamaica, NY Immaculate Conception Monastery.
Powers, James G. *s.j.* '62 (SPK) [C] Spokane, WA Gonzaga University.
Powers, James P. '90 (SUP) Gordon, WI St. Anthony of Padua Church; Minong, WI St. Mary Church; Solon Springs, WI St. Pius X Church.
Powers, Jerome C. '47 (CHR) Retired.
Powers, John *c.p.* '77 (WOR) [N] Shrewsbury, MA Calvery Retreat Center, Passionist Fathers of Shrewsbury, Inc.
Powers, John A. *o.p.* '52 (NO) [25] New Orleans, LA St. Anthony of Padua Church; [N] Metairie, LA Metairie Manor, Metairie II, and Metairie III.
Powers, John J. '51 (CHI) South Holland, IL St. Jude the Apostle Church; Retired.
Powers, Joseph '79 (KC) Raytown, MO Our Lady of Lourdes Church.
Powers, Richard '56 (E) [M] Erie, PA Congregation of the Divine Spirit.
Powers, Richard J. '47 (BO) Senior Priests.
Powers, Richard J. *s.j.* '58 (STA) Interlachen, FL St. John's Church.
Powers, Richard M. '59 (OWN) Fordsville, KY St. John the Baptist Church; Whitesville, KY St. Mary of the Woods Church.
Powers, Msgr. Richard T. '63 (PH) Levittown, PA St. Michael the Archangel Church.
Powers, Msgr. Robert J. '45 (BUR) Retired.
Powers, Robert M. '92 (BRK) [21] Brooklyn, NY Blessed Sacrament Church.
Powers, Thomas *s.j.* '95 (LA) [C] Los Angeles, CA Loyola Marymount University.
Powers, Thomas F. '66 (BO) Wellesley, MA St. John the Evangelist Church.
Powers, Thomas J. (BO) North Reading, MA St. Theresa Church.
Powers, Thomas J. *s.j.* '72 (DET) [P] Clarkston, MI Colombiere Center.
Powers, Thomas M. '49 (CHI) River Grove, IL St. Cyprian Church; Wilmette, IL St. Joseph Church; Retired.
Powers, Thomas M. '62 (ALB) [16] Albany, NY St. Teresa of Avila Church.
Powers, Thomas W. '97 (BGP) [4] Trumbull, CT St. Theresa Church.
Powers, Troy '87 (SAC) Citrus Heights, CA Holy Family Church.

Powers, Msgr. William E. '36 (GR) Retired.
Powers, William V. '58 (PBL) Retired.
Powhida, Robert '78 (ALB) Northville, NY St. Francis of Assisi Church.
Powis, Msgr. John J. '59 (BRK) [15] Brooklyn, NY St. Barbara Church.
Poyatt, Msgr. William F. '49 (CAM) Barrington, NJ St. Francis de Sales Church.
Poynter, Gail A. '51 (CIN) Retired.
Pozdol, Henry '50 (CHI) Summit, IL St. Joseph Church; Retired.
Pozza, Aldo *m.c.c.j.* '66 (CHI) Calumet Park, IL Seven Holy Founders Church.
Pozzoli, Ugo *i.m.c.* '98 (WDC) [V] Washington, DC Consolata Missionaries House of Studies.
Prabell, Paul '72 (LEX) Danville, KY SS. Peter & Paul Church.
Prachar, Andrew '90 (NEW) Livingston, NJ St. Raphael Church.
Pracz, Ted '66 (PEO) Danville, IL Holy Family Church.
Prado, Alfred *o.m.i.* '57 (SAT) [K] San Antonio, TX Oblate Madonna Residence.
Prado, Cletus '58 (CHY) Retired.
Prado, Manuel *c.m.* '62 (PCE) [8] Ponce, PR La Milagrosa Church.
Prado, Teodoro Tim Y. '77 (GAL) [K] Houston, TX The Catholic Chaplain Corps.
Praem, Jude Lucier O. '74 (ORG) Garden Grove, CA St. Callistus Church.
Prager, John P. *c.m.* '82 (FgM) Vincentian Foreign Missions.
Prakaiw, Basil (DEN) [38] Denver, CO Transfiguration of Our Lord Church.
Prakasam, John (BRK) [54] Brooklyn, NY Holy Family Church.
Prakuzhy, Zacharias *c.m.i.* '68 (SHP) Lake Providence, LA St. Patrick Church; Oak Grove, LA Sacred Heart Church.
Prall, Arthur J. *m.m.* '52 (FgM) Maryknoll Foreign Missions.
Pramote, Peter C. *c.s.s.* (NY) [4] White Plains, NY Our Lady of Mt. Carmel Church.
Pramudyarkara, Petrus *s.j.* '92 (MIL) [P] Milwaukee, WI Jesuit Community at Marquette University.
Pranaitis, Mark *c.m.* '93 (CHI) [N] Chicago, IL DePaul Vincentian Residence.
Pranzo, Joseph F. *c.s.* '71 (PRO) [8] Providence, RI St. Bartholomew Church.
Prasad, Gallela (SAN) On Special or Other Diocesan Assignment.
Praski, Jacek '91 (CHI) [189] Chicago, IL St. Stanislaus, Bishop and Martyr Church.
Prass, Charles *o.m.i.* '45 (STP) [W] St. Paul, MN Missionary Oblates of Mary Immaculate.
Prasser, Jeffery A. '89 (MIL) [20] Milwaukee, WI St. Catherine Church.
Prat, Camille *s.j.* '62 (PHX) Chandler, AZ St. Andrew the Apostle Church.
Pratico, Msgr. Patrick J. '79 (SCR) Eynon, PA St. Mary's Czestochowa Church.
Prato, Luis German *s.d.b.* '84 (OAK) [N] Berkeley, CA Salesian Community.
Prats, Charles R. '84 (MET) On Duty Outside the Diocese.
Pratt, Dean '97 (DAL) Special Assignment.
Pratt, Edward C. '72 (ALB) Ushers, NY Corpus Christi Church.
Pratt, James F.X. *s.j.* '86 (BO) [W] Boston, MA The Society of Jesus of New England-Provincial Offices.
Pratt, James F.X. *s.j.* '86 (NSH) [1] Nashville, TN Cathedral of the Incarnation.
Pratt, James L. *s.m.* '46 (SFR) [N] San Francisco, CA Marist Center of the West.
Pratt, Lawrence E. '62 (BO) Melrose, MA Incarnation Church.
Pratt, Oscar J. '96 (BO) [8] Lynn, MA Sacred Heart Church.
Pravetz, Matthew A. *o.f.m.* '79 (NY) [146] Bronx, NY Holy Cross Church.
Pray, Joseph N. '50 (BUR) Retired.
Prebula, David W. *o.s.b.* '44 (SEA) Tacoma, WA Veterans Admin. Medical Center; [L] Lacey, WA St. Martin's Abbey.
Prechtl, Ronald G. '80 (WH) Grafton, WV St. Augustine Church.
Preciado, Rudolph J. '69 (ORG) Garden Grove, CA St. Callistus Church.
Precourt, Peter *a.a.* '76 (PRO) [P] Warwick, RI Augustinians of the Assumption.
Prefontaine, Roger C. *s.s.s.* '53 (SAT) [45] San Antonio, TX St. Joseph Church.
Pregana, Craig '89 (FR) [N] North Dartmouth, MA Catholic Campus Ministry University of Massachusetts Dartmouth.
Pregana, Craig A. '89 (FR) [12] Fall River, MA Sacred Heart Church.
Pregana, David A. '96 (FR) Raynham, MA St. Ann Church.
Prehn, James S. *s.j.* '99 (CLV) [D] Cuyahoga Falls, OH Walsh Jesuit High School.
Prehn, James S. *s.j.* '99 (DET) [K] Detroit, MI Jesuit Provincial Office-Detroit Province of the Society of Jesus.
Preisinger, Robert F. '63 (OM) [8] Sarpy Co., NE St. Bernadette Church.
Preisner, Msgr. A. F. '40 (DOD) Retired.
Premoshis, Gregory F. '68 (GBG) [C] Connellsville, PA Geibel Catholic High School.
Prenatt, David E. '95 (E) [23] Erie, PA St. Luke Church.
Prendergast, Edmond '73 (MIA) [5] Fort Lauderdale, FL St. Bonaventure Church.
Prendergast, Edward F. '51 (CLV) Rocky River, OH St. Christopher Church; Retired.
Prendergast, Fergus '94 (MOB) [3] Montgomery, AL St. Bede Church.
Prendergast, Francis '54 (STO) Turlock, CA Sacred Heart Church; [G] Turlock, CA The McElligott Sacred Heart School Foundation.
Prendergast, Msgr. John J. '76 (PEO) On Duty Outside the Diocese.
Prendergast, Joseph '54 (SJ) [3] Santa Clara, CA St. Justin Church.
Prendergast, Noel '58 (JKS) Clinton, MS Holy Savior Church; [H] Clinton, MS Mississippi College Newman Center.
Prendergast, Richard J. '79 (CHI) Berwyn, IL St. Mary of Celle Church.
Prendergast, Robert E. '22 (PEO) Retired.
Prendergast, Msgr. Thomas '56 (SD) [10] San Diego, CA Mission Basilica San Diego De Alcala Church.
Prendeville, Eugene *o.m.i.* (PEO) Lincoln, IL Lincoln State School.
Prendiville, Edmond P. '63 (PRO) On Duty Outside the Diocese.
Prendiville, Kerry '84 (RC) Spearfish, SD St. Joseph Church.
Prendiville, Thomas *s.d.b.* '56 (SFR) [N] San Francisco, CA Salesian Provincial Residence.
Preneta, Henry S. '67 (GBG) On Duty Outside the Diocese.
Preneta, Henry S. '67 (PIT) [3] Butler, PA St. Paul Church.
Prengaman, Leo P. *s.j.* '93 (SJ) [D] San Jose, CA Bellarmine College Preparatory.
Prengaman, Leo Peter *s.j.* '93 (BAL) [B] Baltimore, MD Loyola College in Maryland.
Prescott, Herbert W. '55 (KNX) Gatlinburg, TN St. Mary Church; Retired.
Preske, Venantius '52 (LR) Retired.
Preskenis, James T. *c.s.c.* '75 (BGP) [P] Bridgeport, CT Provincial Offices of the Priests and Brothers of Holy Cross, Eastern Province.
Presmanes, Jorge *o.p.* '91 (MIA) [18] Miami, FL St. Dominic Church; [H] Miami, FL Dominican Fathers of Miami, Inc.
Presta, James '86 (CHI) [A] Chicago, IL St. Joseph Seminary.
Preston, Larry *m.s.a.* '94 (NOR) [F] Cromwell, CT Society of the Missionaries of the Holy Apostles.
Presume, Marc '93 (MIA) [1] Miami, FL St. Mary's Church.
Presutti, Robert *l.c.* '98 (WDC) [M] Potomac, MD Legionaries of Christ.
Pretto, Franklin D. '72 (SFE) [6] Santa Fe, NM San Isidro Church.
Preuss, David *o.f.m.cap.* '79 (DET) [15] Detroit, MI St. Charles Borromeo Church.
Preuss, Richard *c.m.* '73 (FgM) Vincentian Foreign Missions.
Prevost, Frederick J. '48 (SY) Whitesboro, NY St. Anne Church.
Prevost, Normand *s.a.* '47 (NY) [DD] Garrison, NY Franciscan Friars of the Atonement.
Prevost, Robert F. *o.s.a.* '82 (CHI) [N] Olympia Fields, IL The Augustinians-Provincialate; [N] Olympia Fields, IL Austin Friary.
Prevost, Robert F. *o.s.a.* '82 (FgM) Foreign Missions.
Prevosto, Paul J. '96 (NEW) Mountainside, NJ Our Lady of Lourdes Church.
Prez, Daniel J. '74 (E) Sheffield, PA St. Anthony Church.
Pribek, James M. *s.j.* '99 (MIL) [P] Milwaukee, WI Jesuit Provincial Office, Wisconsin Province.
Pribonic, Phillip '67 (PIT) South Park, PA St. Joan of Arc Church.
Pribula, Duane L. '70 (CR) Warroad, MN St. Mary's Church.
Pribyl, Francis T. '39 (CHI) [5] Chicago, IL St. Agnes of Bohemia Church; Retired.
Pribyl, Ross T. *s.j.* '99 (CHI) [C] Chicago, IL Jesuit Community at Loyola University of Chicago.
Pricco, Richard A. '62 (PEO) Macomb, IL St. Paul's Church.
Price, Basil M. *s.j.* '54 (FgM) Provinces.
Price, Bede *o.s.b.* '96 (STL) [F] Creve Coeur, MO St. Louis Priory School; [P] St. Louis, MO The Abbey of St. Mary and St. Louis.
Price, Msgr. Edward G. '44 (NEW) [6] Elizabeth, NJ St. Genevieve's Church; Roselle Park, NJ The Assumption Church; Retired.
Price, James *c.p.* '94 (BRK) [V] Jamaica, NY Immaculate Conception Monastery; [X] Jamaica, NY Bishop Molloy Retreat House for Laymen.
Price, John R. '66 (CHI) Lansing, IL St. Ann Church.
Price, Rothell '88 (SHP) Bossier City, LA St. Jude Church.
Priebe, Msgr. Norman F. '67 (LA) Arcadia, CA Holy Angels Church.
Priest, Msgr. Gerald '68 (TYL) Texarkana, TX Sacred Heart Church.
Priestly, Joseph *s.m.* '55 (HON) [G] Honolulu, HI Marianist Communities.
Prieto, Frank '64 (SFE) [17] Albuquerque, NM Saint Joseph on the Rio Grande Church.
Prietto, Mario J. *s.j.* '73 (SJ) [B] Santa Clara, CA Santa Clara University; [B] Santa Clara, CA Santa Clara University.
Primeaux, Patrick D. *s.m.* '77 (WDC) [M] Washington, DC Marist Center.
Primich, John '95 (MET) South Plainfield, NJ Sacred Heart Church.
Primozic, Robert *o.carm.* '64 (JOL) [J] Darien, IL Carmelite Provincial Office.
Prince, Gerald '68 (HT) Retired.
Prince, Joseph A. '71 (BGP) Ridgefield, CT St. Elizabeth Seton Church.
Prince, Leo '86 (NY) Pearl River, NY St. Margaret Church.
Prince, Michael J. '98 (DET) Bloomfield Hills, MI St. Regis Church.
Principe, Francis J. '53 (NY) [E] New York, NY Cardinal Spellman High School.
Prindiville, Gerald T. '96 (NEW) On Duty Outside the Archdiocese.
Prindle, Richard '78 (LA) [A] Camarillo, CA St. John's Seminary.
Prinelli, John '78 (RIC) Christiansburg, VA Holy Spirit Catholic Church; Pearisburg, VA Holy Family Church.
Pringle, John R. '72 (MET) Bridgewater, NJ Holy Trinity Church.
Prior, Eugene J. *s.j.* '55 (NY) [F] New York, NY Loyola School; [DD] New York, NY St. Ignatius Loyola Residence.
Prior, Felix *o.carm.* '58 (JOL) Glendale Heights, IL St. Matthew Church.
Prior, Francis X. *c.m.* '51 (BUF) [C] Niagara University, NY Niagara University; [O] Niagara University, NY Vincentian Community at Niagara University.
Prior, James G. *c.m.* '53 (ALN) Roseto, PA Our Lady of Mt. Carmel Church.
Prior, Joseph '90 (PH) [A] Wynnewood, PA Theological Seminary of St. Charles Borromeo, Overbrook.
Prior, Robert J. *c.m.* '94 (CHL) [3] Greensboro, NC St. Mary Church.
Prior, Thomas W. *c.m.* '59 (ALN) Roseto, PA Our Lady of Mt. Carmel Church.
Priscaro, Jerry S. '93 (E) [12] Erie, PA St. Andrew Church.
Prist, Wayne F. '67 (CHI) [176] Chicago, IL Queen of All Saints Basilica Church.
Pritchard, Edward '74 (WDC) Retired.
Pritt, Phillip P. '62 (CLV) Rittman, OH St. Anne Church.
Pritzl, Kurt *o.p.* '91 (WDC) [B] Washington, DC Dominican House of Studies; [C] Washington, DC Catholic University of America, The; [C] Washington, DC Catholic University of America, The.
Prive, Francis R. (BUR) [H] Burlington, VT University of Vermont-The Catholic Center at UVM.
Prive, Francis R. '69 (BUR) Cambridge, VT St. Mary Church; Underhill Center, VT St. Thomas Church.
Privett, John '72 (BO) [W] Cambridge, MA Weston Jesuit Community.
Privett, John A. *s.j.* '72 (BO) [W] Cambridge, MA Weston Jesuit Community.
Privett, Stephen A. *s.j.* '72 (SFR) [N] San Francisco, CA Jesuit Community at University of San Francisco.
Proback, Adrian *o.c.s.o.* '54 (WOR) [N] Spencer, MA St. Joseph's Abbey.
Probst, R. Dean '81 (SFD) Carlinville, IL SS. Mary & Joseph Church.
Probst, Msgr. Robert L. '45 (STP) Retired; [C] St. Paul, MN University of St. Thomas.
Probst, Sergius *o.p.* '73 (OAK) [N] Oakland, CA Dominican Order (Western Province), St. Albert's Priory.
Probstfield, Edgar *o.s.b.* '52 (KC) Trenton, MO St. Joseph's Church.
Probstfield, Regis *o.s.b.* '57 (KC) [J] Conception, MO Conception Abbey.
Procaccini, David C. '93 (PRO) Coventry, RI SS. John and Paul Church.
Procella, Msgr. Paul '87 (GAL) Humble, TX St. Mary Magdalene Church.
Prochaska, John '93 (OAK) [4] San Leandro, CA St. Leander Church.
Prochaski, Adam F. '68 (BRK) Absent on Sick Leave; Absent on Leave.
Procopio, Clement *o.f.m.* '44 (NY) [DD] New York, NY Franciscan Province of the Immaculate Conception.
Procter, John '85 (ORG) Anaheim, CA St. Boniface Church.

Proctor, John G., Jr. '72 (SD) Bonita, CA Corpus Christi Church.
Procyk, Marijan '80 (STF) Buffalo, NY St. Nicholas Church.
Prodehl, Richard B. '66 (JOL) [1] Lockport, IL St. Bernard Church.
Prodywus, Alexander '89 (STN) Absent on Sick Leave.
Proehl, Douglas M. '74 (CLV) Fairview Park, OH St. Angela Merici Church.
Proenca, Luis *s.j.* '91 (LA) [C] Los Angeles, CA Loyola Marymount University.
Proenza, Raphael *o.p.* '96 (FgM) Dominican - Order of Preachers Foreign Missions.
Proenza, Raphael *o.p.* '96 (NO) [P] New Orleans, LA Dominican Friars, Southern Dominican Province of St. Martin de Porres.
Profeta, Salvatore '50 (PMB) Retired.
Proffitt, James D. '91 (BAL) Glyndon, MD Sacred Heart Church.
Profota, James H. '75 (DET) [2] Eastpointe, MI St. Basil Church.
Prohens, James *c.r.* '36 (DEN) [27] Denver, CO St. Cajetan's Church.
Prokes, Francis A. *s.j.* '57 (OM) [K] Omaha, NE Jesuit Community at Creighton University.
Prokop, Roger '87 (LAN) [4] Ann Arbor, MI St. Thomas the Apostle Church.
Prokopiw, Taras *o.s.b.m.* '58 (STF) New York, NY St. George Church.
Promesso, William J. '89 (DET) [74] Detroit, MI St. Thomas Aquinas Church.
Promis, Christopher P. *c.s.sp.* '72 (FgM) Holy Ghost Foreign Missions.
Pronesti, Salvatore J. '67 (PH) Bridgeport, PA Our Lady of Mt. Carmel Church.
Proppe, John *o.f.m.cap.* '47 (NY) Hawthorne, NY Rosary Hill Home; [X] Hawthorne, NY Rosary Hill Home; [EE] Hawthorne, NY Motherhouse & Novitiate of the Sisters of St. Dominic, Congregation of St. Rose of Lima.
Prosen, Anthony J. '71 (LFT) Muncie, IN St. Mary Church; Pendleton, IN Indiana State Reformatory, St. Christopher Chapel; Pendleton, IN Correctional Industrial Complex Ecumenical Chapel; Special Assignment.
Prospero, William F. *s.j.* '98 (MIL) [P] Milwaukee, WI Jesuit Community at Marquette University.
Prost, Charles *c.m.* '78 (KC) [J] Kansas City, MO Vincentian Parish Mission Center.
Protack, Thomas J. '96 (WIL) Wilmington Manor, DE Our Lady of Fatima Church.
Protano, Joseph, Jr. '63 (PRO) [5] Providence, RI St. Anthony Church.
Proterra, Michael *s.j.* '71 (OAK) [N] Oakland, CA Murray Residence Community.
Protopapas, George *o.m.i.* '43 (BO) [W] Lowell, MA Missionary Oblates of Mary Immaculate.
Protopapas, George *o.m.i.* '43 (FgM) Oblates Foreign Missions.
Proud, Albert J. '68 (SY) Clark Mills, NY Church of the Annunciation.
Proulx, Arthur J. '80 (SP) [4] Largo, FL St. Patrick Church.
Proulx, Raymond G. '60 (HRT) Goshen, CT St. Thomas of Villanova Church.
Prout, Thomas S. *s.j.* '92 (NY) [F] New York, NY Loyola School; [DD] New York, NY St. Ignatius Loyola Residence.
Provenza, Msgr. Earl V. *v.f.* '64 (SHP) Bossier City, LA Mary, Queen of Peace Church.
Provenza, John F. '90 (LA) South Gate, CA St. Helen Church.
Provinsal, Thomas G. *s.j.* '75 (FBK) Alakanuk, AK St. Ignatius Church; Emmonak, AK Sacred Heart Church; [E] St. Marys, AK Brother Joe Prince Jesuit Community.
Provinzano, Rocco '66 (NEW) Retired.
Provost, Msgr. Glen John '75 (LAF) [5] Lafayette, LA Our Lady of Fatima Church.
Provost, John T. '73 (ALB) [6] Schenectady, NY Holy Cross Church; [9] Schenectady, NY St. John the Evangelist Church; [12] Schenectady, NY St. Mary Church.
Provost, Robert F. *o.s.a.* '82 (CHI) [N] Olympia Fields, IL Tolentine Monastery at Tolentine Center.
Proxell, Leo '77 (HEL) Conrad, MT St. Michael Church; Dutton, MT St. William Church.
Prozny, Leopold V. '42 (SY) Retired.
Prucha, Francis Paul *s.j.* '57 (MIL) [P] Milwaukee, WI Jesuit Community at Marquette University.
Pruemer, Alexis *o.f.m.* '47 (SFD) Shumway, IL Church of the Annunciation; [H] Effingham, IL St. Anthony's Memorial Hospital; [K] Teutopolis, IL St. Francis Assisi Friary.
Pruett, Bill '79 (OKL) [7] Oklahoma City, OK St. Eugene's Church.
Pruett, John M. '55 (STO) Modesto, CA Our Lady of Fatima Church.
Prunier, Arthur J. '48 (WOR) Retired.
Prunty, Brian *o.praem.* '65 (CHI) [N] Chicago, IL Premonstratensian Fathers and Brothers (Norbertines).
Prus, Edward J. '61 (DET) Retired.
Prus, Msgr. Eugene '64 (MET) Martinsville, NJ Blessed Sacrament Church.
Prusaitis, John P. '78 (BO) [1] Brockton, MA St. Casimir Church.
Prusak, Jacek *s.j.* '00 (BO) [W] Chestnut Hill, MA The Jesuit Community at Boston College.
Prusakowski, Gerald *o.f.m.* '65 (GB) Abrams, WI St. Louis Church; Chase, WI St. Joseph Church; Sobieski, WI St. John Cantius Church.
Pruschowitz, Walter '61 (PAT) [P] Chester, NJ Nazareth Village.
Pruschowitz, Walter M. (PAT) Retired.
Prushinski, Carl T. '64 (SCR) Glen Lyon, PA St. Adalbert's Church; Wanamie, PA St. Mary's Church.
Pruss, Rodney Lee A. '69 (GI) Ravenna, NE Our Lady of Lourdes Church.
Prussing, Charles *s.j.* '55 (LA) [Q] Los Angeles, CA Columbiere House.
Prusynski, Chester *c.s.c.* '62 (P) [B] Portland, OR University of Portland; [L] Portland, OR Holy Cross Fathers & Brothers, C.S.C. - University of Portland.
Pruys, George L. '75 (STN) Wilton, ND SS. Peter and Paul Church.
Prybis, Ray *o.m.i.* '67 (WDC) [M] Washington, DC Oblate College/Center for Mission Studies Community.
Pryor, G. Robert '55 (CR) Retired.
Pryor, Msgr. Thomas P. '37 (PH) Retired.
Przechacki, Casimir J. '44 (MET) Retired.
Przedwiecki, David Ladislaus *o.f.m.* '73 (FAR) [F] Pisek, ND Franciscan Friars of Mary Immaculate.
Przepierski, Frank J. '62 (E) Clarion, PA Immaculate Conception Church.
Przepiora, Vincenty *o.cist.* '90 (DET) [A] Orchard Lake, MI SS. Cyril and Methodius Seminary.
Przewozny, Bernard *o.f.m.conv.* '69 (BAL) [S] Ellicott City, MD Order of Friars Minor Conventual.
Przyblyski, Donald L. '74 (LC) [L] Stevens Point, WI St. Stanislaus Kostka Congregation, Stevens Point Endowment Trust.
Przybocki, Msgr. Bernard A. '58 (ALT) Gallitzin, PA St. Demetrius Church.
Przybyla, Kenneth (COS) Highlands Ranch, CO Pax Christi Catholic Church.
Przybyla, Philip J. '70 (PIT) Canonsburg, PA St. Patrick Church.
Przybylo, William P. '68 (HRT) [10] Hartford, CT SS. Cyril and Methodius Church; [N] Hartford, CT SS. Cyril & Methodius Convent.
Przybylski, Donald L. '74 (LC) [5] Stevens Point, WI St. Stanislaus Church.
Przybysz, Joseph J. '75 (TOL) [23] Toledo, OH St. Hedwig Church.
Przybysz, Mark C. '90 (GR) [22] Grand Rapids, MI St. Stephen's Church; On Special Assignment.
Przydzial, Frederick '56 (ALN) [11] Bethlehem, PA St. Stanislaus Church.
Przygocki, Edward *m.s.a.* '81 (NOR) [F] Cromwell, CT Society of the Missionaries of the Holy Apostles.
Przywara, Gerald A. '67 (RIC) Columbia, VA St. Joseph Church; Palmyra, VA SS. Peter & Paul Church.
Ptacek, Benedict *o.de.m.* (SP) [O] St. Petersburg, FL St. Peter Nolasco Residence.
Ptacek, John P. '55 (DUB) Retired.
Ptak, Walter J. '87 (DET) [4] Wyandotte, MI Our Lady of Mt. Carmel Church.
Ptaszynski, Stephen F. '45 (HRT) Retired.
Ptaszynski, Thomas E. '73 (HRT) New Milford, CT Our Lady of the Lakes Church.
Pu, Matthew C. '53 (B) On Duty Outside the Diocese.
Pu, Matthew C. '53 (BAK) Jordan Valley, OR St. Bernard's Church.
Publicover, James L. '56 (BO) [4] Arlington, MA St. Jerome Church.
Pucci, Alfred J. '54 (NY) [226] Staten Island, NY St. Roch Church.
Pucci, Francis L. '57 (PIT) Retired; [P] Elizabeth, PA Divine Redeemer Motherhouse.
Pucciarelli, George W. '74 (BO) Military & VA Chaplains.
Puccinelli, Alfred *s.m.* '66 (FgM) Marist Foreign Missions.
Puchamkulam, Issac '87 (STA) [1] Gainesville, FL St. Patrick's Church.
Puchenski, Anthony C. '71 (CHI) Tinley Park, IL Saint Julie Billiart Church.
Puchner, Augustine R. *o.praem.* '97 (ORG) [A] Silverado, CA St. Michael's Norbertine Postulancy, Novitiate and Juniorate; [I] Silverado, CA Norbertine Fathers of Orange Inc.
Pucke, Michael U. '73 (CIN) [61] Cincinnati, OH St. Michael Church.
Pudichery, Joseph P. '62 (PIT) Overbrook, PA St. Norbert Church.
Puente, Jose Franciso '00 (SAT) [57] San Antonio, TX St. Matthew's Church.
Puentes, Jesus (CHI) [32] Chicago, IL St. Bronislava Church.
Puerner, John W. '55 (LC) Thorp, WI St. Bernard-St. Hedwig Church.
Puerta, Jorge '89 (MIA) Absent on Sick Leave.
Puetz, Richard W. '45 (LFT) Retired; [D] Delphi, IN St. Elizabeth Healthcare Center.
Pugh, Msgr. Charles '60 (SAT) Retired; [K] San Antonio, TX Padua Place.
Pugh, James L. '67 (MEM) [3] Memphis, TN St. Anne's Church.
Pugliese, Francis A. '68 (NY) Military Chaplains.
Pugliese, Steven J. *s.j.* '93 (NY) [DD] New York, NY Murray-Weigel Hall.
Puglio, Msgr. Guy '71 (BRK) [91] Brooklyn, NY Our Lady of Angels Church.
Puglisi, Msgr. Guy J. (BRK) [E] Brooklyn, NY Office of Religious Education: Evangelization and Catholic Formation.
Puglisi, Msgr. Guy J. '71 (BRK) [E] Brooklyn, NY Office of the Superintendent of Schools.
Puglisi, James *s.a.* '73 (NY) [DD] Garrison, NY Franciscan Friars of the Atonement, Minister General Office.
Puhl, Albert E. '44 (DEN) Retired.
Puhlman, Robert '88 (ORG) Tustin, CA St. Cecilia Church.
Puisis, John C. *c.s.v.* '45 (CHI) [N] Arlington Heights, IL Viatorian Province Center-Clerics of St. Viator.
Puisis, Leonard '52 (MIA) Retired.
Pujdak, Steve *s.c.j.* '69 (BWN) Raymondville, TX Our Lady of Guadalupe Church.
Pulaski, Joseph S. *m.m.* '47 (NY) [DD] Maryknoll, NY Maryknoll Fathers and Brothers.
Puleo, Edward C. '88 (MET) [1] Carteret, NJ St. Joseph Church.
Pulice, John J. '66 (MIL) [74] Milwaukee, WI St. Robert Church.
Pulickal, Sony G. *c.m.f.* '83 (OG) Glenfield, NY St. Mary Church; Houseville, NY St. Hedwig Church; Lowville, NY St. Peter Church.
Pulickal, Thomas *o.c.d.* '83 (SCR) [17] Scranton, PA St. Mary of the Assumption Church.
Pulikoottil, Abraham '65 (BUF) Retired.
Pulikoottil, Berard '62 (BUF) Lancaster, NY St. Mary of the Assumption Church.
Pulivelil, Peter *c.m.i.* '72 (SHP) [B] Shreveport, LA Christus Schumpert Health System.
Pulivelli, Peter *c.m.i.* '72 (SHP) [B] Shreveport, LA Christus Schumpert Health System.
Puljic, Marko *o.f.m.* '00 (DET) [5] Troy, MI St. Lucy Church.
Pulparayil, George '67 (NY) Monroe, NY Sacred Heart Church.
Pulskamp, Msgr. James E. '67 (SR) [2] Santa Rosa, CA Holy Spirit Church.
Pulvermacher, Claude *o.f.m.cap.* '60 (GB) [I] Appleton, WI St. Fidelis Friary.
Pulvermacher, Pius *o.f.m.cap.* '48 (GB) [I] Appleton, WI St. Fidelis Friary.
Puma, Msgr. Vincent E. (PAT) Retired.
Punch, Nicholas W. *o.p.* '66 (SUP) [I] Webster, WI Thomas More Center for Preaching and Prayer, Inc.
Punchekunnel, George J. '57 (LA) Fillmore, CA St. Francis of Assisi Church.
Punderson, Msgr. Joseph R. '76 (TR) On Duty Outside the Diocese.
Pung, Karl L. '97 (LAN) Fowlerville, MI St. Agnes Church.
Pung, Robert *s.v.d.* '44 (FgM) Society of the Divine Word Foreign Missions.
Punke, Msgr. Robert H. '54 (STU) St. Clairsville, OH St. Mary's Church; [I] St. Clairsville, OH Ohio University - Eastern.
Punnakunnel, John '79 (BGP) [1] Bridgeport, CT St. Augustine Church.
Puntal, Pedro (Peter) '82 (ORL) Kissimmee, FL Holy Redeemer Church.
Punti, George '55 (RVC) Elmont, NY St. Boniface Church; Retired.
Puntino, John *s.d.b.* '78 (NY) [DD] New Rochelle, NY Salesian Cooperators of St. John Bosco; [FF] Stony Point, NY Don Bosco Retreat Center and Marian Shrine; [FF] Stony Point, NY Marian Shrine.
Puntrello, Fillippo *r.c.j.* '63 (FRS) Sanger, CA St. Mary Church.
Puopolo, Rocco N. *s.x.* '77 (CHI) [N] Chicago, IL Xaverian Missionaries (S.X.).
Pupin, Vito A. '41 (BRK) Retired.
Pupius, George '63 (OKL) [11] Oklahoma City, OK Immaculate Conception Church.
Pupsys, Adam '52 (NOR) Retired.
Purcell, Arthur D. '79 (BRK) [23] Brooklyn, NY St. Brendan's Church.
Purcell, James '53 (PEO) Retired.
Purcell, Msgr. Lawrence M. '65 (SD) Solana Beach, CA St. James Church.
Purcell, Lee R. '99 (GRY) Munster, IN St. Thomas More Church.
Purcell, Msgr. Paul J. '54 (SCR) [22] Scranton, PA St. Paul's Church.
Purcell, Richard *o.f.m.* '68 (SFR) [8] San Francisco, CA St. Boniface Church.

Purcell, Robert F. *s.j.* '53 (MIL) [P] Wauwatosa, WI Jesuit Community at St. Camillus.
Purcell, Robert H. '74 (ALB) Margaretville, NY Sacred Heart Church.
Purcell, Thomas P. *o.s.a.* '43 (FgM) Foreign Missions.
Purcell, William F. '47 (SCR) Retired; [N] Dunmore, PA Villa St. Joseph.
Purdy, David T. *s.d.b.* '70 (SFR) [46] San Francisco, CA SS. Peter and Paul Church.
Purdy, George *s.j.* '53 (YAK) Naches, WA St. John's Church.
Purfield, James R. '54 (DEN) [2] Denver, CO All Saints Church.
Purta, Jerome J. *o.s.b.* '61 (GBG) [H] Latrobe, PA Saint Vincent Archabbey.
Purtell, John *s.o.l.t.* '95 (CC) [H] Robstown, TX Society of Our Lady of the Most Holy Trinity.
Purtell, John J. '68 (DUB) Hawkeye, IA St. Francis Xavier Church; Sumner, IA Immaculate Conception Church.
Purtell, Thomas J. '61 (CHI) [105] Chicago, IL St. John Fisher Church.
Purtell, Thomas W. '53 (DUB) Retired.
Purvey, J. James '84 (BAL) [63] Baltimore, MD St. Michael Church.
Puryear, Stan '95 (OWN) Stanley, KY St. Peter of Alcantara Church.
Pusak, Ronald '61 (MIA) [30] Miami, FL St. Richard Church.
Pusateri, Christian *o.s.b.* '55 (RCK) [G] Aurora, IL Marmion Abbey-St. Augustine's Abbey.
Pusateri, Joseph *s.m.* '65 (FgM) Marist Foreign Missions.
Pusateri, Joseph E. '54 (GRY) Otis, IN St. Mary Church.
Pusateri, Philip A. *s.j.* '72 (BO) [W] Boston, MA The Society of Jesus of New England-Provincial Offices.
Pusateri, Philip A. *s.j.* '74 (NOR) New London, CT St. Mary, Star of the Sea Church.
Pusateri, Samuel D. *o.s.b.* '79 (PEO) [A] Peru, IL St. Bede Abbey and Academy.
Pusch, Richard '71 (SHP) Shreveport, LA Forcht Wade Correctional Center.
Putano, John P. '70 (SY) Vestal, NY Our Lady of Sorrows Church.
Putera, Vasyl '96 (PHU) Edwardsville, PA St. Vladimir's Church; Wilkes-Barre, PA SS. Peter and Paul Church.
Puthenkulan, Joseph '76 (SFS) Mellette, SD All Saints Church.
Puthenparambil, Jose '78 (NEW) Teaneck, NJ Holy Name Hospital.
Puthenpeedika, George '79 (LAN) [1] Jackson, MI St. John the Evangelist Church.
Puthiyadom, Thomas '94 (HRT) [I] Hartford, CT Saint Francis Hospital and Medical Center.
Puthoff, Chad C. *s.d.s.* '71 (SAC) West Sacramento, CA Holy Cross Church.
Puthoff, Jeffery P. *s.j.* '98 (CAM) [4] Camden, NJ Holy Name Church.
Puthumayil, Chacko '71 (GAL) Sugar Land, TX St. Laurence Church.
Puthuppally, Joseph '66 (SHP) [5] Monroe, LA St. Matthew Church; [B] Monroe, LA St. Francis Medical Center.
Puthusseril, George '79 (MIA) [4] Miami Beach, FL St. Patrick Church.
Puthussery, Anthony S. *c.m.i.* '57 (NSH) [K] Liberty, TN Carmel Center of Spirituality.
Putich, Michael *o.f.m.* '68 (PRO) [P] Providence, RI St. Francis Friary.
Putka, John S. *s.m.* '69 (CIN) [D] Dayton, OH The University of Dayton; [M] Dayton, OH Marianist Provincialate.
Putnam, John T. '92 (CHL) Salisbury, NC Sacred Heart Church.
Putthoff, Jeffrey *s.j.* (CAM) Camden, NJ Riverfront Prison.
Putz, Kenneth G. '73 (PH) [35] Philadelphia, PA St. Christopher Church.
Puza, Paul G. '75 (ALN) Barnesville, PA St. Richard Church.
Puzio, Thomas '70 (DET) [4] Warren, MI St. Dorothy Church.
Puznakoski, Gilbert '75 (PIT) Allegheny County, PA UPMC Shadyside Hospital.
Pwodziunas, John *o.f.m.* '87 (PH) [93] Philadelphia, PA Saint Martha Church.
Pyne, Donald E. '56 (SFR) Retired.
Pyo, Edward J. '85 (PBR) Homer City, PA Holy Protection of Mary, The Mother of God Church.
Pyo, Immanuel '90 (MIL) [Y] Milwaukee, WI Korean Catholic Community.
Pytel, Ronald '73 (BAL) [38] Baltimore, MD Holy Rosary Church.
Pytlik, Conrad E. '66 (LSC) Mesilla, NM St. Albino Church.

Q

Quac Tran, Thomas Hung *s.v.d.* '00 (WH) Gary, WV Our Lady of Victory Church.
Quach, Binh *c.s.sp.* '91 (OAK) [17] Oakland, CA St. Mary, Immaculate Conception-St. Francis de Sales Church.
Quackenbush, Daniel M. *o.f.m.conv.* '88 (R) Siler City, NC St. Julia Church.
Quade, Alvin '54 (SCL) Randall, MN St. James Church.
Quadrini, Angelo '85 (EVN) [E] Jasper, IN Providence Home, Nursing Home for the Needy.
Quaine, Michael W. '85 (DET) [1] Dearborn, MI St. Alphonsus Church.
Quainoo, Clement '82 (VIC) Hillje, TX St. Andrew Church.
Qualizza, Franco *s.x.* '71 (FgM) Xaverian Foreign Missions.
Qualizza, Franco *s.x.* '71 (PAT) [M] Wayne, NJ Xaverian Missionary Fathers.
Quane, Joseph F. *s.j.* '38 (BO) [W] Weston, MA Campion Health Center, Inc.
Quane, Ralph '78 (DET) Absent on Sick Leave.
Quang, Benedict Joseph '91 (NO) Des Allemands, LA St. Gertrude Church.
Quang, John '70 (SAV) Military Chaplains.
Quang, Truc N. '00 (LA) Pasadena, CA St. Andrew Church.
Quang Trinh, Joseph Truong '99 (BLX) [2] Gulfport, MS St. James Church.
Quant, Roberto '91 (OKL) [10] Oklahoma City, OK Holy Angels Church.
Quanz, Paul E. *c.s.b.* '84 (GRY) [B] Merrillville, IN Andrean High School; [J] Merrillville, IN Basilian Fathers Residence.
Quarato, Robert A. '92 (NY) [161] Bronx, NY St. Margaret of Cortona Church.
Quartana, Donald F. '53 (MIL) Retired.
Quartier, Neal E. (SY) [18] Syracuse, NY St. John the Evangelist Church.
Quartier, Neal E. '76 (SY) [1] Syracuse, NY The Cathedral of the Immaculate Conception; Special Assignment.
Quattropane, Joseph *o.f.m. cap.* (SB) Yucaipa, CA St. Frances Xavier Cabrini Church.
Que, Dinh Ngoc *c.ss.r.* '56 (LA) [Q] Baldwin Park, CA Vietnamese Redemptorist Mission.
Quealy, Philip J. '83 (NY) [E] White Plains, NY Archbishop Stepinac High School.
Quebedeaux, Carl *c.m.f.* '82 (CHI) [N] Oak Park, IL Claretian Fathers Headquarters of U.S.A. Eastern Province.
Queen, James T. '65 (SY) [3] Rome, NY St. Paul Church; [C] Rome, NY Rome Catholic Junior-Senior High School.
Quejadas, Mario '00 (JOL) Bolingbrook, IL St. Francis of Assisi Church.
Quenum, Andre (PIT) [27] Pittsburgh, PA St. Mary of Mercy Church.
Quesada Gil, Raul '80 (SJN) [5] Bayamon, PR Nuestra Sra. de los Dolores Church.
Quesnel, Raymond *o.m.i.* '45 (STP) [W] St. Paul, MN Missionary Oblates of Mary Immaculate.
Quesnel, Raymond *o.m.i.* '45 (WIN) Retired.
Quetchenbach, Raymond *s.v.d.* '57 (CHI) [B] Techny, IL Divine Word Residence; [N] Techny, IL Society of the Divine Word, Provincial Headquarter-Chicago Prov.
Quevedo, Alfredo S. *s.j.* '56 (BRK) [62] Brooklyn, NY St. Ignatius Church.
Quevedo-Rodriguez, Hernan '97 (ATL) [3] Marietta, GA St. Joseph Church.
Quezada, Francisco X. '88 (GAL) [4] Spring, TX St. James the Apostle Church.
Quezada, Sixto '81 (NY) [14] New York, NY Ascension Church.
Qui, Vincent '68 (NO) Retired.
Quic, Cristobal Coche '92 (RCK) [G] Aurora, IL Marmion Abbey-St. Augustine's Abbey.
Quiceno, Francisco Jose '72 (SJN) [20] Carolina, PR San Valentin Church.
Quickley, George W. *s.j.* '80 (BAL) [S] Baltimore, MD Jesuit Fathers and Brothers Maryland Provincial Curia.
Quickley, George W. *s.j.* '80 (FgM) Provinces.
Quigg, Harold '60 (SEA) Retired.
Quigley, Bill *c.i.c.m.* '74 (FgM) Missionhurst Foreign Missions.
Quigley, Brian *m.c.c.j.* '77 (CIN) [M] Cincinnati, OH Comboni Missionaries (Verona Fathers)-Comboni Mission Center.
Quigley, J. Joseph '56 (SPR) Retired; [Q] Springfield, MA Newman Apostolates and Campus Ministries.
Quigley, James Ferrer *o.p.* '65 (PRO) [P] Providence, RI St. Thomas Aquinas Priory at Providence College.
Quigley, John *o.f.m.* '72 (CIN) [M] Cincinnati, OH St. Francis Seraph Friary; [V] Cincinnati, OH Franciscans Network.
Quigley, John *o.f.m.* '72 (FgM) Franciscan Foreign Missions.
Quigley, Joseph P. '60 (BRK) [79] Brooklyn, NY St. Mark's Church; Brooklyn, NY Coney Island Hospital.
Quigley, Martin J. '46 (BAK) Retired.
Quigley, Patrick '81 (NY) Absent on Leave.
Quigley, William G. *c.i.c.m.* '74 (ARL) [J] Arlington, VA Missionhurst, C.I.C.M.-Central House and Provincialate.
Quihuis, Luis H. *s.j.* '92 (LA) [3] Santa Barbara, CA Our Lady of Sorrows Church.
Quijano, Antonio *m.s.* '92 (SB) Apple Valley, CA Our Lady of the Desert Church.
Quijano, Carlos *s.j.* '98 (BO) [W] Cambridge, MA Faber House; [W] Cambridge, MA Weston Jesuit Community.
Quijano, Jose Juan '73 (MIA) Higher Studies.
Quijano, Jose Juan '73 (PMB) [A] Boynton Beach, FL St. Vincent de Paul Regional Seminary.
Quill, J. Michael '82 (WDC) Pomfret, MD St. Joseph Church.
Quill, James E. '53 (COV) [2] Covington, KY St. Agnes Church; Retired.
Quill, John '74 (NEW) Summit, NJ Overlook Hospital.
Quillen, Andrew M. '91 (BO) [W] Hingham, MA Glastonbury Abbey.
Quilligan, Maurice '57 (SFD) Retired.
Quilligan, Michael '71 (MIA) West Hollywood, FL Annunciation Church.
Quilty, James B. *m.s.* '65 (WOR) [6] Fitchburg, MA St. Joseph's Church.
Quindlen, Joseph J. '73 (PH) Buckingham, PA Our Lady of Guadalupe Church.
Quinkert, Denis *o.s.b.* '76 (SFS) Milbank, SD St. Lawrence Church.
Quinlan, Edward J. '78 (HBG) Dauphin, PA St. Matthew, Apostle and Evangelist Church.
Quinlan, Eugene '62 (MIA) Retired.
Quinlan, Jack (DET) [1] Clinton Twp., MI St. Claude Church.
Quinlan, Jack '97 (DET) [5] Clinton Twp., MI St. Thecla Church.
Quinlan, James V. '76 (CHI) Maywood, IL St. Eulalia Church.
Quinlan, John J. '70 (PAT) Swartswood, NJ Our Lady of Mt. Carmel Church; Newton, NJ Newton Memorial Hospital.
Quinlan, Joseph M. '52 (NEW) Retired.
Quinlan, Leo F. *s.j.* '45 (BO) [W] Weston, MA Campion Health Center, Inc.
Quinlan, Thomas J. '58 (RIC) [3] Virginia Beach, VA Holy Family Church.
Quinlan, William J. '38 (CHI) Forest Park, IL St. Bernardine Church; Retired.
Quinlan, William M. '99 (BGP) New Fairfield, CT St. Edward the Confessor Church.
Quinlivan, Anthony *c.ss.r.* '71 (ORL) Melbourne, FL Ascension Church.
Quinlivan, Francis *c.s.c.* '70 (FgM) Holy Cross Foreign Missions.
Quinlivan, Thomas J. '72 (BUF) [5] West Seneca, NY Queen of Heaven Church.
Quinlivan, William J. '95 (BUF) Williamsville, NY St. Gregory the Great Church.
Quinn, Alban *o.carm.* '49 (FgM) Carmelite Foreign Missions.
Quinn, Alban *o.carm.* '49 (JOL) [J] Darien, IL Carmelite Provincial Office.
Quinn, Msgr. Andrew F. '35 (NY) [227] Staten Island, NY Sacred Heart Church; Retired.
Quinn, Bernard '53 (HBG) Hanover, PA St. Vincent Church.
Quinn, Bernard J. '72 (LA) [Q] Montebello, CA Vincentian Fathers and Brothers; [Q] Montebello, CA Vincentian Fathers & Brothers.
Quinn, Brendan '74 (NEW) [6] Jersey City, NJ St. Anthony of Padua Church; Elizabeth, NJ Trinitas Hospital.
Quinn, Bruce *o.f.m.cap.* '57 (NOR) [4] Middletown, CT St. Pius X Church; Middletown, CT Middlesex Memorial Hospital.
Quinn, Carroll I. *m.m.* '45 (NY) [DD] Maryknoll, NY Maryknoll Fathers and Brothers.
Quinn, Charles H. '43 (BAL) Retired; [O] Timonium, MD Stella Maris.
Quinn, Charles J. '61 (WIN) Jackson, MN Good Shepherd Church.
Quinn, Charles P. '59 (NY) Pleasant Valley, NY St. Stanislaus Kostka Church.
Quinn, Charles P. '66 (PRO) Glocester, RI St. Eugene Church.
Quinn, Charles T. *o.p.* '55 (NEW) [28] Jersey City, NJ Sacred Heart Church.
Quinn, Desmond *s.s.c.* '54 (FgM) St. Columban's Foreign Mission.
Quinn, Don '83 (IND) [N] Indianapolis, IN Butler University Newman Center; [N] Indianapolis, IN Indiana University-Purdue University, Indianapolis Newman Center; [N] Indianapolis, IN University of Indianapolis Newman Center.
Quinn, Edward I. *s.s.c.* '55 (FgM) St. Columban's Foreign Mission.
Quinn, Edward J. *m.m.* '51 (FgM) Maryknoll Foreign Missions.
Quinn, Frank C. *o.p.* '53 (CHI) [N] Chicago, IL Dominicans (Provincial Office).
Quinn, Frank C. *o.p.* '59 (STL) [B] St. Louis, MO Aquinas Institute of Theology; [P] St. Louis, MO

Dominican Community of St. Louis.
Quinn, Gavin *o.carm.* '65 (JOL) Darien, IL Our Lady of Mount Carmel Church.
Quinn, Gregory J. '85 (WDC) [E] North Bethesda, MD Georgetown Preparatory School.
Quinn, J. Patrick *t.o.r.* '84 (STP) [20] Minneapolis, MN St. Bridget Church; [A] St. Paul, MN The Saint Paul Seminary.
Quinn, Jack '63 (ROC) [57] Rochester, NY St. Theodore Church.
Quinn, James '60 (NY) Absent on Leave.
Quinn, James A. '67 (MIA) Hallandale, FL St. Matthew Church.
Quinn, James A. '67 (SY) [14] Utica, NY St. Peter Church.
Quinn, James E. '54 (MIA) [4] Pompano Beach, FL St. Coleman Church; Retired.
Quinn, James F. '58 (SY) Manlius, NY St. Ann Church; Special Assignment.
Quinn, James J. *s.j.* '50 (OM) [K] Omaha, NE Jesuit Community at Creighton University.
Quinn, James P. '92 (TR) [21] Trenton, NJ St. Raphael Church.
Quinn, Jarlath '96 (NY) [170] Bronx, NY Our Lady of the Assumption Church.
Quinn, John F. '71 (NY) Armonk, NY St. Patrick Church.
Quinn, Msgr. John J. '43 (NY) Retired; [A] Yonkers, NY St. Joseph's Seminary.
Quinn, John J. '50 (HRT) Retired.
Quinn, John J. *s.j.* '54 (SCR) [C] Scranton, PA University of Scranton.
Quinn, John L. '62 (NY) On Special or Other (Arch)Diocesan Assignment.
Quinn, John M. *o.s.a.* '49 (PH) [AA] Villanova, PA St. Thomas Monastery.
Quinn, John M. '57 (SY) New Hartford, NY St. Thomas Church.
Quinn, Msgr. John M. '72 (DET) Special Assignment.
Quinn, Msgr. John P. '68 (MAN) Bedford, NH St. Elizabeth Seton Church.
Quinn, John T. '67 (SD) Retired.
Quinn, John T. *s.j.* '92 (WDC) [M] Washington, DC Leonard Neale House.
Quinn, Msgr. Joseph G. '85 (SCR) [1] Scranton, PA St. Peter's Church.
Quinn, Msgr. Joseph J. '45 (NY) Retired.
Quinn, Joseph L. *s.j.* '66 (SCR) [C] Scranton, PA University of Scranton.
Quinn, Joseph M. *c.s.c.* '50 (BUR) Wallingford, VT St. Patrick Church.
Quinn, Kenneth '71 (BO) Maynard, MA St. Bridget Church.
Quinn, Kevin P. *s.j.* '85 (WDC) [M] Washington, DC The Jesuit Community at Georgetown University.
Quinn, Kieran *o.f.m.cap.* '39 (WH) [2] Charleston, WV St. Anthony Church; [M] Charleston, WV Capuchins-St. Anthony Friary.
Quinn, Lawrence J. '71 (NY) [173] Bronx, NY Our Lady of Mercy Church; [P] New York, NY Catholic Youth Organization of the Archdiocese of New York Inc.
Quinn, Lawrence T. '67 (NY) [195] Staten Island, NY St. Ann Church.
Quinn, Liam '83 (MIA) [A] Miami, FL St. John Vianney College Seminary.
Quinn, Matthew '43 (PRO) [P] Bristol, RI St. Columban's Retirement House.
Quinn, Michael *c.ss.r.* '81 (CHI) [133] Chicago, IL St. Michael Church.
Quinn, Michael F. '70 (JC) Hannibal, MO Holy Family Church.
Quinn, Patrick *t.o.r.* '84 (STP) [C] St. Paul, MN University of St. Thomas.
Quinn, Peter '50 (ORL) Retired.
Quinn, Peter '62 (JKS) On Duty Outside the Diocese.
Quinn, Peter F. '72 (BO) [3] Quincy, MA St. John the Baptist Church.
Quinn, Peter N. '75 (PH) [20] Philadelphia, PA St. Barnabas Church.
Quinn, Peter O. '62 (BLX) [4] Biloxi, MS Our Mother of Sorrows Church.
Quinn, Richard *c.ss.r.* '86 (OM) [19] Omaha, NE Holy Name Church.
Quinn, Richard J. *m.m.* '54 (FgM) Maryknoll Foreign Missions.
Quinn, Msgr. Richard M. '40 (ROC) Retired.
Quinn, Robert C. '61 (ALN) Boyertown, PA St. Columbkill Church.
Quinn, Robert F. *c.s.p.* '53 (NY) [DD] Jamaica Estates, NY Paulist Fathers Generalate.
Quinn, Msgr. Robert J. '34 (SC) Retired.
Quinn, Seamus M. *c.ss.r.* '58 (PH) [136] Philadelphia, PA St. Peter the Apostle Church.
Quinn, Stephen *s.t.* '44 (PAT) [M] Stirling, NJ Holy Spirit Missionary Cenacle.
Quinn, Thomas '62 (SEA) [27] Seattle, WA Our Lady of Fatima Church.
Quinn, Thomas J. *s.j.* '68 (NY) [FF] Staten Island, NY Mount Manresa Jesuit Retreat House.
Quinn, Thomas J. '69 (PBL) Monte Vista, CO St. Joseph Church.
Quinn, Thomas P. '48 (HRT) Retired.
Quinn, Thomas S. '85 (TOL) [2] Toledo, OH Blessed Sacrament Church; [L] Toledo, OH Ursuline Convent of the Sacred Heart.
Quinn, Vincent J. '54 (NEW) Palisades Park, NJ St. Michael's Church; Retired; [N] Caldwell, NJ The Rev. Msgr. James F. Kelley Residence for Retired Priests.
Quinn, Msgr. W. Louis '45 (WDC) [5] Bethesda, MD Our Lady of Lourdes Church; Retired.
Quinn, Walter J. *o.s.a.* '61 (PH) [AA] Villanova, PA St. Thomas Monastery.
Quinn, Msgr. William '62 (CAM) Stone Harbor, NJ St. Paul's Church; Wildwood, NJ St. Ann's Church.
Quinn, Msgr. William J. '41 (CHI) Maywood, IL St. Eulalia Church; Retired.
Quinn, William J. '59 (CHI) [5] Oak Lawn, IL St. Louis De Montfort Church.
Quinn, William P. '55 (SFR) Retired.
Quinnan, Edward J. *s.j.* '87 (NY) [DD] New York, NY Jesuit Provincial's Office.
Quinnan, Edward J. *s.j.* '87 (RVC) [O] Manhasset, NY St. Ignatius Retreat House, Inisfada.
Quinnan, Michael F. '86 (SCR) On Special or Other Diocesan Assignment.
Quinones, Benjamin *c.r.l.* '85 (ARE) Corozal-Palmarito, PR La Milagrosa Church.
Quinones, Francisco '82 (SJN) [B] Santurce, PR Academia Sagrado Corazon.
Quinones, Leoncio '46 (PCE) On Duty Outside the Diocese.
Quinones, Miguel P. '52 (WDC) Retired.
Quinonez, Francisco J. '82 (SJN) [58] San Juan, PR Santa Teresa Jornet Church.
Quinonez-Murillo, Luis H. '97 (SJN) Luquillo, PR Madre del Redentor Church.
Quint, Dennis J. '96 (DUB) Dike, IA St. Mary Church; Grundy Center, IA Sacred Heart Church; Parkersburg, IA St. Patrick's Church; Reinbeck, IA Queen of Heaven Church.
Quintal, Gerald '65 (P) Dallas, OR St. Philip Church.
Quintana, Jose '96 (GR) [6] Grand Rapids, MI St. Francis Xavier Church.
Quinter, Paul S. '82 (PH) [140] Philadelphia, PA St. Raymond of Penafort Church.
Quintero, Francisco *s.d.b.* '50 (SJN) [28] San Juan, PR San Juan Bosco Church.
Quintero, Jose Francisco '89 (SJN) [5] Canovanas, PR San Jose Church.
Quintero, Manuel '81 (LAV) [9] Las Vegas, NV St. Francis de Sales Church.
Quinto, Armand *s.d.b.* '75 (NY) [2] Port Chester, NY Corpus Christi Church.
Quintus, C. A. '80 (ROC) Cohocton, NY Holy Family Catholic Community Church.
Quioque, Roy Milton *c.i.c.m.* '75 (SAT) Uvalde, TX Sacred Heart Church.
Quirk, Kevin M. '93 (WH) [P] Bethany, WV St. John Fisher Catholic Chapel; [P] West Liberty, WV West Liberty State College, St. Thomas Aquinas Campus Ministry.
Quirk, Richard J. '78 (STL) [46] St. Louis, MO Basilica of St. Louis, King of France.
Quiroz, Guido M. '44 (VIC) Retired.
Quispe, Abel '81 (FRS) Dinuba, CA St. Catherine Church.
Quitugua, David C. '84 (AGN) [1] Agana, GU Dulce Nombre de Maria Cathedral - Basilica Church.
Quitugua, David I.A. '64 (AGN) Ordot, GU San Juan Bautista Church.
Quoc Pham, Peter Thang '98 (CHL) [11] Charlotte, NC St. Vincent de Paul Church.
Quyet, Anthony '83 (JKS) Indianola, MS Immaculate Conception Church; Indianola, MS St. Benedict the Moor Church.

R

Raab, John *c.m.f.* '76 (LA) [Q] Los Angeles, CA Claretian Retreat Center Community.
Raab, Ronald Patrick *c.s.c.* (FTW) [M] Notre Dame, IN Our Lady of Fatima Retreat Center.
Raaser, Eric P. '85 (NY) [A] Bronx, NY St. John Neumann Seminary Residence.
Raaz, Paul A. '70 (SAT) [22] San Antonio, TX Resurrection of the Lord Church.
Rabadan, Manuel *c.r.l.* '93 (ARE) Corozal-Palmarito, PR La Milagrosa Church.
Rabalais, Rusty P. '97 (ALX) Fifth Ward, LA Our Lady of Lourdes Church.
Rabaut, Francis D. *s.j.* '44 (DET) [P] Clarkston, MI Colombiere Center.
Rabbat, Robert '95 (NTN) Northlake, IL St. John the Baptist Church; Hammond, IN St. Michael the Archangel Church.
Rabbitte, Martin '60 (AUS) McGregor, TX St. Eugene Church; Moody, TX Our Lady of San Juan Church.
Rabe, David L. '83 (NO) On Duty Outside the Archdiocese.
Rabelo Ortiz, William *o.m.* '95 (SJN) [16] San Juan, PR Ntra. Sra. de Fatima Church.
Rabenecker, David *o.s.b.* '91 (IND) [J] St. Meinrad, IN St. Meinrad Archabbey.
Rabenecker, David *o.s.b.* '91 (SPC) Springfield, MO U.S. Medical Center.
Rabeson, Jocelyn '98 (BO) [W] Cambridge, MA Weston Jesuit Community.
Rabideau, Richard L. '46 (SAG) Retired.
Rable, Cyril J. '56 (SCR) [4] Old Forge, PA St. Stanislaus Church.
Racco, Philip G. '77 (CLV) [30] Cleveland, OH Holy Rosary Church.
Rached, Jose *c.ss.r.* '70 (SJN) [2] San Juan, PR San Agustin Church.
Rachford, Nicholas '71 (PRM) On Special or Other Diocesan Assignment.
Rachunek, Henry C. '62 (GAL) Beasley, TX St. Wenceslaus Church.
Rachunek, Henry C. '62 (VIC) Hungerford, TX St. John the Baptist Church.
Racine, Michael S. '95 (FR) South Dartmouth, MA St. Mary's Church.
Racivitch, Herve P. *s.j.* '62 (NO) [P] New Orleans, LA Ignatius Residence.
Rackensperger, Nobert *o.f.m.conv.* '54 (FRS) Coalinga, CA St. Paul The Apostle Church.
Racki, Leonard E. '62 (PBL) Retired.
Raczek, Kenneth T. '56 (LFT) Elwood, IN St. Joseph Church.
Raczka, Philip '80 (NTN) Akron, OH St. Joseph Church.
Raczynski, Paul L. '72 (MIL) [1] Kenosha, WI St. Anthony Church.
Raczynski, Theodore T. '56 (HRT) Suffield, CT Sacred Heart Church.
Radaich, Thomas '70 (DUL) Grand Rapids, MN St. Joseph's Church.
Radano, Msgr. John A. '65 (NEW) On Duty Outside the Archdiocese.
Radasky, Robert '56 (ALT) [19] Johnstown, PA St. Clement's Church.
Radchuk, Anthony '62 (PHU) Retired.
Radde, James M. *s.j.* '72 (MIL) [P] Milwaukee, WI Jesuit Provincial Office, Wisconsin Province.
Radecki, Albin A. '49 (TOL) Retired.
Radecki, Dane *o.praem.* '77 (GB) [B] De Pere, WI St. Norbert College; [I] De Pere, WI St. Joseph Priory.
Radecky, Stephen F. '45 (CLV) [4] Parma, OH St. Columbkille Church; Retired.
Radek, James '89 (JOL) [2] Naperville, IL St. Elizabeth Seton Church.
Rademacher, Germain P. '58 (NU) Redwood Falls, MN St. Catherine Church.
Rademacher, John R. '70 (GI) [4] Grand Island, NE St. Leo Church.
Rademacher, Raymond M. '62 (LAN) Fowler, MI Most Holy Trinity Church.
Rademacher, Robert *glmy.* '54 (CIN) [M] Cincinnati, OH Headquarters of Glenmary Home Missioners.
Rademacher, Robert B. *glmy.* '55 (RIC) Clintwood, VA St. Joseph Church.
Rademacher, William '54 (LAN) Retired.
Rademaker, Martan *o.f.m.* '55 (GLP) Fort Defiance, AZ Our Lady of Blessed Sacrament Church; St. Michaels, AZ St. Michael Church.
Rader, John S. '91 (SFS) [4] Sioux Falls, SD Our Lady of Guadalupe Church.
Radetic, Msgr. Branimir '52 (Y) Retired.
Radetski, John J. '77 (MIL) [1] Fond du Lac, WI Holy Family Church.
Radetski, Paul J. (GB) Menasha, WI St. John Church.
Radice, Lawrence D. *m.m.* '85 (FgM) Maryknoll Foreign Missions.
Radloff, James A. '93 (BAK) La Pine, OR Holy Redeemer Church.
Radloff, Thomas H. *s.j.* '61 (DET) [K] Detroit, MI Jesuit Provincial Office-Detroit Province of the Society of Jesus.
Radocha, Stephen J. '77 (ALN) Catasauqua, PA St. Andrew Church; Northampton, PA Assumption of the Blessed Virgin Mary Church.
Radomski, Joseph A. '62 (TR) Avon, NJ St. Elizabeth Church.
Radon, Msgr. Eugene M. '47 (BUF) Retired.
Radosevich, George '68 (SFD) Livingston, IL Sacred Heart Church; New Douglas, IL St. Ubaldus Church; Staunton, IL St. Michael Church.
Radtke, Fred '67 (CHI) [N] Chicago, IL St. Peter's Friary.
Radtke, Fred '75 (CHI) [N] Chicago, IL Holy Evangelists Friary.
Radvanski, John M. (MET) Somerset, NJ St. Matthias Church.
Radvansky, Joseph R. '65 (PRM) Marblehead, OH St. Mary Church.
Radvansky, Robert J. '55 (PSC) Edison, NJ St. Nicholas Church; Perth Amboy, NJ St. Nicholas Church.
Raef, Scott '94 (AMA) Gruver, TX Cristo Redentor Church; Spearman, TX Sacred Heart Church.
Raeke, Joseph K. '80 (BO) Holbrook, MA St. Joseph Church.
Rafacz, Joseph J. *v.g.* '56 (LC) [9] La Crosse, WI Mary, Mother of the Church; Special Assignment.
Rafaj, Elias L. '99 (PBR) [3] Pittsburgh, PA St. John the

Baptist Church.
Raffaeta, George J. (HRT) Retired.
Raffaeta, George J. '56 (HRT) Woodmont, CT St. Agnes Church.
Raffel, Godfrey '53 (FRS) Retired.
Rafferty, Brian '94 (RIC) [2] Norfolk, VA Christ the King Church.
Rafferty, Brian M. '62 (BAL) Pasadena, MD Our Lady of the Chesapeake Church.
Rafferty, Colm *s.s.c.* '53 (LA) [57] Los Angeles, CA St. Columban Church.
Rafferty, Gerard F. *s.s.l.* (NY) West Nyack, NY St. Francis of Assisi Church.
Rafferty, Gerard F. *s.s.l.* '79 (NY) [A] Yonkers, NY St. Joseph's Seminary.
Rafferty, James A. '94 (SCR) Carbondale, PA St. Rose of Lima Church; [A] Dalton, PA Saint Pius X Seminary; [D] Carbondale, PA Sacred Heart Junior/Senior High School.
Rafferty, James E. '72 (SD) Escondido, CA Church of St. Timothy.
Rafferty, James F. '63 (BO) Hingham, MA St. Paul Church.
Rafferty, Joseph P. '83 (SCR) Harveys Lake, PA Our Lady of Victory Church.
Rafferty, Lawrence B. '67 (RVC) Elmont, NY St. Boniface Church.
Rafferty, Michael J. '57 (SCR) West Wyoming, PA Our Lady of Sorrows Church.
Rafferty, Raymond J. '54 (PRO) Retired.
Rafferty, Raymond M. '66 (NY) [28] New York, NY Corpus Christi Church; [40] New York, NY St. Gregory Church.
Rafferty, Thomas F. '83 (GAL) [43] Houston, TX St. Justin Martyr Church.
Raffo, Cesar '85 (LA) Carson, CA St. Philomena Church.
Raffo, Frank M. '98 (R) [3] Raleigh, NC Our Lady of Lourdes Church.
Raffo, Frank M., Jr. (R) Fayetteville, NC St. Patrick Church.
Raffo-Rivasplata, Cesar '85 (LA) Torrance, CA L.A. County-Harbor-U.C.L.A. Medical Center.
Raftery, Paul *o.p.* '84 (P) [18] Portland, OR Holy Rosary Parish & Dominican Priory Church.
Raftery, Paul Chrysostom *o.p.* '55 (SFR) [14] San Francisco, CA St. Dominic Church; [N] San Francisco, CA St. Dominic Priory.
Raftery, Thomas J. '44 (CHI) [36] Chicago, IL Christ the King Church; Winnetka, IL Sacred Heart Church; Retired.
Raftery, William J. '45 (WOR) Retired.
Raftery, William J. *s.j.* '57 (FgM) Provinces.
Raftis, J. Duane '47 (DUB) Retired.
Ragan, Gerald P. '79 (SAV) Dublin, GA Immaculate Conception Church.
Ragan, James A. '98 (PBR) Ernest, PA St. Jude Thaddeus Church.
Rager, Patrick F. '85 (PIT) Absent on Sick Leave.
Ragis, Gerald R. '63 (BUR) Charlotte, VT Our Lady of Mount Carmel Church; Hinesburg, VT St. Jude the Apostle Church.
Ragni, Richard '66 (PIT) Washington County, PA Various Nursing Homes.
Ragnoni, James V. '60 (CLV) [2] Akron, OH St. Anthony of Padua Church.
Ragsdale, Patrick J. '72 (SAT) [51] San Antonio, TX St. Luke Church.
Rahilly, James T. *c.s.c.* '64 (FgM) Holy Cross Mission Center(C.S.C.).
Rahilly, James T. *c.s.c.* '64 (FTW) [A] Notre Dame, IN Moreau Seminary; [A] Notre Dame, IN Moreau Seminary.
Rahilly, Paul '81 (RVC) Cedarhurst, NY St. Joachim Church.
Rahm, Harold J. *s.j.* '50 (FgM) Provinces.
Rahn, David C. '94 (ARL) Clifton, VA St. Andrew the Apostle Church.
Rahoy, Nickolas '77 (CI) Lukunor, FM Sacred Heart Church.
Rahrig, Gilbert (LAN) Retired.
Rai, Kevin '74 (AUS) Pflugerville, TX St. Elizabeth Church.
Raible, Daniel *c.pp.s.* '43 (CIN) [B] Carthagena, OH St. Charles.
Raible, Roland *o.f.m.cap.* '35 (PIT) [O] Pittsburgh, PA St. Conrad Friary.
Raica, Msgr. Steven J. '78 (LAN) On Duty Outside the Diocese.
Raich, Stephen *o.f.m.* '43 (CHI) [N] Chicago, IL Croatian Franciscan Custody of the Holy Family.
Raiche, Brian '95 (ALB) Averill Park, NY St. Henry Church.
Raila, Donald *o.s.b.* '83 (GBG) [H] Latrobe, PA Saint Vincent Archabbey.
Raila, Stanislaus '33 (BRK) Retired; [V] Douglaston, NY Bishop Mugavero Residence.
Raimer, Chester J. '74 (GBG) Blairsville, PA SS. Simon and Jude Church; Torrance, PA Torrance State Hospital.
Raimondi, Michele '50 (SFR) Retired.
Raimondo, Msgr. Joseph J. '40 (NY) Harrison, NY St. Gregory the Great Church; Retired.
Rainaldo, John H. *s.j.* '64 (NY) [DD] New York, NY Jesuit Provincial's Office.
Rainaldo, John H. *s.j.* '64 (RVC) [Q] New Hyde Park, NY Apostleship of Prayer, National Office for the U.S.
Rainforth, Thomas G. '73 (PAT) [8] Clifton, NJ St. Philip the Apostle Church.
Rainone, John J. '70 (PRO) [20] Providence, RI St. Joseph Church; Cranston, RI Rhode Island State Institutions.
Rainville, Laurence P. *o.f.m.* '47 (ALB) [B] Loudonville, NY Siena College.
Rainville, Marcel R. *s.s.e.* '67 (BUR) [A] Colchester, VT St. Michael's College.
Rainville, Marcel R. *s.s.e.* '71 (BUR) [E] Colchester, VT Society of St. Edmund.
Rainville, Paul *m.s.* '65 (MAN) Enfield, NH St. Helena Church.
Rainwater, Randall '96 (STO) Stockton, CA Northern California Women's Facility.
Raiser, Jerome K. '58 (COL) Retired.
Raj, Percy Joseph *o.f.m.* '74 (NY) [206] Staten Island, NY Holy Rosary Church.
Raj, Simon (BAL) [M] Baltimore, MD St. Agnes HealthCare, Inc.
Rajacz, Joseph J. *v.c.* '56 (LC) [L] La Crosse, WI Father Joseph Walijewski Orphanage Endowment Trust.
Rajanayagam, Thomas M. '66 (STO) Riverbank, CA St. Frances of Rome Church.
Rajareegam, Paul (ANC) [8] Anchorage, AK St. Patrick Church.
Rajter, Valentine *o.f.m.conv.* '48 (BUF) [21] Buffalo, NY Corpus Christi Church.
Rakaczki, Andor '73 (PSC) White Plains, NY St. Nicholas of Myra Church.
Rakaczky, Basil M. *o.s.b.m.* '60 (PSC) Perth Amboy, NJ St. Michael Church; [A] Matawan, NJ Basilian Fathers of Mariapoch.
Rakoczy, Richard S. '59 (DET) Waterford, MI St. Perpetua Church.
Rakoczy, Walter J. '78 (GRY) Portage, IN Nativity of Our Savior Church.
Rakowicz, William J. *s.j.* '80 (FgM) Provinces.
Rakowiez, William J. *s.j.* '80 (CI) [C] Koror, Palau, PW Manresa Jesuit House.
Ralenkotter, Howard *c.p.* '38 (L) [L] Louisville, KY Sacred Heart Retreat.
Ralko, Martin J. '84 (COL) Dennison, OH Immaculate Conception Church.
Ralph, John '55 (WH) Retired.
Ralph, Msgr. Thomas J. '56 (DUB) Andrew, IA St. John Church; La Motte, IA Holy Rosary Church; Otter Creek, IA St. Lawrence Church; St. Theresa, IA St. Theresa's Church; Sylvia, IA Assumption Church.
Ramacciotti, Gabriel M. *o.s.m.* '51 (CHI) [N] Chicago, IL Order of Friar Servants of Mary (Servites) United States of America Province, Inc.
Ramacciotti, Gabriel M. *o.s.m.* '51 (DEN) [4] Denver, CO Assumption Church.
Ramacciotti, James J. '85 (STL) [23] St. Louis, MO St. Ambrose Church; [A] St. Louis, MO Kenrick-Glennon Seminary.
Ramacher, Edward '45 (SCL) Spring Hill, MN St. Michael's Church; Retired.
Ramadhani, Deshi T.A. *s.j.* '96 (OAK) [N] Berkeley, CA Jesuit Community at Jesuit School of Theology at Berkeley.
Ramaeker, Victor F. '61 (SC) Whittemore, IA St. Michael's Church.
Ramaekers, Timothy '82 (ORG) Placentia, CA St. Joseph Church.
Ramellini, Msgr. P. Lino '47 (GBG) Retired.
Ramelow, Anselm *o.p.* (OAK) [N] Oakland, CA Dominican Order (Western Province), St. Albert's Priory.
Ramen, Paul (NOR) Ashford, CT St. Philip Church.
Ramen, Paul F. '60 (NOR) Retired.
Ramenaden, Ronald '70 (FTW) North Manchester, IN St. Robert Bellarmine Church.
Ramer, James K. '86 (PEO) [1] Rock Island, IL St. Mary Church.
Ramer, Leo '54 (LAN) Retired.
Ramirez, Adalberto *o.f.m.* '64 (CC) [H] Hebbronville, TX Franciscan Friars - O.F.M.
Ramirez, Alberto *ss.cc.* '61 (SJN) [1] Guaynabo, PR Corazon de Jesus Church.
Ramirez, Aldalberto *o.f.m.* '64 (AMA) Hereford, TX San Jose Church.
Ramirez, Alfonso *o.a.r.* (ORG) [3] Santa Ana, CA Our Lady of Guadalupe Church.
Ramirez, Allen A. *o.f.m.conv.* '72 (MRY) [F] Arroyo Grande, CA St. Joseph Cupertino Province, Provincial Center.
Ramirez, Cesar '96 (ARE) [2] Arecibo, PR Church of Sagrado Corazon de Jesus.
Ramirez, Charles J. '87 (LA) Monrovia, CA Immaculate Conception Church.
Ramirez, Cornelio C. *s.a.c.* '67 (LUB) [8] Lubbock, TX St. Patrick Church.
Ramirez, Enrique Espinosa *m.sp.s.* '79 (LA) [3] Oxnard, CA Our Lady of Guadalupe Church.
Ramirez, Fernando '78 (SD) [5] San Diego, CA Good Shepherd Church.
Ramirez, Francisco X. '79 (LA) [85] Los Angeles, CA St. Patrick Church.
Ramirez, Gabriel '85 (ORG) [1] Santa Ana, CA Immaculate Heart of Mary Church.
Ramirez, Gerardo '91 (PCE) Patillas, PR Inmaculado Corazon de Maria Church.
Ramirez, Hernando J. *s.j.* '75 (STL) St. Louis, MO St. Mary's Health Center; [P] St. Louis, MO Jesuit Community Corporation at St. Louis University - Jesuit Hall.
Ramirez, J. Jesus '86 (YAK) Royal City, WA St. Michael the Archangel Church.
Ramirez, Jairo H. '88 (STO) [8] Stockton, CA St. Mary of the Assumption Church.
Ramirez, Jose *s.m.* '69 (STL) [P] St. Louis, MO Marianist Community; [T] Eureka, MO Marianist Retreat & Conference Center.
Ramirez, Jose Nieves '79 (ELP) Absent on Leave.
Ramirez, Mario *m.s.c.* '83 (NY) [209] Staten Island, NY St. John Neumann Church.
Ramirez, Renelmo '84 (CGS) Culebra, PR Nuestra Senora del Carmen Church.
Ramirez, Tulio *m.x.y.* '90 (NY) [179] Bronx, NY Our Saviour Church; [DD] Bronx, NY Yarumal Mission Society, Inc.
Ramirez, Ybain '96 (SP) Brandon, FL Church of the Nativity.
Ramirez-Alejos, Msgr. Pedro '74 (SPK) Pasco, WA St. Patrick Church.
Ramirez-Portugal, Daniel '91 (LAR) [3] Laredo, TX Christ the King Church.
Ramler, Michael '74 (LEX) Frankfort, KY Good Shepherd Church.
Ramon, Gustavo J. '92 (LA) [5] Los Angeles, CA Assumption Church.
Ramon, Robert C. '82 (GAL) Dickinson, TX Shrine of the True Cross Church.
Ramon, Valentin *c.m.f.* '64 (ORG) [2] Orange, CA La Purisima Church.
Ramon-Landry, Ken '87 (BLX) Lumberton, MS Our Lady of Perpetual Help Church.
Ramos, Andre '88 (SD) [4] Chula Vista, CA St. Rose of Lima Church.
Ramos, Angel Roman '90 (MGZ) Hormigueros, PR Shrine of Our Lady of Monserrate Church.
Ramos, Antonio '94 (SFS) Tyndall, SD St. Leo Church; Springfield, SD State Prison.
Ramos, Cipriano '52 (SAC) Retired and in Senior Ministry.
Ramos, Eleuterio '66 (ORG) Inactive Leave.
Ramos, Fausto '35 (PCE) Retired.
Ramos, Fausto '46 (PCE) Villalba, PR Our Lady of Mt. Carmel Church.
Ramos, Gregorio *o.m.i.* '50 (FgM) Oblates Foreign Missions.
Ramos, Justin R. *o.praem* '95 (ORG) [D] Silverado, CA St. Michael's College Preparatory High School.
Ramos, Justin S. *o.praem.* '95 (ORG) [I] Silverado, CA Norbertine Fathers of Orange Inc.
Ramos, Ponciano M. *s.v.d.* '85 (SB) Yucca Valley, CA St. Mary of the Valley Church.
Ramos, Victoriano '54 (SJN) [33] San Juan, PR Santa Luisa de Marillac Church.
Ramoso, Ireneo '89 (SFR) Redwood City, CA St. Pius Church.
Ramsey, Boniface *o.p.* '73 (NEW) [A] South Orange, NJ Immaculate Conception Seminary.
Ramsey, James '84 (GAL) Damon, TX Sts. Cyril and Methodius Church; Needville, TX St. Michael Church.
Ramsey, James Boniface *o.p.* '73 (NY) [121] New York, NY St. Vincent Ferrer Church; [DD] New York, NY St. Vincent Ferrer Priory.
Ramson, Ronald W. *c.m.* '59 (STL) [P] St. Louis, MO Lazarist Residence.
Ranalletti, Richard A. *c.s.b.* '73 (DET) [E] Redford, MI Catholic Central High School.
Ranallo, John E. *o.s.a.* '75 (OAK) Castro Valley, CA Transfiguration Church; Castro Valley, CA Eden Hospital.
Rancourt, Henry *s.m.* '57 (BO) [Y] Framingham, MA The Marist House.
Rancourt, Mauril *o.m.i.* '60 (FgM) Oblates Foreign Missions.
Randall, Msgr. Edward '59 (GAL) [50] Houston, TX St. Michael Church.
Randall, Edward L. *o.m.i.* '50 (LEX) Jenkins, KY St. George Church.
Randall, John F. '53 (PRO) [11] Providence, RI St. Charles Borromeo Church.
Randall, Jude D. *o.s.b.* '60 (JOL) [C] Lisle, IL Benet Academy; [J] Lisle, IL St. Procopius Abbey.
Randall, Kevin '92 (NOR) On Duty Outside the Diocese.
Randall, Robert J. '51 (PRO) Retired.
Randazzo, Anthony J. '86 (NEW) North Caldwell, NJ Notre Dame Church.
Randl, Ewald '98 (NEW) Special Assignment.
Randone, Michael C. (BO) Billerica, MA St. Theresa of Lisieux Church.

Randriamanantena, M.W. '97 (BO) [W] Cambridge, MA Weston Jesuit Community.
Ranek, Jerome M. '91 (SFS) Mobridge, SD St. Joseph Church.
Raneri, Carmine B. '55 (HRT) [6] Waterbury, CT Our Lady of Mt. Carmel Church.
Raney, Isaac *m.ss.a.* '67 (DEN) Greeley, CO St. Peter Church.
Raney, Isaac *m.s.a.* '67 (NOR) [F] Cromwell, CT Society of the Missionaries of the Holy Apostles.
Raney, Richard E. '38 (PEO) Retired.
Ranft, Paul J. '40 (TUC) San Manuel, AZ St. Bartholomew Church; Retired.
Rangel, Maximo *o.f.m.* '96 (ELP) [B] El Paso, TX St. Anthony's School of Theology.
Ranges, Charles H. *s.s.e.* '72 (BUR) Highgate Center, VT St. Louis Church; Swanton, VT Nativity of the Blessed Virgin Mary Church.
Ranieri, John J. '82 (NEW) [B] South Orange, NJ Seton Hall University.
Ranieri, Msgr. Joseph A. '57 (WDC) Pastoral Center Special Ministries.
Ranitz, Richard De *o.p.* '70 (CHI) River Forest, IL St. Vincent Ferrer Church.
Rank, Robert *s.o.l.t.* '67 (CC) [H] Robstown, TX Society of Our Lady of the Most Holy Trinity.
Rank, Robert F. '68 (GB) On Duty Outside the Diocese.
Rank, Ronald G. '58 (MAD) Waterloo, WI St. Joseph Church.
Rankin, James '65 (SD) [37] San Diego, CA St. Vincent de Paul Church; Retired.
Rankin, Joseph M. '79 (L) [27] Louisville, KY St. Francis of Assisi Church.
Rankin, Paul B. *c.s.c.* '48 (AUS) [H] Austin, TX Congregation of Holy Cross - Southern Province.
Rankin, Paul B. *c.s.c.* '48 (FTW) [J] South Bend, IN Congregation of Holy Cross, Indiana Province, Provincial House.
Rankin, Robert '80 (LA) Palmdale, CA St. Mary Church.
Ranly, Ernest W. *c.pp.s.* '56 (CIN) [M] Dayton, OH Provincial Office of the Cincinnati Province of the Society of the Precious Blood.
Rans, Norbert J. *m.m.* '64 (NY) [DD] Maryknoll, NY Maryknoll Fathers and Brothers.
Ransing, Bernard E. *c.s.c.* '35 (FTW) [J] South Bend, IN Congregation of Holy Cross, Indiana Province, Provincial House.
Ransom, Donald B. '64 (NEW) On Duty Outside the Archdiocese.
Ransom, Ralph R. *s.s.j.* '61 (BAL) [S] Baltimore, MD St. Joseph Society of the Sacred Heart House of Central Administration.
Ranzino, Thomas C. '78 (BR) [9] Baton Rouge, LA St. George Church.
Rapaglia, Eric '00 (NY) [221] Staten Island, NY Our Lady Star of the Sea Church.
Raphael, John *s.s.j.* '95 (WDC) [B] Washington, DC St. Joseph's Seminary; [S] Washington, DC Archdiocesan Campus Ministry.
Raphael, Mark S. '98 (NO) [5] Metairie, LA St. Catherine of Siena Church.
Rapin, Cyril W. '46 (OG) Mooers, NY St. Joseph Church; Retired.
Rapose, Mario D. '00 (OM) [40] Omaha, NE St. Robert Bellarmine Church.
Raposo, John A. '77 (FR) Provincetown, MA St. Peter the Apostle Church.
Rapp, Bernard A. '99 (SD) Fallbrook, CA St. Peter Church.
Rapp, Bertrand J. '50 (L) [12] Louisville, KY St. Bartholomew Church; Retired.
Rappold, Norbert Frank '99 (LR) [11] Little Rock, AR Our Lady of the Holy Souls Church.
Raptosh, Richard Joseph '87 (PBR) Monroeville, PA Church of the Resurrection.
Raquepo, Mario '79 (HON) [10] Honolulu, HI Our Lady of the Mount Church; [E] Honolulu, HI St. Francis Healthcare System of Hawaii.
Rareshide, Msgr. Lanaux J. '61 (NO) [4] Slidell, LA St. Margaret Mary Church; Slidell, LA Greenbriar Nursing & Convalescent Home; Slidell, LA Guest House of Slidell Nursing Home; Slidell, LA Greenery Neurologic Rehabilitation Center at Slidell.
Rarus, Boleslaus J. '40 (BGP) Retired; [P] Stamford, CT The Catherine Dennis Keefe Queen of the Clergy Retired Priests' Residence.
Rasby, Msgr. James W. '52 (DEN) Retired.
Rasch, Richard *o.de.m.* '84 (CLV) [57] Cleveland, OH Our Lady of Mount Carmel Church; [O] Cleveland, OH Mercedarians.
Rascher, Joseph C. '81 (BEL) Caseyville, IL St. Stephen Church.
Raschke, Bernard L. '58 (LC) Edgar, WI St. John the Baptist Church.
Raschko, Michael '75 (SEA) Special Assignment.
Rashford, Nicholas J. *s.j.* '71 (PH) [C] Philadelphia, PA St. Joseph's University; [AA] Philadelphia, PA Jesuit Community at St. Joseph's University.
Rasing, Linus E. '53 (DUB) Retired.
Rask, Phillip J. '72 (STP) [A] St. Paul, MN The Saint Paul Seminary; [C] St. Paul, MN University of St. Thomas.
Rasky, Joseph G. *s.m.* '65 (SAT) [F] San Antonio, TX Central Catholic High School; [M] San Antonio, TX Central Catholic Marianist Community.
Rasmussen, John C. '69 (SFS) Elk Point, SD St. Joseph Church.
Rasmussen, Terrence *o.f.m.conv.* (DUB) Jewell, IA Good Shepherd Church.
Rasner, David L. '72 (LFT) Special Assignment.
Rasner, David L. '82 (LFT) Otterbein, IN St. Charles Church.
Raso, Anthony '75 (BRK) [216] Queens, NY Our Lady of Mount Carmel Church.
Raspallo, Domenic '61 (PRO) Retired.
Raspudic, Bruno *o.f.m.* '43 (CHI) [N] Chicago, IL Croatian Franciscan Custody of the Holy Family.
Rasquinha, Ignatius '33 (SB) Joshua Tree, CA St. Christopher of the Desert Church.
Rasquinha, Vincent *s.d.b.* '75 (OAK) [N] Berkeley, CA Salesian Community.
Rassas, George J. '68 (CHI) Lake Forest, IL St. Mary Church.
Rassley, George *c.ss.r.* '53 (DEN) [M] Denver, CO The Redemptorists/Denver Province.
Rassmussen, Terrence *o.f.m.conv.* '79 (DUB) Ames, IA St. Cecilia Church; Gilbert, IA SS. Peter and Paul Church.
Rasura, James I. *s.j.* '56 (SD) [12] San Diego, CA Our Lady of Guadalupe Church; San Diego, CA Central Detention Facility and San Diego City Jail.
Raszeja, Norbert W. *c.r.* '72 (CHI) [N] Chicago, IL Provincial Office of the Congregation of the Resurrection.
Raszewski, Edward J. *c.s.sp.* '47 (FgM) Holy Ghost Foreign Missions.
Raszkowski, Robert P. *s.j.* '46 (FgM) Provinces.
Raszkowski, Robert P. *s.j.* '46 (MIL) [P] Milwaukee, WI Jesuit Provincial Office, Wisconsin Province.
Rataj, Stanley G. '79 (CHI) [140] Chicago, IL St. Nicholas of Tolentine Church.
Ratajczak, Justin *o.f.m.conv.* '77 (BAL) [26] Baltimore, MD St. Clement Mary Hofbauer Church.
Ratajczak, Michael '75 (SD) Spring Valley, CA Santa Sophia Church.
Ratajczak, Richard C. '58 (SAG) Beaver, MI St. Valentine Church.
Ratazak, Bernard A. '76 (RCK) Retired.
Ratchford, Robert J. *s.j.* '61 (NO) Gretna, LA Jefferson Parish Correctional Center; [C] New Orleans, LA Loyola University New Orleans; [P] New Orleans, LA Ignatius Residence.
Raterman, Herbert J *s.j.* '55 (CIN) [M] Cincinnati, OH Faber Jesuit Community.
Raterman, Herbert J. *s.j.* '55 (CIN) [V] Cincinnati, OH Living Monuments of Reparation.
Ratermann, Msgr. David A. '51 (STL) On Duty Outside the Archdiocese.
Ratermann, George H. *m.m.* '47 (NY) [DD] Maryknoll, NY Maryknoll Fathers and Brothers.
Ratermann, Jerome B. '57 (BEL) Retired.
Rath, John G. '36 (Y) Retired.
Rath, Martin *o.s.b.* '83 (NU) Winsted, MN St. Mary's Care Center; [C] Winsted, MN St. Mary's Care Center.
Rath, Martin *o.s.b.* '83 (SCL) [I] Collegeville, MN St. John's Abbey, of the Order of St. Benedict.
Rath, Richard '88 (STL) [6] Florissant, MO St. Ferdinand Church.
Rath, Thomas V. '49 (CLV) Amherst, OH St. Joseph Church; [5] Lorain, OH St. John Church; Retired.
Rathapilly, Emanuel '71 (SJP) Northern Cambria, PA Immaculate Conception Church.
Rathfon, John R. '54 (CLV) Cuyahoga Falls, OH Immaculate Heart of Mary Church; Retired.
Rathgeb, William R. '67 (GBG) [E] Greensburg, PA Clelian Heights School for Exceptional Children; [I] Greensburg, PA Apostles of the Sacred Heart of Jesus.
Rathschmidt, John *o.f.m.cap.* '69 (NY) [C] New Rochelle, NY College of New Rochelle; [DD] White Plains, NY St. Conrad Friary; [GG] New York, NY University Apostolate.
Ratigan, Patrick A. '83 (OG) Military Chaplains.
Ratterman, Kevin '93 (OKL) Special Assignment.
Ratterman, Kevin '94 (OKL) [C] Oklahoma City, OK Mount St. Mary High School.
Ratterman, Kevin J. '93 (OKL) Mangum, OK Sacred Heart Church.
Ratzenberger, Raymond '85 (TUC) Benson, AZ Our Lady of Lourdes Church.
Ratzmann, George '81 (VEN) Sanibel, FL St. Isabel Church.
Rau, Msgr. Donald E. '56 (STL) Bridgeton, MO St. Lawrence the Martyr Church.
Rau, Peter J. '85 (ATL) Cumming, GA Good Shepherd Church.
Rau, Msgr. Raymond '49 (BRK) [55] Brooklyn, NY Holy Family Church.
Rau, Msgr. Raymond '56 (CC) Retired.
Rau, Raymond F. '49 (BRK) Retired; Retired.
Rau, Msgr. Raymond F. '49 (CC) [22] Corpus Christi, TX St. Theresa Church.
Rauch, David E. '70 (STL) [38] St. Louis, MO St. James the Greater Church.
Rauch, Edward L. *o.s.f.s.* '64 (PH) [D] Philadelphia, PA Father Judge High School for Boys; [AA] Philadelphia, PA Father Judge Faculty House.
Raudabaugh, Joseph R. '62 (CIN) Yellow Springs, OH St. Paul Church; [Q] Yellow Springs, OH Antioch College Campus Ministry.
Raulli, Enrico *s.j.* '65 (NEW) [C] Jersey City, NJ St. Peter's Preparatory School.
Raulli, Enrico *s.j.* '65 (NY) [DD] New York, NY West Side Jesuit Community.
Raum, Blair '71 (BAL) Special Assignment.
Raun, Msgr. Douglas A. '82 (SFE) Rio Rancho, NM St. Thomas Aquinas Church.
Rausch, Clyde *o.m.i.* '68 (FgM) Oblates Foreign Missions.
Rausch, Dale J. '68 (DUB) Fayette, IA St. Francis of Assisi Church; West Union, IA Holy Name Church; [N] West Union, IA Upper Iowa University.
Rausch, Dennis '80 (MIA) [6] Fort Lauderdale, FL St. Clement Church.
Rausch, John '72 (CIN) [M] Cincinnati, OH Headquarters of Glenmary Home Missioners.
Rausch, John *o.f.m.* '76 (STL) [C] St. Louis, MO Saint Louis University; [P] St. Louis, MO Franciscan Friary of St. Anthony of Padua.
Rausch, John W. '47 (MIL) Retired.
Rausch, Leon S. *s.j.* '59 (MIL) [P] Wauwatosa, WI Jesuit Community at St. Camillus.
Rausch, Nicholas *o.s.b.* '56 (SEA) [L] Lacey, WA St. Martin's Abbey.
Rausch, Thomas P. *s.j.* '72 (LA) [C] Los Angeles, CA Loyola Marymount University.
Rauscher, Donald F. *s.j.* '68 (FgM) Provinces.
Rauscher, Donald F. *s.j.* '68 (STL) [P] St. Louis, MO Jesuit Community Corporation at St. Louis University - Jesuit Hall.
Rauscher, Msgr. Joseph G. '67 (SCR) [16] Wilkes-Barre, PA St. Nicholas Church.
Rauscher, Msgr. Martin F. '60 (PAT) Morristown, NJ Assumption of the Blessed Virgin Mary Church.
Rauscher, Russell G. '75 (CLV) Medina, OH St. Francis Xavier Church.
Rautenberg, Joseph F. '73 (IND) Beech Grove, IN Holy Name Church; Knightstown, IN St. Rose Church; New Castle, IN St. Anne Church; [F] Indianapolis, IN St. Vincent Hospital and Health Care Center, Inc.
Rauth, Philip J. '59 (LIN) Auburn, NE St. Joseph's Church.
Raux, Redmond P. (BO) Military & VA Chaplains.
Rauzi, Mario *c.s.* '45 (CIN) [76] Cincinnati, OH Sacred Heart Church.
Ravelojaona, Andre '57 (STL) [P] St. Louis, MO La Salette Missionaries.
Raveneau, Ricardo '90 (BRK) [86] Brooklyn, NY St. Michael's Church.
Ravenkamp, Michael *s.j.* '96 (SJ) [17] San Jose, CA Most Holy Trinity Church.
Ravey, Donald J. '61 (BUR) Williston, VT Immaculate Heart of Mary Church.
Ravi, Francis '88 (TR) Marlton, NJ St. Joan of Arc Church.
Ravizza, Mark A. *s.j.* '99 (SJ) [B] Santa Clara, CA Santa Clara University.
Ravlic, Msgr. Cornelius C. '37 (LA) Retired.
Rawa, Jerome D. *s.m.* '55 (WH) Richwood, WV Holy Family Church; Summersville, WV St. John The Evangelist Church.
Rawden, Msgr. John A. '55 (LA) Retired; [J] Santa Barbara, CA St. Francis Medical Center of Santa Barbara.
Rawlins, John J. *s.s.j.* '45 (BAL) [S] Baltimore, MD St. Joseph's Manor.
Ray, James M. '75 (CHI) Other Assignments; [G] Chicago, IL Catholic Charities of the Archdiocese of Chicago-Archdiocesan Offices.
Ray, Robert E. '69 (L) [42] Louisville, KY St. John Vianney Church; Fairdale, KY St. Jerome Church.
Rayappan, Louis '80 (TR) Maple Shade, NJ Our Lady of Perpetual Help Church.
Rayar, Thomas '93 (STP) Clearwater, MN St. Luke Church.
Rayer, Daniel J. '99 (LIN) [8] Lincoln, NE St. Mary Church.
Rayes, Emanuel '54 (EST) Troy, MI St. Joseph Chaldean Church.
Rayes, Joseph *o.f.m.* '57 (CIN) [M] Cincinnati, OH St. Ann Friary.
Raymaker, John *c.i.c.m.* '64 (FgM) Missionhurst Foreign Missions.
Raymond, David R. '89 (SPR) South Hadley, MA St. Patrick's Church; [C] Springfield, MA Cathedral High School; [C] Holyoke, MA Holyoke Catholic High School.
Raymond, Maurice L. '62 (SCR) [2] Hazleton, PA Church of the Most Precious Blood.
Raymond, Wilfred J. *c.s.c.* (HRT) [M] New Haven, CT Priests of the Congregation of Holy Cross.

Raymundo, Gregorio G. '46 (LA) Retired.
Rayson, Robert '99 (PEO) Moline, IL Sacred Heart Church.
Re, Angelo '60 (SJ) Retired.
Rea, John W. '45 (ARL) Falls Church, VA St. Philip Church; Retired.
Read, Denis William *o.c.d.* '52 (MIA) [L] Miami, FL Discalced Carmelite Friars of Miami, Inc.
Read, Ignacio *o.c.d.* '56 (MIL) [P] Milwaukee, WI Provincial Offices - Discalced Carmelites.
Reading, Edward '72 (PAT) On Duty Outside the Diocese.
Ready, Francis P. '50 (BO) Senior Priests.
Ready, Frank J. '59 (ARL) Annandale, VA Holy Spirit Church.
Reagan, Msgr. Donald '47 (Y) Retired.
Real, Fernando *m.id.* '81 (NY) [180] Bronx, NY Santa Maria Church; [DD] Bronx, NY Idente Missionaries - Santa Maria Residence.
Reale, Frank *s.j.* '81 (FgM) Provinces.
Reale, Frank E. *s.j.* '81 (STL) [F] St. Louis, MO St. Louis University High School, George H. Backer Memorial; [P] St. Louis, MO St. Louis University High School Jesuit Community; [P] St. Louis, MO The Jesuits of the Missouri Province.
Reale, Sante *c.pp.s.* '60 (ORL) [6] Orlando, FL St. Andrew Church.
Realmuto, George *m.s.a.* '87 (NOR) [F] Cromwell, CT Society of the Missionaries of the Holy Apostles.
Ream, Gerard J. '54 (ALT) Retired.
Reamer, Mark *o.f.m.* '91 (R) [4] Raleigh, NC St. Francis of Assisi Church.
Reamer, William G. '87 (OG) Plattsburgh, NY Champlain Valley Physicians Hospital Medical Center.
Rearden, Patrick R. *o.p.* '60 (CHI) [N] Chicago, IL Dominicans (Provincial Office).
Reardon, Daniel '97 (KC) On Duty Outside the Diocese.
Reardon, Daniel F. *c.s.v.* '61 (RCK) [G] McHenry, IL Villa Desiderata Retreat House.
Reardon, Dennis A. '72 (PRO) North Kingstown, RI St. Bernard Church.
Reardon, Francis '78 (PMB) [2] Boca Raton, FL Our Lady of Lourdes Church.
Reardon, John D. '73 (PH) Flourtown, PA St. Genevieve Church; Wyndmoor, PA Seven Dolors Church.
Reardon, John F. '50 (NY) [225] Staten Island, NY St. Rita Church.
Reardon, John F. '76 (BO) [7] Boston, MA St. Ann Church.
Reardon, John I. *o.p.* '49 (NO) [30] New Orleans, LA St. Dominic Church.
Reardon, Michael '74 (LA) [5] Long Beach, CA St. Cornelius Church.
Reardon, Patrick *o.p.* '60 (FgM) Dominican - Order of Preachers Foreign Missions.
Reardon, Robert J. '59 (PIT) Upper St. Clair, PA St. John Capistran Church.
Reardon, Thomas J. '51 (LC) Retired.
Reasbeck, Msgr. David E. '56 (STU) Colerain, OH St. Frances Cabrini Church.
Reasoner, Mark J. '98 (DUB) [6] Dubuque, IA Church of the Resurrection.
Reaume, Michael R. *s.m.* '69 (CIN) [M] Dayton, OH Marianist Provincialate.
Reaves, Phillip A. '94 (LR) Texarkana, AR St. Edward's Church.
Rebaldo, Ronald '91 (RVC) Absent on Leave.
Rebamontan, Marito F. '70 (ORG) Anaheim, CA St. Anthony Claret Church.
Rebanal, Msgr. Jeremias R. '55 (NEW) [1] Jersey City, NJ St. Aedan's Church.
Rebaque, Jose *s.a.c.* '70 (BGP) [9] Bridgeport, CT St. George Church; [18] Bridgeport, CT St. Peter Church.
Rebatzki, George M. '64 (MIL) [53] Milwaukee, WI Old St. Mary Church.
Rebeck, Eugene M. '65 (TR) Holmdel, NJ St. Catharine Church.
Rebeiro, Anthony J. '56 (BO) [1] Revere, MA St. Anthony of Padua Church.
Rebel, John W. '65 (PIT) Mars, PA St. Kilian Church.
Rebel, Patrick M. (SP) St. Joseph, FL Sacred Heart Church.
Rebert, Robert '58 (SFD) Special or Other Diocesan Assignment.
Rebeta, James L. *c.s.c.* '73 (BGP) [P] Bridgeport, CT Provincial Offices of the Priests and Brothers of Holy Cross, Eastern Province.
Rebeyro, Lloyd '70 (ALB) [11] Albany, NY St. Mary Church.
Rebman, Msgr. Joseph F. '60 (WIL) Greenville, DE St. Joseph on the Brandywine Church.
Rebol, Anthony '56 (CLV) [42] Cleveland, OH St. Lawrence Church; Brecksville, OH St. Basil the Great Church; Retired.
Rebol, Francis *m.m.* '53 (FgM) Maryknoll Foreign Missions.
Rebold, John '54 (SFE) Retired.
Reboli, John P. *s.j.* '70 (WOR) [N] Worcester, MA Jesuits of Holy Cross College, Inc.
Rebong, Nestor '86 (LA) Whittier, CA St. Gregory the Great Church.
Rebosura, Sabino B., II '87 (HT) Morgan City, LA Sacred Heart of Jesus Church.
Rebovich, John '67 (PRM) Absent on Leave.
Rebuldelha, Alfred '72 (HON) Makawao, HI St. Joseph Church.
Recchuti, William A. *o.s.a.* '61 (ALB) Mechanicville, NY Assumption-St. Paul Church.
Receconi, Edward R. *o.s.b.* '79 (SEA) [L] Lacey, WA St. Martin's Abbey.
Rechenburg, Basil *o.s.b.* '68 (WOR) [N] Still River, MA Benedictine Monks, St. Benedict Abbey.
Rechtein, John *s.m.* '70 (SAT) [C] San Antonio, TX St. Mary's University of San Antonio, Texas; [M] San Antonio, TX Marianist Residence.
Recio, Jesus Perez *o.a.r.* (ELP) [8] El Paso, TX Guardian Angel Church.
Recio, Julio *o.p.* (SFR) [3] San Rafael, CA St. Raphael Church.
Reck, Donald W. *s.j.* '65 (FgM) Provinces.
Reck, Donald W. *s.j.* '65 (STL) [C] St. Louis, MO Saint Louis University; [P] St. Louis, MO Leo Brown Jesuit Community.
Recker, Odo *o.s.b.* '78 (P) [A] St. Benedict, OR Mount Angel Seminary; [L] St. Benedict, OR Mt. Angel Abbey.
Recker, Philip F. '59 (DUB) Osage, IA Sacred Heart Church.
Reckinger, Robert A. '51 (DET) Retired.
Reckker, Stephen C. '63 (DET) Romeo, MI St. Clement of Rome Church.
Rector, Warren *o.f.m.* '68 (CAM) [H] Camden, NJ Our Lady of Lourdes Medical Center, Inc.
Rector, Warren *o.f.m.* '68 (PH) [AA] Philadelphia, PA St. Pius X Friary.
Reczek, Felix J. *o.f.m.* '44 (BUR) Bellows Falls, VT Sacred Heart Church.
Reczek, Felix J. *o.f.m.* '44 (PIT) [O] Ben Avon, PA St. Anthony Friary and Mission House.
Redcay, Christopher '89 (PH) Newtown, PA St. Andrew Church.
Redden, Michael J. (ATL) Fort Oglethorpe, GA St. Gerard Majella Church.
Reddick, E. Peter '72 (SY) [20] Syracuse, NY St. Patrick Church.
Reddington, Benjamin J. '43 (MAD) Retired.
Reddy, Albert F. *s.j.* '58 (BGP) [P] Fairfield, CT The Fairfield Jesuit Community-Fairfield University.
Reddy, Gade Show '91 (CHR) Aiken, SC St. Mary, Help of Christians Church; [H] Aiken, SC University of South Carolina, Aiken Extension.
Reddy, R. Inna '90 (CHR) [2] Columbia, SC St. Joseph Church; [5] Columbia, SC St. John Neumann Church.
Reddy, Reginald J. *o.f.m.* '61 (ALB) [B] Loudonville, NY Siena College.
Redinbo, Joseph *o.f.m.* '59 (SFE) Pena Blanca, NM Nuestra Senora De Guadalupe Church.
Reding, Michael A. '97 (STP) Wayzata, MN St. Bartholomew Church.
Redington, James D. *s.j.* '78 (WDC) [M] Washington, DC Woodstock Jesuit Community; [V] Washington, DC Woodstock Theological Center.
Redlon, Reginald A. *o.f.m.* '49 (NY) [115] New York, NY St. Stephen of Hungary Church.
Redmerski, Stanley J. '58 (LIN) Retired.
Redmond, Arthur S. '55 (LC) Rozellville, WI St. Andrew Church; Retired.
Redmond, Daniel P. '96 (CLV) [76] Cleveland, OH St. Vincent de Paul Church.
Redmond, Donald *o.s.b.* '57 (KCK) Fidelity, KS St. Augustine's Church; Sabetha, KS Sacred Heart Church; Wetmore, KS St. James Church.
Redmond, Lawrence '64 (ORL) Retired.
Redmond, Paul V. '54 (ALB) On Duty Outside the Diocese.
Redmond, Paul V. '54 (BAL) [B] Emmitsburg, MD Mount Saint Mary's College.
Redmond, Sean P. '90 (LIN) Paul, NE St. Joseph's Church.
Redstone, James '98 (NEW) Cedar Grove, NJ St. Catherine of Siena Church.
Redwanski, Dale H. *o.s.c.* '71 (DET) Riverview, MI St. Cyprian Church; [K] Riverview, MI Crosier Community of Riverview.
Redwick, Adolph '59 (DET) [6] Dearborn, MI St. Joseph Church.
Reece, Richard T. *o.s.f.s.* '65 (PH) [AA] Wyndmoor, PA Villa de Sales Oblate Residence.
Reece, Robert *o.s.f.s.* '65 (ALN) [L] Reading, PA St. Joseph Villa.
Reed, Albert *c.pp.s.* '54 (CIN) [B] Carthagena, OH St. Charles.
Reed, Albert A. *c.pp.s.* '54 (CIN) [U] Dayton, OH Community Support Charitable Trust.
Reed, Bruce '93 (RVC) [1] Rockville Centre, NY St. Agnes Church.
Reed, David *s.j.* '64 (FgM) Provinces.
Reed, Dennis L. '69 (DOD) Belpre, KS St. Bernard Church; Larned, KS Sacred Heart Church.
Reed, Douglas '71 (R) Kinston, NC Holy Spirit Catholic Church.
Reed, H. William '62 (NO) [59] New Orleans, LA St. Rose of Lima Church.
Reed, John C. *s.j.* '50 (DET) [P] Clarkston, MI Colombiere Center.
Reed, John Philip *m.afr.* '88 (WDC) [M] Washington, DC Missionaries of Africa.
Reed, Michael V. '84 (PT) [1] Pensacola, FL Cathedral of the Sacred Heart.
Reed, Robert J. '61 (ALN) [10] Bethlehem, PA SS. Simon and Jude Church.
Reed, Robert P. '85 (BO) Whitman, MA Holy Ghost Church.
Reed, Thomas A. '47 (SJ) [L] Los Gatos, CA Sacred Heart Jesuit Center.
Reed, William (NEW) Rahway, NJ Rahway Hospital.
Reed, William C. '71 (NEW) [9] Elizabeth, NJ Our Lady of Most Holy Rosary/St. Michael Church.
Reedy, Francis C. *o.s.b.* '58 (MIL) [P] Benet Lake, WI St. Benedict's Abbey.
Reedy, Gerard *s.j.* '70 (NY) [DD] New York, NY Jesuit Community at Fordham University.
Reedy, John J. '35 (P) Retired.
Reehil, Philip J. '46 (RVC) Setauket, NY St. James Church; Retired.
Reen, Jeremiah *s.d.b.* '71 (PMB) Belle Glade, FL St. Philip Benizi Church.
Reese, Benjamin B. '91 (PEO) [10] Peoria, IL St. Mark's Church.
Reese, Charles T. '49 (CHL) Retired.
Reese, Donald B. '63 (CAM) Retired.
Reese, Edward *s.j.* '73 (PHX) [B] Phoenix, AZ Brophy College Preparatory.
Reese, Francis X. *s.j.* '60 (CHL) Mars Hill, NC St. Andrew the Apostle Church; [J] Charlotte, NC Jesuit Community; [M] Hot Springs, NC Jesuit House of Prayer.
Reese, Robert '89 (ALT) [3] Altoona, PA St. Mark's Church.
Reese, Thomas J. *s.j.* '74 (NY) [DD] New York, NY "America;" Residence and publication office of the America Press; [HH] New York, NY America Press, Inc.
Reeson, David G. '80 (OM) Military Chaplains.
Reeves, Joseph '76 (BAK) On Duty Outside the Diocese.
Reeves, Nathaniel *o.s.b.* '78 (IND) [A] St. Meinrad, IN St. Meinrad Seminary; [J] St. Meinrad, IN St. Meinrad Archabbey.
Refermat, Thomas '94 (CHI) [45] Chicago, IL St. Cornelius Church.
Regado, Justo Beltran '69 (BRK) Brooklyn, NY Woodhull Medical & Mental Health Center.
Regalado, Luis *o.s.b.* '84 (SFE) [I] Abiquiu, NM Monastery of Christ in the Desert.
Regan, Charles '58 (WCH) Retired.
Regan, Columkille *c.p.* '49 (PH) [AA] Philadelphia, PA St. Michael's Passionist Residence.
Regan, Msgr. Dennis M. (RVC) [I] Melville, NY Catholic Health Services of Long Island.
Regan, Msgr. Dennis M. '64 (RVC) Commack, NY Christ the King Church.
Regan, Desmond '46 (BIR) [1] Birmingham, AL St. Paul's Church; Retired.
Regan, Francis A. '53 (BO) Marshfield, MA St. Christine Church.
Regan, Francis A. *s.s.c.* '66 (FgM) St. Columban's Foreign Mission.
Regan, Gerald T. *s.j.* '64 (MOB) [A] Mobile, AL Spring Hill College.
Regan, James J. *s.j.* '67 (FgM) Provinces.
Regan, John '48 (PHX) Luke Air Force Base, AZ Luke Catholic Community.
Regan, Msgr. John D. '53 (HRT) Middlebury, CT St. John of the Cross Church.
Regan, John J. '48 (BO) Senior Priests.
Regan, Matthew R.D. '70 (OAK) [4] San Leandro, CA St. Leander Church.
Regan, Msgr. Michael F. '38 (STL) Retired.
Regan, Michael J. '62 (BO) Permanent Disability.
Regan, Michael J. '64 (BO) Abington, MA St. Bridget Church.
Regan, Richard '85 (SAN) Big Spring, TX Immaculate Heart of Mary Church.
Regan, Richard J. *s.j.* '63 (NY) [DD] New York, NY Jesuit Community at Fordham University.
Regan, Robert F. *s.j.* '59 (BO) [W] Boston, MA The Society of Jesus of New England-Provincial Offices.
Regan, Robert F. *s.j.* '59 (PRT) [9] Portland, ME St. Pius X Church.
Regan, Terrence P. '68 (GF) Stanford, MT St. Rose of Lima Church.
Regan, Thomas J. *s.j.* '87 (BGP) [B] Fairfield, CT Fairfield University; [P] Fairfield, CT The Fairfield Jesuit Community-Fairfield University.
Regan, Timothy J. '91 (DAV) Keota, IA Holy Trinity Church.
Regan, William '56 (SY) [S] Syracuse, NY St. Pius X Home, Inc.
Regan, William P. '56 (SY) Retired.
Regensburger, Edmund *c.ss.r.* '46 (VEN) Wauchula, FL St. Michael Church.
Reger, George L. '69 (BUF) [15] Buffalo, NY Blessed Trinity Church.

Regh, John '53 (SUP) Retired.
Reginald, Edmund *o.m.i.* '92 (WDC) [M] Washington, DC Oblate College/Center for Mission Studies Community.
Reginato, Julian '64 (GR) [9] Grand Rapids, MI Immaculate Heart of Mary Church.
Regnier, William H. '48 (RCK) Retired.
Rego, Richard J. '83 (TUC) Ajo, AZ Immaculate Conception Church.
Regoli, John A. '61 (GBG) West Newton, PA Holy Family Church.
Regotti, Benjamin *o.f.m.cap.* '79 (PH) [80] Philadelphia, PA St. John the Evangelist Church.
Regula, Gary '00 (PHX) Flagstaff, AZ San Francisco de Asis Church.
Regynski, Larry '95 (SFS) Westport, SD Sacred Heart of Westport Church; [H] Aberdeen, SD Aquinas Student Center.
Rehage, Joseph W. *c.s.c.* '46 (AUS) [H] Austin, TX Congregation of Holy Cross - Southern Province.
Rehage, Joseph W. *c.s.c.* '46 (FTW) [J] South Bend, IN Congregation of Holy Cross, Indiana Province, Provincial House.
Rehkemper, Msgr. Robert C. '49 (DAL) Retired.
Rehkemper, Msgr. Robert C. '49 (LR) Hope, AR Our Lady of Good Hope Church.
Rehling, Paul '56 (CIN) [4] Cincinnati, OH St. Aloysius Gonzaga Church.
Rehme, Albert A. '56 (STL) Retired.
Rehrauer, Matthew J. '92 (SPC) Piedmont, MO St. Catherine of Siena Church.
Rehrauer, Stephen *c.ss.r.* '80 (CHI) [N] Chicago, IL Redemptorist Theology Residence.
Reich, John C. '84 (WH) Mullens, WV St. John the Evangelist Church.
Reich, Paul A. *s.m.* '57 (BAL) Sykesville, MD St. Joseph Church.
Reichel, Bill *o.f.m.* '61 (CIN) [M] Cincinnati, OH St. John the Baptist Friary.
Reichenbacher, Charles *o.s.b.* '67 (RCK) [G] Aurora, IL Marmion Abbey-St. Augustine's Abbey.
Reichert, Eldon *s.m.* '52 (CLV) [4] Cleveland, OH St. Aloysius - St. Agatha Church.
Reichert, Henry J. '63 (JC) Tipton, MO St. Andrew Church; Tipton, MO State Correctional Pre-Release Center.
Reichert, J. Lawrence '71 (COL) Groveport, OH St. Mary's Church.
Reichert, James *o.s.b.* '59 (SCL) Avon, MN St. Benedict's Church; [I] Collegeville, MN St. John's Abbey, of the Order of St. Benedict.
Reichert, Msgr. James J. '71 (ALN) West Reading, PA Sacred Heart Church.
Reichert, Kenneth *o.s.b.* '59 (KC) [A] Conception, MO Conception Seminary College; [J] Conception, MO Conception Abbey.
Reichert, Ralph '49 (TOL) Retired.
Reichlin, Urban A. '39 (CLV) [76] Cleveland, OH St. Vincent de Paul Church; Retired.
Reichling, David *o.f.m.cap.* '67 (GF) [4] Billings, MT St. Bernard's Church.
Reichling, Paul *o.f.m.cap.* '65 (GF) [3] Billings, MT Little Flower Church; [5] Billings, MT Our Lady of Guadalupe Church.
Reichmann, James B. *s.j.* '53 (SEA) [A] Seattle, WA Seattle University.
Reicks, Allan '76 (SC) Odebolt, IA St. Martin's Church.
Reicks, Msgr. Leander H. '44 (DUB) Retired.
Reid, David P. *ss.cc.* '66 (FR) [I] Fairhaven, MA Sacred Hearts Provincial House.
Reid, Francis R. '64 (CR) Retired.
Reid, George B. '53 (WDC) Barnesville, MD St. Mary Church and Shrine of Our Lady of Fatima Church; Retired.
Reid, Gerard E. '77 (OAK) [3] Berkeley, CA St. Joseph The Worker Church.
Reid, James H. *s.j.* '46 (NY) [DD] New York, NY Jesuit Community at Fordham University.
Reid, Malcolm '57 (CHY) Rawlins, WY St. Joseph's Church; Rawlins, WY Wyoming State Penitentiary.
Reid, Michael '69 (RVC) [C] Hicksville, NY Holy Trinity.
Reid, Michael P., II '00 (HBG) New Freedom, PA St. John the Baptist Church.
Reid, R. Michael '69 (RVC) Uniondale, NY Holly Patterson Geriatric Center.
Reid, Sean *o.carm.* '33 (NY) [DD] Middletown, NY St. Albert's Priory.
Reidman, John '70 (SFS) Montrose, SD St. Patrick Church.
Reidy, James E. '56 (STP) Retired; [C] St. Paul, MN University of St. Thomas.
Reidy, Richard F. '94 (WOR) [1] Worcester, MA St. Paul's Church.
Reidy, Msgr. Robert '62 (Y) Niles, OH Our Lady of Mt. Carmel Church.
Reidy, Robert J. '75 (CLV) [6] Lorain, OH St. Joseph Church; El Salvador, C.A., OH Parroquial Inmaculada Concepcion.
Reidy, Msgr. Thomas E. '67 (SPC) [2] Springfield, MO Holy Trinity Church.
Reif, John (ROC) [21] Rochester, NY Holy Cross Church.
Reif, Marvin '89 (DOD) Great Bend, KS St. Rose of Lima Church.
Reifel, Mark *t.o.r.* '55 (ALT) [3] Windber, PA St. Anthony of Padua Church.
Reifenberg, Philip D. '79 (MIL) [82] Milwaukee, WI St. Therese Church.
Reiff, Dale C. '67 (SC) Templeton, IA Sacred Heart Church.
Reiff, Dale E. '67 (SC) Halbur, IA St. Augustine's Church; Roselle, IA Holy Angels Church.
Reifsnyder, John A. '41 (COV) Retired.
Reifsnyder, John A. '41 (PIT) [38] Pittsburgh, PA Sacred Heart Church.
Reigel, Joseph P. '97 (E) [1] Erie, PA St. Peter Church.
Reiker, John '78 (STL) [7] St. Louis, MO Immaculate Heart of Mary Church.
Reiker, Robert J. '73 (STL) Dardenne, MO Immaculate Conception Church.
Reikowski, Miroslaw A. '96 (RCK) Apple River, IL St. Joseph Church; Warren, IL St. Ann Church.
Reile, Louis *s.m.* '60 (SAT) [K] San Antonio, TX Marianist Residence: Skilled Nursing.
Reiley, Robert J. *m.m.* '59 (FgM) Maryknoll Foreign Missions.
Reilley, Thomas J. *s.j.* '95 (LA) [F] Los Angeles, CA Loyola High School of Los Angeles.
Reillo, Ricardo *c.ss.r.* (CGS) [1] Caguas, PR Cathedral Dulce Nombre de Jesus Church.
Reilly, Bernard '73 (LAN) [3] Jackson, MI St. Mary, Star of the Sea Church.
Reilly, Cristobal *s.t.* '55 (PCE) Coamo, PR St. Blase Church.
Reilly, David F. '75 (CIN) Shandon, OH St. Aloysius Church.
Reilly, Denis *o.p.* '70 (SLC) [8] Salt Lake City, UT St. Catherine of Siena Church; [H] Salt Lake City, UT University of Utah, Newman Center.
Reilly, Donald F. *o.s.a.* '74 (PH) [C] Villanova, PA Villanova University; [AA] Villanova, PA St. Thomas of Villanova Friary.
Reilly, Msgr. Edward '54 (STL) Mattese, MO Mary, Mother of the Church.
Reilly, F. Joseph '58 (STL) Coffman, MO St. Catherine of Alexandria Church; River Aux Vases, MO SS. Philip and James Church.
Reilly, Francis '80 (SPR) On Duty Outside the Diocese.
Reilly, Francis E. *s.j.* '53 (FgM) Provinces.
Reilly, Gavin *o.f.m.cap.* '54 (NY) [57] New York, NY St. John the Baptist Church.
Reilly, George M. '60 (NEW) Oradell, NJ St. Joseph's Church.
Reilly, James F. '68 (NEW) Palisades Park, NJ St. Michael's Church.
Reilly, James J. '68 (NEW) Harrison, NJ Holy Cross Church; [Q] Bloomfield, NJ Bloomfield College; [Q] Cranford, NJ Union County College.
Reilly, John '48 (SFR) Retired.
Reilly, John '78 (SD) On Duty Outside the Diocese.
Reilly, John C. '39 (BRK) [231] Queens, NY Queen of Peace Church; Retired.
Reilly, John E. *s.j.* '59 (CHI) [C] Chicago, IL Jesuit Community at Loyola University of Chicago.
Reilly, Joseph L. '36 (BO) Senior Priests.
Reilly, Joseph R. '91 (NEW) [C] West Orange, NJ Seton Hall Preparatory School.
Reilly, L. Leo *c.s.b.* '62 (DET) [6] Detroit, MI Ste. Anne Church.
Reilly, Lawrence T. '64 (YAK) Special Assignment.
Reilly, Mark R. '97 (OG) [1] Watertown, NY Holy Family Church; [C] Watertown, NY Immaculate Heart Central High School.
Reilly, Michael P. '92 (NY) [F] New York, NY St. Joseph by the Sea, High School; [S] New York, NY Mission of the Immaculate Virgin.
Reilly, Msgr. Patrick '58 (LA) Burbank, CA St. Robert Bellarmine Church.
Reilly, Msgr. Philip J. '60 (BRK) Special Assignment; [W] Brooklyn, NY Monastery of the Sisters Adorers of the Precious Blood.
Reilly, Rembert F. *o.s.b.* '59 (PAT) [M] Morristown, NJ St. Mary's Abbey.
Reilly, Robert E. '58 (L) [58] Louisville, KY Our Lady Church.
Reilly, Robert F. '55 (COL) Retired.
Reilly, Msgr. Robert J. '45 (E) [25] Erie, PA St. Mary Church.
Reilly, Scott *l.c.* '97 (ATL) [J] Atlanta, GA Legionaries of Christ; [N] Atlanta, GA Home and Family, Inc.
Reilly, Steven *l.c.* '94 (DAL) [D] Irving, TX The Highlands School; [E] Irving, TX The Highland School; [K] Irving, TX Legionaries of Christ.
Reilly, Terence J. *o.p.* '59 (SFR) [14] San Francisco, CA St. Dominic Church; [N] San Francisco, CA St. Dominic Priory.
Reilly, Thomas *m.s.* '72 (SPR) [4] Holyoke, MA Immaculate Conception Church.
Reilly, Thomas *m.afr.* '78 (FgM) Missionaries of Africa Foreign Missions.
Reilly, Thomas J. '00 (BO) [2] Woburn, MA St. Barbara Church.
Reilly, Thomas J. '67 (BO) Foxborough, MA St. Mary Church.
Reilly, Msgr. William J. (NEW) [2] Garfield, NJ Holy Name Church.
Reilly, William L. *s.j.* '45 (NY) [DD] New York, NY Jesuit Community at Fordham University.
Reilman, Thomas J. '61 (DAV) Retired.
Reim, Daniel T. *s.j.* '95 (CLV) [B] Cleveland, OH John Carroll Jesuit Community.
Reimer, Edward J. '67 (SY) [10] Syracuse, NY St. Andrew the Apostle Church; [23] Syracuse, NY St. Therese the Little Flower of Jesus Church; Jamesville, NY Jamesville Penitentiary.
Reimer, Ronald P. '62 (GB) [6] Manitowoc, WI St. Paul Church.
Reina, Nicholas J. *s.d.b.* '78 (FgM) Salesians of Don Bosco Foreign Missions.
Reina, Nicholas J. *s.d.b.* '78 (SFR) [N] San Francisco, CA Salesian Provincial Residence.
Reina, Richard A. '70 (BUF) Kenmore, NY St. John the Baptist Church.
Reinbold, Charles '56 (NEW) On Duty Outside the Archdiocese.
Reinders, David '97 (TUC) [F] Tucson, AZ Regina Cleri Center.
Reinersman, Gerald L. '79 (COV) [N] Covington, KY St. Walburg Monastery.
Reinert, Duane F. *o.f.m.cap.* '76 (KC) [A] Conception, MO Conception Seminary College.
Reinert, Duane F. *o.f.m.cap.* '76 (KCK) Lawrence, KS Haskell Institute; [H] Lawrence, KS St. Conrad's Friary; [J] Lawrence, KS Haskell Catholic Campus Center.
Reinert, Ellis *o.carm.* '49 (NEW) Englewood, NJ St. Cecilia's Church.
Reinert, Msgr. James M. '83 (LIN) On Duty Outside the Diocese.
Reinert, Msgr. James M. '83 (NY) [2] New York, NY St. Agnes Church.
Reinert, Paul C. *s.j.* '40 (STL) [C] St. Louis, MO Saint Louis University; [C] St. Louis, MO Saint Louis University; [P] St. Louis, MO Jesuit Community Corporation at St. Louis University - Jesuit Hall.
Reinhard, William *o.m.i.* '61 (FgM) Oblates Foreign Missions.
Reinhardt, Leo J. '78 (ROC) Clyde, NY St. John the Evangelist Church; Ithaca, NY Immaculate Conception Church.
Reinhardt, Leo S. '55 (BEL) Retired.
Reinhardt, Mark S. '96 (PRT) Rockland, ME St. Bernard's Church.
Reinhart, Blaise R. *o.f.m.* '55 (ALB) [B] Loudonville, NY Siena College.
Reinhart, David A. '98 (TOL) Norwalk, OH St. Paul Church.
Reinhart, Kenneth *o.f.m.cap.* '68 (GB) [3] Appleton, WI St. Joseph Church; [I] Appleton, WI St. Joseph Friary.
Reinhart, Ralph W. '52 (SC) Retired.
Reinhart, Robert C. *c.pp.s.* '53 (LFT) Bryant, IN Holy Trinity Church.
Reinhart, Robert J. '61 (TOL) [2] Toledo, OH Blessed Sacrament Church.
Reinheimer, George '50 (NY) [17] New York, NY St. Bernard Church.
Reinig, Joseph '98 (BAK) Hermiston, OR Our Lady of Angels Church.
Reinke, Frank '57 (GB) Special Assignment.
Reinke, John H. *s.j.* '45 (CHI) [C] Chicago, IL Jesuit Community at Loyola University of Chicago.
Reinke, Robert J. '49 (COV) [3] Covington, KY St. Augustine Church; Retired.
Reinkemeyer, John '57 (WCH) Retired.
Reino, Joseph C. '93 (PH) Retired.
Reinoso, Carlos Alberto *o.r.c.* '96 (PCE) Adjuntas, PR St. Joachim Church.
Reinsfelder, Msgr. John '49 (BAL) [W] Baltimore, MD Legion of Mary.
Reinsfelder, Msgr. John L. '49 (BAL) [36] Baltimore, MD Holy Cross Church; Retired.
Reiran, Eric A. *o.p.* '91 (STL) [P] St. Louis, MO Dominican Community of St. Louis.
Reis, Antonio (OAK) [4] San Leandro, CA St. Leander Church.
Reis, Daniel O. '75 (FR) [6] New Bedford, MA Our Lady of the Immaculate Conception Church.
Reis, Justin J. '69 (COL) Lancaster, OH St. Bernadette Church.
Reis, Lancelot '67 (PAT) Chester, NJ St. Lawrence the Martyr Church.
Reis, Michael J. '67 (COL) Heath, OH St. Leonard Church.
Reis, Raymond H. *s.j.* '37 (STL) [P] St. Louis, MO Jesuit Community Corporation at St. Louis University - Jesuit Hall.
Reis, Timothy P. '86 (FR) [7] Taunton, MA St. Joseph's Church.
Reisch, Msgr. Milton L. '60 (NO) [1] Metairie, LA Our Lady of Divine Providence Church.

Reischl, Fred P. (DM) Retired.
Reischman, Virgil '69 (STU) Barnesville, OH Assumption Church; Temperanceville, OH St. Mary's Church.
Reisdorff, Msgr. Clarence P. '46 (LIN) Retired; [E] Lincoln, NE Bonacum House.
Reiser, Bernard A. '49 (STP) Coon Rapids, MN Church of the Epiphany.
Reiser, John '56 (MIA) Absent on Sick Leave.
Reiser, Richard J. '80 (OM) [18] Omaha, NE Holy Ghost Church.
Reiser, Robert E. *s.j.* '97 (NY) [80] New York, NY Nativity Church; [DD] New York, NY Jesuit Provincial's Office.
Reiser, William *s.j.* '72 (BO) [W] Boston, MA The Society of Jesus of New England-Provincial Offices.
Reiser, William E. *s.j.* '72 (WOR) [N] Worcester, MA Jesuits of Holy Cross College, Inc.; [N] Worcester, MA Jesuits of Holy Cross College, Inc.; [R] Worcester, MA Casa Santa Maria del Camino, Inc.
Reisert, Frederick J. *s.j.* '54 (BUF) [O] Buffalo, NY Canisius Jesuit Community.
Reisert, Gregory *o.f.m.cap.* '64 (NY) [DD] White Plains, NY St. Conrad Friary.
Reising, Raymond '45 (EVN) Retired.
Reisinger, Walter J. *c.m.* '55 (JC) Crocker, MO St. Cornelius Church; Dixon, MO St. Theresa Church.
Reiske, Steven '90 (FAR) Special Assignment; [F] Pisek, ND Franciscan Friars of Mary Immaculate.
Reiss, Francis '66 (DET) Allen Park, MI St. Frances Cabrini Church.
Reiss, John E. *o.f.m.* (Y) [5] Youngstown, OH Our Lady of Hungary Church.
Reiss, John E. *o.f.m.* '69 (Y) [J] Youngstown, OH Mt. Alverna Friary.
Reissmann, Richard A. '63 (WIL) Newark, DE St. John the Baptist-Holy Angels Church.
Reisteter, William *o.f.m.* '71 (ALN) [K] Easton, PA St. Francis Friary; [M] Easton, PA St. Francis Retreat House.
Reisz, Adam '41 (DM) Retired.
Reisz, Leonard '50 (OWN) Non-Parochial Assignments.
Reiter, James E. '90 (ROM) McKeesport, PA St. Mary Church; McKeesport, PA St. Mary Church.
Reites, James W. *s.j.* '71 (LA) [Q] Culver City, CA Ignatius House, The Novitiate of the California Province, Society of Jesus.
Reith, David H. '76 (MIL) Burlington, WI Immaculate Conception Church.
Reith, Herman R. *c.s.c.* '42 (FTW) [B] Notre Dame, IN University of Notre Dame Du Lac; [J] Notre Dame, IN Holy Cross Community, Corby Hall, University of Notre Dame.
Reitter, Frank *s.m.* '84 (BO) [W] Boston, MA Marist Fathers and Brothers Provincial House.
Reitz, Andrew J. *o.f.m.* '71 (TR) Brant Beach, NJ St. Francis of Assisi Church.
Reitz, Joseph A. '53 (GAY) Retired.
Reitz, Louis M. *s.s.* '55 (BAL) [84] Baltimore, MD St. Pius X Church.
Reitz, William J. '47 (GR) Carson City, MI St. Mary's Church; Hubbardston, MI St. John the Baptist Church.
Rejent, Michael *o.s.f.s.* (KAL) [4] Kalamazoo, MI St. Monica Church.
Rejsek, J. Brian '86 (PEO) Mendota, IL Holy Cross Church.
Rekasi, Joseph S. *o.praem.* '46 (GB) [I] De Pere, WI St. Joseph Priory; [O] De Pere, WI Canons Regular of Magnovarad, Ltd.
Reker, Timothy T. '82 (WIN) [5] Rochester, MN St. Francis of Assisi Church.
Rekofke, Robert *s.j.* '59 (SEA) [9] Tacoma, WA Holy Cross Church.
Relihan, Thomas '47 (SAC) Ione, CA Sacred Heart Church.
Reller, Gary W. '71 (HEL) Polson, MT Immaculate Conception Church.
Relyea, Isaac *f.i.* '99 (SY) [W] Maine, NY Mount St. Francis Hermitage, Inc.
Remaklus, Charles W. '47 (LFT) Retired.
Rementeria, Alfonso *o.ss.t.* '76 (PCE) [10] Ponce, PR La Santisima Trinidad Church.
Rementeria, German *o.ss.t.* '61 (PCE) [10] Ponce, PR La Santisima Trinidad Church.
Remillard, Andre N. '70 (WOR) Jefferson, MA St. Mary's Church.
Remillard, Bernard M. *o.p.* '37 (PRT) [I] Lewiston, ME SS. Peter and Paul House.
Remke, Raymond J. '88 (BIR) Montevallo, AL St. Thomas the Apostle Church; [H] Montevallo, AL University of Montevallo.
Remm, George F. '60 (PEO) Urbana, IL St. Patrick's Church.
Remmel, William J. *s.d.s.* '67 (BAL) [85] Baltimore, MD St. Rita Church.
Remmel, William J. *s.d.s.* '67 (WDC) [B] Silver Spring, MD Salvatorian Community.
Remmerswaal, James *o.s.c.* '67 (SCL) [I] Onamia, MN Crosier Monastery.
Remmes, Richard R. '62 (SC) Marcus, IA Holy Name Church.
Remo, Zanatta *c.r.s.* '98 (MAN) [H] Allenstown, NH Pine Haven Boys Center.
Rempe, Melvin L. '65 (LIN) Cambridge, NE St. John's Church.
Remski, Howard *f.s.s.p.* (Y) Vienna, OH Queen of the Holy Rosary Church.
Remski, Howard *f.s.s.p.* '00 (SCR) [M] Elmhurst, PA Priestly Fraternity of St. Peter (F.S.S.P.), North American District Headquarters.
Remy, Adrien T. '34 (SPR) Retired; [K] Holyoke, MA Mont Marie.
Remy, David P. '67 (DUB) Military Chaplains.
Renaldo, Daniel J. *c.m.* '41 (PH) [AA] Philadelphia, PA Congregation of the Mission.
Renard, Eugene C. *s.j.* '60 (PBL) Trinidad, CO Most Holy Trinity, Trinidad Area Catholic Community (Trinidad Cluster) Church; [G] Trinidad, CO Trinidad Area Catholic Community.
Renard, John F. '65 (NEW) Guttenberg, NJ St. John Nepomucene Church.
Renard, Peter J. *o.praem.* '68 (GB) [I] De Pere, WI St. Norbert Abbey.
Renaud, Florian U. '98 (SFE) Chama, NM St. Patrick Church; Albuquerque, NM Lovelace Hospital.
Renaud, Olivier *o.m.i.* '50 (NOR) [F] Willimantic, CT Missionary Oblates of Mary Immaculate; [I] Willimantic, CT Immaculata Retreat House.
Renda, Xavier F. '58 (BGP) Easton, CT Notre Dame of Easton Church.
Render, Msgr. Bernard A. '40 (PEO) Retired; [L] Peoria, IL St. Augustine Manor.
Render, John T. *c.p.* '52 (CHI) [N] Chicago, IL Passionist Community-Immaculate Conception Monastery.
Render, Patrick W. *c.s.v.* '68 (SFD) [9] Springfield, IL St. Joseph Church.
Rendon, Anthony *o.m.i.* '67 (FgM) Oblates Foreign Missions.
Rendon, Luis A. '73 (PAT) [1] Paterson, NJ Cathedral of St. John the Baptist.
Rendon, Matthias *o.f.m.* '92 (BO) [38] Boston, MA St. Leonard of Port Maurice Church.
Rendon, Matthias *o.f.m.* '92 (FgM) Custody of St. Mary of the Angels. Byzantine-Slavonic.
Rendon, Nicolas '76 (LUB) Shallowater, TX St. Phillip Benizi Church.
Rendon, Nicolas A. (LUB) [9] Lubbock, TX St. Theresa's Church.
Rendon, Raul P. *o.s.s.t.* '87 (BAL) [S] Baltimore, MD Holy Trinity Monastery.
Rendon, Samuel '92 (LA) Canoga Park, CA Our Lady of the Valley Church.
Renehan, Msgr. Edmond M. '58 (LA) Santa Clarita, CA St. Clare Church.
Rengers, Christopher *o.f.m.cap.* '42 (RCK) [M] St. Charles, IL Queen of Americas Guild.
Rengers, Christopher *o.f.m.cap.* '42 (WDC) [B] Washington, DC St. Francis Friary-Capuchin College.
Renggli, John '68 (SEA) [11] Tacoma, WA Our Lady, Queen of Heaven Church.
Rengifo, J. Orlando '85 (NEW) [1] Hackensack, NJ Holy Trinity Church.
Renken, John A. (SFD) [8] Springfield, IL St. Katharine Drexel Church.
Renken, John A. '79 (SFD) Riverton, IL St. James Church.
Renkiewicz, Adolphe T. '56 (HRT) [N] Enfield, CT Felician Sisters - Our Lady of the Angels.
Renna, Anton J. *s.j.* '65 (PHX) [B] Phoenix, AZ Brophy College Preparatory.
Rennell, Albert F. '59 (RCK) Retired.
Renner, Christopher A. '91 (DEN) Evergreen, CO Christ the King Church; Julesburg, CO St. Anthony Church.
Renner, Frank G. '81 (EVN) Bicknell, IN St. Philip Neri Church.
Renner, Louis L. *s.j.* '57 (FBK) [C] Fairbanks, AK Jesuit Residence.
Renner, Ralph C. *s.j.* '70 (STL) [C] St. Louis, MO Saint Louis University; [P] St. Louis, MO Jesuit Community Corporation at St. Louis University - Jesuit Hall.
Renninger, Michael A. '93 (RIC) [1] Richmond, VA Cathedral of the Sacred Heart.
Rensing, William F. '55 (BEL) Sparta, IL Our Lady of Lourdes Church.
Renter, Randall *c.s.c.* '90 (NY) [28] New York, NY Corpus Christi Church.
Renter, Randall C. *c.s.c.* '90 (FTW) [J] South Bend, IN Congregation of Holy Cross, Indiana Province, Provincial House.
Renteria, Rudy '79 (DAL) [G] Dallas, TX St. Paul Medical Center.
Renteria, Rudy '79 (FWT) On Duty Outside the Diocese.
Rentino, Pablo (NY) [173] Bronx, NY Our Lady of Mercy Church.
Rento, Richard G. '58 (PAT) Retired.
Rentz, Medicus (CC) [E] Corpus Christi, TX CHRISTUS Spohn Hospital Memorial.
Renz, Christopher J. *o.p.* '97 (OAK) [N] Oakland, CA Dominican Order (Western Province), St. Albert's Priory; [N] Oakland, CA Western Dominican Province.
Repela, Vasyl '86 (PHU) Trenton, NJ St. Josaphat's Church.
Repenshek, Jerry '63 (MIL) [1] Menomonee Falls, WI St. Anthony Church.
Repko, Cyril *o.f.m.cap.* '62 (FgM) Capuchin Foreign Missions.
Repko, Joseph '95 (PRM) Bedford, OH St. Eugene Church; Cleveland, OH Holy Ghost Church.
Replogle, Jack *o.f.m.* '64 (NY) [GG] New York, NY University Apostolate.
Replogle, John *s.j.* (NY) [F] New York, NY Xavier High School.
Repole, Celsus *o.f.m.cap.* '43 (NY) [DD] Yonkers, NY St. Clare Friary.
Repole, Charles *o.f.m.cap.* '43 (NY) [DD] Yonkers, NY St. Clare Friary.
Reppen, Robert B. *o.praem.* '46 (GB) [I] De Pere, WI St. Norbert Abbey.
Reque, Francis M. *o.s.b.* '00 (BIR) [E] Cullman, AL St. Bernard Abbey.
Resch, Gerard F. *c.ss.r.* '44 (STL) [P] Liguori, MO St. Clement Health Care Center.
Resch, Julian C. *o.praem.* '38 (GB) [I] De Pere, WI St. Norbert Abbey.
Reschick, Joseph W. '77 (PIT) [37] Pittsburgh, PA St. Rosalia Church.
Resconich, Emil C. *t.o.r.* '54 (ALT) [A] Loretto, PA St. Francis College; [F] Loretto, PA St. Francis Friary, Third Order Regular of St. Francis of Penance.
Resheske, Florian '55 (GB) Retired.
Reskey, George A. '73 (MOB) On Leave from the Archdiocese.
Reskey, George A. '73 (SP) St. Pete Beach, FL St. John Church.
Resko, Blane L. *o.s.b.* '57 (GBG) [2] Greensburg, PA St. Bruno Church.
Resma, Louis '62 (DET) [13] Detroit, MI St. Brendan Church; [29] Detroit, MI Guardian Angels Church; Farmington, MI Botsford General Hospital; Detroit, MI Saratoga General Hospital.
Resop, Michael A. '79 (MAD) Loreto, WI St. Patrick Church; Plain, WI St. Luke Church.
Respond, Paul *c.s.p.* '81 (LA) Goleta, CA St. Mark University Church.
Ressler, Mark A. '76 (DUB) [A] Dubuque, IA Seminary of St. Pius X; [C] Dubuque, IA Loras College.
Ressler, Wayne A. '64 (DUB) [10] Dubuque, IA Nativity Church.
Resta, Vincent A. '55 (NY) [181] Bronx, NY St. Peter and St. Paul Church.
Restrepo, Francisco '88 (DET) [7] Sterling Heights, MI St. Michael Church.
Restrepo, George *s.j.* '65 (BAL) [91] Baltimore, MD St. Thomas Aquinas Church.
Restrepo, Jairo '92 (B) Fruitland, ID Corpus Christi Church; Weiser, ID St. Agnes Church.
Restrepo, Ruben Dario *c.m.* '97 (PHX) [26] Phoenix, AZ St. Vincent de Paul Church.
Restrick, Jacob *o.p.* '89 (SPR) [K] West Springfield, MA Monastery of the Mother of God, Dominican Nuns (Contemplative).
Resultay, Angel V. '67 (RVC) Farmingdale, NY St. Kilian Church.
Reszel, Marc W. '88 (CHI) Buffalo Grove, IL St. Mary Church.
Reszkowski, Msgr. Joseph V. '54 (E) [9] Erie, PA Our Lady of Mt. Carmel Church.
Reteneller, Charles E. '60 (L) [2] Springfield, KY Holy Rosary Church; [M] St. Catharine, KY St. Catharine of Siena Convent; [M] St. Catharine, KY Sansbury Care Center.
Rethamel, Roger R. '60 (DUB) Alta Vista, IA St. Bernard Church; Elma, IA Immaculate Conception Church; Lourdes, IA Our Lady of Lourdes Church.
Rethinger, Omer '53 (TOL) Retired.
Retortillo, Benito *o.p.* '62 (CC) San Diego, TX St. Francis de Paula Church; [H] San Diego, TX Vicariate of Holy Rosary.
Rettenburg, Basil *o.s.b.* '68 (HRT) [N] Bethlehem, CT Abbey of Regina Laudis.
Rettger, Thaddeus E. *o.s.b.* '74 (GBG) Vandergrift, PA St. Gertrude Church.
Rettig, Donald R. '71 (CIN) [5] Cincinnati, OH St. Aloysius-on-the-Ohio Church; [E] Cincinnati, OH Elder High School.
Rettig, Hermann-Joseph K. *o.praem.* '84 (LA) [91] Los Angeles, CA St. Stephen Church.
Rettig, Hermann-Joseph K. *o.praem.* '84 (ORG) [I] Silverado, CA Norbertine Fathers of Orange Inc.
Retzel, Joseph R. *s.j.* '60 (GF) Hays, MT St. Paul's Indian Church.
Retzner, James P. *o.s.a.* '95 (SD) [34] San Diego, CA St. Patrick Church; San Diego, CA Alvarado, Grossmont and Kaiser Hospitals; [H] San Diego, CA Augustinian Community.
Reuse, Patrick J. *s.j.* '73 (PHX) [11] Phoenix, AZ St. Francis Xavier Church.
Reusing, James (BAL) [41] Baltimore, MD Immaculate Conception Church.

Reusing, James M. '94 (BAL) Special Assignment.
Reuss, Louis L. '38 (RVC) Bohemia, NY St. John Nepomucene Church; Retired.
Reuter, Arnold F. '52 (LC) Retired; [H] La Crosse, WI Holy Cross (Seminary) Diocesan Center.
Reuter, Christian *o.f.m.* '66 (CHI) [46] Chicago, IL Corpus Christi Church.
Reuter, James B. *s.j.* '46 (FgM) Provinces.
Reuter, John F. '67 (GB) On Duty Outside the Diocese.
Reuter, Lawrence *s.j.* '71 (CHI) [C] Chicago, IL Loyola University-Chicago; [C] Chicago, IL Jesuit Community at Loyola University of Chicago; [V] Chicago, IL Ministry in Higher Education.
Reuter, Leon *o.f.m.* '62 (STL) [P] St. Louis, MO Franciscan Friary of St. Anthony of Padua.
Reuter, Lloyd E. '57 (DUB) Retired.
Revak, Msgr. Francis C. '40 (ALN) [C] Allentown, PA Allentown Central Catholic High School; [J] Bethlehem, PA Holy Family Villa.
Revel, Peter '82 (LKC) Westlake, LA St. John Bosco Church.
Revello, James K.I. '73 (DEN) On Duty Outside the Archdiocese.
ReVello, James P. '73 (LAV) Military Chaplains.
Revilla, Francisco '54 (STA) Special Assignment.
Revilla, Isaias *o.s.a.* '60 (MGZ) Aguada, PR St. Francis of Assisi Church.
Rewak, William J. *s.j.* '64 (SJ) [K] Los Altos, CA Jesuit Retreat House.
Rewtiuk, Michael '69 (SJP) Parma, OH St. Josaphat Church.
Rey, Andres *c.m.* '93 (CHI) [N] Chicago, IL DePaul Vincentian Residence.
Reycraft, Robert J. (DEN) [3] Englewood, CO St. Louis Church.
Reyes, Andres J. '70 (NEW) [25] Jersey City, NJ St. Paul of the Cross Church.
Reyes, Francisco *o.f.m.* '42 (SFR) [5] San Francisco, CA St. Anthony of Padua Church.
Reyes, Jaime *o.s.b.* '64 (CGS) [C] Humacao, PR San Antonio Abad Abbey of the Order of St. Benedict.
Reyes, Javier *o.f.m.* (P) [A] Portland, OR Franciscan Formation Community.
Reyes, Jorge A. *o.s.a.* (BO) [7] Lawrence, MA St. Mary Immaculate Conception Church.
Reyes, Jose *o.f.m.conv.* '84 (LSC) Hobbs, NM St. Helena Church.
Reyes, Jose L. '93 (MIA) Absent on Leave.
Reyes, Jose Luis *s.t.* '98 (LA) Compton, CA Our Lady of Victory Church; Compton, CA Sagrado Corazon, Sacred Heart Church.
Reyes, Jose Maria *o.de. m.* '60 (PCE) [13] Ponce, PR Santuario San Judas Tadeo Church.
Reyes, Msgr. Lonnie C. '69 (AUS) [15] Austin, TX St. Julia Church.
Reyes, Marco (BO) [51] Boston, MA Our Lady of Lourdes Church.
Reyes, Oscar Alejandro '97 (ELP) [28] El Paso, TX St. Matthew Church.
Reyes, Ralph *o.c.d.* '69 (SAT) [18] San Antonio, TX Basilica of The National Shrine of Our Lady of Mt. Carmel and St. Therese, Discalced Carmelite Fathers; [M] San Antonio, TX Discalced Carmelites (Prov. of St. Therese).
Reyes, Raymund M. '88 (SFR) [42] San Francisco, CA St. Patrick Church.
Reyes, Reynaldo '93 (LUB) Brownfield, TX St. Anthony's Church.
Reyes, Roberto *o.p.* (LA) [60] Los Angeles, CA St. Dominic Church.
Reyes, Victor J. '94 (ATL) Athens, GA St. Joseph's Church.
Reyes, Xamie M. '00 (CHI) Niles, IL Our Lady of Ransom Church.
Reyes Lebron, Pedro Luis '90 (SJN) [5] Trujillo Alto, PR Bienventurada Virgen Maria de Lourdes Church.
Reyes-Ruiz, Javier *o.f.m.* '98 (PHX) [19] Phoenix, AZ St. Mary's Basilica Church; [23] Phoenix, AZ Sacred Heart Church.
Reyesmedina, Carlos '87 (DET) On Duty Outside the Archdiocese; Retired.
Reyling, Mark D. (BEL) Centreville, IL Immaculate Conception Church.
Reyling, Mark D. '98 (BEL) Cahokia, IL St. Catherine Laboure Church.
Reymann, Albert I. *m.m.* '47 (CLV) [3] Akron, OH St. Bernard Church.
Reymann, Albert I. *m.m.* '47 (NY) [DD] Maryknoll, NY Maryknoll Fathers and Brothers.
Reymann, James J. '58 (CLV) Wellington, OH St. Patrick Church.
Reymerse, Peter (WDC) [4] Rockville, MD St. Raphael Church.
Reyna, Cecilio '93 (LAN) [13] Flint, MI St. Pius X Church.
Reyna, Marcos *o.f.m.conv.* '86 (LSC) Silver City, NM St. Francis Newman Center Church.
Reynolds, Brad R. *s.j.* '77 (P) [L] Portland, OR Jesuit Provincial Office (Society of Jesus, Oregon Prov.); [L] Portland, OR Colombiere Community.
Reynolds, Dan '53 (P) Veneta, OR St. Catherine of Siena Church.
Reynolds, Daniel '53 (P) [2] Eugene, OR St. Mark Church.
Reynolds, Fred G. *s.j.* '78 (LAF) [J] Grand Coteau, LA Jesuit Spirituality Center (St. Charles College).
Reynolds, George L., II '97 (LA) Ventura, CA Our Lady of the Assumption Church.
Reynolds, George S. *o.p.* '59 (PBL) Las Animas, CO St. Mary Church.
Reynolds, J. Patrick '80 (OWN) Sorgho, KY St. Mary Magdalene Church.
Reynolds, Msgr. James B. '50 (MIA) [7] Pompano Beach, FL St. Henry Church.
Reynolds, James J. '84 (BRK) [115] Brooklyn, NY St. Patrick Church.
Reynolds, James L. (SPC) Kennett, MO St. Cecilia Church.
Reynolds, James L. '71 (SPC) Portageville, MO St. Eustachius Church.
Reynolds, Jeffrey '90 (WIL) Perry Point, MD Veterans Admin.
Reynolds, Jeffrie S. '90 (BIR) On Duty Outside the Diocese.
Reynolds, John C. *c.s.p.* '47 (NY) [104] New York, NY St. Paul the Apostle Church; [DD] Jamaica Estates, NY Paulist Fathers Generalate.
Reynolds, John C. '90 (KCK) Alma, KS Holy Family Church; Eskridge, KS St. John Vianney Church; Paxico, KS Sacred Heart Church.
Reynolds, Msgr. John P. '49 (NO) Retired; [S] New Orleans, LA Stella Roman Foundation, Inc.
Reynolds, Joseph F. '59 (NY) Harriman, NY St. Anastasia Church.
Reynolds, Kirk R. *s.j.* '79 (PAT) [I] Morristown, NJ Loyola House of Retreats.
Reynolds, Paul A. *c.s.p.* '94 (BO) [W] Boston, MA Paulist Fathers Residence; [CC] Cambridge, MA Massachusetts Institute of Technology Catholic Community.
Reynolds, Paul F. '65 (PRO) [6] West Warwick, RI St. Mary Church.
Reynolds, Paul H. '62 (ATL) Special or Other (Arch)Diocesan Assignment.
Reynolds, Robert E. '52 (PEO) Rushville, IL St. Rose Church; Retired.
Reynolds, Msgr. Roger A. '43 (NEW) Retired.
Reynolds, Msgr. Roger A., (Retired) '43 (NEW) Harrington Park, NJ Our Lady of Victories Church.
Reynolds, Rubin R. '79 (BR) St. Gabriel, LA St. Gabriel Church.
Reynolds, Stephen B. '89 (GAL) [20] Houston, TX Christ the King Church.
Reynolds, Thomas (RVC) Retired.
Reynolds, Thomas D. '58 (BO) [1] Malden, MA Immaculate Conception Church.
Reynolds, Thomas J. '54 (RVC) Massapequa Park, NY Our Lady of Lourdes Church.
Reynolds, Thomas P. *s.s.c.* '61 (CHI) [N] Chicago, IL Columban Fathers Mission Center.
Reynolds, William E. '81 (DAV) Grinnell, IA St. Mary's Church.
Reynolds, William V. '55 (NY) Nanuet, NY St. Anthony Church.
Rezac, Keith D. '87 (OM) Creighton, NE St. Ludger Church.
Rezac, Robert *i.m.c.* '77 (MET) [H] Somerset, NJ Consolata Society for Foreign Missions.
Rezula, Leon J. '69 (CHI) Elk Grove Village, IL St. Julian Eymard Church.
Rhein, Msgr. George V. '39 (GAL) Retired; [N] Houston, TX St. Dominic Village.
Rhinehart, R. William *c.m.* '79 (COS) Burlington, CO St. Catherine of Siena Church; Stratton, CO St. Charles Borromeo Church.
Rhoades, C. Michael '70 (MAR) Moran, MI Immaculate Conception Church; St. Ignace, MI St. Ignatius Loyola Church.
Rhoades, Kevin C. '83 (BAL) [A] Emmitsburg, MD Mount St. Mary's Seminary; [A] Emmitsburg, MD Mount Saint Mary's Seminary; [B] Emmitsburg, MD Mount Saint Mary's College.
Rhoades, Terance *o.f.m.* '43 (GLP) Zuni, NM St. Anthony, Our Lady of Guadalupe Church.
Rhoden, Raymond '76 (PIT) Sewickley, PA St. James Church.
Rhodes, Msgr. David W. '65 (Y) [11] Youngstown, OH St. Christine's Church.
Rhodes, Edmund L. *s.m.* '41 (CIN) [M] Dayton, OH Marianist Provincialate.
Rhodes, George V. '53 (WIL) Retired.
Rhodes, Joseph '41 (OWN) Retired.
Rhomberg, Thomas W. '53 (DUB) Retired.
Rhyner, Robert E. '59 (GB) [9] Green Bay, WI Holy Martyrs of Gorcum Church.
Riani, Msgr. Peter R. '55 (OG) Elizabethtown, NY St. Elizabeth Church; Westport, NY St. Philip Neri Church.
Riano, Camilo *c.m.f.* '53 (SJN) [9] Bayamon, PR San Jose Church.
Ribando, William R. *c.s.c.* '64 (SCR) [C] Wilkes-Barre, PA Kings College.
Ribas, Isidoro *s.j.* (STL) [P] St. Louis, MO Jesuit Community Corporation at St. Louis University - Jesuit Hall.
Ribaudo, Msgr. Charles A. '67 (RVC) Oyster Bay, NY St. Dominic's Church.
Ribbens, William H. *o.praem.* '62 (GB) [I] De Pere, WI St. Norbert Abbey.
Ribble, Msgr. James M. *ph.d.* '57 (SPK) [1] Spokane, WA Cathedral of Our Lady of Lourdes.
Ribeiro, Alvaro *s.j.* '87 (WDC) [M] Washington, DC The Jesuit Community at Georgetown University.
Ribeiro, George *s.a.* '67 (NY) [14] Yonkers, NY Our Lady of the Rosary Church; [DD] Garrison, NY Franciscan Friars of the Atonement.
Ribeiro, Nelson *c.m.* '54 (HRT) [3] Waterbury, CT Our Lady of Fatima Church.
Ribero, Arthur '50 (OAK) Retired.
Ribezzi, Rinaldo '39 (SPR) [I] Holyoke, MA Mont Marie Health Care Center, Inc.
Ribits, Thomas *o.s.f.s.* '82 (BUF) [T] Buffalo, NY Salesian Studios.
Ribits, Thomas A. *o.s.f.s.* '82 (TOL) [K] Toledo, OH Oblates of St. Francis de Sales.
Ribotta, Michael *s.d.b.* '49 (SFR) [46] San Francisco, CA SS. Peter and Paul Church.
Ricafort, Juvencio D. '82 (SD) [35] San Diego, CA St. Rita Church.
Ricard, David F. '69 (PRO) [2] West Warwick, RI Christ the King Church; Warwick, RI Kent County Memorial Hospital.
Ricard, Joseph M. '64 (NOR) Retired.
Ricard, Richard J. '98 (NOR) North Grosvenordale, CT St. Joseph Church.
Ricard, Rodney Anthony '95 (NO) [54] New Orleans, LA St. Philip the Apostle Church.
Ricardo, John C. (DET) Graduate Studies.
Riccardo, Msgr. Joseph J. '75 (E) West Middlesex, PA Good Shepherd Church.
Ricchini, Joseph *o.f.m.* '64 (CIN) [M] Cincinnati, OH St. Ann Friary.
Ricci, Alfred V. '80 (PRO) [5] Warwick, RI St. Gregory the Great Church.
Ricci, Andrew P. '97 (SUP) Sarona, WI St. Catherine Church; Shell Lake, WI St. Joseph Church; Spooner, WI St. Francis De Sales Church.
Ricci, Daniel A. *c.m.* '74 (STL) [P] St. Louis, MO Vincentian Residence.
Ricci, Philip C. '65 (PH) North Wales, PA Mary, Mother of the Redeemer Church.
Ricciardelli, Albert '84 (TR) [3] Trenton, NJ Holy Angels Church.
Ricciardi, August A. '83 (SCR) Throop, PA St. Anthony's Church; Throop, PA St. Bridget's Church; Throop, PA St. John the Baptist Church.
Ricciardi, Robert P. '79 (HRT) Cheshire, CT St. Bridget's Church; Seymour, CT Good Shepherd Church.
Riccio, Fred A. '77 (OAK) San Ramon, CA St. Joan of Arc Church.
Riccio, Salvatore M. '66 (PH) Springfield, PA St. Francis of Assisi Church.
Riccitelli, Dennis '85 (PHX) [3] Mesa, AZ Holy Cross Church.
Riccomini, Msgr. Dino '57 (FRS) Retired.
Rice, Msgr. Charles O. '34 (PIT) Castle Shannon, PA St. Anne Church; Retired.
Rice, Edward M. '87 (STL) [41] St. Louis, MO St. John the Baptist Church.
Rice, G. Nicholas '67 (L) [59] Louisville, KY Our Lady of Lourdes Church; Louisville, KY Baptist Hospital East.
Rice, John A. '57 (SEA) Retired.
Rice, Joseph P. '77 (NEW) Paramus, NJ Bergen Regional Medical Center.
Rice, Lawrence A. *c.s.p.* '89 (WDC) [B] Washington, DC St. Paul's College; [V] Washington, DC Paulist Media Works.
Rice, Michael D. '64 (KC) Lee's Summit, MO St. Margaret's Catholic Community Church.
Rice, Patrick *s.j.* '72 (BR) [21] Baton Rouge, LA St. Thomas More Church.
Rice, Patrick '74 (PAT) Mountain Lakes, NJ St. Catherine of Siena Church.
Rice, Patrick J. *o.s.a.* '48 (PH) [AA] Villanova, PA St. Thomas Monastery.
Rice, Patrick J. *s.j.* '54 (DET) [E] Detroit, MI University of Detroit Jesuit High School and Academy.
Rice, Richard M. *s.j.* '72 (STP) [6] St. Paul, MN The Immaculate Heart of Mary Church; [Q] St. Paul, MN Loyola.
Rice, Richard P. '60 (PRT) Bath, ME St. Mary Church.
Rice, Robert A. *s.j.* '53 (FgM) Provinces.
Rice, Thomas G. '77 (DET) [7] Warren, MI St. Louise Church.
Rice, William A. '63 (E) Linesville, PA St. Philip Church.
Rice, William G. '00 (E) Grove City, PA Beloved Disciple Church; Hermitage, PA Church of Notre Dame .
Rich, John A. *m.m.* '58 (NY) [DD] Maryknoll, NY Maryknoll Fathers and Brothers.
Rich, Joseph '74 (SJ) On Duty Outside the Diocese.
Rich, Orlando S. '43 (Y) Retired.

Richard, Antonio J. '38 (FAR) Retired.
Richard, Charles J. '46 (OG) Retired.
Richard, Claude *o.p.* '73 (PRT) [I] Lewiston, ME SS. Peter and Paul House.
Richard, Edward '41 (TLS) Retired.
Richard, Edward *m.s.* '91 (STL) [P] St. Louis, MO La Salette Missionaries.
Richard, Edward D. '68 (MAN) Pelham, NH St. Patrick Church.
Richard, Edward J. (STL) [D] St. Louis, MO Paul VI Institute of Catechetical and Pastoral Studies.
Richard, Edward J. '91 (STL) [A] St. Louis, MO Kenrick-Glennon Seminary.
Richard, Joseph *a.a.* '46 (WOR) [N] Worcester, MA Assumptionists (Augustinians of the Assumption).
Richard, Joseph E. '58 (SFR) Lagunitas, CA St. Cecilia Church.
Richard, Louis J. '81 (LAF) Crowley, LA St. Michael Archangel Church.
Richard, Lucien *o.m.i.* '59 (BO) [W] Lowell, MA Missionary Oblates of Mary Immaculate.
Richard, Normand P. '72 (PRT) [1] Old Town, ME Holy Family Church.
Richard, Raymond *o.f.m.cap.* '72 (FgM) Capuchin Foreign Missions.
Richard, Rodney A. '95 (NO) [20] New Orleans, LA Our Lady Star of The Sea Church.
Richard, Theodule *m.s.* '51 (FR) [I] Attleboro, MA La Salette Provincial House.
Richard, Timothy '92 (LAF) Mamou, LA St. Ann Church.
Richard, Msgr. Wayne R. '40 (LAF) Retired.
Richard, William '81 (DAL) Rockwall, TX Our Lady of the Lake Church.
Richards, Damian '92 (SAL) Atwood, KS Sacred Heart Church; Herndon, KS Assumption Church.
Richards, Edward W. '59 (BRK) [217] Queens, NY Our Lady of Perpetual Help Church.
Richards, Fabian '80 (ORG) Inactive Leave.
Richards, George J., Jr. '95 (NOR) Preston, CT St. Catherine of Siena Church.
Richards, John M. '85 (CLV) Wickliffe, OH Our Lady of Mount Carmel Church; Painesville, OH Lake County Memorial Hospital-East; Willoughby, OH Lake County Memorial Hospital-West.
Richards, Joseph D. '90 (CR) Moorhead, MN St. Francis de Sales Church.
Richards, Lawrence '89 (E) [23] Erie, PA St. Luke Church; [C] Erie, PA Cathedral Preparatory School.
Richards, Mark (SAC) [M] Sacramento, CA Catholic Committee on Scouting.
Richards, Peter M. '98 (STP) Burnsville, MN Mary, Mother of the Church.
Richards, Richard E. *a.a.* '50 (BO) [W] Boston, MA Assumptionist Center.
Richardson, Barry (KCK) On Leave of Absence.
Richardson, Donald J. '57 (GLP) Lumberton, NM St. Francis of Assisi Church.
Richardson, Francis X. '93 (ATL) Decatur, GA St. Thomas More Church.
Richardson, James '65 (WIL) [N] Wilmington, DE The Franciscan Center.
Richardson, James *s.c.* '92 (HRT) [1] New Haven, CT Sacred Heart Church.
Richardson, James E. '65 (WIL) Special or Other Diocesan Assignment.
Richardson, John L. '54 (R) Retired.
Richardson, John M. *o.f.m.* '56 (NY) Obernburg, NY St. Mary Church.
Richardson, John T. *c.m.* '49 (CHI) [C] Chicago, IL De Paul University.
Richardson, John T. *c.m.* '49 (FgM) Vincentian Foreign Missions.
Richardson, Matthew Paul '91 (ARL) [6] Alexandria, VA St. Louis Church.
Richardson, Paul *s.s.c.* '54 (FgM) St. Columban's Foreign Mission.
Richardson, Peter *glmy.* '86 (LEX) West Liberty, KY Prince of Peace Church.
Richardson, Robert C. '71 (WDC) Chillum, MD St. John Baptist de la Salle Church.
Richardson, Robert C. '87 (BUR) Ludlow, VT Annunciation Church.
Richardson, Msgr. Ronald (RVC) Bridgehampton, NY Queen of the Most Holy Rosary Church.
Richardson, Msgr. Ronald A. (RVC) Sag Harbor, NY St. Andrew's Church.
Richardson, William A. *s.s.j.* '66 (BAL) [S] Baltimore, MD St. Joseph Society of the Sacred Heart House of Central Administration.
Richardson, William J. *s.j.* '53 (BO) [W] Chestnut Hill, MA The Jesuit Community at Boston College.
Richardson, Msgr. William M. '72 (HBG) [1] Harrisburg, PA Cathedral Parish of St. Patrick Church.
Richardt, J. Lawrence '63 (IND) St. Mary-of-the-Woods, IN St. Mary Church; [K] Saint Mary-of-the-Woods, IN Sisters of Providence General Administration.
Richart, Paul F. '61 (IND) Sellersburg, IN St. Paul Church.
Richel, Michael C. '87 (MAD) Sun Prairie, WI St. Albert the Great Church.
Richers, David E. *s.s.c.* '52 (PRO) [P] Bristol, RI St. Columban's Retirement House.
Richetta, John J. '55 (MIL) [8] Kenosha, WI Our Lady of Mount Carmel Church.
Richey, Msgr. Terrence '64 (LA) [48] Los Angeles, CA St. Basil's Church.
Richman, Randy '82 (DM) [4] Des Moines, IA Holy Trinity Church.
Richmeier, Garry *c.pp.s.* '83 (KC) [7] Kansas City, MO St. Charles Borromeo Church; [A] Liberty, MO Society of the Precious Blood Provincial Offices; [J] Liberty, MO Precious Blood Society Provincial Office.
Richmond, John A. *s.m.* '39 (WDC) [M] Washington, DC Marist Center.
Richstatter, Thomas *o.f.m.* '66 (IND) [A] St. Meinrad, IN St. Meinrad Seminary.
Richter, David A. '00 (BIS) [1] Bismarck, ND Cathedral of the Holy Spirit.
Richter, David T. '86 (SHP) Zwolle, LA St. Joseph Church.
Richter, Helmut W. '94 (OAK) Pittsburg, CA Good Shepherd Church.
Richter, Msgr. James B. '51 (RVC) Huntington, NY St. Patrick's Church; Retired.
Richter, John A. '64 (NU) Lucan, MN Our Lady of Victory Church; Seaforth, MN St. Mary Church; Wabasso, MN St. Anne Church; Wanda, MN St. Mathias Church.
Richter, Kevin M. '88 (SC) [3] Sioux City, IA St. Boniface Church.
Richter, Norbert M. '41 (RCK) Retired.
Richter, Robert J. '67 (MIL) Military Chaplains.
Richter, Thomas J. '96 (BIS) Belfield, ND St. Bernard Church; South Heart, ND St. Mary Church.
Richter, William L. '58 (TOL) Sandusky, OH Holy Angels Church; Retired.
Richtsteig, Erik J. '94 (SLC) Helper, UT St. Anthony's Church.
Ricker, Berthold *o.s.b.* '31 (SCL) [I] Collegeville, MN St. John's Abbey, of the Order of St. Benedict.
Ricker, John Michael '55 (TOL) Retired.
Ricker, John Michael '55 (FgM) Society of St. James the Apostle.
Rickert, William '45 (GB) Retired.
Rickey, James E. '69 (PEO) Dwight, IL St. Patrick's Church; Dwight, IL Dwight Correctional Center.
Rickle, William C. *s.j.* '79 (PH) [83] Philadelphia, PA Old St. Joseph's Church.
Rickles, Gary A. '96 (GAL) New Caney, TX St. John of the Cross Church.
Rickles, Raymond *o.f.m.* '82 (STL) [P] St. Louis, MO Franciscan Friary of St. Anthony of Padua.
Ricks, Paul '78 (SAC) [1] Sacramento, CA Cathedral of the Blessed Sacrament.
Ridella, Joseph '52 (VNN) Retired.
Ridgell, John E. '67 (RIC) Norge, VA St. Olaf, Patron of Norway Church.
Ridgeway, Kenneth *s.m.* '69 (PRT) Brunswick, ME St. John the Baptist Church.
Ridgway, John K. *s.j.* '82 (DEN) [M] Denver, CO Regis Jesuit Community (The Jesuits at Regis University).
Ridi, Pio '47 (P) Retired.
Ridick, George J. '73 (WOR) [20] Worcester, MA St. Catherine of Sweden Church.
Riding, Raymond *s.t.* '75 (PAT) [P] Stirling, NJ Trinity Mission Center.
Ridley, Harold E. *s.j.* '69 (BAL) [B] Baltimore, MD Loyola College in Maryland; [B] Baltimore, MD Loyola College in Maryland; [S] Baltimore, MD Jesuit Community of Loyola College, Inc.
Ridore, Danis '67 (PMB) Fort Pierce, FL Notre Dame Church.
Ridyard, John J. *m.m.* '56 (SJ) [L] Los Altos, CA Maryknoll.
Riebe, Bruce '85 (PRM) Brecksville, OH St. Joseph Church.
Riebe, Todd M. '80 (IND) Richmond, IN Holy Family Church; Richmond, IN St. Andrew Church; Richmond, IN St. Mary Church; Richmond, IN Richmond State Hospital; [N] Richmond, IN Earlham College Newman Center.
Riebe-Estrella, Gary L. *s.v.d.* '71 (CHI) [B] Chicago, IL The Catholic Theological Union at Chicago; [B] Chicago, IL The Catholic Theological Union at Chicago; [B] Techny, IL Divine Word Residence; [B] Techny, IL Divine Word Residence; [N] Chicago, IL Divine Word Theologate; [N] Techny, IL Society of the Divine Word, Provincial Headquarter-Chicago Prov.
Rieck, Raymond '56 (SFD) Retired.
Riedel, Richard R. *c.pp.s.* '52 (CIN) Celina, OH Immaculate Conception of the Blessed Virgin Mary Church.
Riedel, Robert B. '92 (WDC) Valley Lee, MD St. George Church.
Riedemann, Kenneth '64 (SCL) Kensington, MN Our Lady of the Runestone Church; Lake Reno, MN St. John Nepomuk Church.
Rieden, Thomas W. *o.s.f.s.* '68 (LAN) [B] Jackson, MI Lumen Christi High School.
Rieder, David J. '56 (SCL) Perham, MN St. Henry's Church; Perham, MN St. Stanislaus Church.
Rieder, Donald '55 (SCL) Retired.
Rieder, Michael J. '94 (RVC) Central Islip, NY St. John of God Church.
Rieder, Ronald *o.f.m.cap.* '63 (FTW) Huntington, IN SS. Peter and Paul Church.
Riedman, John '62 (SFS) Humboldt, SD St. Ann Church.
Riedman, Joseph G. '56 (IND) [7] Indianapolis, IN Holy Spirit Church.
Riedmann, Boniface *s.a.* '45 (BO) [P] Brockton, MA Chapel of Our Savior-Catholic Pastoral and Information Center; [W] Brockton, MA Chapel of Our Saviour; [BB] Brockton, MA Chapel of Our Saviour.
Riedmueller, Leo A. '48 (LR) Hot Springs National Park, AR St. Mary's of the Springs Church.
Riedy, Robert I. '39 (PH) Spring City, PA St. Joseph Church; Retired.
Rieger, Alan J. *o.c.d.* '61 (MIL) [P] Milwaukee, WI Provincial Offices - Discalced Carmelites.
Riegler, Frederick J. '67 (PH) Quakertown, PA St. Isidore Church.
Riehle, James L. *c.s.c.* '64 (FTW) [B] Notre Dame, IN University of Notre Dame Du Lac; [J] Notre Dame, IN Holy Cross Community, Corby Hall, University of Notre Dame.
Riel, Robert H. '80 (SPR) [3] Chicopee, MA Nativity of the Blessed Virgin Mary Church.
Rielly, John *s.m.* '53 (SJ) [L] Cupertino, CA Marianist Provincial Residence.
Rieman, Richard W. '58 (BO) [V] Chestnut Hill, MA Opus Dei.
Riemer, Robert *s.v.d.* '60 (FgM) Society of the Divine Word Foreign Missions.
Riendeau, Alfred A. '98 (BGP) [1] Greenwich, CT St. Mary Church.
Riendeau, Richard A. '57 (SPR) [1] Holyoke, MA Blessed Sacrament Church.
Riendeau, Walter A. *s.s.s.* '50 (SLC) Eureka, UT St. Patrick's Church; Payson, UT San Andres Church.
Riepe, Charles K. '60 (BAL) Special Assignment; [U] Baltimore, MD Archdiocesan Office-Newman Center.
Riera, John *t.o.r.* '48 (NEW) [20] Newark, NJ Immaculate Heart of Mary Church.
Ries, Carl A. '70 (DUB) Mason City, IA St. Joseph's Church.
Ries, Donald C. '59 (SC) Jefferson, IA St. Joseph's Church.
Ries, James R. '93 (ORG) [3] Orange, CA St. Norbert Church.
Ries, Richard S. '63 (SC) Le Mars, IA St. James Church.
Ries, Victor '45 (CIN) [22] Dayton, OH St. Peter Church.
Ries, Victor F. '45 (CIN) Retired.
Riesbeck, Christian H.F. '96 (GAL) [72] Houston, TX Queen of Peace Church.
Riesberg, Leo L. '57 (SC) Wall Lake, IA St. Joseph's Church.
Riesenberg, John J. '60 (COV) Edgewood, KY St. Pius X Church; Retired.
Riesthuis, Henk *m.h.m.* '59 (LA) [Q] Los Angeles, CA Mill Hill Missionaries Procure.
Rietti, John '57 (JKS) On Duty Outside the Diocese.
Riffle, David '67 (B) Bonners Ferry, ID St. Ann's Church.
Riffle, Donald J. '62 (B) Meridian, ID Holy Apostles Church.
Riffle, Douglas H. '57 (B) Retired.
Riffle, Henry J. '70 (SP) San Antonio, FL St. Anthony of Padua Church.
Riffle, Raymond E. '79 (GBG) Slickville, PA St. Sylvester Church.
Rigali, Joseph *o.f.m.* '58 (GAL) [4] Galveston, TX St. Patrick Church.
Rigali, Norbert *s.j.* '59 (SD) [B] San Diego, CA University of San Diego.
Rigatuso, Leo '94 (OM) Papillion, NE St. Columbkille Church.
Rigdon, Vincent J. '77 (WDC) [8] Silver Spring, MD St. Michael Church; Pastoral Center Special Ministries.
Rigert, James A. *c.s.c.* '66 (FTW) [B] Notre Dame, IN University of Notre Dame Du Lac; [J] Notre Dame, IN Holy Cross Community, Corby Hall, University of Notre Dame.
Rigney, Msgr. Dennis A. (ALN) [P] Orwigsburg, PA Seton Manor, Inc.
Rigney, Msgr. Dennis A. '66 (ALN) [2] Allentown, PA St. Francis of Assisi Church; [H] Bethlehem, PA Holy Family Manor; [I] Bethlehem, PA Holy Family Apartments; [I] Bethlehem, PA Trexler Pavilion, Assisted Living Residence of Holy Family Manor; [I] Orwigsburg, PA Holy Family Assisted Living Residence; [I] Orwigsburg, PA Holy Family Adult Day Care at St. Francis Center; [I] Bethlehem, PA Grace Mansion Assisted Living Residence of Holy Family Manor; [J] Bethlehem, PA Holy Family Villa.
Rigney, Msgr. Philip '49 (CAM) Retired.
Rigney, Msgr. Raymond P. '42 (NY) Retired; [E] White Plains, NY Archbishop Stepinac High School.
Rigoli, Anthony *o.m.i.* '72 (BUF) [C] Buffalo, NY D'Youville College.

Rigoli, Anthony F. *o.m.i.* '72 (BUF) [60] Buffalo, NY St. Rose of Lima Church; [R] Alfred, NY Campus Ministry.
Rigonan, Anthony '88 (BRK) Brooklyn, NY Beth Israel Medical Center/Kings Hgwy.
Rigouts, Alphonse *c.i.c.m.* '48 (FgM) Missionhurst Foreign Missions.
Riha, Francis A. *m.m.* '68 (FgM) Maryknoll Foreign Missions.
Rihn, Msgr. Roy '42 (SAT) Retired; [K] San Antonio, TX Casa De Padres.
Rikteraitis, John E. '56 (HRT) Retired.
Riley, Andrew *p.i.m.e.* '80 (PMB) Hobe Sound, FL St. Christopher Church.
Riley, Daniel J. '84 (BO) [69] Boston, MA St. William Church.
Riley, Daniel P. *o.f.m.* '71 (BUF) [C] St. Bonaventure, NY St. Bonaventure University; [Q] West Clarksville, NY Mount Irenaeus, Franciscan Mountain Retreat & Holy Peace Friary; [R] Alfred, NY Campus Ministry.
Riley, David J. '64 (BGP) [4] Stamford, CT St. Cecilia Church.
Riley, Dennis S. '79 (CHI) [12] Chicago, IL St. Angela Church.
Riley, Edward H. *o.p.* '60 (CHI) [N] Chicago, IL Dominicans (Provincial Office).
Riley, Edward H. *o.p.* '60 (FgM) Dominican - Order of Preachers Foreign Missions.
Riley, Edward M. '00 (BO) [1] Norwood, MA St. Catherine of Siena Church.
Riley, Eric '98 (OWN) [2] Owensboro, KY Blessed Mother Church.
Riley, Finian A. *o.f.m.* '55 (FgM) Franciscan Foreign Missions.
Riley, George F. *o.s.a.* '62 (PH) [C] Villanova, PA Villanova University; [AA] Villanova, PA St. Thomas Monastery.
Riley, J. Norman '57 (CLV) Copley, OH Guardian Angels Church.
Riley, James F. *s.j.* (DET) [K] Detroit, MI Jesuit Provincial Office-Detroit Province of the Society of Jesus.
Riley, James H. '58 (BO) Senior Priests.
Riley, John *c.s.c.* '94 (FTW) [B] Notre Dame, IN University of Notre Dame Du Lac.
Riley, John F. '55 (STP) Retired; [C] St. Paul, MN University of St. Thomas.
Riley, John F. '56 (ALB) Pittstown, NY St. George Church.
Riley, John J. '91 (ARL) [6] Alexandria, VA St. Louis Church.
Riley, John P. *c.s.c.* '94 (FTW) [J] Notre Dame, IN Holy Cross Community, Corby Hall, University of Notre Dame.
Riley, John Patrick *c.s.c.* '94 (FTW) Notre Dame, IN Sacred Heart Church.
Riley, Kenneth A. '92 (KC) [4] Kansas City, MO St. Bernadette's Church.
Riley, Lawrence J. '40 (BO) Senior Priests.
Riley, Leo P. '82 (DUB) Dougherty, IA St. Patrick's Church; Rockford, IA Holy Name Church; Rockwell, IA Sacred Heart Church.
Riley, Malachy *o.s.b.* '42 (KC) [J] Conception, MO Conception Abbey.
Riley, Mark J. '90 (BO) Absent on Leave.
Riley, Mark J. '95 (BO) Boston, MA Children's Hospital.
Riley, Mark R. '95 (CLV) Solon, OH St. Rita Church.
Riley, Miles O'Brien '63 (SFR) Belmont, CA St. Mark Church; Special Assignment.
Riley, Patric '84 (KCK) [8] Topeka, KS St. Matthew Church.
Riley, Patrick '48 (SCL) Retired.
Riley, Placidus H. *o.s.b.* '46 (MAN) [K] Manchester, NH St. Anselm Abbey.
Riley, Robert D. *o.p.* '60 (WDC) [11] Washington, DC St. Dominic Church & Priory Church.
Rilley, John F. '53 (PH) Retired.
Rimassa, Paul S. '83 (TR) [10] Trenton, NJ Our Lady of Sorrows Church; Trenton, NJ Donnelly Memorial Hospital of City of Trenton.
Rimelspach, Jeffrey J. '85 (COL) Powell, OH St. Joan of Arc Church.
Rimes, Robert B. *s.j.* '55 (MOB) [A] Mobile, AL Spring Hill College.
Rimmele, Leo *o.s.b.* '55 (P) [L] St. Benedict, OR Mt. Angel Abbey.
Rimselis, Victor *m.i.c.* '43 (CHI) [N] Chicago, IL Congregation of Marian Fathers of the Immaculate Conception.
Rimshaw, Joseph J. *s.s.j.* '48 (BAL) [S] Baltimore, MD St. Joseph Society of the Sacred Heart House of Central Administration.
Rimshaw, Joseph J. *s.s.j.* '48 (ORL) Retired.
Rinaldi, Francis J. *o.s.f.s.* '69 (WIL) [C] Ridgely, MD The Benedictine School for Exceptional Children; [J] Ridgely, MD St. Gertrude's Monastery, Motherhouse and Novitiate of the Sisters of St. Benedict.
Rinaldi, Nicholas *s.a.c.* (BAL) [54] Baltimore, MD St. Leo Church.
Rinaldo, Joseph *s.c.* '67 (LAN) [E] Chelsea, MI St. Louis Center for Exceptional Children & Adults; [O] Grass Lake, MI The Pious Union of St. Joseph.
Rindos, Paul T. '59 (HBG) Mount Joy, PA Mary, Mother of the Church.
Riney, Maury '77 (OWN) [6] Owensboro, KY St. Pius Tenth Church.
Riney, Philip C. '48 (OWN) Retired.
Riney, W. Jerry '75 (OWN) Bowling Green, KY Holy Spirit Church.
Ring, Msgr. Arthur R. '37 (DM) Retired.
Ring, Daniel J. '68 (TOL) Fostoria, OH St. Wendelin Church.
Ring, John K. '61 (SFR) [54] San Francisco, CA St. Vincent de Paul Church.
Ring, Joseph G. '88 (SFD) Charleston, IL St. Charles Borromeo Church.
Ring, Paul L. (BO) [2] Weymouth, MA St. Francis Xavier Church.
Ring, Robert P. '82 (ROC) Apalachin, NY St. Margaret Mary Church.
Ring, Vincent D. '64 (SFR) San Bruno, CA St. Robert Church.
Ringenback, Gerard A. '72 (RVC) Islip Terrace, NY St. Peter the Apostle Church.
Ringenberger, Harry '69 (MIA) [13] Fort Lauderdale, FL St. Pius X Church.
Ringholz, Benedict E. '45 (TOL) Retired; [H] Sandusky, OH Providence Hospital Inc.
Rini, John '67 (ELP) [19] El Paso, TX Our Lady of the Valley Church.
Rink, George '57 (SEA) Retired.
Rink, Louis W. *c.s.c.* '58 (PHX) [G] Phoenix, AZ Holy Cross Congregation/Casa Santa Cruz.
Rinkowski, George M. '41 (TOL) Retired.
Rinn, Richard A. *c.s.v.* '81 (LAV) [15] Las Vegas, NV St. Viator Church.
Rinzel, Jerome A. '64 (MIL) Muskego, WI St. Leonard Congregation Church.
Riordan, Msgr. Brendan P. '70 (RVC) Great Neck, NY St. Aloysius Church.
Riordan, Brice E. *o.carm.* '44 (NEW) Paramus, NJ Carmelite Chapel of St. Therese Church.
Riordan, Eugene *s.m.a.* '53 (WDC) [M] Takoma Park, MD Society of African Missions (S.M.A.).
Riordan, John B. *o.f.m.cap.* '71 (NY) [17] Yonkers, NY Sacred Heart Church; [17] Yonkers, NY Sacred Heart Church.
Riordan, Patrick '90 (PEO) [2] Streator, IL St. Anthony of Padua Church.
Rios, Angel L. *m.c.* '85 (MGZ) Maricao, PR St. John the Baptist Church.
Rios, Francisco *i.v.e.* '91 (SJ) [14] San Jose, CA St. Leo the Great Church.
Rios, Juan Carlos (PMB) [A] Boynton Beach, FL St. Vincent de Paul Regional Seminary.
Rios, Juan Carlos '93 (MIA) On Duty Outside the Archdiocese.
Rios, Manuel D. '86 (NEW) [2] Jersey City, NJ St. Aloysius Church.
Rios, Teodoro A. *c.m.* '76 (FgM) Vincentian Foreign Missions.
Rios Capiello, Luis B. '81 (ARE) On Duty Outside the Diocese.
Rios Capiello, Luis B. '81 (MGZ) Rincon, PR St. Rose of Lima Church.
Rioux, J. Robert *c.s.c.* '56 (FR) [I] North Dartmouth, MA St. Joseph's Hall.
Rioux, Ray '94 (SR) Middletown, CA St. Joseph Church.
Ripko, DePaul *o.f.m.cap.* '53 (PIT) [O] Herman, PA St. Mary's Friary.
Riplog, Duane T. '84 (CHR) Retired.
Ripoli, Roland R. *o.s.b.* '64 (GBG) [H] Latrobe, PA Saint Vincent Archabbey.
Ripoll, Eduardo Marrugo (R) Wilson, NC Church of St. Therese.
Ripp, Joseph '64 (SFS) Salem, SD St. Mary Church.
Ripper, Thomas J. *m.s.* '68 (STL) Maplewood, MO Immaculate Conception Church.
Ripperger, Chad *f.s.s.p.* '97 (SCR) [M] Elmhurst, PA Priestly Fraternity of St. Peter (F.S.S.P.), North American District Headquarters.
Ripperger, Chad A. *f.s.s.p.* '97 (LIN) [A] Seward, NE St. Gregory the Great Seminary.
Ripperger, Edward J. '61 (IND) Retired.
Ripperger, Harold A. '58 (IND) Lanesville, IN St. Mary Church.
Ripperger, Mark *o.cist.* '93 (DAL) [K] Irving, TX Cistercian Abbey of Our Lady of Dallas.
Ripperger, William '55 (IND) St. Denis, IN St. Denis Church.
Ripperger, William G. '55 (IND) Millhousen, IN Immaculate Conception Church; Napoleon, IN St. Maurice Church.
Rippinger, Joel *o.s.b.* '74 (RCK) [G] Aurora, IL Marmion Abbey-St. Augustine's Abbey.
Rippy, Robert J. '84 (ARL) [6] Arlington, VA Our Lady of Lourdes Church.
Riquelme, Alvaro *c.ss.r.* '97 (ORL) New Smyrna Beach, FL Sacred Heart Church.
Risacher, James (BAL) [42] Baltimore, MD Immaculate Heart of Mary Church.
Risacher, James E. '52 (TOL) Retired.
Rischmann, Edward '48 (NEW) Retired.
Rischmann, Robert J. '61 (NEW) [1] East Orange, NJ Holy Name of Jesus Church.
Risden, George '84 (SR) Crescent City, CA St. Joseph Church.
Rishel, Robert F. '55 (PIT) Retired.
Riski, Bruce *o.f.m.cap.* '53 (GB) [I] Appleton, WI St. Fidelis Friary.
Risley, John C. *o.p.* '65 (MAD) [I] Sinsinawa, WI Dominican Motherhouse.
Risoli, Angelo *c.s.* '69 (SD) Imperial, CA St. Anthony of Padua Church.
Riss, Dennis '84 (RC) Lemmon, SD St. Mary's Church.
Risse, James *s.v.d.* '61 (FgM) Society of the Divine Word Foreign Missions.
Risse, Roger *s.v.d.* '54 (FgM) Society of the Divine Word Foreign Missions.
Ristuccia, Leon *o.f.m.* '45 (HRT) Winsted, CT St. Joseph's Church.
Rita, Carmine J. '94 (NY) Bronxville, NY St. Joseph Church.
Rita, Thomas L. '70 (FR) West Harwich, MA Holy Trinity Church.
Ritacco, Richard '76 (WOR) Absent on Leave.
Ritari, Raymond '83 (PHX) [20] Phoenix, AZ St. Matthew Church.
Ritchey, Samuel E. '73 (COL) [41] Columbus, OH Sacred Heart Church.
Ritchey, Timothy M. '85 (B) Meridian, ID Holy Apostles Church.
Ritchie, Donald E. '59 (BUR) Waitsfield, VT Our Lady of the Snows Church; Retired.
Ritchie, Francis J. '58 (BO) Senior Priests.
Ritchie, Msgr. G. Carlton '32 (E) Retired.
Ritchie, Gerald T. '68 (E) [8] Erie, PA Our Lady of Mercy Church.
Ritchie, Robert T. '71 (NY) [169] Bronx, NY Our Lady of Angels Church; [Q] New York, NY Society of St. Vincent De Paul, Archdiocesan Central Council of New York.
Ritchie, Vincent J. *s.j.* '74 (RVC) Oceanside, NY St. Anthony Church.
Riter, Dennis G. '71 (BUF) [55] Buffalo, NY Our Lady of Perpetual Help Church; [66] Buffalo, NY St. Valentine Church.
Ritt, Paul E. '81 (BO) Sherborn, MA St. Theresa Church; [A] Boston, MA St. John's Seminary School of Theology.
Rittenhouse, Thomas R. '76 (TR) Matawan, NJ St. Clement Church; Retired.
Ritter, Charles F. '67 (TOL) Bryan, OH St. Patrick Church.
Ritter, Edward W. '51 (DET) St. Clair, MI St. Mary Church.
Ritter, Nicholas *o.s.a.* '65 (LAN) Flushing, MI St. Robert Church.
Ritter, Patrick '74 (SEA) Bellevue, WA Sacred Heart Church.
Ritter, Patrick *s.d.s.* '76 (MIL) [P] Milwaukee, WI Salvatorian Provincial Residence.
Rittmeyer, Robert '80 (SP) Retired.
Ritz, Robert G. *c.s.b.* '51 (GAL) Sugar Land, TX St. Theresa Church.
Ritzert, William J. '64 (PIT) Evans City, PA St. Matthias Church; Butler County, PA Department of Veterans Affairs- Deshon Hospital.
Riva, Gerald '68 (JOL) Woodridge, IL St. Scholastica Church.
Riva, Hugo *m.c.c.j.* '50 (CHI) Blue Island, IL St. Donatus Church.
Riva, Paolo *c.r.s.* '96 (MAN) [H] Allenstown, NH Pine Haven Boys Center.
Rivard, Robert *f.m.s.i.* (BO) Norfolk, MA St. Jude Church.
Rivard, Robert *f.m.s.i.* '77 (BO) [B] Framingham, MA Sylva Maria.
Rivard, Roland J. '56 (BUR) [2] Burlington, VT St. Anthony's Church; [3] Burlington, VT Christ the King Church.
Rivas, David '85 (ARE) Corozal-Palos Blancos, PR Christ the King Church.
Rivas, Jorge *o.f.m.* '48 (ELP) [B] El Paso, TX St. Anthony's School of Theology.
Rivas, Juan *l.c.* '82 (LA) [Q] Pasadena, CA Legionaries of Christ; [CC] El Monte, CA Hombre Nuevo.
Rivas, Manuel D. '92 (OWN) Bowling Green, KY St. Joseph's Church.
Rivas, Romeo '59 (MIA) Retired; [K] Miami, FL National Shrine of Our Lady of Charity.
Rivas, Vidal (WDC) [15] Washington, DC St. Gabriel Church.
Rivas-Campiz, Eral Jose '70 (SJN) [61] San Juan, PR Stella Maris Church.
Rive, Gino G. '57 (SB) [E] Morongo Valley, CA St. Michael's of Morongo Valley, Inc.
Rivera, Adalin '77 (PCE) Juana Diaz, PR Santa Teresita Church; [B] Ponce, PR The Pontifical Catholic University of Puerto Rico.
Rivera, Andres *s.d.b.* '74 (SJN) [37] San Juan, PR Maria Auxiliadora Church.

Rivera, Eddie (SJN) Santurce, PR Hospital Del Nino San Jorge.
Rivera, Eddie '90 (SJN) [39] San Juan, PR San Mateo Church.
Rivera, Felix *o.carm.* '91 (JOL) [4] Joliet, IL Mount Carmel Church.
Rivera, Guadalupe '49 (SFE) Retired.
Rivera, Hilario (CGS) Ceiba, PR San Antonio de Padua Church.
Rivera, Jaime Velasco *o.s.b.* '93 (MIL) [P] Benet Lake, WI St. Benedict's Abbey.
Rivera, Jery '00 (PCE) Guayanilla, PR Immaculate Conception Church.
Rivera, Jesus *s.t.* '81 (ARL) [J] Arlington, VA Missionary Servants of the Most Holy Trinity, S.T.
Rivera, Jorge *o.carm.* '96 (SJN) [59] San Juan, PR Santa Teresita Del Nino Jesus Church.
Rivera, Leoncio Quijones '46 (SJN) Retired.
Rivera, Luis '84 (MIA) [11] Miami, FL Our Lady of Divine Providence Church.
Rivera, Luis Antonio '83 (CGS) San Lorenzo, PR Sagrado Corazon de Jesus y 12 Apostoles Church.
Rivera, Miguel '83 (ARE) Corozal-Padilla, PR Our Lady of the Seven Sorrows Church.
Rivera, Orlando '90 (PCE) Arroyo, PR Our Lady of Mt. Carmel Church.
Rivera, Oscar *o.s.b.* '78 (CGS) [C] Humacao, PR San Antonio Abad Abbey of the Order of St. Benedict.
Rivera, Oscar '79 (CGS) [6] Caguas, PR Nuestra Senora del Perpetuo Socorro Church.
Rivera, Raymond L. '86 (PCE) Guayanilla, PR Immaculate Conception Church.
Rivera, Ubladimiro *o.f.m.* '75 (FgM) Franciscan Foreign Missions.
Rivera Ramos, Hector E. '82 (MGZ) [1] Mayaquez, PR Cathedral of Our Lady of Purification.
Rivera Ribo, Francisco J. '54 (SJN) Retired.
Rivera-Martinez, Pius *o.s.c.o.* '53 (WOR) [N] Spencer, MA St. Joseph's Abbey.
Rivero, Andres *o.f.m.* '75 (SD) [H] Oceanside, CA Mission San Luis Rey.
Rivero, Jordi S. '82 (MIA) North Miami, FL Holy Family Church; [K] Miami, FL Respect Life Office.
Rivero, Juan '72 (FWT) Glen Rose, TX St. Rose of Lima Church; Granbury, TX St. Frances Cabrini Church; Denton, TX State School.
Rivero, Julio B. *t.o.r.* '69 (SP) St. Pete Beach, FL St. John Church.
Rivero, Leonides '78 (ELP) [27] El Paso, TX St. Mark Church.
Riveroll, Jesus R. *s.j.* '88 (FgM) Provinces.
Riveros, Wilfredo *o.dem.* '97 (CGS) Cayey, PR Nuestra Senora de la Asuncion Church.
Rivers, Clarence J. '56 (CIN) On Special and Archdiocesan Assignment.
Rivers, Clarence Rufus J. '56 (CIN) [V] Cincinnati, OH Stimuli, Inc.
Rivers, Robert S. *c.s.p.* '68 (WDC) [B] Washington, DC St. Paul's College; [V] Washington, DC Paulist National Catholic Evangelization Assoc.
Rivet, Hilton L. *s.j.* '54 (BR) [11] Baton Rouge, LA Immaculate Conception Church.
Rivi, Geno G. '57 (GBG) Retired.
Rivituso, Mark '88 (STL) [49] St. Louis, MO St. Mary Magdalen Church.
Rivoire, S. Joseph *s.j.* '49 (NO) [P] New Orleans, LA Ignatius Residence.
Rizo, Sergio '89 (FWT) Cleburne, TX St. Joseph Church.
Rizzi, Salvatore '41 (BRK) Retired.
Rizzo, David '00 (ALT) [B] Ebensburg, PA Bishop Carroll High School.
Rizzo, David R. (ALT) Cresson, PA St. Francis Xavier Church; [H] Hollidaysburg, PA Campus Ministry.
Rizzo, Giovanni '00 (NEW) [15] Newark, NJ St. Francis Xavier Church.
Rizzo, John C. '56 (OM) [4] Omaha, NE St. Ann Church; [35] Omaha, NE St. Peter Church.
Rizzo, Mateo J. '73 (BRK) [72] Brooklyn, NY Church of St. Jude.
Rizzo, Robert C. '74 (CHI) Park Ridge, IL St. Paul of the Cross Church.
Rizzotto, Msgr. Vincent M. '56 (GAL) [18] Houston, TX St. Cecilia Church.
Rizzuto, Mariano J. *s.m.* '59 (BR) Convent, LA St. Michael the Archangel Church.
Roa, Mizael '86 (NY) [50] New York, NY Holy Trinity Church.
Roach, Daniel *o.p.* '56 (FgM) Dominican - Order of Preachers Foreign Missions.
Roach, Francis '73 (WOR) Worcester, MA University of Mass Medical Center.
Roach, Francis J. '56 (STP) Retired.
Roach, Francis J. '73 (WOR) [12] Worcester, MA Our Lady of Lourdes Church; [J] Worcester, MA Saint Vincent Hospital, Inc.
Roach, John A. '58 (SPR) Shelburne Falls, MA St. Joseph's Church.
Roach, Joseph (SB) Retired.
Roach, Joseph W. *s.a.g.* '48 (SAG) Retired.
Roach, Joseph W. *s.a.g.* '48 (SB) [E] Morongo Valley, CA St. Michael's of Morongo Valley, Inc.
Roach, Michael '81 (KC) [38] Kansas City, MO St. Therese Church.
Roach, Michael J. '71 (BAL) Manchester, MD St. Bartholomew Church; [A] Emmitsburg, MD Mount St. Mary's Seminary.
Roach, Richard R. *s.j.* '69 (SEA) Vashon, WA St. John Vianney Church; [A] Seattle, WA Seattle University.
Roach, Robert N. *c.s.sp.* '48 (PH) [AA] Bensalem, PA Congregation of the Holy Ghost.
Roach, Thomas E. *s.j.* '70 (BAL) [S] Baltimore, MD Jesuit Fathers and Brothers Maryland Provincial Curia.
Roache, James P. '60 (CHI) [1] Chicago, IL Cathedral of the Holy Name.
Roark, John L. '56 (SY) [11] Syracuse, NY St. Ann Church.
Roark, Michael B. '70 (WIL) Salisbury, MD St. Francis De Sales Church.
Robak, Anthony G. '74 (NEW) North Bergen, NJ Sacred Heart Church.
Robak, Charles P. *m.m.* '70 (FgM) Maryknoll Foreign Missions.
Roban, Myles *s.s.c.* (LA) Hacienda Heights, CA St. John Vianney Church.
Robb, Dennis E. '74 (SEA) Everett, WA Immaculate Conception Church; Everett, WA Our Lady of Perpetual Help Church.
Robb, Kevin Dominic *o.p.* '77 (NY) [DD] New York, NY St. Vincent Ferrer Priory.
Robb, Paul V. *s.j.* '60 (CHI) [C] Chicago, IL Jesuit Community at Loyola University of Chicago; [N] Chicago, IL Chicago Province of the Society of Jesus-Provincial Office.
Robbins, Charles J. *c.pp.s.* '39 (LFT) [A] Rensselaer, IN Saint Joseph's College.
Robbins, John F. *c.s.b.* '72 (GAL) [7] Houston, TX St. Anne Church.
Robbins, Robert J. '74 (NY) [46] New York, NY Holy Family Church.
Robbins, Msgr. Roger P. '63 (SAT) Schertz, TX Church of the Good Shepherd.
Robbins, Thomas P. '74 (COV) Taylor Mill, KY St. Anthony Church; [B] Covington, KY Holy Cross High School.
Robello, Louis J. '65 (SFR) Retired.
Roberge, Francis A. '78 (WOR) West Boylston, MA Our Lady of Good Counsel Church; [Q] Worcester, MA Campus Ministry.
Roberge, Frederick *s.s.s.* '35 (CLV) [O] Cleveland, OH Blessed Sacrament Community.
Roberge, Richard A. '85 (MAN) [2] Berlin, NH Good Shepherd Church.
Roberson, Henry '71 (OKL) Special Assignment.
Roberson, Michael '74 (NO) Edgard, LA St. John the Baptist Church.
Roberson, Ronald G. *c.s.p., s.e.o.d.* '77 (WDC) [B] Washington, DC St. Paul's College.
Robert, Darin '71 (LAN) Ann Arbor, MI University of Michigan Hospitals/Pastoral Care Dept.
Robert, Emile A. '50 (PRO) Retired.
Robert, Rene '89 (STA) [D] St. Augustine, FL Religious Education for Catholic Deaf and Blind.
Roberts, Allan '80 (LA) Glendora, CA St. Dorothy Church.
Roberts, Anthony P. *s.j.* '56 (PH) [AA] Philadelphia, PA Jesuit Community at St. Joseph's University.
Roberts, Art *c.s.b.* '55 (LSC) Truth or Consequences, NM Our Lady of Perpetual Help Church.
Roberts, David *c.p.* '52 (BRK) [V] Jamaica, NY Immaculate Conception Monastery.
Roberts, Don '78 (SFD) Pana, IL St. Patrick Church.
Roberts, Don J. '78 (SFD) Oconee, IL Sacred Heart of Jesus Church.
Roberts, Edward (PEO) Brimfield, IL St. Joseph's Church.
Roberts, Edward *s.s.s.* '60 (CLV) [O] Cleveland, OH Congregation of the Blessed Sacrament Provincial House.
Roberts, Edward A. *s.s.c.* '60 (BO) [W] Quincy, MA St. Columban's Foreign Mission Society.
Roberts, Eugene J. '75 (TR) Marlboro, NJ St. Gabriel Church.
Roberts, G. Richard '91 (LC) Mauston, WI St. Patrick Church.
Roberts, Guy R. '98 (SFE) Roy, NM Holy Family-St. Joseph Church; Wagon Mound, NM Santa Clara Church.
Roberts, Kenneth '66 (DAL) Retired.
Roberts, Mark '83 (LAV) Henderson, NV St. Peter the Apostle Church.
Roberts, Marshall M. '96 (SCR) [M] Shohola, PA Society of Saint John.
Roberts, Ralph *s.s.s.* '75 (CLV) [O] Cleveland, OH Congregation of the Blessed Sacrament Provincial House.
Roberts, Ralph O. '98 (GAL) [29] Houston, TX St. Francis de Sales Church.
Roberts, Randall *o.f.m.* '84 (GB) [I] Pulaski, WI Assumption of B.V.M. Friary.
Roberts, Thomas C. '84 (NEW) Montclair, NJ Our Lady of Mt. Carmel Church; Newark, NJ Northern State Prison.
Roberts, Victor W. *o.s.b.* '69 (OKL) [I] Shawnee, OK St. Gregory's Abbey.
Robertson, Douglas C. '96 (LC) Fountain City, WI Immaculate Conception Church; Rudolph, WI St. Philip Church.
Robertson, Eugene '78 (STL) Farmington, MO St. Joseph Church.
Robertson, Msgr. Glendon E. '57 (CAM) Retired.
Robertson, Msgr. Harold '49 (NY) [E] New York, NY Cardinal Hayes High School.
Robertson, James E. '77 (BO) [8] Quincy, MA Sacred Heart Church.
Robertson, John W. '71 (HEL) Special Assignments.
Robertson, Luke *t.o.r.* '99 (FWT) [8] Fort Worth, TX St. Andrew Church.
Robertson, Thomas M. '65 (STL) Riverview Gardens, MO St. Catherine of Alexandria Church.
Robertson, Msgr. William P. '60 (GAL) [1] Spring, TX Christ the Good Shepherd Church.
Robeson, Stephen P. '84 (STL) [56] St. Louis, MO St. Simon of Cyrene Church.
Robichand, Paul G. *c.s.p.* '75 (NY) [DD] Jamaica Estates, NY Paulist Fathers Generalate.
Robichaud, Armand *s.m.* '50 (BO) [55] Boston, MA Our Lady of Victories Church; [W] Boston, MA Marist Fathers of Our Lady of Victories (Boston Prov.).
Robichaud, George H. '70 (MAN) Wolfeboro, NH St. Cecilia Church.
Robichaud, J. Armand *s.m.* '50 (FgM) Marist Foreign Missions.
Robichaud, James P. *o.m.i.* (PRT) Brownville Junction, ME St. Francis Xavier Church; Dover-Foxcroft, ME St. Thomas Church.
Robichaux, Robie *j.c.l.* '76 (LAF) [14] Lafayette, LA St. Mary, Mother of the Church.
Robicheaux, David J. '98 (NO) [5] Marrero, LA The Visitation of Our Lady Church.
Robida, Raymond A. '48 (FR) Retired.
Robidoux, Dunstan *o.s.b.* (WDC) [M] Washington, DC St. Anselm's Abbey.
Robillard, Joseph R. '84 (ORG) Costa Mesa, CA St. Joachim Church.
Robillard, Raymond A. '66 (FR) Absent on Leave; [I] Fall River, MA Priests' Hostel.
Robillard, Msgr. Thomas J. '44 (OG) Norfolk, NY Visitation of the B.V.M. Church; Retired.
Robin, Richard A. *s.j.* '67 (LA) [C] Los Angeles, CA Loyola Marymount University; [C] Los Angeles, CA Loyola Marymount University.
Robine, Paul M. '59 (ALT) Mundys Corner, PA St. John Vianney's Church.
Robins, Dean L. '87 (NO) [1] Kenner, LA Nativity of Our Lord Church.
Robinson, Charles *o.f.m.cap.* '70 (GF) Crow Agency, MT St. Dennis Church.
Robinson, Christopher S. *c.m.* '89 (STL) [P] Earth City, MO Congregation of the Mission Midwest Province (Vincentians).
Robinson, David C. *s.j.* '92 (SFR) [N] San Francisco, CA Jesuit Community at University of San Francisco.
Robinson, Denis *o.s.b.* '93 (IND) [A] St. Meinrad, IN St. Meinrad Seminary; [J] St. Meinrad, IN St. Meinrad Archabbey.
Robinson, Donald A. '80 (OG) Champlain, NY St. Mary Church.
Robinson, Edmund J. *s.j.* '55 (SPK) [K] Spokane, WA Regis Community.
Robinson, Edward M. *o.p.* '41 (DAL) [K] Irving, TX Dominican Priory of St. Albert the Great.
Robinson, Edwin *o.f.m.* (NY) Dobbs Ferry, NY St. Cabrini Nursing Home; [Z] Dobbs Ferry, NY St. Cabrini Nursing Home.
Robinson, Edwin F.D. *o.f.m.* '68 (PAT) [M] Butler, NJ St. Anthony Friary.
Robinson, Ernest '79 (RVC) Uniondale, NY Holly Patterson Geriatric Center.
Robinson, Fisher *s.v.d.* '56 (LA) [72] Los Angeles, CA St. John, The Evangelist Church.
Robinson, Gerald H. *s.j.* '77 (SAC) [14] Sacramento, CA St. Ignatius of Loyola Church; [J] Applegate, CA Our Lady of the Oaks Villa.
Robinson, Msgr. James P. *s.s.e.* '57 (DET) [1] Detroit, MI Cathedral, Church of the Most Blessed Sacrament.
Robinson, Jerome (MOB) On Leave from the Archdiocese.
Robinson, Jerome R. (LC) Chippewa Falls, WI Notre Dame Church.
Robinson, John '54 (BIR) [21] Birmingham, AL St. Peter the Apostle Church.
Robinson, John A. '71 (CHI) Elk Grove Village, IL Queen of the Rosary Church.
Robinson, John C. '54 (MOB) Retired.
Robinson, Joseph A. '64 (CIN) [17] Cincinnati, OH St. Boniface Church.
Robinson, Joseph P. '68 (BO) Bedford, MA St. Michael Church; Bedford, MA Veterans Administration Hospital Bedford; Military & VA Chaplains.
Robinson, Ken '92 (FWT) Grapevine, TX St. Francis of

Assisi Church.
Robinson, Lawrence F. *s.j.* '65 (P) [D] Portland, OR Jesuit High School.
Robinson, Michael '96 (SD) [26] San Diego, CA St. Didacus Church.
Robinson, Monte E. '75 (MAD) Belmont, WI St. Philomena Church; Calamine, WI St. Michael Church; Truman, WI Immaculate Conception Church.
Robinson, Patrick '91 (PHX) [1] Scottsdale, AZ Blessed Sacrament Church.
Robinson, Perry L. *s.j.* '72 (OM) [K] Omaha, NE Jesuit Community at Creighton University.
Robinson, Richard J. '63 (MIL) [60] Milwaukee, WI Mother of Perpetual Help Church; [81] Milwaukee, WI St. Stephen, Martyr Church.
Robinson, Robert M. '69 (BRK) [224] Queens, NY St. Patrick Church.
Robinson, Tyrone '79 (DET) [46] Detroit, MI Martyrs of Uganda Church.
Robisch, David C. '62 (CIN) [59] Cincinnati, OH St. Mary Church.
Robitaille, Jean C. *m.afr.* '73 (SP) [O] St. Petersburg, FL Missionaries of Africa.
Robitaille, Joseph S. '57 (ALB) [4] Cohoes, NY St. Joseph Church.
Robitaille, Marcel '64 (PRT) [I] Waterville, ME Mt. St. Joseph Priest Retirement Home.
Robitaille, Marcell L. '64 (PRT) Sabbatical.
Robitaille, Raymond '45 (LAF) [G] New Iberia, LA Consolata Home.
Robitaille, Raymond '47 (LAF) Retired.
Robl, Eugene J. '50 (JC) Retired.
Robles, Antonio '61 (CGS) [C] Aibonito, PR Casa Salesiana de Retiros.
Robles, Sergio *c.r.* '99 (PBL) San Luis, CO Sangre de Cristo Church.
Robles, Victor G. '86 (AUS) Bryan, TX Santa Teresa's Church.
Robles, Vidal '98 (BEA) [7] Port Arthur, TX St. Joseph Church; Beaumont, TX Federal Correctional Complex-Penitentiary.
Robles-Sanchez, Jose A. '95 (ALX) Bordelonville, LA St. Peter Church; Rexmere, LA St. Michael Church.
Robling, Landelin A. *o.s.b.* '52 (SCL) [I] Collegeville, MN St. John's Abbey, of the Order of St. Benedict.
Robling, Landelin A. *o.s.b.* '52 (STP) Hastings, MN St. Elizabeth Ann Seton Church.
Robotnik, Lawrence R. '57 (COV) Bellevue, KY Sacred Heart Church.
Robu, Emil *o.f.m.* '98 (LA) Hermosa Beach, CA Our Lady of Guadalupe Church.
Roby, Albin '87 (NY) [200] Staten Island, NY St. Charles Church.
Roby, Brian '96 (OWN) [1] Owensboro, KY St. Stephen Church; [B] Owensboro, KY Owensboro Catholic High School.
Roca, Albert L. '77 (MET) Port Murray, NJ St. Theodore Church.
Roca, Casimiro *s.f.* '43 (SFE) Chimayo, NM Holy Family Church.
Rocca, Gregory *o.p.* '77 (OAK) [A] Berkeley, CA Dominican School of Philosophy and Theology; [A] Berkeley, CA Dominican School of Philosophy and Theology; [N] Oakland, CA Dominican Order, Siena House.
Rocca, Peter *c.s.c.* '94 (FTW) [B] Notre Dame, IN University of Notre Dame Du Lac.
Rocca, Peter D. *c.s.c.* '74 (FTW) [A] Notre Dame, IN Moreau Seminary; [A] Notre Dame, IN Moreau Seminary.
Rocchi, Frank J. '82 (NEW) Maplewood, NJ Immaculate Heart of Mary Church.
Rocco, Daniel '90 (CAM) Haddonfield, NJ Christ the King Church.
Rocco, Msgr. Remigio G. '66 (PAT) Haskell, NJ St. Francis of Assisi Church.
Roccosalvo, Joseph '71 (NY) [DD] New York, NY West Side Jesuit Community.
Rocha, Ivo D. '66 (STO) Tracy, CA St. Bernard's Church.
Rocha, Manuel '30 (SPR) Retired.
Rocha, Michael '88 (LA) Rancho Palos Verdes, CA St. John Fisher Church.
Rocha, Ruben *o.a.r.* '98 (LA) Montebello, CA St. Benedict Church.
Rocha, Victor J. '53 (PIT) Retired.
Roche, David '58 (PEO) [J] Pontiac, IL Saint James Hospital.
Roche, David V. '42 (BUF) Retired; [O] Buffalo, NY Sheehan Residence for Priests.
Roche, Edward C. *s.o.l.t.* '97 (CC) Robstown, TX St. Anthony Church; [H] Robstown, TX Society of Our Lady of the Most Holy Trinity.
Roche, Evan *o.f.m.* (PAT) [M] Ringwood, NJ Holy Name Friary, Inc.
Roche, Evan *o.f.m.* '44 (ALB) [B] Loudonville, NY Siena College.
Roche, John *ss.cc.* '74 (LA) San Dimas, CA Holy Name of Mary Church.
Roche, John *s.d.b.* '86 (MRY) Watsonville, CA Our Lady Help of Christians Church.
Roche, John S. *s.s.c.* '59 (BO) [W] Quincy, MA St. Columban's Foreign Mission Society.
Roche, Joseph L. *s.j.* '58 (FgM) Provinces.
Roche, Msgr. M. Edward '36 (CHI) Chicago Ridge, IL Our Lady of the Ridge Church; Retired.
Roche, Matthew F. *s.j.* '81 (RVC) Oceanside, NY St. Anthony Church.
Roche, Randall H. *s.j.* '68 (HON) [7] Honolulu, HI Newman Center-Holy Spirit Church; [G] Honolulu, HI Jesuit Fathers House.
Roche, Robert *o.s.b.* '62 (ALT) Patton, PA Our Lady of Perpetual Help Church; Patton, PA Queen of Peace Church.
Roche, Ron '61 (PBL) Retired.
Roche, Stanley *o.s.b.* '47 (SCL) [I] Collegeville, MN St. John's Abbey, of the Order of St. Benedict.
Roche, Msgr. William H. '50 (BO) [1] Boston, MA Cathedral of the Holy Cross; Senior Priests.
Roche, Msgr. William M. '55 (ROC) Retired.
Roche, Msgr. William M. '55 (SFR) Redwood City, CA Our Lady of Mount Carmel Church.
Rocheford, Dennis J. '77 (WOR) Clinton, MA St. John the Evangelist Church.
Rochel, Anthony J. *s.j.* '51 (STL) [P] St. Louis, MO Jesuit Community Corporation at St. Louis University - Jesuit Hall.
Rocheleau, Raymond '52 (BR) Retired.
Rochford, Eugene *s.v.d.* '74 (TR) Neptune, NJ Our Lady of Providence Church.
Rochford, John J. '47 (CHI) Country Club Hills, IL St. Emeric Church; Retired.
Rochford, Jude *o.f.m.conv.* '55 (FgM) Conventual Franciscan Foreign Missions.
Rochford, Thomas M. *s.j.* '76 (FgM) Provinces.
Rochon, Bernard M. *s.m.* '58 (SAT) [67] San Antonio, TX St. Timothy's Church.
Rochon, Bernard M. *s.m.* '58 (STL) [P] St. Louis, MO Provincialate of the Society of Mary, Province of St. Louis.
Rochon, Robert A. '74 (FR) [F] Fall River, MA Saint Anne's Hospital.
Rochon, Robert A. '74 (PRO) [1] Central Falls, RI The Holy Spirit Catholic Community Church; On Duty Outside the Diocese.
Rock, John J. '54 (NEW) Retired.
Rock, John J. *s.j.* '87 (SPK) [C] Spokane, WA Gonzaga University.
Rock, Joseph A. '72 (ALN) [H] Bethlehem, PA Holy Family Manor; [J] Bethlehem, PA Holy Family Villa.
Rock, Larry G. '00 (BAL) [3] Baltimore, MD St. Agnes Church.
Rock, Martin *s.j.* '59 (SLC) [4] Ogden, UT St. Mary's Church.
Rock, Michael *o.de.m.* '86 (BUF) [O] LeRoy, NY Order of the BVM of Mercy/Mercedarian Friars.
Rock, Michael R. *o.de.m.* '86 (BUF) Le Roy, NY St. Peter Church; Lime Rock, NY St. Anthony Church.
Rock, Richard J. *c.m.* (PH) [46] Philadelphia, PA St. Francis of Assisi Church.
Rock, Msgr. Russell L. '62 (CAM) Haddon Township, NJ St. Vincent Pallotti Church; [A] Haddonfield, NJ Paul VI High School.
Rock, Stephen B. '74 (BO) Military & VA Chaplains.
Rock, William J. *o.p.* '58 (Y) [13] Youngstown, OH St. Dominic's Church.
Rockenstein, James *o.f.m.* '57 (SAC) Lincoln, CA St. Joseph Church.
Rocker, Stephen R. '79 (OG) Ogdensburg, NY Ogdensburg Correctional Facility; [A] Ogdensburg, NY Wadhams Hall.
Rockers, Alfred '62 (KCK) Leawood, KS Church of the Nativity.
Rocky, Ronald *o.f.m.conv.* '84 (SB) [3] Riverside, CA Queen of Angels Church.
Rodak, Joseph *c.pp.s.* '62 (CIN) [M] Dayton, OH Provincial Office of the Cincinnati Province of the Society of the Precious Blood.
Rodakowski, Louis '42 (P) Retired.
Rodas, Mauro '65 (IND) Retired.
Rodda, Regis *o.f.m.conv.* '59 (SY) [2] Syracuse, NY Assumption B.V.M. Church.
Roddy, James *s.s.c.* '41 (PRO) [P] Bristol, RI St. Columban's Retirement House.
Rodell, Jeremiah J. '47 (CHI) Retired.
Roden, Raymond '81 (BRK) [84] Brooklyn, NY St. Mary, Star of the Sea Church.
Roden-Lucero, Edward G. '82 (ELP) [3] El Paso, TX Blessed Juan Diego Church.
Rodenfels, Jerome P. '74 (COL) Leave of Absence.
Rodenspiel, James '64 (B) Coeur D'Alene, ID St. Thomas Church.
Roder, Terry '88 (SC) Struble, IA St. Joseph's Church.
Roderhero, Jeffery A.G. '84 (STF) Syracuse, NY St. John the Baptist Church.
Rodgers, Arthur E. '65 (PH) Bala Cynwyd, PA St. Matthias Church.
Rodgers, Dermot '91 (FR) [19] Fall River, MA St. Michael's Church.
Rodgers, Francis M. '41 (PIT) Retired; [O] Pittsburgh, PA St. John Vianney Manor.
Rodgers, Kenneth '43 (GB) Retired.
Rodgers, Kieran J. *o.s.b.* '46 (GBG) [H] Latrobe, PA Saint Vincent Archabbey.
Rodgers, Philip F. '81 (ALN) Lehighton, PA SS. Peter and Paul Church.
Rodgers, Thomas M. '44 (PIT) Retired.
Rodgers, Msgr. William J. '49 (BRK) Retired; [S] Queens Village, NY Queen of Peace Residence.
Rodi, Msgr. Thomas J. '78 (NO) On Archdiocesan Assignment.
Rodia, James C. *o.praem.* '72 (PH) [49] Philadelphia, PA St. Gabriel Church; [AA] Philadelphia, PA St. Norbert Priory; [AA] Paoli, PA Daylesford Abbey.
Rodighiero, Dominic *c.s.* '61 (NY) [DD] Staten Island, NY Scalabrinian Missionaries.
Rodighiero, Dominic *c.s.* '61 (WDC) [L] Mitchellville, MD Villa Rosa Nursing Home, Inc.
Rodino, Salvatore A. '80 (ALB) Speigletown, NY St. Bonaventure Church.
Rodis, James '60 (STL) [19] St. Louis, MO St. Agatha Church.
Rodis, Rodney '86 (RIC) Buckner, VA Immaculate Conception Church; Mineral, VA St. Jude Church.
Rodman, Hugh B. *s.j.* '42 (DET) [P] Clarkston, MI Colombiere Center.
Rodney, John *s.v.d.* '60 (WDC) [5] Washington, DC St. Anthony Church; [M] Washington, DC Divine Word College.
Rodney, Joseph C., Jr. *s.s.j.* '68 (NO) Reserve, LA Our Lady of Grace Church.
Rodo, Anthony C. '55 (PH) Retired.
Rodoni, Rick *s.j.* '91 (SJ) [2] Santa Clara, CA St. Clare Church.
Rodrieguez, Tommy '69 (TOL) Sandusky, OH Soldiers and Sailors Home.
Rodrigalvarez, Jose Antonio *o.a.r.* '63 (NEW) [1] Union City, NJ Holy Family Church.
Rodrigo, Charles '86 (NOR) New London, CT St. Joseph Church.
Rodrigo, Marcelo Blazquez '60 (NY) State, NY Woodbourne Correctional Facility.
Rodrigo, Salvador *o.carm.* '62 (SJN) [59] San Juan, PR Santa Teresita Del Nino Jesus Church.
Rodrigo, Stephen '75 (KAL) Battle Creek, MI St. Joseph Church.
Rodrigo, Titus *o.s.b.* '85 (FRS) [4] Bakersfield, CA St. Francis Church.
Rodrigues, Amancio '66 (P) [26] Portland, OR Our Lady of Sorrows Church.
Rodrigues, Anthony '54 (RIC) Big Stone Gap, VA Sacred Heart Church; Pennington Gap, VA Church of the Holy Spirit.
Rodrigues, Carlos '95 (BGP) [5] Stamford, CT St. Clement Church; [K] Stamford, CT St. Camillus Health Center.
Rodrigues, Elias (LA) [8] Los Angeles, CA Christ the King Church.
Rodrigues, Ignatius '66 (SB) Loma Linda, CA St. Joseph the Worker Church.
Rodrigues, Januarius E. '59 (SAC) [9] Sacramento, CA St. Anne Church.
Rodrigues, Joseph *s.d.s.* '93 (MIL) [P] Milwaukee, WI Salvatorian Provincial Residence.
Rodrigues, Sabbas (RVC) Hampton Bays, NY St. Rosalie's Church.
Rodrigues, William M. '00 (FR) Hyannis, MA St. Francis Xavier's Church.
Rodriguez, Alberto (GAL) [77] Houston, TX St. Thomas More Church.
Rodriguez, Alberto *o.p.* '71 (FgM) Dominican - Order of Preachers Foreign Missions.
Rodriguez, Alberto *o.p.* '71 (NO) [25] New Orleans, LA St. Anthony of Padua Church; [P] New Orleans, LA Dominican Friars, Southern Dominican Province of St. Martin de Porres; [P] New Orleans, LA Dominican Friars, Southern Dominican Province of St. Martin de Porres; [S] Metairie, LA Southern Dominican Foundation.
Rodriguez, Alberto *o.ss.t.* '87 (VIC) [4] Victoria, TX Our Lady of Sorrows Church.
Rodriguez, Aloysius M. '66 (BR) Military Chaplains.
Rodriguez, Ambiorix '97 (NY) [95] New York, NY Our Lady Queen of Martyrs Church.
Rodriguez, Anthony *l.c.* '83 (HRT) [B] Cheshire, CT Novitiate of the Legion of Christ.
Rodriguez, Antonio *o.carm.* (ARE) Ciales, PR Holy Rosary Church.
Rodriguez, Antonio '93 (PAT) [5] Passaic, NJ Holy Trinity Church.
Rodriguez, Antonio L. '49 (BUF) [33] Buffalo, NY Immaculate Conception Church.
Rodriguez, Armando J. '55 (GAL) [60] Houston, TX Our Lady of St. John Church.
Rodriguez, Arturo (LAR) Zapata, TX Our Lady of Lourdes Church.
Rodriguez, Arturo '84 (LAR) Zapata, TX Our Lady of Lourdes Church.
Rodriguez, Arturo Perez '72 (CHI) [63] Chicago, IL St. Francis de Sales Church.
Rodriguez, Astor L. '93 (BRK) [116] Brooklyn, NY St. Peter-St. Paul-Our Lady of Pilar Church.
Rodriguez, Ben '91 (PEO) [2] Champaign, IL St. John's Catholic Chapel Church; [P] Champaign, IL St.

John's Catholic Student Chapel and Newman Foundation, University of Illinois.
Rodriguez, Benigno A. '66 (LA) [36] Los Angeles, CA Presentation of the Mary Church.
Rodriguez, Bernardo C. '80 (BGP) [17] Bridgeport, CT St. Patrick Church; Bridgeport, CT Bridgeport Hospital.
Rodriguez, Carlos *o.c.s.o.* '70 (L) [L] Trappist, KY Abbey of Our Lady of Gethsemani, of the Order of Cistercians of the Strict Observance.
Rodriguez, D. Andres G. '36 (RIC) Retired.
Rodriguez, David *o.f.m.* '89 (CHI) [D] Chicago, IL Hales Franciscan High School, Inc.
Rodriguez, Delfin '86 (ARE) [3] Arecibo, PR Nuestra Senora del Carmen Church.
Rodriguez, Domingo *s.t.* '67 (WDC) [M] Adelphi, MD Our Lady Missionary Cenacle.
Rodriguez, Edmundo *s.j.* '66 (SFE) [6] Albuquerque, NM Immaculate Conception Church.
Rodriguez, Eduardo *o.c.s.o.* '69 (ATL) [J] Conyers, GA The Monastery of the Holy Spirit.
Rodriguez, Edwin '95 (ALX) [1] Alexandria, LA St. Francis Xavier Church.
Rodriguez, Msgr. Efrain '74 (SJN) [31] San Juan, PR Nuestra Senora de Lourdes Church.
Rodriguez, Epifanio *o.p.* '54 (CC) Benavides, TX St. Rose of Lima Church; [H] San Diego, TX Vicariate of Holy Rosary.
Rodriguez, Florencio *t.o.r.* '80 (SAT) [60] San Antonio, TX St. Paul Church.
Rodriguez, Francis *o.c.s.o.* '55 (WOR) [N] Spencer, MA St. Joseph's Abbey.
Rodriguez, Gerardo Ibarra *o.s.b.* '97 (MGZ) [6] Mayaquez, PR Sacred Heart Church.
Rodriguez, German *s.v.d.* '77 (WDC) [M] Washington, DC Divine Word College.
Rodriguez, Gilbert '74 (SAN) [2] Odessa, TX St. Anthony Church; [4] Odessa, TX St. Joseph Church.
Rodriguez, Guillermo '56 (SFR) Retired.
Rodriguez, Guillermo '69 (LA) [11] Long Beach, CA St. Matthew Church.
Rodriguez, Guillermo '75 (SAC) Truckee, CA Assumption of the Blessed Virgin Mary Church.
Rodriguez, Henry '86 (SD) [30] San Diego, CA St. Jude Church.
Rodriguez, J. Rigoberto '89 (LA) [94] Los Angeles, CA St. Thomas the Apostle Church.
Rodriguez, Jesus *s.j.* '95 (MOB) [A] Mobile, AL Spring Hill College.
Rodriguez, Jesus A. '93 (ARE) [4] Manati, PR Nuestra Senora del Mar Church.
Rodriguez, Joaquin '89 (MIA) Miami Springs, FL Blessed Trinity Church.
Rodriguez, John '77 (FRS) Los Banos, CA St. Joseph Church.
Rodriguez, John C. (SFE) [5] Santa Fe, NM St. John the Baptist Church.
Rodriguez, Msgr. John F. '59 (SFR) [2] Menlo Park, CA St. Denis Church.
Rodriguez, Jorge '86 (PAT) [10] Paterson, NJ St. Mary's Church.
Rodriguez, Jorge H. (DEN) [4] Aurora, CO St. Therese Church.
Rodriguez, Msgr. Jose A. '64 (SFR) [12] San Francisco, CA St. Charles Borromeo Church.
Rodriguez, Jose A. '80 (ARE) [1] Vega-Baja, PR Holy Rosary Church.
Rodriguez, Jose Andres '95 (WOR) [27] Worcester, MA St. Peter Church.
Rodriguez, Jose Diego '81 (PCE) Villalba, PR Our Lady of Mt. Carmel Church; [B] Ponce, PR The Pontifical Catholic University of Puerto Rico.
Rodriguez, Jose H. '75 (GLP) Retired.
Rodriguez, Jose Trinidad '92 (LA) [16] Los Angeles, CA Immaculate Conception Church.
Rodriguez, Juan '79 (PCE) [B] Ponce, PR The Pontifical Catholic University of Puerto Rico.
Rodriguez, Lawrence '52 (LA) Retired.
Rodriguez, Leonardo J. '90 (SJN) [C] Rio Piedras, PR Seminario Mayor Regional San Juan Bautista.
Rodriguez, Luis *s.j.* '65 (OM) [K] Omaha, NE Jesuit Community at Creighton University.
Rodriguez, Luis R. '93 (HBG) Chambersburg, PA Corpus Christi Church.
Rodriguez, Manuel *c.ss.r.* '71 (CGS) Fajardo, PR Santiago Apostol Church.
Rodriguez, Martin S. *o.r.c.* '92 (SB) Mecca, CA Our Lady of Guadalupe Church; [1] Riverside, CA Our Lady of Guadalupe Church; [E] Riverside, CA Operarios Del Reino De Cristo, O.R.C.
Rodriguez, Mathias '80 (TYL) Longview, TX St. Anthony Church.
Rodriguez, Michael '96 (ELP) [14] El Paso, TX Our Lady of Assumption Church.
Rodriguez, Michael A. '90 (SAN) Eden, TX St. Charles Church.
Rodriguez, Nestor '93 (PMB) [5] West Palm Beach, FL St. Juliana Church.
Rodriguez, P. Ruben *o.carm.* '89 (SJN) [5] San Juan, PR Asuncion de La Virgen Church.
Rodriguez, Msgr. Pablo M. '61 (RVC) Hempstead, NY Our Lady of Loretto Church.
Rodriguez, Peter *c.m.f.* '57 (CHI) [163] Chicago, IL St. Paul Church.
Rodriguez, Rafael '75 (CGS) Yabucoa, PR Santos Angeles Cutodios Church.
Rodriguez, Ray '94 (CHY) Lander, WY Holy Rosary Church.
Rodriguez, Raymond '97 (NEW) Lyndhurst, NJ Sacred Heart Church.
Rodriguez, Reyes G. '67 (SLC) [7] Salt Lake City, UT St. Ann Church; Salt Lake City, UT Veterans Administration Hospital; Salt Lake City, UT Salt Lake County Jail.
Rodriguez, Ricardo *o.f.m.* '82 (ELP) [15] El Paso, TX Our Lady of Guadalupe Church.
Rodriguez, Robert '53 (MIL) Retired.
Rodriguez, Roberto *m.m.* '95 (LA) [Q] Los Angeles, CA Maryknoll Fathers and Brothers.
Rodriguez, Robin E. *c.m.* '73 (BRK) [116] Brooklyn, NY St. Peter-St. Paul-Our Lady of Pilar Church.
Rodriguez, Santos (SFR) [1] South San Francisco, CA All Souls Church.
Rodriguez, Silvestre *o.f.m.* '48 (LAR) Hebbronville, TX Our Lady of Guadalupe Church.
Rodriguez, Victor *c.m.* '69 (BRK) [X] Brooklyn, NY Centro Evangelizacion San Vicente de Paul.
Rodriguez Cotton, Franklin '64 (CGS) Maunabo, PR San Isidor Labrador Church.
Rodriguez-leon, Mario (SJN) [A] Bayamon, PR Bayamon Central University.
Rodriguez-Ochoa, Leonardo '91 (SJN) [3] Trujillo Alto, PR Santa Cruz Church.
Rodriquez, Felix '97 (YAK) Sunnyside, WA St. Joseph's Church.
Rodriquez, Josi Fuentes '45 (SJN) Retired.
Rodriquez, Reyes G. (SLC) Layton, UT St. Rose of Lima Church.
Roebert, Michael '66 (LA) [9] Long Beach, CA St. Lucy Church.
Roebuck, John H. '76 (PH) [2] Drexel Hill, PA St. Bernadette Church.
Roedel, Richard P. '59 (STP) Heidelberg, MN St. Scholastica Church; Lexington, MN St. Joseph Church.
Roedel, Robert H. '56 (PH) Feasterville, PA Assumption B.V.M. Church; Absent on Sick Leave.
Roedig, Robert L. '53 (STL) Richmond Heights, MO Immacolata Church.
Roehrich, David '84 (SFS) Colman, SD St. Peter Church; Flandreau, SD SS. Simon and Jude Church.
Roehrig, Matthew *s.s.p.* '84 (BUF) [O] Derby, NY Society of St. Paul.
Roehrig, Matthew *s.s.p.* '84 (Y) [A] Canfield, OH Society of St. Paul.
Roelke, Joseph Paul *m.s.f.* '81 (STL) [67] St. Louis, MO St. Wenceslaus Church.
Roeltgen, Msgr. Kenneth W. '79 (WDC) [40] Washington, DC St. Stephen Martyr Church.
Roemer, Richard *c.f.r.* (NY) [DD] New York, NY St. Joseph's Friary.
Roensch, Frederick J. '55 (MIL) Retired.
Roensch, Msgr. Roger '57 (WDC) On Duty Outside the Archdiocese.
Roesch, David H. '67 (ALT) Bellwood, PA St. Joseph's Church.
Roesch, Joseph *m.i.c.* '92 (WDC) [B] Washington, DC Marian Fathers Scholasticate.
Roesch, Karl *o.s.b.* '60 (CHR) Hartsville, SC St. Mary the Virgin Mother Church; [H] Hartsville, SC Coker College.
Roesch, Karl J. *o.s.b.* '60 (PAT) [M] Morristown, NJ St. Mary's Abbey.
Roeten, Msgr. Winus '48 (NO) Retired.
Roetzel, Robert E. *c.s.c.* '87 (FTW) [J] South Bend, IN Congregation of Holy Cross, Indiana Province, Provincial House.
Roetzer, James M. '98 (MAR) [1] Marquette, MI St. Peter Church.
Roetzer, Russell G. '64 (MIL) [13] Racine, WI St. Richard of Chichester Church.
Rofrano, Peter J. *s.a.c.* '39 (NY) [91] New York, NY Our Lady of Mt. Carmel Church; [DD] New York, NY Pallottine Fathers.
Rog, Francis *c.r.* '55 (CHI) [86] Chicago, IL St. Hyacinth Church.
Rog, Theodore C. '64 (BUF) [4] Cheektowaga, NY St. Josaphat Church.
Rogaczewski, Daniel '00 (ATL) Duluth, GA St. Benedict Church.
Rogala, Gerard E. '66 (CHI) [198] Chicago, IL St. Thecla Church.
Rogalla, William G. '96 (LAF) Cow Island, LA St. Anne Church.
Rogan, Brian (SB) Retired.
Rogawski, Ralph *o.p.* '59 (AUS) [H] Austin, TX Dominican Friars of Austin.
Roger, Richard G. '64 (WOR) [7] Worcester, MA Notre Dame des Canadiens - St. Joseph Church.
Rogers, Christopher B. '00 (PH) Exton, PA SS. Philip and James Church.
Rogers, Daniel J. '53 (DUB) Retired.
Rogers, Foster P. '66 (ROC) [52] Rochester, NY St. Pius Tenth Church.
Rogers, Francis J. '81 (WIL) Elsmere, DE Corpus Christi Church; Wilmington, DE Delaware Air National Guard.
Rogers, Francis P. '46 (PH) Retired.
Rogers, Gary P. '72 (BRK) [51] Brooklyn, NY St. Gregory the Great Church.
Rogers, Herbert W. *s.j.* '44 (NY) [DD] New York, NY Jesuit Community at Fordham University.
Rogers, James '39 (EVN) Retired.
Rogers, James M. '51 (BO) Senior Priests.
Rogers, Jerry '76 (CR) Detroit Lakes, MN Holy Rosary Church.
Rogers, Joel C. *c.p.m.* '00 (L) Glasgow, KY St. Helen Church.
Rogers, John '84 (RVC) Absent on Leave.
Rogers, Joseph '54 (DAV) Retired; [L] Davenport, IA Kahl Home for the Aged and Infirm.
Rogers, Nicholas P. '55 (MAN) [14] Manchester, NH St. Patrick Church.
Rogers, Patrick W. '82 (COL) [38] Columbus, OH St. Philip The Apostle Church.
Rogers, Paul '77 (RVC) Absent on Leave.
Rogers, Peter S. *s.j.* '74 (NO) [C] New Orleans, LA Loyola University New Orleans.
Rogers, Philip E. '80 (Y) Struthers, OH St. Nicholas Church.
Rogers, Robert C. '92 (HT) Montegut, LA Sacred Heart Church; Pointe-Aux-Chenes, LA St. Charles Borromeo Church.
Rogers, Stephen G. '95 (TOL) [B] Toledo, OH Central Catholic High School.
Rogers, Vincent '93 (KC) [4] St. Joseph, MO St. James Church.
Rogerson, Daniel '77 (SEA) On Duty Outside the Archdiocese.
Rogerson, Dave '82 (P) [A] St. Benedict, OR Mount Angel Seminary.
Rogge, Louis *o.carm.* '54 (JOL) [J] Joliet, IL St. Elias Carmelites.
Rogge, Norman J. *s.j.* '56 (LAF) Grand Coteau, LA St. Charles Borromeo Church; [J] Grand Coteau, LA Jesuit Spirituality Center (St. Charles College).
Rogina, Walter '85 (SR) Occidental, CA St. Philip Church.
Rogliano, Joseph S. '85 (BUF) [1] Lockport, NY St. Anthony Church; [3] Lockport, NY St. Joseph Church.
Rogmans, Gerard *c.i.c.m.* '55 (FgM) Missionhurst Foreign Missions.
Rogusz, Joseph A. *c.s.c.* '46 (FTW) [J] South Bend, IN Congregation of Holy Cross, Indiana Province, Provincial House.
Roh, Raymond V. *o.s.b.* '59 (MRY) [F] San Luis Obispo, CA Monastery of the Risen Christ.
Roh, Robert A. '65 (LIN) Falls City, NE SS. Peter and Paul Church; [C] Falls City, NE Sacred Heart School; [M] Falls City, NE Sacred Heart High School Endowment Fund.
Rohan, John P. '72 (HRT) South Windsor, CT St. Francis of Assisi Church.
Rohen, Patrick J. '96 (TOL) Perrysburg, OH St. Rose Church.
Rohleder, Earl '63 (EVN) New Harmony, IN Holy Angels Church; Special Assignment.
Rohling, Msgr. George W. '39 (NSH) [8] Nashville, TN St. Mary Villa Parish Community Church; [L] Nashville, TN Ladies of Charity Welfare Agency, Inc.
Rohling, Paul *v.c.* '75 (BIR) [6] Birmingham, AL St. Francis Xavier Church; [I] Birmingham, AL Agape Institute of St. Teresa of Jesus.
Rohlinger, Joseph A. *o.praem* '43 (GB) [I] De Pere, WI St. Norbert Abbey.
Rohloff, Ivan *o.f.m.conv.* (LSC) Mesilla Park, NM Shrine and Parish of Our Lady of Guadalupe Church.
Rohmiller, Christian A. '79 (CIN) [Q] Fairborn, OH Catholic Campus Ministry.
Rohr, Jerome M. '94 (DEN) Littleton, CO Light of the World Church.
Rohr, John J. *s.j.* '60 (NEW) [C] Jersey City, NJ St. Peter's Preparatory School.
Rohr, Richard *o.f.m.* '70 (SFE) [M] Albuquerque, NM Center for Action and Contemplation.
Rohrer, Jerome (MIL) [N] Wauwatosa, WI St. Camillus Health Center, Inc.
Rohrer, Jerome E. *s.j.* '54 (MIL) [P] Wauwatosa, WI Jesuit Community at St. Camillus.
Rohrer, Richard '94 (PSC) Cary, NC SS. Cyril & Methodius Byzantine Catholic Church.
Rohrkemper, Charles B. '43 (CIN) Troy, OH St. Patrick Church; Retired.
Roia, Martino *s.x.* '82 (FgM) Xaverian Foreign Missions.
Roia, Martino *s.x.* '82 (PAT) [M] Wayne, NJ Xaverian Missionary Fathers.
Roide, Russell J. *s.j.* '70 (SFR) [2] San Francisco, CA St. Agnes Church.
Roig, Ricardo A. '97 (SJN) [12] Carolina, PR San Juan de Dios Church.
Roig, Vicente Perez '58 (MGZ) Rosario, PR Rosary Church.

Rojas, Alberto '97 (CHI) [94] Chicago, IL Saint Ita Church.
Rojas, Jaime '79 (P) Woodburn, OR St. Luke Church.
Rojas, Jaime Vazquez '83 (SJN) [20] Bayamon, PR Nuestra Senora del Rosario Church.
Rojas, Loreto Businos, Jr. '00 (SAC) Yuba City, CA St. Isidore Church.
Rojas, Manuel I. '64 (NY) [203] Staten Island, NY St. Clement Church; [215] Staten Island, NY St. Michael Church.
Rojas, Melquiades '91 (ARE) [10] Arecibo, PR San Juan Bosco Church.
Rojas, Roberto P. *c.s.b.* '97 (GAL) [Q] Sugar Land, TX Basilian Mission Center.
Rojas, Victor '85 (ARE) [4] Arecibo, PR Santa Ana Church; [A] Arecibo, PR Pontificia Universidad Catholica de Puerto Rico, Recinto de Arecibo.
Rojka, Lubos *s.j.* '96 (BO) [W] Chestnut Hill, MA The Jesuit Community at Boston College.
Rokos, Richard V. '56 (PRT) Bangor, ME St. Joseph's Hospital; [H] Bangor, ME St. Joseph Hospital.
Rokosz, Charles W. '70 (SCR) Duryea, PA Holy Rosary Church.
Rokusek, Robert J. '66 (WDC) [E] Washington, DC Gonzaga College High School.
Rolak, Patrick *o.f.m.conv.* '56 (BAL) [S] Ellicott City, MD Order of Friars Minor Conventual.
Roland, Charles '67 (PT) On Duty Outside the Diocese.
Roland, Charles '67 (SAV) Perry, GA St. Patrick Church.
Roland, Glynn (Bud) '99 (AUS) [1] Austin, TX St. Mary's Church.
Roldan, Basilio '59 (SJN) [54] San Juan, PR Sagrado Corazon de Jesus Church.
Roldan, Juan '56 (SJN) On Duty Outside the Archdiocese.
Rolek, John A. '61 (CHI) Berwyn, IL St. Leonard Church.
Roleke, H. James *s.j.* '62 (BUF) [50] Buffalo, NY St. Michael Church.
Rolewicz, Richard S. *m.m.* '65 (FgM) Maryknoll Foreign Missions.
Rolf, Msgr. John J. '57 (LEX) Retired.
Rolfes, Robert E. '77 (SCL) St. Augusta, MN St. Mary Help of Christians Church.
Rolfs, Richard W. *s.j.* '61 (LA) [C] Los Angeles, CA Loyola Marymount University.
Roll, Bertin *o.f.m.cap.* '42 (PIT) [O] Pittsburgh, PA St. Augustine Friary.
Roll, David H. '70 (SD) Retired.
Roll, Robert J. '77 (CHI) [167] Chicago, IL SS. Peter and Paul Church.
Roll, Ron *o.f.m.conv.* '80 (FgM) Conventual Franciscan Foreign Missions.
Roll, Ronald *o.f.m.conv.* '80 (BAL) [S] Ellicott City, MD Order of Friars Minor Conventual.
Roll, Ronald *o.f.m.conv.* '80 (FgM) Conventual Franciscan Foreign Missions.
Rolland, Daniel J. *o.p.* '93 (TUC) [27] Tucson, AZ St. Thomas More Chapel Church; [I] Tucson, AZ University of Arizona.
Roller, John W. '60 (CHI) [4] Mt. Prospect, IL St. Thomas a Becket Church.
Rolling, Brendan *o.s.b.* '00 (KCK) [H] Atchison, KS St. Benedict's Abbey.
Rollins, Brendan *o.s.b.* '00 (KCK) [A] Atchison, KS Benedictine College.
Rolon, Julio '93 (PCE) Coamo, PR St. Blase Church; [B] Ponce, PR The Pontifical Catholic University of Puerto Rico.
Rolwing, Msgr. Richard C. '53 (SPC) [1] Cape Girardeau, MO Cathedral of St. Mary.
Rom, Gregory A. '75 (CHI) Blue Island, IL St. Isidore Church.
Romage, George '95 (WH) Absent on Leave.
Romagosa, Edward J. *s.j.* '54 (BR) [J] Convent, LA Manresa House of Retreats.
Roman, Carlos '89 (PCE) On Duty Outside the Diocese.
Roman, Charles '70 (HEL) Whitefish, MT St. Charles Church.
Roman, Darrell *s.ch.* (DET) [73] Detroit, MI Sweetest Heart of Mary Church.
Roman, Darrell *s.ch.* '93 (DET) Hamtramck, MI St. Florian Church.
Roman, Julio '73 (LA) Sylmar, CA St. Didacus Church.
Roman, Julio I. '00 (NEW) [3] Jersey City, NJ St. Anne's Church.
Roman, Manuel R. '56 (BAL) [11] Baltimore, MD Ascension Church.
Roman, Paul (ALB) [S] Albany, NY Noonan Community Service Corporation.
Roman, Paul A. '71 (ALB) Oneonta, NY St. Mary Church.
Roman, Paul L. *f.s.s.p.* '99 (CC) [16] Corpus Christi, TX St. Michael the Archangel Latin Mass Community Church.
Roman, Stephen '57 (SEA) Aberdeen, WA St. Mary Church; Aberdeen, WA St. Mary Church; Aberdeen, WA SS. Peter and Paul Church; Hoquiam, WA Our Lady of Good Help Church; Ocean Shores, WA St. Jerome Church.
Roman, Victor '84 (DET) Ecorse, MI St. Francis Xavier Church.
Romanenko, Oleh '95 (LA) [21] Los Angeles, CA Nativity of Blessed Virgin Mary Church.
Romanenko, Oleh '95 (STN) Los Angeles, CA Nativity of B.V.M. Church.
Romani, Joseph '34 (PRT) Retired.
Romano, Blase R. *t.o.r.* '89 (ALT) [3] Windber, PA St. Anthony of Padua Church.
Romano, Charles '79 (RVC) Port Jefferson, NY Infant Jesus Church.
Romano, Eugene L. '57 (PAT) [I] Chester, NJ Hermits of Bethlehem in the Heart of Jesus.
Romano, Harry A. '57 (PH) [2] Coatesville, PA Our Lady of the Rosary Church.
Romano, Joseph '66 (ALB) [5] Albany, NY St. Catherine of Siena Church; Delanson, NY Our Lady of Fatima Church; Coxsackie, NY Greene Correctional Facility.
Romano, Joseph E. '63 (BUR) Pittsford, VT St. Alphonsus Liguori Church.
Romano, Joseph L. '63 (DET) [7] Dearborn Heights, MI St. Sabina Church.
Romano, Joseph R. '66 (ALB) Special Assignment.
Romano, Philip *o.f.m.cap.* (NY) Manhattan, NY Mount Sinai Medical Center.
Romano, Robert J. *m.div.* '77 (BRK) [18] Brooklyn, NY St. Bernadette Church.
Romanoski, Joseph V. '86 (MET) South Amboy, NJ Sacred Heart Church.
Romanowski, Aloysius *o.f.m.conv.* '57 (CHI) [N] Chicago, IL Conventual Franciscans of St. Bonaventure Province.
Romanowski, Jerome C. '64 (CAM) Malaga, NJ St. Mary's Church.
Romanski, Aloysius *o.f.m.conv.* '57 (CHI) [L] Lake Zurich, IL Mt. St. Joseph Home.
Romanski, Edward '75 (CHI) Harvey, IL St. John the Baptist Church.
Romanski, Gregory A. '77 (AUS) [21] Austin, TX St. Theresa Church.
Romansky, Joseph A. '75 (CLV) [M] Cleveland, OH St. Augustine Manor.
Romeo, Peter '72 (LAV) Henderson, NV St. Peter the Apostle Church.
Romeo, Robert A. '87 (RVC) Merrick, NY Cure of Ars Church.
Romero, Alejandro *c.s.b.* '00 (GAL) [Q] Sugar Land, TX Basilian Mission Center.
Romero, David H. *s.j.* '91 (FgM) Provinces.
Romero, David H. *s.j.* '91 (NO) [P] New Orleans, LA Jesuit Provincial Office.
Romero, Domingo *o.f.m.cap.* '00 (FWT) [5] Fort Worth, TX Immaculate Heart of Mary Church.
Romero, Donald '91 (DEN) Akron, CO St. Joseph Church.
Romero, Fortunato (NY) [191] Bronx, NY St. Thomas Aquinas Church.
Romero, J. Robert '75 (LAF) Ville Platte, LA Sacred Heart of Jesus Church; Ville Platte, LA St. Joseph Church.
Romero, Joseph J. '69 (BEA) [4] Port Arthur, TX St. Catherine of Siena Church.
Romero, Juan '64 (LA) Santa Monica, CA St. Clement Church.
Romero, Marcelino *c.m.f.* '59 (SJN) [2] Bayamon, PR San Antonio Maria Claret Church; [A] Bayamon, PR Bayamon Central University.
Romero, Mario '90 (LAF) Cankton, LA St. John Berchmans Church.
Romero, William '67 (VEN) Retired.
Romero Z., Jose *o.s.a.* '77 (LAR) [6] Laredo, TX Holy Redeemer Church.
Romero-Rios, Adolfo '88 (NY) [184] Bronx, NY St. Pius V Church.
Romfh, Paul *o.s.b.* '63 (SP) [O] St. Leo, FL St. Leo Abbey.
Romito, Donald '74 (ORG) Garden Grove, CA St. Columban Church.
Romo, Eugenio *m.g.* '87 (LA) [86] Los Angeles, CA St. Paul Church.
Romo, Sergio '93 (CHI) [102] Chicago, IL St. John Berchmans Church.
Rompa, John '51 (SPK) Retired.
Romza, Msgr. Victor G. '54 (PBR) Campbell, OH St. Michael Church.
Ronaghan, John J. '80 (BO) Melrose, MA St. Mary of the Annunciation Church.
Ronald, Robert *s.j.* '65 (FgM) Provinces.
Ronald, Msgr. Roy K. '60 (BUF) Retired.
Ronan, Charles E. *s.j.* '45 (CHI) [C] Chicago, IL Jesuit Community at Loyola University of Chicago.
Ronan, Eugene *m.s.f.* (STL) [O] St. Louis, MO Little Sisters of the Poor, Home for the Aged.
Ronan, Henry T. '55 (BO) Senior Priests.
Ronan, Msgr. Hugh F. '61 (TR) [6] Trenton, NJ Incarnation Church.
Ronan, James J. '82 (BO) [5] Lawrence, MA Holy Rosary Church.
Roncase, Robert A. '82 (PH) Penndel, PA Our Lady of Grace Church.
Ronchi, Vincenzo *c.s.* (NEW) [12] Newark, NJ St. Columba's Church.
Ronchi, Vincenzo *c.s.* '91 (BRK) [V] Jamaica, NY Saint Charles House of Studies.
Ronchi, Vincenzo *c.s.* '91 (NY) [HH] New York, NY Scalabrini Pastoral Center.
Rondeau, John S. *c.s.sp.* '38 (PIT) [Q] Bethel Park, PA Holy Ghost Animation Center.
Rondeau, Julian *s.m.* '45 (BO) [W] Boston, MA Marist Fathers Lourdes Residence; [BB] Boston, MA Chapel of Our Lady of Lourdes.
Rondeau, Lawrence J. '58 (BO) [5] Salem, MA St. Joseph Church.
Roney, David A. '45 (NU) Retired.
Roney, George '78 (LUB) Woodrow, TX San Ramon Church.
Ronik, Msgr. Michael E. '57 (Y) [2] Youngstown, OH Holy Name Church.
Ronquest, Msgr. John T. '45 (STL) Concord Village, MO St. Simon the Apostle Church; Retired.
Roock, John D. '59 (SY) Endwell, NY Our Lady of Angels Church.
Roodbeen, Henry W. '75 (DET) [2] Livonia, MI St. Colette Church.
Roof, Francis (IND) Terre Haute, IN U.S. Penitentiary.
Roof, Frank '72 (OWN) On Duty Outside the Diocese.
Rook, Paul '47 (TUC) Retired.
Rookey, Peter M. *o.s.m.* '41 (CHI) [N] Chicago, IL Order of Friar Servants of Mary (Servites) United States of America Province, Inc.
Rooks, Charles W. '52 (COV) Retired; [N] Covington, KY St. Joseph Heights Provincialate and Novitiate of the Sisters of Notre Dame.
Rooney, Aidan R. *c.m.* '84 (PH) [156] Philadelphia, PA St. Vincent de Paul Church.
Rooney, Bernard *c.ss.r.* '59 (GR) [3] Grand Rapids, MI St. Alphonsus Church.
Rooney, Bill *o.f.m.* '81 (MEM) [17] Memphis, TN St. Mary's Church.
Rooney, Don '79 (CLV) [1] Parma, OH St. Anthony of Padua Church.
Rooney, Donald J. '94 (ARL) Fairfax, VA St. Leo's Church.
Rooney, Edward '62 (STA) Middleburg, FL St. Luke's Church.
Rooney, Eugene M. *s.j.* '57 (BAL) [S] Baltimore, MD Jesuit Fathers and Brothers Maryland Provincial Curia.
Rooney, Eugene M. *s.j.* '57 (FgM) Provinces.
Rooney, Francis V. *s.j.* '60 (NY) [DD] New York, NY Murray-Weigel Hall.
Rooney, Msgr. Hugh J. '45 (NY) Retired; [DD] New York, NY Our Lady of Consolation Residence.
Rooney, James T. '64 (BRK) [247] Queens, NY Transfiguration Church.
Rooney, John C. '89 (LIN) [A] Seward, NE St. Gregory the Great Seminary.
Rooney, John J. '62 (ALB) [5] Watervliet, NY Sacred Heart of Mary Church.
Rooney, Jordon *o.carm.* '54 (JOL) [J] Darien, IL Carmelite Provincial Office.
Rooney, Joseph S. *s.j.* '66 (SLC) Moab, UT St. Pius X Church; Monticello, UT St. Joseph Church.
Rooney, Kevin E. '62 (BUR) Northfield, VT St. John the Evangelist Church.
Rooney, Martin *m.s.a.* '93 (NOR) [F] Cromwell, CT Society of the Missionaries of the Holy Apostles.
Rooney, Martin '93 (PAT) [J] Paterson, NJ St. Joseph's Hospital and Medical Center.
Rooney, Michael F. *s.j.* '72 (FgM) Provinces.
Rooney, Michael J. *s.m.a.* '41 (BO) [W] Dedham, MA African Mission House.
Rooney, Michael R. '89 (TLS) Miami, OK Sacred Heart Church; [H] Miami, OK Northeastern Oklahoma A & M College Newman Center.
Rooney, Rob '63 (GI) Ord, NE Our Lady of Perpetual Help Church.
Rooney, Sean *s.d.b.* '66 (BIR) [9] Birmingham, AL St. John Bosco Church.
Rooney, Stephen '85 (DET) [5] Monroe, MI St. Michael Church.
Rooney, Msgr. Thaddeus '47 (RVC) Deer Park, NY SS. Cyril and Methodius Church; Retired.
Rooney, Thomas J. '91 (PH) Fallsington, PA St. Joseph the Worker Church.
Rooney, William *o.f.m.* '81 (MEM) [I] Memphis, TN Franciscan Friars (Sacred Heart Prov.) of Memphis.
Roos, Edward M. '66 (NY) [3] White Plains, NY St. Bernard Church.
Roos, H. Jules '56 (PIT) On Duty Outside the Diocese.
Roos, John '55 (ALB) Retired.
Roos, Jules '56 (FgM) Society of St. James the Apostle.
Roos, Lee R. '90 (ARL) Annandale, VA St. Michael's Church.
Roos, Paul '61 (EVN) Mariah Hill, IN Mary, Help of Christians Church; New Boston, IN St. John Chrysostom Church.
Roos, Richard H. *s.j.* '74 (BO) [W] Boston, MA The Society of Jesus of New England-Provincial Offices.
Roos, Richard H. *s.j.* '74 (PRT) [C] Portland, ME Cheverus High School; [I] Portland, ME St. Ignatius Residence.

Roos, Robert E. '54 (ALB) Retired.
Roos, William A. '59 (MET) Retired; [G] Somerset, NJ McCarrick Care Center.
Roost, Joseph F. '89 (DAV) Marengo, IA St. Patrick's Church; Williamsburg, IA St. Mary's Church.
Root, James A. '84 (SAM) Carnegie, PA Our Lady of Victory Church.
Root, Richard '90 (SPK) Absent on Leave.
Ropke, Canon John '78 (SJP) New Kensington, PA St. Vladimir Church.
Roppolo, Msgr. Ignatius M. '54 (NO) [58] New Orleans, LA St. Rita Church; [A] New Orleans, LA Notre Dame Seminary Graduate School of Theology.
Ropposelli, Stephen J. '98 (CAM) Lindenwold, NJ St. Lawrence's Church.
Roque, Alejandro *o.m.i.* '88 (MIA) Opa Locka, FL St. Monica Church.
Rosa, Msgr. Joseph '76 (BRK) [119] Brooklyn, NY Most Precious Blood Church.
Rosa, Salvatore J. '68 (HRT) [10] New Britain, CT St. Mary's Church.
Rosack, Msgr. Edward V. '54 (PBR) Ambridge, PA St. Mary's Church.
Rosaforte, Msgr. Anthony S. '70 (NOR) [1] Norwich, CT St. Patrick Church.
Rosage, Msgr. David E. '43 (SPK) Retired.
Rosales, Angelito *s.d.v.* '96 (NEW) [25] Newark, NJ St. Michael's Church.
Rosales, Cresencio *s.d.b.* '88 (LA) [D] Los Angeles, CA Bishop Mora Salesian High School.
Rosales, Deo G. '82 (WDC) [T] Washington, DC Prelature of the Holy Cross and Opus Dei.
Rosales, Fredi A. '92 (BRK) [99] Brooklyn, NY Our Lady of Loreto Church; [108] Brooklyn, NY Our Lady of the Presentation Church.
Rosales, Fruto '70 (RVC) Hempstead, NY Our Lady of Loretto Church.
Rosales, Ramon '81 (SB) Chino, CA Our Lady of Guadalupe Church.
Rosales, Raul H. '93 (TUC) Clifton, AZ Sacred Heart Church; Morenci, AZ Holy Cross Church.
Rosales, Samuel *s.j.* '73 (SAT) [17] San Antonio, TX Our Lady of Guadalupe Church.
Rosario, Juan *c.ss.r.* '78 (PCE) Guayama, PR St. Anthony of Padua Church.
Rosato, Philip J. *s.j.* '71 (BAL) [S] Baltimore, MD Jesuit Fathers and Brothers Maryland Provincial Curia.
Rosato, Vincenzo *c.s.* (BO) [64] Boston, MA Sacred Heart Church.
Rosca, Paschal *o.de.m.* '63 (CLV) [68] Cleveland, OH St. Rocco Church.
Rosch, James '72 (ALB) Fort Edward, NY St. Joseph Church.
Roscioli, Dominic J. '74 (MIL) Retired.
Roscoe, Keith '92 (RCK) Crystal Lake, IL St. Thomas the Apostle Church.
Rosczewski, Steven M. *o.dem.* '89 (SP) [9] St. Petersburg, FL Transfiguration Church.
Rose, Alphonse G. '56 (BAL) Retired; [W] Linthicum, MD Catholic Daughters of the Americas.
Rose, Msgr. Donald '53 (GB) Retired.
Rose, Frank '90 (NEW) Plainfield, NJ St. Bernard's Church; Plainfield, NJ St. Stanislaus Kostka Church.
Rose, James '57 (FTW) Retired.
Rose, James '57 (LFT) Marion, IN U.S. Veteran's Hospital.
Rose, John '72 (SY) Baldwinsville, NY St. Augustine Church.
Rose, Justin '95 (NTN) San Bernardino, CA St. Philip Church.
Rose, Justin '95 (SB) [9] San Bernardino, CA St. Phillip the Apostle Church.
Rose, Michael F. '81 (WOR) South Grafton, MA St. James Church.
Rose, William J. '96 (TOL) [1] Lima, OH St. Charles Borromeo Church.
Rosebaugh, Lawrence *o.m.i.* '63 (FgM) Oblates Foreign Missions.
Rosebrough, Robert T. '69 (STL) Valley Park, MO Sacred Heart Church.
Roselada, Eulogio '93 (CHI) [N] Chicago, IL Holy Evangelists Friary.
Roselli, Marc J. *s.j.* '85 (FgM) Provinces.
Rosemeyer, John C. '58 (CHI) Westchester, IL Divine Providence Church.
Rosemeyer, Paul F. '52 (CHI) [1] Des Plaines, IL St. Mary Church; Palatine, IL St. Theresa Church; Retired.
Rosen, Cyprian *o.f.m.cap.* '62 (WIL) [I] Wilmington, DE Capuchin Franciscan Friars, St. Francis Renewal Center; [L] Wilmington, DE St. Francis Renewal Center.
Rosenau, Alan '88 (LR) [E] Hot Springs National Park, AR St. Joseph's Regional Health Center.
Rosenbaum, William E. '76 (ALT) [19] Johnstown, PA St. Clement's Church.
Rosendale, Glenn '76 (LUB) Levelland, TX St. Michael's Church.
Rosenfelder, Richard M. *s.j.* '51 (CLV) [D] Cuyahoga Falls, OH Walsh Jesuit High School.
Rosenkranz, George J. '62 (BO) Unassigned.
Rosensteel, William A. '69 (ALT) Newry, PA St. Patrick's Church.
Rosensweig, Msgr. Walter F. '53 (TUC) Absent on Leave; [F] Tucson, AZ Regina Cleri Center.
Rosero, Leo V. '90 (BRK) [181] Queens, NY Immaculate Conception Church.
Roseto, James '90 (E) On Leave of Absence.
Rosette, Fabian Maria *h.o.carm.* '80 (SAN) [A] Christoval, TX Mount Carmel Hermitage.
Rosetti, Fabian Maria *o.carm* (DAL) [N] Dallas, TX The Institute of Divine Mercy, Inc.
Rosetti, Gabriel A. *o.f.m.* '59 (PH) [D] Philadelphia, PA Archbishop Ryan High School; [AA] Philadelphia, PA St. Pius X Friary.
Rosevear, Anthony *o.p.* '78 (OAK) [N] Oakland, CA Dominican Order (Western Province), St. Albert's Priory; [N] Oakland, CA Western Dominican Province.
Rosie, Joseph '90 (TR) [2] Long Branch, NJ Holy Trinity Church.
Rosin, Richard *s.d.b.* '95 (NO) [D] Marrero, LA Archbishop Shaw High School.
Rosing, Paul J. '73 (CLV) [1] Akron, OH Annunciation Church.
Rosing, Robert C. '53 (COV) [8] Covington, KY Church of Our Savior; Retired; [I] Covington, KY St. Elizabeth Medical Center, North; [I] Edgewood, KY St. Elizabeth Medical Center, South; [Q] Erlanger, KY Marydale Retreat Center.
Rosinski, Bernard *s.c.j.* '59 (MIL) [P] Hales Corners, WI Sacred Heart Monastery; [Y] Franklin, WI Congregation of the Priests of the Sacred Heart Support and Maintenance Trust.
Rosinski, Edward B. '63 (CAM) Sicklerville, NJ St. John Neumann Church.
Rosinski, Richard A. '91 (RCK) Dundee, IL St. Catherine of Siena Church.
Rosko, Ladislaus '52 (CLV) Orange Village, OH St. Margaret of Hungary Church.
Rosloniec, Leo S. '54 (GR) Wright Township, MI St. Joseph's Church.
Roslovich, Peter J. *s.j.* '63 (NY) [DD] New York, NY Murray-Weigel Hall.
Roslowski, Romulus *o.f.m. conv.* '74 (ALT) Hooversville, PA Holy Family Church.
Rosolen, Emil '86 (AMA) Absent on Leave.
Rosonke, Steven J. '82 (DUB) [7] Cedar Rapids, IA St. Patrick's Church.
Rosonke, Vince G. '75 (DM) Altoona, IA SS. John and Paul Church.
Rospond, Paul *c.s.p.* '81 (LA) [BB] Los Angeles, CA Archdiocesan Office for Campus Ministry.
Ross, Brenden '87 (NY) Absent on Leave.
Ross, Christopher M. *o.s.m.* '54 (CHI) [N] Chicago, IL Order of Friar Servants of Mary (Servites) United States of America Province, Inc.
Ross, Daniel *s.j.* '66 (FgM) Provinces.
Ross, David M. '75 (TOL) [1] Lima, OH St. Charles Borromeo Church.
Ross, Gregory S. *o.c.d.* '95 (NO) [A] New Orleans, LA Notre Dame Seminary Graduate School of Theology; [B] New Orleans, LA St. John of the Cross, Discalced Carmelite House of Studies.
Ross, James H. '46 (OKL) Retired.
Ross, Joseph *m.s.* '55 (MAN) [K] Enfield, NH Shrine of Our Lady of La Salette.
Ross, Joseph D. '69 (STL) [31] St. Louis, MO St. Cronan Church.
Ross, Joseph R. '69 (OKL) [4] Oklahoma City, OK Christ the King Church.
Ross, Kenneth '92 (ORL) Retired.
Ross, Laurence *s.m.* '43 (BO) [10] Lawrence, MA Sacred Heart Church.
Ross, Lowery A. '97 (CC) Orange Grove, TX St. John of the Cross Church.
Ross, Mark J. '88 (SAV) Vidalia, GA Sacred Heart Church.
Ross, Raymond *c.m.* '48 (STL) Sappington, MO St. Catherine Laboure Church.
Ross, Richard (JOL) Joliet, IL Dept. of Corrections.
Ross, Richard '67 (JOL) [9] Joliet, IL St. Bernard Church.
Ross, Robert *s.d.s.* '58 (WDC) [B] Silver Spring, MD Salvatorian Community.
Ross, Robert J. *s.j.* '72 (CIN) [M] Cincinnati, OH Faber Jesuit Community.
Ross, Robert J. *s.j.* '72 (COV) [I] Covington, KY St. Elizabeth Medical Center, North; [I] Edgewood, KY St. Elizabeth Medical Center, South; [I] Williamstown, KY St. Elizabeth Medical Center, Grant County.
Ross, Stephen-Joseph *o.c.d.* '84 (BO) [W] Boston, MA Carmelite Monastery.
Ross, Theodore *s.j.* '67 (CIN) [B] Cincinnati, OH Mt. St. Mary's Seminary of the West.
Ross, William B. '54 (OKL) Purcell, OK Our Lady of Victory Church.
Rossato, Graziano *s.x.* '66 (FgM) Xaverian Foreign Missions.
Rossato, Graziano *s.x.* '66 (PAT) [M] Wayne, NJ Xaverian Missionary Fathers.
Rossbach, Msgr. George F. '36 (NY) Retired.
Rossbach, J. Robert *c.ss.r.* '47 (STL) [P] Liguori, MO St. Clement Health Care Center.
Rosse, John '54 (ROC) [43] Rochester, NY St. Margaret Mary Church; Retired.
Rossell, Richard *o.f.m.conv.* '61 (TR) Point Pleasant Beach, NJ St. Peter's Church.
Rosselli, Msgr. Charles '36 (NY) Retired.
Rossello, Nicholas A. '60 (BUF) Retired.
Rosser, Aelred *o.s.b.* '67 (KC) [J] Conception, MO Conception Abbey.
Rossetti, Mark T. '85 (NY) Congers, NY St. Paul Church.
Rossetti, Mark T. '85 (SCR) On Duty Outside the Diocese.
Rossetti, Salvatore J. *o.p.* '42 (MET) Edison, NJ St. Helena Church.
Rossetti, Stephen '84 (SY) On Duty Outside the Diocese.
Rossetti, Stephen J. '73 (WDC) [V] Silver Spring, MD Saint Luke Institute, Inc.
Rossey, Stephen J. *o.praem.* '59 (GB) [I] De Pere, WI St. Norbert Abbey.
Rossi, Anthony M. '49 (PH) Retired.
Rossi, Desmond '92 (ALB) Leave of Absence.
Rossi, Domenic A. *o.praem.* '74 (PH) Paoli, PA St. Norbert Church; [AA] Paoli, PA Daylesford Abbey.
Rossi, Dominic *p.i.m.e.* '38 (DET) [K] Detroit, MI P.I.M.E. Missionaries of SS. Peter and Paul.
Rossi, Dominic L. '00 (PH) Plymouth Meeting, PA Epiphany of Our Lord Church.
Rossi, Frank H. '83 (GAL) On Special or Other Diocesan Assignment.
Rossi, Joseph M. '84 (BO) [7] Lynn, MA St. Pius Fifth Church.
Rossi, Joseph S. *s.j.* '80 (BAL) [B] Baltimore, MD Loyola College in Maryland; [S] Baltimore, MD Jesuit Community of Loyola College, Inc.
Rossi, Pat F. '82 (NY) [182] Bronx, NY SS. Philip and James Church.
Rossi, Paul J. '74 (SFR) [3] San Rafael, CA St. Raphael Church; Marin, CA Serra Club of Marin.
Rossi, Philip J. *s.j.* '71 (MIL) [P] Milwaukee, WI Arrupe House Jesuit Community.
Rossi, Raymond R. '58 (LR) Hot Springs Village, AR Sacred Heart of Jesus Church.
Rossi, Robert *o.s.c* '70 (FgM) Crosier Foreign Missions.
Rossi, Thomas J. *o.praem.* '73 (PH) [7] Philadelphia, PA St. Aloysius Church; [85] Philadelphia, PA King of Peace Church; [AA] Paoli, PA Daylesford Abbey.
Rossi, Thomas P. '85 (BO) Tyngsborough, MA St. Mary Magdalen Church.
Rossi, Walter R. '87 (SCR) On Duty Outside the Diocese.
Rossi, Walter R. '87 (WDC) [Q] Washington, DC Basilica of the National Shrine of the Immaculate Conception.
Rossie, Arthur *c.ss.r.* '57 (STP) Brooklyn Center, MN St. Alphonsus Church.
Rossiter, Msgr. Francis S. '42 (BO) Bilerica, MA Middlesex County House of Correction; Cambridge, MA Middlesex County Jail; Senior Priests.
Rossiter, John F. '58 (KCK) [1] Topeka, KS Assumption Church.
Rossito, Joseph V. (BGP) [P] Stamford, CT The Catherine Dennis Keefe Queen of the Clergy Retired Priests' Residence.
Rossitto, Joseph V. '69 (BGP) Retired.
Rossman, George M. '66 (SFR) [S] San Francisco, CA Prelature of the Holy Cross and Opus Dei.
Rossman, Richard '71 (P) Tualatin, OR Church of the Resurrection.
Rosso, Norbert *c.s.sp.* '54 (ALX) Natchitoches, LA St. Anthony Church.
Rosson, John P. '75 (ALB) Cooperstown, NY St. Mary Church.
Rosswog, Ken *o.f.m.* '50 (SFD) Montrose, IL St. Rose of Lima Church.
Rosswog, Kenneth *o.f.m.* '57 (SFD) Teutopolis, IL St. Francis of Assisi Church; [K] Teutopolis, IL St. Francis Assisi Friary.
Rost, Louis B. *m.m.* '55 (FgM) Maryknoll Foreign Missions.
Rost, Robert A. '74 (KC) [5] Independence, MO Nativity of the Blessed Virgin Mary Church.
Roszel, Stephen A. '77 (ARL) Purcellville, VA St. Francis de Sales Church.
Roszko, Edward J. *o.s.f.s.* '70 (ARL) [D] Alexandria, VA Bishop Ireton High School; [J] Alexandria, VA Oblates of St. Francis de Sales Residence.
Roszkowski, Donald '97 (PEO) Campus, IL Sacred Heart Church; Odell, IL St. Paul's Church.
Rotelle, John E. *o.s.a.* '65 (PH) [AA] Villanova, PA Provincial Offices of the Order of St. Augustine, Province of St. Thomas of Villanova; [AA] Villanova, PA St. John Stone Friary.
Roten, Johann B.G. *s.m.* '69 (CIN) [D] Dayton, OH The University of Dayton; [D] Dayton, OH The University of Dayton; [M] Dayton, OH Marianist Provincialate.
Rotert, J. Matthew '94 (KC) Chillicothe, MO St.

Columban Church.
Rotert, Norman '57 (KC) [40] Kansas City, MO Visitation of the Blessed Virgin Mary Church.
Roth, George M. *f.f.i.* '97 (FR) [I] New Bedford, MA Marian Friary of Our Lady, Queen of the Seraphic Order.
Roth, James H. *o.s.f.s.* '95 (TOL) [C] Toledo, OH St. Francis de Sales High School; [K] Toledo, OH Oblates of St. Francis de Sales.
Roth, James V. *m.m.* '54 (FgM) Maryknoll Foreign Missions.
Roth, Msgr. Joseph R. *v.g.* '79 (CHR) Myrtle Beach, SC St. Andrew's Church.
Roth, Robert J. *s.j.* '51 (NY) [DD] New York, NY Jesuit Community at Fordham University.
Roth, Timothy *m.i.c.* '74 (CHI) [N] Chicago, IL Congregation of Marian Fathers of the Immaculate Conception.
Roth, Timothy *m.i.c.* '74 (NOR) [C] Thompson, CT Marianapolis Preparatory School; [F] Thompson, CT Marian Fathers.
Roth, Wallace F. '47 (CLV) South Amherst, OH Nativity of Blessed Virgin Mary Church; Retired.
Rothbauer, Francis J. '66 (STU) Retired.
Rothe, James A. '56 (LA) Retired.
Rothermel, Paul L. (ALN) [2] Allentown, PA St. Francis of Assisi Church.
Rothfuchs, Gregory '95 (JOL) Lombard, IL St. Pius X Church.
Rothrauff, Noel H. *o.s.b.* '54 (FgM) American - Cassinese Congregation Foreign Missions.
Rothrauff, Noel H. *o.s.b.* '54 (GBG) [H] Latrobe, PA Saint Vincent Archabbey.
Rothrock, Theodore D. '83 (LFT) Carmel, IN St. Elizabeth Ann Seton Church.
Rothschild, Paul J. '84 (STL) Overland, MO All Souls Church.
Rothwell, Joseph T. '52 (BO) Senior Priests.
Rotola, Albert C. *s.j.* '68 (STL) [C] St. Louis, MO Saint Louis University; [O] St. Louis, MO Fusz Pavilion.
Rotolo, Michael '51 (STU) Barton, OH Our Lady of Angels Church; Blaine, OH All Saints Church.
Rotondi, Paul *o.f.m.* '56 (HRT) [5] Meriden, CT St. Rose of Lima Church.
Rott, Bernard E. '79 (MAD) Watertown, WI St. Henry Church.
Rottering, Augustine *o.s.b.* '31 (KCK) [H] Atchison, KS St. Benedict's Abbey.
Rotunno, Anthony R. '61 (PRT) Retired.
Rotunno, Floyd '70 (NEW) [2] Orange, NJ Our Lady of the Valley Church.
Rotunno, Philip J. '66 (NEW) West New York, NJ Our Lady of Libera Church.
Rouch, Nicholas J. '89 (E) [B] Erie, PA Gannon University.
Rouech, Chris '96 (GR) Montague, MI St. James Church.
Rougeau, Marc *s.d.b.* '77 (LA) [Q] Los Angeles, CA Dominic Savio Salesian Residence.
Roughan, Richard F. '63 (NOR) Waterford, CT St. Paul Church.
Rouleau, Francis C. '00 (NOR) Pawcatuck, CT St. Michael Church.
Rourke, John C. '63 (VEN) [5] Sarasota, FL St. Michael the Archangel Church.
Rouse, Paul (BO) Avon, MA St. Michael Church.
Rouse, Silvan *c.p.* '49 (ALT) [J] Bedford, PA St. Mary's House of Greater Solitude.
Rouse, Warren *o.f.m.* '57 (LA) [W] Malibu, CA Serra Retreat.
Rousseau, Julian *s.s.s.* '50 (SFE) [25] Albuquerque, NM St. Charles Borromeo Church; Albuquerque, NM Veterans Administration Medical Center.
Rousseau, Peter A. '49 (BUR) Retired.
Rousseau, Richard W. *s.j.* '54 (BO) [W] Boston, MA The Society of Jesus of New England-Provincial Offices.
Rousseau, Richard W. *s.j.* '54 (SCR) [C] Scranton, PA University of Scranton.
Rousseau, Robert J. '67 (HRT) [1] Bristol, CT St. Ann Church.
Rousseau, Sean K. '95 (ARL) Leesburg, VA St. John the Apostle Church.
Rousseau, Msgr. Stanley B. '56 (BGP) [A] Stamford, CT St. John Fisher Seminary Residence; [P] Stamford, CT St. John Fisher Seminary Residence.
Roussel, Matthew G. '99 (LAF) Eunice, LA St. Thomas More Church.
Routhier, Peter A. '78 (BUR) Barre, VT St. Monica Church.
Roux, G. Albert '66 (PRT) Special or Other Diocesan Assignment.
Roux, Philippe '73 (SPR) South Deerfield, MA St. Stanislaus B. and M. Church.
Roux, Randy P. '79 (NO) Lacombe, LA St. John of the Cross Church.
Rovira, Ivan '71 (BWN) [D] San Juan, TX San Juan Nursing Home.
Rowan, Msgr. John '61 (RVC) Sayville, NY St. Lawrence the Martyr Church.
Rowan, John M. '89 (BO) [5] Quincy, MA St. Mary Church.
Rowan, Mark P. '91 (RVC) Lynbrook, NY Our Lady of Peace Church.
Rowan, Stephen '68 (HEL) [B] Helena, MT Carroll College.
Rowan, Stephen '70 (SEA) On Duty Outside the Archdiocese.
Rowe, Charles N. '99 (KC) Lee's Summit, MO Our Lady of the Presentation Church.
Rowe, Donald F. *s.j.* '72 (CHI) [C] Chicago, IL Jesuit Community at Loyola University of Chicago.
Rowe, William J. '64 (BEL) Mount Carmel, IL St. Mary Church.
Rowgh, T. Matthew '75 (WH) Shepherdstown, WV St. Agnes Church.
Rowland, Msgr. Charles H. '70 (CHR) [2] Columbia, SC St. Joseph Church.
Rowland, Edward P. '53 (JOL) [19] Joliet, IL St. Thaddeus Church.
Rowland, Thomas '49 (ELP) On Duty Outside of Diocese.
Rowland, William F. *c.j.m.* '70 (SD) [3] San Diego, CA Blessed Sacrament Church.
Rowntree, Stephen C. *s.j.* '75 (FgM) Provinces.
Rowntree, Stephen C. *s.j.* '75 (NO) [P] New Orleans, LA Jesuit Provincial Office.
Rowsome, Morgan '70 (CC) [19] Corpus Christi, TX St. Peter Prince of Apostles Church.
Roy, Msgr. Allen J. '54 (NO) [10] New Orleans, LA Holy Spirit Church.
Roy, Donald J. '70 (BUR) Graniteville, VT St. Sylvester Church.
Roy, Duane *o.s.b.* '67 (FgM) American - Cassinese Congregation Foreign Missions.
Roy, F. Gilles '57 (WOR) On Duty Outside the Diocese.
Roy, George *o.m.i.* (BO) Special Chaplaincies.
Roy, George *o.m.i.* '73 (BO) [W] Lowell, MA Missionary Oblates of Mary Immaculate.
Roy, George *o.m.i.* '73 (MAN) [K] Les Cayes, Haiti Paroisse Ste. Anne.
Roy, Gregory R. *s.j.* '46 (ALB) [L] Valatie, NY St. Joseph.
Roy, Gregory R. *s.j.* '46 (BO) [W] Boston, MA The Society of Jesus of New England-Provincial Offices.
Roy, J. Jean '56 (WDC) Retired.
Roy, James '61 (ALX) Hessmer, LA St. Alphonsus Church.
Roy, James R. *m.m.* '61 (BO) [W] East Walpole, MA Maryknoll Mission Promotion Department.
Roy, Joe *s.s.s.* '56 (SLC) [7] Taylorsville, UT St. Martin de Porres Church.
Roy, Kenneth J. '78 (ALX) Natchitoches, LA Immaculate Conception Church.
Roy, Louis *o.p.* '72 (BO) [W] Dover, MA St. Stephen Priory.
Roy, Maurice J. '73 (BUR) St. Albans, VT Holy Angels Church.
Roy, Michael J. '75 (WOR) Webster, MA Sacred Heart of Jesus Church.
Roy, Neil J. '86 (WDC) [C] Washington, DC Catholic University of America, The.
Roy, Paul M. *m.s.* '58 (FR) [I] Attleboro, MA La Salette Provincial House.
Roy, Richard *m.afr.* '71 (FgM) Missionaries of Africa Foreign Missions.
Roy, Richard M. '75 (FR) Orleans, MA St. Joan of Arc Church.
Roy, Richard P. '71 (WDC) [M] Washington, DC Missionaries of Africa.
Roy, Robert P. '94 (HRT) [2] Meriden, CT St. Joseph Church; [4] Meriden, CT St. Mary Church.
Roy, Roger *o.m.i.* '49 (BO) [W] Lowell, MA Missionary Oblates of Mary Immaculate.
Roy, Roger *o.m.i.* '49 (FgM) Oblates Foreign Missions.
Roy, Sheldon L. '86 (ALX) Absent on Leave.
Roya-Mojia, Alberto *c.o.* (PH) [48] Philadelphia, PA St. Francis Xavier Church.
Royal, E. Peter '53 (AUS) Lott, TX Sacred Heart Church; Marlin, TX St. Joseph's Church; Marlin, TX V.A. Hospital.
Royal, Kevin T. '85 (BGP) [A] Stamford, CT St. John Fisher Seminary Residence; [P] Stamford, CT St. John Fisher Seminary Residence.
Royce, Thomas R. *s.j.* '56 (YAK) [4] Yakima, WA St. Joseph's Church.
Royer, Msgr. George C. '27 (MOB) Retired; [E] Mobile, AL Little Sisters of the Poor, Home For the Aged, Inc.
Royer, Msgr. Ronald E. '58 (LA) Lakewood, CA St. Pancratius Church.
Royer, Thomas J. '60 (PEO) [3] Champaign, IL St. Mary's Church; Ivesdale, IL St. Joseph's Church.
Royer, Yvon J. '90 (BUR) Derby Line, VT St. Edward Church.
Royo-Mejia, Alberto *c.o.* '89 (PH) [AA] Philadelphia, PA The Philadelphia Congregation of The Oratory of St. Philip Neri.
Royston, Basil '81 (SJ) San Jose, CA O'Connor Hospital; [G] San Jose, CA O'Connor Hospital.
Rozanski, Mitchell T. (BAL) Severna Park, MD St. John the Evangelist Church.
Rozansky, Joseph G. *o.f.m.* '76 (WDC) [B] Silver Spring, MD Holy Name College.
Rozman, Thomas J. '86 (HBG) Marysville, PA Our Lady of Good Counsel Church.
Rozmarynowcz, Michael '95 (PHU) [F] Fox Chase Manor, PA Provincial Motherhouse of the Sisters of St. Basil the Great.
Rozniak, Msgr. Ronald J. '71 (NEW) Ridgewood, NJ Our Lady of Mount Carmel Church.
Roznowski, Thomas *o.s.b.* '76 (SFS) [F] Marvin, SD Blue Cloud Abbey.
Rozum, George A. *c.s.c.* '68 (FTW) [B] Notre Dame, IN University of Notre Dame Du Lac; [J] Notre Dame, IN Holy Cross Community, Corby Hall, University of Notre Dame.
Rozycki, George '70 (SP) Zephyrhills, FL St. Joseph Church.
Rozycki, Isidore '68 (AUS) Tours, TX St. Martin Church.
Ruan, John Ming '97 (WDC) Laurel, MD St. Mary Church.
Ruane, Edward M. *o.p.* '69 (CHI) [N] Chicago, IL Dominicans (Provincial Office); [N] Chicago, IL Dominicans (Provincial Office); [X] Chicago, IL St. Thomas Aquinas Foundation.
Ruane, Edward M. *o.p.* '69 (FgM) Dominican - Order of Preachers Foreign Missions.
Ruane, George '73 (NEW) Edgewater, NJ Holy Rosary Church.
Ruane, John P. *s.j.* '49 (NEW) [B] Jersey City, NJ Saint Peter's College; [N] Jersey City, NJ Jesuits of Saint Peter's College, Inc.
Ruane, Martin '63 (JKS) Pearl, MS St. Jude Church; Pearl, MS Rankin County Prison; Whitfield, MS Mississippi State Hospital.
Ruane, Michael J. '69 (BAL) Poplar Springs, MD St. Michael Church.
Ruba, Msgr. Nicholas J. '51 (SC) Retired.
Rubadue, Paul E. *o.s.b.* '86 (GBG) [H] Latrobe, PA Saint Vincent Archabbey.
Rubaj, Leon '60 (SAT) On Duty Outside the Archdiocese.
Rubbelke, Ronald J. '64 (STL) O'Fallon, MO Assumption Church.
Rubey, Charles T. '66 (CHI) [G] Chicago, IL Catholic Charities of the Archdiocese of Chicago-Archdiocesan Offices; [G] Chicago, IL Catholic Charities of the Archdiocese of Chicago-Archdiocesan Offices; [L] Chicago, IL St. Joseph's Carondelet Child Center.
Rubiano, Cesar *c.j.m.* '96 (SD) [L] San Diego, CA Newman Center - SDSU.
Rubin, Ettore *c.s.* '62 (VEN) Immokalee, FL Our Lady of Guadalupe Church.
Rubino, Vincent A. *o.f.m.conv.* (ATL) Jonesboro, GA St. Philip Benizi Church.
Rubio, Jose Antonio '80 (SJ) [22] San Jose, CA Sacred Heart of Jesus Church; Special Assignment.
Rubsys, Anthony L. *f.s.c.a.* '38 (NY) [DD] New York, NY Brothers of the Christian Schools of Manhattan College, Inc.
Ruby, David (GB) Oconto, WI Holy Trinity Church.
Rucando, Anthony M. '70 (BRK) [98] Brooklyn, NY Our Lady Help of Christians Church.
Ruchgy, Wayne J. '66 (STN) Dearborn, MI St. Michael's Church.
Rucinski, Joseph S. '42 (TR) Retired.
Rucinski, Willard *o.s.f.s.* '65 (R) Fayetteville, NC St. Elizabeth Ann Seton Church.
Ruck, Michael J. *m.m.* '46 (SJ) [L] Los Altos, CA Maryknoll.
Rucker, G. Neville '46 (LA) Pacific Palisades, CA Corpus Christi Church.
Rucker, Lawrence *s.c.j.* '66 (JKS) [F] Nesbit, MS St. Michael Community House.
Rucker, Neville '46 (LA) Retired.
Rudcki, Stanley R. '53 (CHI) Retired.
Rudd, Thad B. '91 (ATL) Calhoun, GA St. Clements Church.
Rudden, Matthew T. '59 (RCK) Retired.
Ruddick, James J. *s.j.* '55 (BUF) [O] Buffalo, NY Canisius Jesuit Community.
Ruddy, Edward J. '40 (PAT) Retired.
Ruddy, H. Paul *o.s.f.s.* '64 (LAN) Hudson, MI Sacred Heart Church.
Rude, James A. *s.j.* '64 (LA) [6] Los Angeles, CA Blessed Sacrament Church.
Rudemiller, Edward L. '58 (CIN) [65] Cincinnati, OH Our Lady of Lourdes Church.
Rudisill, James A. '51 (NSH) Retired.
Rudjak, Joseph '00 (Y) North Canton, OH St. Paul's Church.
Rudnay, Clement A. *o.praem.* '38 (ORG) [I] Silverado, CA Norbertine Fathers of Orange Inc.
Rudnick, Kenneth J. *s.j.* '91 (LA) [A] Camarillo, CA St. John's Seminary College of the Archdiocese of Los Angeles.
Rudnicki, Andrew *m.i.c.* '90 (PMB) Royal Palm Beach, FL Our Lady Queen of the Apostles Church.
Rudnicki, Wladyslaw '56 (RVC) Cutchogue, NY Our Lady of Ostrabrama Church.
Rudnik, John J. '61 (CHI) [204] Chicago, IL Transfiguration of Our Lord Church.
Rudnik, Tadeusz '55 (SY) [22] Syracuse, NY St.

Stephen Church.
Rudolf, Roger G. '92 (IND) Rushville, IN Immaculate Conception/St. Mary Church.
Rudolph, Frederick *s.v.d.* '54 (CHI) [B] Techny, IL Divine Word Residence.
Rudolph, Patrick '88 (LAV) [12] Las Vegas, NV St. Joseph, Husband of Mary Church.
Rudolph, Thomas J. '61 (LC) Rozellville, WI St. Andrew Church; Stratford, WI St. Joseph Church.
Rudolphi, Stephen A. '79 (BEL) Carmi, IL St. Polycarp Church; Enfield, IL St. Patrick Church.
Rudolphi, Timothy C. '89 (STP) Monticello, MN St. Henry Church.
Rudy, Noel T. '53 (SAG) Retired.
Rudy, Richard E. '76 (PH) [103] Philadelphia, PA St. Matthew Church.
Rudy, Theodore '54 (PSC) Dunmore, PA St. Michael Church.
Rudzewicz, Jan '83 (OAK) Pinole, CA St. Joseph's Church.
Rueda, John (NY) [173] Bronx, NY Our Lady of Mercy Church.
Rueda, Juan '99 (BO) [W] Cambridge, MA Weston Jesuit Community.
Ruede, Ernest J. '66 (R) New Bern, NC St. Paul Church.
Ruedel, Richard P. '59 (STP) St. Thomas, MN St. Thomas Church.
Ruedisueli, Robert A. '69 (DET) [8] Warren, MI St. Mark Church.
Ruef, Msgr. James L.T. '78 (COL) [20] Columbus, OH Holy Name Church.
Ruef, John *c.ss.r.* '50 (ALB) [L] Saratoga Springs, NY St. John Neumann Residence.
Rueger, George E. '58 (WOR) [28] Worcester, MA St. Stephen's Church; [R] Worcester, MA Mendon Charitable Corporation, Inc.
Rueger, William J. '75 (BRK) [207] Queens, NY Our Lady of the Blessed Sacrament Church.
Ruehl, William F. '58 (ARL) Front Royal, VA St. John the Baptist Church.
Ruekert, Thomas E. *s.d.b.* '73 (NO) [4] Harvey, LA St. Rosalie Church.
Ruelle, Gerald *o.s.b.* '50 (BIS) Halliday, ND St. Paul Church; Killdeer, ND St. Joseph Church; [A] Richardton, ND Assumption Abbey.
Ruessmann, John J. *m.m.* '79 (FgM) Maryknoll Foreign Missions.
Rueter, Joseph J. '46 (COV) Cold Spring, KY St. Joseph Church; Retired.
Ruetz, Edward J. '62 (FTW) Retired.
Rueve, Charles R. *c.pp.s.* '43 (LFT) [A] Rensselaer, IN Saint Joseph's College.
Ruff, Anthony *o.s.b.* '93 (SCL) [I] Collegeville, MN St. John's Abbey, of the Order of St. Benedict.
Ruff, Charles R. '46 (STL) Retired.
Ruff, Daniel M. *s.j.* '86 (BAL) [A] Baltimore, MD St. Mary's Seminary and University; [S] Baltimore, MD Jesuit Community of Loyola College, Inc.
Ruff, Frank *glmy.* '63 (OWN) Elkton, KY St. Susan Church; Guthrie, KY Sts. Mary & James Church.
Ruffing, Joseph R. '55 (LFT) Retired.
Ruffing, Norman '63 (OAK) Retired.
Ruffo, John *o.f.m.conv.* '74 (R) Burlington, NC Blessed Sacrament Church; [E] Burlington, NC Conventual Franciscans; [H] Elon College, NC Elon College.
Ruffolo, George *c.m.f.* '59 (CHI) [78] Chicago, IL Holy Cross/Immaculate Heart of Mary Church.
Ruge, Kenneth C. '63 (CHI) Other Assignments.
Ruge, Paul *o.f.m.i.* '97 (FAR) [F] Pisek, ND Franciscan Friars of Mary Immaculate.
Rugel, Msgr. James J. (PAT) Retired.
Rugen, Patrick '76 (CHI) [151] Chicago, IL Our Lady of Mercy Church; [C] Chicago, IL Loyola University-Chicago.
Ruggere, Peter *m.m.* '68 (WDC) [B] Washington, DC Maryknoll Fathers and Brothers.
Ruggeri, Joseph A. '65 (BO) [8] Lowell, MA St. Margaret Church.
Ruggeri, Salvatore M. '99 (CLV) [7] Akron, OH St. Hilary Church.
Ruggerio, Salvatore (CLV) [D] Akron, OH St. Vincent-St. Mary High School.
Ruggieri, James T. '95 (PRO) [2] Woonsocket, RI All Saints Catholic Community Church.
Ruggieri, Joseph '95 (Y) [6] Canton, OH St. Joan of Arc Church.
Ruggieri, Pasquale *f.d.p.* '52 (NY) [11] New York, NY St. Ann Church.
Ruggiero, James S. (PIT) [S] Pittsburgh, PA Priests' Benefit Plan of the Diocese of Pittsburgh.
Ruggiero, James S. '70 (PIT) [1] Carnegie, PA St. Elizabeth Ann Seton Church.
Ruglovsky, Robert '61 (PRM) Absent on Leave.
Ruhl, John '64 (ORG) Inactive Leave.
Ruhl, Matthew D. *s.j.* '92 (STL) [52] St. Louis, MO St. Matthew, Apostle Church; [P] St. Louis, MO St. Matthew Jesuit Community.
Ruhl, William J. *o.s.f.s.* '62 (R) Goldsboro, NC St. Mary Church.
Ruhland, Carl J. '45 (DUB) Retired.
Ruhnke, Robert A. *c.ss.r.* '66 (SAT) [M] San Antonio, TX Redemptorists of Texas-San Antonio #1.
Ruisanchez, Jose P. '86 (SFR) [S] San Francisco, CA Prelature of the Holy Cross and Opus Dei.
Ruiz, Msgr. Agustin '56 (BRK) [118] Brooklyn, NY SS. Peter and Paul's Church.
Ruiz, Albert '73 (AUS) Georgetown, TX St. Helen's Church.
Ruiz, Antonio *c.m.* '65 (LA) [96] Los Angeles, CA St. Vincent De Paul Church.
Ruiz, Antonio A. '71 (TUC) Nogales, AZ San Felipe de Jesus Church.
Ruiz, Dominic *o.s.b.* '83 (SCL) Richmond, MN SS. Peter and Paul's Church; [I] Collegeville, MN St. John's Abbey, of the Order of St. Benedict.
Ruiz, Eddie '99 (SD) [1] El Cajon, CA Holy Trinity Church.
Ruiz, Enrique '56 (SAT) On Leave.
Ruiz, Faustino C. '91 (MET) On Duty Outside the Diocese.
Ruiz, Jean-Pierre *s.t.d.* '82 (BRK) [224] Queens, NY St. Patrick Church; Released from Diocesan Assignment.
Ruiz, John '55 (HT) [1] Thibodaux, LA St. Joseph Co-Church.
Ruiz, Jose Domingo '89 (STO) [6] Stockton, CA St. Linus Church; Lockeford, CA St. Joachim Church.
Ruiz, Jose H. '58 (VEN) Sebring, FL St. Catherine Church.
Ruiz, Jose Luis '89 (LA) Bell Gardens, CA St. Gertrude Church.
Ruiz, Joseph B. '66 (CHI) [3] Oak Park, IL St. Edmund Church.
Ruiz, Juan Carlos (PAT) Sparta, NJ Blessed Kateri Tekakwitha Church.
Ruiz, Lorenzo '63 (SJN) [28] San Juan, PR San Juan Bosco Church.
Ruiz, Luis '68 (SAT) [65] San Antonio, TX St. Stephen Church.
Ruiz, Luis '84 (CGS) Naguabo, PR Nuestra Senora del Rosario Church.
Ruiz, Miguel Angel *o.s.a.* '96 (GAL) Baytown, TX Our Lady of Guadalupe Church.
Ruiz, Ricardo '93 (ELP) Alpine, TX Our Lady of Peace Church.
Ruiz, Rudy '79 (MRY) Castroville, CA Our Lady of Refuge Church.
Rukavina, Steven '87 (B) [2] Boise, ID St. Mark's Church.
Rukstalis, Simeon *o.f.m.conv.* '64 (SY) [5] Binghamton, NY SS. Cyril and Method Church.
Ruland, Vernon J. *s.j.* '63 (SFR) [N] San Francisco, CA Jesuit Community at University of San Francisco.
Rule, Philip C. *s.j.* '62 (DET) [K] Detroit, MI Jesuit Provincial Office-Detroit Province of the Society of Jesus.
Rule, Philip C. *s.j.* '62 (WOR) [N] Worcester, MA Jesuits of Holy Cross College, Inc.
Rule, Steven R. '75 (RIC) Roanoke, VA St. Andrew Church.
Rulli, Joseph A. '92 (FTW) [19] Fort Wayne, IN St. Therese Church.
Rumble, Clarence F. '86 (SY) [3] Endicott, NY St. Anthony of Padua Church.
Runde, David H. '57 (MAD) Cottage Grove, WI St. Patrick Church.
Runde, Luis *o.f.m.* '65 (STL) [P] St. Louis, MO Franciscan Friary of St. Anthony of Padua.
Runde, Raymond E. '56 (MAD) Absent on Sick Leave.
Runde, William H. *s.j.* '69 (STL) [P] St. Louis, MO White House Retreat Jesuit Community; [T] St. Louis, MO White House Retreat.
Rundzio, Mark A. '81 (MAN) Center Ossipee, NH St. Joseph Church.
Runge, Msgr. Fenton J. '53 (STL) [50] St. Louis, MO Sts. Mary and Joseph Church.
Runnebaum, Conrad '55 (SFE) Retired.
Runte, Richard M. '73 (SPR) West Springfield, MA St. Thomas the Apostle Church.
Runtz, Anthony *c.j.* '58 (LA) [B] Santa Maria, CA St. Joseph Seminary (Josephite Fathers' Novitiate).
Ruoff, John C. *s.j.* '61 (STL) [P] St. Louis, MO Jesuit Community Corporation at St. Louis University - Jesuit Hall.
Ruoff, Louis '84 (RIC) [3] Richmond, VA Holy Rosary Church.
Rupert, Msgr. Dale R. '77 (SCR) [9] Scranton, PA Holy Rosary Church.
Rupiper, Darrell *o.m.i.* '63 (SFD) [A] Godfrey, IL Immaculate Heart of Mary Novitiate.
Rupp, Daniel James '98 (BUR) Barre, VT St. Monica Church.
Rupp, Daniel N. '66 (MAR) Leave of Absence.
Rupp, Edward F. '60 (CLV) Absent on Leave.
Ruppenkamp, Raymond '50 (DAV) Retired.
Ruppert, Alan E. '78 (BEL) Leave of Absence.
Ruppert, Donald R. '78 (VIC) East Bernard, TX Holy Cross Church.
Rusay, Leonard F.A. '85 (MET) High Bridge, NJ St. Joseph Church.
Ruscetta, Dominic *c.s.s.* '38 (BO) [Z] Waltham, MA Stigmatine Fathers and Brothers.
Rusch, Donald P. '61 (LAN) Clinton, MI St. Dominic's Church.
Ruschman, Albert E. '53 (COV) Fort Thomas, KY St. Thomas Church; Retired.
Rusconi, Msgr. Richard A. '71 (PAT) [4] Paterson, NJ Blessed Sacrament Church.
Ruse, Fred R. '76 (ORL) Winter Haven, FL St. Matthew Church.
Rusek, John '58 (ALN) [J] Bethlehem, PA Holy Family Villa.
Rush, Alfred C. *c.ss.r.* '36 (ALB) [L] Saratoga Springs, NY St. John Neumann Residence.
Rush, Gerald V. '89 (OM) Absent on Leave.
Rush, Msgr. J. Kenneth '71 (RIC) Lynchburg, VA Holy Cross Church.
Rush, James C. '68 (HRT) Retired.
Rush, James P. '72 (CAM) Bridgeton, NJ Immaculate Conception Church.
Rush, Joseph P. '62 (CAM) Pomona, NJ Assumption Church.
Rush, Michael P. '73 (CAM) Mullica Hill, NJ Holy Name of Jesus Church.
Rush, Patrick J. '69 (KC) [34] Kansas City, MO St. Peter's Church; Special Assignment.
Rush, Robert T. *s.j.* '59 (FgM) Provinces.
Rush, Msgr. Vincent '72 (RVC) Huntington Station, NY St. Hugh of Lincoln Church.
Rushford, William A. '55 (BIS) Retired; [G] Bismarck, ND Emmaus Place.
Rushman, John '55 (GAY) Retired.
Rusin, Joseph C. '46 (SCR) Retired.
Rusk, John '68 (SB) Blythe, CA Chuckawalla Valley State Prison.
Rusk, Richard M. '90 (MET) [1] Metuchen, NJ Cathedral of St. Francis; [L] Phillipsburg, NJ The Anawim Community.
Rusk, Richard M. '90 (ROC) [K] Corning, NY Anawim Community Center.
Ruskamp, Florian *o.f.m.cap.* '45 (LC) [H] Marathon City, WI St. Anthony Retreat Center.
Ruskamp, Robert L. '85 (ARL) [2] Arlington, VA St. Agnes Church.
Ruskoski, William '74 (LAF) Arnaudville, LA St. Francis Regis Church; Arnaudville, LA St. Catherine Church.
Ruskowski, Msgr. Clifford F. '62 (DET) Bloomfield Hills, MI St. Owen Church; [A] Detroit, MI Sacred Heart Major Seminary, Inc.
Rusnak, Melvin E. '70 (Y) [22] Youngstown, OH St. Stephen of Hungary Church.
Russ, Francis J. '51 (KC) Retired.
Russ, Joseph '55 (MAN) [M] Enfield, NH La Salette Shrine and Center of Enfield.
Russell, Alfred *o.s.f.s.* '66 (KAL) Portage, MI St. Catherine of Siena Church.
Russell, Anselm *o.s.b.* '97 (IND) [J] St. Meinrad, IN St. Meinrad Archabbey.
Russell, Benjamin J. *o.p.* '60 (CHI) [N] Chicago, IL Dominicans (Provincial Office); [N] Chicago, IL Dominicans (Provincial Office).
Russell, David '64 (MIA) [23] Miami, FL St. John Neumann Church.
Russell, David P. (WDC) North Beach, MD St. Anthony Church.
Russell, Dean Elno '00 (RCK) [2] Aurora, IL Holy Angels Church.
Russell, Edward '83 (NY) [184] Bronx, NY St. Pius V Church.
Russell, J. Christopher '79 (STP) Retired.
Russell, James *s.m.* '64 (SAT) [8] San Antonio, TX Holy Rosary Church; [M] San Antonio, TX Holy Rosary Marianist Community.
Russell, James A. *s.m.* '64 (CIN) [M] Dayton, OH Marianist Provincialate.
Russell, James D. '60 (WIN) Lake City, MN St. Mary's of the Lake Church.
Russell, James M. '70 (BLX) Pass Christian, MS St. Paul Church; Retired.
Russell, John *o.carm.* '60 (NY) [DD] Middletown, NY Brandsma Priory.
Russell, John F. *o.carm.* '60 (NEW) [A] South Orange, NJ Immaculate Conception Seminary.
Russell, Kenneth '58 (OAK) Retired.
Russell, Patrick '86 (B) Boise, ID Chateau de Boise Retirement Center.
Russell, Msgr. Paul F. '87 (BO) On Duty Outside the Archdiocese.
Russell, Raymond R. '56 (BUF) Retired; [O] Buffalo, NY Sheehan Residence for Priests.
Russell, Richard J. '60 (LA) [V] Los Angeles, CA Catholic Kolping House.
Russell, Richard J. '60 (SD) Retired.
Russell, Richard R. '61 (HRT) West Simsbury, CT St. Catherine of Siena Church.
Russell, Samuel *o.s.b.* '94 (KC) [A] Conception, MO Conception Seminary College; [J] Conception, MO Conception Abbey.
Russell, Stanley J. '61 (WIL) Bellefonte, DE St. Helena Church.
Russell, Msgr. W. Joyce '30 (WDC) Retired.

Russell, William C. *s.j.* '65 (BO) [W] Boston, MA Arrupe House.
Russi, Fred F. '66 (LKC) Oakdale, LA Sacred Heart Church.
Russi, John *s.m.* '31 (SJ) [L] Cupertino, CA Marianist Provincial Residence.
Russler, Clint (GAL) On Special or Other Diocesan Assignment.
Russman, Thomas '70 (WDC) [B] Washington, DC St. Francis Friary-Capuchin College.
Russo, Alfred E. '62 (BGP) [L] Trumbull, CT St. Joseph's Manor.
Russo, Anthony J. '00 (BR) [12] Baton Rouge, LA St. Jean Vianney Church.
Russo, Anthony P. *s.c.j.* '66 (MIL) Franklin, WI St. Martin of Tours Church; [P] Franklin, WI St. Francis Residence; [P] Hales Corners, WI Priests of the Sacred Heart; [P] Hales Corners, WI Priests of the Sacred Heart.
Russo, Anthony S. '00 (GR) Rockford, MI Our Lady of Consolation Church.
Russo, Anthony T. *c.ss.r.* '65 (PH) [25] Philadelphia, PA St. Boniface Church; [S] Philadelphia, PA Catholic Center for the Deaf and Hard of Hearing.
Russo, Armando C. '44 (SPR) Russell, MA Our Lady of the Rosary Church.
Russo, Caesar '74 (PMB) [A] Boynton Beach, FL St. Vincent de Paul Regional Seminary.
Russo, Caesar '74 (STA) On Duty Outside the Diocese.
Russo, Msgr. Charles J. (PAT) Retired.
Russo, Francis X. *o.f.m.cap.* '59 (WDC) [39] Washington, DC Shrine of the Sacred Heart Church.
Russo, John W. '78 (TR) Leave of Absence.
Russo, Lawrence J. '80 (BO) Military & VA Chaplains.
Russo, Michael '89 (LAF) Franklin, LA Assumption B.V.M. Church.
Russo, Michael A. '71 (NEW) On Duty Outside the Archdiocese.
Russo, Michael A. '71 (OAK) Moraga, CA St. Monica Church; [B] Moraga, CA St. Mary's College.
Russo, Nicodemus A. '48 (PEO) Retired.
Russo, Peter '76 (ALB) Copake Falls, NY St. Bridget Church.
Russo, Reginald *o.f.m.cap.* (PIT) [P] Pittsburgh, PA Motherhouse and Novitiate of the Vincentian Sisters of Charity.
Russo, Reginald *o.f.m.cap.* '67 (PIT) [30] Pittsburgh, PA Our Lady of the Angels Church.
Russo, Ricardo *o.f.m.* '74 (SFE) Santa Fe, NM New Mexico State Penitentiary; [J] Santa Fe, NM Discalced Carmelite Monastery.
Russo, Richard M. '82 (RCK) [4] Elgin, IL St. Thomas More Church.
Russo, Robert T. '61 (HRT) Retired.
Russo, Romanos '77 (NTN) Cliffside Park, NJ St. Demetrius Church.
Russo, Thomas *o.s.j.* '56 (MRY) [F] Santa Cruz, CA Oblates of St. Joseph Provincial House and Shrine.
Rusteika, John B. '45 (WCH) Retired.
Ruston, Robert L. '76 (ALT) Cassandra, PA St. Agnes Church; Wilmore, PA St. Bartholomew's Church.
Ruszel, Henry *c.r.* '54 (SB) [3] Fontana, CA St. Joseph Church.
Ruszel, Humphrey *c.r.* '46 (SB) [1] Fontana, CA Church of the Resurrection.
Rutan, Albert E. '57 (GF) Retired.
Ruth, John C. '85 (SCR) [20] Scranton, PA Nativity of Our Lord Church; [I] Scranton, PA Mercy Hospital.
Ruth, Robert F. '60 (RIC) Retired.
Ruthenberg, Gari *o.m.i.* '95 (SFS) Sisseton, SD St. Catherine Church; Sisseton, SD St. Peter Church.
Ruthenberg, Michael *o.p.* '88 (CHI) [N] River Forest, IL St. Thomas Aquinas Priory.
Ruther, William E. '90 (LA) [29] Los Angeles, CA Our Lady of Lourdes Church.
Rutherford, Donald L. '81 (ALB) Military Chaplains.
Rutherford, Richard *c.s.c.* '64 (P) [B] Portland, OR University of Portland; [L] Portland, OR Holy Cross Fathers & Brothers, C.S.C. - University of Portland.
Rutkowski, George A. '60 (DET) [54] Detroit, MI Our Lady Help of Christians Church.
Rutkowski, James '77 (STL) On Duty Outside the Archdiocese.
Rutkowski, Ronald J. '69 (GBG) Cardale, PA Madonna of Czestochowa Church; Palmer, PA St. Albert Church.
Rutkowski, Theodore A. '63 (PIT) Scott Township, PA Our Lady of Grace Church.
Rutledge, Arthur F. *s.j.* '51 (SJ) [L] Los Gatos, CA Sacred Heart Jesuit Center.
Rutledge, Robert M. *o.s.f.s.* '89 (ALN) [K] Center Valley, PA Oblates of St. Francis de Sales.
Rutledge, Robert M. *o.s.f.s.* '89 (WDC) [B] Washington, DC Oblates of St. Francis de Sales.
Rutledge, William G. '53 (PIT) Reserve Township, PA St. Aloysius Church.
Rutler, George W. '81 (NY) [2] New York, NY St. Agnes Church; On Duty Outside the Archdiocese; [HH] New York, NY Guild of Catholic Lawyers, The.
Rutowski, William J. '87 (SAG) [9] Bay City, MI St. Stanislaus Church.
Rutten, Paul J. '58 (LIN) [E] Lincoln, NE Madonna Rehabilitation Hospital.
Ruttle, Paul *c.p.* '80 (NY) [DD] Bronx, NY Passionist Residence.
Ruvalcaba, Victor '96 (LA) South Gate, CA St. Helen Church.
Ruvo, Msgr. John A. '54 (NY) [174] Bronx, NY Our Lady of Mt. Carmel Church.
Ruyechan, Matthew *o.f.m.* '80 (E) [2] Sharon, PA St. Anthony Church; [P] Erie, PA Newman Centers and Campus Ministry.
Ruygt, Hans '85 (SR) Healdsburg, CA St. John the Baptist Church.
Ruzich, Boniface *o.ss.t.* '59 (TR) [16] Trenton, NJ St. James Church.
Ruzicka, Gary J. '76 (CHY) [1] Cheyenne, WY St. Mary's Church.
Ruzzo, Paul F. '83 (MAN) [8] Manchester, NH St. Francis of Assisi Church.
Rwechungura, Siffredus B. '99 (NEW) West New York, NJ St. Joseph of the Palisades Church.
Rwegasira, Deogratias *a.j.* '96 (ALN) [3] Shenandoah, PA St. George Church; [5] Shenandoah, PA Our Lady of Mt. Carmel Church.
Rweyemamu, Justinian B. '93 (NOR) Rockville, CT St. Bernard Church.
Ryan, Adam *o.s.b.* '90 (KC) [J] Conception, MO Conception Abbey.
Ryan, Alan J. *m.m.* '60 (NY) [DD] Maryknoll, NY Maryknoll Fathers and Brothers; [DD] Maryknoll, NY Maryknoll Fathers and Brothers.
Ryan, Albert J. '58 (FR) [13] New Bedford, MA St. Francis of Assisi Church.
Ryan, Alphonsus '64 (SD) Retired.
Ryan, Barry '76 (BRK) Absent on Leave.
Ryan, Msgr. Bernard J. '55 (RVC) Bellport, NY Mary Immaculate Church.
Ryan, C. Duane '54 (JC) Laurie, MO Shrine of St. Patrick Church.
Ryan, C. Duane '54 (KC) Retired.
Ryan, Cornelius J. *c.s.c.* '56 (FgM) Holy Cross Foreign Missions.
Ryan, Cornelius J. *c.s.c.* '66 (FTW) [J] South Bend, IN Congregation of Holy Cross, Indiana Province, Provincial House.
Ryan, Daniel J. '89 (TR) Willingboro, NJ Corpus Christi Church.
Ryan, David '79 (CHI) [X] Chicago, IL Catholic Youth, Archdiocese of Chicago.
Ryan, Dennis K. '66 (DEN) Broomfield, CO Nativity of Our Lord Church.
Ryan, Dennis M. '74 (GB) Freedom, WI St. Nicholas Church.
Ryan, Donald L. '63 (L) Fairfield, KY St. Michael Church; Fairfield, KY St. Michael Church.
Ryan, Edmund G. *s.j.* '59 (SY) [B] Syracuse, NY Le Moyne College; [S] Syracuse, NY Jesuits at LeMoyne, Inc.
Ryan, Edmund K. *o.p.* '65 (P) Brookings, OR Star of the Sea Church.
Ryan, Edward '47 (ALB) Retired.
Ryan, Msgr. Edward A. '71 (BRK) [197] Queens, NY Mary's Nativity Church.
Ryan, Edward M. (WOR) [10] Worcester, MA Our Lady of Fatima Church.
Ryan, Eugene '69 (VEN) Absent on Leave.
Ryan, F. Lee '68 (JOL) Watseka, IL St. Edmund Church.
Ryan, Francis '58 (PEO) Retired.
Ryan, Francis J. *c.ss.r.* '44 (STL) [P] Liguori, MO St. Clement Health Care Center.
Ryan, Francis J. *s.j.* '56 (FgM) Provinces.
Ryan, Francis J. '58 (PEO) [L] Peoria, IL St. Joseph's Home of Peoria.
Ryan, Francis X. *s.j.* '84 (CLV) [B] Cleveland, OH John Carroll Jesuit Community.
Ryan, Msgr. Frederick J. '64 (BO) Kingston, MA St. Joseph Church.
Ryan, G. Philip '88 (ATL) Washington, GA St. Joseph's Church.
Ryan, George J. '62 (BRK) [188] Queens, NY St. Joseph Church.
Ryan, Msgr. Gerald E. '55 (DM) [10] Des Moines, IA St. Mary of Nazareth Church.
Ryan, Msgr. Gerald J. '45 (NY) [160] Bronx, NY St. Luke Church; Retired.
Ryan, Herbert J. *s.j.* '62 (LA) [C] Los Angeles, CA Loyola Marymount University.
Ryan, J. Patrick '76 (PAT) Rockaway, NJ St. Cecilia's Church.
Ryan, Jack '76 (HON) Kailua-Kona, HI St. Michael The Archangel Church; Kailua-Kona, HI St. Michael The Archangel Church.
Ryan, James '60 (JUN) Retired.
Ryan, James *s.j.* '69 (RC) Kyle, SD Our Lady of Sorrows Church; Manderson, SD St. Agnes Church; Porcupine, SD Church of Christ the King; [B] Pine Ridge, SD Jesuit Community of Holy Rosary Mission.
Ryan, James *s.j.* '74 (RC) Pine Ridge, SD Holy Rosary Church.
Ryan, James F. *s.s.e.* '56 (MOB) [G] Selma, AL Edmundite Fathers.
Ryan, James G. *o.s.a.* '49 (FWT) Abbott, TX Immaculate Heart of Mary Church.
Ryan, James J. '75 (COV) Elsmere, KY St. Henry Church.
Ryan, James R. '66 (CAM) Ventnor, NJ St. James Church.
Ryan, James W. (BIS) [1] Dickinson, ND Queen of Peace Church.
Ryan, Msgr. James W. '48 (BRK) [39] Brooklyn, NY St. Fortunata Church; Retired.
Ryan, John '45 (MAR) Retired.
Ryan, John '50 (SB) Highland, CA St. Adelaide Church; Highland, CA St. Adelaide Church.
Ryan, John '54 (ALX) Retired.
Ryan, John '64 (JOL) Park Forest, IL St. Mary Church.
Ryan, John '74 (NO) Lafitte, LA St. Anthony Church.
Ryan, John A. '70 (SFR) [21] San Francisco, CA St. Gabriel Church.
Ryan, John Chrysostom *c.p.* '48 (BRK) [V] Jamaica, NY Immaculate Conception Monastery.
Ryan, John J. *c.ss.r.* '53 (BO) [53] Boston, MA Our Lady of Perpetual Help Church.
Ryan, John J. *s.j.* '67 (BUF) [O] Buffalo, NY Canisius Jesuit Community; [R] Alfred, NY Campus Ministry.
Ryan, John J. '71 (ORL) Ormond Beach, FL St. Brendan Church.
Ryan, John J. *c.s.c.* '90 (SCR) [C] Wilkes-Barre, PA Kings College.
Ryan, Msgr. John M. '55 (BUF) Eggertsville, NY St. Benedict Church.
Ryan, John M. '64 (CHI) [3] Waukegan, IL St. Dismas Church.
Ryan, John P. '63 (NEW) Fort Lee, NJ Madonna Church.
Ryan, Msgr. John R. '46 (PAT) Retired; [P] Chester, NJ Nazareth Village.
Ryan, John R. '50 (DM) Retired.
Ryan, Msgr. John T. '56 (IND) [15] Indianapolis, IN St. Anthony Church.
Ryan, John T. *s.j.* '76 (NY) [FF] Staten Island, NY Mount Manresa Jesuit Retreat House.
Ryan, Joseph '58 (SAG) Clare, MI St. Cecilia Church.
Ryan, Joseph '66 (PAT) Mount Arlington, NJ Our Lady of the Lake Church.
Ryan, Joseph *o.s.a.* '83 (PH) [C] Villanova, PA Villanova University.
Ryan, Joseph A. *o.m.i.* '42 (BO) [Z] Tewksbury, MA Immaculate Heart of Mary Infirmary.
Ryan, Joseph D. *s.j.* '43 (NY) [DD] New York, NY Murray-Weigel Hall.
Ryan, Joseph E. '47 (BO) Senior Priests.
Ryan, Joseph F. '46 (SCR) Retired.
Ryan, Joseph J. '51 (STL) Retired.
Ryan, Msgr. Joseph P. '38 (DM) Retired.
Ryan, Kenan *s.t.* '59 (JKS) Philadelphia, MS Holy Cross Church.
Ryan, Kevin *o.s.b.* '42 (HEL) Helmville, MT St. Thomas Church.
Ryan, Kevin *o.s.b.* '42 (IND) [J] St. Meinrad, IN St. Meinrad Archabbey.
Ryan, Kevin E. '70 (SAT) [53] San Antonio, TX St. Mark the Evangelist Church.
Ryan, Laurence D. *s.j.* '77 (BGP) [P] Fairfield, CT The Fairfield Jesuit Community-Fairfield University.
Ryan, Lawrence A. '42 (SAC) Vacaville, CA St. Mary Church; Retired and in Senior Ministry.
Ryan, Lawrence D. *s.j.* '77 (BGP) [E] Fairfield, CT Fairfield College Preparatory School.
Ryan, Msgr. Leo P. '54 (PAT) Retired; [P] Chester, NJ Nazareth Village.
Ryan, Martin E. *s.j.* '48 (BO) [W] Weston, MA Campion Health Center, Inc.
Ryan, Msgr. Martin P. '76 (BGP) New Fairfield, CT St. Edward the Confessor Church; [F] Danbury, CT Catholic Elementary Schools-Region IX and XI.
Ryan, Michael G. '66 (SEA) [1] Seattle, WA St. James Church.
Ryan, Michael J. '68 (SEA) Kent, WA Holy Spirit Church.
Ryan, Michael J. '72 (PH) Oreland, PA Holy Martyrs Church.
Ryan, Milton Fleming *c.m.* '91 (SPC) [2] Cape Girardeau, MO St. Vincent de Paul Church.
Ryan, Noel '63 (LA) [67] Los Angeles, CA St. Gregory Nazianzen Church.
Ryan, Pat (OWN) [A] Owensboro, KY Brescia University.
Ryan, Patrick '70 (STL) On Duty Outside the Archdiocese.
Ryan, Patrick '85 (PMB) On Duty Outside the Diocese.
Ryan, Patrick J. *s.j.* '59 (BO) [W] Chestnut Hill, MA The Jesuit Community at Boston College.
Ryan, Patrick J. *s.j.* '68 (FgM) Provinces.
Ryan, Patrick J. *m.m.* '77 (NY) [DD] Maryknoll, NY Maryknoll Fathers and Brothers.
Ryan, Paul *s.m.* '45 (SAT) [M] San Antonio, TX Marianist Residence.
Ryan, Paul J. '73 (ROC) Hamlin, NY St. Elizabeth Ann Seton Church.
Ryan, Msgr. Paul T. '58 (BO) [23] Boston, MA St. Gregory Church.

Ryan, Peter F. *s.j.* '87 (BAL) [B] Baltimore, MD Loyola College in Maryland; [S] Baltimore, MD Jesuit Community of Loyola College, Inc.
Ryan, Philip J. '57 (SR) Guerneville, CA St. Elizabeth Church.
Ryan, Philip R. '57 (DAV) Keswick, IA Our Lady of Lourdes Church; Sigourney, IA St. Mary's Church.
Ryan, Raymond R. *o.s.a.* '57 (MIL) [14] Racine, WI St. Rita Church; [P] Racine, WI Augustinian Novitiate.
Ryan, Regis J. '66 (PIT) [3] McKees Rocks, PA St. John of God Church.
Ryan, Msgr. Richard '73 (STO) [9] Stockton, CA St. Michael Church.
Ryan, Richard '77 (PHX) Sun City, AZ Church of St. Joachim & St. Anne.
Ryan, Richard R. *c.m.* '69 (DEN) [M] Denver, CO Congregation of the Mission Midwest Province: De Paul House.
Ryan, Robert F. '47 (PH) Retired.
Ryan, Robin C. *c.p.* '84 (BO) [A] Boston, MA St. John's Seminary School of Theology.
Ryan, Stephen D. *o.p.* '93 (BO) [W] Dover, MA St. Stephen Priory.
Ryan, Stephen Desmond '93 (WDC) [B] Washington, DC Dominican House of Studies.
Ryan, Stephen M. *o.s.m.* '55 (CHI) [N] Chicago, IL Order of Friar Servants of Mary (Servites) United States of America Province, Inc.
Ryan, Stephen M. '95 (NY) [199] Staten Island, NY Blessed Sacrament Church.
Ryan, Msgr. T. Peter '62 (RVC) Centerport, NY Our Lady Queen of Martyrs Church.
Ryan, Terrence P. *c.s.p.* '77 (KNX) [4] Knoxville, TN John XXIII University Parish/Catholic Center Church; [J] Knoxville, TN UT-Knoxville, Newman Foundation, Inc.
Ryan, Thomas (BAL) [38] Baltimore, MD Holy Rosary Church; [C] Severn, MD Archbishop Spalding High School.
Ryan, Thomas '68 (FTW) Elkhart, IN St. Thomas the Apostle Church.
Ryan, Thomas A. '64 (GI) [1] Grand Island, NE Cathedral of the Nativity of the Blessed Virgin Mary
Ryan, Thomas F. '93 (MET) [3] Perth Amboy, NJ Holy Trinity Church; [5] Perth Amboy, NJ Our Lady of Hungary Church.
Ryan, Thomas J. '54 (SFS) Retired.
Ryan, Thomas J. '79 (SY) Johnson City, NY St. James Church.
Ryan, Thomas M. *s.j.* '71 (DET) [E] Detroit, MI University of Detroit Jesuit High School and Academy.
Ryan, Thomas P. *c.s.p.* '84 (NY) [104] New York, NY St. Paul the Apostle Church.
Ryan, Msgr. Timothy A. '57 (CAM) Cape May, NJ Our Lady Star of the Sea Church.
Ryan, Timothy K. '62 (SAV) Special Assignment.
Ryan, Vincent B. *s.j.* '45 (SY) [S] Syracuse, NY Jesuits at LeMoyne, Inc.
Ryan, William '55 (JOL) Retired; [I] Naperville, IL St. John Vianney Villa.
Ryan, William *o.s.a.* '66 (P) [L] Sheridan, OR Augustinian Community.
Ryan, William A. (PEO) Retired.
Ryan, William A. *s.j.* '45 (PH) [AA] Philadelphia, PA Jesuit Community at St. Joseph's University.
Ryan, William A. *o.s.a.* '66 (P) Myrtle Creek, OR All Souls Church.
Ryan, William A. '80 (WDC) Gaithersburg, MD St. Martin Church.
Ryan, William Arthur '59 (PEO) Ransom, IL St. Patrick's Church.
Ryan, William B. *o.p.* '47 (HRT) [14] New Haven, CT St. Mary's Priory Church.
Ryan, William F. '62 (CAM) Bellmawr, NJ Annunciation Church.
Ryan, William F. *s.j.* '62 (SPK) [C] Spokane, WA Gonzaga University.
Ryan, Msgr. William H. '48 (ELP) [10] El Paso, TX Immaculate Conception Church.
Ryan, William R. *s.j.* '94 (R) [7] Raleigh, NC St. Raphael Church; [E] Raleigh, NC Jesuit Community.
Ryba, Charles J. '69 (CLV) Columbia Station, OH St. Elizabeth Ann Seton Church; Grafton, OH Grafton Correctional Institution; Lorain, OH Lorain Correctional Institution.
Rybacki, Czeslaw *s.ch.* '85 (SFR) [37] San Francisco, CA Nativity Church.
Rybarczyk, Melvin *c.r.* '69 (VNN) San Diego, CA Holy Angels Church.
Ryberg, James C. '57 (OM) West Point, NE Assumption B.V.M. Church.
Rybicki, Daryl '79 (FTW) [2] South Bend, IN St. Adalbert Church; [4] South Bend, IN St. Augustine Church.
Rybicky, Walter *o.s.b.m.* '83 (STN) Palos Park, IL Nativity of B. V. M. Church.
Rybolt, John E. *c.m.* '67 (STL) [P] St. Louis, MO Vincentian Residence.
Rydelek, Theodore F. '89 (TYL) Buffalo, TX Blessed Kateri Tekakwitha Church.
Ryder, Frederick *c.pp.s.* '63 (CIN) Cassella, OH Nativity of the Blessed Virgin Mary Church; St. Rose, OH St. Rose Church.
Ryder, Joseph F. '46 (DET) Retired.
Ryder, Matthais '62 (ORG) Inactive Leave.
Rydz, Zygmund S. '48 (LIN) Retired.
Rydzewski, Thomas A (BAL) [1] Baltimore, MD Cathedral of Mary Our Queen.
Rydzon, Walter C. '76 (PIT) [55] Pittsburgh, PA St. Justin Church.
Rye, Gary C. *o.s.a.* '65 (LA) [18] Los Angeles, CA Mother of Good Counsel Church.
Ryfinski, Gerald J. '90 (CHR) Georgetown, SC St. Mary's Church; Georgetown, SC St. Cyprian Church.
Rykowski, Jerome A. '55 (PBL) Retired.
Rykowski, Valerian J. '43 (MIL) Retired.
Rykwalder, David L. '85 (GI) St. Libory, NE St. Libory's Church.
Ryland, Raymond '83 (SD) Retired.
Ryland, William A. '98 (LIN) Wahoo, NE St. Wenceslaus Church.
Ryle, Edward J. '56 (PHX) Special Assignment.
Ryle, Edward J. '56 (TUC) On Duty Outside the Diocese.
Ryle, Gerald '68 (SAC) Galt, CA St. Christopher Church.
Rymdeika, Joseph F. '82 (PH) Newtown Square, PA St. Anastasia Church; [A] Wynnewood, PA Theological Seminary of St. Charles Borromeo, Overbrook; [D] Downingtown, PA Bishop Shanahan High School.
Rynda, Reynold *o.f.m.cap.* '54 (GB) [I] Appleton, WI St. Fidelis Friary.
Rynes, Theodore J. *s.j.* '62 (SJ) [B] Santa Clara, CA Santa Clara University.
Rynish, Msgr. John F. '43 (SPC) Retired.
Rynne, Msgr. James J. '59 (CAM) Deptford, NJ St. John Vianney Church.
Rynne, Paul P. '56 (BO) Senior Priests.
Rynne, Thomas J. '56 (PMB) Jensen Beach, FL St. Martin de Porres Church; Retired.
Rys, Paschal *o.f.m.conv.* '51 (OG) Constableville, NY St. Mary Church; Retired.
Ryscavage, Richard J. *s.j.* '77 (FgM) Jesuit Foreign Missions.
Ryscavage, Richard J. *s.j.* '77 (WDC) [M] Washington, DC Leonard Neale House; [V] Washington, DC Jesuit Missions, Inc.; [V] Washington, DC Jesuit Refugee Service.
Rywalt, Lawrence *c.p.* '92 (BRK) [V] Jamaica, NY Immaculate Conception Monastery.
Rzadga, Janusz '95 (PAT) [J] Paterson, NJ St. Joseph's Hospital and Medical Center.
Rzeczkowski, Matthew *o.p.* '69 (WDC) [B] Washington, DC Dominican House of Studies.
Rzepiela, Thomas R. '72 (CHI) [44] Chicago, IL St. Constance Church.
Rzeszutek, Martin *m.i.c.* '51 (WDC) [M] Brookeville, MD Marian Monastery-Brookeville.
Rzonca, Kazimierz '78 (CHI) [112] Chicago, IL St. Ladislaus Church.
Rzonca, Michael W. '73 (PH) Spring City, PA St. Joseph Church; Graterford, PA Graterford State Correctional Institution.

S

Sa, Dominic P. '53 (PT) Panama City, FL SS. Peter & Paul Church.
Saad, Antoun '47 (SAM) Retired.
Saad, Msgr. Richard D. '72 (OLL) Birmingham, AL St. Elias Church; Birmingham, AL Maronite Catholic Community of Mobile Church; New Orleans, LA Maronite Catholic Community Church.
Saade, Bassam '92 (SAM) Utica, NY St. Louis Gonzaga Church.
Saah-Buckman, Michael K. *s.s.j.* '93 (BR) [8] Baton Rouge, LA St. Francis Xavier Church.
Saale, Richard T. '50 (KC) Retired.
Saalfeld, Lawrence '44 (P) Retired.
Saato, Fred '67 (NTN) Yonkers, NY Christ the Savior Church.
Saavedra, Juan de Dios (LAR) [E] Laredo, TX St. John Priory, F.J.
Saavedra, Juan de Dios '89 (CC) [H] Laredo, TX St. John's Priory, (F.J.).
Saba, Joseph '74 (JUN) On Duty Outside the Diocese.
Saba, Joseph '74 (TUC) Tucson, AZ St. Mary's Hospital; [E] Tucson, AZ Carondelet Health Network.
Saba, Joseph J. (BGP) [7] Bridgeport, CT St. Charles Church.
Sabadell, Juan *l.c.* (HRT) [V] Orange, CT Helping Hand Investments, Inc; [V] Orange, CT Horizons Institute, Inc.; [V] Orange, CT LUX ET VITA, INC.; [V] Orange, CT Rossotto, Inc.
Sabadell, Juan *l.c.* (NY) [HH] Thornwood, NY Regina Apostolorum, Inc.; [HH] Thornwood, NY Consolidated Catholic Administrative Services, Inc.
Sabadell, Juan (WDC) [V] Bethesda, MD Leadership Training Corp.
Sabak, James *o.f.m.* '99 (ALB) [B] Loudonville, NY Siena College; [B] Loudonville, NY Siena College; [R] Loudonville, NY Siena College.
Saban, Michael J. '89 (PH) Levittown, PA St. Michael the Archangel Church.
Sabariar, Thobias *h.g.n.* '92 (LEX) Ashland, KY Holy Family Church.
Sabatini, Francis J. '63 (PH) [89] Philadelphia, PA St. Lucy Church.
Sabatini, Lawrence *c.s.* (CHI) [83] Chicago, IL Holy Rosary Church.
Sabatino, Msgr. Robert A. '56 (Y) Ravenna, OH Immaculate Conception Church.
Sabatos, Daniel C. '62 (BRK) Absent on Leave.
Sabatte, Frank *c.s.p.* '80 (BO) [W] Boston, MA Paulist Fathers Residence.
Sabbagh, Stephen F. *o.f.m.* '59 (WDC) [M] Washington, DC Commissariat of the Holy Land, Franciscan Monastery - Mount St. Sepulchre.
Sabella, Charles A. '94 (MET) [L] Phillipsburg, NJ The Anawim Community.
Sabia, Msgr. John B. '64 (BGP) Monroe, CT St. Jude Church.
Sable, Msgr. Robert M. '74 (DET) Special Assignment.
Sable, Thomas F. *s.j.* '75 (SCR) [C] Scranton, PA University of Scranton; [C] Scranton, PA University of Scranton.
Sabo, Edward *t.o.r.* '68 (WH) Stonewood, WV Our Lady of Perpetual Help Church.
Sabo, Gerald J. *s.j.* '80 (CLV) [B] Cleveland, OH John Carroll Jesuit Community.
Sabo, Paul P. '69 (BUF) [68] Buffalo, NY The Visitation of the B.V.M. Church.
Sabog, Henry '60 (HON) Retired.
Sabol, George *o.f.m.conv.* '71 (TR) Riverside, NJ St. Peter Church.
Sabol, Sebastian *o.s.b.m.* '34 (STN) Warren, MI St. Josaphat Church.
Sabourin, Gerard O. '60 (PRO) Exeter, RI Blessed Kateri Tekakwitha Church.
Sabourin, Leo F. '58 (DET) [2] Taylor, MI St. Constance Church.
Sabulis, Paul P. '43 (HRT) Retired.
Saburo, Rusk R. '93 (CI) Koror, FM Sacred Heart Church.
Sacca, Raymond '79 (OAK) Livermore, CA St. Michael Church.
Saccacio, Msgr. Robert J. '61 (RVC) Amityville, NY St. Martin's Church.
Sacco, Carmine J. *s.j.* '57 (SEA) [8] Tacoma, WA St. Rita Church.
Saccoman, Robert D. '57 (NY) Wesley Hills, NY St. Boniface Church.
Sachez, Antero *m.s.c.* '65 (FRS) Earlimart, CA St. Jude Thaddeus Church.
Sachs, John R. *s.j.* '76 (BO) [B] Cambridge, MA Weston Jesuit School of Theology; [W] Cambridge, MA Weston Jesuit Community.
Sackett, Frederick *o.m.i.* '41 (SAT) [C] San Antonio, TX Oblate School of Theology; [M] San Antonio, TX De Mazenod House.
Sackevich, Paul E. '84 (BUR) Chester, VT St. Joseph Church.
Sacks, Msgr. Edward R. '64 (ALN) [8] Bethlehem, PA Our Lady of Perpetual Help Church.
Sacks, Francis *c.m.* (PH) [46] Philadelphia, PA St. Francis of Assisi Church.
Sacks, Francis W. *c.m.* '67 (PH) [B] Philadelphia, PA St. Vincent's Seminary.
Sacksteder, Thomas B. '73 (COV) Florence, KY St. Paul Church.
Sacus, Samuel S. '66 (WH) Beckley, WV St. Francis De Sales Church.
Sadek, Msgr. Ignace '56 (SAM) Brooklyn, NY Cathedral of Our Lady of Lebanon.
Sadie, P. Edward '57 (WH) [1] Charleston, WV Sacred Heart Co-Church.
Sadler, Alfred '34 (DET) Marine City, MI Holy Cross Church.
Sadler, Alfred H. '34 (DET) Retired.
Sadlier, Richard *s.s.j.* (LAF) Crowley, LA St. Theresa Church.
Sadlowski, Ronald F. '72 (SPR) Feeding Hills, MA Sacred Heart Church.
Sadowski, Bob *c.s.p.* '85 (LA) [BB] Los Angeles, CA Archdiocesan Office for Campus Ministry.
Sadowski, Richard *s.d.b.* (CHI) [103] Chicago, IL St. John Bosco Church.
Sadowsky, James A. *s.j.* '57 (NY) [DD] New York, NY Jesuit Community at Fordham University.
Sadsoeitoeboen, Carl *c.i.c.m.* '00 (SAT) Del Rio, TX Sacred Heart Church.
Sadusky, Msgr. Joseph F. '70 (WDC) [37] Washington, DC St. Peter Church; Pastoral Center Special Ministries.
Saelzler, Richard J. '76 (TOL) Bowling Green, OH St. Thomas More University Church; [N] Bowling Green, OH Bowling Green State University Campus Ministry.
Saena, Poao '95 (SEA) [8] Seattle, WA St. Edward Church; [9] Seattle, WA St. George Church; [18] Seattle, WA St. Paul Church.

Saenz, Alonso '97 (PHX) Chandler, AZ St. Mary's Church.
Saenz, David '97 (CC) [E] Corpus Christi, TX CHRISTUS Spohn Hospital Shoreline.
Saenz, Roberto B. *s.j.* '59 (YAK) [3] Yakima, WA Holy Redeemer Church.
Saenz, Urbano *o.s.a.* '70 (MGZ) San German, PR St. Rose of Lima Church.
Saez, Jose '49 (ELP) Retired.
Saez, Raul '82 (SJN) [D] San Juan, PR Santa Ana Chapel.
Saez, Solh '67 (DAL) [13] Dallas, TX St. Augustine Catholic Church.
Saffario, Giovanni *i.m.c.* '65 (SB) [7] Riverside, CA St. Francis de Sales Church.
Safiejko, Edward M. '48 (MIL) Retired.
Safko, Gerard F. '90 (SCR) Drums, PA Church of the Good Shepherd.
Safko, Steven '73 (PSC) Phillipsburg, NJ SS. Peter and Paul Church.
Safranek, William '96 (OM) [38] Omaha, NE St. Pius X Church.
Safraniec, Joseph '76 (STP) Minneapolis, MN Veterans Administration Medical Center.
Safraniec, Joseph '76 (STU) On Duty Outside the Diocese.
Sagala, James F. '61 (PIT) Military Chaplains.
Sagardia, Reinaldo '79 (SJN) [32] San Juan, PR San Lucas Church.
Sagardoy, Angel '60 (LA) [1] Oxnard, CA St. Anthony Church.
Sagili, Msgr. Devadas '79 (CHI) Lyons, IL St. Hugh Church.
Sagorski, Peter A. '95 (ORL) Daytona Beach, FL St. Paul's Church.
Sah, Sushil '87 (DET) [K] Detroit, MI Jesuit Community at the University of Detroit.
Saharic, Michael C. '88 (MET) [1] Metuchen, NJ Cathedral of St. Francis.
Sahlfeld, Francis J. '48 (CIN) Retired.
Sailstad, Kenton (DUL) Duluth, MN Indian Missions Church; Duluth, MN Indian Missions Church.
Sailstad, Kenton '88 (DUL) Carlton, MN St. Francis Church; Cloquet, MN Queen of Peace Church.
Sajda, Michael *o.f.m.conv.* '79 (PMB) [B] Fort Pierce, FL John Carroll High School.
Sajdak, John *s.m.* '71 (DET) [E] Harper Woods, MI Notre Dame High School.
Sajdak, Ronald P. '96 (BUF) [2] Orchard Park, NY St. Bernadette Church.
Saju, P.J. (Steve) (WH) St. Joseph Settlement, WV St. Joseph's Church.
Sakalys, Raphael J. *o.f.m.* '53 (PRT) [I] Kennebunkport, ME St. Anthony's Friary.
Sakano, Msgr. Donald '71 (NY) [47] New York, NY Holy Innocents Church; [HH] New York, NY The Housing Fund of the Archdiocese of New York.
Sakayan, Nerses *o.mech.* (ARM) [A] La Crescenta, CA Mekhitarist School.
Sakevicius, Jonas *m.i.c.* '32 (CHI) [N] Chicago, IL Congregation of Marian Fathers of the Immaculate Conception.
Sakowicz, Gregory '79 (CHI) [129] Chicago, IL St. Mary of the Woods Church.
Saksons, Richard *o.praem.* '91 (BAK) Vale, OR St. Patrick's Church.
Sala, Michael J. *s.j.* '77 (NY) Manhattan, NY Metropolitan Hospital; [DD] New York, NY St. Ignatius Loyola Residence.
Salach, Conrad *o.f.m.conv.* '71 (BO) [6] Lawrence, MA Holy Trinity Church.
Salada, Urbano '59 (SD) Retired.
Saladna, George E. '58 (PIT) Springdale, PA St. Alphonsus Church.
Salah, Michael A. '91 (WDC) [14] Washington, DC St. Francis Xavier Church.
Salamon, John *c.ss.r.* '45 (ALB) [L] Saratoga Springs, NY St. John Neumann Residence.
Salamone, Charles E. '75 (BO) [1] Milton, MA St. Agatha Church.
Salamone, Michael '75 (BRK) [119] Brooklyn, NY Most Precious Blood Church.
Salamoni, Vincent *m.s.a.* '84 (NOR) [F] Cromwell, CT Society of the Missionaries of the Holy Apostles.
Salanitro, Alfred J. '89 (OM) Blair, NE St. Francis Borgia Church.
Salanitro, Carl A. '70 (OM) [30] Omaha, NE Mary Our Queen Church.
Salapata, Andrzej *s.ch.* '97 (CHI) [85] Chicago, IL Holy Trinity Church.
Salas, Raul *o.m.i.* '80 (BEL) [F] Belleville, IL Shrine of Our Lady of the Snows.
Salas, Msgr. Sipio '50 (SFE) Retired.
Salas, Vicente *o.m.* '66 (PCE) [B] Ponce, PR The Pontifical Catholic University of Puerto Rico.
Salatino, John C. '94 (SPR) [4] Westfield, MA St. Mary's Church.
Salazar, Msgr. Alejandro '91 (LAR) [10] Laredo, TX San Martin de Porres Church.
Salazar, Alexander '84 (LA) [92] Los Angeles, CA St. Teresa of Avila Church.
Salazar, Cesar '93 (ORG) [8] Santa Ana, CA St. Joseph's Church.
Salazar, Donald *o.f.m.* '67 (FgM) Franciscan Foreign Missions.
Salazar, Edward *s.j.* '74 (CC) [E] Corpus Christi, TX CHRISTUS Spohn Hospital Shoreline.
Salazar, Fernando Palacio '79 (MGZ) San German, PR San German de Auxerre Church; [C] San German, PR Hospital of the Immaculate Conception.
Salazar, Franklin '75 (RVC) Mastic Beach, NY St. Jude Church.
Salazar, George '67 (SFE) Taos, NM Nuestra Senora De Guadalupe Church.
Salazar, George V. '67 (SFE) Las Vegas, NM Immaculate Conception Church; [L] Las Vegas, NM Highlands University Newman Center.
Salazar, Jairo '91 (SJN) [4] Toa Alta, PR Nuestra Senora de la Medalla Milagrosa Church.
Salazar, Jose *m.s.a.* '77 (NOR) [F] Cromwell, CT Society of the Missionaries of the Holy Apostles.
Salazar, Jose Angel '85 (CC) Mathis, TX Sacred Heart Church.
Salazar, Joseph A. *m.s.a.* '73 (ARL) Woodstock, VA St. John Bosco Church.
Salazar, Mario A. '61 (YAK) Quincy, WA St. Pius X Church.
Salazar, Mario P. '90 (YAK) Granger, WA Our Lady of Guadalupe Church.
Salazar-Jimenez, John '84 (AMA) Tulia, TX Church of the Holy Spirit.
Salberg, James G. '69 (PIT) Center Township, PA St. Andrew Church.
Salca, Louis A. '65 (SD) [4] El Cajon, CA St. Louise de Marillac Church.
Salcedo, Luis G. '89 (WDC) [1] Bethesda, MD St. Bartholomew Church; Retired.
Saldana, Jesus '82 (MIA) [24] Miami, FL St. Kevin Church.
Saldana, Jose '78 (DAL) Absent on Leave.
Saldana, Luis '99 (NY) [31] New York, NY St. Elizabeth Church.
Salditos, Ricardito P. '80 (LUB) Morton, TX St. Ann Church.
Saldivar, Roberto *m.sp.s.* '00 (LA) Huntington Park, CA St. Martha Church.
Salemi, Msgr. Cajetan P. '61 (NEW) Woodcliff Lake, NJ Our Lady Mother of the Church.
Salemi, Paul S. '00 (BUF) Hamburg, NY SS. Peter and Paul Church.
Salera, Alfredo J. '77 (CHI) Round Lake, IL St. Joseph Church.
Salerno, Emilio J. '59 (BRK) [168] Queens, NY St. Francis of Assisi Church.
Salerno, Joseph '80 (SY) [13] Utica, NY St. Mary of Mt. Carmel Church.
Salerno, Joseph A. '65 (CAM) Mantua, NJ Incarnation Church.
Salerno, Michael *s.a.c.* '93 (BAL) [54] Baltimore, MD St. Leo Church.
Saletrik, E. George '96 (GBG) Monessen, PA The Epiphany of Our Lord Church.
Salgado, Jose *f.s.s.p.* (COS) [1] Colorado Springs, CO St. Mary's Church.
Salgado, Jose *f.s.s.p.* (DEN) [3] Arvada, CO Our Lady of Mount Carmel Tridentine Latin Mass Community Church.
Salgado, Jose *f.s.s.p.* '93 (SCR) [M] Elmhurst, PA Priestly Fraternity of St. Peter (F.S.S.P.), North American District Headquarters.
Salgado, Salvador *c.m.f.* '78 (SJN) [2] Bayamon, PR San Antonio Maria Claret Church.
Saliba, John A. *s.j.* '65 (DET) [K] Detroit, MI Jesuit Community at the University of Detroit.
Salim, Anthony J. '74 (OLL) Youngstown, OH St. Maron Church.
Salinas, Octavio Jose *o.f.m.* '83 (NY) [4] Mt. Vernon, NY Our Lady of Mount Carmel Church; [DD] New York, NY Franciscan Province of the Immaculate Conception.
Salinas, Romeo '00 (CC) Mathis, TX Sacred Heart Church.
Salisbury, Paschal Donald *o.p.* '67 (P) Ashland, OR Our Lady of the Mountain Church; White City, OR U.S. Veternan's Affairs Domiciliary.
Salisbury, W. Dayton *s.s.j.* '59 (BAL) [S] Baltimore, MD St. Joseph Society of the Sacred Heart House of Central Administration.
Saliva, Juan J. '90 (PCE) Aguirre, PR Sacred Heart Church.
Salko, John H. '60 (PBR) Scottdale, PA St. John the Baptist Church.
Salkovski, Basil *o.s.b.m.* '88 (STN) Warren, MI St. Josaphat Church.
Saller, Neil *t.o.r.* '56 (PH) [AA] Fairless Hills, PA St. Anthony Friary.
Salles, George *m.afr.* '69 (CHI) [121] Chicago, IL St. Martin De Porres Church.
Salles, Georges *m.afr.* '69 (CHI) [N] Chicago, IL Missionaries of Africa.
Sallese, Albert J. (BO) Hingham, MA Resurrection of Our Lord and Saviour Jesus Christ Church.
Sallis, Steven '80 (SEA) Bothell, WA St. Brendan Church.
Sallot, Steven '80 (ORG) [C] Santa Ana, CA Mater Dei High School.
Salmani, Frank S. '82 (PRO) [22] Providence, RI St. Mary Church.
Salmi, Richard P. *s.j.* '82 (CLV) [B] Cleveland, OH John Carroll University; [B] Cleveland, OH John Carroll Jesuit Community.
Salmon, Charles P. '44 (DEN) Retired.
Salmon, Edward F. *s.j.* '85 (NY) [B] Bronx, NY Ciszek Hall.
Salmon, Edward P. '59 (CHI) [4] Oak Park, IL St. Giles Church.
Salmon, James F. *s.j.* '64 (BAL) [B] Baltimore, MD Loyola College in Maryland; [S] Baltimore, MD Jesuit Community of Loyola College, Inc.
Salmon, William F. '65 (BO) [54] Boston, MA Our Lady of the Presentation Church.
Salnicky, Michael J. '93 (PSC) Old Forge, PA St. Nicholas Church.
Salocks, Stephen E. '80 (BO) [A] Boston, MA St. John's Seminary School of Theology.
Salois, Philip (BO) Jamaica Plain, MA Jamaica Plain; Jamaica Plain, MA Veterans Administration Hospital.
Salomon, Elias *s.s.j.v.* '79 (DET) Plymouth, MI Our Lady of Good Counsel Church.
Salomone, Gregory *o.p.* '72 (RIC) Charlottesville, VA St. Thomas Aquinas Church.
Salomone, Ramon A. *s.j.* '65 (FgM) Provinces.
Saloy, Lee John '72 (NO) [13] Metairie, LA St. Philip Neri Church.
Saloy, Thomas '88 (RVC) West Babylon, NY Our Lady of Grace Church.
Saltarin, Jose '67 (NEW) [18] Jersey City, NJ St. Nicholas Church.
Salter-Smith, Cassandra (BUF) [R] Alfred, NY Campus Ministry.
Saltysiak, Paul M. '92 (WDC) Military Chaplains.
Salus, Jude S. *o.s.b.* '75 (PAT) Cedar Knolls, NJ Notre Dame of Mt. Carmel Church; [M] Morristown, NJ St. Mary's Abbey.
Salvador, Msgr. Antonio (ARE) Retired.
Salvador, John *c.m.f.* '54 (PHX) Prescott, AZ Sacred Heart Church.
Salvador, Stephen B. '74 (FR) [21] Fall River, MA SS. Peter and Paul Church.
Salvagna, Michael *c.p.* '69 (PIT) [O] Pittsburgh, PA St. Paul of the Cross Monastery; [Q] Pittsburgh, PA St. Paul of the Cross Retreat Center.
Salvana, Bonifacio '56 (YAK) Waterville, WA St. Joseph's Church.
Salvas, John *o.f.m.cap.* '88 (CHL) Hendersonville, NC Immaculate Conception Church.
Salvatori, Chris *s.a.c.* '00 (NY) [91] New York, NY Our Lady of Mt. Carmel Church.
Salvi, Americo *c.r.m.* '55 (NEW) Lodi, NJ St. Joseph's Church.
Salwach, Jeffery *o.f.m.* '84 (SAT) [33] San Antonio, TX St. Clare Church; [46] San Antonio, TX St. Joseph Church.
Salwowski, Francis J. *o.f.m.cap.* '45 (PAT) [M] Oak Ridge-Milton, NJ St. Stanislaus B. M. Friary.
Salwowski, John F. *o.f.m.cap.* '45 (MET) [4] New Brunswick, NJ St. Joseph Church.
Saly, Msgr. Robert J. (ALT) [4] Northern Cambria, PA Prince of Peace Church.
Salz, Marv C. '64 (DUB) Waucoma, IA St. Mary's Church.
Salz, Marvin C. '64 (DUB) Lawler, IA Our Lady of Mt. Carmel Church; St. Lucas, IA St. Luke's Church.
Salzmann, George S. *o.s.f.s.* '77 (BO) [11] Cambridge, MA St. Paul Church; [CC] Cambridge, MA Harvard Catholic Student Center.
Salzmann, George S. *o.s.f.s.* '77 (WIL) [I] Wilmington, DE Oblates of St. Francis De Sales.
Samaha, Jeffrey F. '78 (WDC) Camp Springs, MD St. Philip the Apostle Church; Hospital & Nursing Home Ministries.
Samaniego, Eduardo A. *s.j.* '90 (SD) [4] San Diego, CA Christ the King Church.
Samaniego, Tarciscio *l.c.* '65 (HRT) [B] Cheshire, CT Novitiate of the Legion of Christ.
Samay, Sebastian A. '59 (GBG) [H] Latrobe, PA Saint Vincent Archabbey.
Samayoa, Emmanuel G. '89 (ROM) Dearborn, MI St. Mary Church.
Sambor, David R. '78 (SY) [10] Utica, NY St. Joseph and St. Patrick Church; Special Assignment.
Samiano, Marvin '92 (HON) Kailua, HI St. Anthony Church.
Sammon, Msgr. John F. '42 (ORG) Special Assignment.
Sammon, Peter J. '47 (SFR) [51] San Francisco, CA St. Teresa Church.
Sammon, Richard J. *m.m.* '56 (FgM) Maryknoll Foreign Missions.
Sammons, Msgr. Francis L. '47 (SY) East Syracuse, NY St. Matthew Church; Retired.
Sammut, Tito '52 (GB) Retired.
Samonie, Jacob '56 (DET) Retired.

Samperi, Charles J. '96 (GAL) [40] Houston, TX St. John Neumann Church.
Sampietro, Vincent J. *c.s.p.* '45 (NY) [DD] Jamaica Estates, NY Paulist Fathers Generalate.
Sampietro, Vincent J. *c.s.p.* '45 (P) [29] Portland, OR St. Philip Neri Church.
Sample, Alexander K. '90 (MAR) [1] Marquette, MI St. Peter Church; [2] Marquette, MI St. Christopher Church; Special Assignment.
Sampon, Robert G. '53 (MIL) Newburg, WI Holy Trinity Church.
Sampson, Elric '85 (CHI) [N] Chicago, IL St. Peter's Friary.
Sampson, J. Gregory *c.j.m.* '54 (BUF) [1] West Seneca, NY St. Bonaventure Church; [O] West Seneca, NY Eudist Fathers, St. John Eudes Center.
Sampson, James *s.p.* '65 (SFE) Jemez Springs, NM Our Lady of the Assumption Church.
Sampson, Patrick '55 (GF) Retired.
Samra, Basil '86 (NTN) Leave of Absence.
Sams, Ronald W. *s.j.* '59 (BUF) [D] Buffalo, NY Canisius High School; [O] Buffalo, NY Canisius Jesuit Community.
Samsa, Bertin L. *o.f.m.cap.* (GB) Manawa, WI Sacred Heart Church; Weyauwega, WI SS. Peter and Paul Church.
Samsa, John Francis *o.f.m.cap.* '61 (FgM) Capuchin Foreign Missions.
Samson, John F. '61 (SCR) Ashley, PA Holy Rosary Church.
Samson, Robert J. '79 (STL) [9] Florissant, MO St. Sabina Church.
Samter, James '87 (GB) Special Assignment.
Samudio, Francisco *c.m.* '92 (FgM) Vincentian Foreign Missions.
Samuel, Francis '72 (RVC) Seaford, NY St. James Church.
Samway, Patrick H. *s.j.* '69 (NEW) [B] Jersey City, NJ Saint Peter's College; [N] Jersey City, NJ Jesuits of Saint Peter's College, Inc.
Samy, Edward '67 (SJ) Milpitas, CA St. Elizabeth Church.
Samy, S. Anthony '85 (NY) [138] Bronx, NY St. Dominic Church.
San Andres, Vito B. '79 (AGN) Yigo, GU Our Lady of Lourdes Church.
San Fratello, Sennen C. *o.f.m.* '58 (ALB) [B] Loudonville, NY Siena College.
San Llorente, Faustino '41 (ARE) Retired.
San Marco, Salvator J. *s.j.* '53 (MIA) [5] Miami, FL Gesu Church.
San Martin, Miguel Angel *c.p.* '63 (MGZ) San Sebastian, PR San Sebastian Martir Church.
San Nicasio, Julian *s.d.b.* '76 (ARE) Orocovis, PR San Juan Bautista Church.
San Nicolas, Jeffrey '97 (AGN) Yigo, GU Our Lady of Lourdes Church.
Sana, Yoshia '84 (EST) San Jose, CA St. Mary Assyrian-Chaldean Church.
Sanabria, Edgardo *o.p.* '96 (SJN) [8] Bayamon, PR Invencion de la Santa Cruz Church.
Sanahuja, Manuel *sch.p.* '67 (LA) [A] Camarillo, CA St. John's Seminary College of the Archdiocese of Los Angeles.
Sanango, Mauricio '98 (BRK) [24] Brooklyn, NY St. Brigid Church.
Sanches, Joseph A. '70 (ATL) On Duty Outside the Archdiocese.
Sanches, Joseph A. '70 (NSH) [10] Nashville, TN Church of the Most Holy Name; [11] Nashville, TN St. Patrick's Church.
Sanchez, Alejandro (STV) On Duty Outside the Diocese.
Sanchez, Andres Eiroa '88 (SJN) [G] Guaynabo, PR Opus Dei.
Sanchez, Angel '75 (MGZ) Hormigueros, PR El Salvador Church.
Sanchez, Angel '90 (PCE) Salinas, PR Our Lady of Monserrat Church.
Sanchez, Angelo *c.ss.r.* '92 (CGS) Aguas Buenas, PR Church of Tres Santos Reyes.
Sanchez, Antero *m.s.c.* '65 (FRS) McFarland, CA St. Elizabeth Church.
Sanchez, Antonio '90 (MRY) Special Assignment.
Sanchez, Castor G. '61 (TR) [19] Trenton, NJ St. Michael Church.
Sanchez, Eliseo '57 (LA) Retired.
Sanchez, Esquiel '95 (CHI) [180] Chicago, IL Resurrection Church.
Sanchez, Felix '65 (SP) [9] Tampa, FL St. Joseph Church.
Sanchez, Guadalupe *o.s.j.* '60 (FRS) Madera, CA St. Joachim Church.
Sanchez, Hernan J. '98 (GAL) Humble, TX St. Mary Magdalene Church.
Sanchez, J. Antonio '90 (MRY) Watsonville, CA Our Lady of the Assumption Church.
Sanchez, Jose '61 (BRK) [225] Queens, NY St. Paul the Apostle Church; Queens, NY Elmhurst General Hospital.
Sanchez, Jose *c.m.* '62 (PH) [AA] Philadelphia, PA Congregation of the Mission.
Sanchez, Jose *c.m.f.* '95 (LA) San Gabriel, CA San Gabriel Church; [Q] San Gabriel, CA Claretian Missionaries (Missionary Sons of the Immaculate Heart of Mary).
Sanchez, Jose de Jesus *m.sp.s.* '00 (LA) [3] Oxnard, CA Our Lady of Guadalupe Church.
Sanchez, Jose M. '58 (GAL) Freeport, TX St. Henry Church.
Sanchez, Joseph G. '83 (LA) Lynwood, CA St. Philip Neri Church.
Sanchez, Juan Luis '84 (MIA) Absent on Leave.
Sanchez, Msgr. Manuel '54 (LA) Retired.
Sanchez, Msgr. Manuel O. '54 (LA) Pomona, CA Sacred Heart Church.
Sanchez, Miguel Angel '98 (ELP) [1] El Paso, TX St. Patrick's Church.
Sanchez, Msgr. Paul R. '71 (BRK) [2] Brooklyn, NY St. Agatha's Church.
Sanchez, Prudencio *c.m.* '59 (MGZ) [8] Mayaquez, PR San Vicente Church.
Sanchez, Raul '74 (GLP) On Duty Outside of Diocese.
Sanchez, Raul '93 (FRS) [6] Fresno, CA St. Alphonsus Church.
Sanchez, Ricardo F. '99 (CHL) Clemmons, NC Holy Family Church.
Sanchez, Stephen *o.c.d.* '92 (LR) [A] Little Rock, AR Marylake - Carmelite Novitiate.
Sanchez, Stephen A. '82 (SFE) [15] Albuquerque, NM Queen of Heaven Church; Albuquerque, NM Presbyterian Hospital.
Sanchez, Victor '91 (ARE) [2] Manati, PR Our Savior Church.
Sanchez, William E. '83 (SFE) Socorro, NM San Miguel Church.
Sanchez-Espinoza, Juan '93 (CHI) [180] Chicago, IL Resurrection Church.
Sancho, Jesus *o.c.d.* '64 (DAL) [20] Dallas, TX St. Mary of Carmel Church.
Sancho Piquer, Enrique '50 (PCE) On Duty Outside the Diocese.
Sand, John '55 (SPK) Retired.
Sandberg, Stuart '68 (NY) [HH] White Plains, NY Company of St. Paul.
Sandell, John '67 (FAR) Retired.
Sander, Bernard *o.s.b.* '44 (P) [L] St. Benedict, OR Mt. Angel Abbey.
Sander, Francis *o.s.b.* '49 (NO) [P] St. Benedict, LA St. Joseph Abbey.
Sander, Reginald *o.s.b.* '63 (KC) Tarkio, MO St. Paul the Apostle Church.
Sander, Timothy *o.s.b.* '41 (P) [L] St. Benedict, OR Mt. Angel Abbey.
Sanders, Daniel J. (MIL) Fontana, WI St. Benedict Church.
Sanders, Dennis *c.r.* '67 (CHI) [M] Des Plaines, IL Nazarethville; [N] Chicago, IL Provincial Office of the Congregation of the Resurrection.
Sanders, Edwin J. *s.j.* '59 (ALN) [A] Wernersville, PA Jesuit Center.
Sanders, Gary E. *o.s.a.* '75 (LA) Ojai, CA St. Thomas Aquinas Church; [F] Ojai, CA Villanova Preparatory School.
Sanders, Msgr. John C. '73 (BGP) [4] Norwalk, CT St. Mary Church; Retired; [P] Stamford, CT The Catherine Dennis Keefe Queen of the Clergy Retired Priests' Residence.
Sanders, John R. *o.s.a.* '74 (SD) [C] San Diego, CA St. Augustine High School; [H] San Diego, CA Augustinian Community.
Sanders, Joseph P. '61 (ALN) [A] Wernersville, PA Jesuit Center.
Sanders, Lawrence E. *c.ss.r.* '93 (WCH) [F] Wichita, KS Redemptorist Community; [H] Wichita, KS Spiritual Life Center; [H] Wichita, KS Spiritual Life Center.
Sanders, Patrick B. '90 (NO) Reserve, LA St. Peter Church.
Sanders, Peter C. *c.o.* '84 (MRY) [F] Monterey, CA Oratorian Community-Congregation of the Oratory of Pontifical Right.
Sanders, Raymond *s.v.d.* '45 (WDC) [M] Washington, DC Divine Word College.
Sanders, William F. '75 (WOR) [28] Worcester, MA St. Stephen's Church.
Sandersfeld, Msgr. John '66 (SJ) [2] San Jose, CA St. Francis of Assisi Church.
Sanderson, William E. '83 (OM) Coleridge, NE St. Michael Church; Hartington, NE Holy Trinity Church.
Sandford, Stephen *s.j.* '94 (RC) [B] Pine Ridge, SD Jesuit Community of Holy Rosary Mission.
Sandhage, Martin J. '86 (LFT) Portland, IN Immaculate Conception Church.
Sandheinrich, Msgr. Bernard H. '60 (STL) [46] St. Louis, MO Basilica of St. Louis, King of France .
Sandi, Msgr. Thomas (NY) [205] Staten Island, NY Holy Family Church.
Sandi, Thomas P. '73 (NY) Military Chaplains.
Sandman, Gregory '80 (MRY) Watsonville, CA St. Patrick Church.
Sandmann, Augustus C. *o.s.a.* '47 (NY) [216] Staten Island, NY Our Lady of Good Counsel Church.
Sandor, Albert *o.f.m.cap.* '82 (DET) [K] Detroit, MI St. Bonaventure Friary.
Sandor, George *o.f.m.conv.* '72 (SY) [5] Binghamton, NY SS. Cyril and Method Church.
Sandoval, Clarence J. '87 (SLC) Logan, UT St. Thomas Aquinas Church; [H] Logan, UT St. Thomas Aquinas, Newman Center.
Sandoval, Luis '74 (SAT) On Leave.
Sandoval, Victoriano '59 (TR) [3] Long Branch, NJ St. John the Baptist Church.
Sandoz, Robert *o.f.m.* '86 (PAT) Little Falls, NJ Our Lady of the Holy Angels Church.
Sands, Francis *c.ss.r.* '47 (ORL) [F] New Smyrna Beach, FL St. Alphonsus Villa-Redemptorist Fathers and Brothers.
Sands, Joseph C. *s.j.* '92 (BAL) [S] Baltimore, MD Jesuit Fathers and Brothers Maryland Provincial Curia.
Sands, Joseph C. *s.j.* '92 (PH) [83] Philadelphia, PA Old St. Joseph's Church.
Sandstrom, Philip J (NY) [HH] New York, NY St. Ansgar Scandinavian Catholic League.
Sandstrom, Philip J. '62 (NY) Absent on Sick leave.
Sandweg, Michael J. '79 (STL) Portage Des Sioux, MO St. Francis of Assisi Church.
Saner, Daniel J. '69 (COV) Augusta, KY St. Augustine Church; Brooksville, KY St. James Church.
Sanfelippo, Frank J. '58 (MIL) Retired.
Sanfilippo, David '94 (PHX) [8] Phoenix, AZ St. Augustine Church.
Sanfilippo, Ronald J. *s.j.* '76 (SFR) [E] San Francisco, CA St. Ignatius College Preparatory (Coed); [N] San Francisco, CA Jesuit Community at St. Ignatius College Preparatory.
Sanford, James R. '86 (TOL) [C] Toledo, OH St. Francis de Sales High School; [K] Toledo, OH Oblates of St. Francis de Sales.
Sanford, L. Harold *s.j.* '75 (DET) [P] Clarkston, MI Colombiere Center.
Sanford, Mark *o.f.m.* '43 (L) [K] Louisville, KY St. Joseph Home for the Aged.
Sanford, Stephen J *s.j.* '94 (BO) [W] Boston, MA The Society of Jesus of New England-Provincial Offices.
Sanford, Stephen J. *s.j.* '94 (RC) Pine Ridge, SD Sacred Heart Church.
Sanford, Steve *s.j.* '94 (RC) Pine Ridge, SD Holy Rosary Church.
Sang, Andrew Dolinh *c.m.c.* '83 (STP) [28] Minneapolis, MN St. Joseph Hien Church.
Sang, Francis D. '73 (RVC) Deer Park, NY SS. Cyril and Methodius Church.
Sanger, Charles P. '37 (DEN) Retired.
Sangermano, Charles L. '78 (PH) [135] Philadelphia, PA St. Paul Church.
Sangiovanni, William F. '77 (BGP) [4] Trumbull, CT St. Theresa Church; [C] Fairfield, CT Notre Dame Catholic High School.
Sangl, Harry R. '54 (PIT) Chippewa Township, PA Christ the Divine Teacher Church.
Sankoorikal, George '71 (BGP) [6] Fairfield, CT St. Pius X Church.
Sankoorikal, Paul L. '59 (LC) Bangor, WI St. Mary Church; [D] La Crosse, WI Franciscan Skemp Healthcare, Mayo Health System, La Crosse Campus Medical Center.
Sankovitz, Msgr. John P. '47 (STP) Retired; [C] St. Paul, MN University of St. Thomas.
Sanks, T. Howland *s.j.* '65 (OAK) [A] Berkeley, CA The Jesuit School of Theology at Berkeley; [N] Berkeley, CA Jesuit Community at Jesuit School of Theology at Berkeley.
Sanner, Msgr. James E. '59 (E) On Duty Outside Diocese.
Sans, Pablo '53 (BRK) [208] Queens, NY Our Lady of the Cenacle Church; Retired.
Sans, Theodore R. '59 (L) [3] Louisville, KY St. Albert the Great Church.
Sansaricq, Msgr. Carl '51 (NY) Spring Valley, NY St. Joseph Church.
Sansaricq, Guy '60 (BRK) [65] Brooklyn, NY St. Jerome's Church; [U] Brooklyn, NY Catholic Migration & Refugee Office, Catholic Migration Services, Inc.; [Z] Brooklyn, NY National Center of the Haitian Apostolate.
Sansom, Lawrence W. '41 (ROC) Retired.
Sanson, Robert J. '67 (CLV) Strongsville, OH St. Joseph Church.
Sansone, Anthony J. '80 (BRK) [126] Brooklyn, NY St. Rosalia-Regina Pacis Church.
Sansone, Simon *o.c.s.o.* '89 (WOR) [N] Spencer, MA St. Joseph's Abbey.
Santa, Juan '85 (SJN) [17] Bayamon, PR La Resurreccion del Senor Church.
Santa, Michael *o.s.b.* '56 (KCK) [H] Atchison, KS St. Benedict's Abbey.
Santa, Thomas *c.ss.r.* '78 (TUC) [H] Tucson, AZ Redemptorist Picture Rocks Retreat.
Santa Barbara, Robert L. '90 (MET) [7] New Brunswick, NJ St. Mary of Mount Virgin Church.
Santa Maria, Nicanor *s.d.b.* '80 (MIA) [25] Miami, FL St. Kieran Church.

Santa-Bibiana, Joseph *s.d.b.* '66 (NEW) [3] Elizabeth, NJ St. Anthony's Church.
Santa-Bibiana, Joseph *s.d.b.* '66 (NY) [DD] New Rochelle, NY Salesian Provincial House.
Santa-Olaya, Aureliano '63 (VEN) [6] Fort Myers, FL Jesus the Worker Mission (Jesus Obrero) Church; [8] Fort Myers, FL San Jose Church.
Santaella, Esteban '58 (PCE) [3] Ponce, PR Church of the Resurrection; [2] Ponce, PR Church San Patricio Church; [B] Ponce, PR The Pontifical Catholic University of Puerto Rico.
Santamaria, Max '56 (MRY) Retired.
Santamaria, Roberto '98 (NEW) [15] Newark, NJ St. Francis Xavier Church.
Santana, Edward '86 (CGS) [B] San Lorenzo, PR Casa Charlie Rodriguez; [E] San Lorenzo, PR Diocesan Shrine Our Lady of Mount Carmel; [F] Caguas, PR Diocesan Tribunal of Caguas.
Santana, Francisco '68 (MIA) [K] Miami, FL National Shrine of Our Lady of Charity.
Santana, Frank '72 (NY) [72] New York, NY Mary Help of Christians Church.
Santangelo, Christopher *ss.cc.* '99 (FR) [I] Fairhaven, MA Sacred Hearts Provincial House.
Santangelo, Michael '95 (TR) Princeton, NJ St. Paul Church.
Santen, Thomas J. '70 (STL) Manchester, MO St. Joseph Church.
Santerre, Richard R. '82 (BO) Belmont, MA St. Joseph Church; Permanent Disability.
Santiago, Carlos G. *o.r.c.* '89 (PCE) Adjuntas, PR St. Joachim Church.
Santiago, Florentino '78 (HT) Lockport, LA Holy Savior Church.
Santiago, Hiram *s.d.b.* '92 (MGZ) Aguadilla, PR San Jose Obrero Church.
Santiago, Jorge *s.d.b.* '94 (SJN) [28] San Juan, PR San Juan Bosco Church.
Santiago, Jose A. *o.ss.t.* '95 (SJN) [13] Bayamon, PR Ascension Del Senor Church.
Santiago, Leoncio S. '73 (CHI) [67] Chicago, IL St. Genevieve Church.
Santiago, Manuel '85 (PCE) Villalba, PR Our Lady of Mt. Carmel Church.
Santiago, Marciano E. (OAK) Union City, CA St. Anne Church.
Santiago, Msgr. Rafael '69 (PCE) Retired.
Santiago, Samuel '76 (PCE) Ensenada, PR Sacred Heart Church.
Santiago Mateo, Victor *s.t.* '82 (FgM) Trinity Missions.
Santich, Jan Joseph '90 (CHY) Wheatland, WY St. Patrick's Church.
Santillanes, Jose Flavio '65 (SFE) Pojoaque, NM N.S. de Guadalupe del Valle de Pojoaque Church.
Santilli, Francis C. '80 (PRO) [2] Pawtucket, RI St. Cecilia Church.
Santitoro, Francis E. '66 (TR) [4] Toms River, NJ St. Maximilian Kolbe Church.
Santo, Mark '60 (LA) Los Angeles, CA Metropolitan Detention Center; Los Angeles, CA Metropolitan Detention Center.
Santo, Mark '60 (MIL) On Duty Outside the Archdiocese.
Santo, Vincent '45 (SCL) Retired.
Santoalla, Msgr. Jesus '57 (SJN) [25] San Juan, PR San Jorge Church; Santurce, PR Ashford Presbyterian Community Hospital.
Santone, John M. *c.s.c.* '00 (FR) South Easton, MA Holy Cross Church.
Santor, John E. '65 (E) [20] Erie, PA St. Joseph Church; [P] Erie, PA Newman Centers and Campus Ministry.
Santora, Alexander M. '82 (NEW) [19] Jersey City, NJ Our Lady of Czestochowa Church; [Q] Union, NJ Kean University.
Santora, Msgr. Gerard M. '38 (NEW) [11] Jersey City, NJ Holy Rosary Church; Retired; [N] Rutherford, NJ St. John Vianney Residence for Priests.
Santoro, Charles M. *o.p.* '71 (STP) [8] Minneapolis, MN Holy Rosary Church; [15] Minneapolis, MN St. Albert the Great Church; [N] Minneapolis, MN St. Albert the Great Priory.
Santoro, David J. *o.p.* '77 (CHI) [N] River Forest, IL St. Thomas Aquinas Priory.
Santoro, David J. *o.p.* '77 (DM) [10] Des Moines, IA St. Mary of Nazareth Church.
Santoro, Michael C. '80 (NEW) [17] Jersey City, NJ Our Lady of Mt. Carmel Church.
Santorsola, Albert J. '87 (PH) Abington, PA Our Lady Help of Christians Church; [D] Wyncote, PA Bishop McDevitt High School.
Santos, Andrew J. '97 (CHI) Flossmoor, IL Infant Jesus of Prague Church.
Santos, Angel M. '77 (ARE) [9] Arecibo, PR La Milagrosa Church.
Santos, Cesar E. '93 (ARE) [4] Vega-Baja, PR Our Lady of Carmen-Playa Church.
Santos, Gregory *o.c.s.o.* '59 (SLC) [F] Huntsville, UT Abbey of Our Lady of the Holy Trinity of the Order of Cistercians.
Santos, John R. (WIL) [K] Dover, DE Secular Institute of the Two Hearts.
Santos, Jose Nunes (ALN) [4] Bethlehem, PA Holy Infancy Church.
Santos, Maximiano *c.m.* '66 (SJN) [47] San Juan, PR Nuestra Senora del Pilar Church.
Santos, Sergio '85 (SFR) [8] San Francisco, CA St. Boniface Church.
Santos, Tomas '95 (ARE) Morovis, PR St. Paul Apostle Church.
Santos, Ubaldo '87 (SAT) [32] San Antonio, TX St. Cecilia Church.
Santos, Victor *c.m.* '49 (SJN) [60] San Juan, PR San Vicente de Paul Church.
Santos de Dios, Juanito C. (LR) [I] Fort Smith, AR St. Scholastica Monastery-Motherhouse.
Santre, William *t.o.r.* '61 (ALT) [7] Altoona, PA Our Lady of Mt. Carmel Church.
Santry, Robert '86 (HON) Military Chaplains.
Santucci, Hugo *s.d.b.* '55 (LA) [80] Los Angeles, CA St. Mary Church; [Q] Los Angeles, CA Dominic Savio Salesian Residence.
Santucci, Louis '74 (Y) Absent on Leave.
Sanz, Eleutherio '59 (MRY) Retired.
Sanz, Florentino (SJN) Retired.
Sanz, Florentino '65 (SJN) [4] Guaynabo, PR San Juan M. Vianney Church.
Sanz, Jose *d.l.p.* '73 (SB) [A] Riverside, CA Blessed Junipero Serra House of Formation.
Sanz, Jose *d.l.p.* '73 (WDC) On Duty Outside the Archdiocese.
Sanz, Julian '77 (TUC) San Luis, AZ St. Jude Thaddeus Church.
Sanz, Martin '30 (SAT) [12] San Antonio, TX Immaculate Heart of Mary Church.
Saoncella, Valentino *m.c.c.j.* '44 (CHI) [N] La Grange Park, IL Comboni Mission Center.
Saparito, Peter M. '77 (CAM) [1] Vineland, NJ Our Lady of Pompeii Church.
Sapeta, Joseph S. '47 (NEW) Retired.
Sapio, Thadeus M. *o.f.m.* '65 (NY) [146] Bronx, NY Holy Cross Church.
Saplis, Raymond '58 (LA) Granada Hills, CA St. Euphrasia Church.
Saplis, Raymond A. '58 (LA) Retired.
Saporito, Msgr. Cosmo G. '54 (BRK) [18] Brooklyn, NY St. Bernadette Church.
Saporito, Louis R. *s.s.j.* '60 (BAL) [S] Baltimore, MD St. Joseph Society of the Sacred Heart House of Central Administration.
Saporito, Michael '92 (NEW) Paramus, NJ Our Lady of the Visitation Church.
Sapp, James '86 (FTW) [B] Fort Wayne, IN University of Saint Francis.
Sappenfield, John P. '98 (NSH) [6] Nashville, TN St. Henry Church; [B] Nashville, TN Father Ryan High School.
Sapporito, Msgr. Cosmo G. '54 (BRK) Retired.
Saprano, Samuel '71 (STU) Carlisle, OH St. Michael Church; Fulda, OH Immaculate Conception Church.
Sara, Solomon I. *s.j.* '63 (BO) [W] Boston, MA The Society of Jesus of New England-Provincial Offices.
Sara, Solomon I. *s.j.* '63 (WDC) [M] Washington, DC The Jesuit Community at Georgetown University.
Sarachaga, Felix *c.m.* '52 (LA) [32] Los Angeles, CA Our Lady of the Rosary of Talpa Church.
Sarauskas, Msgr. R. George '73 (CHI) On Duty Outside the Archdiocese.
Sardina, John J. '60 (BUF) [10] Cheektowaga, NY Queen of Martyrs Church; [M] Clarence, NY Brothers of Mercy Nursing & Rehabilitation Center; [M] Clarence, NY Brothers of Mercy Sacred Heart Home, Inc.; [O] Clarence, NY Provincial Motherhouse of Brothers of Mercy.
Sardina, Jorge *s.j.* '59 (MIA) [D] Miami, FL Belen Jesuit Preparatory School; [H] Miami, FL Villa Javier.
Sardinas, Jorge '77 (MIA) [B] Opa Locka, FL St. Thomas University.
Sarge, John S. '73 (SAG) [10] Saginaw, MI St. Casimir Church; [11] Saginaw, MI St. George Church.
Sargent, John '53 (Y) Retired.
Sargus, Edward T. (BAL) Emmitsburg, MD St. Anthony Church.
Sargus, Edward T. '39 (BAL) Retired.
Sariego, Francis *o.f.m.cap.* '69 (NEW) [5] Hoboken, NJ St. Ann's Church.
Sarjeant, Francis X. *s.j.* '61 (BO) [W] Boston, MA The Society of Jesus of New England-Provincial Offices.
Sarjeant, Francis X. *s.j.* '61 (SP) [4] Clearwater, FL St. Cecelia Church.
Sarkies, Jeffery L. '65 (SEA) [25] Seattle, WA Holy Rosary Church.
Sarmiento, Oscar '82 (MIA) [2] Miami Beach, FL St. Joseph Church.
Sarmiento, Oscar '82 (PT) On Duty Outside the Diocese.
Sarno, Msgr. Robert J. '73 (BRK) Released from Diocesan Assignment.
Sarosiek, John (DET) [4] Dearborn, MI St. Clement Church.
Sarosiek, John H. '93 (GAY) Retired.
Saroyan, Antoine '85 (ARM) Detroit, MI St. Vartan's Church.
Sarrazin, Victor J. '90 (LA) [Q] Montebello, CA Vincentian Fathers & Brothers; [W] Montebello, CA DePaul Center.
Sarrazine, Kenneth J. '62 (FTW) Nix Settlement, IN St. Catharine Church; Roanoke, IN St. Joseph Church.
Sarro, John A. '79 (WIL) Retired.
Sarsfield, Emmett (YAK) Zillah, WA Resurrection Church.
Sartorelli, Otto J. '50 (MAR) Caspian, MI St. Cecilia Church.
Sartori, Hector *c.s.* '54 (PRO) [4] Johnston, RI St. Rocco Church; Johnston, RI Port of Providence Catholic Chaplain.
Sarweh, Basel R. '98 (SCR) [M] Shohola, PA Society of Saint John.
Sarzynski, Msgr. Edward W. '79 (ALN) [2] Shenandoah, PA St. Casimir Church; [6] Shenandoah, PA St. Stanislaus Church.
Sas, Thomas J. '76 (HRT) [4] West Hartford, CT St. Mark the Evangelist Church.
Sasin, Jan '77 (NEW) [15] Newark, NJ St. Francis Xavier Church.
Saso, Michael '61 (SJ) On Duty Outside the Diocese.
Sass, Donald E. '60 (MIL) Milwaukee, WI St. Luke's Medical Center.
Sassani, John E. '80 (BO) [6] Newton, MA Our Lady Help of Christians Church; [X] Lexington, MA Grey Nuns Provincial Offices.
Sassano, Rock '63 (P) Retired.
Sasso, Frank M. '73 (CHI) [197] Chicago, IL St. Thaddeus Church.
Sasso, Joseph M. '58 (ROC) [4] Rochester, NY St. Anne Church; Retired.
Sasway, Msgr. John R. '62 (ALT) Lilly, PA St. Brigid's Church; Lilly, PA Our Lady of the Alleghenies Church.
Satchell, Martin J. '93 (PH) Absent on Sick Leave.
Satcher, Mikel (BO) Dorchester, MA Carney Hospital.
Sato, Damian *s.a.* '45 (NY) [DD] Garrison, NY Franciscan Friars of the Atonement, Minister General Office.
Satoun, Arbogaste '99 (SCR) [9] Scranton, PA Holy Rosary Church.
Satterfield, Msgr. Carroll E. '54 (BAL) Retired.
Sattler, Frederick F. '70 (ALN) Fountain Hill, PA St. Ursula Church.
Sattler, Henry E. *c.ss.r.* '76 (TOL) [2] Lima, OH St. Gerard Church.
Sattler, Wayne '97 (BIS) Stanley, ND Queen of the Most Holy Rosary Church.
Sauber, A. Michael '69 (STP) Lonsdale, MN Immaculate Conception Church.
Saucci, Ronald R. *m.m.* '65 (FgM) Maryknoll Foreign Missions.
Sauchelli, James J. '63 (TR) Brick Town, NJ Visitation Church.
Saucier, Thomas *o.p.* '96 (CHI) [D] Oak Park, IL Fenwick High School; [N] Oak Park, IL Dominican Community of St. Martin de Porres.
Saudis, Richard B. '55 (CHI) Berwyn, IL St. Odilo Church.
Sauer, Alban '59 (SCL) Retired.
Sauer, Anthony P. *s.j.* '71 (SFR) [E] San Francisco, CA St. Ignatius College Preparatory (Coed); [N] San Francisco, CA Jesuit Community at St. Ignatius College Preparatory.
Sauer, Bonaventure *o.c.d.* '92 (LR) [A] Little Rock, AR Marylake - Carmelite Novitiate.
Sauer, James '77 (EVN) Santa Claus, IN St. Nicholas Church; Special Assignment.
Sauer, James E. '77 (EVN) Chrisney, IN St. Martin Church.
Sauer, John M. '85 (WIN) [1] Winona, MN Cathedral of the Sacred Heart.
Sauer, Steven J. *s.j.* '98 (MOB) [A] Mobile, AL Spring Hill College.
Sauer, Timothy J. '76 (SEA) Ferndale, WA St. Joseph Church; Special Assignment.
Sauerbier, Paul W. *c.m.* '68 (DAL) [6] Dallas, TX Holy Trinity Church.
Saul, James *o.s.b.* '52 (JOL) [J] Lisle, IL St. Procopius Abbey; [J] Lisle, IL St. Procopius Abbey.
Saulenas, Simeon W. '44 (BO) [5] Cambridge, MA Immaculate Conception Church.
Saulino, Joseph '67 (LEX) [5] Lexington, KY St. Elizabeth Ann Seton Church.
Saumell, Amaro '92 (SB) Crestline, CA St. Frances Xavier Cabrini Church.
Saunders, Allan L. '86 (SPC) Monett, MO St. Lawrence Church; Pulaskifield, MO SS. Peter and Paul Church.
Saunders, Charles D. *c.m.* '43 (STL) [P] Perryville, MO Congregation of The Mission.
Saunders, Donald E. *s.j.* '84 (SP) [C] Tampa, FL Jesuit High School.
Saunders, Msgr. Douglas Wm. '65 (LA) [10] Long Beach, CA St. Maria Goretti Church.
Saunders, John A. '40 (BO) Senior Priests.
Saunders, Robert J. '41 (DUB) Retired.
Saunders, Ronald *s.m.* '59 (BUR) White River Junction,

VT St. Anthony Church.
Saunders, William P. '84 (ARL) Potomac Falls, VA Our Lady of Hope Church; [B] Alexandria, VA Notre Dame Graduate School of Christendom College.
Saunter, Scott '00 (FAR) Jamestown, ND The Basilica of St. James.
Sauppe, Timothy J. '92 (PEO) Annawan, IL Sacred Heart Church.
Sauriol, Mark A. '99 (PRO) [7] Cranston, RI St. Paul Church.
Sauro, Frank E. (BRK) [151] Queens, NY St. Ann's Church.
Sauter, David A. *s.j.* '72 (PH) [G] Philadelphia, PA St. Joseph's Preparatory School; [AA] Philadelphia, PA Jesuit Community, Arrupe House.
Sauter, John '85 (GLP) Shiprock, NM Christ the King Church; [A] Chinle, AZ Native American Lay Ministry and Diaconate Program.
Sauter, Thomas M. '47 (DET) Rockwood, MI St. Mary Church.
Savage, James W. '70 (BO) [11] Cambridge, MA St. Paul Church.
Savage, John J. *o.m.i.* '39 (BO) [Z] Tewksbury, MA Immaculate Heart of Mary Infirmary.
Savage, Paul J. '57 (PIT) Beaver Falls, PA Divine Mercy Church; Beaver County, PA Beaver Valley Geriatric Center.
Savage, Robert *s.d.b.* '46 (NY) [DD] New Rochelle, NY Salesian Provincial House.
Savage, Roger A. '77 (MIL) Eldorado, WI Our Risen Savior Church.
Savage, Thomas J. '47 (MAN) Retired.
Savage, Warren J. (SPR) Absent on Leave.
Savage, Warren J. '79 (SPR) [5] Westfield, MA St. Peter's Church.
Savaia, Giuseppe '95 (PMB) [3] Boca Raton, FL St. Joan of Arc Church.
Savard, John D. *s.j.* '91 (BO) [W] Boston, MA The Society of Jesus of New England-Provincial Offices.
Savard, John D. *s.j.* '91 (SFR) [N] San Francisco, CA Jesuit Community at University of San Francisco.
Savard, Wilfred '48 (SFE) Retired.
Savarimuthu, Augustine *s.j.* (RVC) Westbury, NY St. Brigid Church.
Savarimuthu, Pancras '80 (TYL) Athens, TX St. Edward Church.
Savarimuthu, Simon (NY) Staten Island, NY Staten Island University Hospital North.
Savary, James '60 (LR) Retired.
Savastano, Msgr. Anthony J. (RVC) Retired.
Savchyn, Vasyl (STN) The Colony, TX St. Sophia Ukrainian Catholic Church.
Savelesky, Michael '73 (SPK) Walla Walla, WA St. Francis of Assisi Church; Walla Walla, WA St. Patrick Church.
Savelkoul, Leonard '95 (BIS) Parshall, ND St. Bridget Church.
Savial, Clarence J.D. '70 (LAV) [3] Las Vegas, NV Holy Family Church.
Saviano, Frederick L. '68 (BGP) [3] Danbury, CT Our Lady of Guadalupe Church.
Savickas, Michael G. '74 (DET) Walled Lake, MI St. William Church.
Savidge, Peter M. '89 (KC) Odessa, MO St. George Church.
Savilla, Edmund '77 (SFE) [2] Albuquerque, NM Ascension Church.
Savino, Dominic *o.carm.* '65 (LA) [B] Arleta, CA Carmel West Community; [F] Encino, CA Crespi Carmelite High School.
Savino, Michael A. '82 (CIN) Blanchester, OH Holy Name Church; Saint Martin, OH Saint Martin Church.
Savinski, John M. '71 (ALN) [A] Northampton, PA Mary Immaculate Center.
Savinski, John M. '71 (PH) [A] Wynnewood, PA Theological Seminary of St. Charles Borromeo, Overbrook.
Savio, John '67 (CHY) Rock Springs, WY Holy Spirit Catholic Community Church; [F] Rock Springs, WY Rock Springs Catholic School Foundation.
Savio, Michael G. '92 (MIL) [15] Milwaukee, WI Congregation of the Blessed Trinity Church.
Savitt, Alan F. '73 (PAT) [3] Clifton, NJ St. Brendan Church.
Savoie, Johnny S. '95 (MOB) [4] Mobile, AL St. Dominic Church.
Savoree, John M. '63 (SFD) Altamont, IL St. Clare Church; Edgewood, IL St. Anne Church; St. Elmo, IL St. Bonaventure Church; St. Elmo, IL St. Mary Church.
Saw, Benjamin (SAL) Hoxie, KS St. Frances Xavier Cabrini Church.
Sawdy, Wallace E. '51 (HBG) Retired.
Sawicki, Eugene A. '86 (NY) [100] New York, NY Our Lady of Vilnius Church.
Sawicki, Gregory *s.d.s.* '86 (SAT) Cestohowa, TX Nativity of the Blessed Virgin Mary Church; Hobson, TX St. Boniface Church.
Sawyer, Donald '74 (OLL) Baton Rouge, LA Maronite Catholic Community Church; Lake Charles, LA Maronite Catholic Community Church; Austin, TX Our Lady's Maronite Church.
Sawyer, Lucien A. *o.m.i.* '49 (BO) Cambridge, MA Mount Auburn Hospital; [Q] Boston, MA Daughters of Charity National Health System - Boston, Inc.
Sawyer, Michael *o.s.b.* '74 (HON) [G] Waialua, Oahu, HI Benedictine Monastery of Hawaii/Retreat Center.
Sax, Msgr. John C. '73 (NO) [1] New Orleans, LA St. Louis Church.
Saxon, JaVan J. '48 (R) Rocky Mount, NC Our Lady of Perpetual Help Church.
Say, Celestino '58 (VIC) [3] Victoria, TX Our Lady of Lourdes Church.
Say, James K. '60 (TOL) Tiffin, OH St. Joseph Church.
Sayer, Robert J. '99 (CHR) Batesburg, SC St. John of the Cross Church; Lexington, SC Corpus Christi Church.
Sayer, Robert James '99 (CHR) Garden City, SC St. Michael Church.
Sayers, Glen *s.d.s.* (GB) Charlesburg, WI St. Charles Borromeo Church; Charlestown, WI St. Martin Church; Chilton, WI St. Augustine Church; Chilton, WI St. Mary Church; Jericho, WI Holy Trinity Church; Kloten, WI St. Elizabeth Church.
Sayers, James M. '58 (CHI) Homewood, IL St. Joseph Church.
Sayers, Monty '86 (E) Frenchtown, PA St. Hippolyte Church.
Sayers, Raymond J. '64 (DET) [41] Detroit, MI St. Jude Church.
Sayes, Ronald '57 (DET) [1] Westland, MI St. Bernardine Church.
Sayles, Bartholomew *o.s.b.* '48 (SCL) [I] Collegeville, MN St. John's Abbey, of the Order of St. Benedict.
Saylor, Brian '99 (ALT) Altoona, PA Altoona Hospital.
Saylor, Brian R. '99 (ALT) [1] Altoona, PA Cathedral of the Blessed Sacrament.
Saylor, Msgr. Philip (ALT) Retired.
Sazama, Warren J. *s.j.* '77 (MIL) [P] Milwaukee, WI Pere Marquette House Jesuit Community.
Sbordone, Gaetano J. '83 (BRK) [41] Brooklyn, NY St. Frances Cabrini Church.
Scadron, Christopher '83 (RC) Retired.
Scafidi, William A. *m.ss.a.* '83 (NY) [1] New York, NY Cathedral of St. Patrick; [3] Newburgh, NY St. Mary Church.
Scagnelli, Peter J. '76 (PRO) Absent on Leave.
Scahill, James J. '74 (SPR) [16] Springfield, MA St. Mary's Church.
Scala, Thomas A. '73 (HBG) Milton, PA St. Joseph Church.
Scalco, Joseph *c.s.j.* '79 (LA) Lancaster, CA Blessed Junipero Serra Church; [D] Lancaster, CA Paraclete High School.
Scales, Donald F. *o.s.b.* '55 (RIC) [L] Richmond, VA Mary Mother of the Church Abbey.
Scales, George B. (FR) Chatham, MA Holy Redeemer Church.
Scales, Mark P. *s.j.* '97 (WDC) [20] Washington, DC Holy Trinity Church.
Scalese, Mark P. *s.j.* '97 (WDC) [M] Washington, DC Woodstock Jesuit Community.
Scaletty, Thomas F. '63 (WCH) Chanute, KS St. Patrick Church; Humboldt, KS St. Joseph Church.
Scalia, Paul D. '96 (ARL) Fredericksburg, VA St. Patrick's Church.
Scalise, Christopher M. '99 (L) Elizabethtown, KY St. James Church; White Mills, KY St. Ignatius Church.
Scallion, Joseph (MIL) [N] Wauwatosa, WI St. Camillus Health Center, Inc.
Scallon, Joseph D. *s.j.* '57 (MIL) [P] Wauwatosa, WI Jesuit Community at St. Camillus.
Scalone, Jonathan '87 (FWT) Lewisville, TX St. Philip the Apostle Church.
Scanagatta, Joseph *s.d.b.* '47 (SFR) [N] San Francisco, CA Salesian Provincial Residence.
Scanlan, Charles V. '54 (NEW) Retired; [N] Rutherford, NJ St. John Vianney Residence for Priests.
Scanlan, Cornelius *o.m.i.* (GAL) [16] Houston, TX Blessed Sacrament Church.
Scanlan, Cornelius J. *o.m.i.* '59 (SAN) Big Spring, TX Sacred Heart Church; Big Spring, TX St. Thomas Church.
Scanlan, Msgr. Edward J. '53 (BUF) [13] Niagara Falls, NY St. Stanislaus Kostka Church; Retired.
Scanlan, Francis G. '61 (CHI) Oak Forest, IL St. Damian Church.
Scanlan, Msgr. John J. '59 (WDC) Lanham, MD St. Matthias Apostle Church.
Scanlan, Kevin *s.m.a.* '55 (NEW) [N] Tenafly, NJ Society of African Missions, Provincialate, S.M.A. Fathers.
Scanlan, Michael *t.o.r.* '64 (STU) [F] Steubenville, OH Holy Spirit Friary.
Scanlan, Michael J. *o.s.a.* '64 (PH) [AA] Villanova, PA St. John Stone Friary.
Scanlan, Thomas R. '57 (BAK) Retired.
Scanlan, William J. '72 (BO) Military & VA Chaplains.
Scanlin, Joseph T. '89 (HBG) [3] Lebanon, PA St. Cecilia Church.
Scanlon, Msgr. Bernard S. '45 (BGP) Retired; [P] Stamford, CT The Catherine Dennis Keefe Queen of the Clergy Retired Priests' Residence.
Scanlon, Charles *s.v.d.* '54 (FgM) Society of the Divine Word Foreign Missions.
Scanlon, Frank '83 (NY) [27] New York, NY St. Columba Church.
Scanlon, James M. *m.m.* '52 (NY) [DD] Maryknoll, NY Maryknoll Fathers and Brothers.
Scanlon, Msgr. John J. '53 (NY) Scarsdale, NY Immaculate Heart of Mary Church.
Scanlon, Michael *t.o.r.* '64 (STU) [A] Steubenville, OH Franciscan University of Steubenville.
Scanlon, Michael J. *o.s.a.* '64 (PH) [C] Villanova, PA Villanova University.
Scanlon, Michael M. *o.s.m.* '30 (CHI) [N] Chicago, IL Order of Friar Servants of Mary (Servites) United States of America Province, Inc.
Scanlon, Paul *o.p.* '59 (OAK) [N] Oakland, CA Dominican Order (Western Province), St. Albert's Priory.
Scanlon, Peter J. '57 (WOR) [16] Worcester, MA Sacred Heart Church; [Q] Worcester, MA Campus Ministry; [Q] Worcester, MA Campus Ministry; [Q] Worcester, MA Campus Ministry.
Scanlon, Regis *o.f.m.cap.* '72 (DEN) [M] Denver, CO St. Francis of Assisi Friary.
Scanlon, Richard M. '28 (RVC) Blue Point, NY Our Lady of the Snow Church; Retired.
Scanlon, Msgr. Thomas F. '49 (NY) [5] Mt. Vernon, NY SS. Peter and Paul Church.
Scanlon, Msgr. Thomas J. '59 (PH) [5] Norristown, PA St. Titus Church.
Scanlon, William '70 (SFR) Redwood City, CA St. Pius Church.
Scanlon, William J. *s.j.* '70 (NY) [DD] New York, NY St. Ignatius Loyola Residence; [HH] New York, NY Catholic Medical Mission Board, Inc.; [HH] New York, NY Jesuit Seminary and Mission Bureau, Inc.
Scannel, Anthony *o.f.m.cap.* '55 (LA) [F] La Canada Flintridge, CA St. Francis High School.
Scannell, Joseph S. *s.j.* '50 (BO) [W] Weston, MA Campion Health Center, Inc.
Scannell, Msgr. Peter '46 (ORG) Retired.
Scannell, Msgr. Thomas P. '37 (ARL) [2] Arlington, VA St. Agnes Church; Retired.
Scantlebury, Neil '95 (STV) [1] Cruz Bay, VI Our Lady of Mt. Carmel Church.
Scantlin, Joseph S. '59 (FWT) [3] Arlington, TX Most Blessed Sacrament Church.
Scaramella, Renzo L. '95 (NEW) On Duty Outside the Archdiocese.
Scaramuzzo, Peter C. '66 (NY) [1] White Plains, NY St. Anthony Church.
Scarangella, Joseph A. '92 (NEW) Cliffside Park, NJ Epiphany Church.
Scarangello, John (NY) [E] New York, NY Cathedral High School.
Scarangello, John R. *o.f.m.* '81 (NY) [DD] New York, NY Padua Friary.
Scarborough, Henry *o.c.s.o.* '63 (WOR) [N] Spencer, MA St. Joseph's Abbey.
Scarcella, Philip J. '77 (MET) On Duty Outside the Diocese.
Scarcello, Michael S. '56 (B) Retired.
Scarcia, John J. '74 (PH) Pennsburg, PA St. Philip Neri Church.
Scardella, Joseph E. '81 (SY) [7] Syracuse, NY Our Lady of Pompei Church.
Scarfia, Gabriel *o.f.m., s.t.d.* '64 (BUF) [A] East Aurora, NY Christ the King Seminary.
Scarlata, Ronald E. '66 (CHI) Highwood, IL St. James Church; Retired; [M] Des Plaines, IL Holy Family Health Center.
Scepaniak, Russell G. '93 (WIN) Le Roy, MN St. Patrick's Church; Spring Valley, MN St. Ignatius Church.
Scerbo, Joseph *s.a.* '70 (NY) [DD] Garrison, NY Franciscan Friars of the Atonement, Minister General Office.
Scerbo, Joseph *s.a.* '70 (ORG) San Juan Capistrano, CA Mission Basilica Church.
Sceski, Alfred P. '91 (HBG) [K] Harrisburg, PA Catholic Campus Ministry.
Scesney, Everard S. *o.f.m.* '68 (GB) Aniwa, WI St. Boniface Church; Birnamwood, WI St. Philomena Church.
Scezney, Leonard J. '85 (DEN) Absent on Leave.
Schaab, Dennis *c.pp.s.* '68 (KC) Warrensburg, MO Sacred Heart Church.
Schaab, Denny M. '76 (STL) Webster Groves, MO Annunciation Church.
Schaab, R. Michael '71 (PEO) Orion, IL Mary, Our Lady of Peace Church.
Schaab, Thomas J. '74 (STL) Sunset Hills, MO St. Justin Martyr Church; On Medical Leave.
Schaad, Jerome *s.c.j.* '66 (MIL) [P] Hales Corners, WI Priests of the Sacred Heart; [P] Hales Corners, WI Sacred Heart Monastery.
Schaaf, Paul *c.pp.s.* '60 (CIN) [M] Dayton, OH Provincial Office of the Cincinnati Province of the Society of the Precious Blood.

Schaal, John K. '96 (SCR) Unassigned or Leave of Absence.
Schabel, Joseph A. '56 (SAG) Retired.
Schabowski, Henry F. '60 (TR) [15] Trenton, NJ St. Hedwig Church.
Schack, Stephen '99 (PHX) Flagstaff, AZ San Francisco de Asis Church.
Schad, Edward '49 (OM) [H] Omaha, NE Mercy Villa.
Schad, Joseph J. *s.j.* '91 (BO) [W] Boston, MA Loyola House; [W] Boston, MA The Society of Jesus of New England-Provincial Offices.
Schad, Sylvester *o.s.b.* '32 (CC) [H] Sandia, TX Corpus Christi Abbey.
Schaedel, Msgr. Joseph '82 (IND) [6] Indianapolis, IN Holy Rosary Church.
Schaedel, Joseph F. '82 (IND) [1] Indianapolis, IN SS. Peter and Paul Church.
Schaefer, Bernard *o.s.b.* '56 (RCK) [G] Aurora, IL Marmion Abbey-St. Augustine's Abbey.
Schaefer, Msgr. Dennis R. '75 (BEL) Chester, IL St. Mary Help of Christians Church.
Schaefer, Edgar J. '54 (WIN) Retired.
Schaefer, Edward F. '75 (BEL) St. Rose, IL St. Rose Church.
Schaefer, Ferdinand *o.carm.* '48 (JOL) [J] Darien, IL Carmelite Provincial Office.
Schaefer, Francis R. '55 (COL) Retired.
Schaefer, James F. '61 (LC) Dorchester, WI St. Louis Church.
Schaefer, James W. '56 (STL) Ozora, MO Sacred Heart Church.
Schaefer, Kenneth '73 (BEL) Johnston City, IL St. Paul Church.
Schaefer, Msgr. Kenneth J. '74 (BEL) Herrin, IL Our Lady of Mount Carmel Church.
Schaefer, Les F. *c.s.b.* '61 (OAK) [C] Oakland, CA Bishop O'Dowd High School.
Schaefer, Martin T. '92 (WIN) Pipestone, MN St. Leo's Church.
Schaefer, Philip *c.p.* '58 (CHI) [N] Chicago, IL Passionist Community-Immaculate Conception Monastery.
Schaefer, Richard '96 (PMB) Special Assignment; [D] West Palm Beach, FL St. Mary's Foundation of Palm Beach County, Inc.
Schaefer, Roman J. '42 (MIA) [3] Fort Lauderdale, FL Our Lady Queen of Martyrs Church.
Schaefer, Roman J. '42 (NU) Retired.
Schaefer, Thomas '53 (WDC) Retired.
Schaefer, Verne B. '55 (MIL) Retired.
Schaeffer, Bradley M. *s.j.* '77 (CHI) [N] Chicago, IL Chicago Province of the Society of Jesus-Provincial Office.
Schaeffer, Bradley M. *s.j.* '77 (WDC) [M] Washington, DC Leonard Neale House; [V] Washington, DC Jesuit Conference, Inc.
Schaeffer, Richard C. '83 (MAR) Wells, MI St. Anthony Church.
Schaeflein, Msgr. Charles J. '49 (PH) Retired; [V] Philadelphia, PA Mount Nazareth.
Schaeufele, Robert L. '75 (SP) [3] St. Petersburg, FL Holy Cross Church.
Schafer, Dennis *o.f.m.* '80 (SFD) [B] Quincy, IL Quincy University.
Schafer, Dennis R. '89 (BIS) St. Anthony, ND St. Anthony Church.
Schafer, Raymond E. '89 (IND) Jeffersonville, IN Sacred Heart Church.
Schafer, William *s.d.b.* '61 (LA) [Q] Los Angeles, CA Dominic Savio Salesian Residence.
Schaff, Tyrone J. '73 (SPK) [13] Spokane, WA St. John Vianney Church.
Schaffer, Gregory J. '94 (STP) On Duty Outside the Archdiocese.
Schaffer, Msgr. Gregory T. '60 (NU) On Duty Outside the Diocese.
Schaffer, J. Darrell '90 (DEN) [6] Denver, CO Christ the King Church.
Schaffner, Mark *o.carm.* '89 (GAL) [59] Houston, TX Our Lady of Mt. Carmel Church.
Schaffner, William E. '48 (ALN) [A] Wernersville, PA Jesuit Center.
Schaftlein, Stephen '78 (IND) Greensburg, IN St. Mary Church.
Schaible, Donald J. '89 (ALN) Pen Argyl, PA St. Elizabeth of Hungary Church; [C] Bangor, PA Pius X High School.
Schaicoski, Lauro *o.s.b.m.* '95 (STN) Hamtramck, MI Immaculate Conception of B.V.M. Church.
Schak, John R. *s.j.* '61 (FgM) Provinces.
Schak, John R. *s.j.* '61 (MIL) [P] Milwaukee, WI Jesuit Provincial Office, Wisconsin Province.
Schall, James V. *s.j.* '63 (WDC) [M] Washington, DC The Jesuit Community at Georgetown University.
Schallberger, Meinrad '64 (B) [B] Cottonwood, ID St. Mary's Hospital; [C] Jerome, ID Monastery of the Ascension.
Schallenberger, Meinrad *o.s.b.* '64 (B) Cottonwood, ID Monastery of St. Gertrude.
Schaller, Pascal *o.f.m.cap.* '51 (PIT) [O] Pittsburgh, PA St. Augustine Friary.
Schaller, Robert A. '87 (LC) Custer, WI Immaculate Conception Church; [4] Stevens Point, WI St. Peter Church.
Schanberger, J. Lawrence *m.m.* '49 (FgM) Maryknoll Foreign Missions.
Schanz, John P. '50 (E) [B] Erie, PA Gannon University.
Schappert, James P. *s.s.j.* '49 (BAL) [S] Baltimore, MD St. Joseph Society of the Sacred Heart House of Central Administration.
Schappler, Norbert *o.s.b.* '52 (KC) [J] Conception, MO Conception Abbey.
Schardt, William B. '75 (ARL) [3] Arlington, VA St. Ann Church.
Scharf, David E. '85 (PIT) [R] Pittsburgh, PA Office for Campus Ministry.
Scharf, David E.F. '85 (PIT) Beaver Falls, PA St. Philomena Church.
Scharf, Joseph *s.j.* '51 (CLV) [T] Cleveland, OH Jesuit Retreat House.
Scharf, Lawrence C. '65 (TOL) Monroeville, OH St. Joseph Church.
Scharf, T. Patrick '68 (TOL) Napoleon, OH St. Augustine Church.
Scharfenberger, Msgr. Edward B. '73 (BRK) [214] Queens, NY Our Lady of Mercy Church.
Schario, Clayton D. *s.j.* '56 (DET) [P] Clarkston, MI Colombiere Center.
Schario, D. Clayton *s.j.* '56 (DET) [K] Detroit, MI Jesuit Community at the University of Detroit.
Schartz, Kenneth '85 (CIN) Xenia, OH St. Brigid Church.
Schatteman, Rene J. '60 (LA) [X] Los Angeles, CA Prelature of the Holy Cross and Opus Dei.
Schatz, David A. '00 (DUB) [8] Dubuque, IA Holy Ghost Church.
Schatzel, John E. '61 (BO) [2] Brockton, MA St. Colman of Cloyne Church.
Schatzle, Michael J. '74 (BR) New Roads, LA St. Mary of False River Church.
Schauerman, Msgr. Henry J. '51 (E) Meadville, PA St. Agatha Church.
Schaukowitch, James V. *s.j.* '79 (LA) [F] Los Angeles, CA Loyola High School of Los Angeles.
Schaut, Gregory F. '85 (CLV) Chardon, OH St. Mary Church.
Schavitz, Peter *c.ss.r.* (CHI) [133] Chicago, IL St. Michael Church.
Scheaffer, Msgr. Walter T. '66 (ALN) Kutztown, PA St. Mary Church.
Scheble, Carl J. '83 (STL) [33] St. Louis, MO St. Elizabeth, Mother of John the Baptist Church.
Scheckel, Roger J. '84 (LC) [5] La Crosse, WI St. James the Less Church; [C] La Crosse, WI Coulee Catholic Schools.
Scheckenback, Robert C. '89 (RVC) Holbrook, NY Good Shepherd Church.
Schecker, Robert J.W. '71 (TR) Mount Holly, NJ Sacred Heart Church; Burlington, NJ Burlington County Hospital & Extended Care Center; Burlington, NJ Burlington County Jail.
Scheel, Msgr. Daniel '69 (GAL) [39] Houston, TX St. Jerome Church.
Scheeler, Jeffrey *o.f.m.* '80 (CIN) [M] Cincinnati, OH St. Francis Seraph Friary.
Scheer, Allen '95 (SAL) Mankato, KS St. Theresa of Infant Jesus Church.
Scheer, John *s.a.c.* '70 (SUP) Clam Lake, WI St. George Church; Glidden, WI Most Precious Blood Church; Highbridge, WI St. Anthony Church; Mellen, WI Holy Rosary Church.
Scheer, Joseph O. '42 (STL) Retired.
Scheerer, Dominic T. *o.c.d.* '47 (MIL) [26] Milwaukee, WI St. Florian Church.
Scheets, Francis K. *o.s.c.* '51 (DET) Riverview, MI St. Cyprian Church.
Scheetz, Daniel L. '65 (SAL) Ellsworth, KS St. Bernard's Church; Holyrood, KS St. Mary's Church; Kanopolis, KS St. Ignatius Loyola Church.
Scheetz, Joseph '54 (SAL) Retired.
Schefers, Eberhard '64 (SCL) Sartell, MN St. Francis Xavier Church.
Scheffler, Mark *c.ss.r.* '70 (SAT) San Antonio, TX Santa Rosa Hospital System; [H] San Antonio, TX Christus Santa Rosa Health Care Corporation.
Schehr, Timothy P. '73 (CIN) [B] Cincinnati, OH Mt. St. Mary's Seminary of the West.
Scheib, Joseph C. '76 (PIT) [43] Pittsburgh, PA St. Basil Church.
Scheible, Ronald *o.s.a.* '57 (FWT) Abbott, TX Immaculate Heart of Mary Church; Penelope, TX Nativity of the Blessed Virgin Mary Church.
Scheich, Gene '66 (L) [55] Louisville, KY St. Matthias Church.
Scheick, James C. '63 (DET) Grosse Ile, MI Sacred Heart Church.
Scheider, David J. '53 (BUF) East Pembroke, NY Holy Name of Mary Church.
Scheiding, Philip '81 (MIA) On Duty Outside the Archdiocese.
Scheidler, Alfred J. *o.s.b.* '52 (PEO) [A] Peru, IL St. Bede Abbey and Academy.
Scheidler, David J. *c.s.c.* '94 (FTW) [B] Notre Dame, IN University of Notre Dame Du Lac; [J] Notre Dame, IN Holy Cross Community, Corby Hall, University of Notre Dame.
Scheier, Steven '53 (WCH) Bushton, KS Holy Name of Jesus Church; Little River, KS Holy Trinity Church.
Scheierl, LeRoy '91 (SCL) Belgrade, MN St. Francis De Sales Church; Elrosa, MN SS. Peter and Paul Church.
Scheiner, Richard *c.p.* '60 (NY) [DD] New York, NY Passionist Spiritual Center.
Scheinost, Douglas P. '92 (OM) Stuart, NE St. Boniface Church.
Scheip, Michael A. '81 (VEN) [1] Venice, FL Epiphany Church.
Scheip, Michael A. '93 (NEW) On Duty Outside the Archdiocese.
Schelble, T. Michael '61 (LC) Auburndale, WI Nativity of the Blessed Virgin Mary Church; Hewitt, WI St. Michael Church.
Schelble, Thomas M. *s.m.* '46 (SAT) [K] San Antonio, TX Marianist Residence: Skilled Nursing.
Schelich, Anthony T. *o.s.f.s.* '65 (WIL) [G] Newark, DE Jeanne Jugan Residence; [I] Childs, MD Oblates of St. Francis De Sales.
Schelich, Theodosius A. *o.f.m.* '59 (SFD) [H] Litchfield, IL St. Francis Hospital.
Schelich, Theodosius A. *o.f.m.* '59 (STL) [P] St. Louis, MO Franciscan Friary of St. Anthony of Padua.
Schell, Joseph O. *s.j.* '44 (CLV) [B] Cleveland, OH John Carroll Jesuit Community.
Schellemans, Francis *ss.cc.* '49 (HON) Lahaina, HI Maria Lanakila Church.
Schellenberg, James '77 (SAT) San Antonio, TX Brooke Army Medical Center.
Schellenberg, Milton A. '46 (WDC) Retired.
Scheller, Albert J. '61 (EVN) [5] Vincennes, IN St. Vincent de Paul Church.
Scheller, John '58 (OKL) Retired.
Schelling, Michael E. '74 (TOL) Crestline, OH St. Joseph Church; Galion, OH St. Joseph Church.
Schemel, Francis *s.j.* '58 (WDC) [M] Washington, DC The Jesuit Community at Georgetown University.
Schemm, Michael J. '93 (WCH) Parsons, KS St. Patrick Church.
Schenck, Steve *s.d.b.* '81 (PAT) [D] Paterson, NJ Don Bosco Technical High School.
Schendt, Richard L. '63 (CHI) [W] Oak Park, IL Oak Park Study Center.
Schenick, Joseph D. '51 (PRO) Retired; [P] Providence, RI St. John Vianney Residence.
Schenk, Arthur J. *s.j.* '45 (SJ) [L] Los Gatos, CA Sacred Heart Jesuit Center.
Schenk, Francisco *glmy.* '55 (CIN) [M] Cincinnati, OH Headquarters of Glenmary Home Missioners.
Schenk, Francisco *glmy.* '55 (TLS) Idabel, OK St. Francis De Sales Church.
Schenk, Richard *o.p.* '78 (OAK) [A] Berkeley, CA Dominican School of Philosophy and Theology; [N] Oakland, CA Dominican Order (Western Province), St. Albert's Priory; [N] Oakland, CA Western Dominican Province.
Schenkelberg, Edwin J. '51 (CLV) [49] Cleveland, OH St. Mel Church; Retired.
Schenning, Kevin T. (BAL) Pasadena, MD St. Jane Frances de Chantal Church.
Schepers, Frank '55 (KCK) Retired.
Schepers, M. B. *o.p.* '56 (FgM) Dominican - Order of Preachers Foreign Missions.
Scherba, Raymond M. '82 (BGP) [1] Danbury, CT St. Gregory Church.
Scherer, Albert *o.f.m.conv.* '85 (SPR) [10] Chicopee, MA St. Stanislaus Basilica Church.
Scherer, Donald R. '67 (NEW) Retired.
Scherer, Gary *c.pp.s.* '67 (GRY) [4] Whiting, IN St. John the Baptist Church.
Scherer, Gerald N. '54 (RC) Retired.
Scherer, James F. '64 (ATL) On Duty Outside the Archdiocese.
Scherer, Philip M. *o.s.m.* '55 (CHI) [N] Chicago, IL Order of Friar Servants of Mary (Servites) United States of America Province, Inc.
Scherer, Richard '49 (MIA) Retired.
Scherger, Herman F. '58 (TOL) Antwerp, OH St. Mary Church; Cecil, OH Immaculate Conception Church.
Scherman, Charles J. *s.j.* '57 (LC) Chippewa Falls, WI Holy Ghost Church; Springfield, WI St. Bridget Church.
Scherpnenberg, Sergius *o.f.m.* '51 (PEO) [3] Peoria, IL Sacred Heart Church.
Scherrer, Msgr. Carl E. '73 (BEL) Shiloh, IL Corpus Christi Church.
Scherrer, Steven *m.m.* '72 (NY) [DD] Maryknoll, NY Maryknoll Fathers and Brothers.
Scherzer, Edwin J. '50 (L) Retired; [L] Louisville, KY Bishop David Apartments; [Q] Louisville, KY Our Lady's Rosary Makers.
Schetelick, Paul D. '76 (NEW) [34] Newark, NJ Sacred Heart Church.
Schetter, Albert E. '55 (CIN) Retired.
Schettler, Charles H. '54 (OKL) [8] Oklahoma City, OK St. Francis of Assisi Church.

Scheuer, James '59 (DUL) Babbitt, MN St. Pius X Church; Ely, MN St. Anthony's Church.
Scheuerell, Charles A. '57 (MIL) Retired.
Scheuerman, Edward L. '50 (DET) Retired.
Schevers, Joel *o.carm.* '42 (VEN) [1] Venice, FL Epiphany Church; [G] Venice, FL Carmel in Venice.
Schexnayder, Francis F. *m.m.* '64 (FgM) Maryknoll Foreign Missions.
Schexnayder, Gary '69 (LAF) [9] Lafayette, LA St. Edmond Church.
Schexnayder, James '64 (OAK) Retired.
Scheyd, Msgr. William J. '65 (BGP) [7] Norwalk, CT St. Thomas the Apostle Church.
Schiavi, Giulio *p.i.m.e.* '63 (DET) [7] Clinton Twp., MI San Francesco Community Church.
Schiavo, Sylvan *c.s.j.* '63 (LA) San Pedro, CA St. Peter Church.
Schiavone, Alphonse A. *m.m.* '46 (NY) [DD] Maryknoll, NY Maryknoll Fathers and Brothers.
Schiavone, Alphonse A. *m.m.* '46 (RVC) [M] West Hempstead, NY Maryknoll Residence.
Schiavone, Christopher F. '84 (BO) Absent on Leave.
Schiavone, Jeldo J. '52 (LFT) Retired.
Schiavone, Robert W. '69 (GB) On Duty Outside the Diocese.
Schiavone, Robert W. '69 (MIL) [B] Hales Corners, WI Sacred Heart School of Theology.
Schiavonne, John S. '73 (LA) Whittier, CA St. Gregory the Great Church.
Schiblin, Richard *c.ss.r.* '61 (DEN) [M] Denver, CO The Redemptorists/Denver Province.
Schichtel, Kenneth H. '62 (GR) Ludington, MI St. Simon's Church.
Schidel, George E. *c.s.c.* '41 (FTW) [J] South Bend, IN Congregation of Holy Cross, Indiana Province, Provincial House.
Schieber, Brian '99 (KCK) Leawood, KS Cure of Ars Church.
Schieber, Joachim *o.s.b.* '44 (KC) [J] Conception, MO Conception Abbey.
Schieber, Lawrence J. '49 (STL) Moselle, MO St. Mary's Church.
Schiefen, Richard J. *c.s.b.* '61 (GAL) [Q] Houston, TX Residence of the Basilian Fathers of the University of St. Thomas.
Schiefen, Msgr. Robert '46 (VEN) Retired.
Schieffer, Stanley F. '56 (LIN) Red Cloud, NE Sacred Heart Church.
Schiel, Nicholas E. *s.j.* '55 (FgM) Provinces.
Schiel, Nicholas E. *s.j.* '55 (MIL) [P] Milwaukee, WI Jesuit Provincial Office, Wisconsin Province.
Schiele, John D. '93 (PH) Brookhaven, PA Our Lady of Charity Church.
Schifalacqua, Ildebrando E. '43 (PH) [21] Philadelphia, PA St. Bartholomew Church; Retired.
Schifano, James R. *s.c.j.* '75 (JKS) Holly Springs, MS St. Joseph Church.
Schifano, Vincent '00 (RVC) Hicksville, NY Holy Family Church.
Schiffbauer, Rory D. '91 (CHY) Evanston, WY St. Mary Magdalen Church.
Schiffer, James *c.p.* '71 (MET) [H] South River, NJ Passionist Provincial Office.
Schiffer, Thomas E. '63 (WH) Weirton, WV St. Paul's Church.
Schifferli, Jerome F. (ROC) Livonia, NY St. Joseph Church.
Schifferli, Jerome F. '45 (ROC) Retired.
Schik, Jerome *o.s.c.* '75 (STP) Shoreview, MN St. Odilia Church; [N] Shoreview, MN Crosier Community of Shoreview.
Schilder, David M. '68 (COL) On Duty Outside the Diocese.
Schilken, Karl '80 (FWT) Mansfield, TX St. Jude Church.
Schill, Damien '87 (PH) [47] Philadelphia, PA St. Francis de Sales Church; Philadelphia, PA Veterans Administration Medical Center.
Schill, Frederick J. '57 (TOL) Retired.
Schill, Paul A. '80 (E) Greenville, PA St. Michael Church.
Schill, Victor J. '50 (FAR) Retired.
Schiller, Francis E. '65 (NEW) [7] Jersey City, NJ Assumption/All Saints Church; [23] Jersey City, NJ St. Patrick's Church.
Schiller, Thomas A. '55 (GR) Retired.
Schilli, Richard J. '77 (STL) Mattese, MO Assumption Church.
Schillinger, James '84 (ATL) [M] Atlanta, GA Campus Ministry.
Schilly, Joseph '48 (SB) Retired.
Schiltz, Roger J. '68 (WIN) Retired.
Schimelpfening, James *s.m.* (SAT) [8] San Antonio, TX Holy Rosary Church.
Schiml, Ronald J. *c.pp.s.* '55 (LFT) Star City, IN St. Joseph Church.
Schimmelman, Wayne (CHI) [J] Evanston, IL Saint Francis Hospital.
Schimmelman, Wayne *c.m.f.* '86 (CHI) [78] Chicago, IL Holy Cross/Immaculate Heart of Mary Church.
Schimmer, Robert J. '68 (SC) Storm Lake, IA St. Mary's Church.
Schimscheiner, Francis M. *o.s.f.s.* '65 (BUF) [5] Lockport, NY St. Patrick Church.
Schindler, Carl *c.ss.r.* '63 (SAT) [M] San Antonio, TX Redemptorists of Texas-San Antonio #1.
Schindler, John L. '85 (L) [62] Louisville, KY St. Patrick Church.
Schindler, Paul E. '67 (CLV) [3] Akron, OH St. Bernard Church; [W] Cleveland, OH Office of Hispanic Ministry.
Schineller, J. Peter *s.j.* '70 (FgM) Provinces.
Schinelli, Giles *t.o.r.* (ORL) [F] Winter Park, FL San Pedro Center, Third Order Regular of St. Francis.
Schinelli, Giles *t.o.r.* '62 (ORL) [D] Winter Park, FL San Pedro Spiritual Development Center; [F] Winter Park, FL Franciscan Friars, T.O.R., Provincial Residence, San Pedro Friary.
Schinn, Bernard *o.s.b.* '99 (DET) [K] Detroit, MI St. Sylvester Monastery.
Schinski, Msgr. Stanislaus E. '51 (PAT) [1] Wayne, NJ Annunciation Church.
Schipp, John H. '64 (EVN) [2] Vincennes, IN Basilica of St. Francis Xavier; [I] Vincennes, IN Old Cathedral Library & Museum, Inc.
Schipp, Ralph '65 (EVN) Schnellville, IN Sacred Heart Church.
Schiro, Nicholas T. *s.j.* '57 (NO) [F] New Orleans, LA Jesuit High School.
Schirra, Peter M. '37 (PIT) Retired.
Schiska, Paul A. '57 (MAR) Retired.
Schissel, Gregory A. *s.j.* '79 (OM) [K] Omaha, NE Jesuit Community at Creighton University.
Schlachter, Eric A. '81 (JC) Pilot Grove, MO St. Joseph Church.
Schlade, Joseph F. '58 (RCK) Retired.
Schladen, Donald '56 (PEO) [J] Bloomington, IL OSF St. Joseph Medical Center.
Schlaf, John E. '64 (GI) Ogallala, NE St. Luke's Church.
Schlafer, Joseph M. '75 (RVC) Garden City, NY St. Joseph's Church.
Schlageter, Robert *o.f.m.conv.* '84 (BAL) [S] Ellicott City, MD Order of Friars Minor Conventual.
Schlageter, Robert *o.f.m.conv.* '84 (WDC) [C] Washington, DC Catholic University of America, The.
Schlagheck, Regis T. *o.f.m.conv.* '66 (CLV) [1] Lorain, OH St. Anthony of Padua Church.
Schlangen, Louis '57 (SFD) Mendon, IL St. Edward Church.
Schlarb, Gregory J. '97 (LA) [Q] Montebello, CA Vincentian Fathers & Brothers; [W] Santa Barbara, CA St. Mary's Seminary Center.
Schlatter, Fredric *s.j.* '56 (SPK) [C] Spokane, WA Gonzaga University.
Schlattmann, Edward B. '34 (STL) Retired.
Schlautman, Wayne W. '65 (OM) [12] Omaha, NE Christ the King Church.
Schlaver, David *c.s.c.* '71 (PHX) [G] Phoenix, AZ Holy Cross Congregation/Casa Santa Cruz.
Schlax, Charles H. '66 (CHI) [1] Des Plaines, IL St. Mary Church.
Schlegel, Daniel F. '88 (CLV) Rocky River, OH St. Christopher Church.
Schlegel, Msgr. George J. '66 (COL) New Philadelphia, OH Sacred Heart Church.
Schlegel, John P. *s.j.* '73 (OM) [A] Omaha, NE Creighton University; [K] Omaha, NE Jesuit Community at Creighton University.
Schlegel, John P. *s.j.* '73 (SFR) [C] San Francisco, CA University of San Francisco.
Schlegel, Lawrence *o.s.b.* '54 (MAN) [K] Manchester, NH St. Anselm Abbey.
Schleicher, James R. '54 (CLV) [5] Akron, OH St. Francis de Sales Church; [U] Cleveland, OH Society of St. Vincent de Paul, Diocesan Central Council.
Schleisman, Jeffrey A. '00 (SC) [2] Sioux City, IA Blessed Sacrament Church.
Schlenker, Richard J. '56 (MIL) Retired.
Schlert, Msgr. Alfred A. *v.g., j.c.l.* '87 (ALN) [1] Allentown, PA Cathedral of St. Catharine of Siena .
Schlesselmann, Gregory '93 (FAR) Special Assignment.
Schleter, Edward J. '67 (TOL) Bowling Green, OH St. Aloysius Church.
Schlett, Francis J. '70 (PH) [1] Coatesville, PA St. Cecilia Church.
Schleupner, Msgr. G. Michael '72 (BAL) Abingdon, MD St. Francis de Sales Church.
Schlichte, Carl *o.p.* '98 (LA) [60] Los Angeles, CA St. Dominic Church.
Schlick, Regis *o.f.m.cap.* '65 (FgM) Capuchin Foreign Missions.
Schlick, Regis *o.f.m.cap.* '65 (WH) Point Pleasant, WV Sacred Heart Church; [M] Charleston, WV Capuchins-St. Anthony Friary.
Schliessmann, Thomas L. '89 (IND) Salem, IN St. Patrick Church; Scottsburg, IN American Martyrs Church.
Schlight, Harry J. *o.s.f.s.* '44 (FgM) Oblates of St. Francis de Sales Foreign Missions.
Schlim, Robert J. *s.j.* '62 (SPK) [K] Spokane, WA Regis Community.
Schlimm, Chrysostom V. *o.s.b.* '61 (GBG) [H] Latrobe, PA Saint Vincent Archabbey.
Schlitt, Dale *o.m.i.* '69 (FgM) Oblates Foreign Missions.
Schlitt, Dale *o.m.i.* '69 (WDC) [M] Washington, DC Missionary Oblates of Mary Immaculate.
Schlitt, Msgr. Harry '64 (SFR) [T] San Francisco, CA Catholics for Truth & Justice.
Schlitt, Msgr. Harry G. '64 (SFR) Special Assignment.
Schlitt, Robert T. '56 (TLS) Stillwater, OK St. Francis Xavier Church.
Schloeder, Paul '87 (SAC) Awaiting Assignment.
Schloemer, Bernard J. '60 (STL) Sunset Hills, MO St. Justin Martyr Church.
Schloemer, Leo *glmy.* '56 (CIN) [M] Cincinnati, OH Headquarters of Glenmary Home Missioners.
Schloemer, Leo *glmy.* '56 (FWT) Knox City, TX Santa Rosa Church; Rhineland, TX St. Joseph Church.
Schloemer, Thomas N. *s.j.* '68 (OM) [23] Omaha, NE St. John Church; [K] Omaha, NE Jesuit Community at Creighton University.
Schloesser, Stephen *s.j.* '92 (BO) [W] Chestnut Hill, MA The Jesuit Community at Boston College.
Schlosser, Leo R. *o.s.b.* '59 (PBR) Sheffield, PA St. Michael Church.
Schlosser, Richard '74 (GF) [2] Great Falls, MT Holy Spirit Church.
Schloth, Brian D. *m.s.* '89 (NOR) Brooklyn, CT Our Lady of La Salette Church.
Schludecker, Andre *o.f.m.* (CHI) [164] Chicago, IL St. Peter's Church; [N] Chicago, IL St. Peter's Friary.
Schlueter, Clemens M. '58 (TUC) Retired.
Schluter, O. Charles '78 (MAD) Platteville, WI St. Mary Church.
Schmalhofer, John D. '74 (HBG) New Holland, PA Our Lady of Lourdes Church.
Schmaltz, Albert F. '43 (STL) Retired.
Schmaltz, Bernard '73 (NO) Retired.
Schmalzried, Bernard R. '69 (Y) [6] Warren, OH St. Mary's Church.
Schmaus, James E. '92 (CHI) Lake Zurich, IL St. Francis de Sales Church.
Schmeer, John P. '64 (PH) New Hope, PA St. Martin of Tours Church.
Schmeidler, John *o.f.m.cap.* '97 (STL) Arnold, MO Immaculate Conception Church; [P] Arnold, MO Immaculate Conception Friary.
Schmeig, Brennan *o.f.m.* '58 (SUP) Sanborn, WI St. Anne Church.
Schmeising, Julian *o.s.b.* '58 (SCL) [H] Cold Spring, MN Assumption Home; [H] Cold Spring, MN John Paul Apartments; [H] Cold Spring, MN Assumption Court.
Schmelz, Damian *o.s.b.* '58 (IND) [A] St. Meinrad, IN St. Meinrad Seminary; [J] St. Meinrad, IN St. Meinrad Archabbey.
Schmelzer, Msgr. Delbert L. '56 (MAD) Paoli, WI St. William Church; Verona, WI St. Andrew Church.
Schmelzer, Joseph M. '77 (TOL) Van Wert, OH St. Mary Church.
Schmelzer, Linus L. '45 (MIL) Retired.
Schmelzer, Paul '43 (SCL) Retired.
Schmid, Wayne '68 (WCH) Derby, KS St. Mary's Church.
Schmidberger, Richard '57 (DET) Retired.
Schmidlin, Donald L. '57 (IND) [28] Indianapolis, IN St. Matthew Church.
Schmidt, Anthony '50 (SFD) Retired.
Schmidt, Bosco *s.a.* '49 (NY) [DD] Garrison, NY Franciscan Friars of the Atonement.
Schmidt, Carl '50 (SFD) Coffeen, IL St. John the Baptist Church; Panama, IL Sacred Heart Church.
Schmidt, Charles W. *m.m.* '48 (HON) [G] Honolulu, HI Maryknoll Fathers House (M.M.).
Schmidt, Dave '77 (SFD) Hillsboro, IL St. Agnes Church.
Schmidt, David (GB) Kaukauna, WI St. Aloysius Church.
Schmidt, David L. '77 (SFD) Litchfield, IL Holy Family Church.
Schmidt, Dennis C. '80 (STL) Hillsboro, MO Church of the Good Shepherd.
Schmidt, Donald A. '73 (MIL) Belgium, WI St. Mary Church.
Schmidt, Edward *s.j.* '71 (FgM) Provinces.
Schmidt, Edward W. *s.j.* '73 (CHI) [N] Chicago, IL Chicago Province of the Society of Jesus-Provincial Office.
Schmidt, Edwin A. '63 (JC) St. Martins, MO St. Martin Church.
Schmidt, Elmer J. '56 (ROC) Retired.
Schmidt, Eugene '56 (GB) Retired.
Schmidt, Florian J. '61 (DUB) Worthington, IA St. Paul's Church.
Schmidt, Francis J. '58 (MAD) Martinsville, WI St. Martin Church.
Schmidt, Msgr. Francis X. '57 (PH) Bridgeport, PA St. Augustine Church.
Schmidt, Frederick A. *c.s.c.* '37 (FgM) Holy Cross Foreign Missions.

Schmidt, George E., Jr. '70 (KNX) [1] Chattanooga, TN SS. Peter and Paul Church; [K] Chattanooga, TN Mount Olivet.
Schmidt, Msgr. George N. '41 (WCH) Retired.
Schmidt, Gregory L. '61 (STL) Old Monroe, MO Immaculate Conception Church.
Schmidt, Gustav H. *s.j.* '66 (HEL) St. Ignatius, MT St. Ignatius Church.
Schmidt, Henry C. '57 (SFD) [4] Springfield, IL Little Flower Church.
Schmidt, Herbert '75 (SFS) [G] Yankton, SD Sacred Heart Monastery.
Schmidt, Jan Kevin '90 (CIN) [37] Cincinnati, OH Immaculate Heart of Mary Church.
Schmidt, Jerome J. '49 (BRK) Retired.
Schmidt, John *c.ss.r.* '89 (CHI) [133] Chicago, IL St. Michael Church.
Schmidt, John W. '56 (Y) Retired.
Schmidt, Joseph F. '66 (B) Moscow, ID St. Mary's Church.
Schmidt, Kenneth W. '81 (KAL) [5] Kalamazoo, MI St. Thomas More Student Church; [H] Kalamazoo, MI Western Michigan University, Kalamazoo College-Kalamazoo Valley Community College.
Schmidt, Leo C. '56 (COV) [3] Covington, KY St. Augustine Church.
Schmidt, Leslie *glmy.* '61 (RIC) Big Stone Gap, VA Sacred Heart Church; Pennington Gap, VA Church of the Holy Spirit.
Schmidt, Lukas *o.carm* '65 (VEN) [1] Venice, FL Epiphany Church.
Schmidt, Nicholas '67 (ORG) Inactive Leave.
Schmidt, Paul *s.v.d.* '81 (SB) Blythe, CA St. Joan of Arc Church.
Schmidt, Paul J. '64 (OAK) [14] Oakland, CA St. Margaret Mary Church.
Schmidt, Peter *o.c.s.o.* '75 (WOR) [N] Spencer, MA St. Joseph's Abbey.
Schmidt, Ralph G., Jr. '73 (GAL) Texas City, TX St. Mary Church.
Schmidt, Raymond F. '84 (WDC) [10] Washington, DC Blessed Sacrament, Shrine of the Most Church.
Schmidt, Richard C. *s.j.* '61 (WDC) [P] Faulkner, MD Loyola on the Potomac Retreat House.
Schmidt, Robert H. *s.j.* '69 (DET) [E] Detroit, MI University of Detroit Jesuit High School and Academy.
Schmidt, Robert H. *s.j.* '69 (FgM) Provinces.
Schmidt, Msgr. Robert R. '43 (COL) Retired.
Schmidt, Robert W. *s.j.* '42 (CIN) [M] Cincinnati, OH Jesuit Community at Xavier University.
Schmidt, Ronald *s.j.* (NO) [C] New Orleans, LA Loyola University New Orleans.
Schmidt, Sebastian *o.s.b.* '60 (BIS) Glen Ullin, ND Sacred Heart of Jesus Church; [A] Richardton, ND Assumption Abbey.
Schmidt, Thomas *c.ss.r.* '62 (RVC) Bethpage, NY St. Martin of Tours Church.
Schmidt, Thomas '76 (STL) Arnold, MO St. David Church.
Schmidt, Thomas W. '99 (CIN) [7] Dayton, OH St. Charles Borromeo Church.
Schmidt, Msgr. W. Robert '57 (DAV) [5] Davenport, IA St. Anthony's Church.
Schmidt, Wilfred W. '50 (DUB) Retired.
Schmidt, William F. *s.a.* '59 (ARL) Sterling, VA Christ the Redeemer Church.
Schmidt, William T. '76 (BO) Stoneham, MA St. Patrick Church.
Schmidtzinsky, Msgr. Victor '41 (SAT) [K] San Antonio, TX Padua Place.
Schmidtzinsky, Msgr. Victor '41 (VIC) Retired.
Schmied, Msgr. Michael S. '71 (RIC) [6] Richmond, VA St. Augustine Church.
Schmied, Thomas *o.f.m.cap.* '69 (MAR) Special Assignment.
Schmieder, Mark C. '66 (CIN) [79] Cincinnati, OH St. Stephen Church.
Schmieg, Brennan *o.f.m.* '58 (SUP) Washburn, WI St. Louis Church.
Schmiesing, Julian '58 (SCL) [I] Collegeville, MN St. John's Abbey, of the Order of St. Benedict.
Schmit, Arthur G. *o.s.b.* '57 (PEO) [A] Peru, IL St. Bede Abbey and Academy.
Schmit, Fred J. *s.d.s.* '46 (NSH) Sparta, TN St. Andrew Church.
Schmit, George V., Jr. '68 (NU) [1] New Ulm, MN Cathedral of The Holy Trinity.
Schmit, Jerome L. '57 (LA) Altadena, CA Sacred Heart Church.
Schmit, Kenneth A. '79 (ORG) El Toro, CA Santiago de Compostela Church.
Schmit, Louis *c.pp.s.* '63 (CIN) [B] Carthagena, OH St. Charles; [M] Dayton, OH Provincial Office of the Cincinnati Province of the Society of the Precious Blood.
Schmit, Meyrl '65 (JKS) On Duty Outside the Diocese.
Schmit, Msgr. Ralph R. '46 (MIL) Retired.
Schmit, Roger W. *o.s.b.* '62 (CHY) Laramie, WY St. Paul's Newman Center Church; [E] Laramie, WY University of Wyoming.
Schmit, Ronald G. '85 (OAK) Byron, CA St. Anne Church.
Schmit, Stanley J. '94 (OM) Bloomfield, NE St. Andrew Church; [B] Hartington, NE Cedar Catholic High School.
Schmitmeyer, James M. '81 (CIN) North Star, OH St. Louis Church; Osgood, OH St. Nicholas Church.
Schmitt, Adam '57 (FTW) [8] Fort Wayne, IN St. Joseph Church; Retired.
Schmitt, Allen M. '71 (DUB) Dorchester, IA St. Mary's Church; Hanover, IA St. Mary's Church; Waukon, IA St. Patrick's Church.
Schmitt, Bowan '97 (PEO) [14] Peoria, IL St. Thomas Church.
Schmitt, Carl L. '61 (DUB) New Hampton, IA St. Joseph's Church; New Hampton, IA St. Mary's Church; [E] New Hampton, IA St. John's School.
Schmitt, Charles R. '59 (E) Port Allegany, PA St. Gabriel the Archangel Church.
Schmitt, Christopher '60 (PMB) [G] Delray Beach, FL Opus Dei.
Schmitt, Conrad *s.t.* '55 (WDC) [M] University Park, MD Holy Trinity Missionary Cenacle.
Schmitt, David J. '67 (WH) Logan, WV St. Francis of Assisi Church; Man, WV St. Edmund Church.
Schmitt, Donald P. '62 (DUB) Barclay, IA St. Francis Church; Jesup, IA St. Athanasius Church; [D] Gilbertville, IA Don Bosco High School.
Schmitt, Erhard *o.m.i.* '94 (LA) San Fernando, CA St. Ferdinand Church.
Schmitt, Ervin J. (PBL) [E] Pueblo, CO Centura Health-St. Mary-Corwin Medical Center.
Schmitt, Ervin J. '58 (PBL) Retired.
Schmitt, Eugene '00 (EVN) [7] Evansville, IN Holy Redeemer Church.
Schmitt, Eugene A. '45 (WH) Retired.
Schmitt, Frank J. *s.j.* (DEN) [31] Denver, CO St. Ignatius Loyola Church.
Schmitt, Gregory *c.ss.r.* '69 (SEA) [32] Seattle, WA Sacred Heart of Jesus Church.
Schmitt, Harold F. '59 (PEO) [K] Lacon, IL St. Joseph's Nursing Home.
Schmitt, Msgr. J. Harley '40 (DEN) Retired.
Schmitt, James, J. '51 (LAN) Retired.
Schmitt, James C. '66 (GI) [3] Grand Island, NE Resurrection Church; Grand Island, NE Nebraska Veterans Home.
Schmitt, John P. '44 (GB) Retired.
Schmitt, Msgr. Joseph J. '55 (AUS) Lago Vista, TX St. Mary, Our Lady of the Lake Church.
Schmitt, Kent A. '73 (MAD) [7] Madison, WI St. Dennis Church.
Schmitt, Michael T. '71 (ALB) Colonie, NY St. Clare Church.
Schmitt, Phillip E. '56 (DUB) Retired.
Schmitt, Reinhold *c.m.m.* '52 (AUS) Westphalia, TX Visitation Church.
Schmitt, Reinhold *c.m.m.* '52 (DET) [K] Dearborn Heights, MI Our Lady of Grace Monastery.
Schmitt, Silverius '58 (SCL) Retired.
Schmitt, Thomas F. '91 (BO) [A] Weston, MA Pope John XXIII National Seminary.
Schmitt, Thomas F. '91 (SPR) On Duty Outside the Diocese.
Schmitt, Warren J. '42 (MIL) Retired.
Schmitter, Philip '71 (LAN) [14] Flint, MI Sacred Heart Church; Special Assignment.
Schmittgens, Kevin V. '83 (STL) Neier, MO St. Joseph Church.
Schmitz, Aloysius F. *s.j.* '59 (STP) [N] Minneapolis, MN La Storta Jesuit Community.
Schmitz, Bartley *s.v.d.* '44 (FgM) Society of the Divine Word Foreign Missions.
Schmitz, Bernard A. (DEN) Greeley, CO Our Lady of Peace Church.
Schmitz, Msgr. Bernard R. '57 (IND) Milan, IN St. Charles Borromeo Church; Morris, IN St. Anthony of Padua Church; St. Nicholas, IN St. Nicholas Church; St. Pius, IN St. Pius Church.
Schmitz, Charles E. *s.j.* '72 (YAK) [4] Yakima, WA St. Joseph's Church.
Schmitz, Donald J. '80 (WIN) Caledonia, MN St. Mary Church.
Schmitz, Msgr. Donald P. '64 (WIN) [3] Rochester, MN Resurrection Church; [A] Winona, MN Immaculate Heart of Mary Seminary.
Schmitz, Eugene *s.v.d.* '67 (FgM) Society of the Divine Word Foreign Missions.
Schmitz, George '69 (CIN) [4] Cincinnati, OH St. Aloysius Gonzaga Church; [68] Cincinnati, OH Our Lady of Victory Church.
Schmitz, Gerald P. '62 (PRM) Lakewood, OH St. Gregory the Theologian Church.
Schmitz, Gerald T. '48 (MIL) Retired.
Schmitz, Gerard G. '68 (HRT) Madison, CT St. Margaret Church.
Schmitz, James P. '86 (CLV) Amherst, OH St. Joseph Church.
Schmitz, John A. '52 (MIL) Ripon, WI St. Patrick Church.
Schmitz, John J. '91 (JC) Brinktown, MO Guardian Angels Church; Vienna, MO Visitation Church.
Schmitz, Michael D. '96 (OM) Ralston, NE St. Gerald Church.
Schmitz, R. Michael '82 (LC) [H] St. Mary's Ridge, WI Immaculate Conception Priory; [H] Cashton, WI Institute of Christ the King - Sovereign Priest; [N] Cashton, WI Institute of Christ the King-Sovereign Priest.
Schmitz, Robert A. '55 (OM) Tilden, NE Our Lady of Mt. Carmel Church.
Schmitz, Robert E. '75 (CIN) [18] Cincinnati, OH St. Catharine Church.
Schmock, Hilarion *o.c.s.o.* '43 (L) [L] Trappist, KY Abbey of Our Lady of Gethsemani, of the Order of Cistercians of the Strict Observance.
Schmoll, John '85 (FRS) Lamont, CA St. Augustine Church.
Schmuhl, Lawrence R. *s.m.* '47 (ATL) [C] Atlanta, GA Marist School.
Schnacky, Paul '53 (ROC) Hornell, NY St. Ann Church; Retired.
Schnaubelt, Joseph C. *o.s.a.* '57 (PH) [AA] Villanova, PA St. Thomas Monastery.
Schnaus, Urban *o.s.b.* '40 (WDC) [M] Washington, DC St. Anselm's Abbey.
Schneck, Richard *s.j.* '72 (FgM) Provinces.
Schneebeck, Paul Otto *c.m.* '69 (STL) [P] St. Louis, MO Lazarist Residence.
Schneeweis, Joseph E. *s.j.* (NO) [C] New Orleans, LA Loyola University New Orleans.
Schneibel, Jeffrey *c.s.c.* '85 (P) [39] Portland, OR St. Vincent de Paul Church.
Schneible, Peter *o.f.m.* '89 (BUF) [C] St. Bonaventure, NY St. Bonaventure University; [O] St. Bonaventure, NY St. Bonaventure Friary.
Schneider, Adrian *o.f.m.* '41 (CIN) [M] Cincinnati, OH St. Clement Friary.
Schneider, Msgr. Alfred '38 (GB) Retired.
Schneider, Anthony *o.f.m.* '52 (SP) [O] St. Petersburg, FL St. Anthony Friary.
Schneider, Aquinas *o.f.m.* '54 (CIN) [C] Cincinnati, OH St. Anthony Shrine, Franciscan Candidacy; [K] Cincinnati, OH Mercy Health Plaza dba Mercy Franciscan Hospital-Western Hills.
Schneider, Msgr. Arnold J. '51 (BUF) Bowmansville, NY Sacred Heart Church; Retired.
Schneider, Barry *o.f.m.* '56 (SUP) Dauby, WI St. Peter Church; Iron River, WI St. Michael Church.
Schneider, Bernard R. '67 (FAR) Mayville, ND Our Lady of Peace Church.
Schneider, Charles *s.v.d.* '46 (FgM) Society of the Divine Word Foreign Missions.
Schneider, Charles J. '63 (WH) New Martinsville, WV St. Vincent de Paul Church.
Schneider, Chris *o.f.m.* '49 (CIN) [M] Cincinnati, OH St. Clement Friary.
Schneider, Conran *o.f.m.* '51 (STL) [P] St. Louis, MO Franciscan Friary of St. Anthony of Padua.
Schneider, Daniel M. '98 (STP) [T] Lake Elmo, MN Hermits of the Most Blessed Virgin Mary of Mount Carmel.
Schneider, Edward '64 (EVN) Petersburg, IN SS. Peter and Paul Church.
Schneider, Msgr. Ernest '77 (GR) [19] Grand Rapids, MI St. Paul the Apostle Church.
Schneider, Msgr. Francis J. '83 (RVC) Elmont, NY St. Vincent de Paul Church.
Schneider, Fredrick *o.f.m.* '49 (LR) Horseshoe Bend, AR St. Mary of the Mount Church.
Schneider, George D. '56 (FAR) Retired.
Schneider, George P. '45 (PH) Parkesburg, PA Our Lady of Consolation Church; Retired.
Schneider, Gilbert *o.f.m.* '64 (GLP) Laguna, NM St. Joseph Church.
Schneider, Harold '74 (KCK) [3] Topeka, KS Holy Name Church.
Schneider, Harold E. '62 (COL) Retired.
Schneider, Henry W. '53 (BIS) [3] Minot, ND St. John the Apostle Church.
Schneider, Herbert *s.j.* '70 (FgM) Provinces.
Schneider, J. Daniel *m.m.* '45 (NY) [DD] Maryknoll, NY Maryknoll Fathers and Brothers.
Schneider, John '83 (CHL) Boone, NC St. Elizabeth Church.
Schneider, John G. '48 (STL) Retired.
Schneider, John H. '68 (STL) Bonne Terre, MO St. Joseph's Church.
Schneider, Joseph M. '74 (DUB) Meyer, IA Sacred Heart Church; St. Ansgar, IA St. Ansgar Church; Stacyville, IA Church of the Visitation.
Schneider, Juniper *o.f.m.conv.* '72 (P) Roseburg, OR St. Joseph Church; Sutherlin, OR St. Francis Xavier Church.
Schneider, Karl J. '59 (MIL) [4] West Allis, WI Immaculate Heart of Mary Church.
Schneider, Kevin C. *s.j.* '94 (OM) [C] Omaha, NE Creighton Preparatory School.
Schneider, Leo J. '83 (STP) [7] Minneapolis, MN Holy Name Church.
Schneider, Leon J. '53 (MIL) Retired.
Schneider, Mark *o.s.b.* '41 (SCL) [I] Collegeville, MN

St. John's Abbey, of the Order of St. Benedict.
Schneider, Michael '81 (SFS) Howard, SD St. Agatha Church.
Schneider, Michael '94 (GF) Poplar, MT Our Lady of Lourdes Church.
Schneider, Msgr. Nicholas A. '56 (STL) [3] Creve Coeur, MO St. Monica Church.
Schneider, Philip *o.f.m.conv.* '61 (FTW) Angola, IN St. Anthony Church; Clear Lake, IN St. Paul Chapel Church.
Schneider, Ric *o.f.m.* '59 (PEO) [2] Bloomington, IL St. Mary's Church.
Schneider, Msgr. Robert E. '57 (COL) Coshocton, OH Sacred Heart Church.
Schneider, Robert J. (WIN) [C] Albert Lea, MN St. Theodore School.
Schneider, Robert J. '78 (WIN) Albert Lea, MN St. Theodore's Church; [J] Albert Lea, MN St. Theodore Catholic School Endowment.
Schneider, Robert J. '81 (SP) [4] St. Petersburg, FL Holy Family Church.
Schneider, Robert W. *s.j.* (DET) [P] Clarkston, MI Colombiere Center.
Schneider, Ronald '75 (GB) Absent on Leave.
Schneider, Ronald F. '67 (GR) Hart, MI St. Gregory's Church.
Schneider, Stephen *o.f.m.* '39 (CIN) [C] Cincinnati, OH St. Anthony Shrine, Francisan Candidacy.
Schneider, Stephen A. '72 (SPC) [3] Springfield, MO Immaculate Conception Church.
Schneider, Terrance L. '79 (CIN) Oxford, OH St. Mary Church and Catholic Campus Ministry Church; [Q] Oxford, OH Miami University Catholic Campus Ministry.
Schneider, Todd '85 (SCL) Elizabeth, MN St. Elizabeth Church; Pelican Rapids, MN St. Leonard's Church.
Schneider, William T. '63 (TR) [6] Trenton, NJ Incarnation Church.
Schneller, Michael J. '72 (NO) Belle Chasse, LA Our Lady of Perpetual Help Church.
Schnipke, Eugene H. *c.pp.s.* '80 (CIN) [M] Dayton, OH Provincial Office of the Cincinnati Province of the Society of the Precious Blood.
Schnipke, Kenneth R. *c.pp.s.* '90 (ORL) Longwood, FL Church of the Nativity.
Schnoebelen, Kenneth F. '46 (LIN) Retired.
Schnupp, Luzerne A. '57 (NSH) Franklin, TN St. Matthew Church.
Schnur, Edward C. '91 (EVN) Rockport, IN St. Bernard Church.
Schnurr, Msgr. Dennis M. '74 (SC) On Duty Outside the Diocese.
Schnurr, Thomas J. *o.s.b.* '32 (BIR) [E] Cullman, AL St. Bernard Abbey.
Schober, Robert J. '77 (BUF) Bolivar, NY St. Mary Church; Portville, NY Sacred Heart Church.
Schock, Ronald '96 (TOL) [34] Toledo, OH St. Patrick Historic Church.
Schock, William A. *s.j.* '62 (FgM) Provinces.
Schoderbek, Charles *s.v.d.* '47 (CHI) [B] Techny, IL Divine Word Residence.
Schoeberle, Brad *c.s.p.* '00 (LA) [87] Los Angeles, CA St. Paul the Apostle Church.
Schoeberle, John *o.m.i.* '61 (FgM) Oblates Foreign Missions.
Schoellmann, Edward *m.m.* '65 (FgM) Maryknoll Foreign Missions.
Schoemann, Robert L. '66 (DM) Waukee, IA St. Boniface Church.
Schoen, Thomas A. *s.m.* '87 (CIN) [M] Dayton, OH Marianist Provincialate.
Schoen, Timothy *o.s.b.* '64 (KC) [A] Conception, MO Conception Seminary College; [J] Conception, MO Conception Abbey.
Schoenauer, Francis P. '73 (ALN) [8] Reading, PA St. Margaret Church.
Schoenbaechler, Charles *c.r.* '42 (L) [L] Louisville, KY Villa Pacis, Resurrectionist Retirement Home.
Schoenberg, Oscar *o.s.c.* (STP) [N] Anoka, MN Crosier Community of Anoka.
Schoenberg, Oscar *o.s.c.* '48 (STP) Anoka, MN St. Stephen Church.
Schoenberg, Wilfred P. *s.j.* '51 (P) [L] Portland, OR Colombiere Community.
Schoenberger, James T. '57 (STP) North Branch, MN St. Gregory Church; Shakopee, MN Women's State Reformatory; Retired.
Schoenfeldt, Arthur *c.s.c.* '59 (P) [B] Portland, OR University of Portland; [L] Portland, OR Holy Cross Fathers & Brothers, C.S.C. - University of Portland.
Schoenhofen, Darr F. '82 (SY) New Hartford, NY St. John the Evangelist Church.
Schoenhofen, Roger *o.m.i.* '66 (SFD) [1] Alton, IL SS. Peter and Paul Church.
Schoening, Sylvester H. '58 (PBL) Retired.
Schoenstein, Raymond *o.m.i.* (FgM) Oblates Foreign Missions.
Schoenstene, Robert L. '75 (CHI) [A] Mundelein, IL University of St. Mary of the Lake-Mundelein Seminary.
Schoenstene, Robert L. '75 (JOL) On Duty Outside the Diocese.
Schoeppe, Charles K. '49 (GAL) [N] Houston, TX St. Dominic Village.
Schoeppe, F. Warren *s.j.* '58 (SLC) Brigham City, UT St. Henry Church.
Schoettelkotte, Msgr. Charles T. '34 (EVN) Retired.
Schoettelkotte, John B. '60 (IND) St. Croix, IN Holy Cross Church; St. Croix, IN St. Isidore the Farmer Church.
Schoettelkotte, Lawrence L. *s.m.* '70 (CIN) [M] Cincinnati, OH Marianist Community.
Schoettmer, Kenneth J. '68 (CIN) Millville, OH Queen of Peace Church.
Schoffelmeer, Arnold L. '56 (SPK) Retired.
Scholl, William G. *o.s.f.s.* '61 (PH) [AA] Philadelphia, PA Oblates of St. Francis De Sales.
Scholla, Robert *s.j.* '86 (LA) [BB] Los Angeles, CA Archdiocesan Office for Campus Ministry.
Scholla, Robert W. *s.j.* '86 (LA) [C] Los Angeles, CA Loyola Marymount University.
Scholsky, Martin J. '56 (HRT) [5] East Hartford, CT St. Mary's Church.
Scholz, LeRoy '66 (SCL) Clear Lake, MN St. Marcus Church.
Scholz, William J. '52 (PIT) Robinson Township, PA Holy Trinity Church.
Schommer, George P. *o.p.* '94 (PRO) [P] Providence, RI St. Thomas Aquinas Priory at Providence College.
Schommer, Msgr. Mark J. '63 (GB) Bear Creek, WI St. Mary Church; Clintonville, WI St. Rose Church.
Schommer, Michael '93 (FAR) Langdon, ND St. Alphonsus Church; Nekoma, ND St. Edward Church.
Schon, Randy L. '88 (SC) Oyens, IA St. Catherine's Church.
Schons, Msgr. Gerard '47 (SAC) Retired and in Senior Ministry.
Schook, James R. '75 (L) [37] Louisville, KY St. Ignatius Church.
Schooler, William C. '74 (FTW) [10] Fort Wayne, IN St. Jude Church.
Schoone, Raymond L. '58 (SUP) Retired.
Schopfer, John C. '69 (SY) [1] Syracuse, NY The Cathedral of the Immaculate Conception; Special Assignment.
Schopman, Joop *s.j.* '66 (BO) [W] Chestnut Hill, MA The Jesuit Community at Boston College.
Schopp, George L. '74 (CHI) Blue Island, IL St. Benedict Church.
Schoppe, Msgr. Charles K (GAL) Retired.
Schopps, William J. '85 (ARL) Falls Church, VA St. Anthony's Church.
Schork, John *c.p.* '76 (GAL) [Q] Houston, TX Congregation of the Passion, Holy Name Retreat Center; [S] Houston, TX Holy Name Retreat Center.
Schorp, W. Franz *s.m.* '64 (SAT) [C] San Antonio, TX St. Mary's University of San Antonio, Texas; [M] San Antonio, TX Marianist Residence.
Schorr, James D. '68 (CLV) [2] Elyria, OH Holy Cross Church.
Schorr, W. David '73 (PIT) [78] Pittsburgh, PA Most Holy Name of Jesus Church.
Schott, Edward *s.j.* '63 (ELP) [21] El Paso, TX Sacred Heart Church.
Schott, James E. '61 (NO) Retired.
Schott, Kevin J. '90 (NEW) West Orange, NJ St. Joseph's Church.
Schott, Paul *s.j.* '60 (NO) [8] New Orleans, LA Holy Name of Jesus Church.
Schott, Timothy R. '70 (SC) Carroll, IA St. Lawrence Church.
Schott, Valerian *o.f.m.* '32 (STL) Oakville, MO St. Francis of Assisi Church; [P] Oakville, MO St. Francis Friary.
Schott, Victor P. '56 (LFT) Retired.
Schotzko, Philip M. '77 (NU) Bird Island, MN St. Mary Church.
Schouten, Francis L. '55 (CHI) Retired.
Schoutteten, Francis *o.m.i.* '41 (SAT) [K] San Antonio, TX Oblate Madonna Residence.
Schrad, Merlin J. '77 (SC) Lidderdale, IA Holy Family Church; [B] Carroll, IA Kuemper Catholic High School; [G] Carroll, IA Carroll Area Catholic Schools Foundation, Inc.
Schrader, James *c.pp.s.* '56 (KC) [9] Kansas City, MO St. Elizabeth's Church.
Schrader, James C., Jr. '76 (LIN) Campbell, NE St. Anne Church.
Schrader, Robert J. '78 (ROC) [3] Auburn, NY St. Mary Church.
Schrage, Frank (GB) Lena, WI Holy Cross Church.
Schrage, Joseph S. '99 (BEL) [8] Belleville, IL St. Teresa of the Child Jesus Church.
Schramel, Michael J. '80 (ROC) [2] Rochester, NY St. Ambrose Church.
Schramko, Stewart R. *c.s.v.* '64 (LAV) [1] Las Vegas, NV Guardian Angel Church.
Schramm, Charles H. '71 (MIL) [78] Milwaukee, WI St. Sebastian Church.
Schramm, Donald C. '67 (STL) Troy, MO Sacred Heart Church.
Schramm, Edward J. '69 (STL) Kinloch, MO Holy Angels Church.
Schramm, Mark *s.v.d.* '75 (CHI) [B] Techny, IL Divine Word Residence; [N] Chicago, IL Divine Word Theologate; [N] Techny, IL Society of the Divine Word, Provincial Headquarter-Chicago Prov.
Schramm, Robert *o.s.f.s.* '69 (SAG) [4] Saginaw, MI SS. Simon and Jude Church.
Schratz, Martin *o.f.m. cap.* '83 (CHL) [3] Charlotte, NC Our Lady of Consolation Church; [10] Charlotte, NC St. Thomas Aquinas Church.
Schray, Karl '65 (P) North Bend, OR Holy Redeemer Church.
Schreck, Christopher J. '77 (PH) [A] Wynnewood, PA Theological Seminary of St. Charles Borromeo, Overbrook.
Schreck, Christopher J. '77 (SAV) On Duty Outside the Diocese.
Schreck, J. Gerard '83 (SAV) [3] Columbus, GA St. Anne Church; [A] Columbus, GA Pacelli Catholic High School.
Schreck, Joseph *o.f.m.cap.* '55 (ARE) [1] Utuado, PR San Miquel Church.
Schreck, Paul '45 (BUF) Retired.
Schreiber, Bernard G. '47 (LC) Retired.
Schreiber, Edmund J. '44 (CHI) Franklin Park, IL St. Gertrude Church; Retired.
Schreiber, Gerard H. *c.ss.r.* '54 (RIC) [N] Hampton, VA Holy Family Retreat.
Schreiber, Lawrence *o.f.m.* '60 (LSC) Roswell, NM St. Peter Church.
Schreiber, Lawrence *o.f.m.* '60 (SFE) [4] Albuquerque, NM Holy Family Church.
Schreiber, Stephen J. '99 (E) [21] Erie, PA St. Jude the Apostle Church.
Schreiber, William '79 (SC) Arcadia, IA St. John the Baptist Church.
Schreiner, Bernard P. '42 (NU) Retired.
Schreiner, John E. '52 (TOL) Retired.
Schreiner, Robert '89 (ARL) Great Falls, VA St. Catherine of Siena Church.
Schreiner, Robert '89 (CR) On Duty Outside the Diocese.
Schreiner, William M. *c.s.c.* '42 (FTW) [J] South Bend, IN Congregation of Holy Cross, Indiana Province, Provincial House.
Schreiter, Daniel A. '50 (GB) Retired.
Schreiter, John P. '69 (MIL) Dousman, WI St. Bruno Church.
Schreiter, Robert *c.pp.s.* '75 (CHI) [B] Chicago, IL The Catholic Theological Union at Chicago.
Schreitmueller, Henry J. '56 (NEW) [B] South Orange, NJ Seton Hall University.
Schremmer, Robert A. '76 (DOD) Hanston, KS St. Anthony Church; Jetmore, KS St. Lawrence Church; Spearville, KS St. John the Baptist Church.
Schrenger, Arthur C. '75 (MOB) [1] Mobile, AL Cathedral of the Immaculate Conception.
Schrenger, Authur C. '75 (MOB) On Leave from the Archdiocese.
Schriber, Robert T. '96 (R) Garner, NC St. Mary, Mother of the Church.
Schriefer, Msgr. Robert F. '44 (E) Retired.
Schrimpf, Reginald *s.d.s.* '50 (MIL) [P] Milwaukee, WI Salvatorians - Jordan Hall.
Schriver, Ragan '95 (KNX) [2] Knoxville, TN All Saints Catholic Church; [E] Knoxville, TN Columbus Home, Inc.
Schroder, John F. *s.j.* '53 (FgM) Provinces.
Schroder, John F. *s.j.* '53 (NO) [P] New Orleans, LA Jesuit Provincial Office.
Schroeder, Dennis A. '61 (TOL) Bucyrus, OH Holy Trinity Church.
Schroeder, Edward H. '58 (BUF) Clarence Center, NY St. Augustine Church.
Schroeder, Eugene A. '79 (EVN) [19] Evansville, IN St. Joseph Church.
Schroeder, Francis *s.s.j.* '45 (NO) [5] New Orleans, LA Corpus Christi Church.
Schroeder, Fred A. '42 (LFT) Carmel, IN St. Elizabeth Ann Seton Church.
Schroeder, George *o.f.m.conv.* '43 (SAV) St. Simons Island, GA St. Williams Church.
Schroeder, George J. '42 (PEO) [1] Rock Island, IL St. Mary Church; Retired.
Schroeder, George M. '62 (DEN) Steamboat Springs, CO Holy Name Church; [P] Steamboat Springs, CO Colorado Mountain College.
Schroeder, James *s.c.j.* '70 (MIL) [P] Franklin, WI St. Francis Residence.
Schroeder, Jerome *o.f.m.cap.* '70 (MIL) [S] Milwaukee, WI The Dwelling Place.
Schroeder, Kenneth *c.pp.s.* '65 (CIN) [B] Carthagena, OH St. Charles; [M] Dayton, OH Provincial Office of the Cincinnati Province of the Society of the Precious Blood.
Schroeder, Richard F. '45 (CHI) Retired.
Schroeder, Roger P. *s.v.d.* '79 (CHI) [B] Chicago, IL The Catholic Theological Union at Chicago; [B] Techny, IL Divine Word Residence; [N] Chicago, IL Divine Word Theologate; [N] Techny, IL Society of the Divine

Word, Provincial Headquarter-Chicago Prov.
Schroeder, Timothy C. '88 (FAR) [3] Fargo, ND Nativity Church.
Schroeder, Msgr. Walter L. '41 (NY) Armonk, NY St. Patrick Church; Retired.
Schroeppel, Stephen L. *m.m.* '58 (STL) [P] St. Louis, MO Maryknoll House.
Schroer, Joseph *o.c.s.o.* '52 (SLC) [F] Huntsville, UT Abbey of Our Lady of the Holy Trinity of the Order of Cistercians.
Schroer, Thomas A. *s.m.* '72 (CIN) [D] Dayton, OH The University of Dayton; [M] Dayton, OH Marianist Provincialate.
Schroering, Francis A. '59 (EVN) Haubstadt, IN SS. Peter and Paul Church.
Schroering, Raymond A. '49 (EVN) Retired.
Schroll, Bernard A. '69 (DET) [2] Troy, MI St. Alan Church; Retired.
Schroth, Raymond A. *s.j.* '67 (NEW) [B] Jersey City, NJ Saint Peter's College; [N] Jersey City, NJ Jesuits of Saint Peter's College, Inc.
Schu, Walter *l.c.* '94 (HRT) [B] Cheshire, CT Novitiate of the Legion of Christ.
Schubeck, Thomas L. *s.j.* '68 (CLV) [B] Cleveland, OH John Carroll Jesuit Community.
Schubert, Gerard H. *o.s.f.s.* '59 (ALN) [B] Center Valley, PA Desales University; [K] Center Valley, PA Oblates of St. Francis de Sales.
Schubert, Gerold *o.f.m.* '54 (JOL) [J] Joliet, IL St. John the Baptist Friary.
Schubert, Herbert B. '56 (MIL) [1] South Milwaukee, WI St. Adalbert Church.
Schubiger, Albert B. '49 (MAD) Retired.
Schuck, Hugh *o.s.b.* '34 (RCK) [G] Aurora, IL Marmion Abbey-St. Augustine's Abbey.
Schuck, Joseph J. '53 (ALB) Sidney, NY Sacred Heart Church.
Schuck, Joseph J. '53 (BRK) Released from Diocesan Assignment; Retired.
Schuckenbrock, Harry *o.m.i.* '59 (BWN) [7] Brownsville, TX St. Eugene De Mazenod Church.
Schuckman, Kenneth J. '92 (WCH) Newton, KS St. Mary Church; [L] Wichita, KS Serra Club of Wichita - Downtown.
Schudde, Derk M. '89 (OG) Absent on Leave.
Schue, Dennis L. '57 (FAR) Retired; [D] Devils Lake, ND Mercy Hospital.
Schuele, Francis J. '68 (KC) Special Assignment.
Schuele, John '76 (KC) [3] Kansas City, MO St. Anthony Church.
Schueller, Anthony L. *s.s.s.* '77 (CLV) [O] Cleveland, OH Congregation of the Blessed Sacrament Provincial House; [O] Cleveland, OH Blessed Sacrament Community.
Schueller, La Verne L. '66 (DUB) Military Chaplains.
Schueller, Michael G. '97 (DUB) Duncan, IA St. Wenceslaus Church; Garner, IA St. Boniface Church; [G] Mason City, IA Newman Catholic.
Schuer, Robert J. '48 (COL) [2] Columbus, OH St. Agatha Church; Retired.
Schuerger, Anthony J. '77 (CLV) [44] Cleveland, OH Community of St. Malachi Church; [45] Cleveland, OH St. Malachi Church.
Schuerman, James T. '86 (MIL) [A] St. Francis, WI Saint Francis Seminary.
Schuessler, Peter *s.d.s.* '80 (FgM) Salvatorian Foreign Missions.
Schuessler, Peter *s.d.s.* '80 (MIL) [P] Milwaukee, WI Salvatorian Provincial Residence.
Schuessler, William R. '67 (RCK) Carpentersville, IL St. Monica Church.
Schuett, John T. *s.j.* '58 (DET) [P] Bloomfield Hills, MI Manresa Jesuit Retreat House; [P] Clarkston, MI Colombiere Center.
Schuetze, John (GB) Little Chute, WI St. John Church.
Schug, John *o.f.m.cap.* (NY) [B] Beacon, NY St. Lawrence of Brindisi Friary.
Schuh, Earl '43 (GB) Retired.
Schuh, Msgr. John H. '65 (GB) Special Assignment.
Schuhmacher, George J. '57 (COV) Warsaw, KY St. Joseph Church.
Schuler, A. John '74 (STL) Ferguson, MO Our Lady of Guadalupe Church.
Schuler, Emitt *o.f.m.cap.* '69 (PIT) Allegheny County, PA Department of Veterans Affairs Medical Center Aspinwall; Allegheny County, PA Department of Veterans Affairs Medical Center Oakland; [O] Pittsburgh, PA St. Francis Friary.
Schuler, Gregory '77 (LEX) [1] Lexington, KY Cathedral of Christ the King.
Schuler, Msgr. Richard J. '45 (STP) [12] St. Paul, MN St. Agnes Church.
Schuler, Robert J. '89 (JOL) Clarendon Hills, IL Notre Dame Church.
Schuler, Stephen *s.v.d.* '79 (BLX) [A] Bay St. Louis, MS St. Augustine's.
Schuller, Frederick E. *s.j.* '52 (STL) [O] St. Louis, MO Fusz Pavilion.
Schulmeister, Lawrence *o.f.m.* '67 (BAL) Baltimore, MD University of Maryland Hospital.
Schulmeister, Lawrence *o.f.m.* '67 (NY) [DD] New York, NY Franciscan Friars, Order of Friars Minor, Holy Name Province.
Schulte, Bernard C. *s.j.* '47 (STL) [O] St. Louis, MO Fusz Pavilion.
Schulte, Carl G. *c.m.* '48 (KC) [J] Kansas City, MO Vincentian Parish Mission Center.
Schulte, Daniel *c.m.* '87 (SPC) [2] Cape Girardeau, MO St. Vincent de Paul Church.
Schulte, Francisco *o.s.b.* '79 (SCL) [I] Collegeville, MN St. John's Abbey, of the Order of St. Benedict.
Schulte, Gary '72 (DET) [11] Warren, MI St. Sylvester Church.
Schulte, John R. '77 (COV) Walton, KY All Saints Church.
Schulte, Lyle L. '60 (LC) Boyceville, WI St. Luke Church; Menomonie, WI St. Joseph Church.
Schulte, Mark A. '97 (SFD) [5] Springfield, IL St. Agnes Church.
Schulte, Oswald W. '45 (LC) Retired.
Schulte, Robert C. '75 (FTW) [1] Fort Wayne, IN Cathedral of the Immaculate Conception.
Schulte, William P. '52 (NEW) Retired.
Schultenover, David *s.j.* (MIL) [Y] Milwaukee, WI Theological Studies, Inc.
Schultenover, David G. *s.j.* '69 (OM) [K] Omaha, NE Jesuit Community at Creighton University.
Schulterbrandt, Henrique *c.ss.r.* '94 (FgM) Redemptorist Foreign Missions.
Schultheis, Michael J. *s.j.* '65 (FgM) Provinces.
Schultheis, Michael J. *s.j.* '65 (P) [L] Portland, OR Jesuit Provincial Office (Society of Jesus, Oregon Prov.).
Schultheis, Raymond *c.pp.s.* '56 (CIN) [M] Dayton, OH Provincial Office of the Cincinnati Province of the Society of the Precious Blood.
Schultheis, Raymond *c.pp.s.* '56 (CLV) Cleveland, OH Deaconess Hospital.
Schultz, Blaine *o.s.b.* '60 (KCK) [A] Atchison, KS Benedictine College; [H] Atchison, KS St. Benedict's Abbey.
Schultz, Brian '82 (DUL) [14] Duluth, MN St. Michael's Church.
Schultz, Bruce B. *o.p.* '88 (NO) [P] New Orleans, LA Dominican Friars, Southern Dominican Province of St. Martin de Porres.
Schultz, Bruce B. *o.p.* '88 (SAT) [26] San Antonio, TX St. Ann Church.
Schultz, C. Ray '91 (BEL) Special Assignment.
Schultz, Charles F. *s.t.d.* '80 (SB) Ontario, CA St. Elizabeth Ann Seton Church.
Schultz, Joel P. '00 (MEM) [2] Memphis, TN St. Ann Church.
Schultz, John (PEO) Danville, IL Veterans' Administration Hospital.
Schultz, John A. '65 (LC) [5] Eau Claire, WI St. James the Greater Church.
Schultz, John C. '57 (LFT) On Duty Outside the Diocese.
Schultz, Ray '91 (LAV) Laughlin, NV St. John the Baptist Catholic Church.
Schultz, Russell '66 (SAN) Retired.
Schultz, Stephen (SFE) Fort Sumner, NM St. Anthony Church.
Schultz, Stephen C. '99 (SFE) Santa Rosa, NM St. Rose of Lima Church.
Schultz, Msgr. William F. '64 (BGP) [4] Stratford, CT Our Lady of Grace Church.
Schultze, George E. *s.j.* '94 (SFR) [N] San Francisco, CA Jesuit Community at University of San Francisco.
Schulz, Msgr. Donald C. '53 (COL) [4] Columbus, OH St. Aloysius Church; Retired.
Schulz, James W. *s.j.* '77 (GRY) [J] East Chicago, IN Roque Gonzalez Residence-Jesuit Fathers; [O] Hammond, IN Heartland Center.
Schulz, Ronald '68 (PMB) Boynton Beach, FL St. Thomas More Church; Special Assignment.
Schulz, Wilfred *o.s.b.* (PAT) [N] Convent Station, NJ St. Anne Villa.
Schulz, Wilfred G. *o.s.b.* '53 (PAT) [M] Morristown, NJ St. Mary's Abbey.
Schulze, Paul *s.d.s.* '58 (MIL) [P] Milwaukee, WI Salvatorian Provincial Residence.
Schulze, Robert R. '69 (TR) New Egypt, NJ Assumption Church.
Schulzetenberg, Raymond A. '46 (SCL) Gilman, MN SS. Peter and Paul Church.
Schumacher, Andrew '60 (B) Ferdinand, ID Assumption Church.
Schumacher, Andrew '70 (B) Greencreek, ID St. Anthony's Church.
Schumacher, Andrew J. '60 (B) Cottonwood, ID St. Mary's Church.
Schumacher, Anthony J. '60 (MAD) Oregon, WI Holy Mother of Consolation Church.
Schumacher, Charles P. '48 (LC) Bakerville, WI Corpus Christi Church; Retired.
Schumacher, Ernest *c.r.* '41 (L) [Q] New Hope, KY St. Martin De Porres Lay Dominican Community.
Schumacher, Eugene T. '56 (SC) Retired.
Schumacher, Jacob J. '52 (BIS) Retired; [G] Bismarck, ND Emmaus Place.
Schumacher, James '95 (CHY) [1] Cheyenne, WY St. Mary's Church.
Schumacher, John N. *s.j.* '57 (FgM) Provinces.
Schumacher, Msgr. Joseph A. '57 (FWT) [6] Arlington, TX St. Matthew Church.
Schumacher, Kenneth (TLS) [16] Tulsa, OK Resurrection Church.
Schumacher, Msgr. Louis E. '47 (IND) Brookville, IN St. Michael Church; Cedar Grove, IN Holy Guardian Angels Church.
Schumacher, Mark R. '84 (B) Moscow, ID St. Augustine's Church; [F] Moscow, ID St. Augustine Catholic Center.
Schumacher, Patrick A. '93 (BIS) Mandan, ND St. Joseph Church.
Schumacher, Paul '48 (GB) Retired.
Schumacher, Paul A. '62 (NU) Canby, MN St. Peter Church; St. Leo, MN St. Leo Church.
Schumacher, Robert A. '49 (SPC) Sikeston, MO St. Francis Xavier's Church.
Schumacher, William '88 (DAL) Retired.
Schuneman, John P. *c.s.c.* '57 (PHX) [G] Phoenix, AZ Holy Cross Congregation/Casa Santa Cruz.
Schuster, Anthony '70 (GF) Roundup, MT St. Benedict's Church.
Schuster, Charles G. *c.m.* '55 (FgM) Vincentian Foreign Missions.
Schuster, Francis J. *k.h.s.* '63 (ALN) Whitehall, PA St. John the Baptist Church.
Schuster, Frank '99 (SEA) [O] Seattle, WA Campus Ministry.
Schuster, Frank J., Jr. '00 (BIS) Hazelton, ND St. Paul Church; Linton, ND St. Anthony Church.
Schuster, Franklin R. '99 (SEA) Bellingham, WA Sacred Heart Church.
Schuster, Msgr. George M. '57 (BRK) [215] Queens, NY Our Lady of the Miraculous Medal Church.
Schuster, Paul (FAR) [1] Grand Forks, ND Holy Family Church.
Schuster, Paul '93 (FAR) Manvel, ND St. Timothy's Church.
Schuster, Peter '95 (WIN) Lewiston, MN St. Rose of Lima Church.
Schuster, Philip *o.s.b.* '48 (KC) [J] Conception, MO Conception Abbey.
Schuster, Raymond '93 (SAT) [30] San Antonio, TX St. Bonaventure Church.
Schuster, Robert C. '95 (DET) Bloomfield Hills, MI St. Hugo of the Hills Church.
Schuster, Roy R. *o.f.m.cap.* '59 (PIT) [O] Pittsburgh, PA St. Augustine Friary.
Schuster, Roy R. *o.f.m.cap* '59 (WH) Coalton, WV St. Patrick Church; Huttonsville, WV St. John Bosco Church.
Schuster, Troy '99 (STV) [1] St. Thomas, VI Cathedral of Sts. Peter and Paul; [2] Estate Elizabeth, VI Our Lady of Perpetual Help Church.
Schuster, Valery P. '41 (MIL) Retired.
Schuster, Wilfred J. '46 (MAD) Retired; [H] Madison, WI Bishop O'Connor Catholic Pastoral Center.
Schute, Arthur B. '67 (NEW) On Duty Outside the Archdiocese.
Schute, Arthur B. '67 (VEN) [D] Port Charlotte, FL Bon Secours-St. Joseph Hospital.
Schute, Bruce J. *s.a.c.* '60 (MIL) [P] Milwaukee, WI Pallotti House.
Schutte, James R. '79 (CIN) [2] Dayton, OH St. Agnes Church; [8] Dayton, OH Corpus Christi Church.
Schutte, Robert W. '43 (CIN) Retired.
Schutten, Msgr. Marion F. '45 (NO) Retired.
Schutter, Thomas '68 (JOL) Carol Stream, IL St. Luke Church.
Schutty, John J. '83 (JC) Meta, MO St. Cecilia Church; St. Anthony, MO St. Anthony Church.
Schutz, Bruce B. *o.p.* '88 (SAT) [B] San Antonio, TX Dominican Priory of San Juan Macias.
Schuwey, Emil *c.pp.s.* '49 (CIN) [M] Dayton, OH Provincial Office of the Cincinnati Province of the Society of the Precious Blood.
Schuyler, David *s.m.* '60 (SJ) Special Assignment; [L] Cupertino, CA Marianist Provincial Residence.
Schuyler, Henry C. '45 (PH) Trooper, PA Visitation B.V.M. Church; Retired.
Schuyler, Joseph B. *s.j.* '51 (NY) [DD] New York, NY Murray-Weigel Hall.
Schwab, Elwin '60 (P) Forest Grove, OR St. Anthony Church; [P] Portland, OR University of Portland.
Schwab, James A. '81 (JOL) [13] Joliet, IL St. Jude Church.
Schwab, Joseph '48 (OAK) Retired.
Schwab, Joseph C. *o.m.i.* '53 (PT) Madison, FL St. Vincent de Paul Church.
Schwab, Msgr. Robert C. '41 (BUF) Retired.
Schwab, Steven '90 (IND) [10] Indianapolis, IN Nativity of Our Lord Jesus Christ Church.
Schwab, Thomas E. '56 (CHI) Rosemont-Des Plaines, IL Our Lady of Hope Church; Retired.
Schwaegel, Msgr. Joseph R. '65 (BEL) Leave of Absence.
Schwaig, R. John '90 (STL) [3] St. Louis, MO Holy Family Church.

Schwalenberg, Msgr. Martin '45 (BAL) Retired.
Schwalenberg, Msgr. Martin A. (BAL) [22] Baltimore, MD St. Charles Borromeo Church.
Schwalm, Donald '52 (KCK) Retired.
Schwan, Paul Mark *o.c.s.o.* '88 (SAC) [A] Vina, CA Abbey of New Clairvaux, Trappist Seminary; [H] Vina, CA Abbey of New Clairvaux, Trappist.
Schwantes, John A. *s.j.* '69 (STL) [P] St. Louis, MO Jesuit Community Corporation at St. Louis University - Jesuit Hall.
Schwantner, James *o.f.m.* '55 (SP) [O] St. Petersburg, FL St. Anthony Friary.
Schware, Richard A. '75 (ALN) Pen Argyl, PA St. Elizabeth of Hungary Church.
Schwarte, Michael '95 (JUN) Petersburg, AK St. Catherine of Siena Church; Wrangell, AK St. Rose of Lima Church.
Schwarte, Msgr. Michael W. '38 (DM) Retired.
Schwarting, Donald J. (GAL) Retired.
Schwartz, Msgr. Aloysius B. '37 (SFD) Retired.
Schwartz, Charles M. '99 (TR) Lakewood, NJ St. Mary of the Lake Church.
Schwartz, Christopher *o.s.b.* '74 (CLV) Broadview Heights, OH Assumption Church; [O] Cleveland, OH Benedictine Order of Cleveland.
Schwartz, Edwin V. '60 (ALN) Northampton, PA St. Michael Church; Northampton, PA Our Lady of Hungary Church.
Schwartz, Hugh F. '56 (OM) Retired.
Schwartz, James A. '68 (ROC) Pittsford, NY St. Louis Church.
Schwartz, Kevin '93 (SCL) Bluffton, MN St. John the Baptist Church; Butler, MN Holy Cross Church; Menahga, MN The Church of the Assumption of Our Lady of Menahga.
Schwartz, Norman R. '69 (MIL) [K] Milwaukee, WI St. Joseph's Hospital of Franciscan Sisters, Milwaukee, Inc.
Schwartz, Paul E. '53 (CHI) Sauk Village, IL St. James Church; Retired.
Schwartz, Peter *o.s.b.* '62 (SFS) [F] Marvin, SD Blue Cloud Abbey.
Schwartz, Robert M. '67 (STP) Eagan, MN St. John Neumann Church; [H] Eagan, MN Faithful Shepherd Catholic School.
Schwartz, Rodney A. '92 (SFD) [7] Springfield, IL St. Frances Cabrini Church.
Schwartz, William H. '53 (CIN) Retired.
Schwartz, Msgr. William H. '68 (RCK) [1] Rockford, IL St. Peter Church; [B] Rockford, IL Boylan Central Catholic High School.
Schwartz, William J. '68 (PIT) Oakdale, PA St. Patrick Church.
Schwartz, William T. '58 (DUB) Retired.
Schwartzkopf, Gary W. *s.j.* '69 (NY) [EE] Hastings-on-Hudson, NY Sisters of St. Francis.
Schwartzlose, John A. '00 (L) Lebanon, KY St. Augustine Church.
Schwarz, Bernard F. '66 (OKL) Retired.
Schwarz, Carl V. *c.ss.r.* '42 (STL) [P] Liguori, MO St. Clement Health Care Center.
Schwarz, Elmer C. '53 (OKL) Chickasha, OK Holy Name Church; [K] Norman, OK Campus Ministry for the Archdiocese of Oklahoma City.
Schwarz, John *s.j.* '64 (SPK) [K] Spokane, WA Regis Community.
Schwarz, Robert '65 (MRY) Retired.
Schwarzhaupt, Robert '86 (HON) Papaikou, HI Immaculate Heart of Mary Church.
Schwebs, Daniel L. *o.s.j.* '86 (NOR) [5] Middletown, CT St. Sebastian Church.
Schwebs, Daniel L. *o.s.j.* '86 (SCR) [M] Pittston, PA Eastern Province of the Oblates of St. Joseph.
Schweder, Msgr. John F. '60 (DET) [40] Detroit, MI St. Joseph Church.
Schweers, Gregory *o.cist.* '81 (DAL) [K] Irving, TX Cistercian Abbey of Our Lady of Dallas.
Schwehr, Charles L. '76 (LA) [7] Los Angeles, CA Cathedral Chapel Church.
Schweibold, Conrad L. *o.f.m.conv.* '47 (FTW) Angola, IN St. Anthony Church; Big Long Lake, IN St. Mary of the Angels Church.
Schweifler, Michael *o.s.a* (TLS) Coweta, OK St. Vincent de Paul Church.
Schweifler, Michael *o.s.a.* '84 (TLS) [B] Tulsa, OK Cascia Hall Preparatory School.
Schweigardt, Erwin H. '67 (ALB) [4] Watervliet, NY St. Patrick Church.
Schweiger, Troy J. '95 (LIN) Dawson, NE St. Mary's Church; [C] Falls City, NE Sacred Heart School.
Schweihofer, Frederick J. '68 (DET) [9] Sterling Heights, MI St. Rene Goupil Church.
Schweihofer, Walter J. '38 (DET) Retired.
Schweikert, John *m.s.c.* '96 (SB) Upland, CA St. Joseph Church.
Schweiss, Kurt '85 (LA) [54] Los Angeles, CA St. Camillus De Lellis Church; [73] Los Angeles, CA St. Joseph Church.
Schweitzer, Msgr. Francis X. '45 (COL) Retired.
Schweitzer, Gerald H. '71 (GRY) Wanatah, IN Sacred Heart Church.
Schweitzer, Joachim B. *o.s.b.* '58 (PAT) [M] Morristown, NJ St. Mary's Abbey.
Schweitzer, Paul A. *s.j.* '70 (FgM) Provinces.
Schweitzer, Robert J. '67 (PIT) [3] New Castle, PA St. Joseph the Worker Church.
Schweitzer, Thomas '82 (LA) Glendale, CA Church of the Incarnation.
Schweitzer, Tom '82 (LA) Vernon, CA Holy Angels Parish of the Deaf Church.
Schweizer, Paul *o.carm.* '62 (NEW) Bogota, NJ St. Joseph's Church.
Schweizer, Vincent J. '58 (L) Pewee Valley, KY St. Aloysius Church.
Schwemin, Ralph H. '41 (SPK) Retired.
Schwenk, William M. '60 (EVN) Dale, IN St. Joseph Church.
Schwenzer, Ronald G. *c.s.b.* '68 (GAL) [F] Houston, TX St. Thomas High School.
Schwer, Albert *c.p.* '55 (L) [2] Louisville, KY St. Agnes Church; [L] Louisville, KY Sacred Heart Retreat.
Schwermer, Paul '82 (LAN) [5] Flint, MI Holy Rosary Church.
Schwertner, Msgr. Timothy '65 (LUB) [5] Lubbock, TX St. Elizabeth University Church.
Schwet, Edward N. '82 (CLV) Strongsville, OH St. John Neumann Church.
Schwider, John *o.m.i.* '40 (FgM) Oblates Foreign Missions.
Schwieters, Severin '50 (SCL) Retired.
Schwind, Donald F. '46 (BRK) Retired.
Schwinger, Msgr. William A. '58 (BUF) [1] Buffalo, NY St. Joseph's Church; Retired.
Schwinghamer, David J. *m.m.* '73 (NY) [DD] Maryknoll, NY Maryknoll Fathers and Brothers.
Schwinghammer, Claude '35 (SCL) Retired.
Schwinn, Joseph F. '43 (MIL) Retired.
Schwinn, Thomas J. '58 (DUB) Fairfax, IA St. Patrick's Church; Walford, IA Holy Trinity Church.
Scianna, Bernard C. *o.s.a.* '84 (TLS) [B] Tulsa, OK Cascia Hall Preparatory School.
Sciarra, John N. '45 (IND) Retired.
Sciarrotta, Lee L. *s.m.* '67 (CIN) [9] Dayton, OH Emmanuel Church; [M] Dayton, OH Marianist Provincialate.
Sciarrotta, Paul J. '62 (CLV) [P] Chardon, OH Provincial House of the Sisters of Notre Dame, Juniorate, Novitiate.
Sciberras, Ivan '99 (NEW) Ridgewood, NJ Our Lady of Mount Carmel Church.
Sciberras, Michael J. '67 (GBG) [1] Connellsville, PA Immaculate Conception Church.
Sciera, Msgr. Ronald P. '61 (BUF) [56] Buffalo, NY Precious Blood Church.
Scillieri, Charles P. '73 (MET) Jamesburg, NJ St. James the Less Church.
Scioli, Richard A. *c.s.s.* '79 (SPR) [9] Springfield, MA Our Lady of Mt. Carmel Church.
Scirghi, Thomas J. *s.j.* '86 (NY) [DD] New York, NY Jesuit Community at Fordham University.
Sciumbato, Michael R. '99 (SLC) Price, UT Notre Dame de Lourdes Church.
Sciumbato, Mike '92 (SLC) [H] Price, UT College of Eastern Utah, Newman Club.
Sciurba, Salvatore *o.c.d.* '71 (BO) [W] Boston, MA Carmelite Monastery.
Scocco, Victor *o.ss.t.* '81 (VIC) [4] Victoria, TX Our Lady of Sorrows Church.
Scolamiero, Dominic A. '69 (PAT) Unassigned.
Scollard, Joseph *c.r.* '83 (L) [18] Louisville, KY St. Cecilia Church.
Scollen, Msgr. Francis J. '71 (WOR) [27] Worcester, MA St. Peter Church.
Scolozzi, Angelo '65 (BEA) Special Assignment.
Scopa, Joseph A. *c.s.* '48 (BO) [5] Framingham, MA St. Tarcisius Church.
Scopp, Andrew J. *s.j.* '63 (BO) [W] Boston, MA The Society of Jesus of New England-Provincial Offices.
Scopp, Andrew J. *s.j.* '63 (HRT) [K] Enfield, CT The Home for the Aged of the Little Sisters of the Poor.
Scordo, Joseph Anthony *o.p.* '69 (NY) [DD] New York, NY St. Vincent Ferrer Priory.
Scornaienchi, Frank *t.o.r.* '79 (ALT) [7] Altoona, PA Our Lady of Mt. Carmel Church.
Scorzello, Joseph F. '69 (BO) [1] Medford, MA St. Francis of Assisi Church.
Scotchie, David (ORL) [E] Orlando, FL University of Central Florida Catholic Campus Ministry.
Scotchie, David '93 (ORL) Winter Park, FL Saints Peter and Paul Church; [E] Orlando, FL University of Central Florida Newman Center.
Scott, Alfonso '59 (LA) [12] Long Beach, CA Our Lady of Refuge Church; [D] Lakewood, CA Saint Joseph High School.
Scott, Brendan T. *s.j.* '78 (BUF) [O] Buffalo, NY Canisius Jesuit Community.
Scott, Daniel J. *m.s.* '73 (HRT) [10] New Haven, CT St. John the Baptist Church; [M] Hartford, CT Missionaries of LaSalette, Provincial Secretary.
Scott, Daniel V. *m.s.* '73 (HRT) West Haven, CT V.A. CT Health Care System.
Scott, Delroy Thomas '86 (MGZ) Las Marias, PR Immaculate Heart of Mary Church.
Scott, Edward R. '56 (SCR) Lake Ariel, PA St. Thomas More Church.
Scott, Francis '79 (BLX) Retired.
Scott, James C. '74 (PAT) Unassigned.
Scott, John *o.s.b.* '72 (SEA) [L] Lacey, WA St. Martin's Abbey.
Scott, John M. *s.j.* '44 (OM) [K] Omaha, NE Jesuit Community at Creighton University.
Scott, John V. '69 (GRY) Knox, IN St. Thomas Aquinas Church.
Scott, Joseph *s.v.d.* '75 (OAK) [6] Oakland, CA St. Bernard's Church.
Scott, Joseph J. *c.s.p.* '73 (NEW) [S] Mahwah, NJ Paulist Press.
Scott, Joseph J. *c.s.p.* '73 (NY) [104] New York, NY St. Paul the Apostle Church.
Scott, Kenny *o.f.m.* '58 (OAK) [9] Oakland, CA St. Elizabeth's Church; [N] Oakland, CA Franciscan Friars.
Scott, Msgr. Leonard G. '64 (CAM) [2] Cherry Hill, NJ Holy Rosary Church.
Scott, Mark A. *o.c.s.o.* (SPC) [E] Ava, MO Assumption Abbey (Trappist).
Scott, Mark A. *o.c.s.o.* '87 (SPC) [A] Ava, MO Assumption Novitiate (Trappists).
Scott, Michael Craig '96 (ALX) Plaucheville, LA Mater Dolorosa Church.
Scott, Michael P. '87 (MET) [1] Perth Amboy, NJ St. Mary Church.
Scott, Msgr. Patrick J. '60 (PAT) Pompton Plains, NJ Our Lady of Good Counsel Church.
Scott, Philip P. '79 (PSC) Roswell, GA Epiphany Byzantine Church.
Scott, Raymond '48 (DAL) Retired.
Scott, Richard A. '88 (WDC) Clinton, MD Church of St. John the Evangelist.
Scott, Robert *c.s.p.* '49 (AUS) [11] Austin, TX St. Austin Church.
Scott, Samuel V. '95 (BGP) [6] Fairfield, CT St. Pius X Church.
Scott, Stephen (SPR) [G] Springfield, MA CHE - The Mercy Hospital, Inc.
Scott, Vincent J. '75 (OAK) [2] Walnut Creek, CA St. John Vianney Church.
Scotti, P. Paschal *o.s.b.* '89 (PRO) [P] Portsmouth, RI Abbey of St. Gregory the Great.
Scotto, Dominic *t.o.r.* '67 (STU) [A] Steubenville, OH Franciscan University of Steubenville; [F] Steubenville, OH Holy Spirit Friary.
Scrima, Claude *o.f.m.* '61 (BO) [W] Boston, MA St. Christopher Friary.
Scrima, Claude *o.f.m.* '61 (NY) [DD] New York, NY Franciscan Province of the Immaculate Conception.
Scuderi, Carmen *o.f.m.* '83 (PSC) [A] Sybertsville, PA Holy Dormition Friary.
Scuderi, Salvatore A. *m.ss.cc.* '88 (CAM) [8] Camden, NJ Our Lady of Mount Carmel/Fatima Church.
Scull, Msgr. Edward J. '51 (BGP) [6] Fairfield, CT St. Pius X Church.
Scull, James P. *s.j.* '58 (BGP) [P] Fairfield, CT The Fairfield Jesuit Community-Fairfield University.
Scullin, Robert J. *s.j.* '76 (CHI) [N] Chicago, IL Chicago Province of the Society of Jesus-Provincial Office.
Scullin, Robert J. *s.j.* '76 (DET) [K] Detroit, MI Jesuit Provincial Office-Detroit Province of the Society of Jesus; [K] Detroit, MI Jesuit Provincial Office-Detroit Province of the Society of Jesus.
Scullion, James P. *o.f.m.* '80 (WDC) [B] Silver Spring, MD Holy Name College; [B] Washington, DC Washington Theological Union.
Scully, G. Michael *c.s.c.* '58 (FTW) [J] South Bend, IN Congregation of Holy Cross, Indiana Province, Provincial House.
Scully, Msgr. John (SP) Seffner, FL St. Francis of Assisi Church.
Scully, Msgr. John '48 (SP) Retired.
Scully, John J. *s.j.* '57 (NY) [DD] New York, NY Jesuit Community at Fordham University.
Scully, John J. '72 (TR) Matawan, NJ St. Clement Church.
Scully, John T. *s.s.e.* '55 (BUR) Putney, VT Our Lady of Mercy Church.
Scully, Michael *o.f.m.cap.* '65 (SAL) Hays, KS St. Joseph's Church; [D] Hays, KS St. Joseph's Friary.
Scully, Michael G. *s.j.* '86 (SJ) [D] San Jose, CA Bellarmine College Preparatory.
Scully, Patrick A. '56 (SHP) Vivian, LA St. Clement Church.
Scully, Philip A. '42 (PH) Retired.
Scully, Richard D. '78 (AMA) Dumas, TX SS. Peter and Paul Church.
Scully, Robert E. *s.j.* '96 (SY) [S] Syracuse, NY Jesuits at LeMoyne, Inc.
Scully, Timothy R. *c.s.c.* '81 (FTW) [B] Notre Dame, IN University of Notre Dame Du Lac; [J] Notre Dame, IN Holy Cross Community, Corby Hall, University of Notre Dame.
Scully, William *o.f.m.* '67 (PAT) Hewitt, NJ Our Lady Queen of Peace Church.

Scurti, Louis J. '73 (PAT) Totowa, NJ North Jersey Developmental Center; [O] Haledon, NJ William Paterson University of New Jersey.
Seabo, Frank '00 (CHL) Asheville, NC Basilica of St. Lawrence.
Seabold, John P. '88 (CLV) [1] Garfield Heights, OH St. Monica Church.
Seabridge, Thomas L. '88 (SAC) Corning, CA Immaculate Conception Church; Orland, CA St. Dominic Church.
Seagrams, Richard (NY) [8] Yonkers, NY St. Eugene Church.
Seagrave, Thomas L. '68 (SFR) [55] San Francisco, CA Visitacion, Church of the.
Seagraves, Richard '90 (NY) Scarsdale, NY Immaculate Heart of Mary Church.
Seagriff, Edward M. '81 (RVC) Lindenhurst, NY Our Lady of Perpetual Help Church.
Sealy, Robert J. *s.j.* '51 (NY) [DD] New York, NY Jesuit Community at Fordham University.
Seaman, Cyril *o.f.m.* '56 (BO) [BB] Boston, MA St. Anthony Shrine.
Seaman, Paul G. '85 (CHI) Country Club Hills, IL St. Emeric Church.
Searles, Lawrence *s.j.* '87 (SJN) [22] San Juan, PR San Ignacio de Loyola Church.
Searles, Lawrence P. *s.j.* '87 (FgM) Provinces.
Searles, Thaddeus *s.t.* '56 (BLX) Pineville, MS Our Lady of Lourdes Church.
Searles, Wendell H. '55 (BUR) [F] Burlington, VT Mount St. Mary Convent.
Sears, Eugene A. '58 (KAL) St. Joseph, MI St. Joseph Church.
Sears, G. David '63 (NY) [226] Staten Island, NY St. Roch Church.
Sears, G. David '63 (SY) On Duty Outside the Diocese.
Sears, Gerald *o.c.s.o.* '73 (WOR) [N] Spencer, MA St. Joseph's Abbey.
Sears, Michael '94 (LA) Azusa, CA St. Frances of Rome Church.
Sears, Robert T. *s.j.* '66 (CHI) [C] Chicago, IL Jesuit Community at Loyola University of Chicago.
Sears, William F. '84 (PRO) Retired.
Sears, William J. '62 (BRK) Released from Diocesan Assignment.
Seasoltz, Kevin *o.s.b.* '56 (SCL) [I] Collegeville, MN St. John's Abbey, of the Order of St. Benedict.
Seaver, Paul E. *o.p.* '59 (PRO) [P] Providence, RI St. Thomas Aquinas Priory at Providence College.
Seavey, Michael J. '86 (PRT) Augusta, ME St. Andrew's Church.
Seay, Robert (LAF) [2] Lafayette, LA St. Paul The Apostle Church.
Sebaali, George M. '83 (SAM) Glen Allen, VA St. Anthony Church.
Sebahar, John M. '58 (JOL) Glen Ellyn, IL St. James the Apostle Church.
Sebastian, Gregory *o.s.b.* '83 (SCL) [I] Collegeville, MN St. John's Abbey, of the Order of St. Benedict.
Sebastian, Sunny '90 (AUS) Old Washington-on-the Brazos, TX Blessed Virgin Mary Church; Somerville, TX St. Ann's Church.
Sebescak, Gary '94 (BEL) Leave of Absence.
Sebesta, James A. *s.j.* '70 (STL) [C] St. Louis, MO Saint Louis University; [P] St. Louis, MO Jesuit Community Corporation at St. Louis University - Jesuit Hall.
Sebra, Anthony '72 (STA) [13] Jacksonville, FL Resurrection Church.
Seccomb, Daniel *s.m.* '00 (HON) Kapaa, HI St. Catherine Church.
Secondo, Louis J. *t.o.r.* '46 (ALT) [7] Altoona, PA Our Lady of Mt. Carmel Church.
Secor, Gary '77 (HON) [1] Honolulu, HI Cathedral of Our Lady of Peace.
Secora, James L. '75 (DUB) Cedar Falls, IA St. Patrick Church.
Seculoff, James F. '62 (FTW) Bristol, IN St. Mary of the Annunciation Church.
Seda, Jon M. '88 (DUB) Colo, IA St. Mary's Church; Nevada, IA St. Patrick's Church; St. Anthony, IA Sacred Heart Church; State Center, IA St. Joseph's Church; Zearing, IA St. Gabriel Church; Marshalltown, IA Veterans' Home.
Sedar, Adam C. '98 (ALN) Sinking Spring, PA St. Ignatius Loyola Church.
Sederwall, Donald '85 (SFD) Retired; [J] Alton, IL Marian Heights Apartments.
Sedita, Msgr. Vincent '92 (LKC) [1] Sulphur, LA Immaculate Conception of the B.V.M. Church.
Sedlacek, Richard D. '79 (YAK) Kennewick, WA St. Joseph's Church.
Sedlacko, Louis S. *o.s.b.* '44 (GBG) [H] Latrobe, PA Saint Vincent Archabbey.
Sedlak, John A. '82 (GBG) Grindstone, PA St. Cecilia Church; Smock, PA St. Hedwig Church; [K] Smock, PA Ladies of Charity.
Sedlak, Kenneth *c.ss.r.* '72 (CHI) [133] Chicago, IL St. Michael Church.
Sedlak, Valentine G. '44 (PIT) Retired.
Sedley, Joseph *c.p.* '69 (WOR) [N] Shrewsbury, MA Calvery Retreat Center, Passionist Fathers of Shrewsbury, Inc.
Sedlmayer, Lauro C. '85 (MET) [9] Perth Amboy, NJ Our Lady of the Rosary of Fatima Church.
Sedlock, David W. '91 (MAR) Rapid River, MI St. Charles Borromeo Church.
Sedlock, Stephen J. *c.s.c.* '66 (FTW) [9] South Bend, IN Holy Cross Church.
Seeberger, Claude *o.s.b.* '49 (BIS) [3] Dickinson, ND St. Patrick Church; [A] Richardton, ND Assumption Abbey.
Seed, Michael *s.a.* '86 (NY) [DD] Garrison, NY Franciscan Friars of the Atonement, Minister General Office.
Seedorf, Warren H. *c.s.p.* '49 (DEN) Greeley, CO St. Mary Church.
Seedorf, Warren H. *c.s.p.* '49 (NY) [DD] Jamaica Estates, NY Paulist Fathers Generalate.
Seefeldt, Wilbert T. '39 (STP) Retired.
Seegar, Kenneth M. '87 (SCR) Wyalusing, PA St. Mary's Assumption Church.
Seeger, James E. '85 (PIT) On Duty Outside the Diocese.
Seekamp, Walter J. '79 (BGP) Ridgefield, CT St. Elizabeth Seton Church.
Seelaus, William O. *o.s.f.s.* '51 (PH) [D] Philadelphia, PA Father Judge High School for Boys; [AA] Philadelphia, PA Father Judge Faculty House.
Seeley, Burns K. (CHI) [104] Chicago, IL St. John Cantius Church.
Seelman, Patrick *t.o.r.* (ORL) [F] New Smyrna Beach, FL Villa Madonna.
Seeman, Robert L. '79 (PIT) Jefferson Boro, PA St. Thomas A'Becket Church.
Seery, William O. '95 (HRT) Oakville, CT St. Mary Magdalen Church.
Seetch, William D. *c.s.c.* '79 (FTW) [B] Notre Dame, IN University of Notre Dame Du Lac; [B] Notre Dame, IN University of Notre Dame Du Lac; [J] Notre Dame, IN Holy Cross Community, Corby Hall, University of Notre Dame.
Seethaler, Scott *o.f.m.cap.* '70 (PIT) Rochester, PA St. Cecilia Church; [O] Rochester, PA St. Cecilia Friary.
Seeton, Philip '91 (OKL) Lawton, OK Holy Family Church; [K] Norman, OK Campus Ministry for the Archdiocese of Oklahoma City.
Seeton, Philip M. '91 (PBR) Oklahoma City, OK Byzantine Catholic Community of Oklahoma City Church.
Seewald, Carl H. *s.v.d.* '68 (OAK) Martinez, CA St. Catherine of Siena Church.
Sefcik, Dennis L. '65 (SC) Lake City, IA St. Mary's Church; Lohrville, IA St. Joseph's Church.
Segaric, John '48 (LA) [46] Los Angeles, CA St. Anthony Church; Retired; Retired.
Segatta, Bruno '74 (B) On Duty Outside the Diocese.
Seger, Michael '88 (CIN) [B] Cincinnati, OH Mt. St. Mary's Seminary of the West.
Seger, Oscar H '70 (CIN) Fryburg, OH St. John Church.
Seger, Oscar H. '70 (CIN) Egypt, OH St. Joseph Church; Glynwood, OH St. Patrick Church.
Segerson, Thomas M. '69 (MAD) Retired; [H] Madison, WI Bishop O'Connor Catholic Pastoral Center.
Segotta, Vincent *c.p.* (WH) Kingwood, WV St. Sebastian's Church.
Segotta, Vincent *c.p.* '77 (WH) Masontown, WV St. Zita's Church.
Segovia, Norman '67 (SJ) [3] San Jose, CA Christ the King Church.
Segreve, Richard J. *c.s.c.* '61 (FR) [A] North Easton, MA Holy Cross Fathers Religious.
Seguin, Robert J. *c.s.b.* '69 (GAL) [Q] Sugar Land, TX Basilian Mission Center.
Segura, Luis Alfonso *m.s.c.* '99 (FgM) Missionaries of the Sacred Heart Foreign Missions.
Segura, Luis Alfonso *m.s.c.* '99 (RCK) [G] Aurora, IL Missionaries of the Sacred Heart Community.
Seher, Philip O. '65 (CIN) [47] Cincinnati, OH St. Joseph Church.
Sehler, Michael E. *s.j.* '73 (NY) [F] New York, NY Loyola School; [DD] New York, NY "America;" Residence and publication office of the America Press.
Seibert, Gary G. *s.j.* '73 (NY) [45] New York, NY Holy Cross Church; [DD] New York, NY West Side Jesuit Community.
Seibert, Herman *o.f.m.conv.* '45 (SY) [2] Syracuse, NY Assumption B.V.M. Church.
Seibert, James C. *c.pp.s.* '77 (CIN) [B] Carthagena, OH St. Charles; [M] Dayton, OH Provincial Office of the Cincinnati Province of the Society of the Precious Blood.
Seibert, Thomas E. *i.c.* '75 (PEO) Galesburg, IL Corpus Christi Church.
Seichepine, Albert M. *c.s.sp.* '51 (PH) [AA] Bensalem, PA Congregation of the Holy Ghost.
Seidel, George J. *o.s.b.* '58 (SEA) [L] Lacey, WA St. Martin's Abbey.
Seidel, Michael J. '87 (STL) On Medical Leave.
Seidel, Thomas *c.s.c.* '57 (KAL) Bangor, MI Sacred Heart of Jesus Church.
Seidenburg, Msgr. Augustine J. '48 (CAM) Retired.
Seidl, Larry J. '75 (GB) [1] Two Rivers, WI St. Luke Church; [4] Two Rivers, WI St. Mark Church.
Seifert, Michael *s.m.* '85 (BWN) [11] Brownsville, TX San Felipe de Jesus Church.
Seifert, Michael D. '84 (Y) Waynesburg, OH St. James Church.
Seifert, Raymond *c.pp.s.* '44 (CIN) [B] Carthagena, OH St. Charles.
Seifert, William *s.v.d.* '67 (FgM) Society of the Divine Word Foreign Missions.
Seifert, William N. '81 (ALN) [O] Allentown, PA The Newman Center.
Seifferly, Richard R. '63 (GAY) Retired.
Seifner, Thomas J. '92 (JC) Mokane, MO St. Jude Thaddeus Church; Rhineland, MO Church of the Risen Savior; Vandalia, MO Sacred Heart Church.
Seifried, Msgr. Kenneth A. '63 (SC) Granville, IA St. Joseph Church; [B] Granville, IA Spalding Catholic High School.
Seigel, Timothy J. '91 (RCK) Mount Carroll, IL SS. John and Catherine Church; Savanna, IL St. John the Baptist Church.
Seiker, Daniel J. '87 (LIN) [H] Lincoln, NE School Sisters of Christ the King, Villa Regina Motherhouse & Novitiate.
Seiker, Leo V. '91 (LIN) York, NE St. Joseph's Church.
Seiker, Mark E. '84 (LIN) Beatrice, NE St. Joseph's Church.
Seil, Paul D. '89 (BUF) [41] Buffalo, NY St. Lawrence Church.
Seiler, Andrew J. '88 (WCH) Wellington, KS St. Anthony Church; Wellington, KS St. Rose of Lima Church.
Seiler, Gerald L., Jr. '90 (NO) [9] New Orleans, LA Holy Name of Mary (Algiers) Church; [A] New Orleans, LA Notre Dame Seminary Graduate School of Theology.
Seiler, John A. '59 (COV) Fort Thomas, KY St. Luke Hospital East.
Seipp, William J. '63 (MAD) [11] Madison, WI St. Patrick Church.
Seis, Michael '93 (GB) On Duty Outside the Diocese.
Seisser, Edward J. '98 (RCK) St. Charles, IL St. John Neumann Church.
Seiter, George C. '83 (CAM) Merchantville, NJ St. Peter's Church.
Seiter, Joseph A. *c.s.sp.* '62 (LR) Carlisle, AR St. Rose of Lima Church.
Seitz, Cyprian *o.s.b.* '37 (SCL) [I] Collegeville, MN St. John's Abbey, of the Order of St. Benedict.
Seitz, Gilbert J. '82 (BAL) Special Assignment.
Seitz, James J. '94 (WIN) Dodge Center, MN St. John Baptist de La Salle Church.
Seitz, Joseph W. '58 (CHI) Retired.
Seitz, Mark Joseph '80 (DAL) Waxahachie, TX St. Joseph Church.
Seitz, Patrick K. '92 (BWN) San Benito, TX St. Theresa Church.
Seitz, Paul F.X. '58 (CHR) Walterboro, SC St. Anthony's Church.
Seitz, Thomas R. '52 (CHI) [200] Chicago, IL St. Thomas Apostle Church; Retired.
Seiwert, Charles F. '99 (WCH) [1] Wichita, KS Cathedral of the Immaculate Conception.
Sejba, Anthony F. '99 (CLV) Mentor, OH St. John Vianney Church.
Sekellick, Msgr. John T. '69 (PSC) Jessup, PA Holy Ghost Church.
Seland, John *s.v.d.* '68 (FgM) Society of the Divine Word Foreign Missions.
Seleccion, Romeo N. *m.s.* (SB) Lucerne Valley, CA St. Paul Church.
Seleccion, Romeo N. *m.s.* '82 (SB) Apple Valley, CA Our Lady of the Desert Church.
Seli, Msgr. John J. '46 (PIT) Retired.
Seli, William F. *s.m.* '58 (WH) Richwood, WV Holy Family Church; Summersville, WV St. John The Evangelist Church.
Sell, Msgr. Robert L., III '78 (LFT) Special Assignment.
Sella, Donald J. (PAT) [16] Paterson, NJ St. Therese Church.
Sella, Peter *s.d.b.* '68 (NEW) [C] Ramsey, NJ Don Bosco Preparatory High School for Boys.
Sellars, Charles *o.m.i.* '54 (BEA) Silsbee, TX St. Mark the Evangelist Church.
Selle, Paulinus J. *o.s.b.* '39 (GBG) [H] Latrobe, PA Saint Vincent Archabbey.
Selleck, John P. '57 (CAM) Retired.
Selleck, John P. '57 (PT) Blountstown, FL St. Francis of Assisi Church.
Sellentin, Thomas J. '65 (OM) North Bend, NE St. Charles Borromeo Church; Snyder, NE St. Leo Church.
Sellers, Benedict *o.s.b.* '75 (CLV) [O] Cleveland, OH Benedictine Order of Cleveland.
Selvadasan, Albert '91 (PH) [47] Philadelphia, PA St. Francis de Sales Church.
Selvaj, Peter (NY) Staten Island, NY St. Vincent's Medical Center of Richmond.
Selvam, Panneer '81 (P) Stayton, OR Immaculate

Conception Church.
Selvan, Maria Augustine *s.j.* '89 (CHI) [C] Chicago, IL Jesuit Community at Loyola University of Chicago.
Selvaraj, Balappa '86 (ATL) Blairsville, GA St. Francis of Assisi Church.
Selvaraj, Bose Raja '73 (BGP) [4] Trumbull, CT St. Theresa Church.
Selvaraj, Peter '82 (NY) [213] Staten Island, NY St. Mary Church.
Selvaras, Thomas '64 (CHL) [4] Charlotte, NC St. Ann Church.
Selvester, Guy W. '97 (MET) Phillipsburg, NJ St. Philip & St. James Church.
Selzer, Eugene P. '61 (PRM) St. Louis, MO St. Louis Church.
Selzer, Eugene P. '61 (STL) Woodson Terrace, MO St. William Church.
Selzler, Norbert E. '38 (BUF) Retired.
Semaan, Charbel T. '89 (SAM) New Bedford, MA Our Lady of Purgatory Church.
Semancik, Msgr. Joseph F. '53 (GRY) [6] East Chicago, IN Sacred Heart Church.
Semanych, Petro '91 (PHU) Great Meadows, NJ St. Nicholas Church.
Semenych, Petro '91 (PHU) West Easton, PA Holy Ghost Church.
Semien, Gregory '99 (LAF) Eunice, LA St. Anthony of Padua Church.
Seminack, Msgr. Richard '67 (SJP) Carnegie, PA Holy Trinity Church.
Seminara, Ronald S. *s.j.* '74 (RC) Norris, SD Sacred Heart Church; White River, SD St. Ignatius Church; White River, SD Sacred Heart Church; St. Francis, SD Rosebud Reservation Church.
Seminatore, Joseph J. '69 (CLV) [L] Parma, OH CCSC/Parmadale.
Semiraro, Reginald *o.f.m.* '44 (ALB) [A] Catskill, NY St. Anthony Friary.
Semko, Edward '69 (PSC) Carteret, NJ St. Elias Church.
Semler, Albert J. '67 (PIT) Franklin Park Borough, PA Saints John and Paul Church.
Semler, Andrew V. '00 (DAL) Plano, TX St. Elizabeth Ann Seton Church.
Semmer, Dean F. '79 (CHI) Grayslake, IL St. Gilbert Church.
Semonin, James R. '71 (CLV) Cleveland, OH Parma Community Hospital; [L] Parma, OH CCSC/ Parmadale.
Sempa, Msgr. John J. '80 (SCR) [18] Wilkes-Barre, PA Sacred Heart-St. John Church.
Sempko, Walter A. '50 (HBG) [3] Lebanon, PA St. Cecilia Church.
Semple, James '61 (SLC) [10] Salt Lake City, UT St. Thomas More Church.
Semple, Richard '00 (SPK) [9] Spokane, WA St. Augustine Church.
Sena, Charles A. '92 (PBL) La Junta, CO Our Lady of Guadalupe/ St. Patrick Church.
Sena, Sotero A. (SFE) Clovis, NM Our Lady of Guadalupe Church.
Senchur, Becket G. *o.s.b.* '73 (GBG) [H] Latrobe, PA Saint Vincent Archabbey.
Senecal, Gerard *o.s.b.* '54 (KCK) Atchison, KS St. Benedict's Church; Atchison, KS Sacred Heart Church.
Seneschal, Theodore T. *o.s.b.* '70 (OKL) [I] Shawnee, OK St. Gregory's Abbey.
Senetsky, Msgr. Robert *j.c.d.* '60 (PSC) Peekskill, NY SS. Peter and Paul Church.
Senger, Daniel W. *o.f.m.* '93 (HON) [2] Honolulu, HI Co-Cathedral of St. Theresa of the Child Jesus .
Senger, William *m.m.* '73 (FgM) Maryknoll Foreign Missions.
Senghas, Richard E. '98 (PRT) Jay, ME St. Rose of Lima Church.
Senior, Donald *c.p.* '67 (CHI) [B] Chicago, IL The Catholic Theological Union at Chicago; [B] Chicago, IL The Catholic Theological Union at Chicago; [N] Chicago, IL Passionist Community-CTU.
Senior, Msgr. Timothy C. (PH) [FF] Philadelphia, PA Ladies of Charity.
Senior, Msgr. Timothy C. '85 (PH) [K] Philadelphia, PA The Catholic Social Services of the Archdiocese of Philadelphia; [M] Springfield, PA Divine Providence Village.
Seniw, John '82 (PHU) Absent on Leave.
Senk, Christopher L. *o.s.b.* '76 (VEN) Port Charlotte, FL San Antonio Church.
Senko, Martin '56 (P) Retired.
Senn, Edward R. '58 (SUP) Retired.
Senneville, Eugene Joseph '46 (LAF) Retired.
Sennik, Thomas W. '76 (NOR) West Willington, CT St. Jude Church.
Senske, Joseph A. '48 (PH) Retired.
Sepe, Kevin M. '86 (BO) Braintree, MA St. Francis of Assisi Church.
Seper, John M. '83 (STL) Richmond Heights, MO Immacolata Church.
Sepich, Larry '74 (MIL) [75] Milwaukee, WI St. Roman Church.
Sepp, Michael P. '82 (NY) [107] New York, NY Resurrection Church.
Sepulchre, Jaime *o.s.a.* (CHI) [145] Chicago, IL Our Lady of Good Counsel Church.
Sepulveda, Thomas W. *c.s.b.* '74 (GAL) [Q] Sugar Land, TX Basilian Mission Center.
Sequeira, Dominic *s.d.b.* '92 (NY) [99] New York, NY Our Lady of Victory Church.
Sequeira, Glenn N. '91 (LA) Glendale, CA Holy Family Church.
Sequeira, Marcos '91 (NEW) [17] Jersey City, NJ Our Lady of Mt. Carmel Church.
Sequeira, Michael '66 (NOR) Clinton, CT St. Mary of the Visitation Church.
Sera, Enrique '78 (ORG) [1] Santa Ana, CA Immaculate Heart of Mary Church.
Serado, Msgr. William '40 (SR) Retired.
Serafini, Augustine '62 (GB) [I] Oshkosh, WI Community of Our Lady.
Seramur, Leo J. '45 (MIL) Retired.
Serano, Joseph A. *o.praem.* '69 (PH) [B] Paoli, PA Daylesford Abbey; [AA] Paoli, PA Daylesford Abbey.
Serban, Ron '93 (SB) Military Chaplains.
Serban, Ron '93 (SR) Military Chaplains.
Seremet, Hyacinth '51 (SY) [4] Utica, NY Sacred Heart Church.
Serena, Edward T. '68 (BO) Marshfield, MA St. Ann Church.
Sereno, David A. '86 (SD) Escondido, CA Church of the Resurrection.
Sergi, Michael D. *c.ss.r.* '79 (BAL) [68] Baltimore, MD Our Lady of Fatima Church.
Sergott, Joseph *o.p.* '96 (ANC) [1] Anchorage, AK Holy Family Church.
Serio, Anthony M. '67 (NO) Westwego, LA Our Lady of Prompt Succor Church.
Serio, John J. *s.d.b.* '82 (BO) [E] Boston, MA Savio Preparatory High School.
Sermak, Ronald *o.f.m.conv.* '60 (BAL) [S] Ellicott City, MD Order of Friars Minor Conventual.
Sermak, Ronald *o.f.m.conv.* '60 (BUF) [P] Hamburg, NY Immaculate Conception Convent.
Serna, F. Mark *o.s.b.* '86 (PRO) [E] Portsmouth, RI Portsmouth Abbey School.
Serna, Jose Juan '00 (STO) Tracy, CA St. Bernard's Church.
Serna, Luis '96 (DAL) [7] Dallas, TX Mary Immaculate Church.
Serour, George J. '59 (SAG) Pigeon, MI St. Francis Borgia Church; Sebewaing, MI Holy Family Church.
Serowik, James P. '87 (SY) [5] Endicott, NY St. Joseph Church.
Serra, Dominic '72 (NY) On Duty Outside the Archdiocese.
Serra, Dominic '72 (STP) [A] St. Paul, MN The Saint Paul Seminary; [C] St. Paul, MN University of St. Thomas.
Serra, Dominic F. *s.t.d.* '72 (WDC) [C] Washington, DC Catholic University of America, The.
Serra, Javier *c.m.* (BRK) [116] Brooklyn, NY St. Peter-St. Paul-Our Lady of Pilar Church.
Serra, Javier Antonio *c.m.* '99 (BRK) [X] Brooklyn, NY Centro Evangelizacion San Vicente de Paul; [Z] Brooklyn, NY Jornada Movement.
Serraglio, Msgr. Mario A. '58 (COL) [3] Columbus, OH St. Agnes Church.
Serraino, Frederick *c.s.c.* (ORL) Retired.
Serrano, Dionisio '97 (PCE) On Duty Outside the Diocese.
Serrano, Edgar '87 (HON) Papaaloa, HI St. Anthony Church.
Serrano, Heriberto '67 (SAC) Maxwell, CA Sacred Heart Church; Willows, CA St. Monica Church.
Serrano, John J. '42 (RVC) Retired; [M] Uniondale, NY St. Pius X Residence.
Serrano, Jose '95 (NY) [31] New York, NY St. Elizabeth Church.
Serrano, Macario P. *o.r.c.* '89 (PCE) Castaner, PR Our Lady of the Miraculous Medal Church.
Serrano, Salvador V. '85 (PMB) [G] Delray Beach, FL Opus Dei.
Serratelli, Arthur J. '68 (NEW) [B] South Orange, NJ Seton Hall University.
Serrick, James K. *s.j.* '62 (DET) [P] Bloomfield Hills, MI Manresa Jesuit Retreat House.
Serva, Donald M. *s.j.* '78 (DET) [K] Detroit, MI Jesuit Provincial Office-Detroit Province of the Society of Jesus.
Serva, Donald M. *s.j.* '78 (WH) [A] Wheeling, WV Wheeling Jesuit University.
Servatius, Msgr. Robert R. '64 (SLC) [6] Sandy, UT Blessed Sacrament Church.
Service, Msgr. Gerald H. '69 (OG) Canton, NY St. Mary Church.
Servinsky, Msgr. Michael E. '70 (ALT) Coupon, PA St. Joseph's Church.
Servodidio, Msgr. John T. '54 (NY) [210] Staten Island, NY St. Joseph Church.
Serwa, Greg *s.a.c.* '70 (MIL) [86] Milwaukee, WI St. Vincent Pallotti Church.
Serwa, Gregory P. *s.a.c.* '70 (MIL) [P] Milwaukee, WI Pallotti House.
Sesana, Joseph *i.m.c.* '74 (MET) [H] Somerset, NJ Consolata Society for Foreign Missions.
Sescon, Esteban '77 (ELP) [23] El Paso, TX St. Francis Xavier Church.
Sessa, Eugene *s.j.* '97 (DAL) [D] Dallas, TX Jesuit College Preparatory School.
Sessions, Phillip D. '80 (LAN) On Duty Outside the Diocese.
Sessions, Phillip D. '80 (SD) [29] San Diego, CA St. John the Evangelist Church.
Sestito, Joseph N. '59 (OG) On Duty Outside the Diocese.
Sesto, Gennaro *s.d.b.* '50 (NY) [FF] Stony Point, NY Don Bosco Retreat Center and Marian Shrine; [FF] Stony Point, NY Marian Shrine.
Setelik, James '84 (RNO) Carson City, NV Corpus Christi Church.
Setter, H. '88 (WCH) Goddard, KS Holy Spirit Church.
Settle, Anthony P. '90 (NY) [1] Mt. Vernon, NY Sacred Heart Church.
Settles, Dennis F. '65 (JOL) [1] Kankakee, IL St. Martin of Tours Church.
Setzer, Frank A. *s.m.m.* '37 (BRK) Retired.
Seubert, August *o.f.m.cap.* '57 (FgM) Capuchin Foreign Missions.
Seubert, Xavier J. *o.f.m.* '71 (BUF) [C] St. Bonaventure, NY St. Bonaventure University; [O] St. Bonaventure, NY St. Bonaventure Friary.
Seuferling, George '56 (KCK) Shawnee, KS Good Shepherd Church.
Seuntjens, LeRoy L. '98 (SC) Hawarden, IA St. Mary's Church.
Sevcik, Lawrence *o.s.b.* '53 (CLV) [O] Cleveland, OH Benedictine Order of Cleveland.
Severson, Richard '82 (ALB) Wilton, NY Mount McGregor Correctional Facility; Special Assignment.
Severt, William '74 (CLV) Cleveland, OH University Hospitals.
Sevick, John M. '73 (CHI) Other Assignments.
Sevigny, Michael E. *o.f.m.cap.* '78 (MAN) [5] Manchester, NH Blessed Sacrament Church.
Sevilla, Dennis '69 (SEA) Bainbridge Island, WA St. Cecilia Church.
Sevola, Frank *o.f.m.* '91 (HRT) [15] Hartford, CT St. Patrick-St. Anthony Church.
Sewar, Dennis R. '83 (ROC) [5] Rochester, NY Church of the Annunciation.
Sewell, Jack '78 (ORG) San Clemente, CA Our Lady of Fatima Church.
Sewvello, Robert (YAK) On Duty Outside the Diocese.
Sewvello, Robert '94 (GF) [1] Billings, MT St. Patrick's Co-Church; Special Assignment.
Sexstone, James H. '69 (ATL) [4] Atlanta, GA Immaculate Heart of Mary Church.
Sexton, Charles E. '38 (IND) Retired.
Sexton, John '36 (SPR) [I] Holyoke, MA Sisters of Providence Care Centers, Inc.
Sexton, John J. '36 (SPR) Retired.
Sexton, Msgr. Michael *v.g.* '61 (BIR) Madison, AL St. John the Baptist Church; [I] Madison, AL St. John's Educational Foundation.
Sexton, Patrick D. '77 (BRK) Absent on Leave.
Sexton, Thomas *s.j.* '49 (SEA) [C] Tacoma, WA Bellarmine Preparatory School.
Seyer, James A. '50 (SPC) Retired.
Seyer, Lawrence '97 (LA) [3] Long Beach, CA St. Barnabas Church.
Seymour, Francis J. '61 (LA) Retired.
Seymour, Msgr. Francis R. '63 (NEW) Kearny, NJ St. Cecilia's Church.
Seymour, James P. '97 (BO) [8] Lawrence, MA St. Patrick Church.
Seymour, James W. '87 (OG) Graduate Studies.
Seymour, John J. *s.t.* '70 (ORG) [I] Santa Ana, CA Trinitarian Missionaries/Missionary Servants of the Most Holy Trinity.
Seymour, Scott R. '99 (OG) Malone, NY Notre Dame Church.
Seynaeve, Jaak *m.afr.* '44 (BR) Special Assignment.
Sezzi, Michael '96 (LA) Moorpark, CA Holy Cross Church.
Sgarbossa, Lino *s.x.* '64 (CHI) [N] Chicago, IL Xaverian Missionaries (S.X.).
Sgarioto, Michael *o.carm.* '85 (FgM) Carmelite Foreign Missions.
Sgarioto, Michael *o.carm.* '85 (JOL) [J] Darien, IL Carmelite Provincial Office.
Sgueglia, Charles J.M. '52 (SPR) Retired.
Shackelford, Christopher '91 (GAL) [24] Houston, TX St. Cyril of Alexandria Church.
Shad, Joseph J. *s.j.* '91 (BGP) [W] Fairfield, CT Newman Centers - Campus Ministry.
Shadeg, Norbert *s.v.d.* '49 (FgM) Society of the Divine Word Foreign Missions.
Shadeg, Werner *s.v.d.* '45 (FgM) Society of the Divine Word Foreign Missions.
Shadwell, Damian E. '90 (WDC) Leonardtown, MD St. Aloysius Church.
Shaefer, Konrad *o.s.b.* '80 (FgM) American - Cassinese Congregation Foreign Missions.
Shafer, Drake R. '73 (DAV) [B] Davenport, IA St.

Ambrose University; [B] Davenport, IA St. Ambrose University.
Shafer, James A. '75 (FTW) [4] Fort Wayne, IN St. Elizabeth Ann Seton Church.
Shafer, Richard '46 (GB) Retired.
Shafer, Robert J. '99 (DET) Rochester, MI St. Andrew Church.
Shaffer, G. Scott '89 (TR) Jackson, NJ St. Aloysius Gonzaga Church.
Shafran, Stephen *s.d.b.* (NEW) [C] Ramsey, NJ Don Bosco Preparatory High School for Boys.
Shafter, Drake R. (DAV) [K] Davenport, IA St. Vincent Center.
Shaheen, Joseph '59 (SAM) Unassigned.
Shaheen, Robert J. '64 (OLL) Columbia, MO Maronite Catholic Community Church; St. Louis, MO St. Raymond Church.
Shaiibetter, Martin '69 (STP) Deephaven, MN St. Therese Church.
Shaji, Jose (FAR) Orrin, ND Sacred Heart Church.
Shaji, Jose *s.d.b.* '92 (FAR) Balta, ND Our Lady of Mount Carmel Church.
Shakalis, Peter A. '47 (BO) Senior Priests.
Shaldone, Robert *s.o.l.t.* '97 (CC) Robstown, TX St. Anthony Church; [H] Robstown, TX Society of Our Lady of the Most Holy Trinity.
Shallow, Edmund J. '81 (MET) [2] Carteret, NJ Holy Family Church.
Shamleffer, John B. '83 (STL) Warson Woods, MO Ste. Genevieve Du Bois Church.
Shamon, Albert J. '40 (ROC) Fleming, NY St. Isaac Jogues Church; Retired.
Shamsher, Paul '67 (HRT) [1] New Haven, CT Sacred Heart Church; Retired.
Shanahan, Daniel A. *o.p.* '62 (DAL) [K] Irving, TX Dominican Priory of St. Albert the Great.
Shanahan, John D. '50 (SFR) Larkspur, CA St. Patrick Church.
Shanahan, Michael *ss.cc.* '62 (FR) [I] Fairhaven, MA Sacred Hearts Provincial House.
Shanahan, Michael J. '92 (CHI) [120] Chicago, IL St. Mark Church.
Shanahan, Thomas J. *s.j.* '67 (OM) [K] Omaha, NE Jesuit Community at Creighton University.
Shane, Donald R. '54 (RVC) Retired; [M] Uniondale, NY St. Pius X Residence.
Shane, Donald W. '69 (OM) [40] Omaha, NE St. Robert Bellarmine Church.
Shaner, Edward G. '96 (MET) On Duty Outside the Diocese.
Shaner, Simon *o.s.p.p.e.* '96 (PH) [AA] Doylestown, PA Pauline Fathers Monastery, Shrine of Our Lady of Czestochowa.
Shanfelt, Thomas '78 (ALN) Tresckow, PA St. Bartholomew Church; Tresckow, PA St. Michael Church.
Shangraw, Philip A. '79 (GR) Sparta, MI Holy Family Church; On Special Assignment.
Shanks, Thomas E. *s.j.* '77 (SJ) [B] Santa Clara, CA Santa Clara University.
Shanley, Albert J. *m.s.* '38 (STP) Taylors Falls, MN St. Joseph's Church.
Shanley, Brian J. *o.p.* '87 (WDC) [B] Washington, DC Dominican House of Studies; [C] Washington, DC Catholic University of America, The.
Shanley, Charles M. *c.m.* '55 (PH) [B] Philadelphia, PA DePaul Novitiate.
Shanley, Gerry *ss.cc.* '61 (BWN) [1] Pharr, TX St. Anne, Mother of Mary Church.
Shanley, James A. '80 (HRT) Rocky Hill, CT St. Elizabeth Seton Church.
Shanley, Joseph D. '43 (PRO) Retired; [M] Woonsocket, RI Saint Francis House.
Shanley, Kevin *o.carm.* '56 (JOL) Darien, IL Our Lady of Mount Carmel Church; [J] Darien, IL Carmelite Community; [L] Darien, IL Carmelite Spiritual Center.
Shanley, Matthew R. '55 (HRT) East Haven, CT Our Lady of Pompeii Church.
Shanley, Matthias *ss.cc.* '65 (BWN) [3] Harlingen, TX Queen of Peace Church.
Shanley, Owen F. '53 (ALB) Corinth, NY Immaculate Conception Church.
Shanley, Paul R. '60 (BO) Senior Priests.
Shannon, Albert C. *o.s.a.* '44 (PH) [AA] Villanova, PA St. Thomas Monastery.
Shannon, Bernard E. *s.j.* '80 (NY) [DD] New York, NY Murray-Weigel Hall.
Shannon, Brendan '62 (MIA) Retired.
Shannon, Brendon '62 (MIA) Coconut Grove, FL St. Hugh Church.
Shannon, David *c.ss.r.* '48 (STP) Brooklyn Center, MN St. Alphonsus Church.
Shannon, Francis '87 (BRK) [76] Brooklyn, NY St. Lucy-St. Patrick Church; [104] Brooklyn, NY Our Lady of Monserrate-St. Ambrose Church.
Shannon, Joseph E. '64 (CAM) On Sick Leave.
Shannon, Joseph L. *o.s.a.* '37 (PH) [AA] Villanova, PA St. Thomas Monastery.
Shannon, Joseph P. *c.s.b.* '48 (GAL) [Q] Sugar Land, TX Basilian Mission Center.
Shannon, Michael T. *s.j.* '44 (SPK) [C] Spokane, WA Gonzaga University.
Shannon, Patrick J. '72 (HBG) Lewisburg, PA Sacred Heart of Jesus Church.
Shannon, Richard J. '59 (CHI) [5] Lemont, IL St. Patrick Church.
Shannon, Timothy '75 (STU) [1] Steubenville, OH Holy Name Church; [6] Steubenville, OH St. Anthony of Padua Church.
Shannon, Timothy T. *s.j.* '88 (DET) [E] Detroit, MI University of Detroit Jesuit High School and Academy.
Shannon, William '71 (HON) Kahului, HI Christ the King Church.
Shannon, Msgr. William H. '43 (ROC) Retired; [J] Rochester, NY Sisters St. Joseph Motherhouse; [L] Rochester, NY Censores Librorum.
Shappard, Christopher *o.s.b.* '62 (IND) [J] St. Meinrad, IN St. Meinrad Archabbey.
Shappard, Christopher *o.s.b.* '62 (PHX) Gilbert, AZ St. Anne Church.
Shappelle, James '48 (CIN) [14] Cincinnati, OH St. Bernard Church; [63] Cincinnati, OH Mother of Christ Church.
Sharanevych, Emile '32 (STF) Retired.
Sharbel, Joseph M. '85 (KC) [34] Kansas City, MO St. Peter's Church.
Sharkey, Gregory C. *s.j.* '88 (BO) [W] Boston, MA The Society of Jesus of New England-Provincial Offices.
Sharkey, Gregory C. *s.j.* '88 (SJ) [B] Santa Clara, CA Santa Clara University.
Sharkey, Msgr. John A. '56 (PH) [96] Philadelphia, PA Old St. Mary's Church.
Sharkey, Owen *c.p.* '45 (HRT) [M] West Hartford, CT Holy Family Monastery/Retreat.
Sharkey, Peter *s.j.* '74 (CIN) [M] Cincinnati, OH Faber Jesuit Community.
Sharkey, Philip J. '98 (HRT) [6] Hamden, CT St. Rita's Church.
Sharkey, Robert Urban *o.p.* '63 (NY) [DD] New York, NY St. Vincent Ferrer Priory.
Sharkey, Msgr. Thomas H. '48 (CAM) Retired; [G] Northfield, NJ The Sharkey Family Charitable Trust.
Sharkey, Thomas P. *c.s.sp.* '50 (VEN) Bradenton, FL Sacred Heart Church.
Sharland, David '99 (FR) Seekonk, MA Our Lady of Mt. Carmel Church.
Sharman, Robert F. '84 (HBG) New Bloomfield, PA St. Bernard Church.
Sharon, Charles *s.a.* '72 (NY) [DD] New York, NY Atonement Friars; [DD] Garrison, NY Franciscan Friars of the Atonement, Minister General Office.
Sharon, Norbert *s.t.* (LA) [30] Los Angeles, CA Our Lady of Victory Church.
Sharp, David L. *c.s.b.* '70 (PHX) Special Assignment; [I] Phoenix, AZ Office of Youth and Young Adult Ministries.
Sharp, Edward A. *s.j.* '53 (OM) [K] Omaha, NE Jesuit Community at Creighton University.
Sharp, George '89 (NEW) Nutley, NJ St. Mary's Church; Elizabeth, NJ Elizabeth Detention Center.
Sharp, James R. '84 (DAL) [4] Garland, TX St. Michael the Archangel Church.
Sharp, Kenneth W. '81 (PH) [125] Philadelphia, PA Our Lady of Mt. Carmel Church.
Sharpe, John O'M. *c.m.* '38 (PHX) [26] Phoenix, AZ St. Vincent de Paul Church.
Sharpe, Patrick F. '42 (E) Retired.
Sharrett, Victor F. '65 (PH) Kennett Square, PA St. Patrick Church.
Sharrock, David J. *c.ss.r.* '55 (ORL) New Smyrna Beach, FL Sacred Heart Church.
Sharum, Peter *o.s.b.* '52 (LR) Charleston, AR Sacred Heart Church.
Shashy, Daniel '91 (STA) Retired.
Shatzel, Richard (ROC) Hammondsport, NY St. Gabriel Church.
Shatzel, Richard J. '69 (ROC) Bath, NY St. Mary Church.
Shaughnessy, James E. '73 (KCK) Lawrence, KS Corpus Christi Church.
Shaughnessy, James M. *s.j.* '79 (BO) Boston, MA New England Medical Center; [W] Boston, MA Loyola House.
Shaughnessy, John H. *c.ss.r.* '49 (STL) [P] Liguori, MO St. Clement Health Care Center.
Shaughnessy, Martin G. *s.j.* '63 (BGP) [E] Fairfield, CT Fairfield College Preparatory School; [P] Fairfield, CT The Fairfield Jesuit Community-Fairfield University.
Shaughnessy, Paul J. *s.j.* '87 (BAL) [S] Baltimore, MD Jesuit Fathers and Brothers Maryland Provincial Curia.
Shaughnessy, Thomas *o.f.m.* '60 (SAT) [70] San Antonio, TX San Jose y San Miguel Church.
Shaughnessy, Thomas *s.s.c.* '66 (FgM) St. Columban's Foreign Mission.
Shaughnessy, William *o.f.m.* '73 (PHX) [H] Scottsdale, AZ Franciscan Renewal Center, Inc. (Casa de Paz Y Bien).
Shaughnessy, William G. '92 (TR) [R] Princeton, NJ Opus Dei.
Shaules, Patrick R. *s.j.* '48 (PH) [AA] Philadelphia, PA Jesuit Community at St. Joseph's University; [AA] Philadelphia, PA Jesuit Community at St. Joseph's University.
Shaum, David W. '46 (BAL) Retired; [B] Emmitsburg, MD Mount Saint Mary's College.
Shaunessy, Francis W. '45 (CHI) [54] Chicago, IL St. Eugene Church; Retired.
Shaver, James R. '89 (LAN) [1] Jackson, MI St. John the Evangelist Church.
Shaw, Brian A. '66 (HRT) [5] Bristol, CT St. Stanislaus Church.
Shaw, Charles E. '51 (HRT) Retired.
Shaw, David '68 (SR) [4] Santa Rosa, CA Resurrection Church.
Shaw, Dennis '74 (ROC) [36] Rochester, NY Our Lady of Mount Carmel Church.
Shaw, Dennis J. '74 (ROC) [25] Rochester, NY Holy Redeemer-St. Francis Xavier Church; [47] Rochester, NY St. Michael Church.
Shaw, Eugene F. *s.j.* '60 (MIL) [P] Milwaukee, WI Jesuit Community at Marquette University.
Shaw, John '57 (YAK) White Swan, WA St. Mary's Church.
Shaw, Kenneth *s.d.b.* '78 (NY) [FF] Stony Point, NY Don Bosco Retreat Center and Marian Shrine; [FF] Stony Point, NY Marian Shrine.
Shaw, Michael '96 (PT) [2] Tallahassee, FL Blessed Sacrament Church.
Shaw, Richard '68 (ALB) Coxsackie, NY Coxsackie Correctional Facility; Special Assignment.
Shaw, William E. '57 (YAK) Wapato, WA St. Peter Claver Church.
Shay, Michael *s.d.s.* '73 (TUC) Green Valley, AZ Our Lady of the Valley Church.
Shay, Robert M. *s.t.* '59 (MOB) Holy Trinity, AL St. Joseph Church.
Shea, Arthur F. *s.j.* '38 (FgM) Provinces.
Shea, Baldwin *o.c.s.o.* '53 (SLC) [F] Huntsville, UT Abbey of Our Lady of the Holy Trinity of the Order of Cistercians.
Shea, Bernard J. (BO) Melrose, MA St. Mary of the Annunciation Church.
Shea, Daniel B. '69 (HEL) [3] Helena, MT Our Lady of the Valley Church; [B] Helena, MT Carroll College.
Shea, Msgr. Donald (HEL) [H] Butte, MT Montana College of Mineral Science and Technology.
Shea, Donald *c.pp.s.* '53 (TOL) [M] Bellevue, OH Sorrowful Mother Shrine.
Shea, Msgr. Donald W. '62 (HEL) [1] Butte, MT Butte Catholic Community North Church; [4] Butte, MT Immaculate Conception Church; [9] Butte, MT St. Joseph Church; [11] Butte, MT St. Patrick Church.
Shea, Edward *o.f.m.* '87 (JOL) [11] Joliet, IL St. John the Baptist Church; [J] Joliet, IL St. John the Baptist Friary.
Shea, Evan P. '86 (CHY) Lusk, WY St. Leo's Church.
Shea, James *c.ss.r.* '65 (KC) [31] Kansas City, MO Our Lady of Perpetual Help Church; [J] Kansas City, MO Redemptorists of Kansas City; [N] Kansas City, MO Our Lady of Perpetual Help Charitable Trust.
Shea, James J. *sch.p.* '92 (PH) [AA] Devon, PA Piarist Fathers (Order of the Pious Schools).
Shea, James M. *s.j.* '75 (BO) [W] Boston, MA The Society of Jesus of New England-Provincial Offices.
Shea, James M. *s.j.* '75 (WDC) [K] Washington, DC Georgetown University Hospital; [M] Washington, DC The Jesuit Community at Georgetown University.
Shea, James M. '85 (WOR) [14] Worcester, MA Our Lady of the Rosary Church.
Shea, James P. *sch.p.* '92 (PH) [G] Devon, PA Devon Preparatory School.
Shea, John J. '45 (SPR) Granby, MA Immaculate Heart of Mary Church.
Shea, John J. '61 (BO) [4] Plymouth, MA St. Peter Church.
Shea, John J. *s.j.* '75 (SCR) [C] Scranton, PA University of Scranton.
Shea, Joseph '57 (STL) [P] St. Louis, MO La Salette Missionaries.
Shea, Joseph '78 (LA) Glendale, CA Holy Family Church.
Shea, Joseph C. *m.s.* '57 (STL) Maplewood, MO Immaculate Conception Church.
Shea, L. M. *o.p.* '52 (FgM) Dominican - Order of Preachers Foreign Missions.
Shea, Leo A. '64 (MAN) Retired.
Shea, Leo B. *m.m.* '66 (NY) [DD] Maryknoll, NY Maryknoll Fathers and Brothers.
Shea, Lewis M. *o.p.* '52 (FgM) Dominican - Order of Preachers Foreign Missions.
Shea, Lewis M. *o.p.* '66 (CHI) [N] Chicago, IL Dominicans (Provincial Office).
Shea, Michael *c.ss.r.* '64 (FgM) Redemptorist Foreign Missions.
Shea, Michael J. *c.m.* '70 (GR) [I] Spring Lake, MI St. Lazare Retreat House.
Shea, Michael J. '76 (SFE) [2] Santa Fe, NM Our Lady of Guadalupe Church.
Shea, Michael M. *c.m.* '70 (PH) [AA] Philadelphia, PA

Congregation of the Mission.
Shea, Peter D. '75 (WOR) West Brookfield, MA Sacred Heart of Jesus Church.
Shea, Peter G. *c.s.p.* '62 (SFR) [32] San Francisco, CA Old St. Mary's Church.
Shea, Msgr. Richard J. '61 (BGP) [2] Trumbull, CT St. Catherine of Siena Church.
Shea, Robert F. '55 (R) Retired.
Shea, Roy *c.i.c.m.* '86 (FgM) Missionhurst Foreign Missions.
Shea, Thomas '49 (SJ) Retired.
Shea, Thomas *c.s.c.* '67 (FgM) Holy Cross Foreign Missions.
Shea, Thomas '73 (PEO) Absent on Leave.
Shea, Thomas F. '64 (PH) Retired.
Shea, Thomas J. *o.s.a.* '52 (PH) [AA] Villanova, PA St. Thomas Monastery.
Shea, Thomas J. *m.m.* '67 (FgM) Maryknoll Foreign Missions.
Shea, Thomas M. '66 (SPR) [4] Springfield, MA Holy Cross Church.
Shea, Thomas W. '46 (NOR) On Duty Outside the Diocese.
Shea, Timothy J. '61 (BO) [3] Woburn, MA St. Charles Church.
Shea, Vincent *o.f.m.* '51 (PAT) [M] Ringwood, NJ Holy Name Friary, Inc.
Shea, William *s.v.d.* '64 (DUB) [B] Epworth, IA Divine Word College.
Shea, Msgr. William B. '46 (BO) Senior Priests.
Sheaffer, John '93 (SPR) [4] Springfield, MA Holy Cross Church.
Sheahan, Msgr. Donal C. '60 (SD) [17] San Diego, CA Our Mother of Confidence Church.
Sheahan, John A. '60 (ORG) Retired.
Sheahan, John F. '46 (SFD) Retired.
Sheahan, Kevin '88 (CHI) Other Assignments.
Sheahan, Richard D. '69 (PRO) [2] Cranston, RI Holy Apostles Church.
Shean, William F. '73 (RVC) Centereach, NY Assumption of the Blessed Virgin Mary Church.
Shear, Michael P. '64 (PSC) Harrisburg, PA St. Ann Church.
Shearer, Thomas M. '78 (CIN) [4] Dayton, OH St. Anthony of Padua Church.
Shebuski, Charles '65 (GB) Absent on Leave.
Shecterle, Ross A. '86 (MIL) [A] St. Francis, WI Saint Francis Seminary.
Shedlock, John '94 (SFE) Santa Fe, NM Hospital & Prison Ministry.
Sheedlo, Walter J. '71 (MAR) Leave of Absence.
Sheeds, Gerald E. '68 (KCK) Gardner, KS Sacred Heart Church.
Sheedy, Edward J. '72 (BUF) On Duty Outside the Diocese.
Sheedy, Edward J. '72 (OG) [A] Ogdensburg, NY Wadhams Hall.
Sheedy, Patrick J. (ORL) [A] Ocala, FL Trinity Catholic High School.
Sheedy, Patrick J. '65 (ORL) [1] Ocala, FL Blessed Trinity Church.
Sheedy, Timothy J. '76 (DAV) [4] Fort Madison, IA Sacred Heart Church.
Sheedy, Val (ORL) Retired.
Sheehan, Augustine J. (RVC) Retired.
Sheehan, Augustine J. '55 (RVC) Northport, NY Veteran's Administration Hospital.
Sheehan, Bernard *o.s.b.* '68 (OM) [K] Elkhorn, NE Mount Michael Abbey.
Sheehan, Daniel *c.p.m.* '46 (OWN) [F] South Union, KY Fathers of Mercy.
Sheehan, Daniel F. '51 (BO) [14] Boston, MA St. Brigid Church.
Sheehan, Daniel J. '53 (BO) Senior Priests.
Sheehan, David M. *s.s.c.* '53 (FgM) St. Columban's Foreign Mission.
Sheehan, Msgr. Dennis F. '63 (BO) [11] Cambridge, MA St. Paul Church; [CC] Cambridge, MA Harvard Catholic Student Center.
Sheehan, Donald P. '68 (NEW) Ridgefield, NJ St. Matthew's Church.
Sheehan, Edward *s.m.* '61 (PRT) Brunswick, ME St. John the Baptist Church.
Sheehan, George F. '61 (SY) [S] East Syracuse, NY Vianney House.
Sheehan, George F. '63 (SY) [C] East Syracuse, NY Bishop Grimes Jr./Sr. High School.
Sheehan, Gerald *s.o.l.t.* '85 (CC) [H] Robstown, TX Society of Our Lady of the Most Holy Trinity.
Sheehan, Gerald P. '64 (BUF) Forestville, NY St. Rose of Lima Church; Sheridan, NY St. John Bosco Church.
Sheehan, Gerard J. *s.o.l.t.* '98 (CC) Robstown, TX St. John Nepomucene Church.
Sheehan, J. Peter '56 (BIR) Retired.
Sheehan, J. William *o.m.i.* '65 (WDC) [M] Washington, DC Oblate College/Center for Mission Studies Community.
Sheehan, James '79 (NY) [GG] New York, NY University Apostolate; [GG] New York, NY University Apostolate.
Sheehan, James C. '79 (NY) [159] Bronx, NY St. Lucy Church.
Sheehan, James T. *s.j.* '59 (BO) [W] Weston, MA Campion Jesuit Community; [W] Weston, MA Campion Health Center, Inc.
Sheehan, John F.X. *s.j.* '64 (BO) [W] Boston, MA The Society of Jesus of New England-Provincial Offices.
Sheehan, John F.X. *s.j.* '64 (STL) [P] St. Louis, MO Jesuit Community Corporation at St. Louis University - Jesuit Hall.
Sheehan, Msgr. John J. '37 (BO) Senior Priests.
Sheehan, John J. '54 (NY) [219] Staten Island, NY Our Lady, Queen of Peace Church.
Sheehan, John P. '89 (NY) [142] Bronx, NY St. Frances of Rome Church; [155] Bronx, NY St. John Chrysostom's Church.
Sheehan, John R. *s.j.* '92 (FgM) Provinces.
Sheehan, Joseph *o.carm.* '63 (SFS) [A] Aberdeen, SD Presentation College.
Sheehan, Joseph A. '59 (ALN) [4] Easton, PA St. Joseph Church.
Sheehan, Joseph G. '48 (NEW) [3] Linden, NJ St. John the Apostle Church; Retired.
Sheehan, Justin R. *o.c.s.o.* '91 (ROC) [I] Piffard, NY Abbey of the Genesee.
Sheehan, Lawrence A. *s.j.* '47 (RVC) Massapequa, NY St. Rose of Lima Church; Retired.
Sheehan, Mark S. '63 (BO) Bedford, MA St. Michael Church.
Sheehan, Maurice *o.f.m.cap.* '55 (NOR) [A] Cromwell, CT Holy Apostles College and Seminary.
Sheehan, Maurice *o.f.m.cap.* '55 (PIT) [O] Pittsburgh, PA St. Francis Friary.
Sheehan, Michael J. '64 (PH) [145] Philadelphia, PA Sacred Heart of Jesus Church.
Sheehan, Michael J. '78 (NEW) Paramus, NJ Annunciation Church.
Sheehan, Myles N. *s.j.* '94 (BO) [W] Boston, MA The Society of Jesus of New England-Provincial Offices.
Sheehan, Myles N. *s.j.* '94 (CHI) [C] Chicago, IL Jesuit Community at Loyola University of Chicago.
Sheehan, Paul M. *s.j.* '52 (FgM) Provinces.
Sheehan, Richard *o.m.i.* '61 (BWN) [1] Brownsville, TX Immaculate Conception Church.
Sheehan, Thomas *o.f.m.* '60 (BUF) [A] East Aurora, NY Christ the King Seminary.
Sheehan, Thomas *s.j.* '97 (NO) New Orleans, LA Memorial Medical Center.
Sheehan, Thomas J. *s.j.* (NO) [C] New Orleans, LA Loyola University New Orleans.
Sheehan, Thomas J. '53 (WDC) [37] Washington, DC St. Peter Church; Retired.
Sheehan, Thomas J. *s.j.* '97 (BO) [W] Boston, MA The Society of Jesus of New England-Provincial Offices.
Sheehan, Thomas W. '70 (CLV) Retired.
Sheehan, William *o.m.i.* '42 (FgM) Oblates Foreign Missions.
Sheehan, William *o.m.i.* '58 (BO) [DD] Tewksbury, MA The Society of Oblate Fathers for Missions Among the Poor Formation Charitable Trust.
Sheehan, William *o.m.i.* '65 (BO) [DD] Tewksbury, MA The Society of Oblate Fathers Continuing Support Fund.
Sheehan, William *o.m.i.* '65 (CHI) [N] Chicago, IL The Oblate House of Theology.
Sheehan, William J. *s.j.* '65 (BO) [W] Weston, MA Campion Health Center, Inc.
Sheehan, William J. *c.s.b.* '66 (ROC) [I] Rochester, NY Basilian Residence.
Sheehey, Robert J. *s.s.e.* '47 (MOB) [G] Selma, AL Edmundite Fathers.
Sheehy, Charles I. '44 (BO) Braintree, MA St. Francis of Assisi Church; Senior Priests.
Sheehy, Dennis E. '68 (GBG) Clymer, PA Church of the Resurrection.
Sheehy, Joseph T. '53 (BO) Swampscott, MA St. John the Evangelist Church.
Sheehy, Paul E. '54 (LIN) Hebron, NE Sacred Heart Church.
Sheehy, Sean O. '70 (BR) [K] Hammond, LA St. Albert the Great Catholic Student Center.
Sheehy, Vincent J. '61 (VEN) [2] Venice, FL Our Lady of Lourdes Church.
Sheehy, Wilfred '60 (SR) Retired.
Sheehy, Yvon *s.c.j.* '78 (RC) Lower Brule, SD St. Mary's Church; Lower Brule, SD Lower Brule Reservation Church; [B] Lower Brule, SD SCJ Community House.
Sheehy, Yvon *s.c.j.* '78 (SFS) Fort Thompson, SD St. Joseph Church; Stephan, SD Immaculate Conception Church.
Sheekey, Philip P. '64 (WIL) [8] Wilmington, DE St. Mary of the Immaculate Conception Church; [9] Wilmington, DE St. Patrick Church; [G] Wilmington, DE Franciscan Health System/Care at Wilmington; [G] Hockessin, DE Franciscan Health System/Care at Brackenville.
Sheeran, Fintan *ss.cc.* '55 (WDC) Seat Pleasant, MD St. Margaret Church.
Sheeran, Kevin J. *o.s.b.* '65 (JOL) [A] Lisle, IL Benedictine University; [J] Lisle, IL St. Procopius Abbey.
Sheeran, Michael J. *s.j.* '70 (DEN) [B] Denver, CO Regis University; [M] Denver, CO Regis Jesuit Community (The Jesuits at Regis University).
Sheeran, Msgr. Robert T. '70 (NEW) [A] South Orange, NJ Immaculate Conception Seminary; [A] South Orange, NJ Seton Hall University College Seminary; [B] South Orange, NJ Seton Hall University; [B] South Orange, NJ Seton Hall University.
Sheerin, James O. '56 (NEW) Retired.
Sheerin, Philip F. *m.m.* '44 (SJ) [L] Los Altos, CA Maryknoll.
Sheets, James P. '75 (SAC) Sacramento, CA Sutter General Hospital; Sacramento, CA Sutter Memorial Hospital.
Sheets, John R. *s.j.* '53 (OM) [K] Omaha, NE Jesuit Community at Creighton University.
Sheets, Joseph B. '57 (IND) Brownstown, IN Our Lady of Providence Church; Seymour, IN St. Ambrose Church.
Sheffield, Walter N. '82 (GAL) [66] Houston, TX St. Paul Church.
Sheffler, Mark *c.ss.r.* '70 (SAT) [M] San Antonio, TX Redemptorists of Texas-San Antonio #1.
Sheganoski, Fabian *t.o.r.* '65 (ORL) Bushnell, FL St. Lawrence Church.
Sheherd, Eugene '78 (AUS) Chappell Hill, TX St. Stanislaus Church.
Sheil, James '66 (CLV) Military Chaplains.
Shelander, Donald E. '70 (CIN) Newport, OH SS. Peter and Paul Church.
Shelby, Charles F. *c.m.* '68 (STL) [P] Perryville, MO Congregation of The Mission; [V] Perryville, MO Association of the Miraculous Medal.
Shelden, Denis '95 (FBK) Alakanuk, AK St. Ignatius Church.
Sheldon, William W. *c.m.* '52 (PH) [B] Philadelphia, PA St. Vincent's Seminary; [AA] Philadelphia, PA Congregation of the Mission; [AA] Philadelphia, PA Congregation of the Mission.
Sheley, John '73 (SPC) Dexter, MO Sacred Heart Church.
Shellem, John J. '52 (PH) Newtown Square, PA St. Anastasia Church.
Shelley, John J. (PH) Warminster, PA Nativity of Our Lord Church.
Shelley, Jon P. '95 (STP) Mahtomedi, MN St. Jude of the Lake Church.
Shelley, Owen *o.f.m.cap.* '45 (NY) [DD] Yonkers, NY St. Clare Friary.
Shelley, Msgr. Thomas '62 (NY) [118] New York, NY St. Thomas More Church.
Shelley, William M. '50 (NY) [2] New York, NY St. Agnes Church.
Shellito, Edward D. *m.m.* '80 (FgM) Maryknoll Foreign Missions.
Shellman, Richard L. '86 (HRT) Bethlehem, CT Church of the Nativity.
Shelly, Otto *s.v.d.* '42 (FgM) Society of the Divine Word Foreign Missions.
Shelly, Roy *s.d.b.* '77 (OAK) [N] Berkeley, CA Salesian Community.
Shelly, Thomas J. '62 (NY) On Duty Outside the Archdiocese.
Shelton, Charles *o.f.m.conv.* '81 (RNO) [1] Reno, NV St. Thomas Aquinas Church.
Shelton, Charles M. *s.j.* '82 (DEN) [M] Denver, CO Regis Jesuit Community (The Jesuits at Regis University).
Shelton, Henry '69 (JKS) Tupelo, MS St. James Church.
Shelton, Lawrence '66 (LA) [45] Los Angeles, CA St. Anselm Church.
Sheltz, Anton R. '76 (GAL) [26] Houston, TX St. Dominic Church.
Sheltz, Msgr. George '71 (GAL) The Woodlands, TX St. Anthony of Padua Church.
Shema, George T. '67 (PAT) Retired; [P] Chester, NJ Nazareth Village.
Shemayer, Roman P. *o.p.* '00 (MAD) [3] Madison, WI Blessed Sacrament Church.
Shemuga, Kevin L. '83 (CLV) [11] Lorain, OH St. Stanislaus Church.
Shen, Raphael *s.j.* '70 (DET) [K] Detroit, MI Jesuit Community at the University of Detroit.
Shenk, Bertrand J. '37 (TOL) Retired.
Shenosky, Joseph T. '00 (PH) Lansdale, PA St. Stanislaus Church.
Shenoy, Leslie F. '76 (FRS) Rosamond, CA St. Mary Church.
Shenrock, Msgr. Joseph C. '53 (TR) Whiting, NJ St. Elizabeth Ann Seton Church.
Shepanski, Don C. '62 (SAT) [57] San Antonio, TX St. Matthew's Church.
Shepard, Thomas B. '77 (HRT) Rocky Hill, CT St. James Church.
Shepard, Timothy J. *s.j.* '82 (DET) [B] Berkley, MI Loyola House.
Sheperd, Raymond C. '57 (TOL) [13] Toledo, OH Regina Coeli Church.

Shepherd, Maurice *s.o.l.t.* '88 (CC) [H] Robstown, TX Society of Our Lady of the Most Holy Trinity.
Shepherd, Maurice *s.o.l.t.* '88 (NO) [28] New Orleans, LA St. Cecilia Church.
Shepherd, Thomas N. '45 (BUF) [46] Buffalo, NY St. Martin Church; Retired.
Shepler, Charles C. '43 (DAV) Retired.
Shepley, Brian J. '92 (DAV) Wilton, IA St. Mary's Church.
Shepley, Brian J.. '92 (DAV) Blue Grass, IA St. Andrew Church.
Sherba, Girard M. '79 (R) [1] Raleigh, NC Cathedral of the Sacred Heart.
Sherbno, John C. '49 (TOL) Retired.
Sherbo, Albert G. '87 (DM) [3] Des Moines, IA Christ the King Church.
Sherburne, Richard F. *s.j.* '56 (MIL) [P] Milwaukee, WI Jesuit Community at Marquette University.
Sherdel, Lawrence W. (HBG) McSherrystown, PA Annunciation of the Blessed Virgin Mary Church.
Sherer, Richard B. '58 (HRT) Retired.
Sheridan, Brian R. *m.s.* '83 (ORL) [3] Orlando, FL Good Shepherd Church.
Sheridan, Daniel P. '79 (RVC) Elmont, NY St. Vincent de Paul Church.
Sheridan, Denis J. (RVC) Retired.
Sheridan, Denis J. '81 (RVC) [M] Uniondale, NY St. Pius X Residence.
Sheridan, Edward J. '63 (CHL) Hickory, NC St. Aloysius Church.
Sheridan, Eugene '45 (NY) Retired.
Sheridan, Eugene F. *c.m.* '68 (BRK) [66] Brooklyn, NY St. John the Baptist Church; [V] Brooklyn, NY St. John the Baptist Rectory.
Sheridan, James B. '50 (PH) Retired.
Sheridan, James J. *o.s.a.* '61 (TLS) [B] Tulsa, OK Cascia Hall Preparatory School.
Sheridan, John (BO) Ashland, MA St. Cecilia Church.
Sheridan, John F. '87 (ALN) Retired; [J] Bethlehem, PA Holy Family Villa.
Sheridan, John J. *o.s.a.* '85 (PH) [AA] Villanova, PA Provincial Offices of the Order of St. Augustine, Province of St. Thomas of Villanova; [AA] Villanova, PA St. Thomas Monastery.
Sheridan, Msgr. John V. '43 (LA) Malibu, CA Our Lady of Malibu Church; Retired.
Sheridan, Mark *o.s.b.* '65 (WDC) [M] Washington, DC St. Anselm's Abbey.
Sheridan, Matthew W. '54 (BRK) [64] Brooklyn, NY Immaculate Heart of Mary Church; Retired.
Sheridan, Michael '75 (PRT) [M] Machias, ME University of Maine at Machias.
Sheridan, Michael J. '71 (STL) [58] St. Louis, MO St. Raphael The Archangel Church.
Sheridan, Michael J. '75 (PRT) Machias, ME Holy Name of Jesus Church.
Sheridan, Patrick L. '98 (CIN) [37] Cincinnati, OH Immaculate Heart of Mary Church.
Sheridan, Paul G. *s.j.* '75 (STL) [F] St. Louis, MO St. Louis University High School, George H. Backer Memorial; [P] St. Louis, MO St. Louis University High School Jesuit Community.
Sheridan, Msgr. Paul W. '56 (SFD) Pierron, IL Immaculate Conception Church; Pocahontas, IL St. Nicholas Church.
Sheridan, Peter C. *o.f.m.* '41 (WDC) [B] Silver Spring, MD Holy Name College.
Sheridan, Philip A. '51 (HRT) Retired.
Sheridan, Thomas '64 (CHY) Rock Springs, WY Holy Spirit Catholic Community Church.
Sheridan, Thomas L. *s.j.* '57 (NEW) [B] Jersey City, NJ Saint Peter's College; [N] Jersey City, NJ Jesuits of Saint Peter's College, Inc.
Sheridan, William H. '54 (CHI) [168] Chicago, IL St. Philip Neri Church; Retired.
Sheridan, William J. '72 (CHI) [1] Chicago, IL Cathedral of the Holy Name.
Sheridan, William P. '89 (NEW) [A] South Orange, NJ Seton Hall University College Seminary; [B] South Orange, NJ Seton Hall University.
Sherliza, Michael S. '99 (ATL) Woodstock, GA St. Michael the Archangel Church.
Sherlock, Alexander '66 (MOB) [1] Montgomery, AL St. Peter Church.
Sherlock, James C. '64 (PH) [122] Philadelphia, PA Our Lady of Lourdes Church.
Sherlock, John '69 (WCH) [B] Wichita, KS Kapaun Mt. Carmel Catholic High School.
Sherlock, John P. '69 (WCH) Colwich, KS Sacred Heart Church.
Sherlock, R. Marc '79 (CIN) [64] Cincinnati, OH Nativity of Our Lord Church.
Sherman, Msgr. Anthony F. '70 (BRK) [199] Queens, NY St. Matthias Church.
Sherman, Daniel J. *m.m.* '47 (NY) [DD] Maryknoll, NY Maryknoll Fathers and Brothers.
Sherman, Daniel M. '77 (CAM) Egg Harbor City, NJ St. Nicholas Church.
Sherman, Edward '56 (FAR) St. Michael, ND St. Michael's Church; St. Michael, ND St. Michael's Indian Church.
Sherman, Gary '85 (TLS) [4] Tulsa, OK St. Catherine Church; [E] Tulsa, OK St. John Medical Center, Inc.
Sherman, Kenneth '80 (NTN) Rochester, NY St. Nicholas Church.
Sherman, Richard '00 (SLC) [C] Ogden, UT St. Joseph Regional School.
Sherman, Richard T. '00 (SLC) [3] Ogden, UT St. Joseph's Church.
Sherman, Thomas P. *s.j.* '87 (LA) [C] Los Angeles, CA Loyola Marymount University.
Sherman, William C. '55 (FAR) [3] Grand Forks, ND St. Michael's Church; Grand Forks, ND School for the Blind.
Sherrer, Charles D. *c.s.c.* '61 (P) [B] Portland, OR University of Portland; [L] Portland, OR Holy Cross Fathers & Brothers, C.S.C. - University of Portland.
Sherry, Brendan '52 (AMA) Retired.
Sherry, Bryan W. *j.c.l.* '62 (TUC) Special Assignment.
Sherry, Edward F. '68 (BO) Merrimac, MA Nativity Church.
Sherry, Peter Thomas *o.carm.* '38 (BO) [P] Peabody, MA Catholic Information Center; [BB] Peabody, MA St. Theresa Carmelite Chapel.
Sherry, Robert N. '66 (RCK) McHenry, IL Church of Holy Apostles.
Shershanovich, Michael '74 (SPR) [7] Pittsfield, MA St. Joseph's Church.
Sherwood, Lan S. '75 (PHX) Unassigned.
Sherwood, Stephen K. *c.m.f.* '71 (SAT) [B] San Antonio, TX Immaculate Heart Claretian Seminary; [C] San Antonio, TX Oblate School of Theology.
Sherwood, Timothy H. '93 (SP) [4] St. Petersburg, FL Holy Family Church.
Sherzer, Msgr. William J. '46 (DET) Retired.
Sheslo, Charles '61 (SD) Retired.
Shetler, Msgr. Carl A. '47 (EVN) Retired.
Shetler, John '92 (PHX) Prescott Valley, AZ St. Germaine Church.
Shetler, John E. '57 (ORG) Irvine, CA St. John Neumann Church.
Shevlin, John *s.v.d.* '60 (SB) [A] Riverside, CA Divine Word Seminary.
Shevlin, Msgr. Raymond R. '44 (BRK) [122] Brooklyn, NY Resurrection Church; Retired.
Shibley, Amel A. '62 (SPC) Fredericktown, MO St. Michael Church; Retired.
Shidler, Anthony *o.s.b.* '64 (SPC) [6] Springfield, MO St. Joseph's Church; [C] Springfield, MO St. John's Regional Health Center; [J] Springfield, MO St. John's Regional Health Center.
Shields, David *s.j.* (MIL) [Y] Milwaukee, WI Casa Romero Renewal Center, Inc.
Shields, David M. *s.j.* '73 (MIL) [67] Milwaukee, WI St. Patrick Church.
Shields, Hugh Joseph '72 (BO) [W] Boston, MA The Society of St. James the Apostle, Inc.; [BB] Boston, MA St. Stephen.
Shields, Hugh Joseph '72 (FgM) Society of St. James the Apostle.
Shields, Hugh Joseph '72 (PH) On Duty Outside the Archdiocese.
Shields, Msgr. James J. '63 (PH) [13] Philadelphia, PA St. Anselm Church.
Shields, James P. '52 (CHI) [6] Waukegan, IL Immaculate Conception B.V.M. Church; Retired.
Shields, Msgr. Joseph A. '49 (PH) Gladwyne, PA St. John Baptist Vianney Church; Retired.
Shields, Joseph E. '36 (MAN) Newmarket, NH St. Mary Church; Retired.
Shields, Lester O. *s.j.* '94 (BO) [W] Boston, MA The Society of Jesus of New England-Provincial Offices.
Shields, Msgr. Maurice L. '57 (MOB) [11] Mobile, AL Little Flower Church.
Shields, Michael '79 (ANC) On Duty Outside Archdiocese.
Shields, Patrick J. '64 (CLV) [7] Lorain, OH St. Ladislaus Church.
Shields, Robert J. '64 (YAK) Retired.
Shields, Stephen L. '74 (CLV) Sheffield Lake, OH St. Thomas the Apostle Church.
Shields, W. Bry '84 (MOB) [7] Mobile, AL St. Ignatius Church; [B] Mobile, AL McGill-Toolen Catholic High School.
Shields, William J. '52 (CHI) Mundelein, IL Santa Maria Del Popolo Church; Retired.
Shiffer, Jim *s.s.c.* '65 (LA) [Q] Los Angeles, CA Columban Fathers, Procure House.
Shiffler, John C. '78 (TOL) Fayette, OH Our Lady of Mercy Church; Lyons, OH Our Lady of Fatima Church.
Shigo, Francis L. *s.v.d.* '60 (LA) [J] Torrance, CA Little Company of Mary Hospital; [J] Torrance, CA Little Company of Mary Hospital; [Q] Los Angeles, CA Society of the Divine Word Missionaries, Western Province.
Shih, John M. '49 (NEW) Fort Lee, NJ Madonna Church; Retired.
Shikany, Paul M. '79 (IND) Edinburgh, IN Holy Trinity Church; Franklin, IN St. Rose of Lima Church; [N] Franklin, IN Franklin College Newman Center.
Shillcox, Timothy D. *o.praem.* (GB) Dyckesville, WI St. Louis Church.
Shillcox, Timothy D. *o.praem.* '87 (GB) Bay Settlement, WI Holy Cross Church; [I] De Pere, WI St. Joseph Priory.
Shimanek, Joseph '54 (JOL) Retired.
Shimnowski, Gaylord '59 (KAL) [4] Kalamazoo, MI St. Monica Church.
Shimotsu, John '94 (ORG) Military Chaplains.
Shindelar, Vincent J. '56 (RCK) Retired.
Shine, Edward J. '57 (CIN) [42] Cincinnati, OH St. John the Baptist Church.
Shine, Francis J. *c.m.* '55 (STL) St. Louis, MO Regional Hospital; [P] St. Louis, MO Vincentian Residence.
Shine, John V. *c.m.* '63 (PHX) [26] Phoenix, AZ St. Vincent de Paul Church.
Shine, Robert W. '55 (SAG) Albee, MI St. Mary Church.
Shine, Sean '52 (ORL) Retired.
Shinney, Robert J. *s.j.* '68 (SJ) [D] San Jose, CA Bellarmine College Preparatory.
Shinnick, Edward P. '56 (GF) Retired.
Shinnick, James F. '39 (B) Retired.
Shinos, Robert '63 (ALB) Herkimer, NY St. Anthony-St. Joseph Church.
Shipe, William '61 (Y) [3] Canton, OH Sacred Heart Church.
Shipley, Msgr. William '54 (SD) [B] San Diego, CA University of San Diego.
Shipp, Edmund M. '61 (SFR) [45] San Francisco, CA St. Peter Church; San Francisco, CA San Francisco General Hospital; Special Assignment.
Shipper, Carl A. '68 (SFR) Absent on Leave.
Shipps, Frank Bede *o.p.* (FgM) Dominican - Order of Preachers Foreign Missions.
Shipps, Frank Bede *o.p.* '85 (NY) [22] New York, NY St. Catherine of Siena Church.
Shiraki, Gabriel *s.a.* '89 (NY) [DD] Garrison, NY Franciscan Friars of the Atonement, Minister General Office.
Shiras, Natalie '82 (BGP) [J] Bridgeport, CT St. Vincent's Medical Center.
Shirey, John W. '43 (CHI) [111] Chicago, IL St. Kilian Church; Retired.
Shirey, Joseph E. *s.j.* '56 (P) White City, OR U.S. Veternan's Affairs Domiciliary; [J] Medford, OR Providence Medford Medical Center.
Shirilla, Gerald '68 (DET) Absent on Leave.
Shirley, John T. *o.s.a.* '65 (MIL) [14] Racine, WI St. Rita Church.
Shirley, Msgr. Richard '67 (CC) [21] Corpus Christi, TX St. Pius X Church.
Shirley, Ronald R. '73 (MRY) [4] Salinas, CA Madonna Del Sasso Church.
Shiroda, Donald L. '59 (MAR) Retired.
Shiverski, John J. '68 (MAR) Negaunee, MI St. Paul Church.
Shlesinger, Bernard (Ned), III '96 (R) Newton Grove, NC Our Lady of Guadalupe Church.
Shmaruk, Richard J. '65 (BO) [18] Boston, MA St. Columbkille Church.
Shmauz, Donald A. '60 (MIL) On Duty Outside the Archdiocese.
Shnob, Alan D. '78 (OG) Massena, NY St. Mary Church.
Shoback, Edward J. '67 (SCR) [23] Scranton, PA SS. Peter and Paul Church.
Shoback, Thomas P. '77 (SCR) Montoursville, PA Our Lady of Lourdes Church.
Shockey, David P. '56 (COV) Retired; [N] Walton, KY St. William Convent.
Shocklee, Msgr. John A. '42 (STL) Retired.
Shoda, D. Brian '87 (WH) Inwood, WV St. Leo Church.
Shoda, Richard W. '78 (WH) Ronceverte, WV St. Catherine of Siena Church.
Shoemaker, David M. '00 (MOB) Dothan, AL St. Columba Church.
Shoemaker, Msgr. Samuel E. '66 (PH) Yardley, PA St. Ignatius of Antioch Church.
Shoemaker, Thomas '90 (FTW) [5] Fort Wayne, IN St. Henry Church; [18] Fort Wayne, IN Sacred Heart Church; [C] Fort Wayne, IN Bishop Luers High School.
Sholander, Anthony E. *s.j.* '84 (SJ) [L] Los Gatos, CA California Province of the Society of Jesus, Jesuit Provincial Office.
Shonebarger, Thomas '69 (COL) [40] Columbus, OH St. Timothy Church.
Shonis, Anthony '71 (OWN) Bowling Green, KY St. Joseph's Church.
Shonis, Anthony J. '71 (OWN) [A] Owensboro, KY Brescia University.
Shore, Zachary J. '81 (SFR) [36] San Francisco, CA Most Holy Redeemer Church.
Shori, Nicholas R. '74 (Y) New Middletown, OH St. Paul the Apostle Church.
Short, Anthony J. *s.j.* '71 (DEN) [M] Denver, CO Xavier Jesuit Center.
Short, Gregory *o.m.v.* '79 (BO) [W] Milton, MA Oblate Residence (St. Joseph House).
Short, James M. *s.j.* '61 (FgM) Provinces.
Short, John '99 (SFS) Highmore, SD St. Mary Church.
Short, Joseph '90 (SFS) Hoven, SD St. Anthony of

Padua Church.
Short, Redemptus *o.c.d.* '47 (MIL) [P] Holy Hill, WI Discalced Carmelite Monastery.
Shortall, Robert '74 (DAL) Plano, TX St. Elizabeth Ann Seton Church.
Shortall, Robert '74 (DAV) On Duty Outside the Diocese.
Shorter, Melvin *c.p.* '86 (ATL) [11] Atlanta, GA St. Paul of the Cross Church.
Shorter, Melvin *c.p.* '86 (MET) [H] South River, NJ Passionist Provincial Office.
Shortt, David J. '89 (PBR) [2] Youngstown, OH St. Nicholas Church.
Shortt, Patrick J. '66 (JC) Kirksville, MO Mary Immaculate Church.
Shott, Stephen E. *o.s.f.s.* '95 (WIL) [B] Wilmington, DE Salesianum School.
Shoup, Steven L. '84 (CIN) Fort Loramie, OH St. Michael's Church.
Shovelton, Gerald T. '56 (FR) Retired.
Shovelton, William J. '46 (FR) Retired.
Showalter, Joseph *s.j.* '75 (SPK) [E] Spokane, WA Gonzaga Preparatory School.
Showalter, Msgr. Paul E. '66 (PEO) [4] Rock Island, IL St. Pius X Church.
Showalter, Thomas *s.o.l.t.* '97 (CC) [H] Robstown, TX Society of Our Lady of the Most Holy Trinity.
Showfety, Msgr. Joseph S. '55 (CHL) [2] Greensboro, NC St. Benedict Church.
Shrader, Dwight E. '82 (RIC) [6] Virginia Beach, VA St. John the Apostle Church.
Shreenan, Timothy J. *o.f.m.* '84 (NY) [35] New York, NY St. Francis of Assisi Church.
Shreve, Msgr. Thomas F. '61 (RIC) [2] Richmond, VA Church of the Epiphany.
Shroeder, Danielmose *o.f.m.* '91 (FgM) Custody of St. Mary of the Angels. Byzantine-Slavonic.
Shubiak, Stephen '88 (NY) Bronx, NY U.S.V.A. Medical Center.
Shubiak, Stephen '88 (STF) Special Assignment.
Shuck, Joseph J. '53 (ALB) Special Assignment.
Shuda, Paul R. '60 (HBG) [8] Harrisburg, PA Our Lady of the Blessed Sacrament Church.
Shuda, Msgr. Robert J. '59 (GBG) Greensburg, PA Westmoreland Hospital; [I] Greensburg, PA Benedictine Sisters (Eichstatt, Bavaria).
Shugrue, Paul S. '70 (BO) Braintree, MA St. Clare Church.
Shugrue, Msgr. Timothy J. '73 (NEW) Montclair, NJ Immaculate Conception Church.
Shuhler, Ralph V. *o.s.a.* '39 (PH) [AA] Villanova, PA St. Thomas Monastery.
Shuley, Keith *c.c.* '92 (CC) Military Chaplains.
Shuley, Keith *c.c.* '92 (SR) Petaluma, CA U.S. Coast Guard Training Center.
Shulik, Bernard P. '74 (PIT) [O] Pittsburgh, PA St. John Vianney Manor.
Shultz, John M. '82 (E) [10] Erie, PA Our Lady of Peace Church.
Shultz, Msgr. William E. '70 (ALT) Roaring Spring, PA St. Thomas More Church.
Shuman, Killian E. *t.o.r.* '59 (E) Ramey, PA Holy Trinity Church.
Shuppert, William T.J. '71 (TUC) On Duty Outside the Diocese.
Shurer, Ralph C. *o.s.a.* '54 (PH) [C] Villanova, PA Villanova University; [AA] Villanova, PA St. Thomas Monastery.
Shurtleff, F. James '66 (OG) [2] Ogdensburg, NY Notre Dame Church.
Shurtleff, Robert M. '70 (OG) Clayton, NY St. Mary of Clayton Church; Lafargeville, NY St. John the Evangelist Church.
Shutt, Paul-Alexander *o.s.b.* '98 (GBG) [H] Latrobe, PA Saint Vincent Archabbey.
Shuttleworth, Edward J. '90 (LC) Prescott, WI St. Joseph Church.
Siani, Angelo *o.m.i.* '65 (FgM) Oblates Foreign Missions.
Sibel, John J. '72 (PH) [97] Philadelphia, PA St. Mary of the Assumption Church.
Sibenik, Simeon B. '81 (PBR) Du Bois, PA Nativity of the Mother of God Church; Sykesville, PA Holy Trinity Church.
Sibilano, Joseph D. *o.s.j.* '65 (SCR) [8] Pittston, PA St. Rocco Church; [B] Pittston, PA St. Joseph's Oblate Seminary.
Sibley, Bryce Andrew '00 (LAF) On Special Assignment.
Sica, Joseph F. '82 (SCR) Clarks Summit, PA Our Lady of the Snows Church; La Plume, PA Keystone Junior College.
Sicard, Kenneth *o.p.* '90 (PRO) [P] Providence, RI St. Thomas Aquinas Priory at Providence College.
Sicari, Joseph J. '82 (BUF) Snyder, NY Christ the King Church; [H] Buffalo, NY The Catholic Charities of the Diocese of Buffalo; [H] Buffalo, NY The Catholic Charities of the Diocese of Buffalo.
Sichko, James '98 (LEX) Special Assignment; [A] Lexington, KY Lexington Catholic High School.
Sicilia, Msgr. Pablo '60 (SAT) Dilley, TX St. Joseph's Church.
Siciliano, Donald E. '93 (JC) Absent on Leave.
Siciliano, John '82 (WOR) Absent on Leave.
Siciliano, Jude *o.p.* '69 (OAK) [N] Oakland, CA Order of Preachers (Southern Province).
Siciliano, Jude *o.p.* '69 (R) [E] Raleigh, NC Dominican Community.
Siciliano, Ronald A. *o.f.m.* '49 (BO) [W] Boston, MA St. Christopher Friary.
Sickler, Robert *m.s.a.* '87 (NOR) [A] Cromwell, CT Holy Apostles College and Seminary; [F] Cromwell, CT Society of the Missionaries of the Holy Apostles.
Sickler, Thomas G. *m.s.* '73 (NOR) Danielson, CT St. James Church.
Sicoli, David C. '75 (PH) [64] Philadelphia, PA Holy Spirit Church.
Siconolfi, Msgr. Constantine V. '59 (SCR) [7] Scranton, PA Holy Family Church; [R] Scranton, PA St. Francis of Assisi Kitchen.
Siconolfi, Michael T. *s.j.* '72 (SY) [S] Syracuse, NY Jesuits at LeMoyne, Inc.
Siconolfi, Thomas J. *c.ss.r.* '70 (RVC) Bethpage, NY St. Martin of Tours Church.
Sidera, Joseph A. *c.s.c.* '68 (SCR) [C] Wilkes-Barre, PA Kings College.
Sidler, Fred '92 (DAL) [17] Dallas, TX St. Elizabeth Church.
Sidler, Gordon L. (ATL) Released from Archdiocesan Assignment.
Sidney, Walter T. *s.j.* '78 (DEN) [D] Aurora, CO Regis Jesuit High School; [M] Aurora, CO Regis Jesuit High School - Jesuit Community.
Sidoti, Anthony '40 (ALB) [8] Albany, NY St. James Church; Retired.
Sidoti, James *o.carm.* '92 (NY) Middletown, NY Our Lady of Mt. Carmel Church.
Siebenaler, John M. '61 (STP) Retired.
Siebenaler, Leonard '59 (STP) St. Michael, MN St. Michael Church.
Siebenaler, Martin J. '59 (STP) Waconia, MN St. Joseph Church.
Siebenand, Ambrose F. '41 (NU) Retired.
Siebenand, John N. '38 (NU) Retired.
Siebenand, Paul Alcuin '60 (LA) Avalon, CA St. Catherine of Alexandria Church.
Siebenand, Richard '67 (LA) [29] Los Angeles, CA Our Lady of Lourdes Church.
Siebers, Glen F. *o.praem* '50 (GB) [I] De Pere, WI St. Norbert Abbey.
Siebert, Anthony G. '59 (STL) On Duty Outside the Archdiocese.
Siebert, David (Thomas) '81 (PHU) [E] Washington, DC Monastery of the Holy Cross.
Siebert, Edward J. *s.j.* '97 (DET) [K] Detroit, MI Jesuit Provincial Office-Detroit Province of the Society of Jesus.
Siebert, Edward J. *s.j.* '97 (LA) [C] Los Angeles, CA Loyola Marymount University.
Siebert, Hieromonk David '81 (PHU) [A] Washington, DC St. Josaphat Seminary.
Siebert, Paul S. '86 (E) Emporium, PA St. Mark Church.
Siebert, William P. '79 (DET) [2] Roseville, MI St. Athanasius Church.
Siebold, Gerry *c.ss.r.* '58 (LAF) Crowley, LA Immaculate Heart of Mary Church.
Siebor, John '58 (RVC) Hempstead, NY St. Ladislaus Church.
Sieczynski, Jersy '00 (SAT) [57] San Antonio, TX St. Matthew's Church.
Siedlecki, Edmund J. '52 (CHI) [58] Chicago, IL Five Holy Martyrs Church; Retired; [T] Mundelein, IL Cardinal Stritch Retreat House.
Siefer, Richard R. '75 (E) Du Bois, PA St. Catherine Church; Du Bois, PA St. Joseph Church.
Siefert, John S. '89 (STL) Clayton, MO St. Joseph Church.
Siefert, Ralph *s.m.* (STL) [P] St. Louis, MO Provincialate of the Society of Mary, Province of St. Louis.
Siefert, Ralph A. *s.m.* '73 (STL) [F] Creve Coeur, MO Chaminade College Preparatory School Inc.; [G] Creve Coeur, MO Chaminade College Preparatory.
Sieg, Leslie M. '76 (P) Tigard, OR St. Anthony Church.
Sieg, Robert *o.f.m.* '75 (STL) [P] St. Louis, MO Franciscan Friary of St. Anthony of Padua.
Sieg, Robert C. *o.f.m.* (STL) [25] St. Louis, MO St. Anthony of Padua Church.
Sieg, Thomas H. '71 (STP) Edina, MN St. Patrick Church.
Siegel, Joseph '88 (JOL) [1] Joliet, IL The Cathedral of St. Raymond.
Siegel, Kenan *o.f.m.cap.* '56 (MIL) [B] Mount Calvary, WI St. Lawrence Seminary; [P] Mount Calvary, WI St. Lawrence Friary.
Siekaniec, Ladislas *o.f.m.* '40 (SFD) [K] Sherman, IL Our Lady of Angels Friary.
Siekierski, Msgr. John J. '67 (GRY) [13] East Chicago, IN St. Stanislaus Church.
Siekierski, Matthew J. '77 (WDC) La Plata, MD Sacred Heart Church.
Sielski, Joseph *m.i.c.* '41 (WDC) [B] Washington, DC Marian Fathers Scholasticate.
Siemanowski, John S. '89 (CHI) Chicago Heights, IL St. Agnes Church.
Siener, Albert L. '46 (NSH) Retired.
Siener, Msgr. Leo C. '48 (KNX) Retired.
Sienkiewicz, Matthew '59 (FTW) Retired.
Siepka, Richard W. '82 (BUF) [A] East Aurora, NY Christ the King Seminary.
Siepker, Daniel E. '93 (DM) Corning, IA St. Patrick's Church; [D] Corning, IA Mercy Midlands: Mercy Hospital.
Sieracki, Aloysius A. *o.carm.* '59 (CHI) [N] Chicago, IL Brandsma House.
Sieradski, Alfred *c.ss.r.* '49 (ORL) [F] New Smyrna Beach, FL St. Alphonsus Villa-Redemptorist Fathers and Brothers.
Sierminski, Vernon '56 (SAG) Retired.
Sierocki, Paul E. '44 (DET) Retired.
Sierra, Angel A. '80 (SFD) [4] Alton, IL St. Matthew Church.
Sierra, Francis A. '46 (SD) Retired.
Sierra, John A. *s.f.* '40 (WDC) [B] Silver Spring, MD Holy Family Seminary.
Sierra, Jose '96 (FRS) Clovis, CA Our Lady of Perpetual Help Church.
Sierra, Luis (CGS) Yabucoa, PR Santos Angeles Cutodios Church.
Sierra-Posada, Pedro J. '76 (ALX) [1] Alexandria, LA St. Francis Xavier Church; Glenmora, LA St. Louis Church.
Sievel, Thomas A. '78 (HRT) [2] Manchester, CT St. Bartholomew's Church.
Sieverding, Dale '89 (SFS) On Leave of Absence.
Siffert, Etienne *s.m.* '58 (SFR) [38] San Francisco, CA Notre Dame des Victoires Church.
Siffrin, Msgr. Robert '79 (Y) [9] Youngstown, OH St. Brendan's Church.
Sigaran, Mamerto '60 (SFR) [43] San Francisco, CA St. Paul Church.
Sigler, Gary L. '79 (FTW) Huntington, IN St. Mary Church.
Sigman, Louis A. '67 (PHX) Retired.
Sigmund, Andrew J. '64 (STL) Kimmswick, MO St. Joseph Church.
Signey, Lawrence '87 (LA) La Canada Flintridge, CA St. Bede the Venerable Church.
Signiski, Michael M. '66 (CAM) [2] Cherry Hill, NJ Holy Rosary Church.
Signorelli, Francis *s.x.* '58 (BO) [W] Holliston, MA Xaverian Missionaries.
Siguenza, Francisco *o.a.r.* '56 (ELP) [12] El Paso, TX Saint Therese of the Little Flower Church.
Siguere, Robert *o.f.m.* '73 (FgM) Franciscan Foreign Missions.
Sihuay, Francis X. *o.f.m.* '51 (WDC) [M] Washington, DC Commissariat of the Holy Land, Franciscan Monastery - Mount St. Sepulchre.
Sikandar, Anthony '90 (BRK) [151] Queens, NY St. Ann's Church; [U] Brooklyn, NY Catholic Migration & Refugee Office, Catholic Migration Services, Inc.
Siklodi, Sandor '71 (CLV) [22] Cleveland, OH St. Emeric Church.
Sikon, Michael '96 (GBG) Indiana, PA St. Bernard Church.
Sikora, Eric L. '81 (BUF) [1] Orchard Park, NY Nativity of Our Lord Church.
Sikora, James R. '67 (GF) [A] Great Falls, MT University of Great Falls; [A] Great Falls, MT University of Great Falls.
Sikora, Stanley J. '57 (HRT) [A] Bloomfield, CT St. Thomas Seminary.
Sikora, Thomas More *o.s.b.* '97 (GBG) [H] Latrobe, PA Saint Vincent Archabbey.
Sikorski, Harold R. '56 (SAG) Retired.
Sikorski, Jeffery P. '73 (TOL) Maumee, OH St. Joseph Church.
Sikorski, Leszek '97 (VEN) Punta Gorda, FL Sacred Heart Church.
Sikorski, Louis S. '64 (GAL) Anderson, TX St. Stanislaus Church.
Silayo, Constantine (RIC) [1] Virginia Beach, VA Church of the Ascension.
Silcox, John D., Jr. '95 (PH) Highland Park, PA St. Laurence Church.
Sileo, Joseph R. '71 (WDC) [37] Washington, DC St. Peter Church; Special Ministries.
Siler, Francis A. '63 (PIT) [27] Pittsburgh, PA St. Mary of Mercy Church.
Siler, Paschal *o.f.m.cap.* '60 (GF) Ashland, MT St. Labre's Church.
Silgvero, Cecilio '92 (LAN) [E] Chelsea, MI St. Louis Center for Exceptional Children & Adults.
Siliako, Petelo '86 (SPP) [1] Pago Pago, AS Cathedral of the Holy Family.
Silio, Antonio R. '88 (MIA) Pembroke Pines, FL St. Boniface Church.
Silipigni, Stephan A. '81 (PRO) [3] North Providence, RI Mary, Mother of Mankind Church.
Silk, John D. '59 (BO) Amesbury, MA Holy Family Church; Senior Priests.

Silk, William J. '60 (WDC) [5] Bethesda, MD Our Lady of Lourdes Church.
Silko, Herbert *o.f.m.* '55 (MIL) [P] Burlington, WI Queen of Peace Friary.
Sill, Theodore K. '89 (COL) London, OH St. Patrick Church.
Silva, Alvaro (BO) [1] Quincy, MA St. Ann Church.
Silva, Alvaro (SJN) [B] Bayamon, PR Sagrada Familia.
Silva, Alvaro '87 (SJN) [22] Bayamon, PR Sagrada Familia Church.
Silva, Caesar '74 (HT) [3] Houma, LA Maria Immacolata Church.
Silva, David E. '54 (CLV) Retired.
Silva, Edwin Lugo '89 (MGZ) [5] Mayaquez, PR Nuestra Senora De Fatima Church.
Silva, Eusebio F. '66 (MAN) [1] Nashua, NH St. Aloysius Church.
Silva, Francis J. *s.j.* '42 (SJ) [L] Los Gatos, CA Sacred Heart Jesuit Center.
Silva, Frank (BO) Wayland, MA St. Ann Church.
Silva, George '97 (SFE) Clayton, NM St. Francis Xavier Church.
Silva, Hilary *o.m.i.* '89 (FRS) [5] Bakersfield, CA St. Joseph Church.
Silva, Ismael *m.c.c.j.* '79 (ORG) Costa Mesa, CA St. Joachim Church.
Silva, James M. '67 (PRO) Retired.
Silva, John F. '34 (BO) Senior Priests.
Silva, Jose D. '51 (HRT) [4] Hartford, CT Our Lady of Fatima Church.
Silva, Juan '92 (LA) Pomona, CA Sacred Heart Church.
Silva, Langes J. '95 (SLC) [1] Salt Lake City, UT Cathedral of the Madeleine.
Silva, Larry '75 (OAK) [7] Fremont, CA St.Leonard-Santa Paula Church.
Silva, Luis P. '98 (CR) Stephen, MN St. Stephen's Church.
Silva, Miguel '84 (SAC) Corning, CA Immaculate Conception Church; Orland, CA St. Dominic Church.
Silva, Pedro *o.f.m.cap.* '75 (ARE) [1] Utuado, PR San Miquel Church.
Silva, Raul '21 (LA) [83] Los Angeles, CA San Miguel Church.
Silva, Robert J. '65 (STO) [1] Stockton, CA Cathedral of the Annunciation.
Silveira, Eduino '87 (SAC) [12] Sacramento, CA St. Elizabeth Church; Special Assignment.
Silver, Bertram *o.m.i.* '54 (FgM) Oblates Foreign Missions.
Silver, E. John '92 (OG) Rosiere, NY St. Vincent de Paul Church.
Silver, E. John '93 (OG) Cape Vincent, NY St. Vincent of Paul Church.
Silver, Jeffrey P. '84 (CIN) [3] Hamilton, OH St. Julie Billiart Church.
Silver, Martin J. '54 (NEW) [3] Hackensack, NJ St. Joseph's Church.
Silveri, Donato P. '64 (PH) Spring City, PA St. Joseph Church; Spring City, PA Southeastern Pennsylvania Veterans Center.
Silverio, Gilbert *o.f.m.* '59 (NY) [DD] New York, NY Franciscan Province of the Immaculate Conception.
Silverman, Msgr. Robert '67 (SAT) [44] San Antonio, TX St. John Neumann Church; [U] San Antonio, TX The Blue Army.
Silvers, Rudolph M. '75 (PIT) Bulger, PA St. Ann Church.
Silvester, George E. *c.s.b.* '46 (GAL) Sugar Land, TX St. Theresa Church.
Silvester, Peter *s.v.d.* '78 (TR) [M] Bordentown, NJ Society of the Divine Word.
Silvestrini, Dino F. '85 (MAR) Menominee, MI Resurrection Church.
Sima, John Ross *s.j.* '71 (CHI) [87] Chicago, IL St. Ignatius Church.
Simard, Robert '56 (BAK) Merrill, OR St. Augustine Church; Retired.
Simas, Msgr. Manuel C. '61 (OAK) [4] Fremont, CA St. Joseph Church.
Simboli, Ronald L. '75 (GBG) Rostraver, PA St. Anne Church.
Simburger, R. Joseph '79 (SFD) Unassigned.
Simcox, Thomas *s.c.j.* '40 (MIL) [P] Franklin, WI Villa Maria.
Simeone, Francis P. '61 (FRS) Lone Pine, CA Santa Rosa Church.
Simeone, Gary F. '75 (HRT) East Haven, CT St. Vincent de Paul's Church.
Simeone, Ronald P. '82 (PRO) [5] Woonsocket, RI St. Anthony Church.
Simington, Ralph P. '62 (DUB) Greeley, IA St. Joseph's Church; Manchester, IA St. Mary's Church; Ryan, IA St. Patrick's Church; [E] Manchester, IA St. Paul's School of Religion.
Simko, James G. '91 (DEN) Estes Park, CO Our Lady of the Mountains Church.
Simko, Michael S. (NEW) Retired.
Simlik, Frank P. '54 (PHX) Sun City, AZ Church of St. Joachim & St. Anne.
Simmons, Msgr. Donald W. '43 (B) Retired.
Simmons, Franklin '79 (GAL) [5] Houston, TX St. Ambrose Church; [K] Houston, TX The Catholic Chaplain Corps.
Simmons, Hilary F. '43 (LC) Retired; Retired.
Simmons, Jerome S. '68 (E) [11] Erie, PA Sacred Heart Church; [O] Erie, PA Ecclesia Center/Renewal Center.
Simmons, Joseph C. '61 (BAL) Joppa, MD Church of the Holy Spirit.
Simmons, Msgr. Walter E. (RVC) Retired.
Simmons, Msgr. Walter E. '55 (RVC) Port Washington, NY St. Peter of Alcantara Church.
Simmons, William *c.s.c.* '52 (FTW) [B] Notre Dame, IN University of Notre Dame Du Lac; [J] Notre Dame, IN Holy Cross Community, Corby Hall, University of Notre Dame.
Simmons, William B. *c.s.c.* '52 (FTW) [L] Notre Dame, IN Holy Cross Mission House.
Simms, Robert A. *s.j.* '46 (FgM) Provinces.
Simms, William '62 (BAL) [91] Baltimore, MD St. Thomas Aquinas Church; Special Assignment.
Simo, Philip *o.s.b.* '97 (WDC) [M] Washington, DC St. Anselm's Abbey.
Simon, Akan S. '98 (RCK) Loves Park, IL St. Bridget Church.
Simon, Ambrose *o.f.m.cap.* '50 (GB) [I] Appleton, WI St. Fidelis Friary.
Simon, Brian '96 (SFS) Bowdle, SD St. Augustine Church.
Simon, Carl A. '71 (LAN) Brooklyn, MI St. Joseph's Church.
Simon, David '67 (ROC) Webster, NY St. Paul Church.
Simon, George H. '57 (LAF) Scott, LA Saint Martin de Porres Church.
Simon, John L. '73 (MIL) Clyman, WI St. John Church; Elba, WI St. Columbkille Church; Reeseville, WI Holy Family Church.
Simon, Joseph D. *s.v.d.* '61 (LAF) Maurice, LA St. Joseph Church.
Simon, Joseph M. '71 (STL) Webster Groves, MO Holy Redeemer Church.
Simon, Raphael *o.c.s.o.* '47 (WOR) [N] Spencer, MA St. Joseph's Abbey.
Simon, Richard T. '75 (CHI) [201] Chicago, IL St. Thomas of Canterbury Church.
Simon, Robert *c.ss.r.* (DEN) [33] Denver, CO St. Joseph's Church.
Simon, Robert G. *c.s.c.* '61 (FgM) Holy Cross Foreign Missions.
Simon, Robert J. '90 (SCR) [4] Scranton, PA St. David's Church.
Simon, Thomas *m.ss.a* '79 (HRT) [2] Waterbury, CT Immaculate Conception Church.
Simon, Thomas *m.s.a.* '79 (NOR) [F] Cromwell, CT Society of the Missionaries of the Holy Apostles.
Simon, Vincent J. '46 (DUB) Retired.
Simonar, Mathew (GB) Baileys Harbor, WI St. Mary of the Lake Church; Egg Harbor, WI St. John the Baptist Church; Fish Creek, WI St. Paul Church; Jacksonport, WI St. Michael Church; Sister Bay, WI St. Rosalia Church.
Simonds, Donald D. *m.s.* '63 (NOR) Danielson, CT St. James Church.
Simonds, Tom *s.j.* '99 (RC) Pine Ridge, SD Holy Rosary Church; [B] Pine Ridge, SD Jesuit Community of Holy Rosary Mission.
Simone, Earl Francis '77 (CIN) [22] Dayton, OH St. Peter Church.
Simone, Michael A. *m.m.* '56 (NY) [DD] Maryknoll, NY Maryknoll Fathers and Brothers.
Simoneau, Norman J. (MAN) Nashua, NH Southern N.H. Regional Medical Center and Nursing Homes.
Simoneau, Norman J. '67 (MAN) Hudson, NH St. John the Evangelist Church.
Simoneau, Roland L. '78 (PRO) [4] Burrillville, RI St. Theresa of the Child Jesus Church.
Simoneaux, Jody '82 (LAF) [11] Lafayette, LA St. Genevieve Church.
Simonelli, Gerald '90 (JOL) Glen Ellyn, IL St. Petronille Church.
Simonetti, Albino *s.d.b.* '68 (MIA) [25] Miami, FL St. Kieran Church.
Simoni, Salvador '80 (CHI) Northlake, IL St. John Vianney, Cure of Ars Church.
Simonin, Msgr. John A. '47 (CHR) Retired.
Simonini, Michael F. '75 (GB) [2] Appleton, WI St. Bernard Church.
Simonini, Michael F. '75 (RCK) Active Outside the Diocese.
Simonnet, Philippe *s.s.e.* '52 (BUR) [E] Colchester, VT Society of St. Edmund.
Simonnet, Philippe *s.s.e.* '52 (FgM) Edmundite Foreign Missions.
Simons, Derek *s.v.d.* '70 (CHI) [B] Techny, IL Divine Word Residence; [N] Chicago, IL Divine Word Theologate; [N] Techny, IL Society of the Divine Word, Provincial Headquarter-Chicago Prov.
Simons, James A. '00 (CIN) [38] Cincinnati, OH St. James the Greater Church.
Simons, Lawrence D. '48 (HEL) Retired.
Simons, Msgr. Richard J. '38 (PH) Newtown Square, PA St. Anastasia Church; Retired.
Simons, Thomas G. '77 (GR) [2] Muskegon, MI St. Francis de Sales Church.
Simonson, Earl C. '69 (STP) [22] Minneapolis, MN St. Clement Church.
Simpson, Brian L. '72 (CHI) Military Chaplains.
Simpson, David *o.carm.* '70 (NEW) [P] Mahwah, NJ Carmel Retreat House.
Simpson, Gerald T. '57 (STL) Union, MO Immaculate Conception Church.
Simpson, Kenneth C. '78 (CHI) [V] Chicago, IL Ministry in Higher Education.
Simpson, Mark '79 (CHI) Winnetka, IL Sacred Heart Church.
Simpson, Mauro *o.s.b.* '52 (CGS) Humacao, PR Maria Reina de la Paz Church.
Simpson, Robert A. '65 (RNO) [4] Reno, NV St. Albert the Great Church.
Simpson, Roger '52 (SFD) Retired.
Sims, Paul *c.r.* '86 (CHI) [A] Chicago, IL Archbishop Quigley Preparatory Seminary; [D] Chicago, IL Gordon Tech High School.
Sims, Robert W. '71 (IND) [36] Indianapolis, IN St. Simon Church.
Simutowe, Patrick '96 (BAL) [S] Baltimore, MD Sulpician Provincial House.
Sinasac, Alvin A. *c.s.b.* '78 (GAL) [B] Houston, TX Casa San Basilio.
Sinatra, Leonard '67 (PHU) Pottstown, PA St. Michael's Church; Reading, PA Nativity of Blessed Virgin Mary Church.
Sinatra, William D. '64 (DET) [4] Southfield, MI St. Ives Church.
Sinclair, Alexander B. '57 (KC) [35] Kansas City, MO St. Raphael the Archangel Church.
Sinclair, Roger A. (BO) Jamaica Plain, MA Jamaica Plain; Jamaica Plain, MA Veterans Administration Hospital.
Sinclair, Roger A. '74 (GBG) Military Chaplains.
Sindik, George '59 (PT) [1] Pensacola, FL Cathedral of the Sacred Heart.
Sindik, Matthew A. '62 (MOB) [6] Montgomery, AL St. Jude Church; [E] Montgomery, AL City of St. Jude, Inc., The; [K] Montgomery, AL The City of St. Jude, Inc.
Singarayar, Philip *o.m.i.* '64 (CHI) [N] Chicago, IL The Oblate House of Theology.
Singarayer, Lawrence Maria '66 (NY) [1] New Rochelle, NY Blessed Sacrament Church.
Singelyn, Robert K. '60 (DET) On Duty Outside the Archdiocese.
Singer, Charles '84 (CIN) [B] Cincinnati, OH Mt. St. Mary's Seminary of the West.
Singer, Jerome C. '63 (DET) [51] Detroit, MI Nativity of Our Lord Church.
Singer, Thomas *o.m.i.* (CHI) [X] Chicago, IL Oblates for International Pastoral.
Singer, Thomas *o.m.i.* '57 (SAT) [M] San Antonio, TX Missionary Oblates of Mary Immaculate; [M] San Antonio, TX Missionary Oblates of Mary Immaculate.
Singer, Thomas *o.m.i.* '57 (WDC) [M] Washington, DC Missionary Oblates of Mary Immaculate.
Singlar, Charles E. '84 (TOL) Special Assignment.
Singler, James E. '82 (CLV) Cleveland Heights, OH St. Ann Church.
Singler, John P. '82 (CLV) Willowick, OH St. Mary Magdalene Church.
Singleton, William V. '50 (RVC) East Rockaway, NY St. Raymond's Church; Retired.
Sinibaldi, Daniel J. '96 (MAN) Lisbon, NH St. Catherine of Siena Church; Woodsville, NH St. Joseph Church.
Sinisi, Daniel *t.o.r.* '66 (BAL) [30] Baltimore, MD St. Elizabeth of Hungary Church.
Siniskey, Joseph M. '48 (ALB) East Greenbush, NY Holy Spirit Church; Retired.
Sinkele, W. T. *o.p.* '73 (FgM) Dominican - Order of Preachers Foreign Missions.
Sinkler, Michael D. '81 (LR) Bentonville, AR St. Stephen Church.
Sinnema, Paul *o.f.m.* '63 (NEW) East Rutherford, NJ St. Joseph's Church; Wood-Ridge, NJ Our Lady of the Assumption Church.
Sinner, Msgr. Emil E. '42 (SAL) Retired.
Sinner, Richard W. '52 (FAR) Retired.
Sinnerud, James A. *s.j.* '72 (OM) [C] Omaha, NE Creighton Preparatory School.
Sinnott, Andrew R. '99 (SCR) Honesdale, PA St. John the Evangelist Church.
Sinnott, James P. *m.m.* '60 (NY) [DD] Maryknoll, NY Maryknoll Fathers and Brothers.
Sinnott, Thomas '00 (SCR) [D] Scranton, PA Bishop Hannan High School.
Sinnott, Thomas G. '00 (SCR) [1] Scranton, PA St. Peter's Church.
Sinor, Michael J. '88 (SD) Ramona, CA Immaculate Heart of Mary Church.
Sinski, Norbert J. *c.s.c.* '77 (FTW) [J] South Bend, IN Congregation of Holy Cross, Indiana Province, Provincial House.
Sinz, Eugene R. '60 (STL) High Ridge, MO St. Anthony

of Padua Church.
Siok, Slawomir *s.a.c.* '90 (BRK) [43] Brooklyn, NY St. Frances de Chantal Church.
Siola, Roman *o.f.m.conv.* '56 (BUF) [21] Buffalo, NY Corpus Christi Church.
Sioleti, Andrew *o.f.m.* (NY) Manhattan, NY Cabrini Medical Center.
Sioli, Joseph E. *c.o.* '97 (PIT) [O] Pittsburgh, PA Congregation of the Oratory of St. Philip Neri; [R] Pittsburgh, PA Office for Campus Ministry; [R] Pittsburgh, PA Office for Campus Ministry; [R] Pittsburgh, PA Office for Campus Ministry.
Sipaco, Cecilio E. '67 (MET) [F] New Brunswick, NJ St. Peter's University Hospital.
Sipe, Robert J. '59 (STP) Forest Lake, MN St. Peter Church.
Sipitkowski, James A. '74 (SPR) Easthampton, MA Sacred Heart Church.
Siple, Donald M. *o.s.m.* '92 (CHI) [157] Chicago, IL Our Lady of Sorrows, Basilica of; [N] Chicago, IL Order of Friar Servants of Mary (Servites) United States of America Province, Inc.
Siple, William P. '92 (PIT) Perrysville, PA St. Teresa of Avila Church.
Sippel, Bernard S. '65 (MIL) Germantown, WI St. Boniface Church.
Sippel, Edward F. '47 (MIL) Retired.
Sipperly, Edward '53 (ALB) [8] Amsterdam, NY St. Stanislaus Church.
Sipulski, Vianney C. *o.f.m.* '60 (GAY) Atlanta, MI Jesus the Good Shepherd Church; Hillman, MI St. Augustine Church.
Siracuse, Aloysius *o.f.m.* '47 (FgM) Franciscan Foreign Missions.
Siracuse, Guy F. '67 (BUF) [4] Buffalo, NY St. Agnes Church.
Sirba, Joseph '87 (DUL) Aurora, MN Holy Rosary Church; Hoyt Lakes, MN Queen of Peace Church.
Sirba, Paul D. '86 (STP) [7] St. Paul, MN Maternity of the Blessed Virgin Church.
Siriani, Klaus-Werner J. '78 (WDC) Military Chaplains.
Sirianni, Anthony J.. '89 (MET) Three Bridges, NJ St. Elizabeth Ann Seton Church.
Sirianni, Jasper F. '46 (DET) Emmett, MI Our Lady of Mount Carmel Church; Retired.
Sirianni, Louis A. '74 (ROC) [4] Rochester, NY St. Anne Church; [18] Rochester, NY Guardian Angels Church.
Sirianni, Richard D. '78 (P) Gresham, OR St. Henry Church.
Sirianni, Sam A. '84 (TR) [3] Trenton, NJ Holy Angels Church.
Sirico, Robert '89 (KAL) [E] Kalamazoo, MI St. Philip Neri House.
Sirois, Gerald *s.d.s.* '61 (GB) St. Nazianz, WI St. Gregory Church; School Hill, WI Holy Trinity Church.
Sirois, Msgr. Joseph V. '51 (WOR) [5] Worcester, MA Holy Name of Jesus Church.
Siroki, David '93 (PSC) Leave of Absence.
Sirolli, Francis A. *o.s.a.* '65 (PH) [AA] Malvern, PA Augustinian Friars (O.S.A.).
Siroskey, P. Larry '80 (DET) [2] Wyandotte, MI St. Helena Church.
Sirvent, Francisco '88 (PCE) On Duty Outside the Diocese.
Siry, Philip L. '62 (WIL) Delaware City, DE St. Paul Church; Delaware City, DE Governor Bacon Health Center.
Sis, Michael J. '86 (AUS) College Station, TX St. Mary's Church; [M] College Station, TX St. Mary's Catholic Center.
Sisco, Michael A. '97 (PRO) [2] East Providence, RI St. Francis Xavier Church; Providence, RI Rhode Island Hospital.
Sise, John '45 (ALB) Retired.
Siska, Ernest J. '60 (TR) Retired; [M] Trenton, NJ Villa Vianney.
Sison, Alden J. '87 (LA) Canoga Park, CA Our Lady of the Valley Church.
Sison, Bernabe '65 (NY) [94] New York, NY Our Lady of Pompeii Church.
Sistare, John A. '00 (PRO) On Duty Outside the Diocese.
Sisul, Paul *c.m.* '72 (CHI) [N] Chicago, IL DePaul Vincentian Residence.
Sitar, Richard T. '79 (GAY) Retired.
Sitko, Joseph S. '68 (SCR) Mayfield, PA Sacred Heart of Jesus Church.
Sito, Joseph '62 (DET) Retired.
Sitter, Leonard F. *s.j.* '61 (SPK) [C] Spokane, WA Gonzaga University.
Sittinger, Eduardo *s.t.* '77 (SJN) Loiza, PR Santiago Apostol, El Mayor Church.
Sitzmann, Eugene E. '62 (SC) Cherokee, IA St. Dymphna Chapel Church; Maryhill, IA Visitation of the B.V.M. Church; Cherokee, IA State Mental Health Institute.
Sitzmann, Richard A. '62 (SC) [3] Sioux City, IA St. Boniface Church; Sioux City, IA Mercy Medical Center; [C] Sioux City, IA Mercy Medical Center - Sioux City.
Siu, Peter Kin Chung *s.j.* '93 (SFR) [E] San Francisco, CA St. Ignatius College Preparatory (Coed); [N] San Francisco, CA Jesuit Community at St. Ignatius College Preparatory.
Siu, Robert K.C. '54 (CHY) Lander, WY Holy Rosary Church; In Residence.
Siu, Robert K.C. '54 (HON) Retired.
Sivalon, John C. *m.m.* '75 (FgM) Maryknoll Foreign Missions.
Sivillo, Msgr. Nicholas W. '64 (BRK) [212] Queens, NY Our Lady of Hope Church.
Sivinsky, Wasyl '92 (PHU) [6] Philadelphia, PA St. Josaphat's Church.
Sivore, Victor J. '64 (CHI) [3] Lemont, IL SS. Cyril and Methodius Church.
Siwek, Daniel S. '73 (CHI) [A] Mundelein, IL University of St. Mary of the Lake-Mundelein Seminary.
Siwek, Jerome S. '56 (CHI) [181] Chicago, IL St. Richard Church; Retired.
Sizelove, Michael Dennis '90 (NO) On Leave.
Sizemore, David W. '96 (COL) [1] Columbus, OH St. Joseph Church.
Sizing, Theodore C. '55 (SY) [24] Syracuse, NY St. Vincent de Paul Church.
Skach, Charles J. '51 (CHI) [3] Mt. Prospect, IL St. Raymond de Penafort Church; Retired.
Skaff, Elias B. '36 (NTN) Retired.
Skagen, Robert '70 (PHX) [2] Glendale, AZ St. Helen Church.
Skager, Robert (NTN) Phoenix, AZ St. John of the Desert Church.
Skaj, John P. *c.s.sp.* '63 (PIT) Emsworth, PA Sacred Heart Church.
Skala, John J. '97 (ROM) Canton, OH St. George Church.
Skalski, Francis S. '56 (DET) [34] Detroit, MI St. Hyacinth Church.
Skalsky, Ted A. '72 (DOD) [2] Dodge City, KS Our Lady of Guadalupe Church.
Skarbek, Richard *m.s.a.* '86 (NOR) [F] Cromwell, CT Society of the Missionaries of the Holy Apostles.
Skarich, William '99 (DUL) Brainerd, MN St. Francis Church.
Skaskiw, Bohdan '80 (STN) Retired.
Skechus, Francis E. *s.j.* '75 (PH) [G] Philadelphia, PA St. Joseph's Preparatory School; [AA] Philadelphia, PA Jesuit Community at St. Joseph's University.
Skeehan, William K. '60 (TLS) Bartlesville, OK The Community of St. James Church.
Skehan, James W. *s.j.* '54 (BO) [W] Chestnut Hill, MA The Jesuit Community at Boston College.
Skehan, John A. '52 (PMB) [4] Delray Beach, FL St. Vincent Ferrer Church.
Skehan, John R. '86 (PRT) Special or Other Diocesan Assignment.
Skehan, Msgr. Martin O. '44 (YAK) Moses Lake, WA Our Lady of Fatima Church; Retired.
Skeldon, John Robert '00 (FWT) [6] Arlington, TX St. Matthew Church.
Skelly, Francis G. *c.ss.r.* '72 (NY) [23] New York, NY St. Cecilia Church.
Skelly, Msgr. John J. (RVC) Retired.
Skelly, Msgr. John J. '53 (RVC) Manhasset, NY St. Mary's Church.
Skelly, Msgr. Richard J. '54 (PH) Morton, PA Our Lady of Perpetual Help Church.
Skelskey, David *s.j.* '80 (BO) [W] Chestnut Hill, MA The Jesuit Community at Boston College.
Skelskey, David A. *s.j.* '80 (FgM) Provinces.
Skelton, Paul H. '64 (SFD) Hume, IL St. Michael Church; Villa Grove, IL Sacred Heart Church.
Skenderovic, Ivan '76 (BUF) Alden, NY St. John the Baptist Church.
Skeris, Robert A. '61 (MIL) Retired.
Skerl, Alphonse '55 (GRY) [3] East Chicago, IN Holy Trinity Church.
Skerry, Donald *s.v.d.* '62 (BO) [W] Boston, MA Divine Word Missionaries.
Skertich, Mark J. '77 (PIT) California, PA St. Thomas Aquinas Church; [R] Pittsburgh, PA Office for Campus Ministry.
Skiba, Andrew *o.f.m.conv.* '47 (SPR) [5] Holyoke, MA Mater Dolorosa Church.
Skiba, Walter F. '56 (SCR) Wyoming, PA St. Joseph's Church.
Skidmore, Harold G. *c.m.* '50 (FgM) Vincentian Foreign Missions.
Skillin, Harmon D. *j.c.d.* '60 (STO) [7] Stockton, CA St. Luke Church.
Skillingstad, M. Delmar '60 (SPK) [C] Spokane, WA Gonzaga University.
Skindeleski, Thomas J. '71 (PMB) Royal Palm Beach, FL Our Lady Queen of the Apostles Church.
Skinner, Charles D. '53 (E) Retired.
Skinta, Stephen J. *o.s.b.m.* '59 (PSC) New Brunswick, NJ St. Joseph Church; [A] Matawan, NJ Basilian Fathers of Mariapoch.
Skirtich, John '90 (PIT) [6] Ambridge, PA Good Samaritan Church.
Skitski, Francis P. '70 (SCR) [16] Wilkes-Barre, PA St. Nicholas Church.
Skluzacek, Michael C. '80 (STP) Stillwater, MN St. Mary Church; Stillwater, MN St. Michael Church; [H] Stillwater, MN St. Croix Catholic Educational Programs.
Skluzacek, Richard F. (STP) Retired.
Skoczylas, Walter '75 (CR) On Duty Outside the Diocese.
Skok, Charles D. '52 (SPK) [13] Spokane, WA St. John Vianney Church.
Skoneki, William J. '87 (MOB) [4] Mobile, AL St. Dominic Church.
Skonezny, Ray '61 (ORG) Irvine, CA St. John Neumann Church.
Skonny, Thomas F. *o.c.s.o.* '51 (ATL) [J] Conyers, GA The Monastery of the Holy Spirit.
Skonseng, Dennis A. '82 (FAR) Special Assignment; [A] Fargo, ND Cardinal Muench Seminary.
Skornia, Bernard L. '57 (SAG) Retired.
Skorup, Ildephonse *o.f.m.* '59 (CHI) [63] Chicago, IL St. Francis de Sales Church; [N] Countryside, IL St. Gratian Friary, Franciscan Friars.
Skotek, Thomas D. '63 (SCR) Mocanaqua, PA St. Mary, Our Lady of Perpetual Help Church.
Skotnicki, Andrew *o.carm.* '77 (JOL) [J] Darien, IL Carmelite Provincial Office.
Skotnicki, Andrew *o.carm.* '77 (SJ) San Jose, CA Santa Clara County Jail.
Skriba, Raymond F. '57 (CHI) Round Lake, IL St. Joseph Church.
Skrocki, Michael '00 (NTN) Waterford, CT St. Ann Church.
Skrypek, Gregory A. '70 (STP) Stillwater, MN Minnesota State Prison.
Skrzypiec, Andrzej '82 (SLC) [3] Magna, UT Our Lady of Lourdes Church.
Skudlarek, William *o.s.b.* '64 (FgM) American - Cassinese Congregation Foreign Missions.
Skudlarek, William *o.s.b.* '64 (SCL) [I] Collegeville, MN St. John's Abbey, of the Order of St. Benedict.
Skufca, Ronald J. '79 (MAR) Menominee, MI Holy Redeemer Church.
Skupien, Edward D. '37 (CHI) Retired.
Skupien, Msgr. Francis M. '51 (BUF) Retired.
Skupien, Msgr. Joseph F. '47 (BUF) Retired.
Skura, Mark David *ofm conv.* '82 (BUF) [D] Athol Springs, NY St. Francis High School; [O] Athol Springs, NY St. Francis of Assisi Friary.
Skurla, Anthony *o.f.m.* '54 (PSC) [A] Sybertsville, PA Holy Dormition Friary.
Skurla, Robert J. '56 (PSC) Jersey City, NJ St. Mary's Church.
Skurla, William '87 (VNN) Tucson, AZ St. Melany Church.
Skwara, John M. '59 (MET) South Plainfield, NJ Our Lady of Czestochowa Church.
Skwor, Donald *s.d.s.* '53 (WDC) [B] Silver Spring, MD Salvatorian Community.
Skylstad, William S. '48 (NY) [HH] New York, NY Catholic Medical Mission Board, Inc.
Slaby, Joseph A. *m.m.* '66 (FgM) Maryknoll Foreign Missions.
Slacke, Varin *o.f.m.* '44 (CIN) [M] Cincinnati, OH St. John the Baptist Friary.
Sladek, Robert '47 (GB) Retired.
Sladicka, Phillip J. '76 (SCR) Olyphant, PA St. Patrick's Church.
Slafkosky, Andrew L. '38 (ORL) Retired.
Slafkosky, Andrew L. '38 (PH) Pottstown, PA Holy Trinity Church; Retired.
Slampak, John A. '66 (RCK) Special Assignment.
Slane, Anthony *c.ss.r.* '42 (SEA) [32] Seattle, WA Sacred Heart of Jesus Church.
Slate, William '55 (SEA) Retired.
Slater, Edward *o.f.m.* '83 (CIN) [24] Cincinnati, OH St. Francis Seraph Church; [M] Cincinnati, OH St. Francis Seraph Friary.
Slater, Msgr. John J. '52 (E) Retired.
Slater, William T. '77 (RVC) New Hyde Park, NY Notre Dame Church.
Slatterie, Leo (LIN) [G] Crete, NE Our Lady of the Sacred Heart Cistercian Monastery.
Slatterie, Leo '51 (LAV) Caliente, NV Holy Child Church; Retired.
Slatterie, Leo '51 (P) [Q] Beaverton, OR Our Lady of Peace Institute in Catholic Teaching.
Slattery, Edmund *s.s.s.* '40 (CLV) [O] Cleveland, OH Blessed Sacrament Community.
Slattery, Edmund *s.s.s.* '40 (NY) Manhattan, NY Lenox Hill Hospital.
Slattery, James F. '41 (ROC) Retired.
Slattery, John '57 (COS) Retired.
Slattery, Joseph A. '66 (RIC) On Duty Outside the Diocese.
Slattery, Kenneth '94 (SP) New Port Richey, FL Our Lady Queen of Peace Church.
Slattery, Kenneth F. *c.m.* '48 (BRK) [V] Jamaica, NY Vincentian Residence.
Slattery, Kevin '86 (JKS) Canton, MS Sacred Heart Church; Carthage, MS St. Anne Church.
Slattery, Maurice C. '55 (NY) Absent on Sick leave; [DD] New York, NY Our Lady of Consolation Residence.

Slattery, Michael *o.m.i.* '41 (SAT) [K] San Antonio, TX Oblate Madonna Residence.
Slattery, Michael *o.s.a.* '77 (JOL) New Lenox, IL St. Jude Church.
Slattery, Michael J. '62 (LA) Santa Clarita, CA Blessed Kateri Tekakwitha Church.
Slaughter, Martin '85 (LA) Culver City, CA St. Augustine Church.
Slaven, Donald J. '67 (SC) Salix, IA St. Joseph's Church.
Slaven, Msgr. Frederick '59 (Y) Streetsboro, OH St. Joan of Arc Church.
Slavish, Richard '59 (PEO) Matherville, IL St. Anthony's Church.
Sleasman, Martin J. *c.m.* '42 (BUF) [C] Niagara University, NY Niagara University; [O] Niagara University, NY Vincentian Community at Niagara University.
Sledesky, Stephen M. '93 (HRT) [2] Torrington, CT Sacred Heart Church; [4] Torrington, CT St. Peter's Church.
Sledzaus, Alexander L. '50 (RVC) Patchogue, NY Our Lady of Mt. Carmel Church; Retired.
Sledziona, John S. *c.m.* '70 (HRT) [M] Manchester, CT DePaul Provincial Residence.
Slejzer, Ferdinand E. '53 (BO) Senior Priests.
Slemba, Dominic *o.f.m.conv.* '51 (BAL) [S] Ellicott City, MD Order of Friars Minor Conventual.
Slemba, Dominic *o.f.m.conv.* '51 (FgM) Conventual Franciscan Foreign Missions.
Slepicka, Msgr. Joseph J. '55 (DUB) Retired.
Slesinski, Robert '76 (PSC) On Duty Outside Diocese.
Slesinski, Sebastian *o.f.m.conv.* '51 (FR) [8] New Bedford, MA Our Lady of Perpetual Help Church.
Slevin, Henry '62 (WDC) [13] Washington, DC St. Francis de Sales Church; On Duty Outside the Archdiocese.
Slevin, Patrick C. '57 (MIA) [13] Fort Lauderdale, FL St. Pius X Church.
Sleyman, Kenneth *m.m.* (STL) [3] Creve Coeur, MO St. Monica Church.
Sleyman, Kenneth C. *m.m.* '90 (FgM) Maryknoll Foreign Missions.
Slezak, Raymond P. '74 (ALN) Sheppton, PA St. Joseph Church.
Slight, William *m.s.* '65 (MAN) [K] Enfield, NH Shrine of Our Lady of La Salette; [M] Enfield, NH La Salette Shrine and Center of Enfield.
Sliney, Michael *l.c.* '98 (WDC) [M] Potomac, MD Legionaries of Christ.
Slinger, Msgr. Joseph T. '70 (NEW) Paramus, NJ Our Lady of the Visitation Church.
Slipe, Robert H. '73 (NEW) River Edge, NJ St. Peter the Apostle Church.
Slipski, William P. '46 (Y) Retired.
Slisz, Charles E. '71 (BUF) Kenmore, NY St. Andrew Church.
Slivonik, Stanley '69 (ARL) Retired.
Sliwak, Msgr. Stanley A. '66 (LAR) [2] Laredo, TX Blessed Sacrament Church.
Sliwinski, Phillip A. '97 (GR) Howard City, MI Christ the King Church; Lakeview, MI St. Francis de Sales Church.
Sloan, Daniel '82 (MET) Manville, NJ Christ the King Church.
Sloan, James D. *c.pp.s.* '62 (OAK) [N] Berkeley, CA Society of the Precious Blood; [N] San Leandro, CA Society of the Precious Blood.
Slobig, John '90 (PHX) [4] Glendale, AZ St. Louis The King Church.
Sloboda, Michael J. *m.m.* '85 (STA) [H] Jacksonville, FL Maryknoll Fathers & Brothers.
Slobogin, Roland D. '73 (PH) [47] Philadelphia, PA St. Francis de Sales Church; [108] Philadelphia, PA Most Blessed Sacrament Church.
Slocum, Samuel B. '80 (E) Eldred, PA St. Raphael Church; Shinglehouse, PA St. Theresa Church.
Slodowski, Bronislaw '68 (MIL) [N] Kenosha, WI St. Joseph's Home for the Aged.
Slomba, Eugene S. '64 (BUF) [4] Batavia, NY Sacred Heart Church; Albion, NY Albion Correctional Facility.
Slominski, Fabian B. '48 (DET) Pontiac, MI St. Joseph Church; Retired.
Slominski, George A. '38 (CHI) Retired.
Slominski, Leon '58 (SCL) Luxemburg, MN St. Wendelin's Church.
Slomski, Joseph P. '53 (WCH) Chase, KS St. Mary Church.
Slonecki, Michael *o.f.m.conv.* '41 (SPR) [5] Chicopee, MA St. Anthony's Church.
Sloneker, Patrick L. '97 (CIN) Sidney, OH Holy Angels Church.
Slosarcik, Edward A. (CHI) Retired.
Slota, Frederick V. '53 (PRO) [2] Providence, RI St. Adalbert Church.
Slough, Charles R. '56 (HBG) Elysburg, PA Queen of the Most Holy Rosary Church.
Slovacek, Emil C. '54 (DAL) Retired.
Slovikovski, John (ALT) [A] Cresson, PA Mount Aloysius College.
Slovikovski, John J. '96 (ALT) [H] Hollidaysburg, PA Campus Ministry.
Slowey, John P. '57 (SUP) Retired.
Slowiak, Allan L. '73 (LC) Rothschild, WI St. Mark Church.
Slowik, Joseph S. '72 (RIC) Portsmouth, VA St. Paul Church.
Slowinski, Jerome '90 (DET) [1] Warren, MI St. Anne's Church; Special Assignment.
Slowinski, Thomas '81 (DET) Clawson, MI Guardian Angels Church.
Sloyan, Gerard S. '44 (TR) Retired.
Slubecky, Msgr. David S. '73 (BUF) [3] West Seneca, NY Fourteen Holy Helpers Church.
Slusser, Michael S. '66 (STP) On Duty Outside the Archdiocese.
Smail, Brian E. *o.f.m.* '99 (BO) [BB] Boston, MA St. Anthony Shrine.
Smaistrla, Benjamin '72 (GAL) [5] Houston, TX St. Ambrose Church; [76] Houston, TX St. Theresa Church.
Small, Edward J. *s.j.* '70 (BGP) [4] Stratford, CT Our Lady of Grace Church; [P] Fairfield, CT The Fairfield Jesuit Community-Fairfield University.
Small, Edward J. *s.j.* '70 (BO) [W] Boston, MA The Society of Jesus of New England-Provincial Offices.
Small, James *c.ss.r.* '54 (HBG) [2] Lancaster, PA St. Anthony of Padua Church.
Small, James *c.ss.r.* '54 (NY) [DD] Esopus, NY Redemptorist Priests and Brothers C.Ss.R. (Province of Baltimore); [FF] Esopus, NY Mount St. Alphonsus Redemptorist Retreat Center.
Small, Jeffrey '93 (PEO) Carthage, IL Immaculate Conception Church.
Small, Joseph F. *s.j.* '48 (DET) [P] Clarkston, MI Colombiere Center.
Small, Joseph H. *s.j.* '60 (FgM) Provinces.
Small, Joseph H. *s.j.* '60 (P) [L] Portland, OR Jesuit Provincial Office (Society of Jesus, Oregon Prov.).
Small, William T. '77 (PH) Broomall, PA St. Pius X Church.
Smalley, William R. '55 (NEW) [4] Irvington, NJ St. Paul the Apostle Church; Retired.
Smar, Michael J. '69 (Y) Champion, OH St. William Church.
Smarsh, Charles F. '64 (NY) On Duty Outside the Archdiocese.
Smart, Raymond W. '70 (PH) Absent on Sick Leave.
Smegal, John T. '77 (SPR) Lanesboro, MA North American Martyrs Church.
Smegelsky, John J. '66 (SY) Central Square, NY St. Michael Church.
Smet, Joachim *o.carm.* '42 (JOL) [J] Darien, IL Carmelite Provincial Office.
Smet, Leroy R. '59 (GB) Winneconne, WI St. Mary Church.
Smetana, Brendan L. *o.s.b.* '40 (GBG) [H] Latrobe, PA Saint Vincent Archabbey.
Smetana, Joseph *o.f.m.cap.* '56 (MIL) [27] Milwaukee, WI St. Francis of Assisi Church.
Smetanka, Gary T. '82 (DET) [1] Clinton Twp., MI St. Claude Church; [5] Clinton Twp., MI St. Thecla Church.
Smialowski, Raymond S. '82 (HRT) Newington, CT Holy Spirit Church; [R] Hartford, CT University of Hartford Newman Center.
Smiciklas, Msgr. Nicholas X. '56 (PBR) [6] Pittsburgh, PA St. Pius X Church.
Smiech, Charles *o.f.m.* (ALN) [K] Easton, PA St. Francis Friary.
Smiga, George '75 (CLV) Willoughby Hills, OH St. Noel Church.
Smigiel, Edgar '47 (MIL) [P] Burlington, WI Queen of Peace Friary.
Smigiel, Walter J. '50 (PBL) Retired.
Smilanic, Daniel A. '73 (CHI) Park Ridge, IL St. Paul of the Cross Church.
Smiley, Douglas J. '00 (R) Jacksonville, NC Shrine of the Infant of Prague, Church of the Holy Spirit .
Smilga, Zenon A. '50 (NOR) Retired.
Smink, Edward *o.h.* (SFR) San Francisco, CA Catholic Healthcare West/Bay Area Region.
Smiroldo, Msgr. Onofrio R. '53 (BUF) [5] Tonawanda, NY St. Edmund Church.
Smit, Gerard C. '50 (LKC) Retired.
Smith, A. Philip *o.p.* '68 (PRO) [P] Providence, RI St. Thomas Aquinas Priory at Providence College.
Smith, Alberic *o.f.m.* '58 (LA) [Q] Santa Barbara, CA Franciscan Friary, Order of Friars Minor (Old Mission).
Smith, Albert J. *o.s.f.s.* '65 (PH) [C] Philadelphia, PA Holy Family College; [AA] Wyndmoor, PA Villa de Sales Oblate Residence.
Smith, Alexei R. '87 (LA) El Segundo, CA St. Andrew Church.
Smith, Alexei R. '87 (NTN) El Segundo, CA St. Paul Church.
Smith, Alfred E. '56 (BAL) Williamsport, MD St. Augustine Church.
Smith, Alphonsus M. '56 (WDC) Retired.
Smith, Andrew T. *o.s.b.* (PAT) [M] Morristown, NJ St. Mary's Abbey.
Smith, Anthony *c.ss.r.* '84 (DEN) [M] Denver, CO The Redemptorists/Denver Province.
Smith, Anthony *c.ss.r.* '84 (TUC) [H] Tucson, AZ Redemptorist Picture Rocks Retreat.
Smith, Aquinas '59 (SD) Retired.
Smith, Arthur F. *o.s.a.* '54 (PH) [AA] Villanova, PA St. Thomas Monastery.
Smith, Arthur J. '71 (BUF) [64] Buffalo, NY St. Thomas Aquinas Church.
Smith, Bernard *o.f.m.cap.* '64 (FgM) Capuchin Foreign Missions.
Smith, Bernard *o.f.m.cap.* '64 (NY) [DD] White Plains, NY St. Conrad Friary.
Smith, Msgr. Bernard E. '33 (TOL) Retired.
Smith, Bernardine J. *t.o.r.* '59 (SP) [6] St. Petersburg, FL St. Mary Our Lady of Grace Church.
Smith, Brendan *s.t.* '54 (ORG) Orange, CA Juvenile Hall; Orange, CA Theo Lacy Minimum Security Facility; [I] Santa Ana, CA Trinitarian Missionaries/Missionary Servants of the Most Holy Trinity.
Smith, Brian '98 (SJ) On Leave of Absence.
Smith, Brian P. '87 (STL) [8] Florissant, MO St. Norbert Church.
Smith, Charles *s.v.d.* '88 (IND) [34] Indianapolis, IN St. Rita Church.
Smith, Msgr. Charles A. '45 (WCH) Retired.
Smith, Charles C. *c.s.b.* '60 (DET) [E] Redford, MI Catholic Central High School.
Smith, Charles Clyde '95 (FBK) Alakanuk, AK St. Ignatius Church.
Smith, Charles D. '65 (PH) [95] Philadelphia, PA St. Martin of Tours Church.
Smith, Charles F. '76 (FRS) [5] Fresno, CA Sacred Heart Church.
Smith, Chester *s.v.d.* '88 (IND) [34] Indianapolis, IN St. Rita Church.
Smith, Christopher H. '78 (ORG) [8] Santa Ana, CA St. Joseph's Church.
Smith, Clifford G. '96 (DAL) Grand Prairie, TX St. Michael the Archangel Church.
Smith, Cyril J. *o.s.a.* '55 (MIA) [C] Miami, FL Msgr. Edward Pace High School; [H] Miami, FL Casa San Lorenzo.
Smith, D. Stephen '73 (MAD) Cross Plains, WI St. Francis Xavier Church.
Smith, Daniel *o.carm.* '46 (NEW) Paramus, NJ Carmelite Chapel of St. Therese Church.
Smith, David '82 (MIA) Special Assignment.
Smith, David A. *m.m.* '85 (FgM) Maryknoll Foreign Missions.
Smith, David G. '73 (BAL) Absent on Leave.
Smith, David L. *c.s.sp.* '58 (PIT) [B] Pittsburgh, PA Duquesne University of the Holy Ghost.
Smith, David L. *s.j.* '85 (OM) [K] Omaha, NE Jesuit Community at Creighton University.
Smith, David W. '64 (STP) [C] St. Paul, MN University of St. Thomas.
Smith, Dean M. '99 (RCK) [10] Rockford, IL St. Rita Church.
Smith, Dennis '75 (FWT) Keller, TX St. Elizabeth Ann Seton Church.
Smith, Donald C. '61 (NEW) [B] South Orange, NJ Seton Hall University.
Smith, Donald R. '57 (SC) Retired.
Smith, Douglas '57 (GAL) [39] Houston, TX St. Jerome Church.
Smith, Edmund *o.s.b.* '65 (P) Mt. Angel, OR St. Mary Church; [L] St. Benedict, OR Mt. Angel Abbey.
Smith, Edward '82 (CIN) [B] Cincinnati, OH Mt. St. Mary's Seminary of the West.
Smith, Edward E. '82 (MOB) On Leave from the Archdiocese.
Smith, Edward J. *o.praem.* (GB) [O] Green Bay, WI Green Bay Area Catholic High School Foundation, L.T.D.
Smith, Edward J. '63 (BRK) [157] Queens, NY Blessed Sacrament Church.
Smith, Edward J. *o.praem.* '73 (WIL) [I] Claymont, DE Immaculate Conception Priory of the Canons Regular of Premontre; [I] Claymont, DE Norbertine Fathers of Delaware, Inc.
Smith, Edward P. '82 (CIN) Milford, OH St. Andrew Church.
Smith, Elmer W. '50 (CIN) [19] Cincinnati, OH St. Cecilia Church; [V] Cincinnati, OH Legion of Mary.
Smith, Ermin R. *o.s.b.* '45 (GBG) Latrobe, PA Latrobe Area Hospital; [H] Latrobe, PA Saint Vincent Archabbey.
Smith, Eugene M. *o.s.m.* '84 (CHI) [N] Chicago, IL Order of Friar Servants of Mary (Servites) United States of America Province, Inc.
Smith, Eugene M. *o.s.m.* '88 (CHI) [N] Chicago, IL Order of Friar Servants of Mary (Servites) United States of America Province, Inc.
Smith, Eugene M. *o.s.m.* '88 (ORG) [D] Anaheim, CA Servite High School; Servite High School Development Fund; [I] Anaheim, CA Servite Fathers and Brothers; [I] Buena Park, CA Order of Friar Servants of Mary (Servites); [I] Buena Park, CA Order of Friar Servants of Mary (Servites).

Smith, Eugene P. '50 (LC) Boyd, WI Sacred Heart of Jesus-St. Joseph Church; Retired.
Smith, F. Harold '50 (L) Retired.
Smith, Francis J. *s.j.* '52 (CLV) [B] Cleveland, OH John Carroll Jesuit Community.
Smith, Msgr. Francis J. '67 (ELP) [31] El Paso, TX St. Raphael Church.
Smith, Francis R. *s.j.* '70 (SJ) [B] Santa Clara, CA Santa Clara University.
Smith, Francis X.J. '64 (ORL) Melbourne, FL Ascension Church.
Smith, Gabriel J. '82 (CHR) [12] Charleston, SC St. Joseph Church.
Smith, Gary N. *s.j.* '71 (FgM) Provinces.
Smith, Gary N. *s.j.* '71 (P) [39] Portland, OR St. Vincent de Paul Church; [L] Portland, OR Jesuit Provincial Office (Society of Jesus, Oregon Prov.).
Smith, Gene F. '84 (CHI) Winnetka, IL SS. Faith, Hope and Charity Church.
Smith, Geoffrey C. '74 (HRT) [6] Hamden, CT St. Rita's Church; New Haven, CT Yale-New Haven Hospital.
Smith, Gerald S. '64 (PH) North Wales, PA St. Rose of Lima Church.
Smith, Glen E. *s.j.* '63 (FgM) Provinces.
Smith, Gregory J. '74 (GB) Howard, WI St. John the Baptist Church.
Smith, Msgr. Gregory M. '67 (BGP) [16] Bridgeport, CT Our Lady of Good Counsel Church; [X] Fairfield, CT The Institute for Religious Education and Pastoral Studies (REAPS).
Smith, Herbert F. *s.j.* '62 (PH) [AA] Philadelphia, PA Jesuit Community at St. Joseph's University; [FF] Philadelphia, PA Apostleship of Prayer.
Smith, Howard C. *s.m.* '72 (WDC) [M] Washington, DC Marist Center.
Smith, Ignatius E. *o.f.m.* '56 (NY) Callicoon, NY Holy Cross Church.
Smith, Ignatius J. *o.s.b.* '46 (PBL) [G] Canon City, CO Holy Cross Abbey.
Smith, Ivan E. '91 (GB) Special Assignment.
Smith, James A. '52 (CLV) Retired.
Smith, James A.D. '56 (PAT) Succasunna, NJ St. Therese Church.
Smith, James B. '85 (WIL) Dover, DE Holy Cross Church.
Smith, James D. '87 (STP) Oakdale, MN Transfiguration Church.
Smith, James E. *c.m.* '61 (ALB) [M] Menands, NY De Paul Provincial House.
Smith, James E. *c.m.* '61 (BRK) [V] Jamaica, NY Vincentian Residence.
Smith, James F. *s.j.* '62 (SY) [S] Syracuse, NY Jesuits at LeMoyne, Inc.
Smith, James G. *o.praem.* '77 (ORG) [D] Silverado, CA St. Michael's College Preparatory High School; [I] Silverado, CA Norbertine Fathers of Orange Inc.
Smith, James H. '63 (HRT) Derby, CT St. Mary's Church.
Smith, James R. '67 (SC) Breda, IA St. Bernard's Church.
Smith, James T. '56 (BRK) [189] Queens, NY St. Kevin Church.
Smith, James T. '65 (COL) [31] Columbus, OH St. Matthias Church.
Smith, Jerome (PEO) On Duty Outside the Diocese.
Smith, Jerry A. '65 (AUS) [1] Austin, TX St. Mary's Church.
Smith, John *s.s.c.* (CHI) [N] Chicago, IL Korean Catholic Center.
Smith, John B. '59 (STP) Military Chaplains.
Smith, John D. *s.j.* '59 (FgM) Provinces.
Smith, John F.X. '61 (NY) Tuxedo, NY Our Lady of Mt. Carmel Church.
Smith, Msgr. John J. '59 (FR) South Yarmouth, MA St. Pius Tenth Church.
Smith, John P. '42 (DUB) Retired.
Smith, Joseph A. '96 (SAV) [9] Savannah, GA St. James Church.
Smith, Joseph F. '35 (PH) [35] Philadelphia, PA St. Christopher Church; Retired.
Smith, Joseph J. *s.j.* '57 (FgM) Provinces.
Smith, Msgr. Joseph P.T. '60 (ALN) [3] Reading, PA St. Catharine of Siena Church.
Smith, Joseph S. *m.m.* '51 (NY) [DD] Maryknoll, NY Maryknoll Fathers and Brothers.
Smith, Jude *o.f.m.* (PAT) [M] Ringwood, NJ Holy Name Friary, Inc.
Smith, Jude *o.f.m.* '53 (PAT) [M] Butler, NJ St. Anthony Friary.
Smith, Karl Bartholomew '98 (WDC) [2] Silver Spring, MD St. Bernadette Church.
Smith, Kenneth A. '63 (BR) [20] Baton Rouge, LA Sacred Heart of Jesus Church.
Smith, Kenneth G. '84 (HBG) Columbia, PA St. Peter Church.
Smith, Kenneth J. '64 (NY) [17] New York, NY St. Bernard Church; [120] New York, NY St. Veronica Church.
Smith, Kevin M. '88 (RVC) Manhasset, NY St. Mary's Church; East Meadow, NY Nassau County, Fire Chiefs, Council of.
Smith, Lawrence '97 (DAV) Clinton, IA Jesus Christ, Prince of Peace Church.
Smith, Lawrence C. *s.j.* '82 (BO) [W] Boston, MA The Society of Jesus of New England-Provincial Offices.
Smith, Lawrence C. *s.j.* '82 (GLP) Acoma, NM San Esteban, Acoma Catholic Indian Church.
Smith, Lawrence H.F. '68 (MET) Parlin, NJ St. Bernadette Church.
Smith, Lawrence R. '76 (PIT) [3] McKees Rocks, PA St. John of God Church.
Smith, Leland J. '53 (WIN) Retired.
Smith, Leroy '78 (SPR) Pittsfield, MA Berkshire Medical Center.
Smith, LeRoy J. '78 (BRK) Released from Diocesan Assignment.
Smith, Lester E. '75 (SY) Marathon, NY St. Stephen Church.
Smith, Malachy *o.carm.* '43 (JOL) [J] Darien, IL Carmelite Provincial Office.
Smith, Mark C. '83 (JC) Absent on Leave.
Smith, Mark S. '96 (JC) Columbia, MO St. Thomas More Newman Center, University of Missouri Church; [F] Columbia, MO University of Missouri-Columbia, Campus Ministry.
Smith, Martin D. '79 (STU) On Duty Outside the Diocese.
Smith, Martin L. *o.s.a.* (CAM) [C] Richland, NJ St. Augustine Preparatory School.
Smith, Maury *o.f.m.* '66 (SAT) [70] San Antonio, TX San Jose y San Miguel Church.
Smith, Michael B. '74 (CLV) [8] Akron, OH Immaculate Conception Church.
Smith, Michael H. '66 (SAV) McRae, GA Holy Redeemer Church.
Smith, Michael M. '77 (HEL) Stevensville, MT St. Mary Church.
Smith, Michael N. *s.j.* '67 (PBL) Paonia, CO Sacred Heart Church.
Smith, Michael S. (NOR) Hebron, CT The Church of the Holy Family.
Smith, Michel Robert '00 (SP) [8] St. Petersburg, FL St. Raphael Church.
Smith, Myles H. '70 (IND) [24] Indianapolis, IN St. Lawrence Church; On Special or Other Archdiocesan Assignment.
Smith, Neil B. '48 (MAR) Retired.
Smith, Nicholas P. '65 (PRO) South Kingstown, RI St. Francis of Assisi Church; South Kingstown, RI South County Hospital.
Smith, Nicholas W. '94 (STL) [5] Lemay, MO St. Martin of Tours Church.
Smith, Norman '50 (GLP) Retired.
Smith, Norman N. '70 (CLV) [66] Cleveland, OH St. Philip Neri Church; Kirtland, OH Divine Word Church.
Smith, Paschal *c.p.* '51 (NY) [DD] Pelham Manor, NY St. Vincent's Residence; [HH] Pelham, NY Passionist Communications, Inc.
Smith, Patrick '67 (PHX) [5] Scottsdale, AZ St. Daniel the Prophet Church; Scottsdale, AZ Scottsdale Memorial Hospital.
Smith, Patrick A. '90 (WDC) [41] Washington, DC St. Teresa of Avila Church.
Smith, Paul '59 (ALB) Altamont, NY St. Lucy Church; Special Assignment; [D] Albany, NY Academy of the Holy Names Upper, Middle and Lower Schools.
Smith, Paul F. '73 (CLV) Thompson, OH St. Patrick Church.
Smith, Paul O. '64 (COL) [11] Columbus, OH St. Christopher Church.
Smith, Paul R. '59 (ALB) [B] Albany, NY Maria College.
Smith, Peter J. '51 (BWN) Retired.
Smith, Peter J. '51 (NY) [Z] Rhinebeck, NY Ferncliff Nursing Home.
Smith, Philip A. *o.p.* '68 (PRO) [B] Providence, RI Providence College.
Smith, Philip T. *o.praem.* '84 (ORG) Fountain Valley, CA Holy Spirit Church; [I] Silverado, CA Norbertine Fathers of Orange Inc.
Smith, R. Douglas *o.s.f.s.* '62 (CAM) [M] Pittsgrove, NJ Villa St. Joseph.
Smith, R. Leroy '54 (COV) Retired.
Smith, Ramon *o.f.m.* '53 (LSC) Roswell, NM St. Peter Church.
Smith, Raymond J. '50 (CLV) [11] Akron, OH St. Mary Church.
Smith, Raymond K. '56 (SFR) Special Assignment; On Duty Outside the Archdiocese; [M] Petaluma, CA Silver Penny Farm Retreat Center.
Smith, Raynard '86 (MET) [F] New Brunswick, NJ St. Peter's University Hospital.
Smith, Richard '00 (WIL) Sherwood Park, DE St. John the Beloved Church.
Smith, Richard '76 (JOL) Channahon, IL St. Ann Church.
Smith, Richard '84 (JKS) Forest, MS St. Michael Church; Paulding, MS St. Michael Church; [H] Forest, MS East Central Community College Newman Center.
Smith, Richard '97 (NY) Haverstraw, NY St. Peter Church.
Smith, Richard '98 (FRS) On Leave.
Smith, Richard A. '56 (MAN) Bennington, NH St. Patrick Church.
Smith, Richard E. '66 (BAL) Ellicott City, MD Our Lady of Perpetual Help Church.
Smith, Richard J. '60 (BO) Norwell, MA St. Helen Church.
Smith, Richard P. *m.m.* '76 (NY) [DD] Maryknoll, NY Maryknoll Fathers and Brothers.
Smith, Robert '53 (ROC) Retired.
Smith, Robert D. '56 (BO) [3] Haverhill, MA St. James Church.
Smith, Robert J. '55 (OM) Retired.
Smith, Msgr. Robert J. '70 (E) [J] Erie, PA Bishop Michael J. Murphy Residence for Retired Priests.
Smith, Robert J. '83 (RVC) [A] Huntington, NY Diocesan Seminary of the Immaculate Conception.
Smith, Robert V. '61 (CAM) Glassboro, NJ St. Bridget's Church.
Smith, Roger J. '73 (SEA) Morton, WA Sacred Heart Church.
Smith, Roger R. '76 (CC) [17] Corpus Christi, TX St. Patrick Church.
Smith, Ronald T. '73 (HRT) [4] New Britain, CT St. Andrew's Church; New Britain, CT New Britain General Hospital.
Smith, Russell E. '80 (RIC) Quinton, VA St. Elizabeth Ann Seton Church.
Smith, S. Douglas *c.s.c.* '76 (FTW) [J] South Bend, IN Congregation of Holy Cross, Indiana Province, Provincial House.
Smith, Msgr. Sherrill '55 (SAT) Retired; [K] San Antonio, TX Casa De Padres.
Smith, Simon E. *s.j.* (BO) [W] Boston, MA Arrupe House.
Smith, Simon E. *s.j.* '61 (BO) [E] Boston, MA Boston College High School & Jesuit Community; [H] Boston, MA Nativity Preparatory School.
Smith, Stanley C. *o.s.a.* '60 (PH) [B] Villanova, PA St. Augustine Friary.
Smith, Steve *o.p.* (R) [E] Raleigh, NC Dominican Community.
Smith, Terrance W. '73 (CIN) Loveland, OH St. Columban Church.
Smith, Terrence *t.o.r.* '73 (ALT) [5] Johnstown, PA St. Clare of Assisi Church.
Smith, Terrence T. *t.o.r.* '73 (WH) Stonewood, WV Our Lady of Perpetual Help Church.
Smith, Theodore R. *o.praem.* '91 (ORG) [I] Silverado, CA Norbertine Fathers of Orange Inc.
Smith, Thomas *o.f.m. conv.* (L) [L] Louisville, KY St. Francis Friary.
Smith, Thomas '51 (ORL) Altamonte Springs, FL St. Mary Magdalen Church; Retired.
Smith, Thomas *o.f.m.conv.* '79 (STP) [Q] Prior Lake, MN Franciscan Retreat House.
Smith, Thomas A. '83 (L) Flaherty, KY St. Martin of Tours Church; Vine Grove, KY St. Brigid Church.
Smith, Thomas Bernard *o.p.* '58 (L) [4] Springfield, KY St. Rose Church; [M] St. Catharine, KY Sansbury Care Center.
Smith, Thomas E. '51 (PIT) Retired.
Smith, Thomas E. '67 (E) [27] Erie, PA St. Patrick/St. Hedwig Church.
Smith, Thomas E. *s.j.* '74 (FgM) Provinces.
Smith, Thomas E. *s.j.* '74 (NY) [DD] New York, NY Jesuit Provincial's Office; [DD] New York, NY St. Ignatius Loyola Residence.
Smith, Thomas F. *o.c.s.o.* '58 (ATL) [J] Conyers, GA The Monastery of the Holy Spirit.
Smith, Msgr. Thomas H. '57 (HBG) [5] Lancaster, PA St. Joseph Church.
Smith, Thomas J. *o.s.f.s.* '58 (LAN) Michigan Center, MI Our Lady of Fatima Church.
Smith, Thomas J. '60 (LC) [F] La Crosse, WI St. Joseph's Nursing Home; [F] La Crosse, WI Bethany-St. Joseph Care Center; [H] La Crosse, WI Holy Cross (Seminary) Diocesan Center.
Smith, Thomas J. '73 (PH) Springfield, PA St. Francis of Assisi Church.
Smith, Thomas J. '82 (NOR) New London, CT St. Mary, Star of the Sea Church.
Smith, Thomas R. '81 (CLV) [5] Lorain, OH St. John Church.
Smith, Thomas W. *c.s.c.* '72 (FgM) Holy Cross Foreign Missions.
Smith, Thomas W. *c.s.c.* '72 (FTW) [J] South Bend, IN Congregation of Holy Cross, Indiana Province, Provincial House.
Smith, Vernon '90 (FAR) Harvey, ND St. Cecilia's Church.
Smith, Vincent E. *o.s.f.s.* '85 (PH) [AA] Philadelphia, PA Oblates of St. Francis De Sales.
Smith, Msgr. Vincent J. '55 (HBG) Mechanicsburg, PA Saint Katharine Drexel Church; Retired.
Smith, Vincent Leo '66 (DEN) Breckenridge, CO St. Mary Church.
Smith, W. Andrew '80 (LR) Pine Bluff, AR St. Joseph's Church.
Smith, Walter J. *s.j.* '72 (BO) [W] Boston, MA The Society of Jesus of New England-Provincial Offices.

Smith, Walter J. *s.j.* '72 (NY) [DD] New York, NY "America;" Residence and publication office of the America Press.
Smith, Walter N. '68 (CAM) Woodbury, NJ St. Patrick's Church.
Smith, Wilfred T. '56 (CLV) Mentor, OH St. Mary of the Assumption Church.
Smith, Willaim A. '74 (BRK) [100] Brooklyn, NY Our Lady of Lourdes Church.
Smith, William *glmy.* '47 (CIN) [M] Cincinnati, OH Headquarters of Glenmary Home Missioners.
Smith, William *o.carm.* '54 (FgM) Carmelite Foreign Missions.
Smith, William *o.carm.* '54 (JOL) [J] Darien, IL Carmelite Provincial Office.
Smith, William '78 (BRK) [59] Brooklyn, NY Holy Rosary Church.
Smith, Msgr. William B. '66 (NY) [A] Yonkers, NY St. Joseph's Seminary.
Smith, William C. '45 (HRT) Retired.
Smith, William F. '52 (JOL) Gibson City, IL Our Lady of Lourdes Church.
Smith, William J. '47 (PH) Downingtown, PA St. Joseph Church; Retired.
Smith, Msgr. William J. '60 (NY) [130] Bronx, NY St. Athanasius Church.
Smith, William J. '81 (MET) Blairstown, NJ St. Jude Church.
Smith, William L. *c.s.p.* (DEN) Glenwood Springs, CO St. Stephen Church.
Smith, William P. (BO) Lexington, MA St. Brigid Church; Tewksbury, MA St. William Church.
Smith, Wilton S. '58 (SFR) [4] South San Francisco, CA St. Veronica Church.
Smits, Joseph B. *c.i.c.m.* '56 (PH) [C] Gwynedd Valley, PA Gwynedd-Mercy College.
Smits, Kenneth *o.f.m.cap.* '64 (MAD) [F] Madison, WI St. Marys Hospital Medical Center.
Smits, Lambert H. '48 (DET) Royal Oak, MI Shrine of the Little Flower Church.
Smits, Pete *s.v.d.* '41 (BLX) [A] Bay St. Louis, MS St. Augustine's.
Smochko, Basil '46 (PRM) Retired.
Smolarski, Dennis C. *s.j.* '79 (SJ) [B] Santa Clara, CA Santa Clara University.
Smolenski, Stanley '68 (HRT) [4] Enfield, CT St. Martha's Church.
Smoley, Rudolph F. '69 (PIT) [1] Carnegie, PA St. Elizabeth Ann Seton Church.
Smolich, Thomas H. *s.j.* '86 (FgM) Jesuit Foreign Missions.
Smolich, Thomas H. *s.j.* '86 (SJ) [L] Los Gatos, CA California Province of the Society of Jesus, Jesuit Provincial Office; [L] Los Gatos, CA California Province of the Society of Jesus, Jesuit Provincial Office; [L] Los Gatos, CA Sacred Heart Jesuit Center.
Smolinski, Arcadius *o.f.m.* '47 (GB) [I] Pulaski, WI Assumption of B.V.M. Friary.
Smolinski, Clarence D. '53 (GAY) Retired.
Smolinski, Joseph J. '48 (NY) Retired.
Smolko, John F. '57 (BGP) On Duty Outside the Diocese.
Smolko, John F. '57 (WDC) [C] Washington, DC Catholic University of America, The.
Smolley, Robert J. '82 (STF) Terryville, CT St. Michael Church.
Smoot, K. Robert '95 (STL) Richmond Heights, MO St. Luke the Evangelist Church.
Smuda, Alfred J. *o.s.f.s.* '66 (FgM) Oblates of St. Francis de Sales Foreign Missions.
Smulders, Raphael *ss.cc.* '34 (HON) [G] Kaneohe, HI Sacred Hearts Center.
Smullen, Martin J. '82 (NO) [16] New Orleans, LA Our Lady of Good Counsel Church.
Smutelovic, Peter '95 (NEW) North Arlington, NJ Queen of Peace Church.
Smutko, Gregory *o.f.m.cap.* '58 (FgM) Capuchin Foreign Missions.
Smutny, Jan '42 (GI) Retired.
Smutny, Wenceslaus J. *c.ss.r.* '53 (PH) [25] Philadelphia, PA St. Boniface Church.
Smyer, Msgr. Francis (AMA) [10] Amarillo, TX St. Mary's Church.
Smyka, James *o.f.m.conv.* '73 (BGP) [14] Bridgeport, CT St. Michael The Archangel Church.
Smylie, Benjamin '85 (TYL) Longview, TX St. Anthony Church.
Smyth, Henry J. '50 (PH) Retired.
Smyth, James '56 (NY) Hastings-on-Hudson, NY St. Matthew Church.
Smyth, James '57 (NY) Retired.
Smyth, John *c.ss.r.* '64 (CHL) Concord, NC St. James Church.
Smyth, John P. '62 (CHI) [H] Des Plaines, IL Maryville Academy; [X] Chicago, IL Catholic Youth, Archdiocese of Chicago.
Smyth, Joseph P. '59 (BO) Senior Priests.
Sneck, William J. *s.j.* '71 (ALN) [A] Wernersville, PA Jesuit Center; [N] Wernersville, PA Jesuit Center for Spiritual Growth.
Sneck, William J. *s.j.* '71 (BAL) [B] Baltimore, MD Loyola College in Maryland.
Snedeker, Arthur '74 (CLV) Cleveland, OH Metro Health Medical Center & Rehabilitation Center.
Snell, Roger K. '72 (FAR) Retired.
Sneyd, Derrick '70 (FTW) [3] Mishawaka, IN St. Monica Church.
Snider, Harold *o.f.m.cap.* (LA) [F] La Canada Flintridge, CA St. Francis High School.
Snieg, Marion J. '55 (CHI) [M] Wheeling, IL Addolorata Villa.
Snieg, Peter '93 (CHI) [153] Chicago, IL Our Lady of Mount Carmel Church; [A] Chicago, IL Archbishop Quigley Preparatory Seminary.
Sniezyk, Msgr. Richard S. '62 (SPR) [16] Springfield, MA St. Mary's Church.
Snincak, Stephen A. '35 (WH) Retired.
Sniosek, Jaroslav '98 (VEN) Port Charlotte, FL St. Charles Borromeo Church.
Snipes, Roy Lee *o.m.i.* '80 (BWN) [1] Mission, TX Our Lady of Guadalupe Church.
Snock, Bernard C. '62 (GAL) Frydek, TX St. Mary's Church.
Snock, Francis '50 (Y) Retired.
Snodgrass, Thomas A. '76 (CIN) [1] Cincinnati, OH St. Peter in Chains Church.
Snoeren, Cornelius M. *m.h.m.* '52 (NY) [DD] Hartsdale, NY Mill Hill Fathers Residence.
Snoich, Stephen *o.s.b.* '72 (IND) [J] St. Meinrad, IN St. Meinrad Archabbey.
Snoke, F. Richard '65 (COL) Danville, OH St. Luke Church.
Snouffer, Philip T. '62 (BAL) Retired.
Snow, Glen *o.carm.* '89 (CHI) [D] Chicago, IL Mt. Carmel High School; [N] Chicago, IL Carmelite Priory of St. Cyril.
Snow, Msgr. Harry K. '77 (OG) [1] Ogdensburg, NY St. Mary's Church.
Snow, J. Lee '55 (OG) Retired.
Snow, Lorn *s.j.* '99 (CLV) University Heights, OH Gesu Church.
Snyder, Alexander '59 (OAK) Retired.
Snyder, Brian '79 (SEA) Special Assignment.
Snyder, Chester P. '77 (HBG) Mechanicsburg, PA St. Joseph Church.
Snyder, Clatus E. '34 (BUF) Retired.
Snyder, Donald E. '73 (CLV) Westlake, OH St. Ladislas Church.
Snyder, Edward J. *s.j.* '52 (NEW) [C] Jersey City, NJ St. Peter's Preparatory School.
Snyder, Edward J. *s.j.* '52 (NY) [DD] New York, NY Jesuit Provincial's Office.
Snyder, Frederick '52 (GI) Retired.
Snyder, Gary B. (SC) [7] Sioux City, IA St. Joseph Church.
Snyder, Joachim J. *o.carm.* '48 (NY) [DD] Scarborough, NY Carmelite Fathers, NY Prov. of St. Elias.
Snyder, John F. *s.j.* '55 (STL) [P] St. Louis, MO Jesuit Community Corporation at St. Louis University - Jesuit Hall; [V] St. Louis, MO Jesuit Community - Ministries.
Snyder, Msgr. John R. '54 (E) Retired.
Snyder, Larry J. '88 (STP) Special Assignment.
Snyder, Michael E. '97 (BLX) [6] Biloxi, MS St. John Church; [7] Biloxi, MS St. Louis Church.
Snyder, Michael J. *m.m.* '78 (FgM) Maryknoll(M.M.).
Snyder, Michael J. *m.m.* '78 (NY) [DD] Maryknoll, NY Maryknoll Fathers and Brothers.
Snyders, William J. *s.j.* '66 (STL) [P] St. Louis, MO De Smet Jesuit High School Community.
Snyderwine, L. Thomas '68 (E) [23] Erie, PA St. Luke Church; Erie, PA Erie County Geriatric Center Annex.
Snyers, Peter '53 (SCL) [6] St. Cloud, MN St. John Cantius Church.
Soares, Bernaro Manuel '54 (MRY) Retired.
Soares, John P. '92 (PRO) [S] South Kingstown, RI University of Rhode Island Catholic Center.
Soares, Manuel (FRS) [C] Los Banos, CA New Bethany.
Soares, Msgr. Nicholas J. '64 (NY) [203] Staten Island, NY St. Clement Church; [215] Staten Island, NY St. Michael Church.
Sobczak, Marek W. '81 (HRT) [4] Ansonia, CT St. Joseph's Church.
Sobejano, Jesus *o.a.r.* '51 (NY) [DD] New York, NY Augustinian Recollects Provincial Residence, Province of St. Nicholas of Tolentine.
Soberal, Jose Diman (SJN) [A] Bayamon, PR Bayamon Central University.
Soberick, George J. '62 (MAN) Lakeport, NH Our Lady of the Lakes Church.
Sobhasundar, Isaac (ATL) Lawrenceville, GA St. Marguerite D'Youville Church.
Sobiech, Stanley *o.f.m.conv.* '62 (BO) [6] Lawrence, MA Holy Trinity Church.
Sobiecki, Peter S. '66 (HRT) [2] New Britain, CT Holy Cross Church.
Sobierajski, Msgr. Edward J. '61 (BUF) Retired; [O] Tonawanda, NY O'Hara Residence.
Sobierajski, Joseph A. *s.j.* '74 (CHL) [9] Charlotte, NC St. Peter Church; [J] Charlotte, NC Jesuit Community.
Sobiesiak, Msgr. Joseph R. '76 (ALN) [6] Allentown, PA Our Lady of Mt. Carmel Church; [9] Allentown, PA Sacred Heart of Jesus Church; [C] Allentown, PA Allentown Central Catholic High School.
Sobolewski, Edward F. '69 (CAM) National Park, NJ St. Matthew's Church.
Sobon, Walter A. '67 (PIT) Ingram, PA Ascension Church.
Sobotka, DePaul *o.f.m.* '63 (GB) [J] Manitowoc, WI Holy Family Convent of Franciscan Sisters of Christian Charity.
Sobr, Clement *o.s.b.* '51 (JOL) [J] Lisle, IL St. Procopius Abbey.
Sobr, Clement *o.s.b.* '51 (SUP) [C] Fifield, WI King of Martyrs Priory.
Sobus, James M. '86 (WH) [10] Wheeling, WV St. Michael's Church.
Socha, Bronislaw F. *o.c.d.* '89 (GRY) [J] Munster, IN Discalced Carmelite Fathers Monastery.
Socha, Mikolaj *o.s.p.p.e.* '93 (PH) [AA] Doylestown, PA Pauline Fathers Monastery, Shrine of Our Lady of Czestochowa.
Sochacki, Pawel '93 (NY) [228] Staten Island, NY St. Stanislaus Kostka Church.
Sochacki, Walter L. '68 (STP) Roseville, MN St. Rose of Lima Church.
Socias, James '78 (CHI) [W] Chicago, IL Northview University Center.
Sockol, Timothy '77 (PMB) On Duty Outside the Diocese.
Sodano, Ralph H. '67 (PAT) Schooley's Mountain, NJ Our Lady of the Mountain Church.
Sodano, Thomas M. '91 (PH) [32] Philadelphia, PA St. Cecilia Church.
Soderlund, David '65 (ALN) Unassigned.
Sodini, Pierre G. '68 (PIT) Avella, PA St. Michael Church.
Sodja, Richard H. '65 (HEL) Bigfork, MT St. Catherine Church.
Sodomora, John *c.ss.r.* '78 (BAL) Annapolis, MD St. Mary Church; [S] Annapolis, MD Saint Mary Rectory.
Sodoro, Carl F. '77 (OM) [5] Omaha, NE St. Anthony Church; [L] Omaha, NE Sisters of the Annunciation of the Archdiocese of Omaha.
Soehner, Mark *o.f.m.* '87 (DET) [3] Detroit, MI St. Aloysius Church.
Soerries, Denis *o.s.b.* '56 (LR) Paris, AR St. Joseph's Church.
Sofie, J. Francis, Jr. '94 (MOB) Eufaula, AL Holy Redeemer Church; Clayton, AL Ventress Correctional Institution; Union Springs, AL Bullock County Correctional Facility.
Sogliuzzo, Gerard W. '79 (NEW) Union, NJ St. Michael's Church.
Sogliuzzo, Louis P. *s.j.* '87 (PAT) [I] Morristown, NJ Loyola House of Retreats.
Soha, Roderick *t.o.r.* '95 (ORL) [2] Lakeland, FL St. Anthony's Church; [E] Lakeland, FL Florida Southern College Newman Center.
Sohm, John E. '58 (SFD) Sullivan, IL St. Columcille Church.
Soileau, Charles '57 (LKC) Retired.
Soisson, Clifford F. '37 (PIT) Retired; [O] Pittsburgh, PA St. John Vianney Manor.
Sojka, Jeremiusz H. '95 (RIC) Salem, VA Our Lady of Perpetual Help Church.
Sojka, Louis L. *o.s.b.* '90 (OM) [C] Elkhorn, NE Mount Michael High School; [K] Elkhorn, NE Mount Michael Abbey.
Sokalski, Michael *o.f.m.conv.* '59 (BRK) [61] Brooklyn, NY Most Holy Trinity Church.
Sokol, Stanley '85 (SPR) [10] Springfield, MA Our Lady of the Rosary Church.
Sokolowski, Bernard T. '45 (BUF) [4] Cheektowaga, NY St. Josaphat Church; Retired.
Sokolowski, Edward V. '44 (SCR) Retired.
Sokolowski, Robert S. '61 (WDC) [C] Washington, DC Catholic University of America, The.
Sokolowski, Msgr. Robert S. '65 (HRT) On Duty Outside the Archdiocese.
Sokolowski, Thomas J. '79 (SCR) East Stroudsburg, PA St. Matthew's Church.
Sokolowski, Waclaw *o.f.m.conv.* '84 (PAT) [6] Clifton, NJ St. John Kanty Church.
Sokolowski, William R. '65 (HRT) Wolcott, CT St. Maria Goretti Church.
Sokolski, John '55 (SAT) [K] San Antonio, TX Oblate Madonna Residence.
Sola, Jeronimo *c.m.* '35 (SJN) [60] San Juan, PR San Vicente de Paul Church.
Solan, Lawrence T. '80 (COS) Highlands Ranch, CO St. Mark Church.
Solana, Fermin '70 (MIA) [11] Miami, FL Our Lady of Divine Providence Church.
Solano, Julio '93 (MIA) [5] Pompano Beach, FL St. Elizabeth of Hungary Catholic Church.
Solano-Uribe, Jose Maria '96 (SJN) [5] Toa Baja, PR San Pedro Apostol Church.
Solari, James K. '55 (CHL) Retired.
Solarski, Jack '76 (DAL) [J] Irving, TX Opus Dei.

Solazzo, Michael J. '76 (CHI) Evanston, IL St. Mary Church.
Solcia, Louis M. *c.r.s.p.* '57 (SD) [15] San Diego, CA Our Lady of the Rosary Church.
Soldo, Slavko *o.f.m.* '72 (CHI) [N] Chicago, IL Croatian Franciscan Custody of the Holy Family.
Soler, Lawrence *t.o.r.* '51 (AUS) [1] Waco, TX Sacred Heart Church.
Soler, Luis A. '67 (SP) Plant City, FL St. Clement Church.
Soler, Roberto '62 (MGZ) Aguada, PR Santuario Protomartires de la Concepcion Church.
Soles, John '64 (BRK) [U] Brooklyn, NY Catholic Migration & Refugee Office, Catholic Migration Services, Inc.
Soles, Juan '64 (NY) [75] New York, NY St. Michael Chapel Church; Federal, NY Metropolitan Correctional Center.
Soleta, Chester A. *c.s.c.* '42 (FTW) [J] South Bend, IN Congregation of Holy Cross, Indiana Province, Provincial House.
Soley, Roger A. '78 (WDC) Huntingtown, MD Jesus the Divine Word Church.
Solis, Marco T. '97 (LA) Lomita, CA St. Margaret Mary Alacoque Church.
Solis, Oscar '79 (HT) [1] Thibodaux, LA St. Joseph Co-Church; [6] Thibodaux, LA St. Luke Church.
Solis, Ralph, Jr. '93 (ELP) Horizon City, TX Holy Spirit Church.
Solis, Sergio '00 (CHI) [4] Waukegan, IL Holy Family Church.
Solivan, Roberto '88 (CGS) Comerio, PR Santo Cristo de la Salud Church.
Solla, Santiago '53 (PCE) Juana Diaz, PR St. Raymond Nonato Church.
Solma, Martin A. *s.m.* '78 (CIN) [M] Dayton, OH Marianist Provincialate.
Soloman, Louis E. *s.j.* '64 (NY) [DD] New York, NY Murray-Weigel Hall.
Solomia, Paul '59 (DM) [D] Des Moines, IA Mercy Medical Center.
Soloranzo, Miguel A. '93 (GAL) [70] Houston, TX St. Philip of Jesus Church.
Solors, Stephen '91 (DUL) Bigfork, MN Our Lady of the Snows Church.
Solorzano, Marcelo *o.p.* '95 (SAT) [26] San Antonio, TX St. Ann Church; [B] San Antonio, TX Dominican Priory of San Juan Macias.
Soltis, John F. *m.m.* '62 (FgM) Maryknoll Foreign Missions.
Soltys, Daniel F. '68 (OM) Gretna, NE St. Patrick Church.
Soltys, Raymond A. '79 (SPR) [1] Ludlow, MA Christ the King Church.
Somarriba, Marcos '93 (MIA) [33] Miami, FL St. Timothy Church.
Somers, Eldon K. '51 (E) Retired.
Somers, Michael '82 (GB) Absent on Leave.
Somers, Richard '66 (JKS) Greenville, MS St. Joseph Church.
Somerville, Alvin *o.f.m.conv.* '58 (ALB) [4] Albany, NY St. Casimir Church; [12] Albany, NY Our Lady of Angels Church.
Somerville, Walter F. (CHI) Retired.
Somma, James E. '59 (PIT) Pitcairn, PA St. Michael Church; Allegheny County, PA West Penn Allegheny Health System-Forbes Regional.
Sommer, Allan J. '66 (MIL) Port Washington, WI St. Mary Church.
Sommer, Gerald J. *m.s.c.* '47 (Y) [9] Canton, OH St. Mary Church; [A] Youngstown, OH Sacred Heart Retreat House & Renewal Center.
Sommer, Harold *s.j.* '65 (CIN) [M] Cincinnati, OH Faber Jesuit Community.
Sommer, Msgr. Jerome '40 (JC) Retired.
Sommer, Msgr. Jerome '40 (STL) Retired.
Sommer, Kenneth J. *s.m.* '59 (CIN) [M] Dayton, OH Marianist Provincialate.
Sommer, Ralph '83 (RVC) Hauppauge, NY St. Thomas More Church.
Sommermeyer, Gary '91 (BRK) [58] Brooklyn, NY Holy Name Church.
Sommers, Edward P. '73 (CAM) [4] Vineland, NJ St. Isidore Church; On Sick Leave.
Sommerville, Conrad *o.f.m.conv.* '54 (SY) [2] Syracuse, NY Assumption B.V.M. Church.
Sommerville, William '93 (GAL) Freeport, TX St. Mary: Star of the Sea Church.
Somos, Joseph '59 (STL) Retired.
Somoza, Jose I. *o.f.m.* '65 (WDC) [33] Washington, DC Our Lady Queen of the Americas Church.
Son, Kyungsu *m.m.* '79 (FgM) Maryknoll Foreign Missions.
Son, Nguyen Thanh *c.ss.r.* '85 (LA) [Q] Baldwin Park, CA Vietnamese Redemptorist Mission.
Son, Nguyen That '90 (WH) Oak Hill, WV SS. Peter and Paul Church.
Son Le, Peter Ha '74 (LA) Santa Fe Springs, CA St. Pius X Church.
Sondergeld, Theodore '59 (SEA) Retired.
Sonderman, Msgr. James '45 (AMA) [D] Panhandle, TX St. Ann's Nursing Home.
Sonderman, Msgr. James W. '45 (AMA) Retired.
Sondgeroth, Louis *o.m.i.* '57 (DUL) International Falls, MN St. Thomas Aquinas Church; Littlefork, MN St. Columban Church.
Sonefeld, Raymond G. '48 (KAL) Retired.
Songy, David *o.f.m.cap.* '87 (DEN) [M] Denver, CO St. Francis of Assisi Friary.
Songy, Msgr. Donald J. '53 (BR) [20] Baton Rouge, LA Sacred Heart of Jesus Church; Retired.
Songy, Msgr. James B. '54 (HT) Retired.
Sonnberger, Albert W. '56 (LC) Retired.
Sonnier, Cedric (LAF) Henry, LA St. John Church.
Sonnier, Cedric '97 (LAF) Abbeville, LA St. Mary Magdalen Church.
Sonnier, Charles '64 (VIC) Koerth, TX St. John the Baptist Church; Sweet Home, TX Queen of Peace Church.
Sonnier, T. Alcide '56 (LAF) Chataignier, LA Our Lady of Mount Carmel Church; Retired.
Sontheimer, Msgr. W. Wendell '47 (NO) Retired.
Soo Kim, Andrew Moon '98 (BRK) [36] Brooklyn, NY St. Ephrem's Church.
Soon-Sin Park, Francis X. '82 (ARL) Fairfax, VA St. Paul Chung Church.
Soper, Paul R. '90 (BO) [15] Lowell, MA St. Rita Church; [CC] Lowell, MA The Catholic Center U Mass, Lowell.
Sopiak, Donald A. '78 (DET) [59] Detroit, MI Our Lady Queen of Heaven Church.
Sopke, Philip *c.s.c.* '88 (OAK) [3] Hayward, CA St. Clement Church.
Sopoliga, Michael '79 (PSC) Fort Pierce, FL SS. Cyril and Methodius Church.
Sopp, Michael '75 (SJP) Ford City, PA St. Mary Church.
Soprano, Ernest R. '79 (CAM) [3] Vineland, NJ St. Francis of Assisi Church.
Soprych, Marion '75 (CHI) [24] Chicago, IL St. Bede the Venerable Church.
Soranno, Joseph M. '74 (SPR) Wilbraham, MA St. Cecilia's Church.
Sorce, John J. '61 (CHR) Absent On Leave.
Sorci, Msgr. Francis P. '42 (BUF) Retired.
Sordillo, Ronald T. '74 (PAT) Parsippany, NJ St. Peter the Apostle Church.
Sorensen, Bartley A. '76 (PIT) Bairdford, PA St. Victor Church.
Sorgie, Anthony '82 (NY) [133] Bronx, NY St. Benedict Church.
Sorgon, Rey N. '82 (LUB) O'Donnell, TX St. Pius X Church.
Soria, Manuel B. '81 (SAC) Yuba City, CA St. Isidore Church.
Soria, Santiago *o.c.d.* '59 (PCE) [12] Ponce, PR San Jose Church.
Soriano, Danilo '78 (JOL) [5] Naperville, IL St. Margaret Mary Church.
Soriano, Eugene '52 (BRK) [154] Queens, NY St. Bartholomew's Church; [U] Brooklyn, NY Catholic Migration & Refugee Office, Catholic Migration Services, Inc.
Soriano, Jesus '70 (SAC) Vallejo, CA St. Catherine of Siena Church.
Soriso, Emmanuel A. '93 (NEW) Nutley, NJ Our Lady of Mount Carmel Church.
Sork, Msgr. David A. '70 (LA) Rancho Palos Verdes, CA St. John Fisher Church.
Sorohan, Msgr. David V. '59 (COL) [8] Columbus, OH St. Catharine Church.
Sors, Vladimir '28 (PEO) Retired.
Sorvillo, Mark B. '78 (CHI) [118] Chicago, IL St. Margaret Mary Church.
Sosa, Carlos '89 (MIL) On Leave.
Sosa, Juan J. '72 (MIA) [17] Miami, FL St. Catherine of Siena Church.
Sosa, Philip *m.s.f.* '68 (BWN) Donna, TX St. Joseph Church.
Soseman, Richard '92 (PEO) Princeville, IL St. Mary of the Woods Church.
Sosinski, Thomas P. '58 (MAD) Absent on Sick Leave.
Sostrich, John L. '62 (SD) Retired.
Sota, P. Pascual *c.m.* '56 (SJN) [60] San Juan, PR San Vicente de Paul Church.
Sotak, Donald J. '62 (PIT) Natrona, PA St. Joseph Church.
Sotak, John J. *o.s.a.* '92 (TLS) [B] Tulsa, OK Cascia Hall Preparatory School.
Sotelo, A. Richard *s.j.* '87 (BAL) [S] Baltimore, MD Jesuit Fathers and Brothers Maryland Provincial Curia.
Sotelo, Andrew *s.j.* '82 (SB) [B] San Bernardino, CA Aquinas High School.
Sotelo, Angel '91 (FRS) Frazier Park, CA Our Lady of the Snows Church.
Sotelo-Pena, Fabio '99 (ATL) [1] Atlanta, GA Cathedral of Christ the King.
Sotiroff, Stephen T. '81 (SFD) Vandalia, IL Mother of Dolors Church.
Sotiroff, Steven '81 (SFD) Ramsey, IL St. Joseph Church.
Soto, Calixto '85 (SJN) [3] Toa Alta, PR San Jose Church.
Soto, Carlos R. '99 (CGS) Las Piedras, PR Inmaculada Concepcion Church.
Soto, Charles *o.f.m.* '70 (NY) [DD] New York, NY Franciscan Province of the Immaculate Conception.
Soto, Edward '58 (LA) Maywood, CA St. Rose of Lima Church.
Soto, Gilberto '90 (DEN) Longmont, CO St. John the Baptist Church.
Soto, Jose *m.d.r.* '79 (NY) [135] Bronx, NY St. Brendan Church.
Soto, Jose L. *m.d.r.* '80 (NY) [172] Bronx, NY Our Lady of Grace Church.
Soto, Roberto Angel '95 (CGS) Gurabo, PR San Jose Church.
Soto Barreto, Angel L. '92 (MGZ) Rincon, PR St. Rose of Lima Church.
Sottek, James J. *o.s.f.s.* '57 (TOL) [K] Toledo, OH Oblates of St. Francis de Sales.
Soucey, Louis A. '74 (MAN) North Conway, NH Our Lady of the Mountains Church; Retired.
Soucie, Edward *s.j.* '62 (MI) Ebeye, MH Queen of Peace Church.
Soucie, Edward A. *s.j.* '62 (FgM) Provinces.
Soucy, A. Francis *o.f.m.* '67 (PAT) [M] Ringwood, NJ Holy Name Friary, Inc.
Soucy, Bertrand *s.m.* '53 (FgM) Marist Foreign Missions.
Soucy, D. Wilfrid '30 (PRT) Retired.
Soucy, Neil *s.m.* '62 (FgM) Marist Foreign Missions.
Soucy, Robert P. '62 (BO) Senior Priests.
Soucy, Timothy J. '73 (OG) Lake Clear, NY St. John in the Wilderness Church; Saranac Lake, NY St. Bernard Church.
Soukup, Gervase *o.s.b.* '45 (SCL) [I] Collegeville, MN St. John's Abbey, of the Order of St. Benedict.
Soukup, Gregory *o.s.b.* '41 (SCL) [I] Collegeville, MN St. John's Abbey, of the Order of St. Benedict.
Soukup, Paul A. *s.j.* '79 (SJ) San Jose, CA Catholic Scouting; [B] Santa Clara, CA Santa Clara University.
Soule, Becket *o.p.* '93 (WDC) [11] Washington, DC St. Dominic Church & Priory Church.
Soulliere, Richard '76 (MIA) Retired.
Soupos, Christopher '80 (SB) Colton, CA Immaculate Conception Church; On Leave.
Sousa, Douglas H. '91 (FR) Absent on Leave.
Sousa, Eugene W. *o.p.* '58 (SAC) Benicia, CA St. Dominic Church.
Sousa, Jose '85 (FR) [20] Fall River, MA St. Patrick's Church.
Sousa, Manuel F. '80 (STO) Turlock, CA Our Lady of the Assumption of the Portuguese Church.
Sousa, Peter E. *c.ss.r.* '78 (BRK) [C] Whitestone, NY St. Alphonsus Formation Residence.
Souse, Stephen J. *o.s.b.* '40 (PEO) [A] Peru, IL St. Bede Abbey and Academy; [C] Peru, IL St. Bede Academy.
Southerton, Gary '88 (SEA) Puyallup, WA Holy Disciples Church.
Soutiere, Ronald A. '74 (BUR) Milton, VT St. Ann Church.
Soutus, Hugo '94 (STN) Phoenix, AZ Assumption of B.V.M. Church.
Soutuyo, Raul '93 (MIA) [16] Miami, FL St. Brendan Church.
Souva, Eileen *o.p.* (LAN) [1] Jackson, MI St. John the Evangelist Church.
Souza, Jason A. '98 (LA) Norwalk, CA St. John of God Church.
Sowada, Arlie '73 (SCL) Brown's Valley, MN St. Anthony's Church.
Sowinski, Albin (MIL) [N] Wauwatosa, WI St. Camillus Health Center, Inc.
Sowinski, Albin F. '51 (MIL) Retired.
Sowinski, Richard E. '74 (BUF) Kenmore, NY St. Paul Church.
Soy, Esteban '52 (VEN) Retired.
Soyka, Giles *o.f.m.cap.* '50 (GB) [I] Appleton, WI St. Fidelis Friary.
Spacek, Frank W. '97 (BRK) [204] Queens, NY Nativity of the Blessed Virgin Mary Church.
Spacek, William F. (BAL) [5] Baltimore, MD St. Alphonsus, Shrine of Church.
Spacek, William F. '95 (BAL) Baltimore, MD University of Maryland Hospital; Special Assignment.
Spacht, Andres *c.ss.r.* (CGS) [1] Caguas, PR Cathedral Dulce Nombre de Jesus Church.
Spadaro, Thomas L. '64 (RVC) Holbrook, NY Good Shepherd Church.
Spadini, Marian '62 (JKS) On Duty Outside the Diocese.
Spadini, Marian '62 (MEM) [22] Memphis, TN Our Lady Of Perpetual Help Church.
Spagnolia, D. George '68 (BO) [13] Lowell, MA St. Patrick Church.
Spagnolo, Michael G. '00 (CAM) Blackwood, NJ St. Agnes Church.
Spagnolo, Nicholas *c.s.s.* '52 (BO) [W] Waltham, MA Stigmatine House.
Spahn, James *o.p.* '81 (FgM) Dominican - Order of

Preachers Foreign Missions.
Spahn, James A. *o.p.* '81 (CHI) [N] Chicago, IL Dominicans (Provincial Office).
Spahn, James S. '00 (DEN) Centennial, CO St. Thomas More Church.
Spahn, Steve *s.j.* (BAL) [B] Baltimore, MD Loyola College in Maryland.
Spahr, Matthew '92 (SD) [B] San Diego, CA University of San Diego.
Spahr, Matthew D. '92 (SD) Alpine, CA Queen of Angels Church.
Spain, John H. *m.m.* '70 (FgM) Maryknoll Foreign Missions.
Spain, P. Arnold '47 (BIS) Retired.
Spajic, Zdenko '94 (WDC) [9] Washington, DC St. Blaise Church.
Spalatin, Christopher A. *s.j.* '71 (FgM) Provinces.
Spalding, Francis Larry '80 (L) On Special Assignment.
Spalding, J. Mark '91 (L) LaGrange, KY Immaculate Conception Church.
Spalding, Leon C. '59 (L) [1] Springfield, KY St. Dominic Church.
Spalding, William '45 (GB) Retired.
Spanel, Hubert J. '59 (GI) Hemingford, NE St. Bridget Church.
Spanier, Marian '81 (NEW) [4] Garfield, NJ St. Stanislaus Kostka Church.
Spanjers, John J. '59 (SUP) Turtle Lake, WI St. Ann Church.
Spanley, Anthony L. '68 (GRY) Hamlet, IN Holy Cross Church.
Spano, Philip F. '82 (BR) Gonzales, LA St. Theresa of Avila Church.
Sparacino, Thomas A. '98 (PIT) Ross Township, PA St. Sebastian Church.
Sparklin, Paul (BAL) [41] Baltimore, MD Immaculate Conception Church.
Sparks, Joseph R. '66 (DAV) Solon, IA St. Mary's Church.
Sparks, Kenneth A. '95 (PIT) Canonsburg, PA St. Patrick Church.
Sparks, Richard *c.s.p.* '78 (OAK) [2] Berkeley, CA Holy Spirit Parish/Newman Hall Church.
Sparks, Timothy H. *o.p.* '30 (CHI) [N] River Forest, IL St. Thomas Aquinas Priory.
Sparough, J. Michael *s.j.* '78 (CHI) [C] Chicago, IL Jesuit Community at Loyola University of Chicago.
Spatorico, Joseph S. '66 (BUF) [1] Batavia, NY St. Anthony Church.
Spatt, John *c.pp.s.* '43 (CIN) [B] Carthagena, OH St. Charles.
Spaulding, Donald E. '57 (EVN) Retired.
Spaulding, John '71 (PHX) [25] Phoenix, AZ St. Thomas the Apostle Church.
Speaks, John '74 (OWN) Non-Parochial Assignments; [E] Owensboro, KY Carmel Home.
Speaks, Sidney *s.s.j.* '99 (BEA) [7] Beaumont, TX Our Mother of Mercy Church.
Specht, Joseph E. *s.j.* '69 (HON) [E] Honolulu, HI St. Francis Healthcare System of Hawaii; [G] Honolulu, HI Jesuit Fathers House.
Specht, Terry W. '96 (ARL) Fairfax, VA St. Leo's Church; [D] Fairfax, VA Paul VI High School.
Speck, Gregory M. *s.c.j.* '76 (BWN) Raymondville, TX Our Lady of Guadalupe Church.
Speck, James A. '50 (WIN) Retired.
Speckman, Harry *o.f.m.* '61 (GAY) Indian River, MI Cross in the Woods Catholic Church.
Speer, Patrick J. '41 (BGP) [L] Trumbull, CT St. Joseph's Manor.
Speer, Patrick J. '41 (HRT) Retired.
Speerstra, William F. '59 (SUP) Retired.
Speice, Msgr. Lawrence T. '61 (E) Cambridge Springs, PA St. Anthony Church; [A] Erie, PA St. Mark's Seminary.
Speicher, Charles W. '75 (PIT) Unity, PA St. John the Baptist Church.
Speicher, David J. '86 (LAN) East Lansing, MI St. Thomas Aquinas Church.
Speichinger, Lawrence '55 (KC) Retired.
Speier, Francis J. '75 (TOL) [27] Toledo, OH St. John the Baptist Church.
Speier, Thomas *o.f.m.* '58 (CIN) [22] Cincinnati, OH Corpus Christi Church.
Speiser, Allan '48 (SCL) Retired.
Speiser, Thomas M. '77 (DAL) Plano, TX St. Mark the Evangelist Church.
Speitel, Edmond J. '55 (PH) Retired.
Spekschate, John '42 (LAF) Retired.
Spelgatti, Msgr. David P. '41 (MAR) Retired.
Spellen, Lawrence M. '46 (SLC) Retired.
Spellerberg, Joseph R. *s.j.* '53 (BUF) [50] Buffalo, NY St. Michael Church.
Spellman, Francis J. '40 (CHI) [4] Cicero, IL Mary, Queen of Heaven Church; Retired.
Spellman, John P. *o.s.f.s.* '66 (WIL) [B] Wilmington, DE Salesianum School; [I] Wilmington, DE Oblates of St. Francis De Sales.
Spellman, Robert M. '74 (WOR) Berlin, MA St. Joseph the Good Provider Church.
Spenard, James *o.s.a.* '72 (ALB) [2] Troy, NY St. Augustine Church.
Spencer, F. Richard '88 (BAL) Military Chaplains.
Spencer, Francis M. *m.s.* '50 (MAN) [2] Nashua, NH St. Casimir Church.
Spencer, Gregory D. '89 (R) Morehead City, NC St. Egbert Church.
Spencer, Jeremiah L. '65 (KCK) [5] Kansas City, KS Holy Name Church; Kansas City, KS K.U. Medical Center and Chapel.
Spencer, John *s.j.* '79 (BO) [W] Chestnut Hill, MA The Jesuit Community at Boston College.
Spencer, Robert '58 (CC) On Special Assignment.
Spencer, Robert A. '98 (CHR) [17] Charleston, SC Christ Our King Church.
Spencer, Robert M. '82 (RIC) Petersburg, VA St. Joseph Church.
Spencer, William *o.f.m.* '74 (SHP) [6] Shreveport, LA St. Catherine of Siena Church.
Spendov, Vendelin *o.f.m.* '47 (CHI) [N] Lemont, IL The Slovene Franciscan Fathers, Order of Friars Minor, Commissariat of the Holy Cross.
Spengler, Msgr. James F. (BRK) [161] Queens, NY St. Catherine of Sienna Church.
Spenner, Jerome I. '64 (OM) [9] Omaha, NE St. Bernard Church.
Speno, Eugene '60 (SB) Retired.
Spera, James F. '77 (NEW) [B] South Orange, NJ Seton Hall University; [B] South Orange, NJ Seton Hall University.
Sperber, Timothy '78 (HBG) On Duty Outside the Diocese.
Sperger, Herbert J. '79 (PH) [69] Philadelphia, PA Immaculate Conception Church; [104] Philadelphia, PA St. Michael Church.
Sperl, August J. '54 (SFD) Palmyra, IL Holy Rosary Church; Virden, IL Sacred Heart Church.
Sperlak, Charles S. '64 (ALN) [4] Reading, PA SS. Cyril and Methodius Church.
Sperry, Msgr. James E. '41 (E) Retired.
Spexarth, Daniel J. '84 (WCH) [19] Wichita, KS St. Thomas Aquinas Church.
Spexarth, Fred N. (WCH) [B] Wichita, KS Kapaun Mt. Carmel Catholic High School.
Spexarth, James '55 (WCH) Retired.
Spexarth, Joachim *o.s.b.* '65 (OKL) [I] Shawnee, OK St. Gregory's Abbey.
Speyrer, Jules '45 (LAF) Retired.
Spezia, Leo J. '76 (STL) [41] St. Louis, MO St. John the Baptist Church.
Spezzano, James '97 (YAK) Benton City, WA St. Frances Xavier Cabrini Church.
Spicer, Kevin *c.s.c.* '92 (FR) [A] North Easton, MA Stonehill College.
Spicer, Kevin P. *c.s.c.* '92 (FR) [A] North Easton, MA Holy Cross Fathers Religious.
Spicer, Leo M. *o.s.m.* '76 (CHI) [N] Chicago, IL Order of Friar Servants of Mary (Servites) United States of America Province, Inc.
Spicer, Richard J. '86 (SEA) Arlington, WA Immaculate Conception Church.
Spicuzza, Anthony P. '46 (IND) Brazil, IN Annunciation of the Blessed Virgin Mary Church.
Spiece, Msgr. Lawrence T. '61 (E) [F] Fairview, PA Camp Notre Dame.
Spiegel, John D. '76 (DAV) Ottumwa, IA St. Patrick's Church.
Spiegel, Msgr. Robert H. '66 (DAV) Military Chaplains.
Spiegel, Thomas J. '67 (DAV) Bettendorf, IA Our Lady of Lourdes Church.
Spiekermeier, Michael '69 (DAV) [8] Davenport, IA St. Paul the Apostle Church.
Spieler, Joseph G. *s.j.* '75 (MIL) [67] Milwaukee, WI St. Patrick Church.
Spielman, Paul E. (STL) [51] St. Louis, MO St. Mary of Victories Church.
Spielmann, Henry V. *o.s.a.* '39 (TLS) [B] Tulsa, OK Cascia Hall Preparatory School.
Spielmann, Paul '61 (STL) [42] St. Louis, MO St. John Nepomuk Church.
Spier, Mathias *o.s.b.* '58 (SCL) [I] Collegeville, MN St. John's Abbey, of the Order of St. Benedict.
Spiers, Msgr. Edward F. '39 (COL) Retired.
Spiess, Kevin J. '86 (CHI) [1] Lemont, IL St. Alphonsus Church.
Spilka, Anthony F. *o.f.m.conv.* '69 (E) [4] Sharon, PA St. Stanislaus Kostka Church.
Spillane, Emmanuel *o.c.s.o.* '44 (SLC) [F] Huntsville, UT Abbey of Our Lady of the Holy Trinity of the Order of Cistercians.
Spillane, Michael '68 (BAL) Special Assignment.
Spillane, Walter J. '60 (KAL) Retired.
Spillane, William *c.ss.r.* (CGS) [1] Caguas, PR Cathedral Dulce Nombre de Jesus Church.
Spillett, Thomas '64 (SP) Plant City, FL St. Clement Church.
Spilly, Alphonse *c.pp.s.* '67 (CHI) [B] Chicago, IL The Catholic Theological Union at Chicago.
Spilly, Alphonse *c.pp.s.* '67 (CIN) [M] Dayton, OH Provincial Office of the Cincinnati Province of the Society of the Precious Blood.
Spilly, William V. '74 (ROC) [29] Rochester, NY St. John the Evangelist Church.
Spilman, Robert D. '96 (PEO) Colfax, IL St. Joseph's Church.
Spina, Douglas J. '76 (PRO) [2] Johnston, RI Our Lady of Grace Church.
Spine, William J. *s.j.* '73 (CHI) [C] Chicago, IL Jesuit Community at Loyola University of Chicago.
Spinelli, Joseph A. *o.s.a.* '55 (VEN) Golden Gate, FL St. Elizabeth Seton Church.
Spinler, Ruben C. '94 (WIN) Rose Creek, MN St. Peter's Church.
Spino, John '91 (NEW) Roselle, NJ Church of St. Joseph the Carpenter.
Spinos, Vincent J. *t.o.r.* '50 (STP) [20] Minneapolis, MN St. Bridget Church.
Spinosa, Anthony (OLL) Toledo, OH Maronite Catholic Community Church.
Spinosa, Anthony S. '83 (OLL) Flint, MI Our Lady of Lebanon Church.
Spirko, Nicholas A. '72 (PIT) [2] Bridgeville, PA Holy Child Church.
Spisak, Paul G. '73 (PIT) Allegheny County, PA Vincentian Regency Home; Allegheny County, PA Vincentian Home for the Chronically Ill; [K] Pittsburgh, PA Vincentian Home Inc.; [L] Allison Park, PA Vincentian Regency.
Spisak, Stephen M. '82 (CLV) North Olmsted, OH St. Brendan Church.
Spisak, Thomas M. '77 (Y) [6] Warren, OH St. Mary's Church.
Spishak, Carl A. '59 (ALT) [5] Altoona, PA Holy Rosary Church.
Spitale, John '26 (Y) Retired.
Spiteri, George '70 (NY) Cortlandt Manor, NY St. Columbanus Church; [3] White Plains, NY St. Bernard Church.
Spiteri, Laurence J. *j.c.l.* '78 (LA) Simi Valley, CA St. Rose of Lima Church.
Spittler, Ernest G. *s.j.* '62 (CLV) [B] Cleveland, OH John Carroll Jesuit Community.
Spitz, Gregory M. '67 (MIL) Mequon, WI St. James Church.
Spitzer, Michael H. '98 (PH) Ardsley, PA Queen of Peace Church.
Spitzer, Robert J. *s.j.* '83 (SPK) [C] Spokane, WA Gonzaga University.
Spitzig, Msgr. Joseph '42 (CLV) Retired.
Spitzley, Denis R. '75 (LAN) Charlotte, MI St. Mary Church.
Splain, Thomas E. *s.j.* '71 (FgM) Provinces.
Splawski, Bernard J. *o.f.m.* '63 (PAT) West Milford Township, NJ St. Joseph Church.
Spleet, Julius A. '62 (SAG) Ithaca, MI St. Paul the Apostle Church; Retired.
Splonskowski, Wilfred '52 (GF) Miles City, MT Sacred Heart Church.
Splonskowski, Wilfrid J. *o.s.b.* '52 (BIS) [A] Richardton, ND Assumption Abbey.
Spodnik, A. Leo '48 (HRT) Retired.
Spoletini, Pasquale M. *s.j.* '54 (SEA) [31] Seattle, WA Our Lady of Mount Virgin Church; [L] Seattle, WA Jesuit House, Seattle.
Spolny, Joseph R. '78 (CLV) [1] Lakewood, OH St. Clement Church.
Sponder, John '93 (JOL) Westmont, IL Holy Trinity Church.
Spong, William '79 (FWT) On Duty Outside the Diocese.
Spong, William '79 (ROC) [C] Rochester, NY McQuaid Jesuit High School.
Spontak, James A. '75 (PBR) Charleroi, PA Holy Ghost Church.
Spors, Roman '58 (DUL) Emily, MN St. Emily's Church.
Spotswood, Cecil '97 (MOB) Atmore, AL St. Robert Bellarmine Church.
Sprague, George Raymond '34 (PEO) Retired; [L] Peoria, IL St. Augustine Manor.
Spranger, William J. '56 (GRY) San Pierre, IN All Saints Church; [H] San Pierre, IN Holy Cross Care Services dba Little Company of Mary Health Facility, Inc.
Sprecace, Msgr. Francis A. '55 (CAM) Retired.
Spreen, John W. '53 (SFD) Ashland, IL St. Augustine Church.
Sprenger, Alan H. '60 (COL) Retired.
Sprenger, Alan M. '60 (COL) Westerville, OH St. Paul the Apostle Church.
Spriet, Jules *c.i.c.m.* '34 (FgM) Missionhurst Foreign Missions.
Sprietsma, Leo *o.f.m.* '53 (LA) [Q] Santa Barbara, CA Franciscan Friary, Order of Friars Minor (Old Mission); [Q] Santa Barbara, CA St. Anthony's Seminary.
Spriggs, Robert W. '65 (SFD) Highland, IL St. Paul Church.
Sprigler, William A. '75 (NU) Hutchinson, MN Church of St. Anastasia.
Spring, Mark P. '80 (DAV) Knoxville, IA St. Anthony's Church.
Spring, Mark P. '99 (DAV) Melcher, IA Sacred Heart Church.

Springer, Francis *s.m.* '55 (SFR) [N] San Francisco, CA Marist Center of the West.
Springer, Lawrence F. '59 (CHI) [4] Des Plaines, IL St. Zachary Church.
Springer, Robert *s.j.* '48 (NY) [DD] New York, NY West Side Jesuit Community.
Springer, William A. '72 (SD) [10] San Diego, CA Mission Basilica San Diego De Alcala Church.
Springman, Donald W. '67 (L) [3] Valley Station, KY Our Lady of Consolation Church.
Sprinkle, R. Russell *m.m.* '35 (FgM) Maryknoll Foreign Missions.
Sprott, Robert *o.f.m.* '80 (CHI) [N] Chicago, IL St. Joseph Interprovincial Post-Novitiate Formation House.
Sprouffske, Matthew *o.carm.* '54 (JOL) [J] Darien, IL Carmelite Provincial Office.
Sproul, John M. '63 (SD) La Mesa, CA St. Martin of Tours Church.
Sprute, Mel '69 (B) Kellogg, ID St. Rita's Church; Wallace, ID St. Alphonsus Church.
Spuhler, Gregory *o.f.m.conv.* (CHL) Winston-Salem, NC Our Lady of Mercy Church; [L] Charlotte, NC Diocesan Office of Campus Ministry.
Spychala, Daniel S. '84 (ARL) Falls Church, VA St. Philip Church.
Spyrka, Edward C. *o.c.d.* '62 (GRY) [J] Munster, IN Discalced Carmelite Fathers Monastery.
Squeo, Eugene P. '71 (NEW) [7] Jersey City, NJ Assumption/All Saints Church; [23] Jersey City, NJ St. Patrick's Church.
Squiller, Msgr. John '56 (STF) [A] Stamford, CT St. Basil College.
Srebernak, Francis '37 (LAN) Retired.
Sreboth, Michael J. '86 (MOB) [1] Mobile, AL Cathedral of the Immaculate Conception.
Sredzinski, Joseph L. '70 (GBG) Point Marion, PA St. Hubert Church.
Srenn, Thomas E. '77 (CHI) [97] Chicago, IL St. Jane de Chantal Church.
Srion, Charles '78 (RVC) East Meadow, NY St. Raphael Church.
Srnec, Msgr. Stanley J. '42 (STP) Retired.
Sroba, Andrew (WDC) [1] Rockville, MD St. Elizabeth Church.
Srode, John S. *c.pp.s.* '72 (CIN) [M] Dayton, OH Provincial Office of the Cincinnati Province of the Society of the Precious Blood.
Sroka, Gerald A. '60 (GRY) La Porte, IN Sacred Heart Church.
Srumpf, David *o.f.m.* '90 (CHI) [6] Lemont, IL Blessed A.M. Slomsek Slovenian Catholic Church; [N] Lemont, IL The Slovene Franciscan Fathers, Order of Friars Minor, Commissariat of the Holy Cross.
Ssebadduka, George '78 (LAN) [J] Adrian, MI Motherhouse of the Sisters of St. Dominic.
Ssekiranda, Remigious '98 (VEN) [9] Fort Myers, FL St. Peter Claver Church.
Ssekiwala, Maximus (CHI) [203] Chicago, IL St. Timothy Church.
Ssemakula, Luke '97 (OAK) [1] Hayward, CA All Saints Church.
Sserwanga, George '68 (STP) [C] St. Paul, MN University of St. Thomas.
St-Godard, Edward G. '64 (PRO) [7] Woonsocket, RI Holy Family Church.
St-Pierre, Michel J. '57 (BUR) [2] Burlington, VT St. Anthony's Church.
St. Amand, Ken '69 (NEW) Plainfield, NJ St. Mary Church.
St. Charles, Paul W. '66 (MEM) Retired.
St. Clair, Robert L. *s.j.* '58 (SJ) [B] Santa Clara, CA Santa Clara University; [L] Los Gatos, CA California Province of the Society of Jesus, Jesuit Provincial Office.
St. Cyr, John *o.m.i.* '61 (FgM) Oblates Foreign Missions.
St. Cyr, Richard E. '66 (PRT) Augusta, ME St. Augustine's Church.
St. George, John P. *s.j.* '66 (NEW) [B] Jersey City, NJ Saint Peter's College; [N] Jersey City, NJ Jesuits of Saint Peter's College, Inc.
St. George, Peter T. '95 (CIN) Military Chaplains.
St. Germain, Andre (NTN) On Special Projects.
St. Germain, Brian '88 (PRM) Absent on Leave.
St. Jacques, Clement *s.a.* '45 (WDC) [B] Washington, DC Atonement Seminary-Franciscan Friars of the Atonement.
St. James, Paul F. '68 (BUR) Essex Junction, VT St. Lawrence, Martyr Church.
St. Jean, M. Kidney '92 (MIA) [8] Pompano Beach, FL St. Joseph Church.
St. Jean, Marcel '96 (BGP) Riverside, CT St. Catherine of Siena Church.
St. John, George G. '52 (ALB) East Greenbush, NY Holy Spirit Church.
St. John, Norman *s.v.d.* '62 (TR) Freehold, NJ St. Rose of Lima Church.
St. John, Norman R. *s.v.d.* '62 (MET) Belle Mead, NJ Carrier Clinic.
St. John, Norman R. *s.v.d.* '62 (TR) [M] Bordentown, NJ Society of the Divine Word.
St. Jules, Stephen '79 (RCK) Batavia, IL Holy Cross Church.
St. Laurent, Daniel (MAN) [N] Manchester, NH Campus Ministries.
St. Laurent, Daniel A. '71 (MAN) Durham, NH St. Thomas More Church; [N] Durham, NH St. Thomas More Catholic Student Center at the University of New Hampshire.
St. Louis, Richard E., Jr. '00 (MAN) Exeter, NH St. Michael Church.
St. Marie, Denis L. '59 (CLV) Independence, OH St. Michael Church; El Salvador, C.A., OH The Catholic Center.
St. Marie, Michael '93 (B) Idaho Falls, ID Holy Rosary Church.
St. Martin, Robert (PRM) Cleveland, OH St. Mary Church.
St. Martin, Robert J. '56 (HRT) North Haven, CT St. Frances Cabrini Church.
St. Onge, Omer *s.m.* '46 (BUR) Bradford, VT Our Lady of Perpetual Help Church.
St. Onge, Msgr. Paul J. '41 (NOR) New London, CT St. Joseph Church; Retired.
St. Peter, Lawrence '59 (DEN) Absent on Leave.
St. Pierre, Msgr. Leo L. '39 (MAN) Retired.
St. Pierre, Roland *o.m.i.* '52 (MAN) [K] Colebrook, NH Shrine of Our Lady of Grace.
St. Pierre, Romeo A. '54 (PRT) Retired.
St. Pierre, Ronald L. '83 (BO) Tyngsborough, MA St. Mary Magdalen Church.
St. Pierre, Thomas J. '80 (RVC) Brentwood, NY St. Anne's Church.
St. Sure, Donald F. *s.j.* '39 (SJ) [L] Los Gatos, CA Sacred Heart Jesuit Center.
Staab, Gregory *o.m.v.* '84 (LA) Hawaiian Gardens, CA St. Peter Chanel Church.
Staak, John *o.m.i.* '95 (FgM) Oblates Foreign Missions.
Staal, David E. '90 (OAK) Livermore, CA St. Michael Church; [S] Oakland, CA The Roman Catholic Cemeteries of the Diocese of Oakland.
Staar, Robert J. '77 (NY) Stony Point, NY Immaculate Conception Church.
Stab, Herbert J. '59 (MET) Piscataway, NJ Our Lady of Fatima Church.
Stabene, Edmondo '45 (STU) Retired.
Stabeno, John M. '00 (CAM) Washington Township, NJ Holy Family Church.
Stabile, Thomas *t.o.r.* '87 (VEN) [3] Sarasota, FL Our Lady Queen of Martyrs Church.
Stacer, John *s.j.* '63 (FgM) Provinces.
Stacer, John R. *s.j.* '63 (NO) [P] New Orleans, LA Jesuit Provincial Office.
Stachacz, James '98 (RVC) Westbury, NY St. Brigid Church.
Stacherczak, Idzi '75 (CHI) [33] Chicago, IL St. Bruno Church.
Stachewicz, Msgr. Henry J. '47 (BUF) Retired.
Stachnik, Kenneth R. '86 (GAY) [3] Alpena, MI St. John the Baptist Church.
Stachowiak, Conrad P. '74 (BUF) [1] Depew, NY St. Augustine Church.
Stachura, Thaddeus X. '64 (WOR) [9] Worcester, MA Our Lady of Czestochowa Church.
Stachurski, David *o.f.m.conv.* '80 (SAV) Statesboro, GA St. Matthew Church.
Stack, Aquinas *o.carm.* '84 (NY) [GG] New York, NY University Apostolate.
Stack, Christopher '66 (PMB) Retired.
Stack, Christopher *o.carm.* '85 (PMB) [5] Boca Raton, FL St. Jude Church.
Stack, Daniel '82 (ATL) Monroe, GA St. Anna's Church.
Stack, Gabriel D. *o.praem.* '82 (ORG) [D] Silverado, CA St. Michael's College Preparatory High School; [I] Silverado, CA Norbertine Fathers of Orange Inc.
Stack, George J. '61 (BRK) [220] Queens, NY Our Lady of the Snows Church.
Stack, Gilbert *o.s.b.* '39 (KC) [J] Conception, MO Conception Abbey.
Stack, James M. '86 (WDC) Hyattsville, MD St. Jerome Church.
Stack, Jerome *c.pp.s.* '72 (LA) Norwalk, CA Metropolitan State Hospital.
Stack, John (DAV) [N] Clinton, IA The Canticle.
Stack, John G. *s.j.* '71 (DAL) [D] Dallas, TX Jesuit College Preparatory School.
Stack, John J. '53 (HRT) [6] West Hartford, CT St. Thomas the Apostle Church; [C] West Hartford, CT Saint Joseph College.
Stack, John J. '88 (DAV) [J] Clinton, IA Mercy Medical Center - Clinton.
Stack, John P. '55 (WDC) Chaptico, MD Our Lady of the Wayside Church.
Stack, John P. *o.s.a.* '74 (PH) [C] Villanova, PA Villanova University; [AA] Villanova, PA St. Thomas Monastery.
Stack, Joseph O. *o.m.i.* '34 (BO) [Z] Tewksbury, MA Immaculate Heart of Mary Infirmary.
Stack, Msgr. Richard J. '56 (E) [28] Erie, PA St. Paul Church.
Stack, Thomas Mannix '73 (MIA) [11] Fort Lauderdale, FL St. Mark Church.
Stack, Msgr. William E. '48 (MAD) Retired.
Stackpoole, Edward V. *s.j.* '56 (SFR) [N] San Francisco, CA Jesuit Community at University of San Francisco.
Stadler, Robert G. '48 (SFR) Retired.
Stadmeyer, Raymond '97 (DET) [15] Detroit, MI St. Charles Borromeo Church.
Stadtmueller, Msgr. Fred '40 (SFE) Retired.
Stadtmueller, Roman *s.d.s.* '54 (WDC) [B] Silver Spring, MD Salvatorian Community.
Staebell, James A. '57 (BUF) Angola, NY Most Precious Blood Church; Retired.
Staehler, Adrian *o.f.m.cap.* '67 (MIL) [P] Milwaukee, WI St. Conrad Friary.
Staes, Robert *o.p.* '71 (DEN) [35] Denver, CO St. Mary Magdalene's Church.
Staff, Stephen M. '90 (MOB) On Leave from the Archdiocese.
Stafford, Dennis '91 (CHI) [2] Mt. Prospect, IL St. Emily Church.
Stafford, Edward *t.o.r.* (ALT) [H] Hollidaysburg, PA Campus Ministry.
Stafford, Edward *t.o.r.* '00 (ALT) [F] Loretto, PA Mount Assisi Friary.
Stafford, Edward *t.o.r.* '99 (ALT) [A] Loretto, PA St. Francis College.
Stafford, James D.M. '61 (OKL) Lawton, OK Blessed Sacrament Church.
Stafford, Msgr. Joseph L. '57 (BRK) [178] Queens, NY Holy Family Church.
Stafford, Michael *o.s.b.* '58 (PRO) [P] Portsmouth, RI Abbey of St. Gregory the Great.
Stafford, Msgr. Raymond W. '59 (BRK) [203] Queens, NY Most Precious Blood Church.
Stagaman, David J. *s.j.* '66 (OAK) [A] Berkeley, CA The Jesuit School of Theology at Berkeley; [N] Berkeley, CA Jesuit Community at Jesuit School of Theology at Berkeley.
Stagg, Robert B. '75 (NEW) Springfield, NJ St. James Church.
Stagnaro, John J. '76 (BO) [3] Framingham, MA St. Jeremiah Church.
Stahel, Thomas H. *s.j.* (NO) [P] New Orleans, LA Jesuit Provincial Office.
Stahl, Allen '75 (ORL) On Duty Outside the Diocese.
Stahl, David (DEN) [1] Denver, CO Cathedral of the Immaculate Conception.
Stahl, David '91 (DEN) [12] Denver, CO Holy Ghost Church.
Stahl, David A. '91 (DEN) [23] Denver, CO Presentation of Our Lady Church.
Stahura, Joseph L. '81 (HBG) Greencastle, PA St. Mark the Evangelist Church.
Staib, Donald F. '61 (R) Apex, NC St. Mary Magdalene Church.
Staigers, P. Del '87 (CIN) [20] Dayton, OH Our Lady of Mercy Church.
Staijkowski, James '73 (STL) [P] St. Louis, MO La Salette Missionaries.
Stajkowski, James '73 (MIL) [P] Twin Lakes, WI La Salette Missionaries Shrine.
Stajkowski, Leo S. '66 (ALN) [9] Reading, PA St. Mary Church.
Stake, Ronald P. '85 (CHI) Military Chaplains.
Stakel, Thomas *s.j.* '71 (NO) [11] New Orleans, LA Immaculate Conception Church.
Stakem, Gary *o.f.m.cap.* '51 (PIT) [O] Herman, PA St. Mary's Friary.
Stakem, Ward *o.f.m.cap.* '78 (PIT) Rochester, PA St. Cecilia Church; [O] Rochester, PA St. Cecilia Friary.
Stalavicz, George P. '51 (SCR) Retired.
Staley, Robert P. '95 (R) Roxboro, NC SS. Mary and Edward Church.
Stallings, Donald E. '76 (BEL) Harrisburg, IL St. Mary Church.
Stallings, Msgr. John E. '50 (BEL) Retired.
Stallings, Michael W. '74 (TUC) Patagonia, AZ St. Theresa Church.
Stalter, Cal '94 (AMA) Wellington, TX Our Mother of Mercy Church; Wellington, TX Our Mother of Mercy Church.
Stalzer, Joseph '59 (JOL) Itasca, IL St. Peter the Apostle Church.
Stampiglia, Fausto *s.a.c.* '60 (VEN) [4] Sarasota, FL St. Martha Church; [F] Sarasota, FL St. Martha's Housing, Inc.; [F] Sarasota, FL St. Martha's Housing II, Inc.
Stamschror, Robert P. '61 (WIN) Retired.
Stanbery, Stephen L. '80 (TOL) New Bavaria, OH Sacred Heart of Jesus Church; North Creek, OH St. Joseph Church.
Stanchik, Dennis P. '59 (LC) Adams, WI St. Joseph Church; Brooks, WI St. Ann Church.
Stander, Charles J. *s.m.* '81 (CIN) [M] Dayton, OH Marianist Provincialate.
Stander, Edwin L. '63 (LIN) [5] Lincoln, NE Sacred Heart Church; Lincoln, NE Nebraska Penal Complex.
Stanfield, Francis E. '80 (GLP) Retired.
Stanfield, George *c.p.* '68 (LA) [Q] Pasadena, CA

Passionist Community; [W] Sierra Madre, CA Mater Dolorosa Retreat Center.
Stanfield, William L. '76 (MIL) Oak Creek, WI St. Matthew Church.
Stang, Charles L. *s.j.* '67 (MIL) [E] Milwaukee, WI Marquette University High School; [P] Milwaukee, WI Arrupe House Jesuit Community.
Stang, Mark '90 (SCL) Long Prairie, MN St. Mary of Mt. Carmel Church.
Stang, William J. *c.pp.s.* '77 (LFT) [A] Rensselaer, IN Saint Joseph's College.
Stange, Henry A. (ALT) Retired.
Stange, James R. '95 (P) Scappoose, OR St. Wenceslaus Church.
Stangel, Mark J. '65 (MIL) Retired.
Stanger, Edward J. '91 (STL) Oakville, MO Queen of All Saints Church.
Stanger, Harold B. '77 (CHI) Deerfield, IL Holy Cross Church.
Stangl, Alfred '63 (SCL) St. Cloud, MN U.S. Veteran's Hospital.
Stangl, Alfred '67 (SCL) Special Assignment.
Stangl, Frank J. '53 (JC) Retired.
Stangnelli, Msgr. Anthony M. '79 (RVC) New Hyde Park, NY Holy Spirit Church.
Stanialus, John Peter '91 (TYL) Clarksville, TX St. Joseph Church.
Stanibula, Christopher '95 (FR) Seekonk, MA St. Mary's Church.
Stanichar, Joseph '68 (VNN) Seattle, WA St. John Chrysostom Church.
Stanievich, J. Walter '46 (DET) Retired.
Stanion, Robert *c.f.r.* '92 (NY) [DD] Yonkers, NY St. Felix Friary.
Staniskis, Daniel '84 (PSC) Flanders, NJ Holy Wisdom Church.
Staniszewski, Ignatius *s.s.p.* '64 (NY) [B] New York, NY Society of St. Paul.
Staniszewski, Stanley *c.m.* '63 (HRT) [M] Manchester, CT DePaul Provincial Residence.
Staniszewski, Stanley *c.m.* '64 (BGP) [7] Stamford, CT Holy Name of Jesus Church.
Stanizewski, Stanley '74 (SFS) [5] Sioux Falls, SD St. Lambert Church.
Stankard, Albert H. '59 (BO) [4] Framingham, MA St. Stephen Church.
Stankavage, Joseph G. '90 (WDC) Absent On Leave.
Stanko, Andrew C. '70 (ALT) [7] Johnstown, PA St. Stephen, First King of Hungary Church.
Stankus, Gregory A. '78 (BRK) [47] Brooklyn, NY St. Francis Xavier Church.
Stanley, Brian L. '96 (KAL) Coldwater, MI St. Charles Borromeo Church; Coldwater, MI Florence Crane Correctional Facility for Women; Coldwater, MI Camp Branch; Coldwater, MI Lakeland Correctional Facility for Men.
Stanley, Charles '71 (FgM) Society of St. James the Apostle.
Stanley, Charles R. '71 (BO) Society of St. James the Apostle.
Stanley, Colm *s.s.c.* '69 (OM) [K] St. Columbans, NE St. Columban's Foreign Mission Society.
Stanley, Matthew D. '91 (SJ) [7] San Jose, CA Holy Family Church.
Stanley, Melvin *o.f.m.* '52 (OAK) [N] Oakland, CA Franciscan Friars.
Stanley, Michael H. *o.s.a.* '81 (FgM) Foreign Missions.
Stanley, Richard D. '74 (BO) [BB] Boston, MA Immaculate Conception Church.
Stanley, Richard J. *s.j.* '74 (BGP) [W] Fairfield, CT Newman Centers - Campus Ministry.
Stanley, Richard J. *s.j.* '74 (BO) [W] Boston, MA Loyola House; [W] Boston, MA The Society of Jesus of New England-Provincial Offices.
Stanley, Ronald A. *o.p.* '67 (MET) [H] New Brunswick, NJ De Porres House; [M] New Brunswick, NJ Catholic Center at Rutgers University.
Stanley, Thomas A. *s.m.* '50 (CIN) [M] Dayton, OH Marianist Provincialate.
Stanley, William S. *m.m.* '92 (FgM) Maryknoll Foreign Missions.
Stano, Luke M. *o.s.m.* '61 (CHI) [N] Chicago, IL Order of Friar Servants of Mary (Servites) United States of America Province, Inc.
Stano, Luke M. *o.s.m.* '61 (DET) [37] Detroit, MI St. John Berchmans-St. Juliana Church.
Stanonik, Anthony '82 (SD) On Duty Outside the Diocese.
Stanosz, Paul A. '84 (MIL) Graduate Studies.
Stansberry, Richard D., Jr. '92 (OKL) Kingfisher, OK SS. Peter and Paul Church.
Stansley, Ralph W. '73 (TR) Hopewell, NJ St. Alphonsus Church.
Stanton, Finbarr P. '67 (SAV) Albany, GA St. Teresa Church.
Stanton, Francis M. '59 (COL) Crooksville, OH Church of the Atonement.
Stanton, Joseph E. '51 (COL) [29] Columbus, OH St. Mary Church; Retired.
Stanton, Joseph F. *o.c.s.o.* '84 (ROC) [I] Piffard, NY Abbey of the Genesee.
Stanton, Terence *o.s.b.* '43 (RCK) [G] Aurora, IL Marmion Abbey-St. Augustine's Abbey.
Stanton, Thomas J. '91 (BO) Westford, MA St. Catherine of Alexandria Church.
Stanton, Msgr. William G. '49 (BUF) Retired.
Stanton, William J. '52 (PH) Retired.
Stanton, Msgr. William J. '56 (SPC) Sikeston, MO St. Francis Xavier's Church.
Stapenhorst, Verne P. '61 (SC) [1] Sioux City, IA Cathedral of the Epiphany; [B] Sioux City, IA Catholic Schools of Sioux City.
Staples, Terrence R. '95 (ARL) [6] Alexandria, VA St. Louis Church.
Stapleton, Edward J. *s.s.s.* '60 (CLV) [O] Cleveland, OH Congregation of the Blessed Sacrament Provincial House; [O] Cleveland, OH Blessed Sacrament Community.
Stapleton, Gerard P. '85 (NO) Port Sulphur, LA St. Patrick Church.
Stapleton, James *c.s.p.* '74 (BRK) [239] Queens, NY Sacred Heart Church.
Starasinich, James E. '99 (NEW) Westfield, NJ Holy Trinity Church.
Starbuck, James '48 (OAK) Retired.
Starbuck, James '90 (DUB) Cedar Falls, IA St. Patrick Church.
Staricek, Andrew '40 (RC) Retired.
Stark, Paul V. *s.j.* '85 (DEN) [D] Aurora, CO Regis Jesuit High School.
Stark, Paul V. *s.j.* '85 (STL) [C] St. Louis, MO Saint Louis University.
Stark, Robert *s.s.s.* '77 (SFE) [25] Albuquerque, NM St. Charles Borromeo Church.
Stark, Ronald P. *o.f.m.* '66 (NY) [35] New York, NY St. Francis of Assisi Church; [115] New York, NY St. Stephen of Hungary Church; [HH] New York, NY St. Francis Counseling Center, Inc.; [HH] New York, NY Franciscan Missionary Charities, Inc.; [HH] New York, NY St. Francis Monastery Breadline for the Poor, Inc.
Starkloff, Carl F. *s.j.* '65 (STL) [P] St. Louis, MO Jesuit Community Corporation at St. Louis University - Jesuit Hall.
Starks, R. Mansfield '42 (ALB) Glenville, NY Immaculate Conception Church; Retired.
Starmann, Joseph W. '63 (JC) Retired.
Staron, Stanley R. '74 (HRT) [I] Waterbury, CT St. Mary Hospital.
Starostka, John C. '61 (OM) [15] Omaha, NE St. Francis Assisi Church.
Starus, Ralph E. '69 (CHI) Midlothian, IL St. Christopher Church.
Starzynski, Stefan '96 (ARL) [7] Alexandria, VA St. Mary's Church.
Stash, Robert '82 (PRM) Bay City, MI Saint George Church; Omer, MI St. John Church.
Stashek, Leonard C. '56 (LC) Milan, WI St. Thomas Church; Wuerzburg, WI St. John the Baptist Church.
Stasiak, Kurt *o.s.b.* '80 (IND) [A] St. Meinrad, IN St. Meinrad Seminary; [J] St. Meinrad, IN St. Meinrad Archabbey.
Stasik, Thaddeus '60 (NEW) [5] Jersey City, NJ St. Ann's Church.
Stasiowski, John S. '65 (FWT) Bowie, TX St. Jerome Church; Henrietta, TX St. Mary Church; Montague, TX St. William Church; Nocona, TX St. Joseph Church.
Stasker, R. Louis '65 (GR) Ada, MI St. Robert Church.
Stasyszen, Lawrence *o.s.b.* (OKL) [A] Shawnee, OK St. Gregory's University.
Stasyszen, Lawrence R. *o.s.b.* '94 (OKL) [I] Shawnee, OK St. Gregory's Abbey.
Staszak, Bernard C. '65 (BUF) French Creek, NY St. Matthias Church; Panama, NY Our Lady of the Snows Church.
Staszewski, Joseph P. '64 (E) Brookville, PA Immaculate Conception Church.
Staszewski, Robert M. '72 (PIT) [3] Butler, PA St. Paul Church.
Statkus, Msgr. Francis J. '46 (PH) Ardmore, PA St. Colman Church; Retired.
Statnick, Roger A. '73 (GBG) Derry, PA St. Joseph Church.
Statt, Thomas R. (ROC) [12] Rochester, NY St. Charles Borromeo Church.
Statt, Thomas R. '58 (ROC) [40] Rochester, NY Our Mother of Sorrows Church.
Stattmiller, John E. '66 (COL) [12] Columbus, OH Corpus Christi Church; [26] Columbus, OH St. Ladislas Church.
Statz, James '84 (SCL) Brooten, MN St. Donatus Church; Padua, MN Church of St. Anthony of Padua
Staub, Eugene J. *c.ss.r.* '52 (BR) [H] Baton Rouge, LA Redemptorist Vice Province.
Stauber, James (SB) Retired.
Staublin, Daniel J. '82 (IND) Brownsburg, IN St. Malachy Church.
Staud, Msgr. Sylvester W. '42 (WH) Retired.
Staudenmaier, John M. *s.j.* '70 (DET) [K] Detroit, MI Jesuit Community at the University of Detroit.
Staudenmaier, Wilbert '43 (GB) Retired.
Stauder, Paul W. '48 (BEL) Retired.
Stauder, William V. *s.j.* '52 (STL) [P] St. Louis, MO Jesuit Community Corporation at St. Louis University - Jesuit Hall; [P] St. Louis, MO The Jesuits of the Missouri Province.
Staudinger, Greg '81 (GF) Sidney, MT St. Matthew Church.
Staudt, Joseph W. '78 (RVC) Commack, NY Christ the King Church.
Staunton, Msgr. Patrick J. '60 (LA) La Puente, CA St. Joseph Church.
Stauter, Andrew '57 (MOB) [E] Mobile, AL Little Sisters of the Poor, Home For the Aged, Inc.
Stavoy, Stephen J. '79 (SCR) White Haven, PA St. Patrick's Church.
Stawasz, James '53 (HON) Retired.
Stawasz, John B. '53 (HON) Kailua-Kona, HI St. Michael The Archangel Church.
Staysniak, Dale W. '75 (CLV) [1] Parma, OH St. Anthony of Padua Church.
Ste. Marie, Adrien *c.s.c.* '50 (P) [L] Portland, OR Holy Cross Fathers & Brothers, C.S.C. - University of Portland.
Stead, Julian *o.s.b.* '52 (PRO) [P] Portsmouth, RI Abbey of St. Gregory the Great.
Stead, Mell '56 (P) Lincoln City, OR St. Augustine Church.
Stearns, Joseph E. '72 (VEN) [4] Naples, FL St. William Church.
Steber, Michael J. '86 (MAR) Escanaba, MI St. Anne Church.
Stec, Emil *c.r.* '48 (CHI) [190] Chicago, IL St. Stanislaus Kostka Church.
Stec, John '74 (MET) [2] Perth Amboy, NJ St. Stephen Church.
Stec, Joseph C. '57 (PH) [87] Philadelphia, PA St. Laurentius Church; Retired.
Stec, Mark D. '88 (BEL) Equality, IL St. Joseph Church; Pond Settlement, IL St. Patrick Church; Ridgway, IL St. Joseph Church; Shawneetown, IL St. Mary Church.
Stec, Michael S. '94 (LIN) Syracuse, NE St. Paulinus Church.
Stec, Robert '88 (CLV) [A] Wickliffe, OH Borromeo Seminary.
Stecher, John E. '72 (DAV) [H] Iowa City, IA Newman Catholic Student Center; [M] Iowa City, IA O'Keefe Hall.
Stecher, Kenneth C. '68 (DUB) Fairbank, IA Immaculate Conception Church; Independence, IA Mental Health Institute.
Steck, Christopher W. *s.j.* '94 (WDC) [M] Washington, DC The Jesuit Community at Georgetown University.
Steckel, Gregory A. '81 (DAV) On Duty Outside the Diocese.
Stecklein, Warren L. '90 (DOD) Great Bend, KS St. Patrick Church.
Steckler, Gerard *s.j.* '57 (P) Waldport, OR St. Anthony Church.
Steckler, Kenneth '96 (EVN) [18] Evansville, IN St. Joseph Church; Special Assignment; [A] Evansville, IN Mater Dei High School.
Stecz, Jeffrey M. '99 (PH) Exton, PA SS. Philip and James Church.
Steed, Donald R. *m.m.* '54 (NY) [DD] Maryknoll, NY Maryknoll Fathers and Brothers.
Steeg, Mark Vander (GB) [5] Appleton, WI St. Pius X Church.
Steel, Mark Richard *o.f.m.conv.* '89 (WDC) [B] Washington, DC St. Bonaventure Friary.
Steele, Christopher A. '00 (NSH) Madison, TN St. Joseph's Church.
Steele, John *c.s.c.* '97 (FTW) [B] Notre Dame, IN University of Notre Dame Du Lac.
Steele, Joseph S. '97 (LIN) Grant, NE Mother of Sorrows Church.
Steele, Michael J. '77 (BO) Wakefield, MA St. Joseph Church.
Steele, Philip G. *s.j.* '80 (STL) [P] St. Louis, MO Leo Brown Jesuit Community; [P] St. Louis, MO The Jesuits of the Missouri Province.
Steele, Steven G. '90 (MAD) Bloomington, WI St. Mary Church; Patch Grove, WI St. John Church.
Steele, Thomas J. *s.j.* '64 (SFE) [6] Albuquerque, NM Immaculate Conception Church.
Steen, Charles A. *o.f.m.* '64 (FgM) Franciscan Foreign Missions.
Steen, Raymond *o.m.i.* '60 (BO) [Z] Tewksbury, MA Immaculate Heart of Mary Infirmary.
Steenken, George W. *s.j.* '54 (CHI) [T] Barrington, IL Bellarmine Hall.
Stefanelli, Joseph *s.m.* (SJ) [L] Cupertino, CA Villa Saint Joseph.
Stefaniak, James J. *m.m.* '50 (FgM) Maryknoll Foreign Missions.
Stefanko, Paul F. '76 (PRT) Yarmouth, ME Sacred Heart Church.
Stefanski, Gery W. '79 (CHI) [J] Evanston, IL Saint Francis Hospital.

Stefanski, Walter '40 (CHI) Retired.
Steffan, Paul *o.f.m.cap.* '57 (NOR) [4] Middletown, CT St. Pius X Church.
Steffen, Arnold *s.v.d.* '57 (FgM) Society of the Divine Word Foreign Missions.
Steffen, Carl J. '58 (HBG) Buchanan Valley, PA St. Ignatius Loyola Church.
Steffen, Francis J. '57 (MAD) Dickeyville, WI Holy Ghost Church.
Steffen, Kenneth C. '84 (SFD) Riverton, IL St. James Church.
Steffenes, Gerard (BAL) Westminster, MD St. John Church.
Steffens, Terrence J. '82 (GRY) Crown Point, IN St. Matthias Church.
Steffensmeier, Ralph J. '59 (OM) Cedar Rapids, NE St. Anthony Church.
Steffes, James D. *s.c.j.* '63 (GAL) [56] Houston, TX Our Lady of Guadalupe Church.
Steffes, James P. '93 (WIN) [A] Winona, MN Immaculate Heart of Mary Seminary.
Steffes, Joseph *c.ss.r.* '40 (BR) [5] Baton Rouge, LA St. Charles Borromeo Church; [10] Baton Rouge, LA St. Gerard Majella Church.
Steffes, LuVerne W. '95 (OM) Atkinson, NE St. Joseph Church.
Steffes, Marvin J. *c.pp.s.* '58 (MRY) Los Gatos, CA Christ Child Church.
Steffes, Raymond *o.s.c.* '58 (SCL) Hillman, MN St. Rita's Church; Wahkon, MN Sacred Heart Church; [I] Onamia, MN Crosier Monastery.
Steffey, John M. (KAL) Retired.
Steffy, David *l.c.* '94 (MAN) [A] Center Harbor, NH Immaculate Conception Apostolic School.
Stefula, Salvator *t.o.r.* '74 (FWT) [16] Fort Worth, TX St. Thomas Church.
Stefun, Bonaventure *o.f.m.cap.* '56 (PIT) Allegheny County, PA St. Francis Medical Center; [O] Pittsburgh, PA St. Augustine Friary.
Steger, Francis R. *o.c.s.o.* '56 (ROC) [I] Piffard, NY Abbey of the Genesee.
Steger, John J. '51 (ROC) [32] Rochester, NY St. Jude the Apostle Church.
Steggert, Bruce A. *s.j.* '93 (WDC) [E] Washington, DC Gonzaga College High School.
Stegman, Leonard F. '40 (ELP) Retired.
Stegman, Thomas D. *s.j.* '95 (ATL) [L] Atlanta, GA Ignatius House.
Stegman, Thomas D. *s.j.* '95 (MIL) [P] Milwaukee, WI Jesuit Community at Marquette University.
Stegman, Vincent G. *c.s.sp.* '62 (FgM) Holy Ghost Foreign Missions.
Stegmann, Robert (GB) [2] Oshkosh, WI St. Mary Church; [3] Oshkosh, WI St. Josaphat Church.
Stehlik, Thomas *c.m.* '96 (DAL) [6] Dallas, TX Holy Trinity Church.
Stehling, Lawrence J. '88 (AUS) [1] Austin, TX St. Mary's Church; Austin, TX State Hospital; [F] Austin, TX Seton Medical Center.
Stehly, Dennis R. '77 (STL) Mehlville, MO St. Margaret Mary Alacoque Church.
Stehly, James '83 (LA) Camarillo, CA St. Mary Magdalen Church.
Stehly, Mark '66 (SEA) Special Assignment.
Stehly, Thomas J. '61 (LA) Retired.
Stehr, James P. *s.j.* '75 (NY) [DD] New York, NY "America;" Residence and publication office of the America Press.
Steibel, Gary '63 (MIA) Miramar, FL St. Bartholomew Church.
Steichen, John A. '54 (OKL) Union City, OK St. Joseph's Church.
Steidle, Mark A. '93 (COV) Leave of Absence.
Steier, Charles '73 (SAL) Gorham, KS St. Mary's Church; Russell, KS St. Mary's Church.
Steiger, Msgr. Richard A. '67 (PAT) Andover, NJ Good Shepherd Church.
Steigmeyer, Robert C. *c.s.c.* '47 (FTW) [5] South Bend, IN St. Casimir Church; [19] South Bend, IN St. Stephen Church.
Steik, Dennis J. *s.m.* '69 (ATL) [J] Atlanta, GA Marist Provincial Office, Society of Mary - Washington Province.
Steimel, Craig E. '89 (DUB) Buffalo Center, IA St. Patrick's Church; Forest City, IA St. James Church; Lake Mills, IA St. Patrick Church.
Steimel, Msgr. Paul T. '52 (DUB) Retired.
Stein, Benjamin *o.s.b.* '36 (SCL) [I] Collegeville, MN St. John's Abbey, of the Order of St. Benedict.
Stein, C. William *c.m.* '39 (STL) [P] Perryville, MO Congregation of The Mission.
Stein, E. John *o.f.m.* '85 (CIN) [21] Cincinnati, OH St. Clement Church; [M] Cincinnati, OH St. Clement Friary.
Stein, James *o.praem.* '86 (CHI) [N] Chicago, IL Premonstratensian Fathers and Brothers (Norbertines).
Stein, Jerry '66 (AMA) Retired.
Stein, Norbert W. *s.s.j.* '61 (LAF) Cecilia, LA St. Rose of Lima Church.
Stein, Robert '78 (MRY) Hollister, CA Sacred Heart/St. Benedict Catholic Community Church.
Stein, Robert E. '81 (CLV) [14] Akron, OH St. Paul Church.
Stein, Ron (DUB) [H] Mason City, IA Mercy Medical Center-North Iowa.
Stein, Timothy P. '84 (ALT) Chest Springs, PA St. Monica's Church.
Steinauer, Carl J. '76 (SAC) Absent on Leave.
Steinbacher, Wilfred '62 (NSH) [H] Nashville, TN Glenmary Home Missioners.
Steinbauer, Joseph R. '79 (TOL) Rossford, OH All Saints Church.
Steinbeisser, Joseph A. '86 (NU) Willmar, MN St. Mary Church.
Steinberger, Edward J. '45 (WCH) Caney, KS Sacred Heart Church; Moline, KS St. Mary's Church; Sedan, KS St. Robert Bellarmine Church.
Steinbicker, Carl '33 (CIN) [L] Cincinnati, OH Archbishop Leibold Home for the Aged.
Steinbicker, Carl R. '34 (CIN) Retired.
Steinbock, Leo E. '54 (LA) [74] Los Angeles, CA St. Kevin Church.
Steinbrunner, Jerry *c.pp.s.* '74 (CIN) [55] Cincinnati, OH St. Mark Church.
Steinbugler, Thomas B. *s.j.* '61 (FgM) Provinces.
Steiner, Bernard J. '61 (NU) Green Isle, MN St. Brendan Church.
Steiner, Msgr. Carl '55 (GB) Retired.
Steiner, Daniel R. '79 (CHI) Other Assignments.
Steiner, Edward F., III '82 (NSH) Madison, TN St. Joseph's Church.
Steiner, Msgr. John M. '69 (SPK) [19] Spokane, WA St. Thomas More Church.
Steiner, John W. '74 (LC) Alma, WI St. Lawrence Church; Waumandee, WI St. Boniface Church.
Steiner, Luke *o.s.b.* '56 (SCL) [A] Collegeville, MN St. John's Seminary; [B] Collegeville, MN St. John's University; [I] Collegeville, MN St. John's Abbey, of the Order of St. Benedict.
Steiner, William *c.ss.r.* '54 (FgM) Redemptorist Foreign Missions.
Steingraeber, John *c.ss.r.* '74 (DEN) [M] Denver, CO The Redemptorists/Denver Province.
Steingreaber, Paul *o.s.b.* '65 (KCK) [H] Atchison, KS St. Benedict's Abbey.
Steinhauser, Kenneth B. '70 (BRK) Released from Diocesan Assignment.
Steinhilber, Richard *s.s.c.* '51 (OM) [K] St. Columbans, NE St. Columban's Foreign Mission Society.
Steinhoff, Henry '67 (B) Retired.
Steinhoff, Henry '67 (HEL) Eureka, MT Our Lady of Mercy Church.
Steinkirchner, Edward '49 (ROC) East Rochester, NY St. Jerome Church.
Steinkirchner, Edward E. '49 (ROC) Penfield, NY St. Joseph Church; Retired.
Steinle, Christopher C. *o.s.a.* '98 (CHI) [N] Olympia Fields, IL The Augustinians-Provincialate.
Steinle, Christopher C. *o.s.a.* '98 (FgM) Foreign Missions.
Steinle, David G. '79 (DAV) [4] Davenport, IA St. Alphonsus Church; Buffalo, IA St. Peter's Church.
Steinle, James '53 (TOL) Retired.
Steinman, Robert E. *o.s.a.* '50 (PH) [AA] Villanova, PA St. Thomas Monastery.
Steinmetz, Paul B. *s.j.* '59 (MIL) [P] Milwaukee, WI Jesuit Community at Marquette University.
Steinmetz, Ricardo *s.j.* '55 (FgM) Provinces.
Steinmiller, Alexander *c.p.* '70 (CHI) [N] Chicago, IL Passionist Provincial Office.
Steinmiller, Alexander *c.p.* '70 (GAL) [Q] Houston, TX Congregation of the Passion, Holy Name Retreat Center.
Steinwachs, Boniface *o.s.b.* '00 (SP) [O] St. Leo, FL St. Leo Abbey.
Stella, Livio *c.s.* '75 (LA) Sun Valley, CA Our Lady of the Holy Rosary Church.
Stella, Thomas A. *c.s.c.* '72 (COS) [F] Cascade, CO Holy Cross Novitiate.
Stella, Tom '72 (COS) [C] Colorado Springs, CO Penrose-St. Francis Health Services.
Steller, Paul W. '65 (BUF) [R] Alfred, NY Campus Ministry.
Stelling, William F. '64 (MEM) [15] Memphis, TN St. Joseph's Church.
Stelmach, Jerome J. '80 (BUF) Limestone, NY St. Patrick Church; Olean, NY Transfiguration Church.
Stelmach, Michael '70 (STN) Minneapolis, MN St. Constantine Church.
Stelmaszczyk, Miroslaw '77 (PIT) Creighton, PA Holy Family Church.
Stelten, Anthony Mary *m.f.v.a.* '00 (BIR) [E] Birmingham, AL Franciscan Missionaries of the Eternal Word, A Public Association of the Christian Faithful.
Stelten, Leo F. '50 (FAR) Retired.
Steltenkamp, Michael F. *s.j.* '76 (DET) [K] Detroit, MI Jesuit Provincial Office-Detroit Province of the Society of Jesus.
Steltenkamp, Michael F. *s.j.* '76 (WH) [A] Wheeling, WV Wheeling Jesuit University.
Stelter, Richard T. '80 (RVC) Amityville, NY St. Martin's Church.
Stelzer, Mark S. '83 (SPR) [12] Springfield, MA Sacred Heart Church.
Stembler, James G. (CC) [18] Corpus Christi, TX St. Paul the Apostle Church.
Stemler, Bruno *f.s.s.p.* '98 (SCR) [E] Moscow, PA St. Gregory's Academy; [M] Elmhurst, PA Priestly Fraternity of St. Peter (F.S.S.P.), North American District Headquarters.
Stemman, Joseph '63 (LAF) Henderson, LA Our Lady of Mercy Church.
Stemmann, Joseph '63 (LAF) Retired.
Stempora, Daniel F. '60 (JOL) Oswego, IL St. Anne Church.
Stempsey, William E. *s.j.* '92 (WOR) [N] Worcester, MA Jesuits of Holy Cross College, Inc.
Stencil, Rallen H. '63 (GB) Hilbert, WI St. Mary Church.
Stencil, Steven G. '81 (TUC) [19] Tucson, AZ St. Mark The Evangelist Church.
Stengel, Msgr. Charles G. '56 (NEW) [12] Jersey City, NJ St. John the Baptist Church.
Stengel, Mark '72 (LR) [A] Subiaco, AR Subiaco Monastery.
Stengel, Michael Joseph *c.p.* '57 (CHI) [N] Chicago, IL Passionist Community-Immaculate Conception Monastery.
Stengel, Msgr. Paul F. '59 (BUF) Boston, NY St. John the Baptist Church.
Stengel, William '57 (GB) Retired.
Stenger, James R. '81 (CLV) [4] Parma, OH St. Columbkille Church.
Stenger, Joseph *c.ss.r.* '57 (FgM) Redemptorist Foreign Missions.
Stenger, William J., Sr. '94 (WH) Glen Dale, WV St. Jude Church.
Stenson, Brian '77 (LAV) Overton, NV St. John the Evangelist Church.
Stenson, Patrick J. *m.s.c.* '63 (CHR) Pawleys Island, SC Precious Blood of Christ Church.
Stenson, Patrick J. *m.s.c.* '63 (SAT) [M] San Antonio, TX Missionaries of the Sacred Heart.
Stenson, Paul J. '98 (PH) [84] Philadelphia, PA St. Katherine of Siena Church.
Stenzel, Duane (HT) [4] Houma, LA Our Lady of the Most Holy Rosary Church.
Stenzel, Eugene F. '67 (WIN) Wells, MN St. Casimir's Church.
Stenzel, William J. '75 (CHI) La Grange, IL St. Francis Xavier Church.
Stepanich, Martin *o.f.m.* '41 (CHI) [N] Lemont, IL The Slovene Franciscan Fathers, Order of Friars Minor, Commissariat of the Holy Cross.
Stepanski, Thomas K. '62 (IND) Danville, IN Mary Queen of Peace Church.
Stepek, Robert A. '81 (CHI) Burbank, IL St. Albert the Great Church.
Stephan, George J. '62 (BUF) [25] Buffalo, NY St. Francis Xavier Church; [37] Buffalo, NY St. John the Baptist Church.
Stephan, Matthew J. '83 (CC) Falfurrias, TX Sacred Heart Church.
Stephen, John *c.r.* '38 (CHI) [D] Chicago, IL Gordon Tech High School.
Stephens, Gerald '63 (FWT) Retired.
Stephens, James '97 (BAK) Madras, OR St. Patrick's Church.
Stephens, Rod '74 (ORG) [1] Orange, CA Cathedral of the Holy Family.
Stephens, Timothy J. *s.j.* '99 (WDC) [P] Faulkner, MD Loyola on the Potomac Retreat House.
Stephenson, Alphonse J. '75 (PAT) On Duty Outside the Diocese.
Stephenson, Lloyd F. '80 (RIC) Newport News, VA St. Vincent de Paul Church; Hampton, VA VA Medical Center.
Stephenson, Patrick '68 (SR) American Canyon, CA Holy Family Church.
Stephenson, Robert B. '78 (SY) [3] Binghamton, NY St. Catherine of Siena Church; [H] Syracuse, NY Bishop Joseph T. O'Keefe, Inc.
Stepien, Allen F. '65 (PAT) Long Valley, NJ St. Mark the Evangelist Church.
Steri, Efisio *o.f.m.conv.* '60 (FgM) Conventual Franciscan Foreign Missions.
Steriti, Edward *o.c.s.o.* '57 (WOR) [N] Spencer, MA St. Joseph's Abbey.
Sterk, Francis R. '65 (CLV) [1] Euclid, OH St. Christine Church.
Sterling, Donald A. '74 (BAL) [4] Baltimore, MD The New All Saints Church.
Sterling, John J. '96 (COV) Crescent Springs, KY St. Joseph Church.
Sterling, John K. (DAV) On Duty Outside the Diocese.
Sterling, John K. '94 (WDC) [42] Washington, DC St. Thomas Apostle Church.
Stern, Jerome F. '63 (LEX) London, KY St. William/St. Sylvester Church.
Stern, Msgr. Robert L. '58 (NY) [HH] New York, NY Catholic Near East Welfare Association (CNEWA).
Sternemann, Reinhard *o.s.a.* '66 (FWT) Gainesville, TX

St. Mary Church.
Sterner, James M. '70 (HBG) Littlestown, PA St. Aloysius Church.
Sterns, Msgr. Robert L. (TR) [T] Lincroft, NJ The Bethlehem University Foundation, Inc.
Sterowski, Scott P. '91 (SCR) Olyphant, PA St. Patrick's Church; [D] Dunmore, PA Bishop O'Hara High School.
Stessman, Msgr. Gerald J. '59 (DM) [4] Des Moines, IA Holy Trinity Church.
Stetson, William H. '62 (WDC) [T] Washington, DC Prelature of the Holy Cross and Opus Dei.
Stetz, Allan *o.s.b.* '66 (JC) Mexico, MO St. Brendan Church.
Stetz, Mark '90 (MRY) Los Osos, CA St. Elizabeth Ann Seton Church.
Steuer, James '63 (ALB) Mohawk, NY Blessed Sacrament Church.
Steuernol, E. Slider '96 (P) Gresham, OR St. Henry Church.
Steuterman, James M. '75 (WOR) North Oxford, MA St. Ann's Church.
Stevens, Clifford J. '56 (OM) Retired.
Stevens, David '98 (SFS) [3] Sioux Falls, SD Holy Spirit Church.
Stevens, Gladstone H. '00 (L) [69] Louisville, KY St. Rita Church.
Stevens, Michael J. '80 (STP) [11] St. Paul, MN St. Adalbert Church; Special Assignment.
Stevensky, Msgr. John '60 (SJP) Conyers, GA Mother of God Church.
Stevenson, Alden F. *s.j.* '46 (SJ) [L] Los Gatos, CA Sacred Heart Jesuit Center.
Stevenson, Anthony '81 (OWN) Bardwell, KY St. Charles Church; Fancy Farm, KY St. Denis Church.
Stevenson, Dennis E. *j.c.l.* '88 (COL) [4] Columbus, OH St. Aloysius Church.
Stevenson, R. Francis '92 (SAC) On Duty Outside the Diocese.
Stevenson, William J. '82 (LAN) Saline, MI St. Andrew Church.
Stevenson, William P. '86 (SD) Santa Ysabel, CA Santa Ysabel Indian Church.
Stevko, Victor *s.v.d.* '57 (FgM) Society of the Divine Word Foreign Missions.
Stewart, August '94 (COS) [11] Colorado Springs, CO St. Gabriel the Archangel Church.
Stewart, Columba *o.s.b.* '90 (SCL) [I] Collegeville, MN St. John's Abbey, of the Order of St. Benedict.
Stewart, Edward R. '89 (BRK) [36] Brooklyn, NY St. Ephrem's Church.
Stewart, George R. '94 (NY) [185] Bronx, NY St. Raymond Church.
Stewart, J. David *s.j.* '95 (CHI) [C] Chicago, IL Jesuit Community at Loyola University of Chicago.
Stewart, J. Keith (MEM) [1] Memphis, TN Cathedral of the Immaculate Conception.
Stewart, J. Patrick *s.j.* '61 (P) [L] Portland, OR Colombiere Community; [Q] Portland, OR Jesuit Development & Communications Office.
Stewart, James *o.f.m.cap.* '85 (NY) Valhalla, NY Westchester County Medical Center; [DD] White Plains, NY St. Conrad Friary.
Stewart, Jonathan '91 (IND) [37] Indianapolis, IN St. Therese of the Infant Jesus (Little Flower) Church.
Stewart, Kenneth *o.f.m.cap.* (CHI) [68] Chicago, IL St. George Church.
Stewart, Michael L. '75 (MEM) [6] Memphis, TN St. Brigid Church.
Stewart, Patrick F. '78 (LEX) Richmond, KY St. Mark Church; [L] Richmond, KY St. Stephen Newman Center-St. Mark Church.
Stewart, Paul E. '73 (PT) [4] Tallahassee, FL St. Louis Church.
Stewart, Robert *o.f.m.* '80 (BUF) [C] St. Bonaventure, NY St. Bonaventure University; [O] St. Bonaventure, NY St. Bonaventure Friary.
Stewart, Robert H. '82 (KC) [15] Kansas City, MO Holy Family Church.
Stewart, Msgr. Terrence L. '70 (GR) Marne, MI St. Mary's Church; On Special Assignment.
Sthokal, Edward S. *s.j.* '54 (STP) [Q] Lake Elmo, MN Jesuit Retreat House.
Sticco, Peter T. *s.a.c.* '69 (NEW) Fairview, NJ Our Lady of Grace Church.
Stickle, William '50 (RIC) Retired.
Stieferman, Lowell '76 (OKL) Special Assignment.
Stieferman, Lowell L. '63 (OKL) [6] Oklahoma City, OK Church of the Epiphany of the Lord.
Stiefvater, Robert X. '77 (MIL) Special Assignment.
Stiegeler, A. Francis '78 (SFR) [E] San Francisco, CA St. Ignatius College Preparatory (Coed); [N] San Francisco, CA Jesuit Community at St. Ignatius College Preparatory.
Stieger, Msgr. Joseph '50 (MRY) Retired.
Stiene, Paul *i.c.* '90 (PEO) Elmwood, IL St. Patrick's Church; Farmington, IL St. Matthew's Church.
Stier, Timothy '79 (OAK) [1] Fremont, CA Corpus Christi Church.
Stika, Msgr. Richard F. (STL) [V] St. Louis, MO Friends of the Archbishop.
Stika, Msgr. Richard F. '85 (STL) Special Assignment.
Stikel, Roman '88 (MIL) [3] Kenosha, WI St. Elizabeth Church.
Stiles, J. Roy '63 (L) [24] Louisville, KY St. Elizabeth of Hungary Church; [72] Louisville, KY St. Therese Church.
Stiles, Wallis '61 (SAT) D'Hanis, TX Holy Cross Church.
Stiller, Ludwig F. *s.j.* '62 (FgM) Provinces.
Stillmank, John G. '93 (MAD) Mount Horeb, WI St. Ignatius Church; Perry, WI Holy Redeemer Church.
Stillmark, John C. '93 (MAD) [H] Madison, WI Bishop O'Connor Catholic Pastoral Center.
Stillmock, Martin *c.ss.r.* '58 (STP) Brooklyn Center, MN St. Alphonsus Church.
Stillmunks, Steven J. '77 (OM) Papillion, NE St. Columbkille Church.
Stillwell, Msgr. William J. '67 (BUF) Retired.
Stilwell, Dennis R. '71 (GAY) Cheboygan, MI St. Mary-St. Charles Church.
Stine, Robert F. '73 (BR) St. Amant, LA Holy Rosary Church.
Stineman, William F. '49 (IND) Retired.
Stingel, Louis F. '60 (MET) Jamesburg, NJ St. James the Less Church.
Stingle, Lawrence A. '41 (GB) Retired.
Stinson, James G. *s.j.* '94 (BO) [W] Boston, MA The Society of Jesus of New England-Provincial Offices.
Stirniman, Jeffrey D. '95 (PEO) [3] Bloomington, IL St. Patrick's Church.
Stirpe, Carlo '65 (SY) Fulton, NY Immaculate Conception Church.
Stislow, Louis *o.f.m.* '61 (PH) [D] Philadelphia, PA Archbishop Ryan High School.
Stiteler, Francis Michael *o.c.s.o.* '83 (ATL) [J] Conyers, GA The Monastery of the Holy Spirit.
Stites, John F. '76 (TOL) [B] Oregon, OH Cardinal Stritch High School.
Stitz, John '53 (KCK) Retired.
Stivason, Paul R. '89 (GBG) Smithton, PA St. Timothy Church; Yukon, PA Seven Dolors Church.
Stluka, Jerome D. '69 (COL) [18] Columbus, OH Holy Cross Church.
Stobba, Joseph G. *o.s.a.* '59 (MIL) [14] Racine, WI St. Rita Church.
Stober, Msgr. William P. '73 (PAT) Branchville, NJ Our Lady Queen of Peace Church.
Stobie, Steve (P) Absent on Leave.
Stochl, John J. *s.j.* '54 (FgM) Provinces.
Stochmal, Marek '95 (DET) Absent on Leave.
Stock, Augustine *o.s.b.* '48 (KC) [J] Conception, MO Conception Abbey.
Stock, Thomas E. '98 (CLV) Wickliffe, OH Our Lady of Mount Carmel Church.
Stockelman, William R. '78 (CIN) Batavia, OH Holy Trinity Church; Williamsburg, OH St. Ann Church.
Stocker, Bede *o.s.b.* '42 (RCK) [G] Aurora, IL Marmion Abbey-St. Augustine's Abbey.
Stockert, Harold '63 (PSC) Granville, NY SS. Peter and Paul Church.
Stockhausen, Paul G. *s.j.* '40 (MIL) [P] Wauwatosa, WI Jesuit Community at St. Camillus.
Stocking, Joseph R. *s.j.* '67 (SEA) [8] Seattle, WA St. Edward Church; [9] Seattle, WA St. George Church; [18] Seattle, WA St. Paul Church; [A] Seattle, WA Seattle University.
Stockinger, Tony '63 (JOL) Retired.
Stocklosa, J. Walter '40 (BO) Senior Priests.
Stockman, Gerald '64 (JC) On Duty Outside the Diocese.
Stockmeyer, Basil *c.p.* '40 (BAL) [11] Baltimore, MD Ascension Church; [S] Baltimore, MD St. Joseph's Passionist Community.
Stockus, Edward S. '91 (CHI) [1] Oak Lawn, IL St. Catherine of Alexandria Church.
Stockwell, C. Robert '53 (LAN) Retired.
Stodola, Francis '89 (LAR) [11] Laredo, TX Santa Margarita de Escocia Independent Church.
Stoeber, Charles L *s.f.* '56 (SFE) [30] Albuquerque, NM St. Therese of the Infant Jesus of the Little Flower Church.
Stoegbauer, Carlton C. '82 (CAM) Absecon, NJ St. Elizabeth Ann Seton Church.
Stoeger, James A. *s.j.* '75 (CHI) [C] Chicago, IL Jesuit Community at Loyola University of Chicago; [N] Chicago, IL Chicago Province of the Society of Jesus-Provincial Office.
Stoeger, John D. '72 (LA) [A] Camarillo, CA St. John's Seminary; [A] Camarillo, CA St. John's Seminary.
Stoeger, William R. *s.j.* '72 (TUC) [F] Tucson, AZ Jesuit Community of the Vatican Observatory.
Stoerlein, Msgr. Joseph G. '49 (CAM) Retired.
Stoetzel, Charles D. '80 (LC) Marshfield, WI St. John the Baptist Church; Spencer, WI Christ the King Church.
Stofcik, John A. '40 (GBG) Retired.
Stoffel, Msgr. Jerome C. '36 (SLC) Retired.
Stoffel, Richard J. '79 (MIL) [7] Racine, WI St. Joseph Church.
Stoffer, Patrick *o.f.m.conv.* '97 (PEO) [2] Peoria, IL Holy Family Church.
Stohrer, Walter J. *s.j.* '60 (MIL) [P] Milwaukee, WI Jesuit Community at Marquette University.
Stokes, David *s.j.* '63 (RIC) [5] Richmond, VA Sacred Heart Church.
Stokes, Thomas A. *s.m.* '63 (SP) [7] Tampa, FL Our Lady of Perpetual Help Church.
Stokowski, Lucjan '77 (CLV) [37] Cleveland, OH St. John Cantius Church.
Stolcis, Ronald '68 (CHY) Sheridan, WY Holy Name Church.
Stoley, Lawrence J. '91 (LIN) Rulo, NE Immaculate Conception Church; [C] Falls City, NE Sacred Heart School.
Stolinksi, Dennis R. '69 (OM) Bellevue, NE St. Matthew The Evangelist Church of Bellevue.
Stolinski, Robert A. '70 (BUF) [62] Buffalo, NY St. Stephen Church; Buffalo, NY Erie County Medical Center.
Stoll, Eugene *s.v.d.* '30 (CHI) [B] Techny, IL Divine Word Residence.
Stoll, Kenneth *s.c.j.* '45 (JKS) [F] Nesbit, MS St. Michael Community House.
Stoll, Mark J. '92 (SC) Neptune, IA St. Joseph Church.
Stollenwerk, Charles J. '73 (CLV) North Olmsted, OH St. Richard Church.
Stolowski, Stephen '79 (NSH) [I] Nashville, TN Mercy Convent.
Stoltz, John J. '90 (L) Edmonton, KY Christ the Healer Church.
Stoltz, Joseph H. '73 (L) [75] Louisville, KY St. William Church; Louisville, KY Caritas Medical Center; [H] Louisville, KY Caritas Medical Center.
Stoltz, Richard L. '74 (STL) Richmond Heights, MO St. Luke the Evangelist Church.
Stolz, Paul L. '61 (CIN) Retired.
Stolz, William K. *s.j.* '62 (SAC) [C] Sacramento, CA Jesuit High School; [H] Carmichael, CA Jesuit High School Community of Sacramento.
Stolze, Edward B. '72 (CIN) Morrow, OH St. Philip the Apostle Church.
Stolzer, Vincent A. '56 (STL) Retired.
Stolzman, William F. '71 (STP) Shakopee, MN St. Mark Church.
Stommel, Russell J. '67 (MIL) Neosho, WI St. Matthew Church; Rubicon, WI St. John Church; Woodland, WI St. Mary Church.
Stone, Carl '42 (ALB) Retired.
Stone, Colm *o.c.d.* '62 (SEA) Stanwood, WA St. Cecilia Church.
Stone, Francis Mary *m.f.v.a.* '98 (BIR) [E] Birmingham, AL Franciscan Missionaries of the Eternal Word, A Public Association of the Christian Faithful.
Stone, Harold *s.t.* '59 (FgM) Trinity Missions.
Stone, Harold *s.t.* '59 (SJN) Loiza, PR San Patricio Church.
Stone, Michael J. (ALN) [P] Orwigsburg, PA Seton Manor, Inc.
Stone, Michael J. '68 (ALN) Schuylkill Haven, PA St. Ambrose Church.
Stone, Robert '90 (KC) [6] Kansas City, MO St. Catherine of Siena Church.
Stone, Robert J. *c.m.* '77 (BIR) Alexander City, AL St. John the Apostle Church.
Stone, Theodore '52 (CHI) Park Ridge, IL Mary, Seat of Wisdom Church.
Stone, Msgr. William (BAK) The Dalles, OR St. Peter's Church.
Stone, Msgr. William S. '43 (BAK) Retired.
Stoneberg, Jeff '90 (JOL) Glen Ellyn, IL St. James the Apostle Church.
Stoner, John Bosco *o.s.b.* '76 (LA) [Q] Valyermo, CA St. Andrew's Abbey.
Stoner, Tim '96 (GI) Kearney, NE St. James Church.
Stonich, Raymond '56 (JOL) Wheaton, IL St. Michael Church.
Stookey, Gerald L. *o.p.* '78 (CHI) [N] Chicago, IL Dominicans (Provincial Office).
Stopponi, John '38 (DET) [32] Detroit, MI Holy Family Church; [K] Detroit, MI St. Sylvester Monastery.
Stopyra, David M. *o.f.m.conv.* '60 (FR) [1] Taunton, MA Our Lady of the Holy Rosary Church.
Storan, William P. '61 (SAC) Vallejo, CA St. Basil Church.
Storck, Edward J. '52 (WIL) Nursing Homes.
Storey, John R. '47 (CLV) Retired.
Stormes, James R. *s.j.* '79 (BAL) [S] Baltimore, MD Jesuit Fathers and Brothers Maryland Provincial Curia; [S] Baltimore, MD Ferdinand Wheeler Jesuit Community.
Stormes, James R. *s.j.* '79 (FgM) Jesuit Foreign Missions.
Storms, Francis *o.f.m.* '75 (BUF) [C] St. Bonaventure, NY St. Bonaventure University; [C] St. Bonaventure, NY St. Bonaventure University; [O] St. Bonaventure, NY St. Bonaventure Friary.
Storms, Louis B. *c.m.* (BAL) Emmitsburg, MD St. Joseph Church.
Storms, Louis B. *c.m.* '40 (BAL) [S] Emmitsburg, MD Vincentian House.
Stortz, Donald L. '64 (OM) Absent on Sick Leave.
Stortz, Mario '49 (AMA) Retired.

Stott, Thomas D. '83 (CHL) Mount Airy, NC Holy Angels Church.
Stout, O. Hugh '61 (CAM) On Duty Outside the Diocese.
Stout, O. Hugh '61 (NO) [7] New Orleans, LA Holy Ghost Church.
Stout, Richard E. *c.s.c.* '71 (FgM) Holy Cross Foreign Missions.
Stout, Richard E. *c.s.c.* '71 (FTW) [J] South Bend, IN Congregation of Holy Cross, Indiana Province, Provincial House.
Stout, Thomas '77 (BEL) Red Bud, IL St. John the Baptist Church.
Stouvenel, Gerald E. '72 (DAV) West Burlington, IA SS. Mary and Patrick Church.
Stover, James M. '00 (PIT) Ross Township, PA St. Sebastian Church.
Stoviak, Leonard W. '73 (GBG) Scottdale, PA St. John the Baptist Church.
Stovik, Raphael *o.s.b.* '56 (BIS) [A] Richardton, ND Assumption Abbey.
Stowe, John *o.f.m.conv.* '95 (ELP) [17] El Paso, TX Our Lady of Mt. Carmel Church.
Stoyle, James F. '91 (FTW) [13] South Bend, IN St. Jude Church.
Strabala, Matthew T. *o.p.* '00 (SFE) [31] Albuquerque, NM St. Thomas Aquinas University Church; [L] Albuquerque, NM St. Thomas Aquinas (Newman Center) University Parish.
Strachota, Dennis '67 (BAK) Pendleton, OR St. Mary's Church.
Strachota, Michael D. '79 (MIL) [22] Milwaukee, WI Corpus Christi Church.
Strader, Mark A. '91 (LA) Tujunga, CA Our Lady of Lourdes Church.
Stradinger, Stephen J. '74 (MIL) [9] Racine, WI St. Mary by the Lake Church.
Stradomski, Ryszard '83 (SP) Temple Terrace, FL Corpus Christi Church.
Strafalace, Francis *s.c.j.* '65 (GAL) [56] Houston, TX Our Lady of Guadalupe Church.
Strahan, Msgr. Francis V. '59 (BO) [1] Framingham, MA St. Bridget Church.
Strain, Eugene '53 (DET) Rochester Hills, MI St. Mary's of the Hills Church.
Straka, Francis P. '90 (ALN) West Reading, PA Sacred Heart Church.
Straley, Michael '83 (PHX) Flagstaff, AZ San Francisco de Asis Church.
Stram, Msgr. Gideon '38 (AUS) Retired.
Strand, Ralph S. '64 (CHI) Other Assignments.
Strange, Michael *s.s.* (SFR) [K] San Francisco, CA Home for the Aged of the Little Sisters of the Poor.
Strange, Michael *s.s.* '65 (SFR) San Francisco, CA St. Anne's Home.
Strano, Antonio *o.m.i.* '51 (SAT) [K] San Antonio, TX Oblate Madonna Residence.
Strano, Msgr. Edward '56 (TR) Retired.
Stransky, Thomas F. *c.s.p.* '57 (NY) [DD] Jamaica Estates, NY Paulist Fathers Generalate.
Strass, Richard *c.ss.r.* '60 (ANC) Seward, AK Sacred Heart Church.
Strass, Richard *c.ss.r.* '60 (DEN) [M] Denver, CO The Redemptorists/Denver Province.
Strasser, John R. '76 (DOD) [1] Dodge City, KS Cathedral of the Sacred Heart.
Strassle, Paul '58 (LR) Retired.
Strassner, Henry E. '47 (ALN) Tamaqua, PA St. Jerome Church.
Strasz, James G. *s.m.* '80 (BO) [Y] Framingham, MA The Marist House.
Stratman, Ambrose F. '48 (STL) Retired.
Stratman, Joseph '77 (BEA) [6] Beaumont, TX Our Lady of the Assumption Church; Retired.
Stratman, Raymond '55 (LEX) Retired.
Stratman, Thomas F. '50 (DAV) [1] Davenport, IA Sacred Heart Church; Retired.
Stratman, William J. '56 (DAV) Retired; [B] Davenport, IA St. Ambrose University.
Straub, David R. '94 (CHI) [27] Chicago, IL St. Benedict the African (West) Church.
Straub, Msgr. Edward F. '65 (NY) Liberty, NY St. Peter Church.
Strausser, George '77 (PH) [3] Philadelphia, PA St. Agatha-St. James Church.
Stravinskas, Peter M.J. '77 (B) On Duty Outside the Diocese.
Stravinskas, Peter M.J. '77 (SCR) [M] Mount Pocono, PA Newman House.
Strawn, Nicholas *s.v.d.* '62 (FgM) Society of the Divine Word Foreign Missions.
Strebel, Roger '66 (GB) Wagner, WI St. Edward Church; Walsh, WI St. Joseph Church.
Strebig, John J. '52 (GRY) Retired.
Strebler, Charles F. '94 (CLV) North Royalton, OH St. Albert the Great Church.
Strecok, Lubomir '98 (ALT) On Special or Other Diocesan Assignment.
Strecok, Lubomir J. '98 (ALT) [J] Hollidaysburg, PA Conference of Slovak Clergy.
Stredny, Anthony G. '57 (GAL) Retired.
Streichardt, Wolfgang '82 (SAG) Bannister, MI St. Cyril Church.
Streicher, Bernard J. *s.j.* '60 (CLV) [D] Cleveland, OH St. Ignatius High School.
Streider, Leon '76 (GAL) [A] Houston, TX St. Mary's Seminary.
Streifel, Keith N. '99 (BIS) [4] Minot, ND St. Leo Church.
Streit, David *s.v.d.* '69 (FgM) Society of the Divine Word Foreign Missions.
Streit, Joseph C. '60 (SCR) [I] Wilkes-Barre, PA Mercy Hospital.
Streit, Thomas G. *c.s.c.* '86 (FTW) [B] Notre Dame, IN University of Notre Dame Du Lac; [J] Notre Dame, IN Holy Cross Community, Corby Hall, University of Notre Dame.
Strelick, Charles J. '56 (MAR) Retired.
Strelinski, Ernest '65 (PIT) Allison Park, PA St. Ursula Church.
Stremel, Adolph '36 (WCH) Retired.
Strempeck, Msgr. Martin R. '55 (BAL) Hydes, MD St. John the Evangelist Church; Retired.
Stremski, John P. '60 (SUP) Retired.
Streng, Msgr. James E. '51 (BUF) Retired.
Strenski, Joseph A. '45 (MIL) Retired.
Stretch, Daniel P. '53 (STL) On Duty Outside the Archdiocese.
Stretton, Noel '59 (DUL) [10] Duluth, MN St. Joseph's Church; Duluth, MN Duluth Federal Prison.
Streveler, Robert A. '69 (LC) Rothschild, WI St. Therese of the Child Jesus Church; Weston, WI St. Agnes Church.
Streza, Charles V. '43 (ROM) Retired.
Stricker, Robert A. '48 (CIN) [81] Cincinnati, OH St. Therese, The Little Flower Church; Retired.
Strickland, Msgr. Joseph E. '85 (TYL) [1] Tyler, TX Cathedral of the Immaculate Conception.
Strieder, Leon '76 (AUS) On Duty Outside the Diocese.
Striedl, Max, Jr. '96 (RCK) Dundee, IL St. Catherine of Siena Church.
Striedl, Max J. '96 (RCK) [B] Elgin, IL St. Edward Central Catholic High School.
Striegel, Robert M. '73 (DAV) Ottumwa, IA St. Mary of the Visitation Church.
Stringini, John L. '79 (RCK) [3] Rockford, IL St. Bernadette Church.
Stripe, Keith '96 (TOL) Sycamore, OH St. Pius X Church.
Stripe, Keith A. '96 (TOL) Tiffin, OH St. Mary Church.
Strish, Andrew F. '67 (SCR) [3] Pittston, PA St. John the Baptist Church.
Stritch, Morris G. '42 (MEM) Retired.
Strittmatter, Andre *t.o.r.* '61 (ALT) [A] Loretto, PA St. Francis College; [F] Loretto, PA Mount Assisi Friary.
Strittmatter, J. Joseph '56 (ALT) Retired.
Strittmatter, Lawrence R. '57 (CIN) [3] Dayton, OH St. Albert the Great Church.
Strittmatter, Paul J. *s.j.* '77 (DM) Dunlap, IA St. Patrick Church; Woodbine, IA Sacred Heart Church.
Strittmatter, Paul J. *s.j.* '77 (OM) [K] Omaha, NE Jesuit Community at Creighton University.
Strittmatter, Robert '66 (FWT) [1] Fort Worth, TX St. Patrick Church.
Stroba, Marek *o.m.i.* '85 (STP) [27] St. Paul, MN St. Mary Church.
Strobel, Charles '70 (NSH) Absent on Leave.
Strock, Richard M. '65 (LR) Siloam Springs, AR St. Mary's Church.
Strohmeyer, George E. '64 (E) [B] Erie, PA Gannon University.
Strollo, Charles P. *c.m.* '73 (PH) [B] Philadelphia, PA St. Vincent's Seminary; [B] Philadelphia, PA DePaul Novitiate; [AA] Philadelphia, PA Congregation of the Mission.
Strom, Charles W. '72 (HEL) Retired.
Stromberg, Floyd G. '59 (TUC) [9] Tucson, AZ Our Lady, Queen of All Saints Church.
Stromberg, James S. '57 (STP) Retired; [C] St. Paul, MN University of St. Thomas.
Strommer, James G. *c.p.* '70 (CHI) [N] Chicago, IL Passionist Provincial Office.
Strommer, James G. *c.p.* '70 (SAC) [H] Citrus Heights, CA Christ the King Retreat.
Strommer, Jim *c.p.* '70 (SAC) [J] Citrus Heights, CA Christ the King Retreat Center.
Stromski, Adam F.X. '46 (MIA) [12] Miami, FL Our Lady of the Holy Rosary Church.
Stromski, Adam F.X. '46 (STU) Retired.
Strong, Barry R. *o.s.f.s.* '84 (R) Wilmington, NC Immaculate Conception Church.
Stronkowski, John '85 (BGP) [1] Danbury, CT St. Gregory Church.
Stroot, Ralph E. '60 (STL) Gardenville, MO St. George Church; Retired.
Stroot, Thomas J. '70 (WCH) Pittsburg, KS Our Lady of Lourdes Church; [B] Pittsburg, KS St. Mary-Colgan High School.
Stroud, J. Francis *s.j.* '61 (NY) [DD] New York, NY Jesuit Community at Fordham University.
Stroup, Edmund F. '49 (BAL) Retired.
Strub, Herman A. '34 (DAV) [L] Davenport, IA Kahl Home for the Aged and Infirm.
Struc, Marian '69 (PHU) Jersey City, NJ SS. Peter and Paul Church.
Struik, Felix A.P. *o.p.* '58 (SJN) Catano, PR Nuestra Senora del Carmen Church; [A] Bayamon, PR Bayamon Central University.
Strumski, Matthew J. '48 (PRO) [2] Warren, RI St. Casimir Church.
Strupp, James A. '67 (MIL) Retired.
Strupp, Joachim *o.f.m.cap.* '63 (MIL) [N] Fond du Lac, WI St. Francis Home for Aged; [P] Mount Calvary, WI St. Lawrence Friary.
Strus, Walter A. '94 (CHI) Other Assignments.
Struzik, Edward J. '85 (MET) Plainsboro, NJ Queenship of Mary Church.
Struzynski, Robert *o.f.m.* '63 (BUF) [59] Buffalo, NY SS. Rita & Patrick Church.
Struzzieri, Andrew L. '75 (BRK) [85] Brooklyn, NY St. Matthew's Church.
Struzzo, John A. *c.s.c.* '65 (FTW) [J] South Bend, IN Congregation of Holy Cross, Indiana Province, Provincial House.
Strycharz, Stanley '91 (VEN) Graduate Studies.
Stryjewski, John J. '85 (MOB) On Leave from the Archdiocese.
Stryker, Peter R. *c.p.m.* '98 (L) Glasgow, KY St. Helen Church.
Strykowski, Msgr. John J. '63 (BRK) Released from Diocesan Assignment.
Strzadala, Wieslaw P. *s.d.s.* '90 (BRK) [93] Brooklyn, NY Our Lady of Consolation Church.
Strzalkowski, Dariusz Z. '00 (DET) Allen Park, MI St. Frances Cabrini Church.
Strzelec, Thaddeus '42 (HBG) [G] Danville, PA Holy Family Convent and Infirmary.
Strzok, James J. *s.j.* '70 (OM) [C] Omaha, NE Creighton Preparatory School.
Stua, Ronald *c.m.f.* (CHI) [79] Chicago, IL Holy Family Church.
Stuardi, Msgr. J. Edwin '41 (MOB) Retired; [E] Daphne, AL Mercy Medical; [K] Daphne, AL Apostleship of Prayer.
Stuart, Francis *o.s.b.* '61 (SAL) Sharon Springs, KS Holy Ghost Church.
Stuart, George '89 (WDC) [3] Bethesda, MD Little Flower Church.
Stuart, George E. '89 (WDC) Pastoral Center Special Ministries.
Stubbs, Msgr. Charles W. '63 (BGP) Leave of Absence.
Stubbs, Michael C. '78 (KCK) Lansing, KS St. Francis de Sales Church.
Stubeda, Anthony J. '85 (NU) On Special or Other Diocesan Assignment.
Stubna, Kris D. '85 (PIT) Scott Township, PA SS. Simon and Jude Church.
Stuchlik, Richard '68 (WCH) Hutchinson, KS St. Teresa Church; Wichita, KS Veterans Administration Hospital.
Stucklie, Eugene '60 (BRK) [245] Queens, NY St. Thomas Apostle Church.
Stuczko, Richard J. '54 (SY) Oriskany, NY Oneida County Jail; Retired.
Studeny, Colman *o.f.m.cap.* '61 (FgM) Capuchin Foreign Missions.
Studer, Louis B. *o.m.i.* '76 (BEL) [F] Belleville, IL Shrine of Our Lady of the Snows; [J] Belleville, IL Missionary Association of Mary Immaculate-Missionary Oblates of Mary Immaculate.
Studerus, Gregory J. '80 (NEW) [24] Jersey City, NJ Parish of the Resurrection Church.
Studniewski, Gary R. '95 (WDC) Military Chaplains.
Studwell, Joachim C. *o.f.m.* '87 (PIT) [O] Ben Avon, PA St. Anthony Friary and Mission House.
Studzinski, Lambert V. '40 (FAR) Retired.
Studzinski, Raymond *o.s.b.* '69 (IND) [J] St. Meinrad, IN St. Meinrad Archabbey.
Studzinski, Raymond *o.s.b.* '69 (WDC) [C] Washington, DC Catholic University of America, The.
Stuebben, Anthony A. *c.ss.r.* '48 (STL) [P] Liguori, MO St. Clement Health Care Center.
Stuebben, Msgr. George '54 (SAT) Retired.
Stuebben, Lawrence '55 (SAT) [24] San Antonio, TX St. Agnes Church.
Stueber, Edwin *o.s.b.* '46 (SCL) [I] Collegeville, MN St. John's Abbey, of the Order of St. Benedict.
Stuecker, Henry C. '38 (L) Retired; [L] Louisville, KY Bishop David Apartments.
Stuempel, Robert L. '75 (L) [44] Louisville, KY St. Lawrence Church.
Stueve, Bernard C. *s.m.* '38 (CIN) [M] Dayton, OH Marianist Provincialate.
Stulb, Joseph A. '61 (NEW) Retired.
Stulens, Cyriel *c.i.c.m.* '65 (FgM) Missionhurst Foreign Missions.
Stump, David X. *s.j.* '71 (NEW) [B] Jersey City, NJ Saint Peter's College; [N] Jersey City, NJ Jesuits of Saint Peter's College, Inc.
Stump, James *o.f.m.cap* '88 (SFR) [B] San Francisco, CA Capuchin House of Studies; [R] San Francisco, CA Newman Center, University of California Medical Center.

Stumpf, Thomas W. *o.s.b.* '52 (RIC) [H] Richmond, VA St. Joseph's Home for the Aged; [L] Richmond, VA Mary Mother of the Church Abbey.
Stumpf, William F. '85 (IND) [1] Indianapolis, IN SS. Peter and Paul Church; Nashville, IN St. Agnes Church.
Stunek, Howard *o.f.m.* '57 (LAN) Milan, MI Federal Correctional Institution.
Stunek, Leonard *o.f.m.* '60 (SAG) [18] Saginaw, MI St. Thomas Aquinas Church.
Stupca, Edward L. '61 (HEL) Madison, MT Madison County Catholic Community Church.
Sturm, Donald E. '58 (KC) Hirlingen, MO Seven Dolors Church.
Sturm, George *c.m.f.* '37 (SAT) [12] San Antonio, TX Immaculate Heart of Mary Church.
Sturm, John G. *s.j.* '50 (BUF) [50] Buffalo, NY St. Michael Church.
Sturm, Michael O. '69 (MIL) Special Assignment.
Sturm, Samuel L. '99 (KNX) [2] Knoxville, TN All Saints Catholic Church.
Sturmer, Jeffrey J. '94 (BUF) [4] Tonawanda, NY St. Christopher Church.
Sturmer, Jeffrey M. '94 (BUF) [D] Buffalo, NY Nardin Academy High School.
Sturn, Michael '77 (SB) Chino, CA St. Margaret Mary Church.
Sturtz, Richard S. '56 (OG) Olmstedville, NY St. Joseph Church; Schroon Lake, NY Our Lady of Lourdes Church.
Stutz, Edward J. '46 (E) Retired.
Styczen, Emil '55 (SP) Holiday, FL St. Vincent De Paul Church.
Styles, Kenneth A. *s.j.* '72 (CLV) [D] Cleveland, OH St. Ignatius High School.
Su, Stanislaus *c.s.j.b.* '69 (BRK) [V] Astoria, NY Congregation of St. John the Baptist of China.
Su, Stanislaus *c.s.j.b.* '69 (LA) [CC] Monterey Park, CA Congregation of St. John the Baptist.
Su, Msgr. Tomas '50 (SJN) [53] San Juan, PR Sagrada Familia Church.
Suan, Charito '85 (SFR) [18] San Francisco, CA Church of the Epiphany.
Suarez, Carlos *o.s.b.* '86 (BIS) [A] Richardton, ND Assumption Abbey.
Suarez, Carlos *o.s.b.* '86 (FgM) American - Cassinese Congregation Foreign Missions.
Suarez, Msgr. Jose V. '54 (SJ) [13] San Jose, CA St. Julie Billiart Church.
Suarez, Leo '88 (STO) [3] Stockton, CA St. Edward Church.
Suarez, Michael F. *s.j.* '94 (NY) [DD] New York, NY Jesuit Community at Fordham University.
Suarez, Octavio '64 (TYL) Nacogdoches, TX Sacred Heart Church.
Suarez, Pedro A. *s.j.* '72 (MIA) [B] Miami, FL Barry University; [H] Miami, FL Villa Arrieta.
Suarez, Walter *i.v.e.* '96 (SJ) [14] San Jose, CA St. Leo the Great Church.
Suaybaguio, Evangelio R. '75 (NY) [211] Staten Island, NY St. Joseph, St. Thomas Church.
Suazo, Rafael '64 (SJN) [7] Carolina, PR San Felipe Apostol Church.
Subb, Victor *glmy.* '87 (SAV) Swainsboro, GA Holy Trinity Church.
Suberlak, Donald *c.r.* '67 (KAL) Three Oaks, MI St. Mary of the Assumption Church.
Subitowski, Joseph A. *s.j.* (DET) [P] Bloomfield Hills, MI Manresa Jesuit Retreat House.
Subocz, Adam C. '86 (HRT) East Windsor, CT St. Philip's Church.
Suchan, Robert J. *s.j.* '56 (FgM) Provinces.
Suchan, William T. *s.j.* '58 (AGN) [H] Mangilao, GU Campus Ministry, Newman Center, University of Guam.
Suchan, William T. *s.j.* '58 (FgM) Provinces.
Sucharski, Michael M. *s.v.d.* '83 (LAF) Broussard, LA St. Joseph Church.
Sucher, Frederick *c.p.* '44 (CHI) [N] Chicago, IL Passionist Community-Immaculate Conception Monastery.
Suchnicki, Michael *o.f.m.cap.* '88 (SAL) Hays, KS St. Joseph's Church; [D] Hays, KS St. Joseph's Friary.
Suchocki, James A. '62 (GAY) Bay Shore, MI St. Francis Solanus Church; Petoskey, MI St. Francis Xavier Church.
Suchocki, Marek '86 (NY) [228] Staten Island, NY St. Stanislaus Kostka Church.
Sucholet, James Joseph '91 (NOR) Voluntown, CT St. Thomas Apostle Church.
Suchy, Theodore D. *o.s.b.* '67 (JOL) [A] Lisle, IL Benedictine University; [J] Lisle, IL St. Procopius Abbey.
Sudano, Glenn *c.f.r.* '84 (NY) [18] Yonkers, NY Most Holy Trinity Church; [DD] Yonkers, NY St. Felix Friary.
Sudekum, Msgr. Edward J. '61 (STL) [3] University City, MO Our Lady of Lourdes Church.
Sudhoff, Leonard *c.pp.s.* '39 (CIN) [B] Carthagena, OH St. Charles.
Suding, Steve *o.f.m.* (STL) [P] St. Louis, MO Franciscan Friary of St. Anthony of Padua.
Sudlik, Leonard '76 (GR) [8] Grand Rapids, MI Holy Spirit Church.
Sudlik, Richard *o.m.i.* '72 (MIA) [7] Miami, FL Holy Redeemer Church.
Sudlik, Richard *o.m.i.* '72 (WDC) [M] Washington, DC Missionary Oblates of Mary Immaculate.
Sudol, Gerard J. (NEW) [11] Jersey City, NJ Holy Rosary Church.
Sudol, Gerard J. '80 (NEW) Hoboken, NJ St. Mary's Hospital; Jersey City, NJ St. Francis Community Health Center; [S] Jersey City, NJ Bon Secours New Jersey Health System.
Suehr, Philip *o.s.c.* '66 (STP) [N] Shoreview, MN Crosier Provincial House Province of St. Odilia.
Suehr, Philip *o.s.c.* '69 (TOL) Sandusky, OH Holy Angels Church.
Suellentrop, Anthony J. '73 (DOD) Kiowa, KS St. John the Apostle Church; Medicine Lodge, KS Holy Rosary Church; Sharon, KS St. Boniface Church.
Suellentrop, Bernard A. '45 (STL) Shrewsbury, MO St. Michael Church.
Suellentrop, Bernard A. '46 (STL) Retired.
Suellentrop, Daniel M. *o.s.b.* '51 (OKL) [I] Shawnee, OK St. Gregory's Abbey.
Suelzer, Msgr. John N. '65 (FTW) [3] Fort Wayne, IN St. Charles Borromeo Church.
Sueper, Alban *s.s.c.* '53 (OM) [K] St. Columbans, NE St. Columban's Foreign Mission Society.
Suess, Milton M. '63 (GB) Champion, WI St. Joseph Church; Luxemburg, WI Immaculate Conception Church.
Suffredini, Louis '57 (MOB) Dauphin Island, AL St. Edmund-by-the-Sea Church; Retired.
Sugrue, John F. '62 (CAM) Mays Landing, NJ St. Vincent de Paul Church.
Sugrue, Patrick *o.c.d.* '64 (SB) [G] Redlands, CA El Carmelo Retreat House.
Sugrue, Timothy F. *s.m.* '63 (WDC) [M] Washington, DC Marist Center.
Suh, Daniel *s.j.* (BRK) [235] Queens, NY St. Robert Bellarmine Church.
Suh, Steven Kang-Jin '85 (RIC) [1] Hampton, VA Catholic Community of the Korean Martyrs Church.
Suhaka, Peter '86 (MET) Pittstown, NJ St. Catherine of Siena Church.
Suhoza, John E. '68 (PIT) Mt. Lebanon, PA St. Bernard Church.
Suibielski, Kenneth J. '77 (PRO) [8] Pawtucket, RI St. Maria Goretti Church.
Suing, Benedict *o.s.b.* '54 (P) [L] St. Benedict, OR Mt. Angel Abbey.
Suit, Robert J. '74 (STL) De Soto, MO St. Rose of Lima Church.
Sujka, Andrew *o.f.m.conv.* '75 (BO) [50] Boston, MA Our Lady of Czestochowa Church.
Sukovaty, G. L. *o.p.* '51 (FgM) Dominican - Order of Preachers Foreign Missions.
Sukup, Joseph G. '56 (MIL) Retired.
Sulahian, Mesrop (ARM) [C] Glendale, CA Mekhitarian Educational Foundation.
Sulaiman, Selwan A. (OLD) Jacksonville, FL St. Ephrem Church.
Sularz, Tom '71 (JOL) Addison, IL St. Philip The Apostle Church.
Sulavik, Athanasius *o.p.* '95 (NY) [DD] New York, NY St. Vincent Ferrer Priory.
Sulkowski, Anthony P. '86 (DET) [4] Monroe, MI St. Mary's Church.
Sullivan, Alan *o.f.m.* '56 (NY) [DD] New York, NY Franciscan Friars, Order of Friars Minor, Holy Name Province.
Sullivan, Andrew A. '94 (BIR) Tuscaloosa, AL St. Francis of Assisi University Church; [H] Tuscaloosa, AL Diocesan Campus Ministry Office; [H] Tuscaloosa, AL University of Alabama in Tuscaloosa.
Sullivan, Andrew J. '47 (WOR) Retired.
Sullivan, Brendan J. '78 (BO) Health Leave.
Sullivan, Brendan V. '60 (CAM) Ventnor, NJ St. James Church.
Sullivan, C. Otis (CHI) Retired.
Sullivan, Charles '65 (SPR) Retired.
Sullivan, Charles D. *s.j.* '72 (NY) [F] New York, NY Fordham Preparatory School; [DD] New York, NY Jesuit Community at Fordham University.
Sullivan, Charles J. '66 (PH) [23] Philadelphia, PA St. Bernard Church.
Sullivan, Charles K. '64 (VEN) [4] Fort Myers, FL St. Columbkille Church.
Sullivan, D. Edward '42 (CHL) Retired.
Sullivan, Dan *c.p.* '68 (PIT) [O] Pittsburgh, PA St. Paul of the Cross Monastery; [O] Pittsburgh, PA St. Paul of the Cross Monastery.
Sullivan, Daniel '75 (TR) Hainesport, NJ Our Lady Queen of Peace Church.
Sullivan, Daniel F. '57 (CHI) Arlington Heights, IL St. Edna Church.
Sullivan, Daniel J. *c.m.* '53 (BRK) [V] Jamaica, NY Vincentian Residence.
Sullivan, Daniel J. '53 (CHI) Retired.
Sullivan, Daniel J. *s.j.* '61 (NY) [DD] New York, NY Jesuit Community at Fordham University.
Sullivan, Daniel J. '72 (SJ) [D] San Jose, CA Bellarmine College Preparatory.
Sullivan, Daniel J. '77 (PH) [61] Philadelphia, PA Holy Innocents Church.
Sullivan, Daniel James '63 (HRT) [3] Hamden, CT Our Lady of Mt. Carmel Church.
Sullivan, Daniel Jeremiah '63 (HRT) South Windsor, CT St. Margaret Mary Church.
Sullivan, David D. '58 (STL) [K] Creve Coeur, MO St. John's Mercy Medical Center.
Sullivan, Msgr. Dennis J. '71 (NY) [116] New York, NY St. Teresa Church; Manhattan, NY Gouverneur Hospital.
Sullivan, Donal '64 (STA) Green Cove Springs, FL Sacred Heart Church.
Sullivan, E. Hartrick *c.m.* '46 (DEN) [M] Denver, CO Congregation of the Mission Midwest Province: De Paul House.
Sullivan, E. Paul (BO) Topsfield, MA St. Rose of Lima Church.
Sullivan, Edward *o.f.m.* (NY) [W] Warwick, NY St. Anthony Community Hospital, Inc.; [FF] Warwick, NY Franciscan Sisters of the Poor Convent.
Sullivan, Edward G. '55 (RVC) Uniondale, NY St. Martha Church.
Sullivan, Edward J. *o.f.m.* '45 (PAT) [M] Butler, NJ St. Anthony Friary.
Sullivan, Edward P. *s.j.* '46 (BUF) [O] Buffalo, NY Canisius Jesuit Community.
Sullivan, Msgr. Edwin V. '46 (NEW) Retired; [B] South Orange, NJ Seton Hall University.
Sullivan, Emmanuel *o.c.d.* '52 (BO) [W] Boston, MA Carmelite Monastery.
Sullivan, Emmanuel *s.a.* '55 (NY) [DD] Garrison, NY Franciscan Friars of the Atonement.
Sullivan, Eugene P. '59 (CHY) Sheridan, WY Holy Name Church.
Sullivan, Eugene P. '68 (BO) [2] Weymouth, MA St. Francis Xavier Church.
Sullivan, F. Norman '63 (BUF) [5] Cheektowaga, NY Most Holy Redeemer Church.
Sullivan, Francis A. *s.j.* '51 (BO) [W] Chestnut Hill, MA The Jesuit Community at Boston College.
Sullivan, Francis D. *o.f.m.* '43 (BUF) [5] Cheektowaga, NY Most Holy Redeemer Church.
Sullivan, Francis E. *c.ss.r.* '59 (ALB) Saratoga Springs, NY St. Clement Church.
Sullivan, Francis E. '88 (BO) [3] Malden, MA Sacred Hearts Church.
Sullivan, Francis J. '30 (SPR) Retired; [I] Springfield, MA St. Michael's Residence.
Sullivan, Francis X. '48 (SPR) Retired.
Sullivan, Frederick '53 (NY) Cold Spring-on-Hudson, NY Our Lady of Loretto Church.
Sullivan, Gael *s.d.b.* '76 (LA) Bellflower, CA St. Dominic Savio Church.
Sullivan, George *o.f.m.conv.* '74 (CHL) Winston-Salem, NC Our Lady of Mercy Church.
Sullivan, George '76 (LA) [1] Oxnard, CA St. Anthony Church.
Sullivan, George R. *s.j.* '75 (LA) [Q] Los Angeles, CA Columbiere House.
Sullivan, Gerald A. '59 (CHY) [2] Cheyenne, WY Holy Trinity Church.
Sullivan, Gerald P. *s.j.* '62 (SJ) [B] Santa Clara, CA Santa Clara University.
Sullivan, J. Bernard '44 (HEL) Retired.
Sullivan, J. David *m.m.* '60 (FgM) Maryknoll Foreign Missions.
Sullivan, J. Richard '77 (L) Elizabethtown, KY St. James Church; White Mills, KY St. Ignatius Church.
Sullivan, James '47 (SFD) Retired.
Sullivan, James '53 (BO) [Z] Tewksbury, MA Immaculate Heart of Mary Infirmary.
Sullivan, James *o.m.i.* '53 (FgM) Oblates Foreign Missions.
Sullivan, James B. '58 (NEW) Fort Lee, NJ Holy Trinity Church.
Sullivan, James E. '46 (BRK) [179] Queens, NY Holy Trinity Church; Retired.
Sullivan, James F. '87 (PH) King of Prussia, PA Mother of Divine Providence Church.
Sullivan, James H. *s.m.a.* '60 (NEW) [N] Tenafly, NJ Society of African Missions, Provincialate, S.M.A. Fathers.
Sullivan, James K. '65 (SAT) [C] San Antonio, TX Oblate School of Theology.
Sullivan, James L. '43 (BO) Senior Priests.
Sullivan, James M. '60 (HEL) On Duty Outside the Diocese.
Sullivan, James M. '60 (OM) [24] Omaha, NE St. John Vianney Church.
Sullivan, James M. '66 (STL) Hazelwood, MO Our Lady of Mercy Church.
Sullivan, Msgr. James P. '70 (NY) [E] New York, NY Cardinal Spellman High School.
Sullivan, James T. *o.p.* '45 (PRO) [P] Providence, RI St. Thomas Aquinas Priory at Providence College.
Sullivan, Jan C. '91 (COL) Washington Court House, OH St. Colman Church.

Sullivan, Jeremiah *c.s.p.* '59 (LA) [87] Los Angeles, CA St. Paul the Apostle Church.
Sullivan, Jeremiah T. '62 (HEL) [B] Helena, MT Carroll College.
Sullivan, John *o.p.* (NY) Orangeburg, NY Rockland Psychiatric Center.
Sullivan, John '54 (JOL) Glen Ellyn, IL St. Petronille Church.
Sullivan, John *o.f.m.* '59 (SFD) [K] Sherman, IL Our Lady of Angels Friary.
Sullivan, John *s.m.* '65 (HON) [15] Honolulu, HI Star of the Sea Church.
Sullivan, John *o.c.d.* '68 (WDC) [B] Washington, DC Discalced Carmelite Friars; [V] Washington, DC Institute of Carmelite Studies and ICS Publications.
Sullivan, John A. (PAT) Retired.
Sullivan, John Andrew '78 (LAV) [6] Las Vegas, NV St. Anne Church.
Sullivan, John B. '61 (NY) [164] Bronx, NY St. Mary Church.
Sullivan, John E. '49 (TR) Retired.
Sullivan, John J. *s.j.* '44 (BO) [W] Weston, MA Campion Health Center, Inc.
Sullivan, Msgr. John J. '51 (SLC) [7] Salt Lake City, UT St. Ann Church.
Sullivan, John J. *m.m.* '60 (FgM) Maryknoll Foreign Missions.
Sullivan, John J. '66 (DET) Plymouth, MI Our Lady of Good Counsel Church.
Sullivan, John J. '67 (CLV) Mentor, OH St. Bede the Venerable Church.
Sullivan, John J. '77 (CHI) Glenwood, IL St. John Church.
Sullivan, John J. *o.s.f.s.* '81 (PH) [AA] Philadelphia, PA Oblates of St. Francis De Sales.
Sullivan, John James *o.p.* '39 (NY) [DD] New York, NY St. Vincent Ferrer Priory.
Sullivan, John L. '49 (PRO) [29] Providence, RI St. Pius V Church; [P] Providence, RI St. Pius Priory.
Sullivan, John L. '52 (BO) Senior Priests.
Sullivan, John L. '52 (FgM) Society of St. James the Apostle.
Sullivan, John L. '71 (SPR) [15] Springfield, MA St. Joseph's Church.
Sullivan, John L. '74 (BO) [A] Boston, MA St. John's Seminary School of Theology.
Sullivan, John M. '91 (BO) Melrose, MA St. Mary of the Annunciation Church.
Sullivan, John P. '65 (HRT) [12] New Haven, CT St. Joseph's Church; [R] New Haven, CT Southern Connecticut State University Catholic Center.
Sullivan, John P. *m.s.* '70 (HRT) [M] Hartford, CT Missionaries of LaSalette, Provincial Secretary.
Sullivan, John P. '72 (SAC) El Dorado Hills, CA Holy Trinity Church; Retired and in Senior Ministry.
Sullivan, Msgr. John P. '81 (RVC) Wading River, NY St. John Baptist Church.
Sullivan, John R. '94 (LIN) [2] Lincoln, NE Blessed Sacrament Church.
Sullivan, John W. *s.j.* '47 (BO) [W] Weston, MA Campion Health Center, Inc.
Sullivan, Joseph *o.f.m.* '56 (WDC) [B] Silver Spring, MD Holy Name College.
Sullivan, Msgr. Joseph A. '58 (BGP) [3] Greenwich, CT St. Paul Church.
Sullivan, Joseph D. '56 (NY) Montgomery, NY Holy Name of Mary Church.
Sullivan, Msgr. Joseph P. '53 (SFR) Retired.
Sullivan, Joseph T. '52 (BUR) Retired.
Sullivan, Kenneth J. *m.m.* '57 (FgM) Maryknoll Foreign Missions.
Sullivan, Kevin B. '63 (SFD) Bethalto, IL Our Lady Queen of Peace Church.
Sullivan, Msgr. Kevin L. '76 (NY) [28] New York, NY Corpus Christi Church; [40] New York, NY St. Gregory Church; [I] New York, NY The Catholic Charities of the Archdiocese of New York; [I] New York, NY The Catholic Charities of the Archdiocese of New York; [HH] New York, NY Carmel Housing Development Fund Co., Inc.; [HH] New York, NY The Housing Fund of the Archdiocese of New York; [HH] New York, Ny Cor Mariae Development Fund Corporation; [HH] New York, NY Cor Mariae Housing Development Fund, Inc.
Sullivan, Lawrence F. *o.c.d.* '60 (BO) Chelsea, MA Quigley Memorial Hospital; [W] Boston, MA Carmelite Monastery.
Sullivan, Lawrence J. '92 (CHI) Elmwood Park, IL St. Celestine Church.
Sullivan, Msgr. Leo F. '41 (STL) Retired.
Sullivan, Matthew *ss.cc.* (FR) [H] Fairhaven, MA Our Lady's Haven of Fairhaven Inc.
Sullivan, Matthew *ss.cc.* '55 (FR) New Bedford, MA Bristol Co. House of Correction & Eastern Massachusetts Correctional Alcohol Center; [I] Fairhaven, MA Sacred Hearts Provincial House.
Sullivan, Mervyn '69 (SJ) On Leave of Absence.
Sullivan, Michael (MIA) Sabbatical.
Sullivan, Michael (STP) Maple Grove, MN St. Joseph the Worker Church.
Sullivan, Michael '66 (MIA) Deerfield Beach, FL Our Lady of Mercy Church.
Sullivan, Michael '81 (CR) On Duty Outside the Diocese.
Sullivan, Michael Bruce *c.s.c.* '75 (FTW) [B] Notre Dame, IN University of Notre Dame Du Lac; [J] Notre Dame, IN Holy Cross Community, Corby Hall, University of Notre Dame.
Sullivan, Michael D. '45 (BO) Senior Priests.
Sullivan, Michael D. '91 (TR) Bayville, NJ St. Barnabas Church.
Sullivan, Michael J. '79 (SCR) Wellsboro, PA St. Peter's Church.
Sullivan, Michael J. *o.f.m.cap.* '84 (MIL) [Y] Milwaukee, WI Franciscan Peacemakers, Inc., Milwaukee.
Sullivan, Michael P. *o.s.a.* '67 (PH) [AA] Villanova, PA St. Thomas Monastery.
Sullivan, Neil S. '97 (HBG) Camp Hill, PA Good Shepherd Church.
Sullivan, Patrick *o.f.m.cap.* (MAN) Manchester, NH Hillsborough County Jail.
Sullivan, Patrick '62 (DEN) Retired.
Sullivan, Patrick *o.f.m.cap.* '71 (MAN) [2] Manchester, NH St. Anne Church.
Sullivan, Patrick *o.f.m. cap.* '72 (MAN) [4] Manchester, NH St. Augustin Church.
Sullivan, Patrick A. *s.j.* '45 (BO) [W] Weston, MA Campion Health Center, Inc.
Sullivan, Patrick A. '82 (CR) Red Lake, MN St. Mary's Church; [A] Red Lake, MN St. Mary's Mission School.
Sullivan, Patrick H. '55 (LA) [81] Los Angeles, CA St. Mary Magdalen Church.
Sullivan, Patrick J. *s.j.* '50 (NY) [DD] New York, NY Jesuit Community at Fordham University.
Sullivan, Patrick J. *c.s.c.* '56 (BGP) [P] Bridgeport, CT Provincial Offices of the Priests and Brothers of Holy Cross, Eastern Province.
Sullivan, Patrick J. *c.s.c.* '56 (SCR) [C] Wilkes-Barre, PA Kings College.
Sullivan, Patrick J. '71 (PAT) [I] Morristown, NJ Loyola House of Retreats.
Sullivan, Patrick M. *o.s.b.* '87 (MAN) [K] Manchester, NH St. Anselm Abbey.
Sullivan, Patrick T. *s.j.* '64 (NY) [DD] New York, NY Murray-Weigel Hall.
Sullivan, Paul M. *s.j.* '83 (BO) [W] Boston, MA The Society of Jesus of New England-Provincial Offices.
Sullivan, Paul M. *s.j.* '83 (PRT) Eastport, ME St. Joseph Church.
Sullivan, Paul V. '50 (NY) [10] Yonkers, NY St. Joseph Church; Retired.
Sullivan, Paul V. '52 (BO) Senior Priests.
Sullivan, Peter J., III '70 (ALB) [7] Albany, NY Church of the Holy Cross; Special Assignment.
Sullivan, R. William *o.s.a.* '67 (JOL) New Lenox, IL St. Jude Church.
Sullivan, Raymond F. *m.m.* '54 (NY) [DD] Maryknoll, NY Maryknoll Fathers and Brothers.
Sullivan, Richard H. *c.s.c.* '38 (FR) [K] North Easton, MA Holy Cross Fathers Retreat House.
Sullivan, Msgr. Richard J. '58 (E) [12] Erie, PA St. Andrew Church.
Sullivan, Robert *o.m.i.* '41 (FgM) Oblates Foreign Missions.
Sullivan, Robert *s.j.* '67 (COS) [6] Colorado Springs, CO Our Lady of Guadalupe Church.
Sullivan, Robert *s.s.j.* '72 (BLX) Pascagoula, MS St. Peter the Apostle Church.
Sullivan, Robert E. (FTW) [B] Notre Dame, IN University of Notre Dame Du Lac.
Sullivan, Robert E. '80 (BO) On Duty Outside the Archdiocese.
Sullivan, Robert J. *s.j.* '40 (BO) [W] Weston, MA Campion Health Center, Inc.
Sullivan, Robert J. '63 (SY) Special Assignment; [V] Vestal, NY Binghamton University Newman Center.
Sullivan, Robert J. '78 (BO) Pembroke, MA St. Thecla Church.
Sullivan, Robert J. '93 (BIR) Demopolis, AL St. Leo Church; Livingston, AL St. Francis of Assisi Church.
Sullivan, Sean *t.o.r.* '57 (VEN) [3] Sarasota, FL Our Lady Queen of Martyrs Church.
Sullivan, Terence *o.s.b.* '56 (KCK) Hiawatha, KS St. Ann's Church.
Sullivan, Msgr. Terrence J. '64 (SJ) Campbell, CA St. Lucy Church.
Sullivan, Thomas '53 (BIS) Retired.
Sullivan, Thomas D. *s.s.e.* '38 (VEN) [G] Englewood, FL Society of St. Edmund Residence.
Sullivan, Thomas F. '41 (CLV) Retired; [M] Akron, OH Francesca Residence; [P] Akron, OH Provincial Motherhouse and Novitiate of the Daughters of Divine Charity.
Sullivan, Thomas G. *c.ss.r.* '72 (HRT) [5] Enfield, CT St. Patrick's Church.
Sullivan, Thomas J. '77 (WOR) [N] Leicester, MA Father James Fitton House of Priestly Formation.
Sullivan, Thomas K. '52 (STA) [19] Jacksonville, FL St. Paul's Church.
Sullivan, Timothy *s.a.* '90 (NY) [DD] Garrison, NY Franciscan Friars of the Atonement, Minister General Office.
Sullivan, Msgr. Timothy E. '37 (BO) Senior Priests.
Sullivan, Timothy F. *c.s.p.* '85 (NY) [104] New York, NY St. Paul the Apostle Church.
Sullivan, Vincent B. *s.j.* '76 (NEW) [24] Jersey City, NJ Parish of the Resurrection Church; [C] Jersey City, NJ St. Peter's Preparatory School.
Sullivan, Msgr. W. Jerome '61 (BUF) Hamburg, NY St. Mary of the Lake Church.
Sullivan, William *s.j.* '66 (MI) Kwajalein, MH Blessed Sacrament Church.
Sullivan, William '72 (FTW) Elkhart, IN St. Thomas the Apostle Church.
Sullivan, William *o.ss.t.* '81 (BAL) [S] Baltimore, MD Holy Trinity Monastery.
Sullivan, William F. *s.s.c.* '56 (PRO) [P] Bristol, RI St. Columban's Retirement House.
Sullivan, William J. *o.s.b.* (MAN) [A] Manchester, NH St. Anselm Abbey Seminary.
Sullivan, William J. '59 (HBG) Rohrerstown, PA St. Leo the Great Church.
Sullivan, William J. *s.j.* '61 (SEA) [A] Seattle, WA Seattle University.
Sullivan, William J. *o.s.b.* '71 (MAN) [K] Manchester, NH St. Anselm Abbey.
Sullivan, William J. *o.ss.t.* '81 (WDC) [E] Hyattsville, MD (De Matha) Catholic High School.
Sullivan, William M. *s.j.* '66 (FgM) Provinces.
Sullivan, William M. '81 (BO) Westford, MA St. Catherine of Alexandria Church.
Sullivan, Msgr. William P. '39 (BO) Senior Priests.
Sullivan, Msgr. William V. '66 (RIC) Ashland, VA St. Ann Church.
Sullivan,, Patrick J., V.F. '63 (BIR) [21] Birmingham, AL St. Peter the Apostle Church.
Sullivant, Raymond L. *s.j.* '66 (FgM) Provinces.
Sumampong, Jed '84 (SFR) [3] South San Francisco, CA St. Augustine Church.
Sumler, Kevin '82 (BEA) Absent On Leave.
Sumler, Paul '80 (BEA) Buna, TX St. Francis of Assisi Church.
Sumler, Paul E. '80 (BEA) Kountze, TX Holy Spirit Church; Lumberton, TX Infant Jesus Church.
Summers, Bryan F. *c.o.* '72 (PIT) [O] Pittsburgh, PA Congregation of the Oratory of St. Philip Neri; [R] Pittsburgh, PA Office for Campus Ministry; [R] Pittsburgh, PA Office for Campus Ministry; [R] Pittsburgh, PA Office for Campus Ministry.
Summers, John '54 (Y) Retired.
Summers, Msgr. R. Emmett '52 (KC) Retired.
Summitt, James A. '81 (BIR) Absent on Leave.
Sumpter, Gary '79 (SR) Napa, CA St. Thomas Aquinas Church.
Sunberg, David A. '92 (CIN) Mount Repose, OH St. Elizabeth Ann Seton Church.
Sundborg, Stephen V. *s.j.* '74 (SEA) [A] Seattle, WA Seattle University.
Sunderland, James C. *s.j.* '58 (DEN) [M] Denver, CO Xavier Jesuit Center.
Sundholm, Conrad '55 (ROC) Retired.
Sunds, Elvin '73 (JKS) Meridian, MS St. Patrick Church; Meridian, MS St. Joseph Church; Meridian, MS East Mississippi State Hospital.
Sung, Anthony Ki-Hong (OKL) [14] Oklahoma City, OK Korean Martyrs Church.
Sung, Thomas *c.s.j.b.* '51 (BRK) [209] Queens, NY Our Lady of China Chapel Church; [U] Brooklyn, NY Catholic Migration & Refugee Office, Catholic Migration Services, Inc.; [V] Astoria, NY Congregation of St. John the Baptist of China.
Sung-ho, Benedict Kim *s.j.* '95 (NY) [DD] New York, NY Jesuit Provincial's Office.
Sunhwa, Gaspar *s.j.* '95 (OAK) [N] Berkeley, CA Jesuit Community at Jesuit School of Theology at Berkeley.
Suntum, James J. *s.f.* '84 (WDC) Takoma Park, MD Our Lady of Sorrows Church.
Supancheck, Norm '68 (LA) Santa Clarita, CA Our Lady of Perpetual Help Church.
Super, David J. '80 (CR) [1] Crookston, MN Cathedral of the Immaculate Conception Church; [E] Crookston, MN Marywood Residential Community.
Superiaso, Jose '85 (SFE) [1] Santa Fe, NM The Cathedral of San Francisco de Asis.
Supnet, Romeo '84 (SD) Imperial, CA Centinela State Prison.
Suppa, F. Thomas '78 (E) Union City, PA St. Teresa of Avila Church.
Suppe, Bernard A. *s.j.* '56 (BAL) [M] Baltimore, MD Mercy Health Services Inc.
Supple, Edmund R. *c.s.sp.* '38 (PIT) [B] Pittsburgh, PA Duquesne University of the Holy Ghost.
Supple, Msgr. James A. '36 (DUB) Ames, IA St. Thomas Aquinas Church (and Catholic Student Center) Church; Retired; [N] Ames, IA St. Thomas Aquinas Church and Catholic Student Center (Iowa State University).
Suquilvide, Abel '55 (LA) Guadalupe, CA Our Lady of Guadalupe Church.
Surace, Robert J. '79 (NY) Absent on Leave.

Surafka, Michael *o.f.m.* '91 (CLV) [72] Cleveland, OH St. Stanislaus Church.
Suran, Joachim '49 (BRK) Retired.
Suran, Joaquin '50 (BRK) [190] Queens, NY St. Leo Church.
Surban, Edmundo A. '61 (NEW) Jersey City, NJ Jersey City Medical Center.
Suren, John '58 (STL) Weingarten, MO Our Lady Help of Christians Church.
Suren, Richard H. '53 (STL) High Ridge, MO St. Anthony of Padua Church.
Surette, John E. *s.j.* '67 (FgM) Provinces.
Surges, Robert F. '64 (MIL) Big Bend, WI St. Joseph Church.
Suriani, Raymond N. '85 (PRO) [3] Westerly, RI St. Pius X Church.
Suriano, Thomas M. '64 (MIL) [64] Milwaukee, WI Our Lady of Lourdes Church.
Surman, Stanley '56 (SAG) Retired.
Surmay, Rafael *c.s.* '98 (SJ) [6] San Jose, CA Holy Cross Church.
Surmeier, William J. '65 (SAL) Hays, KS St. Nicholas of Myra Church; Munjor, KS St. Francis of Assisi Church.
Surowiec, Jude *o.f.m.conv.* '75 (SPR) [A] Granby, MA St. Hyacinth College and Seminary.
Surprenant, John L. '78 (NOR) Absent on Leave.
Surprenant, Paul W. '73 (WIN) [7] Rochester, MN St. Pius X Church.
Surufka, Michael *o.f.m.* '91 (CLV) [O] Cleveland, OH St. Stanislaus Friary.
Survil, Bernard '67 (GBG) On Duty Outside the Diocese.
Surwilo, Msgr. Edward R. '63 (BGP) [14] Stamford, CT Our Lady Star of the Sea Church.
Susa, Robert P. '61 (E) [B] Erie, PA Gannon University.
Susai-Marion, Francis '80 (NY) [7] Yonkers, NY St. Denis Church.
Susann, Robert F. *m.s.* '63 (ATL) [2] Marietta, GA Church of St. Ann.
Susi, Msgr. Joseph M. '50 (ALX) Special Assignment; Retired.
Suskey, Robert G. '90 (PH) Warrington, PA St. Joseph Church.
Susko, Msgr. Martin S. '61 (Y) Girard, OH St. Rose Church.
Suslenko, Mark S. '86 (HRT) [1] West Haven, CT Our Lady of Victory Church.
Suslowicz, Michael S. '80 (PIT) Kennedy Township, PA St. Malachy Church.
Susnik, Bernardin *o.f.m.* '59 (CHI) [N] Lemont, IL The Slovene Franciscan Fathers, Order of Friars Minor, Commissariat of the Holy Cross.
Suss, Thomas '73 (SEA) McNeil Island, WA McNeil Island Correction Center.
Sustarsic, John (DUL) Retired.
Sustarsic, John '52 (DUL) Babbitt, MN St. Pius X Church.
Sustayta, Paul A. '91 (LA) [14] Los Angeles, CA Holy Spirit Church.
Suszek, Eugene A. '87 (SPR) [1] Pittsfield, MA Holy Family Church.
Sutherland, Thomas J. '60 (DET) Shelby Twp., MI St. Therese of Lisieux Church.
Sutherland, Msgr. William E. '83 (E) [17] Erie, PA St. Hedwig/St. Patrick Church; [27] Erie, PA St. Patrick/ St. Hedwig Church.
Sutherland, Msgr. William J. '33 (BUF) Retired.
Sutil, Florencio (SJN) On Duty Outside the Archdiocese.
Sutman, Frank I. *o.p.* '85 (FgM) Dominican - Order of Preachers Foreign Missions.
Sutphin, Carl M. '58 (LA) [1] Los Angeles, CA Cathedral Residence Church.
Sutter, Conrad *o.f.m.conv.* '93 (TOL) Carey, OH Our Lady of Consolation, Basilica-National Church; Frenchtown, OH St. Nicholas Church.
Sutter, Raymond A. '73 (CLV) [7] Parma, OH St. Matthias Church.
Sutton, Alphonsus M. *f.f.i.* '57 (FR) [I] New Bedford, MA Marian Friary of Our Lady, Queen of the Seraphic Order.
Sutton, Donald (DEN) [1] Denver, CO Cathedral of the Immaculate Conception.
Sutton, Donald '81 (DEN) [12] Denver, CO Holy Ghost Church.
Sutton, John H. '56 (PBL) Retired.
Sutton, John V. '87 (BO) [5] Weymouth, MA Sacred Heart Church.
Sutton, ST '96 (OLD) Special Assignment.
Sutton, Stephen R. '84 (BAL) [49] Baltimore, MD St. Joseph Church.
Sutton, Thomas E. '73 (SAG) Auburn, MI St. Joseph Church.
Sutula, Leo S. '49 (NOR) Retired.
Suvakeen, Peter A. '89 (BRK) [14] Brooklyn, NY St. Augustine Church.
Suver, Robert J. '40 (CIN) Retired.
Suvokeen, Peter (NEW) Cedar Grove, NJ Essex County Hospital Center.
Suwala, Stanislaw *c.r.* (CHI) [86] Chicago, IL St. Hyacinth Church.
Suwalsky, David J. *s.j.* '95 (STL) [P] St. Louis, MO Jesuit Community Corporation at St. Louis University - Jesuit Hall.
Suwinski, Leo S. '43 (BGP) Retired.
Svarczkopf, Msgr. Mark '74 (IND) On Duty Outside the Archdiocese.
Sveher, Philip *o.s.b.* '69 (TOL) [H] Sandusky, OH Providence Hospital Inc.
Svenram, John M. *o.c.d.* '87 (DAL) [I] Dallas, TX Mount Carmel Center.
Sviokla, Msgr. Edmond J. '51 (BO) [2] Everett, MA Immaculate Conception Church.
Svirskas, Joseph J. '51 (BO) Senior Priests.
Svitan, Martin '39 (NY) [59] New York, NY St. John Nepomucene Church.
Svobodny, Aloysius *o.m.i.* '49 (STP) [Q] Buffalo, MN Christ the King Retreat Center.
Swacha, Stanley J. '79 (E) Falls Creek, PA St. Bernard Church.
Swade, Thomas J. '61 (CHI) Other Assignments.
Swain, Kenneth J. '72 (ALB) Fort Plain, NY St. James Church.
Swain, Msgr. Paul J. '88 (MAD) [H] Madison, WI Bishop O'Connor Catholic Pastoral Center.
Swain, Robert J. '59 (BRK) [V] Jamaica, NY Vincentian Residence.
Swalina, Msgr. Michael F. '70 (SPC) New Madrid, MO Immaculate Conception Church.
Swaminathan, John Peter '93 (SCR) Dickson City, PA Visitation of the Blessed Virgin Mary Church.
Swaner, Msgr. James (PEO) Eureka, IL St. Luke's Church.
Swaner, James J. '61 (PEO) Washington, IL St. Patrick's Church; [B] Peoria, IL Notre Dame High School.
Swanson, Charles F. '66 (OM) [16] Omaha, NE Holy Cross Church.
Swanson, James *l.c.* '94 (WDC) [M] Potomac, MD Legionaries of Christ.
Swanson, Mark W. '81 (DAV) Richmond, IA Holy Trinity Church; Riverside, IA St. Mary of the Assumption Church; Wellman, IA St. Joseph Church.
Swartvagher, Marc (BRK) [33] Brooklyn, NY St. Dominic Church.
Swartz, Joseph M. '75 (EVN) [1] Vincennes, IN Sacred Heart Church.
Swartz, Lawrence *o.c.s.o.* '34 (ATL) [J] Conyers, GA The Monastery of the Holy Spirit.
Swartz, Michael R. '87 (BUF) Absent on Leave.
Swast, George W. '80 (GBG) New Kensington, PA St. Joseph Church.
Sweany, Thomas M. '80 (CLV) Chesterland, OH St. Anselm Church.
Swearingen, Eric '87 (FRS) Lemoore, CA St. Peter Church.
Sweeney, Callistus *o.f.m.* (FgM) Franciscan Foreign Missions.
Sweeney, Charles J. *s.j.* '62 (TOL) [C] Toledo, OH St. John's Jesuit High School.
Sweeney, Msgr. Cornelius '50 (MRY) Morro Bay, CA St. Timothy Church; Retired.
Sweeney, D. Gilbert *s.j.* '54 (ALN) [A] Wernersville, PA Jesuit Center.
Sweeney, Daniel L. '82 (PIT) [11] Pittsburgh, PA Epiphany Church.
Sweeney, Daniel R. *s.j.* '94 (WDC) [M] Washington, DC The Jesuit Community at Georgetown University.
Sweeney, Denis *c.ss.r.* '81 (BAL) [S] Annapolis, MD Saint Mary Rectory.
Sweeney, Denis J. *c.ss.r.* (BAL) Annapolis, MD St. Mary Church.
Sweeney, Edward '88 (AMA) Friona, TX St. Teresa of Jesus Church.
Sweeney, Edward J. *s.j.* '46 (NY) [DD] New York, NY Jesuit Community at Fordham University.
Sweeney, Ernest S. *s.j.* '63 (LA) [C] Los Angeles, CA Loyola Marymount University.
Sweeney, Eugene *s.m.* '78 (FWT) Denton, TX St. Mark Church.
Sweeney, Eugene J. '65 (PBL) Retired.
Sweeney, Francis M. *c.s.p.* '61 (BO) [W] Boston, MA Paulist Fathers Residence.
Sweeney, Francis W. *s.j.* '44 (BO) [W] Chestnut Hill, MA The Jesuit Community at Boston College.
Sweeney, Frederick E. '52 (BO) [4] Haverhill, MA St. John the Baptist Church.
Sweeney, James '45 (MRY) Retired.
Sweeney, James E. '59 (ALN) Retired; [J] Bethlehem, PA Holy Family Villa.
Sweeney, James H. '81 (BRK) [101] Brooklyn, NY Our Lady of Mercy Church.
Sweeney, James P. '63 (BRK) [V] Jamaica, NY Parsons Manor.
Sweeney, Msgr. John A. '41 (STP) Retired.
Sweeney, John D. '56 (NEW) West Orange, NJ St. Joseph's Church; Retired.
Sweeney, John M. *f.p.o.* '98 (FR) [I] New Bedford, MA Franciscans of Primitive Observance.
Sweeney, John P. '73 (PIT) Aliquippa, PA St. Titus Church.
Sweeney, John T. '70 (GBG) Apollo, PA St. James the Greater Church.
Sweeney, Joseph F. *s.j.* '57 (WDC) [M] Washington, DC The Jesuit Community at Georgetown University.
Sweeney, Joseph J. '61 (PH) Absent on Sick Leave; [U] Philadelphia, PA Nazareth Hospital.
Sweeney, Msgr. Kenny C. '53 (IND) Retired.
Sweeney, Kevin '94 (ORG) Military Chaplains.
Sweeney, Kevin '97 (BRK) [U] Brooklyn, NY Catholic Migration & Refugee Office, Catholic Migration Services, Inc.
Sweeney, Kevin J. '97 (BRK) [205] Queens, NY St. Nicholas of Tolentine Church.
Sweeney, Lawrence P. '54 (SLC) [1] Ogden, UT Holy Family Church.
Sweeney, Leo C. *s.j.* '49 (CHI) [C] Chicago, IL Jesuit Community at Loyola University of Chicago.
Sweeney, Liam *s.a.c.* '77 (FWT) Weatherford, TX St. Stephen Church.
Sweeney, Michael '79 (KNX) Harriman, TN Blessed Sacrament Church; Lancing, TN St. Ann Church.
Sweeney, Michael *o.p.* '79 (OAK) [N] Oakland, CA Western Dominican Province.
Sweeney, Michael *o.p.* '79 (SEA) [22] Seattle, WA Blessed Sacrament Church.
Sweeney, Patrick E. '72 (PH) [11] Philadelphia, PA St. Anne Church.
Sweeney, Peter J. '61 (WDC) Damascus, MD St. Paul Church.
Sweeney, Robert J. '69 (RCK) Pecatonica, IL St. Mary Church.
Sweeney, Robert J. '82 (NY) Greenwood Lake, NY Holy Rosary Church.
Sweeney, Robert L. '48 (BWN) Retired.
Sweeney, Robert P. *s.s.c.* '59 (FgM) St. Columban's Foreign Mission.
Sweeney, Timothy *o.s.b.* '61 (IND) [J] St. Meinrad, IN St. Meinrad Archabbey.
Sweeney, Timothy *o.s.b.* '61 (OWN) [3] Owensboro, KY The Immaculate Church.
Sweeney, William *s.s.c.* '75 (OM) [K] St. Columbans, NE St. Columban's Foreign Mission Society.
Sweeney, William F. '81 (BRK) [163] Queens, NY St. Clare Church; [G] Fresh Meadows, NY St. Francis Preparatory School.
Sweeny, Msgr. Edward A. '57 (RVC) Long Beach, NY St. Ignatius Martyr Church.
Sweeny, Msgr. John J. '48 (SJ) [5] Santa Clara, CA Our Lady of Peace Church; [A] Santa Clara, CA Shrine of Our Lady of Peace.
Sweeny, Richard R. '86 (TR) Fair Haven, NJ Nativity Church.
Sweet, Douglas S. '95 (PRO) Absent on Leave.
Sweitzer, Raymond M. *s.j.* '75 (NY) [F] New York, NY Fordham Preparatory School; [DD] New York, NY Jesuit Community at Fordham University.
Swencki, John T. '79 (BO) Emergency Response Group.
Swengros, William '91 (SP) On Duty Outside the Diocese.
Swenson, Frederick O. '67 (LAF) Church Point, LA Our Lady of the Sacred Heart Church.
Swenson, James L. '74 (LAV) [7] Las Vegas, NV St. Bridget Church.
Swenson, Msgr. Roger A. '70 (NO) [5] Metairie, LA St. Catherine of Siena Church; [A] New Orleans, LA Notre Dame Seminary Graduate School of Theology.
Swenson, Walter J.F. '50 (NEW) [22] Jersey City, NJ Our Lady of Victories Church; Retired.
Swetland, Msgr. Stuart W. '91 (PEO) [2] Champaign, IL St. John's Catholic Chapel Church; [P] Champaign, IL St. John's Catholic Student Chapel and Newman Foundation, University of Illinois.
Swetnam, James H. *s.j.* '58 (FgM) Provinces.
Swetnam, R. William '73 (STL) Military Chaplains.
Swett, Charles J. '57 (TLS) Retired.
Swett, Msgr. Ronald J. '67 (FRS) [6] Bakersfield, CA St. Philip the Apostle Church.
Swiader, Msgr. James P. '75 (RVC) Merrick, NY Cure of Ars Church.
Swiat, James R. '67 (LAN) Grand Blanc, MI Holy Family Church.
Swiatecki, Emilian '56 (VEN) Moore Haven, FL St. Joseph the Worker Church.
Swiatek, Emil P. '65 (BUF) Elma, NY Annunciation of the Blessed Virgin Mary Church.
Swiatek, Nicholas *o.f.m. conv.* '68 (BAL) [S] Ellicott City, MD Order of Friars Minor Conventual.
Swiatek, Nicholas *o.f.m.conv.* '68 (FgM) Conventual Franciscan Foreign Missions.
Swiatkowski, Msgr. Francis M. '44 (BUF) Retired; [O] Tonawanda, NY O'Hara Residence.
Swiatocha, Bruno '56 (RVC) Retired.
Swichtenberg, William '83 (GB) Howard, WI St. John the Baptist Church.
Swickard, John L. '74 (COL) [6] Columbus, OH Saint Anthony Church.
Swicox, Thomas (MIL) [N] Wauwatosa, WI St. Camillus Health Center, Inc.
Swiderski, Gregory C. '72 (PIT) Wildwood, PA St. Catherine of Sweden Church.
Swiderski, Stan *s.d.s* '63 (LR) Mountain Home, AR St. Peter the Fisherman Church.

Swierczynski, Joseph E. '64 (PIT) [17] Pittsburgh, PA Immaculate Heart of Mary Church.
Swierz, Michael '85 (Y) Campbell, OH St. Joseph the Provider Church.
Swierzbinski, Edward '51 (NEW) Retired.
Swierzbiolek, Waclav *s.d.b.* '62 (NY) [DD] New Rochelle, NY Salesian Provincial House.
Swierzbolek, Waclaw (NY) Chester, NY St. Columba Church.
Swierzowski, Stanislaus J. '56 (ALB) [1] Amsterdam, NY St. Casimir Church; [2] Amsterdam, NY St. John the Baptist Church.
Swierzy, Michael W. '75 (PH) Absent on Leave.
Swietek, Walter '62 (VEN) Lehigh Acres, FL St. Raphael Church.
Swietochowski, Andrew K. '78 (SFS) Jefferson, SD St. Peter Church.
Swift, Daniel '89 (TR) Leave of Absence.
Swift, Gerald *s.t.* '46 (WDC) [M] Adelphi, MD Missionary Servants of the Most Holy Trinity.
Swift, James E. *c.m.* '78 (STL) [A] St. Louis, MO Kenrick-Glennon Seminary; [P] St. Louis, MO Lazarist Residence.
Swift, John *s.v.d.* '75 (CHI) [B] Techny, IL Divine Word Residence.
Swift, Walter A. '69 (SPR) Brimfield, MA St. Christopher's Church.
Swift, William J. '44 (TLS) [10] Tulsa, OK Church of St. Mary.
Swift, William V. '44 (TLS) Retired.
Swiger, Msgr. Charles W. '63 (RVC) Farmingdale, NY St. Kilian Church.
Swing, R. John '70 (LC) Nekoosa, WI Sacred Heart of Jesus Church; Port Edwards, WI St. Alexander Church.
Swirski, Thaddeus M. '54 (CLV) [6] Akron, OH St. Hedwig Church.
Swisshelm, Germain *o.s.b.* '60 (IND) [J] St. Meinrad, IN St. Meinrad Archabbey.
Swistovich, John '98 (FWT) [11] Fort Worth, TX St. John the Apostle Church.
Switalksi, Casimir S. '40 (SPR) Retired.
Switalski, Bruno '33 (CHI) [195] Chicago, IL St. Tarcissus Church.
Switalski, Casimir S. '40 (SPR) [I] Holyoke, MA Sisters of Providence Care Centers, Inc.
Switanowski, Robert Joseph *o.f.m.conv.* '90 (MIL) [47] Milwaukee, WI Basilica of St. Josaphat.
Swoger, Msgr. John W. '63 (E) Emlenton, PA St. Michael Church; [3] Oil City, PA St. Joseph Church; Rouseville, PA St. Venantius Church.
Swoger, Mark S. '85 (E) Du Bois, PA St. Michael Church; [C] Du Bois, PA Du Bois Area Catholic Schools; [K] Du Bois, PA Christ the King Manor, Inc.
Swolek, Richard J. '63 (OM) [48] Douglas Co., NE St. Wenceslaus Church.
Swope, John W. *s.j.* '86 (WDC) [M] Washington, DC The Jesuit Community at Georgetown University.
Swope, Mark G. '90 (PH) Springfield, PA Holy Cross Church.
Swope, Timothy J. '66 (ALT) Loretto, PA Basilica of St. Michael the Archangel.
Swyschuk, Msgr. Jaroslaw '51 (STN) [1] Chicago, IL St. Nicholas Ukrainian Catholic Church.
Sybertz, Donald F. *m.m.* '55 (FgM) Maryknoll Foreign Missions.
Sye, Angelo Y. *s.s.p.* '93 (Y) [A] Canfield, OH Society of St. Paul.
Sykes, Gregory '77 (OG) Military Chaplains.
Sykora, Paul *m.m.* (DEN) [M] Denver, CO Maryknoll Fathers, Catholic Foreign Mission Society of America (Legal Title).
Sylva, Eugene R. '93 (PAT) [5] Wayne, NJ Our Lady of the Valley Church; [C] Wayne, NJ De Paul High School.
Sylva, Joseph W. '72 (BO) Westwood, MA St. Denis Church.
Sylvester, Gary (DET) [6] St. Clair Shores, MI St. Margaret of Scotland Church.
Sylvester, Sean E. '99 (DET) [33] Detroit, MI Holy Redeemer Church.
Sylvestre, Ernest *o.m.i.* '61 (PT) Madison, FL St. Vincent de Paul Church; Monticello, FL St. Margaret Church.
Sylvia, Albert A. '66 (BO) [9] Lawrence, MA SS. Peter and Paul Church.
Symes, Joseph J. *c.m.* '50 (PH) [AA] Philadelphia, PA Congregation of the Mission.
Symolon, Lawrence '75 (HRT) [5] West Haven, CT St. Paul's Church.
Synek, Roger A. '98 (BIS) Center, ND St. Martin Church.
Sypek, Msgr. Stanislaus T. '43 (BO) [2] Boston, MA St. Adalbert Church.
Syracuse, Ross *o.f.m.conv.* '78 (BAL) [20] Baltimore, MD St. Casimir Church.
Sys, Joseph *m.afr.* '41 (SP) [O] St. Petersburg, FL Missionaries of Africa.
Syslo, Alan M. *c.s.v.* '66 (CHI) [N] Arlington Heights, IL Viatorian Province Center-Clerics of St. Viator.
Sysol, Steven M. *o.f.m.* '79 (ALB) [A] Catskill, NY St. Anthony Friary.
Syverson, David B. '99 (FAR) [4] Fargo, ND SS. Anne & Joachim Church.
Syverstad, Daniel *o.p.* '82 (FgM) Dominican - Order of Preachers Foreign Missions.
Syverstad, Daniel *o.p.* '82 (OAK) [4] Berkeley, CA St. Mary Magdalen Church; [N] Oakland, CA Western Dominican Province.
Szabelski, Joseph R. '70 (CHI) Other Assignments.
Szabo, Msgr. Julius J. '36 (BUF) Retired; [O] Tonawanda, NY O'Hara Residence.
Szabo, Marcel '71 (PSC) Passaic, NJ St. Michael Church.
Szada, John '77 (HBG) [3] Harrisburg, PA St. Francis of Assisi Church.
Szada, John A., Jr. '78 (HBG) Harrisburg, PA Harrisburg Hospital; Harrisburg, PA Polyclinic Medical Clinic.
Szafranski, Richard T. '75 (SAG) Carrollton, MI St. John the Baptist Church; Zilwaukee, MI St. Matthew Church.
Szakaly, Anthony V. *c.s.c.* '92 (FTW) [12] South Bend, IN St. Joseph Church.
Szal, George L. *s.m.* '75 (BO) [4] Methuen, MA St. Theresa Church.
Szal, Ignatius J. '44 (PH) Oreland, PA Holy Martyrs Church; Retired.
Szamocki, Piotr '91 (CAM) [6] Camden, NJ St. Joseph's Church.
Szamreta, John *o.f.m.cap.* '81 (FgM) Capuchin Foreign Missions.
Szanto, Hubert S. *o.praem.* '48 (ORG) [A] Silverado, CA St. Michael's Norbertine Postulancy, Novitiate and Juniorate; [D] Silverado, CA St. Michael's College Preparatory High School; [I] Silverado, CA Norbertine Fathers of Orange Inc.
Szantyr, Eugene R. '78 (BGP) [5] Fairfield, CT Holy Family Church.
Szantyr, John '57 (WOR) Absent on Leave.
Szanyi, Mark *o.f.m.conv.* '78 (PMB) Boynton Beach, FL St. Mark Church.
Szarek, Eugene *c.r.* '67 (CHI) [72] Chicago, IL St. Hedwig Church.
Szarek, Mitchell '54 (DET) Retired.
Szarek, Mitchell '57 (DET) [62] Detroit, MI SS. Peter and Paul Church.
Szarnicki, Henry A. '55 (PIT) Retired; [O] Pittsburgh, PA St. John Vianney Manor.
Szarnicki, Zygmunt V. '45 (PIT) Retired; [O] Pittsburgh, PA St. John Vianney Manor.
Szaroleta, Andrew L. '77 (MET) Clinton, NJ Immaculate Conception Church; Clinton, NJ Hunterdon State School.
Szarwark, Stan *c.i.c.m.* '64 (FgM) Missionhurst Foreign Missions.
Szatkowski, Casimir M. '50 (CHI) Retired.
Szczapa, Stanley J. '71 (NOR) Vernon, CT Sacred Heart Church.
Szczepanik, John J. '88 (MET) Lambertville, NJ St. John the Evangelist Church.
Szczepankiewicz, Gary '75 (BUF) [1] North Tonawanda, NY Ascension Church.
Szczerbicki, Thaddeus P. '40 (LC) Retired.
Szczesniak, Harry F. '72 (BUF) [8] Cheektowaga, NY Our Lady of Czestochowa Church.
Szczesny, John S. '75 (GBG) Youngwood, PA Holy Cross Church.
Szczesny, Michael S. '36 (GI) Retired.
Szczesny, Walter '90 (BUF) [A] East Aurora, NY Christ the King Seminary.
Szczesny, Walter J. '90 (BUF) West Falls, NY St. George Church.
Szczotka, Krzysztof *s.d.s.* '88 (NEW) [2] Elizabeth, NJ St. Adalbert's Church.
Szczurek, Victor S. *o.praem.* '00 (ORG) [D] Silverado, CA St. Michael's College Preparatory High School.
Szczygiel, Edwin A. '47 (DET) [38] Detroit, MI St. John Cantius Church.
Szczykutowicz, Francis S. '58 (PT) Sunny Hills, FL St. Theresa Church.
Szebenyi, Andrew L. *s.j.* '61 (SY) [S] Syracuse, NY Jesuits at LeMoyne, Inc.
Szekula, Augustin *o.mech.* '44 (ARM) [A] La Crescenta, CA Mekhitarist School.
Szelest, Theodore A. '47 (NEW) Dumont, NJ St. Mary's Church; Retired.
Szeman, Stephen '53 (SEA) Kirkland, WA Holy Family Church; Retired.
Szemborski, Chester *s.d.b.* '50 (NY) [FF] Stony Point, NY Don Bosco Retreat Center and Marian Shrine; [FF] Stony Point, NY Marian Shrine.
Szemla, Patrick *o.f.m.* '42 (GB) [I] Pulaski, WI Assumption of B.V.M. Friary.
Szendrey, J. Edward *m.m.* '62 (FgM) Maryknoll Foreign Missions.
Szepe, Ladislaus *s.f.o.* '35 (GB) [I] Pulaski, WI Assumption of B.V.M. Friary.
Szewczyk, Grzegorz *s.d.s.* '91 (BRK) [93] Brooklyn, NY Our Lady of Consolation Church.
Szewczyk, Grzegorz *s.d.s.* '91 (NEW) [N] Verona, NJ The Salvatorian Fathers.
Szewczyk, Joseph '55 (DET) New Boston, MI St. Stephen Church; [H] Pontiac, MI St. Joseph Mercy - Oakland.
Szews, George R. '78 (LC) [2] Eau Claire, WI Newman Community Church; [K] Eau Claire, WI Newman Parish.
Szippl, Richard *s.v.d.* '81 (FgM) Society of the Divine Word Foreign Missions.
Szivos, Charles '99 (NY) [145] Bronx, NY St. Helena Church.
Szklarski, Joseph '62 (NEW) Lyndhurst, NJ St. Michael's Church.
Szkulaski, John *s.v.d.* (DUB) [B] Epworth, IA Divine Word College.
Szlanga, Edmund S. '48 (CHI) [33] Chicago, IL St. Bruno Church; [194] Chicago, IL St. Symphorosa and Seven Sons Church; Retired.
Szleszinski, Peter F. '56 (SUP) Hudson, WI St. Patrick Church.
Szlezak, Emeric *o.f.m.* '44 (BGP) [3] Fairfield, CT St. Emery Church.
Szmutko, Stephen *s.v.d.* '44 (TR) [M] Bordentown, NJ Society of the Divine Word.
Szmyd, John '96 (CHI) Wilmette, IL St. Joseph Church.
Szostak, Msgr. Danile J. '54 (BUF) Retired.
Szott, Timothy J. '70 (DET) Utica, MI St. Lawrence Church.
Szpiech, Edward P. '67 (NEW) [4] Garfield, NJ St. Stanislaus Kostka Church.
Szpieg, Edmund L. '94 (PMB) Port St. Lucie, FL St. Elizabeth Ann Seton Church.
Szpilski, Joseph *c.m.* '56 (HRT) [4] Ansonia, CT St. Joseph's Church.
Sztorc, Richard E. '69 (CHI) Northbrook, IL Our Lady of the Brook Church.
Sztybel, Jaroslaw '97 (SP) Tarpon Springs, FL St. Ignatius Church.
Szudarek, Ronald J. '81 (CLV) [19] Cleveland, OH Corpus Christi Church.
Szudera, Ted '77 (GF) Centerville, MT Holy Trinity Church.
Szudera, Ted F. '77 (GF) Belt, MT St. Mark the Evangelist Church.
Szufel, Adam *o.f.m.* '64 (GB) [I] Pulaski, WI Assumption of B.V.M. Friary.
Szukalski, John *s.v.d.* '97 (CHI) [B] Techny, IL Divine Word Residence; [N] Techny, IL Society of the Divine Word, Provincial Headquarter-Chicago Prov.
Szulecki, Raymond '46 (MET) [H] Somerset, NJ Maria Regina Residence.
Szulecki, Raymond L. '46 (MET) Retired.
Szulwach, Joseph '87 (MET) Laurence Harbor, NJ St. Lawrence Church.
Szumilo, Julian *c.m.* '50 (HRT) [M] Manchester, CT DePaul Provincial Residence.
Szupa, Joseph '92 (PHU) Passaic, NJ St. Nicholas Church.
Szupper, Michael F. '57 (WIL) Newark, DE St. Thomas More Oratory Church; Dover, DE Wesley College; Newark, DE University of Delaware; [O] Newark, DE Univ. of Delaware Newman Center; [O] Newark, DE Univ. of Delaware Newman Center.
Szura, Carl '71 (FWT) [8] Fort Worth, TX St. Andrew Church.
Szura, John *o.s.a.* (CHI) [N] Chicago, IL St. John Stone Friary.
Szura, Thomas *c.m.m.* '78 (DET) [K] Dearborn Heights, MI Our Lady of Grace Monastery.
Szwach, Joseph F. '55 (WOR) Dudley, MA St. Andrew Bobola Church.
Szybka, Joseph P. '83 (TOL) Attica, OH SS. Peter and Paul Church; Republic, OH St. Aloysius Church; St. Stephen, OH St. Stephen Church.
Szybka, Stanley S. '80 (TOL) Lexington, OH Resurrection Church.
Szych, Mark *o.f.m.* '53 (GAY) Mio, MI St. Mary Church.
Szydlowski, Gregory *o.cist.* '63 (CHI) [N] Willow Springs, IL Cistercian Fathers, Our Lady Mother of the Church.
Szydlowski, Joel F. *o.f.m.* '67 (PH) [AA] Philadelphia, PA St. Pius X Friary.
Szydlowski, Joel F. *o.f.m.* '67 (TR) Trenton, NJ St. Francis Medical Center; [I] Trenton, NJ St. Francis Medical Center.
Szydlowski, Robert L. '62 (STL) [50] St. Louis, MO Sts. Mary and Joseph Church.
Szymanski, Edward S. '99 (BAL) Annapolis, MD St. Andrew by the Bay Church.
Szymanski, Msgr. John B. '57 (MET) Old Bridge, NJ St. Thomas the Apostle Church.
Szymaszek, Leszek '97 (BGP) Ridgefield, CT St. Mary Church.
Szymkowiak, Gerard J. *c.ss.r.* '68 (HBG) Lititz, PA St. James Church; [H] Ephrata, PA St. Clement's Mission House.
Szymusiak, Bruno '59 (SP) Retired.
Szyszko, Brian J. '83 (MIL) [6] Sheboygan, WI St. Peter Claver Church.

T

Ta, Binh Thanh *c.ss.r.* '93 (NO) [23] New Orleans, LA St. Alphonsus Church.
Taaffe, Charles '55 (P) Retired.
Tabbert, Robert D. '79 (VEN) [1] Naples, FL St. Ann Church; [K] Naples, FL St. Ann School Foundation, Inc.
Tabbot, Mark (CHI) [J] Hoffman Estates, IL St. Alexius Medical Center.
Taberski, Richard M. '64 (HRT) Union City, CT St. Mary's Church.
Tabing, Omar '77 (OKL) Calumet, OK Immaculate Heart of Mary Church.
Tabon, Raymond *o.s.j.* '60 (SCR) Exeter, PA St. Anthony of Padua Church.
Tabone, Marcel M. '85 (CAM) Sea Isle City, NJ St. Joseph's Church.
Tabor, Kenneth F. '75 (CHI) Other Assignments.
Tabor, Paul J. *s.j.* '88 (BO) [W] Boston, MA The Society of Jesus of New England-Provincial Offices.
Tabor, Paul J. *s.j.* '88 (NY) [DD] New York, NY St. Ignatius Loyola Residence.
Tabujara, Oscar D. '75 (SJ) Mountain View, CA St. Joseph Church.
Tacelli, Ronald K. *s.j.* '82 (BO) [W] Chestnut Hill, MA The Jesuit Community at Boston College.
Tachias, Alfred A. '59 (GLP) [A] Gallup, NM Diocesan Diaconate and Lay Ecclesial Ministry Formation Program; [E] Gallup, NM Villa Guadalupe Home for the Aged.
Tacito, Nicholas M. *o.praem.* '96 (ORG) [I] Silverado, CA Norbertine Fathers of Orange Inc.
Tack, Theodore E. *o.s.a.* '53 (TLS) [B] Tulsa, OK Cascia Hall Preparatory School.
Tackaberry, John P. *c.m.* '41 (STL) [P] Perryville, MO Congregation of The Mission.
Tackney, John P. '74 (BO) [13] Cambridge, MA Sacred Heart of Jesus Church.
Taddy, Jerome J. (GB) Elcho, WI Holy Family Church.
Tadeo, Abran R. '00 (TUC) [12] Tucson, AZ St. Ambrose Church.
Tadeusz, Majcher *s.d.s.* '87 (NEW) [N] Verona, NJ The Salvatorian Fathers.
Tadia, Casmir *c.r.* '48 (SB) [3] Fontana, CA St. Joseph Church.
Tadyszak, Leonard *s.c.j.* '51 (SP) [O] Pinellas Park, FL Priests of the Sacred Heart.
Taft, Robert F. *s.j.* '63 (BO) [W] Boston, MA The Society of Jesus of New England-Provincial Offices.
Taft, William A. '94 (TUC) Kearny, AZ Infant Jesus of Prague Church.
Tagg, Joseph L., III '88 (MEM) [14] Memphis, TN St. John's Church.
Taggart, Bruce *o.carm.* '97 (WDC) [B] Washington, DC Whitefriars Hall.
Taggart, Frederick H. *o.s.a.* '65 (LAN) [11] Flint, MI St. Matthew Church.
Taggart, James E. *o.m.i.* (BO) [12] Lowell, MA Nuestra Senora del Carmen Church.
Taggart, John L. '70 (WIL) Milford, DE St. John the Apostle Church.
Taggart, Msgr. Paul J. '51 (WIL) Retired.
Tague, Charles *s.t.* '44 (WDC) [M] Adelphi, MD Missionary Servants of the Most Holy Trinity.
Taheny, Mark V. '95 (SFR) San Bruno, CA St. Robert Church.
Taheny, Robert R. *s.j.* '59 (SJ) [25] San Jose, CA St. Victor Church; [L] Los Gatos, CA Sacred Heart Jesuit Center.
Taheny, Theodore T. *s.j.* '56 (FgM) Provinces.
Taheny, Theodore T. *s.j.* '56 (SFR) [E] San Francisco, CA St. Ignatius College Preparatory (Coed).
Tahney, Theodore *s.j.* '56 (SFR) [N] San Francisco, CA Jesuit Community at St. Ignatius College Preparatory.
Taillez, Daniel *o.m.i.* '63 (STP) [27] St. Paul, MN St. Mary Church.
Taillon, Marcel L. '94 (PRO) [A] Providence, RI Seminary of Our Lady of Providence; [C] Warwick, RI Bishop Hendricken High School.
Tajak, Ralph *o.s.b.* '94 (GBG) Youngstown, PA Sacred Heart Church.
Takach, Brinstan G. *o.s.b.* '48 (GBG) Bovard, PA St. Bede Church; [H] Latrobe, PA Saint Vincent Archabbey.
Takeuchi, Osamu *s.j.* '96 (OAK) [N] Berkeley, CA Jesuit Community at Jesuit School of Theology at Berkeley.
Takuski, Walter J. '95 (CHI) [56] Chicago, IL St. Ferdinand Church.
Talafous, Don *o.s.b.* '52 (SCL) [I] Collegeville, MN St. John's Abbey, of the Order of St. Benedict.
Talamo, John *s.d.b.* (NEW) [C] Ramsey, NJ Don Bosco Preparatory High School for Boys.
Talar, Charles J.T. '79 (BAL) [A] Baltimore, MD St. Mary's Seminary and University; [S] Baltimore, MD Sulpician Provincial House.
Talar, Charles J.T. '79 (BGP) On Duty Outside the Diocese.
Talarico, Anthony '70 (CHI) Other Assignments.
Talaska, Richard J. '68 (MIL) Greenfield, WI St. John the Evangelist Church.
Talavera, Carlos S. '97 (HT) Thibodaux, LA Thibodaux General Hospital.
Talbot, Felix F. *s.j.* '44 (BO) [W] Weston, MA Campion Health Center, Inc.
Talbot, James F. *s.j.* '68 (BO) [W] Weston, MA Campion Jesuit Community.
Talbot, John F. *s.j.* '59 (SJN) [C] Rio Piedras, PR Jesuit Novitiate.
Talbot, Ronald *o.f.m.cap.* (SB) [E] Burlington, CA Capuchin Franciscans.
Talbott, Ronald *o.f.m.cap.* '81 (SFR) [N] Burlingame, CA Capuchin Provincial House.
Talcott, Peter '75 (SR) Unassigned.
Talesfore, John J. '89 (SFR) [9] San Francisco, CA St. Brendan Church; Special Assignment.
Taliercio, Pasquale *m.s.a.* '92 (NOR) [F] Cromwell, CT Society of the Missionaries of the Holy Apostles.
Talkin, Ralph H. *s.j.* '57 (CHY) Glenrock, WY St. Louis Church.
Tallarida, Thomas *c.s.c.* '51 (FTW) [B] Notre Dame, IN University of Notre Dame Du Lac; [J] Notre Dame, IN Holy Cross Community, Corby Hall, University of Notre Dame.
Talley, Charles *o.f.m.* (P) [6] Portland, OR Ascension Church.
Talley, David P. '89 (ATL) Special or Other (Arch)Diocesan Assignment.
Tallman, Gilmary *o.f.m.cap.* '60 (STL) Arnold, MO Immaculate Conception Church; [P] Arnold, MO Immaculate Conception Friary.
Tallman, John '88 (ALB) [5] Albany, NY St. Catherine of Siena Church; Albany, NY St. Peter's Hospital; Special Assignment; [H] Albany, NY Mercycare Corporation, St. Peter's Hospital.
Tallman, Stephen '59 (HEL) Retired.
Talloen, Jerome G. '45 (OKL) Retired.
Talocci, Peter '86 (PH) Croydon, PA St. Thomas Aquinas Church.
Tam, Francis '87 (TR) Keyport, NJ St. Joseph Church.
Tam, Thomas '50 (STP) [18] St. Paul, MN St. Columba Church.
Tamayo, Alfredo '77 (SAC) Folsom, CA St. John the Baptist Church.
Tamayo, Msgr. Elias '72 (PAT) Dover, NJ Our Lady Queen of the Most Holy Rosary Church.
Tamborino, James *s.o.l.t.* '91 (CC) [H] Robstown, TX Society of Our Lady of the Most Holy Trinity.
Tamburello, Dennis *o.f.m.* '80 (ALB) [B] Loudonville, NY Siena College.
Tamburello, John Dominic *o.p.* (TYL) [C] Lufkin, TX Monastery of the Infant Jesus.
Tamburrini, Joseph '64 (Y) Retired.
Tamburrino, James *o.carm.* '98 (NY) Middletown, NY Our Lady of Mt. Carmel Church.
Tamburro, Francis J. '74 (HBG) Berwick, PA Immaculate Conception of the Blessed Virgin Mary Church.
Tamburro, Joseph '99 (SJP) Pittsburgh, PA St. John the Baptist Church.
Tamm, Thaddeus *c.p.* '39 (CHI) [N] Chicago, IL Daneo Hall.
Tamminga, Robert G. '71 (TUC) [15] Tucson, AZ St. Francis de Sales Church.
Tampe, Eric *s.a.* '49 (NY) [DD] Garrison, NY Franciscan Friars of the Atonement, Minister General Office.
Tamulis, John J. '40 (GAY) Retired.
Tanch, Norman C. *c.s.b.* '74 (ROC) [13] Rochester, NY Christ the King Church.
Tancrede, Msgr. Roland '47 (MAN) [11] Manchester, NH St. John the Baptist Church; Retired.
Tancredi, Carl T. '67 (HBG) [4] York, PA St. Rose of Lima Church; York, PA York Hospital; [K] Harrisburg, PA Catholic Campus Ministry; [K] Harrisburg, PA Catholic Campus Ministry.
Tancrell, Luke *o.p.* '59 (COL) [36] Columbus, OH St. Patrick Church.
Tandoh, Francis *c.s.sp.* '93 (CIN) [26] Dayton, OH St. James/Resurrection of Our Lord Church.
Taney, Francis J. *m.m.* '58 (NY) [DD] Maryknoll, NY Maryknoll Fathers and Brothers.
Tang, Emery *o.f.m.* '52 (ORG) [3] Huntington Beach, CA SS. Simon and Jude Church.
Tanghal, Alberto R. '91 (CHI) Other Assignments.
Tanguay, Andre *o.m.i.* '53 (FgM) Oblates Foreign Missions.
Tanguay, Andre *o.m.i.* '53 (MIA) Homestead, FL Sacred Heart Church.
Tanguay, William H. '69 (CHL) Hickory, NC St. Aloysius Church.
Tanguay, William H. '69 (PRO) [11] Pawtucket, RI Sacred Heart of Jesus Church; On Duty Outside the Diocese.
Tanilong, Msgr. Gerardo J. '62 (ORG) [2] Santa Ana, CA Our Lady of Guadalupe Church.
Tank, Thomas '67 (KCK) [1] Kansas City, KS Cathedral of St. Peter the Apostle.
Tansaeng, Haet (STO) Permanent Deacons.
Taormina, Msgr. Andrew C. '62 (NO) [9] Metairie, LA St. Francis Xavier Church.
Tape, Bernard '00 (SAC) Special Assignment.
Tapella, Joseph J. '78 (JOL) [1] Joliet, IL The Cathedral of St. Raymond.
Taphorn, Joseph C. '97 (OM) Graduate Studies.
Tapia, Gilberto Mora (SEA) LaConner, WA Sacred Heart Church.
Tapia, Gilberto Mora '88 (SEA) Burlington, WA St. Charles Church; Mount Vernon, WA Immaculate Conception Church; Sedro Woolley, WA Immaculate Heart of Mary Church.
Tapp, John G. '84 (SP) [16] Tampa, FL St. Timothy Church; [F] Tampa, FL St. Timothy Catholic Early Childhood Learning Center.
Tappe, Walter J. '85 (WDC) Kensington, MD Holy Redeemer Church; Pastoral Center Special Ministries.
Tapper, John W. '61 (CHI) Hanover Park, IL St. Ansgar Church.
Tarabay, Nahed '93 (OLL) [A] Ann Arbor, MI Maronite Order of Blessed Virgin Mary.
Taraborelli, Arthur I. '64 (PH) [152] Philadelphia, PA St. Thomas Aquinas Church.
Taraborelli, Carmen F. '70 (PH) Absent on Leave.
Tarallo, Philip *s.s.j.* '36 (BR) New Roads, LA St. Augustine Church.
Taran, Peter *s.a.* '60 (NY) [DD] Garrison, NY Franciscan Friars of the Atonement, Minister General Office.
Tarantino, James '81 (SFR) Tiburon, CA St. Hilary Church.
Tarantino, James A. '72 (NO) [19] New Orleans, LA Our Lady of The Rosary Church.
Tarantino, John F. '78 (PAT) Montville, NJ St. Pius X Church.
Taranto, James '81 (KC) [24] Kansas City, MO St. Matthew The Apostle Church.
Tarasi, Carlo DiNatale '72 (CHL) Monroe, NC Our Lady of Lourdes Church.
Tarasiw, Ihor '90 (STF) Riverhead, NY St. John the Baptist Church.
Tardiff, Edward *c.ss.r.* '42 (ALB) [L] Saratoga Springs, NY St. John Neumann Residence.
Tardiff, Mark *p.i.m.e.* '80 (DET) [K] Detroit, MI P.I.M.E. College Community.
Tardivo, Mario *c.s.* '38 (BO) [64] Boston, MA Sacred Heart Church.
Targonski, Conrad *o.f.m.* '75 (GB) [I] Pulaski, WI Assumption of B.V.M. Friary.
Tarlizzo, David *o.m.i.* '68 (SAT) Nixon, TX St. Joseph's Church; Smiley, TX St. Philip Benizi Church.
Tarlton, Allen *o.s.b.* '55 (SCL) [I] Collegeville, MN St. John's Abbey, of the Order of St. Benedict.
Tarnawski, Wiktor '80 (ARE) Ciales, PR N.S. Madre del Redentor Church.
Tarran, Peter *s.a.* '60 (NY) [DD] Garrison, NY Franciscan Friars of the Atonement, Minister General Office.
Tarrant, Msgr. Edward L. '50 (RVC) Hicksville, NY St. Ignatius Loyola Church; Mineola, NY Corpus Christi Church; Retired.
Tarrant, Patrick J. '53 (GF) Retired.
Tarrier, William Brandon *o.p.* '47 (L) [4] Springfield, KY St. Rose Church.
Tarrillion, Joseph A. *s.m.* '66 (SAT) [F] San Antonio, TX Central Catholic High School; [M] San Antonio, TX Chaminade Community House.
Tartaglia, Paul '58 (ALB) Retired.
Tartaglia, Richard V. '72 (PAT) Denville, NJ St. Mary's Church.
Tasch, Hugh *o.s.b.* '48 (KC) [J] Conception, MO Conception Abbey.
Taschetta, Anthony '71 (JOL) [5] Kankakee, IL St. Teresa Church.
Tascon, Wilson *m.s.c.* '90 (FgM) Missionaries of the Sacred Heart Foreign Missions.
Tascon, Wilson *m.s.c.* '90 (RCK) [G] Aurora, IL Missionaries of the Sacred Heart Community.
Tash, Msgr. Joseph T. '62 (AMA) [11] Amarillo, TX St. Thomas the Apostle Church.
Tasker, Franklin R. *o.carm.* '56 (VEN) [G] Nokomis, FL Carmel at Mission Valley.
Tasler, Mark A. '90 (LIN) Nebraska City, NE St. Benedict's Church.
Tassone, Salvatore A. *s.j.* '63 (SJ) [B] Santa Clara, CA Santa Clara University.
Tasto, Harold J. '68 (STP) Blaine, MN St. Timothy's Church.
Tasto, John P. *o.s.a.* '67 (CHI) [N] Olympia Fields, IL The Augustinians-Provincialate.
Tasto, John P. *o.s.a.* '67 (FgM) Foreign Missions.
Tasy, Msgr. Francis G. *v.s.* '52 (FRS) Reedley, CA St. Anthony Church.
Tatarczuk, Msgr. Vincent A. '49 (PRT) Retired.
Tate, Joseph H. *c.s.c.* '81 (BUR) Readsboro, VT St. Joachim Church.
Tatel, Orlando '65 (STP) [3] St. Paul, MN Blessed Sacrament Church.
Taton, Thomas P. '60 (BUF) Buffalo, NY Millard Fillmore Hospital.
Taton, Thomas P. '61 (BUF) [10] Buffalo, NY Assumption Church.

Tatro, Joseph C. '00 (WCH) [3] Wichita, KS Blessed Sacrament Church.
Tatro, Kenneth J. '76 (SPR) [4] Westfield, MA St. Mary's Church.
Tatro, Timothy M. '99 (JC) [3] Jefferson City, MO Immaculate Conception Church.
Tatum, Gregory T. *o.p.* '81 (OAK) [A] Berkeley, CA Dominican School of Philosophy and Theology.
Tatum, Gregory T. *o.p.* '81 (SFR) [14] San Francisco, CA St. Dominic Church; [N] San Francisco, CA St. Dominic Priory.
Taube, Sylvester '64 (DET) Birmingham, MI St. Columban Church.
Tauber, Gregory J. *s.t.l.* '77 (ALN) Bath, PA Sacred Heart Church.
Taubitz, Leo A. '56 (KAL) Dowagiac, MI Holy Maternity of Mary Church.
Taufen, Daniel '56 (SCL) Special Assignment.
Taufen, Msgr. Daniel J. *s.t.l.* '56 (SCL) Rockville, MN Mary of the Immaculate Conception Church.
Taugher, Timothy J. '78 (SY) Johnson City, NY Wilson Memorial Hospital; Special Assignment.
Taurasi, David '88 (CC) Sinton, TX Our Lady of Guadalupe Church.
Tauscher, Donald *o.s.b.* '65 (SCL) [I] Collegeville, MN St. John's Abbey, of the Order of St. Benedict.
Tavai, Van Camp '89 (SPP) [9] Pago Pago, AS Church of the Holy Cross.
Tavard, George *a.a.* '47 (BO) [W] Boston, MA Assumptionist Center.
Tavares, Antonino C. '43 (FR) [7] New Bedford, MA Our Lady of Mt. Carmel Church; Retired.
Tavares, Msgr. John E. '55 (PRO) Retired.
Tavarro, Elly S. '81 (ORG) [G] Orange, CA St. Joseph Hospital of Orange.
Tavella, Thomas A. *c.s.p.* '81 (NY) [104] New York, NY St. Paul the Apostle Church.
Tavis, Gordon *o.s.b.* '58 (SCL) [D] Collegeville, MN St. John's Preparatory School; [I] Collegeville, MN St. John's Abbey, of the Order of St. Benedict.
Tay, Msgr. Peter '54 (PBR) [2] Pittsburgh, PA Holy Ghost Church.
Taylor, Anthony B. '80 (OKL) Edmond, OK St. Monica Church; Special Assignment.
Taylor, Augustus R., Jr. '66 (PIT) On Duty Outside the Diocese.
Taylor, Benedict M. *o.f.m.* '60 (NY) [DD] New York, NY Franciscan Friars, Order of Friars Minor, Holy Name Province.
Taylor, Charles F. '53 (CHY) Buffalo, WY St. John the Baptist Church.
Taylor, Daniel '75 (TUC) Absent on Leave.
Taylor, David H. '74 (PIT) [8] Pittsburgh, PA St. Charles Lwanga Church.
Taylor, Donn J. '53 (KAL) Battle Creek, MI St. Joseph Church; Retired.
Taylor, Douglas D. '97 (TOL) Findlay, OH St. Michael Church.
Taylor, Gordon A. '85 (B) Salmon, ID St. Charles Church; Retired.
Taylor, James B. '54 (BLX) Pascagoula, MS Sacred Heart Church; Retired.
Taylor, James E. *o.m.i.* '56 (BEL) [F] Belleville, IL Missionary Oblates of Mary Immaculate - St. Henry's Oblate Residence; [J] Belleville, IL Missionary Association of Mary Immaculate-Missionary Oblates of Mary Immaculate.
Taylor, Jon '64 (GF) Special Assignment; [A] Great Falls, MT University of Great Falls.
Taylor, Jon '64 (LAN) On Duty Outside the Diocese.
Taylor, Joseph C. '53 (CHI) [50] Chicago, IL St. Edward Church; Retired.
Taylor, Kenneth E. '78 (IND) [8] Indianapolis, IN Holy Trinity Church; [O] Indianapolis, IN Archdiocesan Black Catholics Concerned.
Taylor, Mel *o.s.b.* '67 (FgM) American - Cassinese Congregation Foreign Missions.
Taylor, Mel *o.s.b.* '67 (SCL) [I] Collegeville, MN St. John's Abbey, of the Order of St. Benedict.
Taylor, Michael (SY) [O] Syracuse, NY St. Joseph's Hospital Health Center.
Taylor, Michael '86 (SY) [2] Syracuse, NY Assumption B.V.M. Church.
Taylor, Michael G. '93 (ARL) Springfield, VA St. Bernadette's Church.
Taylor, Michael J. *s.j.* '54 (SEA) [A] Seattle, WA Seattle University.
Taylor, Michael S. '97 (MAN) [6] Manchester, NH St. Catherine Church.
Taylor, Paul R. *o.s.b.* '92 (GBG) [H] Latrobe, PA Saint Vincent Archabbey.
Taylor, Peter '74 (GB) On Duty Outside the Diocese.
Taylor, Peter '74 (PHX) Prescott, AZ Sacred Heart Church.
Taylor, Robert H. *s.j.* '52 (LA) [C] Los Angeles, CA Loyola Marymount University.
Taylor, Robert H. '56 (WIN) Absent on Leave.
Taylor, Roger H. '64 (MAD) Avoca, WI St. Joseph Church; Muscoda, WI St. John the Baptist Church.
Taylor, Samuel '82 (NY) [107] New York, NY Resurrection Church.
Taylor, Senan *o.f.m.cap.* '70 (NY) [DD] Yonkers, NY St. Clare Friary.
Taylor, Thomas '83 (PEO) Lincoln, IL Holy Family Church.
Taylor, Vincent A. *s.j.* '45 (NY) [F] New York, NY Xavier High School.
Taylor, William '64 (B) Saint Maries, ID St. Mary's Church.
Taylor, William R. '67 (SAG) [2] Saginaw, MI Holy Family Church.
Tchingui, Antonio Jorge (CHI) [130] Chicago, IL Maternity of the Blessed Virgin Mary Church.
Teague, Bruce N. '80 (SPR) Amherst, MA St. Brigid's Church; [Q] Springfield, MA Newman Apostolates and Campus Ministries.
Teague, James '87 (NY) [E] Somers, NY John F. Kennedy High School.
Teahan, Timothy J. '70 (BRK) [50] Brooklyn, NY Good Shepherd Church.
Teall, Richard S. *c.s.c.* (AUS) [H] Austin, TX Brother Andre House.
Teall, Richard S. *c.s.c.* '50 (AUS) [H] Austin, TX Congregation of Holy Cross - Southern Province.
Teater, Kristian C. '00 (STL) Graduate Studies.
Tebangura, Francis '68 (SFD) Granite City, IL St. Elizabeth Church.
Tebbe, Francis S. *o.f.m.* '75 (CHI) [U] Chicago, IL National Organization for Continuing Education of Roman Catholic Clergy, Inc.
Tebbe, Francis S. *o.f.m.* '75 (CIN) [M] Cincinnati, OH St. Francis Seraph Friary.
Tebes, Stephen J. '68 (CHI) Norridge, IL Divine Savior Church.
Teczar, Thomas '80 (WOR) Absent on Leave.
Tederous, Elias *m.m.* '55 (HON) [G] Honolulu, HI Maryknoll Fathers House (M.M.).
Tedesco, Joseph A. '79 (TR) Medford, NJ St. Mary of the Lakes Church.
Tedesco, Joseph P. *s.m.* '83 (CIN) [C] Dayton, OH Marianist Novitiate; [M] Dayton, OH Marianist Provincialate; [M] Dayton, OH Marianist Provincialate.
Tedone, Michael '91 (BRK) [72] Brooklyn, NY Church of St. Jude.
Teeling, John P. *s.j.* '55 (DEN) [M] Denver, CO Regis Jesuit Community (The Jesuits at Regis University).
Tegeder, Michael '78 (STP) Bloomington, MN St. Edward Church.
Tegeder, Vincent *o.s.b.* '37 (SCL) [I] Collegeville, MN St. John's Abbey, of the Order of St. Benedict.
Tegeler, Herbert L. '53 (DUB) Earlville, IA St. Joseph's Church.
Tegels, Aelred *o.s.b.* '48 (SCL) [I] Collegeville, MN St. John's Abbey, of the Order of St. Benedict.
Teichert, Isaiah *o.s.b.cam.* '90 (MRY) [F] Big Sur, CA New Camaldoli Hermitage.
Tejada, Denis '72 (LSC) [5] Las Cruces, NM St. Genevieve Church.
Tejada, Francisco R. (ARE) [1] Vega-Baja, PR Holy Rosary Church.
Tejeda, Jose F. '74 (PCE) [G] Alhambra, Ponce, PR Prelature of the Holy Cross and Opus Dei.
Tejedor, Gonzalo *s.d.b.* (CHI) [103] Chicago, IL St. John Bosco Church.
Tekippe, Msgr. Terry T. '65 (NO) [A] New Orleans, LA Notre Dame Seminary Graduate School of Theology.
Teles, Dennis J. '65 (GRY) [4] Merrillville, IN Ss. Peter and Paul Church.
Telesz, Msgr. Leo '39 (CLV) [14] Cleveland, OH St. Casimir Church.
Teletchea, Msgr. Joseph L. '44 (WDC) Hyattsville, MD St. Jerome Church; Retired.
Teletchen, Msgr. Joseph L. '44 (WDC) [L] Washington, DC Cardinal O'Boyle Residence for Priests.
Telken, Paul E. '73 (STL) St. Clair, MO St. Clare Church.
Tellers, Marven *o.s.c.* '50 (STP) Shoreview, MN St. Odilia Church; [N] Shoreview, MN Crosier Community of Shoreview.
Telles, John '75 (ELP) [A] El Paso, TX St. Charles Seminary College Program.
Tellez, Eric '86 (PHX) [7] Scottsdale, AZ St. Patrick Church.
Tellez, Jairo '62 (SAT) Military Chaplains.
Telnack, Methodius *o.c.s.o.* '57 (ATL) [J] Conyers, GA The Monastery of the Holy Spirit.
Telthorst, Msgr. James T. '68 (STL) [1] St. Louis, MO Cathedral Basilica of Saint Louis.
Teluma, Lukas Bao *s.v.d.* '75 (LA) [Q] Los Angeles, CA Casa Guadalupe.
Temba, Camillus *a.l.c.p.* '91 (B) Pocatello, ID St. Joseph's Church; Pocatello, ID St. Anthony's Church.
Tempel, Theodore G. '64 (EVN) [6] Evansville, IN Good Shepherd Church.
Temple, Matthew *o.carm.* '82 (ROC) [I] Rochester, NY Whitefriars Priory.
Templeton, Edward J. *s.m.* '53 (WDC) [M] Washington, DC Marist Center.
Templeton, Robert '88 (NEW) [4] Elizabeth, NJ Blessed Sacrament Church.
Templin, Kenneth A. *s.m.* '79 (CIN) [D] Dayton, OH The University of Dayton; [M] Dayton, OH Marianist Provincialate; [Q] Dayton, OH University of Dayton Campus Ministry.
Tenbarge, Timothy '73 (EVN) St. Anthony, IN St. Anthony Church.
Tengler, Msgr. Alvin '49 (CC) Retired.
Tenhundfeld, Paul F. '54 (COV) Fort Mitchell, KY Blessed Sacrament Church; Retired.
Tenorio, Michael *o.f.m.cap.* '99 (AGN) Sinajana, GU Saint Jude Thaddeus Church.
Tenorio, Roger P.T. '93 (CHK) San Vicente Village, District 10, MP San Vicente Church; San Vicente Village, District 10, MP San Vicente Church; [A] Saipan, MP Santa Soledad Catholic School.
Tensi, Lawrence R. '77 (CIN) On Special and Archdiocesan Assignment.
Tentori, Franco *o.s.m.* '54 (ELP) [24] El Paso, TX St. Ignatius of Loyola Church.
Teonrio, Michael *o.f.m.cap.* '99 (AGN) [F] Agana Heights, GU St. Fidelis Friary.
Terdine, Richard '65 (PIT) Allegheny County, PA UPMC University of Pittsburgh Medical Center.
Terentieff, Robert J. '62 (BGP) On Duty Outside the Diocese.
Terga, Richard '73 (NY) [85] New York, NY Our Lady of Good Counsel Church.
Terico, Nicholas R. *o.praem.* '89 (PH) [AA] Paoli, PA Daylesford Abbey.
Terlecky, John '76 (STF) Stamford, CT St. Vladimir Church; [A] Stamford, CT St. Basil College.
Termine, Vincent J. '44 (BRK) Retired.
Termini, Mario '79 (BR) Retired.
Termyna, James J. '70 (PAT) Boonton, NJ SS. Cyril and Methodius Church.
Ternes, Cletus *o.m.i.* '61 (FgM) Oblates Foreign Missions.
Ternes, Gary '79 (SFS) [6] Sioux Falls, SD St. Mary Church; [D] Sioux Falls, SD Avera McKennan.
Ternullo, Joseph P. '73 (SAC) North Highlands, CA St. Lawrence Church.
Tero, Richard D. '74 (ANC) Soldotna, AK Our Lady of Perpetual Help Church.
Terra, Joseph *f.s.s.p.* '89 (SCR) [M] Elmhurst, PA Priestly Fraternity of St. Peter (F.S.S.P.), North American District Headquarters.
Terra, Msgr. Russell G. '62 (SAC) Redding, CA St. Joseph Church.
Terranova, Robert P. *o.s.a.* '73 (FgM) Foreign Missions.
Terrebonne, Burnick J. '77 (NO) [3] Marrero, LA St. Joachim Church.
Terrera, C. Bernardo '89 (SCR) [M] Shohola, PA Society of Saint John.
Terrien, Douglas J. '79 (DET) Lapeer, MI Immaculate Conception of the Blessed Virgin Mary Church.
Terrill, Richard F. '54 (IND) Retired.
Terrillion, Albert *o.s.b.* '96 (NO) [P] St. Benedict, LA St. Joseph Abbey.
Terriquez, Enrique '63 (B) Caldwell, ID St. Mary Church; [F] Caldwell, ID Albertson's College of Idaho.
Terry, Christopher *o.p.* '89 (P) [18] Portland, OR Holy Rosary Parish & Dominican Priory Church.
Terry, John S. '75 (SCR) Sugar Notch, PA Holy Family Church; [Q] Wilkes-Barre, PA Catholic Youth Center.
Tertzakian, Hovhannes *o. mech.* '48 (ARM) New York, NY St. Ann's Church.
Terza, William R. '69 (PIT) [54] Pittsburgh, PA St. John Vianney Church; Allegheny County, PA State Correctional Institute at Pittsburgh.
Terzano, John D. '74 (CLV) Peninsula, OH Mother of Sorrows Church.
Tesek, Albert J. '51 (CLV) North Royalton, OH St. Albert the Great Church; Retired.
Teske, Roland J. *s.j.* '65 (MIL) [P] Milwaukee, WI Jesuit Community at Marquette University.
Teslovic, Eugene J. '77 (RIC) [7] Virginia Beach, VA St. Luke Church.
Tessmer, Richard A. (CHI) Retired.
Testa, David '67 (ALB) On Duty Outside the Diocese.
Testa, Genaro J. '47 (HRT) Retired.
Testa, Jess '88 (JOL) Lombard, IL Sacred Heart Church.
Testa, Richard '67 (ALB) Special Assignment.
Testa, Msgr. Steve J. *v.f.* '64 (ALX) Bunkie, LA St. Anthony of Padua Church.
Testagrossa, Joseph *o.f.m.cap.* '57 (SP) [O] Seminole, FL Capuchin Franciscan Residence.
Teta, Michael J. '74 (TUC) Absent on Leave.
Teter, Patrick A. '92 (SPC) Billings, MO St. Joseph Church.
Teti, James V. '97 (NEW) [1] Newark, NJ Cathedral Basilica of the Sacred Heart.
Tetlow, John H. '84 (STA) [3] Jacksonville, FL Christ the King Church.
Tetlow, Joseph A. *s.j.* '60 (NO) [P] New Orleans, LA Jesuit Provincial Office.
Tetrault, Ralph D. '65 (FR) Retired.
Tetrault, Raymond L. '60 (PRO) [32] Providence, RI St. Teresa of Avila Church.
Tetreault, Msgr. Jean C. '49 (BGP) Retired.

Tetreault, Maynard *o.f.m.* '60 (CIN) [V] Cincinnati, OH Franciscan Central Purchasing.
Tetreault, Maynard *o.f.m.* '60 (LEX) Cumberland, KY St. Stephen Church.
Tetreault, Raymond A. '71 (PRO) North Smithfield, RI St. John the Evangelist Church.
Tetu, Richard P. '69 (MAN) [12] Manchester, NH St. Marie Church.
Tevaga, Emani '86 (SPP) [2] Pago Pago, AS Co-Cathedral of St. Joseph the Worker.
Teverzczuk, William J. (PH) Lenni, PA St. Francis de Sales Church.
Tevington, Thomas *o.s.a.* '34 (ORG) Buena Park, CA St. Pius V Church.
Tewes, Msgr. Thomas '63 (BAL) Retired.
Texada, David Ker '80 (NO) Retired.
Texlemariam, Tesfamariam *c.m.* '92 (CHI) [N] Chicago, IL DePaul Vincentian Residence.
Tey, Jose R. *s.j.* '59 (MIA) [D] Miami, FL Belen Jesuit Preparatory School; [H] Miami, FL Villa Javier.
Tezie, John '59 (CLV) Cleveland, OH St. Michael Hospital.
Tezie, William F. '56 (CLV) [38] Cleveland, OH St. John Nepomucene Church; Retired.
Thaar, Gerald *o.s.c.* '65 (DET) Royal Oak, MI St. Dennis Church; [K] Riverview, MI Crosier Community of Riverview.
Thachet, Joseph '60 (KAL) Retired.
Thaden, Roy W. *s.j.* '73 (FgM) Provinces.
Thaden, William A. '88 (CLV) [4] Lorain, OH Sacred Heart Chapel Church; El Salvador, C.A., OH Parroquial Inmaculada Concepcion; [W] Cleveland, OH Office of Hispanic Ministry.
Thadeu, Joseph S. '47 (PRO) Retired.
Thai, Thomas Vu Minh '54 (LEX) Carlisle, KY Shrine of Our Lady of Guadalupe Church; Paris, KY Annunciation of the Blessed Virgin Mary Church.
Thai Minh Tran, Joseph *s.s.s.* '94 (SFE) [25] Albuquerque, NM St. Charles Borromeo Church.
Thalanany, Joseph *v.c.* '67 (SFS) Emery, SD St. Martin Church; [F] Emery, SD Vincentian Congregation.
Thaler, Joseph L. *m.m.* '77 (FgM) Maryknoll Foreign Missions.
Thall, Apollinaris I. *s.j.* '83 (CI) Nemar, FM St. Mary Church.
Thalman, Eugene A. *m.m.* '60 (FgM) Maryknoll Foreign Missions.
Thamert, Mark *o.s.b.* '79 (SCL) [I] Collegeville, MN St. John's Abbey, of the Order of St. Benedict.
Thames, Robert '64 (FWT) On Duty Outside the Diocese.
Thanh, Mark Tran-Xuan '59 (IND) [22] Indianapolis, IN St. Joseph Church.
Thanh, Nguyen Duc *c.ss.r.* '96 (LA) [Q] Baldwin Park, CA Vietnamese Redemptorist Mission.
Thanh Hung, John B. '54 (MIL) [8] Milwaukee, WI St. Anthony Church; Retired.
Thannickal, Joseph *s.d.b.* '83 (SJ) Los Altos, CA St. Simon Church.
Thanugundla, Joji '94 (CHI) [92] Chicago, IL Immaculate Heart of Mary Church.
Thapwa, Stephen M. '76 (WCH) Cherryvale, KS St. Francis Xavier's Church; Independence, KS St. Andrew Church.
Tharakan, Jose '94 (LR) Fort Smith, AR Immaculate Conception Church.
Tharakan, Martin *o.i.c.* '88 (SB) Lake Elsinore, CA St. Frances of Rome Church.
Tharappel, Augustine '70 (TYL) [1] Tyler, TX Cathedral of the Immaculate Conception.
Tharayil, John *c.m.i.* '74 (PH) Croydon, PA St. Thomas Aquinas Church.
Tharp, Larry R. '77 (CIN) [80] Cincinnati, OH St. Teresa Church.
Tharp, Shane I. '00 (OKL) [3] Oklahoma City, OK St. Charles Borromeo Church.
Thatcher, John R. *s.j.* '47 (SPK) [K] Spokane, WA Regis Community.
Thawale, P.J. (NY) [8] Yonkers, NY St. Eugene Church.
Thayer, David D. *s.s.* '75 (HRT) On Duty Outside the Archdiocese.
Thayer, David D. *s.s.* '75 (WDC) [A] Washington, DC Theological College of the Catholic University of America.
Thayer Tewes, J. Edwin '96 (ARL) Chantilly, VA St. Timothy Church.
Thayil, Matthew *m.s.f.s.* '67 (ATL) Norcross, GA Saint Patrick's Church.
The Pham, Vincent Tung '85 (PH) Bristol, PA St. Mark Church.
Thein, Edward '79 (ATL) [1] Marietta, GA Holy Family Church.
Theiryoung, John '96 (PEO) Tiskilwa, IL St. Mary's Church.
Theis, Gerald *s.v.d.* '80 (FgM) Society of the Divine Word Foreign Missions.
Theis, Gerard J. *o.s.a.* '53 (CHI) [N] Olympia Fields, IL The Augustinians-Provincialate.
Theisen, Donald J. '42 (LC) Retired.
Theisen, Eugene A. *m.m.* '53 (FgM) Maryknoll Foreign Missions.
Theisen, Eugene J. '99 (STP) Minnetonka, MN Immaculate Heart of Mary Church.
Theisen, John J. '59 (MIL) Retired.
Theisen, Kenneth *o.s.b.* '84 (RCK) [A] Aurora, IL Marmion Abbey; [G] Aurora, IL Marmion Abbey-St. Augustine's Abbey.
Theisen, Paul J. '98 (WOR) [2] Fitchburg, MA St. Bernard's Church.
Theisen, Roman G. *m.m.* '54 (FgM) Maryknoll Foreign Missions.
Theisen, Wilfred *o.s.b.* '56 (SCL) [I] Collegeville, MN St. John's Abbey, of the Order of St. Benedict.
Theiss, Daniel *c.m.* '90 (CHI) [N] Chicago, IL Vincentian Community, Congregation of the Mission, Midwest Province.
Thekkan, Pauly *c.m.i.* '89 (MET) Edison, NJ John F. Kennedy Medical Center.
Thekkattayil, Varghese '95 (PRO) [K] North Providence, RI St. Joseph Health Services of Rhode Island - Our Lady of Fatima Hospital.
Thekkedam, George '60 (LUB) Special Assignment; [B] Lubbock, TX St. Mary of the Plains Hospital.
Thekkel, Thomas J. *m.s.t.* '82 (MAR) Trenary, MI St. Rita Church.
Thekkeveetil, Bonaventure '63 (RVC) Dix Hills, NY St. Matthew Church.
Thekkummattathil, George *c.s.c.* (BO) Brighton, MA Vencor Hospital Boston.
Thekumthala, Ouseph '75 (TYL) Canton, TX St. Therese Church.
Thelakkatt, Xavier '80 (STP) [A] St. Paul, MN St. John Vianney Seminary; [C] St. Paul, MN University of St. Thomas.
Thelen, Albert R. *s.j.* '68 (OM) [K] Omaha, NE Jesuit Community at Creighton University.
Thelen, Bert *s.j.* '68 (OM) [23] Omaha, NE St. John Church.
Thelen, Frederick L. '80 (LAN) [9] Lansing, MI Cristo Rey Church.
Thelen, Jerome *o.f.m.* '66 (SHP) Ruston, LA St. Thomas Aquinas Church; [G] Ruston, LA E. Donn Piatt Catholic Student Center at Louisiana Tech University.
Thelen, Msgr. Robert J. '70 (BRK) [204] Queens, NY Nativity of the Blessed Virgin Mary Church.
Thell, Richard *o.s.b.* '74 (OM) [C] Elkhorn, NE Mount Michael High School; [K] Elkhorn, NE Mount Michael Abbey.
Thelly, Matthew '71 (SY) Utica, NY St. Elizabeth Hospital.
Thelly, Matthew '71 (TR) Deal, NJ St. Mary of the Assumption Church.
Then Henriquez, Christian Jose *s.d.b.* '85 (MGZ) Aguadilla, PR San Jose Obrero Church.
Thenen, James '58 (NY) Retired.
Thenen, John T. '58 (NY) [224] Staten Island, NY St. Peter Church.
Thennattil, George *t.o.r.* '76 (FWT) Carrollton, TX St. Catherine of Siena Church.
Thennes, Clarence J. '38 (RCK) Retired; [E] Freeport, IL St. Vincent's Community Living Facility and Supported Living Arrangement; [F] Freeport, IL Provena St. Joseph Center; [F] Freeport, IL Provena St. Joseph Adult Day Care Services.
Theobald, Charles F. '58 (NEW) Lodi, NJ St. Francis de Sales Church.
Theobald, Vincent *s.v.d.* '49 (NO) [N] New Orleans, LA St. John Berchmans Manor.
Theoret, Glenn A. '99 (MAR) Grand Marais, MI Holy Rosary Church.
Thepe, Theodore C. *s.j.* '55 (CIN) [M] Cincinnati, OH Jesuit Community at Xavier University.
Theraux, Normand *m.s.* '54 (FR) [I] Attleboro, MA La Salette Shrine.
Theriault, A. Francis *s.v.d.* '55 (BLX) Bay St. Louis, MS St. Rose De Lima Church.
Theriault, H. *m.div.* '60 (NY) Tivoli, NY St. Sylvia Church.
Theriot, Donald C. '57 (LAF) Abbeville, LA St. Mary Magdalen Church.
Theroux, Bertrand '67 (PRO) North Kingstown, RI St. Francis De Sales Church.
Theroux, Denis B. '90 (DET) Redford Township, MI St. Robert Bellarmine Church.
Theroux, J. Raymond '65 (PRO) [3] Cumberland, RI St. John Baptist Mary Vianney Church.
Theroux, Normand *m.s.* '54 (FR) [K] Attleboro, MA La Salette Center for Christian Living.
Theroux, Msgr. Paul D. '77 (PRO) [25] Providence, RI Our Lady of Lourdes Church.
Therriault, Ronald P. (PRT) Special or Other Diocesan Assignment.
Therrien, Shawn M. '87 (MAN) Charlestown, NH St. Catherine Church; North Walpole, NH St. Peter Church.
Thesing, Gilbert *o.p.* '75 (FgM) Dominican - Order of Preachers Foreign Missions.
Thesing, Gilbert J. *o.p.* '75 (CHI) [N] Chicago, IL Dominicans (Provincial Office).
Thesing, Kenneth F. *m.m.* '69 (FgM) Maryknoll Foreign Missions.
Thesing, Mark *c.s.c.* '86 (FTW) [B] Notre Dame, IN University of Notre Dame Du Lac; [J] Notre Dame, IN Holy Cross Community, Corby Hall, University of Notre Dame.
Thesing, Mark B. *c.s.c.* '86 (FTW) [A] Notre Dame, IN Moreau Seminary; [J] South Bend, IN Congregation of Holy Cross, Indiana Province, Provincial House.
Thesing, Robert J. *s.j.* '76 (CIN) [26] Cincinnati, OH St. Francis Xavier Church; [M] Cincinnati, OH Jesuit Community at St. Xavier High School; [V] Cincinnati, OH St. Xavier Church Property Corporation.
Thess, William C. '00 (STL) Des Peres, MO St. Clement Church.
Thessing, Charles '88 (LR) Morrilton, AR Sacred Heart Church.
Thevarkunnel, Anselm (DUL) Duluth, MN Indian Missions Church; Duluth, MN Indian Missions Church.
Thevarkunnel, Anselm '57 (DUL) Ball Club, MN St. Joseph's Church.
Thevenin, Georgereau '92 (RVC) Elmont, NY St. Boniface Church.
Thi, Andrew '85 (NY) [102] New York, NY St. Patrick Old Church.
Thibault, Armand *s.m.* '85 (BO) [55] Boston, MA Our Lady of Victories Church; [W] Boston, MA Marist Fathers and Brothers Provincial House; [W] Boston, MA Marist Fathers of Our Lady of Victories (Boston Prov.).
Thibault, Camillus *a.a.* '56 (BO) [W] Boston, MA Assumptionist Center.
Thibault, Donald P. *o.p.* '68 (WDC) [11] Washington, DC St. Dominic Church & Priory Church.
Thibeau, Richard *s.v.d.* '57 (FgM) Society of the Divine Word Foreign Missions.
Thibeault, W. Timothy '72 (MAN) Penacook, NH Immaculate Conception Church.
Thibedeau, Vianney *o.f.m.cap.* '88 (GB) [I] Appleton, WI St. Fidelis Friary.
Thibodeau, Andre M. '71 (MAN) Hillsboro, NH St. Mary Church; [N] Henniker, NH New England College Newman Center.
Thibodeau, Clement D. '58 (PRT) Gardiner, ME St. Joseph's Church.
Thibodeau, Kenneth *s.m.* '68 (BO) [W] Boston, MA Marist Fathers and Brothers Provincial House; [W] Boston, MA Marist Fathers of Our Lady of Victories (Boston Prov.).
Thibodeau, Kenneth *s.m.* '86 (BO) [55] Boston, MA Our Lady of Victories Church.
Thibodeau, Raynold *o.f.m.cap.* '85 (NY) New Paltz, NY St. Joseph Church; [DD] New Paltz, NY St. Joseph Friary; [GG] New York, NY University Apostolate.
Thibodeau, Richard *c.ss.r.* '76 (DEN) [M] Denver, CO The Redemptorists/Denver Province.
Thibodeau, Richard *c.ss.r.* '76 (FgM) Redemptorist Foreign Missions.
Thibodeau, Scott A. '98 (DET) Farmington, MI Our Lady of Sorrows Church.
Thibodeaux, Charles B. *s.j.* '59 (FgM) Provinces.
Thibodeaux, Charles B. *s.j.* '59 (NO) [P] New Orleans, LA Jesuit Provincial Office.
Thibodeaux, Paul '48 (LAF) Retired.
Thibodeaux, Roger '79 (BEA) Corrigan, TX St. Martin de Porres Church; Livingston, TX St. Joseph Church.
Thiel, Cris *o.f.m.cap.* '90 (LA) [F] La Canada Flintridge, CA St. Francis High School.
Thiel, Harold J. *c.ss.r.* '56 (DEN) [M] Denver, CO The Redemptorists/Denver Province.
Thiel, Harold J. *c.ss.r.* '56 (FgM) Redemptorist Foreign Missions.
Thiel, Lloyd *o.f.m.cap.* (DET) [K] Detroit, MI St. Bonaventure Friary.
Thiel, Lloyd *o.f.m. cap.* '56 (DET) Detroit, MI Beaumont Hospital.
Thiele, Richard *c.ss.r.* '54 (DEN) [M] Denver, CO The Redemptorists/Denver Province.
Thiele, Richard *c.ss.r.* '54 (FgM) Redemptorist Foreign Missions.
Thiele, Robert A. '55 (SC) Retired.
Thielen, Jeffrey M. '74 (MIL) [8] Racine, WI St. Lucy Church.
Thielen, Martin '35 (P) Retired.
Thielman, Kenneth '55 (SCL) Retired.
Thieman, Donald J. *c.pp.s.* '53 (CIN) [M] Dayton, OH Provincial Office of the Cincinnati Province of the Society of the Precious Blood.
Thien, Peter Van Hoang *o.p.* '72 (GAL) [58] Houston, TX Our Lady of Lourdes Church.
Thiers, George G. *c.o.* '70 (PH) [48] Philadelphia, PA St. Francis Xavier Church; [AA] Philadelphia, PA The Philadelphia Congregation of The Oratory of St. Philip Neri.
Thieryoung, John '96 (PEO) Bradford, IL St. John the Baptist Church.
Thies, Jeffrey '83 (ORG) Inactive Leave.
Thiessen, Dennis D. *s.d.s.* '78 (MIL) [P] Milwaukee, WI Salvatorian Provincial Residence.
Thilburger, Chad *s.j.* (STL) [52] St. Louis, MO St. Matthew, Apostle Church.
Thill, Richard '81 (PBL) Absent on Leave.
Thillo, Marcel Van *c.i.c.m.* '56 (ARL) [J] Arlington, VA

Missionhurst, C.I.C.M.-Central House and Provincialate.
Thimm, Donald H. '76 (MIL) Pleasant Prairie, WI St. Anne Church.
Thimmesh, Hilary *o.s.b.* '54 (SCL) [I] Collegeville, MN St. John's Abbey, of the Order of St. Benedict.
Thinnes, John M. '64 (CHI) Glenview, IL Our Lady of Perpetual Help Church.
Thirumangalam, George *c.m.i.* '76 (SAN) Brady, TX St. Patrick's Church.
Thissen, Donald R. '70 (WCH) Arma, KS St. Joseph Church; Girard, KS St. Michael Church.
Thissen, Kevin C. *o.p.* '63 (GAL) Sugar Land, TX St. Thomas Aquinas Church.
Thoa, Ngo Dinh *c.ss.r.* '62 (LA) [Q] Baldwin Park, CA Vietnamese Redemptorist Mission.
Thodukayil, Philip Joseph (CHI) Chicago, IL Knanite Syro-Malabar Catholic Mission of the Archdiocese of Chicago Church.
Thodukayil, Phillip (CHI) [92] Chicago, IL Immaculate Heart of Mary Church.
Thoennes, James '64 (SCL) Special Assignment.
Thoennes, Roger '90 (SCL) Harding, MN Holy Cross Church; Lastrup, MN St. John Nepomuk Church.
Thole, Simeon J. *o.s.b.* '62 (SCL) [I] Collegeville, MN St. John's Abbey, of the Order of St. Benedict.
Thole, Simeon J. *o.s.b.* '62 (SP) [O] St. Leo, FL St. Leo Abbey.
Thole, Thomas *o.s.b.* '58 (SCL) [I] Collegeville, MN St. John's Abbey, of the Order of St. Benedict.
Tholen, John '62 (YAK) Retired.
Thom, Elmer D. '43 (SC) Retired.
Thom, William V. *s.j.* '58 (SJ) [L] Los Gatos, CA Sacred Heart Jesuit Center.
Thoman, Dwayne J. '76 (DUB) [1] Dubuque, IA St. Raphael's Church; [D] Dubuque, IA Wahlert High School.
Thoman, James *c.p.* '75 (DET) [K] Detroit, MI St. Paul of the Cross Community, Congregation of the Passion; [P] Detroit, MI St. Paul of the Cross Retreat Center.
Thoman, Robert A. '41 (PH) [AA] Philadelphia, PA Jesuit Community at St. Joseph's University.
Thomas, Alan E. '92 (ALT) [1] Johnstown, PA St. John Gualbert Church.
Thomas, Alan E. '92 (GBG) [A] Latrobe, PA St. Vincent Seminary.
Thomas, Antoine '92 (PEO) [N] Peoria, IL Congregation of St. John; [P] Peoria, IL Newman Foundation at Bradley University & Illinois Central College.
Thomas, Aquinas *s.a.* '48 (NY) [O] Barryville, NY New Hope Manor; [DD] Garrison, NY Franciscan Friars of the Atonement; [HH] Barryville, NY New Hope Manor.
Thomas, Msgr. Arthur S. (NU) Retired.
Thomas, Charles Theodore '73 (COL) Mt. Vernon, OH St. Vincent de Paul Church; [J] Columbus, OH Campus Ministry.
Thomas, Curtis R. '87 (NO) [5] Metairie, LA St. Catherine of Siena Church.
Thomas, Msgr. Daniel E. '85 (PH) On Duty Outside the Archdiocese.
Thomas, David T. '52 (STL) [2] Creve Coeur, MO St. John Bosco Church; Retired.
Thomas, Dominic *m.c.b.s.* '87 (HRT) Guilford, CT St. George Church.
Thomas, Donald '85 (HON) Retired.
Thomas, Donald N. '68 (SAM) Retired.
Thomas, Ephrem *s.j.* '74 (CHI) [C] Chicago, IL Jesuit Community at Loyola University of Chicago.
Thomas, Gary R. '83 (SJ) Los Altos, CA St. Nicholas Church.
Thomas, George L. '48 (SFR) [2] Menlo Park, CA St. Denis Church; Retired.
Thomas, Jacob '76 (ALX) [2] Alexandria, LA Our Lady of Prompt Succor Church; Glenmora, LA St. Louis Church.
Thomas, James J. '76 (ALN) Military Chaplains.
Thomas, James P. (BEL) [J] Scott AFB, IL Scott Air Force Base.
Thomas, Jeffrey F. '00 (HBG) Gettysburg, PA St. Francis Xavier's Church.
Thomas, Jerald '56 (SR) Retired.
Thomas, John '93 (IND) [A] St. Meinrad, IN St. Meinrad Seminary.
Thomas, John '93 (OWN) On Duty Outside the Diocese.
Thomas, John D. '54 (WOR) Paxton, MA St. Columba's Church.
Thomas, John E. '50 (BO) Senior Priests.
Thomas, John M. '66 (SC) Vail, IA St. Ann's Church.
Thomas, Joseph S. '52 (CHI) Northlake, IL St. John Vianney, Cure of Ars Church; Retired.
Thomas, Juniper J. '70 (RVC) Glen Cove, NY St. Rocco Church; Glen Cove, NY North Shore Community Hospital at Glen Cove.
Thomas, Kevin '88 (DET) [5] Dearborn, MI Divine Child Church.
Thomas, LaVerne, III '86 (SHP) [7] Shreveport, LA St. Elizabeth Ann Seton Church.
Thomas, Mark A. '96 (PIT) Glenshaw, PA St. Bonaventure Church.
Thomas, Mark L. '93 (PIT) Ellwood City, PA Holy Redeemer Church.
Thomas, Merwyn J. *c.s.c.* '67 (FTW) [B] Notre Dame, IN University of Notre Dame Du Lac; [J] Notre Dame, IN Holy Cross Community, Corby Hall, University of Notre Dame.
Thomas, Michael G. '83 (SAM) Miami, FL Our Lady of Lebanon Church.
Thomas, Milton '64 (LIN) [6] Lincoln, NE St. John the Apostle Church.
Thomas, Norman P. '55 (DET) [69] Detroit, MI Sacred Heart of Jesus Church.
Thomas, P. T. '64 (CHI) [208] Chicago, IL St. Walter Church; [J] Blue Island, IL St. Francis Hospital and Health Center.
Thomas, Paschal *o.s.b.* '57 (KC) [J] Conception, MO Conception Abbey.
Thomas, Paul '42 (ALT) Retired.
Thomas, Paul '63 (BAL) Special Assignment.
Thomas, Paul *o.s.b.* '82 (P) [L] St. Benedict, OR Mt. Angel Abbey.
Thomas, Philip *o.c.d.* '79 (MIL) [26] Milwaukee, WI St. Florian Church.
Thomas, Ralph W. '65 (CLV) Gates Mills, OH St. Francis of Assisi Church.
Thomas, Raymond J. '72 (Y) Conneaut, OH St. Mary's Church; Conneaut, OH St. Frances Cabrini Church.
Thomas, Richard L. '66 (GB) Oneida Township, WI Immaculate Conception Church.
Thomas, Richard M. *s.j.* '58 (ELP) [N] El Paso, TX Our Lady's Youth Center.
Thomas, Robert '61 (FgM) Society of St. James the Apostle.
Thomas, Robert R. '60 (TOL) Retired.
Thomas, Robert W. '76 (BO) Society of St. James the Apostle.
Thomas, Msgr. Royce R. '69 (LR) Fort Smith, AR Christ the King Church; [B] Fort Smith, AR Trinity Junior High.
Thomas, Siby *h.g.n.* '99 (LEX) Louisa, KY St. Jude Church.
Thomas, Sylvester J. '55 (LA) Retired; [CC] San Pedro, CA Apostleship of the Sea, Catholic Maritime Ministry.
Thomas, Wilbur N. '73 (CHL) Asheville, NC Basilica of St. Lawrence; Special Assignment.
Thomas, William '78 (LAN) Hamburg, MI Holy Spirit Church.
Thomas, William F. '93 (LR) West Memphis, AR St. Michael's Church.
Thomas, William V. '62 (CIN) Jamestown, OH St. Augustine Church; South Charleston, OH St. Charles Borromeo Church.
Thome, Edward '51 (WIN) [A] Winona, MN Immaculate Heart of Mary Seminary.
Thome, Edwin A. '54 (GAY) Retired.
Thome, Edwin J. '51 (LC) Onalaska, WI St. Patrick Church; Retired.
Thome, Frank '89 (MRY) Retired.
Thome, John J. '46 (SAG) Retired.
Thompson, Andrew *c.ss.r.* '81 (FgM) Redemptorist Foreign Missions.
Thompson, August L. '57 (ALX) Retired.
Thompson, Augustine '85 (RIC) Charlottesville, VA St. Thomas Aquinas Church.
Thompson, Charles C. '87 (L) Lebanon, KY St. Augustine Church.
Thompson, D. Timothy '82 (FWT) [11] Fort Worth, TX St. John the Apostle Church.
Thompson, Damien *o.c.s.o.* '61 (L) [L] Trappist, KY Abbey of Our Lady of Gethsemani, of the Order of Cistercians of the Strict Observance.
Thompson, David '92 (WDC) Forestville, MD Mt. Calvary Church.
Thompson, Dennis '89 (STP) St. Louis Park, MN Most Holy Trinity Church.
Thompson, Edward C. '59 (NEW) Dumont, NJ St. Mary's Church.
Thompson, Edward J. '51 (ORL) Altamonte Springs, FL St. Mary Magdalen Church.
Thompson, Garrett J. '81 (BO) Boston, MA St. Elizabeth's Medical Center; Graduate Studies; [Q] Boston, MA St. Elizabeth's Hospital of Boston.
Thompson, George M. '52 (PEO) Retired.
Thompson, Msgr. George P. '65 (NY) [60] New York, NY St. John the Martyr Church.
Thompson, J. Noel '54 (SD) Retired.
Thompson, J. Timothy *s.j.* '70 (FgM) Provinces.
Thompson, J. Vincent *c.s.b.* '49 (GAL) [Q] Sugar Land, TX Basilian Mission Center.
Thompson, James *o.s.a.* '71 (CHI) [N] Chicago, IL St. John Stone Friary.
Thompson, James A. '44 (TR) Lakehurst, NJ St. John Church; Retired.
Thompson, James W. '44 (L) Retired; [L] Louisville, KY Bishop David Apartments.
Thompson, Jefferson *c.s.b.* (GAL) [C] Houston, TX University of St. Thomas.
Thompson, Jefferson M. *c.s.b.* '91 (GAL) [Q] Houston, TX Residence of the Basilian Fathers of the University of St. Thomas; [T] Houston, TX University of St. Thomas Campus Ministry.
Thompson, Jerald '94 (LA) Whittier, CA St. Gregory the Great Church.
Thompson, Jerome F. '66 (MIL) On Duty Outside the Archdiocese.
Thompson, Jerome H. '60 (LA) Retired.
Thompson, John *s.d.b.* '79 (FgM) Salesians of Don Bosco Foreign Missions.
Thompson, John A. '79 (BRK) [166] Queens, NY St. Elizabeth's Church.
Thompson, Kevin *o.f.m.cap.* '97 (BAL) [45] Baltimore, MD St. Jerome Church; [58] Baltimore, MD St. Martin Church; [80] Baltimore, MD St. Peter the Apostle Church.
Thompson, Kizito *o.c.s.o.* '70 (WOR) [N] Spencer, MA St. Joseph's Abbey.
Thompson, Matthew E. '79 (WDC) Hilltop, MD St. Ignatius Loyola Church; McConchie, MD St. Catherine of Alexandria Church.
Thompson, Melvin F. '67 (DEN) [3] Lakewood, CO Our Lady of Fatima Church.
Thompson, Michael '96 (STA) Palm Coast, FL St. Elizabeth Ann Seton Church.
Thompson, Msgr. Patrick '60 (LA) Lomita, CA St. Margaret Mary Alacoque Church; Pacoima, CA Mary Immaculate Church.
Thompson, Philip E. '78 (DUB) [3] Cedar Rapids, IA John XXIII Church.
Thompson, Richard *o.s.c.* '78 (DET) [K] Riverview, MI Crosier Community of Riverview.
Thompson, Richard B. '69 (MAN) Meredith, NH St. Charles Church.
Thompson, Richard B. '95 (P) Astoria, OR St. Mary, Star of the Sea Church.
Thompson, Richard J. '96 (PIT) Wexford, PA St. Alphonsus Church.
Thompson, Richard R. '59 (SY) Fulton, NY Holy Family Church; Fulton, NY St. Michael Church.
Thompson, Thomas '82 (SD) La Jolla, CA All Hallows Church; San Diego, CA Scripps Hospital; La Jolla, CA Thornton Hospital.
Thompson, Thomas A. *s.m.* '68 (CIN) [D] Dayton, OH The University of Dayton; [M] Dayton, OH Marianist Provincialate.
Thompson, Thomas E. '92 (SUP) Balsam Lake, WI Our Lady of the Lakes Church; Centuria, WI St. Patrick Church; Osceola, WI St. Joseph Church.
Thompson, Thomas W. '64 (LAN) Williamston, MI St. Mary Church.
Thompson, William D. '69 (BGP) Military Chaplains.
Thompson, William J. '71 (WDC) [2] Silver Spring, MD St. Bernadette Church.
Thompson, William L. *o.s.b.* '44 (PBL) [G] Canon City, CO Holy Cross Abbey.
Thompson, Msgr. William P.A. (CC) Retired.
Thomsen, Stephen '86 (LAN) On Duty Outside the Diocese.
Thomson, Edward A. '80 (PRT) Windham, ME Our Lady of Perpetual Help Church.
Thomson, Richard *c.p.* '69 (FgM) Mission Procurators.
Thon, Andrew J. *s.j.* '74 (MIL) [C] Milwaukee, WI Marquette University; [P] Milwaukee, WI Jesuit Community at Marquette University.
Thong, Nguyen Duc *c.ss.r.* '56 (LA) [Q] Baldwin Park, CA Vietnamese Redemptorist Mission.
Thoni, Philip F. '49 (KNX) Retired.
Thoni, Phillip F. '49 (KNX) Cleveland, TN St. Therese of Lisieux Church.
Thoomkuzhy, George '72 (STP) Cologne, MN St. Bernard Church.
Thoonkuzhy, Joseph '58 (BEL) Special Assignment.
Thoonkuzhy, Joseph '58 (TLS) [E] Tulsa, OK Saint Francis Hospital, Inc.
Thorburn, Msgr. Timothy J. '83 (LIN) [13] Lincoln, NE Bishop Bonacum Chancery Church; [K] Lincoln, NE Chancery.
Thoren, Guy S. '71 (MAR) [4] Marquette, MI St. Louis Church.
Thorn, Robert *o.f.m. cap.* '99 (LC) Marathon City, WI Nativity of the Blessed Virgin Mary Church.
Thorne, Carrol *c.p.* '60 (MET) [H] South River, NJ Passionist Provincial Office.
Thorne, Stephen D. '98 (PH) [2] Chester, PA Saint Katharine Drexel Church; [EE] Philadelphia, PA Newman Center at Drexel University.
Thorne, Thomas P. '76 (BGP) Westport, CT Assumption Church.
Thorne, Vance *s.v.d.* '53 (TR) [M] Bordentown, NJ Society of the Divine Word.
Thornsberry, Michael (BAL) [24] Baltimore, MD St. Clare Church.
Thornton, Lawrence *s.v.d.* '54 (CHI) [B] Techny, IL Divine Word Residence.
Thornton, Msgr. Michael '69 (JKS) [I] Jackson, MS Parroquia De San Miguel Del Arcangel.
Thorsen, Henry '53 (BIR) Retired.
Thorsen, Robert J. '56 (CIN) Retired.
Thottankara, Raju D. '95 (CC) [2] Kingsville, TX St. Gertrude Church.
Thottapally, James J. '71 (OAK) [7] Fremont, CA St.Leonard-Santa Paula Church.

Thottiyil, Mathew '78 (BIR) Demopolis, AL St. Leo Church; Livingston, AL St. Francis of Assisi Church.
Thottungal, Thomas '70 (NEW) [2] Jersey City, NJ St. Aloysius Church.
Thrasher, Robert W. '62 (SPR) [3] Holyoke, MA Holy Family Church.
Thro, Linus J. *s.j.* '44 (STL) [P] St. Louis, MO Jesuit Community Corporation at St. Louis University - Jesuit Hall.
Thro, Thomas F. *s.j.* '51 (STL) [O] St. Louis, MO Fusz Pavilion.
Thuan, Dominic Phuc Nguyen *s.s.s.* '68 (GAL) [25] Houston, TX Corpus Christi Church.
Thuc, John Bosco Pham Trung *c.m.c.* (BO) [58] Boston, MA St. Peter Church.
Thuer, William J. '46 (HRT) Retired.
Thueraf, Jason '99 (TUC) Yuma, AZ St. Francis of Assisi Church.
Thuerauf, Jeffrey P. '89 (TUC) Coolidge, AZ St. James Church.
Thul, Joseph T. '55 (MET) Retired; [H] Somerset, NJ Maria Regina Residence.
Thul, Robert C. *s.j.* '61 (CHI) [D] Chicago, IL St. Ignatius College Prep; [D] Chicago, IL St. Ignatius Jesuit Community.
Thuma, Clifton M. '96 (BO) [3] Peabody, MA St. John the Baptist Church.
Thumma, Albin Reddy '85 (NY) [206] Staten Island, NY Holy Rosary Church.
Thumma, Aloysius *s.t.d.* '80 (NY) [170] Bronx, NY Our Lady of the Assumption Church.
Thumma, Jacob '93 (NY) Pearl River, NY St. Aedan Church.
Thuong, Msgr. Philippe Le-Xuan *j.c.d.* '70 (GAL) [15] Houston, TX Christ, The Incarnate Word Church.
Thurmond, Benton A. '46 (VIC) Inez, TX St. Joseph's Church.
Thurn, Brian R. '98 (NU) Absent on Leave.
Thurner, Robert M. '51 (STP) Retired.
Thurston, Anthony '82 (WH) Weirton, WV St. Paul's Church.
Thury, Gerald '67 (SFS) Woonsocket, SD St. Wilfrid Church.
Thuy, Pham Quang '73 (RIC) On Duty Outside the Diocese.
Thychary, George '60 (LAF) Morrow, LA St. Peter Church.
Thymootil, Paul *c.m.i.* (NY) [3] Kingston, NY St. Joseph Church.
Thymoutil, Paul (NY) State, NY Wallkill Correctional Facility.
Tiano, Christopher M. '89 (HRT) [1] New Britain, CT All Saints Church; [5] New Britain, CT St. Ann Church; Special and other Archdiocesan Assignment.
Tiba Kunirwa, John C. (AUS) [H] Austin, TX St. Joseph Hall.
Tibay, Ernesto '76 (NEW) Bergenfield, NJ St. John the Evangelist Church.
Tibbett, Richard K. '98 (ATL) Toccoa, GA St. Mary's Church.
Tibbs, Thomas T. '74 (GRY) Kouts, IN St. Mary Church.
Tibesar, Leo J. '68 (STP) [24] Minneapolis, MN St. Frances Cabrini Church; Minneapolis, MN Riverside Medical Center.
Tiblier, Edgar J. *s.j.* '56 (GAL) [42] Houston, TX St. Joseph Church.
Tiboni, Vito '69 (BRK) Brooklyn, NY Veterans Administration Medical Center.
Tiboni, Vito '69 (NEW) Military Chaplains.
Tibudan, Tomasito '73 (AGN) Dededo, GU Santa Barbara Church.
Tice, Cecil W. '81 (CHL) Winston-Salem, NC St. Leo's Church.
Tichacek, Charles P. '94 (STL) On Duty Outside the Archdiocese.
Tickerhoof, Bernard *t.o.r.* (PIT) [Q] Pittsburgh, PA Franciscan Spirit and Life Center.
Tickerhoof, Bernard *t.o.r.* '77 (PIT) [O] Pittsburgh, PA Franciscan Friars, T.O.R.; [O] Pittsburgh, PA Third Order Regular of Saint Francis - Province of the Most Sacred Heart of Jesus.
Tickerhoof, David *t.o.r.* '67 (SFS) Marty, SD St. Paul's Church.
Tickle, John '67 (LSC) [1] Las Cruces, NM Cathedral of Immaculate Heart of Mary.
Tiedeman, Edmund '66 (SC) Mapleton, IA St. Mary's Church.
Tiedemann, Neil *c.p.* '75 (BRK) [145] Brooklyn, NY Visitation of the Blessed Virgin Mary Church.
Tiedemann, Neil *c.p.* '75 (MET) [H] South River, NJ Passionist Provincial Office.
Tiefenbrunn, Ronald R. '60 (STL) Retired.
Tiegs, James R. (OM) [O] Omaha, NE New Cassel Foundation.
Tiegs, James R. '74 (OM) [H] Omaha, NE New Cassel Retirement Center.
Tiel, Florian *o.f.m. conv.* '68 (L) [K] Louisville, KY Franciscan Health Care Center.
Tiell, Maurice J. '50 (OWN) Eddyville, KY St. Mark Church.
Tien, Msgr. Peter Nguyen Duc '60 (ORG) [H] Santa Ana, CA Vietnamese Catholic Center.
Tiercelin, Harry (NY) [122] New York, NY St. Vincent de Paul Church.
Tiercelin, Harry '47 (NY) Retired.
Tiernan, John F. *m.s.f.s.* '98 (ATL) Norcross, GA Saint Patrick's Church.
Tierney, Berard *c.p.* '48 (SCR) [M] Scranton, PA Saint Ann's Passionist Monastery.
Tierney, Charles *o.m.i.* '73 (FgM) Oblates Foreign Missions.
Tierney, Francis J. *s.j.* '42 (NY) [DD] New York, NY Murray-Weigel Hall.
Tierney, Gary M. '67 (DET) [2] Troy, MI St. Alan Church.
Tierney, Msgr. James E. '50 (BO) [Z] Boston, MA Regina Cleri, Inc.
Tierney, Joseph P. '86 (NY) [A] Yonkers, NY St. Joseph's Seminary.
Tierney, Michael E. '69 (KC) Lee's Summit, MO Holy Spirit Church.
Tierney, Michael J. '67 (RCK) Algonquin, IL St. Margaret Mary Church.
Tierney, Patrick '89 (DEN) [H] Denver, CO St. Joseph Hospital.
Tierney, Patrick J. *v.f.* '69 (BIR) Tuscumbia, AL Our Lady of the Shoals Church.
Tierney, Msgr. Patrick M. '57 (CAM) Avalon, NJ Maris Stella Church.
Tierney, Robert G. '57 (VEN) Bradenton, FL St. Joseph Church.
Tierney, Thomas J. *s.j.* '62 (RC) [B] Howes, SD Kino Jesuit Community.
Tierney, Thomas M. '70 (WOR) [2] Fitchburg, MA St. Bernard's Church; Gardner, MA Massachusetts Correctional Institution.
Tiesi, Samuel *t.o.r.* '63 (STU) [A] Steubenville, OH Franciscan University of Steubenville; [F] Steubenville, OH Holy Spirit Friary.
Tietjen, Kenneth F. *o.c.s.o.* '56 (DUB) [K] Peosta, IA New Melleray Abbey, Order of Cistercians of the Strict Observance.
Tiffany, Eugene W. '72 (STP) Lakeville, MN All Saints Church.
Tifft, Thomas W. '69 (CLV) [A] Wickliffe, OH St. Mary Seminary and Graduate School of Theology.
Tigga, Ranjit *s.j.* '96 (MIL) [P] Milwaukee, WI Jesuit Community at Marquette University.
Tigges, James '71 (SC) Alton, IA St. Mary's Church; Hospers, IA St. Anthony's Church.
Tighe, Msgr. Benedict F. '59 (BGP) [10] Stamford, CT St. Leo Church.
Tighe, Msgr. Emmett F. '51 (WIN) Retired.
Tighe, James '70 (BRK) [231] Queens, NY Queen of Peace Church.
Tighe, Leonard J. (BO) Jamaica Plain, MA Lemuel Shattuck Hospital; Jamaica Plain, MA Shattuck Hospital Correctional Unit.
Tighe, Philip M. '00 (R) Cary, NC St. Michael the Archangel Church.
Tighe, Timothy P. *c.s.p.* '69 (NY) [104] New York, NY St. Paul the Apostle Church.
Tigreros, Ernesto *s.s.p.* '66 (NY) [B] New York, NY Society of St. Paul.
Tigyer, Jeffrey E. '00 (COL) Powell, OH St. Joan of Arc Church.
Tigyer, Paul '54 (PSC) Retired.
Tijerina, Richard J. '85 (AUS) Austin, TX Seton Hospital.
Tikalsky, Russell F. '56 (MIL) [K] Milwaukee, WI St. Mary's Hospital of Milwaukee.
Tildon, Louise G. (BAL) [35] Baltimore, MD St. Gregory the Great Church.
Tilford, John E. '66 (CHI) [136] Chicago, IL St. Michael the Archangel Church.
Till, Joseph E. '46 (GRY) Retired.
Tilley, Charles J. *s.j.* '85 (MRY) San Luis Obispo, CA San Luis Obispo Church; [B] San Luis Obispo, CA Mission College Preparatory Catholic High School.
Tillia, Marc '59 (KCK) On Duty Outside the Archdiocese.
Tillman, Richard H. '65 (BAL) Columbia, MD St. John the Evangelist Church.
Tillman, Richard J. '65 (STL) [1] St. Charles, MO St. Charles Borromeo Church.
Tillman, Robert J. *s.j.* '77 (OM) [C] Omaha, NE Creighton Preparatory School.
Tillman, Stanley C. *s.j.* '45 (DET) [P] Clarkston, MI Colombiere Center.
Tillolson, Fred *o.carm.* '69 (TUC) [A] Tucson, AZ Salpointe Catholic High School.
Tillotson, Frederick *o.carm.* '69 (TUC) [F] Tucson, AZ Carmelite Priory.
Tillrock, Raymond J. '69 (CHI) [21] Chicago, IL St. Barnabas Church.
Tillyer, Msgr. Herbert K. '68 (PAT) Parsippany, NJ St. Peter the Apostle Church; [P] Paterson, NJ Riese Corporation; [P] Paterson, NJ Martin de Porres Village Corporation.
Tilp, John R. '69 (DUB) Clutier, IA Immaculate Conception Church; Traer, IA St. Paul's Church; Vining, IA St. Mary's Church.
Timar, Frank John *m.s.c.* '58 (RCK) Sycamore, IL St. Mary Church; [G] Aurora, IL Missionaries of the Sacred Heart Community.
Timbre, Roland '61 (HT) Chackbay, LA Our Lady of Prompt Succor Church.
Timby, Bryan P. '83 (MEM) [10] Memphis, TN Holy Rosary Church.
Timchak, Robert M. '92 (SCR) West Hazleton, PA Transfiguration Church.
Timko, Philip S. *o.s.b.* '69 (JOL) [A] Lisle, IL Benedictine University; [J] Lisle, IL St. Procopius Abbey.
Timlin, Anthony J. '56 (SB) Palm Desert, CA Sacred Heart Church.
Timlin, John P. *c.m.* '79 (PH) [B] Philadelphia, PA DePaul Novitiate.
Timm, Richard W. *c.s.c.* '49 (FgM) Holy Cross Foreign Missions.
Timmel, Gerald L. '56 (L) Retired.
Timmerman, David W. '93 (MAD) McFarland, WI Christ the King Church.
Timmerman, Gerard W. *s.m.* '75 (MAN) Ashland, NH St. Agnes Church; Plymouth, NH St. Matthew Church.
Timmerman, Randy '87 (MAD) [6] Madison, WI Our Lady, Queen of Peace Church.
Timmerman, Randy J.. '93 (MAD) [12] Madison, WI St. Paul University Church.
Timmermans, Msgr. John '52 (ALX) Retired; [E] Moreauville, LA St. John's Village.
Timmers, Jozef *o.f.m.capuchin* (CHI) [63] Chicago, IL St. Francis de Sales Church; [68] Chicago, IL St. George Church.
Timmings, Thomas '70 (FRS) Atwater, CA St. Anthony Church.
Timock, Ronald K. '83 (MAR) Gwinn, MI St. Anthony Church.
Timone, Donald '60 (NY) [4] Newburgh, NY Sacred Heart Church.
Timone, Richard F. *s.j.* '64 (NY) [DD] New York, NY Murray-Weigel Hall.
Timoney, Brian '56 (OAK) Pleasant Hill, CA Christ the King Church.
Timoney, Christopher *o.c.d.* '62 (SAT) [18] San Antonio, TX Basilica of The National Shrine of Our Lady of Mt. Carmel and St. Therese, Discalced Carmelite Fathers; [M] San Antonio, TX Discalced Carmelites (Prov. of St. Therese).
Timoney, Conan H. '68 (BAL) [11] Baltimore, MD Ascension Church; Baltimore, MD Veterans Hospital, Fort Howard; Baltimore, MD Veterans Hospital, Baltimore; [W] Baltimore, MD Catholic War Veterans, Inc.
Timoney, Conan H. '68 (PSC) Baltimore, MD Patronage of the Mother of God Church.
Timoney, Francis '69 (LAV) [5] Las Vegas, NV Prince of Peace Church.
Timp, Frederick *s.v.d.* '71 (FgM) Society of the Divine Word Foreign Missions.
Timperman, Robert *c.i.c.m.* '49 (SAT) [K] San Antonio, TX Padua Place.
Timperman, Robert A. *c.i.c.m.* '49 (ARL) [J] Arlington, VA Missionhurst, C.I.C.M.-Central House and Provincialate.
Tin, Urbano '87 (SAL) Manhattan, KS Seven Dolors Church.
Tinajero, Frank *s.v.d.* '88 (LAV) [12] Las Vegas, NV St. Joseph, Husband of Mary Church.
Tindall, Harold '78 (SD) Retired.
Tindall, William H. '89 (DET) Newport, MI St. Charles Borromeo Church.
Tinder, Msgr. F. Dennis (BAL) [41] Baltimore, MD Immaculate Conception Church.
Tingerthal, James *o.s.b.* '61 (SCL) [I] Collegeville, MN St. John's Abbey, of the Order of St. Benedict.
Tinh, Joseph Nguyen '57 (SJ) On Duty Outside the Diocese.
Tinney, Edward J. *s.j.* '44 (PH) [AA] Philadelphia, PA Jesuit Community at St. Joseph's University.
Tinney, Richard W. '65 (BUR) Fair Haven, VT Our Lady of Seven Dolors Church.
Tino, Robert '71 (SEA) Steilacoom, WA Western State Hospital.
Tino, Robert F. '71 (MIL) On Duty Outside the Archdiocese.
Tinsley, Msgr. Edmond T. '51 (WOR) [I] Leicester, MA McAuley Nazareth Home for Boys; [R] Worcester, MA Monsignor Thomas Griffin Foundation.
Tintle, Raymond *o.f.m.* '69 (LA) [73] Los Angeles, CA St. Joseph Church.
Tiongson, Joselito '92 (SD) [13] San Diego, CA Our Lady of Mt. Carmel Church.
Tippmann, Laurence '69 (FTW) [8] Fort Wayne, IN St. Joseph Church.
Tipton, Grover B. '96 (STA) Special Assignment.
Tipton, Paul S. (MOB) On Leave from the Archdiocese.
Tirabassi, Camillo '59 (FTW) [7] South Bend, IN Corpus Christi Church.
Tirado, Orlando *c.m.* (SJN) Military Services.
Tirado, Ramon Orlando '99 (SJN) [43] San Juan, PR San Pablo Church.
Tirkey, Dominic '98 (LAN) East Lansing, MI St.

Thomas Aquinas Church.
Tirpak, Adrian *t.o.r.* '60 (ALT) [3] Windber, PA St. Anthony of Padua Church.
Tiscornia, Thomas A. *m.m.* '73 (FgM) Maryknoll Foreign Missions.
Tiso, Francis Vi '88 (SFR) Mill Valley, CA Our Lady of Mt. Carmel Church.
Titko, Stephen J. '79 (GRY) Saint John, IN St. John Evangelist Church.
Titland, Peter R. *s.j.* '70 (FgM) Provinces.
Titmas, William D. '63 (CAM) [M] Cherry Hill, NJ Vianney Villa.
Tito, Joseph '88 (NOR) Baltic, CT St. Mary of the Immaculate Conception Church.
Tito, Joseph '96 (CHI) [193] Chicago, IL St. Sylvester Church.
Tito, Rocco A. '55 (E) Titusville, PA St. Walburga Church.
Titone, Robert '71 (BRK) [170] Queens, NY St. Gabriel Church.
Titotto, Carlo *c.s.* '67 (GAL) [44] Houston, TX St. Leo the Great Church.
Titta, Santino '60 (ALB) Retired.
Tittler, Leo R. '63 (BAL) Emmitsburg, MD St. Anthony Church; Thurmont, MD Our Lady of Mount Carmel Church.
Titus, Austin E. '92 (NY) [225] Staten Island, NY St. Rita Church.
Titus, John M. '89 (SFD) [6] Springfield, IL St. Aloysius Church.
Titus, Rodney A. '95 (PMB) Port St. Lucie, FL Holy Family Church.
Tiu, Jimmy '00 (FAR) Jamestown, ND State Hospital.
Tiu, Jimmy Lim '00 (FAR) Jamestown, ND The Basilica of St. James.
Tivadar, Vasile (STF) Ozone Park, NY St. Mary Protectress Church.
Tivenan, John J. '72 (BRK) Released from Diocesan Assignment.
Tivnan, Paul J. '63 (BO) Permanent Disability.
Tivy, Gerald '64 (JOL) Lisle, IL St. Joan of Arc Church.
Tivy, Thomas A. '62 (CHI) [146] Chicago, IL Our Lady of Grace Church; [169] Chicago, IL St. Philomena Church.
Tix, Michael '92 (STP) Richfield, MN Assumption of the B.V.M. Church.
Tizio, John G. *c.ss.r.* '85 (BAL) Annapolis, MD St. Mary Church; [S] Annapolis, MD Saint Mary Rectory.
Tizio, Joseph C. *c.ss.r.* '75 (NY) [78] New York, NY Most Holy Redeemer Church.
Tizio, Joseph C. *c.ss.r.* '75 (PH) [136] Philadelphia, PA St. Peter the Apostle Church.
Tkach, Norman A. '56 (SLC) On Duty Outside the Diocese.
Tkachuk, William '81 (CHI) Schaumburg, IL Church of the Holy Spirit.
Tlapa, Richard J. (CHI) Retired.
Tlucek, Edward G. *o.f.m.* '78 (GRY) [J] Cedar Lake, IN San Damiano Friary.
To, Joseph Lien *i.c.m.* '62 (BR) [H] Baton Rouge, LA Incarnatio Consecratio Mission.
Toal, James '58 (LA) [J] Burbank, CA Providence Saint Joseph Medical Center; [J] Burbank, CA Providence Health System.
Toal, James '75 (ALB) [B] Loudonville, NY Siena College; [B] Loudonville, NY Siena College.
Toale, Thomas E. '81 (DUB) Temple Hill, IA St. Peter's Church.
Toan, Francis '34 (MRY) Retired.
Toan, John Hoang Minh '68 (GAL) [79] Houston, TX Vietnamese Martyrs Church.
Tobia, David (OAK) [S] Berkeley, CA Maria House.
Tobias, Humphrey *o.f.m.* '48 (GB) [I] Pulaski, WI Assumption of B.V.M. Friary.
Tobias, Joseph *m.s.c.* '66 (PH) Ottsville, PA St. John the Baptist Church.
Tobin, Chuck '68 (KC) Maryville, MO St. Gregory Barbarigo Church.
Tobin, Eamon '72 (ORL) Cocoa Beach, FL Church of Our Saviour.
Tobin, James *s.m.* (STL) [P] St. Louis, MO Provincialate of the Society of Mary, Province of St. Louis.
Tobin, James E. *c.s.c.* '47 (FR) [A] North Easton, MA Holy Cross Fathers Religious.
Tobin, James M. *s.m.* '69 (STL) [4] Creve Coeur, MO Our Lady of the Pillar Church.
Tobin, Jeremy *o.praem.* '63 (JKS) [F] Jackson, MS Priory of St. Moses the Black.
Tobin, Joseph *c.ss.r.* '62 (LA) Whittier, CA St. Mary of the Assumption Church; [Q] Whittier, CA Redemptorist Fathers Mission House.
Tobin, Joseph W. *c.ss.r.* '78 (DEN) [M] Denver, CO The Redemptorists/Denver Province; [M] Denver, CO The Redemptorists/Denver Province.
Tobin, Msgr. Neil W. '57 (DUB) Castle Grove, IA Immaculate Conception Church; Monticello, IA Sacred Heart Church.
Tobin, Patrick '56 (KC) [38] Kansas City, MO St. Therese Church.
Tobin, Paul R. '64 (Y) Geneva, OH Assumption B.V.M. Church.
Tobin, Robert E. *m.m.* '57 (FgM) Maryknoll Foreign Missions.
Tobin, T. Michael '93 (L) [66] Louisville, KY St. Pius X Church.
Tobin, Terence *o.f.m.conv.* '55 (FgM) Conventual Franciscan Foreign Missions.
Tobin, Thomas '59 (GF) Baker, MT St. John the Evangelist Church.
Tobin, Thomas F. *s.j.* '65 (FgM) Provinces.
Tobin, Thomas H. *s.j.* '73 (CHI) [C] Chicago, IL Jesuit Community at Loyola University of Chicago.
Tobin, Thomas J. *c.s.c.* '55 (FR) [I] North Dartmouth, MA Holy Cross Mission House.
Tobin, Vincent *o.s.b.* '59 (IND) [J] St. Meinrad, IN St. Meinrad Archabbey.
Tobolski, James F. '84 (SUP) [5] Superior, WI St. Francis Xavier Church.
Tobolski, Robert *m.s.c.* '55 (ALN) [K] Reading, PA Missionaries of the Sacred Heart.
Toborowski, Jonathan S. '98 (MET) Basking Ridge, NJ St. James Church.
Tocco, Msgr. Anthony M. '65 (DET) Bloomfield Hills, MI St. Hugo of the Hills Church.
Tochtrop, Randolph '96 (SPC) [3] Springfield, MO Immaculate Conception Church.
Toczek, Melchior *o.f.m.* '49 (CHI) [N] Chicago, IL Chaplains:.
Toczek, Melchoir *o.f.m.* (CLV) [O] Cleveland, OH St. Jude Friary.
Toczex, Melchior *o.f.m.* (CLV) Warrensville Heights, OH St. Jude Church.
Todd, Richard J. *c.m.f.* '55 (CHI) [163] Chicago, IL St. Paul Church.
Todd, Terence N. *s.j.* (FgM) Provinces.
Todd, Wilmer L. '63 (HT) [4] Thibodaux, LA St. Genevieve Church.
Toepfer, John *o.f.m.cap.* '86 (DEN) [3] Denver, CO Annunciation Church; [1] Aurora, CO Queen of Peace Church; [M] Denver, CO Annunciation Friary.
Tofani, Msgr. Richard L. '79 (TR) [2] Trenton, NJ Blessed Sacrament Church.
Togni, Peter J. *s.j.* '85 (SFR) [N] San Francisco, CA Jesuit Community at University of San Francisco.
Tokarczyk, Joseph '79 (NY) Florida, NY St. Joseph Church.
Tokarski, Stanley '93 (DET) [62] Detroit, MI SS. Peter and Paul Church.
Tokarski, Stephen L. '69 (GF) [6] Billings, MT St. Pius X Church.
Tokarz, David J. '91 (MOB) [3] Montgomery, AL St. Bede Church.
Tokarz, John '39 (SPR) Retired; [I] Springfield, MA St. Michael's Residence.
Tokarz, Thomas M. '77 (WOR) [2] Gardner, MA St. Joseph's Church.
Tokaz, John *o.f.m.cap.* '78 (PRT) [3] Portland, ME St. Joseph's Church; [A] Standish, ME Saint Joseph's College; [M] Standish, ME Saint Joseph's College.
Tokus, William J. *m.m.* '60 (NY) [DD] Maryknoll, NY Maryknoll Fathers and Brothers.
Tolaas, Gregory '83 (STP) [32] Minneapolis, MN St. Philip Church.
Toland, Charles M. *o.s.m.* '56 (CHI) [N] Chicago, IL Order of Friar Servants of Mary (Servites) United States of America Province, Inc.
Toland, Eugene W. *m.m.* '64 (FgM) Maryknoll Foreign Missions.
Toland, Paul L. '53 (BO) Senior Priests.
Toland, Terrence *s.j.* '52 (SCR) [C] Scranton, PA University of Scranton.
Tolang, Jaime '58 (SEA) [26] Seattle, WA Immaculate Conception Church; Retired.
Tolbert, George T. *s.j.* '45 (DET) [P] Clarkston, MI Colombiere Center.
Tolczyk, Marion M. *o.f.m.conv.* '54 (BUF) [O] Athol Springs, NY Father Justin Rosary Hour Radio Apostolate.
Tolentino, Eddie, III '84 (WDC) [16] Washington, DC Holy Comforter—St. Cyprian Church.
Tolentino, Thomas (NY) [DD] New York, NY Our Lady of Consolation Residence.
Tolentino, Virgilio '82 (MET) Old Bridge, NJ St. Ambrose Church.
Tolentino de la Rosa, Lorenzo Maria, Jr. *o.cart.* '92 (BUR) [E] Arlington, VT Carthusian Foundation, Charterhouse of the Transfiguration.
Toliusis, Msgr. Casimir '36 (SFD) Retired.
Tolland, Cyril E. '44 (BO) Senior Priests.
Tollini, Frederick P. *s.j.* '65 (SJ) [B] Santa Clara, CA Santa Clara University.
Toloczko, Msgr. Bernard A. '58 (SCR) [2] Nanticoke, PA Holy Trinity Church; [J] Nanticoke, PA Mercy Health Care Center.
Tolosa, Braulio '64 (DM) [D] Des Moines, IA Mercy Medical Center.
Tolve, Paul *o.f.m.cap.* '84 (NY) County, NY Westchester County Jail; Valhalla, NY Westchester County Medical Center; [DD] White Plains, NY St. Conrad Friary.
Tomaino, Peter *s.a.* '47 (NY) [DD] Garrison, NY Franciscan Friars of the Atonement, Minister General Office.
Tomalonis, John '51 (PBL) Retired.
Toman, Edward A. *s.d.s.* '83 (NEW) [N] Verona, NJ The Salvatorian Fathers.
Tomas, Peter '95 (SJP) Lorain, OH St. John the Baptist Church.
Tomasek, Richard J. *s.j.* '73 (COL) [A] Columbus, OH Pontifical College Josephinum.
Tomaselli, Msgr. Samuel J. '59 (ALT) Somerset, PA St. Peter's Church.
Tomasi, Lydio *c.s.* '63 (NY) [DD] Staten Island, NY Scalabrinian Missionaries.
Tomasiewicz, Edward J. *c.m.* '74 (CHI) [N] Chicago, IL DePaul Vincentian Residence.
Tomasiewicz, Frank S. '65 (SCL) Kimball, MN Church of Saint Anne.
Tomasiewicz, Mark A. '91 (OM) Laurel, NE St. Mary Church.
Tomasko, Andrew J. '91 (DET) [53] Detroit, MI Our Lady of Good Counsel Church; [66] Detroit, MI St. Raymond Church.
Tomaskovic, Emil *s.a.* (NY) [DD] Garrison, NY Franciscan Friars of the Atonement.
Tomasone, Richard C. '80 (E) [4] Farrell, PA St. Ann Church; [C] Hermitage, PA Kennedy Christian High School.
Tomasovich, Msgr. John A. '48 (NO) Retired.
Tomassetti, Berard *o.f.m.cap.* '53 (SAL) [D] Victoria, KS St. Fidelis Friary.
Tomasso, Paul J. '81 (ROC) [6] Rochester, NY St. Anthony of Padua Church; [15] Rochester, NY St. Francis Assisi Church; [20] Rochester, NY Holy Apostles Church; [22] Rochester, NY Holy Family Church; [L] Rochester, NY Family Rosary For Peace, Inc.
Tomasulo, Anthony *o.s.a.* '61 (MIA) Dania, FL Church of the Resurrection.
Tomaszewski, Msgr. Michael J. '58 (GRY) Retired.
Tomatis, Christopher *o.f.m.* '65 (MRY) San Miguel, CA San Miguel Church; [F] San Miguel, CA Franciscan Friars, O.F.M.; [F] San Miguel, CA Novitiate House for the Franciscan Friars, O.F.M.
Tombasco, Anthony R. '51 (SCR) [6] Dunmore, PA St. Rocco's Church.
Tomc, Victor N. '43 (CLV) [47] Cleveland, OH St. Mary Church; Retired.
Tomei, Joseph A. *c.s.c.* '50 (AUS) [H] Austin, TX Congregation of Holy Cross - Southern Province.
Tomiak, Walter L. '40 (BUF) Retired.
Tomich, Daniel M. '76 (CHI) Riverdale, IL Queen of Apostles Church.
Tomichek, Msgr. George *d.c.* '74 (PH) [136] Philadelphia, PA St. Peter the Apostle Church.
Tomicky, Ronald '75 (CLV) Retired.
Tomiczek, Damien *s.d.s.* '82 (SAT) St. Hedwig, TX Annunciation of the Blessed Virgin Mary Church.
Tomkin, Robert '88 (SB) On Duty Outside the Diocese.
Tomkins, Robert '88 (SEA) Burlington, WA St. Charles Church; LaConner, WA Sacred Heart Church; Mount Vernon, WA Immaculate Conception Church.
Tomkins, Terry '82 (OAK) [2] Fremont, CA Holy Spirit Church.
Tomkosky, Richard B. '00 (ALT) Ebensburg, PA Holy Name Church.
Tomlinson, Brian *o.f.m. cap.* (NEW) [4] Hackensack, NJ Church of St. Francis of Assisi.
Tomlinson, Brian *o.f.m.cap.* '65 (PAT) [M] Lafayette, NJ St. Francis Center.
Tompkins, John Mary '93 (RIC) [5] Virginia Beach, VA St. Gregory the Great Church.
Tompkins, Regis C. *o.c.s.o.* '54 (ROC) [I] Piffard, NY Abbey of the Genesee.
Tompkins, Robert '88 (SEA) Sedro Woolley, WA Immaculate Heart of Mary Church.
Tompson, Harry W. *s.j.* '67 (NO) [11] New Orleans, LA Immaculate Conception Church.
Tomzik, Fred W. '84 (CHI) La Grange Park, IL St. Louise de Marillac Church.
Ton, Anthony '66 (SEA) [P] Seattle, WA Seattle, Vietnamese Catholic Center.
Tonary, David *m.s.f.* '81 (CC) [15] Corpus Christi, TX St. Joseph Church.
Tonelli, Robert F. '72 (CHI) Streamwood, IL St. John the Evangelist Church.
Toner, Donald *c.s.s.* '62 (BO) [W] Waltham, MA Stigmatine Fathers & Brothers Provincial House.
Toner, Edward R. '52 (COV) Retired.
Toner, Msgr. Francis X. '55 (NY) [132] Bronx, NY St. Barnabas Church.
Toner, John G. *m.s.* '44 (HRT) [M] Hartford, CT Missionaries of LaSalette, Provincial Secretary.
Toner, Oliver '71 (VEN) [2] Fort Myers, FL Church Of The Resurrection Of Our Lord.
Toner, Patrick A. '75 (COL) Plain City, OH St. Joseph Church; London, OH London Correctional Institution.
Toner, Raphael F. *s.t.* '41 (JKS) Philadelphia, MS Holy Rosary Church.
Tong, Chak-Long '00 (BO) [W] Cambridge, MA Weston Jesuit Community.

Tong, Peter *o.c.s.o.* '68 (L) [L] Trappist, KY Abbey of Our Lady of Gethsemani, of the Order of Cistercians of the Strict Observance.

Tongatani, Celestin *c.i.c.m.* '96 (SAT) [7] San Antonio, TX Holy Redeemer Church.

Tonne, Msgr. Arthur '32 (WCH) Retired.

Tonos, Joseph '94 (JKS) [F] Jackson, MS Priory of St. Moses the Black.

Tonry, Patrick J. *s.m.* '65 (BAL) Sykesville, MD St. Joseph Church.

Tonsmiere, Sidney A. *s.j.* '43 (NO) [P] New Orleans, LA Ignatius Residence.

Toof, Daniel R. '94 (ATL) Fayetteville, GA St. Gabriel Church.

Toohey, Timothy J. '65 (STL) Clover Bottom, MO St. Ann's Church; Washington, MO St. John's Hospital; [K] Washington, MO St. John's Mercy Hospital.

Toohig, Timothy E. *s.j.* '65 (BO) [W] Boston, MA The Society of Jesus of New England-Provincial Offices; [W] Chestnut Hill, MA The Jesuit Community at Boston College.

Toohy, Msgr. William J. '61 (NY) [18] New York, NY Blessed Sacrament Church; [I] New York, NY The Catholic Charities of the Archdiocese of New York; [I] New York, NY The Catholic Charities of the Archdiocese of New York.

Toolan, David S. *s.j.* '67 (NY) [DD] New York, NY West Side Jesuit Community.

Toolan, John A. *c.s.v.* '43 (CHI) [N] Arlington Heights, IL Viatorian Province Center-Clerics of St. Viator.

Toole, Arthur A. '58 (ALB) Voorheesville, NY St. Matthew Church.

Toole, Lawrence E. '67 (PRO) [6] Cumberland, RI St. Patrick Church.

Toolis, Martin '70 (GR) Retired.

Tooman, Robert E. '77 (NEW) North Bergen, NJ St. Brigid Church; [5] Union City, NJ St. Rocco's Church.

Toomey, John M. '61 (BO) Health Leave; Senior Priests.

Toomey, Kevin G. '78 (BO) [4] Medford, MA St. Raphael Church.

Toomey, Msgr. Leonard R. '48 (TR) Retired; [M] Trenton, NJ Villa Vianney.

Toomey, Thomas *o.s.b.* '50 (PAT) [M] Clifton, NJ Holy Face of Jesus Monastery.

Toonen, Harvey H. *o.praem.* '41 (GB) [I] De Pere, WI St. Joseph Priory.

Topel, L. John *s.j.* '65 (SEA) [A] Seattle, WA Seattle University.

Topf, Thomas J. '63 (SC) Schaller, IA St. Joseph's Church.

Topmoeller, William G. '52 (DET) [P] Clarkston, MI Colombiere Center.

Topolewski, Jaroslaw (ATL) Smyrna, GA St. Thomas the Apostle Church.

Topper, Charles J. '68 (HBG) On Duty Outside the Diocese.

Topper, Charles J. '68 (HRT) [C] West Hartford, CT Saint Joseph College.

Topper, John *o.s.m.* '87 (CHI) [N] Chicago, IL Order of Friar Servants of Mary (Servites) United States of America Province, Inc.

Topper, John M. *o.s.m.* '87 (CHI) [N] Chicago, IL Order of Friar Servants of Mary (Servites) United States of America Province, Inc.

Topper, John M. *o.s.m.* '87 (P) [L] Portland, OR The Grotto, The National Sanctuary of Our Sorrowful Mother.

Topper, Msgr. Vincent J. '36 (HBG) [2] Harrisburg, PA St. Catherine Laboure Church; Retired.

Topping, Msgr. Joseph '47 (SD) Retired.

Torba, Jason '91 (CHI) [44] Chicago, IL St. Constance Church.

Torborg, Elmer '55 (SCL) Retired.

Torgerson, Msgr. Lloyd A. '65 (LA) Santa Monica, CA St. Monica Church.

Torina, Ronald F. *s.j.* '76 (DET) [E] Detroit, MI University of Detroit Jesuit High School and Academy.

Torm, Agustin '93 (CHR) Military Chaplains.

Torma, Andrew *m.s.c.* '76 (OG) [2] Watertown, NY Our Lady of the Sacred Heart Church; [F] Watertown, NY Missionaries of the Sacred Heart.

Tormey, Daniel '55 (ROC) Retired.

Tormey, James D. '78 (SY) [12] Binghamton, NY St. Thomas Aquinas Church.

Tornes, Dale F. '70 (STU) Belle Valley, OH Corpus Christi Church; Caldwell, OH St. Stephen Church.

Torney, Msgr. John R. *p.a.* '39 (MET) Bernardsville, NJ Our Lady of Perpetual Help Church; Retired; [H] Somerset, NJ Maria Regina Residence.

Toro, Carlos Perez '88 (SJN) Graduate Studies.

Toro, Msgr. Emilio '60 (SJN) Luquillo, PR San Jose Church.

Torok, Msgr. Dezso '48 (Y) East Palestine, OH Our Lady of Lourdes Church; Retired.

Torok, George J. '58 (NY) [HH] Sparkill, NY Hallel Institute.

Torpey, Charles L. '69 (GI) Kearney, NE St. James Church.

Torpey, James M. '83 (ALN) Summit Hill, PA St. Joseph Church; Summit Hill, PA St. Stanislaus Church.

Torpey, Matt G. *o.c.s.o.* '56 (ATL) [J] Conyers, GA The Monastery of the Holy Spirit.

Torpey, Michael J. '68 (RVC) Sea Cliff, NY St. Boniface Martyr Church.

Torralba, Antolin B. '48 (LA) Retired.

Torralba, Julio *sch.p.* '58 (PCE) [C] Coto Laurel, PR Colegio Ponceno.

Torre, Emilio Diaz *l.c.* '93 (HRT) [V] Orange, CT Legion of Christ, Inc.

Torre, Emilio Diaz *l.c.* '93 (NY) [HH] Thornwood, NY Helping Hands Medical Missions, Inc.

Torre, Jesse *o.f.m.cap.* '61 (DAL) [8] Dallas, TX Our Lady of Lourdes Church.

Torrelas, Eduardo '85 (CGS) [C] Humacao, PR San Antonio Abad Abbey of the Order of St. Benedict.

Torrente, Lorenzo '75 (RNO) Lovelock, NV St. John the Baptist Church.

Torres, Adrian '75 (PMB) Vero Beach, FL St. Helen Church.

Torres, Alfonso G. '72 (BWN) Escobares, TX Sacred Heart Church.

Torres, Daniel '96 (LKC) De Ridder, LA St. Joseph's Church.

Torres, Eduardo '87 (PCE) [B] Ponce, PR The Pontifical Catholic University of Puerto Rico.

Torres, Ernesto '72 (DAL) [13] Dallas, TX St. Augustine Catholic Church.

Torres, Fernado *sch.p.* '93 (PCE) [C] Coto Laurel, PR Colegio Ponceno.

Torres, Frank D. '94 (GRY) [4] Gary, IN Holy Rosary Church.

Torres, Gabriel M. '95 (ARE) Ciales, PR Holy Rosary Church.

Torres, Gilberto *m.s.p.* '93 (LA) [22] Los Angeles, CA Our Lady of Solitude Church.

Torres, Hipolito '85 (CGS) Naranjito, PR San Miguel Arcangel Church.

Torres, Ivan '89 (SJN) On Duty Outside the Archdiocese.

Torres, Jose *o.m.i.* '74 (FgM) Oblates Foreign Missions.

Torres, Luis Angel '85 (SJN) [17] Carolina, PR Santisima Trinidad Church.

Torres, Mario '96 (LA) [20] Los Angeles, CA Nativity Church; [58] Los Angeles, CA St. Columbkille Church.

Torres, Marioalberto A. *s.j.* (SFR) [N] San Francisco, CA Jesuit Community at University of San Francisco.

Torres, Martin Betances '87 (NY) [96] New York, NY Our Lady of the Rosary Church.

Torres, P.L. Orlando *s.j.* '73 (SJN) [C] Rio Piedras, PR Jesuit Novitiate.

Torres, Robert A. '66 (LR) Retired.

Torres, Victor *o.m.i.* '95 (SJN) [7] San Juan, PR Ntr. Sra. de la Caridad del Cobre Church.

Torres, William '91 (SJN) Graduate Studies.

Torres-Ortiz, Anibal R. '00 (SJN) [38] San Juan, PR Santa Maria de Los Angeles Church.

Torres-Tarazona, P. Demetrio *o.m.i.* '99 (SJN) [8] San Juan, PR Nuestra Senora del Carmen Church.

Torretto, Joseph '75 (RIC) Scottsville, VA St. George Church.

Torrez, Basil '56 (SAL) Retired.

Torrez, John '98 (KCK) [1] Kansas City, KS Cathedral of St. Peter the Apostle; [B] Kansas City, KS Bishop Ward High School.

Torsiello, Ralph C. '58 (WDC) Bryantown, MD St. Mary Church.

Torson, Daniel L. *c.pp.s.* '90 (COL) [B] Columbus, OH Ohio Dominican College.

Tortell, Alexander '00 (BO) [W] Cambridge, MA Weston Jesuit Community.

Tortora, James '72 (NEW) [22] Jersey City, NJ Our Lady of Victories Church.

Tortora, Raymond '52 (RVC) Retired.

Tortorelli, Kevin *o.f.m.* '73 (NY) [35] New York, NY St. Francis of Assisi Church.

Tortorici, James D. '95 (PH) Downingtown, PA St. Joseph Church.

Tortorici, Joseph *o.p.* '72 (WDC) [B] Washington, DC Dominican House of Studies.

Toruno, Jorge R. *s.j.* '44 (FgM) Provinces.

Tos, Aldo J. '53 (NY) [61] New York, NY St. Joseph Church.

Tosatto, Lawrence *f.d.p.* '65 (BO) [U] Boston, MA Don Orione Nursing Home.

Toscani, Peter J. *o.s.a.* '47 (PH) [B] Villanova, PA St. Augustine Friary.

Toscano, Pasquale A. '44 (HRT) Retired.

Toschi, Larry *o.s.j.* '76 (FRS) Madera, CA St. Joachim Church.

Tosco, Lawrence *c.s.j.* '70 (CLV) [O] Avon, OH Congregation of St. Joseph.

Tosco, Lorenzo *c.s.j.* '70 (CLV) [A] Wickliffe, OH St. Mary Seminary and Graduate School of Theology.

Tosello, Matthew '62 (PIT) Prospect, PA St. Christopher at the Lake Church.

Tosi, Msgr. John C. '73 (BRK) [1] Brooklyn, NY The Cathedral-Basilica of St. James; [Z] Brooklyn, NY St. James Cathedral Foundation, Inc.

Toste, Frank A. *c.s.c.* '60 (BGP) [P] Bridgeport, CT Provincial Offices of the Priests and Brothers of Holy Cross, Eastern Province.

Tosti, Anthony F. '65 (SY) Canastota, NY St. Agatha Church.

Tosti, Msgr. Ronald A. '62 (FR) Mashpee, MA Christ The King Church.

Tosto, Louis F. '97 (RCK) Fulton, IL Immaculate Conception Church.

Totah, Sami '71 (NY) [9] Yonkers, NY Immaculate Conception Church; [9] Yonkers, NY Immaculate Conception Church.

Totaro, Dominic J. *s.j.* '67 (BAL) [S] Baltimore, MD Jesuit Fathers and Brothers Maryland Provincial Curia.

Totaro, Dominic J. *s.j.* '67 (FgM) Provinces.

Toth, Julius *o.f.m.conv.* '53 (TR) Riverside, NJ St. Peter Church.

Toth, Michael A. '74 (OG) Mineville, NY The Church of All Saints; Port Henry, NY St. Patrick Church.

Toth, Simon J. *o.s.b.* '59 (GBG) [5] Latrobe, PA St. Boniface Church; [H] Latrobe, PA Saint Vincent Archabbey.

Toth, Victor '48 (HT) Retired.

Totten, Raymond F. '48 (COL) Retired.

Tottle, Gregg '91 (SP) Safety Harbor, FL Espiritu Santo Church.

Tou, John '57 (NY) On Duty Outside the Archdiocese.

Tou, Louis A. '56 (WDC) Retired.

Touchette, Marc L. '57 (ALB) [3] Cohoes, NY St. Bernard Church.

Tougas, Paul J. '64 (WOR) Boylston, MA St. Mary of the Hills Church.

Tougas, Roger *a.a.* '60 (BO) [W] Boston, MA Assumptionist Center.

Toups, David L. '97 (SP) Spring Hill, FL St. Frances Xavier Cabrini Church.

Toups, Earl *c.ss.r.* '48 (BLX) [E] Biloxi, MS St. John Neumann Residence.

Tourigney, Ernest E. '61 (BO) Senior Priests.

Tourigny, William '80 (SPR) [11] Springfield, MA Our Lady of the Sacred Heart Church.

Tourneir, Msgr. Andre '48 (SFR) [K] San Rafael, CA Nazareth House.

Tournier, Msgr. Andre '48 (SR) Retired.

Touzin, Yves-Michel *c.s.* (NEW) [12] Newark, NJ St. Columba's Church.

Tovar, Emilio *c.m.* '43 (ARE) [1] Manati, PR La Candelaria Church.

Tovar, Francisco Hernandez '80 (SAC) [19] Sacramento, CA St. Peter Church.

Tovar, Ireneo Lopez '50 (CAM) Retired.

Towey, Cyprian *c.p.* '42 (CHI) [N] Chicago, IL Daneo Hall.

Towey, Damian *c.p.* '56 (PMB) [H] North Palm Beach, FL Our Lady of Florida Spiritual Center.

Towle, Joseph C. *s.j.* '66 (NY) [DD] New York, NY Jesuit Provincial's Office.

Towle, Joseph W. *m.m.* '65 (NY) [DD] Maryknoll, NY Maryknoll Fathers and Brothers.

Townsend, C. Frederick '83 (KC) Leave of Absence.

Townsend, Charles P. '91 (LIN) Mead, NE St. James Church; [C] Wahoo, NE Bishop Neumann Jr.-Sr. High School.

Townsend, Joe C. '88 (TLS) Pawnee, OK St. John Church; Stillwater, OK St. John University Parish and Catholic Student Center Church; [H] Stillwater, OK St. John's University Parish and Catholic Student Center.

Townsend, Ralph V. *o.p.* '50 (NEW) [28] Jersey City, NJ Sacred Heart Church.

Towsley, Peter J. '91 (BGP) Newtown, CT St. Rose of Lima Church.

Toye, D. Richard *s.j.* '65 (GAL) [F] Houston, TX Strake Jesuit College Preparatory Inc.

Tra, John *s.v.d.* '44 (DUB) [B] Epworth, IA Divine Word College.

Trabold, Alphonsus A. *o.f.m.* '51 (BUF) [C] St. Bonaventure, NY St. Bonaventure University; [O] St. Bonaventure, NY St. Bonaventure Friary.

Trabold, Msgr. George R. '73 (NEW) Short Hills, NJ St. Rose of Lima Church.

Trac, Peter Vu Dinh '54 (ORG) Retired.

Tracey, Bernard M. *c.m.* '74 (BRK) [D] Staten Island, NY St. John's University, Staten Island Campus; [D] Jamaica, NY St. John's University; [V] Jamaica, NY St. Vincent's House.

Tracey, Michael '72 (BLX) Bay St. Louis, MS Our Lady of the Gulf Church.

Tracey, Terence '52 (SFD) Retired; [L] Springfield, IL St. Francis Convent.

Tracey, Thomas S. '63 (CAM) Wildwood Crest, NJ Assumption B.V.M. Church.

Tracy, Charles '63 (SR) Retired.

Tracy, David W. '63 (BGP) On Duty Outside the Diocese.

Tracy, Eugene '91 (SPK) [18] Spokane, WA St. Peter Church.

Tracy, Msgr. George E. '84 (PRT) Retired.

Tracy, Msgr. James R. '60 (CAM) [4] Cherry Hill, NJ St. Pius X Church.

Tracy, John A. '52 (NEW) Retired.

Tracy, John P. '48 (HRT) Retired; [A] Bloomfield, CT St. Thomas Seminary.

Tracy, Joseph '92 (PH) [11] Philadelphia, PA St. Anne Church.
Tracy, Laurence '66 (ROC) [25] Rochester, NY Holy Redeemer-St. Francis Xavier Church; [36] Rochester, NY Our Lady of Mount Carmel Church; [47] Rochester, NY St. Michael Church.
Tracy, Norbert J. *s.j.* '55 (MIL) [P] Milwaukee, WI Jesuit Community at Marquette University.
Tracy, Philip A. '88 (PRT) Waterville, ME Parish of the Holy Spirit Church; [M] Waterville, ME Colby College; [M] Waterville, ME Thomas College.
Tracy, Philip Michael '60 (PRT) South Berwick, ME St. Michael Church.
Tracy, Robert D. *o.carm.* '63 (NY) Tarrytown, NY Transfiguration Church.
Tracy, Robert P. *o'carm.* '63 (NY) Castle Point, NY Veterans Administration Medical Center.
Tracy, T. Shawn *o.s.a.* '66 (PH) [C] Villanova, PA Villanova University; [AA] Villanova, PA St. John Stone Friary.
Tracy, Theodore J. *s.j.* '50 (CHI) [C] Chicago, IL Jesuit Community at Loyola University of Chicago.
Trad, John '41 (OLL) Retired.
Trader, William A. '74 (PH) Westtown, PA St. Maximilian Kolbe Church.
Traeger, Gregory *o.s.b.* '42 (SP) [O] St. Leo, FL St. Leo Abbey.
Traenkle, Mark *s.a.* '56 (OG) Olmstedville, NY St. Joseph Church.
Trahan, C. Nicholas '81 (LAF) [1] Lafayette, LA Cathedral of St. John the Evangelist.
Trahan, Harold '69 (LAF) [10] Lafayette, LA St. Elizabeth Seton Church.
Trahan, Romeo A. *s.s.e.* '45 (BUR) [E] Colchester, VT Society of St. Edmund.
Trahon, Basil *c.p.* '62 (HRT) [M] West Hartford, CT Holy Family Monastery/Retreat.
Trainer, Eugene '58 (STO) Hughson, CA St. Anthony Church.
Trainor, Daniel M. '61 (PRO) [6] Providence, RI Assumption of the Blessed Virgin Mary Church.
Trainor, Henry J. '73 (SFR) [42] San Francisco, CA St. Patrick Church.
Trainor, James F. '64 (WIL) [8] Wilmington, DE St. Mary of the Immaculate Conception Church; [9] Wilmington, DE St. Patrick Church; [G] Wilmington, DE St. Patrick's House, Inc.
Trainor, Msgr. Patrick '44 (SP) St. Pete Beach, FL St. John Church; Retired.
Trainor, Richard F. '75 (WOR) [18] Worcester, MA St. Bernard Church.
Trainor, Msgr. Robert M. '57 (NY) [125] Bronx, NY St. Ann Church.
Tran, Andrew *s.c.j.* '98 (MIL) [P] Hales Corners, WI Priests of the Sacred Heart.
Tran, Anthony Doan (BLX) Pass Christian, MS Sacred Heart Church.
Tran, Anthony Hung Ngoc *o.p.* '92 (GAL) [Q] Houston, TX Dominican Fathers and Brothers, St. Mark Priory, Inc.
Tran, Anthony Lan '70 (SEA) [3] Vancouver, WA St. James Church.
Tran, Augustine Hoa T. '98 (ATL) Decatur, GA St. Thomas More Church.
Tran, Augustine Hoa Trung '98 (ATL) Atlanta, GA Atlanta Veterans Administration Hospital.
Tran, Binh K. '92 (PEO) Ohio, IL Immaculate Conception Church; Walnut, IL St. John's Church.
Tran, Cong Bang *s.v.d.* '00 (FgM) Society of the Divine Word Foreign Missions.
Tran, Dac Tat *o.f.m.* '89 (BO) Boston, MA New England Medical Center; [BB] Boston, MA St. Anthony Shrine.
Tran, Dominic Dat '99 (PT) [11] Pensacola, FL St. Mary Church.
Tran, Hung *o.p.* '86 (GAL) [K] Houston, TX The Catholic Chaplain Corps.
Tran, Hung '98 (LA) Redondo Beach, CA St. James Church.
Tran, John *c.s.j.b.* '92 (BRK) [V] Astoria, NY Congregation of St. John the Baptist of China.
Tran, John Chinh Chan (GAL) Retired.
Tran, John Dam '95 (NY) [125] Bronx, NY St. Ann Church; Bronx, NY Montefiore Medical Center.
Tran, John Kha '89 (GAL) [A] Houston, TX St. Mary's Seminary.
Tran, John Nghi '71 (LA) Claremont, CA Our Lady of the Assumption Church.
Tran, John R. '00 (L) [28] Louisville, KY St. Gabriel the Archangel Church.
Tran, John Tinh '96 (SY) [7] Syracuse, NY Our Lady of Pompei Church.
Tran, John-Hue *s.v.d.* '95 (DUB) [B] Epworth, IA Divine Word College.
Tran, Joseph '74 (LAN) [6] Lansing, MI St. Andrew Dung-Lac Church.
Tran, Joseph '95 (NY) [168] Bronx, NY St. Nicholas of Tolentine Church.
Tran, Joseph Huynh *s.v.d.* '93 (FgM) Society of the Divine Word Foreign Missions.
Tran, Joseph Thang Dinh '96 (NO) [12] Metairie, LA St. Mary Magdalen Church.
Tran, Joseph Tu '99 (HT) Chauvin, LA St. Joseph Church.
Tran, Kiem Van '91 (ORG) [7] Santa Ana, CA St. Barbara's Church.
Tran, Luan Q. '94 (P) Rainier, OR Nativity B.V.M. Church.
Tran, Luc *s.v.d.* (SB) Yucca Valley, CA St. Mary of the Valley Church.
Tran, Luong Quang '89 (BEA) China, TX Our Lady of Sorrows Church; [G] Beaumont, TX St. Thomas More Society of Southeast Texas.
Tran, Martin D. *s.s.* '90 (SFR) [A] Menlo Park, CA St. Patrick Seminary.
Tran, Michael Mai *c.m.c.* '93 (BEA) [2] Port Arthur, TX Queen of Vietnam Church.
Tran, Michael X. '93 (SD) [4] Chula Vista, CA St. Rose of Lima Church.
Tran, Paul Tam X. '00 (WDC) Gaithersburg, MD St. John Neumann Church.
Tran, Peter '73 (RIC) Newport News, VA Our Lady of Mount Carmel Church.
Tran, Peter Tam *s.v.d.* '98 (FgM) Society of the Divine Word Foreign Missions.
Tran, Philip P. '92 (NY) [6] Poughkeepsie, NY St. Martin de Porres Church; Military Chaplains.
Tran, Quan H. '96 (PH) [125] Philadelphia, PA Our Lady of Mt. Carmel Church; [D] Philadelphia, PA St. John Neumann High School.
Tran, Quynh '93 (SPR) [6] Springfield, MA Holy Name Church.
Tran, Sang V. '92 (LA) Sepulveda, CA Our Lady of Peace Church.
Tran, Tan Van '92 (DM) Bayard, IA St. Patrick Church.
Tran, Thomas *s.v.d.* '00 (WH) Powhatan, WV Sacred Heart Church.
Tran, Tuan Quoc '97 (ATL) Riverdale, GA Our Lady of Vietnam Church.
Tran Cao Tuong, Andrew '75 (NO) [2] Marrero, LA St. Agnes Le Thi Thanh Church.
Tran Dien, Peter (SPC) [E] Carthage, MO Congregation of the Mother Co-Redemptrix, United States Assumption Province.
Tran Hung Long, Francis M. *c.m.c.* (SPC) [E] Carthage, MO Congregation of the Mother Co-Redemptrix, United States Assumption Province.
Tran Ngoc Diep, Joseph M. *c.m.c.* '83 (SPC) [E] Carthage, MO Congregation of the Mother Co-Redemptrix, United States Assumption Province.
Tran Ngoc Thoai, Aloysius M. *c.m.c.* '92 (SB) [E] Corona, CA Congregation of the Mother Coredemptrix.
Tran Thanh Liem, Aloysius M. *c.m.c.* (SPC) [E] Carthage, MO Congregation of the Mother Co-Redemptrix, United States Assumption Province.
Tran Van Dong, Alphonsus '63 (BGP) [1] Bridgeport, CT St. Augustine Church.
Tran-cong-Ly, Hilary M. *c.m.c.* '77 (FWT) [6] Arlington, TX St. Matthew Church.
Tran-Khac-Hy, Hilarius '57 (WDC) Retired.
Trance, F. Raymond '94 (PIT) [1] McKeesport, PA St. Martin de Porres Church.
Tranchida, Blaise *o.f.m.* '50 (NY) [DD] New York, NY Franciscan Province of the Immaculate Conception.
Tranchina, Joseph '68 (NO) Retired.
Trancone, Gerard A. '69 (WDC) Special Ministries; [S] Washington, DC Archdiocesan Campus Ministry; [V] Landover Hills, MD Catholic Deaf Center.
Tranel, Daniel D. '56 (RCK) Galena, IL St. Mary Church; Galena, IL St. Michael Church.
Tranel, Dorrance E. '49 (RCK) Wonder Lake, IL Christ the King Church.
Trang, Vang C. '83 (RIC) [N] Hampton, VA Holy Family Retreat.
Trapani, Anthony '73 (RVC) Priests Released from Diocesan Assignment; Military Chaplains.
Trapasso, Msgr. Thomas J. '49 (PAT) Morristown, NJ St. Margaret's Church; Retired.
Trapp, Arthur L. *c.m.* '56 (STL) [P] Perryville, MO Congregation of The Mission.
Trapp, Daniel J. '84 (DET) [11] Detroit, MI St. Augustine and St. Monica Church; [A] Detroit, MI Sacred Heart Major Seminary, Inc.
Trapp, Joseph J., II '96 (COL) Hilliard, OH St. Brendan Church.
Trapp, Joseph L. '59 (BEL) Benton, IL St. Joseph Church.
Traser, Anthony *c.pp.s.* '40 (CIN) [B] Carthagena, OH St. Charles.
Trask, David R. '86 (CLV) Macedonia, OH Our Lady of Guadalupe Church.
Traub, George W. *s.j.* '67 (CIN) [P] Milford, OH Milford Spiritual Center.
Traub, Robert '39 (FTW) Retired; [H] Fort Wayne, IN Saint Anne Home & Retirement Community.
Traudt, Robert *o.carm.* '82 (NEW) Leonia, NJ St. John the Evangelist's Church.
Traufler, John F. '57 (WIN) Winnebago, MN St. Mary's Church.
Trauger, Francis X. '72 (PH) Levittown, PA St. Michael the Archangel Church.
Traupman, Robert '69 (ORL) On Duty Outside the Diocese.
Trausch, Dennis '78 (DM) Carter Lake, IA Our Lady of Carter Lake Church.
Trautner, Kevin C. '74 (PH) [1] Norristown, PA St. Francis of Assisi Church.
Travaglione, Fidelis *o.f.m.* '66 (NY) [DD] New York, NY Franciscan Province of the Immaculate Conception.
Travaglione, Michael *o.f.m.* '66 (BO) [P] Andover, MA Franciscan Center; [W] Andover, MA St. Francis Friary; [Y] Andover, MA Franciscan Center - Retreat House.
Travassos, Horace J. '73 (FR) Westport, MA Our Lady of Grace Church.
Travers, Alan '83 (NY) Military Chaplains.
Travers, David O. *s.j.* '68 (BO) [W] Boston, MA The Society of Jesus of New England-Provincial Offices.
Travers, David O. *s.j.* '68 (HON) [17] Honolulu, HI Saints Peter and Paul Church.
Travers, Gerard P. '65 (NY) Highland Mills, NY St. Patrick Church.
Travers, John J. *c.ss.r.* '59 (BRK) [107] Brooklyn, NY Our Lady of Perpetual Help Basilica Church.
Travers, Joseph A. *o.s.f.s.* (FgM) Oblates of St. Francis de Sales Foreign Missions.
Travers, Joseph A. *o.s.f.s.* '48 (CAM) [M] Pittsgrove, NJ Villa St. Joseph.
Travers, Luke L. *o.s.b.* '86 (PAT) [D] Morristown, NJ Delbarton School; [M] Morristown, NJ St. Mary's Abbey.
Travers, Patrick *ss.cc.* '62 (LA) [D] La Verne, CA Damien High School; [Q] La Verne, CA Congregation of the Sacred Hearts of Jesus and Mary.
Travers, Patrick J. '93 (JUN) Ketchikan, AK Holy Name Church.
Travers, Tomas *c.ss.r.* (SJN) [I] San Juan, PR Casa San Clemente.
Travers, Tomas J. *c.ss.r.* '62 (SJN) [2] San Juan, PR San Agustin Church.
Traverso, Leonard '72 (SJ) Milpitas, CA St. Elizabeth Church.
Travieso, Ernesto *s.j.* '73 (OM) [K] Omaha, NE Jesuit Community at Creighton University.
Travis, Francis J. '81 (CHR) Pickens, SC Holy Cross Church.
Travis, Herbert A. '42 (BRK) [10] Brooklyn, NY St. Anselm's Church; Retired.
Travis, James M. '67 (TUC) [23] Tucson, AZ Saints Peter and Paul Church.
Travis, Leo *c.ss.r.* '54 (FgM) Redemptorist Foreign Missions.
Travnikar, Rock *o.f.m.* '76 (CIN) [M] Cincinnati, OH St. Francis Seraph Friary.
Travnikar, Rock *o.f.m.* '76 (HT) [C] Schriever, LA Lumen Christi Retreat Center.
Trawick, Gregory G. '85 (OWN) St. Joseph, KY St. Alphonsus Church.
Trawinski, Joseph *o.f.m.conv.* '40 (BUF) [21] Buffalo, NY Corpus Christi Church.
Traxl, William L. '60 (HRT) Glastonbury, CT St. Dunstan Church.
Trayers, Kevin '52 (WCH) Cherryvale, KS St. Francis Xavier's Church; Retired.
Traylor, William A. '76 (EVN) [3] Vincennes, IN St. John the Baptist Church; [4] Vincennes, IN St. Thomas The Apostle Church.
Traynor, Anthony '58 (SAC) [6] Sacramento, CA Our Lady of Lourdes Church; Special Assignment.
Traynor, John J. '45 (RVC) Retired.
Traynor, Joseph P. '82 (GBG) Clymer, PA Church of the Resurrection.
Traynor, Patrick *c.s.p.* (NY) [104] New York, NY St. Paul the Apostle Church.
Traynor, Scott '00 (SFS) [1] Sioux Falls, SD St. Joseph Church.
Treacy, Canice '52 (WDC) Olney, MD St. Peter Church; Retired.
Treacy, Jerome F. '61 (DET) [P] Clarkston, MI Colombiere Center.
Treacy, John R. *s.j.* '90 (SFR) [N] San Francisco, CA Jesuit Community at University of San Francisco.
Treacy, William '44 (SEA) Burlington, WA St. Charles Church; LaConner, WA Sacred Heart Church; Mount Vernon, WA Immaculate Conception Church; Sedro Woolley, WA Immaculate Heart of Mary Church; Retired.
Treanor, Boniface J. *o.s.b.* '56 (NEW) [N] Newark, NJ Newark Abbey.
Trebtoske, Everett '59 (AUS) Wimberley, TX St. Mary Church.
Trejo, Horacio *o.s.j.* '97 (SAC) [A] Loomis, CA Mount St. Joseph Novitiate and Seminary.
Trejo, Ramiro '77 (CC) [14] Corpus Christi, TX SS. Cyril and Methodius Church.
Trejo, Ramiro M. *o.f.m.cap.* '77 (CHI) [6] Cicero, IL Our Lady of the Mount Church.
Trela, Norman J. '66 (CHI) [194] Chicago, IL St. Symphorosa and Seven Sons Church.
Trela, Tadeusz '82 (NEW) [3] Irvington, NJ Sacred Heart of Jesus Church.
Treleaven, Michael *s.j.* '83 (SPK) [C] Spokane, WA

Gonzaga University.
Treloar, John L. *s.j.* '70 (MIL) [P] Milwaukee, WI Arrupe House Jesuit Community.
Tremblay, Albert J., Jr. '97 (MAN) Belmont, NH St. Joseph Church.
Tremblay, Eugene *o.m.i.* '38 (STP) [W] St. Paul, MN Missionary Oblates of Mary Immaculate.
Tremblay, Eugene *o.m.i.* '74 (BUF) [27] Buffalo, NY Holy Angels Church.
Tremblay, J. Normand '53 (WOR) Charlton City, MA St. Joseph's Church.
Tremblay, Jean A. '54 (MAN) Retired.
Tremblay, Leger '48 (SHP) Retired.
Tremblay, Marc P. '80 (FR) Somerset, MA St. Patrick's Church.
Tremblay, Nellis '54 (ALB) Retired.
Trementozzi, Paul *o.c.d.* '55 (BO) [W] Boston, MA Carmelite Monastery.
Tremie, Eugene R. '71 (LAF) [1] Opelousas, LA St. Landry Church.
Treml, Richard L. '99 (DET) [6] St. Clair Shores, MI St. Margaret of Scotland Church.
Tremmel, Benjamin *o.s.b.* '66 (KCK) [H] Atchison, KS St. Benedict's Abbey.
Tremonte, Pasquale *c.ss.r.* '81 (WIL) Seaford, DE Our Lady of Lourdes Church.
Tremonti, Joseph *c.s.v.* '41 (JOL) [2] Kankakee, IL St. Patrick Church; [I] Bourbonnais, IL Provena Our Lady of Victory.
Tremonti, Joseph B. '41 (CHI) [N] Arlington Heights, IL Viatorian Province Center-Clerics of St. Viator.
Trempe, James F. '96 (LC) Plover, WI St. Bronislava Church; [L] Plover, WI St. Bronislava Parish, Plover Endowment Trust.
Trench, Msgr. Edmond J. (RVC) Retired.
Trench, Msgr. Edmond J. '57 (RVC) Southampton, NY Sacred Hearts of Jesus and Mary Church.
Trenchard, Dawson D. (HRT) Retired.
Trenchard, Dawson D. '58 (HRT) Yalesville, CT Our Lady of Fatima Church.
Trenchera, Manuel '80 (AGN) Malojlo, GU San Isidro Church.
Trenchs, Juan *sch.p.* '40 (LA) [Q] Los Angeles, CA Piarist Fathers.
Trenier, Anthony S. '66 (MIL) Retired; [Y] Milwaukee, WI Archdiocesan Marian Shrine.
Trenor, Msgr. Edward F. '58 (COL) [10] Columbus, OH Christ the King Church; Columbus, OH Regency Manor.
Trent, James '62 (SR) Fortuna, CA St. Joseph Church.
Trent, James F. '62 (DET) On Duty Outside the Archdiocese.
Trepanier, James R. *c.s.c.* '55 (FTW) [A] Notre Dame, IN Moreau Seminary.
Trepanier, Thomas J. '64 (PRO) Lincoln, RI St. Ambrose Church.
Treppa, Terence '67 (DET) [4] Westland, MI St. Richard Church.
Trese, John A. '48 (DET) Retired.
Tressic, David L. '96 (ALB) Gloversville, NY Sacred Heart Church.
Tressler, Msgr. David L. '85 (SCR) Hudson, PA St. Joseph's Church; Plains, PA Sacred Heart Church; [D] Wilkes-Barre, PA Bishop Hoban High School.
Tressler, Robert '80 (ORG) Inactive Leave.
Treston, Msgr. James A. '60 (ALN) Sinking Spring, PA St. Ignatius Loyola Church.
Treston, Kevin *o.f.m.* '81 (WDC) [M] Washington, DC Commissariat of the Holy Land, Franciscan Monastery - Mount St. Sepulchre.
Trevett, Msgr. Cyril I. '48 (BUF) Retired.
Trevino, Alberto T. *m.s.f.* '80 (SAT) Seguin, TX Our Lady of Guadalupe Church.
Trevizo, Raul P. '88 (TUC) [16] Tucson, AZ St. John the Evangelist Church.
Trexler, Donald P. '98 (GBG) Belle Vernon, PA St. Sebastian Church.
Treyes, Reynaldo '78 (JOL) West Chicago, IL St. Mary Church.
Trezza, Richard *o.f.m.* '87 (NY) [48] New York, NY Holy Name of Jesus Church.
Tri Van Vu, Joseph *s.v.d.* '85 (FgM) Society of the Divine Word Foreign Missions.
Triano, Joseph A. *s.s.p.* '59 (DET) [K] Dearborn, MI Society of St. Paul.
Tribou, Msgr. George W. '49 (LR) [B] Little Rock, AR Catholic High School.
Tribuiani, Raymond F. '73 (PH) Oreland, PA Holy Martyrs Church.
Trick, James F. '60 (CIN) Botkins, OH Immaculate Conception Church; Rhine, OH St. Lawrence Church.
Trieu Ngoc Le, '58 (PIT) Verona, PA St. Joseph Church.
Triggs, Thomas J. '75 (TR) Cinnaminson, NJ St. Charles Borromeo Church.
Trigilio, John, Jr. '88 (HBG) Middletown, PA Seven Sorrows of the Blessed Virgin Mary Church.
Trigueros, Raul '69 (ELP) [7] El Paso, TX Cristo Rey Church.
Trimaglio, John *c.s.j.* '68 (LA) San Pedro, CA St. Peter Church; [Q] Los Angeles, CA Congregation of St. Joseph Casa Nazareth.
Trimbur, Edwin H. '51 (COV) Retired.
Trimbur, John S. '74 (Y) Campbell, OH St. John the Baptist Church.
Trimbur, Lee Francis '54 (LEX) Middlesboro, KY St. Julian Church.
Trinchard, Paul '66 (NO) Retired.
Trindade, Leonard J. '87 (FRS) Gustine, CA Our Lady of Miracles Church.
Tringhese, James D. '74 (GBG) Trafford, PA St. Regis Church.
Trinh, Dominic Huy The *o.p.* '75 (GAL) [58] Houston, TX Our Lady of Lourdes Church.
Trinh, Joseph T. '91 (PH) [55] Philadelphia, PA St. Helena Church.
Trinh, Loc '92 (GR) Newaygo, MI St. Bartholomew's Church.
Trinh, Paul H. '90 (CAM) Gibbsboro, NJ St. Andrew the Apostle Church.
Trinh, Thai '90 (OAK) [17] Oakland, CA St. Mary, Immaculate Conception-St. Francis de Sales Church.
Trinh, Thai Q. '90 (RIC) Graduate Studies.
Trinidad, Mel *s.d.b.* '85 (LA) [F] Bellflower, CA St. John Bosco High School.
Trinidad, Nelson (LA) [82] Los Angeles, CA St. Michael Church.
Trinidad-Fonseca, Miguel Angel '00 (SJN) [3] Toa Baja, PR Espiritu Santo Church.
Trinity, Msgr. Bernard J. '54 (PH) Southampton, PA Our Lady of Good Counsel Church.
Trinka, Joseph C. '59 (SUP) Clear Lake, WI St. John Church; Stanton, WI St. Bridget Church.
Trinkle, Clarence M. '92 (ARL) Woodstock, VA St. John Bosco Church.
Trinkle, Donald F. '63 (CAM) [3] Cherry Hill, NJ St. Peter Celestine Church.
Tripi, Ronald R. *c.s.c.* '62 (FTW) [18] South Bend, IN St. Stanislaus Church.
Tripodi, Frank J. '88 (RCK) Absent on Leave.
Tripole, Martin R. *s.j.* '67 (PH) [C] Philadelphia, PA St. Joseph's University; [AA] Philadelphia, PA Jesuit Community at St. Joseph's University.
Trippel, Edward G. '55 (CIN) [8] Cincinnati, OH Annunciation of the Blessed Virgin Mary Church; Retired.
Trippel, Jack '95 (LFT) [4] Lafayette, IN St. Lawrence Church.
Trisco, Msgr. Robert F. '54 (CHI) On Duty Outside the Archdiocese.
Trisco, Msgr. Robert F. '54 (WDC) [C] Washington, DC Catholic University of America, The.
Trisolini, John *s.d.b.* '67 (FgM) Salesians of Don Bosco Foreign Missions.
Triulzi, Daniel *s.m.* (STL) [P] St. Louis, MO Provincialate of the Society of Mary, Province of St. Louis.
Trivison, Louis J. '48 (CLV) Solon, OH Resurrection of Our Lord Church; Retired.
Trocha, Lukasz Pawel '00 (BRK) [199] Queens, NY St. Matthias Church.
Trocinski, LaVern E. '60 (WIN) [2] Rochester, MN Pax Christi Church.
Troiano, Msgr. Leonard F. '79 (TR) Lavallette, NJ St. Bonaventure Church.
Troiano, Louis *o.f.m.* '57 (NY) [DD] New York, NY Padua Friary.
Trojan, Columban *o.s.b.* (JOL) [J] Lisle, IL St. Procopius Abbey.
Trojcak, Ron (JKS) [H] Holly Springs, MS Rust College Newman Center.
Trojcak, Ronald '62 (SFD) On Duty Outside the Diocese.
Trombetta, Jonah P. *o.s.b.* '79 (BO) [W] Hingham, MA Glastonbury Abbey.
Trombetta, Paul N. '79 (BRK) Released from Diocesan Assignment.
Trombley, Joseph P. '65 (OG) Ellenburg, NY St. Edmund Church; Altona, NY Altona Correctional Facility; [G] Ellenburg Center, NY Our Lady of the Adirondack's Inc. House of Prayer.
Trompeter, Msgr. Arthur J. '33 (KCK) Retired.
Troncale, F. Charles '65 (MOB) [4] Montgomery, AL Church of the Holy Spirit.
Trong, John T.B. '71 (ARL) Springfield, VA St. Bernadette's Church.
Trong, Joseph (LAV) [4] Las Vegas, NV Our Lady of Las Vegas Church.
Trong, Joseph '46 (SB) Retired.
Trong, Joseph Nguyen '69 (SFR) On Duty Outside the Archdiocese.
Trong, Joseph Tuoc *s.j.* '89 (STL) [P] St. Louis, MO Jesuit Community Corporation at St. Louis University - Jesuit Hall.
Trosch, David '82 (MOB) On Leave from the Archdiocese.
Troska, Llewelyn J. '86 (CR) Leave of Absence.
Trosley, Anthony J. '78 (PEO) [4] Champaign, IL St. Matthew Church.
Trotta, Louis P. *c.m.* '52 (BUF) [C] Niagara University, NY Niagara University; [O] Niagara University, NY Vincentian Community at Niagara University.
Trouille, Alan P. '97 (LKC) [5] Lake Charles, LA St. Margaret Church.
Troung, Dien *c.pp.s.* '97 (KC) Liberty, MO St. James Church.
Troung, Peter '99 (PMB) North Palm Beach, FL St. Paul of the Cross Church.
Trout, Richard W. '85 (ORL) Sanford, FL All Souls Church.
Troutman, Richard E. '68 (TUC) [21] Tucson, AZ Saint Odilia Church.
Trovato, Joseph A. *c.s.b.* '56 (ROC) [13] Rochester, NY Christ the King Church.
Troxell, Christopher E. '92 (LA) Alhambra, CA All Souls Church.
Troy, Gabriel '66 (BO) [32] Boston, MA St. Joseph Church.
Troy, Gabriel '66 (FgM) Society of St. James the Apostle.
Troy, Henry A. '41 (CHI) Retired.
Troy, Joseph F. *c.s.p.* '34 (NY) [DD] Jamaica Estates, NY Paulist Fathers Generalate.
Troy, Leander *o.carm.* '42 (CHI) [D] Chicago, IL Mt. Carmel High School; [N] Chicago, IL Carmelite Priory of St. Cyril.
Trucksis, Fred '64 (Y) [5] Warren, OH St. Joseph Church.
Trudeau, Marc V. '91 (LA) Pasadena, CA St. Philip the Apostle Church.
Trudel, Lionel G. *m.m.* '56 (NY) Kingston, NY Benedictine Hospital; [W] Kingston, NY Benedictine Hospital; [DD] Maryknoll, NY Maryknoll Fathers and Brothers.
True, David '88 (OKL) Absent on Sick Leave.
True, Isaac *o.s.b.* '66 (KC) [A] Conception, MO Conception Seminary College; [J] Conception, MO Conception Abbey.
Truhan, Luke *o.c.s.o.* '82 (WOR) [A] Spencer, MA St. Joseph's Abbey School of Theology and Institute of Monastic Studies; [N] Spencer, MA St. Joseph's Abbey.
Trujillo, Carlos B. '76 (PBL) Absent on Leave.
Trujillo, Daniel '53 (SJN) [7] Bayamon, PR Santa Elena Church.
Trujillo, Eloy *o.r.c.* '89 (SB) [5] Riverside, CA St. Anthony Church.
Trujillo, Ivan R. '85 (BUF) [3] Batavia, NY St. Mary Church; Buffalo, NY Erie County Holding Center; Attica, NY Attica Correctional Facility.
Trujillo, Vincent *o.s.b.* '82 (P) Mt. Angel, OR St. Mary Church; [L] St. Benedict, OR Mt. Angel Abbey.
Trujillo-Cano, Amando *t.o.r.* '88 (SAT) [50] San Antonio, TX St. Leonard's Church.
Trujillo-Luna, Jesus D. '98 (ATL) Alpharetta, GA St. Thomas Aquinas Church.
Trunk, Vincent E. *c.m.* '52 (PH) [AA] Philadelphia, PA Congregation of the Mission.
Truong, Dien *c.pp.s.* '96 (KC) [J] Liberty, MO Precious Blood Center.
Truong, James Thuc Vam *o.s.b.* (SPC) [E] Carthage, MO Congregation of the Mother Co-Redemptrix, United States Assumption Province.
Trupia, Msgr. Robert C. '73 (TUC) Absent on Leave.
Trupkovich, Joseph V. '97 (GBG) [3] Greensburg, PA Our Lady of Grace Church.
Trupkovich, Thomas '97 (GBG) Irwin, PA Immaculate Conception Church.
Trupkovich, Thomas S. (GBG) North Huntingdon, PA St. Elizabeth Ann Seton Church.
Trupkovich, Thomas S. '97 (GBG) North Huntingdon, PA St. Agnes Church.
Trussel, Christopher '92 (SCL) Special Assignment; [C] St. Cloud, MN Cathedral High and John XXIII Middle School.
Trutter, Carl B. *o.p.* '60 (NO) [25] New Orleans, LA St. Anthony of Padua Church; [P] New Orleans, LA Dominican Friars, Southern Dominican Province of St. Martin de Porres; [P] New Orleans, LA Dominican Friars, Southern Dominican Province of St. Martin de Porres; [S] Metairie, LA Southern Dominican Foundation.
Trzeciakowski, Edward J. '55 (PIT) Retired; [O] Pittsburgh, PA St. John Vianney Manor.
Trzecieski, Stephen *c.m.* (BAL) Emmitsburg, MD St. Joseph Church.
Trzecieski, Stephen P. *c.m.* '60 (BAL) [S] Emmitsburg, MD Vincentian House.
Trzil, Louis J. '50 (DUB) Cherry Mound, IA St. Pius Church; Harpers Ferry, IA St. Ann-St. Joseph Church; Wexford, IA Immaculate Conception Church.
Tsang, Augustine *s.j.* '94 (BO) [W] Cambridge, MA Faber House; [W] Cambridge, MA Weston Jesuit Community.
Tsang, Peter '59 (LA) Retired.
Tsau, Paul (BAL) [M] Baltimore, MD St. Agnes HealthCare, Inc.
Tsau, Paul '64 (WDC) [3] Rockville, MD St. Mary Church.
Tschakert, Gregory '82 (SFS) Aberdeen, SD St. Mary Church.
Tscherne, David D. '77 (TOL) Junction, OH St. Mary Church; St. Michael's Ridge, OH St. Michael Church.
Tschudi, Michael '84 (PMB) Special Assignment.
Tseszczuk, Cyril *o.s.b.m.* '84 (RVC) [M] Glen Cove, NY

St. Josaphat's Monastery, Novitiate and Retreat House.
Tseu, Msgr. Andrew '56 (LA) Pomona, CA St. Madeleine Church.
Tshibambe, Henri '81 (DEN) Louisville, CO St. Louis Church.
Tshikele, Roger *c.i.c.m.* '87 (FgM) Missionhurst Foreign Missions.
Tshikolu, Kazadi *s.j.* '00 (OAK) [N] Berkeley, CA Jesuit Community at Jesuit School of Theology at Berkeley.
Tsung, Basil *o.f.m.* '53 (FgM) Franciscan Foreign Missions.
Tsung-Li-Chuen, Basil *o.f.m.* '53 (STL) [P] St. Louis, MO Franciscan Friary of St. Anthony of Padua.
Tu, Raymond '95 (KC) [14] Kansas City, MO Holy Cross Church; [16] Kansas City, MO Church of the Holy Martyrs.
Tuan, Bui quang *c.ss.r.* '96 (LA) [Q] Baldwin Park, CA Vietnamese Redemptorist Mission.
Tuan, Camillus M. Nguyen Duc *c.m.c.* (SPC) [E] Carthage, MO Congregation of the Mother Co-Redemptrix, United States Assumption Province.
Tuan Nguyen, Anh Tran '98 (ORG) Westminster, CA Blessed Sacrament Church.
Tubbs, Leo *o.p.* '66 (OAK) [N] Oakland, CA Dominican Order, Siena House.
Tubianosa, Jose '86 (NY) [79] New York, NY Most Precious Blood Church.
Tubridy, James J. '53 (NY) Retired.
Tucceri, Robert A. '79 (TOL) Bellevue, OH Immaculate Conception Church.
Tucci, Bruno M. '71 (ALN) Nesquehoning, PA Immaculate Conception of B.V.M. Church; Nesquehoning, PA Our Lady of Mount Carmel Church.
Tucci, Italo '48 (DET) Retired.
Tuchalski, Stanley (WH) On Duty Outside the Diocese.
Tuchalski, Stanley T. '90 (WH) [1] Fairmont, WV St. Peter the Fisherman Church.
Tucker, James *s.s.* '69 (SJ) Special Assignment.
Tucker, James S. '69 (LA) On Duty Outside the Archdiocese.
Tucker, Lawrence E. *s.o.l.t.* '97 (CC) [H] Robstown, TX Society of Our Lady of the Most Holy Trinity.
Tucker, Mark E. *c.ss.r.* (WDC) Hyattsville, MD St. Jerome Church.
Tucker, Michael '77 (SEA) Unassigned.
Tucker, Patrick M. '74 (CHI) Forest Park, IL St. Bernardine Church.
Tucker, Richard '58 (SY) Retired.
Tucker, Rick '76 (LFT) Dunkirk, IN St. Mary Church.
Tucker, Robert *s.c.j.* '82 (GAL) [48] Houston, TX St. Matthew the Evangelist Church.
Tucker, Robert F. '70 (HRT) Litchfield, CT St. Anthony's Church.
Tucker, Robert G. '89 (LIN) [1] Lincoln, NE Cathedral of the Risen Christ.
Tucker, Thomas J. *o.s.f.s.* '66 (WIL) [B] Wilmington, DE Salesianum School.
Tueth, Michael V. *s.j.* '71 (NY) [DD] New York, NY Xavier Jesuit Community.
Tufaro, Douglas J. '83 (BGP) [1] Bridgeport, CT St. Augustine Church.
Tuffour, Louis '86 (DET) [H] Livonia, MI St. Mary Hospital.
Tufo, Berard *o.f.m.* '51 (FR) [I] Onset, MA St. Joseph Friary-Franciscan Friars.
Tufts, Donn P. '80 (GR) Brunswick, MI St. Michael's Church.
Tugwell, Msgr. Michael W. '75 (PT) [13] Pensacola, FL St. Paul Church.
Tuite, Howard A. '54 (CHI) Retired.
Tuite, Thomas P. '86 (RVC) Massapequa, NY St. Rose of Lima Church.
Tuite, Thomas P., Jr. '86 (RVC) Hicksville, NY Our Lady of Mercy Church.
Tull, Terry *c.ss.r.* '85 (CGS) Aguas Buenas, PR Church of Tres Santos Reyes.
Tuller, Eugene *o.f.m.cap.* '49 (MIL) [P] Mount Calvary, WI St. Lawrence Friary.
Tuller, John '84 (CHL) Morganton, NC St. Charles Borromeo Church; Retired.
Tulley, Edward M. '39 (CLV) Parma Heights, OH St. John Bosco Church; Retired.
Tullius, Richard '73 (DAL) Absent on Leave.
Tully, Eugene D. '68 (BO) Billerica, MA St. Theresa of Lisieux Church.
Tully, Eugene M. '73 (PH) [28] Philadelphia, PA St. Callistus Church.
Tully, Gerard P. *c.s.p.* '94 (TUC) [13] Tucson, AZ St. Cyril of Alexandria Church.
Tully, Henry F. '77 (IND) [7] Indianapolis, IN Holy Spirit Church.
Tully, James *s.x.* '75 (FgM) Xaverian Foreign Missions.
Tully, James *s.x.* '75 (PAT) [M] Wayne, NJ Xaverian Missionary Fathers.
Tully, James J. '44 (BRK) Retired.
Tully, John P. '69 (Y) Dungannon, OH St. Philip Neri Church; Salineville, OH St. Patrick's Church; Summitville, OH St. John's Church.
Tully, Raymond M. *s.j.* '40 (STL) [P] St. Louis, MO Hallahan House.
Tully, Msgr. Ronald J. '66 (PAT) Dover, NJ Sacred Heart Church.
Tully, Terence '42 (SPK) Retired.
Tuma, Anthony F. '31 (OM) Retired.
Tumicki, Ted '97 (NOR) On Duty Outside the Diocese.
Tumino, Frank C. '98 (BRK) [240] Queens, NY St. Sebastian Church.
Tumminelli, Lawrence *b.s.o.* '96 (NTN) [B] Methuen, MA Basilian Salvatorian Order.
Tumosa, John Joseph '69 (CAM) Newfield, NJ St. Rose of Lima Church.
Tumulty, Matt *o.f.m.* '59 (P) [Q] Portland, OR Franciscan Ministry Network.
Tumulty, Michael J. *c.m.* '51 (BUF) [C] Niagara University, NY Niagara University; [O] Niagara University, NY Vincentian Community at Niagara University.
Tunacao, Paul (BRK) [131] Brooklyn, NY Sacred Hearts of Jesus and Mary and St. Stephen Church.
Tungol, Eugene D. '75 (SFR) [3] South San Francisco, CA St. Augustine Church.
Tunink, Wilfrid *o.s.b.* '45 (SFE) [I] Pecos, NM Our Lady of Guadalupe Abbey; [K] Pecos, NM Our Lady of Guadalupe Olivetan Benedictine Abbey.
Tunney, Ken (ALB) [8] Schenectady, NY St. John the Baptist Church.
Tunney, Michael F. *s.j.* '88 (BUF) [O] Buffalo, NY Canisius Jesuit Community.
Tunney, Thomas P. *c.s.sp.* '60 (NY) [69] New York, NY St. Mark the Evangelist Church.
Tunny, Kenneth J. '63 (ALB) [16] Schenectady, NY St. Paul the Apostle Church; Special Assignment.
Tuoc, Ignatius '71 (SP) [3] Tampa, FL Epiphany Church.
Tuohey, John F. '81 (SPR) On Duty Outside the Diocese.
Tuohy, Edward *s.v.d.* '58 (BO) [W] Duxbury, MA Society of the Divine Word.
Tuohy, Msgr. Francis R. '61 (IND) [2] Indianapolis, IN Christ The King Church.
Tuozzolo, Leonard *c.s.sp.* '59 (ARL) [7] Arlington, VA Our Lady, Queen of Peace Church.
Tuozzolo, Leonard J. *c.s.sp.* '59 (WDC) [V] Wheaton, MD U.S. Foundation for the Congregation of the Holy Ghost and the Immaculate Heart of Mary, Inc. (The Spirit.
Tupa, Jerome *o.s.b.* '82 (SCL) [I] Collegeville, MN St. John's Abbey, of the Order of St. Benedict.
Tupa, Michael J. '91 (SUP) Bloomville, WI St. John the Baptist Church; Harrison, WI St. Augustine Church; Pier-Willow, WI St. Francis of Assisi Church; Tomahawk, WI St. Mary Church.
Tupper, Dale E. '67 (WIN) [1] Rochester, MN Holy Spirit Church.
Tupper, John B. '60 (GAY) Retired.
Tuptynski, Marek S. '97 (FR) [7] Fall River, MA Notre Dame de Lourdes Church.
Turati, Fortunato *s.c.* '67 (LAN) [E] Chelsea, MI St. Louis Center for Exceptional Children & Adults.
Turchich, Ronald R. *o.s.a.* '58 (KAL) Douglas, MI St. Peter Church.
Turcich, Ronald R. *o.s.a.* '58 (KAL) [E] Douglas, MI Order of St. Augustine.
Turco, Alfredo *s.x.* '88 (MIL) [B] Franklin, WI Xaverian Missionary Fathers College Seminary.
Turczany, Christopher J. '83 (BRK) [194] Queens, NY St. Mary Church.
Turek, Michael E. '76 (STL) [8] Florissant, MO St. Norbert Church.
Turek, Ronald '74 (CLV) [52] Cleveland, OH Our Lady of Angels Church.
Tureman, Thomas *s.d.s.* '88 (SAC) Orangevale, CA Divine Savior Church.
Turgeon, Armand A. '43 (MAN) Retired.
Turi, John J. '55 (SCR) Matamoras, PA St. Joseph's Church.
Turillo, B. Samuel '46 (PRO) Retired.
Turk, Damian C. *o.c.s.o.* '69 (ATL) [J] Conyers, GA The Monastery of the Holy Spirit.
Turley, Daniel T. *o.s.a.* '68 (CHI) [N] Olympia Fields, IL The Augustinians-Provincialate.
Turley, Sean F. '71 (WIL) On Duty Outside the Diocese.
Turlik, Andrew J. '46 (PIT) Retired.
Turlo, Walter J. '70 (CHI) Bridgeview, IL St. Fabian Church.
Turnbull, John B. *o.f.m.* '55 (CIN) Centerville, OH St. Francis of Assisi Church.
Turnbull, Paul E. '73 (ALT) [10] Altoona, PA St. John the Evangelist Church.
Turnbull, William '67 (ALB) [11] Troy, NY St. Paul the Apostle Church; Troy, NY Seton Health.
Turner, Bernard '77 (ALB) Glens Falls, NY St. Mary Church.
Turner, David *o.s.b.* '63 (JOL) [A] Lisle, IL Benedictine University; [J] Lisle, IL St. Procopius Abbey.
Turner, Edward '66 (HON) Retired.
Turner, George F. '60 (LR) Retired.
Turner, James '84 (PHX) [6] Glendale, AZ St. Thomas More Church.
Turner, James M. *o.s.f.s.* '81 (ARL) Vienna, VA Our Lady of Good Counsel Church.
Turner, Jerome R. '64 (MAD) Retired.
Turner, Joseph *s.d.s.* '58 (WDC) [B] Silver Spring, MD Salvatorian Community.
Turner, Patrick '72 (BEA) Orangefield, TX St. Helen Church.
Turner, Paul '79 (KC) [21] Kansas City, MO St. John Francis Regis Church.
Turner, Richard M. '80 (SPR) South Hadley, MA St. Patrick's Church.
Turner, Richard W. '65 (R) Rocky Mount, NC Our Lady of Perpetual Help Church.
Turner, Robert '62 (GR) On Duty Outside the Diocese.
Turner, Robert '88 (GLP) On Duty Outside of Diocese.
Turner, Robert D. '82 (SPK) On Duty Outside the Diocese.
Turner, Robert D. '88 (MIL) [14] Milwaukee, WI Blessed Sacrament Church.
Turner, Robert G. '59 (PIT) [4] West Mifflin, PA Resurrection Church.
Turner, Thomas W. '82 (KC) Leave of Absence; [M] Kansas City, MO Bishop Sullivan Center.
Turner, Wayne A. '50 (MAD) Retired.
Turner, William J. '75 (IND) New Alsace, IN St. Paul Church; Yorkville, IN St. Martin Church.
Turner, William J. '79 (LAN) Chelsea, MI St. Mary Church.
Turon, L. L. *o.p.* '55 (FgM) Dominican - Order of Preachers Foreign Missions.
Turowski, Joseph *m.m.* '84 (BUF) [O] Buffalo, NY Maryknoll House.
Turro, Msgr. James C. '48 (NEW) Park Ridge, NJ Our Lady of Mercy Church; Retired; [A] South Orange, NJ Immaculate Conception Seminary; [B] South Orange, NJ Seton Hall University.
Tuscan, Joseph *o.f.m.cap.* '97 (FgM) Capuchin Foreign Missions.
Tushar, David '76 (DUL) [1] Duluth, MN Cathedral of Our Lady of the Rosary.
Tusky, Richard J. '73 (PIT) Burgettstown, PA Our Lady of Lourdes Church.
Tustin, Joseph E. *o.s.f.s.* '67 (CHL) Kernersville, NC Holy Cross Church.
Tutds, Stephen *s.m.* (SJ) [L] Cupertino, CA Villa Saint Joseph.
Tutokie, Msgr. Michael E. '45 (E) Winburne, PA SS. Cyril and Methodius Church; Retired.
Tutone, John J. '71 (RVC) Island Park, NY Sacred Heart Church.
Tuttle, Arthur *c.ss.r.* '65 (ALB) Saratoga Springs, NY St. Clement Church.
Tuttle, Charles W. '74 (BEL) Sandoval, IL St. Lawrence Church; [A] Breese, IL Mater Dei High School.
Tuttle, Patrick E. *o.f.m.* '94 (R) [3] Durham, NC Immaculate Conception Church.
Tuttle, Richard '76 (STU) [2] Steubenville, OH Holy Family Church.
Tuxbury, James C. *o.f.m.* '63 (FR) Buzzards Bay, MA St. Margaret Church.
Tuyn, William R. '62 (BUF) North Evans, NY St. Vincent Church.
Tuzeneu, Kenard J. '79 (TR) Barnegat, NJ St. Mary Church.
Tuzicka, Fred M. '51 (DOD) Retired.
Tuzik, Robert L. '73 (CHI) Rolling Meadows, IL St. Colette Church.
Tvrdik, Roy *s.m.m.* '93 (BRK) [V] Ozone Park, NY Montfort Missionaries Provincialate (Missionaries of the Company of Mary) - Formation Community.
Tvrdy, Julius '73 (LIN) [5] Lincoln, NE Sacred Heart Church.
Twaddell, Gerald E. '67 (COV) Camp Springs, KY St. Joseph Church.
Twardzik, Francis M. *s.d.b.* '70 (PSC) Scranton, PA St. Mary's Church.
Twardzik, Michael W.T. '70 (SPR) [2] North Adams, MA Notre Dame Church; [4] North Adams, MA Our Lady of Mercy Church; [5] North Adams, MA Our Lady of Mercy Church; [7] North Adams, MA St. Francis Church.
Twarog, Jerome *c.r.* '82 (CHI) Northlake, IL St. John Vianney, Cure of Ars Church.
Twarog, Theodore S. '50 (SD) Retired.
Twele, Robert *o.f.m.conv.* '81 (BAL) [S] Ellicott City, MD Order of Friars Minor Conventual.
Twiddy, Paul '52 (WDC) Retired.
Twigg-Porter, George M. *s.j.* '53 (SFR) [K] San Francisco, CA Home for the Aged of the Little Sisters of the Poor; [T] San Francisco, CA Apostleship of Prayer.
Twigg-Porter, Geroge M. *s.j.* '53 (SFR) San Francisco, CA San Francisco Fire Department.
Twiggs, Matthew J. '73 (PAT) Stockholm, NJ St. John Vianney Church.
Twlko, Richard J. *o.f.m.* '64 (PH) [93] Philadelphia, PA Saint Martha Church.
Twohig, Christopher T. '50 (WDC) On Duty Outside the Archdiocese.
Twohig, Michael J. '83 (SPR) West Springfield, MA Immaculate Conception Church; West Springfield, MA St. Louis de France Church.
Twohig, Richard H. *s.j.* '65 (DET) [K] Detroit, MI Jesuit

Provincial Office-Detroit Province of the Society of Jesus; [T] Detroit, MI Jesuit Seminary Association.
Twohig, Richard H. *s.j.* '65 (FgM) Provinces.
Twohy, Patrick *s.j.* '70 (SEA) LaConner, WA St. Paul Church.
Twomey, Daniel F. '75 (BO) Natick, MA St. Patrick Church.
Twomey, Dermot *s.c.j.* '76 (JKS) Senatobia, MS St. Gregory the Great Church; [H] Senatobia, MS Northwest Mississippi Community College Newman Center.
Twomey, Dermot J. *s.c.j.* '76 (JKS) Walls, MS Sacred Heart Church; [F] Nesbit, MS St. Michael Community House.
Twomey, Gerald S. '81 (RVC) Brentwood, NY St. Anne's Church.
Twomey, John E. '52 (MIL) Retired.
Twomey, Msgr. John P. '63 (LA) [3] Long Beach, CA St. Barnabas Church.
Twomey, Simon '70 (SAC) Grass Valley, CA St. Patrick Church.
Twomey, Thomas '65 (NOR) Absent on Leave.
Twomey, Vincent *s.v.d.* '70 (BO) [W] Boston, MA Divine Word Missionaries.
Tydlacka, Msgr. George '44 (AUS) Retired.
Tykhovytch, Ivan '94 (STF) Spring Valley, NY SS. Peter and Paul Church.
Tyl, Albert '54 (FWT) [1] Fort Worth, TX St. Patrick Church.
Tylawskyj, Mitrat Iwan '50 (SJP) North Port, FL Entrance of B.V.M. into the Temple Church; Retired.
Tylenda, Joseph N. *s.j.* '60 (WDC) [M] Washington, DC The Jesuit Community at Georgetown University; [V] Washington, DC Woodstock Theological Center.
Tyler, Bernard '61 (LAN) Fenton, MI St. John Church.
Tyler, Thomas L. '79 (E) North East, PA St. Gregory Thaumaturgus Church.
Tylka, Louis J. '96 (CHI) Orland Park, IL St. Michael Church.
Tyma, John A. *o.s.a.* '59 (CHI) [N] Olympia Fields, IL The Augustinians-Provincialate.
Tyma, John A. *o.s.a.* '59 (FgM) Foreign Missions.
Tyman, Gary '86 (ROC) Fairport, NY Assumption of the Blessed Virgin Mary Church.
Tyminski, Joseph *s.d.b.* (NY) [2] Port Chester, NY Corpus Christi Church.
Tynan, Desmond '67 (FgM) Society of St. James the Apostle.
Tynan, Desmond A. '67 (BO) Society of St. James the Apostle.
Tynan, John C. *m.m.* '62 (FgM) Maryknoll Foreign Missions.
Tynan, Joseph F. *o.c.s.o.* '47 (ATL) [J] Conyers, GA The Monastery of the Holy Spirit.
Tyne, John *s.s.j.* (MOB) [15] Mobile, AL Most Pure Heart of Mary Church.
Tynski, Robert '89 (TR) [B] Trenton, NJ Notre Dame High School.
Tynski, Robert M. '89 (TR) [11] Trenton, NJ Sacred Heart Church.
Tyrasinski, Lucius *o.s.p.p.e.* '56 (PH) [AA] Doylestown, PA Pauline Fathers Monastery, Shrine of Our Lady of Czestochowa.
Tyrell, Michael A. *s.j.* '76 (SEA) Kent, WA Holy Spirit Church.
Tyrell, Patrick *s.j.* (CHI) Glenview, IL Our Lady of Perpetual Help Church.
Tyrell, Robert D. '67 (BO) Weston, MA St. Julia Church.
Tyrrell, Anthony *f.s.s.p.* (OKL) [3] Oklahoma City, OK St. Charles Borromeo Church; [16] Oklahoma City, OK St. Michael Tridentine Community Church.
Tyrrell, Anthony (PCE) On Duty Outside the Diocese.
Tyrrell, Anthony *f.s.s.p.* '95 (SCR) [M] Elmhurst, PA Priestly Fraternity of St. Peter (F.S.S.P.), North American District Headquarters.
Tyrrell, Bernard J. *s.j.* '65 (SPK) [C] Spokane, WA Gonzaga University.
Tyrrell, Joseph J. '89 (NY) [89] New York, NY Our Lady of Lourdes Church.
Tyrrell, Michael A. *s.j.* '76 (P) [L] Portland, OR Jesuit Provincial Office (Society of Jesus, Oregon Prov.).
Tyrrell, Michael A. *s.j.* '76 (SEA) [C] Tacoma, WA Bellarmine Preparatory School.
Tyrrell, Wilfred *s.a.* '94 (LA) [84] Los Angeles, CA St. Odilia Church.
Tyson, David T. *c.s.c.* '75 (FTW) [J] South Bend, IN Congregation of Holy Cross, Indiana Province, Provincial House.
Tyson, David T. *c.s.c.* '75 (P) [B] Portland, OR University of Portland; [L] Portland, OR Holy Cross Fathers & Brothers, C.S.C. - University of Portland.
Tyson, Joseph J. '89 (SEA) [8] Seattle, WA St. Edward Church; [9] Seattle, WA St. George Church; [18] Seattle, WA St. Paul Church.
Tyson, Joseph V. *s.s.j.* '55 (LAF) Eunice, LA St. Mathilda Church.
Tyson, Michael *o.f.m.* '67 (WDC) [3] Silver Spring, MD St. Camillus Church.
Tywoniak, Robert F. '83 (MIA) [7] Fort Lauderdale, FL St. George Church.
Tzanakas, George M. '62 (AUS) Retired.

U

Ubalde, Ulysses L. '93 (NEW) Fort Lee, NJ Madonna Church.
Ubel, John L. '89 (STP) [E] St. Paul, MN The Saint Thomas Academy.
Uboldi, Victor '45 (SD) Retired.
Ucbaghiorghis, Teclezghi *o.cist.* '78 (TR) Mount Laurel, NJ St. John Neumann Church; [M] Mount Laurel, NJ Cistercian Monastery of Our Lady of Fatima.
Uchendu, Cajetan '92 (RVC) Manhasset, NY St. Mary's Church.
Udegbulem, Cyriacus (LAR) Laredo, TX Mercy Health Center.
Udick, William S. *s.j.* '55 (DEN) [M] Denver, CO Xavier Jesuit Center.
Udo, Aloysius '84 (GAL) [2] Galveston, TX Holy Rosary Church.
Udo, Emmanuel '80 (MIL) [4] Wauwatosa, WI St. Jude the Apostle Church.
Udoh, Cletus C.U. *m.s.p.* '92 (BAL) [83] Baltimore, MD St. Pius V Church.
Udoh, Ernest P. '88 (ROC) [5] Rochester, NY Church of the Annunciation.
Udovic, Edward R. *c.m.* '84 (CHI) [C] Chicago, IL De Paul University; [C] Chicago, IL De Paul University; [N] Chicago, IL Vincentian Community, Congregation of the Mission, Midwest Province.
Udulutsch, Irvin *o.f.m.cap.* (GB) Kaukauna, WI St. Mary of the Annunciation Church.
Udulutsch, Robert *o.f.m.cap.* '56 (GB) Kaukauna, WI St. Mary of the Annunciation Church.
Uebler, Michael G. '82 (BUF) Arcade, NY SS. Peter and Paul Church; East Arcade, NY St. Mary's Church.
Uecker, Joseph H. *c.pp.s.* '68 (SAN) [3] Abilene, TX St. Francis of Assisi Church; [4] Abilene, TX St. Vincent Pallotti Church.
Uehlein, Christopher *o.s.b.* '60 (SFS) [F] Marvin, SD Blue Cloud Abbey.
Ufomadu, Charles '97 (LA) Culver City, CA St. Augustine Church.
Uftring, Richard A. '76 (BO) [22] Boston, MA Gate of Heaven Church; [BB] East Boston, MA Our Lady of the Airways Chapel.
Ugah, Gregory '78 (PIT) [8] Pittsburgh, PA St. Charles Lwanga Church.
Ugliano, Bruno A. *o.s.b.* '67 (PAT) [M] Morristown, NJ St. Mary's Abbey.
Ugliano, Bruno A. *o.s.b.* '67 (TR) [S] Princeton, NJ Campus Ministry for the Diocese of Trenton; [S] Princeton, NJ Campus Ministry for the Diocese of Trenton.
Uglietto, Peter J. '77 (BO) [A] Weston, MA Pope John XXIII National Seminary.
Ugochukwu, John '84 (BRK) [217] Queens, NY Our Lady of Perpetual Help Church.
Ugochukwu, Sebastian A. (LC) Tomah, WI Veterans Administration Medical Center.
Ugolik, Richard '54 (DET) Retired.
Ugwoji, Matthew (NY) [122] New York, NY St. Vincent de Paul Church.
Ugwuanya, Valentine '94 (NEW) [3] Newark, NJ Blessed Sacrament/St. Charles Borromeo Church.
Ugwuegbu, Ambrose '87 (SAC) Carmichael, CA St. John the Evangelist Church.
Uhde, Peter M. '81 (NEW) [13] Newark, NJ Epiphany Church; [16] Newark, NJ Holy Trinity Church.
Uhen, Cletus V. '42 (MIL) Retired.
Uhen, Timothy J. '96 (WDC) [T] Washington, DC Prelature of the Holy Cross and Opus Dei.
Uhl, Anthony C. '68 (COS) Salida, CO St. Joseph Church.
Uhlenkott, Gary D. *s.j.* '80 (SPK) [C] Spokane, WA Gonzaga University.
Uhler, Carl A. '56 (CLV) West Salem, OH St. Stephen Church.
Uhlman, Laurence *t.o.r.* '90 (ALT) [F] Loretto, PA Mount Assisi Friary.
Uhlman, Laurence *t.o.r.* '90 (STU) [A] Steubenville, OH Franciscan University of Steubenville.
Uhlman, Laurence R. *t.o.r.* '90 (ALT) [F] Loretto, PA St. Bonaventure Friary.
Uhran, Vernon '69 (ORL) Sabbatical.
Uhrig, A. Gregory '73 (MET) Iselin, NJ St. Cecelia Church.
Uitendaal, Pius *o.f.m.conv.* '63 (FgM) Conventual Franciscan Foreign Missions.
Ukaegbu, Lloyd '62 (LA) Hacienda Heights, CA St. John Vianney Church.
Ukanide, Anietie Akama *m.s.p.* '91 (MOB) [5] Mobile, AL St. Francis Xavier Church; Plateau, AL Our Mother of Mercy Church.
Uko, Joseph '81 (MIL) [4] Wauwatosa, WI St. Jude the Apostle Church.
Ukomadu, Linus '90 (LR) Arkadelphia, AR St. Mary's Church; Hot Springs National Park, AR St. John the Baptist Church.
Ukpong, Justin S. '67 (CHR) Greenville, SC St. Mary's Church.
Ukwe, Charles E. *o.p.* '89 (HBG) Rohrerstown, PA St. Leo the Great Church.
Ukwe, Stan U. *o.p.* '94 (HBG) [1] Lebanon, PA Assumption of the Blessed Virgin Mary Church.
Ulak, Robert T. '70 (NEW) Park Ridge, NJ Our Lady of Mercy Church.
Ulam, Richard *o.s.b.* '82 (PIT) [81] Pittsburgh, PA St. Peter Church.
Ulaszeski, Msgr. Edward J. '52 (BUF) Retired.
Ulincy, Andrew A. '66 (ALN) [10] Reading, PA St. Paul Church.
Uline, Cyprian *o.f.m.conv.* '70 (IND) [I] Mount Saint Francis, IN Mount Saint Francis Friary and Retreat Center.
Ullery, Kirk '65 (SFR) [41] San Francisco, CA Our Lady of Lourdes Church.
Ullman, Earl L. '38 (SD) Retired.
Ulloa, Daniel *o.p.* '70 (NY) [82] New York, NY Notre Dame Church; [GG] New York, NY University Apostolate.
Ullrich, David *o.m.i.* '71 (WDC) [M] Washington, DC Missionary Oblates of Mary Immaculate; [M] Washington, DC Oblate College/Center for Mission Studies Community.
Ullrich, John R. *o.f.m.* '76 (BO) [BB] Boston, MA St. Anthony Shrine; [BB] Boston, MA St. Anthony Shrine.
Ullrich, Mark C. '78 (STL) [15] St. Louis, MO Our Lady of the Holy Cross Church.
Ullrich, Peter *o.s.b.* '87 (KC) [A] Conception, MO Conception Seminary College; [J] Conception, MO Conception Abbey.
Ulm, John '58 (GAL) [49] Houston, TX St. Maximilian Kolbe Church.
Ulman, Stanley A. '73 (DET) Hamtramck, MI St. Ladislaus Church.
Ulrich, Carl G. '43 (SCR) Retired; [N] Dunmore, PA Villa St. Joseph.
Ulrich, David *o.m.i.* (CHI) [X] Chicago, IL Oblates for International Pastoral.
Ulrich, Eugene P. '74 (BUF) Almond, NY SS. Brendan and Jude Church; [R] Alfred, NY Campus Ministry; [R] Alfred, NY Campus Ministry.
Ulrich, James E. '60 (CIN) [39] Cincinnati, OH St. James of the Valley Church.
Ulrich, John *s.m.* '86 (AUS) [B] Waco, TX Reicher Catholic High School; [H] Waco, TX Marist Community; [M] Waco, TX Catholic Student Center at Baylor University.
Ulrich, Steve '90 (OWN) Absent on Leave.
Ulrick, Stephen D. '82 (STP) Chanhassen, MN St. Hubert Church.
Ulses, Eugene J. '69 (SC) Gilmore City, IA St. John's Church; Humboldt, IA St. Mary's Church.
Ulshafer, Thomas *s.s.* '70 (WDC) On Duty Outside the Archdiocese.
Ulshafer, Thomas R. *s.s.* '70 (BAL) [A] Baltimore, MD St. Mary's Seminary and University; [S] Baltimore, MD Sulpician Provincial House.
Ulto, Victor A. '80 (PMB) Stuart, FL St. Joseph Church.
Umaga, Alfred *m.s.p.* '33 (LAF) Lebeau, LA Immaculate Conception Church.
Umana, Miguel '96 (WDC) Absent On Leave.
Umana, Pedro *o.f.m.* '89 (FRS) [F] Three Rivers, CA St. Anthony's Retreat House.
Umberg, Andrew J. '91 (CIN) On Duty Outside the Archdiocese.
Umberger, Patrick A. '80 (LC) Arcadia, WI Holy Family Church.
Umbras, Thomas *s.v.d.* '81 (FgM) Society of the Divine Word Foreign Missions.
Ume, Michael '93 (LA) [61] Los Angeles, CA St. Eugene Church.
Umhoefer, Stephen J. '66 (MAD) Monroe, WI St. Victor Church.
Umrahn, Kaleem '65 (BRK) [18] Brooklyn, NY St. Bernadette Church.
Umwech, Adalbert '97 (CI) Tbl, FM Assumption of the Blessed Virgin Mary Church.
Underdahl, Mark J. '96 (STP) Bayport, MN St. Charles Church.
Underwood, Gary E. '80 (TUC) On Duty Outside the Diocese.
Underwood, Joseph '63 (BIR) Retired.
Underwood, Scott J. *o.s.b.* '76 (NO) [P] St. Benedict, LA St. Joseph Abbey.
Ungashick, Thomas J. '76 (Y) Leetonia, OH St. Patrick's Church.
Unger, John M. '42 (PIT) Retired; [O] Pittsburgh, PA St. John Vianney Manor.
Unger, John M. '65 (STL) [R] St. Louis, MO School Sisters of Notre Dame.
Unger, Robert P. '99 (FAR) Park River, ND St. Mary's Church.
Unger, Steve (RVC) Stony Brook, NY Stony Brook University Hospital.
Unger, Todd '82 (BAK) The Dalles, OR St. Peter's Church.
Ungerleider, David L. *s.j.* '77 (BAL) [S] Baltimore, MD Jesuit Fathers and Brothers Maryland Provincial Curia.
Ungerleider, David L. *s.j.* '77 (FgM) Provinces.
Uniowski, Peter '75 (ORL) [3] Lakeland, FL St. John Neumann Church.

Universal, Patrick J. '75 (GLP) [1] Gallup, NM Cathedral of the Sacred Heart; Crownpoint, NM St. Paul Church.
Unni, John '83 (BO) Danvers, MA St. Richard Church.
Unsworth, John E. '76 (PRO) [1] East Providence, RI St. Brendan Church.
Unterreiner, James J. '70 (SPC) Ironton, MO Ste. Marie Du Lac Church.
Unverdorben, Ernest *o.c.d.* '66 (MIL) [P] Holy Hill, WI Discalced Carmelite Monastery.
Unverferth, Steven R. '89 (BEL) Leave of Absence.
Unwin, Rick '79 (CIN) Piqua, OH St. Boniface Church.
Unz, Thomas E. '83 (CHI) Stickney, IL St. Pius X Church.
Uong, Luong *c.ss.r.* '95 (NO) [23] New Orleans, LA St. Alphonsus Church.
Upah, William J. '98 (R) Cary, NC St. Michael the Archangel Church.
Uppena, Msgr. James J. '68 (MAD) Milton, WI St. Mary Church.
Upson, Michael G. '76 (BRK) Released from Diocesan Assignment.
Upson, Michael G. '76 (ROC) [27] Rochester, NY Immaculate Conception Church.
Upton, Edward F. '69 (CHI) Orland Park, IL St. Francis of Assisi Church.
Upton, John C. '83 (GAL) [1] Spring, TX Christ the Good Shepherd Church.
Uralikunnel, George V. '67 (PBL) Lamar, CO St. Francis De Sales-Our Lady of Guadalupe Church.
Uram, Msgr. Kenneth '59 (STU) Amsterdam, OH St. Joseph Church; Richmond, OH St. John Fisher Church.
Urarte, Carmelo '59 (ARE) Quebradillas, PR Sacred Heart Church.
Urasa, Rogation *a.l.c.p.* '83 (B) [1] Boise, ID Cathedral of St. John the Evangelist.
Urbain, Joseph V. '32 (CIN) Retired.
Urban, Anthony M. '73 (SCR) Bear Creek Township, PA St. Elizabeth Church.
Urban, Carl A. '66 (ALB) [1] Schenectady, NY Church of St. Adalbert.
Urban, Charles T. *o.praem.* '54 (PH) [AA] Paoli, PA Daylesford Abbey.
Urban, John L. '59 (MAD) Boscobel, WI Immaculate Conception Church; Castle Rock, WI St. John Nepomucene Church.
Urban, Joseph '72 (NEW) [10] Newark, NJ St. Casimir's Church.
Urban, Lawrence *s.d.b.* '77 (SP) [E] Tampa, FL Mary Help of Christians School.
Urban, Lonnie A. '67 (AUS) Taylor, TX St. Mary's Church.
Urban, Peter '58 (DEN) [15] Denver, CO Montbello Catholic Parish-Church of the Ascension.
Urban, Reginald A. '77 (GI) Loup City, NE St. Josaphat's Church.
Urban, Robert M. '60 (SUP) Retired.
Urbanek, Raymond J. '68 (LAN) Mount Morris, MI St. Mary Church.
Urbaniak, Msgr. Bernard J. '68 (E) [29] Erie, PA St. Stanislaus Church.
Urbaniak, Jan *c.m.* '71 (BRK) [134] Brooklyn, NY St. Stanislaus Kostka Church.
Urbaniak, Lawrence M. '61 (RCK) Retired.
Urbaniak, Lucian '85 (SY) [11] Utica, NY St. Mark Church.
Urbanowski, Konrad *s.ch.* '23 (DET) [8] Sterling Heights, MI Our Lady of Czestochowa Church.
Urbanski, Louis '64 (P) Portland, OR Oregon Health Sciences University.
Urbanski, Louis J. '64 (P) [13] Portland, OR St. Elizabeth of Hungary Church.
Urbine, Gordon *o.f.m.* '42 (LA) [Q] Santa Barbara, CA Franciscan Friary, Order of Friars Minor (Old Mission).
Urbine, Gordon *o.f.m.* '42 (OAK) [9] Oakland, CA St. Elizabeth's Church.
Urbine, Richard '48 (FTW) Retired.
Urbonas, Msgr. Ignatius L. '35 (CHI) [2] Lemont, IL Blessed Jurgis Matulaitis Church.
Urbonas, Msgr. Ignatius L. '35 (GRY) Retired.
Urcia, Daniel C. *c.r.s.* '89 (SJ) Milpitas, CA St. John the Baptist Church.
Urdiain, Angelo *c.r.* '66 (DEN) [A] Denver, CO St. Andrew's Theatine Religious House.
Ureel, Wayne G. '90 (DET) Dryden, MI St. Cornelius Church.
Urell, Msgr. John (ORG) Garden Grove, CA St. Callistus Church.
Urian, Thomas R. '90 (PH) Secane, PA Our Lady of Fatima Church; [D] Springfield, PA Cardinal O'Hara High School.
Uribe, Arturo *c.ss.r.* '95 (LA) Whittier, CA St. Mary of the Assumption Church; [Q] Whittier, CA Redemptorist Fathers Mission House.
Uribe, Saul de Jesus '80 (ELP) [34] El Paso, TX Sts. Peter and Paul Church.
Uribe-Villa, Luis (SP) [5] Tampa, FL Incarnation Church.
Urizalqui, Richard '77 (FRS) Tulare, CA St. Aloysius Church.
Urlage, Robert J. '58 (COV) Retired.
Urmston, Benjamin J. *s.j.* '59 (CIN) [M] Cincinnati, OH Jesuit Community at Xavier University.
Urnick, Charles B. '74 (NEW) Norwood, NJ Immaculate Conception Church.
Uroda, Stanley *s.v.d.* '74 (CHI) [B] Techny, IL Divine Word Residence; [N] Techny, IL Society of the Divine Word, Provincial Headquarter-Chicago Prov.; [N] Techny, IL Society of the Divine Word, Provincial Headquarter-Chicago Prov.
Uroda, Stanley *s.v.d.* '74 (FgM) Society of the Divine Word Foreign Missions.
Urrea, Miguel '87 (SB) [2] San Bernardino, CA Christ the King Church.
Urrea, Miguel A. '87 (SB) Redlands, CA St. Mary Church.
Urriza, Luis *o.s.a.* '44 (BEA) [4] Beaumont, TX Cristo Rey Church.
Urrutigoity, Carlos '91 (SCR) [M] Shohola, PA Society of Saint John.
Urtubia, Jorge *c.s.c.* '95 (FTW) [J] South Bend, IN Congregation of Holy Cross, Indiana Province, Provincial House.
Uschold, Raymond F. '64 (BUF) Delevan, NY Blessed Sacrament Church; Machias, NY Holy Family Church.
Useche, Teofilo '84 (VEN) Palmetto, FL Holy Cross Church.
Useldinger, Karl '77 (COS) On Duty Outside Diocese.
Usenza, Robert J. '61 (BGP) Retired.
Ustaski, William B. *c.r.i.c.* '77 (LA) Santa Clarita, CA St. Clare Church; [B] Los Angeles, CA Canons Regular of the Immaculate Conception-Novitiate.
Uter, Frank M. '69 (BR) Gramercy, LA Most Sacred Heart of Jesus Church; Paulina, LA St. Joseph Church.
Utrup, Eugene E. '59 (STL) Chesterfield, MO Incarnate Word Church.
Utz, Raymond M. '63 (PIT) [1] Carnegie, PA St. Elizabeth Ann Seton Church.
Uvietta, Joseph *s.m.* (STL) [P] St. Louis, MO Provincialate of the Society of Mary, Province of St. Louis.
Uvietta, Joseph *s.m.* '61 (STL) [T] Eureka, MO Marianist Retreat & Conference Center.
Uwando, Marcellius (NY) Bronx, NY St. Barnabas Hospital.
Uzdrowski, Mel R. *o.s.b.* '56 (JOL) [J] Lisle, IL St. Procopius Abbey.
Uzoh, Louis '73 (BRK) [163] Queens, NY St. Clare Church; [U] Brooklyn, NY Catholic Migration & Refugee Office, Catholic Migration Services, Inc.
Uzzilio, Robert A. '65 (BGP) [6] Stamford, CT St. Gabriel Church.

V

V., Gustavo Quintero '80 (STO) [6] Stockton, CA St. Linus Church.
Vaca, Jacinto *s.d.b.* (PAT) [3] Paterson, NJ St. Anthony's Church.
Vaca, Modesto *o.de.m.* '56 (PCE) [13] Ponce, PR Santuario San Judas Tadeo Church.
Vacca, Bernard '52 (Y) Retired.
Vacca, Dan (WCH) [D] Wichita, KS Via Christi Regional Medical Center, Inc.
Vaccarella, Sam *t.o.r.* '77 (CAM) [O] Blackwood, NJ St. Pius X Retreat House.
Vaccari, Andrew J. '86 (BRK) [215] Queens, NY Our Lady of the Miraculous Medal Church.
Vaccari, Peter I. '77 (BRK) Released from Diocesan Assignment.
Vaccari, Peter I. '77 (RVC) [A] Huntington, NY Diocesan Seminary of the Immaculate Conception.
Vaccaro, Guy '78 (JOL) Winfield, IL St. John the Baptist Church.
Vaccaro, Joseph V. '58 (STP) [T] Lake Elmo, MN Hermits of the Most Blessed Virgin Mary of Mount Carmel.
Vacco, James *o.f.m.* '82 (BUF) [C] St. Bonaventure, NY St. Bonaventure University; [O] St. Bonaventure, NY St. Bonaventure Friary; [R] Alfred, NY Campus Ministry.
Vacek, Carl *t.o.r.* '79 (ORL) [D] Winter Park, FL San Pedro Spiritual Development Center; [F] Winter Park, FL San Pedro Center, Third Order Regular of St. Francis; [F] Winter Park, FL Franciscan Friars, T.O.R., Provincial Residence, San Pedro Friary.
Vacek, Edward V. *s.j.* '73 (BO) [W] Cambridge, MA Weston Jesuit Community.
Vachon, Robert *m.s.* '55 (FR) [I] Attleboro, MA La Salette Provincial House.
Vadakin, Msgr. Royale M. '64 (LA) [43] Los Angeles, CA St. Anastasia Church.
Vadakkedath, Vincent '72 (LKC) Grand Chenier, LA St. Eugene Church.
Vadakkekara, J. Philip '69 (MET) Fords, NJ Our Lady of Peace Church.
Vadakkekudy, Jacob '61 (HEL) Retired.
Vader, Anthony J. '52 (CHI) [81] Chicago, IL Holy Name of Mary Church; [187] Chicago, IL Sacred Heart Mission of Holy Name of Mary Church; Retired.
Vadino, Joseph A. '63 (PH) Strafford, PA Our Lady of the Assumption Church.
Vadja, Jordan *o.p.* '98 (OAK) [N] Oakland, CA Western Dominican Province.
Vaeth, Paul *c.p.* '68 (PIT) [Q] Pittsburgh, PA St. Paul of the Cross Retreat Center.
Vaeth, Paul *c.p.* '69 (PIT) [O] Pittsburgh, PA St. Paul of the Cross Monastery.
Vaghetto, Benedetto P. '78 (PIT) [10] New Castle, PA St. Vincent de Paul Church.
Vaghi, Msgr. Peter J. '85 (WDC) [36] Washington, DC St. Patrick Church; [V] Washington, DC The John Carroll Society.
Vaglienty, Felipe '00 (CHI) [5] Chicago, IL St. Agnes of Bohemia Church.
Vago, John C. '70 (ALT) Bedford, PA St. Thomas Church.
Vail, Nathan '94 (SCR) [M] Elmhurst, PA Priestly Fraternity of St. Peter (F.S.S.P.), North American District Headquarters.
Vail, Thomas '51 (ALB) Retired.
Vaillancourt, Raymond *m.s.* '89 (FR) [I] Attleboro, MA La Salette Shrine.
Vaillancourt, Joseph *o.m.i.* '46 (FgM) Oblates Foreign Missions.
Vaillancourt, Mark G. '94 (NY) [A] New York, NY Cathedral Preparatory Seminary; [A] New York, NY Cathedral Preparatory Seminary; [A] Yonkers, NY St. Joseph's Seminary; [DD] Yonkers, NY Cathedral Preparatory Seminary Residence; [DD] Yonkers, NY Bishop Ford Residence.
Vaillencourt, Robert C. '82 (PRT) Bridgton, ME St. Joseph Church.
Vainavicz, Anthony C. '61 (GR) Spring Lake, MI St. Mary's Church.
Vairo, Carmine *s.d.b.* '64 (LA) [C] Rosemead, CA Don Bosco Technical Institute; [D] Rosemead, CA Don Bosco Technical Institute.
Vaisnoras, Boniface *m.i.c.* '47 (JOL) Plano, IL St. Mary Church.
Vaisnys, Juozas *s.j.* '43 (CHI) [N] Chicago, IL Lithuanian American Jesuits.
Vajda, Jordan *o.p.* '96 (PHX) [G] Tempe, AZ Dominicans (Dominican Community-Jordan House); [I] Phoenix, AZ Office of Youth and Young Adult Ministries.
Vakoc, Henry T. '92 (STP) Military Chaplains.
Vakulskas, John A., Jr. '69 (SC) Larchwood, IA St. Mary Church.
Vala, John B. '40 (NY) Retired.
Valades, Reuben '70 (RC) Retired.
Valainis, Vitolds '66 (DAV) Iowa City, IA State University of Iowa Hospital.
Valasek, Donald '74 (PBR) Northern Cambria, PA St. John the Baptist Church.
Valastro, Msgr. George J. '56 (NY) Middletown, NY St. Joseph Church.
Valayathil, Thomas '89 (MAR) Ewen, MI Sacred Heart Church; Watersmeet, MI Immaculate Conception Church; Watersmeet, MI Lac Vieux Desert Reservation Church.
Valdazo, Stephen '58 (BRK) [184] Queens, NY St. Joan of Arc Church.
Valderrama, Viliulfo '96 (TUC) [20] Tucson, AZ St. Monica Church.
Valdes, Msgr. Angel (SJN) Resident Chaplains.
Valdes, Msgr. Angel '38 (SJN) [E] Rio Piedras, PR Hospital del Maestro.
Valdes, Msgr. Angel Valdes '38 (SJN) Retired.
Valdes, Bert W. '62 (WH) Ona, WV St. Stephen Church.
Valdes, Luis '45 (SB) Retired.
Valdes, Nicanor '60 (SJN) [30] San Juan, PR San Juan Evangelista Church; [30] San Juan, PR San Juan Evangelista Church.
Valdes, Pedro '98 (LA) Pico Rivera, CA St. Hilary Church.
Valdez, Angel L. '94 (FTW) [15] Fort Wayne, IN St. Paul Church.
Valdez, John '91 (AMA) Pampa, TX St. Vincent de Paul Church.
Valdez, Jose Pedro '69 (LSC) Hobbs, NM Our Lady of Guadalupe Church.
Valdez, Patrick *c.r.* (DEN) [A] Denver, CO St. Andrew's Theatine Religious House.
Valdez, Patrick M. *c.r.* '75 (PBL) San Luis, CO Sangre de Cristo Church.
Valdez, Paul R. '82 (MRY) Boulder Creek, CA St. Michael Church.
Valdez, Salvador *o.f.m.* '97 (STP) [10] St. Paul, MN Sacred Heart Church.
Valdivia, Msgr. Adolfo A. '81 (SAT) [48] San Antonio, TX St. Lawrence Church.
Valdivia, Antonio A. '63 (OAK) Richmond, CA St. Cornelius Church.
Valdivia, Sergio '83 (MRY) Santa Cruz, CA Holy Cross Church.
Valencheck, John A. '98 (CLV) Brunswick, OH St. Ambrose Church.
Valencia, Thaddeus T. *c.s.b.* '79 (GAL) Missouri City, TX Holy Family Church.

Valenciano, Luis C. '77 (SD) National City, CA St. Mary Church.
Valenta, John G. '62 (STL) [P] St. Louis, MO Jesuit Community Corporation at St. Louis University - Jesuit Hall.
Valenta, Stephen *o.f.m.conv.* '51 (NY) [B] Staten Island, NY St. Francis Friary.
Valente, Michael '58 (JOL) Winfield, IL St. John the Baptist Church; Winfield, IL Central DuPage Hospital.
Valente, Palmo *s.f.* '52 (WDC) [B] Silver Spring, MD Holy Family Seminary.
Valenti, Thomas J. '76 (NY) [82] New York, NY Notre Dame Church; [GG] New York, NY University Apostolate.
Valenti, Thomas J. '76 (ROC) On Duty Outside the Diocese.
Valentine, Charles R. '54 (TR) Englishtown, NJ Our Lady of Mercy Church.
Valentine, Daniel A. '74 (PIT) [2] West Mifflin, PA Holy Spirit Church; Allegheny County, PA Southwestern Nursing and Rehabilitation Center; [R] Pittsburgh, PA Office for Campus Ministry.
Valentine, Joseph R. *f.s.s.p.* '93 (CHL) On Duty Outside the Diocese.
Valentine, Joseph R. *f.s.s.p.* '93 (SCR) [M] Elmhurst, PA Priestly Fraternity of St. Peter (F.S.S.P.), North American District Headquarters.
Valentine, Keveny M. '73 (WDC) Hospital & Nursing Home Ministries.
Valentine, Lambert F. *o.f.m.* '43 (NY) [35] New York, NY St. Francis of Assisi Church.
Valentine, Leroy A. '77 (STL) [10] Florissant, MO St. Thomas the Apostle Church.
Valentine, Richard A. '74 (PRO) Smithfield, RI St. Michael Church.
Valentine, Timothy *s.j.* '85 (NY) [DD] New York, NY Jesuit Community at Fordham University.
Valentini, Francis M. '44 (CLV) Retired.
Valentino, Dominic '47 (JOL) Retired.
Valentino, Francis *s.j.* '68 (NY) [96] New York, NY Our Lady of the Rosary Church.
Valentino, Msgr. Frederick A. '50 (TR) Retired.
Valenzano, Msgr. Arthur F. '75 (BAL) Westminster, MD St. John Church.
Valenzuela, Luciano '87 (SAC) Winters, CA St. Anthony Church.
Valenzuela, Pablo '53 (SJN) [11] San Juan, PR Corpus Christi Church.
Valera, Ramon '75 (LA) Woodland Hills, CA St. Mel Church.
Valerio, Raymond A. '59 (MAR) Retired.
Valero, Isidro G. '73 (SJN) [38] San Juan, PR Santa Maria de Los Angeles Church.
Valero, Leonardo (CGS) Gurabo, PR San Jose Church.
Valero, Pedro Ruiz *o.m.* '88 (CGS) Cayey, PR Nuestra Senora de la Asuncion Church.
Valiquette, Hilaire *o.f.m.* '64 (SFE) Pena Blanca, NM Nuestra Senora De Guadalupe Church.
Valiquette, Thomas M. *s.j.* '64 (DEN) [M] Aurora, CO Regis Jesuit High School - Jesuit Community.
Valit, Robert L. '61 (STP) Edina, MN Our Lady of Grace Church.
Valker, Richard J. '57 (CHI) Northbrook, IL St. Norbert Church.
Valko, George J. '77 (ALT) St. Michael, PA St. Michael's Church.
Valko, Robert A. '65 (PIT) Military Chaplains.
Valla, Dominic J. '63 (HRT) Oxford, CT St. Thomas the Apostle Church.
Valladares, Alejandro E. '00 (MOB) [7] Mobile, AL St. Ignatius Church.
Vallamattam, Thomas *s.j.* '64 (FgM) Provinces.
Valle, Msgr. Fernando '56 (LA) Retired.
Valle, Francisco (RIC) Onley, VA St. Peter's the Apostle Church.
Vallecorsa, Daniel '93 (PIT) [35] Pittsburgh, PA St. Raphael Church.
Vallee, Robert '87 (MIA) [A] Miami, FL St. John Vianney College Seminary.
Vallelonga, J. Stephen '90 (WH) Hurricane, WV Catholic Church of the Ascension.
Valleroy, Paul '74 (KNX) Signal Mountain, TN St. Augustine Church.
Valleroy, Rickey J. '93 (STL) Valley Park, MO Sacred Heart Church.
Valles, Carlos R. *c.ss.r.* '67 (SJN) [2] San Juan, PR San Agustin Church.
Valley, John '60 (CLV) Released from Diocesan Assignment.
Valley, Paul *s.p.* '64 (SFE) [I] Jemez Springs, NM Our Lady of Lourdes Novitiate.
Vallier, John '87 (GR) Coopersville, MI St. Michael's Church.
Vallier, John F. '87 (GR) [J] Coopersville, MI Grand Valley State University Catholic Campus Ministry.
Valliere, Romeo J. '63 (MAN) Absent on Sick Leave.
Valliere, Timothy C. '91 (NOR) Somersville, CT All Saints Church.
Vallieres, Jean-Joseph *o.m.i.* '39 (BO) [W] Lowell, MA Missionary Oblates of Mary Immaculate.
Vallina, Alfredo *o.p.* '57 (PCE) Yauco, PR Holy Rossary Church.
Vallina, Msgr. Emilio '52 (MIA) [22] Miami, FL St. John Bosco Church.
Valliquette, Thomas *s.j.* '64 (DEN) [D] Aurora, CO Regis Jesuit High School.
Vallone, Louis A. '48 (BUF) Retired.
Vallone, Louis F. '73 (PIT) [56] Pittsburgh, PA St. Mary of the Mount Church.
Vallooran, Joseph '59 (SR) Crescent City, CA Pelican Bay State Prison.
Vallooran, Pius *c.m.i.* '63 (LAF) Mamou, LA St. Ann Church.
Valls, Richard G. '57 (KAL) Delton, MI St. Ambrose Church.
Valois, Normand W. '46 (PRO) [1] Providence, RI Cathedral of SS. Peter and Paul; Retired.
Valone, Fred '94 (GAL) Tomball, TX St. Anne Church.
Valoret, Joseph '83 (MIA) Retired.
Valtierra, David D. *c.o.* '76 (CHR) [E] Rock Hill, SC Oratory of St. Philip Neri, Congregation of the Oratory of Pontifical Rite; [H] Rock Hill, SC Winthrop University, York Co. Tech Center.
Valtierra, J. Antonio '79 (GRY) [1] Hammond, IN All Saints Church.
Valukaran, Thomas *s.d.b.* '88 (NEW) [3] Elizabeth, NJ St. Anthony's Church.
Vamos, Joseph E. '66 (GRY) [1] Merrillville, IN Our Lady of Consolation Church.
Vamos, Joseph L. '61 (TOL) [16] Toledo, OH St. Agnes Church.
Van Abel, John W. '72 (MIL) On Duty Outside the Archdiocese.
Van Acker, Michael R. '81 (PEO) [J] Galesburg, IL St. Mary Medical Center.
van Ackeren, Leonard J. *o.s.b.* '38 (MIL) [P] Benet Lake, WI St. Benedict's Abbey.
Van Alstyne, Donald *m.i.c.* '81 (SPR) [J] Stockbridge, MA Congregation of Marians of The Immaculate Conception of the BVM.
Van Ban, Martin Tran *c.m.c.* '98 (DEN) Wheat Ridge, CO Queen of Vietnamese Martyrs Church.
Van Beck, Alfred F. '50 (MIL) Retired.
van Beeck, Frans J. *s.j.* '63 (CHI) [C] Chicago, IL Jesuit Community at Loyola University of Chicago.
Van Beek, Alois R. '73 (MIL) St. Lawrence, WI St. Lawrence Church.
Van Beek, Dennis E. '69 (MIL) Plymouth, WI St. John the Baptist Church.
Van Bergen, Francis G. '56 (CLV) South Euclid, OH St. Gregory the Great Church.
Van Boxel, Msgr. W. H. '40 (LAF) Retired.
Van Breda, William C. *o.s.a.* '50 (PH) [AA] Villanova, PA St. Thomas Monastery.
Van Bui, Joseph Dung '95 (ORL) [7] Orlando, FL St. Charles Borromeo Church.
Van Cauwenbergh, Roger *c.i.c.m.* '51 (ARL) [J] Arlington, VA Missionhurst, C.I.C.M.-Central House and Provincialate.
Van Chinh, Pierre Pham '71 (SP) [5] St. Petersburg, FL St. Joseph Church.
Van Coillie, Paul *c.i.c.m.* '47 (SAT) [M] San Antonio, TX Missionhurst Community Residence.
Van De Kreeke, William L. '63 (GB) [4] Oshkosh, WI St. Vincent de Paul Church; [5] Oshkosh, WI St. John Church.
Van De Loo, Willard '55 (GB) Special Assignment.
Van De Paer, John *c.i.c.m.* '47 (PH) Parkesburg, PA Our Lady of Consolation Church.
Van De Ven, Kenneth A. '71 (PHX) [3] Glendale, AZ St. James Church.
Van De Voord, Simeon *o.s.b.* (B) Boise, ID Elks Rehabilitation.
Van De Voord, Simeon *o.s.b.* '61 (B) Retired.
Van Del, Curtis E. *s.j.* '65 (SAL) [E] Concordia, KS Nazareth Convent & Academy Coporation Sisters of St. Joseph of Concordia.
Van Del, Curtis E. *s.j.* '65 (STL) [P] St. Louis, MO The Jesuits of the Missouri Province.
Van den Bussche, Hugo *o.m.i.* '53 (BWN) Roma, TX Our Lady of Refuge Church.
Van den Eynde, Stephen *ss.cc.* '48 (HON) [G] Kaneohe, HI Sacred Hearts Center.
Van der Linden, Peter J. '55 (DET) Retired.
Van Der Paalen, Pieter *c.i.c.m.* '55 (SAT) [M] San Antonio, TX Missionhurst Community Residence.
Van Der Peet, Michael *s.c.j.* '53 (MIL) [B] Hales Corners, WI Sacred Heart School of Theology; [P] Franklin, WI Villa Maria.
Van der Werff, Msgr. Martin '50 (NO) Retired.
Van Der Zanden, Edmund '38 (P) Retired.
Van Deuren, John H. '59 (GB) Special Assignment.
Van Doan, Vincent H. '86 (LAN) Blissfield, MI St. Peter the Apostle Church.
van Dyk, John *c.s.sp.* '51 (SB) [E] Hemet, CA Holy Ghost Fathers.
Van Dyke, James R. *s.j.* '93 (BUF) [D] Buffalo, NY Canisius High School; [O] Buffalo, NY Canisius Jesuit Community.
Van Gastel, William *m.h.m.* '59 (LA) South Gate, CA St. Helen Church.
Van Guilder, Alphonse *o.f.m.conv.* '64 (RNO) [B] Reno, NV St. Mary's Regional Medical Center.
Van Hoof, Achilles E. *o.praem.* '48 (GB) [I] De Pere, WI St. Norbert Abbey.
Van Hoof, Gordon *o.s.c.* '53 (CHI) [J] Chicago, IL Resurrection Medical Center.
Van Hoof, Gordon *o.s.c.* '53 (DET) [K] Riverview, MI Crosier Community of Riverview.
Van Hook, John E. *o.f.m.* '55 (ALB) [B] Loudonville, NY Siena College.
Van Horn, David *c.pp.s.* '54 (CIN) [M] Dayton, OH Provincial Office of the Cincinnati Province of the Society of the Precious Blood.
Van Houtteghem, Paul *c.i.c.m.* '48 (FgM) Missionhurst Foreign Missions.
Van Kempen, Robert A. '93 (FTW) [9] Fort Wayne, IN St. Joseph Church.
Van Kunnel, Joseph Muda (MOB) [11] Mobile, AL Little Flower Church.
Van Kuren, Corey S. '86 (SY) [10] Binghamton, NY St. Paul Church.
Van Lai, Joseph Khuyen '74 (SD) [6] San Diego, CA Holy Family Church.
van Lare, John *c.m.* '47 (LAR) Cotulla, TX Sacred Heart Church.
Van Leeuwen, Joseph *c.p.* '64 (CHI) [N] Chicago, IL Passionist Provincial Office.
Van Lente, Richard J. '66 (GR) Fremont, MI All Saints Church.
Van Liefde, Msgr. Christian M. '73 (LA) Panorama City, CA St. Genevieve Church; Los Angeles, CA L.A. City Fire Dept.
Van Linden, Philip A. '70 (LA) [Q] Montebello, CA Vincentian Fathers & Brothers; [W] Montebello, CA DePaul Center.
Van Mullekom, Richard '56 (SAG) Retired.
Van Natta, Todd Robert '00 (MAD) [6] Madison, WI Our Lady, Queen of Peace Church.
Van Nevel, Msgr. Albert H. '42 (GRY) Retired.
Van Nguyen, Peter '60 (PMB) [1] Lake Worth, FL Sacred Heart Church.
Van Nguyen, Peter Phan *c.ss.r.* '93 (CC) Rockport, TX St. Peter Indo-Chinese Church.
Van Nguyen, Phuong '93 (WOR) [4] Worcester, MA Christ the King Church.
Van Ommeren, Msgr. William '52 (SPK) Retired; [M] Spokane, WA Immaculate Heart Retreat Center.
Van Oosbree, Christian J. (SC) Fort Dodge, IA Corpus Christi Church.
Van Oss, James R. '64 (BEL) Posen, IL Our Lady of Perpetual Help Church; Todd's Mill, IL St. Mary Magdalen Church; [J] Belleville, IL Catholic Committee on Scouting of the Diocese of Belleville.
Van Overbeck, Gerald J. *o.s.a.* (CHI) [105] Chicago, IL St. John Fisher Church.
Van Overbeel, Gerald *o.s.a.* (CHI) [J] Chicago, IL Holy Cross Hospital.
Van Phung, Joseph '00 (DAV) [1] Iowa City, IA St. Mary Church.
Van Phuong, Msgr. Francis Pham '66 (ATL) Riverdale, GA Our Lady of Vietnam Church.
Van Roo, William A. *s.j.* '47 (MIL) [P] Wauwatosa, WI Jesuit Community at St. Camillus.
Van Sickler, Robert '93 (BAK) John Day, OR St. Elizabeth's Church.
van Sloun, Eugene G. '48 (DOD) Retired.
Van Sloun, Michael *o.s.c.* '95 (STP) Anoka, MN St. Stephen Church; [N] Anoka, MN Crosier Community of Anoka.
van Smoorenburg, Matthew *l.c.* '94 (DET) [T] Bloomfield Hills, MI Logos, Inc. (Michigan).
Van Stone, John J. '48 (PH) Retired.
van Straaten, Werenfried P. *o.praem.* '40 (ORG) [I] Silverado, CA Norbertine Fathers of Orange Inc.
Van Thanh, Louis '94 (NY) [1] Newburgh, NY St. Patrick Church.
Van Thong, Pierre Nguyen (GAL) [17] Houston, TX St. Catherine of Siena Church.
Van Thuyne, Dennis G. '77 (PH) Absent on Sick Leave.
Van Tran, John-Nhan '92 (NO) [1] Metairie, LA Our Lady of Divine Providence Church.
Van Tran, Peter Nam '84 (NO) Avondale, LA St. Bonaventure Church.
Van Ty, Nguyen '85 (HT) [2] Thibodaux, LA St. Charles Borromeo Church.
Van Vlaenderen, Leonard S. '88 (MIL) Special Assignment.
Van Vliet, Charles *f.s.s.p.* '96 (LIN) [A] Denton, NE Our Lady of Guadalupe Seminary.
Van Vurst, James *o.f.m.* '61 (CIN) [L] Centerville, OH The Franciscan at St. Leonard.
Van Winkle, Charles *c.s.c.* '78 (AUS) Copperas Cove, TX Holy Family Church.
Van Winkle, Charles E. *c.s.c.* '78 (AUS) [H] Austin, TX Congregation of Holy Cross - Southern Province.
Van Wormer, Giles *o.f.m.conv.* '57 (ALB) [12] Albany, NY Our Lady of Angels Church.
Van-Hoorn, Leo '55 (ALX) Retired.
VanAmburgh, Donald C. '61 (SY) [4] Binghamton, NY St. Christopher Church.
Vanasse, Bernard '78 (FR) [H] Taunton, MA Marian

Manor Inc.; [I] Fall River, MA Priests' Hostel.
Vanasse, Henry *f.i.c.* '85 (PRT) [I] Alfred, ME Notre Dame Institute.
Vanasse, Hervey '77 (SEA) Buckley, WA St. Aloysius Church.
Vanasse, Roman R. *o.praem.* '60 (GB) [I] De Pere, WI St. Norbert Abbey.
Vance, Charle P. (PH) Lafayette Hill, PA St. Philip Neri Church.
Vance, Gregory D. *s.j.* '98 (SEA) [C] Tacoma, WA Bellarmine Preparatory School.
Vance, James L. '63 (SFE) Raton, NM St. Patrick/St. Joseph Church.
Vance, Leslie A. '76 (SAT) [31] San Antonio, TX St. Brigid Church.
Vancik, Vladimir '34 (PRM) Retired.
Vandal, Roland *m.s.* '49 (FR) [I] Attleboro, MA La Salette Provincial House.
VanDamme, Larry P. '93 (MAR) Houghton, MI St. Albert the Great University Church; [G] Houghton, MI St. Albert the Great, University Parish.
VanDane, Louis L. *m.s.* '45 (STL) [P] St. Louis, MO La Salette Missionaries.
Vande Hey, Robert *o.praem.* '49 (GB) [I] De Pere, WI St. Joseph Priory.
Vandeberg, Joseph '89 (SCL) Villard, MN St. Bartholomew's Church; West Union, MN St. Alexius Church.
Vandebroek, Felix J. *ss.cc.* '54 (HON) Koloa, HI St. Raphael Church.
Vandegrift, John Raymond *o.p.* '60 (NY) [DD] New York, NY St. Vincent Ferrer Priory.
Vandegrift, William S. '80 (CAM) Penns Grove, NJ St. James Church.
Vandehey, Ervin S. '46 (P) Retired.
Vandehey, Kelly '96 (P) [10] Portland, OR St. Charles Church.
Vandehey, Scott '66 (P) Beaverton, OR St. Cecilia Church.
Vandeloo, Msgr. Melvin (BEL) Dubois, IL St. Charles Borromeo Church.
Vandeloo, Msgr. Melvin '53 (BEL) Tamaroa, IL Immaculate Conception Church.
Vanden Boogard, Steven J. *o.praem* '88 (GB) [I] De Pere, WI St. Norbert Abbey.
Vanden Hogen, Msgr. James '64 (GB) [O] Green Bay, WI The Diocesan Charismatic Renewal Center.
Vanden Hogen, Paul '54 (GB) Retired.
Vandenberg, James '77 (PBL) Absent on Leave.
Vandenberg, Robert H. '58 (GB) Combined Locks, WI St. Paul Church.
Vandenberg, Thomas L. '62 (SEA) Federal Way, WA St. Vincent De Paul Church.
VandenBossche, John V. *c.s.c.* '51 (FTW) [J] South Bend, IN Congregation of Holy Cross, Indiana Province, Provincial House.
VandenHogen, Msgr. James '64 (GB) Little Chute, WI St. John Church.
Vander Heyden, William F. '70 (CHI) North Chicago, IL Veterans Affairs Medical Center.
Vander Heyden, William F. '70 (GB) On Duty Outside the Diocese.
Vander Woude, Thomas P. '92 (ARL) [2] Arlington, VA St. Agnes Church.
Vandergeest, Peter J. '40 (ALN) Retired; [J] Bethlehem, PA Holy Family Villa.
Vanderholt, James '57 (BEA) [5] Port Arthur, TX St. James Church; Sabine Pass, TX St. Paul Church.
VanDerHorst, John G. (GB) [13] Green Bay, WI SS. Peter and Paul Church.
Vanderkolk, Peter J. '83 (LFT) Delphi, IN St. Joseph Church.
VanderLey, Louis *o.s.b.* '66 (OKL) Edmond, OK St. John the Baptist Church; [I] Shawnee, OK St. Gregory's Abbey; [K] Norman, OK Campus Ministry for the Archdiocese of Oklahoma City.
Vanderlin, Philip *o.s.b.* '70 (BIS) [A] Richardton, ND Assumption Abbey.
Vanderlin, Philip *o.s.b.* '80 (FgM) American - Cassinese Congregation Foreign Missions.
VanderVennett, Timothy *o.c.s.o.* '35 (SAC) [A] Vina, CA Abbey of New Clairvaux, Trappist Seminary; [H] Vina, CA Abbey of New Clairvaux, Trappist.
VanderWeel, Richard L. *s.s.e.* '62 (BUR) [E] Colchester, VT Society of St. Edmund.
VanDeuren, John H. (GB) [16] Green Bay, WI St. Elizabeth Ann Seton Church.
VandeVelde, J. Richard *s.j.* '68 (CHI) [C] Chicago, IL Jesuit Community at Loyola University of Chicago.
VanDeVoord, Simeon *o.s.b.* '61 (B) [C] Jerome, ID Monastery of the Ascension.
Vandewalle, Matthew J. '00 (LIN) Plattsmouth, NE Church of the Holy Spirit.
VandeWalle, Victor '40 (OKL) Retired.
VandeWeyer, Vincent *c.i.c.m.* '48 (FgM) Missionhurst Foreign Missions.
VanDorpe, Ray *c.m.* '82 (PBL) [K] Pueblo, CO Deacon Candidate Formation Council.
VanDurme, Patrick '00 (ROC) Graduate Studies.
vanDyk, John *c.s.sp.* '88 (SB) Hemet, CA Our Lady of the Valley Church.
Vanecko, William E. '65 (CHI) [111] Chicago, IL St. Kilian Church.
Vanegas, Albeyro *c.s.v.* '90 (CHI) [N] Arlington Heights, IL Viatorian Province Center-Clerics of St. Viator.
Vang, Chue Ying '92 (STP) [35] St. Paul, MN St. Vincent de Paul Church.
VanGuilder, Alphonse *o.f.m.conv.* '64 (RNO) [1] Reno, NV St. Thomas Aquinas Church.
VanHaverbeke, Kenneth S. '91 (WCH) [5] Wichita, KS Church of the Magdalen.
Vanin, Dino S. *p.i.m.e.* '72 (COL) [H] Newark, OH P.I.M.E. Mission & Retreat Center.
Vanitvelt, Milton H. '49 (MAR) Retired.
Vankeirsbilck, Paul *e.c.* '90 (STU) [F] Bloomingdale, OH Holy Family Hermitage.
VanLeeuwen, Joseph *c.p.* '64 (FgM) Mission Procurators.
VanLente, Richard J. '66 (GR) White Cloud, MI St. Joseph's Church.
VanLoon, Msgr. Neil J. *v.f.* '79 (SCR) Kingston, PA St. Ignatius Church.
Vann, Alfred *ss.cc.* '43 (HON) [G] Kaneohe, HI Sacred Hearts Center.
Vann, John C. '42 (MIA) Retired.
Vann, Kevin W. '81 (SFD) [2] Decatur, IL Our Lady of Lourdes Church.
VanNufflen, Albert *c.i.c.m.* '41 (ORL) Retired.
Vano, Roque P. '79 (SD) Brawley, CA St. Margaret Mary Church.
Vanoncini, Robert R. '63 (FRS) Dos Palos, CA Sacred Heart Church.
Vanorny, Ed '98 (RC) Bison, SD Blessed Sacrament Church.
Vanrell, Bartolome '53 (SJN) [E] San Juan, PR Centro Medico de P.R.
Vanthu, Joseph N. '71 (SJ) [4] Sunnyvale, CA Church of The Resurrection.
VanTrieste, Martin *s.t.* '45 (WDC) [M] Adelphi, MD Missionary Servants of the Most Holy Trinity.
VanWiel, John E. *c.s.v.* '66 (CHI) [D] Arlington Heights, IL St. Viator High School.
Vanyo, Leo V. '52 (PIT) [1] Pittsburgh, PA St. Paul Church.
Vanzillotta, Gino *o.m.* '54 (LA) [3] Los Angeles, CA All Saints Church; [Q] Los Angeles, CA Minim Fathers.
Vap, Gerald F. '65 (LIN) Orleans, NE St. Mary's Church.
Vap, Msgr. Ivan F. '54 (LIN) Geneva, NE St. Joseph's Church.
Varady, Michael *c.ss.r.* '87 (CHR) Sumter, SC St. Jude Church; [H] Sumter, SC Morris College.
Varakukala, George '62 (SAN) Eldorado, TX Our Lady of Guadalupe Church.
Varano, Andrew R. '58 (BRK) [46] Brooklyn, NY St. Francis of Paola Church.
Varas, Felix '50 (SJN) [50] San Juan, PR Maria Reina del Mundo Church.
Varble, Edward F. '50 (Y) Middlebranch, OH St. Therese Little Flower Church; Retired.
Varela, Jose *o.r.c.* '90 (SB) [5] San Bernardino, CA Our Lady of Guadalupe Church; [E] Riverside, CA Operarios Del Reino De Cristo, O.R.C.
Varettoni, Msgr. Julian B. '55 (PAT) [1] Clifton, NJ Sacred Heart Church.
Varga, Andrew G. '78 (BGP) Westport, CT St. Luke Church.
Varga, Luis '98 (SJ) [22] San Jose, CA Sacred Heart of Jesus Church.
Varga, Wayne M. '74 (PAT) Parsippany, NJ St. Peter the Apostle Church.
Vargas, Eric P. *s.v.d.* '75 (WDC) [M] Washington, DC Divine Word College.
Vargas, Gabriel (ALN) [11] Reading, PA St. Peter Church.
Vargas, Gabriel '90 (B) St. Anthony, ID Mary Immaculate Church.
Vargas, John C. *c.ss.r.* '73 (STL) [P] Liguori, MO Alphonsian Foundation Office.
Vargas, John C. *c.ss.r.* '78 (BR) [H] Baton Rouge, LA Redemptorist Vice Province.
Vargas, Jose Carlos '92 (PCE) Guanica, PR St. Anthony Abbot Church.
Vargas, Leonel '91 (LA) Palmdale, CA St. Mary Church.
Vargas, Luis '98 (SJ) [15] San Jose, CA St. Maria Goretti Church.
Vargas, Ramon *m.c.c.j.* '92 (CHI) [N] Chicago, IL Comboni Missionaries Theologate (M.C.C.J.), Verona Fathers.
Vargas Oliveras, Jose C. '92 (PCE) [B] Ponce, PR The Pontifical Catholic University of Puerto Rico.
Varghese, Chacko Thadathil '79 (PH) [72] Philadelphia, PA Incarnation of Our Lord Church.
Vargo, Robert B. '89 (HRT) Poquonock, CT St. Joseph's Church; Special and other Archdiocesan Assignment.
Varkey, Joseph (CHI) [56] Chicago, IL St. Ferdinand Church.
Varkey, Varghese P. '81 (TYL) New Boston, TX St. Mary of the Cenacle Church.
Varley, John J. '59 (SPR) [10] Pittsfield, MA St. Teresa Church.
Varna, Msgr. Leons '29 (BRK) [Z] Brooklyn, NY Latvian Roman Catholic Mission.
Varney, Lawrence F. '64 (TOL) Assumption, OH St. Mary of Assumption Church.
Varno, John '66 (ALB) Schenectady, NY Ellis Hospital.
Varno, John N. '66 (ALB) Special Assignment.
Varnorny, Ed '98 (RC) Buffalo, SD St. Anthony Church.
Varo, Jose Luis '56 (FRS) Hanford, CA Immaculate Heart Church.
Varone, Normand G. '75 (SPC) Benton, MO St. Denis Church; New Hamburg, MO St. Lawrence Church.
Varsanyi, Msgr. William I. '46 (PRO) [24] Providence, RI Our Lady of Charity Church; [M] Pawtucket, RI Jeanne Jugan Residence.
Varsanyi, Msgr. William I. '52 (NY) [HH] New York, NY Hungarian Catholic League of America, Inc.
Varuvel, Paul L. *s.t.d.* '72 (BUF) [A] East Aurora, NY Christ the King Seminary.
Varvaro, Msgr. William A. '63 (BRK) [192] Queens, NY St. Margaret Church.
Varvaro, Msgr. William A. '63 (NY) [HH] Middle Village, NY National Italian Apostolate Conference.
Vas, Joseph S. '79 (OKL) Special Assignment; [E] Oklahoma City, OK St. Anthony Hospital; [F] Oklahoma City, OK Bone and Joint Hospital.
Vasaturo, Anthony J. '55 (BO) [5] Medford, MA Sacred Heart Church; Senior Priests.
Vaschetto, Bernardo *o.f.m.cap.* '62 (BO) [56] Boston, MA St. Patrick Church.
Vasek, Stephen *o.m.i.* '71 (BUF) [27] Buffalo, NY Holy Angels Church.
Vashon, Randall J. '00 (MET) Bound Brook, NJ St. Joseph Church.
Vasil, James '74 (GBG) Sutersville, PA St. Charles Borromeo Church.
Vasile, Louis A. '72 (ROC) [4] Auburn, NY St. Alphonsus Church.
Vasilj, Kvirin *o.f.m.* '40 (CHI) [N] Chicago, IL Croatian Franciscan Custody of the Holy Family.
Vaske, Martin O. *s.j.* '47 (OM) [K] Omaha, NE Jesuit Community at Creighton University.
Vasko, Christopher P. '83 (TOL) Cloverdale, OH St. Barbara Church; Continental, OH St. John the Baptist Church.
Vasko, Peter *o.f.m.* '87 (FgM) Custody of St. Mary of the Angels. Byzantine-Slavonic.
Vasquez, Edwin '96 (BO) [W] Cambridge, MA Weston Jesuit Community.
Vasquez, Joe S. '84 (SAN) [5] San Angelo, TX St. Joseph Church.
Vasquez, Jorge I. (LA) Huntington Park, CA St. Matthias Church.
Vasquez, Luis '87 (RCK) South Beloit, IL St. Peter Church.
Vasquez, Paul L. '98 (OM) [33] Omaha, NE Our Lady of Lourdes Church.
Vasquez, Perfecto '98 (RCK) Crystal Lake, IL St. Elizabeth Ann Seton Church.
Vasquez, Raymundo Chavez '00 (TYL) [1] Tyler, TX Cathedral of the Immaculate Conception.
Vasquez, Reinalo Terrero '85 (SJN) [45] San Juan, PR Ntra. Sra. del Perpetuo Socorro Church.
Vass, Robert *s.d.v.* '87 (PAT) [M] Florham Park, NJ Father Justin Vocationary.
Vasti, Michael J. *m.s.c.* '56 (ALN) [A] Center Valley, PA Missionaries of the Sacred Heart; [G] Allentown, PA Sacred Heart Hospital.
Vasyliv, Stepan '94 (STN) Grand Rapids, MI St. Michael's Church.
Vater, Robert L. '45 (COV) Fort Thomas, KY St. Catherine of Siena Church; Retired.
Vath, William R. '72 (LFT) [3] Lafayette, IN St. Boniface Church; Special Assignment.
Vathalloor, Joseph *c.m.i.* '74 (SAN) [3] San Angelo, TX St. Margaret Church; [5] San Angelo, TX St. Joseph Church.
Vattakudiyil, Francis P. '63 (RVC) Kings Park, NY St. Joseph's Church.
Vattakunnel, Jose '90 (LKC) Elton, LA St. Joseph's Church; [D] Elton, LA Herald of Good News, Inc.
Vattaparambil, Thomas Varughese '83 (CHI) [71] Chicago, IL St. Gregory Church.
Vatter, Joseph E. '78 (BUF) Angelica, NY Sacred Heart Church; Belmont, NY St. Mary Church; Scio, NY St. Joseph Church.
Vattothuparambil, Thomas '63 (PH) Ambler, PA St. Anthony of Padua Church.
Vaudreuil, Paul '64 (WOR) Fiskdale, MA St. Anne's and St. Patrick's Church.
Vaughan, Gregory D. '72 (TR) [21] Trenton, NJ St. Raphael Church.
Vaughan, James '50 (ALB) [13] Troy, NY Sacred Heart Church; Retired.
Vaughan, Msgr. John J. '67 (MIA) [4] Miami Beach, FL St. Patrick Church; [L] Miami Shores, FL Archdiocese of Miami Millennium Appeal, Inc.; [L] Miami Shores, FL Archdiocese of Miami, Inc.
Vaughan, John R. '74 (OWN) [1] Owensboro, KY St. Stephen Church.
Vaughan, Msgr. Richard '47 (AMA) Retired; [D] Panhandle, TX St. Ann's Nursing Home.
Vaughan, Richard P. *s.j.* '50 (LA) [C] Los Angeles, CA Loyola Marymount University.

Vaughan, Roger (NY) Staten Island, NY St. Vincent's Medical Center of Richmond.
Vaughan, Thomas *s.s.c.* '56 (OM) [K] St. Columbans, NE St. Columban's Foreign Mission Society.
Vaughan, William L. '95 (SFR) Daly City, CA Our Lady of Mercy Church.
Vaughey, Msgr. James K. (NY) On Special or Other (Arch)Diocesan Assignment.
Vaughey, Msgr. James K. '65 (NY) Briarcliff Manor, NY St. Theresa Church.
Vaughn, John *o.f.m.* '55 (MRY) [F] San Miguel, CA Franciscan Friars, O.F.M.; [F] San Miguel, CA Novitiate House for the Franciscan Friars, O.F.M.
Vaughn, Mason L. '50 (SAG) Bridgeport, MI St. Christopher Church.
Vaughn, Robert William *o.p.* '71 (NY) [DD] New York, NY St. Vincent Ferrer Priory.
Vaughn, Roger *o.s.c.* '77 (NY) [DD] New York, NY Crosier (Canons Regular of the Order of the Holy Cross).
Vaughn, Roland '71 (LKC) Hackberry, LA St. Peter Apostle Church.
Vaught, Michael R. '73 (OKL) Clinton, OK St. Mary's Church.
Vavasseur, Henry C. '58 (BR) Port Allen, LA Holy Family Church.
Vaverek, Gavin '90 (TYL) Longview, TX St. Mary Church.
Vaverek, Hayden J. '94 (CHR) Moncks Corner, SC St. Philip Benizi Church.
Vaverek, Timothy V. '85 (AUS) [5] Waco, TX St. Joseph Church.
Vavonese, Charles S. '73 (SY) Dewitt, NY Holy Cross Church; Special Assignment.
Vavra, Clarence '65 (STP) Shieldsville, MN St. Patrick Church.
Vavra, Clarence J. '65 (STP) Montgomery, MN Holy Redeemer Church.
Vavrina, Kenneth P. '62 (OM) [39] Omaha, NE St. Richard Church; [45] Omaha, NE St. Therese of the Child Jesus Church.
Vayalil, Thomas C. (CHI) [J] Evanston, IL Saint Francis Hospital.
Vaz, Francis F. '61 (MET) Oxford, NJ St. Rose of Lima Church.
Vaze Parampil, Thomas '69 (LUB) Retired.
Vazhapilly, Paul '61 (BRK) [133] Brooklyn, NY SS. Simon and Jude Church; [U] Brooklyn, NY Catholic Migration & Refugee Office, Catholic Migration Services, Inc.
Vazhappilly, Mathew *c.m.i.* '74 (SFS) Conde, SD St. John the Baptist Church.
Vazhupaclickal, Joseph Ouseph *s.a.c.* '79 (LUB) Spur, TX St. Mary Church.
Vazquez, Albert M. *c.m.f.* '55 (LA) [31] Los Angeles, CA Our Lady Queen of the Angels Church.
Vazquez, Carlos R. '89 (WIL) [1] Wilmington, DE Cathedral of St. Peter; New Castle, DE Delaware Psychiatric Hospital.
Vazquez, Harry Lopez '93 (MGZ) [7] Mayaquez, PR Santa Teresita Church.
Vazquez, Jose '89 (Y) Absent on Leave.
Vazquez, Luis A. '91 (ARE) [12] Arecibo, PR Church of Santa Teresita.
Vazquez, Msgr. Perfecto '56 (BRK) [52] Brooklyn, NY Guardian Angel Church.
Vazquez, Virginio C. '73 (GAL) Huntsville, TX Eastham Unit.
Vazquez, Virginio C. '73 (TYL) Lovelady, TX Eastham Unit, Texas Department of Corrections.
Vazquez-Colon, Antonio Jose '90 (SJN) [10] Guaynabo, PR Santa Rosa de Lima Church.
Vazquez-Vega, Edwin '95 (PCE) Salinas, PR Our Lady of Monserrat Church.
Vead, Victor P. '92 (ALX) Isle Brevelle, LA St. Augustine's Church.
Vecchio, Egidio *m.s.* '55 (BEA) Woodville, TX Our Lady of the Pines Church.
Vecchio, Giovanni *p.i.m.e.* '97 (DET) [K] Detroit, MI P.I.M.E. Missionaries of SS. Peter and Paul.
Vecchio, Michael J. '50 (PIT) Retired.
Vecsey, Stephen N. '73 (LA) Retired.
Vedro, James A. *o.s.c.* '65 (DET) Trenton, MI St. Joseph Church; [K] Riverview, MI Crosier Community of Riverview.
Veeneman, Dismas J. *o.f.m.conv.* '69 (IND) Clarksville, IN St. Anthony of Padua Church.
Veerkamp, Teodoro *o.p.* (SJN) [A] Bayamon, PR Bayamon Central University.
Vega, Carlos '89 (MIA) Miami Shores, FL St. Rose of Lima Church.
Vega, Donald '65 (SJN) [22] San Juan, PR San Ignacio de Loyola Church.
Vega, Fernando *c.m.f.* '40 (FRS) [8] Fresno, CA St. Anthony Mary Claret Church.
Vega, Hector R. '74 (MIL) [T] Waukesha, WI Secular Institute of Schoenstatt Fathers.
Vega, Jose L. *o.m.* '69 (LA) [3] Los Angeles, CA All Saints Church; [Q] Los Angeles, CA Minim Fathers.
Vega, Jose Luis '54 (FRS) Cutler, CA St. Mary Church.
Vega, Raymond *s.c.j.* '73 (SP) [O] Pinellas Park, FL Priests of the Sacred Heart.
Vega, Richard '83 (LA) Lompoc, CA La Purisima Concepcion Church.
Vega, Roberto '87 (ARE) [1] Arecibo, PR Cathedral of San Felipe Apostol.
Vehovec, Valentine '43 (SB) Retired.
Veich, Vincent J. '71 (BGP) [2] Stamford, CT Saint Benedict and Our Lady of Montserrat Church.
Veigas, Albert '80 (CLV) [3] Garfield Heights, OH St. Therese Church.
Veik, Al *o.f.m.cap.* '67 (MIL) [Y] Milwaukee, WI House of Peace.
Veit, David John '98 (JC) Columbia, MO Our Lady of Lourdes Church.
Veith, William E. '70 (CHI) [J] Elk Grove Village, IL Alexian Brothers Medical Center.
Vela, Fabian '56 (MRY) Hollister, CA Sacred Heart/St. Benedict Catholic Community Church; Retired.
Vela, Jesus *o.f.m.cap.* '98 (LA) [75] Los Angeles, CA St. Lawrence of Brindisi Church.
Vela, William *c.s.b.* '90 (GAL) [F] Houston, TX St. Thomas High School.
Velas, Vincent P. '64 (PIT) [6] McKeesport, PA St. Patrick Church.
Velasco, Arturo '86 (LA) [68] Los Angeles, CA St. Ignatius of Loyola Church.
Velasco, Jose *o.m.i.* '58 (SAT) [K] San Antonio, TX Oblate Madonna Residence.
Velasco, Jose' J. *s.j.* '57 (LA) Monterey Park, CA St. Stephen Church.
Velasquez, Charles '85 (CHY) On Leave of Absence.
Velasquez, Jose '67 (ELP) Canutillo, TX St. Patrick Church.
Velasquez, Marcos C. '89 (TUC) Nogales, AZ Sacred Heart Church.
Velasquez, Rodrigo '59 (NY) [DD] Bronx, NY Yarumal Mission Society, Inc.
Velazquez, Carlos B. '90 (SAT) [43] San Antonio, TX St. John Berchmans Church.
Velazquez, David *m.sp.s.* '80 (LA) Ventura, CA San Buenaventura Church.
Velazquez, Francisco *v.d.m.f.* '90 (SAC) North Highlands, CA St. Lawrence Church.
Velazquez, Luis '78 (ARE) [7] Vega-Baja, PR Our Lady of Mt. Carmel Church.
Velazquez, Mario '85 (SJN) [16] San Juan, PR Ntra. Sra. de Fatima Church; [19] Carolina, PR Ntra. Sra. de Fatima Church.
Velazquez Heredia, P. Mario '85 (SJN) [3] Guaynabo, PR Maria Madre de Mi Senor Church.
Velez, Andrew '96 (PAT) Dover, NJ Sacred Heart Church.
Velez, Carlos Felipe '00 (B) Idaho Falls, ID Holy Rosary Church.
Velez, Guillermo (PAT) Dover, NJ Our Lady Queen of the Most Holy Rosary Church.
Velie, Richard '79 (MIA) Absent on Leave.
Vella, Msgr. Desmond J. '59 (NY) [52] New York, NY Immaculate Conception Church.
Vella, Edward *c.ss.r.* '85 (DEN) [M] Denver, CO The Redemptorists/Denver Province.
Vella, Francis '55 (OAK) On Special Assignment.
Vella, Francis M. (HRT) Newington, CT Department of Veteran Affairs Medical Center.
Vella, Francis M. '55 (OAK) Retired.
Vella, Joseph C. (BRK) [166] Queens, NY St. Elizabeth's Church.
Vella, Joseph C. '68 (BRK) Military Chaplains.
Vellankal, James '58 (LAF) [2] Opelousas, LA Our Lady of Mercy Church; On Special Assignment.
Vellappellil, Thomas M. *m.s.* (TYL) Lufkin, TX St. Patrick Church.
Vellaramparampil, Aaron T. '66 (RVC) Glen Cove, NY St. Rocco Church.
Vellardita, Guy *o.f.m.* '58 (FgM) Franciscan Foreign Missions.
Vellenga, R. Stephen '81 (CLV) Painesville, OH St. Mary Church; [W] Cleveland, OH Office of Hispanic Ministry.
Vellorattil, George '78 (CHI) Highland Park, IL Immaculate Conception Church.
Vellucci, Dennis C. '75 (LA) Retired.
Velo, Msgr. Kenneth '73 (CHI) [U] Chicago, IL Catholic Church Extension Society, aka Catholic Extension.
Velo, Kenneth J. '73 (CHI) Rosemont-Des Plaines, IL Our Lady of Hope Church.
Velozo, Msgr. Donald D. '65 (CAM) Northfield, NJ St. Bernadette Church.
Velten, Robert *o.s.b.* '54 (SP) [O] St. Leo, FL St. Leo Abbey.
Veltri, Dennis J. '93 (E) Greenville, PA St. Michael Church.
Veltrie, James V. *s.j.* '65 (STL) [C] St. Louis, MO Saint Louis University; [P] St. Louis, MO Jesuit Community Corporation at St. Louis University - Jesuit Hall.
Velutis, John '32 (CHI) Retired.
Vendetti, Michael A. '64 (BRK) Released from Diocesan Assignment.
Venditti, J. Michael '87 (MET) On Duty Outside the Diocese.
Venditti, J. Michael '87 (PSC) Dunellen, NJ St. Nicholas Church; East Brunswick, NJ Nativity of Our Lord Church.
Vendramin, Aldo *c.s.* '75 (CHI) [N] Oak Park, IL Missionaries of Saint Charles.
Venegoni, John L. '95 (BEL) Pinckneyville, IL St. Bruno Church.
Veneklase, Michael G. *o.c.d.* '93 (GRY) [J] Munster, IN Discalced Carmelite Fathers Monastery.
Veneroso, Joseph R. *m.m.* '78 (NY) [DD] Maryknoll, NY Maryknoll Fathers and Brothers.
Venette, Howard J. '84 (OG) Colton, NY St. Patrick Church.
Venezia, Arthur '71 (PMB) North Palm Beach, FL St. Paul of the Cross Church.
Venganinna, David '66 (FAR) Oakwood, ND Sacred Heart Church.
Vengayil, Thomas '59 (PMB) Tequesta, FL St. Jude Church.
Venglarik, Daniel M. '73 (Y) Boardman, OH St. Charles Borromeo's Church.
Venker, Josef V. *s.j.* '87 (SEA) [A] Seattle, WA Seattle University.
Venne, Douglas F. *m.m.* '59 (FgM) Maryknoll Foreign Missions.
Venne, R. Thomas '62 (MIL) [2] Pewaukee, WI St. Anthony Church.
Venne, Samuel J. '78 (BUF) Pendleton, NY Good Shepherd Church.
Venneri, Michael D. '82 (SPK) Special Ministry; [G] Spokane, WA Sacred Heart Medical Center.
Vennitti, Thomas A. '73 (STU) Cadiz, OH St. Teresa Church; Hopedale, OH Sacred Heart Church.
Vennix, James F. '56 (GB) Waupaca, WI St. Mary Magdalene Church.
Venters, Darrell '89 (OWN) [I] Bowling Green, KY Western Kentucky University Newman Center.
Ventiquattro, Jude *t.o.r.* '88 (ARL) [J] White Post, VA Sacred Heart Friary.
Ventura, Anthony '78 (HRT) [A] Bloomfield, CT St. Thomas Seminary.
Ventura, Anthony C. '78 (HRT) Retired.
Ventura, Gennaro J. '43 (ROC) Cohocton, NY Holy Family Catholic Community Church; Retired.
Ventura, John '68 (BIR) Absent on Leave.
Ventura, Thomas F. '61 (CHI) Winnetka, IL SS. Faith, Hope and Charity Church.
Venus, Charles C., Jr. '80 (BLX) Leakesville, MS South Mississippi Correctional Institution.
Venuti, Angelo A. '61 (BRK) [81] Brooklyn, NY St. Mary Mother of Jesus Church.
Venvertloh, Ken J. '67 (SFD) Jacksonville, IL Our Saviour Church; Virginia, IL St. Luke Church.
Venza, Felix F. '72 (TR) Florence, NJ St. Clare Church.
Venzor, Jesse C. '80 (FRS) Woodlake, CA St. Frances Cabrini Church.
Ver Bust, Richard M. '58 (GB) Special Assignment.
Ver'Schneider, Neil L. *s.j.* '66 (PH) [AA] Philadelphia, PA Jesuit Community, Arrupe House.
Ver-Schneider, Neil *s.j.* '66 (PH) [I] Philadelphia, PA The Gesu School.
Vera, Julio '98 (MGZ) San German, PR San German de Auxerre Church.
Vera, Luis *o.s.a.* (CHI) [N] Chicago, IL St. John Stone Friary.
Vera, Romulo E. *c.s.c.* '89 (FTW) [J] South Bend, IN Congregation of Holy Cross, Indiana Province, Provincial House.
Vera, Vincente Antonio '85 (TOL) Mansfield, OH St. Peter Church.
Veras, Richard '96 (NY) [211] Staten Island, NY St. Joseph, St. Thomas Church.
Verbeke, Albert *c.i.c.m.* '46 (FgM) Missionhurst Foreign Missions.
Verber, Thomas *o.s.a.* '99 (SD) [H] San Diego, CA Augustinian Community.
Verber, Tom *o.s.a.* '99 (SD) [C] San Diego, CA St. Augustine High School.
Verberg, Richard R. '71 (MIL) Greenfield, WI St. John the Evangelist Church.
Verbest, Stephen *o.c.s.o.* '98 (DUB) [K] Peosta, IA New Melleray Abbey, Order of Cistercians of the Strict Observance.
Verboomen, Willy *c.i.c.m.* '63 (BWN) McCook, TX Immaculate Conception Church; San Isidro, TX St. Isidore Church.
Verbrugghe, Albert E. '50 (TUC) [F] Tucson, AZ Regina Cleri Center.
Verbryke, William L. *s.j.* '83 (CIN) [F] Cincinnati, OH St. Xavier High School; [M] Cincinnati, OH Jesuit Community at St. Xavier High School.
Vercek, Alphonse *sch.p.* '38 (BUF) [O] Lackawanna, NY Piarist Fathers.
Vercellone, Anthony (LAV) [G] Las Vegas, NV Serra House (Formation Residence).
Verdegan, Albert L. '60 (SUP) Retired.
Verdelotti, Anthony W. '86 (PRO) East Greenwich, RI Our Lady of Mercy Church.
Verdelotti, James J. '78 (PRO) Bristol, RI Our Lady of Mount Carmel Church.
Verdi, Ralph C. *c.pp.s.* '71 (LFT) [A] Rensselaer, IN

Saint Joseph's College.
Verdia, Carlos *c.m.f.* '85 (SJN) [5] Toa Alta, PR N. Sra. de la Providencia Church.
Verdick, James *o.f.m.* '40 (MIL) [P] Burlington, WI Queen of Peace Friary.
Verdick, Jerome F. '58 (WIN) Retired.
Verdoon, Cornelius '51 (SPK) Retired.
Verdun, Gerald J. '72 (PEO) Delavan, IL St. Mary's Church.
Vereb, Jerome *c.p.* '72 (FgM) Passionist Foreign Missions.
Vereb, John '47 (PMB) [4] West Palm Beach, FL St. John Fisher Church; Retired.
VerEecke, Robert F. *s.j.* '78 (BO) [3] Newton, MA St. Ignatius Church.
Vereker, Tobias '58 (SAC) Retired and in Senior Ministry.
Verespy, Joseph D. '79 (SCR) Dupont, PA Sacred Heart of Jesus Church.
Vergara, Armando '73 (STO) Linden, CA Holy Cross Church.
Vergara, Jaime *c.m.* '56 (SJN) [54] San Juan, PR Sagrado Corazon de Jesus Church.
Vergauwen, Peter '42 (SAN) Retired.
Vergauwen, Peter '42 (SAT) [K] San Antonio, TX Padua Place.
Verghese, Benedict *c.m.i.* '60 (BRK) [109] Brooklyn, NY Our Lady of Refuge Church.
Verhaeghe, Ronald '92 (KC) Special Assignment; [H] Blue Springs, MO St. Mary's Manor.
Verhagen, Donald *s.d.s.* '45 (MIL) [P] Milwaukee, WI Salvatorians - Jordan Hall.
Verhagen, Norbert M. *m.m.* '39 (SJ) [L] Los Altos, CA Maryknoll.
Verhalen, Charles J. '47 (MIL) Retired.
Verhalen, David H. *c.s.c.* '54 (FTW) [J] South Bend, IN Congregation of Holy Cross, Indiana Province, Provincial House.
Verhalen, Peter *o.cist.* '81 (DAL) [D] Irving, TX Cistercian Preparatory School; [E] Irving, TX Cistercian Preparatory School; [K] Irving, TX Cistercian Abbey of Our Lady of Dallas.
Verhalin, David *c.s.c.* '54 (TYL) [B] Palestine, TX Hermitage.
Verhasselt, David A. '89 (MIL) Mapleton, WI St. Catherine Church.
Verheggen, Peter A. *o.f.m.* '49 (LSC) Tularosa, NM St. Francis de Paula Church.
Verhelst, Steven J. '90 (NU) Benson, MN St. Francis Church; Clara City, MN St. Clara Church; Clontarf, MN St. Malachy Church; Danvers, MN Church of the Visitation; De Graff, MN St. Bridget Church; Murdock, MN Church of the Sacred Heart .
Verhoff, Melvin T. '91 (TOL) Plymouth, OH St. Joseph Church; Willard, OH St. Francis Xavier Church.
Verhoff, Werner *c.pp.s.* '43 (CIN) [B] Carthagena, OH St. Charles.
Verhoye, Gerard A. '49 (PEO) Retired.
Verkamp, Bernard J. '64 (EVN) On Leave of Absence.
Verley, Jude *o.s.c.* '79 (DET) Riverview, MI St. Cyprian Church; [K] Riverview, MI Crosier Community of Riverview.
Vermiglio, Tom *m.c.c.j.* '72 (CHI) [N] La Grange Park, IL Comboni Mission Center.
Vernon, Donald '55 (LFT) [C] Lafayette, IN St. Elizabeth Medical Center.
Vernon, John E. '54 (OM) [46] Omaha, NE St. Thomas More Church.
Vernon, William F. '97 (HEL) Shelby, MT St. William Church.
Veronesi, Giulio *c.r.s.* '75 (HRT) [6] Hartford, CT Sacred Heart Church.
Verrett, Joseph C. *s.s.j.* '55 (BAL) [S] Baltimore, MD St. Joseph Society of the Sacred Heart House of Central Administration; [S] Baltimore, MD St. Joseph Society of the Sacred Heart House of Central Administration.
Verretti, Joseph C. *s.s.j.* (BAL) [33] Baltimore, MD St. Francis Xavier Church.
Verrier, John (PEO) Henry, IL St. Joseph's Church; Henry, IL St. Mary's Church.
Verrier, John M. '95 (PEO) Lacon, IL Immaculate Conception Church.
Verrigni, Robert J. '77 (NY) Larchmont, NY SS. John and Paul Church.
Verrill, Wendell '63 (BO) [4] Waltham, MA St. Mary Church.
Verrilli, William F. '79 (BGP) On Duty Outside the Diocese.
Verruni, Samuel A. '86 (PH) Exton, PA SS. Philip and James Church; [EE] Philadelphia, PA Newman Center at Drexel University.
Vershaeve, C. Michael '77 (DET) Ortonville, MI St. Anne Church.
Verstreken, Alfred *c.j.* '73 (LA) [D] Santa Barbara, CA Bishop Garcia Diego High School.
Verstynen, Robert J. '47 (RCK) Retired.
Verswyvel, Joseph *c.i.c.m.* '52 (FgM) Missionhurst Foreign Missions.
Vertiz, Fico Barahona *o.p.* '88 (WDC) [11] Washington, DC St. Dominic Church & Priory Church.
Vertzelis, George D. '53 (BO) Wellesley, MA St. James the Great Church.
Vesbit, Thomas S. '64 (GR) [15] Grand Rapids, MI St. Jude Church.
Vesely, James J. '54 (CLV) Brooklyn, OH St. Thomas More Church.
Vesely, Stanley G. *o.s.b.* '40 (JOL) [J] Lisle, IL St. Procopius Abbey.
Vesey, John E. '68 (BRK) [53] Brooklyn, NY Holy Cross Church.
Vesga, Mario '62 (SD) [2] Chula Vista, CA Our Lady of Guadalupe Church.
Vessels, John L. *s.j.* '57 (ATL) [L] Atlanta, GA Ignatius House.
Vest, Joseph E. '81 (L) [15] Louisville, KY St. Bernard Church.
Veszelovszky, Albin V. *o.praem.* '44 (GB) [I] De Pere, WI St. Norbert Abbey; [O] De Pere, WI Canons Regular of Magnovarad, Ltd.
Vetrano, Anthony *o.f.m.cap.* '92 (NY) [DD] Garrison, NY St. Francis Friary.
Vetrano, Michael A. '79 (RVC) West Islip, NY Our Lady of Lourdes Church.
Vetter, Austin '93 (BIS) [3] Dickinson, ND St. Patrick Church.
Vetter, Joseph G. '73 (R) [H] Durham, NC Newman Catholic Student Center Duke University.
Vetter, Matthew *c.p.* '38 (FgM) Mission Procurators.
Vetter, Msgr. Wendelyn *v.g.* '60 (FAR) Hillsboro, ND St. Rose of Lima Church.
Vettese, Donald *s.j.* '82 (TOL) [C] Toledo, OH St. John's Jesuit High School.
Veverka, Floribert *o.f.m.* '48 (SFD) [K] Sherman, IL Our Lady of Angels Friary.
Vevik, Paul '77 (SPK) [12] Spokane, WA St. Francis Xavier Church.
Vezhaparambil, Paul *c.m.i.* '64 (NY) Bronxville, NY St. Joseph Church; Bronxville, NY Lawrence Hospital.
Via, Anthony P. *s.j.* '62 (P) [L] Portland, OR Jesuit Provincial Office (Society of Jesus, Oregon Prov.).
Via, Anthony P. *s.j.* '62 (SPK) [C] Spokane, WA Gonzaga University.
Viall, James A. '54 (CLV) [69] Cleveland, OH St. Rose of Lima Church.
Viall, John L. '59 (CLV) North Royalton, OH St. Albert the Great Church.
Viallis, Didier-Marie Dugas (LAR) [E] Laredo, TX St. John Priory, F.J.
Viallis, Didier-Marie Dugas '94 (CC) [H] Laredo, TX St. John's Priory, (F.J.).
Vialpando, Kenneth L. '91 (SLC) [2] Salt Lake City, UT Our Lady of Guadalupe Church.
Viana, Carlos Sergio '00 (BO) [W] Cambridge, MA Weston Jesuit Community.
Vianney, John M. '88 (LA) Santa Maria, CA St. Mary of the Assumption Church.
Viau, Msgr. Roger '43 (SPR) Retired; [I] Springfield, MA St. Michael's Residence.
Viberti, Victor L. *s.s.p.* '38 (NY) [B] New York, NY Society of St. Paul.
Vicari, Marc A. '97 (NEW) South Orange, NJ Our Lady of Sorrows Church.
Vicedo, Hermenegildo '63 (SJN) [49] San Juan, PR Nuestra Senora de la Providencia Church.
Vicente, Francisco '49 (OAK) Antioch, CA Holy Rosary Church.
Vicente, Isidore V. *o.p.* '64 (GAL) [Q] Houston, TX Dominican Fathers and Brothers, St. Mark Priory, Inc.
Vicentini, Joseph *c.s.* '55 (KC) [17] Kansas City, MO Holy Rosary Church.
Vichas, Walter A. '49 (HRT) [1] Waterbury, CT Blessed Sacrament Church.
Vichich, Michael T. '74 (MAR) Hermansville, MI St. John Neumann Church.
Vick, James L. '99 (KNX) [2] Chattanooga, TN Our Lady of Perpetual Help Church.
Vickery, Richard F. '48 (MAN) Retired.
Victor, Ronald J. '78 (DET) Centerline, MI St. Clement Church.
Victoria, Robert '91 (LA) [38] Los Angeles, CA Sacred Heart Church.
Vida, Msgr. George N. '57 (VNN) Anaheim, CA Annunciation Church.
Vidal, Gustavo A. '97 (SLC) Provo, UT St. Francis of Assisi Church.
Vidal, Robert S. '66 (ORG) Seal Beach, CA St. Anne's Church.
Vidiella, Felix '52 (CC) Retired.
Vidmar, John C. *o.p.* '80 (WDC) [B] Washington, DC Dominican House of Studies.
Vidra, Msgr. Thomas J. '59 (SD) El Centro, CA St. Mary Church.
Vidrine, Richard '95 (LAF) Military Chaplains.
Vieages, Harold '64 (RNO) Leave of Absence.
Vieck, Hilary F. '55 (EVN) Bloomfield, IN Holy Name Church; Linton, IN St. Peter Church.
Viefhues, Ludger *s.j.* '95 (BO) [W] Cambridge, MA Faber House.
Viefhus, Ludger '95 (BO) [W] Cambridge, MA Weston Jesuit Community.
Viego, Carlos '98 (NEW) West New York, NJ St. Joseph of the Palisades Church.
Vieira, John S. '97 (SB) [2] Corona, CA St. Edward Church; Hesperia, CA Holy Family Church.
Vieira, Victor M. '67 (PRO) [2] East Providence, RI St. Francis Xavier Church.
Vielgus, Thaddeus A. '54 (MET) Retired.
Vien, John Rogers '93 (STL) Kirkwood, MO St. Peter Church.
Viera, Manuel *o.f.m.* '82 (SFE) [4] Albuquerque, NM Holy Family Church.
Vierling, Ronald M. *m.f.c.* '92 (PH) Roslyn, PA St. John of the Cross Church.
Vierra, Theodore A. '60 (LA) [87] Los Angeles, CA St. Paul the Apostle Church.
Vieson, Paul F. *s.m.* '84 (CIN) [D] Dayton, OH The University of Dayton; [M] Dayton, OH Marianist Provincialate.
Viet Tran, Bac-Hai '84 (NO) Pearl River, LA SS. Peter and Paul Church.
Viet-Chau, Joachim *s.s.s.* '72 (CLV) [O] Cleveland, OH Congregation of the Blessed Sacrament Provincial House.
Vietes, Jesus *ss.cc.* '62 (SJN) [8] Guaynabo, PR Nuestra Senora de la Paz Church.
Vieweg, Robert R. '64 (CLV) Grafton, OH Immaculate Conception Church.
Vigeant, Wilfrid J. *s.j.* '46 (BO) [W] Weston, MA Campion Health Center, Inc.
Vigil, Joe '80 (SFE) [9] Albuquerque, NM Our Lady of Guadalupe Church.
Vigil, Michael A. '85 (GLP) On Duty Outside of Diocese.
Vigil, Paul E. '91 (LA) [4] Los Angeles, CA Ascension Church.
Vigilanti, John A. '72 (NY) Chappaqua, NY St. John and St. Mary Church; [GG] New York, NY University Apostolate.
Vigliotta, Thomas F. *o.f.m.* '85 (CHR) Anderson, SC St. Mary of the Angels Church.
Vigliotta, William J. *s.m.m.* '54 (RVC) [M] Eastport, NY Shrine of Our Lady of the Island.
Vignoe, Joseph M. '58 (BUR) Retired.
Vignola, Robert R. *c.m.* '50 (BRK) [V] Jamaica, NY St. Vincent's House.
Vignone, John J. '75 (CAM) Landisville, NJ Our Lady of Victories Church; Minotola, NJ St. Michael's Church.
Vigues, Gabriel '93 (MIA) Coral Springs, FL St. Andrew Church.
Vijayan, Joseph (NY) [149] Bronx, NY Holy Spirit Church.
Viladesau, Richard R. *s.t.d.* '69 (RVC) Saltaire, NY Our Lady Star of the Sea, Mission Chapel Church; Priests Released from Diocesan Assignment.
Vilakkunnel, Joseph *s.j.* '95 (CHI) [C] Chicago, IL Jesuit Community at Loyola University of Chicago.
Vilano, Anthony (SAT) Charlotte, TX St. Rose of Lima Church.
Vilaplana, Jose *s.j.* '63 (NY) [3] White Plains, NY St. Bernard Church.
Vilar, Juan Diaz '69 (NEW) [B] Jersey City, NJ Saint Peter's College.
Vileo, Stephen '87 (DET) New Baltimore, MI St. Mary Queen of Creation Church; [A] Detroit, MI Sacred Heart Major Seminary, Inc.
Vilie, Richard '79 (PMB) Hobe Sound, FL St. Christopher Church.
Villa, Aurelio *o.f.m.* '64 (SR) Boyes Hot Springs, CA St. Leo Church.
Villa, Eduardo '80 (BWN) [2] Pharr, TX St. Frances Xavier Cabrini Church.
Villa, James *o.f.m.* '69 (NY) [4] Mt. Vernon, NY Our Lady of Mount Carmel Church.
Villa, Joseph '97 (IND) Clinton, IN Sacred Heart Church; Universal, IN St. Joseph Church.
Villa, Leonard F. '86 (NY) [8] Yonkers, NY St. Eugene Church.
Villa, Nemorio '56 (LA) Retired.
Villabon, German *o.s.a.* '54 (RVC) [1] Rockville Centre, NY St. Agnes Church.
Villacis, Jose H. '81 (LA) Retired.
Villada, Luis E. '82 (SJN) [2] Canovanas, PR Resurreccion del Senior Church.
Villafan, Ignacio '99 (FRS) Porterville, CA St. Anne Church.
Villafranca, Eugenio *c.m.* '53 (SJN) [24] San Juan, PR Jesus Maestro Church.
Villagomez, Jose *o.f.m.cap.* '74 (AGN) Agat, GU Our Lady of Mount Carmel Church; [F] Agat, GU Capuchin Fraternity.
Villalba, Angel *o.m.i.* '39 (CC) [4] Kingsville, TX St. Martin Church.
Villalobos, Alberto '85 (LA) Pacoima, CA Guardian Angel Church; [D] Mission Hills, CA Alemany High School.
Villalobos, David '96 (SR) [3] Santa Rosa, CA St. Rose of Lima Church.
Villalobos, W.R. Suarez *s.j.* '79 (NY) [DD] New York, NY St. Ignatius Loyola Residence.
Villalon, Jose '89 (BWN) [C] Brownsville, TX Jail Ministry.

Villalon, Jose M. '89 (BWN) [4] Brownsville, TX Holy Family Church.
Villamide, Msgr. Aniceto '67 (BGP) [18] Bridgeport, CT St. Peter Church; [X] Bridgeport, CT Hispanic Social Ministries of Fairfield County, Inc.
Villani, Ralph A. '68 (NY) Mt. Kisco, NY St. Francis of Assisi Church.
Villani, Msgr. Rocco D. '61 (BRK) [81] Brooklyn, NY St. Mary Mother of Jesus Church.
Villano, Mark A. *c.s.p.* '88 (COL) [J] Columbus, OH Campus Ministry.
Villano, Richard R. '58 (STP) [26] Minneapolis, MN St. Helena Church.
Villanova, Richard A. '67 (NEW) Hillside, NJ St. Catherine of Siena Church.
Villanueva, Alfred '96 (ELP) Van Horn, TX Our Lady of Fatima Church.
Villanueva, Jose A. '63 (SAT) Rocksprings, TX Sacred Heart of Mary Church.
Villao, Roberto *s.v.d.* '93 (SB) [7] San Bernardino, CA St. Anthony Church.
Villar, Msgr. Demetrio '46 (RVC) Retired.
Villareal, Carlos Alberto '00 (BWN) [3] Brownsville, TX Church of the Good Shepherd.
Villaronga, Angel *o.f.m.* '51 (MIA) [H] Miami, FL Franciscan Fathers' Residence.
Villarreal, Louis J. *o.m.i.* '65 (BEA) Anahuac, TX Our Lady of Light Church; Mont Belvieu, (1991) Holy Trinity Church.
Villarreal, Manuel '78 (GAL) [S] Dickinson, TX Christian Renewal Center.
Villarreal, Ricardo A. '98 (YAK) Wenatchee, WA St. Joseph's Church.
Villarroya, Ernesto '63 (DAL) [1] Garland, TX Good Shepherd Church.
Villarroya, Pedro '59 (LA) [Q] Montebello, CA Vincentian Fathers & Brothers.
Villarruel, Salvador M. *m.s.c.* '79 (LA) Cudahy, CA Sagrado Corazon y Santa Maria de Guadalupe Church.
Villarubia, Roger '99 (HT) [1] Houma, LA Cathedral of St. Francis De Sales.
Villaruel, Alvin '94 (SR) [3] Santa Rosa, CA St. Rose of Lima Church.
Villaruel, Alvin M. '94 (SR) [B] Santa Rosa, CA Cardinal Newman High School.
Villaverde, Tirso S. '96 (CHI) Niles, IL St. Isaac Jogues Church.
Villegas, Efraim *o.s.b.* '88 (BIS) [A] Richardton, ND Assumption Abbey.
Villegas, Efraim *o.s.b.* '88 (FgM) American - Cassinese Congregation Foreign Missions.
Villegas, Gonzalo J. '92 (TUC) Casa Grande, AZ St. Anthony of Padua Church.
Villegas, Hernando '57 (MIA) Coral Gables, FL Little Flower Church; Retired.
Villegas, Jorge C. '66 (E) [30] Erie, PA St. Stephen Church.
Villegas, Juan C. *s.j.* '75 (FgM) Provinces.
Villegas, Rafael '90 (ORL) Kissimmee, FL Holy Redeemer Church.
Villegas, Robert *c.s.c.* '63 (LSC) Chamberino, NM San Luis Rey Church.
Villegas, Samuel C. '56 (LA) Huntington Park, CA St. Matthias Church; Retired.
Villemaire, Arthur '51 (SP) Retired.
Villerot, Henry E. '41 (DET) Retired.
Villerot, Msgr. Thomas H. '43 (DET) Royal Oak, MI St. Mary Church; Retired.
Vima, Amalor '71 (TLS) McAlester, OK St. John Church.
Vima, Amalorpavam '71 (TLS) Krebs, OK St. Joseph's Church.
Vincent, Msgr. Amos J. '49 (LKC) Retired.
Vincent, David P. '64 (CIN) [3] Springfield, OH St. Mary Church.
Vincent, John *o.s.c.* '58 (PHX) [G] Phoenix, AZ Crosier Community of Phoenix (Canons Regular of the Order of the Holy Cross).
Vincent, John F. '54 (WIN) Retired.
Vincent, Michael A. *s.j.* '82 (CLV) [D] Cleveland, OH St. Ignatius High School.
Vincent, Msgr. Robert G. '57 (NO) La Place, LA St. Joan of Arc Church.
Vincenzo, Dennis J. '91 (HRT) [3] Manchester, CT St. Bridget's Church.
Vinci, Msgr. Guy S. '59 (NY) Harrison, NY St. Gregory the Great Church.
Vinci, Terzo *s.a.c.* '58 (NY) [13] Yonkers, NY Our Lady of Mt. Carmel Church.
Vincke, Gerald '99 (LAN) [L] De Witt, MI St. Francis Retreat Center.
Vincke, Gerald L. '99 (LAN) [4] Ann Arbor, MI St. Thomas the Apostle Church.
Vincze, Michael A. '40 (MET) Retired.
Vincze, Michael M. '40 (MET) Woodbridge, NJ Our Lady of Mount Carmel Church.
Vinsko, John J. *m.m.* '62 (SJ) [L] Los Altos, CA Maryknoll.
Vinslauski, Robert B. '71 (SFS) Madison, SD St. Thomas Aquinas Church.
Viola, William L. (BAL) Odenton, MD St. Joseph Church.
Violette, Lawrence M. '93 (ARL) Woodbridge, VA Our Lady of Angels Church.
Violette, Tex '75 (HT) On Leave.
Virella, Miguel A. *s.v.d.* '96 (TR) Freehold, NJ St. Rose of Lima Church.
Virgen, Javier G. '93 (SLC) [4] Midvale, UT St. Therese of the Child Jesus Church.
Virginia, Stephen G. '79 (COL) [35] Columbus, OH Our Lady of Victory Church.
Virnig, Laurn '63 (SCL) Royalton, MN Holy Trinity Church.
Virtue, William D. '75 (BAL) [A] Emmitsburg, MD Mount St. Mary's Seminary.
Virtue, William D. '75 (PEO) On Duty Outside the Diocese.
Virus, Keith M. '92 (GRY) Schererville, IN St. Michael Church.
Visbisky, Richard W. '62 (BO) Brockton, MA Good Samaritan Medical Center; [Q] Brockton, MA Good Samaritan Medical Center.
Viscardi, Christopher J. *s.j.* '76 (MOB) [A] Mobile, AL Spring Hill College.
Viscardi, Robert *i.m.c.* '63 (SB) [7] Riverside, CA St. Francis de Sales Church.
Visconti, Luciano M. *c.r.s.p.* '42 (BUF) [B] Youngstown, NY St. Anthony M. Zaccaria Seminary.
Visich, Eduard C. '53 (BRK) Absent on Leave.
Visperas, Joseph '86 (LA) Palmdale, CA St. Mary Church.
Vistal, Felix, Jr. '86 (DAL) Bonham, TX St. Elizabeth Church; Bonham, TX Veterans Administration Hospital.
Vita, Mariano L. '42 (CHI) Bellwood, IL St. Simeon Church; Retired.
Vitacolonna, Xavier *c.p.* (NEW) [N] Union City, NJ Congregation of the Passion (Passionists)-St. Michael's Residence.
Vitaglione, Robert '76 (BRK) [70] Brooklyn, NY St. Joseph's Church.
Vitale, Louis *o.f.m.* (SFR) San Francisco, CA St. Francis Hospital.
Vitale, Louis *o.f.m.* '63 (SFR) [8] San Francisco, CA St. Boniface Church.
Vitali, James V. *o.s.a.* '81 (VEN) Golden Gate, FL St. Elizabeth Seton Church.
Vitali, John *c.r.s.* '71 (MAN) [H] Allenstown, NH Pine Haven Boys Center.
Vitali, Theodore *c.p.* '69 (MET) [H] South River, NJ Passionist Provincial Office.
Vitaliano, Dominic (PEO) On Duty Outside the Diocese.
Vitela, Francisco '68 (LA) El Monte, CA Our Lady of Guadalupe Church.
Vithanage, Denzil *s.s.s.* (TYL) Longview, TX St. Mary Church.
Vitillo, Robert J. '72 (PAT) On Duty Outside the Diocese.
Vitka, Stephen G. '41 (HRT) Retired.
Vito, Alfred J. '84 (SCR) Canadensis, PA St. Bernadette Church.
Vitro, Thomas J. '66 (CHI) Other Assignments.
Vitte, Jules '49 (NO) Retired.
Vittengl, Donald '56 (ALB) Cherry Valley, NY St. Thomas the Apostle Church.
Vittengl, Donald J. *m.m.* '56 (FgM) Maryknoll Foreign Missions.
Vittengl, Donald J. *m.m.* '56 (NY) [DD] Maryknoll, NY Maryknoll Fathers and Brothers.
Vitturino, Saverio T. '67 (WDC) Benedict, MD St. Francis de Sales Church.
Vitucci, James '72 (MIA) Pembroke Pines, FL St. Maximilian Kolbe Church.
Vituj, George L. '48 (CLV) [M] Cleveland, OH Sts. Mary and Joseph Home for the Aged.
Vitus, Frank '75 (JOL) Wilmington, IL St. Rose Church.
Viveiros, Joseph F. '74 (FR) [1] Swansea, MA St. Dominic's Church.
Vivero, David, Jr. '90 (ORL) Winter Park, FL St. Margaret Mary Church.
Viviano, Benedict T. *o.p.* '66 (CHI) [N] Chicago, IL Dominicans (Provincial Office); [N] Chicago, IL Dominicans (Provincial Office).
Viviano, Charles '89 (ORL) Titusville, FL St. Teresa Church.
Viviano, Nino '64 (ALX) On Duty Outside the Diocese.
Vivona, Anthony '53 (BRK) Retired.
Vivona, Francis '69 (VNN) Las Vegas, NV Our Lady of Wisdom Italo-Greek Church.
Vivona, Francis M. '69 (LAV) [8] Las Vegas, NV St. Elizabeth Ann Seton Church.
Vizcaino, Mario B. *sch.p.* '60 (MIA) [K] Miami, FL Southeast Pastoral Institute; [K] Miami, FL Southeast Regional Office for Hispanic Ministry, Inc.; [L] Miami, FL SEPI Evangelization and Education Foundation, Inc.
Vizcaino, Mario B. *sch.p.* '60 (PH) [AA] Devon, PA Piarist Fathers (Order of the Pious Schools).
Vizcaino, Mario B. *sch.p.* '60 (WDC) [B] Washington, DC Queen of Pious Schools House of Studies-Piarist Fathers.
Vizcarra, Angel '46 (DAL) [K] Irving, TX Dominican Priory of St. Albert the Great.
Vizzard, Msgr. James J. '48 (PH) Retired.
Vjecha, Michael J. *s.j.* '87 (STP) [N] Minneapolis, MN La Storta Jesuit Community.
Vlaenderen, Leonard Van (MIL) [65] Milwaukee, WI Our Lady, Queen of Peace Church.
Vlasz, Melvyn J. '63 (RCK) Retired.
Vlaun, James C. '79 (RVC) [C] West Islip, NY St. John the Baptist.
Vlaun, James C. '88 (RVC) West Islip, NY Our Lady of Lourdes Church.
Vliet, Charles Van *f.s.s.p.* '96 (SCR) [M] Elmhurst, PA Priestly Fraternity of St. Peter (F.S.S.P.), North American District Headquarters.
Vo, Peter De Ta *s.v.d.* '87 (CHI) [N] Chicago, IL Divine Word Theologate.
Vo, Peter Phong '88 (NEW) On Duty Outside the Archdiocese.
Vo., John K. '86 (LA) El Monte, CA Nativity Church.
Vodoklys, Edward J. *s.j.* '91 (WOR) [N] Worcester, MA Jesuits of Holy Cross College, Inc.
Voegele, Fridolin *o.f.m.* '58 (CIN) [M] Cincinnati, OH St. John the Baptist Friary.
Voelker, David A. '74 (BEL) Military Chaplains.
Voelker, David A. '74 (RC) Ellsworth, SD Ellsworth AFB.
Voelker, Harold H. '54 (STL) Gardenville, MO St. George Church.
Voelker, James A. '69 (BEL) [3] East St. Louis, IL St. Joseph Church; [5] East St. Louis, IL St. Philip Church.
Voelker, Karl *s.j.* '72 (WIN) [1] Mankato, MN SS. Peter and Paul's Church.
Voelker, Lawrence '66 (IND) [5] Indianapolis, IN Holy Cross Church; [31] Indianapolis, IN St. Patrick Church; Indianapolis, IN Indiana Women's Prison.
Voelker, Peter H. *c.ss.r.* '61 (GAL) [34] Houston, TX Holy Ghost Church.
Voellmecke, Francis W. '59 (CIN) [B] Cincinnati, OH Mt. St. Mary's Seminary of the West.
Vogan, Howard L. '69 (DET) [4] Livonia, MI St. Genevieve Church.
Vogan, Robert C. '70 (PH) Aston, PA St. Joseph Church.
Vogel, Arthur '57 (SCL) Retired.
Vogel, Charles P. '43 (BRK) [137] Brooklyn, NY St. Sylvester Church; Retired.
Vogel, F. Philip *s.d.s.* '69 (BAL) Baltimore, MD Spring Grove Center Hospital.
Vogel, F. Philip *s.d.s.* '69 (WDC) [B] Silver Spring, MD Salvatorian Community.
Vogel, Gerhard *s.v.d.* '65 (TR) Asbury Park, NJ St. Peter Claver Church.
Vogel, J. Carl '50 (DAL) McKinney, TX St. Michael Church.
Vogel, John J. '86 (LA) Lancaster, CA Sacred Heart Church.
Vogel, Joseph '87 (SFS) [7] Sioux Falls, SD St. Michael Church.
Vogel, Marcel J. '89 (GF) Chinook, MT St. Gabriel's Church; Special Assignment.
Vogel, Walter J. '58 (MIL) Greendale, WI St. Alphonsus Church.
Vogel, Walter P. *o.s.a.* '63 (SD) San Diego, CA R.J. Donovan Correctional Facility; [B] San Diego, CA Austin House; [H] San Diego, CA Augustinian Community.
Vogel, William '49 (DOD) Kinsley, KS St. Nicholas Church; Offerle, KS St. Joseph Church.
Vogel, William *s.j.* '75 (YAK) [4] Yakima, WA St. Joseph's Church.
Vogelpohl, Daniel J. '75 (COV) Fort Mitchell, KY Blessed Sacrament Church.
Vogelpohl, Msgr. Henry J. '39 (CIN) Retired.
Vogelpohl, Herbert '39 (LR) [A] Subiaco, AR Subiaco Monastery.
Vogelsang, Clifford R. '63 (IND) Jeffersonville, IN St. Augustine Church.
Vogl, John C. '00 (YAK) Grandview, WA Blessed Sacrament Church.
Vogl, Msgr. Robert R. '47 (DUB) Retired; [C] Dubuque, IA Loras College; [I] Dubuque, IA Marian Hall Infirmary.
Vogler, Jean '70 (EVN) [2] Evansville, IN Holy Trinity Church.
Voglio, John *s.d.b.* '87 (NY) [136] Bronx, NY St. Clare of Assisi Church.
Vogrin, Joseph '44 (SCL) Retired.
Vogt, Dick *s.j.* (STL) Ferguson, MO Our Lady of Guadalupe Church.
Vogt, Emmerich *o.p.* '78 (OAK) [N] Oakland, CA Dominican Order, Siena House.
Vogt, Emmerich W. *o.p.* '78 (P) [18] Portland, OR Holy Rosary Parish & Dominican Priory Church.
Vogt, Eric T. *o.s.b.* '79 (ALT) Summerhill, PA St. John Church.
Vogt, Francis H. '38 (ROC) Palmyra, NY St. Anne Church; Canandaigua, NY Veteran's Hospital; Retired.

Vogt, John '62 (PHX) Prescott, AZ Sacred Heart Church; Wickenburg, AZ St. Anthony of Padua Church.
Vogt, Otto J. '50 (ROC) [34] Rochester, NY Our Lady of Lourdes Church; Retired.
Vogt, Richard J. *s.j.* '63 (STL) [35] St. Louis, MO St. Francis Xavier Church; [P] St. Louis, MO Jesuit Community Corporation at St. Louis University - Jesuit Hall.
Vogt, Robert H. *s.j.* '61 (NY) [DD] New York, NY Murray-Weigel Hall.
Vogt, Robert W. '62 (BUF) Retired.
Vogt, William '56 (FRS) Faculties Only.
Vogt, William E. '46 (GRY) Retired.
Vohsing, William J. '78 (ORG) Anaheim, CA San Antonio Church.
Voigt, Richard '78 (LAR) [17] Laredo, TX St. Patrick Church.
Voiland, Msgr. George T. '50 (BRK) [203] Queens, NY Most Precious Blood Church; Retired.
Voiss, James K. *s.j.* '88 (STL) [C] St. Louis, MO Saint Louis University; [P] St. Louis, MO Jesuit Community Corporation at St. Louis University - Jesuit Hall.
Voity, Maurice '79 (SAN) [1] San Angelo, TX Cathedral of the Sacred Heart.
Vojtek, John '76 (PIT) Etna, PA All Saints Church.
Vojtik, James (MIL) [Y] Kenosha, WI St. Mark Latin American Center.
Vojtik, James P. '62 (MIL) [6] Kenosha, WI St. Mark Church.
Volertas, Vytautas '93 (BRK) [247] Queens, NY Transfiguration Church.
Volino, Michael J. '92 (ROC) [41] Rochester, NY St. Lawrence Church.
Volk, Msgr. Marvin C. '74 (BEL) [2] Belleville, IL Blessed Sacrament Church.
Volk, Michael '92 (MRY) Gonzales, CA St. Theodore Church.
Volk, Norman *o.m.i.* '68 (SUP) [G] River Falls, WI St. Thomas More Newman Center.
Volkert, James T. '90 (MIL) Brighton, WI St. Francis Xavier Church; Paris, WI St. John the Baptist Church.
Volkmer, Michael *c.pp.s.* '68 (KC) [3] St. Joseph, MO St. Francis Xavier Church.
Voll, Walter Urban *o.p.* '49 (PRO) [P] Providence, RI St. Thomas Aquinas Priory at Providence College.
Vollenweider, Roy W. *s.j.* '47 (NO) [P] New Orleans, LA Ignatius Residence.
Vollkommer, Andrew J. '86 (CHR) Chapin, SC Our Lady of the Lake Church.
Vollmer, Anthony *c.pp.s.* '53 (CIN) [B] Carthagena, OH St. Charles.
Vollmer, Caron *o.f.m.* '47 (GLP) Lukachukai, AZ St. Isabel Church; [F] Gallup, NM Southwest Indian Foundation.
Vollmer, Gary L. '77 (LAV) [3] Las Vegas, NV Holy Family Church.
Vollmer, Gary L. '77 (STL) On Duty Outside the Archdiocese.
Vollmer, Gene '78 (RVC) Seaford, NY St. James Church.
Vollmer, Raymond A. '40 (PIT) Retired.
Vollmer, William C. '58 (COS) Retired.
Vollor, John '79 (JKS) West Point, MS Immaculate Conception Church.
Vollor, William '63 (BLX) Hattiesburg, MS Holy Rosary Church.
Volmi, Dennis G. '75 (WIL) Military Chaplains.
Volpe, Alphonse M. '83 (LKC) Cameron, LA Our Lady Star of the Sea Church.
Volpert, Robert C. '61 (L) On Special Assignment.
Volskis, Aloyzas '85 (DET) [3] Southfield, MI Divine Providence Church.
Voltaggio, Fred '71 (CAM) Berlin, NJ Our Lady of Mt. Carmel Church.
Volungis, Alphonse A. '45 (WOR) [15] Worcester, MA Our Lady of Vilna Church.
Volz, Anthony '85 (IND) [29] Indianapolis, IN St. Michael the Archangel Church.
Volz, Edward *o.s.p.p.e.* '88 (GBG) Cadogan, PA St. Lawrence Church; [H] Kittanning, PA Pauline Fathers Monastery.
Volz, Jerry '92 (KCK) [J] Emporia, KS Didde Catholic Campus Center, Emporia State University.
Vomund, Jeffrey G. (STL) [D] St. Louis, MO Paul VI Institute of Catechetical and Pastoral Studies.
Vomund, Jeffrey G. '97 (STL) [A] St. Louis, MO Kenrick-Glennon Seminary.
Von Ah, Richard J. (DAV) Retired.
Von Ah, Richard J. '58 (DAV) [L] Davenport, IA Kahl Home for the Aged and Infirm.
Von Arx, Jeffrey *s.j.* (NY) [C] Bronx, NY Fordham University.
von Arx, Jeffrey P. *s.j.* '81 (NY) [DD] New York, NY Jesuit Community at Fordham University.
von Behren, Thomas R. *c.s.v.* '83 (CHI) [D] Arlington Heights, IL St. Viator High School; [N] Arlington Heights, IL Viatorian Province Center-Clerics of St. Viator.
von Drehle, James '81 (DET) [H] Pontiac, MI St. Joseph Mercy - Oakland.
von Duerbeck, Julian *o.s.b.* '76 (JOL) [A] Lisle, IL Benedictine University; [J] Lisle, IL St. Procopius Abbey.
Von Essen, Pacificus *s.a.* '53 (NY) [DD] Garrison, NY Franciscan Friars of the Atonement, Minister General Office.
Von Essen, Peter *o.f.m.cap.* '56 (FgM) Capuchin Foreign Missions.
Von Euw, Vincent P. '66 (BO) [4] Boston, MA St. Ambrose Church.
von Fauer, Stephen C. '41 (BUR) Retired.
von Fauer, Stephen C. '41 (STF) [E] West Burke, VT Mary Theotokos Centre.
Von Hagel, Davin W. *o.f.m.* '47 (GLP) Navajo, NM St. Berard Church.
Von Kaenel, George E. *s.j.* '58 (CHI) [C] Chicago, IL Jesuit Community at Loyola University of Chicago; [N] Chicago, IL Chicago Province of the Society of Jesus-Provincial Office; [X] Chicago, IL Jesuit International Missions, Inc.
Von Kaenel, George E. *s.j.* '58 (FgM) Provinces.
Von Kerssenbrock, Joachim *s.j.* '59 (NY) [HH] Bronx, NY American St. Boniface Society, Incorporated.
Von Kobs, Allan G. *o.f.m.* '82 (NY) [35] New York, NY St. Francis of Assisi Church.
Von Kobs, Allan G. *o.f.m.* '82 (PAT) [P] Paterson, NJ St. Anthony's Guild.
Von Lehmen, Jeffrey D. '85 (COV) Taylor Mill, KY St. Patrick Church; [C] Covington, KY Villa Madonna High School.
von Nell, Boniface *o.s.b.* '91 (WDC) [M] Washington, DC St. Anselm's Abbey.
Von Son, Msgr. Henry A. '49 (LA) Retired.
von Tobel, James E. *s.j.* (DET) [K] Detroit, MI Jesuit Provincial Office-Detroit Province of the Society of Jesus.
Von Tobel, James E. *s.j.* '67 (CLV) University Heights, OH Gesu Church.
Vona, Michael S. '68 (TR) Farmingdale, NJ St. Catherine of Siena Church.
Vonderhaar, Eugene F. '59 (CIN) Russia, OH St. Remy Church.
Vonderhaar, Ralph E. *s.j.* '57 (STL) [P] St. Louis, MO Hallahan House.
VonderHaar, Msgr. Roland '48 (LSC) Retired.
Vondras, John J. '85 (NY) [2] Newburgh, NY St. Francis of Assisi Church.
Vonnahmen, Robert J. '56 (BEL) Retired.
Voor, Joseph H. '50 (L) [17] Louisville, KY St. Brigid Church; [40] Louisville, KY St. James Church; Louisville, KY Vencor Hospital; Retired.
Voorhes, Msgr. Fred R. '71 (BUF) [P] Williamsville, NY Sisters of St. Francis of the Third Order Regular, St. Mary of the Angels.
Voorhies, Bennett J. '83 (LAF) On Duty Outside the Diocese.
Voorhies, Bennett J. '83 (SFE) Pecos, NM St. Anthony Church.
Voorhies, Louis '67 (ALX) Retired.
Voorhies, Thomas P. '90 (LAF) Delcambre, LA Our Lady of the Lake Church; Delcambre, LA Saint Martin de Porres Church.
Voors, David '81 (FTW) [13] Fort Wayne, IN Our Lady of Good Hope Church.
Vorderlandwehr, Adrian *o.s.b.* '67 (OKL) Prague, OK St. Wenceslaus, National Shrine of the Infant Jesus of Prague Church.
Voris, Francis *o.f.m.cap.* '86 (SAG) Sanford, MI St. Agnes Church; [G] Saginaw, MI Queen of Angels Friary and Retreat House.
Vorisek, Rudolph T. *c.s.p.* '56 (NY) [104] New York, NY St. Paul the Apostle Church; [DD] Jamaica Estates, NY Paulist Fathers Generalate.
Vorwald, Aloysius J. '64 (DUB) Independence, IA St. John Evangelist Church; Rowley, IA All Saints Church.
Vorwek, James *s.v.d.* '69 (FgM) Society of the Divine Word Foreign Missions.
Vorwoldt, James F. *s.j.* '71 (CHI) [D] Chicago, IL St. Ignatius Jesuit Community.
Vorwoldt, James S. *s.j.* '70 (CHI) [D] Chicago, IL St. Ignatius College Prep.
Vos, Jude '96 (FAR) Special Assignment.
Vos, Thomas *o.f.m.* '61 (KNX) Mountain City, TN St. Anthony of Padua Catholic Church; [F] Mountain City, TN Franciscan Friars.
Vos, William '64 (SCL) Mora, MN St. Mary's Church; Ogilvie, MN St. Kathryn's Church.
Vosen, Gerald P. '61 (MAD) Baraboo, WI St. Joseph Church.
Vosko, Richard '69 (ALB) Special Assignment.
Voss, Msgr. Bernard L. '66 (BEL) [5] Belleville, IL St. Henry Church; [J] Belleville, IL Serra Club of St. Clair County.
Voss, Dennis F. '64 (BEL) Lively Grove, IL St. Anthony Church; St. Libory, IL St. Liborius Church.
Voss, Donald J. '93 (PBR) Clarence, PA St. Mary's Church; Hawk Run, PA St. John the Baptist Church.
Voss, Marcus *o.s.b.* (BIR) [I] Cullman, AL St. Bernard Foundation.
Voss, Marcus J. *o.s.b.* '71 (BIR) [B] Cullman, AL St. Bernard Preparatory School Educational Foundation; [E] Cullman, AL St. Bernard Abbey.
Voss, Robert '70 (PHX) [4] Scottsdale, AZ St. Bernard of Clairvaux Church.
Voss, Robert D. *s.j.* '72 (FgM) Provinces.
Vossler, Brian E. '91 (E) Galeton, PA St. Bibiana Church.
Vota, Paul *m.j.* '85 (PCE) On Duty Outside the Diocese.
Votraw, Thomas G. '60 (OG) Absent on Sick Leave.
Votraw, Wilbur J. '55 (SY) [24] Syracuse, NY St. Vincent de Paul Church; Syracuse, NY Loretto Geriatric Center.
Votraw, William J. '55 (SY) Special Assignment.
Votruba, George L. '54 (SUP) Retired.
Votto, Salvano P. *s.j.* '73 (SJ) [L] Los Gatos, CA Sacred Heart Jesuit Center.
Vouk, William, III '86 (SCL) St. Anthony, MN St. Anthony's Church; St. Francis, MN St. Francis of Assisi Church.
Vowells, John J. *s.j.* '90 (DEN) [M] Denver, CO Regis Jesuit Community (The Jesuits at Regis University); [P] Denver, CO Regis University (Denver).
Vowels, G. Timothy '77 (STL) Hazelwood, MO St. Martin de Porres Church.
Voyt, Stephen A. '85 (PT) Military Chaplains.
Voytek, John *o.f.m.conv.* '82 (HBG) [5] Shamokin, PA Mother Cabrini Church.
Voytek, Leonard E. '74 (ALT) [1] Windber, PA St. John Cantius Church; [4] Windber, PA St. Mary's Church.
Voytko, Geo. '49 (STU) Retired.
Vrabel, George A. '87 (CLV) North Olmsted, OH St. Richard Church.
Vrabely, George M. '53 (GRY) La Porte, IN St. Peter Church.
Vrablic, Cyril *o.s.b.* '51 (IND) [J] St. Meinrad, IN St. Meinrad Archabbey.
Vrana, Francis R. '53 (STP) Retired.
Vrana, John G. '67 (CLV) Concord Twp., OH St. Gabriel Church.
Vrana, John P. '56 (OKL) Retired.
Vrana, Joseph L. '65 (VIC) Wharton, TX Holy Family Church.
Vrazel, Edward *o.m.i.* '58 (LAR) [7] Laredo, TX Our Lady of Guadalupe Church.
Vrba, James J. '77 (DAV) [2] Iowa City, IA St. Patrick's Church.
Vreteau, Robert *o.m.i.* '46 (SAT) [K] San Antonio, TX Oblate Madonna Residence.
Vu, An '95 (WDC) Upper Marlboro, MD Saint Mary of the Assumption Church.
Vu, Hoat Dinh '60 (BAL) Retired.
Vu, Ignatius '94 (NY) [5] White Plains, NY Our Lady of Sorrows Church.
Vu, John Baptist Han '65 (NO) [2] Marrero, LA St. Agnes Le Thi Thanh Church.
Vu, John Francis *s.j.* '97 (LA) [F] Los Angeles, CA Loyola High School of Los Angeles.
Vu, Joseph (BRK) [U] Brooklyn, NY Catholic Migration & Refugee Office, Catholic Migration Services, Inc.
Vu, Joseph '90 (BRK) [10] Brooklyn, NY St. Anselm's Church.
Vu, Joseph Dao *s.v.d.* '88 (IND) [34] Indianapolis, IN St. Rita Church.
Vu, Joseph Duc (DET) Detroit, MI Veterans Administration Hospital.
Vu, Lieu '91 (SJ) [19] San Jose, CA St. Patrick Church.
Vu, Louis Lam '85 (LAF) Youngsville, LA St. Anne Church.
Vu, Minh '94 (STP) Lino Lakes, MN St. Joseph Church.
Vu, Peter '97 (GR) Portland, MI St. Patrick's Church.
Vu, Peter Duc '96 (ATL) [2] Atlanta, GA Holy Cross Church.
Vu, Than N. '84 (BR) [6] Baton Rouge, LA Christ the King Church; [K] Baton Rouge, LA Christ the King Parish and Catholic Student Center.
Vu, Trung '94 (BO) [W] Cambridge, MA Weston Jesuit Community.
Vu Dinh Huyen, Leo M. *c.m.c.* '94 (SB) [E] Corona, CA Congregation of the Mother Coredemptrix.
Vu Kim Ngan, Joseph M. *c.m.c.* (SPC) [E] Carthage, MO Congregation of the Mother Co-Redemptrix, United States Assumption Province.
Vu Thanh Thien, Cyril M. *c.m.c.* (SPC) [E] Carthage, MO Congregation of the Mother Co-Redemptrix, United States Assumption Province.
Vu Van Vanh, Francis M. *c.m.c.* (SPC) [E] Carthage, MO Congregation of the Mother Co-Redemptrix, United States Assumption Province.
Vucinovich, Albert P. '64 (SFR) Burlingame, CA St. Catherine of Siena Church.
Vuelvas-Arias, David '75 (ORG) Westminster, CA Blessed Sacrament Church.
Vujs, Joseph E. '57 (HRT) [3] Enfield, CT St. Bernard's Church.
Vujs, Robert W. *m.m.* '61 (FgM) Maryknoll Foreign Missions.
Vuketich, Donald F. *t.o.r.* '53 (PH) [AA] Fairless Hills, PA St. Anthony Friary.

Vuoso, Pasquale *c.r.i.c.* '87 (LA) Santa Paula, CA St. Sebastian Church; Santa Paula, CA Our Lady of Guadalupe Church; [Q] Los Angeles, CA Canons Regular of the Immaculate Conception.
Vuturo, Paul '73 (MIA) Miramar, FL St. Bartholomew Church.
Vye, Francis W. *s.j.* '65 (BO) [W] Chestnut Hill, MA The Jesuit Community at Boston College.
Vytautas, Msgr. Balciunas '33 (NOR) Retired.
Vyverman, Mark J. '93 (KAL) [1] Kalamazoo, MI St. Augustine Church.

W

Wach, Anthony J. *s.j.* '72 (FgM) Provinces.
Wach, Anthony J. *s.j.* '72 (MIL) [P] Milwaukee, WI Jesuit Provincial Office, Wisconsin Province.
Wachala, John M. '79 (CLV) [14] Cleveland, OH St. Casimir Church.
Wachdorf, Paul H. '75 (CHI) [A] Mundelein, IL University of St. Mary of the Lake-Mundelein Seminary.
Wachowiak, Duane A. '98 (GAY) Acme, MI Christ the King Church.
Wachter, Robert B. '76 (WCH) [4] Wichita, KS Christ the King Church.
Wack, William A. *c.s.c.* '94 (FTW) [A] Notre Dame, IN Moreau Seminary; [B] Notre Dame, IN University of Notre Dame Du Lac; [J] Notre Dame, IN Holy Cross Community, Corby Hall, University of Notre Dame.
Wackerman, John F. '98 (PH) Quakertown, PA St. Isidore Church.
Waclawik, Leszek '84 (LAR) [2] Laredo, TX Blessed Sacrament Church.
Waclawski, Msgr. Joseph P. '42 (BUF) Retired.
Waczula, Michael F. '66 (GBG) On Duty Outside the Diocese.
Wadas, Msgr. Ignatius C. (ALT) Retired.
Wadas, Joseph S. '91 (MOB) Enterprise, AL St. John Church.
Wadas, Raymond J. '72 (WDC) Hillcrest Heights, MD Holy Family Church.
Waddell, Chrysogonus *o.c.s.o.* '58 (L) [L] Trappist, KY Abbey of Our Lady of Gethsemani, of the Order of Cistercians of the Strict Observance.
Waddill, Dale T. '64 (P) [28] Portland, OR St. Peter Church.
Wade, Ed '72 (GAL) [U] Houston, TX Catholic Charismatic Center.
Wade, Ed '92 (GAL) [72] Houston, TX Queen of Peace Church.
Wade, Edward C. '72 (CAM) On Duty Outside the Diocese.
Wade, Gerald T. *s.j.* '68 (SJ) [D] San Jose, CA Bellarmine College Preparatory.
Wade, Hubert, Jr. '77 (SAN) Ballinger, TX St. Mary Star of the Sea Church.
Wade, Jarrell D. *s.j.* '65 (FgM) Provinces.
Wade, John '56 (TLS) [E] Tulsa, OK St. John Medical Center, Inc.
Wadell, John '40 (SB) Retired.
Wadell, Paul *c.p.* '78 (CHI) [N] Chicago, IL Passionist Provincial Office.
Wadowicz, Msgr. Joseph M. '45 (STU) Retired.
Wadsworth, Msgr. James '41 (DM) Retired.
Waechter, Ernest *o.f.m.conv.* '59 (TOL) Carey, OH Our Lady of Consolation, Basilica-National Church; Salem Twp., OH St. Joseph Church.
Wafzig, James E. '55 (L) [9] Louisville, KY St. Athanasius Church; Louisville, KY University Hospital; Retired; [O] Louisville, KY Catholic Charismatic Renewal.
Wagay, Gideon '93 (NY) [185] Bronx, NY St. Raymond Church.
Wagay, Gideon G. '94 (NY) [148] Bronx, NY Holy Rosary Church.
Wagener, John M. '61 (NU) Military Chaplains.
Wagenhoffer, Josef A. '65 (CAM) Somers Point, NJ St. Joseph's Church.
Wager, Terence J. *o.s.b.* '64 (SEA) Yelm, WA St. Columban Church.
Waggenor, William L. '52 (HEL) Retired.
Wagman, Msgr. Cletus H. '42 (HBG) [5] Lancaster, PA St. Joseph Church.
Wagman, Stephen *o.s.b.* '48 (SCL) [I] Collegeville, MN St. John's Abbey, of the Order of St. Benedict.
Wagner, Alan *s.d.s.* '76 (TUC) Vail, AZ Shrine of St. Rita in the Desert Church.
Wagner, Alfred S. '48 (STP) Retired.
Wagner, Bernard *o.f.m.cap.* '63 (FgM) Capuchin Foreign Missions.
Wagner, Cyril *o.f.m.* '67 (MEM) [L] Memphis, TN Charismatic Prayer Groups.
Wagner, Dennis A. '76 (GR) On Special Assignment.
Wagner, Donald '87 (SCL) St. Wendel, MN St. Columbkille's Church; Special Assignment.
Wagner, Ed *o.ss.t.* (BAL) Poplar Springs, MD St. Michael Church.
Wagner, Edward *o.ss.t.* '80 (BAL) [S] Baltimore, MD Holy Trinity Monastery.
Wagner, Eugene L. '40 (BUF) Olcott, NY St. Charles Borromeo Church; Retired.
Wagner, Frank *o.m.i.* '57 (SD) [1] Chula Vista, CA Most Precious Blood Church.
Wagner, Greta '91 (TOL) [H] Lima, OH St. Rita's Medical Center.
Wagner, Msgr. Harold '55 (BUF) [F] Buffalo, NY Cantalician Center for Learning, Inc.
Wagner, Jerome A. '72 (MIL) [1] Fond du Lac, WI Holy Family Church.
Wagner, John '49 (SAT) Retired.
Wagner, John '64 (SB) Temecula, CA St. Catherine Church.
Wagner, John A. '49 (SAT) [57] San Antonio, TX St. Matthew's Church.
Wagner, John C. '73 (MIL) On Leave.
Wagner, John J., III '87 (RIC) [4] Norfolk, VA Sacred Heart Church.
Wagner, John P. '62 (SY) Baldwinsville, NY St. Elizabeth Ann Seton Church.
Wagner, Joseph '65 (SFS) Military Chaplains.
Wagner, Joseph F. '44 (CLV) [46] Cleveland, OH St. Mark Church; Brunswick, OH St. Colette Church; Retired.
Wagner, Joseph F. *s.j.* '98 (CHI) [N] Chicago, IL Chicago Province of the Society of Jesus-Provincial Office.
Wagner, Joseph F. *s.j.* '98 (OAK) [N] Berkeley, CA Jesuit Community at Jesuit School of Theology at Berkeley.
Wagner, Lawrence *s.v.d.* '44 (FgM) Society of the Divine Word Foreign Missions.
Wagner, Lawrence L. *o.s.b.* '54 (BIS) Lefor, ND St. Elizabeth Church; Lefor, ND St. Elizabeth Church.
Wagner, Leon R. '49 (CHI) Riverside, IL St. Mary Church; Retired.
Wagner, Mark '88 (STO) Ripon, CA St. Patrick Church.
Wagner, Philip *o.m.i.* '98 (MIA) Opa Locka, FL St. Monica Church.
Wagner, Raymond J. '52 (LC) Retired; [H] La Crosse, WI Holy Cross (Seminary) Diocesan Center.
Wagner, Richard '61 (DM) [8] Des Moines, IA Basilica of Saint John.
Wagner, Richard F. *s.s.j.* '59 (LAF) Breaux Bridge, LA St. Francis of Assisi Church.
Wagner, Robert *s.d.s.* '46 (BIR) [3] Huntsville, AL St. Joseph's Church.
Wagner, Robert F. '60 (SPR) Monson, MA State Hospital; [O] Holyoke, MA Bureau for Exceptional Children and Adults Inc.
Wagner, Robert J. '57 (LC) Galesville, WI St. Mary Church; Trempealeau, WI St. Bartholomew Church.
Wagner, Ronald F. '79 (SAG) [1] Saginaw, MI St. Mary Church.
Wagner, Terence *o.s.b.* '64 (SEA) [L] Lacey, WA St. Martin's Abbey.
Wagner, Thomas A. '83 (PIT) Braddock, PA Good Shepherd Church; Braddock Hills, PA Sacred Heart Church.
Wagner, Urban S. *o.f.m.conv.* '41 (STP) Bloomington, MN St. Bonaventure Church.
Wagner, Van A. '61 (TUC) [23] Tucson, AZ Saints Peter and Paul Church; Special Assignment.
Wagner, Vernon *o.f.m.cap.* '53 (SAG) [G] Saginaw, MI Queen of Angels Friary and Retreat House.
Wagner, Walter *o.p.* '93 (CIN) [28] Cincinnati, OH St. Gertrude Church; [M] Cincinnati, OH St. Gertrude Priory.
Wagner, Walter C. *o.p.* '54 (CIN) [C] Cincinnati, OH Dominican Novitiate.
Wagner, Walter C. *o.p.* '93 (BO) [W] Dover, MA St. Stephen Priory.
Wagner, Wilbert *s.v.d.* '40 (FgM) Society of the Divine Word Foreign Missions.
Wagner, William C. '73 (CIN) Milford, OH St. Andrew Church.
Wagner, William F. '63 (L) [70] Louisville, KY SS. Simon and Jude Church.
Wagoner, Gordon P. (IND) Indianapolis, IN Veterans' Administration Hospital.
Waguespack, Clarence J. '62 (BR) Pierre Part, LA St. Joseph the Worker Church.
Wahl, Joseph A. *c.o.* '56 (CHR) [E] Rock Hill, SC Oratory of St. Philip Neri, Congregation of the Oratory of Pontifical Rite.
Wahl, Raymond J. '37 (ROC) Retired.
Wahl, Msgr. Raymond J. '52 (RCK) [4] Rockford, IL St. Edward Church.
Wahl, Richard A. *c.s.b.* '72 (GAL) [F] Houston, TX St. Thomas High School.
Wahl, Thomas *o.s.b.* '58 (FgM) American - Cassinese Congregation Foreign Missions.
Wahl, Thomas *o.s.b.* '58 (SCL) [I] Collegeville, MN St. John's Abbey, of the Order of St. Benedict.
Wahmhoff, Andrew *o.s.b.* '58 (RCK) [G] Aurora, IL Marmion Abbey-St. Augustine's Abbey.
Waibel, Kenneth '84 (LEX) Mt. Sterling, KY St. Patrick Church; Winchester, KY St. Joseph Church.
Waibel, Philip *o.s.b.* '83 (P) [A] St. Benedict, OR Mount Angel Seminary; [L] St. Benedict, OR Mt. Angel Abbey.
Waickman, Thomas L. '84 (JC) Louisiana, MO St. Joseph Church.
Waid, Edward *s.v.d.* '50 (STL) [65] St. Louis, MO St. Thomas of Aquin Church.
Wainwright, Walter '65 (ROC) [2] Elmira, NY St. Patrick Church.
Wainwright, Walter L. '65 (ROC) Canandaigua, NY St. Mary Church; [7] Elmira, NY St. Anthony Church.
Waiss, John R. '87 (LA) [X] Los Angeles, CA Prelature of the Holy Cross and Opus Dei.
Wait, Dennis '72 (KCK) Special Assignment.
Waite, Patrick J. '54 (SC) Retired.
Waitekus, Christopher '90 (SPR) [9] Chicopee, MA St. Rose de Lima Church.
Waiwood, Richard '73 (ELP) Retired.
Wajda, Edward J. '56 (PHX) Retired.
Wajda, Joseph L. '73 (STP) Special Assignment.
Wake, John F. '74 (TR) Maple Shade, NJ Our Lady of Perpetual Help Church.
Wakefield, Alan J. '75 (LAN) Mason, MI St. James Church.
Wakefield, Christopher L. '96 (ALN) [11] Reading, PA St. Peter Church.
Wakefield, Michael '81 (LA) Granada Hills, CA St. Euphrasia Church.
Wakeman, Msgr. John J. '56 (ALX) Retired.
Wakim, Rodolph '96 (SAM) Roanoke, VA St. Elias Church.
Wakitsch, Randall '89 (RCK) Absent on Leave.
Wal, Eduardo '79 (SP) [4] Clearwater, FL St. Cecelia Church.
Walas, Joseph '59 (RVC) Riverhead, NY St. Isidore's Church.
Walaszek, Luke A. *o.p.* '58 (NOR) Willimantic, CT St. Joseph Church.
Walch, John '45 (OKL) Retired.
Walck, Edward F. *m.m.* '56 (NY) [DD] Maryknoll, NY Maryknoll Fathers and Brothers.
Walczak, Donald J. '63 (LC) [2] Stevens Point, WI St. Casimir Church; Torun, WI St. Mary Church.
Walczak, Melvin '68 (ROC) Absent on Leave.
Wald, Jeffrey '92 (FAR) Devils Lake, ND St. Joseph's Church; Rutten, ND St. Benedict Church; Devils Lake, ND School for the Deaf; [J] Devils Lake, ND UND-Lake Region.
Wald, John *s.v.d.* '43 (FgM) Society of the Divine Word Foreign Missions.
Wald, Kenneth '57 (BIS) Kenmare, ND St. Agnes Church.
Walden, Msgr. Ellsworth R. '71 (RVC) Hauppauge, NY St. Thomas More Church.
Waldie, Paul *o.m.i.* '65 (SEA) [4] Seattle, WA St. Benedict Church.
Walding, Eugene F. '66 (SC) Fort Dodge, IA Trinity Regional Hospital; [D] Fort Dodge, IA The Marian Home.
Waldmann, Pablo *i.v.e.* '97 (NY) [103] New York, NY St. Paul Church.
Waldmann, Robert J. '46 (B) Retired.
Waldon, Clarence R. '64 (IND) [4] Indianapolis, IN Holy Angels Church.
Waldow, Msgr. Harold L. '70 (AMA) [3] Amarillo, TX Blessed Sacrament Church; [K] Amarillo, TX Monsignor B.A. Erpen Trust Fund.
Waldrep, Jeffrey '90 (JKS) Starkville, MS St. Joseph Church; [H] Starkville, MS Mississippi State University Catholic Student Association.
Waldrep, John W. *m.m.* '90 (FgM) Maryknoll Foreign Missions.
Waldron, John '66 (P) Beaverton, OR Holy Trinity Church.
Waldron, Msgr. John E. '66 (BRK) Retired; [A] Douglaston, NY Immaculate Conception Center.
Waldron, John F. '58 (ALB) Colonie, NY Our Lady of Mercy Church.
Waldron, John R. '56 (NEW) Retired.
Waldron, Richard P. '61 (HBG) Mechanicsburg, PA St. Elizabeth Ann Seton Church.
Waldron, Robert J. '68 (BO) [3] Waltham, MA St. Jude Church.
Waldron, Walter J. '64 (BO) [31] Boston, MA St. Joseph Church; [56] Boston, MA St. Patrick Church.
Waldrop, Gregory *s.j.* '99 (OAK) [N] Berkeley, CA Jesuit Community at Jesuit School of Theology at Berkeley.
Waldschmidt, Donald L. '55 (DAV) Retired; [M] Davenport, IA St. Vincent Center.
Waldschmidt, Valens J. *o.f.m.* '47 (CIN) [M] Cincinnati, OH St. Clement Friary; [V] Cincinnati, OH St. Dymphna Ministry.
Waldspurger, Daniel-Zachary *o.s.b.* '90 (GBG) [H] Latrobe, PA Saint Vincent Archabbey.
Walega, Stanley J. '64 (MET) Bound Brook, NJ St. Mary of Czestochowa Church.
Walick, Stephen J. '69 (CLV) Maple Heights, OH St. Wenceslas Church; Cleveland, OH University Hospitals Bedford Medical Center; Cleveland, OH South Pointe Hospital.
Walijewski, Joseph A. '50 (LC) Retired.
Walk, Donald J. '67 (VEN) Absent on Leave.
Walk, Edward J. '78 (E) [C] Du Bois, PA Du Bois Area Catholic Schools.
Walker, Anselm '56 (GAL) Retired.
Walker, Benjamin R. *o.s.b.* '60 (PIT) [81] Pittsburgh, PA

St. Peter Church; [R] Pittsburgh, PA Office for Campus Ministry.
Walker, Brian *o.m.i.* (FgM) Oblates Foreign Missions.
Walker, Brian G. *o.p.* '86 (CHI) [23] Chicago, IL St. Basil/Visitation Church.
Walker, Carlos *i.v.e.* '83 (BRK) [48] Brooklyn, NY St. Gabriel The Archangel Church.
Walker, Charles D. '81 (L) [66] Louisville, KY St. Pius X Church.
Walker, Msgr. David M. '64 (HRT) [6] Hamden, CT St. Rita's Church.
Walker, Donald L. '58 (DET) [7] Dearborn, MI St. Martha Church.
Walker, Douglas '99 (FRS) Visalia, CA St. Mary Church.
Walker, Earl G. '48 (LA) [7] Los Angeles, CA Cathedral Chapel Church; Retired.
Walker, Edmund *o.f.m.cap.* '63 (WIL) [I] Wilmington, DE Capuchin Franciscan Friars, St. Francis Renewal Center; [L] Wilmington, DE St. Francis Renewal Center.
Walker, Msgr. Edward J. '36 (BUF) Retired.
Walker, Fabian *o.f.m.* (MRY) [H] San Juan Bautista, CA St. Francis Retreat Center.
Walker, Francisco '87 (BRK) [154] Queens, NY St. Bartholomew's Church.
Walker, Francisco J. '87 (BRK) [153] Queens, NY Ascension Church.
Walker, Gerald B. '48 (LA) Retired.
Walker, Henry B. *o.m.i.* '85 (GAL) [65] Houston, TX St. Patrick Church.
Walker, J. Kenneth '81 (EVN) Newburgh, IN St. John the Baptist Church; Special Assignment.
Walker, J. Patrick '88 (STO) [9] Stockton, CA St. Michael Church.
Walker, James E. '99 (GLP) [1] Gallup, NM Cathedral of the Sacred Heart; [A] Gallup, NM Diocesan Diaconate and Lay Ecclesial Ministry Formation Program.
Walker, James P. '77 (Y) [3] Warren, OH SS. Cyril and Methodius Church.
Walker, Kent '89 (ORL) St. Cloud, FL St. Thomas Aquinas Church.
Walker, Michael '62 (KC) Mission Duty.
Walker, Michael '99 (P) Corvallis, OR St. Mary Church.
Walker, Paul '72 (STU) McConnelsville, OH St. James Church.
Walker, Robert F. '65 (CAM) Pleasantville, NJ St. Peter's Church.
Walker, Robert L. *o.p.* '56 (WDC) [11] Washington, DC St. Dominic Church & Priory Church.
Walker, Ronald *o.m.i.* '61 (FgM) Oblates Foreign Missions.
Walker, Thomas (MIL) [2] Cudahy, WI Nativity of the Lord Church.
Walker, Thomas J. '89 (MIL) Special Assignment.
Walker, Thomas J. '90 (STP) Red Wing, MN St. Joseph Church.
Walker, Ward W. '99 (FBK) St. Michael, AK St. Michael Church; Stebbins, AK St. Bernard Church; Unalakleet, AK Church of the Holy Angels.
Walkiewicz, Jacek *s.ch.* (CHI) Chicago, IL Cook County Hospital.
Walkowiak, David J. '79 (CLV) [A] Wickliffe, OH St. Mary Seminary and Graduate School of Theology.
Wall, Antoninus *o.p.* '50 (OAK) [N] Oakland, CA Dominican Order (Western Province), St. Albert's Priory.
Wall, Augustine *s.v.d.* '91 (CHI) [N] Techny, IL Society of the Divine Word, Provincial Headquarter-Chicago Prov.
Wall, Barry W. '62 (FR) [10] Fall River, MA Our Lady of the Holy Rosary Church.
Wall, Damian '65 (CGS) [1] Caguas, PR Cathedral Dulce Nombre de Jesus Church; [B] Aguas Buenas, PR Casa Cristo Redentor.
Wall, G. Warren '76 (MOB) [7] Mobile, AL St. Ignatius Church.
Wall, Gus *s.v.d.* '91 (DUB) [B] Epworth, IA Divine Word College.
Wall, James '98 (PHX) [24] Phoenix, AZ St. Theresa Church.
Wall, Msgr. James E. '63 (BUF) [Q] Derby, NY St. Columban's Center.
Wall, Msgr. John A. '60 (R) Cary, NC St. Michael the Archangel Church.
Wall, John E. '57 (CIN) [54] Cincinnati, OH St. Margaret Mary Church.
Wall, John J. '68 (CHI) [162] Chicago, IL St. Patrick Church.
Wall, Sherman B. *o.m.i.* '57 (SPC) Willow Springs, MO Sacred Heart Church.
Wallace, Basil J. *o.s.b.* '78 (PAT) [M] Newton, NJ St. Paul's Abbey.
Wallace, Cavana '92 (SD) [24] San Diego, CA St. Charles Borromeo Church.
Wallace, Donald '62 (JC) [F] Fayette, MO Central Methodist College.
Wallace, Donald L. '62 (JC) Fayette, MO St. Joseph Church; Columbia, MO University Hospital & Clinics.
Wallace, Francis K. *s.j.* '46 (FgM) Provinces.
Wallace, Msgr. Francis T. '63 (LA) La Canada Flintridge, CA St. Bede the Venerable Church.
Wallace, Francis X. '47 (FR) Retired.
Wallace, George *s.m.* '57 (PH) [U] Langhorne, PA St. Mary Medical Center; [AA] Langhorne, PA Society of Mary, Marist Fathers.
Wallace, Harry '56 (ORL) Retired.
Wallace, Harry C. '56 (SY) On Duty Outside the Diocese.
Wallace, James *c.ss.r.* '70 (WDC) [M] Washington, DC Holy Redeemer College.
Wallace, John *f.m.s.i.* '60 (BO) [B] Framingham, MA Sylva Maria.
Wallace, Joseph '85 (CAM) [1] Cherry Hill, NJ St. Mary's Church.
Wallace, Kenneth F '00 (CLV) [6] Parma, OH Holy Family Church.
Wallace, Kenneth F. '00 (CLV) [6] Parma, OH Holy Family Church.
Wallace, Leonard P. '55 (DET) Retired.
Wallace, Msgr. Murrough C. '60 (SAC) South Lake Tahoe, CA St. Theresa Church.
Wallace, Philip D. '65 (SEA) Bellevue, WA St. Louise Church.
Wallace, Regis P. *o.s.b.* (PAT) Mountain Lakes, NJ St. Catherine of Siena Church.
Wallace, Regis P. *o.s.b.* '60 (PAT) [M] Morristown, NJ St. Mary's Abbey.
Wallace, Richard J. '86 (P) Oregon City, OR St. John the Apostle Church.
Wallace, Thomas '80 (SB) Murrieta, CA St. Martha Church.
Wallace, William J. *o.s.a.* '74 (NY) [168] Bronx, NY St. Nicholas of Tolentine Church.
Wallaik, William H. '49 (MIL) Mequon, WI St. James Church; Retired.
Walle, Msgr. Julius G. '56 (ALX) Cheneyville, LA St. Joseph Church; Retired.
Walleman, Kenneth T. *s.j.* '59 (MIL) [P] Wauwatosa, WI Jesuit Community at St. Camillus.
Wallen, Charles L. *c.s.c.* '54 (BUR) Wilmington, VT Our Lady of Fatima Church.
Wallen, Charles L. *c.s.c.* '54 (FR) [I] North Dartmouth, MA Holy Cross Mission House.
Wallen, Clarence J. *s.j.* '51 (LA) [C] Los Angeles, CA Loyola Marymount University.
Wallenfelsz, Scott *s.d.s.* '69 (MIL) [P] Greendale, WI Salvatorian Formation Community.
Waller, Charles J. '73 (PAT) [16] Paterson, NJ St. Therese Church.
Waller, Robert C. '75 (CIN) [46] Cincinnati, OH St. John Neumann Church.
Wallin, Msgr. Kevin W. '84 (BGP) [5] Danbury, CT St. Peter Church; [S] Bridgeport, CT Inner-City Foundation for Charity & Education.
Walling, Gerald C. *s.j.* '61 (CHI) [N] Chicago, IL Chicago Province of the Society of Jesus-Provincial Office.
Walling, Lawrence E. *o.s.m.* (DEN) [22] Denver, CO Our Lady of Mt. Carmel Church.
Walling, Lawrence M. *o.s.m.* '79 (CHI) [N] Chicago, IL Order of Friar Servants of Mary (Servites) United States of America Province, Inc.
Walling, Norman *s.j.* '61 (FgM) Provinces.
Walling, Richard W. '78 (CIN) [5] Springfield, OH St. Teresa of the Child Jesus Church.
Wallis, William H. '82 (SPR) Great Barrington, MA St. Peter's Church.
Walljasper, Mark A. '55 (LC) Retired.
Wallner, Francis A. *s.j.* '51 (ALN) [A] Wernersville, PA Jesuit Center.
Wallner, Gerhard '89 (FBK) Leave of Absence.
Wallroth, Joseph *o.carm.* '70 (JOL) [J] Darien, IL Carmelite Provincial Office.
Walls, Msgr. David E. '60 (PH) Bryn Mawr, PA St. John Neumann Church; Absent on Leave.
Walmesley, Jack '74 (SEA) Covington, WA St. John the Baptist Church.
Walpole, Donald *o.s.b.* '43 (IND) [J] St. Meinrad, IN St. Meinrad Archabbey.
Walsh, Aidan (BO) [2] Milton, MA St. Elizabeth Church.
Walsh, Aidan J. '70 (BO) Bedford, MA Veterans Administration Hospital Bedford.
Walsh, Albert '92 (GAL) [77] Houston, TX St. Thomas More Church.
Walsh, Andrew J. '66 (NY) Hopewell Junction, NY St. Columba Church.
Walsh, Arthur '85 (CC) On Duty Outside the Diocese.
Walsh, Arthur '85 (NY) Rye, NY Resurrection Church.
Walsh, Austin *s.t.* '65 (ARL) [J] Arlington, VA Missionary Servants of the Most Holy Trinity, S.T.
Walsh, Austin *s.t.* '65 (FgM) Trinity Missions.
Walsh, Bernard '55 (SY) Retired.
Walsh, Brendan J. '93 (LAN) Dexter, MI St. Joseph Church.
Walsh, Brendan J. *s.a.c.* '98 (LUB) [7] Lubbock, TX St. Joseph's Church.
Walsh, Broderick M. *c.s.p.* '92 (KNX) [3] Knoxville, TN Immaculate Conception Church.
Walsh, Msgr. Bryan O. '54 (MIA) Retired.
Walsh, Msgr. Charles '51 (WCH) Retired.
Walsh, Christopher J. '87 (BGP) [4] Norwalk, CT St. Mary Church; [P] Stamford, CT St. John Fisher Seminary Residence.
Walsh, Christopher M. '99 (PH) [127] Philadelphia, PA Our Lady of Ransom Church.
Walsh, Clyde J. '51 (PRO) Retired; [P] Providence, RI St. John Vianney Residence.
Walsh, Daniel *c.s.sp.* '91 (SD) [19] San Diego, CA St. Agnes Church.
Walsh, Daniel M. '59 (SHP) [1] Shreveport, LA St. John Berchmans Church.
Walsh, Daniel P. '68 (BUF) [38] Buffalo, NY St. John the Evangelist Church.
Walsh, David *c.ss.r.* '47 (CC) [8] Corpus Christi, TX Our Lady of Perpetual Help Church; On Special Assignment.
Walsh, Denis '66 (TYL) [B] Palestine, TX Hermitage.
Walsh, Dennis '92 (TOL) Sandusky, OH St. Mary Church.
Walsh, Donal C. '55 (SD) Julian, CA St. Elizabeth Church.
Walsh, E. Corbett *s.j.* '71 (BO) [W] Weston, MA Campion Jesuit Community.
Walsh, Edward J. '64 (CAM) Retired.
Walsh, Edward J. '91 (RVC) Franklin Square, NY St. Catherine of Sienna Church.
Walsh, Edward P. '93 (BIR) On Duty Outside the Diocese.
Walsh, Flannan J. '65 (STA) On Duty Outside the Diocese.
Walsh, Flavian A. *o.f.m.* '56 (WIL) [10] Wilmington, DE St. Paul's Church.
Walsh, Francis *s.j.* '53 (SEA) [C] Tacoma, WA Bellarmine Preparatory School.
Walsh, Francis E. '66 (SPR) Military Chaplains.
Walsh, Francis M. *c.s.c.* '56 (FR) [A] North Easton, MA Stonehill College; [A] North Easton, MA Holy Cross Fathers Religious.
Walsh, Francis M. '67 (WDC) On Duty Outside the Archdiocese.
Walsh, Francis P. '57 (CLV) [5] Lakewood, OH St. Luke Church.
Walsh, Frederick P. *o.s.b.* '38 (BR) [I] Tickfaw, LA Our Lady Queen Contemplative Monastery.
Walsh, Frederick P. *o.s.b.* '38 (IND) [J] St. Meinrad, IN St. Meinrad Archabbey.
Walsh, George J. '52 (PH) Retired.
Walsh, Gerald '95 (CHI) Tinley Park, IL St. George Church.
Walsh, Msgr. Gerald J. '55 (BIS) Retired.
Walsh, Gerard P. '74 (WOR) Oxford, MA St. Roch's Church.
Walsh, Gerard W. '46 (NEW) Nutley, NJ St. Mary's Church.
Walsh, Harry A. '60 (STP) Special Assignment.
Walsh, J. B. '65 (SAC) West Sacramento, CA Our Lady of Grace Church.
Walsh, J. Daniel *c.s.c.* '60 (BR) [2] Baton Rouge, LA St. Agnes Church; Jackson, LA East Feliciana Chronic Disease Hospital and Rehabilitation Center.
Walsh, J. Gerald *c.s.sp.* '42 (PIT) [Q] Bethel Park, PA Holy Ghost Animation Center.
Walsh, J. Patrick *s.j.* (DEN) [31] Denver, CO St. Ignatius Loyola Church.
Walsh, J. Patrick *s.j.* '66 (PBL) Springfield, CO Annunciation Church.
Walsh, James '69 (SJ) [11] San Jose, CA St. Christopher Church.
Walsh, James A. '54 (TOL) Milan, OH St. Anthony Church.
Walsh, James F. *s.j.* '72 (BO) [W] Boston, MA The Society of Jesus of New England-Provincial Offices; [W] Boston, MA The Society of Jesus of New England-Provincial Offices.
Walsh, James J. '68 (CIN) [23] Cincinnati, OH St. Dominic Church.
Walsh, James J. *s.j.* '72 (BO) [W] Boston, MA The Society of Jesus of New England-Provincial Offices.
Walsh, James J. '73 (SCR) Jermyn, PA Sacred Heart of Mary Church.
Walsh, James J. '93 (ALB) Loudonville, NY St. Pius X Church; Special Assignment.
Walsh, James P. *s.j.* (DEN) [M] Denver, CO Xavier Jesuit Center.
Walsh, James P. *s.j.* '62 (BO) [W] Weston, MA Campion Health Center, Inc.; [Y] Weston, MA Campion Renewal Center.
Walsh, James P. '73 (MAN) [6] Manchester, NH St. Catherine Church; [N] Manchester, NH Campus Ministries.
Walsh, James P.M. *s.j.* '70 (WDC) [M] Washington, DC The Jesuit Community at Georgetown University.
Walsh, Jeffrey J. '94 (SCR) Lake Winola, PA St. Mary of the Lake Church; [A] Dalton, PA Saint Pius X Seminary.
Walsh, Jeffrey T. '89 (HRT) [1] East Hartford, CT Blessed Sacrament Church.
Walsh, Jerome '69 (DET) On Duty Outside the Archdiocese.

Walsh, Joachim *o.s.b.* '37 (IND) [J] St. Meinrad, IN St. Meinrad Archabbey.
Walsh, Joachim E. *o.s.b.* '37 (BR) [I] Tickfaw, LA Our Lady Queen Contemplative Monastery.
Walsh, John '55 (SAL) Norton, KS St. Francis of Assisi Church.
Walsh, John A. '61 (SCR) On Duty Outside the Diocese.
Walsh, John A. '80 (E) Conneautville, PA St. Peter Church.
Walsh, John B. '57 (MAD) Johnson Creek, WI St. Mary Magdalene Church; Lake Mills, WI St. Francis Xavier Church.
Walsh, John D. *m.m.* '56 (FgM) Maryknoll Foreign Missions.
Walsh, John F. '70 (BRK) Absent on Leave.
Walsh, John F. '76 (PIT) [11] Pittsburgh, PA Epiphany Church; Allegheny County, Pa UPMC Southside Hospital.
Walsh, John F. '85 (BO) Plainville, MA St. Martha Church.
Walsh, John J. (DUB) Blairstown, IA St. John Church; Newhall, IA St. Paul's Church; Van Horne, IA Immaculate Conception Church.
Walsh, John J. *c.s.sp.* '48 (GAL) [B] Houston, TX Holy Ghost Fathers and Brothers.
Walsh, John J. *m.m.* '61 (NY) [DD] Maryknoll, NY Maryknoll Fathers and Brothers.
Walsh, John Joseph *s.j.* '71 (BO) [E] Boston, MA Boston College High School & Jesuit Community; [W] Boston, MA The Society of Jesus of New England-Provincial Offices.
Walsh, John M. '47 (PH) Retired.
Walsh, John P. '77 (ATL) Peachtree City, GA Holy Trinity Catholic Church.
Walsh, John T. *m.div.* '44 (ROC) [38] Rochester, NY Our Lady Queen of Peace Church; Retired.
Walsh, Joseph E. '47 (PH) Lenni, PA St. Francis de Sales Church; Retired.
Walsh, Joseph M. '86 (LIN) [11] Lincoln, NE St. Teresa's Church; [L] Lincoln, NE Catholic Social Services; [M] Lincoln, NE Catholic Social Services.
Walsh, Joseph R. '64 (SFR) [50] San Francisco, CA St. Stephen Church.
Walsh, Kenneth *c.p.* '50 (SCR) [2] Scranton, PA St. Ann's Basilica Church; [M] Scranton, PA Saint Ann's Passionist Monastery.
Walsh, Kevin B. '92 (ARL) Falls Church, VA St. James Church; [A] Arlington, VA Marymount University; [M] Arlington, VA Marymount University.
Walsh, Laurence '45 (NO) Retired.
Walsh, Msgr. Lawrence '54 (SAT) [16] San Antonio, TX Our Lady of Grace Church.
Walsh, Msgr. Lawrence J. '63 (STL) [39] St. Louis, MO St. Joan of Arc Church.
Walsh, Leo '94 (ANC) Eagle River, AK St. Andrew Church.
Walsh, Marion C. *o.s.b.* '42 (BR) [I] Tickfaw, LA Our Lady Queen Contemplative Monastery.
Walsh, Marion C. *o.s.b.* '42 (IND) [J] St. Meinrad, IN St. Meinrad Archabbey.
Walsh, Martin *o.p.* '50 (OAK) [N] Oakland, CA Dominican Order (Western Province), St. Albert's Priory.
Walsh, Martin *o.m.i.* '54 (BO) Tewksbury, MA St. William Church.
Walsh, Martin *o.p.* '69 (OAK) [N] Oakland, CA Western Dominican Province.
Walsh, Msgr. Martin E. '43 (OAK) Military Chaplains; Retired; [M] Oakland, CA Bishop Begin Villa.
Walsh, Martin J. '74 (BO) Absent on Leave.
Walsh, Matthias *o.p.* '58 (MAD) [I] Sinsinawa, WI Dominican Motherhouse.
Walsh, Maurice b. *s.j.* '46 (BO) [W] Weston, MA Campion Health Center, Inc.
Walsh, Michael (DEN) [37] Denver, CO St. Vincent De Paul Church.
Walsh, Msgr. Michael '38 (LA) Retired.
Walsh, Michael '53 (DEN) Centennial, CO St. Thomas More Church.
Walsh, Michael *o.f.m.cap.* '58 (BAK) Bend, OR St. Francis of Assisi Church.
Walsh, Michael A. '72 (PAT) Succasunna, NJ St. Therese Church.
Walsh, Michael E. *s.j.* '62 (SEA) [P] Tacoma, WA Catholic Pastoral Care-Hospital Tacoma Ministry.
Walsh, Michael F. *c.m.* '72 (LA) [96] Los Angeles, CA St. Vincent De Paul Church.
Walsh, Michael J. '56 (CHI) Retired.
Walsh, Michael J. '70 (BRK) [242] Queens, NY St. Stanislaus Kostka Church.
Walsh, Msgr. Michael J. '73 (TR) Lakewood, NJ St. Mary of the Lake Church.
Walsh, Michael L. '45 (PH) Retired; [V] Immaculata, PA Camilla Hall Nursing Home.
Walsh, Michael P. *m.m.* '88 (FgM) Maryknoll Foreign Missions.
Walsh, Miles D. '80 (BR) [15] Baton Rouge, LA Most Blessed Sacrament Church.
Walsh, Milton T. '78 (SFR) San Francisco, CA Knights of Malta; [A] Menlo Park, CA St. Patrick Seminary; [A] Menlo Park, CA St. Patrick Seminary.
Walsh, Patrick *o.p.* '34 (WDC) [11] Washington, DC St. Dominic Church & Priory Church.
Walsh, Patrick '69 (SC) [G] Fort Dodge, IA Fort Dodge Catholic Grade System Foundation; [G] Fort Dodge, IA St. Edmund High School Foundation; [G] Fort Dodge, IA Fort Dodge Catholic Schools Foundation.
Walsh, Patrick '72 (P) Springfield, OR St. Alice Church.
Walsh, Patrick *c.s.c.* '81 (PRT) Saco, ME Most Holy Trinity Church.
Walsh, Patrick *l.c.* '91 (MAN) [A] Center Harbor, NH Immaculate Conception Apostolic School.
Walsh, Patrick A. *s.m.a.* '65 (NY) Tuckahoe, NY Immaculate Conception Church; Tuckahoe, NY Assumption Church.
Walsh, Patrick E. *s.j.* '60 (MIL) [31] Milwaukee, WI Gesu Church.
Walsh, Patrick J. '58 (LA) [61] Los Angeles, CA St. Eugene Church.
Walsh, Patrick R. '69 (SC) [B] Fort Dodge, IA Fort Dodge Catholic Schools, Inc.
Walsh, Msgr. Paul '66 (RVC) Smithtown, NY St. Patrick Church.
Walsh, Peter '59 (JC) Retired.
Walsh, Peter *o.f.m.* '82 (NY) [DD] New York, NY Padua Friary.
Walsh, Peter J. *c.s.c.* '89 (FR) [A] North Easton, MA Holy Cross Fathers Religious.
Walsh, Raymond D. '54 (BUR) Retired.
Walsh, Raymond E. '54 (BUR) [D] Rutland, VT Loretto Home for Aged.
Walsh, Richard '68 (ORL) Winter Park, FL St. Margaret Mary Church; Special Assignment.
Walsh, Richard '83 (JOL) Romeoville, IL St. Andrew the Apostle Church.
Walsh, Richard A. '62 (PRO) [M] Newport, RI St. Clare Home.
Walsh, Msgr. Richard J. '44 (ALT) Retired.
Walsh, Richard J. *c.s.p.* '44 (NY) [104] New York, NY St. Paul the Apostle Church; [DD] Jamaica Estates, NY Paulist Fathers Generalate.
Walsh, Msgr. Robert '46 (LA) Arcadia, CA Holy Angels Church; Retired.
Walsh, Robert '77 (CHI) [J] Chicago, IL Our Lady of the Resurrection Medical Center.
Walsh, Robert T. *s.j.* '80 (LA) [F] Los Angeles, CA Loyola High School of Los Angeles.
Walsh, Seamus '66 (DUL) Brainerd, MN St. Francis Church.
Walsh, Sebastian *o.praem* (ORG) [D] Silverado, CA St. Michael's College Preparatory High School.
Walsh, Stephen M. *o.f.m.* '50 (BO) [Z] Boston, MA Saint Anthony Residence.
Walsh, Terrance G. *s.j.* '82 (BO) [W] Boston, MA The Society of Jesus of New England-Provincial Offices.
Walsh, Theodore *c.p.* '59 (BRK) [V] Jamaica, NY Immaculate Conception Monastery.
Walsh, Thomas *s.s.c.* '57 (FgM) St. Columban's Foreign Mission.
Walsh, Thomas *c.o.* '94 (MET) [M] New Brunswick, NJ Catholic Center at Rutgers University.
Walsh, Thomas A. '42 (PHX) [3] Scottsdale, AZ St. Bernadette Church; Retired.
Walsh, Thomas E. *o.f.m.conv.* '80 (BAL) [C] Baltimore, MD Archbishop Curley High School; [S] Baltimore, MD Immaculate Heart of Mary Friary.
Walsh, Thomas F. '45 (PH) Valley Forge, PA St. Teresa of Avila Church; Retired.
Walsh, Thomas F. *s.j.* '55 (PAT) [I] Morristown, NJ Loyola House of Retreats.
Walsh, Thomas J. *o.carm* '50 (VEN) [G] Nokomis, FL Carmel at Mission Valley.
Walsh, Thomas J. '67 (BO) Franklin, MA St. Mary Church.
Walsh, Thomas J. *c.o.* '94 (MET) [H] Somerset, NJ The Metuchen Oratory, Congregation of the Oratory of St. Philip Neri.
Walsh, Thomas P. '72 (STA) [4] St. Augustine, FL San Sebastian Church.
Walsh, Thomas P. '86 (CHI) [172] Chicago, IL Presentation Church.
Walsh, Thomas R. '53 (CHL) Retired.
Walsh, Thomas R. '94 (LIN) [5] Lincoln, NE Sacred Heart Church.
Walsh, Thomas V. '67 (WOR) Clinton, MA St. John the Evangelist Church.
Walsh, Ulich (WCH) Retired.
Walsh, Msgr. Vincent M. '62 (PH) Wynnewood, PA Presentation B.V.M. Church.
Walsh, William *s.j.* '67 (BAL) [S] Baltimore, MD Ferdinand Wheeler Jesuit Community.
Walsh, William D. '66 (BO) [12] Cambridge, MA St. Peter Church.
Walsh, William F. *o.s.f.s.* '68 (PH) [AA] Wyndmoor, PA Villa de Sales Oblate Residence.
Walsh, William K. '49 (SAC) Rio Vista, CA St. Joseph Church; Retired and in Senior Ministry.
Walsh, William M. '71 (BO) Danvers, MA St. Mary of the Annunciation Church.
Walsh, William P. *s.j.* '67 (RVC) [O] Manhasset, NY St. Ignatius Retreat House, Inisfada.
Walski, Adalbert *t.o.r.* (ALT) Johnstown, PA Conemaugh Memorial Medical Center; Johnstown, PA UPMC Lee Hospital.
Walsman, Paul *o.f.m.* '58 (CIN) [K] Cincinnati, OH Mercy Health Plaza dba Mercy Franciscan Hospital-Western Hills.
Walter, Andrew W. (BGP) Bethel, CT St. Mary Church.
Walter, Anthony *o.f.m.* '59 (BR) [F] Baton Rouge, LA Our Lady of the Lake Regional Medical Center; [H] Baton Rouge, LA Franciscan Residence.
Walter, Charles *m.c.c.j.* '66 (CHI) [N] La Grange Park, IL Comboni Mission Center.
Walter, Charles W. '74 (MIL) Retired.
Walter, Chris B. '58 (BIS) [4] Minot, ND St. Leo Church.
Walter, David A. '63 (STL) On Medical Leave.
Walter, Eugene *s.d.b.* '83 (NY) [FF] Stony Point, NY Don Bosco Retreat Center and Marian Shrine; [FF] Stony Point, NY Marian Shrine.
Walter, Francis *o.f.m.* '77 (TR) Roebling, NJ Holy Assumption Church.
Walter, James A. '62 (COL) Sunbury, OH St. John Neumann Church.
Walter, James A. '69 (BUF) Springbrook, NY St. Vincent Church.
Walter, John F. '44 (MIL) Retired.
Walter, Joseph J. *s.j.* '45 (NY) [F] New York, NY Xavier High School; [DD] New York, NY Xavier Jesuit Community.
Walter, Joseph L. *c.s.c.* '61 (FTW) [B] Notre Dame, IN University of Notre Dame Du Lac; [J] Notre Dame, IN Holy Cross Community, Corby Hall, University of Notre Dame.
Walter, Marius *o.s.b.* '98 (P) [L] St. Benedict, OR Mt. Angel Abbey.
Walter, Mark J. '88 (CHI) [3] Oak Lawn, IL St. Germaine Church.
Walter, Raymond F. *c.ss.r.* '41 (STL) [P] Liguori, MO St. Clement Health Care Center.
Walter, Msgr. Robert J. '45 (DAV) Retired.
Walter, Steven P. '77 (CIN) [71] Cincinnati, OH Our Mother of Sorrows Church.
Walter, William P. *c.pp.s.* '61 (DAV) Albia, IA St. Mary's Church.
Walter, William P. *c.pp.s.* '61 (KC) [A] Liberty, MO Society of the Precious Blood Provincial Offices.
Walters, Frederick '87 (PAT) McAfee, NJ St. Francis de Sales Church.
Walters, Gary R. (TOL) [19] Toledo, OH St. Catherine of Siena Church.
Walters, Hilarion *c.p.* '47 (FgM) Passionist Foreign Missions.
Walters, James '59 (LR) Retired.
Walters, James L. *s.c.j.* '78 (RC) Lower Brule, SD St. Mary's Church; Lower Brule, SD Lower Brule Reservation Church; [B] Lower Brule, SD SCJ Community House.
Walters, James L. *s.c.j.* '78 (SFS) Stephan, SD Immaculate Conception Church.
Walters, Jim L. *s.c.j.* '78 (SFS) Fort Thompson, SD St. Joseph Church.
Walters, Michael M. '81 (NEW) [2] East Orange, NJ Holy Spirit-Our Lady Help of Christians Church.
Walters, Neil G. '89 (CLV) [2] Euclid, OH St. Felicitas Church.
Walters, Ronald F. *o.f.m.* '78 (GRY) [J] Cedar Lake, IN San Damiano Friary.
Walters, Theodore W. *s.j.* '56 (DET) [K] Detroit, MI Jesuit Provincial Office-Detroit Province of the Society of Jesus.
Walters, Theodore W. *s.j.* '56 (FgM) Provinces.
Walters, Thomas J. *o.f.m.* '80 (NY) [35] New York, NY St. Francis of Assisi Church.
Walters, Vincent '54 (SB) Retired.
Walther, James '95 (SFD) [2] Alton, IL Immaculate Conception-St. Mary's Church.
Walton, James *o.f.m.* '91 (CHI) [N] Countryside, IL St. Gratian Friary, Franciscan Friars.
Walton, James *o.f.m.* '91 (JOL) Hinsdale, IL Hinsdale Hospital.
Walton, Msgr. Robert '74 (SAC) Elk Grove, CA St. Joseph Church.
Walyaula, Joseph '89 (NY) Sleepy Hollow, NY St. Teresa of Avila Church.
Walz, Julius J. '46 (FAR) Retired.
Walz, Richard *o.s.b.* '67 (FgM) American - Cassinese Congregation Foreign Missions.
Walz, Richard '88 (SCL) Special Assignment.
Walz, Msgr. W. Dean '53 (DUB) [1] Waterloo, IA St. Joseph's Church; On Special or Other Archdiocesan Assignment.
Wambach, John W. *s.j.* '64 (LC) Prairie du Chien, WI St. Gabriel Church; Prairie du Chien, WI St. John Nepomucene Church.
Wambach, Joseph G. *s.d.s.* '67 (MIL) [P] Milwaukee, WI Salvatorian Provincial Residence.
Wampach, Frank J. '84 (STP) Watertown, MN Immaculate Conception Church.
Wamsher, Ronald '77 (SPR) Belchertown, MA St. Francis of Assisi Church.
Wanat, Mitchell J. *c.m.* '71 (MAN) [2] Concord, NH St. Peter Church.
Wanaurny, John '59 (OM) [K] St. Columbans, NE St.

Columban's Foreign Mission Society.
Wancewicz, Wally G. '92 (OM) [20] Omaha, NE Immaculate Conception, B.V.M. Church.
Wancewicz, Walter G. '92 (OM) [25] Omaha, NE St. Joseph Church.
Wanda, Michael J. '91 (CHI) La Grange Park, IL St. Louise de Marillac Church.
Wander, Paul '90 (B) Gooding, ID St. Elizabeth's Church; Shoshone, ID St. Peter's Church.
Wandless, John '97 (KC) [8] Kansas City, MO Christ the King Church.
Wang, Barnabas '52 (BRK) Retired; [V] Douglaston, NY Bishop Mugavero Residence.
Wang, Francis X. *s.j.* '52 (SJ) [L] Los Gatos, CA Sacred Heart Jesuit Center.
Wang, Msgr. Ignatius '59 (SFR) [24] San Francisco, CA Holy Name of Jesus Church; Special Assignment.
Wang, John '54 (HEL) Retired.
Wangaih, Paul '85 (JKS) Shelby, MS St. Mary Church; Parchman, MS Mississippi State Penitentiary.
Wangbu, John K. '83 (TUC) Green Valley, AZ Our Lady of the Valley Church.
Wangler, Msgr. Alex '41 (SAT) Retired.
Wangler, Brian *o.s.b.* '69 (BIS) Richardton, ND St. Mary Church; [A] Richardton, ND Assumption Abbey.
Wangler, Msgr. Donald L. '57 (BUF) [2] Lockport, NY St. John the Baptist Church.
Wangler, Leonard '70 (LR) [A] Subiaco, AR Subiaco Monastery.
Wangler, Msgr. William O. '63 (BUF) Olean, NY St. John Church.
Wanjura, Victor '99 (LUB) On Duty Outside the Diocese.
Wanjura, Victor '99 (WDC) Hyattsville, MD St. Mark Church.
Wankerl, Gary A. '80 (MAD) De Forest, WI St. Olaf Church; East Bristol, WI St. Joseph Church.
Wannemuehler, Robert '51 (EVN) Retired.
Wanser, George V. *s.j.* '76 (SAC) [C] Sacramento, CA Jesuit High School; [H] Carmichael, CA Jesuit High School Community of Sacramento.
Wantland, Thomas '67 (MAR) On Duty Outside the Diocese.
Wantland, Thomas '67 (VEN) Port Charlotte, FL St. Charles Borromeo Church.
Wanzong, Gary F. '82 (GAL) [N] Houston, TX St. Dominic Village.
Wapen, Francis A. '70 (SY) Taberg, NY St. Patrick Church.
Waraksa, Alex J. '90 (KNX) Alcoa, TN Our Lady of Fatima Church.
Warczynski, Leon '42 (BAL) [88] Baltimore, MD Sacred Heart of Mary Church; Retired.
Ward, Austin T. '70 (STP) Maplewood, MN Holy Redeemer Church.
Ward, Bernardine *o.f.m.* '42 (FgM) Franciscan Foreign Missions.
Ward, Bruce *s.t.* '60 (FgM) Trinity Missions.
Ward, Daniel *o.s.b.* '71 (SCL) [I] Collegeville, MN St. John's Abbey, of the Order of St. Benedict.
Ward, Donal '63 (BUR) Vergennes, VT St. Peter Church.
Ward, Donald M. *s.j.* '70 (BAL) [S] Baltimore, MD Jesuit Fathers and Brothers Maryland Provincial Curia.
Ward, Donald M. *s.j.* '70 (FgM) Provinces.
Ward, Edward *o.m.i.* '67 (LAR) [7] Laredo, TX Our Lady of Guadalupe Church.
Ward, Edward *o.carm* '73 (NEW) Teaneck, NJ St. Anastasia's Church.
Ward, Gary '80 (NEW) [2] Bayonne, NJ St. Andrew's Church.
Ward, George *o.f.m.* (SFE) [I] Albuquerque, NM San Antonio Provincial Friary.
Ward, Gerald T. '79 (PEO) [4] Bloomington, IL St. Patrick Church of Merna.
Ward, James Garcia *c.m.* '77 (NO) [61] New Orleans, LA St. Stephen Church.
Ward, James J. '73 (ALN) Palmerton, PA Sacred Heart Church.
Ward, Jerome A. *o.m.i.* '67 (CHR) Kingstree, SC St. Ann's Church.
Ward, John *o.m.i.* '49 (GAL) [S] Dickinson, TX Christian Renewal Center.
Ward, John A. *s.s.* '39 (BAL) [O] Baltimore, MD St. Charles Villa; [S] Baltimore, MD St. Charles Villa.
Ward, John A. *o.m.i.* '67 (CHR) Lake City, SC St. Philip's Church.
Ward, John B. (BAL) [70] Baltimore, MD Our Lady of Hope Church.
Ward, Msgr. John C. '45 (NU) Retired.
Ward, John F. '58 (HEL) Three Forks, MT Holy Family Church.
Ward, John J. '55 (SFR) Retired; [D] Kentfield, CA Marin Catholic College Preparatory (Coed).
Ward, John J. *c.s.b.* '70 (DET) [E] Redford, MI Catholic Central High School.
Ward, John P. '65 (CAM) Pine Hill, NJ St. Edward's Church.
Ward, Mark *c.p.* '76 (WH) Kingwood, WV St. Sebastian's Church; Masontown, WV St. Zita's Church.
Ward, Michael *o.f.m.* (CHI) [D] Chicago, IL Hales Franciscan High School, Inc.
Ward, Michael '97 (NEW) Kearny, NJ St. Cecilia's Church.
Ward, Neal A. '57 (WDC) Morganza, MD St. Joseph Church.
Ward, Richard '93 (SEA) Snohomish, WA St. Michael Church.
Ward, Richard E. '68 (PIT) Scott Township, PA SS. Simon and Jude Church; Allegheny County, PA Manorcare Health Services.
Ward, Robert *o.m.i.* '61 (FgM) Oblates Foreign Missions.
Ward, Robert A. '74 (BO) Health Leave.
Ward, Sebastian *o.f.m.cap.* '47 (LA) [B] Santa Ynez, CA San Lorenzo Novitiate and Seminary.
Ward, Serge E. (ATL) [M] Atlanta, GA Campus Ministry.
Ward, Serge E. '95 (ATL) Gainesville, GA St. Michael's Church.
Ward, Thomas '62 (KC) Retired.
Ward, Thomas '97 (SY) [5] Endicott, NY St. Joseph Church.
Ward, Thomas R. '65 (OM) [12] Omaha, NE Christ the King Church.
Ward, William G. '50 (BUF) Retired.
Ward, Msgr. William P. '57 (SCR) Milford, PA St. Vincent de Paul Church.
Wardanski, Msgr. Joseph V. '67 (E) [27] Erie, PA St. Patrick/St. Hedwig Church; [K] Erie, PA St. Mary's Home of Erie.
Warden, Daniel L. '66 (GAL) Rosenberg, TX Holy Rosary Church.
Warden, Joel M *c.o.* '99 (BRK) [V] Brooklyn, NY Oratory of Saint Philip Neri, Congregation Pontifical Rite.
Warden, Joel M. *c.o.* '99 (BRK) [22] Brooklyn, NY St. Boniface Church.
Warden, T. Patrick *c.s.b.* '65 (GAL) [Q] Houston, TX Residence of the Basilian Fathers of the University of St. Thomas.
Wardenski, Robert W. '72 (BUF) [4] West Seneca, NY St. William Church.
Wardrope, Juan *c.m.* '89 (FgM) Vincentian Foreign Missions.
Ware, Donald *c.p.* '72 (NY) [DD] New York, NY Passionist Spiritual Center.
Ware, Joseph F. '48 (ATL) Retired.
Ware, Joseph F. '48 (SAV) [8] Savannah, GA St. Frances Xavier Cabrini Church.
Wargel, William J. '65 (EVN) Ferdinand, IN St. Ferdinand Church.
Wargo, Msgr. Robert J. '72 (ALN) Orefield, PA St. Joseph The Worker Church.
Waris, Gerald '67 (KC) [33] Kansas City, MO St. Patrick Church.
Warkulwiz, Victor *m.s.s.* '91 (PH) [4] Bensalem, PA Our Lady of Fatima Church.
Warman, William '64 (MET) Lyons, NJ U.S. Veterans Medical Center.
Warman, William C. '64 (BAL) On Duty Outside the Archdiocese.
Warmuz, Gregory W. *o.cist.* (CHI) Berwyn, IL St. Odilo Church.
Warnakula, Anthony B. *c.h.s.p.* '88 (SAC) Susanville, CA California Correctional Center.
Warner, James L. '69 (GI) Mullen, NE St. Mary's Church.
Warner, John '70 (Y) [19] Youngstown, OH SS. Peter and Paul's Church.
Warner, John B. *s.j.* '74 (FgM) Provinces.
Warner, Richard V. *c.s.c.* '66 (FTW) [B] Notre Dame, IN University of Notre Dame Du Lac; [J] Notre Dame, IN Holy Cross Community, Corby Hall, University of Notre Dame.
Warnimont, Ronald R. '76 (TOL) [1] Toledo, OH Queen of the Most Holy Rosary Church; [32] Toledo, OH St. Mary of the Assumption Church.
Warnisher, Maximilian M. *f.f.i.* '94 (FR) [I] New Bedford, MA Marian Friary of Our Lady, Queen of the Seraphic Order.
Warnock, Damian J. *o.s.b.* '79 (GBG) [H] Latrobe, PA Saint Vincent Archabbey.
Warnstedt, Mark A. '96 (LA) Lakewood, CA St. Pancratius Church.
Warosh, James B. *s.j.* '67 (LC) Prairie du Chien, WI St. Gabriel Church; Prairie du Chien, WI St. John Nepomucene Church.
Warren, Arthur '63 (LAF) Retired.
Warren, Clarence A. *s.s.p.* '85 (NY) [B] New York, NY Society of St. Paul.
Warren, Edward V. *s.j.* '52 (SJ) [B] Santa Clara, CA Santa Clara University.
Warren, Martin L. '78 (STP) [28] St. Paul, MN St. Matthew Church.
Warren, Paul F. '78 (SFR) [50] San Francisco, CA St. Stephen Church.
Warren, Robert '64 (RIC) Clifton Forge, VA St. Joseph Church; Retired.
Warren, Robert *s.a.* '81 (NY) [DD] Garrison, NY Franciscan Friars of the Atonement; [DD] Garrison, NY St. Christopher's Friary.
Warren, Robert J. (RIC) Fincastle, VA Church of the Transfiguration.
Warren, Ronald J. '62 (BAK) Chiloquin, OR Our Lady of Mt. Carmel Church.
Warren, Thomas '66 (LA) On Sick Leave.
Warsey, Robert M. *o.s.m.* '85 (CHI) [N] Chicago, IL Order of Friar Servants of Mary (Servites) United States of America Province, Inc.; [N] Chicago, IL Order of Friar Servants of Mary (Servites) United States of America Province, Inc.
Warthen, Michael *(baptist)* '95 (MIA) [G] Fort Lauderdale, FL Holy Cross Hospital.
Warzocha, Frank S. '53 (BUR) West Rutland, VT St. Stanislaus Kostka Church.
Wasek, Piotr (CHI) [96] Chicago, IL St. James Church.
Wasek, Stanislaus *c.p.* '53 (BRK) [V] Jamaica, NY Immaculate Conception Monastery.
Waseline, Nicholas R. *o.s.f.s.* '80 (PH) [D] Philadelphia, PA Northeast Catholic High School for Boys; [AA] Philadelphia, PA Oblates of St. Francis De Sales.
Waser, Frank A. '79 (RCK) Absent on Leave.
Washabaugh, Robert '78 (NOR) [1] Middletown, CT St. Francis Church.
Washburn, Thomas *o.f.m.* '00 (MAN) Derry, NH St. Thomas Aquinas Church.
Washko, Robert M. '77 (GBG) Everson, PA St. Joseph Church.
Washko, Stephen G. '78 (VNN) Phoenix, AZ St. Stephen Church.
Wasiecko, Allan *o.f.m.cap.* '68 (FgM) Capuchin Foreign Missions.
Wasiel, Michael '33 (CHI) Harvey, IL St. John the Baptist Church.
Wasiel, Michael J. '33 (CHI) Retired.
Wasielewski, Henry R. '64 (PHX) Retired.
Wasikowski, Ronald S. '75 (OM) Elkhorn, NE St. Patrick Church.
Wasilewski, John D. '97 (CAM) Bridgeton, NJ Immaculate Conception Church.
Wasinger, Msgr. Alfred J. '44 (SAL) Retired.
Wasinger, Mark S. '94 (STP) [19] Minneapolis, MN St. Boniface Church; [23] Minneapolis, MN SS. Cyril & Methodius Church.
Waska, Raymond '95 (FBK) Emmonak, AK Sacred Heart Church.
Wasko, Anthony J. *o.s.a.* '58 (SD) [34] San Diego, CA St. Patrick Church; [H] San Diego, CA Augustinian Community.
Waskowiak, Harlon D. '98 (LIN) Hastings, NE St. Michael's Church.
Waslo, Msgr. Peter '86 (SJP) Parma, OH St. Andrew Church.
Wasnewski, Richard P. '53 (BO) Senior Priests.
Wasnie, Blane *o.s.b.* '66 (SCL) [I] Collegeville, MN St. John's Abbey, of the Order of St. Benedict.
Wasowski, Ronald *c.s.c.* '73 (P) [B] Portland, OR University of Portland; [L] Portland, OR Holy Cross Fathers & Brothers, C.S.C. - University of Portland.
Wassel, Msgr. Anthony F. '60 (ALN) [5] Mahanoy City, PA St. Joseph Church.
Wassel, Eugene A. '52 (PH) [30] Philadelphia, PA St. Casimir Church; Retired.
Wassell, John E. '97 (NEW) [9] Elizabeth, NJ Our Lady of Most Holy Rosary/St. Michael Church.
Wasser, James *m.s.f.* '74 (SAT) New Braunfels, TX Holy Family Church.
Wassie, Stephen M. '79 (Y) Jefferson, OH St. Joseph Calasanctius Church.
Wassmuth, Dennis '73 (B) [4] Boise, ID Our Lady of the Rosary Church.
Wastag, Michael *o.carm.* '97 (NEW) [P] Mahwah, NJ Carmel Retreat House.
Waszak, Norbert J. '53 (CHI) Retired.
Waszczenko, Andrew *s.d.s.* '89 (RVC) Copiague, NY Our Lady of the Assumption Church.
Waszczenko, Andrzej *s.d.s.* '89 (NEW) [N] Verona, NJ The Salvatorian Fathers.
Watanabe, Philip '77 (KC) Montrose, MO Immaculate Conception Church.
Watanabe, Msgr. Terrence A.M. '77 (HON) [12] Honolulu, HI St. Philomena Church.
Waterfall, Richard A. '49 (SB) Retired.
Waterman, Gerald *o.f.m.conv.* (ATL) Lithia Springs, GA St. John Vianney Church.
Waterman, Gerald *o.f.m.conv.* '85 (BGP) [6] Danbury, CT Sacred Heart Church.
Waters, J. Kevin *s.j.* '64 (SPK) [C] Spokane, WA Gonzaga University.
Waters, John *s.j.* '64 (PBL) [8] Pueblo, CO Our Lady of Mt. Carmel Church.
Waters, Joseph '56 (CHL) Lenoir, NC St. Francis of Assisi Church.
Waters, Joseph L. *s.s.j.* '45 (WDC) [B] Washington, DC St. Joseph's Seminary.
Waters, Joseph L. *s.s.j.* '49 (BAL) [S] Baltimore, MD St. Joseph Society of the Sacred Heart House of Central Administration.
Waters, Joseph L. '87 (SP) Temple Terrace, FL Corpus Christi Church.

Waters, Mark S. '90 (STA) Fernandina Beach, FL St. Michael's Church.
Waters, Philip J. *o.s.b.* '72 (NEW) [23] Newark, NJ St. Mary's Church; [N] Newark, NJ Newark Abbey.
Waters, Robert E. '69 (BUF) Corfu, NY St. Francis of Assisi Church; Crittenden, NY St. Patrick Church.
Waters, Robert J. '60 (SC) Merrill, IA Assumption Church.
Waters, William F. *o.s.a.* (BO) [7] Lawrence, MA St. Mary Immaculate Conception Church.
Wathen, Ambrose G. *o.s.b.* '65 (NO) [P] St. Benedict, LA St. Joseph Abbey.
Wathier, Douglas O. '84 (DUB) [C] Dubuque, IA Loras College; [L] Dubuque, IA Mt. Loretto Convent.
Watkins, Clarence N. '67 (ARL) Retired.
Watkins, James D. '89 (WDC) [1] Washington, DC St. Matthew Church.
Watkins, Jean '82 (ORG) [G] Fullerton, CA St. Jude Medical Center.
Watkins, Mark T. '91 (CIN) [1] Cincinnati, OH St. Peter in Chains Church.
Watkins, Paul D. *o.p.* '90 (NO) [P] New Orleans, LA Dominican Friars, Southern Dominican Province of St. Martin de Porres.
Watkins, Thomas F. '74 (R) Wendell, NC St. Eugene Church.
Watrin, Clarence E. *c.s.b.* '59 (GAL) [Q] Sugar Land, TX Basilian Mission Center.
Watrin, Eugene L. *s.j.* '52 (FgM) Provinces.
Watroba, Boleslaus M. '35 (ALB) [2] Watervliet, NY Immaculate Conception Church; Retired.
Watson, Cletus M. *t.o.r.* '66 (STA) [4] Jacksonville, FL Church of the Crucifixion.
Watson, David E. *s.j.* '92 (TOL) [6] Toledo, OH Gesu Church.
Watson, Douglas *s.c.j.* '83 (MIL) [P] Hales Corners, WI Priests of the Sacred Heart.
Watson, J. Vincent *o.p.* '63 (CIN) [28] Cincinnati, OH St. Gertrude Church; [M] Cincinnati, OH St. Gertrude Priory.
Watson, Msgr. James P. '58 (MAN) Retired.
Watson, Joseph '92 (PH) West Chester, PA SS. Simon and Jude Church.
Watson, Joseph T. *s.j.* '52 (NEW) [C] Jersey City, NJ St. Peter's Preparatory School.
Watson, Mark '96 (SHP) On Special Assignment.
Watson, Michael B. '86 (COL) [5] Columbus, OH St. Andrew Church.
Watson, Timothy *c.ss.r.* (DEN) [33] Denver, CO St. Joseph's Church.
Watson, Walter *s.j.* '70 (DEN) [2] Arvada, CO St. Joan of Arc Church.
Watson, William A. '62 (PEO) [14] Peoria, IL St. Thomas Church.
Watson, William M. *s.j.* '85 (SPK) [C] Spokane, WA Gonzaga University.
Watt, Joseph '68 (MRY) Retired.
Watters, Timothy J. '71 (CHR) Absent On Leave.
Watters, William J. *s.j.* '65 (BAL) [39] Baltimore, MD St. Ignatius Church; [J] Baltimore, MD St. Ignatius Loyola Academy; [W] Baltimore, MD Radio Mass of Baltimore, Inc.
Watterson, John E. '62 (PRO) [9] Pawtucket, RI St. Mary of the Immaculate Conception Church.
Wattigny, Patrick B. '94 (NO) [3] Kenner, LA St. Elizabeth Ann Seton Church.
Watts, Albert W. '59 (BGP) [M] Norwalk, CT Notre Dame Convalescent Home; [Q] Norwalk, CT Regional House of Sisters of St. Thomas of Villanova.
Watts, Msgr. Roger J. '59 (BGP) Retired.
Watts, Thomas H. '57 (ROC) Van Etten, NY St. Pius the Tenth Church; Waverly, NY St. James Church.
Watts, Trent L. '93 (R) Wilson, NC Church of St. Therese.
Watts, Wayne F. '90 (CHI) [176] Chicago, IL Queen of All Saints Basilica Church; [A] Chicago, IL Archbishop Quigley Preparatory Seminary.
Watzke, James N. *c.s.c.* '63 (FTW) [J] South Bend, IN Congregation of Holy Cross, Indiana Province, Provincial House.
Waudby, Lawrence '90 (BAL) Special Assignment.
Waudby, Lawrence A., Jr. (BAL) [5] Baltimore, MD St. Alphonsus, Shrine of Church.
Waugh, John G. '55 (PEO) Wedron, IL St. Joseph's Church; Sheridan, IL Illinois Industrial School for Boys.
Wawerski, Msgr. Edward '61 (RVC) Hempstead, NY St. Ladislaus Church.
Wawiorka, Ray W. '56 (MIL) Retired.
Wawrzycki, Andrew '70 (ORL) Clermont, FL Blessed Sacrament Church.
Wawrzyniakowski, Edward J. '57 (MIL) Cedarburg, WI St. Francis Borgia Church.
Wawrzynski, Edward A. '60 (YAK) Retired.
Way, Edmund J. *o.p.* '43 (WDC) [11] Washington, DC St. Dominic Church & Priory Church.
Wayda, Henry A. '41 (SCR) Retired.
Wayne, David A. *s.j.* '68 (DEN) [D] Aurora, CO Regis Jesuit High School; [M] Aurora, CO Regis Jesuit High School - Jesuit Community.
Waznak, Robert J. *s.s.* '64 (SCR) On Duty Outside the Diocese.
Waznak, Robert P. *s.s.* '64 (BAL) [S] Baltimore, MD Sulpician Provincial House.
Wdowiak, Boleslaw '65 (SAC) Retired and in Senior Ministry.
Wdzieczny, Gilbert *o.f.m.conv.* '42 (HRT) [K] New Britain, CT St. Lucian's Residence, Inc.
Wdzieczyny, Gilbert *o.f.m.conv.* '42 (HRT) [M] New Britain, CT Conventual Franciscans.
Wea, Raymundus Bhia *s.v.d.* '82 (LA) [Q] Los Angeles, CA Casa Guadalupe.
Weakley, Robert *o.f.m.* '68 (PEO) Metamora, IL St. Mary of Lourdes Church.
Wearden, Msgr. Francis G. '54 (GAL) Retired.
Wearsch, Ronald '92 (CLV) Willowick, OH St. Mary Magdalene Church.
Weary, William M. '84 (HBG) Danville, PA St. Joseph Church.
Weaver, Cyprian *o.s.b.* '72 (FgM) American - Cassinese Congregation Foreign Missions.
Weaver, Cyprian *o.s.b.* '72 (SCL) [I] Collegeville, MN St. John's Abbey, of the Order of St. Benedict.
Weaver, Jeffrey M. '82 (CLV) North Royalton, OH St. Albert the Great Church.
Weaver, John G. '70 (HRT) [1] Torrington, CT St. Francis of Assisi Church; [3] Torrington, CT St. Mary's Church.
Weaver, Mark *o.f.m.conv.* '77 (FgM) Conventual Franciscan Foreign Missions.
Weaver, Patrick '63 (CAM) On Leave of Absence.
Weaver, Richard '63 (DAL) [2] Dallas, TX All Saints Church.
Webb, Raymond J. '67 (CHI) [A] Mundelein, IL University of St. Mary of the Lake-Mundelein Seminary.
Webber, Donald *c.p.* '73 (CHI) [N] Chicago, IL Passionist Provincial Office; [N] Chicago, IL Passionist Community-Immaculate Conception Monastery.
Webber, Msgr. Donald S. '62 (SB) Special or Other Diocesan Assignment.
Webber, Lawrence *o.f.m.cap.* (CHI) [N] Chicago, IL St. Clare Friary.
Webber, Lawrence *o.f.m.cap.* '80 (FgM) Capuchin Foreign Missions.
Weber, Alan '84 (SP) [T] Tampa, FL Catholic Student Center, University of South Florida.
Weber, Allen *o.f.m.* '65 (BUF) [C] St. Bonaventure, NY St. Bonaventure University; [O] St. Bonaventure, NY St. Bonaventure Friary.
Weber, Arnold *o.s.b.* '52 (SCL) [I] Collegeville, MN St. John's Abbey, of the Order of St. Benedict.
Weber, Arnold *o.s.b.* '52 (STP) Wayzata, MN Holy Name Church.
Weber, Bernard *c.p.* '81 (GAL) [Q] Houston, TX Congregation of the Passion, Holy Name Retreat Center.
Weber, Charles E. '53 (COV) Retired.
Weber, Charles P. '57 (BO) Senior Priests.
Weber, Chuck (WCH) [H] Wichita, KS Spiritual Life Center.
Weber, Daniel C. *s.j.* '60 (P) [Q] Portland, OR Jesuit Development & Communications Office.
Weber, Daniel C. *s.j.* '60 (SEA) [C] Tacoma, WA Bellarmine Preparatory School.
Weber, David C. '77 (CLV) [1] Cleveland, OH Cathedral of St. John the Evangelist; [Y] Cleveland, OH St. John Cathedral Endowment Trust.
Weber, Dennis M. *s.c.* '97 (PH) [M] Springfield, PA Cardinal Krol Center.
Weber, Donald C. '53 (BUF) Sheldon, NY St. Cecilia Church.
Weber, Donald E. '58 (GR) [7] Grand Rapids, MI Holy Name of Jesus Church; On Special Assignment.
Weber, Donald N. '47 (MIL) Retired.
Weber, Edward J. '76 (NY) West Nyack, NY St. Francis of Assisi Church.
Weber, Eugene J. '72 (WH) Romney, WV Our Lady of Grace Church.
Weber, Fidelis F. *t.o.r.* '55 (PH) [D] Fairless Hills, PA Conwell-Egan Catholic High School; [AA] Fairless Hills, PA St. Anthony Friary.
Weber, Msgr. Francis J. '59 (LA) Mission Hills, CA San Fernando Rey Church.
Weber, Frank (GB) New Holstein, WI Holy Rosary Church; St. Anna, WI St. Ann Church.
Weber, Frank W. '62 (PAT) [3] Clifton, NJ St. Brendan Church.
Weber, Gabriel M. *o.s.m.* '49 (CHI) [N] Chicago, IL Order of Friar Servants of Mary (Servites) United States of America Province, Inc.
Weber, Gabriel M. *o.s.m.* '49 (DEN) [22] Denver, CO Our Lady of Mt. Carmel Church.
Weber, George A. '60 (CAM) Retired.
Weber, George J. *c.m.* '54 (DAL) Terrell, TX St. John Church; Terrell, TX State Hospital; [K] Dallas, TX Congregation of the Mission, Southern Province.
Weber, George J. *c.m.* '54 (FgM) Vincentian Foreign Missions.
Weber, Gerard *o.m.i.* '62 (SAT) [M] San Antonio, TX Oblate Benson Residence (Southwest Area); [T] San Antonio, TX Oblate Lourdes Grotto Shrine of the Southwest, Tepeyac de San Antonio.
Weber, Gerard P. '43 (CHI) Retired; [X] Chicago, IL Foundation for Adult Catechetical Teaching Aids.
Weber, Gordon A. '52 (MIL) Retired.
Weber, Harold J. *s.j.* '44 (FgM) Provinces.
Weber, Herbert F. '74 (TOL) Mansfield, OH St. Peter Church.
Weber, Jacques *s.j.* '49 (GAL) [18] Houston, TX St. Cecilia Church.
Weber, James H. '43 (E) Retired.
Weber, Jerome '67 (HT) Grand Caillou, LA Holy Family Church; Theriot, LA St. Eloi Church.
Weber, Jerome F. '56 (SY) [3] Utica, NY Our Lady of Lourdes Church.
Weber, John (LSC) Mesilla, NM St. Albino Church.
Weber, Msgr. John George '43 (SAL) Retired.
Weber, John R. *c.s.sp.* '61 (PIT) [3] Millvale, PA Holy Spirit Church.
Weber, Joseph A. '76 (PRM) St. Louis, MO St. Louis Church.
Weber, Joseph A. '76 (STL) New Melle, MO Immaculate Heart of Mary Church.
Weber, Joseph J. '66 (BRK) [57] Brooklyn, NY Holy Innocents Church.
Weber, Joseph O. '57 (SCR) Carverton, PA St. Frances Cabrini Church.
Weber, Keith '83 (SAL) Manhattan, KS St. Isidore Church; [G] Manhattan, KS St. Isidore's Catholic Student Center.
Weber, Kevin '92 (SAL) Ellis, KS St. Mary's Church.
Weber, Leo F. *s.j.* '56 (FgM) Provinces.
Weber, Mark *s.v.d.* '82 (CHI) [15] Chicago, IL St. Anselm Church.
Weber, Mark E. *s.v.d.* '82 (CHI) [B] Techny, IL Divine Word Residence; [N] Techny, IL Society of the Divine Word, Provincial Headquarter-Chicago Prov.
Weber, Matthew *s.c.* '90 (LAN) [E] Chelsea, MI St. Louis Center for Exceptional Children & Adults.
Weber, Michael J. *o.praem.* '77 (GB) [I] De Pere, WI St. Norbert Abbey.
Weber, Norbert B. *m.s.c.* '57 (RCK) Lee, IL St. James Church; [G] Aurora, IL Missionaries of the Sacred Heart Community.
Weber, Randall '91 (SAL) Abilene, KS St. Andrew's Church.
Weber, Robert C. '81 (SY) Holland Patent, NY St. Leo Church; Marcy, NY Mid-State Correctional Facility; Special Assignment.
Weber, Robert P. (CAM) Bridgeton, NJ Southwoods State Prison.
Weber, Robert P. '65 (CAM) Bridgeton, NJ Immaculate Conception Church; Delmont, NJ Southern State Correctional Facility.
Weber, Samuel *o.s.b.* '96 (IND) [J] St. Meinrad, IN St. Meinrad Archabbey.
Weber, Terry '85 (SFS) Miller, SD St. Ann Church.
Weber, Theodore '55 (P) Retired.
Weber, Thomas H. '57 (CLV) Retired.
Weber, Thomas L. '74 (CLV) [43] Cleveland, OH St. Leo the Great Church.
Webster, Andrew J. '00 (DET) Canton, MI Saint John Neumann Church.
Webster, John C. '76 (SFR) Pacifica, CA St. Peter Church.
Webster, Robert E. '86 (ORL) Daytona Beach, FL St. Paul's Church; Special Assignment.
Wechter, David *o.c.s.o.* '58 (WIN) [G] Houston, MN Hermits of St. Mary of Carmel, H.S.M.C.
Weckbach, Hanford E. *s.j.* '43 (LA) [C] Los Angeles, CA Loyola Marymount University.
Weckerle, Leo F. '58 (BAK) Redmond, OR St. Thomas Church.
Weckert, Paul *o.s.b.* '99 (SEA) Olympia, WA St. Michael Church.
Weckert, Paul M. *o.s.b.* '99 (SEA) [L] Lacey, WA St. Martin's Abbey.
Weckesser, James R. *m.m.* '55 (FgM) Maryknoll Foreign Missions.
Wedeking, Patrick '88 (GLP) Waterflow, NM Sacred Heart Church.
Wedig, James M. '93 (CIN) Wilmington, OH St. Columbkille Church; [Q] Wilmington, OH Wilmington College Campus Ministry.
Wedig, Mark *o.p.* '86 (MIA) [18] Miami, FL St. Dominic Church; [B] Miami, FL Barry University; [H] Miami, FL Dominican Fathers of Miami, Inc.
Weeden, Richard '63 (MIL) [K] Milwaukee, WI St. Joseph's Hospital of Franciscan Sisters, Milwaukee, Inc.
Weeg, Edmund J. '45 (DAV) Retired; [M] Davenport, IA St. Vincent Center.
Weeke, James L. '86 (OM) [11] Omaha, NE St. Bridget Church.
Weekly, Christopher *s.j.* '99 (SPK) [6] Spokane, WA St. Aloysius Church.
Weeks, Leonard (COS) [E] Colorado Springs, CO The Medalion (East); [E] Colorado Springs, CO The Medalion (West).
Weerakkody, Don Oliver '65 (AUS) Austin, TX Brackenridge Hospital; [F] Austin, TX Seton Medical Center.

Weerasinghe, Felix '64 (RVC) Syosset, NY St. Edward Confessor Church.
Weezorak, Dennis R. '86 (MET) South Amboy, NJ St. Mary Church.
Wegg, Mark R. '87 (NEW) On Duty Outside the Archdiocese.
Wegg, Mark R. '87 (ORL) [2] Ocala, FL Our Lady of the Springs Church.
Wegher, William F. '91 (LAN) [12] Flint, MI St. Michael Church.
Wegierski, Blase *o.f.m.conv.* '71 (BAL) [S] Ellicott City, MD Order of Friars Minor Conventual.
Weglicki, Michael '79 (LEX) Lancaster, KY St. William Church; Ottenheim, KY St. Sylvester Church.
Wegman, Richard H. '90 (MAN) Alton, NH St. Joan of Arc Church.
Wegner, Gary *o.f.m.cap.* '89 (MIL) [B] Mount Calvary, WI St. Lawrence Seminary; [P] Mount Calvary, WI St. Lawrence Friary.
Wegner, Laurian *o.f.m.* '78 (FgM) Franciscan Foreign Missions.
Wehage, Robert C. '71 (COV) Edgewood, KY St. Pius X Church.
Wehby, Albert *b.a.o.* '63 (NTN) North Hollywood, CA St. Anne Church.
Wehinger, Thomas E. '61 (TOL) [11] Toledo, OH Our Lady of Lourdes Church.
Wehman, Jack W. '80 (CIN) [67] Cincinnati, OH Our Lady of the Sacred Heart Church.
Wehn, Timothy Clark '79 (LAV) Ely, NV Sacred Heart Church.
Wehner, Edwin P. '69 (BIS) [4] Bismarck, ND St. Anne Church.
Wehner, Eugene C. *o.c.d.* '75 (MIL) [P] Milwaukee, WI Provincial Offices - Discalced Carmelites.
Wehner, James A. '95 (PIT) Graduate Studies.
Wehnert, Donald R. '63 (JOL) [2] Kankakee, IL St. Patrick Church.
Wehri, Francis *o.s.b.* '61 (BIS) [A] Richardton, ND Assumption Abbey.
Wehri, Francis *o.s.b.* '61 (FgM) American - Cassinese Congregation Foreign Missions.
Wehrle, Jonathan '78 (LAN) Okemos, MI St. Martha Church.
Wehrle, Peter G. '99 (NEW) Oradell, NJ St. Joseph's Church.
Wehrlen, Msgr. John B. '59 (PAT) Flanders, NJ St. Elizabeth Ann Seton Church.
Wehrlin, Leo J. '93 (Y) [10] Canton, OH St. Michael the Archangel Church.
Wehrmeyer, Richard *c.m.* '91 (PBL) Gardner, CO Sacred Heart Church; Walsenburg, CO St. Mary Church.
Wei, Luke '60 (BRK) [38] Brooklyn, NY St. Finbar's Church.
Weibel, George L. '48 (DEN) Retired.
Weibel, John F. '72 (E) Coudersport, PA St. Eulalia Church.
Weibl, Nicholas '64 (TOL) Sandusky, OH Holy Angels Church.
Weible, Thomas C. '59 (LA) Retired.
Weider, Gregory '63 (ALB) [9] Troy, NY Our Lady of Victory Church.
Weider, Gregory S. '63 (ALB) Johnsonville, NY St. Monica's Church; Schaghticoke, NY St. John the Baptist Church.
Weider, William *t.o.r.* '41 (PIT) [O] Pittsburgh, PA Franciscan Friars, T.O.R.
Weidert, Richard J. '95 (BEL) Modoc, IL St. Leo Church; Ruma, IL St. Patrick Church; [G] Ruma, IL Province Center, Adorers of the Blood of Christ, United States Province.
Weidie, Kent *s.t.* '98 (LA) Compton, CA Our Lady of Victory Church; Compton, CA Sagrado Corazon, Sacred Heart Church.
Weidman, Michael J. '95 (CHI) Orland Park, IL St. Francis of Assisi Church.
Weidner, Halbert *c.o.* '74 (CHR) [E] Rock Hill, SC Oratory of St. Philip Neri, Congregation of the Oratory of Pontifical Rite.
Weidner, Halbert *c.o.* '74 (HON) [8] Honolulu, HI Holy Trinity Church.
Weidner, Larry W. '80 (PHX) [14] Phoenix, AZ St. Joan of Arc Church.
Weidner, Mark *o.c.s.o.* '54 (P) [L] Lafayette, OR The Cistercian (Trappist) Abbey of Our Lady of Guadalupe.
Weier, Msgr. John A. '43 (DET) Retired.
Weigand, Dom Peter *o.s.b.* '70 (WDC) [E] Washington, DC St. Anselm's Abbey School.
Weigand, John J. '67 (CLV) [4] Lakewood, OH St. James Church.
Weigand, Joseph C. '62 (CLV) [4] Elyria, OH St. Mary Church.
Weigand, Peter *o.s.b.* '70 (WDC) [M] Washington, DC St. Anselm's Abbey.
Weigel, Edmund *c.pp.s.* '58 (KC) [J] Liberty, MO Precious Blood Center.
Weigel, Jovian C. *o.f.m.* '48 (CIN) [L] Cincinnati, OH Archbishop Leibold Home for the Aged.
Weiglein, John *s.m.* '50 (WH) [H] Wheeling, WV Good Shepherd Nursing Home.
Weigman, Joseph A. '91 (IND) [A] St. Meinrad, IN St. Meinrad Seminary.
Weigman, Joseph A. '91 (TOL) Special Assignment.
Weiher, Charles *c.s.c.* '53 (FTW) [J] Notre Dame, IN Holy Cross Community, Corby Hall, University of Notre Dame.
Weiher, Charles F. *c.s.c.* '53 (FTW) [B] Notre Dame, IN University of Notre Dame Du Lac.
Weiksnar, William J. *o.f.m.* '94 (BUF) [C] St. Bonaventure, NY St. Bonaventure University; [O] St. Bonaventure, NY St. Bonaventure Friary.
Weiksner, Jerome M. '55 (GBG) Retired.
Weil, Frank *o.carm.* '67 (JOL) [J] Darien, IL Carmelite Provincial Office.
Weil, Robert L. '88 (MET) [H] Asbury, NJ Lanteri House.
Weiler, Anthony '90 (SAM) [E] Shelbourne, VT Blessed Rafka Retreat Center.
Weiler, Michael F. *s.j.* '88 (SJ) [B] Santa Clara, CA Santa Clara University.
Weimer, Msgr. John '58 (BUF) [A] East Aurora, NY Christ the King Seminary.
Weimer, Msgr. John C. '58 (BUF) [R] Alfred, NY Campus Ministry.
Weinberger, Paul L. '89 (DAL) [3] Dallas, TX Blessed Sacrament Church.
Weiner, James J. '88 (NEW) Cranford, NJ St. Michael's Church.
Weiner, Philip '91 (STF) Yonkers, NY St. Michael Church.
Weinert, Allan *c.ss.r.* '72 (STL) [P] Liguori, MO Liguori Mission House/Redemptorists.
Weingartz, Francis '54 (DET) North Branch, MI St. Mary's Burnside Church.
Weingartz, Francis A. '54 (DET) Retired.
Weinholtz, Bernard *o.f.m.* '40 (PAT) [M] Ringwood, NJ Holy Name Friary, Inc.
Weinlader, Wayne T. *m.m.* '68 (NY) [DD] Maryknoll, NY Maryknoll Fathers and Brothers.
Weinlich, Alfred J. '35 (BRK) Retired; [S] Queens Village, NY Queen of Peace Residence.
Weinzapfel, Msgr. Thomas '45 (DAL) Retired.
Weir, Bernard E. '86 (DAV) [3] Muscatine, IA SS. Mary and Mathias of Muscatine Church; [4] Muscatine, IA Our Lady of Guadalupe Catholic Church.
Weirauch, William P. '35 (PIT) Retired; [O] Pittsburgh, PA St. John Vianney Manor.
Weis, Denis P. '63 (MIL) [7] West Allis, WI St. Mary, Help of Christians Church.
Weis, Earl A. *s.j.* '54 (CHI) [C] Chicago, IL Jesuit Community at Loyola University of Chicago.
Weis, Earl A. *s.j.* '54 (DET) [K] Detroit, MI Jesuit Provincial Office-Detroit Province of the Society of Jesus.
Weis, Eugene R. '62 (ROC) Waterloo, NY St. Mary Church.
Weis, Ivan '80 (BLX) White Cypress, MS St. Matthew the Apostle Church.
Weis, John '66 (SAG) Rapson, MI St. Joseph Church.
Weis, John H. '66 (PAT) On Duty Outside the Diocese.
Weis, Patrick *s.j.* (DEN) [31] Denver, CO St. Ignatius Loyola Church.
Weis, Patrick J. *s.j.* '94 (DEN) [M] Denver, CO Regis Jesuit Community (The Jesuits at Regis University).
Weis, Paul L. '57 (DUB) Bankston, IA St. Clement's Church.
Weisbeck, Paul P. '70 (SJ) [8] San Jose, CA Holy Spirit Church.
Weisbecker, Thomas '96 (OM) Columbus, NE St. Bonaventure Church.
Weiscopf, Daniel '90 (BRK) [218] Queens, NY Our Lady, Queen of Martyrs Church.
Weise, David *c.s.b.* '82 (OAK) [C] Oakland, CA Bishop O'Dowd High School.
Weise, Melvern A.. '57 (OM) Leigh, NE St. Mary Church.
Weise, Thomas D. '62 (MOB) Phenix City, AL St. Patrick Church; Phenix City, AL Mother Mary Church.
Weisenbaugh, Robert D. *s.j.* '71 (CHL) [J] Charlotte, NC Jesuit Community.
Weisenbeck, Jude *s.d.s.* '60 (MIL) [P] Milwaukee, WI Salvatorian Provincial Residence.
Weisenberger, Gary '77 (SEA) Gig Harbor, WA St. Nicholas Church.
Weisenberger, Leon *m.s.c.* '59 (FgM) Missionaries of the Sacred Heart Foreign Missions.
Weisenberger, Leon *m.s.c.* '59 (RCK) [G] Aurora, IL Missionaries of the Sacred Heart Community.
Weisenberger, Raymond *s.v.d.* '39 (MIL) [P] East Troy, WI Divine Word Seminary.
Weisenberger, Richard J. '79 (LFT) Marion, IN St. Paul Church.
Weisenburger, Edward J. '87 (OKL) Okarche, OK Holy Trinity Church.
Weisensel, Cyril O. '67 (MAD) Benton, WI St. Patrick Church; Hazel Green, WI St. Francis de Sales Church.
Weiser, Charles B. '66 (TR) [4] Long Branch, NJ St. Michael Church.
Weishaar, Leo '84 (MOB) [D] Mobile, AL Providence Hospital.
Weishaar, Ralph '44 (LA) [Q] Santa Barbara, CA Franciscan Friary, Order of Friars Minor (Old Mission).
Weishar, John A. '43 (PEO) Retired.
Weishar, Paul M. '48 (MIL) Retired.
Weisman, Raymond F. '76 (WIL) Pocomoke City, MD Holy Name of Jesus Church.
Weisner, Mark D. '95 (OAK) Pleasanton, CA The Catholic Community of Pleasanton Church.
Weiss, James F. '90 (E) On Leave of Absence.
Weiss, Jerome P. '77 (DUL) [9] Duluth, MN St. John's Church.
Weiss, John C. '67 (KC) [8] Kansas City, MO Christ the King Church.
Weiss, Joseph E. *s.j.* '85 (FTW) [B] Notre Dame, IN University of Notre Dame Du Lac.
Weiss, Nicholas *o.f.m.conv.* '58 (ALB) [12] Albany, NY Our Lady of Angels Church.
Weiss, Peter C. *s.s.j.* '79 (NO) [39] New Orleans, LA St. Joan of Arc Church.
Weiss, Richard '80 (ELP) [14] El Paso, TX Our Lady of Assumption Church.
Weiss, Robert *c.p.* '65 (DET) [K] Detroit, MI St. Paul of the Cross Community, Congregation of the Passion.
Weiss, Robert E. '73 (BGP) Newtown, CT St. Rose of Lima Church.
Weiss, Robert F. *s.j.* '59 (STL) [P] St. Louis, MO Hallahan House; [P] St. Louis, MO The Jesuits of the Missouri Province.
Weissbeck, Reinhold B. '72 (DEN) Brighton, CO St. Augustine Church.
Weisse, Thomas A. *s.s.s.* '75 (GAL) [25] Houston, TX Corpus Christi Church.
Weist, Edward F. '69 (CLV) Litchfield, OH Our Lady Help of Christians Church.
Weitensteiner, Joseph M. '66 (SPK) [H] Spokane, WA Morning Star Boys' Ranch, Inc.
Weithman, Martin V. '80 (COL) Pickerington, OH Seton Church.
Weithman, Raymond *c.ss.r.* '56 (NY) [DD] Esopus, NY Redemptorist Priests and Brothers C.Ss.R. (Province of Baltimore).
Weithman, Robert J. '55 (TOL) [3] Fremont, OH St. Casimir Church.
Weitzel, Eugene J. *c.s.v.* '59 (SFD) Arenzville, IL St. Fidelis Church; Beardstown, IL St. Alexius Church.
Weitzel, Stephen D. '90 (HBG) Mechanicsburg, PA St. Joseph Church.
Weitzel, Theodore '68 (JOL) Hinsdale, IL St. Isaac Jogues Church.
Weixelman, Richard *o.m.i.* '65 (FgM) Oblates Foreign Missions.
Wekerle, Ron '90 (B) Jerome, ID St. Jerome's Church.
Welbers, Thomas '68 (LA) Claremont, CA Our Lady of the Assumption Church.
Welch, Bernard J. '81 (PRT) Military Chaplains.
Welch, Christopher (DET) Detroit, MI Beaumont Hospital.
Welch, Christopher '85 (ALB) [C] Saratoga Springs, NY Saratoga Central Catholic High School.
Welch, Christopher '94 (ALB) Ushers, NY Corpus Christi Church; [R] Saratoga, NY Skidmore College.
Welch, D. Michael '70 (IND) [18] Indianapolis, IN St. Christopher Church.
Welch, Eugene A. *s.j.* '60 (BAL) [S] Baltimore, MD Jesuit Fathers and Brothers Maryland Provincial Curia.
Welch, Eugene A. *s.j.* '60 (FgM) Provinces.
Welch, Gregory T. '67 (STP) [18] Minneapolis, MN St. Austin Church.
Welch, J. Paul *s.s.* '39 (BAL) [O] Baltimore, MD St. Charles Villa; [S] Baltimore, MD St. Charles Villa.
Welch, John *o.carm.* '65 (WDC) [B] Washington, DC Whitefriars Hall; [V] Washington, DC Carmelite Institute.
Welch, John E. *m.s.* '60 (NOR) Danielson, CT St. James Church.
Welch, John J. *s.j.* '55 (FgM) Provinces.
Welch, Joseph *c.s.s.* '37 (BO) [Z] Waltham, MA Stigmatine Fathers and Brothers.
Welch, Joseph '91 (OAK) [4] Concord, CA Queen of All Saints Church.
Welch, Robert J. *s.j.* '60 (LA) [C] Los Angeles, CA Loyola Marymount University.
Welch, Thomas David '56 (RIC) Retired.
Welch, William F. '36 (DET) Retired.
Welch, William J. '55 (GLP) Snowflake, AZ Our Lady of the Snows Church.
Weldgen, Msgr. Francis G. '59 (BUF) [4] Tonawanda, NY St. Christopher Church.
Welding, Brian J. '91 (PIT) Graduate Studies.
Weldishofer, Bernard '92 (CIN) [69] Cincinnati, OH Our Lady of Visitation Church.
Weldom, Michael *o.f.m.* '81 (MRY) [H] San Juan Bautista, CA St. Francis Retreat Center.
Weldon, Eric M. '00 (WCH) Pittsburg, KS Our Lady of Lourdes Church.
Weldon, James F. '98 (WCH) [13] Wichita, KS St. Francis of Assisi Church.

Weldon, Michael *o.f.m.* (OAK) [N] Oakland, CA Franciscan Friars Provincial Office, Province of St. Barbara.
Weling, John B. *s.j.* (NO) [C] New Orleans, LA Loyola University New Orleans.
Welk, Thomas *c.pp.s.* '69 (WCH) [G] Wichita, KS Adorers of the Blood of Christ.
Welkie, Paul P. '57 (ALN) Nesquehoning, PA Sacred Heart Church; Retired.
Wellar, Thomas '80 (CC) Ingleside, TX Our Lady of the Assumption Church.
Welle, Jacob *m.s.c.* '50 (ALN) Nazareth, PA Holy Family Church; [A] Center Valley, PA Missionaries of the Sacred Heart.
Wellems, Bruce *c.m.f.* '86 (CHI) [78] Chicago, IL Holy Cross/Immaculate Heart of Mary Church; [N] Oak Park, IL Claretian Fathers Headquarters of U.S.A. Eastern Province.
Weller, Andre *o.f.m.cap.* '63 (FgM) Capuchin Foreign Missions.
Weller, Arnold *o.c.s.o.* '38 (P) [L] Lafayette, OR The Cistercian (Trappist) Abbey of Our Lady of Guadalupe.
Weller, Harold E. '45 (LFT) Retired.
Weller, Joseph W. '64 (KAL) Retired.
Wellisch, Robert B. '69 (STP) [C] St. Paul, MN University of St. Thomas.
Wellman, Msgr. Dale L. '64 (PEO) Milan, IL St. Ambrose Church.
Wellmeier, Herbert J. '56 (SAV) Richmond Hill, GA St. Anne Church.
Wells, Jack M. '72 (P) Newport, OR Sacred Heart Church.
Wells, James *o.f.m.* '82 (NY) [DD] New York, NY Franciscan Province of the Immaculate Conception.
Wells, Morris F. *o.carm.* (VEN) Englewood, FL St. Raphael Church.
Wells, Msgr. Patrick R. '93 (GAL) [30] Houston, TX St. Francis of Assisi Church.
Wells, Peter B. '91 (TLS) On Duty Outside the Diocese.
Wells, Peter VB. '84 (PAT) Madison, NJ St. Vincent Martyr Church.
Wells, Philip '83 (SAC) Elk Grove, CA Good Shepherd Catholic Church; Elk Grove, CA Rio Consumnes Correctional Center.
Wells, Robert '86 (MIL) On Leave.
Welna, Floyd '50 (SAG) Retired.
Welp, Msgr. Harry J. '45 (COV) Retired.
Welsch, Gerard R. '66 (STL) [2] Creve Coeur, MO St. John Bosco Church.
Welsch, John '46 (Y) Retired.
Welschmeyer, Joseph J. '00 (STL) Fenton, MO St. Paul Church.
Welsh, Msgr. Aloysius J. '40 (NEW) Retired; [N] Caldwell, NJ The Rev. Msgr. James F. Kelley Residence for Retired Priests.
Welsh, Bartholomew '43 (LA) [Q] Santa Barbara, CA Franciscan Friary, Order of Friars Minor (Old Mission).
Welsh, Charles *s.j.* '72 (FgM) Provinces.
Welsh, Msgr. James F. '56 (CAM) Retired.
Welsh, John *s.j.* '56 (LAF) Grand Coteau, LA St. Charles Borromeo Church.
Welsh, Joseph L. '66 (BO) Abington, MA St. Nicholas Church.
Welsh, Patrick J. '00 (PH) Media, PA Nativity of the Blessed Virgin Mary Church.
Welsh, Patrick J. '98 (CIN) [30] Cincinnati, OH Guardian Angels Church.
Welsh, Peter J. '80 (PH) [2] Chester, PA Saint Katharine Drexel Church.
Welsh, Richard '60 (DET) [4] Warren, MI St. Dorothy Church.
Welsh, Msgr. Robert E. '44 (BRK) Retired.
Welsh, Robert J. *s.j.* (DET) [K] Detroit, MI Jesuit Provincial Office-Detroit Province of the Society of Jesus.
Welsh, Timothy L. *o.c.s.o.* '51 (DUB) [K] Peosta, IA New Melleray Abbey, Order of Cistercians of the Strict Observance.
Welsh, Vincent F. '89 (PH) [135] Philadelphia, PA St. Paul Church.
Welsh, William P. '60 (CHI) Skokie, IL St. Lambert Church.
Welshons, Glendon R. *s.j.* '62 (RC) St. Francis, SD Rosebud Reservation Church.
Welsmiller, Francis F. '44 (SAG) Retired.
Welstead, Flavian *o.f.m.cap.* '67 (SFR) [N] Burlingame, CA Capuchin Provincial House.
Welter, Charles J. *c.m.* '45 (CHI) [N] Chicago, IL DePaul Vincentian Residence.
Weltin, Richard W. '83 (SFD) Oblong, IL Our Lady of Lourdes Church; Robinson, IL St. Elizabeth Church.
Welton, Arthur T. '69 (NY) [143] Bronx, NY St. Francis Xavier Church.
Weltzer, Arthur '32 (SAV) [1] Columbus, GA Holy Family Church; Retired.
Welzbacher, George A. '51 (STP) New Market, MN St. Nicholas Church; [C] St. Paul, MN University of St. Thomas.
Wempe, Michael '66 (LA) [17] Los Angeles, CA Immaculate Heart of Mary Church; Los Angeles, CA Cedar Sinai Medical Center.
Wempe, Richard C. '52 (KCK) Retired.
Wendel, Alfred W. '78 (ATL) [4] Atlanta, GA Immaculate Heart of Mary Church.
Wendel, Alfred W. '78 (CHY) On Duty Outside the Diocese.
Wendel, Paul G. *c.s.c.* '55 (FTW) [L] Notre Dame, IN Holy Cross Mission House; [M] Notre Dame, IN Our Lady of Fatima Retreat Center.
Wendelken, Robert M. '61 (CLV) Solon, OH St. Rita Church.
Wenderoth, Joseph R. '62 (BAL) Retired.
Wendrychowicz, John B. '53 (PH) [82] Philadelphia, PA St. Josaphat Church.
Wendrychowicz, John B. '73 (PH) [86] Philadelphia, PA St. Ladislaus Church.
Wendt, Frank '70 (PSC) [C] Miami, FL Holy Cross Community.
Wendt, Patrick R. '79 (MIL) West Bend, WI Immaculate Conception Church.
Wendzikowski, Msgr. Mecislaus S. '59 (BUF) Retired.
Wenger, Sean A. '95 (GAL) [72] Houston, TX Queen of Peace Church; [U] Houston, TX Catholic Charismatic Center.
Wenig, Laurin J. '73 (MIL) Whitefish Bay, WI Holy Family Church.
Weninger, Ronald *c.ss.r.* '49 (FgM) Redemptorist Foreign Missions.
Wenke, Leonard C. '79 (CIN) [9] Cincinnati, OH St. Anthony Church.
Wenning, Grigion *o.f.m.cap.* '54 (GB) [I] Appleton, WI St. Fidelis Friary.
Wenning, Paul A. '45 (SPK) Retired.
Wenninger, Magnus *o.s.b.* '45 (SCL) [I] Collegeville, MN St. John's Abbey, of the Order of St. Benedict.
Wenninger, William '54 (SUP) Retired.
Wensing, Michael G. *s.t.l.* (BAL) [A] Emmitsburg, MD Mount St. Mary's Seminary.
Wenting, Msgr. James J. '46 (JC) [A] Hannibal, MO St. Thomas Aquinas Seminary.
Wentink, William R. '70 (RCK) [D] Rockford, IL Saint Anthony Medical Center.
Wentz, Aelred W. *o.c.s.o.* '85 (ROC) [I] Piffard, NY Abbey of the Genesee.
Wenz, Robert '82 (CLV) Bedford, OH St. Pius X Church.
Wenzel, Edward J. '51 (MAR) Retired.
Wenzel, James *o.s.a.* '56 (BO) [C] North Andover, MA Merrimack College; [CC] North Andover, MA Merrimack College Campus Ministry Center.
Wenzel, Kamil *o.f.m.conv.* '66 (FgM) Conventual Franciscan Foreign Missions.
Wenzel, Timothy '66 (SCL) Sauk Centre, MN St. Paul's Church.
Wenzinger, George E. '78 (TOL) Defiance, OH St. John the Evangelist Church.
Wenzinger, Mark Edward *o.s.b.* '95 (GBG) [H] Latrobe, PA Saint Vincent Archabbey.
Wenzinger, Robert (FRS) [H] Fresno, CA Fresno District Council.
Wenzinger, Robert D. '82 (FRS) [5] Bakersfield, CA St. Joseph Church.
Werbicki, Walter '57 (BUF) [4] Dunkirk, NY St. Elizabeth Ann Seton Church; Lakeview, NY Lakeview Shock Incarceration Correctional Facility.
Werbylo, Walter M. *c.s.b.* '90 (GAL) [Q] Houston, TX Residence of the Basilian Fathers of the University of St. Thomas.
Werling, Keith V. '99 (JOL) Downers Grove, IL St. Mary of Gostyn Church.
Werner, Ben '64 (LAN) Ann Arbor, MI University of Michigan Hospitals/Pastoral Care Dept.
Werner, Msgr. Cyril J. '45 (OM) Retired.
Werner, George J. *s.m.m.* '57 (RVC) [M] Bay Shore, NY Montfort Missionaries.
Werner, Gerald *o.c.d.* '74 (SJ) [L] San Jose, CA Carmelite Monastery, Novitiate.
Werner, John J. '00 (MET) Alpha, NJ St. Mary Church.
Werner, John P. '51 (COV) Retired; [I] Edgewood, KY St. Elizabeth Medical Center, South.
Werner, Jon K. '82 (SY) [1] Liverpool, NY Christ the King Church.
Werner, Justin '58 (GB) Retired.
Werner, Leo E. '51 (WH) Retired.
Werner, Steven A. '98 (SPK) Oroville, WA Immaculate Conception Church; Tonasket, WA Holy Rosary Church.
Werning, David H. '98 (WDC) [3] Bethesda, MD Little Flower Church.
Werr, Donald *o.f.m.* '46 (FWT) [H] Crowley, TX St. Francis Village, Inc.; [I] Crowley, TX St. Maximilian Kolbe Friary.
Werra, Bogdan '81 (KAL) Mattawan, MI St. John Bosco Church.
Wert, William *o.carm.* '86 (CHI) [D] Chicago, IL Mt. Carmel High School.
Wertanen, Steven '97 (DET) Northville, MI Our Lady of Victory Church.
Werth, Alvin '62 (SAL) Phillipsburg, KS SS. Philip and James Church.
Werth, Charles M. '53 (BUF) Retired.
Werth, Jerome *o.s.b.* '99 (KC) [A] Conception, MO Conception Seminary College; [J] Conception, MO Conception Abbey.
Werth, Loren '56 (SAL) Retired.
Werth, Robert T. '79 (ROC) [48] Rochester, NY St. Monica Church; [49] Rochester, NY Roman Catholic Community of the 19th Ward Church.
Werthman, Robert R. '60 (PIT) Allegheny County, PA Marian Manor, Inc.; [L] Pittsburgh, PA Marian Manor Corp.
Wertin, George P. '63 (STP) [27] Minneapolis, MN St. Joan of Arc Church.
Wertman, Raymond '72 (OG) On Duty Outside the Diocese.
Wertz, Gerald *s.d.b.* '88 (OAK) [E] Richmond, CA Salesian High School.
Wesdock, Thomas J. '00 (PBR) [1] Youngstown, OH Assumption of the Blessed Virgin Church.
Wesely, Eugene L. '57 (CR) Lake Eunice Township, MN St. Mary of the Lakes Church.
Wesely, Mark '93 (SAL) Elmo, KS St. Columba's Church; Herington, KS St. John the Evangelist Church; Hope, KS St. Phillip's Church.
Weseman, Alan R. '86 (NO) Madisonville, LA St. Anselm Church.
Wesley, Andrew '80 (DET) [75] Detroit, MI Transfiguration Church.
Weslin, Norman U. *o.s.* '86 (PCE) On Duty Outside the Diocese.
Wesloh, Ferdinand J. '64 (STL) [3] Florissant, MO St. Angela Merici Church.
Wesnofske, Matthias *o.f.m.cap.* '67 (NY) [57] New York, NY St. John the Baptist Church.
Wesoloski, Richard J. '72 (PIT) Imperial, PA St. Columbkille Church.
Wesolowski, Anthony P. *o.s.b.* '72 (SAV) [B] Savannah, GA Benedictine Military School; [F] Savannah, GA The Benedictine Priory.
Wesolowski, Edmund C. '48 (PH) [69] Philadelphia, PA Immaculate Conception Church; Retired.
Wessel, John F. '57 (CLV) Retired.
Wessels, Cletus J. *o.p.* '57 (STP) [15] Minneapolis, MN St. Albert the Great Church.
Wesselsky, Msgr. Emil J. '56 (SAT) [40] San Antonio, TX St. Henry Church.
Wessling, Floyd A. '64 (OM) Clarkson, NE SS. Cyril and Methodius Church.
Wessling, John E. '58 (CIN) [69] Cincinnati, OH Our Lady of Visitation Church; [F] Cincinnati, OH Ursuline Academy of Cincinnati.
West, Donald J. '90 (CIN) Bethel, OH St. Mary Church.
West, Gerald '59 (BAL) Retired; [T] Baltimore, MD Franciscan Sisters of Baltimore-General Motherhouse and Novitiate.
West, H. Gregory '93 (CHR) Bluffton, SC St. Gregory the Great Church.
West, James P. '86 (LR) Hot Springs National Park, AR St. John the Baptist Church.
West, John H. '80 (DET) Special Assignment; [P] Plymouth, MI St. John Center for Youth and Family; [Q] Detroit, MI St. Vincent de Paul Society.
West, Joseph *o.f.m.conv.* '92 (IND) [4] Terre Haute, IN St. Joseph Church.
West, Mauricio W. '79 (CHL) Special Assignment.
West, Norbert '56 (SUP) Retired.
West, Norbert R. '57 (Y) [I] Canton, OH House of Loreto.
West, Patrick J. '81 (BRK) [117] Brooklyn, NY St. Peter Claver Church; [120] Brooklyn, NY Queen of All Saints Church; [F] Brooklyn, NY Bishop Loughlin Memorial High School.
West, Peter '69 (NEW) On Duty Outside the Archdiocese.
West, Peter J. '91 (NY) [207] Staten Island, NY Immaculate Conception Church.
West, Stephen C. '79 (GBG) Derry, PA St. Joseph Church.
West, Thomas *o.f.m.* '86 (OAK) [A] Berkeley, CA Franciscan School of Theology; [N] Oakland, CA Franciscan Friars.
West, William (HRT) [I] New Haven, CT Hospital of St. Raphael.
West, Msgr. Willis W. '63 (NOR) Willimantic, CT St. Joseph Church.
Westbrook, J. Severyn '62 (SPK) Retired.
Wester, Charles H. '59 (MIL) Le Roy, WI St. Andrew Church; Mayville, WI St. Mary Church.
Wester, Donald R. '78 (STL) Bellefontaine Neighbors, MO Our Lady of Good Counsel Church.
Wester, John C. '76 (SFR) Special Assignment.
Wester, Kevin J. '90 (MIL) Armstrong, WI Good Shepherd Church.
Westerhoff, Ralph A. '62 (CIN) [50] Cincinnati, OH St. Lawrence Church.
Westfall, Joseph B. '93 (LFT) On Duty Outside the Diocese.
Westfield, Carlton J. '71 (BUF) Fredonia, NY St. Anthony Church.
Westhoven, Thomas *s.c.j.* '66 (RC) Eagle Butte, SD All Saints Church; Eagle Butte, SD Cheyenne River Reservation Church; [B] Eagle Butte, SD Sacred

Heart Community House.
Westhues, Msgr. John H. '48 (SPC) [1] Springfield, MO Cathedral of St. Agnes.
Weston, Thomas C. *s.j.* '78 (OAK) [N] Oakland, CA Murray Residence Community.
Westray, Kenneth M. '81 (SFR) Greenbrae, CA St. Sebastian Church.
Wetmore, John J. '73 (STL) Manchester, MO St. Joseph Church.
Wetter, Msgr. Richard L. '57 (BUF) Clarence, NY Our Lady of Peace Church.
Wetterer, Msgr. Edward V. '64 (BRK) [201] Queens, NY St. Michael Church.
Wetterholm, Lawrence J. '56 (BO) [1] Ipswich, MA Our Lady of Hope Church.
Wetzel, Leo *o.m.i.* '52 (BO) [Z] Tewksbury, MA Immaculate Heart of Mary Infirmary.
Wetzel, William I. '55 (STL) Retired.
Wetzler, Daniel E. '63 (SPK) [16] Spokane, WA St. Paschal Church.
Wevita, Bede '91 (LAV) North Las Vegas, NV St. John Neumann Church.
Wewer, Andrew '43 (LR) [A] Subiaco, AR Subiaco Monastery.
Wewers, William *o.s.b.* '67 (LR) Clarksville, AR Holy Redeemer Church; Morrison Bluff, AR SS. Peter and Paul Church.
Wey, Richard '50 (SCL) Retired.
Weyand, John '62 (ALB) Greenfield Center, NY St. Joseph Church.
Weydert, Donald D. '43 (DUB) Retired.
Weyer, John T. '73 (GAL) Sugar Land, TX St. Laurence Church.
Weyhing, John '51 (L) Retired.
Weyker, James *s.d.s.* '69 (FgM) Salvatorian Foreign Missions.
Weyls, Richard C. '93 (COL) [15] Columbus, OH St. Francis of Assisi Church.
Weymes, Gerald '74 (ARL) Chantilly, VA St. Timothy Church.
Weyrens, Ronald '82 (SCL) Waite Park, MN St. Joseph's Church.
Whalan, Thomas J. '81 (BO) Unassigned.
Whalen, Charles W. '44 (DUB) Retired.
Whalen, Daniel W. '00 (PIT) Crafton, PA St. Philip Church.
Whalen, David M. *o.s.f.s.* '71 (TOL) [K] Toledo, OH Oblates of St. Francis de Sales.
Whalen, Msgr. Earl L. '40 (CIN) Retired.
Whalen, Msgr. Edmund J. '84 (NY) [A] Yonkers, NY St. Joseph's Seminary; [A] Bronx, NY St. John Neumann Seminary Residence; [HH] New York, NY North American College of Rome, Alumni Assoc. of.
Whalen, Frank J. '68 (CIN) Military Chaplains.
Whalen, James R. '47 (GI) Retired.
Whalen, James W. '58 (STP) Coates, MN St. Agatha Church; Retired; [C] St. Paul, MN University of St. Thomas.
Whalen, John J. '69 (DAV) North English, IA St. Joseph's Church; Parnell, IA St. Joseph's Church.
Whalen, John J. '94 (BUR) Bethel, VT St. Anthony Church.
Whalen, John J. '94 (OM) Absent on Leave.
Whalen, John P. '53 (ALB) Retired.
Whalen, John T. (ALN) Frackville, PA SCI-Mahoney.
Whalen, Joseph E. '89 (GI) On Duty Outside the Diocese.
Whalen, Joseph E. '89 (LEX) [D] Lexington, KY St. Joseph Hospital.
Whalen, Joseph E. '99 (STP) [1] Minneapolis, MN The Basilica of St. Mary Co-.
Whalen, Joseph F. *m.s.* '89 (HRT) Rocky Hill, CT Veterans' Home and Hospital; [M] Hartford, CT Missionaries of LaSalette, Provincial Secretary.
Whalen, Joseph T. '71 (ALN) [4] Pottsville, PA St. Patrick Church.
Whalen, Michael D. *c.m.* '83 (BRK) [V] Jamaica, NY Vincentian Residence.
Whalen, Norman M. '54 (TUC) Retired.
Whalen, Paul A. '82 (GBG) Farmington, PA St. Joan of Arc Church.
Whalen, Robert B. '51 (BUR) Retired.
Whalen, Msgr. Thomas J. '67 (BGP) Shelton, CT St. Margaret Mary Church.
Whalen, Timothy (DET) [E] Orchard Lake, MI St. Mary's Preparatory.
Whalen, Timothy F. '78 (PIT) On Duty Outside the Diocese.
Whalen, William F. '55 (ALB) Retired.
Whalen, William H. '59 (MIL) [13] Milwaukee, WI St. Bernadette Church.
Wharton, Joseph E. '92 (WIL) [6] Wilmington, DE St. Hedwig Church.
Wharton, Paul J. '82 (WH) Montgomery, WV Immaculate Conception Church.
Whatley, Christopher '70 (BAL) [57] Baltimore, MD St. Mark Church.
Whatley, Francis *o.ss.t.* '88 (NO) [N] New Orleans, LA Mary-Joseph Residence for the Elderly.
Wheatley, Carroll '75 (OWN) Military Chaplains.
Wheatley, Dennis F. *o.f.m.* '84 (BO) [6] Waltham, MA Sacred Heart Church.
Wheatley, Herbert *o.f.m.* '67 (P) [J] Portland, OR Providence Portland Medical Center.
Wheatly, Charles J. '68 (MIL) Delavan, WI St. Andrew Church.
Wheaton, William F. '92 (SLC) [2] Kearns, UT St. Francis Xavier Church; [C] Kearns, UT St. Francis Xavier Regional School.
Whedbee, Dominic *o.c.s.o.* '77 (WOR) [A] Spencer, MA St. Joseph's Abbey School of Theology and Institute of Monastic Studies; [N] Spencer, MA St. Joseph's Abbey.
Whedbee, George *c.m.f.* '69 (LA) [Q] Los Angeles, CA Claretian Retreat Center Community.
Wheelahan, Michael '80 (OKL) Medford, OK St. Mary's Church.
Wheeland, Thomas H. '66 (ROC) [21] Rochester, NY Holy Cross Church.
Wheeler, Ambrose J. *c.s.c.* '47 (PHX) [G] Phoenix, AZ Holy Cross Congregation/Casa Santa Cruz.
Wheeler, Arthur F. *c.s.c.* '84 (P) [B] Portland, OR University of Portland; [L] Portland, OR Holy Cross Fathers & Brothers, C.S.C. - University of Portland.
Wheeler, Charles '79 (JOL) [3] Kankakee, IL St. Rose of Lima Church.
Wheeler, Clarence '54 (JC) Retired.
Wheeler, Daniel '75 (LAN) Tecumseh, MI St. Elizabeth Church.
Wheeler, Msgr. David A. '52 (DUB) [4] Dubuque, IA St. Mary's Church; Retired.
Wheeler, Florence (BGP) [X] Fairfield, CT The Institute for Religious Education and Pastoral Studies (REAPS).
Wheeler, James *o.f.m.* '66 (SFD) [5] Quincy, IL St. Francis Solanus Church; [K] Quincy, IL St. Francis Solanus Friary.
Wheeler, James D. *s.j.* '54 (KC) [B] Kansas City, MO Rockhurst University; [J] Kansas City, MO Rockhurst Jesuit Community.
Wheeler, James J. *s.j.* '68 (NY) [DD] New York, NY Murray-Weigel Hall.
Wheeler, James J. *s.j.* '68 (RVC) [O] Patchogue, NY St. Joseph's Prayer Center.
Wheeler, John '47 (SD) Coronado, CA Sacred Heart Church; Retired.
Wheeler, John P. *c.s.b.* '68 (DET) [E] Redford, MI Catholic Central High School.
Wheeler, Thomas *s.j.* '62 (PH) [AA] Philadelphia, PA Jesuit Community at St. Joseph's University.
Wheeler, Thomas F.X. *s.j.* '62 (PH) [BB] Merion Station, PA Religious Sisters of Mercy.
Wheeler, Thomas FX *s.j.* '62 (PH) [AA] Philadelphia, PA Jesuit Community at St. Joseph's University.
Wheeler, Wayne B., Jr. '79 (GR) Big Rapids, MI St. Paul's Campus Church.
Wheelock, Joseph P. '96 (OG) Lake Clear, NY St. John in the Wilderness Church; Saranac Lake, NY St. Bernard Church.
Wheelock, Robert *o.f.m.cap.* '64 (MIL) [Y] Milwaukee, WI Franciscan Peacemakers, Inc., Milwaukee.
Whelan, Charles M. *s.j.* '58 (NY) [DD] New York, NY "America;" Residence and publication office of the America Press; [HH] New York, NY America Press, Inc.
Whelan, Dennis '65 (RVC) Franklin Square, NY St. Catherine of Sienna Church.
Whelan, Edward J. *m.m.* '61 (FgM) Maryknoll Foreign Missions.
Whelan, Fintan *o.f.m.cap.* '60 (LA) [B] Santa Ynez, CA San Lorenzo Novitiate and Seminary.
Whelan, Gerald J. *c.s.c.* '55 (FgM) Holy Cross Foreign Missions.
Whelan, Gerald J. *c.s.c.* '55 (FTW) [J] South Bend, IN Congregation of Holy Cross, Indiana Province, Provincial House.
Whelan, James J. '73 (PH) Manoa, PA Sacred Heart Church.
Whelan, James P. '93 (NEW) Midland Park, NJ Nativity Church.
Whelan, John F. '58 (RVC) Malverne, NY Our Lady of Lourdes Church.
Whelan, Robert J. '83 (BRK) [14] Brooklyn, NY St. Augustine Church.
Whelan, Robert L. *s.j.* '44 (SPK) [C] Spokane, WA Gonzaga University.
Whelan, Steve *s.d.b.* '69 (SFR) [46] San Francisco, CA SS. Peter and Paul Church.
Whelan, William S. '57 (OM) Schuyler, NE St. Augustine Church.
Whelton, Daniel P. '70 (SR) Healdsburg, CA St. John the Baptist Church.
Whetstone, Richard J. *j.c.o.l.* '83 (PBR) Uniontown, PA St. John the Baptist Church.
Whipkey, Robert (DEN) Erie, CO St. Scholastica Church; Frederick, CO St. Theresa Church.
Whipkey, Robert G., Jr. '83 (DEN) Iliff, CO St. Catherine of Siena Church; Peetz, CO Sacred Heart Church; [P] Sterling, CO Northeastern Junior College (Sterling).
Whipple, Donald W. *c.s.c.* '57 (ORL) Retired; [F] Cocoa Beach, FL Holy Cross Fathers, Eastern Priests Province.
Whistle, Brad '81 (OWN) [5] Owensboro, KY Precious Blood Church.
Whitacre, John (SD) [F] San Diego, CA Scripps Mercy Hospital.
White, A. Paul '59 (BO) [22] Boston, MA Gate of Heaven Church.
White, Alan '84 (NSH) Absent on Leave.
White, Anthony J. '55 (NO) [50] New Orleans, LA St. Patrick Church.
White, Bernard (ALT) Huntingdon, PA State Correctional Institution.
White, Bernard C. '52 (CHI) Elmwood Park, IL St. Celestine Church; Retired.
White, Bernard L. '77 (ALT) Williamsburg, PA St. Joseph Church; Smithfield, PA State Correctional Institution.
White, Charles H. '65 (BRK) [248] Queens, NY St. Virgilius Church.
White, Charles S. *c.s.p.* '48 (NY) [DD] Jamaica Estates, NY Paulist Fathers Generalate.
White, Clark S. '74 (OG) Brasher Falls, NY St. Patrick Church; North Lawrence, NY St. Lawrence Church.
White, Cosmas *o.s.b.* '61 (P) Silverton, OR St. Paul Church; [L] St. Benedict, OR Mt. Angel Abbey.
White, Daniel C. '93 (LA) Westlake Village, CA St. Jude Church.
White, David '52 (SEA) Retired.
White, David F. *s.j.* '67 (NY) [F] New York, NY Xavier High School.
White, David P. (BO) Society of St. James the Apostle.
White, Denis E. '67 (JOL) Hopkins Park, IL Sacred Heart Church; Momence, IL St. Patrick Church.
White, Douglas '00 (PT) [13] Pensacola, FL St. Paul Church.
White, Msgr. Francis A. '49 (OG) Retired.
White, Francis P. *c.s.v.* '44 (LAV) [1] Las Vegas, NV Guardian Angel Church.
White, Gale '56 (DAL) Retired.
White, George M. *o.m.i.* '45 (HRT) [2] Waterbury, CT Immaculate Conception Church.
White, George M. *o.m.i.* '45 (NY) [FF] Newburgh, NY Our Lady of Hope Center.
White, Gervase F. *o.f.m.* '54 (BUF) [C] St. Bonaventure, NY St. Bonaventure University; [O] St. Bonaventure, NY St. Bonaventure Friary.
White, Gregory A. '96 (PAT) Absent on Leave.
White, James *c.ss.r.* '81 (MIL) [S] Oconomowoc, WI The Redemptorist Retreat Center.
White, James D. '69 (TLS) Skiatook, OK Sacred Heart Church.
White, Msgr. James E. '83 (NY) [134] Bronx, NY Blessed Sacrament Church.
White, James J. *s.j.* '71 (STL) [P] St. Louis, MO The Jesuits of the Missouri Province.
White, James R. '80 (NEW) Mahwah, NJ Immaculate Conception Church; [C] Oradell, NJ Bergen Catholic.
White, John *s.j.* (CLV) [D] Cleveland, OH St. Ignatius High School.
White, John '83 (RVC) Absent on Leave.
White, John J. '55 (NOR) Rockville, CT St. Bernard Church.
White, John J. '57 (BO) Senior Priests.
White, John L. *s.m.* '45 (CHI) [2] Oak Lawn, IL St. Gerald Church.
White, John R. '81 (CIN) Greenville, OH St. Mary Church.
White, John V. *s.j.* (DET) [K] Detroit, MI Jesuit Provincial Office-Detroit Province of the Society of Jesus.
White, Joseph L. *s.s.* '33 (BAL) [O] Baltimore, MD St. Charles Villa; [S] Baltimore, MD St. Charles Villa.
White, Joseph M. '92 (BO) Hull, MA St. Mary of the Assumption Church.
White, Kenneth R. '68 (PIT) Bethel Park, PA St. Thomas More Church; Allegheny County, PA Mt. Lebanon Manor Convalescent Center; Allegheny County, PA Manorcare Health Services.
White, Kevin '99 (BO) [W] Cambridge, MA Weston Jesuit Community.
White, Kris '41 (SB) Retired.
White, Msgr. Lawrence E. '70 (CC) [14] Corpus Christi, TX SS. Cyril and Methodius Church.
White, Leland J. '65 (CHR) On Duty Outside the Diocese.
White, Leo J. (BRK) Retired.
White, Msgr. Leo J. '56 (BRK) Released from Diocesan Assignment.
White, Leroy E. '56 (KAL) Retired.
White, Leroy E. '56 (LAN) Davison, MI St. John Church.
White, Lloyd W. '58 (SC) Retired.
White, Michael *c.s.sp.* (SD) [B] San Diego, CA University of San Diego.
White, Michael *c.s.sp.* '83 (SD) [C] San Diego, CA University of San Diego High School.
White, Michael J. '48 (BIR) Retired.
White, Michael J. '84 (BAL) Timonium, MD Church of the Nativity.
White, Paul *s.s.c.* '58 (LA) [67] Los Angeles, CA St.

Gregory Nazianzen Church.
White, Paul '83 (PT) [13] Pensacola, FL St. Paul Church.
White, Paul C. '89 (RCK) Sterling, IL Sacred Heart Church; [B] Sterling, IL Newman Central Catholic High School.
White, Paul R. *c.pp.s.* '53 (LFT) Francesville, IN St. Francis Solano Church; Medaryville, IN St. Henry Church; [A] Rensselaer, IN Saint Joseph's College.
White, Peter H. '62 (WOR) Rochdale, MA St. Aloysius-St. Jude Church.
White, Philip '85 (PT) Retired.
White, Ralph *o.f.m.conv.* '83 (SY) Bridgeport, NY St. Francis of Assisi Church.
White, Raymond F. *c.m.* '45 (CHI) [N] Chicago, IL DePaul Vincentian Residence.
White, Robert '70 (SD) On Duty Outside the Diocese.
White, Robert A. *s.j.* '62 (FgM) Provinces.
White, Robert H. *o.f.m.* '51 (BUF) [C] St. Bonaventure, NY St. Bonaventure University; [O] St. Bonaventure, NY St. Bonaventure Friary.
White, Robert H. '60 (DEN) Absent on Leave.
White, Robert K. '61 (SFR) Tomales, CA Church of the Assumption.
White, Robert L. '74 (STP) Victoria, MN St. Victoria Church.
White, Robert S. *c.s.s.* '73 (BO) [W] Waltham, MA Stigmatine House.
White, Roger *o.f.m.cap.* '65 (FgM) Capuchin Foreign Missions.
White, Stephen (DUL) Duluth, MN Indian Missions Church.
White, Stephen '98 (DUL) Grand Marais, MN St. John's Church.
White, Stephen C. '86 (PH) [34] Philadelphia, PA Christ the King Church.
White, Thomas '64 (BLX) [8] Biloxi, MS St. Mary Church.
White, Thomas '78 (LA) Palmdale, CA St. Mary Church.
White, Thomas J. '59 (JOL) Wheaton, IL St. Daniel the Prophet Church.
White, Tomas '78 (LA) Lancaster, CA California State Prison, L.A. County.
White, Msgr. William '58 (NY) On Duty Outside the Archdiocese.
White, Msgr. William '58 (PMB) [A] Boynton Beach, FL St. Vincent de Paul Regional Seminary.
White, William A. '90 (NY) Pine Plains, NY St. Anthony Church.
White, William J. '52 (CHI) [2] Oak Lawn, IL St. Gerald Church; Retired.
Whited, Msgr. Walter M. '66 (STL) Cottleville, MO St. Joseph Church.
Whiteing, Richard '80 (OM) Jackson, NE St. Patrick Church.
Whiteing, Richard J. '80 (OM) South Sioux City, NE St. Michael Church.
Whiteside, Daniel '92 (CHI) [2] Oak Park, IL St. Catherine of Siena-St. Lucy Church.
Whiteside, David '97 (PEO) [4] Rock Island, IL St. Pius X Church.
Whitestone, David A. '89 (ARL) Fairfax, VA St. Mary of Sorrows Church.
Whitley, Edward D. *c.s.p.* '51 (NY) [DD] Jamaica Estates, NY Paulist Fathers Generalate.
Whitley, John R. *c.s.b.* '54 (GAL) [Q] Sugar Land, TX Basilian Mission Center.
Whitley, Rufus J. *o.m.i.* (CHI) [X] Chicago, IL Oblates for International Pastoral.
Whitley, Rufus J. *o.m.i.* '76 (WDC) [M] Washington, DC Oblate College/Center for Mission Studies Community.
Whitlock, Joseph E. '55 (PRT) [1] Portland, ME Cathedral of the Immaculate Conception; Retired.
Whitman, Andrew P. *s.j.* '63 (TUC) [F] Tucson, AZ Jesuit Community of the Vatican Observatory.
Whitman, Dan G. '83 (KNX) Clinton, TN St. Therese Church; Helenwood, TN St. Jude Church; [K] Knoxville, TN Diocesan Council of Catholic Women.
Whitman, Glenn R. '75 (E) Girard, PA St. John the Evangelist Church.
Whitman, Mark (STL) [7] St. Louis, MO Immaculate Heart of Mary Church.
Whitman, Thomas J. '87 (E) [26] Erie, PA St. Matthew in the Woods Church; Waterford, PA St. Cyprian Church.
Whitmore, James R. *m.m.* '59 (SJ) [L] Los Altos, CA Maryknoll.
Whitmore, Msgr. Paul E. '54 (OG) Port Leyden, NY St. Martin Church.
Whitney, A. Peter '84 (GAL) La Marque, TX Our Lady Queen of Peace Church.
Whitney, John D. *s.j.* '94 (SEA) [L] Seattle, WA Jesuit Community.
Whitney, Patrick J. '68 (RVC) Lake Ronkonkoma, NY St. Elizabeth Ann Seton Church.
Whitney, Msgr. Paul J. '58 (BUF) Medina, NY St. Mary Church.
Whitney, Peter A. '84 (TYL) Retired.
Whitney, Msgr. Philip '47 (HT) Retired.
Whitney, Richard P. '87 (RVC) West Islip, NY Our Lady of Lourdes Church.
Whitsell, John '96 (TYL) Kilgore, TX Christ the King Church.
Whitson, Robley E. '58 (NY) On Duty Outside the Archdiocese.
Whitt, D. Reginald *o.p.* '76 (FTW) [B] Notre Dame, IN University of Notre Dame Du Lac.
Whittaker, Kenneth '77 (MIA) Deerfield Beach, FL St. Ambrose Church.
Whitten, Carlton *s.j.* '61 (MRY) San Luis Obispo, CA San Luis Obispo Church.
Whittier, James E. '53 (BO) Senior Priests.
Whittier, William O. '61 (STP) Retired.
Whittington, Justin *s.j.* '99 (PH) [G] Philadelphia, PA St. Joseph's Preparatory School; [AA] Philadelphia, PA Jesuit Community, Arrupe House.
Whittington, Kenneth L. '88 (CHL) Morganton, NC St. Charles Borromeo Church.
Whittington, Paul *o.p.* '97 (CHI) River Forest, IL St. Vincent Ferrer Church; [D] Oak Park, IL Fenwick High School.
Wholey, John *o.m.i.* '39 (BO) [Z] Tewksbury, MA Immaculate Heart of Mary Infirmary.
Whorton, David '98 (LA) Burbank, CA St. Robert Bellarmine Church.
Whyte, Edmond F. '64 (MIA) [11] Fort Lauderdale, FL St. Mark Church; [C] Fort Lauderdale, FL Archbishop Edward A. McCarthy High School.
Wiant, George '61 (ROC) Victor, NY St. Patrick Church.
Wiatrowski, Ralph E. '74 (CLV) [5] Lakewood, OH St. Luke Church.
Wible, Charles (BAL) Cockeysville, MD St. Joseph Church.
Wichlan, David L. '57 (STL) Vinita Park, MO St. Rita Church.
Wichman, Edwin J. '80 (PIT) Verona, PA St. Joseph Church.
Wichmann, Edward W. '52 (PBL) Retired.
Wichmanowski, Walter F. '52 (PIT) Retired; [O] Pittsburgh, PA St. John Vianney Manor.
Wicht, Robert *s.d.s.* '67 (TUC) Vail, AZ Shrine of St. Rita in the Desert Church.
Wickenhauser, Gerald M. *m.m.* '62 (FgM) Maryknoll Foreign Missions.
Wicker, Paul F. '63 (COS) [4] Colorado Springs, CO Holy Apostles Church.
Wickers, Amideus M. *o.s.m.* '49 (CHI) [N] Chicago, IL Order of Friar Servants of Mary (Servites) United States of America Province, Inc.
Wickey, Harold '55 (KCK) Retired.
Wickham, William E. *c.s.c.* '81 (P) Portland, OR Department of Veterans' Affairs Medical Center.
Wicklum, Paul R. '61 (LFT) De Motte, IN St. Cecilia Church.
Wickman, Robert T. '49 (RVC) Retired.
Wickowski, Leroy A. '66 (CHI) [4] Oak Park, IL St. Giles Church.
Wickrematunge, Vernon P. '87 (NY) Peekskill, NY Assumption Church.
Wicks, W. Jared *s.j.* '62 (DET) [K] Detroit, MI Jesuit Provincial Office-Detroit Province of the Society of Jesus.
Widera, Siegfried '67 (ORG) Inactive Leave.
Widhammer, Nicholas *o.f.m.cap.* '63 (FgM) Capuchin Foreign Missions.
Widmann, Phillip A. '77 (FTW) [2] Fort Wayne, IN St. Andrew Church; [16] Fort Wayne, IN St. Peter Church; [N] Fort Wayne, IN Cathedral Museum.
Widner, Thomas C. *s.j.* '69 (CHI) [N] Chicago, IL Chicago Province of the Society of Jesus-Provincial Office.
Widner, Thomas C. *s.j.* '69 (WDC) [M] Washington, DC Leonard Neale House.
Widomski, Stanislaus '62 (FgM) Franciscan Foreign Missions.
Wieber, Donald A. '57 (KAL) Watervliet, MI St. Joseph Church.
Wieber, Elmer F. '54 (KAL) Retired.
Wieber, Robert *o.s.b.* '67 (SCL) [I] Collegeville, MN St. John's Abbey, of the Order of St. Benedict.
Wiecaszek, Leszek *s.a.c.* '88 (BRK) [43] Brooklyn, NY St. Frances de Chantal Church.
Wiecek, Ronald P. *c.pp.s.* '71 (MRY) Soledad, CA Our Lady of Solitude Church; Special Assignment.
Wiecki, Donald J. '58 (MAD) Doylestown, WI St. Patrick Church; Rio, WI St. Joseph Church.
Wieckowski, Msgr. John F. '38 (CAM) Retired.
Wieczorek, Edward R. '65 (Y) Randolph Township, OH St. Joseph Church.
Wieczorek, Matthew S. '57 (SY) [4] Endicott, NY St. Casimir Church.
Wiedel, Thomas L. '90 (LIN) Steinauer, NE St. Anthony Church.
Wieder, Henry '89 (OWN) LaCenter, KY St. Mary Church; [4] Paducah, KY St. Thomas More Church.
Wieder, William *t.o.r.* '41 (PIT) [O] Pittsburgh, PA Third Order Regular of Saint Francis - Province of the Most Sacred Heart of Jesus.
Wiederholt, Clarence '55 (JC) Hermitage, MO St. Bernadette Church.
Wiederholt, Clarence E. '55 (JC) Mary's Home, MO Our Lady of the Snows Church.
Wiederholt, Thomas W. '63 (KC) [32] Kansas City, MO Our Lady of Sorrows Church.
Wiedmann, Paul A. '63 (PH) Levittown, PA Queen of the Universe Church.
Wiegenstein, Francis J. '59 (HEL) Whitehall, MT St. Teresa Church.
Wieging, James F. '67 (DET) River Rouge, MI Our Lady of Lourdes Church.
Wiejata, Sylwester '96 (PH) Absent on Leave.
Wiekierak, Joseph F. '46 (GAY) Retired.
Wieland, Dennis J. '91 (CR) Thief River Falls, MN St. Bernards Church.
Wieland, Edward R. '56 (MIL) Retired.
Wielebski, John T. '78 (BAL) Laurel, MD Resurrection of Our Lord Church.
Wielgus, Msgr. Bronislaw '62 (NEW) [4] Linden, NJ St. Theresa of the Child Jesus Church.
Wieliczko, Christopher *o.s.p.* '87 (NY) [113] New York, NY St. Stanislaus Church.
Wieling, Raymond P. '49 (SC) Retired.
Wielinski, Alan '84 (SCL) Morris, MN Assumption of the Blessed Virgin Mary Church.
Wielosinski, Robert J. '80 (CHI) [156] Chicago, IL Our Lady of the Snows Church.
Wielunski, Gregory '78 (BRK) [192] Queens, NY St. Margaret Church.
Wiemeyer, Raymond G. '52 (CIN) Retired.
Wienhoff, Paul R. '78 (BEL) Nashville, IL St. Ann Church.
Wiera, Stefan '68 (SAT) [G] San Antonio, TX Mount Sacred Heart School.
Wierichs, Paul *c.p.* '78 (NEW) [N] Union City, NJ Congregation of the Passion (Passionists)-St. Michael's Residence.
Wiersgalla, Joseph '51 (SCL) Retired.
Wierzbicki, Melvin *o.f.m.* '53 (GB) [I] Pulaski, WI Assumption of B.V.M. Friary.
Wiese, Miro *o.f.m.* '57 (GAY) Klacking Creek, MI Holy Family Church.
Wiese, Stephen *s.c.j.* (PRM) [C] Kenosha, WI Byzantine Catholic Center.
Wiese, Steve *s.c.j.* '63 (MIL) [P] Franklin, WI Villa Maria.
Wieseler, Lawrence A. '69 (CR) Warren, MN SS. Peter and Paul Church.
Wiesenbaugh, Robert D. *s.j.* '71 (BAL) [S] Baltimore, MD Jesuit Fathers and Brothers Maryland Provincial Curia.
Wiesenbaugh, Robert D. *s.j.* '71 (FgM) Provinces.
Wieser, Francis '44 (SB) Retired.
Wieser, Stanley '68 (SCL) Dumont, MN St. Peter's Church; Wheaton, MN Ave Maria Church.
Wieslaw, Strzadala *s.d.s.* '90 (NEW) [N] Verona, NJ The Salvatorian Fathers.
Wiesler, Willard F. '47 (TUC) Nogales, AZ Sacred Heart Church; Retired.
Wiesmann, Gary '83 (MIA) [5] Pompano Beach, FL St. Elizabeth of Hungary Catholic Church.
Wiesner, James F. *c.s.p.* '83 (MEM) [20] Memphis, TN St. Patrick's Church; [I] Memphis, TN Paulist Fathers (New York); [L] Memphis, TN St. Patrick's Center.
Wiesner, Louis J. *s.m.* '40 (CIN) [M] Dayton, OH Marianist Provincialate.
Wiest, Msgr. John J. '41 (RVC) Manhasset, NY St. Mary's Church; Retired.
Wieszczek, Rudolph *o.f.m.* '54 (PH) [AA] Philadelphia, PA St. Pius X Friary.
Wieszczek, Rudolph *o.f.m.* '54 (TR) Trenton, NJ St. Francis Medical Center.
Wietensteiner, Joseph M. '66 (SPK) Retired.
Wigand, William J. '83 (STL) [1] Jennings, MO Corpus Christi Church.
Wiggins, Charles W. '85 (WIL) Garfield Park, DE Holy Spirit Church.
Wiggins, Frank '86 (RIC) Onley, VA St. Peter's the Apostle Church.
Wigginton, Ellsworth T. '76 (FWT) [13] Fort Worth, TX St. Paul Church.
Wiggs, Msgr. Joel M. '49 (MEM) Retired.
Wight, Jonathan C. '86 (TOL) [24] Toledo, OH St. Hyacinth Church; [C] Toledo, OH St. Francis de Sales High School.
Wightman, John H. '43 (NEW) Retired.
Wightman, Paul *o.m.i.* '55 (SPC) Mansfield, MO Immaculate Heart of Mary Church.
Wightman, William *s.m.* (STL) [P] St. Louis, MO Provincialate of the Society of Mary, Province of St. Louis.
Wightman, William R. *s.m.* '59 (STL) [F] Kirkwood, MO St. John Vianney High School.
Wijanarko, Robertus *c.m.* '96 (CHI) [N] Chicago, IL DePaul Vincentian Residence.
Wiktor, Ronald A. *c.m.* '63 (HRT) Derby, CT St. Michael Church.
Wiktorek, Wladyslaw *c.ss.r.* '81 (MET) Manville, NJ Sacred Heart of Jesus Church; Somerville, NJ Somerset Medical Center.
Wilber, Stewart A. '91 (ATL) Douglasville, GA St.

Theresa Church.
Wilbers, Msgr. Michael J. '72 (JC) Lake Ozark, MO Our Lady of the Lake Church.
Wilborn, Jeffrey W. '00 (DEN) Graduate Studies.
Wilbricht, Stephen *c.s.c.* '97 (PHX) [12] Phoenix, AZ St. Gregory Church.
Wilbright, Stephen Sullivan *c.s.c.* '97 (FTW) On Duty Outside the Diocese.
Wilcox, C. Thomas *m.m.* '51 (FgM) Maryknoll Foreign Missions.
Wilczek, Walter *c.r.* '53 (CHI) [72] Chicago, IL St. Hedwig Church.
Wilczynski, Casimir J. *c.r.* '40 (MOB) [8] Montgomery, AL Resurrection Catholic Church.
Wilczynski, Richard J. '55 (SY) [2] Utica, NY Holy Trinity Church.
Wild, Alexander (OM) [46] Omaha, NE St. Thomas More Church.
Wild, Alexander '89 (DUB) Unassigned.
Wild, David D. '53 (FAR) Retired.
Wild, J. Jerome '81 (PH) Maple Glen, PA St. Alphonsus Church.
Wild, Jon '82 (DUL) [6] Duluth, MN St. Benedict's Church.
Wild, Michael L. '84 (MIL) Fox Lake, WI Annunciation Church.
Wild, Paul *o.f.m.* '72 (CIN) [M] Cincinnati, OH St. Clement Friary.
Wild, Robert A. '67 (BUF) On Duty Outside the Diocese.
Wild, Robert A. *s.j.* '70 (MIL) [C] Milwaukee, WI Marquette University; [P] Milwaukee, WI Jesuit Community at Marquette University.
Wilde, Adrian *o.carm.* '72 (GAL) [14] Houston, TX St. Bernadette Soubirous Church.
Wilde, Dennis G. *o.s.a.* '70 (PH) [AA] Villanova, PA St. Thomas Monastery.
Wildeman, Richard J. '77 (EVN) On Duty Outside the Diocese.
Wilder, Alfred W. *o.p.* '65 (NO) [P] New Orleans, LA Dominican Friars, Southern Dominican Province of St. Martin de Porres.
Wilder, Daniel '96 (PEO) [4] Ottawa, IL St. Patrick's Church.
Wilder, Daniel J. '96 (PEO) [P] Macomb, IL St. Francis of Assisi Newman Center.
Wilder, Frank T. *o.a.r.* (NY) [B] Suffern, NY Tagaste Monastery.
Wilderotter, Paul C. '74 (CHL) On Duty Outside the Diocese.
Wildes, Kevin W. *s.j.* '86 (WDC) [M] Washington, DC The Jesuit Community at Georgetown University.
Wildonger, Lawrence H. *m.s.c.* '79 (ALN) [K] Reading, PA Missionaries of the Sacred Heart.
Wiles, Arthur W. '67 (COL) [11] Columbus, OH St. Christopher Church.
Wiley, James A. '58 (E) Grove City, PA Beloved Disciple Church.
Wiley, Leo A. '56 (OG) Croghan, NY St. Stephen Church.
Wiley, Robert *s.m.* '63 (STP) Waverly, MN St. Mary Church.
Wilgenbusch, Lyle L. '66 (DUB) [11] Dubuque, IA St. Joseph the Worker Church.
Wilger, Donald F. '57 (LC) [D] Marshfield, WI Saint Joseph's Hospital of Marshfield, Inc.
Wilger, John J. *t.o.r.* '48 (ALT) [F] Loretto, PA Mount Assisi Friary.
Wilger, Norbert J. '49 (LC) Altoona, WI St. Mary Church.
Wilhelm, Chad F. '94 (FAR) Gwinner, ND St. Vincent Church; Lisbon, ND St. Aloysius Church; Lisbon, ND Soldier's Home.
Wilhelm, Dean E. '88 (AUS) College Station, TX St. Thomas Aquinas Church.
Wilhelm, Edward *c.ss.r.* '47 (CHI) [133] Chicago, IL St. Michael Church.
Wilhelm, H. Joseph *s.m.* '59 (WH) [11] Wheeling, WV St. Vincent de Paul's Church.
Wilhelm, Patrick R.C. '71 (NEW) Kearny, NJ Our Lady of Sorrows Church.
Wilhelm, Paul W. *o.m.i.* '68 (LA) San Fernando, CA Santa Rosa Church.
Wilhelm, Ray *o.m.i.* '58 (SAN) [2] Midland, TX Our Lady of Guadalupe Church.
Wilhelm, Robert J. '59 (TOL) [12] Toledo, OH Our Lady of Perpetual Help Church.
Wilhite, Philip A. *s.t.l.* '90 (GAL) [3] Houston, TX St. Albert of Trapani Church.
Wilimek, Louis J. '50 (MIL) Kohler, WI St. John Evangelist Church.
Wilk, Joseph M. '81 (CHI) Schaumburg, IL St. Matthew Church.
Wilk, Meiczyslaw *o.f.m. conv.* '83 (CHI) Bridgeview, IL St. Fabian Church.
Wilk, Mitchell S. '70 (SPC) Military Chaplains.
Wilke, David M. '95 (BEL) Fairmont City, IL Holy Rosary Church.
Wilke, James B. '89 (STL) Concord Village, MO St. Simon the Apostle Church.
Wilkening, David F. '79 (DAV) Farmington, IA St. Boniface Church; West Point, IA Assumption of the Blessed Virgin Mary Church.
Wilkening, Henry '47 (JOL) Carol Stream, IL Corpus Christi Church; Retired.
Wilkenson, Richard S. *c.s.c.* '79 (AUS) [A] Austin, TX St. Edward's University.
Wilker, Ronald H. '71 (CIN) Coldwater, OH Holy Trinity Church.
Wilkerson, Msgr. Jerome F. '50 (STL) [2] Creve Coeur, MO St. John Bosco Church; Retired.
Wilkerson, Wayne '99 (GAL) Pearland, TX St. Helen Church.
Wilkie, John J. '92 (SEA) [4] Tacoma, WA St. Joseph Church; [10] Tacoma, WA Holy Rosary Church.
Wilkie, William E. '54 (DUB) [C] Dubuque, IA Loras College.
Wilkie, William E., Ph.D. '54 (DUB) Retired.
Wilkiemeyer, Victor L. '43 (SJ) [4] Santa Clara, CA St. Lawrence the Martyr Church; Retired.
Wilkins, Bernard J. '61 (STL) Brentwood, MO St. Mary Magdalen Church.
Wilkinson, Bruce W. '81 (ATL) [5] Atlanta, GA Most Blessed Sacrament Church.
Wilkinson, James '42 (WCH) Retired.
Wilkinson, Msgr. John '48 (NY) Retired; [E] White Plains, NY Archbishop Stepinac High School.
Wilkinson, John H. '59 (BRK) [24] Brooklyn, NY St. Brigid Church; Queens, NY Queens House of Detention.
Wilkinson, John H. '59 (NY) City, NY Adolescent Remand & Detention Center.
Wilkinson, Msgr. John V. (NY) Hartsdale, NY Sacred Heart Church.
Wilkinson, Neal '00 (RC) St. Francis, SD Rosebud Reservation Church.
Wilkinson, Neal J. *s.j.* '00 (RC) Parmelee, SD St. Agnes Church.
Wilkosz, William '95 (CHI) [36] Chicago, IL Christ the King Church.
Wilks, Bede *o.p.* '62 (P) [6] Eugene, OR St. Thomas More Church.
Wilkuski, Leonard F. '64 (SAG) [1] Bay City, MI Holy Trinity Church.
Will, Anthony *o.f.m.cap.* '47 (MIL) [P] Mount Calvary, WI St. Lawrence Friary; [Q] Fond du Lac, WI Convent of the Sisters of St. Agnes.
Will, Carl G. '49 (CIN) Retired.
Will, Lowell C. '68 (EVN) Washington, IN Immaculate Conception Church.
Will, Ronald *c.pp.s.* '75 (KC) Liberty, MO St. James Church; [J] Liberty, MO Precious Blood Center.
Willard, Stephen A. '93 (PEO) [3] Bloomington, IL St. Patrick's Church; [B] Bloomington, IL Central Catholic High School.
Willathgamuwa, Flavian *c.m.f.* '83 (LA) [Q] Rancho Dominguez, CA Dominguez Seminary Inc.
Wille, Arthur H. *m.m.* '51 (FgM) Maryknoll Foreign Missions.
Wille, Carol (BUF) [K] Buffalo, NY Sisters of Charity Hospital of Buffalo, NY.
Willemsen, Andrew J. '54 (AUS) Retired.
Willenborg, Henry *o.f.m.* '76 (STL) [P] St. Louis, MO Franciscan Friary of St. Anthony of Padua.
Willenbring, Mark '57 (SCL) Princeton, MN St. Edward's Church.
Willenburg, Msgr. Francis J. '54 (SY) [5] Utica, NY St. Agnes Church.
Willett, John *c.ss.r.* '61 (DEN) [M] Denver, CO The Redemptorists/Denver Province.
Willett, John *c.ss.r.* '61 (FgM) Redemptorist Foreign Missions.
Willett, Robert '68 (OWN) Uniontown, KY St. Agnes Church; Waverly, KY Sacred Heart Church; Waverly, KY St. Peter Church.
Willett, William D. '79 (OWN) Military Chaplains.
Willette, Donald '84 (DEN) Longmont, CO Spirit of Peace Church; Louisville, CO St. Louis Church.
Willey, Dennis B. '94 (CHR) [11] Charleston, SC Church of the Nativity.
Willger, Gerard I. '86 (SUP) Barron, WI St. Joseph Church; Cameron, WI St. Peter Church; Chetek, WI St. Boniface Church.
Willhite, Robert J. '63 (RCK) [8] Aurora, IL St. Rita of Cascia Church.
William, Herbert J. '57 (GAY) East Jordan, MI St. Joseph Church.
Williams, Alfred '39 (P) Retired.
Williams, Anthony C. '83 (KCK) Olathe, KS St. Paul's Church.
Williams, Bruce A. *o.p.* '67 (BO) [W] Dover, MA St. Stephen Priory.
Williams, Clarence E. *c.pp.s.* '78 (DET) Special Assignment; [T] Detroit, MI The Black Catholic Televangelization Network.
Williams, David '98 (AUS) Brenham, TX St. Mary of the Immaculate Conception Church.
Williams, Dennis T. '91 (NY) [34] New York, NY Epiphany Church.
Williams, Donald J. '83 (SCR) Elmhurst, PA St. Eulalia Church.
Williams, Edward *o.m.i.* '57 (FgM) Oblates Foreign Missions.
Williams, Edward J. '93 (SCR) [L] Wilkes-Barre, PA Little Flower Manor of the Diocese of Scranton; [L] Wilkes-Barre, PA Little Flower Manor of the Diocese of Scranton.
Williams, Edward T. '69 (CIN) Retired.
Williams, Ernest (BUF) [K] Buffalo, NY Sisters of Charity Hospital of Buffalo, NY.
Williams, Francis '77 (LAN) Retired.
Williams, Gary G. '81 (VIC) [2] Victoria, TX Holy Family of Joseph, Mary & Jesus Church.
Williams, George J. '39 (BO) Senior Priests.
Williams, George S. *s.j.* '72 (ALN) [A] Wernersville, PA Jesuit Center; [N] Wernersville, PA Jesuit Center for Spiritual Growth.
Williams, George W. '96 (DET) Graduate Studies.
Williams, Germain *o.f.m.conv.* '48 (ALB) [12] Albany, NY Our Lady of Angels Church.
Williams, Glenn F. *s.j.* '56 (CLV) [D] Cleveland, OH St. Ignatius High School.
Williams, H. Brendan '65 (TR) Howell Township, NJ St. Veronica Church.
Williams, Henry (BRK) [222] Queens, NY St. Pancras Church.
Williams, Ian J. '96 (GRY) [5] Hammond, IN St. John Bosco Church.
Williams, J. Craig '83 (PT) Niceville, FL Christ Our Redeemer Church.
Williams, James A. '65 (SEA) [5] Seattle, WA St. Bernadette Church.
Williams, James C. *s.m.* '87 (RVC) [D] Mineola, NY Chaminade High School (Boys).
Williams, James C. *s.m.* '98 (RVC) [M] Mineola, NY Provincial Residence and Novitiate.
Williams, James M. '70 (MAR) Mackinac Island, MI Ste. Anne de Michilimackinac Church.
Williams, Jerry *o.carm.* '80 (CHI) [N] Chicago, IL Carmelite Priory of St. Cyril.
Williams, Jim '97 (COS) Salida, CO St. Joseph Church.
Williams, John '78 (R) Clinton, NC Immaculate Conception Church.
Williams, John L. '91 (HRT) [16] Waterbury, CT St. Patrick Church.
Williams, John Mark '89 (PEO) On Duty Outside the Diocese.
Williams, Jonathan *o.f.m.cap.* '71 (FgM) Capuchin Foreign Missions.
Williams, Joseph *c.m.* '87 (PBL) [11] Pueblo, CO St. Francis Xavier Church; [E] Pueblo, CO Centura Health-St. Mary-Corwin Medical Center.
Williams, Kenneth '63 (SHP) Noble, LA St. Ann Church.
Williams, Manuel *c.r.* '87 (MOB) [8] Montgomery, AL Resurrection Catholic Church; [8] Montgomery, AL Resurrection Catholic Church; [E] Marbury, AL Resurrection Catholic Nursing Home; [E] Montgomery, AL Father Walter Memorial Center for Handicapped Children.
Williams, Matthew *o.c.d.* '90 (LA) Alhambra, CA St. Therese Church.
Williams, McKinley '83 (RIC) On Duty Outside the Diocese.
Williams, Michael '97 (OWN) Fordsville, KY St. John the Baptist Church.
Williams, Michael A. *s.j.* '75 (MOB) [A] Mobile, AL Spring Hill College.
Williams, Michael J. '95 (LAN) Adrian, MI St. Joseph Church.
Williams, Michael S. '64 (STA) [2] Gainesville, FL Holy Faith Church.
Williams, Mike '97 (OWN) Whitesville, KY St. Mary of the Woods Church.
Williams, Oliver F. *c.s.c.* '70 (FTW) [B] Notre Dame, IN University of Notre Dame Du Lac; [J] Notre Dame, IN Holy Cross Community, Corby Hall, University of Notre Dame.
Williams, Patrick J. '93 (NO) [A] New Orleans, LA Notre Dame Seminary Graduate School of Theology.
Williams, Paul D., Jr. '95 (ATL) Griffin, GA Sacred Heart Church.
Williams, Paul M. *o.f.m.* '86 (CHR) Greenville, SC St. Anthony of Padua Church; [H] Greenville, SC Furman University.
Williams, Peter A. '83 (SY) Camillus, NY St. Joseph Church; Special Assignment.
Williams, Peter Y. '87 (BUR) Fairfield, VT St. Patrick Church; [G] Burlington, VT Camp Holy Cross, Inc.
Williams, Ray '97 (CHL) Bryson City, NC St. Joseph Church.
Williams, Rayner F. *o.f.m.* '56 (NY) [35] New York, NY St. Francis of Assisi Church.
Williams, Rayner F. *o.f.m.* '56 (PAT) [P] Paterson, NJ St. Anthony's Guild.
Williams, Richard B. *o.p.* '71 (NO) [30] New Orleans, LA St. Dominic Church; [65] New Orleans, LA St. Thomas More Church; New Orleans, LA Tulane-Newcomb.
Williams, Richard C. '65 (PH) Chester Heights, PA St. Thomas the Apostle Church.
Williams, Richard S. '99 (OG) Massena, NY Sacred Heart Church.
Williams, Robert '91 (DAL) Corsicana, TX Immaculate

Conception Church; [N] Dallas, TX Commission on Ecumenism.
Williams, Robert Hayes '82 (DET) Hazel Park, MI St. Justin Church; Special Assignment.
Williams, Robert L. '68 (LFT) Anderson, IN St. Mary Church.
Williams, Ronald R. '79 (DET) [48] Detroit, MI St. Mary's of Redford Church.
Williams, Steven T. '91 (MOB) [12] Mobile, AL St. Mary Church; [B] Mobile, AL McGill-Toolen Catholic High School.
Williams, Thomas G. *s.j.* '60 (SEA) [C] Tacoma, WA Bellarmine Preparatory School.
Williams, Msgr. William E. '59 (NY) Centerville, NY St. John the Evangelist Church.
Williams, William G. '69 (BO) Hull, MA St. Mary of the Assumption Church.
Williams, William M. '96 (ATL) Greensboro, GA Christ Our King and Savior Church.
Williams, William W. *s.j.* '68 (COS) [F] Sedalia, CO Sacred Heart Jesuit Community; [H] Sedalia, CO Sacred Heart Jesuit Retreat House.
Williamson, Bruce *o.m.v.* '82 (BO) [B] Boston, MA Oblate Provincialate.
Williamson, Christopher '88 (ATL) Blue Ridge, GA St. Anthony's Church.
Williamson, G. Michael '86 (CLV) [10] Lorain, OH St. Peter Church.
Williamson, John A. (BAL) Pasadena, MD St. Jane Frances de Chantal Church.
Williamson, Msgr. Robert J. '62 (BUF) Akron, NY St. Teresa of Avila Church.
Williamson, Thomas '96 (CHL) Absent On Leave.
Willig, James M. '77 (CIN) [72] Cincinnati, OH Sts. Peter and Paul Church.
Willingham, Charles W. *o.praem.* '95 (ORG) Costa Mesa, CA Fairview Developmental Center; [D] Silverado, CA St. Michael's College Preparatory High School; [I] Silverado, CA Norbertine Fathers of Orange Inc.
Willingham, Jeffrey R. '97 (MET) Sayreville, NJ Our Lady of Victories Church; [A] South Amboy, NJ St. Mary Regional High School.
Willis, Eugene F. '55 (ALB) Walton, NY St. John the Baptist Church.
Willis, Glen *s.d.s.* '69 (WDC) [B] Silver Spring, MD Salvatorian Community; [G] Rockville, MD The Frost Center, Society of the Divine Savior; [V] Silver Spring, MD Camp St. Charles, Inc.
Willis, Kevin L. (FAR) Wishek, ND St. Patrick Church.
Willis, Kevin L. '93 (FAR) Oakes, ND St. Charles Borromeo Church; Verona, ND St. Raphael Church.
Willis, Lawrence R. *o.s.b.* '66 (CHL) [J] Belmont, NC Belmont Abbey.
Willis, Nathan S. '66 (Y) Kingsville, OH St. Andrew Church.
Willis, Thomas S. '84 (STA) [10] Jacksonville, FL Most Holy Redeemer Church.
Willlard, Stephen A.. '93 (PEO) Downs, IL St. Mary's Church.
Willman, Herbert J. '57 (GAY) Praga, MI St. John Nepomucene Church.
Willmann, Robert E. '92 (COL) [2] Columbus, OH St. Agatha Church.
Willmering, John H. *s.j.* '68 (FgM) Provinces.
Willmes, James *glmy.* '52 (CIN) [M] Cincinnati, OH Headquarters of Glenmary Home Missioners.
Willmes, Joseph F. *s.j.* '48 (FgM) Provinces.
Willmes, Robert J. *s.j.* '40 (DET) [P] Clarkston, MI Colombiere Center.
Willoughby, Malcolm Sylvester *o.p.* '49 (WDC) [B] Washington, DC Dominican House of Studies.
Wilmot, John P. '77 (WIN) Easton, MN Our Lady of Mount Carmel Church; Minnesota Lake, MN St. John the Baptist Church.
Wilmoth, James R. '65 (IND) [35] Indianapolis, IN St. Roch Church; Indianapolis, IN Marion County Sheriff Department.
Wilson, Alan *o.f.m.cap.* (FRS) Fresno, CA Community Hospital, Veterans' Hospital & University Medical Center.
Wilson, Albert L. '51 (L) Rhodelia, KY St. Theresa Church; Retired.
Wilson, Anthony *o.f.m.* '87 (FgM) Franciscan Foreign Missions.
Wilson, Cedric M. *o.s.a.* '78 (WDC) [B] Silver Spring, MD Austin Friars Hall, Order of St. Augustine.
Wilson, David J. '88 (E) Johnsonburg, PA Holy Rosary Church.
Wilson, Dennis M. *o.f.m.* '92 (NY) [35] New York, NY St. Francis of Assisi Church; [HH] New York, NY Franciscans of Holy Name Province Benevolence Trust, Inc.
Wilson, Edward M. '56 (E) Retired.
Wilson, Eugene C. '00 (PH) Trooper, PA Visitation B.V.M. Church.
Wilson, F. Philip *o.s.b.* '53 (PRO) [P] Portsmouth, RI Abbey of St. Gregory the Great.
Wilson, Gene *c.pp.s.* '60 (OAK) Newark, CA St. Edward's Church.
Wilson, George '92 (WDC) [L] Washington, DC Jeanne Jugan Residence-St. Joseph's Villa.
Wilson, George B. *s.j.* '59 (CIN) [M] Cincinnati, OH Jesuit Community at Xavier University.
Wilson, George W. '92 (WDC) Retired.
Wilson, Guy *s.t.* '78 (FgM) Trinity Missions.
Wilson, James E. (DAV) Retired.
Wilson, James R. '54 (B) Retired.
Wilson, Msgr. John F. '48 (BRK) [58] Brooklyn, NY Holy Name Church; Retired.
Wilson, John H. *c.s.c.* '41 (FTW) [J] South Bend, IN Congregation of Holy Cross, Indiana Province, Provincial House.
Wilson, Joseph B. '94 (SCR) [I] Williamsport, PA Divine Providence Hospital of the Sisters of Christian Charity.
Wilson, Joseph F. '86 (BRK) [191] Queens, NY St. Luke Church.
Wilson, Kent '90 (NY) Fishkill, NY Church of St. Mary, Mother of the.
Wilson, Method *o.f.m.* '52 (LFT) [F] Kokomo, IN Maria Regina Mater Monastery.
Wilson, Michael '75 (WDC) [4] Rockville, MD St. Raphael Church.
Wilson, Ser Khu '79 (WCH) Arkansas City, KS Sacred Heart Church.
Wilson, Stuart T. (BAL) Retired.
Wilson, Stuart T. '67 (BAL) Military Chaplains.
Wilson, Thomas R. '75 (PIT) Wireton, PA St. Catherine of Siena Church.
Wilson, Thomas W. '96 (STP) Coon Rapids, MN Church of the Epiphany.
Wilson, William P. '69 (NEW) On Duty Outside the Archdiocese.
Wilt, George A. '59 (PIT) Mt. Lebanon, PA St. Bernard Church.
Wilt, John E. '57 (GBG) Seward, PA Holy Family Church.
Wiltgen, Ralph *s.v.d.* '50 (MIL) [P] East Troy, WI Divine Word Seminary.
Wilton, David M. *c.p.m.* '93 (OWN) [F] South Union, KY Fathers of Mercy.
Wiltz, George *s.j.* '65 (FWT) [K] Lake Dallas, TX Montserrat Jesuit Retreat House; [K] Lake Dallas, TX Montserrat Jesuit Retreat House.
Wilus, Msgr. John M. '37 (TR) Retired.
Wilutis, John P. '55 (RVC) Retired; [M] Uniondale, NY St. Pius X Residence.
Wilwerding, Anthony P. '46 (OM) Retired.
Wilwerding, Jim '92 (DM) Leave of Absence.
Wilz, John C. '64 (PH) Horsham, PA St. Catherine of Siena Church.
Wimett, Leo J. '60 (SY) North Bay, NY St. John Church.
Wimmer, Joseph F. *o.s.a.* '64 (PH) [C] Villanova, PA Villanova University.
Wimmer, Joseph F. *o.s.a.* '64 (WDC) [B] Silver Spring, MD Austin Friars Hall, Order of St. Augustine.
Wimsett, Scott J. '88 (L) Mount Washington, KY St. Francis Xavier Church.
Winance, Eleutherius *o.s.b.* '35 (LA) [Q] Valyermo, CA St. Andrew's Abbey.
Winca, Msgr. George F. '38 (Y) Retired.
Winca, Harry S. '45 (CLV) Middlefield, OH St. Lucy Church; Parkman, OH St. Edward Church.
Winchester, George P. *s.j.* '65 (BO) Boston, MA Brigham and Women's Hospital; [W] Boston, MA Jesuit Urban Center & Immaculate Conception Community.
Windbacher, Ambrose *o.p.* '54 (FgM) Dominican - Order of Preachers Foreign Missions.
Windbacher, Ambrose P. *o.p.* '54 (CHI) [N] Chicago, IL Dominicans (Provincial Office).
Windhaus, Edward A. '72 (PH) [5] Norristown, PA St. Titus Church.
Windholtz, Barry '88 (CIN) [75] Cincinnati, OH St. Rose of Lima Church.
Windisch, Adolf M. *s.m.* '60 (CIN) [M] Dayton, OH Marianist Provincialate.
Windisch, Adolf M. *s.m.* '60 (STL) [P] St. Louis, MO Provincialate of the Society of Mary, Province of St. Louis.
Windle, John J. '43 (CHI) Retired.
Windle, Raymond L. *s.j.* '59 (STL) [P] St. Louis, MO Jesuit Community Corporation at St. Louis University - Jesuit Hall.
Windolph, George *o.f.m.* '48 (SFD) [B] Quincy, IL Quincy University.
Windolph, Joseph '48 (CHI) [N] Chicago, IL St. Peter's Friary.
Windolph, Michael *o.f.m.* '51 (CHI) [N] Chicago, IL Chaplains:.
Windolph, Nestor *o.f.m.* '55 (FgM) Franciscan Foreign Missions.
Windy, Jeff '96 (PEO) Sheffield, IL St. Patrick's Church.
Winel, Msgr. Roland T. '39 (COL) Retired.
Wing, Kenneth A. '59 (GR) Retired.
Wingert, D. William '60 (SC) Retired.
Wingert, Gerald R. '47 (SC) Retired.
Wingfield, Harvey J. *o.s.b.* '81 (SEA) [L] Lacey, WA St. Martin's Abbey.
Winiarski, James *m.s.* '66 (MIL) [68] Milwaukee, WI St. Paul Church; [P] Milwaukee, WI La Salette Fathers.
Winikates, Thomas '70 (CHI) Westchester, IL Divine Infant Church.
Winkel, Thomas J. '71 (CLV) Bedford, OH St. Mary Church.
Winkelbauer, Phillip J. '75 (KCK) Bendena, KS St. Benedict's Church; Troy, KS St. Charles Church; Wathena, KS St. Joseph's Church.
Winkels, Michael *o.p.* '76 (CHI) [N] Oak Park, IL Dominican Community of St. Martin de Porres.
Winkels, Michael A. *o.p.* '76 (CHI) [D] Oak Park, IL Fenwick High School.
Winkels, Robert H. *m.m.* '41 (NY) [DD] Maryknoll, NY Maryknoll Fathers and Brothers.
Winkler, Edward J. '86 (VIC) Eagle Lake, TX Parish of the Nativity Church.
Winkler, Eugene D. '50 (MIL) Lima, WI St. Rose Church; St. George, WI St. George Church.
Winkler, Jude *o.f.m.conv.* '81 (BAL) [S] Ellicott City, MD St. Joseph Cupertino Friary, Friars Minor Conventual of St. Francis of Assisi; [S] Ellicott City, MD Friary of St. Joseph Cupertino.
Winkler, Kenneth H. '81 (RVC) Mineola, NY Corpus Christi Church.
Winkowski, Eugene R. '71 (CHI) [159] Chicago, IL Our Lady of Victory Church.
Winkowski, Michael J. *c.pp.s* '70 (FTW) Walkerton, IN St. Patrick Church.
Winn, Frank A. '98 (BGP) [2] Stratford, CT St. James Church.
Winne, George R. '83 (ALN) [9] Allentown, PA Sacred Heart of Jesus Church.
Winnenberg, John O. '55 (WDC) Retired.
Winrich, Walter W. *m.m.* '50 (NY) [DD] Maryknoll, NY Maryknoll Fathers and Brothers.
Winshman, Alfred O. *s.j.* '65 (BO) [W] Boston, MA Loyola House.
Winslow, Patrick J. '99 (ALB) [3] Albany, NY Blessed Sacrament Church.
Winston, William L. '86 (PAT) Morris Plains, NJ St. Virgilius Church.
Winter, Donald *c.ss.r.* '55 (RIC) [3] Hampton, VA St. Joseph Church.
Winter, Harry E. *o.m.i.* '65 (BUF) [60] Buffalo, NY St. Rose of Lima Church.
Winterer, Michael J. '60 (SLC) Cedar City, UT Christ the King Church.
Winterlin, John R. '68 (GRY) [2] Hammond, IN Our Lady of Perpetual Help Church.
Wintermyer, John S. '62 (WDC) [13] Washington, DC St. Francis de Sales Church; Washington, DC Washington Hospital Center; Hospital & Nursing Home Ministries.
Winters, Alfred H. '62 (CLV) [1] Lakewood, OH St. Clement Church.
Winters, Bartholomew S. '83 (CHI) [71] Chicago, IL St. Gregory Church.
Winters, Darvin Edwin, Jr. '99 (IND) Greenwood, IN Our Lady of the Greenwood Church.
Winters, Martin N. '52 (CHI) Retired; [O] Oak Forest, IL Our Lady of Sorrows Priory, Benedictine Sisters of Pontifical Jurisdiction.
Winters, Richard *s.v.d.* '41 (SB) [A] Riverside, CA Divine Word Seminary.
Winters, Sean '87 (MET) [7] Perth Amboy, NJ Holy Spirit Church; Perth Amboy, NJ Raritan Bay Medical Center.
Winters, Vaughn '93 (LA) [2] North Hollywood, CA St. Charles Borromeo Church.
Winters, William *o.f.m.cap.* '64 (RVC) East Patchogue, NY St. Joseph the Worker Church.
Wintz, Jack R. *o.f.m.* '63 (CIN) [M] Cincinnati, OH Pleasant Street Friary.
Winzenburg, George E. *s.j.* '74 (MIL) [31] Milwaukee, WI Gesu Church.
Wiorkiewicz, Marek *s.d.s.* '89 (NEW) [4] Garfield, NJ St. Stanislaus Kostka Church; [N] Verona, NJ The Salvatorian Fathers.
Wipf, Terrance R. '00 (BIS) Fort Yates, ND St. Peter - Catholic Indian Church; Selfridge, ND St. Philomena Church.
Wippel, Msgr. John '60 (STU) On Duty Outside the Diocese.
Wippel, Msgr. John '60 (WDC) [C] Washington, DC Catholic University of America, The.
Wirkes, Stephen P. '80 (SY) Mexico, NY St. Mary, Star of the Sea Church.
Wironen, John *c.s.c.* '79 (P) [J] Portland, OR Providence Portland Medical Center.
Wirth, Geoffrey '67 (RCK) Crystal Lake, IL St. Thomas the Apostle Church.
Wirth, Jerry E. '68 (BEL) Olney, IL St. Joseph Church.
Wirth, John J. '52 (STP) Retired.
Wirth, Richard P. '56 (STP) Retired.
Wirth, Robert *c.ss.r.* '64 (DEN) [M] Denver, CO The Redemptorists/Denver Province.
Wirth, Robert *c.ss.r.* '64 (FgM) Redemptorist Foreign Missions.
Wischmeyer, Amos H. '51 (LAN) Swartz Creek, MI St. Mary Church.
Wisdom, Andrew Carl *o.p.* '87 (STL) [P] St. Louis, MO St. Dominic Priory.

Wise, Carl *c.pp.s.* '55 (CIN) [B] Carthagena, OH St. Charles.
Wise, Kenneth F. '47 (COL) Dennison, OH Immaculate Conception Church; Retired.
Wise, Marcos *c.ss.r.* '72 (CGS) [B] Aguas Buenas, PR Casa Cristo Redentor.
Wise, Paul C. '74 (CAM) [5] Atlantic City, NJ Our Lady Star of the Sea Church.
Wise, Richard P. '81 (ATL) Decatur, GA Sts. Peter and Paul Church.
Wise, Thomas F. *c.s.v.* '56 (SFD) Granite City, IL Holy Family Church.
Wiseman, James A. *o.s.b.* '70 (WDC) [C] Washington, DC Catholic University of America, The; [M] Washington, DC St. Anselm's Abbey.
Wiseman, Joseph F. '52 (BRK) [197] Queens, NY Mary's Nativity Church; Retired.
Wiseman, Vincent *o.p.* '71 (WDC) [B] Washington, DC Dominican House of Studies.
Wishard, John W. '62 (LA) Retired.
Wiskirchen, George C. *c.s.c.* '55 (FTW) [B] Notre Dame, IN University of Notre Dame Du Lac; [J] Notre Dame, IN Holy Cross Community, Corby Hall, University of Notre Dame.
Wisner, John H. '72 (KCK) Roeland Park, KS St. Agnes Church.
Wisneske, S. Patrick '50 (MAR) Menominee, MI Holy Spirit Church.
Wisneski, Edward '67 (NOR) Retired.
Wisneski, John A. '57 (LC) Blenker, WI St. Kilian Church; Junction City, WI St. Michael Church; Milladore, WI St. Wenceslaus Church.
Wisneski, John J. '64 (GR) [5] Grand Rapids, MI Blessed Sacrament Church.
Wisneski, Jonathan J. '98 (GBG) [1] Greensburg, PA Blessed Sacrament Church.
Wisniefski, Robert W. '80 (PAT) [9] Paterson, NJ St. Joseph's Church.
Wisniewski, David '81 (OG) Glenfield, NY St. Mary Church; Houseville, NY St. Hedwig Church; Lowville, NY St. Peter Church.
Wisniewski, Joseph *c.m.* '65 (BRK) [134] Brooklyn, NY St. Stanislaus Kostka Church.
Wisniewski, Robert W. '89 (CLV) [1] Barberton, OH St. Augustine Church.
Wisniewski, Stanley *s.j.* '64 (CHI) [D] Chicago, IL St. Ignatius Jesuit Community; [D] Chicago, IL Cristo Rey Jesuit High School, Inc.
Wisniewski, Thomas '76 (MIA) Parkland, FL Mary Help of Christians Church.
Wisniewski, Thomas '80 (NEW) Maplewood, NJ St. Joseph's Church.
Wisniewski, Thomas J. '74 (PH) Penn Valley, PA St. Justin Martyr Church.
Wissel, Msgr. Francis C. '77 (BGP) [U] Bridgeport, CT St. Peter's Parish, St. Maximillian Kolbe House of Studies.
Wissel, Msgr. Frank C. '77 (BGP) [1] Greenwich, CT St. Mary Church.
Wissler, Thomas J. '83 (STL) Farmington, MO St. Joseph Church.
Wissman, J. Patrick '64 (SPC) Bolivar, MO Sacred Heart Church.
Wister, Msgr. Robert J. '68 (NEW) [A] South Orange, NJ Immaculate Conception Seminary; [B] South Orange, NJ Seton Hall University.
Wisz, Dominic *o.f.m.conv.* '47 (RCK) [2] Rockford, IL St. Anthony of Padua Church.
Witalec, Dennis J. '82 (PH) [79] Philadelphia, PA St. John Cantius Church.
Witcoski, Stanley '93 (CAM) North Cape May, NJ St. John of God Church.
Witczak, Michael G. '77 (MIL) [A] St. Francis, WI Saint Francis Seminary.
Witek, John W. *s.j.* '65 (WDC) [M] Washington, DC The Jesuit Community at Georgetown University.
Witek, Stanley '87 (KAL) Niles, MI St. Mary Church.
With, William A. '72 (BRK) [98] Brooklyn, NY Our Lady Help of Christians Church.
Withers, Mark *c.s.j.* '79 (LA) Lancaster, CA Blessed Junipero Serra Church; [D] Lancaster, CA Paraclete High School.
Witherup, Ronald D. *s.s.* '76 (BAL) [S] Baltimore, MD Sulpician Provincial House.
Withrow, Justin *o.s.b.* '90 (GBG) Greensburg, PA Westmoreland Hospital; Latrobe, PA Latrobe Area Hospital; Jeannette, PA Jeannette District Memorial Hospital; Jeannette, PA Monsour Medical Center; [F] Jeannette, PA Jeannette District Memorial Hospital; [H] Latrobe, PA Saint Vincent Archabbey.
Witkowski, Msgr. Bernard E. '62 (PH) [102] Philadelphia, PA Maternity B.V.M. Church.
Witkowski, Phillip J. '75 (GR) [7] Muskegon, MI St. Thomas the Apostle Church.
Witkowski, Raymond A. '42 (MIL) Retired.
Witkowski, Robert J. '61 (DET) [5] Warren, MI St. Edmund Church.
Witmer, Joseph W. '67 (Y) Aurora, OH Our Lady of Perpetual Help Church.
Witon, Russell F. '63 (MIL) Retired.
Witsken, Gary J. (CIN) New Richmond, OH St. Peter Church.
Witt, Edward G. *s.j.* '91 (MIL) [E] Milwaukee, WI Marquette University High School; [P] Milwaukee, WI Pere Marquette House Jesuit Community.
Witt, Michael '90 (STL) Brentwood, MO St. Mary Magdalen Church.
Witt, Michael J. '90 (STL) [A] St. Louis, MO Kenrick-Glennon Seminary.
Witt, Paul K. '71 (LIN) [8] Lincoln, NE St. Mary Church.
Witt, Robert G. '50 (COV) Retired.
Witt, William '49 (Y) Retired.
Witte, Clarence J. *m.m.* '35 (FgM) Maryknoll Foreign Missions.
Witte, Msgr. John C. '45 (GRY) Retired.
Witte, Mark G. '95 (COV) Fort Mitchell, KY Blessed Sacrament Church; [C] Covington, KY Academy of Notre Dame.
Witte, Steven D. '92 (BEL) Leave of Absence.
Wittemann, Paul J. '56 (MIL) Retired.
Wittenbrink, Boniface *o.m.i.* '41 (BEL) [F] Belleville, IL Missionary Oblates of Mary Immaculate - St. Henry's Oblate Residence.
Witthauer, Paul G. '60 (BAL) [70] Baltimore, MD Our Lady of Hope Church.
Witting, Martin *o.s.b.* '51 (RCK) [G] Aurora, IL Marmion Abbey-St. Augustine's Abbey.
Wittliff, Thomas F. '64 (MIL) [10] Milwaukee, WI St. Augustine Church.
Wittman, Christopher *s.m.* '94 (CIN) [E] Dayton, OH Chaminade-Julienne High School.
Wittman, Karl M. '46 (STP) Retired.
Wittman, Michael A. '88 (CLV) East Cleveland, OH Christ the King Church.
Wittman, Peter C. '75 (STP) Savage, MN St. John the Baptist Church.
Wittmann, Christopher T. *s.m.* '94 (CIN) [M] Dayton, OH Marianist Provincialate.
Wittouck, Frank *s.c.j.* '65 (GAL) [27] Houston, TX St. Elizabeth Ann Seton Church.
Wittreich, John A. '47 (CLV) Norton, OH St. Andrew the Apostle Church; Retired.
Wittrock, Daniel '94 (OM) Dodge, NE St. Wenceslaus Church; Olean, NE Sacred Heart Church.
Wittstock, John J. '36 (DET) Retired.
Wittstock, Joseph *o.c.s.o.* '84 (ARL) [J] Berryville, VA Cistercian Abbey of Our Lady of the Holy Cross.
Witz, Dennis M. '76 (MIL) [44] Milwaukee, WI Immaculate Conception Church.
Witzemann, Gerald B. '61 (COV) Retired.
Witzmann, Hugh *o.s.b.* '55 (SCL) [I] Collegeville, MN St. John's Abbey, of the Order of St. Benedict.
Wixted, Matthew O. '62 (SLC) Tooele, UT St. Marguerite's Church.
Wizeman, William L. *s.j.* '98 (NY) [DD] New York, NY Jesuit Provincial's Office.
Wleczyk, Msgr. Leo '65 (GAL) Lake Jackson, TX St. Michael Church.
Wlodyka, Stanley *o.f.m.conv.* '41 (SPR) [A] Granby, MA St. Hyacinth College and Seminary.
Wocken, Jeffrey *s.d.s.* '99 (SAC) Orangevale, CA Divine Savior Church.
Wodarski, Msgr. John P. *s.t.d.* '31 (HRT) [5] Bristol, CT St. Stanislaus Church; Retired.
Wodniak, John L. '43 (CHI) [96] Chicago, IL St. James Church; Retired.
Wodziak, Michael '48 (RVC) Retired.
Woefl, Paul A. *s.j.* '44 (TOL) [6] Toledo, OH Gesu Church.
Woempner, Michael A. '79 (MAR) White Pine, MI St. Jude Church.
Woerter, Dennis C. *o.p.* '97 (CHI) [N] Chicago, IL Dominicans (Provincial Office).
Woerter, Dennis C. *o.p.* '97 (DEN) [29] Denver, CO St. Dominic's Church.
Woerth, Thomas J. '66 (DEN) Denver, CO Veterans Hospital.
Woerz, Christian H. *s.d.b.* '76 (OAK) [E] Richmond, CA Salesian High School.
Woestman, William *o.m.i.* (CHI) [83] Chicago, IL Holy Rosary Church.
Wohinc, Karl R. '63 (WH) Shinnston, WV St. Ann's Church.
Wohlrab, Paul G. '41 (ROC) Spencerport, NY St. John the Evangelist Church; Retired; [L] Spencerport, NY Legion of Mary.
Wohlwend, Paul W. *c.pp.s.* '54 (CIN) Fort Recovery, OH Mary Help of Christians Church.
Wojcicki, Miroslaus A. '62 (PIT) East Pittsburgh, PA Holy Cross Church.
Wojcicki, Ted J. '75 (STL) [A] St. Louis, MO Kenrick-Glennon Seminary.
Wojcicki, Msgr. Ted L. '75 (STL) [62] St. Louis, MO St. Stanislaus Kostka Church.
Wojcicki, Wojciech '90 (DET) [5] Warren, MI St. Edmund Church.
Wojciechowski, Christian *o.f.m.conv.* '53 (TR) [22] Trenton, NJ St. Stanislaus Church.
Wojciechowski, Edward C. '81 (PRM) Minneapolis, MN St. John the Baptist Church.
Wojciechowski, Richard P. '63 (BAL) [23] Baltimore, MD Christ the King Church.
Wojciechowski, Robert J. '83 (DET) [22] Detroit, MI St. Francis D'Assisi Church.
Wojciechowski, Thomas *o.f.m.* '75 (GB) [H] Manitowoc, WI St. Mary's Home for the Aged; [I] Pulaski, WI Assumption of B.V.M. Friary; [I] Pulaski, WI Assumption of B.V.M. Friary.
Wojciehowski, Msgr. Thaddeus J. '36 (TR) Retired; [M] Trenton, NJ Villa Vianney.
Wojcik, Eugene J. '74 (BEL) Tipton, IL St. Patrick Church.
Wojcik, Joseph J. '69 (CHI) [11] Chicago, IL St. Andrew Church; [A] Chicago, IL Archbishop Quigley Preparatory Seminary.
Wojcik, Richard J. '49 (CHI) Retired; [A] Mundelein, IL University of St. Mary of the Lake-Mundelein Seminary.
Wojcinski, Anthony A. '85 (PBL) [1] Pueblo, CO Sacred Heart Church.
Wojtewicz, Eugene E. '57 (DET) Southgate, MI St. Hugh Church.
Wojtowicz, Edward L. '44 (NU) Retired.
Wojtowicz, John *o.f.m.* '80 (MIL) [P] Milwaukee, WI Francis and Clare House.
Wojtunik, Henry *m.s.* '60 (MIL) [P] Twin Lakes, WI La Salette Missionaries Shrine.
Wojtus, Anthony '58 (WH) Retired.
Wojtycha, Msgr. Edward F. '38 (NEW) [2] Bayonne, NJ St. Andrew's Church; Retired.
Wolak, Edmund '92 (SY) [7] Oswego, NY St. Stephen the King Church.
Wolanski, Edward *c.p.* '72 (WOR) [N] Shrewsbury, MA Calvery Retreat Center, Passionist Fathers of Shrewsbury, Inc.
Wolbach, Msgr. Richard A. '56 (OM) Retired.
Wolber, Ferdinand A. '40 (DET) Retired.
Woldai, Ghebriel (OAK) [3] Berkeley, CA St. Joseph The Worker Church.
Woldum, Richard *o.m.v.* '77 (BO) [B] Boston, MA Oblate Provincialate.
Wolensky, Paul '94 (STF) Brooklyn, NY Holy Ghost Church.
Wolesky, John '67 (SAL) Gypsum, KS St. Patrick's Church; Solomon, KS Immaculate Conception Church.
Wolf, Adam *o.f.m.* (CHI) Oak Forest, IL Oak Forest Hospital.
Wolf, Anthony J. '96 (LC) Bakerville, WI Corpus Christi Church; Marshfield, WI Sacred Heart of Jesus Church.
Wolf, Charles E. *s.j.* '49 (BAL) [S] Baltimore, MD Jesuit Fathers and Brothers Maryland Provincial Curia.
Wolf, Charles E. *s.j.* '49 (FgM) Provinces.
Wolf, David *o.s.b.* '52 (BIS) [A] Richardton, ND Assumption Abbey.
Wolf, Dennis G. '72 (BUF) Wellsville, NY Immaculate Conception Church.
Wolf, Donald J. '81 (OKL) Duncan, OK Assumption Church.
Wolf, Eugene *o.f.m.cap.* '54 (MIL) [P] Mount Calvary, WI St. Lawrence Friary.
Wolf, Eugene J. '63 (LC) Seneca, WI St. Patrick Church; Wauzeka, WI Sacred Heart Church.
Wolf, George *o.s.b.* '44 (FgM) American - Cassinese Congregation Foreign Missions.
Wolf, George *o.s.b.* '44 (SCL) [I] Collegeville, MN St. John's Abbey, of the Order of St. Benedict.
Wolf, George '80 (P) Salem, OR Queen of Peace Church.
Wolf, George C. '63 (RNO) Sparks, NV Holy Cross Catholic Community Church.
Wolf, James '48 (SFS) Retired.
Wolf, James *o.f.m.cap.* '57 (DET) [K] Detroit, MI St. Bonaventure Friary; [K] Detroit, MI St. Bonaventure Friary.
Wolf, Msgr. James J. '69 (FTW) Warsaw, IN Sacred Heart Church; [H] Fort Wayne, IN St. Anne Home of the Diocese of Fort Wayne - South Bend, Inc.
Wolf, John *c.pp.s.* '69 (KC) [7] Kansas City, MO St. Charles Borromeo Church.
Wolf, Msgr. John V. '45 (COL) Retired.
Wolf, Joseph *o.f.m.cap.* '64 (FgM) Capuchin Foreign Missions.
Wolf, Joseph A. '68 (MIL) [62] Milwaukee, WI Our Lady of Good Hope Church.
Wolf, Joseph B. '54 (STL) Retired.
Wolf, Joseph D. '87 (BUF) [3] Orchard Park, NY Our Lady of the Sacred Heart Church.
Wolf, Joseph M. '94 (DAV) [M] Davenport, IA St. Vincent Center.
Wolf, Lawrence Robert *o.s.b.m.* '75 (PSC) Roebling, NJ St. Nicholas Church; [A] Matawan, NJ Basilian Fathers of Mariapoch.
Wolf, Michael H. '42 (SAG) Essexville, MI St. John the Evangelist Church; Retired.
Wolf, Paul L. '83 (NU) Winsted, MN Holy Trinity Church; Winsted, MN Holy Trinity Church.
Wolf, Robert J. '44 (MIL) Retired.
Wolf, Ronald D. *s.j.* '74 (SJ) [L] Los Gatos, CA Sacred Heart Jesuit Center.
Wolf, Stephen J. '97 (NSH) Old Hickory, TN St. Stephen Church.

Wolf, Werner *o.f.m.cap.* '58 (GB) [M] Appleton, WI Monte Alverno Retreat Center.
Wolfe, Allan F. '92 (HBG) [3] Lancaster, PA Assumption of the Blessed Virgin Mary Church; [J] Lancaster, PA Iglesia de San Juan Bautista.
Wolfe, James '55 (ROC) Retired.
Wolfe, Joseph M. *m.f.v.a.* '93 (BIR) [E] Birmingham, AL Franciscan Missionaries of the Eternal Word, A Public Association of the Christian Faithful.
Wolfe, Robert A. *o.carm.* '75 (NEW) Englewood, NJ St. Cecilia's Church.
Wolfe, William P. '70 (LA) West Hollywood, CA St. Ambrose Church.
Wolfee, Robert '98 (NEW) Verona, NJ Our Lady of the Lake Church.
Wolfel, Daniel L. '54 (E) St. Marys, PA Sacred Heart of Jesus Church.
Wolfer, Paul J. '45 (CIN) [65] Cincinnati, OH Our Lady of Lourdes Church; Retired.
Wolfer, Robert R. '48 (CIN) [65] Cincinnati, OH Our Lady of Lourdes Church; Retired.
Wolff, Alec J. '81 (CHI) Graduate Studies; [X] Wilmette, IL Musica Pacis.
Wolff, Msgr. Robert C. '50 (CLV) Copley, OH Guardian Angels Church; Retired.
Wolfgram, Daniel '97 (SFS) [7] Sioux Falls, SD St. Michael Church.
Wolford, Donald L. '79 (SFD) [3] Decatur, IL St. Patrick Church.
Wolfram, Frank *s.d.b.* '62 (NY) [FF] Stony Point, NY Don Bosco Retreat Center and Marian Shrine; [FF] Stony Point, NY Marian Shrine.
Wolken, Gary P. '93 (STL) [14] St. Louis, MO Our Lady of Sorrows Church.
Wolken, Louis J. *m.m.* '46 (FgM) Maryknoll Foreign Missions.
Wolkovich, William L. '53 (BO) [2] Norwood, MA St. George Church.
Wolkovits, Paul '93 (LA) Graduate Studies.
Woll, Peter J. '44 (CLV) [31] Cleveland, OH Holy Trinity - St. Edward Church; [5] Euclid, OH St. Robert Bellarmine Church; Retired.
Wollering, Carl J. '66 (CIN) [30] Cincinnati, OH Guardian Angels Church; [40] Cincinnati, OH St. Jerome Church.
Wollersheim, David '77 (GLP) Absent on Leave.
Wollesen, Charles A. *s.j.* '52 (SEA) [A] Seattle, WA Seattle University.
Wollmering, Bruce *o.s.b.* '67 (SCL) [I] Collegeville, MN St. John's Abbey, of the Order of St. Benedict.
Wolnik, James G. '79 (STP) [4] St. Paul, MN Holy Childhood Church.
Wolnowski, Kenneth J. '65 (CLV) [10] Lorain, OH St. Peter Church.
Woloszczuk, Wolodymyr '81 (SJP) North Port, FL Entrance of B.V.M. into the Temple Church.
Woloszyk, Ignatius J. '38 (SAG) Retired.
Wolski, Adalbert *t.o.r.* '58 (ALT) [5] Johnstown, PA St. Clare of Assisi Church.
Wolski, Adalbert *t.o.r.* '59 (ALT) [F] Hollidaysburg, PA St. Joseph Friary.
Wolski, Mark J. '67 (BUF) Hamburg, NY SS. Peter and Paul Church.
Wolter, Allan *o.f.m.* '40 (BUF) [C] St. Bonaventure, NY St. Bonaventure University; [O] St. Bonaventure, NY St. Bonaventure Friary.
Wolter, Allan *o.f.m.* '40 (STL) [P] St. Louis, MO Franciscan Friary of St. Anthony of Padua.
Wolter, Martin *o.f.m.* '46 (STL) [P] St. Louis, MO Franciscan Friary of St. Anthony of Padua.
Wolter, Richard J. '59 (STP) Retired.
Wolter, Thomas '66 (JOL) Elmhurst, IL Mary, Queen of Heaven Church; Elmhurst, IL Elmhurst Memorial Hospital.
Wolters, Gilbert *o.s.b.* '34 (KCK) [H] Atchison, KS St. Benedict's Abbey.
Wolverton, R. Ambrose *o.s.b.* '65 (PRO) [P] Portsmouth, RI Abbey of St. Gregory the Great.
Womack, Emil *c.p.* '44 (SAC) [H] Citrus Heights, CA Christ the King Retreat.
Womack, Warren *c.p.* (CHI) [N] Chicago, IL Passionist Community-Immaculate Conception Monastery.
Womack, Warren *c.p.* '49 (ORL) [F] Orlando, FL Bethany House of Beutel.
Won, Msgr. John P. '58 (LA) West Covina, CA St. Christopher Church.
Wong, George *s.j.* '51 (SJ) [L] Los Gatos, CA Sacred Heart Jesuit Center.
Wong, Joseph *o.s.b.cam.* '74 (MRY) [F] Big Sur, CA New Camaldoli Hermitage.
Wong, Victor '50 (WDC) [5] Washington, DC St. Anthony Church.
Wood, Charles '00 (P) [17] Portland, OR Holy Redeemer Church.
Wood, Dennis Mark '87 (LR) Mountain Home, AR St. Peter the Fisherman Church.
Wood, Edson J. *o.s.a.* '72 (PH) [C] Villanova, PA Villanova University.
Wood, Gregg D. *s.j.* '75 (FBK) Chevak, AK Sacred Heart Church; Hooper Bay, AK Little Flower of Jesus Church; Scammon Bay, AK Blessed Sacrament Church; [E] St. Marys, AK Brother Joe Prince Jesuit Community.
Wood, James L. '72 (RVC) Bohemia, NY St. John Nepomucene Church.
Wood, John M. '83 (SY) [1] Rome, NY St. John the Baptist Church.
Wood, Kenneth E. '89 (RIC) Harrisonburg, VA Blessed Sacrament Church.
Wood, Michael (NOR) [C] Baltic, CT Academy and Boarding-School of the Holy Family; [G] Baltic, CT Holy Family Motherhouse.
Wood, Michael '84 (AMA) Absent on Leave.
Wood, Norbert J. *o.praem.* '81 (ORG) [I] Silverado, CA Norbertine Fathers of Orange Inc.
Wood, Paul '80 (BRK) [E] Brooklyn, NY Office of Religious Education: Evangelization and Catholic Formation.
Wood, Paul A. '80 (BRK) [189] Queens, NY St. Kevin Church.
Wood, Peter N. '82 (PT) On Leave of Absence.
Wood, Raymond B. '64 (SY) Jamesville, NY St. Mary Church.
Wood, Robert *c.m.* '56 (FgM) Vincentian Foreign Missions.
Wood, Robert T. '87 (OKL) [12] Oklahoma City, OK St. James Church.
Wood, Robert W. '74 (BUF) Elma, NY Annunciation of the Blessed Virgin Mary Church.
Wood, Simon *c.p.* '43 (BAL) [S] Baltimore, MD St. Joseph's Passionist Community.
Wood, Simon Paul *c.p.* (HRT) [M] West Hartford, CT Holy Family Monastery/Retreat.
Wood, Steven R. *m.m.* '67 (NY) [DD] Maryknoll, NY Maryknoll Fathers and Brothers.
Wood, William Andrew '73 (GAL) Sugar Land, TX St. Laurence Church.
Wood, William T. *s.j.* '48 (NY) [DD] New York, NY Murray-Weigel Hall.
Woodarek, Richard *c.s.s.* '57 (BO) [W] Waltham, MA Stigmatine Fathers & Brothers Provincial House.
Woodcock, Michael '73 (PMB) Fort Pierce, FL St. Anastasia Church.
Woodeshick, Martin E. '69 (PH) Sharon Hill, PA Holy Spirit Church.
Woodhall, Jonathan A. '99 (R) [1] Raleigh, NC Cathedral of the Sacred Heart.
Woodka, Raymond *s.s.j.* (BAL) [81] Baltimore, MD St. Peter Claver Church.
Woodka, Raymond A. *s.s.j.* '66 (BAL) [S] Baltimore, MD St. Joseph Society of the Sacred Heart House of Central Administration.
Woodland, Stephen '88 (LA) Inglewood, CA St. John Chrysostom Church.
Woodman, Gerald '78 (SEA) Chehalis, WA St. Joseph Church; Toledo, WA St. Francis Xavier Church; Winlock, WA Sacred Heart Church.
Woodruff, Mark '72 (SAN) [3] Odessa, TX St. Elizabeth Ann Seton Church.
Woodruff, William F. '82 (NY) Mahopac, NY St. John the Evangelist Church.
Woods, Curtis W. '80 (SHP) [1] Shreveport, LA St. John Berchmans Church.
Woods, Msgr. Earl C. '57 (NO) Retired.
Woods, James A. *s.j.* '61 (BO) [C] Chestnut Hill, MA Boston College; [C] Chestnut Hill, MA Boston College; [W] Chestnut Hill, MA The Jesuit Community at Boston College.
Woods, Keith '95 (WDC) Olney, MD St. Peter Church.
Woods, Michael A. '66 (ATL) On Duty Outside the Archdiocese.
Woods, Michael A. '66 (KNX) Oak Ridge, TN St. Mary Church.
Woods, Patrick F. *c.ss.r.* '75 (BRK) [V] Brooklyn, NY Our Lady of Good Counsel Residence.
Woods, Richard J. *o.p.* '69 (CHI) [N] Chicago, IL Dominicans (Provincial Office).
Woods, Walter J. '70 (BO) Acton, MA St. Elizabeth of Hungary Church.
Woods, Warren '50 (SFR) [K] San Rafael, CA Nazareth House.
Woods, Warren L. '50 (SFR) Special Assignment.
Woodward, John B. *s.j.* '58 (WDC) [E] Washington, DC Gonzaga College High School.
Woolever, James '74 (SJ) Palo Alto, CA St. Thomas Aquinas Church.
Woolever, James '74 (SY) On Duty Outside the Diocese.
Woollett, D. Mathew '82 (ALX) Cottonport, LA St. Mary Assumption Church.
Woolley, Michael J. '99 (PRO) [4] Cranston, RI St. Mark Church.
Woolsey, Msgr. John G. '65 (NY) [60] New York, NY St. John the Martyr Church; [190] Bronx, NY St. Theresa of the Infant Jesus Church.
Woolson, Herbert '82 (LFT) Fishers, IN St. Louis de Montfort Church.
Woolway, John S. '80 (LA) Los Nietos, CA Our Lady of Perpetual Help Church.
Woost, David G. '91 (CLV) Concord Twp., OH St. Gabriel Church; [C] Mentor, OH Lake Catholic High.
Woost, Michael '84 (CLV) Mentor, OH St. Bede the Venerable Church.
Woost, Michael G. '84 (CLV) [A] Wickliffe, OH St. Mary Seminary and Graduate School of Theology.
Woost, Thomas G. '97 (CLV) Cuyahoga Falls, OH Immaculate Heart of Mary Church.
Wooton, Jerry A. '96 (ARL) Lake Ridge, VA St. Elizabeth Ann Seton Church.
Wopperer, Thomas J. '64 (BUF) [4] Dunkirk, NY St. Elizabeth Ann Seton Church.
Woracek, Msgr. Thomas J. '46 (STL) Retired.
Worcester, Thomas W. *s.j.* '91 (WOR) [N] Worcester, MA Jesuits of Holy Cross College, Inc.
Worch, Donald P. '67 (WDC) Derwood, MD St. Francis of Assisi Church.
Worczak, Paul F. '68 (OG) Norwood, NY St. Andrew Church.
Wordekemper, Thomas *o.s.b.* '94 (BIS) [A] Richardton, ND Assumption Abbey.
Worley, Jason C. '99 (BAL) [57] Baltimore, MD St. Mark Church.
Worm, Paul '88 (LR) Fayetteville, AR St. Joseph's Church; Fayetteville, AR St. Thomas Aquinas University Church; [J] Fayetteville, AR Catholic Campus Ministries.
Worman, Jeremiah F. '67 (GB) Antigo, WI St. Mary Church; Neva, WI St. Wenceslaus Church.
Wormek, Joseph E. '76 (STL) Manchester, MO Christ, Prince of Peace Church.
Worn, G. Peter '77 (SY) Cazenovia, NY St. James Church.
Worner, William H. '45 (SFR) Special Assignment; Retired.
Woroniewicz, Michael A. '85 (DET) Royal Oak, MI St. Mary Church.
Worry, Benedict M. *o.s.b.* '87 (PAT) [M] Morristown, NJ St. Mary's Abbey.
Worry, Benedict Michael *o.s.b.* '87 (NEW) [1] Linden, NJ St. Elizabeth's Church.
Worschak, George D. '78 (PHU) Absent on Leave.
Worsley, Stephen C. '84 (R) Ahoskie, NC St. Charles Borromeo Church.
Worster, John '87 (B) Buhl, ID Immaculate Conception Church.
Worthley, John '90 (RVC) Port Jefferson, NY Infant Jesus Church.
Worthy, Donald '62 (DET) [H] Pontiac, MI St. Joseph Mercy - Oakland.
Wortmann, Edgar J. '48 (OM) [10] Omaha, NE Blessed Sacrament Church.
Wortmann, Joseph F. '58 (NEW) [B] South Orange, NJ Seton Hall University; [C] West Orange, NJ Seton Hall Preparatory School.
Worzalla, Dennis A. '50 (GB) Retired.
Worzalla, Dennis A. '50 (LC) [4] Stevens Point, WI St. Peter Church.
Wosman, Richard *s.m.* (STL) [P] St. Louis, MO Provincialate of the Society of Mary, Province of St. Louis.
Wosman, Richard *s.m.* '93 (STL) [F] Kirkwood, MO St. John Vianney High School.
Woster, Msgr. Michael '82 (RC) [1] Rapid City, SD Cathedral of Our Lady of Perpetual Help; [D] Rapid City, SD Priest Retirement and Aid Association.
Wotelko, Matthew S. *o.s.b.* '67 (NEW) [N] Newark, NJ Newark Abbey.
Woulfe, Cornelius C. *c.s.sp.* '44 (NY) Kingston, NY Kingston City Hospital.
Woy, Msgr. Richard '79 (BAL) Special Assignment.
Woytek, Robert '91 (PSC) New Britain, CT Holy Trinity Church.
Woytyna, Chistopher *o.s.b.m.* '61 (STF) Long Island City, NY Holy Cross Church.
Wozniak, Aloysius '52 (LC) [H] La Crosse, WI Holy Cross (Seminary) Diocesan Center.
Wozniak, Aloysius A. '52 (LC) Retired.
Wozniak, Casimir J. '68 (E) [B] Erie, PA Gannon University.
Wozniak, James E. '97 (GRY) Saint John, IN St. John Evangelist Church.
Wozniak, Msgr. Louis '51 (AUS) Retired.
Wozniak, Phillip '49 (CHI) [N] Libertyville, IL Marytown, Our Lady of Fatima Friary.
Wozniak, Richard *c.m.f.* '52 (AUS) San Marcos, TX St. John the Evangelist Church.
Wozniak, Robert A. '88 (BUF) Ripley, NY St. Thomas More Church; Westfield, NY St. James Church.
Wozniak, Ronald E. *s.j.* '77 (BO) [W] Weston, MA Campion Jesuit Community; [W] Weston, MA Campion Health Center, Inc.
Wozniak, Tim '74 (STP) Burnsville, MN Church of the Risen Savior.
Wozniczka, Stephen Z. *o.s.p.p.e.* '60 (PH) [AA] Doylestown, PA Pauline Fathers Monastery, Shrine of Our Lady of Czestochowa.
Wraszczak, Chester '43 (P) Retired.
Wray, Joseph M. '96 (OM) [13] Omaha, NE St. Elizabeth Ann Church.
Wreisner, Hugh *o.p.* '88 (CHI) [N] River Forest, IL St. Thomas Aquinas Priory.
Wrenn, Lawrence G. '53 (HRT) Special and other Archdiocesan Assignment.
Wrenn, Msgr. Michael J. '61 (NY) [58] New York, NY St. John the Evangelist Church.

Wright, Addison G. *s.s.* '60 (BAL) [S] Baltimore, MD Sulpician Provincial House.
Wright, Arthur F. '67 (BO) [6] Cambridge, MA Immaculate Conception Church.
Wright, Bryan B. '00 (SCR) [4] Pittston, PA St. John the Evangelist Church.
Wright, Charles *o.s.b.* '70 (SD) [H] Oceanside, CA Prince of Peace Abbey, Benet Hill.
Wright, D. Ralph *o.s.b.* '70 (STL) [F] Creve Coeur, MO St. Louis Priory School; [P] St. Louis, MO The Abbey of St. Mary and St. Louis.
Wright, David F. *o.p.* '68 (CHI) [N] Chicago, IL Dominicans (Provincial Office); [N] Chicago, IL Dominicans (Provincial Office).
Wright, Msgr. Edward S. '54 (RCK) North Aurora, IL Blessed Sacrament Church.
Wright, Francis W. *c.s.sp.* '49 (WDC) [V] Washington, DC Holy Childhood Association.
Wright, Frank Allen *s.m.a.* '93 (FgM) Society of African Missions.
Wright, Gary R. *s.j.* '80 (DET) [K] Detroit, MI Jesuit Community at the University of Detroit; [S] Detroit, MI University of Detroit Mercy University Ministry.
Wright, Gerald *o.m.v.* '80 (BO) [W] Milton, MA Oblate Residence (St. Joseph House).
Wright, James B. '69 (DET) Farmington Hills, MI St. Alexander Church.
Wright, John A. '56 (CHY) Retired.
Wright, John A. '82 (MAN) Retired.
Wright, John H. '52 (SPK) [C] Spokane, WA Gonzaga University.
Wright, John H. '62 (HBG) [H] Ephrata, PA St. Clement's Mission House.
Wright, John J. '78 (CLV) [4] Garfield Heights, OH St. Timothy Church; [Z] Cleveland, OH The Greater Cleveland/Akron Corporation United for Education; [Z] Cleveland, OH Ninth Street CDC.
Wright, Msgr. John M. '62 (IND) Retired.
Wright, Joseph R. *c.m.* '54 (PH) [AA] Philadelphia, PA Congregation of the Mission.
Wright, Michael H. '95 (SEA) Castle Rock, WA St. Mary Church; Kelso, WA Immaculate Heart of Mary Church.
Wright, Patrick J. '54 (SFD) [5] Springfield, IL St. Agnes Church.
Wright, Richard J. '45 (PH) Ardmore, PA St. Colman Church; Retired.
Wright, Robert '54 (SY) Retired.
Wright, Robert *o.m.i.* '74 (SAT) [M] San Antonio, TX Joseph Gerard House.
Wright, Robert E. *o.m.i.* '74 (SAT) [C] San Antonio, TX Oblate School of Theology.
Wright, Msgr. Rupert A. '56 (BUF) Williamsville, NY St. Gregory the Great Church.
Wright, Tennant C. *s.j.* '62 (SJ) [B] Santa Clara, CA Santa Clara University.
Wright, Thomas '55 (RNO) Retired.
Wright, Thomas *s.m.a.* '92 (NEW) [N] Tenafly, NJ Society of African Missions, Provincialate, S.M.A. Fathers.
Wright, Thomas *s.m.a.* '92 (WDC) [M] Takoma Park, MD Society of African Missions (S.M.A.).
Wright, Vincent L. '57 (BUF) Retired.
Wright, Warren J. *s.j.* '82 (SFR) [E] San Francisco, CA St. Ignatius College Preparatory (Coed); [N] San Francisco, CA Jesuit Community at St. Ignatius College Preparatory.
Wright, William *c.ss.r.* '60 (FgM) Redemptorist Foreign Missions.
Wright, William A. '65 (PH) [2] Drexel Hill, PA St. Bernadette Church.
Wrightington, Charles G. *s.j.* '00 (NY) [DD] New York, NY St. Ignatius Loyola Residence.
Wrightson, Mark J. *o.s.f.s* '86 (PH) [D] Philadelphia, PA Northeast Catholic High School for Boys; [AA] Philadelphia, PA Oblates of St. Francis De Sales.
Wrigley, Franklin '52 (OKL) Retired.
Wrobleski, Edward D. *c.s.p.* '62 (LA) [87] Los Angeles, CA St. Paul the Apostle Church.
Wroblewski, Anthony *o.m.i.* '95 (BEL) [F] Belleville, IL Shrine of Our Lady of the Snows.
Wroblewski, Brendan *o.f.m.* (GB) Pulaski, WI Assumption of the Blessed Virgin Mary Church.
Wroblewski, Edward D. *c.s.p.* '62 (NY) [DD] Jamaica Estates, NY Paulist Fathers Generalate.
Wroblewski, Edward M. *m.m.* '52 (NY) [DD] Maryknoll, NY Maryknoll Fathers and Brothers.
Wroblewski, John J. '92 (NY) [196] Staten Island, NY St. Anthony Church.
Wroblewski, Lawrence J. *s.j.* '74 (ROC) [C] Rochester, NY McQuaid Jesuit High School.
Wroblewski, Marion *c.r.* '65 (CHI) [189] Chicago, IL St. Stanislaus, Bishop and Martyr Church.
Wroblewski, Sergius *o.f.m.* '46 (FgM) Franciscan Foreign Missions.
Wroblewski, Sergius *o.f.m.* '46 (GB) [I] Pulaski, WI Assumption of B.V.M. Friary.
Wroblicky, Theodore '99 (STN) Sacramento, CA St. Andrew the Apostle Church.
Wrozek, Timothy A. '88 (FTW) Wabash, IN St. Bernard Church.
Wrynn, John F. *s.j.* '70 (NEW) [N] Jersey City, NJ Jesuits of Saint Peter's College, Inc.
Wrynn, John P. '70 (NEW) [B] Jersey City, NJ Saint Peter's College.
Wszolek, Stanislaw '83 (DET) [A] Detroit, MI Sacred Heart Major Seminary, Inc.
Wtorek, Krzysztof '94 (CAM) Runnemede, NJ St. Teresa of the Infant Jesus Church.
Wtulich, John S. '72 (BRK) [26] Brooklyn, NY St. Catharine of Alexandria Church.
Wtyklo, Jacek S. '98 (MAR) DeTour, MI Sacred Heart Church; Goetzville, MI St. Stanislaus Kostka Church.
Wu, Peter A. *m.m.* '61 (FgM) Maryknoll Foreign Missions.
Wu, Stanley '60 (SFR) Retired.
Wu, Stanley '76 (SFR) [52] San Francisco, CA St. Thomas the Apostle Church.
Wudarski, Dariusz P. '96 (SPR) Longmeadow, MA St. Mary's Church; [Q] Springfield, MA Newman Apostolates and Campus Ministries.
Wuellner, George E. '54 (PEO) Seymour, IL St. Boniface Church; Retired.
Wuerth, James E. *m.s.f.* '71 (SAT) Seguin, TX Our Lady of Guadalupe Church.
Wuertz, Richard A. '68 (YAK) Chelan, WA St. Francis de Sales Church.
Wueste, Andrew *o.m.i.* '54 (SAT) [M] San Antonio, TX Oblate Benson Residence (Southwest Area).
Wulinski, Stanley F. '80 (BRK) Released from Diocesan Assignment.
Wulsch, Michael A. '72 (CHI) [137] Chicago, IL St. Monica Church.
Wummer, Robert P. '56 (WDC) Fort Washington, MD St. Ignatius Church.
Wunderlich, Dale P. '74 (STL) [2] St. Louis, MO Epiphany of Our Lord Church.
Wunderlich, Donulus *o.f.m.* '46 (SFD) [K] Sherman, IL Our Lady of Angels Friary.
Wunsch, Richard J. *c.s.c.* '66 (FgM) Holy Cross Foreign Missions.
Wunsch, Richard J. *c.s.c.* '66 (FTW) [J] South Bend, IN Congregation of Holy Cross, Indiana Province, Provincial House.
Wurm, Robert L. '60 (DET) Ferndale, MI St. James Church.
Wurm, William *o.s.b.* '79 (GBG) [H] Latrobe, PA Saint Vincent Archabbey.
Wurst, Wayne H. '80 (CHI) Oak Forest, IL Oak Forest Hospital.
Wurth, Elmer P. *m.m.* '56 (FgM) Maryknoll Foreign Missions.
Wurth, Mary Philip *o.c.d.* '59 (SAT) [18] San Antonio, TX Basilica of The National Shrine of Our Lady of Mt. Carmel and St. Therese, Discalced Carmelite Fathers; [M] San Antonio, TX Discalced Carmelites (Prov. of St. Therese).
Wurth, Richard W. '99 (COV) Edgewood, KY St. Pius X Church; [B] Covington, KY Covington Catholic High School; [B] Newport, KY Newport Central Catholic High School.
Wurtz, Camillus *o.s.b.* '52 (KCK) [C] Atchison, KS Maur Hill Prep School.
Wurtz, Msgr. Robert C. '58 (BUF) [1] Lackawanna, NY Basilica of Our Lady of Victory; [J] Lackawanna, NY Baker Victory Services; [T] Lackawanna, NY Our Lady of Victory Homes of Charity.
Wurz, George E. '60 (SY) [3] Oswego, NY St. Louis Church; [6] Oswego, NY St. Peter Church.
Wurzel, Richard T. '59 (TOL) Sylvania, OH St. Joseph Church.
Wutscheck, John '61 (MIL) West Bend, WI Holy Angels Church.
Wyczawski, Stanley '73 (DET) Port Huron, MI St. Mary Church.
Wydeven, John (OAK) Military Chaplains.
Wyen, Larry *c.pp.s.* '69 (CIN) St. Henry, OH St. Henry Church.
Wyffels, Robert J. '60 (NU) Morgan, MN St. Michael Church.
Wykes, John *o.m.v.* '98 (SFD) [2] Alton, IL Immaculate Conception-St. Mary's Church; [H] Alton, IL Saint Anthony's Health Center; [N] Alton, IL Saint Anthony's Health System, Inc.; [N] Alton, IL Saint Clare's Hospital.
Wymelenberg, M. John *s.j.* '60 (OM) [K] Omaha, NE Jesuit Community at Creighton University.
Wymes, John F. *m.m.* '54 (NY) [DD] Maryknoll, NY Maryknoll Fathers and Brothers.
Wymes, John F. *m.m.* '54 (RVC) Malverne, NY Our Lady of Lourdes Church.
Wynants, Paul G. *c.i.c.m.* '51 (ARL) [N] Vienna, VA Mount Tabor Society, Inc.
Wyndaele, William *c.i.c.m.* '59 (ARL) [J] Arlington, VA Missionhurst, C.I.C.M.-Central House and Provincialate.
Wyndham, Thomas F. '69 (BO) [4] Weymouth, MA St. Jerome Church.
Wynne, James J. *o.m.i.* '55 (BEL) [F] Belleville, IL Missionary Oblates of Mary Immaculate - St. Henry's Oblate Residence.
Wynne, Robert F. *m.m.* '68 (HON) Kamuela, HI Church of the Annunciation; [G] Honolulu, HI Maryknoll Fathers House (M.M.).
Wynne, William J. *o.s.a.* '44 (BO) [C] North Andover, MA Merrimack College.
Wynnycky, John P. '92 (DET) Pontiac, MI St. Joseph Church; Pontiac, MI St. Michael Church; Pontiac, MI St. Vincent de Paul Church.
Wypych, Andrew P. '79 (CHI) [160] Chicago, IL St. Pancratius Church.
Wyrostek, Andrzej Stanislaw '00 (RC) [2] Rapid City, SD Blessed Sacrament Church.
Wyrsch, Thomas W. '78 (STL) [16] St. Louis, MO Resurrection of Our Lord Church; [V] St. Louis, MO Archdiocesan Stewardship Education Committee.
Wyse, James B. '87 (GR) [3] Muskegon, MI St. Jean Baptiste Church.
Wysochansky, Constantine *o.s.b.m.* '62 (STN) Hamtramck, MI Immaculate Conception of B.V.M. Church.
Wysochansky, Demetrius *o.s.b.m.* '59 (STN) Palos Park, IL Nativity of B. V. M. Church.
Wysochansky, John '57 (PHU) St. Clair, PA St. Nicholas Church; St. Clair, PA Holy Trinity Church.
Wysochansky, Walter (SJP) Ambridge, PA Ss. Peter and Paul Church.
Wysocki, James R. '67 (DET) Harsens Island, MI St. Mark Church; Marine City, MI Holy Cross Church.
Wysocki, Joseph A. '71 (SCR) On Duty Outside the Diocese.
Wysocki, Mark B. '85 (NEW) Wallington, NJ Most Sacred Heart of Jesus Church.
Wysocki, Paul J. '64 (CLV) Orrville, OH St. Agnes Church.
Wysocki, Paul P. '54 (HRT) [3] New Britain, CT Sacred Heart of Jesus Church.
Wysong, William H. '72 (CIN) [J] Cincinnati, OH St. Rita School for the Deaf.
Wyszynski, Darius W. '58 (LAN) [5] Jackson, MI St. Stanislaus Kostka Church.
Wytish, Michael Jude '90 (PBR) Morgantown, WV St. Mary Holy Protection Church; [D] Uniontown, PA Motherhouse and Novitiate of the Sisters of St. Basil the Great.
Wytrwal, Alexander J. '50 (DET) New Boston, MI St. Stephen Church.
Wyvill, Christopher *o.s.b.* '65 (WDC) [M] Washington, DC St. Anselm's Abbey.
Wyzgoski, Robert F. '59 (DET) Birmingham, MI Our Lady Queen of Martyrs Church.
Wyzykiewicz, Richard S. *sch.p.* '71 (PH) [G] Devon, PA Devon Preparatory School; [AA] Devon, PA Piarist Fathers (Order of the Pious Schools).

X

Xavier, Antony '60 (RVC) Manhasset, NY North Shore Univ. Hospital.
Xavier, Francis '41 (WOR) [N] Still River, MA Benedictine Monks, St. Benedict Abbey.
Xavier, Godwin '85 (SAC) Downieville, CA Immaculate Conception Church.
Xavier, Lawrence '79 (NY) Rhinebeck, NY The Good Shepherd Church.
Xuereb, Paul '45 (DET) Retired.
Xuereb, Publius '68 (FWT) The Colony, TX Holy Cross Church.

Y

Yabao, William '68 (NEW) [22] Jersey City, NJ Our Lady of Victories Church.
Yabes, Arthur *s.v.d.* '87 (SJ) [12] San Jose, CA St. John Vianney Church.
Yablonsky, Gabriel '59 (Y) Retired.
Yackanich, Eugene P. '65 (PBR) Munhall, PA St. Elias Church.
Yacobi, Francis *o.f.m.cap.* '90 (WDC) [B] Washington, DC St. Francis Friary-Capuchin College.
Yacyshyn, Gregory '98 (RVC) Greenlawn, NY St. Francis of Assisi Church.
Yadegar, Benn Beth '93 (EST) On Assignment Outside the Diocese.
Yadron, Michael J. '83 (GRY) [3] Michigan City, IN Queen of All Saints Church.
Yadron, Raymond A. '63 (CHI) Palatine, IL St. Thomas of Villanova Church.
Yaeger, Joseph J. '89 (R) Fayetteville, NC St. Ann Church.
Yager, James P. '41 (GR) Retired.
Yagesh, Richard C. '78 (PIT) Military Chaplains.
Yaghi, Milad T. *m.l.m.* '88 (OLL) Houston, TX Our Lady of the Cedars Maronite Church; [A] Houston, TX The Congregation of Maronite Lebanese Missionaries.
Yagley, Carl J. '53 (DET) Centerline, MI St. Clement Church.
Yagley, Carl J. '54 (DET) Retired.
Yahner, Gordon A. '63 (CLV) [7] Akron, OH St. Hilary Church.
Yakaitis, Michael T. '78 (CHI) [20] Chicago, IL St. Barbara Church; [138] Chicago, IL Nativity of the Blessed Virgin Mary Church.

Yaksick, Michael L. '94 (PIT) Bellevue, PA Assumption of the Blessed Virgin Mary on the Beautiful River Church.
Yallaly, Jules G. *c.m.* '36 (STL) [P] St. Louis, MO Lazarist Residence.
Yamada, John *ss.cc.* '71 (FR) [I] Fairhaven, MA Sacred Hearts Provincial House.
Yanas, John '84 (ALB) Frankfort, NY Our Lady Queen of Apostles Church.
Yance, Eugenio '92 (SLC) Wendover, UT San Felipe Church.
Yander, Steven L. '74 (ATL) [H] Atlanta, GA Saint Joseph's Hospital of Atlanta, Inc.
Yandrisevits, Philip *m.s.c.* '42 (ALN) [A] Center Valley, PA Missionaries of the Sacred Heart.
Yanez, Aurelio '74 (NEW) [5] Elizabeth, NJ Immaculate Conception Church.
Yanez, Horacio '75 (SEA) Marysville, WA St. Mary Church.
Yanez, Jaime *o.f.m.* '47 (ELP) [B] El Paso, TX St. Anthony's School of Theology.
Yanez, Jose *c.m.* (SJN) [54] San Juan, PR Sagrado Corazon de Jesus Church.
Yang, Paul '48 (RVC) Retired.
Yangas, Peter M. '64 (CHI) Schaumburg, IL St. Marcelline Church.
Yaniak, Frank J. '49 (MIL) Retired.
Yanju, Henry M. (BO) [4] Waltham, MA St. Mary Church.
Yankauskas, Albin J. '51 (WOR) Retired.
Yankevitch, Robert J. *s.j.* '69 (R) Lumberton, NC St. Francis De Sales Church; [E] Raleigh, NC Jesuit Community.
Yannarell, James J. *s.j.* '71 (NY) [DD] New York, NY Murray-Weigel Hall.
Yanos, Richard M. '83 (CHI) Lake Villa, IL Prince of Peace Church.
Yanovski, Stepan '90 (STF) Bridgeport, CT Protection of B.V.M. Church.
Yanta, John W. (AMA) [K] Amarillo, TX Monsignor B.A. Erpen Trust Fund.
Yanus, Gary D. '81 (CLV) [33] Cleveland, OH St. Ignatius of Antioch Church.
Yaoch, Felix K. *s.j.* '67 (CI) Koror, FM Sacred Heart Church; [C] Koror, Palau, PW Manresa Jesuit House.
Yarbrough, Msgr. Michael H. '80 (SAT) [57] San Antonio, TX St. Matthew's Church.
Yarce, Eugenio '92 (SLC) Tooele, UT St. Marguerite's Church.
Yardemian, Dadjad *o.mech.* '71 (ARM) [C] Glendale, CA Mekhitarian Educational Foundation.
Yargeau, Ronald G. '73 (SPR) Greenfield, MA Holy Trinity Church.
Yarno, Kenneth *c.s.v.* '59 (JOL) St. George, IL St. George Church.
Yarnovitz, Msgr. Robert '57 (PRM) Parma, OH Saint John the Baptist, Church.
Yaro, James '92 (BRK) [138] Brooklyn, NY St. Teresa of Avila Church.
Yaroch, Kenneth E. '67 (SAG) Caro, MI Sacred Heart Church.
Yaroch, Paul *o.f.m.cap.* '64 (MIL) [P] Mount Calvary, WI St. Lawrence Friary.
Yarrish, Msgr. Bernard E. '76 (SCR) [3] Wilkes-Barre, PA St. Boniface Church.
Yarrosh, Ronald J. '74 (ALN) Cumbola, PA St. Anthony of Padua Church; New Philadelphia, PA Holy Family Church; New Philadelphia, PA Sacred Heart Church.
Yasso, Jacob O. '60 (DET) [68] Detroit, MI Sacred Heart-Chaldean Church.
Yasso, Jacob O. '60 (EST) Detroit, MI Sacred Heart Chaldean Church.
Yast, Robert A. '56 (FTW) [2] Mishawaka, IN St. Joseph Church.
Yastishock, Charles '77 (PSC) Toms River, NJ Our Lady of Perpetual Help Church.
Yaszcz, Thomas A. '75 (SCR) On Special or Other Diocesan Assignment.
Yates, John *c.s.sp.* '54 (LR) Conway, AR St. Joseph's Church.
Yates, M. Clark *s.m.a.* '56 (NEW) [N] Tenafly, NJ Society of African Missions, Provincialate, S.M.A. Fathers.
Yates, Msgr. Robert J. '41 (MIA) [4] Hollywood, FL St. Bernadette Church.
Yates, Msgr. Robert J. '41 (TOL) Retired; [J] Oregon, OH Sacred Heart Home.
Yates, Simeon *o.f.m.conv.* '63 (IND) [I] Mount Saint Francis, IN Mount Saint Francis Friary and Retreat Center.
Yatkauskas, Matthew '89 (NY) Croton-on-Hudson, NY Holy Name of Mary Church.
Yavarone, Mark *o.m.v.* '00 (MET) Avenel, NJ St. Andrew Church.
Yavorsky, James A. '34 (CLV) Retired.
Yavorsky, Stephen T. *s.j.* '77 (FgM) Provinces.
Ybarra, Manuel *o.f.m.* '86 (WDC) [M] Washington, DC Commissariat of the Holy Land, Franciscan Monastery - Mount St. Sepulchre.
Ycoback, John D. '60 (PBR) [1] Youngstown, OH Assumption of the Blessed Virgin Church.
Ye Swe, Zeno '79 (DOD) Fowler, KS St. Anthony Church; Meade, KS St. John the Baptist Church; Plains, KS St. Patrick Church.
Yeager, James (ROC) Canisteo, NY St. Joachim Church; Rexville, NY St. Mary Church.
Yeager, Robert J. '62 (TOL) Special Assignment; [O] Waterville, OH Diocesan Fiscal Management Conference - National Office.
Yeaglin, Armand *o.f.m.cap* '38 (PIT) [O] Pittsburgh, PA St. Augustine Friary.
Yeakel, James R. *o.s.f.s.* '79 (WDC) [B] Washington, DC Oblates of St. Francis de Sales.
Yeazel, J. Robert '67 (SY) Dewitt, NY Holy Cross Church; Special Assignment.
Yebra, Bernardino S. (CHR) Cheraw, SC St. Peter's Church.
Yee Mon, Ronald '85 (FAR) Towner, ND St. Cecilia's Church.
Yehl, Msgr. Addison *m.s.* '51 (E) [B] Erie, PA Gannon University.
Yelenc, Joseph *t.o.r.* '71 (STU) [A] Steubenville, OH Franciscan University of Steubenville; [F] Steubenville, OH Holy Spirit Friary.
Yelinko, Flavian G. *o.s.b.* '33 (GBG) [H] Latrobe, PA Saint Vincent Archabbey.
Yelle, Ronald R. '79 (HRT) Granby, CT St. Therese's Church.
Yender, Basil *o.s.b.* '71 (RCK) [C] Aurora, IL Marmion Academy; [G] Aurora, IL Marmion Abbey-St. Augustine's Abbey.
Yenkevich, Daniel J. '90 (SCR) East Stroudsburg, PA St. Matthew's Church.
Yennock, Msgr. Eugene M. '50 (SY) [15] Syracuse, NY St. Daniel Church.
Yenushosky, Daniel J. '77 (ALN) [5] Allentown, PA Our Lady Help of Christians Church.
Yeo, Augustine H.K. (GAL) [R] Houston, TX Handmaids of the Sacred Heart of Jesus (H.S.H.).
Yeo, Augustine Hyeok-Ku '96 (GAL) [6] Houston, TX St. Andrew Kim Church.
Yeo, Wilfred '58 (NEW) Hoboken, NJ St. Mary's Hospital; Jersey City, NJ St. Francis Community Health Center; [S] Jersey City, NJ Bon Secours New Jersey Health System; [S] Jersey City, NJ Bon Secours New Jersey Health System.
Yetmar, J. Charles '57 (SC) Rock Rapids, IA Holy Name Church.
Yetsko, Robert K. *t.o.r.* (PBR) Punxsutawney, PA SS. Peter and Paul Church.
Yetter, Robert M. '73 (BUF) Swormville, NY St. Mary Church.
Yiengst, Msgr. George B. '62 (BUF) Getzville, NY St. Pius X Church.
Yiftheg, Cuthbert '89 (CI) Ulithi and Neighboring Islands, FM Queen of Heaven Church.
Yim, Joseph (SB) Ontario, CA St. George Church.
Yim, Louis H. '57 (HON) Retired.
Yina, Mark *m.s.p.* (LA) Covina, CA St. Louise de Marillac Church.
Yncierto, Frank S. '75 (LAV) [9] Las Vegas, NV St. Francis de Sales Church.
Yocis, David A. '87 (BGP) Leave of Absence.
Yock, Peter *o.s.b.* '95 (IND) [A] St. Meinrad, IN St. Meinrad Seminary; [J] St. Meinrad, IN St. Meinrad Archabbey.
Yockey, Gregory *o.s.b.* '88 (CC) [H] Sandia, TX Corpus Christi Abbey.
Yockey, John G. '70 (MIL) Oconomowoc, WI St. Jerome Church; [B] Hales Corners, WI Sacred Heart School of Theology.
Yogus, Ronald B. '75 (ALT) [4] Portage, PA St. John the Baptist Church; Cresson, PA State Correctional Institution.
Yohe, Robert A. '89 (HBG) [K] Harrisburg, PA Catholic Campus Ministry.
Yohe, Robert A., Jr. '89 (HBG) Shippensburg, PA Our Lady of the Visitation Church.
Yom, Lawrence *s.j.* '97 (BAL) [B] Baltimore, MD Loyola College in Maryland.
Yonkovig, John R. '77 (OG) [5] Plattsburgh, NY St. Peter Church.
Yontz, Msgr. George W. '59 (STU) [7] Steubenville, OH St. Peter's Church; [9] Steubenville, OH St. Stanislaus Church.
Yontz, Msgr. William C. '50 (STU) Byesville, OH Holy Trinity Church.
Yore, Lambert *o.carm.* '45 (WDC) [B] Washington, DC Whitefriars Hall.
Yori, Robert O. (CAM) Retired.
York, Edward '47 (WCH) Retired.
York, Kenneth J. (BEL) Fayetteville, IL St. Pancratius Church.
York, Kenneth J. '88 (BEL) [1] East St. Louis, IL Immaculate Conception Church; Smithton, IL St. John the Baptist Church.
York, Patrick '90 (WCH) Schulte, KS St. Peter's Church.
York, Paul '64 (LIN) Ashland, NE St. Mary's Church.
York, Richard R. '73 (PH) [27] Philadelphia, PA St. Bridget Church; [EE] Philadelphia, PA Newman Center at Drexel University; [EE] Philadelphia, PA Newman Center at Drexel University; [EE] Philadelphia, PA Newman Center at Drexel University.
York, Vincent P. '68 (ALN) Fountain Hill, PA St. Ursula Church.
Yossa, Kenneth F. '88 (ROM) Special Assignment or On Duty Outside the Diocese.
Yost, Charles *s.c.j.* '58 (JKS) [F] Nesbit, MS St. Michael Community House; [I] Walls, MS Sacred Heart League.
Yost, Herbert C. *c.s.c.* '75 (FTW) [J] South Bend, IN Congregation of Holy Cross, Indiana Province, Provincial House.
Yost, Richard J. *o.s.f.s.* '76 (DET) [Q] Warren, MI St. John's Deaf Center.
Young, Anthony J. '44 (MAD) Retired.
Young, Arthur *o.f.m.conv.* '49 (TOL) Carey, OH Our Lady of Consolation, Basilica-National Church.
Young, Bernard L. '63 (NO) Retired.
Young, Christopher Joseph '99 (FTW) [3] Fort Wayne, IN St. Charles Borromeo Church.
Young, Clyde *o.f.m.* '54 (CIN) [C] Cincinnati, OH St. Anthony Shrine, Franciscan Candidacy.
Young, Daniel A. '95 (BUF) Harris Hill, NY Nativity of the Blessed Virgin Mary Church.
Young, David (MI) Special Assignment.
Young, David E. '95 (COL) Otway, OH Our Lady of Lourdes Church; West Portsmouth, OH Our Lady of Sorrows Church.
Young, Dennis M. '80 (HBG) Lebanon, PA Veterans Administration Hospital.
Young, Dennis M. '80 (STA) On Duty Outside the Diocese.
Young, DeSales *o.f.m.cap.* '48 (PIT) [O] Pittsburgh, PA St. Augustine Friary; [P] Millvale, PA St. Francis Convent.
Young, Dismas *o.f.m.cap.* '66 (GBG) Export, PA St. Mary Church.
Young, Dominic '79 (LFT) Monterey, IN St. Anne Church.
Young, Edward J. '53 (SC) Retired.
Young, Edward P. '83 (STF) Rochester, NY St. Josaphat Church.
Young, Eugene '86 (PHX) [5] Scottsdale, AZ St. Daniel the Prophet Church.
Young, Frank '70 (SY) North Syracuse, NY St. Rose of Lima Church.
Young, Gary *c.r.* '76 (L) St. Mary, KY St. Charles Church; [M] Nazareth, KY Generalate, Motherhouse and Novitiate of the Sisters of Charity of Nazareth.
Young, Gerald A. '72 (DEN) Wray, CO St. Andrew Church; Yuma, CO St. John Church.
Young, Gerald A. '72 (LA) On Duty Outside the Archdiocese.
Young, Gerard F. '63 (BR) [1] Baton Rouge, LA St. Joseph Church.
Young, James *s.m.* '45 (SAT) [K] San Antonio, TX Marianist Residence: Skilled Nursing.
Young, Msgr. James E. '74 (TYL) Nacogdoches, TX Sacred Heart Church.
Young, James G. '69 (PIT) Washington, PA Immaculate Conception Church.
Young, Jerome *o.s.b.* '86 (P) [L] St. Benedict, OR Mt. Angel Abbey.
Young, John *s.c.j.* '74 (JKS) Olive Branch, MS Queen of Peace Church.
Young, John E. '57 (KAL) South Haven, MI St. Basil Church.
Young, John L. *c.s.c.* '71 (BGP) [P] Bridgeport, CT Provincial Offices of the Priests and Brothers of Holy Cross, Eastern Province.
Young, Msgr. John M. '47 (LA) Retired.
Young, Larry E. '81 (OAK) Rodeo, CA St. Patrick's Church.
Young, Peter G. '47 (PRO) [2] North Providence, RI St. Lawrence Church; Retired.
Young, Peter G. '59 (ALB) Bolton Landing, NY Blessed Sacrament Church.
Young, Richard K. '95 (ATL) [4] Atlanta, GA Immaculate Heart of Mary Church.
Young, Robert '94 (SP) Zephyrhills, FL St. Joseph Church.
Young, Robert J. '53 (BRK) Retired; [V] Douglaston, NY Bishop Mugavero Residence.
Young, Ronald E. (DAV) On Duty Outside the Diocese.
Young, Ronald W. *o.m.i.* '88 (SAT) [C] San Antonio, TX Oblate School of Theology; [M] San Antonio, TX De Mazenod House.
Young, Samuel V. (BAL) Aberdeen, MD St. Joan of Arc Church.
Young, Msgr. Terry W. '72 (ATL) Sabbatical.
Young, Valentine *o.f.m.cap.* '49 (STL) [54] St. Louis, MO St. Patrick Church; [P] St. Louis, MO St. Patrick Friary; [V] St. Louis, MO Catholic Information Center.
Young, Valentine *o.f.m.* '56 (RC) [1] Rapid City, SD Cathedral of Our Lady of Perpetual Help.
Young, Valentine *o.f.m.* '56 (SCR) [M] Elmhurst, PA Priestly Fraternity of St. Peter (F.S.S.P.), North American District Headquarters.
Young, Vincent J. '78 (SCR) [M] Little Meadows, PA St. Joseph's House.

Young, William E. '90 (NY) On Duty Outside the Archdiocese.
Young, William E. '90 (SFE) Questa, NM St. Anthony Church.
Young, William J. *c.s.b.* '51 (GAL) [C] Houston, TX University of St. Thomas; [Q] Houston, TX Residence of the Basilian Fathers of the University of St. Thomas.
Young, Msgr. William L., III '70 (GAL) [77] Houston, TX St. Thomas More Church.
Young, William T. *s.s.s.* '64 (CLV) [O] Cleveland, OH Blessed Sacrament Community.
Young, William W. '76 (SFR) [36] San Francisco, CA Most Holy Redeemer Church.
Young- Keu Sin, Peter '91 (CLV) [1] Cleveland, OH Cathedral of St. John the Evangelist.
Youngberg, Vincent *c.p.* '67 (NY) [DD] Pelham Manor, NY St. Vincent's Residence.
Youngkamp, Vincent J. *s.s.c.* '59 (FgM) St. Columban's Foreign Mission.
Youngs, Fred '90 (BR) Baker, LA St. Isidore the Farmer Church.
Youssef, Youssef A. *b.s.o.* '86 (NTN) Lawrence, MA St. Joseph Church; [D] Lawrence, MA St. Joseph's Plains Community Center.
Youtz, Msgr. Richard A. '66 (HBG) [4] Lancaster, PA St. John Neumann Church.
Yoya, Louis '79 (NY) Kingston, NY Benedictine Hospital.
Yrarrazaval, Diego J. *c.s.c.* '84 (FTW) [J] South Bend, IN Congregation of Holy Cross, Indiana Province, Provincial House.
Yrigan, Msgr. Pedro '47 (ORG) Retired.
Yrlas, Raynaldo, Jr. '97 (CC) Alice, TX Our Lady of Guadalupe Church.
Yslas, Martin *o.s.b.* '87 (LA) [Q] Valyermo, CA St. Andrew's Abbey.
Ytsen, Robert A. *s.j.* '82 (CHI) [D] Wilmette, IL Loyola Academy.
Yu, Celso A. *m.f.* (AUS) [H] Bremond, TX Clerical Congregation Missionaries of Faith.
Yu, Celso A. '92 (AUS) Bremond, TX St. Mary's Church.
Yu, Inchang '56 (PH) [57] Philadelphia, PA Holy Angels Church.
Yu, Reynaldo '55 (SEA) Everett, WA St. Mary Magdalen Church.
Yu, Reynaldo '83 (SEA) Bellingham, WA Assumption B.V.M. Church; Bellingham, WA Sacred Heart Church.
Yuchung, Romeo *s.m.* (BO) [55] Boston, MA Our Lady of Victories Church.
Yudin, Raynald *o.f.m.conv.* '62 (TR) [5] Trenton, NJ Immaculate Conception Church.
Yuen, Thomas '58 (SCR) [21] Scranton, PA St. Patrick's Church.
Yuenger, Paul D. '00 (WH) [10] Wheeling, WV St. Michael's Church.
Yuhaus, Cassian J. *c.p.* '51 (SCR) [M] Scranton, PA Saint Ann's Passionist Monastery; [R] Clarks Summit, PA Ministry for Religious Research and Consultancy.
Yulfo, Nestor '93 (SJN) [1] Carolina, PR San Andres Church.
Yuliantoro, Antionius Eko *s.v.d.* '94 (WDC) [M] Washington, DC Divine Word College.
Yunk, Msgr. Michael J. '57 (BUF) Retired.
Yurchak, Thomas D. '76 (P) Canby, OR St. Patrick Church.
Yurco, Roy *ss.cc.* '62 (FR) [I] Fairhaven, MA Sacred Hearts Provincial House.
Yurgel, Robert *o.f.m.cap.* '96 (NY) [DD] New York, NY Immaculate Conception Friary.
Yurista, Michael '67 (PSC) Bayonne, NJ St. John the Baptist Church.
Yurkovic, Dale E. '91 (GF) Livingston, MT St. Mary's Church.

Z

Z, Ray (OAK) [4] Oakland, CA St. Augustine's Church.
Zabala, Efrain '67 (CGS) [12] Barrio Hormigas, PR Santisima Trinidad Church.
Zabala, Luis *o.f.m.* '57 (SJN) [51] San Juan, PR Resurreccion del Senor Church.
Zaballa, Pedro '57 (SJN) [38] San Juan, PR Santa Maria de Los Angeles Church.
Zaballa, Pedro L. '57 (SJN) [E] San Juan, PR Centro Medico de P.R.
Zabelskas, John A. '56 (GAL) Highlands, TX St. Jude Thaddeus Church.
Zabler, Charles G. '77 (MIL) West Allis, WI West Allis Memorial Hospital.
Zablotski, Vladimir '99 (PSC) Hillsborough Township, NJ St. Mary's Church.
Zaborowski, Edward *m.s.f.* '63 (SAT) [K] San Antonio, TX Padua Place.
Zaborowski, Paul *o.f.m.cap.* '97 (WDC) [39] Washington, DC Shrine of the Sacred Heart Church.
Zabrocki, Patrick R. '88 (GF) [6] Great Falls, MT St. Joseph's Church; [8] Great Falls, MT St. Luke the Evangelist Church; [K] Great Falls, MT St. Joseph's Education Trust.
Zabrocki, Stephen J. '89 (GF) Wolf Point, MT Immaculate Conception Church.
Zacarias, Carlos *s.t.* '97 (LA) [30] Los Angeles, CA Our Lady of Victory Church.
Zaccagnigno, Raffaele '68 (BRK) Retired.
Zaccagnini, Kenneth G. '82 (GBG) [4] Uniontown, PA St. Therese, the Little Flower of Jesus Church.
Zaccardo, Msgr. Peter J. '64 (NEW) Nutley, NJ Holy Family Church.
Zaccone, Paul *o.m.* '87 (HON) [11] Honolulu, HI St. Patrick Church.
Zaccone, Paul C. '87 (OM) Absent on Leave.
Zach, Charles *o.s.b.* '73 (OM) [C] Elkhorn, NE Mount Michael High School; [K] Elkhorn, NE Mount Michael Abbey.
Zach, Kenneth M. '81 (RVC) Massapequa, NY St. Rose of Lima Church.
Zach, Placidus *o.s.b.* '56 (P) [L] St. Benedict, OR Mt. Angel Abbey.
Zachariadis, Nicholas '86 (VNN) [A] Newberry Springs, CA Holy Resurrection Monastery.
Zachariah, Boban '84 (NEW) [12] Jersey City, NJ St. John the Baptist Church.
Zacheis, Dennis B. '75 (STL) Krakow, MO St. Gertrude Church.
Zachman, Charles *o.m.i.* '48 (BEL) [F] Belleville, IL Missionary Oblates of Mary Immaculate - St. Henry's Oblate Residence.
Zacker, Mark *m.s.c.* '96 (RCK) [G] Aurora, IL Missionaries of the Sacred Heart Community.
Zadora, Bill *s.d.s.* '75 (SAT) Kosciuszko, TX St. Ann's Church.
Zadora, Charles J. '67 (BUF) Fredonia, NY St. Joseph Church.
Zafe, Peter V. '64 (TOL) [16] Toledo, OH St. Agnes Church.
Zagar, Janko *o.p.* '48 (OAK) [N] Oakland, CA Dominican Order (Western Province), St. Albert's Priory.
Zagar, John T. '61 (OKL) Retired.
Zagarella, John C. *o.praem.* '86 (PH) [AA] Philadelphia, PA St. Norbert Priory; [AA] Paoli, PA Daylesford Abbey.
Zagone, Frederick P. *s.j.* '93 (MIL) [P] Milwaukee, WI Jesuit Community at Marquette University.
Zagorc, Francis D. *c.s.c.* '58 (FTW) [J] South Bend, IN Congregation of Holy Cross, Indiana Province, Provincial House.
Zahler, Paul J. *o.s.b.* '62 (OKL) [I] Shawnee, OK St. Gregory's Abbey; [L] Shawnee, OK Oklahoma Benedictine Institute on Mental Retardation, Inc.
Zahn, George E. '68 (RIC) [17] Richmond, VA St. Paul Church.
Zahn, John '72 (LFT) Logansport, IN All Saints Church.
Zahn, John H. (LFT) Lucerne, IN St. Elizabeth Church.
Zahn, Robert R. *m.m.* '55 (FgM) Maryknoll Foreign Missions.
Zahner, William '45 (L) Retired.
Zahorchak, Michael '56 (STU) Retired.
Zaiats, Volodymyr '73 (STN) Milwaukee, WI St. Michaels Church.
Zaidan, Abdallah E. *m.l.m.* '86 (OLL) Los Angeles, CA Our Lady of Mt. Lebanon-St. Peter Church; Los Angeles, CA St. Jude Church; Denver, CO Maronite Catholic Community of Denver Church; [A] Houston, TX The Congregation of Maronite Lebanese Missionaries.
Zajac, Richard E. '76 (BUF) [K] Buffalo, NY Sisters of Charity Hospital of Buffalo, NY.
Zajdel, Bernard *o.f.m.conv.* '64 (STP) Bloomington, MN St. Bonaventure Church.
Zajdel, Robert J. '80 (PIT) Braddock, PA Good Shepherd Church.
Zak, Msgr. Casimir A. '45 (BUF) Retired; [O] Tonawanda, NY O'Hara Residence.
Zak, Daniel J. '67 (TOL) Swanton, OH St. Richard Church.
Zak, Stan '75 (OAK) Danville, CA St. Isidore's Church.
Zak, Steven B. '88 (LA) On Duty Outside the Archdiocese.
Zak, Timothy *s.d.b.* '91 (NY) [3] Port Chester, NY Our Lady of the Rosary Church.
Zakarauskas, Anthony J. '41 (CHI) [138] Chicago, IL Nativity of the Blessed Virgin Mary Church; Retired.
Zake, Louis J. '60 (CHI) [13] Chicago, IL St. Ann Church; [A] Chicago, IL Archbishop Quigley Preparatory Seminary.
Zakens, Michael W. '45 (ALB) [12] Schenectady, NY St. Mary Church; Retired.
Zakowicz, Giles *o.f.m.conv.* '75 (BAL) [S] Ellicott City, MD Order of Friars Minor Conventual.
Zakowicz, Giles *o.f.m.conv.* '75 (FgM) Conventual Franciscan Foreign Missions.
Zakshesky, Francis '81 (TYL) Absent on Sick Leave.
Zalecki, Dennis M. '76 (CHI) [A] Mundelein, IL University of St. Mary of the Lake-Mundelein Seminary.
Zalecki, Marian *o.s.p.p.e.* '62 (PH) [AA] Doylestown, PA Pauline Fathers Monastery, Shrine of Our Lady of Czestochowa.
Zalenski, Gary '77 (STU) Neffs, OH Sacred Heart Church.
Zaleski, Daniel '80 (DET) [1] Dearborn Heights, MI St. Albert the Great Church.
Zaleswki, Peter L. '97 (PT) Panama City, FL St. Dominic Church.
Zalewski, Francis '78 (TR) [20] Trenton, NJ SS. Peter and Paul Church; [23] Trenton, NJ St. Stephen Church.
Zalewski, Thomas *o.carm.* '79 (PMB) [B] Boca Raton, FL Pope John Paul II High School; [H] Boca Raton, FL St. Elias Priory-Order of Carmelites, NY.
Zallo, Huytham Bashir (OLD) North Hollywood, CA Sacred Heart Syriac Church.
Zaloga, Daniel S. '67 (MAR) Iron Mountain, MI St. Mary and St. Joseph Church.
Zalonis, Jerome A. *m.i.c.* '59 (CHI) [N] Chicago, IL Congregation of Marian Fathers of the Immaculate Conception.
Zalonis, Jerome A. *m.i.c.* '59 (JOL) Plano, IL St. Mary Church.
Zamborsky, Bill '74 (ORL) Mims, FL Holy Spirit Church.
Zamborsky, Leonard J. '76 (CLV) Cleveland Heights, OH St. Louis Church.
Zamborsky, Stephen A. *c.s.sp.* '36 (PH) [AA] Bensalem, PA Congregation of the Holy Ghost.
Zammit, Francis X. '66 (ORL) Retired.
Zammit, Msgr. Joseph J. '56 (NY) [105] New York, NY St. Peter Church; New York, NY New York Police Department; Bronx, NY U.S.V.A. Medical Center.
Zamora, Marcos *c.s.p.* '90 (NY) [41] New York, NY Good Shepherd Church.
Zamorski, Msgr. Robert J. '72 (MET) Fords, NJ Our Lady of Peace Church.
Zampelli, Michael A. *s.j.* '93 (SJ) [B] Santa Clara, CA Santa Clara University.
Zampino, Ignatius *o.f.m.cap.* '61 (CHL) [10] Charlotte, NC St. Thomas Aquinas Church.
Zanatta, Albert *c.r.s.* '74 (HRT) [6] Hartford, CT Sacred Heart Church.
Zanavich, Albert J. '41 (HRT) [1] Ansonia, CT Assumption Church; Retired.
Zancan, Robert D. '82 (BUF) Retired.
Zandri, William A. '84 (RC) Lead, SD St. Patrick's Church.
Zandy, Edward J. '70 (SY) [1] Endicott, NY Our Lady of Good Counsel Church.
Zanetti, Humberto C. *o.f.m.* '55 (SD) [3] Oceanside, CA St. Mary, Star of the Sea Church.
Zang, Richard P. *c.s.c.* '69 (FTW) [J] South Bend, IN Congregation of Holy Cross, Indiana Province, Provincial House.
Zangari, Salvatore V. '44 (HBG) Retired.
Zaniewski, Jaroslaw '93 (NEW) [6] Bayonne, NJ Mt. Carmel Church.
Zaniolo, Michael G. '88 (CHI) Calumet City, IL St. Andrew the Apostle Church.
Zankl, Angelo *o.s.b.* '26 (SCL) [I] Collegeville, MN St. John's Abbey, of the Order of St. Benedict.
Zanni, Frank L. '90 (Y) Vienna, OH St. Vincent de Paul Church.
Zanni, James '96 (Y) Boardman, OH St. Charles Borromeo's Church.
Zanon, Romano '66 (BRK) [239] Queens, NY Sacred Heart Church; [Z] Flushing, NY Mount St. Mary.
Zanoni, Charles *c.s.* '62 (WDC) [19] Washington, DC Holy Rosary Church.
Zanoni, John J. '60 (JOL) Rockdale, IL St. Joseph Church.
Zanoni, Richard J. *s.j.* '75 (BUF) [50] Buffalo, NY St. Michael Church; [D] Buffalo, NY Canisius High School.
Zanotti, Charles F. '53 (NY) Glasco, NY St. Joseph Church.
Zanotti, Richard *c.s.* '80 (CHI) Melrose Park, IL Our Lady of Mount Carmel Church.
Zanotto, Luigi *m.c.c.j.* '68 (LA) [56] Los Angeles, CA St. Cecilia Church.
Zant, Louis *o.f.m.* '73 (FgM) Franciscan Foreign Missions.
Zaorski, Edward F. '90 (DET) [2] Detroit, MI All Saints Church; [5] Detroit, MI SS. Andrew and Benedict Church.
Zapalac, David *c.s.b.* '93 (GAL) Missouri City, TX Holy Family Church.
Zapalac, William *o.m.i.* '70 (SAT) [K] San Antonio, TX Oblate Madonna Residence.
Zapata, Antonio '68 (ORG) Anaheim, CA St. Justin Martyr Church.
Zapata, Emiliano *o.p.* '95 (SAT) [26] San Antonio, TX St. Ann Church; [B] San Antonio, TX Dominican Priory of San Juan Macias.
Zapata, Pedro J. '99 (ORL) Altamonte Springs, FL St. Mary Magdalen Church.
Zapf, Albert L. '80 (PIT) Harwick, PA Our Lady of Victory Church.
Zapfel, Robert E. '81 (BUF) On Duty Outside the Diocese.
Zapotocki, Henry E. '48 (SCR) Retired.
Zapp, John '72 (Y) Uniontown, OH Holy Spirit Church.

Zappa, James C., Jr. '76 (STP) Burnsville, MN Mary, Mother of the Church.
Zappitelli, Francis R. '62 (PHX) [5] Scottsdale, AZ St. Daniel the Prophet Church.
Zarama, Luis '93 (ATL) Clarkesville, GA St. Mark Church.
Zarate-Suarez, Jose Edmundo '96 (SD) Calexico, CA Our Lady of Guadalupe Church.
Zarati, Ramon *s.d.b.* '90 (LA) Bellflower, CA St. Dominic Savio Church.
Zareski, Joseph S. '80 (SY) [3] Syracuse, NY Blessed Sacrament Church.
Zarichny, Steven '78 (SJP) Cleveland, OH Ss. Peter and Paul Church.
Zarkoski, Donald *s.d.b.* '62 (MIA) [25] Miami, FL St. Kieran Church.
Zarlenga, Vincent I. *o.p.* '51 (CHI) River Forest, IL St. Vincent Ferrer Church; [N] Chicago, IL Dominicans (Provincial Office).
Zartaga, Msgr. George F. '68 (BRK) [V] Douglaston, NY Bishop Mugavero Residence.
Zasacki, Robert E. '67 (STP) Robbinsdale, MN Sacred Heart Church.
Zastawny, Kazimierz '57 (BO) [5] Lynn, MA St. Michael Church.
Zastoupil, Stephen R. '61 (BIS) [3] Bismarck, ND Corpus Christi Church.
Zastrow, John A. '56 (LIN) Retired; [E] Lincoln, NE Bonacum House.
Zatalava, James D. '70 (ALT) State College, PA Our Lady of Victory Church.
Zatina, Gregory E.J. '87 (SPC) Leave of Absence.
Zauala, Antonio *o.a.r.* '95 (ORG) Fullerton, CA St. Mary's Church.
Zaucha, Finian *o.f.m.* '68 (GB) [I] Pulaski, WI Assumption of B.V.M. Friary.
Zavacki, Richard A. '58 (SCR) Kingston, PA St. Hedwig's Church.
Zavala, Genaro *m.s.p.* '97 (LA) [22] Los Angeles, CA Our Lady of Solitude Church.
Zavaski, William J. '69 (CHI) Arlington Heights, IL St. James Church.
Zavattaro, Gabriel J. *s.d.b.* '34 (SFR) [46] San Francisco, CA SS. Peter and Paul Church.
Zavell, Edward '61 (PRM) Fairview Park, OH St. Mary Magdalene Church.
Zavodny, Msgr. Francis J. '51 (ALN) [4] Allentown, PA St. John the Baptist Church.
Zawacki, Casimir J. '50 (GAY) Retired.
Zawacki, Robert '77 (JKS) Fayette, MS St. Anne Church; Natchez, MS Holy Family Church.
Zawada, Jerome *o.f.m.* '64 (MIL) [P] Milwaukee, WI Francis and Clare House.
Zawada, Joseph F. *o.c.d.* '64 (STA) [J] Bunnell, FL Discalced Carmelite Fathers of Florida.
Zawadzki, Justin '68 (SJ) Los Gatos, CA St. Mary of the Immaculate Conception Church.
Zawadzki, Piotr '97 (VEN) [1] Venice, FL Epiphany Church; Graduate Studies.
Zawadzki, Victor C. '50 (SCR) Retired.
Zawistanowicz, Norbert J. '49 (CHI) [92] Chicago, IL Immaculate Heart of Mary Church; [159] Chicago, IL Our Lady of Victory Church; Retired.
Zawodniak, Edward J. '47 (SCR) Retired.
Zayas, Antonio '59 (PCE) On Duty Outside the Diocese.
Zazella, Msgr. Thomas J. (PAT) Retired.
Zbieranski, Roman *o.f.m.* '61 (GB) [3] Manitowoc, WI St. Mary Church.
Zbin, Raphael *o.s.b.* '47 (CLV) [5] Cleveland, OH St. Andrew Church; [O] Cleveland, OH Benedictine Order of Cleveland.
Zborowski, Richard M. '78 (CHI) Hoffman Estates, IL St. Hubert Church.
Zdancewicz, Carl *o.f.m. conv.* '77 (ATL) Lithia Springs, GA St. John Vianney Church.
Zdilla, Valentine '96 (LA) Santa Clarita, CA St. Clare Church.
Zdrodowski, Francis '43 (DET) Retired.
Zebron, Sam *o.f.m. conv.* '58 (SAV) Macon, GA Holy Spirit Church.
Zebrowski, Arnold '73 (VEN) Cape Coral, FL St. Andrew Church.
Zebrowski, Roy *o.f.m.* '58 (GAY) Lake City, MI St. Stephen Church; Manton, MI St. Theresa Church.
Zeck, George '70 (DUL) Pequot Lakes, MN St. Alice's Church.
Zedar, Thomas J. '65 (VEN) Port Charlotte, FL San Antonio Church.
Zeder, Msgr. John M. (SY) Retired.
Zee, Louis C. '59 (DUB) On Duty Outside the Archdiocese.
Zee, Louis C. '59 (GAL) [10] Houston, TX Ascension Chinese Church.
Zeeb, Charles '56 (DET) Retired.
Zega, Eugene M. *o.s.a.* '36 (PH) [AA] Villanova, PA St. Thomas Monastery.
Zegar, David '79 (P) Woodburn, OR St. Luke Church.
Zegers, Paul A. *ss.cc.* '49 (HON) Hana, HI St. Mary Church.
Zehe, Ralph *o.f.m.cap.* '50 (PIT) [30] Pittsburgh, PA Our Lady of the Angels Church; Allegheny County, PA Department of Veterans Affairs Medical Center Aspinwall; Allegheny County, PA Department of Veterans Affairs Medical Center Oakland.
Zeihen, Joseph N. '50 (MIL) Retired.
Zeimet, Richard E. *m.m.* '64 (FgM) Maryknoll Foreign Missions.
Zeis, Gabriel *t.o.r.* '80 (PH) [AA] Fairless Hills, PA St. Anthony Friary.
Zeis, Gabriel '80 (TR) [S] Princeton, NJ Campus Ministry for the Diocese of Trenton.
Zeisig, B. Thomas '57 (CLV) Cuyahoga Falls, OH St. Eugene Church.
Zeisler, Warren *o.f.m.* '50 (CIN) [P] Cincinnati, OH Friarhurst Retreat Center.
Zeitler, Msgr. Edward J. '58 (E) Grove City, PA Beloved Disciple Church.
Zeitler, Msgr. John W. '64 (BUF) Lake View, NY Our Lady of Perpetual Help Church.
Zekas, Msgr. Stanley '49 (STU) Retired.
Zeleznik, Clement *o.s.b.* '59 (CLV) Broadview Heights, OH Assumption Church; [O] Cleveland, OH Benedictine Order of Cleveland.
Zelik, Richard J. *o.f.m.cap.* '70 (WH) [2] Charleston, WV St. Anthony Church; [M] Charleston, WV Capuchins-St. Anthony Friary.
Zelinski, James *o.f.m.cap.* '61 (DET) [K] Detroit, MI St. Bonaventure Friary; [K] Detroit, MI St. Mary's Friary.
Zelinski, James *o.f.m.cap.* '61 (FgM) Capuchin Foreign Missions.
Zelinski, Thomas *o.f.m.cap.* '72 (SAG) [G] Saginaw, MI Queen of Angels Friary and Retreat House.
Zelker, Thomas '83 (ALB) Granville, NY Roman Catholic Community of Granville Church.
Zell, Charles Felix *o.c.s.o.* '80 (ATL) [J] Conyers, GA The Monastery of the Holy Spirit.
Zeller, Leonard H. '73 (BAL) Military Chaplains.
Zelonis, Richard *s.c.j.* '79 (SP) [O] Pinellas Park, FL Priests of the Sacred Heart.
Zemaitis, Kestutis '65 (CLV) [M] Cleveland, OH Jennings Hall Center for Older Adults.
Zeman, Gerald L. '63 (SC) Sutherland, IA Sacred Heart Church.
Zemanick, Peter *o.c.s.o.* '44 (SP) [L] St. Petersburg, FL Bon Secours-Maria Manor Nursing Care Center, Inc.
Zemanick, Peter *o.c.s.o.* '44 (WOR) [N] Spencer, MA St. Joseph's Abbey.
Zemanik, Edward S. '81 (ALN) Kelayres, PA Immaculate Conception Church; [1] McAdoo, PA St. Kunegunda Church; [3] McAdoo, PA St. Patrick Church.
Zembal, Theodore E. *s.j.* '68 (SEA) [A] Seattle, WA Seattle University.
Zembrzuski, Michael *o.s.p.p.e.* '34 (PH) [AA] Doylestown, PA Pauline Fathers Monastery, Shrine of Our Lady of Czestochowa.
Zemeikis, Alfred '63 (NEW) [13] Elizabeth, NJ SS. Peter and Paul's Church.
Zemelko, John J. '87 (GRY) [3] Whiting, IN St. Adalbert Church.
Zender, Gary '86 (SEA) Renton, WA St. Anthony Church.
Zendzian, Peter '79 (BRK) [177] Queens, NY Holy Cross Church.
Zendzian, Peter W. '79 (BRK) [U] Brooklyn, NY Catholic Migration & Refugee Office, Catholic Migration Services, Inc.
Zengierski, Patrick '91 (BUF) [2] Cheektowaga, NY Infant of Prague Church.
Zeni, Msgr. Dino M. '59 (BRK) [126] Brooklyn, NY St. Rosalia-Regina Pacis Church.
Zenk, Donald W. '54 (WIN) Twin Lakes, MN St. James Church; Retired.
Zenk, Msgr. Richard E. '54 (SC) Akron, IA St. Patrick Church.
Zenkel, Edward B. '62 (ROC) Honeoye, NY St. Mary, Our Lady of the Hills Church.
Zenorini, Henry J. *s.j.* '61 (NY) [DD] New York, NY Xavier Jesuit Community.
Zens, Roger A. '57 (MIL) Retired.
Zensen, Gerald '24 (SC) Mapleton, IA St. Mary's Church.
Zensen, Gerald F. '49 (SC) Retired.
Zenz, Msgr. John P. '82 (DET) Special Assignment; [Q] Detroit, MI Catholic Community Services of the Archdiocese of Detroit, Inc.; [T] Detroit, MI Christ Child Society.
Zepczyk, Gabriel C. '62 (SUP) Ino, WI St. Florian Church; Moquah, WI Ss. Peter and Paul Church.
Zepecki, Ronald P. '95 (HRT) Union City, CT St. Hedwig Church; [18] Waterbury, CT St. Stanislaus Kostka Church.
Zepp, Anthony '56 (CLV) Retired.
Zepp, Anthony W. '56 (CLV) [2] Garfield Heights, OH SS. Peter and Paul Church.
Zeps, Michael J. *s.j.* '71 (MIL) [P] Milwaukee, WI Jesuit Community at Marquette University.
Zercie, David *m.s.a.* '69 (NOR) [A] Cromwell, CT Holy Apostles College and Seminary; [F] Cromwell, CT Society of the Missionaries of the Holy Apostles.
Zerfas, Msgr. Herman H. '47 (GR) Retired.
Zerhusen, Msgr. Henry F. '53 (BAL) [57] Baltimore, MD St. Mark Church; [O] Timonium, MD Stella Maris.
Zeringue, Guy P. '75 (HT) Bourg, LA St. Ann Church.
Zerkel, Donald F. '57 (MIL) Retired.
Zermeno, Joseph *o.f.m.* '68 (SJ) [18] San Jose, CA Our Lady of Guadalupe Church.
Zerr, Gary '97 (P) Tillamook, OR Sacred Heart Church.
Zerr, Maurice J. *m.m.* '51 (FgM) Maryknoll Foreign Missions.
Zerwas, Rick '91 (SFE) Los Lunas, NM St. Clement Church.
Zeth, Allen '86 (ALT) [14] Johnstown, PA Our Mother of Sorrows Church.
Zettel, David H. '66 (L) [B] Louisville, KY Trinity High School.
Zetzl, Ralph '65 (SFD) [K] Sherman, IL Our Lady of Angels Friary.
Zeugner, Raymond J. '67 (MAR) Crystal Falls, MI Guardian Angels Church.
Zeuner, Karl A. '71 (PH) [3] Philadelphia, PA St. Agatha-St. James Church.
Zevola, Giovanni *o.m.i.* '90 (WDC) [M] Washington, DC Oblate College/Center for Mission Studies Community.
Zewe, M. Donald *s.j.* '56 (SY) [S] Syracuse, NY Jesuits at LeMoyne, Inc.
Zeyack, John *s.t.l.* '65 (PSC) Rahway, NJ St. Thomas the Apostle Church.
Zeyen, Charles *m.s.f.* '53 (SAT) [K] San Antonio, TX Padua Place.
Zeyen, Thomas E. *s.j.* '54 (P) [L] Portland, OR Jesuit Provincial Office (Society of Jesus, Oregon Prov.).
Zglejszewski, Andrzej '90 (RVC) West Hempstead, NY St. Thomas, the Apostle Church.
Zgunda, Ronald '77 (EVN) [7] Evansville, IN Holy Redeemer Church.
Zhang, Dehua *c.s.j.b.* '76 (BRK) [V] Astoria, NY Congregation of St. John the Baptist of China.
Zibognon, Marcel *o.p.* (DEN) [3] Fort Collins, CO John XXIII University Church.
Ziccardi, C. Anthony '90 (NEW) [A] South Orange, NJ Immaculate Conception Seminary; [B] South Orange, NJ Seton Hall University.
Zickert, John *o.f.m.cap.* (GB) Greenville, WI St. Mary Church.
Zidek, Vincent E. *o.s.b.* '91 (ALT) Carrolltown, PA St. Benedict's Church.
Zieba, Jerzy *c.r.* '92 (CHI) [N] Chicago, IL Provincial Office of the Congregation of the Resurrection.
Zieba, Jerzy *c.r.* '92 (PT) Panama City, FL St. John the Evangelist Church.
Zieba, Jerzy *c.r.* '92 (RCK) Woodstock, IL Resurrection Church.
Ziebacz, Wieslaw M. '92 (SCR) [2] Hazleton, PA Church of the Most Precious Blood.
Ziebert, George M. *s.j.* '41 (FgM) Provinces.
Ziegelmaier, David A. '60 (LC) Alma Center, WI Immaculate Conception Church; Fairchild, WI St. John Cantius Church; Fairview, WI St. Joseph Church.
Ziegler, John A. '96 (ARL) Winchester, VA Sacred Heart of Jesus Church.
Ziegler, Thomas G. '69 (Y) Columbiana, OH St. Jude Church.
Ziegmann, Msgr. Leonard M. '59 (SC) Laurens, IA Sacred Heart Church.
Zielezienski, Ray '81 (OAK) [4] Hayward, CA St. Joachim Church.
Zielinski, Brian *o.praem.* (BAL) [76] Baltimore, MD Our Lady, Queen of Peace Church.
Zielinski, Casimir *o.carm.* '52 (WDC) [B] Washington, DC Whitefriars Hall.
Zielinski, Chad W. '96 (GAY) Empire, MI St. Philip Neri Church; Maple City, MI St. Rita-St. Joseph Church.
Zielinski, Francis A. '62 (DET) Columbus, MI St. Philip Neri Church.
Zielinski, Martin '78 (CHI) [A] Mundelein, IL University of St. Mary of the Lake-Mundelein Seminary.
Zielinski, Sylwan *o.c.d.* '65 (GRY) [J] Munster, IN Discalced Carmelite Fathers Monastery.
Zielke, Michael *o.f.m.conv.* '83 (BAL) [S] Ellicott City, MD Order of Friars Minor Conventual.
Zielke, Michael *o.f.m.conv.* '83 (BGP) [6] Danbury, CT Sacred Heart Church; [W] Fairfield, CT Newman Centers - Campus Ministry.
Zielonka, Dariusz J. '95 (BGP) New Canaan, CT St. Aloysius Church.
Ziemba, Herman J. *o.f.m.* '48 (GB) [I] Pulaski, WI Assumption of B.V.M. Friary.
Ziemba, Howard '79 (Y) Absent on Leave.
Ziemba, Walter J. '51 (DET) Retired; [A] Orchard Lake, MI SS. Cyril and Methodius Seminary.
Ziemkiewicz, Frank *o.s.b.* '84 (E) St. Marys, PA St. Mary Church.
Ziemnicki, Edward '96 (HRT) [2] New Britain, CT Holy Cross Church.
Zientek, Msgr. Benedict '58 (SAN) Brownwood, TX St. Mary's Church.
Zientek, Msgr. Boleslaus '59 (GAL) Danbury, TX St. Anthony de Padua Church.
Zientek, Theodore '00 (STN) [A] Redwood Valley, CA Holy Transfiguration Monastery.

Ziezulewicz, George F. (HRT) Retired.
Ziezulewicz, George J. '64 (HRT) [1] Hartford, CT Cathedral of St. Joseph.
Zigmond, Kenneth *o.s.b.* '57 (JOL) Lisle, IL St. Joan of Arc Church; [J] Lisle, IL St. Procopius Abbey.
Zigrang, Stephen P. *j.c.l.* '78 (GAL) Channelview, TX St. Andrew Church.
Ziliak, Jerome *s.v.d.* '47 (MIL) [P] East Troy, WI Divine Word Seminary.
Ziliak, Joseph L. '62 (EVN) Newburgh, IN St. John the Baptist Church.
Zilimu, Johndamascene '95 (PEO) [2] Champaign, IL St. John's Catholic Chapel Church; [P] Champaign, IL St. John's Catholic Student Chapel and Newman Foundation, University of Illinois.
Zillo, Hay Tham '91 (LA) [1] North Hollywood, CA Sacred Heart Syriac Catholic Church.
Zilonka, Paul *c.p.* (BAL) [A] Baltimore, MD St. Mary's Seminary and University.
Zilonka, Paul *c.p.* '71 (MET) [H] South River, NJ Passionist Provincial Office.
Ziminski, James C. '91 (MAR) [5] Marquette, MI St. Michael Church; Special Assignment; [G] Marquette, MI Catholic Campus Ministry-Northern Michigan University.
Zimmer, Anthony J. '86 (MIL) [21] Milwaukee, WI St. Charles Borromeo Church.
Zimmer, David L. '88 (BIS) New Salem, ND St. Pius V Church.
Zimmer, Edward A. '47 (ROC) [29] Rochester, NY St. John the Evangelist Church; Retired.
Zimmer, Ellis *o.f.m.cap.* '55 (GB) [M] Appleton, WI Monte Alverno Retreat Center.
Zimmer, Eric A. *s.j.* '94 (DET) [K] Detroit, MI Jesuit Provincial Office-Detroit Province of the Society of Jesus.
Zimmer, James '76 (SFS) Huron, SD Holy Trinity Church.
Zimmer, Nicholas M. '57 (SCL) Braham, MN St. Peter & Paul Church.
Zimmer, Thomas J. '52 (LFT) Retired.
Zimmer, William E. (CHI) [1] Cicero, IL St. Anthony Church.
Zimmerman, Albert J. '45 (GRY) Retired.
Zimmerman, David (GB) Peshtigo, WI St. Mary Church.
Zimmerman, David '97 (SFD) Farmersville, IL St. Mary Church; Girard, IL St. Patrick Church.
Zimmerman, Donald D. '73 (SAL) Hays, KS Immaculate Heart of Mary Church.
Zimmerman, Msgr. Donald F. '73 (DAL) [4] Dallas, TX Christ the King Church.
Zimmerman, Eugene F. *s.j.* '51 (GB) [M] Oshkosh, WI Jesuit Retreat House.
Zimmerman, John F. *c.m.* '34 (STL) [P] Perryville, MO Congregation of The Mission.
Zimmerman, Joseph *o.f.m.* '62 (SFD) [B] Quincy, IL Quincy University.
Zimmerman, Ralph '76 (SCL) Big Lake, MN Our Lady of the Lake Church.
Zimmerman, Rex A. '67 (LC) Bevent, WI St. Ladislaus Church; Galloway, WI St. Joseph Church.
Zimmerman, Msgr. Roland G. '51 (LA) Arcadia, CA Annunciation Church; Retired.
Zimmers, Eugene R. *s.j.* '51 (OAK) [A] Oakland, CA Graduate School of Theology, School of Applied Theology.
Zimmers, Eugene R. *s.j.* '51 (SJ) [L] Los Gatos, CA Sacred Heart Jesuit Center.
Zimmers, Michael J. *s.j.* '54 (SJ) [L] Los Gatos, CA Sacred Heart Jesuit Center.
Zimmerschied, Daniel (DEN) Holyoke, CO St. Patrick Church.
Zimney, Robert J. *c.m.* '42 (STL) [P] Perryville, MO Congregation of The Mission.
Zimpfer, Eugene A. *s.j.* '65 (BUF) [D] Buffalo, NY Canisius High School; [O] Buffalo, NY Canisius Jesuit Community.
Zina, George '86 (SAM) Orlando, FL St. Jude Church.
Zingales, Jonathan *o.s.b.* '76 (SP) [O] St. Leo, FL St. Leo Abbey.
Zingales, Jonathan A. '76 (CLV) Released from Diocesan Assignment.
Zingaro, Joseph J. '78 (PH) [79] Philadelphia, PA St. John Cantius Church.
Zink, David L. '90 (CIN) St. Paris, OH Sacred Heart Church; Urbana, (1853) St. Mary Church; [Q] Urbana, OH Urbana University Campus Ministry.
Zink, Harold G. *c.s.c.* '51 (AUS) [13] Austin, TX St. Ignatius Martyr Church.
Zink, William F. '68 (GR) Remus, MI St. Michael's Church.
Zinkan, Matthias *o.s.b.* '40 (FgM) American - Cassinese Congregation Foreign Missions.
Zinkan, Matthias *o.s.b.* '40 (RCK) [G] Aurora, IL Marmion Abbey-St. Augustine's Abbey.
Zinkle, Ronald T. *s.j.* '59 (LC) Lyndon Station, WI St. Mary Church.
Zinkula, Thomas R. '90 (DUB) Balltown, IA St. Francis of Assisi Church; Rickardsville, IA St. Joseph's Church; Sherrill, IA SS. Peter and Paul Church.
Zinn, Donald *c.r.* '72 (CHI) [D] Chicago, IL Gordon Tech High School.
Zinnamon, Brian F. *s.j.* '79 (NY) [DD] New York, NY West Side Jesuit Community.
Zinno, Henry P., Jr. '82 (PRO) [2] Tiverton, RI Holy Ghost Church.
Zins, Charles '77 (BIS) Beulah, ND St. Joseph Church; Hazen, ND St. Martin Church.
Zinser, Robert E. '68 (STL) [64] St. Louis, MO St. Teresa of Avila Church.
Zint, Russell R. '00 (IND) Brownsburg, IN St. Malachy Church.
Zinthefer, Neil G. '69 (MIL) Fredonia, WI St. Rose of Lima Church; Holy Cross, WI Holy Cross Church; Little Kohler, WI Mother of Sorrows Church.
Zinzer, Walter A. '64 (STL) Military Chaplains.
Ziobro, Joseph M. '73 (SCR) Tunkhannock, PA Nativity of Blessed Virgin Mary Church.
Ziolkowski, Adam *o.f.m.conv.* '72 (SPR) [5] Holyoke, MA Mater Dolorosa Church.
Ziomek, David F. (BO) Wakefield, MA St. Joseph Church.
Ziomek, Dennis A. '78 (CHI) [156] Chicago, IL Our Lady of the Snows Church; [A] Chicago, IL Archbishop Quigley Preparatory Seminary.
Zipay, Michael J. '68 (SCR) [3] Swoyersville, PA Holy Trinity Church.
Zirnheld, Matthew J. '93 (BUF) [1] Lackawanna, NY Basilica of Our Lady of Victory.
Zitek, Brad '89 (LIN) Seward, NE St. Vincent de Paul Church.
Zito, Thomas '98 (CAM) Merchantville, NJ St. Peter's Church.
Zitz, Nicholas *c.p.* '56 (BRK) [V] Jamaica, NY Immaculate Conception Monastery.
Ziuraitis, Gary *c.ss.r.* '78 (STL) [22] St. Louis, MO St. Alphonsus Liguori Church; [P] St. Louis, MO St. Alphonsus Rectory of the Redemptorist.
Zivic, Richard A. '94 (ATL) [8] Atlanta, GA Sacred Heart of Jesus Church.
Zivkovic, Robert M. *o.s.m.* '66 (CHI) [N] Chicago, IL Order of Friar Servants of Mary (Servites) United States of America Province, Inc.
Zlock, Charles '94 (PH) Jamison, PA St. Cyril of Jerusalem Church; [D] Warminster, PA Archbishop Wood Catholic High School.
Zlotkowski, Francis *c.s.c.* '76 (FR) [8] Taunton, MA St. Mary's Church.
Zmerlicki, Andrew '92 (NEW) Hasbrouck Heights, NJ Corpus Christi Church.
Zmozynski, Francis J. '57 (BUF) [11] Niagara Falls, NY Prince of Peace Church.
Znotinas, John '40 (WDC) Retired.
Zodrow, Nathan *o.s.b.* (P) [A] St. Benedict, OR Mount Angel Seminary.
Zodrow, Nathan *o.s.b.* '88 (P) [L] St. Benedict, OR Mt. Angel Abbey.
Zoeller, Ben '65 (OKL) Yukon, OK St. John Nepomuk Church.
Zoeller, Eugene L. '58 (L) [A] Louisville, KY Bellarmine University.
Zoellner, Mark *c.f.o.* (CIN) [V] Cincinnati, OH Franciscan Ministry Services.
Zoellner, Michael *o.s.b.* '80 (KCK) [H] Atchison, KS St. Benedict's Abbey; [I] Leavenworth, KS Motherhouse of the Sisters of Charity of Leavenworth.
Zogby, Edward G. *s.j.* '67 (NY) [DD] New York, NY West Side Jesuit Community.
Zoghby, James F. '71 (MOB) [3] Mobile, AL Corpus Christi Church.
Zoghby, Paul G. '93 (MOB) [12] Mobile, AL St. Mary Church.
Zogheib, Hares '54 (SAM) Retired.
Zohlen, Ray J. '53 (SFR) Retired.
Zohnerowicz, Nicholas *s.s.s.* '62 (CLV) [O] Cleveland, OH Congregation of the Blessed Sacrament Provincial House.
Zollinger, Msgr. Richard '55 (GRY) Retired.
Zolnerowicz, Nicholas *f.s.s.p.* '62 (SCR) [M] Elmhurst, PA Priestly Fraternity of St. Peter (F.S.S.P.), North American District Headquarters.
Zolnowski, Wojciech J. '96 (DET) [2] Dearborn, MI St. Barbara Church.
Zolverowicz, Nicholas *f.s.s.p.* '62 (PAT) Pequannock, NJ Our Lady of Fatima Chapel (Tridentine) Church.
Zombe, Omer-Luzolo Lwa-Lu *o.p.* '90 (SB) Chino, CA St. Margaret Mary Church.
Zoni, Pierino *s.x.* '61 (FgM) Xaverian Foreign Missions.
Zoni, Pierino *s.x.* '61 (PAT) [M] Wayne, NJ Xaverian Missionary Fathers.
Zonneveld, Leo J. *c.i.c.m.* '58 (ARL) Culpeper, VA Precious Blood Church.
Zoph, John L. '36 (SFR) Retired.
Zorbach, Msgr. Francis X. '52 (BAL) Linthicum Heights, MD St. Philip Neri Church.
Zore, Richard I (IND) Retired.
Zorichak, William '39 (DUL) Retired.
Zoromski, Herbert P. '51 (LC) Retired.
Zotter, Thomas A. '76 (SFE) [24] Albuquerque, NM St. Bernadette Church.
Zoubek, Ronald J. '85 (BAL) Absent on Sick Leave.
Zoucha, Carl '98 (OM) Fremont, NE St. Patrick Church.
Zoufal, Michael L. '87 (CHI) Argo, IL St. Blase Church.
Zowada, Stanley *o.m.i.* '00 (CHI) [N] Chicago, IL The Oblate House of Theology.
Zsolczai, Raymond (MIL) [P] Burlington, WI Queen of Peace Friary.
Zube, Joseph '53 (PEO) Special Residence.
Zuber, Thaddeus F. '50 (NEW) Retired; [N] Rutherford, NJ St. John Vianney Residence for Priests.
Zuberbueler, Matthew '96 (ARL) [1] Alexandria, VA Blessed Sacrament Church.
Zubik, Rudolf '64 (NEW) Harrison, NJ Our Lady of Czestochowa Church.
Zubizarreta, Jose Ramon *c.p.* '72 (SJN) [46] San Juan, PR Nuestra Senora de la Piedad Church.
Zubovic, Robert (BRK) [U] Brooklyn, NY Catholic Migration & Refugee Office, Catholic Migration Services, Inc.
Zubovic, Robert '92 (BRK) [203] Queens, NY Most Precious Blood Church.
Zuchowski, Robert J. '72 (GAY) Elk Rapids, MI Sacred Heart Church.
Zuckerman, Eric *s.j.* '98 (SPK) [K] Spokane, WA Regis Community.
Zuckerman, Erik *s.j.* '98 (SPK) [6] Spokane, WA St. Aloysius Church.
Zudaire, Claudio *o.f.m.cap.* '54 (FWT) [6] Fort Worth, TX Our Lady of Guadalupe Church.
Zuelke, Michael *o.f.m.cap.* '74 (MIL) [27] Milwaukee, WI St. Francis of Assisi Church.
Zuercher, Jack *s.j.* (OM) [P] Omaha, NE Christian Life Community-North Central Region (CLC).
Zuercher, John D. *s.j.* '59 (OM) [K] Omaha, NE Jesuit Community at Creighton University.
Zuerlein, Damian '81 (OM) [3] Omaha, NE St. Agnes Church; [32] Omaha, NE Our Lady of Guadalupe Church.
Zuern, Theodore F. *s.j.* '57 (WDC) [M] Washington, DC Leonard Neale House.
Zuffoletto, Michael P. '72 (BUF) Military Chaplains.
Zugelter, Alvin T. '46 (CIN) Retired.
Zugger, Christopher L. '81 (VNN) Albuquerque, NM Our Lady of Perpetual Help Church.
Zukas, Stephen P. '93 (BO) [59] Boston, MA St. Peter Church.
Zukowski, Nicholas '82 (DET) New Baltimore, MI St. Mary Queen of Creation Church.
Zuleger, Donald M. '76 (GB) [5] Appleton, WI St. Pius X Church.
Zuleta, Nondier '92 (B) Fruitland, ID Corpus Christi Church; Weiser, ID St. Agnes Church.
Zuliani, Vincent *s.d.b.* '56 (NY) [DD] New Rochelle, NY Salesian Provincial House.
Zulkie, Lambert *o.carm.* '88 (BO) [P] Peabody, MA Catholic Information Center.
Zulkie, Lambert *o.carm.* '88 (JOL) Darien, IL Our Lady of Mount Carmel Church.
Zuluaga, Carlos Alberto '93 (NY) [131] Bronx, NY St. Augustine Church.
Zuluaga, Jose Omar '84 (PRO) [5] Pawtucket, RI St. John the Baptist Church.
Zumaya, David '77 (SAT) Retired.
Zuniga, Carlos '98 (BWN) La Feria, TX St. Francis Xavier Church.
Zuniga, Domingo *c.m.f.* '52 (LA) [31] Los Angeles, CA Our Lady Queen of the Angels Church.
Zuniga, Juan M. *m.m.* '88 (NY) [DD] Maryknoll, NY Maryknoll Fathers and Brothers.
Zunmas, Oby J. '00 (OKL) Duncan, OK Assumption Church.
Zunno, Michael O. *m.m.* '53 (FgM) Maryknoll Foreign Missions.
Zupa, Msgr. Emil P. '48 (BUF) Le Roy, NY St. Joseph Church.
Zupez, John H. *s.j.* '67 (FgM) Provinces.
Zupka, Anselm *o.s.b.* '67 (CLV) [D] Cleveland, OH Benedictine High School; [O] Cleveland, OH Benedictine Order of Cleveland.
Zurat, Hugh *o.f.m.* '62 (CHI) [O] Chicago, IL Mother of Good Counsel Provincialate.
Zurat, Hugh *o.f.m.* '62 (FgM) Franciscan Foreign Missions.
Zuraw, Msgr. John A. '87 (Y) [3] Youngstown, OH Immaculate Conception Church.
Zurawski, Lawrence '85 (DET) [2] Westland, MI St. Damian Church.
Zurcher, Thomas K. *c.s.c.* '72 (PHX) [12] Phoenix, AZ St. Gregory Church.
Zurek, Lawrence W. *o.f.m.* '85 (DET) [5] Southfield, MI St. Michael Church.
Zuromskis, John D. '41 (BO) Senior Priests.
Zuschmidt, Joseph C. *o.s.f.s.* '65 (CHL) High Point, NC Immaculate Heart of Mary Church.
Zusy, Dennis R. *o.p.* '55 (DEN) [A] Denver, CO St. Dominic Priory.
Zusy, James *o.p.* '59 (LEX) [6] Lexington, KY St. Paul Church.

Zuziak, Joseph R. *s.d.s.* '66 (GRY) [J] Merrillville, IN Salvatorian Fathers (Society of the Divine Savior).
Zuzik, John '91 (Y) [5] Canton, OH St. Benedict Church.
Zuzik, John E. (Y) [11] Canton, OH St. Paul's Church.
Zvarych, Petro '00 (PHU) Elizabeth, NJ St. Vladimir's Church.
Zvijak, John *c.pp.s.* '63 (CLV) [53] Cleveland, OH Our Lady of Good Counsel Church.
Zvinklys, Antanas '39 (LC) Retired.
Zwack, Jeffrey '84 (BIS) Bowman, ND St. Charles Church.
Zwahl, Eugene *o.f.m.conv.* '42 (TR) Seaside Park, NJ St. Catharine of Siena Church.
Zwaska, Victor L. '56 (MIL) Retired.
Zweber, Benedict A. *m.m.* '59 (FgM) Maryknoll Foreign Missions.
Zweber, Clement J. '49 (STP) Retired.
Zweber, Raymond J. '54 (STP) Retired.
Zwers, John B. '50 (DET) Retired.
Zwiefka, William L. '83 (GAY) Manistee, MI St. Joseph Church.
Zwifka, David A. '81 (BUF) Absent on Leave.
Zwinger, Msgr. Leonard '51 (SFS) Retired.
Zwirn, Ralph H. '85 (CHI) [205] Chicago, IL St. Turibius Church.
Zwolenkiewicz, Raphael *o.f.m.conv.* '79 (SPR) [5] Holyoke, MA Mater Dolorosa Church.
Zych, Janusz *s.ch.* '90 (JOL) Bensenville, IL St. Charles Borromeo Church.
Zygadlo, Mitchell '82 (ROC) Military Chaplains.
Zyla, Jeff (OM) Beemer, NE Holy Cross Church.
Zyla, Jeffrey L. '92 (OM) Wisner, NE St. Joseph Church.
Zylla, Paul '45 (SCL) Retired.
Zylla, Robert V. *o.s.c.* '51 (BAL) [A] Emmitsburg, MD Mount St. Mary's Seminary.
Zylla, Robert V. *o.s.c.* '51 (PHX) [G] Phoenix, AZ Crosier Community of Phoenix (Canons Regular of the Order of the Holy Cross).
Zywan, Paul J. '86 (PIT) Wexford, PA St. Alexis Church.
Zywiec, David *o.f.m.cap.* (CHI) [68] Chicago, IL St. George Church; [110] Chicago, IL St. Kevin Church.
Zywiec, David *o.f.m.cap.* '74 (FgM) Capuchin Foreign Missions.

Necrology

BISHOPS

✠ Garner, Most Rev. Robert F., D.D. (NEW) (Retired). —Died Dec. 25, 2000
✠ Graham, Most Rev. John J. (PH) Retired Auxiliary Bishop. —Died Aug. 4, 2000
✠ Herrmann, Most Rev. Edward J. (COL) (Retired). —Died Dec. 22, 1999
✠ Kaniecki, Most Rev. Michael J., *s.j.* (FBK) Fairbanks, AK Bishop of Fairbanks. —Died Aug. 6, 2000
✠ Krawczak, Most Rev. Arthur H. (DET) Retired Bishop of Denver. —Died Jan. 13, 2000
✠ Malone, Most Rev. James W. (Y) (Retired). —Died April 9, 2000
✠
✠ Marino, Most Rev. Eugene Antonio, *s.s.j.* (ATL) Atlanta, GA Archbishop Emeritus of Atlanta. —Died Nov. 12, 2000
✠ McGarry, Most Rev. Urban, *t.o.r.* (FgM) Bishop Emeritus of Bhagalpur, Bihar, India. —Died Sept. 16, 2000
✠ McGrath, Most Rev. Mark G., *c.s.c.* (FgM) Archbishop Emeritus of Panama. —Died Aug. 4, 2000
✠ McHugh, Most Rev. James T. (RVC) Bishop of Rockville Centre. —Died Dec. 10, 2000
✠ O'Keefe, Most Rev. Gerald F. (DAV) Retired Bishop of Davenport. —Died April 12, 2000
✠ Ryan, Most Rev. Joseph T. (ALB) (Retired). —Died Oct. 9, 2000
✠ Sheehan, Most Rev. Daniel E. (OM) (Retired). —Died Oct. 24, 2000
✠ Vaughan, Most Rev. Austin B. (NY) (Retired). —Died June 25, 2000

ABBOTS

✠ Coggin, Rt. Rev. Walter A., *o.s.b.* (CHL) Belmont, NC Belmont Abbey. —Died Dec. 28, 1999
✠ Coriston, Rt. Rev. Charles V., *o.s.b.* (PAT) Newton, NJ St. Paul's Abbey. —Died Jan. 7, 2000
✠ Killeen, Rt. Rev. Sylvester M., *o.praem.* (GB) De Pere, WI St. Norbert Abbey. —Died Dec. 8, 2000
✠ Mardelli, Maximos (NTN) (Retired). —Died Oct. 2000
✠ McCarthy, Rt. Rev. Gerald, *o.s.b.* (MAN) Manchester, NH St. Anselm Abbey. —Died Feb. 5, 2000
✠ Skluzacek, Rt. Rev. Valentine, *o.s.b.* (JOL) Lisle, IL St. Procopius Abbey. —Died Oct. 16, 2000
✠ Skutecky, Rt. Rev. Pascal, *o.c.s.o.* (WOR) Spencer, MA St. Joseph Abbey. —Died Feb. 3, 2000

PRIESTS

† Aaron, James (SAN) (Retired). —Died Dec. 12, 1999
† Abi-Nader, Maron (OLL) (Retired). —Died Dec. 19, 1996
† Adomaitis, John J. (GAY) Mackinaw City, MI St. Anthony of Padua. —Died Nov. 10, 1999
† Aleman, Rev. Msgr. Vernon P. (NO) (Retired). —Died July 8, 2000
† Allen, Thomas E. (SPC) Lamar, MO St. Mary. —Died Jan. 29, 2000
† Antoci, Mario J. (LA) Downey, CA Our Lady of Perpetual Help. —Died Jan. 1, 2000
† Applegate, Rev. Msgr. Bennett (COL) (Retired). —Died March 22, 2000
† Arentsen, Edwin F. (BEL) (Retired). —Died Jan. 3, 2000
† Aresserial, Xavier (B) Pocatello, ID St. Anthony. —Died Feb. 2, 2000
† Arquitt, William (DUB) Manly, IA Sacred Heart. —Died March 9, 2000
† Aschenbrenner, George F. (CHI) (Retired). —Died Dec. 15, 1999
† Attridge, Rev. Msgr. Terence J. (NY) Dobbs Ferry, NY Sacred Heart Church. —Died April 20, 2000
† Auer, Paul A. (SEA) (Retired). —Died Sept. 26, 2000
† Averman, Melvin, *o.f.m.cap.* (PIT) Herman, PA St. Mary's Friary. —Died April 26, 2000
† Avila, Lourenco (SB) Onatrio, CA St. Elizabeth Ann Seton. —Died Feb. 11, 2000
† Axtmann, Joseph S. (FAR) Munich, ND St. Mary. —Died July 4, 2000
† Bablitch, Michael (GB) (Retired). —Died Jan. 29, 2000
† Babula, Benjamin S. (GBG) Connellsville, PA Holy Trinity. —Died July 6, 2000
† Bacevicius, John A. (FAR) Kintyre, ND St. Boniface. —Died March 15, 2000
† Bachmann, Leonard, *s.t.* (WDC) Adelphi, MD Holy Trinity Missionary Cenacle. —Died Jan. 20, 2000
† Bachnak, Francis J. (KC) (Retired). —Died April 16, 2000
† Bailey, Rev. Msgr. Joseph G. (OG) (Retired). —Died April 17, 2000
† Ball, David F. (CHI) Chap., US Navy. —Died Nov. 26, 1999
† Balog, John (PSC) Wilkes-Barre, PA St. John the Baptist Church. —Died June 11, 2000
† Balogh, Donald J. (CLV) Parma, OH St. Francis de Sales. —Died Nov. 19, 2000
† Banach, Joseph S. (MET) (Retired). —Died June 26, 2000
† Baptista, Michael, *s.d.b.* (LA) Bellflower, CA St. John Bosco High School. —Died Jan. 11, 2000
† Barlog, Raymond M. (CHI) (Retired). —Died Jan. 17, 2000
† Barrett, M. Stephen, *s.s.* (BAL) Baltimore, MD Sulpician Provincial House. —Died Nov. 17, 2000
† Barron, Harold R., *o.p.* (COL) Columbus, OH Mohun Health Care Center, St. Mary of the Springs. —Died April 23, 2000
† Barrus, Paul W. (DAL) Plano, TX St. Elizabeth Seton. —Died Jan. 3, 2000
† Barry, Rev. Msgr. Denis L. (LIN) (Retired). —Died Nov. 10, 2000
† Barry, James H., *s.j.* (BO) Weston, MA Campion Center. —Died Jan. 4, 2000
† Barry, Joseph A. (STA) (Retired). —Died Aug. 17, 2000
† Bartos, Rev. Msgr. John V. (PH) Sellersville, PA St. Agnes. —Died Sept. 9, 2000
† Bauer, Francis J. (EVN) (Retired). —Died Feb. 5, 2000
† Bauer, Joseph O. (SAG) (Retired). —Died April 23, 2000
† Bauer, Paul (SD) Chula Vista, CA St. Pius X. —Died March 30, 2000
† Baum, Rev. Msgr. Charles James (CHR) (Retired). —Died Dec. 19, 2000
† Bauwens, Joseph, *o.c.s.o.* (DUB) Peosta, IA New Melleray Abbey. —Died May 23, 2000
† Beausang, Rev. Msgr. Charles C. (CAM) (Retired). —Died Aug. 24, 2000
† Becker, Charles J., *s.s.* (CAM) Camden, NJ St. Joseph. —Died May 18, 2000
† Beckers, Rev. Msgr. Henry F. (ALX) (Retired). —Died Jan. 5, 2000
† Bedicek, Valerian Vincent (GF) (Retired). —Died April 4, 2000
† Beiter, Rev. Msgr. Lambert M. (ALT) (Retired). —Died Dec. 2, 1999
† Bellavista, Jose B. (LA) Los Angeles, CA St. Aloysius Gonzaga. —Died March 11, 2000
† Bender, Joseph J. (ALT) (Retired). —Died Aug. 7, 2000
† Beno, John R. (PBL) (Retired). —Died Dec. 5, 2000
† Berbusse, Edward J., *s.j.* (NY) Bronx, NY Province Infirmary. —Died July 20, 2000
† Berk, Aloysius B. (PIT) Beechview, PA St. Catherine of Siena. —Died Aug. 27, 1999
† Bernard, Rev. Msgr. Murphy J. (LKC) (Retired). —Died Sept. 4, 2000
† Bialas, Andrew, *c.s.v.* (JOL) Kankakee, IL St. Patrick. —Died Aug. 26, 2000
† Biecker, Thomas C., *s.j.* (DET) Clarkston, MI Colombiere Center. —Died Jan. 23, 2000
† Bihler, Joseph J. (BRK) (Retired). —Died Feb. 28, 2000
† Billimek, Alvin Otto, *c.ss.r.* (STL) Liguori, MO St. Clement Health Care Center. —Died June 19, 2000
† Binder, Albert H. (FAR) (Retired). —Died Feb. 27, 2000
† Biondino, Joseph Patrick (BGP) Schenectady, NY St. Joseph. —Died Jan. 8, 2001
† Bishop, Patrick, *s.m.* (OAK) Fremont, CA Holy Spirit. —Died Dec. 27, 1999
† Blasovich, Joseph D. (HBG) Elizabethtown, PA St. Peter. —Died Dec. 12, 1999
† Blighton, Francis E. (ROC) Rochester, NY St. Charles Borromeo Prayer Center. —Died Jan. 11, 2000
† Bloom, R. Frederick (WDC) (Retired). —Died Sept. 4, 2000
† Bogel, William A., *c.m.* (DEN) Denver, CO Holy Ghost. —Died March 17, 2000
† Bolduc, Rev. Msgr. Norman P. (MAN) Auburn, NH St. Peter. —Died Sept. 30, 2000
† Bombardier, Gerald (BUR) Winooski, VT St. Stephen. —Died Sept. 3, 2000
† Bombardier, Wilfrid F. (MAN) (Retired). —Died Sept. 16, 2000
† Bones, James J. (PH) Levittown, PA Immaculate Conception. —Died March 18, 2000
† Boreczky, John V. (CHI) (Retired). —Died Aug. 23, 2000
† Borowiak, Henry M. (BUF) (Retired). —Died July 27, 2000
† Borucki, Wallace T. (BUF) Cattaraugus, NY St. Mary. —Died Sept. 9, 2000
† Bosio, August P., *s.d.b.* (SP) Tampa, FL Mary Help of Christians School. —Died 2000
† Boucher, Nelson (MAN) (Retired). —Died June 21, 2000
† Boul, Walter M. (STL) (Retired). —Died July 14, 2000
† Bourbon, Arthur (PHX) (Retired). —Died Jan. 18, 2000
† Boyle, James A. (FWT) (Retired). —Died Dec. 26, 2000
† Boyle, William E., *s.j.* (NY) Bronx, NY Loyola Hall, Fordham University. —Died May 15, 2000
† Bradley, Gary J., *s.j.* (FgM) Provinces. —Died June 4, 2000
† Bradley, Richard, *o.carm.* (NEW) Paramus, NJ Carmelite Chapel of St. Therese. —Died Nov. 18, 1999
† Brady, Daniel J. (NY) Armonk, NY St. Patrick. —Died March 8, 2000
† Brannon, Bernard I., *s.j.* (SJ) Los Gatos, CA Sacred Heart Jesuit Center. —Died Jan. 31, 2000
† Brasley, Rev. Msgr. Lucean R. (CC) (Retired). —Died Dec. 16, 1999
† Bray, Kevin M., *o.s.b.* (PAT) Morristown, NJ St. Mary's Abbey. —Died April 14, 2000
† Bray, William A. (HRT) (Retired). —Died Nov. 15, 2000
† Breen, John P. (NY) (Retired). —Died Nov. 30, 2000
† Brennan, Edward C. (BRK) Douglaston, NY Immaculate Conception Center. —Died Jan. 19, 2000
† Brennan, Robert E. (PH) Norristown, PA St. Titus. —Died July 11, 2000
† Brennan, Roderick, *o.f.m.cap.* (FgM) Capuchin Foreign Mission. —Died Oct. 1, 2000
† Brennan, William V., *c.m.* (CHI) Chicago, IL DePaul Vincentian Community. —Died Jan. 8, 2000
† Bretz, Rev. Msgr. John W. (SFD) Chap. Springfield, St. Joseph's Home. —Died Aug. 9, 2000
† Brinkman, Norbert C. (CIN) (Retired). —Died April 3, 2000
† Broderick, Rev. Msgr. John A. (BO) (Retired). —Died Aug. 21, 2000
† Brodhead, Martin, *t.o.r.* (ALT) Loretto, PA Mount Assisi Monastery. —Died July 16, 2000
† Broome, Robert C., *s.j.* (DET) Clarkston, MI Colombiere Center. —Died April 17, 2000
† Brosius, Alfred G. (DUB) Delhi, IA St. John. —Died Feb. 26, 2000
† Brouillard, Donald, *s.s.s.* (NY) New York, NY St. Jean Baptiste. —Died July 23, 2000
† Brown, Ferdinand L., *c.s.c.* (FTW) Notre Dame, IN Holy Cross House. —Died May 14, 2000
† Brzoska, Anthony B., *s.j.* (LA) Los Angeles, CA Loyola Marymount University. —Died July 24, 2000
† Bua, Antonio, *c.s.* (LA) Sun Valley, CA St. Charles Residence. —Died April 17, 2000
† Buchanan, Scott James Allen (CHR) Holly Hill, SC St. Ann. —Died Jan. 8, 2001
† Burkardt, Rev. Msgr. Harold J. (ALT) Newry, PA St. Patrick. —Died March 17, 2000
† Burns, Lawrence J., *m.m.* (NY) Maryknoll, NY Maryknoll Fathers & Brothers. —Died Oct. 27, 1999

† Burns, Timothy L. (BIR) Huntsville, AL Our Lady, Queen of the Universe. —Died Jan. 1, 1999
† Burt, Julian F., *o.s.b.* (GBG) Latrobe, PA St. Vincent Archabbey. —Died Feb. 14, 2000
† Buschmiller, Robert J. (CIN) Cincinnati, OH St. Cecilia Parish. —Died May 27, 2000
† Butler, Bede John, *o.s.b.* (PBL) Canon City, CO Holy Cross Abbey. —Died June 28, 2000
† Butler, Henry J., *s.j.* (BO) Weston, MA Campion Center. —Died Jan. 29, 2000
† Buzynski, Laurin, *o.f.m.* (STL) St. Louis, MO Franciscan Friary of St. Anthony of Padua. —Died Dec. 18, 1999
† Byrd, Thomas (BAL) (Retired). —Died Jan. 5, 2000
† Byrne, James F. (IND) (Retired). —Died Jan. 23, 2000
† Byrne, Pierce D. (NEW) (Retired). —Died March 21, 2000
† Cain, John T. (SPR) West Springfield, MA St. Thomas the Apostle. —Died April 20, 2000
† Calhoun, George, *o.c.s.o.* (WOR) Spencer, MA St. Joseph's Abbey. —Died Oct. 6, 1999
† Calkins, Gerard M., *o.s.m.* (ORG) Anaheim, CA Servite Fathers & Brothers. —Died June 21, 2000
† Callahan, Edward R., *s.j.* (BO) Chestnut Hill, MA Boston College. —Died April 27, 2000
† Calme, Stephen J. (CIN) (Retired). —Died Feb. 10, 2000
† Calpin, Thomas J. (PH) Pastor Emeritus Morrisville, PA Holy Trinity. —Died Jan. 6, 2000
† Calvo, Rev. Msgr. Oscar L. (AGN) (Retired). —Died July 28, 2000
† Camacho, Gilbert (ELP) (Retired). —Died 2000
† Cameron, Albert S. (MAN) (Retired). —Died Jan. 3, 2001
† Campbell, Joseph Thomas, *c.ss.r.* (STL) Liguori, MO St. Clement's Health Care Center. —Died April 14, 2000
† Canfield, F. Joseph (SUP) (Retired). —Died Feb. 10, 2000
† Capozzelli, Anthony (E) (Retired). —Died Dec. 23, 2000
† Carey, Thomas, *s.m.* (CLV) Retired. —Died Aug. 13, 2000
† Carey, Thomas F. (PIT) Scott Township, PA SS. Simon and Jude. —Died Sept. 9, 1999
† Carpenter, Ralph T., *c.s.p.* (NY) Jamaica Estates, NY Paulist Fathers Generalate. —Died 2000
† Carr, Bernard J. (LFT) Anza, CA Sacred Heart. —Died Dec. 1, 2000
† Carriere, David, *o.f.m.* (LA) Santa Barbara, CA Old Mission. —Died Aug. 4, 2000
† Carson, Paul C. (KC) (Retired). —Died Feb. 23, 2000
† Carta, Umberto (CAM) (Retired). —Died March 6, 2000
† Carton, Rev. Msgr. George A. (PEO) (Retired). —Died March 18, 2000
† Carton, Leo F. (CHI) (Retired). —Died Nov. 26, 1999
† Casey, Daniel, *o.p.* (DET) Detroit, MI St. Dominic. —Died Jan. 3, 2000
† Casey, John F., *o.s.a.* (PH) Villanova, PA St. Thomas Monastery. —Died Sept. 7, 2000
† Casey, Thomas M., *o.s.a.* (BO) North Andover, MA Merrimack College. —Died Sept. 12, 2000
† Cassian, Kieran, *o.f.m.* (PAT) Butler, NJ St. Anthony. —Died March 3, 2000
† Cassidy, Jeremiah, *o.f.m.cap.* (FgM) Capuchin Foreign Mission. —Died Feb. 17, 2000
† Cattelona, Jude, *o.carm.* (NEW) Demarest, NJ St. Joseph's. —Died Aug. 10, 2000
† Cau, Leon (NO) (Retired). —Died Sept. 29, 2000
† Cavanagh, Rev. Msgr. James M. (BRK) Brooklyn, NY Our Lady of Angels. —Died June 21, 2000
† Cesario, Victor, *o.f.m.* (NY) Bronx, NY Workmen's Circle Multicultural Center. —Died Aug. 9, 2000
† Chagas, Virgilio P. (NEW) (Retired). —Died Jan. 15, 2000
† Chapman, A. James (PH) Pastor Emeritus Philadelphia, PA St. Irenaeus. —Died Feb. 23, 2000
† Chess, Rev. Msgr. Edwin R. (CHI) (Retired). —Died June 13, 2000
† Clancy, Frederick J. (TR) (Retired). —Died Jan.4, 2000
† Clark, C. Thomas (L) (Retired). —Died May 21, 2000
† Clark, James W. (FR) (Retired). —Died Dec. 7, 2000
† Clarkson, John T., *o.m.i.* (SAT) Retired. —Died Dec. 31, 1999
† Clifford, A. Jerome, *s.j.* (CLV) Cleveland, OH John Carroll Jesuit Community. —Died Jan. 28, 2000
† Clifford, David K. (NY) Valhalla, NY Holy Name of Jesus. —Died March 7, 2000
† Clinton, Kenneth J. (WIN) (Retired). —Died Dec. 19, 1999
† Coady, Edward L. (BAL) (Retired). —Died Aug. 15, 2000
† Cobb, Daniel, *o.s.b.* (NO) St. Benedict, LA St. Joseph Abbey. —Died July 11, 2000
† Cobeaga, Victoriano (ARE) Vega-Baja, PR Our Lady of Lourdes Church. —Died Dec. 16, 1999
† Coffey, William H. (OG) (Retired). —Died Sept. 8, 2000
† Cohen, Gerald P., *c.s.c.* (NOR) Willimantic, CT Campus Ministry. —Died May 6, 2000
† Colbert, Joseph (BRK) Glendale, NY St. Pancras. —Died Oct. 10, 2000
† Collins, Francis W., *m.m.* (FgM) Maryknoll Foreign Mission. —Died Aug. 23, 2000
† Condon, John F.X., *s.j.* (NY) Bronx, NY Province Infirmary. —Died July 17, 2000
† Conlan, William J., *o.p.* (WDC) Washington, DC Dominican House of Studies. —Died Aug. 26, 2000
† Conley, Philip P. (Y) Poland, OH Holy Family. —Died May 9, 2000
† Conneen, Laurence J., *o.s.a.* (PH) Villanova, PA St. Thomas Monastery. —Died July 7, 2000
† Connell, James C., *m.m.* (NY) Maryknoll, NY Maryknoll Fathers & Brothers. —Died Dec. 30, 1999
† Conner, John, *o.f.m.cap.* (NY) New York, NY St. John Friary. —Died Aug. 19, 2000
† Connors, Edward P. (CHI) (Retired). —Died Oct. 25, 2000
† Conrad, Arthur D. (RIC) Richmond, VA Holy Rosary. —Died Jan. 5, 2000
† Conro, Ronald J. (RCK) (Retired). —Died Nov. 13, 2000
† Conroy, Cyril J. (BO) Beverly, MA St. Margaret. —Died May 26, 2000
† Conroy, Edward M. (NY) Bronx, NY St. Raymond. —Died Feb. 5, 2000
† Conroy, Peter C. (PRT) Lewiston, ME Holy Family Church. —Died Nov. 18, 1999
† Considine, Rev. Msgr. John J. (NY) Bronx, NY St. Barnabas. —Died July 29, 2000
† Cooper, R. John (CLV) (Released from Diocesan Assignment). —Died Dec. 28, 1999
† Corcoran, Albert C., *s.j.* (SFR) San Francisco, CA University of San Francisco. —Died April 28, 2000
† Corcoran, Mel M., *o.s.m.* (ORG) Anaheim, CA Seven Holy Founders Priory. —Died March 14, 2000
† Cormier, Allen L., *c.s.c.* (AUS) Austin, TX Congregation of Holy Cross - Southern Providence. —Died July 4, 2000
† Cosgrove, Francis J., *s.j.* (NY) New York, NY St. Ignatius Residence. —Died Jan. 27, 2000
† Cosgrove, James R. (ROC) Chap. Rochester, NY St. Mary's Hospital/Unity Health System. —Died Nov. 2, 1999
† Costelloe, M. Joseph, *s.j.* (MIL) Wauwatosa, WI Jesuit Community at St. Camillus. —Died May 28, 2000
† Cotto Rodriguez, Carlos N. (CGS) Ceiba, Puerto Rico San Antonio de Padua. —Died March 11, 2000
† Courtney, Humphrey (HEL) (Retired). —Died Nov. 22, 1999
† Cowgill, Rev. Msgr. Francis (ANC) Anchorage, AK St. Anthony. —Died Oct. 16, 2000
† Coyle, T. William, *c.ss.r.* (STL) Liguori, MO St. Clement's Health Care Center. —Died Jan. 26, 2000
† Crocenzi, George A., *c.s.s.p.* (VEN) Sarasota, FL Congregation of Holy Ghost. —Died Jan. 25, 2000
† Cronin, David (VEN) Punta Gorda, FL Sacred Heart Parish. —Died Feb. 13, 2000
† Crowley, Charles E. (TOL) (Retired). —Died Feb. 15, 2000
† Crowley, John D. (BO) Cambridge, MA St. Mary of the Annunciation. —Died Nov. 6, 2000
† Cubells, Joseph, *s.f.* (WDC) Silver Spring, MD Holy Family Seminary. —Died Dec. 4, 1999
† Culliton, Leo (VEN) Lake Placid, FL St. James Parish. —Died Jan. 18, 2000
† Curley, Patrick J. (JKS) (Retired). —Died May 15, 2000
† Curran, John W. (CHI) (Retired). —Died March 28, 2000
† Curtiss, John B. (LC) (Retired). —Died Sept. 8, 2000
† D'Agostino, Lorenzo, *s.s.e.* (BUR) Colchester, VT Society of St. Edmund. —Died Jan. 5, 2000
† D'Alessandro, Francis X., *o.f.m.* (NY) New York, NY Padua Friary. —Died July 22, 2000
† D'Elia, Michael Anthony (BGP) Chap. Bridgeport, CT Dinan Center. —Died Oct. 29, 2000
† Daley, Wallace J. (ORG) (On Duty Outside the Diocese). —Died April 8, 2000
† Daly, Lowrie J., *s.j.* (STL) St. Louis, MO Mercy Medical Center. —Died July 1, 2000
† Day, Edward E. (BWN) Raymondville, TX St. Anthony. —Died Aug. 19, 2000
† Deasy, Edward (ALX) (Retired). —Died Feb. 13, 2000
† DeForke, John C. (GAL) (Retired). —Died Sept. 15, 2000
† DeFrancesco, Albert J. (CIN) (Retired). —Died March 8, 2000
† Del Rio, Oscar (LUB) Anson, TX St. Michael. —Died Sept. 10, 2000
† Dempsey, J. Richard, *s.j.* (DET) Clarkston, MI Colombiere Center. —Died May 14, 2000
† DeMunnik, Shawn (NY) New York, NY St. Mary. —Died Sept. 28, 2000
† Dennis, Henry Clay (SFE) (Retired). —Died Oct. 27, 2000
† Devlin, Eugene J., *s.j.* (NEW) Jersey City, NJ St. Peter's College. —Died Feb. 10, 2000
† Didas, James F., *s.s.j.* (BAL) Baltimore, MD St. Joseph's Manor. —Died Aug. 29, 2000
† Diemer, Charles J. (CHI) (Retired). —Died Jan. 24, 2000
† Diersam, Carl G. (NY). —Died Jan. 10, 2001
† Diezel, Joseph (SB) (Retired). —Died Aug. 9, 2000
† Dillon, Thomas J., *o.s.a.* (PH) Villanova, PA St. Thomas Monastery. —Died Jan. 2, 2000
† Dismachek, Francis M. (PIT) (Retired). —Died Feb. 4, 2000
† Dittami, Mark, *o.carm.* (BO) Peabody, MA Catholic Information Center. —Died Feb. 12, 2000
† Dittman, Rev. Msgr. Harold J. (WIN) (Retired). —Died Dec. 25, 1999
† Diviney, Rev. Msgr. Charles E. (BRK) Brooklyn, NY St. Charles Borromeo. —Died June 28, 2000
† Dobosiewicz, Stephen J. (E) (Retired). —Died March 9, 2000
† Dodd, Rev. Msgr. Richard F. (COL) (Retired). —Died Feb. 26, 2000
† Doga, Rev. Msgr. Allen R. (GAL) Spring, TX St. Edward. —Died Dec. 15, 1999
† Dolan, Francis H., *o.m.i.* (FgM) Oblates Foreign Missions. —Died Sept. 29, 2000
† Donaghue, Joseph, *s.v.d.* (BO) Retired. —Died April 16, 2000
† Donelin, John M. (BO) (Retired). —Died June 2, 2000
† Donohoe, Thomas C., *s.j.* (OM) Omaha, NE Health Care Ministry. —Died Feb. 3, 2000
† Donovan, Vincent, *c.s.s.p.* (CHL) Monroe, NC Our Lady of Lourdes. —Died May 13, 2000
† Doran, William (DAL) Meyersville, TX St. Peter & Paul. —Died May 25, 2000
† Doran, William (VIC) Meyersville, TX Ss. Peter & Paul. —Died May 25, 2000
† Dore, Dennis W. (BRK) Rosedale, NY St. Pius X. —Died Dec. 5, 2000
† Dougherty, Joseph A., *o.s.f.s.* (PH) Philadelphia, PA Father Judge High School for Boys. —Died Feb. 29, 2000
† Dowling, John (SAC). —Died April 5, 2000
† Dowling, Rev. Msgr. Thomas C. (NO) (Retired). —Died Aug. 12, 2000
† Doyle, Denis (SR) Ferndale, CA Assumption of Blessed Virgin Mary. —Died Sept. 18, 2000
† Drain, William A (CIN) Cincinnati, OH St. Matthias. —Died June 29, 2000
† Driscoll, William M., *s.j.* (BAL) Timonium, MD Stella Maris. —Died Jan. 29, 2000
† Drolet, Francis K., *s.j.* (NY) Bronx, NY Province Infirmary. —Died March 30, 2000
† Drummond, Robert T., *o.s.a.* (PH) Villanova, PA St. Thomas Monastery. —Died Sept. 2, 2000
† Dudley, Francis R. (STP) (Retired). —Died Jan. 26, 2000
† Duffy, Michael J., *m.m.* (NY) Maryknoll, NY Maryknoll Fathers & Brothers. —Died Nov. 16, 1999
† Duffy, Patrick (FAR) (Retired). —Died Dec. 30, 1999
† Duffy, Roger K., *c.s.s.p.* (GAL) Bellville, TX SS. Peter & Paul. —Died July 31, 2000
† Dumas, Rev. Msgr. Edmund H. (OG) (Retired). —Died Aug. 7, 2000
† Dumminger, Urban, *c.pp.s.* (CIN) Carthagena, OH St. Charles. —Died Feb. 25, 2000
† Dunn, Rev. Msgr. Meinrad M. (BEL) (Retired). —Died May 15, 2000
† Durette, Constant H., *m.afr.* (SP) St. Petersburg, FL Missionaries of Africa. —Died 2000
† Durkee, John, *c.s.v.* (CHI) Lemont, IL Viatorian Residence. —Died April 14, 2000
† Duschinsky, Vitus, *o.f.m.* (SFD) Teutopolis, IL St. Francis of Assisi. —Died Jan. 21, 2000
† Dwyer, Albert (SAL) Junction City, KS St. Francis Xavier. —Died Feb. 29, 2000
† Dych, William V., *s.j.* (NY) New York, NY Jesuit Community at Fordham University. —Died May 9, 2000
† Dyer, Ralph J., *s.m.* (SAT) San Antonio, TX Marianist Residence. —Died Dec. 23, 1999
† Dynes, Leo (STP) (Retired). —Died Jan. 1, 2000
† Dziadosz, Rev. Msgr. Henry J. (NOR) Moodus, CT St. Bridget of Kildare. —Died May 28, 2000
† Dzuban, Giles, *o.c.d.* (BO) Brighton, MA Carmelite Monastery. —Died Jan. 16, 2000
† Dzurenda, Thomas J. (MET) Watchung, NJ St. Mary-Stony Hill Church. —Died Feb. 29, 2000
† Eaton, Vincent M., *s.s.* (BAL) Baltimore, MD St. Charles Villa. —Died Nov. 14, 1999
† Edwards, Thomas, *t.o.r.* (ALT) Loretto, PA Mt. Assisi Friary. —Died March 8, 2000
† Eeles, Justin, *o.f.m.* (PAT) Ringwood, NJ Holy Name Friary. —Died July 29, 2000
† Egan, Daniel, *s.a.* (NY) Garrison, NY Drug Prevention Work Office at Graymoor. —Died Feb. 10, 2000
† Egan, Joseph M. (ROC) (Retired). —Died Dec. 20, 1999
† Eggleston, William J., *m.m.* (NY) Maryknoll, NY Maryknoll Fathers & Brothers. —Died June 8, 2000

† Eiardi, Anthony J., *s.j.* (BGP) Fairfield, CT Fairfield Jesuit Community. —Died Feb. 10, 2000
† Ellspermann, Gerard, *o.s.b.* (IND) St. Meinrad, IN St. Meinrad Archabbey. —Died Feb. 12, 2000
† Emling, Bertin L., *o.s.b.* (GBG) Latrobe, PA St. Vincent Archabbey. —Died Feb. 16, 2000
† Emmenegger, Rev. Msgr. Joseph (MIL) (Retired). —Died Jan. 15, 2000
† Engler, Rev. Msgr. Francis V. (BUF) (Retired). —Died Oct. 24, 2000
† Ennis, James E. (LC) Hillsboro, WI St. Aloysius Parish. —Died Feb. 11, 2000
† Erwin, James M., *o.p.* (CHI) River Forest, IL St. Thomas Aquinas Priory. —Died March 6, 2000
† Evans, Alan A., *o.p.* (COL) Columbus, OH Mohun Health Care Center, St. Mary of the Springs. —Died Nov. 17, 1999
† Evanstock, Matthew C., *c.s.s.p.* (SB) Hemet, CA Holy Ghost Fathers. —Died May 15, 2000
† Every, Robert Louis, *o.p.* (NO) New Orleans, LA St. Anthony of Padua. —Died April 8, 2000
† Exley, Thomas G. (NU) (Retired). —Died Aug. 10, 2000
† Eyckmans, A. John (CHR) (Retired). —Died Aug. 24, 2000
† Fabachet, Ignatius M., *s.j.* (LAF) Lafayette, LA Village du Lac, Inc. —Died March 18, 2000
† Fagan, Rev. Msgr. Daniel E. (RVC) Valley Stream, NY Holy Name of Mary. —Died April 25, 2000
† Fahy, Rev. Msgr. John J. (NEW) (Retired). —Died Nov. 18, 2000
† Fairbairn, Frank E. (BO) Boston, MA Society of St. James the Apostle. —Died Sept. 14, 2000
† Fairbanks, Florian, *o.s.b.* (BIS) Richardton, ND Assumption Abbey. —Died May 14, 2000
† Falaniko, Mikaele (SPP) Lauli'i, Ss. Peter & Paul. —Died Oct. 21, 1999
† Fallon, Francis H., *s.s.j.* (BAL) Baltimore, MD St. Joseph. —Died July 3, 2000
† Fanelli, Rev. Msgr. Eugene A. (NEW) (Retired). —Died May 9, 2000
† Fanning, Gerard F. (RNO) (Retired). —Died Oct. 15, 2000
† Fannon, Rev. Msgr. Robert C. (Y) (Retired). —Died April 5, 2000
† Faraone, David J. (ROC) Sodus, NY Church of the Epiphany. —Died Dec. 19, 1999
† Farragher, Leo J., *s.s.j.* (BAL) Baltimore, MD St. Joseph Medical Center. —Died Nov. 10, 1999
† Farrelly, Thomas J. (NY) Bronx, NY Blessed Sacrament. —Died Aug. 25, 2000
† Fasching, Felix J. (NU) (Retired). —Died Aug. 28, 2000
† Fealey, Edward J. (CHI) Orland Park, IL St. Michael. —Died May 26, 2000
† Federal, Most Rev. Joseph Lennox (SLC) (Retired). —Died Aug. 31, 2000
† Feghali, Chorbishop Joseph (OLL) (Retired). —Died Dec. 29, 1998
† Feichter, Paul, *o.f.m.* (PAT) Ringwood, NJ Holy Name Friary. —Died Feb. 27, 2000
† Feliz, Felix (SJN) (Retired). —Died May 12, 2000
† Femenia, Nicholas (SAN) (Retired). —Died Dec. 28, 1999
† Fenton, Patrick, *s.s.s.* (CLV) Cleveland, OH Blessed Sacrament Community. —Died Dec. 2, 1999
† Fergus, Edward L., *s.j.* (DET) Clarkston, MI Colombiere Center. —Died Feb. 14, 2000
† Ferhatian, Basil, *c.m.vd.* (ARM) Los Angeles, CA Our Lady Queen of Martyrs. —Died Dec. 19, 1999
† Fernandez, Rev. Msgr. Orlando (MIA) (Retired). —Died Jan. 13, 2000
† Ferran, Michael, *i.c.* (SP) Seminole, FL Blessed Sacrament. —Died Feb. 2, 1999
† Ferrick, Robert T., *s.j.* (BO) Weston, MA Campion Center. —Died April 9, 2000
† Ficko, Anthony D. (GRY) Whiting, IN Immaculate Conception. —Died Aug. 23, 2000
† Field, Rev. Msgr. William N. (NEW) South Orange, NJ Seton Hall Univ.. —Died Dec. 3, 2000
† Figol, Reverend Father Wolodymyr (STF) (Retired). —Died Dec. 27, 1999
† Filteau, Jerome E. (FAR) (Retired). —Died March 19, 2000
† Finnegan, Peter J. (WCH) (Retired). —Died June 26, 2000
† Finnigan, Joyce, *o.f.m.* (GLP) Grants, NM St. Teresa. —Died May 27, 2000
† Finnigan, Rev. Msgr. Thomas J. (DET) Detroit, MI St. Cecilia.
† Firneno, Ralph, *s.a.c.* (WDC) West Hyattsville, MD Pallottine Seminary at Green Hill. —Died March 17, 2000
† Fitzpatrick, Jerome B., *o.s.b.* (PAT) Morristown, NJ St. Mary's Abbey. —Died July 20, 2000
† Flahaven, Robert J., *s.j.* (MIL) Milwaukee, WI Pray for Church and Society. —Died April 18, 2000
† Flannery, Michael J. (NY) (Retired). —Died Jan. 16, 2000
† Flour, Anton (SPK) (Retired). —Died March 13, 1999
† Flynn, Joseph D. (BO) Hingham, MA St. Paul. —Died Oct. 8, 2000
† Flynn, Rev. Msgr. Martin J. (RVC) (Retired). —Died Nov. 8, 2000
† Flynn, Vincent J. (HRT) (Retired). —Died Nov. 8, 2000
† Foley, Daniel P., *s.j.* (DET) Clarkston, MI Colombiere Center. —Died Aug. 13, 2000
† Foley, Ignatius L., *c.m.* (NO) New Orleans, LA Vincentian Fathers. —Died Feb. 1, 2000
† Foran, Edward R. (HRT) (Retired). —Died May 23, 2000
† Fortier, Harvey J. (ALX) Evergreen, LA Little Flower of Jesus. —Died Dec. 10, 1999
† Fosselman, David H., *c.s.c.* (FTW) Notre Dame, IN Holy Cross House. —Died June 11, 2000
† Fossier, Ignatius, *o.s.b.* (NO) Mandeville, LA Southeast Louisiana Hospital. —Died Nov. 19, 1999
† Foster, Edward C. (BUR) (Retired). —Died April 14, 2000
† Foster, Robert L. (GI) (Retired). —Died Dec. 27, 2000
† Fox, Francis J. (ALN) (Retired). —Died Feb. 23, 2000
† Fox, Peter D., *s.j.* (DET) Clarkston, MI Colombiere Center. —Died Feb. 10, 2000
† Foxen, Bertin, *o.f.m.* (LA) Santa Barbara, CA Old Mission. —Died March 1, 2000
† Franczek, Walter J. (MAR) (Retired). —Died Dec. 20, 1999
† Frederick, Edwin J. (GAY) (Retired). —Died Jan. 4, 2000
† Fredette, Albert, *m.s.* (FR) Attleboro, MA La Salette Shrine. —Died June 26, 2000
† Freyaldenhoven, George P. (LR) (Retired). —Died June 5, 2000
† Fryberger, Paul E., *c.s.c.* (FTW) Notre Dame, IN Holy Cross House. —Died Dec. 2, 1999
† Frye, Kenneth Alan, *c.p.m.* (L) Glasgow, KY St. Helen. —Died May 24, 2000
† Furlong, James (LUB) Chap. Lubbock, TX St. Mary's Hospital. —Died Aug. 2, 2000
† Galdon, Richard M. (NEW) (Retired). —Died June 26, 2000
† Gallagher, Rev. Msgr. James (PT) Pensacola, FL Holy Spirit. —Died Feb. 8, 2000
† Galvin, Bartholomew J., *m.m.* (NY) Maryknoll, NY Maryknoll Fathers & Brothers. —Died Nov. 16, 1999
† Ganss, George E., *s.j.* (STL) St. Louis, MO Fusz Pavilion. —Died June 7, 2000
† Gara, Rev. Msgr. Robert (LA) Sierra Madre, CA St. Rita. —Died June 10, 2000
† Gardner, Louis C. (OG) (Retired). —Died Sept. 5, 2000
† Garrity, Francis A. (CHI) (Retired). —Died May 8, 2000
† Gately, Alfred A., *o.p.* (COL) Columbus, OH Mohun Health Care Center, St. Mary of the Springs. —Died April 7, 2000
† Gates, Martin, *o.f.m.* (FgM) Franciscan Foreign Mission. —Died July 27, 2000
† Geary, Edward A., *s.j.* (PH) Philadelphia, PA Jesuit Community at St. Joseph's University. —Died Aug. 29, 2000
† Gensert, Bernon, *o.f.m.* (STL) St. Louis, MO Franciscan Friary of St. Anthony of Padua. —Died Aug. 24, 2000
† Gerety, Rev. Msgr. John L. (MET) South Amboy, NJ St. Mary Church. —Died Jan. 25, 2000
† Gessner, Kurt, *o.f.m.cap.* (GB) Appleton, WI St. Joseph. —Died Sept. 24, 2000
† Giblin, Bernard, *o.f.m.* (PAT) Ringwood, NJ Holy Name Friary. —Died June 26, 2000
† Gieranowski, William (FTW) (Retired). —Died April 24, 2000
† Gildea, Joseph J., *o.s.a.* (PH) Villanova, PA St. Thomas Monastery. —Died July 12, 2000
† Gilmore, Brendan, *o.carm.* (NEW) Englewood, NJ St. Cecilia's. —Died Sept. 15, 2000
† Giroux, Rev. Msgr. Robert J. (OG) (Retired). —Died Sept. 4, 2000
† Glancy, Alfred P. (NY) Kingston, NY St. Joseph Church. —Died Jan. 22, 2001
† Gleason, William J., *s.j.* (NY) Bronx, NY Province Infirmary. —Died Aug. 1, 2000
† Glick, George W. (BAL) Hancock, MD St. Peter. —Died May 15, 2000
† Goce, Lauro (SD) (Retired). —Died Sept. 8, 2000
† Goedken, Nestor B. (DUB) Castle Grove, IA Immaculate Conception; Prairieburg, IA St. Joseph. —Died May 23, 2000
† Gogel, Odo, *o.s.b.* (SFS) Marvin, SD Blue Cloud Abbey. —Died Nov. 28, 1999
† Going, Joseph Gregory, *o.p.* (PT) Pensacola, FL St. John the Evangelist. —Died Sept. 26, 2000
† Gonser, Francis, *o.f.m.* (STL) Retired. —Died July 9, 2000
† Gonzales, George (ORG) El Toro, CA Santiago de Compostela Church. —Died Jan. 21, 2000
† Gonzalez, Miguel (PCE) Ponce, PR Cathedral of Our Lady of Guadalupe. —Died Nov. 17, 1999
† Gorra, Edward M., *o.s.a.* (LAN) Flint, MI St. Matthew's. —Died Aug. 30, 2000
† Gough, James F. (PH) (Retired). —Died Jan. 10, 2000
† Grace, Gerald P., *s.j.* (CHI) Chicago, IL Chicago Province of the Society of Jesus-Provincial Office Center. —Died Dec. 1, 1999
† Graham, William F., *s.j.* (ALN) Wernersville, PA Jesuit Center. —Died Dec. 30, 1999
† Grande, Alphonsus, *c.p.* (HRT) West Hartford, CT Holy Family Monastery. —Died May 17, 2000
† Gratsch, Edward J. (CIN) Cincinnati, OH Mt. St. Mary Seminary. —Died July 21, 2000
† Grenier, Carlton, *s.m.* (WDC) Washington, D.C. Marist Center. —Died Sept. 18, 2000
† Grieco, Charles (PAT) (Retired). —Died March 17, 2000
† Griffin, Bertram F. (P) Portland, OR St. Michael the Archangel. —Died July 28, 2000
† Grondalski, Thaddeus J. (WH) (Retired). —Died Dec. 3, 1999
† Grotzinger, Alfred L., *o.s.b.* (GBG) Latrobe, PA St. Vincent Archabbey. —Died July 30, 2000
† Guandalini, Julius S. (HRT) (Retired). —Died Jan. 19, 2000
† Guillaume, Lionel (ALB) (Retired). —Died May 2, 2000
† Guirsch, Bernard G. (CHI) (Retired). —Died Dec. 16, 1999
† Guzman, Rev. Msgr. Raul (PAT) Pastor Emeritus Passaic, NJ Our Lady of Fatima. —Died Aug. 24, 2000
† Habenicht, James F., *m.m.* (SJ) Los Altos, CA Maryknoll. —Died Feb. 28, 2000
† Hacker, George, *s.d.b.* (SFR) San Francisco, CA Salesian Provincial Residence. —Died Feb. 8, 2000
† Haggerty, Charles, *o.carm.* (NY) Middletown, NY St. Albert's Priory. —Died Oct. 22, 2000
† Halaburda, Walter A. (HBG) Lebanon, PA Assumption of the B.V.M.. —Died Oct. 22, 2000
† Halata, William (VIC) La Grange, TX Holy Rosary. —Died June 11, 2000
† Halpin, Raymond (ALB) (Retired). —Died April 24, 2000
† Hamel, Joseph, *o.m.i.* (SAT) Retired. —Died Jan. 23, 2000
† Hamel, Roland, *o.m.i.* (MAN) Colebrook, NH Shrine of Our Lady of Grace. —Died Jan. 28, 2000
† Hammer, Rev. Msgr. Edward (NY) Haverstraw, NY St. Mary. —Died April 4, 2000
† Haney, Richard M. (DET) (Retired). —Died May 18, 2000
† Hankinson, Aquin, *o.f.m.conv.* (SY) Syracuse, NY Assumption B.V.M. —Died June 1999
† Hanley, John J. (LA) Los Angeles, CA Nazareth House. —Died Sept. 29, 2000
† Hanlon, Thomas C. (CHI) (Retired). —Died Dec. 1, 1999
† Hannon, Michael G. (BRK) Whitestone, NY St. Luke. —Died Jan.19, 2000
† Hanrahan, John Alphonsus (GF) (Retired). —Died Sept. 12, 2000
† Hargarten, Joseph F. (GI) (Retired). —Died Jan. 29, 2000
† Harland, Norman E., *s.j.* (CHI) Wilmette, IL Loyola Academy. —Died Sept. 22, 2000
† Harley, Ronald P. (ROC) Avon, NY St. Agnes Church. —Died Sept. 26, 2000
† Harney, Peter P. (WIL) Greenville, DE St. Joseph on the Brandywine. —Died April 16, 2000
† Hart, Harry J. (SAG) (Retired). —Died Sept. 16, 1999
† Hart, Rev. Msgr. James G. (ALB) (Retired). —Died Jan. 13, 2000
† Hart, James P. (BO) (Retired). —Died Nov. 20, 2000
† Hartke, Florian, *c.pp.s.* (CIN) Carthagena, OH St. Charles. —Died April 7, 2000
† Hartlove, Walter J., *o.s.f.s.* (FgM) Oblates of St. Francis de Sales Foreign Mission. —Died Jan. 8, 2000
† Hartman, Donald (MAR) (Retired). —Died Nov. 15, 1999
† Hary, Melvin J. (OAK) (Retired). —Died Nov. 5, 2000
† Hasenfuss, Louis B., *o.s.b.* (TUC) St. David, AZ Holy Trinity Monastery. —Died Feb. 28, 2000
† Hayes, Canisius, *s.t.* (B) Greencreek, ID St. Anthony's. —Died Oct. 7, 2000
† Hayes, John E. (CHI) (Retired). —Died Dec. 25, 1999
† Healey, John C., *s.s.c.* (PRO) Bristol, RI St. Columban's Retirement House. —Died 2000
† Hebein, James M. (MAR) (Retired). —Died Jan. 19, 2000
† Heile, Edwin B. (COV) Elsmere, KY St. Henry. —Died Oct. 24, 2000
† Heintschel, Rev. Msgr. Donald E. (TOL) (Retired). —Died Aug. 23, 2000
† Heisse, John R., *m.m.* (CHI) Chicago, IL Maryknoll Fathers & Brothers. —Died March 10, 2000
† Helget, Venard, *o.s.b.* (KCK) Atchison, KS St. Benedict's Abbey. —Died Jan. 14, 2000
† Helldorfer, J. Nicholas, *c.ss.r.* (ALB) Saratoga Springs, NY St. John Neumann Residence. —Died Jan. 7, 2000

† Hellmann, George, *o.f.m.* (CIN) Cincinnati, OH St. John the Baptist Friary. —Died April 2, 2000
† Henady, Martin (TOL) (Retired). —Died Jan. 2, 2000
† Henle, Robert J., *s.j.* (STL) St. Louis, MO Fusz Pavilion. —Died Jan. 20, 2000
† Hennes, Paul R. (DET) (Retired). —Died April 24, 2000
† Henry, Joseph A. (PH) Pastor Emeritus Riegelsville, PA St. Lawrence. —Died Dec. 7, 1999
† Henry, Thomas J. (NEW) (Retired). —Died Jan. 17, 2000
† Herlihy, Charles E. (BO) Marlborough, MA Immaculate Conception. —Died Dec. 24, 1999
† Hernandez, Antonio (SJN). —Died Jan. 16, 1998
† Hernandez, Antonio, *s.t.* (SJN) Loiza, PR San Patricio. —Died Jan. 16, 1998
† Herold, Carl A. (IND) (Retired). —Died Nov. 26, 1999
† Herrera, David S. (LA) Carpinteria, CA St. Joseph. —Died Jan. 15, 2000
† Hesseldenz, Rev. Msgr. Clarence H. (STL) (Retired). —Died Oct. 25, 1999
† Hickey, Most Rev. Dennis W. (ROC) (Retired Auxiliary Bishop). —Died Oct. 6, 1999
† Hickey, John F., *c.m.* (CHI) Chicago, IL DePaul Vincentian Community. —Died March 28, 2000
† Hietpas, Raymond W. (GB) (Retired). —Died April 20, 2000
† Highland, Rev. Msgr. Charles F. (STU) Churchtown, OH St. John the Baptist. —Died May 30, 2000
† Hill, Richard A., *s.j.* (SJ) Los Gatos, CA Sacred Heart Jesuit Center. —Died Jan. 29, 2000
† Hinckley, Christopher J. (FTW) (Retired). —Died May 9, 2000
† Hines, Bartholomew F., *s.s.j.* (BAL) Baltimore, MD St. Joseph's Manor. —Died Aug. 7, 2000
† Hiney, Thomas (ALB) (Retired). —Died Nov. 20, 1999
† Hite, Clarence (OWN) (Retired). —Died Dec. 11, 2000
† Hoek, John F., *s.j.* (NY) Bronx, NY Province Infirmary. —Died Feb. 9, 2000
† Hoenig, George B. (DAV) (Retired). —Died July 19, 2000
† Hogan, Cornelius J. (BO) (Retired). —Died Jan. 29, 2000
† Hogan, Most Rev. Joseph L. (ROC) (Retired). —Died Aug. 27, 2000
† Hogan, Rev. Msgr. Robert J. (BUF) (Retired). —Died April 17, 2000
† Hogan, Rev. Msgr. William F. (NEW) (Retired). —Died May 19, 2000
† Holberton, William B. (ROC) (Retired). —Died March 6, 2000
† Holzer, Rev. Msgr. Ambrose W. (MAD) (Retired). —Died March 10, 2000
† Horan, F. Joseph (NOR) Versailles, CT St. Joseph. —Died Feb. 16, 2000
† Horgan, John J. (NEW). —Died May 19, 2000
† Horvath, Martin A. (FTW) (Retired). —Died Sept. 20, 2000
† Hoshock, Richard J. (TOL) (Retired). —Died April 2, 2000
† Houle, Cecil (STP) (Retired). —Died April 25, 2000
† Hourihan, Brendan, *o.carm.* (NY) Middletown, NY St. Albert's Priory. —Died March 18, 2000
† Howard, Thomas C. (SAG) (Retired). —Died Oct. 14, 1999
† Howley, Leo W. (STP) (Retired). —Died Aug. 17, 2000
† Hubert, James, *c.i.c.m.* (SAT) San Antonio, TX Mount Sacred Heart School. —Died Dec. 5, 1999
† Hughes, Joseph Arthur (DUL) Duluth, MN St. John. —Died May 21, 2000
† Hughes, Joseph (KC) Savannah, MO St. Rose of Lima. —Died July 13, 2000
† Hughes, Martin (B) (Retired). —Died Dec. 28, 1999
† Huguet, Dean M. (PEO) Westville, IL Church of St. Mary. —Died April 20, 2000
† Huhn, Bernard F. (STL) (Retired). —Died March 7, 2000
† Humanitzki, Reverend Father Theodore (STF) (Retired). —Died April 7, 2000
† Hunkins, Richard C. (JC) Stoutsville, MO Special Ministry. —Died April 27, 2000
† Hunt, Michael J. (BRK) Brooklyn, NY St. Frances de Chantal. —Died Nov. 4, 2000
† Hunt, Ted J. (SFE) Espanola, NM Sacred Heart. —Died July 26, 2000
† Huntington, Rev. Msgr. Christopher (RVC) (Retired). —Died March 10, 2000
† Hurley, Paul T. (PRO) Burrillville, RI St. Theresa of the Child Jesus Church. —Died Jan. 29, 2000
† Hynes, Francis, *s.m.a.* (BO) Dedham, MA African Mission House. —Died March 10, 2000
† Igoe, John T. (BIR) Birmingham, AL St. Joseph. —Died Jan. 13, 2000
† Inkel, Roland (BIR) (Retired). —Died Sept. 24, 2000
† Jablonovsky, John C., *c.p.* (CHI) Chicago, IL Passionist Community - Immaculate Conception Monastery. —Died Dec. 23, 1999
† Jackson, Donald F. (TUC) Oracle, AZ St. Helen Mission. —Died Oct. 17, 2000
† Jackson, Edward W., *c.ss.r.* (HBG) Ephrata, PA St. Clement's Mission House. —Died 2000
† Jakubik, Emil (SY) (Retired). —Died Dec. 14, 1999
† Janiak, Anthony J. (CHI) (Retired). —Died Nov. 21, 2000
† Jansonis, Alphonse B. (BO). —Died May 13, 2000
† Jelly, Frederick M., *o.p.* (BAL) Emmitsburg, MD Mount St. Mary's Seminary. —Died April 14, 2000
† Jones, Robert C., *c.ss.r.* (BAL) Baltimore, MD St. Ursula. —Died April 6, 2000
† Jordan, Patrick J. (NY) (Sick Leave). —Died May 1, 2000
† Joseph, Louis John (FR) (Retired). —Died Jan. 8, 2000
† Joseph, Ramon A. (RVC) (Retired). —Died Sept. 13, 2000
† Joyce, John, *o.m.i.* (SAT) San Antonio, TX Oblate School of Theology. —Died March 11, 2000
† Joyce, John (STP) (Retired). —Died Oct. 15, 2000
† Joyce, Pierce J. (CHI) (Retired). —Died March 1, 2000
† Jozwiak, Zygmunt (SP) (Retired). —Died Nov. 12, 2000
† Jurgelaitis, Anthony A., *o.p.* (PRO) Providence, RI St. Thomas Aquinas Priory at Providence College. —Died 2000
† Kaczkowski, Leon (BAL) (Retired). —Died Feb. 5, 2000
† Kalayjian, Rev. Msgr. Joseph (ARM) Detroit, MI St. Vartan Church. —Died Nov. 20, 1999
† Kaminski, Henry T. (NEW) (Retired). —Died Aug. 17, 2000
† Kane, John, *c.ss.r.* (TUC) Tucson, AZ Desert House of Prayer. —Died Feb. 13, 2000
† Katrij, Julian, *o.s.b.m.* (STF) Glen Cove, NY Basilian Fathers Novitiate of the Order of St. Basil the Great. —Died July 8, 2000
† Kautzky, Jon (DM) Red Oak, IA St. Mary. —Died Jan. 17, 2000
† Keane, John F. (SAT) On Leave.
† Keefe, John W. (ALB) Latham, NY Our Lady of Hope. —Died Oct. 30, 2000
† Keefner, James, *o.f.m.* (SFD) Madison, IL Our Lady of Czestochowa. —Died Aug. 15, 2000
† Keegan, Gregory J., *m.m.* (NY) Maryknoll, NY Maryknoll Fathers & Brothers. —Died June 6, 2000
† Kelleher, James P. (DAV) (Retired). —Died Sept. 20, 2000
† Kelley, Thomas J.C., *s.j.* (BO) Weston, MA Campion Center. —Died Sept. 30, 1999
† Kelley, William F., *s.j.* (OM) Omaha, NE Jesuit Community at Creighton University. —Died May 2, 2000
† Kelly, Edward J., *c.s.s.p.* (ARL) Arlington, VA Our Lady, Queen of Peace. —Died July 10, 2000
† Kelly, Rev. Msgr. Edward (DM). —Died June 12, 2000
† Kelly, Rev. Msgr. J. Morgan (MET) East Brunswick, NJ St. Bartholomew Church. —Died Aug. 3, 2000
† Kelly, Joseph A., *o.praem.* (HBG) Lykens, PA Our Lady Help of Christians. —Died 2000
† Kelty, Charles J. (L) (Retired). —Died Jan. 18, 2000
† Kennedy, Rev. Msgr. John S. (HRT) (Retired). —Died Oct. 3, 2000
† Kenney, Martin F., *s.s.j.* (BAL) Baltimore, MD St. Joseph's Manor. —Died Aug. 4, 2000
† Kesting, Philip A. (CIN) (Retired). —Died Sept. 19, 2000
† Kieran, Benet, *c.p.* (LA) Pasadena, CA Passionist Community. —Died May 1, 2000
† Kikowski, Zdzislaw, *o.s.p.p.e.* (PH) Doylestown, PA Pauline Fathers Monastery. —Died Jan. 5, 2000
† King, William (LAN) (Unassigned). —Died May 26, 2000
† Kinlough, Rev. Msgr. William C. (CC) (Retired). —Died Sept. 29, 2000
† Kinzig, James J. (JOL) (Retired). —Died May 2, 2000
† Kirchmyer, Thomas B., *m.m.* (NY) Maryknoll, NY Maryknoll Fathers & Brothers. —Died June 3, 2000
† Klauder, Francis, *s.d.b.* (NEW) Orange, NJ The Salesian Community. —Died Jan. 28, 2000
† Klein, Robert William (DUL) (On Leave). —Died Feb. 16, 2000
† Klein, Rev. Msgr. Sylvester P. (LFT) Tipton, IN St. Joseph Center. —Died Sept. 6, 2000
† Kleiser, Rev. Msgr. William J. (MEM) (Retired). —Died June 5, 2000
† Kliche, Anthony S., *c.s.s.p.* (PH) Bensalem, PA Congregation of the Holy Ghost. —Died Feb. 2, 2000
† Kobularik, Robert J. (HBG) New Freedom, PA St. John the Baptist. —Died Dec. 30, 1999
† Koegel, Victor C. (CIN) (Retired). —Died March 8, 2000
† Koehler, C. Ralph, *c.s.b.* (GAL) Sugar Land, TX Basilian Mission Center. —Died 2000
† Koelzer, Bonaventure, *s.a.* (NY) Garrison, NY Franciscan Friars of the Atonement. —Died June 2, 2000
† Kolesar, Casimir, *o.f.m.* (PEO) Peoria, IL Sacred Heart. —Died March 17, 2000
† Kollar, Edmund V. (ARL) (Retired). —Died Aug. 1, 2000
† Konoske, Rev. Msgr. Paul M. (LA) (Retired). —Died March 11, 2000
† Kos, Joseph S. (IND) Chap. Indianapolis, IN Wishard Memorial Hospital. —Died Aug. 9, 2000
† Kost, Harold J. (SCL) Belle Prairie, MN Holy Family Church. —Died Aug. 20, 2000
† Kotyuk, Stephen J. (E) (Retired). —Died Nov. 27, 2000
† Kowalewski, Vincent J., *o.s.f.s.* (WIL) Childs, MD Oblates of St. Francis De Sales. —Died Jan. 3, 2000
† Kraker, John J. (CLV) Euclid, OH St. Felicitas. —Died Feb. 20, 2000
† Kram, Charles (VIC) Chap. Yoakum, TX Yoakum Community Hospital. —Died Aug. 13, 2000
† Krastel, Francis W. (WDC) St. Mary's City, MD St. Cecilia. —Died July 3, 2000
† Kratz, Lawrence, *o.s.b.* (SFS) Marvin, SD Blue Cloud Abbey. —Died July 10, 2000
† Kriege, Roger L. (COV) Vicar Gen. & Chancellor Erlanger, KY The Catholic Center. —Died Feb. 13, 2000
† Krische, Otto, *o.f.m.* (CIN) Cincinnati, OH St. Clement Friary. —Died June 26, 2000
† Krizmanich, Germain, *o.f.m.* (CIN) Cincinnati, OH St. Francis Center. —Died Sept. 8, 2000
† Kromer, Stanley, *o.carm.* (VEN) Englewood, FL St. Raphael. —Died Nov. 17, 1999
† Krumpe, William F. (CIN) Cincinnati, OH Our Lady of Victory. —Died Aug. 29, 2000
† Krusling, Lawrence R. (CIN) Cincinnati, OH St. Rose. —Died Feb. 22, 2000
† Kubacki, Anthony (SJP) Johnstown, PA St. John the Baptist Church. —Died Dec. 9, 1999
† Kuberski, Leonard, M.A. (PSC) Dunellen, NJ St. Nicholas of Myra Church. —Died Aug. 18, 2000
† Kuntz, Aloysius G. (BUF) (Retired). —Died Oct. 30, 2000
† Kutz, Rev. Msgr. Ralph G. (JC) Argyle, MO St. Aloysius. —Died July 5, 2000
† Kvedrovicz, Richard J. (SCR). —Died July 18, 2000
† Labadie, Carmel, *o.f.m.cap.* (GB) Appleton, WI St. Fidelis Friary. —Died Sept. 29, 2000
† LaCerra, Rev. Msgr. Gerard T. (MIA) Miami, FL St. Timothy. —Died July 25, 2000
† Lacey, Thomas E. (SFR) Redwood City, CA St. Matthias Church. —Died Aug. 13, 2000
† Lackamp, Franklin J. (KC) (Retired). —Died June 26, 2000
† Lambing, Gregory, *o.c.s.o.* (L) Trappist, KY Abbey of Our Lady of Gethsemani. —Died June 18, 2000
† Landoll, Rev. Msgr. Gilbert J. (SAL) Solomon, KS Immaculate Conception. —Died Sept. 1, 2000
† Lane, John H., *s.j.* (CHI) Chicago, IL Resurrection Health Center. —Died Feb. 21, 2000
† Lane, Rev. Msgr. William (MRY) (Retired). —Died Feb. 26, 2000
† Lange, Matthew J. (FTW) (Retired). —Died Dec. 31, 1999
† Langely, Joseph W. (BO) (Retired). —Died April 26, 2000
† Larguier, Everett H., *s.j.* (NO) New Orleans, LA Ignatius Residence. —Died Sept. 20, 2000
† Larkin, Joseph M., *s.j.* (BO) Chestnut Hill, MA Boston College. —Died May 17, 2000
† Lash, Theodore, *o.f.m.conv.* (SY) Utica, NY St. Joseph and St. Patrick. —Died Oct. 1999
† Lassuy, Raymond J. (PEO) (Retired). —Died Aug. 17, 2000
† Later, Morse (B) (Retired). —Died June 1, 2000
† Latimer, Rev. Msgr. Edward H. (E) (Retired). —Died Aug. 10, 2000
† Laurenzano, Roch M. (NY) (Retired). —Died June 19, 2000
† Lazzaro, NIcholas A. (PH) Pastor Emeritus Conshohocken, PA SS. Cosmas/Damian. —Died Nov. 15, 1999
† Leary, Edward A., *s.s.e.* (VEN) Englewood, FL Society of St. Edmund. —Died April 4, 2000
† Leary, Rev. Msgr. Joseph W. (CAM) (Retired). —Died July 30, 2000
† Leinfelder, Philip (LC) (Retired). —Died May 2, 2000
† Lembo, Philip (SY) North Syracuse, St. Rose of Lima. —Died April 16, 2000
† Lenk, Edward, *o.f.m.conv.* (SY) Retired. —Died Sept. 2000
† Leonard, William J., *s.j.* (BO) Chestnut Hill, MA Boston College. —Died Feb. 11, 2000
† Lesco, Francis J. (HRT) (Retired). —Died July 6, 2000
† Leskiw, Rt. Rev. Mitred Msgr Peter (STN) (Retired). —Died Feb. 12, 2000
† Linskey, Thomas J., *s.j.* (ALN) Wernersville, PA Jesuit Center. —Died 2000
† Lippert, Alexander W. (STL) Ozora, MO Sacred Heart. —Died April 16, 2000
† Lloyd, Ronald, *s.m.m.* (HRT) Litchfield, CT Montfort Missionaries. —Died Oct. 31, 1999

† Loftus, Rev. Msgr. Robert B. (NY) (Retired). —Died Aug. 5, 2000
† Logue, Louis (BUR) (Retired). —Died Dec. 28, 1999
† Lorenz, Rev. Msgr. Victor O. (DET) (Retired). —Died Jan. 29, 2000
† Low, Rev. Msgr. Albert W. (BO) (Retired). —Died Aug. 22, 2000
† Lowery, William R. (SFR) San Mateo, CA St. Bartholomew Church. —Died May 15, 2000
† Lucko, Aidan, *o.f.m.cap.* (PIT) Pittsburgh, PA St. Conrad Friary. —Died July 16, 2000
† Lukas, Michael (SEA) (Retired). —Died May 7, 2000
† Lukaszewski, Joseph C. (RVC) (Retired). —Died April 26, 2000
† Lustig, Victor (B) (Retired). —Died March 18, 2000
† Lynch, Daniel G. (BO) (Retired). —Died Oct. 25, 2000
† Lynch, Richard D. (E) Erie, PA St. Mark the Evangelist. —Died April 21, 2000
† Lyons, Timothy, *o.f.m.conv.* (TR) Seaside Park, NJ St. Catharine of Siena. —Died Jan. 1999
† Lyons, William P. (CLV) Akron, OH St. Matthew. —Died Nov. 10, 2000
† Lysaght, John, *o.c.d.* (SR) Oakville, CA Carmelite House of Prayer. —Died Sept. 17, 2000
† MacCarthy, Peter (BIR) Leeds, AL St. Theresa. —Died Aug. 23, 2000
† MacGillivray, Arthur R., *s.j.* (BO) Chestnut Hill, MA Boston College. —Died June 17, 2000
† Machovec, Frank J. (LIN) (Retired). —Died July 30, 2000
† Maciejewski, Richard J. (STU) (Retired). —Died Feb. 24, 2000
† Mackin, Gerard, *m.s.f.* (SAT) Seguin, TX Our Lady of Guadalupe. —Died April 25, 2000
† Madrid, Ramon (NY) Rhinebeck, NY The Good Shepherd. —Died Feb. 2, 2000
† Maguire, James F., *s.j.* (DET) Clarkston, MI Colombiere Center. —Died Jan. 10, 2000
† Maguire, John J. (BO) (Retired). —Died March 25, 2000
† Magyar, Ladislaus, *sch.p.* (PH) Devon, PA Piarist Fathers. —Died 2000
† Maher, Rev. Msgr. Thomas J. (ALT) Loretto, PA Basilica of St. Michael the Archangel. —Died Dec. 31, 1999
† Mahoney, Rev. Msgr. Francis X. (NY) (Retired). —Died Sept. 29, 2000
† Mahoney, John F. (RVC) (Retired). —Died June 4, 2000
† Maiza, Felix A., *s.j.* (LA) Duarte, CA Santa Teresita Hospital. —Died Dec. 30, 1999
† Maley, William Austin (CHR) Hartsville, SC St. Mary. —Died Sept. 22, 2000
† Mallon, John F. (ALB) (Retired). —Died Nov. 11, 2000
† Malloy, Rev. Msgr. Faber J. (ALT) Ebensburg, PA Holy Name. —Died June 1, 2000
† Malone, James P., *s.j.* (ROC) Rochester, NY McQuaid Jesuit High School. —Died Feb. 9, 2000
† Maloney, Raymond G. (BUR) (Retired). —Died Nov. 12, 1999
† Manning, Edward J., *m.m.* (NY) Maryknoll, NY Maryknoll Fathers & Brothers. —Died Aug. 11, 2000
† Manning, Joseph (SEA). —Died Feb. 22, 2000
† Marcantonio, Robert A. (PRO). —Died Oct. 20, 1999
† Marciulionis, Benedict J. (GAY) (Retired). —Died May 5, 2000
† Marheuser, Richard A. (CIN) Cincinnati, OH Mt. St. Mary Seminary. —Died March 30, 2000
† Marks, Kenneth L. (NY) Bronx, NY St. Benedict. —Died July 29, 2000
† Marlow, Ransom A., *s.j.* (NO) New Orleans, LA Loyola University New Orleans. —Died Jan. 16, 2000
† Marsh, Dwaine Joseph, *c.ss.r.* (STL) Liguori, MO St. Clement's Health Care Center. —Died May 17, 2000
† Marszalek, Francis G. (PH) King of Prussia, PA Mother of Divine Providence. —Died Jan. 3, 2000
† Martin, Edward L., *o.p.* (BRK) Bayside, NY Ozanam Hall of Queens Nursing Home. —Died Aug. 23, 2000
† Martin, Francis M., *o.s.m.* (CHI) Chicago, IL Resurrection Life Center. —Died Jan. 8, 2000
† Martin, John H., *s.j.* (SJ) Los Gatos, CA Sacred Heart Jesuit Center. —Died Aug. 20, 2000
† Martin, Vincent, *o.s.b.* (LA) Valyermo, CA St. Andrew's Abbey. —Died 2000
† Martis, Albin A. (WH) (Retired). —Died Feb. 23, 1999
† Masterson, John J. (WIL) Bethany Beach, DE St. Ann. —Died June 19, 2000
† Mateo, Miguel, *s.f.* (SFE) Chimayo, NM Holy Family. —Died Dec. 4, 1999
† Matsko, John M. (PH) Pastor Emeritus Bridgeport, PA Our Mother of Sorrows. —Died Dec. 31, 1999
† Mattei, Rev. Msgr. Saverio C. (RVC) Dix Hills, NY St. Matthew. —Died April 10, 2000
† Matulis, Albert J. (NEW) (Retired). —Died Jan. 16, 2000
† Mazzocchia, George, *o.f.m.* (NY) New York, NY Padua Friary. —Died April 1, 2000
† Mc G.A. Nugent, Frank, *s.j.* (ALN) Wernersville, PA Novitiate of St. Isaac Jogues. —Died 2000
† McArdle, Rev. Msgr. Joseph G. (MOB) (Retired). —Died Aug. 23, 2000
† McBrearty, William J., *s.j.* (SY) Syracuse, NY LeMoyne College Community. —Died Dec. 23, 1999
† McCaffrey, Gerard D. (PH) (Retired). —Died March 9, 2000
† McCall, Robert E., *s.s.j.* (BAL) Baltimore, MD St. Joseph's Manor. —Died July 5, 2000
† McCarron, Francis, *o.m.i.* (BO) Tewksbury, MA Immaculate Heart of Mary Infirmary. —Died Feb. 12, 2000
† McCarthy, Francis J., *s.s.j.* (BEA) Beaumont, TX Blessed Sacrament. —Died Jan. 30, 2000
† McCartney, Marcellus, *o.f.m.* (NY) New York, NY St. Francis. —Died July 2, 2000
† McCormack, Thomas A., *s.s.c.* (PRO) Bristol, RI St. Columban's Retirement House. —Died Jan. 7, 2000
† McCormick, George C. (CAM) (Retired). —Died March 16, 2000
† McCormick, Richard A., *s.j.* (FTW) Notre Dame, IN University of Notre Dame Du Lac. —Died Feb. 12, 2000
† McDermott, Francis A. (PH) Pastor Emeritus Philadelphia, PA Assumption B.V.M.. —Died Sept. 9, 2000
† McDermott, Paul B. (PEO) (Absent on Leave). —Died May 19, 2000
† McDonald, J. Robert (DUB) Newhall, IA St. Paul. —Died Nov. 18, 1999
† McDonald, Raphael, *o.f.m.* (PAT) Ringwood, NJ Holy Name Friary. —Died July 11, 2000
† McDonnell, Cyril (CAM) (Retired). —Died May 17, 2000
† McEntee, Paul H. (BO) Watertown, MA Sacred Heart. —Died Oct. 11, 2000
† McEvoy, John (MRY) (Retired). —Died July 27, 2000
† McGinnity, Ambrose T. (GRY) (Retired). —Died Feb. 27, 2000
† McGovern, Arthur F., *s.j.* (DET) Detroit, MI Jesuit Community at the University of Detroit. —Died May 24, 2000
† McGrane, Rev. Msgr. Walter J. (SPC) (Retired). —Died Nov. 5, 2000
† McGuigan, Francis W., *s.j.* (FBK) Fairbanks, AK Monroe Foundation, Inc. —Died June 3, 2000
† McGuire, Michael A. (MET) South Plainfield, NJ Sacred Heart Church. —Died March 10, 2000
† McGuirk, Raymond A. (BRK) Brooklyn, NY Holy Innocents. —Died Nov. 30, 2000
† McKenna, James D. (SPR) (Retired). —Died Oct. 7, 2000
† McKeon, Alexander P. (PT). —Died Feb. 3, 2000
† McLoughlin, John, *c.p.* (HRT) West Hartford, CT Holy Family Monastery. —Died Oct. 9, 2000
† McMahon, John B. (WDC) (Retired). —Died April 9, 2000
† McManimon, Rev. Msgr. James (TR) Lawrenceville, NJ Morris Hall. —Died Aug. 31, 2000
† McManus, John E., *c.s.b.* (GAL) Houston, TX University of St. Thomas. —Died March 27, 2000
† McManus, Martin (SD) (Retired). —Died March 28, 2000
† McNamara, Thomas L., *o.s.f.s.* (TOL) Toledo, OH Oblates of St. Francis de Sales. —Died March 1, 2000
† McNelis, Patrick J. (BRK) Babylon, NY Immaculate Heart of Mary. —Died Oct. 19, 2000
† McSweeney, Placid, *o.s.c.o.* (WOR) Spencer, MA St. Joseph's Abbey. —Died March 20, 2000
† McSweeny, James (GI) (Retired). —Died Jan. 22, 2000
† McTarsney, John F. (DUB) Fairbank, IA Immaculate Conception. —Died June 6, 2000
† McVinney, Paul, *s.v.d.* (CHI) Techny, IL Divine Word Residence. —Died July 30, 2000
† Meany, Stephen J., *s.j.* (NY) Bronx, NY Murray-Weigel Hall. —Died Sept. 3, 2000
† Meder, James R. (L) (Retired). —Died July 23, 2000
† Merlucci, Michael A. (NEW) Scotch Plains, NJ St. Bartholow. —Died Feb. 5, 2000
† Merz, Fabiano, *o.f.m.* (SFD) Sherman, IL Our Lady of Angels Friary. —Died 2000
† Middendorf, Frederic G., *s.j.* (CIN) Cincinnati, OH St. Francis Xavier. —Died Feb. 20, 2000
† Mikulich, Joseph, *o.f.m.* (SJ) San Jose, CA St. Mary of the Assumption. —Died March 15, 2000
† Miller, Francis N. (BUF) (Retired). —Died Feb. 21, 2000
† Miller, Robert, *c.m.f.* (LA) Rancho Dominguez, CA Dominguez Seminary, Inc. —Died Aug. 5, 2000
† Missler, Othmar, *c.pp.s.* (CIN) Carthagena, OH St. Charles. —Died Nov. 22, 1999
† Monteleone, Raphael D. (RVC) (Retired). —Died Nov. 23, 1999
† Montgomery, Rev. Msgr. James F. (WDC) Washington, DC Church of the Annunciation. —Died Sept. 10, 2000
† Moore, Michael (YAK) (Retired). —Died Jan. 12, 2000
† Moran, Howard L., *s.j.* (SPK) Spokane, WA Gonzaga University. —Died July 13, 2000
† Moreau, Ernest P. (SPR) (Retired). —Died Sept. 5, 2000
† Moriarty, Joseph T. (CLV) Parma Heights, OH Incarnate Word Academy. —Died July 27, 2000
† Morris, Robert J. (PAT) (Retired). —Died May 30, 2000
† Morris, William, *s.m.* (FgM) Marianist Provincialate. —Died Dec. 22, 1999
† Morrison, Harry B. (OAK) Walnut Creek, CA St. Stephen Church. —Died April 10, 2000
† Morrissey, William F. (RCK) Aurora, IL St. Mary. —Died Nov. 4, 2000
† Morrow, Lambert, *o.s.b.* (PBL) Canon City, CO Holy Cross Abbey. —Died Nov. 25, 2000
† Morse, Guy E. (CHL) (Retired). —Died June 6, 2000
† Mosovsky, James J. (CLV) Avon Lake, OH Holy Spirit. —Died Jan. 25, 2000
† Moynahan, Joseph A. (WOR) Worcester, St. Christopher Parish. —Died Mar. 13, 2000
† Moynihan, Eugene, *s.m.m.* (RVC) Bay Shore, NY Montfort Missionaries. —Died Jan. 27, 2000
† Moynihan, Paul V. (BO) (Retired). —Died June 24, 2000
† Mulhall, Emmanuel F., *o.praem.* (GB) De Pere, WI St. Norbert Abbey. —Died Aug. 7, 2000
† Mullen, John (ALB). —Died April 5, 2000
† Mullen, L. James (PH) Chap. Philadelphia, PA St. John Neumann Nursing Home. —Died June 2, 2000
† Mungari, Joseph, *s.a.c.* (CAM) Pennsauken, NJ Bishop Eustace Prep. School. —Died Jan. 6, 2000
† Murphy, Francis W. (NOR) Essex, CT Our Lady of Sorrows. —Died Jan. 28, 2000
† Murphy, James F. (PH) (Retired). —Died Oct. 19, 2000
† Murphy, John B., *o.s.f.s.* (CHL) High Point, NC Maryfield Nursing Home. —Died July 24, 2000
† Murphy, John T. (LC) (Retired). —Died July 23, 2000
† Murphy, Kenneth J. (IND) (Retired). —Died Nov. 24, 1999
† Murphy, Patrick J. (BIR) Birmingham, AL St Mark the Evangelist. —Died Sept. 16, 2000
† Murphy, William, *s.a.* (NY) Garrison, NY Franciscan Friars of the Atonement. —Died March 16, 2000
† Murray, John J. (NY) Port Jervis, NY Immaculate Conception. —Died Nov. 30, 2000
† Murray, Maximillian (SEA) (Retired). —Died March 29, 2000
† Musselman, Joseph, *s.j.* (NY) New York, NY Xavier Jesuit Community. —Died Nov. 30, 1999
† Nadeau, J.H. Normand (BUR) Brattleboro, VT St. Michael. —Died Aug. 3, 2000
† Naffah, Rev. Msgr. John (OLL) (Retired). —Died Sept. 9, 1999
† Nagler, Robert (SB) San Diego, CA St. Michael's. —Died May 18, 2000
† Najdowski, Rev. Msgr. John A. (GR) (Retired). —Died Oct. 26, 2000
† Natali, Alfred, *o.s.a.* (PH) Philadelphia, PA St. Mary Magdalen de Pazzi. —Died Dec. 14, 1999
† Nealy, Francis D., *o.p.* (PRO) Providence, RI St. Thomas Aquinas Priory at Providence College. —Died Nov. 12, 1999
† Neumann, August (MET) (Retired). —Died Dec. 29, 1998
† Nienhaus, Bernard J. (STL) Hawk Point, MO St. Mary. —Died Nov. 8, 2000
† Nikolai, William V. (LC) (Retired). —Died Oct. 19, 2000
† Nolan, Rev. Msgr. William L. (MAN) (Retired). —Died May 1, 2000
† Noll, Joseph, *c.ss.r.* (ALB) Saratoga Springs, NY St. John Neumann Residence. —Died Jan. 12, 2000
† Norris, Frank B., *s.s.* (SFR) Menlo Park, CA St. Patrick's Seminary. —Died Jan. 7, 2000
† Noto, James (RIC) (Retired). —Died March 6, 2000
† Novacki, Michael L., *o.p.* (COL) Columbus, OH Mohun Health Care Center, St. Mary of the Springs. —Died March 25, 2000
† Nowakowski, Francis (ALB) (Retired). —Died Oct. 1, 2000
† O'Boyle, Andrew F. (CLV) Newbury, OH St. Helen. —Died Dec. 31, 1999
† O'Brien, Rev. Msgr. Cornelius M. (NY) Port Chester, NY Our Lady of Mercy. —Died Dec. 18, 2000
† O'Brien, Edward J. (PRT) (Retired). —Died Dec. 28, 1999
† O'Brien, Joseph A. (WDC) Rector Washington, DC Cardinal O'Boyle Residence for Priests. —Died Sept. 19, 2000
† O'Brien, Patrick, *o.m.i.* (SAT) Retired. —Died Oct. 15, 2000
† O'Connell, Brian J., *c.m.* (WDC) Washington, DC Providence Hospital. —Died Feb. 28, 2000
† O'Connell, John Quentin, *c.m.* (DEN) Denver, CO Kateri Mission. —Died Aug. 29, 1999

† O'Connell, Luke, *o.f.m.* (BO) Boston, MA St. Anthony Residence. —Died Sept. 1, 2000
† O'Connell, Rev. Msgr. Patrick Hayes (BEA) (Retired). —Died Oct. 16, 2000
† O'Connor, Francis A. (SPR) (Retired). —Died Feb. 27, 2000
† O'Connor, Rev. Msgr. Patrick C. (MOB) Gulf Shores, AL Our Lady of the Gulf Church. —Died Nov. 29, 2000
† O'Connor, Thomas M., *o.m.i.* (STP) St. Paul, MN Missionary Oblates of Mary Immaculate. —Died Sept. 20, 2000
† O'Curneen, Hugh (SD) (Retired). —Died April 19, 2000
† O'Dea, James J. (HRT) Beacon Falls, CT St. Michael. —Died Oct. 4, 2000
† O'Dea, John (SPK) (Retired). —Died July 21, 1999
† O'Donnell, Richard Joseph (PMB) (Retired). —Died Oct. 20, 2000
† O'Donovan, Rickard J. (BO) Wilmington, MA St. Dorothy. —Died Aug. 7, 2000
† O'Farrell, Michael J. (RVC) Northport, NY St. Philip Neri. —Died Feb. 13, 2000
† O'Grady, James W. (TOL) (Retired). —Died June 1, 2000
† O'Grady, John G. (ALB) (Retired). —Died May 31, 2000
† O'Hara, Arthur T. (TLS) Pryor, OK St. Mark. —Died Jan. 17, 2000
† O'Heron, Edward J. (SY) Newman Chap. Cortland, NY State University of New York. —Died Nov. 20, 1999
† O'Meara, James (KAL) (Retired). —Died Aug. 18, 2000
† O'Neil, Lewis B., *s.j.* (SFR) San Francisco, CA St. Vincent de Paul. —Died Sept. 20, 2000
† O'Neil, Maurice L. (OG) (On Duty Outside of the Diocese). —Died Nov. 27, 1999
† O'Neil, Maurice L., *s.s.* (TUC) Green Valley, AZ Our Lady of the Valley. —Died Nov. 27, 1999
† O'Neill, Desmond R. (ROC) Leicester, NY St. Thomas Aquinas/St Lucy. —Died March 31, 2000
† O'Reilly, Rev. Msgr. John Lawrence (WH) (Retired). —Died Oct. 1, 1999
† O'Rourke, Thomas P., *m.m.* (NY) Maryknoll, NY Maryknoll Fathers & Brothers. —Died Jan. 21, 2000
† O'Shea, John F., *s.j.* (STL) St. Louis, MO Fusz Pavilion. —Died May 6, 2000
† O'Sullivan, John J. (BRK) Babylon, NY St. Joseph. —Died Oct. 29, 2000
† Ober, Anselm A., *o.s.b.* (RIC) Virginia Beach, VA St. Gregory the Great. —Died Aug. 13, 2000
† Obmann, Rev. Msgr. Russell J. (STL) (Retired). —Died Sept. 21, 2000
† Olkovikas, Rev. Msgr. Albert W., P.A. (MAN) Manchester, NH NH Monastery of the Precious Blood. —Died May 13, 2000
† Opalenick, Rev. Msgr. John, O.E.S.L. (PSC) Old Forge, PA St. Nicholas of Myra Church. —Died June 19, 2000
† Oravecz, John (BRK) Woodburg, NY Holy Name of Jesus. —Died March 22, 2000
† Ortner, John M., *s.j.* (NY) Bronx, NY Loyola Hall, Fordham University. —Died March 27, 2000
† Oryshkewych, Ostap, Ph.D. (PHU) Philadelphia, PA St. Andrew. —Died Jan. 13, 2000
† Ottensmeyer, Hilary, *o.s.b.* (IND) Beech Grove, IN Our Lady of Grace Monastery. —Died May 17, 2000
† Ouellette, Lionel P. (BO) Marlborough, MA St. Mary. —Died Sept. 4, 2000
† Pacacha, Joseph (NY) (Retired). —Died May 8, 2000
† Padovano, Louis A., *s.j.* (NY) New York, NY St. Ignatius Community. —Died Sept. 20, 2000
† Pagan, Joaquin Rivera (SJN) Carolina, P.R. San Fernando Parish. —Died July 12, 1999
† Pagone, Joseph J. (WDC) (Retired). —Died July 11, 2000
† Pakalniskis, John L. (BRK) Brooklyn, NY Annunciation. —Died June 26, 2000
† Pakulniewicz, Rev. Msgr. Raphael F. (NY) Staten Island, NY St. Anthony. —Died May 8, 2000
† Palmieri, John A. (BO) (Retired). —Died Nov. 17, 2000
† Pastorius, Vance, *o.f.m.cap.* (BAL) Cumberland, MD SS. Peter and Paul. —Died Oct. 4, 2000
† Pavlak, Robert P., *s.s.j.* (NO) New Orleans, LA Josephite Fathers and Brothers. —Died June 14, 2000
† Pavlick, Clement, *c.p.* (PIT) Pittsburgh, PA St. Paul of the Cross Monastery. —Died April 2, 2000
† Pawlicki, Joseph F., *c.s.c.* (SB) Coachella, CA Valley Missionary Program. —Died Dec. 13, 1999
† Pelleteri, Manuel J., *c.m.* (CHI) Chicago, IL DePaul Vincentian Community. —Died Oct. 24, 2000
† Pellicore, Rev. Msgr. Edward M. (CHI) (Retired). —Died Dec. 28, 1999
† Penzimas, Joseph A. (NU) (Retired). —Died June 21, 2000
† Pereda, Guillermo (SJN) (Retired). —Died Oct. 17, 1999
† Perpete, Louis M., *m.s.* (HRT) Hartford, CT Missionaries of LaSalette. —Died Dec. 3, 1999
† Perry, Daniel, *ss.cc.* (FgM) Provincial House. —Died Feb. 6, 2000
† Perry, Michael, *o.f.m.* (PAT) Ringwood, NJ Holy Name Friary. —Died Sept. 19, 2000
† Peruti, John J. (HRT) Hartford, CT St. Luke. —Died Sept. 28, 2000
† Peter, Rev. Msgr. Paul F. (OM) (Retired). —Died Oct. 15, 2000
† Peters, Raymond (LC) (Retired). —Died June 27, 2000
† Pfeiffer, Raymond, *o.s.b.* (KCK) Atchison, KS St. Benedict's Abbey. —Died July 30, 2000
† Pfender, Terrence, *o.carm.* (NEW) Cresskill, NJ St. Therese of Lisieux. —Died Dec. 31, 1999
† Phelan, Rev. Msgr. John F. (BAK) (Retired). —Died Nov. 22, 1999
† Phillips, Joseph, *s.p.* (Y) Canton, OH House of Loreto. —Died Nov. 12, 1999
† Phillips, Thomas R. (NY) (Retired). —Died Nov. 30, 2000
† Piatkowski, Robert J. (NEW) Springfield, NJ St. James. —Died Nov. 20, 2000
† Pierce, Justin, *s.d.s.* (GB) Manitowoc, WI Silver Lake College of the Holy Family. —Died Sept. 9, 2000
† Pinci, August, *o.ss.t.* (FgM) Province of the Immaculate Heart of Mary. —Died Jan. 27, 2000
† Pineau, Gerard P. (BO) Braintree, MA St. Francis of Assisi. —Died Oct. 20, 2000
† Pinho, Antonio M. (NEW) (Military Chaplain). —Died July 6, 2000
† Pisanelli, Humbert D. (NY) (Retired). —Died July 23, 2000
† Pitruzzello, Raymond S. (HRT) Waterbury, CT Immaculate Conception. —Died Jan. 7, 2000
† Plante, Albert R. (OG) (Retired). —Died Aug. 31, 2000
† Pollard, Daniel E. (PRT) (Retired). —Died May 22, 2000
† Pollone, Ralph A. (SPR) Pittsfield, MA St. Mary the Morning Star. —Died Feb. 9, 2000
† Porada, Charles, *o.f.m.conv.* (FR) New Bedford, MA Our Lady of Perpetual Help. —Died Nov. 26, 2000
† Porten, Henry Francis, *c.ss.r.* (STL) Liguori, MO St. Clement's Health Care Center. —Died May 17, 2000
† Posco, Raphael A. (SPR) (Retired). —Died Jan. 14, 2000
† Poulin, Robert P. (WOR) Southbridge, Notre Dame Parish. —Died Sept. 23, 2000
† Power, Joseph L. (SFS) (Retired). —Died Jan. 5, 2000
† Powers, Joseph M., *s.j.* (OAK) Berkeley, CA Jesuit School of Theology. —Died Sept. 6, 2000
† Pranckus, Rev. Msgr. Francis John (BGP) (Retired). —Died Sept. 6, 2000
† Prestera, Vincent (NEW) (Retired). —Died April 22, 2000
† Price, Francis R. (OM) (Retired). —Died March 5, 2000
† Price, Wolfe, *o.f.m.* (STL) Retired. —Died March 7, 2000
† Priester, Robert E. (BUF) (Retired). —Died Sept. 3, 2000
† Privitera, Rev. Msgr. Santi J. (BRK) Brooklyn, NY St. Bernadette. —Died Sept. 4, 2000
† Procaccini, Joseph J. (TR) Allentown, NJ St. John. —Died Feb. 17, 2000
† Proeller, Ulric J. (FAR) (Retired). —Died April 15, 2000
† Provost, James H. (HEL) Washington, D.C. The Catholic University of America. —Died Aug. 26, 2000
† Pucci, Joseph, *o.m.i.* (PMB) West Palm Beach, FL St. John Fisher. —Died Oct. 12, 2000
† Puccini, Alfred V. (BO) Malden, MA St. Peter. —Died Jan. 18, 2000
† Pugevicius, Casimir (BAL) (Retired). —Died Feb. 29, 2000
† Quinn, J. Patrick (JC) Rich Fountain, MO Sacred Heart; Belle, MO St. Alexander. —Died Nov. 17, 1999
† Quirk, Rev. Msgr. Edward J. (NY) Pearl River, NY St. Aedan. —Died Jan. 9, 2001
† Rafalowski, Leonard (SEA) (Retired). —Died Dec. 13, 1999
† Rafferty, Thomas A. (WH) (Retired). —Died June 17, 1999
† Readance, Frederick F., *s.j.* (DET) Retired. —Died March 1, 2000
† Reardon, Robert, *o.m.i.* (FgM) Oblates Foreign Missions. —Died Nov. 18, 1999
† Reddy, Thomas, *o.m.i.* (BO) Tewksbury, MA Immaculate Heart of Mary Infirmary. —Died April 25, 2000
† Reding, Aquinas, *o.f.m.* (NY) Obernburg, NY St. Mary. —Died Jan. 4, 2000
† Reece, Frederick (DM) (Retired). —Died Aug. 29, 2000
† Reed, Robert A. (BAL) (Retired). —Died Dec. 11, 1999
† Regan, James M., *o.p.* (CHI) River Forest, IL St. Thomas Aquinas Priory. —Died March 30, 2000
† Reiman, Frederick M., *o.s.m.* (FgM) Our Lady of Perpetual Help Mission. —Died Sept. 22, 2000
† Reimer, Elroy (GB) Wrightstown, WI St. Paul. —Died July 19, 2000
† Reiner, Charles J., *o.s.b.* (MOB) Foley, AL St. Margaret. —Died April 27, 2000
† Renaud, Roland A. (SPR) (Retired). —Died Feb. 26, 2000
† Reynolds, Ignatius C. (PH) Pastor Emeritus Gladwyne, PA St. John Baptist Vianney. —Died Aug. 6, 2000
† Reynolds, Ray, *o.f.m.conv.* (TR) Point Pleasant Beach, NJ St. Peter. —Died Dec. 1999
† Rhatigan, Rev. Msgr. John (SD) (Retired). —Died Sept. 19, 2000
† Ribeiro, Arthur (OAK) (Retired). —Died Oct. 18, 2000
† Richman, Bertrand N. (PRO) Tiverton, RI St. Theresa Church. —Died July 3, 2000
† Richter, Raynor (JOL) (Retired). —Died Feb. 8, 2000
† Riede, Clifford A. (L) (Retired). —Died June 18, 2000
† Rigney, Rev. Msgr. James F. (NY) (Retired). —Died Aug. 31, 2000
† Riley, James L. (SY) (Retired). —Died June 6, 2000
† Ring, Francis J., *s.j.* (MIL) Milwaukee, WI Jesuit Provincial Office. —Died 2000
† Riordan, Rev. Msgr. Daniel F. (BO) (Retired). —Died May 10, 2000
† Riotte, Rt. Rev. Mitred Msgr Jules (STN) (Retired). —Died May 10, 2000
† Risley, L. Thomas (RCK) Carpentersville, IL St. Monica. —Died Jan. 22, 2000
† Robards, Charles P. (PEO) Thomasboro, IL Church of St. Elizabeth. —Died Dec. 31, 1999
† Roca, William W., *s.j.* (NO) Metairie, LA Rummel High School. —Died Dec. 6, 1999
† Rogers, Furman (MOB) (Retired). —Died June 3, 2000
† Romero, Michael C. (PIT) Carrick, PA St. Basil. —Died June 17, 2000
† Rooney, William A. (NY) Monroe, NY Sacred Heart Church. —Died Nov. 13, 2000
† Rosner, William F., *c.ss.r.* (HBG) Ephrata, PA St. Clement's Mission House. —Died 2000
† Ross, Rev. Msgr. Charles R. (IND) (Retired). —Died Aug. 25, 2000
† Roth, Jacob P. (DUB) Fort Atkinson, IA St. John Nepomucene; Festina, IA Our Lady of Seven Dolors. —Died April 1, 2000
† Roueche, Rev. Msgr. John F. (CHL) (Retired). —Died June 1, 2000
† Rubba, John C., *o.p.* (PRO) Providence, RI St. Thomas Aquinas Priory at Providence College. —Died June 7, 2000
† Ruddy, Rev. Msgr. Donald J. (LA) Whittier, CA St. Gregory the Great. —Died Sept. 27, 2000
† Ruppert, Nelson, *o.f.m.cap.* (NY) White Plains, NY St. Conrad Friary. —Died March 11, 2000
† Ruskamp, Florian, *o.f.m.cap.* (LC) Marathon, WI St. Anthony Retreat Center. —Died Feb. 11, 2000
† Russell, Paul M. (L) (Retired). —Died Jan. 30, 2000
† Russo, Carmen T., *c.s.s.* (FgM) Stigmatine Fathers and Brothers. —Died Aug. 2, 2000
† Ruth, Ronald A. (RIC) Richmond, VA St. Edward. —Died March 9, 2000
† Ryan, Rev. Msgr. Edward J. (SY) Liverpool, Immaculate Heart of Mary. —Died Nov. 5, 2000
† Ryan, John J. (PEO) (Absent on Leave). —Died Feb. 19, 2000
† Ryan, Kenneth T. (STP) (Retired). —Died April 25, 2000
† Ryan, LeRoy F., *s.j.* (DET) Clarkston, MI Colombiere Community. —Died Nov. 24, 1999
† Ryan, Thomas J. (OAK) Berkeley, CA St. Ambrose Church. —Died Jan. 25, 2000
† Sadaba, Eugenio, *c.m.* (SJN) San Juan, PR San Vicente de Paul. —Died May 20, 2000
† Salem, George J., *o.s.b.* (BIR) Cullman, AL St. Bernard Abbey. —Died Nov. 7, 2000
† Salomon, Jean Francois (NEW) Union City, NJ St. Anthony. —Died Jan. 20, 2000
† Sammons, Joseph F. (SCR) Athens, GA St. Joseph's. —Died Dec. 30, 1999
† Sampson, William P., *s.j.* (WDC) Washington, DC Gonzaga College High School. —Died July 29, 2000
† Savage, Charles H. (WH) (Retired). —Died July 14, 2000
† Savoie, Albert J., *s.j.* (DET) Retired. —Died Oct. 3, 1999
† Scahill, John J. (PRT) Portland, ME Cathedral of the Immaculate Conception. —Died Feb. 26, 2000
† Scanlan, Lambert D. (GB) (Retired). —Died July 9, 2000
† Scanlon, John J. (PIT) East McKeesport, PA St. Robert Bellarmine. —Died Nov. 22, 1999
† Scanlon, Thomas, *t.o.r.* (SP) St. Petersburg, FL St. Mary Our Lady of Grace. —Died July 12, 2000
† Scannell, Richard J., *s.j.* (NO) New Orleans, LA Ignatius Residence. —Died Aug. 16, 2000

† Schackmuth, William A. (CHI) (Retired). —Died April 17, 2000
† Schaefer, Joseph P., *o.s.f.s.* (CAM) Pittsgrove, NJ Villa St. Joseph. —Died June 5, 2000
† Schaefer, Vernon J. (WIN) (Retired). —Died Nov. 16, 2000
† Scheible, Alan D., *o.praem.* (GB) De Pere, WI Norbertine Center for Spirituality, St. Norbert Abbey. —Died Jan. 30, 2000
† Scheller, Raymund (FAR) (Retired). —Died July 30, 2000
† Schemel, George J., *s.j.* (SCR) Scranton, PA University of Scranton. —Died June 18, 2000
† Schexnayder, Daniel (LAF) Leonville, LA St. Leo the Great. —Died June 19, 2000
† Schiller, David Joseph (CHR) (Retired). —Died June 10, 2000
† Schilling, Francis X. (KNX) Gatlinburg, TN St. Mary. —Died July 9, 2000
† Schilly, Rev. Msgr. Adolph M. (STL) (Retired). —Died Jan. 12, 2000
† Schindler, John (YAK) (Retired). —Died April 13, 2000
† Schmidt, Frederick N. (MIL) (Retired). —Died Feb. 3, 2000
† Schmidt, Gerald, *o.f.m.cap.* (GB) Wabeno, WI St. Ambrose. —Died May 13, 2000
† Schmidt, William, *o.f.m.* (STL) St. Louis, MO Franciscan Friary of St. Anthony of Padua. —Died Dec. 19, 1999
† Schneider, George E. (COV) Newport, KY Holy Spirit. —Died Jan. 16, 2000
† Schneider, Ralph, *c.pp.s.* (CIN) Montezuma, OH Our Lady of Guadalupe. —Died Feb. 24, 2000
† Schneweis, Emil, *o.f.m.cap.* (MIL) Mt. Calvary, WI St. Lawrence Friary. —Died Jan. 16, 2000
† Schnitzius, Donald (STP) (Retired). —Died Jan. 12, 2000
† Schoming, Henry C., *c.s.s.p.* (PIT) Bethel Park, PA Bethel Animation Center. —Died Dec. 16, 2000
† Schultz, Rev. Msgr. Raymond T. (PIT) Beaver, PA SS. Peter and Paul. —Died Oct. 27, 1999
† Schulz, Albert H., *s.j.* (STL) St. Louis, MO Jesuit Hall. —Died May 23, 2000
† Schwab, Jerome Frederick (CHR) Lexington, SC Corpus Christi. —Died Nov. 15, 2000
† Schwellenbach, Aloysius (SFD) On Leave. —Died Sept. 15, 2000
† Seeger, Francis J. (BRK) Flushing, NY Holy Family. —Died Jan. 25, 2000
† Segrue, Joseph D. (SY) Syracuse, Blessed Sacrament. —Died Dec. 20, 1999
† Seib, Herbert, *o.c.s.o.* (L) Trappist, KY Abbey of Our Lady of Gethsemani. —Died Sept. 11, 2000
† Sennott, Rev. Msgr. Robert J. (BO) (Retired). —Died Feb. 19, 2000
† Setzer, Frank, *s.m.m.* (FgM) Montfort Missionaries. —Died April 16, 2000
† Sexton, Charles E. (IND) (Retired). —Died Oct. 18, 2000
† Shannon, Robert J. (CHI) (Retired). —Died July 25, 2000
† Sharpe, Patrick F. (E) (Retired). —Died Jan. 15, 2000
† Shaughnessy, John A., *c.m.* (STL) St. Louis, MO Lazarist Residence. —Died Dec. 22, 1999
† Sheahan, Gerald R., *s.j.* (STL) St. Louis, MO Province Offices. —Died Aug. 29, 2000
† Sheedy, Rev. Msgr. Mateo E. (SJ) San Jose, Sacred Heart of Jesus. —Died Oct. 20, 2000
† Sheehan, George, *s.d.s.* (MIL) Milwaukee, WI Salvatorians - Jordan Hall. —Died May 28, 2000
† Sheehan, Thomas Damian, *o.p.* (GAL) Houston, TX St. Mark Priory. —Died July 24, 2000
† Sheehan, William J., *s.j.* (BO) Weston, MA Campion Center. —Died Sept. 28, 2000
† Shevlin, Rev. Msgr. John G. (NY) Bangall, NY Immaculate Conception. —Died May 21, 2000
† Shields, William J. (ALN) (Retired). —Died Aug. 27, 2000
† Silvestri, Luke A. (SCR) (On Duty Outside the Diocese). —Died July 18, 2000
† Silvestri, Vincent A. (MIL) (Retired). —Died July 17, 2000
† Simon, Martin M. (MIL) (Retired). —Died Sept.15, 2000
† Simons, Edward J., *o.s.f.s.* (WIL) Childs, MD Oblates of St. Francis De Sales. —Died Dec. 31, 1999
† Skalko, John Dominic, *o.p.* (PRO) Providence, RI St. Thomas Aquinas Priory at Providence College. —Died July 25, 2000
† Skarohild, Robert F. (FAR) Lakota, ND St. Mary. —Died Feb. 20, 2000
† Skrapits, John (BUF) Buffalo, NY St. Elizabeth. —Died March 29, 2000
† Slikas, William (JOL) Joliet, IL Holy Cross. —Died Oct. 22, 2000
† Sloan, Daniel, *i.c.* (SP) Seffner, FL St. Francis of Assisi. —Died Feb. 5, 1999
† Sloup, Ernest O. (LIN) (Retired). —Died Aug. 30, 2000
† Smith, Conor, *c.p.* (HRT) Farmington, CT Holy Family Monastery. —Died July 18, 2000
† Smith, Martin G. (PH) (Retired). —Died Dec. 22, 1999
† Smith, Michael (SD) (Retired). —Died April 28, 2000
† Smith, Paul (PHX) (Retired). —Died July 8, 2000
† Smithes, Donald F. (RCK) Polo, IL St. Mary. —Died Aug. 9, 2000
† Snella, Adolp A. (ARL) (Retired). —Died May 4, 2000
† Sonntag, Luis, *o.f.m.cap.* (MIL) Mount Calvary, WI St. Lawrence Friary. —Died Feb. 22, 2000
† Sorento, Armand, *o.f.m.conv.* (TR) Seaside Park, NJ St. Catharine of Siena. —Died Oct. 1999
† Sosnowski, Rev. Msgr. Stanley (ALN) Emmaus, PA St. Ann. —Died April 6, 2000
† Spaits, George S. (PH) (Retired). —Died March 29, 2000
† Spalding, William A. (LEX) Danville, KY SS. Peter & Paul Church. —Died May 23, 2000
† Spraker, Rev. Msgr. Gerard W. (BAL) (Retired). —Died March 3, 2000
† St. Clair, Joseph A. (PH) Pastor Emeritus Ardmore, PA St. Colman. —Died March 9, 2000
† Staiger, Charles (RVC) (Retired). —Died April 24, 2000
† Stalzer, David (JOL) Joliet, IL St. Mary Magdalene. —Died June 18, 2000
† Stanek, Rev. Msgr. Wenceslaus (CHI) (Retired). —Died June 24, 2000
† Staniszewski, Jerome Benedict, *o.f.m.* (PIT) Ben Avon, PA St. Anthony Friary & Mission House. —Died March 21, 2000
† Stankiewicz, John A., *s.s.e.* (BUR) Colchester, VT Society of St. Edmund. —Died Jan. 12, 2000
† Stark, John W. (DUB) Masonville, IA Immaculate Conception. —Died Dec. 6, 1999
† Statkus, Edward (GR) (Retired). —Died Dec. 26, 1999
† Staub, Rev. Msgr. Edward F. (BAL) Severna Park, MD St. John the Evangelist. —Died May 12, 2000
† Stearns, Rev. Msgr. John D. (CR). —Died Dec. 1, 1999
† Steckbauer, Linus (GB) (Retired). —Died April 21, 2000
† Stegmann, Rev. Msgr. Raymond V. (RVC) (Retired). —Died June 9, 2000
† Steinbicker, Carl L. (CIN) (Retired). —Died Nov. 27, 2000
† Stemac, Rev. Msgr. Louis Vincent (LR) (Retired). —Died Oct. 8, 2000
† Stephan, George J. (LA) Los Angeles, CA St. John the Evangelist. —Died Jan. 2, 2000
† Stephan, George, *s.v.d.* (LA) Los Angeles, CA St. John the Evangelist. —Died Jan. 2, 2000
† Stevenson, Rev. Msgr. Frederick J. (PH) Pastor Emeritus Wallingford, PA St. John Chrysostom. —Died Feb. 13, 2000
† Stokes, Edward J., *s.j.* (DET) Clarkston, MI Colombiere Center. —Died July 30, 2000
† Stonebridge, John H. (BRK) Glendale, NY Sacred Heart. —Died June 13, 2000
† Storey, Finan, *c.p.* (CHI) Chicago, IL Daneo Hall. —Died May 8, 2000
† Stotenbur, Rev. Msgr. David (LAN) East Lansing, MI St. Thomas Aquinas. —Died May 29, 2000
† Strahl, Ernest (IND) (Retired). —Died Jan. 3, 2000
† Streff, Joseph (STP) (Retired). —Died April 26, 2000
† Strub, Herman A. (DAV) (Retired). —Died July 10, 2000
† Studney, J. Edward (WDC) (Retired). —Died Oct. 12, 2000
† Stump, Reinhard Bartholomew, *c.ss.r.* (STL) Liguori, MO St. Clement Health Care Center. —Died Dec. 29, 1999
† Suchan, William T., *s.j.* (FgM) Campus Ministry. —Died May 21, 2000
† Sullivan, Rev. Msgr. Arthur A. (PRO) (Retired). —Died Jan. 30, 2000
† Sullivan, Cletus, *o.carm.* (CHI) Mundelein, IL Carmelite Monastery. —Died July 5, 2000
† Sullivan, Cornelius O. (CHI) (Retired). —Died Oct. 26, 2000
† Sullivan, Rev. Msgr. Daniel L. (NY) Staten Island, NY Blessed Sacrament. —Died June 6, 2000
† Sullivan, Rev. Msgr. Donald E. (STL) (Retired). —Died July 1, 2000
† Sullivan, James J. (HRT) (Retired). —Died Aug. 13, 2000
† Sullivan, John J. (NOR) Portland, CT St. Mary. —Died May 15, 2000
† Sutton, John Joseph (PMB) Boca Raton, St. Joan of Arc. —Died Aug. 30, 2000
† Sweeney, Sean, *s.m.a.* (BO) Dedham, MA African Mission House. —Died Dec. 9, 1999
† Sweeny, Louis L. (STO) Newman, CA St. Joachim Church. —Died Feb. 8, 2000
† Synowiak, Rev. Msgr. Edward F. (BUF) Buffalo, NY St. Florian. —Died Oct. 23, 2000
† Szarka, Balthasar S., *o.cist.* (DAL) Irving, TX Cistercian Abbey of Our Lady of Dallas. —Died April 1, 2000
† Tamulis, Anthony (SFD) (Retired). —Died Nov. 23, 2000
† Tardiff, Charles, *m.afr.* (SP) St. Petersburg, FL Missionaries of Africa. —Died 2000
† Tavares, Evaristo (FR) Fall River, MA Our Lady of the Angels Church. —Died Jan. 8, 2000
† Taylor, Vincent A., *s.j.* (NY) New York, NY Xavier High School. —Died March 29, 2000
† Teknipp, Robert J. (CLV) Green, OH Queen of Heaven. —Died Feb. 28, 2000
† Terwilliger, Rev. Msgr. John G. (SAC) (Retired). —Died Oct. 7, 2000
† Thielemann, William A., *s.s.* (BAL) Baltimore, MD St. Charles Villa. —Died Sept. 12, 2000
† Thoma, Anthony, *o.f.m.cap.* (GB) Appleton, WI St. Fidelis Friary. —Died April 29, 2000
† Thomas, Rev. Msgr. Gartland A. (NY) (Retired). —Died Jan. 8, 2000
† Thompson, Robert B. (GB) (On Duty Outside Diocese). —Died Nov. 26, 1999
† Thomson, Paul van K. (PRO) (Retired). —Died Dec. 22, 1999
† Thomson, Richard, *o.s.c.* (DET) Romulus, MI St. Aloysius. —Died Jan. 19, 2000
† Thro, Edward A., *s.j.* (STL) St. Louis, MO Fusz Pavilion. —Died Feb. 18, 2000
† Tobin, Flavian, *o.f.m.* (PAT) Ringwood, NJ Holy Name Friary. —Died July 21, 2000
† Tomasi, Noel, *s.x.* (FgM) Xaverian Foreign Mission. —Died Oct. 4, 1999
† Toomey, Gregory, *o.f.m.* (PAT) Ringwood, NJ Holy Name Friary. —Died May 10, 2000
† Toomey, Sylvester, *o.s.b.* (PAT) Clifton, NJ Holy Face Monastery. —Died Sept. 27, 2000
† Toulas, James, *c.ss.r.* (PH) Philadelphia, PA St. Peter the Apostle. —Died May 3, 2000
† Towell, Stephen A. (CLV) South Euclid, OH St. Gregory the Great. —Died June 9, 2000
† Trainor, John J., *c.m.* (BUF) Niagara University, NY Vincentian Community. —Died Sept. 12, 2000
† Traynor, Vincent dePaul, *o.s.b.* (OKL) Shawnee, OK St. Gregory's Abbey. —Died March 3, 2000
† Trombley, Jerome E. (SAG) (Retired). —Died June 26, 2000
† Trutter, Richard S., *o.p.* (SFD) Taylorville, IL St. Vincent Hospital. —Died Feb. 5, 2000
† Turcotte, Ulric H., *o.m.i.* (BO) Tewksbury, MA Immaculate Heart of Mary Infirmary. —Died Jan. 31, 2000
† Turk, John P. (Y) Warren, OH St. Joseph. —Died March 9, 2000
† Turnbull, Robert, *o.s.a.* (PH) Villanova, PA St. Thomas Monastery. —Died Feb. 21, 2000
† Turula, Juan E., *s.j.* (BAK) Hermiston, OR Our Lady of Angels. —Died March 15, 2000
† Twohy, Richard E., *s.j.* (SPK) Spokane, WA Gonzaga University. —Died March 16, 2000
† Uhrich, Hugh, *c.pp.s.* (CIN) Carthagena, OH St. Charles. —Died Aug. 17, 2000
† Underwood, O. Fred, *c.s.c.* (AUS) Austin, TX Congregation of Holy Cross - Southern Providence. —Died Feb. 25, 2000
† Urbine, Richard (FTW) (Retired). —Died Oct. 31, 2000
† Vail, John D. (WDC) Newburg, MD Holy Ghost. —Died Jan. 7, 2000
† Van Hoomissen, Bernard, *c.ss.r.* (STL) Liguori, MO St. Clement's Health Care Center. —Died Dec. 22, 1999
† Varnskuhler, Paschal, *o.f.m.* (CIN) Cincinnati, OH St. Francis Seraph Friary. —Died June 8, 2000
† Vela, Santiago (SJN) (Retired). —Died Aug. 25, 1999
† Ventre, Armand V. (PRO) North Providence, RI Our Lady of Fatima Hospital. —Died Dec. 27, 1999
† Ventresca, A. Andrew (HRT) (Retired). —Died Sept. 14, 2000
† Vidrine, Rev. Msgr. Curtis S. (LKC) (Retired). —Died Oct. 23, 2000
† Vier, Rev. Msgr. Henry J. (NY) (Retired). —Died Jan. 10, 2001
† Villar, Vincent, *s.d.b.* (MIA) Miami, FL St. Kieran. —Died Aug. 2, 2000
† Vogel, Edward A. (MIL) (Retired). —Died March 23, 2000
† Vogelgesang, John, *s.v.d.* (CHI) Techny, IL Divine Word Residence. —Died March 30, 2000
† Vollmer, Rev. Msgr. Roman F. (EVN) (Retired). —Died Jan. 22, 2000
† Voors, Rev. Msgr. William J. (FTW) (Retired). —Died March 9, 2000
† Wackenheim, Apollinaris, *o.f.m.* (SFD) Sherman, IL Our Lady of Angels Friary. —Died 2000
† Wagener, Clarence M., *s.j.* (OM) Omaha, NE Jesuit Community at Creighton University. —Died April 28, 2000
† Wagner, Cyril, *o.f.m.* (MEM) Memphis, TN St. Louis. —Died June 19, 2000

† Wahl, Raymond J. (ROC) (Retired). —Died Dec. 24, 1999
† Walker, James B. (SAV) (Retired). —Died Sept. 23, 2000
† Walker, John H. (CLV) Sheffield, OH St. Teresa of Avila. —Died June 11, 2000
† Walsh, David I., *m.m.* (NY) Maryknoll, NY Maryknoll Fathers & Brothers. —Died Oct. 13, 1999
† Walsh, Rev. Msgr. Gerard W. (NEW) (Retired). —Died Nov. 14, 2000
† Walsh, John J., *s.j.* (BO) Weston, MA Campion Center. —Died April 27, 2000
† Walsh, Patrick, *s.a.* (NY) New York, NY Franciscan Friars of the Atonement. —Died Feb. 8, 2000
† Wanstreet, Rev. Msgr. Jospeh W. (WH) (Retired). —Died Aug. 27, 1999
† Ward, Martin DePorres, *o.f.m.conv.* (FgM) Conventual Franciscan Foreign Mission. —Died June 1999
† Ward, William J. (STP) Minneapolis, MN Our Lady of Lourdes. —Died Nov. 17, 2000
† Warren, William (NY) Bronx, NY St. Margaret of Cortona. —Died April 18, 2000
† Watrin, Bernardo, *o.s.b.* (CGS) Humacao, PR San Antonio Abad Abbey of the Order of St. Benedict. —Died 2000
† Watson, Edwin, *o.s.b.* (KCK) Basehor, KS Holy Angels. —Died Oct. 22, 1999
† Weber, Charles A., *o.s.b.* (GBG) Latrobe, PA St. Vincent Archabbey. —Died April 14, 2000
† Weber, Rev. Msgr. John A. (BR) (Retired). —Died Feb. 22, 2000
† Weeks, William H., *s.j.* (BO) Weston, MA Campion Center. —Died April 9, 2000
† Welch, J. Paul, *s.s.* (BAL) Baltimore, MD St. Charles Villa. —Died Sept. 23, 2000
† Wells, Rev. Msgr. Thomas M. (WDC) Germantown, MD Mother Seton. —Died June 8, 2000
† Welsh, David B. (NY) (Retired). —Died Sept. 6, 2000
† Welton, Paul D. (STU) Shadyside, OH St. Mary. —Died July 27, 2000
† Werring, Edward J. (RVC) Rockville Centre, NY Our Lady of Mt. Carmel. —Died June 13, 2000
† White, Cajetan, *o.s.b.* (IND) St. Meinrad, IN St. Meinrad Seminary. —Died July 14, 2000
† White, Joseph L., *s.s.* (BAL) Baltimore, MD St. Charles Villa. —Died Sept. 27, 2000
† Wierzbinski, Zeno, *o.f.m.conv.* (SPR) Granby, MA St. Hyacinth College and Seminary. —Died March 9, 2000
† Wildgruber, Francis C. (BRK) Syosset, NY St. Edward the Confessor. —Died April 30, 2000
† Will, Rev. Msgr. Irvin Ross (SFD) (Retired). —Died March 20, 2000
† Williams, Rev. Msgr. Charles M. (NSH) Vicar Gen. Emeritus. —Died Nov. 21, 1999
† Wilson, Leland P. (LA) Pomona, CA Sacred Heart. —Died Aug. 25, 2000
† Wingert, LaVern (DM) Griswold, IA Wakonda Prayer House. —Died Dec. 17, 1999
† Winters, Arthur Cornelis, *s.v.d.* (BLX) Bay St. Louis, MS St. Augustine's. —Died July 28, 2000
† Winters, Daniel H., *s.m.* (CIN) Cincinnati, OH Marianist Community. —Died April 23, 2000
† Wisnieski, Rev. Msgr. Theodore (BAL) (Retired). —Died Feb. 1, 2000
† Wolf, Rev. Msgr. Michael O.J. (EVN) Evansville, IN Little Sisters of the Poor. —Died March 26, 2000
† Wood, Robert J. (NOR) Groton, CT Sacred Heart. —Died Jan. 6, 2000
† Wordeman, John J. (LEX) Ashland, KY Holy Family Church. —Died May 3, 2000
† Wozny, William J. (CHI) (Retired). —Died Jan. 31, 2000
† Wright, John C., *s.j.* (MRY) Salinas, CA Villa Sierra Retirement Home. —Died June 2, 2000
† Wunderlich, Daniel (LAN) DeWitt, MI St. Jude. —Died Dec. 15, 1999
† Wylie, Stephen (DOD) (Retired). —Died Jan. 6, 2000
† Yavorsky, James A. (CLV) Barberton, OH SS. Cyril and Methodius. —Died May 31, 2000
† Yuskauskas, Raymond B. (HRT) (Retired). —Died Feb. 12, 2000
† Zachar, Rev. Msgr. Albert L. (DUB) Blairstown, IA St. John. —Died Dec. 30, 1999
† Zarate, Raymond, *c.pp.s.* (LFT) Rensselaer, IN St. Joseph College. —Died May 7, 2000
† Zaratti, Elio (SB) San Diego, CA Nazareth House. —Died June 11, 2000
† Zimmer, William H. (GB) Manitowoc, WI Sacred Heart. —Died Nov. 25, 1999
† Zimmerman, Lee B., *c.m.* (NO) New Orleans, LA Vincentian Fathers. —Died April 17, 2000
† Ziter, Nelson B., *s.s.e.* (MOB) Selma, AL Edmundite Fathers. —Died July 7, 2000
† Zitko, Rev. Msgr. Aloysius (OAK) (Retired). —Died June 15, 2000
† Zusy, Dennis R., *o.p.* (DEN) Denver, CO St. Dominic Priory. —Died Aug. 6, 2000

	*Mobile AL	Birmingham AL	ALABAMA TOTAL	*Anchorage AK	Fairbanks AK	Juneau AK	2001 U.S. GRAND TOTAL
Cardinals	–	–	–	–	–	–	11
Archbishops	1	–	1	2	–	–	45
Bishops	–	1	1	–	1	1	373
Abbots	–	3	3	–	–	–	115
Diocesan Priests	112	67	179	18	7	7	30,655
Religious Priests	41	41	82	12	17	2	15,386
Total Priests in Diocese	153	108	261	30	24	9	46,075
Newly Ordained Priests	7	2	9	–	–	–	536
Total Permanent Deacons	37	48	85	18	40	5	13,348
Total Brothers	12	33	45	1	4	–	5,565
Total Sisters	181	143	324	42	16	7	79,462
Number of Parishes	76	57	133	19	41	10	19,544
Missions	14	18	32	8	7	14	3,075
Pastoral Centers	3	–	3	–	1	–	984
New Parishes	–	–	–	–	–	–	59
Catholic Hospitals	1	1	2	3	–	1	596
Patients Assisted Annually	215,039	167,189	382,228	403,479	–	50,105	78,996,656
Health Care Centers	2	1	3	2	–	–	544
Patients Assisted Annually	4,762	242,431	247,193	462	–	–	6,022,667
Specialized Homes	3	–	3	7	–	1	1,454
Total Assisted Annually	365	–	365	3,765	–	128	590,981
Residential Care of Children (Orphanages)	1	–	1	–	–	–	165
Total Assisted Annually	200	–	200	–	–	–	74,478
Day Care and Extended Day Care Centers	4	–	4	–	–	1	1,100
Total Assisted Annually	245	–	245	–	–	100	118,958
Special Centers for Social Services	9	9	18	5	1	1	2,290
Total Assisted Annually	62,432	59,539	121,971	22,091	2,020	7,829	20,953,944
Diocesan Seminaries	–	–	–	–	–	–	77
Students	–	–	–	–	–	–	3,400
Religious Seminaries	–	–	–	–	–	2	141
Students	–	5	5	–	–	–	1,517
Colleges and Universities	1	–	1	–	–	–	235
Total Students	1,005	–	1,005	–	–	–	705,059
High Schools, Diocesan and Parish	3	4	7	–	1	–	801
Total Students	1,525	1,491	3,016	–	216	–	386,476
High Schools, Private	–	1	1	1	–	–	795
Total Students	–	133	133	115	–	–	294,471
Elementary Schools, Diocesan and Parish	22	20	42	2	1	1	6,697
Total Students	5,973	5,224	11,197	348	268	100	1,940,698
Elementary Schools, Private	–	1	1	1	–	–	364
Total Students	–	147	147	79	–	–	117,776
Non–residential Schools for the Disabled	–	1	1	–	–	–	80
Total Students	–	126	126	–	–	–	18,120
Religious Education High School Students	791	1,965	2,756	938	607	237	782,102
Religious Education Elementary Students	3,585	6,402	9,987	3,145	1,746	599	3,617,181
Priests Teaching	1	–	1	–	–	–	1,934
Scholastics Teaching	–	–	–	–	–	–	41
Brothers Teaching	–	–	–	–	–	–	1,093
Sisters Teaching	13	21	34	2	2	–	8,201
Lay Teachers	411	503	914	48	43	9	156,470
Infant Baptisms	1,136	1,678	2,814	614	405	107	1,031,243
Adult Baptisms	239	237	476	71	43	20	83,234
Received into Full Communion	409	561	970	70	38	12	95,299
First Communions	1,230	1,488	2,718	614	433	116	909,779
Confirmations	1,137	1,239	2,376	571	299	216	651,443
Marriages	409	447	856	176	69	24	269,034
Deaths	628	408	1,036	151	126	24	479,034
Totals Catholics	66,325	90,590	156,915	32,364	17,132	5,453	63,683,030
Total Population	1,600,020	2,769,842	4,369,862	370,376	155,224	73,302	278,849,034
Catholic Population Percentage	4	3	4	9	11	7	23

Archdioceses = 36; Dioceses = 164; Apostolates = 3

2001 GENERAL SUMMARY

	ALASKA TOTAL	Samoa-Pago Pago AS	Phoenix AZ	Tucson AZ	ARIZONA TOTAL	Little Rock AR	2001 U.S. GRAND TOTAL
Cardinals	–	–	–	–	–	–	**11**
Archbishops	2	–	1	–	1	–	**45**
Bishops	2	1	2	1	3	2	**373**
Abbots	–	–	–	–	–	2	**115**
Diocesan Priests	32	9	132	115	247	80	**30,655**
Religious Priests	31	2	98	66	164	57	**15,386**
Total Priests in Diocese	63	11	230	181	411	137	**46,075**
Newly Ordained Priests	–	–	5	3	8	–	**536**
Total Permanent Deacons	63	17	207	121	328	76	**13,348**
Total Brothers	5	–	9	10	19	32	**5,565**
Total Sisters	65	11	233	250	483	298	**79,462**
Number of Parishes	70	11	87	71	158	90	**19,544**
Missions	29	–	27	30	57	43	**3,075**
Pastoral Centers	1	–	–	–	–	–	**984**
New Parishes	–	–	1	–	1	–	**59**
Catholic Hospitals	4	–	1	3	4	13	**596**
Patients Assisted Annually	453,584	–	415,019	363,129	778,148	1,171,195	**78,996,656**
Health Care Centers	2	–	1	1	2	6	**544**
Patients Assisted Annually	462	–	97,000	36,803	133,803	26,461	**6,022,667**
Specialized Homes	8	1	19	–	19	34	**1,454**
Total Assisted Annually	3,893	26	1,338	–	1,338	1,294	**590,981**
Residential Care of Children (Orphanages)	–	–	–	–	–	–	**165**
Total Assisted Annually	–	–	–	–	–	–	**74,478**
Day Care and Extended Day Care Centers	1	1	27	–	27	7	**1,100**
Total Assisted Annually	100	95	1,012	–	1,012	417	**118,958**
Special Centers for Social Services	7	1	10	1	11	1	**2,290**
Total Assisted Annually	31,940	400	2,128,679	400,000	2,528,679	227	**20,953,944**
Diocesan Seminaries	–	–	–	–	–	–	**77**
Students	–	–	–	–	–	–	**3,400**
Religious Seminaries	2	–	–	–	–	–	**141**
Students	–	–	–	–	–	–	**1,517**
Colleges and Universities	–	–	–	–	–	–	**235**
Total Students	–	–	–	–	–	–	**705,059**
High Schools, Diocesan and Parish	1	1	4	4	8	3	**801**
Total Students	216	229	2,868	1,664	4,532	984	**386,476**
High Schools, Private	1	–	1	2	3	2	**795**
Total Students	115	–	1,196	209	1,405	775	**294,471**
Elementary Schools, Diocesan and Parish	4	2	25	19	44	31	**6,697**
Total Students	716	426	8,087	5,244	13,331	6,432	**1,940,698**
Elementary Schools, Private	1	–	–	2	2	1	**364**
Total Students	79	–	–	241	241	75	**117,776**
Non-residential Schools for the Disabled	–	–	–	–	–	–	**80**
Total Students	–	–	–	–	–	–	**18,120**
Religious Education High School Students	1,782	180	6,727	3,588	10,315	2,657	**782,102**
Religious Education Elementary Students	5,490	1,700	34,185	19,805	53,990	5,737	**3,617,181**
Priests Teaching	–	–	13	4	17	6	**1,934**
Scholastics Teaching	–	–	3	–	3	–	**41**
Brothers Teaching	–	–	1	2	3	3	**1,093**
Sisters Teaching	4	5	43	47	90	45	**8,201**
Lay Teachers	100	69	619	400	1,019	597	**156,470**
Infant Baptisms	1,126	301	10,838	7,127	17,965	2,076	**1,031,243**
Adult Baptisms	134	107	563	366	929	319	**83,234**
Received into Full Communion	120	18	1,033	753	1,786	555	**95,299**
First Communions	1,163	210	8,143	6,244	14,387	1,855	**909,779**
Confirmations	1,086	180	4,118	3,021	7,139	1,515	**651,443**
Marriages	269	43	1,879	1,221	3,100	637	**269,034**
Deaths	301	28	3,609	2,535	6,144	945	**479,034**
Totals Catholics	54,949	12,250	462,780	304,060	766,840	93,480	**63,683,030**
Total Population	598,902	62,000	3,335,125	1,348,371	4,683,496	2,551,373	**278,849,034**
Catholic Population Percentage	9	20	14	23	16	4	**23**

*Indicates Archdioceses.

†Certain Dioceses traverse state lines.

	*Los Angeles CA	*San Francisco CA	Fresno CA	Monterey in California CA	Oakland CA	Orange in California CA	2001 U.S. GRAND TOTAL
Cardinals	1	–	–	–	–	–	**11**
Archbishops	–	2	–	–	–	–	**45**
Bishops	7	2	1	3	1	3	**373**
Abbots	1	–	–	1	–	2	**115**
Diocesan Priests	582	215	114	70	157	182	**30,655**
Religious Priests	580	185	37	21	110	89	**15,386**
Total Priests in Diocese	1,162	400	151	91	267	271	**46,075**
Newly Ordained Priests	14	3	1	–	2	5	**536**
Total Permanent Deacons	188	72	9	2	99	67	**13,348**
Total Brothers	173	45	4	34	25	12	**5,565**
Total Sisters	1,878	801	121	108	340	360	**79,462**
Number of Parishes	287	90	85	46	87	55	**19,544**
Missions	7	11	40	9	2	3	**3,075**
Pastoral Centers	1	5	–	–	15	4	**984**
New Parishes	–	–	–	–	–	–	**59**
Catholic Hospitals	19	3	3	1	1	3	**596**
Patients Assisted Annually	1,569,850	513,000	743,635	1,000	80,000	362,032	**78,996,656**
Health Care Centers	5	–	–	3	–	–	**544**
Patients Assisted Annually	15,422	–	–	13,500	–	–	**6,022,667**
Specialized Homes	18	13	3	3	8	6	**1,454**
Total Assisted Annually	5,215	3,000	335	396	26,000	625	**590,981**
Residential Care of Children (Orphanages)	2	16	–	–	–	–	**165**
Total Assisted Annually	604	15,000	–	–	–	–	**74,478**
Day Care and Extended Day Care Centers	82	5	–	–	5	2	**1,100**
Total Assisted Annually	5,264	363	–	–	1,500	171	**118,958**
Special Centers for Social Services	80	8	14	–	3	3	**2,290**
Total Assisted Annually	352,006	16,500	382,431	–	26,500	2,639,227	**20,953,944**
Diocesan Seminaries	2	1	–	–	–	–	**77**
Students	143	103	–	–	–	–	**3,400**
Religious Seminaries	12	–	1	1	–	–	**141**
Students	96	4	–	2	71	–	**1,517**
Colleges and Universities	5	3	–	–	3	–	**235**
Total Students	10,484	11,098	–	–	4,500	–	**705,059**
High Schools, Diocesan and Parish	29	4	2	2	3	3	**801**
Total Students	16,652	3,666	1,423	646	1,979	4,658	**386,476**
High Schools, Private	22	10	–	2	6	3	**795**
Total Students	13,658	4,538	–	977	4,518	1,088	**294,471**
Elementary Schools, Diocesan and Parish	218	60	23	11	51	38	**6,697**
Total Students	66,754	18,004	5,423	3,360	14,895	14,673	**1,940,698**
Elementary Schools, Private	9	5	–	3	–	2	**364**
Total Students	2,644	1,849	–	765	–	725	**117,776**
Non-residential Schools for the Disabled	–	–	–	–	–	–	**80**
Total Students	–	–	–	–	–	–	**18,120**
Religious Education High School Students	30,000	1,733	7,343	1,750	2,000	15,086	**782,102**
Religious Education Elementary Students	230,200	15,572	26,067	14,012	11,000	37,515	**3,617,181**
Priests Teaching	109	43	2	1	–	10	**1,934**
Scholastics Teaching	1	1	–	–	–	–	**41**
Brothers Teaching	28	18	–	4	18	10	**1,093**
Sisters Teaching	357	39	29	19	31	40	**8,201**
Lay Teachers	4,185	1,436	326	303	1,064	984	**156,470**
Infant Baptisms	82,869	7,831	15,789	6,620	9,964	17,291	**1,031,243**
Adult Baptisms	2,340	611	581	191	759	710	**83,234**
Received into Full Communion	4,703	527	458	385	1,217	632	**95,299**
First Communions	56,422	5,312	9,730	3,944	8,063	13,082	**909,779**
Confirmations	18,013	3,245	3,847	1,202	3,275	11,281	**651,443**
Marriages	12,406	1,869	2,360	1,068	1,722	3,303	**269,034**
Deaths	13,268	3,063	3,264	1,094	2,951	2,948	**479,034**
Totals Catholics	4,148,720	422,500	360,574	313,405	429,477	1,044,191	**63,683,030**
Total Population	11,055,000	1,760,000	2,324,650	949,300	2,348,723	2,760,948	**278,849,034**
Catholic Population Percentage	38	24	16	33	18	38	**23**

Archdioceses = 36; Dioceses = 164; Apostolates = 3

2001 GENERAL SUMMARY

	Sacramento CA	San Bernardino CA	San Diego CA	San Jose in California CA	Santa Rosa in California CA	Stockton CA	2001 U.S. GRAND TOTAL
Cardinals	–	–	–	–	–	–	**11**
Archbishops	–	–	–	–	–	–	**45**
Bishops	3	1	2	2	3	2	**373**
Abbots	2	–	2	–	–	–	**115**
Diocesan Priests	163	133	202	116	83	64	**30,655**
Religious Priests	72	111	102	169	17	12	**15,386**
Total Priests in Diocese	235	244	304	285	100	76	**46,075**
Newly Ordained Priests	5	3	–	2	1	2	**536**
Total Permanent Deacons	115	89	105	8	38	33	**13,348**
Total Brothers	31	19	20	68	38	4	**5,565**
Total Sisters	184	154	355	401	78	64	**79,462**
Number of Parishes	98	97	98	48	42	32	**19,544**
Missions	42	13	17	3	21	12	**3,075**
Pastoral Centers	–	–	2	1	13	2	**984**
New Parishes	–	–	–	–	–	–	**59**
Catholic Hospitals	6	2	1	2	5	3	**596**
Patients Assisted Annually	427,059	185,174	20,000	195,438	563,975	647,837	**78,996,656**
Health Care Centers	–	–	1	–	–	1	**544**
Patients Assisted Annually	–	–	17,000	–	–	2,447	**6,022,667**
Specialized Homes	2	3	16	2	1	2	**1,454**
Total Assisted Annually	141	3,100	79,157	143	53	322	**590,981**
Residential Care of Children (Orphanages)	1	–	3	–	1	–	**165**
Total Assisted Annually	21	–	428	–	107	–	**74,478**
Day Care and Extended Day Care Centers	3	–	1	1	2	–	**1,100**
Total Assisted Annually	1,289	–	594	215	80	–	**118,958**
Special Centers for Social Services	8	67	10	–	12	1	**2,290**
Total Assisted Annually	109,150	68,000	88,845	–	26,237	19,258	**20,953,944**
Diocesan Seminaries	–	1	1	–	–	–	**77**
Students	–	10	18	–	–	–	**3,400**
Religious Seminaries	1	–	–	–	–	–	**141**
Students	12	–	–	–	–	–	**1,517**
Colleges and Universities	–	–	1	1	–	–	**235**
Total Students	–	–	6,806	7,668	–	–	**705,059**
High Schools, Diocesan and Parish	4	2	3	2	3	2	**801**
Total Students	1,831	942	2,118	1,828	998	1,484	**386,476**
High Schools, Private	3	–	2	4	3	–	**795**
Total Students	2,450	–	1,374	4,136	1,015	–	**294,471**
Elementary Schools, Diocesan and Parish	47	34	43	29	12	12	**6,697**
Total Students	12,752	8,117	13,872	10,392	2,850	3,485	**1,940,698**
Elementary Schools, Private	–	1	1	–	1	–	**364**
Total Students	–	343	359	–	31	–	**117,776**
Non-residential Schools for the Disabled	–	–	1	–	–	–	**80**
Total Students	–	–	220	–	–	–	**18,120**
Religious Education High School Students	2,631	16,030	9,039	3,067	1,053	1,261	**782,102**
Religious Education Elementary Students	16,267	39,928	31,473	15,878	6,709	9,514	**3,617,181**
Priests Teaching	13	3	23	1	4	2	**1,934**
Scholastics Teaching	2	–	–	–	–	–	**41**
Brothers Teaching	7	–	1	1	–	2	**1,093**
Sisters Teaching	23	21	52	26	8	4	**8,201**
Lay Teachers	860	480	1,450	492	290	263	**156,470**
Infant Baptisms	9,326	12,691	11,488	9,977	3,065	4,945	**1,031,243**
Adult Baptisms	691	2,490	1,145	752	104	382	**83,234**
Received into Full Communion	848	2,040	982	493	189	–	**95,299**
First Communions	7,049	13,564	9,495	5,720	1,976	4,057	**909,779**
Confirmations	5,218	6,799	4,456	2,879	741	1,984	**651,443**
Marriages	1,704	2,540	2,422	1,741	869	876	**269,034**
Deaths	2,724	3,706	2,994	1,918	989	–	**479,034**
Totals Catholics	477,330	899,416	896,105	411,855	146,024	205,350	**63,683,030**
Total Population	3,020,340	3,212,000	3,056,800	1,647,419	751,312	1,102,053	**278,849,034**
Catholic Population Percentage	16	28	29	25	19	19	**23**

*Indicates Archdioceses.

†Certain Dioceses traverse state lines.

	CALIFORNIA TOTAL	The Caroline Islands CI	*Denver CO	Colorado Springs CO	Pueblo CO	COLORADO TOTAL	2001 U.S. GRAND TOTAL
Cardinals	1	–	1	–	–	1	**11**
Archbishops	2	–	2	–	–	2	**45**
Bishops	30	2	1	1	2	4	**373**
Abbots	8	–	–	–	2	2	**115**
Diocesan Priests	2,081	12	163	36	71	270	**30,655**
Religious Priests	1,505	14	128	22	30	180	**15,386**
Total Priests in Diocese	3,586	26	291	58	101	450	**46,075**
Newly Ordained Priests	38	–	6	–	2	8	**536**
Total Permanent Deacons	825	40	147	25	25	197	**13,348**
Total Brothers	473	3	22	2	7	31	**5,565**
Total Sisters	4,844	31	459	127	111	697	**79,462**
Number of Parishes	1,065	26	114	32	52	198	**19,544**
Missions	180	4	37	9	56	102	**3,075**
Pastoral Centers	43	–	–	–	–	–	**984**
New Parishes	–	5	–	1	–	1	**59**
Catholic Hospitals	49	–	3	2	5	10	**596**
Patients Assisted Annually	5,309,000	–	372,000	265,232	882,933	1,520,165	**78,996,656**
Health Care Centers	10	–	8	2	–	10	**544**
Patients Assisted Annually	48,369	–	4,500	109	–	4,609	**6,022,667**
Specialized Homes	77	–	13	2	2	17	**1,454**
Total Assisted Annually	118,487	–	2,021	103	1,400	3,524	**590,981**
Residential Care of Children (Orphanages)	23	–	1	–	–	1	**165**
Total Assisted Annually	16,160	–	60	–	–	60	**74,478**
Day Care and Extended Day Care Centers	101	–	24	–	–	24	**1,100**
Total Assisted Annually	9,476	–	1,305	–	–	1,305	**118,958**
Special Centers for Social Services	206	–	4	–	3	7	**2,290**
Total Assisted Annually	3,728,154	–	136,000	–	3,800	139,800	**20,953,944**
Diocesan Seminaries	5	–	1	–	–	1	**77**
Students	274	–	63	–	6	69	**3,400**
Religious Seminaries	15	–	–	–	–	–	**141**
Students	185	–	1	–	–	1	**1,517**
Colleges and Universities	13	–	1	–	–	1	**235**
Total Students	40,556	–	12,360	–	–	12,360	**705,059**
High Schools, Diocesan and Parish	59	3	2	1	1	4	**801**
Total Students	38,225	481	857	374	90	1,321	**386,476**
High Schools, Private	55	2	3	–	1	4	**795**
Total Students	33,754	317	2,161	–	65	2,226	**294,471**
Elementary Schools, Diocesan and Parish	578	4	36	5	4	45	**6,697**
Total Students	174,577	1,537	11,302	1,459	691	13,452	**1,940,698**
Elementary Schools, Private	22	1	3	–	1	4	**364**
Total Students	6,716	230	504	–	392	896	**117,776**
Non-residential Schools for the Disabled	1	–	–	–	–	–	**80**
Total Students	220	–	–	–	–	–	**18,120**
Religious Education High School Students	90,993	230	3,797	2,780	2,172	8,749	**782,102**
Religious Education Elementary Students	454,135	750	24,309	7,252	4,820	36,381	**3,617,181**
Priests Teaching	211	4	6	–	2	8	**1,934**
Scholastics Teaching	4	3	–	–	–	–	**41**
Brothers Teaching	89	2	7	–	4	11	**1,093**
Sisters Teaching	649	21	22	1	10	33	**8,201**
Lay Teachers	12,133	160	712	114	80	906	**156,470**
Infant Baptisms	191,856	1,667	9,994	1,543	1,868	13,405	**1,031,243**
Adult Baptisms	10,756	295	925	184	157	1,266	**83,234**
Received into Full Communion	12,474	65	1,670	207	327	2,204	**95,299**
First Communions	138,414	1,308	8,536	1,504	1,367	11,407	**909,779**
Confirmations	62,940	929	4,248	943	870	6,061	**651,443**
Marriages	32,880	566	2,295	347	360	3,002	**269,034**
Deaths	38,919	–	2,796	390	1,376	4,562	**479,034**
Totals Catholics	9,754,947	70,185	373,500	86,951	109,129	569,580	**63,683,030**
Total Population	33,988,545	135,831	2,719,200	749,355	601,000	4,069,555	**278,849,034**
Catholic Population Percentage	29	52	14	12	18	14	**23**

Archdioceses = 36; Dioceses = 164; Apostolates = 3

2001 GENERAL SUMMARY

	*Hartford CT	Bridgeport CT	† Norwich CT	CONNECTICUT TOTAL	† Wilmington DE	† *Washington DC	2001 U.S. GRAND TOTAL
Cardinals	–	–	–	–	–	2	**11**
Archbishops	1	–	–	1	–	–	**45**
Bishops	2	1	1	4	2	2	**373**
Abbots	–	–	–	–	–	3	**115**
Diocesan Priests	380	268	139	787	126	318	**30,655**
Religious Priests	138	67	64	269	85	647	**15,386**
Total Priests in Diocese	518	335	203	1,056	211	965	**46,075**
Newly Ordained Priests	2	4	3	9	3	6	**536**
Total Permanent Deacons	308	87	48	443	45	226	**13,348**
Total Brothers	48	–	23	71	25	137	**5,565**
Total Sisters	941	466	269	1,676	270	748	**79,462**
Number of Parishes	218	87	78	383	56	140	**19,544**
Missions	3	2	10	15	21	9	**3,075**
Pastoral Centers	–	–	23	23	8	1	**984**
New Parishes	1	–	–	1	–	–	**59**
Catholic Hospitals	3	1	–	4	1	3	**596**
Patients Assisted Annually	777,990	167,172	–	945,162	217,707	427,376	**78,996,656**
Health Care Centers	1	–	–	1	2	5	**544**
Patients Assisted Annually	60	–	–	60	1,050	99,181	**6,022,667**
Specialized Homes	3	5	3	11	7	21	**1,454**
Total Assisted Annually	386	868	242	1,496	779	1,666	**590,981**
Residential Care of Children (Orphanages)	1	–	–	1	4	1	**165**
Total Assisted Annually	69	–	–	69	99	203	**74,478**
Day Care and Extended Day Care Centers	3	18	–	21	2	5	**1,100**
Total Assisted Annually	170	340	–	510	252	647	**118,958**
Special Centers for Social Services	–	24	1	25	18	65	**2,290**
Total Assisted Annually	–	11,353	165	11,518	338,951	91,767	**20,953,944**
Diocesan Seminaries	1	1	–	2	–	1	**77**
Students	6	10	–	16	–	96	**3,400**
Religious Seminaries	1	–	1	2	–	30	**141**
Students	114	–	30	144	–	137	**1,517**
Colleges and Universities	2	3	–	5	–	3	**235**
Total Students	5,706	11,191	–	16,897	–	20,277	**705,059**
High Schools, Diocesan and Parish	4	5	3	12	5	1	**801**
Total Students	1,947	2,603	1,013	5,563	2,942	612	**386,476**
High Schools, Private	6	3	3	12	3	16	**795**
Total Students	3,106	1,160	1,147	5,413	1,712	8,388	**294,471**
Elementary Schools, Diocesan and Parish	67	33	22	122	25	79	**6,697**
Total Students	17,882	9,709	4,543	32,134	9,825	23,576	**1,940,698**
Elementary Schools, Private	3	2	–	5	4	9	**364**
Total Students	380	507	–	887	1,050	1,481	**117,776**
Non–residential Schools for the Disabled	–	1	–	1	1	1	**80**
Total Students	–	8	–	8	100	175	**18,120**
Religious Education High School Students	12,422	3,257	2,581	18,260	1,117	2,264	**782,102**
Religious Education Elementary Students	59,416	26,423	17,466	103,305	10,313	21,435	**3,617,181**
Priests Teaching	18	19	8	45	18	23	**1,934**
Scholastics Teaching	–	–	–	–	–	12	**41**
Brothers Teaching	43	1	1	45	5	13	**1,093**
Sisters Teaching	45	52	19	116	48	78	**8,201**
Lay Teachers	105	992	–	1,097	910	2,071	**156,470**
Infant Baptisms	10,194	6,149	3,237	19,580	3,028	7,084	**1,031,243**
Adult Baptisms	330	154	153	637	353	890	**83,234**
Received into Full Communion	363	118	291	772	315	734	**95,299**
First Communions	10,421	5,809	2,979	19,209	2,953	6,472	**909,779**
Confirmations	7,830	4,275	2,245	14,350	1,893	6,330	**651,443**
Marriages	2,856	1,885	908	5,649	881	2,261	**269,034**
Deaths	8,841	3,660	2,289	14,790	1,527	2,930	**479,034**
Totals Catholics	745,069	364,685	225,016	1,334,770	205,000	510,000	**63,683,030**
Total Population	1,805,278	841,334	633,722	3,280,334	1,137,988	2,436,407	**278,849,034**
Catholic Population Percentage	41	43	36	41	18	21	**23**

*Indicates Archdioceses.
†Certain Dioceses traverse state lines.

	*Miami FL	Orlando FL	Palm Beach FL	Pensacola-Tallahassee FL	St. Augustine FL	St. Petersburg FL	2001 U.S. GRAND TOTAL
Cardinals	–	–	–	–	–	–	11
Archbishops	2	–	–	–	–	–	45
Bishops	3	2	2	1	1	3	373
Abbots	–	–	–	–	–	–	115
Diocesan Priests	258	124	95	73	91	131	30,655
Religious Priests	109	42	38	9	28	134	15,386
Total Priests in Diocese	367	166	133	82	119	265	46,075
Newly Ordained Priests	3	2	6	2	1	3	536
Total Permanent Deacons	140	116	43	53	26	93	13,348
Total Brothers	54	15	5	5	2	50	5,565
Total Sisters	316	124	156	51	111	341	79,462
Number of Parishes	108	71	48	50	51	73	19,544
Missions	7	10	4	9	8	4	3,075
Pastoral Centers	1	–	–	–	–	1	984
New Parishes	–	1	1	–	–	–	59
Catholic Hospitals	2	–	1	1	1	2	596
Patients Assisted Annually	679,886	–	230,000	–	229,596	182,875	78,996,656
Health Care Centers	3	–	–	–	–	7	544
Patients Assisted Annually	19,175	–	–	–	–	35,000	6,022,667
Specialized Homes	14	2	2	3	2	11	1,454
Total Assisted Annually	20,235	325	256	210	43,548	2,099	590,981
Residential Care of Children (Orphanages)	2	–	–	–	–	5	165
Total Assisted Annually	417	–	–	–	–	11,000	74,478
Day Care and Extended Day Care Centers	7	10	–	–	–	14	1,100
Total Assisted Annually	3,862	900	–	–	–	1,500	118,958
Special Centers for Social Services	64	6	23	4	6	10	2,290
Total Assisted Annually	938,420	45,658	13,005	21,968	60,000	15,000	20,953,944
Diocesan Seminaries	1	–	1	–	–	–	77
Students	58	–	86	–	–	–	3,400
Religious Seminaries	–	–	–	–	–	–	141
Students	5	–	–	–	–	–	1,517
Colleges and Universities	2	–	–	–	–	1	235
Total Students	11,639	–	–	–	–	2,708	705,059
High Schools, Diocesan and Parish	9	5	3	1	2	3	801
Total Students	8,518	2,466	2,219	612	2,012	2,110	386,476
High Schools, Private	4	–	–	–	–	2	795
Total Students	2,954	–	–	–	–	960	294,471
Elementary Schools, Diocesan and Parish	55	31	14	8	24	29	6,697
Total Students	24,385	12,753	5,568	2,457	7,978	11,200	1,940,698
Elementary Schools, Private	2	–	2	–	–	4	364
Total Students	888	–	581	–	–	1,190	117,776
Non-residential Schools for the Disabled	2	1	–	1	1	2	80
Total Students	11,648	60	–	16	115	145	18,120
Religious Education High School Students	5,090	4,342	3,088	1,266	8,282	2,400	782,102
Religious Education Elementary Students	29,957	21,342	13,761	5,346	1,501	19,000	3,617,181
Priests Teaching	18	1	6	–	2	11	1,934
Scholastics Teaching	–	–	–	–	–	2	41
Brothers Teaching	25	–	–	–	–	5	1,093
Sisters Teaching	52	35	18	9	19	60	8,201
Lay Teachers	2,350	855	460	202	540	841	156,470
Infant Baptisms	17,544	5,878	4,624	1,258	2,242	4,869	1,031,243
Adult Baptisms	1,228	537	342	–	415	741	83,234
Received into Full Communion	1,282	737	384	1,730	660	623	95,299
First Communions	14,581	5,474	3,760	1,251	2,329	5,329	909,779
Confirmations	8,733	4,365	2,307	990	1,967	3,684	651,443
Marriages	3,319	1,596	1,137	388	770	1,646	269,034
Deaths	4,542	3,583	2,691	593	1,035	4,258	479,034
Totals Catholics	816,207	340,448	244,771	67,425	142,886	371,714	63,683,030
Total Population	3,791,043	3,177,046	1,482,026	1,274,000	1,598,247	2,478,095	278,849,034
Catholic Population Percentage	22	11	17	5	9	15	23

Archdioceses = 36; Dioceses = 164; Apostolates = 3

2001 GENERAL SUMMARY

	Venice FL	FLORIDA TOTAL	*Atlanta GA	Savannah GA	GEORGIA TOTAL	*Agana GUAM	2001 U.S. GRAND TOTAL
Cardinals	–	–	–	–	–	–	**11**
Archbishops	–	2	1	–	1	1	**45**
Bishops	1	13	–	2	2	–	**373**
Abbots	–	–	3	–	3	–	**115**
Diocesan Priests	96	868	146	63	209	33	**30,655**
Religious Priests	73	433	70	29	99	16	**15,386**
Total Priests in Diocese	169	1,301	216	92	308	49	**46,075**
Newly Ordained Priests	2	19	12	1	13	–	**536**
Total Permanent Deacons	78	549	137	31	168	7	**13,348**
Total Brothers	24	155	1	15	16	1	**5,565**
Total Sisters	120	1,219	119	129	248	125	**79,462**
Number of Parishes	51	452	77	51	128	24	**19,544**
Missions	5	47	21	27	48	–	**3,075**
Pastoral Centers	8	10	1	–	1	–	**984**
New Parishes	1	3	2	1	3	–	**59**
Catholic Hospitals	2	9	2	3	5	–	**596**
Patients Assisted Annually	441,499	1,763,856	244,723	300,000	544,723	–	**78,996,656**
Health Care Centers	8	18	2	–	2	–	**544**
Patients Assisted Annually	44,455	98,630	20,176	–	20,176	–	**6,022,667**
Specialized Homes	11	45	6	1	7	12	**1,454**
Total Assisted Annually	38,900	105,573	381	20	401	658	**590,981**
Residential Care of Children (Orphanages)	–	7	–	1	1	–	**165**
Total Assisted Annually	–	11,417	–	51	51	–	**74,478**
Day Care and Extended Day Care Centers	2	33	–	–	–	3	**1,100**
Total Assisted Annually	73	6,335	–	–	–	136	**118,958**
Special Centers for Social Services	17	130	33	20	53	1	**2,290**
Total Assisted Annually	48,000	1,142,051	40,000	117,875	157,875	8,496	**20,953,944**
Diocesan Seminaries	–	2	–	–	–	1	**77**
Students	–	144	–	–	–	14	**3,400**
Religious Seminaries	–	–	–	–	–	1	**141**
Students	–	5	–	–	–	5	**1,517**
Colleges and Universities	–	3	–	–	–	–	**235**
Total Students	–	14,347	–	–	–	–	**705,059**
High Schools, Diocesan and Parish	3	26	3	2	5	2	**801**
Total Students	1,652	19,589	1,479	495	1,974	788	**386,476**
High Schools, Private	–	6	1	3	4	244	**795**
Total Students	–	3,914	1,028	1,385	2,413	1,032	**294,471**
Elementary Schools, Diocesan and Parish	9	170	15	16	31	7	**6,697**
Total Students	3,664	68,005	5,309	4,608	9,917	2,114	**1,940,698**
Elementary Schools, Private	–	8	2	–	2	–	**364**
Total Students	–	2,659	860	–	860	–	**117,776**
Non–residential Schools for the Disabled	–	7	–	–	–	–	**80**
Total Students	–	11,984	–	–	–	–	**18,120**
Religious Education High School Students	621	25,089	5,942	1,142	7,084	–	**782,102**
Religious Education Elementary Students	9,979	100,886	27,216	5,223	32,439	–	**3,617,181**
Priests Teaching	5	43	12	–	12	1	**1,934**
Scholastics Teaching	–	2	–	–	–	–	**41**
Brothers Teaching	2	32	2	3	5	–	**1,093**
Sisters Teaching	13	206	2	15	17	41	**8,201**
Lay Teachers	318	5,566	412	254	666	220	**156,470**
Infant Baptisms	4,597	41,012	7,865	1,742	9,607	2,272	**1,031,243**
Adult Baptisms	215	3,478	617	251	868	14	**83,234**
Received into Full Communion	343	5,759	1,192	703	1,895	42	**95,299**
First Communions	2,756	35,480	5,211	1,456	6,667	1,349	**909,779**
Confirmations	2,311	24,357	3,701	1,251	4,952	873	**651,443**
Marriages	801	9,657	1,932	503	2,435	264	**269,034**
Deaths	2,512	19,214	975	656	1,631	462	**479,034**
Totals Catholics	181,941	2,165,392	250,999	76,048	327,047	150,563	**63,683,030**
Total Population	1,453,244	15,253,701	5,241,325	3,385,646	8,626,971	167,292	**278,849,034**
Catholic Population Percentage	13	14	5	2	4	90	**23**

*Indicates Archdioceses.

†Certain Dioceses traverse state lines.

	Honolulu HI	Boise ID	*Chicago IL	Belleville IL	Joliet in Illinois IL	Peoria IL	2001 U.S. GRAND TOTAL
Cardinals	–	–	1	–	–	–	11
Archbishops	–	–	–	–	–	–	45
Bishops	2	1	10	2	2	1	373
Abbots	–	–	1	–	2	2	115
Diocesan Priests	70	86	897	135	194	247	30,655
Religious Priests	72	13	817	34	101	49	15,386
Total Priests in Diocese	142	99	1,714	169	295	296	46,075
Newly Ordained Priests	–	3	24	–	5	3	536
Total Permanent Deacons	32	34	618	32	152	81	13,348
Total Brothers	54	4	361	13	92	21	5,565
Total Sisters	155	92	3,340	241	669	321	79,462
Number of Parishes	66	57	378	124	120	165	19,544
Missions	24	32	12	1	12	39	3,075
Pastoral Centers	–	24	7	–	–	5	984
New Parishes	–	–	–	–	–	–	59
Catholic Hospitals	2	5	22	8	3	8	596
Patients Assisted Annually	365,373	613,998	2,965,798	705,498	669,656	1,409,004	78,996,656
Health Care Centers	15	–	1	–	–	–	544
Patients Assisted Annually	35,136	–	5,000	–	–	–	6,022,667
Specialized Homes	2	–	47	5	13	6	1,454
Total Assisted Annually	120	–	5,814	594	8,659	500	590,981
Residential Care of Children (Orphanages)	–	–	3	–	–	1	165
Total Assisted Annually	–	–	3,682	–	–	55	74,478
Day Care and Extended Day Care Centers	1	4	34	6	4	2	1,100
Total Assisted Annually	105	143	3,726	395	991	349	118,958
Special Centers for Social Services	13	15	99	3	5	1	2,290
Total Assisted Annually	12,016	68,015	369,116	41,074	25,011	16,921	20,953,944
Diocesan Seminaries	–	–	3	–	–	–	77
Students	–	–	457	–	–	–	3,400
Religious Seminaries	1	–	1	–	–	–	141
Students	1	–	155	–	–	–	1,517
Colleges and Universities	1	–	6	–	3	1	235
Total Students	2,812	–	43,032	–	11,375	150	705,059
High Schools, Diocesan and Parish	3	1	7	3	4	6	801
Total Students	1,173	672	2,194	1,729	2,556	2,588	386,476
High Schools, Private	5	–	37	–	4	1	795
Total Students	2,406	–	29,055	–	3,279	331	294,471
Elementary Schools, Diocesan and Parish	32	13	264	37	56	47	6,697
Total Students	7,386	2,478	95,604	6,978	19,549	12,440	1,940,698
Elementary Schools, Private	3	–	2	–	–	–	364
Total Students	406	–	529	–	–	–	117,776
Non-residential Schools for the Disabled	–	–	6	–	–	–	80
Total Students	–	–	516	–	–	–	18,120
Religious Education High School Students	2,223	3,164	10,655	1,290	4,723	2,744	782,102
Religious Education Elementary Students	8,034	7,465	105,300	7,166	54,338	10,616	3,617,181
Priests Teaching	59	–	58	–	20	16	1,934
Scholastics Teaching	–	–	–	–	–	–	41
Brothers Teaching	8	–	43	–	24	2	1,093
Sisters Teaching	83	1	281	9	43	40	8,201
Lay Teachers	817	162	5,782	403	1,659	1,033	156,470
Infant Baptisms	2,502	2,652	41,083	1,540	10,284	2,729	1,031,243
Adult Baptisms	302	402	2,008	275	370	455	83,234
Received into Full Communion	226	241	1,756	283	999	517	95,299
First Communions	1,970	2,184	30,237	1,685	10,218	2,515	909,779
Confirmations	1,052	1,288	21,516	2,025	7,571	3,041	651,443
Marriages	754	602	10,367	676	2,261	923	269,034
Deaths	1,447	727	18,252	1,422	3,627	2,011	479,034
Totals Catholics	124,987	130,500	2,394,000	107,425	591,706	221,932	63,683,030
Total Population	1,185,497	1,310,000	5,803,000	849,925	1,609,740	1,440,518	278,849,034
Catholic Population Percentage	11	10	41	13	37	15	23

Archdioceses = 36; Dioceses = 164; Apostolates = 3

2001 GENERAL SUMMARY

	Rockford IL	Springfield in Illinois IL	ILLINOIS TOTAL	*Indianapolis IN	Evansville IN	Fort Wayne - South Bend IN	2001 U.S. GRAND TOTAL
Cardinals	–	–	1	–	–	–	**11**
Archbishops	–	–	–	1	–	–	**45**
Bishops	3	2	20	–	1	4	**373**
Abbots	3	–	8	3	–	–	**115**
Diocesan Priests	157	143	1,773	161	100	95	**30,655**
Religious Priests	58	62	1,121	115	8	170	**15,386**
Total Priests in Diocese	215	205	2,894	276	108	265	**46,075**
Newly Ordained Priests	8	–	40	2	1	4	**536**
Total Permanent Deacons	112	4	999	–	21	22	**13,348**
Total Brothers	16	18	521	48	2	100	**5,565**
Total Sisters	260	690	5,521	758	308	656	**79,462**
Number of Parishes	105	164	1,056	139	70	87	**19,544**
Missions	–	–	64	13	–	–	**3,075**
Pastoral Centers	1	–	13	–	6	2	**984**
New Parishes	–	–	–	1	–	–	**59**
Catholic Hospitals	3	8	52	2	2	5	**596**
Patients Assisted Annually	499,606	895,689	7,145,251	1,259,463	390,776	375,430	**78,996,656**
Health Care Centers	21	–	22	–	1	1	**544**
Patients Assisted Annually	43,752	–	48,752	–	60	20,000	**6,022,667**
Specialized Homes	9	4	84	8	3	5	**1,454**
Total Assisted Annually	1,041	467	17,075	1,621	242	71	**590,981**
Residential Care of Children (Orphanages)	–	1	5	–	–	–	**165**
Total Assisted Annually	–	140	3,877	–	–	–	**74,478**
Day Care and Extended Day Care Centers	1	1	48	3	1	2	**1,100**
Total Assisted Annually	56	100	5,617	110	285	648	**118,958**
Special Centers for Social Services	10	–	118	7	9	4	**2,290**
Total Assisted Annually	303,832	–	755,954	125,311	130,500	18,836	**20,953,944**
Diocesan Seminaries	–	–	3	–	–	–	**77**
Students	–	–	457	–	–	–	**3,400**
Religious Seminaries	–	1	2	1	–	1	**141**
Students	–	7	162	6	–	37	**1,517**
Colleges and Universities	–	2	12	2	–	5	**235**
Total Students	–	1,484	56,041	3,226	–	14,811	**705,059**
High Schools, Diocesan and Parish	6	2	28	6	4	4	**801**
Total Students	3,335	573	12,975	3,236	1,643	3,020	**386,476**
High Schools, Private	2	5	49	3	–	–	**795**
Total Students	895	2,158	35,718	2,025	–	–	**294,471**
Elementary Schools, Diocesan and Parish	41	54	499	62	24	41	**6,697**
Total Students	12,181	11,071	157,823	18,125	6,044	11,164	**1,940,698**
Elementary Schools, Private	–	–	2	–	–	–	**364**
Total Students	–	–	529	–	–	–	**117,776**
Non-residential Schools for the Disabled	–	–	6	–	1	–	**80**
Total Students	–	–	516	–	22	–	**18,120**
Religious Education High School Students	5,329	2,573	27,314	2,994	2,036	1,860	**782,102**
Religious Education Elementary Students	26,958	8,673	213,051	13,197	7,615	10,319	**3,617,181**
Priests Teaching	12	1	107	4	2	2	**1,934**
Scholastics Teaching	–	–	–	–	–	–	**41**
Brothers Teaching	2	–	71	7	2	1	**1,093**
Sisters Teaching	22	22	417	42	14	21	**8,201**
Lay Teachers	838	668	10,383	1,345	468	761	**156,470**
Infant Baptisms	6,105	2,384	64,125	4,196	1,407	2,799	**1,031,243**
Adult Baptisms	254	353	3,715	844	173	458	**83,234**
Received into Full Communion	428	505	4,488	920	205	480	**95,299**
First Communions	6,347	2,679	53,681	3,967	1,456	3,132	**909,779**
Confirmations	4,352	2,805	41,310	3,093	1,628	3,069	**651,443**
Marriages	1,435	1,018	16,680	1,378	569	984	**269,034**
Deaths	2,153	1,862	29,327	2,148	927	1,466	**479,034**
Totals Catholics	363,430	154,931	3,833,424	227,501	90,812	166,108	**63,683,030**
Total Population	1,298,208	1,106,124	12,107,515	2,359,104	486,500	1,170,337	**278,849,034**
Catholic Population Percentage	28	14	32	10	19	14	**23**

*Indicates Archdioceses.

†Certain Dioceses traverse state lines.

2001 GENERAL SUMMARY

	Gary IN	Lafayette in Indiana IN	INDIANA TOTAL	*Dubuque IA	Davenport IA	Des Moines IA	2001 U.S. GRAND TOTAL
Cardinals	–	–	–	–	–	–	**11**
Archbishops	–	–	1	2	–	–	**45**
Bishops	1	1	7	–	1	1	**373**
Abbots	–	–	3	3	–	–	**115**
Diocesan Priests	123	122	601	245	146	107	**30,655**
Religious Priests	47	19	359	33	3	11	**15,386**
Total Priests in Diocese	170	141	960	278	149	118	**46,075**
Newly Ordained Priests	1	–	8	5	2	1	**536**
Total Permanent Deacons	39	5	87	59	42	65	**13,348**
Total Brothers	15	2	167	25	1	7	**5,565**
Total Sisters	117	88	1,927	889	228	107	**79,462**
Number of Parishes	75	63	434	211	85	85	**19,544**
Missions	4	–	17	2	1	1	**3,075**
Pastoral Centers	6	–	14	1	1	–	**984**
New Parishes	–	–	1	1	–	–	**59**
Catholic Hospitals	6	7	22	7	2	3	**596**
Patients Assisted Annually	830,567	698,740	3,554,976	1,195,315	794,135	1,073,775	**78,996,656**
Health Care Centers	–	–	2	4	–	–	**544**
Patients Assisted Annually	–	–	20,060	306	–	–	**6,022,667**
Specialized Homes	4	3	23	5	3	2	**1,454**
Total Assisted Annually	1,149	334	3,417	446	441	2,127	**590,981**
Residential Care of Children (Orphanages)	3	–	3	–	–	–	**165**
Total Assisted Annually	93	–	93	–	–	–	**74,478**
Day Care and Extended Day Care Centers	2	–	8	1	–	–	**1,100**
Total Assisted Annually	500	–	1,543	42	–	–	**118,958**
Special Centers for Social Services	7	–	27	–	–	4	**2,290**
Total Assisted Annually	10,000	–	284,647	–	–	65,724	**20,953,944**
Diocesan Seminaries	–	–	–	1	1	–	**77**
Students	–	–	–	1	4	–	**3,400**
Religious Seminaries	1	–	3	1	–	–	**141**
Students	4	–	47	80	–	–	**1,517**
Colleges and Universities	1	3	11	3	2	1	**235**
Total Students	978	9,338	28,353	4,337	3,629	432	**705,059**
High Schools, Diocesan and Parish	3	1	18	7	7	2	**801**
Total Students	1,705	339	9,943	3,133	1,206	1,456	**386,476**
High Schools, Private	–	–	3	–	–	–	**795**
Total Students	–	–	2,025	–	–	–	**294,471**
Elementary Schools, Diocesan and Parish	27	24	178	53	21	17	**6,697**
Total Students	7,350	4,760	47,443	13,732	4,604	4,839	**1,940,698**
Elementary Schools, Private	1	–	1	–	–	–	**364**
Total Students	112	–	112	–	–	–	**117,776**
Non-residential Schools for the Disabled	–	–	1	–	–	–	**80**
Total Students	–	–	22	–	–	–	**18,120**
Religious Education High School Students	705	3,505	11,100	6,745	3,628	2,536	**782,102**
Religious Education Elementary Students	11,950	10,321	53,402	16,836	11,137	9,970	**3,617,181**
Priests Teaching	3	–	11	5	6	3	**1,934**
Scholastics Teaching	–	–	–	–	–	–	**41**
Brothers Teaching	4	–	14	–	–	–	**1,093**
Sisters Teaching	19	–	96	31	9	10	**8,201**
Lay Teachers	489	266	3,329	1,027	525	383	**156,470**
Infant Baptisms	2,473	1,887	12,762	3,392	1,782	2,052	**1,031,243**
Adult Baptisms	200	361	2,036	138	269	234	**83,234**
Received into Full Communion	285	381	2,271	510	206	351	**95,299**
First Communions	2,504	2,198	13,257	3,708	2,177	1,925	**909,779**
Confirmations	2,082	1,967	11,839	3,355	2,028	1,836	**651,443**
Marriages	814	588	4,333	1,424	706	609	**269,034**
Deaths	1,985	845	7,371	2,189	1,172	764	**479,034**
Totals Catholics	186,800	96,791	768,012	219,195	113,535	96,492	**63,683,030**
Total Population	761,912	1,144,222	5,922,075	923,000	730,544	671,091	**278,849,034**
Catholic Population Percentage	25	8	13	24	16	14	**23**

Archdioceses = 36; Dioceses = 164; Apostolates = 3

2001 GENERAL SUMMARY

	Sioux City IA	IOWA TOTAL	*Kansas City in Kansas KS	Dodge City KS	Salina KS	Wichita KS	2001 U.S. GRAND TOTAL
Cardinals	–	–	–	–	–	–	11
Archbishops	–	2	2	–	–	–	45
Bishops	2	4	1	3	2	1	373
Abbots	–	3	3	–	–	–	115
Diocesan Priests	168	666	100	42	67	128	30,655
Religious Priests	–	47	66	1	11	8	15,386
Total Priests in Diocese	168	713	166	43	78	136	46,075
Newly Ordained Priests	1	9	2	–	2	4	536
Total Permanent Deacons	38	204	–	3	–	2	13,348
Total Brothers	–	33	16	–	1	–	5,565
Total Sisters	96	1,320	712	108	222	332	79,462
Number of Parishes	124	505	119	50	92	92	19,544
Missions	–	4	–	–	–	–	3,075
Pastoral Centers	1	3	–	–	–	–	984
New Parishes	–	1	–	–	–	–	59
Catholic Hospitals	3	15	4	3	–	6	596
Patients Assisted Annually	405,780	3,469,005	491,040	97,618	–	421,013	78,996,656
Health Care Centers	–	4	4	–	–	2	544
Patients Assisted Annually	–	306	21,168	–	–	32,011	6,022,667
Specialized Homes	4	14	4	–	4	3	1,454
Total Assisted Annually	313	3,327	440	–	297	447	590,981
Residential Care of Children (Orphanages)	–	–	–	–	–	–	165
Total Assisted Annually	–	–	–	–	–	–	74,478
Day Care and Extended Day Care Centers	–	1	–	–	–	1	1,100
Total Assisted Annually	–	42	–	–	–	183	118,958
Special Centers for Social Services	4	8	10	4	–	1	2,290
Total Assisted Annually	5,874	71,598	15,500	257,775	–	19,851	20,953,944
Diocesan Seminaries	–	2	–	–	–	–	77
Students	–	5	–	–	–	–	3,400
Religious Seminaries	–	1	–	2	–	–	141
Students	–	80	2	–	–	–	1,517
Colleges and Universities	1	7	3	–	–	1	235
Total Students	937	9,335	3,489	–	–	1,967	705,059
High Schools, Diocesan and Parish	8	24	5	–	4	4	801
Total Students	2,413	8,208	3,320	–	468	2,143	386,476
High Schools, Private	–	–	2	–	1	–	795
Total Students	–	–	277	–	441	–	294,471
Elementary Schools, Diocesan and Parish	26	117	43	10	12	32	6,697
Total Students	5,369	28,544	11,684	1,114	2,023	8,150	1,940,698
Elementary Schools, Private	–	–	1	–	–	–	364
Total Students	–	–	30	–	–	–	117,776
Non–residential Schools for the Disabled	–	–	–	–	–	–	80
Total Students	–	–	–	–	–	–	18,120
Religious Education High School Students	4,233	17,142	3,844	2,540	2,090	3,141	782,102
Religious Education Elementary Students	7,871	45,814	14,772	3,189	5,316	7,095	3,617,181
Priests Teaching	7	21	–	–	3	3	1,934
Scholastics Teaching	–	–	–	–	–	–	41
Brothers Teaching	–	–	–	–	–	–	1,093
Sisters Teaching	19	69	23	9	4	21	8,201
Lay Teachers	546	2,481	990	76	202	514	156,470
Infant Baptisms	1,868	9,094	4,256	968	999	2,533	1,031,243
Adult Baptisms	107	748	457	364	90	348	83,234
Received into Full Communion	272	1,339	805	98	185	486	95,299
First Communions	1,670	9,480	4,051	740	822	2,513	909,779
Confirmations	1,564	8,783	3,353	440	896	1,840	651,443
Marriages	692	3,431	1,197	253	392	849	269,034
Deaths	1,201	5,326	1,362	361	603	902	479,034
Totals Catholics	97,413	526,635	197,190	42,566	50,113	114,539	63,683,030
Total Population	468,549	2,793,184	1,174,500	212,332	318,359	947,499	278,849,034
Catholic Population Percentage	21	19	17	20	16	12	23

*Indicates Archdioceses.

†Certain Dioceses traverse state lines.

2001 GENERAL SUMMARY

	KANSAS TOTAL	*Louisville KY	Covington KY	Lexington KY	Owensboro KY	KENTUCKY TOTAL	2001 U.S. GRAND TOTAL
Cardinals	–	–	–	–	–	–	11
Archbishops	2	1	–	–	–	1	45
Bishops	7	1	2	1	1	5	373
Abbots	3	2	–	–	–	2	115
Diocesan Priests	337	186	111	48	83	428	30,655
Religious Priests	86	65	2	19	20	106	15,386
Total Priests in Diocese	423	251	113	67	103	534	46,075
Newly Ordained Priests	8	6	1	1	6	14	536
Total Permanent Deacons	5	107	25	37	–	169	13,348
Total Brothers	17	83	6	4	4	97	5,565
Total Sisters	1,374	987	418	152	226	1,783	79,462
Number of Parishes	353	112	47	60	79	298	19,544
Missions	–	12	10	5	–	27	3,075
Pastoral Centers	–	3	–	–	2	5	984
New Parishes	–	–	–	–	–	–	59
Catholic Hospitals	13	2	3	6	1	12	596
Patients Assisted Annually	1,009,671	185,428	369,025	929,666	300,000	1,784,119	78,996,656
Health Care Centers	6	1	–	4	2	7	544
Patients Assisted Annually	53,179	2,400	–	71,436	8,000	81,836	6,022,667
Specialized Homes	11	6	3	1	2	12	1,454
Total Assisted Annually	1,184	877	734	82	170	1,863	590,981
Residential Care of Children (Orphanages)	–	2	2	–	–	4	165
Total Assisted Annually	–	100	112	–	–	212	74,478
Day Care and Extended Day Care Centers	1	1	1	1	3	6	1,100
Total Assisted Annually	183	150	113	80	209	552	118,958
Special Centers for Social Services	15	8	4	1	2	15	2,290
Total Assisted Annually	293,126	30,000	70,833	8,200	16,000	125,033	20,953,944
Diocesan Seminaries	–	–	–	–	–	–	77
Students	–	–	–	–	–	–	3,400
Religious Seminaries	2	–	–	–	–	–	141
Students	2	–	–	–	–	–	1,517
Colleges and Universities	4	3	1	–	1	5	235
Total Students	5,456	4,290	1,325	–	750	6,365	705,059
High Schools, Diocesan and Parish	13	4	7	1	3	15	801
Total Students	5,931	2,153	2,555	874	1,091	6,673	386,476
High Schools, Private	3	6	2	2	–	10	795
Total Students	718	4,220	718	80	–	5,018	294,471
Elementary Schools, Diocesan and Parish	97	57	28	14	19	118	6,697
Total Students	22,971	17,764	8,596	3,018	4,122	33,500	1,940,698
Elementary Schools, Private	1	2	2	1	–	5	364
Total Students	30	498	573	206	–	1,277	117,776
Non–residential Schools for the Disabled	–	1	1	–	–	2	80
Total Students	–	48	28	–	–	76	18,120
Religious Education High School Students	11,615	1,117	356	740	1,299	3,512	782,102
Religious Education Elementary Students	30,372	6,391	4,375	2,781	2,941	16,488	3,617,181
Priests Teaching	6	9	–	2	6	17	1,934
Scholastics Teaching	–	–	–	–	–	–	41
Brothers Teaching	–	8	1	–	–	9	1,093
Sisters Teaching	57	29	53	16	13	111	8,201
Lay Teachers	1,782	1,745	667	246	401	3,059	156,470
Infant Baptisms	8,756	3,107	1,306	780	1,008	6,201	1,031,243
Adult Baptisms	1,259	483	445	119	176	1,223	83,234
Received into Full Communion	1,574	555	169	232	263	1,219	95,299
First Communions	8,126	3,065	1,791	806	1,016	6,678	909,779
Confirmations	6,529	2,695	1,492	803	1,058	6,048	651,443
Marriages	2,691	1,132	552	267	427	2,378	269,034
Deaths	3,228	1,919	905	248	559	3,631	479,034
Totals Catholics	404,408	196,910	86,031	42,345	51,152	376,438	63,683,030
Total Population	2,652,690	1,215,069	452,484	1,421,558	778,235	3,867,346	278,849,034
Catholic Population Percentage	15	16	19	3	7	10	23

Archdioceses = 36; Dioceses = 164; Apostolates = 3

2001 GENERAL SUMMARY

	*New Orleans LA	Alexandria LA	Baton Rouge LA	Houma-Thibodaux LA	Lafayette LA	Lake Charles LA	2001 U.S. GRAND TOTAL
Cardinals	–	–	–	–	–	–	**11**
Archbishops	2	–	–	–	–	–	**45**
Bishops	3	1	1	1	2	1	**373**
Abbots	1	–	–	–	–	–	**115**
Diocesan Priests	225	63	79	78	141	46	**30,655**
Religious Priests	190	16	42	5	57	12	**15,386**
Total Priests in Diocese	415	79	121	83	198	58	**46,075**
Newly Ordained Priests	2	–	3	1	2	–	**536**
Total Permanent Deacons	192	6	26	29	76	24	**13,348**
Total Brothers	123	3	12	7	27	1	**5,565**
Total Sisters	834	49	114	32	148	25	**79,462**
Number of Parishes	146	48	70	39	121	36	**19,544**
Missions	8	24	–	5	32	25	**3,075**
Pastoral Centers	1	1	–	–	–	–	**984**
New Parishes	–	–	–	–	–	–	**59**
Catholic Hospitals	–	2	2	–	1	1	**596**
Patients Assisted Annually	–	108,490	212,012	–	81,000	117,653	**78,996,656**
Health Care Centers	4	–	–	–	1	–	**544**
Patients Assisted Annually	120,037	–	–	–	16,000	–	**6,022,667**
Specialized Homes	28	2	9	3	12	1	**1,454**
Total Assisted Annually	5,507	164	855	65	3,500	62	**590,981**
Residential Care of Children (Orphanages)	2	–	–	–	–	–	**165**
Total Assisted Annually	116	–	–	–	–	–	**74,478**
Day Care and Extended Day Care Centers	17	–	–	1	–	1	**1,100**
Total Assisted Annually	2,234	–	–	96	–	65	**118,958**
Special Centers for Social Services	57	18	6	4	6	1	**2,290**
Total Assisted Annually	92,643	92,215	123,285	22,000	188,000	11,781	**20,953,944**
Diocesan Seminaries	2	–	–	–	–	–	**77**
Students	225	–	–	–	–	–	**3,400**
Religious Seminaries	3	–	7	–	1	–	**141**
Students	23	–	–	–	7	–	**1,517**
Colleges and Universities	3	–	1	–	–	–	**235**
Total Students	10,420	–	1,047	–	–	–	**705,059**
High Schools, Diocesan and Parish	10	3	6	3	9	1	**801**
Total Students	6,541	669	2,713	1,937	3,775	574	**386,476**
High Schools, Private	13	–	2	–	1	–	**795**
Total Students	9,896	–	1,665	–	133	–	**294,471**
Elementary Schools, Diocesan and Parish	72	9	25	10	29	7	**6,697**
Total Students	32,925	2,501	12,406	4,233	10,485	2,594	**1,940,698**
Elementary Schools, Private	8	–	–	–	2	–	**364**
Total Students	1,677	–	–	–	664	–	**117,776**
Non–residential Schools for the Disabled	1	–	1	–	–	–	**80**
Total Students	211	–	34	–	–	–	**18,120**
Religious Education High School Students	4,244	1,366	5,170	2,910	10,771	2,656	**782,102**
Religious Education Elementary Students	18,275	2,649	11,530	6,545	21,468	6,492	**3,617,181**
Priests Teaching	48	–	–	–	–	–	**1,934**
Scholastics Teaching	–	–	–	–	–	–	**41**
Brothers Teaching	36	2	2	–	2	–	**1,093**
Sisters Teaching	127	13	23	–	21	–	**8,201**
Lay Teachers	3,521	211	1,002	–	926	221	**156,470**
Infant Baptisms	6,784	753	3,043	1,759	5,578	1,479	**1,031,243**
Adult Baptisms	395	156	208	48	204	103	**83,234**
Received into Full Communion	335	283	412	147	305	223	**95,299**
First Communions	6,125	792	3,030	1,573	4,954	1,367	**909,779**
Confirmations	5,679	603	2,831	1,304	4,143	1,271	**651,443**
Marriages	2,260	293	1,007	474	1,900	465	**269,034**
Deaths	4,332	722	1,702	1,013	3,480	936	**479,034**
Totals Catholics	489,652	48,050	215,929	126,000	335,700	80,199	**63,683,030**
Total Population	1,331,561	401,211	831,478	202,000	546,000	259,425	**278,849,034**
Catholic Population Percentage	37	12	26	62	61	31	**23**

*Indicates Archdioceses.

†Certain Dioceses traverse state lines.

	Shreveport LA	LOUISIANA TOTAL	Portland (In Maine) ME	Marshall Islands	*Baltimore MD	*Boston MA	2001 U.S. GRAND TOTAL
Cardinals	–	–	–	–	1	1	**11**
Archbishops	–	2	–	–	2	–	**45**
Bishops	1	10	3	–	6	7	**373**
Abbots	–	1	–	–	–	1	**115**
Diocesan Priests	43	675	174	–	301	932	**30,655**
Religious Priests	16	338	45	6	304	842	**15,386**
Total Priests in Diocese	59	1,013	219	6	605	1,774	**46,075**
Newly Ordained Priests	1	9	1	–	7	8	**536**
Total Permanent Deacons	6	359	19	2	184	190	**13,348**
Total Brothers	5	178	30	–	74	105	**5,565**
Total Sisters	51	1,253	416	16	1,233	2,877	**79,462**
Number of Parishes	32	492	136	4	155	369	**19,544**
Missions	13	107	51	–	9	–	**3,075**
Pastoral Centers	2	4	–	1	–	2	**984**
New Parishes	–	–	–	–	–	1	**59**
Catholic Hospitals	2	8	3	–	6	10	**596**
Patients Assisted Annually	938	520,093	156,432	–	1,251,895	833,311	**78,996,656**
Health Care Centers	3	8	1	–	–	6	**544**
Patients Assisted Annually	705,884	841,921	830	–	–	4,181	**6,022,667**
Specialized Homes	3	58	8	–	21	33	**1,454**
Total Assisted Annually	472	10,625	1,025	–	1,828	4,404	**590,981**
Residential Care of Children (Orphanages)	–	2	–	–	–	1	**165**
Total Assisted Annually	–	116	–	–	–	430	**74,478**
Day Care and Extended Day Care Centers	2	21	4	–	4	11	**1,100**
Total Assisted Annually	80	2,475	353	–	251	1,675	**118,958**
Special Centers for Social Services	21	113	7	–	44	43	**2,290**
Total Assisted Annually	13,400	543,324	4,116	–	721,081	203,792	**20,953,944**
Diocesan Seminaries	–	2	–	–	2	4	**77**
Students	–	225	–	–	231	184	**3,400**
Religious Seminaries	–	11	–	–	–	4	**141**
Students	–	30	–	–	–	152	**1,517**
Colleges and Universities	–	4	1	–	3	7	**235**
Total Students	–	11,467	3,941	–	11,049	21,457	**705,059**
High Schools, Diocesan and Parish	2	34	1	–	23	15	**801**
Total Students	700	16,909	279	–	10,510	5,941	**386,476**
High Schools, Private	–	16	2	–	12	20	**795**
Total Students	–	11,694	745	–	7,265	11,159	**294,471**
Elementary Schools, Diocesan and Parish	8	160	17	6	73	119	**6,697**
Total Students	2,046	67,190	4,032	1,325	23,374	36,329	**1,940,698**
Elementary Schools, Private	–	10	1	–	9	9	**364**
Total Students	–	2,341	171	–	1,866	2,626	**117,776**
Non–residential Schools for the Disabled	–	2	–	–	1	3	**80**
Total Students	–	245	–	–	129	343	**18,120**
Religious Education High School Students	681	27,798	2,241	24	3,184	31,128	**782,102**
Religious Education Elementary Students	2,091	69,050	13,812	250	25,317	125,954	**3,617,181**
Priests Teaching	–	48	–	–	17	6	**1,934**
Scholastics Teaching	–	–	1	–	–	–	**41**
Brothers Teaching	1	43	–	–	24	33	**1,093**
Sisters Teaching	8	192	15	6	156	468	**8,201**
Lay Teachers	213	6,094	252	75	3,069	3,092	**156,470**
Infant Baptisms	567	19,963	2,737	70	8,051	29,301	**1,031,243**
Adult Baptisms	74	1,188	354	–	676	575	**83,234**
Received into Full Communion	231	1,936	464	52	–	383	**95,299**
First Communions	457	18,298	3,132	42	8,216	24,735	**909,779**
Confirmations	597	16,428	5,589	12	5,684	15,748	**651,443**
Marriages	257	6,656	1,275	34	2,590	7,534	**269,034**
Deaths	336	12,521	2,782	10	5,315	18,847	**479,034**
Totals Catholics	38,929	1,334,459	212,253	4,427	486,607	2,038,032	**63,683,030**
Total Population	778,633	4,350,308	1,227,927	50,894	2,870,150	3,857,751	**278,849,034**
Catholic Population Percentage	5	31	17	9	17	53	**23**

Archdioceses = 36; Dioceses = 164; Apostolates = 3

2001 GENERAL SUMMARY

	Fall River MA	Springfield in Massachusetts MA	Worcester MA	MASS. TOTAL	*Detroit MI	Gaylord MI	2001 U.S. GRAND TOTAL
Cardinals	–	–	–	1	1	–	11
Archbishops	–	–	–	–	–	–	45
Bishops	1	2	2	12	7	1	373
Abbots	–	–	3	4	–	–	115
Diocesan Priests	167	189	241	1,529	485	73	30,655
Religious Priests	130	41	111	1,124	294	16	15,386
Total Priests in Diocese	297	230	352	2,653	779	89	46,075
Newly Ordained Priests	7	2	–	17	5	1	536
Total Permanent Deacons	62	49	76	377	146	12	13,348
Total Brothers	26	9	85	225	130	1	5,565
Total Sisters	314	580	446	4,217	1,900	49	79,462
Number of Parishes	106	130	126	731	308	81	19,544
Missions	11	15	–	26	4	–	3,075
Pastoral Centers	–	1	–	3	–	–	984
New Parishes	1	–	–	2	1	–	59
Catholic Hospitals	1	1	1	13	12	3	596
Patients Assisted Annually	85,270	198,000	185,000	1,301,581	1,671,343	369,365	78,996,656
Health Care Centers	1	10	–	17	9	–	544
Patients Assisted Annually	102	92,602	–	96,885	13,128	–	6,022,667
Specialized Homes	9	12	9	63	21	1	1,454
Total Assisted Annually	1,210	6,881	25,285	37,780	4,652	633	590,981
Residential Care of Children (Orphanages)	1	1	1	4	8	2	165
Total Assisted Annually	160	–	20	610	1,407	29	74,478
Day Care and Extended Day Care Centers	2	1	6	20	2	–	1,100
Total Assisted Annually	105	126	1,750	3,656	700	–	118,958
Special Centers for Social Services	6	3	10	62	12	19	2,290
Total Assisted Annually	42,007	62,909	32,000	340,708	21,182	4,433	20,953,944
Diocesan Seminaries	–	–	1	5	2	–	77
Students	–	–	6	190	84	–	3,400
Religious Seminaries	–	–	–	4	2	–	141
Students	10	–	4	166	9	–	1,517
Colleges and Universities	1	2	3	13	4	–	235
Total Students	2,165	1,075	6,501	31,198	19,226	–	705,059
High Schools, Diocesan and Parish	4	4	4	27	18	4	801
Total Students	2,731	1,637	2,726	13,035	5,271	596	386,476
High Schools, Private	–	–	4	24	16	–	795
Total Students	–	–	1,557	12,716	8,472	–	294,471
Elementary Schools, Diocesan and Parish	24	28	22	193	127	17	6,697
Total Students	5,987	7,561	5,494	55,371	39,811	2,686	1,940,698
Elementary Schools, Private	–	1	2	12	7	–	364
Total Students	–	51	638	3,315	1,580	–	117,776
Non–residential Schools for the Disabled	–	–	1	4	–	–	80
Total Students	–	–	80	423	–	–	18,120
Religious Education High School Students	5,603	8,657	7,581	52,969	7,899	1,888	782,102
Religious Education Elementary Students	32,270	23,417	26,135	207,776	73,963	5,423	3,617,181
Priests Teaching	22	1	1	30	11	–	1,934
Scholastics Teaching	–	–	–	–	–	–	41
Brothers Teaching	4	–	8	45	14	–	1,093
Sisters Teaching	23	38	32	561	144	6	8,201
Lay Teachers	676	413	649	4,830	2,700	210	156,470
Infant Baptisms	4,920	3,836	4,416	42,473	16,763	1,078	1,031,243
Adult Baptisms	121	153	145	994	1,535	177	83,234
Received into Full Communion	233	238	242	1,096	1,767	155	95,299
First Communions	4,847	3,883	4,622	38,087	15,600	1,134	909,779
Confirmations	3,737	2,919	2,936	25,340	11,720	1,539	651,443
Marriages	1,908	1,411	1,231	12,084	5,299	531	269,034
Deaths	6,073	4,264	3,722	32,906	10,286	944	479,034
Totals Catholics	348,549	275,899	306,213	2,968,693	1,431,565	82,835	63,683,030
Total Population	787,876	792,195	790,705	6,228,527	4,266,650	458,130	278,849,034
Catholic Population Percentage	44	35	39	48	34	18	23

*Indicates Archdioceses.

†Certain Dioceses traverse state lines.

	Grand Rapids MI	Kalamazoo MI	Lansing MI	Marquette MI	Saginaw MI	MICHIGAN TOTAL	2001 U.S. GRAND TOTAL
Cardinals	–	–	–	–	–	1	**11**
Archbishops	–	–	–	–	–	–	**45**
Bishops	3	2	2	2	1	18	**373**
Abbots	–	–	–	–	–	–	**115**
Diocesan Priests	121	56	143	100	112	1,090	**30,655**
Religious Priests	20	13	32	13	15	403	**15,386**
Total Priests in Diocese	141	69	175	113	127	1,493	**46,075**
Newly Ordained Priests	2	–	4	1	–	13	**536**
Total Permanent Deacons	18	23	73	22	14	308	**13,348**
Total Brothers	2	3	12	–	–	148	**5,565**
Total Sisters	294	155	484	59	125	3,066	**79,462**
Number of Parishes	91	46	95	74	108	803	**19,544**
Missions	12	13	–	23	–	52	**3,075**
Pastoral Centers	2	1	2	–	–	5	**984**
New Parishes	–	–	–	–	–	1	**59**
Catholic Hospitals	2	3	4	1	1	26	**596**
Patients Assisted Annually	397,374	628,992	1,388,260	80,043	263,120	4,798,497	**78,996,656**
Health Care Centers	–	–	3	–	1	13	**544**
Patients Assisted Annually	–	–	7,102	–	10,750	30,980	**6,022,667**
Specialized Homes	2	2	6	1	2	35	**1,454**
Total Assisted Annually	669	246	687	123	1,362	8,372	**590,981**
Residential Care of Children (Orphanages)	–	–	–	–	4	14	**165**
Total Assisted Annually	–	–	–	–	191	1,627	**74,478**
Day Care and Extended Day Care Centers	–	8	1	–	7	18	**1,100**
Total Assisted Annually	–	293	100	–	274	1,367	**118,958**
Special Centers for Social Services	15	5	13	6	–	70	**2,290**
Total Assisted Annually	222,840	30,825	165,899	2,083	–	447,262	**20,953,944**
Diocesan Seminaries	1	–	–	–	–	3	**77**
Students	5	–	–	–	–	89	**3,400**
Religious Seminaries	–	–	–	–	–	2	**141**
Students	–	–	–	–	–	9	**1,517**
Colleges and Universities	1	–	2	–	–	7	**235**
Total Students	2,605	–	3,877	–	–	25,708	**705,059**
High Schools, Diocesan and Parish	4	3	4	–	3	36	**801**
Total Students	1,916	827	2,483	–	1,138	12,231	**386,476**
High Schools, Private	–	–	2	–	–	18	**795**
Total Students	–	–	176	–	–	8,648	**294,471**
Elementary Schools, Diocesan and Parish	41	22	37	10	30	284	**6,697**
Total Students	8,133	3,672	9,809	1,669	5,007	70,787	**1,940,698**
Elementary Schools, Private	–	–	5	–	–	12	**364**
Total Students	–	–	710	–	–	2,290	**117,776**
Non–residential Schools for the Disabled	–	–	–	–	–	–	**80**
Total Students	–	–	–	–	–	–	**18,120**
Religious Education High School Students	2,120	767	3,100	3,086	2,362	21,222	**782,102**
Religious Education Elementary Students	14,863	5,461	21,700	5,998	9,790	137,198	**3,617,181**
Priests Teaching	–	–	6	–	1	18	**1,934**
Scholastics Teaching	–	–	–	–	–	–	**41**
Brothers Teaching	1	–	1	–	–	16	**1,093**
Sisters Teaching	11	5	18	8	19	211	**8,201**
Lay Teachers	509	286	636	113	303	4,757	**156,470**
Infant Baptisms	3,137	1,644	4,041	990	1,928	29,581	**1,031,243**
Adult Baptisms	298	295	695	66	251	3,317	**83,234**
Received into Full Communion	–	–	1,344	127	252	3,645	**95,299**
First Communions	2,928	1,586	4,829	959	2,125	29,161	**909,779**
Confirmations	2,352	1,522	3,778	973	3,401	25,285	**651,443**
Marriages	982	558	1,521	537	738	10,166	**269,034**
Deaths	1,410	922	2,045	1,244	1,680	18,531	**479,034**
Totals Catholics	158,050	117,523	224,166	70,237	142,505	2,226,881	**63,683,030**
Total Population	1,167,900	917,327	1,722,146	309,000	685,532	9,526,685	**278,849,034**
Catholic Population Percentage	14	13	13	23	21	23	**23**

Archdioceses = 36; Dioceses = 164; Apostolates = 3

2001 GENERAL SUMMARY

	*St. Paul and Minneapolis MN	Crookston MN	Duluth MN	New Ulm MN	St. Cloud MN	Winona MN	2001 U.S. GRAND TOTAL
Cardinals	–	–	–	–	–	–	11
Archbishops	2	–	–	–	–	–	45
Bishops	3	1	1	1	2	2	373
Abbots	–	–	–	–	3	–	115
Diocesan Priests	343	50	78	83	137	128	30,655
Religious Priests	160	2	12	1	116	8	15,386
Total Priests in Diocese	503	52	90	84	253	136	46,075
Newly Ordained Priests	8	1	–	–	–	3	536
Total Permanent Deacons	173	12	27	1	34	5	13,348
Total Brothers	52	1	2	–	76	22	5,565
Total Sisters	1,090	171	165	85	646	449	79,462
Number of Parishes	222	69	92	80	139	118	19,544
Missions	5	–	3	2	–	1	3,075
Pastoral Centers	4	–	–	–	–	2	984
New Parishes	–	–	–	–	–	–	59
Catholic Hospitals	3	3	2	2	4	2	596
Patients Assisted Annually	94,685	61,584	308,067	13,619	215,011	71,207	78,996,656
Health Care Centers	–	–	–	–	–	1	544
Patients Assisted Annually	–	–	–	–	–	4,100	6,022,667
Specialized Homes	8	3	2	6	14	10	1,454
Total Assisted Annually	1,025	284	305	356	1,298	957	590,981
Residential Care of Children (Orphanages)	1	–	–	–	2	–	165
Total Assisted Annually	4,100	–	–	–	157	–	74,478
Day Care and Extended Day Care Centers	–	1	1	–	–	3	1,100
Total Assisted Annually	–	70	120	–	–	9,500	118,958
Special Centers for Social Services	5	–	–	–	7	7	2,290
Total Assisted Annually	–	–	–	–	401,706	13,001	20,953,944
Diocesan Seminaries	2	–	–	–	–	1	77
Students	180	–	–	–	–	57	3,400
Religious Seminaries	–	–	–	–	1	–	141
Students	–	–	–	–	1	–	1,517
Colleges and Universities	3	–	1	–	2	1	235
Total Students	17,305	–	2,010	–	4,044	1,364	705,059
High Schools, Diocesan and Parish	10	1	–	3	1	4	801
Total Students	7,228	166	–	510	589	1,396	386,476
High Schools, Private	2	–	–	–	1	–	795
Total Students	429	–	–	–	292	–	294,471
Elementary Schools, Diocesan and Parish	91	8	12	19	33	28	6,697
Total Students	28,017	1,175	2,033	2,641	5,493	5,020	1,940,698
Elementary Schools, Private	1	1	–	–	–	–	364
Total Students	264	68	–	–	–	–	117,776
Non–residential Schools for the Disabled	–	–	–	–	–	–	80
Total Students	–	–	–	–	–	–	18,120
Religious Education High School Students	–	2,825	3,450	3,736	7,722	4,838	782,102
Religious Education Elementary Students	65,422	3,701	3,800	7,330	15,717	12,114	3,617,181
Priests Teaching	22	–	–	–	30	7	1,934
Scholastics Teaching	–	–	–	–	–	–	41
Brothers Teaching	14	–	–	–	8	1	1,093
Sisters Teaching	57	7	3	6	35	17	8,201
Lay Teachers	2,031	119	112	223	803	362	156,470
Infant Baptisms	11,202	704	1,057	1,038	2,382	1,881	1,031,243
Adult Baptisms	480	23	49	43	84	77	83,234
Received into Full Communion	1,702	106	180	142	237	232	95,299
First Communions	10,869	637	1,206	1,240	2,684	1,948	909,779
Confirmations	7,887	698	977	1,215	2,774	2,166	651,443
Marriages	3,690	306	472	415	1,040	752	269,034
Deaths	4,967	496	1,063	766	1,483	1,122	479,034
Totals Catholics	769,135	40,646	78,235	70,835	147,047	150,370	63,683,030
Total Population	2,831,931	235,145	475,000	281,065	488,181	528,303	278,849,034
Catholic Population Percentage	27	17	16	25	30	28	23

*Indicates Archdioceses.

†Certain Dioceses traverse state lines.

2001 GENERAL SUMMARY

	MINNESOTA TOTAL	Biloxi MS	Jackson MS	MISSISSIPPI TOTAL	*St. Louis MO	Jefferson City MO	2001 U.S. GRAND TOTAL
Cardinals	–	–	–	–	–	–	11
Archbishops	2	–	–	–	1	–	45
Bishops	10	2	1	3	4	2	373
Abbots	3	–	–	–	2	–	115
Diocesan Priests	819	58	65	123	456	110	30,655
Religious Priests	299	24	30	54	381	9	15,386
Total Priests in Diocese	1,118	82	95	177	837	119	46,075
Newly Ordained Priests	12	2	–	2	8	1	536
Total Permanent Deacons	252	19	7	26	225	63	13,348
Total Brothers	153	32	12	44	157	5	5,565
Total Sisters	2,606	59	240	299	2,106	89	79,462
Number of Parishes	720	44	74	118	228	95	19,544
Missions	11	15	29	44	8	15	3,075
Pastoral Centers	6	–	–	–	–	–	984
New Parishes	–	–	–	–	–	–	59
Catholic Hospitals	16	–	1	1	10	1	596
Patients Assisted Annually	764,173	–	85,799	85,799	1,180,000	281,999	78,996,656
Health Care Centers	1	–	2	2	–	14	544
Patients Assisted Annually	4,100	–	9,271	9,271	–	149,012	6,022,667
Specialized Homes	43	7	8	15	51	2	1,454
Total Assisted Annually	4,225	7,656	2,225	9,881	34,000	210	590,981
Residential Care of Children (Orphanages)	3	–	3	3	9	–	165
Total Assisted Annually	4,257	–	350	350	1,200	–	74,478
Day Care and Extended Day Care Centers	5	–	2	2	16	–	1,100
Total Assisted Annually	9,690	–	550	550	1,700	–	118,958
Special Centers for Social Services	19	4	5	9	35	1	2,290
Total Assisted Annually	414,707	62,325	12,500	74,825	124,043	15,573	20,953,944
Diocesan Seminaries	3	–	–	–	2	1	77
Students	237	–	–	–	103	26	3,400
Religious Seminaries	1	–	–	–	5	–	141
Students	1	–	–	–	55	–	1,517
Colleges and Universities	7	–	1	1	2	–	235
Total Students	24,723	–	24	24	13,172	–	705,059
High Schools, Diocesan and Parish	19	4	4	8	14	2	801
Total Students	9,889	1,185	1,224	2,409	6,649	976	386,476
High Schools, Private	3	1	–	1	15	–	795
Total Students	721	571	–	571	9,052	–	294,471
Elementary Schools, Diocesan and Parish	191	14	16	30	139	37	6,697
Total Students	44,379	3,331	3,779	7,110	41,469	6,536	1,940,698
Elementary Schools, Private	2	–	–	–	8	–	364
Total Students	332	–	–	–	1,842	–	117,776
Non–residential Schools for the Disabled	–	–	–	–	9	1	80
Total Students	–	–	–	–	328	37	18,120
Religious Education High School Students	22,571	2,238	870	3,108	970	2,607	782,102
Religious Education Elementary Students	108,084	3,384	3,980	7,364	24,327	4,993	3,617,181
Priests Teaching	59	–	2	2	39	5	1,934
Scholastics Teaching	–	–	–	–	1	–	41
Brothers Teaching	23	11	2	13	12	5	1,093
Sisters Teaching	125	20	17	37	174	20	8,201
Lay Teachers	3,650	444	349	793	3,569	454	156,470
Infant Baptisms	18,264	821	798	1,619	6,940	1,415	1,031,243
Adult Baptisms	756	406	161	567	1,568	245	83,234
Received into Full Communion	2,599	236	312	548	8,669	355	95,299
First Communions	18,584	1,246	667	1,913	8,454	1,586	909,779
Confirmations	15,717	619	488	1,107	7,908	1,603	651,443
Marriages	6,675	409	290	699	2,662	619	269,034
Deaths	9,897	789	411	1,200	4,413	895	479,034
Totals Catholics	1,256,268	68,043	47,873	115,916	555,621	86,826	63,683,030
Total Population	4,839,625	748,433	1,980,025	2,728,458	2,089,000	807,921	278,849,034
Catholic Population Percentage	26	9	2	4	27	11	[illegible]

Archdioceses = 36; Dioceses = 1[illegible]

2001 GENERAL SUMMARY

	Kansas City-St. Joseph MO	Springfield-Cape-Girardeau MO	MISSOURI TOTAL	Great Falls - Billings MT	Helena MT	MONTANA TOTAL	2001 U.S. GRAND TOTAL
Cardinals	–	–	–	–	–	–	11
Archbishops	–	–	1	–	–	–	45
Bishops	2	1	9	1	1	2	373
Abbots	2	2	6	–	–	–	115
Diocesan Priests	122	75	763	69	82	151	30,655
Religious Priests	94	71	555	14	10	24	15,386
Total Priests in Diocese	216	146	1,318	83	92	175	46,075
Newly Ordained Priests	1	5	15	–	2	2	536
Total Permanent Deacons	57	10	355	3	34	37	13,348
Total Brothers	32	82	276	1	1	2	5,565
Total Sisters	279	110	2,584	77	48	125	79,462
Number of Parishes	85	65	473	66	58	124	19,544
Missions	14	19	56	47	39	86	3,075
Pastoral Centers	–	2	2	–	14	14	984
New Parishes	–	–	–	–	–	–	59
Catholic Hospitals	3	4	18	2	3	5	596
Patients Assisted Annually	263,364	525,380	2,250,743	153,629	180,996	334,625	78,996,656
Health Care Centers	–	–	14	1	–	1	544
Patients Assisted Annually	–	–	149,012	18,507	–	18,507	6,022,667
Specialized Homes	16	2	71	–	–	–	1,454
Total Assisted Annually	1,134	368	35,712	–	–	–	590,981
Residential Care of Children (Orphanages)	–	–	9	–	–	–	165
Total Assisted Annually	–	–	1,200	–	–	–	74,478
Day Care and Extended Day Care Centers	13	1	30	7	3	10	1,100
Total Assisted Annually	346	45	2,091	609	130	739	118,958
Special Centers for Social Services	2	1	39	3	–	3	2,290
Total Assisted Annually	24,000	1,187	164,803	22,745	–	22,745	20,953,944
Diocesan Seminaries	–	–	3	–	1	1	77
Students	–	–	129	–	3	3	3,400
Religious Seminaries	1	2	8	–	–	–	141
Students	3	30	88	–	–	–	1,517
Colleges and Universities	2	–	4	1	1	2	235
Total Students	5,163	–	18,335	1,054	1,292	2,346	705,059
High Schools, Diocesan and Parish	4	3	23	2	2	4	801
Total Students	1,515	878	10,018	375	418	793	386,476
High Schools, Private	3	–	18	1	–	1	795
Total Students	1,941	–	10,993	166	–	166	294,471
Elementary Schools, Diocesan and Parish	34	23	233	8	4	12	6,697
Total Students	10,364	3,793	62,162	1,430	889	2,319	1,940,698
Elementary Schools, Private	1	–	9	4	–	4	364
Total Students	338	–	2,180	1,204	–	1,204	117,776
Non-residential Schools for the Disabled	–	–	10	–	–	–	80
Total Students	–	–	365	–	–	–	18,120
Religious Education High School Students	998	1,692	6,267	2,085	1,692	3,777	782,102
Religious Education Elementary Students	8,992	3,998	42,310	4,518	5,669	10,187	3,617,181
Priests Teaching	3	1	48	2	10	12	1,934
Scholastics Teaching	–	–	1	–	–	–	41
Brothers Teaching	2	1	20	–	–	–	1,093
Sisters Teaching	17	5	216	7	10	17	8,201
Lay Teachers	861	266	5,150	215	200	415	156,470
Infant Baptisms	2,572	734	11,661	945	1,060	2,005	1,031,243
Adult Baptisms	328	520	2,661	164	185	349	83,234
Received into Full Communion	480	219	9,723	176	125	301	95,299
First Communions	2,746	1,205	13,991	1,044	1,078	2,122	909,779
Confirmations	1,958	1,020	12,489	2,396	763	3,159	651,443
Marriages	980	428	4,689	313	276	589	269,034
Deaths	1,259	590	7,157	776	871	1,647	479,034
Totals Catholics	158,089	59,038	859,574	57,429	67,500	124,929	63,683,030
Total Population	1,394,040	1,187,339	5,478,300	391,360	424,372	815,732	278,849,034
olic Population Percentage	11	5	16	15	16	15	23

* ... Archdioceses.

... traverse state lines.

2001 GENERAL SUMMARY

	Chalan Kanoa MP	*Omaha NE	Grand Island NE	Lincoln NE	NEBRASKA TOTAL	Las Vegas NV	2001 U.S. GRAND TOTAL
Cardinals	–	–	–	–	–	–	11
Archbishops	–	1	–	–	1	–	45
Bishops	1	1	2	1	4	–	373
Abbots	–	2	–	–	2	–	115
Diocesan Priests	13	217	76	149	442	31	30,655
Religious Priests	2	115	–	10	125	21	15,386
Total Priests in Diocese	15	332	76	159	567	52	46,075
Newly Ordained Priests	–	5	–	5	10	–	536
Total Permanent Deacons	3	142	–	2	144	7	13,348
Total Brothers	–	21	–	3	24	3	5,565
Total Sisters	9	306	91	127	524	26	79,462
Number of Parishes	11	138	43	135	316	24	19,544
Missions	2	16	40	1	57	7	3,075
Pastoral Centers	–	2	–	–	2	–	984
New Parishes	–	–	–	–	–	–	59
Catholic Hospitals	–	5	–	3	8	1	596
Patients Assisted Annually	–	349,495	–	197,890	547,385	101,528	78,996,656
Health Care Centers	–	1	2	–	3	–	544
Patients Assisted Annually	–	1,287	164,473	–	165,760	–	6,022,667
Specialized Homes	–	5	1	3	9	–	1,454
Total Assisted Annually	–	1,000	75	271	1,346	–	590,981
Residential Care of Children (Orphanages)	–	–	–	–	–	–	165
Total Assisted Annually	–	–	–	–	–	–	74,478
Day Care and Extended Day Care Centers	–	6	–	1	7	1	1,100
Total Assisted Annually	–	5,500	–	4,923	10,423	8,400	118,958
Special Centers for Social Services	1	14	–	21	35	19	2,290
Total Assisted Annually	2,960	124,230	–	14,294	138,524	1,000,000	20,953,944
Diocesan Seminaries	–	–	–	1	1	–	77
Students	–	–	–	19	19	–	3,400
Religious Seminaries	–	–	–	1	1	–	141
Students	–	–	–	62	62	–	1,517
Colleges and Universities	–	2	–	–	2	–	235
Total Students	–	7,218	–	–	7,218	–	705,059
High Schools, Diocesan and Parish	1	12	4	6	22	1	801
Total Students	239	3,557	808	1,590	5,955	996	386,476
High Schools, Private	–	5	–	–	5	–	795
Total Students	–	2,440	–	–	2,440	–	294,471
Elementary Schools, Diocesan and Parish	4	62	7	25	94	7	6,697
Total Students	408	16,097	871	5,910	22,878	2,531	1,940,698
Elementary Schools, Private	–	2	–	–	2	–	364
Total Students	–	195	–	–	195	–	117,776
Non-residential Schools for the Disabled	–	1	–	1	2	–	80
Total Students	–	40	–	18	58	–	18,120
Religious Education High School Students	626	3,414	3,263	2,375	9,052	2,433	782,102
Religious Education Elementary Students	1,650	16,708	5,361	5,353	27,422	10,124	3,617,181
Priests Teaching	–	34	1	32	67	1	1,934
Scholastics Teaching	–	2	–	–	2	–	41
Brothers Teaching	–	3	–	–	3	–	1,093
Sisters Teaching	7	46	4	36	86	–	8,201
Lay Teachers	47	2,588	129	398	3,115	177	156,470
Infant Baptisms	760	4,280	1,063	1,438	6,781	4,997	1,031,243
Adult Baptisms	17	444	123	180	747	296	83,234
Received into Full Communion	–	625	175	182	982	221	95,299
First Communions	680	4,610	1,179	1,576	7,365	3,233	909,779
Confirmations	405	4,247	773	1,247	6,267	1,044	651,443
Marriages	96	1,553	408	473	2,434	739	269,034
Deaths	144	1,935	608	677	3,220	780	479,034
Totals Catholics	53,066	214,046	56,879	89,225	360,150	406,000	63,683,030
Total Population	66,559	830,522	295,176	538,527	1,664,225	1,400,000	278,849,034
Catholic Population Percentage	80	26	19	17	22	29	[illegible]

Archdioceses = 36; Dioceses [illegible]

2001 GENERAL SUMMARY

	Reno NV	NEVADA TOTAL	Manchester NH	*Newark NJ	Camden NJ	Metuchen NJ	2001 U.S. GRAND TOTAL
Cardinals	–	–	–	–	–	–	**11**
Archbishops	–	–	–	1	–	–	**45**
Bishops	1	1	3	5	2	2	**373**
Abbots	–	–	1	1	–	–	**115**
Diocesan Priests	24	55	235	722	314	205	**30,655**
Religious Priests	12	33	85	239	46	42	**15,386**
Total Priests in Diocese	36	88	320	961	360	247	**46,075**
Newly Ordained Priests	–	–	3	11	4	3	**536**
Total Permanent Deacons	7	14	25	251	122	102	**13,348**
Total Brothers	3	6	26	96	17	20	**5,565**
Total Sisters	38	64	688	1,374	328	418	**79,462**
Number of Parishes	28	52	131	235	127	108	**19,544**
Missions	8	15	38	–	5	–	**3,075**
Pastoral Centers	–	–	–	172	24	–	**984**
New Parishes	–	–	–	–	1	–	**59**
Catholic Hospitals	1	2	2	8	1	1	**596**
Patients Assisted Annually	199,234	300,762	258,562	829,735	247,886	105,617	**78,996,656**
Health Care Centers	3	3	–	114	2	2	**544**
Patients Assisted Annually	199,234	199,234	–	21,247	11,216	6,525	**6,022,667**
Specialized Homes	–	–	9	15	6	6	**1,454**
Total Assisted Annually	–	–	501	871	2,088	227	**590,981**
Residential Care of Children (Orphanages)	–	–	2	–	1	–	**165**
Total Assisted Annually	–	–	41	–	11	–	**74,478**
Day Care and Extended Day Care Centers	2	3	–	145	2	6	**1,100**
Total Assisted Annually	233	8,633	–	5,199	192	557	**118,958**
Special Centers for Social Services	7	26	–	242	12	9	**2,290**
Total Assisted Annually	32,250	1,032,250	–	130,232	9,113	20,366	**20,953,944**
Diocesan Seminaries	–	–	–	3	–	–	**77**
Students	–	–	–	139	–	–	**3,400**
Religious Seminaries	–	–	–	1	–	–	**141**
Students	–	–	2	21	–	–	**1,517**
Colleges and Universities	–	–	5	4	–	–	**235**
Total Students	–	–	5,533	16,629	–	–	**705,059**
High Schools, Diocesan and Parish	1	2	3	17	8	4	**801**
Total Students	655	1,651	1,590	8,264	4,861	3,496	**386,476**
High Schools, Private	–	–	2	20	3	2	**795**
Total Students	–	–	951	7,783	1,317	1,080	**294,471**
Elementary Schools, Diocesan and Parish	4	11	34	132	59	43	**6,697**
Total Students	1,123	3,654	6,939	40,474	16,276	15,569	**1,940,698**
Elementary Schools, Private	–	–	3	7	1	1	**364**
Total Students	–	–	929	1,618	42	38	**117,776**
Non–residential Schools for the Disabled	–	–	–	6	2	–	**80**
Total Students	–	–	–	397	844	–	**18,120**
Religious Education High School Students	1,162	3,595	5,756	3,141	672	2,221	**782,102**
Religious Education Elementary Students	4,357	14,481	29,456	69,004	35,784	39,723	**3,617,181**
Priests Teaching	–	1	1	164	20	–	**1,934**
Scholastics Teaching	–	–	–	–	–	–	**41**
Brothers Teaching	1	1	5	29	12	2	**1,093**
Sisters Teaching	4	4	62	245	90	71	**8,201**
Lay Teachers	115	292	766	4,321	998	667	**156,470**
Infant Baptisms	1,839	6,836	4,587	17,618	6,894	7,168	**1,031,243**
Adult Baptisms	143	439	191	436	666	202	**83,234**
Received into Full Communion	120	341	–	599	721	364	**95,299**
First Communions	1,359	4,592	4,916	14,782	6,932	7,421	**909,779**
Confirmations	681	1,725	3,168	10,826	5,367	5,674	**651,443**
Marriages	318	1,057	1,257	4,804	1,913	1,786	**269,034**
Deaths	340	1,120	2,608	11,743	4,351	4,012	**479,034**
Totals Catholics	71,997	477,997	325,674	1,319,558	430,867	522,719	**63,683,030**
Total Population	573,630	1,973,630	1,201,000	2,655,985	1,294,470	1,253,288	**278,849,034**
Catholic Population Percentage	13	24	27	50	33	42	**23**

* ... Archdioceses.

... traverse state lines.

	Paterson NJ	Trenton NJ	NEW JERSEY TOTAL	*Santa Fe NM	† Gallup NM	Las Cruces NM	2001 U.S. GRAND TOTAL
Cardinals	–	–	–	–	–	–	11
Archbishops	–	–	1	2	–	–	45
Bishops	1	2	12	–	1	1	373
Abbots	8	–	9	2	–	–	115
Diocesan Priests	258	235	1,734	111	63	31	30,655
Religious Priests	199	59	585	92	28	51	15,386
Total Priests in Diocese	457	294	2,319	203	91	82	46,075
Newly Ordained Priests	–	1	19	4	2	–	536
Total Permanent Deacons	158	268	901	146	26	25	13,348
Total Brothers	48	66	247	86	13	2	5,565
Total Sisters	853	440	3,413	254	139	45	79,462
Number of Parishes	111	127	708	92	56	44	19,544
Missions	–	14	19	217	35	45	3,075
Pastoral Centers	5	–	201	4	–	2	984
New Parishes	–	–	1	–	–	–	59
Catholic Hospitals	3	1	14	4	–	–	596
Patients Assisted Annually	747,657	139,705	2,070,600	13,806	–	–	78,996,656
Health Care Centers	–	1	119	1	–	3	544
Patients Assisted Annually	–	3,940	42,928	6,646	–	35,000	6,022,667
Specialized Homes	10	16	53	7	3	–	1,454
Total Assisted Annually	14,425	26,843	44,454	1,554	138	–	590,981
Residential Care of Children (Orphanages)	3	1	5	–	–	–	165
Total Assisted Annually	244	15	270	–	–	–	74,478
Day Care and Extended Day Care Centers	6	5	164	1	3	3	1,100
Total Assisted Annually	561	475	6,984	274	66	226	118,958
Special Centers for Social Services	13	15	291	5	24	1	2,290
Total Assisted Annually	90,000	41,320	291,031	281,412	30,861	7,600	20,953,944
Diocesan Seminaries	–	–	3	–	–	–	77
Students	–	–	139	–	–	–	3,400
Religious Seminaries	2	–	3	–	–	–	141
Students	5	–	26	18	–	–	1,517
Colleges and Universities	2	1	7	1	–	–	235
Total Students	1,852	2,420	20,901	1,774	–	–	705,059
High Schools, Diocesan and Parish	5	8	42	1	–	–	801
Total Students	2,512	6,414	25,547	1,041	–	–	386,476
High Schools, Private	5	3	33	1	3	–	795
Total Students	1,568	1,122	12,870	758	357	–	294,471
Elementary Schools, Diocesan and Parish	57	51	342	16	–	4	6,697
Total Students	16,783	20,169	109,271	4,187	–	624	1,940,698
Elementary Schools, Private	3	2	14	–	10	–	364
Total Students	519	584	2,801	–	1,540	–	117,776
Non–residential Schools for the Disabled	–	1	9	–	–	–	80
Total Students	–	17	1,258	–	–	–	18,120
Religious Education High School Students	8,473	962	15,469	5,694	1,345	2,564	782,102
Religious Education Elementary Students	36,908	65,238	246,657	18,729	3,771	8,333	3,617,181
Priests Teaching	24	–	208	–	2	–	1,934
Scholastics Teaching	–	–	–	–	–	–	41
Brothers Teaching	14	–	57	5	–	–	1,093
Sisters Teaching	133	43	582	25	31	2	8,201
Lay Teachers	1,129	–	7,115	346	135	60	156,470
Infant Baptisms	8,959	10,571	51,210	7,136	962	2,414	1,031,243
Adult Baptisms	225	464	1,993	391	267	232	83,234
Received into Full Communion	364	590	2,638	675	119	94	95,299
First Communions	7,943	12,374	49,452	5,891	974	2,142	909,779
Confirmations	4,411	9,359	35,637	3,443	647	1,664	651,443
Marriages	2,060	2,851	13,414	1,499	237	443	269,034
Deaths	3,720	6,898	30,724	2,939	639	984	479,034
Totals Catholics	407,932	728,314	3,409,390	286,155	54,306	132,646	63,683,030
Total Population	1,093,309	1,367,348	7,664,400	1,071,238	379,555	484,637	278,849,034
Catholic Population Percentage	37	53	44	27	14	27	23

Archdioceses = 36; Dioceses = 164; Apostolates = 3

2001 GENERAL SUMMARY

	NEW MEXICO TOTAL	*New York NY	Albany NY	Brooklyn NY	Buffalo NY	Ogdensburg NY	2001 U.S. GRAND TOTAL
Cardinals	–	1	–	–	–	–	11
Archbishops	2	–	–	–	–	–	45
Bishops	2	10	2	6	4	1	373
Abbots	2	–	–	–	–	–	115
Diocesan Priests	205	838	292	649	424	164	30,655
Religious Priests	171	911	77	78	179	13	15,386
Total Priests in Diocese	376	1,749	369	727	603	177	46,075
Newly Ordained Priests	6	10	1	5	3	3	536
Total Permanent Deacons	197	343	90	152	100	56	13,348
Total Brothers	101	250	94	153	41	12	5,565
Total Sisters	438	3,490	946	1,326	1,362	171	79,462
Number of Parishes	192	412	184	217	266	120	19,544
Missions	297	–	34	–	10	25	3,075
Pastoral Centers	6	–	–	6	2	–	984
New Parishes	–	–	–	–	–	–	59
Catholic Hospitals	4	17	4	4	6	–	596
Patients Assisted Annually	13,806	2,089,079	668,100	944,645	1,417,252	–	78,996,656
Health Care Centers	4	3	15	30	1	–	544
Patients Assisted Annually	41,646	166,890	51,000	862,413	1,100	–	6,022,667
Specialized Homes	10	23	22	41	17	4	1,454
Total Assisted Annually	1,692	23,150	2,564	14,850	2,506	974	590,981
Residential Care of Children (Orphanages)	–	13	–	6	–	–	165
Total Assisted Annually	–	4,500	–	8,334	–	–	74,478
Day Care and Extended Day Care Centers	7	15	7	20	3	–	1,100
Total Assisted Annually	566	1,255	517	2,143	216	–	118,958
Special Centers for Social Services	30	147	25	92	4	6	2,290
Total Assisted Annually	319,873	322,850	175,000	87,329	263,920	14,000	20,953,944
Diocesan Seminaries	–	3	–	1	2	1	77
Students	–	140	–	20	37	19	3,400
Religious Seminaries	–	3	–	2	1	–	141
Students	18	100	–	–	–	–	1,517
Colleges and Universities	1	12	3	3	7	–	235
Total Students	1,774	44,904	4,000	19,080	15,251	–	705,059
High Schools, Diocesan and Parish	1	27	4	4	–	2	801
Total Students	1,041	15,654	1,194	1,949	–	559	386,476
High Schools, Private	4	28	3	16	17	–	795
Total Students	1,115	13,427	870	15,300	5,972	–	294,471
Elementary Schools, Diocesan and Parish	20	228	37	152	89	26	6,697
Total Students	4,811	76,763	8,555	54,607	21,561	3,996	1,940,698
Elementary Schools, Private	10	15	2	2	4	–	364
Total Students	1,540	4,165	12,181	351	1,000	–	117,776
Non–residential Schools for the Disabled	–	6	–	1	1	–	80
Total Students	–	222	–	113	629	–	18,120
Religious Education High School Students	9,603	5,845	9,273	1,150	13,148	2,015	782,102
Religious Education Elementary Students	30,833	103,438	31,211	52,795	39,539	9,985	3,617,181
Priests Teaching	2	54	6	14	62	2	1,934
Scholastics Teaching	–	–	–	–	–	–	41
Brothers Teaching	5	49	17	60	11	2	1,093
Sisters Teaching	58	105	65	271	129	25	8,201
Lay Teachers	541	3,539	898	3,830	2,554	266	156,470
Infant Baptisms	10,512	33,979	4,623	21,901	6,741	1,593	1,031,243
Adult Baptisms	890	983	143	927	485	196	83,234
Received into Full Communion	888	980	324	1,375	527	103	95,299
First Communions	9,007	28,037	5,298	15,598	7,890	1,795	909,779
Confirmations	5,754	20,527	2,963	11,167	5,842	1,502	651,443
Marriages	2,179	6,984	1,759	4,141	2,688	744	269,034
Deaths	4,562	15,944	5,232	10,898	7,380	1,878	479,034
Totals Catholics	473,107	2,388,047	400,000	1,651,304	725,452	143,084	63,683,030
Total Population	1,935,430	5,276,900	1,386,200	4,268,939	1,553,471	450,982	278,849,034
Catholic Population Percentage	24	45	29	39	47	32	23

*Indicates Archdioceses.

†Certain Dioceses traverse state lines.

	Rochester NY	Rockville Centre NY	Syracuse NY	NEW YORK TOTAL	Charlotte NC	Raleigh NC	2001 U.S. GRAND TOTAL
Cardinals	–	–	–	1	–	–	11
Archbishops	–	–	–	–	–	–	45
Bishops	1	4	3	31	2	2	373
Abbots	2	–	–	2	1	–	115
Diocesan Priests	251	402	286	3,306	93	87	30,655
Religious Priests	31	74	60	1,423	96	53	15,386
Total Priests in Diocese	282	476	346	4,729	189	140	46,075
Newly Ordained Priests	2	2	1	27	7	2	536
Total Permanent Deacons	126	219	73	1,159	63	23	13,348
Total Brothers	37	94	16	697	3	9	5,565
Total Sisters	666	1,433	497	9,891	134	77	79,462
Number of Parishes	157	134	172	1,662	68	75	19,544
Missions	11	1	15	96	23	12	3,075
Pastoral Centers	–	–	20	28	4	5	984
New Parishes	1	–	–	1	–	1	59
Catholic Hospitals	2	4	3	40	–	–	596
Patients Assisted Annually	280,000	1,219,082	670,000	7,288,158	–	–	78,996,656
Health Care Centers	2	34	1	86	5	–	544
Patients Assisted Annually	900	175,725	300	1,258,328	238,600	–	6,022,667
Specialized Homes	11	10	57	185	4	–	1,454
Total Assisted Annually	2,000	10,788	60	56,892	281	–	590,981
Residential Care of Children (Orphanages)	2	4	10	35	–	–	165
Total Assisted Annually	40	10,562	150	23,586	–	–	74,478
Day Care and Extended Day Care Centers	1	102	–	148	5	–	1,100
Total Assisted Annually	120	4,322	–	8,573	502	–	118,958
Special Centers for Social Services	42	21	8	345	–	12	2,290
Total Assisted Annually	85,000	48,706	62,800	1,059,605	–	46,508	20,953,944
Diocesan Seminaries	1	1	–	9	–	1	77
Students	5	38	–	259	–	3	3,400
Religious Seminaries	–	–	–	6	–	–	141
Students	–	5	–	105	–	–	1,517
Colleges and Universities	1	2	1	29	2	–	235
Total Students	149	5,358	2,915	91,657	925	–	705,059
High Schools, Diocesan and Parish	1	4	5	47	2	1	801
Total Students	132	3,851	3,039	26,378	1,228	862	386,476
High Schools, Private	6	8	1	79	–	–	795
Total Students	3,454	7,365	737	47,125	–	–	294,471
Elementary Schools, Diocesan and Parish	49	59	39	679	15	29	6,697
Total Students	11,951	28,057	7,345	212,835	6,075	6,943	1,940,698
Elementary Schools, Private	5	4	1	33	–	–	364
Total Students	927	1,072	14	19,710	–	–	117,776
Non–residential Schools for the Disabled	–	3	–	11	–	–	80
Total Students	–	103	–	1,067	–	–	18,120
Religious Education High School Students	4,420	3,319	7,777	46,947	2,480	2,730	782,102
Religious Education Elementary Students	30,936	116,331	31,003	415,238	13,706	14,061	3,617,181
Priests Teaching	3	12	4	157	4	6	1,934
Scholastics Teaching	–	–	–	–	–	–	41
Brothers Teaching	16	53	6	214	1	4	1,093
Sisters Teaching	61	174	63	893	7	14	8,201
Lay Teachers	1,096	1,952	727	14,862	479	386	156,470
Infant Baptisms	5,250	22,522	5,522	102,131	3,733	3,998	1,031,243
Adult Baptisms	398	627	357	4,116	209	263	83,234
Received into Full Communion	714	517	655	5,195	638	418	95,299
First Communions	5,012	22,181	5,293	91,104	3,305	2,898	909,779
Confirmations	4,860	16,595	4,054	67,510	2,322	1,470	651,443
Marriages	2,011	6,365	2,029	26,721	839	887	269,034
Deaths	4,239	13,098	4,717	63,386	673	1,006	479,034
Totals Catholics	338,501	1,404,361	345,736	7,396,485	129,385	167,537	63,683,030
Total Population	1,470,304	3,008,203	1,174,887	18,589,886	3,984,578	3,697,588	278,849,034
Catholic Population Percentage	23	47	29	40	3	5	23

Archdioceses = 36; Dioceses = 164; Apostolates = 3

2001 GENERAL SUMMARY

	NORTH CAROLINA TOTAL	Bismarck ND	Fargo ND	NORTH DAKOTA TOTAL	*Cincinnati OH	Cleveland OH	2001 U.S. GRAND TOTAL
Cardinals	–	–	–	–	–	–	11
Archbishops	–	–	–	–	1	–	45
Bishops	4	1	1	2	1	3	373
Abbots	1	3	–	3	–	1	115
Diocesan Priests	180	71	147	218	324	480	30,655
Religious Priests	149	27	9	36	242	142	15,386
Total Priests in Diocese	329	98	156	254	566	622	46,075
Newly Ordained Priests	9	6	5	11	4	10	536
Total Permanent Deacons	86	59	24	83	137	174	13,348
Total Brothers	12	24	8	32	164	71	5,565
Total Sisters	211	142	143	285	1,150	1,479	79,462
Number of Parishes	143	62	160	222	231	235	19,544
Missions	35	38	–	38	–	1	3,075
Pastoral Centers	9	–	–	–	–	2	984
New Parishes	1	–	1	1	–	–	59
Catholic Hospitals	–	4	8	12	10	3	596
Patients Assisted Annually	–	208,350	60,798	269,148	1,223,000	475,971	78,996,656
Health Care Centers	5	–	6	6	2	–	544
Patients Assisted Annually	238,600	–	757	757	349	–	6,022,667
Specialized Homes	4	5	5	10	13	31	1,454
Total Assisted Annually	281	664	485	1,149	2,570	4,958	590,981
Residential Care of Children (Orphanages)	–	–	–	–	1	1	165
Total Assisted Annually	–	–	–	–	24	197	74,478
Day Care and Extended Day Care Centers	5	–	35	35	–	6	1,100
Total Assisted Annually	502	–	280	280	–	950	118,958
Special Centers for Social Services	12	–	–	–	6	23	2,290
Total Assisted Annually	46,508	–	–	–	45,480	516,318	20,953,944
Diocesan Seminaries	1	–	1	1	1	2	77
Students	3	–	16	16	40	45	3,400
Religious Seminaries	–	–	–	–	–	–	141
Students	–	1	–	1	–	4	1,517
Colleges and Universities	2	1	–	1	4	3	235
Total Students	925	2,343	–	2,343	22,939	6,483	705,059
High Schools, Diocesan and Parish	3	3	1	4	10	7	801
Total Students	2,090	1,143	286	1,429	12,934	4,130	386,476
High Schools, Private	–	–	–	–	4	16	795
Total Students	–	–	–	–	2,960	10,294	294,471
Elementary Schools, Diocesan and Parish	44	12	12	24	109	132	6,697
Total Students	13,018	1,656	2,129	3,785	40,356	47,289	1,940,698
Elementary Schools, Private	–	–	–	–	4	8	364
Total Students	–	–	–	–	1,375	2,639	117,776
Non-residential Schools for the Disabled	–	–	–	–	–	2	80
Total Students	–	–	–	–	–	183	18,120
Religious Education High School Students	5,210	3,260	3,856	7,116	6,689	6,317	782,102
Religious Education Elementary Students	27,767	7,320	7,010	14,330	34,219	43,723	3,617,181
Priests Teaching	10	5	1	6	11	28	1,934
Scholastics Teaching	–	–	–	–	–	–	41
Brothers Teaching	5	–	6	6	22	30	1,093
Sisters Teaching	21	7	4	11	96	225	8,201
Lay Teachers	865	163	159	322	2,975	3,637	156,470
Infant Baptisms	7,731	1,047	1,231	2,278	8,182	9,228	1,031,243
Adult Baptisms	472	145	43	188	982	2,455	83,234
Received into Full Communion	1,056	147	172	319	1,087	957	95,299
First Communions	6,203	1,190	1,314	2,504	9,039	12,162	909,779
Confirmations	3,792	1,325	1,303	2,628	8,554	9,971	651,443
Marriages	1,726	514	540	1,054	2,997	4,152	269,034
Deaths	1,679	685	809	1,494	4,712	8,685	479,034
Totals Catholics	296,922	68,484	98,960	167,444	513,469	816,912	63,683,030
Total Population	7,682,166	254,426	391,000	645,426	2,805,557	2,818,711	278,849,034
Catholic Population Percentage	4	27	25	26	18	29	23

*Indicates Archdioceses.

†Certain Dioceses traverse state lines.

	Columbus OH	Steubenville OH	Toledo OH	Youngstown OH	OHIO TOTAL	*Oklahoma City OK	2001 U.S. GRAND TOTAL
Cardinals	–	–	–	–	–	–	11
Archbishops	–	–	–	–	1	2	45
Bishops	1	2	3	2	12	–	373
Abbots	–	–	–	–	1	4	115
Diocesan Priests	193	111	206	184	1,498	96	30,655
Religious Priests	38	18	54	24	518	25	15,386
Total Priests in Diocese	231	129	260	208	2,016	121	46,075
Newly Ordained Priests	2	3	1	3	23	2	536
Total Permanent Deacons	59	7	192	71	640	61	13,348
Total Brothers	3	8	10	20	276	13	5,565
Total Sisters	376	82	712	236	4,035	154	79,462
Number of Parishes	107	73	162	116	924	71	19,544
Missions	5	3	–	2	11	43	3,075
Pastoral Centers	–	–	11	–	13	1	984
New Parishes	1	–	–	–	1	2	59
Catholic Hospitals	4	2	7	3	29	5	596
Patients Assisted Annually	1,274,425	256,232	1,012,844	955,152	5,197,624	641,916	78,996,656
Health Care Centers	–	–	2	5	9	–	544
Patients Assisted Annually	–	–	717	159,638	160,704	–	6,022,667
Specialized Homes	17	1	2	12	76	5	1,454
Total Assisted Annually	1,955	87	330	941	10,841	571	590,981
Residential Care of Children (Orphanages)	–	–	1	–	3	–	165
Total Assisted Annually	–	–	61	–	282	–	74,478
Day Care and Extended Day Care Centers	1	–	–	3	10	2	1,100
Total Assisted Annually	126	–	–	395	1,471	332	118,958
Special Centers for Social Services	8	1	14	7	59	1	2,290
Total Assisted Annually	291,400	14,788	14,788	312,976	1,195,750	700	20,953,944
Diocesan Seminaries	1	–	–	–	4	–	77
Students	102	–	–	–	187	–	3,400
Religious Seminaries	–	–	–	–	–	–	141
Students	–	–	–	–	4	–	1,517
Colleges and Universities	1	1	2	1	12	1	235
Total Students	2,191	2,154	1,513	1,580	36,860	755	705,059
High Schools, Diocesan and Parish	11	3	10	6	47	2	801
Total Students	4,912	733	3,843	2,686	29,238	942	386,476
High Schools, Private	–	–	4	–	24	–	795
Total Students	–	–	2,726	–	15,980	–	294,471
Elementary Schools, Diocesan and Parish	45	–	83	44	413	17	6,697
Total Students	13,874	–	21,427	11,418	134,364	3,557	1,940,698
Elementary Schools, Private	2	14	3	–	31	2	364
Total Students	337	2,685	657	–	7,693	292	117,776
Non–residential Schools for the Disabled	–	–	1	–	3	–	80
Total Students	–	–	75	–	258	–	18,120
Religious Education High School Students	941	755	1,981	3,190	19,873	3,037	782,102
Religious Education Elementary Students	24,678	2,778	10,434	15,398	131,230	8,893	3,617,181
Priests Teaching	1	4	3	3	50	–	1,934
Scholastics Teaching	–	–	–	–	–	–	41
Brothers Teaching	1	–	–	–	53	–	1,093
Sisters Teaching	20	13	81	29	464	7	8,201
Lay Teachers	953	255	1,739	761	10,320	252	156,470
Infant Baptisms	4,083	596	3,815	3,061	28,965	2,111	1,031,243
Adult Baptisms	522	239	600	322	5,120	349	83,234
Received into Full Communion	711	119	671	548	4,093	469	95,299
First Communions	4,214	818	5,239	3,457	34,929	2,102	909,779
Confirmations	3,506	904	7,897	2,904	33,736	1,555	651,443
Marriages	1,263	321	1,803	1,316	11,852	677	269,034
Deaths	1,634	776	3,097	3,057	21,961	868	479,034
Totals Catholics	198,116	40,541	335,909	262,020	2,166,967	98,225	63,683,030
Total Population	2,283,842	522,253	1,481,725	1,217,333	11,129,421	2,224,000	278,849,034
Catholic Population Percentage	9	8	23	22	19	4	23

Archdioceses = 36; Dioceses = 164; Apostolates = 3

2001 GENERAL SUMMARY

	Tulsa OK	OKLAHOMA TOTAL	*Portland in Oregon OR	Baker OR	OREGON TOTAL	*Philadelphia PA	2001 U.S. GRAND TOTAL
Cardinals	–	–	–	–	–	1	**11**
Archbishops	–	2	1	–	1	–	**45**
Bishops	1	1	1	2	3	4	**373**
Abbots	–	4	3	–	3	2	**115**
Diocesan Priests	75	171	152	37	189	773	**30,655**
Religious Priests	20	45	181	6	187	407	**15,386**
Total Priests in Diocese	95	216	333	43	376	1,180	**46,075**
Newly Ordained Priests	5	7	4	1	5	11	**536**
Total Permanent Deacons	52	113	26	15	41	188	**13,348**
Total Brothers	8	21	79	1	80	125	**5,565**
Total Sisters	103	257	531	28	559	3,711	**79,462**
Number of Parishes	80	151	125	36	161	283	**19,544**
Missions	–	43	26	27	53	7	**3,075**
Pastoral Centers	–	1	1	–	1	20	**984**
New Parishes	–	2	1	–	1	3	**59**
Catholic Hospitals	2	7	9	5	14	8	**596**
Patients Assisted Annually	237,045	878,961	2,063,583	276,384	2,339,967	830,526	**78,996,656**
Health Care Centers	–	–	5	–	5	9	**544**
Patients Assisted Annually	–	–	2,867	–	2,867	235	**6,022,667**
Specialized Homes	4	9	13	1	14	25	**1,454**
Total Assisted Annually	262	833	4,957	110	5,067	8,562	**590,981**
Residential Care of Children (Orphanages)	–	–	–	–	–	5	**165**
Total Assisted Annually	–	–	–	–	–	926	**74,478**
Day Care and Extended Day Care Centers	–	2	4	3	7	2	**1,100**
Total Assisted Annually	–	332	3,163	286	3,449	165	**118,958**
Special Centers for Social Services	2	3	14	7	21	15	**2,290**
Total Assisted Annually	4,555	5,255	1,028,589	25,218	1,053,807	93,530	**20,953,944**
Diocesan Seminaries	–	–	1	–	1	1	**77**
Students	–	–	148	–	148	145	**3,400**
Religious Seminaries	–	–	–	–	–	1	**141**
Students	–	–	36	–	36	20	**1,517**
Colleges and Universities	–	1	2	–	2	11	**235**
Total Students	–	755	4,549	–	4,549	33,161	**705,059**
High Schools, Diocesan and Parish	1	3	3	–	3	22	**801**
Total Students	953	1,895	1,535	–	1,535	23,148	**386,476**
High Schools, Private	1	1	6	–	6	15	**795**
Total Students	569	569	3,365	–	3,365	7,259	**294,471**
Elementary Schools, Diocesan and Parish	10	27	41	3	44	214	**6,697**
Total Students	2,359	5,916	8,938	644	9,582	81,672	**1,940,698**
Elementary Schools, Private	1	3	1	–	1	20	**364**
Total Students	1,167	1,459	382	–	382	5,205	**117,776**
Non-residential Schools for the Disabled	–	–	–	–	–	5	**80**
Total Students	–	–	–	–	–	356	**18,120**
Religious Education High School Students	1,500	4,537	3,090	1,417	4,507	7,596	**782,102**
Religious Education Elementary Students	5,000	13,893	13,092	2,395	15,487	51,007	**3,617,181**
Priests Teaching	–	–	49	–	49	148	**1,934**
Scholastics Teaching	–	–	–	–	–	–	**41**
Brothers Teaching	1	1	9	–	9	55	**1,093**
Sisters Teaching	4	11	62	1	63	746	**8,201**
Lay Teachers	39	291	1,388	36	1,424	9,091	**156,470**
Infant Baptisms	1,157	3,268	5,591	776	6,367	18,074	**1,031,243**
Adult Baptisms	245	594	760	182	942	1,296	**83,234**
Received into Full Communion	314	783	763	145	908	684	**95,299**
First Communions	1,190	3,292	4,206	932	5,138	15,308	**909,779**
Confirmations	828	2,383	2,433	338	2,771	13,610	**651,443**
Marriages	420	1,097	1,357	237	1,594	6,509	**269,034**
Deaths	535	1,403	1,982	326	2,308	12,896	**479,034**
Totals Catholics	62,673	160,898	297,841	36,179	334,020	1,430,161	**63,683,030**
Total Population	1,500,000	3,724,000	2,869,750	425,650	3,295,400	3,707,238	**278,849,034**
Catholic Population Percentage	4	4	10	9	10	39	**23**

*Indicates Archdioceses.

†Certain Dioceses traverse state lines.

	Allentown PA	Altoona-Johnstown PA	Erie PA	Greensburg PA	Harrisburg PA	Pittsburgh PA	2001 U.S. GRAND TOTAL
Cardinals	–	–	–	–	–	–	11
Archbishops	–	–	–	–	–	–	45
Bishops	2	2	2	1	1	4	373
Abbots	–	–	–	1	–	–	115
Diocesan Priests	244	154	238	151	160	479	30,655
Religious Priests	66	62	14	77	36	123	15,386
Total Priests in Diocese	310	216	252	228	196	602	46,075
Newly Ordained Priests	3	3	1	3	4	6	536
Total Permanent Deacons	100	30	16	–	61	52	13,348
Total Brothers	–	6	2	27	–	37	5,565
Total Sisters	505	89	479	409	491	1,606	79,462
Number of Parishes	153	103	127	105	89	216	19,544
Missions	9	5	20	–	8	–	3,075
Pastoral Centers	–	–	1	–	–	–	984
New Parishes	–	–	–	–	–	2	59
Catholic Hospitals	3	1	1	1	1	7	596
Patients Assisted Annually	962,822	115,851	60,000	110,488	168,827	1,039,870	78,996,656
Health Care Centers	1	1	–	–	–	–	544
Patients Assisted Annually	32,940	200	–	–	–	–	6,022,667
Specialized Homes	12	3	6	2	9	18	1,454
Total Assisted Annually	3,138	267	1,060	132	1,098	8,643	590,981
Residential Care of Children (Orphanages)	–	–	–	–	1	–	165
Total Assisted Annually	–	–	–	–	123	–	74,478
Day Care and Extended Day Care Centers	39	–	2	–	–	22	1,100
Total Assisted Annually	1,593	–	209	–	–	2,139	118,958
Special Centers for Social Services	14	2	9	7	11	11	2,290
Total Assisted Annually	74,010	57,449	103,204	3,982	1,674	92,638	20,953,944
Diocesan Seminaries	–	–	1	–	–	1	77
Students	–	–	16	–	–	9	3,400
Religious Seminaries	–	–	–	1	–	–	141
Students	–	–	–	20	–	–	1,517
Colleges and Universities	2	2	2	2	–	3	235
Total Students	3,305	3,993	6,290	2,559	–	13,829	705,059
High Schools, Diocesan and Parish	9	3	5	2	7	8	801
Total Students	4,140	1,221	1,837	771	3,784	3,574	386,476
High Schools, Private	–	–	2	–	–	3	795
Total Students	–	–	1,281	–	–	630	294,471
Elementary Schools, Diocesan and Parish	53	29	41	24	39	106	6,697
Total Students	13,749	4,733	9,669	5,543	11,162	26,078	1,940,698
Elementary Schools, Private	–	–	1	3	1	4	364
Total Students	–	–	393	220	114	950	117,776
Non-residential Schools for the Disabled	3	–	–	–	–	2	80
Total Students	138	–	–	–	–	154	18,120
Religious Education High School Students	1,444	4,328	6,827	3,787	2,164	6,862	782,102
Religious Education Elementary Students	17,700	9,066	11,942	10,476	21,218	50,154	3,617,181
Priests Teaching	11	6	24	23	1	5	1,934
Scholastics Teaching	–	–	–	–	–	–	41
Brothers Teaching	–	–	–	6	–	9	1,093
Sisters Teaching	78	17	28	34	72	95	8,201
Lay Teachers	910	561	784	562	808	1,946	156,470
Infant Baptisms	3,658	1,512	2,188	1,993	3,272	8,598	1,031,243
Adult Baptisms	175	133	286	134	337	378	83,234
Received into Full Communion	–	229	305	373	534	776	95,299
First Communions	4,056	1,750	3,023	2,375	3,564	8,797	909,779
Confirmations	4,270	1,818	2,616	2,503	3,226	9,083	651,443
Marriages	1,169	747	1,111	1,005	1,123	3,258	269,034
Deaths	3,210	1,656	2,699	2,699	2,238	9,699	479,034
Totals Catholics	264,373	110,651	230,016	188,710	240,495	753,147	63,683,030
Total Population	1,125,349	641,763	867,197	680,152	1,940,954	1,939,656	278,849,034
Catholic Population Percentage	23	17	27	28	12	39	23

Archdioceses = 36; Dioceses = 164; Apostolates = 3

2001 GENERAL SUMMARY

	Scranton PA	PENN. TOTAL	*San Juan, Puerto Rico	Arecibo, Puerto Rico	Caguas, Puerto Rico	Mayaguez, Puerto Rico	2001 U.S. GRAND TOTAL
Cardinals	–	1	1	–	–	–	**11**
Archbishops	–	–	1	–	–	–	**45**
Bishops	2	18	2	2	2	1	**373**
Abbots	–	3	–	–	2	–	**115**
Diocesan Priests	347	2,546	91	119	73	41	**30,655**
Religious Priests	96	881	205	41	51	31	**15,386**
Total Priests in Diocese	443	3,427	296	160	124	72	**46,075**
Newly Ordained Priests	3	34	5	16	4	–	**536**
Total Permanent Deacons	51	498	273	11	69	4	**13,348**
Total Brothers	11	208	23	8	18	3	**5,565**
Total Sisters	760	8,050	506	163	154	135	**79,462**
Number of Parishes	198	1,274	154	59	43	29	**19,544**
Missions	85	134	178	230	–	–	**3,075**
Pastoral Centers	25	46	–	1	–	154	**984**
New Parishes	–	5	–	–	–	–	**59**
Catholic Hospitals	7	29	1	–	–	1	**596**
Patients Assisted Annually	916,372	4,204,756	180	–	–	80,000	**78,996,656**
Health Care Centers	3	14	2	–	–	–	**544**
Patients Assisted Annually	96,832	130,207	7,880	–	–	–	**6,022,667**
Specialized Homes	13	88	34	5	3	1	**1,454**
Total Assisted Annually	2,344	25,244	588	9,525	654	133	**590,981**
Residential Care of Children (Orphanages)	5	11	7	3	–	–	**165**
Total Assisted Annually	983	2,032	55	69	–	–	**74,478**
Day Care and Extended Day Care Centers	9	74	36	–	–	–	**1,100**
Total Assisted Annually	438	4,544	7,674	–	–	–	**118,958**
Special Centers for Social Services	13	82	4	2	–	1	**2,290**
Total Assisted Annually	198,763	625,250	41,852	13,518	–	1,780	**20,953,944**
Diocesan Seminaries	1	4	1	1	1	–	**77**
Students	17	187	16	4	12	–	**3,400**
Religious Seminaries	1	3	15	–	–	–	**141**
Students	–	40	37	–	–	–	**1,517**
Colleges and Universities	4	26	2	1	–	1	**235**
Total Students	11,365	74,502	8,361	867	–	1,750	**705,059**
High Schools, Diocesan and Parish	9	65	20	14	1	3	**801**
Total Students	3,455	41,930	4,397	2,617	113	635	**386,476**
High Schools, Private	2	22	26	–	6	4	**795**
Total Students	779	9,949	6,611	–	3,896	1,394	**294,471**
Elementary Schools, Diocesan and Parish	50	556	28	14	4	3	**6,697**
Total Students	12,044	164,650	9,683	4,286	670	924	**1,940,698**
Elementary Schools, Private	–	29	40	–	13	7	**364**
Total Students	–	6,882	13,539	–	4,164	3,043	**117,776**
Non–residential Schools for the Disabled	1	11	–	–	–	–	**80**
Total Students	19	667	–	–	–	–	**18,120**
Religious Education High School Students	10,835	43,843	–	3,996	4,102	12,500	**782,102**
Religious Education Elementary Students	23,123	194,686	–	12,990	5,670	–	**3,617,181**
Priests Teaching	14	232	36	7	19	5	**1,934**
Scholastics Teaching	–	–	–	–	4	–	**41**
Brothers Teaching	–	70	23	3	4	3	**1,093**
Sisters Teaching	94	1,164	80	40	17	6	**8,201**
Lay Teachers	884	15,546	2,191	478	370	315	**156,470**
Infant Baptisms	4,131	43,426	11,397	3,515	6,188	4,547	**1,031,243**
Adult Baptisms	435	3,174	1,353	258	500	132	**83,234**
Received into Full Communion	395	3,296	–	83	–	–	**95,299**
First Communions	5,573	44,446	6,925	3,180	5,670	3,485	**909,779**
Confirmations	8,225	45,351	3,675	2,196	4,102	3,083	**651,443**
Marriages	1,832	16,754	2,161	764	1,267	993	**269,034**
Deaths	5,408	40,505	–	1,670	2,248	1,683	**479,034**
Totals Catholics	337,454	3,555,007	1,007,197	386,874	515,000	360,000	**63,683,030**
Total Population	1,032,536	11,934,845	1,393,611	609,690	653,012	491,518	**278,849,034**
Catholic Population Percentage	33	30	72	63	79	73	**23**

*Indicates Archdioceses.

†Certain Dioceses traverse state lines.

2001 GENERAL SUMMARY

	Amarillo TX	Austin TX	Beaumont TX	Brownsville TX	Corpus Christi TX	Dallas TX	2001 U.S. GRAND TOTAL
Cardinals	–	–	–	–	–	–	11
Archbishops	–	–	–	–	–	–	45
Bishops	2	2	1	2	2	2	373
Abbots	–	–	–	–	2	1	115
Diocesan Priests	64	131	46	58	100	104	30,655
Religious Priests	6	93	28	38	46	72	15,386
Total Priests in Diocese	70	224	74	96	146	176	46,075
Newly Ordained Priests	1	1	1	3	2	3	536
Total Permanent Deacons	45	181	30	81	63	147	13,348
Total Brothers	–	43	4	14	24	4	5,565
Total Sisters	132	107	41	127	193	153	79,462
Number of Parishes	35	101	44	64	66	65	19,544
Missions	13	26	9	43	33	7	3,075
Pastoral Centers	–	1	–	1	1	–	984
New Parishes	–	1	–	1	–	–	59
Catholic Hospitals	1	4	3	–	6	1	596
Patients Assisted Annually	22,300	587,487	386,358	–	559,931	18,800	78,996,656
Health Care Centers	1	4	1	1	–	–	544
Patients Assisted Annually	750	80,054	80,000	111	–	–	6,022,667
Specialized Homes	3	3	–	2	3	1	1,454
Total Assisted Annually	606	745	–	250	237	44	590,981
Residential Care of Children (Orphanages)	–	1	–	–	–	–	165
Total Assisted Annually	–	4,000	–	–	–	–	74,478
Day Care and Extended Day Care Centers	3	4	–	2	3	3	1,100
Total Assisted Annually	170	200	–	175	251	447	118,958
Special Centers for Social Services	4	1	2	4	2	15	2,290
Total Assisted Annually	35,000	240	53,854	33,591	11,490	62,720	20,953,944
Diocesan Seminaries	–	–	–	–	–	1	77
Students	–	–	–	–	–	45	3,400
Religious Seminaries	–	–	–	–	–	–	141
Students	–	–	–	–	–	–	1,517
Colleges and Universities	–	1	–	–	1	1	235
Total Students	–	3,669	–	–	29	3,100	705,059
High Schools, Diocesan and Parish	1	2	1	–	–	4	801
Total Students	118	274	567	–	–	1,689	386,476
High Schools, Private	–	2	–	2	1	4	795
Total Students	–	461	–	721	349	1,996	294,471
Elementary Schools, Diocesan and Parish	7	15	6	7	15	30	6,697
Total Students	1,085	3,400	1,286	2,278	2,406	14,186	1,940,698
Elementary Schools, Private	–	3	–	2	2	2	364
Total Students	–	625	–	683	478	584	117,776
Non–residential Schools for the Disabled	–	–	–	–	–	1	80
Total Students	–	–	–	–	–	125	18,120
Religious Education High School Students	1,718	3,200	2,303	7,836	3,255	4,779	782,102
Religious Education Elementary Students	4,380	17,000	6,287	28,665	10,271	33,887	3,617,181
Priests Teaching	–	4	–	3	1	29	1,934
Scholastics Teaching	–	–	–	–	–	–	41
Brothers Teaching	–	2	–	6	–	2	1,093
Sisters Teaching	8	13	5	15	40	28	8,201
Lay Teachers	87	379	130	381	200	996	156,470
Infant Baptisms	1,230	7,337	1,480	4,393	3,426	13,838	1,031,243
Adult Baptisms	111	629	126	4,095	163	658	83,234
Received into Full Communion	146	992	310	368	598	778	95,299
First Communions	1,363	5,958	1,408	6,569	2,903	8,662	909,779
Confirmations	1,617	4,167	1,085	3,023	885	5,201	651,443
Marriages	275	1,714	356	1,027	820	2,458	269,034
Deaths	264	1,712	809	2,321	1,803	1,451	479,034
Totals Catholics	54,208	266,838	95,397	799,217	165,921	630,156	63,683,030
Total Population	401,261	2,027,192	588,265	940,255	548,198	2,979,840	278,849,034
Catholic Population Percentage	14	13	16	85	30	21	23

Archdioceses = 36; Dioceses = 164; Apostolates = 3

2001 GENERAL SUMMARY

	El Paso TX	Fort Worth TX	Galveston—Houston TX	Laredo TX	Lubbock TX	San Angelo TX	2001 U.S. GRAND TOTAL
Cardinals	–	–	–	–	–	–	11
Archbishops	–	–	–	–	–	–	45
Bishops	1	1	3	1	1	1	373
Abbots	–	–	–	–	–	–	115
Diocesan Priests	92	60	198	16	36	39	30,655
Religious Priests	42	55	212	24	9	16	15,386
Total Priests in Diocese	134	115	410	40	45	55	46,075
Newly Ordained Priests	–	2	4	–	–	–	536
Total Permanent Deacons	14	63	296	23	49	40	13,348
Total Brothers	16	13	11	20	–	–	5,565
Total Sisters	247	100	498	83	30	30	79,462
Number of Parishes	58	86	151	25	34	49	19,544
Missions	22	3	8	26	28	24	3,075
Pastoral Centers	–	–	17	–	1	–	984
New Parishes	–	–	–	–	–	–	59
Catholic Hospitals	–	1	3	1	1	–	596
Patients Assisted Annually	–	160,000	455,315	195,544	223,400	–	78,996,656
Health Care Centers	1	1	5	–	35	–	544
Patients Assisted Annually	20,319	2,394	75,879	–	451,000	–	6,022,667
Specialized Homes	3	5	7	2	–	–	1,454
Total Assisted Annually	173	754	3,678	1,895	–	–	590,981
Residential Care of Children (Orphanages)	–	–	3	1	–	–	165
Total Assisted Annually	–	–	2,508	62	–	–	74,478
Day Care and Extended Day Care Centers	1	1	38	–	–	–	1,100
Total Assisted Annually	81	80	4,025	–	–	–	118,958
Special Centers for Social Services	5	16	10	1	–	–	2,290
Total Assisted Annually	81,411	35,000	811,278	576	–	–	20,953,944
Diocesan Seminaries	1	–	1	–	–	–	77
Students	3	–	46	–	–	–	3,400
Religious Seminaries	2	–	3	–	–	–	141
Students	25	–	35	–	–	–	1,517
Colleges and Universities	–	–	1	–	–	–	235
Total Students	–	–	2,897	–	–	–	705,059
High Schools, Diocesan and Parish	1	4	2	1	–	–	801
Total Students	673	1,560	328	631	–	–	386,476
High Schools, Private	2	–	6	–	–	–	795
Total Students	352	–	3,216	–	–	–	294,471
Elementary Schools, Diocesan and Parish	9	14	44	5	2	3	6,697
Total Students	3,612	4,887	14,051	1,064	411	818	1,940,698
Elementary Schools, Private	3	1	6	1	–	–	364
Total Students	867	260	11,946	721	–	–	117,776
Non-residential Schools for the Disabled	–	–	–	–	–	–	80
Total Students	–	–	–	–	–	–	18,120
Religious Education High School Students	5,398	8,273	14,803	1,299	5,768	4,078	782,102
Religious Education Elementary Students	13,527	19,333	66,255	5,232	3,607	9,068	3,617,181
Priests Teaching	6	1	35	1	–	–	1,934
Scholastics Teaching	–	4	–	–	–	–	41
Brothers Teaching	7	11	–	–	–	–	1,093
Sisters Teaching	40	–	29	20	–	1	8,201
Lay Teachers	299	484	1,493	143	33	60	156,470
Infant Baptisms	9,033	6,015	19,630	3,416	2,064	2,143	1,031,243
Adult Baptisms	136	470	1,374	71	284	186	83,234
Received into Full Communion	273	793	1,078	249	142	343	95,299
First Communions	5,742	4,974	16,392	3,124	1,573	2,046	909,779
Confirmations	3,842	2,798	8,062	2,184	993	1,595	651,443
Marriages	1,344	1,248	3,977	554	453	510	269,034
Deaths	1,955	1,109	3,631	1,122	438	679	479,034
Totals Catholics	630,573	228,649	951,360	217,707	55,701	78,557	63,683,030
Total Population	798,763	2,490,147	4,528,005	286,457	451,995	687,730	278,849,034
Catholic Population Percentage	79	9	21	76	12	11	23

*Indicates Archdioceses.

†Certain Dioceses traverse state lines.

	Tyler TX	Victoria in Texas TX	TEXAS TOTAL	Salt Lake City UT	Burlington VT	St. Thomas Virgin Islands	2001 U.S. GRAND TOTAL
Cardinals	–	–	–	–	–	–	11
Archbishops	–	–	1	–	–	–	45
Bishops	1	1	24	1	1	2	373
Abbots	–	–	3	1	–	–	115
Diocesan Priests	32	56	1,183	57	131	12	30,655
Religious Priests	20	8	876	27	51	5	15,386
Total Priests in Diocese	86	64	2,093	84	182	17	46,075
Newly Ordained Priests	2	2	27	2	–	–	536
Total Permanent Deacons	47	19	1,382	39	45	18	13,348
Total Brothers	4	–	244	12	18	4	5,565
Total Sisters	60	135	2,855	52	219	17	79,462
Number of Parishes	40	50	1,012	47	87	8	19,544
Missions	28	19	321	15	43	2	3,075
Pastoral Centers	2	–	26	–	1	–	984
New Parishes	5	–	7	3	–	–	59
Catholic Hospitals	4	–	29	–	–	–	596
Patients Assisted Annually	310,264	–	3,077,708	–	–	–	78,996,656
Health Care Centers	42	–	94	–	–	–	544
Patients Assisted Annually	639,894	–	1,350,401	–	–	–	6,022,667
Specialized Homes	–	1	42	1	4	–	1,454
Total Assisted Annually	–	59	9,458	750	129	–	590,981
Residential Care of Children (Orphanages)	–	–	8	–	–	–	165
Total Assisted Annually	–	–	6,701	–	–	–	74,478
Day Care and Extended Day Care Centers	–	–	74	9	–	–	1,100
Total Assisted Annually	–	–	5,429	387	–	–	118,958
Special Centers for Social Services	1	–	69	3	1	4	2,290
Total Assisted Annually	120	–	1,125,280	289,191	6,377	808	20,953,944
Diocesan Seminaries	–	–	4	–	–	–	77
Students	–	–	130	–	–	–	3,400
Religious Seminaries	–	–	14	–	–	–	141
Students	–	–	103	–	–	–	1,517
Colleges and Universities	–	–	8	–	3	–	235
Total Students	–	–	21,153	–	4,685	–	705,059
High Schools, Diocesan and Parish	1	2	21	3	2	2	801
Total Students	176	149	6,940	1,479	738	240	386,476
High Schools, Private	–	1	26	–	–	–	795
Total Students	–	393	10,710	–	–	–	294,471
Elementary Schools, Diocesan and Parish	4	11	210	10	12	3	6,697
Total Students	938	2,058	63,679	3,690	2,037	558	1,940,698
Elementary Schools, Private	–	1	25	–	3	–	364
Total Students	–	382	18,291	–	719	–	117,776
Non–residential Schools for the Disabled	–	–	1	–	–	–	80
Total Students	–	–	125	–	–	–	18,120
Religious Education High School Students	1,259	3,006	78,860	1,507	2,856	297	782,102
Religious Education Elementary Students	5,373	6,932	267,008	6,905	9,688	720	3,617,181
Priests Teaching	–	–	117	6	2	–	1,934
Scholastics Teaching	–	–	6	–	–	–	41
Brothers Teaching	1	–	57	–	–	1	1,093
Sisters Teaching	4	22	354	2	9	3	8,201
Lay Teachers	90	234	6,388	310	412	64	156,470
Infant Baptisms	1,758	1,606	90,676	3,308	1,679	347	1,031,243
Adult Baptisms	188	92	9,121	439	138	16	83,234
Received into Full Communion	321	111	7,138	269	160	13	95,299
First Communions	1,402	1,447	74,117	2,031	1,830	290	909,779
Confirmations	800	1,212	43,814	1,162	1,196	189	651,443
Marriages	357	502	18,273	636	728	109	269,034
Deaths	316	1,031	23,850	580	1,581	158	479,034
Totals Catholics	53,776	107,804	5,015,576	107,000	148,712	30,000	63,683,030
Total Population	1,215,918	210,831	20,104,363	2,130,000	590,883	110,000	278,849,034
Catholic Population Percentage	4	51	25	5	25	27	23

Archdioceses = 36; Dioceses = 164; Apostolates = 3

2001 GENERAL SUMMARY

	Arlington VA	Richmond VA	VIRGINIA TOTAL	*Seattle WA	Spokane WA	Yakima WA	2001 U.S. GRAND TOTAL
Cardinals	–	–	–	–	–	–	11
Archbishops	–	–	–	2	–	–	45
Bishops	1	1	2	2	2	1	373
Abbots	4	1	5	2	1	–	115
Diocesan Priests	154	165	319	179	89	65	30,655
Religious Priests	80	39	119	117	99	11	15,386
Total Priests in Diocese	234	204	438	296	188	76	46,075
Newly Ordained Priests	4	2	6	3	6	3	536
Total Permanent Deacons	41	29	70	74	48	25	13,348
Total Brothers	17	12	29	13	12	8	5,565
Total Sisters	171	198	369	495	299	55	79,462
Number of Parishes	66	143	209	139	78	41	19,544
Missions	5	7	12	30	3	4	3,075
Pastoral Centers	–	2	2	–	1	2	984
New Parishes	1	–	1	1	–	–	59
Catholic Hospitals	–	10	10	8	7	3	596
Patients Assisted Annually	–	619,549	619,549	1,500,000	368,925	305,306	78,996,656
Health Care Centers	–	–	–	11	2	–	544
Patients Assisted Annually	–	–	–	310,000	18,011	–	6,022,667
Specialized Homes	–	15	15	18	13	–	1,454
Total Assisted Annually	–	2,733	2,733	61	1,998	–	590,981
Residential Care of Children (Orphanages)	–	2	2	–	–	–	165
Total Assisted Annually	–	460	460	–	–	–	74,478
Day Care and Extended Day Care Centers	–	9	9	7	14	2	1,100
Total Assisted Annually	–	867	867	675	993	391	118,958
Special Centers for Social Services	8	8	16	24	4	5	2,290
Total Assisted Annually	38,624	10,000	48,624	51,608	17,022	36,570	20,953,944
Diocesan Seminaries	–	–	–	–	1	–	77
Students	–	–	–	–	5	–	3,400
Religious Seminaries	–	–	–	–	–	–	141
Students	–	–	–	–	–	–	1,517
Colleges and Universities	4	–	4	2	1	–	235
Total Students	4,935	–	4,935	7,408	4,602	–	705,059
High Schools, Diocesan and Parish	3	6	9	3	1	–	801
Total Students	3,474	1,382	4,856	2,358	239	–	386,476
High Schools, Private	2	3	5	6	2	1	795
Total Students	576	869	1,445	3,165	1,035	140	294,471
Elementary Schools, Diocesan and Parish	34	22	56	53	16	6	6,697
Total Students	13,585	8,519	22,104	15,275	3,032	1,888	1,940,698
Elementary Schools, Private	1	1	2	3	–	1	364
Total Students	191	431	622	855	–	135	117,776
Non-residential Schools for the Disabled	1	1	2	–	–	–	80
Total Students	100	140	240	–	–	–	18,120
Religious Education High School Students	5,122	5,922	11,044	5,451	532	2,031	782,102
Religious Education Elementary Students	30,618	18,779	49,397	34,744	2,074	5,815	3,617,181
Priests Teaching	9	4	13	–	5	–	1,934
Scholastics Teaching	–	–	–	–	1	–	41
Brothers Teaching	3	–	3	–	4	8	1,093
Sisters Teaching	16	7	23	–	2	5	8,201
Lay Teachers	1,065	740	1,805	–	281	117	156,470
Infant Baptisms	7,103	3,538	10,641	6,794	1,241	3,312	1,031,243
Adult Baptisms	848	701	1,549	1,268	323	135	83,234
Received into Full Communion	552	1,134	1,686	773	208	122	95,299
First Communions	7,072	3,619	10,691	6,238	798	2,161	909,779
Confirmations	5,392	1,917	7,309	4,714	329	933	651,443
Marriages	1,949	1,277	3,226	1,758	424	593	269,034
Deaths	1,463	1,545	3,008	2,914	1,802	443	479,034
Totals Catholics	353,367	200,342	553,709	525,040	76,691	62,587	63,683,030
Total Population	2,317,773	4,555,139	6,872,912	4,526,200	720,569	461,600	278,849,034
Catholic Population Percentage	15	4	8	12	11	14	23

*Indicates Archdioceses.
†Certain Dioceses traverse state lines.

	WASHINGTON TOTAL	Wheeling-Charleston WV	*Milwaukee WI	Green Bay WI	La Crosse WI	Madison WI	2001 U.S. GRAND TOTAL
Cardinals	–	–	–	–	–	–	**11**
Archbishops	2	–	1	–	–	–	**45**
Bishops	4	2	1	3	2	2	**373**
Abbots	3	–	2	3	1	–	**115**
Diocesan Priests	333	157	445	220	201	151	**30,655**
Religious Priests	227	57	293	136	27	13	**15,386**
Total Priests in Diocese	560	214	738	356	228	164	**46,075**
Newly Ordained Priests	12	–	2	1	2	5	**536**
Total Permanent Deacons	147	28	163	87	35	5	**13,348**
Total Brothers	33	13	68	38	6	7	**5,565**
Total Sisters	849	260	2,764	622	494	321	**79,462**
Number of Parishes	258	112	234	191	168	137	**19,544**
Missions	37	25	–	4	–	–	**3,075**
Pastoral Centers	3	4	17	13	–	–	**984**
New Parishes	1	–	8	–	2	–	**59**
Catholic Hospitals	18	3	11	8	9	4	**596**
Patients Assisted Annually	2,174,231	407,954	2,322,939	1,074,636	582,416	288,750	**78,996,656**
Health Care Centers	13	2	1	–	–	2	**544**
Patients Assisted Annually	328,011	10,215	13,800	–	–	346	**6,022,667**
Specialized Homes	31	5	32	14	18	5	**1,454**
Total Assisted Annually	2,059	670	10,277	8,097	13,523	605	**590,981**
Residential Care of Children (Orphanages)	–	1	–	–	–	–	**165**
Total Assisted Annually	–	25	–	–	–	–	**74,478**
Day Care and Extended Day Care Centers	23	4	5	1	2	29	**1,100**
Total Assisted Annually	2,059	440	538	60	200	2,685	**118,958**
Special Centers for Social Services	33	8	40	8	2	7	**2,290**
Total Assisted Annually	105,200	9,627	241,181	188,437	3,125	30,250	**20,953,944**
Diocesan Seminaries	1	–	1	–	1	–	**77**
Students	5	–	25	–	8	–	**3,400**
Religious Seminaries	–	9	1	1	–	–	**141**
Students	–	–	2	5	–	–	**1,517**
Colleges and Universities	3	1	5	2	1	1	**235**
Total Students	12,010	1,497	27,065	6,455	2,106	1,909	**705,059**
High Schools, Diocesan and Parish	4	7	7	5	7	–	**801**
Total Students	2,597	1,668	4,565	1,521	1,745	–	**386,476**
High Schools, Private	9	1	6	1	–	1	**795**
Total Students	4,340	184	3,075	757	–	639	**294,471**
Elementary Schools, Diocesan and Parish	75	26	133	78	76	44	**6,697**
Total Students	20,195	5,186	30,881	12,379	9,817	7,015	**1,940,698**
Elementary Schools, Private	4	1	2	–	–	1	**364**
Total Students	990	184	112	–	–	281	**117,776**
Non-residential Schools for the Disabled	–	–	2	–	–	–	**80**
Total Students	–	–	11	–	–	–	**18,120**
Religious Education High School Students	8,014	1,182	13,840	8,739	8,448	8,961	**782,102**
Religious Education Elementary Students	42,633	4,334	31,205	24,325	15,855	15,524	**3,617,181**
Priests Teaching	5	2	19	–	5	–	**1,934**
Scholastics Teaching	1	–	1	–	–	–	**41**
Brothers Teaching	12	2	8	–	–	2	**1,093**
Sisters Teaching	7	12	96	42	27	31	**8,201**
Lay Teachers	398	185	2,422	812	752	559	**156,470**
Infant Baptisms	11,347	969	9,156	4,844	2,874	3,359	**1,031,243**
Adult Baptisms	1,726	257	358	206	122	586	**83,234**
Received into Full Communion	1,103	352	712	298	341	–	**95,299**
First Communions	9,197	1,440	8,943	4,900	3,464	3,035	**909,779**
Confirmations	5,976	1,522	6,312	3,535	3,328	2,642	**651,443**
Marriages	2,775	535	3,153	1,809	1,305	1,213	**269,034**
Deaths	5,159	1,133	5,503	3,247	2,063	1,707	**479,034**
Totals Catholics	664,318	97,232	685,004	388,093	209,426	264,536	**63,683,030**
Total Population	5,708,369	1,815,787	2,222,364	924,032	831,042	903,212	**278,849,034**
Catholic Population Percentage	12	5	31	42	25	29	**23**

Archdioceses = 36; Dioceses = 164; Apostolates = 3

2001 GENERAL SUMMARY

	Superior WI	WISCONSIN TOTAL	† Cheyenne WY	EASTERN RITE *Philadelphia	*Pittsburgh	Armenian	2001 U.S. GRAND TOTAL
Cardinals	–	–	–	–	–	–	11
Archbishops	–	1	–	1	1	–	45
Bishops	1	9	2	1	–	2	373
Abbots	–	6	–	–	1	–	115
Diocesan Priests	76	1,093	52	59	64	6	30,655
Religious Priests	15	484	9	6	8	7	15,386
Total Priests in Diocese	91	1,577	61	65	72	13	46,075
Newly Ordained Priests	1	11	1	1	2	–	536
Total Permanent Deacons	48	338	14	6	–	1	13,348
Total Brothers	1	120	1	–	4	–	5,565
Total Sisters	111	4,312	24	81	104	15	79,462
Number of Parishes	114	844	36	74	86	7	19,544
Missions	–	4	42	–	–	–	3,075
Pastoral Centers	1	31	–	–	–	–	984
New Parishes	–	10	–	–	–	–	59
Catholic Hospitals	5	37	–	–	–	–	596
Patients Assisted Annually	137,752	4,406,493	–	–	–	–	78,996,656
Health Care Centers	–	3	–	–	–	–	544
Patients Assisted Annually	–	14,146	–	–	–	–	6,022,667
Specialized Homes	–	69	3	–	2	–	1,454
Total Assisted Annually	–	32,502	286	–	488	–	590,981
Residential Care of Children (Orphanages)	–	–	–	–	–	–	165
Total Assisted Annually	–	–	–	–	–	–	74,478
Day Care and Extended Day Care Centers	2	39	7	2	–	–	1,100
Total Assisted Annually	260	3,743	325	120	–	–	118,958
Special Centers for Social Services	2	59	10	–	–	–	2,290
Total Assisted Annually	380	463,373	11,000	–	–	–	20,953,944
Diocesan Seminaries	–	2	–	1	1	–	77
Students	–	33	–	9	7	–	3,400
Religious Seminaries	–	2	–	–	–	–	141
Students	–	7	–	–	–	–	1,517
Colleges and Universities	–	9	–	–	–	–	235
Total Students	–	37,535	–	–	–	–	705,059
High Schools, Diocesan and Parish	–	19	–	–	–	–	801
Total Students	–	7,831	–	–	–	–	386,476
High Schools, Private	–	8	1	1	–	–	795
Total Students	–	4,471	53	352	–	–	294,471
Elementary Schools, Diocesan and Parish	17	348	6	7	2	4	6,697
Total Students	2,879	62,971	998	1,020	374	1,005	1,940,698
Elementary Schools, Private	–	3	–	–	–	–	364
Total Students	–	393	–	–	–	–	117,776
Non-residential Schools for the Disabled	–	2	–	–	–	–	80
Total Students	–	11	–	–	–	–	18,120
Religious Education High School Students	3,125	43,113	1,900	215	517	–	782,102
Religious Education Elementary Students	7,114	94,023	6,050	1,120	1,823	–	3,617,181
Priests Teaching	–	24	–	2	–	2	1,934
Scholastics Teaching	–	1	–	–	–	–	41
Brothers Teaching	1	11	–	–	–	–	1,093
Sisters Teaching	7	203	2	15	5	15	8,201
Lay Teachers	172	4,717	100	325	20	85	156,470
Infant Baptisms	990	21,223	932	210	308	68	1,031,243
Adult Baptisms	286	1,558	173	19	26	1	83,234
Received into Full Communion	–	1,351	162	35	60	69	95,299
First Communions	1,329	21,671	976	214	530	55	909,779
Confirmations	1,006	16,823	898	202	401	69	651,443
Marriages	497	7,977	338	98	137	23	269,034
Deaths	1,195	13,715	616	413	584	35	479,034
Totals Catholics	88,715	1,635,774	48,781	67,800	64,986	25,000	63,683,030
Total Population	401,631	5,282,281	480,000	–	–	–	278,849,034
Catholic Population Percentage	22	31	10	–	–	–	23

*Indicates Archdioceses.

†Certain Dioceses traverse state lines.

2001 GENERAL SUMMARY

	EASTERN RITE (Cont.)						
	Lady of Deliverance	Lady of Lebanon	Newton	Parma	Passaic	Romanian	2001 U.S. GRAND TOTAL
Cardinals	–	–	–	–	–	–	11
Archbishops	–	–	–	–	–	–	45
Bishops	1	1	2	1	2	2	373
Abbots	–	–	–	–	–	–	115
Diocesan Priests	9	31	44	38	88	15	30,655
Religious Priests	–	9	17	3	11	2	15,386
Total Priests in Diocese	9	40	61	41	99	17	46,075
Newly Ordained Priests	–	–	1	1	–	1	536
Total Permanent Deacons	–	8	–	4	15	–	13,348
Total Brothers	–	–	–	–	2	–	5,565
Total Sisters	–	8	3	14	19	–	79,462
Number of Parishes	8	29	35	37	93	15	19,544
Missions	2	10	7	1	6	4	3,075
Pastoral Centers	–	–	–	1	–	–	984
New Parishes	2	2	–	–	–	–	59
Catholic Hospitals	–	–	–	–	–	–	596
Patients Assisted Annually	–	–	–	–	–	–	78,996,656
Health Care Centers	–	–	–	–	–	–	544
Patients Assisted Annually	–	–	–	–	–	–	6,022,667
Specialized Homes	–	1	–	–	–	–	1,454
Total Assisted Annually	–	55	–	–	–	–	590,981
Residential Care of Children (Orphanages)	–	–	–	–	–	–	165
Total Assisted Annually	–	–	–	–	–	–	74,478
Day Care and Extended Day Care Centers	–	–	–	2	–	–	1,100
Total Assisted Annually	–	–	–	93	–	–	118,958
Special Centers for Social Services	–	–	–	2	–	–	2,290
Total Assisted Annually	–	–	–	8,500	–	–	20,953,944
Diocesan Seminaries	–	–	1	–	–	–	77
Students	–	–	–	–	–	–	3,400
Religious Seminaries	–	–	1	–	–	–	141
Students	–	–	–	–	–	–	1,517
Colleges and Universities	–	–	–	–	–	–	235
Total Students	–	–	–	–	–	–	705,059
High Schools, Diocesan and Parish	–	–	–	–	–	–	801
Total Students	–	–	–	–	–	–	386,476
High Schools, Private	–	–	–	–	–	–	795
Total Students	–	–	–	–	–	–	294,471
Elementary Schools, Diocesan and Parish	–	–	–	2	2	–	6,697
Total Students	–	–	–	339	245	–	1,940,698
Elementary Schools, Private	–	–	–	–	–	–	364
Total Students	–	–	–	–	–	–	117,776
Non–residential Schools for the Disabled	–	–	–	–	–	–	80
Total Students	–	–	–	–	–	–	18,120
Religious Education High School Students	130	–	362	193	384	6	782,102
Religious Education Elementary Students	260	–	1,260	693	1,863	10	3,617,181
Priests Teaching	–	–	–	–	–	–	1,934
Scholastics Teaching	–	–	–	–	–	–	41
Brothers Teaching	–	–	–	–	–	–	1,093
Sisters Teaching	–	–	–	4	5	–	8,201
Lay Teachers	–	–	–	23	15	–	156,470
Infant Baptisms	66	457	394	120	287	19	1,031,243
Adult Baptisms	2	23	18	13	15	–	83,234
Received into Full Communion	18	–	4	29	39	16	95,299
First Communions	72	339	407	85	304	–	909,779
Confirmations	68	480	431	96	266	–	651,443
Marriages	18	133	161	59	123	17	269,034
Deaths	22	181	183	224	606	12	479,034
Totals Catholics	12,100	24,411	27,394	12,572	32,860	5,000	63,683,030
Total Population	–	–	–	–	–	–	278,849,034
Catholic Population Percentage	–	–	–	–	–	–	23

Archdioceses = 36; Dioceses = 164; Apostolates = 3

2001 GENERAL SUMMARY

	EASTERN RITE (Cont.)						2001 U.S. GRAND TOTAL
	St. Josephat	St. Maron	St. Nicholas	St. Thomas	Stamford	Van Nuys	
Cardinals	–	–	–	–	–	–	11
Archbishops	–	1	–	–	–	–	45
Bishops	1	1	2	1	1	1	373
Abbots	–	–	2	–	–	–	115
Diocesan Priests	40	65	26	22	30	21	30,655
Religious Priests	1	12	13	–	12	5	15,386
Total Priests in Diocese	41	77	39	22	42	26	46,075
Newly Ordained Priests	–	–	–	–	–	1	536
Total Permanent Deacons	7	13	12	–	5	4	13,348
Total Brothers	10	7	2	–	5	7	5,565
Total Sisters	10	2	4	–	38	4	79,462
Number of Parishes	38	33	37	13	51	18	19,544
Missions	3	4	7	–	4	–	3,075
Pastoral Centers	–	–	–	–	1	1	984
New Parishes	–	–	1	–	–	–	59
Catholic Hospitals	–	–	–	–	–	–	596
Patients Assisted Annually	–	–	–	–	–	–	78,996,656
Health Care Centers	–	–	–	–	–	–	544
Patients Assisted Annually	–	–	–	–	–	–	6,022,667
Specialized Homes	2	–	–	3	1	–	1,454
Total Assisted Annually	146	–	–	–	28	–	590,981
Residential Care of Children (Orphanages)	–	–	–	–	–	–	165
Total Assisted Annually	–	–	–	–	–	–	74,478
Day Care and Extended Day Care Centers	–	–	–	–	1	–	1,100
Total Assisted Annually	–	–	–	–	44	–	118,958
Special Centers for Social Services	–	–	–	–	2	–	2,290
Total Assisted Annually	–	–	–	–	250	–	20,953,944
Diocesan Seminaries	–	1	–	–	1	–	77
Students	–	1	–	–	28	–	3,400
Religious Seminaries	–	–	–	–	–	–	141
Students	–	–	–	–	–	–	1,517
Colleges and Universities	–	–	–	–	–	–	235
Total Students	–	–	–	–	–	–	705,059
High Schools, Diocesan and Parish	–	–	1	–	1	–	801
Total Students	–	–	82	–	165	–	386,476
High Schools, Private	–	–	–	–	–	–	795
Total Students	–	–	–	–	–	–	294,471
Elementary Schools, Diocesan and Parish	2	–	2	–	3	–	6,697
Total Students	307	–	380	–	331	–	1,940,698
Elementary Schools, Private	–	–	–	–	–	–	364
Total Students	–	–	–	–	–	–	117,776
Non–residential Schools for the Disabled	–	–	–	–	–	–	80
Total Students	–	–	–	–	–	–	18,120
Religious Education High School Students	65	299	150		359	165	782,102
Religious Education Elementary Students	575	1,503	310		795	437	3,617,181
Priests Teaching	–	–	–	–	6	–	1,934
Scholastics Teaching	–	–	–	–	–	–	41
Brothers Teaching	–	–	–	–	–	–	1,093
Sisters Teaching	2	–	4	–	4	–	8,201
Lay Teachers	29	–	52	–	29	–	156,470
Infant Baptisms	112	447	244	1,078	213	102	1,031,243
Adult Baptisms	6	20	10	3	3	22	83,234
Received into Full Communion	4	13	4		5	20	95,299
First Communions	99	286	230	1,029	168	151	909,779
Confirmations	121	280	260		219	171	651,443
Marriages	62	140	74	405	60	23	269,034
Deaths	240	216	240	191	350	43	479,034
Totals Catholics	11,299	30,000	10,000	85,800	15,501	3,121	63,683,030
Total Population	–	–	–	–	–	–	278,849,034
Catholic Population Percentage	–	–	–	–	–	–	23

*Indicates Archdioceses.

†Certain Dioceses traverse state lines.

	EASTERN RITE TOTAL	*Military Archdiocese			1991 GRAND TOTALS	2000 GRAND TOTALS	2001 U.S. GRAND TOTAL
Cardinals	–	–			7	9	11
Archbishops	3	2			47	50	45
Bishops	19	4			367	366	373
Abbots	3	–			111	114	115
Diocesan Priests	558	–			34,598	30,940	30,655
Religious Priests	106	–			18,488	15,465	15,386
Total Priests in Diocese	664	–			53,088	46,603	46,075
Newly Ordained Priests	7	–			620	463	536
Total Permanent Deacons	75	–			10,120	12,862	13,348
Total Brothers	37	–			6,896	5,736	5,565
Total Sisters	302	–			101,911	81,161	79,462
Number of Parishes	574	–			19,946	19,627	19,544
Missions	48	–			3,696	2,965	3,075
Pastoral Centers	3	–			1,129	1,147	984
New Parishes	5	–			43	49	59
Catholic Hospitals	–	–			640	593	596
Patients Assisted Annually	–	–			44,031,842	77,006,804	78,996,656
Health Care Centers	–	–			216	557	544
Patients Assisted Annually	–	–			1,674,063	5,868,006	6,022,667
Specialized Homes	9	–			1,350	1,414	1,454
Total Assisted Annually	717	–			820,629	504,558	590,981
Residential Care of Children (Orphanages)	–	–			197	149	165
Total Assisted Annually	–	–			78,807	78,858	74,478
Day Care and Extended Day Care Centers	5	–			749	1,152	1,100
Total Assisted Annually	257	–			128,336	108,240	118,958
Special Centers for Social Services	4	–			1,701	2,271	2,290
Total Assisted Annually	8,750	–			12,220,300	20,134,669	20,953,944
Diocesan Seminaries	5	–			76	74	77
Students	45	–			4,777	3,088	3,400
Religious Seminaries	1	–			152	113	141
Students	–	–			1,705	1,437	1,517
Colleges and Universities	–	–			235	235	235
Total Students	–	–			650,314	701,240	705,059
High Schools, Diocesan and Parish	2	–			890	796	801
Total Students	247	–			380,466	381,311	386,476
High Schools, Private	1	–			531	557	795
Total Students	352	–			259,617	303,544	294,471
Elementary Schools, Diocesan and Parish	24	–			7,246	6,721	6,697
Total Students	4,001	–			1,929,184	1,940,285	1,940,698
Elementary Schools, Private	–	–			271	360	364
Total Students	–	–			59,313	92,967	117,776
Non–residential Schools for the Disabled	–	–			105	82	80
Total Students	–	–			9,767	18,342	18,120
Religious Education High School Students	2,845	21,000			770,257	821,833	782,102
Religious Education Elementary Students	10,649	44,200			3,252,779	3,607,108	3,617,181
Priests Teaching	10	–			3,352	1,794	1,934
Scholastics Teaching	–	–			104	49	41
Brothers Teaching	–	–			1,797	1,135	1,093
Sisters Teaching	54	12			18,098	9,255	8,201
Lay Teachers	578	220			142,930	150,561	156,470
Infant Baptisms	4,125	10,399			–	1,022,014	1,031,243
Adult Baptisms	181	1,304			–	83,157	83,234
◆ Receptions into the Church					1,147,976	–	–
Received into Full Communion	316	493			–	87,799	95,299
First Communions	3,969	7,478			876,809	884,570	909,779
Confirmations	3,064	5,098			510,860	629,762	651,443
Marriages	1,533	1,570			336,645	267,517	269,034
Deaths	3,540	–			457,337	473,724	479,034
Totals Catholics	427,844	–			58,568,015	62,391,484	63,683,030
Total Population	–	–			252,175,844	273,961,528	278,849,034
Catholic Population Percentage	–	–			24	23	23

◆ **Combination of Infant and Adult Baptisms**

Archdioceses = 36; Dioceses = 164; Apostolates = 3

1. U.S. Census Bureau estimate of Total Population as of Jan. 1, 2001: 281,421,906
2. U.S. Census Bureau estimate of Total Population as of Jan. 1, 2000: 274,023,981
3. U.S. Census Bureau estimate of Total Population as of Jan. 1, 1991: 250,870,030

The Official Catholic Directory

Products & Services Guide

2001

P.J. Kenedy & Sons
121 Chanlon Road, New Providence, NJ 07974
(908) 665-3543

THE OFFICIAL CATHOLIC DIRECTORY
PRODUCTS & SERVICES GUIDE
TABLE OF CONTENTS

AUDIO & VIDEO

GOLDEN DOME MEDIA

GOLDEN DOME MEDIA
P.O. Box 1616
South Bend, IN 46637-3357
Tel.: 800-782-7979; FAX: 219-631-1212
E-mail: goldendome@wndu.com
Web Site: www.goldendomemedia.com

Personnel:

Patrick Palella..Director
Jim Ford, Lisa Gillespie,
Michael O' Leary, Betsy Tavernier ....Account Executives

Type of Business:

Golden Dome Media is a diverse group of professional storytellers with an award-winning talent for presenting ideas, products and services. Golden Dome Media is a full service production house with twenty years experience which offers everything from building sets to producing documentaries, from staging live events to producing video and interactive services. We work hand-in-hand with you to inform, educate and inspire.

PATRICK BAKER & SONS

PATRICK BAKER & SONS, INC.
1650 West Street
Southington, CT 06489
Tel.: 860-628-5566; FAX: 860-276-9438

Personnel:

Patrick A. Baker ....Chairman
Brian T. Baker ....President
Michael P. Baker ....Vice President
Maureen Kelly ....Secretary

Type of Business:

- Religious Supplies
- Church Goods
- Church Renovations

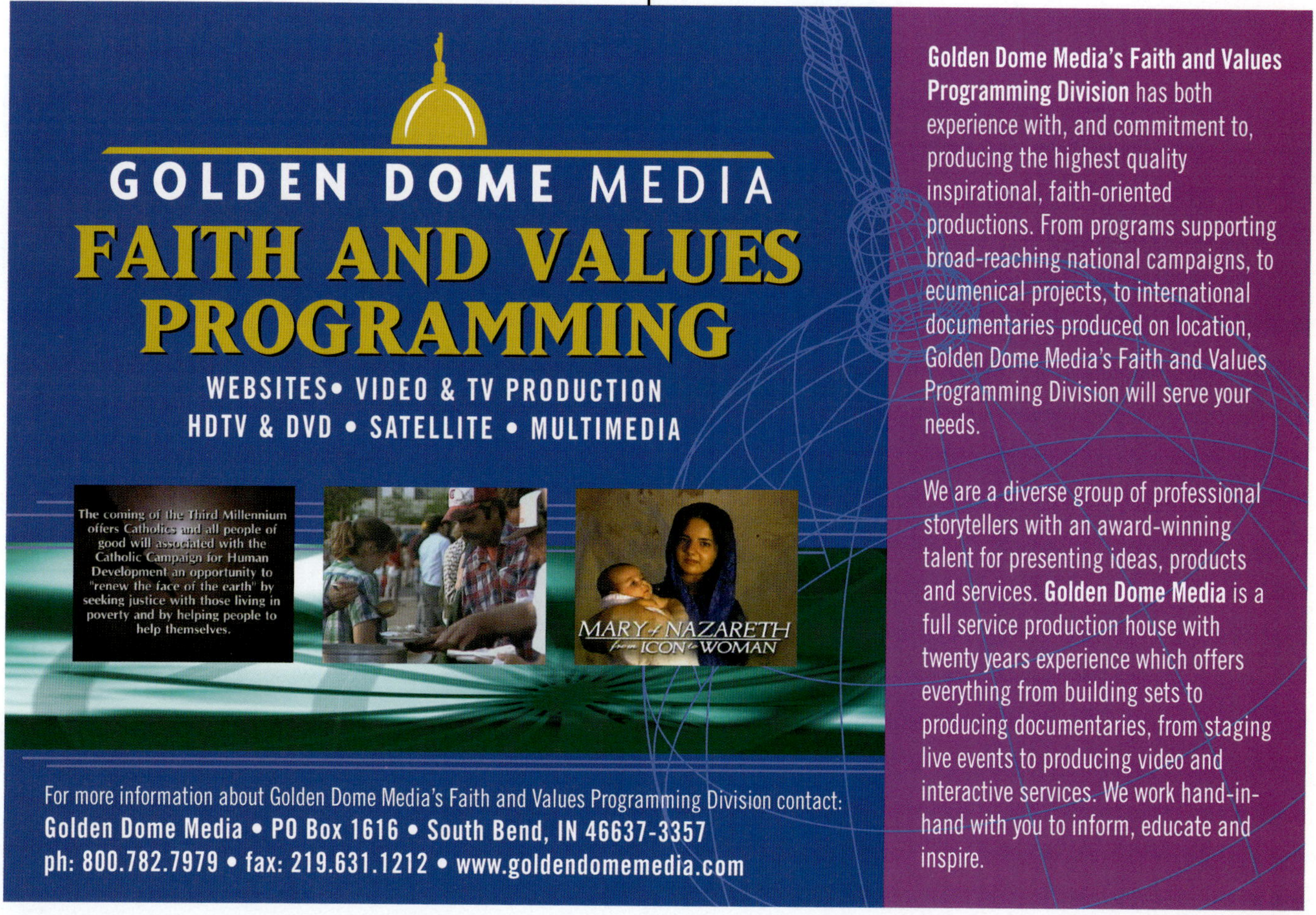

CASSETTES, AUDIO & VIDEO

Pauline
BOOKS & MEDIA
www.pauline.org

PAULINE BOOKS & MEDIA
50 Saint Paul's Avenue
Boston, MA 02130
Tel.: 617-522-8911; FAX: 617-541-9805
Web Site: www.pauline.org

Type of Business:
PAULINE Books & Media is the publishing house of the Daughters of St. Paul, an international Congregation of women religious who serve the Church with the communications media. The Daughters of St. Paul operate twenty bookstores in the U.S. and Canada. Visit our website, www.pauline.org, to access our online catalog and for a complete listing of our bookstores.

PRE-RECORDED CASSETTES & VIDEO

AMERICAN BIBLE SOCIETY

AMERICAN BIBLE SOCIETY
1865 Broadway
New York, NY 10023
Tel.: 800-784-6579; FAX 860-828-4773

Personnel:
Charlie Krueger....................Group Director
Bill Sinclair....................National Sales Manager

Type of Business:
ABS publishes and distributes a wide variety of low cost English, Spanish, and foreign language bibles for Catholic readers, including The Good News Bible, The New Revised Standard, New Jerusalem Bible, Contemporary English Version, Dios Habla Hoy and more. Outstanding resources for children, youth, and adults. The Bible on audio cassettes, video, and CD-ROM, Kingsley's Meadow Children's Videos, Resources for pastors, Bible study software. Call for a free catalog.

BUSINESS & FINANCE

AON RELIGIOUS INSTITUTIONS ALLIANCE (ARIA)
1 Market, Spear Tower, Suite 2100
San Francisco, CA 94105
Tel.: 415-512-3040; FAX: 415-543-5436

Personnel:
James M. Crowley....................Managing Consultant
Gregory S. Perez....................Senior Vice President
Russell B. Sands....................Chairman

Type of Business:
The Aon Religious Institution Alliance is an initiative of Aon Corporation, a world leader in insurance and consulting services with over $7 billion in revenues and a global history going back to 1680. ARIA works with religious institutions to provide: superior service, reduce costs, solve problems and provide financial risk management, and prudent analysis of the general risks that affect structure and operations. We serve with a sense of urgency in an atmosphere of commitment and trust.

TARGET CORPORATION
33 South 6th Street CC-19A
Minneapolis, MN 55402
Tel.: 612-304-1991
Web Site: www.target.com

Type of Business:
Target supports education with nearly $20 million in 2000. The Take Charge of Education initiative is a collection of programs created to help schools nationwide address a wide range of student needs. There are four programs available to both students and schools: School Fundraising, All-Around Scholarships, Teachers' Scholarships, and AAS in Education Grants. For more information visit us at Target.com or call 1-800-316-6142.

CAPITAL CAMPAIGNS

Guidance In Giving

GUIDANCE IN GIVING, INC.
225 Snedecor Ave.
Bayport, NY 11705
Tel.: 888-757-5444; FAX: 631-472-6109

8164 Sea Water Path
Columbia, MD 21045
Tel.: 888-869-5522; FAX: 410-799-9155

8465 Entreken Way
San Diego, CA 92129
Tel.: 800-993-3335; FAX: 858-484-0132

4110 Wellington Woods Circle #203
Kissimmee, FL 34741
Tel.: 888-575-6005; FAX: 562-920-0149

(continued)

(Guidance in Giving Continued)

Personnel:

Michael R. Cusack ....CEO and President
Joseph W. Zamorano ....Executive Vice President
Michael V. Goodwin ....Executive Vice President

Type of Business:

Guidance In Giving is a Catholic Development and Stewardship firm specializing in Diocesan and Parish capital campaigns, annual appeals, and stewardship programs. Additionally, the firm assists Catholic schools with their development and fund raising programs. Executives of the firm have been conducting successful campaigns since 1980 and understand and respect the Mission of the Church. We welcome the opportunity to spend a day at your diocese, parish or school to discuss your development and stewardship efforts. We will prepare an honest objective appraisal of your program at no cost to you. If you are considering counsel, please call one of our office locations.

CHURCH REGISTERS & PARISH OFFICE FORMS

F. J. REMEY CO., INC.
121 Willis Ave.
Mineola, NY 11501-0589
Tel.: 516-741-5112; FAX: 516-741-0523
Toll Free: 1-877-FJ REMEY (357-3639)

Type of Business:

Serving Catholic parishes since 1921 by providing the following products: Offering Envelope Mailing Systems, Annual Offering Envelope Boxsets, Bulk Collection Envelopes, Computer Recording, Collection Baskets, Parish Census, Church Record Books, Parish Office Forms, Church Stationery, Mass Cards, Raffle Tickets and Tuition Supplies.

CHURCH SYSTEMS

JP CONSULTING (CORNERSTONE)
2101 S. College #1
Bryan, TX 77801
Phone: 800-866-0250
Fax: 979-823-7028
Website:www.jpconsulting.net
E-mail: jpconsulting@yahoo.com

Personnel:

James Youngblood........................President
Mike Hnatt........................Vice President
Andrew Youngblood........................Vice President/Marketing
Jack Youngblood........................Vice President/Operations

Type of Business:

Cornerstone software products are used in 4 countries and 35 US states. Prices start at $99 and all programs include free networking. All Cornerstone products run in Windows 95, 98, NT, 2000. Call for a FREE demonstration CD.
Products include:
- Diocesan Certification Tracking
- Conference Tracking and Billing
- Parish Census/ Pledge/ Sacramental
- Facility/ Event/ Calendar Scheduling
- Ministry/ Intention Scheduling
- Religious Education, Youth Ministry, School Management

T L C CHURCH SOFTWARE
1045 Wildwood Boulevard SW
Issaquah, WA 98027-4506
Phone: 425-392-9592
Fax: 425-392-9592
Web Site:www:tlccommunications.com
E-mail: info@tlccommunications.com

Personnel:

Bob Liebscher........................President
Kate Poulson........................Sr. Technical Support
Rosemarie Olsen........................Marketing

Type of Business:

T L C Communications, Inc. is a software development company which has been in business since 1984. We produce user-friendly Windows based church management software (written for catholic churches) for census and contribution recording including time, treasure & talent, multi-year campaigns/drives, sacraments, user-defined lists, certificates, etc. We have a scheduling system for ministries and facilities and a religious education system for the administrative side of religious education.

COMMEMORATIVE KEEPSAKES

MESSERSMITH PROMOTIONS, INC.
P.O. Box 247
New Hampton, IA 50659-0247
Tel.: 800-726-1206; FAX: 641-394-4556
E-mail: bob@messersmithpromo.com
Web Site: www.messersmithpromo.com

Personnel:

Bob Messersmith

Type of Business:

For over 30 years supplying churches with keepsakes to commemorate anniversaries. A large selection of mugs, plates, ornaments, etc.

COMPUTERS & SOFTWARE

CHURCH MANAGEMENT RESOURCES
7120 South Division Avenue
Grand Rapids, MI 49548
Tel.: 877-455-9300; 616-988-1015; FAX 616-988-1093
Website: http://churchmgt.catholicweb.com

Offices in Michigan, Ohio, Pennsylvania, Florida, & Texas

Personnel:

Carl Grant........................President
Vicki Wells Bedard........................National Director

Type of Business:

Parish, School, & Religious Education Consulting: certified, licensed vendors of Churchmouse Suite Software™ and Parish Data Systems, Inc.™ software and provider of Catholicweb.com™ webware for church, school and religious education offices. Training, installation, seminars, newsletter, user group associations, stewardship appeals, scanning services, custom report writing and much more . . .
We know your needs. We exist to service those needs and to provide a network of resources to assist you in administering to the geographical and new "virtual" Internet parish.

Free demos and informational packets available.

ROHN
DESIGN GROUP

ROHN DESIGN GROUP
5075 Clairton Blvd, Suite 301
Pittsburgh, PA 15236
Tel: (412) 561-1228; (800) 245-1288; Fax: (412) 561-8129
E-mail: rohnstudio@aol.com
Web Site: www.rohndesign.com

Personnel:

A full service team of U.S. and international artisans & craftsmen.
Rolf R. Rohn ....Principal Consultant/Director/Artist
Kathleen L. Maglicco ....Principal Interior Design
Sister Janet Baxendale, S.C..Education

Type of Business:
Experience spanning 4 decades in renovation/restoration, conservation, and design of new worship environments. A valuable partner in over 1,300 commissions throughout the U.S., Canada and Europe.

We offer:
-Conservation, Preservation & Restoration
-Self Study Programs
-Ecclesiastical Artwork, Appointments & Furnishings
-Fundraising & Marketing
-Construction Management
-Estimates & Appraisals
-Interior Design and more....
Please see our ads on the divider pages for "General Summary" and "Products & Services." For other services look under "Construction, Maintenance & Renovation", "Church Furnishings" and "Liturgical & Church Goods".
www.rohndesign.com

FINANCIAL SERVICES

F. L. PUTNAM INVESTMENT MANAGEMENT COMPANY
Langley Place
10 Langley Road
Newton Centre
Boston, MA 02459
Tel.: 800-344-3435

1184 Lexington Court
San Luis Obispo, CA 93401
Tel.: 800-640-3770

Two City Center
Portland, ME 04101
Tel.: 800-356-1781

Type of Business:
F. L. Putnam is a diversified and integrated investment management firm with offices in Massachusetts, Maine, and California. We provide comprehensive investment advisory, counsel, fiduciary (trust) and supervisory services, along with related custodial and securities transaction and financial planning activity, to all types of investors. Since the 1950's we have specialized in the application of religious, ethical, and social justice criteria to the investment accounts of Church-affiliated institutions and other Clients concerned with this activity. Our services are tailored to the requirements of each Clients' accountants, securities brokers and other existing service providers.

SMART TUITION MANAGEMENT SERVICES
95 Wall Street, Suite 2300
New York, NY 10005
Tel.: 800-762-7808; FAX: 212-858-8043
E-mail: info@smarttuition.com
Web Site: www.smarttuition.com

Personnel:
Sam Rosen ....President

Type of Business:
SMART is a complete tuition management service that is designed to take schools out of the tuition collection business. The SMART program helps to reduce delinquencies, increase cash flow, and decrease the administrative workload. SMART serves more than 1,700 schools nationwide. SMART also has a Tuition Aid Analysis Service (TAAS) that determines how much families can afford to pay.

FUND-RAISING COUNSELING

Guidance In Giving

GUIDANCE IN GIVING, INC.
225 Snedecor Ave.
Bayport, NY 11705
Tel.: 888-757-5444; FAX: 631-472-6109

8164 Sea Water Path
Columbia, MD 21045
Tel.: 888-869-5522; FAX: 410-799-9155

8465 Entreken Way
San Diego, CA 92129
Tel.: 800-993-3335; FAX: 858-484-0132

4110 Wellington Woods Circle #203
Kissimmee, FL 34741
Tel.: 888-575-6005; FAX: 562-920-0149

Personnel:
Michael R. Cusack ....CEO and President
Joseph W. Zamorano ....Executive Vice President
Michael V. Goodwin ....Executive Vice President

Type of Business:
Guidance In Giving is a Catholic Development and Stewardship firm specializing in Diocesan and Parish capital campaigns, annual appeals, and stewardship programs. Additionally, the firm assists Catholic schools with their development and fund raising programs. Executives of the firm have been conducting successful campaigns since 1980 and understand and respect the Mission of the Church. We welcome the opportunity to spend a day at your diocese, parish or school to discuss your development and stewardship efforts. We will prepare an honest objective appraisal of your program at no cost to you. If you are considering counsel, please call one of our office locations.

HOLYBEARS, INC.
8550 Westland West Blvd.
Houston, TX 77041
Tel.: 281-469-4880; FAX 281-469-1030
E-mail: info@holybears.com
Web Site: www.holybears.com

Personnel:
Robert S. LeClair .... Founder

Type of Business:
HolyBears, Inc. produces the most appealing religious-themed fundraising and retail gift items in the industry. Our comprehensive fundraising program is designed to help churches, schools and other organizations easily achieve their fundraising goals. Our cuddly and inspiring teddy bears, complemented by our line of chocolates, giftwrap, and other traditional fundraising products, will instantly earn the endorsement and support of your community.

On the retail side, we offer a complete line of branded items supported by an array of display and promotional materials and backed by a strong Customer Service program.

RSI-KETCHUM, INC.
12270 Merit Drive #900
Dallas, TX 75251
Tel: 800-529-0803; FAX: 972-450-4477

Personnel:
Schuyler Lehman .... Senior Vice-President
Dan Conway .... Senior Vice-President
Vito Napoletano .... Vice-President

Type of Business:
RSI-Ketchum, Inc. provides to Catholic institutions uniquely tailored fund-raising campaigns with a spiritual stewardship perspective. The Catholic Services Group is dedicated to meeting the exclusive needs of Archdioceses, Dioceses, Parishes, schools and other Catholic organizations.

FUND-RAISING SERVICES

AMERICAN CITY BUREAU
1721 Moon Lake Blvd.
Hoffman Estates, IL 60194
Tel.: 800-786-GOAL (4625); FAX: 847-490-5860
E-mail: success@acb-inc.com
Web Site: www.acb-inc.com

Personnel:
Leslie Biggins Mollsen .... President
Daniel C. Mollsen .... Vice President

Type of Business:
Now celebrating its 88th year of service to Catholic dioceses, orders of men and women religious, basilicas, shrines, seminaries, hospitals, elementary schools, high schools and colleges. American City Bureau is the oldest, most experienced fund-raising consulting firm in the country. Since 1913, we have helped raise **billions** for our clients with services such as:

- Developmental/feasibility Studies
- Major Gift/Planned
- Communication Services
- Development Office Audits
- Capital Campaign Direction
- Gift/Endowment Development
- Video Productions
- Strategic Planning

CARGILL ASSOCIATES, INC.
4701 Altamesa Blvd.
Fort Worth, TX 76133
Tel.: 888-640-7020; FAX 817-292-9631
Web Site: www.cargillassociates.com

Personnel:
Steve Cargill .... CEO
Pat Graham .... President, Church Division
Wayne Vaughn .... President, Institution Division
Cade Garrison .... Director, Marketing

Type of Business:
Since 1976, Cargill Associates faith based program has raised over 3 billion dollars for churches, parishes, and other Christian causes. Cargill consultants work with parishes to craft programs to fit their spiritual needs. Other clients include universities, colleges, seminaries, hospitals, children's homes, retirement homes, and other institutions.

- Feasibility Studies
- Capital Campaigns
- Vision Workshops
- Financial & Spiritual Renewal
- Planned Giving
- Offertory Enhancement

www.cargillassociates.com

CATHEDRAL CORPORATION
Griffiss Technology Park
632 Ellsworth Road
Rome, NY 13441
Phone: (315) 338-0021
Fax: (315) 338-5874
Web Site: www:cathedralstewardship.com
E-mail: sales@cathedralstewardship.com

Personnel:
Marianne W. Gaige ....President and COO
Larry J. Beasley ....Director of Marketing
Ronald P. Blakeman ....Director of Sales

Business description:

Cathedral Corporation is a leader in the creation, printing, personalization, and high volume mailing of church envelopes and stewardship programs. Our customer base has grown for more than six decades. Today we serve churches nationwide with a full range of stewardship resources and electronic services for the internet.

CATHOLIC CONNECT
CROSS THE BRIDGE

Catholic Connect, Inc.
PO Box 15511
Pittsburgh, PA 15244
ph: 412.809.9710
fx: 412.809.9711
www.catholicconnect.com
info@catholicconnect.com

CATHOLIC CONNECT, INC.
P. O. Box 15511
Pittsburgh, PA 15244
Phone: 412-809-9710
Fax: 412-809-9711

Personnel:
Kathy A. Gennuso .... Co-founder
Richard F. Gennuso .... Co-founder

Type of Business:
On November 1st, 2000 www.catholicconnect.com was launched with the goal of encouraging Catholics to "Cross The Bridge". Catholic Connect is approaching it's objective in four ways.

-Provides information about Saints and a virtual look at the place where they lived.
-Sells fine religious giftware, artwork, and books
-Organizes custom design pilgrimages
-Donates 100% of after tax profit to charity

As a way to assist Catholic organizations, Catholic Connect will donate 10% of sales from the site's e-store to a registered association. Please contact us at: info@catholicconnect.com or 412-809-9710.

Your Supplier of Fine Ecclesiastical Interiors
CAVE CO.

CAVE COMPANY
P.O. Box 211
Old Westbury, NY 11568
Tel.: 800-989-CAVE / 516-676-1231; FAX: 516-676-9695
E-mail: caveco33@aol.com
Web Site: www.churchconstruction.com/caveco/

Personnel:
Gregory P. Cave ....President

Type of Business:
Our company is a fourth-generation business whose specialty is in the ecclesiastical interior design and restoration field. Our staff prides itself in the complete restoration and decoration of the smallest chapel to the largest cathedral, offering such unique services and products as our "Tree of Life" for fund raising, and electrical devotional candle stands. Our true specialty is the personalized service we are committed to bring our customers in the professional fashion they deserve.
We specialize in:
- Tree of Life
- Electric Devotional Candles
- Painting & Decorating
- Poor Boxes
- Kneelers & Pews; Restoration & New
- Gold Leaf
- Statuary & Sculpture; Repair & Restoration
- Challices & Ciboria; 24 Karat Gold Plating

Church Management Resources
"Serving the Church professional through information management."

CHURCH MANAGEMENT RESOURCES
7120 South Division Avenue
Grand Rapids, MI 49548
Tel.: 877-455-9300; 616-988-1015; FAX 616-988-1093
Website: http://churchmgt.catholicweb.com

Offices in Michigan, Ohio, Pennsylvania, Florida, & Texas

Personnel:
Carl Grant ....President
Vicki Wells Bedard..National Director

Type of Business:
Parish, School, & Religious Education Consulting: certified, licensed vendors of Churchmouse Suite Software™ and Parish Data Systems, Inc.™ software and provider of Catholicweb.com™ webware for church, school and religious education offices. Training, installation, seminars, newsletter, user group associations, stewardship appeals, scanning services, custom report writing and much more . . .
We know your needs. We exist to service those needs and to provide a network of resources to assist you in administering to the geographical and new "virtual" Internet parish.

Free demos and informational packets available.

C C S

COMMUNITY COUNSELLING SERVICE CO., INC.
350 Fifth Avenue, Suite 7210
New York, NY 10118
Tel.: 800-223-6733; FAX: 212-967-6451
Web Site: www.ccsfundraising.com

Personnel:

William B. Hanrahan .... President
Robert Kissane .... Executive Vice President
Patrick W. Moughan ...... Managing Director, Midwest Division
Joseph F. X. Lee .... Vice President

Type of Business:

CCS celebrates over 50 years of service to the Church. We have become one of the largest, most widely recommended fund raising firms in the world. CCS has successfully planned and managed fund raising campaigns for a variety of Catholic dioceses, parishes, universities, colleges, high schools, hospitals, homes for the aged, social service agencies, seminaries and religious communities. Regional offices in Chicago, San Francisco, London, Toronto and Dublin. Call 1-800-223-6733 for an estimate of your potential.

COSGRIFF COMPANY
Share Our Tradition of Success

COSGRIFF COMPANY
209 South 19th Street
Omaha, NE 68102
Tel.: 800-456-9902; FAX: 402-341-8590
E-mail: cosgriff@alltel.net
Web Site: www.cosgriffco.com

Personnel:

Michael J. Fitzpatrick .... President & CEO
Janet Wilson .... Vice President, Administration
Richard Spitler .... Vice President, Field Operations
M.J. Fitzpatrick, Jr. .... Director of Marketing
John Keeley .... Vice President, Sales Training

Type of Business:

Established in 1960, The Cosgriff Company provides a time proven, successful approach to fund-raising and capital campaigns. We are specialists in leadership motivation, fund-raising education, donor participation strategy and low-key solicitation. We provide on-site direction and executive supervision during your campaign, as well as consultative service before and after the campaign with a total service program. The Cosgriff Company has been an outstanding leader in Catholic projects all around the country, having raised over $3 billion for our clients through the years. We can make it happen for you!

**IN CATHOLIC FUND-RAISING,
COSGRIFF IS #1 AND RISING!**

Serving Catholic Parishes for Twenty Years
20 Years

CUNNEEN PARISH FUNDRAISING SERVICES, INC.
24 Rossotto Drive
Hamden, CT 06514
Tel: 800.842.4488 Fax: 203.407.5848
Web Site: www.cunneenfundraising.com
E-mail: info@cunneenfundraising.com

Personnel:

Frank J. Cunneen .... President
John F. Cunneen .... Vice President
James F. Cunneen .... Director of Operations
Gerard E. Kenney .... New England Director
Kevin R. Mancini .... Mid-Atlantic Director
Daniel J. Wendt .... Mid-Western Director

Type of Business:

Cunneen Parish Fundraising began serving Catholic parishes in 1981. Our approach is to provide the most effective, innovative and creative Fundraising campaigns for client Catholic parishes. All of our services, whether Offertory Enhancement, Stewardship, In-Pew Capital Campaigns, On-Site Capital Campaigns, Feasibility Studies or PRS-Pledge Redemption Service are infused with a commitment to providing fundraising that is firmly grounded in the principles of Biblical Stewardship. Over the past twenty years, Cunneen has assisted over 5,500 Catholic parishes in all-50 states and Canada.

GRAHAM
GP
PELTON
CONSULTING

GRAHAM-PELTON CONSULTING
16 Maple Street, Suite 5
Summit, NJ 07901
Tel.: 800-562-3695; FAX: 908-608-1520
Web Site: www.grahampelton.com

Type of Business:

Graham-Pelton Consulting is a full-service fund-raising and non-profit management firm specializing in capital campaigns for religious, healthcare, educational and social service organizations. Graham-Pelton offers a team of seasoned fund-raising and public relations executives who have raised over 385 million dollars for the Catholic community including Catholic colleges, universities, secondary schools, dioceses and parishes. Graham-Pelton provides resident campaign management as well as a full range of consulting services.

Guidance In Giving

GUIDANCE IN GIVING, INC.
225 Snedecor Ave.
Bayport, NY 11705
Tel.: 888-757-5444; FAX: 631-472-6109

8164 Sea Water Path
Columbia, MD 21045
Tel.: 888-869-5522; FAX: 410-799-9155

8465 Entreken Way
San Diego, CA 92129
Tel.: 800-993-3335; FAX: 858-484-0132

4110 Wellington Woods Circle #203
Kissimmee, FL 34741
Tel.: 888-575-6005; FAX: 562-920-0149

Personnel:
Michael R. Cusack ....CEO and President
Joseph W. Zamorano ....Executive Vice President
Michael V. Goodwin ....Executive Vice President

Type of Business:
Guidance In Giving is a Catholic Development and Stewardship firm specializing in Diocesan and Parish capital campaigns, annual appeals, and stewardship programs. Additionally, the firm assists Catholic schools with their development and fund raising programs. Executives of the firm have been conducting successful campaigns since 1980 and understand and respect the Mission of the Church. We welcome the opportunity to spend a day at your diocese, parish or school to discuss your development and stewardship efforts. We will prepare an honest objective appraisal of your program at no cost to you. If you are considering counsel, please call one of our office locations.

See our ad on the opposite page.

HARVEST DEVELOPMENT, INC.
Touching Hearts Through Philanthropy

HARVEST DEVELOPMENT, INC.
200 Executive Way
Ponte Vedra Beach, FL 32082
Tel.: 888-828-9250; 904-543-0117; Fax: 904-543-0364
Web Site: www.HARVESTDEVELOPMENT.com

Personnel:
Paul D'Alessandro CEO

Type of Business:
A full-service development consulting firm dedicated to helping our Catholic clients successfully achieve their development, strategic planning and campaign goals. Our services include:
- Long Range & Strategic Planning
- Campaign Readiness Assessments
- Campaign Planning & Management
- Case Statement Development
- Board & Volunteer Training
- Prospect Research Services
- Major Gift Solicitation
- Planned Giving

The Original Holy Bears

HOLYBEARS, INC.
8550 Westland West Blvd.
Houston, TX 77041
Tel.: 281-469-4880; FAX 281-469-1030
E-mail: info@holybears.com
Web Site: www.holybears.com

Personnel:
Robert S. LeClair ....Founder

Type of Business:
HolyBears, Inc. produces the most appealing religious-themed fundraising and retail gift items in the industry. Our comprehensive fundraising program is designed to help churches, schools and other organizations easily achieve their fundraising goals. Our cuddly and inspiring teddy bears, complemented by our line of chocolates, giftwrap, and other traditional fundraising products, will instantly earn the endorsement and support of your community.

On the retail side, we offer a complete line of branded items supported by an array of display and promotional materials and backed by a strong Customer Service program.

John V. McCarthy and Associates
16250 Northland Drive, Suite 200
Southfield, Michigan 48075-5266

Development and Fundraising Consultants

800-444-1840 E-mail: jvmfund@aol.cor
Fax: 248-552-0857 Website: jvmfundraising.cor

Personnel:
Frank J. Krajca ....Marketing/Sales
Thomas A. Parker ....Operations
Joseph H. Schram ....Follow-up Service

Type of Business:
Specialists in development and fundraising: exclusively for Catholic parishes, dioceses, schools and other institutions. Individual campaign timetables are designed to allow for the composition of the parish or institution. Since 1954 John V. McCarthy has been a major partner in the successful development and growth of ministries within the Catholic community through the application of proven principles of fundraising. We charge a flat fee with no additional costs for travel or living expenses. Our assigned Account Executive is on site full-time, except for small parish campaigns which can be designed on a consultation basis. We provide unmatched follow-up service for all clients.
Help is as close as our website.
If you feel that we can be of service to you in your develop-ment and fundraising needs, just visit our website and use the convenient response form to contact us.
A partner where "Your Priorities Become Ours."

KELLY

KELLY PROFESSIONAL FUND RAISING CONSULTANTS
203 W. 7TH St.
Traverse City, MI 49684
Tel.: 800-567-4660; FAX: 231-922-8120
E-mail: kpfrc@aol.com
Web Site: www.kpfrc.com

Personnel:
Joe Kelly ....President & CEO
Al Kelly ....Executive Director (C.F.R.E.)
Paul Kelly ....Vice President, Operations
Lynne Green ....Vice President, Campaign Development

Our Mission: To Serve Your Mission. We want to be your Financial Partner.

(Continued)

(Kelly Professional Fund Raising Consultants continued)

Type of Business:
We offer a variety of innovative financial-growth services to help you remove the fiscal barriers to your mission:
- Capital Campaigns
- Stewardship Programs/Annual Renewals
- Major Gifts
- Comprehensive Appeal
- Continuous Guidance
- Planned Giving
- Endowment Campaigns
- Feasibility Studies
- Development Office Establishment & Training

Call Kelly for a free appraisal of your financial future.

Services to Archdioceses, Dioceses, large and small Parishes, elementary and secondary schools, consolidated school systems. We work nationally, we succeed locally.

Celebrating 32 years in service to the Catholic Community.

Kirby Smith
Associates, Inc.
Ministry of Church Finance

KIRBY-SMITH ASSOCIATES, INC.
5 Fawn Dr.
Quarryville, PA 17566
Tel.: 1-800-762-3996; 717-284-3100; FAX: 717-284-3659
Web Site: http://www.kirbysmith.com
email: kirbysmith@aol.com

Personnel:
C. Eugene Musser .... President
Dale Bateman .... Executive Vice President

Type of Business:
Since our founding in 1938, Kirby-Smith Associates has served more than 10,000 parishes and schools, and has raised more than three billion dollars. Our campaigns include detailed on-site counseling, organizational guidance, comprehensive materials, as well as long-term consultation and stewardship training. We offer a full range of services to better meet the needs of your parish or school; Capital and Budget Campaigns, Feasibility Studies, Pre-Campaign Planning and Strategic Planning. Meeting the needs of the Catholic community we serve is our ministry and the service we bring to you.

THE MARTIN J. MORAN CO.

Washington D.C. • San Diego • North Palm Beach • Boston
Catholic Fund-Raising Counsel

MARTIN J. MORAN CO.
One Pennsylvania Plaza
New York, NY 10119
Tel.: 212-736-9550; FAX: 212-736-7122

Type of Business:
The Moran Co. has been raising great amounts of money for its clients for a variety of needs. The key to success has been the design and conduct of a proven, time-tested Moran Co. Plan for generating both dollars and a high level of participation.

MESSERSMITH PROMOTIONS, INC.
P.O. Box 247
New Hampton, IA 50659-0247
Tel.: 800-726-1206; FAX: 641-394-4556
E-mail: bob@messersmithpromo.com
Web Site: www.messersmithpromo.com

Personnel:
Bob Messersmith

Type of Business:
For over 30 years supplying churches with keepsakes to commemorate anniversaries. A large selection of mugs, plates, ornaments, etc.

RUOTOLO
ASSOCIATES INC.
The Right Direction

RUOTOLO ASSOCIATES INC.
Horizon Square
29 Broadway, Ste. 210
Cresskill, NJ 07626
Tel.: 201-568-3898; FAX: 201-568-8783

Personnel:
George C. Ruotolo, Jr. .... C.F.R.E., President

Type of Business:
Comprehensive development programs, capital campaigns, annual funds, planned giving, feasibility/planning studies, executive search, student recruitment, and marketing/public relations efforts. Specializing in service to Catholic institutions, including dioceses, schools, churches, religious orders, and social service and health organizations, serving the country through our four regional offices.

TARGET CORPORATION
33 South 6th Street CC-19A
Minneapolis, MN 55402
Tel.: 612-304-1991
Web Site: www.target.com

Type of Business:
Target supports education with nearly $20 million in 2000. The Take Charge of Education initiative is a collection of programs created to help schools nationwide address a wide range of student needs. There are four programs available to both students and schools: School Fundraising, All-Around Scholarships, Teachers' Scholarships, and AAS in Education Grants. For more information visit us at Target.com or call 1-800-316-6142.

Walsh & Associates
"Helping Catholic Causes Reach New Heights"

WALSH & ASSOCIATES
12700 Nicollet Ave. So., Ste. 216
Burnsville, MN 55337
Tel.: 800-894-3863; FAX: 952-882-5270
E-mail: walshandassc@mciworldcom.net

Personnel:
Michael A. Walsh ....President

Type of Business:
Walsh & Associates has been helping Catholic causes reach new heights since 1984 with our high quality, cost effective fund development and stewardship enhancement services. Our services include capital campaigns, feasibility/planning studies, stewardship education and enhancement efforts, planned giving programs and a variety of other services to help meet our clients' needs. So if you're ready to reach new heights in your fund development and stewardship efforts, give us a call. We'd be happy to help.

ALPINE AIR PURIFIER
CHARLES DUNN SYSTEMS
400 School Street
Woodbridge, NJ 07095
Phone: 732-969-2708
Fax: 732-634-5411

Type of Business:
A terrific fund raiser.
Learn how parishioner can enjoy purified air for their families at virtually no cost. Bingo halls, rectory rest are.s, homes - wherever there is a smoke or order problem. Alpine Air Purifier: A terrific fund raiser – on its own. Learn how parishioners can enjoy purified air for their families at virtually no cost.

. Improves Business
. Eliminates Smoke
. Eliminates Odors
. No Installation Cost
. No Filters to Buy
. No Monthly Service Contracts
. Great part-time job

Our Free Trial will make you a believer. Introducing our new Flair Air Purifier at only $360.00. Call 1-800-575-2454 for information or free literature.

FUND-RAISING SUPPLIES

AmericanChurch

AMERICANCHURCH
365 McClurg Road, Youngstown, OH 44512
Tel: 800-250-7112 – fax: 888-763-8772
E-mail: sales@americanchurch.com
Web Site: www.americanchurch.com

Personnel:
Christine J. Dailey ....Executive V.P. of Sales & Marketing

Type of Business:
For nearly 100 years, AmericanChurch has been dedicated to serving the needs of the Catholic Community. We are the largest church offering envelope manufacturer in the world, with the most comprehensive range of Adult and Children's Stewardship Resources available:

* Mailed Offering Envelope Systems
* Annual Boxed Envelopes
* Bulk Collection Envelopes
* Stewardship Fundraising Programs
  Capital Campaigns
  Increased Offertory Collections
  Pledge Drives & School Tuition Programs
* Direct Mail Services
* Fulfillment Services
* Electronic Church Giving
* Computerized Contribution Recording
* Specialty Imprinted Fund Raising Products

www.americanchurch.com

BC
BARTON-COTTON

BARTON COTTON
1405 Parker Rd.
Baltimore, MD 21227
Tel.: 800-638-4652; FAX; 800-807-2954

Personnel:
Denise J. Payne ....Vice President, Marketing and Sales

Type of Business:
For over 70 years, Barton-Cotton, Inc. has been proud to offer the finest selection of quality religious stationery products to the Catholic Clergy and Religious. Over 300 products are available including Mass cards, Sacramental certificates, Christmas and Easter cards, Mother's/Father's Day sets, Ordination/Jubilee products, Way of the Cross booklets, Rosary folders, Holy cards, Bulletins, Offering Envelopes, Bookmarks and more. Products can be personalized with your name, church name, address, or special message. For a FREE catalog, call 1-800-638-4652.

CARROLL ART, INC.
710 NE 26th St.
Fort Lauderdale, FL 33305
Tel.: 800-876-4569; FAX: 954-561-4098

Personnel:
David Nagle..President Designer
Liza Palmer ....Sales Manager
Wayne Palmer...Sales Representative
Robert Perkins ....Sales Representative

Type of Business:
Carroll Art has been in business for 12 years. We design and custom build all types of plaques and memorials including the tree of life, plaques, recognition systems, church signs, donor plates, custom sculptures, and memorials are just a few of our products. We can provide you with the perfect fund raising tool.

CATHEDRAL CORPORATION
Griffiss Technology Park
632 Ellsworth Road
Rome, NY 13441
Phone: (315) 338-0021
Fax: (315) 338-5874
Web Site: www:cathedralstewardship.com
E-mail: sales@cathedralstewardship.com

Personnel:
Marianne W. Gaige ....President and COO
Larry J. Beasley ....Director of Marketing
Ronald P. Blakeman ....Director of Sales

Business description:

Cathedral Corporation is a leader in the creation, printing, personalization, and high volume mailing of church envelopes and stewardship programs. Our customer base has grown for more than six decades. Today we serve churches nationwide with a full range of stewardship resources and electronic services for the internet.

F. J. REMEY CO., INC.
121 Willis Ave.
Mineola, NY 11501-0589
Tel.: 516-741-5112; FAX: 516-741-0523
Toll Free: 1-877-FJ REMEY (357-3639)

Type of Business:
Serving Catholic parishes since 1921 by providing the following products: Offering Envelope Mailing Systems, Annual Offering Envelope Boxsets, Bulk Collection Envelopes, Computer Recording, Collection Baskets, Parish Census, Church Record Books, Parish Office Forms, Church Stationery, Mass Cards, Raffle Tickets and Tuition Supplies.

The Original Holy Bears™

HOLYBEARS, INC.
8550 Westland West Blvd.
Houston, TX 77041
Tel.: 281-469-4880; FAX 281-469-1030
E-mail: info@holybears.com
Web Site: www.holybears.com

Personnel:
Robert S. LeClair..Founder

Type of Business:
HolyBears, Inc. produces the most appealing religious-themed fundraising and retail gift items in the industry. Our comprehensive fundraising program is designed to help churches, schools and other organizations easily achieve their fundraising goals. Our cuddly and inspiring teddy bears, complemented by our line of chocolates, giftwrap, and other traditional fundraising products, will instantly earn the endorsement and support of your community.

On the retail side, we offer a complete line of branded items supported by an array of display and promotional materials and backed by a strong Customer Service program.

THE PRINTERY HOUSE
Conception Abbey · CONCEPTION · MISSOURI 64433

THE PRINTERY HOUSE
Conception Abbey
PO Box 12
Conception, MO 64433
Tel.: 800-889-0105; 660-944-2632; FAX: 888-556-8262
E-mail: sales@printeryhouse.org
Web Site: printeryhouse.org

Personnel:
Br. William Buchholz, O.S.B ....Director
Ron Riggs ....Director of Sales and Marketing
Br. Jeremiah Tuttle, O.S.B ....Marketing Associate
Br. Michael Marcotte, O.S.B ....Art Director

Type of Business:
Manufacture and market Christian/Catholic Greeting cards and icons. Customized Christmas and other cards to enhance your development programs are our forte`! The Printery House is a not-for-profit extension of the apostolate of the monks of Conception Abbey.

Call 800-889-0105 or fax 888-556-8262 for free samples, catalogs and quantity discount schedules.

THE ARTIST'S HAND MAKES THE DIFFERENCE

SANFORD WERFEL- ARTIST

SANFORD WERFEL - ARTIST
425 Old Georges Rd.
North Brunswick, NJ 08902
Tel.: 800-443-3744; 732-297-1166; FAX: 732-297-7770
E-mail: werfelart@aol.com
Web Site: http://www.sanfordwerfelartist.com

Type of Business:

Since 1968, Mr. Werfel's sculptures have been helping parishes to INSPIRE and MOTIVATE GIVING through the use of his original sculptures. Building drives, capital or endowment funds, sacrificial giving, and tithing programs all benefit from using Donor Recognition Sculptures. Call or write for FREE INFORMATION. Included will be costs and designs as well as a "HOW-TO-USE" guide that tells how your parish can use sculpture to raise funds. Good art is forever.

Visit our Website at: http://www.SanfordWerfelArtist.com
email us at: WerfelArt@aol.com

TESTAMINTS™

TESTAMINTS, INC.
1248 Sussex Turnpike, Unit C-1
Randolph, NJ 07869
Tel.: 973-895-0400; FAX: 973-895-3742

Personnel:

Al Poe .... President/CEO
Tom Ryder .... V.P. Sales
Vilma Hampton .... Product Manager

Type of Business:

Testamints, Inc., Pl the message in Catholic School Fund-Raising, Promote the Gospel *tastefully* using testamints Brand Fund-Raising Products: Promise Pop Brand Lollipops, Sugar free and Surgared mints, Fruit Flavored Candies, Sour Fruit Candies, and Collector's Tins. Great Tasting, Profitable and Fully-Refundable. All products are creatively packaged and wrapped with Scripture Verses!

Please call: 1-888-879-0400 or 973-895-5041 for a free brochure.

INSURANCE

ABERCROMBIE, BURNS, MCKIERNAN & CO. INSURANCE, INC.
581 Post Road
Darien, CT 06820-1125
Tel.: 203-655-7468
FAX: 203-656-2540

See our display ad on page 25r.

AON RELIGIOUS INSTITUTIONS ALLIANCE (ARIA)
1 Market, Spear Tower, Suite 2100
San Francisco, CA 94105
Tel.: 415-512-3040; FAX: 415-543-5436

Personnel:

James M. Crowley .... Managing Consultant
Gregory S. Perez .... Senior Vice President
Russell B. Sands .... Chairman

Type of Business:

The Aon Religious Institution Alliance is an initiative of Aon Corporation, a world leader in insurance and consulting services with over $7 billion in revenues and a global history going back to 1680. ARIA works with religious institutions to provide: superior service, reduce costs, solve problems and provide financial risk management, and prudent analysis of the general risks that affect structure and operations. We serve with a sense of urgency in an atmosphere of commitment and trust.

See our display ad on page 23r.

INVESTMENT ADVISORS

CBIS Christian Brothers Investment Services, Inc.

CHRISTIAN BROTHERS INVESTMENT SERVICES, INC.
90 Park Avenue, 29th floor
New York, NY 10016
Tel: 800-592-8890
Fax: 212-490-6092
Web Site: www.cbisonline.com

Personnel:
Michael W. O'Hern, FSC ....President & CEO
Donald E. Platner ....Vice President – Head of Sales and Marketing
Phone: (800) 592-8890 Fax: (212) 490-6092

Type of Business:
For 20 years, Christian Brothers Investment Services, Inc. (CBIS), has been a registered Catholic faith-based investment advisory firm solely dedicated to serving the financial needs of Catholic institutions worldwide. We currently work with over 1,000 Catholic organizations representing total assets under management of $2.6 billion.

CBIS is committed to a Catholic faith-based socially responsible investing strategy emphasizing active ownership, through dialogue with corporate management, shareholder resolutions, proxy voting and principled purchasing. We and our clients/participants believe that investing should reflect our Catholic values. We have been able to integrate a comprehensive Catholic SRI program into all of our 10 equity and fixed income diversified funds as well as our individually managed accounts. Performance overall has been very competitive. We welcome inquiries from representatives of any Catholic organizations. Please contact Donald Platner at 1-800-592-8890.

F. L. PUTNAM INVESTMENT MANAGEMENT COMPANY
Langley Place
10 Langley Road
Newton Centre
Boston, MA 02459
Tel.: 800-344-3435

1184 Lexington Court
San Luis Obispo, CA 93401
Tel.: 800-640-3770

Two City Center
Portland, ME 04101
Tel.: 800-356-1781

Type of Business:
F. L. Putnam is a diversified and integrated investment management firm with offices in Massachusetts, Maine, and California. We provide comprehensive investment advisory, counsel, fiduciary (trust) and supervisory services, along with related custodial and securities transaction and financial planning activity, to all types of investors. Since the 1950's we have specialized in the application of religious, ethical, and social justice criteria to the investment accounts of Church-affiliated institutions and other Clients concerned with this activity. Our services are tailored to the requirements of each Clients' accountants, securities brokers and other existing service providers.

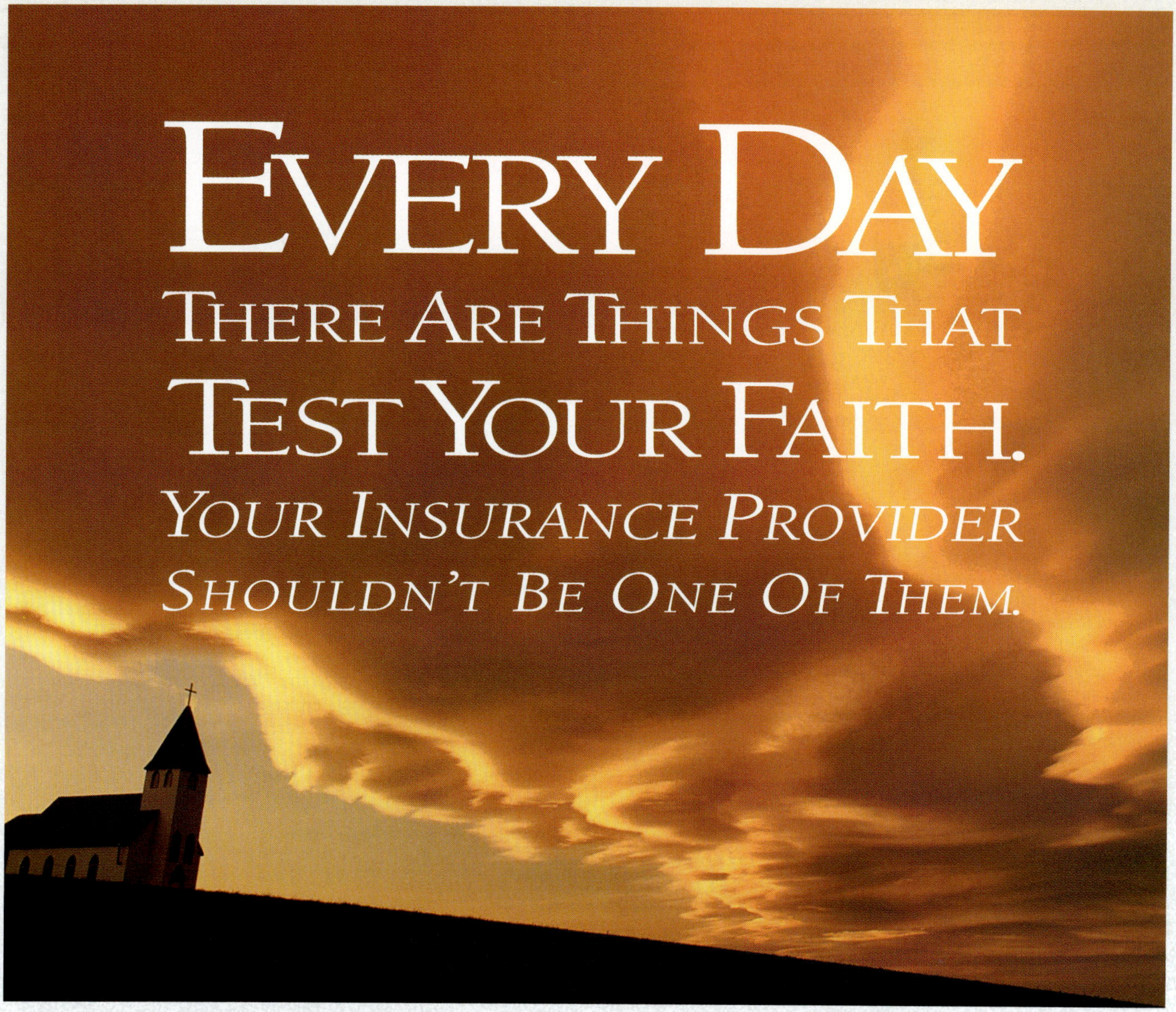

Aon understands. Ministering to the spiritual needs of humanity takes many forms, from sanctuaries and hospitals to campgrounds and inner-city youth work. And for each and every form your ministry takes, there are risks to manage, assets to protect, funds to invest, and employee needs to be met.

Helping you respond to these many challenges takes knowledge and skills of unusual depth and breadth. That's why the Aon Religious Institutions Alliance was created. We bring together the dedication, expertise and experience of Aon's 40,000 employees and focus them on the special needs that religious ministries present.

Aon is a strong leader among insurance and consulting organizations worldwide, with a history dating back to 1680, yearly revenues of $5.8 billion and offices in 100 countries. Through the Aon Religious Institutions Alliance, all the best of this strength is coordinated to "benefit and build" in cooperation with those, like you, who work toward the fulfillment of God's purpose for this creation.

You can learn more about us by visiting our Web site at www.aria.aon.com or by calling us at 1-800-669-9460 or (415) 512-3040. AON *Aon Religious Institutions Alliance*

INVESTMENT MANAGEMENT

F. L. PUTNAM INVESTMENT MANAGEMENT COMPANY
Langley Place
10 Langley Road
Newton Centre
Boston, MA 02459
Tel.: 800-344-3435

1184 Lexington Court
San Luis Obispo, CA 93401
Tel.: 800-640-3770

Two City Center
Portland, ME 04101
Tel.: 800-356-1781

Type of Business:

F. L. Putnam is a diversified and integrated investment management firm with offices in Massachusetts, Maine, and California. We provide comprehensive investment advisory, counsel, fiduciary (trust) and supervisory services, along with related custodial and securities transaction and financial planning activity, to all types of investors. Since the 1950's we have specialized in the application of religious, ethical, and social justice criteria to the investment accounts of Church-affiliated institutions and other Clients concerned with this activity. Our services are tailored to the requirements of each Clients' accountants, securities brokers and other existing service providers.

MINISTRY OF CHURCH FINANCE

CATHEDRAL CORPORATION
Griffiss Technology Park
632 Ellsworth Road
Rome, NY 13441
Phone: (315) 338-0021
Fax: (315) 338-5874
Web Site: www:cathedralstewardship.com
E-mail: sales@cathedralstewardship.com

Personnel:

Marianne W. Gaige ....President and COO
Larry J. Beasley ....Director of Marketing
Ronald P. Blakeman ....Director of Sales

Business description:

Cathedral Corporation is a leader in the creation, printing, personalization, and high volume mailing of church envelopes and stewardship programs. Our customer base has grown for more than six decades. Today we serve churches nationwide with a full range of stewardship resources and electronic services for the internet.

MUTUAL FUNDS

F. L. PUTNAM INVESTMENT MANAGEMENT COMPANY
Langley Place
10 Langley Road
Newton Centre
Boston, MA 02459
Tel.: 800-344-3435

1184 Lexington Court
San Luis Obispo, CA 93401
Tel.: 800-640-3770

Two City Center
Portland, ME 04101
Tel.: 800-356-1781

Type of Business:

F. L. Putnam is a diversified and integrated investment management firm with offices in Massachusetts, Maine, and California. We provide comprehensive investment advisory, counsel, fiduciary (trust) and supervisory services, along with related custodial and securities transaction and financial planning activity, to all types of investors. Since the 1950's we have specialized in the application of religious, ethical, and social justice criteria to the investment accounts of Church-affiliated institutions and other Clients concerned with this activity. Our services are tailored to the requirements of each Clients' accountants, securities brokers and other existing service providers.

PLANNED GIVING

CARDINAL GLENNON CHILDREN'S HOSPITAL
Office of Gift Planning
1465 South Grand Blvd.
St. Louis, MO 63104
Tel.: 314-577-5605
FAX: 314-268-6416

Personnel:

Jim Orsund ....Executive Vice President
Roya Bromell ....Director of Gift Planning

Type of Business:

As America's only full-service, free-standing, Catholic Children's Hospital, Cardinal Glennon Children's Hospital meets the medical needs of children regardless of race, religion, or ability to pay.

TRUST AND CUSTODY SERVICES

F. L. PUTNAM INVESTMENT MANAGEMENT COMPANY
Langley Place
10 Langley Road
Newton Centre
Boston, MA 02459
Tel.: 800-344-3435

1184 Lexington Court
San Luis Obispo, CA 93401
Tel.: 800-640-3770

Two City Center
Portland, ME 04101
Tel.: 800-356-1781

Type of Business:
F. L. Putnam is a diversified and integrated investment management firm with offices in Massachusetts, Maine, and California. We provide comprehensive investment advisory, counsel, fiduciary (trust) and supervisory services, along with related custodial and securities transaction and financial planning activity, to all types of investors. Since the 1950's we have specialized in the application of religious, ethical, and social justice criteria to the investment accounts of Church-affiliated institutions and other Clients concerned with this activity. Our services are tailored to the requirements of each Clients' accountants, securities brokers and other existing service providers.

CHURCH FURNISHINGS

TOUJOURS
ADRIAN HAMERS®
CHURCH INTERIORS

ADRIAN HAMERS INC.
2 Madison Avenue
Larchmont, NY 10538
Tel.: 914-834-7780; FAX: 914-834-0712

Type of Business:
Custom designers and manufacturers of Sacred Vessels. Since 1887, the Hamers name has been synonymous with expert Silversmithing throughout the world in the field of Liturgical Art. Please contact us for those hard to find items, as we always have a large selection of Adrian Hamers Estate Collection pieces in stock. We are experts in: Church Interiors from design to execution, Renovations, Altars, Sacred Vessels, Gold and Silver Plating & Repairing, Appraisals, Tabernacles, Marble, Statuary, Woodwork & Woodcarving, Stained Glass, Pews & Chairs, Gold Leafing, Frescoes, Restoration, Trompe-l' oeuil, Wall Murals (repair and conservation cleaning), Ornamental Plaster, Heraldic Designs & Bishop Regalia. Please call us for a free 24 page Sacred Vessels color catalog, or our free 80 page color Woodcarvings catalog.

BOTTI STUDIO OF
ARCHITECTURAL ARTS, INC.

BOTTI STUDIO OF ARCHITECTURAL ARTS, INC.
919 Grove St.
Evanston, IL 60201
Tel.: 800-524-7211; FAX: 847-869-5996; 847-869-5933
E-mail: botti@bottistudio.com
Web Site: www.bottistudio.com

East Coast Studio
3104 S. Osprey Ave.
Sarasota, FL 33577
Tel.: 941-951-0978; FAX: 941-953-9078

West Coast Studio
1038 N. Highway 101
Encinitas, CA 92024
Tel.: 760-753-0705; FAX: 760-753-0705
Agropoli, Italy

Personnel:
Staff includes internationally recognized artists and designers working in conjunction with our highly skilled artisans and craftsmen.
Italo G. Botti .... President

Type of Business:
For generations Botti Studio has had a reputation for embodying all that is artistically creative in the traditional and contemporary ecclesiastical field. This field includes design and fabrication of stained and faceted glass windows, restoration/conservation of windows, church interiors, appointments, murals, sculpture, mosaic and marble. We are completely dedicated to both quality and satisfying our clients needs spiritually and liturgically. Botti Studio , established in 1864, is nationwide, offering consultation and designs without obligation. Member of the Stained Glass Association of America.

CARROLL ELECTRONICS INCORPORATED
710 Northeast 26th St.
Wilton Manors, FL 33305
Tel.: 800-331-0444; FAX: 954-561-4098

Personnel:
David Nagle .... President
Liza Palmer .... Sales Manager
Bob Perkins .... Sales Representative
Donna Spencer .... Service Engineer

Type of Business:
Carroll Electronics has been in business for 20 years designing and building Electronic Votive Candle Stands for thousands of churches throughout the United States.

Chagall Design Limited©

Designers of Custom Liturgical Vestments, Stoles, Dalmatics, Banners and Sanctuary Accessories.

CHAGALL DESIGN LTD.
910 south Los Angeles Street
Los Angeles, CA 90015
Tel: 1-800-947-7923 fax: 213-624-8036
E-mail Address: CHAGALL@IX.NETCOM.COM
Web: WWW.CHAGALLDESIGN.COM

Personnel:

Jacques de Groot..President
Mannix Delfino ....Vice President

Type of Business:

Designers of custom liturgical Vestments, Stoles, Dalmatics Banners and sanctuary accessories. The finest import fabrics, and custom embroidery's are used in a blend of traditional elegance and modern design. Our attention to detail makes each vestment, and banner unique. All our banners are custom made in design and size; we also offer a line of Tabernacles, Candlesticks, Chalices, Ciborium's that are imported from Italy, Spain and France. Please review our accompanying catalog with the Catholic Directory.

ARCHITECTURAL FEATURES
CREATED BY *Madden*

CHARLES L. MADDEN
CREATING ARCHITECTURAL FEATURES
1245 E. Butler Pike
Ambler, PA 19002-6032 U.S.A.
Tel.: 215-646-8919; FAX: 215-643-7272
email: cmadden@concentric.net

Personnel:

Charles L. Madden ....Owner/Creative Director

Type of Business:

Architectural Features by definition is a single art resource for consultation, design, fabrication, and installation in creating spaces of liturgical and meditative inspiration with sacred art and beautiful materials of fine substance and detailing. Our worldwide commissions in bronze sculpture, mosaic, marble, stained glass, tapestry, and fine woods are custom created to extend our client's vision. Whether you are a Diocesan, Community, Institutional, or Architectural client - we are pleased to put our vast creative and computer technological resources at the service of your building and renovational vision.

COKESBURY
201 Eighth Avenue, South
P.O. Box 801
Nashville, TN 37202-0801
Tel.: 800-672-1789; FAX: 800-445-8189
Web Site: www.cokesbury.com

Personnel:

Neil Alexander.......................................President and Publisher
Edward R. Kowalski ....Senior Vice President of Marketing and Sales

Type of Business:

Cokesbury has been serving the needs of clergy, religious educators, and churches for over 200 years. We offer a wide variety of church furnishings, both standard and customized, including chancel sets, pulpits, pews and pew cushions, guest registry and memorial desks, baptismal fonts, lecterns, classroom furnishings, and indoor and outdoor signs. All are backed by our 100% satisfaction guarantee.

Look for Cokesbury's 2001 Liturgical Catalog, mailing February 28. If you haven't received your catalog by the end of March, please call 1-800-672-1789 and request a free copy. Ask for catalog number CL1-508895.

Conrad Schmitt Studios Inc.

CONRAD SCHMITT STUDIOS, INC.
2405 S. 162nd St.
New Berlin, WI 53151
Tel.: 800-969-3033; 414-786-3030; FAX: 414-786-9036

Personnel:

Heidi Gruenke Emery........Vice President & Marketing Director

Type of Business:

Since 1889, this family-owned Studio has restored and decorated hundreds of interiors across the country. Their scope of work includes the investigation and documentation of original decorative schemes; the restoration of those schemes through the application of various decorative techniques including gilding, glazing, marbleizing, stenciling, and graining, as well as the design, fabrication, conservation or replication of murals and stained glass. The Studio can assist projects in the early stages with architectural samples and rendering for fund-raising. Recently completed projects include St. Josaphat's Basilica, Milwaukee, WI; St. Ann's, Napoleanville, LA; and St. Bernard's, Akron, OH.

HOLY ART STUDIOS

DOMUSDEI

SINCE 1963 TO HOLY ART SERVICE.
WE CREATE CHURCH INTERIOS, STAINED GLASS WINDOWS, MOSAICS, BRONZE CASTINGS WITH LOST WAX PROCESS, FIBERGLASS MASTERPIECES, RESTAURATIONS

▲ **Stained glass window of holy spirit with bronze frame of angels**
Artist: F. Serangeli

▲ **Mr. Alessandro del Monte, president and founder of Domudei company with His Holiness the Pope during a meeting.**

▲**Stained glass window made in modern style.**
Artist: G. Luzzietti

▲ **Apsidal mosaic made with enamels and marbles.**
Artist: A. Fumagalli

▲ **Big bronze masterpiece dedicaded to St. Vitale made for Card. Maida archbishop of Detroit**
Artist: L. Andreuzzi

FACTORY: Via dei Tulipani 48 - 00040 CECCHINA DI ALBANO (ROMA) - ITALY
TEL: 011-39-06-9343369 - FAX: 011-39-06-9344971
SHOW ROOM: Via Scossacavalli 3/9 - 00193 ROMA - ITALY - Tel. 011-39-06-6868090
E-MAIL: info@domusdei.it - m.delmonte@domusdei.it
HTTP:/www.domusdei.it

DOMUSDEI HOLY ART STUDIOS

DOMUSDEI HOLY ART STUDIOS

DOMUSDEI HOLY ART STUDIOS
FACTORY: Via dei Tulipani, 48 - 00040 CECCHINA DI ALBANO (RM) - ITALY
Tel: 011-39-06-9343369
FAX: 011-39-06-9344971

SHOW ROOM: Via Scossacavalli 3/9 - 00193 - ROMA - ITALY
Tel: 011-39-06-6868090
FAX: 011-39-06-6869806
E-Mail: info@domusdei.it
m.delmonte@domusdei.it
Web Site: www.domusdei.it

Personnel:
Alessandro Del Monte ....President
Massimiliano Del Monte ....Executive Director
Aldo Del Monte .... Assistant President

Type of Business:
Founded in 1963, Domusdei Studio has restored thousands of church interiors all over the world. Specializing in designing and manufacturing stained glass windows, mosaics, bronze and fiberglass statues, altars, bronze doors, lecterns, baptismal fonts, candlesticks, flower holders, tabernacles.
We are also experts in silver and gold plating and the restoration of wood and metal masterpieces.

EZELL COMPANY
1569 Wilmington Blvd.
Wilmington, CA 90744
Tel.: 800-643-4400; FAX: 310-834-4857
E-mail: ezellcompany@aol.com

Type of Business:
Ezell Company is a third generation, family owned and operated business since 1957. Ezell is a member of the Association of Christian Schools International and has satisfied customers across the U.S. with quality furniture, customer service and low prices. Whether your needs are for your school, church, or office, we will be glad to service you.

MAAS ROWE

MAAS-ROWE CARILLONS, INC.
2255 Meyers Ave.
Escondido, CA 92029
Tel.: 800-854-2023; FAX: 760-747-2677

Personnel:
Paul Rowe ....President
Craig Johnson ....National Sales Manager
Joel Bloom............................ Sales and Marketing Coordinator

Type of Business:
Established 1922. Manufacturers of automatic (computerized) Carillon and Church Bell Systems using compact discs for ultra high quality sound. Factory direct sales, service and installation. Sales—National and International. Upgrading of older carillon systems (any brand) to compact disc with computer control. Producers of compact discs featuring carillon and organ church music designed to play automatically or manually in computer controlled carillon equipment. Manufacturers of Musical Handbells. Importers of European Cast Bronze Church Bells and accessories. Manufacturer of Tower Clocks.

P. J. McDERMOTT & CO.
P.O. Box 950101
Fort Tilden, NY 11695
Tel.: 718-634-5583

Personnel:
Patrick J. McDermott ....President

Type of Business:
We are a major supplier of Ready-made suits, coats, slacks, blazers, R.J. Toomey Co. shirt fronts, French-cuff shirts, clerical vests ... "Beau-Veste" and Gammarelli (Rome) albs, surplices and rochets ... Fully custom tailored cassocks ... We are considered the leader in the U.S. and specialize in Bishops and Monsignors robes, all of which are custom tailored here. We also supply all Episcopal accessories; mitres, zuchettos, birettas, rochets, albs, pectoral cross, chains and cross cords, bishops rings, croziers.
HAVE TAPE MEASURE — WILL TRAVEL

PATRICK BAKER & SONS

PATRICK BAKER & SONS, INC.
1650 West Street
Southington, CT 06489
Tel.: 860-628-5566; FAX: 860-276-9438

Personnel:
Patrick A. Baker ....Chairman
Brian T. Baker ....President
Michael P. Baker ....Vice President
Maureen Kelly ....Secretary

Type of Business:
- Religious Supplies
- Church Goods
- Church Renovations

ROHN DESIGN GROUP

ROHN DESIGN GROUP
5075 Clairton Blvd, Suite 301
Pittsburgh, PA 15236
Tel: (412) 561-1228; (800) 245-1288; Fax: (412) 561-8129
E-mail: rohnstudio@aol.com
Web Site: www.rohndesign.com

Personnel:

A full service team of U.S. and international artisans & craftsmen.
Rolf R. Rohn ....Principal Consultant/Director/Artist
Kathleen L. Maglicco ....Principal Interior Design
Sister Janet Baxendale, S.C...Education

Type of Business:
Experience spanning 4 decades in renovation/restoration, conservation, and design of new worship environments. A valuable partner in over 1,300 commissions throughout the U.S., Canada and Europe.

We offer:
-Altars
-Tabernacles
-Bronze/Stonework
-Artwork, multi-mediums
-Statuary
-Baptismal Fonts
-Ambo-Lecterns
-Mosaics
-Pews/Choirs
-Lamps and Lighting
-Liturgical Design
and more....
Please see our ads on the divider pages for "General Summary" and "Products & Services." For other services look under "Construction, Maintenance & Renovation", "Consultants" and "Liturgical & Church Goods".
www.rohndesign.com

SN STADELMAIER NIJMEGEN

STADELMAIER-NIJMEGEN-HOLLAND
P.O. Box 7063
6503 GN Nijmegen
Nijmegen, Holland 6503 GN
Tel.: 31-24-3791170; FAX: 31-24-3791171
e-mail: info@stadelmaier.com

Type of Business:
SN-Antiques offers, for the re-use in the Cath. Liturgy;
Completely restored, original, devotional interior-pieces. Altars, stations, candlesticks, perpetual lights, statues, reliquaries, ciboria, chalices, monstrances, censers, mission crosses, processional crosses, Saints, paintings, etc.
Different styles and age: Roman, baroque, neo-gothic, etc.
Please describe your interest directly to Mrs. Annemieke Drijber.

RAMBUSCH

RAMBUSCH
40 West 13th St.
New York, NY 10011
Tel.: 212-675-0400; FAX: 212-620-4687

Personnel:
Viggo Bech Rambusch ....Senior Project Director
Martin V. Rambusch ....Stained Glass Director

Type of Business:
Since 1898, creating church interiors, liturgical furnishings, and art work. Fine restoration of church interiors. In-house studios and shops for designing and executing stained glass, church lighting systems, art metal work, and decorative painting.

Vermont Church Supply Co.

VERMONT CHURCH SUPPLY CO.
676 Pine Street, P.O. Box 368
Burlington, VT 05401
Tel.: 802-862-6486, 800-451-3453; FAX: 802-862-5765
E-mail: vcs@together.net

Personnel:
Neil Clark ....President

Type of Business:
Since our inception in 1946 by W. Barrett Clark and Doris Clark, Vermont Church Supply has offered the highest quality products and the best service to the Church and the Clergy. We have a wide range of products including Candles, Church Furniture, Metalware and Vestments. Our founders' Sons, Neil, John, Thomas and Robert, along with the third generation Anthony Clark, continue to provide services such as refinishing Sacred Vessels, Candlesticks and abernacles and also the execution of hand carved wood and marble Statuary. Whether your needs are small or large, we can give the best personalized service to our Customers.

ALTARS, TABERNACLES, ETC.

TOUJOURS

ADRIAN HAMERS®
CHURCH INTERIORS

ADRIAN HAMERS INC.
2 Madison Avenue
Larchmont, NY 10538
Tel.: 914-834-7780; FAX: 914-834-0712

Type of Business:
Custom designers and manufacturers of Sacred Vessels. Since 1887, the Hamers name has been synonymous with expert Silversmithing throughout the world in the field of Liturgical Art. Please contact us for those hard to find items, as we always have a large selection of Adrian Hamers Estate Collection pieces in stock. We are experts in: Church Interiors from design to execution, Renovations, Altars, Sacred Vessels, Gold and Silver Plating & Repairing, Appraisals, Tabernacles, Marble, Statuary, Woodwork & Woodcarving, Stained Glass, Pews & Chairs, Gold Leafing, Frescoes, Restoration, Trompe-l' oeuil, Wall Murals (repair and conservation cleaning), Ornamental Plaster, Heraldic Designs & Bishop Regalia. Please call us for a free 24 page Sacred Vessels color catalog, or our free 80 page color Woodcarvings catalog.

Conrad Schmitt Studios Inc.

CONRAD SCHMITT STUDIOS, INC.
2405 S. 162nd St.
New Berlin, WI 53151
Tel.: 800-969-3033; 414-786-3030; FAX: 414-786-9036

Personnel:
Heidi Gruenke Emery........Vice President & Marketing Director

Type of Business:
Since 1889, this family-owned Studio has restored and decorated hundreds of interiors across the country. Their scope of work includes the investigation and documentation of original decorative schemes; the restoration of those schemes through the application of various decorative techniques including gilding, glazing, marbleizing, stenciling, and graining, as well as the design, fabrication, conservation or replication of murals and stained glass. The Studio can assist projects in the early stages with architectural samples and rendering for fund-raising. Recently completed projects include St. Josaphat's Basilica, Milwaukee, WI; St. Ann's, Napoleanville, LA; and St. Bernard's, Akron, OH.

D.C. RIGGOTT INC.
3540 Neal Ave.
Afton, MN 55001
Tel.: 800-479-8777; FAX: 651-436-4769
E-mail: dcriggottinc@aol.com

Personnel:
Don Riggott ....Owner/President

Type of Business:
Specializing in vintage church accessories, architectural ornamentation and liturgical furnishings.
Stained Glass Windows • Altars • Lighting • Statuary • Stations of the Cross • Tabernacles • Monstrances • Fonts • Pews • Steeple Bells • Vestments • Books • Furniture • Candlesticks • Chalices
Please contact us with specific requests. We will be happy to send you photographs and specifics on any items in our inventory. You may have items in storage or not being used, please contact us as we are actively searching for vintage items to purchase for re-use in liturgical spaces.

TAG GRANDA.
LITURGICAL ARTS

GRANDA LITURGICAL ARTS, INC.
990 Grove Street, Suite 203
Evanston, IL 60201
Tel.: 800-425-0828; FAX: 847-492-1374
email: ruf4granda@aol.com
Website: www.hispacom.es/granda

Personnel:
Karen Johnson...Business Manager

Type of Business:
GRANDA LITURGICAL ARTS, Inc. is the USA branch of the largest supplier of church goods in the world: TALLERES DE ARTE GRANDA, S.A.
With 65 employees and sales all over the world, we can offer our experience in the manufacture of:
— metalware: chalices, tabernacles, etc.
— vestments
— wood carvings
— church decoration, interior design
Since 1891, we have been serving the church, combining modern techniques (computer aided design, projects in 3D ...) with artistic values.
Special custom orders are our specialty, styled and priced according to your needs.

INSPIRED ARTISANS, Ltd.

INSPIRED ARTISANS, LTD.
816 W. National Avenue
Milwaukee, WI 53204
Tel.: 414-672-9478; 1-888-442-9141; FAX: 414-672-9479
Website: www.inspiredart.com

Personnel:
Old and New World Artists and Craftpeople
Gianfranco Tassara ....President & Art Director

Type of Business:
Inspired Artisans has been serving the church with quality Liturgical Art such as Baptismal Fonts, Crypt Fronts, Decorating, Floor Plan Layout, Fund Raising Items, Iconography, Liturgical Fitments, Memorials, Mosaics, Murals, Restorations, Sculptures, Stained, Etched, Faceted Glass and Terra Cotta. Our work can be seen in many locations in Alabama, California, Connecticut, Galapagos/Ecuador, Colorado, Georgia, Illinois, Minnesota and Wisconsin. See our display ad under the "Art, Statuary & Decorations" category or contact us for a complete list of our past commissions, and brochures.

Marklin Candle Design

MARKLIN CANDLE DESIGN
PO Box 182
Contoocook, NH 03229-0182
Tel.: 603-746-2211; FAX 603-746-2070
E-mail: info@marklincandle.com
Websites: www.marklincandle.com; www.liturgy2000.com

Type of Business:
The artisans of Marklin Candle Design commit themselves to create liturgical candles and appointments of outstanding craftmanship and unmatched elegance.

Our goal shall be to help foster full, active, and conscious participation in liturgical celebrations. To this end, our designs will boldly proclaim the symbols for which they stand; and our products will embody authentic and noble materials.

Each and every product that we sell will bear the mark of human hands in the production process.

We shall offer our customers excellent value, and we shall stand behind our products without question.

NEW HOLLAND Church-Furniture™
If You Can Imagine It We Can Build It!

NEW HOLLAND CHURCH FURNITURE
313 Prospect Street
New Holland, PA 17557
Phone 800-220-1465 Fax 717-354-2481
Web Site http://www.newhollandwood.com

Personnel:
Donald Long ....President
Richard Ragan ....Marketing & Sales Director

Type Of Business
New Holland Church Furniture is the nations leading manufacturer of Radius Curved Pews. In addition to our Radius Curved Pews, New Holland also manufactures a complete line of Straight and Mitered solid wood pews, upholstered pews available in a wide variety of styles and finishes.. In addition to pews New Holland also manufactures a complete line of high quality interlocking wood chairs or flexible seating. We will be happy to work with your designer and Architect to find the best possible seating solution for your church. New Holland is also the nations leading manufacturer of Custom Altar, Tabernacle, and Platform Furniture. Since our beginning in 1919 our tag line has been "If you can imagine it, we can build it." TM

RAMBUSCH

RAMBUSCH
40 West 13th St.
New York, NY 10011
Tel.: 212-675-0400; FAX: 212-620-4687

Personnel:
Viggo Bech Rambusch ....Senior Project Director
Martin V. Rambusch ....Stained Glass Director

Type of Business:
Since 1898, creating church interiors, liturgical furnishings, and art work. Fine restoration of church interiors. In-house studios and shops for designing and executing stained glass, church lighting systems, art metal work, and decorative painting.

St. Anthony's CHURCH SUPPLIES

ST. ANTHONY'S CHURCH SUPPLIES
3121 McCart Ave.
Fort Worth, TX 76110
Tel: 800-772-5928
E-mail: books4u@airmail.net
Web Site: www.StellaMarisBooks.com

Type of Business:
We can supply your church or chapel with the finest sanctuary appointments available. We offer a full line of ecclesiastical goods from clerical shirts and vestments, to chalices and tabernacles, to church statuary and stained glass windows, to Catholic books and other media, to furniture for churches, church offices, classrooms, and cafeterias.

We offer great service with a smile and look forward to making new friends.

Please use our toll free number or e-mail to contact John Heitzenrater or Richard Myers.

ANNOUNCEMENT & BULLETIN BOARDS

ATD-AMERICAN CO.

ATD-AMERICAN CO.
135 Greenwood Avenue
Wyncote, PA 19095-1396
Tel.: 888-283-2487; FAX: 800-283-7363
E-mail: american@atd.com
Web Site: www.atd.com

Personnel:
Bob Roche....................Marketing
Sal Catanese....................Sales

Type of Business:
For four generations, ATD-AMERICAN has supplied Furniture and Equipment to Churches, Organizations and Institutions nationally and worldwide. Since 1931, it has been our tradition to deliver high quality products and personal service at the lowest competitive prices. ATD offers a wide range of products to meet all of the needs of your Church and School. Our comprehensive catalog includes the following: Announcement and Bulletin Boards, Audio-Visual Equipment, Classroom Furniture, Computer Furniture, Daycare Furniture, Display Cases, Folding Chairs, Folding Tables, Lecterns, Library Furniture, Office Furniture, Outdoor Equipment, Pews and Pulpit Furniture, Room Dividers and Partitions, Stacking Chairs, and Stages and Risers.

For a FREE Wholesale Furniture Catalog, call us toll-free 888-283-2487 or fax us at 800-283-7363. You can also visit our website at http://www.atd.com or email us at atd.com.

SPECIAL OFFER FOR CATHOLIC DIRECTORY SUBSCRIBERS: Mention offer code 6557 and receive a special 10% discount on your first order.

ANTIQUES, RELIGIOUS

TOUJOURS

ADRIAN HAMERS® CHURCH INTERIORS

ADRIAN HAMERS INC.
2 Madison Avenue
Larchmont, NY 10538
Tel.: 914-834-7780; FAX: 914-834-0712

Type of Business:
Custom designers and manufacturers of Sacred Vessels. Since 1887, the Hamers name has been synonymous with expert Silversmithing throughout the world in the field of Liturgical Art. Please contact us for those hard to find items, as we always have a large selection of Adrian Hamers Estate Collection pieces in stock. We are experts in: Church Interiors from design to execution, Renovations, Altars, Sacred Vessels, Gold and Silver Plating & Repairing, Appraisals, Tabernacles, Marble, Statuary, Woodwork & Woodcarving, Stained Glass, Pews & Chairs, Gold Leafing, Frescoes, Restoration, Trompe-l' oeuil, Wall Murals (repair and conservation cleaning), Ornamental Plaster, Heraldic Designs & Bishop Regalia. Please call us for a free 24 page Sacred Vessels color catalog, or our free 80 page color Woodcarvings catalog.

D.C. RIGGOTT INC.
3540 Neal Ave.
Afton, MN 55001
Tel.: 800-479-8777; FAX: 651-436-4769
E-mail: dcriggottinc@aol.com

Personnel:
Don Riggott....................Owner/President

Type of Business:
Specializing in vintage church accessories, architectural ornamentation and liturgical furnishings.
Stained Glass Windows • Altars • Lighting • Statuary • Stations of the Cross • Tabernacles • Monstrances • Fonts • Pews • Steeple Bells • Vestments • Books • Furniture • Candlesticks • Chalices
Please contact us with specific requests. We will be happy to send you photographs and specifics on any items in our inventory. You may have items in storage or not being used, please contact us as we are actively searching for vintage items to purchase for re-use in liturgical spaces.

Mark W. Read Studio & Gallery

MARK W. READ STUDIO
1898 Broadstone Road
P.O. Box 671
Valle Crucis, NC 28691
Phone & Fax (828) 963-8191
Web Site: www.markreadstudio.com

Type of Business:

Liturgical Jewelry	Sculpture
Architectural Pieces	Sacred Vessels
Utensils	Urns
Holloware/Chalices	Gem Setting
Gold & Silver Plating	Museum Quality Restoration

Mark Read is an artist craftsman of 30 years experience. Trained in old world and traditional methods he possesses the patience and skill to master the precise craftsmanship that goes into each custom project or restoration piece. Whether his exquisite one-of-a-kind creations are to purely inspire the beholder or serve as a functional piece, Marks creative gifts, unique approach and special sensitivity ensures that each commission works in harmony with its architectural surroundings.

From gold, silver, bronze, titanium to iron and beyond...the possibilities are endless.

Research and consulting is his first priority for restoration projects, thereby ensuring a clear understanding of the steps that must be taken to restore your piece back to its original glory. All types of restoration are accepted.

Please visit our website with the special section for Liturgical pieces.

See our display ad on page 107r.

GREG SPIESS & CO.

SPIESS ARCHITECTURAL ANTIQUES
230 East Washington St.
Joliet, IL 60433
Tel.: 815-722-5639; FAX: 815-722-0171

Type of Business:
Specializing in older and antique church furniture. Gothic, Romanesque and Classical styles in marble, wood, bronze etc. Altars, pews, communion rails, stained glass, lecterns, baptismals, vestment cases, confessionals, Stations of the Cross statuary. Lighting Pew and wood restoration available.

SN STADELMAIER NIJMEGEN

STADELMAIER-NIJMEGEN-HOLLAND
P.O. Box 7063
6503 GN Nijmegen
Nijmegen, Holland 6503 GN
Tel.: 31-24-3791170; FAX: 31-24-3791171
e-mail: info@stadelmaier.com

Type of Business:
SN-Antiques offers, for the re-use in the Cath. Liturgy;
Completely restored, original, devotional interior-pieces. Altars, stations, candlesticks, perpetual lights, statues, reliquaries, ciboria, chalices, monstrances, censers, mission crosses, processional crosses, Saints, paintings, etc.
Different styles and age: Roman, baroque, neo-gothic, etc.
Please describe your interest directly to Mrs. Annemieke Drijber.

ART, STATUARY & DECORATIONS

ABBOTT

ABBOTT INC.
Showroom 1515 Route 38
Cherry Hill, NJ 08002
Tel.: 800-522-2688; 856-662-6959; FAX: 856-665-5109
Website: http://www.abbottsinc.com
email: acg.inc@cwixmail.com

Personnel:
Daniel J. Castonguay .... President
Joseph F. McKeaney .... General Manager
Michael W. Wasyluk .... Customer Service

Type of Business:
Purveyors of the Finest Vesture, Paraments, Statuary & Metalware since 1962. Unique and original creations, our specialty. Custom designs to complement your liturgical environment. Exclusive representatives of Slabbinck Master Collection & Original Collection.

FRATRES TOUJOURS

ADRIAN HAMERS® CHURCH INTERIORS

ADRIAN HAMERS INC.
2 Madison Avenue
Larchmont, NY 10538
Tel.: 914-834-7780; FAX: 914-834-0712

Type of Business:
Custom designers and manufacturers of Sacred Vessels. Since 1887, the Hamers name has been synonymous with expert Silversmithing throughout the world in the field of Liturgical Art. Please contact us for those hard to find items, as we always have a large selection of Adrian Hamers Estate Collection pieces in stock. We are experts in: Church Interiors from design to execution, Renovations, Altars, Sacred Vessels, Gold and Silver Plating & Repairing, Appraisals, Tabernacles, Marble, Statuary, Woodwork & Woodcarving, Stained Glass, Pews & Chairs, Gold Leafing, Frescoes, Restoration, Trompe-l' oeuil, Wall Murals (repair and conservation cleaning), Ornamental Plaster, Heraldic Designs & Bishop Regalia. Please call us for a free 24 page Sacred Vessels color catalog, or our free 80 page color Woodcarvings catalog.

THE BLACK FOREST BUILDING COMPANY

ANTHONY JOHN BELLOMO / THE BLACK FOREST CO.
310 Euclid
Mt. Clemens, MI 48043
Tel.: 810-954-4800; FAX: 810-954-4806

Personnel:
Anthony Bellomo .... President

Type of Business:
Anthony John Bellomo is a sculptor. He works in a wide variety of materials from wood and bronze to fibers, stone and living plant materials. Over the past twenty-five years he has developed the Black Forest Company. Black Forest is a group of artists and artisans, who along with Bellomo, design and build contemporary sculpture and furniture for liturgical spaces. He has developed a series of redwood sand carved exterior pieces for outdoor chapels and meditation gardens. Anthony, along with his team of dedicated crafts persons, pride themselves in listening to the individual community, designing and building pieces to help make their worship a deeper experience.

Berlinger Company

THE BERLINGER COMPANY
2605 N. Sheridan Road
Peoria, IL 61604
Tel.: 888-688-1781; 309-688-1771
Website: www.theberlingercompany.com

Personnel:
Michael Berlinger .... President
John Lingenfelter .... Vice-President
Jeff Walters .... Office Manager

Type of Business:
Church interior design and consultants
Interior restoration
New church designs
New liturgical whole goods—domestic and imported
Custom manufacturers
Liturgical Antiquities—domestic and imported

BOTTI STUDIO OF ARCHITECTURAL ARTS, INC.

BOTTI STUDIO OF ARCHITECTURAL ARTS, INC.
919 Grove St.
Evanston, IL 60201
Tel.: 800-524-7211; FAX: 847-869-5996; 847-869-5933
E-mail: botti@bottistudio.com
Website: www.bottistudio.com

East Coast Studio
3104 S. Osprey Ave.
Sarasota, FL 33577
Tel.: 941-951-0978; FAX: 941-953-9078

West Coast Studio
1038 N. Highway 101
Encinitas, CA 92024
Tel.: 760-753-0705; FAX: 760-753-0705
Agropoli, Italy

Personnel:
Staff includes internationally recognized artists and designers working in conjunction with our highly skilled artisans and craftsmen.
Italo G. Botti .... President

Type of Business:
For generations Botti Studio has had a reputation for embodying all that is artistically creative in the traditional and contemporary ecclesiastical field. This field includes design and fabrication of stained and faceted glass windows, restoration/conservation of windows, church interiors, appointments, murals, sculpture, mosaic and marble. We are completely dedicated to both quality and satisfying our clients needs spiritually and liturgically. Botti Studio , established in 1864, is nationwide, offering consultation and designs without obligation. Member of the Stained Glass Association of America.

CARROLL ART, INC.
710 NE 26th St.
Fort Lauderdale, FL 33305
Tel.: 800-876-4569; FAX: 954-561-4098

Personnel:
David Nagle....................President Designer
Liza Palmer....................Sales Manager
Wayne Palmer....................Sales Representative
Robert Perkins....................Sales Representative

Type of Business:
Carroll Art has been in business for 12 years. We design and custom build all types of plaques and memorials including the tree of life, plaques, recognition systems, church signs, donor plates, custom sculptures, and memorials are just a few of our products. We can provide you with the perfect fund raising tool.

Conrad Schmitt Studios Inc.

CONRAD SCHMITT STUDIOS, INC.
2405 S. 162nd St.
New Berlin, WI 53151
Tel.: 800-969-3033; 414-786-3030; FAX: 414-786-9036

Personnel:
Heidi Gruenke Emery........Vice President & Marketing Director

Type of Business:
Since 1889, this family-owned Studio has restored and decorated hundreds of interiors across the country. Their scope of work includes the investigation and documentation of original decorative schemes; the restoration of those schemes through the application of various decorative techniques including gilding, glazing, marbleizing, stenciling, and graining, as well as the design, fabrication, conservation or replication of murals and stained glass. The Studio can assist projects in the early stages with architectural samples and rendering for fund-raising. Recently completed projects include St. Josaphat's Basilica, Milwaukee, WI; St. Ann's, Napoleanville, LA; and St. Bernard's, Akron, OH.

D.C. RIGGOTT INC.
3540 Neal Ave.
Afton, MN 55001
Tel.: 800-479-8777; FAX: 651-436-4769
E-mail: dcriggottinc@aol.com

Personnel:
Don Riggott....................Owner/President

Type of Business:
Specializing in vintage church accessories, architectural ornamentation and liturgical furnishings.
Stained Glass Windows • Altars • Lighting • Statuary • Stations of the Cross • Tabernacles • Monstrances • Fonts • Pews • Steeple Bells • Vestments • Books • Furniture • Candlesticks • Chalices
Please contact us with specific requests. We will be happy to send you photographs and specifics on any items in our inventory. You may have items in storage or not being used, please contact us as we are actively searching for vintage items to purchase for re-use in liturgical spaces.

DAPRATO RIGALI STUDIOS, INC.

DAPRATO RIGALI STUDIOS, INC.
7956 Oakton St.
Niles, IL 60714
Tel.: 847-692-6350; FAX: 847-692-3445

Personnel:
John Rigali
Robert Rigali
Lisa Rigali Galvin
Mike Rigali

Type of Business:
Daprato Rigali Studios Inc. has been beautifying Churches in America since 1860.
Today we find the Rigali Family restoring and renovating the churches originally decorated by their Great-Grandfather, John E. Rigali; aware of his reputation to create spiritually moving environments with quality material and craftsmanship.
Some of their most recent jobs include: decoration and stained glass restoration at St. Mary of the Lake Seminary, Mundelein, IL.; Marble renovation and decoration, St. Elizabeth's Mother House, Allegany, N.Y.; and General Contracting for complete renovation of St. Bernadette's Church, Rockford, IL.
The Daprato Rigali staff is equipped to take your project from start to finish. If you're interested in working with a fine interior design studio experienced in Ecclesiastical Artistries please call for consultation at no obligation. We deliver what we design.

EGAN'S RELIGIOUS ART & CHURCH FURNISHINGS
Showrooms:
612 Gallivan Blvd. Boston, MA 02124
120 Slade Ferry Ave., Somerset, MA 02726
Office Danbury CT
Tel.: 1-800-235-0003; FAX (free): 1-888-217-3690
Web Sites: www.EGANCHURCHSUPPLY.com
E-mail: egans@eganchurchsupply.com
Type of Business:

Over 40 years of service to the Religious. Specializing in Quality Liturgical Furnishings and Interior Restorations. Radius Pews and Solid Oak chairs, Tabernacles, Woodcarvings, Marble Statuary, Candlesticks, Stadelmaier & Slabbinck Paraments, Stained Glass, Church Painting, Faux and Decorative Painting.

Call "Egan's When Quality Counts".

EverGreene
PAINTING STUDIOS, INC.

EVERGREENE PAINTING STUDIOS, INC.

450 West 31st Street, 7th Fl.
New York, NY 10001
Tel.: 212-244-2800
FAX: 212-244-6204

323 South Blvd.
Oak Park, IL 60302
Tel.: 708-358-1656
Fax: 708-358-1656

E-mail: info@evergreene.com
Web Site: www.evergreene.com

Personnel:
Jeff Greene .... President

Type of Business:

EverGreene is a full-service decorative arts studio committed to preserving the integrity of historic sacred spaces through conservation, restoration, and compatible new design. Services include investigation and analysis of original finishes; consultations, renderings, budgets and samples to support decision-making and capital campaigns; design of color schemes and architectural ornament; specifications; and execution of work by our staff of experienced project managers, artists, artisans and conservators.

EverGreene is accomplished in all types of decorative painting and gilding; conservation, replication, and new design of murals and mosaics; ornamental plaster and scagliola; and allied crafts including wood refinishing, interior stone cleaning, metal patination, art glass, tile work and other architectural arts.

Established in 1978, EverGreene undertakes projects large and small around the country. Recently completed works include St. Cecilia's Cathedral, Omaha; St. Peter Church, San Francisco; Our Lady of Perpetual Help (Redemptorist Church), Kansas City; and St. John's Seminary Chapel, Brighton, MA. Among current projects are St. Joseph's Church in Burlington, VT and Assumption Abbey, ND.

TAG GRANDA
LITURGICAL ARTS

GRANDA LITURGICAL ARTS, INC.
990 Grove Street, Suite 203
Evanston, IL 60201
Tel.: 800-425-0828; FAX: 847-492-1374
email: ruf4granda@aol.com
Website: www.hispacom.es/granda

Personnel:
Karen Johnson

Type of Business:
GRANDA LITURGICAL ARTS, Inc. is the USA branch of the largest supplier of church goods in the world: TALLERES DE ARTE GRANDA, S.A.
With 65 employees and sales all over the world, we can offer our experience in the manufacture of:
— metalware: chalices, tabernacles, etc.
— vestments
— wood carvings
— church decoration, interior design
Since 1891, we have been serving the church, combining modern techniques (computer aided design, projects in 3D ...) with artistic values.
Special custom orders are our specialty, styled and priced according to your needs.

GREENE & COMPANY, RA, INC.
PO Box 220371
61 Greenpoint Avenue 5th Floor
Brooklyn, NY 11222
E-mail: jgreene102@aol.com
Website: www.greene-inc.com

Type of Business:
Greene & Company offers the largest variety of Devotional articles and religious gifts in the United States today. Call for a catalog or visit our website to browse our selection of rosaries, crucifixes, crosses, candles, statuary, holy water fonts, prayer cards, greeting cards, prints, and communion and confirmation gifts.

INSPIRED ARTISANS, Ltd.

INSPIRED ARTISANS, LTD.
816 W. National Avenue
Milwaukee, WI 53204
Tel.: 414-672-9478; 1-888-442-9141; FAX: 414-672-9479
Website: www.inspiredart.com

Personnel:
Old and New World Artists and Craftpeople
Gianfranco Tassara ....President & Art Director

Type of Business:
Inspired Artisans has been serving the church with quality Liturgical Art such as Baptismal Fonts, Crypt Fronts, Decorating, Floor Plan Layout, Fund Raising Items, Iconography, Liturgical Fitments, Memorials, Mosaics, Murals, Restorations, Sculptures, Stained, Etched, Faceted Glass and Terra Cotta. Our work can be seen in many locations in Alabama, California, Connecticut, Galapagos/Ecuador, Colorado, Georgia, Illinois, Minnesota and Wisconsin. See our display ad under the "Art, Statuary & Decorations" category or contact us for a complete list of our past commissions, and brochures.

INSTITUTIONAL STATUARY
637 E. 132nd St.
Bronx, NY 10450
Tel.: 718-665-1125 / 800-847-3622 FAX: 718-665-0956

Type of Business:
Distinctive religious works of art: Designers-Sculptors-Manufacturers. Full color catalog available upon request.

Mark W. Read Studio & Gallery

MARK W. READ STUDIO
1898 Broadstone Road
P.O. Box 671
Valle Crucis, NC 28691
Phone & Fax (828) 963-8191
Web Site: www.markreadstudio.com

Type of Business:

Liturgical Jewelry	Sculpture
Architectural Pieces	Sacred Vessels
Utensils	Urns
Holloware/Chalices	Gem Setting
Gold & Silver Plating	Museum Quality Restoration

Mark Read is an artist craftsman of 30 years experience. Trained in old world and traditional methods he possesses the patience and skill to master the precise craftsmanship that goes into each custom project or restoration piece. Whether his exquisite one-of-a-kind creations are to purely inspire the beholder or serve as a functional piece, Marks creative gifts, unique approach and special sensitivity ensures that each commission works in harmony with its architectural surroundings.

From gold, silver, bronze, titanium to iron and beyond...the possibilities are endless.

Research and consulting is his first priority for restoration projects, thereby ensuring a clear understanding of the steps that must be taken to restore your piece back to its original glory. All types of restoration are accepted.

Please visit our website with the special section for Liturgical pieces.

See our display ad on page 107r.

MAZZOLINI ARTCRAFT CO., INC.
1607 East 41st Street
Cleveland, OH 44103
Tel.: 888-437-4499; 216-431-7529; FAX: 216-431-7531
E-mail: mazzart@aol.com
Web Site: www.mazzart.com

Personnel:
John Mazzolini ....President
Barbara Mazzolini ....Customer Service

Type of Business:
Largest Statue Manufacturer/Distributor in the United States of America. Established in 1904; Celebrating 97th year in business. Importers of Statuary from Italy, Spain and Portugal. Specializes in Woodcarved, Bronze, Marble and Fiberglass figures. Deals direct with Studios.
Domestically manufactures over 270 different religious subjects, from 9in. through 5ft., for Church, School, and Home use. Ships throughout the U.S.A. and Canada.
Visit the Website at mazzart.com.

RAMBUSCH

RAMBUSCH
40 West 13th St.
New York, NY 10011
Tel.: 212-675-0400; FAX: 212-620-4687

Personnel:
Viggo Bech Rambusch ....Senior Project Director
Martin V. Rambusch ....Stained Glass Director

Type of Business:
Since 1898, creating church interiors, liturgical furnishings, and art work. Fine restoration of church interiors. In-house studios and shops for designing and executing stained glass, church lighting systems, art metal work, and decorative painting.

RESTORATIONS PLUS
5427 Virginia Avenue
Saint Louis, Missouri 63111
Tel.: 314-481-3268; FAX: 314-481-3268
E-mail: rplus@kwd.zzn.com

Type of Business:

Our service offers restoration of statuary, old or new, we'll determine the original artist palette through an historical color analysis if necessary, or repair areas as needed. We can replicate the statue back to original or repaint to an existing or new palette. We manufacture and distribute a wonderful selection of ecclesiastical pieces, and replicate finishes from statuary of old using the same methodologies of over 100 years ago. We have a placement service for statuary /artifacts that are no longer being used and place into a new or existing Church or Religious Institution. Also, we can replicate any architectural element or statue as needed with latex rubber molds and gypsum plaster.

Also offered are restoration services of vestments. Fragile treasured ornamentation from older vestments are carefully removed and hand-sewn onto vestment fabric of your choice. Custom labor is our specialty.

SN
STADELMAIER
NIJMEGEN

STADELMAIER-NIJMEGEN-HOLLAND
P.O. Box 7063
6503 GN Nijmegen
Nijmegen, Holland 6503 GN
Tel.: 31-24-3791170; FAX: 31-24-3791171
e-mail: info@stadelmaier.com

Type of Business:

SN-Antiques offers, for the re-use in the Cath. Liturgy;
Completely restored, original, devotional interior-pieces. Altars, stations, candlesticks, perpetual lights, statues, reliquaries, ciboria, chalices, monstrances, censers, mission crosses, processional crosses, Saints, paintings, etc.
Different styles and age: Roman, baroque, neo-gothic, etc.
Please describe your interest directly to Mrs. Annemieke Drijber.

BAPTISMAL FONTS

Conrad Schmitt Studios Inc.

CONRAD SCHMITT STUDIOS, INC.
2405 S. 162nd St.
New Berlin, WI 53151
Tel.: 800-969-3033; 414-786-3030; FAX: 414-786-9036

Personnel:

Heidi Gruenke Emery........Vice President & Marketing Director

Type of Business:

Since 1889, this family-owned Studio has restored and decorated hundreds of interiors across the country. Their scope of work includes the investigation and documentation of original decorative schemes; the restoration of those schemes through the application of various decorative techniques including gilding, glazing, marbleizing, stenciling, and graining, as well as the design, fabrication, conservation or replication of murals and stained glass. The Studio can assist projects in the early stages with architectural samples and rendering for fund-raising. Recently completed projects include St. Josaphat's Basilica, Milwaukee, WI; St. Ann's, Napoleanville, LA; and St. Bernard's, Akron, OH.

D.C. RIGGOTT INC.
3540 Neal Ave.
Afton, MN 55001
Tel.: 800-479-8777; FAX: 651-436-4769
E-mail: dcriggottinc@aol.com

Personnel:

Don Riggott ....Owner/President

Type of Business:

Specializing in vintage church accessories, architectural ornamentation and liturgical furnishings.
Stained Glass Windows • Altars • Lighting • Statuary • Stations of the Cross • Tabernacles • Monstrances • Fonts • Pews • Steeple Bells • Vestments • Books • Furniture • Candlesticks • Chalices
Please contact us with specific requests. We will be happy to send you photographs and specifics on any items in our inventory. You may have items in storage or not being used, please contact us as we are actively searching for vintage items to purchase for re-use in liturgical spaces.

DAPRATO RIGALI STUDIOS, INC.

DAPRATO RIGALI STUDIOS, INC.
7956 Oakton St.
Niles, IL 60714
Tel.: 847-692-6350; FAX: 847-692-3445

Personnel:
John Rigali
Robert Rigali
Lisa Rigali Galvin
Mike Rigali

Type of Business:
Daprato Rigali Studios Inc. has been beautifying Churches in America since 1860.
Today we find the Rigali Family restoring and renovating the churches originally decorated by their Great-Grandfather, John E. Rigali; aware of his reputation to create spiritually moving environments with quality material and craftsmanship.
Some of their most recent jobs include: decoration and stained glass restoration at St. Mary of the Lake Seminary, Mundelein, IL.; Marble renovation and decoration, St. Elizabeth's Mother House, Allegany, N.Y.; and General Contracting for complete renovation of St. Bernadette's Church, Rockford, IL.
The Daprato Rigali staff is equipped to take your project from start to finish. If you're interested in working with a fine interior design studio experienced in Ecclesiastical Artistries please call for consultation at no obligation. We deliver what we design.

WATER STRUCTURES COMPANY
182 High Street
Newburyport, MA 01950
Tel: 800-747-0168 Fax 978-463-8210

Personnel:
Kim Noble ....Owner

Type of Business:
Water Structures is a full service manufacturer of baptisteries offering baptistery equipment, design consultation, and optional equipment. Custom baptisteries are offered in almost any size, shape or finish. Water Structures' baptistery equipment features an odorless water purification system, quiet run pumps and heaters. Beneath Water Structures' attractive natural stone or ceramic tile front pool lies a rugged leak-proof fibercement shell. Water Structures offers a number of quiet run water features with our custom fonts, including wet walls, water steps, and a baffled waterfall system.

BELLS, CARILLONS, ETC.

BELLTRON USA

BELLTRON USA
PO Box 428
Manlius, NY 13104-0428
Tel.: 800-962-3003; FAX 315-682-4913
Website: www.belltronusa.com
E-Mail: sales@belltronusa.com

Personnel:
Lance M. Fisher ....President

Type of Business:
Belltron Manufacturing, located in Italy, is the largest producer of bell products in the world. From cast bell swingers, strikers, and hammers, to electronic carillons with no moving parts. Belltron USA offers equipment for almost any need. Belltron USA offers full cast bell upgrades and repair, as well as provide the actual sound of bronze bells in the form of a moderately priced digital carillon. Call for a free demonstration or sales video.

BROSAMER'S BELLS
207 Irwin Street
Brooklyn, MI 49230
Tel.: 517-592-9030; FAX: 517-592-4511
Website: www.brosamersbells.com

Personnel:
R.C. Brosamer and family

Type of Business:
BUYS & SELLS USED BELLS
We will purchase pre-owned bells and remove bells that are no longer needed by churches or other organizations. The bells will then be restored and kept until they are called on to serve someone else's needs. Our pre-owned cast bells are affordable. Check on new, then call us.

CHIME MASTER™ SYSTEMS
Automation ♦ Chimes ♦ Bells ♦ Carillons
America's Best Value
USA Toll Free 800-344-7464
CAN Toll Free 800-432-3977
www.ChimeMaster.com

CHIME MASTERS SYSTEMS
P.O. Box 936
Lancaster, OH 43130
Tel.: 800-344-7464; FAX: 740-746-9566
E-mail: cmsinfo@ChimeMaster.com
Website: www.ChimeMaster.com

Type of Business:

Chime Master Systems is a leading manufacturer of electronic carillons and bell control equipment. In 1999 Chime Master Systems celebrated forty years in business.

Chime Master Systems features a complete line of digital electronic carillons available as complete new installations or to renovate older existing carillon equipment. Chime Master Carillons are designed and built in the USA, and carry a 5-year parts and labor warranty, with ZERO maintenance required, and 100% satisfaction customer care.

Chime Master Systems is pleased to announce a complete line of automatic electric bell ringing equipment. The Chime Master 2006 Cast Bell Control is designed for up to 6 bells and the Chime Master Millenium Cast Bell Control is available for sets of bells greater than six. Ringing equipment available for stationary or swinging bells.

Chime Master Systems can supply new tower bells (from America's only foundry casting tuned carillon style bronze bells), tower and street clocks, fiberglass steeples, and free standing steel bell towers.

Contact us for free information or quote.

D.C. RIGGOTT INC.
3540 Neal Ave.
Afton, MN 55001
Tel.: 800-479-8777; FAX: 651-436-4769
E-mail: dcriggottinc@aol.com

Personnel:

Don Riggott ....Owner/President

Type of Business:

Specializing in vintage church accessories, architectural ornamentation and liturgical furnishings.
Stained Glass Windows • Altars • Lighting • Statuary • Stations of the Cross • Tabernacles • Monstrances • Fonts • Pews • Steeple Bells • Vestments • Books • Furniture • Candlesticks • Chalices
Please contact us with specific requests. We will be happy to send you photographs and specifics on any items in our inventory. You may have items in storage or not being used, please contact us as we are actively searching for vintage items to purchase for re-use in liturgical spaces.

MAAS ROWE

MAAS-ROWE CARILLONS, INC.
2255 Meyers Ave.
Escondido, CA 92029
Tel.: 800-854-2023; FAX: 760-747-2677

Personnel:

Paul Rowe ....President
Craig Johnson ....National Sales Manager
Joel Bloom............................. Sales and Marketing Coordinator

Type of Business:

Established 1922. Manufacturers of automatic (computerized) Carillon and Church Bell Systems using compact discs for ultra high quality sound. Factory direct sales, service and installation. Sales—National and International. Upgrading of older carillon systems (any brand) to compact disc with computer control. Producers of compact discs featuring carillon and organ church music designed to play automatically or manually in computer controlled carillon equipment. Manufacturers of Musical Handbells. Importers of European Cast Bronze Church Bells and accessories. Manufacturer of Tower Clocks.

Schulmerich Bells
Electronic Carillons • Cast Bell Carillons
Handbells • MelodyChime® Instruments
Carillon Hill • PO Box 903 • Sellersville, PA • 18960-0903
215/257-2771 • 800/772-3557 • Fax: 215/257-1910

SCHULMERICH BELLS
Carillon Hill • P.O. Box 903
Sellersville, PA 18960-0903
Tel.: 215-257-2771 • 800-772-3557; FAX: 215-257-1910
E-mail: homeoffice@schulmerichbells.com
Web Site: www.schulmerichbells.com

Personnel:
Bern E. Deichmann .... President & CEO

Type of Business:

World Leader in Bells

Cast bells - Electronic & Cast Bell Carillons - Handbells - Hand Held Chimes
Enhance your worship easily and affordably with the sound of Schulmerich Bells, the world leader in bells since 1935. For more information, visit our website at: www.Schulmerichbells.com.

VERDIN V SINCE 1842

THE VERDIN CO.
444 Reading Rd.
Cincinnati, OH 45202
Tel.: 800-543-0488; 531-241-4010; FAX: 531-241-1855

Personnel:
Robert Verdin .... CEO
James Verdin .... President
David Verdin .... Vice President
Suzanne Sizer .... Sales/Mkt. Mgr.

Type of Business:
Combining 155 years of experience and tradition with 20th Century technical expertise makes The Verdin Company the leading supplier and manufacturer of bells, bell ringing equipment, carillons and clocks in the nation.

BENCHES, LECTERNS, PEWS

Hamlin
ATWOOD-HAMLIN MANUFACTURING

ATWOOD-HAMLIN MFG., INC.
P.O. Box 578
Richmond, IL 60071
Tel.: 800-545-8964

Type of Business:
Since 1948, Atwood-Hamlin Manufacturing has been your source for church furnishing. Our products include the famous **Hamlin Folding Pew Kneeler** as well as their replacement upholstered pads and parts. For your pews we also offer our comfortable, non-slip **Pew-Form Cushions** that do not have to be fastened to your pews. All reversible styles available. Our solid oak, stacking pew-chairs top our line of seating products. All upholstered products are available in hundreds of colors and fabric choices. We also offer pew refinishing services. Call for free product information.

D.C. RIGGOTT INC.
3540 Neal Ave.
Afton, MN 55001
Tel.: 800-479-8777; FAX: 651-436-4769
E-mail: dcriggottinc@aol.com

Personnel:
Don Riggott .... Owner/President

Type of Business:
Specializing in vintage church accessories, architectural ornamentation and liturgical furnishings.
Stained Glass Windows • Altars • Lighting • Statuary • Stations of the Cross • Tabernacles • Monstrances • Fonts • Pews • Steeple Bells • Vestments • Books • Furniture • Candlesticks • Chalices
Please contact us with specific requests. We will be happy to send you photographs and specifics on any items in our inventory. You may have items in storage or not being used, please contact us as we are actively searching for vintage items to purchase for re-use in liturgical spaces.

IMPERIAL WOODWORKS, INC.
PO Box 7835
Waco, TX 76714-7835
E-mail: smsmith@hot1.net
Website: www.imperialww.com

Type of Business:
Manufacturer serving the nation since 1960 constructing hand crafted Pews, Ambos, Lecterns, Altars, etc. You will be pleased with the craftsmenship of our products and the quality of our people. WE GUARANTEE IT!

NEW HOLLAND
Church-Furniture™
If You Can Imagine It We Can Build It!

NEW HOLLAND CHURCH FURNITURE
313 Prospect Street
New Holland, PA 17557
Phone 800-220-1465 Fax 717-354-2481
Web Site http://www.newhollandwood.com

Personnel:
Donald Long .... President
Richard Ragan .... Marketing & Sales Director

Type Of Business
New Holland Church Furniture is the nations leading manufacturer of Radius Curved Pews. In addition to our Radius Curved Pews, New Holland also manufactures a complete line of Straight and Mitered solid wood pews, upholstered pews available in a wide variety of styles and finishes.. In addition to pews New Holland also manufactures a complete line of high quality interlocking wood chairs or flexible seating. We will be happy to work with your designer and Architect to find the best possible seating solution for your church. New Holland is also the nations leading manufacturer of Custom Altar, Tabernacle, and Platform Furniture. Since our beginning in 1919 our tag line has been "If you can imagine it, we can build it." ™

SAUDER®
MANUFACTURING COMPANY

SAUDER MANUFACTURING COMPANY
930 W. Barre Road
Archbold, OH 43502
Tel.: 1-800-537-1530; FAX: 419-446-3697
Website: www.saudermfg.com

Personnel:
Virgil Miller .... President
Kelvin Friesen .... V.P. Sales & Marketing
Bob Borcherdt .... Sales Manager

Type of Business:
Sauder Manufacturing Company is the leading U.S. manufacturer of church furniture, including pews, chairs, sanctuary furniture, and re-upholstery service. Upholstered and non-upholstered pews are available in a wide selection of styles, finish colors, and fabrics. Chairs provide flexible seating and are available in a variety of styles to complement pews and the worship area decor.
Visit our Website at www.saudermfg.com.

Serenity® CHURCH FURNITURE

WALTER JACOBI AND SONS, INC.
1400 Elmer St. / P.O. Box 471
Belmont, CA 94002
Tel.: 800-522-6241; FAX: 650-592-2434
website: http://www.serenity-wjs.com

Personnel:
Arno M. Jacobi .... Sales
Albert O. Jacobi .... Sales

Type of Business:
Since 1921, MANUFACTURER: Devotional - Reverential - Furniture. MADE TO ORDER: Conducive to MEDITATION and PRAYER - ALL Wood, Cushion-loc, and Conventional Upholstered - Pews, Pewchairs, PewCHAR, Presider Chair, Clergy Chairs, Serenity Kneelers, Premium Kneelers, SKE Hydraulics, Kneeler Maintenance, Kneeler Parts and Repairs, Altar, Ambo, Lectern, Candlesticks, Crosses, Carvings. Seating Consultants to Church and/or Architect. Computer Layouts - send Plans or CAD Disk.

BISHOP'S REGALIA

TOUJOURS

ADRIAN HAMERS® CHURCH INTERIORS

ADRIAN HAMERS INC.
2 Madison Avenue
Larchmont, NY 10538
Tel.: 914-834-7780; FAX: 914-834-0712

Type of Business:
Custom designers and manufacturers of Sacred Vessels. Since 1887, the Hamers name has been synonymous with expert Silversmithing throughout the world in the field of Liturgical Art. Please contact us for those hard to find items, as we always have a large selection of Adrian Hamers Estate Collection pieces in stock. We are experts in: Church Interiors from design to execution, Renovations, Altars, Sacred Vessels, Gold and Silver Plating & Repairing, Appraisals, Tabernacles, Marble, Statuary, Woodwork & Woodcarving, Stained Glass, Pews & Chairs, Gold Leafing, Frescoes, Restoration, Trompe-l' oeuil, Wall Murals (repair and conservation cleaning), Ornamental Plaster, Heraldic Designs & Bishop Regalia. Please call us for a free 24 page Sacred Vessels color catalog, or our free 80 page color Woodcarvings catalog.

P. J. McDERMOTT & CO.
P.O. Box 950101
Fort Tilden, NY 11695
Tel.: 718-634-5583

Personnel:
Patrick J. McDermott .... President

Type of Business:
We are a major supplier of Ready-made suits, coats, slacks, blazers, R.J. Toomey Co. shirt fronts, French-cuff shirts, clerical vests ... "Beau-Veste" and Gammarelli (Rome) albs, surplices and rochets ... Fully custom tailored cassocks ... We are considered the leader in the U.S. and specialize in Bishops and Monsignors robes, all of which are custom tailored here. We also supply all Episcopal accessories; mitres, zuchettos, birettas, rochets, albs, pectoral cross, chains and cross cords, bishops rings, croziers. HAVE TAPE MEASURE — WILL TRAVEL

SN STADELMAIER NIJMEGEN

STADELMAIER-NIJMEGEN-HOLLAND
P.O. Box 7063
6503 GN Nijmegen
Nijmegen, Holland 6503 GN
Tel.: 31-24-3791170; FAX: 31-24-3791171
e-mail: info@stadelmaier.com

Type of Business:
SN-Antiques offers, for the re-use in the Cath. Liturgy;
Completely restored, original, devotional interior-pieces. Altars, stations, candlesticks, perpetual lights, statues, reliquaries, ciboria, chalices, monstrances, censers, mission crosses, processional crosses, Saints, paintings, etc.
Different styles and age: Roman, baroque, neo-gothic, etc.
Please describe your interest directly to Mrs. Annemieke Drijber.

INTERIOR DESIGN & RESTORATION

Your Supplier of Fine Ecclesiastical Interiors

CAVE CO.

CAVE COMPANY
P.O. Box 211
Old Westbury, NY 11568
Tel.: 800-989-CAVE / 516-676-1231; FAX: 516-676-9695
E-mail: caveco33@aol.com
Web Site: www.churchconstruction.com/caveco/

Personnel:

Gregory P. Cave ....President

Type of Business:

Our company is a fourth-generation business whose specialty is in the ecclesiastical interior design and restoration field. Our staff prides itself in the complete restoration and decoration of the smallest chapel to the largest cathedral, offering such unique services and products as our "Tree of Life" for fund raising, and electrical devotional candle stands. Our true specialty is the personalized service we are committed to bring our customers in the professional fashion they deserve.

Cave Company Continued

We specialize in:
- Tree of Life
- Electric Devotional Candles
- Painting & Decorating
- Poor Boxes
- Kneelers & Pews; Restoration & New
- Gold Leaf
- Statuary & Sculpture; Repair & Restoration
- Chalices & Ciboria; 24 Karat Gold Plating

D.C. RIGGOTT INC.
3540 Neal Ave.
Afton, MN 55001
Tel.: 800-479-8777; FAX: 651-436-4769
E-mail: dcriggottinc@aol.com

Personnel:
Don Riggott ....Owner/President

Type of Business:
Specializing in vintage church accessories, architectural ornamentation and liturgical furnishings.
Stained Glass Windows • Altars • Lighting • Statuary • Stations of the Cross • Tabernacles • Monstrances • Fonts • Pews • Steeple Bells • Vestments • Books • Furniture • Candlesticks • Chalices
Please contact us with specific requests. We will be happy to send you photographs and specifics on any items in our inventory. You may have items in storage or not being used, please contact us as we are actively searching for vintage items to purchase for re-use in liturgical spaces.

EGAN'S RELIGIOUS ART & CHURCH FURNISHINGS
120 Slade Ferry Avenue
Somerset, MA 02726
612 Gallivan Blvd.
Boston, MA 02124
Tel.: 800-235-0003; FAX: 508-673-4268
Websites: www.eganchurchsupply.com & www.egansart.com

Personnel:
Dennis P. Egan ....President and Project Manager
Robert J. Egan ....Vice President and Project Manager
James C. Egan.............................Treasurer and Project Manager

Type of Business:
Egan's Religious Art and Church Furnishing has been serving the religious for over 40 years. We have two show rooms and a convenient web address for you to visit. We represent: Frederick Hart Studios, Creator of the "Cross of the Millennium" and Christ Rising, Demetz Art and Conrad Moroder Studios, Slabbinck Millennium Vestments and Tapestries, Stadelmaier Paraments, New Holland Custom Pews (Radius) and Chairs, Fontanni Nativity's, Hamlin Kneelers, Art Paintings, Icons Paintings and Mosaics, etc.

EVERGREENE
PAINTING STUDIOS, INC.

EVERGREENE PAINTING STUDIOS, INC.

450 West 31st Street, 7th Fl.	323 South Blvd.
New York, NY 10001	Oak Park, IL 60302
Tel.: 212-244-2800	Tel.: 708-358-1656
FAX: 212-244-6204	Fax: 708-358-1656

E-mail: info@evergreene.com
Web Site: www.evergreene.com

Personnel:
Jeff Greene ....President

Type of Business:
EverGreene is a full-service decorative arts studio committed to preserving the integrity of historic sacred spaces through conservation, restoration, and compatible new design. Services include investigation and analysis of original finishes; consultations, renderings, budgets and samples to support decision-making and capital campaigns; design of color schemes and architectural ornament; specifications; and execution of work by our staff of experienced project managers, artists, artisans and conservators.

EverGreene is accomplished in all types of decorative painting and gilding; conservation, replication, and new design of murals and mosaics; ornamental plaster and scagliola; and allied crafts including wood refinishing, interior stone cleaning, metal patination, art glass, tile work and other architectural arts.

Established in 1978, EverGreene undertakes projects large and small around the country. Recently completed works include St. Cecilia's Cathedral, Omaha; St. Peter Church, San Francisco; Our Lady of Perpetual Help (Redemptorist Church), Kansas City; and St. John's Seminary Chapel, Brighton, MA. Among current projects are St. Joseph's Church in Burlington, VT and Assumption Abbey, ND.

TAG GRANDA LITURGICAL ARTS

GRANDA LITURGICAL ARTS, INC.
990 Grove Street, Suite 203
Evanston, IL 60201
Tel.: 800-425-0828; FAX: 847-492-1374
email: ruf4granda@aol.com
Website: www.hispacom.es/granda

Personnel:
Karen Johnson

Type of Business:
GRANDA LITURGICAL ARTS, Inc. is the USA branch of the largest supplier of church goods in the world: TALLERES DE ARTE GRANDA, S.A.
With 65 employees and sales all over the world, we can offer our experience in the manufacture of:
— metalware: chalices, tabernacles, etc.
— vestments
— wood carvings
— church decoration, interior design
Since 1891, we have been serving the church, combining modern techniques (computer aided design, projects in 3D ...) with artistic values.
Special custom orders are our specialty, styled and priced according to your needs.

Kosinski
Liturgical Design
Architecture
Interior Design
Construction Management
800-260-8149
www.keiarch.com

KOSINSKI ENTERPRISES, INC.

1212 Main Street
Branford, CT 06405
Tel.: 203-488-7733;
FAX: 203-483-7066
1-800-260-8149

20401 N.W. Second Avenue, Suite 308
Miami, FL 33169
Tel.: 305-770-3971;
FAX: 305-770-3910

Website: http://www.keiarch.com

Personnel:
Peter R. Kosinski,.................. AIA Liturgical Design Consultant

Type of Business:
Kosinski has offered architectural and liturgical design services for 32 years. Our extensive knowledge of architecture and the liturgy allows us to provide our clients with exceptional services. Our full range of in-house professional services, including the design of all liturgical elements, interior design and construction management, gives our clients a single point of contact for complete project delivery. We emphasize a team approach in which the client participates actively in design and project delivery.

LAMPS & LIGHTING

CAPITOL LIGHTING DESIGN & RESTORATION
1800 D Industrial Park Drive
Grand Haven, MI 49417
Tel.: 616-844-5000; FAX: 616-844-2228

CAPITOL LIGHTING DESIGN, INC.
333 N. Michigan Avenue, Suite 1330
Chicago, IL 60601
Tel.: 312-332-7400; FAX: 312-332-2764
Website: www.capitollighting.com

Personnel:
Brenda Hoyt...... Managing Director — Sales and Marketing
John Fuchs .... Managing Director — Design

Type of Business:
CAPITOL LIGHTING & RESTORATION is a company whose two founders and senior business associates have a history in the lighting industry dating back to the 1950's. It is a company totally dedicated to supplying quality products and delivering them on schedule. Due to the background of its founders, CAPITOL LIGHTING is sensitive to the needs of its clients. Designers need accurate drawings and information on time. Owners and contractors need adherence to schedules with equipment delivered in good condition and in conformance with approved coordination drawings.
CAPITOL LIGHTING & RESTORATION is owned and operated by Brenda Hoyt and John Fuchs. Both bring their own unique talents to the organization making it unrivaled in the lighting industry. CAPITOL LIGHTING's associates include a metal sculptor with a Master of Fine Arts degree; another metal sculptor whose special interest is 19th century gas and oil lighting fixtures and their early conversion to electric usage; two foundry specialists, one for short custom production runs, the other for production runs using the traditional lost wax process. In this process, CAPITOL LIGHTING & RESTORATION is able to offer bronze chandeliers of extraordinary quality. CAPITOL LIGHTING & RESTORATION has also successfully modified existing and antique lighting equipment to make use of newly developed light sources. It has always been a corporate philosophy to restore old fixtures rather than discard them and supply new replacements — it is a philosophy much appreciated by sensitive clients.
In addition to restoring and supplying ornamental lighting equipment, CAPITOL LIGHTING DESIGN has carved a niche for itself in the design of special lighting equipment largely unavailable from other suppliers. Whether it is the design of ornamental exit signs or small accent lights to be installed in very limited spaces — CAPITOL LIGHTING & RESTORATION has always prevailed in the face of difficult design challenges.
It is safe to say that no other ornamental lighting fixture supplier can claim to have this type of expertise at its disposal or within its own corporate structure — it is a fertile environment conducive to the promotion and fulfillment of the design process.

D.C. RIGGOTT INC.
3540 Neal Ave.
Afton, MN 55001
Tel.: 800-479-8777; FAX: 651-436-4769
E-mail: dcriggottinc@aol.com

Personnel:
Don Riggott ....Owner/President

Type of Business:
Specializing in vintage church accessories, architectural ornamentation and liturgical furnishings.
Stained Glass Windows • Altars • Lighting • Statuary • Stations of the Cross • Tabernacles • Monstrances • Fonts • Pews • Steeple Bells • Vestments • Books • Furniture • Candlesticks • Chalices
Please contact us with specific requests. We will be happy to send you photographs and specifics on any items in our inventory. You may have items in storage or not being used, please contact us as we are actively searching for vintage items to purchase for re-use in liturgical spaces.

RAMBUSCH

RAMBUSCH
40 West 13th St.
New York, NY 10011
Tel.: 212-675-0400; FAX: 212-620-4687

Personnel:
Viggo Bech Rambusch ....Senior Project Director
Martin V. Rambusch ....Stained Glass Director

Type of Business:
Since 1898, creating church interiors, liturgical furnishings, and art work. Fine restoration of church interiors. In-house studios and shops for designing and executing stained glass, church lighting systems, art metal work, and decorative painting.

LITURGICAL DESIGN

Kosinski
Liturgical Design
Architecture
Interior Design
Construction Management
800-260-8149
www.keiarch.com

KOSINSKI ENTERPRISES, INC.
1212 Main Street
Branford, CT 06405
Tel.: 203-488-7733;
FAX: 203-483-7066
1-800-260-8149

20401 N.W. Second Avenue, Suite 308
Miami, FL 33169
Tel.: 305-770-3971;
FAX: 305-770-3910

Website: http://www.keiarch.com

Personnel:
Peter R. Kosinski,.................. AIA Liturgical Design Consultant

Type of Business:
Kosinski has offered architectural and liturgical design services for 32 years. Our extensive knowledge of architecture and the liturgy allows us to provide our clients with exceptional services. Our full range of in-house professional services, including the design of all liturgical elements, interior design and construction management, gives our clients a single point of contact for complete project delivery. We emphasize a team approach in which the client participates actively in design and project delivery.

BOTTI STUDIO OF ARCHITECTURAL ARTS, INC.

BOTTI STUDIO OF ARCHITECTURAL ARTS, INC.
919 Grove St.
Evanston, IL 60201
Tel.: 800-524-7211; FAX: 847-869-5996; 847-869-5933
E-mail: botti@bottistudio.com
Web Site: www.bottistudio.com

East Coast Studio
3104 S. Osprey Ave.
Sarasota, FL 33577
Tel.: 941-951-0978; FAX: 941-953-9078

West Coast Studio
1038 N. Highway 101
Encinitas, CA 92024
Tel.: 760-753-0705; FAX: 760-753-0705
Agropoli, Italy

Personnel:

Staff includes internationally recognized artists and designers working in conjunction with our highly skilled artisans and craftsmen.

Italo G. Botti ....President

Type of Business:

For generations Botti Studio has had a reputation for embodying all that is artistically creative in the traditional and contemporary ecclesiastical field. This field includes design and fabrication of stained and faceted glass windows, restoration/conservation of windows, church interiors, appointments, murals, sculpture, mosaic and marble. We are completely dedicated to both quality and satisfying our clients needs spiritually and liturgically. Botti Studio , established in 1864, is nationwide, offering consultation and designs without obligation. Member of the Stained Glass Association of America.

MOSAICS

ARCHITECTURAL FEATURES CREATED BY Madden

CHARLES L. MADDEN
CREATING ARCHITECTURAL FEATURES
1245 E. Butler Pike
Ambler, PA 19002-6032 U.S.A.
Tel.: 215-646-8919; FAX: 215-643-7272
email: cmadden@concentric.net

Personnel:

Charles L. Madden ....Owner/Creative Director

Type of Business:

Architectural Features by definition is a single art resource for consultation, design, fabrication, and installation in creating spaces of liturgical and meditative inspiration with sacred art and beautiful materials of fine substance and detailing. Our worldwide commissions in bronze sculpture, mosaic, marble, stained glass, tapestry, and fine woods are custom created to extend our client's vision. Whether you are a Diocesan, Community, Institutional, or Architectural client - we are pleased to put our vast creative and computer technological resources at the service of your building and renovational vision.

Conrad Schmitt Studios Inc.

CONRAD SCHMITT STUDIOS, INC.
2405 S. 162nd St.
New Berlin, WI 53151
Tel.: 800-969-3033; 414-786-3030; FAX: 414-786-9036

Personnel:

Heidi Gruenke Emery ....Vice President & Marketing Director

Type of Business:

Since 1889, this family-owned Studio has restored and decorated hundreds of interiors across the country. Their scope of work includes the investigation and documentation of original decorative schemes; the restoration of those schemes through the application of various decorative techniques including gilding, glazing, marbleizing, stenciling, and graining, as well as the design, fabrication, conservation or replication of murals and stained glass. The Studio can assist projects in the early stages with architectural samples and rendering for fund-raising. Recently completed projects include St. Josaphat's Basilica, Milwaukee, WI; St. Ann's, Napoleanville, LA; and St. Bernard's, Akron, OH.

EVERGREENE PAINTING STUDIOS, INC.

EVERGREENE PAINTING STUDIOS, INC.
450 West 31st Street, 7th Fl. 323 South Blvd.
New York, NY 10001 Oak Park, IL 60302
Tel.: 212-244-2800 Tel.: 708-358-1656
FAX: 212-244-6204 Fax: 708-358-1656
E-mail: info@evergreene.com
Web Site: www.evergreene.com

Personnel:
Jeff Greene .... President

Type of Business:
EverGreene is a full-service decorative arts studio committed to preserving the integrity of historic sacred spaces through conservation, restoration, and compatible new design. Services include investigation and analysis of original finishes; consultations, renderings, budgets and samples to support decision-making and capital campaigns; design of color schemes and architectural ornament; specifications; and execution of work by our staff of experienced project managers, artists, artisans and conservators.

EverGreene is accomplished in all types of decorative painting and gilding; conservation, replication, and new design of murals and mosaics; ornamental plaster and scagliola; and allied crafts including wood refinishing, interior stone cleaning, metal patination, art glass, tile work and other architectural arts.

Established in 1978, EverGreene undertakes projects large and small around the country. Recently completed works include St. Cecilia's Cathedral, Omaha; St. Peter Church, San Francisco; Our Lady of Perpetual Help (Redemptorist Church), Kansas City; and St. John's Seminary Chapel, Brighton, MA. Among current projects are St. Joseph's Church in Burlington, VT and Assumption Abbey, ND.

RAMBUSCH

RAMBUSCH
40 West 13th St.
New York, NY 10011
Tel.: 212-675-0400; FAX: 212-620-4687

Personnel:
Viggo Bech Rambusch .... Senior Project Director
Martin V. Rambusch .... Stained Glass Director

Type of Business:
Since 1898, creating church interiors, liturgical furnishings, and art work. Fine restoration of church interiors. In-house studios and shops for designing and executing stained glass, church lighting systems, art metal work, and decorative painting.

ORGANS & PIANOS

Allen organs®

ALLEN ORGAN COMPANY
PO BOX 36
Macungie, PA 18062-0036
Tel.: 610-966-2202; FAX 610-965-3098
E-mail: aosales@allenorgan.com
Website: www.allenorgan.com

Personnel:
Barry Holben .... Vice President Sales and Marketing

Type of Business:
Manufacturer of digital, electronic, classical, and theatrical organs.

THE ORGAN CLEARING HOUSE, L.L.C.
P.O. Box 219
Lexington, MA 02420
Tel.: 866-827-3055
E-mail: john@organclearinghouse.com
Web Site: www.organclearinghouse.com

Personnel:
John Bishop .... Executive Director
Amory Atkin .... Associate
Joshua Wood .... Associate

Type of Business:
We are purveyors of existing pipe organs of high quality and distinction which are made available through church closings and mergers. Since 1959, we have arranged for the relocation and renovation of more than 2000 pipe organs. Restored, these instruments are generally available for around half the cost of an equivalent new organ. Currently we have more than 200 organs available for sale. Contact us if you wish to buy or sell.

RODGERS®

RODGERS INSTRUMENT CORPORATION
1300 N.E. 25th Ave.
Hillsboro, OR 97124
Tel.: 503-648-4181; FAX: 503-681-0444

Personnel:

- Dennis Houlihan .... President
- Jonas Nordwall .... Product Marketing Manager
- Donna Parker .... Marketing Administrator
- David Tomb .... Sales & Marketing Development Manager

Type of Business:

Rodgers Instrument Corporation is respected worldwide for technical leadership in the manufacturing of digital electronic, pipe and electronic/pipe combination organs using PDI (Parallel Digital Imaging) technology for church, home, schools, and concert halls. Rodgers also builds digital keyboards, MIDI sound modules and sequencers.

WICKS PIPE ORGAN COMPANY

WICKS ORGAN CO.
1100 Fifth St.
Highland, IL 62249
Tel.: 618-654-2191; FAX: 618-654-3770
Web Site: www.wicks.com

Personnel:

- Martin Wick .... President
- Scott Wick .... Sales Manager
- Mark Wick .... Sales
- Darren Meskill .... Purchasing
- Mary Wick Haberer .... Custom Church Furnishings

Type of Business:

Custom designed pipe organs and combination instruments to fit your space and budget. 100+ years experience in over 6,000 churches worldwide. Free on-site evaluations and proposal drawings. Highest levels of professionalism from beginning to end. 10-year warranty. Specialists in DIRECT-ELECTRIC™ and Mechanical Action organs. Financially sound company, AAA-#1 Dunn & Bradstreet rating. Also, pre-designed compact models for limited space, time or budget. Some available for immediate delivery. Literature and video available for committees and indi viduals.

Call Wicks Organ Co. at 800-444-WICK or 618-654-2191.

PEW CUSHIONS

Hamlin

ATWOOD-HAMLIN MANUFACTURING

ATWOOD-HAMLIN MFG., INC.
P.O. Box 578
Richmond, IL 60071
Tel.: 800-545-8964

Type of Business:

Since 1948, Atwood-Hamlin Manufacturing has been your source for church furnishing. Our products include the famous **Hamlin Folding Pew Kneeler** as well as their replacement upholstered pads and parts. For your pews we also offer our comfortable, non-slip **Pew-Form Cushions** that do not have to be fastened to your pews. All reversible styles available. Our solid oak, stacking pew-chairs top our line of seating products. All upholstered products are available in hundreds of colors and fabric choices. We also offer pew refinishing services. Call for free product information.

PLAQUES & MEMORIALS

CARROLL ART, INC.
710 NE 26th St.
Fort Lauderdale, FL 33305
Tel.: 800-876-4569; FAX: 954-561-4098

Personnel:

David Nagle....................President Designer
Liza Palmer....................Sales Manager
Wayne Palmer....................Sales Representative
Robert Perkins....................Sales Representative

Type of Business:

Carroll Art has been in business for 12 years. We design and custom build all types of plaques and memorials including the tree of life, plaques, recognition systems, church signs, donor plates, custom sculptures, and memorials are just a few of our products. We can provide you with the perfect fund raising tool.

CAVE CO.
Your Supplier of Fine Ecclesiastical Interiors

CAVE COMPANY
P.O. Box 211
Old Westbury, NY 11568
Tel.: 800-989-CAVE / 516-676-1231; FAX: 516-676-9695
E-mail: caveco33@aol.com
Web Site: www.churchconstruction.com/caveco/

Personnel:

Gregory P. Cave....................President

Type of Business:

Our company is a fourth-generation business whose specialty is in the ecclesiastical interior design and restoration field. Our staff prides itself in the complete restoration and decoration of the smallest chapel to the largest cathedral, offering such unique services and products as our "Tree of Life" for fund raising, and electrical devotional candle stands. Our true specialty is the personalized service we are committed to bring our customers in the professional fashion they deserve.

We specialize in:
- Tree of Life
- Electric Devotional Candles
- Painting & Decorating
- Poor Boxes
- Kneelers & Pews; Restoration & New
- Gold Leaf
- Statuary & Sculpture; Repair & Restoration
- Challices & Ciboria; 24 Karat Gold Plating

INSPIRED ARTISANS, Ltd.

INSPIRED ARTISANS, LTD.
816 W. National Avenue
Milwaukee, WI 53204
Tel.: 414-672-9478; 1-888-442-9141; FAX: 414-672-9479
Website: www.inspiredart.com

Personnel:

Old and New World Artists and Craftpeople
Gianfranco Tassara....................President & Art Director

Type of Business:

Inspired Artisans has been serving the church with quality Liturgical Art such as Baptismal Fonts, Crypt Fronts, Decorating, Floor Plan Layout, Fund Raising Items, Iconography, Liturgical Fitments, Memorials, Mosaics, Murals, Restorations, Sculptures, Stained, Etched, Faceted Glass and Terra Cotta. Our work can be seen in many locations in Alabama, California, Connecticut, Galapagos/Ecuador, Colorado, Georgia, Illinois, Minnesota and Wisconsin. See our display ad under the "Art, Statuary & Decorations" category or contact us for a complete list of our past commissions, and brochures.

Mark W. Read Studio & Gallery

MARK W. READ STUDIO
1898 Broadstone Road
P.O. Box 671
Valle Crucis, NC 28691
Phone & Fax (828) 963-8191
Web Site: www.markreadstudio.com

Type of Business:

Liturgical Jewelry	Sculpture
Architectural Pieces	Sacred Vessels
Utensils	Urns
Holloware/Chalices	Gem Setting
Gold & Silver Plating	Museum Quality Restoration

Mark Read is an artist craftsman of 30 years experience. Trained in old world and traditional methods he possesses the patience and skill to master the precise craftsmanship that goes into each custom project or restoration piece. Whether his exquisite one-of-a-kind creations are to purely inspire the beholder or serve as a functional piece, Marks creative gifts, unique approach and special sensitivity ensures that each commission works in harmony with its architectural surroundings.

From gold, silver, bronze, titanium to iron and beyond...the possibilities are endless.

Research and consulting is his first priority for restoration projects, thereby ensuring a clear understanding of the steps that must be taken to restore your piece back to its original glory. All types of restoration are accepted.

Please visit our website with the special section for Liturgical pieces.

See our display ad on page

THE ARTIST'S HAND MAKES THE DIFFERENCE

SANFORD WERFEL- ARTIST

SANFORD WERFEL - ARTIST
425 Old Georges Rd.
North Brunswick, NJ 08902
Tel.: 800-443-3744; 732-297-1166; FAX: 732-297-7770
E-mail: werfelart@aol.com
Web Site: http://www.sanfordwerfelartist.com

Type of Business:

Since 1968, Mr. Werfel's sculptures have been helping parishes to INSPIRE and MOTIVATE GIVING through the use of his original sculptures. Building drives, capital or endowment funds, sacrificial giving, and tithing programs all benefit from using Donor Recognition Sculptures. Call or write for FREE INFORMATION. Included will be costs and designs as well as a "HOW-TO-USE" guide that tells how your parish can use sculpture to raise funds. Good art is forever.

Visit our Website at: http://www.SanfordWerfelArtist.com
email us at: WerfelArt@aol.com

ZAX

ZAX SIGNAGE
30 Otterson Street
Nashua, NH 03061
Tel: 800-258-1566 FAX: 603-883-6395
Web Site: www.zaxcorp.com
E-mail: info@zaxcorp.com
Personnel:
Patrick Walsh .... President

Type of Business:

The Zax Corporation of Nashua, NH has a distinguished history of providing the highest quality recognition products throughout North America. Our recognition products represent not only fine materials and craftsmanship, but the highest standards of design excellence for meeting your specific needs.

Zax manufactures an array of products such as Donor Walls, Books of Memories, Trees of Life, Add-On Donor Plaques, MarbleGraph, ClassBrass Multi-Plate/Multi-Name Plaques, Bronze Tablets, Incentive Awards and Signage Products.

For detailed information on our product line, or help in designing a donor wall of distinction, our expert staff can help you with your donor recognition needs. Call us at 1-800-258-1566 for help or to request our recognition catalog.

We pledge Service, Value, Quality, and our Commitment to you, to help you express your gratitude to your donors, and at the same time...increase donations.

TABLES & CHAIRS

ATD-AMERICAN CO.

ATD-AMERICAN CO.
135 Greenwood Avenue
Wyncote, PA 19095-1396
Tel.: 888-283-2487; FAX: 800-283-7363
E-mail: american@atd.com
Web Site: www.atd.com

Personnel:
Bob Roche....................Marketing
Sal Catanese....................Sales

Type of Business:
For four generations, ATD-AMERICAN has supplied Furniture and Equipment to Churches, Organizations and Institutions nationally and worldwide. Since 1931, it has been our tradition to deliver high quality products and personal service at the lowest competitive prices. ATD offers a wide range of products to meet all of the needs of your Church and School. Our comprehensive catalog includes the following: Announcement and Bulletin Boards, Audio-Visual Equipment, Classroom Furniture, Computer Furniture, Daycare Furniture, Display Cases, Folding Chairs, Folding Tables, Lecterns, Library Furniture, Office Furniture, Outdoor Equipment, Pews and Pulpit Furniture, Room Dividers and Partitions, Stacking Chairs, and Stages and Risers.

For a FREE Wholesale Furniture Catalog, call us toll-free 888-283-2487 or fax us at 800-283-7363. You can also visit our web-site at http://www.atd.com or email us at atd.com.

SPECIAL OFFER FOR CATHOLIC DIRECTORY SUBSCRIBERS: Mention offer code 6557 and receive a special 10% discount on your first order.

SAUDER®
MANUFACTURING COMPANY

SAUDER MANUFACTURING COMPANY
930 W. Barre Road
Archbold, OH 43502
Tel.: 1-800-537-1530; FAX: 419-446-3697
Website: www.saudermfg.com

Personnel:
Virgil Miller....................President
Kelvin Friesen....................V.P. Sales & Marketing
Bob Borcherdt....................Sales Manager

Type of Business:
Sauder Manufacturing Company is the leading U.S. manufacturer of church furniture, including pews, chairs, sanctuary furniture, and re-upholstery service. Upholstered and non-upholstered pews are available in a wide selection of styles, finish colors, and fabrics. Chairs provide flexible seating and are available in a variety of styles to complement pews and the worship area decor.
Visit our Website at www.saudermfg.com.

CLERICAL APPAREL

Chagall Design Limited©
Designers of Custom Liturgical Vestments, Stoles, Dalmatics, Banners and Sanctuary Accessories.

CHAGALL DESIGN LTD.
910 south Los Angeles Street
Los Angeles, CA 90015
Tel: 1-800-947-7923 fax: 213-624-8036
E-mail Address: CHAGALL@IX.NETCOM.COM
Web: WWW.CHAGALLDESIGN.COM

Personnel:
Jacques de Groot....................President
Mannix Delfino....................Vice President

Type of Business:
Designers of custom liturgical Vestments, Stoles, Dalmatics Banners and sanctuary accessories. The finest import fabrics, and custom embroidery's are used in a blend of traditional elegance and modern design. Our attention to detail makes each vestment, and banner unique. All our banners are custom made in design and size; we also offer a line of Tabernacles, Candlesticks, Chalices, Ciborium's that are imported from Italy, Spain and France. Please review our accompanying catalog with the Catholic Directory.

DQ
DUFFY & QUINN
Apparel for the Clergy

DUFFY & QUINN
307 5th Ave.
New York, NY 10016
Tel.: 800-425-3466; 212-725-0213; FAX: 212-685-3503

Personnel:
John M. McGuinness....................Manager
Marvin Goldman....................Owner

Type of Business:
Duffy & Quinn is a leading supplier of religious apparel and accessories to the Reverend clergy — featuring suits, coats, clerical shirts, ready-made and custom-tailored cassocks. Monsignors and Bishops robes are made to order, with careful attention to detail, quality and on-time delivery. Full stocks of R.J. Toomey, Beau Veste, Gammarelli, and Barbiconi merchandise available for shipment at once. Mitres, zuchettos, birettas, vestments, pectoral crosses, chains, cross cords and Bishop's rings are our specialty.

P. J. McDERMOTT & CO.
P.O. Box 950101
Fort Tilden, NY 11695
Tel.: 718-634-5583

Personnel:
Patrick J. McDermott ....President

Type of Business:
We are a major supplier of Ready-made suits, coats, slacks, blazers, R.J. Toomey Co. shirt fronts, French-cuff shirts, clerical vests ... "Beau-Veste" and Gammarelli (Rome) albs, surplices and rochets ... Fully custom tailored cassocks ... We are considered the leader in the U.S. and specialize in Bishops and Monsignors robes, all of which are custom tailored here. We also supply all Episcopal accessories; mitres, zuchettos, birettas, rochets, albs, pectoral cross, chains and cross cords, bishops rings, croziers.
HAVE TAPE MEASURE — WILL TRAVEL

See our ad on this page.

PATRICK BAKER & SONS

PATRICK BAKER & SONS, INC.
1650 West Street
Southington, CT 06489
Tel.: 860-628-5566; FAX: 860-276-9438

Personnel:
Patrick A. Baker ....Chairman
Brian T. Baker ....President
Michael P. Baker ....Vice President
Maureen Kelly ....Secretary

Type of Business:
- Religious Supplies
- Church Goods
- Church Renovations

Vermont Church Supply Co.

VERMONT CHURCH SUPPLY CO.
676 Pine Street, P.O. Box 368
Burlington, VT 05401
Tel.: 802-862-6486, 800-451-3453; FAX: 802-862-5765
E-mail: vcs@together.net

Personnel:
Neil Clark ....President

Type of Business:
Since our inception in 1946 by W. Barrett Clark and Doris Clark, Vermont Church Supply has offered the highest quality products and the best service to the Church and the Clergy. We have a wide range of products including Candles, Church Furniture, Metalware and Vestments. Our founders' Sons, Neil, John, Thomas and Robert, along with the third generation Anthony Clark, continue to provide services such as refinishing Sacred Vessels, Candlesticks and abernacles and also the execution of hand carved wood and marble Statuary. Whether your needs are small or large, we can give the best personalized service to our Customers.

CLERGY SHIRTS

C. M. ALMY & SON, INC.
Three American Lane
P.O. Box 2644
Greenwich, CT 06836-2644
Tel.: 800-225-2569; FAX: 800-426-2569
E-mail: almyaccess@almy.com

Showrooms in:
Old Greenwich, CT: 203-637-2739 and
Pittsfield, ME: 207-487-3232

Type of Business:
Almy was founded in 1892. We design and make virtually all of our products in our Maine shop. It is our mission to design furnishings that will grace your worship and to ensure their value by making them with the highest quality materials and craftsmanship. We make a complete line of vestments, haberdashery, choir robes, candles, communion bread, linens, processional and altar appointments, and eucharistic vessels. We also offer custom design and fabrication of all Almy products, and repair and refurbishing of old metal appointments. Quik Ship© delivery of many popular items. All orders backed by The Almy Guarantee. Call, write, or email for a free catalog.

STADELMAIER-NIJMEGEN-HOLLAND
P.O. Box 7063
6503 GN Nijmegen
Nijmegen, Holland 6503 GN
Tel.: 31-24-3791170; FAX: 31-24-3791171
e-mail: info@stadelmaier.com

Type of Business:
SN-Antiques offers, for the re-use in the Cath. Liturgy;
Completely restored, original, devotional interior-pieces. Altars, stations, candlesticks, perpetual lights, statues, reliquaries, ciboria, chalices, monstrances, censers, mission crosses, processional crosses, Saints, paintings, etc.
Different styles and age: Roman, baroque, neo-gothic, etc.
Please describe your interest directly to Mrs. Annemieke Drijber.

ROBES, VESTMENTS, ETC.

ABBOTT INC.
Showroom 1515 Route 38
Cherry Hill, NJ 08002
Tel.: 800-522-2688; 856-662-6959; FAX: 856-665-5109
Website: http://www.abbottsinc.com
email: acg.inc@cwixmail.com

Personnel:
Daniel J. Castonguay .... President
Joseph F. McKeaney .... General Manager
Michael W. Wasyluk .... Customer Service

Type of Business:
Purveyors of the Finest Vesture, Paraments, Statuary & Metalware since 1962. Unique and original creations, our specialty. Custom designs to complement your liturgical environment. Exclusive representatives of Slabbinck Master Collection & Original Collection.

ART STUDIO SLABBINCK
Headquarters:
L. Bauwensstraat 18
8200 Brugge, Belgium
Tel.: 32-50-312557; FAX: 32-50-318358

Type of Business:
Belgian made vestments (chasubles, stoles, albs, copes, deaconstoles, dalmatics, altar and lectern covers, altar linens and cloths, tapestries and banners). Chalices, ciboria, patens and pyxes also available. Slabbinck Speed Service offered for many items as advertised in our catalog. Also Dirk Slabbinck Master Collection, an exclusive collection of vestments and paraments created from the inspired imagination of master designer Dirk Slabbinck, or according to your own specifications. For information on the dealer nearest you, call 800-423-3224 or FAX 800-284-9000.

T.M.

Bringing the Art Back into the Craft

BRAMANTE STUDIO
20 Queen Street North
Kitchener, Ontario, Canada N2H 2G8
Phone: 519-570-2908 Fax: 519-570-2706
1-800-295-6902

Personnel:
Abraham Mathew ....Owner/President

Type of Business:
Bramante is a unique arts and crafts studio specializing in fine quality, one of a kind liturgical art specifically for church worship environments. Our artisans, in conjunction with the individual church staff, design each piece to work in harmony with the church as a whole. We are able to offer such a high level of personalized service because all our work is done in house. From weaving our own fabric, to laminating the wood used for each sculpture, each piece is completely hand made. Whether it is a simple stole, a wall to wall tapestry, or a larger than life hand carved sculpture, each piece is created with your worship environment in mind.

CM ALMY

C. M. ALMY & SON, INC.
Three American Lane
P.O. Box 2644
Greenwich, CT 06836-2644
Tel.: 800-225-2569; FAX: 800-426-2569
E-mail: almyaccess@almy.com

Showrooms in:
Old Greenwich, CT: 203-637-2739 and
Pittsfield, ME: 207-487-3232

Type of Business:
Almy was founded in 1892. We design and make virtually all of our products in our Maine shop. It is our mission to design furnishings that will grace your worship and to ensure their value by making them with the highest quality materials and craftsmanship. We make a complete line of vestments, haberdashery, choir robes, candles, communion bread, linens, processional and altar appointments, and eucharistic vessels. We also offer custom design and fabrication of all Almy products, and repair and refurbishing of old metal appointments. Quik Ship© delivery of many popular items. All orders backed by The Almy Guarantee. Call, write, or email for a free catalog.

Chagall Design Limited ©

Designers of Custom Liturgical Vestments, Stoles, Dalmatics, Banners and Sanctuary Accessories.

CHAGALL DESIGN LTD.
910 south Los Angeles Street
Los Angeles, CA 90015
Tel: 1-800-947-7923 fax: 213-624-8036
E-mail Address: CHAGALL@IX.NETCOM.COM
Web: WWW.CHAGALLDESIGN.COM

Personnel:
Jacques de Groot...President
Mannix Delfino ....Vice President

Type of Business:
Designers of custom liturgical Vestments, Stoles, Dalmatics Banners and sanctuary accessories. The finest import fabrics, and custom embroidery's are used in a blend of traditional elegance and modern design. Our attention to detail makes each vestment, and banner unique. All our banners are custom made in design and size; we also offer a line of Tabernacles, Candlesticks, Chalices, Ciborium's that are imported from Italy, Spain and France. Please review our accompanying catalog with the Catholic Directory.

GRANDA LITURGICAL ARTS, INC.
990 Grove Street, Suite 203
Evanston, IL 60201
Tel.: 800-425-0828; FAX: 847-492-1374
email: ruf4granda@aol.com
Website: www.hispacom.es/granda

Personnel:
Karen Johnson

Type of Business:
GRANDA LITURGICAL ARTS, Inc. is the USA branch of the largest supplier of church goods in the world: TALLERES DE ARTE GRÁNDA, S.A.
With 65 employees and sales all over the world, we can offer our experience in the manufacture of:
— metalware: chalices, tabernacles, etc.
— vestments
— wood carvings
— church decoration, interior design
Since 1891, we have been serving the church, combining modern techniques (computer aided design, projects in 3D ...) with artistic values.
Special custom orders are our specialty, styled and priced according to your needs.

THE HOLY ROOD GUILD
St. Joseph's Abbey
167 North Spencer Rd.
Spencer, MA 01562-1233
Tel.: 508-885-8750; FAX: 508-885-8758
E-mail: holyrood@holyroodguild.com
Website: www.holyroodguild.com

Type of Business:
Designers and crafters of ecclesiastical vesture for over 40 years. Inspired by our monastic tradition, we seek to unite in our work simplicity in design, quality in materials and excellence in craftsmanship. The result is vesture that enhances the liturgical celebration with visual grace and order. Our artists—both monks and laypersons—are available for custom design work and consultation. We also provide an extensive selection of ready made items.

HOUSE OF HANSEN
4223 W. Irving Park Rd.
Chicago, IL 60641
Tel.: 773-736-5858; FAX: 773-736-6715

Type of Business:
Clerical tailoring specialists for over 85 years. We specialize in Prelatial Appointments and Custom Tailored cassocks made by our professional staff. Custom tailored vestments and albs. A full line of ready-made clerical apparel. See our ad in the front section of this book.

See our ad on the next page.

MURPHY VESTMENTS
Murphy Cap & Gown Co.
4200 31st St. North
St. Petersburg, FL 33714
Tel.: 727-527-0696; FAX: 727-526-3528
Web Site: www.murphyrobes.com
E-mail: murphyrb@gte.net

Personnel:
Don Camp .... President
Gary Bergamo .... Sales Manager
George Shahine .... Administrative Manager
Josephine DeFeo .... Vestment Designer

Type of Business:
Manufacturer of vestments, albs, cassocks, choir and acolyte robes and accessories, all value priced with guaranteed fit and quality. We supply a complete line of liturgical attire, custom tailored as well as many styles in stock and ready to ship within 24 hours of receipt of order. Available through your church goods dealer, or call or write for more information.

CUSTOM TAILORED
CLERICAL APPAREL
SINCE 1907

Priest Cassocks, **Prelatial Garments** & Appointments, Clerical Vests, Vestments, etc.

READYMADE: **CLERICAL SUITS**, PRIEST CASSOCKS SHIRTS, VESTMENTS, SUPPLIES, ALBS, CLERGY VESTS, ETC.

RELIGIOUS GOODS AND CHURCH SUPPLIES

THE HOUSE OF HANSEN

TOLL FREE (outside Illinois): **1-800-522-1457**
In Illinois: (312) 372-8750
(773) 736-5858

4223 W. Irving Park Rd. - Chicago, IL 60641

Personal appointments can be arranged.

the symbol of Regal Splendor

Robert Gaspard Co.

ROBERT GASPARD CO., INC.
200 N. Janacek Rd.
Brookfield, WI 53045-6101
Tel.: 800-784-6868; 262-784-6800; FAX: 262-784-7567
E-mail: robertgaspard.com
Web Site: www.robertgaspardco.com

Personnel:
Rose Gaspard .... President
John Andorfer .... Vice President
Jason R. Gaspard .... Sales & Marketing Mgr.

Type of Business:
The Robert Gaspard Co. was established in 1954. Over the past 47 years, we have grown to be a nationally-known company. We pride ourselves on the ability to create original custom designs to enrich your worship needs. Our complete line consists of all ecclesiastical vesture, as well as paraments, mass and altar linens, stoles, banners, chasubles, funeral palls, albs, cossacks, surplices, choir robes, acolyte robes and many accessories. Complimentary catalogs and fabric swatches sent on request.

St. Anthony's CHURCH SUPPLIES

ST. ANTHONY'S CHURCH SUPPLIES
3121 McCart Ave.
Fort Worth, TX 76110
Tel: 800-772-5928
E-mail: books4u@airmail.net
Web Site: www.StellaMarisBooks.com

Type of Business:
We can supply your church or chapel with the finest vestature available including chasubles, albs, clergy shirts, and choir robes. We offer a full line of ecclesiastical goods from chalices and tabernacles, to church statuary and stained glass windows, to Catholic books and other media, to furniture for churches, church offices, classrooms, and cafeterias.

We offer great service with a smile and look forward to making new friends.

Please use our toll free number or e-mail to contact John Heitzenrater or Richard Myers.

SN
STADELMAIER
NIJMEGEN

STADELMAIER-NIJMEGEN-HOLLAND
P.O. Box 7063
6503 GN Nijmegen
Nijmegen, Holland 6503 GN
Tel.: 31-24-3791170; FAX: 31-24-3791171
e-mail: info@stadelmaier.com

Type of Business:
SN-Antiques offers, for the re-use in the Cath. Liturgy; Completely restored, original, devotional interior-pieces. Altars, stations, candlesticks, perpetual lights, statues, reliquaries, ciboria, chalices, monstrances, censers, mission crosses, processional crosses, Saints, paintings, etc.
Different styles and age: Roman, baroque, neo-gothic, etc.
Please describe your interest directly to Mrs. Annemieke Drijber.

SUITS, COATS & CASSOCKS

P. J. McDERMOTT & CO.
P.O. Box 950101
Fort Tilden, NY 11695
Tel.: 718-634-5583

Personnel:
Patrick J. McDermott ....President

Type of Business:
We are a major supplier of Ready-made suits, coats, slacks, blazers, R.J. Toomey Co. shirt fronts, French-cuff shirts, clerical vests ... "Beau-Veste" and Gammarelli (Rome) albs, surplices and rochets ... Fully custom tailored cassocks ... We are considered the leader in the U.S. and specialize in Bishops and Monsignors robes, all of which are custom tailored here. We also supply all Episcopal accessories; mitres, zuchettos, birettas, rochets, albs, pectoral cross, chains and cross cords, bishops rings, croziers.
HAVE TAPE MEASURE — WILL TRAVEL

CONSTRUCTION, MAINTENANCE & RENOVATION

The Art of Glass, Inc.

THE ART OF GLASS, INC.
316 Media Station Road
Media, PA 19037
Tel.: 610-891-7813; FAX: 610-891-0150

Personnel:
Kathy Jordan ....President

Type of Business:
The Art of Glass, Inc. provides quality design and fabrication services and is committed to the efficient completion of new construction and the ethical restoration and preservation of historic windows. Our reputation and experience in the field is well documented. We would be pleased to assist you in the early stages of planning (and design), working with your architect and/or committee to achieve your desired goals.

Berlinger Company

THE BERLINGER COMPANY
2605 N. Sheridan Road
Peoria, IL 61604
Tel.: 888-688-1781; 309-688-1771
Website: www.theberlingercompany.com

Personnel:
Michael Berlinger ....President
John Lingenfelter ....Vice-President
Jeff Walters ....Office Manager

Type of Business:
Church interior design and consultants
Interior restoration
New church designs
New liturgical whole goods—domestic and imported
Custom manufacturers
Liturgical Antiquities—domestic and imported

BOTTI STUDIO OF ARCHITECTURAL ARTS, INC.

BOTTI STUDIO OF ARCHITECTURAL ARTS, INC.
919 Grove St.
Evanston, IL 60201
Tel.: 800-524-7211; FAX: 847-869-5996; 847-869-5933
E-mail: botti@bottistudio.com
Website: www.bottistudio.com

East Coast Studio
3104 S. Osprey Ave.
Sarasota, FL 33577
Tel.: 941-951-0978; FAX: 941-953-9078

West Coast Studio
1038 N. Highway 101
Encinitas, CA 92024
Tel.: 760-753-0705; FAX: 760-753-0705
Agropoli, Italy

Personnel:

Staff includes internationally recognized artists and designers working in conjunction with our highly skilled artisans and craftsmen.

Italo G. Botti .... President

Type of Business:

For generations Botti Studio has had a reputation for embodying all that is artistically creative in the traditional and contemporary ecclesiastical field. This field includes design and fabrication of stained and faceted glass windows, restoration/conservation of windows, church interiors, appointments, murals, sculpture, mosaic and marble. We are completely dedicated to both quality and satisfying our clients needs spiritually and liturgically. Botti Studio, established in 1864, is nationwide, offering consultation and designs without obligation. Member of the Stained Glass Association of America.

Guidance In Giving

GUIDANCE IN GIVING, INC.
225 Snedecor Ave.
Bayport, NY 11705
Tel.: 888-757-5444; FAX: 631-472-6109

8164 Sea Water Path
Columbia, MD 21045
Tel.: 888-869-5522; FAX: 410-799-9155

8465 Entreken Way
San Diego, CA 92129
Tel.: 800-993-3335; FAX: 858-484-0132

4110 Wellington Woods Circle #203
Kissimmee, FL 34741
Tel.: 888-575-6005; FAX: 562-920-0149

Personnel:

Michael R. Cusack .... CEO and President
Joseph W. Zamorano .... Executive Vice President
Michael V. Goodwin .... Executive Vice President

Type of Business:

Guidance In Giving is a Catholic Development and Stewardship firm specializing in Diocesan and Parish capital campaigns, annual appeals, and stewardship programs. Additionally, the firm assists Catholic schools with their development and fund raising programs. Executives of the firm have been conducting successful campaigns since 1980 and understand and respect the Mission of the Church. We welcome the opportunity to spend a day at your diocese, parish or school to discuss your development and stewardship efforts. We will prepare an honest objective appraisal of your program at no cost to you. If you are considering counsel, please call one of our office locations.

Kosinski

Liturgical Design
Architecture
Interior Design
Construction Management

800-260-8149
www.keiarch.com

KOSINSKI ENTERPRISES, INC.

1212 Main Street	20401 N.W. Second Avenue, Suite 308
Branford, CT 06405	Miami, FL 33169
Tel.: 203-488-7733;	Tel.: 305-770-3971;
FAX: 203-483-7066	FAX: 305-770-3910
1-800-260-8149	

Website: http://www.keiarch.com

Personnel:

Peter R. Kosinski,.................. AIA Liturgical Design Consultant

Type of Business:

Kosinski has offered architectural and liturgical design services for 32 years. Our extensive knowledge of architecture and the liturgy allows us to provide our clients with exceptional services. Our full range of in-house professional services, including the design of all liturgical elements, interior design and construction management, gives our clients a single point of contact for complete project delivery. We emphasize a team approach in which the client participates actively in design and project delivery.

PATRICK BAKER & SONS

PATRICK BAKER & SONS, INC.

1650 West Street
Southington, CT 06489
Tel.: 860-628-5566; FAX: 860-276-9438

Personnel:

Patrick A. Baker ....Chairman
Brian T. Baker ....President
Michael P. Baker ....Vice President
Maureen Kelly ....Secretary

Type of Business:

- Religious Supplies
- Church Goods
- Church Renovations

See our ad on the next page.

RAMBUSCH

RAMBUSCH

40 West 13th St.
New York, NY 10011
Tel.: 212-675-0400; FAX: 212-620-4687

Personnel:

Viggo Bech Rambusch ....Senior Project Director
Martin V. Rambusch ....Stained Glass Director

Type of Business:

Since 1898, creating church interiors, liturgical furnishings, and art work. Fine restoration of church interiors. In-house studios and shops for designing and executing stained glass, church lighting systems, art metal work, and decorative painting.

ROHN
DESIGN GROUP

ROHN DESIGN GROUP

5075 Clairton Blvd, Suite 301
Pittsburgh, PA 15236
Tel: (412) 561-1228; (800) 245-1288; Fax: (412) 561-8129
E-mail: rohnstudio@aol.com
Web Site: www.rohndesign.com

Personnel:

A full service team of U.S. and international artisans & craftsmen.

Rolf R. Rohn ....Principal Consultant/Director/Artist
Kathleen L. Maglicco ....Principal Interior Design
Sister Janet Baxendale, S.C ....Education

Type of Business:

Experience spanning 4 decades in renovation/restoration, conservation, and design of new worship environments. A valuable partner in over 1,300 commissions throughout the U.S., Canada and Europe.

We offer:
-Altars
-Tabernacles
-Bronze/Stonework
-Artwork, multi-mediums
-Statuary
-Baptismal Fonts
-Ambo-Lecterns
-Mosaics
-Pews/Choirs
-Lamps and Lighting
-Liturgical Design
and more....

Please see our ads on the divider pages for "General Summary" and "Products & Services." For other services look under "Construction, Maintenance & Renovation", "Consultants" and "Liturgical & Church Goods".
www.rohndesign.com

Vermont Church Supply Co.

VERMONT CHURCH SUPPLY CO.
676 Pine Street, P.O. Box 368
Burlington, VT 05401
Tel.: 802-862-6486, 800-451-3453; FAX: 802-862-5765
E-mail: vcs@together.net

Personnel:
Neil Clark ....President

Type of Business:
Since our inception in 1946 by W. Barrett Clark and Doris Clark, Vermont Church Supply has offered the highest quality products and the best service to the Church and the Clergy. We have a wide range of products including Candles, Church Furniture, Metalware and Vestments. Our founders' Sons, Neil, John, Thomas and Robert, along with the third generation Anthony Clark, continue to provide services such as refinishing Sacred Vessels, Candlesticks and abernacles and also the execution of hand carved wood and marble Statuary. Whether your needs are small or large, we can give the best personalized service to our Customers.

ARCHITECTS

ARCHITECTURAL FEATURES CREATED BY Madden

CHARLES L. MADDEN
CREATING ARCHITECTURAL FEATURES
1245 E. Butler Pike
Ambler, PA 19002-6032 U.S.A.
Tel.: 215-646-8919; FAX: 215-643-7272
email: cmadden@concentric.net

Personnel:
Charles L. Madden ....Owner/Creative Director

Type of Business:
Architectural Features by definition is a single art resource for consultation, design, fabrication, and installation in creating spaces of liturgical and meditative inspiration with sacred art and beautiful materials of fine substance and detailing. Our worldwide commissions in bronze sculpture, mosaic, marble, stained glass, tapestry, and fine woods are custom created to extend our client's vision. Whether you are a Diocesan, Community, Institutional, or Architectural client - we are pleased to put our vast creative and computer technological resources at the service of your building and renovational vision.

Conrad Schmitt Studios Inc.

CONRAD SCHMITT STUDIOS, INC.
2405 S. 162nd St.
New Berlin, WI 53151
Tel.: 800-969-3033; 414-786-3030; FAX: 414-786-9036

Personnel:
Heidi Gruenke Emery........Vice President & Marketing Director

Type of Business:
Since 1889, this family-owned Studio has restored and decorated hundreds of interiors across the country. Their scope of work includes the investigation and documentation of original decorative schemes; the restoration of those schemes through the application of various decorative techniques including gilding, glazing, marbleizing, stenciling, and graining, as well as the design, fabrication, conservation or replication of murals and stained glass. The Studio can assist projects in the early stages with architectural samples and rendering for fund-raising. Recently completed projects include St. Josaphat's Basilica, Milwaukee, WI; St. Ann's, Napoleanville, LA; and St. Bernard's, Akron, OH.

DUNCAN G. STROIK, ARCHITECT

DUNCAN G. STROIK, ARCHITECT
52488 Briarcliff Lane
South Bend, Indiana 46635
Tel. & Fax: 219/ 271-0522
E-mail: dstroik@nd.edu

Personnel:
Duncan G. Stroik ....Principal

Type of Business:
Duncan G. Stroik, Architect is a full service design firm focused on creating carefully detailed and proportioned ecclesiastical and institutional buildings. Projects are undertaken with the intent to create works of art which ennoble those who come in contact with them. The firm is a leader in the renaissance of traditional Catholic architecture, basing its work on the ancient principles of firmitas (durability), utilitas (function) and venustas (beauty). We believe that buildings must fulfill all three of these requirements to be considered true works of architecture.

Kosinski
Liturgical Design
Architecture
Interior Design
Construction Management
800-260-8149
www.keiarch.com

KOSINSKI ENTERPRISES, INC.

1212 Main Street
Branford, CT 06405
Tel.: 203-488-7733;
FAX: 203-483-7066
1-800-260-8149

20401 N.W. Second Avenue, Suite 308
Miami, FL 33169
Tel.: 305-770-3971;
FAX: 305-770-3910

Website: http://www.keiarch.com

Personnel:
Peter R. Kosinski,.................. AIA Liturgical Design Consultant

Continued

Kosinski Enterprises, Inc. Continued

Type of Business:
Kosinski has offered architectural and liturgical design services for 32 years. Our extensive knowledge of architecture and the liturgy allows us to provide our clients with exceptional services. Our full range of in-house professional services, including the design of all liturgical elements, interior design and construction management, gives our clients a single point of contact for complete project delivery. We emphasize a team approach in which the client participates actively in design and project delivery.

ARTISTS & DECORATORS

Berlinger Company

THE BERLINGER COMPANY
2605 N. Sheridan Road
Peoria, IL 61604
Tel.: 888-688-1781; 309-688-1771
Website: www.theberlingercompany.com

Personnel:
Michael Berlinger ....President
John Lingenfelter ....Vice-President
Jeff Walters...Office Manager

Type of Business:
Church interior design and consultants
Interior restoration
New church designs
New liturgical whole goods—domestic and imported
Custom manufacturers
Liturgical Antiquities—domestic and imported

BOTTI STUDIO OF ARCHITECTURAL ARTS, INC.

BOTTI STUDIO OF ARCHITECTURAL ARTS, INC.
919 Grove St.
Evanston, IL 60201
Tel.: 800-524-7211; FAX: 847-869-5996; 847-869-5933
E-mail: botti@bottistudio.com
Website: www.bottistudio.com

East Coast Studio
3104 S. Osprey Ave.
Sarasota, FL 33577
Tel.: 941-951-0978; FAX: 941-953-9078

West Coast Studio
1038 N. Highway 101
Encinitas, CA 92024
Tel.: 760-753-0705; FAX: 760-753-0705
Agropoli, Italy

Personnel:
Staff includes internationally recognized artists and designers working in conjunction with our highly skilled artisans and craftsmen.
Italo G. Botti ....President

Continued

RAMBUSCH

RAMBUSCH
40 West 13th St.
New York, NY 10011
Tel.: 212-675-0400; FAX: 212-620-4687

Personnel:
Viggo Bech Rambusch ....Senior Project Director
Martin V. Rambusch ....Stained Glass Director

Type of Business:
Since 1898, creating church interiors, liturgical furnishings, and art work. Fine restoration of church interiors. In-house studios and shops for designing and executing stained glass, church lighting systems, art metal work, and decorative painting.

BRONZE MILLENIUM DOORS

ARCHITECTURAL FEATURES CREATED BY Madden

CHARLES L. MADDEN
CREATING ARCHITECTURAL FEATURES
1245 E. Butler Pike
Ambler, PA 19002-6032 U.S.A.
Tel.: 215-646-8919; FAX: 215-643-7272
email: cmadden@concentric.net

Personnel:
Charles L. Madden ....Owner/Creative Director

Type of Business:
Architectural Features by definition is a single art resource for consultation, design, fabrication, and installation in creating spaces of liturgical and meditative inspiration with sacred art and beautiful materials of fine substance and detailing. Our worldwide commissions in bronze sculpture, mosaic, marble, stained glass, tapestry, and fine woods are custom created to extend our client's vision. Whether you are a Diocesan, Community, Institutional, or Architectural client - we are pleased to put our vast creative and computer technological resources at the service of your building and renovational vision.

DOMUSDEI HOLY ART STUDIOS

DOMUSDEI HOLY ART STUDIOS

DOMUSDEI HOLY ART STUDIOS
FACTORY: Via dei Tulipani, 48 - 00040 CECCHINA
DI ALBANO (RM) - ITALY
Tel: 011-39-06-9343369
FAX: 011-39-06-9344971

SHOW ROOM: Via Scossacavalli 3/9 - 00193 - ROMA - ITALY
Tel: 011-39-06-6868090
FAX: 011-39-06-6869806
E-Mail: info@domusdei.it
m.delmonte@domusdei.it
Web Site: www.domusdei.it

Personnel:
Alessandro Del Monte ....President
Massimiliano Del Monte ....Executive Director
Aldo Del Monte ....Assistant President

Type of Business:
Founded in 1963, Domusdei Studio has restored thousands of church interiors all over the world. Specializing in designing and manufacturing stained glass windows, mosaics, bronze and fiberglass statues, altars, bronze doors, lecterns, baptismal fonts, candlesticks, flower holders, tabernacles.
We are also experts in silver and gold plating and the restoration of wood and metal masterpieces.

CHURCH SIGNS & BANNERS

Chagall Design Limited©
Designers of Custom Liturgical Vestments, Stoles, Dalmatics, Banners and Sanctuary Accessories.

CHAGALL DESIGN LTD.
910 south Los Angeles Street
Los Angeles, CA 90015
Tel: 1-800-947-7923 fax: 213-624-8036
E-mail Address: CHAGALL@IX.NETCOM.COM
Web: WWW.CHAGALLDESIGN.COM

Personnel:
Jacques de Groot..........President
Mannix Delfino ....Vice President

Type of Business:
Designers of custom liturgical Vestments, Stoles, Dalmatics Banners and sanctuary accessories. The finest import fabrics, and custom embroidery's are used in a blend of traditional elegance and modern design. Our attention to detail makes each vestment, and banner unique. All our banners are custom made in design and size; we also offer a line of Tabernacles, Candlesticks, Chalices, Ciborium's that are imported from Italy, Spain and France. Please review our accompanying catalog with the Catholic Directory.

the symbol of Regal Splendor
Robert Gaspard Co.

ROBERT GASPARD CO., INC.
200 N. Janacek Rd.
Brookfield, WI 53045-6101
Tel.: 800-784-6868; 262-784-6800; FAX: 262-784-7567
E-mail: robertgaspard.com
Web Site: www.robertgaspardco.com

Personnel:
Rose Gaspard ....President
John Andorfer ....Vice President
Jason R. Gaspard ....Sales & Marketing Mgr.

Type of Business:
The Robert Gaspard Co. was established in 1954. Over the past 47 years, we have grown to be a nationally-known company. We pride ourselves on the ability to create original custom designs to enrich your worship needs. Our complete line consists of all ecclesiastical vesture, as well as paraments, mass and altar linens, stoles, banners, chasubles, funeral palls, albs, cossacks, surplices, choir robes, acolyte robes and many accessories. Complimentary catalogs and fabric swatches sent on request.

CONSERVATIONS

The Art of Glass, Inc.

THE ART OF GLASS, INC.
316 Media Station Road
Media, PA 19037
Tel.: 610-891-7813; FAX: 610-891-0150

Personnel:
Kathy Jordan ....President

Type of Business:
The Art of Glass, Inc. provides quality design and fabrication services and is committed to the efficient completion of new construction and the ethical restoration and preservation of historic windows. Our reputation and experience in the field is well documented. We would be pleased to assist you in the early stages of planning (and design), working with your architect and/or committee to achieve your desired goals.

Conrad Schmitt Studios Inc.

CONRAD SCHMITT STUDIOS, INC.
2405 S. 162nd St.
New Berlin, WI 53151
Tel.: 800-969-3033; 414-786-3030; FAX: 414-786-9036

Personnel:
Heidi Gruenke Emery . . . Vice President & Marketing Director

Type of Business:
Since 1889, this family-owned Studio has restored and decorated hundreds of interiors across the country. Their scope of work includes the investigation and documentation of original decorative schemes; the restoration of those schemes through the application of various decorative techniques including gilding, glazing, marbleizing, stenciling, and graining, as well as the design, fabrication, conservation or replication of murals and stained glass. The Studio can assist projects in the early stages with architectural samples and rendering for fund-raising. Recently completed projects include St. Josaphat's Basilica, Milwaukee, WI; St. Ann's, Napoleanville, LA; and St. Bernard's, Akron, OH.

EverGreene Painting Studios, Inc.

EVERGREENE PAINTING STUDIOS, INC.
450 West 31st Street, 7th Fl.
New York, NY 10001
Tel.: 212-244-2800
FAX: 212-244-6204

323 South Blvd.
Oak Park, IL 60302
Tel.: 708-358-1656
Fax: 708-358-1656

E-mail: info@evergreene.com
Web Site: www.evergreene.com

Personnel:
Jeff Greene .... President

Type of Business:
EverGreene is a full-service decorative arts studio committed to preserving the integrity of historic sacred spaces through conservation, restoration, and compatible new design. Services include investigation and analysis of original finishes; consultations, renderings, budgets and samples to support decision-making and capital campaigns; design of color schemes and architectural ornament; specifications; and execution of work by our staff of experienced project managers, artists, artisans and conservators.

EverGreene is accomplished in all types of decorative painting and gilding; conservation, replication, and new design of murals and mosaics; ornamental plaster and scagliola; and allied crafts including wood refinishing, interior stone cleaning, metal patination, art glass, tile work and other architectural arts.

Established in 1978, EverGreene undertakes projects large and small around the country. Recently completed works include St. Cecilia's Cathedral, Omaha; St. Peter Church, San Francisco; Our Lady of Perpetual Help (Redemptorist Church), Kansas City; and St. John's Seminary Chapel, Brighton, MA. Among current projects are St. Joseph's Church in Burlington, VT and Assumption Abbey, ND.

Mark W. Read Studio & Gallery

MARK W. READ STUDIO
1898 Broadstone Road
P.O. Box 671
Valle Crucis, NC 28691
Phone & Fax (828) 963-8191
Web Site: www.markreadstudio.com

Type of Business:

Liturgical Jewelry	Sculpture
Architectural Pieces	Sacred Vessels
Utensils	Urns
Holloware/Chalices	Gem Setting
Gold & Silver Plating	Museum Quality Restoration

Mark Read is an artist craftsman of 30 years experience. Trained in old world and traditional methods he possesses the patience and skill to master the precise craftsmanship that goes into each custom project or restoration piece. Whether his exquisite one-of-a-kind creations are to purely inspire the beholder or serve as a functional piece, Marks creative gifts, unique approach and special sensitivity ensures that each commission works in harmony with its architectural surroundings.

From gold, silver, bronze, titanium to iron and beyond...the possibilities are endless.

Research and consulting is his first priority for restoration projects, thereby ensuring a clear understanding of the steps that must be taken to restore your piece back to its original glory. All types of restoration are accepted.

Please visit our website with the special section for Liturgical pieces.

See our display ad on page 107r.

DOORS & PARTITIONS

ATD-AMERICAN CO.

ATD-AMERICAN CO.
135 Greenwood Avenue
Wyncote, PA 19095-1396
Tel.: 888-283-2487; FAX: 800-283-7363
E-mail: american@atd.com
Web Site: www.atd.com

Personnel:
Bob Roche....................Marketing
Sal Catanese....................Sales

Type of Business:
For four generations, ATD-AMERICAN has supplied Furniture and Equipment to Churches, Organizations and Institutions nationally and worldwide. Since 1931, it has been our tradition to deliver high quality products and personal service at the lowest competitive prices. ATD offers a wide range of products to meet all of the needs of your Church and School. Our comprehensive catalog includes the following: Announcement and Bulletin Boards, Audio-Visual Equipment, Classroom Furniture, Computer Furniture, Daycare Furniture, Display Cases, Folding Chairs, Folding Tables, Lecterns, Library Furniture, Office Furniture, Outdoor Equipment, Pews and Pulpit Furniture, Room Dividers and Partitions, Stacking Chairs, and Stages and Risers.

For a FREE Wholesale Furniture Catalog, call us toll-free 888-283-2487 or fax us at 800-283-7363. You can also visit our web-site at http://www.atd.com or email us at atd.com.

SPECIAL OFFER FOR CATHOLIC DIRECTORY SUBSCRIBERS: Mention offer code 6557 and receive a special 10% discount on your first order.

HUFCOR

HUFCOR INC.
P.O. Box 591
Janesville, WI 53547
Tel.: 800-542-2371, ext. 214; FAX: 608-758-8253

Personnel:
Elaine Masters....................Marketing Coordinator

Type of Business:
Hufcor operable and accordion partitions allow you the flexibility to create large or small spaces, fast. Our wide selection of models, sound control ratings, configurations, options, and finishes, lets you choose the right product for your budget and needs. Hufcor partitions are available through local, factory-trained Distributors who offer free design assistance as well as installation and service. Hufcor is a ISO 9001 registered company. Call our toll free number for the name of your nearest representative.

FACETED GLASS

Conrad Schmitt Studios Inc.

CONRAD SCHMITT STUDIOS, INC.
2405 S. 162nd St.
New Berlin, WI 53151
Tel.: 800-969-3033; 414-786-3030; FAX: 414-786-9036

Personnel:
Heidi Gruenke Emery........Vice President & Marketing Director

Type of Business:
Since 1889, this family-owned Studio has restored and decorated hundreds of interiors across the country. Their scope of work includes the investigation and documentation of original decorative schemes; the restoration of those schemes through the application of various decorative techniques including gilding, glazing, marbleizing, stenciling, and graining, as well as the design, fabrication, conservation or replication of murals and stained glass. The Studio can assist projects in the early stages with architectural samples and rendering for fund-raising. Recently completed projects include St. Josaphat's Basilica, Milwaukee, WI; St. Ann's, Napoleanville, LA; and St. Bernard's, Akron, OH.

GENERAL CONTRACTORS

DAPRATO RIGALI STUDIOS, INC.

DAPRATO RIGALI STUDIOS, INC.
7956 Oakton St.
Niles, IL 60714
Tel.: 847-692-6350; FAX: 847-692-3445

Personnel:
John Rigali
Robert Rigali
Lisa Rigali Galvin
Mike Rigali

Type of Business:
Daprato Rigali Studios Inc. has been beautifying Churches in America since 1860.
Today we find the Rigali Family restoring and renovating the churches originally decorated by their Great-Grandfather, John E. Rigali; aware of his reputation to create spiritually moving environments with quality material and craftsmanship.
Some of their most recent jobs include: decoration and stained glass restoration at St. Mary of the Lake Seminary, Mundelein, IL.; Marble renovation and decoration, St. Elizabeth's Mother House, Allegany, N.Y.; and General Contracting for complete renovation of St. Bernadette's Church, Rockford, IL.
The Daprato Rigali staff is equipped to take your project from start to finish. If you're interested in working with a fine interior design studio experienced in Ecclesiastical Artistries please call for consultation at no obligation. We deliver what we design.

EVERGREENE
PAINTING STUDIOS, INC.

EVERGREENE PAINTING STUDIOS, INC.

450 West 31st Street, 7th Fl.
New York, NY 10001
Tel.: 212-244-2800
FAX: 212-244-6204

323 South Blvd.
Oak Park, IL 60302
Tel.: 708-358-1656
Fax: 708-358-1656

E-mail: info@evergreene.com
Web Site: www.evergreene.com

Personnel:

Jeff Greene .... President

Type of Business:

EverGreene is a full-service decorative arts studio committed to preserving the integrity of historic sacred spaces through conservation, restoration, and compatible new design. Services include investigation and analysis of original finishes; consultations, renderings, budgets and samples to support decision-making and capital campaigns; design of color schemes and architectural ornament; specifications; and execution of work by our staff of experienced project managers, artists, artisans and conservators.

EverGreene is accomplished in all types of decorative painting and gilding; conservation, replication, and new design of murals and mosaics; ornamental plaster and scagliola; and allied crafts including wood refinishing, interior stone cleaning, metal patination, art glass, tile work and other architectural arts.

Established in 1978, EverGreene undertakes projects large and small around the country. Recently completed works include St. Cecilia's Cathedral, Omaha; St. Peter Church, San Francisco; Our Lady of Perpetual Help (Redemptorist Church), Kansas City; and St. John's Seminary Chapel, Brighton, MA. Among current projects are St. Joseph's Church in Burlington, VT and Assumption Abbey, ND.

MONUMENTAL CHURCH ENTRANCES

THE BAUT STUDIOS, INC.
ECCLESIASTICAL CRAFTSMEN

THE BAUT STUDIOS INC.

1095 Main St.
Swayersville, PA 18704
Tel.: 800-326-9421; FAX: 570-288-0380
E-mail: info@baut.com
Web Site: www.baut.com

Personnel:

Conrad Dismas .... Baut President
Gerhard Francis .... Baut Master Sculptor
Heide Baut Cebrick .... Artist/Designer
Karen Baut Klemm .... Business Manager

Type of Business:

The STAINED GLASS of the FUTURE is here NOW!

The Baut Studios, Inc., established in 1927, is a full service ecclesiastical studio that has been manufacturing and installing their own patented STRUCTURAL STAINED GLASS* in windows and doors for over 40 years. A unique non-sagging construction never needing structural repairs, STRUCTURAL STAINED GLASS is LEAD FREE, and CUSTOM DESIGNED to fit many tastes and budgets. Pricing is competitive with leaded and stained glass but with many more advantages when combined with the BAUT WINDOW and DOOR SYSTEMS. Beautiful, long lasting, environmentally and financially sound, and virtually maintenance free, STRUCTURAL STAINED GLASS is featured in over 5000 churches worldwide.

Other products include Single, Double and Triple Glazed Church Windows and Ventilators. Heavy Duty Doors, Restoration/New Traditional Stained Glass, Altars and Appointments, Crosses, Steeples, Glass Mosaics and church Lighting. All Baut products are custom made to your sizes and shapes, and designed to match your décor.

* U.S. Patent No. 3,064,380

RESTORATION / REFINISHING

TOUJOURS

ADRIAN HAMERS®
CHURCH INTERIORS

ADRIAN HAMERS INC.
2 Madison Avenue
Larchmont, NY 10538
Tel.: 914-834-7780; FAX: 914-834-0712

Type of Business:

Custom designers and manufacturers of Sacred Vessels. Since 1887, the Hamers name has been synonymous with expert Silversmithing throughout the world in the field of Liturgical Art. Please contact us for those hard to find items, as we always have a large selection of Adrian Hamers Estate Collection pieces in stock. We are experts in: Church Interiors from design to execution, Renovations, Altars, Sacred Vessels, Gold and Silver Plating & Repairing, Appraisals, Tabernacles, Marble, Statuary, Woodwork & Woodcarving, Stained Glass, Pews & Chairs, Gold Leafing, Frescoes, Restoration, Trompe-l' oeuil, Wall Murals (repair and conservation cleaning), Ornamental Plaster, Heraldic Designs & Bishop Regalia. Please call us for a free 24 page Sacred Vessels color catalog, or our free 80 page color Woodcarvings catalog.

The Art of Glass, Inc.

THE ART OF GLASS, INC.
316 Media Station Road
Media, PA 19037
Tel.: 610-891-7813; FAX: 610-891-0150

Personnel:

Kathy Jordan .... President

Type of Business:

The Art of Glass, Inc. provides quality design and fabrication services and is committed to the efficient completion of new construction and the ethical restoration and preservation of historic windows. Our reputation and experience in the field is well documented. We would be pleased to assist you in the early stages of planning (and design), working with your architect and/or committee to achieve your desired goals.

Berlinger Company

THE BERLINGER COMPANY
2605 N. Sheridan Road
Peoria, IL 61604
Tel.: 888-688-1781; 309-688-1771
Website: www.theberlingercompany.com

Personnel:

Michael Berlinger .... President
John Lingenfelter .... Vice-President
Jeff Walters .... Office Manager

Type of Business:

Church interior design and consultants
Interior restoration
New church designs
New liturgical whole goods—domestic and imported
Custom manufacturers
Liturgical Antiquities—domestic and imported

BOTTI STUDIO OF ARCHITECTURAL ARTS, INC.

BOTTI STUDIO OF ARCHITECTURAL ARTS, INC.
919 Grove St.
Evanston, IL 60201
Tel.: 800-524-7211; FAX: 847-869-5996; 847-869-5933
E-mail: botti@bottistudio.com
Website: www.bottistudio.com

East Coast Studio
3104 S. Osprey Ave.
Sarasota, FL 33577
Tel.: 941-951-0978; FAX: 941-953-9078

West Coast Studio
1038 N. Highway 101
Encinitas, CA 92024
Tel.: 760-753-0705; FAX: 760-753-0705
Agropoli, Italy

Personnel:
Staff includes internationally recognized artists and designers working in conjunction with our highly skilled artisans and craftsmen.
Italo G. Botti ....President

Type of Business:
For generations Botti Studio has had a reputation for embodying all that is artistically creative in the traditional and contemporary ecclesiastical field. This field includes design and fabrication of stained and faceted glass windows, restoration/conservation of windows, church interiors, appointments, murals, sculpture, mosaic and marble. We are completely dedicated to both quality and satisfying our clients needs spiritually and liturgically. Botti Studio, established in 1864, is nationwide, offering consultation and designs without obligation. Member of the Stained Glass Association of America.

ARCHITECTURAL FEATURES CREATED BY Madden

CHARLES L. MADDEN
CREATING ARCHITECTURAL FEATURES
1245 E. Butler Pike
Ambler, PA 19002-6032 U.S.A.
Tel.: 215-646-8919; FAX: 215-643-7272
email: cmadden@concentric.net

Personnel:
Charles L. Madden ....Owner/Creative Director

Type of Business:
Architectural Features by definition is a single art resource for consultation, design, fabrication, and installation in creating spaces of liturgical and meditative inspiration with sacred art and beautiful materials of fine substance and detailing. Our worldwide commissions in bronze sculpture, mosaic, marble, stained glass, tapestry, and fine woods are custom created to extend our client's vision. Whether you are a Diocesan, Community, Institutional, or Architectural client - we are pleased to put our vast creative and computer technological resources at the service of your building and renovational vision.

Conrad Schmitt Studios Inc.

CONRAD SCHMITT STUDIOS, INC.
2405 S. 162nd St.
New Berlin, WI 53151
Tel.: 800-969-3033; 414-786-3030; FAX: 414-786-9036

Personnel:
Heidi Gruenke Emery........Vice President & Marketing Director

Type of Business:
Since 1889, this family-owned Studio has restored and decorated hundreds of interiors across the country. Their scope of work includes the investigation and documentation of original decorative schemes; the restoration of those schemes through the application of various decorative techniques including gilding, glazing, marbleizing, stenciling, and graining, as well as the design, fabrication, conservation or replication of murals and stained glass. The Studio can assist projects in the early stages with architectural samples and rendering for fund-raising. Recently completed projects include St. Josaphat's Basilica, Milwaukee, WI; St. Ann's, Napoleanville, LA; and St. Bernard's, Akron, OH.

DAPRATO RIGALI STUDIOS, INC.

DAPRATO RIGALI STUDIOS, INC.
7956 Oakton St.
Niles, IL 60714
Tel.: 847-692-6350; FAX: 847-692-3445

Personnel:
John Rigali
Robert Rigali
Lisa Rigali Galvin
Mike Rigali

Type of Business:
Daprato Rigali Studios Inc. has been beautifying Churches in America since 1860.
Today we find the Rigali Family restoring and renovating the churches originally decorated by their Great-Grandfather, John E. Rigali; aware of his reputation to create spiritually moving environments with quality material and craftsmanship.
Some of their most recent jobs include: decoration and stained glass restoration at St. Mary of the Lake Seminary, Mundelein, IL.; Marble renovation and decoration, St. Elizabeth's Mother House, Allegany, N.Y.; and General Contracting for complete renovation of St. Bernadette's Church, Rockford, IL.
The Daprato Rigali staff is equipped to take your project from start to finish. If you're interested in working with a fine interior design studio experienced in Ecclesiastical Artistries please call for consultation at no obligation. We deliver what we design.

STONE RESTORATION OF NEW YORK ®

Office: (716) 896-5960 Fax: (716) 896-5966

Natural Stone Care Specialists **Restore • Clean • Polish & Seal**

Mr. Rubin Cruz, president, applies a sub-sealer on a stone at St. John Evangelist Parish, in Buffalo, to protect it from dirt and moisture penetration.

Mr. Bob Cardarelli of Stone Restoration polishes a terrazzo floor at St. Josaphat Parish in Cheektowaga. No wax or coating is ever used.

Mr. Chris Webber (in background) and Mr. Rubin Cruz sand oak pews at St. Josaphat Parish.

"We Take Pride in Our Craftsmanship"

There is no reason for your terrazzo floors not to look beautiful…or your white Carrara statues and oak pews, either!

The care and maintenance of stone is a specialized craft and should not be trusted to your general janitorial staff.

BEFORE **AFTER**

White Carrara statues at St. John the Evangelist Parish in Buffalo

Stone Restoration specializes in the care and maintenance of marble, travertine, terrazzo, granite, and related stones. With Stone Restoration's refinishing process, these materials can be restored to "like new" beauty and luster without wax or coatings which cause unsightly discoloration.

In loving memory of
Henry Falkowski

EVERGREENE PAINTING STUDIOS, INC.

EVERGREENE PAINTING STUDIOS, INC.
450 West 31st Street, 7th Fl.
New York, NY 10001
Tel.: 212-244-2800
FAX: 212-244-6204

323 South Blvd.
Oak Park, IL 60302
Tel.: 708-358-1656
Fax: 708-358-1656

E-mail: info@evergreene.com
Web Site: www.evergreene.com

Personnel:
Jeff Greene ....President

Type of Business:
EverGreene is a full-service decorative arts studio committed to preserving the integrity of historic sacred spaces through conservation, restoration, and compatible new design. Services include investigation and analysis of original finishes; consultations, renderings, budgets and samples to support decision-making and capital campaigns; design of color schemes and architectural ornament; specifications; and execution of work by our staff of experienced project managers, artists, artisans and conservators.

EverGreene is accomplished in all types of decorative painting and gilding; conservation, replication, and new design of murals and mosaics; ornamental plaster and scagliola; and allied crafts including wood refinishing, interior stone cleaning, metal patination, art glass, tile work and other architectural arts.

Established in 1978, EverGreene undertakes projects large and small around the country. Recently completed works include St. Cecilia's Cathedral, Omaha; St. Peter Church, San Francisco; Our Lady of Perpetual Help (Redemptorist Church), Kansas City; and St. John's Seminary Chapel, Brighton, MA. Among current projects are St. Joseph's Church in Burlington, VT and Assumption Abbey, ND.

KOLEY'S, INC.
2951 Harney St.
Omaha, NE 68131
Tel.: 402-341-9795; FAX: 402-341-5857

Personnel:
Tom Koley
Terry Goehring

Type of Business:
Quality, Care and Craftsmanship. For four generations these words have described Koley's, Inc. Since our very beginning in 1919, we have endeavored to serve the churches and clergy in repairing, polishing and replating of sacred vessels or other items of metal found in the Church. Our craftsmen strive to restore your cherished ecclesiastical items to its original condition whenever possible. We take pride in knowing that you have entrusted us with your items. Free estimates.

RAMBUSCH

RAMBUSCH
40 West 13th St.
New York, NY 10011
Tel.: 212-675-0400; FAX: 212-620-4687

Personnel:
Viggo Bech Rambusch ....Senior Project Director
Martin V. Rambusch ....Stained Glass Director

Type of Business:
Since 1898, creating church interiors, liturgical furnishings, and art work. Fine restoration of church interiors. In-house studios and shops for designing and executing stained glass, church lighting systems, art metal work, and decorative painting.

RESTORATIONS PLUS
5427 Virginia Avenue
Saint Louis, Missouri 63111
Tel.: 314-481-3268; FAX: 314-481-3268
E-mail: rplus@kwd.zzn.com

Type of Business:
Our service offers restoration of statuary, old or new, we'll determine the original artist palette through an historical color analysis if necessary, or repair areas as needed. We can replicate the statue back to original or repaint to an existing or new palette. We manufacture and distribute a wonderful selection of ecclesiastical pieces, and replicate finishes from statuary of old using the same methodologies of over 100 years ago. We have a placement service for statuary /artifacts that are no longer being used and place into a new or existing Church or Religious Institution. Also, we can replicate any architectural element or statue as needed with latex rubber molds and gypsum plaster.

Also offered are restoration services of vestments. Fragile treasured ornamentation from older vestments are carefully removed and hand-sewn onto vestment fabric of your choice. Custom labor is our specialty.

ROHLF'S STAINED & LEADED GLASS STUDIO, INC.
783 South Third Ave.
Mt. Vernon, NY 10550
Tel.: 914-699-4848; FAX: 914-699-7091
Website: www.rohlfstudio.com

Personnel:
Peter Hans Rohlf .... President
Gregory Rohlf .... Vice President
Rich Widmer .... Secretary/Treasurer

Type of Business:
For Three Generations our family owned and operated Studio together with our affiliate, George L. Payne Studio have been dedicated to excellence in Stained Glass Art. Our team of International designers and Master Craftspersons have created stained glass windows for over a thousand Churches and Institutions Worldwide. Our reputation and experience in the field of Restoration, Replication and Preservation is well known. We would be pleased to assist you in the early stages of planning and design, working with your Architect and/or committee to achieve your desired goals.
From concept to completion, we are dedicated to serve you.

Stained Glass Associates

STAINED GLASS ASSOCIATES
P.O. Box 1531
Raleigh, NC 27602-1531
Tel.: 919-266-2493

Personnel:
Robert J. Wysocki .... Owner

Type of Business:
• Design, Fabrication and Installation of:
– Leaded, Faceted and Painted Glass
• Restoration and Repair
– Replacement Frames
– Fire Damage
• Appraisals
About SGA:
– Established in 1958
– Studio Member of Stained Glass Association of America
– 1,024 Installations Nationally and Internationally
Stained Glass Associates is committed to maintaining the highest of ecclesiastical standards and the complete satisfaction of every client.

STAINED GLASS STUDIOS, LTD.
RR # 1 Pleasantville
2102 West LaHave, NS BOR 1GO
Tel.: 1-902-688-1156; Fax: 1-902-688-1475
Web Site: www.sattlerglas.com
E-mail: Sattler@atcon.com

Personnel:
Norbert Sattler .... President
Helga Sattler .... Vice President, Sales & Marketing Mngr.

Type of Business:
Over 33 years experience. Sattler's Stained Glass Studio has developed working partnerships with many artists from all over the world, exploring traditional and innovative applications of glass in the production of art works. Sattler's studio takes care of your project from taking the measurements, to fabricating and the installation.
STAINED GLASS
Fabrication of stained glass in collaboration with artists, designers and architects: religious, profane, modern, traditional, artistic, craft.
GLASS RESTORATION
in all traditional and historical stained glass: restore, renovate, copy.
PROJECTS IN COMBINATION WITH GLASS WOOD AND METAL. WE TAKE CARE OF: measurments, advise for framing and technical support to install glass purchase (antique glass) flashed, opal, opaque, etc. 1:1 Cartoon, ready for transfer of the design, painting, printing, etching, sandblasting, glazing and installation.

STONE RESTORATION OF NEW YORK®
Natural Stone Care Specialists

STONE RESTORATION OF NEW YORK
54 Marlene Drive
Buffalo, NY 14225
Tel.: 716-896-5960; FAX: 716-681-9538
E-mail: info@srony.com
Web Site: www.srony.com

Type of Business:
Special Craft Brings New Life and Beauty to Churches
Stone Restoration of New York brings an art to the Catholic diocese that would make Michaelangelo happy. Mr. Rubin Cruz is president of Stone Restoration of New York. Originally from New York City, Mr. Cruz has been working in Buffalo and western New York for the past seven years, with seventeen years of outstanding service.

His company specializes in the care and maintenance of marble-terrazzo-travertine-granite-and brick & masonry restoration. They travel at times around the northeast, consulting with architects and interior decorators as well as construction attorneys.

See our ad on the page 76r.

SCULPTOR

ARCHITECTURAL FEATURES CREATED BY Madden

CHARLES L. MADDEN
CREATING ARCHITECTURAL FEATURES
1245 E. Butler Pike
Ambler, PA 19002-6032 U.S.A.
Tel.: 215-646-8919; FAX: 215-643-7272
email: cmadden@concentric.net

Personnel:
Charles L. Madden ....Owner/Creative Director

Type of Business:
Architectural Features by definition is a single art resource for consultation, design, fabrication, and installation in creating spaces of liturgical and meditative inspiration with sacred art and beautiful materials of fine substance and detailing. Our worldwide commissions in bronze sculpture, mosaic, marble, stained glass, tapestry, and fine woods are custom created to extend our client's vision. Whether you are a Diocesan, Community, Institutional, or Architectural client - we are pleased to put our vast creative and computer technological resources at the service of your building and renovational vision.

See our ad on page 80r.

STAINED GLASS

The Art of Glass, Inc.

THE ART OF GLASS, INC.
316 Media Station Road
Media, PA 19037
Tel.: 610-891-7813; FAX: 610-891-0150

Personnel:
Kathy Jordan ....President

Type of Business:
The Art of Glass, Inc. provides quality design and fabrication services and is committed to the efficient completion of new construction and the ethical restoration and preservation of historic windows. Our reputation and experience in the field is well documented. We would be pleased to assist you in the early stages of planning (and design), working with your architect and/or committee to achieve your desired goals.

THE BAUT STUDIOS, INC.
ECCLESIASTICAL CRAFTSMEN

BAUT

THE BAUT STUDIOS INC.
1095 Main St.
Swayersville, PA 18704
Tel.: 800-326-9421; FAX: 570-288-0380
E-mail: info@baut.com
Web Site: www.baut.com

Personnel:
Conrad Dismas ....Baut President
Gerhard Francis ....Baut Master Sculptor
Heide Baut Cebrick ....Artist/Designer
Karen Baut Klemm ....Business Manager

Type of Business:
The STAINED GLASS of the FUTURE is here NOW!
The Baut Studios, Inc., established in 1927, is a full service ecclesiastical studio that has been manufacturing and installing their own patented STRUCTURAL STAINED GLASS* in windows and doors for over 40 years. A unique non-sagging construction never needing structural repairs, STRUCTURAL STAINED GLASS is LEAD FREE, and CUSTOM DESIGNED to fit many tastes and budgets. Pricing is competitive with leaded and stained glass but with many more advantages when combined with the BAUT WINDOW and DOOR SYSTEMS. Beautiful, long lasting, environmentally and financially sound, and virtually maintenance free, STRUCTURAL STAINED GLASS is featured in over 5000 churches worldwide.

Other products include Single, Double and Triple Glazed Church Windows and Ventilators. Heavy Duty Doors, Restoration/New Traditional Stained Glass, Altars and Appointments, Crosses, Steeples, Glass Mosaics and church Lighting. All Baut products are custom made to your sizes and shapes, and designed to match your decor.

* U.S. Patent No. 3,064,380

Berlinger Company

THE BERLINGER COMPANY
2605 N. Sheridan Road
Peoria, IL 61604
Tel.: 888-688-1781; 309-688-1771
Website: www.theberlingercompany.com

Personnel:
Michael Berlinger ....President
John Lingenfelter ....Vice-President
Jeff Walters...Office Manager

Type of Business:
Church interior design and consultants
Interior restoration
New church designs
New liturgical whole goods—domestic and imported
Custom manufacturers
Liturgical Antiquities—domestic and imported

BOTTI STUDIO OF ARCHITECTURAL ARTS, INC.

BOTTI STUDIO OF ARCHITECTURAL ARTS, INC.
919 Grove St.
Evanston, IL 60201
Tel.: 800-524-7211; FAX: 847-869-5996; 847-869-5933
E-mail: botti@bottistudio.com
Website: www.bottistudio.com

East Coast Studio
3104 S. Osprey Ave.
Sarasota, FL 33577
Tel.: 941-951-0978; FAX: 941-953-9078

West Coast Studio
1038 N. Highway 101
Encinitas, CA 92024
Tel.: 760-753-0705; FAX: 760-753-0705
Agropoli, Italy

Personnel:
Staff includes internationally recognized artists and designers working in conjunction with our highly skilled artisans and craftsmen.
Italo G. Botti ....President

Type of Business:
For generations Botti Studio has had a reputation for embodying all that is artistically creative in the traditional and contemporary ecclesiastical field. This field includes design and fabrication of stained and faceted glass windows, restoration/conservation of windows, church interiors, appointments, murals, sculpture, mosaic and marble. We are completely dedicated to both quality and satisfying our clients needs spiritually and liturgically. Botti Studio, established in 1864, is nationwide, offering consultation and designs without obligation. Member of the Stained Glass Association of America.

Century Art Glass Company Inc.

CENTURY ART GLASS COMPANY, INC.
11864 Dorsett Road
St. Louis, MO 63043
Tel.: 314-344-4447; FAX: 314-344-4449

Personnel:
William A. Sumner .... President
Matthew V. Sumner .... Vice President
Richard J. Loveless .... Creative Director

Type of Business:
Our family-owned stained glass firm, founded in 1908, proudly maintains the distinguished tradition of spiritually inspired, conceptually designed stained glass artworks for churches, chapels, mausoleums, and other religious environments. Our attention to every detail in the design, structure, manufacturing and installation of stained, faceted, beveled, etched and other diverse art glass windows in traditional or contemporary styles is what our reputation is built on. We also offer a full line of restoration products and services, such as releading of bowed stained glass windows, repair of broken stained glass pieces, window frame restoration or replacement, and energy-efficient protective storm coverings.

Our Goal: To highlight and preserve the highest spiritual, artistic and craftsmanship capabilities in the art of stained glass. Custom designs available - please inquire. Estimates available nationwide without obligation.

ARCHITECTURAL FEATURES CREATED BY Madden

CHARLES L. MADDEN
CREATING ARCHITECTURAL FEATURES
1245 E. Butler Pike
Ambler, PA 19002-6032 U.S.A.
Tel.: 215-646-8919; FAX: 215-643-7272
email: cmadden@concentric.net

Personnel:
Charles L. Madden .... Owner/Creative Director

Type of Business:
Architectural Features by definition is a single art resource for consultation, design, fabrication, and installation in creating spaces of liturgical and meditative inspiration with sacred art and beautiful materials of fine substance and detailing. Our worldwide commissions in bronze sculpture, mosaic, marble, stained glass, tapestry, and fine woods are custom created to extend our client's vision. Whether you are a Diocesan, Community, Institutional, or Architectural client - we are pleased to put our vast creative and computer technological resources at the service of your building and renovational vision.

Conrad Schmitt Studios Inc.

CONRAD SCHMITT STUDIOS, INC.
2405 S. 162nd St.
New Berlin, WI 53151
Tel.: 800-969-3033; 414-786-3030; FAX: 414-786-9036

Personnel:
Heidi Gruenke Emery .... Vice President & Marketing Director

Type of Business:
Since 1889, this family-owned Studio has restored and decorated hundreds of interiors across the country. Their scope of work includes the investigation and documentation of original decorative schemes; the restoration of those schemes through the application of various decorative techniques including gilding, glazing, marbleizing, stenciling, and graining, as well as the design, fabrication, conservation or replication of murals and stained glass. The Studio can assist projects in the early stages with architectural samples and rendering for fund-raising. Recently completed projects include St. Josaphat's Basilica, Milwaukee, WI; St. Ann's, Napoleanville, LA; and St. Bernard's, Akron, OH.

D.C. RIGGOTT INC.
3540 Neal Ave.
Afton, MN 55001
Tel.: 800-479-8777; FAX: 651-436-4769
E-mail: dcriggottinc@aol.com

Personnel:
Don Riggott .... Owner/President

Type of Business:
Specializing in vintage church accessories, architectural ornamentation and liturgical furnishings.
Stained Glass Windows • Altars • Lighting • Statuary • Stations of the Cross • Tabernacles • Monstrances • Fonts • Pews • Steeple Bells • Vestments • Books • Furniture • Candlesticks • Chalices
Please contact us with specific requests. We will be happy to send you photographs and specifics on any items in our inventory. You may have items in storage or not being used, please contact us as we are actively searching for vintage items to purchase for re-use in liturgical spaces.

DAPRATO RIGALI STUDIOS, INC.

DAPRATO RIGALI STUDIOS, INC.
7956 Oakton St.
Niles, IL 60714
Tel.: 847-692-6350; FAX: 847-692-3445

Personnel:

John Rigali
Robert Rigali
Lisa Rigali Galvin
Mike Rigali

Type of Business:

Daprato Rigali Studios Inc. has been beautifying Churches in America since 1860.

Today we find the Rigali Family restoring and renovating the churches originally decorated by their Great-Grandfather, John E. Rigali; aware of his reputation to create spiritually moving environments with quality material and craftsmanship.

Some of their most recent jobs include: decoration and stained glass restoration at St. Mary of the Lake Seminary, Mundelein, IL.; Marble renovation and decoration, St. Elizabeth's Mother House, Allegany, N.Y.; and General Contracting for complete renovation of St. Bernadette's Church, Rockford, IL.

The Daprato Rigali staff is equipped to take your project from start to finish. If you're interested in working with a fine interior design studio experienced in Ecclesiastical Artistries please call for consultation at no obligation. We deliver what we design.

DOMUSDEI HOLY ART STUDIOS

DOMUSDEI HOLY ART STUDIOS

DOMUSDEI HOLY ART STUDIOS

FACTORY: Via dei Tulipani, 48 - 00040 CECCHINA DI ALBANO (RM) - ITALY
Tel: 011-39-06-9343369
FAX: 011-39-06-9344971

SHOW ROOM: Via Scossacavalli 3/9 - 00193 - ROMA - ITALY
Tel: 011-39-06-6868090
FAX: 011-39-06-6869806
E-Mail: info@domusdei.it
m.delmonte@domusdei.it
Web Site: www.domusdei.it

Personnel:

Alessandro Del Monte ....President
Massimiliano Del Monte ....Executive Director
Aldo Del Monte... Assistant President

Type of Business:

Founded in 1963, Domusdei Studio has restored thousands of church interiors all over the world. Specializing in designing and manufacturing stained glass windows, mosaics, bronze and fiberglass statues, altars, bronze doors, lecterns, baptismal fonts, candlesticks, flower holders, tabernacles.

We are also experts in silver and gold plating and the restoration of wood and metal masterpieces.

EverGreene Painting Studios, Inc.

EVERGREENE PAINTING STUDIOS, INC.

450 West 31st Street, 7th Fl.
New York, NY 10001
Tel.: 212-244-2800
FAX: 212-244-6204

323 South Blvd.
Oak Park, IL 60302
Tel.: 708-358-1656
Fax: 708-358-1656

E-mail: info@evergreene.com
Web Site: www.evergreene.com

Personnel:

Jeff Greene..President

Type of Business:

EverGreene is a full-service decorative arts studio committed to preserving the integrity of historic sacred spaces through conservation, restoration, and compatible new design. Services include investigation and analysis of original finishes; consultations, renderings, budgets and samples to support decision-making and capital campaigns; design of color schemes and architectural ornament; specifications; and execution of work by our staff of experienced project managers, artists, artisans and conservators.

EverGreene is accomplished in all types of decorative painting and gilding; conservation, replication, and new design of murals and mosaics; ornamental plaster and scagliola; and allied crafts including wood refinishing, interior stone cleaning, metal patination, art glass, tile work and other architectural arts.

Established in 1978, EverGreene undertakes projects large and small around the country. Recently completed works include St. Cecilia's Cathedral, Omaha; St. Peter Church, San Francisco; Our Lady of Perpetual Help (Redemptorist Church), Kansas City; and St. John's Seminary Chapel, Brighton, MA. Among current projects are St. Joseph's Church in Burlington, VT and Assumption Abbey, ND.

HIGGINS &
ASSOCIATES
DEVELOPERS OF RELIGIOUS ENVIRONMENTS
PO Box 1334, Front Royal, VA 22630

25 years experience

Specialties:
custom stained glass windows, restoration/ preservation, framing systems, protective covering

Our own designers –
Experts in **iconography**

Our own artists –
Experts in **painted glass art** and **religious art** in the **style of the old masters**
Tiffany & **contemporary styles**
Leaded & **faceted** stained glass

Sensitive to clients' needs, religious traditions, architectural style, unique spirituality

♦800 636 3756♦FAX 540 636 6114 ♦
e-mail: haglass@rma.edu
www.higgins.thomasregister.com

HIGGINS &
ASSOCIATES
DEVELOPERS OF RELIGIOUS ENVIRONMENTS

HIGGINS & ASSOCIATES
P.O. Box 1334
Front Royal, VA 22630
Tel.: 800-636-3756; FAX: 540-636-6114
E-mail: haglass@rma.edu
Web Site: www.hastainedglass.com

Type of Business:
Higgins & Associates are uniquely talented individuals with one goal: to provide exceptional products and services. We are sensitive to each client's needs, religious traditions, architectural style, and expression of the spiritual. Our specialties are custom stained glass windows, on-site restoration/preservation, new frames, and protective covering.
Our designers are experts in iconography. They masterfully blend liturgical colors and designs that are esthetically striking and powerfully meaningful legacies of art. Our artists specialize in the old masters' style of religious art, painted glass art, Tiffany and contemporary styles; faceted stained glass, and restoration.
For information or on-site consultation, please write, call or visit us.

Winterich's
DESIGNERS AND CRAFTSMEN

JOHN W. WINTERICH & ASSOCIATES, INC.
9545 Midwest Ave. Ste. M
Cleveland, OH 44125
Tel.: 800-255-4544; FAX: 216-662-2509
Website: www.winterichs.com

Personnel:
Greg Winterich
Richard Winterich
Beth Winterich

Type of Business:
Founded in 1913, the Winterich Studio of Liturgical Art provides complete interior design and fabrication services for all aspects of new church projects and restorations and renovations. The award winning work of Winterich's is known nationwide. Our on-staff architect, liturgical consultants, designers and craftsmen are dedicated to excellence in Liturgical Art.

LYNCHBURG STAINED GLASS CO.
P.O. Box 4453
Lynchburg, VA 24502
Tel.: 800-237-6161; FAX: 804-525-6168

Type of Business:

Products Offered: Custom designed leaded and faceted stained glass windows. Aluminum frames and protective coverings.
Services Offered: On site design and consultation service. Complete delivery and installation. Repair and restoration service.
Recent Clients: Holy Spirit, Atlanta, GA; St. Joseph's, Cockeysville, MD; St. Andrew the Apostle, Silver Springs, MD; Immaculate Conception, Towson, MD; St. Anthonys, Atlanta, GA.
Free Information: Call for a free packet of information.

See our ad on the opposite page.

RAMBUSCH

RAMBUSCH
40 West 13th St.
New York, NY 10011
Tel.: 212-675-0400; FAX: 212-620-4687

Personnel:

Viggo Bech Rambusch ....Senior Project Director
Martin V. Rambusch ....Stained Glass Director

Type of Business:

Since 1898, creating church interiors, liturgical furnishings, and art work. Fine restoration of church interiors. In-house studios and shops for designing and executing stained glass, church lighting systems, art metal work, and decorative painting.

REINARTS STAINED GLASS STUDIOS INC.
73 Washington Street
Winona, MN 55987
Tel.: 507-452-4465; FAX: 507-452-4649
E-mail: reinarts@luminet.net
Web Site: www.reinarts.com

Personnel:

William A. Reinarts ....President

Type of Business:

Design, Manufacture and Install Stained Glass and Faceted Glass. Restoration and Re-Leading of Stained Glass. Protective, Insulative Covering of Stained Glass. Repair and Replacement of Window Frames.

ROHLF'S STAINED & LEADED GLASS STUDIO, INC.
783 South Third Ave.
Mt. Vernon, NY 10550
Tel.: 914-699-4848; FAX: 914-699-7091
Website: www.rohlfstudio.com

Personnel:
Peter Hans Rohlf ....President
Gregory Rohlf ....Vice President
Rich Widmer ....Secretary/Treasurer

Type of Business:
For Three Generations our family owned and operated Studio together with our affiliate, George L. Payne Studio have been dedicated to excellence in Stained Glass Art. Our team of International designers and Master Craftspersons have created stained glass windows for over a thousand Churches and Institutions Worldwide. Our reputation and experience in the field of Restoration, Replication and Preservation is well known. We would be pleased to assist you in the early stages of planning and design, working with your Architect and/or committee to achieve your desired goals.
From concept to completion, we are dedicated to serve you.

STAINED GLASS EXCELLENCE

80 years of creating art for yesterday's and today's environment.

Cemetery of the Ascension Mausoleum Chapel Window, Monsey, NY.

We service the religious and architectural communities, WORLDWIDE with an international team of designers and craftspeople.

Rohlf's is also one of the most respected stained glass Studios in Historic Preservation

ESTABLISHED 1920
ROHLF's
STAINED & LEADED GLASS
783 So. 3rd Avenue, Mount Vernon, NY 10550
(914) 699-4848 • 800-969-4106
Fax: (914) 699-7091 • E-mail: Rohlf1@aol.com

Traditional • Contemporary • Restoration

GREG SPIESS & CO.

SPIESS ARCHITECTURAL ANTIQUES
230 East Washington St.
Joliet, IL 60433
Tel.: 815-722-5639; FAX: 815-722-0171

Type of Business:
Specializing in older and antique church furniture. Gothic, Romanesque and Classical styles in marble, wood, bronze etc. Altars, pews, communion rails, stained glass, lecterns, baptismals, vestment cases, confessionals, Stations of the Cross statuary. Lighting. Pew and wood restoration available.

St. Anthony's CHURCH SUPPLIES

ST. ANTHONY'S CHURCH SUPPLIES
3121 McCart Ave.
Fort Worth, TX 76110
Tel: 800-772-5928
E-mail: books4u@airmail.net
Web Site: www.StellaMarisBooks.com

Type of Business:
We can supply your church or chapel with the finest available in stained glass windows. We offer a full line of ecclesiastical goods from clerical shirts and vestments, to chalices and tabernacles, to church statuary and other appointments, to Catholic books and other media, to furniture for churches, church offices, classrooms, and cafeterias.

We offer great service with a smile and look forward to making new friends.

Please use our toll free number or e-mail to contact John Heitzenrater or Richard Myers.

Stained Glass Associates

STAINED GLASS ASSOCIATES
P.O. Box 1531
Raleigh, NC 27602-1531
Tel.: 919-266-2493

Personnel:
Robert J. Wysocki ....Owner

Type of Business:
- Design, Fabrication and Installation of:
- – Leaded, Faceted and Painted Glass
- Restoration and Repair
- – Replacement Frames
- – Fire Damage
- Appraisals

About SGA:
– Established in 1958
– Studio Member of Stained Glass Association of America
– 1,024 Installations Nationally and Internationally

Stained Glass Associates is committed to maintaining the highest of ecclesiastical standards and the complete satisfaction of every client.

STAINED GLASS STUDIOS, LTD.
RR # 1 Pleasantville
2102 West LaHave, NS BOR 1GO
Tel.: 1-902-688-1156; Fax: 1-902-688-1475
Web Site: www.sattlerglas.com
E-mail: Sattler@atcon.com

Personnel:
Norbert Sattler ....President
Helga Sattler ....Vice President, Sales & Marketing Mngr.

Type of Business:
Over 33 years experience. Sattler's Stained Glass Studio has developed working partnerships with many artists from all over the world, exploring traditional and innovative applications of glass in the production of art works. Sattler's studio takes care of your project from taking the measurements, to fabricating and the installation.

STAINED GLASS
Fabrication of stained glass in collaboration with artists, designers and architects: religious, profane, modern, traditional, artistic, craft.

GLASS RESTORATION
in all traditional and historical stained glass: restore, renovate, copy.

PROJECTS IN COMBINATION WITH GLASS WOOD AND METAL. WE TAKE CARE OF: measurments, advise for framing and technical support to install glass purchase (antique glass) flashed, opal, opaque, etc. 1:1 Cartoon, ready for transfer of the design, painting, printing, etching, sandblasting, glazing and installation.

The Willet Stained Glass Studios

WILLET STAINED GLASS STUDIOS
10 East Moreland Avenue
Philadelphia, PA 19118
Tel.: 215-247-5721; toll free: 877-709-4106; FAX: 215-247-2951
Web Site: www.willetglass.com

Type of Business:
The Willet Stained Glass Studios offer a full range of established stained glass techniques--from leaded, faceted, and sand carved to sculptured gold. Willet creations are designed to complement their architectural setting, and the extensive Willet design experience offers depth and competence in a diversity of artistic styles.

Since 1898, the Willet Studios have executed hundreds of commissions for Catholic churches and cathedrals around the nation. This year will mark new Catholic works in Fremont, Nebraska and the Bahamas.

The Willet national sales team can meet at your location to understand firsthand the goals you wish to achieve and to provide the information necessary to make a sound stained glass purchase decision.

The Willet Stained Glass Studios
E. Crosby Willet, President
...a division of Hauser Art Glass, Inc.

EDUCATION

Human Life International · HLI

HUMAN LIFE INTERNATIONAL
4 Family Drive
Front Royal VA 22630
Tel.: 540-635-7884; FAX: 540-636-7363

Type of Businee:
Human Life International promotes the sanctity of life from conception to natural death. We promote chastity and parenthood, while also exposing modern day threats to life and family. HLI is the world's largest apostolate, with chapters in the United States and a network of international branches and affliates serving 90 countries. HLI publishes a wealth of material on life and family issues, and holds national and international conferences.

See our ad on the next page.

For the very best mailing lists and database information, go to the source...

The Official Catholic Directory

ORDER DIRECT FROM THE PUBLISHER!

P.J. Kenedy & Sons, publishers of **The Official Catholic Directory**, is your #1 source for the most accurate and up-to-date mailing lists and databased information. All lists come with our exclusive 100% *deliverability guarantee.*

When you order your mailing list or database directly from the publisher, you can choose only those selections and options you need:

SELECTIONS:

The Hierarchy
Provincials of Religious Orders

Roman Catholic Priests
Eastern Rite Priests
Diocesan & Religious Order Priests

Pastors
Associate Pastors
Chaplains
Brothers
Nuns

Religious Education Directors
Lay persons

Parishes
Diocesan Offices
Convents
Monasteries

Hospitals
Newman Centers
Nursing Homes
Retreat Centers
Specialized Homes & Centers

Elementary Schools
High Schools
Colleges & Universities
Seminaries & Novitiates

Addressing: Cheshire Labels, Pressure Sensitive or Labels.
Magnetic Tape and Diskettes are available for 1-year use.

For the latest counts, or to order your list or database, please call:
Virginia Ricablanca at 800-521-8110 ext. 3566

The Official Catholic Directory – Mailing List Department
P.J. Kenedy & Sons, Publishers
121 Chanlon Road • New Providence, NJ 07974
800-521-8110 ext. 3566 • 908-665-3566 • FAX: 908-665-2894

EDUCATIONAL FUNDING

TUITION PROGRAM, INC.
PO Box 571
Livingston, NJ 07039
Tel.: 800-828-9944 / 973-535-2776
FAX: 800-432-9994 / 973-533-0086

Personnel:
Brendon & Cecilia Devlin

Type of Business:
Founded in 1985 by Catholic parents to serve Catholic Schools. There is absolutely no charge to the school. There is no charge to parents if payments are on time. Each student receives a Tuition Credit Line for present and future use. The school receives 100% tuition. Call today 1-800-828-9944 or fax 1-800-432-9994 or email: info@tuitionprogram.com
Financial Aid service included.

EDUCATIONAL OPPORTUNITIES

Guest House

GUEST HOUSE, INC.
1601 Joslyn Rd., P.O. Box 420
Lake Orion, MI 48361
Tel.: 800-626-6910; 248-391-4445; FAX:248-391-0210
email: info@guesthouse.org

LAKE ORION CENTER
(For Women Religious)
P.O. Box 68
Lake Orion, MI 48361
Tel.: 800-626-6910; 248-391-3100; FAX: 248-391-1553
email: guestmae@ic.net

ROCHESTER TREATMENT CENTER
(For priests, deacons, brothers & seminarians)
P.O. Box 954
Rochester, MN 55903
Tel.: 800-634-4155; 507-288-4693; FAX: 507-288-1240
email: ghousemn@infonet.isl.net

Personnel:
Daniel A. Kidd..................President and Chief Executive Officer
Sr. Mae Kierans, CSJ ....Director, Lake Orion, MI
Bill Morgan, C.C.D.C.R. ....VP Clinical Oper., Rochester, MN
Gerard O'Connor..Director of Marketing

Type of Business:
Guest House, Inc. is a lay-owned, lay-operated nonprofit corporation established in 1956. With the approbation of the Catholic hierachy, it operates special residential treatment centers for alcoholic Catholic priests, deacons, brothers, sisters and seminarians from all over the world.

Catholic women religious are treated in Guest House in Lake Orion, Michigan. The facility in Rochester, Minnesota has treatment programs for priests, deacons, brothers and seminarians. An important part of the treatment is the beautiful environment of our facilities. Residents respond to the quiet serenity of the surroundings to help in their recovery not only physically and emotionally, but spiritually as well.

Surveys are conducted regularly to determine how our graduates are doing. The 1997 survey shows that after a year and a half, over 90% report they are doing well and abstaining from all drugs and alcohol.

Generous donors have established an endowment fund to provide financial assistance for any diocese or religious community needing assistance with the costs of treatment. Treatment is provided without regard to financial consideration.

The facilities are accredited by JCAHO (Joint Commission on Accreditation of Healthcare Organizations) and licensed by the Department of Public Health in the states of Michigan and Minnesota respectively.

Guest House also offers educational programs, seminars, and workshops on addition-related topics.

SETON HALL UNIVERSITY, IMMACULATE CONCEPTION SEMINARY SCHOOL OF THEOLOGY
400 South Orange Avenue
South Orange, NJ 07079
Tel.: 973-761-9633; FAX: 973-761-9577
E-mail: theology@shu.edu
Web Site: http://theology.shu.edu

Personnel:

Reverend Monsignor John W. Flesey, STD ....Rector/Dean
Reverend Monsignor Robert F. Coleman,JCD ....Vice Rector/ Business Manager
Reverend C. Anthony Ziccardi, SSL .... Associate Dean
Dianne M. Traflet, JD, STD ....Assistant Dean

Type of Business:

Immaculate Conception Seminary School of Theology (ICSST) is the graduate school of theology of Seton Hall University and the major seminary of the Catholic Archdiocese of Newark. With a 139-year tradition of preparing committed Catholics for service to the Church, ICSST admits both seminarians studying for the Catholic priesthood and lay students. ICSST offers three graduate degree programs: the Master of Arts in Theology, the Master of Arts in Pastoral Ministry and the Master of Arts in Divinity.

EDUCATIONAL SYSTEMS & SOFTWARE

Church Management Resources
"Serving the Church professional through information management."

CHURCH MANAGEMENT RESOURCES
7120 South Division Avenue
Grand Rapids, MI 49548
Tel.: 877-455-9300; 616-988-1015; FAX 616-988-1093
Website: http://churchmgt.catholicweb.com

Offices in Michigan, Ohio, Pennsylvania, Florida, & Texas

Personnel:

Carl Grant ....President
Vicki Wells Bedard..National Director

Type of Business:

Parish, School, & Religious Education Consulting: certified, licensed vendors of Churchmouse Suite Software™ and Parish Data Systems, Inc.™ software and provider of Catholicweb.com™ webware for church, school and religious education offices. Training, installation, seminars, newsletter, user group associations, stewardship appeals, scanning services, custom report writing and much more . . .
We know your needs. We exist to service those needs and to provide a network of resources to assist you in administering to the geographical and new "virtual" Internet parish.

Free demos and informational packets available.

COMPUTER RESOURCES, INCORPORATED
94 Route 125, P.O. Box 60
Barrington, NH 03825
Tel.: 888-665-4046; FAX: 603-664-5864
E-mail: sales@cri-mms.com
Web Site: www.cri-mms.com

Type of Business:

Computer Resources, Inc. publishes MMS 2000—the Modular Management System for Schools. MMS 2000 is school administrative software for Windows or Macintosh, stand-alone or networked computers. The student biographical database seamlessly integrates with modules for Student Scheduling, Attendance, Grade Reporting, Discipline, Health, Fee Accounting, and Internet Access. We offer an economical software package especially for Catholic schools. Call us toll-free to learn about the custom features we've included in this special offer.

INSTRUCTIONAL MANAGEMENT & STUDENT RECORD SYSTEMS

Church Management Resources
"Serving the Church professional through information management."

CHURCH MANAGEMENT RESOURCES
7120 South Division Avenue
Grand Rapids, MI 49548
Tel.: 877-455-9300; 616-988-1015; FAX 616-988-1093
Website: http://churchmgt.catholicweb.com

Offices in Michigan, Ohio, Pennsylvania, Florida, & Texas

Personnel:

Carl Grant ....President
Vicki Wells Bedard..National Director

Type of Business:

Parish, School, & Religious Education Consulting: certified, licensed vendors of Churchmouse Suite Software™ and Parish Data Systems, Inc.™ software and provider of Catholicweb.com™ webware for church, school and religious education offices. Training, installation, seminars, newsletter, user group associations, stewardship appeals, scanning services, custom report writing and much more . . .
We know your needs. We exist to service those needs and to provide a network of resources to assist you in administering to the geographical and new "virtual" Internet parish.

Free demos and informational packets available.

MINISTRY OPPORTUNITIES

AIR FORCE Chaplain SERVICE

AIR FORCE CHAPLAIN RECRUITING SERVICE
HQ AFRS/RSOCC
550 D Street West Ste 1
Randolph AFB TX 78150-4527
Tel.: 800-803-2452
john.kinney@rs.af.mil / howard.stendahl@rs.af.mil

Personnel:
Ch, Lt. Col. Howard D. Stendahl ....Chief, Chaplain Accessions Section
Ch, Maj. John M. Kinney ....Deputy, Chaplain Accessions Section

Air Force Chaplain Service continued

Type of Business:
Air Force chaplains ensure the free exercise of religion for the globally engaged Air Force community. Catholics make up approximately 30% of the military. Priest chaplains are particularly responsible for the spiritual and the sacramental needs of Catholics in the military setting. Because the Catholic Chaplain lives the same challenging demands of military life, he can truly respond. The Air Force offers the qualified priest many opportunities to serve both the Church and the country in a pluralistic global environment.
Chaplains remain steadfast witnesses of the holy in a changing world environment. Consider the possibility of serving as a priest and an officer in the United States Air Force. For more information, please contact the above office.

SPIRITUAL ENRICHMENT

HUMAN LIFE INTERNATIONAL
4 Family Drive
Front Royal VA 22630
Tel.: 540-635-7884; FAX: 540-636-7363

Type of Business:
Human Life International promotes the sanctity of life from conception to natural death. We promote chastity and parenthood, while also exposing modern day threats to life and family. HLI is the world's largest apostolate, with chapters in the United States and a network of international branches and affiliates serving 90 countries. HLI publishes a wealth of material on life and family issues, and holds national and international conferences.

TUITION FINANCING

TUITION PROGRAM, INC.
PO Box 571
Livingston, NJ 07039
Tel.: 800-828-9944 / 973-535-2776
FAX: 800-432-9994 / 973-533-0086

Personnel:
Brendon & Cecilia Devlin

Type of Business:
Founded in 1985 by Catholic parents to serve Catholic Schools. There is absolutely no charge to the school. There is no charge to parents if payments are on time. Each student receives a Tuition Credit Line for present and future use. The school receives 100% tuition. Call today 1-800-828-9944 or fax 1-800-432-9994 or email: info@tuitionprogram.com
Financial Aid service included.

TUITION MANAGEMENT SERVICES

SMART TUITION MANAGEMENT SERVICES
95 Wall Street, Suite 2300
New York, NY 10005
Tel.: 800-762-7808; FAX: 212-858-8043
E-mail: info@smarttuition.com
Website: www.smarttuition.com

Personnel:
Sam Rosen..............President

Type of Business:
SMART is a complete tuition management service that is designed to take schools out of the tuition collection business. The SMART program helps to reduce delinquencies, increase cash flow, and decrease the administrative workload. SMART serves more than 1,700 schools nationwide. SMART also has a Tuition Aid Analysis Service (TAAS) that determines how much families can afford to pay.

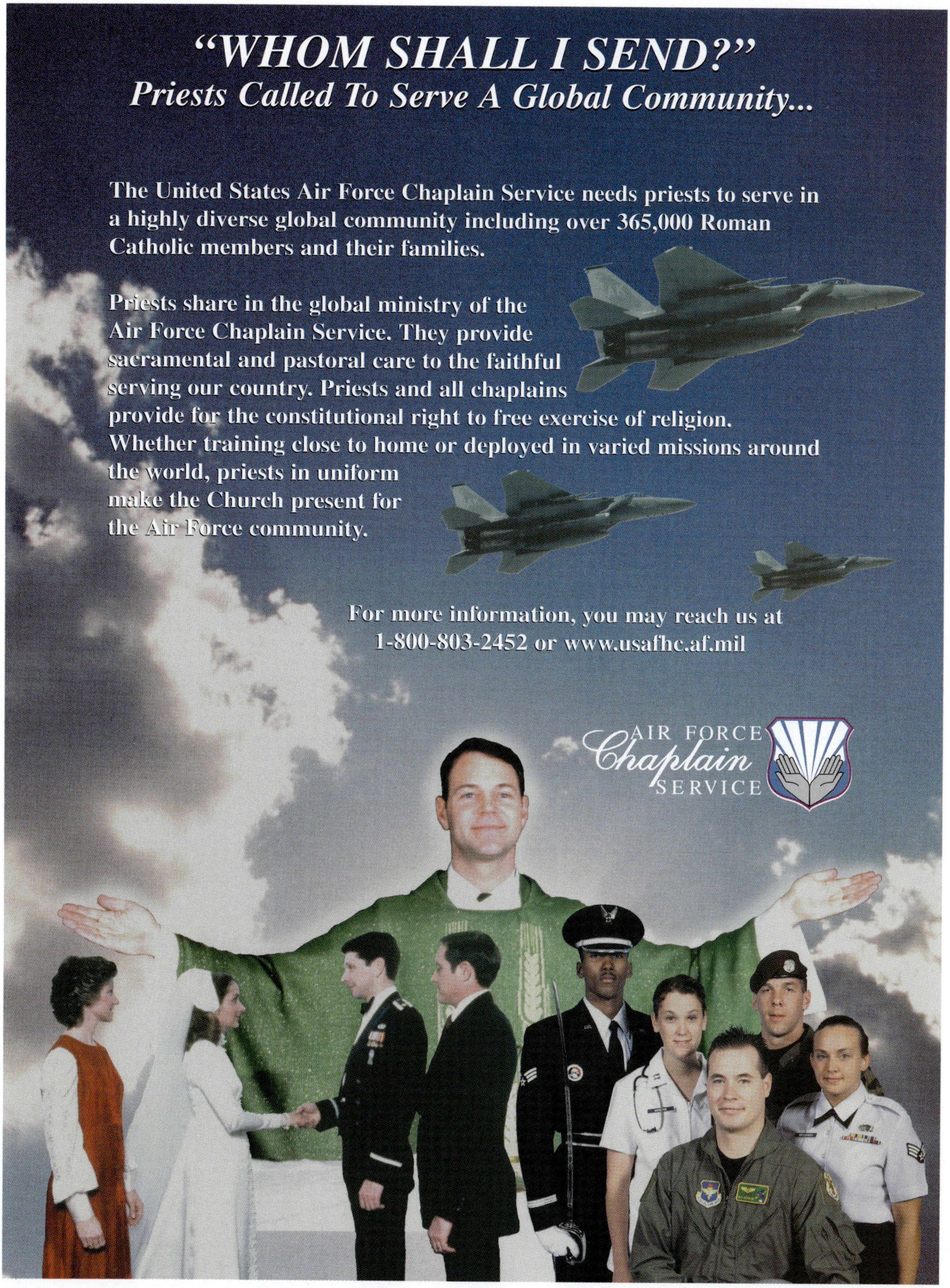
"WHOM SHALL I SEND?"
Priests Called To Serve A Global Community...
The United States Air Force Chaplain Service needs priests to serve in a highly diverse global community including over 365,000 Roman Catholic members and their families.
Priests share in the global ministry of the Air Force Chaplain Service. They provide sacramental and pastoral care to the faithful serving our country. Priests and all chaplains provide for the constitutional right to free exercise of religion. Whether training close to home or deployed in varied missions around the world, priests in uniform make the Church present for the Air Force community.
For more information, you may reach us at 1-800-803-2452 or www.usafhc.af.mil
AIR FORCE
Chaplain
SERVICE

EMPLOYMENT

NAVY
accelerate your life

NAVY CHAPLAIN CORPS
Commander, Navy Recruiting Command
5722 Integrity Drive, Bldg. 784
Millington, TN 38054-5057
Tel: (901) 874-9216 or Toll Free: 866-484-5232
E-mail: CarrG@cnrc.navy.mil
Web Site: www.navy.com/professionals

Personnel:

CDR Gary Carr, CHC, USN ....Program Manager
LCDR Michael Parisi, CHC, USN ....Chaplain Recruiter
ParisiM@cnrc.navy.mil
LCDR Herb Griffin, CHC, USN ....Chaplain Recruiter
GriffinH@cnrc.navy.mil
LT Heinz Malon, CHC, USN.........................Chaplain Recruiter
MalonH@cnrc.navy.mil
LT Kimberly Sawatsky, CHC, USN ....Chaplain Recruiter
SawatskyK@cnrc.navy.mil

Type of Business:

Navy Chaplains serve both the Church and Country in diverse ministry settings. Chaplains provide spiritual guidance to members of the Navy, Marine Corps and Coast Guard. We offer leadership positions in ministry for the spiritual well being of the whole community. Priest Chaplains provide sacramental and spiritual support for Catholics in the military and care for all. Working closely with clergy from other faith traditions, we cooperate with each other without compromising our own faith and practice. Navy Chaplains experience the joy of ministry with young people. We have a program for seminarians, the Naval Reserve, and for full-time, active-duty positions. Contact the chaplain recruiters listed above for more information.

www.navy.com 1-800-USA-NAVY

CHAPLAIN SERVICE

AIR FORCE
Chaplain
SERVICE

AIR FORCE CHAPLAIN RECRUITING SERVICE
HQ AFRS/RSOCC
550 D Street West Ste 1
Randolph AFB TX 78150-4527
Tel.: 800-803-2452
john.kinney@rs.af.mil / howard.stendahl@rs.af.mil

Personnel:

Ch, Lt. Col. Howard D. Stendahl
....Chief, Chaplain Accessions Section
Ch, Maj. John M. Kinney
....Deputy, Chaplain Accessions Section

Type of Business:

Air Force chaplains ensure the free exercise of religion for the globally engaged Air Force community. Catholics make up approximately 30% of the military. Priest chaplains are particularly responsible for the spiritual and the sacramental needs of Catholics in the military setting. Because the Catholic Chaplain lives the same challenging demands of military life, he can truly respond. The Air Force offers the qualified priest many opportunities to serve both the Church and the country in a pluralistic global environment.

Chaplains remain steadfast witnesses of the holy in a changing world environment. Consider the possibility of serving as a priest and an officer in the United States Air Force. For more information, please contact the above office.

LITURGICAL & CHURCH GOODS

ABBOTT INC.
Showroom 1515 Route 38
Cherry Hill, NJ 08002
Tel.: 800-522-2688; 856-662-6959; FAX: 856-665-5109
Website: http://www.abbottsinc.com
email: acg.inc@cwixmail.com

Personnel:
Daniel J. Castonguay .... President
Joseph F. McKeaney .... General Manager
Michael W. Wasyluk .... Customer Service

Type of Business:
Purveyors of the Finest Vesture, Paraments, Statuary & Metalware since 1962. Unique and original creations, our specialty. Custom designs to complement your liturgical environment. Exclusive representatives of Slabbinck Master Collection & Original Collection.

ADRIAN HAMERS INC.
2 Madison Avenue
Larchmont, NY 10538
Tel.: 914-834-7780; FAX: 914-834-0712

Type of Business:
Custom designers and manufacturers of Sacred Vessels. Since 1887, the Hamers name has been synonymous with expert Silversmithing throughout the world in the field of Liturgical Art. Please contact us for those hard to find items, as we always have a large selection of Adrian Hamers Estate Collection pieces in stock. We are experts in: Church Interiors from design to execution, Renovations, Altars, Sacred Vessels, Gold and Silver Plating & Repairing, Appraisals, Tabernacles, Marble, Statuary, Woodwork & Woodcarving, Stained Glass, Pews & Chairs, Gold Leafing, Frescoes, Restoration, Trompe-l' oeuil, Wall Murals (repair and conservation cleaning), Ornamental Plaster, Heraldic Designs & Bishop Regalia. Please call us for a free 24 page Sacred Vessels color catalog, or our free 80 page color Woodcarvings catalog.

CARROLL ART, INC.
710 NE 26th St.
Fort Lauderdale, FL 33305
Tel.: 800-876-4569; FAX: 954-561-4098

Personnel:
David Nagle .... President Designer
Liza Palmer .... Sales Manager
Wayne Palmer .... Sales Representative
Robert Perkins .... Sales Representative

Type of Business:
Carroll Art has been in business for 12 years. We design and custom build all types of plaques and memorials including the tree of life, plaques, recognition systems, church signs, donor plates, custom sculptures, and memorials are just a few of our products. We can provide you with the perfect fund raising tool.

CARROLL ELECTRONICS INCORPORATED
710 Northeast 26th St.
Wilton Manors, FL 33305
Tel.: 800-331-0444; FAX: 954-561-4098

Personnel:
David Nagle .... President
Liza Palmer .... Sales Manager
Bob Perkins .... Sales Representative
Donna Spencer .... Service Engineer

Type of Business:
Carroll Electronics has been in business for 20 years designing and building Electronic Votive Candle Stands for thousands of churches throughout the United States.

COKESBURY
201 Eighth Avenue, South
P.O. Box 801
Nashville, TN 37202-0801
Tel.: 800-672-1789; FAX: 800-445-8189
Web Site: www.cokesbury.com

Personnel:
Neil Alexander .... President and Publisher
Edward R. Kowalski .... Senior Vice President of Marketing and Sales

Type of Business:
Cokesbury has been serving the needs of clergy, religious educators, and churches for over 200 years. We're your one-stop shop for a vast array of communion supplies and altarware, paraments, apparel and vestments, Bibles and books for church leaders, candles and accessories, offering envelopes, bulletins, and music resources. All are backed by our 100% satisfaction guarantee.

DOMUSDEI

HOLY ART STUDIOS

DOMUSDEI HOLY ART STUDIOS

DOMUSDEI HOLY ART STUDIOS

FACTORY: Via dei Tulipani, 48 - 00040 CECCHINA DI ALBANO (RM) - ITALY
Tel: 011-39-06-9343369
FAX: 011-39-06-9344971

SHOW ROOM: Via Scossacavalli 3/9 - 00193 - ROMA - ITALY
Tel: 011-39-06-6868090
FAX: 011-39-06-6869806
E-Mail: info@domusdei.it
m.delmonte@domusdei.it
Web Site: www.domusdei.it

Personnel:

Alessandro Del Monte ....President
Massimiliano Del Monte ....Executive Director
Aldo Del Monte.. Assistant President

Type of Business:

Founded in 1963, Domusdei Studio has restored thousands of church interiors all over the world. Specializing in designing and manufacturing stained glass windows, mosaics, bronze and fiberglass statues, altars, bronze doors, lecterns, baptismal fonts, candlesticks, flower holders, tabernacles.
We are also experts in silver and gold plating and the restoration of wood and metal masterpieces.

THE holy+ROOD GUILD

THE HOLY ROOD GUILD

St. Joseph's Abbey
167 North Spencer Rd.
Spencer, MA 01562-1233
Tel.: 508-885-8750; FAX: 508-885-8758
E-mail: holyrood@holyroodguild.com
Website: www.holyroodguild.com

Type of Business:

Designers and crafters of ecclesiastical vesture for over 40 years. Inspired by our monastic tradition, we seek to unite in our work simplicity in design, quality in materials and excellence in craftsmanship. The result is vesture that enhances the liturgical celebration with visual grace and order. Our artists—both monks and laypersons—are available for custom design work and consultation. We also provide an extensive selection of ready made items.

PATRICK BAKER & SONS

PATRICK BAKER & SONS, INC.

1650 West Street
Southington, CT 06489
Tel.: 860-628-5566; FAX: 860-276-9438

Personnel:

Patrick A. Baker ....Chairman
Brian T. Baker ....President
Michael P. Baker ....Vice President
Maureen Kelly ....Secretary

Type of Business:

- Religious Supplies
- Church Goods
- Church Renovations

ROHN DESIGN GROUP

ROHN DESIGN GROUP

5075 Clairton Blvd, Suite 301
Pittsburgh, PA 15236
Tel: (412) 561-1228; (800) 245-1288; Fax: (412) 561-8129
E-mail: rohnstudio@aol.com
Web Site: www.rohndesign.com

Personnel:

A full service team of U.S. and international artisans & craftsmen.
Rolf R. Rohn ....Principal Consultant/Director/Artist
Kathleen L. Maglicco ....Principal Interior Design
Sister Janet Baxendale, S.C...Education

Type of Business:

Experience spanning 4 decades in renovation/restoration, conservation, and design of new worship environments. A valuable partner in over 1,300 commissions throughout the U.S., Canada and Europe.

We offer:
-Metal Ware
-Fabric Art Hangings & Tapestries
-Gold & Silver Plating
-Brass Restoration & Repairs
-Sacred Vessels
and more....

Please see our ads on the divider pages for "General Summary" and "Products & Services." For other services look under "Construction, Maintenance & Renovation", "Consultants" and "Church Goods."

www.rohndesign.com

St. Anthony's CHURCH SUPPLIES

ST. ANTHONY'S CHURCH SUPPLIES
3121 McCart Ave.
Fort Worth, TX 76110
Tel: 800-772-5928
E-mail: books4u@airmail.net
Web Site: www.StellaMarisBooks.com

Type of Business:

We can supply your church or chapel with the finest sanctuary appointments available. We offer a full line of ecclesiastical goods from clerical shirts and vestments, to chalices and tabernacles, to church statuary and stained glass windows, to Catholic books and other media, to furniture for churches, church offices, classrooms, and cafeterias.

We offer great service with a smile and look forward to making new friends.

Please use our toll free number or e-mail to contact John Heitzenrater or Richard Myers.

Vermont Church Supply Co.

VERMONT CHURCH SUPPLY CO.
676 Pine Street, P.O. Box 368
Burlington, VT 05401
Tel.: 802-862-6486, 800-451-3453; FAX: 802-862-5765
E-mail: vcs@together.net

Personnel:

Neil Clark ....President

Type of Business:

Since our inception in 1946 by W. Barrett Clark and Doris Clark, Vermont Church Supply has offered the highest quality products and the best service to the Church and the Clergy. We have a wide range of products including Candles, Church Furniture, Metalware and Vestments. Our founders' Sons, Neil, John, Thomas and Robert, along with the third generation Anthony Clark, continue to provide services such as refinishing Sacred Vessels, Candlesticks and abernacles and also the execution of hand carved wood and marble Statuary. Whether your needs are small or large, we can give the best personalized service to our Customers.

See our ad on the next page.

ALTAR BREADS

CM ALMY

C. M. ALMY & SON, INC.
Three American Lane
P.O. Box 2644
Greenwich, CT 06836-2644
Tel.: 800-225-2569; FAX: 800-426-2569
E-mail: almyaccess@almy.com

Showrooms in:
Old Greenwich, CT: 203-637-2739 and
Pittsfield, ME: 207-487-3232

Type of Business:

Almy was founded in 1892. We design and make virtually all of our products in our Maine shop. It is our mission to design furnishings that will grace your worship and to ensure their value by making them with the highest quality materials and craftsmanship. We make a complete line of vestments, haberdashery, choir robes, candles, communion bread, linens, processional and altar appointments, and eucharistic vessels. We also offer custom design and fabrication of all Almy products, and repair and refurbishing of old metal appointments. Quik Ship© delivery of many popular items. All orders backed by The Almy Guarantee. Call, write, or email for a free catalog.

SN STADELMAIER NIJMEGEN

STADELMAIER-NIJMEGEN-HOLLAND
P.O. Box 7063
6503 GN Nijmegen
Nijmegen, Holland 6503 GN
Tel.: 31-24-3791170; FAX: 31-24-3791171
e-mail: info@stadelmaier.com

Type of Business:

SN-Antiques offers, for the re-use in the Cath. Liturgy;
Completely restored, original, devotional interior-pieces. Altars, stations, candlesticks, perpetual lights, statues, reliquaries, ciboria, chalices, monstrances, censers, mission crosses, processional crosses, Saints, paintings, etc.
Different styles and age: Roman, baroque, neo-gothic, etc.
Please describe your interest directly to Mrs. Annemieke Drijber.

ALTAR LINENS, LACES

CM ALMY

C. M. ALMY & SON, INC.
Three American Lane
P.O. Box 2644
Greenwich, CT 06836-2644
Tel.: 800-225-2569; FAX: 800-426-2569
E-mail: almyaccess@almy.com

Showrooms in:
Old Greenwich, CT: 203-637-2739 and
Pittsfield, ME: 207-487-3232

Type of Business:
Almy was founded in 1892. We design and make virtually all of our products in our Maine shop. It is our mission to design furnishings that will grace your worship and to ensure their value by making them with the highest quality materials and craftsmanship. We make a complete line of vestments, haberdashery, choir robes, candles, communion bread, linens, processional and altar appointments, and eucharistic vessels. We also offer custom design and fabrication of all Almy products, and repair and refurbishing of old metal appointments. Quik Ship© delivery of many popular items. All orders backed by The Almy Guarantee. Call, write, or email for a free catalog.

the symbol of Regal Splendor

Robert Gaspard Co.

ROBERT GASPARD CO., INC.
200 N. Janacek Rd.
Brookfield, WI 53045-6101
Tel.: 800-784-6868; 262-784-6800; FAX: 262-784-7567
E-mail: robertgaspard.com
Web Site: www.robertgaspardco.com

Personnel:
Rose Gaspard .... President
John Andorfer .... Vice President
Jason R. Gaspard .... Sales & Marketing Mgr.

Type of Business:
The Robert Gaspard Co. was established in 1954. Over the past 47 years, we have grown to be a nationally-known company. We pride ourselves on the ability to create original custom designs to enrich your worship needs. Our complete line consists of all ecclesiastical vesture, as well as paraments, mass and altar linens, stoles, banners, chasubles, funeral palls, albs, cossacks, surplices, choir robes, acolyte robes and many accessories. Complimentary catalogs and fabric swatches sent on request.

SN STADELMAIER NIJMEGEN

STADELMAIER-NIJMEGEN-HOLLAND
P.O. Box 7063
6503 GN Nijmegen
Nijmegen, Holland 6503 GN
Tel.: 31-24-3791170; FAX: 31-24-3791171
e-mail: info@stadelmaier.com

Type of Business:
SN-Antiques offers, for the re-use in the Cath. Liturgy;
Completely restored, original, devotional interior-pieces. Altars, stations, candlesticks, perpetual lights, statues, reliquaries, ciboria, chalices, monstrances, censers, mission crosses, processional crosses, Saints, paintings, etc.
Different styles and age: Roman, baroque, neo-gothic, etc.
Please describe your interest directly to Mrs. Annemieke Drijber.

BIBLE STUDY SOFTWARE

AMERICAN BIBLE SOCIETY

AMERICAN BIBLE SOCIETY
1865 Broadway
New York, NY 10023
Tel.: 800-784-6579; FAX 860-828-4773

Personnel:
Charlie Krueger .... Group Director
Bill Sinclair .... National Sales Manager

Type of Business:
ABS publishes and distributes a wide variety of low cost English, Spanish, and foreign language bibles for Catholic readers, including The Good News Bible, The New Revised Standard, New Jerusalem Bible, Contemporary English Version, Dios Habla Hoy and more. Outstanding resources for children, youth, and adults. The Bible on audio cassettes, video, and CD-ROM, Kingsley's Meadow Children's Videos, Resources for pastors, Bible study software. Call for a free catalog.

BIBLES, HYMNALS, MISSALETTES

AMERICAN BIBLE SOCIETY

AMERICAN BIBLE SOCIETY
1865 Broadway
New York, NY 10023
Tel.: 800-784-6579; FAX 860-828-4773

Personnel:
Charlie Krueger..Group Director
Bill Sinclair..National Sales Manager

Type of Business:
ABS publishes and distributes a wide variety of low cost English, Spanish, and foreign language bibles for Catholic readers, including The Good News Bible, The New Revised Standard, New Jerusalem Bible, Contemporary English Version, Dios Habla Hoy and more. Outstanding resources for children, youth, and adults. The Bible on audio cassettes, video, and CD-ROM, Kingsley's Meadow Children's Videos, Resources for pastors, Bible study software. Call for a free catalog.

CARIBE BETANIA EDITORES

CARIBE-BETANIA EDITORES
P.O. Box 141000
Nashville, TN 37214
Tel: 615-902-2370; FAX: 615-883-9376

Personnel:
Phil Stoner..President
Ruben DePeña...Sales Director
Maria Hoyos...Sales Representative
Marcela Gómez...Marketing Manager

Type of Business:
Our Betania imprint is regarded as the Spanish Christian industry's leading publisher in the areas of family and Christian life. The Caribe imprint focuses on developing fine reference materials and bibles, including the "Precious Moments" bible in Dios Habla Hoy version.

OXFORD UNIVERSITY PRESS
198 Madison Ave.
New York, NY 10016-4314
Tel.: 800-451-7556; FAX: 919-677-1303
Website: www.oup-usa.org

Type of Business:
Oxford University Press publishes many books and Bibles for Roman Catholic readers. Among these are *The NRSV Catholic Edition* (with a concordance and section of Catholic prayers and devotions); *The Catholic Study Bible*, *NAB* (the first true study Bible for Catholics); *The Catholic Bible: Personal Study Edition*, *NAB* (ideal for RCIA participants and other first-time Scripture students); and, *The Complete Parallel Bible* (featuring the texts of the New Revised Standard Version, Revised English Bible, New American Bible & New Jerusalem Bible).

BOOKS & RELIGIOUS ARTICLES

CARIBE BETANIA EDITORES

CARIBE-BETANIA EDITORES
P.O. Box 141000
Nashville, TN 37214
Tel: 615-902-2370; FAX: 615-883-9376

Personnel:
Phil Stoner..President
Ruben DePeña...Sales Director
Maria Hoyos...Sales Representative
Marcela Gómez...Marketing Manager

Type of Business:
Our Betania imprint is regarded as the Spanish Christian industry's leading publisher in the areas of family and Christian life. The Caribe imprint focuses on developing fine reference materials and bibles, including the "Precious Moments" bible in Dios Habla Hoy version.

Affordable Catholic Products for everyone!

1.

2.

1. Good News Catholic Jubilee Edition Bible *with Imprimatur*
Contains Deuterocanonicals/Apocrypha and the Daily Roman Catholic Lectionary Guide. New articles by African American Catholic Scholars include: history of Africa American Catholics, racial reconciliation from the African American Catholic perspective, evangelization and education of African American Catholics. 1,836 p. (6 x 9 in.)
✠ #110806 $ 39.95 single copy Green Padded Hardcover
✠ #109875 $ 39.95 single copy Black Padded Hardcover

2. Good News Hardcover Bible w/Lectionary Guide
An exceptional value. This sturdy hardcover edition makes a fine pew or study Bible. *With Imprimatur* 1,865 p. (5½ x 8¼ in.)
✠ #109879 Hardcover $9.95

3. Bilingual Bible *Versión Popular/ Good News Bible*
Includes Deuterocanonicals/Apocryphal Books A wonderful bilingual Bible for those who enjoy the Word of God in Spanish as well as English. With CELAM endorsement. 3,008 p. (5½ x 8¼ in.)
✠#107901 $24.95 Black Hardcover
✠#107902 $24.95 Burgundy Hardcover
✠#107899 $34.95 Black bonded-leather
✠#107900 $34.95 Burgundy bonded-leather

3.

4.

4. A Very Popular Spanish Bible
Dios Habla Hoy
La Biblia *Versión Popular, 2nd Edition*
Illustrated throughout, this popular hardcover Bible is ideal for all pastoral ministry programs. With CELAM endorsement. 1,856 p. (5½ x 8¼ in.) Hardcover
✠ #103349 $10.15

For further information

Call the toll-free number of the ABS Ministry Representative in your area to receive "personalized" customer service care

Bob Camburn, Northeast Region
1-800-424-2573

Delores Burnett, Mid Atlantic Region
1-888-918-8088

Glenn Herndon, Southern Region
1-800-673-6237

Bill Kuykendall, Central Region
1-800-784-6579

John Andersen, South Central Region
1-800-647-9028

Joe Lachnit, Northwest Region
1-877-719-2221

John Walker, Western Region
1-888-386-7117

5. Kingsley's Meadow Videos

Join Kingsley, a friendly lion, in his musical kingdom. Kids will learn virtues and values in this colorful extravaganza of exciting animation, beautiful scenery, upbeat songs and fun Bible stories. Get all SIX titles!

5.

Also available in Spanish!

Hang in There! #107720-$12.95
Wise Guy #107721-$12.95
Funny Money Video #107723-$12.95
Munch, Munch, Where's My Lunch? #107722-$12.95
1-2-3 Count on Me #110403-$12.95
Just the Facts, Mac #110404-$12.95

Kingsley's Meadow Fun Activity Books are the perfect companion. (English only)

AMERICAN BIBLE SOCIETY

6.

7.

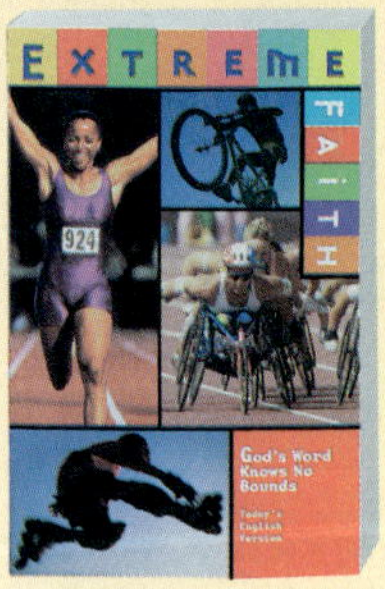

6. Good News Study Bible *with Deuterocanonicals/Apocrypha and Imprimatur*
This comprehensive hardcover study Bible in the GNB translation includes a wide variety of materials to aid in the study of Scriptures in church, in school and in the home. With index, chronology of the Bible, maps and many other features. 1,456 p. (6¾ x 9¼ in.)
✠ #109241 $32.95

7. Good News Bible for Youth
This colorful youth Bible will be treasured by teens of all ages. Includes reader's aids and supplements. 1,408 p. (5¼ x 8¼ in.) *With Imprimatur.*
✠ #107593 Paperback $4.25

8. Good News Bible for Children
A Bible young ones will cherish for years to come. 32 full-color illustrations. 1,888 p. (5¼ x 8¼ in.) *With Imprimatur.*
✠# 107613
Paperback $9.95

8.

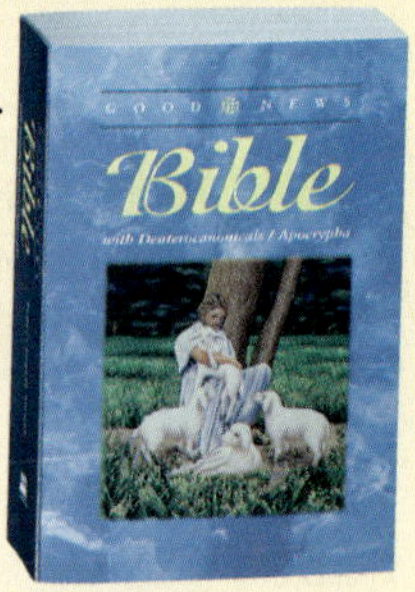

9.

9. An Illustrated New Testament Bible for Today's Family *Contemporary English Version*
Printed in larger type for young readers, this New Testament for children contains 200 black and white drawings. (8 x 10 in.) *With Imprimatur.*
✠ #104783 Paperback $6.15

D.C. RIGGOTT INC.
3540 Neal Ave.
Afton, MN 55001
Tel.: 800-479-8777; FAX: 651-436-4769
E-mail: dcriggottinc@aol.com

Personnel:
Don Riggott .... Owner/President

Type of Business:
Specializing in vintage church accessories, architectural ornamentation and liturgical furnishings.
Stained Glass Windows • Altars • Lighting • Statuary • Stations of the Cross • Tabernacles • Monstrances • Fonts • Pews • Steeple Bells • Vestments • Books • Furniture • Candlesticks • Chalices
Please contact us with specific requests. We will be happy to send you photographs and specifics on any items in our inventory. You may have items in storage or not being used, please contact us as we are actively searching for vintage items to purchase for re-use in liturgical spaces.

LITURIGICAL PUBLICATIONS, INC.
2875 S. James Drive
New Berlin, WI 53151
Tel.: 800-876-4574; FAX: 414-785-9567
Website: www.litpub.com

Personnel:
Craig Polack .... President
Glenn Roskilly .... Chief Operating Officer
Bill Knaapen .... Chief Financial Officer
Michelle Jacobson .... Vice President of Administration

Type of Business:
For over a quarter of a century, Liturgical Publications, Inc. has been helping thousands of churches and 100,000 advertisers deliver their message. We provide all the tools, training, resources, and assistance for you to communicate more effectively and economically. To learn more about how we can help you, call us, or visit our Website at: www.litpub.com.

SAN FRANCIS IMPORTS, INC.
1919 N. Victory Place
Burbank, CA 91504-3425
Tel.: 800-882-4916; FAX: 800-692-9129
Web Site: www.sanfrancis.com

Personnel:
Tirso George .... President
Carlos George .... Vice President Sales
Joseph Gamgene .... Marketing

Type of Business:
San Francis Imports is an importer and manufacturer of fine religious articles. For the retailer we carry the most complete line offering for the American and Hispanic market for baby, baby shower, Baptism, First Communion, Confirmation, Quinceañera, wedding and memorial remembrances. We guarantee the widest selection of gifts at the lowest competitive prices.

BULLETINS & CALENDARS

LITURIGICAL PUBLICATIONS, INC.
2875 S. James Drive
New Berlin, WI 53151
Tel.: 800-876-4574; FAX: 414-785-9567
Website: www.litpub.com

Personnel:
Craig Polack .... President
Glenn Roskilly .... Chief Operating Officer
Bill Knaapen .... Chief Financial Officer
Michelle Jacobson .... Vice President of Administration

Type of Business:
For over a quarter of a century, Liturgical Publications, Inc. has been helping thousands of churches and 100,000 advertisers deliver their message. We provide all the tools, training, resources, and assistance for you to communicate more effectively and economically. To learn more about how we can help you, call us, or visit our Website at: www.litpub.com.

CANDLES, INCENSE

ROOT CANDLES

THE A.I. ROOT CANDLE CO.
623 W. Liberty St.
Medina, OH 44258
Tel.: 800-289-7668; FAX: 330-725-5624
Website: www.airoot.com
E-mail: church@airoot.com

Personnel:
John Holodnak .... Sales Manager

Type of Business:
• Merchandise Handled: Full line of altar candles, Advent, wedding and sacrament candles. Devotional lights, sanctuary lights, altar wine/bread, palms/ashes, and church supplies.
•Services Offered: Replating/refinishing services. Personalized sales representation in most states. Two factory locations: Medina, OH; San Antonio, TX.
•Recent Clients: Serving over 12,000 churches nationwide.
•Statement: Craftsmen in wax since 1869. Root Quality–Root Service.
•Free Literature: Free color catalog, 800-BUY-ROOT.

ACADIAN Candle Company

ACADIAN CANDLE COMPANY
1920 West 94th Street
Bloomington, MN 55431
Tel.: 888-424-9425; FAX: 952-888-6465
Web Site: www.acadiancandles.com

Personnel:
Scott Evenson........ President
Judy Hechtl........ Customer Service

Type of Business:
Handcrafted, custom candles poured in layers of colors lathed to give them their unique and distinctive look. Slow-burning and dripless, our candles are made of the finest raw materials available. Candles for every occasion — Paschal, Advent, Lent, RCIA, Baptism, Confirmation, Weddings, or custom silkscreened candles to fit any commemorative celebration or event. Call for a complete free color brochure.
Acadian Candles — Quality Candles Crafted By Hand.

CM ALMY

C. M. ALMY & SON, INC.
Three American Lane
P.O. Box 2644
Greenwich, CT 06836-2644
Tel.: 800-225-2569; FAX: 800-426-2569
E-mail: almyaccess@almy.com

Showrooms in:
Old Greenwich, CT: 203-637-2739 and
Pittsfield, ME: 207-487-3232

Type of Business:
Almy was founded in 1892. We design and make virtually all of our products in our Maine shop. It is our mission to design furnishings that will grace your worship and to ensure their value by making them with the highest quality materials and craftsmanship. We make a complete line of vestments, haberdashery, choir robes, candles, communion bread, linens, processional and altar appointments, and eucharistic vessels. We also offer custom design and fabrication of all Almy products, and repair and refurbishing of old metal appointments. Quik Ship© delivery of many popular items. All orders backed by The Almy Guarantee. Call, write, or email for a free catalog.

CARROLL ELECTRONICS INCORPORATED
710 Northeast 26th St.
Wilton Manors, FL 33305
Tel.: 800-331-0444; FAX: 954-561-4098

Personnel:
David Nagle .... President
Liza Palmer .... Sales Manager
Bob Perkins .... Sales Representative
Donna Spencer .... Service Engineer

Type of Business:
Carroll Electronics has been in business for 20 years designing and building Electronic Votive Candle Stands for thousands of churches throughout the United States.

CATHEDRAL CANDLE CO.
Now in stock at your nearest Church Goods dealer.

Type of Business:
Classical symbolism and expressive liturgical design in the luxurious hand decorated artistry of SCULPTWAX ... created and mastercrafted here in the United States, exclusively at Cathedral Candle Co.

CANDLE STUDIOS LLC
249 Windsor Street
Kearny, NJ 07032
Phone: 800-648-4229, 201-998-3648
Fax: 201-991-3419
E-mail: candlestudios@msn.com

Type of Business:

We design and manufacture the highest quality, reasonably priced automatic electronic candle systems on today's market. Pictured on this page is our latest state of the art Soft Glow model. It's like nothing you have ever seen before. The lights look so much like actual candles it's amazing. We offer custom units, at stock prices. Our state-of-the-art electronic circuitry is like no other.

What is different about us is:

- State of the art simplicity – plug it in, select your timing and you are ready to go
- Simple Maintenance – each and every part is snap in, snap out repair parts
- The most realistic imitation candle on the market
- Custom made cabinetry of wood or metal
- Service – fast, courteous, prompt and continuous

There has never been a better time to get into electric candles or replace your old units.
We offer sales and service of all makes and models, so give us a call today.

CAVE CO. Your Supplier of Fine Ecclesiastical Interiors

CAVE COMPANY
P.O. Box 211
Old Westbury, NY 11568
Tel.: 800-989-CAVE / 516-676-1231; FAX: 516-676-9695
E-mail: caveco33@aol.com
Web Site: www.churchconstruction.com/caveco/

Personnel:

Gregory P. Cave ....President

Type of Business:

Our company is a fourth-generation business whose specialty is in the ecclesiastical interior design and restoration field. Our staff prides itself in the complete restoration and decoration of the smallest chapel to the largest cathedral, offering such unique services and products as our "Tree of Life" for fund raising, and electrical devotional candle stands. Our true specialty is the personalized service we are committed to bring our customers in the professional fashion they deserve.
We specialize in:
- Tree of Life
- Electric Devotional Candles
- Painting & Decorating
- Poor Boxes
- Kneelers & Pews; Restoration & New
- Gold Leaf
- Statuary & Sculpture; Repair & Restoration
- Challices & Ciboria; 24 Karat Gold Plating

Marklin
Candle Design

MARKLIN CANDLE DESIGN
PO Box 182
Contoocook, NH 03229-0182
Tel.: 603-746-2211; FAX 603-746-2070
E-mail: info@marklincandle.com
Websites: www.marklincandle.com; www.liturgy2000.com

Type of Business:

The artisans of Marklin Candle Design commit themselves to create liturgical candles and appointments of outstanding craftmanship and unmatched elegance.

Our goal shall be to help foster full, active, and conscious participation in liturgical celebrations. To this end, our designs will boldly proclaim the symbols for which they stand; and our products will embody authentic and noble materials.

Each and every product that we sell will bear the mark of human hands in the production process.

We shall offer our customers excellent value, and we shall stand behind our products without question.

emkay

MUENCH KREUZER CANDLE CO.
P.O. Box 4969
Syracuse, NY 13221
Tel.: 315-471-4515; FAX: 315-471-4581

Type of Business:

Manufacturers of Church candles, altar, sanctuary, sacramental, votive & devotional candles of the highest quality. Emkay Candles ... available through your nearest Church Goods Dealer.

See our ad on the next page.

CHALICES, CROSSES, METALWARE

ADRIAN HAMERS®
CHURCH INTERIORS

ADRIAN HAMERS INC.
2 Madison Avenue
Larchmont, NY 10538
Tel.: 914-834-7780; FAX: 914-834-0712

Type of Business:

Custom designers and manufacturers of Sacred Vessels. Since 1887, the Hamers name has been synonymous with expert Silversmithing throughout the world in the field of Liturgical Art. Please contact us for those hard to find items, as we always have a large selection of Adrian Hamers Estate Collection pieces in stock. We are experts in: Church Interiors from design to execution, Renovations, Altars, Sacred Vessels, Gold and Silver Plating & Repairing, Appraisals, Tabernacles, Marble, Statuary, Woodwork & Woodcarving, Stained Glass, Pews & Chairs, Gold Leafing, Frescoes, Restoration, Trompe-l' oeuil, Wall Murals (repair and conservation cleaning), Ornamental Plaster, Heraldic Designs & Bishop Regalia. Please call us for a free 24 page Sacred Vessels color catalog, or our free 80 page color Woodcarvings catalog.

Cut out the mess.
Toss the candle.
Emkay introduces
Emitte Elite:
The first completely disposable & recyclable oil-filled candle.
Emkay has taken oil-filled candles to the next level with the introduction of our new Emitte Elite disposable candle. Less expensive than beeswax and more convenient than conventional oil-burning candles, the Emitte Elite offers the best features of both candles.
emkay
Followers and adapters sold separately.
7/8"
1 1/8"
2"
1 1/2"
APE
Patent Pending

CM ALMY

C. M. ALMY & SON, INC.
Three American Lane
P.O. Box 2644
Greenwich, CT 06836-2644
Tel.: 800-225-2569; FAX: 800-426-2569
E-mail: almyaccess@almy.com

Showrooms in:
Old Greenwich, CT: 203-637-2739 and
Pittsfield, ME: 207-487-3232

Type of Business:
Almy was founded in 1892. We design and make virtually all of our products in our Maine shop. It is our mission to design furnishings that will grace your worship and to ensure their value by making them with the highest quality materials and craftsmanship. We make a complete line of vestments, haberdashery, choir robes, candles, communion bread, linens, processional and altar appointments, and eucharistic vessels. We also offer custom design and fabrication of all Almy products, and repair and refurbishing of old metal appointments. Quik Ship© delivery of many popular items. All orders backed by The Almy Guarantee. Call, write, or email for a free catalog.

D.C. RIGGOTT INC.
3540 Neal Ave.
Afton, MN 55001
Tel.: 800-479-8777; FAX: 651-436-4769
E-mail: dcriggottinc@aol.com

Personnel:
Don Riggott ....Owner/President

Type of Business:
Specializing in vintage church accessories, architectural ornamentation and liturgical furnishings.
Stained Glass Windows • Altars • Lighting • Statuary • Stations of the Cross • Tabernacles • Monstrances • Fonts • Pews • Steeple Bells • Vestments • Books • Furniture • Candlesticks • Chalices
Please contact us with specific requests. We will be happy to send you photographs and specifics on any items in our inventory. You may have items in storage or not being used, please contact us as we are actively searching for vintage items to purchase for re-use in liturgical spaces.

GRANDA LITURGICAL ARTS

GRANDA LITURGICAL ARTS, INC.
990 Grove Street, Suite 203
Evanston, IL 60201
Tel.: 800-425-0828; FAX: 847-492-1374
email: ruf4granda@aol.com
Website: www.hispacom.es/granda

Personnel:
Karen Johnson

Type of Business:
GRANDA LITURGICAL ARTS, Inc. is the USA branch of the largest supplier of church goods in the world: TALLERES DE ARTE GRANDA, S.A.
With 65 employees and sales all over the world, we can offer our experience in the manufacture of:
— metalware: chalices, tabernacles, etc.
— vestments
— wood carvings
— church decoration, interior design
Since 1891, we have been serving the church, combining modern techniques (computer aided design, projects in 3D ...) with artistic values.
Special custom orders are our specialty, styled and priced according to your needs.

THE HOLY+ROOD GUILD

THE HOLY ROOD GUILD
St. Joseph's Abbey
167 North Spencer Rd.
Spencer, MA 01562-1233
Tel.: 508-885-8750; FAX: 508-885-8758

Type of Business:
Designers and crafters of ecclesiastical vesture for over 40 years. Inspired by our monastic tradition, we seek to unite in our work simplicity in design, quality in materials and excellence in craftsmanship. The result is vesture that enhances the liturgical celebration with visual grace and order. Our artists—both monks and laypersons—are available for custom design work and consultation. We also provide an extensive selection of ready made items.

Mark W. Read Studio & Gallery

MARK W. READ STUDIO
1898 Broadstone Road
P.O. Box 671
Valle Crucis, NC 28691
Phone & Fax (828) 963-8191
Web Site: www.markreadstudio.com

Type of Business:

Liturgical Jewelry	Sculpture
Architectural Pieces	Sacred Vessels
Utensils	Urns
Holloware/Chalices	Gem Setting
Gold & Silver Plating	Museum Quality Restoration

Mark Read is an artist craftsman of 30 years experience. Trained in old world and traditional methods he possesses the patience and skill to master the precise craftsmanship that goes into each custom project or restoration piece. Whether his exquisite one-of-a-kind creations are to purely inspire the beholder or serve as a functional piece, Marks creative gifts, unique approach and special sensitivity ensures that each commission works in harmony with its architectural surroundings.

From gold, silver, bronze, titanium to iron and beyond...the possibilities are endless.

Research and consulting is his first priority for restoration projects, thereby ensuring a clear understanding of the steps that must be taken to restore your piece back to its original glory. All types of restoration are accepted.

Please visit our website with the special section for Liturgical pieces.

See our display ad on this page.

St. Anthony's CHURCH SUPPLIES

ST. ANTHONY'S CHURCH SUPPLIES
3121 McCart Ave.
Fort Worth, TX 76110
Tel: 800-772-5928
E-mail: books4u@airmail.net
Web Site: www.StellaMarisBooks.com

Type of Business:

We can supply your church or chapel with the finest sanctuary appointments available. We offer a full line of ecclesiastical goods from clerical shirts and vestments, to chalices and tabernacles, to church statuary and stained glass windows, to Catholic books and other media, to furniture for churches, church offices, classrooms, and cafeterias.

We offer great service with a smile and look forward to making new friends.

Please use our toll free number or e-mail to contact John Heitzenrater or Richard Myers.

STADELMAIER NIJMEGEN

STADELMAIER-NIJMEGEN-HOLLAND
P.O. Box 7063
6503 GN Nijmegen
Nijmegen, Holland 6503 GN
Tel.: 31-24-3791170; FAX: 31-24-3791171
e-mail: info@stadelmaier.com

Type of Business:

SN-Antiques offers, for the re-use in the Cath. Liturgy;
Completely restored, original, devotional interior-pieces. Altars, stations, candlesticks, perpetual lights, statues, reliquaries, ciboria, chalices, monstrances, censers, mission crosses, processional crosses, Saints, paintings, etc.
Different styles and age: Roman, baroque, neo-gothic, etc.
Please describe your interest directly to Mrs. Annemieke Drijber.

CHOIR ROBES

CM ALMY

C. M. ALMY & SON, INC.
Three American Lane
P.O. Box 2644
Greenwich, CT 06836-2644
Tel.: 800-225-2569; FAX: 800-426-2569
E-mail: almyaccess@almy.com

Showrooms in:
Old Greenwich, CT: 203-637-2739 and
Pittsfield, ME: 207-487-3232

Type of Business:

Almy was founded in 1892. We design and make virtually all of our products in our Maine shop. It is our mission to design furnishings that will grace your worship and to ensure their value by making them with the highest quality materials and craftsmanship. We make a complete line of vestments, haberdashery, choir robes, candles, communion bread, linens, processional and altar appointments, and eucharistic vessels. We also offer custom design and fabrication of all Almy products, and repair and refurbishing of old metal appointments. Quik Ship© delivery of many popular items. All orders backed by The Almy Guarantee. Call, write, or email for a free catalog.

MURPHY VESTMENTS

MURPHY VESTMENTS
Murphy Cap & Gown Co.
4200 31st St. North
St. Petersburg, FL 33714
Tel.: 727-527-0696; FAX: 727-526-3528
Web Site: www.murphyrobes.com
E-mail: murphyrb@gte.net

Personnel:

Don Camp .... President
Gary Bergamo .... Sales Manager
George Shahine .... Administrative Manager
Josephine DeFeo .... Vestment Designer

Type of Business:

Manufacturer of vestments, albs, cassocks, choir and acolyte robes and accessories, all value priced with guaranteed fit and quality. We supply a complete line of liturgical attire, custom tailored as well as many styles in stock and ready to ship within 24 hours of receipt of order. Available through your church goods dealer, or call or write for more information.

the symbol of Regal Splendor

Robert Gaspard Co.

ROBERT GASPARD CO., INC.
200 N. Janacek Rd.
Brookfield, WI 53045-6101
Tel.: 800-784-6868; 262-784-6800; FAX: 262-784-7567
E-mail: robertgaspard.com
Web Site: www.robertgaspardco.com

Personnel:

Rose Gaspard .... President
John Andorfer .... Vice President
Jason R. Gaspard .... Sales & Marketing Mgr.

Type of Business:

The Robert Gaspard Co. was established in 1954. Over the past 47 years, we have grown to be a nationally-known company. We pride ourselves on the ability to create original custom designs to enrich your worship needs. Our complete line consists of all ecclesiastical vesture, as well as paraments, mass and altar linens, stoles, banners, chasubles, funeral palls, albs, cossacks, surplices, choir robes, acolyte robes and many accessories. Complimentary catalogs and fabric swatches sent on request.

CHURCH REGISTERS

Serving Catholic Parishes since 1873.

D.P. MURPHY CO., INC.
1221 Walt Whitman Rd.
Melville, NY 11747-3090
Tel.: 631-673-9400; FAX: 631-673-1851

Personnel:
Peter Q. Murphy..President

Type of Business:
Envelope mailing systems specifically designed to meet the needs of your parish - available at any frequency . . . monthly, bi-monthly, quarterly, semi-annual, yearly sets. FREE List Maintenance. Contribution recording via fax, phone, mail, diskette, modem or E-Mail. Census, stewardship, tithing, and fundraising programs. Church stationary, registers, record books, mass cards and certificates. Specialists in old register binding.

F. J. REMEY CO., INC.
121 Willis Ave.
Mineola, NY 11501-0589
Tel.: 516-741-5112; FAX: 516-741-0523
Toll Free: 1-877-FJ REMEY (357-3639)

Type of Business:
Serving Catholic parishes since 1921 by providing the following products: Offering Envelope Mailing Systems, Annual Offering Envelope Boxsets, Bulk Collection Envelopes, Computer Recording, Collection Baskets, Parish Census, Church Record Books, Parish Office Forms, Church Stationery, Mass Cards, Raffle Tickets and Tuition Supplies.

CLIP ART

LITURIGICAL PUBLICATIONS, INC.
2875 S. James Drive
New Berlin, WI 53151
Tel.: 800-876-4574; FAX: 414-785-9567
Website: www.litpub.com

Personnel:
Craig Polack .... President
Glenn Roskilly .... Chief Operating Officer
Bill Knaapen .... Chief Financial Officer
Michelle Jacobson .... Vice President of Administration

Type of Business:
For over a quarter of a century, Liturgical Publications, Inc. has been helping thousands of churches and 100,000 advertisers deliver their message. We provide all the tools, training, resources, and assistance for you to communicate more effectively and economically. To learn more about how we can help you, call us, or visit our Website at: www.litpub.com.

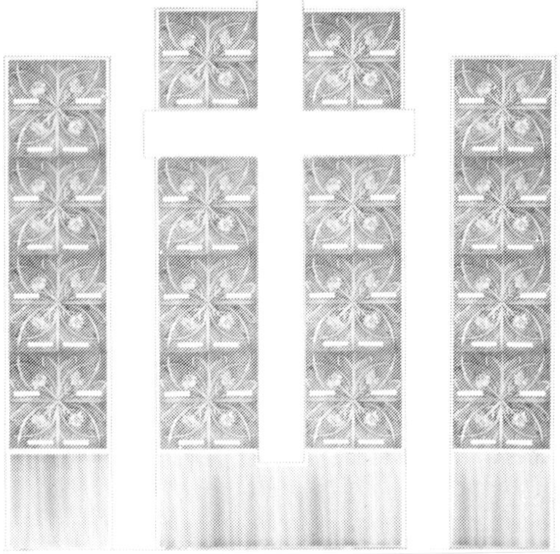

COLUMBARIUM

ARMENTO LITURGICAL ARTS, INC.
1011 Military Road, P.O. Box 39
Buffalo, NY 14217-0039
Tel.: 716-875-2423; FAX: 716-875-8011
Toll Free: 866-276-3686
E-mail: armento@aol.com
Web Site: www.armento-columbarium.com

Personnel:
Louis S. Armento .... Founder
Robert W. Pierce .... President
M. Colletta Harrower .... Vice-President

Type of Business:
Established in 1947. We Design and Fabricate Traditional and Contemporary Liturgical Art work. The Armento Columbarium for the cremated remains of the faithful deceased is designed with an understanding of and respect for the denominational needs and architectural style of the church. The Bronze Face Plates are sculptured bas-reliefs of liturgical meaning. The modular construction encourages integrity of design and makes possible the precise use of space.

We make it easy to plan and to select. We make it easy to install. We ship the Columbarium substantially assembled for ease of installation at the church.

See our ad on this page.

FABRIC ART HANGINGS & TAPESTRIES

ABBOTT INC.
Showroom 1515 Route 38
Cherry Hill, NJ 08002
Tel.: 800-522-2688; 856-662-6959; FAX: 856-665-5109
Website: http://www.abbottsinc.com
email: acg.inc@cwixmail.com

Personnel:
Daniel J. Castonguay .... President
Joseph F. McKeaney .... General Manager
Michael W. Wasyluk .... Customer Service

Type of Business:
Purveyors of the Finest Vesture, Paraments, Statuary & Metalware since 1962. Unique and original creations, our specialty. Custom designs to complement your liturgical environment. Exclusive representatives of Slabbinck Master Collection & Original Collection.

T.M.

Bringing the Art Back into the Craft

BRAMANTE STUDIO
20 Queen Street North
Kitchener, Ontario, Canada N2H 2G8
Phone: 519-570-2908 Fax: 519-570-2706
1-800-295-6902

Personnel:
Abraham Mathew ....Owner/President

Type of Business:
Bramante is a unique arts and crafts studio specializing in fine quality, one of a kind liturgical art specifically for church worship environments. Our artisans, in conjunction with the individual church staff, design each piece to work in harmony with the church as a whole. We are able to offer such a high level of personalized service because all our work is done in house. From weaving our own fabric, to laminating the wood used for each sculpture, each piece is completely hand made. Whether it is a simple stole, a wall to wall tapestry, or a larger than life hand carved sculpture, each piece is created with your worship environment in mind.

CM ALMY

C. M. ALMY & SON, INC.
Three American Lane
P.O. Box 2644
Greenwich, CT 06836-2644
Tel.: 800-225-2569; FAX: 800-426-2569
E-mail: almyaccess@almy.com

Showrooms in:
Old Greenwich, CT: 203-637-2739 and
Pittsfield, ME: 207-487-3232

Type of Business:
Almy was founded in 1892. We design and make virtually all of our products in our Maine shop. It is our mission to design furnishings that will grace your worship and to ensure their value by making them with the highest quality materials and craftsmanship. We make a complete line of vestments, haberdashery, choir robes, candles, communion bread, linens, processional and altar appointments, and eucharistic vessels. We also offer custom design and fabrication of all Almy products, and repair and refurbishing of old metal appointments. Quik Ship© delivery of many popular items. All orders backed by The Almy Guarantee. Call, write, or email for a free catalog.

STADELMAIER NIJMEGEN

STADELMAIER-NIJMEGEN-HOLLAND
P.O. Box 7063
6503 GN Nijmegen
Nijmegen, Holland 6503 GN
Tel.: 31-24-3791170; FAX: 31-24-3791171
e-mail: info@stadelmaier.com

Type of Business:
SN-Antiques offers, for the re-use in the Cath. Liturgy;
Completely restored, original, devotional interior-pieces. Altars, stations, candlesticks, perpetual lights, statues, reliquaries, ciboria, chalices, monstrances, censers, mission crosses, processional crosses, Saints, paintings, etc.
Different styles and age: Roman, baroque, neo-gothic, etc.
Please describe your interest directly to Mrs. Annemieke Drijber.

GLASSWARE

STADELMAIER NIJMEGEN

STADELMAIER-NIJMEGEN-HOLLAND
P.O. Box 7063
6503 GN Nijmegen
Nijmegen, Holland 6503 GN
Tel.: 31-24-3791170; FAX: 31-24-3791171
e-mail: info@stadelmaier.com

Type of Business:
SN-Antiques offers, for the re-use in the Cath. Liturgy;
Completely restored, original, devotional interior-pieces. Altars, stations, candlesticks, perpetual lights, statues, reliquaries, ciboria, chalices, monstrances, censers, mission crosses, processional crosses, Saints, paintings, etc.
Different styles and age: Roman, baroque, neo-gothic, etc.
Please describe your interest directly to Mrs. Annemieke Drijber.

GOLD/SILVER PLATING, BRASS RESTORATION

TOUJOURS

ADRIAN HAMERS®
CHURCH INTERIORS

ADRIAN HAMERS INC.
2 Madison Avenue
Larchmont, NY 10538
Tel.: 914-834-7780; FAX: 914-834-0712

Type of Business:
Custom designers and manufacturers of Sacred Vessels. Since 1887, the Hamers name has been synonymous with expert Silversmithing throughout the world in the field of Liturgical Art. Please contact us for those hard to find items, as we always have a large selection of Adrian Hamers Estate Collection pieces in stock. We are experts in: Church Interiors from design to execution, Renovations, Altars, Sacred Vessels, Gold and Silver Plating & Repairing, Appraisals, Tabernacles, Marble, Statuary, Woodwork & Woodcarving, Stained Glass, Pews & Chairs, Gold Leafing, Frescoes, Restoration, Trompe-l' oeuil, Wall Murals (repair and conservation cleaning), Ornamental Plaster, Heraldic Designs & Bishop Regalia. Please call us for a free 24 page Sacred Vessels color catalog, or our free 80 page color Woodcarvings catalog.

CM ALMY

C. M. ALMY & SON, INC.
Three American Lane
P.O. Box 2644
Greenwich, CT 06836-2644
Tel.: 800-225-2569; FAX: 800-426-2569
E-mail: almyaccess@almy.com

Showrooms in:
Old Greenwich, CT: 203-637-2739 and
Pittsfield, ME: 207-487-3232

Type of Business:
Almy was founded in 1892. We design and make virtually all of our products in our Maine shop. It is our mission to design furnishings that will grace your worship and to ensure their value by making them with the highest quality materials and craftsmanship. We make a complete line of vestments, haberdashery, choir robes, candles, communion bread, linens, processional and altar appointments, and eucharistic vessels. We also offer custom design and fabrication of all Almy products, and repair and refurbishing of old metal appointments. Quik Ship© delivery of many popular items. All orders backed by The Almy Guarantee. Call, write, or email for a free catalog.

MUELLER KAISER PLATING CO.
Since 1911
5815 Hampton Avenue • St. Louis, MO 63109 • (314) 832-3553

MUELLER KAISER PLATING CO.
5815 Hampton Ave.
St. Louis, MO 63109
Tel.: 314-832-3553
Web Site: www.mueller-kaiserplating.com

Type of Business:
One of the OLDEST liturgical metalware platers and refinishers in the U.S.A., offering a distinguished tradition of Master Metal Craftsmanship in the expert restoration, plating and refinishing of Sacred Vessels and Metalware in GOLD, SILVER, BRASS, COPPER and BRONZE SINCE 1911. Customers should ship chalices, ciboria, monstrances, candelabra and other sacred metalware to us by U.P.S. (insured) for estimates and work. (Note: return ship items without work at customer expense.) We also offer OLD CHALICES, CIBORIA, MONSTRANCES, CANDELABRA and other FITMENTS to Catholic clergy, religious and churches for ONLY the cost of refinishing. Inquire for selection and price. Ecclesiastical Authorization. Awards from recognized religious, arts and cultural organizations. CELEBRATING 90 YEARS OF MASTER CRAFTSMANSHIP in the LITURGICAL METAL ARTS!

GOLD LEAFING & PAINTED MURALS

TOUJOURS

ADRIAN HAMERS®
CHURCH INTERIORS

ADRIAN HAMERS INC.
2 Madison Avenue
Larchmont, NY 10538
Tel.: 914-834-7780; FAX: 914-834-0712

Type of Business:
Custom designers and manufacturers of Sacred Vessels. Since 1887, the Hamers name has been synonymous with expert Silversmithing throughout the world in the field of Liturgical Art. Please contact us for those hard to find items, as we always have a large selection of Adrian Hamers Estate Collection pieces in stock. We are experts in: Church Interiors from design to execution, Renovations, Altars, Sacred Vessels, Gold and Silver Plating & Repairing, Appraisals, Tabernacles, Marble, Statuary, Woodwork & Woodcarving, Stained Glass, Pews & Chairs, Gold Leafing, Frescoes, Restoration, Trompe-l' oeuil, Wall Murals (repair and conservation cleaning), Ornamental Plaster, Heraldic Designs & Bishop Regalia. Please call us for a free 24 page Sacred Vessels color catalog, or our free 80 page color Woodcarvings catalog.

OFFERING ENVELOPES

AMERICANCHURCH
365 McClurg Road, Youngstown, OH 44512
Tel: 800-250-7112 – fax: 888-763-8772
E-mail: sales@americanchurch.com
Web Site: www.americanchurch.com

Personnel:
Christine J. Dailey ....Executive V.P. of Sales & Marketing

Type of Business:
For nearly 100 years, AmericanChurch has been dedicated to serving the needs of the Catholic Community. We are the largest church offering envelope manufacturer in the world, with the most comprehensive range of Adult and Children's Stewardship Resources available:

* Mailed Offering Envelope Systems
* Annual Boxed Envelopes
* Bulk Collection Envelopes
* Stewardship Fundraising Programs
  Capital Campaigns
  Increased Offertory Collections
  Pledge Drives & School Tuition Programs
* Direct Mail Services
* Fulfillment Services
* Electronic Church Giving
* Computerized Contribution Recording
* Specialty Imprinted Fund Raising Products

www.americanchurch.com

CATHEDRAL CORPORATION
Griffiss Technology Park
632 Ellsworth Road
Rome, NY 13441
Phone: (315) 338-0021
Fax: (315) 338-5874
Web Site: www:cathedralstewardship.com
E-mail: sales@cathedralstewardship.com

Personnel:
Marianne W. Gaige ....President and COO
Larry J. Beasley ....Director of Marketing
Ronald P. Blakeman ....Director of Sales

Business description:

Cathedral Corporation is a leader in the creation, printing, personalization, and high volume mailing of church envelopes and stewardship programs. Our customer base has grown for more than six decades. Today we serve churches nationwide with a full range of stewardship resources and electronic services for the internet.

Serving Catholic Parishes since 1873.

D.P. MURPHY CO., INC.
1221 Walt Whitman Rd.
Melville, NY 11747-3090
Tel.: 631-673-9400; FAX: 631-673-1851

Personnel:
Peter Q. Murphy..President

Type of Business:
Envelope mailing systems specifically designed to meet the needs of your parish - available at any frequency . . . monthly, bi-monthly, quarterly, semi-annual, yearly sets. FREE List Maintenance. Contribution recording via fax, phone, mail, diskette, modem or E-Mail. Census, stewardship, tithing, and fundraising programs. Church stationary, registers, record books, mass cards and certificates. Specialists in old register binding.

F. J. REMEY CO., INC.
121 Willis Ave.
Mineola, NY 11501-0589
Tel.: 516-741-5112; FAX: 516-741-0523
Toll Free: 1-877-FJ REMEY (357-3639)

Type of Business:
Serving Catholic parishes since 1921 by providing the following products: Offering Envelope Mailing Systems, Annual Offering Envelope Boxsets, Bulk Collection Envelopes, Computer Recording, Collection Baskets, Parish Census, Church Record Books, Parish Office Forms, Church Stationery, Mass Cards, Raffle Tickets and Tuition Supplies.

NATIONAL CHURCH SUPPLY CO.
P.O. Box 269
Chester, WV 26034
Tel.: 304-387-5200; FAX: 304-387-5266

Personnel:
Ms. Kathy Myers ....Sales & Advertising Coordinator

Type of Business:
Nurturing Stewardship Growth in churches is a tradition at Catholic Envelope Service. A division of National Church Supply Co., we have been serving the Christian community for over 80 years. Every person in our family owned organization has the same goal: to help every church customer find the best possible solution to today's and tomorrow's stewardship challenges. Our innovative church offering envelopes and stewardship systems are geared to increase communications while improving parishioner commitment and response.

ONE WRITE COMPANY

ONE-WRITE COMPANY
P.O. Box 628
Lancaster, OH 43130
Tel.: 1-800-268-6070; FAX: 800-504-2260

Type of Business:
Book Offering Envelopes, Tuition Payment Books, Mailing Plan for Offering Envelopes, and Contribution Report Forms. We invite you to compare the features and prices of the Book Offering Envelopes with your current system. The savings will be considerable. Write or call for a free catalog and quote today.

Our Sunday Visitor, Inc.

OUR SUNDAY VISITOR, INC.
200 Noll Plaza
Huntington, IN 46750
Tel.: 800-348-2886; 219-356-8400
FAX: 800-442-0669; 219-356-8472
Web Site: www.osv.com

Personnel:
Greg Erlandson ....President, Publishing Division
Kyle Hamilton..................President, Offering Envelope Division
Jill Kurtz ....Marketing Director, Publishing Division
Julie Kenny .....Marketing Manager, Offering Envelope Division

Type of Business:
Our Sunday Visitor, Inc. is a not-for-profit organization providing thousands of parishes with a wide variety of Catholic:
- Books
- Magazines
- Offering Envelope Products and Services
- Religious Education Products
- Stewardship Products and Services

See our display ad on the next page.

ONE WRITE COMPANY
P.O. Box 628
Lancaster, Ohio 43130

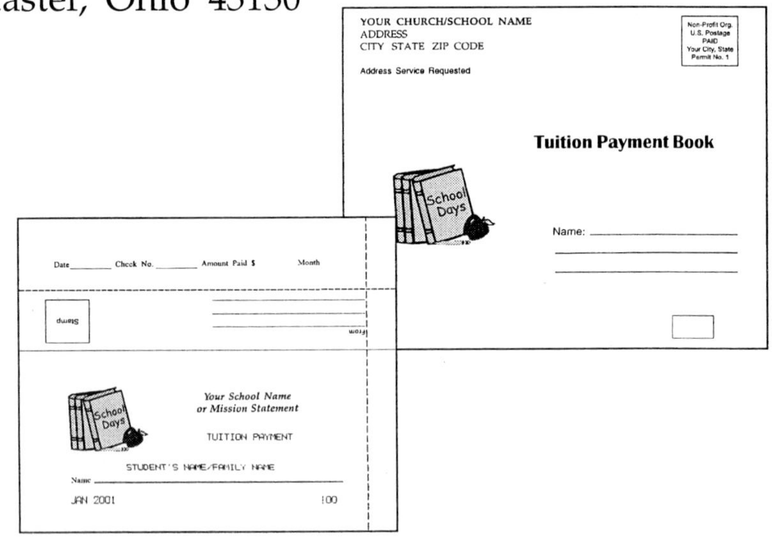

Adult Offering Books

Special Campaign Books

Youth Offering Books

Stock Offering Books

Offering Envelope Mailing Plan
(Monthly -- Bi-Monthly -- Quarterly)

Custom Printed Bulk Envelopes

Tuition Payment Books

Call or write today for a free catalog, quote, or samples.
Tel. 1-800-268-6070 Fax 1-800-504-2260

SACRED VESSELS

TOUJOURS

ADRIAN HAMERS®
CHURCH INTERIORS

ADRIAN HAMERS INC.
2 Madison Avenue
Larchmont, NY 10538
Tel.: 914-834-7780; FAX: 914-834-0712

Type of Business:

Custom designers and manufacturers of Sacred Vessels. Since 1887, the Hamers name has been synonymous with expert Silversmithing throughout the world in the field of Liturgical Art. Please contact us for those hard to find items, as we always have a large selection of Adrian Hamers Estate Collection pieces in stock. We are experts in: Church Interiors from design to execution, Renovations, Altars, Sacred Vessels, Gold and Silver Plating & Repairing, Appraisals, Tabernacles, Marble, Statuary, Woodwork & Woodcarving, Stained Glass, Pews & Chairs, Gold Leafing, Frescoes, Restoration, Trompe-l'oeuil, Wall Murals (repair and conservation cleaning), Ornamental Plaster, Heraldic Designs & Bishop Regalia. Please call us for a free 24 page Sacred Vessels color catalog, or our free 80 page color Woodcarvings catalog.

CM ALMY

C. M. ALMY & SON, INC.
Three American Lane
P.O. Box 2644
Greenwich, CT 06836-2644
Tel.: 800-225-2569; FAX: 800-426-2569
E-mail: almyaccess@almy.com

Showrooms in:
Old Greenwich, CT: 203-637-2739 and
Pittsfield, ME: 207-487-3232

Type of Business:

Almy was founded in 1892. We design and make virtually all of our products in our Maine shop. It is our mission to design furnishings that will grace your worship and to ensure their value by making them with the highest quality materials and craftsmanship. We make a complete line of vestments, haberdashery, choir robes, candles, communion bread, linens, processional and altar appointments, and eucharistic vessels. We also offer custom design and fabrication of all Almy products, and repair and refurbishing of old metal appointments. Quik Ship© delivery of many popular items. All orders backed by The Almy Guarantee. Call, write, or email for a free catalog.

D.C. RIGGOTT INC.
3540 Neal Ave.
Afton, MN 55001
Tel.: 800-479-8777; FAX: 651-436-4769
E-mail: dcriggottinc@aol.com

Personnel:
Don Riggott .... Owner/President

Type of Business:
Specializing in vintage church accessories, architectural ornamentation and liturgical furnishings.
Stained Glass Windows • Altars • Lighting • Statuary • Stations of the Cross • Tabernacles • Monstrances • Fonts • Pews • Steeple Bells • Vestments • Books • Furniture • Candlesticks • Chalices
Please contact us with specific requests. We will be happy to send you photographs and specifics on any items in our inventory. You may have items in storage or not being used, please contact us as we are actively searching for vintage items to purchase for re-use in liturgical spaces.

TAG GRANDA.
LITURGICAL ARTS

GRANDA LITURGICAL ARTS, INC.
990 Grove Street, Suite 203
Evanston, IL 60201
Tel.: 800-425-0828; FAX: 847-492-1374
email: ruf4granda@aol.com
Website: www.hispacom.es/granda

Personnel:
Karen Johnson

Type of Business:
GRANDA LITURGICAL ARTS, Inc. is the USA branch of the largest supplier of church goods in the world: TALLERES DE ARTE GRANDA, S.A.
With 65 employees and sales all over the world, we can offer our experience in the manufacture of:
— metalware: chalices, tabernacles, etc.
— vestments
— wood carvings
— church decoration, interior design
Since 1891, we have been serving the church, combining modern techniques (computer aided design, projects in 3D ...) with artistic values.
Special custom orders are our specialty, styled and priced according to your needs.

Mark W. Read Studio & Gallery

MARK W. READ STUDIO
1898 Broadstone Road
P.O. Box 671
Valle Crucis, NC 28691
Phone & Fax (828) 963-8191
Web Site: www.markreadstudio.com

Type of Business:

Liturgical Jewelry	Sculpture
Architectural Pieces	Sacred Vessels
Utensils	Urns
Holloware/Chalices	Gem Setting
Gold & Silver Plating	Museum Quality Restoration

Mark Read is an artist craftsman of 30 years experience. Trained in old world and traditional methods he possesses the patience and skill to master the precise craftsmanship that goes into each custom project or restoration piece. Whether his exquisite one-of-a-kind creations are to purely inspire the beholder or serve as a functional piece, Marks creative gifts, unique approach and special sensitivity ensures that each commission works in harmony with its architectural surroundings.

From gold, silver, bronze, titanium to iron and beyond...the possibilities are endless.

Research and consulting is his first priority for restoration projects, thereby ensuring a clear understanding of the steps that must be taken to restore your piece back to its original glory. All types of restoration are accepted.

Please visit our website with the special section for Liturgical pieces.

See our display ad on page 107r.

MK MUELLER KAISER PLATING CO.
Since 1911
5815 Hampton Avenue • St. Louis, MO 63109 • (314) 832-3553

MUELLER KAISER PLATING CO.
5815 Hampton Ave.
St. Louis, MO 63109
Tel.: 314-832-3553
Web Site: www.mueller-kaiserplating.com

Type of Business:

One of the OLDEST liturgical metalware platers and refinishers in the U.S.A., offering a distinguished tradition of Master Metal Craftsmanship in the expert restoration, plating and refinishing of Sacred Vessels and Metalware in GOLD, SILVER, BRASS, COPPER and BRONZE SINCE 1911. Customers should ship chalices, ciboria, monstrances, candelabra and other sacred metalware to us by U.P.S. (insured) for estimates and work. (Note: return ship items without work at customer expense.) We also offer OLD CHALICES, CIBORIA, MONSTRANCES, CANDELABRA and other FITMENTS to Catholic clergy, religious and churches for ONLY the cost of refinishing. Inquire for selection and price. Ecclesiastical Authorization. Awards from recognized religious, arts and cultural organizations. CELEBRATING 90 YEARS OF MASTER CRAFTSMANSHIP in the LITURGICAL METAL ARTS!

SN STADELMAIER NIJMEGEN

STADELMAIER-NIJMEGEN-HOLLAND
P.O. Box 7063
6503 GN Nijmegen
Nijmegen, Holland 6503 GN
Tel.: 31-24-3791170; FAX: 31-24-3791171
e-mail: info@stadelmaier.com

Type of Business:

SN-Antiques offers, for the re-use in the Cath. Liturgy;
Completely restored, original, devotional interior-pieces. Altars, stations, candlesticks, perpetual lights, statues, reliquaries, ciboria, chalices, monstrances, censers, mission crosses, processional crosses, Saints, paintings, etc.
Different styles and age: Roman, baroque, neo-gothic, etc.
Please describe your interest directly to Mrs. Annemieke Drijber.

STATIONERY & GREETING CARDS

ARTCRAFT DISTRIBUTING CO.
25462 S. Hwy. 213
Mulino, OR 97042
Tel.: 800-547-6890; FAX: 503-632-3194
Web Site: www.artcraft-dist.com
E -mail: info@artcraft-dist.com

Personnel:
Larry Baughman ....CEO and President
Maxine Baughman ....Executive Vice-President

Type of Business:
Artcraft Distributing Co., has been in business for over 50 years. We offer a distinctive line of over 200 Religious, Spiritually moving note cards embossed/gold foiled messages and attractive Welcome Folders also embossed and gold foiled. Fits neatly into jacket pocket or purse. We offer a unique line of stained leaded glass window décor for gifts or fund raising.

Artcraft has a reputation for quality and service. We offer you the power to touch someone with Grace and Peace.
www.artcraft-dist.com
email: info@artcraft-dist.com

BARTON-COTTON

BARTON COTTON
1405 Parker Rd.
Baltimore, MD 21227
Tel.: 800-638-4652; FAX; 800-807-2954

Personnel:
Denise J. Payne ....Vice President, Marketing and Sales

Type of Business:
For over 70 years, Barton-Cotton, Inc. has been proud to offer the finest selection of quality religious stationery products to the Catholic Clergy and Religious. Over 300 products are available including Mass cards, Sacramental certificates, Christmas and Easter cards, Mother's/Father's Day sets, Ordination/Jubilee products, Way of the Cross booklets, Rosary folders, Holy cards, Bulletins, Offering Envelopes, Bookmarks and more. Products can be personalized with your name, church name, address, or special message. For a FREE catalog, call 1-800-638-4652.

THE PRINTERY HOUSE
Conception Abbey · CONCEPTION · MISSOURI 64433

THE PRINTERY HOUSE
Conception Abbey
PO Box 12
Conception, MO 64433
Tel.: 800-889-0105; 660-944-2632; FAX: 888-556-8262
E-mail: sales@printeryhouse.org
Web Site: printeryhouse.org

Personnel:
Br. William Buchholz, O.S.B ....Director
Ron Riggs ....Director of Sales and Marketing
Br. Jeremiah Tuttle, O.S.B ....Marketing Associate
Br. Michael Marcotte, O.S.B ....Art Director

Type of Business:
Manufacture and market Christian/Catholic Greeting cards and icons. Customized Christmas and other cards to enhance your development programs are our forte`! The Printery House is a not-for-profit extension of the apostolate of the monks of Conception Abbey.

Call 800-889-0105 or fax 888-556-8262 for free samples, catalogs and quantity discount schedules.

SHAW CARTIER

SHAW CARTIER
PO Box 51746
Phoenix, AZ 85076
Tel.: 602-437-4360 vm; 602-470-0060
E-mail: sc1@shawcartier.com/
Web Site: http://www.shawcartier.com/

Type of Business:
Web intra/internet design and development, with unique graphic presentation exclusive to each site. We will also maintain and update preexisting web sites. Design, prep and distribution of CD brochure-ware, and postcard production. Holy cards are designed and produced in quantities starting at 5,000. All business services are free to papal cloisters. Catholic-related web sites may also be added to our Catholic portal free of charge.

STEWARDSHIP

NCS Envelope Service™

NATIONAL CHURCH SUPPLY CO.
P.O. Box 269
Chester, WV 26034
Tel.: 304-387-5200; FAX: 304-387-5266

Personnel:
Ms. Kathy Myers......................Sales & Advertising Coordinator

Type of Business:
Nurturing Stewardship Growth in churches is a tradition at Catholic Envelope Service. A division of National Church Supply Co., we have been serving the Christian community for over 80 years. Every person in our family owned organization has the same goal: to help every church customer find the best possible solution to today's and tomorrow's stewardship challenges. Our innovative church offering envelopes and stewardship systems are geared to increase communications while improving parishioner commitment and response.

Our Sunday Visitor, Inc.

OUR SUNDAY VISITOR, INC.
200 Noll Plaza
Huntington, IN 46750
Tel.: 800-348-2886; 219-356-8400
FAX: 800-442-0669; 219-356-8472
Web Site: www.osv.com

Personnel:
Greg Erlandson ....President, Publishing Division
Kyle Hamilton..................President, Offering Envelope Division
Jill Kurtz ....Marketing Director, Publishing Division
Julie Kenny .....Marketing Manager, Offering Envelope Division

Type of Business:
Our Sunday Visitor, Inc. is a not-for-profit organization providing thousands of parishes with a wide variety of Catholic:

- Books
- Magazines
- Offering Envelope Products and Services
- Religious Education Products
- Stewardship Products and Services

PUBLISHERS

ALBA HOUSE PUBLISHERS
2187 Victory Blvd.
Staten Island, NY 10314
Tel.: 800-343-ALBA (2522); FAX: 718-698-8390
email: albahouse@aol.com
Website: http://www.albahouse.org

Personnel:
Rev. Ignatius Staniszewski, ...SSP Publisher
Rev. Edmund Lane, ...SSP Managing Editor
Rev. Anthony Warren, ...SSP Marketing/Sales Director

Type of Business:
Alba House is a ministry of the Society of St. Paul. The specific mission of the Pauline Family (6 religious congregations and 3 secular institutes world wide) is evangelization through the media of social communications. Alba House Book Publishers is one of the instruments used for the propagation of the faith. We are ministers who are responsible for accompanying the people of God towards His Kingdom, following the teaching of the universal and local Church.

COKESBURY
201 Eighth Avenue, South
P.O. Box 801
Nashville, TN 37202-0801
Tel.: 800-672-1789; FAX: 800-445-8189
Web Site: www.cokesbury.com

Personnel:
Neil Alexander.......................................President and Publisher
Edward R. Kowalski ....Senior Vice President of Marketing and Sales

Type of Business:
Cokesbury has been serving the needs of clergy, religious educators, and churches for over 200 years. We're your one-stop shop for a vast array of communion supplies and altarware, paraments, apparel and vestments, Bibles and books for church leaders, candles and accessories, offering envelopes, bulletins, and music resources. All are backed by our 100% satisfaction guarantee.

THE CROSSROAD PUBLISHING COMPANY
370 Lexington Avenue
New York, NY 10017
Tel.: 212-532-3650; FAX: 212-532-4922

Type of Business:
Crossroads is a book publishing company in the area of religion and spirituality, religious studies, theology, and parish and pastoral materials. We publish under the Crossroad Classic, Crossroad General Interest, Herder and Herder, and Faith and Formation Imprints.

Liguori PUBLICATIONS

LIGUORI PUBLICATIONS
One Liguori Drive
Liguori, MO 63057
Phone: 800-325-9521
Fax: 800-325-9526
Web site: www.liguori.org
E-mail: liguori@liguori.org

Personnel:
Rev. Harry Grile, C.Ss.R .... President/Publisher
Mr. Mark Schmersahl .... Director of Marketing & Sales

Type of Business:
Liguori Publications is an apostolate of the Redemptorist priests and brothers, who, together with a dedicated group of lay people, are devoted to spreading the Good News of Jesus Christ. Publications range from Liguorian magazine, an award-winning general interest Catholic magazine, to Liguori books, pamphlets, bulletins, catechetical resources, videos, software, and PastoraLink, a subscription website for pastoral ministers and preachers. Our Spanish-language imprint, Libros Liguori, publishes books, pamphlets and catechetical resources for the growing Hispanic community.

THE LITURGICAL PRESS
P.O. Box 7500, St. John's Abbey
Collegeville, MN 56321
Tel.: 800-858-5450; 320-363-2213; FAX: 800-445-5899
E-mail: sales@litpress.org
Web Site: www.litpress.org

Personnel:
Ed Vessel .... Bookstore Sales
Carmen Donabauer .... Customer Service
Nancy Fiedler .... Customer Service
Pat Kampa .... Customer Service
Diane Sobania .... Customer Service

Type of Business:
For 75 years, suppliers of liturgical, biblical, ritual, and instructional material to English-speaking countries. Products offered: Celebrating the Eucharist Mass Guide, the New Lectionary, Bible and Liturgy Sunday Bulletins, books, leaflets, video and audio cassettes, Sacra Pagina, Butler's Lives of the Saints, Berit Olam, the Focus on Theology study program, the International Bible Commentary, The Bible Today, Sister's Today, Worship, New Theology Review, Liturgical Ministry, and Journal of Hispanic/Latino Theology magazines. Call for a free catalog.

LTP
LITURGY TRAINING PUBLICATIONS

LITURGY TRAINING PUBLICATIONS
1800 N. Hermitage Avenue
Chicago, IL 60622-1101
Tel.: 800-933-1800; FAX: 800-933-7094
email: orders@ltp.org

Personnel:
Gabe Huck .... Director
John D. Wright .... General Manager
Jennifer Odegard .... Marketing Director

Type of Business:
LTP provides materials that assist parishes, institutions and households in the preparation and celebration of liturgy in Christian life. In its products and its operation, LTP strives to express the justice and beauty that are fundamental to the church and to its liturgy. Publications include Workbook for Lectors and Gospel Readers, Sourcebook for Sundays and Seasons, At Home with the Word, Children's Daily Prayer, The Basics of Ministry Series, Catechumenate magazine, Rite, E&A Newsletter and ¡Gracias!.

LORETO PUBLICATIONS
P.O. Box 603
Fitzwilliam, New Hampshire 03447
Tel.: 603-239-6671
Fax: 603-239-6127
E-Mail: loretopubs@myexcel.com

Personnel:
Douglas Bersaw ....President
Brian Kelly ....Bookstore Sales
Joshua Smart...Retail Sales
Christopher Sarsfield ....Production

Type of Business:
Loreto publishes and distributes Catholic Books of all types for the retail and wholesale trade. Recent titles include: The Roman Martyrology, The Liturgical Year by Dom Guéranger, Our Glorious Popes by Sr. Catherine MICM, The Continuity of Religion by Bishop Boussuet, The Catena Aurea of St. Thomas Aquinas, The Commentary on the Psalms by St. Robert Bellarmine, Fish on Friday by Fr. Leonard Feeney, The Sacred Heart by St. John Eudes, and many others.

Call or write for a listing of titles.

MAETA

MAETA
PO Box 6012
Metairie, LA 70009-6012
Tel.: 888-577-4428; FAX: 504-833-5272

Personnel:
V.A. Muller ....Director

Type of Business:
Pamphlets, books and audio-visual material, especially Bible study; apologetics; traditional (indult) Mass, including missals and priest-related study and other relevant issues. MAETA distributes a selection of other books such as THERESE' & LISIEUX, a unique book, featuring poignant glimpes into the spirituality of St. Therese', a chronology around her life, brief family genealogy, plus 600 colored photos. $75. Buy it because it's beautiful--for that special someone! Also excellent, JACINTA, $3 plus others.

See our display ad this page.

MAETA

MAETA
PO BOX 6012
METAIRIE LA 70009-6012
Toll Free: 1-888-577-4428 Fax: 504-833-5272

Personnel: V. A. Muller .... Director

Type of business:
Pamphlets, books, audio-visual material, especially Bible study; apologetics; traditional (indult) Mass, including missals and priest-related study and other relevant issues.

Bookstore discounts: 20--50% A few books: GOD'S WORD (Hardback $16); THE MASS THAT MADE PADRE PIO $15; The ABBOT on LITURGY $12; Holy MARY Holy MASS $10; MY BASIC MISSAL $8. Pamphlets: Canonized Mass History & Law; Faith Hope Charity; Keep the Faith; Gestating into Heaven. $3 each. Books are easy reading, large print, ideal for school and seminary libraries. YES, we have Fr. Stedman's MY SUNDAY MISSAL! $10

MAETA distributes a selection of other books such as THERESE' & LISIEUX, a unique book, featuring poignant glimpses into the spirituality of St. Therese`, a chronology around her life, brief family genealogy, plus 600 colored photos. $75. Buy it because it's beautiful-- for that special someone! Also excellent, JACINTA, $3 plus others.

Our Sunday Visitor, Inc.

OUR SUNDAY VISITOR, INC.
200 Noll Plaza
Huntington, IN 46750
Tel.: 800-348-2886; 219-356-8400
FAX: 800-442-0669; 219-356-8472
Web Site: www.osv.com

Personnel:
Greg Erlandson ....President, Publishing Division
Kyle Hamilton..................President, Offering Envelope Division
Jill Kurtz ....Marketing Director, Publishing Division
Julie Kenny .....Marketing Manager, Offering Envelope Division

Type of Business:
Our Sunday Visitor, Inc. is a not-for-profit organization providing thousands of parishes with a wide variety of Catholic:

- Books
- Magazines
- Offering Envelope Products and Services
- Religious Education Products
- Stewardship Products and Services

Pauline BOOKS & MEDIA
www.pauline.org

PAULINE BOOKS & MEDIA
50 Saint Paul's Avenue
Boston, MA 02130
Tel.: 617-522-8911; FAX: 617-541-9805
Website: www.pauline.org

Type of Business:
PAULINE Books & Media is the publishing house of the Daughters of St. Paul, an international Congregation of women religious who serve the Church with the communications media. The Daughters of St. Paul operate twenty bookstores in the U.S. and Canada. Visit our website, www.pauline.org, to access our on line catalog and for a complete listing of our bookstores.

PAULIST PRESS
997 Macarthur Blvd.
Mahwah, NJ 07430
Tel.: 201-825-7300; FAX: 201-825-8345
Web Site: www.paulistpress.com

Personnel:
Rev. Lawrence Boadt, CSP ....Publisher
John A. Thomas ....Director of Marketing and Sales
Maria L. Maggi..Managing Editor

Type of Business:
Paulist Press, a leading publisher of theology, spirituality, self-help, ethics and children's books, provides quality Catholic magazines and inexpensive religious paperbacks to parishes through its Unified Magazine Program and Guaranteed Paperback Service.

APOLOGETICS

CAI

CATHOLIC APOLOGETICS INTERNATIONAL
P.O. Box 7146
Alexandria, VA 22307
Tel.: 800-531-6393
Web Site: www.catholicintl.com

Personnel:
Robert Sungenis M.A ....President
John Pacheco...V.P. Canada
Michael Lopez ....Apologist
John Dorcy..Apologist

Type of Business:
Catholic Apologetics International is a theologically conservative apostolate, teaching and defending the faith as defined by the Catholic Magisterium. CAI produces programs on EWTN with host Robert Sungenis; radio programs on the Catholic Family Network; books through Queenship Publishing; the Internet Bible Study; audio and video tapes; formal debates; seminars and conferences across North America; and personal counseling by telephone and email. All of our services can be found at our website: www.catholicintl.com.

BOOKS & RELIGIOUS ARTICLES

MAETA

MAETA
PO Box 6012
Metairie, LA 70009-6012
Tel.: 888-577-4428; FAX: 504-833-5272

Personnel:
V.A. Muller ....Director

Type of Business:
Pamphlets, books and audio-visual material, especially Bible study; apologetics; traditional (indult) Mass, including missals and priest-related study and other relevant issues. MAETA distributes a selection of other books such as THERESE' & LISIEUX, a unique book, featuring poignant glimpes into the spirituality of St. Therese', a chronology around her life, brief family genealogy, plus 600 colored photos. $75. Buy it because it's beautiful--for that special someone! Also excellent, JACINTA, $3 plus others.

See our display ad on page 121r.

Our Sunday Visitor, Inc.

OUR SUNDAY VISITOR, INC.
200 Noll Plaza
Huntington, IN 46750
Tel.: 800-348-2886; 219-356-8400
FAX: 800-442-0669; 219-356-8472
Web Site: www.osv.com

Personnel:
Greg Erlandson ....President, Publishing Division
Kyle Hamilton..................President, Offering Envelope Division
Jill Kurtz ....Marketing Director, Publishing Division
Julie Kenny .....Marketing Manager, Offering Envelope Division

Type of Business:
Our Sunday Visitor, Inc. is a not-for-profit organization providing thousands of parishes with a wide variety of Catholic:
- Books
- Magazines
- Offering Envelope Products and Services
- Religious Education Products
- Stewardship Products and Services

Pauline
BOOKS & MEDIA
www.pauline.org

PAULINE BOOKS & MEDIA
50 Saint Paul's Avenue
Boston, MA 02130
Tel.: 617-522-8911; FAX: 617-541-9805
Website: www.pauline.org

Type of Business:
PAULINE Books & Media is the publishing house of the Daughters of St. Paul, an international Congregation of women religious who serve the Church with the communications media. The Daughters of St. Paul operate twenty bookstores in the U.S. and Canada. Visit our website, www.pauline.org, to access our on line catalog and for a complete listing of our bookstores.

PRESERVING CHRISTIAN PUBLICATIONS, INC.
P.O. Box 221
Boonville, New York 13309-0221
Tel.: 315-942-6338; FAX: 315-942-6938
E-mail: info@pcbooks.com

Personnel:
Gerard Maicher..President
John Parrot...Secretary
Brian Pouliot ....Treasurer

Type of Business:
DON'T THROW OUT YOUR CATHOLIC BOOKS! We will purchase your used/old Catholic books. Since 1988, we have provided hundreds of institutions, as well as individuals, with an outlet for their no-longer needed Catholic books. We in turn will find a new home for these books. The purpose of our work is to preserve our Catholic literary heritage by collecting and redistributing Catholic books that might be discarded. If you would like to sell your Catholic books, please contact us.

SFI

SAN FRANCIS IMPORTS, INC.
1919 N. Victory Place
Burbank, CA 91504-3425
Tel.: 800-882-4916; FAX: 800-692-9129
Web Site: www.sanfrancis.com

Personnel:
Tirso George ....President
Carlos George ....Vice President Sales
Joseph Gamgene...Marketing

Type of Business:
San Francis Imports is an importer and manufacturer of fine religious articles. For the retailer we carry the most complete line offering for the American and Hispanic market for baby, baby shower, Baptism, First Communion, Confirmation, Quinceañera, wedding and memorial remembrances. We guarantee the widest selection of gifts at the lowest competitive prices.

MAGAZINES & JOURNALS

INSIDE THE VATICAN / URBI ET ORBI COMMUNICATIONS

3050 Gap Knob Rd.
New Hope, KY 40052
Tel.: 800-789-9494; FAX: 270-325-3091

ROME office:
Via delle Mura Aurelie 7c
00165 Rome Italy
Tel.: 39-06-3938-7471; FAX: 39-06-638-1316
E-mail: editor@insidethevatican.com
Website: www.insidethevatican.com

Personnel:
Robert Moynihan ....Editor of "Inside the Vatican"
Genevieve Kineke ....Editor of "Canticle"
Robert Moynihan ....President, Urbi Et Orbi Communications

Type of Business:
"Inside the Vatican" has become the world's leading English-language magazine reporting from the Vatican. Its editorial thrust is not based on liberal or conservative agendas. Award-winning photography and artwork make this publication one of the most beautiful as well as informative magazines in print. Also Available: "Catechism of the Catholic Church" and beautiful papal calendars with photos by Gzegorz Galazka. Our sister publication: "Canticle"- The Voice of Today's Catholic Woman.

LITURIGICAL PUBLICATIONS, INC.
2875 S. James Drive
New Berlin, WI 53151
Tel.: 800-876-4574; FAX: 414-785-9567
Website: www.litpub.com

Personnel:
Craig Polack ....President
Glenn Roskilly ....Chief Operating Officer
Bill Knaapen ....Chief Financial Officer
Michelle Jacobson ....Vice President of Administration

Type of Business:
For over a quarter of a century, Liturgical Publications, Inc. has been helping thousands of churches and 100,000 advertisers deliver their message. We provide all the tools, training, resources, and assistance for you to communicate more effectively and economically. To learn more about how we can help you, call us, or visit our Website at: www.litpub.com.

NATIONAL CATHOLIC REPORTER PUBLISHING CO.
115 E. Armour Blvd.
Kansas City, MO 64111
Tel.: 800-333-7373 (customer service); 800-444-8910 (list rental and advertising); FAX: 816-968-2268
E-mail: ncrsub@natcath.com
Website: www.natcath.com

Personnel:
Tom Fox...Publisher
Joyce Ford..List Rental
Vicki Breashears ....Advertising

Type of Business:
National Catholic Reporter, the independent and courageous newsweekly, is the first place to find injustices unveiled, changes fought for and hope restored. Your source for news on the church and the world.

Celebration, an ecumenical worship resource, provides unparalleled scripture exegesis, liturgical ideas and ground-breaking articles.

Eucharistic Minister, The Catechist's Connection and The Caring Community effectively train, support and inspire your valued volunteers each month.

Mailing lists available: Ideal for fundraisers, publishers and religious goods.

Pauline
BOOKS & MEDIA
www.pauline.org

PAULINE BOOKS & MEDIA
50 Saint Paul's Avenue
Boston, MA 02130
Tel.: 617-522-8911; FAX: 617-541-9805
Website: www.pauline.org

Type of Business:
PAULINE Books & Media is the publishing house of the Daughters of St. Paul, an international Congregation of women religious who serve the Church with the communications media. The Daughters of St. Paul operate twenty bookstores in the U.S. and Canada. Visit our website, www.pauline.org, to access our online catalog and for a complete listing of our bookstores.

THE TABLET
the international Catholic weekly

THE TABLET PUBLISHING COMPANY LTD.
1 King St. Cloisters
Clifton Walk
London W6 OQZ
United Kingdom
Tel.: (011 44) 20 8 748 8484; FAX: (011 44) 20 8 563 7644
E-mail: market@tablet.netkonect.co.uk
Web Site: www.thetablet.co.uk

Personnel:
Hugh Kealy .... Publisher
Eva Langan .... Subscriptions
Matthew Blythe .... Advertising Manager
Sarah Blackburn .... Back issues, binders & indexes

Type of Business:
The Tablet is the international Catholic weekly, reporting on world Church news as well as informing and entertaining on issues of the day. The discussion of politics, current affairs, religion, science, literature and biography provides a forum for international debate and is combined with a comprehensive books and arts review section.
Parish Sales:
Copies can be supplied for sale in the parish. Please call Hugh Lally (collect) at Paulist Press on 0-201-825-7300.

WLP WORLD LIBRARY PUBLICATIONS

WORLD LIBRARY PUBLICATIONS
3825 N. Willow Road
Schiller Park, IL 60176
Tel.: 800-566-6150; FAX: 800-621-5197
Web Site: www.wlp.jspaluch.com

Personnel:
Mary Prete .... General Manager
Mary Beth Kunde Anderson .... Editorial Director
Fred Vipond .... Marketing Director
Peter Caragiulo .... Sales Representative

Type of Business:
World Library Publications exists to provide worship and music resources of the highest quality. Faithful to its heritage as a pioneer in liturgical renewal, WLP continues to support, assist and form worship and music leaders. publisher of the nation's finest missals- Seasonal Missalette, We Celebrate, and Celebremos! - WLP also produces the We Celebrate Hymnal,Peoples Mass Book, and Voices as One. In addition, WLP publishes music for worship including choral octavos, mass settings, songbooks and instrument scores, and produces quality recordings of music for wirship meditation and spiritual norishment. WLP's innovative website facilitates complete liturgical planning.

PARISH DIRECTORIES

Lifetouch® CHURCH DIRECTORIES AND PORTRAITS

LIFETOUCH CHURCH DIRECTORIES AND PORTRAITS
11000 Viking Drive, Suite 460
Eden Prairie, MN 55344-7244
Tel.: 877-703-9483; Fax: 952-826-4226
Website: www.lifetouch.com

Personnel:
Jay Johnston .... Director of Sales and Operation Development
Renee Belina .... Director of Marketing

Type of Business:
A parish pictorial directory highlights your ministries and activities, documents your history, and best of all, connects your parishioners. Entrust your parish directory and family portraits to the best, Lifetouch. With our new Fellowship Directory™ Program, producing a directory is easy, fast, and fun. *Added Bonuses*: Your directory is provided to your parish *at no cost*. Plus, every family photographed recieves a FREE directory and a FREE custom 8x10 portrait!

olan mills® PORTRAIT STUDIOS We Make It Special

OLAN MILLS CHURCH DIVISION
4325 Amnicola Highway
Chattanooga, TN 37406
Tel.: 800-845-1157; FAX: 423-629-8106
Website: www.olanmills.com

Personnel:
A. W. Lanford .... Vice President, Sales

Type of Business:
You can trust America's largest Church Directory publisher. A full color pictorial directory by Olan Mills, IS the Number One Parish communication tool. It's delivered in 45 days and we help you all the way. Each family receives an Olan Mills custom 8x10 portrait AND a copy of the directory FREE.

Special 1999-2000 Millennium directories: Mention this offer: Code KEN 599 and receive 2 Extra Color pages plus 50 additional directories FREE.

PHOTOGRAPHY

Lifetouch®

CHURCH DIRECTORIES AND PORTRAITS

LIFETOUCH CHURCH DIRECTORIES AND PORTRAITS
11000 Viking Drive, Suite 460
Eden Prairie, MN 55344-7244
Tel.: 877-703-9483; Fax: 952-826-4226
Website: www.lifetouch.com

Personnel:
Jay Johnston........Director of Sales and Operation Development
Renee Belina..Director of Marketing

Type of Business:
Lifetouch, the largest employee-owned photography company in the world, has provided high quality portraits and services to families for nearly 65 years. Our customer-friendly portrait experience and our commitment to quality and service ensure your parish members loving portrait memories they will treasure for years to come. We offer your families a variety of poses, portrait finishes and sizes, and even frames- all at attractive prices!

olan mills®

PORTRAIT STUDIOS

We Make It Special

OLAN MILLS, INC.
4325 Amnicola Highway
Chattanooga, TN 37406
Tel.: 800-845-1157; FAX: 423-629-8106
Website: www.olanmills.com

Personnel:
Richard Restiano ....Director, of Marketing

Type of Business:
Olan Mills is the premier portrait company in America, with studios across the nation. Families, for over 65 years, have enjoyed our professionalism and exceptional quality.
The Church Division provides this same quality product when photographing your families for a parish directory. All work is 100% satisfaction guaranteed. Special discount prices are made available to parish families.

SUNDAY BULLETINS

DIOCESAN PUBLICATIONS
TRINITY PUBLICATIONS
" Communication specialists dedicated to serving the Church"

DIOCESAN PUBLICATIONS & TRINITY PUBLICATIONS

Diocesan Publications	Trinity Publications
7120 South Division Avenue	8416 N. Interregional Hwy.
Grand Rapids, MI 49548	Austin, TX 78753
Tel.: 800-783-1623	Tel.: 800-633-1122
FAX 616-455-7700	FAX 512-835-0886
Website: www.diocesan.com	www.trinitypublications.com

Offices in Michigan, Ohio, Pennsylvania, Florida, & Texas

Personnel:
Carl Galant .... President
Kevin Stapleton .... Executive Vice President
Vicki Wells Bedard .... Director, CMR

Type of Business:
Weekly Sunday Bulletin Publishing: Telecommunications & publishing software, full color covers, multi-page layout, inserts, flyers. On-site training.
Church Management Resources: certified, licensed Churchmouse Software™ and Parish Data System, Inc. vendor and CatholicWeb.com™ distributor. Quality church, school & religious education management software. Training, installation, newsletter, custom reports, data transfers, scanning services, CASS certification, and more . . .

Free demos and informational packets available.

YEARBOOKS

olan mills
PORTRAIT STUDIOS
We Make It Special

OLAN MILLS CHURCH DIVISION
4325 Amnicola Highway
Chattanooga, TN 37406
Tel.: 800-845-1157; FAX: 423-629-8106
Website: www.olanmills.com

Personnel:
Richard Restiano .... Director of Marketing

Type of Business:
Olan Mills is the nation's leading producer of full color pictorial parish directories. Each edition can commemorate a significant Anniversary, or become the special Jubilee 2000 Millennium edition. It will become a treasured keepsake for years to come. There is no cost to the parish and each family photographed receives a free copy of the directory and a free color 8x10 portrait. Mention this ad - KEN599 to receive an additional bonus.

School Annual
THE YEARBOOK SPECIALISTS

SCHOOL ANNUAL PUBLISHING COMPANY
545 Walnut Street, P.O. Box 58
Coshocton, OH 43812
Tel.: 800-436-6030; FAX: 800-436-6048
E-mail: yearbook@schoolannual.com
Web Site: www.schoolannual.com

Personnel:
Nancy Stone .... Vice President, Chief Operating Officer
Jackie Ogle .... Manager, Inquiry Services

Type of Business:
School Annual Publishing Company introduces full color yearbooks to the current line of high quality black and white yearbooks. Our new color yearbooks are designed to be every bit as colorful as the memories within them. Our yearbooks are a great value - providing you with high quality books at great prices... And with 53 years of experience, School Annual Publishing represents... *all you need to remember.*

For more information, visit us at www.schoolannual.com or call us at 800-436-6030 to request a FREE information kit *and samples!*

WEBSITE HOSTING & DEVELOPMENT

CatholicWeb.com
www.CatholicWeb.com
Connecting the Catholic Faith Online!

CATHOLICWEB.COM
108 Chapman Avenue
Sanford, FL 32771
Tel.: 407-322-8654; FAX 407-322-1714
E-mail: support@CatholicWeb.com

Type of Business:
CatholicWeb.com offers FREE Web sites to Catholic churches, organizations and schools, Web-based E-mail, and online National Catholic Directories. Update your parish mass times, contact information, and pastor/staff listing instantly! Visit CatholicWeb.com for other services like online Prayer Intentions, Catholic Media Partners, and Fund-raising programs. Your parish can now get a powerful and professional Internet presence! It's easy to set-up and easy to maintain. No web authorizing skills required- anyone can do it!

For more information E-mail: support@catholicweb.com

Powered by EZWebonline.com™, a division of CompBiz, Inc.

GOLDEN DOME MEDIA
P.O. Box 1616
South Bend, IN 46637-3357
Tel.: 800-782-7979; FAX: 219-631-1212
E-mail: goldendome@wndu.com
Web Site: www.goldendomemedia.com

Personnel:
Patrick Palella .... Director
Jim Ford, Lisa Gillespie,
Michael O' Leary, Betsy Tavernier .... Account Executives

Type of Business:
Golden Dome Media is a diverse group of professional storytellers with an award-winning talent for presenting ideas, products and services. Golden Dome Media is a full service production house with twenty years experience which offers everything from building sets to producing documentaries, from staging live events to producing video and interactive services. We work hand-in-hand with you to inform, educate and inspire.

SHAW CARTIER

SHAW CARTIER
PO Box 51746
Phoenix, AZ 85076
Tel.: 602-437-4360 vm; 602-470-0060
E-mail: sc1@shawcartier.com/
Website: http://www.shawcartier.com/

Type of Business:
Web intra/internet design and development, with unique graphic presentation exclusive to each site. We will also maintain and update preexisting web sites. Design, prep and distribution of CD brochure-ware, and postcard production. Holy cards are designed and produced in quantities starting at 5,000. All business services are free to papal cloisters. Catholic-related web sites may also be added to our Catholic portal free of charge.

INTERNET SERVICES

CATHEDRAL CORPORATION
Griffiss Technology Park
632 Ellsworth Road
Rome, NY 13441
Phone: (315) 338-0021
Fax: (315) 338-5874
Web Site: www:cathedralstewardship.com
E-mail: sales@cathedralstewardship.com

Personnel:
Marianne W. Gaige .... President and COO
Larry J. Beasley .... Director of Marketing
Ronald P. Blakeman .... Director of Sales

Business description:

Cathedral Corporation is a leader in the creation, printing, personalization, and high volume mailing of church envelopes and stewardship programs. Our customer base has grown for more than six decades. Today we serve churches nationwide with a full range of stewardship resources and electronic services for the internet.

GOLDEN DOME MEDIA
P.O. Box 1616
South Bend, IN 46637-3357
Tel.: 800-782-7979; FAX: 219-631-1212
E-mail: goldendome@wndu.com
Web Site: www.goldendomemedia.com

Personnel:
Patrick Palella .... Director
Jim Ford, Lisa Gillespie,
Michael O' Leary, Betsy Tavernier .... Account Executives

Type of Business:
Golden Dome Media is a diverse group of professional storytellers with an award-winning talent for presenting ideas, products and services. Golden Dome Media is a full service production house with twenty years experience which offers everything from building sets to producing documentaries, from staging live events to producing video and interactive services. We work hand-in-hand with you to inform, educate and inspire.

PROFESSIONAL ASSOCIATIONS & ORGANIZATIONS

NAVY
accelerate your life

NAVY CHAPLAIN CORPS
Commander, Navy Recruiting Command
5722 Integrity Drive, Bldg. 784
Millington, TN 38054-5057
Tel: (901) 874-9216 or Toll Free: 866-484-5232
E-mail: CarrG@cnrc.navy.mil
Web Site: www.navy.com/professionals

Personnel:

CDR Gary Carr, CHC, USN ....Program Manager
LCDR Michael Parisi, CHC, USN ....Chaplain Recruiter
ParisiM@cnrc.navy.mil
LCDR Herb Griffin, CHC, USN ....Chaplain Recruiter
GriffinH@cnrc.navy.mil
LT Heinz Malon, CHC, USN.........................Chaplain Recruiter
MalonH@cnrc.navy.mil
LT Kimberly Sawatsky, CHC, USN ....Chaplain Recruiter
SawatskyK@cnrc.navy.mil

Type of Business:

Navy Chaplains serve both the Church and Country in diverse ministry settings. Chaplains provide spiritual guidance to members of the Navy, Marine Corps and Coast Guard. We offer leadership positions in ministry for the spiritual well being of the whole community. Priest Chaplains provide sacramental and spiritual support for Catholics in the military and care for all. Working closely with clergy from other faith traditions, we cooperate with each other without compromising our own faith and practice. Navy Chaplains experience the joy of ministry with young people. We have a program for seminarians, the Naval Reserve, and for full-time, active-duty positions. Contact the chaplain recruiters listed above for more information.

www.navy.com 1-800-USA-NAVY

Priests For Life

PRIESTS FOR LIFE
PO Box 141172
Staten Island, NY 10314
Tel: 888-PFL-3448 or 718-980-4400; FAX: 718-980-6515
E-mail: mail@priestsforlife.org
Web Site: www.priestsforlife.org

Type of Business:

Priests for Life exists to help you preach sensitively and challenge effectively, in the context of Sacred Scripture, and of a consistent ethic of life.

- Resources:
- Networking with Priests Worldwide
- Seminars on Abortion
- Regular Newsletter
- Pro-Life Strategies
- Consultation
- Organizing Activities

Subscribe to our bi-weekly column (free) at:
subscribe@priestsforlife.org

FRATERNAL ORGANIZATIONS

AIR FORCE Chaplain SERVICE

AIR FORCE CHAPLAIN RECRUITING SERVICE
HQ AFRS/RSOCC
550 D Street West Ste 1
Randolph AFB TX 78150-4527
Tel.: 800-803-2452
john.kinney@rs.af.mil / howard.stendahl@rs.af.mil

Personnel:

Ch, Lt. Col. Howard D. Stendahl
....Chief, Chaplain Accessions Section
Ch, Maj. John M. Kinney
....Deputy, Chaplain Accessions Section

Type of Business:

Air Force chaplains ensure the free exercise of religion for the globally engaged Air Force community. Catholics make up approximately 30% of the military. Priest chaplains are particularly responsible for the spiritual and the sacramental needs of Catholics in the military setting. Because the Catholic Chaplain lives the same challenging demands of military life, he can truly respond. The Air Force offers the qualified priest many opportunities to serve both the Church and the country in a pluralistic global environment.

Chaplains remain steadfast witnesses of the holy in a changing world environment. Consider the possibility of serving as a priest and an officer in the United States Air Force. For more information, please contact the above office.

KNIGHTS OF COLUMBUS
Supreme Council Office
1 Columbus Plaza
New Haven, CT 06510-3326
Tel.: 203-772-2130
Web Site: www.kofc.org

Supreme Council Officers:
- Carl A. Anderson................Supreme Knight
- Bishop Thomas V. Daily................Supreme Chaplain
- Jean B. Migneault................Deputy Supreme Knight
- Charles H. Foos................Supreme Secretary
- Kenneth N. Ryan................Supreme Treasurer
- Pat A. Cipollone................Supreme Advocate
- Terry Archbold................Supreme Warden

Type of Business:
The Knights of Columbus is the world's largest Catholic family fraternal service organization. Father Michael J. McGivney (1852-90), assistant pastor at St. Mary's Church, New Haven, Conn., founded the fraternal benefit society in 1882 with a group of parishioners. The organization was chartered to assist the widows and orphans of deceased members through a life insurance program and instill in members a heightened sense of pride in their Catholic faith. Since then, the Knights has grown into a worldwide organization with more than 1.6 million members and their families. Annually, Knights orderwide raise and contribute more than $100 million and volunteer more than 50 million hours of service to Church and community charities. The Order's insurance program consistently receives top ratings from independent review services.

PRIVATE ASSOCIATIONS OF LAY FAITHFUL

ST. LAWRENCE MISSION
14951 Haggerty Rd.
Plymouth, MI 48170
Tel.: 734-207-1751

Personnel:
- Judy LaManna................Chair
- Katharine O. Alberts................Founder
- Randy Eiffa................Vice Chairman
- Lawrence Sutherland................Trustee
- Joe Wood................Treasurer
- Sue Brukewinski................Secretary
- Father Tuffuor................Chaplain

Type of Business:
St. Lawrence Mission, knowing that God is in charge, ministers to the poor in body, mind or spirit by providing a link to any help and services they need.
This includes but is not limited to:
- aid of support groups that are already in place
- providing access to temporal and spiritual services
- providing for emergencies
- coordinating community concerns, resources, programs and projects
- supporting individuals with needs
- performing other appropriate tasks as needed

CLASSROOM SEATING

ATD-AMERICAN CO.

ATD-AMERICAN CO.
135 Greenwood Avenue
Wyncote, PA 19095-1396
Tel.: 888-283-2487; FAX: 800-283-7363
E-mail: american@atd.com
Web Site: www.atd.com

Personnel:
- Bob Roche................Marketing
- Sal Catanese................Sales

Type of Business:
For four generations, ATD-AMERICAN has supplied Furniture and Equipment to Churches, Organizations and Institutions nationally and worldwide. Since 1931, it has been our tradition to deliver high quality products and personal service at the lowest competitive prices. ATD offers a wide range of products to meet all of the needs of your Church and School. Our comprehensive catalog includes the following: Announcement and Bulletin Boards, Audio-Visual Equipment, Classroom Furniture, Computer Furniture, Daycare Furniture, Display Cases, Folding Chairs, Folding Tables, Lecterns, Library Furniture, Office Furniture, Outdoor Equipment, Pews and Pulpit Furniture, Room Dividers and Partitions, Stacking Chairs, and Stages and Risers.

For a FREE Wholesale Furniture Catalog, call us toll-free 888-283-2487 or fax us at 800-283-7363. You can also visit our website at http://www.atd.com or email us at atd.com.

SPECIAL OFFER FOR CATHOLIC DIRECTORY SUBSCRIBERS: Mention offer code 6557 and receive a special 10% discount on your first order.
See our ad on the opposite page.

St. Anthony's CHURCH SUPPLIES

ST. ANTHONY'S CHURCH SUPPLIES
3121 McCart Ave.
Fort Worth, TX 76110
Tel: 800-772-5928
E-mail: books4u@airmail.net
Web Site: www.StellaMarisBooks.com

Type of Business:
We can supply your church or chapel with the finest sanctuary appointments available. We offer a full line of ecclesiastical goods from clerical shirts and vestments, to chalices and tabernacles, to church statuary and stained glass windows, to Catholic books and other media, to furniture for churches, church offices, classrooms, and cafeterias.

We offer great service with a smile and look forward to making new friends.

Please use our toll free number or e-mail to contact John Heitzenrater or Richard Myers.

The problem is the disease, not the priest.

Alcoholism and addiction breed isolation, confusion, anger, and despair. The chemically dependent clergyman or religious is often very defensive and resistant to accepting help. He will put the blame for his problems on everything but the substance that he abuses. His disease tells him he cannot live without it. And he believes his disease. That's why he can't seem to change. He needs professional help in a safe, affirming environment.

Guest House treats both the problem and the priest.

- The Guest House program is designed to effectively treat chemical dependency in an atmosphere which affirms the special nature of the priesthood.
- We base our treatment on the 12-step recovery program of Alcoholics Anonymous.
- Our recovery rate is outstanding. A recent study shows that more than 90% of those who undergo primary treatment at Guest House are still abstinent after 18 months (Chart 1). A majority of vicars and superiors rate the Guest House experience as excellent (Chart 2).
- We provide an evaluation for any Catholic priest or religious in order to determine the extent of an addiction – or if indeed there is an addiction.
- We use the medical resources of the world-renowned Mayo Clinic.
- **No priest is turned away because of the inability to pay.**

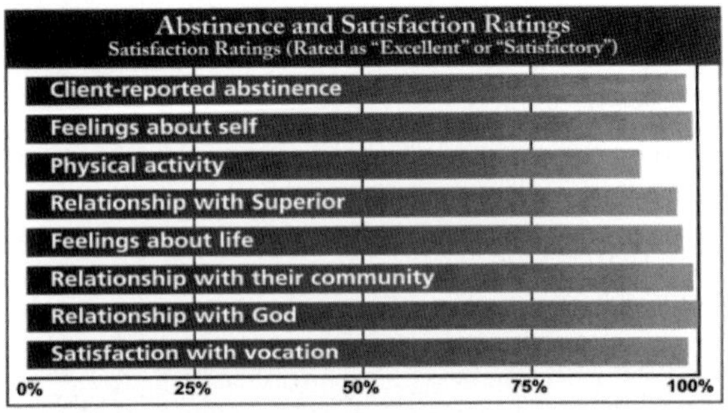

Chart 2.

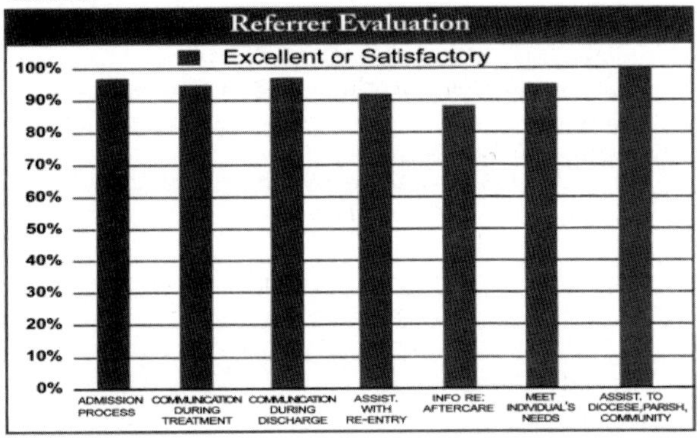

The Staff: The treatment team includes certified chemical dependency counselors, physicians, nurses, psychiatrists, psychologists, a dietician, and an exercise instructor.

The facility: Our environment is friendly, non-threatening, and spiritually affirming. The grounds and buildings are attractive and non-clinical. The atmosphere of quiet serenity is conducive to recovery.

The Mission: For more than four decades we have been dedicated to treating clergy and religious for addictive disease and restoring them to productive, spirit-filled lives.

Interventions:

Before confronting an alcoholic or an addict, you should get professional advice. Interventions can be difficult for all involved. But they can save lives and vocations. We have the expertise to advise and help you.

Call us 24 hours a day, 7 days a week at:

1-800-634-4155

GuestHouse®

SPECIAL CARE FACILITIES

GUEST HOUSE, INC.
1601 Joslyn Rd., P.O. Box 420
Lake Orion, MI 48361
Tel.: 800-626-6910; 248-391-4445; FAX:248-391-0210
email: info@guesthouse.org

LAKE ORION CENTER
(For Women Religious)
P.O. Box 68
Lake Orion, MI 48361
Tel.: 800-626-6910; 248-391-3100; FAX: 248-391-1553
email: guestmae@ic.net

ROCHESTER TREATMENT CENTER
(For priests, deacons, brothers & seminarians)
P.O. Box 954
Rochester, MN 55903
Tel.: 800-634-4155; 507-288-4693; FAX: 507-288-1240
email: ghousemn@infonet.isl.net

Personnel:
Daniel A. Kidd..................President and Chief Executive Officer
Sr. Mae Kierans, CSJ............................Director, Lake Orion, MI
Bill Morgan, C.C.D.C.R. ....VP Clinical Oper., Rochester, MN
Gerard O'Connor..Director of Marketing

Type of Business:

Guest House, Inc. is a lay-owned, lay-operated nonprofit corporation established in 1956. With the approbation of the Catholic hierachy, it operates special residential treatment centers for alcoholic Catholic priests, deacons, brothers, sisters and seminarians from all over the world.

Catholic women religious are treated in Guest House in Lake Orion, Michigan. The facility in Rochester, Minnesota has treatment programs for priests, deacons, brothers and seminarians. An important part of the treatment is the beautiful environment of our facilities. Residents respond to the quiet serenity of the surroundings to help in their recovery not only physically and emotionally, but spiritually as well.

Surveys are conducted regularly to determine how our graduates are doing. The 1997 survey shows that after a year and a half, over 90% report they are doing well and abstaining from all drugs and alcohol.

Generous donors have established an endowment fund to provide financial assistance for any diocese or religious community needing assistance with the costs of treatment. Treatment is provided without regard to financial consideration.

The facilities are accredited by JCAHO (Joint Commission on Accreditation of Healthcare Organizations) and licensed by the Department of Public Health in the states of Michigan and Minnesota respectively.

Guest House also offers educational programs, seminars, and workshops on addition-related topics.

CHILDREN'S HOSPITALS

CARDINAL GLENNON CHILDREN'S HOSPITAL
Office of Gift Planning
1465 South Grand Blvd.
St. Louis, MO 63104
Tel.: 314-577-5605
FAX: 314-268-6416

Personnel:
Jim Orsund...Executive Vice President
Roya Bromell......................................Director of Gift Planning

Type of Business:

As America's only full-service, free-standing, Catholic Children's Hospital, Cardinal Glennon Children's Hospital meets the medical needs of children regardless of race, religion, or ability to pay.

See our ad on the next page.

TRAVEL & TOURISM

206 TOURS
325 Middle Country Road
Smithtown, NY 11787
Tel.: 800-206-TOURS; FAX: 516-361-3682
e-mail: info@206tours.com
Website: www.206tours.com

Personnel:
Milanka Pauciullo ....CTC President, 206 Tours
Elena Gorham-Rossi..Manager
Maria Ufret...Sales
Jennifer Hangley..Sales

Type of Business:

206 Tours have serviced hundreds of thousands of Catholic pilgrims to Medjugorje, Lourdes, the Holy Land, Italy and Fatima since 1985. We are dedicated to the needs of the Catholic pilgrim and are unparalleled in our service to these individuals who participate in these journeys of faith. Please feel free to call us for upcoming special Pilgrimages for the year 2000.

BEST CATHOLIC PILGRIMAGES

BEST CATHOLIC PILGRIMAGES
1 East Superior Street
Chicago, IL 60611
Tel.: 800-908-BEST (2378); FAX: 312-944-3352
E-mail: info@bestcatholic.com

Type of Business:

Best Catholic Pilgrimages is a tour operator and land Destination management company that specializes in Customized religious/cultural tours world-wide.

Our professional and highly skilled staff headquartered in Chicago handles with consummate precision, to every detail of our tours, land/air itineraries. Our priorities are directed to our clients' high expectations, personalized needs and total satisfaction.

Plus...ask about our Preferred Partnership Program which develops outstanding Fund Raising events that benefit and bond all participants toward a mutually beneficial goal...Call Today for more information.

Blue Army Tours

P.O. Box 582
Broadway, NJ 08808
Toll-free: 877-513-1917
Tel: 908-689-0971
Fax: 908-689-2489
Website: www.bluearmy.com
E-mail: bluearmytours@juno.com

We are the only official and authorized Blue Army Pilgrimage operator. Our reputation is known, recognized and respected by Catholic pilgrims everywhere.

Type of Business:

We specialize in arranging pilgrimages to the Catholic shrines in Europe. Though our name says tour, make no mistake about it, we are a pilgrimage operator. When you travel with us, your needs for an enriching pilgrimage experience are our concern. All our pilgrimages include the following:

Daily Mass, Travelers Insurance, Round trip airfare from USA to Europe, Double occupancy hotel room, Two meals a day/Three in Fatima, Bus costs in Europe, Porterage/Baggage Handling, Multilingual Tour guide, Blue Army Tours flight bag, Package of assorted religious articles, etc.

PILGRIMAGE
INTERNATIONAL
Catholic Pilgrimage Tours™

PILGRIMAGE INTERNATIONAL—CATHOLIC PILGRIMAGE TOURS
5711 Constitution Avenue
Colorado Springs, CO 80915
Tel.: 800-455-5514; FAX: 719-622-1400

Personnel:
David Roth, MA, STL, STD ....Founder and Chairman
Joel Samy...President
Kevin J. Wright ....Senior Pilgrimage Planner
Assisted by staff and associates across the US, and in Rome, Jerusalem, and elsewhere.

Type of Business:
Pilgrimage International is America's only travel company founded and overseen by a Catholic theologian whose full-time ministry is devoted to pilgrimage. Our senior planner is the best-selling author of Catholic Shrines of Western Europe and Catholic Shrines of Central and Eastern Europe (Liguori, 1997, 1999). Also, we sponsor research and study on pilgrimage and house the largest specialized pilgrimage library in the U.S. We provide top-quality, bona fide Catholic Pilgrimage Tours to the Holy Land, Rome, Fatima, Lourdes, Santiago de Compostela, Our Lady of Guadalupe, and other holy sites around the world, as well as parish and diocesan fund-raising getaways and vacations.

Check out our website, or call us at 1-800-455-5514.

Catholic Travel Centre
Worldwide Tours and Pilgrimages

CATHOLIC TRAVEL CENTRE
444 Riverside Drive, Suite 301
Burbank, CA 91505
Tel.: 800-553-5233; FAX: 818-848-0712
E-mail: info@GoCatholicTravel.com
Website: www.GoCatholicTravel.com

Personnel:
J. Scott Scherer .... President
Carol Jones .... Assistant to the President
Inga Duranovic ....Director of Operations
Natalie Carr...Operations Assistant
Henry Nassim .... CFO
Geri Lemoine...Finance Assistant

Type of Business:
A reputation for extraordinary quality has made Catholic Travel Centre the choice of groups that demand exacting service and exceptional attention to detail.

With meticulous detail, we will plan a one-of-a-kind pilgrimage tour catering to your group's specific interests. We can work within the constraints of any budget.

Our client list includes prestigious Catholic institutions nationwide, returning year-after-year to Catholic Travel Centre. We will gladly provide a reference list.

In the Year 2001, we are celebrating our 10th Anniversary of exceptional service to the traveling Catholic community, and we invite your group's inquiry. Please call us at (800) 553-5233. Or visit our website at: www.GoCatholicTravel.com

CLASSIC PILGRIMAGES
101 Limekiln Pike
Glenside, PA 19038
Tel.: 800-682-3377; FAX 215-886-2228
E-mail: ZS@Gate1Travel.com
Website: www.Gate1Travel.com

Personnel:
Dani Pipano....................President and CEO
Zlatko Stoparic....................Managing Director

Type of Business:
For 19 years Classic Pilgrimages has been organizing quality religious journeys throughout the world for the American Catholic community.

We plan pilgrimages for groups and individuals to the Holyland, Italy, France, Portugal, Spain, Ireland, Greece, Turkey, Egypt and Jordan.

Pilgrimage organizers benefit from our "Best Price Guarantee", generous complimentary policy, special group insurance rates and the services of our offices abroad, including Rome and the Holyland.

Classic Pilgrimages is a proud member of the United States Tour Operators Association and their $1 Million Consumer Protection Plan, assuring our commitment to the highest standard of travel services abroad and the financial security of every passenger.

Please call us to discuss your next pilgrimage plans.

EF EXPLORE AMERICA
EF Center Boston
One Education Street
Cambridge, MA 02141
Tel.: 1-800-297-0298; FAX: 617-619-1805
E-mail: explore@ef.com
Website: www.efamerica.com

Personnel:
Phillip R. Johnson....................President

Type of Business:
EF Explore America will work with you to create the perfect program and itinerary for your World Youth Day group. Thousands of participants have traveled with EF to World Youth Days in Paris and Rome. Our dedication to high quality service and value will make planning your trip easy and your travel experience safe and secure. Our reasonable prices and flexibility allow groups of all sizes to participate in World Youth Day 2002. Call us today to begin planning for this special event.

ISRAEL TOURISM INFORMATION CENTER, N.A.
800 2nd Ave.
New York, NY 10017
Tel.: 888-77-ISRAEL; FAX: 212-499-5665

Type of Business:
Only Israel can offer you the chance to actually experience the wonders of The Bible. From walking the Vin Dolorosa to enjoying a sunset on the Mount of the Beatitudes, Israel has it all. Come visit the land that feels your body and soul. Israel. No one belongs here more than you. For more information on travel to Israel call toll-free 888-77-ISRAEL or visit us at www.goisrael.com.

ITS INTERNATIONAL TOURS
3013 20th Street, Suite B
Metairie, LA 70002
Tel.: 800-359-1931; FAX: 504-837-2920

Personnel:
James Hyland

Type of Business:
ITS is a Catholic Tour Company specializing in pilgrimage travel to the Holy Land and Catholic Shrines around the world. ITS offers monthly catalog departures to the Holy Land, Fatima, Lourdes, Medjugorje, and Rome. ITS can make arrangements for Jubilee Events, Beautification or Canonization Ceremonies, Passion Play tickets at Oberammergau. Free places for Spiritual Directors with as little as 5 paying passengers. All passengers protected by $1Million Dollar USTOA Consumer Protection Plan.

See our display ad in the Pilgrimage Destination Guide

JOURNEYS UNLIMITED
500 Eighth Ave.
New York, NY 10018
Tel.: 800-486-8359; 212-736-2028; FAX: 212-736-8959
email: holytours@worldnet.att.net
Website: http://www.journeys-unlimited.com

West Coast Office:
220 State Street
Los Altos, CA
800-473-HOLY

Personnel:
- Nicholas Mancino............President
- Raymond Masillo............Vice President
- Lucille Sciabarassi............Travel Consultant
- Everett Mansfield............Group Sales
- Total Staff 20

Type of Business:
Serving the Church through Travel. Journeys Unlimited was founded by Raymond Masillo & Nicholas Mancino in 1990. The Management has been arranging Pilgrimages since 1969.
The company's philosophy is that each Pilgrimage be escorted by a spiritual leader in order to transform our tours into Pilgrimages. Our Pilgrimages have been designed to give each participant comfort for recreation and spiritual guidance for RENEWAL.
We also offer tours to Italy, Greece, Turkey, Egypt, Syria, Fatima, Lourdes, Oberammergau, and other Marian Shrines, Jubilee 2000, and World Youth Day.

NAWAS INTERNATIONAL TRAVEL
777 Post Road, Third Floor
Darien, CT 06820-4721
Tel.: 800-221-4984; FAX: 203-655-1577
E-mail: Nawastvl@aol.com

On the West Coast:
1100 Alma Street, Suite 100
Menlo Park, CA 94025-3344
Tel.: 800-288-2688; FAX: 650-322-6485
E-mail: Nawastrvl.aol.com

Personnel:
- Soli Nawas............President
- George Khoury............Executive Vice President (Darien, CT)
- Sami Nawas............Vice President
- Neil Dellis............Vice President

Type of Business:
Nawas International has designed and operated pilgrimages to Rome, the Shrines of Italy, Fatima, Lourdes, the Shrines of Europe, Ireland, the Holy Land and more since 1949. With our dedication to delivering high quality programs at very competitive prices and on-site quality control via our local, Nawas-owned offices, we provide the finest pilgrimages available. We also offer excellent tour host benefits - you can travel FREE with as few as five paying passengers! Thousands of church leaders have organized their travel plans through Nawas. Call us toll-free and we'll show you how to do it, too!

MARANATHA TOURS
13825 N. 32nd Street, Suite 28
Phoenix, AZ 85032
Tel.: 800-545-5533; FAX: 602-788-6182
E-mail: mti@maranathatours.com
Website: www.maranathatours.com

Type of Business:
Marantha Tours, Inc. is the leader in customized Christian pilgrimages, specializing in tours to the Holy Land, Italy, Greece, Spain and Portugal, as well as other sacred sites. With over 30 years experience, our family owned business offers you the opportunity to celebrate Jubilee Year 2000 in Italy or to walk where Jesus walked, letting Him touch your heart as you travel where it all began 2000 years ago. Whether you are an individual wanting to join a group, or are wanting to lead your own group, you can feel confident that Marantha Tours will provide quality service at affordable prices.

PAT TOURS
1285 Riverdale Street
West Springfield, MA 01089
Tel.: 413-747-7702; FAX: 413-747-8114

Type of Business:
Specialists on travel to Poland and Eastern Europe. Twenty seven years experience in operating Pilgrimages for Catholic groups. Divine Mercy Pilgrimages to Poland and Lithuania. Call today for promotional brochures and assistance.

SELECT International

SELECT INTERNATIONAL TOURS & CRUISES
916 Somerset Street
Watchung, NJ 07069
Tel.: 800-571-0884; 908-412-0044; FAX: 908-412-0099

Personnel:
Edita Krunic....................President
Maryanna Kosorich....................Manager

Type of Business:
For the past 15 years, our company has created programs for Catholic churches, choirs, schools and organizations to Europe, Holy Land, and Latin America. In addition to the 60 page catalogue featuring over 45 different itineraries we also offer cruises for groups and custom designed itineraries, based on the group's interests and preferences.
With affiliate offices throughout Europe, Holy Land and Latin America and with a staff that has visited each destination we feature, you will benefit by receiving assistance for your groups from an experienced and friendly staff, staying at excellent hotels, traveling with knowledgeable guides and all at a superior value.

CONFERENCE CENTERS

LifeWay Glorieta Conference Center

LIFEWAY GLORIETA CONFERENCE CENTER
P.O. Box 8, I-25 North Exit 299
Glorieta, NM 87535
Tel.: 1-888-366-5676 x4270; FAX: 505-757-4385
Web Site: www.glorieta.com

Type of Business:
Lifeway Glorieta Conference Center is the perfect setting for conferences, conventions, and church retreats. With three auditoriums ranging from 400 to 2,800 capacities and 60+ conference rooms. Glorieta offers ten distinctive styles of accommodations. Our professional staff will take care of your needs from audio-visual equipment to extra blankets. Glorieta's commitment to you: Our ministry is to serve your ministry, in a safe, secure Christian environment.

SAN DAMIANO CONFERENCE AND RETREAT CENTER
Rt. 1, Box 106
Golconda, IL 62938
Tel.: 618-385-3507; FAX: 618-285-3508

Personnel:
Mark Migas....................Manager
Margie Douglas....................Reservationist
Reverend Robert Vonnahmen....................Director
Craig Simoneaux....................Assistant Director

Type of Business:
San Damiano Retreat Center and Shrine of the Good Shepherd is located in Southern Illinois' Shawnee National Forest high on the bluffs overlooking the Ohio River and Western Kentucky. The shrine hosts seminars, retreats, concerts, conferences, and workshops for groups of all faiths. Featured on the grounds are 26 cottages, 35 foot bronze Good Shepherd statue, XXIII Psalm, Meditation Garden, Stations of the Cross, book and video library as well as conference and visitor center.
San Damiano is independent of Camp Ondessonk and Diocese of Belleville.

PILGRIMAGES

206 Tours

206 TOURS
325 Middle Country Road
Smithtown, NY 11787
Tel.: 800-206-TOURS; FAX: 516-361-3682
e-mail: info@206tours.com
Website: www.206tours.com

Personnel:
Milanka Pauciullo....................CTC President, 206 Tours
Elena Gorham-Rossi....................Manager
Maria Ufret....................Sales
Jennifer Hangley....................Sales

Type of Business:
206 Tours have serviced hundreds of thousands of Catholic pilgrims to Medjugorje, Lourdes, the Holy Land, Italy and Fatima since 1985. We are dedicated to the needs of the Catholic pilgrim and are unparalleled in our service to these individuals who participate in these journeys of faith. Please feel free to call us for upcoming special Pilgrimages for the year 2000.

BEST CATHOLIC PILGRIMAGES

BEST CATHOLIC PILGRIMAGES
1 East Superior Street
Chicago, IL 60611
Tel.: 800-908-BEST (2378); FAX: 312-944-3352
E-mail: info@bestcatholic.com

Type of Business:

Best Catholic Pilgrimages is a tour operator and land Destination management company that specializes in Customized religious/cultural tours world-wide.

Our professional and highly skilled staff headquartered in Chicago handles with consummate precision, to every detail of our tours, land/air itineraries. Our priorities are directed to our clients' high expectations, personalized needs and total satisfaction.

Plus...ask about our Preferred Partnership Program which develops outstanding Fund Raising events that benefit and bond all participants toward a mutually beneficial goal...Call Today for more information.

Blue Army Tours

P.O. Box 582
Broadway, NJ 08808
Toll-free: 877-513-1917
Tel: 908-689-0971
Fax: 908-689-2489
Website: www.bluearmy.com
E-mail: bluearmytours@juno.com

We are the only official and authorized Blue Army Pilgrimage operator. Our reputation is known, recognized and respected by Catholic pilgrims everywhere.

Type of Business:

We specialize in arranging pilgrimages to the Catholic shrines in Europe. Though our name says tour, make no mistake about it, we are a pilgrimage operator. When you travel with us, your needs for an enriching pilgrimage experience are our concern. All our pilgrimages include the following:

Daily Mass, Travelers Insurance, Round trip airfare from USA to Europe, Double occupancy hotel room, Two meals a day/Three in Fatima, Bus costs in Europe, Porterage/Baggage Handling, Multilingual Tour guide, Blue Army Tours flight bag, Package of assorted religious articles, etc.

PILGRIMAGE INTERNATIONAL
Catholic Pilgrimage Tours™

PILGRIMAGE INTERNATIONAL—CATHOLIC PILGRIMAGE TOURS
5711 Constitution Avenue
Colorado Springs, CO 80915
Tel.: 800-455-5514; FAX: 719-622-1400

Personnel:

David Roth, MA, STL, STD ....Founder and Chairman
Joel Samy ....President
Kevin J. Wright ....Senior Pilgrimage Planner
Assisted by staff and associates across the US, and in Rome, Jerusalem, and elsewhere.

Type of Business:

Pilgrimage International is America's only travel company founded and overseen by a Catholic theologian whose full-time ministry is devoted to pilgrimage. Our senior planner is the best-selling author of Catholic Shrines of Western Europe and Catholic Shrines of Central and Eastern Europe (Liguori, 1997, 1999). Also, we sponsor research and study on pilgrimage and house the largest specialized pilgrimage library in the U.S. We provide top-quality, bona fide Catholic Pilgrimage Tours to the Holy Land, Rome, Fatima, Lourdes, Santiago de Compostela, Our Lady of Guadalupe, and other holy sites around the world, as well as parish and diocesan fund-raising getaways and vacations.

Check out our website, or call us at 1-800-455-5514.

Catholic Travel Centre
Worldwide Tours and Pilgrimages

CATHOLIC TRAVEL CENTRE
444 Riverside Drive, Suite 301
Burbank, CA 91505
Tel.: 800-553-5233; FAX: 818-848-0712
E-mail: info@GoCatholicTravel.com
Website: www.GoCatholicTravel.com

Personnel:
J. Scott Scherer .... President
Carol Jones .... Assistant to the President
Inga Duranovic .... Director of Operations
Natalie Carr .... Operations Assistant
Henry Nassim .... CFO
Geri Lemoine .... Finance Assistant

Type of Business:
A reputation for extraordinary quality has made Catholic Travel Centre the choice of groups that demand exacting service and exceptional attention to detail.

With meticulous detail, we will plan a one-of-a-kind pilgrimage tour catering to your group's specific interests. We can work within the constraints of any budget.

Our client list includes prestigious Catholic institutions nationwide, returning year-after-year to Catholic Travel Centre. We will gladly provide a reference list.

In the Year 2001, we are celebrating our 10th Anniversary of exceptional service to the traveling Catholic community, and we invite your group's inquiry. Please call us at (800) 553-5233. Or visit our website at: www.GoCatholicTravel.com

Classic Pilgrimages
International Travel Services

CLASSIC PILGRIMAGES
101 Limekiln Pike
Glenside, PA 19038
Tel.: 800-682-3377; FAX 215-886-2228
E-mail: ZS@Gate1Travel.com
Website: www.Gate1Travel.com

Personnel:
Dani Pipano .... President and CEO
Zlatko Stoparic .... Managing Director

Type of Business:
For 19 years Classic Pilgrimages has been organizing quality religious journeys throughout the world for the American Catholic community.

We plan pilgrimages for groups and individuals to the Holyland, Italy, France, Portugal, Spain, Ireland, Greece, Turkey, Egypt and Jordan.

Pilgrimage organizers benefit from our "Best Price Guarantee", generous complimentary policy, special group insurance rates and the services of our offices abroad, including Rome and the Holyland.

Classic Pilgrimages is a proud member of the United States Tour Operators Association and their $1 Million Consumer Protection Plan, assuring our commitment to the highest standard of travel services abroad and the financial security of every passenger.

Please call us to discuss your next pilgrimage plans.

club europa™

CLUB EUROPA
U.S. Office
802 West Oregon
Urbana, IL 61801
Tel.: 217-344-5863; FAX: 217-344-4072
E-mail: clubeuropa@compuserve.com

Personnel:
Andreas Benz
Marti Auler

Type of Business:
In operation since 1959, CLUB EUROPA is one of the foremost leaders in group travel and Pilgrimages to Europe. We arrange trips for all budgets - from modest to deluxe - and for all ages - youths or senior citizens. If your group has a special European travel program in mind, we can provide a customized itinerary that will satisfy all of its goals. Please call our experienced staff to request a proposal for your next religious tour.

EF Religious Tours

EF EXPLORE AMERICA
EF Center Boston
One Education Street
Cambridge, MA 02141
Tel.: 1-800-297-0298; FAX: 617-619-1805
E-mail: explore@ef.com
Website: www.efamerica.com

Personnel:
Phillip R. Johnson .... President

Type of Business:
EF Explore America will work with you to create the perfect program and itinerary for your World Youth Day group. Thousands of participants have traveled with EF to World Youth Days in Paris and Rome. Our dedication to high quality service and value will make planning your trip easy and your travel experience safe and secure. Our reasonable prices and flexibility allow groups of all sizes to participate in World Youth Day 2002. Call us today to begin planning for this special event.

GOLDEN FRONTIER
4100 North Illinois St.
Swansea, IL 62226-1834
Tel.: 618-234-1445; FAX: 618-234-9861

Personnel:
Linda Davinroy .... Domestic Reservations
Sharron Malloy .... International Reservations
Reverend Robert Vonnahmen .... Director
Craig Simoneaux .... Assistant Director

Type of Business:
Golden Frontier has provided 22 years of spiritual renewal through travel to religious destinations throughout the world. A professional and knowledgeable staff are on hand here and at overseas destinations to assure your travel experience will be rewarding and uplifting. A priest chaplain accompanies each group to offer Holy Mass and spiritual guidance along the way. Customized group programs are available for parish groups and other religious organizations. See our ad in the Pilgrimage Guide.

Golden Frontier is independent of Camp Ondessonk and Diocese of Belleville.

ISRAEL
NO ONE BELONGS HERE MORE THAN YOU.

ISRAEL TOURISM INFORMATION CENTER, N.A.
800 2nd Ave.
New York, NY 10017
Tel.: 888-77-ISRAEL; FAX: 212-499-5665

Type of Business:
Only Israel can offer you the chance to actually experience the wonders of The Bible. From walking the Vin Dolorosa to enjoying a sunset on the Mount of the Beatitudes, Israel has it all. Come visit the land that feels your body and soul. Israel. No one belongs here more than you. For more information on travel to Israel call toll-free 888-77-ISRAEL or visit us at www.goisrael.com.

ITS

ITS INTERNATIONAL TOURS
3013 20th Street, Suite B
Metairie, LA 70002
Tel.: 800-359-1931; FAX: 504-837-2920

Personnel:
James Hyland

Type of Business:
ITS is a Catholic Tour Company specializing in pilgrimage travel to the Holy Land and Catholic Shrines around the world. ITS offers monthly catalog departures to the Holy Land, Fatima, Lourdes, Medjugorje, and Rome. ITS can make arrangements for Jubilee Events, Beautification or Canonization Ceremonies, Passion Play tickets at Oberammergau. Free places for Spiritual Directors with as little as 5 paying passengers. All passengers protected by $1Million Dollar USTOA Consumer Protection Plan.

See our display ad in the Pilgrimage Destination Guide

JOURNEYS UNLIMITED
500 Eighth Ave.
New York, NY 10018
Tel.: 800-486-8359; 212-736-2028; FAX: 212-736-8959
email: holytours@worldnet.att.net
Website: http://www.journeys-unlimited.com

West Coast Office:
220 State Street
Los Altos, CA
800-473-HOLY

Personnel:
Nicholas Mancino....................President
Raymond Masillo....................Vice President
Lucille Sciabarassi....................Travel Consultant
Everett Mansfield....................Group Sales
Total Staff 20

Type of Business:
Serving the Church through Travel. Journeys Unlimited was founded by Raymond Masillo & Nicholas Mancino in 1990. The Management has been arranging Pilgrimages since 1969.
The company's philosophy is that each Pilgrimage be escorted by a spiritual leader in order to transform our tours into Pilgrimages. Our Pilgrimages have been designed to give each participant comfort for recreation and spiritual guidance for RENEWAL.
We also offer tours to Italy, Greece, Turkey, Egypt, Syria, Fatima, Lourdes, Oberammergau, and other Marian Shrines, Jubilee 2000, and World Youth Day.

MARANATHA TOURS
13825 N. 32nd Street, Suite 28
Phoenix, AZ 85032
Tel.: 800-545-5533; FAX: 602-788-6182
E-mail: mti@maranathatours.com
Website: www.maranathatours.com

Type of Business:
Marantha Tours, Inc. is the leader in customized Christian pilgrimages, specializing in tours to the Holy Land, Italy, Greece, Spain and Portugal, as well as other sacred sites. With over 30 years experience, our family owned business offers you the opportunity to celebrate Jubilee Year 2000 in Italy or to walk where Jesus walked, letting Him touch your heart as you travel where it all began 2000 years ago. Whether you are an individual wanting to join a group, or are wanting to lead your own group, you can feel confident that Marantha Tours will provide quality service at affordable prices.

UNITOURS, INC.
411 W. Putnam Ave.
Greenwich, CT 06830
Tel.: 800-777-7432; 203-629-3900; FAX: 203-629-1905
E-mail: UnitoursUS@aol.com
Web Site: www.Unitours.com

Type of Business:
Unitours is the "world leader in quality Christian travel. This reputation is based upon 45 years of experience in designing and leading custom pilgrimages to the Holy Land, Europe and more. Unitours' professionals will design a tour that includes the intinerary, sights, masses, and accommodations that meet your religious, spiritual and financial needs. You also benefit from knowledgeable guides who help make your pilgrimage a memorable experience. Scheduled departures tours for smaller groups are also available.

SHRINES

206 TOURS
325 Middle Country Road
Smithtown, NY 11787
Tel.: 800-206-TOURS; FAX: 516-361-3682
e-mail: info@206tours.com
Website: www.206tours.com

Personnel:
Milanka Pauciullo....................CTC President, 206 Tours
Elena Gorham-Rossi....................Manager
Maria Ufret....................Sales
Jennifer Hangley....................Sales

Type of Business:
206 Tours have serviced hundreds of thousands of Catholic pilgrims to Medjugorje, Lourdes, the Holy Land, Italy and Fatima since 1985. We are dedicated to the needs of the Catholic pilgrim and are unparalleled in our service to these individuals who participate in these journeys of faith. Please feel free to call us for upcoming special Pilgrimages for the year 2000.

BEST CATHOLIC PILGRIMAGES

BEST CATHOLIC PILGRIMAGES
1 East Superior Street
Chicago, IL 60611
Tel.: 800-908-BEST (2378); FAX: 312-944-3352
E-mail: info@bestcatholic.com

Type of Business:

Best Catholic Pilgrimages is a tour operator and land Destination management company that specializes in Customized religious/cultural tours world-wide.

Our professional and highly skilled staff headquartered in Chicago handles with consummate precision, to every detail of our tours, land/air itineraries. Our priorities are directed to our clients' high expectations, personalized needs and total satisfaction.

Plus...ask about our Preferred Partnership Program which develops outstanding Fund Raising events that benefit and bond all participants toward a mutually beneficial goal...Call Today for more information.

THE BLUE ARMY OF OUR LADY OF FATIMA, U.S.A

Shrine of the Immaculate Heart of Mary

PO. Box 976 - Mountain View Road
Washington, N.J. 07882 (Warren County)
Tel.: 908-689-7079; FAX: 908-689-0721
E-mail: service@bluearmy.com
Website: http://www.bluearmy.com

Personnel:
President - Most Rev.James S. Sullivan, Bishop of Fargo
Type of Business:
The Blue Army is a Church-approved non-profit Catholic organization with divisions in 70 United States dioceses. Our famous shrine honors Our Lady of Fatima. Perched upon a majestic country hillside, our shrine offers 72 acres of well-maintained countryside where you, or your group, can walk, pray and meditate. Mass and Confession are available daily. Expositon of the Blessed Sacrament daily. A unique Rosary Garden and Way of the Cross allow an environment for outdoor prayer. There many special events and ceremonies available for pilgrimage groups, especilally from May through October. A Gift Shop with assorted religious articles, etc.

ISRAEL
NO ONE BELONGS HERE MORE THAN YOU

ISRAEL TOURISM INFORMATION CENTER, N.A.
800 2nd Ave.
New York, NY 10017
Tel.: 888-77-ISRAEL; FAX: 212-499-5665

Type of Business:

Only Israel can offer you the chance to actually experience the wonders of The Bible. From walking the Vin Dolorosa to enjoying a sunset on the Mount of the Beatitudes, Israel has it all. Come visit the land that feels your body and soul. Israel. No one belongs here more than you. For more information on travel to Israel call toll-free 888-77-ISRAEL or visit us at www.goisrael.com.

ITS

ITS INTERNATIONAL TOURS
3013 20th Street, Suite B
Metairie, LA 70002
Tel.: 800-359-1931; FAX: 504-837-2920

Personnel:
James Hyland

Type of Business:

ITS is a Catholic Tour Company specializing in pilgrimage travel to the Holy Land and Catholic Shrines around the world. ITS offers monthly catalog departures to the Holy Land, Fatima, Lourdes, Medjugorje, and Rome. ITS can make arrangements for Jubilee Events, Beautification or Canonization Ceremonies, Passion Play tickets at Oberammergau. Free places for Spiritual Directors with as little as 5 paying passengers. All passengers protected by $1Million Dollar USTOA Consumer Protection Plan.

See our display ad in the Pilgrimage Destination Guide

MARANATHA TOURS
13825 N. 32nd Street, Suite 28
Phoenix, AZ 85032
Tel.: 800-545-5533; FAX: 602-788-6182
E-mail: mti@maranathatours.com
Website: www.maranathatours.com

Type of Business:

Marantha Tours, Inc. is the leader in customized Christian pilgrimages, specializing in tours to the Holy Land, Italy, Greece, Spain and Portugal, as well as other sacred sites. With over 30 years experience, our family owned business offers you the opportunity to celebrate Jubilee Year 2000 in Italy or to walk where Jesus walked, letting Him touch your heart as you travel where it all began 2000 years ago. Whether you are an individual wanting to join a group, or are wanting to lead your own group, you can feel confident that Marantha Tours will provide quality service at affordable prices.

RAMBUSCH
40 West 13th St.
New York, NY 10011
Tel.: 212-675-0400; FAX: 212-620-4687

Personnel:

Viggo Bech Rambusch .... Senior Project Director
Martin V. Rambusch .... Stained Glass Director

Type of Business:

Since 1898, creating church interiors, liturgical furnishings, and art work. Fine restoration of church interiors. In-house studios and shops for designing and executing stained glass, church lighting systems, art metal work, and decorative painting.

TOURS

CATHOLIC TRAVEL CENTRE
444 Riverside Drive, Suite 301
Burbank, CA 91505
Tel.: 800-553-5233; FAX: 818-848-0712
E-mail: info@GoCatholicTravel.com
Website: www.GoCatholicTravel.com

Personnel:

J. Scott Scherer .... President
Carol Jones .... Assistant to the President
Inga Duranovic .... Director of Operations
Natalie Carr .... Operations Assistant
Henry Nassim .... CFO
Geri Lemoine .... Finance Assistant

Type of Business:

A reputation for extraordinary quality has made Catholic Travel Centre the choice of groups that demand exacting service and exceptional attention to detail.

With meticulous detail, we will plan a one-of-a-kind pilgrimage tour catering to your group's specific interests. We can work within the constraints of any budget.

Our client list includes prestigious Catholic institutions nationwide, returning year-after-year to Catholic Travel Centre. We will gladly provide a reference list.

In the Year 2001, we are celebrating our 10th Anniversary of exceptional service to the traveling Catholic community, and we invite your group's inquiry. Please call us at (800) 553-5233. Or visit our website at: www.GoCatholicTravel.com

YOUTH MINISTRY

LIFE TEEN, INC.
1730 W. Guadalupe Rd.
Mesa, AZ 85202
Tel.: 480-820-7001; FAX: 480-820-8653
E-mail: kdemalja@lifeteen.com
Website: www.lifeteen.com

Personnel:

Rev. Dale Fushek .... Founder/President
Phil Baniewicz .... Executive Director
Randy Raus .... National Director

Type of Business:

As one of the fastest growing youth ministries in the country, LIFE TEEN is a comprehensive program designed to lead teens and their families closer to Christ. Open to high school teens of all faiths, this Catholic-centered ministry is focused on the Liturgy, especially the true presence of Christ in the Eucharist. Every Sunday, more than 75,000 teenagers attend LIFE TEEN Masses and LIFE Nights in nearly 700 parishes worldwide. In addition to these powerful liturgies and challenging youth meetings, there are retreats, outreach, prayer groups and weekly activities for teens that deepen their relationship with Christ and each other. LIFE TEEN also provides youth rallies for high school teens, Training Conferences and Advanced Training Certificate Programs for our youth leaders on a national level. Ministry products and resources available include introductory training packages, quarterly LIFE Support for parishes, Mass and promo videos, a nine-video Training Conference resource, seven-video Right of Confirmation Package, three-video Legacy Series on vocations to the priesthood, books and music. For more information check out our website or call our National Office at 480-820-7001.

Index to Advertisers